A CONCORDANCE

TO THE

POEMS OF WILLIAM WORDSWORTH

A CONCORDANCE

TO THE

POEMS OF

WILLIAM WORDSWORTH

EDITED FOR THE CONCORDANCE SOCIETY

BY

LANE COOPER

NEW YORK / RUSSELL & RUSSELL

1965

FIRST PUBLISHED IN 1911
REISSUED, 1965, BY RUSSELL & RUSSELL
BY ARRANGEMENT WITH THE ESTATE OF LANE COOPER
L.C. CATALOG CARD NO: 65—18799
PRINTED IN THE UNITED STATES OF AMERICA

PREFACE

FOLLOWING a similar work on Thomas Gray, A CONCORDANCE TO THE POEMS OF WILLIAM WORDSWORTH is the second volume to appear under the auspices of The Concordance Society. Of the subvention requested by the publishers, in order to decrease the pecuniary risk attending so large and costly a venture, The Concordance Society has contributed one-third; for a part of the remainder the editor is indebted to the generosity of his mother and his two brothers. It should be added that, in all their dealings with the editor and The Concordance Society, the publishers have shown themselves friendly, in an unusual measure, to the interests of scholarship as represented in this work.

Function of the Concordance. The labour of compiling this index to the language of Wordsworth was begun, and has been finished, in the well-considered belief that, after Chaucer, Spenser, Shakespeare, and Milton, he is the fifth of the great English poets; that the notion of discarding any large section of his writings as if they were of relatively little value, or unnecessary to the comprehension of the rest, is as pestilent an error as the same notion would be if applied to Lucretius or Plato; that a study of the whole is indispensable to an understanding of the parts, and *vice versa*; that the study of Wordsworth, having passed beyond the stage of naïve appreciation, could not now make any essential advance if a concordance were lacking; and that probably no recent English author has employed so large a vocabulary with so much precision.

The main function of the Concordance is to aid 'the attentive reader', whose coming is anticipated in Wordsworth's Preface to The Excursion, in discovering the vital relation between the longer poems, which are likened to the antechapel and the body of a Gothic church, and the 'minor pieces' which correspond 'to the little cells, oratories, and sepulchral recesses, ordinarily included in those edifices.'

Plan and Execution. The enterprise of this concordance having been announced at a meeting of The Modern Language Association of America in December, 1907, the plan was elaborated by the editor in the following October. A set of 'Instructions to Collaborators'* was drawn up, submitted to the scrutiny both of specialists in the study of Wordsworth and of other competent judges, again rendered as exact and comprehensive as possible, and then, together with the necessary materials, put into the hands of those who had agreed to assist the editor in his undertaking. The Oxford Wordsworth, edited by Mr. Thomas Hutchinson, and bearing the imprint of the year 1907, was adopted as the basic text. Loose sheets of this were obtained in a sufficient number to provide eight complete sets of each allotment of pages; and the work of excerpting was actually begun in November, 1908. The concordance-words were written in the upper left-hand corner of slips of paper of a uniform size (three inches by five); the line of poetry containing each word was cut out of the printed text, and pasted on the corresponding slip; by the use of rubber stamps, the number of the page on which the word and line occur in the text was added in the upper right-hand corner of the slip; by the same device, the title of the poem was indicated in the lower right-

---

* The editor will be pleased to give a copy of these 'Instructions' to any one who intends to engage in a similar undertaking.

hand corner; and then the number of the line was commonly added in script. Cross-references for hyphenated words were made on separate slips.

In this way, it was hoped, a high degree of accuracy would be secured in the copy; for the slips thus prepared were sent to the printer without transcription.

Each collaborator received from one-fortieth to one-eightieth of the Oxford Wordsworth for his share of text. The editor of the Concordance copied the lines for a number of anomalous passages in the basic text, and also for certain poems which are not contained in the Oxford Wordsworth, but appear in the edition of Mr. Nowell Smith, the Eversley Edition of Professor William Knight, or Professor Knight's Letters of the Wordsworth Family (the choice here being in favour of the text of Mr. Nowell Smith where a choice was possible); and, in addition, he assisted a few of his collaborators who, for one reason or another, were unable to complete their assignments within the time desired.

In most cases, the finished slips for each section of the work were alphabetically arranged before they were returned to the editor, to be incorporated in one main alphabetical list. This final arrangement of all the slips (about 211,000, including the cross-references) was completed before the end of May, 1909, so that the whole task of preparing the copy was accomplished, through careful planning, the division of the burden, the employment of labour-saving devices, and an exceptional spirit of co-operation, in the space of less than seven months. Some delay was encountered in finding a publisher; but this obstacle being suddenly and happily overcome, in part through the kind offices of Mr. Gordon Wordsworth, the printers set to work about the beginning of May, 1910. At the date of this Preface it is two years and three months since the excerpting commenced; had there been no loss of time in discovering the right publisher, the Concordance might have been before the public within eighteen months after its inception.

Collaborators. The following persons freely gave their services in recording the quotations:—

PROFESSOR ARTHUR ADAMS, TRINITY COLLEGE, HARTFORD.
DR. CARROLL S. ALDEN, UNITED STATES NAVAL ACADEMY, ANNAPOLIS.
MR. ADOLPH C. BAEBENROTH, SYRACUSE UNIVERSITY.
DR. ELMER J. BAILEY, CORNELL UNIVERSITY.
MR. DANE L. BALDWIN, CASCADILLA SCHOOL, ITHACA.
MISS MARY M. BELDEN, ELMIRA COLLEGE.
MISS EDITH BENTLEY, LINCOLN, NEBRASKA.
MR. LESLIE N. BROUGHTON, CORNELL UNIVERSITY.
MR. LLEWELLYN BUELL, CORNELL UNIVERSITY.
PROFESSOR ALBERT S. COOK, YALE UNIVERSITY.
*MRS. ALBERT S. COOK. (*Died December* 31, 1908.)
MISS MILDRED E. COOK, NEW HAVEN, CONNECTICUT.
DR. EDWARD G. COX, CORNELL UNIVERSITY.
MR. WILLARD W. ELLIS, CORNELL UNIVERSITY LIBRARY.
MRS. WILLARD W. ELLIS, ITHACA.
PROFESSOR ROBERT H. FLETCHER, IOWA COLLEGE.
MR. ALLAN H. GILBERT, CORNELL UNIVERSITY.
MISS ANTOINETTE GREENE, ELMIRA COLLEGE.
MISS ELSIE L. GWYN, CORNELL UNIVERSITY.
DR. JOHN LOUIS HANEY, CENTRAL HIGH SCHOOL, PHILADELPHIA.
MISS JULIA HARRIS, CORNELL UNIVERSITY.

Dr. Charles M. Hathaway, Jr., United States Naval Academy, Annapolis.
Mrs. Samuel P. Hayes, South Hadley, Massachusetts.
Professor Charles W. Hodell, Goucher College, Baltimore.
Miss Cecilia A. Law, Ithaca.
Miss Ernestine Laurence Miller, Sayre Institute, Lexington, Kentucky.
Miss Mary A. Molloy, Winona Seminary, Winona, Minnesota.
Miss Mary Morrison, Nooksack, Washington.
Miss Edith J. Munsell, Cornell University.
Dr. Herbert S. Murch, Princeton University.
Professor Irene T. Myers, Transylvania University, Lexington, Kentucky.
Professor Paul R. Pope, Cornell University.
Mrs. Paul R. Pope, Ithaca.
Mrs. George F. Reinhardt, Berkeley, California.
Professor Robert K. Root, Princeton University.
Professor Hubert G. Shearin, Transylvania University, Lexington, Kentucky.
*Miss Emma F. Skinner. (Died September 30, 1910.)
Mr. George S. Spohn, Western Maryland College, Westminster, Maryland.
Mr. Benjamin F. Stelter, The University of Kansas.
Mrs. Henry L. Stephenson, Portland, Oregon.
Miss Frances N. Stevens, New Brunswick, New Jersey.
Professor William Strunk, Jr., Cornell University.
Mrs. William Strunk, Jr., Ithaca.
Dr. George B. Tennant, Paterson, New Jersey.
Miss Mary Rebecca Thayer, Oakland, Maryland.
Miss Mabel F. Yeomans, Oneonta, New York.

The most of these persons had no previous experience in the making of concordances. The editor's experience had been limited to a certain amount of proof-reading in connection with the Concordance to Gray.

Alphabetizing. The following persons took part in the final arrangement of the slips :—

Miss Rose Abel.
Mr. Dane L. Baldwin.
Mrs. Madison Bentley.
Professor Albert S. Cook.
Miss Mildred E. Cook.
Mr. Sidney A. Cook.
Mr. Howard T. Foulkes.
Miss Margaret Fowler.
Mr. Allan H. Gilbert.
Miss Elizabeth G. Hopper.
Mr. Gerard E. Jensen.
Mr. Alexander C. Judson.
Mr. John T. McCants.
Miss Bessie Marriott.
Miss Elizabeth Merrill.
Mr. Sherman B. Neff.
Mr. Dominic Ruotolo.
Mr. William E. Schultz.
Miss Edith B. Sloat.
Miss Mary W. Smyth.
Mr. Benjamin F. Stelter.
*Mr. William S. Whittle-sey. (Died January 19, 1910.)
Miss Frances B. van Zandt.
The Editor.

Proof-reading. The following assisted the editor in the proof-reading :—

Professor Arthur Adams.
Miss Emily H. Hall.
Miss Elizabeth G. Hopper.
Miss Roca Leland.
Professor Charles G. Osgood.
Mr. Dominic Ruotolo.
Miss Edith B. Sloat.
Miss Mary Rebecca Thayer.
Professor Hubert G. Shearin.

Quotations. Save in the case of two passages from The Borderers, the quotations from Wordsworth, as in Neve's Concordance to Cowper, consist in every instance of a single line of poetry ; care has been taken to preserve any mark of punctuation at the end of a line. The different method of excerpting which was employed in the Concordance to Gray seems not, on the whole, to have produced a much happier result in the way of intelligibility ; could not have been so exactly carried out for Wordsworth if the printed text was to be cut and pasted ; would inevitably break down if the attempt were made to apply it to the long periodic sentences that are found in The Prelude and The Excursion ; and would tend to swell immoderately the size of the work.

Lines 1903–2008 and 2217–2224 of The Borderers are in prose, much of it closely approximating blank verse. For the purposes of the Concordance, it has been assumed that the prose of the first passage gives way to actual verse at line 2009, beginning with ' We are betrayed !' The line-numbering of these two passages being arbitrary, words cited from them are accompanied by what seems to be the most germane bit of context, a part of which may be taken from the line preceding or following.

Omitted Words. No quotations accompany the following words in this Concordance :—

A	BY	HIM	OF	THEIR	US
ALSO	FOR	HIS	OH	THEM	WE
AN	FROM	IF	ON	THERE	WHICH
AND	HAD	IN	OR	THEY	WITH
ARE	HAS	IT	OUR	THIS	YE
AS	HAVE	ITS	OUT	THOU	YOU
AT	HE	NO	SHE	TO	YOUR
BE	HER	NOT	THAT	TOO	
BUT	HERE	O	THE	UP	

This list is mainly based upon a similar list in the Concordance to Gray, and has its sanction from the practice in Strong's Exhaustive Concordance of The Bible. In the Concordance to Wordsworth, however, it will be observed that the personal pronouns and pronominal adjectives I, ME, MINE, and MY, which are of unusual interest in a subjective poet, are not included in the list of omissions, but belong in another category, which is indicated by the term Partial List. The attempt has been made to include all the occurrences of these four words that have any special significance in connection with the poet.

Partial Lists. In order to lessen the cost of publication, only some of the occurrences of each of the following words have been recorded :—

ABOUT	EVEN	NEITHER	THOSE
ABOVE	EVER	NEVER	THOUGH
AFTER	EVERY	NOR	THRO'
AGAIN	FORTH	NOW	THROUGH
AGAINST	'GAINST	O'ER	THUS
AH	HADST	OFF	THY
ALL	HAST	OFT	TILL
ALONG	HATH	OFTEN	'TILL
ALTHOUGH	HE'S	ONCE	'TIS
AM	HIMSELF	ONE	'TWAS
AMID	HOW	ONLY	'TWERE
AMONG	HOWEVER	OURS	'TWILL
ANY	I	OVER	UNDER
AROUND	I'D	OWN	UNTIL
ART	I'LL	ROUND	UPON
AWAY	I'M	SAID	VERY
BEEN	INDEED	SAY	WAS
BEFORE	INTO	SAYS	WERE
BEHIND	IS	SHALL	WE'RE
BELOW	IT'S	SHALT	WERT
BENEATH	ITSELF	SHE'S	WHAT
BETWEEN	I'VE	SHOULD	WHEN
BOTH	LESS	SHOULDST	WHENCE
CAN	LET	SO	WHERE
CANNOT	LIKE	SOME	WHETHER
CANST	MAY	STILL	WHILE
COULD	MAY'ST	SUCH	WHO
COULDST	ME	TH'	WHOM
DID	MID	THAN	WHOSE
DO	'MID	THAT'S	WHY
DOES	MIGHT	THEE	WILL
DONE	MIGHT'ST	THEIRS	WILT
DOST	MINE	THEN	WITHIN
DOTH	MORE	THENCE	WITHOUT
DOWN	MOST	THEREFORE	WOULD
EACH	MUST	THERE'S	WOULDST
E'ER	MY	THESE	YES
EITHER	MYSELF	THINE	YET
ERE	NE'ER	THO'	YOURS

The formation of such a list is to some extent arbitrary. The quotations for most of these words were recorded by two of the more experienced and rapid workers, Professor Arthur Adams and Mrs. George F. Reinhardt, whose sections of text, as it happens, were not very characteristic in their substance, though interesting for their peculiarities of syntax. A valuable collection of similes is included in the quotations under the word LIKE. The references to WERE are restricted to the use of this word as a proper name.

Concordance-titles. In order to facilitate the use of the Concordance by persons who may not own the Oxford Wordsworth, it has been necessary to employ no fewer than 728 combinations of words in italics to indicate the titles of the poems. The selection of these catch-titles was very difficult. Wordsworth is often so circumstantial in naming his poems that no significant catchword is discernible ; in other cases, the poems have no names ; in others, two poems have the same name, or names very similar. In still others, it was found that two or more of the editors of Wordsworth, who give an alphabetical list of titles, had not hit upon the same catchword for their arrangement. For various reasons, therefore, it has often been necessary to refer to a poem by words enough from the opening line to identify it in such an index of first lines as the recent editions of this poet contain. Though some of the concordance-titles may seem unfamiliar or awkward, it must not be supposed that the choice of them was made at random ; there is a reason for the particular form in virtually all cases.

Variants. No truly exhaustive collection of the variant readings in the successive editions of Wordsworth's text has ever been published. The editor of the Concordance, having solicited advice from those who were most able to give it, was confirmed in his opinion that he ought not to attempt a labour which would greatly delay the appearance of the whole work, as well as materially increase a pecuniary outlay already becoming formidable. In general, therefore, variant readings have not been recorded, with the exception of those which are included in the standard text of Mr. Hutchinson. In the case of one stanza in each of the poems referred to as *Dion*, *Duty*, and *Louisa*, the variant quotations were provided with no line-numbers in the Concordance, because of the confusion which would otherwise result through the similar numbering of contiguous passages in the same text. The variants in *There was a Boy* (Oxford Wordsworth, p. 183), and similar extracts from The Prelude (pp. 89, 186, 208), have been noted according to the page, but otherwise the quotations in these extracts are referred to their place in the complete poem ; Vaudracour and Julia, however, has been treated in all respects as a separate work, so that there are a few unimportant repetitions as between this and The Prelude, Book 9. In the case of An Evening Walk and Descriptive Sketches, it has been the intention that the final text should be fully recorded ; and, for the first or 'Quarto' editions of these poems, the purpose has been to include quotations only for those lines which show a verbal difference from the final text—not merely a difference in the use of capital letters or marks of punctuation. Yet differences in the compounding of words by means of a hyphen have been noted, as well as a few anomalous forms like IT'S. The delicate task of recording the variants in the 'Quarto' editions of these two poems was entrusted to Professor Robert K. Root, of Princeton University.

Concerning The Recluse, Book First, Part First, it is to be observed that the Concordance accepts the readings of the Eversley Edition in matters of spelling and punctuation, as far as and including line 753, and that the line-numbering of quotations from the extracts published by Wordsworth and his nephew follows that of the canto as a whole. Verbal differences in the Oxford Wordsworth are noted, however, and all the quotations from these extracts are referred to their proper pages (pp. 218, 621, 622, 755) in this text. The text of the Eversley Wordsworth as far as line 753 is said to be based upon a new and careful examination of the original manuscript. From line 754 the text of the quotations in the Concordance is that of the Oxford Wordsworth, and the page-number (755) of this edition is preserved, but the line-numbering, again, is that of the canto as a whole.

Variants and Additional Poems. Of the ostensibly new material from Wordsworth which has been printed by Mr. Nowell Smith and Professor Knight, it must be said that these passages have come before the public in spite of such utterances as the poet is known to have made to Alexander Dyce : ' You know what importance I attach to following strictly the last copy of the text of an author ' (Letters of the Wordsworth Family 2. 420). Concerning his adaptations from Juvenal he wrote to Francis Wrangham : ' The verses which you have of mine I should wish to be destroyed ' (1. 253). But where recognized editors have shown the way, the maker of a concordance has little choice but to follow. As a result, the present work admits a full list of quotations from these additional sources, even in certain cases where Mr. Nowell Smith and Professor Knight have not clearly differentiated between fresh discoveries and mere variants, or additional or rejected manuscript passages of poems already known. The present writer has discussed several of these cases in Notes and Queries during the autumn of 1910.

One sonnet, attributed to Wordsworth, and published in The Home Journal, New York, October, 1847, is referred to in the Concordance without an accompanying page-number, by the title *A sad.

Homographs. This work makes no pretence of uniting the functions of a lexicon with those of a concordance pure and simple. A lexical concordance to Wordsworth, with an equal number of references, would require a volume probably one-third or one-half as large again as the present. As in the Concordance to Gray, in a few cases only has a distinction been indicated in the meaning of different words which are spelled in the same way. Where such a distinction is made, the attention of the reader will be called to it by a departure from the normal ordering of references according to page-numbers, the form having the fewer references being put first under the common head-word. Under CAN, for example, the quotations containing the noun precede those containing the auxiliary verb ; and the case is similar with MUSIC, the name of a dog, and MUSIC, a common noun.

Cross-references. When two or more verbal elements are compounded in the text of Wordsworth by means of a hyphen, the occurrences of the entire word are arranged in their proper place in the alphabet, and cross-reference is made to this whole word from the second element, or second and third elements, of the compound, except in most cases where these elements, being particles and the like, would as single words fall under the rule of partial or complete omissions.

Wordsworth, however, seems to be very inconsistent in the use of the hyphen : within the limits even of a short poem he may print the same combination of elements as a single word and as a compound (see, for example, the references to GREENHOUSE, GREEN-SWARD, NOONTIDE) ; or he may join the same elements with a hyphen at one time, and at another print them as separate words (compare BATTLE, BATTLE-FIELD, LITTLE, LITTLE-ONE, and various combinations under COTTAGE and MOUNTAIN). He is also at times inconsistent in his spelling (see CRECY, CRESSY, FORBODE, FOREBODE). It is improbable that all of these variations have been discovered in the proof-reading. And though an attempt has been made to normalize the cross-references in page-proof, it has been impossible to obtain a complete uniformity in this matter ; for one thing, the unusual demands upon particular fonts have made it necessary that the earlier letters of the alphabet should be printed off, in order to release the type for later ones. Moreover, the editor is doubtful whether any system could have been devised which should exactly provide for all of these petty abnormalities. As the industrious Cruden remarked in his second preface : ' Though it be called . . . "A Complete Concordance", poor sinful man can do nothing absolutely perfect and complete, and therefore the word " complete " is only to be taken in a comparative sense.'

Errors in the Basic Text. In the preparation of this

Concordance, the following errors have been noted in the basic text :—

108 *Indolence* 31, *read* Than *for* Then
209 *Laod.* 4, *read* required : *for* required
245 *P. B.* 775, *read* Bell. *for* Bell
789 *Excursion* 3. 194, *read* " One *for* " One
858 *Excursion* 7. 87, *read* fortune-telling *for* foretune-telling.

In some few instances, the word *sic*, or a mark of interrogation, or a word which should be substituted, has been inserted in brackets in the text of a quotation, in order to draw the attention of the reader to an abnormality ; but the paramount aim has been to reproduce with the utmost fidelity the text of Wordsworth as it appears in the editions which have been quoted.

It only remains for the editor to express his sense of deep obligation to all those persons who by their advice, or direct participation in the labour, have aided in the advancement of this work. To Professor Albert S. Cook, President of The Concordance Society, both for counsel in the planning and manifold help in the making, the volume owes a debt too extensive to be well expressed. And from Professor William Strunk, Jr., of Cornell University, the editor has received endless assistance in difficulties both small and great. Mr. George William Harris, the Librarian of Cornell University, provided the manuscript of the Concordance with a place of safe-keeping for the better part of a year. To Miss Elizabeth G. Hopper, of the Library of Congress, Miss Mary Rebecca Thayer, of Oakland, Maryland, Miss Edith B. Sloat, of Ithaca, and Mr. Dominic Ruotolo, of the Yale University Library, special thanks are due for a devotion to the interests of the Concordance which has been quite incommensurate with the compensation which they received for their labours.

LANE COOPER

ITHACA, NEW YORK
February 8, 1911.

ERRATA

Under **Anguish,** 867 *Excursion* 7. 676, *read* them all ! *for* then all !
Under **Barge,** 547 *Rude is 18, *read* up-piled *for* uppiled
Under **Beautiful,** K. 8. 237 *Recluse* I. 1. 49, *read* it had *for* had it
Below **Breath-like,** *insert* **Breath's.**
Read **Brother-shepherds.** *for* **Brother-Shepherds.**
Under **Cheer,** *insert* I may not trust thy placid cheer ! 112 *Lament* 9
Instead of **Comest,** *with a cross-reference, the quotations for* **Com'st** *should appear on p.* 153.
Under **Eminently,** *the quotation should be entirely in the second space.*
Under **Highway,** 651 *Prelude* 3. 128, *read* high-way *for* highway

The following corrected, or additional, cross-references are to be noted :

Apprentice. *See* **'Prentice.** **Boat.** *See* **Steam-boat.** **Bred.** *See* **Thorough-bred.** **Briar.** *See* **Sweet-briar.** **Bright.** *See* **Star-bright.** **Bucks.** *See* **Roe-bucks.** **Bud.** *See* **Rose-bud.** **Cat.** *See* **Wild-cat.** **Cemented.** *See* **Time-cemented ;** *delete* **Lime-cemented.** **Changed.** *Delete See* **Unchanged.** **Clamor.** *See* **Clamour.** **Clamour.** *See* **Clamor.** **Course.** *See* **Water-course.** **Crow.** *See* **Scare-crow.** **Crecy.** *See* **Cressy.** **Cressy.** *See* **Crecy.** **Dale.** *See* **Tiviot-dale ;** *delete* **Teviot-dale.** **Falls.** *Delete See* **Waterfalls.** **Fold.** *See* **Twofold.** **Nymph's.** *See* **Wood-nymph's.** **Nymphs.** *Delete See* **Wood-nymphs.** **'Prentice.** *See* **Apprentice.**

LIST OF TITLES

[The following is an alphabetical list of the catchwords used in this Concordance to designate titles or first lines in the Poetical Works of Wordsworth. The full titles which here accompany the catchwords are taken, as far as possible, from the Table of Contents in the Oxford Wordsworth; and the page-numbers v, 1–756, indicate the pages in the Oxford Wordsworth on which the poems begin. S. 3, with a page-number, refers to Nowell Smith's edition, Volume 3; K. 8, with a page-number, to Knight's Eversley Wordsworth, Volume 8; and similarly L. 1, L. 2, and L. 3, refer to the three volumes of Knight's Letters of the Wordsworth Family. A preceding asterisk signifies that the catchwords are taken from the first line of a poem; a dagger, that the poem, although included in his works by Wordsworth. is by another hand, for example, that of his sister; and a mark of interrogation, that the ascription of the poem to Wordsworth is to some extent doubtful.]

A CONCORDANCE

TO THE

POEMS OF WILLIAM WORDSWORTH

A, omitted.
Aäliza. When Lady Aäliza mourned . . . . . 398 White Doe 226
Aar. Thunders through echoing pines the headlong Aar ; . . . 16 Desc. Sk. 337
Abandoned. To winds abandoned and the prying stars, . . . 272 Ruins 10
Cast off—abandoned by thy rugged Sire, . . . 290 Kilchurn 10
That less should scorn the abandoned clay ; . . 301 Bran 83
All trust abandoned in the healing might . . . 363 *The world forsaken 3
For him abandoned to blank awe, ... 411 White Doe 1387
By Rome abandoned ; vain are suppliant cries, . 420 Ecc. Sonn. 1. 9. 9
Renounced, abandoned by degenerate Men . . 515 Penn. 12
On his wet bed, abandon'd and alone. . . . . 613 Desc.Sk.Quarto 613
Abandoned, and the pride of public vice ; . . 693 Prelude 7. 387
Who was not lost, abandoned, selfish, proud, . 713 Prelude 9. 285
The hut itself abandoned to decay, ... 763 Excursion 1. 509
Abandoning. Abandoning and all his showy friends, 859 Excursion 7. 132
Abandons. Pronounces, ne'er abandons Charity. . 429 Ecc. Sonn. 2. 1. 14
Abased. By public power abased, to fatal crime, . 717 Prelude 9. 570
Abasement. See Self-abasement.
'Mid much abasement, what he had received . . 775 Excursion 2. 273
Abashed. Abashed, Sir Dinas turned away ; . . 373 Eg. Maid 271
Too long abashed thy Name is like a rose . . 584 *With copious 46
Her trappings here, should strip them off abashed 654 Prelude 3. 393
Would have abashed those impious crests—have quelled . . . . 721 Prelude 10. 212
Was less upraised in spirit than abashed ; . . 805 Excursion 4. 256
Abashed, and tender pity overawed." . . . 865 Excursion 7. 515
Abate. Or till the storm abate. He has restored you, 53 Bord. 864
I looked at her again, nor did my pride abate. . 119 Sailor's Mother 12
" Abate this unbecoming pride, ... 167 Pilgrim's Dream 34
His mid-day warmth abate not, seeming less . . 219 Haunted Tree 2
One tender claim abate ; . . . . . 223 Wishing-gate 15
And, to a point of just relief, abate . . . 255 *Grief, thou 13
Which neither force shall check nor time abate ! . 271 Henry : Portrait 14
Will that, or deeper thoughts, abate . . . 372 Eg. Maid 219
To sap your hardy virtue, and abate . . . 420 Ecc. Sonn. 1. 8. 6
Echoed in Heaven, cries out, " Ye Chiefs, abate . 429 Ecc. Sonn. 2. 4. 9
By objects, which might force the soul to abate . 493 Hap. War. 19
When the fierce orbs abate their glare ;— . . 526 *The soaring 37
Loose livers he can make abate their vice, . . 557 Cuck. and Night. 14
Would have inclined each to abate his zeal . . 845 Excursion 6. 462
Have caused her to abate the virgin pride, . . 882 Excursion 8. 510
Abated. Thus is the storm abated by the craft . 432 Ecc. Sonn. 2. 16. 1
In most, abated or suppressed ; in some, . . 646 Prelude 2. 263
Was fallen, the rain abated, but the hills . . 784 Excursion 2. 808
Abated not ; and all that time the boy . . . K.8. 229 *I will 137
Abatement. Except for that abatement which is paid 68 Bord. 1685
Abates. He stands, backed by the wall ;—he abates not his din ; . . . . 188 Music 25
Abates the perils of a stormy night ; . . . 459 *Wanderer! that 16
Abating. Or pride of heart abating : and, whene'er 813 Excursion 4. 841
Abbey. And lo ! a statelier pile, the Abbey of St. Bees. 466 St. Bees 63
Nursed in the quiet Abbey of St. Bees. . . 467 St. Bees 108
An abbey in its lone recess, ... 472 Ossian 13
As church or abbey furnisheth. . . . . 550 Hermit's Cell 2. 12
To the next Abbey him they bare away ; . . 555 Prioress 173
Of that large abbey, where within the Vale . . 643 Excursion 2. 103
Abbey's. To crown their abbey's sanctity. . . 301 Bran 61
Of a clear brook ;—beneath an abbey's roof . . 771 Excursion 2. 7
Abbey-walls. These find, 'mid ivied abbey-walls, . 168 Wren's Nest 17
Abbey-windows. And mosques, and spires, and abbey-windows, ... 244 P. B. 684
Abbot. See Stone-abbot.
Soon after, the good Abbot of St. Cuthbert's . . 41 Bord. 199
The Abbot with his convent's company . . . 555 Prioress 186
" This Abbot, for he was a holy man, . . . 555 Prioress 191
" This holy Monk, this Abbot—him mean I, . . 556 Prioress 219

Abbot—continued.
And, when the Abbot had this wonder seen, . . 556 Prioress 222
And the stone abbot, after circuit made . . . 727 Prelude 10. 599
Abbot's. Nor wants the holy Abbot's gliding Shade 393 Inglewood 9
Abdicate. The noblest-born must abdicate ; . . 390 Highland Broach 36
A-bed. Old Susan lies a-bed in pain, . . . 126 Idiot Boy 24
A-bed or up, to young or old ; . . . . 537 Goody Blake 122
A-bed or up, by night or day ; . . . . 537 Goody Blake 125
Whether he's up or a-bed. . . . . S. 3. 424 Tinker 50
Abel. The Death of Abel, Shakspeare, and the Bard . 695 Prelude 7. 564
Of him who cooked the death of Abel, . . . S. 3. 432 *A German 2
Abel's. Of harmless Abel's death, by murdering Cain. . . . . S. 3. 432 *Critics, right 4
Aberdeen. And far as Aberdeen. . . . . 239 P. B. 220
Aberrations. Those aberrations—had the clamorous friends . . . . 731 Prelude 11. 260
Abhor. All Powers and Places that abhor the light 513 *Said Secrecy 12
They who bewail not, must abhor, the sneer . . 514 *Portentous change 5
Which, now, as infamous, I should abhor— . . 798 Excursion 3. 815
To acts which they abhor ; though I bewail . . 805 Excursion 4. 301
Abhorred. To that abhorred den of brutish vice !— 47 Bord. 546
Though of a lineage once abhorred, ... 232 Jew. Fam. 39
Stalks round—abhorred by Heaven, a terror to the Earth ! . . . . 311 *Who rises 20
Shun not this Rite, neglected, yea abhorred, . . 447 Ecc. Sonn. 3. 29. 1
So dreaded, so abhorred. The day deserves . . 725 Prelude 10. 513
Abhorrence. Nor—touched with due abhorrence of their guilt . . . . 321 *Here pause 10
Until abhorrence and contempt are things . . 819 Excursion 4. 1225
Abide. To abide the issue of my act, alone. . . 65 Bord. 1519
Unfettered as bees that in gardens abide ; . . 116 Repentance 10
Where by the week he doth abide, . . . 126 Idiot Boy 28
For what was now so obvious. To abide, . . 150 *When, to 52
With us openly abide, ... 171 Kitten 61
The waters of the pools where they abide. . . 197 Resolution 123
Calm pleasures there abide—majestic pains. . . 210 Laod. 72
No trace of pain or languor could abide . . . 258 *Even so 5
Through fields whose thrifty occupants abide . . 275 *Chatsworth ! thy 5
St. Francis, far from Man's resort, to abide . . 362 *List—'twas 37
In the cloud-piercing rocks doth her grandeur abide, 364 Vallomb. 11
I feel how in their presence doth abide . . . 365 *Rapt above 10
And now, if men with men in peace abide, . . 383 Duddon 27. 12
I see what was, and is, and will abide ; . . . 384 Duddon 34. 4
That " bliss with mortal Man may not abide : ". 395 WhiteDoe: Ded. 23
In resignation to abide . . . . 407 White Doe 1070
" Hope," said the old Man, " must abide . . 408 White Doe 1394
Receive the faith, and in the hope abide. . . 419 Ecc. Sonn. 1. 3. 14
His thin autumnal locks where Monks abide . . 424 Ecc. Sonn. 1. 21. 5
Do in the supernatural world abide . . . 425 Ecc. Sonn. 1. 28. 11
But not till They, with all that do abide . . . 446 Ecc. Sonn. 3. 25. 5
So exquisite ; but here do they abide, . . . 509 F. Stone 87
Ah, think how one compelled for life to abide . 519 Pun. Death 11. 1
If such do on this earth abide, ... 534 *Blest is 62
That there she may abide . . . . 543 Russ. Fug. 150
No longer would I in my bed abide . . . 557 Cuck. and Night. 57
Of that false Bird whom Love can not abide. . 561 Cuck.andNight.270
Established in the land where they abide . . . 568 Cumb. Beg. 137
A power that never ceased to abide in him, . . 584 Ch. Lamb 34
Of the clear flood, from things which there abide 662 Prelude 4. 266
To abide in the great City, where I found . . 721 Prelude 10. 245
Among the fallen of nations, dost abide . . . 732 Prelude 11. 376
In which the everlasting stars abide . . . 787 Excursion 5. 37
The spots where such abide ! But happier still . 823 Excursion 5. 37
Who here abide, the persons like the place. . . K.8. 245 Recluse 1.1.315
Abides. True dignity abides with him alone . . 23 Yew-tree 61
Is present and perpetually abides . . . . 118 Maternal Grief 4
In that enjoyment which with You abides, . . 333 Ded. Tour 11
Methinks that there abides in thee . . . . 485 *Bright Flower 5

Above—*continued.*
Some ground not mine; and, strong her strength above, 208 *It is no 15
(Above the convex of the watery globe) 219 *This Height 19
(Above the general roar of woods and crags) 219 Haunted Tree 23
Above the hermit's long-forsaken cell!" 220 Triad 40
High is her aim as heaven above, 222 Triad 145
Streaming from founts above the starry sky, 229 Cuckoo-clock 39
Lodged above the starry pole; 234 Power of Sound 109
" Haste! and above Siberian snows 237 P. B. 91
(Above it shivering aspens play) 246 P.B. 922
To flesh and blood; no Goddess from above, 252 *Her only 13
Even here below, but more in heaven above. 257 *No mortal 14
Even on this earth, above the reach of Time! 272 Lady E. B. 14
From the dread chasm, woods climbing above woods, 272 Devil's Bridge 10
The Eagle, he was lord above, 291 Rob Roy 59
Above the tossing surge. 296 Highland Boy 125
The thing which ought to be; is raised *above* 305 *The Voice 10
Or seek, from saints above, miraculous aid— 311 *Who rises 52
Now (for, though Truth descending from above 325 Ode 1814 118
Blest, above measure blest, 329 Ode 1815 125
Shall live enrolled above the starry spheres. 330 Ode: Thanks. 66
Above whose heads the tide so long hath rolled, 333 Fish-women 4
Hovered in air above the far-famed Spot. 334 *A winged 5
" What know we of the Blest above 338 Brientz 1
To chant, as Angels do above, 338 Brientz 16
Clear shines the glorious sun above; 339 *Meek Virgin 39
Each narrowing above each;—the wings, 343 Eclipse 50
Impetuous motion to the Stars above her. 346 Gemmi 8
From sorrow, like the sky above our heads. 353 Aquap. 65
Rapt though He were above the power of sense, 362 *List—'twas 49
Hands clasped above the crucifix he wore 362 *List—'twas 79
And seeking consolation from above; 363 *Grieve for 2
Rapt above earth by power of one fair face, 365 *Rapt above 1
God reigns above, and Spirits strong 370 Eg. Maid 81
And mysteries above her years. 407 White Doe 1032
" But oh! thou Angel from above, 407 White Doe 1044
Above the loftiest ridge or mound 409 White Doe 1165
Raised far above the law of kind; 416 White Doe 1878
Woman! above all women glorified, 434 Ecc. Sonn. 2. 25. 3
Then, like the mountain, thundering from above 439 Ecc. Sonn. 2. 44. 4
(As yours above all offices is high) 444 Ecc. Sonn. 3. 16. 2
Looks on, and Grace descendeth from above 445 Ecc. Sonn. 3. 20. 7
By a bright ladder to the world above. 451 Ecc. Sonn. 3. 42. 10
Warbled, for heaven above and earth below, 457 *Had this 14
Stage above stage) would sit this Island's King, 470 Tynwald 3
Towering above the sea and little ships; 471 Ailsa Crag 7
Above his head uplifted in vain prayer 475 *Here on their 9
Above sea-clouds, the Peaks of Arran rose; 475 *There! said 6
About, below, above, 483 Sister 34
The lark above the hill, 487 Fountain 38
My spirit seems to mount above 498 *The sylvan 22
Lost above all, ye labouring multitude! 505 Warning 112
May He pour round you, from worlds far above 505 Warning 134
Its living roof above our heads. 506 Lab. Hymn 20
Above a world that deems itself most wise 512 *Who rashly 41
Above thy knowledge as they dared to go, 513 Newspaper 13
Above all grandeur, a pure life uncrossed 528 *Those breathing 89
Then, with a blessing granted from above 529 *Those breathing 137
Through its meek influence, from above, 534 *Blest is 93
The cold, cold moon above her head, 537 Goody Blake 101
Above a murmuring brook. 543 Russ. Fug. 120
Above his antlered head; 544 Russ. Fug. 268
And, if she trust the stars above 550 Hermit's Cell 5. 7
For love of God, run fast above thy sphere; 564 Troilus 138
Himself above each lower thought uplifting, 576 Chiabrera 9. 15
These mortal spheres above, 582 Invoc. Earth 31
Above the babe, unseen; 628 Installation 32
When first, above the yells of bigot strife, 629 Installation 101
Above the raven's nest, by knots of grass 637 Prelude 1. 331
Extended high above a dusky grove. 649 Prelude 3. 6
Hast placed me high above my best deserts, 653 Prelude 3. 318
Lifted above the ground by airy fancies, 674 Prelude 5. 567
Above, behind, far stretching and before; 690 Prelude 7. 247
Above the press and danger of the crowd, 697 Prelude 7. 684
Above all height! like an aerial cross 703 Prelude 8. 273
And above all—for this was more than all— 729 Prelude 11. 164
To things above all art; but more,—for this, 736 Prelude 12. 112
On which he dwells, above this frame of things 752 Prelude 14. 450
Brooding above the fierce confederate storm 755 Recluse 1. 1. 831
The shadows of the breezy elms above 762 Excursion 1. 440
Of heath-plant, under and above him strewn, 784 Excursion 2. 819
I stand—the chasm of sky above my head 787 Excursion 3. 94
Above what rules can teach, or fancy feign; 792 Excursion 3. 434
To an Authority enthroned above 794 Excursion 3. 569
Above our human region, or below, 802 Excursion 4. 82
On human nature from above imposed. 803 Excursion 4. 129
And that unless above himself he can 806 Excursion 4. 330
—Jehovah—shapeless Power above all Powers, 811 Excursion 4. 651
Above the summits of the highest hills, 824 Excursion 5. 136
Hovered above our destiny on earth: 826 Excursion 5. 247
Of ancient minster lifted above the cloud 838 Excursion 6. 21
Shedding sweet influence from above; or pure 841 Excursion 6. 187
Above the centre of the Vale, a voice 849 Excursion 6. 762
Above this transitory world, allow 877 Excursion 8. 193
And would preserve as things above all price, 877 Excursion 8. 235
Of increase and the mandate from above 889 Excursion 9. 367
Above the darkened hills stood boldly forth 895 Excursion 9. 764
Thoughts raised above the Earth while here he sits S. 3. 435 *The doubt 140

Above—*continued.*
Of vale below, a height of hills above. K.8. 237 Recluse 1. 1. 21
A task above my skill; the silent mind K.8. 248 Recluse 1. 1. 424
Scrub lives a genuine Marquess above stairs, L. 1. 95 Juvenal 3. 17
Abraham. To Abraham of old. The supper done, 681 Prelude 6. 397
Abraham's. Thou liest in Abraham's bosom all the year; 258 *It is a 12
Abridge. And to abridge my sorrow's violence, 562 Cuck. and Night. 308
Abridged. With love abridged the day; 544 Russ. Fug. 214
By which our toilsome journey was abridged, 680 Prelude 6. 355
And their place knew them not. Meanwhile, abridged 764 Excursion 1. 546
Abroad. And eve's mild hour invites my steps abroad. 3 Ev. Wk. 89
Dissolved the Barons' League, and sent abroad 56 Bord. 1023
Surely some evil Spirit abroad to-night 67 Bord. 1664
The tale was spread abroad; my power at once 69 Bord. 1761
have kept me abroad to-night till this hour? 72 Bord. 1950
Wandering by stealth abroad, he chanced to hear 104 Artegal 107
There's neither horse nor man abroad, 128 Idiot Boy 175
There's not a single soul abroad." 129 Idiot Boy 281
And who is she, betimes abroad, 130 Idiot Boy 409
One summer morning we had walked abroad 147 Joanna 36
When falcons were abroad for prey. 204 Brougham 101
And quickly spread themselves abroad, 398 White Doe 160
Come forth, ye drooping old men, look abroad, 458 *Had this 53
In sleep She sometimes walked abroad, 479 Somnamb. 82
Nor hedge-row screen invites my steps abroad; 521 Epist. Beaumont 13
" Thy name in this large world is spread abroad! 552 Prioress 2
To tell abroad thy mighty worthiness, 553 Prioress 30
Fair Spirits are abroad; in sportive chase 598 Ev. Wk. Quarto 347
Tumbles, the wildering Thunder slips abroad; 605 Desc. Sk. Quarto 204
Had run abroad in wantonness, to sport, 636 Prelude 1. 299
By royal visages. Meanwhile abroad 640 Prelude 1. 535
Of high endeavours, daily spreads abroad 661 Prelude 4. 170
Why, gifted with such powers to send abroad 666 Prelude 5. 48
Was yellowing the hill tops, I went abroad 674 Prelude 5. 560
Abroad, how cheeringly the sunshine lay 682 Prelude 6. 479
That owned him; living cheerfully abroad 688 Prelude 7. 74
And thirst for bloody spoils abroad is paired 714 Prelude 9. 353
That a benignant spirit was abroad 717 Prelude 9. 519
And spread abroad the wings of Liberty, 731 Prelude 11. 253
Abroad on many nations, are no more 733 Prelude 11. 411
They from their native selves can send abroad 747 Prelude 14. 93
His restless mind to look abroad with hope. 761 Excursion 1. 321
In summer, ere the mower was abroad 764 Excursion 1. 525
The shade, and look abroad. On this old bench 769 Excursion 1. 879
With sparing hand. Then trust yourself abroad 819 Excursion 4. 1193
The herds and flocks are yet abroad to crop 823 Excursion 5. 70
The Mother, oft as she was sent abroad, 853 Excursion 6. 984
Wretched at home, he gained no peace abroad; 855 Excursion 6. 1098
Of old Helvellyn spread their arms abroad K.8. 225 *I will 33
Abrogate. Should abrogate his human privilege 123 V. and J. 117
Abrupt. His prey, through tracts abrupt of desolate space, 16 Desc. Sk. 306
Dead pause abrupt of midnight winds, 225 Present. 41
Through all thy most abrupt transitions 300 Bran 32
No more: the end is sudden and abrupt, 394 *No more 1
Abrupt—as without preconceived design 394 *No more 2
From those abrupt and perilous rocks 491 Fidelity 42
For pastime plunge—into the " abrupt abyss," 496 *A little 31
Dismantled, but by violence abrupt— 716 Prelude 9. 469
Supplied a boundary less abrupt and close; 776 Excursion 2. 336
Through what perplexing labyrinths, abrupt 800 Excursion 3. 982
Abruptly. Abruptly spreading to depart, 154 Flower Garden 50
Abruptly paused the strife;—the field throughout 322 Germans 1
Of slow endeavour! or abruptly cast 379 Duddon 15. 10
And thus abruptly spake;—" We yield 405 White Doe 809
Oh! severed, too abruptly, from delights 583 *With copious 26
Thrust out abruptly into Fortune's way 656 Prelude 3. 525
Abruptly into some sequestered nook, 689 Prelude 7. 170
Abruptly, with the view (a sight not rare) 696 Prelude 7. 638
With needful knowledge, had abruptly passed 711 Prelude 9. 93
Abruptly, and indeed before my time: 728 Prelude 11. 78
Said the old man, abruptly breaking silence,— 777 Excursion 2. 383
I was abruptly summoned by the sound 826 Excursion 5. 239
Abruptly broken off. The ruddy boys 883 Excursion 8. 592
Abruptly here, but with a graceful air, 890 Excursion 9. 416
Absence. *See* **Half-absence.**
His absence, he hath sought, whate'er his aim, 37 Bord. 7
Thy absence, till old age and fresh infirmities 41 Bord. 203
I did not think that, during that long absence, 41 Bord. 205
Were with him:—his long absence, cherished hopes, 102 Brothers 422
Absence and death how differ they! and how 118 Maternal Grief 8
Through a long absence, have not been to me 206 Tintern 23
Of absence, these steep woods and lofty cliffs, 207 Tintern 157
Of absence withers what was once so fair? 277 *Why art 3
For a brief absence, proves that love is true; 284 Departure 30
The drooping mind of absence, by vows sworn 383 Duddon 28. 12
Of absence! but they will not stay, 478 Somnamb. 62
Thou strikest—absence perisheth, 583 *O for a 50
Though for brief absence. But farewell! the page 627 *The star 9
After long absence, thither I repaired, 642 Prelude 2. 37
After an eight-days' absence. For (to omit 661 Prelude 4. 196
Restored . me—such absence that she seemed 678 Prelude 6. 202
No absence scarcely can there be, for those 678 Prelude 6. 246
After short absence, curiously I scanned 688 Prelude 7. 94
Absent. His absent Brother still was at his heart. 100 Brothers 348
One rarely absent from thy train 217 Enterprise 135
How slackly for the absent mind permits 509 F. Stone 55

Absent—*continued.*
That absent was, 'gan sing as ye may hear. . . . 564 *Troilus* 119
I found that she was absent. In the shade, . . 767 *Excursion* 1. 711
The spiritual presences of absent things. . . . 819 *Excursion* 4. 1234
Absolute. The extremes of suffering meet in absolute peace. . . . . 76 *Bord.* 2216
Blended in absolute serenity, ... 226 *Vernal Ode* 35
For his field-pastime high and absolute, . . . 313 **Go back* 13
Of a deliverance absolute and pure . . . . 322 **By Moscow* 7
Absolute stillness, poised aloft in air, . . . 390 *Glencroe* 11
The absolute, the world-absorbing One, . . . 392 **Though joy* 7
For thought—dominion vast and absolute . . 489 *Illus. Books* 4
Whose absolute rule permits not to withstand . 518 *Pun. Death* 4. 13
Or see of absolute accomplishment . . . . 636 *Prelude* 1. 263
Not as our glory and our absolute boast, . . . 645 *Prelude* 2. 213
For objects hitherto the absolute wealth . . 662 *Prelude* 4. 234
The absolute presence of reality, ... 690 *Prelude* 7. 233
Love for the human creature's absolute self, . . 701 *Prelude* 8. 123
Hatred of absolute rule, where will of one . . 717 *Prelude* 9. 502
In absolute dominion. Gladly here, . . . 736 *Prelude* 12. 131
Is but another name for absolute power . . 749 *Prelude* 14. 190
Claimed absolute dominion for the day. . . 772 *Excursion* 2. 89
But for its absolute self; a life of peace, . . 791 *Excursion* 3. 38
Faith absolute in God, including hope, . . 801 *Excursion* 4. 22
And, least of all, is absolute despair. . . 803 *Excursion* 4. 164
But is that bounty absolute?—His gifts, . . 817 *Excursion* 4. 1093
Have not been starved by absolute neglect; . . 885 *Excursion* 9. 97
And sway with absolute controul . . . . S. 3. 439 **Avaunt this* 5
The boon is absolute; surpassing grace . . K.8. 239 *Recluse* I. I. 103
Contemplating perfection absolute . . . . K.8. 245 *Recluse* I. I. 307
Absolve. "Ere I absolve thee, stoop! that on thy neck . . . . 428 *Ecc. Sonn.* 1. 38. 3
Absolved. For Justice hath absolved the innocent, . 442 *Ecc. Sonn.* 3. 8. 3
Stands at the Bar, absolved by female eyes . . 442 *Ecc. Sonn.* 3. 11. 6
Though pitied among men, absolved by God, . . 855 *Excursion* 6. 1112
Absorbed. From finite cares, to rest absorbed in Thee! . . . . 454 **The Sun, that* 26
Absorbing. *See* **World-absorbing.**
Absorbs. That absorbs time, space, and number; . 90 *Longest Day* 47
Abstain. abstain from conjecture till you see me. . 76 *Bord.* 2221
Nor doth the general voice abstain from prayer, . 213 *Dion* 39
Abstemiousness. Led in abstemiousness a studious life; . . . . 655 *Prelude* 3. 449
Abstinence. In this cold abstinence from evil deeds, 568 *Cumb. Beg.* 144
Abstract. A slender abstract of the Arabian tales; 672 *Prelude* 5. 462
Against all systems built on abstract rights, . . 695 *Prelude* 7. 524
That promised to abstract the hopes of Man . . 730 *Prelude* 11. 225
But turned to abstract science, and there sought . 732 *Prelude* 11. 328
Which an abstract intelligence supplies; . . . 802 *Excursion* 4. 75
Abstract those gleaming relics, and uplift them, . S. 3. 434 **The doubt* 56
Abstracted. Or Archimedes, pure abstracted soul! . 733 *Prelude* 11. 435
So moulded, joined, abstracted, so endowed . 747 *Prelude* 14. 83
And from the stillness of abstracted thought . . 760 *Excursion* 1. 292
Upstirring but, abstracted by a charm . . S. 3. 435 **The doubt* 99
Abstraction. Of calm abstraction? Can the ruling thought . . . . 508 *F. Stone* 43
Of calm abstraction through the face diffused . 509 *F. Stone* 72
Little, in this abstraction, did I see; . . . 660 *Prelude* 4. 161
The idea, or abstraction of the kind. . . . 706 *Prelude* 8. 502
"From that abstraction I was roused,—and how? 796 *Excursion* 3. 706
All that Abstraction furnished for my needs . 797 *Excursion* 3. 796
In some abstraction;—gracefully he stood, . . 825 *Excursion* 5. 214
Abstractions. Abstractions, and by lifeless fact to fact . . . . 357 *Aquap.* 327
On the relation those abstractions bear . . . 677 *Prelude* 6. 123
Of those abstractions to a mind beset . . . 677 *Prelude* 6. 159
Give us, for our abstractions, solid facts; . . 832 *Excursion* 5. 637
Amid his calm abstractions, would admit . . . 877 *Excursion* 8. 228
Abstruse. Or pains abstruse—to elevate the will, . 315 **Alas! what* 3
Abstruse, nor wanting punctual service high, . . 632 *Prelude* 1. 44
Thy subtle speculations, toils abstruse . . . 679 *Prelude* 6. 297
Toil, say I, for it leads to thoughts bstruse— 715 *Prelude* 9. 397
And from those transports, and these toils abstruse, ... 796 *Excursion* 3. 702
And virtue, difficult, abstruse, and dark; . . . 887 *Excursion* 9. 234
Abstruser. Entering upon abstruser argument, . 736 *Prelude* 12. 132
Abstrusest. Abstrusest matter, reasonings of the mind . . . . 757 *Excursion* 1. 65
Abundance. Abundance; and that, feeling as we do K.8. 254 *Recluse* I. I. 639
Abundant. Abundant recompense. For I have learned . . . . 207 *Tintern* 88
Guide, from thy love's abundant source, . . . 506 *Lab. Hymn* 27
Abundant recompense for every want. . . . 833 *Excursion* 5. 721
Abundant exercise for thought and speech, . . 844 *Excursion* 6. 385
Conscious of that abundant favour showered . . 895 *Excursion* 9. 738
Had ever more abundant cause to speak . . . K.8. 239 *Recluse* I. I. 99
Abuse. *See* **Self-abuse.**
Nay, you abuse my friendship! Heaven forbid!— 42 *Bord.* 271
And shrieks, that revel in abuse . . . . . 232 *Power of Sound* 9
Had filled the astonished world with such abuse . 330 *Ode: Thanks.* 96
Abuse hath cleared from vain imaginings; . . 433 *Ecc. Sonn.* 2. 18. 12
Till the arched roof, with resolute abuse . . 433 *Ecc. Sonn.* 2. 20. 12
His gracious help, or give what we abuse. . . 455 **Not in the lucid* 31
Avaunt this vile abuse of pictured page! . . . 489 *Illus. Books* 12
Then, moved by needless fear of past abuse, . . 520 *Pun. Death* 13. 11
Abused. Is that I have my inner self abused, . . 32 *Guilt* 439
(Abused, betrayed, but how it matters not) . . 76 *Bord.* 2208
As ye were more and more abused: . . . . 175 *Waggoner* 1. 129
When Art's abused inventions were unknown; . 256 *Easter* 12
Which old idolatry abused. . . . . 301 *Bran* 93
Tho' miserably, oft monstrously, abused . . . 429 *Ecc. Sonn.* 2. 2. 13

Abused—*continued.*
From Rite and Ordinance abused they fled . . 443 *Ecc. Sonn.* 3. 14. 1
Abused, as all possessions *are* abused . . . . 792 *Excursion* 3. 435
Used or abused, as selfishness may prompt. . . 886 *Excursion* 9. 119
Of some abused Festivity—so be it. . . . . K.8. 246 *Recluse* I. I. 346
Abysmal. A fixed, abysmal, gloomy, breathing-place— . . . . 747 *Prelude* 14. 58
Abyss. Hang o'er the abyss, whose else impervious gloom . . . . 13 *Desc. Sk.* 164
And yet, in plumbing the abyss for judgment, . 51 *Bord.* 782
In time's abyss, are privileged to endure . . . 152 **Forth from* 21
And sharp, and bright, along the dark abyss . . 184 *Night-piece* 16
What a vast abyss is there! . . . . 217 **Inmate of* 10
Down to the unapproachable abyss, ... 230 *Clouds* 35
Each other in the vast abyss, ... 237 *P. B.* 44
Opening to view the abyss in which she feeds . 313 **Clouds, lingering* 10
Who through the abyss of weakness dive. . . . 330 *Ode: Thanks.* 86
Avoid these sights; nor brood o'er Fable's dark abyss! . . . . 347 *Processions* 72
A comfort in the dark abyss. . . . . . . 402 *White Doe* 537
And when she from the abyss returned . . . 416 *White Doe* 1821
For pastime plunge—into the "abrupt abyss," . 496 **A little* 31
To breathless Nature's dark abyss; . . . . 581 **Loud is* 18
Be chained for ever to the black abyss! . . . 582 *Invoc. Earth* 32
Bend o'er th' abyss?—the else impervious gloom 605 *Desc. Sk. Quarto* 186
In trepidation, from the blank abyss . . . . 682 *Prelude* 6. 470
That awful Power rose from the mind's abyss . 684 *Prelude* 6. 594
On towns and cities, wallowing in the abyss . . 724 *Prelude* 10. 442
To illuminate the abyss of ages past, . . . 735 *Prelude* 12. 63
Over the dark abyss, intent to hear . . . 747 *Prelude* 14. 72
Of that profound abyss a solemn voice, . . . 777 *Excursion* 2. 373
Or to pass through; but rather an abyss . . 787 *Excursion* 3. 97
Not less than that huge Pile (from some abyss . 788 *Excursion* 3. 143
That one, poor, finite object, in the abyss . . 816 *Excursion* 4. 993
To expire; yet from the abyss is caught again, . 819 *Excursion* 4. 1186
Majestic circuit, beautiful abyss, ... 822 *Excursion* 5. 9
Of earth, the great abyss, and be no more; . . 868 *Excursion* 7. 712
With correspondent wings the abyss of air. . . 891 *Excursion* 9. 494
Abysses. As, through the abysses of a joyless heart, 213 *Dion* 61
Abodes of Naiads, calm abysses pure, ... 379 *Duddon* 12. 6
Her Son in Wharf's abysses drowned, ... 398 *White Doe* 229
Abyssinian. Poured from his fount of Abyssinian clouds . . . . 684 *Prelude* 6. 615
Of Abyssinian privacy. I spake . . . . . 685 *Prelude* 6. 662
Acacia. The embowering rose, the acacia, and the pine, ... 546 **The embowering* 1
Academe. Fell round him in the grove of Academe, 212 *Dion* 10
Academic. By frame of Academic discipline . . 656 *Prelude* 3. 536
Internally from academic cares; . . . . . 675 *Prelude* 6. 26
Ceased, had I left those academic bowers . . . 679 *Prelude* 6. 277
An Idler among academic bowers, ... 706 *Prelude* 8. 503
Derived from academic institutes . . . . . 713 *Prelude* 9. 224
Oh, sweet it is, in academic groves, . . . 715 *Prelude* 9. 390
From academic groves, that have for thee . . 787 *Excursion* 3. 105
From academic bowers. He loved the spot— . . 824 *Excursion* 5. 115
Academus'. Emerging slow from Academus' grove 618 *School Ex.* 13
Accent. And shrill and fierce in accent!—Fear it not: . . . . 333 *Fish-women* 9
Accents. Those accents were his last. . . . . 155 *Waterfall* 56
Assumes the accents of our native tongue; . . 435 *Ecc. Sonn.* 2. 29. 3
His voice shall chant, in accents clear, . . . 507 **While from* 61
Through all my frame the pleasing accents ran. . 618 *School Ex.* 28
In slender accents of sweet verse, some tale . . 668 *Prelude* 5. 179
Had caught the accents of my native speech . . 721 *Prelude* 10. 240
Do I declare—in accents which, from truth . . 748 *Prelude* 14. 144
Accept. Lies on your way; accept us as your Guides. . . . . 43 *Bord.* 357
Accept, O Friend, for praise or blame, . . . 182 *Waggoner* 4. 197
Accept the gift, behold him face to face!" . . 209 *Laod.* 24
Accept, mute Captives! thanks and praise; . . 527 **The soaring* 53
Deign, Sovereign Mistress! to accept a lay, . . 628 **Deign, Sovereign* 1
The high and tender Muses shall accept . . . 757 *Excursion* 1. 105
Nor for their bodies would accept release; . . 839 *Excursion* 6. 68
That, from his dying hand, she would accept . . 841 *Excursion* 6. 203
And patient listening, thanks accept from me. . 874 *Excursion* 8. 9.
The radiant Cherubim;—accept the thanks . . 893 *Excursion* 9. 622
Acceptable. Night is than day more acceptable; sleep . . . . 790 *Excursion* 3. 277
Some acceptable lesson to their minds . . . . 820 *Excursion* 4. 1237
Acceptance. Stretched out for my acceptance,—but Death came. . . . . 574 *Chiabrera* 3. 16
Acceptation. Like acceptation from the World will find. . . . . 314 **I dropped* 8
Accepted. Accepted of the offer. . . . . . . 620 *Birth of Love* 37
Our prayers have been accepted; thou wilt stand . . . . 734 *Prelude* 11. 453
Accepts. Accepts from your bold hands the proffered crown . . . . 477 *Steamboats* 13
And he accepts the punctual hymn . . . . 506 *Lab. Hymn* 3
Thee she accepts as for her service fit! . . . 562 *Cuck. and Night.* 301
Access. When every hour brings palpable access . 646 *Prelude* 2. 286
Find easier access to the pious mind, ... 648 *Prelude* 2. 420
In such access of mind, in such high hour . . . 759 *Excursion* 1. 211
Without access of unexpected strength. . . . 804 *Excursion* 4. 221
The colours of the sun. Access for you . . . 818 *Excursion* 4. 1126
Was no access for wain, heavy or light. . . . 858 *Excursion* 7. 62
Accident. The moving accident is not my trade; . 202 *Hart-leap* 97
'Mid direst shocks of mortal accident— . . . 326 **Intrepid sons* 11
A marvellous study of wild accident; . . . . 428 *Ecc. Sonn.* 1. 37. 3
The hour of accident or crippling age, ... 764 *Excursion* 1. 555
Of accident. But when the rising sun . . . 772 *Excursion* 2. 85

Accident—*continued.*
Sickness, or accident, or grief, or pain. . . . 777 *Excursion* 2. 369
Security from shock of accident, ... 791 *Excursion* 3. 363
To the blind walk of mortal accident; . . . . 812 *Excursion* 4. 758
Of sickness, accident, and helpless age. . . . 834 *Excursion* 5. 811
Of strange or tragic accident, hath helped . . 858 *Excursion* 7. 40
Passing, as accident or fancy led, ... 882 *Excursion* 8. 523
Accidental. Is not an accidental quality, . . . 57 *Bord.* 1074
Occasional, an accidental grace, ... 704 *Prelude* 8. 355
Accidents. For accidents and changes such as these, 97 *Brothers* 146
Through accidents of peace or war, ... 181 *Waggoner* 4. 110
All accidents of time and place; . . . . . 224 *'*Tis gone* 56
By chance collisions and quaint accidents . . . 641 *Prelude* 1. 589
All accidents, and to the very road . . . . 671 *Prelude* 5. 356
By change of accidents, or even, to speak . . 677 *Prelude* 6. 186
And accidents as children do with cards, . . . 679 *Prelude* 6. 290
And all the accidents of life were pressed . . . 723 *Prelude* 10. 349
From Nature's way by outward accidents, . . 731 *Prelude* 11. 291
Revolving with the accidents of life, . . . 748 *Prelude* 14. 148
All accidents, converting them to good. . . . 801 *Excursion* 4. 17
All accidents, and judges were of all. . . . 812 *Excursion* 4. 717
And local accidents, shall tend alike . . . . 820 *Excursion* 4. 1241
Subject, you deem, to vital accidents; . . . 831 *Excursion* 5. 566
Acclaim. The people answered with a loud acclaim: 105 *Artegal* 226
The sight was hailed with loud acclaim . . . 400 *White Doe* 415
Acclamation. Glad acclamation by which the air was rent! . . . . 312 **A Roman* 6
And acclamation, crowds in open air . . . 797 *Excursion* 3. 750
Accompanied. Accompanied his steps, by anxious love . . . . 125 *V. and J.* 250
I, who accompanied with faithful pace . . . 418 *Ecc. Sonn.* 1. 1. 1
And open day; accompanied its course . . . 749 *Prelude* 14. 197
Accompanied by feelings of delight . . . . 755 *Recluse* 1. 1. 757
Accompanied those strains of apt discourse, . . 772 *Excursion* 2. 38
Accompanied these musings; fervent thanks . . 823 *Excursion* 5. 50
Softly accompanied the tuneful harp, ... 843 *Excursion* 6. 337
Accompanied, still extant, in a wreath . . . 872 *Excursion* 7. 972
The stately fence accompanied our steps; . . . 881 *Excursion* 8. 454
Accompanies. The wanderer accompanies her flight . . . . 819 *Excursion* 4. 1183
Accompany. To accompany the verse? The mountain blast . . . . 230 *Clouds* 61
Accomplish. To accomplish there her loveliness: . 344 **How blest* 23
And, with life, power to accomplish aught of worth, ... 751 *Prelude* 14. 389
Accomplish:—this is our high argument. . . . 755 *Recluse* 1. 1. 824
(And Heaven was pleased to accomplish the desire) . . . . 845 *Excursion* 6. 501
—Accomplish, then, their number; and conclude 893 *Excursion* 9. 634
Accomplished. Accomplished under friendly shade of night. . . . . 123 *V. and J.* 86
A work accomplished by the brotherhood . . . 147 *Joanna* 69
Accomplished in the showman's part; . . . . 178 *Waggoner* 2. 126
That Man may be accomplished for a task . . 311 **Who rises* 53
His task accomplished to his mind, ... 543 *Russ. Fug.* 121
Accomplished, giving thus unto events . . . 711 *Prelude* 9. 104
Accomplished; minds whose faculties are then . 743 *Prelude* 13. 258
By some accomplished Master, while he sate . . 857 *Excursion* 7. 12
Fulfilled, the hope accomplished; and thy praise 894 *Excursion* 9. 677
Camoëns, he the accomplished and the good, . . S. 3. 442 **Vasco, whose* 9
Accomplishes. Labour accomplishes, or patience bears— . . . . 363 **The world forsaken* 5
Accomplishment. Or see of absolute accomplishment 636 *Prelude* 1. 263
Yet wanting the accomplishment of verse, . . 757 *Excursion* 1. 80
Accomplishments. Those rare accomplishments, and varied powers, ... 583 **With copious* 15
Accord. Who, in the open air, with due accord . 95 *Brothers* 24
Do with the service of this Day accord. . . . 329 *Ode: Thanks.* 26
Then well may their accord be true, ... 415 *White Doe* 1728
Cathedral pomp and grace, in apt accord . . . 477 **Lowther! in* 2
That, with a perfect will in one accord . . . 500 *Humanity* 37
Whose offering gladly would accord . . . . 534 **Blest is* 89
Failing, we finally shall make accord. . . . 562 *Cuck.andNight.*280
With one accord our voices raise, ... 578 **I come* 50
Long months of peace (if such bold word accord . 632 *Prelude* 1. 24
Your beauty with me, a serene accord . . . . 685 *Prelude* 6. 678
Of thanks and expectation, in accord . . . . 797 *Excursion* 3. 755
Our inquest turns.—Accord, good Sir! the light 829 *Excursion* 5. 481
As with her office would but ill accord) . . . 853 *Excursion* 6. 959
A happy consummation! an accord . . . . 861 *Excursion* 7. 255
Accordance. Your praise in meet accordance with your claims . . . . 352 *Aquap.* 5
Touched by accordance of thy placid cheer, . . 460 **Wanderer! that* 56
Accordant. —Now o'er the soothed accordant heart we feel . . . . 8 *Ev. Wk.* 315
Sight that inspired accordant thoughts; and speech I thus renewed: . . . . . . 92 *Poet's Dream* 48
With accordant steps, or gathering . . . . . 141 *Arm. Lady* 93
And singing, while the accordant hand . . . 234 *Power of Sound* 140
Accordant to the measure. . . . . 302 *Yarrow V.* 80
Accordant meditations, which in times . . . 358 *Aquap.* 364
Gives to that rapture an accordant Rhyme. . . 426 *Ecc. Sonn.* 1. 30. 11
Sung to the Virgin while accordant oars . . . 454 *Sea-side* 25
Accordant to the sweet Birds' harmony; . . . 558 *Cuck. and Night.* 83
But o'er the sooth'd accordant heart we feel . . 599 *Ev. Wk. Quarto* 381
Accordant to the cheek's unquiet glow; . . . 604 *Desc. Sk. Quarto* 153
A kindling eye:—accordant feelings rushed . . 808 *Excursion* 4. 506
Feelings with these accordant; love, esteem, . . 848 *Excursion* 6. 648
Was cleared, I dipped, with arms accordant, oars 891 *Excursion* 9. 489
Accorded. To you accorded, never be withdrawn, 143 **High bliss* 7
To saints accorded in their mortal hour. . . . 272 **Where holy* 14

Accorded—*continued.*
Up to the measure of accorded might, ... 311 **Who rises* 44
False tints too well accorded with the glare . . 692 *Prelude* 7. 345
Accorded little with his present mind; . . . . 791 *Excursion* 3. 358
According. Yet seek thy firm support, according to their need. . . . . 492 *Duty* 24
Still act according to the voice . . . . . . 492 *Duty*
From word to word according to the note: . . . 554 *Prioress* 96
Redeemed, according to example given . . . 721 *Prelude* 10. 220
That are not prized according to their worth. . 792 *Excursion* 3. 436
But ill according. An heraldic shield, ... 824 *Excursion* 5. 160
Accordingly. Knowledge was given accordingly; my trust . . . . 740 *Prelude* 13. 55
Accordingly he by degrees perceives . . . . 819 *Excursion* 4. 1218
Accords. And with that voice accords the soothing sound . . . . 16 *Desc. Sk.* 356
With Him who made the Work that Work accords . . . . 365 **Rapt above* 5
That which is done accords with what is known . 826 *Excursion* 5. 256
Accords with nature's language;—the soft voice . 846 *Excursion* 6. 524
Accost. He took his way, impatient to accost . . 95 *Brothers* 36
Came up the hollow:—him did I accost . . . 202 *Hart-leap* 119
Accosted. Nor, if accosted now, in thought engrossed, ... 26 *Guilt* 97
A blind old Greybeard and accosted him, . . . 45 *Bord.* 447
Was thus accosted by the Dame: . . . . . 371 *Eg. Maid* 167
Account. And, finding that he can account . . 245 *P. B.* 802
Numbers exceeding credible account . . . . 347 *Processions* 51
Who shall complain, or call thee to account? . . 455 *Rydal Mere* 36
High as the Sun, that he could take account . . 511 **So fair* 8
Oh! much have they to account for, who could tear, ... 722 *Prelude* 10. 300
Accoutred. He, on his part, accoutred for the worst, 715 *Prelude* 9. 423
Accoutred with his burthen and his staff; . . 772 *Excursion* 2. 26
Of prophecy, accoutred to fulfil . . . . . . S. 3. 437 **The doubt* 192
Accoutrement. Motley accoutrement, of power to smile . . . . 185 *Nutting* 12
Accumulated. Accumulated feelings pressed his heart . . . . 760 *Excursion* 1. 281
Than that accumulated store of gold . . . . 809 *Excursion* 4. 567
Languished beneath accumulated years, . . . 871 *Excursion* 7. 937
Accursed. His banner in accursed league with France, ... 313 *Prophecy* 13
That an accursed thing it is to gaze . . . . 321 **Here pause* 8
In hideous usages, and rights accursed, . . . 378 *Duddon* 8. 7
The blood cries out on your accursèd deed. . . 554 *Prioress* 127
And him among the accursèd Jews she sought. . 555 *Prioress* 148
Accurst. A mortal malady. I am accurst: . . 76 *Bord.* 2204
Into main Ocean they, this deed accurst . . . 433 *Ecc. Sonn.* 2. 17. 11
Accusation. Should cease; and open accusation lead . . . . 717 *Prelude* 9. 537
Accusations. Disclose, had accusations to prefer . 798 *Excursion* 3. 860
Accuse. "I, Robespierre, accuse thee!" Well is known . . . . 720 *Prelude* 10. 113
Probed, vexed, and criticised?—Accuse me not . 816 *Excursion* 4. 978
Accused. *See* **Self-accused.**
At which I half accused the God in Heaven.— . 45 *Bord.* 427
Appeal was made to the great Judge: the Accused . . . . 62 *Bord.* 1384
What though the Accused, upon his own appeal . 500 *Humanity* 1
Accuses. And then betrays; accuses and inflicts . 827 *Excursion* 5. 326
Accustomed. Ere, from accustomed paths, familiar fields, ... 353 *Aquap.* 33
Wanting accustomed food, must pass from earth, . 531 *Octogen.* 4
With the accustomed garb of daily life) . . . 653 *Prelude* 3. 271
In my accustomed bed, more welcome now . . 659 *Prelude* 4. 82
On his accustomed journey. The delight, . . 687 *Prelude* 7. 26
With my accustomed load; in heat and cold, . . 766 *Excursion* 1. 698
Of one accustomed to desires that feed . . . 820 *Excursion* 4. 1290
Not long accustomed to this breathing world; . 826 *Excursion* 5. 262
Detains him after his accustomed hour . . . 834 *Excursion* 5. 765
All her accustomed offices and cares . . . . S. 3. 437 **The doubt* 187
Ace. Roared in the tempest, was within an ace . 50 *Bord.* 736
The paramount ace, a moon in her eclipse, . . 640 *Prelude* 1. 532
Achates. Achates, with the gifts to Carthage hied; 624 *Æneid* 54
Ache. When my heart does not ache to think of it!— . . . . 57 *Bord.* 1098
With agony his eye-balls ache . . . . . . 247 *P. B.* 933
And made her poor old bones to ache, ... 537 *Goody Blake* 58
Ached. Now I could laugh till my ribs ached. Oh, Fool! . . . . 59 *Bord.* 1218
And clasped her to my heart, my heart that ached 62 *Bord.* 1361
Till my ribs ached I'd laugh at you! . . . . 236 *P. B.* 20
That any heart had ached to hear her, begged . 769 *Excursion* 1. 866
Aches. *See* **Heart-aches.**
Sore aches she needs must have! but less . . 194 *Ruth* 232
And with an infinite pain the spirit aches, . . 330 *Ode: Thanks.* 102
Achieve. Had power as lofty actions to achieve . 325 *Ode 1814* 140
Content to observe, to achieve, and to enjoy. . 676 *Prelude* 6. 65
To achieve its higher triumph. Not unfelt . . 695 *Prelude* 7. 545
The worst that human reasoning can achieve, . 804 *Excursion* 4. 198
Such triumph over sin and guilt achieve? . . 894 *Excursion* 9. 674
Achieved. Achieved their separation: and once more . . . . 124 *V. and J.* 173
And perfect harmony of notes, achieved . . . 261 **I heard* (*alas* 6
Achieved, this closing deed magnificent, . . . 327 *Ode 1815* 6
"Thou hast achieved, fair Dame! what none . . 371 *Eg. Maid* 153
The day when he achieved that matchless feat, . 373 *Eg. Maid* 315
(So might they dream) till victory was achieved, . 423 *Ecc. Sonn.* 1. 17. 7
Wrought in men's minds, like miracles achieved; 466 *St. Bees* 47
Doth melt away; but for those palms achieved . 665 *Prelude* 5. 8

Achieved—*continued.*
Of conquest over sense, hourly achieved . . . 682 *Prelude* 6. 458
In sign of conquest by his wit achieved . . . 816 *Excursion* 4. 999
One who achieved a humbler victory, ... 841 *Excursion* 6. 213
Achievement. Seeking less bold achievement, where he will ! . . . . 377 *Duddon* 4. 14
Achievements. Those high achievements ; even as she arrayed . . . . 324 *Ode 1814* 96
Achieves. Walks, and achieves his wonders, from the eye . . . . 691 *Prelude* 7. 282
Achilles. How looked Achilles—their dread paramount— . . . . 625 *Æneid* 138
Where Achilles swift of feet . . . . S. 3. 442 *Harmodius* 13
Achilles—but, O Queen, the whole relate. . . . L. 2. 123 *Frag. Æneid* 3. 4

Aching. 'Tis a strange aching that, when we would curse . . . . 70 *Bord.* 1845
And all its aching joys are now no more, . . . 206 *Tintern* 84
Assiduously—to soothe her aching breast ; . . 255 **Grief, thou* 12
And though an aching and a barren sense . . 658 *Prelude* 3. 624
Mirth that to aching ribs will not submit . . . L. 1. 95 *Juvenal* 3. 19
Acidalian. His Acidalian mother, by degrees . 625 *Æneid* 90
Acknowledge. So seemed it,—now I thankfully acknowledge, ... 721 *Prelude* 10. 223
Acknowledge when thus moved, which Nature thus . . . . 747 *Prelude* 14. 87
Acknowledge, then, that whether by the side . . 813 *Excursion* 4. 826
And did acknowledge, wheresoe'er they moved, . 815 *Excursion* 4. 926
Acknowledge that to Nature's humbler power . 819 *Excursion* 4. 1190
Acknowledge reason's law ? A living power . . 829 *Excursion* 5. 471
The sacred truth to acknowledge, linger still ; . 894 *Excursion* 9. 654
Acknowledged. *See* **World-acknowledged.**
And cease the acknowledged purpose to withstand ; . . . . 22 *Desc. Sk.* 662
With thy acknowledged glories ;—No ! . . . . 167 *Pilgrim's Dream* 44
By a continuous and acknowledged tie . . . 394 **No more* 5
Who cast not off the acknowledged guide, . . 473 *Ossian* 55
When all the world acknowledged elfin sway ? . 529 *Poor Robin* 19
He was acknowledged : and the blast, . . . 535 *Egremont* 15
And written lore, acknowledged my liege lord, . 654 *Prelude* 3. 376
And, to acknowledged law rebellious, still, . . 732 *Prelude* 11. 318
For calm subjection to acknowledged law ; . . 790 *Excursion* 3. 268
Which all acknowledged. The dark winter night, 864 *Excursion* 7. 448
And so acknowledged with a tremulous joy . . 867 *Excursion* 7. 640
That shall be like the acknowledged voice of life, K. 8. 247 *Recluse* 1. 1. 403
Acknowledges. Acknowledges God's grace, his mercy feels, ... 586 *Ch. Lamb* 119
Acknowledging. Acknowledging no task-master, at will . . . . 366 *Lombardy* 5
Acknowledging a grace in this, ... 402 *White Doe* 536
God's glory ; and acknowledging thy share . . 461 **Queen of* 43
Acknowledging dependency sublime. . . . . 706 *Prelude* 8. 494
Their rights acknowledging he felt for all. . . 772 *Excursion* 2. 47
Acknowledging, and grievous self-reproach, . . 804 *Excursion* 4. 200
Acknowledgment. And glad acknowledgment, of lawful sway. . . . . 383 *Duddon* 29. 14
By some acknowledgment of thanks and praise, . 454 *Sea-side* 23
Strains followed of acknowledgment addressed . 794 *Excursion* 3. 568
As a brute mean, without acknowledgment . . 886 *Excursion* 9. 117
With zeal, acknowledgment that with the gift . K. 8. 255 *Recluse* 1. 1. 671
Acknowledgments. Acknowledgments of gratitude sincere . . . . 823 *Excursion* 5. 49
To those acknowledgments subscribed his own, . 874 *Excursion* 8. 2
Acorn. Now here, now there, an acorn, from its cup 633 *Prelude* 1. 83
Acquaintance. *See* **Chance-acquaintance.**
The one that held acquaintance with the stars, . 667 *Prelude* 5. 103
Through his acquaintance with the ways of truth, 823 *Excursion* 5. 42
Or wraps an old acquaintance up in clay, . . . 826 *Excursion* 5. 236
Acquaintance as they sweep from cloud to cloud. K. 8. 250 *Recluse* 1. 1. 520
Acquaintances. Some friends I had, acquaintances who there . . . . 649 *Prelude* 3. 19
Friendships, acquaintances, were welcome all. . 652 *Prelude* 3. 247
Acquaintances of every little child, ... 662 *Prelude* 4. 246
Acquainted. Now first acquainted with distress and grief, ... 118 *Maternal Grief* 50
Make thy young thoughts acquainted with the grave ; . . . . 465 **Thou look'st* 10
Acquiescence. That lives but in the torpid acquiescence . . . . 64 *Bord.* 1489
Such acquiescence neither doth imply, ... 790 *Excursion* 3. 264
By acquiescence in the Will supreme . . . . 801 *Excursion* 4. 20
Acquiescences. Not only acquiescences of faith . 724 *Prelude* 10. 456
Acquire. It was denied them to acquire, through lack . . . . 757 *Excursion* 1. 82
Like this our honoured Friend ; and thence acquire . . . . 828 *Excursion* 5. 387
By your authority. But how acquire . . . . 831 *Excursion* 5. 571
Acquired. Acquired by traffic 'mid the Indian Isles, 96 *Brothers* 67
Given or acquired, to raise us from the mire, . . 358 *Aquap.* 346
Intensely brooded, even till they acquired . . 758 *Excursion* 1. 147
And whence they flowed ; and from them he acquired . . . . 759 *Excursion* 1. 238
By sounding titles, hath acquired the name . . 788 *Excursion* 3. 130
To what an alien spirit had acquired . . . . 795 *Excursion* 3. 625
Acquisition. By acquisition of sincere delight, . . 892 *Excursion* 9. 524
Acquisitions. This, of all acquisitions, first awaits 698 *Prelude* 7. 737
Acre. Pray tell me what this land is worth by the acre. . . . . 60 *Bord.* 1278
Or reap an acre of his neighbour's corn. . . . 95 *Brothers* 10
Acre's. To see an acre's breadth of that wide cliff . 97 *Brothers* 150
Acres. Strews twenty acres of good meadow-ground 60 *Bord.* 1230

Acrid. These natural council-seats your acrid blood 268 **Dogmatic Teachers* 6
Across. *See* **'Cross.**
Across the gloomy valley flings her light, . . . 8 *Ev. Wk.* 335
Sound of closed gate, across the water borne, . . 9 *Ev. Wk.* 373
Of Deep that calls to Deep across the hills, . . 16 *Desc. Sk.* 355
Across the pebbly road a little runnel strayed. . 34 *Guilt* 540
One happy thought has passed across my mind. . 61 *Bord.* 1326
With staff in hand across the cleft . . . . . 85 *Shepherd-boys* 56
Pine not like them with arms across, ... 109 **Ere with* 9
And one across the bosom lies— . . . . . 112 **How rich* 15
I'll follow you across the snow ; . . . . . 114 *Ind. Wom.* 51
" Across the waters I am come, ... 120 *Emigrant Mother* 25
While across her virgin cheek pure blushes strayed, ... 141 *Arm. Lady* 137
Across the wave, a Rover brave . . . . . 161 *Binnorie* 14
Across the welkin seemed to spread . . . . 167 *Pilgrim's Dream* 50
That he was lame) across the floor— . . . . 177 *Waggoner* 2. 104
Across yon meadowy bottom look, ... 180 *Waggoner* 4. 40
That wild with glee across the lawn . . . . 187 **Three years* 14
They dart across my path—but lo, ... 191 *Beggars* 37
With him to sail across the sea, ... 193 *Ruth* 101
To Time's first step across the bound . . . . 223 *Wishing-gate* 68
Across the deep and quiet spot . . . . . . 240 *P. B.* 381
Across a shady lane ; his chest . . . . . . 247 *P. B.* 983
Across the harp, with soul-engrossing speed ; . . 274 **Wait, prithee* 4
Across the setting sun and all the fiery west. . 311 **Who rises* 29
Across her burning breast, ... 327 *Ode 1815* 26
Across thy long deep Valley, furious Rhone ! . . 350 *Des. Stanzas* 29
Ploughs her bold course across the wondering seas ; 432 *Ecc. Sonn.* 2. 15. 11
Shall bound across The Strid ? . . . . . . 494 *Force of Prayer* 28
Across the slender wrist of the left arm . . . 509 *F. Stone* 53
Across the marsh, the game in view, ... 544 *Russ. Fug.* 273
The massy Ways, carried across these heights . 549 **The massy* 1
Had placed his staff across the broad smooth stone 566 *Cumb. Beg.* 7
Small cottage lights across the water stream, . . 598 *Ev. Wk. Quarto* 374
Went single in his ministry across . . . . . 635 *Prelude* 1. 209
To cut across the reflex of a star . . . . . 638 *Prelude* 1. 450
Ships he can guide across the pathless sea, . . 670 *Prelude* 5. 316
Across the watery vale, and shout again, . . . 671 *Prelude* 5. 375
With shield and stone-axe, stride across the wold ; 744 *Prelude* 13. 323
Across a bare wide Common I was toiling . . . 756 *Excursion* 1. 21
Across the lawn and through the darksome grove, 814 *Excursion* 4. 866
Fetched by a neighbouring brook.—Across the vale 881 *Excursion* 8. 453
Of the still evening. Right across the lake . . 892 *Excursion* 9. 560
Act. For act and suffering, to the city straight . 36 *Guilt* 650
Which with the motion of a virtuous act . . . 40 *Bord.* 170
A thing worth further notice, we must act . . 42 *Bord.* 292
Stoop for a moment ; 'tis an act of justice ; . . 48 *Bord.* 638
Are hushed to sleep, by your own act and deed, . 55 *Bord.* 956
To abide the issue of my act, alone. . . . . 65 *Bord.* 1519
Act of soul-devoted homage, ... 142 *Arm. Lady* 141
" Stranger, 'tis no act of courage . . . . . 163 *Hint* 17
In act embodied, my deliverance wrought. . . 211 *Laod.* 138
These moralists could act and comprehend : . . 307 **Great men* 5
Gave specious colouring to aim and act, . . . 313 **Go back* 10
Checked in the very act and deed of blood, . . 322 *Germans* 3
To act the God among external things, . . . 347 *Processions* 66
Drawn to his side by look or act of love . . . 362 **List—'twas* 58
To live, and act, and serve the future hour ; . . 384 *Duddon* 34. 11
The act were justified to-day." . . . . . . 401 *White Doe* 451
Merciless act of sorrow infinite ! . . . . . 439 *Ecc. Sonn.* 2. 42. 11
Still act according to the voice . . . . . 492 *Duty*
And what in quality or act is best . . . . . 493 *Hap. War.* 31
We act as if we joyed in the sad tune . . . . 505 *Warning* 144
And some, we know, when they by wilful act . . 517 *Pun. Death* 3. 9
He feels how far the act would derogate . . . 518 *Pun. Death* 5. 10
In act, as hovering Angels when they spread . . 518 *Pun. Death* 6. 4
To every act, word, thought, and look of love, . 529 **Those breathing* 138
A single Act endears to high and low . . . . 540 *Grace Darl.* 8
Upon the act a blessing I implore, ... 582 *Invoc. Earth* 24
Pushed from the shore. It was an act of stealth 637 *Prelude* 1. 361
Such was the tenour of the second act . . . . 652 *Prelude* 3. 256
To manage books, and things, and make them act 671 *Prelude* 5. 351
Save when realities of act and mien, ... 694 *Prelude* 7. 477
But for her guidance—one who was to *act*, . . 707 *Prelude* 8. 522
In anything, save only as the act . . . . . 711 *Prelude* 9. 138
Acted, or seemed at least to act, like men . . 728 *Prelude* 11. 63
As selfish passion urged, would act amiss ; . . 732 *Prelude* 11. 319
Of act and circumstance, and visible form, . . 744 *Prelude* 13. 288
Her body was subdued. In every act . . . . 768 *Excursion* 1. 795
All act of inquisition whence we rise, ... 789 *Excursion* 3. 235
The test of act and suffering, to provoke . . . 792 *Excursion* 3. 418
And, therefore, not to act—convinced that all 799 *Excursion* 3. 893
Whether to act, judge, suffer, or enjoy. . . . 799 *Excursion* 3. 924
They act, or they recede, observe, and feel ; . . 806 *Excursion* 4. 323
And courteously, as if the act removed, . . . 816 *Excursion* 4. 1012
' This single act is all that we demand.' . . . 817 *Excursion* 4. 1082
And act in that obedience, he shall gain . . . 830 *Excursion* 5. 519
By act of naked reason. Moral truth . . . . 831 *Excursion* 5. 562
Announced, as a preparatory act . . . . . 839 *Excursion* 6. 89
That in the act of preference he had been . . . 840 *Excursion* 6. 135
Ye wished for act and circumstance, that make . 874 *Excursion* 8. 17
The happy Island where ye think and act ; . . 890 *Excursion* 9. 412
An act of courage, and the thing itself . . . . K. 8. 238 *Recluse* 1. 1. 61
Sometimes in act, and evermore in thought. . . K. 8. 256 *Recluse* 1. 1. 714
Acted. Acted, or seemed at least to act, like men . 728 *Prelude* 11. 63
Have acted, suffered, travelled far, observed . . 809 *Excursion* 4. 563
Acting. Acting, in furtherance of the Father's will, 123 *V. and J.* 128
Rebellious, acting in a devious mood ; . . . . 647 *Prelude* 2. 364

Acting—*continued*.
Never forsaken, that, by acting well, . . . 707 *Prelude* 8. 527
These, if these only, acting in despite . . . 828 *Excursion* 5. 419

Action. Action is transitory—a step, a blow, . . 65 *Bord.* 1539
I saw that every possible shape of action . 69 *Bord.* 1780
From action up to action with a mind . . 69 *Bord.* 1789
This action ? Innocent !—oh breaking heart !— 71 *Bord.* 1880
That strenuous action follow both, . . . 224 *'Tis gone 52
Yet, with deliberate action slow, . . . 241 *P. B.* 422
With action, were as nothing, patriot Friend ! 261 *Retirement* 3
For action born, existing to be tried, . . 361 *For action 1
Of virtuous action ; all that courage dares, . 363 *The world forsaken 4

Had mortal action e'er a nobler scope ? . . 442 *Ecc. Sonn.* 3. 9. 9
All principles of action that transcend . . . 514 *Portentous change 13

That by the regular action of the world . . 647 *Prelude* 2. 361
And busy with an action far advanced. . . 711 *Prelude* 9. 95
In action, give it outwardly a shape, . . . 715 *Prelude* 9. 402
Of action from without and from within ; . . 745 *Prelude* 13. 376
Of civil action, yielded to a power . . . 798 *Excursion* 3. 825
Which bears the name of action, howsoe'er . 799 *Excursion* 3. 894
Is meditated action ; robbed of this . . . 884 *Excursion* 9. 21
Of life, and hope, and action. And 'tis known 886 *Excursion* 9. 128

Actions. Of actions, and their laws and tendencies. 60 *Bord.* 1227
Great actions move our admiration, chiefly . 65 *Bord.* 1536
Had power as lofty actions to achieve . . 325 *Ode 1814* 140
His actions witness, venerate his mien, . . 368 *Trajan* 27
Symbols or actions. but of my own heart . 651 *Prelude* 3. 175
Of Fairy, or some dream of actions wrought . 714 *Prelude* 9. 301
Unhallowed actions—planted like a crown . 775 *Excursion* 2. 269
With empty actions and vain passions stuffed, . 835 *Excursion* 5. 851
Kind wishes, and good actions, and pure thoughts. 887 *Excursion* 9. 242

Active. The bending body of my active sire ; . 28 *Guilt* 218
As active round the hollow dome, . . . 300 *Bran* 18
If e'er, on wings which active fancy gave, . 630 [?] *O Moon 5
Of active days urged on by flying hours,— . 632 *Prelude* 1. 42
An inmate of this active universe . . . 646 *Prelude* 2. 254
More active even than " best society "— . . 646 *Prelude* 2. 295
Her frenzy only active to extol . . . 723 *Prelude* 10. 353
An active partisan, I thus convoked . . . 729 *Prelude* 11. 153
Most active when they are most eloquent, . 743 *Prelude* 13. 259
An active power to fasten images . . . 758 *Excursion* 1. 145
As makes the nations groan. This active course 761 *Excursion* 1. 381
Active and nervous was his gait ; his limbs . 762 *Excursion* 1. 424
With such an active countenance, an eye . 765 *Excursion* 1. 616
Of a quick fancy and an active heart, . . 810 *Excursion* 4. 583
To steal from active duties, and embrace . . 822 *Excursion* 5. 27
Meek to admit ; the active energy, . . . 831 *Excursion* 5. 574
Too little checked. An active, ardent mind ; . 859 *Excursion* 7. 116
" An *active* Principle :—howe'er removed . . 884 *Excursion* 9. 3
Our active powers, those powers themselves become . 886 *Excursion* 9. 131
Active as lambs, and overcome with joy. . . K.8. 251 *Recluse* 1.1.549

Activities. And animal activities, and all . 704 *Prelude* 8. 344

Activity. And take delight in its activity ; . . 80 *Loving she 10
Their jubilant activity evolves . . . 218 *Recluse* 1. 1. 212
The languid mind into activity. . . . 488 *Pers. Talk* 18
By scars which his activity has left . . . 788 *Excursion* 3. 175

Actor. The little Actor cons another part ; . 589 *Immortality* 102
Or could perform ; a zealous actor, hired . . 842 *Excursion* 6. 284

Acts. A pledge of endless bliss in acts of early piety, 93 *Poet's Dream* 74
Had fed or sheltered, linking to such acts . 132 *Michael* 72
To acts of tenderness ; and he had rocked . 133 *Michael* 157
His little, nameless, unremembered, acts . . 206 *Tintern* 34
Of Britain's acts,—may catch it with rapt ear, 325 *Ode 1814* 129
Of Britain's acts would sing, . . . 330 *Ode : Thanks.* 68
His acts, his wrongs, his final sacrifice ; . . 351 *Des. Stanzas* 71
To localise heroic acts—could look . . . 356 *Aquap.* 273
But element and orb on *acts* did wait . . 469 *Bold words 12
Judgments and aims and acts whose higher source 517 *Pun. Death* 2. 11
Of wrongful acts. Downward it is and broad, 519 *Pun. Death* 8. 5
To acts of love ; and habit does the work . 567 *Cumb. Beg.* 100
In acts of love to those with whom they dwell, 568 *Cumb. Beg.* 139
Reflective acts to fix the moral law . . . 650 *Prelude* 3. 84
Of natural rights and civil ; and to acts . . 712 *Prelude* 9. 201
In thought or conversation, public acts, . . 717 *Prelude* 9. 543
The Senate's language, and the public acts . 727 *Prelude* 11. 8
Of a majestic intellect, its acts . . . 747 *Prelude* 14. 67
Hence cheerfulness for acts of daily life, . . 747 *Prelude* 14. 121
This spiritual Love acts not nor can exist . 749 *Prelude* 14. 188
These acts of mind, and memory, and heart, . 794 *Excursion* 3. 574
To acts which they abhor ; though I bewail . 805 *Excursion* 4. 301
And emanations were perceived ; and acts . 812 *Excursion* 4. 738
For acts of service ? Can his love extend . 817 *Excursion* 4. 1095
And her uncharitable acts, I trust, . . . 850 *Excursion* 6. 775

Actual. Of present, actual, superficial life, . . 706 *Prelude* 8. 506
The actual world of our familiar days, . . 745 *Prelude* 13. 357
Actual, divine, and true. To fear and love, . 748 *Prelude* 14. 162
(Whether of actual vision, sensible . . . 811 *Excursion* 4. 642

Actuates. From that which *is* and actuates, by forms, 357 *Aquap.* 326

Adage. The adage on all tongues, " Murder will out," 518 *Pun. Death* 6. 10

Adam. Could Father Adam open his eyes . . 162 *Art thou the 12
Young Adam Bruce beside her lay, . . . 287 *Ellen Irwin* 5
Fair parks spread wide where Adam Bell might deign 393 *Inglewood* 6
That I sing of old Adam, the pride of old men. 569 *Farmer* 4
Yet Adam was far as the farthest from ruin, . 569 *Farmer* 17

Adam—*continued*.
Yet Adam prized little the feast and the bowl,— 569 *Farmer* 21
For Adam was simple in thought ; and the poor, 569 *Farmer* 25
All trades, as need was, did old Adam assume,— 570 *Farmer* 49
Old Adam will smile at the pains that have made 570 *Farmer* 75
Like a magnet, the heart of old Adam can draw ; 570 *Farmer* 78
Now farewell, old Adam ! when low thou art laid, 571 *Farmer* 89
The mind of Adam, yet in Paradise . . . 709 *Prelude* 8. 659

Adamant. Ay, we are coupled by a chain of adamant ; 70 *Bord.* 1854
Against a Champion cased in adamant. . . 442 *Ecc. Sonn.* 3. 7. 14

Adamantine. Yea, all the adamantine holds of truth 666 *Prelude* 5. 39

Adam's. The quiet of nature was Adam's delight. . 569 *Farmer* 24

Adapt. Can portion out his pleasures, and adapt, 813 *Excursion* 4. 803

Add. And doth call out for vengeance. Do not add, 75 *Bord.* 2125
That skill or means of his could add, but the architect had wrought 91 *Norman Boy* 18
And bear with their transgression, when I add . 122 *V. and J.* 65
In silence, though my memory could add . . 124 *V and J* 177
And I to this would add another tale. . . . 202 *Hart-leap* 96
Great is their glee while flake they add to flake . 280 *Intent on 4
And add your voices to the quire . . . 286 *Sons of Burns* 26
Add every charm the Universe can show . . . 455 *Not in the lucid 22
Nor add to it a flower ! . . . . 508 *May* 92
To express what then I saw ; and add the gleam, 578 *Peele Castle* 14
And to my Friend who knows me I may add, . 643 *Prelude* 2. 73
Add that whate'er of Terror or of Love . . 651 *Prelude* 3. 133
Here must we pause : this only let me add . 674 *Prelude* 5. 584
—To time thus spent, add multitudes of hours . 677 *Prelude* 6. 179
Add to these exhibitions, mute and still, . . 691 *Prelude* 7. 260
Taking my seat, I saw (nor blush to add, . . 691 *Prelude* 7. 270
Add also, that among the multitudes . . . 709 *Prelude* 8. 665
Devoured by locusts,—Carra, Gorsas,—add . 712 *Prelude* 9. 176
Add unto this, subservience from the first . . 713 *Prelude* 9. 233
Whom no one owned, sate silent, shall I add, . 722 *Prelude* 10. 298
Suffice it here to add, that, somewhat stern . 731 *Prelude* 11. 275
With half a harvest. It pleased Heaven to add . 764 *Excursion* 1. 538
Loud echoing, add your speed to the pursuit ; . 808 *Excursion* 4. 502
Forgive me if I add another claim, . . . K.8. 255 *Recluse* 1.1.692
And months, and let me add the long year through, K.8. 265 *Brook, that 2

Added. " And from your doom," he added, " now I wait, 36 *Guilt* 652
Another grave was added.—He had found . . 96 *Brothers* 84
But added, that, the evening being calm, . . 102 *Brothers* 416
To which, requests were added, that forthwith . 136 *Michael* 310
A Lady added to my court . . . . 372 *Eg. Maid* 231
Six months to six years added he remained . . 576 *Six months 1
While every moment added doubt to doubt, . 683 *Prelude* 6. 578
With vice at home. We added dearest themes— 714 *Prelude* 9. 354
I added, work of safety : from all doubt . . 720 *Prelude* 10. 143
Added no farewell to his parting counsel, . . 726 *Prelude* 10. 538
Was added to the troubles of a time . . . 764 *Excursion* 1. 557
Foretold, and added prayer to prophecy ; . . 797 *Excursion* 3. 765
Year after year is added to his store . . . 866 *Excursion* 7. 565

Adding. And adding, with a hope to be forgiven, 102 *Brothers* 431
Knocked here—and knocked there, pounds still adding to pounds. 570 *Farmer* 36
Adding immortal labours of his own— . . . 587 *Crosth.* 6
A Being, who by adding love to peace . . 764 *Excursion* 1. 518

Address. With backward will ; but, wanting not address 874 *Excursion* 8. 31

Addressed. *See* **Addrest, Re-addressed.**
Her he addressed in words of cheering sound ; . 27 *Guilt* 185
His neighbour thus addressed :— . . . 156 *Oak and Broom* 20
The Queen of Beauty thus her court address'd) . 620 *Birth of Love* 11
A calm resolve of mind, firmly addressed . . 654 *Prelude* 3. 346
Whether for gorgeous tournament addressed, . 689 *Prelude* 7. 140
To his fraternal sympathy addressed, . . . 762 *Excursion* 1. 419
In solitude : and mutually addressed . . . 792 *Excursion* 3. 441
Strains followed of acknowledgment addressed 794 *Excursion* 3. 568
Was pointedly addressed ; and to the thoughts . 880 *Excursion* 8. 436
This universal plea in vain addressed, . . . 889 *Excursion* 9. 322
To Lowther Castle she addressed . . . S.3. 431 *The Scottish 9

Addressing. To that same child, addressing tenderly 789 *Excursion* 3. 227

Addrest. *See* **Addressed.**
Thus spake—and lo ! a Fleet, for Gaul addrest, . 432 *Ecc. Sonn.* 2. 15. 10
To feats of arms addrest ! . . . . 499 *This Lawn 12
Aspires to thee addrest, ... 506 *While from 46
A Titian's hand, addrest to picture forth . . 850 *Excursion* 6. 828
For prouder service were addrest ; but each, . 891 *Excursion* 9. 479

Adequate. The Wanderer said :—" One adequate support 801 *Excursion* 4. 10

Adhere. The spots that to my soul adhere ; . . 214 *Dion* 97
I should adhere, and seeming to possess . . 688 *Prelude* 7. 59

Adhered. Of mortified presumption, I adhered . . 730 *Prelude* 11. 216
She mused, resolved, adhered to her resolve ; . 849 *Excursion* 6. 720

Adheres. And to the rock the root adheres . . 224 *Primrose* 17

Adieu. But now farewell to each and all—adieu . 13 *Desc. Sk.* 127
Experience forces—then adieu ! . . . 237 *P. B.* 115
—Then why these lingering steps ?—A bright adieu, 284 *Departure* 29
This parting glance, no negligent adieu ! . . 377 *Duddon* 4. 2
Adieu, Rydalian Laurels ! that have grown . . 463 *Adieu, Rydalian 1
And looked a blind adieu. . . . 478 *Somnamb.* 45

Adjoining. From an adjoining pasture, overhung . 826 *Excursion* 5. 228

Adjusted. *See* **Ill-adjusted.**

Administered. In its degree of power, administered 686 *Prelude* 6. 747

Administering. —Preaching, administering, in every work 862 *Excursion* 7. 334

Administration. Administration of the holy rite . 836 *Excursion* 5. 950

Admiral. On which brave Admiral Nelson stood— 178 *Waggoner* 2. 129

Admirals. Land-warriors, kings, or admirals of the sea, ... 689 *Prelude* 7. 165
Admiration. Great actions move our admiration, chiefly . . . . 65 *Bord.* 1536
In speechless admiration. I, a witness . . . 151 **Forth from* 12
In willing admiration and respect, ... 290 *Kilchurn* 29
With admiration I behold . . . . . . 294 *Jedbor.* 37
Of admiration sprung from truth ; . . . . . 301 *Bran.* 114
With praise, as genuine admiration prompts. . . 356 *Aquap.* 246
Sage Merlin gazed with admiration : . . . . 369 *Eg. Maid.* 14
In admiration or dismay, ... 411 *White Doe* 1344
The noblest drops to admiration known, . . . 436 *Ecc. Sonn.* 2. 32. 10
A theme for praise and admiration high. . . . 517 *Pun. Death* 3. 4
And admiration lost, by change of place . . . 527 **Those breathing* 23
Of admiration and respectful love, ... 539 **Lady ! a* 29
Of tremulous admiration. Such true fame . . 540 *Grace Darl.* 13
From *silent* admiration wins relief. . . . . . 584 **With copious* 45
All genuine admiration unimpaired. . . . . 653 *Prelude* 3. 274
With admiration of her modest mien . . . . 691 *Prelude* 7. 307
Looked out for admiration. Folly, vice, . . . 695 *Prelude* 7. 578
To measured admiration, or to aught . . . . 737 *Prelude* 12. 186
For admiration and mysterious awe. . . . . 784 *Excursion* 2. 869
Of admiration, and all sense of joy ? " . . . . 791 *Excursion* 3. 356
The admiration winning of the crowd ; . . . 797 *Excursion* 3. 766
" We live by Admiration, Hope, and Love ; . . 812 *Excursion* 4. 763
" Love, Hope, and Admiration—are they not . . 812 *Excursion* 4. 768
Love, admiration, fear, desire, and hate, . . . 830 *Excursion* 5. 496
And admiration ; lifting up a veil, ... 848 *Excursion* 6. 649
With admiration would he lift his eyes . . . 868 *Excursion* 7. 747
Of admiration and delightful awe, ... 872 *Excursion* 7 950
For with the sense of admiration blends . . . 877 *Excursion* 8. 208
He gazed, with admiration unsuppressed, . . . 882 *Excursion* 8. 534
Wonder, and admiration, things that wrought . K.8. 230 **I will* 187
Admirations. That gentle admirations raise . . 527 **The soaring* 55
And admirations that were there, of God . . K.8. 227 **I will* 96
Admire. Meanwhile untroubled I admire . . . 236 *P. B.* 16
Others look up, and with fixed eyes admire . . 283 **Well have* 8
Fronting the noontide sun. We paused to admire 881 *Excursion* 8. 464
Admired. And pleased to be admired ! . . . . 165 *Parrot* 28
Most dainty, most admired, ... 170 *Rural Ill.* 22
Peep forth, and are admired. . . . . . . 508 *May* 88
Admired and envied. Oh ! the beating heart, . 694 *Prelude* 7. 493
And elevated most when most admired. . . . 743 *Prelude* 13. 260
Admired for beauty, for her sweetness praised ; . 774 *Excursion* 2. 188
To be admired, than coveted and loved. . . . 848 *Excursion* 6. 690
Admires. Unworthily admires. . . . . 194 *Ruth* 156
Admiring. While silent stands the admiring crowd below, ... 6 *Ev. Wk.* 205
In solemn shapes before the admiring eye . . . 14 *Desc. Sk.* 222
Unless, while with admiring eye . . . . . 164 **Glad sight* 7
And the whole world, not envious but admiring, . 325 *Ode 1814* 137
That moved in long array before admiring eyes. . 346 *Processions* 9
Admiring, loving, and with grief and pride . . 547 **Ye Lime* 17
While silent stands th' admiring vale below ; . . 595 *Ev. Wk. Quarto* 188
Or sate reclined ; admiring quietly . . . . . 893 *Excursion* 9. 582
Shall pause, the skill admiring that can work . . S. 3. 433 **The doubt* 45
Admission. Derived—find no admission. Then it was— . . . . 732 *Prelude* 11. 333
Admit. Should in his love admit no rivalship, . . 42 *Bord.* 269
Did not admit of stronger evidence ; . . . . 53 *Bord.* 881
Shall I admit that nothing can restore . . . . 118 *Maternal Grief* 9
Admit no bondage and my words have wings. . 230 *Clouds* 59
And in the soul admit of no decay, ... 260 **High is* 12
Though not unwilling here to admit . . . . 302 *Yarrow V.* 23
Admit me in the equipage . . . . . . 406 *White Doe* 919
Listeners who not unwillingly admit . . . . 538 **In desultory* 50
Her doors to admit this homeless Pensioner ; . . 783 *Excursion* 2. 744
Meek to admit ; the active energy, ... 831 *Excursion* 5. 574
Or with too brief a warning, to admit . . . . 836 *Excursion* 5. 949
Is in controlling Providence, admit . . . . 846 *Excursion* 6. 561
Amid his calm abstractions, would admit . . . 877 *Excursion* 8. 228
While she exacts allegiance, shall admit . . . 888 *Excursion* 9. 296
Admits. That doth reject all show of pride, admits no outward sign, ... 189 *Star-gazers* 27
Where height, or depth, admits not the approach 795 *Excursion* 3. 643
" O blest seclusion ! when the mind admits . . 816 *Excursion* 4. 1035
Admittance. Admittance was denied. The young man spake . . . . 125 *V. and J.* 265
Admitted. No pause admitted, no design avowed ! 213 *Dion* 80
Sole light admitted here, a small cascade, . . . 593 *Ev. Wk. Quarto* 79
Admitted more habitually a mild . . . . . 750 *Prelude* 14. 288
And in what age admitted and confirmed ? . . 827 *Excursion* 5. 348
Admitting. Admitting no resistance, bends alike 57 *Bord.* 1089
Approachable, admitting fellowship . . . . 676 *Prelude* 6. 62
Admonish. Could teach, admonish ; suffered with the rest . . . . 703 *Prelude* 8. 290
Admonished. But be admonished by his grave, . 287 *Sons of Burns* 47
Admonished by these truths, and quench all pain 317 **Call not* 13
Admonished not without some sense of fear, . . 355 *Aquap.* 181
Admonished, from his silent grave, ... 577 **By playful* 20
Simonides, admonished by the ghost, ... 623 **I find* 9
And, by these thoughts admonished, will pour out . . . . 669 *Prelude* 5. 225
As if admonished from another world. . . . . 697 *Prelude* 7. 649
Admonished thus, the sweet hour coming on. . . 771 *Excursion* 1. 961
Admonished of the days of love to come . . . K.8. 252 *Recluse* 1. 1. 580
Admonishing. Admonishing the man who walks below . . . . K.8. 240 *Recluse* 1. 1. 132
Admonishment. The same admonishment, have called the place . . . . 149 * *A narrow* 76
To give me human strength, by apt admonishment. 197 *Resolution* 112

Admonishment—*continued.*
Grateful for that admonishment, I hushed . . 660 *Prelude* 4. 125
Admonishments. Were its admonishments, nor lightly heard . . . . 695 *Prelude* 7. 546
Remembrances and dim admonishments. . . . 719 *Prelude* 10. 77
Admonition. Would, with imperious admonition, then . . . . 172 *Infant Daughter* 25
He starts—and takes, at the admonition, . . 175 *Waggoner* 1. 158
First admonition that the sun is down ! . . . 208 **It is no* 5
By admonition from this prostrate Stone ! . . 345 **Ambition—following* 6
Of sudden admonition—like a brook . . . 732 *Prelude* 11. 337
Shrinking from admonition, like a man . . . 805 *Excursion* 4. 257
Admonitions. In admonitions of thy softest voice ! 454 **The Sun, that* 20
With peaceful admonitions for the heart . . . 876 *Excursion* 8. 163
Admonitory. Admonitory texts inscribed the walls, 824 *Excursion* 5. 150
Ado. " Come ! come ! " cried one, and without more ado . . . . 191 *Beggars* 47
Adonis. So drooped Adonis, bathed in sanguine dew 169 *Love lies Bleeding* 12
Adopt. Joy, as her holiest language, shall adopt ; . 173 *Infant Daughter* 77
Adopt your homely ways, and dress, ... 288 *Highland Girl* 51
Adopted. Or run, my own adopted bride, . . . 193 *Ruth* 94
Nor by soft Peace adopted ; though, in place . 290 *Kilchurn* 11
Tended at need, the adopted Plant may thrive . 445 *Ecc. Sonn.* 3. 21. 8
From youth our own adopted, he had passed . 660 *Prelude* 4. 99
Adopts. Superior, magisterially adopts . . . . 73x *Prelude* 11. 242
Adoration. Her tuneful adoration ! . . . . 112 **How rich* 10
Breathless with adoration ; the broad sun . . 258 **It is a* 3
To a soft breeze, in lowly adoration. . . . . 431 *Ecc. Sonn.* 2. 11. 8
Her adoration was not your demand, ... 434 *Ecc. Sonn.* 2. 24. 5
For kneeling adoration ;—while—above, . . . 450 *Ecc. Sonn.* 3. 39. 12
Of adoration, with an eye of love. . . . . 648 *Prelude* 2. 414
For adoration thou endur'st ; endure . . . . 802 *Excursion* 4. 94
From mortal adoration or regard, ... 811 *Excursion* 4. 665
Adorations. These humbler adorations will receive. 337 *Aar* 14
Adore. Thee I adore, and find my rest in faith. . 53 *Bord.* 854
This is idolatry ; and these we adore : . . . . 307 **O Friend* 10
To adore the Invisible, and Him alone. . . . 431 *Ecc. Sonn.* 2. 11. 11
The Druid-priest the hallowed Oak adore ; . . 500 *Humanity* 8
To kneel together, and adore their God ! . . . 534 **Blest is* 100
The knee that bends to adore . . . . . . 545 *Russ. Fug.* 294
And offices humane, intent to adore . . . . 551 **If thou in* 11
That tempts us to adore. . . . . 583 **O for a* 54
And ye adore ! But blessèd be the God . . . 703 *Prelude* 8. 301
It teaches less to love, than to adore ; . . . 806 *Excursion* 4. 349
Adore, and worship, when you know it not ; . . 818 *Excursion* 4. 1148
Are yet exalted, and in soul adore ! . . . . 893 *Excursion* 9. 627
Adored. A vision, and adored the thing he saw. 122 *V. and J.* 38
His God may be adored. . . . . 341 *San Salv.* 12
Union significant of God adored, ... 477 **Lowther ! in* 4
Britain, who long her warriors had adored, . . 619 *School Ex.* 53
Father, and king, and judge, adored and feared ! 794 *Excursion* 3. 573
Bow to the watery element, adored . . . . S. 3. 435 **The doubt* 123
Adores. And mocks whom he adores. . . . . 374 *Eg. Maid* 358
Love that adores, but on the knees of prayer, . 748 *Prelude* 14. 183
Adorn. —Did Sabine grace adorn my living line, . 3 *Ev. Wk.* 72
For him sod-seats the cottage-door adorn ; . . 11 *Desc. Sk.* 19
Or holy festal pomps adorn, ... 164 **Fair Lady* 7
" 'Tis known," cried they, " that he, who would adorn . . . . 312 **When, far* 5
Making the precincts ye adorn . . . . . . 366 **Ye Trees* 17
Just limits ; but yon Tower, whose smiles adorn . 469 **The feudal* 5
With gleaming lights more gracefully adorn . . 471 *Ailsa Crag* 3
High will he hang thee up, well pleased to adorn . 490 *Spade* 31
Then did the Penitent adorn . . . . . . 543 *Russ. Fug.* 185
Green dewy lights adorn the freshen'd mead, . . 607 *Desc. Sk. Quarto* 272
As thou art wont, thy sovereignty adorn . . . 628 **Deign, Sovereign* 13
She came, no more a phantom to adorn . . . 750 *Prelude* 14. 268
How she her station doth adorn : the pool . . 868 *Excursion* 7. 720
To help it and adorn. . . . . S. 3. 425 **No whimsy* 6
Adorned. Of beauty, by the changing moon adorned, 172 *Infant Daughter* 24
Adorned with wreaths of myrtle ; . . . . . 287 *Ellen Irwin* 4
Float with its crest of trees adorned . . . . 531 †*Float. Isl.* 11
Adorned, and shady boughs. . . . . . . 543 *Russ. Fug.* 104
Not so enriched, not so adorned, to thee . . . 585 *Ch. Lamb* 77
That wish for something loftier, more adorned, . 674 *Prelude* 5. 575
And occupations which her beauty adorned, . . 701 *Prelude* 8. 127
And its invisible counterpart, adorned . . . . 812 *Excursion* 4. 712
For this occasion daintily adorned, ... 826 *Excursion* 5. 278
Out of the living rock, to be adorned . . . . 855 *Excursion* 6. 1145
And flowering shrubs, protected and adorned : . 881 *Excursion* 8. 470
Adorning. Or with a milder grace adorning . . 182 *Waggoner* 4. 230
And now the stars adorning. . . . . . . 237 *P. B.* 95
Or a spider's web adorning . . . . . . 549 *Hermit's Cell* 1. 3
Enriching and adorning. Unto thee, ... 585 *Ch. Lamb* 76
While Earth herself is adorning, ... 588 *Immortality* 43
Adorning flowery gardens, 'mid vast squares ; . 689 *Prelude* 7. 135
Adorns. Supports, adorns, and over all presides ; . 368 *Trajan* 52
Adorns, in which the good Man's ancestors . . 824 *Excursion* 5. 125
Whose window, somewhat sadly, it adorns. . . 852 *Excursion* 6. 938
Adown. Whirled adown the rocky channel, . . 93 *Westmoreland Girl* 13
Adown a rocky maze ; . . . . 190 **Lyre ! though* 32
The brook adown the rocky steeps. . . . . 215 *Kirkstone* 76
This cry—that floats adown the flood, ... 243 *P. B.* 629
Wafted adown the wind from lake or stream ; . 261 **I heard (alas* 4
Broke forth in concert flung adown the dells, . . 267 *St. Cath.* 3
Pace the long avenue, or glide adown . . . . 270 **Ye sacred* 12

Aerial—*continued.*
Looking far forth from his aerial cell. . . . . 362 *List—'twas* 85
Aerial keystone haughtily secure ; . . . . 435 *Ecc. Sonn.* 2. 26. 4
Above all height ! like an aerial cross . . . 703 *Prelude* 8. 273
Of some aerial Down, while there he halts . . 709 *Prelude* 9. 10
Of aspect, with aerial softness clad, . . . 773 *Excursion* 2. 95
Aerial, or in green secluded vale, ... 792 *Excursion* 3. 394
Not giddy yet aerial, with a depth . . . K.8. 237 *Recluse* 1. 1. 20
Through that aerial fir-grove, could preserve . K.8. 248 *Recluse* 1.1.415
Aery. Where the eagle builds her aery, . . 220 *Triad* 39
Upon its aëry summit crowned with heath, . . 101 *Brothers* 369
How quickly from that aëry hold unbound, . . 259 *A volant* 4
O'er Limbo lake with aëry flight to steer, . . 284 *Departure* 11
Anxious an aëry name to immortalize. . . . 313 *Go back* 8
Of aëry voices locked in unison,— . . . . 346 *Gemmi* 11
Of yon pure waters, from their aëry height . . 380 *Duddon* 19. 4
And griefs whose aëry motion comes not near . 395 *White Doe : Ded.* 35
And aëry harvests crown the fertile lea. . . 429 *Ecc. Sonn.* 2. 3. 14
Glance to and fro, like aëry Sprites . . . 499 *This Lawn* 11
Fruitless as those of aëry alchemists . . . 832 *Excursion* 5. 633
Drawn from her cottage, on that aëry height, . 834 *Excursion* 5. 758
Aery's. From a bold headland, their loved aery's guard, ... 388 *Eagles* 7
Æson. And Æson stood a youth 'mid youthful peers. 210 *Laod.* 84
Æther's. And pours a deeper blue to Æther's bound ; 8 *Ev. Wk.* 328
And pouring deeper blue to Æther's bound, . 599 *Ev. Wk. Quarto* 394
Ætolians. The rough Ætolians smiled with bitter scorn. . . . . . . 312 *When, far* 4
Afar. Afar, his tail he closes and unfurls ; . . 5 *Ev. Wk.* 151
Sweet are the sounds that mingle from afar . . 7 *Ev. Wk.* 279
Toy with the sun and glitter from afar. . . 11 *Desc. Sk.* 51
To where afar rich orange lustres glow . . 13 *Desc. Sk.* 160
Now couch thyself where, heard with fear afar, . 16 *Desc. Sk.* 336
O thou ! whose fancies from afar are brought ; . 88 *H. C.* 1
I see thee glittering from afar— . . . . 159 *With little* 33
And *That* which glittered from afar ; . . . 167 *Pilgrim's Dream* 21
Old as the hills that feed it from afar, . . 184 *Airey-force* 5
Like a glory from afar, ... 205 *Brougham* 155
Catches sometimes from afar— . . . . 209 *Yes, it* 18
Yea ! even the Stranger from afar. . . . 223 *Wishing-gate* 31
The peaceful pageant advancing from afar. . . 327 *Ode 1815* 51
(Stilled from afar—such marvel story tells— . 362 *List—'twas* 55
And blue-topped hills, behold him from afar ; . 384 *Duddon* 32. 11
Hath watched the Banner from afar, . . . 404 *White Doe* 758
Whose fervent exhortations from afar . . . 429 *Ecc. Sonn.* 2. 5. 6
Piercing the Papal darkness from afar ! . . 436 *Ecc. Sonn.* 2. 31. 14
Stilled by thy voice ! But quickly from afar . 438 *Ecc. Sonn.* 2. 38. 5
Seem fixed, to eyes that watch them from afar ; . 444 *Ecc. Sonn.* 3. 17. 4
And cometh from afar : . . . . . 588 *Immortality* 61
Asleep on Bunker's charnel hill afar ; . . 596 *Ev. Wk. Quarto* 254
If, in that country, where there dwells afar . 596 *Ev. Wk. Quarto* 265
Hence shall we turn where, heard with fear afar, 609 *Desc.Sk.Quarto* 414
Retiring or approaching from afar . . . 716 *Prelude* 9. 448
When from afar invoked by anxious love ? . . 733 *Prelude* 11. 423
The welcome of an Inmate from afar, . . . 772 *Excursion* 2. 60
One after one, collected from afar, . . . 792 *Excursion* 3. 395
The cawing rooks, and sea-mews from afar, . 808 *Excursion* 4. 451
An iron knell ! with echoes from afar . . 819 *Excursion* 4. 1181
By that unwearied signal, kenned afar ; . . 834 *Excursion* 5. 761
Of pious sentiment diffused afar, . . . 838 *Excursion* 6. 28
Alone and devious from afar he came ; . . K.8. 236 *Recluse* 1. 1. 6
Partaking this day's pleasure ? From afar . K.8. 243 *Recluse* 1.1.240
Affair. But what has brought you hither ? A slight affair, ... 43 *Bord.* 339
Esteemed you worthy to conduct the affair . . 53 *Bord.* 870
" When we arranged the affair, she wept a little . 59 *Bord.* 1195
Affairs. See **House-affairs.**
Intense, and frugal, apt for all affairs, . . 131 *Michael* 45
From shop to shop about my own affairs, . . 649 *Prelude* 3. 27
Affect. Affect my native habitations ; . . 226 *Vernal Ode* 27
Though the bold wings of Poesy affect . . 270 *Though the bold* 1
Which, heard in foreign lands, the Swiss affect . 339 *Ranz* 3
Sad fancies do we then affect, . . . 497 *Lycoris* 23
Be Folly and False-seeming free to affect . 655 *Prelude* 3. 401
Affectations. By affectations interchanged, . . 301 *Bran* 108
Affected. Of trespasses, affected to provoke . 80 *Loving she* 5
Affecting. See **Soul-affecting.**
Affecting type of him I mourn ! . . . 580 *John Words.* 17
Of poesy, affecting private shades . . . 660 *Prelude* 4. 104
Affecting more emotion than I felt ; . . . 710 *Prelude* 9. 73
And I am conscious of affecting thoughts . . 755 *Recluse* 1. 1. 759
Gay, and affecting graceful gaiety ; . . . 774 *Excursion* 2. 182
Was best, the most affecting eloquence. . . 807 *Excursion* 4. 415
From some affecting images and thoughts, . 826 *Excursion* 5. 240
Might almost think, at this affecting hour, . 895 *Excursion* 9. 716
Affectingly. Affectingly set forth, more than elsewhere . . . . . . 709 *Prelude* 8. 667
Affection. Entire affection for all human kind. . 3 *Ev. Wk.* 85
For that another in his Child's affection . . 38 *Bord.* 56
Whose natural affection doubts enslave, . . 104 *Artegal* 124
And, from this triumph of affection pure, . . 106 *Artegal* 240
The brood of chaste affection. . . . 302 *Yarrow V.* 64
And I by my affection was beguiled : . . . 308 *When I* 11
Of dutiful affection. . . . . . 337 *Thun* 8
Of joy immortal and of pure affection. . . 370 *Eg. Maid* 78
With what entire affection do they prize . . 438 *Ecc. Sonn.* 2. 40. 3
She calls them near, and with affection sweet . 595 *Ev. Wk. Quarto* 215
Some lingering fragrance of the pure affection, . 627 *We gaze* 13
There are who think that strong affection, love . 742 *Prelude* 13. 186
The nearest in affection or in blood ; . . 780 *Excursion* 2. 572
Friendship betrayed, affection unreturned, . . 791 *Excursion* 3. 377

Affection—*continued.*
The fond affection. She no more could bear . . 852 *Excursion* 6. 942
Affectionate. And from affectionate observance gain . 212 *Dion* 16
Affectionate and true, ... 487 *Fountain* 2
Affectionate without disquietude, . . . 661 *Prelude* 4. 223
Frugal, affectionate, sober, and withal . . 764 *Excursion* 1. 522
Affectionately. Is styled, when most affectionately praised. . . . . . . 824 *Excursion* 5. 103
Affection's. Say, will my friend, with soft affection's ear, ... 592 *Ev. Wk. Quarto* 51
Affections. And search the affections to their inmost cell ; . . . . . . 19 *Desc. Sk.* 523
Of her affections ? so they blindly asked . . 125 *V. and J.* 224
Strong hold on his affections, were to him . . 132 *Michael* 75
But affections higher, holier, ... 141 *Arm. Lady* 79
To guide your speech and your affections. . . 142 †*Lov. and Lik.* 4
And while these right affections play, . . . 143 †*Lov. and Lik.* 59
In memory of affections old and true, . . 148 *Joanna* 81
The affections, to exalt them or refine ; . . 172 *Infant Daughter* 35
In which the affections gently lead us on,— . 206 *Tintern* 42
Be thy affections raised and solemnised. . . 211 *Laod.* 144
She, in benign affections pure, . . . 222 *Triad* 159
For if of our affections none finds grace . . 256 *Yes ! hope* 3
To old affections, had been heard to plead . . 274 *Wait, prithee* 8
Dwells in the affections and the soul of man . 315 *O'er the* 2
Affections which, if put to proof, are kind ; . 319 *Avaunt all* 8
Of agonised affections ; . . . . 324 *Ode 1814* 86
Divine affections ; and with beast and bird . 362 *List—'twas* 54
Plays false with our affections ; . . . 386 *Yarrow Rev.* 90
The chaste affections tremble to fulfil . . 425 *Ecc. Sonn.* 1. 28. 8
To calm the affections, elevate the soul, . . 496 *A little* 56
Of right affections climbing or descending . . 500 *Humanity* 28
Affections pure and holy in their source . . 503 *Warning* 14
Called forth by those affections that endear . 510 *Among a* 15
Affections lose their object ; Time brings forth . 531 *Octogen.* 1
Have waited—till the affections could no more . 539 *Lady ! a* 30
Her soothed affections clung, ... 544 *Russ. Fug.* 210
By vain affections unenthralled, . . . 576 *Cenotaph* 1
Affections, warm as sunshine, free as air ; . . 584 *Ch. Lamb* 10
But for those first affections, ... 589 *Immortality* 152
Were fastened to the affections. I began . . 641 *Prelude* 1. 612
The props of my affections were removed, . . 646 *Prelude* 2. 279
And all my young affections out of doors. . . 688 *Prelude* 7. 76
For me, when my affections first were led . . 701 *Prelude* 8. 121
Was Man in my affections and regards . . 704 *Prelude* 8. 350
Loose and disjointed, and the affections left . 711 *Prelude* 9. 106
Or our infirm affections Nature pleads, . . 721 *Prelude* 10. 189
To rivet my affections ; nor did now . . 722 *Prelude* 10. 255
Diffusing only those affections wider . . 729 *Prelude* 11. 169
The affections and the spirit of the place, . . 736 *Prelude* 12. 120
Of the affections, and to Nature's self . . 743 *Prelude* 13. 200
And all affections by communion raised . . 747 *Prelude* 14. 117
Foremost in my affections, had fallen back . 749 *Prelude* 14. 258
Spontaneously had his affections thriven . . 761 *Excursion* 1. 351
Their lost affections unto thee and thine ! " . 801 *Excursion* 4. 31
And such benign affections cultivates . . 806 *Excursion* 4. 357
Corrupt affections, covetous desires, . . 826 *Excursion* 5. 286
And to the best affections that proceed . . 836 *Excursion* 5. 905
For Man's affections—else betrayed and lost, . 837 *Excursion* 5. 1006
Affections seated in the mother's breast, . . 875 *Excursion* 8. 74
Of pure affections, shedding upon joy . . K.8. 237 *Recluse* 1. 1. 51
In my affections. Witness the delight . . K.8. 251 *Recluse* 1. 1. 544
Affiance. Affiance in each other ; faith more firm . 805 *Excursion* 4. 306
Affianced. See **Heart-affianced.**
Affinities. To those first-born affinities that fit . 640 *Prelude* 1. 555
By observation of affinities . . . . 647 *Prelude* 2. 384
Affirm. The wise man, I affirm, can find no rest . 257 *No mortal* 9
I now affirm of Nature and of Truth, . . 816 *Excursion* 4. 983
We safely may affirm that human life . . 830 *Excursion* 5. 526
Affirmed. Bold words affirmed, in days when faith was strong . . . . . 468 *Bold words* 1
Discoloured, then divested. 'Tis affirmed . . 840 *Excursion* 6. 161
Affixed. Here stood an Oak, that long had borne affixed . . . . . . 393 *Hart's-horn* 1
Afflict. Afflict, or injuries assail, . . . 457 *Had this* 42
To humble or afflict whome'er he will, . . 557 *Cuck. and Night.* 18
The God of Love afflict thee with all teen, . . 560 *Cuck. and Night.* 187
Afflicted. " Hither the Afflicted come, as thou hast heard thy Mother say, . . . 92 *Poet's Dream* 49
And feel, thou Earth, for this afflicted Race ! . 306 *We had* 14
To hide her poor afflicted head ? . . . 413 *White Doe* 1556
Of Pagan night. Afflicted and dismayed, . . 421 *Ecc. Sonn.* 1. 11. 5
Beside the afflicted ; to sustain with prayer, . 447 *Ecc. Sonn.* 3. 28. 6
Of poor humanity's afflicted will . . . 846 *Excursion* 6. 556
Afflicting. And afflicting moans she fetches, . . 490 *Incident : Dog* 35
Affliction. Our hopes such harvest of affliction reap, 29 *Guilt* 295
From which affliction—when the grace . . 398 *White Doe* 231
Dear daughter of affliction, say . . . 408 *White Doe* 1080
Such strength as, if ever affliction and pain . 482 *Character* 6
If from the affliction somewhere do not grow . 725 *Prelude* 10. 466
A worse affliction in the plague of war ! . . 764 *Excursion* 1. 539
Whether affliction be the foe, or guilt ! . . 792 *Excursion* 3. 420
But worse affliction must be borne—far worse ; . 853 *Excursion* 6. 965
With such, in their affliction.—Ellen's fate, . 854 *Excursion* 6. 1073
Tending to patience when affliction strikes ; . 873 *Excursion* 7. 1055
Affliction's. Wreaths that endure affliction's heaviest shower, ... 259 *Weak is* 13
Afflictions. But, surely, if severe afflictions borne . 143 *High bliss* 2
Nor Duty struggling with afflictions strange— . 262 *Not Love* 3

Ages—*continued.*
A knot of spiry trees for ages grew . . . . . 212 *Laod.* 169
The brightest star of ages yet to be, ... 220 *Triad* 6
Of ages coming, ages gone ; . . . . 227 *Vernal Ode* 94
As laboured minstrelsies through ages wear ! . . 235 *Power of Sound* 174
Whole ages if I here should roam, ... 237 *P. B.* 52
Lies fixed for ages on his conscious neck ; . . . 278 *Wellington* 4
Go back to antique ages, if thine eyes . . . . 313 **Go back* 1
England's illustrious sons of long, long ages ; . . 328 *Ode 1815* 62
Perchance, in future ages, here may stop ; . . . 345 **Ambition—following* 4
Departed ages, shedding where he flew . . . 380 *Duddon* 17. 4
That, in the lapse of ages, hath crept o'er . . . 419 *Ecc. Sonn.* 1. 3. 6
Ages ere Valdo raised his voice to preach . . . 431 *Ecc. Sonn.* 2. 12. 3
In classic ages men perceived a soul . . . 456 **The leaves* 26
Enshrined for ages. Is not then the Art . . . 509 *F. Stone* 88
True freedom where for ages they have lain . . 515 **Ah why* 3
Which for ages there had hung. . . . . . 535 *Egremont* 4
And through ages, heirs of heirs, ... 536 *Egremont* 110
On strangers, of all ages ; the quick dance . . 689 *Prelude* 7. 154
A weight of ages did at once descend . . . . 707 *Prelude* 8. 552
The experience of past ages, as, through help . 714 *Prelude* 9. 335
For a paradise of ages, the blind rage . . . . 723 *Prelude* 10. 345
Friends, enemies, of all parties, ages, ranks, . . 723 *Prelude* 10. 361
To illuminate the abyss of ages past, ... 735 *Prelude* 12. 63
Time with his retinue of ages fled . . . . . 744 *Prelude* 13. 318
Through a long course of later ages, drove, . . 791 *Excursion* 3. 368
" Once more to distant ages of the world . . . 814 *Excursion* 4. 847
Have dwelt through ages—Patrons of this Cure. . 824 *Excursion* 5. 126
Shall cause to fade, till ages pass away ; . . . 842 *Excursion* 6. 252
And the best ages of the world prescribe. . . . 862 *Excursion* 7. 333
Aggravate. With me to aggravate his crimes, and heaped . . . . 77 *Bord.* 2263
To quicken, and to aggravate—to feed . . . 788 *Excursion* 3. 141
To multiply and aggravate the din ? . . . . 863 *Excursion* 7. 366
Aggravated. Or lastly, aggravated by the times . 737 *Prelude* 12. 198
Aggravates. Combat, while darkness aggravates the groans : . . . . 464 **Greta, what* 4
Aggravation. But drop the rest :—this aggravation, 181 *Waggoner* 4. 177
Aggressive. Tides of aggressive war, oft served as well . . . . 469 **The feudal* 3
Aghast. And, wildly pausing, oft she hangs aghast, 15 *Desc. Sk.* 267
The Soldier's Widow heard and stood aghast ; . . 33 *Guilt* 476
Once raised, remains aghast, and will not fall ! . 214 *Dion* 93
And then aghast, as at the world . . . . . 234 *Power of Sound* 103
Aghast within its gloomy cavity . . . . . 439 *Ecc. Sonn.* 2. 42. 5
Aghast and prayerless. Into a deep wood . . 718 *Prelude* 9. 578
The Senate stood aghast, her prudence quenched, 723 *Prelude* 10. 351
Aghast we might behold this crystal Mere . . . 894 *Excursion* 9. 701
Agile. Like a bold Girl, who plays her agile pranks 260 **How sweet* 6
By Youth's surviving spirit ? What agile grace ! 540 **Lady ! a* 70
Agitate. Or rouse and agitate his labouring soul ? . 15 *Desc. Sk.* 292
Could thus have dared the grave to agitate, . . 275 *Gravestone* 8
Words that can soothe, more than they agitate ; . 510 *F. Stone* 124
Agitated. Were agitated ; and commotions, strife . 712 *Prelude* 9. 163
Was agitated ; yea, I could almost . . . . . 720 *Prelude* 10. 134
The agitated scene before his eye . . . . . 863 *Excursion* 7. 414
Agitating. Blow fiercely, agitating earth and sky, 795 *Excursion* 3. 651
Agitation. While, with increasing agitation, . 176 *Waggoner* 1. 225
In foamy agitation ; . . . . 385 *Yarrow Rev.* 18
Rash schemes, to abjure all selfish agitation, . . 516 **As leaves* 6
In agitation said, " 'Tis against *that* . . . . 717 *Prelude* 9. 517
In clamorous agitation, round the crest . . . 786 *Excursion* 3. 3
Of endless agitation. Here you stand, . . . 818 *Excursion* 4. 1147
To the agitation of a brook that runs . . . . 849 *Excursion* 6. 735
Agitations. To agitations less severe, ... 376 **The Minstrels* 76
Too high, or idle agitations lull ! . . . . 394 **How profitless* 4
Of kindred agitations for thy sake ; . . . . 440 *Ecc. Sonn.* 3. 2. 5
And gentle agitations of the mind . . . . 646 *Prelude* 2. 298
Wakes in me agitations like its own, . . . 687 *Prelude* 7. 47
Some inward agitations thence are brought, . . 739 *Prelude* 12. 332
For other agitations, or be calm ; . . . . . K.8. 256 *Recluse* 1.1.727
Aglaia. To fair Aglaia ; by what envy moved, . 575 *Chiabrera* 7. 4
Ago. (For many years ago I passed this road) . . 97 *Brothers* 132
Your love hath been, nor long ago, ... 111 *A Complaint* 2
And Betty, half an hour ago, ... 127 *Idiot Boy* 157
Celandine ! and long ago, ... 161 **Pleasures newly* 7
Said I, " not half an hour ago . . . . . . 191 *Beggars* 39
But a few hours ago, had been . . . . . . 246 *P. B.* 879
And battles long ago : . . . . 289 *Sol. Reap.* 20
Bandusia, prattling as when long ago . . . . 376 *Duddon* 1. 3
I should have died, yea many hours ago ; . . . 556 *Prioress* 200
For it was done a little while ago— . . . . 556 *Prioress* 235
" Not twenty years ago, but you I think . . . 764 *Excursion* 1. 535
Twelve tedious years ago, ... S. 3. 431 **The Scottish* 2
Agonies. Pray in ghostly agonies. . . . . . 204 *Brougham* 68
Thy friends are exultations, agonies, ... 305 *Toussaint* 13
—O prostrate Lands, consult your agonies ! . . 330 *Ode : Thanks.* 126
Woven out of passion's sharpest agonies, . . . 467 *St. Bees* 74
Agonised. Of agonised affections ; . . . . . 324 *Ode 1814* 86
Agonizing. An agonizing sorrow to transmute ; 803 *Excursion* 4. 168
Agony. *See* **Heart-agony.**
While prayer contends with silenced agony, . . 20 *Desc. Sk.* 549
Disease and famine, agony and fear, ... 29 *Guilt* 299
Hope died, and fear itself in agony was lost ! . . 30 *Guilt* 351
In all things like ourselves but in the agony . . 68 *Bord.* 1730
Of agony had pressed the Sufferer down : . . . 125 *V. and J.* 226
Is love, though oft to agony distrest, ... 210 *Laod.* 89
With agony his eye-balls ache . . . . . . 247 *P. B.* 933
In agony of silent grief— . . . . 248 *P. B.* 1077
From Bethlehem, from the Mounts of Agony . . 426 *Ecc. Sonn.* 1. 33. 3

Agony—*continued.*
Was Duty,—Duty calmed his agony. . . . . 517 *Pun. Death* 3. 8
Where every parting agony is hushed, ... 540 *Grace Darl.* 41
When Virtue weeps in agony of woe, ... 619 *School Ex.* 91
And from all agony of mind . . . . 623 *G. and S. Green* 25
Of her composure, felt that agony, ... 723 *Prelude* 10. 382
Love with despair, or grief in agony ;— . . . 791 *Excursion* 3. 378
But in her stead—fear—doubt—and agony ! " . 792 *Excursion* 3. 461
Of wife and children stung to agony. . . . . 855 *Excursion* 6. 1097
Agra. Erewhile went forth from Agra or Lahore, . 718 *Prelude* 10. 19
Agravaine. Sir Agravaine advanced ; no sign he won 373 *Eg. Maid* 269
Agree. " But, if my looks did with my words agree, 104 *Artegal* 147
His steed and he right well agree ; . . . . . 127 *Idiot Boy* 107
She thought again—and did agree . . . . . 193 *Ruth* 100
(And all do in this tale agree) . . . . . . 194 *Ruth* 226
But all and each agree, ... 200 *Thorn* 207
As doth with mellowing years agree, ... 217 *Enterprise* 134
If in this book Fancy and Truth agree ; . . . 281 *Valedict.* 11
England ! all nations in this charge agree : . . 309 **England ! the* 9
If with his vows this object ill agree ; . . . . 363 **The world forsaken* 10
Spake bitter words ; words that did ill agree . . 367 **As indignation* 2
Harsh thoughts with her high mood agree— . . 399 *White Doe* 261
Fear hath a hundred eyes that all agree . . . 439 *Ecc. Sonn.* 2. 42. 1
How in thy mind and moral frame agree . . . 478 **Lonsdale ! it* 6
All in one duteous task agree. . . . . . . 531 †*Float. Isl.* 4
With learnèd ears may ill agree, ... 577 **I come* 30
Agreed. Said one, " It is agreed on. The blind Man 59 *Bord.* 1184
On making (so the Lovers had agreed) . . . 123 *V. and J.* 104
Agreeing. And, with this silent gloom agreeing, . 413 *White Doe* 1579
I said, " My thoughts, agreeing, Sir, with yours, . 791 *Excursion* 3. 332
Of human-kind—the tone agreeing . . . . . S. 3. 439 **Avaunt this* 11
Agrees. Wanderers whose course no longer now agrees. . . . . 34 *Guilt* 533
With thy stern aspect better far agrees . . . 466 *St. Bees* 25
Musing, the lone spot with my soul agrees . . S. 3. 417 **Sweet was* 10
Ah. (*Partial list.*)
Ah ! what is here ? Oh ! Gentlemen, I thank you ; 44 *Bord.* 396
The God of Love—*ah, benedicite !* . . . . . 556 *Cuck. and Night.* 1
Ah ! good sweet Nightingale ! for my heart's cheer, 558 *Cuck.andNight.* 101
Ah, fool ! quoth she, wist thou not what it is ? . 559 *Cuck.andNight.* 126
Aid. *See* **Ayde.**
Rouse hell's own aid and wrap thy fields in fire : 22 *Desc. Sk.* 643
In an impartial balance, give thine aid . . . 22 *Desc. Sk.* 653
Her dwelling in his dreams. By Fancy's aid . . 25 *Guilt* 59
To him we turned :—we had no other aid : . . 29 *Guilt* 257
And begged a little aid for charity : . . . . 45 *Bord.* 473
Nor was there wanting other aid— . . . . . 85 *Shepherd-boys* 83
Suppliant for aid his kingdom to regain ; . . . 103 *Artegal* 83
Farewell desire of human aid, ... 113 *Lament* 57
And blasts of heaven will aid their flight ; . . 117 *Affl. Marg.* 44
Tormented ? by such aid you may conceive . . 123 *V. and J.* 144
Why of your further aid bereave me ? . . . . 130 *Idiot Boy* 344
With like command of beauty—grant your aid . 152 **Forth from* 23
Had to a Primrose looked for aid . . . . . 168 *Wren's Nest* 39
By her sweet farewell looks, I longed to aid. . . 190 **Lyre ! though* 7
Their very wishes wanted aid . . . . . . 224 **'Tis gone* 29
Which by their aid re-clothe the naked lawn . . 230 *Clouds* 67
How, with the Muse's aid, her love attest ? . . 253 **Aerial Rock* 6
Not while—to aid the spirit of the place— . . 270 **Shame on* 3
Or seek, from saints above, miraculous aid— . . 311 **Who rises* 52
Which, without aid of numbers, I sustain, . . 314 **I dropped* 7
Now, surely, hath that gracious aid . . . . 338 *Brientz* 9
While she, by aid of Nature, climbs— . . . . 341 *San Salv.* 17
Nice aid maternal fingers lend ; . . . . . . 344 **How blest* 24
A not unwelcome aid may lend, ... 348 **Lulled by* 76
Aid, with congenial influence, to uphold . . . 351 *Des. Stanzas* 76
And enter, with prompt aid from the Most High, 361 *Alban Hills* 13
Both feel, when he renews the wished-for aid : . 378 *Duddon* 10. 10
With native Fancy her fresh aid, ... 386 *Yarrow Rev.* 55
Yea, trusting in God's holy aid, ... 401 *White Doe* 488
Weep, if that aid thee ; but depend . . . . 402 *White Doe* 542
From Naworth come ; and Howard's aid . . . 405 *White Doe* 801
On you, if room for mortal aid . . . . . . 408 *White Doe* 1088
For promise fails of Howard's aid ; . . . . . 408 *White Doe* 1134
Nor wants the cause the panic-striking aid . . 421 *Ecc. Sonn.* 1. 11. 1
Nor scorn the aid which Fancy oft doth lend . . 423 *Ecc. Sonn.* 1. 18. 1
Nor leaves her Speech one word to aid the sigh . 425 *Ecc. Sonn.* 1. 25. 11
Aid, glorious Martyrs, from your fields of light, . 437 *Ecc. Sonn.* 2. 36. 1
Of thee to visit them with lenient aid. . . . . 460 **Queen of* 32
To aid the Votaress, miracles believed . . . . 466 *St. Bees* 46
Leapt from this rock, and but for timely aid . . 469 **A youth* 4
Received my proffered aid. . . . . 484 *Simon Lee* 84
To aid a covert purpose, cried—" O ye . . . 495 *Fact* 3
So might he ken how by his sovereign aid . . 511 **So fair* 10
Their spirit mounted, crying, " God us aid ! " . 513 *General Fast* 8
This high repute, with bounteous Nature's aid, . 515 *Penn.* 6
And aid my verse, content with local bounds . . 522 *Epist. Beaumont* 52
To aid the work, what time these walks and bowers 546 **Oft is* 15
Not to withhold his bounteous aid, Sebeto . . 575 *Chiabrera* 7. 11
Rouze Hell's own aid, and wrap thy hills in fire. . 616 *Desc. Sk. Quarto* 781
But unto Faith and Loyalty comes aid . . . . 628 *Eagle and Dove* 15
Or by its aid leaping from crag to crag, . . . 703 *Prelude* 8. 247
Diffused through time and space, with aid derived 708 *Prelude* 8. 611
That Heaven's best aid is wasted upon men . . 720 *Prelude* 10. 119
They had left behind ? So feeling comes in aid . 738 *Prelude* 12. 269
From every combination which might aid . . . 748 *Prelude* 14. 156
Of culture and the inspiring aid of books, . . . 757 *Excursion* 1. 83
Of pleasure move without the aid of hope : . . 792 *Excursion* 3. 457
How willingly their aid they would unite . . . 793 *Excursion* 3. 529
Or through dependence upon mutual aid, . . . 807 *Excursion* 4. 442

Aid—*continued.*
With virtuous friendship's soul-sustaining aid, 823 Excursion 5. 58
Of feeling to produce them, without aid 837 Excursion 5. 985
And, by that whiskered tabby's aid, set forth 858 Excursion 7. 91
To aid him, and in Song resound his joy. K.8. 239 Recluse 1.1.102
By Nature's kind and ever-present aid K.8. 249 Recluse 1.1.455
Prompt aid, forgiveness speedy and entire. K.8. 266 *Rid of 14
Aided. By brave Corineus aided, he subdued, 102 Artegal 17
Of morning, aided by exhaling dew, 773 Excursion 2. 135
The sport of Nature, aided by blind Chance 788 Excursion 3. 126
—Aided by this appearance, I at length 853 Excursion 6. 1003
Though aided by wild winds, the groans and shrieks 894 Excursion 9. 696
Aiding. To words the Church prescribes aiding the lip 448 Ecc. Sonn. 3. 30. 10
For its keen breath, was aiding to our steps, 622 Recluse 1. 1. 159
Aids. That aids or supersedes our grosser sight, 226 Vernal Ode 4
Forms, images, nor numerous other aids 634 Prelude 1. 155
Quickens the slumbering mind, and aids the thoughts, 698 Prelude 7. 759
How long, and by what kindly outward aids, 864 Excursion 7. 474
Ailed. Shine calmly as if nothing ailed the sky : 45 Bord. 426
What ailed thee, Robin, that thou couldst pursue 162 *Art thou the 24
Aileth. Rest, little young One, rest ; what is't that aileth thee ? 87 Pet-lamb 24
Ailments. Beneath worse ailments of the mind. 294 Jedbor. 75
Ails. I hung this belt. Mercy of Heaven ! What ails you ! 67 Bord. 1642
"What ails you, child ?"—she sobbed, "Look here !" 82 Alice Fell 25
"What ails thee, young One ? what ? Why pull so at thy cord ? 87 Pet-lamb 21
What ails you ? wherefore weep you so ?" 115 Last of Flock 16
"What ails you, that you must come creeping to me !" 116 Repentance 20
For what she ails they cannot guess. 126 Idiot Boy 26
'Tis a note of enchantment ; what ails her ? She sees 188 Poor Susan 5
But something ails it now : the spot is curst. 202 Hart-leap 124
What ails you now, my little Bess ? 243 P. B. 626
What is 't that ails young Harry Gill ? 536 Goody Blake 2
What ! quoth she then, what is 't that ails thee now ? 558 Cuck. and Night. 116
Ailsa. Appeared the Crag of Ailsa, ne'er did morn 471 Ailsa Crag 2
Aim. At least, not owning to himself an aim 10 Desc. Sk. 13
His absence, he hath sought, whate'er his aim 37 Bord. 7
She dances, runs without an aim, 81 †Mother's Return 23
Thou liv'st with less ambitious aim, 158 *In youth 29
In perfect fitness for its aim, 168 Wren's Nest 10
Pursue thee with their deadly aim ! 214 Dion 105
High is her aim as heaven above, 222 Triad 145
But your smooth motions suit a peaceful aim ; 230 Clouds 15
And no one could have guessed his aim,— 247 P. B. 993
Some path of steep ascent and lofty aim ; 261 *Fair Prime 12
Was the aim frustrated by force or guile, 269 Malham 1
To live and die, the peace of heaven his aim ; 272 Lady E. B. 6
But a bold Knight, the selfish aim 301 Bran 68
Meek, destitute, as seemed, of hope or aim 305 *We had 5
Gave specious colouring to aim and act, 313 *Go back 10
Could they, poor Shepherds, have preserved an aim, 316 *It was a 3
To whose all-pondering mind a noble aim, 317 *Brave Schill 12
Thy saintly rapture with celestial aim : 326 Sobieski 5
Gracious to service hallowed by its aim ;— 332 Ode : Thanks. 226
And to his Father give its own unerring aim. 339 Tell 27
The guerdon of the steadiest aim. 342 Ital. Itin. 62
Peace greets us ;—rambling on without an aim 349 Val. Dover 5
Of bounty infinite. Between Powers that aim 354 Aquap. 144
Sword dropped not, javelin kept its deadly aim.— 361 *When here 4
What aim had they, the Pair of Monks, in size 363 *What aim 1
That, when his age was measured with his aim, 368 Trajan 61
Whose aim is pleasure light and fugitive : 395 White Doe : Ded. 58
Bold proof that with no selfish aim, 410 White Doe 1298
What feebler means had failed to give, one aim 430 Ecc. Sonn. 2. 9. 3
Defiance breathes with more malignant aim ; 438 Ecc. Sonn. 2. 38. 6
Like those aspirants let us soar—our aim, 462 *Where lies the truth 12
When Europe prostrate lay, the Conqueror's aim, 471 *Despond who 7
Tranquillity ! the sovereign aim wert thou 476 *Tranquillity ! the 1
To sit without emotion, hope, or aim, 488 Pers. Talk 11
Keeps faithful with a singleness of aim ; 493 Hap. War. 40
How happy at all seasons, could like aim 512 *Who rashly 36
Was fondly grafted with a virtuous aim, 515 Penn. 11
Is one great aim of penalty, extend 519 Pun. Death 9. 2
Would tempt me to renounce that humble aim. 521 Epist. Beaumont 37
Far happier they who, fixing hope and aim 529 *Those breathing 126
With heavenly inspiration ; such the aim 538 *In desultory 31
Whose virtues called them forth. That aim is missed ; 585 Ch. Lamb 43
And no unworthy aim, 588 Immortality 80
And told him not to sail as was his aim, 623 *I find 7
Let the new Church be worthy of its aim, 627 *When Severn's 11
And help life onward in its noblest aim. 628 *Deign, Sovereign 28
To brace myself to some determined aim, 633 Prelude 1. 115
More palpable, as best might suit her aim. 637 Prelude 1. 356
Nor is my aim neglected if I tell 643 Prelude 2. 94
St. Peter's Church ; or, more aspiring aim, 691 Prelude 7. 252
The indecision on their part whose aim 720 Prelude 10. 130
Below its aim, or meets with, from without, 720 Prelude 10. 177
Even when the public welfare is their aim, 741 Prelude 13. 69
Tamper with conscience from a private aim ; 748 Prelude 14. 151
To aim and purpose, he consumed his days, 774 Excursion 2. 208
As the prime object of a wise man's aim, 791 Excursion 3. 362

Aim—*continued.*
Yet not to be diverted from his aim, 805 Excursion 4. 259
An effort only, and a noble aim ; 830 Excursion 5. 502
Miss not the humbler good at which they aim, 835 Excursion 5. 857
This is the genuine course, the aim, and end 837 Excursion 5. 1008
Till the heart sickened. So, each loftier aim 859 Excursion 7. 131
Were subject to young Oswald's steady aim, 869 Excursion 7. 756
Aimed. Aimed at the White Man's ignorance the while, 380 Duddon 16. 5
Aimed at the laggards slumbering within doors ; 701 Prelude 8. 149
Of rustic homeliness ; they only aimed 846 Excursion 6. 508
Of Desolation, aimed : to slow decline 872 Excursion 7. 994
The Dalesmen may have aimed the deadly tube, K.8. 244 Recluse 1.1.266
Aims. She knows that only from high aims ensue 22 Desc. Sk. 650
Who aims but at our purse ; and shall this Parricide— 53 Bord. 895
Fit aims, with courage to begin, 224 *'Tis gone 47
All anguish ; Saint that evil thoughts and aims 253 *Fond words 7
By some weak aims at services assigned 262 Retirement 13
With something more propitious to high aims 357 Aquap. 286
Their aims I utterly forswear ; 401 White Doe 509
Slowly the cormorant aims her heavy flight, 419 Ecc. Sonn. 1. 3. 4
With ill-matched aims the Architect who planned— 451 Ecc. Sonn. 3. 43. 2
Less humble, draws her lessons, aims, and rules. 468 St. Bees 155
While he struck his desolate harp without hopes or aims. 474 *Ye shadowy 8
Good aims lie down, and perish in the road 504 Warning 72
If in the aims of men the surest test 504 Warning 89
Millions from glorious aims. Our chains to sever 516 *Hard task 6
Judgments and aims and acts whose higher source 517 Pun. Death 2. 11
Wide were his aims, yet in no human breast 587 Crosth. 13
And loose indifference, easy likings, aims 653 Prelude 3. 325
(If with unworldly ends and aims compared) 712 Prelude 9. 203
Enjoining, as may best promote the aims 721 Prelude 10. 186
Disgusted therefore, or appalled, by aims 797 Excursion 3. 773
Of military sway. The shifting aims, 798 Excursion 3. 822
With the gross aims and body-bending toil 875 Excursion 8. 41
Air. Air listens, like the sleeping water, still, 9 Ev. Wk. 367
But lo ! the Alps, ascending white in air, 11 Desc. Sk. 50
Whether some old Swiss air hath checked her haste, 15 Desc. Sk. 268
Awful the light, and holy is the air. 18 Desc. Sk. 456
Tremble in ever-varying tints of air. 19 Desc. Sk. 469
For creatures doomed to breathe terrestrial air : 22 Desc. Sk. 647
Help from the staff he bore ; for mien and air 24 Guilt 4
We breathed a pestilential air, that made 29 Guilt 283
And looked, and fed upon the silent air 30 Guilt 341
In open air forgetful would I sit 32 Guilt 431
The jolting road and morning air severe. 34 Guilt 553
Beneath their roof, but to the open air 36 Guilt 646
That you are thus the fault is mine ; for the air 39 Bord. 115
That died the moment the air breathed upon it. 47 Bord. 557
The moon shone clear, the air was still, so still 47 Bord. 575
The spirit of vengeance seemed to ride the air. 51 Bord. 794
Is blithe society, who fills the air 80 *Loving she 13
She had a rustic, woodland air, 83 We are Seven 9
To brood on air than on an earthly stream ; 88 H. C. 8
Air blackened, thunder growled, fire flashed from clouds that hid the sky, 91 Poet's Dream 3
And while around it storm as fierce seemed troubling earth and air, 91 Poet's Dream 7
And bore him high through yielding air my debt of love to pay, 92 Poet's Dream 19
Like a Spirit of air she moved, 94 Westmoreland Girl 42
Rapid and gay, as if the earth were air, 95 Brothers 3
Who, in the open air, with due accord 95 Brothers 24
Hanging in the open air—but, O good Sir ! 100 Brothers 314
Their branches in mid air. 109 *Ere with 12
For thou dost haunt the air with sounds 111 *'Tis said that some 31
For thus to see thee nodding in the air, 111 *'Tis said that some 41
In sky, air, earth, and ocean. 112 *Yes ! thou 12
Of Infancy, but still did breathe the air 118 Maternal Grief 15
And cheered ; and now together breathe fresh air 119 Maternal Grief 64
Protected from this cold damp air ?" 119 Sailor's Mother 16
Which liberty and love dispersed in air. 123 V. and J. 153
The owlet, in the moonlight air, 126 Idiot Boy 3
The common air ; hills, which with vigorous step 132 Michael 66
The air or laugh upon a precipice ; 139 Widow 35
Driven in by Autumn's sharpening air 143 *Driven in 1
Such an entire contentment in the air 146 *It was an 13
Or like some natural produce of the air, 146 *It was an 29
Was fettered, and the air by storm disturbed, 150 *When, to 40
The sight is free as air—or crost 154 Flower Garden 29
Then—all at once the air was still, 154 *A whirl-blast 3
There's not a breeze—no breath of air— 155 *A whirl-blast 14
Their nuptial song, a gladsome air ; 157 Oak and Broom 97
Self-poised in air thou seem'st to rest ;— 159 *With little 38
That breath'st with me in sun and air, 159 *With little 45
A Life, a Presence like the Air, 159 Green Linnet 21
And fly about in the air together ! 163 *Art thou the 34
Bees, wafted on the breezy air, 165 Danish Boy 17
No trace of a ferocious air, 166 Danish Boy 46
Clouds that love through air to hasten, 166 Wand. Jew 5
Of his death-wound, when he from innocent air 169 Love lies Bleeding 15
Or with the language of the viewless air 170 *Never enlivened 15
Through the calm and frosty air 170 Kitten 7
And the air is calm in vain ; 171 Kitten 86
The air, as in a lion's den, 173 Waggoner 1. 15
The air was now without a breath— 175 Waggoner 1. 154

Alas—*continued*.
Alas ! where'er the current tends, 285 *Grave of Burns* 37
Alas that ever he was born ! 287 *Ellen Irwin* 21
Alas ! and when he felt their hands—— 297 *Highland Boy* 206
Alas ! what boots the long laborious quest 315 **Alas ! what* 1
Alas ! it may not be : for earthly fame 317 **Brave Schill* 9
Alas ! that from the lips of abject Want 336 *Staub-bach* 10
—Alas ! that One thus disciplined could toil 368 *Trajan* 58
" Alas ! and I have caused this woe ; 372 *Eg. Maid* 223
Alas ! the bright Ship floated, 374 *Eg. Maid* 361
Alas ! thought he, and I have borne 405 *White Doe* 845
Too oft, alas ! by her whose head 405 *White Doe* 883
How soon—alas ! did Man, created pure— 428 *Ecc. Sonn.* 2. 1. 1
And speak the word ——" Alas ! of fearful things 433 *Ecc. Sonn.* 2. 18. 10
The hospitality—the alms (alas ! 434 *Ecc. Sonn.* 2. 23. 11
Alas ! the Genius of our age, from Schools 468 *St. Bees* 154
Alas ! too busy Rival of old Tyre, 475 *Greenock* 9
Alas ! the gratitude of men 484 *Simon Lee* 95
Alas ! how he fumbles about the domains 484 **A plague* 11
" Alas ! that cannot be." 488 *Fountain* 64
Alas for thee, bright Galaxy of Isles, 501 *Humanity* 69
Alas ! with most, who weigh futurity 516 **As leaves* 9
Half hid in native trees. Alas 'tis not, 524 *Epist. Beaumont* 193
Alas ! they pined, they languished while they shone ; 527 **Those breathing* 21
Though I, alas ! may ne'er enjoy 530 †*Redbreast* 5
With numbers near, alas ! no company. 530 **I know* 4
Alas ! that such perverted zeal 534 **Blest is* 71
Alas ! 'twas hardly worth the telling, 536 *Goody Blake* 27
Alas ! that day for Harry Gill ! 537 *Goody Blake* 108
But take it in good part :—alas ! the poor 547 **Rude is* 5
How hard, alas ! to bear, I only know. 557 *Cuck. and Night.* 40
And said, Alas ! that ever I was born, 560 *Cuck.and Night.*208
Alas, alas ! my very heart will break, 560 *Cuck.and Night.*211
Alas, poor Book ! for thy unworthiness, 562 *Cuck.and Night.*298
And to himself full oft he said, alas ! 564 *Troilus* 88
Alas, and there I took of her my leave ; 564 *Troilus* 93
It saith, Alas, why severed are we twain ? 565 *Troilus* 161
Alas ! the twentieth April of his life 575 *Chiabrera* 8. 10
By playful smiles, (alas ! too oft 577 **By playful* 1
Alas ! what idle words ; but take 577 **I come* 26
Alas, how feebly ! but our feelings rise 583 **With copious* 3
Her seat scarce left, she strives, alas ! in vain, 596 *Ev. Wk. Quarto* 248
Alas ! such high emotion touched not me. 654 *Prelude* 3. 342
Might sit and sun himself.—Alas ! alas ! 655 *Prelude* 3. 441
I, too, have been a wanderer ; but, alas ! 678 *Prelude* 6. 252
Power growing under weight : alas ! I feel 707 *Prelude* 8. 555
Alas ! to few in this untoward world, 741 *Prelude* 13. 121
I treat the matter lightly, but, alas ! 783 *Excursion* 2. 780
Not worth the trouble of a thought ?—alas ! 783 *Excursion* 2. 792
Alas ! the endowment of immortal power 804 *Excursion* 4. 205
Alas ! such wisdom bids a creature fly 817 *Excursion* 4. 1083
" Alas ! before to-morrow's sun goes down 840 *Excursion* 6. 113
To fix her eyes—alas ! 'twas hard to bear ! 853 *Excursion* 6. 964
" Alas ! what differs more than man from man ! 887 *Excursion* 9. 206
Alas ! the nations, who of yore received 894 *Excursion* 9. 652
Alas for this Hero ! S. 3. 440 **Said red-ribboned* 21
Alas ! how quiet, and how deep ! K.8. 220 **The snow-tracks* 26
Alas that one beloved, forlorn, K.8. 220 **The snow-tracks* 36
Alas ! 'twas other cause than lack of years L.1. 96 *Juvenal* 3. 61
Alban. And dreadful respite. Thus was Alban tried, 420 *Ecc. Sonn.* 1. 6. 9
The Alban Sites and walls of lofty Rome. K. 8. 281 **Arms and* 9
Albano's. Albano's dripping Ilex avenue, 360 *Albano* 3
Albeit. Albeit of a stern unbending mind, 133 *Michael* 161
For joy and rest, albeit to find them only 231 *Clouds* 93
(Albeit of effect profound) 324 *Ode 1814* 92
Albeit lifting human to divine, 357 *Aquap.* 308
Albeit his deep-worn channel doth immure 379 *Duddon* 12. 2
Albeit sickness, lingering yet, 386 *Yarrow Rev.* 45
Albeit labouring for a scanty band 451 *Ecc. Sonn.* 3. 43. 3
Albeit oft the Virgin-mother mild 465 **The cattle* 12
Of sunset ever there, albeit streams 470 *Bala-Sala* 11
Albeit shattered and impaired) 472 *Ossian* 21
Albeit uninspired by love, 498 **The sylvan* 8
Buildings, albeit rude, that have maintained 547 **Rude is* 2
Albeit putting forth a fainter light. 622 **Among all* 12
Albeit lifeless then, and doomed to sleep 641 *Prelude* 1. 594
Albeit long after the importunate bell 653 *Prelude* 3. 306
And measured passions of the stage, albeit 693 *Prelude* 7. 405
Even as this setting sun (albeit the Vale 706 *Prelude* 8. 471
Than to do wrong, albeit themselves have erred. 854 *Excursion* 6. 1071
That one, albeit of these degenerate times, 875 *Excursion* 8. 37
Such pleasure now is mine, albeit forced, K.8. 250*Recluse* 1.1.491
Albert. Albert, in thy race we cherish 629 *Installation* 95
Albinos. Are here—Albinos, painted Indians, Dwarfs, 697 *Prelude* 7. 707
Albion. Intrepid sons of Albion ! not by you 325 **Intrepid sons* 1
Albion's. And Albion's giants quelled, 102 *Artegal* 14
Such is Albion's fame and glory, 628 *Installation* 17
Beat against Albion's shore, since ear of mine 721 *Prelude* 10. 239
On Albion's noble Race in freedom born, 890 *Excursion* 9. 393
Albogasio's. To Albogasio's olive bowers, 343 *Eclipse* 35
Alcæus. When the live chords Alcæus smote, 499 **Departing summer* 38
Alcairo. Alcairo, Babylon, or Persepolis ; 688 *Prelude* 7. 81
Alcestis. Alcestis, a reanimated corse, 210 *Laod.* 81
Alchemists. Fruitless as those of aery alchemists, 832 *Excursion* 5. 633
Alcove. And shrubs—to hang upon the warm alcove, 264 **Lady ! the* 4
For instant flight ; the Sage in yon alcove 393 **The Lovers* 4
When here, in this remote alcove, 407 *White Doe* 1027
Nor lacking, for fit company, alcove, 547 **Rude is* 12'
Alder. Upon that alder sit ; 111 **'Tis said that some* 27
And, from his alder shades and rocky falls, 636 *Prelude* 1. 272
Where two tall hedge-rows of thick alder boughs 763 *Excursion* 1. 460
Aldermen. And *worship* Mayors, Tipstaffs, Aldermen and all. L. 1. 88 *Juvenal* 1. 18
Alders. Beneath the alders, near the river ; 242 *P. B.* 532
For Thee, green alders have together wound 377 *Duddon* 5. 6
And sail that glides the well-known alders by. 592 *Ev. Wk. Quarto* 48
Ale. Offered a greeting of good ale 174 *Waggoner* 1. 54
While the warm hearth exalts the mantling ale, 379 *Duddon* 13. 12
Of the silver-rimmed horn whence he dealt his mild ale ! 569 *Farmer* 16
Right good ale he bowses ; S. 3. 423 *Tinker* 15
Ale-house. Every ale-house should then have a feast on its walls. 571 *Avarice* 8
Alert. When thou art up, alert and gay, 158 **In youth* 58
But thou, perhaps, (alert as free 341 *Ital. Itin.* 19
Turned this way—that way ! sportive and alert 693 *Prelude* 7. 438
Alert to follow as the Pastor led, 892 *Excursion* 9. 569
Alfred. The pious ALFRED, King to Justice dear ! 425 *Ecc. Sonn.* 1. 26. 2
Of Alfred boasts remote Jerusalem, 425 *Ecc. Sonn.* 1. 26. 12
In sacred converse gifts with Alfred shares. 425 *Ecc. Sonn.* 1. 26. 14
The Race of Alfred covet glorious pains 425 *Ecc. Sonn.* 1. 27. 5
That orb whose beams round Saxon Alfred shone : 471 **Despond who* 11
Her darling Alfred, *might* have spoken ; 495 *Fact* 26
Of Saxon liberty that Alfred wore, 504 *Warning* 59
Alfred, dear Babe, thy great Progenitor ! 504 *Warning* 60
For ever.—The Spirit of Alfred, at the head 516 **Young England* 6
Sir Alfred Irthing, with appropriate words 872 *Excursion* 7. 971
Alice. And said, " My name is Alice Fell ; 82 *Alice Fell* 43
Of Alice and her grief I told ; 82 *Alice Fell* 54
The little orphan, Alice Fell ! 82 *Alice Fell* 60
Alien. Shall on some lovely Alien set 164 **Fair Lady* 14
On motley bands of alien flowers 301 *Bran* 122
And alien storms with home-bred ferments claim 438 *Ecc. Sonn.* 2. 38. 7
By monstrous theories of alien growth, 514 **Long-favoured* 2
Lest alien frenzy seize thee, waxing wroth, 514 **Long-favoured* 3
Into the tumult sent an alien sound 638 *Prelude* 1. 443
A sort of alien scattered from the clouds. 692 *Prelude* 7. 350
To what an alien spirit had acquired 795 *Excursion* 3. 625
The unhappy alien hoping to obtain 844 *Excursion* 6. 398
Alienation. To wilful alienation from the right, 653 *Prelude* 3. 323
Aliens. Aliens, is God's good winter for their haunts. 431 *Ecc. Sonn.* 2. 12. 14
Alight. Which, they foresee, must soon alight 181 *Waggoner* 4. 91
There to alight upon crisp moss and range, 353 *Aquap.* 38
From the warm breeze that bears thee on, alight 455 *Rydal Mere* 33
Through humbleness, the Spirit that did alight 552 *Prioress* 18
Alighted. Or descend where the ark alighted, 218 **Inmate of* 31
Alighted, there the Stranger stood alone ; 226 *Vernal Ode* 15
Ere on firm ground the car alighted ; 372 *Eg. Maid* 194
And where'er their strokes alighted, 535 *Egremont* 43
And at the *Hoop* alighted, famous Inn. 649 *Prelude* 3. 17
Alighting. Forthwith alighting on the ground, 82 *Alice Fell* 17
Alights. And there alights 'mid that aerial host 343 *Eclipse* 39
Alike. Alike, when first the bittern's hollow bill 2 *Ev. Wk.* 19
Alike in whelming snows and roaring waves. 14 *Desc. Sk.* 207
Be scorn and fear and hope alike forgot 22 *Desc. Sk.* 666
In Palestine ? Where he despised alike 37 *Bord.* 18
Doth prey alike on two distracted Countries, 41 *Bord.* 209
Admitting no resistance, bends alike 57 *Bord.* 1089
To occupy—both fools, or wise alike, 60 *Bord.* 1238
Learn how she can feel alike 94 *Westmoreland Girl* 50
But hand and voice alike are still ; 112 **How rich* 11
Alike indulged to all, we paused, one now, 148 **A narrow* 27
Alike are vain. 284 *Grave of Burns* 12
Of hearts and hands alike " prepared 342 *Ital. Itin.* 67
The glorious temple—did alike proceed 354 *Aquap.* 142
All kinds alike seemed favourites of Heaven. 377 *Duddon* 6. 14
Studied alike in palace and in cot. 393 **The Lovers* 14
Confirmed alike in progress and decline. 431 *Ecc. Sonn.* 2. 10. 14
As will be owned alike by bad and good, 478 **Lonsdale ! it* 12
There's indifference, alike when he fails or succeeds, 482 *Character* 9
Be Thou to love and praise alike impelled, 511 **So fair* 20
Cheerful alike if bare of flowers as now, 530 *Poor Robin* 27
Rivals in effort ; and, alike intent 541 *Grace Darl.* 52
Upon its mother) may be both alike 586 *Ch. Lamb* 115
Alike, when first the vales the bittern fills, 592 *Ev. Wk. Quarto* 25
Fostered alike by beauty and by fear : 636 *Prelude* 1. 302
We rested in the shade, all pleased alike, 643 *Prelude* 2. 68
Both silent and both motionless alike ; 643 *Prelude* 2. 112
And now and then, alike from need of theirs 669 *Prelude* 5. 253
One spirit ruling in each heart ; alike 711 *Prelude* 9. 131
Alike to body and to mind : his port, 711 *Prelude* 9. 146
Faithful alike in forwarding a day 752 *Prelude* 14. 440
Cast out, alike of person and of thing. 775 *Excursion* 2. 242
The wandering Herbalist,—who, clear alike 788 *Excursion* 3. 161
Earnest alike, let both from hill to hill 789 *Excursion* 3. 191
Her annual, her diurnal, round alike 795 *Excursion* 3. 613
And local accidents, shall tend alike 820 *Excursion* 4. 1241
And uncorrupted senators, alike 825 *Excursion* 5. 177
Dear Youth, by young and old alike beloved, 868 *Excursion* 7. 706
Gifts nobler are vouchsafed alike to all ; 887 *Excursion* 9. 221
Granted alike in the outset of their course 888 *Excursion* 9. 271
Been shown, alike to body and to mind." 888 *Excursion* 9. 289

Alone—*continued.*
In which he sate alone, with unclosed eyes, 548 *Stay, bold 28
And peace was given,—nor peace alone, 550 Hermit's Cell 5. 19
For not alone by men of dignity 552 Prioress 3
Forth did I go, alone and fearlessly, 557 Cuck. and Night. 59
To breathe and live but for himself alone, 568 Cumb. Beg. 165
And this alone—the life which now I live 573 Chiabrera 1. 4
And mourn when thou art all alone, 577 *I come 35
For charity's sweet sake alone. 578 *I come 68
Farewell, farewell the heart that lives alone, 579 Peele Castle 53
In works of love, in these alone, 582 *O for a 29
Thy virtues *He* must judge, and He alone, 584 *With copious 63
To me alone there came a thought of grief: 588 Immortality 22
But Death alone their vain regret destroys. 598 Ev. Wk. Quarto 362
But now with other soul I stand alone 609 Desc.Sk.Quarto 366
On his wet bed, abandon'd and alone. 613 Desc.Sk.Quarto 613
Alone ascends that mountain nam'd of white 614 Desc.Sk.Quarto 690
The charge belong'd to her alone) 620 Birth of Love 29
But the poor Cripple was alone 621 Andrew Jones 14
Standing alone, and at his feet 621 Andrew Jones 24
And not by strangers to our blood alone, 627 *We gaze 6
Were bronzed with deepest radiance, stood alone 636 Prelude 1. 296
Were shining o'er my head. I was alone, 636 Prelude 1. 315
While on the perilous ridge I hung alone, 637 Prelude 1. 336
Alone upon the rock—oh, then, the calm 644 Prelude 2. 170
From unknown causes. I was left alone 646 Prelude 2. 277
Sublimer joy; for I would walk alone, 646 Prelude 2. 302
Have something to pursue. And not alone, 646 Prelude 2. 322
Alone upon some jutting eminence, 647 Prelude 2. 343
Voyaging through strange seas of Thought, alone. 650 Prelude 3. 63
And as I paced alone the level fields 650 Prelude 3. 93
That spells seemed on me when I was alone, 652 Prelude 3. 229
Standing alone, as from a rampart's edge, 658 Prelude 4. 4
Alone, continuing there to muse: the slopes 661 Prelude 4. 178
Where an old man had used to sit alone, 661 Prelude 4. 202
Rising or setting, would he stand alone 671 Prelude 5. 368
While I was roving up and down alone, 672 Prelude 5. 431
Alone, beneath this fairy work of earth. 676 Prelude 6. 94
Of greatness, love, and beauty. Not alone, 679 Prelude 6. 305
Pacing, two social pilgrims, or alone 683 Prelude 6. 548
Alone, within the valley, at a point 684 Prelude 6. 642
Checked our unwearied steps. Let this alone 686 Prelude 6. 731
Of Savoyards; or, single and alone, 689 Prelude 7. 179
Stationed alone upon a spiry rock 703 Prelude 8. 274
Alone, that something of a better life 703 Prelude 8. 313
Not in my single self alone I found, 722 Prelude 10. 266
Not favoured spots alone, but the whole Earth, 729 Prelude 11. 117
And that alone, my office upon earth; 732 Prelude 11. 348
One great society alone on earth: 733 Prelude 11. 394
"The Wealth of Nations," *where* alone that wealth 741 Prelude 13. 78
With overweening trust alone we give 742 Prelude 13. 170
For this alone is genuine liberty: 748 Prelude 14. 132
Rest, and be not alone, but have thou there 748 Prelude 14. 177
Him had I marked the day before—alone 756 Excursion 1. 38
Grow larger in the darkness; all alone 758 Excursion 1. 128
To feed such appetite—nor this alone 758 Excursion 1. 152
Nor we alone, but that which each man loved 763 Excursion 1. 471
And she was left alone. She now, released 769 Excursion 1. 857
Alone, through half the vacant sabbath day; 769 Excursion 1. 877
Through the long winter, reckless and alone; 770 Excursion 1. 905
And her discernment; not alone in rights, 775 Excursion 2. 237
Than the mute agents stirring there:—alone 782 Excursion 2. 724
Who at her bidding early and alone, 783 Excursion 2. 786
The moment I was seated here alone, 783 Excursion 2. 802
Fast anchored in the desert?—Not alone 791 Excursion 3. 372
And those wild paths were left to me alone. 794 Excursion 3. 556
Quick change of objects; and, to laugh alone, 799 Excursion 3. 903
And reason's steadfast rule—thou, thou alone 802 Excursion 4. 91
With no inferior power. You dwell alone; 809 Excursion 4. 558
You walk, you live, you speculate alone; 809 Excursion 4. 559
Alone or mated, solitude was not. 810 Excursion 4. 633
That poor men's children, they, and they alone, 813 Excursion 4. 786
For succour; but perhaps he sits alone 817 Excursion 4. 1086
Blind were we without these: through these alone 830 Excursion 5. 497
Not for gross good alone which ye produce, 831 Excursion 5. 616
—Alone within her solitary hut; 833 Excursion 5. 704
While traversing alone yon mountain-pass. 833 Excursion 5. 735
Not from the naked *Heart* alone of Man 837 Excursion 5. 979
And all desisted, all, save him alone. 841 Excursion 6. 218
Round his domain, desirous not alone 844 Excursion 6. 394
Alone, with loitering step, and upward eye 849 Excursion 6. 760
Alone, within her widowed Mother's house. 851 Excursion 6. 854
To think of one, blind and alone, advancing 864 Excursion 7. 492
This transfer is permitted,—not alone 865 Excursion 7. 522
When he had risen alone! No braver Youth 869 Excursion 7. 811
The Mother left alone,—no helping hand 878 Excursion 8. 267
Tossed on the waves alone, or 'mid a crew 891 Excursion 9. 487
But is the property of him alone 891 Excursion 9. 515
From human converse to frequent alone S.3. 436 *The doubt 169
For ever left alone am I. K.8. 219 *The snow-tracks 3
I might have dropp'd, and died alone K.8. 220 *The snow-tracks 29
Had left his fellows, made his way alone K.8. 229 *I will 145
Meantime the father had returned alone K.8. 229 *I will 159
The fields and mountains, not alone for this K.8. 230 *I will 206
Alone and devious from afar he came; K.8. 236 Recluse 1. 1. 6
Not upon me alone hath been bestowed, K.8. 243 Recluse 1. 1. 232
Inseparable, not for these alone, K.8. 243 Recluse 1. 1. 251
No, we are not alone, we do not stand, K.8. 248 Recluse 1. 1. 427

Alone—*continued.*
Whose lustre we alone participate, K.8. 248 Recluse 1. 1. 437
Which shines dependent upon us alone, K.8. 248 Recluse 1. 1. 438
Where these things are. He truly is alone, K.8. 252 Recluse 1. 1. 593
I grant that not in parents' hearts alone L. 1. 96 Juvenal 3. 57

Along. (*Partial list.*)
Along the confines of the Esk and Tweed 38 Bord. 62
You paced along, when the bewildering moonlight 39 Bord. 111
Trotting alone along the beaten road, 44 Bord. 411
Come to him thus, and drove the weary Wight along. 108 Indolence 36
And down the rocks can leap along 108 Louisa 5
Along the margin of a bay: 187 *I wandered 10
Felt in the blood, and felt along the heart; 206 Tintern 28
Rolled audibly!—it swept along, 245 P. B. 836
Along the nether region's rugged frame! 452 Ecc. Sonn. 3. 46. 8
His eyes are turned, and, as he moves along, 567 Cumb. Beg. 46
They move along the ground; and, evermore, 567 Cumb. Beg. 47
That peck along the road, regard him not. 572 Animal Tran. 2
Along that very Loire, with festal mirth 716 Prelude 9. 431

Alongside. Might trudge it alongside each other!" 179 Waggoner 3. 55

Aloof. Have dared to keep aloof; 168 Turtledove 12
So may all trace and sign of deeds aloof 361 *When here 9
Belike less happy.—Stand no more aloof! 390 Highland Hut 14
He did not arm, he walked aloof! 412 White Doe 1466

Aloud. She cried aloud; and forth ran out in haste 34 Guilt 557
And oft he groaned aloud, "O God, that I were dead!" 36 Guilt 639
And Johnny burrs, and laughs aloud; 130 Idiot Boy 377
He sobbed aloud. The old Man grasped his hand, 136 Michael 358
That ravishment of mine, and laughed aloud. 147 Joanna 53
"Bring forth another horse!" he cried aloud. 200 Hart-leap 4
Aloud she shrieked! for Hermes re-appears! 211 Laod. 151
To hill and vale proclaims aloud, 215 Kirkstone 84
"Repent! repent!" he cries aloud, 247 P. B. 946
Of them that were before us.—Sing aloud 315 *The Land 9
City and field and flood;—aloud it cried— 323 Ode 1814 28
Present your prayers—go—and rejoice aloud— 332 Ode: Thanks. 229
Aloud, saluted by her voice! 344 *How blest 45
They shout aloud—but Heaven decreed 408 White Doe 1145
The roving bee proclaims aloud 526 *The soaring 3
Pain's wild rebellious burst proclaims her rights aloud. 614 Desc.Sk.Quarto 653
Smitten, the precipices rang aloud; 638 Prelude 1. 440
He left me: I called after him aloud; 667 Prelude 5. 133
Aloud, with fervour irresistible 687 Prelude 7. 5
Of a new master; bleat the flocks aloud. 699 Prelude 8. 24
Her solitary infant cried aloud; 767 Excursion 1. 736
By him that utters it, exclaim aloud, 809 Excursion 4. 535

Aloys. The name of Aloys Reding. 337 Thun 4

Alp. To pant slow up the endless Alp of life. 613 Desc. Sk.Quarto 593

Alpine. Or wild Aosta lulled by Alpine rills, 15 Desc. Sk. 294
O'er the curled waters Alpine measures swell, 19 Desc. Sk. 522
The tall sun, pausing on an Alpine spire, 20 Desc. Sk. 553
Thou from thy Alpine holds at length art driven, 306 *Two Voices 7
Through Alpine vale, or champaign wide, 337 Cath. Cantons 15
Remembering, and green Alpine pastures decked 340 Ranz 6
Blithe Paragon of Alpine grace, 344 *How blest 46
Enwrapt—and winding, between Alpine trees 347 Processions 43
Led on till an Alpine strait confined our view 366 *Fair Land 5
Heedless of Alpine torrents thundering 376 Duddon 1. 7
Niagaras, Alpine passes, and anon 379 Duddon 12. 5
When Alpine Vales threw forth a suppliant cry, 441 Ecc. Sonn. 3. 7. 1
Through Alpine vapours. Such appalling rite 450 Ecc. Sonn. 3. 40. 6
Or like the Alpine Mount, that takes its name 452 Ecc. Sonn. 3. 46. 5
Oft-times from Alpine *chalets* sends a greeting. 524 Epist. Beaumont 206
Strange "weeds" and alpine plants her helm entwine, 608 Desc.Sk.Quarto 329
—The tall Sun, tip-toe on an Alpine spire, 614 Desc.Sk.Quarto 662
Was Nature's, uttered from her Alpine throne; 681 Prelude 6. 431
As aromatic flowers on Alpine turf, 714 Prelude 9. 297

Alps. But lo! the Alps, ascending white in air, 11 Desc. Sk. 50
The eagle of the Alps o'ershades her prey. 16 Desc. Sk. 335
Of the Alps the Chamois bound, 166 Wand. Jew 10
Alps or Andes—they are thine! 217 *Inmate of 18
Through the grey clouds; the Alps are here, 237 P. B. 59
Through the long chain of Alps from mound to mound 314 *Advance—come 4
That all the Alps may gladden in thy might, 315 *Advance—come 13
Among the herdsmen of the Alps, have wrought 315 *Alas! what 12
Among the interior Alps, gigantic crew, 350 Des. Stanzas 20
Caught the far-winding barrier Alps among. 367 *As indignation 11
Down from the Pennine Alps how fiercely sweeps 476 Nunnery 2
To where the Alps, ascending white in air, 603 Desc. Sk. Quarto 51
Wide o'er the Alps a hundred streams unfold, 608 Desc. Sk.Quarto 342
The eagle of the Alps o'ershades his prey. 609 Desc.Sk.Quarto 407
Alps overlooking Alps their state upswell; 612 Desc.Sk.Quarto 563
Bound to the distant Alps. A hardy slight 680 Prelude 6. 326
Ended in this,—*that we had crossed the Alps.* 684 Prelude 6. 591
That, stretching far among the Alps, assumed 685 Prelude 6. 690
So lately, journeying toward the snow-clad Alps. 710 Prelude 9. 35
My own delights; the lordly Alps themselves, 733 Prelude 11. 409
And afterwards, when through the gorgeous Alps 737 Prelude 12. 191
"As 'mid some happy valley of the Alps," 823 Excursion 5. 92

Already. Prepared already for the sacrifice. 57 Bord. 1093
Already I've been punished to the height 67 Bord. 1638
I prithee, to the harm thou'st done already. 75 Bord. 2126
As I already have in thought devised; 105 Artegal 216
Whom I already loved;—not verily 131 Michael 24

Already—*continued.*
'Tis already like a hill — 157 *Sexton* 4
Already hast survived that great decay, — 172 *Infant Daughter* 6
Behold, already they forget to shine, — 278 **The most* 7
Inviting words—perchance already flung — 332 *Ode : Thanks.* 212
Already gathered in this favoured Land — 354 *Aquap.* 105
Their guide in flight—already she — 408 *White Doe* 1124
Perhaps already to his home ; — 411 *White Doe* 1359
Already half his race hath run ; — 506 *Lab. Hymn* 22
And breathing life of flesh, as if already — 510 **Among a* 7
Thy faults, where not already gone — 578 **I come* 66
Grew dear to me : already I began — 644 *Prelude* 2. 177
Too weak to gather it, already love — 645 *Prelude* 2. 246
Hath beautified that flower ; already shades — 646 *Prelude* 2. 248
What is already written in the hearts — 668 *Prelude* 5. 185
If not already from the woods retired — 705 *Prelude* 8. 444
Already hinted at, of other mould— — 714 *Prelude* 9. 289
He, on that ministry already bound, — 715 *Prelude* 9. 411
Already said of patriotic love, — 731 *Prelude* 11. 274
Of Nature, and already was prepared, — 759 *Excursion* 1. 192
Already formed upon the village-green. — 773 *Excursion* 2. 125
Too much of frailty hath already dropped ; — 793 *Excursion* 3. 496
Gone forth already to the far-off seat — 834 *Excursion* 5. 803
From every mind !—Already had the sun, — 893 *Excursion* 9. 590
My Son ! behold the Tide already spent — S. 3. 427 **My Son* 1
It is too late already for such hope, — K. 8. 244 *Recluse* 1. 1. 265
For they are blest already. None would give — K. 8. 244 *Recluse* 1. 1. 280
Already have I gained. The inward frame — K. 8. 249 *Recluse* 1. 1. 472
Already hath sprung up within my heart — K. 8. 250 *Recluse* 1. 1. 504
Already with a stranger whom we love — K. 8. 254 *Recluse* 1. 1. 653

Also, *omitted.*

Altar. Before the Altar. What, if he were sick, — 57 *Bord.* 1070
There be who pray nightly before the Altar. — 67 *Bord.* 1655
Shrine, Altar, Image, Offerings hung in sign of gratitude ; — 92 *Poet's Dream* 47
Upon the altar, to the Maid he loved. — 123 *V. and J.* 119
While incense from the altar breathes — 228 *Devot. Incit.* 30
Had pledged his troth before the altar — 246 *P. B.* 904
Of stagnant waters : altar, sword, and pen, — 307 **Milton ! thou* 3
He knows that from a holier altar came — 329 *Ode : Thanks.* 51
The altar, to deride the fane, — 337 *Cath. Cantons* 4
Marched round the altar—to commemorate — 346 *Processions* 12
They round his altar bore the hornèd God, — 346 *Processions* 24
When toward the altar from her bower — 374 *Eg. Maid* 352
Or altar, whence the cross was rent, — 397 *White Doe* 124
Lo ! Discord at the altar dares to stand — 420 *Ecc. Sonn.* 1. 9. 4
Temple and Altar sink, to hide their shame — 423 *Ecc. Sonn.* 1. 17. 9
Then he, who to the altar had been led, — 428 *Ecc. Sonn.* 1. 38. 5
Down to the humbler altar, which the Knight — 430 *Ecc. Sonn.* 2. 6. 5
The Vested Priest before the Altar stands ; — 446 *Ecc. Sonn.* 3. 26. 1
The Altar calls ; come early under laws — 446 *Ecc. Sonn.* 3. 25. 11
May-garlands, there let the holy altar stand — 450 *Ecc. Sonn.* 3. 39. 11
And humble altar, 'mid your sumptuous aisles — 451 *Ecc. Sonn.* 3. 42. 4
Shed round the altar a celestial calm ; — 500 *Humanity* 5. 24
An altar is in each man's cot, — 506 *Lab. Hymn* 18
Before the Altar, where the Sacrament — 520 *Pun. Death* 12. 7
To the high altar its determined place ; — 534 **When in* 12
Our Christian altar faithful to the east, — 535 **When in* 23
From the altar of this sacrifice, — 544 *Russ. Fug.* 239
Before the altar while the Mass doth last : — 555 *Prioress* 185
It is the sacrificial altar, fed — 744 *Prelude* 13. 331
A fragment, like an altar, flat and smooth : — 787 *Excursion* 3. 60
Altar and image, and the inclusive walls — 811 *Excursion* 4. 672
Shrine, altar, image, and the massy piles — 814 *Excursion* 4. 899
Even like an altar lit by fire from heaven, — 818 *Excursion* 4. 1121
When grove was felled, and altar was cast down, — 870 *Excursion* 7. 814
Altar, and cross, and church of solemn roof, — 873 *Excursion* 7. 1024
On the dim altar burned continually, — 877 *Excursion* 8. 189
From her own lonely altar ? Do not think — 885 *Excursion* 9. 44

Altars. With altars undisturbed of mossy stone, — 185 *Yew-trees* 30
Altars for Druid service fit ; — 214 *Kirkstone* 13
Did incense-bearing altars rise, — 216 *Enterprise* 40
The priests are from their altars thrust ; — 228 *Devot. Incit.* 50
How oft above their altars have been hung — 326 **Emperors and* 3
Altars that piety neglects ; — 366 **Ye Trees* 2
Even for our Altars—for the prize — 403 *White Doe* 652
The darksome altars would have blazed — 410 *White Doe* 1265
Of prostrate altars, shrines defaced, — 416 *White Doe* 1890
Again with frankincense the altars smoke — 436 *Ecc. Sonn.* 2. 33. 11
Their altars they forego, their homes they quit, — 441 *Ecc. Sonn.* 3. 6. 9
From altars threatened, levelled, or defiled, — 449 *Ecc. Sonn.* 3. 36. 3
Keep watch before the altars of St. Bees. — 467 *St. Bees* 72
Wherever Christian altars have been raised, — 584 *Ch. Lamb* 25
Who tend her altars, wait upon her throne, — 810 *Excursion* 4. 597
Of those pure altars worthy ; ministers — 839 *Excursion* 6. 44
(As books and haply votive altars vouch) — S. 3. 435 **The doubt* 125

Altar-stone. Where altar-stone and rock-hewn seat — 301 *Bran* 65

Altar-window. Imbued the altar-window ; fixed aloft — 825 *Excursion* 5. 162

Alteration. Strange alteration wrought on every side — 96 *Brothers* 97
Whence alteration in the forms of things, — 873 *Excursion* 7. 1011

Alterations. Of alterations human hands might make — K. 8. 227 **I will* 102

Altered. Desponding Father ! mark this altered bough, — 266 **Desponding Father* 1
To fit proportion with my altered state ! — 267 **As the* 10
As lightly, though of altered hue. — 343 *Eclipse* 15
An altered look upon the advancing Stranger — 369 *Eg. Maid* 26

Altered—*continued.*
And recognised it, though an altered form, — 571 **There is a Flower* 10

Altering. Of hue and altering shape that charmed all eyes. — 527 **Those breathing* 20

Alternate. Alternate empire in the shades below— — 460 **Queen of* 5
Alternate ; carrying holy thoughts and prayers — 500 *Humanity* 30
Alternate, all a summer's day, or scoured — 636 *Prelude* 1. 292
Alternate and revolving ! How benign, — 790 *Excursion* 3. 316
Alternate progress and impediment, — K. 8. 250 *Recluse* 1. 1. 489

Alternately. Alternately they mount her back, and rest — 6 *Ev. Wk.* 230
Alternately relieves their weary feet ; — 595 *Ev. Wk. Quarto* 216
Alternately, and plain below, while breath — 745 *Prelude* 13. 347
That rule alternately the weary hours, — 790 *Excursion* 3. 276
Two several souls alternately had lodged, — 842 *Excursion* 6. 288
Stealing alternately at them and us — 882 *Excursion* 8. 566

Alternating. Brisk toil, alternating with ready ease, — 11 *Desc. Sk.* 17

Alternations. When alternations came of rage — 391 *Highland Broach* 49

Alternative. For ever—sad alternative ! preferred, — 125 *V. and J.* 237
Desperate alternative ! what fiend could dare — 381 *Duddon* 22. 11
The last alternative of Life or Death. — 518 *Pun. Death* 5. 14

Although. (*Partial list.*) *See* **'Tho'.**
Although I for my Primer shall be shent, — 554 *Prioress* 90
Although I cannot quaver so in vain — 559 *Cuck. and Night.* 119
Although for pain thou may'st be like to die, — 561 *Cuck. and Night.* 244

Altitude. To measure the altitude of some tall crag — 760 *Excursion* 1. 274

Altogether. Had altogether yielded to the sun, — 148 **A narrow* 8
But, altogether as we go, — 179 *Waggoner* 3. 77

Alway. Was taken up, singing his song alway ; — 555 *Prioress* 171
After my knowledge I have loved alway ; — 556 *Prioress* 206
Unless it alway stay with him, I wis — 560 *Cuck. and Night.* 179

Always. And Leonard being always by his side — 100 *Brothers* 333
And we have always used him well ; — 129 *Idiot Boy* 304
And for this cause not always, I believe, — 134 *Michael* 190
And I will always be thy guide, — 145 *Her Eyes* 53
The blind Boy always had his share ; — 295 *Highland Boy* 72
Not always is the heart unwise, — 334 **In Bruges* 25
For change, to whom the new looks always green ! — 436 *Ecc. Sonn.* 2. 33. 3
That makes the path before him always bright : — 493 *Hap. War.* 7
And mind always that thou be good and true, — 561 *Cuck. and Night.* 246
I pray to God with her always to be, — 561 *Cuck. and Night.* 257
Giving him always hope, that she the morrow — 565 *Troilus* 167
Sits brooding, lives not always to that end, — 634 *Prelude* 1. 141
Unmoved. I could not always lightly pass — 652 *Prelude* 3. 261
In mournful thoughts, and always might be found, — 765 *Excursion* 1. 633
Not always from intolerable pangs — 791 *Excursion* 3. 379

Am. (*Partial list.*)
Unless I differ from the thing I am — 43 *Bord.* 319
Well as the wreck I am permits. And you, Sir ? — 43 *Bord.* 336
A stone than what I am.—But two nights gone, — 45 *Bord.* 422
An inch, till I am answered. Know you aught — 46 *Bord.* 497
Now I *do* love thee. I am thunderstruck. — 46 *Bord.* 528
Thou wilt relate the story. Am I neither — 49 *Bord.* 648
Since that Man left me.—No, I am not lost. — 52 *Bord.* 803
Fallen am I, and worn out, a useless Man ; — 52 *Bord.* 824
Which way soe'er I turn, I am perplexed. — 53 *Bord.* 878
Weak ! I am weak—there does my torment lie, — 53 *Bord.* 884
Might envy, and am now,—but he shall know — 54 *Bord.* 939
What I am now— Praying or parleying ?—tut ! — 54 *Bord.* 940
I am of flesh and blood, and may I perish — 57 *Bord.* 1097
I am your hearer. This I caught, and more — 59 *Bord.* 1198
Young as I am, I might go forth a teacher, — 59 *Bord.* 1223
Old am I, and to genial pleasure slow ; — 557 *Cuck. and Night.* 37
Not one word have I now, I am so forlorn,— — 560 *Cuck. and Night.* 209
When next May comes, if I am not afraid. — 561 *Cuck. and Night.* 235
Since I am wholly at thy will ? what joy — 563 *Troilus* 69
I am right sorry Troilus will die : — 564 *Troilus* 109
And said, I am in constant dread I trow, — 564 *Troilus* 145
That stripped of arms I to my end am brought — 575 *Chiabrera* 6. 11

Amain. His bosom heaves, his Spirit towers amain, — 18 *Desc. Sk.* 459
Deluge of tender thoughts then rushed amain, — 33 *Guilt* 494
Silent he stood ; then laughed amain,— — 81 †*Mother's Return* 7
She led him home, and wept amain, — 297 *Highland Boy* 236
And long privation, now dissolves amain, — 441 *Ecc. Sonn.* 3. 3. 7
That tears burst forth amain. Did gleams appear ? — 446 *Ecc. Sonn.* 3. 24. 9
To viewless realms his Spirit towers amain, — 612 *Desc. Sk. Quarto* 548
Suspended by the blast that blew amain, — 637 *Prelude* 1. 334
I bounded down the hill shouting amain — 658 *Prelude* 4. 12
His front against the blast, and runs amain, — 723 *Prelude* 10. 373
Spinning amain, as if to overtake — 856 *Excursion* 6. 1180

Amalek. These sons of Amalek, or laid them low !"— — 427 *Ecc. Sonn.* 1. 33. 8

Amaracus. Where he on soft *amaracus* is laid, — 624 *Æneid* 51

Amaranth. Bright Spirit, not with amaranth crowned — 345 **How blest* 70
Immortal amaranth and palms abound. — 418 *Ecc. Sonn.* 1. 1. 14

Amaranthine. 'Tis hers to pluck the amaranthine flower — 259 **Weak is* 11
Those palms and amaranthine wreaths — 324 *Ode 1814* 50
Garlands shall wear of amaranthine bloom, — 474 **On to* 13
An amaranthine crown of flowers forlorn— — K. 8. 325 [?] **The vestal* 7

Amassed. Till our joint savings had amassed enough — 672 *Prelude* 5. 472

Amazed. At houses, men, and common light, amazed. — 31 *Guilt* 401
With a dim eye, distracted and amazed ; — 34 *Guilt* 563
Confounded and amazed— — 104 *Artegal* 119

Amazed—*continued.*
Awed, delighted, and amazed ! . . . . . . 217 **Inmate of* 4
Amazement. Amazement runs before the towering casque . . . . 421 *Ecc. Sonn.* 1. 10. 5
Amazement strikes the crowd : while many turn . 428 *Ecc. Sonn.* 1. 38. 10
Amazement rose to pain, ... 545 *Russ. Fug.* 354
And with amazement smote ;—thereby to assert . 811 *Excursion* 4. 661
Amazonian. To lead those ancient Amazonian files ; 190 *Beggars* 11
Amber. (Like clouds of sunset) into lucid amber. . 371 *Eg. Maid* 180
With amber honey from the mountain's breast ; . 525 *Epist. Beaumont* 243
Ambient. With ambient streams more pure and bright . . . . 375 **The Minstrels* 50
Ambiguous. Ambiguous, neither wholly thine nor theirs. . . . . 290 *Kilchurn* 5
Ambition. Thy office, thy ambition, be henceforth 78 *Bord.* 2303
Him, in whose wretched heart ambition failed, . 103 *Artegal* 86
Whom she to young Ambition bore, ... 215 *Enterprise* 21
If like ambition be *their* guide. . . . . . . 228 *Devot. Incit.* 12
Thou, with ambition modest yet sublime, . . . 252 *Picture* 11
Or with a new ambition raised ; . . . . . 298 *Brownie's Cell* 9
Ambition—following down this far-famed slope . 345 **Ambition—following* 1
Of checked ambition, tyranny controlled, . . . 349 *Boulogne* 11
By no profane ambition, Powers that thrive . . 354 *Aquap.* 146
Urged by Ambition, who with subtlest skill . . 425 *Ecc. Sonn.* 1. 28. 1
By blind ambition, be this tribute paid. . . . 429 *Ecc. Sonn.* 2. 2. 14
For, sooth to say, ambition, in the breast . . 432 *Ecc. Sonn.* 2. 15. 12
Greedy ambition, armed to treat with scorn . . 469 **The feudal* 4
Ambition frames and heart-humilities. . . . 472 **Arran ! a* 12
Enough of climbing toil !—Ambition treads . . 497 **Enough of climbing* 1
I saw (ambition quickening at the view) . . . 532 **Once I* 13
Her bed, his mountains mad Ambition piles ; . . 617 *Desc. Sk. Quarto* 799
Of zeal and just ambition, than to live . . . 636 *Prelude* 1. 256
Through fond ambition of that hour, I strove . 685 *Prelude* 6. 671
By personal ambition unenslaved, ... 688 *Prelude* 7. 63
Though like ambition, such was he, O Friend ! . 715 *Prelude* 9. 418
Of low ambition or distempered love ? " . . . 735 *Prelude* 12. 74
Ambition to attempt, and skill to win. . . . 774 *Excursion* 2. 190
Wretched ambition drops astounded, fell . . . 795 *Excursion* 3. 674
Into the dewy clouds. Ambition reigns . . . 807 *Excursion* 4. 394
Has, through ambition of his soul, given way . 809 *Excursion* 4. 542
Of ill-advised Ambition and of Pride . . . . K.8. 255 *Recluse* 1.1.673
Ambition's. They shrunk, insane ambition's barren goal— . . . . 321 **Humanity, delighting* 16
Ambitious. Beware of rousing an ambitious thought ; 104 *Artegal* 164
On aught of more ambitious show . . . . . 113 *Lament* 32
Rising to no ambitious height ; yet both, . . . 151 **Forth from* 4
Thou liv'st with less ambitious aim, ... 158 **In youth* 29
Ambitious to be seen or heard, ... 165 *Parrot* 27
O most ambitious Star ! an inquest wrought . . 208 **It is no* 9
And sometimes with ambitious wing that soars . 218 *Recluse* 1. 1. 207
Take with you some ambitious Youth ! . . . 237 *P. B.* 128
But, with a less ambitious sympathy, ... 282 **While beams* 5
Her skill she tried with less ambitious views. . . 333 *Ded. Tour* 8
And guide the Bard, ambitious to be One . . . 389 *Tyndrum* 10
Troubling the last holds of ambitious Rome, . . 394 **How profitless* 2
If unreproved the ambitious eagle mount . . . 527 **Those breathing* 37
Sometimes the ambitious Power of choice, mistaking . . . . 634 *Prelude* 1. 166
Whether the Painter, whose ambitious skill . . 690 *Prelude* 7. 240
Ambitious projects, pleased me less ; I sought . 741 *Prelude* 13. 61
Not less ambitious once among the wilds . . . 744 *Prelude* 13. 313
Where youth's ambitious feet might move at large ; 794 *Excursion* 3. 539
Be joyless as the blind ? Ambitious spirits— . . 815 *Excursion* 4. 947
To follow reason's least ambitious course ; . . 831 *Excursion* 5. 595
And by ambitious longings undisturbed ; . . . 839 *Excursion* 6. 47
Ambitiously. Ambitiously the office tried ; . . . 182 *Waggoner* 4. 190
That, while they most ambitiously set forth . . 743 *Prelude* 13. 217
Ambitiously collected. Yet the sigh, ... 842 *Excursion* 6. 266
Ambles. And deftly ambles towards the south. . 243 *P. B.* 610
Ambrose. Stood Richard, Ambrose, Christopher, . 401 *White Doe* 477
To Ambrose that ! and then a knell . . . . 411 *White Doe* 1369
Ambrosio. True is it that Ambrosio Salinero . . 574 *Chiabrera* 5. 1
Ambush. Into the ambush of despair ; . . . . 232 *Power of Sound* 13
Amended. Yet if I live it shall amended be, . . 561 *Cuck.and Night.*234
Amendeth. For evermore his servants Love amendeth, ... 560 *Cuck.and Night.*191
Amends. Has made amends. Thanks to you both ; but, Oh Sir !. . . . . 45 *Bord.* 431
If such the bright amends at last. . . . . . 177 *Waggoner* 2. 75
The frosty wind, as if to make amends . . . 622 *Recluse* 1. 1. 158
Five rivers broad and vast, made rich amends, . 683 *Prelude* 6. 532
Last look, to make the best amends he may : . 709 *Prelude* 9. 16
Amenities. Even here, where her amenities are sown 819 *Excursion* 4. 1192
Amerdale. In the deep fork of Amerdale ; . . . 415 *White Doe* 1707
America. And, when America was free . . . . 192 *Ruth* 28
America, the Hunter-Indian ; Moors ; . . . . 690 *Prelude* 7. 226
American. With the American (a thought which suits . . . . 789 *Excursion* 3. 240
Amiable. Youth amiable ; O friend so true of soul . 575 *Chiabrera* 7. 3
Amicable. Life, Death, in amicable interchange ;— 350 *Des. Stanzas* 43
An amicable smile retained the life . . . . . 779 *Excursion* 2. 523
Amicably. " These grassy heaps lie amicably close," 857 *Excursion* 7. 31
Amid. (*Partial list.*) *See* **Mid.**
Amid the cypress with which Dante crowned . . 260 **Scorn not* 8
France, humbled France, amid her wild disorders, . 327 *Ode 1815* 41
Amid oblivious weeds. " *O come to me,* . . . 423 *Ecc. Sonn.* 1. 17. 10
And watch from pike to pike amid the sky . . 609 *Desc. Sk.Quarto* 368

Amidst. And stands amidst you now an armèd creature, ... 311 **Who rises* 16
Amiss. Through Death,—so judging we should judge amiss. . . . . 139 *Widow* 31
Now should you say I judge amiss, ... 177 *Waggoner* 2. 76
Seen fairly, is not much amiss ! . . . . . . 179 *Waggoner* 3. 75
To gentle Natures, thanks not Heaven amiss. . . 262 *Retirement* 14
Hence, prayers are shaped amiss, and dirges sung 423 *Ecc. Sonn.* 1. 20. 8
Shall ye, by Poets even, be judged amiss ! . . 477 *Steamboats* 3
Who sees, foresees ; who cannot judge amiss, . 519 *Pun. Death* 11. 13
Whoever against Love mean aught amiss. . . 559 *Cuck.and Night.*130
And dread of shame that will not do amiss ; . . 559 *Cuck.and Night.*158
His too fond father's car amiss to drive. . . . 564 *Troilus* 147
And is half pleased with things that are amiss, . 729 *Prelude* 11. 151
As selfish passion urged, would act amiss ; . . 732 *Prelude* 11. 319
Ah ! let not aught amiss within dispose . . . 816 *Excursion* 4. 1018
Amity. And in the excess of amity, ... 179 *Waggoner* 3. 49
Haunts of a strengthening amity . . . . . 415 *White Doe* 1712
With amity and glee ; we bore a name . . . 681 *Prelude* 6. 402
Of amity, whose living threads should stretch . 797 *Excursion* 3. 747
Religion tells of amity sublime . . . . . . 817 *Excursion* 4. 1089
Of amity and gratitude." " Thus sanctioned," . 848 *Excursion* 6. 645
Strangers to all particular amity, ... K.8. 251 *Recluse* 1.1.534
Ammonian. The priests and damsels of Ammonian Jove . . . . 346 *Processions* 21
Amnesty. An amnesty for what is past ; . . . 110 *Forsaken* 4
Among. (*Partial list.*) *See* **'Mong.**
Her last death-shriek, distinct among a thousand. 40 *Bord.* 187
" Among these children was a Widow's son, . . 553 *Prioress* 50
And him among the accursèd Jews she sought. . 555 *Prioress* 148
How among them it was a common tale, . . . 557 *Cuck. and Night.* 48
There sate I down among the fair fresh flowers, . 558 *Cuck. and Night.* 66
Among the farms and solitary huts, ... 567 *Cumb. Beg.* 96
Hazard or toil ; among the sands was seen . . 575 *Chiabrera* 6. 5
Amorous. And amorous music on the water dies. . 12 *Desc. Sk.* 106
Whose amorous water multiplies . . . . . 497 *Lycoris* 13
Soft as the gentle kiss of amorous maid . . . 630 [?] **O Moon* 11
Of amorous passion. And that gentle Bard, . . 653 *Prelude* 3. 278
Amphibious. To a floating island, an amphibious spot . . . . 654 *Prelude* 3. 333
Amphion. The Gift to king Amphion . . . . 234 *Power of Sound* 129
Amphitrite. As the pearly car of Amphitrite, . . 296 *Highland Boy* 119
Ample. And in her ample heart loving even me— . 57 *Bord.* 1106
Or duty sanctions. We will have ample justice. . 57 *Bord.* 1113
What wonder, then, if in such ample field . . . 103 *Artegal* 57
Of an industrious life, and ample means ; . . . 134 *Michael* 212
Is ample, and some little might be stored . . . 149 **A narrow* 53
From east to west, in ample vest . . . . 180 *Waggoner* 4. 55
Nor harsh nor grating, though of ample power . 207 *Tintern* 92
More ample than the time-dismantled Oak . . 219 *Haunted Tree* 7
Into two ample horns his forehead wide," . . . 251 **Pelion and* 5
An ample sovereignty of eye and ear. . . . . 267 **Though narrow* 4
A shell of ample size, and light . . . . . 296 *Highland Boy* 118
And bade the Snow their ample backs bestride, . 321 **Humanity, delighting* 30
Lugano ! on thy ample bay ; . . . . . . 343 *Eclipse* 32
Ample for a wingèd hope, ... 503 **Like a* 65
And thou, O Friend ! who in thy ample mind . 653 *Prelude* 3. 317
With ample recompense) giants and dwarfs, . . 691 *Prelude* 7. 271
Of Leven's ample estuary lay . . . . . . 725 *Prelude* 10. 515
A twilight of its own, an ample shade, ... 756 *Excursion* 1. 12
Up through an ample vale, with higher hills . . 772 *Excursion* 2. 91
O'er the smooth surface of an ample crag, . . 787 *Excursion* 3. 41
This knowledge ample recompense affords . . 813 *Excursion* 4. 814
Her native brightness. As the ample moon, . . 817 *Excursion* 4. 1062
With ample shadows, seemingly, no less . . . 821 *Excursion* 4. 1304
Beneath his ample brow, in darkness paired,— . 865 *Excursion* 7. 508
Among his fellows, while an ample map . . . 869 *Excursion* 7. 784
Ampler. An ampler ether, a diviner air, . . . 211 *Laod.* 105
A circuit ampler than the lake beneath, . . . 218 *Recluse* 1. 1. 209
Obtaining ampler boon, at every step, ... 353 *Aquap.* 39
Beneath an ampler sky a region wide . . . . 384 *Duddon* 32. 9
There is an ampler page for man to quote, . . 393 **The Lovers* 12
Maeonides of ampler mind ; . . . . 473 *Ossian* 80
He comes not back ; an ampler space . . . . 479 *Somnamb.* 68
For One who speaks in numbers ; ampler scope . 520 *Pun. Death* 14. 2
Of ampler or more varied argument, ... 641 *Prelude* 1. 643
To see the river flow with ampler range . . . 656 *Prelude* 3. 496
Amplest. Derived from clouds and storms !) the amplest range . . . . 219 **This Height* 3
The broad full visage, chest of amplest mould, . 270 *Henry : Portrait* 3
The amplest share of heavenly favour gives ; . . 433 *Ecc. Sonn.* 2. 19. 11
Amplitude. A correspondent amplitude of mind ; . 708 *Prelude* 8. 606
And clearest insight, amplitude of mind, . . . 749 *Prelude* 14. 191
Amused. Attention was engrossed ; and, thus amused, ... 711 *Prelude* 9. 85
Amusement. Amusement, where the Mother does not miss . . . . 119 *Maternal Grief* 70
With that amusement, and a simple look . . . 707 *Prelude* 8. 535
Amusements. *See* **Home-amusements.**
Amusing. Amusing, yet uneasy, novelty, . . . 764 *Excursion* 1. 575
Amusive. A grave proficient in amusive feats . . 826 *Excursion* 5. 269
An, *omitted.*
Analogies. From strict analogies by thought supplied 651 *Prelude* 3. 125
Analogous. Analogous, the moon to me was dear ; 645 *Prelude* 2. 191
Analogy. Analogy to uproar and misrule, . . . 707 *Prelude* 8. 516
Analyse. Hard task, vain hope, to analyse the mind, 645 *Prelude* 2. 228
Analysed. Have solved the elements, or analysed 815 *Excursion* 4. 952
Analytic. Than analytic industry to me . . . 647 *Prelude* 2. 379

Anarchy. Striking through English breasts the anarchy . . . . 309 **What if* 4
For eyes and ears ! what anarchy and din, . . 697 *Prelude* 7. 686
Who from the anarchy of dreaming sleep, . . . 802 *Excursion* 4. 87
Anathemas. Than to allay. Anathemas are hurled 437 *Ecc. Sonn.* 2. 36. 9
Anatomise. To anatomise the frame of social life ; . 731 *Prelude* 11. 280
Ancestor. Like that Wise ancestor of thine . . . 629 *Installation* 99
Ancestors. To his ancestors restored . . . . 205 *Brougham* 153
Which all his glorious ancestors approve : . . . 305 **The Voice* 13
Think ye your British Ancestors forsook . . . 515 **Men of* 3
Adorns, in which the good Man's ancestors . . 824 *Excursion* 5. 125
Our ancestors, within the still domain . . . . 877 *Excursion* 8. 186
Or where their ancestors erected huts, ... 879 *Excursion* 8. 367
Ancestral. Uprisen—to lodge among ancestral kings ; 325 *Enghien* 2
In his ancestral palace, where, from morn . . . 359 **They—who* 4
Hearths loved in childhood, and ancestral floors ;. 458 *Sea-shore* 11
She heard the ancestral stream ; . . . . . . 544 *Russ. Fug.* 254
Our dim ancestral Past in vision clear ; . . . 744 *Prelude* 13. 320
The Sultan hides deep in ancestral tombs. . . 809 *Excursion* 4. 569
Who, with ancestral feeling, can perceive . . . 838 *Excursion* 6. 25
Ancestry. How fragile ! yet of ancestry . . . 227 *Vernal Ode* 116
The eagle worthy of her ancestry ? . . . . . 350 *Des. Stanzas* 47
Who counts among her ancestry . . . . . 399 *White Doe* 262
Honouring the hope of noble ancestry. . . . 504 *Warning* 46
With all his ancestry. Then peace to him, . . 548 **Stranger ! this* 23
And customs of our rural ancestry . . . . . 780 *Excursion* 2. 551
Anchor. The skiffs, at anchor where with umbrage wide . . . . 4 *Ev. Wk.* 106
Fixed on the anchor left by Him who saves . . 14 *Desc. Sk.* 206
Much sorrow ere the fleet its anchor weighed ; . 29 *Guilt* 281
The anchor of my purest thoughts, the nurse, . 207 *Tintern* 109
Some lying fast at anchor in the road, ... 258 **With Ships* 3
Or, in the hollow surge, at anchor rocked . . . 454 *Sea-side* 14
While that stout Ship at anchor lay . . . . 579 **Sweet Flower* 16
The skiffs with naked masts at anchor laid, . . 593 *Ev. Wk. Quarto* 105
Or drops his anchor down with plunge profound ; 597 *Ev. Wk. Quarto* 320
Toss like a ship at anchor, rocked by storms ; . 710 *Prelude* 9. 51
The torch, the star, the anchor ; nor except . . 827 *Excursion* 5. 336
Or ride at anchor in her sounds and bays ; . . 876 *Excursion* 8. 138
Anchorage. Of trusty anchorage, or scudding o'er . 369 *Eg. Maid* 41
Anchored. Our boat is safely anchored by the shore, 106 *Farewell* 9
For ever anchored in her sheltering bay. . . . 252 *Picture* 8
Against an anchored vessel's side ; . . . . . 397 *White Doe* 145
Fast anchored in the desert ?—Not alone . . . 791 *Excursion* 3. 372
Anchoress. And there, a saintly Anchoress, she dwelt 267 *St. Cath.* 13
No saintly anchoress . . . . 543 *Russ. Fug.* 158
Anchorite. Nor would the nicest Anchorite exclude 379 *Duddon* 14. 3
Anchorites. Her anchorites, like piety of old ; . 823 *Excursion* 5. 31
Anchors. Anchors her placid beauty. Not a leaf, . 842 *Excursion* 6. 295
Ancient. *See* **Antient.**
And who, that walks where men of ancient days . 15 *Desc. Sk.* 289
It was a spot where, ancient vows fulfilled, . . 27 *Guilt* 148
Led by its murmur, to the ancient oak . . . 62 *Bord.* 1357
The ancient spirit is not dead ; . . . . . . 119 *Sailor's Mother* 7
That in our ancient uncouth country style . . 133 *Michael* 111
Of her who in my heart still holds her ancient place. 141 *Arm. Lady* 114
And the ancient church was filled with light, . . 144 **Driven in* 54
Their ancient neighbour, the old steeple-tower, . 147 *Joanna* 20
That ancient Woman seated on Helm-crag . . 147 *Joanna* 56
Of ancient mountains, or my ear was touched . 148 *Joanna* 70
Our walk was far among the ancient trees : . . 149 *M. H.* 1
What wonder ? at her bidding, ancient lays . . 153 *Morn. Ex.* 19
Of ancient ether was no more, ... 168 *Pilgrim's Dream* 58
With no one but the ANCIENT WOMAN,. . . . 175 *Waggoner* 1. 175
To lead those ancient Amazonian files ; . . . 190 *Beggars* 11
The words of ancient time I thus translate, . . 203 *Brougham* 3
Sigh forth their ancient melodies ! . . . . . 215 *Kirkstone* 40
What though this ancient Earth be trod . . . 216 *Enterprise* 43
The ancient faith disclaim ? . . . . 223 *Wishing-gate* 39
His ancient dower Olympus hath not sold ; . . 251 **Pelion and* 3
Heed not the pillage of man's ancient heart. . . 255 *S. H.* 14
Is ancient Piety for ever flown ? . . . . . 256 *Decay of Piety* 11
In which some ancient Chieftain finds repose . . 262 **Mark the* 8
Day's mutable distinctions.—Ancient Power ! . . 265 **Hail, Twilight* 4
Leaving an ancient dome, and towers like these, . 292 **Degenerate Douglas* 7
Have forfeited their ancient English dower . . 307 **Milton ! thou* 5
Whether, as bards have told in ancient song, . . 312 **Who rises* 65
In due observance of an ancient rite, ... 318 **In due* 1
Our ancient freedom ; else 'twere worse than vain 318 *Biscayan* 3
Guardians of Biscay's ancient liberty. . . . . 319 *Guernica* 14
Hither, like yon ancient Tower . . . . . . 336 **Jesu ! bless* 13
And of the ancient hills ! . . . . 341 *San Salv.* 30
Descend, and, on the brow of ancient Rome . . 357 *Aquap.* 292
Flattery in Ancient Rome's pure-minded style : . 359 **Complacent Fictions* 10
From ancient Rome, downwards through that bright dream . . . . 359 **They—who* 11
And habit of his vow. That ancient Man— . . 362 **List—'twas* 82
Hail, ancient Manners ! sure defence, ... 376 **The Minstrels* 55
And lasting terror through that ancient Hold. . 383 *Duddon* 27. 8
Round strath and mountain, stamped by the ancient tongue . . . . 389 *Sound of Mull* 3
To be looked down upon by ancient hills, . . . 389 *Breadalb.* 11
The forest huge of ancient Caledon . . . . . 392 *Inglewood* 1
The Lovers took within this ancient grove . . 393 **The Lovers* 1
That ancient voice which wont to call . . . . 396 *White Doe* 23
The rites of ancient piety . . . . 400 *White Doe* 371
Be parted from his ancient ground : . . . . 402 *White Doe* 553
All ancient honour in the realm. . . . . . 403 *White Doe* 645
—This bring I from an ancient hearth, . . . 403 *White Doe* 664

Ancient—*continued.*
And in Saint Cuthbert's ancient seat . . . . 404 *White Doe* 712
And privilege of ancient love ; . . . . . . 409 *White Doe* 1250
While, in their ancient habitation . . . . . 413 *White Doe* 1573
Ancient of days ! that to the eternal Sire, . . 419 *Ecc. Sonn.* 1. 4. 6
Like ivy, round some ancient elm, they twine . 424 *Ecc. Sonn.* 1. 21. 11
Old laws, and ancient customs to derange, . . 426 *Ecc. Sonn.* 1. 31. 13
The ancient thrones of Christendom are stuff . . 428 *Ecc. Sonn.* 1. 39. 11
Forthwith that ancient Voice which Streams can hear . . . . 432 *Ecc. Sonn.* 2. 17. 5
Against the ancient pine-trees of the grove . . 439 *Ecc. Sonn.* 2. 44. 5
And Faith preserved her ancient purity. . . . 441 *Ecc. Sonn.* 3. 7. 4
Against her ancient virtue. HIGH and LOW, . . 443 *Ecc. Sonn.* 3. 11. 9
Bowing with reverence to the ancient creed, . . 444 *Ecc. Sonn.* 3. 15. 3
Now, ruin, beauty, ancient stillness, all . . 449 *Ecc. Sonn.* 3. 35. 3
Around their ancient grove) with cawing noise . 455 *Rydal Mere* 11
That ancient Fable did to thee assign, ... 460 **Queen of* 2
Forth from their cells ; their ancient House laid low 468 *St. Bees* 147
Where ancient trees this convent-pile enclose, . 470 *Bala-Sala* 3
Of ancient honour ; whence that goodly state . 477 **Lowther ! in* 6
And the most ancient heavens, through Thee, are fresh and strong. . . . . 492 *Duty* 48
That, for the functions of an ancient State— . . 514 **Blest Statesman* 11
How shall your ancient warnings work for good . 518 *Pun. Death* 6. 11
And ancient ordinance, shall endure, ... 534 **Blest is* 98
Ancient castle, woods, and mountains . . . . 536 *Egremont* 83
Of Lowther to this ancient Line, bear witness . 539 **Lady ! a* 24
'Tis sung in ancient minstrelsy . . . . . . 543 *Russ. Fug.* 177
Thin silver hairs, and ancient hamlet fame ; . . 595 *Ev. Wk. Quarto* 176
Who walks, where honour'd men of ancient days . 608 *Desc. Sk. Quarto* 354
Who sang in ancient Greece his loving lay, . . 623 **I find* 13
In ancient times, and ere the Hall was built . . 644 *Prelude* 2. 145
The ghostly language of the ancient earth, . . 646 *Prelude* 2. 309
Of ancient times revive, and youth be trained . 655 *Prelude* 3. 411
To see again, was one by ancient right . . . 659 *Prelude* 4. 94
In ancient story versed, whose breast had heaved 695 *Prelude* 7. 541
Take one,—that ancient festival, the Fair, . . 697 *Prelude* 7. 676
Perennial of the ancient hills ; nor less . . . 698 *Prelude* 7. 757
With looking on, some ancient wedded pair . . 699 *Prelude* 8. 46
Retaineth more of ancient homeliness, ... 712 *Prelude* 9. 216
Of ancient loyalty, and chartered rights, . . . 714 *Prelude* 9. 324
Of ancient Story, thought of each bright spot, . 715 *Prelude* 9. 365
Of Romorentin, home of ancient kings, . . . 716 *Prelude* 9. 481
By ancient lawgivers. In this frame of mind, . 721 *Prelude* 10. 221
Wantoned, fast rooted on the ancient tower . . 722 *Prelude* 10. 279
In which apostasy from ancient faith . . . . 722 *Prelude* 10. 309
But as the ancient Prophets, borne aloft . . . 724 *Prelude* 10. 437
Of ancient Institutions said and done . . . . 731 *Prelude* 11. 261
Of ancient heroes. If I suffered grief . . . . 733 *Prelude* 11. 383
An ancient servant of my father's house . . . 737 *Prelude* 12. 229
Didst chaunt the vision of that Ancient Man, . . 751 *Prelude* 14. 399
Was wholly ignorant that my ancient Friend— . 783 *Excursion* 2. 785
Of a small chapel, where, in ancient time, . . . 784 *Excursion* 2. 814
Of ancient inspiration serving me, ... 797 *Excursion* 3. 763
Beats to the heroic song of ancient days ; . . . 813 *Excursion* 4. 832
Enquire of ancient Wisdom ; go, demand . . . 815 *Excursion* 4. 957
The ancient rural character, composed . . . 824 *Excursion* 5. 117
My ancient Friend and I together took . . . 826 *Excursion* 5. 231
Of ancient minster lifted above the cloud . . . 838 *Excursion* 6. 21
The fire of ancient Caledonia burned : . . . . 844 *Excursion* 6. 415
That ancient story of Prometheus chained . . 846 *Excursion* 6. 539
Drawn from the chords of the ancient British harp 857 *Excursion* 7. 11
Futurity was thought, in ancient times, . . . 865 *Excursion* 7. 532
England, the ancient and the free, appeared . . 870 *Excursion* 7. 856
Sent by the ancient Soul of this wide land, . . 871 *Excursion* 7. 896
For ancient worth and honourable things, . . 872 *Excursion* 7. 960
Or straggling burgh, of ancient charter proud, . 875 *Excursion* 8. 101
Among the clouds, and roars through the ancient woods ; . . . . 878 *Excursion* 8. 304
Lamenting ancient virtues overthrown, . . . 888 *Excursion* 9. 252
And mountains bare, or clothed with ancient woods, 891 *Excursion* 9. 506
The home and ancient birthright of their flock. . K.8. 228 **I will* 132
Which had been sighed for, ancient thought fulfilled K.8. 239 *Recluse* 1.1.107
And if those eagles to their ancient hold . . . K.8. 250 *Recluse* 1.1.517
Thy ancient honours when shalt thou resume ? . L. 1. 94 *Juvenal* 2. 17
Of ancient Ares. . . . . L. 2. 318 *Frag. Æneid* 4. 12

And, *omitted.*
Andates. Or to Andates, female Power ! who gave . 894 *Excursion* 9. 708
Andes. Alps or Andes—they are thine ! . . . 217 **Inmate of* 18
Old Andes thrusts yon craggy spear . . . . 237 *P. B.* 58
Of Andes—frozen gulfs became its bridge— . . 327 *Ode 1815* 22
Andrew. His simple truths did Andrew glean . . 155 *Oak and Broom* 1
His youngest born did Andrew hold : . . . . 156 *Oak and Broom* 7
Andrew there, and Susan here, ... 157 *Sexton* 27
I hate that Andrew Jones : he'll breed . . . 621 *Andrew Jones* 1
It chanc'd that Andrew pass'd that way . . . 621 *Andrew Jones* 21
Quoth Andrew, " Under half-a-crown, ... 621 *Andrew Jones* 28
Andrew's. Andrew's whole fire-side is there. . . 157 *Sexton* 12
And *hence* I say, that Andrew's boys . . . . 621 *Andrew Jones* 31
Anet's. O'er Anet's hopeless seas of marsh to stray, 615 *Desc. Sk. Quarto* 715
Aneurin. Rise !—they *have* risen : of brave Aneurin ask . . . . 421 *Ecc. Sonn.* 1. 10. 1
Anew. And said : I wis, when thou art horn'd anew, 564 *Troilus* 132
And wakes anew life's glimmering trembling fires, 619 *School Ex.* 100
He should depart, to plant himself anew. . . . 864 *Excursion* 7. 430
Angel. The Chapel Oak of Allonville ; good Angel, show it me ! " . . . . 92 *Poet's Dream* 28
And belike a guardian angel . . . . . . 93 *Westmoreland Girl* 23

Another—*continued.*
Softly she glides, another home to seek. . . . 434 *Ecc. Sonn.* 2. 22. 8
These vespers of another year, ... 498 **The sylvan* 20
"Another year is ours;" . . . . 507 *May* 30
Another takes its place. . . . . 507 *May* 64
Another was on Thursday brought, ... 537 *Goody Blake* 111
Some with their notes another manner feigned; . 558 *Cuck. and Night.* 74
Another time he took into his head, ... 564 *Troilus* 106
The little Actor cons another part; . . . . 589 *Immortality* 102
Another race hath been, and other palms are won. . . . . 590 *Immortality* 203
With it's own Virtues springs another earth: . . 616 *Desc.Sk.Quarto* 783
If this be error, and another faith . . . . 648 *Prelude* 2. 419
With clearer knowledge; with another eye . . 661 *Prelude* 4. 214
And bore the semblance of another stream . . 664 *Prelude* 4. 382
As if it appertained to another mind, ... 676 *Prelude* 6. 98
Without unkindness, in another place. . . . . 677 *Prelude* 6. 187
Above all joys, that seemed another morn. . . 678 *Prelude* 6. 197
Another maid there was, who also shed . . . 678 *Prelude* 6. 224
With children gathered round; another street . 689 *Prelude* 7. 175
Another lies at length, beside a range . . . . 690 *Prelude* 7. 205
As if admonished from another world. . . . . 697 *Prelude* 7. 649
Into another region. As a light . . . . . 722 *Prelude* 10. 276
One victory with another, higher far,— . . . 727 *Prelude* 11. 19
My deeper feelings, but another cause, . . . 736 *Prelude* 12. 123
For future restoration.—Yet another . . . . 738 *Prelude* 12. 286
Is but another name for absolute power . . . 749 *Prelude* 14. 190
One deeper than another, self-condemned . . . 818 *Excursion* 4. 1110
To the green meadows of another vale. . . . 823 *Excursion* 5. 66
Another tablet registered the death, ... 825 *Excursion* 5. 185
Was wedded to another, and his heart . . . . 840 *Excursion* 6. 129
Though from another sprung, different in kind: . 843 *Excursion* 6. 368
Methinks, would better suit another place. . . 851 *Excursion* 6. 843
Full blest he was, 'Another Margaret Green,'. . 867 *Excursion* 7. 672
Another and the same! Most beautiful, . . . 890 *Excursion* 9. 442
Of yet another summer's day, not loth . . . 895 *Excursion* 9. 777
And o'er the mountain-wastes. "Another sun," 896 *Excursion* 9. 779
Another sun, and peradventure more; . . . . 896 *Excursion* 9. 781
The journey of another night, ... K.8. 220 **The snow-tracks* 39
I could have lived another day. . . . . . K.8. 220 **The snow-tracks* 41
Faithful companions, yet another year . . . K.8. 243 *Recluse* 1.1.262
First one and then another silver spout, . . . K.8. 251 *Recluse* 1.1.555
Forgive me if I add another claim, ... K.8. 255 *Recluse* 1.1.692

Another's. When trusted to another's care, . . 175 *Waggoner* 1. 123
Another's praise from envy clear. . . . . . 344 **How blest* 13
Another's first, and then her own?) . . . . 344 **How blest* 19
Or by another's sympathy was led, ... 353 *Aquap.* 68
Another's need to suit, ... 582 **O for a* 27
Which was the captive of another's toil . . . 637 *Prelude* 1. 320
She lives another's wishes to complete,— . . . 840 *Excursion* 6. 140

Answer. No voice made answer, he could only hear 25 *Guilt* 34
Recovering heart, like answer did she make; . . 27 *Guilt* 186
Answer these questions, from our common knowledge, ... 38 *Bord.* 39
I'll answer for it that our four-legged friend . . 51 *Bord.* 774
To stay behind!—Hearing at first no answer, . 52 *Bord.* 811
And spake to you, why did you give no answer? 55 *Bord.* 959
'Twas a strange answer that he made; he said, . 63 *Bord.* 1446
No answer—hush—lost wretch, he lifts his hand . 67 *Bord.* 1669
A wicked Man should answer for his crimes. . . 75 *Bord.* 2123
Made answer to that plaintive sound. . . . . 85 *Shepherd-boys* 77
The Boy no answer made by words, but, so earnest was his look, ... 93 *Poet's Dream* 69
One that will answer to my mind; . . . . . 117 *Affl. Marg.* 69
No answer, only took the mother's hand . . . 125 *V. and J.* 232
To this did Johnny answer make, ... 126 *Idiot Boy* 62
Made answer, like a traveller bold, ... 131 *Idiot Boy* 448
The Youth made answer with a jocund voice; . 135 *Michael* 299
The Jay makes answer as the Magpie chatters; . 195 *Resolution* 6
A gentle answer did the old Man make, . . . 196 *Resolution* 85
Shall answer, for our song is of the Clouds, . . 230 *Clouds* 65
A simple answer! but even so forth springs, . . 252 **Why, Minstrel* 5
"Wait, prithee, wait!" this answer Lesbia threw 274 **Wait, prithee* 1
No sign of answer made by word or face: . . . 306 **We had* 9
There would the Indian answer with a smile . . 380 *Duddon* 16. 4
The tombs—which hear and answer that brief cry, 445 *Ecc. Sonn.* 3. 20. 11
And some a bold unerring answer made: . . . 445 *Ecc. Sonn.* 3. 22. 7
The tear in answer flows; . . . . 479 *Somnamb.* 78
And she made answer "ENDLESS SORROW!" . . 494 *Force of Prayer* 7
No answer did the Matron give, ... 542 *Russ. Fug.* 29
Concise in answer; solemn and sublime . . . 665 *Prelude* 4. 441
He with a smile made answer, that in truth . . 666 *Prelude* 5. 52
That they might answer him; and they would shout. . . . . 671 *Prelude* 5. 374
Nor had I power to answer ere she told . . . 766 *Excursion* 1. 660
Prompt answer; they proclaim the annual Wake, 773 *Excursion* 2. 120
And have an answer—thither come, and shape . 782 *Excursion* 2. 715
We shouted—but no answer! Darkness fell . . 783 *Excursion* 2. 798
And, with that ready answer satisfied, ... 789 *Excursion* 3. 183
To appear and answer; to the grave I spake . . 796 *Excursion* 3. 689
But what is error?"—"Answer he who can!" . 812 *Excursion* 4. 766
This answer followed.—"You have turned my thoughts . . . . 815 *Excursion* 4. 919
Amid these wilds, this answer may suffice; . . 842 *Excursion* 6. 300
"Though," said the Priest in answer, "these be terms . . . . 846 *Excursion* 6. 558
And answer flowed, the fetters of reserve . . . 882 *Excursion* 8. 525

Answered. An inch, till I am answered. Know you aught . . . . 46 *Bord.* 497

Answered—*continued.*
"To Durham," answered she, half wild— . . . 82 *Alice Fell* 35
She answered, "Seven are we;" . . . . . . 83 *We are Seven* 18
The people answered with a loud acclaim: . . 105 *Artegal* 226
She answered, soon as she the question heard, . 119 *Sailor's Mother* 17
—Thus answered Johnny in his glory, ... 131 *Idiot Boy* 452
The Housewife answered, talking much of things . 136 *Michael* 318
And Fairfield answered with a mountain tone; . 147 *Joanna* 60
"That cannot be," one answered—"she is dead:"— 191 *Beggars* 41
And requiems answered by the pulse that beats . 232 *Power of Sound* 15
"Then Francis answered—'Trust thy Son, . . 410 *White Doe* 1309
With quickening impulse answered their mute pleas, 466 *St. Bees* 62
"Fear not," quickly answered Hubert; . . . . 535 *Egremont* 33
Answered him thus:—'This song, I have heard say, 553 *Prioress* 80
He answered, "to the Person suited well, . . . 778 *Excursion* 2. 459
He answered, "has been here; but could not well 779 *Excursion* 2. 543
Answered the sick Man with a careless voice— . 780 *Excursion* 2. 612
"Far happiest," answered the desponding Man, . 789 *Excursion* 3. 207
And where they lie, how answered and appeased. 813 *Excursion* 4. 813
"I blame them not," he calmly answered—"no; 827 *Excursion* 5. 309
The Solitary answered: "Such a Form . . . 839 *Excursion* 6. 102
"He loved," the Vicar answered, "deeply loved, . 840 *Excursion* 6. 118
Of Wilfred Armathwaite?" The Vicar answered, 854 *Excursion* 6. 1079
The Vicar answered,—"No disdainful pride . . 858 *Excursion* 7. 38
The Pastor answered, "You have read him well. 866 *Excursion* 7. 564

Answering. *See* **Faintly-answering.**
While o'er the desert, answering every close, . . 16 *Desc. Sk.* 344
With answering vows. Plebeian was the stock, . 121 *V. and J.* 14
Answering to the shouting Cuckoo, ... 209 **Yes, it* 3
That, answering to thy touch, will sound the hour; 229 *Cuckoo-clock* 6
More thrilling melodies; Witch answering Witch, 336 *Staub-bach* 7
Right gladly answering signals we displayed, . . 524 *Epist. Beaumont* 213
Turrets and pinnacles in answering files, . . . 649 *Prelude* 3. 5
Answering the question which himself had asked, 802 *Excursion* 4. 68
With answering constellations, under earth, . . 812 *Excursion* 4. 713
With answering brightness in the hearts of all . 828 *Excursion* 5. 416
Were met with answering sympathy and love. . 864 *Excursion* 7. 462
In answering to itself; or like a hound . . . K.8. 245 *Recluse* 1.1.323
Keeps pace, a harvest answering to the seed— . K.8. 255 *Recluse* 1.1.672

Answers. Answers, and we know not whence; . . 209 **Yes, it* 14
Whose current answers to the heart's desire, . . 395 *White Doe: Ded.* 4
Answers with more than Indian fortitude, . . . 437 *Ecc. Sonn.* 2. 35. 9
That answers unexpectedly awry, ... 688 *Prelude* 7. 101
As the mind answers to them, or the heart . . 697 *Prelude* 7. 670
Strange question, yet it answers not itself. . . K.8. 255 *Recluse* 1.1.681

Antechapel. The antechapel where the statue stood 650 *Prelude* 3. 60

Antedate. Or rather rose the day to antedate, . . 432 *Ecc. Sonn.* 2. 14. 3

Anthem-book. The whilst the rest their anthem-book repeat . . . . 553 *Prioress* 67

Anthems. Of human anthems,—choral song, or burst 818 *Excursion* 4. 1163

Ant-hill. Rise up, thou monstrous ant-hill on the plain . . . . 689 *Prelude* 7. 149

Antic. Or dromedary, with an antic pair . . . 689 *Prelude* 7 177

Anticipate. To anticipate the privilege of Age. . . 791 *Excursion* 3. 327

Anticipated. Had seen the anticipated quarry turned 718 *Prelude* 10. 25

Anticipations. Lacked not anticipations, tender dreams, ... 675 *Prelude* 6. 45

Antics. Were her antics played in the eye . . . 171 *Kitten* 33.
The antics striving to outstrip each other, . . 693 *Prelude* 7. 431
And, fraught with antics as the Indian bird . . 842 *Excursion* 6. 290

Antient. *See* **Ancient.**
Till Egypt sees her antient fame outvied. . . . L. 1. 88 *Juvenal* 1. 20

Antioch. When, Antioch blazing to her topmost towers, ... 40 *Bord.* 178

Antiparos. The Grotto of Antiparos, or the Den . 707 *Prelude* 8. 562

Antipodes. Antipodes unconscious of each other, . 890 *Excursion* 9. 449
Through him the Antipodes in thy name delight. S. 3. 442 **Vasco, whose* 14

Antiquarian. The antiquarian humour, and am pleased . . . . 788 *Excursion* 3. 134

Antiquarian's. Exclaimed—"The sagest Antiquarian's eye . . . . 871 *Excursion* 7. 921

Antiquarians. While poring Antiquarians search the ground . . . . 275 **While poring* 1

Antiquated. From hour to hour the antiquated Earth 304 **Jones! as* 6

Antique. Where antique roots its bustling course o'erlook, ... 3 *Ev. Wk.* 67
And antique castles seen through gleamy showers. 14 *Desc. Sk.* 225
What seems an antique castle spreading wide; . 26 *Guilt* 114
Of antique form; this large, for spinning wool; . 132 *Michael* 83
Go back to antique ages, if thine eyes . . . . 313 **Go back* 1
By antique Fancy trimmed—though lowly, bred . 339 *Schwytz* 1
And marvel not that antique Faith inclined . . 347 *Processions* 68
No fiction was it of the antique age: . . . . 378 *Duddon* 11. 1
As story says, in antique days . . . . . . 478 *Somnamb.* 12
And antique towers nodded their foreheads high, . 529 **Those breathing* 118
When in the antique age of bow and spear . . 534 **When in* 1
Antique, and Cottage with verandah graced, . . 547 **Rude is* 11
Where antique roots its bustling path o'erlook, . 593 *Ev. Wk. Quarto* 82
And antique castles seen thro' drizzling show'rs. 607 *Desc.Sk.Quarto* 282
The Druids worshipped, or the antique walls . . 643 *Prelude* 2. 102
In the antique market-village where was passed . 757 *Excursion* 1. 53
Crowned by its antique summer-house—descends, 881 *Excursion* 8. 492

Antiquity. Want, through neglect of hoar Antiquity. 253 **Aerial Rock* 12
Strains—which, as sage Antiquity believed, . . 261 **I heard (alas* 2
Of the world's praise, from dark antiquity . . 307 **It is not* 3
The Spirit of Antiquity—enshrined . . . . 334 **The Spirit* 1
That oft befriends Antiquity, ... 391 *Highland Broach* 88
To days of dim antiquity; . . . . 398 *White Doe* 225

Antiquity—*continued.*
Antiquity salutes him with a smile, ... 463 **Why should the* 4
Before antiquity and steadfast truth . . . . 654 *Prelude* 3. 394
Stand near the worthiest of Antiquity) . . . 715 *Prelude* 9. 420
See as they have been taught—Antiquity . . . 729 *Prelude* 11. 160
Antiquity's. No sign of hoar Antiquity's esteem . 376 *Duddon* 3. 10
Antlered. Above his antlered head ; . . . . . 544 *Russ. Fug.* 268
Antlers. The leafy antlers sprout ; . . . . . 168 *Wren's Nest* 36
The palmy antlers of a hunted Hart, ... 393 *Hart's-horn* 4
And glistening antlers are descried ; . . . . 457 **Had this* 31
Antony. Down to the suburbs of St. Antony, . . 710 *Prelude* 9. 46
Anubis. The reverence by the fierce Anubis lost. . L. 1. 89 *Juvenal* 1. 26
Anxieties. The anxieties of human love, . . . 498 **The sylvan* 23
Anxiety. Anxiety lest mischief should befall her . 41 *Bord.* 234
Is pregnant with anxiety, ... 404 *White Doe* 767
That maniac's fond anxiety, and go . . . . 668 *Prelude* 5. 160
In quietness, without anxiety : . . . . . . 692 *Prelude* 7. 323
I looked in such anxiety of hope ; . . . . . 739 *Prelude* 12. 313
And manhood's vain anxiety dismissed ; . . . 816 *Excursion* 4. 1040
Of turbulence, anxiety, and fear— . . . . . 863 *Excursion* 7. 369
Anxious. *See* **Fondly-anxious, Over-anxious, Too-anxious.**
And the poor Boy was busier still, with work of anxious heed. . . . . 91 *Norman Boy* 12
Accompanied his steps, by anxious love . . . 125 *V. and J.* 250
The mourner is cheered, and the anxious have rest ; 188 *Music* 11
Who leads them on ?—The anxious people see . 213 *Dion* 22
Come with each anxious hope subdued . . . . 222 *Triad* 180
Anxious for far-off children, where . . . . . 224 **'Tis gone* 34
Anxious an aery name to immortalize. . . . . 313 **Go back* 8
The patriot Mother's weight of anxious cares ! . 344 **How blest* 52
" The Wizard of the North," with anxious hope . 353 *Aquap.* 57
How fluttered then thy anxious heart for me, . 445 *Ecc. Sonn.* 3. 22. 8
A care more anxious, or a heavier grief ? . . . 461 **Where lies the truth* 3
In anxious bondage, to such nice array . . . 497 **Enough of climbing* 10
Anxious duty hindering, ... 503 *Warning* 10
Be strong in faith, bid anxious thoughts lie still ; 505 *Warning* 160
We started, looked again with anxious eyes, . . 523 *Epist. Beaumont* 129
Now dupes me, trusting to an anxious eye . . 635 *Prelude* 1. 247
That anxious visitation ;—moon and stars . . 636 *Prelude* 1. 314
From anxious fear of error or mishap, ... 670 *Prelude* 5. 280
Drew to the spot an anxious crowd ; some looked 672 *Prelude* 5. 444
And clomb with eagerness, till anxious fears . . 683 *Prelude* 6. 575
When from afar invoked by anxious love ? . . 733 *Prelude* 11. 423
By worldly-mindedness or anxious care ; . . . 762 *Excursion* 1. 393
Was ended, that long anxious day, I learned, . 766 *Excursion* 1. 674
An anxious duty ! which the lofty site, . . . 834 *Excursion* 5. 762
That Father was, and filled with anxious fear, . 855 *Excursion* 6. 1132
The obligation of an anxious mind, ... 866 *Excursion* 7. 571
Not seldom over anxious to make known . . . 893 *Excursion* 9. 584
Anxiously. " We've waited anxiously and long," . 238 *P. B.* 178
Conqueror beloved ! expected anxiously ! . . . 442 *Ecc. Sonn.* 3. 9. 12
Anxiousness. Reverence the hope whose vital anxiousness . . . . 568 *Cumb. Beg.* 177
Of anxiousness with which they are combined. . K. 8. 249 *Recluse* 1. 1. 458
Any. (*Partial list.*)
For any lady I have seen this twelvemonth. . . 43 *Bord.* 314
Nor moves her hands to any needful work : . . 44 *Bord.* 385
In a deep wood remote from any town. . . . 50 *Bord.* 698
Nor any half so sure. This Stripling's mind . . 58 *Bord.* 1162
That may not be retold to any ear. . . . . 59 *Bord.* 1199
Against him dare not any wight say nay ; . . . 557 *Cuck. and Night.* 17
That any living heart should sleepy be . . . 557 *Cuck. and Night.* 44
Anything. You have not *buried* anything ? . . . 72 *Bord.* 1919
Be anything, sweet Rill, but that which thou art now. . . . . 111 **'Tis said that some* 36
Earth has not anything to show more fair : . . 269 *Westm. Bridge* 1
Thy Father—anything to thee ! . . . . . . 288 *Highland Girl* 61
Nor know we anything so fair . . . . . . 492 *Duty* 43
Why think of anything but present good ? " . . 633 *Prelude* 1. 100
As, more than anything we know, instinct . . 706 *Prelude* 8. 492
In anything, save only as the act . . . . . 711 *Prelude* 9. 138
Grief call it not, 'twas anything but that,— . . 722 *Prelude* 10. 289
Anywhere. And find, find anywhere, a right . 411 *White Doe* 1399
Found scarcely anywhere in like degree ! . . . 491 *Tribute : Dog* 26
Deep vale, or anywhere, the home of both, . . 741 *Prelude* 13. 126
Heard anywhere ; but in a place like this . . . 780 *Excursion* 2. 549
Aosta. Or wild Aosta lulled by Alpine rills, . . 15 *Desc. Sk.* 294
Apace. Slant watery lights, from parting clouds, apace . . . . 4 *Ev. Wk.* 92
A flood of tears that flowed apace . . . . . 414 *White Doe* 1663
Gliding apace, with shadows in their train, . . 814 *Excursion* 4. 874
Apart. From ringing team apart and grating wain— 12 *Desc. Sk.* 82
And, while they stood upon the plain apart, . . 104 *Artegal* 128
"Whence the undeserved mistrust ? Too wide apart 140 *Arm. Lady* 47
Apart from happy Ghosts, that gather flowers . 212 *Laod.* 162
Apart she tolls within the chosen ring ; . . . 259 **A volant* 9
But metaphor dismissed, and thanks apart, . . 281 *Valedict.* 9
Thy soul was like a Star, and dwelt apart ; . . 307 **Milton ! thou* 9
And one brief day is rightly set apart . . . . 330 *Ode : Thanks.* 88
Apart, beside his silent goats, ... 342 *Ital. Itin.* 86
A few short steps (painful they were) apart . . 353 *Aquap.* 83
Apart, some little space, was made . . . . . 412 *White Doe* 1524
And stood apart from human cares : . . . . 416 *White Doe* 1859
Apart—like glow-worms on a summer night : . 441 *Ecc. Sonn.* 3. 5. 10
Apart, to overlook the circle vast— . . . . 477 *Long Meg* 7
Sees that, apart from magnanimity, ... 514 **Blest Statesman* 3
This Stone is sacred. Here he lies apart . . . 584 *Ch. Lamb* 2

Apart—*continued.*
Hadst shared, when, from profane regards apart,. 682 *Prelude* 6. 474
For patrimonial honour set apart, ... 714 *Prelude* 9. 327
To all mankind. But, these things set apart, . 717 *Prelude* 9. 532
Apart from all that leads to wealth, or even . . 751 *Prelude* 14. 365
Apart from benefits received or done . . . . 810 *Excursion* 4. 579
Standing apart ; with curvèd arm reclined . . 825 *Excursion* 5. 211
And still remain self-governed, and apart, . . 828 *Excursion* 5. 386
Of a rough precipice ; and some, apart, . . . 835 *Excursion* 5. 867
These that in trembling hope are laid apart ; . . 836 *Excursion* 5. 953
Apart from old temptations, and constrained . . 859 *Excursion* 7. 148
Lay thy diadem apart, ... L. 2. 190 **Queen and* 13
Apartment. My school-time, an apartment he had owned, ... 757 *Excursion* 1. 54
And reached a small apartment dark and low, . 781 *Excursion* 2. 648
Apartments. To such apartments as they found ; . 298 *Brownie's Cell* 8
Apathy. A people sunk in apathy and fear. . . 319 *Biscayan* 9
Be lost, through apathy, or scorn, or fear, . . 442 *Ecc. Sonn.* 3. 10. 10
May season apathy with scorn, ... 534 **Blest is* 63
If, 'mid indifference and apathy, ... 648 *Prelude* 2. 434
An uncomplaining apathy displaced . . . . 774 *Excursion* 2. 206
Ape. Homeward or schoolward, ape what ye behold ; 339 *Tell* 8
Impostors, drivellers, dotards, as the ape . . . 673 *Prelude* 5. 525
From every clime; and, next, those sights that ape 690 *Prelude* 7. 232
Apennine. White as the snows of Apennine . . 343 *Eclipse* 41
(Not Apennine can boast of fairer), hills . . 353 *Aquap.* 41
Among these sterile heights of Apennine, . . . 362 **List—'twas* 38
Apennines. Ye Apennines ! with all your fertile vales 352 *Aquap.* 1
Apex. Upon the apex of that lofty cone . . . 226 *Vernal Ode* 14
Bending its apex toward a paler self . . . . S. 3. 434 **The doubt* 69
A-pilfering. Between them, and both go a-pilfering together. . . . . 572 *Avarice* 16
Apis. The thundering Thurlow, Apis ! shall rejoice L. 1. 88 *Juvenal* 1. 21
Apocalypse. Characters of the great Apocalypse, . 684 *Prelude* 6. 638
Apollo. Never golden-haired Apollo, ... 181 *Waggoner* 4. 108
For is she not the votary of Apollo ? . . . . 261 **I heard (alas* 9
Pan or Apollo, veiled in human form : . . . . 868 *Excursion* 7. 730
Apostasy. In which apostasy from ancient faith . 722 *Prelude* 10. 309
Apostle. The Apostle of the Gentiles ; both prepared 357 *Aquap.* 312
Apostolic. Patriots informed with Apostolic light . 444 *Ecc. Sonn.* 3. 15. 1
An apostolic hand, and with prayer seals . . . 446 *Ecc. Sonn.* 3. 23. 10
Apostolical. *Who* comes with functions apostolical ? 422 *Ecc. Sonn.* 1. 15. 4
Thy function apostolical . . . . 486 **Bright Flower* 23
Appal. Not to appal me have the gods bestowed . 210 *Laod.* 35
That thought is one which neither can appal . . 305 **The Voice* 8
A Man whose aspect doth at once appal . . . 422 *Ecc. Sonn.* 1. 15. 8
Appalled. Appalled she may not be, and cannot yield. 330 *Ode : Thanks.* 82
The appalled Discoverer with a sigh . . . . 491 *Fidelity* 40
By the deep quiet gloom appall'd, she sighs, . . 606 *Desc. Sk. Quarto* 221
Disgusted therefore, or appalled, by aims . . . 797 *Excursion* 3. 773
Appalling. *See* **Soul-appalling.**
Appalling havoc ! but serene his brow, . . . 21 *Desc. Sk.* 581
Appalling process ! I have marked . . . . 245 *P. B.* 826
Man to curse man, (thought monstrous and appalling). . . . . 447 *Ecc. Sonn.* 3. 29. 3
Through Alpine vapours. Such appalling rite . 450 *Ecc. Sonn.* 3. 40. 6
Appanage. No appanage of human kind, . . . 214 *Kirkstone* 6
Apparel. Who of thy words dost make a mock apparel, ... 88 *H. C.* 2
Wheeled her back in full apparel ; . . . . . 178 *Waggoner* 2. 161
Her tackling rich, and of apparel high. . . . 258 **With Ships* 8
Of quaint apparel for a half-spoilt boy ; . . . 388 **The pibroch's* 3
Apparelled. Apparelled in celestial light, . . . 587 *Immortality* 4
Apparent. Apparent at his feet. . . . . . . 167 *Pilgrim's Dream* 16
Apparent now beside his team— . . . . . . 180 *Waggoner* 4. 67
(Then first apparent from the Pincian Height) . 358 *Pine : Rome* 13
Between the orbs of our apparent sphere . . . 812 *Excursion* 4. 711
Its most apparent home. The food of hope . . 884 *Excursion* 9. 20
Apparently. Even to the dust ; apparently, through weight . . . . 803 *Excursion* 4. 166
Apparition. A lovely Apparition, sent . . . . 186 **She was* 3
My Soul, an Apparition in the place, ... 208 **It is no* 16
The apparition that before thee shone . . . . 222 *Triad* 214
Resplendent Apparition ! if in vain . . . . . 338 *Engelberg* 15
The Apparition ; evil thoughts are stayed . . 423 *Ecc. Sonn.* 1. 19. 10
An Apparition more divinely bright ! . . . . 434 *Ecc. Sonn.* 2. 22. 10
In glorious apparition, Powers on whom . . . 735 *Prelude* 12. 98
The apparition faded not away, ... 785 *Excursion* 2. 880
Bright apparition, suddenly put forth, ... 808 *Excursion* 4. 462
Apparitions. Strange apparitions mocked the shepherd's sight. . . . . 6 *Ev. Wk.* 195
Strange apparitions mock the village sight. . . 595 *Ev. Wk. Quarto* 178
Appeal. Appeal was made to the great Judge : the Accused . . . . 62 *Bord.* 1384
Give ear, O Man ! to their appeal, ... 228 *Devot. Incit.* 23
O sovereign Nature ! I appeal to thee, ... 231 **The gentlest Poet* 14
From thy remonstrance would be no appeal ; . . 262 *Retirement* 4
And angry Ocean roars a vain appeal. . . . . 428 *Ecc. Sonn.* 1. 37. 14
What though the Accused, upon his own appeal . 500 *Humanity* 1
That Europe knows, would echo this appeal ; . . 509 *F. Stone* 94
Did we appeal ; and, finally, beheld . . . . 715 *Prelude* 9. 381
To him appeal was made as to a judge ; . . . 772 *Excursion* 2. 75
From higher judgment-seats make no appeal . . 816 *Excursion* 4. 1022
To whom the appeal couched in its closing words . 880 *Excursion* 8. 435
Appear. *See* **Re-appear.**
Like a black wall, the mountain-steeps appear. . 8 *Ev. Wk.* 314
How fair its lawns and sheltering woods appear ! . 8 *Ev. Wk.* 349
That like to leaning masts of stranded ships appear. 18 *Desc. Sk.* 412
The traces of primeval Man appear ; . . . . 18 *Desc. Sk.* 442
While ghastly faces through the gloom appear, . 20 *Desc. Sk.* 547
Before thy face did ever wretch appear, . . . 26 *Guilt* 124

Appear—*continued.*
I thought the Convent never would appear ; — 39 *Bord.* 113
Heavy his low-hung lip did oft appear, — 108 *Indolence* 42
Appear not more shut out than they. — 154 *Flower Garden* 42
Though she appear not, and be sought in vain. — 165 *Parrot* 40
Though habitation none appear, — 215 *Kirkstone* 65
And oft in splendour dost appear — 215 *Enterprise* 16
" Appear !—obey my lyre's command ! — 220 *Triad* 15
Appear ; a calm descent of sky conducting — 230 *Clouds* 34
As they themselves appear to be, — 235 *Power of Sound* 182
The Pleiads, that appear to kiss — 237 *P. B.* 43
Appear so lovely, never, never ;— — 237 *P. B.* 72
More like themselves the rocks appear — 242 *P. B.* 494
To thee appear not an unmeaning voice, — 255 *Detraction* 12
Will thank you. Faultless does the Maid appear ; — 256 *Marriage : Friend* 9
If thou appear untouched by solemn thought, — 258 **It is a* 10
Soul-smitten ; for, that instant did appear — 264 *Storm* 10
Rise into life and in thy train appear : — 268 **Pure element* 4
And thou forbidden to appear ? — 284 *Grave of Burns* 8
To the perception of this Age, appear — 290 *Kilchurn* 39
And from that Infant's face let joy appear ; — 294 **Fly, some* 9
But thou, that didst appear so fair. — 302 *Yarrow V.* 41
Of righteous Vengeance side by side appear, — 318 **Is there* 8
The aspiring heads of future things appear, — 326 **The Bard* 7
Where towns and cities thick as stars appear, — 327 *Ode 1815* 29
To his omniscience will appear — 332 *Ode : Thanks.* 242
Each ministering to each, didst thou appear — 355 *Aquap.* 206
Appear to sight still more forlorn. — 366 **Ye Trees* 18
Of facts divulged, wherein appear — 398 *White Doe* 200
Than ghosts are fabled to appear — 407 *White Doe* 1047
Of speediest wing, should he appear. — 411 *White Doe* 1376
Than they appear to holy Gregory ; — 421 *Ecc. Sonn.* 1. 13. 7
The full-orbed Moon, slow-climbing, doth appear — 426 *Ecc. Sonn.* 1. 29. 10
Though pride's least lurking thought appear a wrong — 444 *Ecc. Sonn.* 3. 18. 6
That tears burst forth amain. Did gleams appear ? — 446 *Ecc. Sonn.* 3. 24. 9
And gilded flocks appear. — 457 **Had this* 32
Not uninspired appear their simplest ways ; — 500 *Humanity* 15
Till the first silver star appear, — 507 **While from* 63
Portentous change when History can appear — 514 **Portentous change* 1
Will flow, and on a welcome page appear — 522 *Epist. Beaumont* 57
To appear before my Lady ? but a sense — 562 *Cuck.and Night.*294
How fair it's lawn and silvery woods appear ! — 599 *Ev. Wk.Quarto* 417
And emerald isles to spot the heights appear, — 610 *Desc.Sk.Quarto* 445
Like leaning masts of stranded ships appear — 611 *Desc.Sk.Quarto* 500
Dim dreadful faces thro' the gloom appear, — 614 *Desc.Sk.Quarto* 650
As might appear to the eye of fleeting time, — 666 *Prelude* 5. 17
Among all regions ; chiefly where appear — 698 *Prelude* 7. 743
And this same city, that did then appear — 725 *Prelude* 10. 504
Souls that appear to have no depth at all — 742 *Prelude* 13. 167
—Now, by thy care befriended, I appear — 753 **Oft, through* 5
Doth, in my estimate of good, appear — 790 *Excursion* 3. 278
To appear and answer ; to the grave I spake — 796 *Excursion* 3. 689
And when that sacred spirit shall appear, — 806 *Excursion* 4. 318
From east to west, before you will appear — 830 *Excursion* 5. 536
To some, too lightly minded, might appear — 830 *Excursion* 5. 550
Too delicate employ, as would appear, — 839 *Excursion* 6. 98
Such and so glorious did this Youth appear ; — 868 *Excursion* 7. 723
Who, in his very childhood, should appear — 879 *Excursion* 8. 319
Invests the thriving churl, his legs appear, — 880 *Excursion* 8. 404
Forest and field, and hill and dale appear, — 885 *Excursion* 9. 61

Appearance. Of his forlorn appearance, could not fail — 39 *Bord.* 81
So helpless in appearance, that for him — 566 *Cumb. Beg.* 25
Thy every-day appearance, as it strikes— — 689 *Prelude* 7. 152
In person and appearance ; but her house — 768 *Excursion* 1. 821
And, of the sad appearance which at once — 779 *Excursion* 2. 521
The appearance, instantaneously disclosed, — 784 *Excursion* 2. 834
That an appearance which hath raised your minds — 788 *Excursion* 3. 153
—Aided by this appearance, I at length — 853 *Excursion* 6. 1003

Appearances. In second-sight appearances, or crost — 523 *Epist. Beaumont* 149
Collateral objects and appearances, — 641 *Prelude* 1. 593
Or could more bright appearances create — 676 *Prelude* 6. 91
But something must have felt. Call ye these appearances— — 703 *Prelude* 8. 293
That in life's every-day appearances — 745 *Prelude* 13. 368
The appearances of things ! From such, how changed — 894 *Excursion* 9. 712

Appeared. *See* **Re-appeared.**
The world, and human life, appeared a scene — 23 *Yew-tree* 41
Appeared the genuine colour of his soul— — 41 *Bord.* 233
For bodied forth before my eyes the cross-crowned hut appeared ; — 91 *Poet's Dream* 6
Of this rude church-yard, till the stars appeared — 97 *Brothers* 114
Appeared but seldom ; oftener was he seen — 124 *V. and J.* 212
And all the ensuing week the house appeared — 135 *Michael* 305
Appeared, and spiritual presence gained a power — 139 *Widow* 26
Which I till then had heard appeared the voice — 146 **It was an* 24
Of that one beech, appeared a thrush's nest ; — 150 **When, to* 20
This Flower, that first appeared as summer's guest, — 169 **Never enlivened* 4
In his deportment, shape, and mien, appeared — 211 *Laod.* 94
Appeared, in presence of the spiritual eye — 226 *Vernal Ode* 3
" And wheresoever he appeared, — 238 *P. B.* 203
The broad blue heavens appeared to glimmer, — 241 *P. B.* 484
Appeared, set forth in strange array, — 244 *P. B.* 753
Forthwith a little Girl appeared. — 247 *P. B.* 1000
Appeared upon his tender cheek) — 342 *Ital. Itin.* 84
Appeared—to govern Christian pageantries : — 346 *Processions* 38
Till the bright Star appeared in eastern skies, — 351 *Des. Stanzas* 69
Those vernal charms of sight and sound, appeared — 356 *Aquap.* 223
And soon Caerleon's towers appeared, — 372 *Eg. Maid* 189

Appeared—*continued.*
Brisk Youth appeared, the Morn of Youth, — 385 *Yarrow Rev.* 25
Past, present, future, all appeared — 385 *Yarrow Rev.* 29
Appeared, with free and open hate — 404 *White Doe* 705
And Officers appeared in state — 410 *White Doe* 1314
Appeared the Crag of Ailsa, ne'er did morn — 471 *Ailsa Crag* 2
A stern-browed house appeared ; — 478 *Somnamb.* 13
If, mixed with what appeared of rock, lawn, wood, — 524 *Epist. Beaumont* 187
All that appeared was suitable to One — 532 **Once I* 9
Appeared unwelcome dawn. — 542 *Russ. Fug.* 16
A thousand times more beautiful appeared — 586 *Ch. Lamb* 127
Last Industry appear'd with steady pace, — 618 *School Ex.* 23
The icy brooks, as on we passed, appeared — 622 *Recluse* 1. 1. 166
Of happiness, my blood appeared to flow — 645 *Prelude* 2. 187
Appeared like something in myself, a dream, — 647 *Prelude* 2. 351
Appeared a different aspect of old age ; — 657 *Prelude* 3. 549
The things which were the same and yet appeared — 661 *Prelude* 4. 197
With like success, nor often have appeared — 662 *Prelude* 4. 273
No living thing appeared in earth or air, — 664 *Prelude* 4. 385
He stood, and in his very dress appeared — 664 *Prelude* 4. 401
Though weak his step and cautious, he appeared — 665 *Prelude* 4. 431
Close at my side, an uncouth shape appeared — 666 *Prelude* 5. 75
Appeared distinctly on the opposite shore — 672 *Prelude* 5. 436
So gracefully ; even then when it appeared — 677 *Prelude* 6. 163
Of soul-affecting *solitude* appeared — 681 *Prelude* 6. 421
Appeared more touching. One will I select ; — 696 *Prelude* 7. 602
Appeared to recompense the traveller's pains — 710 *Prelude* 9. 76
Born in a land whose very name appeared — 712 *Prelude* 9. 189
Appeared unfit for the repose of night, — 719 *Prelude* 10. 92
With all the sorrow that it brought, appeared — 739 *Prelude* 12. 310
When at my feet the ground appeared to brighten, — 746 *Prelude* 14. 35
Into the main Atlantic, that appeared — 746 *Prelude* 14. 47
Reflected, it appeared to me the type — 747 *Prelude* 14. 66
Appeared a roofless Hut ; four naked walls — 756 *Excursion* 1. 30
O then how beautiful, how bright, appeared — 759 *Excursion* 1. 222
And when these lofty elms once more appeared — 766 *Excursion* 1. 644
And strolled into her garden. It appeared — 767 *Excursion* 1. 720
Pertaining to her house-affairs, appeared — 768 *Excursion* 1. 796
No ridges there appeared of clear black mould, — 769 *Excursion* 1. 836
Appeared an idle dream, that could maintain, — 770 *Excursion* 1. 952
To the wide world's astonishment, appeared — 774 *Excursion* 2. 211
And mortal sickness on her face appeared, — 775 *Excursion* 2. 276
Not ceasing, forth appeared in view a band — 777 *Excursion* 2. 386
Than it appeared when from the beetling rock — 781 *Excursion* 2. 642
Right in the midst, where interspace appeared — 784 *Excursion* 2. 861
Barren the tablet, yet thereon appeared — 787 *Excursion* 3. 61
Find entrance ;—high or low appeared no trace — 787 *Excursion* 3. 68
For to my judgment such they then appeared, — 790 *Excursion* 3. 291
Disbanded—or in hostile ranks appeared ; — 797 *Excursion* 3. 771
" Long wished-for sight, the Western World appeared ; — 798 *Excursion* 3. 870
Appeared, of high pretensions—unreproved — 799 *Excursion* 3. 898
I found him not. There, in his stead, appeared — 800 *Excursion* 3. 952
The solemn voice appeared to issue, startling — 807 *Excursion* 4. 407
Of God ; and Angels to his sight appeared — 810 *Excursion* 4. 635
They came and go, appeared and disappear, — 813 *Excursion* 4. 838
On the stream's bank, and everywhere, appeared — 823 *Excursion* 5. 87
Sepulchral stones appeared, with emblems graven — 825 *Excursion* 5. 168
One might be likened : flourishing appeared, — 829 *Excursion* 5. 458
High in the gloom appeared, too high, methought, — 833 *Excursion* 5. 740
Within the heart no outward sign appeared — 840 *Excursion* 6. 155
A sun-like beauty, and appeared divine ! — 854 *Excursion* 6. 1037
With righteous Joshua ; nor appeared in arms — 870 *Excursion* 7. 813
England, the ancient and the free, appeared — 870 *Excursion* 7. 856
If there were not, before those arts appeared, — 879 *Excursion* 8. 338
That charm all eyes. So bright, so fair, appeared — 882 *Excursion* 8. 516
Appeared, confusion checking their delight. — 882 *Excursion* 8. 546
Was wanting ; but inferior lights appeared — 895 *Excursion* 9. 762

Appear'st. Or rather thou appear'st a glistering snake, — 377 *Duddon* 4. 5

Appearing. *See* **Re-appearing, Scarce-appearing.**
From the sage Nymph appearing at his wish — 498 **Enough of climbing* 29
Set off, and to our ken appearing fair — 773 *Excursion* 2. 94

Appears. *See* **Re-appears.**
An edge all flame, the broadening sun appears ; — 5 *Ev. Wk.* 169
The form appears of one that spurs his steed — 6 *Ev. Wk.* 196
Anon, appears a brave, a gorgeous show — 6 *Ev. Wk.* 200
Appears a scanty plot of smiling green, — 14 *Desc. Sk.* 235
Confused the Marathonian tale appears, — 15 *Desc. Sk.* 287
And all the world appears unkind. — 117 *Affl. Marg.* 70
An undistinguishable style appears — 118 *Maternal Grief* 34
Appears along the moonlight road ; — 128 *Idiot Boy* 174
Appears a straggling heap of unhewn stones ! — 131 *Michael* 17
And often, when no cause appears, — 166 *Danish Boy* 40
By breathing mist ; and thine appears to be — 173 *Infant Daughter* 63
Again appears to be — 184 **O blithe* 30
At the corner of Wood Street, when daylight appears, — 187 *Poor Susan* 1
Her habitable shores, but now appears — 219 **This Height* 21
Oft as appears a grove, or obvious hill, — 267 **As the* 3
Which hold, whate'er to common sight appears, — 279 **All praise* 13
O joy when the girdle of England appears ! — 346 *Stanzas : Simplon* 30
Appears *his* lot, to the small Worm's compared, — 366 *Lombardy* 3
Appears, and none of modern Fortune's care ; — 376 *Duddon* 3. 11
Appears to cherish most that Torrent white, — 381 *Duddon* 19. 8
Appears a joyless human Being, — 413 *White Doe* 1580
Appears to shine, by miracle restored ; — 458 **Had this* 76
Appears, on Morven's lonely shore, — 473 *Ossian* 77

Appears—*continued.*
A Moralist perchance appears ; — 485 *Poet's Epitaph* 25
The tide of things has borne him, he appears . — 568 *Cumb. Beg.* 164
It's edge all flame, the broad'ning sun appears ; — 594 *Ev. Wk. Quarto* 152
A desperate form appears, that spurs his steed, — 595 *Ev. Wk. Quarto* 179
On my corporeal frame, so wide appears — 642 *Prelude* 2. 28
Science appears but what in truth she is, — 645 *Prelude* 2. 212
Even now appears before the mind's clear eye — 671 *Prelude* 5. 398
Had vanity (quick Spirit that appears — 688 *Prelude* 7. 103
Which yet survive in memory, appears — 692 *Prelude* 7. 335
Over still mountains, or appears in dreams ; — 696 *Prelude* 7. 634
As it appears to unaccustomed eyes. — 737 *Prelude* 12. 183
No evidence appears that they who rest — 847 *Excursion* 6. 602
And in his humble dwelling, he appears — 862 *Excursion* 7. 337
That your praise appears to me — S. 3. 438 **My Lord* 27
Appease. To appease the Gods ; or public thanks to yield ; — 346 *Processions* 1
She knelt in prayer—the waves their wrath appease ; — 466 *St. Bees* 34
Ask not of me, whose tongue can best appease — 522 *Epist. Beaumont* 65
And conscience her tortures appease, — 621 *Convict* 30
Counsel is given ; contention they appease — 875 *Excursion* 8. 78
Of human victims, offered up to appease — 894 *Excursion* 9. 697
Appeased. Yet loathing life—till anger is appeased — 78 *Bord.* 2352
Our tumults appeased, and our strifes passed away! — 340 *Fort Fuentes* 20
Appeased his yearning :—in the after-day — 758 *Excursion* 1. 153
And where they lie, how answered and appeased. — 813 *Excursion* 4. 813
Those troubles had appeased, he sought and gained, — 844 *Excursion* 6. 424
Appellations. Thy appellations. — 158 **With little* 24
Appendage. Who now, with no appendage but a staff, — 762 *Excursion* 1. 435
Appended. Appended to his bosom, and lips closed — 362 **List—'twas* 80
Appertained. Bred in this vale, to which he appertained — 548 **Stranger ! this* 22
Yea, appertained by a peculiar right — 645 *Prelude* 2. 196
As if it appertained to another mind, — 676 *Prelude* 6. 98
And to his moral being appertained : — 853 *Excursion* 6. 1014
Appertains. And to that simple object appertains — 131 *Michael* 18
(For such in truth it is, and appertains — 858 *Excursion* 7. 56
Appetite. An appetite ; a feeling and a love, — 206 *Tintern* 80
Or prest together by the appetite, — 312 **Who rises* 67
Such food a Tyrant's appetite demands ; — 319 *Spaniard* 4
Hath preyed with ruthless appetite — 472 *Ossian* 33
To feed such appetite—nor this alone — 758 *Excursion* 1. 152
Which appetite required—a blind dull nook, — 783 *Excursion* 2. 746
And nurse ' the dreadful appetite of death ? ' — 810 *Excursion* 4. 602
With keener appetite (if that might be) — 840 *Excursion* 6. 153
And to produce, with appetite as keen — 875 *Excursion* 8. 93
Appetites. And call of her own natural appetites, — 669 *Prelude* 5. 254
Dumb yearnings, hidden appetites, are ours, — 673 *Prelude* 5. 506
May with such heinous appetites be compared), — 723 *Prelude* 10. 366
Our animal appetites and daily wants, — 741 *Prelude* 13. 91
Among wild appetites and blind desires, — K. 8. 256 *Recluse* 1. 1. 706
Applaud. And charm of colours ; *I* applaud those signs — 277 **Haydon ! let* 3
For once I burst my bands, and cry, applaud ! " — 513 **Said Secrecy* 8
Applauded. Caressed, applauded, upon dainties fed, — 165 *Parrot* 45
Applauding. *See* **Self-applauding.**
Applauds. That heaven-deserted man applauds ; — 301 *Bran* 110
Applause. *See* **Self-applause.**
Of popular applause. I now perceived — 70 *Bord.* 1822
Not on the breath of popular applause, — 213 *Dion* 47
She trained her Burns to win applause — 286 *Nith* 41
His breath in confidence of Heaven's applause : — 494 *Hap. War.* 83
Loud shouts,—the Trojans echo the applause. — 625 *Æneid* 131
As vanity and fondness for applause, — 775 *Excursion* 2. 225
Apple. Where the green apple shrivels on the spray, — 15 *Desc. Sk.* 258
Fair hangs the apple frae the rock, — 293 *Yarrow Unv.* 35
Whose head the ruddy apple tops, while he — 339 *Tell* 22
And apple sickens pale in summer's ray, — 608 *Desc. Sk. Quarto* 322
Apples. Studded with apples, a beautiful show ! — 80 †*Address : Child* 27
Apple-tree. Feeding in the apple-tree ; — 171 *Kitten* 66
Of a young apple-tree, lay at its root ; — 769 *Excursion* 1. 841
Apple-trees. Where apple-trees in blossom made a bower, — 107 *Indolence* 25
Application. Safer, of universal application, such — 730 *Prelude* 11. 204
Applied. Proverbial words of comfort he applied, — 32 *Guilt* 458
Made, to his ear attentively applied, — 108 *Indolence* 57
To archangelic lips applied, — 235 *Power of Sound* 215
Nor was applied nor could be, Ledbury bells — 267 *St. Cath.* 2
A standard, often usefully applied, — 676 *Prelude* 6. 103
May with fit reverence be applied—that peace — 748 *Prelude* 14. 126
So grounded, so applied, that it was heard — 772 *Excursion* 2. 79
Applies. When she applies her annual test — 299 *Brownie's Cell* 82
Apply. And chafe her temples, careful hands apply. — 34 *Guilt* 571
Which to the sun of truth he can apply, — 813 *Excursion* 4. 809
Applying. And many anodynes applying, — 245 *P.B.* 799
Of inland ground, applying to his ear — 818 *Excursion* 4. 1134
Appointed. *See* **Well-appointed.**
That unto him, where'er shall lie his life's appointed way, — 91 *Norman Boy* 31
Which, when the appointed season hath arrived, — 173 *Infant Daughter* 76
Was doomed to wear out her appointed time, — 212 *Laod.* 161
But in calm peace the appointed Victim slept, — 214 *Dion* 112
They move ; but soon the appointed way — 233 *Power of Sound* 58
Then pays submissively the appointed debt — 261 **I watch* 8
At God's appointed hour to them who tread — 278 **Lo ! where she* 10
Peasant and lord, in their appointed seat, — 319 *Guernica* 13
Appointed by man's common heritage, — 354 *Aquap.* 92
To meditate upon his own appointed tasks, — 354 *Aquap.* 124
Its bloom, unfolding at the appointed day ; — 393 *Countess' Pillar* 3
And so will keep the appointed ground — 404 *White Doe* 727
The Priest bestows the appointed consecration ; — 431 *Ecc. Sonn.* 2. 11. 4

Appointed—*continued.*
To keep with faithful step the appointed way — 461 **Queen of* 51
Yet may outstrip me in the appointed race, — 464 **A point* 10
Each at the appointed hour — 535 *Egremont* 13
In thy appointed way, and bear in mind — 575 *Chiabrera* 6. 15
To cup or viand its appointed place. — 624 *Æneid* 70
To its appointed close : the discipline — 750 *Prelude* 14. 303
The appointed task and duties of the day, — 773 *Excursion* 2. 148
Man's only dwelling, sole appointed seat, — 777 *Excursion* 2. 362
The appointed seat of equitable law — 796 *Excursion* 3. 715
In their appointed place. The pale Recluse — 825 *Excursion* 5. 224
Their life's appointed prison ; not more free — 846 *Excursion* 6. 535
His own appointed hour will come at last ; — 867 *Excursion* 7. 629
Humanity's appointed shroud, enwraps — 872 *Excursion* 7. 998
And at the appointed hour a bell is heard, — 877 *Excursion* 8. 170
The will, the instincts, and appointed needs — 889 *Excursion* 9. 376
Shall be—divested at the appointed hour — 893 *Excursion* 9. 632
The guide appointed, and the ransom paid. — 894 *Excursion* 9. 651
Appointment. 'Tis God's appointment who must sway, — 291 *Rob Roy* 51
He by appointment waited for me here, — 757 *Excursion* 1. 50
Apposite. Is to that other state more apposite, — 831 *Excursion* 5. 553
Apprehension. Some apprehension ; — 158 **In youth* 44
With words of apprehension and despair : — 308 **These times* 3
Sore stress of apprehension, with a mind — 449 *Ecc. Sonn.* 3. 37. 6
Methought, with apprehension that these rites — 777 *Excursion* 2. 396
Than apprehension and bewildering thoughts. — 784 *Excursion* 2. 826
For apprehension those transcendent truths — 802 *Excursion* 4. 96
A fearful apprehension from the owl — 810 *Excursion* 4. 616
The clearest apprehension of those truths, — 830 *Excursion* 5. 520
A tardy apprehension. From a fount — 834 *Excursion* 5. 786
Apprehensions. And apprehensions dark and criminal. — 104 *Artegal* 125
My apprehensions come in crowds ; — 117 *Affl. Marg.* 64
Though apprehensions crossed me that my zeal — 874 *Excursion* 8. 21
'Mid all his apprehensions, cares, and fears,— — 884 *Excursion* 9. 35
Thy apprehensions—blush thou for them all. — K. 8. 238 *Recluse* 1. 1. 64
Apprehensive. Yet some with apprehensive ear shall drink — 314 **I dropped* 9
But shrunk with apprehensive jealousy — 748 *Prelude* 14. 155
And gave the Mind that apprehensive power — 758 *Excursion* 1. 167
Apprehensiveness. In fits of kindliest apprehensiveness, — 708 *Prelude* 8. 603
Apprentice. Youngest apprentice in the school of art ! — 789 *Excursion* 3. 199
Apprenticed. Now happily apprenticed.—' I perceive — 767 *Excursion* 1. 762
Approach. Her sad approach, and stole away to find, — 118 *Maternal Grief* 52
Approach the spot when she is there." — 198 *Thorn* 99
Ascending, they approach—I hear their wings — 218 *Recluse* 1. 1. 219
Approach ;—and, thus invited, crown with rest — 219 *Haunted Tree* 18
Does joy approach ? they meet the coming tide ; — 278 **Life with* 3
We can approach, thy sorrow to behold, — 316 **Hail, Zaragoza* 2
Love wound his way by soft approach, — 391 *Highland Broach* 47
Skilled to approach or to retire,— — 415 *White Doe* 1720
At his approach and low-bowed necks entreat — 423 *Ecc. Sonn.* 1. 19. 11
Approach, come gladly, ye prepared, in sight — 446 *Ecc. Sonn.* 3. 26. 2
At the approach of all-involving night. — 452 *Ecc. Sonn.* 3. 46. 14
Prelude of night's approach with soothing dreams. — 453 **The Sun, that* 4
Approach ; yet, Doctor, not too near, — 485 *Poet's Epitaph* 11
Could fearlessly approach the shade ? — 497 *Lycoris* 8
And soon approach Diana's Looking-glass ! — 524 *Epist. Beaumont* 165
At our approach, a jealous watch-dog's bark, — 525 *Epist. Beaumont* 233
More imminent. Not unseen do they approach ; — 541 *Grace Darl.* 63
To something that resembles an approach — 656 *Prelude* 3. 519
Contemplating in soberness the approach — 668 *Prelude* 5. 157
To chant your praise ; nor can approach you now — 685 *Prelude* 6. 672
To wait upon the storms : of their approach — 702 *Prelude* 8. 224
Open ; I would approach them, but they close. — 738 *Prelude* 12. 280
Approach this door but she who dwelt within — 763 *Excursion* 1. 498
The Stoic's heart against the vain approach — 791 *Excursion* 3. 355
Approach the embowered abode—our chosen seat— — 793 *Excursion* 3. 521
Where height, or depth, admits not the approach — 795 *Excursion* 3. 643
Removed from all approach of living sight — 812 *Excursion* 4. 714
At night's approach bring down the unclouded sky, — 818 *Excursion* 4. 1159
Our little Page : the rustic pair approach ; — 821 *Excursion* 4. 1310
The Pastor learned that his approach had given — 829 *Excursion* 5. 463
Approach their reverend graces, unopposed ; — 838 *Excursion* 6. 31
Of thunder daunting those who would approach — 876 *Excursion* 8. 144
Till the swift vehicle approach, they stand ; — 880 *Excursion* 8. 378
To his own home, and now at the approach — K. 8. 229 **I will* 160
Approachable. Approachable, admitting fellowship — 676 *Prelude* 6. 62
Approached. As we approached, a solitary crow — 74 *Bord.* 2102
When Leonard had approached his home, his heart — 96 *Brothers* 77
Approached ; he recognised the Priest at once, — 97 *Brothers* 117
While they were speaking, Vaudracour approached ; — 126 *V. and J.* 294
Thus talking of that Peasant, we approached — 149 **A narrow* 55
And now, as he approached a vassal's door, — 200 *Hart-leap* 3
Approached this glory of the firmament ; — 265 **The Shepherd* 12
That we approached the Seat of Charlemaine ? — 335 *Aix* 2
As we approached the Convent gate, aloft — 362 **List—'twas* 84
Changed, as the pair approached the light, — 371 *Eg. Maid* 178
Which whosoe'er approached of strength was shorn, — 373 *Eg. Maid* 317
Whom now he had approached, he said— — 401 *White Doe* 453
As she approached yon rustic Shed — 407 *White Doe* 1022
Approached, and, greeting her, thus spake ; — 408 *White Doe* 1077
These shores if he approached them bent on wrong ; — 468 **Bold words* 4
Has but approached the gates of womanhood, — 509 *F. Stone* 48
Proportions more harmonious, and approached — 547 **Rude is* 3
Approached within the length of half his staff. — 566 *Cumb. Beg.* 21
With giddy motion. But the time approached — 642 *Prelude* 2. 48

Arch —continued.

To dignify arch looks and laughing eyes ; . . .	80 *Loving she 3
The middle of the arch.	85 Shepherd-boys 59
To see thy arch thus stretch and bend, . .	111 *'Tis said that some 42
And thy arch and wily ways, ...	161 *Pleasures newly 31
Arch, volatile, a sportive bird	165 Parrot 25
An arch thrown back between luxuriant wings	212 Dion
When, through this Height's inverted arch, .	215 Kirkstone 43
Turning them inside out with arch audacity. .	221 Triad 127
Hell to the lyre bowed low ; the upper arch .	234 Power of Sound 126
Swiftly thereon a rainbow arch to build .	261 *Fair Prime 4
Faith had her arch—her arch, when winds blow loud, ...	282 *In my 8
That wide-spanned arch, wondering how it was raised, ...	283 *Well have 9
Of lurking cloistral arch, through trees espied .	335 Rhine 9
Arch that here rests upon the granite ridge .	350 Des. Stanzas 30
And, from that arch, down-looking on the Vale	350 Des. Stanzas 33
Life slips from underneath us, like that arch .	351 Des. Stanzas 84
From fractured arch and mouldering wall— .	366 *Ye Trees 14
Crossed ever and anon by plank or arch ; . .	378 Duddon 9. 3
Who through the silent portal arch	386 Yarrow Rev. 99
Under an arch of that forlorn abode ; . . .	391 Brownie 4
Beneath the arch with ivy bound, ...	396 White Doe 53
From some lofty arch or wall, ...	397 White Doe 89
Finds entrance through yon arch, where way .	416 White Doe 1887
Through " Nature's hollow arch " that voice resounds.	427 Ecc. Sonn. 1. 33. 14
Age after age to the arch of Christendom .	435 Ecc. Sonn. 2. 26. 3
Of that arch fancy which would round him play,	583 *With copious 10
Proud of the varying arch and moveless form of snow.	595 Ev. Wk. Quarto 206
Stands yet a mouldering pile with fractured arch,	643 Prelude 2. 105
How arch his notices, how nice his sense .	670 Prelude 5. 310
Some vagrant mother, whose arch little ones, .	705 Prelude 8. 402
And freak put on, and arch word dropped—to swell	858 Excursion 7. 83
Hung in his rustic hall. One ivied arch .	872 Excursion 7. 962
Fanning his temples under heaven's blue arch.	878 Excursion 8. 308
To see the arch grimace of Marquis Scrub, . .	L. 1. 95 Juvenal 3. 11
Crams through the arch, and bellies o'er the ridge ?	L. 1. 95 Juvenal 3. 26

Archangelic. To archangelic lips applied, . . 235 Power of Sound 215

Arch-despot. The bold Arch-despot re-appeared ;— again . . . . 331 Ode : Thanks. 148

Arch-druid's. Screams round the Arch-druid's brow the sea-mew—white . . . . 419 Ecc. Sonn. 1. 3. 1

Arched. See High-arched, Over-arched.

Till the arched roof, with resolute sweep . . 433 Ecc. Sonn. 2. 20. 12

Archer. Of Sherwood's Archer, or in caves of Wallace— . . . . 221 Triad 70
Of archer, there was tried ; . . . . 543 Russ. Fug. 108

Archer-god. By the blind Archer-god ; her fancy free : . . . . 509 F. Stone 50

Archery. For Tell's dread archery renowned, . . 342 Ital. Itin. 60
To practise games and archery : . . . 409 White Doe 1179

Arches. To thank me for this service. Rainbow arches, ... 54 Bord. 930
The visionary Arches are not there, . . . 252 *The fairest 10
O'er mutilated arches shed their seeds ; . . 367 Trajan 2
Through ice-built arches radiant as heaven's bow ; | 376 Duddon 1. 8
Pillars, and arches,—not in vain time-proof, . 387 Roslin 7
Thence creeping under sylvan arches cool, . 424 Ecc. Sonn. 1. 22. 7

Archetype. From this fair Portrait's fleshly Archetype, ... 509 F. Stone 83
But that pure archetype of human greatness, . 799 Excursion 3. 951

Archibald. Seven daughters had Lord Archibald, . 161 Binnorie 1

Archimago's. In days of old romance at Archimago's gate. . . . . 523 Epist. Beaumont 153

Archimedes. With Archimedes also he conversed . 576 Chiabrera 9. 11
Or Archimedes, pure abstracted soul ! . . 733 Prelude 11. 435
—Call Archimedes from his buried tomb . 877 Excursion 8. 220

Arch-impostor. The Arch-impostor—— Treat him gently, Oswald . . . . 39 Bord. 86

Architect. That skill or means of his could add, but the architect had wrought . . . 91 Norman Boy 18
With ill-matched aims the Architect who planned— . 451 Ecc. Sonn. 3. 43. 2
That made the worlds, the sovereign Architect, . 473 *We saw 13

Architects. Of cloistered Architects, free their souls to fill . . . . 467 St. Bees 119

Architecture. Of stateliest architecture, where the Forms . . . . 334 *Bruges I 13

Architrave. But ye, bright Flowers, on frieze and architrave . . . . 474 *Hope smiled 7

Archway. Brightening the archway of revered St. Bees. . . . . 467 St. Bees

Arcs. Flowers left to wither on triumphal arcs, . 680 Prelude 6. 352

Arcturus. He chaunts Arcturus,—that fraternal twain . . . . 625 Æneid 126

Arden. Of Arden—amid sunshine or in shade . 701 Prelude 8. 139

Arden's. That in wild Arden's brakes was ever heard, 523 Epist. Beaumont 161

Ardent. The Stream, so ardent in its course before, 146 *It was an 22
That from his ardent countenance are flung, . . 624 Æneid 75
And ardent meditation. Later years . . 693 Prelude 7. 393
And hissing Factionists with ardent eyes, . . 710 Prelude 9. 59
Who have as ardent hearts as he had then. . . 716 Prelude 9. 430
In dreams, in study, and in ardent thought, . . 760 Excursion 1. 301
And, like an ardent hunter, I forgot, . . . 788 Excursion 3. 122
Too little checked. An active, ardent mind ; . 859 Excursion 7. 116
This ardent sally pleased the mild good Man, . 880 Excursion 8. 434

Ardour. Yet filled with ardour and on triumph bent 326 *Intrepid sons 10

Ardour—continued.

Health, meekness, ardour, quietness secure, . . 489 Spade 9
And ranged, with ardour heretofore unfelt, . . 719 Prelude 10. 49
To meditate with ardour on the rule . . 728 Prelude 11. 99
So, with more ardour than an unripe girl . . . 781 Excursion 2. 654

Arduous. We know the arduous strife, the eternal laws . . . . 316 *O'er the 10
And of more arduous duties thence imposed . . 332 Ode : Thanks. 236
For such an arduous work, I through myself . . 634 Prelude 1. 147
Nor arduous, yet will not be scorned by them, . 694 Prelude 7. 460
I deem not arduous ; but must needs confess . . 803 Excursion 4. 135
" That for this arduous office you possess . . 813 Excursion 4. 780

Are, omitted.

Area. This castle has another Area—come, . . 50 Bord. 732
O'er the blank Area of sacred earth . . . 355 Aquap. 158
An area level as a Lake and spread . . . 525 Epist. Beaumont 227
Of the wide area, twinkles, is alive . . 697 Prelude 7. 690
I crossed the square (an empty area then !) . . 719 Prelude 10. 55

Ares. Of ancient Ares. . . . . L. 2. 318 Frag. Æneid 4. 12

Arethuse. Thou wilt recline of pastoral Arethuse ; . 734 Prelude 11. 465

Argentiere. Below the icy bed of bright ARGENTIERE. 347 Processions 45

Argo. ARGO—exalted for that daring feat . . 336 Danube 13

Argos. To Argos. So wills angry Jupiter, . . . L. 2. 121 Frag. Æneid 2. 5.

Argued. So have we argued ; reaping for our pains 832 Excursion 5. 626

Argument. For such high argument. . . . . 245 P. B. 790
Of ampler or more varied argument, ... 641 Prelude 1. 643
This is, in truth, heroic argument, . . . 651 Prelude 3. 181
In this late portion of my argument, . . . 679 Prelude 6. 275
Nor checked by aught of tamer argument, . . 688 Prelude 7. 50
Our argument. Enough is said to show . . 693 Prelude 7. 401
Thrice needful to the argument which now . . 710 Prelude 9. 21
Entering upon abstruser argument, . . . 736 Prelude 12. 132
Coleridge ! with this my argument, of thee . 750 Prelude 14. 276
Accomplish :—this is our high argument. . . 755 Recluse 1. 824
To outward argument ; the passive will . . 831 Excursion 5. 573
From trivial themes to general argument . . 882 Excursion 8. 522
The compass of his argument—began . . 883 Excursion 8. 600

Arguments. Enough of humble arguments ; recall, 706 Prelude 8. 476
Arguments sent from Heaven to prove the cause . 713 Prelude 9. 283
In arguments of civil polity. . . . . 728 Prelude 11. 77

Arid. Ye dewy mists the arid rocks o'er-spread . 609 Desc. Sk. Quarto 392

Aright. And when he might his time aright espy, . 563 Troilus 38
The ingenuous mind, apt to be set aright ; . . 831 Excursion 5. 581 1

Arimathean. Arimathean Joseph's wattled cells. . 434 Ecc. Sonn. 2. 21. 1

Arion. Was for belief no dream :—thy skill, Arion ! 234 Power of Sound 134

Arise.—Cast off your bonds, awake, arise, . . 228 Devot. Incit. 38
Arise superior to the Siren's power, . . . 619 School Ex. 95
Sharp contradictions may arise, by doom . . 792 Excursion 3. 447

Aristogiton. And his compeer Aristogiton, known . 721 Prelude 10. 199
As Aristogiton bore, ... S. 3. 442 Harmodius 4
As Aristogiton bore, ... S. 3. 442 Harmodius 18
Dear Aristogiton, bore ! . . . . S. 3. 442 Harmodius 24

Arithmetic. The arithmetic of babes, must foreign hordes, ... 309 *What if 2

Ark. (Slow-moving ark of all his hopes !) that veiled 125 V. and J. 255
The happiest bird that sprang out of the Ark ! . 153 Morn. Ex. 30
Or descend where the ark alighted, . . . 218 *Inmate of 31
The Ark, her melancholy voyage done ! . . . 348 Sky-prosp. 3
Brought to the ark are coming evermore, . . 360 *Near Anio's 10
On earth, enshrined within the wandering ark ; . 811 Excursion 4. 655
Into the second ark, Christ's church, with trust . 826 Excursion 5. 282

Arm. Have wrought, with godlike arm the deeds of praise, ... 15 Desc. Sk. 290
Half raised, for well his arm might lose its force . 27 Guilt 179
We'll stroll into the wood ; lean on my arm. . . 43 Bord. 363
You say he was asleep,—look at this arm, . . 52 Bord. 796
And when I felt your hand upon my arm . . 55 Bord. 958
But I had once a spirit and an arm— . . . 62 Bord. 1346
Upon this arm. You led him towards the Convent ? 76 Bord. 2228
No, not by stroke of arm. But learn the process : . 77 Bord. 2257
Why should a thrust of the arm have such a power, 77 Bord. 2270
I said, and took him by the arm, . . . 86 Anecdote 30
While still I held him by the arm, . . . 86 Anecdote 34
One upright arm sustains the cheek, . . . 112 *How rich 14
And here it lies upon my arm, ... 116 Last of Flock 97
And, with this basket on his arm, the lad . . 135 Michael 263
She has a baby on her arm, ... 144 Her Eyes 5
The babe I carry on my arm, ... 145 Her Eyes 47
The uplifted arm of Suicide ; . . . . 233 Power of Sound 93
Arm at its blast for deadly wars) . . . 235 Power of Sound 214
At length, by Peter's arm sustained, ... 248 P. B. 1056
And wondrous length and strength of arm : . . 291 Rob Roy 10
Thine arm from peril guards the coasts . . . 328 Ode 1815 110
An angry arm that snatches good away, . . . 357 Aquap. 320
Neither put forth that way Thy arm severe ; . . 366 *Eternal Lord 11
Stood He, whose arm yet lacks the power . . 401 White Doe 482
He did not arm, he walked aloof ! . . . 412 White Doe 1466
He, whose strong arm the Orient could not check, 428 Ecc. Sonn. 1. 38. 6
Across the slender wrist of the left arm . . 509 F. Stone 53
Then trust thy cause to the arm of Fortitude, . 515 *Ah why 13
And fiercely by the arm he took her, . . . 537 Goody Blake 89
And by the arm he held her fast, . . . 537 Goody Blake 90
And fiercely by the arm he shook her, . . . 537 Goody Blake 91
While Harry held her by the arm— . . . 537 Goody Blake 98
And the Babe leaps up on his Mother's arm :— . 588 Immortality 49
Shakes her numb arm that slumbers with its weight, 596 Ev. Wk. Quarto 251
My care, if the arm of the mighty were mine, . 621 Convict 51
He rose, and with a lean and wasted arm . . 664 Prelude 4. 413

Arm—*continued.*
A lance he bore, and underneath one arm . . . 666 *Prelude* 5. 78
With freight of slippers piled beneath his arm ! . 690 *Prelude* 7. 218
From far, with basket, slung upon her arm, . . 699 *Prelude* 8. 28
Tied to her arm, and picking thus from the lane . 717 *Prelude* 9. 513
Were baffled ; nor could my weak arm disperse . 756 *Excursion* 1. 23
But wrought with mightier arm than now prevails. 787 *Excursion* 3. 91
Standing apart ; with curvèd arm reclined . . 825 *Excursion* 5. 211
Whizzed from the Stripling's arm ! If touched by him, ... 868 *Excursion* 7. 741
Hence a dread arm of floating power, a voice . . 876 *Excursion* 8. 143
Who, bearing each a basket on his arm, . . . 891 *Excursion* 9. 476
The tyrant felt their arm sublime. . . . . . S. 3. 442 *Harmodius* 20
A Pym's brave heart, or stir a Hampden's arm ? . L. 1. 94 *Juvenal* 2. 6
The nobler badge shall glitter on *his arm*. . . . L. 1. 96 *Juvenal* 3. 38

Armath's. On Armath's pleasant fields. And now they came, ... K. 8. 225 **I will* 51

Armathwaite. Of Wilfred Armathwaite ?" The Vicar answered, ... 854 *Excursion* 6. 1079

Armed. He to an armèd fleet was forced away . 25 *Guilt* 51
About your Daughter ! Troops of armed men, 61 *Bord.* 1330
Was made to seize him by three armèd men, . . 123 *V. and J.* 127
As soon as he had armed himself with strength . 134 *Michael* 221
Each crowned with flowers, and armed with spear and shield, ... 212 *Dion* 19
And armed with living spear for mortal fight ; . 227 *Vernal Ode* 104
And stands amidst you now an armèd creature, . 311 **Who rises* 16
Like a Champion, armed I come ; . . . . . 323 *Ode 1814* 30
With all her armèd Powers, ... 331 *Ode : Thanks.* 150
Alone, the armèd Multitude. . . . . . . 402 *White Doe* 593
Well-pleased, the armèd Company . . . . . 402 *White Doe* 601
Rides forth, an armèd man, and hurls a spear . 422 *Ecc. Sonn.* 1. 17. 3
Of Justice armed, and Pride to be laid low. . . 433 *Ecc. Sonn.* 2. 18. 14
Encounters, armed for work of pain and death. . 448 *Ecc. Sonn.* 3. 30. 12
Greedy ambition, armed to treat with scorn . . 469 **The feudal* 4
Armed to repel them ? Every hazard faced . 541 *Grace Darl.* 76
His being armed with strength that cannot fail. . 661 *Prelude* 4. 171
Now meeting on his road an armed knight, . . 771 *Excursion* 2. 5
And armèd warrior ; and in every grove . . . 812 *Excursion* 4. 742

Armenian. Hear now of a fair Armenian, . . . 139 *Arm. Lady* 3
Constant to the fair Armenian, ... 142 *Arm. Lady* 145

Armies. Than twenty armies. How ? The old blind Man, ... 51 *Bord.* 760
Opposed to armies, not a nerve would tremble : . 51 *Bord.* 779
To chase mankind, with men in armies packed . 313 **Go back* 12
Of perilous war her weightiest armies fail, . . 316 **Say, what* 7
Armies or kingdoms. We have heard a strain . 317 **The martial* 5
On fleets and armies, and external wealth : . . 320 **O'erweeningStatesmen* 2
The power of Armies is a visible thing, . . . 321 **The power* 1
And laurelled armies, not to be withstood— . . 450 *Ecc. Sonn.* 3. 38. 2
We crossed the Brabant armies on the fret . . 686 *Prelude* 6. 764
Armies of clouds,—even so, its powers and aspects 698 *Prelude* 7. 753
Than sentinels, between two armies, set, . . . 846 *Excursion* 6. 536

Arming. Thou Power supreme ! who, arming to rebuke . . . . 454 **The Sun, that* 13

Arminius. Arminius !—all the people quaked like dew . . . . 313 *Prophecy* 4

Armorial. Figures with armorial signs of race and birth, ... 142 *Arm. Lady* 155

Armorica. In old Armorica, whose secret springs . 102 *Artegal* 10

Armour. Armour rusting in his halls . . . . 205 *Brougham* 142
Armour divine, and conquer in your cause ! . . 446 *Ecc. Sonn.* 3. 25. 14
Cased in the unfeeling armour of old time, . . 579 *Peele Castle* 51
Broke forth in armour of resplendent words, . . 695 *Prelude* 7. 539
The boxer's armour, the dishonoured *Glove*. . . L. 1. 94 *Juvenal* 2. 26

Armoury. Armoury of the invincible Knights of old : 307 **It is not* 10

Arm's. But, with the plaything at arm's length, he sets . . . . 723 *Prelude* 10. 372

Arms. Their frozen arms her neck no more can fold ; 7 *Ev. Wk.* 272
Thy breast their death-bed, coffined in thine arms ! 7 *Ev. Wk.* 278
The cloister startles at the gleam of arms. . . 11 *Desc. Sk.* 60
With few in arms, innumerable foes, ... 18 *Desc. Sk.* 452
And the short thunder, and the flash of arms ; . 21 *Desc. Sk.* 617
With its dark arms to form a circling bower, . . 23 *Yew-tree* 11
The happy husband flies, his arms to throw . . 25 *Guilt* 60
Left by gigantic arms—at length surveys . . . 26 *Guilt* 113
My husband's arms now only served to strain . 29 *Guilt* 275
Whole hours, with idle arms in moping sorrow knit. . . . . 33 *Guilt* 432
Died in his arms ; and with those thanks a prayer 36 *Guilt* 643
I felt thy infant brother in her arms ; . . . . 40 *Bord.* 184
I took thee in my arms and we began . . . 40 *Bord.* 194
I bore her in my arms ; her looks won pity ; . . 53 *Bord.* 846
And arms to fold her to my heart. Submissively . 53 *Bord.* 853
Is brave. To Clifford's arms he would have led . 54 *Bord.* 912
To stretch her arms, and dim the gladsome light . 56 *Bord.* 1046
His pleading face, and feel his clasping arms, . 66 *Bord.* 1609
But take me to your arms—this breast, alas ! . 66 *Bord.* 1619
And in the arms of a stranger I must die. . . 67 *Bord.* 1672
But standing, walking, stretching forth his arms, . 68 *Bord.* 1729
and he had died in my arms !—— . . . . . 72 *Bord.* 1969
His senses play him false ; and see, his arms . 73 *Bord.* 2024
To weep that I am gone. Brothers in arms ! . 78 *Bord.* 2325
They hug the infant in my arms, ... 81 †*Mother's Return* 27
Into their arms the lamb they took, ... 85 *Shepherd-boys* 93
"He took thee in his arms, and in pity brought thee home : . . . . 87 *Pet-lamb* 37

Arms—*continued.*
Me had the dream equipped with wings, so I took him in my arms, ... 92 *Poet's Dream* 17
His arms have a perpetual holiday ; . . . . 96 *Brothers* 107
Pine not like them with arms across, ... 109 **Ere with* 9
When from my arms my Babe they took, . . . 114 *Ind. Wom.* 33
And then he stretched his arms, how wild ! . . 114 *Ind. Wom.* 39
And in his arms a Lamb he had. . . . . . 114 *Last of Flock* 10
I cannot keep thee in my arms ; . . . . . 121 *Emigrant Mother* 62
Upon the nursling which his arms embraced. . . 125 *V. and J.* 261
She looks again—her arms are up— . . . . 130 *Idiot Boy* 372
Old Michael, while he was a babe in arms, . . 133 *Michael* 153
With outspread arms and fallen upon her knees . 139 *Widow* 39
Thee, Baby, laughing in my arms, ... 171 *Kitten* 106
While she dandles the Babe in her arms to the sound. . . . . 189 *Music* 40
The trees were grey, with neither arms nor head ; 202 *Hart-leap* 109
For blue Ether's arms, flung round thee, . . . 217 **Inmate of* 7
Their own far-stretching arms and leafy heads 220 *Haunted Tree* 38
Nor of her arms ashamed. . . . . 232 *Jew. Fam.* 32
While Soldiers, weary of the arms they wield, 268 **Four fiery* 12
And now entwine their arms ; but ne'er again 276 *Oker Hill* 10
Back turned, arms folded, the unapparent face 277 **Haydon ! let* 9
Through the beloved retreats your arms enfold ! . 283 **Proud were* 8
And, falling into Bruce's arms, ... 287 *Ellen Irwin* 33
And useless arms, a trunk of man, ... 294 *Jedbor* 18
And spreads her arms, as if the general air . . 311 **Who rises* 11
That which we *would* perform in arms—we must ! 315 **The Land* 5
Resting upon his arms each warrior stood, . . 322 *Germans* 2
Glory to arms ! But, conscious that the nerve . 326 **Emperors and* 9
Infants in arms, and ye, that as ye go . . . . 339 *Tell* 7
By skeleton arms, that, from the mountain's trunk 353 *Aquap.* 44
The clang of arms is heard, and phantoms glide, . 361 **For action* 7
Whose infant arms enclasp the shrine . . . . 366 **Ye Trees* 3
Their foliage ; ashes flung their arms around ; . 377 *Duddon* 5. 7
And din of arms and minstrelsy, ... 400 *White Doe* 416
And Captains known for worth in arms ; . . . 403 *White Doe* 630
Now was the North in arms :—they shine . . . 403 *White Doe* 688
And thus, in arms, a zealous Band . . . . . 404 *White Doe* 709
To spread its arms, and stand for aye. . . . . 410 *White Doe* 1269
Her arms, or over-deeply breathed, ... 415 *White Doe* 1725
Dissension, checking arms that would restrain . 425 *Ecc. Sonn.* 1. 29. 2
And has a Champion risen in arms to try . . . 426 *Ecc. Sonn.* 1. 32. 9
Their tents, and check the current of their arms. . 427 *Ecc. Sonn.* 1. 34. 8
Of good, o'er manners arts and arms, diffused : . 429 *Ecc. Sonn.* 2. 2. 10
Creep round its arms through centuries unborn. . 450 *Ecc. Sonn.* 3. 40. 14
But, from the arms of silence—list ! O list ! . . 451 *Ecc. Sonn.* 3. 44. 9
That fascinate the very Babe in arms, ... 460 **Queen of* 18
By Social Order's watchful arms embraced ; . . 463 *Why should the* 10
Struggling for life, into its saving arms ! . . . 469 **The feudal* 10
They fail, thy saving arms, dread Power ! around them cast. . . . . 492 *Duty* 16
That every man in arms should wish to be ? . . 493 *Hap. War.* 2
That every Man in arms should wish to be. . . 494 *Hap. War.* 85
The Boy is in the arms of Wharf, ... 494 *Force of Prayer* 33
His arms, as swimmers use, and plunge—dread thought, ... 496 **A little* 30
To feats of arms addrest ! . . . . 499 **This Lawn* 12
And in Death's arms has long reposed the Friend . 525 **Soon did* 3
The dusky Shape within her arms imbound, . . 532 **Once I* 4
Their arms still strengthening with the strengthening heart, ... 541 *Grace Darl.* 61
And every season has soft arms . . . . . . 545 *Russ. Fug.* 303
That stripped of arms I to my end am brought . 575 *Chiabrera* 6. 11
In the chaste arms of thy belovèd Love ! . . . 575 *Chiabrera* 7. 13
Stretched forth his little arms and smil'd. . . 620 *Birth of Love* 27
Thee to her arms, and kisses interweave . . . 624 *Æneid* 39
Clasps in her arms, nor weens (O lot unblest !) 625 *Æneid* 87
What arms the son of bright Aurora wore ;— . 625 *Æneid* 135
Uplifted in his arms the child, ... 629 *Installation* 42
Where I was looking on, a babe in arms, . . . 636 *Prelude* 1. 276
Nursed in his Mother's arms, who sinks to sleep, . 645 *Prelude* 2. 235
In arms, now rosy prattlers at the feet . . . 661 *Prelude* 4. 204
Long were his arms, pallid his hands ; his mouth 664 *Prelude* 4. 395
Arms flashing, and a military glare . . . . 681 *Prelude* 6. 424
And stumping on his arms. In sailor's garb . . 690 *Prelude* 7. 204
He took no heed ; but in his brawny arms . . 696 *Prelude* 7. 612
Men, Women, three-years' Children, Babes in arms. 698 *Prelude* 7. 721
To augment the band of emigrants in arms . . 712 *Prelude* 9. 183
Surrounded by adventurers in arms, ... 715 *Prelude* 9. 413
What, then, were my emotions, when in arms . 722 *Prelude* 10. 263
The Herculean Commonwealth had put forth her arms, ... 724 *Prelude* 10. 391
Shaken by arms of mighty bone, in strength, . . 744 *Prelude* 13. 325
—Margaret stood near, her infant in her arms, . 769 *Excursion* 1. 843
—In rugged arms how softly does it lie, . . . 777 *Excursion* 2. 358
How Nature hems you in with friendly arms ! . 786 *Excursion* 3. 14
And, so consumed, she melted from my arms ; . 796 *Excursion* 3. 678
A broad oak, stretching forth its leafy arms . . 825 *Excursion* 5. 227
That lovingly consigns the babe to the arms . . 836 *Excursion* 5. 951
Of arms, the crown which bigotry had lost, . . 844 *Excursion* 6. 418
Against his conscience rose in arms, and, braving 855 *Excursion* 6 1092
And in remotest vales was heard—to arms ! . . 869 *Excursion* 7. 762
With righteous Joshua ; nor appeared in arms . 870 *Excursion* 7. 813
Was cleared, I dipped, with arms accordant, oars 891 *Excursion* 9. 489
For baffled lips and disappointed arms . . . S. 3. 434 **The doubt* 79
Of old Helvellyn spread their arms abroad . . K. 8. 225 **I will* 33
Of glory, fronted multitudes in arms. . . . . K. 8. 256 *Recluse* 1. 1. 720
Arms and the Man I sing, the first who bore . . K. 8. 281 **Arms and* 1
Slap-dash, tail foremost, as his arms shall drive. . L. 1. 96 *Juvenal* 3. 32
What arms the son of bright Aurora wore, . . L. 2. 123 *Frag. Æneid* 3. 2

Art—*continued.*
For thou art worse than mad a thousand fold; . 560 *Cuck.and Night.*188
O Palace whilom day that now art night, . . . 563 *Troilus* 26
And said: I wis, when thou art horn'd anew, . 564 *Troilus* 132
In him it was scarcely a business of art, . . . 570 *Farmer* 43
Now farewell, old Adam! when low thou art laid, 571 *Farmer* 89
That never art secure from dolorous change! . . 573 *Chiabrera* 2. 14
Or Fancy, disciplined by studious art, ... 587 *Crosth.* 9
Shaped by himself with newly-learned art; . . 589 *Immortality* 92
The confidence of Youth our only Art, . . . 625 **The confidence* 1
Yet, blessed Art, we yield not to dejection; . . 627 **We gaze* 9
No Laureate offering of elaborate art; . . . . 628 **Deign, Sovereign* 2
Of Grecian art, and purest poesy. . . . . . 672 *Prelude* 5. 459
In summer, making quest for works of art, . . 677 *Prelude* 6. 190
Where tones of Nature smoothed by learned Art . 685 *Prelude* 6. 674
When Art was young; dramas of living men, . 691 *Prelude* 7. 290
And to book-notions and the rules of art . . . 704 *Prelude* 8. 370
And all the nicely-guarded shows of art, . . . 710 *Prelude* 9. 31
Liking; by rules of mimic art transferred . 736 *Prelude* 12. 111
To things above all art; but more,—for this, . 736 *Prelude* 12. 112
Of courteous usages refined by art. . . . . . 742 *Prelude* 13. 194
Reared by the industrious hand of human art . 787 *Excursion* 3. 102
Youngest apprentice in the school of art! . . . 789 *Excursion* 3. 199
True, the intelligence of social art . . . . 799 *Excursion* 3. 925
Of art, this palpable array of sense, ... 812 *Excursion* 4. 730
Art to outstrip in her peculiar walk. . . . . 842 *Excursion* 6. 303
A work of art more sumptuous than might seem . 846 *Excursion* 6. 506
Shall find apt subjects for her highest art. . . 846 *Excursion* 6. 552
Had learned the art of pleasing, and had now . 882 *Excursion* 8. 531
A Youth, I practised this delightful art; . . . 891 *Excursion* 9. 486
An art, a music, and a strain of words K.8. 247*Recluse* 1.1.402
Artegal. He died, whom Artegal succeeds—his son; 103 *Artegal* 74
Feebly returned by daunted Artegal; . . . . 104 *Artegal* 123
A while the astonished Artegal stood mute, . . 104 *Artegal* 138
Then Artegal thus spake: "I only sought . . 104 *Artegal* 162
The reinstated Artegal became . . . . . . 105 *Artegal* 228
Artful. Together,—'mid trim walks and artful bowers, ... 389 *Breadalb.* 10
And there he planned an artful Cot . . . . 543 *Russ. Fug.* 111
With preparation artful and benign, ... 687 *Prelude* 7. 24
Artfully. With caution, sift the matter artfully. . 42 *Bord.* 293
Arthur. *See* **Stone-Arthur.**
The feats of Arthur and his knightly peers; . . 103 *Artegal* 52
Of Arthur,—who, to upper light restored, . . 103 *Artegal* 53
In silence did King Arthur gaze . . . . 374 *Eg. Maid* 337
King Arthur led the Egyptian Maid, ... 374 *Eg. Maid* 353
Of Arthur, bearing through the stormy field . . 421 *Ecc. Sonn.* 1. 10. 6
Arthur's. Soon will the Knights of Arthur's Table . 370 *Eg. Maid* 86
May yet to Arthur's court be borne . . . . 370 *Eg. Maid* 101
Thence northward did they pass by Arthur's seat, K.8. 225 **I will* 23
Articulate. The Child, as if the thunder's voice spake with articulate call, ... 92 *Poet's Dream* 9
Which yet I understood, articulate sounds, . . 667 *Prelude* 5. 94
Articulate music. Above all, one thought . . 688 *Prelude* 7. 115
Articulate prattle—Child as beautiful . . . . 692 *Prelude* 7. 339
And haply sometimes with articulate voice, . . 809 *Excursion* 4. 533
He heard, borne on the wind, the articulate voice 810 *Excursion* 4. 634
The ready Organ of articulate sounds K.8. 246*Recluse* 1.1.343
Artificer. As the supreme Artificer ordained. . . 474 **Hope smiled* 14
(The Artificer was to the elbow bare, ... 696 *Prelude* 7. 613
But by the great Artificer endowed . . . . 809 *Excursion* 4. 557
Artificial. The surfaces of artificial life . . . . 657 *Prelude* 3. 559
By artificial lights; how they debase . . . . 743 *Prelude* 13. 210
Artillery. And whole artillery of the western blast, 474 **Hope smiled* 4
Artisans. With care and sorrow: shoals of artisans 764 *Excursion* 1. 559
Artist. "A cunning artist will I have to frame . . 201 *Hart-leap* 61
Might some aspiring artist dare . . . . . . 301 *Bran* 78
Or more mechanic artist represent . . . . . 691 *Prelude* 7. 248
Artist's. Of long companionship, the artist's hand, 831 *Excursion* 5. 608
Artists. Like Grecian Artists, give thee human cheeks, 268 **Brook! whose* 8
Artless. Trained to health and artless beauty; . . 629 *Installation* 46
An artless rustic's notice, this way less, . . . 657 *Prelude* 3. 586
And wooed the artless daughter of the hills, . . 691 *Prelude* 7. 300
Art's. When Art's abused inventions were unknown; 256 *Easter* 12
Art's noblest relics, history's rich bequests, . . 354 *Aquap.* 96
Arts. Yet are thy softer arts with power indued 13 *Desc. Sk.* 141
And droop, while no Italian arts are thine, . . 21 *Desc. Sk.* 589
Who, through most wicked arts, was made an orphan . . . . 78 *Bord.* 2330
With goodly arts and usages refined; . . . . 102 *Artegal* 20
To freeze the blood I have no ready arts: . . . 202 *Hart-leap* 98
Spake of heroic arts in graver mood . . . . 211 *Laod.* 101
By Art's bold privilege Warrior and War-horse stand . . . . 278 *Wellington* 1
Her arts, her strength, her iron, and her gold. . 320 **Avaunt all* 14
Honour to word-preserving Arts, and hail . . . 356 *Aquap.* 250
By civil arts and labours of the pen, ... 389 *Sound of Mull* 10
Yet peaceful Arts did entrance gain . . . . 390 *Highland Broach* 11
Their arts, their customs, ebb and flow; . . . 391 *Highland Broach* 62
Of your redemption. Shun the insidious arts . 420 *Ecc. Sonn.* 1. 8. 9
Whose arts and honours in the dust are laid . . 421 *Ecc. Sonn.* 1. 11. 8
With all their Arts,—but classic lore glides on . 425 *Ecc. Sonn.* 1. 25. 13
Of good, o'er manners arts and arms, diffused: . 429 *Ecc. Sonn.* 2. 2. 11
With a bad world, and foil the Tempter's arts. . 447 *Ecc. Sonn.* 3. 28. 14
Not by black arts but magic natural! . . . . 474 **Ye shadowy* 12
Then Arts, which still had drawn a softening grace 476 **Tranquillity! the* 10
Of neighbourhood and intermingling arts, . . . 524 *Epist. Beaumont* 198
Yet, arts are thine that rock th' unsleeping heart . 605 *Desc.Sk.Quarto* 162
While no Italian arts their charms combine . . 615 *Desc.Sk.Quarto* 707

Arts—*continued.*
To the mild influence of the finer arts; . . . 619 *School Ex.* 60
Arts yet untried, upon new counsels bent, . . 624 *Æneid* 2
Then seeks the queen; with her his arts he tries; 625 *Æneid* 85
And left their usuages, their arts and laws, . . 635 *Prelude* 1. 193
To thee, unblinded by these formal arts, . . . 645 *Prelude* 2. 220
Have made me pay to science and to arts . . . 654 *Prelude* 3. 375
O seat of Arts! renowned throughout the world! 655 *Prelude* 3. 458
Of arts and letters—but be that forgiven)— . . 671 *Prelude* 5. 410
With arts and laws so tempered, that their lives . 701 *Prelude* 8. 130
Polished in arts, and in punctilio versed; . . . 711 *Prelude* 9. 117
Of strenuous champions, in scholastic arts . . 839 *Excursion* 6. 57
In their own arts outdone, their fame eclipsed, . 843 *Excursion* 6. 348
Hands apt for all ingenious arts and games; . . 859 *Excursion* 7. 119
Spread with the spreading of her wealthy arts, . 870 *Excursion* 7. 855
By importation of unlooked-for arts, ... 875 *Excursion* 8. 68
Owes to alliance with these new-born arts! . . 876 *Excursion* 8. 132
And the Arts died by which they had been raised. 877 *Excursion* 8. 219
Those arts, and high inventions, if unpropped . 877 *Excursion* 8. 226
I said, "And, did in truth those vaunted Arts . 877 *Excursion* 8. 232
Of household occupation; no nice arts . . . 878 *Excursion* 8. 271
If there were not, before those arts appeared, . 879 *Excursion* 8. 338
A Little-one, subjected to the arts . . . . . 886 *Excursion* 9. 157
Arts, in themselves beneficent and kind, . . . 887 *Excursion* 9. 189
With civil arts, that shall breathe forth their fragrance, ... 890 *Excursion* 9. 390
What arts had better claim with wrath to warm . L. 1. 94 *Juvenal* 2. 5
Do arts like these a royal mind evince? . . . L. 1. 94 *Juvenal* 2. 11
Arve. While roars the sullen Arve in anger by, 21 *Desc. Sk.* 585
When roar'd the sullen Arve in anger by, . . . 615 *Desc. Sk.Quarto* 703
As, *omitted.*
Ascanius. To young Ascanius, should assume his place; . . . . 624 *Æneid* 4
His young Ascanius to the Tyrian walls; . . . 624 *Æneid* 28
The true Ascanius steep'd in placid rest; . . . 624 *Æneid* 48
Ascend. Aerial pines from loftier steeps ascend, . 14 *Desc. Sk.* 232
Winds our deep Vale, two heath-clad Rocks ascend 151 **Forth from* 2
"Learn, by a mortal yearning, to ascend . . . 211 *Laod.* 145
So be it!—but let praise ascend . . . . . 294 *Jedbor.* 76
Shall praises be poured forth, and thanks ascend, 328 *Ode 1815* 122
Or thanks and praises to His throne ascend . . 331 *Ode: Thanks.* 180
His volant Spirit will, he trusts, ascend . . . 366 *Lombardy* 13
Ascend, with lineaments in air not lost: . . . 367 *Trajan* 14
Blest while their Spirits from the woods ascend . 443 *Ecc. Sonn.* 3. 13. 12
And tempting Fancy to ascend, ... 458 **Had this* 47
In his mind's eye thy crescent horns ascend, . . 460 **Wanderer! that* 71
Thy mental vision further and ascend . . . . 519 *Pun. Death* 9. 3
—As thro' th' astonish'd woods the notes ascend, 598 *Ev. Wk. Quarto* 351
Shade above shade the desert pines ascend, . . 607 *Desc.Sk.Quarto* 290
Up to the loftiest towers of Pride ascend, . . . 681 *Prelude* 6. 446
Conspicuous invitation to ascend . . . . . 683 *Prelude* 6. 572
Fresh from a toilette of two hours, ascend . . 695 *Prelude* 7. 552
In dignity of being we ascend. . . . . . . 812 *Excursion* 4. 765
And the clear hills, as high as they ascend . . K.8. 252*Recluse* 1.1.578
Ascendant. And, as the Moon, o'er some dark hill ascendant, ... 369 *Eg. Maid* 8
Ascended. The Water-wraith ascended thrice— . . 302 *Yarrow V.* 31
Ascended, with his staff and faithful dog; . . 863 *Excursion* 7. 420
Ascending. But lo! the Alps, ascending white in air, 11 *Desc. Sk.* 50
That dark mysterious gulf ascending, sound . . 18 *Desc. Sk.* 415
And up the craggy hill ascending . . . . . 174 *Waggoner* 1. 35
The stately waggon is ascending, ... 180 *Waggoner* 4. 65
A mountain ascending, a vision of trees; . . . 188 *Poor Susan* 6
And now, ascending, after one dark hour . . . 192 *Gipsies* 17
Ascending, they approach—I hear their wings . 218 *Recluse* 1. 1. 219
Ascending from behind the motionless brow . . 229 *Clouds* 2
Skyward ascending from a woody dell. . . . 262 **Not Love* 8
But aye ascending, restless in her pride . . . 327 *Ode 1815* 2
Aloft ascending, and descending deep, ... 395 *White Doe: Ded.*44
To where the Alps, ascending white in air, . . 603 *Desc.Sk.Quarto* 51
—Breaking th' ascending roar of desert floods, . 606 *Desc.Sk.Quarto* 223
Ascending, nearer howls the famish'd wolf, . . 606 *Desc.Sk.Quarto* 240
Loud thro' that midway gulf ascending, sound . 611 *Desc.Sk.Quarto* 504
That, from the rural school ascending, play . . 671 *Prelude* 5. 405
Ascending, as if distance had the power . . . 699 *Prelude* 8. 3
Ascending, overlooked them both, far stretched; . 738 *Prelude* 12. 294
Ascending at loose distance each from each, . . 746 *Prelude* 14. 33
Deep—and, aloft ascending, breathe in worlds . 755 *Recluse* 1. 1. 782
In clearest air ascending, showed far off . . . 756 *Excursion* 1. 4
Was heard ascending; mournful, deep, and slow 777 *Excursion* 2. 375
To loftiest heights ascending, from their tops, . 811 *Excursion* 4. 674
A veil of glory for the ascending moon; . . . 866 *Excursion* 7. 599
Ascending! For on that superior height . . . 885 *Excursion* 9. 69
Ascends. Honour ascends among the humblest poor, 138 *Widow* 2
A voice to Peter's ear ascends, ... 247 *P. B.* 939
Huge Criffel's hoary top ascends . . . . . 285 *Grave of Burns* 39
The "trumpery" that ascends in bare display— 435 *Ecc. Sonn.* 2. 28. 6
Heavenward ascends with all her charities, . . 467 *St. Bees* 116
That from the vale ascends. . . . . 583 **O for a* 48
While loud and dull ascends the weeping cry, . 614 *Desc.Sk.Quarto* 658
Alone ascends that mountain nam'd of white . . 614 *Desc.Sk.Quarto* 690
In the waste wilderness: the Soul ascends . . 807 *Excursion* 4. 395
Below, from which the curling smoke ascends. . 832 *Excursion* 5. 645
Commingling with the incense that ascends, . . 885 *Excursion* 9. 42
Yet not for meek of heart. The smoke ascends . 887 *Excursion* 9. 245
That from the humblest floor ascends to heaven, . 889 *Excursion* 9. 326
Ascension. And glorified Ascension? Warriors, go, 427 *Ecc. Sonn.* 1. 33. 4
Ascent. *See* **Re-ascent.**
Then up the steep ascent they hied, ... 85 *Shepherd-boys* 95
Your feet must struggle; in such bold ascent . 131 *Michael* 4
The long ascent of Dunmail-raise . . . . . 174 *Waggoner* 1. 100

Asketh—*continued.*
This matter asketh counsel good as grave, . . 562 *Cuck.andNight.*272
Asking. No pity asking, on the group she gazed . 34 *Guilt* 562
Nor asking more, on that delicious Bay, . . . 356 *Aquap.* 264
Asks. That flatters us, because it asks not thought : 56 *Bord.* 1034
Asks of the clouds what occupants they hide :— . 220 *Triad* 29
He asks with insecure delight, ... 398 *White Doe* 195
Asks of himself, and doubts,—and still . . . 398 *White Doe* 196
" And shall," the Pontiff asks, " profaneness flow 426 *Ecc. Sonn.* 1. 33. 1
That asks for daily bread. . . . . . . 530 *Gleaner* 34
A timid voice, that asks in whispers, ... 586 *Hogg* 27
And asks of me why I am here. . . . . . . 621 *Convict* 44
That asks not speed, a traveller might bestow . 696 *Prelude* 7. 591
The wisdom of the prayer that daily asks . . 813 *Excursion* 4. 788
Asleep. You say he was asleep,—look at this arm, 52 *Bord.* 796
I could have dropped asleep upon his breast. . . 53 *Bord.* 892
Murder—perhaps asleep, blind, old, alone, . . 54 *Bord.* 901
Asleep upon their beds they lie ; . . . . . 82 †*Mother's Return* 54
He there had fallen asleep ; that in his sleep . 101 *Brothers* 398
The breeze had better been asleep, ... 156 *Oak and Broom* 43
As if they'd fall asleep embracing ! . . . . . 179 *Waggoner* 3. 47
Nor all asleep—in his extreme old age : . . . 196 *Resolution* 65
And oftentimes, when all are fast asleep, . . . 202 *Hart-leap* 135
" Here on the grass perhaps asleep he sank, . . 203 *Hart-leap* 149
Almost suspended, we are laid asleep . . . . 206 *Tintern* 45
Or, tired with sport, wouldst sink asleep . . . 216 *Enterprise* 34
Through years that have been long asleep ! . . 248 *P. B.* 1094
Dear God ! the very houses seem asleep ; . . . 269 *Westm. Bridge* 13
When earthly cares are laid asleep ! . . . . 288 *Highland Girl* 14
Asleep on ZURICH's shore ! . . . . 348 **Lulled by* 24
That lulled me asleep, bids me listen once more. . 364 *Vallomb.* 4
Not all asleep and yet not waking wholly ; . . 558 *Cuck. and Night.*88
Lulling the mourner's best good thoughts asleep, 576 **By a* 17
Asleep on Bunker's charnel hill afar ; . . . . 596 *Ev. Wk. Quarto* 254
And threshold steps were empty ; fast asleep . 642 *Prelude* 2. 12
That, in an easy temper lulled asleep, ... 658 *Prelude* 3. 614
And loved the book, when she had dropped asleep 661 *Prelude* 4. 229
The whole creative powers of man asleep !— . . 697 *Prelude* 7. 681
With waters running, falling, or asleep. . . . 700 *Prelude* 8. 97
To lay the inner faculties asleep. . . . . 736 *Prelude* 12. 147
Recumbent in the shade, as if asleep ; . . . . 756 *Excursion* 1. 36
By sorrow laid aside ; or borne away, ... 768 *Excursion* 1. 786
Is Common-sense asleep ? has she no wand . . L. 1. 88 *Juvenal* 1. 15
Christophe now is laid asleep . . . . . . L. 2. 190 **Queen and* 2
Aspect. And death's dire aspect daily he surveyed, 25 *Guilt* 56
With aspect so inviting. Why forbid me . . . 55 *Bord.* 970
And fling him to the ravens. But his aspect, . 57 *Bord.* 1067
Shocked at his savage aspect, from the place . . 126 *V. and J.* 298
Of form and aspect too magnificent . . . . 184 *Yew-trees* 12
Of aspect more sublime ; that blessed mood, . . 206 *Tintern* 37
And hideous aspect, stalking round and round ! . 213 *Dion* 68
And in the aspect of each radiant orb ;— . . . 226 *Vernal Ode* 32
The heavens, whose aspect makes our minds as still 235 *Power of Sound* 181
" As the cold aspect of a sunless way . . . . 267 **As the* 1
Of aspect winning and serene ; . . . . . . 299 *Brownie's Cell* 76
Before the ominous aspect of her spear ; . . . 311 **Who rises* 24
And scattered rural farms of aspect bright ; . . 323 *Ode 1814* 12
—Well does thine aspect usher in this Day ; . . 329 *Ode : Thanks.* 14
And splendid aspect yon emblazonings . . . 335 *Cologne* 7
From the fierce aspect of this River, throwing . 336 *Aar* 1
The aspect I behold of every zone ; . . . . 350 *Des Stanzas* 34
By Fiends of aspect more malign ; . . . . 369 *Eg. Maid* 35
What aspect bore the Man who roved or fled, . 378 *Duddon* 8. 1
Aught that more surely by its aspect fills . . 387 *Manse* 8
A choice that wears the aspect of a doom ; . . 391 *Brownie* 10
Bold is his aspect ; but his eye . . . . . . 404 *White Doe* 766
One star of aspect heavenly bright ; . . . . 411 *White Doe* 1357
Of aspect such as if the waste . . . . . 413 *White Doe* 1581
A Man whose aspect doth at once appal . . . 422 *Ecc. Sonn.* 1. 15. 8
Wonder that aught of aspect so serene . . . 439 *Ecc. Sonn.* 2. 43. 4
Of sapience in thy aspect, headless Owl ! . . . 456 **The leaves* 27
Yet thy mild aspect does not, cannot, cease . . 460 **Queen of* 35
With thy stern aspect better far agrees . . . 466 *St. Bees* 25
An aspect tenderly illumed, ... 498 **Departing summer* 2
Fiends in your aspect, yet beneficent . . . . 518 *Pun. Death* 6. 3
Whose studious aspect should have bent me down 654 *Prelude* 3. 373
Appeared a different aspect of old age ; . . . 657 *Prelude* 3. 549
Than is the common aspect, daily garb, . . . 674 *Prelude* 5. 576
Of modest sympathy. Such aspect now, . . . 676 *Prelude* 6. 63
Thou canst put on an aspect most severe ; . . 707 *Prelude* 8. 531
Of aspect, with aerial softness clad, ... 773 *Excursion* 2. 95
Owes that presiding aspect which might well . . 824 *Excursion* 5. 129
To trust the smiling aspect of this fair . . . 828 *Excursion* 5. 422
Death and its two-fold aspect ! wintry—one, . 831 *Excursion* 5. 554
In aspect and forbidding, yet a point . . . 885 *Excursion* 9. 53
On every shore whose aspect favours hope . . 889 *Excursion* 9. 380
The general aspect of the scene ; but each . . 893 *Excursion* 9. 583
And gentle aspect oft has ministered . . . . S. 3. 433 **The doubt* 20
Aspects. Of moral qualities in their diverse aspects ; 59 *Bord.* 1226
With aspects novel to my sight ; but still . . . 361 **List—'twas* 13
Two aspects bears Truth needful for salvation ; . 447 *Ecc. Sonn.* 3. 29. 9
Through every change its aspects undergo— . . 455 **Not in the lucid* 23
Armies of clouds,—even so, its powers and aspects 698 *Prelude* 7. 753
Still roll ; where all the aspects of misery . . 806 *Excursion* 4. 327
Their aspects lend, and mingle in their turn . . 809 *Excursion* 4. 537
And, by their aspects, signifying works . . . 812 *Excursion* 4. 705
Unusual aspects, or by questions apt . . . . K. 8. 230 **I will* 192
Aspen. " You see these lifeless stumps of aspen wood— . . . . 202 *Hart-leap* 125

Aspen—*continued.*
If from a golden perch of aspen spray . . . . 388 *Trosachs* 10
Aspen's. There doth the twinkling aspen's foliage sleep, ... 4 *Ev. Wk.* 116
Aspens. Through rustling aspens heard from side to side, ... 21 *Desc. Sk.* 625
Three aspens at three corners of a square ; . . 202 *Hart-leap* 103
(Above it shivering aspens play) . . . . . 246 *P. B.* 922
Aspirant. Full soon the Aspirant of the plough, . 285 *Grave of Burns* 27
For some Aspirant of our short-lived race, . . . 313 **Go back* 7
Here may the aspirant find a trysting-place . . S. 3. 436 **The doubt* 148
Aspirants. Like those aspirants let us soar—our aim, 462 **Where lies the truth* 12
Aspiration. Vain aspiration of an earnest will ! . 395 *White Doe : Ded.* 61
Of Christian aspiration, deigned to fill . . . . 436 *Ecc. Sonn.* 2. 30. 11
Till breath departs in blissful aspiration : . . . 437 *Ecc. Sonn.* 2. 35. 11
My last and favourite aspiration, mounts . . . 635 *Prelude* 1. 228
A noble aspiration ! *yet* I feel . . . . . . 731 *Prelude* 11. 255
The aspiration, nor shall ever cease . . . . 731 *Prelude* 11. 257
Aspirations. Meek aspirations please her, lone endeavour, ... 262 **Not Love* 9
Oh that with aspirations more intense, . . . 513 *General Fast* 9
Thee kindred aspirations moved . . . . . 533 **Blest is* 17
The views and aspirations of the soul . . . . 698 *Prelude* 7. 755
To aspirations then of our own minds . . . . 715 *Prelude* 9. 380
In hope, and trained to noble aspirations, . . . 720 *Prelude* 10. 166
Poured forth his aspirations, and announced . . 805 *Excursion* 4. 240
Not without aspirations, evermore . . . . . 827 *Excursion* 5. 302
Of aspirations that *have* been, of foes . . . . K. 8. 256 *Recluse* 1. 1. 738
Aspire. 'Cross the calm lake's blue shades the cliffs aspire, ... 5 *Ev. Wk.* 174
The dull-red steeps, and, darkening still, aspire . 13 *Desc. Sk.* 159
" But not for this do I aspire . . . . . . 167 *Pilgrim's Dream* 41
Or, while the wings aspire, are heart and eye . . 209 **Ethereal minstrel* 3
Mount from the earth ; aspire ! aspire ! . . . 228 *Devot. Incit.* 26
For deepest sorrows that aspire . . . . . . 411 *White Doe* 1352
These jealous Ministers of law aspire, ... 419 *Ecc. Sonn.* 1. 4. 7
And straightway cease to aspire, than God disdain 465 **Pastor and* 13
Aspire to more than earthly destinies ; . . . 467 *St. Bees* 125
The generous course, aspire, and still aspire ; . . 529 **Those breathing* 129
With growing faculties she doth aspire, . . . 646 *Prelude* 2. 319
Things that aspire to unconquerable life ; . . . 666 *Prelude* 5. 20
Yet cease I not to struggle, and aspire . . . 803 *Excursion* 4. 126
By story be confounded ! Ye aspire . . . . 805 *Excursion* 4. 289
Nor would their reason, tutored to aspire . . . 877 *Excursion* 8. 192
Aspired. That not in vain aspired . . . . . 170 *Rural Ill.* 20
For him who to divinity aspired, ... 213 *Dion* 46
Who neither grovelled nor aspired : . . . . 298 *Brownie's Cell* 26
Aspires. He tamed, who foolishly aspires ; . . . 291 *Rob Roy* 46
Aspires to thee addrest, ... 506 **While from* 46
While Faith aspires to seats in that domain . . 533 **Once I* 41
In brighter rows her table wealth aspires, . . 615 *Desc.Sk.Quarto* 732
Aspiring. " Such it is ; the aspiring creature . . 163 *Hint* 25
Aspiring Road ! that lov'st to hide . . . . 215 *Kirkstone* 49
The aspiring Virgin kneels ; and, pale . . . 216 *Enterprise* 55
To pause at last on more aspiring heights . . . 230 *Clouds* 21
Aspiring Votary, ere thy hand present . . . . 270 **Though the bold* 12
Might some aspiring artist dare . . . . . . 301 *Bran* 78
And to the like aspiring, ... 325 *Ode 1814* 138
The aspiring heads of future things appear, . . 326 **The Bard* 7
Who dwells in heaven ! But that aspiring heat . 335 *Cologne* 5
Aspiring thoughts, by memory reclaimed, . . . 340 *Ranz* 12
Or some aspiring rock, that shrouds . . . . 413 *White Doe* 1562
The aspiring Mountains and the winding Streams, 459 **Wanderer ! that* 23
Go, single—yet aspiring to be joined . . . . 538 **In desultory* 17
St. Peter's Church ; or, more aspiring aim, . . 691 *Prelude* 7. 252
The fence where that aspiring shrub looked out . 763 *Excursion* 1. 452
Upon the insolent aspiring brow . . . . . 775 *Excursion* 2. 270
Or too aspiring, thankless at the best) . . . . 790 *Excursion* 3. 292
Fresh, youthful, and aspiring ! What are these . 799 *Excursion* 3. 885
That are not lofty as her rights ; aspiring . . . 806 *Excursion* 4. 315
At her aspiring outset. Mark the babe . . . 826 *Excursion* 5. 261
These inward feelings, and the aspiring vows . . 827 *Excursion* 5. 312
Ass. My Ass and fifty things beside,— . . . . 176 *Waggoner* 1. 260
Pursues, with Ass and all his store, ... 176 *Waggoner* 1. 276
Re-yoked her to the Ass :—anon . . . . . 178 *Waggoner* 2. 163
Says Benjamin, " That Ass of thine, ... 179 *Waggoner* 3. 50
The Ass, uplifting a hind hoof, ... 179 *Waggoner* 3. 106
And, O indignity ! an Ass, ... 181 *Waggoner* 4. 162
A solitary Ass. . . . . 240 *P. B.* 385
But still the Ass his station kept. . . . . . 241 *P. B.* 400
Only the Ass, with motion dull, ... 241 *P. B.* 413
—Once more the Ass, with motion dull, . . . 241 *P. B.* 418
The poor Ass staggered with the shock ; . . . 241 *P. B.* 426
And east and west, the Ass sent forth . . . . 241 *P. B.* 464
Once more the Ass did lengthen out . . . . 241 *P. B.* 478
He scans the Ass from limb to limb, ... 242 *P. B.* 491
The Ass is by the river-side, ... 242 *P. B.* 533
Full suddenly the Ass doth rise ! . . . . . 242 *P. B.* 560
The little Ass his neck extends, ... 242 *P. B.* 564
The Ass looks on—and to his work . . . . 242 *P. B.* 571
And he whom the poor Ass had lost, ... 243 *P. B.* 577
Of this poor miserable Ass ! " . . . . . . 243 *P. B.* 585
Upon the pleased and thankful Ass ; . . . . 243 *P. B.* 597
And there the Ass four days had been, . . . 243 *P. B.* 604
The Ass is startled—and stops short . . . . 243 *P. B.* 621
The listening Ass conjectures well ; . . . . 243 *P. B.* 652
But Peter—when he saw the Ass . . . . . 243 *P. B.* 656
Meanwhile the Ass to reach his home . . . . 244 *P. B.* 666
And while the Ass pursues his way . . . . . 244 *P. B.* 686

Ass—*continued.*
Where, as before, the enduring Ass 244 *P. B.* 712
He thought,—of thee, O faithful Ass ! 244 *P. B.* 732
An Ass like this was worth the stealing !" 245 *P. B.* 815
The Ass turned round his head and *grinned.* 245 *P. B.* 825
The unheeding Ass moves slowly on, 246 *P. B.* 866
Meanwhile the persevering Ass 247 *P. B.* 981
Along the lane the trusty Ass 247 *P. B.* 991
The poor Ass standing by her side, 248 *P. B.* 1024
The Ass in that small meadow-ground ; 248 *P. B.* 1037
She calls the poor Ass by his name, 248 *P. B.* 1044
He lifts his head—and sees the Ass 248 *P. B.* 1096
He sees the Ass—and nothing living 249 *P. B.* 1107
Forth to the gentle Ass he springs, 249 *P. B.* 1111
And many years did this poor Ass, 249 *P. B.* 1126
—Rocked by the motion of a trusty ass 858 *Excursion* 7. 72
Assail. Oh ! when the sleety showers her path assail, 7 *Ev. Wk.* 269
Which now with freezing thoughts did all her powers assail ; 27 *Guilt* 171
Afflict, or injuries assail, 457 **Had this* 42
Oh ! when the bitter showers her path assail, 597 *Ev. Wk. Quarto* 279
Till Death's cold touch her cistern-wheel assail, 615 *Desc. Sk. Quarto* 742
Assailants. The Assailants, turning round and round ; 412 *White Doe* 1484
Assailed. Dire poverty assailed ; 103 *Artegal* 87
But, one by one, the hand of death assailed 139 *Widow* 13
Over that tender Spirit—assailed 405 *White Doe* 882
Of self-reproach familiarly assailed ; 793 *Excursion* 3. 490
Of disputation, shrunk not, though assailed 839 *Excursion* 6. 63
Assails. Where Horror-led his sea of ice assails, 615 *Desc. Sk. Quarto* 694
Assault. From rash assault ? Schemes of retirement sown 282 *Railway* 2
No courage can repel the dire assault ; 322 **Humanity, delighting* 33
She saw the desperate assault 408 *White Doe* 1126
"Though fierce the assault, and shattered the defence, 471 **Despond who* 2
Unhurt, the assault of Time with all his hours, 474 **Hope smiled* 13
Suffices ; and unshaken bears the assault 833 *Excursion* 5. 701
Screen'd from assault of every bitter blast ; 860 *Excursion* 7. 201
Was loth to assault the majesty he loved : 868 *Excursion* 7. 749
Assaulting. Assaulting without ruth 330 *Ode : Thanks.* 107
Assaulting and defending, and the wind, 813 *Excursion* 4. 796
Assaults. As if, to rough assaults unknown, 348 **Lulled by* 9
All worse assaults may safely be defied. 383 *Duddon* 27. 14
With patient care. What tho' assaults run high, 514 **Blest Statesman* 6
Assaults the pride she strove in vain to quell. 519 *Pun. Death* 12. 4
Fearless of all assaults that would her brood molest. 525 *Epist. Beaumont* 231
Fate harder still ! had he to endure assaults 574 *Chiabrera* 5. 4
Against the dire assaults of papacy 844 *Excursion* 6. 433
Assemblage. And for itself, the assemblage, grand and fair 355 *Aquap.* 185
Who, looking round the fair assemblage, feels 446 *Ecc. Sonn.* 3. 23. 13
Uncouth assemblage was it, where no few 640 *Prelude* 1. 521
That gay assemblage. Round them and above, 773 *Excursion* 2. 128
The mild assemblage of the starry heavens ; 808 *Excursion* 4. 464
A grave assemblage, seated while they shear 866 *Excursion* 7. 619
Where, in assemblage with the flower and choice 869 *Excursion* 7. 769
And full assemblage of a barbarous host ; 894 *Excursion* 9. 707
Assemblages. Whate'er assemblages of new and old, 362 **List—'twas* 25
Assembled. *See* **Re-assembled.**
Assembled, He, by a herald's voice, proclaims 312 **A Roman* 3
Of time to Lords and Ladies thus assembled. 373 *Eg. Maid* 282
Spirits of Power, assembled there, complain 386 *Scott* 4
Of an assembled Senate unredeemed 439 *Ecc. Sonn.* 2. 42. 9
Assembled with their children and their wives, 699 *Prelude* 8. 9
Boldly assembled,—here is shadowed forth 707 *Prelude* 8. 582
Into the hearing of assembled tribes, 820 *Excursion* 4. 1279
To the assembled spirits of just men 864 *Excursion* 7. 453
With shouts the *assembled* people rend the skies L. 1. 96 *Juvenal* 3. 33
Assembly. What an eager assembly ! what an empire is this ! 188 *Music* 9
And all the assembly own a law 399 *White Doe* 320
"God willeth it," the whole assembly cry ; 427 *Ecc. Sonn.* 1. 33. 9
From the assembly ; through a length of streets, 653 *Prelude* 3. 303
Assembly-room. A smart Assembly-room usurped the ground 642 *Prelude* 2. 39
Assent. Assent is power, belief the soul of fact. 359 **Those old* 14
That, if the Priest should yield assent 412 *White Doe* 1518
Then spake one Bird, and full assent all gave ; 562 *Cuck. and Night.* 271
That, in assent or opposition, rose 880 *Excursion* 8. 437
Assert. With weapons grasped in fearless hands, to assert 315 **The Land* 13
That I should here assert their rights, attest 669 *Prelude* 5. 216
When Reason seemed the most to assert her rights 729 *Prelude* 11. 113
And with amazement smote ;—thereby to assert 811 *Excursion* 4. 661
Asserts. And, for yourself, in plain terms he asserts 38 *Bord.* 64
Asses. With panniered asses driven from door to door ; 32 *Guilt* 407
And he had lain beside his asses 239 *P. B.* 224
Assiduous. Assiduous, through the length of sixty years. 642 *Prelude* 2. 46
The most assiduous of her ministers ; 648 *Prelude* 2. 464
Assiduously. Assiduously — to soothe her aching breast ; 255 **Grief, thou* 12
Which thus assiduously she paces, 397 *White Doe* 107
Assign. That ancient Fable did to thee assign, 460 **Queen of* 2
For the presumptuous thoughts that would assign 473 **Thanks for* 2
And cannot fall beneath ; that do assign 806 *Excursion* 4. 340
Which did to him assign a pensive lot— 873 *Excursion* 7. 1013

Assigned. In his providence, assigned 90 *Longest Day* 34
That a retreat might be assigned to him, 125 *V. and J.* 268
Who wants the glorious faculty assigned 259 **Weak is* 6
By some weak aims at services assigned 262 *Retirement* 13
Nought but that word assigned to the unknown, 275 *Gravestone* 3
Vouchsafed in pity or in wrath assigned ; 347 *Processions* 70
In those bold fictions that, by deeds assigned 357 *Aquap.* 280
As that by dreaming Bards to Love assigned, 428 *Ecc. Sonn.* 1. 39. 5
Until they reach the bounds by Heaven assigned." 495 *Fact* 43
Are well assigned to Memory 499 *Memory* 3
But who (though neither reckoning ills assigned 504 *Warning* 47
Assigned to it in future worlds. Thou, too, 510 **Among a* 10
Assigned to them and given them for their own 553 *Prioress* 38
Oh ! tremble, ye, to whom hath been assigned 792 *Excursion* 3. 452
" Nor higher place can be assigned to him 816 *Excursion* 4. 995
Of less particular notices assigned 825 *Excursion* 5. 201
" To every Form of being is assigned," 884 *Excursion* 9. 1
Until they reach the bounds by Heaven assigned. S. 3. 427 **My Son* 14
Assigns. One to whom Heaven assigns that mournful part 531 *Octogen.* 11
Assist. I will assist you to lay hands upon him. 73 *Bord.* 2031
Assist me, God, their boundaries to know, 118 *Maternal Grief* 12
Assist me to detain 190 **Lyre ! though* 4
That bloom—those eyes—can they assist to bind 363 **Grieve for* 9
And gurgling rills, assist her in the work 497 **Enough of climbing* 15
Hear, and assist ;—the father's mandate calls 624 *Æneid* 27
A prime enchantress—to assist the work, 729 *Prelude* 11. 115
Thus was he reared ; much wanting to assist 760 *Excursion* 1. 302
Assistance. Now, gentle Muses, your assistance grant, 103 *Artegal* 61
Not without such assistance could the use 837 *Excursion* 5. 994
Assisted. That mutually assisted they may live 446 *Ecc. Sonn.* 3. 26. 7
Assisted, led me back through opening day 732 *Prelude* 11. 352
To Nature's care, assisted in her office 841 *Excursion* 6. 183
Assisting. There did I sit, assisting. If, with noise 797 *Excursion* 3. 749
Assisting, lucid well-spring ! thou revealest S. 3. 435 **The doubt* 103
Associate. Associate with the simply meek, 341 *San Salv.* 22
This one Associate that disproves 415 *White Doe* 1789
Associate all in the calm Pool beneath, 524 *Epist. Beaumont* 180
Thy dark Associate ever I discern ; 532 **Once I* 32
Fletcher's Associate, Jonson's Friend beloved. 546 **The embowering* 21
Associate with his children and his wife 719 *Prelude* 10. 52
And I, associate with such labour, steeped 752 *Prelude* 14. 402
Associates. Associates in that eager chase ; 191 *Seq. Beggars* 33
Happy Associates breathing air remote 252 **Her only* 8
Thy pleased associates :—light as endless May 377 *Duddon* 5. 13
Associates, and, unscared by blustering winds, 687 *Prelude* 7. 30
Of my associates : some of these wore swords 711 *Prelude* 9. 127
Of my associates stood prepared for flight 712 *Prelude* 9. 182
Among associates who have power of speech, 781 *Excursion* 2. 614
My two Associates, in the morning sunshine 823 *Excursion* 5. 63
Associates in the joy of purest minds, K. 8. 249 *Recluse* 1. 1. 460
Association. Enough ! for see, with dim association 431 *Ecc. Sonn.* 2. 11. 1
Assoil. Ne'er assoil my cobwebbed shield ! 140 *Arm. Lady* 52
Assoiled. Assoiled from all encumbrance of our time, 326 **The Bard* 9
Ass's. The goslings green, the ass's colt, 81 †*Mother's Return* 43
What feats an Ass's hoof can do ! 181 *Waggoner* 4. 176
He stoops the Ass's neck to seize 242 *P. B.* 497
Such life is in the Ass's eyes, 242 *P. B.* 566
Where he had struck the Ass's head ; 244 *P. B.* 727
Close to the Ass's feet she fell ; 247 *P. B.* 1013
Assuage. Suffering what no endurance could assuage, 35 *Guilt* 578
For the distracted Mother to assuage 378 *Duddon* 11. 8
Threats come which no submission may assuage, 433 *Ecc. Sonn.* 2. 21. 1
By wingèd Love inscribed, to assuage 499 **Departing summer* 44
That victims yet were wanting to assuage L. 1. 95 *Juvenal* 3. 3
Assume. *See* **Re-assume.**
On Mona settle, and the shapes assume 468 **Ranging the* 5
Shall man assume a property in man ? 501 *Humanity* 79
All trades, as need was, did old Adam assume,— 570 *Farmer* 49
The long-protected to assume the part 585 *Ch. Lamb* 90
To young Ascanius, should assume his place ; 624 *Æneid* 4
Play on her streamers, fails she to assume 882 *Excursion* 8. 514
Assumed. Departing summer hath assumed 498 **Departing summer* 1
Assumed a voice of deep portentous sound, 629 *Installation* 103
That, stretching far among the Alps, assumed 685 *Prelude* 6. 690
Assumed the body and venerable name 718 *Prelude* 10. 40
Honour assumed or given : and him, the Wonderful, 862 *Excursion* 7. 344
Assumes. Unto itself, the Crown assumes a voice 435 *Ecc. Sonn.* 2. 28. 13
Assumes the accents of our native tongue ; 435 *Ecc. Sonn.* 2. 29. 3
When, for the night deserted, it assumes 664 *Prelude* 4. 368
Assuming. Profusion bright ! and every flower assuming 881 *Excursion* 8. 471
Assumption. From false assumption rose, and fondly hailed 429 *Ecc. Sonn.* 2. 2. 1
Assurance. I am your friend. What need of this assurance 64 *Bord.* 1478
The bright assurance, visibly return : 258 **Even so* 12
To think that such assurance can stand fast ! 317 **The martial* 14
Some blest assurance, from this cloud emerging, 372 *Eg. Maid* 258
That confident assurance may be read ; 429 *Ecc. Sonn.* 2. 3. 6
Or seek to make assurance doubly sure. 445 *Ecc. Sonn.* 3. 21. 12
Stricken by this ill assurance, 535 *Egremont* 51
Than Fancy gave assurance of some work 633 *Prelude* 1. 78
The assurance which then cheered some heavy thoughts 687 *Prelude* 7. 13

Attended—*continued.*
Shall be attended with a bolder prayer— . . . 582 *Invoc. Earth* 29
Is on his way attended ; . . . . 588 *Immortality* 74
Attended, doubtless, with a little pride, . . . 659 *Prelude* 4. 74
Attended ; then, my spirit was entranced . . . 803 *Excursion* 4. 118

Attending. *See* **Close-attending.**
With faithful Benjamin attending, ... 180 *Waggoner* 4. 66
No dog attending, by no staff sustained, . . . 664 *Prelude* 4. 400
Grow weary of attending on a track . . . 694 *Prelude* 7. 504

Attends. Attends your pleasure. We are ready— Sir! 49 *Bord.* 665
Attends on goodness with dominion decked, . . 105 *Artegal* 188
" Him only pleasure leads, and peace attends, . 214 *Dion* 122
" But where attends thy chariot—where ? " . . 371 *Eg. Maid* 169
Attends the motions of the viewless winds, . . 674 *Prelude* 5. 596
Attends us, if but once we have been strong. . . 738 *Prelude* 12. 271
We came, and roused the shepherd who attends . 746 *Prelude* 14. 8
The charm more superficial that attends . . . 750 *Prelude* 14. 317
The Man, whom, furthermore, a hope attends . 823 *Excursion* 5. 38

Attention. A pleased attention I may win . . . 376 **The Minstrels* 75
And attention full ten times as much as there needs ; 482 *Character* 10
On that through which I passed. Attention springs, 698 *Prelude* 7. 740
Attention was engrossed ; and, thus amused, . . 711 *Prelude* 9. 85
Was vested with attention or respect . . . . 713 *Prelude* 9. 221
Seemed present ; and, attention now relaxed, . 765 *Excursion* 1. 618

Attentive. It's drowsy tinklings on th' attentive hills ; 598 *Ev. Wk. Quarto* 354
To an attentive eye. For progress meet, . . . 750 *Prelude* 14. 329
Attentive audience. But, oh ! gentle Friends, . 794 *Excursion* 3. 600
The Christian promise with attentive ear ; . . 866 *Excursion* 7. 578

Attentively. Made, to his ear attentively applied, . 108 *Indolence* 57

Attest. Myriads of notes attest her subtle skill ; . 153 *Morn. Ex.* 14
How, with the Muse's aid, her love attest ? . . 253 **Aerial Rock* 6
When human touch (as monkish books attest) . 267 *St. Cath.* 1
As soon we shall be, may these words attest . . 282 **Wansfell ! this* 11
Are faces that attest the same ; . . . . . . 292 *Rob Roy* 118
Where every passion shall the sway attest . . 315 **Alas ! what* 5
Of peaceful civic virtue : they attest . . . . 316 **Hail, Zaragoza* 7
Here must a high attest be given, ... 372 *Eg. Maid* 249
To attest my Faith, if not restore. . . . . . 410 *White Doe* 1285
So does her Unity its power attest . . . . . 430 *Ecc. Sonn.* 2. 9. 5
Yet be unmoved with wishes to attest . . . . 478 **Lonsdale ! it* 5
That I should here assert their rights, attest . . 669 *Prelude* 5. 216
That may attest her prowess, blest in thoughts . 684 *Prelude* 6. 611
And would have fought, even to the death, to attest 728 *Prelude* 11. 81
" Rites which attest that Man by nature lies . 826 *Excursion* 5. 294
Whose grateful owner can attest these truths, . 855 *Excursion* 6. 1140
Of Castaly attest that Woman's heart . . . . S.3. 436 **The doubt* 162
Let homelier words without offence attest . . K.8. 301 **And oh* 2
The whip, the cap, and spurs, thy praise attest ; . L. 1. 94 *Juvenal* 2. 22

Attestation. Emblem of faith untouched, miraculous attestation ! . . . . 437 *Ecc. Sonn.* 2. 35. 14

Attests. Their badge, attests the holy fight they wage. 628 *Eagle and Dove* 12

Attic. Such conversation, under Attic shades, . . 715 *Prelude* 9. 408

Attica. Mourn, hills and groves of Attica ! and mourn 213 *Dion* 42

Attire. When market-morning came, the neat attire 28 *Guilt* 221
Had put on boy's attire, did Michael love, . . 133 *Michael* 160
Is reached, where, forfeiting his bright attire, . 261 **I watch* 6
Joined with the lustre of her rich attire . . . 306 **We had* 12
Attire the peaceful corse in vestments white . . 318 **In due* 4
Unmarred, unstripped of her attire, ... 371 *Eg. Maid* 137
How Una, sad of soul—in sad attire, ... 395 *White Doe : Ded.* 6
And Romish priest, in priest's attire. . . . . 404 *White Doe* 708
Put on, to welcome spring, their best attire, . . 529 *Poor Robin* 4
The rhymes so homely in attire . . . . . . 577 **I come* 29
The transformation wrought by gay attire. . . 659 *Prelude* 4. 76
And all the attire of ordinary life, ... 711 *Prelude* 9. 84
The shady forest of its green attire,— . . . . 790 *Excursion* 3. 309
Ten hardy Striplings, all in bright attire, . . . 869 *Excursion* 7. 766
Figure and mien, complexion and attire, . . . 879 *Excursion* 8. 358
—Not brothers they in feature or attire, . . . 882 *Excursion* 8. 547

Attired. Attired in peasant's garb, who stood alone, 149 **A narrow* 48
When one, who was in shepherd's garb attired, . 202 *Hart-leap* 118
Spreads o'er this tuft of heath, which now, attired 219 *Haunted Tree* 8
Bruges I saw attired with golden light . . . . 333 **Bruges I* 1
Her sisters, soon like her to be attired . . . . 353 *Aquap.* 28
Is happy as a Lover ; and attired . . . . . . 493 *Hap. War.* 51
No sooner stand attired . . . . 508 *May* 86
With emblematic purity attired . . . . . . 508 *F. Stone* 12
Behold me rich in monies, and attired . . . . 649 *Prelude* 3. 37
Bare-headed, and all decently attired ! . . . . 777 *Excursion* 2. 392
Who, in old time, attired with snakes and whips . 798 *Excursion* 3. 851
Came on a war-horse sumptuously attired, . . . 871 *Excursion* 7. 925

Attitude. Caught in their fairest, happiest, attitude ! 891 *Excursion* 9. 464

Attract. Attract us still, and passionate exercise 445 *Ecc. Sonn.* 3. 19. 2
Survive for inspiration, shall attract . . . . 734 *Prelude* 11. 463
Attract your notice ; statelier than could else . 824 *Excursion* 5. 130

Attracted. Chanter by heaven attracted, whom no bars . . . . 154 *Morn. Ex.* 55

Attraction. Quaint stories of the bird's attraction ! 174 *Waggoner* 1. 96
The attraction of a country in romance ! . . . 729 *Prelude* 11. 112

Attractions. When, to the attractions of the busy world . . . . 150 **When, to* 1
Attractions manifold ;—and this he chose. . . 761 *Excursion* 1. 337
In the sublime attractions of the grave." . . . 804 *Excursion* 4. 238

Attractive. Not more attractive to the dazzled sight 434 *Ecc. Sonn.* 2. 22. 11
Nor less attractive when by glimpses seen . . . 460 **Queen of* 11
Boyle, Shakspeare, Newton, or the attractive head 689 *Prelude* 7. 166
Howe'er attractive, Fellow voyager ! . . . . 717 *Prelude* 9. 563
And guardian rocks !—Farewell, attractive seat ! 822 *Excursion* 5. 3
And that attractive brightness is its own. . . . 832 *Excursion* 5. 678

Attractive—*continued.*
That *was* attractive, and hath ceased to be ! . . 843 *Excursion* 6. 318

Attribute. Than that most noble attribute of man, 674 *Prelude* 5. 573
Discourse was deemed Man's noblest attribute, . 489 *Illus. Books* 1
A crown, an attribute of sovereign power, . . . 830 *Excursion* 5. 503

Attributes. And in her Catholic attributes, hath trod : 281 *Chris. Words.* 6
With attributes from History derived, ... 357 *Aquap.* 283
And all those attributes of modest grace, . . . 460 **Queen of* 13
With these ennobling attributes conjoined . . 540 **Lady ! a* 68
Where wanted most : " The lordly attributes . 731 *Prelude* 11. 309
This is her glory ; these two attributes . . . 740 *Prelude* 13. 3
The varied functions and high attributes . . . 798 *Excursion* 3. 824
Retired from notice, lost in attributes . . . . 862 *Excursion* 7. 318
To thy obscure and modest attributes, . . . S. 3. 437 **The doubt* 205

Attune. From snowy peak and cloud, attune . . 235 *Power of Sound* 200
Peace let us seek,—to steadfast things attune . 278 **The most* 11
Pleased to renounce, does this dear Thrush attune 279 **'Tis he* 6
As may attune his soul to meet the dower . . 458 **Had this* 59

Attuned. Softly responsive ; and, attuned to all . 356 *Aquap.* 222
Attuned to words with sacred wisdom fraught ; . 395 *White Doe: Ded.* 18
Thou hast attuned thy murmurings ; . . . . 399 *White Doe* 327
Attuned to verse that, crowning light Distress 528 **Those breathing* 98
By gusts of vernal storm, attuned his song . . 537 **In desultory* 4
Fitly attuned to all that gratitude . . . . . 541 *Grace Darl.* 89
Attuned, or sprightly fife resounding far. . . . 702 *Prelude* 8. 201
The inferior creatures, beast or bird, attuned . . 704 *Prelude* 8. 357
Worthy of poets who attuned their harps . . . 734 *Prelude* 11. 457
That was the best, to that she was attuned . . 736 *Prelude* 12. 160
She pondered murmurs that attuned her ear . . S. 3. 436 **The doubt* 174
The idle breath of softest pipe attuned . . . K.8. 247 *Recluse* 1. 1. 408

Attunes. That sparkling thrids the rocks, attunes his voice . . . . 856 *Excursion* 6. 1171

Atween. Atween his downy wings be furnished, there 382 *Duddon* 25. 6

Audacious. At this audacious blasphemy, I thought 51 *Bord.* 793
And reason govern that audacious flight . . . 261 **From the dark* 8
Prompting the world's audacious vanities ! . . . 313 **Go back* 4

Audacity. Turning them inside out with arch audacity. . . . . 221 *Triad* 127
Reckless audacity extol, and jeer . . . . . 514 **Portentous change* 3

Audible. Of music, audible to him alone. . . . 220 *Triad* 51
Audible tears, from some invisible source . . . 498 **Enough of climbing* 37
Was audible ; and sate among the woods . . . 647 *Prelude* 2. 342
One song they sang, and it was audible, . . . 648 *Prelude* 2. 415
Most audible, then, when the fleshly ear, . . . 648 *Prelude* 2. 416
Then stopped for years ; not audible again . . 687 *Prelude* 7. 11
To make the sounds more audible ? What crowd 699 *Prelude* 8. 4
And audible seclusions, dashing lakes, ... 708 *Prelude* 8. 636
His respiration quick and audible ; . . . . . 879 *Excursion* 8. 312
Audible praise, to thee, omniscient Mind, . . . 895 *Excursion* 9. 753

Audibly. Is cropping audibly his later meal : . . 1 *Early Youth* 4
Main ocean, breaking audibly, and stretched . . 219 **This Height* 14
Rolled audibly !—it swept along, ... 245 *P. B.* 836
Strike audibly the noblest of your lyres, . . . 325 *Ode 1814* 125
Methinks, if audibly repeated now . . . . . 457 **Had this* 16

Audience. Now, to a maturer Audience, . . . 93 *Westmoreland Girl* 25
'Mid that strange audience, he bestrides . . . 234 *Power of Sound* 138
Due audience, how for aught but scorn defy . . 365 **The Baptist* 4
A Tuscan audience : but full soon was called . . 573 *Chiabrera* 2. 17
Of the plain Burghers, who in audience stood . 653 *Prelude* 3. 313
If willing audience fail not, Nature's self, . . . 732 *Prelude* 11. 350
I sing :—' fit audience let me find though few !' . 755 *Recluse* 1. 1. 776
Attentive audience. But, oh ! gentle Friends, . 794 *Excursion* 3. 600

Auditors. Rapt auditors ! from thy most eloquent tongue— . . . . 695 *Prelude* 7. 517

Augean. Could cleanse the Augean stable, by the might . . . . 726 *Prelude* 10. 585

Aught. *See* **Ought.**
An inch, till I am answered. Know you aught . 46 *Bord.* 497
And if I have in aught offended you, ... 61 *Bord.* 1317
I did not think that aught was left in me . . . 61 *Bord.* 1324
Nor aught else like it, could be heard. . . . . 82 *Alice Fell* 12
The hut stood finished by his pains, nor seemingly lacked aught . . . . 91 *Norman Boy* 17
Was nothing, scarcely can be aught, yet 'twas bounteously bestowed, ... 93 *Poet's Dream* 78
Which then it had ! Nay, Sir, for aught I know, 97 *Brothers* 136
Are aught of what makes up a mother's heart, . 99 *Brothers* 233
A pretty flock, and which, for aught I know, . . 100 *Brothers* 302
Aught that my feeble nature could perform, . . 105 *Artegal* 179
On aught of more ambitious show . . . . . 113 *Lament* 32
If aught which he had owned might still remain for me. . . . . 119 *Sailor's Mother* 24
Surpasses aught these elements can show. . . . 139 *Widow* 22
Nor did aught of future days that kiss belie, . . 142 *Arm. Lady* 143
Alone I tread this path ;—for aught I know, . . 151 **When, to* 105
I listened, nor aught else could hear ; . . . . 155 *Waterfall* 54
A boding sound—for aught but sleep unfit ! . . 167 *Pilgrim's Dream* 51
Had aught of sylvan growth been there), . . . 175 *Waggoner* 1. 186
Can aught on earth impede delight, ... 178 *Waggoner* 3. 24
Was aught ever heard like his fiddle and him ? . 188 *Music* 8
And he perhaps, for aught we know, was born . 203 *Hart-leap* 155
With aught that breathes the ethereal element, . 213 *Dion* 55
Her voice would utter, aught ensue . . . . 222 *Triad* 157
Points she to aught ?—the bliss draws near, . . 223 *Wishing-gate* 5
If aught on earth have heavenly might, . . . 238 *P. B.* 149
Of limpid water, humbler far than aught . . . 251 **There is a little* 2
As aught that song records of Robin Hood ; . . 255 *Detraction* 3
More efficaciously than aught that flows . . . 255 **Grief, thou* 6
His heart to aught which doth on time depend. . 257 **No mortal* 11

Aught—*continued.*
If there be aught of pure, or good, or great, 259 *Calvert* 10
If aught be in them of immortal seed, 261 **From the dark* 8
Nor aught of mutual joy or sorrow knew 276 *Oker Hill* 12
But are we aught enriched in love and meekness? 281 **What strong* 8
Aught dost thou see, bright Star! of pure and wise 281 **What strong* 9
To him, and aught that hides his clay 284 *Grave of Burns* 17
Aught good were destined, thou wouldst step between. 309 **England! the* 8
By aught redeemed out of the hollow grave: 325 *Enghien* 9
Than aught dependent on the fickle skies. 329 *Ode: Thanks.* 56
Thus after Man had fallen (if aught 343 *Eclipse* 55
Nor more, for aught that time supplies, 348 **Lulled by* 27
More touching far than aught which on the walls 355 *Aquap.* 165
As aught that marvellous coast thro' all its length 355 *Aquap.* 208
From mortal change, aught that is born on earth 356 *Aquap.* 230
If to the future aught of good must come 358 *Aquap.* 350
Nor giving heed to aught that passed the while, 365 **Under the* 3
Due audience, how for aught but scorn defy 365 **The Baptist* 4
In aught that ye would grace or hide— 366 **Ye Trees* 8
Heard them, unchecked by aught of saddening hue, 367 **If with* 12
Or aught in Syrian deserts left to save 367 *Trajan* 11
On aught by which another is deprest. 368 *Trajan* 57
Aught that was ever shown in magic glass; 369 *Eg. Maid* 16
Nor aught that troubles us, the fools of Nature. 370 *Eg. Maid* 60
Nor saw of wreck or ruin aught 371 *Eg. Maid* 124
Aught of the fading year's inclemency! 381 *Duddon* 21. 14
His sky-born warblings—does aught meet your ken 387 *Manse* 6
Aught that more surely by its aspect fills 387 *Manse* 8
For aught the wisest know or comprehend; 423 *Ecc. Sonn.* 1. 18. 5
Than aught the sky's fantastic element, 428 *Ecc. Sonn.* 1. 37. 7
By aught that mingled with the tragic scene 435 *Ecc. Sonn.* 2. 26. 11
Wonder that aught of aspect so serene 439 *Ecc. Sonn.* 2. 43. 4
Disgraced by aught that seems content to sit 439 *Ecc. Sonn.* 2. 41. 7
If aught impair thy beauty or destroy, 440 *Ecc. Sonn.* 3. 2. 9
If aught unworthy be my choice, 458 **Had this* 71
To aught of highest, holiest, influence— 461 **Queen of* 45
Nor aught that makes men's promises a blank, 470 **A youth* 12
Or aught that watchful Love to Nature owes 471 *Ailsa Crag* 13
If aught (intrusted to the pen 472 *Ossian* 19
Of aught transacted there in bay or creek; 522 *Epist. Beaumont* 80
Not soon does aught to which mild fancies cling 527 **Those breathing* 3
Could strip, for aught the prospect yields 533 **Blest is* 57
Whoever against Love mean aught amiss. 559 *Cuck.andNight.* 130
That least of all can aught—that ever owned 567 *Cumb. Beg.* 80
O dread reverse! if aught *be* so, which proves 576 **By a* 5
In aught to earth pertaining? Death has proved 581 **Why should we* 6
When aught had suffered wrong,— 583 **O for a* 33
When aught that breathes had felt a wound; 583 **O for a* 34
Aught of these bowers and whence their pleasures flow; 583 **With copious* 35
In these lone vales, if aught of faith may claim, 595 *Ev.Wk.Quarto* 175
Do fall around him upon aught that bears 646 *Prelude* 2. 250
Or looked that way for aught that might be clothed 652 *Prelude* 3. 238
As aught by wooden images performed 657 *Prelude* 3. 571
By aught, I fear, of genuine desert— 677 *Prelude* 6. 169
Nor checked by aught of tamer argument, 688 *Prelude* 7. 50
That aught external to the living mind 707 *Prelude* 8. 550
The region left behind him; and, if aught 709 *Prelude* 9. 12
I clearly saw that neither these nor aught 725 *Prelude* 10. 474
Can aught be more ignoble than the man 735 *Prelude* 12. 71
But most intensely; never dreamt of aught 737 *Prelude* 12. 177
To measured admiration, or to aught 737 *Prelude* 12. 186
Or aught of heavier or more deadly weight, 737 *Prelude* 12. 212
And, with life, power to accomplish aught of worth, 751 *Prelude* 14. 389
Nor aught of blinder vacancy, scooped out 755 *Recluse* 1. 1. 790
And, being still unsatisfied with aught 758 *Excursion* 1. 143
Most happy, if, from aught discovered there 770 *Excursion* 1. 898
Nor in the other region, nor in aught 789 *Excursion* 3. 217
With aught, as more desirable and fair, 790 *Excursion* 3. 319
Of various intercourse, nor wishing aught 794 *Excursion* 3. 587
At aught, however fair, that bore the mien 797 *Excursion* 3. 780
Aught that deserves respect: for I exist, 800 *Excursion* 3. 966
Of aught unworthily conceived, endured 801 *Excursion* 4. 25
By aught that innocently satisfies 806 *Excursion* 4. 353
Ah! let not aught amiss within dispose 816 *Excursion* 4. 1018
So deeply, that, unsatisfied with aught 819 *Excursion* 4. 1214
Is aught so certain as that man is doomed 831 *Excursion* 5. 587
That sparkling decked the morning grass; or aught 843 *Excursion* 6. 317
A mind by nature indisposed to aught 849 *Excursion* 6. 730
Aught by these perishable heavens disclosed 850 *Excursion* 6. 769
Aught of romantic interest, it is gone. 875 *Excursion* 8. 85
Nor crowded city can be taxed with aught 880 *Excursion* 8. 422
And whether aught, of tendency as good 896 *Excursion* 9. 791
Not from such hope, or aught of such belief K. 8. 245 *Recluse* 1. 1. 316
Scattered about us, nor through dearth of aught K. 8. 254 *Recluse* 1. 1. 636
Could aught but envy now his pride rebuke? L. 1. 96 *Juvenal* 3. 29
Augment. To augment the band of emigrants in arms 712 *Prelude* 9. 183
Augmented. The choirs of Angels spread, triumphantly augmented. 582 *Invoc. Earth* 18
Augmented and sustained. Yet is a path 646 *Prelude* 2. 272
Augments. Yet, while each useful Art augments her store, 466 *St. Bees* 28
Auguries. For her consult the auguries of time, 314 **Not 'mid* 11
To watch for undelusive auguries:— 500 *Humanity* 14
Augurs. Where Augurs stand, the Future questioning, 419 *Ecc. Sonn.* 1. 3. 3
Nor what it augurs of the life to come; 673 *Prelude* 5. 511
August. Display august of man's inheritance, 219 **This Height* 33
A landscape more august than happiest skill 323 *Ode 1814* 6
Filling the soul with sentiments august— 351 *Des. Stanzas* 80

August—*continued.*
That o'er the channel holds august command, 470 **Did pangs* 7
Raised by many a hand august, 629 *Installation* 78
Augusta. High-born Augusta! Witness, Towers and Groves! 539 **Lady! a* 22
Augustin. The pictured Saviour!—By Augustin led, 422 *Ecc. Sonn.* 1. 14. 6
Aulis. What time the fleet at Aulis lay enchained. 211 *Laod.* 120
Aurora. Pleasure's Aurora, Day of gladsomeness! 562 *Cuck.andNight.* 312
What arms the son of bright Aurora wore;— 625 *Æneid* 135
The Hours, like young Aurora, to his car: 694 *Prelude* 7. 502
What arms the son of bright Aurora wore, L. 2. 123 *Frag. Æneid* 3. 2
Aurora's. Precursors to Aurora's car, 191 *Beggars* 34
Auspicious. Comes Faith that in auspicious hours 225 *Present.* 20
Of this auspicious day— 629 *Installation* 68
If two auspicious magpies crossed my way;— 810 *Excursion* 4. 618
Auspiciously. A hopeful reign, auspiciously begun, 103 *Artegal* 76
Auster. Like Auster whirling to and fro, 213 *Dion* 71
Of Auster and Boötes. Fifty years 574 *Chiabrera* 4. 13
Austere. Softening their inbred dignity austere— 212 *Dion* 11
May feed on thoughts though pensive not austere; 264 **Lady! I* 12
Is of the grave; and of austere 289 *Glen-Al.* 28
Then question not that, 'mid the austere Band, 362 **List—'twas* 66
In the pines pointing heavenward her beauty austere; 364 *Vallomb.* 12
Thanks to the austere and simple Devotees, 467 *St. Bees* 70
In symphony austere; 491 *Fidelity* 28
Pure livers were they all, austere and grave, 758 *Excursion* 1. 113
He clothed the nakedness of austere truth. 760 *Excursion* 1. 269
Austerities. Dare they confront the lean austerities 364 **What aim* 5
Austral. Through him her course along the Austral flood S. 3. 442 **Vasco, whose* 12
Australian. But, exiled from Australian bowers, 165 *Parrot* 17
Austria. Austria a Daughter of her Throne hath sold! 317 **The martial* 10
Austrian. Of fatal Austrian spears. 341 *San Salv.* 36
Authentic. The very Angels whose authentic lays, 338 *Engelberg* 11
Of battle meets him in authentic form! 368 *Trajan* 44
Authentic words be given, or none! 472 *Ossian* 30
With what ye symbolise; authentic Story. 477 **Lowther! in* 13
Authentic history been set forth of Rome, 688 *Prelude* 7. 80
Have their authentic comment; that even these 755 *Recluse* 1. 1. 834
Authentic tidings of invisible things; 818 *Excursion* 4. 1144
Authentic epitaphs on some of these 832 *Excursion* 5. 651
With eloquence, and such authentic power, 865 *Excursion* 7. 513
Authoritative. And questions in authoritative tone, 859 *Excursion* 7. 101
Authorities. To your serene authorities conform; 827 *Excursion* 5. 352
Authority. The like authority, with grace 413 *White Doe* 1598
As when, arrayed in Christ's authority, 444 *Ecc. Sonn.* 3. 18. 10
As all Authority in earth depends 518 *Pun. Death* 5. 6
Loses her just authority, falls beneath 655 *Prelude* 3. 421
And known authority of office served 656 *Prelude* 3. 538
And blind Authority beating with his staff 657 *Prelude* 3. 605
Of zeal, by an authority Divine 715 *Prelude* 9. 406
Her innocent authority was wrought, 723 *Prelude* 10. 379
From that time forth, Authority in France 727 *Prelude* 11. 1
To an Authority enthroned above 794 *Excursion* 3. 569
Gracing his doctrine with authority 820 *Excursion* 4. 1288
By your authority. But how acquire 831 *Excursion* 5. 571
Authors. And meditative, authors of delight 567 *Cumb. Beg.* 107
Authorship. Of printed books and authorship, began 676 *Prelude* 6. 59
Autocracy. Yet do not deem the Autocracy prevailed 429 *Ecc. Sonn.* 2. 2. 3
Autumn. The very brightest Sunday Autumn saw, 99 *Brothers* 269
And Autumn, melancholy Wight! 157 **In youth* 14
Nor Autumn, when the viewless wren 299 *Brownie's Cell* 89
Taught by his summer spent, his autumn gone, 388 *Trosachs* 3
And Autumn to the Spring. 497 *Lycoris* 22
May pensive Autumn ne'er present 497 *Lycoris* 49
What pensive beauty autumn shows, 502 *Seasons* 13
So may our Autumn blend 502 *Seasons* 18
'Twas autumn, and a clear and placid day, 633 *Prelude* 1. 65
The woods of autumn, and their hazel bowers 639 *Prelude* 1. 484
What spring and autumn, what the winter snows, 647 *Prelude* 2. 353
The labouring time of autumn, winter, spring, 658 *Prelude* 3. 630
Were flown, and autumn brought its annual show 664 *Prelude* 4. 371
The twilight more than dawn, autumn than spring; 677 *Prelude* 6. 175
With cheerful hope, until the second autumn, 764 *Excursion* 1. 550
Of summer, autumn, winter, and of spring. 764 *Excursion* 1. 577
—'Blow winds of autumn!—let your chilling breath 790 *Excursion* 3. 307
"Life's autumn past, I stand on winter's verge; 810 *Excursion* 4. 611
And mellow Autumn, charged with bounteous fruit, 828 *Excursion* 5. 400
Such universal change as autumn makes 840 *Excursion* 6. 159
Autumnal. Waves the ripe harvest in the autumnal gale; 21 *Desc. Sk.* 587
Driven by the autumnal whirlwind to and fro. 123 *V. and J.* 140
Preserves her beauty 'mid autumnal leaves, 169 **Never enlivened* 5
How sweet, on this autumnal day, 302 *Yarrow V.* 65
And in fit measure cheers autumnal days. 336 *Rhine* 14
O'er twilight fields the autumnal gossamer? 378 *Duddon* 11. 14
His thin autumnal locks where Monks abide 424 *Ecc. Sonn.* 1. 21. 5
Through summer heat, autumnal cold, 507 *May* 15
Trilled by the redbreast, when autumnal leaves 539 **Lady! a* 34
The last autumnal crocus, 'twas my joy 636 *Prelude* 1. 309
Prolonged till sprinklings of autumnal snow 686 *Prelude* 6. 730
In man's autumnal season is set forth 828 *Excursion* 5. 404
Dark on my road the autumnal evening fell, 833 *Excursion* 5. 736
Of life's autumnal season.—Shall I tell 849 *Excursion* 6. 742
On those high peaks, the first autumnal snow, 861 *Excursion* 7. 249
Decked with autumnal berries, that outshine 868 *Excursion* 7. 717
At the first falling of the autumnal snows, K. 8. 224 **I will* 5
Autumn's. To the green corn of summer, autumn's hue. 8 *Ev. Wk.* 338

Autumn's—*continued.*
Driven in by Autumn's sharpening air . . . . 143 **Driven in* 1
Blithe Autumn's purple crown, and Winter's icy mail ! . . . . 350 *Des. Stanzas* 36
Dwindles the pear on autumn's latest spray, . . 608 *Desc.Sk.Quarto* 321
Autumns. Of many autumns in the cave had piled. 50 *Bord.* 706
Autumn-winds. When Autumn-winds are sobbing ? 162 **Art thou the* 5
Auvergne. Among the vine-clad mountains of Auvergne, ... 121 *V. and J.* 11
Auxiliar. Mixed with auxiliar Rocks, three hundred Forms ; . . . . 612 *Desc.Sk.Quarto* 539
With which it communed. An auxiliar light . . 647 *Prelude* 2. 368
Auxiliar to divine. That change shall clothe . . 820 *Excursion* 4. 1249
Auxiliars. Druids descend, auxiliars of the Cross ; . 421 *Ecc. Sonn.* 1. 10. 11
For mighty were the auxiliars which then stood . 728 *Prelude* 11. 106
Avail. But what can all avail to clear him, . . . 181 *Waggoner* 4. 154
But what do his desires avail ? . . . . . 295 *Highland Boy* 81
Sea, desert, what do these avail ? . . . . . 413 *White Doe* 1565
Is tender pity then of no avail ? . . . . . 423 *Ecc. Sonn.* 1. 20. 3
When Prayer is of no avail ? . . . . . . 494 *Force of Prayer* 4
That, might a wish avail, would never fade, . . 500 *Humanity* 22
May not avail, nor prayer have for God's ear . . 519 *Pun. Death* 10. 7
What may your ill intentions you avail ? . . . 554 *Prioress* 124
What profit riches ? what does youth avail ? . . 575 *Chiabrera* 7. 14
Dear Liberty ! Yet what would it avail . . . 632 *Prelude* 1. 31
For neither unremitting rains avail . . . . . S. 3. 433 **The doubt* 27
Availed. Availed against the mighty ; never more 76 *Bord.* 2196
(When all that Man could do availed no more) . 448 *Ecc. Sonn.* 3. 30. 4
But all availed not ; by a mandate given . . . 468 *St. Bees* 145
Availed not to my Vessel's overthrow. . . . . 574 *Chiabrera* 4. 20
And their disastrous issues. What availed, . . 735 *Prelude* 12. 52
Of a relenting soul, have now availed ; . . . 853 *Excursion* 6. 1009
Avails. Best eloquence avails not, Inspiration . . 233 *Power of Sound* 67
Avails those modulations to detect, ... 339 *Ranz* 2
Ah, what avails heroic deed ? . . . . . . 342 *Ital. Itin.* 91
Ah ! what avails that she was fair, ... 370 *Eg. Maid* 51
But what avails the bold intent ? . . . . . 404 *White Doe* 784
But what to them avails the land . . . . . 483 *Simon Lee* 47
What avails the kindly shelter . . . . . . 550 *Hermit's Cell* 4. 5
Within this court full seldom Truth avails, . . 560 *Cuck.andNight.*204
Ah ! what avails imagination high . . . . . 789 *Excursion* 3. 209
Prove a degraded Race ? and what avails . . . 815 *Excursion* 4. 954
Avalanche. Save when the avalanche breaks loose, to rend . . . . 16 *Desc. Sk.* 312
But list ! the avalanche—the hush profound . . 350 *Des. Stanzas* 44
And here the avalanche of Death destroy . . . 613 *Desc.Sk.Quarto* 600
Avarice. Delights us. Rapine, avarice, expense, . 307 **O Friend* 9
If cloistered Avarice scruple not to wrong . . . 433 *Ecc. Sonn.* 2. 19. 5
Nor avarice, nor over-anxious care. . . . . 449 *Ecc. Sonn.* 3. 34. 6
Sublime o'er Conquest, Avarice, and Pride, . . 617 *Desc.Sk.Quarto* 793
Avaricious. An unremitting, avaricious thrift ; . . 849 *Excursion* 6. 709
Avast. I've had a glimpse of you—*avast !* . . . 176 *Waggoner* 1. 238
Avaunt. " Avaunt, inexplicable Guest !—avaunt," 213 *Dion* 81
Avaunt all specious pliancy of mind . . . . 319 **Avaunt all* 1
Sad thoughts,avaunt!—partake we their blithe cheer 381 *Duddon* 23. 1
Avaunt this vile abuse of pictured page ! . . . 489 *Illus. Books* 12
" With such foundations laid, avaunt the fear . 889 *Excursion* 9. 363
Avaunt this economic rage ! . . . . S. 3. 439 **Avaunt this* 1
Ave. A choral *Ave Marie* shall beguile, ... 233 *Power of Sound* 59
Ave Marie, as he goeth by the way. . . . . 553 *Prioress* 56
Avenge. Of angry Nature to avenge her God. . . 17 *Desc. Sk.* 402
May gather to avenge this wrong . . . . . 370 *Eg. Maid* 82
To avenge their own insulted majesty. . . . 816 *Excursion* 4. 1034
Yea, to avenge her violated rights, ... 876 *Excursion* 8. 155
Avenged. Shall Nature be avenged. 'Tis nobly thought ; . . . . 58 *Bord.* 1123
And slight Hope *will* be avenged ; and, when . 792 *Excursion* 3. 459
Avenger. Avenger you of outraged innocence ! . . 55 *Bord.* 983
Not long the Avenger was withstood— . . . 204 *Brougham* 26
And ofttimes Death, avenger of the past, . . . 886 *Excursion* 9. 124
Avenger's. Crimes which the great Avenger's hand provoke, ... 345 **Ambition—following* 12
Avengers. Into avengers, from whose wrath they fled 718 *Prelude* 10. 26
Avenging. Last night, when moved to lift the avenging steel, ... 59 *Bord.* 1213
For deep as hell itself, the avenging draught . . 432 *Ecc. Sonn.* 2. 16. 8
Or is the painted staffs [? staff's] avenging host . L. 1. 97 *Juvenal* 3. 85
Avenue. Pace the long avenue, or glide adown 270 **Ye sacred* 12
Down the main avenue my sight can range : . . 350 *Des. Stanzas* 38
Albano's dripping Ilex avenue, ... 360 *Albano* 3
Louvet walked single through the avenue, . . . 720 *Prelude* 10. 111
The narrow avenue of daily toil . . . . . 831 *Excursion* 5. 600
Avenues. Obscure not yet these silent avenues 334 **Bruges I* 12
League after league, and cloistral avenues, . . 685 *Prelude* 6. 668
In avenues disposed ; there, towers begirt . . 784 *Excursion* 2. 843
(Prized avenues ere others had been shaped . . 876 *Excursion* 8. 107
Aver. Never heed them ; I aver . . . . . . 160 **Pansies, lilies* 35
Yet all do still aver . . . . 200 *Thorn* 229
Averr'd. 'Tis said ENJOYMENT (who averr'd . . 620 *Birth of Love* 28
Averse. Ever averse to pantomime, ... 300 *Bran* 34
Aversion. That savoured of aversion to thy name . 41 *Bord.* 232
More than we see, or whence this strong aversion ? 41 *Bord.* 254
Yet whence this strange aversion ? You are a man 42 *Bord.* 290
Of unbenign aversion or contempt, ... 816 *Excursion* 4. 1014
His feelings of aversion softened down ; . . . 819 *Excursion* 4. 1219
Avert. They are labouring to avert . . . . . 181 *Waggoner* 4. 89
Come ye—who, if (which Heaven avert !) the Land 310 *Invasion* 1
No sacrifice avert, no power dispute ; . . . . 433 *Ecc. Sonn.* 2. 21. 2
Cause should recur, which righteous Heaven avert ! 839 *Excursion* 6. 60
And prudent caution needful to avert . . . . 889 *Excursion* 9. 356
Avoid. Whose footsteps superstitiously avoid . . 219 *Haunted Tree* 20

Avoid—*continued.*
And sullenness avoid, as now they shun . . . 278 **Life with* 4
Avoid these sights; nor brood o'er Fable's dark abyss ! . . . . 347 *Processions* 72
To imitate, not wise enough to avoid ; . . . . 728 *Prelude* 11. 69
To be instructed what they must avoid : . . . 886 *Excursion* 9. 147
Avoids. The limpid mountain-rill avoids it not ; . 390 *Highland Hut* 5
Avon. Avon—a precious, an immortal name ! . . 392 *Avon* 1
Into the Avon, Avon to the tide . . . . . 432 *Ecc. Sonn.* 2. 17. 9
Avow. I will avow before the face of day. . . . 71 *Bord.* 1878
This will I here avow, not dreading thy despite.". 104 *Artegal* 145
Dare I avow that wish was mine to see, . . . 735 *Prelude* 12. 57
Avowed. No pause admitted, no design avowed ! . 213 *Dion* 80
Are but the avowed attire . . . . 330 *Ode : Thanks.* 104
Await. Enjoins, while firm resolves await . . . 224 **'Tis gone* 50
On those revolving motions did await . . . . 255 **Grief, thou* 11
Us humbler ceremonies now await ; . . . . 332 *Ode : Thanks.* 220
Await my steps when they the breezy height . . 356 *Aquap.* 253
Heart-killing luxury, on your steps await. . . 420 *Ecc. Sonn.* 1. 8. 2
You, on whose progress dazzling trains await . . 433 *Ecc. Sonn.* 2. 18. 3
Than even now await her prest, ... 503 **Like a* 81
And silence did await upon these thoughts . . 677 *Prelude* 6. 140
Awaited. And infant's smile awaited my return. . 794 *Excursion* 3. 583
Awaits. Awaits on virtuous life, and ever most 105 *Artegal* 187
What joy awaits you, when the breeze . . . 106 **I've watched* 7
That bliss awaits her which the ungenial Hollow . 261 **I heard (alas* 11
Such doom awaits us. Nay, forbid it Heaven ! . 316 **O'er the* 9
Awaits you then, if they were rightly taught . . 444 *Ecc. Sonn.* 3. 16.13
Awaits her *now* ; but, verily, good deeds . . 540 *Grace Darl.* 14
This, of all acquisitions, first awaits . . . . 698 *Prelude* 7. 737
Awaits us ! Oh, how much unlike the past ! . . 710 *Prelude* 9. 22
Of evil hap and good as oft awaits . . . . . 833 *Excursion* 5. 733
Belike no higher destiny awaits . . . . . . 888 *Excursion* 9. 276
Awake. From such romantic dreams, my soul, awake 14 *Desc. Sk.* 226
And thus, to keep herself awake, ... 156 *Oak and Broom* 53
Keep the sprightly soul awake, ... 172 *Kitten* 123
Playthings that keep the eyes awake . . . . 214 *Kirkstone* 31
—Cast off your bonds, awake, arise, ... 228 *Devot. Incit.* 38
Listen ! the mighty Being is awake, ... 258 **It is a* 6
Awake ! the majesty of God revere ! . . . . 332 *Ode : Thanks.* 227
Of the world's hopes, dare to fulfil ; awake, . . 366 **Fair Land* 13
Give to devotion, wheresoe'er awake, ... 430 *Ecc. Sonn.* 2. 9. 12
Early awake, by Siloa's brook, to sing . . . . 440 *Ecc. Sonn.* 2. 46. 5
Of light, which tells that Morning is awake. . . 440 *Ecc. Sonn.* 3. 2. 8
Must Man, with labour born, awake to sorrow . 462 **Wherelies the truth* 6
Awake to silent joy : . . . . 506 **While from* 28
Their own significance for hearts awake, . . . 525 *Epist. Beaumont* 267
—He hears a noise—he's all awake— . . . . 537 *Goody Blake* 77
Awake, awake ! and snatch the slumbering lyre, . 619 *School Ex.* 109
Had lain awake on summer nights to watch . . 659 *Prelude* 4. 87
A human being destined to awake . . . . . 768 *Excursion* 1. 787
Him, sleeping or awake, the robber spared ; . . 771 *Excursion* 2. 12
Right gladly would I lie awake . . . . . . K. 8. 262 **Ah ! if* 3
Awaked. As if awaked from sleep, the Nations hailed . . . . 686 *Prelude* 6. 757
They first of all that breathe should have awaked 732 *Prelude* 11. 381
Awaken. Ah then, lest you awaken me, speak low. . S. 3. 441 **Grateful is sleep ; my* 5
Awakened. As if awakened, summoned, roused, constrained, ... 650 *Prelude* 3. 105
From sleep awakened, and misled by sound . . 685 *Prelude* 6. 692
Before our eyes, awakened in my mind . . . 857 *Excursion* 7. 3
Awakener. To be the awakener of divinest thoughts, 870 *Excursion* 7. 823
Awakening. *See* **Soul-awakening.**
Awakening, chastening an intemperate grief, . . 813 *Excursion* 4. 840
Awakenings. Gentle awakenings, visitations meek ; 460 **Wanderer ! that* 60
Awakens. Whom Morn awakens, among dews and flowers . . . . 894 *Excursion* 9. 670
Awakes. Earth awakes from wintry sleep : . . . 628 *Installation* 26
Award. And, proud of her award, ... 629 *Installation* 70
Aware. As Benjamin is now aware, ... 176 *Waggoner* 2. 24
The pleased Enchanter was aware . . . . . 369 *Eg. Maid* 3
Gives rights to error ; and aware, no less, . . . 729 *Prelude* 11. 161
Away. (*Partial list.*) *See* **Castaway.**
It seemed to move away from us : and yet . . 39 *Bord.* 114
To fling't away from you : you make no use . . 39 *Bord.* 127
The name of Marmaduke is blown away : . . . 39 *Bord.* 138
For this good deed !—Well, Sirs, this passed away ; 44 *Bord.* 409
And smothered all that's man in me ?—away !— 53 *Bord.* 873
Away ! away !—— Nay, I have done with you : 54 *Bord.* 903
On which it should be touched, would melt away. 250 *Admon.* 14
We have given our hearts away, a sordid boon ! . 259 **The world is* 4
And from our earthly memory fade away. . . 262 **Dark and* 14
Fame tells of groves—from England far away— . 271 **Fame tells* 1
The house that cannot pass away be ours. . . 278 **The most* 14
His native superstitions melt away. . . . . 426 *Ecc. Sonn.* 1. 29. 8
To wantonness.—Away, Circean revels ! . . . 441 *Ecc. Sonn.* 3. 3. 9
Mourns less for what age takes away . . . . 487 *Fountain* 35
And, when Thou art past service, worn away, . 489 *Spade* 27
As he breaks the ice away. . . . . 490 *Incident : Dog* 36
Such greeting heard, away with sighs . . . . 507 *May* 57
O cursèd folk ! away, ye Herods new ! . . . 554 *Prioress* 123
To the next Abbey him they bare away ; . . . 555 *Prioress* 173
Touched then his tongue, and took away the grain ; 556 *Prioress* 220
And he for dread did fly away full fast ; . . . 560 *Cuck.and Night.*219
Till he was far, all out of sight, away. . . . . 561 *Cuck.and Night.*225
Ere he has passed the door, will turn away, . . 567 *Cumb. Beg.* 62
What less may mislead you, they took it away. . 569 *Farmer* 28
Thus might we wear a midnight hour away, . . 746 *Prelude* 14. 32

Away—*continued.*

From natural wisdom turn our hearts away ; .	765 *Excursion* 1. 601
Then, like a blast that dies away self-stilled, .	767 *Excursion* 1. 737
By sorrow laid asleep ; or borne away, .	768 *Excursion* 1. 786
It seemed the better part were gnawed away .	769 *Excursion* 1. 838
" The glory of the times fading away— .	776 *Excursion* 2. 293
And their immortal soul, may waste away." .	886 *Excursion* 9. 152
And steal away, and for a while deceive .	K.8. 245 *Recluse* 1.1.304
That must not die, that must not pass away. .	K.8. 255 *Recluse* 1.1.676

Awe. Now, with religious awe, the farewell light

	7 *Ev. Wk.* 287
Awe in his breast with holiest love unites, .	19 *Desc. Sk.* 476
Were yet with pensive fear and gentle awe	118 *Maternal Grief* 59
With awe, receives the hallowed veil, .	216 *Enterprise* 56
The mercy, goodness, have not failed to awe .	342 *Last Sup.* 4
Tempered with awe, and sweetened by compassion	354 *Aquap.* 89
Deep was the awe, the rapture high, .	374 *Eg. Maid* 331
Was on the wing ; stooping, he struck with awe	388 *Eagles* 5
Of orderly respect and awe ; .	399 *White Doe* 321
Inspiring universal awe, .	410 *White Doe* 1332
For him abandoned to blank awe, .	411 *White Doe* 1387
The unconverted soul with awe submit. .	430 *Ecc. Sonn.* 2. 9. 14
An awe and supernatural horror breeds ; .	431 *Ecc. Sonn.* 2. 11. 6
(Swerves not, how blest if by religious awe .	442 *Ecc. Sonn.* 3. 9. 5
Peasant and mail-clad Chief with pious awe ; .	467 *St. Bees* 122
A weight of awe, not easy to be borne, .	477 *Long Meg* 1
Of reverential awe will chiefly seek .	496 **A little* 40
To awe the lightness of humanity. .	498 **Enough of climbing* 40
If generous Loyalty must stand in awe .	504 *Warning* 101
To a like salutary sense of awe .	510 **Among a* 24
In after-thought, for Him who stood in awe .	517 *Pun. Death* 2. 4
Copying with awe the one Paternal mind. .	518 *Pun. Death* 5. 8
Awe struck, the kneeling peasant scarce surveys ;	606 *Desc.Sk.Quarto* 254
Humility and modest awe themselves .	635 *Prelude* 1. 243
Of the whole place should bear a stamp of awe ;	655 *Prelude* 3. 434
Of awe or tremulous dread, that had given way .	662 *Prelude* 4. 253
To melt away ; and further, the dread awe .	676 *Prelude* 6. 60
With Indian awe and wonder, ignorance pleased .	677 *Prelude* 6. 121
With wonder heightened, or sublimed by awe— .	689 *Prelude* 7. 153
Out of its leafy brow, the more to awe .	695 *Prelude* 7. 521
But that one tutored thus should look with awe .	713 *Prelude* 9. 239
But, even if that were not, amid the awe . .	724 *Prelude* 10. 454
Be hallowed, love that breathes not without awe ; .	748 *Prelude* 14. 182
By help of dreams—can breed such fear and awe	755 *Recluse* 1. 1. 791
And human reason dictated with awe. .	762 *Excursion* 1. 413
Inly distressed or overpowered with awe, .	779 *Excursion* 2. 539
For admiration and mysterious awe. .	784 *Excursion* 2. 869
The heart, in concert with that temperate awe .	824 *Excursion* 5. 142
And look upon the dust of man with awe." .	832 *Excursion* 5. 657
Not, as before, like one oppressed with awe, .	839 *Excursion* 6. 92
Tho', in this Vale, remembered with deep awe." .	850 *Excursion* 6. 777
Of admiration and delightful awe, .	872 *Excursion* 7. 950
Not without awe. Thence passing on, she said .	891 *Excursion* 9. 457

Awed. Awed sober Reason till she crouched in fear ?

	11 *Desc. Sk.* 55
The Chamois-chaser awed in vain .	216 *Enterprise* 65
Awed, delighted, and amazed ! .	217 **Inmate of* 4
Or awed he weeps, struggling to quell dismay.	234 *Power of Sound* 107
For she returns not.—Awed by her own knell, .	420 *Ecc. Sonn.* 1. 9. 11
And awed to piety. .	479 *Somnamb.* 153
Awed by the theme's peculiar sanctity .	585 *Ch. Lamb* 56
Aw'd, while below the Genii hold their state. .	598 *Ev.Wk. Quarto* 358
Youth should be awed, religiously possessed .	654 *Prelude* 3. 387
Awed have I been by strolling Bedlamites ; .	742 *Prelude* 13. 157

Awe-inspiring. The impregnable and awe-inspiring fort

	190 **Lyre ! though* 9
The simple shepherd's awe-inspiring God ! "	814 *Excursion* 4. 887

Awes. And awes like night with mercy-tempered frown

	425 *Ecc. Sonn.* 1. 26. 8

Awe-stricken. Awe-stricken she beholds the array

	343 *Eclipse* 43
Awe-stricken stood both Knights and Dames .	372 *Eg. Maid* 193
And, in awe-stricken Countries far and nigh, .	427 *Ecc. Sonn.* 1. 33. 13

Awe-struck. Of awe-struck wisdom droops : or let my path

	452 *Ecc. Sonn.* 3. 45. 7

Awful. —Is there who 'mid these awful wilds has seen

	16 *Desc. Sk.* 340
Stand motionless, to awful silence bound : .	17 *Desc. Sk.* 410
Awful the light, and holy is the air. .	18 *Desc. Sk.* 456
Within a temple stands an awful shrine, .	20 *Desc. Sk.* 542
—There doth she ken the awful form .	180 *Waggoner* 4. 18
But every awful note in unison .	227 *Vernal Ode* 97
And solemn rites and awful forms .	228 *Devot. Incit.* 52
Will be an awful thought, if life have one." .	251 **Beloved Vale* 5
An unexampled voice of awful memory ! .	271 *George : Death* 14
And claim, among the dead, this awful crown ; .	275 *Gravestone* 9
These Shapes of awful phantasy ? .	300 *Cora Linn* 29
And neither awful Voice be heard by thee ! .	306 **Two Voices* 14
Of awful prudence, keep the unvanquished soul : .	316 **It was a* 11
The awful light of heavenly innocence .	319 *Biscayan* 11
Within its awful caves.—From year to year .	321 **The power* 10
Soft notes, awful as the omen .	328 *Ode 1815* 72
But Man is Thy most awful instrument, .	328 *Ode 1815* 106
Saw ye the soft yet awful veil .	344 *Eclipse* 76
A product of that awful Mountain seem, .	347 *Processions* 57
That follows—yet more awful than that awful sound ! .	350 *Des. Stanzas* 45
That awful name to Thee, thee, simple Cuckoo,	363 **List—'twas* 97
Thee hath some awful Spirit impelled to leave, .	379 *Duddon* 14. 9
Verily so to live was an awful choice— .	391 *Brownie* 9
With awful cheer a voice of praise ; .	397 *White Doe* 157
In deep and awful channel runs .	401 *White Doe* 469
He from the pulpit lifts his awful hand ; .	444 *Ecc. Sonn.* 3. 18. 11

Awful—*continued.*

Of awful notes, whose concord shall not fail ; .	449 *Ecc. Sonn.* 3. 34. 3
What awful perspective ! while from our sight .	451 *Ecc. Sonn.* 3. 44. 1
Come links for social order's awful chain. .	475 **Here on their* 14
To humbler functions, awful Power ! .	492 *Duty* 49
Some awful moment to which Heaven has joined .	493 *Hap. War.* 49
More awful, where, advancing hand in hand, .	496 **A little* 54
An awful balancing of loss and gain, .	514 **Who ponders* 2
In silence and the awful modesties .	516 **Feel for* 7
Strike not from Law's firm hand that awful rod, .	520 *Pun. Death* 13. 12
'Mid these more awful feelings, to infuse .	534 **When in* 18
That may recall to mind that awful Pile .	546 **Ye Lime* 6
Deepening her echoing torrents' awful peal .	603 *Desc. Sk.Quarto* 76
' Soften'd the terrors of her awful mien.' .	618 *School Ex.* 16
But from this awful burthen I full soon .	635 *Prelude* 1. 234
Incumbencies more awful, visitings .	650 *Prelude* 3. 116
O Heavens ! how awful is the might of souls, .	651 *Prelude* 3. 177
Soul awful—if the earth has ever lodged .	653 *Prelude* 3. 286
An awful soul—I seemed to see him here .	653 *Prelude* 3. 287
Kept the same awful steadiness—at his feet .	664 *Prelude* 4. 407
And thought that, in the blind and awful lair .	668 *Prelude* 5. 151
Rested within an awful *solitude :* .	681 *Prelude* 6. 419
That awful Power rose from the mind's abyss .	684 *Prelude* 6. 594
The awful truths delivered thence by tongues .	695 *Prelude* 7. 547
Man suffering among awful Powers and Forms ; .	701 *Prelude* 8. 165
Companionless your awful solitudes ! .	702 *Prelude* 8. 222
Though with such awful proof before their eyes .	728 *Prelude* 11. 66
'Mid circumstances awful and sublime, .	747 *Prelude* 14. 80
And that most awful scripture which declares .	780 *Excursion* 2. 577
At thy command, how awful ! Shall the Soul, .	802 *Excursion* 4. 36
When piety more awful had relaxed, .	812 *Excursion* 4. 744
Received a shock of awful consciousness, .	818 *Excursion* 4. 1157
Within the bosom of her awful pile, .	842 *Excursion* 6. 265
A type and shadow of an awful truth ; .	865 *Excursion* 7. 527
Its cities, temples, fields, its awful power, .	871 *Excursion* 7. 898
In awful sovereignty ; a place of power, .	885 *Excursion* 9. 55
More awful than the chambers of dark earth .	S. 3. 436 **The doubt* 178
Which I have felt this day. An awful voice, .	K.8. 245 *Recluse* 1.1.318
Awful as ever stray Demoniac uttered, .	K.8. 246 *Recluse* 1.1.337
When, such the awful will of heaven, she died .	K.8. 275 **These vales* 3

Awfully. And awfully impenetrable. .

	414 *White Doe* 1628

Awfulness. Of awfulness, is in her face,—

	413 *White Doe* 1599
So much I felt the awfulness of life, .	780 *Excursion* 2. 555

Awhile. Not yet in sight !—We'll saunter here awhile ;

	38 *Bord.* 48
You are quite exhausted. Let us rest awhile .	39 *Bord.* 130
Spare me awhile that greeting. It may be .	64 *Bord.* 1507
That she is innocent. Leave that thought awhile	67 *Bord.* 1678
Listen yet awhile ;—with patience .	94 *Westmoreland Girl* 57
Be loth that we should breathe awhile exempt .	382 *Duddon* 24. 11
Stay, bold Adventurer ; rest awhile thy limbs .	548 **Stay, bold* 1
Those lofty hopes awhile, for present gifts .	634 *Prelude* 1. 133
Leaving us at the board ; awhile we lingered, .	683 *Prelude* 6. 567
That flowed awhile with unabating strength, .	687 *Prelude* 7. 10
But let him pause awhile, and look again, .	707 *Prelude* 8. 577
Therein, with our simplicity awhile .	802 *Excursion* 4. 85
Awhile they stood in conference, and I guess .	829 *Excursion* 5. 446
Over both minds, when they awhile had marked .	845 *Excursion* 6. 481
Till the spectator, who awhile was pleased .	874 *Excursion* 8. 26

Awning. And pleasant awning. On the moss-grown wall

	826 *Excursion* 5. 230

Awoke. Awoke a fainter sense of moral grief ; .

	22 *Desc. Sk.* 633
The father, and relenting thoughts awoke ; .	33 *Guilt* 501
Awoke to new life from its ashes and dust ; .	345 *Stanzas : Simplon* 14
So loudly, that I with that song awoke. .	562 *Cuck.and Night.* 290
Awoke a fainter pang of moral grief ; .	616 *Desc. Sk. Quarto* 769

Awry. His body, dwindled and awry, . .

	483 *Simon Lee* 34
That answers unexpectedly awry, .	688 *Prelude* 7. 101

Axe. See **Battle-axe, Stone-axe.**
Stretched on the block the glittering axe recoils ;

	252 **Why, Minstrel* 10
Saved from the sordid axe by Beaumont's care, .	358 *Pine : Rome* 7
Than the bare axe more luminous and keen. .	435 *Ecc. Sonn.* 2. 26. 14
Whose shades have never felt the encroaching axe, .	799 *Excursion* 3. 916
His sentence to the axe would doom them all. .	867 *Excursion* 7. 624

Axis. On its own axis restlessly revolving, . .

	810 *Excursion* 4. 629

Axle-tree. Or forest, fetched the enormous axle-tree . . .

	866 *Excursion* 7. 606

Ay. *See* **Aye.**

You must forgive me. Ay, and if you think .	45 *Bord.* 428
Ay, Sir, there's nobody that feels for us. .	45 *Bord.* 445
At Herbert's door. Ay ; and if truth were known	46 *Bord.* 480
Ay, what is it you mean ? Harkee, my Friends ;—	56 *Bord.* 1037
But hear the proofs—— Ay, prove that when two peas .	59 *Bord.* 1176
Feed on her leaves. You knewher well—ay, there, .	61 *Bord.* 1312
But they will soon be lightened. Ay, look up—	65 *Bord.* 1533
Ay, we are coupled by a chain of adamant ; .	70 *Bord.* 1854
Ay, and his head was bare ; .	72 *Bord.* 1983
Ay, and say at once that I murdered him ! .	72 *Bord.* 1990
Ay, in the word a thousand scorpions lodge ; .	74 *Bord.* 2094
Ay, come to me and weep. Yes, Varlet, look, .	76 *Bord.* 2189
Ay, what shall we encounter next ? This issue—	77 *Bord.* 2284
Ay, thought the Vicar, smiling to himself, .	96 *Brothers* 104
Ay, there, indeed, your memory is a friend .	97 *Brothers* 138
Ay—you may turn that way—it is a grave .	99 *Brothers* 238
Ay, more than once I have seen him, mid-leg deep, .	99 *Brothers* 261

Ay—*continued.*
Then they could write, ay, and speak too, as well 99 *Brothers* 279
Ay, Sir, that passed away: we took him to us; 100 *Brothers* 342
Ay, that he did— And all went well with him?— 101 *Brothers* 385
"Ay," said the Tar, "through fair and foul— 179 *Waggoner* 3. 97
Ay, quoth the Cuckoo, that is a quaint law, 559 *Cuck.andNight.*136
Ayde. Their sabbath music—"God us ayde!" 415 *White Doe* 1762
With vocal music, "God us ayde;" 415 *White Doe* 1774
Aye. Descending, shuts for aye his prison door. 16 *Desc. Sk.* 331
And so will gallop on for aye, 129 *Idiot Boy* 335
And there, my babe, we'll live for aye." 145 *Her Eyes* 100
Of nature trusts the Mind that builds for aye; 259 **A volant* 6
Set, like his fortunes; but not set for aye. 277 **Haydon! let* 12
The Olympian summit hath destroyed for aye 325 *Ode 1814* 119
But aye ascending, restless in her pride 327 *Ode 1815* 2
That through the realms of glory shines for aye. 365 **Rapt above* 14
To spread its arms, and stand for aye. 410 *White Doe* 1269
And aye, methinks, this hoary Pile, 417 *White Doe* 1905
'Mid Heaven-born flowers that shall for aye endure, 428 *Ecc. Sonn.* 2. 1. 7
Which did Thee bear, and is a Maid for aye, 552 *Prioress* 10
To worship aye, and he forgat it not; 553 *Prioress* 59
Saint Nicholas in my presence standeth aye, 553 *Prioress* 63
Now may'st thou sing for aye before the throne, 554 *Prioress* 129
Loving is aye an office of despair, 560 *Cuck.andNight.*176
And as he flew, the Cuckoo, ever and aye, 561 *Cuck.andNight.*221
Aye as he rode, to Pandarus he told 563 *Troilus* 39
Aye, think on that, my heart, and cease to stir, 622 *Recluse* 1. 80
To endure for aye. The Vicar, taking note 871 *Excursion* 7. 919
Ayr. All through the bonny shire of Ayr; 239 *P. B.* 219
Azincour. And drew their sounding bows at Azincour, 184 *Yew-trees* 7
Azure. In robes of azure, fleecy-white, and gold. 8 *Ev. Wk.* 330
The hills, while gleams below the azure tide; 9 *Ev. Wk.* 360
Bright stars of ice and azure fields of snow; 19 *Desc. Sk.* 467
At the spectator's feet.—Yon azure ridge, 219 **This Height* 23
But let thy love, upon that azure field 222 *Triad* 194
An azure disc—shield of Tranquillity; 264 *Storm* 12
The azure brooks, where Dian joys to lave 264 **Lady! I* 5
That through the texture of yon azure dome 322 *Germans* 6
The azure sea upswelled upon the sight. 323 *Ode 1814* 14
The sky an azure field displayed; 343 *Eclipse* 21
Peering in air and backed by azure sky, 355 *Aquap.* 171
Floating through the azure sky. 415 *White Doe* 1742
A land whose azure mountain-tops are seats 501 *Humanity* 73
Whose azure depth their colour emulates, 508 *F. Stone* 33
One chimney smoking and its azure wreath, 524 *Epist. Beaumont* 179
O'er azure pikes serene and still, they go, 610 *Desc.Sk.Quarto* 458
Bright stars of ice and azure worlds of snow, 612 *Desc.Sk.Quarto* 557
From the green fields, and from yon azure sky. 632 *Prelude* 1. 4
To the broad ocean and the azure heavens 651 *Prelude* 3. 161
Yon azure smoke betrays the lurking town; 658 *Prelude* 4. 24
Of azure without cloud, and at my feet 746 *Prelude* 14. 41
Is heaven's profoundest azure; no domain 787 *Excursion* 3. 95
Inverted trees, rocks, clouds, and azure sky; 800 *Excursion* 3. 972
Of azure heaven, the unenduring clouds, 884 *Excursion* 9. 6

B

Babble. And babble of her pastime!—On, dread Power! 315 **Advance—come* 9
Babbled. That babbled on through groves and meadows green; 34 *Guilt* 517
Babbling. And all the babbling brooks are liquid gold; 5 *Ev. Wk.* 189
In every babbling brook he finds a friend; 11 *Desc. Sk.* 26
We have no time for this, my babbling Gossip; 44 *Bord.* 407
Beside the babbling rills; 155 *Oak and Broom* 2
Though babbling only to the Vale, 183 **O blithe* 9
To a babbling wanderer sent; 209 **Yes, it* 6
Of babbling winds as they go by, 405 *White Doe* 850
"The babbling flatteries 542 *Russ. Fug.* 58
Babe. A nursling babe her only comforter; 13 *Desc. Sk.* 176
The heart of living creature.—My poor Babe 44 *Bord.* 398
But there are Mothers who can see the Babe 45 *Bord.* 440
I overtook him, Sirs, my Babe and I, 45 *Bord.* 472
A little Infant, and instruct the Babe, 56 *Bord.* 1041
Of this poor Babe, and taught its innocent tongue 56 *Bord.* 1051
Yields, could not chuck his babe beneath the chin, 60 *Bord.* 1243
While in my lap I held my little Babe 62 *Bord.* 1360
I had a better guide—that innocent Babe— 62 *Bord.* 1368
Helpless and harmless as a babe: a Man 75 *Bord.* 2164
When from my arms my Babe they took, 114 *Ind. Wom.* 33
But thou, dear Babe, art far away, 114 *Ind. Wom.* 69
Such things as she unto the Babe might say: 120 *EmigrantMother*12
"Dear Babe, thou daughter of another, 120 *EmigrantMother*15
And I have left a babe at home: 120 *EmigrantMother*26
Sweet Babe! and they will let him die. 121 *EmigrantMother*46
The babe and mother near me dwell: 121 *EmigrantMother*70
Until the babe was born. When morning came, 122 *V. and J.* 73
Of Julia's travail. When the babe was born, 124 *V. and J.* 187
The Babe was drawing in its quiet food. 124 *V. and J.* 216
In which the Babe was carried. To a hill, 125 *V. and J.* 247
And thither took with him his motherless Babe, 125 *V. and J.* 274
Old Michael, while he was a babe in arms, 133 *Michael* 153
While thou, a feeding babe, didst in thy joy 136 *Michael* 348
"Sweet babe! they say that I am mad, 144 *Her Eyes* 11
"Suck, little babe, oh suck again! 145 *Her Eyes* 31
It comes to cool my babe and me. 145 *Her Eyes* 40
The babe I carry on my arm, 145 *Her Eyes* 47

Babe—*continued.*
Without me my sweet babe would die. 145 *Her Eyes* 50
From him no harm my babe can take; 145 *Her Eyes* 77
My little babe! thy lips are still, 145 *Her Eyes* 83
And there, my babe, we'll live for aye." 145 *Her Eyes* 100
Here, for neither Babe nor me, 171 *Kitten* 43
Once up, once down the hill, one journey, Babe, 172 *Infant Daughter* 56
She and her Babe, which to her breast 176 *Waggoner* 1. 245
Not to speak of babe and mother; 181 *Waggoner* 4. 167
While she dandles the Babe in her arms to the sound. 189 *Music* 40
The little Babe was buried there, 200 *Thorn* 208
The shadow of a babe you trace, 200 *Thorn* 216
The little Babe lies buried there, 200 *Thorn* 230
The last she to her Babe did say: 204 *Brougham* 83
She called her babe unborn. 246 *P. B.* 910
Of some sweet Babe—Flower stolen, and coarse Weed left 378 *Duddon* 11. 7
That fascinate the very Babe in arms, 460 **Queen of* 18
Her new-born Babe; dire ending of bright hope! 476 *Howard* 2
Lies the Babe, in helplessness 502 **Like a* 3
To the babe, whate'er betide, 503 **Like a* 58
For the unconscious Babe so prompt a love!)— 503 *Warning* 29
Alfred, dear Babe, thy great Progenitor! 504 *Warning* 60
Can such a One, dear Babe! though glad and proud 504 *Warning* 78
And the Babe leaps up on his Mother's arm:— 588 *Immortality* 49
His father helpless as the babe he rocks, 612 *Desc.Sk.Quarto* 575
Laid snares to make the babe her own. 620 *Birth of Love* 31
Above the babe, unseen; 628 *Installation* 32
Where I was looking on, a babe in arms, 636 *Prelude* 1. 276
Hath no beginning. Blest the infant Babe, 645 *Prelude* 2. 232
Our Being's earthly progress,) blest the Babe, 645 *Prelude* 2. 234
In which, a Babe, by intercourse of touch 646 *Prelude* 2. 267
Or in some sheltering vale, was seen a babe 692 *Prelude* 7. 355
With envy on thy nameless babe that sleeps, 692 *Prelude* 7. 380
This One Man, with a sickly babe outstretched 696 *Prelude* 7. 608
Eyed the poor babe with love unutterable. 696 *Prelude* 7. 618
The mother from the cradle of her babe, 723 *Prelude* 10. 359
I took my staff, and, when I kissed her babe, 768 *Excursion* 1. 809
As they had chanced to fall. Her infant Babe 768 *Excursion* 1. 829
If I had any hope:—but for her babe 769 *Excursion* 1. 848
She told me that her little babe was dead, 769 *Excursion* 1. 856
At her aspiring outset. Mark the babe 826 *Excursion* 5. 261
That lovingly consigns the babe to the arms 836 *Excursion* 5. 951
To rock the cradle of the slumbering babe: 867 *Excursion* 7. 668
To rock the cradle of her peevish babe; 878 *Excursion* 8. 268
This sacred right, the lisping babe proclaims 888 *Excursion* 9. 311
The trees (her first-born child being then a babe) K. 8. 247 *Recluse* 1. 1. 391
But, Babe! there's none to work for me, K. 8. 262 **Ah! if* 6
Babel. Go back, and see the Tower of Babel rise; 313 **Go back* 5
Babel-like. Hence could I see how Babel-like their task, 727 *Prelude* 11. 35
Babe's. From the babe's first cry to voice of regal city, 234 *Power of Sound*163
Her babe's small cry, that leads him to his prey. 606 *Desc.Sk.Quarto* 242
Babes. Weak roof a cowering form two babes to shield, 7 *Ev. Wk.* 273
Three lovely babes had lain upon my breast; 29 *Guilt* 264
And babes in wet and starveling plight; 182 *Waggoner* 4. 260
Thou, while thy babes around thee cling, 218 *Young Lady* 10
The arithmetic of babes, must foreign hordes, 309 **What if* 2
Let Babes and Sucklings be thy oracles. 516 **Young England*14
Two Babes were laid in earth before she died; 576 **By a* 9
Hath dragg'd her babes along this weary way; 596 *Ev. Wk. Quarto* 244
For thy poor babes that, hurrying from the door, 615 *Desc.Sk.Quarto* 709
Now vacant; pale-faced babes whom I had left 661 *Prelude* 4. 203
Men, Women, three-years' Children, Babes in arms. 698 *Prelude* 7. 721
One while he would speak lightly of his babes, 765 *Excursion* 1. 585
That I should follow with my babes, and sink 766 *Excursion* 1. 680
Baby. Or own we baby S[illegible]ts? Genuine courage 57 *Bord.* 1073
For thee, sweet Baby!—th[illegible] hast tried, 120 *Emigrant Mother* 31
My baby and its dwelling-pl[illegible], 121 *EmigrantMother*40
Dear Baby! I must lay thee down; 121 *EmigrantMother*59
Your grown-up and your baby brother; 143 †*Lov. and Lik.* 56
She has a baby on her arm, 144 *Her Eyes* 5
Then, lovely baby, do not fear! 144 *Her Eyes* 15
My lovely baby! thou shalt be: 144 *Her Eyes* 18
Thy lips I feel them, baby! they 145 *Her Eyes* 33
'Tis thine, sweet baby, there to rest; 145 *Her Eyes* 62
Thee, Baby, laughing in my arms, 171 *Kitten* 106
Sleeping by her sleeping Baby. 177 *Waggoner* 2. 91
She hanged her baby on the tree; 200 *Thorn* 204
A baby and a baby's face, 200 *Thorn* 217
The baby looks at you again. 200 *Thorn* 220
Baby-faces. They guard, with winged baby-faces. 144 **Driven in* 57
Baby-houses. Of baby-houses, curiously arranged; 778 *Excursion* 2. 425
Babylon. Truth, their immortal Una? Babylon, 425 *Ecc. Sonn.* 1. 25. 9
Alcairo, Babylon, or Persepolis; 688 *Prelude* 7. 81
Babylonian. After the Babylonian harlot; 247 *P. B.* 953
Yielding his soul, the Babylonian framed 811 *Excursion* 4. 682
Baby's. A baby and a baby's face, 200 *Thorn* 217
There, by her innocent Baby's precious grave, 850 *Excursion* 6. 811
Baby-show. What a pretty baby-show! 170 *Kitten* 2
Baby-treat. 'Tis a pretty baby-treat; 171 *Kitten* 41
Bacchanal. Dance, like a Bacchanal, from rock to rock, 381 *Duddon* 20. 13
Bacchanals. Of giddy Bacchanals belong? 344 **How blest* 36
Bacchus. Young Bacchus was conveyed—to lie 299 *Brownie's Cell* 95
While Bacchus, clothed in semblance of a Friar, 433 *Ecc. Sonn.* 2. 20. 4
Let Bacchus, donor of soul-quick'ning cheer, 625 *Æneid* 112
Bachelor. The Bachelor, that loves to sun himself, 690 *Prelude* 7. 208
There have I seen a comely bachelor, 695 *Prelude* 7. 551

Backward—*continued.*
With backward steps. Yet ever as there passed . 769 *Excursion* 1. 887
With backward will; but, wanting not address . 874 *Excursion* 8. 31
Among the mazy streams that backward went, . S. 3. 427 **My Son* 4
Backward-looking. The strength of backward-looking thoughts is scorned. 477 **Lowther! in* 11
Backwardness. Or a nice backwardness afraid of shame) 757 *Excursion* 1. 85
Backwards. And, looking backwards when he looked, mine eyes 667 *Prelude* 5. 127
Backwards, nor checked his flight until I saw 744 *Prelude* 13. 319
Bacon. The very bacon shows its feeling, 177 *Waggoner* 2. 68
Bacon's. Now honour'd Edward's less than Bacon's name. 619 *School Ex.* 56
Bad. Then the milk-thistle bad those herds demand 611 *Desc.Sk.Quarto* 484
"Bad is the world, and hard is the world's law . 33 *Guilt* 505
Henceforth it shall be said that bad men only . 54 *Bord.* 910
I thought there was no harm: but that bad Man, 77 *Bord.* 2245
—So bad proceeded propagating worse; 330 *Ode: Thanks.* 121
That even bad men had vainly striven 412 *White Doe* 1457
With a bad world, and foil the Tempter's arts. 447 *Ecc. Sonn.* 3. 28. 14
As will be owned alike by bad and good, 478 **Lonsdale! it* 12
Of their bad influence, and their good receives: 493 *Hap. War.* 18
Great issues, good or bad for human kind, 493 *Hap. War.* 50
Of good or bad (whate'er be sought for or profest) 504 *Warning* 89
The bad man's restless walk, and haunt his bed— 518 *Pun. Death* 6. 2
Far oftener then, bad ushering worse event, 519 *Pun. Death* 8. 7
But turn we from these "bold bad" men; 534 **Blest is* 81
This Provost doth for those bad Jews prepare 555 *Prioress* 178
Small jealousies, and triumphs good or bad— 650 *Prelude* 3. 72
No fear had they of bad becoming worse, 711 *Prelude* 9. 135
In their unhallowed principles; the bad 805 *Excursion* 4. 307
Mid such bad daring sought a coward's name. L. 1. 96 *Juvenal* 3. 56
Bade. *See* **Bad.**
She rose and bade farewell! and, while her heart. 34 *Guilt* 534
The cry, I bade him halt again, 82 *Alice Fell* 16
And bade them better mind their trade. 85 *Shepherd-boys* 99
And bade the Snow their ample backs bestride, 321 **Humanity, delighting* 30
Darkens the sun, hath bade the forest sink, 328 *Ode 1815* 95
Saved by His care who bade the tempest cease; 454 *Sea-side* 16
Which done, he bade that they the Jews should bind. 555 *Prioress* 169
Nor that vile wretch who bade the tender age 618 *School Ex.* 9
I bade farewell; and, one among the youth 675 *Prelude* 6. 3
Returned from that excursion, soon I bade 688 *Prelude* 7. 52
For those that bade them fall. They found their joy, 723 *Prelude* 10. 363
Pointing towards a sweet-briar, bade me climb 763 *Excursion* 1. 451
Toward him, bade him leap, which word scarce said K. 8. 230 **I will* 176
But me hath Nature tamed, and bade to seek K. 8. 256 *Recluse* 1. 1. 726
Badge. Their badge, attests the holy fight they wage. 628 *Eagle and Dove* 12
Of those who lived distinguished by the badge 656 *Prelude* 3. 534
Than as they were a badge glossy and fresh 662 *Prelude* 4. 285
The nobler badge shall glitter on *his arm.* L. 1. 96 *Juvenal* 3. 38
Badger. To hunt the badger and unearth the fox 660 *Prelude* 4. 97
Baffle. To baffle me—it put me to my prayers. 55 *Bord.* 987
Baffle the threat, bright Scene, from Orrest-head 282 *Railway* 9
Redeemed to baffle that imperial Slave, 318 **Ah! where* 7
To baffle all that may her strength impair; 438 *Ecc. Sonn.* 2. 40. 5
That has power to baffle death— 502 **Like a* 42
To baffle, as he might, the watery storm: 784 *Excursion* 2. 820
Baffled. *See* **Long-baffled.**
He hears the chiding of the baffled wind, 19 *Desc. Sk.* 489
Where ours are baffled. I had been deceived. 69 *Bord.* 1753
It took effect—and yet I baffled it, 75 *Bord.* 2144
"You shall be baffled in your mad intent 123 *V. and J.* 120
And, baffled thus, though earth from day to day. 150 **When, to* 39
How baffled projects on the spirit prey, 458 *Sea-shore* 3
Was baffled still, the crumbs in little showers 566 *Cumb. Beg.* 18
On the dark earth the baffl'd vision fails, 598 *Ev. Wk. Quarto* 364
Secure, the chiding of the baffled wind, 612 *Desc.Sk.Quarto* 579
Baffled and plagued by a mind that every hour 636 *Prelude* 1. 257
Of silence came and baffled his best skill, 671 *Prelude* 5. 380
Baffled my understanding: how men lived 688 *Prelude* 7. 116
With spiteful gratitude the baffled League, 718 *Prelude* 10. 36
Were baffled; nor could my weak arm disperse 756 *Excursion* 1. 23
For baffled lips and disappointed arms S. 3. 434 **The doubt* 79
A baffled conqueror's deeply searching rage, L. 1. 95 *Juvenal* 3. 4
Baffling. Might else have triumphed, baffling prayer, 391 *Highland Broach* 54
Bag. Than the height of a counsellor's bag; 86 *Rural Arch.* 3
That overlays the pile; and, from a bag 566 *Cumb. Beg.* 8
Bagdad's. In his still haunt on Bagdad's summit high; 252 **The fairest* 6
Bagpipe. The bag-pipe dinning on the midnight moor 32 *Guilt* 410
Cheered by the Highland bagpipe, as they marched 774 *Excursion* 2. 176
Bagpipers. Of bagpipers on distant Highland hills. 132 *Michael* 52
Bagpipes. And then the bagpipes he could blow— 295 *Highland Boy* 41
Bait. Was playing with some inward bait. 240 *P. B.* 310
Remains without an Heir, the bait 403 *White Doe* 639
Baits. Wages of folly—baits of crime, 214 *Kirkstone* 29
Baker's. And the pale-visaged Baker's, with basket on back. 188 *Music* 16
Balance. In an impartial balance, give thine aid 22 *Desc. Sk.* 653
Would balance claim with claim, and right with right? 105 *Artegal* 171
Restless with fixed to balance, high with low, 153 *Morn. Ex.* 32
O for a balance fit the truth to tell. 235 *Power of Sound* 175
(The balance trembling between night and morn. 279 **'Tis he* 10
Yes, ye were startled;—and, in balance true, 283 **Proud were* 11
Are weighed by Providence, in balance even; 331 *Ode: Thanks.* 156
How in still air the balance trembled— 373 *Eg. Maid* 278
A skill—to balance and supply; 497 *Lycoris* 41
The balance of delight. 506 **While from* 16

Balance—*continued.*
In such an even balance, that the heart 586 *Ch. Lamb* 118
Might fix the wavering balance of my mind, 641 *Prelude* 1. 622
As in a balance! of excessive hopes, 650 *Prelude* 3. 70
The balance, and with firm hand weighed myself. 660 *Prelude* 4. 159
A balance, an ennobling interchange 745 *Prelude* 13. 375
The excess, by which the balance is destroyed. 804 *Excursion* 4. 178
Balanced. Balanced in ether he will never tarry, 472 *Dunolly Eagle* 11
More justly balanced; partly at their feet, 488 *Pers. Talk* 24
To take his sentence from the balanced Block, 500 *Humanity* 5
Balanced by vigilance for others' weal. 539 **Lady! a* 66
Balanced these contemplations in his mind; 714 *Prelude* 9. 330
And balanced by pathetic truth, by trust 750 *Prelude* 14. 296
Balancing. And, balancing the hopes that are the dearest 66 *Bord.* 1614
Of seasons balancing their flight 228 *Devot. Incit.* 56
A State—which, balancing herself between 450 *Ecc. Sonn.* 3. 37. 13
An awful balancing of loss and gain, 514 **Who ponders* 2
Balbi. Pause, courteous Spirit!—Balbi supplicates 575 *Chiabrera* 9. 1
Bald. Couched on the bald top of an eminence; 196 *Resolution* 58
Murmuring submission, and bald government, 657 *Prelude* 3. 602
Baleful. Portending ruin to each baleful rite 419 *Ecc. Sonn.* 1. 3. 5
With cheeks o'erspread by smiles of baleful glow, 617 *Desc.Sk.Quarto* 790
Balked. And Tyranny is balked of her desire: 442 *Ecc. Sonn.* 3. 8. 4
Ball. *See* **Eyeball.**
The Ball whizz'd by,—it grazed his ear, S. 3. 441 **The ball* 1
Ballad. And it seemed, as I retraced the ballad line by line, 88 *Pet-lamb* 63
Of which we in the Ballad read. 143 **Driven in* 10
And crowded street resound with ballad strains, 540 *Grace Darl.* 3
The milkmaid stops her ballad, and her pail 598 *Ev. Wk. Quarto* 355
Stretched under wayside hedge-rows, ballad tunes, 668 *Prelude* 5. 210
Here files of ballads dangle from dead walls; 690 *Prelude* 7. 193
Ballad-singer. An English ballad-singer. Private courts, 689 *Prelude* 7. 180
Ballad-singer's. The English ballad-singer's joy! 290 *Rob Roy* 2
Balloon. There's something in a huge balloon; 236 *P. B.* 2
The bravest traveller in balloon, 296 *Highland Boy* 168
Ballot-box. Hurrah for ——— [Grote], hugging his Ballot-box! 513 **Said Secrecy* 14
Balls. *See* **Eye-balls, Foam-balls.**
A Juggler's balls old Time about him tossed; 251 **Beloved Vale* 12
Yon eddying balls of foam, these arrowy gleams 268 **Dogmatic Teachers* 10
Yet, like to eddying balls of foam 551 **Behold an* 3
Balm. His good works will be balm and life to him. 67 *Bord.* 1632
In that delicious hour of balm, 182 *Waggoner* 4. 238
And hers shall be the breathing balm, 187 **Three years* 16
A balm of expectation? 224 **'Tis gone* 33
In rich reward all suffering; Balm that tames 253 **Fond words* 6
Balmy. My story may begin) O balmy time, 121 *V. and J.* 2
Thy spirits will seem to feed on balmy air: 229 *Cuckoo-clock* 15
So the balmy minutes pass, 397 *White Doe* 152
That day of balmy April weather, 414 *White Doe* 1682
And hums the balmy air to still 506 **While from* 15
The story might begin,) oh, balmy time, 717 *Prelude* 9. 554
In balmy spring-time full of rising flowers 748 *Prelude* 14. 171
Baltic. And, from the wide and open Baltic, rise 454 *Sea-side* 31
To the flat margin of the Baltic sea, 889 *Excursion* 9. 337
Ban. With scorn, invoking a vindictive ban 428 *Ecc. Sonn.* 1. 38. 12
Lay on the moral will a withering ban? 501 *Humanity* 80
Laws that lay under Heaven's perpetual ban 514 **Portentous change* 12
Banbury. Who dragged Earl Pembroke from Banbury church 399 *White Doe* 252
Band. *See* **Faggot-band.**
True; and, remembering how the Band have proved 37 *Bord.* 11
Let us begone—the Band may else be foiled. 37 *Bord.* 20
Repair to Liddesdale, and tell the Band 38 *Bord.* 41
Is rooted in his mind; this Band of ours, 38 *Bord.* 60
Till all the band of playmates wept together; 39 *Bord.* 94
Your single virtue has transformed a Band 48 *Bord.* 610
Obey you more. Your weakness, to the Band, 55 *Bord.* 980
We come by order of the Band. Belike 56 *Bord.* 1021
Commissioned by the Band, burst in upon us. 59 *Bord.* 1212
A band of Pirates in the Norway seas; 63 *Bord.* 1443
Pledge of an eternal band: 142 *Arm. Lady* 142
About that tight and deadly band 145 *Her Eyes* 37
Make all one band of paramours, 159 *Green Linnet* 18
Herald of a mighty band, 160 **Pansies, lilies* 59
And hark! the Leader of the band 161 *Binnorie* 19
The gladdest of the gladsome band, 177 *Waggoner* 2. 93
Is touched—and all the band take flight. 180 *Waggoner* 4. 35
Of the pleasure it spreads through so thankful a band; 188 *Music* 30
Which stopped that band of travellers on their way, 252 *Picture* 5
And so the bright immortal Theban band, 265 **When haughty* 12
Or hath not Pindus fed thee, where the band 272 *Devil's Bridge* 4
Full sure they were a happy band, 297 *Highland Boy* 222
Unfit for men; and that in one great band 308 **One might* 3
Wise, upright, valiant; not a servile band, 310 **Another year* 12
A loyal band to follow their liege Lord 329 *Ode: Thanks.* 60
Then, glittering like a star, she joins the festal band. 344 **How blest* 26
Bear to the glacier band—those Shapes aloft descried. 347 *Processions* 63
Than question not that, 'mid the austere Band, 362 **List—'twas* 66
Kept watch, a viewless band; 374 *Eg. Maid* 380
So stout and hardy were the band 375 **The Minstrels* 11
But some—a variegated band 398 *White Doe* 162
All followed him, a gallant band! 400 *White Doe* 413
That Norton with his band is near! 402 *White Doe* 598

Band—*continued.*
"Uplift it!" cried once more the Band, . . . 403 *White Doe* 678
And thus, in arms, a zealous Band . . . . . 404 *White Doe* 709
From Norton and his filial band; . . . . . 408 *White Doe* 1150
And reverently the Band went forth. . . . . 410 *White Doe* 1321
—'Tis Sir George Bowes who leads the Band: . 412 *White Doe* 1446
The Banner clenched; till, from out the Band, . 412 *White Doe* 1489
Firm as the stake to which with iron band . . 437 *Ecc. Sonn.* 2. 35. 5
Of genuine Faith. Where, haply, 'mid this band 450 *Ecc. Sonn.* 3. 39. 9
Albeit labouring for a scanty band . . . . . 451 *Ecc. Sonn.* 3. 43. 3
Our little Band would thrid this mountain-way, . 524 *Epist. Beaumont* 210
Loving the dewy shade,—a humble band, . . . 539 **Lady! a* 19
The happiest of the band! . . . . 544 *Russ. Fug.* 248
The Tyrians rushing in, an eager band, . . . 624 *Æneid* 71
No little band of yet remembered names . . . 634 *Prelude* 1. 161
Nor saw a band in happiness and joy . . . 639 *Prelude* 1. 481
Among the band of my compeers was one . . . 653 *Prelude* 3. 293
Following a band of muleteers, we reached . . 683 *Prelude* 6. 564
Of monkeys on his back; a minstrel band . . 689 *Prelude* 7. 178
From house and home, the courtly band whose fortunes . . . . 701 *Prelude* 8. 137
A band of military Officers, ... 711 *Prelude* 9. 125
To augment the band of emigrants in arms . . 712 *Prelude* 9. 183
Among that band of Officers was one, ... 714 *Prelude* 9. 288
And cheerful, but the foremost of the band . . 726 *Prelude* 10. 570
In wantonness of heart, a joyous band . . . 727 *Prelude* 10. 600
The humblest of this band who dares to hope . 744 *Prelude* 13. 306
And I, as chanced, the foremost of the band; . 746 *Prelude* 14. 34
Not ceasing, forth appeared in view a band . . 777 *Excursion* 2. 386
"Can it be thus among so small a band . . . 780 *Excursion* 2. 608
For her defence, replenished with a band . . . 839 *Excursion* 6. 56
High in these mountains, that allured a band . 841 *Excursion* 6. 215
Not one of all the band, a full-blown flower. . . 855 *Excursion* 6. 1130
Like a bright star, amid the lowly band . . . 872 *Excursion* 7. 954
A fresh band meets them, at the crowded door— 877 *Excursion* 8. 176
A servile band among the lordly free! . . . . 888 *Excursion* 9. 310
For you, in presence of this little band . . . 895 *Excursion* 9. 729
And in and all about that playful band, . . . K.8. 252 *Recluse* 1.1.583
And must be, with God's will, a happy band. . K.8. 254 *Recluse* 1.1.663
Banded. Ye banded instruments of wind and chords; 235 *Power of Sound* 194
Here, there, a banded few who loathe the chain . 515 **Ah why* 6
Was soon defrauded, and the banded host . . 633 *Prelude* 1. 97
Banded beneath the Great Mogul, when he . . 718 *Prelude* 10. 18
Bandied. When Echo bandied, round and round, . 483 *Simon Lee* 11
And bandied up and down by love and hate; . 671 *Prelude* 5. 413
Bandit's. Or ruling Bandit's wife among the Grecian isles. . . . . 190 *Beggars* 12
Banditti. And, far beneath, Banditti voices talk; . 606 *Desc.Sk.Quarto* 234
Bands. Sink with his servile bands, to rise no more! 22 *Desc. Sk.* 664
In shoals and bands, a morrice train, ... 158 **In youth* 17
"The Minstrels of Pygmean bands, ... 164 *Needlecase* 21
Some are sleeping; some in bands . . . . 171 *Kitten* 55
Not loth to furnish weapons for the bands . . 184 *Yew-trees* 4
Had roamed about, with vagrant bands . . . 193 *Ruth* 119
And heard his viewless bands . . . . . . 222 *Triad* 172
Like bands of ministering Spirits, or when they lie, 230 *Clouds* 74
More welcome notes to weary bands . . . . 289 *Sol. Reap.* 10
On motley bands of alien flowers . . . . . 301 *Bran* 122
Which spurns the check of salutary bands, . . 307 **It is not* 6
Where all the brave lie dead. But, when of bands 319 *Spaniard* 8
The roving Spanish Bands are reached at last, . 320 **Hunger, and* 5
Advance in order the redoubted Bands, . . . 324 *Ode 1814* 56
But 'tis a rueful thought that willow bands . . 325 *Enghien* 12
The sacred ENGELBERG, celestial Bands, . . . 338 *Engelberg* 7
To wash the fleece, where haply bands of rock, . 381 *Duddon* 23. 3
And blooming thickets; nor by rocky bands . . 384 *Duddon* 32. 3
Then followed the Waldensian bands, whom Hate 432 *Ecc. Sonn.* 2. 14. 6
Solemnly joined. Now sanctify the bands . . 446 *Ecc. Sonn.* 3. 26. 5
For once I burst my bands, and cry, applaud!", 513 **Said Secrecy* 8
All strength—all terror, single or in bands, . . 755 *Recluse* 1. 1. 784
Closed up each chink, and with fresh bands of straw 770 *Excursion* 1. 903
Bandusia. Bandusia, prattling as when long ago . 376 *Duddon* 1. 3
Bandusian. Of his Bandusian fount; or I invoke . 356 *Aquap.* 257
Bandusia's. Bandusia's praise, wild stream, should yield to thine! . . . . 3 *Ev. Wk.* 73
Or when the prattle of Bandusia's spring . . . 528 **Those breathing* 104
Bane. The bane of all that dread the devil! . . 129 *Idiot Boy* 336
The most familiar bane of life . . . . . . 191 *Seq. Beggars* 20
"Thou Enemy, my bane and blight! . . . . 406 *White Doe* 924
Her bane, her vital energies recruit. . . . . 431 *Ecc. Sonn.* 2. 10. 8
Plague from this union spread, whose subtle bane 775 *Excursion* 2. 243
For Mutability is Nature's bane; . . . . . 792 *Excursion* 3. 458
For England's bane.—When soothing darkness spreads . . . . 876 *Excursion* 8. 156
Into an instrument of deadly bane . . . . . 878 *Excursion* 8. 258
Baneful. That rules o'er Britain like a baneful star, 283 **Proud were* 5
This baneful diligence:—at early morn . . . 840 *Excursion* 6. 168
Bangor's. The sword from Bangor's walls, and guard the store . . . . 421 *Ecc. Sonn.* 1. 12. 6
Banish. Banish the thought, crush it, and be at peace. . . . . 69 *Bord.* 1750
To banish listlessness and irksome care; . . . 108 *Indolence* 51
And banish melancholy . . . . 221 *Triad* 63
Sad thought, which I would banish, ... 302 *Yarrow V.* 84
"Oh, banish far such wisdom as condemns . . 878 *Excursion* 8. 297
Banished. Of banished bliss, by fancy loved too well. 17 *Desc. Sk.* 400
Though martial songs have banished songs of love, 21 *Desc. Sk.* 614
Banished that dismal thought; and now the wind 27 *Guilt* 191
Banished from human intercourse, exist . . . 66 *Bord.* 1577

Banished—*continued.*
No more—the guilt is banished, ... 330 *Ode: Thanks.* 127
Banished, nor ever, haply, be restored . . . . 509 *F. Stone* 85
Book-learning and books should be banished the land: . . . . 571 *Avarice* 6
Darkness is banished from the realms of death, . 865 *Excursion* 7. 529
Banishment. Slackening the pains of ruthless banishment . . . . 273 **When Philoctetes* 7
As in a dear and chosen banishment, ... 275 **Chatsworth! thy* 6
And, the main fear once doomed to banishment, . 519 *Pun. Death* 8. 6
To summon back from lonesome banishment, . 634 *Prelude* 1. 163
Fell Human-kind—to banishment condemned . 811 *Excursion* 4. 647
And from long banishment recall Saint Giles, . 815 *Excursion* 4. 911
Bank. *See* **Cowslip-bank, Faro-bank.**
That on the noon-day bank of leisure lie. . . . 19 *Desc. Sk.* 507
On this green bank. Idonea, you are silent, . . 39 *Bord.* 131
They followed from the snowy bank . . . . 83 *Lucy Gray* 53
Leapt from this steep bank to follow . . . . 93 *Westmoreland Girl* 3
Though Christian rites be wanting! From what bank . . . . 387 *Roslin* 8
Upon a primrose bank, her throne . . . . . 413 *White Doe* 1583
Beside her, on some sunny bank! . . . . . 415 *White Doe* 1735
On a green bank a creature stood forlorn . . . 523 *Epist. Beaumont* 122
Meanwhile the stream, whose bank I sate upon, . 558 *Cuck. and Night.* 81
Beneath the trees, or on a grassy bank . . . 569 *Cumb. Beg.* 193
Sparkling from out a copse-clad bank that rose . 705 *Prelude* 8. 409
When on its sunny bank the primrose flower . . 768 *Excursion* 1. 815
On the stream's bank, and everywhere, appeared . 823 *Excursion* 5. 87
"As on a sunny bank, a tender lamb . . . . 850 *Excursion* 6. 787
Of a green hill or bank of rugged stream. . . . 876 *Excursion* 8. 104
A twofold image; on a grassy bank . . . . 890 *Excursion* 9. 440
At noon, the bank and hedgerows all the way . S. 3. 417 **Sweet was* 2
When every field and bank and brae . . . . S. 3. 431 **The Scottish* 27
To either bank, nor could he summon up . . . K.8. 229 **I will* 154
Devoured with keenness ere to grove or bank . K.8. 245 *Recluse* 1.1.333
Banked. And banked with woody risings; but the Plain . . . . 702 *Prelude* 8. 192
Banks. Or seek at eve the banks of Tusa's stream, 13 *Desc. Sk.* 156
And banks of ragged earth; beneath the shade . 34 *Guilt* 539
From the Great Gavel, down by Leeza's banks, . 100 *Brothers* 310
Our pathway led us on to Rotha's banks; . . 147 *Joanna* 41
Along the banks of Rydal Mere . . . . . 174 *Waggoner* 1. 30
And all their fellow banks and braes, ... 175 *Waggoner* 1. 141
Upon the banks of Windermere; . . . . . 179 *Waggoner* 3. 121
And, coming to the Banks of Tone, ... 194 *Ruth* 214
For thou art with me here upon the banks . . 207 *Tintern* 114
That on the banks of this delightful stream . . 207 *Tintern* 150
Along the river's winding banks . . . . . 240 *P. B.* 326
On Deva's banks, ye have abode so long; . . . 272 *Lady E. B.* 12
Had trod the banks of Clyde, and Tay, . . . 292 *Yarrow Unv.* 3
On Yarrow's banks let herons feed, ... 292 *Yarrow Unv.* 13
Which, gathering round, did on the banks . . 297 *Highland Boy* 223
Along thy banks, at dead of night . . . . . 300 *Cora Linn* 19
Who rises on the banks of Seine, ... 311 **Who rises* 1
On rampart, and the banks of all her streams. . 318 **Ah! where* 14
That tunes on Duddon's banks her slender voice. 377 *Duddon* 7. 14
Along the banks of crystal Wharf, ... 396 *White Doe* 6
Marching down the banks of Were. . . . . 402 *White Doe* 602
A strong Hold on the banks of Tees; . . . . 405 *White Doe* 798
Of a HOLY RIVER, on whose banks are found . . 418 *Ecc. Sonn.* 1. 1. 10
This Valdo brooks not. On the banks of Rhone . 431 *Ecc. Sonn.* 2. 11. 9
Decks, on thy sinuous banks, her thousand thrones, 464 **Greta, what* 10
Dreams on the banks, and to the river talks. . . 477 *Nunnery* 12
Ere on its banks the few grey cabins rose . . . 524 *Epist. Beaumont* 168
And the skill which he learned on the banks of the Tyne, ... 571 *Avarice* 2
On Tiber's banks my youth was dedicate . . . 573 *Chiabrera* 3. 5
Of Lybia; and not seldom, on the banks . . . 575 *Chiabrera* 6. 6
When last along its banks I wandered, . . . 586 *Hogg* 5
To people the steep rocks and river banks, . . 635 *Prelude* 1. 218
And all the shadowy banks on either side . . . 639 *Prelude* 1. 454
The leaves were fading when to Esthwaite's banks 675 *Prelude* 6. 1
A gift then first bestowed. The varied banks . 678 *Prelude* 6. 203
Lay a few steps, and then along its banks; . . 683 *Prelude* 6. 583
Long springs and tepid winters, on the banks . 701 *Prelude* 8. 174
Thy banks, Cephisus, he again hath trod, . . . 812 *Excursion* 4. 749
By beds and banks Arcadian of gay flowers . . 881 *Excursion* 8. 469
Banner. Till the last banner of their long array 6 *Ev. Wk.* 208
Thy three-striped banner fluctuate on the breeze; 21 *Desc. Sk.* 613
Fresh as a banner bright, unfurled . . . . . 194 *Ruth* 170
"They came with banner, spear, and shield; . . 204 *Brougham* 24
His banner in accursed league with France, . . 313 *Prophecy* 13
The banner of our joy we will erect, ... 332 *Ode: Thanks.* 222
A Banner, fashioned to fulfil . . . . . . 400 *White Doe* 352
For on this Banner had her hand . . . . . 400 *White Doe* 354
And that same Banner, on whose breast . . . 400 *White Doe* 374
That Banner, waiting for the Call, ... 400 *White Doe* 378
The Banner touch not, stay your hand, . . . 400 *White Doe* 393
As on the banner which stood near . . . . 400 *White Doe* 402
As that unhallowed Banner grew . . . . . 401 *White Doe* 501
He took the Banner, and unfurled . . . . . 403 *White Doe* 658
Who saw the Banner reared on high . . . . 403 *White Doe* 682
Hath watched the Banner from afar, ... 404 *White Doe* 758
This Banner raised with joyful pride, ... 405 *White Doe* 846
This night,—the Banner shall be planted!" . . 408 *White Doe* 1140
This Banner (for such vow I made) . . . . 410 *White Doe* 1275
The Banner strive thou to regain; . . . . . 410 *White Doe* 1288
And, with that rueful Banner borne . . . . 410 *White Doe* 1325

Bare—*continued.*
" A basket on her head she bare ; . . . . . 487 **We walked* 45
No cliff so bare but on its steeps . . . . 507 *May* 43
From this bare eminence thereon have cast . . 517 *Pun. Death* 1. 12
By deeds the blackest purpose to lay bare— . . 518 *Pun. Death* 4. 3
Of this unfinished house—a Fortress bare, . . 521 *Epist. Beaumont* 22
Cheerful alike if bare of flowers as now, . . 530 *Poor Robin* 27
This child did him beseech on his bare knees. . 553 *Prioress* 78
To the next Abbey him they bare away ; . . . 555 *Prioress* 173
Along a bare and open valley, ... 586 *Hogg* 3
Look round her when the heavens are bare, . . 587 *Immortality* 13
Bare steeps, where Desolation stalks, afraid, . . 606 *Desc.Sk.Quarto* 251
Or summer hamlet, flat and bare, on high . . . 610 *Desc.Sk.Quarto* 428
Nor Hunger forc'd the herds from pastures bare . 611 *Desc.Sk.Quarto* 482
Where needle peaks of granite shooting bare . . 612 *Desc.Sk.Quarto* 558
From his bare nest amid the storms of heaven . 613 *Desc.Sk.Quarto* 618
Forc'd from my native mountains bleak and bare ; 615 *Desc.Sk.Quarto* 714
To the bare earth dropped with a startling sound. 633 *Prelude* 1. 85
Was crossed, a bare ridge clomb, upon whose top 658 *Prelude* 4. 3
Old Ocean, in his bed left singed and bare, . . 666 *Prelude* 5. 33
Exposed on the bare fell, were scattered love, . 678 *Prelude* 6. 235
From a bare ridge we also first beheld . . . . 683 *Prelude* 6. 524
Of daylight, the bare thought of where I was . . 694 *Prelude* 7. 453
(The Artificer was to the elbow bare, ... 696 *Prelude* 7. 613
Bare hills and valleys, full of caverns, rocks, . . 708 *Prelude* 8. 635
Then, reascending the bare common, saw . . . 738 *Prelude* 12. 248
Trackless and smooth, or paced the bare white roads 744 *Prelude* 13. 316
Across a bare wide Common I was toiling . . . 756 *Excursion* 1. 21
The Mother followed :—miserably bare . . . 774 *Excursion* 2. 201
And one bare dwelling ; one abode, no more ! . 776 *Excursion* 2. 339
Whence the bare road descended rapidly . . . 823 *Excursion* 5. 65
And the owl's prey ; from these bare haunts, to which . . . . 843 *Excursion* 6. 328
To the bare rock, on frozen Caucasus ; . . . . 846 *Excursion* 6. 540
Through bare enclosures stretches, 'till its line . 858 *Excursion* 7. 44
By an unthought-of patron. Bleak and bare . . 859 *Excursion* 7. 136
" ' All gone, all vanished ! he deprived and bare, . 861 *Excursion* 7. 263
Of that tall pine, the shadow of whose bare . . 863 *Excursion* 7. 396
Of some bare hill, with wonder kenned from far. . 876 *Excursion* 8. 116
Their slender ditties when the trees are bare. . . 881 *Excursion* 8. 483
As of a final Eminence ; though bare . . . . 885 *Excursion* 9. 52
Where the bare columns of those lofty firs, . . 891 *Excursion* 9. 499
And mountains bare, or clothed with ancient woods, 891 *Excursion* 9. 506
Lie loose on the bare turf, some half-o'ergrown . K.8. 226 **I will* 65
And those bare rocks, if you had asked if he . . K.8. 230 **I will* 200
In the bare twigs, each little budding place . . K.8. 252 *Recluse* 1.1.565
Now would you be content with bare release . . L.1. 97 *Juvenal* 3. 69
Bared. And the sharp wind his head he oft hath bared ; . . . . 25 *Guilt* 47
Bare-headed. Bare-headed, and all decently attired ! 777 *Excursion* 2. 392
Barely. What if our numbers barely could defy . 309 **What if* 1
Hath hitherto been barely touched upon, . . . 750 *Prelude* 14. 316
One that hath barely learned to shape a smile, . 826 *Excursion* 5. 263
Bareness. Yet would I not be of such wintry bareness . . . . 793 *Excursion* 3. 491
Bares. This Sea that bares her bosom to the moon ; 259 **The world is* 5
Barge. Coasts, with industrious oar, the charcoal barge. . . . . 4 *Ev. Wk.* 127
And lures from bay to bay the vocal barge. . . 13 *Desc. Sk.* 140
Or float with music in the festal barge ; . . . 273 **While Anna's* 3
So have I done ; as trusty as thy barge . . . 371 *Eg. Maid* 171
While his free Barge skims the smooth flood along, 426 *Ecc. Sonn.* 1. 30. 10
His pinnace, a small vagrant barge, uppiled . . 547 **Rude is* 18
And winds between thine isles the vocal barge. . 605 *Desc.Sk.Quarto* 161
Bark. Their watch-dog ne'er his angry bark forgoes, 15 *Desc. Sk.* 242
The bark of dogs, the heifer's tinkling bell, . . 18 *Desc. Sk.* 419
To charm the surly house-dog's faithful bark, . 32 *Guilt* 417
In his bark the polar sea ; . . . . 161 **Pleasures newly* 52
Now—like a tempest-shattered bark, ... 242 *P. B.* 556
Why have I crowded this small bark with you . 252 **Her only* 10
And showed the Bark upon the glassy flood . . 252 *Picture* 7
Is with me at thy farewell, joyous Bark ! . . . 258 **Where lies the Land* 14
Guide our Bark among the waves ; . . . . . 336 **Jesu ! bless* 19
In a frail bark urged by two slender oars . . . 354 *Aquap.* 120
Shun, like a shattered bark, the storm, and flee . 366 **Eternal Lord* 3
" On Christian service this frail Bark . . . 370 *Eg. Maid* 73
Whom Obloquy pursues with hideous bark : . . 432 *Ecc. Sonn.* 2. 14. 8
Light as a buoyant bark from wave to wave, . . 438 *Ecc. Sonn.* 2. 39. 2
Urge the slow bark along Calabrian shores ; . . 454 *Sea-side* 26
That no adventurer's bark had power to gain . 468 **Bold words* 3
For many a voyage made in her swift bark, . . 475 **Homeward we* 7
At our approach, a jealous watch-dog's bark, . . 525 *Epist. Beaumont* 233
Till pitying Saints conduct her bark . . . . 544 *Russ. Fug.* 235
To the confiding Bark, untrue ; . . . . . . 550 *Hermit's Cell* 5. 6
The bark of dogs, the drowsy tinkling bell, . . 611 *Desc.Sk.Quarto* 508
There in her mooring-place I left my bark,— . 638 *Prelude* 1. 388
His bark to land upon the wished-for shore, . . 656 *Prelude* 3. 487
The doleful sequel. But our little bark . . . 717 *Prelude* 9. 559
The bark was nibbled round by truant sheep. . 769 *Excursion* 1. 842
And arbitrary rule. But launch thy bark . . 844 *Excursion* 6. 434
And thus the bark, meandering with the shore, . 892 *Excursion* 9. 566
Like a frail Bark, weary I turn to Thee,— . . K.8. 266 **Rid of* 3
Barking. The dog, loud barking, 'mid the glittering rocks, ... 5 *Ev. Wk.* 184
Nor can it be a barking fox, ... 243 *P. B.* 618
Of barking dogs, and bleatings from strange fear. 382 *Duddon* 23. 8
A barking sound the Shepherd hears, ... 491 *Fidelity* 1
Weary of barking at him. Boys and girls, . . 567 *Cumb. Beg.* 63
That, barking busy 'mid the glittering rocks, . . 594 *Ev.Wk. Quarto* 167
Barking-fit. The stranger till its barking-fit I checked ; 28 *Guilt* 224
Barkings. Thy hungry barkings to the hymn . . 235 *Power of Sound* 201
His coiled-up prey with barkings turbulent. . . 746 *Prelude* 14. 24
Barks. Low barks the fox : by Havoc rouz'd the bear, ... 606 *Desc.Sk.Quarto* 231
Barley. And once, behind a rick of barley, . . . 537 *Goody Blake* 73
Barn. *See* **Cottage-barn.**
In barn uplighted ; and companions boon, . . 32 *Guilt* 411
A Barn her *winter* bed supplies ; . . . . . 194 *Ruth* 223
Clustering, with barn and byre, and spouting mill ! 379 *Duddon* 13. 3
When at a country-playhouse, some rude barn . 694 *Prelude* 7. 449
Barnard's. Are now besieging Barnard's Towers,— 408 *White Doe* 1116
Barns. Of vagrant poverty ; from rifted barns . . 843 *Excursion* 6. 326
Baron. The Baron Herbert perish in the waves . 38 *Bord.* 76
The Baron Herbert. Mercy, the Baron Herbert ! 43 *Bord.* 333
With Henry, our good King ;—the Baron might . 43 *Bord.* 348
You have been insolent. And there's the Baron, ... 46 *Bord.* 490
Of this mock Father's guilt. The Baron Herbert . . . . 49 *Bord.* 664
The Baron Herbert, who, as was supposed, . . 49 *Bord.* 681
To waken our stray Baron. Were there not . . 51 *Bord.* 766
To have heard your voice. Your couch, I fear, good Baron, ... 53 *Bord.* 859
Herbert ! since you will have it, Baron Herbert ; 55 *Bord.* 975
Good Baron, have you ever practised tillage ? . 60 *Bord.* 1277
Baronial. Baronial halls the opprobrious insult feel ; 428 *Ecc. Sonn.* 1. 37. 13
With the baronial castle's sterner mien ; . . . 477 **Lowther ! in* 3
Baronial court or royal ; cheered with gifts . . 771 *Excursion* 2. 3
Baronies. The genuine owners of such Lands and Baronies . . . . 56 *Bord.* 1025
Barons. Fraternity of Barons old ; . . . . . 405 *White Doe* 820
Came Barons bold, with store of gold, ... 478 *Somnamb.* 21
Barons'. Dissolved the Barons' League, and sent abroad . . . . 56 *Bord.* 1023
Barony. The tale of this his quondam Barony . . 39 *Bord.* 79
He shall be seated in his Barony, ... 54 *Bord.* 906
Now, for a word about your Barony : . . . . 62 *Bord.* 1347
Barred. " Barred every comfort labour could procure, 35 *Guilt* 577
Lo ! ships, from seas by nature barred, . . . 391 *Highland Broach* 69
All further progress here was barred ;—And who, 787 *Excursion* 3. 43
Barren. What if the bee love not these barren boughs? 22 *Yew-tree* 4
And on these barren rocks, with fern and heath, . 23 *Yew-tree* 28
That haunt some barren island of the north, . . 47 *Bord.* 559
The barren Moor, hangs from a beetling rock . . 49 *Bord.* 658
Violets, a barren kind, ... 79 *Foresight* 19
My unassisted heart is barren clay, ... 257 **The prayers* 3
To barren heath, bleak moor, and quaking fen, . 298 *Brownie's Cell* 1
They shrunk, insane ambition's barren goal— . 321 **Humanity, delighting* 16
A barren and ungrateful soil. . . . . . . 375 **The Minstrels* 24
The encircling turf into a barren clod ; . . . 465 **The cattle* 3
Who with the ploughshare clove the barren moors, 468 *St. Bees* 136
Close up those barren leaves ; . . . . . . 482 *Tables Turned* 30
Long, barren silence, square with my desire ; . . 488 *Pers. Talk* 10
And mountain-tops, a barren ridge we scale ; . . 524 *Epist. Beaumont* 224
Where, from the barren wall's unshelter'd end, . 592 *Ev. Wk. Quarto* 59
And though an aching and a barren sense . . . 658 *Prelude* 3. 624
Is law for all, and of that barren pride . . . 717 *Prelude* 9. 503
Or barren intermeddling subtleties, ... 736 *Prelude* 12. 155
By reason, barren of all future good. . . . . 765 *Excursion* 1. 631
Barren the tablet, yet thereon appeared . . . 787 *Excursion* 3. 61
The obstreperous city ; on the barren seas . . 806 *Excursion* 4. 369
From peace like exiles on some barren rock, . . 846 *Excursion* 6. 534
He sees the barren wilderness erased, ... 876 *Excursion* 8. 129
These barren rocks, your stern inheritance ; . . 895 *Excursion* 9. 743
Barrenness. With stony barrenness, a shining speck 832 *Excursion* 5. 672
Barricadoed. Of sorrow, barricadoed evermore . 755 *Recluse* 1. 1. 832
Barrier. This flimsy barrier you have overleaped. . 66 *Bord.* 1585
Tracing the lofty barrier with my eye . . . . 147 *Joanna* 44
Come, blessed barrier between day and day, . . 254 **A flock* 13
Some barrier with which Nature, from the birth . 284 *Departure* 17
I shrunk ; for verily the barrier flood . . . . 306 **Inland, within* 5
The barrier Rhine hath flashed, through battle-smoke, ... 322 *Germans* 9
It found no barrier on the ridge . . . . . 327 *Ode 1815* 21
Caught the far-winding barrier Alps among. . . 367 **As indignation* 11
But that enormous barrier holds it fast. . . . 491 *Fidelity* 33
I shuddered, for a barrier seemed at once . . . 693 *Prelude* 7. 388
Diffused adown that barrier of steep rock, . . . 787 *Excursion* 3. 70
Once to the verge of yon steep barrier came . . K.8. 236 *Recluse* 1. 1. 1
Barriers. These mighty barriers, and the gulf between ; . . . . 265 **Hail, Twilight* 12
Against all barriers which his labour meets . . 520 *Pun. Death* 14. 7
The barriers disregarding that surround . . . 807 *Excursion* 4. 390
Who seems, by these stupendous barriers cast . 844 *Excursion* 6. 393
And as these lofty barriers break the force . . K.8. 247 *Recluse* 1.1. 374
Barrow. *See* **Wheel-barrow.**
The Lass with her barrow wheels hither her store ;— 188 *Music* 22
Content, if foss, and barrow, and the girth . . 421 *Ecc. Sonn.* 1. 11. 13
Barrows. The barrows glistered bright with drops of rain, ... 30 *Guilt* 327
Bars. *See* **Prison-bars.**
So many bars between his present state . . . 122 *V. and J.* 58
Chanter by heaven attracted, whom no bars . . 154 *Morn. Ex.* 55
But He hath overleaped the eternal bars ; . . . 213 *Dion* 53
Clouds, lingering yet, extend in solid bars . . . 313 **Clouds, lingering* 1
True, as inexorable winds, or bars . . . . . 586 *Ch. Lamb* 105
Why may not millions be ? What bars are thrown 741 *Prelude* 13. 89
That bars the traveller's road, she often stood, . 769 *Excursion* 1. 895

Bays—*continued.*
The sands of Westmoreland, the creeks and bays . 640 *Prelude* 1. 567
Lake, islands, promontories, gleaming bays, . . 658 *Prelude* 4. 8
Or ride at anchor in her sounds and bays ; . . 876 *Excursion* 8. 138
Be, *omitted.*
Beach. *See* **Beech, Sea-beach.**
Far o'er the secret water dark with beach, . . 607 *Desc.Sk.Quarto* 288
On Grasmere's beach, than Naiad by the side . 149 **A narrow* 36
Her Hero slain upon the beach of Troy ? . . . 209 *Laod.* 15
Driving some vessel toward a dangerous beach— . 336 *Staub-bach* 6
Well—let him pace this noted beach once more, . 349 *Boulogne* 5
Traced on the beach, his work the Sorcerer urges ; . 369 *Eg. Maid* 32
But a carved Lotus cast upon the beach . . . 371 *Eg. Maid* 125
Are safely borne, landed upon the beach, . . . 541 *Grace Darl.* 81
Along the beach of this small isle and thought . 551 **If thou in* 20
From the same beach one ocean to explore . . 586 *Ch. Lamb* 103
Over the shadowy lake, and to the beach . . . 644 *Prelude* 2. 166
On sea-shells that bestrew the sandy beach, . . 696 *Prelude* 7. 592
Upon the beach, rolls back into the sea. . . 823 *Excursion* 5. 76
Where is it now ?—Deserted on the beach— . . 892 *Excursion* 9. 551
Beacon. I took it for the blaze of Cheviot Beacon : 50 *Bord.* 742
Light up this beacon. You shall be obeyed. . . 64 *Bord.* 1465
As the first flash of beacon light ; . . . . . 215 *Enterprise* 9
Till, but the lonely beacon all is fled, ... 595 *Ev. Wk. Quarto* 189
And o'er the Border Beacon, and the waste . . 678 *Prelude* 6. 233
The beacon on the summit, and, more near, . . 738 *Prelude* 12. 250
The beacon crowning the lone eminence, . . . 738 *Prelude* 12. 259
And on the melancholy beacon, fell . . . . 738 *Prelude* 12. 265
Beacon's. Of splendour—save the beacon's spiry head . . . . 6 *Ev. Wk.* 210
Red on the hills her beacon's far-seen blaze ; . . 22 *Desc. Sk.* 639
When not a twinkling star or beacon's light . . 459 **Wanderer! that* 15
Red on his hills his beacon's comet blaze ; . . 616 *Desc.Sk.Quarto* 775
Beacons. *See* **Love-beacons.**
Bead-drops. Till thou with crystal bead-drops didst encrust . . . . S. 3. 434 **The doubt* 53
Bead-roll. Its bead-roll of midnight, ... 176 *Waggoner* 2. 9
A bead-roll, in his hand a claspèd book, . . . 423 *Ecc. Sonn.* 1. 21. 2
Beads. Ere with cold beads of midnight dew . . 109 **Ere with* 1
Like beads of glossy jet her eyes ; . . . . . 165 *Parrot* 5
No hermit with his beads and glass ? . . . . 240 *P. B.* 377
Whose memory, spotless as the crystal beads . . 330 *Ode : Thanks.* 64
The solace beads and masses yield, ... 478 *Somnamb.* 53
Hopes what are they ?—Beads of morning . . 549 *Hermit's Cell* 1. 1
The whole world over, tight as beads of dew . . 670 *Prelude* 5. 321
Amid the untrodden desert, tells his beads, . . 862 *Excursion* 7. 303
Cased with its several beads, what myriads there . K. 8. 252 *Recluse* 1. 1. 566
Beak. The soaring eagle's curvèd beak ; . . . 227 *Vernal Ode* 120
Pounced,—and the Dove, which from its ruthless beak . . . . 274 **Wait, prithee* 13
His prominent feature like an eagle's beak ; . . 422 *Ecc. Sonn.* 1. 15. 7
Which turned an angry beak against the down . 798 *Excursion* 3. 818
Beam. Though to the vale no parting beam . . . 1 *Extract* 11
Shed from their sides, that face the sun's slant beam, 4 *Ev. Wk.* 108
And now the van reflects the solar beam ; . . . 6 *Ev. Wk.* 203
From gulf of parting clouds one friendly beam, . 26 *Guilt* 131
Together smoking in the sun's slant beam, . . 33 *Guilt* 461
On Dion's virtues, while the lunar beam . . . 212 *Dion* 8
Aloft, beneath the moon's pale beam, ... 300 *Cora Linn* 22
Whether the mighty beam, in scorn upheld, . . 311 **Who rises* 25
Thy glory meets me with the earliest beam . . 440 *Ecc. Sonn.* 3. 2. 7
Where thy deep voice could lull me ! Faint the beam . . . . 464 *Derwent* 4
Sapped by the very beam that gilds. . . . . 550 *Hermit's Cell* 2. 24
And now the van is gilt with evening's beam . . 595 *Ev.Wk. Quarto* 185
Unbreathing Justice her still beam surveys : . . 616 *Desc.Sk.Quarto* 787
She sheds her beam, and, lo ! the shades dissolve ; 618 *School Ex.* 48
If e'er thy beam, as Symrna's shepherds tell, . . 630 [?] **O Moon* 10
Their sports together in the solar beam, . . . 808 *Excursion* 4. 447
Beamed. Beamed from that gracious countenance ; 416 *White Doe* 1828
And beam'd on Britain's sons a brighter day ; . 618 *School Ex.* 36
Beaming. *See* **Far-beaming.**
Her earnest tone, and look beaming with faith, . 541 *Grace Darl.* 45
A smile sat beaming on her pensive face. . . . 618 *School Ex.* 24
And hence, a beaming Goddess with her Nymphs, 814 *Excursion* 4. 865
Eyes beaming courtesy and mild regard ; . . . 834 *Excursion* 5. 783
His beaming eye that had been raised to Heaven, . 894 *Excursion* 9. 681
Beamless. Faint types of suffering in thy beamless face. . . . . 460 **Queen of* 38
An Eagle with stretched wings, but beamless eye— 472 **The captive* 7
Beams. And they that from the zenith dart their beams, ... v **If thou indeed* 5
There, objects, by the searching beams betrayed, . 4 *Ev. Wk.* 102
Bright beams the lonely mountain-horse illume . 4 *Ev. Wk.* 132
Deep yellow beams the scattered stems illume, . 5 *Ev. Wk.* 180
And beams of evening, slipping in between, . . 14 *Desc. Sk.* 212
Shorn of its beams, insufferably white, . . . 16 *Desc. Sk.* 324
Yet when faint beams of light that ruin showed, . 27 *Guilt* 156
Is now, by beams of dawning light imprest, . . 30 *Guilt* 335
Beholds her own bright beams . . . . . . 112 **What heavenly* 6
Reflected beams of that celestial light . . . . 118 *Maternal Grief* 17
Will holy Church disperse by beams of gospel-light." 141 *Arm. Lady* 120
Smiles are beginning, like the beams of dawn, . 173 *Infant Daughter* 67
To overshade than multiply his beams . . . 219 *Haunted Tree* 3
That no to-morrow shall our beams restore ! . . 261 **I watch* 14
Of noontide suns :—and even the beams that play 262 **Mark the* 3
While beams of orient light shoot wide and high, . 282 **While beams* 1
With matchless beams. . . . . 285 *Grave of Burns* 24
When, far and wide, swift as the beams of morn . 312 **When, far* 1
Bright shines the Sun, as if his beams would wake 332 *Ode : Thanks.* 207

Beams—*continued.*
That beams from his ingenuous face, ... 342 *Ital. Itin.* 38
Nor is least pleased, we trust, when golden beams, 354 *Aquap.* 111
Than his unmitigated beams allow, ... 356 *Aquap.* 228
With those bright beams yet hid it not, must steer 359 **Those old* 8
Black as the clouds its beams dispersed, while shone, ... 438 *Ecc. Sonn.* 2. 38. 13
Empress of Night ! are gladdened by thy beams ; . 459 **Wanderer! that* 24
Spares thy mild splendour ; still those far-shot beams . . . . 460 **Queen of* 23
The old Tower's brow yellowed as with the beams 470 *Bala-Sala* 10
That orb whose beams round Saxon Alfred shone : 471 **Despond who* 11
Still on her sons the beams of mercy shine ; . . 474 **How sad* 10
In the still summer noon, while beams of light, . 496 **A little* 41
Swift as the rising sun his beams extends . . 503 *Warning* 26
How faint their portion of his vital beams ! . . 528 **Those breathing* 57
Turn a broad front full on his flattering beams : . 539 **Lady ! a* 17
With thy bright beams to guide me but one hour, 564 *Troilus* 125
Deep yellow beams the scattered boles illume, . 594 *Ev. Wk. Quarto* 163
The beams of evening, slipping soft between, . . 607 *Desc.Sk.Quarto* 267
Shorn of his beams, insufferably white, . . . 609 *Desc.Sk.Quarto* 387
Loitering, I watched the golden beams of light . 706 *Prelude* 8. 463
Determined and unmoved, with steady beams . 756 *Excursion* 1. 7
And beautified with morning's purple beams. . 773 *Excursion* 2. 96
By this dark hill protected from thy beams ! . . 773 *Excursion* 2. 112
Exclude a power to enjoy the vital beams . . 790 *Excursion* 3. 298
And round our path darted oppressive beams. . 824 *Excursion* 5. 137
His beams ; which, unexcluded in their fall, . . 830 *Excursion* 5. 542
To intercept the sun's glad beams—may ne'er . 838 *Excursion* 6. 23
This goodly Matron, shining in the beams . . 882 *Excursion* 8. 517
From under thee hath vanished, and slant beams, S. 3. 435 **The doubt* 101
Mistakes for sorrow darting beams of light . . K. 8. 238 *Recluse* 1. 1. 54
Beamy. Of beamy radiance, that imbues . . . 457 **Had this* 27
Of beamy lustre from a tower of strength ; . . 466 *St. Bees* 42
To ride the ring, or toss the beamy lance ; . . 619 *School Ex.* 58
Bear. If the sad grave of human ignorance bear . 20 *Desc. Sk.* 551
So in they bear her to the chimney seat, . . . 34 *Guilt* 568
Sir Host ! by all the love you bear to courtesy, . 42 *Bord.* 306
To bear a part in this Man's punishment, . . . 49 *Bord.* 649
That were most dear to me, and some will bear . 49 *Bord.* 651
Are still forthcoming ; some which, though they bear 65 *Bord.* 1526
Ill can I bear that look—Plead for me, Oswald ! . 66 *Bord.* 1603
A day it was when I could bear . . . . . 85 *Anecdote* 13
Such wings as, when our Saviour calls, shall bear us up to heaven." . . . . 93 *Poet's Dream* 68
Which will bear looking at. These boys—I hope 99 *Brothers* 239
A place in which he could not bear to live : . . 102 *Brothers* 426
Sabrina,—vowing that the stream should bear . 103 *Artegal* 39
Disturbs me till the sight is more than I can bear." 111 **'Tis said that some* 44
Yet bear me up—else faltering in the rear . . 112 **O dearer* 11
" What is it," said I, " that you bear, ... 119 *Sailor's Mother* 14
I bear it with me, Sir ;—he took so much delight in it." . . . . 119 *Sailor's Mother* 36
One Child did it bear, and that Child was his last. . 120 *Childless Father* 12
And bear with their transgression, when I add . 122 *V. and J.* 65
May'st bear in mind the life thy Fathers lived, . 137 *Michael* 410
And bear thy memory with me to the grave." . . 137 *Michael* 417
" Yes, kind Lady ! otherwise man could not bear . 140 *Arm. Lady* 17
Your kind's first seed did bear ; . . . . . . 156 *Oak and Broom* 42
Bear for me to my native land . . . . . . 164 **Fair Lady* 39
Their burdens do they bear ; . . . . . . 165 *Danish Boy* 20
With thine, and gave the mournful name which thou wilt ever bear. . . . . 169 *Love lies Bleeding* 24
And forced unworthy stripes to bear, ... 175 *Waggoner* 1. 122
His board with lawful joy, and bear . . . . 193 *Ruth* 113
Bear me to the heart of France, ... 205 *Brougham* 145
And, in their anguish, bear what other minds have borne ! " . . . . 213 *Dion* 89
Nor grieves—tho' doomed thro' silent night to bear 216 *Enterprise* 95
But why solicit more than sight could bear, . . 220 *Triad* 30
Bear witness ye who seldom passed . . . . . 224 **'Tis gone* 7
Might bear thee to this glen, ... 231 *Jew. Fam.* 2
Of memory ?—O that ye might stoop to bear . . 235 *Power of Sound* 172
Are delegates of harmony, and bear . . . . 235 *Power of Sound* 190
The joy was more than he could bear !— . . . 247 *P. B.* 959
Rise, Gillies, rise : the gales of youth shall bear . 260 **From the dark* 3
Since thou dost bear it,—a memorial theme . . 275 *Rotha Q.* 12
When kindred thoughts and yearnings bear . . 286 *Nith* 62
Hath Nature strung your nerves to bear . . . 286 *Sons of Burns* 13
I bear away my recompense. . . . . 288 *Highland Girl* 65
Bear witness many a pensive sigh . . . . . 292 *Rob Roy* 113
Bear witness, rueful Yarrow ! . . . . . . 302 *Yarrow V.* 40
There is a bondage worse, far worse, to bear . . 308 **There is a bondage* 1
Of Terror, bear us to the ground, and tie . . . 309 **What if* 5
Oh, bear the infant covered to his grave ! . . . 319 *Biscayan* 7
That he has power to inflict what we lack strength to bear. . . . . 319 *Spaniard* 14
Bear through the world these tidings of delight ! . 327 *Ode 1815* 10
Or through our hamlets thou wilt bear . . . 341 *Ital. Itin.* 11
Bear to the glacier band—those Shapes aloft descried. . . . . 347 *Processions* 63
And yon resplendent Church are proud to bear. . 360 **Long has* 14
Will bear me on from wave to wave, ... 370 *Eg. Maid* 105
Bear with me, Brother ! quench the thought . . 376 **The Minstrels* 61
Would lodge her, and the cherished burden bear . 382 *Duddon* 25. 7
Bear witness, Ye, whose thoughts that day . . 386 *Yarrow Rev.* 97
Yet is it one that other rivulets bear . . . . 392 *Avon* 2
Did meekly bear the pang unmerited ; . . . . 395 *White Doe : Ded* 12
The five dear wounds our Lord did bear ; . . . 400 *White Doe* 357
To Durham first their course they bear ; . . . 404 *White Doe* 711

Beat. *See* **Sea-beat.**
For then the inexperienced heart would beat . . 2 *Ev. Wk.* 23
Beat round to clear the streets of want and pain. 29 *Guilt* 274
Beat hard upon my head—and yet I saw . . . 45 *Bord.* 424
You could not hear, for the foam beat the rocks . 51 *Bord.* 746
The least of which would beat out a man's brains; 56 *Bord.* 1008
Her fires, that like mysterious pulses beat . . 123 *V. and J.* 98
As ever tempest beat ! . . . . 156 *Oak and Broom* 12
When cross-winds on her quarter beat ; . . . 179 *Waggoner* 3. 87
No fears to beat away—no strife to heal— . . 211 *Laod.* 99
Nor let thy genuine impulse fail to beat . . . 217 *Enterprise* 123
While Fauns and Satyrs beat the ground . . . 234 *Power of Sound* 150
Beat back the roaring storm—but how subdued . 279 *'Tis he 2
And heard the water beat the shore . . . . 295 *Highland Boy* 49
Beat like the heart of Man : songs, garlands, mirth, 304 **Jones ! as* 7
And greet your sons ! drums beat and trumpets blow ! . . . . 310 *Anticip.* 7
Should beat too strongly, both may be betrayed. . 378 *Duddon* 10. 12
The One for whom my heart shall ever beat . . 382 *Duddon* 25. 4
Some island which the wild waves beat— . . . 413 *White Doe* 1560
Of learning, where thou heard'st the billows beat . 424 *Ecc. Sonn.* 1. 23. 7
So high their hearts would beat ; . . . . . 544 *Russ. Fug.* 220
Beat his grey locks against his withered face. . . 568 *Cumb. Beg.* 176
Long time his pulse hath ceased to beat ; . . . 578 **I come* 57
For then, ev'n then, the little heart would beat . 592 *Ev. Wk. Quarto* 33
Who faint, and beat by summer's breathless ray, . 596 *Ev. Wk. Quarto* 243
Dim were my swimming eyes—my pulse beat slow, 619 **She wept* 3
We beat with thundering hoofs the level sand. . 644 *Prelude* 2. 137
Of contemplation almost failed to beat. . . . 654 *Prelude* 3. 331
Can beat never will I forget thy name. . . . 659 *Prelude* 4. 32
Roar, and the rain beat hard ; where I so oft . 659 *Prelude* 4. 86
Coarse manners, vulgar passions, that beat in . 704 *Prelude* 8. 320
Beat high, and filled the fancy with fair forms, . 712 *Prelude* 9. 207
Shall beat no more. Thou, also, there may'st read, 717 *Prelude* 9. 568
Beat against Albion's shore, since ear of mine . 721 *Prelude* 10. 239
Through months, through years, long after the last beat . . . . 724 *Prelude* 10. 399
We beat with thundering hoofs the level sand. . 727 *Prelude* 10. 603
Beat on my roof, or, haply, at noon-day, . . . 739 *Prelude* 12. 328
That made her heart beat quick. You see that path, ... 769 *Excursion* 1. 882
A stirring foot, a head which beat at nights . . 860 *Excursion* 7. 211
Or as the Norman Curfew's regular beat, . . . K. 8. 246 *Recluse* 1. 1. 339
And beat the passive water with their wings. . . K. 8. 251 *Recluse* 1. 1. 551

Beaten. *See* **Storm-beaten, Weather-beaten.**
Trotting alone along the beaten road, ... 44 *Bord.* 411
She finds familiar names, a beaten way . . . 258 **Where lies the Land* 7
She gave, if Faith might tread the beaten ways . 322 **By Moscow* 8
At this he from the beaten road . . . . . 412 *White Doe* 1476
And lowly huts, near beaten ways, ... 508 *May* 85
And shall be beaten three times in an hour, . . 554 *Prioress* 91
Black drizzling craggs, that beaten by the din, . 606 *Desc. Sk. Quarto* 249
Of lighthouse, beaten by Atlantic waves ; . . . 664 *Prelude* 4. 365
Then paced the beaten downward way that led . 683 *Prelude* 6. 568
When the world travels in a beaten road, . . . 728 *Prelude* 11. 97
To quit the beaten track of life, and soar . . . 789 *Excursion* 3. 213
Beaten by lonely billows, hear the songs . . . 890 *Excursion* 9. 388

Beatific. Visions with all but beatific light . . . 231 *Clouds* 86
The beatific crown— . . . . 343 *Eclipse* 48

Beating. Thy heart these two weeks has been beating fast. . . . . 137 *Michael* 397
Yet still the bosom beating high, ... 216 *Enterprise* 47
Thus beating up against the wind. . . . . . 288 *Highland Girl* 46
Protect from beating sunbeams, and the sweep . 395 *White Doe : Ded.* 46
To plague her beating heart ; and there is one . 439 *Ecc. Sonn.* 2. 42. 2
—*There* swims, of blazing sun and beating shower . 527 **Those breathing* 13
Beating on one of those disastrous isles— . . . 540 *Grace Darl.* 31
Those steadfast eyes, that beating breasts inspire . 604 *Desc. Sk. Quarto* 150
Feverish with weary joints and beating minds. . 642 *Prelude* 2. 18
And blind Authority beating with his staff . . 657 *Prelude* 3. 605
Admired and envied. Oh ! the beating heart, . 694 *Prelude* 7. 493
The fluttering nerves composed ; the beating heart 841 *Excursion* 6. 194
This vestige, neither force of beating rain, . . 842 *Excursion* 6. 250

Beatings. Have hung upon the beatings of my heart— . . . . 206 *Tintern* 54
A grandeur in the beatings of the heart. . . . 638 *Prelude* 1. 414

Beatitude. Strong in herself and in beatitude . . 684 *Prelude* 6. 613
Therefore to serve was high beatitude ; . . . 724 *Prelude* 10. 433
Of Spirits in beatitude : my heart . . . . . 784 *Excursion* 2. 874
With joy exalted to beatitude ; . . . . . . 803 *Excursion* 4. 119

Beats. Wisdom, if Justice speak the word, beats down . . . . 57 *Bord.* 1077
The storm beats hard—Mercy for poor or rich, . 71 *Bord.* 1882
Returning from their Feast—my heart beats so— 71 *Bord.* 1889
Till heart with heart in concord beats, ... 111 **Let other* 11
And requiems answered by the pulse that beats . 232 *Power of Sound* 15
Beats with a fancy running high, ... 344 **How blest* 3
Beats frequent on thy satiate ear, ... 376 **The Minstrels* 74
Nine beats distinctly to each other bound . . . 453 **Calm is the* 12
Where moans the blast, or beats the wave, . . 472 *Ossian* 26
And, serving Truth, the heart more strongly beats 520 *Pun. Death* 14. 6
That with intrusive restlessness beats off . . . 635 *Prelude* 1. 248
Or beats the gladsome air ; o'er all that glides . 648 *Prelude* 2. 407
Beats to the heroic song of ancient days ; . . . 813 *Excursion* 4. 832

Beaumont. Beaumont ! it was thy wish that I should rear . . . . 251 *Appleth.* 1
And should these slacken, honoured BEAUMONT ! still 251 *Appleth.* 9
Then haply, Beaumont ! words in current clear . 522 *Epist. Beaumont* 56
Ah, Beaumont ! when an opening in the road . 524 *Epist. Beaumont* 171

Beaumont—*continued.*
Yet, Beaumont, thou wilt not, I trust, reprove . 525 *Epist. Beaumont* 274
Did Francis Beaumont sport, an eager child ; . 547 **Beneath yon* 10
Then, Beaumont, Friend ! who would have been the Friend, ... 579 *Peele Castle* 41
Ill-worthy, Beaumont ! were the grief . . . . 582 **O for a* 10
Such offering BEAUMONT dreaded and forbade, . 583 **With copious* 5

Beaumont's. Saved from the sordid axe by Beaumont's care, ... 358 *Pine : Rome* 7
Planted by Beaumont's and by Wordsworth's hands. . . . . 546 **The embowering* 4

Beaupuy. Of whom I speak. So BEAUPUY (let the name . . . . 715 *Prelude* 9. 419

Beauteous. The beauty, still more beauteous ! Nor, that time, ... 23 *Yew-tree* 37
An object beauteous to behold ; . . . . . 117 *Affl. Marg.* 16
The beauteous forms of nature wrought, . . . 193 *Ruth* 134
A beauteous heap, a hill of moss, ... 198 *Thorn* 36
So fresh in all its beauteous dyes, ... 198 *Thorn* 51
This pond, and beauteous hill of moss, . . . 198 *Thorn* 57
The Hermit sits alone. These beauteous forms, . 206 *Tintern* 22
Of all that is most beauteous—imaged there . . 211 *Laod.* 103
As light and beauteous as a squirrel, ... 246 *P. B.* 889
As beauteous and as wild ! . . . . 246 *P. B.* 890
It is a beauteous evening, calm and free, . . . 258 **It is a* 1
Thus died the beauteous Ellen, ... 287 *Ellen Irwin* 34
Wild Relique ! beauteous as the chosen spot . . 299 *Brownie's Cell* 91
And beauteous as the silver moon . . . . . 396 *White Doe* 60
Mis-shapes the beauteous forms of things :— . . 481 *Tables Turned* 27
Till of the beauteous court, at length, a voice . 620 *Birth of Love* 25
Sees many beauteous sights—weeds, fishes, flowers, 662 *Prelude* 4. 261
At last, the dead man, 'mid that beauteous scene . 672 *Prelude* 5. 448
Solemn or gay : whether some beauteous dame . 693 *Prelude* 7. 413
A silent station in this beauteous world. . . . 740 *Prelude* 13. 47
The beauteous girl, whose cheek was flushed with joy. . . . . 890 *Excursion* 9. 428

Beauteously. Amid his fellows beauteously revealed 313 **Clouds, lingering* 6

Beauties. Thy open beauties, or thy lone retreats ; 12 *Desc. Sk.* 108
Of Beauties yet unborn—the rustic Lodge . . 547 **Rude is* 10
Soon fades her cheek, her blushing beauties fly, . 619 *School Ex.* 97
Loch Lomond's beauties to discuss, ... S. 3. 438 **My Lord* 12

Beautified. Had beautified Elysium ! But these chains . . . . 381 *Duddon* 20. 6
And there, by fresh hopes beautified, ... 401 *White Doe* 481
Enriched and beautified his studious mind : . . 576 *Chiabrera* 9. 10
Hath beautified that flower ; already shades . . 646 *Prelude* 2. 248
Of morning beautified, or purple eve ; . . . . 678 *Prelude* 6. 219
And Nature and her objects beautified . . . 704 *Prelude* 8. 374
And beautified with morning's purple beams. . . 773 *Excursion* 2. 96

Beautifies. That beautifies the fairest shore, . . 233 *Power of Sound* 55
Or beautifies, like changes undergoes, ... S. 3. 434 **The doubt* 63

Beautiful. A face (no cherub's face more beautiful) 50 *Bord.* 717
As beautiful, and gentle and benign, ... 57 *Bord.* 1105
Studded with apples, a beautiful show ! . . . 80 †*Address : Child* 27
Thy limbs, are they not strong ? And beautiful thou art : . . . . 87 *Pet-lamb* 26
How beautiful is holiness !—what wonder if the sight, ... 92 *Poet's Dream* 13
Fair in thyself and beautiful alone, ... 107 *Farewell* 39
Those beautiful fields, the delight of the day, . . 116 *Repentance* 2
Shady as night, and beautiful as heaven, . . . 123 *V. and J.* 109
How beautiful when up a lofty height . . . . 138 *Widow* 1
Looked the beautiful Deliverer . . . . . . 141 *Arm. Lady* 135
Then think of her beautiful gliding form, . . . 142 †*Lov. and Lik.* 45
The star of Jove, so beautiful and large . . . 148 **There is an* 10
Unknown to them ; but it is beautiful ; . . . 149 *M. H.* 17
Beautiful in yourselves, and richly graced . . . 152 **Forth from* 22
A beautiful creature, ... 162 **Art thou the* 25
His beautiful wings in crimson are drest, . . . 163 **Art thou the* 35
So warm, so beautiful withal, ... 168 *Wren's Nest* 9
Was beautiful to see—a weed of glorious feature. . 191 *Beggars* 18
So beautiful, through savage lands . . . . . 193 *Ruth* 118
How beautiful the world below ; . . . . . . 215 *Kirkstone* 74
Couch beautiful as e'er for earthly use . . . . 219 *Haunted Tree* 10
How beautiful his eyes, ... 232 *Jew. Fam.* 18
My gay and beautiful Canoe, ... 237 *P. B.* 112
One beautiful November night, ... 240 *P. B.* 323
Though clad in colours beautiful and pure, . . 263 **Those words* 10
So beautiful of late, with sunshine warmed, . . 266 **Desponding Father* 2
Such age how beautiful ! O Lady bright, . . . 274 **Such age* 1
As welcome, and as beautiful—in sooth . . . 279 **Though I* 9
More beautiful, as being a thing more holy : . . 279 **Though I* 10
Plead for thy peace, thou beautiful romance . . 282 *Railway* 11
For thee who art so beautiful ? . . . . . . 288 *Highland Girl* 48
Fresh risen, and beautiful within !—there meet . 327 *Ode 1815* 53
And such a beautiful creation makes . . . . 338 *Engelberg* 3
Of the beautiful countenance, twine round his neck ; 340 *Fort Fuentes* 8
The beautiful, the brave, the holy, and the just ! . 351 *Des. Stanzas* 81
How beautiful ! how worthy to be sung . . . 367 **As indignation* 7
The enrapt, the beautiful, the young, ... 373 *Eg. Maid* 310
(So beautiful is Clyde) forgot to mourn . . . . 392 *Bothwell* 2 8
In the beautiful form of this innocent Doe : . . 398 *White Doe* 237
If thou art beautiful, and youth . . . . . 402 *White Doe* 581
A Doe most beautiful, clear-white, ... 414 *White Doe* 1646
So beautiful the timid Thrall . . . . . . 416 *White Doe* 1805
Beautiful strangers, stand within the pale . . . 421 *Ecc. Sonn.* 1. 13. 2
How beautiful your presence, how benign, . . 423 *Ecc. Sonn.* 1. 19. 1
A *dawn* she has both beautiful and bright, . . 455 *Rydal Mere* 22

Bed—*continued.*
To make a bed for me !—My Girl will weep . . 52 *Bord.* 817
It should be told you pinioned in your bed, . . 56 *Bord.* 1011
Holla ! to bed, good Folks, within ! O save us ! . 71 *Bord.* 1884
Dragged from his bed, was cast into a dungeon, . 71 *Bord.* 1892
Not yet in bed, Eleanor !— . . . . 71 *Bord.* 1903
Tranquil as he had died in his own bed. . . . 75 *Bord.* 2140
The home and sheltered bed, ... 79 *Sparrow's Nest* 6
Make your bed, or make your bower ; . . . . 79 *Foresight* 14
That he's left, for a bed, to beggars or thieves ! . 80 †*Address : Child* 19
—Come now we'll to bed ! and when we are there 81 †*Address : Child* 38
To bed the children must depart ; . . . . . . 81 †*Mother's Return* 46
In bed she moaning lay, ... 84 *We are Seven* 50
Is it not well with thee ? well both for bed and board ? . . . . 87 *Pet-lamb* 22
Our hearth shall be thy bed, our house shall be the fold. . . . . 88 *Pet-lamb* 48
That often, rising from his bed at night, . . . 101 *Brothers* 351
Or, if the grave be now thy bed, ... 116 *Affl. Marg.* 4
Scarcely a soul is out of bed ; . . . . . . 126 *Idiot Boy* 12
Cried Betty, rising from the bed, ... 128 *Idiot Boy* 185
And, grumbling, he went back to bed ! . . . 129 *Idiot Boy* 261
She turned, she tossed herself in bed, ... 130 *Idiot Boy* 417
Did Susan rise up from her bed, ... 130 *Idiot Boy* 425
From twig or bed an humbler flower, even for your sake ! " . . . . 139 *Arm. Lady* 12
Blessing the bed she lies upon ? " . . . . . 144 **Driven in* 46
The leaves that make the softest bed : . . . . 145 *Her Eyes* 56
And a small bed of water in the woods. . . . 149 *M. H.* 7
You stirred me on my rocky bed— . . . . 155 *Waterfall* 25
What keeps her thus reclined upon her lonesome bed ? . . . . 170 **Never enlivened* 10
Couched on a casual bed of moss and leaves, . . 172 *Infant Daughter* 19
The Sailor gathers up his bed, ... 176 *Waggoner* 1. 272
The mists, that o'er the streamlet's bed . . . 180 *Waggoner* 4. 57
Their bed of straw and blanket-walls. . . . . 192 *Gipsies* 8
A Barn her *winter* bed supplies ; . . . . . 194 *Ruth* 223
And nightly tosses on a bed of pain ; . . . . 229 *Cuckoo-clock* 24
Made the warm earth his lazy bed. . . . . . 239 *P. B.* 260
And this one Beast, that from the bed . . . . 240 *P. B.* 393
Head-foremost from the river's bed . . . . . 243 *P. B.* 579
Beside that luckless river's bed . . . . . . 248 *P. B.* 1039
If he had died upon his bed ! . . . . . . 248 *P. B.* 1047
Her doom it is to press a weary bed— . . . . 273 **While Anna's* 5
For *he* is safe, a quiet bed . . . . . . 285 *Grave of Burns* 67
And stirring in its bed. . . . . 295 *Highland Boy* 55
His bed perchance was yon smooth mound . . . 302 *Yarrow V.* 27
And hang like dreams around his guilty bed. . . 320 **Hunger, and* 14
Watching o'er the River's bed, ... 336 **Jesu ! bless* 14
Below the icy bed of bright ARGENTIERE. . . . 347 *Processions* 45
And *that* which marks thy bed. . . . . . . 348 **Lulled by* 72
A light around his mossy bed ; . . . . . . 373 *Eg. Maid* 304
Along his path ? His unprotected bed . . . 378 *Duddon* 8. 5
But when, from out their viewless bed, . . . 391 *Highland Broach* 79
Lie quiet in your churchyard bed ! . . . . . . 397 *White Doe* 68
Upon a bed of herbage green, ... 407 *White Doe* 1004
Crisp, yellow leaves my bed ; the hooting owl . . 424 *Ecc. Sonn.* 1. 22. 11
A Growth from sinful Nature's bed of weeds !— . 445 *Ecc. Sonn.* 3. 20. 4
And now with thankful heart to bed doth creep, . 453 **Calm is the* 18
As on a bed of death ? Some lodge in peace, . 454 *Sea-side* 15
Rumble along thy bed, block after block : . . 464 **Greta, what* 2
If Life were slumber on a bed of down, . . . 465 *St. Bees* 1
Along its foaming bed. . . . . 479 *Somnamb.* 135
The bad man's restless walk, and haunt his bed— 518 *Pun. Death* 6. 2
And the rough bed of many an unbridged brook ? 523 *Epist. Beaumont* 106
The bed we give him, though of softest down ; . 528 **Those breathing* 74
With a hard bed and scanty nourishment, . . 529 *Poor Robin* 8
Who, whether from their lowly bed . . . . 530 *Gleaner* 29
And bright the Lady is who shares his bed. . . 535 *Egremont* 72
For very cold to go to bed ; . . . . 536 *Goody Blake* 47
She left her fire, or left her bed, ... 537 *Goody Blake* 63
And on that simple bed, ... 542 *Russ. Fug.* 38
Of his own Household : nor, while from his bed . 547 **Rude is* 26
But tossing lately on a sleepless bed, ... 557 *Cuck. and Night.* 46
No longer would I in my bed abide, ... 557 *Cuck. and Night.* 57
" It grows upon its native bed . . . . . . 580 *John Words.* 53
Is but a lonely bed without the sense or sight . 589 *Immortality* 122
His torch, and shew them slumbering in their bed, 597 *Ev. Wk. Quarto* 298
Silent the hedge or steaming rivulet's bed, . . 599 *Ev. Wk. Quarto* 390
O'er-walk the chasmy torrent's foam-lit bed, . . 610 *Desc.Sk.Quarto* 464
Bloom'd with the snow-drops of Man's narrow bed, 613 *Desc.Sk.Quarto* 595
On his wet bed, abandon'd and alone. . . . . 613 *Desc.Sk.Quarto* 613
To cull her dinner from it's garden bed, . . . 615 *Desc.Sk.Quarto* 729
And whiter is the hospitable bed. . . . . . 615 *Desc.Sk.Quarto* 739
Her bed, his mountains mad Ambition piles ; . . 617 *Desc.Sk.Quarto* 799
Edged the black clouds, home and to bed we went, 642 *Prelude* 2. 17
In a sea-river's bed at ebb of tide, ... 652 *Prelude* 3. 216
I overlooked the bed of Windermere, ... 658 *Prelude* 4. 5
In my accustomed bed, more welcome now . . 659 *Prelude* 4. 82
That lowly bed whence I had heard the wind . . 659 *Prelude* 4. 85
Old Ocean, in his bed left singed and bare, . . 666 *Prelude* 5. 33
A bed of glittering light : I asked the cause : . . 667 *Prelude* 5. 129
That roars along the bed of Jewish song, . . . 668 *Prelude* 5. 203
Upon a bed of heath ;—full many a spot . . . 776 *Excursion* 2. 351
See, rooted in the earth, her kindly bed, . . . 793 *Excursion* 3. 522
That yields such kindly product. He, whose bed 835 *Excursion* 5. 880
Within these precincts, a capacious bed . . . 836 *Excursion* 5. 912
There lies the channel, and original bed, . . . 837 *Excursion* 5. 1004
How on her bed of death the Matron lay, . . . 849 *Excursion* 6. 743
Until dark night dismissed her to her bed ! . . 852 *Excursion* 6. 903

Bed—*continued.*
Within the garden, like the rest, a bed . . . 856 *Excursion* 6. 1162
In what may now be called a peaceful bed. . . 868 *Excursion* 7. 694
Glares, like a troubled spirit, in its bed . . . 877 *Excursion* 8. 179
He sings the sun to bed ; . . . . S. 3. 423 *Tinker* 19
Compare ! thy earthly bed a moment past . . S. 3. 434 **The doubt* 95
From open ground to covert, from a bed . . . K.8. 237 *Recluse* 1. 1. 41
Bedded. Lay bedded in a quickening soul, and all . 651 *Prelude* 3. 131
Lay bedded, changing oftentimes its form . . . 685 *Prelude* 6. 706
Bedded among rich plumes of tropic birds ; . . 700 *Prelude* 8. 94
Bedded for good and evil in a gulf . . . . . 826 *Excursion* 5. 295
Bede. Thy hovering Shade, O venerable Bede ! . 424 *Ecc. Sonn.* 1. 23. 4
Bedeck. Why bedeck her temples less . . . . 221 *Triad* 109
" How gay the habitations that bedeck . . . 828 *Excursion* 5. 411
Bedecked. Of orange-trees bedecked with glowing fruit . . . . 361 **List—'twas* 18
As sound—blithe race ! whose mantles were bedecked . . . . 790 *Excursion* 3. 249
Upon a Charger gorgeously bedecked . . . . 872 *Excursion* 7. 945
Bedewed. Of universal grief bedewed his honoured bier. . . . . 105 *Artegal* 233
My leaves you freshened and bedewed ; . . . 155 *Waterfall* 28
Bedewed with toil, ... 287 *Sons of Burns* 34
Bedewed with meditative tears . . . . . . 473 *Ossian* 61
Bedfords. The Bedfords, Glosters, Salisburys, of old 694 *Prelude* 7. 497
Bedim. Bedim, the grand terraqueous spectacle, . 548 **Stay, bold* 10
Bedimmed. Even till long gazing hath bedimmed his eye, ... 460 **Wanderer! that* 54
With my true self ; for, though bedimmed and changed . . . . 732 *Prelude* 11. 342
Hidden by clouds, and oft bedimmed by haze, . 849 *Excursion* 6. 704
Bedimmed with smoke, in wreaths voluminous, . 894 *Excursion* 9. 702
Bedimming. Of a bedimming sleep, or as a lamp . 266 **Even as* 2
Bedims. If, while a half-slumber his memory bedims, 621 *Convict* 35
Bedlam. Bedlam, and those carved maniacs at the gates, ... 689 *Prelude* 7. 132
Bedlamites. Awed have I been by strolling Bedlamites ; . . . . 742 *Prelude* 13. 157
Bedouin. He seemed an Arab of the Bedouin tribes : 666 *Prelude* 5. 77
Bedrop. Shall with a thankful tear bedrop its latest page. . . . . 529 **Those breathing* 140
Bedropped. On the window pane bedropped with rain : . . . . 118 †*Cottager* 13
Pale and bedropped with everflowing tears. . . 710 *Prelude* 9. 80
Bedropped with tears. 'Twill please you to be told 851 *Excursion* 6. 893
Bedrowsed. Daunt him—if his Companions, now bedrowsed . . . . 392 *Daniel* 12
Beds. I heard my neighbours in their beds complain 31 *Guilt* 390
Asleep upon their beds they lie ; . . . . . 82 †*Mother's Return* 54
Or peeped they often from their beds, ... 154 *Flower Garden* 13
Through beds of matted fern, and tangled thickets, 185 *Nutting* 15
And culled, from sundry beds, a lucid store . . 264 **Lady ! I* 3
While I was shaping beds for winter flowers ; . . 264 **Lady ! the* 2
Each kind in several beds of one parterre ; . . 281 *Valedict.* 4
Down their steep beds, that never shall be still : . 314 **Not 'mid* 8
With lawns and beds of flowers, and shades . . 407 *White Doe* 985
Flowers laugh before thee on their beds . . . 492 *Duty* 45
Like beds of moonlight shifting on the brine. . . 522 *Epist. Beaumont* 76
As from the beds and borders of a garden . . . 549 **The massy* 16
Unthought of : in their woodland beds the flowers 670 *Prelude* 5. 339
And while below, along their several beds, . . 681 *Prelude* 6. 438
Among the cottages by beds of flowers. . . . 683 *Prelude* 6. 540
Shut up in lesser lakes or beds of lawn . . . 702 *Prelude* 8. 194
And o'er the brawling beds of unbridged streams. 703 *Prelude* 8. 248
On these soft beds of thyme-besprinkled turf, . 789 *Excursion* 3. 247
By beds and banks Arcadian of gay flowers . . 881 *Excursion* 8. 469
Upon their grassy beds lay couch'd in sleep, . . S. 3. 427 **Through Cumbrian* 13
Bee. What if the bee love not these barren boughs ? 22 *Yew-tree* 4
A bee came darting, which the Child with joy . 44 *Bord.* 404
Does the dim-eyed curious Bee, ... 161 **Pleasures newly* 43
To the soft murmur of the vagrant Bee. . . . 227 *Vernal Ode* 90
At which the desert trembles.—Humming Bee ! . 227 *Vernal Ode* 124
With low soft murmur, like a distant bee, . . 445 *Ecc. Sonn.* 3. 22. 5
Rapt into upper regions, like the bee . . . . 503 *Warning* 32
The roving bee proclaims aloud . . . . . . 526 **The soaring* 3
When hums the mountain bee in May's glad ear, . 610 *Desc. Sk. Quarto* 444
New pleasure like a bee among the flowers. . . 640 *Prelude* 1. 580
A humming bee—a little tinkling rill— . . . 786 *Excursion* 3. 1
Upon their tops, adventurous as a bee . . . . 808 *Excursion* 4. 495
Murmured the labouring bee. When stormy winds 863 *Excursion* 7. 409
Beech. *See* **Beach.**
Far o'er the water, hung with groves of beech ; . 14 *Desc. Sk.* 231
This beech is standing by, its covert thou canst gain; 87 *Pet-lamb* 30
Of that one beech, appeared a thrush's nest ; . . 150 **When, to* 20
Into a gloomy grove of beech, ... 244 *P. B.* 672
Beechen. Would elevate my dreams. A beechen bowl, ... 424 *Ecc. Sonn.* 1. 22. 9
More toilsome than to carve a beechen bowl . . 702 *Prelude* 8. 206
Beeches. With all its beeches, we have named from You ! . . . . 150 *M. H.* 24
Some say that they are beeches, others elms— . 202 *Hart-leap* 126
Beneath the budding beeches. . . . . . . 287 *Ellen Irwin* 8
Has peered o'er the beeches, their work is begun : 572 *Avarice* 34
Beech-tree. Hither repaired.—A single beech-tree grew. . . . . 150 **When, to* 18
Been. (*Partial list.*)
Your natural breathing has been troubled. Nay . 39 *Bord.* 105
I found how my domains had been usurped, . . 40 *Bord.* 193
After his death. I have been much deceived. . 41 *Bord.* 235

Been—*continued.*
You know, Sir, I have been too long your guard — 43 *Bord.* 315
I have been waiting in the wood hard by — 43 *Bord.* 355
But here he is, it must have been a dream. — 44 *Bord.* 415
You have been insolent. And there's the Baron, — 46 *Bord.* 490
Speak out. Oh, Sir, I've been a wicked Woman. — 46 *Bord.* 505
He has been two years in his grave. Enough. — 46 *Bord.* 514
That I have been his comforter till now! — 50 *Bord.* 720
That would have been a vile mischance. It would. — 50 *Bord.* 738
Justice had been most cruelly defrauded. — 50 *Bord.* 739
Why so? a roofless rock had been a comfort, — 52 *Bord.* 814
No doubt you have been nobly entertained? — 53 *Bord.* 865
Do never dream of. I *have* been what he— — 54 *Bord.* 937
Is he not eyeless? He has been half-dead — 54 *Bord.* 941
Takes fire:—The men that have been reappear; — 275 **While poring* 3
And still he lay as if he had been bound. — 556 *Prioress* 225
Within a little time, as hath been found, — 556 *Cuck. and Night.* 6
I in so fair a one had never been. — 557 *Cuck. and Night.* 62
And she hath been before thee with her song; — 558 *Cuck.andNight.*104
Who had been nought, if Love had never been. — 560 *Cuck.andNight.*190
O cause of woe, that cause has been of bliss: — 563 *Troilus* 32
When they can know and feel that they have been, — 568 *Cumb. Beg.* 149
For his hive had so long been replenished with honey, — 570 *Farmer* 34
When hailstones have been falling, swarm on swarm, — 571 **There is a Flower* 5
It is not now as it hath been of yore;— — 587 *Immortality* 6

Bees. Where hum on busier wing her happy bees; — 21 *Desc. Sk.* 607
Where the bees hummed, and chair by winter fire; — 28 *Guilt* 220
Unfettered as bees that in gardens abide; — 116 *Repentance* 10
That instant brought two stripling bees — 157 *Oak and Broom* 99
Bees, wafted on the breezy air, — 165 *Danish Boy* 17
Sit blithe and happy; bees that soar for bloom, — 250 **Nuns fret* 5
One after one; the sound of rain, and bees — 253 **A flock* 2
Bees fill their hives; — 286 *Nith* 46
And, earlier still, was heard the hum of bees; — 377 *Duddon* 6. 4
The people work like congregated bees; — 424 *Ecc. Sonn.* 1. 24. 2
For some rare plant, yon Headland of St. Bees. — 466 *St. Bees* 9
Firm as the towering Headlands of St. Bees. — 466 *St. Bees* 18
As millions thus shall do, the Headlands of St. Bees. — 466 *St. Bees* 27
Rose, where she touched the strand, the Chantry of St. Bees. — 466 *St. Bees* 36
Like the fixed Light that crowns yon Headland of St. Bees, — 466 *St. Bees* 45
From her religious Mansion of St. Bees. — 466 *St. Bees* 54
And lo! a *statelier* pile, the Abbey of St. Bees. — 466 *St. Bees* 63
Keep watch before the altars of St. Bees. — 467 *St. Bees* 72
That best unlock the secrets of St. Bees. — 467 *St. Bees* 81
Nor hear the loudest surges of St. Bees. — 467 *St. Bees* 90
Brightening the archway of revered St. Bees. — 467 *St. Bees* 99
Nursed in the quiet Abbey of St. Bees. — 467 *St. Bees* 108
Taught by the hooded Celibates of St. Bees. — 467 *St. Bees* 117
Witness yon Pile that greets us from St. Bees. — 467 *St. Bees* 126
To bear thy part in this good work, St. Bees. — 468 *St. Bees* 135
Poured from the bosom of thy Church, St. Bees! — 468 *St. Bees* 144
Prosper the new-born College of St. Bees! — 468 *St. Bees* 153
That furthered the first teaching of St. Bees. — 468 *St. Bees* 162
As from the hive where bees in summer dwell, — 475 *Greenock* 6
And his fingers as busy as bees in a hive. — 570 *Farmer* 56
While hum with busier joy her happy bees; — 615 *Desc. Sk. Quarto* 731
A humming sound, less tuneable than bees, — 649 *Prelude* 3. 50
Like bees they swarmed, gaudy and gay as bees; — 681 *Prelude* 6. 391
I hear thee tell how bees with honey fed — 733 *Prelude* 11. 443
Of bees around their range of sheltered hives — 856 *Excursion* 6. 1169
An easy passage to the industrious bees — 889 *Excursion* 9. 370

Bees'. From out the rocks, the wild bees' safe abode: — 17 *Desc. Sk.* 389

Beetle. The beetle panoplied in gems and gold, — 108 *Indolence* 60
The beetle loves his unpretending track, — 528 **Those breathing* 71

Beetling. The barren Moor, hangs from a beetling rock — 49 *Bord.* 658
Each beetling rampart, and each tower sublime, — 335 *Rhine* 7
Than it appeared when from the beetling rock — 781 *Excursion* 2. 642

Beeves. "Let beeves and home-bred kine partake — 293 *Yarrow Unv.* 41

Befall. Anxiety lest mischief should befall her — 41 *Bord.* 234
This charge of thine, then ill befall thee!—Look, — 42 *Bord.* 304
Come home again, whate'er befall, — 126 *Idiot Boy* 60
Befall thee, I shall love thee to the last, — 137 *Michael* 416
Ill befall the yellow flowers, — 160 **Pansies, lilies* 49
Blest Pair! whate'er befall you, — 374 *Eg. Maid* 383
To meet such need as might befall— — 391 *Highland Broach* 57
Was in its birth, sustained as might befall — 642 *Prelude* 2. 6
Drooping or blithe of heart, as might befall; — 766 *Excursion* 1. 701

Befallen. What has befallen you? A stranger has done this, — 67 *Bord.* 1671
What has befallen you? — 71 *Bord.* 1906
From what has just befallen me I have cause — 74 *Bord.* 2120
some signal judgment has befallen the man — 76 *Bord.* 2218

Befalls. First cam'st into the world—as oft befalls — 136 *Michael* 340
Of what befalls;—be this your task— — 408 *White Doe* 1105
As oft befalls, prevent or turn aside — 517 *Pun. Death* 2. 10

Befell. What once to me befell. — 109 **Strange fits* 4
But half of what to him befell; — 129 *Idiot Boy* 340
Whate'er befell she could not grieve or pine; — 139 *Widow* 24
And this was my reply:—"As it befell, — 147 *Joanna* 35
Yet it befell that, in this lonely place, — 196 *Resolution* 52
Which ever till this night befell. — 243 *P. B.* 665
That strange adventure which befell — 295 *Highland Boy* 9
Ye soon shall know how this befell) — 296 *Highland Boy* 97
That dwelt among them. Sometimes it befell — 636 *Prelude* 1. 317

Befell—*continued.*
To Tutor or to Tailor, as befell, — 649 *Prelude* 3. 28
It befell — K. 8. 224 **I will* 4

Befit. Hail countless Temples! that so well befit — 430 *Ecc. Sonn.* 2. 9. 9
Lycoris (if such name befit — 497 *Lycoris* 27
Less than might well befit my youth, the cause — 713 *Prelude* 9. 245

Befits. His Power is this way tending. It befits us — 56 *Bord.* 1027
It ill befits us to disdain — 337 *Cath. Cantons* 3
—Ah who (and with such rapture as befits — 863 *Excursion* 7. 374

Befitting. With dignity befitting his proud hope; — 879 *Excursion* 8. 318

Befooled. Slaves, vile as ever were befooled by words, — 309 **What if* 3

Before. (*Partial list.*)
And I had heard the like before: in sooth — 38 *Bord.* 78
She is gone before, to spare my weariness. — 43 *Bord.* 338
Tied by a woollen cord, moves on before — 45 *Bord.* 456
Must never come before a mortal judgment-seat, — 55 *Bord.* 1001
Dissolve before a twinkling atom!—Oswald, — 59 *Bord.* 1220
Seem to meet with little gain, seem less happy than before: — 189 *Star-gazers* 30
"Before me shone a glorious world— — 194 *Ruth* 169
Before me in my endless way. — 289 *Stepping West.* 26
Thou goest before in thy benignity, — 552 *Prioress* 26
"Through all the Jewry (this before said I) — 554 *Prioress* 100
Now may'st thou sing for aye before the throne, — 554 *Prioress* 129
Before the Lamb singing continually, — 554 *Prioress* 133
Before the altar while the Mass doth last: — 555 *Prioress* 185
And she hath been before thee with her song; — 558 *Cuck.andNight.*104
This May-time, every day before thou dine, — 561 *Cuck.andNight.*242
Before the chamber-window of the Queen, — 562 *Cuck.andNight.*284
Twice as fast as before does his blood run about; — 570 *Farmer* 54
Than treading a path trod by thousands before. — 572 *Avarice* 28
Such sights, or worse, as are before me here.— — 579 *Peele Castle* 59
Though with such awful proof before their eyes — 728 *Prelude* 11. 66

Beforehand. A pile beforehand, turf or stick, — 536 *Goody Blake* 55

Befriend. Like Angels from their bowers, our virtues to befriend; — 456 **Soft as* 23
(Which doth at once befriend us and betray) — 779 *Excursion* 2. 533

Befriended. Not knowing that he had befriended — 177 *Waggoner* 2. 111
—Now, by thy care befriended, I appear — 753 **Oft, through* 5

Befriends. Befriends the observance, readily they join — 119 *Maternal Grief* 67
The local Genius ne'er befriends — 223 *Wishing-gate* 40
That oft befriends Antiquity, — 391 *Highland Broach* 88

Beg. The stone-cutters, 'tis true, might beg their bread — 98 *Brothers* 175
This would I beg; but on my mind — 408 *White Doe* 1086
His means are run out,—he must beg, or must borrow. — 569 *Farmer* 32
A lame man or a blind, the one to beg, — 699 *Prelude* 8. 26

Bega. When Bega sought of yore the Cumbrian coast, — 466 *St. Bees* 32

Began. *See* **'Gan.**
And I believe that, soon as I began — 28 *Guilt* 201
When we began to tire of childish play, — 28 *Guilt* 248
Stretched on the ground, began a piteous tale; — 33 *Guilt* 471
I took thee in my arms, and we began — 40 *Bord.* 194
So was it when my life began; — 79 **My heart* 3
Our pleasant home when spring began, — 85 *Anecdote* 11
The dew was falling fast, the stars began to blink; — 87 *Pet-lamb* 1
That he began to doubt; and even to hope — 96 *Brothers* 88
End happily, as they began!" These gleams — 124 *V. and J.* 211
The little birds began to stir, — 130 *Idiot Boy* 405
And with the owls began my song, — 131 *Idiot Boy* 435
When Michael, telling o'er his years, began — 132 *Michael* 88
When I began, my purpose was to speak — 135 *Michael* 242
Began his journey, and, when he had reached — 137 *Michael* 426
Wrought at the Sheep-fold. Meantime Luke began — 138 *Michael* 442
The Broom began to doze, — 156 *Oak and Broom* 52
Two ravens now began to croak — 157 *Oak and Broom* 96
Before their eyes began to stir! — 200 *Thorn* 226
Began the pencil's strife, — 231 **The gentlest Poet* 25
Began the promised Tale. — 238 *P. B.* 190
I loitered long ere I began: — 245 *P. B.* 792
In supplication to the Child began — 555 *Prioress* 193
Began to honour May with all their powers. — 558 *Cuck. and Night.* 70
And thus it was that she began her tale. — 561 *Cuck.andNight.*265
Next morning Troilus began to clear — 562 *Troilus* 1
Beneath yon roof began her heavenly reign? — 618 *School Ex.* 4
When lo! the heavenly goddess thus began, — 618 *School Ex.* 27
She wept.—Life's purple tide began to flow — 619 **She wept* 1
Were fastened to the affections. I began — 641 *Prelude* 1. 612
Grew dear to me: already I began — 644 *Prelude* 2. 177
At evening, when the earliest stars began — 671 *Prelude* 5. 366
Of printed books and authorship, began — 676 *Prelude* 6. 59
I had my face turned toward the truth, began — 704 *Prelude* 8. 323
When I began in youth's delightful prime — 724 *Prelude* 10. 416
Began to spin, with toil, my earliest songs. — 726 *Prelude* 10. 552
Guide faithful as is needed—I began — 728 *Prelude* 11. 98
And things to hope for! Not with these began — 734 *Prelude* 12. 7
Take note of this? When I began to enquire, — 742 *Prelude* 13. 160
But, undiscouraged, we began to climb — 746 *Prelude* 14. 14
A slant and mellow radiance, which began — 771 *Excursion* 1. 958
But, in the process, I began to feel — 797 *Excursion* 3. 790
Began in honour, gradually obtained — 849 *Excursion* 6. 707
To keep two hearts together, that began — 851 *Excursion* 6. 875
"If ye, by whom invited I began — 874 *Excursion* 8. 5
The compass of his argument—began — 883 *Excursion* 8. 600
Began to fall upon the mountain tops, — K. 8. 228 **I will* 135
Began to fail, this sheep by hunger pressed — K. 8. 229 **I will* 144
Childless, until the time when he began — K. 8. 231 **I will* 214
In times of heavy snow." She then began — K. 8. 247 *Recluse* 1. 1. 399

Begat. Dreams not unlike to those which once begat — 688 *Prelude* 7. 111

Beget. And listen, till I do beget — 184 **O blithe* 27
Beget strange themes; and to freaks give birth — K. 8. 301 **And oh* 9

Beheld—*continued.*
And older eyes than theirs beheld, 215 Kirkstone 46
Beheld in your impetuous march the likeness 229 Clouds 12
As he beheld the Woman lie 247 P. B. 1016
Smooth way ; and I beheld the face of one 257 *Methought I 10
Though I beheld at first with blank surprise 279 *Though I 1
I once beheld, a Templar Knight ; 301 Bran 47
When first mine eyes beheld that famous Hill 338 Engelberg 6
Beheld what I had feared to see, 386 Yarrow Rev. 77
His voice—beheld his speaking face ; 479 Somnamb. 142
Right glad was he when he beheld her : 537 Goody Blake 81
Beheld with wonder ; whether floor or path 540 *Lady ! a 72
The soul's pure brightness he beheld 545 Russ. Fug. 323
Beheld their only Child returned 545 Russ. Fug. 359
On regal decks beheld ! yet in the end 574 Chiabrera 4. 22
While Friends beheld thee give with eye, voice, mien, 583 *With copious 32
With rapture she beheld Britannia smile, 618 School Ex. 45
Beheld not vales more beautiful than ours ; 639 Prelude 1. 480
Beheld her breast the wind, then suddenly 639 Prelude 1. 497
By its own spirit ! All that I beheld 646 Prelude 2. 281
That I beheld respired with inward meaning. 651 Prelude 3. 132
Could have beheld,—with undelighted heart, 652 Prelude 3. 217
Glorious as e'er I had beheld—in front, 663 Prelude 4. 325
To travel without pain, and I beheld, 665 Prelude 4. 432
This Arab phantom, which I thus beheld, 667 Prelude 5. 142
Than I beheld loitering on calm clear nights 676 Prelude 6. 93
Far distant, thus beheld from year to year 679 Prelude 6. 273
Beheld the Convent of Chartreuse, and there 681 Prelude 6. 418
Issued, and with uplifted eyes beheld, 682 Prelude 6. 482
From a bare ridge we also first beheld 683 Prelude 6. 524
Whate'er in this wide circuit we beheld, 683 Prelude 6. 541
Beheld her serving at the cottage inn ; 691 Prelude 7. 305
The lovely Boy as I beheld him then 692 Prelude 7. 367
Which I beheld of shepherds in my youth, 703 Prelude 8. 294
Did we appeal ; and, finally, beheld 715 Prelude 9. 381
To mingle, I beheld the vessels lie, 722 Prelude 10. 317
Beheld long-bearded teachers, with white wands 745 Prelude 13. 345
There I beheld the emblem of a mind 747 Prelude 14. 70
The transitory Being that beheld 755 Recluse 1. 1. 850
Beheld the stars come out above his head, 758 Excursion 1. 129
Of some bold headland, he beheld the sun 759 Excursion 1. 199
She opened—found no writing, but beheld 766 Excursion 1. 669
That we beheld ; and lend the listening sense 773 Excursion 2. 106
Such as by Hebrew Prophets were beheld 784 Excursion 2. 867
Whence, unmolested wanderers, we beheld 794 Excursion 3. 540
When, from the blind mist issuing, I beheld 796 Excursion 3. 719
Intruder ne'er beheld, he thence surveys 799 Excursion 3. 937
Of some huge hill, expectant, I beheld 803 Excursion 4. 113
With a submissive reverence they beheld ; 811 Excursion 4. 700
Like those celestial messengers beheld 812 Excursion 4. 716
Those dark rocks hide it !' Entering, I beheld 834 Excursion 5. 768
And when, mature in manhood, he beheld 864 Excursion 7. 431
In fertile pastures—was beheld with eyes 872 Excursion 7. 949
Beheld without compassion, yea, with praise ! 887 Excursion 9. 194
Of blooming Boys (whom we beheld even now) 888 Excursion 9. 257
Who hath beheld it, noted it with care, 891 Excursion 9. 516
Else had Morality beheld her line L. I. 97 Juvenal 3. 63

Behest. At whose behest uprose on British ground 477 Long Meg 11
Of boundless suffrage, at whose sage behest 505 Warning 126
That spake the Norman Conqueror's stern behest— 877 Excursion 8. 172
The high behest, and every heart obey ; 893 Excursion 9. 642

Behests. For Him upon whose high behests 533 *Blest is 19
And in the order of sublime behests : 724 Prelude 10. 453

Behind. (*Partial list.*)
Lingers behind his disappearing wain. 3 Ev. Wk. 71
Gives one bright glance, and drops behind the hill. 5 Ev. Wk. 191
Behind his sail the peasant shrinks, to shun 15 Desc. Sk. 281
There, safely guarded by the woods behind, 19 Desc. Sk. 488
The little fool is loth to stay behind. 42 Bord. 305
Stay you behind ; and, when the sun is down, 64 Bord. 1464
Daisies leave no fruit behind 80 Foresight 21
Sitting behind the chaise, alone. 82 Alice Fell 20
And never looks behind ; 83 Lucy Gray 62
As visions still more bright have done, and left no trace behind. 93 Poet's Dream 72
The other, left behind, is flowing still. 97 Brothers 145
The humour of the moment, lagged behind. 101 Brothers 363
When down behind the cottage roof, 109 *Strange fits 23
" Oh, move, thou Cottage, from behind that oak ! 110 *'Tis said that some 13
When last he sailed, he left the bird behind ; 119 Sailor's Mother 29
A whirl-blast from behind the hill 154 *A whirl-blast 1
Some close behind, some side by side, 162 Binnorie 45
The evil One is left behind. 174 Waggoner 1. 115
The VANGUARD, following close behind, 179 Waggoner 3. 68
" The pleasure-house is dust :—behind, before, 203 Hart-leap 169
He leaves behind a moon-illumined wake : 212 Dion
For service hung behind thy chamber-door ; 229 Cuckoo-clock 8
Ascending from behind the motionless brow 229 Clouds 2
Companions, fear ye to be left behind, 229 Clouds 6
Among the rocks, behind the trees ; 243 P. B. 643
—A withered leaf is close behind, 244 P. B. 703
Perchance without one look behind me cast, 284 Departure 16
The Gordon, couched behind a thorn, 287 Ellen Irwin 22
Behind, all gloomy to behold ; 289 Stepping West. 10
Live, and take comfort. Thou hast left behind 305 Toussaint 9
Our hands behind our backs with felon cords ? 309 *What if 6
But, touched from behind by the Sun, it now shines 345 Stanzas : Simplon 23
Moments, to cast a look behind, 376 *The Minstrels 69

Behind—*continued.*
And each tumultuous working left behind 384 Duddon 33. 11
Whatever fate remain behind, 406 White Doe 921
Made halt—but hark ! a noise behind 412 White Doe 1443
But from behind with treacherous wound 412 White Doe 1485
Darkness before and danger's voice behind ; 441 Ecc. Sonn. 3. 4. 8
Could leave both man and horse behind ; 483 Simon Lee 18
Full thirty years behind. 486 *We walked 24
Than what it leaves behind. 487 Fountain 36
Pacing behind along the silent lane. 523 Epist. Beaumont 119
Rich prospect left behind of stream and vale, 524 Epist. Beaumont 223
And once, behind a rick of barley, 537 Goody Blake 73
He stood behind a bush of elder, 537 Goody Blake 83
(Winds behind, and rocks before !) 549 Hermit's Cell 1. 30
Him even the slow-paced waggon leaves behind. 567 Cumb. Beg. 66
Strength in what remains behind ; 590 Immortality 184
Crouded behind the swain, in mute distress, 592 Ev. Wk. Quarto 67
Nought else of man or life remains behind 598 Ev. Wk. Quarto 375
Behind her hill the Moon, all crimson, rides, 606 Desc.Sk.Quarto 235
Shakes from behind the clouds his flashing shield. 608 Desc.Sk.Quarto 337
Behind his sail the peasant strives to shun 608 Desc.Sk.Quarto 344
And drag their length of deluge train behind. 615 Desc.Sk.Quarto 697
Nor even DELICACY stayed behind : 620 Birth of Love 17
How fast that length of way was left behind, 622 Recluse 1. 1. 156
Leaving behind her still, on either side, 637 Prelude 1. 364
When, from behind that craggy steep till then 637 Prelude 1. 377
Behind me did they stretch in solemn train, 639 Prelude 1. 461
Till he was left an arrow's flight behind. 649 Prelude 3. 12
Darkness before, and danger's voice behind, 653 Prelude 3. 285
Even when we look behind us, and best things 656 Prelude 3. 480
Looked ghastly in the moonlight : from behind, 664 Prelude 4. 396
Some monument behind me which pure hearts 676 Prelude 6. 56
Leaves far behind life's treacherous vanities, 682 Prelude 6. 453
Above, behind, far stretching and before ; 690 Prelude 7. 247
Would leave behind a dance of images, 700 Prelude 8. 114
The region left behind him ; and, if aught 709 Prelude 9. 12
Behind the summer clouds. By birth he ranked 714 Prelude 9. 302
Rising behind a thick and lofty grove, 817 Excursion 4. 1064
Leaving behind of yellow radiance spread 820 Excursion 4. 1302
Lingering behind my comrades, thus I breathed 822 Excursion 5. 14
And, close behind, the comely Matron rode, 858 Excursion 7. 77
She, far behind him in the race of years, 861 Excursion 7. 226
Retired behind the mountain-tops or veiled 893 Excursion 9. 594
Shame of such dye, but worse remains behind. L. I. 97 Juvenal 3. 80

Behold. One I behold who, 'cross the foaming flood, 17 Desc. Sk. 380
Yes, I must see you when ye first behold 20 Desc. Sk. 563
When I behold the ruins of that face, 39 Bord. 135
My heart leaps up when I behold 79 *My heart 1
Behold, within the leafy shade, 79 Sparrow's Nest 1
Behold the hunter train ! 104 Artegal 111
And all the gorgeous sights which fairies do behold. 108 Indolence 63
An object beauteous to behold ; 117 Affl. Marg. 16
I should behold his face again ! 121 EmigrantMother54
Where they may live, with no one to behold 123 V. and J. 110
A perilous wound—he shuddered to behold 123 V. and J. 132
Behold thee, and my misery is complete ! " 124 V. and J. 162
To living thing—not even to her.—Behold ! 125 V. and J. 293
To behold thy captive state ; 139 Arm. Lady 14
Fresh from the crowded city, to behold 143 *High bliss 10
We can behold it from our orchard seat ; 148 *There is an 3
Here in my blossoms to behold 156 Oak and Broom 83
The shape will vanish—and behold 159 *With little 29
Behold him perched in ecstasies, 159 Green Linnet 27
The life of all that we behold 164 *Glad sight 3
Behold yon Prisoners three, 166 Stray Pleasures 3
Hath this conception, grateful to behold, 173 Infant Daughter 61
Again behold them on their way ! 178 Waggoner 2. 166
Behold the mighty Moon ! this way 192 Gipsies 19
Behold her how She smiles to-day 204 Brougham 17
Do I behold these steep and lofty cliffs, 205 Tintern 5
And mountains ; and of all that we behold 207 Tintern 104
May I behold in thee what I was once, 207 Tintern 120
Our cheerful faith, that all which we behold 207 Tintern 133
What doth she look on ?—whom doth she behold ? 209 Laod. 14
Accept the gift, behold him face to face ! " 209 Laod. 24
' Behold they tremble !—haughty their array, 211 Laod. 134
Behold ! the mantling spirit of reserve 212 Dion
—Behold !—as with a gushing impulse heaves 212 Dion
Which they behold, whom vengeful Furies haunt ; 213 Dion 86
Do we behold the line of Erin's coast ? 219 *This Height 25
—She comes !—behold 220 Triad 41
" Long have I loved what I behold, 238 P. B. 131
Right through the quarry ;—and behold 240 P. B. 361
While not an English Mountain we behold 251 *Pelion and 7
No mortal object did these eyes behold 256 *No mortal 1
Shall soon behold this border thickly set 264 Snowdrop 9
The self-same Vision which we now behold, 265 *Hail, Twilight 10
Recumbent : Him thou may'st behold, who hides 269 Gordale 10
Are yet before me ; yet do I behold 270 Henry : Portrait 2
As in life's morn ; permitted to behold, 272 Devil's Bridge 9
When I behold thy blanched unwithered cheek, 274 *Such age 6
Behold, already they forget to shine, 278 *The most 7
And having rights in all that we behold. 284 Departure 28
At thought of what I now behold : 284 Grave of Burns 2
As fair before me shall behold, 288 Highland Girl 75
Behind, all gloomy to behold ; 289 Stepping West. 10
Behold her, single in the field, 289 Sol. Reap. 1
With us who now behold the light, 292 Rob Roy 106
With admiration I behold 294 Jedbor. 37

Being—*continued.*
Diffused through all the mysteries of our Being, . 538 **In desultory* 26
Yet, being inwardly unstained, ... 542 *Russ. Fug.* 79
A life and soul, to every mode of being . . . 567 *Cumb. Beg.* 78
In childhood, from this solitary Being, . . . 567 *Cumb. Beg.* 110
—Such pleasure is to one kind Being known, . . 568 *Cumb. Beg.* 154
But its necessity in being old. . . . . . . 571 **There is a Flower* 16
Still, at the centre of his being, lodged . . . 584 *Ch. Lamb* 30
Our noisy years seem moments in the being . . 589 *Immortality* 158
Of unknown modes of being ; o'er my thoughts . 638 *Prelude* 1. 393
Can I forget you, being as you were . . . 639 *Prelude* 1. 501
And, in our dawn of being, constitute . . . 640 *Prelude* 1. 557
And of some other Being. A rude mass . . . 642 *Prelude* 2. 33
Emphatically such a Being lives, ... 646 *Prelude* 2. 252
Great birthright of our being, was in me . . 646 *Prelude* 2. 271
I felt the sentiment of Being spread . . . 648 *Prelude* 2. 401
With our own inner being are forgot. . . . 656 *Prelude* 3. 508
His being armed with strength that cannot fail. . 661 *Prelude* 4. 171
Of my own private being and no more ; . . . 662 *Prelude* 4. 235
It gives, to think that our immortal being . . 666 *Prelude* 5. 23
Reverence was due to a being thus employed ; . 668 *Prelude* 5. 150
Being itself benign. My drift I fear . . . 670 *Prelude* 5. 293
I guess not what this tells of Being past, . . 673 *Prelude* 5. 510
That frame of social being, which so long . . 681 *Prelude* 6. 427
His hour being not yet come. Far less had then . 704 *Prelude* 8. 356
Of dust, and kindred to the worm ; a Being, . . 706 *Prelude* 8. 488
This notwithstanding, being brought more near . 706 *Prelude* 8. 510
Being written in a tongue he cannot read, . . 719 *Prelude* 10. 61
Forgot, at seasons, whence they had their being ; . 723 *Prelude* 10. 376
Of pity and sorrow to a state of being . . . 724 *Prelude* 10. 450
The very being of the immortal soul. . . . 730 *Prelude* 11. 222
" What are they but a mockery of a Being . . 732 *Prelude* 11. 311
Those mysteries of being which have made, . . 735 *Prelude* 12. 85
And various trials of our complex being, . . 736 *Prelude* 12. 149
In such a being ; for, her common thoughts . . 736 *Prelude* 12. 172
A sensitive being, a *creative* soul. . . . . 737 *Prelude* 12. 207
Salutes the being at his birth, where grace . . 742 *Prelude* 13. 196
Of being understood at once, or else . . . 743 *Prelude* 13. 214
Which do both give it being and maintain . . 745 *Prelude* 13. 374
Being over and forgotten, on we wound . . . 746 *Prelude* 14. 27
Where is the favoured being who hath held . . 748 *Prelude* 14. 133
Of human Being, Eternity, and God. . . . . 749 *Prelude* 14. 205
The transitory Being that beheld . . . . 755 *Recluse* 1. 1. 850
And, being still unsatisfied with aught . . . 758 *Excursion* 1. 143
His animal being ; in them did he live, . . . 759 *Excursion* 1. 209
What wonder if his being thus became . . . 759 *Excursion* 1. 233
From years of youth ; which, like a Being made . 762 *Excursion* 1. 430
A Being, who by adding love to peace . . . 764 *Excursion* 1. 518
A human being destined to awake . . . . . 768 *Excursion* 1. 787
That passing shows of Being leave behind, . . 770 *Excursion* 1. 951
The ends of being would secure, and win . . 791 *Excursion* 3. 349
Sad or disturbed, is ordered by a Being . . . 801 *Excursion* 4. 14
That in the scale of being fill their place ; . . 802 *Excursion* 4. 81
As he must bear, being powerless to redress ; . . 806 *Excursion* 4. 329
Of Life continuous, Being unimpaired ; . . . 812 *Excursion* 4. 755
In dignity of being we ascend. . . . . . 812 *Excursion* 4. 765
Of infinite Being, twinkling restlessly ! . . . 816 *Excursion* 4. 994
Has not the soul, the being of your life, . . . 818 *Excursion* 4. 1156
—So build we up the Being that we are ; . . . 820 *Excursion* 4. 1264
For future states of being ; and the wings . . 826 *Excursion* 5. 245
The being one, and one the element. . . . 837 *Excursion* 5. 1003
From my good Host, that being crazed in brain . 839 *Excursion* 6. 108
In his dividual being, self-reviewed, ... 844 *Excursion* 6. 386
And to his moral being appertained : . . . . 853 *Excursion* 6. 1014
The infant Being in itself, and makes . . . 878 *Excursion* 8. 290
Of no mean Being ? One who should be clothed 879 *Excursion* 8. 317
" To every Form of being is assigned," . . . 884 *Excursion* 9. 1
Run o'er with gladness ; whence the Being moves 886 *Excursion* 9. 135
Of effort with the end of Being. . . . . . S. 3. 439 **Avaunt this* 13
Was that same young and happy being) became . K. 8. 237 *Recluse* 1. 1. 48
—What Being, therefore, since the birth of man . K. 8. 239 *Recluse* 1. 1. 98
The trees (her first-born child being then a babe) . K. 8. 247 *Recluse* 1. 1. 391
They lift the animal being, do themselves . . . K. 8. 249 *Recluse* 1. 1. 454
She being herself a Mother, happy Beast . . . K. 8. 251 *Recluse* 1. 1. 529
Each being has his office, lowly some . . . . K. 8. 255 *Recluse* 1. 1. 669
Being's. And by all nations. In that Being's sight 172 *Infant Daughter* 8
Conscience, the timid being's inmost light, . . 467 *St. Bees* 82
And to one purpose cleave, their Being's godlike mate ! . . . . 529 **Those breathing* 132
Of heaven-born freedom on thy being's height, . 589 *Immortality* 126
Our Being's earthly progress,) blest the Babe, . 645 *Prelude* 2. 234
Our destiny, our being's heart and home, . . . 684 *Prelude* 6. 604
Even to thy Being's infinite majesty ! . . . . 802 *Excursion* 4. 99
Beings. *See* **Fellow-beings.**
Would he forget those Beings to whose minds . 23 *Yew-tree* 39
In dim relation to imagined Beings. . . . . 64 *Bord.* 1455
The living Beings by your own fire-side, . . . 147 *Joanna* 4
Of human Beings, in the self-same spot ! . . . 192 *Gipsies* 2
Invoke we those bright Beings one by one ; . . 220 *Triad* 32
Dread Beings ! and your empire show . . . . 245 *P. B.* 774
When the Being of Beings shall summon her hence. 364 *Vallomb.* 36
Ye shadowy Beings, that have rights and claims . 473 **Ye shadowy* 1
To Beings else forlorn and blind ! . . . . . 481 *Expost.* 6
And to such beings temperately deal forth . . 634 *Prelude* 1. 122
As natural beings in the strength of Nature. . . 652 *Prelude* 3. 193
Predestined, if two beings ever were, ... 679 *Prelude* 6. 257
The measure of themselves, these favoured Beings, 757 *Excursion* 1. 88
Of many Beings, he had wondrous skill . . . 762 *Excursion* 1. 431
Kind and degree, among all visible Beings ; . . 806 *Excursion* 4. 337
" Beings like these present ! But proof abounds 865 *Excursion* 7. 518

Belated. A lonely Spital, the belated swain . . . 27 *Guilt* 150
I am belated, and you must know the cause— . 71 *Bord.* 1907
Haunts him belated on the silent plains ! . . . 265 **There is a pleasure* 8
Belated and by sickness overcome. . . . . . 665 *Prelude* 4. 452
Beleaguered. A Camp, and a beleaguered Town, 406 *White Doe* 940
Toward the beleaguered city, in the might . . S. 3. 437 **The doubt* 191
Beleaguering. Against the pressure of beleaguering war. . . . . 811 *Excursion* 4. 693
Belfries. The tapers shall be quenched, the belfries mute, ... 433 *Ecc. Sonn.* 2. 21. 3
Belfry. Belfry, and images, and living trees ; . . 643 *Prelude* 2. 106
Belfry's. Had, with its belfry's humble stock, . . 176 *Waggoner* 2. 3
Belgic. Stooped to the Victory on that Belgic field 327 *Ode 1815* 5
Belie. Nor did aught of future days that kiss belie, 142 *Arm. Lady* 143
Thou, whose exterior semblance doth belie . . 589 *Immortality* 108
Belied. Why is the Past belied with wicked art, 505 *Warning* 140
Belief. Confirmed by hoary hairs, belief may claim ; 5 *Ev. Wk.* 193
To win belief, such as my plot requires. . . . 44 *Bord.* 369
A scale and table of belief—as thus— . . . 58 *Bord.* 1147
But, whether blithe or sad, 'tis my belief . . . 100 *Brothers* 347
Such earnest vigils, that belief prevailed . . . 139 *Widow* 11
Be but a vain belief, yet, oh ! how oft— . . . 206 *Tintern* 50
'Tis gone—with old belief and dream . . . . 223 *'*Tis gone* 1
At their own fond belief. . . . . 224 *'*Tis gone* 42
Was for belief no dream :—thy skill, Arion ! . . 234 *Power of Sound* 131
And for the boldest tale belief commands. . . 338 *Engelberg* 5
Assent is power, belief the soul of fact. . . . 359 **Those old* 14
Belief sank deep into the crowd . . . . . 373 *Eg. Maid* 311
To the heart's fond belief ; though some there are 463 **They called* 6
If eyes be still sworn vassals of belief, ... 474 **Ye shadowy* 13
If this belief from heaven be sent, ... 482 *Lines : Spring* 21
This sad belief, the happiest that is left . . . 531 *Octogen.* 6
Now say—in such belief I'll live and die ; . . . 559 *Cuck. and Night.* 162
And live and die I will in thy belief ; . . . . 563 *Troilus* 75
And paramount belief ; there, recognised . . . 677 *Prelude* 6. 132
In the belief, that my maturer age, ... 679 *Prelude* 6. 310
To note the laws and progress of belief ; . . . 691 *Prelude* 7. 276
In what we *may* become ; induce belief . . . 709 *Prelude* 8. 650
Of wild belief engrafted on their names . . . 725 *Prelude* 10. 475
Of mine can give it life,) in firm belief . . . 751 *Prelude* 14. 356
Shaped his belief, as grace divine inspired, . . 762 *Excursion* 1. 412
With their belief, I sang Saturnian rule . . . 797 *Excursion* 3. 756
Exists—one only ; an assured belief . . . . 801 *Excursion* 4. 12
Hope, below this, consists not with belief . . . 804 *Excursion* 4. 191
Hope, below this, consists not with belief . . . 804 *Excursion* 4. 194
Of one in whom persuasion and belief . . . . 820 *Excursion* 4. 1293
" Vague thoughts are these ; but, if belief may rest 872 *Excursion* 7. 941
Not from such hope, or aught of such belief . . K. 8. 245 *Recluse* 1. 1. 316
Beliefs. As one of those beliefs which in their hearts 68 *Bord.* 1679
And ye, Beliefs ! coiled serpent-like about . . 518 *Pun. Death* 6. 9
Believe. And I believe that, soon as I began . . 28 *Guilt* 201
And thee, my Child ! Believe me, honoured Sire ! . . . . 40 *Bord.* 144
It struck me at the time—yet I believe . . . 42 *Bord.* 273
What can I do ? believe me, gentle Sirs, . . . 47 *Bord.* 535
I scarcely can believe it. Myself, I heard . . 49 *Bord.* 678
Has driven him out of harbour ? I believe . . 53 *Bord.* 867
But listen, for my peace—— Why, I *believe* you. . . . . 59 *Bord.* 1175
I did believe all things were shadows—yea, . . 59 *Bord.* 1214
I do believe he weeps—I could weep too— . . 61 *Bord.* 1319
I sate me down, and cannot but believe— . . 62 *Bord.* 1359
Yet calm.—I could believe that there was here . 64 *Bord.* 1467
Some terrible phantom I believe is now . . . 73 *Bord.* 2026
I left him. I believe that there are phantoms, . 74 *Bord.* 2083
And you believe, then, that his mind was easy ?— 101 *Brothers* 387
" Believe it not," said Elidure ; " respect . . . 105 *Artegal* 186
Dear Maid, this truth believe, ... 112 **Yes ! thou* 6
And for this cause not always, I believe, . . . 134 *Michael* 190
Have lutes (believe my words) . . . . . . 164 *Needlecase* 26
Kind Spirits ! may we not believe . . . . . 191 *Seq. Beggars* 36
Have followed ; for such loss, I would believe, . 207 *Tintern* 87
One might believe that natural miseries . . . 308 **One might* 1
So shall the people gather and believe . . . . 325 *Ode 1814* 135
Where what we gladliest would believe . . . 345 **How blest* 68
And let me believe that when nightly the Muse . 364 *Vallomb.* 21
Lone Sufferer ! will not she believe . . . . 414 *White Doe* 1676
Where Piety, as they believe, obtains . . . . 424 *Ecc. Sonn.* 1. 24. 4
Informs my spirit, ne'er can I believe . . . . 457 **Had this* 35
Nor can I not believe but that hereby . . . . 488 *Pers. Talk* 43
Until I cannot but believe that they— . . . 510 *F. Stone* 116
Yet further.——Many, I believe, there are . . 568 *Cumb. Beg.* 133
With calmness suffer and believe, ... 580 *John Words.* 18
Must keep to all, as fondly all believe, ... 656 *Prelude* 3. 482
Yet in themselves less grateful, I believe, . . . 662 *Prelude* 4. 284
On summer evenings, I believe that there . . . 671 *Prelude* 5. 395
Loth to believe what we so grieved to hear, . . 684 *Prelude* 6. 586
Have stopped, as some believe, the kindliest growths. . . . . 692 *Prelude* 7. 372
Of utter ruin. How might we believe . . . . 728 *Prelude* 11. 44
Her prospects, nor did he believe,—he *saw.* . . 759 *Excursion* 1. 232
" Do not believe it ; never could that be ! " . . 840 *Excursion* 6. 117
She spake, yet, I believe, not unsustained . . . 849 *Excursion* 6. 767
Is satisfied, I cannot but believe, ... 885 *Excursion* 9. 104
And frustrate all the rest ! Believe it not : . . 887 *Excursion* 9. 23
Hard to believe, yet could they well discern . . K. 8. 225 **I will* 41
Believed. Was, I believed, prime Agent. The wind fell ; . . . . 68 *Bord.* 1692

Beloved—*continued.*
Of those belovèd fields she oft — 544 *Russ. Fug.* 249
Fletcher's Associate, Jonson's Friend beloved. — 546 **The embowering* 21
In earnest converse with belovèd Friends, — 549 **The massy* 14
Far from St. Cuthbert his belovèd Friend, — 551 **If thou in* 26
Heard I my most beloved Lady dear, — 563 *Troilus* 58
Weep not, belovèd Friends ! nor let the air — 573 *Chiabrera* 1. 1
In the chaste arms of thy belovèd Love ! — 575 *Chiabrera* 7. 13
A brother's Child, most tenderly beloved ! — 575 *Chiabrera* 8. 5
Holy, and ever dutiful —beloved — 581 **Why should we* 3
Lady ! devoutly honoured and beloved — 628 **Deign, Sovereign* 9
In that belovèd Vale to which erelong — 636 *Prelude* 1. 304
About its narrow precincts all beloved, — 659 *Prelude* 4. 42
And Jupiter, my own beloved star ! — 662 *Prelude* 4. 247
Where had we been, we two, belovèd Friend ! — 669 *Prelude* 5. 233
Oh, most belovèd Friend ! a glorious time, — 686 *Prelude* 6. 754
Before last primrose-time. Belovèd Friend ! — 687 *Prelude* 7. 12
Yet still a stranger and beloved as such ; — 713 *Prelude* 9. 280
Useless, and even, beloved Friend ! a soul — 721 *Prelude* 10. 235
Of my belovèd country, wishing not — 722 *Prelude* 10. 280
That the belovèd Sister in whose sight — 732 *Prelude* 11. 335
When thinking on my own beloved friend, — 733 *Prelude* 11. 442
Is all uncertain : but, beloved Friend ! — 751 *Prelude* 14. 392
Beloved and honoured—far as he was known. — 757 *Excursion* 1. 97
To the degree that he desired, beloved. — 772 *Excursion* 2. 56
Thankful for my belovèd child's return. — 812 *Excursion* 4. 748
A virtuous Lady tenderly beloved — 825 *Excursion* 5. 194
" She loved, and fondly deemed herself beloved. — 851 *Excursion* 6. 844
Dear Youth, by young and old alike beloved, — 868 *Excursion* 7. 706
Alas that one beloved, forlorn, — K.8. 220 **The snow-tracks* 36
Beloved Grasmere (let the Wandering Streams — K.8. 238 *Recluse* 1. 1. 57

Below. (*Partial list.*)
And vainly eyed below the tempting flood, — 3 *Ev. Wk.* 50
While silent stands the admiring crowd below, — 6 *Ev. Wk.* 205
The hills, while gleams below the azure tide ; — 9 *Ev. Wk.* 360
Were there, below, a spot of holy ground — 10 *Desc. Sk.* 1
Rich golden verdure on the lake below. — 12 *Desc. Sk.* 102
And hear the rattling thunder far below ; — 17 *Desc. Sk.* 377
Reclined, he sees, above him and below, — 19 *Desc. Sk.* 466
Glitter the stars above, and all is black below. — 21 *Desc. Sk.* 583
The gulf is deep below ; — 85 *Shepherd-boys* 53
Only in the lake below. — 93 *Westmoreland Girl* 16
Below him, in the bosom of the deep, — 96 *Brothers* 61
Watching below till he had disappeared — 125 *V. and J.* 252
In high and low, above, below, — 128 *Idiot Boy* 207
And do not dread the waves below, — 145 *Her Eyes* 43
Our blest re-union in the shades below. — 211 *Laod.* 142
How beautiful the world below ; — 215 *Kirkstone* 74
Upon the lake below, — 224 **'Tis gone* 9
Even here below, but more in heaven above. — 257 **No mortal* 14
The lake below reflects it not ; the sky — 266 **Even as* 6
Below the white-rimmed bonnet, far-descried. — 271 *Henry : Portrait* 8
And earth below, they best can serve true gladness — 280 **'Tis he* 13
Thou " poor Inhabitant below," — 285 *Grave of Burns* 50
And Rob was lord below. — 291 *Rob Roy* 60
Reflected in the pool below. — 301 *Bran* 73
Upon a princely company below, — 324 *Ode 1814* 79
To us who tread below), — 329 *Ode : Thanks.* 25
Below the icy bed of bright Argentière. — 347 *Processions* 45
Earth stretched below, heaven in our neighbourhood. — 351 *Des. Stanzas* 86
And prospect right below of deep coves shaped — 353 *Aquap.* 43
Of the Jerusalem below, her sin — 365 **The Baptist* 6
From the bowers of earth below ; — 397 *White Doe* 76
Warbled, for heaven above and earth below, — 457 **Had this* 14
Alternate empire in the shades below— — 460 **Queen of* 5
About, below, above, — 483 *Sister* 34
That he below may rest in peace, — 485 *Poet's Epitaph* 23
A silent tarn below ! — 491 *Fidelity* 20
Each weary step, dwarfing the world below, — 497 **Enough of climbing* 6
Unshaded, eying far below, the flood, — 592 *Ev. Wk. Quarto* 66
While silent stands th' admiring vale below ; — 595 *Ev. Wk. Quarto* 188
Aw'd, while below the Genii hold their state. — 598 *Ev. Wk. Quarto* 358
Rich golden verdure on the waves below. — 604 *Desc. Sk. Quarto* 111
The death-dog, howling loud and long, below ; — 606 *Desc. Sk. Quarto* 226
Below, the echo of his parting oar, — 607 *Desc. Sk. Quarto* 314
He looks below with undelighted eye. — 611 *Desc. Sk. Quarto* 511
Below its aim, or meets with, from without, — 720 *Prelude* 10. 177
Above our human region, or below, — 802 *Excursion* 4. 82
Hope, below this, consists not with belief — 804 *Excursion* 4. 194
Wherever laid, who living fell below — 842 *Excursion* 6. 268
From the full river in the vale below, — 885 *Excursion* 9. 68
Or fret and labour on the Plain below. — 885 *Excursion* 9. 92
Then fell below zero, — S. 3. 440 **Said red-ribboned* 23
Of vale below, a height of hills above. — K.8. 237 *Recluse* 1. 1. 21
Admonishing the man who walks below — K.8. 240 *Recluse* 1. 1. 132
Yon curling smoke from the grey cot below, — K.8. 247 *Recluse* 1. 1. 390
Heavenward, so piercing deep the lake below. — K.8. 252 *Recluse* 1. 1. 579

Belt. I hung this belt. Mercy of Heaven ! What ails you ! — 67 *Bord.* 1642
And, haply, far within the marble belt — 269 **Pure element* 11
Its warfare's bourn, its travel's belt ! — 298 *Brownie's Cell* 40
They belt him round with hearts undaunted — 408 *White Doe* 1142
Whose white belt scared him thence, or wind that blew — 656 *Prelude* 3. 489
Orion with his belt, and those fair Seven, — 662 *Prelude* 4. 245
Of the warm summer, from a belt of hemp — 769 *Excursion* 1. 885

Belus. Then she, as Belus wont, and all the line — 625 *Æneid* 105
From Belus, filled it to the brim with wine ; — 625 *Æneid* 106
That Belus, nightly to his splendid couch — 811 *Excursion* 4. 686

Belying. Of promise, nor belying the kind hope — 726 *Prelude* 10. 550

Bemazed. Stock-still there he stands like a traveller bemazed : — 484 **A plague* 16

Bemoan. And must he too the ruthless change bemoan — 282 *Railway* 6
" If there be one who need bemoan — 487 *Fountain* 49
In secret did, we trust, her loss bemoan. — 627 **When Severn's* 8

Bemock. Hills, torrents, woods, embodied to bemock — 314 *Hofer* 13

Bemocked. And by a train of flying clouds bemocked ; — 454 *Sea-side* 13

Bemocking. 'Mid spectral lakes bemocking thirsty men, — 435 *Ecc. Sonn.* 2. 27. 13
To stretch his limbs, bemocking, as might seem, — 826 *Excursion* 5. 267

Bench. *See* **Cottage-bench.**
They came to lowly bench or sculptured stall, — 256 *Decay of Piety* 7
No chair remained before the doors ; the bench — 642 *Prelude* 2. 11
With long long ways before, by cottage bench, — 742 *Prelude* 13. 139
The voice was silent. From the bench I rose ; — 767 *Excursion* 1. 738
The shade, and look abroad. On this old bench — 769 *Excursion* 1. 879
And this rude bench, one torturing hope endeared, — 770 *Excursion* 1. 913
From that low bench, rising instinctively — 770 *Excursion* 1. 918
We sate on that low bench : and now we felt, — 771 *Excursion* 1. 960

Benches. Was occupied by oaken benches ranged — 824 *Excursion* 5. 155

Bend. Three years a wanderer now my course I bend— — 32 *Guilt* 445
She saw the carman bend to scoop the flood — 34 *Guilt* 543
To see thy arch thus stretch and bend, — 111 **'Tis said that some* 42
The way my friends their course did bend, — 114 *Ind. Wom.* 46
Bend with the breeze their heads, beside a crystal stream. — 141 *Arm. Lady* 96
But ne'er could Fancy bend the buoyant Lark — 153 *Morn. Ex.* 23
Hither his flight he would bend ; — 162 **Art thou the* 16
To her ; for her the willow bend ; — 187 **Three years* 20
Wherever sportive breezes bend — 227 *Vernal Ode* 69
Bending, as you or I might bend — 244 *P. B.* 741
But hardier far, once more I see thee bend — 264 *Snowdrop* 2
Why should we bend in grief, to sorrow cling, — 271 *George : Death* 8
With first-fruit offerings crowd to bend the knee — 303 **Is it* 6
In splendour : what strength was, that would not bend — 307 **Great men* 8
Who never did to Fortune bend the knee ; — 317 **Call not* 2
Where simple Sufferers bend, in trust — 337 *Cath. Cantons* 5
Bend that way herdesires. The dew, the storm— — 354 *Aquap.* 133
" Though here I bend a suppliant knee — 406 *White Doe* 897
Her own thoughts loved she ; and could bend — 416 *White Doe* 1854
Not unforgiven the suppliant knee might bend, — 434 *Ecc. Sonn.* 2. 25. 10
In freedom. Men they were who could not bend ; — 443 *Ecc. Sonn.* 3. 13. 9
To which our souls must bend ; — 497 *Lycoris* 40
And can earthward bend an ear — 503 **Like a* 66
Works not the righteousness of God ? Oh bend, — 514 **Portentous change* 10
Bend, ye Perverse ! to judgments from on High, — 514 **Portentous change* 11
Must bend the sceptred Potentates of earth. — 574 *Chiabrera* 3. 20
Was ever Spirit that could bend — 582 **O for a* 25
Bend o'er th' abyss ?—the else impervious gloom — 605 *Desc. Sk. Quarto* 186
Bend o'er the smoke that curls beneath the rocks. — 605 *Desc. Sk. Quarto* 191
Again to bend the Sabbath of that time — 633 *Prelude* 1. 104
To bend at last to the same discipline, — 679 *Prelude* 6. 256
To bend as doth a slender blade of grass — 705 *Prelude* 8. 398
The shape of theirs, my understanding bend — 713 *Prelude* 9. 253
Bend the complying heads of lordly pines, — 734 *Prelude* 12. 16
Here might I pause, and bend in reverence — 743 *Prelude* 13. 224
Nor would I bend to it ; who should have grieved — 797 *Excursion* 3. 779
To this would rather bend than see and hear — 810 *Excursion* 4. 619
Your cherished sullenness is forced to bend — 819 *Excursion* 4. 1191
To bend, he stoutly re-addressed himself, — 840 *Excursion* 6. 151

Bended. A Prelate's blessing ask on bended knees. — 442 *Ecc. Sonn.* 3. 8. 14
Where a few villagers on bended knees — 444 *Ecc. Sonn.* 3. 17. 13

Bending. *See* **Body-bending, Down-bending, Meekly-bending.**
There, bending o'er the stream, the listless swain — 3 *Ev. Wk.* 70
Or, from the bending rocks, obtrusive cling, — 12 *Desc. Sk.* 85
The bending body of my active sire ; — 28 *Guilt* 218
Bending low before the Donor, — 90 *Longest Day* 75
He sees the bending multitude, He hears the choral rites, — 93 *Poet's Dream* 63
Hither he his course is bending ;— — 174 *Waggoner* 1. 33
Ilissus, bending o'er thy classic urn ! — 213 *Dion* 43
Bending, as you or I might bend — 244 *P. B.* 741
And o'er the sickle bending ;— — 289 *Sol. Reap.* 28
His look and bending figure, all bespeak — 572 *Animal Tran.* 5
Low bending o'er the colour'd water, fold — 593 *Ev. Wk. Quarto* 103
And, bending, water'd with the human tear, — 606 *Desc. Sk. Quarto* 258
Bending beneath our life's mysterious weight — 672 *Prelude* 5. 418
In different quarters of the bending sky, — 682 *Prelude* 6. 483
He held the child, and, bending over it, — 696 *Prelude* 7. 615
When, in the congregation bending all — 722 *Prelude* 10. 293
Whose flexile boughs low bending with a weight — 881 *Excursion* 8. 443
Bending its apex toward a paler self — S. 3. 434 **The doubt* 69
To linger, bending over thee : for now, — S. 3. 434 **The doubt* 93

Bends. Admitting no resistance, bends alike — 57 *Bord.* 1089
She bends) at leisure may be seen — 221 *Triad* 136
Bends to the favourite burthen. Moon and stars — 230 *Clouds* 71
While Peter o'er the river bends, — 242 *P. B.* 563
For more than Fancy to the influence bends — 262 **Mark the* 12
A blue sky bends o'er Yarrow vale, — 302 *Yarrow V.* 17
Still stronger, bends him to his course. — 401 *White Doe* 466
Who bends to happier duties, who more wise — 528 **Those breathing* 87

Benjamin—*continued.*
It is a doubt with Benjamin — 174 *Waggoner* 1. 68
The place to Benjamin right well — 174 *Waggoner* 1. 83
While Benjamin in earnest mood — 175 *Waggoner* 1. 146
By solitary Benjamin; — 175 *Waggoner* 1. 181
And Benjamin is groping near them, — 175 *Waggoner* 1. 192
Benjamin can faintly hear — 176 *Waggoner* 1. 217
And Benjamin, without a question, — 176 *Waggoner* 1. 232
Through help of honest Benjamin; — 176 *Waggoner* 1. 244
Then Benjamin entreats the Man — 176 *Waggoner* 1. 253
To courteous Benjamin replied, — 176 *Waggoner* 1. 257
As Benjamin is now aware, — 176 *Waggoner* 2. 24
And Benjamin is wet and cold, — 177 *Waggoner* 2. 37
Come, come," cries he to Benjamin! — 177 *Waggoner* 2. 48
And Benjamin—ah, woe is me! — 177 *Waggoner* 2. 49
All care with Benjamin is gone— — 177 *Waggoner* 2. 80
To Benjamin, who rubs his eyes, — 177 *Waggoner* 2. 110
Cries Benjamin, "a draught of length! — 178 *Waggoner* 2. 146
When Benjamin had seized the bowl, — 178 *Waggoner* 2. 149
For Benjamin, triumphant soul! — 178 *Waggoner* 2. 153
Cries Benjamin, "We must be gone." — 178 *Waggoner* 2. 164
That Benjamin, with clouded brains, — 178 *Waggoner* 3. 12
Says Benjamin, "That Ass of thine, — 179 *Waggoner* 3. 50
I like," said Benjamin, "her shape and stature: — 179 *Waggoner* 3. 72
—Said Benjamin, "This whip shall lay — 179 *Waggoner* 3. 116
Benjamin, among the stars, — 180 *Waggoner* 3. 139
With faithful Benjamin attending, — 180 *Waggoner* 4. 66
And sooth for Benjamin a vein — 180 *Waggoner* 4. 75
Benjamin, this outward glory — 181 *Waggoner* 4. 121
Him Benjamin, with lucky glance, — 181 *Waggoner* 4. 141
On both sides, Benjamin the good, — 181 *Waggoner* 4. 182
Which Benjamin had ceased to drive: — 182 *Waggoner* 4. 188
Which robbed us of good Benjamin;— — 182 *Waggoner* 4. 267

Benoni. Benoni, or the child of sorrow, — 246 *P.B.* 909

Bent. *See* **Bow-bent.**
Bent o'er the groaning flood that sweeps away his tears. — 11 *Desc. Sk.* 62
With which, though bent on haste, myself I decked; — 28 *Guilt* 222
And female cries. Their course they thither bent, — 33 *Guilt* 467
Yet still, while over her the husband bent, — 36 *Guilt* 627
Lank as a ghost and tall, his shoulders bent, — 45 *Bord.* 461
Here is a tree, ragged, and bent, and bare, — 61 *Bord.* 1294
Anglers, bent on reckless pastime, — 94 *Westmoreland Girl* 49
I to her cottage bent my way, — 109 **Strange fits* 7
A sister Queen, against the bent — 113 *Lament* 51
Reached speedily the native threshold, bent — 123 *V. and J.* 103
But Betty's bent on her intent; — 126 *Idiot Boy* 17
Her thoughts are bent on deadly sin, — 129 *Idiot Boy* 293
That gives to all the self-same bent — 162 **Who fancied* 17
On barbarous plunder bent, — 169 *Wren's Nest* 64
Thus leans, with hanging brow and body bent — 169 *Love lies Bleeding* 7
When the malicious Fates are bent — 181 *Waggoner* 4. 117
Bent earthwards; he looks up—the clouds are split — 184 *Night-piece* 11
His body was bent double, feet and head — 196 *Resolution* 66
So close, you'd say that they are bent — 197 *Thorn* 18
(Each hero following his peculiar bent) — 211 *Laod.* 116
His strong hand on the wind, if it were bent — 221 *Triad* 74
For sorrow that had bent — 225 *Primrose* 38
So toward the stream his head he bent, — 242 *P. B.* 553
With brow in penitential sorrow bent! — 270 **Though the bold* 14
Calais is not: and I have bent my way — 304 **Festivals have* 7
Yet filled with ardour and on triumph bent — 326 **Intrepid sons* 10
Even as if bent on perishing. There lives — 357 *Aquap.* 341
Bent by a load of Mulberry leaves!—most hard — 366 *Lombardy* 2
The secret thou art bent on keeping: — 372 *Eg. Maid* 248
Whose Guardians bent the knee to Jove and Mars: — 380 *Duddon* 17. 11
Or the Indian tree whose branches, downward bent, — 383 *Duddon* 31. 7
Of love on which his soul was bent. — 401 *White Doe* 520
To London were the Chieftains bent; — 404 *White Doe* 783
And tremblingly her course she bent — 413 *White Doe* 1541
I saw a Mother's eye intensely bent — 446 *Ecc. Sonn.* 3. 24. 1
The shepherd, bent on rising with the sun, — 453 **Calm is the* 16
Untaught that meekness is the cherished bent — 455 **Not in the lucid* 14
And, to the sinner, mercifully bent; — 464 **A point* 6
These shores if he approached them bent on wrong; — 468 **Bold words* 4
Bent in quick turns each other to undo, — 513 *Newspaper* 7
And, though no longer upon rapine bent, — 523 *Epist. Beaumont* 127
Shall tottering Age, bent earthward, hear — 533 **Blest is* 37
While over her the Matron bent — 542 *Russ. Fug.* 45
I bent before Thy gracious throne, — 550 *Hermit's Cell* 5. 17
And on his purpose bent so fast to ride, — 563 *Troilus* 20
When to that Ship he bent his way, — 579 **Sweet Flower* 9
His black matted hair on his shoulder is bent, — 620 *Convict* 13
Arts yet untried, upon new counsels bent, — 624 *Æneid* 2
Whose studious aspect should have bent me down — 654 *Prelude* 3. 373
Were bent upon undoing what was done: — 711 *Prelude* 9. 133
Bent overmuch on superficial things, — 736 *Prelude* 12. 116
In silence as before. With forehead bent — 746 *Prelude* 14. 28
Flowed in the bent of Nature. Having now — 751 *Prelude* 14. 369
In youth I roamed, on youthful pleasures bent; — 753 **Oft, through* 2
Bent as he moves, and needing frequent rest; — 761 *Excursion* 1. 325
My spirits, that they were bent on enterprise; — 788 *Excursion* 3. 121
I bent my way; and, roaming far and wide, — 799 *Excursion* 3. 945
Are scarcely told, since, on a service bent — 808 *Excursion* 4. 469
And lifts his wilful hand on mischief bent, — 889 *Excursion* 9. 317
But, on harshness are you bent, — S. 3. 438 **I, whose* 28
And of his works: or, yielding to the bent — K.8. 227 **I will* 97

Benumb. And comfortless despairs the soul benumb. — 427 *Ecc.Sonn.* 1. 36. 14

Benumbed. Distracted, spiritless, benumbed, and blind, — 322 **Humanity, delighting* 34

Bequeathed. Since parting Innocence bequeathed — 191 *Seq. Beggars* 21
"Where are your books?—that light bequeathed — 481 *Expost.* 5
Ashes to ashes, dust bequeathed to dust, — 780 *Excursion* 2. 569
But, blessing God and praising him, bequeathed — 839 *Excursion* 6. 69

Bequest. I feel my strength returning. The bequest, — 40 *Bord.* 155
By a bequest sufficient for my needs — 751 *Prelude* 14. 359
Than those resplendent lights, his rich bequest; — 821 *Excursion* 4. 1305

Bequests. Art's noblest relics, history's rich bequests — 354 *Aquap.* 96

Bereave. Why of your further aid bereave me? — 130 *Idiot Boy* 344
Is busiest to confer and to bereave; — 269 *Gordale* 3

Bereaves. Your sound my heart of rest bereaves, — 111 *'Tis said that some* 23
When winter the grove of its mantle bereaves, — 340 *Fort Fuentes* 10
Controls them and subdues, transmutes, bereaves — 493 *Hap. War.* 17

Bereft. The Lover, thus bereft, stung with his loss, — 122 *V. and J.* 74
Though of both leaf and flower bereft, — 155 *Waterfall* 45
Which would have led him, if bereft — 295 *Highland Boy* 38
Of one deep bliss thine ear hath been bereft: — 306 **Two Voices* 9
And pine, of human hope bereft, — 338 **Meek Virgin* 17
Grieve for the Man who hither came bereft, — 363 **Grieve for* 1
Bereft Ones, and in lowly anguish weep — 387 **Part fenced* 7
For woman, even of tears bereft, — 391 *Highland Broach* 59
That she, of him and all bereft, — 415 *White Doe* 1787
But, oh the heavy change!—bereft — 483 *Simon Lee* 25
For all that seem neglected or bereft; — 530 *Poor Robin* 34
To thousands, share not Thou; howe'er bereft, — 531 *Octogen.* 7
By his bereft, his lonely, Chiabrera. — 574 *Chiabrera* 5. 18
That the bereft their recompense may win; — 865 *Excursion* 7. 523

Berne. Majestic BERNE, high on her guardian steep, — 339 *Schwytz* 9

Berries. *See* **Whortle-berries.**
Lurking berries, ripe and red, — 80 *Foresight* 29
With unrejoicing berries—ghostly Shapes — 185 *Yew-trees* 25
All bright with berries ripe and red, — 243 *P. B.* 637
There berries ripen, flowerets bloom; — 532 †*Float. Isl.* 14
Or berries of the wood; — 542 *Russ. Fug.* 20
Decked with autumnal berries, that outshine — 868 *Excursion* 7. 717

Berry-bearing. Green herbs, bright flowers, and berry-bearing plants, — 268 **Pure element* 3

Berth. Within that warm and peaceful berth, — 177 *Waggoner* 2. 88

Beseech. Can its eyes beseech?—no more — 502 **Like a* 7
This child did him beseech on his bare knees. — 553 *Prioress* 78
Beseech her meekly with all lowliness, — 562 *Cuck.andNight.* 305

Beseeching. Cast up the Stream or down at her beseeching, — 190 **Lyre! though* 26

Beseem. And well might it beseem that mighty Town — 327 *Ode 1815* 46
As might beseem the fairest Fair, — 390 *HighlandBroach* 25
As might beseem a stately embassy, — 394 **No more* 10
Some pensive musings which might well beseem — 706 *Prelude* 8. 457
Are these the studies that beseem a prince? — L. 1. 94 *Juvenal* 2. 12

Beseemed. It might have well beseemed me to repeat — 668 *Prelude* 5. 177

Beseems. With such embellishment as well beseems — 824 *Excursion* 5. 121

Beseen. Fie, quoth she, on thy name, Bird ill beseen! — 560 *Cuck.andNight.* 186
Under a maple that is well beseen, — 562 *Cuck.andNight.* 283

Beset. When the troublesome Tempter beset us, said I, — 116 *Repentance* 5
And many dreadful fears beset her, — 130 *Idiot Boy* 413
Is hardly worse beset than mine, — 179 *Waggoner* 3. 86
For he it was—dread Winter! who beset, — 321 **Humanity, delighting* 13
For such a One beset with cloistral snares. — 363 **The world forsaken* 8
Ere hope declines:—their union is beset — 437 *Ecc. Sonn.* 2. 37. 8
How fancy sickens by vague hopes beset; — 458 *Sea-shore* 2
More hurtful here beset him, doomed though free, — 470 **Did pangs* 12
Through crags, and smoothing paths beset with danger, — 477 *Nunnery* 10
Cares entangle, sins beset, — 503 **Like a* 54
But 'twas a splendid place, the door beset — 644 *Prelude* 2. 142
Beset me, and to height unusual rose, — 666 *Prelude* 5. 62
Of those abstractions to a mind beset — 677 *Prelude* 6. 159
And thus, on every side beset with foes, — 723 *Prelude* 10. 335
Standing before the multitude, beset — 793 *Excursion* 3. 467
For fixed annoyance; and full oft beset — 817 *Excursion* 4. 1055
As virtue's self; like virtue is beset — 830 *Excursion* 5. 494
And hindrances with which they stand beset — 835 *Excursion* 5. 861
Frequented, and beset with howling winds. — 859 *Excursion* 7. 144

Beshrew. "Beshrew all them that are in love untrue." — 561 *Cuck.andNight.* 250

Beside. Each with its household boat beside the door; — 12 *Desc. Sk.* 112
Starts, like a horse, beside the glaring road— — 13 *Desc. Sk.* 182
To lisp, he made me kneel beside my bed, — 28 *Guilt* 202
A cart and horse beside the rivulet stood; — 34 *Guilt* 541
Torn from our hut, that stood beside the sea — 35 *Guilt* 591
At Herbert's door—and when he stood beside — 47 *Bord.* 539
Beside a human door! — 82 *Lucy Gray* 8
My boy beside me tripped, so slim — 86 *Anecdote* 25
Risen from his seat, beside the snow-white ridge — 95 *Brothers* 31
Beside the springs of Dove, — 109 **She dwelt* 2
Beside an English fire. — 109 **I travelled* 12
The water which beside it stood: — 114 *Ind. Wom.* 56
Might see and notice not. Beside the brook — 131 *Michael* 16
Then old, beside him, lying at his feet. — 138 *Michael* 469
That grew beside their door; and the remains — 138 *Michael* 480
Beside the boisterous brook of Green-head Ghyll. — 138 *Michael* 482
Bend with the breeze their heads, beside a crystal stream. — 141 *Arm. Lady* 96
Angling beside the margin of the lake. — 149 **A narrow* 49
Beside the babbling rills; — 155 *Oak and Broom* 2

Best—continued.
Best pleased with what is aptliest framed . . . 499 *Departing summer 29
And seem to love it best. . . . . 507 May 48
With life's best sinews more and more unknit. . 515 *Ah why 5
How cold the quarter that the wind best loves, . 521 Epist. Beaumont 19
Ask not of me, whose tongue can best appease . 522 Epist. Beaumont 65
On best or worst which they and Nature give? . 528 *Those breathing 70
You, whom, though long deserted, he loved best; . 529 *Those breathing 124
Put on, to welcome spring, their best attire, . . 529 Poor Robin 4
To see or not to see, as best may please . . . 532 *Once I 29
Go forth upon a mission best fulfilled . . . . 538 *In desultory 20
Of goodness, next her Son, our soul's best boot. . 552 Prioress 14
Methought that it was the best melody . . . 558 Cuck. and Night. 84
For of all good she is the best alive. 562 Cuck.andNight.297
For of all good she is the best alive. 562 Cuck.andNight.304
For of all good she is the best alive. 562 Cuck.andNight.311
Since of all good you are the best alive. . . . 562 Cuck.andNight.316
The occasion of his woe, as best he might; . . 564 Troilus 114
He gave them the best that he had; or, to say . 569 Farmer 27
Has from Savona torn her best delight? . . . 573 Chiabrera 7. 7
Lulling the mourner's best good thoughts asleep, 576 *By a 17
Ne'er will the best of all your train . . . . 577 *I come 13
Thou best Philosopher, who yet dost keep . . 589 Immortality 110
But by our best descendants be unknown, . . 627 *We gaze 7
That best betoken patriot loyalty. . . . . . 629 Installation 85
Unmanageable thoughts: his mind, best pleased . 634 Prelude 1. 139
More palpable, as best might suit her aim. . . 637 Prelude 1. 356
One is there, though the wisest and the best . . 642 Prelude 2. 22
(For with my best conjecture I would trace . . 645 Prelude 2. 233
More active even than "best society"— . . . 646 Prelude 2. 295
Hast placed me high above my best deserts, . . 653 Prelude 3. 318
Even when we look behind us, and best things . 656 Prelude 3. 480
Detain me from the best of other guides . . . 668 Prelude 5. 168
Of silence came and baffled his best skill, . . . 671 Prelude 5. 380
The deepest and the best, what keen research, . 675 Prelude 6. 40
Culled the best fruits of Time's uncounted hours, 701 Prelude 8. 140
As sometimes to the best of feeble means . . . 707 Prelude 8. 523
Last look, to make the best amends he may: . . 709 Prelude 9. 16
Great rendezvous of worst and best, the walk . 710 Prelude 9. 55
And ill could brook, beholding that the best . . 712 Prelude 9. 213
As best, the government of equal rights . . . 713 Prelude 9. 242
That Heaven's best aid is wasted upon men . . 720 Prelude 10. 119
Seemed best, and the straightforward path of those 720 Prelude 10. 131
Enjoining, as may best promote the aims . . . 721 Prelude 10. 186
Meets foes irreconcilable, and at best . . . . 721 Prelude 10. 207
From the best youth in England their dear pride, 722 Prelude 10. 302
The best of names, when patriotic love . . . 722 Prelude 10. 305
What there is best in individual man, ... 728 Prelude 11. 83
I summoned my best skill, and toiled, intent . . 731 Prelude 11. 279
That their best virtues were not free from taint . 735 Prelude 12. 65
That was the best, to that she was attuned . . 736 Prelude 12. 160
His best and purest friend; from her receives . 740 Prelude 13. 7
As found among the best of those who live— . . 743 Prelude 13. 242
The excellence, pure function, and best power . 745 Prelude 13. 377
Emotions which best foresight need not fear, . 748 Prelude 14. 122
Lifted, in union with the purest, best, ... 748 Prelude 14. 185
Told what best merits mention, further pains . . 751 Prelude 14. 370
As I grew up, it was my best delight . . . . 757 Excursion 1. 60
Of humble industry that promised best . . . 761 Excursion 1. 310
That in our best experience he was rich, . . . 761 Excursion 1. 372
Was their best hope, next to the God in heaven. . 764 Excursion 1. 534
My best companions now the driving winds, . . 766 Excursion 1. 702
Of my best prayers to bring me back again.' . . 767 Excursion 1. 756
With the best hope and comfort I could give: . . 768 Excursion 1. 811
And reverence for himself; and, last and best, . 775 Excursion 2. 289
But now ye shall be feasted with our best." . . 781 Excursion 2. 653
Or too aspiring, thankless at the best) . . . 790 Excursion 3. 292
In the best quiet to her course allowed; . . . 800 Excursion 3. 988
Most frequently call forth, and best sustain, . . 806 Excursion 4. 367
Was best, the most affecting eloquence. . . . 807 Excursion 4. 415
Whom the best might of faith, wherever fixed, . 828 Excursion 5. 360
And all the laboured novelties at best . . . . 829 Excursion 5. 437
Reason, best reason, is to imperfect man . . . 830 Excursion 5. 501
We may not doubt that who can best subject . . 830 Excursion 5. 517
Your instances; for they are both best known, . 832 Excursion 5. 648
And that best gift of heaven hath fallen on them; 833 Excursion 5. 720
And to the best affections that proceed . . . 836 Excursion 5. 905
Its best attainment fits of such repose . . . . 849 Excursion 6. 739
And the best ages of the world prescribe. . . . 862 Excursion 7. 333
That venerable clay. Meanwhile the best . . . 863 Excursion 7. 390
Each by the thoughts best suited to his years: . 867 Excursion 7. 658
Was a true patriot, hopeful as the best . . . 869 Excursion 7. 805
And such as my best judgment could select . . 874 Excursion 8. 19
And best protection, this imperial Realm, . . . 888 Excursion 9. 295
Prevail, 'tis best to neither hear nor see. . . . S.3. 441 *Grateful is sleep, more 3

Bestir. Bestir them in good deeds. Now, fare thee well— . . . . 137 Michael 412
Bestow. That choice lacked courage to bestow! . 215 Kirkstone 60
Nor such fine skill as did the meed bestow . . 339 Tell 2
And his dear Daughter on a Knight bestow . . 372 Eg. Maid 227
Heaven's breathing influence failed not to bestow 395 White Doe: Ded. 29
Nor more regard doth She bestow . . . . . 407 White Doe 1010
The unblemished good they only can bestow. . 516 *As leaves 8
For the least boon that freedom can bestow? . 528 *Those breathing 80
Who did on thee the hardiness bestow 562 Cuck.andNight.293
That asks not speed, a traveller might bestow . 696 Prelude 7. 591
Of mighty Poets: upon me bestow . . . . 755 Recluse 1. 1. 840
As choice as musing Leisure can bestow; . . . 799 Excursion 3. 906

Bestow—continued.
Spare them, they shall continue to bestow, . . 838 Excursion 6. 36
For the least boon that pity can bestow. . . . 879 Excursion 8. 361
On me can Time no happier state bestow . . . S.3. 441 *Grateful is sleep; my 3

Bestowed. While chastening thoughts of sweetest use, bestowed . . . . 11 Desc. Sk. 27
Was nothing, scarcely can be aught, yet 'twas bounteously bestowed, ... 93 Poet's Dream 78
Of fond correction and reproof bestowed . . . 133 Michael 173
Not to appal me have the gods bestowed . . . 210 Laod. 35
And hath bestowed on thee a safer good; . . . 268 *Brook! whose 13
Have I received this proof of pains bestowed . . 281 Chris. Words. 2
Upon the Lakes of Asia 'tis bestowed— . . . 327 Ode 1815 24
Bestowed by Nature, or from man's great deeds . 352 Aquap. 6
From every sympathy that Man bestowed! . . 419 Ecc. Sonn. 1. 4. 4
His be a welcome cordially bestowed!" . . . 422 Ecc. Sonn. 1. 16. 14
Alms may be needed) which that House bestowed? 434 Ecc. Sonn. 2. 23. 12
Ever bestowed to equalize and bless . . . . 435 Ecc. Sonn. 2. 29. 10
Bestowed on this transcendent hour! . . . . 458 *Had this 60
Are with a ready heart bestowed . . . . . 506 Lab. Hymn 15
For all his bounties upon man bestowed: . . . 517 Pun. Death 1. 7
For opportunity bestowed . . . . 534 *Blest is 99
The Czar bestowed a dower; . . . . 545 Russ. Fug. 366
Full many a glimpse (but sparingly bestowed . . 548 *Stay, bold 18
For what hath been bestowed, then where, where then . . . . 622 Recluse 1. 1. 84
Bestowed new splendour; the melodious birds, . 647 Prelude 2. 370
Bestowed composure on a neighbourhood . . . 676 Prelude 6. 75
A gift then first bestowed. The varied banks . 678 Prelude 6. 203
Hath dropped all functions by the gods bestowed, 732 Prelude 11. 368
—His Parents on the enterprise bestowed . . . 761 Excursion 1. 338
For studious fancy, his quick hand bestowed . . 812 Excursion 4. 726
Called on the lovely wanderer who bestowed . . 814 Excursion 4. 863
Bestowed; were gladsome,—and their moral sense 815 Excursion 4. 938
Have been bestowed, through course of common chance, ... 824 Excursion 5. 131
Of joyful greeting were on him bestowed, . . . 843 Excursion 6. 320
His introverted spirit; and bestowed . . . . 864 Excursion 7. 446
And in return for sympathy bestowed . . . . 874 Excursion 8. 8
From culture, unexclusively bestowed . . . . 890 Excursion 9. 392
Then, intermingling thanks, on each bestowed . 895 Excursion 9. 771
Not upon me alone hath been bestowed, . . . K.8. 243 Recluse 1.1.232
Unprofitable kindliness, bestowed . . . . . K.8. 248 Recluse 1.1.432
On much repentance Grace will be bestow'd. . . K.8. 266 *Rid of 5
Bestowing. Thy quiet soul on all bestowing, . . 9 Collins 6
But, gradually a calmer look bestowing, . . . 337 Aar 4
Bestows. The firm protection she bestows; . . . 154 Flower Garden 46
Be thanks poured out to Him whose Hand bestows, 226 Vernal Ode 45
And exquisite, that sleep alone bestows . . . 324 Ode 1814 71
The thousandth part of what the Nymph bestows; 377 Duddon 7. 8
So may the Soul, through powers that Faith bestows, ... 390 Glencroe 13
The Priest bestows the appointed consecration; . 431 Ecc. Sonn. 2. 11. 4
Go forth, great King! claim what thy birth bestows; . . . . 432 Ecc. Sonn. 2. 15. 6
Through all the colours which the sun bestows, . 690 Prelude 7. 222
The gladsome child bestows at his request; . . 881 Excursion 8. 496
Bestrew. Loose fragments of wild wailing, that bestrew . . . . 380 Duddon 17. 5
On sea-shells that bestrew the sandy beach, . . 696 Prelude 7. 592
Bestrewn. Though with the wreck of loftier years bestrewn. . . . . 733 Prelude 11. 391
Bestrews. Or strip the bough whose mellow fruit bestrews . . . . 335 Namur 8
Bestride. And bade the Snow their ample backs bestride, ... 321 *Humanity, delighting 30
Henceforth bestride;—triumphantly . . . . 404 White Doe 729
How tempting to bestride! . . . . 494 Force of Prayer 18
Of the fleet coursers they bestride, to raise . . 773 Excursion 2. 100
Bestrides. 'Mid that strange audience, he bestrides 234 Power of Sound 138
Bestriding. The Beast bestriding thus, he reached . 246 P. B. 851
Their steeds bestriding,—every mimic shape . . 689 Prelude 7. 138
Bestrode. Of the unwieldy creature he bestrode, . 667 Prelude 5. 132
Bestrown. He looks on festal ground with fruits bestrown; . . . . 213 Dion 36
Heaved less for thy bright plains and hills bestrown 360 Alban Hills 2
His church with monumental wreck bestrown; . 393 Inglewood 10
The dewy turf with flowers bestrown; . . . . 397 White Doe 139
O'er chasms with new-fallen obstacles bestrown, . 431 Ecc. Sonn. 2. 12. 12
Bestrows. In a dry nook where fern the floor bestrows 27 Guilt 161
Bestudded. See **Rock-bestudded.**
Bethesda's. Into Bethesda's pool, with healing virtue 510 F. Stone 126
Bethgelert's. I left Bethgelert's huts at couching-time, ... 746 Prelude 14. 4
Bethink. Bethink you of the hour when on your shoulder . . . . 67 Bord. 1641
Bethink you of your own good name: . . . . 400 White Doe 385
Bethinking. Bethinking him of this, again the boy. K.8. 228 *I will 128
Bethlehem. See **Star-of-Bethlehem.**
From Bethlehem, from the Mounts of Agony . . 426 Ecc. Sonn. 1. 33. 3
The Star of Bethlehem from its sphere invites . 467 St. Bees 113
Bethought. My frame, and I bethought me of two things . . . . 40 Bord. 142
So you bethought you of the many ways . . . 61 Bord. 1289
Bethought him, and he to himself would say, . . 132 Michael 54
And I bethought me of the playful hare: . . . 195 Resolution 30
Bethought him, angry and ashamed, ... 412 White Doe 1450
Betide. What must be done? what will betide? . 126 Idiot Boy 31
For I must have, whate'er betide, ... 176 Waggoner 1. 259
"Whate'er betide, we'll turn aside, ... 292 Yarrow Unv. 7

Betide—*continued.*
With all of us, whate'er betide. 408 *White Doe* 1093
To the babe, whate'er betide, 503 **Like a* 58
Betimes. And who is she, betimes abroad, 130 *Idiot Boy* 409
Who gathered in betimes the unshorn flock 381 *Duddon* 23. 2
Enter betimes with more than martial fire 529 **Those breathing* 128
Though I had learnt betimes to stand unpropped, 652 *Prelude* 3. 227
Uprisen betimes, our journey we renewed, 684 *Prelude* 6. 649
Shepherds and tillers of the ground—betimes 699 *Prelude* 8. 8
Betoken. Air, earth, sea, sky, and heaven, success betoken." 371 *Eg. Maid* 156
That best betoken patriot loyalty. 629 *Installation* 85
Betokens. A calmness that betokens strength to bear [?] **A sad* 6
Betook. At midnight, I betook me to the Churchyard: 47 *Bord.* 574
And his old Father both betook themselves 132 *Michael* 104
The weary Sun betook himself to rest;— 192 *Gipsies* 13
I to the sport betook myself again. 673 *Prelude* 5. 490
Betray. Of fainter gold, a purple gleam betray. 5 *Ev. Wk.* 177
Betray the Elf that loves to dwell 143 **Driven in* 25
The silent company betray: 180 *Waggoner* 4. 32
That might his trespasses betray. 181 *Waggoner* 4. 153
Doth she betray us when they're seen? or are they but a name? 189 *Star-gazers* 16
Knowing that Nature never did betray 207 *Tintern* 122
Betray not by the cozenage of sense 233 *Power of Sound* 85
That might his steps betray. 240 *P. B.* 340
That might thy sylvan confidence betray. 273 **Wild Redbreast* 8
Feel not that Conscience never can betray, 441 *Ecc. Sonn.* 3. 6. 7
Nor thought of tender happiness betray; 494 *Hap. War.* 73
To hide what they betray! 543 *Russ. Fug.* 168
Betray me, serving often for a cloak 635 *Prelude* 1. 244
Frail human will, dependent should betray 720 *Prelude* 10. 180
(Which doth at once befriend us and betray) 779 *Excursion* 2. 533
Betray to sight the motion of the stream, 800 *Excursion* 3. 976
So cowardly, so ready to betray, K.8. 238 *Recluse* 1. 1. 66
Betray their occupation, rising up, K.8. 251 *Recluse* 1. 1. 554
Betrayed. *See* **Self-betrayed.**
There, objects, by the searching beams betrayed, 4 *Ev. Wk.* 102
Betrayed, in darkness! Here to strike the blow— 54 *Bord.* 902
We wonder at ourselves like men betrayed: 65 *Bord.* 1542
No more was heard of? I had been betrayed. 69 *Bord.* 1755
And cannot.—You have betrayed me—I have done— 70 *Bord.* 1846
Have you betrayed me? Speak to that. The mask, 70 *Bord.* 1860
We are betrayed! His Daughter!—God have mercy! 72 *Bord.* 2009
(Abused, betrayed, but how it matters not) 76 *Bord.* 2208
By friends deceived, by foes betrayed, 113 *Lament* 59
Check with thy notes the impulse which, betrayed 190 **Lyre! though* 6
To hearts so oft by hope betrayed; 224 **'Tis gone* 28
His peace hath no offence betrayed; 247 *P. B.* 937
Never before to human sight betrayed. 252 **The fairest* 8
Things incomplete and purposes betrayed 269 *Malham* 12
Wandering with timid footsteps oft betrayed, 272 *Ruins* 2
While glory seemed betrayed, while patriot-zeal 334 **A wingèd* 11
And therefore are betrayed. 348 **Lulled by* 30
Should beat too strongly, both may be betrayed. 378 *Duddon* 10. 12
He looked about like one betrayed: 411 *White Doe* 1393
No Spirit was she; *that* my heart betrayed, 440 *Ecc. Sonn.* 3. 1. 5
Some spake, by thought-perplexing fears betrayed; 445 *Ecc. Sonn.* 3. 22. 6
He, by the alluring element betrayed, 470 **A youth* 5
When novel trusts by folly are betrayed,— 504 *Warning* 69
Betrayed by mockery of holy fear. 514 **Portentous change* 8
Won confidence, now ruthlessly betrayed 515 *Penn.* 7
Who had betrayed their country. The stern word 517 *Pun. Death* 3. 2
A steadfast peace that might not be betrayed. 578 *Peele Castle* 32
Such sympathies, though rarely, were betrayed 651 *Prelude* 3. 144
Or left (by mere timidity betrayed) 728 *Prelude* 11. 70
And the errors into which I fell, betrayed 731 *Prelude* 11. 287
Friendship betrayed, affection unreturned, 791 *Excursion* 3. 377
For Man's affections—else betrayed and lost, 837 *Excursion* 5. 1006
But not betrayed by tenderness of mind K.8. 245 *Recluse* 1. 1. 309
Betrayer. Cast off by her Betrayer, she dwells alone, 44 *Bord.* 384
She was reserved by me her life's betrayer; 372 *Eg. Maid* 236
The rash betrayer could not face the shame 853 *Excursion* 6. 1006
Betraying. Till a betraying sickliness was seen 840 *Excursion* 6. 156
Betrays. The rear through iron brown betrays a sullen gleam. 6 *Ev. Wk.* 204
A last infirmity betrays, 216 *Enterprise* 50
Remembrance persecutes, and Hope betrays; 259 **Weak is* 2
Yon azure smoke betrays the lurking town; 658 *Prelude* 4. 24
And then betrays; accuses and inflicts 827 *Excursion* 5. 326
That tires not, nor betrays. Our life is turned 885 *Excursion* 9. 113
Betrothèd. Which with the dear Betrothèd *was* to come; 458 *Sea-shore* 14
To be waylaid by her betrothèd, peace S. 3. 436 **The doubt* 143
Better. Be better fed. Ne'er may I own the heart 38 *Bord.* 67
Our march of yesterday had better suited 39 *Bord.* 107
Shall squire you, (would it not be better, Sir?) 43 *Bord.* 312
He should have used me better!—Charity! 45 *Bord.* 449
You'd better like we should descend together, 51 *Bord.* 771
Felt warm as a wren's nest. You'd better turn 53 *Bord.* 862
The deeper malady is better hid; 56 *Bord.* 1035
And I, no coward in my better days, 61 *Bord.* 1287
I had a better guide—that innocent Babe— 62 *Bord.* 1368
Would have been better timed. Alone, I see; 64 *Bord.* 1471

Better—*continued.*
These stifling blasts—God help me! Better this bare rock, 67 *Bord.* 1658
Lovers lock up as pearls, though oft no better 68 *Bord.* 1680
The wider space the better—we may find 78 *Bord.* 2307
Far better than the sages' books, 85 *Shepherd-boys* 85
And bade them better mind their trade. 85 *Shepherd-boys* 99
For better lore would seldom yearn, 86 *Anecdote* 58
I now can see with better eyes; 117 *Affl. Marg.* 40
Her body—it grew better. 130 *Idiot Boy* 416
Her body still grew better. 130 *Idiot Boy* 421
'Twere better to be dumb than to talk thus. 134 *Michael* 241
To see a better day. At eighty-four 137 *Michael* 389
The breeze had better been asleep, 156 *Oak and Broom* 43
There is a better and a best; 168 *Wren's Nest* 30
The better fortune or the worse; 178 *Waggoner* 3. 17
And so were better manners bred, 179 *Waggoner* 3. 108
And, to be the better seen, 181 *Waggoner* 4. 144
Of thoughts with better thoughts at strife, 191 *Seq. Beggars* 19
Regard not her:—oh, better wrong and strife 192 *Gipsies* 21
With men to whom no better law 194 *Ruth* 146
Nor better life was known; 194 *Ruth* 147
Full soon that better mind was gone: 194 *Ruth* 181
Better provide thee with a Cuckoo-clock, 229 *Cuckoo-clock* 7
That taints the purer, better, mind; 233 *Power of Sound* 88
Would not a whit the better be; 237 *P. B.* 54
And make no better use of it; 237 *P. B.* 79
Was heart or head the better. 239 *P. B.* 240
Who mad'st at length the better life thy choice, 255 *Detraction* 10
The world which we inhabit? Better plea 256 **Yes! hope* 5
If ye would give the better will 286 *Sons of Burns* 11
Without a better guide. 295 *Highland Boy* 40
Still better pleased as more and more 296 *Highland Boy* 153
And tongues that uttered wisdom—better none: 307 **Great men* 2
The truth should now be better understood; 309 **England! the* 3
Fair seed-time, better harvest might have been 309 **England! the* 5
I better like a blunt indifference, 319 **Avaunt all* 3
Of Ilex, or, if better suited to the hour, 361 **List—'twas* 20
Better to breathe at large on this clear height 376 *Duddon* 1. 11
If not, O Mortals, better cease to live! 388 **The pibroch's* 14
Better to thank a dear and long-past day 392 *Bothwell* 9
To have no seat for thought were better doom, 394 **How profitless* 6
Thy place be on my better hand;— 400 *White Doe* 409
That shows, ev'n on its better side, the might 437 *Ecc. Sonn.* 2. 36. 5
A better will; and, in the imagined view 447 *Ecc. Sonn.* 3. 27. 13
With thy stern aspect better far agrees 466 *St. Bees* 25
Better, if Reason's triumphs match with these, 468 *St. Bees* 160
Better than such discourse doth silence long, 488 *Pers. Talk* 9
Better fate have Prince and Swallow— 490 *Incident: Dog* 25
From well to better, daily self-surpast: 494 *Hap. War.* 76
So shall the truth be better understood, 515 **Men of* 13
Crime might lie better hid. And, should the change 519 *Pun. Death* 8. 9
A blooming Lass—who in her better hand 523 *Epist. Beaumont* 107
For thy better memory. 535 *Egremont* 20
Yet, since I may no better, would I kiss 563 *Troilus* 33
The fields better suited the ease of his soul: 569 *Farmer* 22
Let not our times halt in their better choice. 627 **When Severn's* 14
Be nothing better than a wandering cloud, 632 *Prelude* 1. 17
Sometimes it suits me better to invent 635 *Prelude* 1. 221
Ah! better far than this, to stray about 635 *Prelude* 1. 250
Far better never to have heard the name 636 *Prelude* 1. 255
O'erpowered my better reason, and the bird 637 *Prelude* 1. 319
With better knowledge how the heart was framed 641 *Prelude* 1. 628
From the remembrances of better things, 652 *Prelude* 3. 240
A boy, no better, with his rosy cheeks 653 *Prelude* 3. 290
Did better suit my visionary mind, 656 *Prelude* 3. 523
Far better, than to have been bolted forth, 656 *Prelude* 3. 524
For permanent possession, better fruits, 656 *Prelude* 3. 529
Far better had it been to exalt the mind 663 *Prelude* 4. 304
When from our better selves we have too long 663 *Prelude* 4. 354
Sprinkling this talk with questions, better spared, 665 *Prelude* 4. 438
Rises to lead him toward a better clime, 670 *Prelude* 5. 333
A better eye than theirs, most prodigal 671 *Prelude* 5. 361
With a dear friend, and for the better part 674 *Prelude* 5. 561
I was a better judge of thoughts than words, 676 *Prelude* 6. 106
Alone, that something of a better life 703 *Prelude* 8. 313
Of Kings, their vices and their better deeds, 716 *Prelude* 9. 494
In framing their own laws; whence better days 717 *Prelude* 9. 531
And perfect triumph for the better cause. 718 *Prelude* 10. 30
No better than a landsman on the deck 721 *Prelude* 10. 227
Untired, the better, surely, would preserve 727 *Prelude* 11. 26
And can reap nothing better,—child-like longed 728 *Prelude* 11. 68
The plain straight road, for one no better chosen 728 *Prelude* 11. 71
When erring, erring on the better part, 729 *Prelude* 11. 157
Through want of better knowledge in the heads 743 *Prelude* 13. 215
That, whatsoever falls my better mind, 748 *Prelude* 14. 147
Express the image of a better time, 755 *Recluse* 1. 1. 856
The better portion of his time; and there 761 *Excursion* 1. 350
Ere we built up a pile of better thoughts, 766 *Excursion* 1. 687
It seemed the better part were gnawed away 769 *Excursion* 1. 838
Of pain were keen as those of better men, 775 *Excursion* 2. 279
No dearer relique, and no better stay, 778 *Excursion* 2. 483
"Nor could your coming have been better timed; 779 *Excurs* 2. 526
I love it better than a snail his house. 781 *Excursion* 2. 652
Can be attained,—a better sanctuary 789 *Excursion* 3. 223
A better state than waking; death than sleep: 790 *Excursion* 3. 279
Of better entertainment:—let us hence!" 791 *Excursion* 3. 320
Change manifold, for better or for worse: 803 *Excursion* 4. 125
"You have known lights and guides better than these. 816 *Excursion* 4. 1017

Blame—*continued.*
I give to thee, for praise or blame, ... 158 *With little 14
As much as may be of the blame, ... 181 Waggoner 4. 90
Accept, O Friend, for praise or blame, ... 182 Waggoner 4. 197
Praise, blame, love, kisses, tears, and smiles. . . 186 *She was 20
Yet, Showman, where can lie the cause? Shall thy Implement have blame, ... 189 Star-gazers 9
What matters it?—I blame them not . . . . 289 Glen-Al. 19
Yet downcast as a woman fearing blame; . . 305 *We had 4
But gently, gently blame her— . . . . . . 374 Eg. Maid 373
Such wrong; nor need *we* blame the licensed joys, 382 Duddon 23. 12
Than blame the present, that our wish hath crost. 392 Bothwell 11
Tree, flower, and green herb, feeding without blame. . . . . 392 Avon 8
And blame not me if my heart and sight . . . 397 White Doe 71
They might deserve a good Man's blame; . . 409 White Doe 1224
Then blame not those who, by the mightiest lever 427 Ecc. Sonn. 1. 34. 9
Of worship, glory and grace, which who shall blame 430 Ecc. Sonn. 2. 9. 7
Had wondered at the work. But blame him not, 548 *Stranger! this 20
This work of thine I blame not, but commend; . 579 Peele Castle 43
Nor wilt thou blame an aged Poet's prayer, . . 628 *Deign, Sovereign 21
Fearless of blame, that hence for future days . . 643 Prelude 2. 74
To puissant efforts. Nor was this the blame . . 654 Prelude 3. 347
With any thought that looks at others' blame; . 669 Prelude 5. 262
For this unnatural growth the trainer blame, . . 670 Prelude 5. 328
This I repeat, was mine; mine be the blame. . 677 Prelude 6. 189
The blame is ours, not Nature's. When a taunt . 725 Prelude 10. 470
Objects unseen before, thou wilt not blame . . 744 Prelude 13. 305
In holiness and truth." "You cannot blame," . 826 Excursion 5. 292
"I blame them not," he calmly answered—" no; 827 Excursion 5. 309
Who saw enough for blame and pitying love. . . 843 Excursion 6. 362
What boots the sculptured tomb? And who can blame, ... 847 Excursion 6. 615
Of mortals (if such fables without blame . . . 868 Excursion 7. 733
A conquest? who must bear the blame? sage man K.8. 238 Recluse 1. 1. 62
Is past we blame it not for having come. . . . K.8. 244 Recluse 1. 1. 291

Blamed. I had, my Country—am I to be blamed? . 308 *When I 5
With me is now such passion, to be blamed . . 634 Prelude 1. 144

Blameless. She flung her blameless child, . . . 103 Artegal 38
Of blameless debt. On evil Fortune's spite . . 138 Widow 5
Ye, who within the blameless mind . . . . 191 Seq. Beggars 34
Why should it daunt a blameless prayer? . . . 217 Enterprise 121
While flowing rivers yield a blameless sport, . . 254 Complete Angler 1
From stain or taint; in which thy blameless mind 264 *Lady! I 11
The blameless Muse, who trains her Sons . . . 386 Yarrow Rev. 43
The blameless Lady had exprest . . . . . 400 White Doe 375
And live at home in blameless ease; . . . . 400 White Doe 395
Blameless—with them that shuddered o'er his grave, 517 Pun. Death 2. 13
As blameless pleasure, not without some tears, . 526 *Soon did 14
The blameless cause lay in the Theme itself. . . 539 *Lady! a 11
The blameless inmates, and belike subvert . . 681 Prelude 6. 426
Have quarrelled with that blameless spectacle . 725 Prelude 10. 508
Blameless, so intimate with love and joy . . . 796 Excursion 3. 682
They stayed not long.—The blameless Infant grew; 852 Excursion 6. 930
Capacious and serene; his blameless life, . . . 854 Excursion 6. 1066
Of whose society the blameless Man . . . . 864 Excursion 7. 441

Blanc. Unveiled the summit of Mont Blanc, and grieved . . . . 683 Prelude 6. 525

Blanch. And blanch, without the owner's crime, . 113 Lament 41
Blanch, Swift, and Music, noblest of their kind, . 201 Hart-leap 19

Blanched. When I behold thy blanched unwithered cheek, ... 274 *Such age 6

Bland. The bland composure of eternal youth! . 221 Triad 140
Freely as in youth's season bland, ... 286 Nith 26
That sense, the bland philosophy of life, . . . 583 *With copious 13
Then Summer lengthen'd out his season bland, . 611 Desc.Sk.Quarto 476
Of bland entreaty at her court detains; . . . 624 Æneid 20
As bland as the reed of peace: . . . . 629 Installation 37

Blandishment. Hired minstrel of voluptuous blandishment; . . . . 843 Excursion 6. 355

Blank. Now, in this blank of things, a harmony, . 1 Early Youth 7
Was lost, though still he looked, in the blank sky. 24 Guilt 23
But what is done will save you from the blank . 71 Bord. 1870
On the blank plains,—the coldness of the night, . 172 Infant Daughter 22
'Mid the blank world of snow and ice, ... 216 Enterprise 63
By this blank wall, from every eye, ... 223 *'Tis gone 5
Cleaves the blank air, Life flies: now every day . 270 *If these 9
That unencumbered whole of blank and still, . . 277 *Haydon! let 5
Though I beheld at first with blank surprise . . 279 *Though I 1
She vanished; leaving prospect blank and cold . 334 *A winged 6
O'er the blank Area of sacred earth . . . . 355 Aquap. 158
When the blank day is over, garreted . . . . 359 *They—who 3
A gloomy NICHE, capacious, blank, and cold; . . 379 Duddon 15. 3
In the blank earth, neglected and forlorn, . . . 383 Duddon 29. 10
The notes, in prelude, ROSLIN! to a blank . . 387 Roslin 5
For him abandoned to blank awe, ... 411 White Doe 1387
Of blank astonishment; . . . . 457 *Had this 4
Nor aught that makes men's promises a blank, . 470 *A youth 12
Blank ocean and mere sky, support that mood . 488 Pers. Talk 31
Espied him on his legs sustained, blank, mute, . 523 Epist. Beaumont 140
Blank misgivings of a Creature . . . . . . 589 Immortality 148
Locks every function up in blank reserve, . . . 635 Prelude 1. 246
Or blank desertion. No familiar shapes . . . 638 Prelude 1. 395
In trepidation, from the blank abyss . . . . 682 Prelude 6. 470
Oh, blank confusion! true epitome . . . . . 698 Prelude 7. 722
And, in the blank and solitude of things, . . . 798 Excursion 3. 848
The blank air—for the region all around . . . 807 Excursion 4. 408
Incongruous, impotent, and blank.—But, oh! . 827 Excursion 5. 317
An unillumined, blank, and dreary, plain, . . . 830 Excursion 5. 537

Blank—*continued.*
Cold, sullen, blank, from hope and joy shut out; . 831 Excursion 5. 555
To the blank margin of a Valentine, ... 851 Excursion 6. 892
To save themselves from blank forgetfulness!" . 877 Excursion 8. 230
Wide, sluggish, blank, and ignorant, and strange— 880 Excursion 8. 410
And blank dissociation from a world . . . . S. 3. 435 *The doubt 116

Blanket. He has a blanket on his back, ... 536 Goody Blake 7

Blankets. And blankets were about him pinned; . 537 Goody Blake 114

Blanket-walls. Their bed of straw and blanket-walls. 192 Gipsies 8

Blankness. A sudden blankness overspreads his face. 63 Bord. 1439

Blarney. And wished, at least, to hear the blarney S. 3. 438 *My Lord 13

Blaspheme. They paused, and heard a hoarser voice blaspheme, ... 33 Guilt 466

Blasphemy. —The voice of blasphemy the fane alarms, ... 11 Desc. Sk. 59
At this audacious blasphemy, I thought . . . 51 Bord. 793
That shall protect from blasphemy the Land. . . 450 Ecc. Sonn. 3. 39. 14
And Blasphemy the shuddering fane alarms; . . 603 Desc. Sk. Quarto 61
The voice of woman utter blasphemy— . . . 693 Prelude 7. 385

Blast. *See* **Sea-blast, Whirl-blast.**
Or thrill of Spartan life is caught between the blast. 15 Desc. Sk. 269
Ran mountains high before the howling blast, . 29 Guilt 291
The cold blast struck me. 'Twas a foolish question. . . . . 52 Bord. 838
But, hearing soon upon the blast . . . . . 82 Alice Fell 15
Within the eddy of a common blast, ... 122 V. and J. 27
To keep at bay the howling blast, ... 144 *Driven in 66
That, for protection from the nipping blast, . . 150 *When, to 17
There came a furious blast; . . . . 157 Oak and Broom 102
We've weathered many a furious blast; . . . 179 Waggoner 3. 80
Perchance was on the blast, ... 215 Kirkstone 42
To accompany the verse? The mountain blast . 230 Clouds 61
Mounts with a tune, that travels like a blast . . 233 Power of Sound 68
Arm at its blast for deadly wars) . . . . . 235 Power of Sound 214
Down from the far-seen mount. No blast might kill 276 Oker Hill 8
Yes, I will forth, bold Bird! and front the blast, . 279 *Hark! 'tis 9
Oh! spare to sweep, thou mournful blast, . . 285 Grave of Burns 59
The prophecy,—like that of this wild blast, . . 314 *I dropped 12
Hunger, and sultry heat, and nipping blast . . 320 *Hunger, and 1
The trumpet blew a universal blast! . . . . 331 Ode: Thanks. 152
While the tubed engine feels the inspiring blast, . 332 Ode: Thanks. 216
Dread hour! when, upheaved by war's sulphurous blast, ... 340 Fort Fuentes 1
Green boughs were borne, while, for the blast that shook . . . . 346 Processions 16
Through Europe, echoing from the newsman's blast, 349 Val. Dover 3
Anon the breeze became a blast, ... 369 Eg. Maid 29
No meaner Poet than the whistling Blast, . . . 376 Duddon 2. 7
Into rude shape by fire, with roaring blast . . . 379 Duddon 15. 11
The blast will sweep us all away— . . . . . 402 White Doe 554
The faintest note to echo which the blast . . . 440 Ecc. Sonn. 2. 46. 2
Where now the ships that drove before the blast, 454 Sea-side 11
Where moans the blast, or beats the wave, . . 472 Ossian 26
And whole artillery of the western blast, . . . 474 *Hope smiled 4
And sunbeams; and the sounding blast, . . . 491 Fidelity 31
From every hurtful blast, ... 502 Seasons 2
But now, when every sharp-edged blast . . . 507 May 37
On old temptations, might for ever blast. . . . 520 Pun. Death 12. 14
He was acknowledged: and the blast, ... 535 Egremont 15
A blast was uttered from the Horn, ... 535 Egremont 79
Hubert! though the blast be blown . . . . 536 Egremont 85
Her fancy rode the blast; . . . . 544 Russ. Fug. 244
A death-proclaiming blast; . . . . 544 Russ. Fug. 276
Now standing forth an offering to the blast, . . 571 *There is a Flower 11
And blast of trumpets. He who hath been doomed 574 Chiabrera 4. 5
Oh, fled for ever! vanished like a blast . . . 583 *With copious 17
While thrills the "Spartan fife" between the blast. 608 Desc.Sk.Quarto 331
Havoc and Chaos blast a thousand vales, . . . 615 Desc.Sk.Quarto 695
Parted and re-united by the blast. . . . . . 622 Recluse 1. 1. 162
Suspended by the blast that blew amain, . . . 637 Prelude 1. 334
A loud prophetic blast of harmony; . . . . 667 Prelude 5. 95
His front against the blast, and runs amain, . . 723 Prelude 10. 373
Distempered, till they found, in every blast . . 727 Prelude 11. 41
Then, like a blast that dies away self-stilled, . . 767 Excursion 1. 737
Like smoke, along the level of the blast, . . . 782 Excursion 2. 703
Without remission of the blast or shower, . . . 783 Excursion 2. 799
In spite of many a rough untoward blast, . . . 828 Excursion 5. 396
By blast of trumpet?' Plenteous was the growth 858 Excursion 7. 94
Screen'd from assault of every bitter blast; . . 860 Excursion 7. 201
A guardian planted to fence off the blast, . . . 866 Excursion 7. 613
A dull forbidding blast, ... S.3. 431 *The Scottish 18

Blasted. And *blasted* quarry thunders, heard remote! 4 Ev. Wk. 141
And think that they were blasted for my sake, . 39 Bord. 137
She saw my blasted face—a tide of soldiers . . 40 Bord. 185
I will not murmur; blasted as I have been, . . 53 Bord. 851
Move where the blasted soil is not unworn, . . 213 Dion 88
Had blasted France, and made of it a land . . 308 *One might 2
A dark plume fetch me from yon blasted yew, . 380 Duddon 17. 1
The last leaf on a blasted tree; . . . . . . 402 White Doe 567
Maid of the blasted family, ... 416 White Doe 1867
Unsteadfast, by a blasted yew upstay'd; . . . 606 Desc.Sk.Quarto 252
Upon my left a blasted hawthorn stood; . . . 738 Prelude 12. 301
The single sheep, and the one blasted tree, . . 739 Prelude 12. 319
Death blasted all. Death suddenly o'erthrew . 774 Excursion 2. 199
Remote from Europe; from her blasted hopes; . 798 Excursion 3. 833

Blasts. *See* **Sea-blasts.**
These stifling blasts—God help me! Better this bare rock, ... 67 Bord. 1658
And blasts of heaven will aid their flight; . . . 117 Affl. Marg. 44

Blessings—*continued.*
For the dear blessings of a lowly couch, . . . 528 *Those breathing 84
His present blessings, and to husband up . . . 568 Cumb. Beg. 130
Of some small blessings; have been kind to such 568 Cumb. Beg. 151
And blessings half a century old. . . . . . 578 *I come 64
While Freedom's farthest hamlets blessings share, 615 Desc.Sk.Quarto 724
Saw blessings spread around me like a sea. . . 648 Prelude 2. 395
Of blessings, and most studious of our good, . . 671 Prelude 5. 362
With my first blessings. Nevertheless, on these . 704 Prelude 8. 362
The ability to spread the blessings wide . . . 820 Excursion 4. 1243
And with the blessings of domestic love. . . . 823 Excursion 5. 59
From whom all gifts descend, all blessings flow!" 895 Excursion 9. 754

Blest. *See* **Blessed, Heaven-blest.**
How blest, delicious scene! the eye that greets . 12 Desc. Sk. 107
Was blest as free—for he was Nature's child. . . 18 Desc. Sk. 434
And, blest within himself, he shrinks not from the sound. . . . . 19 Desc. Sk. 491
"We lived in peace and comfort; and were blest 29 Guilt 262
As quiet all within me. I was blest, ... 30 Guilt 340
"Be blest: by sight of thee from heaven was sent . . . . 36 Guilt 629
May you in age be blest with such a daughter!— 52 Bord. 827
May become a blest example . . . . . . 94 Westmoreland Girl 83
At this blest moment led me, if I speak . . . 104 Artegal 152
Blest was I then all bliss above! . . . . . 111 A Complaint 8
With "sober certainties" of love is blest. . . . 112 *O dearer 8
Which, in her own blest nature, rooted deep, . . 118 Maternal Grief 21
And how blest the Reunited, ... 141 Arm. Lady 127
Blest, though every tear that falls . . . . 141 Arm. Lady 130
Then happy lie; for blest am I; . . . . . 145 Her Eyes 49
Hail, blest above all kinds!—Supremely skilled . 153 Morn. Ex. 31
Ah! would you think, even yet how blest . . 155 Waterfall 43
In all this covert of the blest: . . . . . . 159 Green Linnet 10
Too blest with any one to pair; . . . . . 159 Green Linnet 23
The lovely Danish Boy is blest . . . . . . 166 Danish Boy 49
Who was blest as bird could be, ... 171 Kitten 65
But Heaven has blest a good endeavour; . . . 174 Waggoner 1. 113
And weary expectation, have been blest . . . 185 Nutting 28
O blest are the hearers, and proud be the hand . 188 Music 29
This precious boon; and blest a sad abode." . . 210 Laod. 36
Our blest re-union in the shades below. . . . 211 Laod. 142
Or blest procession (to the Immortals dear) . . 213 Dion 29
Blest is that ground, where, o'er the springs . . 224 *'Tis gone 13
Blest times when mystery is laid bare, . . . 226 Present. 68
So shall the seventh be truly blest, ... 228 Devot. Incit. 76
Blest be the song that brightens . . . . . 233 Power of Sound 49
Is Harmony, blest queen of smiles and tears, . . 235 Power of Sound 219
The appropriate calm of blest eternity. . . . 252 Picture 14
The mantling triumphs of a day too blest. . . 255 *Grief, thou 14
A blest estate when piety sublime . . . . . 255 Easter 9
And, haply, there the spirits of the blest . . . 266 *The stars 2
Sweet tones, and caught by a noble Lady blest . 267 St. Cath. 5
Conqueror, 'mid some sad thoughts, divinely blest! 278 Wellington 14
And seems, as more incited, still more blest. . . 279 *Hark! 'tis 5
To thy heart's wish, thy labour blest by God! . 281 Chris. Words. 8
Endears that Lingerer. And how blest her sway, 282 *While beams 9
That such are blest. . . . . 285 Grave of Burns 72
Beholds them blest and blessing. . . . . . 287 Ellen Irwin 24
With heroes, 'mid the islands of the Blest, . . 317 *Brave Schill 3
Blest, above measure blest, ... 329 Ode 1815 125
"What know we of the Blest above . . . . 338 Brientz 1
How blest the souls who when their trials come . 339 Tell 19
And, therefore, art thou blest with peace, serene . 339 Schwytz 6
How blest the Maid whose heart—yet free . . 344 *How blest 1
How blest (if truth may entertain . . . . . 344 *How blest 27
The blest tranquillity that sunk so deep . . . 355 Aquap. 153
For by her Son's blest hand the seed was sown. . 360 Albano 14
And folds thy pinions up in blest repose. . . . 363 *List—'twas 112
For he and he only with wisdom is blest . . . 365 Vallomb. 37
I mingle with the blest on those pure heights . . 365 *Rapt above 3
Some blest assurance, from this cloud emerging, . 372 Eg. Maid 258
Blest Pair! whate'er befall you, ... 374 Eg. Maid 383
Blest its humane Memorial's fond endeavour; . . 394 Countess' Pillar 12
And thus, with short oblivion blest, ... 404 White Doe 776
This dying prayer, and be thou blest!' . . . 410 White Doe 1309
Breathed to a Son forgiven, and blest . . . . 411 White Doe 1423
Oh, moment ever blest! O Pair . . . . . 414 White Doe 1665
Into a soul which now was blest . . . . . 415 White Doe 1756
Blest be the unconscious shore on which ye tread, 422 Ecc. Sonn. 1. 14. 2
And blest the silver Cross, which ye, instead . . 422 Ecc. Sonn. 1. 14. 3
In the blest soil of gospel truth, the Tree, . . . 431 Ecc. Sonn. 2. 10. 2
Blest Prisoners They, whose spirits were at large! 432 Ecc. Sonn. 2. 13. 14
That master them. How enviably blest . . . 438 Ecc. Sonn. 2. 37. 12
Hath blest, respiring from that dismal war . . 438 Ecc. Sonn. 2. 38. 4
By men and angels blest, the glorious light? . . 438 Ecc. Sonn. 2. 38. 14
Near spicy shores of Araby the blest, ... 438 Ecc. Sonn. 2. 39. 10
(Swerves not, how blest if by religious awe . . 442 Ecc. Sonn. 3. 9. 5
Blest Pilgrims, surely, as they took for guide . . 443 Ecc. Sonn. 3. 13. 10
Blest while their Spirits from the woods ascend . 443 Ecc. Sonn. 3. 13. 12
Blest Rite for him whose heart in faith, "I know . 448 Ecc. Sonn. 3. 31. 5
In that blest charge; let us—without offence . 461 *Queen of 44
And under one blest ensign serve the Lord . . 467 St. Bees 104
Blest in their pious ignorance, though weak . . 468 *Ranging the 13
Blest work it is of love and innocence, ... 469 *The feudal 7
Yet blest was Emma when she heard . . . . 478 Somnamb. 55
As blest and as glad, in this desolate gloom, . . 484 *A plague 28
Children are blest, and powerful; their world lies 488 Pers. Talk 23
Mother! blest be thy calm ease; . . . . . 503 *Like a 60
Blest the starry promises,— . . . . 503 *Like a 61
On proud towers, like this humble cottage, blest . 503 Warning 37

Blest—*continued.*
Blest are the moments, doubly blest, ... 506 Lab. Hymn 13
Time was, blest Power! when youths and maids . 506 *While from 17
She bears for *us*—for us how blest, ... 512 *Who rashly 35
Blest Statesman He, whose Mind's unselfish will . 514 *Blest Statesman 1
The soaring lark is blest as proud . . . . . 526 *The soaring 1
Blest is this Isle—our native Land; . . . . 533 *Blest is 1
By a blest Husband guided, Mary came . . . 576 *By a 1
But Heaven is now, blest Child, thy Spirit's home: 581 *Why should we 11
To the blest world where parting is unknown. . 586 Ch. Lamb 131
Mighty Prophet! Seer blest! . . . . . . 589 Immortality 114
For that which is most worthy to be blest; . . 589 Immortality 139
On earth to goodness blest by grace divine. . . 628 *Deign, Sovereign 8
Ever blest wherever seen, ... 629 Installation 114
Hath no beginning. Blest the infant Babe, . . 645 Prelude 2. 232
Our Being's earthly progress,) blest the Babe, . 645 Prelude 2. 234
Of my own native region, and was blest . . . 678 Prelude 6. 195
Risen on mid noon; blest with the presence, Friend! . . . . 678 Prelude 6. 198
That may attest her prowess, blest in thoughts . 684 Prelude 6. 611
By reason, blest by faith: what we have loved, . 752 Prelude 14. 446
Huts where his charity was blest; his voice . . 772 Excursion 2. 63
And they, if blest with health and hearts at ease, 773 Excursion 2. 102
Oh! blest are they who live and die like these, . 780 Excursion 2. 591
"O blest seclusion! when the mind admits . . 816 Excursion 4. 1035
That promises to the end a blest old age!" . . 828 Excursion 5. 389
Blest with a kindly faculty to blunt . . . . 835 Excursion 5. 858
"And blest are they who sleep; and we that know, 836 Excursion 5. 922
The pensive silence, saying:—"Blest are they . . . . 854 Excursion 6. 1069
In one blest moment. Like a shadow thrown . 861 Excursion 7. 283
Full blest he was, 'Another Margaret Green,' . 867 Excursion 7. 672
Holy and blest? and where the winning grace . 878 Excursion 8. 249
Upon the brighter scene. How blest that pair . 888 Excursion 9. 256
Blest in their several and their common lot! . . 888 Excursion 9. 258
And ne'er to fail? Shall that blest day arrive . 894 Excursion 9. 666
The worshippers how innocent and blest! . . . 895 Excursion 9. 714
In the islands of the blest, ... S. 3. 442 Harmodius 12
For they are blest already. None would give . K. 8. 244 Recluse 1. 1. 280
—Blest as they are—to furnish a reply, . . . K. 8. 255 Recluse 1. 1. 684
And Truth had blest the logic of his sword. . . L. 1. 97 Juvenal 3. 66
Issued the blest Redeemer of our race . . . . [?] *A sad 11

Blew. If once they blew a horn this side the Tweed. 50 Bord. 730
As if the wind blew many ways, ... 82 Alice Fell 5
From the peak of the crag blew the giant away. . 86 Rural Arch. 16
And blew with the same breath through days and weeks, ... 96 Brothers 51
When, whether it blew foul or fair, they two . . 96 Brothers 74
Fair blew the wished-for wind—the voyage sped; 103 Artegal 90
Carried the Lady's voice,—old Skiddaw blew . . 147 Joanna 62
That blew us hither!—let him dance, ... 177 Waggoner 2. 44
The wind blew from the mountain-peak, . . . 199 Thorn 156
He neither cracked his whip, nor blew his horn, . 201 Hart-leap 35
The Thing became a trumpet; whence he blew . 260 *Scorn not 13
The trumpet blew a universal blast! . . . . 331 Ode: Thanks. 152
Soft was the wind, that landward blew; . . . 369 Eg. Maid 7
Gales sweet as those that over Eden blew! . . 434 Ecc. Sonn. 2. 24. 14
Nor paused, till o'er the stag he blew . . . . 544 Russ. Fug. 275
Blew softly o'er the russet heath, ... 550 Hermit's Cell 2. 10
Suspended by the blast that blew amain, . . . 637 Prelude 1. 334
And rowed off gently, while he blew his flute . 644 Prelude 2. 169
Whose white belt scared him thence, or wind that blew . . . . 656 Prelude 3. 489
Blew mimic hootings to the silent owls, . . . 671 Prelude 5. 373
"Fresh blew the wind, when o'er the Atlantic Main 798 Excursion 3. 835
And Gideon blew the trumpet, soul-inflamed, . . 870 Excursion 7. 815
But from the Castle turret blew . . . . . S. 3. 431 *The Scottish 17

Blight. A constant interchange of growth and blight! . . . . 212 Laod. 174
Scorching blight or noxious dew, ... 226 Vernal Ode 26
Or blight that fond memorial;—the trees grew, . 276 Oker Hill 9
Must perish;—how can they this blight endure? . 282 Railway 5
Enough of sorrow, wreck, and blight; . . . . 286 Nith 19
"Thou Enemy, my bane and blight! . . . . 406 White Doe 924
Haughty the Bard: can these meek doctrines blight . . . . 419 Ecc. Sonn. 1. 3. 8
How *could* we feel it? each the other's blight, . 473 *We saw 3
Mishap by worm and blight; . . . . . . 507 May 66
Whispering of promise, where no blight . . . 530 Gleaner 11
From meditated blight; . . . . 542 Russ. Fug. 12
The Rose of England suffers blight, ... 628 Installation 21

Blighted. *See* **Sin-blighted.**
All pride; by which all happiness is blighted. . 372 Eg. Maid 198
(Blighted or scathed tho' many branches be, . . 431 Ecc. Sonn. 2. 10. 3
That he was blighted, pale, and waxen less . . 564 Troilus 100
And they had blighted him, had eaten away . . 711 Prelude 9. 144
Like blighted buds; or clouds that mimicked land 843 Excursion 6. 315
How art thou blighted for the poor Man's heart! 878 Excursion 8. 264

Blighting. How canst thou flourish at this blighting hour? . . . . 319 Guernica 5
Two blighting seasons, when the fields were left . 764 Excursion 1. 537

Blights. That all too often are but fiery blights, . 448 Ecc. Sonn. 3. 33. 7

Blind. *See* **Stone-blind.**
To end her wrongs. But if the blind Man's tale . . . . 38 Bord. 72
Blind as the grave, but, as you oft have told me, 40 Bord. 180
And the blind Man was told how you had rescued 42 Bord. 285
A blind old Greybeard and accosted him, . . . 45 Bord. 447
The blind Man—at the silent Girl he looked . . 47 Bord. 540
Of truth, enough to dazzle and to blind, . . . 47 Bord. 564

Bliss—*continued.*
The bliss of walking daily in life's prime . . . 741 *Prelude* 13. 122
For they are Powers ; and hence the highest bliss 747 *Prelude* 14. 113
The measure of my soul was filled with bliss, . . 803 *Excursion* 4. 120
With lip almost as pure.—Domestic bliss . . . 878 *Excursion* 8. 262
The penetrating bliss ; oh surely these . . . K.8. 243 *Recluse* 1.1.234
Blisses. And all these innocent blisses ? . . . . 457 **The sun has* 14
Behold the Child among his new-born blisses, . . 588 *Immortality* 85
Blissful. Of Eden's blissful wilderness, ... 154 *Flower Garden* 4
Does, then, a deep and earnest thought the blissful mind employ . . . . 189 *Star-gazers* 25
Even as these blissful creatures do I fare ; . . 195 *Resolution* 32
Blissful Mary, Mother mild, ... 204 *Brougham* 69
Of blissful quiet 'mid unfading bowers. . . 212 *Laod.* 163
Which makes of thine a blissful state ; . . . 294 *Jedbor.* 82
Held with all Kinds in Eden's blissful bowers. . 362 **List—'twas* 65
Of God, and Heaven's pure Queen—the blissful Mary. . . . . 374 *Eg. Maid* 342
From blissful transport some—from clefts of woe 436 *Ecc. Sonn.* 2. 32. 3
Till breath departs in blissful aspiration : . . . 437 *Ecc. Sonn.* 2. 35. 11
Opened a vision of that blissful place . . . . 446 *Ecc. Sonn.* 3. 24. 10
Of blissful infancy. . . . . 458 **Had this* 64
They knelt in prayer, or sang to blissful Mary. . 477 *Nunnery* 8
Her eyes grew bright with blissful light, . . . 479 *Somnamb.* 138
And they a blissful course may hold . . . . 492 *Duty* 21
For the blissful calm, the peace . . . . . . 502 **Like a* 21
" My knowledge is so weak, O blissful Queen ! . 553 *Prioress* 29
Our blissful Lady, Jesu's Mother dear, . . . 553 *Prioress* 58
Was fashioned for our blissful Lady free ; . . . 553 *Prioress* 81
In honour of that blissful Maiden free, . . . 556 *Prioress* 213
The blissful sound ; and in that very place . . 563 *Troilus* 62
O blissful God of Love ! then thus he cried, . . 563 *Troilus* 64
Now, blissful Lord, so cruel do not be . . . . 563 *Troilus* 81
O would the blissful God now for his joy, . . . 564 *Troilus* 90
Without whose blissful influence Paradise . . . 585 *Ch. Lamb* 67
If e'er they pointed forth the blissful way . . . 619 *School Ex.* 105
Of blissful gratitude and fearless love ? . . . 735 *Prelude* 12. 56
—I, long before the blissful hour arrives, . . . 755 *Recluse* 1. 1. 809
Which those most blissful days reverberate. . . 795 *Excursion* 3. 606
And she lies conscious, in a blissful rest, . . . 867 *Excursion* 7. 646
By all,—a blissful immortality, ... 887 *Excursion* 9. 226
Of blissful Eden this was neither given, . . . K.8. 239 *Recluse* 1.1.105
Blissfully. And I will mate and match him blissfully. 220 *Triad* 7
I yonder saw her eke full blissfully ; . . . . 563 *Troilus* 52
Blithe. And quickens the blithe sound of oars that pass . . . . 13 *Desc. Sk.* 125
Is blithe society, who fills the air . . . . . 80 **Loving she* 13
But, whether blithe or sad, 'tis my belief . . . 100 *Brothers* 347
With others round them, earnest all and blithe, . 133 *Michael* 171
Blithe ravens croak of death ; and when the owl . 153 *Morn. Ex.* 7
" Her voice was blithe, her heart was light ; . . 157 *Oak and Broom* 91
Blithe of heart, from week to week . . . . 161 **Pleasures newly* 33
And many a blithe day they have past. . . . 166 *Stray Pleasures* 12
And this vale, so blithe a place ; . . . . . 171 *Kitten* 52
" Blithe souls and lightsome hearts have we . . 177 *Waggoner* 2. 52
—Blithe spirits of her own impel . . . . . 180 *Waggoner* 4. 11
O blithe New-comer ! I have heard, ... 183 **O blithe* 1
Yet *they*, so blithe of heart, seemed fit . . . . 191 *Beggars* 31
And she was blithe and gay, ... 198 *Thorn* 108
So, truant in waste woods, the blithe Euphrosyne ! 221 *Triad* 106
Will to composure lead—or make thee blithe as bird in bower. . . . . 229 *Cuckoo-clock* 11
Sit blithe and happy ; bees that soar for bloom, . 250 **Nuns fret* 5
Made blithe with plough and harrow : . . . . 293 *Yarrow Unv.* 22
Knit the blithe dance upon the soft green grass ; 322 **Ye Storms* 9
That stream in blithe succession from the throats 329 *Ode : Thanks.* 40
Blithe Paragon of Alpine grace, ... 344 **How blest* 46
Blithe as the lark on sun-gilt wings . . . . 348 **Lulled by* 57
Blithe Autumn's purple crown, and Winter's icy mail ! . . . . 350 *Des. Stanzas* 36
Luminous, blithe, and debonair ? . . . . . . 370 *Eg. Maid* 52
Sad thoughts, avaunt !—partake we their blithe cheer . . . . 381 *Duddon* 23. 1
While Tweed, best pleased in chanting a blithe strain, ... 387 *Scott* 6
What sprinklings of blithe company ! . . . . 396 *White Doe* 10
And hark ! how blithe the throstle sings ! . . . 481 *Tables Turned* 13
As blithe a man as you could see . . . . . 486 **We walked* 7
Catch the blithe music as it sinks and swells, . . 504 *Warning* 43
Blithe Flora from her couch upstarts, ... 506 **While from* 3
Since thou, blithe May, wert born, ... 507 *May* 2
Blithe hopes and happy musings soon took flight, . 523 *Epist. Beaumont* 120
Whence the blithe hail ? behold a Peasant stand . 524 *Epist. Beaumont* 207
The emancipated captive through blithe air . . 528 **Those breathing* 68
Of those emancipated, a blithe host . . . . 681 *Prelude* 6. 387
With these blithe friends our voyage we renewed 681 *Prelude* 6. 407
Drooping or blithe of heart, as might befall ; . . 766 *Excursion* 1. 701
Blithe notes of music, suddenly let loose . . . 773 *Excursion* 2. 118
And, with blithe air of open fellowship, . . . 785 *Excursion* 2. 898
As sound—blithe race ! whose mantles were bedecked . . . . 790 *Excursion* 3. 249
Who happier for the moment—who more blithe . 843 *Excursion* 6. 341
Winds pipe through fading woods ; but those blithe notes . . . . 851 *Excursion* 6. 859
Tender or blithe ; now, as the varying mood . . 857 *Excursion* 7. 16
Pageant and revels of blithe elves—to her . . S. 3. 436 **The doubt* 172
Blither. Not blither is the mountain roe : . . . 83 *Lucy Gray* 25
To blither tasks did Simon rouse . . . . . 483 *Simon Lee* 15
That sport among green leaves, a blither train. . K.8. 243 *Recluse* 1.1.237

Block. Into a chasm a mighty block . . . . 85 *Shepherd-boys* 51
Reposed upon the block ! . . . . 113 *Lament* 70
" Dost thou presume my course to block ? . . 155 *Waterfall* 11
This ponderous block was caught by me, . . . 156 *Oak and Broom* 38
This block—and yon, whose church-like frame . 215 *Kirkstone* 47
Stretched on the block the glittering axe recoils ; 252 **Why, Minstrel* 10
Rumble along thy bed, block after block : . . 464 **Greta, what* 2
Stilled by the ensanguined block of Fotheringay ! 465 **Dear to* 14
To take his sentence from the balanced Block, . 500 *Humanity* 5
The block on which these lines are traced, perhaps, 548 **Stranger ! this* 14
Was but a block hewn from a mighty quarry— . 672 *Prelude* 5. 465
Instinct with vital functions, but a block . . . 703 *Prelude* 8. 299
Ripe for the block that might have spared his son, L. 1. 96 *Juvenal* 3. 48
Blockade. Till storm and driving ice blockade him there. . . . . 19 *Desc. Sk.* 487
Blocks. Blocks out the forms of nature, preconsumes 878 *Excursion* 8. 288
Blois. To the imperial edifice of Blois, ... 716 *Prelude* 9. 482
Blood. *See* **Life-blood.**
He met a traveller, robbed him, shed his blood ; . 25 *Guilt* 70
I feel my error ; shedding human blood . . . 55 *Bord.* 994
I am of flesh and blood, and may I perish . . 57 *Bord.* 1097
We all are of one blood, our veins are filled . . 69 *Bord.* 1739
Did constant meditation dry my blood ; . . . 69 *Bord.* 1773
Light to thy path, warmth to thy blood !—Together 70 *Bord.* 1852
With a few drops of blood cut short the business ; 71 *Bord.* 1868
that is the blood of an unhappy Man. . . . . 71 *Bord.* 1908
I saw the stains of blood upon my clothes— . . 72 *Bord.* 1933
But, for the stains of blood—— . . . . . 72 *Bord.* 1942
His head was bruised, and there was blood about him—— . . . . 74 *Bord.* 2075
At remembrance whereof my blood sometimes will flag ; . . . . 86 *Rural Arch.* 22
Engendering in the blood of hale four-score. . . 98 *Brothers* 203
That besprinkled the field ; 'twas like youth in my blood ! . . . . 116 *Repentance* 32
Desperate the Maid—the Youth is stained with blood ; . . . . 123 *V. and J.* 146
Fond spirit that blindly works in the blood of all— 133 *Michael* 145
Is of royal eastern blood, ... 141 *Arm. Lady* 116
My little boy of flesh and blood ; . . . . . 144 *Her Eyes* 28
It cools my blood ; it cools my brain ; . . . . 145 *Her Eyes* 32
Yet seems a form of flesh and blood ; . . . . 165 *Danish Boy* 24
A sight that would have roused your blood ! . . 178 *Waggoner* 2. 130
And thus, and through distempered blood . . 181 *Waggoner* 4. 181
From Indian blood you deem him sprung : . . 192 *Ruth* 25
And such impetuous blood. . . . . 193 *Ruth* 126
With drops of that poor infant's blood ; . . . 200 *Thorn* 211
To freeze the blood I have no ready arts : . . . 202 *Hart-leap* 98
And blood cries out for blood : but, for my part, 203 *Hart-leap* 138
Earth helped him with the cry of blood : . . . 204 *Brougham* 27
On the blood of Clifford calls ;— . . . . . 205 *Brougham* 143
Felt in the blood, and felt along the heart ; . . 206 *Tintern* 28
And even the motion of our human blood . . . 206 *Tintern* 44
Mine the first blood that tinged the Trojan sand. 211 *Laod.* 126
Hath stained the robes of civil power with blood, 213 *Dion* 56
Too potent over nerve and blood, ... 225 *Present.* 14
A stain—as of a drop of blood . . . . . 244 *P. B.* 721
He knows not how the blood comes there— . . 244 *P. B.* 724
He sees the blood, knows what it is,— . . . 244 *P. B.* 728
" Blood drops—leaves rustle—yet," quoth he, . 245 *P. B.* 808
To flesh and blood ; no Goddess from above, . . 252 **Her only* 13
Nor heat, at Tam o'Shanter's name, their blood) . 255 *Detraction* 6
With purer robes than those of flesh and blood, . 268 **Brook ! whose* 12
These natural council-seats your acrid blood . . 268 **DogmaticTeachers* 6
Than flesh and blood ; whene'er thou meet'st my sight, ... 274 **Such age* 5
Suns that through blood their western harbour sought, ... 299 *Brownie's Cell* 61
Of Earth's first blood, have titles manifold. . . 307 **It is not* 14
Blood flowed before thy sight without remorse ; . 316 **Hail, Zaragoza* 9
Descend on all that issues from our blood. . . 319 *Biscayan* 14
For whose dire ends tears flow, and blood is spilt, 321 **Here pause* 11
Nor spared the reverend blood that feebly runs ; . 321 **Humanity, delighting* 23
Of dreadful sacrifice ; by Russian blood . . . 322 **By Moscow* 2
Checked in the very act and deed of blood, . . 322 *Germans* 3
—A gentle Boy (perchance with blood . . . . 342 *Ital. Itin.* 79
The blood of Heroes runs its race ! . . . . . 344 **How blest* 48
Save in this Rill that took from blood the name . 361 **When here* 7
Wash with Thy blood my sins ; thereto incline . 366 **Eternal Lord* 12
Anguish, and death : full oft where innocent blood 392 *Avon* 10
Our noblest blood is given in trust, ... 403 *White Doe* 647
The infant Heir of Mowbray's blood— . . . 405 *White Doe* 823
That grey-haired Man of gentle blood, ... 409 *White Doe* 1201
That he was born of gentle blood ; . . . . . 413 *White Doe* 1528
Of victory mounts high, and blood is quaffed . . 432 *Ecc. Sonn.* 2. 16. 5
Which showers of blood seem rather to incite . . 437 *Ecc. Sonn.* 2. 36. 8
The blood of Huguenots through Paris streamed. . 439 *Ecc. Sonn.* 2. 42. 14
And Russell's milder blood the scaffold wet ; . . 442 *Ecc. Sonn.* 3. 10. 4
That Fortitude, whose blood disdains to freeze . 466 *St. Bees* 16
But *she* is innocent of blood,— . . . . . . 479 *Somnamb.* 86
Between life and death his blood freezes and thaws ; 484 **A plague* 23
Round these, with tendrils strong as flesh and blood, 488 *Pers. Talk* 35
With thy own blood, which tears in torrents shed 514 **Long-favoured* 5
If for deliberate shedder of man's blood . . . 518 *Pun. Death* 6. 13
Blood would be spilt that in his dark abode . . 519 *Pun. Death* 8. 8
A nest of children come of Christian blood, . . 553 *Prioress* 45
The blood cries out on your accursèd deed. . . 554 *Prioress* 127
Unto the blood of Troy, I pray of thee, . . . 563 *Troilus* 82
As Juno was unto the Theban blood, ... 563 *Troilus* 83

Blood—*continued.*
Their kindred, and the children of their blood. 568 *Cumb. Beg.* 140
The freshness of the valleys ; let his blood 568 *Cumb. Beg.* 173
Twice as fast as before does his blood run about ; 570 *Farmer* 54
Within Savona's walls, of gentle blood. 573 *Chiabrera* 3. 4
O flower of all that springs from gentle blood, 575 *Chiabrera* 7. 1
And not by strangers to our blood alone, 627 **We gaze* 6
Which, like a tempest, works along the blood 640 *Prelude* 1. 584
Of happiness, my blood appeared to flow 645 *Prelude* 2. 187
Childless, yet by the strangers to thy blood 659 *Prelude* 4. 38
Through claims of wealth or blood ; nor was it least 713 *Prelude* 9. 222
Upon the traffickers in Negro blood ; 721 *Prelude* 10. 249
A river of Blood, and preached that nothing else 726 *Prelude* 10. 584
A kerchief sprinkled with his master's blood, 778 *Excursion* 2. 478
The nearest in affection or in blood ; 780 *Excursion* 2. 572
There flowed no Gallic blood, nor had I breathed 796 *Excursion* 3. 742
And all the nice regards of flesh and blood) 809 *Excursion* 4. 511
Founded in truth ; by blood of Martyrdom 838 *Excursion* 6. 9
Turned into blood before her heart-sick eye. S.3. 436 **The doubt* 185
Cleanse with thy blood my sins, to this incline K.8. 266 **Rid of* 12
That moistened Dunkirk's sands with blood and tears, L. 1. 96 *Juvenal* 3. 62

Blood-drop. As a blood-drop from my heart. 'Twas even so. 66 *Bord.* 1601
Blood-drop.. Point to his wife the blood-drops on his pillow ! 76 *Bord.* 2184
Like blood-drops from my heart they dropped. 115 *Last of Flock* 64
Bloodiest. In bloodiest battle since the days of Mars ! 180 *Waggoner* 3. 143
Bloodless. Those watery locks, that bloodless cheek ! 372 *Eg. Maid* 215
Blood-red. Flings o'er the desert blood-red streams of fire. 614 *Desc.Sk.Quarto* 663
Decanters, glasses, and the blood-red wine. 644 *Prelude* 2. 144
Blood-reeking. When from the dark synod, or blood-reeking field, 621 *Convict* 25
Bloodshed. And bloodshed, longed in quiet to be laid 320 **They seek* 13
And Fear, and Bloodshed, miserable train ! 493 *Hap. War.* 13
Blood-stained. The blood-stained Writing is for ever torn ; 312 *Clarkson* 11
Else shall your blood-stained hands in frenzy reap 505 *Warning* 138
Blood-thirsty. For the blood-thirsty mead of Odin's riotous Hall. 359 **Complacent Fictions* 14
Bloody. This Boy—when he comes forth with bloody hands— 54 *Bord.* 938
From bloody deeds his thoughts are far ; 166 *Danish Boy* 51
"Cruel of heart were they, bloody of hand," 466 *St. Bees* 37
And thirst for bloody spoils abroad is paired 714 *Prelude* 9. 353
Outrage and bloody power, and—in despite 721 *Prelude* 10. 213
Bloom. And bloom unnoticed even to this late hour ? 103 *Artegal* 60
That kill the bloom before its time ; 113 *Lament* 40
It falls not *here* on bud or bloom. 154 *Flower Garden* 18
That in Madeira bloom and fade, 164 **Fair Lady* 2
Fresh as the bloom upon his face. 166 *Danish Boy* 33
When files of stateliest plants have ceased to bloom, 169 **Never enlivened* 7
For mercy and immortal bloom ? 192 *Seq. Beggars* 42
Shall here put on her beauty and her bloom. 203 *Hart-leap* 172
Given back to dwell on earth in vernal bloom ? 210 *Laod.* 82
In the whole fulness of its bloom, affords 219 *Haunted Tree* 9
Tenderest bloom is on her cheek ; 222 *Triad* 191
The roseate bloom on woman's cheek ; 227 *Vernal Ode* 119
Sit blithe and happy ; bees that soar for bloom, 250 **Nuns fret* 5
Be gracious as the music and the bloom 264 **Lady ! the* 13
How does the Meadow-flower its bloom unfold ? 277 **A Poet* 9
Eyes unbedimmed, see bloom that cannot fade, 279 **All praise* 5
The flowers in pearly dews their bloom renewing ! 283 **Here, where* 8
Where bud, and bloom, and fruitage, glowed, 299 *Brownie's Cell* 97
Fair scenes for childhood's opening bloom, 302 *Yarrow V.* 57
And there shall bloom, with Thee allied, 345 **How blest* 76
Garden and field all decked with orange bloom, 356 *Aquap.* 217
Shall they no longer bloom upon the stock 359 **Those old* 2
That bloom—those eyes—can they assist to bind 363 **Grieve for* 9
But with closed eyes,—of breath and bloom forsaken. 371 *Eg. Maid* 138
So, for the favoured One, the Flower may bloom 372 *Eg. Maid* 255
The lonely Primrose yet renews its bloom, 381 *Duddon* 22. 13
Its bloom, unfolding at the appointed day ; 393 *Countess' Pillar* 3
The fostered hyacinths spread their purple bloom. 425 *Ecc. Sonn.* 1. 27. 14
For everlasting bloom. Benign and pure 445 *Ecc. Sonn.* 3. 21. 9
Garlands shall wear of amaranthine bloom, 474 **On to* 13
There's thought and no thought, and there's paleness and bloom 482 *Character* 3
There berries ripen, flowerets bloom ; 532 †*Float. Isl.* 14
Of the fields, he collected that bloom, when a boy ; 569 *Farmer* 10
Of symmetry and light and bloom, expressed, 711 *Prelude* 9. 150
A residence afford them, 'mid the bloom 879 *Excursion* 8. 373
Of humanised society ; and bloom 890 *Excursion* 9. 389
When good Jemima perished in her bloom ; K.8. 275 **These vales* 2
Bloomed. Where they bloomed singly, or in scattered knots,) 280 *Valedict.* 3
There bloomed the strawberry of the wilderness ; 377 *Duddon* 6. 9
Bloom'd with the snow-drops of Man's narrow bed, 613 *Desc.Sk.Quarto* 595
Of virtues bloomed beneath this lowly roof. 763 *Excursion* 1. 512
Blooming. And with wild flowers and blooming orchards blend ;— 20 *Desc. Sk.* 572
As if a blooming face it ought to be ; 108 *Indolence* 41
The blooming heath their couch, gazed side by side, 151 **Forth from* 11
Come, blooming Hero, place thee by my side ! 210 *Laod.* 62
Inflamed by thee, the blooming Boy 216 *Enterprise* 59
Or blooming thicket moist with morning dews ; 227 *Vernal Ode* 80
Sits blooming like a flower. 238 *P. B.* 160
I see a blooming Wood-boy there, 243 *P. B.* 631
Ye sacred Nurseries of blooming Youth ! 270 **Ye sacred* 1

Blooming—*continued.*
A crest of blooming heather ! 302 *Yarrow V.* 68
O'er blooming fields and gushing springs 338 **Meek Virgin* 28
And blooming thickets ; nor by rocky bands 384 *Duddon* 32. 3
(Ripe men, or blooming in life's spring) 404 *White Doe* 721
And many a blooming, many a lovely, cheek 446 *Ecc. Sonn.* 3. 23. 7
A blooming Girl, whose hair was wet 487 **We walked* 43
A blooming Lass—who in her better hand 523 *Epist. Beaumont* 107
Laden from blooming grove or flowery field, 733 *Prelude* 11. 446
A blooming Lady—a conspicuous flower, 774 *Excursion* 2. 187
Have scarcely disappeared." "This blooming Child," 779 *Excursion* 2. 536
A claim that shattered all.—Our blooming girl, 795 *Excursion* 3. 638
To range her blooming bowers, and spacious fields, 819 *Excursion* 4. 1194
Those blooming Boys, whose hearts are almost sick 884 *Excursion* 9. 29
Of blooming Boys (whom we beheld even now) 888 *Excursion* 9. 257
Blooms. So blooms this lonely Plant, nor dreads 224 *Primrose* 23
Of outward change, there blooms a deathless flower, 256 **Yes ! hope* 13
Of the unfaded rose that still blooms on his cheek. 569 *Farmer* 8
'Mid the dark pines a little orchard blooms, 607 *Desc.Sk.Quarto* 296
Of infancy first blooms upon his cheek ; 836 *Excursion* 5. 958
Beholds the gulf beneath.—No floweret blooms 865 *Excursion* 7. 498
(For all the blooms on Bird-nest brae S.3.431 **The Scottish* 11
Blossom. *See* **Strawberry-blossom.**
Where apple-trees in blossom made a bower, 107 *Indolence* 25
Have they, who nursed the blossom, seen 344 **How blest* 59
A blossom from thy crown to drop, 508 *May* 91
A fly may settle, or a blossom fall. 527 **Those breathing* 12
To utter, above showers of blossom swept 537 **In desultory* 7
"The blossom you so fondly praised 542 *Russ. Fug.* 65
Would plant thee where yet thou might'st blossom again." 621 *Convict* 52
Again the Tree a blossom bears ; 628 *Installation* 27
Blossoming. For everlasting blossoming : 203 *Brougham* 10
Blossoms. *See* **Strawberry-blossoms.**
Bringing thee chosen plants and blossoms blown 106 *Farewell* 34
Spread here his careless blossoms, here 156 *Oak and Broom* 69
Here in my blossoms to behold 156 *Oak and Broom* 83
Their snow-white blossoms on my head, 159 *Green Linnet* 2
Were only blossoms dropped from twigs 170 *Rural Ill.* 23
Her blossoms which, though shed, out-brave 170 *Rural Ill.* 27
Turning blossoms inside out ; 171 *Kitten* 68
Their blossoms, through a boundless range 193 *Ruth* 56
That rifles blossoms on a tree, 221 *Triad* 126
Its blossoms shrivelled, and its fruit, if formed, 266**Desponding Father* 4
He smote the blossoms of their warrior youth ; 321 **Humanity, delighting* 20
Sing ye, with blossoms crowned, and fruits, and flowers, 322 **Ye Storms* 6
With golden blossoms opening at the feet 353 *Aquap.* 29
'Mid new-born blossoms that soft airs were wooing, 360 **Near Anio's* 3
Displayed her richest blossoms among files 361 **List—'twas* 17
From blossoms wild of fancies innocent. 395 *White Doe: Ded.* 32
Where the wild rose blossoms fair ; 397 *White Doe* 123
Delightful blossoms for the *May* 478 *Somnamb.* 61
While blossoms and the budding spray 497 *Lycoris* 51
Of the same face, blossoms upon one tree ; 684 *Prelude* 6. 637
And hopeful blossoms of a second spring : 727 *Prelude* 11. 6
Blossoms of piety and innocence. 774 *Excursion* 2. 169
There blossoms, strong in health, and will be soon 855 *Excursion* 6. 1152
Spring's richest blossoms ; and ye may have marked, 868 *Excursion* 7. 718
When many plants strange blossoms bore S. 3. 431 **The Scottish* 3
A wreath she twines of blossoms lowly born— K.8. 325[?]**The vestal* 6
Blot. Like wreaths of vapour without stain or blot. 390 *Highland Hut* 4
Glad Hearts ! without reproach or blot ; 492 *Duty* 13
When life would be a blot. 544 *Russ. Fug.* 200
—Without one hope her written griefs to blot, 614 *Desc.Sk.Quarto* 676
Blots. Blots out Sichæus, studious to remove 625 *Æneid* 91
Blots from the human countenance all trace 648 *Prelude* 2. 459
Blotted. And saw the tears with which she blotted it. 38 *Bord.* 54
All institutes for ever blotted out 717 *Prelude* 9. 525
Blow. The churlish gales of penury, that blow 19 *Desc. Sk.* 504
As if each blow were deadlier than the last, 33 *Guilt* 474
Betrayed, in darkness ! Here to strike the blow— 54 *Bord.* 902
That half a word should blow it to the winds ! 58 *Bord.* 1144
Action is transitory—a step, a blow, 65 *Bord.* 1539
Fresh flowers blow as flowers have blown, 90 *Longest Day* 38
Which blow at daybreak, droop ere even-song ; 110 **Look at* 2
Whatever wind may blow ?" 198 *Thorn* 103
To blow against thee : and, in after years, 207 *Tintern* 137
He dealt a sturdy blow. 241 *P. B.* 425
Ever before her, and a wind to blow. 258 **Where lies the Land* 8
Or hear old Triton blow his wreathèd horn. 259 **The world is* 14
Must blow to-night his bugle horn. Had I 266 **With how* 8
Of human life : a Stripling's graces blow, 267 **Desponding Father* 9
Faith had her arch—her arch, when winds blow loud, 282 **In my* 8
Have sate and talked where gowans blow, 285 *Grave of Burns* 53
And then the bagpipes he could blow— 295 *Highland Boy* 41
Virtuous and wise. Winds blow, and waters roll, 306 **Inland, within* 10
And greet your sons ! drums beat and trumpets blow ! 310 *Anticip.* 7
Another year !—another deadly blow ! 310 **Another year* 1
Though plenteous flowers around thee blow, 338 **Meek Virgin* 20
Shouts rise, and storms of sound from lifted trumpets blow ! 346 *Processions* 18
Careless of flowers that in perennial blow 376 *Duddon* 1. 5

Blow—*continued.*
Sheds on the flowers that round her blow . . . 397 *White Doe* 104
Must come and ask permission when to blow, . 428 *Ecc. Sonn.* 1. 39. 2
For where, but on *this* River's margin, blow . . 430 *Ecc. Sonn.* 2. 7. 6
I struck, and with a single blow . . . . . 484 *Simon Lee* 85
And lilies face the March-winds in full blow, . . 529 *Poor Robin* 2
By night or day, blow foul or fair, ... 577 **I come* 12
Though, from the widely-sweeping blow, . . . 582 *Invoc. Earth* 17
The cataracts blow their trumpets from the steep; 588 *Immortality* 25
The churlish gales, that unremitting blow . . . 613 *Desc.Sk.Quarto* 604
Blow through my ear ! the sky seemed not a sky 637 *Prelude* 1. 338
Still as a sheltered place when winds blow loud ! . 689 *Prelude* 7. 171
Then, if a widow, staggering with the blow . . 704 *Prelude* 8. 384
Do of itself blow fresh, and make the vanes . . 723 *Prelude* 10. 370
Blow keen upon an eminence that gave . . . 729 *Prelude* 11. 166
And hence a blow that, in maturer age, . . . 730 *Prelude* 11. 186
—'Blow winds of autumn !—let your chilling breath 790 *Excursion* 3. 307
Blow fiercely, agitating earth and sky, ... 795 *Excursion* 3. 651
A calendar of flowers, plucked as they blow . . 841 *Excursion* 6. 174
And sorrow and care blow over him, ... S. 3. 424 *Tinker* 49
With *yellow* in full blow. . . . . S. 3. 431 **The Scottish* 8
Unsettled by a wanton blow from foot. . . . K.8. 226 **I will* 67
To shout with transport o'er a knock-down blow, L. 1. 94 *Juvenal* 2. 14
Blowing. As many will be blowing here. . . . 80 *Foresight* 24
Hues ever fresh, in rocky fortress blowing : . . 337 *Aar* 8
List, the winds of March are blowing ; . . . . 503 *Warning* 1
Its green untrodden turf, and blowing flowers ; . 585 *Ch. Lamb* 54
Was blowing on my body, felt within . . . . 632 *Prelude* 1. 34
Upon the stretch, when winds are blowing fair : . 682 *Prelude* 6. 499
Against the blowing wind. It was, in truth, . . 738 *Prelude* 12. 253
When winds are blowing strong. The traveller slaked . . . . 814 *Excursion* 4. 871
In anger blowing from the distant sea. . . . 833 *Excursion* 5. 703
That flattering breezes blowing thence . . . . S. 3. 431 **The Scottish* 13
Blown. *See* **Full-blown, Half-blown, New-blown.**
The name of Marmaduke is blown away : . . . 39 *Bord.* 138
Blown to you from a trumpet. Why talk thus ? . 56 *Bord.* 1013
By man and nature ;—if a breeze had blown, . . 68 *Bord.* 1700
Fresh flowers blow as flowers have blown, . . . 90 *Longest Day* 38
Bringing thee chosen plants and blossoms blown . 106 *Farewell* 34
Hath blown his bugle horn. . . . . 161 *Binnorie* 20
The bugles that so joyfully were blown ? . . . 201 *Hart-leap* 26
Though a breath made it) like a bubble blown . 250 **Happy the* 3
As when their earliest flowers of hope were blown, 282 *Railway* 4
While the thrill of her fifes thro' the mountains was blown : . . . . 340 *Fort Fuentes* 16
And pleasant course ; flower after flower has blown, 361 **List—'twas* 11
O'er Rylstone's fair domain have blown ; . . . 413 *White Doe* 1569
Yea, like a ship at random blown . . . . . 414 *White Doe* 1615
To be blown off at will, by Power that spares it . 505 *Warning* 109
If expectations newly blown . . . . . . 507 *May* 67
Hubert ! though the blast be blown . . . . 536 *Egremont* 85
Of hopeful life,—by battle's whirlwind blown . . 582 *Invoc. Earth* 12
Within our hearts, the love whose flower hath blown 627 **We gaze* 3
Just three parts blown—a cottage-child—if e'er, . 692 *Prelude* 7. 353
Blown from their favourite resting-place, or mists 699 *Prelude* 8. 16
Blown back upon themselves ; their reason seemed 713 *Prelude* 9. 258
The budding rose above the rose full blown. . . 729 *Prelude* 11. 121
Pleasant as roses in the thickets blown, . . . 773 *Excursion* 2. 109
Blows. And orange gale that o'er Lugano blows ; . 21 *Desc. Sk.* 596
For sight of a warm fire. The wind blows keen ;. 50 *Bord.* 726
And, when the stormy wind blows o'er the peak, 73 *Bord.* 2056
Shine hot, or wind blows troublesome and strong ; 151 **When, to* 89
Fresh blows the wind, a western wind, . . . 161 *Binnorie* 12
And, while he talked of blows and scars, . . . 180 *Waggoner* 3. 138
And every wind that blows ; . . . . . . 198 *Thorn* 70
Blows keenly, it sends forth a creaking sound . 219 *Haunted Tree* 22
And the blows fell with heavier weight . . . 238 *P. B.* 194
And glance, while wantonly the rough wind blows, 262 **Mark the* 4
Whose proffered beauty in safe shelter blows . . 466 *St. Bees* 6
More than the feeblest wind that idly blows. . . 524 *Epist. Beaumont* 170
To me the meanest flower that blows can give . 590 *Immortality* 206
On tiptoe rear'd he blows his clarion throat, . . 594 *Ev. Wk. Quarto* 137
Blows not a Zephyr but it whispers joy ; . . . 602 *Desc. Sk. Quarto* 18
A tournament of blows, some hardly dealt . . 657 *Prelude* 3. 583
Blue. *See* **Black-blue, Clear-blue, Dark-blue, Pale-blue, Sky-blue.**
A blue rim borders all the lake's still brink ; . . 4 *Ev. Wk.* 115
Into blue spots, and slowly lengthening streaks ; . 4 *Ev. Wk.* 119
Blue pomp of lakes, high cliffs and falling floods, 5 *Ev. Wk.* 143
A long blue bar its ægis orb divides, ... 5 *Ev. Wk.* 170
'Cross the calm lake's blue shades the cliffs aspire, 5 *Ev. Wk.* 174
On cold blue nights, in hut or straw-built shed, . 7 *Ev. Wk.* 257
And pours a deeper blue to Æther's bound ; . . 8 *Ev. Wk.* 328
Stretch o'er the pictured mirror broad and blue, . 12 *Desc. Sk.* 94
—Thy lake that, streaked or dappled, blue or grey, 12 *Desc. Sk.* 119
Those fast-receding depths of sable blue . . . 16 *Desc. Sk.* 326
Faint wail of eagle melting into blue . . . 17 *Desc. Sk.* 358
A single chasm, a gulf of gloomy blue, ... 18 *Desc. Sk.* 413
Fell where the blue flood rippled into white ; . . 21 *Desc. Sk.* 627
The gloomy lantern, and the dim blue match, . 32 *Guilt* 419
Those bright blue eggs together laid ! . . . . 79 *Sparrow's Nest* 2
And, while the broad blue wave and sparkling foam 96 *Brothers* 56
With their comely blue aprons, and caps white as snow, ... 120 *Childless Father* 7
The moon is up,—the sky is blue, ... 126 *Idiot Boy* 2
The owlets through the long blue night . . . 129 *Idiot Boy* 287
Helvellyn far into the clear blue sky . . . . 147 *Joanna* 61
But in the storm 'tis fresh and blue . . . . 166 *Danish Boy* 30
In the blue depth, like Lucifer . . . . . . 167 *Pilgrim's Dream* 55

Blue—*continued.*
Red, green, and blue ; a moment's sight ! . . . 180 *Waggoner* 4. 33
And is as happy in his night, for the heavens are blue and fair ; . . . . 189 *Star-gazers* 6
Blue sky prevailing ; . . . . 190 *March* 19
'Mid silver clouds, and openings of blue sky . . 190 **Lyre ! though* 23
When the blue daylight's in the skies, ... 198 *Thorn* 72
When the blue daylight's in the sky . . . . 198 *Thorn* 83
Through half the clear blue sky will go ; . . . 199 *Thorn* 193
And the blue sky, and in the mind of man : . . 207 *Tintern* 99
For blue Ether's arms, flung round thee, . . . 217 **Inmate of* 7
Far into silent regions blue and pale ;— . . . 219 **This Height* 15
Profound of night's ethereal blue ; . . . . . 226 *Vernal Ode* 31
Or racing o'er your blue ethereal field . . . . 229 *Clouds* 7
Flung back, and, in the sky's blue caves, reborn— 233 *Power of Sound* 36
Through many a long blue field of ether, . . . 236 *P. B.* 33
The soft blue sky did never melt . . . . . 239 *P. B.* 263
The witchery of the soft blue sky ! . . . . . 239 *P. B.* 265
Where blue and grey, and tender green, . . . 240 *P. B.* 363
Beneath the clear blue sky he saw . . . . . 240 *P. B.* 366
The broad blue heavens appeared to glimmer, . 241 *P. B.* 484
Blue ether still surrounds him—yet—and yet ; . . 261 **I watch* 4
Hurrying and sparkling through the clear blue heaven ; . . . . 266 **With how* 12
And rolls the planets through the blue profound ; 273 **Wild Redbreast* 12
A blue sky bends o'er Yarrow vale, ... 302 *Yarrow V.* 17
As stretches a blue bar of solid cloud . . . . 311 **Who rises* 28
When morn returns, beneath the clear blue sky, . 322 **Humanity, delighting* 37
The sky was blue, the air was mild ; . . . . 348 **Lulled by* 7
In vain ; the sky will change to sunny blue, . . 360 *Albano* 7
The trembling eyebright showed her sapphire blue, 377 *Duddon* 6. 10
And Thou, blue Streamlet, murmuring yield'st no more . . . . 378 *Duddon* 8. 10
The starry treasure from the blue profound . . 381 *Duddon* 22. 7
To the blue ether and bespangled plain ; . . . 420 *Ecc. Sonn.* 1. 7. 4
Bards, nursed on blue Plinlimmon's still abode, . 421 *Ecc. Sonn.* 1. 10. 12
Before her wane begins on heaven's blue coast ; . 434 *Ecc. Sonn.* 2. 25. 8
Soft as a cloud is yon blue Ridge—the Mere . . 456 **Soft as* 1
Varying her crowded peaks and ridges blue ; . . 471 **Arran ! a* 3
Eyeing the sea's blue depths. Poor Bird ! even so 472 *Dunolly Eagle* 12
And his two pretty pinions of blue dusky gauze . 484 **A plague* 24
Unruffled doth the blue lake lie, ... 498 **The sylvan* 5
If yon ethereal blue . . . . 507 *May* 18
Till they were plucked together ; a blue flower . 509 *F. Stone* 60
As if their lustre flowed from ether's purest blue. 525 *Epist. Beaumont* 257
Break forth,—again to walk the clear blue sky. . 532 **How beautiful the* 8
And the blue sky, one little span of earth . . . 567 *Cumb. Beg.* 50
And pouring deeper blue to Æther's bound ; . . 599 *Ev. Wk. Quarto* 394
Stretch, o'er their pictur'd mirror, broad and blue, 604 *Desc.Sk.Quarto* 103
—Thy lake, mid smoking woods, that blue and grey 604 *Desc.Sk.Quarto* 138
Th' interminable sea of sable blue. . . . . . 609 *Desc.Sk.Quarto* 389
A gulf of gloomy blue, that opens wide . . . 611 *Desc.Sk.Quarto* 498
Of feudal sway, the bright blue river passed . . 636 *Prelude* 1. 285
That streamlet whose blue current works its way 678 *Prelude* 6. 192
The torrents shooting from the clear blue sky, . 684 *Prelude* 6. 629
O'er the blue firmament a radiant white, . . . 709 *Prelude* 8. 663
More keenly than elsewhere in night's blue vault, 782 *Excursion* 2. 721
Once more beneath the concave of a blue . . . 786 *Excursion* 3. 9
Or heaven's blue vault, is suffered to put forth . 789 *Excursion* 3. 211
Athwart the concave of the dark blue dome, . . 819 *Excursion* 4. 1179
Whose blue roofs ornament a distant reach . . 844 *Excursion* 6. 408
Covered the smooth blue slabs of mountain-stone 860 *Excursion* 7. 189
A plain blue stone, a gentle Dalesman lies, . . 863 *Excursion* 7. 400
Bright was the sun, the sky a cloudless blue— . 871 *Excursion* 7. 876
Fanning his temples under heaven's blue arch. . 878 *Excursion* 8. 308
Between his hands he holds a smooth blue stone, 882 *Excursion* 8. 556
The silvery lake is streaked with placid blue ; . 890 *Excursion* 9. 421
Of the blue firmament—aloft, and wide : . . . 893 *Excursion* 9. 596
And put forth *Blue* at last. . . . . S. 3. 431 **The Scottish* 24
While faction Blue from shops and booths . . S. 3. 431 **The Scottish* 29
Of blue unfrozen water, where they lodged, . . K.8. 243 *Recluse* 1. 1. 259
And see the blue beyond.—Type of that grace . [?] **A sad* 9
Blue-breeched. Blue-breeched, pink-vested, with high-towering plumes.— . . . . . . 697 *Prelude* 7. 705
Blue-cap. Blue-cap, with his colours bright, . . 171 *Kitten* 64
Blue-eyed. Whose zeal outruns his promise ! Blue-eyed May . . . . 264 *Snowdrop* 8
Blue-topped. And blue-topped hills, behold him from afar ; . . . . 384 *Duddon* 32. 11
Blunder. Or happy blunder triumphed, bursts of glee 644 *Prelude* 2. 163
Blunt. I better like a blunt indifference, . . . 319 **Avaunt all* 3
Rang with its blunt unceremonious voice, . . . 676 *Prelude* 6. 72
Blest with a kindly faculty to blunt . . . . 835 *Excursion* 5. 858
By notice indirect, or blunt demand . . . . 859 *Excursion* 7. 105
That with blunt repetition of your words . . . K.8. 230 **I will* 180
All plain blunt sense, all subtlety of thought. . . L. 1. 88 *Juvenal* 1. 8
Blush. And never blush was on my face. . . . 117 *Affl. Marg.* 21
Nor blush if o'er your heart be stealing . . . 142 †*Lov. and Lik.* 29
At Nature's call, nor blush to lean . . . . . 223 *Wishing-gate* 59
Shall blush ; and may not we with sorrow say, . 315 **Alas ! what* 10
The thyme her purple, like the blush of Even ; . 377 *Duddon* 6. 11
A shame-faced blush of glowing red ! . . . . 398 *White Doe* 183
Shall Percy blush, then, for his name ? . . . 405 *White Doe* 825
And some, coeval with the earliest blush . . . 436 *Ecc. Sonn.* 2. 32. 5
And reprehended, by a fancied blush . . . . 539 **Lady ! a* 38
To blush for me. Thou, loiter not nor halt . . 575 *Chiabrera* 6. 14
Taking my seat, I saw (nor blush to add, . . . 691 *Prelude* 7. 270
With him can talk ; nor blush to waste a word . 834 *Excursion* 5. 818
Could break from out those languid eyes, or a blush 879 *Excursion* 8. 314

Blush—*continued.*
The boy of plainer garb, whose blush survives . 882 *Excursion* 8. 552
Thy apprehensions—blush thou for them all. . K.8. 238 *Recluse* 1.1. 64
Need only blush for what they once have been, . L.1. 96 *Juvenal* 3. 54
Blush Pride to see a farmer's wife produce . . L.1. 97 *Juvenal* 3. 96
Blushed. He blushed with shame, nor made reply ; 86 *Anecdote* 46*j*
Hung back, and smiled, and blushed for joy, . . 398 *White Doe* 182
Blushes. While across her virgin cheek pure blushes strayed, ... 141 *Arm. Lady* 137
But her blushes are joy-flushes ; . . . . . 222 *Triad* 164
By blushes yet untamed ; . . . . 232 *Jew. Fam.* 30
In Heaven ; hence no one blushes for thy name, . 278 *Wellington* 13
Our groans, our blushes, our pale cheeks declare . 319 *Spaniard* 13
Suffused with blushes of celestial hue, ... 434 *Ecc. Sonn.* 2. 22. 6
And high her blushes mounted ; . . . . . 478 *Somnamb.* 58
Blushing. I stood, of simple shame the blushing Thrall ; . . . . 251 **Beloved Vale* 10
Blushing she eyes the dizzy flood askance ; . . 378 *Duddon* 10. 4
Her blushing cheek, love-vows upon her lip, . . 427 *Ecc. Sonn.* 1. 35. 6
Soon fades her cheek, her blushing beauties fly, . 619 *School Ex.* 97
The blushing mien and downcast look ; . . . 620 *Birth of Love* 33
Of her new office, blushing restlessly. . . . 699 *Prelude* 8. 43
Feeding on sunshine—to the blushing girl . . . S. 3. 435 **The doubt* 141
Blustering. *See* **Hollow-blustering.**
Where leafy shades fence off the blustering gale, . 6 *Ev. Wk.* 234
Associates, and, unscared by blustering winds, . 687 *Prelude* 7. 30
And if the blustering wind that drives the clouds 834 *Excursion* 5. 820
Tricks out her blustering powers, ... S. 3. 431 **The Scottish* 30
Boar. From which the tusky wild boar flies in fear ; 104 *Artegal* 109
Made room where wolf and boar were used to range ? 468 *St. Bees* 139
Board. *See* **Sign-board, Supper-board.**
Of thrice ten summers dignify the board. . . . 19 *Desc. Sk.* 499
No board inscribed the needy to allure . . . 24 *Guilt* 13
Dried up, despairing, desolate, on board . . . 30 *Guilt* 305
It was a rustic inn ;—the board was spread, . . 34 *Guilt* 528
Is it not well with thee ? well both for bed and board ? . . . . 87 *Pet-lamb* 22
His board with lawful joy, and bear . . . . 193 *Ruth* 113
But chiefly from above the board . . . . 204 *Brougham* 21
Pursues the Enthusiast to the social board, . . 265 **There is a pleasure* 7
And hand reposing on the board in ruth . . . 343 *Last Sup.* 11
The Master of whose humble board . . . . 414 *White Doe* 1690
A genial hearth, a hospitable board, ... 444 *Ecc. Sonn.* 3. 18. 1
At his board by these surrounded, ... 535 *Egremont* 75
Of thrice ten summers consecrate the board. . . 613 *Desc.Sk.Quarto* 589
By clearer taper lit a cleanlier board . . . 615 *Desc.Sk.Quarto* 736
On board a ship then ready for the seas. . . . 623 **I find* 8
Set sail, was wrecked, and all on board was lost. . 623 **I find* 11
While round a vacant board the chiefs recline, . 625 *Æneid* 97
She spake and shed an offering on the board ; . 625 *Æneid* 116
Oh, with what echoes on the board they fell ! . 640 *Prelude* 1. 526
Of the old grey stone, from her scant board, supplied. 643 *Prelude* 2. 88
And, hand in hand, danced round and round the board ; . . . . 681 *Prelude* 6. 400
And round and round the board we danced again. 681 *Prelude* 6. 406
Leaving us at the board ; awhile we lingered, . 683 *Prelude* 6. 567
By Nature's gift so favoured. Upon a board . 692 *Prelude* 7. 356
While on the board she spread our evening meal, 767 *Excursion* 1. 757
By which it had been bleached, o'erspread the board ; . . . . 781 *Excursion* 2. 675
Of country 'squire ; or at the statelier board . . 859 *Excursion* 7. 124
Of his own board, where sat his gentle Mate . . 859 *Excursion* 7. 161
Theirs was a hospitable board, and theirs . . 860 *Excursion* 7. 168
—Seven lusty Sons sate daily round the board . 867 *Excursion* 7. 636
Spread on the never-empty board, and drink . . 867 *Excursion* 7. 654
Of unexpected pleasure.—Soon the board . . . 882 *Excursion* 8. 518
Upon the board he lays the sky-blue stone . . 882 *Excursion* 8. 561
So long unthanked) hast cheered a simple board . S. 3. 433 **The doubt* 16
Boards. From time to time, the solid boards, and makes them . . . . 693 *Prelude* 7. 427
Boast. Of any wonder Normandy, or all proud France, can boast ! " . . . . . . 92 *Poet's Dream* 26
Which stands the universal empire's boast ; . . 105 *Artegal* 189
The happiest lovers Arcady might boast, . . . 110 **Look at* 14
Object uncouth ! and yet our boast, ... 174 *Waggoner* 1. 89
France would have had her present Boast, . . 292 *Rob Roy* 95
Hadst this to boast of ; thou didst love . . . 292 *Rob Roy* 103
He, whose heaped waves confounded the proud boast . . . . 322 **By Moscow* 12
Heaven upon earth's an empty boast ; . . . . 337 **Oh Life* 9
(Not Apennine can boast of fairer), hills . . . 353 *Aquap.* 41
Still do our very children boast . . . . . 405 *White Doe* 813
Our tainted nature's solitary boast ; . . . . . 434 *Ecc. Sonn.* 2. 25. 4
" Slaves cannot breathe in England "—yet that boast . . . . 501 *Humanity* 83
Meet them half way." Vain boast ! for These, the more . . . . 513 *Newspaper* 3
Soon the relapsing penitent may boast . . . 519 *Pun. Death* 11. 7
And boast that they alone are free . . . . . 534 **Blest is* 79
O, of all houses once the crownèd boast ! . . . 563 *Troilus* 29
Was the boast of the country for excellent cheer ; 569 *Farmer* 14
What steeds the car of Diomed could boast ; . . 625 *Æneid* 136
Not as our glory and our absolute boast, . . . 645 *Prelude* 2. 213
Nor made unto myself a secret boast . . . . 696 *Prelude* 7. 586
Such palms I boast not ;—no ! to me, who find, . 790 *Excursion* 3. 270
Indifferent judges. 'Spite of proudest boast, . . 830 *Excursion* 5. 500
—Such the too frequent tenour of his boast . . 843 *Excursion* 6. 359
Nature (I but repeat your favourite boast) . . 875 *Excursion* 8. 59
Bishops, of milder Spanish breed, shall boast . . L. 1. 89 *Juvenal* 1. 25
Would More or Henry boast the general voice ? . L. 1. 96 *Juvenal* 3. 42

Boasted. Tokens, once kept as boasted wealth, . . 391 *Highland Broach* 67
A crown for Hope !—I dread the boasted lights . 448 *Ecc. Sonn.* 3. 33. 6
Where now that boasted liberty ? No welcome . 798 *Excursion* 3. 856
Boaster. I hate a boaster ; but to thee . . . . 179 *Waggoner* 3. 83
A boaster that, when he is tried, fails, and is put to shame ? . . . . 189 *Star-gazers* 10
Boastful. Boastful Idolatress of formal skill . . 468 *St. Bees* 158
Beginning to mistrust their boastful guides, . . 695 *Prelude* 7. 515
Of France a boastful Tyrant hurled his threats ; . 869 *Excursion* 7. 758
Oh ! shame ! is this thy service boastful plume ? L. 1. 94 *Juvenal* 2. 18
Boasts. Of Alfred boasts remote Jerusalem, . . 425 *Ecc. Sonn.* 1. 26. 12
Yes, shall the fine immunities she boasts . . . 791 *Excursion* 3. 341
Boat. *See* **Steamboat.**
Sounds from the water-side the hammered boat ; . 4 *Ev. Wk.* 140
The boat her silent course pursues ! . . . . 9 *Lines : Boat* 4
Each with its household boat beside the door ; . 12 *Desc. Sk.* 112
The cries he uttered might have stopped the boat 68 *Bord.* 1733
In such clear water, that thy boat . . . . . 88 *H. C.* 6
Our boat is safely anchored by the shore, . . . 106 *Farewell* 9
Like travellers shouting for a boat. . . . . . 179 *Waggoner* 3. 125
Long is it as a barber's pole, or mast of little boat, 189 *Star-gazers* 3
Until I have a little Boat, ... 236 *P. B.* 4
And now I *have* a little Boat, ... 236 *P. B.* 6
Fast through the clouds my Boat can sail ; . . 236 *P. B.* 8
Both for my little Boat and me ! . . . . . 236 *P. B.* 15
Away we go, my Boat and I— . . . . . . 236 *P. B.* 21
Up goes my Boat among the stars . . . . . 236 *P. B.* 31
Up goes my little Boat so bright ! . . . . . 236 *P. B.* 35
" Shame on you ! " cried my little Boat, . . . 237 *P. B.* 76
Within a living Boat to sit, ... 237 *P. B.* 78
A Boat twin-sister of the crescent-moon ! . . . 237 *P. B.* 80
Off flew the Boat—away she flees, ... 238 *P. B.* 171
Her only pilot the soft breeze, the boat . . . 251 **Her only* 1
In sailor's ship, or fisher's boat, ... 295 *Highland Boy* 84
A boat is ready to pursue ; . . . . 297 *Highland Boy* 182
Leapt, from his storm-vext boat, to land, . . . 300 *Cora Linn* 46
Jesu ! bless our slender Boat, ... 336 **Jesu ! bless* 1
Homeward in their rugged Boat, ... 338 *Brientz* 6
To chant, as glides the boat along, ... 338 *Brientz* 14
" My pearly Boat, a shining Light, ... 370 *Eg. Maid* 103
One boat there was, but it will touch the shore . 453 **Calm is the* 28
And thus from day to day my little boat . . . 489 *Pers. Talk* 49
A silver boat launched on a boundless flood ; . . 532 **Once I* 14
To launch the boat ; and with her blessing cheered, 541 *Grace Darl.* 48
Placed in the little boat, then o'er the deep . . 541 *Grace Darl.* 80
The talking boat that moves with pensive sound, 597 *Ev. Wk. Quarto* 319
Each with his household boat beside the door, . 604 *Desc.Sk.Quarto* 127
A little boat tied to a willow tree . . . . . 637 *Prelude* 1. 358
Of mountain-echoes did my boat move on ; . . 637 *Prelude* 1. 363
And, as I rose upon the stroke, my boat . . . 637 *Prelude* 1. 375
I did not step into the well-known boat . . . 658 *Prelude* 4. 16
Of a slow-moving boat, upon the breast . . . 662 *Prelude* 4. 257
While from a boat others hung o'er the deep, . . 672 *Prelude* 5. 446
On stormy waters, tossed in a little boat . . . 817 *Excursion* 4. 1087
To the lake's margin, where a boat lies moored . 890 *Excursion* 9. 425
Free from obstruction ; and the boat advanced . 891 *Excursion* 9. 490
In twinkling lustre, ere the boat attained . . . 895 *Excursion* 9. 765
Boat-house. Yon chestnuts half the latticed boat-house hide, ... 4 *Ev. Wk.* 107
Before the boat-house peeping thro' the shade ; . 593 *Ev. Wk. Quarto* 106
Boatman. But, lo ! the boatman, overawed, before 15 *Desc. Sk.* 285
And where the boatman of the Western Isles . . 419 *Ecc. Sonn.* 1. 5. 6
Boatmen. Of the sly boatmen of Killarney, . . S. 3. 438 **My Lord* 14
Boat's. The boat's first motion—made with dashing oar ; . . . . 9 *Ev. Wk.* 372
Boats. Come boats and ships that safely ride . . 295 *Highland Boy* 67
To tend their silent boats and ringing wains, . . 335 *Namur* 7
When full five hundred boats in trim array, . . 522 *Epist. Beaumont* 71
Old Roman boats and figures thro' the shade, . 604 *Desc.Sk.Quarto* 117
Bodied. *See* **Feeble-bodied.**
Even such a Man my fancy bodied forth . . . 61 *Bord.* 1321
For bodied forth before my eyes the cross-crowned hut appeared ; . . . . 91 *Poet's Dream* 6
Mere Mortals, bodied forth in vision still, . . . 220 *Triad* 12
Bodied forth and evanescent, ... 550 *Hermit's Cell* 3. 3
Had bodied forth the ghostliness of things . . 681 *Prelude* 6. 428
Bodies. While feeding on their bodies. Would that Idonea . . . . 48 *Bord.* 588
To give their bodies to the family mould. . . . 137 *Michael* 370
Of the dead bodies.—'Twas a day of shame . . 293 *Killicranky* 8
A vault where the bodies are buried upright ! . 398 *White Doe* 245
Their warrant. Bodies fall by wild sword-law ; . 442 *Ecc. Sonn.* 3. 7. 12
Our bodies feel, where'er they be, ... 481 *Expost.* 19
When we had given our bodies to the wind, . . 639 *Prelude* 1. 453
Of many minds, of minds and bodies too ; . . . 761 *Excursion* 1. 376
Nor for their bodies would accept release ; . . 839 *Excursion* 6. 68
Nor bodies crushed by unremitting toil ; . . . 885 *Excursion* 9. 98
Of heavenly bodies shining in their spheres. . . 889 *Excursion* 9. 350
Bodiless. Living or dead all things were bodiless, . 59 *Bord.* 1215
Bodily. Than bodily weariness. While here we sit 40 *Bord.* 154
And what are a few throes of bodily suffering . 62 *Bord.* 1400
Even with the organs of his bodily eye, . . . 96 *Brothers* 60
His bodily frame had been from youth to age . 131 *Michael* 43
His bodily frame had been from youth to age . 138 *Michael* 454
Our bodily life, some plead, that life the shrine . 519 *Pun. Death* 10. 1
The bodily frame. That beauty is laid low . . 581 **Why should we* 9
Would overspread my soul, that bodily eyes . . 647 *Prelude* 2. 349
It was no madness, for the bodily eye . . . . 651 *Prelude* 3. 155
Who through that bodily image hath diffused, . 666 *Prelude* 5. 16
To look with bodily eyes, and be consoled." . . 682 *Prelude* 6. 471
Or saw, like other men, with bodily eyes, . . . 724 *Prelude* 10. 444

Bold—*continued.*
And bold transfigurations, more untrue . . . 428 *Ecc. Sonn.* 1. 37. 5
Ploughs her bold course across the wondering seas; 432 *Ecc. Sonn.* 2. 15. 11
How the bold Teacher's Doctrine, sanctified . . 433 *Ecc. Sonn.* 2. 17. 13
Their liquid world, for bold discovery, ... 434 *Ecc. Sonn.* 2. 23. 7
The Other gains a confidence as bold; . . . . 437 *Ecc. Sonn.* 2. 34. 7
Down a swift Stream, thus far, a bold design . . 443 *Ecc. Sonn.* 3. 12. 1
And some a bold unerring answer made: . . . 445 *Ecc. Sonn.* 3. 22. 7
I, of his bold wing floating on the gale, . . 464 *Derwent* 3
Through my green courts; or climbing, a bold suitor, ... 465 **Thou look'st* 12
Bold as if men and creatures of the Deep . . . 466 *St. Bees* 20
Her flight before the bold credulities . . . . 468 *St. Bees* 161
Bold words affirmed, in days when faith was strong 468 **Bold words* 1
And thy bold rocks are worthy of their fame. . 476 *Eden* 8
Accepts from your bold hands the proffered crown 477 *Steamboats* 13
Came Barons bold, with store of gold, ... 478 *Somnamb.* 21
Or when a bold heroic lay . . . . 478 *Somnamb.* 59
Bold in maternal Nature's care, ... 485 **Bright Flower* 2
Even now, who, not unwisely bold, ... 492 *Duty* 22
And what if hence a bold desire should mount . 511 **So fair* 7
Knows that this prophecy is not too bold. . . 516 **Young England* 8
Skilful and bold, the horse and burthened *sled* 523 *Epist. Beaumont* 110
But turn we from these "bold bad" men; . . 534 **Blest is* 81
Wherefore, bold as day, the Murderer . . . . 535 *Egremont* 59
But bold Hubert lives in glee: . . . . . . 535 *Egremont* 69
Was yet not bold enough to write of Thee. . . 539 **Lady! a* 9
The bold good Man his labour sped . . . . 543 *Russ. Fug.* 115
Stay, bold Adventurer; rest awhile thy limbs . 548 **Stay, bold* 1
Bold settlers on some foreign shore, ... 577 **I come* 46
And Hope gay Pilot of the bold design, . . . 625 **The confidence* 2
As clear and bold as the trumpet's clang, . . . 629 *Installation* 36
In that bold form and impress high . . . . 629 *Installation* 84
Long months of peace (if such bold word accord . 632 *Prelude* 1. 24
Remembering the bold promise of the past, . . 634 *Prelude* 1. 128
Those bold imaginations in due time . . . . 689 *Prelude* 7. 142
These, bold in conscious merit, lower down; . . 690 *Prelude* 7. 196
Delusion bold! and how can it be wrought? . . 691 *Prelude* 7. 285
Rough, bold, as Grecian comedy displayed . . 691 *Prelude* 7. 289
The one bold man, whose voice the attack had sounded, ... 720 *Prelude* 10. 116
And therefore bold to look on painful things, . . 731 *Prelude* 11. 277
Free likewise of the world, and thence more bold, . 731 *Prelude* 11. 278
Of some bold headland, he beheld the sun . . 759 *Excursion* 1. 199
Chase the wild goat; and if the bold red deer . 808 *Excursion* 4. 500
Of doubt and bold denial hourly urged . . . 812 *Excursion* 4. 734
Over the mountain-sides, in contrast bold . . . 820 *Excursion* 4. 1303
The thinking, thoughtless, school-boy; the bold youth . . . . 836 *Excursion* 5. 959
Struggling and bold, and shining from the west . 861 *Excursion* 7. 232
Towards one, whose bold contrivances and skill, . 866 *Excursion* 7. 591
Save at worst need, from bold impetuous force, . 873 *Excursion* 7. 1031
Easy and bold, that penetrate the gloom . . . 876 *Excursion* 8. 110
With bold projections and recesses deep; . . . 881 *Excursion* 8. 462
To a bold brook that splits for better speed, . . 883 *Excursion* 8. 578
Or bold adventure; promising to skill . . . . 889 *Excursion* 9. 381
Shaggy and bold, and wreathèd horns superb, . 890 *Excursion* 9. 444
A prayer both bold and sly . . . . S.3. 431 **The Scottish* 10
Oft help to make bold fancy's flight more bold; . K.8. 301 **And oh* 8
Bolder. Only their fire seems bolder, yielding light, 192 *Gipsies* 5
With bolder than Icarian flight? . . . . . 216 *Enterprise* 70
Smile on his Mother now with bolder cheer. . . 294 **Fly, some* 14
Coy fancy with a bolder strain) . . . . . . 344 **How blest* 28
With wishes of still bolder scope . . . . . 403 *White Doe* 650
Imagination works with bolder hope . . . . 520 *Pun. Death* 14. 4
Shall be attended with a bolder prayer— . . . 582 *Invoc. Earth* 29
Had burst innocuous. Say in bolder words, . . 718 *Prelude* 10. 16
A bolder transport seizes. From the side . . . 867 *Excursion* 7. 649
Boldest. And for the boldest tale belief commands. 338 *Engelberg* 5
Ne'er could the boldest Eulogist have dared . . 359 **Complacent Fictions* 5
Harp! couldst thou venture, on thy boldest string, 440 *Ecc. Sonn.* 2. 46. 1
No natural bond between the boldest schemes . 471 **Arran! a* 11
Of boldest projects, and a peaceful end . . . 661 *Prelude* 4. 175
Boldest of plants that ever faced the wind, . . 787 *Excursion* 3. 85
Which foot of boldest stranger would attempt, . 822 *Excursion* 5. 13
Boldly. To reach a small wood-hut hung boldly on the steep. . . . . 15 *Desc. Sk.* 237
And what was boldly promised, truly shall be done. 220 *Triad* 33
So taught, so trained, we boldly face . . . . 224 **'Tis gone* 55
Did Peter boldly press his way . . . . . . 240 *P. B.* 360
With that resolve he boldly mounts . . . . 243 *P. B.* 596
Pecked, as at mine, thus boldly, Love might say, 272 **Wild Redbreast* 2
And boldly urged a general plea, ... 400 *White Doe* 370
By some too boldly named "the Jaws of Hell:" . 475 *Greenock* 3
Hence am I checked: but let me boldly say, . . 669 *Prelude* 5. 264
Boldly assembled,—here is shadowed forth . . 707 *Prelude* 8. 582
On a strong river boldly hath been launched; . 717 *Prelude* 9. 560
Him who too boldly trusted them, I felt . . . 720 *Prelude* 10. 181
Or boldly seeking pleasure nearer heaven . . . 735 *Prelude* 12. 36
Deal boldly with substantial things; in truth . 743 *Prelude* 13. 235
May boldly take his way among mankind . . . 744 *Prelude* 13. 296
To known restraints; and who most boldly drew 775 *Excursion* 2. 258
Was of a mighty city—boldly say . . . . . 784 *Excursion* 2. 835
That, stretching boldly from the mountain side, . 855 *Excursion* 6. 1117
Past or to come; yea, boldly might I say, . . 866 *Excursion* 7. 567
Proclaiming boldly that they never drew . . . 880 *Excursion* 8. 411
Above the darkened hills stood boldly forth . . 895 *Excursion* 9. 764
Boldly and bear away to softer life; . . . . S.3. 436 **The doubt* 158
I, thus boldly looking at you, ... S.3. 437 **I, whose* 4

Boldly—*continued.*
Say boldly then that solitude is not . . . . K.8. 252 *Recluse* 1. 1. 592
Boldly-winding. A copious stream with boldly-winding course; . . . . 823 *Excursion* 5. 84
Boldness. If she, a timid Maid, hath put such boldness on. . . . . 141 *Arm. Lady* 84
Boles. Deep yellow beams the scatter'd boles illume, 594 *Ev. Wk. Quarto* 163
Bologna's. Such course he held! Bologna's learned schools . . . . 573 *Chiabrera* 2. 9
Bolt. The obstinate bolt of a small iron door . . 59 *Bord.* 1200
Till the fatal bolt is shot! . . . . 549 *Hermit's Cell* 1. 8
Of trees and hills and water, bolt upright . . . 672 *Prelude* 5. 449
Whether the bolt of childhood's Fancy shot . . 688 *Prelude* 7. 88
Bolted. For when he saw her doors fast bolted all, 562 *Troilus* 13
Far better, than to have been bolted forth, . . 656 *Prelude* 3. 524
Bolton. New life in Bolton Priory; . . . . . 410 *White Doe* 1271
Bear it to Bolton Priory, ... 410 *White Doe* 1292
Could see the Tower of Bolton rise. . . . . 412 *White Doe* 1441
In Bolton, on the field of Wharf, ... 495 *Force of Prayer* 55
Bolton's. From Bolton's old monastic tower . . 396 *White Doe* 1
To Bolton's mouldering Priory. . . . . . . 396 *White Doe* 16
Of Bolton's dear fraternity; . . . . 399 *White Doe* 296
Toward Bolton's ruined Priory. . . . . . . 413 *White Doe* 1542
But most to Bolton's sacred Pile, ... 416 *White Doe* 1811
Bolts. When madding Power her bolts had hurled, 298 *Brownie's Cell* 22
To sulphurous bolts a sacrifice, ... 341 *San Salv.* 5
The giant-quelling bolts of Jove, I flee, . . . 624 *Æneid* 13
Bomb's. Driven by the bomb's incessant thunder-stroke . . . . 30 *Guilt* 349
Bond. The bond of nature, all unkindness cease, . 33 *Guilt* 508
A cheerful mind,—and buffeted with bond, . . 98 *Brothers* 214
Between us there was little other bond . . . 151 **When, to* 74
('Twixt thee and thine a never-failing bond), . . 153 *Morn. Ex.* 45
Frail is the bond by which we hold . . . . 156 *Oak and Broom* 58
Are Sisters in the bond of love; . . . . . 220 *Triad* 18
No natural bond between the boldest schemes . 471 **Arran! a* 11
In bond of peace, in bond of love, ... 623 *G. and S. Green* 35
Upon this hour, the bond to celebrate!" . . . 625 *Æneid* 115
The bond of union between life and joy. . . . 640 *Prelude* 1. 558
The gravitation and the filial bond . . . . . 645 *Prelude* 2. 243
Were then made for me; bond unknown to me . 663 *Prelude* 4. 335
And wedded soul to soul in purest bond . . . 667 *Prelude* 5. 104
And she herself from the maternal bond . . . 669 *Prelude* 5. 249
One sadness, they and I. For them a bond . . 763 *Excursion* 1. 486
The bond of brotherhood, when he sees them go, . 780 *Excursion* 2. 562
For signs and tokens of a mutual bond; . . . 806 *Excursion* 4. 362
An unrelaxing bond, a mutual need; . . . . 853 *Excursion* 6. 1017
By the pure bond of independent love, . . . 864 *Excursion* 7. 434
Bondage. Earth's noblest penitent; from bondage freed . . . . 105 *Artegal* 229
Thee from bondage would I rescue . . . . . 140 *Arm. Lady* 21
That self might be annulled; her bondage prove . 211 *Laod.* 149
Admit no bondage and my words have wings. . 230 *Clouds* 59
But from that bondage when her thoughts were freed . . . . 274 **Wait, prithee* 5
A bondage sweetly brooked, a strife . . . . 288 *Highland Girl* 42
There is a bondage worse, far worse, to bear . . 308 **There is a bondage* 1
Triumph, and thoughts no bondage can restrain. . 314 **Not 'mid* 14
From bondage threatened by the embattled East, 326 *Sobieski* 7
To these glad eyes from bondage freed, again . . 496 **A little* 50
In anxious bondage, to such nice array . . . 497 **Enough of climbing* 10
Or, if the soul to bondage be subdued, ... 501 *Humanity* 67
Bondage, the other to build liberty . . . . 715 *Prelude* 9. 359
In bondage; and the palace, lately stormed . . 719 *Prelude* 10. 53
By partial bondage. In his steady course, . . 761 *Excursion* 1. 358
A bondage lurking under shape of good,— . . 887 *Excursion* 9. 188
Bondman. The vacillating Bondman of the Pope . 442 *Ecc. Sonn.* 3. 9. 13
And in the light of truth thy Bondman let me live! 493 *Duty* 56
Bonds. Her bonds and chains, which make the mighty feeble. . . . . 57 *Bord.* 1091
The bonds of our humanity. . . . . 81 †*Mother's Return* 20
—Cast off your bonds, awake, arise, ... 228 *Devot. Incit.* 38
Wear rather in thy bonds a cheerful brow: . . 305 *Toussaint* 7
Europe is yet in bonds; but let that pass, . . 306 **Here, on our* 9
May pass in hope, and, though from mortal bonds 396 **Action is* 11
Or He, whose bonds dropped off, whose prison doors 419 *Ecc. Sonn.* 1. 2. 9
And airy bonds are hardest to disown; . . . . 435 *Ecc. Sonn.* 2. 28. 11
Than that the Soul, freed from the bonds of Sense, 436 *Ecc. Sonn.* 2. 30. 2
The bonds of indolent society . . . . . . 675 *Prelude* 6. 20
As from restraints and bonds. Yet who can tell— 675 *Prelude* 6. 35
Of love and marriage bonds. These words to thee 691 *Prelude* 7. 302
A young enthusiast, who escaped these bonds; . 736 *Prelude* 12. 152
The thankful captive of maternal bonds; . . . 794 *Excursion* 3. 555
"But all was quieted by iron bonds . . . . 798 *Excursion* 3. 821
Or, less reluctantly to bonds of sense . . . . 811 *Excursion* 4. 681
As bonds, on grave philosopher imposed . . . 812 *Excursion* 4. 741
Prevailed; and, from those bonds released, she went 853 *Excursion* 6. 1004
For chastisement, and custody, and bonds, . . 886 *Excursion* 9. 123
Preferring bonds and darkness to a state . . . 894 *Excursion* 9. 655
Bond-slave. Thy destined bond-slave? No! though earth be dust . . . . 235 *Power of Sound* 222
And here was Labour, his own bond-slave; Hope, 657 *Prelude* 3. 595
Bondsmen. One of Love's simple bondsmen—the soft chain . . . . 70 *Bord.* 1841
Bone. In thy bone-house bone on bone? . . . 157 *Sexton* 3
She to the very bone was worn, ... 246 *P. B.* 913
With sights the ruefullest that flesh and bone . 257 **Methought I* 5
"'My throat is cut unto the bone, I trow,' . . 556 *Prioress* 198
Shaken by arms of mighty bone, in strength, . . 744 *Prelude* 13. 325

Books—*continued.*
That pressed upon his brother's house ; for books 864 *Excursion* 7. 439
(As books and haply votive altars vouch) . . . S. 3. 435 **The doubt* 125
Book-stalls. Than for the humble book-stalls in the streets, ... 710 *Prelude* 9. 32
Boon. In barn uplighted ; and companions boon, . 32 *Guilt* 411
With which he gave the boon—I see it now ! . . 54 *Bord.* 920
Kind Nature's gentlest boon ! . . . . . . 109 **Strange fits* 18
Bright boon of pitying Heaven !—alas, . . . 112 *Lament* 8
And yet a boon I gave her, for the creature . . 191 *Beggars* 17
This precious boon ; and blest a sad abode." . . 210 *Laod.* 36
That wretched boon, days lengthened by mistrust. 214 *Dion* 117
Whether this boon be granted us or not, . . . 251 *Appleth.* 12
We have given our hearts away, a sordid boon ! . 259 **The world is* 4
Is there no debt to pay, no boon to grant ? . . 277 **Why art* 4
Not loth to thank each moment for its boon . . 278 **The most* 9
A poor old Dame will bless them for the boon : . 280 **Intent on* 3
Ah ! that a *boon* could shed such rapturous joys ! 312 **A Roman* 12
Then might the passing Monk receive a boon . . 339 *Tell* 16
Obtaining ampler boon, at every step, ... 353 *Aquap.* 39
O'er man and beast a not unwelcome boon . . 360 **Long has* 2
Announces to the thirsty fields a boon . . . . 381 *Duddon* 19. 13
Rite to perform, or boon to ask ? . . . . . 397 *White Doe* 109
Of mountain-quiet and boon nature's grace ; . . 418 *Ecc. Sonn.* 1. 1. 4
Transcendent Boon ! noblest that earthly King . 435 *Ecc. Sonn.* 2. 29. 9
On the bare coast ; nor do they grudge the boon . 467 *St. Bees* 93
Whatever boon is granted or withheld. . . . 511 **So fair* 21
For the least boon that freedom can bestow ? . 528 **Those breathing* 80
Then, little Bird, this boon confer, ... 530 †*Redbreast* 13
For which I ask for guerdon but one boon, . . 563 *Troilus* 76
Of myriads and boon nature's lavish help ; . . 700 *Prelude* 8. 81
And intellectual strength so rare a boon— . . 742 *Prelude* 13. 178
To speak the word—with rapture ! Nature's boon, 792 *Excursion* 3. 432
He gives it—the boon produce of a soil . . . 855 *Excursion* 6. 1137
" Oh ! pang unthought of, as the precious boon . 867 *Excursion* 7. 674
For the least boon that pity can bestow. . . . 879 *Excursion* 8. 361
No mystery is here ! Here is no boon . . . 887 *Excursion* 9. 243
The boon is absolute ; surpassing grace . . . K.8. 239 *Recluse* 1.1.103
Boons. His hat gives him vigour, with boons dropping in, ... 188 *Music* 26
But for some precious boons vouchsafed to thee, . 491 *Tribute : Dog* 25
By casual boons and formal charities ; . . . . 516 **Feel for* 10
Of each recalling his peculiar boons, ... 568 *Cumb. Beg.* 126
The laggard Rustic ; and repay with boons . . 773 *Excursion* 2. 123
Boons inexhaustible ? Who, hurrying on . . S. 3. 433 **The doubt* 43
Their little boons of animating thought . . . K.8. 249 *Recluse* 1.1.467
Boor. Of boor or burgher, as they marched along. 858 *Excursion* 7. 97
Boorish. In air high-towering with a boorish pomp, 880 *Excursion* 8. 428
Boors. Art thou the Peter of Norway Boors ? . . 162 **Art thou the* 6
Boot. There is no need of boot or spur, . . . 126 *Idiot Boy* 47
Of goodness, next her Son, our soul's best boot. . 552 *Prioress* 14
Boötes. Of Auster and Boötes. Fifty years . . 574 *Chiabrera* 4. 13
Booths. A Parliament of Monsters. Tents and Booths . . . . 698 *Prelude* 7. 718
Booths are there none ; a stall or two is here ; . 699 *Prelude* 8. 25
While faction Blue from shops and booths . . S.3. 431 **The Scottish* 29
Bootless. " What is good for a bootless bene ? " . . 494 *Force of Prayer* 1
" What is good for a bootless bene ? " . . . . 494 *Force of Prayer* 5
Boots. Alas ! what boots it ?—who can hide, . . 181 *Waggoner* 4. 116
What boots the enquiry ?—Neither friend nor foe 258 **Where lies the Land* 5
Alas ! what boots the long laborious quest . . 315 **Alas ! what* 1
" What boots," continued she, " to mourn ? . . 370 *Eg. Maid* 97
How little boots that precedent of good, . . . 442 *Ecc. Sonn.* 3. 7. 5
What boots the gain if Nature should lose more ? 466 *St. Bees* 29
What boots the sculptured tomb ? And who can blame, ... 847 *Excursion* 6. 615
Booty. Will be the Tinker's booty ; . . . . . S. 3. 424 *Tinker* 41
Border. Of their rich Spoil, ere they recross the Border. . . . . 37 *Bord.* 3
Through border wilds where naked Indians stray, 153 *Morn. Ex.* 13
Shall soon behold this border thickly set . . . 264 *Snowdrop* 9
Renowned in Border story. . . . . 302 *Yarrow V.* 56
Of the old minstrels and the border bards.— . . 353 *Aquap.* 52
Great Minstrel of the Border ! . . . . . . 385 *Yarrow Rev.* 8
Of border tunes was played to cheer . . . . 406 *White Doe* 890
And o'er the Border Beacon, and the waste . . 678 *Prelude* 6. 233
Bordering. A frog leaps out from bordering grass, . 142 †*Lov. and Lik.* 17
Prolonged beneath the bordering deep ; . . . 299 *Brownie's Cell* 88
With bordering lines of intervening gloom, . . 598 *Ev. Wk. Quarto* 342
Border-lines. Had broken their trim border-lines, and straggled . . . . 767 *Excursion* 1. 723
Border-minstrel. My steps the Border-minstrel led. 586 *Hogg* 8
Borders. *See* **Mountain-borders.**
A blue rim borders all the lake's still brink ; . . 4 *Ev. Wk.* 115
Who here, upon the borders of the Tweed, . . 41 *Bord.* 208
Why art thou here ? Wallace, upon these Borders, 78 *Bord.* 2323
Whom from the borders of the Lake we brought, 106 *Farewell* 23
Even the proud Realm, from whose distracted borders . . . . 327 *Ode 1815* 39
As from the beds and borders of a garden . . 549 **The massy* 16
By the still borders of the misty lake, ... 674 *Prelude* 5. 563
Upon the borders of the Rhine, and leagued . . 712 *Prelude* 9. 184
Upon the borders of the unhappy Loire, . . . 715 *Prelude* 9. 425
Border-song. With some old border-song, or catch 487 *Fountain* 11
Border-war. Such as in unsafe times of border-war 833 *Excursion* 5. 698
Bore. Help from the staff he bore ; for mien and air 24 *Guilt* 4
" There were we long neglected, and we bore . . 29 *Guilt* 280
He bore within a breast where dreadful quiet reigned. . . . . 36 *Guilt* 648

Bore—*continued.*
Where now we dwell.—For many years I bore . 41 *Bord.* 202
I bore her in my arms ; her looks won pity ; . . 53 *Bord.* 846
That bore us through the water—— You returned 68 *Bord.* 1734
And bore him high through yielding air my debt of love to pay, ... 92 *Poet's Dream* 19
With other burthens than the crop it bore. . . 98 *Brothers* 212
He bore the lasting name of " pious Elidure ! " . 106 *Artegal* 241
What love I bore to thee. . . . . 109 **I travelled* 4
Turned upon her who bore him, she would stoop . 118 *Maternal Grief* 60
And the vain rank the pilgrims bore while yet on earth. . . . . 142 *Arm. Lady* 156
Gave the baptismal name each Sister bore. . . 151 **Forth from* 15
What love they bore each other. . . . . . 161 *Binnorie* 4
The Porter sits down on the weight which he bore; 188 *Music* 21
And bore a soldier's name ; . . . . 192 *Ruth* 27
"The good Lord Clifford" was the name he bore. 205 *Brougham* 172
Whom she to young Ambition bore, ... 215 *Enterprise* 21
Whose countenance bore resemblance to the sun, 226 *Vernal Ode* 6
Was the worst pang that sorrow ever bore, . . 257 **Surprised by* 10
The music in my heart I bore, ... 289 *Sol. Reap.* 31
And bore it on his head. . . . . 296 *Highland Boy* 145
Of triumph, how the labouring Danube bore . . 317 **The martial* 6
For him who bore the world ! . . . . . . 341 *Ital. Itin.* 16
They round his altar bore the hornèd God, . . 346 *Processions* 24
But in his breast the mighty Poet bore . . . 365 **Under the* 11
But worthy of the name she bore . . . . . 369 *Eg. Maid* 37
A fairer than herself she bore, ... 370 *Eg. Maid* 63
What aspect bore the Man who roved or fled, . 378 *Duddon* 8. 1
Ere the meek Saint, Columba, bore . . . . 390 *Highland Broach* 3
To guard the Standard which he bore. . . . 404 *White Doe* 725
He bore a heart of timid frame ; . . . . . 404 *White Doe* 794
That bore it, compassed round by a bold . . . 405 *White Doe* 819
Bore instantly his Charge away." . . . . . 411 *White Doe* 1345
Proudly the Horsemen bore away . . . . . 412 *White Doe* 1499
Bore it, or led, to Rylstone-hall . . . . . . 416 *White Doe* 1809
Her sanction inwardly she bore, ... 416 *White Doe* 1858
Charged with these offerings which their fathers bore 448 *Ecc. Sonn.* 3. 32. 10
As if she for no purpose bore you ; . . . . . 481 *Expost.* 10
Bore a light switch, her sceptre of command . . 523 *Epist. Beaumont* 108
Of chieftains sprung, who stoutly bore . . . 533 **Blest is* 12
And bore her toward the fields of France, . . . 544 *Russ. Fug.* 245
Faith bore her up through pains in mercy given, . 576 **By a* 7
And bore him to the grave. . . . . 579 **Sweet Flower* 56
Had been derived the name he bore—a name, . 584 *Ch. Lamb* 24
That the shield bore, so glorious was the strife ; . 634 *Prelude* 1. 179
And bore the semblance of another stream . . 664 *Prelude* 4. 382
A lance he bore, and underneath one arm . . . 666 *Prelude* 5. 78
With amity and glee ; we bore a name . . . 681 *Prelude* 6. 402
A Father—for he bore that sacred name— . . 696 *Prelude* 7. 603
Into the turmoil, bore a sounder judgment . . 714 *Prelude* 9. 332
That bore it—on the plains of Liberty . . . . 718 *Prelude* 10. 15
Too justly bore a part. A veil had been . . . 731 *Prelude* 11. 266
An intimation how she bore herself . . . . 736 *Prelude* 12. 170
A girl, who bore a pitcher on her head, . . . 738 *Prelude* 12. 251
Or Cambrian solitudes. A youth—(he bore . . 751 *Prelude* 14. 354
Bore stars—illumination of all gems ! . . . . 784 *Excursion* 2. 845
That with united shoulders bore aloft . . . . 787 *Excursion* 3. 59
At aught, however fair, that bore the mien . . 797 *Excursion* 3. 780
She bore a secret burthen ; and full soon . . . 851 *Excursion* 6. 851
Who bore me ; and hath prayed for me in vain ;— 852 *Excursion* 6. 926
Of friends and kindred bore him from his home . 864 *Excursion* 7. 466
And in the various conversation bore . . . 882 *Excursion* 8. 528
It bears no sounding name, nor ever bore ; . . 887 *Excursion* 9. 184
When many plants strange blossoms bore . . . S. 3. 431* *The Scottish* 3
As Aristogiton bore, ... S. 3. 442 *Harmodius* 4
As Aristogiton bore, ... S. 3. 442 *Harmodius* 18
Arms and the Man I sing, the first who bore . . K.8. 281**Arms and* 1
Boreal. We'll sport amid the boreal morning ; . . 237 *P. B.* 92
The medley less when boreal Lights . . . . 499 **This Lawn* 10
Boreas. Or Boreas when he scours the snow . . 213 *Dion* 73
Born. *See* **Borne, Cloud-born, Earth-born, First-born, Free-born, Heart-born, Heaven-born, High-born, Low-born, New-born, Noblest-born, Sea-born, Self-born, Sky-born, Well-born.**
All newly born ! both earth and sky . . . . 84 *Shepherd-boys* 28
" My Mother," said the Boy, " was born near to a blessèd Tree, ... 92 *Poet's Dream* 27
A child is born or christened, a field ploughed, . 97 *Brothers* 158
Who has been born and dies among the mountains. 98 *Brothers* 183
And hills on which we all of us were born, . . 99 *Brothers* 265
How changed from him who, born to highest place, 103 *Artegal* 94
Born all too high, by wedlock raised . . . . 113 *Lament* 29
Well born, well bred ; I sent him forth . . . 117 *Affl. Marg.* 17
Until the babe was born. When morning came, . 122 *V. and J.* 73
Of Julia's travail. When the babe was born, . 124 *V. and J.* 187
Go !—'tis a town where both of us were born ; . 124 *V. and J.* 196
An only Child, who had been born to them . . 132 *Michael* 87
And that the old Man's heart seemed born again ? 134 *Michael* 203
His youngest born did Andrew hold : . . . . 156 *Oak and Broom* 7
And beauty born of murmuring sound . . . . 187 **Three years* 29
Nay—if a child to her was born . . . . . 199 *Thorn* 148
And if 'twas born alive or dead, ... 199 *Thorn* 150
And he perhaps, for aught we know, was born . 203 *Hart-leap* 155
When the fatherless was born— . . . . . 204 *Brougham* 56
" Last of the Three, though eldest born, . . . 222 *Triad* 174
And see the town where I was born ! . . . . 237 *P. B.* 66
And, ere that little child was born, ... 246 *P. B.* 914
Alas that ever he was born ! . . . . . . 287 *Ellen Irwin* 21

Born—*continued.*
Of mortal parents is the Hero born . . . . 314 *Hofer* 1
Triumphant wrong, battle of battle born, . . . 326 **Emperors and* 5
Nor pity idly born, ... 334 **In Bruges* 26
Announcing, ONE was born mankind to free ; . . 351 *Des. Stanzas* 70
From mortal change, aught that is born on earth 356 *Aquap.* 230
For action born, existing to be tried, ... 361 **For action* 1
The ground where we were born and reared ! . . 375 **The Minstrels* 54
I am your son, your eldest born ; . . . . . 400 *White Doe* 390
I, by the right of eldest born, ... 401 *White Doe* 484
That he was born of gentle blood ; . . . . . 413 *White Doe* 1528
That ever he was born, a glance of mind . . . 447 *Ecc. Sonn.* 3. 27. 11
That they were born for immortality. . . . . 451 *Ecc. Sonn.* 3. 43. 14
Must Man, with labour born, awake to sorrow . 462 **Where lies the truth* 6
Born to be lost in Derwent flowing near ; . . . 465 **The cattle* 5
Born only to depart. . . . . 478 *Somnamb.* 63
With weary feet by all of woman born)— . . . 504 *Warning* 50
Since thou, blithe May, wert born, ... 507 *May* 2
Would that the little Flowers were born to live, . 511 **So fair* 2
Born of Conceit, Power's blind Idolater ; . . . 514 **Portentous change* 6
A creature born of time, that keeps one eye . . 519 *Pun. Death* 9. 6
That touchingly bespeaks thee born . . . . 530 *Gleaner* 27
Mindful of Him Who in the Orient born . . . 534 **When in* 13
Yea, to the stars, if they were born . . . . 541 *Russ. Fug.* 7
And said, Alas ! that ever I was born, ... 560 *Cuck.and Night.*208
Which man is born to—sink, howe'er depressed, . 567 *Cumb. Beg.* 82
'Twill be no fruitless moment. I was born . . 573 *Chiabrera* 3. 3
Born deaf, and living deaf and dumb. . . . . 577 **I come* 40
When Love was born of heavenly line, . . . 620 *Birth of Love* 1
They tell that your future Queen is born. . . . 628 *Installation* 30
Beneath the sky, as if I had been born . . . 636 *Prelude* 1. 297
That dwell among the hills where I was born. . 648 *Prelude* 2. 426
Where he was born ; the grassy churchyard hangs 671 *Prelude* 5. 392
And human nature seeming born again. . . . 680 *Prelude* 6. 341
Pleased (though to hardship born, and compassed round . . . . 682 *Prelude* 6. 509
Upon the spot where she was born and reared ; . 692 *Prelude* 7. 321
Upon the allegiance to which men are born— . . 695 *Prelude* 7. 530
As, of all visible natures, crown, though born . . 706 *Prelude* 8. 487
Born in a land whose very name appeared . . 712 *Prelude* 9. 189
For, born in a poor district, and which yet . . 712 *Prelude* 9. 215
Hence Genius, born to thrive by interchange . . 740 *Prelude* 13. 5
Among the hills of Athol he was born ; . . . 758 *Excursion* 1. 108
The twain within our happy cottage born, . . 794 *Excursion* 3. 589
And learning's solid dignity ; though born . . 824 *Excursion* 5. 112
That they were ever born to ! In due time . . 826 *Excursion* 5. 273
Who to your dull society are born, ... 832 *Excursion* 5. 619
Among her higher creatures born and trained . 835 *Excursion* 5. 848
Thus are they born, thus fostered, thus maintained ; 837 *Excursion* 5. 996
" The other, born in Britain's southern tract, . . 844 *Excursion* 6. 427
When that poor Child was born. Upon its face . 852 *Excursion* 6. 907
" Though born a younger brother, need was none 864 *Excursion* 7. 428
Which tells her that a living child is born ; . . 867 *Excursion* 7. 645
Of furze-clad commons ; such are born and reared 879 *Excursion* 8. 364
To Britons born and bred within the pale . . . 880 *Excursion* 8. 392
Thus would have lived, or never have been born. 887 *Excursion* 9. 205
Them who are born to serve her and obey ; . . 888 *Excursion* 9. 298
On Albion's noble Race in freedom born, . . . 890 *Excursion* 9. 393
And that the old man's heart seem'd born again ? K. 8. 226 **I will* 83
Untainted manners ; born among the hills, . . K. 8. 246 *Recluse* 1. 1. 348
A wreath she twines of blossoms lowly born— . K. 8. 325[?]**The vestal* 6
Were Kings a free born work, a people's choice. . L. 1. 96 *Juvenal* 3. 41

Borne. Sound of closed gate, across the water borne, 9 *Ev. Wk.* 373
The crows rushed by in eddies, homeward borne. 25 *Guilt* 40
" Borne to a hospital, I lay with brain . . . 31 *Guilt* 388
Borne gently to a bed, in death she lay ; . . . 36 *Guilt* 626
I have borne my burthen to its destined end. . . 66 *Bord.* 1588
But had he strength to walk? I could have borne him . . . . 74 *Bord.* 2077
It must be told, and borne. I am the man, . . 76 *Bord.* 2207
The cataract had borne him down . . . . . 85 *Shepherd-boys* 69
She saw him down the torrent borne ; . . . . 85 *Shepherd-boys* 72
On whose breast are thither borne . . . . 90 *Longest Day* 50
Which to an only brother he has borne . . . 96 *Brothers* 72
(Such it may seem) if I thy crown have borne, . 104 *Artegal* 134
But, surely, if severe afflictions borne . . . . 143 **High bliss* 2
The gallant ship is borne ; . . . . 161 *Binnorie* 17
Three leaps have borne him from this lofty brow 201 *Hart-leap* 55
And, in their anguish, bear what other minds have borne ! " . . . . 213 *Dion* 89
That she had borne a heavy yoke, ... 294 *Jedbor.* 72
When I have borne in memory what has tamed . 307 **When I* 1
Of Jesus goes before, the child is borne . . . 318 **In due* 10
—Hours, Days, and Months, *have* borne them in the sight . . . . 327 *Ode 1815* 11
Borne gaily o'er the sea, ... 334 **In Bruges* 38
Green boughs were borne, while, for the blast that shook . . . . 346 *Processions* 16
The Cross, in calm procession, borne aloft . . . 346 *Processions* 39
But many a benefit borne upon his breast . . 357 *Aquap.* 317
How patient y the weight of wrong is borne ; . . 359 **They—who* 8
Borne by the Muse from rills in shepherds' ears . 368 *Trajan* 23
May yet to Arthur's court be borne . . . . 370 *Eg. Maid* 101
Here stood an Oak, that long had borne affixed . 393 *Hart's-horn* 1
Alas ! thought he, and have I borne . . . . 405 *White Doe* 845
While to the prison they are borne, ... 409 *White Doe* 1242
And, with that rueful Banner borne . . . . 410 *White Doe* 1325
The mighty sorrow hath been borne, ... 414 *White Doe* 1621
Have long borne witness as the Scriptures teach ?— 431 *Ecc. Sonn.* 2. 12. 2

Borne—*continued.*
Than his who sees, borne forward by the Rhine, . 443 *Ecc. Sonn.* 3. 12. 3
Meed of some Roman chief—in triumph borne . 464 *Derwent* 11
Rightfully borne ; for Nature gives thee flowers . 476 *Eden* 6
A weight of awe, not easy to be borne, . . . 477 *Long Meg* 1
A thousand years hath it borne that name, . . 494 *Force of Prayer* 23
Borne in their hands the lily and the palm . . 500 *Humanity* 23
Up to the throne of God is borne . . . . . 506 *Lab. Hymn* 1
Strong as could then be borne. A Master meek . 518 *Pun. Death* 7. 5
Had the House of Lucie born, ... 535 *Egremont* 10
Thou tread ; or sweep—borne on the managed steed— . . . . 540 **Lady ! a* 73
Are safely borne, landed upon the beach, . . . 541 *Grace Darl.* 81
The tide of things has borne him, he appears . 568 *Cumb. Beg.* 164
FRANCESCO was the name the Youth had borne, . 575 *Chiabrera* 8. 6
And frequent sights of what is to be borne ! . . 579 *Peele Castle* 58
Or clock, that blind against the wanderer born, . 597 *Ev. Wk. Quarto* 313
Slow swells the service o'er the water born, . . 604 *Desc. Sk. Quarto*146
That the weight can no longer be borne, . . . 621 *Convict* 34
Pellucid water for the hands is borne, . . . 624 *Æneid* 61
Within my mind, should e'er have borne a part, . 637 *Prelude* 1. 347
Else sooner ended, I have borne in mind . . . 679 *Prelude* 6. 260
But as the ancient Prophets, borne aloft . . 724 *Prelude* 10. 437
By sorrow laid asleep ; or borne away, . . . 768 *Excursion* 1. 786
Is raised from the church-aisle, and forward borne 780 *Excursion* 2. 570
Ill borne in earlier life ; but his was now . . 783 *Excursion* 2. 749
And from the cottage hath been borne to-day. . 785 *Excursion* 2. 895
Your heart had borne a pitiable share . . . . 793 *Excursion* 3. 484
With bodily eyes, they are borne down by love . 804 *Excursion* 4. 172
He heard, borne on the wind, the articulate voice 810 *Excursion* 4. 634
And sufferings meekly borne—I, for my part, . 847 *Excursion* 6. 630
But worse affliction must be borne—far worse ; . 853 *Excursion* 6. 965
These titles emperors and chiefs have borne, . . 862 *Excursion* 7. 343
Into its graveyard will ere long be borne . . . 862 *Excursion* 7. 351
The Knight arrived, with spear and shield, and borne . . . . 872 *Excursion* 7. 944
Borne by yon clustering cottages, that sprang . 872 *Excursion* 7. 968
With them I think I could have borne . . . . K. 8. 220 **The snow-tracks* 38
And was borne headlong by the roaring flood. . K. 8. 229 **I will* 151
Thy kindred and thy friends such travail borne . L. 2. 318 *Frag. Æneid* 4. 5

Borrow. From Scripture she a name did borrow ; . 246 *P. B.* 908
Seemed from each other a faint warmth to borrow. 374 *Eg. Maid* 330
And loved to borrow, ornament ; . . . . . 390 *Highland Broach* 42
A solace she might borrow . . . . 494 *Force of Prayer* 42
His means are run out,—he must beg, or must borrow. . . . . 569 *Farmer* 32

Borrowdale. Are those fraternal Four of Borrowdale, 185 *Yew-trees* 14

Borrowed. In the street that from Oxford hath borrowed its name. . . . . . . 188 *Music* 4
The tone of voice which wedded borrowed words 353 *Aquap.* 73
Upon a living staff, with borrowed sight. . . . 496 **A little* 10
The vanquished Whig, under a borrowed name, . 845 *Excursion* 6. 451

Borrowing. While, borrowing helps where'er he may, 178 *Waggoner* 2. 139
From blended colours also borrowing help, . . 691 *Prelude* 7. 250
And borrowing more their spirit, and their shape K. 8. 249 *Recluse* 1. 1. 451

Borrows. Benevolence is mild ; nor borrows help, . 873 *Excursion* 7. 1030

Bosom. No tears can chill them, and no bosom warms, 7 *Ev. Wk.* 277
Gleams that upon the lake's still bosom fall ; . . 7 *Ev. Wk.* 294
Triumphant on the bosom of the storm, . . . 15 *Desc. Sk.* 275
His bosom heaves, his Spirit towers amain, . . 18 *Desc. Sk.* 459
Nor pain nor pity in my bosom raised. . . . 31 *Guilt* 398
Fill your lap and fill your bosom ; . . . . . 79 *Foresight* 15
Upon the bosom of a placid lake. . . . . . 80 **Loving she* 21
Below him, in the bosom of the deep, ... 96 *Brothers* 61
Into thy bosom we again shall creep. . . . . 107 *Farewell* 64
And one across the bosom lies— . . . . . 112 **How rich* 15
Though at my bosom nursed ; this woeful gain . 118 *Maternal Grief* 2
Find place within his bosom.—Once again . . 124 *V. and J.* 171
Upon the Mother's bosom ; resting thus . . . 124 *V. and J.* 214
In Robin's bosom, as a chosen cell. . . . . 143 **Driven in* 26
Thrills not the less the bosom of the plain : . . 153 *Morn. Ex.* 46
A bosom to the sun endeared ? . . . . . . 154 *Flower Garden* 16
In the bosom of the cliff. . . . . 166 *Wand. Jew* 20
Ruffles the bosom of this leafy glen. . . . . 184 *Airey-force* 2
Her virgin bosom swell ; . . . . 187 **Three years* 33
Her bosom heaves and spreads, her stature grows; 209 *Laod.* 11
Might in the universal bosom reign, ... 212 *Dion* 15
A deep delight the bosom thrills, ... 214 *Kirkstone* 2
Yet still the bosom beating high, ... 216 *Enterprise* 47
FLOWER OF THE WINDS, beneath her bosom worn— 221 *Triad* 117
And in the bosom of the firmament . . . . 230 *Clouds* 50
Lodged in the bosom of eternal things ? . . . 231 *Clouds* 94
Happy the feeling from the bosom thrown . . 250 **Happy the* 1
Of his full bosom, gladsome Piety ! . . . . 254 *Complete Angler* 14
Thou liest in Abraham's bosom all the year ; . . 258 **It is a* 12
This Sea that bares her bosom to the moon ; . . 259 **The world is* 5
Reflected in my bosom all too late !— . . . . 267 **As the* 12
On England's bosom ; yet well pleased to rest, . 303 **Fair Star* 4
Into whose bosom earth's best treasures flow, . 327 *Ode 1815* 47
Along the bosom of this favoured Nation, . . . 331 *Ode : Thanks.* 190
But in the bosom, with devout respect . . . 332 *Ode : Thanks.* 221
And quits the bosom of the deep . . . . . 344 **How blest* 31
Appended to his bosom, and lips closed . . . 362 **List—'twas* 80
The bosom half, and half concealed, ... 371 *Eg. Maid* 130
Spreading his bosom under Kentish downs, . . 384 *Duddon* 32. 13
Yet still the female bosom lent, ... 390 *Highland Broach* 41
Till in the bosom of our rustic Cell . . . . 395 *White Doe : Ded.* 21
That swells the bosom of our passing sail ! . . 430 *Ecc. Sonn.* 2. 7. 5
Mother ! whose virgin bosom was uncrost . . . 434 *Ecc. Sonn.* 2. 25. 1

Bosom—*continued.*
Henceforth, as on the bosom of a stream . . . 443 *Ecc. Sonn.* 3. 12. 10
Which whoso travels in her bosom eyes, . . . 445 *Ecc. Sonn.* 3. 19. 7
THAT STREAM upon whose bosom we have passed 452 *Ecc. Sonn.* 3. 47. 6
Poured from the bosom of thy Church, St. Bees ! 468 *St. Bees* 144
From the dread bosom of the unknown past, . . 477 *Long Meg* 3
For precious tremblings in your bosom found ! . 480 *Cordelia* 14
Far in the bosom of Helvellyn, ... 491 *Fidelity* 21
Out of the bosom of a wiser vow. . . . . . 510 **Among a* 23
Tossed on the bosom of a stormy sea. . . . . 516 **As leaves* 14
Swells like the bosom of a man set free ; . . . 527 **Those breathing* 31
Reader ! if to thy bosom cling the pain . . 576 **By a* 13
Within thy bosom. "Wonderful" hath been . 585 *Ch. Lamb* 62
Slow lights upon the lake's still bosom fall, . . 598 *Ev. Wk. Quarto* 336
From out the bosom of a modest home . . . 627 **Son of* 12
Deep in the bosom of the wilderness ; . . . . 664 *Prelude* 4. 361
Into the bosom of the steady lake. . . . . . 671 *Prelude* 5. 388
Upon the bosom of the gentle Saone . . . . 680 *Prelude* 6. 376
The maiden from the bosom of her love, . . . 723 *Prelude* 10. 358
Guarded within the bosom of Thy will. . . . 724 *Prelude* 10. 432
From out the bosom of the night, come ye : . . 726 *Prelude* 10. 581
Not safe within its bosom. Thus prepared, . . 728 *Prelude* 11. 92
The seat and bosom of pure innocence, . . . 781 *Excursion* 2. 624
Darken the silver bosom of the crag, ... 786 *Excursion* 3. 27
Into my bosom, whence these words broke forth : 808 *Excursion* 4. 507
Within the bosom of yon crystal Lake, . . . 836 *Excursion* 5. 920
Would o'er the bosom of a joyful land . . . . 839 *Excursion* 6. 79
Within the bosom of her awful pile, ... 842 *Excursion* 6. 265
Out of the bosom of simplicity . . . . . . 862 *Excursion* 7. 331
Were working the broad bosom of the lake . . 863 *Excursion* 7. 410
Lodged in her bosom ; and, by science led, . . 865 *Excursion* 7. 505
Within the bosom of his native vale. . . . . 888 *Excursion* 9. 280
From out the bosom of these troubled times . . 890 *Excursion* 9. 401
When, on thy bosom, spacious Windermere ! . . 891 *Excursion* 9. 485
The Valley, opening out her bosom, gave . . . 892 *Excursion* 9. 571
Then, in the bosom of yon mountain-cove, . . 894 *Excursion* 9. 688
But, from thy bosom, should some venturous hand S. 3. 434 **The doubt* 55
Ye the tyrant's bosom gor'd, ... S. 3. 442 *Harmodius* 26
Bosom-child. Dear Bosom-child we call thee, that dost steep . . . . 253 **Fond words* 5
Bosomed. Of Como, bosomed deep in chestnut groves. . . . . 12 *Desc. Sk.* 78
Where, bosom'd deep, the shy Winander peeps . 591 *Ev. Wk. Quarto* 13
The bosom'd cabin's lyre enliven'd gloom ; . . 604 *Desc.Sk.Quarto* 101
Bosom'd in gloomy woods, her golden fields, . . 614 *Desc.Sk.Quarto* 681
Bosom's. "Lightly for both the bosom's lord did sit 435 *Ecc. Sonn.* 2. 26. 9
In the true filial bosom's inmost fold . . . 516 **Young England* 5
He felt ; but his parental bosom's lord . . . 517 *Pun. Death* 3. 7
Of passion at the bosom's inmost seat. . . . 624 *Æneid* 6
Bosoms. Soft bosoms breathe around contagious sighs, ... 12 *Desc. Sk.* 105
By diving for it into their own bosoms. . . . 64 *Bord.* 1487
Lodged in their innocent bosoms, and the spirit . 118 *Maternal Grief* 36
For sheltered places, bosoms, nooks, and bays, . 292 **Degenerate Douglas* 12
And there how many bosoms panted ! . . . . 373 *Eg. Maid* 284
On infant bosoms lonely Nature lies. . . . . 377 *Duddon* 5. 14
In gentle bosoms, while sere leaves . . . . . 385 *Yarrow Rev.* 11
In thankful bosoms to a modest pride. . . . 456 *Rydal Mere* 44
How savage bosoms melted at the sound . . . 466 *St. Bees* 51
To saintly bosoms !—Glorious is the blending . 500 *Humanity* 27
And her cold back their colder bosoms thrill ; . 597 *Ev. Wk. Quarto* 284
So shall our bosoms feel a covert growth . . S. 3. 437 **The doubt* 203
Bosom-weight. The bosom-weight, your stubborn gift, 225 *Present.* 25
Bosphorus. Of ease, the narrow Bosphorus will disdain ; . . . . 427 *Ecc. Sonn.* 1. 34. 6
Boss. A silver shield with boss of gold, ... 159 **With little* 30
Bosworth-field. And it was proved in Bosworth-field. 204 *Brougham* 25
In civil conflict met on Bosworth-field ; . . . 546 **The embowering* 18
Botanize. One that would peep and botanize . . 485 *Poet's Epitaph* 19
Both. (*Partial list.*)
Traitor to both. Oh, could you hear his voice ! . 41 *Bord.* 210
'Twere wrong to trouble you. God speed you both. 41 *Bord.* 222
Has made amends. Thanks to you both; but, Oh Sir ! . . . . 45 *Bord.* 431
What harvest it would bring us both ; and so . 46 *Bord.* 507
God bless and thank you both, my gentle Masters. 46 *Bord.* 526
More of contempt than hatred ; both are flown ; . 47 *Bord.* 554
Both soul and body—— 'Tis too horrible ; . . 57 *Bord.* 1065
To occupy—both fools, or wise alike, ... 60 *Bord.* 1238
On both sides, Benjamin the good, ... 181 *Waggoner* 4. 182
The morning that must wed them both ; . . . 199 *Thorn* 112
When silent were both voice and chords, . . . 334 **In Bruges* 13
Both hot and cold, and heart-aches every day,— 557 *Cuck. and Night.* 39
And had good knowing both of their intent, . . 558 *Cuck.andNight.* 109
For mine's a song that is both true and plain,— . 559 *Cuck.andNight.* 118
Is gone who held us both in sovereignty. . . . 563 *Troilus* 28
Both his new sorrow and his joys of old, . . . 563 *Troilus* 40
For I'd take my last leave both of verse and of prose. . . . . 571 *Avarice* 4
Between them, and both go a-pilfering together. . 572 *Avarice* 16
So reverenced by us both. O'er paths and fields 678 *Prelude* 6. 230
Unite the graceful qualities of both, ... 883 *Excursion* 8. 586
Even as she shares the pride and joy of both. . 883 *Excursion* 8. 587
Bothnic. Howling in troops along the Bothnic Main. 640 *Prelude* 1. 543
Bothwell's. Immured in Bothwell's towers, at times the Brave . . . . 392 *Bothwell* 1
Bottom. And down into the bottom cast his eye, . 73 *Bord.* 2016
For at the bottom of the brow, ... 174 *Waggoner* 1. 52
Across yon meadowy bottom look, ... 180 *Waggoner* 4. 40
Out of the bottom of his heart. . . . . . . 245 *P. B.* 760

Bottom—*continued.*
Verily, in the bottom of my heart, ... 308 **When I* 7
On the smooth bottom of this clear bright sea, . 469 **A youth* 2
With the green bottom strewing o'er the wave ; . 596 *Ev. Wk. Quarto* 236
Beneath him in the bottom of the deep, . . . 662 *Prelude* 4. 260
Came to a bottom, where in former times . . . 737 *Prelude* 12. 235
Or grassy bottom, all, with little hills— . . . 807 *Excursion* 4. 435
On height or bottom did they see, in flocks . . K.8. 225 **I will* 39
Bottomless. And bottomless, divides the midway tide. 611 *Desc.Sk.Quarto* 499
Bough. *See* **Holly-bough, Olive-bough.**
A brook to murmur or a bough to wave, . . . 16 *Desc. Sk.* 308
Sit near us on the bough ! . . . . 106 **I've watched* 15
If still beneath that pine-tree's ragged bough . . 111 **'Tis said that some* 33
The heavier substance of a leaf-clad bough, . . 123 *V. and J.* 142
Yet as the troubled seed and tortured bough . . 123 *V. and J.* 148
He shakes the green bough in his hand. . . . 126 *Idiot Boy* 51
The green bough motionless and dead : . . . 127 *Idiot Boy* 79
Feather, or leaf, or weed, or withered bough, . . 148 **A narrow* 14
Through sunshine flitting from the bough . . . 170 *Rural Ill.* 5
Upon bough or grassy blade) . . . . . . 171 *Kitten* 48
Unvisited, where not a broken bough . . . . 185 *Nutting* 17
And dragged to earth both branch and bough, with crash . . . . 185 *Nutting* 44
Words cannot paint the o'ershadowing yew-tree bough, ... 254 *Wild Duck's Nest* 9
Desponding Father ! mark this altered bough, . 266 **Desponding Father* 1
The clouds, or night-bird sang from shady bough ; 270 **Shame on* 5
With buds on every bough ! . . . . 291 *Rob Roy* 68
The chosen sceptre is a withered bough, . . . 321 **Humanity, delighting* 9
Or strip the bough whose mellow fruit bestrews . 335 *Namur* 8
O bounteous Heaven ! signs true as dove and bough 360 **Near Anio's* 9
Were on the bough, or falling ; . . . . . . 385 *Yarrow Rev.* 12
As at that moment, with a bough . . . . . 487 **We walked* 59
And yellow on the bough :— . . . . 498 **Departing summer* 15
All brighten on the bough ; . . . . 502 *Seasons* 12
Untouched the hawthorn bough, ... 506 **While from* 22
And many a rotten bough about. . . . . . 536 *Goody Blake* 52
Are thin upon the bough. Mine, only mine, . . 539 **Lady ! a* 35
Her crest a bough of Winter's bleakest pine, . . 608 *Desc.Sk.Quarto* 328
That flutters on the bough, lighter than he ; . . 842 *Excursion* 6. 296
Boughs. Its darkening boughs and leaves in stronger lines ; . . . . 6 *Ev. Wk.* 215
What if the bee love not these barren boughs ? . 22 *Yew-tree* 4
In solitude.—Stranger ! these gloomy boughs . . 23 *Yew-tree* 24
With rotten boughs and leaves, such as the winds 50 *Bord.* 705
Let not flowers, or boughs fruit-laden, ... 90 *Longest Day* 43
The wide-spread boughs, for view of door, window, and stair that wound . . . . . . 92 *Poet's Dream* 38
Beneath these fruit-tree boughs that shed . . 159 *Green Linnet* 1
With boughs above them closing, ... 161 *Binnorie* 24
And rudely canopied by leafy boughs . . . . 172 *Infant Daughter* 20
A soft eye-music of slow-waving boughs, . . . 184 *Airey-force* 14
Of boughs, as if for festal purpose decked . . . 185 *Yew-trees* 24
Of whitest garniture, like fir-tree boughs . . . 212 *Dion*
Darkling, among the boughs and leaves. . . . 240 *P. B.* 345
Of hardy laurel and wild holly boughs— . . . 324 *Ode 1814* 45
Thick boughs of palm, and willows from the brook, 346 *Processions* 11
Green boughs were borne, while, for the blast that shook . . . . 346 *Processions* 16
Then, not in vain, under these chestnut boughs . 358 *Aquap.* 358
Their darksome boughs on either side, ... 407 *White Doe* 993
That used to spread its boughs, and ring . . . 413 *White Doe* 1588
Beneath the boughs that heard their vows, . . 479 *Somnamb.* 102
Or listens to its play among the boughs . . . 522 *Epist. Beaumont* 48
(Among reflected boughs of leafy trees) . . . 527 **Those breathing* 43
From tossing boughs, the promise of a calm, . . 537 **In desultory* 8
Adorned, and shady boughs. . . . . . . 543 *Russ. Fug.* 104
A garland of immortal boughs . . . . . . 582 **O for a* 4
Their moveless boughs and leaves like threads of gold ; . . . . 593 *Ev. Wk.Quarto* 104
The oak its dark'ning boughs and foliage twines, . 595 *Ev. Wk.Quarto* 194
—Bursts from the troubl'd Larch's giant boughs . 606 *Desc.Sk.Quarto* 229
Between the pine's enormous boughs descry'd . 615 *Desc.Sk.Quarto* 698
The chamber hearth with fresher boughs is spread, 615 *Desc.Sk.Quarto* 738
Breaks from the rustling boughs, ... 626 †*Cento* 14
With sinuous trunk, boughs exquisitely wreathed, 676 *Prelude* 6. 77
Tossing in sunshine its dark boughs aloft, . . . 687 *Prelude* 7. 45
Maturer years. A grove there is whose boughs . 706 *Prelude* 8. 458
How widely spread the boughs, of that old tree . 717 *Prelude* 9. 550
Piping on boughs, or sporting on fresh fields, . . 735 *Prelude* 12. 35
Where two tall hedge-rows of thick alder boughs . 763 *Excursion* 1. 460
Of dews fast melting on their leafy boughs . . 773 *Excursion* 2. 132
Of yon black Yew-tree, whose protruded boughs . 786 *Excursion* 3. 26
With gentle whisper. Withered boughs grotesque, 814 *Excursion* 4. 879
Upon the boughs of sheltering leisure hung . . 816 *Excursion* 4. 1042
Whose flexile boughs low bending with a weight . 881 *Excursion* 8. 443
That, disentangled from the shady boughs . . 891 *Excursion* 9. 492
With the myrtle's boughs arrayed, ... S. 3. 442 *Harmodius* 2
With the myrtle [? myrtle's] boughs arrayed, . S. 3. 442 *Harmodius* 16
Bought. Here at my breast, and ask me where I bought it : . . . . 45 *Bord.* 441
Yet, so it was, an ewe I bought ; . . . . . 115 *Last of Flock* 24
And bought my little children bread, ... 115 *Last of Flock* 52
And halfpennies, wherewith the neighbours bought 135 *Michael* 261
Which neither can be overturned nor bought. . . 316 **It was a* 8
Bounced. Bounced, leapt, and pawed the air ; or mumbling sire, ... 693 *Prelude* 7. 422

Bowers—*continued.*
For ever broke, the sabbath of her bowers. . . . 12 *Desc. Sk.* 76
The green light sparkles;—the dim bowers recede. 14 *Desc. Sk.* 219
Close by my mother in their native bowers; . . 28 *Guilt* 240
And pleasure's sumptuous bowers; . . . . 102 *Artegal* 22
And wild notes warbled among leafy bowers; . 107 *Farewell* 61
The bowers where Lucy played; . . . . . 109 **I travelled* 14
There dwelt we, as happy as birds in their bowers; 116 *Repentance* 9
And if, amid those once-bright bowers, our fate . 124 *V. and J.* 198
Thou, ranging up and down the bowers, . . . 159 *Green Linnet* 19
And the children build their bowers, ... 161 **Pleasures newly* 19
I who ne'er sate within their bowers, ... 164 **Fair Lady* 3
But, exiled from Australian bowers, ... 165 *Parrot* 17
They stand the wonder of the bowers . . . . 193 *Ruth* 59
Into those favoured bowers. . . . . 193 *Ruth* 138
Of blissful quiet 'mid unfading bowers. . . . 212 *Laod.* 163
To bowers in which thy fortune may be tried, . 222 *Triad* 217
Amid your pleasant bowers to sit, ... 227 *Vernal Ode* 73
Great Jove is full of stately bowers; . . . . 237 *P. B.* 47
And streams, and bowers, and ladies fair, . . . 237 *P. B.* 104
While I was planting green unfading bowers, . . 264 **Lady! the* 3
And these perennial bowers and murmuring pines 264 **Lady! the* 12
And volatile their love of transient bowers, . . 278 **The most* 13
The greenest bowers, the most inviting ways, . . 333 *Ded. Tour* 6
But, for the bowers of Eden lost, ... 337 **Oh Life* 10
To Albogasio's olive bowers, ... 343 *Eclipse* 35
Free were the streams and green the bowers; . 348 **Lulled by* 8
Held with all Kinds in Eden's blissful bowers. . 362 **List—'twas* 65
To bowers of endless love! . . . . 374 *Eg. Maid* 386
To humbler streams, and greener bowers. . . . 376 **The Minstrels* 66
It lacked not old remains of hawthorn bowers, . 377 *Duddon* 6. 2
Transferred to bowers imperishably green, . . 381 *Duddon* 20. 5
Together,—'mid trim walks and artful bowers, . 389 *Breadalb.* 10
Whether she be of forest bowers, ... 397 *White Doe* 75
From the bowers of earth below; . . . . . 397 *White Doe* 76
Among the rocks and holly bowers. . . . . 399 *White Doe* 273
This Mansion and these pleasant bowers, . . . 402 *White Doe* 547
With weeds; the bowers are overthrown, . . . 413 *White Doe* 1571
From fields where good men walk, or bowers wherein they rest. . . . . 438 *Ecc. Sonn.* 2. 39. 14
The birds, of late so noisy in their bowers, . . 453 **Calm is the* 7
Like Angels from their bowers, our virtues to befriend; . . . . 456 **Soft as* 23
For summer wandering quit their household bowers; . . . . 463 **Adieu, Rydalian* 10
That have no rivals among British bowers; . . 476 *Eden* 7
Thy brook, and bowers of holly; . . . . . 478 *Somnamb.* 29
Through dewy grass, nor small birds hushed in bowers, ... 501 **The unremitting* 4
Choose from the bowers of virgin earth . . . 507 *May* 51
'Mid that soft air, those long-lost bowers, . . . 530 *Gleaner* 24
Harass the mind and strip from off the bowers . 538 **In desultory* 35
She saw the hereditary bowers, ... 544 *Russ. Fug.* 253
To aid the work, what time these walks and bowers 546 **Oft is* 15
And saw the birds come tripping from their bowers, 558 *Cuck. and Night.* 67
Drew TITUS from the depth of studious bowers, . 573 *Chiabrera* 2. 2
And loved you glittering in your bowers, . . . 579 **Sweet Flower* 27
Might have their record among sylvan bowers. . 583 **With copious* 16
Aught of these bowers and whence their pleasures flow; . . . . 583 **With copious* 35
While in soft gloom the scattering bowers recede, 607 *Desc. Sk. Quarto* 271
Prince, in these collegiate bowers, ... 629 *Installation* 73
The woods of autumn, and their hazel bowers . 639 *Prelude* 1. 484
Once more should I have made those bowers resound, ... 668 *Prelude* 5. 174
Ceased, had I left those academic bowers . . . 679 *Prelude* 6. 277
Yea, when a glimpse of those imperial bowers . 700 *Prelude* 8. 111
An Idler among academic bowers, ... 706 *Prelude* 8. 503
Among the bowers of Paradise itself) . . . . 729 *Prelude* 11. 120
To range her blooming bowers, and spacious fields, 819 *Excursion* 4. 1194
From academic bowers. He loved the spot— . 824 *Excursion* 5. 115
And that contents him; bowers that hear no more 828 *Excursion* 5. 406
(With shame I speak it) to her guilty bowers . . 843 *Excursion* 6. 352
To me hath been vouchsafed; among the bowers K.8. 239 *Recluse* 1.1.104
Bowery. His head in sunbeams or a bowery cloud, 503 *Warning* 35
Bowes. —'Tis Sir George Bowes who leads the Band: 412 *White Doe* 1446
Bowing. Bowing with reverence to the ancient creed, 444 *Ecc. Sonn.* 3. 15. 3
Bowing her head before her sister Faith . . . 650 *Prelude* 3. 86
Bowl. Our treat shall be a friendly bowl!" . . 177 *Waggoner* 2. 46
A steaming bowl, a blazing fire, ... 177 *Waggoner* 2. 70
With bowl that sped from hand to hand, . . . 177 *Waggoner* 2. 92
"A bowl, a bowl of double measure," . . . . 178 *Waggoner* 2. 145
When Benjamin had seized the bowl, ... 178 *Waggoner* 2. 149
Would elevate my dreams. A beechen bowl, . . 424 *Ecc. Sonn.* 1. 22. 9
Over the bowl, whose silver lip hath won . . . 433 *Ecc. Sonn.* 2. 20. 7
Yet Adam prized little the feast and the bowl,— 569 *Farmer* 21
Shall love, 'till Life has broke her golden bowl, . 615 *Desc. Sk. Quarto* 741
A bowl of state is offered to her hand: . . . 625 *Æneid* 104
Then sipp'd the bowl whence she the wine had pour'd . . . . 625 *Æneid* 117
He rais'd the bowl, and took a long deep draught; 625 *Æneid* 119
More toilsome than to carve a beechen bowl . . 702 *Prelude* 8. 206
The useless fragment of a wooden bowl, . . . 763 *Excursion* 1. 493
To cope with stoutest champions of the bowl; . 859 *Excursion* 7. 121
Bowling-green. Of a small bowling-green; beneath us stood . . . . 644 *Prelude* 2. 157
Daily, its bowling-green with harmless strife; . 845 *Excursion* 6. 466
Bowls. Again the jolly Tinker bowls . . . . S. 3. 424 *Tinker* 25
Bows. Bows his young head with sorrow to the grave. 20 *Desc. Sk.* 527
And drew their sounding bows at Azincour, . . 184 *Yew-trees* 7
Bows his young hairs with sorrow to the grave. . 613 *Desc. Sk. Quarto* 631

Bowscale-tarn. Through Bowscale-tarn did wait on him; . . . . 205 *Brougham* 123
Bowses. Right good ale he bowses; . . . . . S. 3. 423 *Tinker* 15
Box. *See* **Ballot-box, Salt-box, Tobacco-box.**
In a close Box, covert for Justice meet. . . . 626 *Ballot* 8
A box, perchance, is from your casement hung . 807 *Excursion* 4. 388
The box resound on Viscount Buffo's ear. . . . L. 1. 95 *Juvenal* 3. 13
Boxed. The famous brook, who, soon as he was boxed 659 *Prelude* 4. 51
Pulling the strings of his boxed raree-show; . . 699 *Prelude* 8. 33
Boxer's. Wedged in with blacklegs at a boxer's show L. 1. 94 *Juvenal* 2. 13
The boxer's armour, the dishonoured *Glove*. . . L. 1. 94 *Juvenal* 2. 26
Box-wood. Fresh sprigs of green box-wood, not six months before, ... 120 *Childless Father* 9
Boy. *See* **Cottage-boy, Errand-boy, Herd-boy, Mountain-boy, Parish-boy, Ploughboy, Post-boy, Schoolboy, Sheep-boy, Shepherd-boy, Stable-boy, Wood-boy.**
Save when, a stranger seen below, the boy . . 17 *Desc. Sk.* 364
With face to earth; and, as the boy turned round 33 *Guilt* 488
Yet happy thou, poor boy! compared with me, . 33 *Guilt* 498
To love him. I remember, when a Boy . . . 39 *Bord.* 89
Will give me quiet lodging. You have a boy, good Host, ... 43 *Bord.* 353
But how's the day?—I fear, my little Boy, . . 46 *Bord.* 494
Here's for your little boy, and when you christen him 46 *Bord.* 520
He had a Guide, a Shepherd's boy; but grieved . 49 *Bord.* 688
This Boy—when he comes forth with bloody hands— 54 *Bord.* 938
It said, "I will be with thee." A little boy, . . 62 *Bord.* 1364
Was with me when a boy: . . . . 79 *Sparrow's Nest* 16
"Nay, patience! patience, little boy; . . . . 81 †*Mother's Return* 11
At length I to the boy called out; . . . . . 82 *Alice Fell* 9
The boy then smacked his whip, and fast . . 82 *Alice Fell* 13
The Boy recovered heart, and told . . . . . 85 *Shepherd-boys* 80
I have a boy of five years old; . . . . . . 85 *Anecdote* 1
My boy beside me tripped, so slim . . . . . 86 *Anecdote* 25
At this my boy hung down his head, ... 86 *Anecdote* 45
Then did the boy his tongue unlock, ... 86 *Anecdote* 53
O dearest, dearest boy! my heart . . . . . 86 *Anecdote* 57
Served, tending a few sheep and goats, a ragged Norman Boy. . . . . 91 *Norman Boy* 4
And the poor Boy was busier still, with work of anxious heed. . . . . 91 *Norman Boy* 12
The innocent Boy, else shelterless, his lonely head must hide. . . . . 91 *Norman Boy* 24
I saw, within, the Norman Boy kneeling alone in prayer. . . . . 91 *Poet's Dream* 8
It came with sleep and showed the Boy, no cherub, not transformed, ... 92 *Poet's Dream* 15
"My Mother," said the Boy, "was born near to a blessèd Tree, ... 92 *Poet's Dream* 27
Forth from his eyes, when first the Boy looked down on that huge oak, ... 92 *Poet's Dream* 34
Past softly, leading in the Boy; and while from roof to floor, ... 92 *Poet's Dream* 42
Far happier lot, dear Boy, than brings full many to this shrine; . . . . 92 *Poet's Dream* 54
The Boy no answer made by words, but, so earnest was his look, ... 93 *Poet's Dream* 69
Alas the dream, to thee, poor Boy! to thee from whom it flowed, ... 93 *Poet's Dream* 77
For the boy loved the life which we lead here; . 100 *Brothers* 296
Noisy he was, and gamesome as a boy; . . . . 108 *Indolence* 47
And tottering spirit. And full oft the Boy, . . 118 *Maternal Grief* 49
Or art can fashion, shall you deck our boy, . . 124 *V. and J.* 201
Him whom you love, your Idiot Boy? . . . 126 *Idiot Boy* 11
Him whom she loves, her Idiot Boy. . . . . 126 *Idiot Boy* 41
The Boy, who is her best delight, ... 126 *Idiot Boy* 53
On which her Idiot Boy must ride, ... 126 *Idiot Boy* 70
Oh! then for the poor Idiot Boy! . . . . . 127 *Idiot Boy* 73
The silence of her Idiot Boy, ... 127 *Idiot Boy* 92
What speedy help her Boy will bring, ... 127 *Idiot Boy* 124
And I have lost my poor dear Boy, ... 129 *Idiot Boy* 255
Oh carry back my Idiot Boy! . . . . . . 129 *Idiot Boy* 300
And cannot find her Idiot Boy. . . . . . . 130 *Idiot Boy* 361
Him whom she loves, her Idiot Boy. . . . . 130 *Idiot Boy* 366
He whom you love, your Idiot Boy. . . . . 130 *Idiot Boy* 371
And fast she holds her Idiot Boy. . . . . . 130 *Idiot Boy* 376
To hear again her Idiot Boy. . . . . . . 130 *Idiot Boy* 381
Him whom she loves, her Idiot Boy; . . . . 130 *Idiot Boy* 388
The Pony, Betty, and her Boy, ... 130 *Idiot Boy* 407
And hence this Tale, while I was yet a Boy . . 131 *Michael* 27
And in a later time, ere yet the Boy . . . . 133 *Michael* 159
And when by Heaven's good grace the boy grew up 134 *Michael* 177
And gave it to the Boy; wherewith equipt . . 134 *Michael* 184
Were dearer now? that from the Boy there came 134 *Michael* 200
Thus in his Father's sight the Boy grew up: . . 134 *Michael* 204
Who, out of many, chose the trusty boy . . . 135 *Michael* 265
If he *could* go, the Boy should go to-night." . . 135 *Michael* 282
His utmost for the welfare of the Boy; . . . 136 *Michael* 309
Lack any pleasure which a boy can know." . . 136 *Michael* 356
Nay, Boy, be of good hope;—we both may live . 137 *Michael* 388
Before I knew thy face.—Heaven bless thee, Boy! 137 *Michael* 396
Ere the night fell:—with morrow's dawn the Boy 137 *Michael* 425
Of Luke and his well-doing: and the Boy . . 138 *Michael* 432
I waked, and saw my little boy, ... 144 *Her Eyes* 27
My little boy of flesh and blood; . . . . . 144 *Her Eyes* 28
"Oh! love me, love me, little boy! . . . . 145 *Her Eyes* 41
"Then do not fear, my boy! for thee . . . . 145 *Her Eyes* 51
If his sweet boy he could forsake, ... 145 *Her Eyes* 75
"I'll teach my boy the sweetest things: . . . . 145 *Her Eyes* 81
The shadow of a Danish Boy. . . . . . . 165 *Danish Boy* 11

Brain—*continued.*
In heart as dull in brain—while pacing ground . 356 *Aquap.* 270
No heart had she, no busy brain ; . . . . . 370 *Eg. Maid* 57
His brain will burn, his stout heart split asunder. 372 *Eg. Maid* 222
Of the world's flatteries if the brain be full, . . 394 **How profitless* 5
From his distracted brain was cast, ... 406 *White Doe* 894
To stay the precious waste. Through every brain 433 *Ecc. Sonn.* 2. 20. 9
To fiercer mood the frenzy-stricken brain, . . 459 **Wanderer! that* 42
And doubts and scruples seldom teased the brain, 468 **Bold words* 2
Though brain would swim, and eyes grow dim, . 478 *Somnamb.* 57
That spectacle, for many days, my brain . . . 638 *Prelude* 1. 391
Depicted on the brain, and to the eye . . . . 641 *Prelude* 1. 601
And gratitude grew dizzy in a brain . . . . 653 *Prelude* 3. 300
On men suspected to be crazed in brain. . . . 660 *Prelude* 4. 130
When Wisdom, like the Goddess from Jove's brain, 695 *Prelude* 7. 538
Labouring, a brain confounded, and a sense, . . 724 *Prelude* 10. 413
No composition of the brain, but man . . . . 741 *Prelude* 13. 82
Upon his brain ; and on their pictured lines . . 758 *Excursion* 1. 146
From my good Host, that being crazed in brain . 839 *Excursion* 6. 108
Through fancy's heat redounding in the brain, . 863 *Excursion* 7. 380

Brains. The least of which would beat out a man's brains ; . . . . 56 *Bord.* 1008
And all particulars that dull brains require . . 58 *Bord.* 1156
That Benjamin, with clouded brains, ... 178 *Waggoner* 3. 12

Brake. *See* **Fern-brake, Forest-brake, Furze-brake.**
A voice of uttermost joy brake out : . . . . 403 *White Doe* 684
I followed on from brake to bush ; . . . . 79 **Stay near* 16
In bush and brake, in black and green ; . . . 128 *Idiot Boy* 210
He trudged along through copse and brake . . 240 *P. B.* 331
Close by a brake of flowering furze . . . . . 246 *P. B.* 921
And startled only by the rustling brake, . . . 262 *Retirement* 11
Intent on gathering wool from hedge and brake . 280 **Intent on* 1
Dwarf willows gliding, and by ferny brake. . . 377 *Duddon* 4. 8
The White Doe, in the hawthorn brake ; . . . 405 *White Doe* 877
Retreated towards a brake of thorn, ... 412 *White Doe* 1477
A stirring in a brake of fern ; . . . . . . 491 *Fidelity* 6
Seven days she lurked in brake and field, . . . 542 *Russ. Fug.* 17
Good Cuckoo, seek some other bush or brake, . 558 *Cuck.andNight.*112
Fixed in the centre of a prickly brake, . . . 835 *Excursion* 5. 842

Brakes. At thorns, and brakes, and brambles,— and in truth . . . . 185 *Nutting* 13
That in wild Arden's brakes was ever heard, . . 523 *Epist. Beaumont* 161

Bramble. Deep in its tomb :—the bramble crept . 390 *Highland Broach* 32
The gadding bramble hang her purple fruit ; . . 433 *Ecc. Sonn.* 2. 21. 6
Thy fragments to the bramble and the rose ; . . 549 **Stranger ! this* 33

Bramble-leaf. A bramble-leaf or blade of grass. . 244 *P. B.* 715

Brambles. At thorns, and brakes, and brambles,—and in truth . . . . 185 *Nutting* 13
To couch in this thicket of brambles alone, . . 340 *Fort Fuentes* 4
'Mid thorns and brambles ; or a bird that breaks 886 *Excursion* 9. 171

Bran. Upon thy margin, roaring Bran !— . . . 301 *Bran* 87

Brancepeth. Of Brancepeth look in doubt and fear, . 402 *White Doe* 595
And, mixed with these, to Brancepeth came . . 403 *White Doe* 628

Branch. And dragged to earth both branch and bough, with crash . . . . 185 *Nutting* 44
Grasping a hawthorn branch in hand, ... 243 *P. B.* 636
Perched on an olive branch, and heard her cooing 360 **Near Anio's* 2
Godlike, a humble branch of the divine, . . . 509 *F. Stone* 89
The trunk and every master branch were green . 676 *Prelude* 6. 81
And this most rotten branch of human shame, . 722 *Prelude* 10. 260
The veins that branch through every frame of life, 724 *Prelude* 10. 423
No natural branch ; despondency far less ; . . 803 *Excursion* 4. 163

Branches. Among the branches of the leafless trees; v **If thou indeed* 13
While thick above the rill the branches close, . 3 *Ev. Wk.* 57
And cracked the branches, and strewn them about; 80 †*Address: Child* 23
There *was* he, where of branches rent and withered and decayed, ... 91 *Norman Boy* 13
Like branches when strong winds the trees annoy. 108 *Indolence* 49
Their branches in mid air. . . . . 109 **Ere with* 12
Beneath the branches—of itself had made . . 149 *M. H.* 5
My branches are so fresh and gay . . . . . 156 *Oak and Broom* 78
But in the branches of the oak . . . . . . 157 *Oak and Broom* 95
Under the branches of the tree : . . . . . 162 **Art thou the* 18
In spikes, in branches, and in stars, ... 198 *Thorn* 47
Among thy branches safe he lay, ... 204 *Brougham* 99
He lay beneath the branches high, ... 239 *P. B.* 262
Which should extend thy branches on the ground, 319 *Guernica* 10
Aloft, where pines their branches toss ! . . . 337 *Cath. Cantons* 10
Or the Indian tree whose branches,downward bent, 383 *Duddon* 31. 7
Among its withering topmost branches mixed, . 393 *Hart's-horn* 3
The root sincere, the branches bold to strive . . 425 *Ecc. Sonn.* 1. 27. 9
(Blighted or scathed tho' many branches be, . . 431 *Ecc. Sonn.* 2. 10. 3
And proudly did its branches wave ; . . . . 495 *Force of Prayer* 50
With branches intertwined, ... 543 *Russ. Fug.* 142
Bounding through branches interlaced, . . . 544 *Russ. Fug.* 263
And when its potent branches, wide outthrown, . 546 **The embowering* 11
And see the budding leaves the branches throng, 557 *Cuck.and Night.* 27
That,round his trunk and branches,might have clung 585 *Ch. Lamb* 75
To where, while thick above the branches close, . 592 *Ev. Wk. Quarto* 73
Stand like an oak whose stag-horn branches start 695 *Prelude* 7. 520
Upon my naked branches :—lively thoughts . . 793 *Excursion* 3. 493

Branching. These lofty pillars, spread that branching roof . . . . 451 *Ecc. Sonn.* 3. 43. 9
Of pillars, branching off from year to year, . . 546 **Ye Lime* 4

Branchy. And all its branchy vales, and all that lurks 350 *Des. Stanzas* 39

Brand. Bare to the sky, with threatening brand . 301 *Bran* 71
Uplifting toward high Heaven her fiery brand, . 420 *Ecc. Sonn.* 1. 9. 5
Michael, and thou, St. George, whose flaming brand 434 *Ecc. Sonn.* 2. 24. 8

Brandished. Brandished his crutch against the mountain tops ; . . . . 180 *Waggoner* 3. 137

Brandishes. Which yet he brandishes for future war, 103 *Artegal* 55

Brass. Here's neither head nor foot-stone, plate of brass, ... 98 *Brothers* 170
By plate of monumental brass . . . . . . 417 *White Doe* 1895
And shining effigies of brass inlaid. . . . . . 825 *Excursion* 5. 170

Bravado. Or with bravado insolent and hard, . . 504 *Warning* 103

Brave. Anon, appears a brave, a gorgeous show . 6 *Ev. Wk.* 200
Poison, which not a frame of steel can brave, . 20 *Desc. Sk.* 526
Rejoice, brave Land, though pride's perverted ire 22 *Desc. Sk.* 642
I long for news of our brave Comrades ; Lacy . 50 *Bord.* 728
Are brave : Clifford is brave ; and that old Man . 54 *Bord.* 911
Is brave. To Clifford's arms he would have led . 54 *Bord.* 912
Shall be proclaimed : brave Men, they all shall hear it. . . . . 55 *Bord.* 981
Let me speak of this brave Child . . . . . 93 *Westmoreland Girl* 26
By brave Corineus aided, he subdued, ... 102 *Artegal* 17
With two brave sheep-dogs tried in many a storm, 132 *Michael* 91
Hardships for the brave encountered . . . . 140 *Arm. Lady* 33
Across the wave, a Rover brave . . . . . 161 *Binnorie* 14
His brave spirit with the war in . . . . . 163 *Hint* 7
Heaped over brave King Dunmail's bones, . . 176 *Waggoner* 1. 210
On which brave Admiral Nelson stood— . . . 178 *Waggoner* 2. 129
Wert kind as resolute, and good as brave ; . . 210 *Laod.* 56
Or through the clouds, and brave the light . . 216 *Enterprise* 69
The prompt, the brave, ... 285 *Grave of Burns* 28
Be independent, generous, brave ; . . . . . 287 *Sons of Burns* 44
She has her brave Rob Roy ! . . . . . . 291 *Rob Roy* 5
In honour of that Hero brave ! . . . . . . 291 *Rob Roy* 8
Yet was Rob Roy as *wise* as brave ; . . . . 291 *Rob Roy* 13
Say, then, that he was wise as brave ; . . . . 291 *Rob Roy* 17
I would not wrong thee, Champion brave ! . . 292 *Rob Roy* 98
Strength to the brave, and Power, and Deity ; . 306 **Inland, within* 11
Even rich men, brave by nature, taint the air . 308 **These times* 2
And hear you shouting forth your brave intent. . 309 *Men of Kent* 8
Sons of the brave who fought at Marathon, . . 312 **When, far* 10
Whose factions lead astray the wise and brave— . 314 **Not 'mid* 4
By Palafox, and many a brave compeer, . . . 315 **And is it* 10
Brave Schill ! by death delivered, take thy flight 317 **Brave Schill* 1
Methinks that we shall hail thee, Champion brave, 318 **Ah ! where* 6
Where all the brave lie dead. But, when of bands 319 *Spaniard* 8
Which a brave People into light can bring . . 321 **The power* 4
Fit garlands for the brave, ... 323 *Ode 1814* 40
O murdered Prince ! meek, loyal, pious, brave ! . 325 *Enghien* 10
Fuentes once harboured the good and the brave, 340 *Fort Fuentes* 13
The beautiful, the brave, the holy, and the just ! 351 *Des. Stanzas* 81
By hands of men, humble as brave, who fought . 355 *Aquap.* 161
From death the memory of the good and brave. . 367 *Trajan* 12
Yet, to the loyal and the brave, who lie . . . 383 *Duddon* 29. 9
While we, the brave, the mighty, and the wise, . . 384 *Duddon* 34. 7
Immured in Bothwell's towers, at times the Brave 392 *Bothwell* 1
Like the brave Lion slain in her defence. . . . 395 *White Doe: Ded.*16
He spake, and eight brave sons straightway . . 400 *White Doe* 412
Of this brave man, when he shall see . . . 401 *White Doe* 443
—Brave Earls ! to whose heroic veins . . . . 403 *White Doe* 646
Would breed us thousands brave as they." . . 405 *White Doe* 861
—The noble Francis—wise as brave, ... 408 *White Doe* 1111
Swayed the brave man to his wrong. . . . . 411 *White Doe* 1411
And where full many a brave tree stood, . . . 413 *White Doe* 1587
And sculptured Forms of Warriors brave : . . 417 *White Doe* 1897
Rise !—they *have* risen : of brave Aneurin ask . 421 *Ecc. Sonn.* 1. 10. 1
When she would tell how Brave, and Good, and Wise, ... 430 *Ecc. Sonn.* 2. 8. 13
Children of Summer ! Ye fresh Flowers that brave 474 **Hope smiled* 2
A loving creature she, and brave ! . . . . . 490 *Incident : Dog* 31
More brave for this, that he hath much to love :— 494 *Hap. War.* 64
Dive, at thy choice, or brave the freshening gale! 527 **Those breathing* 36
Oh ! can a brave Man wish to take . . . . 535 *Egremont* 47
Pious and pure, modest and yet so brave, . . . 541 *Grace Darl.* 94
" Silence ! " the brave Commander cried ; . . . 579 **Sweet Flower* 43
A meek man and a brave ! . . . . 580 **Sweet Flower* 66
The meek, the brave, the good, was gone ; . . . 580 *John Words.* 38
Strong poison not a form of steel can brave . . 613 *Desc.Sk.Quarto* 630
The seats of learning brave the distant skies. . . 619 *School Ex.* 64
Brave hearts ! to shameful flight. It was a grief,— 722 *Prelude* 10. 288
Upon our brave Progenitors, who rose . . . . 815 *Excursion* 4. 920
Near this brave Knight his Father lay entombed ; 825 *Excursion* 5. 188
With his brave sword endeavoured to prevent . 844 *Excursion* 6. 420
For, like brave Philip Sidney, ... S.3. 440 **Said red-ribboned* 6
Than that brave vessel, though she sailed so far ;. S.3.442 **Vasco, whose* 11
And the brave Tydides meet. . . . . . . S.3. 442 *Harmodius* 14
Of two brave vessels matched in deadly fight, . K.8.256*Recluse* 1.1.722
A Pym's brave heart, or stir a Hampden's arm ? . L.1.94 *Juvenal* 2. 6

Braved. Whose fierce wrath the Girl had braved ; . 93 *Westmoreland Girl* 18
Discord in hearts of men till they have braved . 105 *Artegal* 236
Thus, after he had fondly braved . . . . . 297 *Highland Boy* 241
But Francis, soon as he had braved . . . . 410 *White Doe* 1340

Bravely. For them who bravely stood unhurt, or bled 328 *Ode 1815* 80
" Gone are they, bravely, though misled ; . . . 401 *White Doe* 461
And there stood bravely, though forlorn. . . . 412 *White Doe* 1479
As bravely as the foe was keenly sought. . . . 458 *Sea-shore* 24
Sister of Mercy, bravely hast thou won . . . K.8.325[?]**The vestal* 9

Braver. When he had risen alone ! No braver Youth 869 *Excursion* 7. 811

Bravery. With all its bravery on ; in times . . . 294 *Jedbor.* 31
Of all this outside bravery, within, ... 775 *Excursion* 2. 285

Braves. And, as a Coracle that braves . . . . 296 *Highland Boy* 121
The Helvetian Girl—who daily braves, . . . 344 **How blest* 29
Or like the invincible Rock itself that braves, . 540 *Grace Darl.* 25

Braves—*continued.*
But did not fall ; for Virtue braves all shocks, . 574 *Chiabrera* 3. 11
I love to see the look with which it braves, . . 579 *Peele Castle* 50
Bravest. "Supreme of Heroes—bravest, noblest, best ! 210 *Laod.* 49
The bravest traveller in balloon, ... 296 *Highland Boy* 168
Were crowded with the bravest youth of France,. 713 *Prelude* 9. 263
Braving. Against his conscience rose in arms, and, braving . . . . 855 *Excursion* 6. 1092
Brawl. Filled with its fray or brawl, how eagerly . 693 *Prelude* 7. 436
Brawling. And o'er the brawling beds of unbridged streams. . . . . 703 *Prelude* 8. 248
Brawls. Where the brook brawls along the public road 7 *Ev. Wk.* 262
Whose nursling current brawls o'er mossy stones, 475 *Greenock* 13
Where the brook brawls along the painful road, . 596 *Ev. Wk. Quarto* 271
I mean the brawls of lawyers in their courts . . 694 *Prelude* 7. 490
Issuing when shame hath ceased to check the brawls K.8. 246 *Recluse* 1.1.345
Brawny. He took no heed ; but in his brawny arms 696 *Prelude* 7. 612
Bray. A long and clamorous bray ! . . . . . 241 *P. B.* 465
The hard dry see-saw of his horrible bray ! . . 241 *P. B.* 480
Brazen. To king and people true. A brazen plate, . 825 *Excursion* 5. 178
Breach. Or tempt them to an hour of sabbath breach. 99 *Brothers* 272
Had saved him from that breach of faith ! . . 199 *Thorn* 132
Then would I seek the Pyrenean Breach . . . 335 *Aix* 11
Pain entered through a ghastly breach— . . . 337 **Oh Life* 7
No breach of promise in the fruit ? . . . . . 344 **How blest* 60
The breach is open—on the wall, ... 408 *White Doe* 1139
He made by wilful breach of law divine. . . . 428 *Ecc. Sonn.* 2. 1. 4
Of sottish vice or desperate breach of law, . . 880 *Excursion* 8. 423
Bread. *See* **Convent-bread.**
Bread has he none, the snow must be his drink ; . 16 *Desc. Sk.* 333
With daily bread, by constant toil supplied. . . 29 *Guilt* 263
And lustily the master carved the bread, . . . 34 *Guilt* 530
Our heavenly Father granted each day's bread ; . 35 *Guilt* 598
Was crying, as I thought, crying for bread . . 44 *Bord.* 399
And begged our daily bread from door to door. . 50 *Bord.* 692
The stone-cutters, 'tis true, might beg their bread 98 *Brothers* 175
Never did worthier lads break English bread ; . 99 *Brothers* 268
Shelter and daily bread,—the sum of his desires. . 104 *Artegal* 105
Whereof to buy us bread. . . . . 115 *Last of Flock* 48
And bought my little children bread, ... 115 *Last of Flock* 52
Her shelter and her bread. . . . . 194 *Ruth* 210
For shelter, and a poor man's bread ! . . . . 204 *Brougham* 79
That not by bread alone we live, ... 228 *Devot. Incit.* 72
Lived thankful for day's light, for daily bread, . 278 **Lo ! where she* 13
The bread which without industry they find. . . 315 **And is it* 14
Roof, raiment, bread, or burial : . . . . . 391 *Highland Broach* 58
Thanks given to God for daily bread, and here . 509 *F. Stone* 110
That asks for daily bread. . . . . 530 *Gleaner* 34
Came not, but in a lane partook his bread. . . 531 **I know* 8
Was reared and taught ; and humbly earned his bread, ... 584 *Ch. Lamb* 4
Deny'd the bread of life the foodful ear, . . . 608 *Desc.Sk.Quarto* 320
No bread to feed him, and the snow his drink, . 609 *Desc.Sk.Quarto* 405
Meantime in canisters is heap'd the bread, . . 624 *Æneid* 60
Sought daily bread from public charity, . . . 764 *Excursion* 1. 561
Of dainties,—oaten bread, curd, cheese, and cream ; 781 *Excursion* 2. 677
Relinquished, lived dependent for his bread . . 783 *Excursion* 2. 739
For daily bread. A consciousness is yours . . 813 *Excursion* 4. 789
For daily bread." "Yes," buoyantly exclaimed . 831 *Excursion* 5. 601
And, through Heaven's blessing, thus we gain the bread . . . . 834 *Excursion* 5. 809
As there to linger, there to eat his bread, . . . 843 *Excursion* 6. 354
The bread they eat. A sample should I give . . 880 *Excursion* 8. 395
To every day's demand for daily bread, . . . K.8. 249 *Recluse* 1.1.450
Breadth. *See* **Hair-breadth.**
To see an acre's breadth of that wide cliff . . . 97 *Brothers* 150
Break. *See* **Day-break, Water-break.**
In timely sleep ; and when, at break of day, . . 22 *Desc. Sk.* 667
That break against the shore, shall lull thy mind 22 *Yew-tree* 6
To break my dream the vessel reached its bound ; 31 *Guilt* 367
And under covert rest till break of day, . . . 53 *Bord.* 863
Then shatter the delusion, break it up . . . . 54 *Bord.* 934
But will return to you by break of day. . . . 67 *Bord.* 1650
As if her innocent heart would break ; . . . . 82 *Alice Fell* 23
I chanced to see at break of day . . . . . 82 *Lucy Gray* 3
Sleep—and at break of day I will come to thee again ! " . . . . 88 *Pet-lamb* 60
Never did worthier lads break English bread ; . 99 *Brothers* 268
Friendships that will not break, and love that cannot roam. . . . . 102 *Artegal* 24
Would overset the brain, or break the heart : . 138 *Michael* 450
At break of day, Joanna and myself. . . . . 147 *Joanna* 37
At break of day I ventured forth, ... 157 *Oak and Broom* 103
Break forth into thanksgiving, ... 235 *Power of Sound* 193
Or that he could not break the chain, ... 241 *P. B.* 472
His eyes will burst—his heart will break— . . 242 *P. B.* 528
Nor ever once did break his fast : . . . . . 243 *P. B.* 605
And, with due care, ere break of day, ... 249 *P. B.* 1124
Fresh as a lark mounting at break of day, . . 258 **Where lies the Land* 2
Would break the silence of this Dell : . . . . 289 *Glen-Al.* 24
Which he will break for us he dares to speak, . 319 *Spaniard* 9
Break forth at thought of laying down his head, . 359 **They—who* 2
When thou, uprisen, shalt break thy double yoke, 361 *Alban Hills* 12
The Monks relax or break these iron chains ; . . 429 *Ecc. Sonn.* 2. 4. 7
And some break forth when others' sorrows crush 436 *Ecc. Sonn.* 2. 32. 8
Why should we break Time's charitable seals ? . 449 *Ecc. Sonn.* 3. 35. 12
Voices, thy winds break forth in prophecy, . . 471 *Tynwald* 12
Let us break off all commerce with the Muse : . 480 **Most sweet* 10
Would through the clouds break forth on human sight ! . . . . 511 **So fair* 15

Break—*continued.*
May rise to break it : effort worse than vain . . 515 **Ah why* 7
Let us break forth in tempest now or never !— . 516 **Hard task* 7
Nor chide the Muse that stooped to break a spell 525 *Epist. Beaumont* 276
Break forth,—again to walk the clear blue sky. . 532 **How beautiful the* 8
The twain ere break of day . . . . 543 *Russ. Fug.* 122
Alas, alas ! my very heart will break, ... 560 *Cuck.and Night.* 211
His eyes from sleep, at the first break of day, . 562 *Troilus* 2
Him thought his sorrowful heart would break in two ; . . . . 562 *Troilus* 12
Now is there not good reason to break forth . . 575 *Chiabrera* 8. 17
To break the quiet of the village shade . . . 615 *Desc.Sk.Quarto* 745
To break, the vales where Death with Famine scow'rs, ... 617 *Desc.Sk.Quarto* 794
Severely honest, break no plighted trust, . . . 619 *School Ex.* 87
To break upon the sabbath of her rest . . . . 669 *Prelude* 5. 261
Halted without an effort to break through ; . . 684 *Prelude* 6. 597
But here I must break off, and bid farewell . . 686 *Prelude* 6. 727
To times, when half the city shall break out . . 697 *Prelude* 7. 672
That shall break in upon his sleep for weeks ; . 700 *Prelude* 8. 115
Capable of clear truth, the one to break . . . 714 *Prelude* 9. 358
For, like a plague, will memory break out ; . . 798 *Excursion* 3. 847
Of a command which they have power to break, . 807 *Excursion* 4. 379
Break down all grandeur, still unsatisfied . . . 815 *Excursion* 4. 964
Did never break the stillness that prevails . . 818 *Excursion* 4. 1166
That seemed to break from an expanding heart, . 835 *Excursion* 5. 839
Break from the maddened nations at the sight . 873 *Excursion* 7. 1038
Could break from out those languid eyes, or a blush 879 *Excursion* 8. 314
And as these lofty barriers break the force . . . K.8. 247 *Recluse* 1.1.374
Break up, and are beginning to recede ; . . . K.8. 249 *Recluse* 1.1.477
Breaker. From such a desperate breaker of the peace? L. 1. 97 *Juvenal* 3. 70
Breakers. With breakers roaring to the gales . . 217 *Enterprise* 154
Threatened by angry breakers as they passed ; . 454 *Sea-side* 12
Breakfast. Their breakfast done, the pair, though loth, must part ; . . . . 34 *Guilt* 532
Breakfasts. And breakfasts with his dog. When they have stolen, ... 702 *Prelude* 8. 238
Breaking. *See* **Heart-breaking.**
Where sparkling eyes and breaking smiles illume . 13 *Desc. Sk.* 133
This action ? Innocent !—oh breaking heart !— 71 *Bord.* 1880
He suffered—breaking down in heart and mind ! . 124 *V. and J.* 184
Till, breaking in upon the dying strain, . . . 175 *Waggoner* 1. 203
Main ocean, breaking audibly, and stretched . . 219 **This Height* 14
Where mists are breaking up or gone, ... 233 *Power of Sound* 42
Breaking the silence of the seas . . . . . . 289 *Sol. Reap.* 15
Of the waves breaking on the chalky shore ;— . 306 **Here, on our* 5
Come, weak as is a breaking wave ! . . . . . 485 *Poet's Epitaph* 58
Thus innocently sported, breaking forth . . . 584 *Ch. Lamb* 19
Pleas'd thro' the dusk their breaking smiles to view, 596 *Ev. Wk. Quarto* 274
Where sparkling eyes and breaking smiles illume . 604 *Desc.Sk.Quarto* 100
—Breaking th' ascending roar of desert floods, . 606 *Desc.Sk.Quarto* 223
In breaking up a long-continued frost, ... 632 *Prelude* 1. 40
Said the old man, abruptly breaking silence,— . 777 *Excursion* 2. 383
Wantonly breaking in upon the Swiss, ... 823 *Excursion* 5. 94
Was left to tremble for a breaking vow,— . . 851 *Excursion* 6. 852
Breaks. *See* **Water-breaks.**
And now, on every side, the surface breaks . . 4 *Ev. Wk.* 118
In foamy breaks the rill, with merry song, . . 4 *Ev. Wk.* 136
And breaks the spreading of its golden tides ; . 5 *Ev. Wk.* 171
Save when the avalanche breaks loose, to rend . 16 *Desc. Sk.* 312
The ice breaks up and sweeps away a bridge ; . 97 *Brothers* 156
Oft, when light breaks through clouds or waving trees, ... 139 *Widow* 38
Such a light of gladness breaks, ... 171 *Kitten* 101
When in some great extremity breaks out . . 309 **What if* 11
Europe breaks forth ; then, Shepherds ! shall ye rise 316 **It was a* 13
Of Time, breaks forth triumphant Memory ; . . 381 *Duddon* 21. 10
Needful when o'er wide realms the tempest breaks, 395 *White Doe: Ded.* 53
Breaks into dimples small and bright ; . . . 406 *White Doe* 968
Breaks—and the greyhound, DART, is overhead ! 490 *Incident : Dog* 24
As he breaks the ice away. . . . . 490 *Incident : Dog* 36
It breaks, and all is clear : . . . . 491 *Fidelity* 45
Breaks off the dreadful kiss with angry shriek. . 597 *Ev. Wk. Quarto* 288
And breaks the mirror of the circling deeps ; . . 597 *Ev. Wk. Quarto* 312
Breaks on the shade, the shade upon the light, . 598 *Ev. Wk. Quarto* 346
The pie, and chattering breaks the night's repose. 606 *Desc.Sk.Quarto* 230
Breaks from the rustling boughs, ... 626 †*Cento* 14
Where the salt sea innocuously breaks, . . . 793 *Excursion* 3. 516
Breaks from a many-windowed fabric huge ; . . 877 *Excursion* 8. 169
'Mid thorns and brambles ; or a bird that breaks 886 *Excursion* 9. 171
Breast. *See* **Redbreast.**
Thy breast their death-bed, coffined in thine arms ! 7 *Ev. Wk.* 278
Creep hushed into the tranquil breast of death. . 8 *Ev. Wk.* 354
How richly glows the water's breast . . . . 9 *Lines : Boat* 1
When, from the sunny breast of open seas, . . 17 *Desc. Sk.* 366
Awe in his breast with holiest love unites, . . 19 *Desc. Sk.* 476
In mute devotion on the thankful breast ! . . 20 *Desc. Sk.* 568
Three lovely babes had lain upon my breast ; . 29 *Guilt* 264
I too forgot the heavings of my breast. . . . 30 *Guilt* 338
He bore within a breast where dreadful quiet reigned. . . . . 36 *Guilt* 648
Here at my breast, and ask me where I bought it : 45 *Bord.* 441
Back on herself, I think, again—my breast . . 51 *Bord.* 784
I could have dropped asleep upon his breast. . . 53 *Bord.* 892
Whate'er the monster brooding in your breast . 56 *Bord.* 1014
But take me to your arms—this breast, alas ! . 66 *Bord.* 1619
No strife disturbs his sister's breast ; . . . . 81 †*Mother's Return* 17
On whose breast are thither borne . . . . . 90 *Longest Day* 50
In her breast, unruly fire, ... 94 *Westmoreland Girl* 74

Breath—*continued.*

A Being breathing thoughtful breath, 186 *She was 23
As with the breath of one sweet flower,— 191 Seq. Beggars 16
But breath and eyesight fail; and, one by one, 201 Hart-leap 23
And with the last deep groan his breath had fetched 201 Hart-leap 43
Until, the breath of this corporeal frame 206 Tintern 43
As when their breath enriched Thessalian air. 210 Laod. 60
Not on the breath of popular applause, 213 Dion 47
—And though to every draught of vital breath, 226 Vernal Ode 48
Unscorned the peasant's whistling breath, that lightens 233 Power of Sound 51
Breathes into him a second breath, 248 P. B. 1074
More searching than the breath of spring. 248 P. B. 1075
Though a breath made it) like a bubble blown 250 *Happy the 3
Its waste.—Though crumbling with each breath of air, 276 Filial Piety 11
He sang of battles, and the breath 288 Glen-Al. 5
Obedient to my breath." 292 Rob Roy 92
To dead and living; when her breath 299 Brownie's Cell 83
Is breathed upon by Hope's perpetual breath; 308 *These times 11
No parleying now. In Britain is one breath; 309 Men of Kent 12
The breath of Heaven has drifted them like snow, 310 Anticip. 3
Internal darkness and unquiet breath; 318 *Look now 11
Of Winter's breath surcharged with sleety showers, 322 *Ye Storms 7
With breath suspended, like a listening scout. 322 Germans 4
Of locusts travels on his breath; 328 Ode 1815 90
They suck—from breath that, threatening to destroy, 337 Aar 9
The breath of an Helvetian Maid. 344 *How blest 39
The breath of air can be where earth had else 356 Aquap. 215
Mingling with thy soft breath! That morning too, 367 *If with 9
But with closed eyes,—of breath and bloom forsaken. 371 Eg. Maid 138
Allowed a soft and flower-like breath, 374 Eg. Maid 334
And if the breath of some to no caress 377 Duddon 6. 12
Falls upon her like a breath, 397 White Doe 88
If not in vain we breathed the breath 402 White Doe 568
Led on, and yielded up their breath; 410 White Doe 1338
The last dear service of thy passing breath! 424 Ecc. Sonn. 1. 23. 14
Till breath departs in blissful aspiration: 437 Ecc. Sonn. 2. 35. 11
On a true Penitent. When breath departs 447 Ecc. Sonn. 3. 28. 9
In vain who, for a rightful cause, give breath 448 Ecc. Sonn. 3. 30. 9
Of thy soft breath!—Less vivid wreath entwined 464 Derwent 9
Fanned by the breath of foes. 478 Somnamb. 40
Too weak to stand against its sportive breath, 491 Tribute: Dog 19
His breath in confidence of Heaven's applause: 494 Hap. War. 83
Less than they heed a breath of wanton air. 495 Fact 8
Something like the faintest breath 502 *Like a 41
Whose first-drawn breath from bush and tree 506 *While from 7
Earth's sweetness in thy breath. 507 May 40
No tempest from his breath, their promised rest 512 *Who rashly 39
Nay, said a voice, soft as the south wind's breath, 515 *Men of 9
That never more shall hang upon her breath 518 Pun. Death 5. 13
Whose breath would labour at the flute in vain, 521 Epist. Beaumont 29
So that the very heaving of his breath 523 Epist. Beaumont 142

'Tis the breath of good Sir Eustace! 536 Egremont 81
The breath of the cows you may see him inhale, 571 Farmer 87
And when his breath was fled, 577 *I come 6
A breath, a sound, and scarcely heard. 580 John Words. 36
From the great city where he first drew breath, 584 Ch. Lamb 3
Plunge with the Russ embrown'd by Terror's breath, 606 Desc. Sk. Quarto 245
And as on glorious ground he draws his breath, 612 Desc. Sk. Quarto 536
'Till Hope-deserted, long in vain his breath 613 Desc. Sk. Quarto 642
To the low-warbled breath of twilight lute, 615 Desc. Sk. Quarto 749
And deep is the sigh of his breath, 620 Convict 14
Or an *unseen* companionship, a breath, 622 Recluse 1. 1. 93
For its keen breath, was aiding to our steps, 622 Recluse 1. 1. 159
These children claim thee for their sire; the breath 627 Eagle and Dove 5
For I, methought, while the sweet breath of heaven 632 Prelude 1. 33
Frost, and the breath of frosty wind, had snapped 636 Prelude 1. 308
That givest to forms and images a breath 638 Prelude 1. 403
Disowned by memory—ere the breath of spring 641 Prelude 1. 615
Than Nature's self, which is the breath of God, 669 Prelude 5. 221
Might waste their breath in chiding. Under hills— 680 Prelude 6. 374
Fanned by the breath of angry Providence. 681 Prelude 6. 447
Alternately, and plain below, while breath 745 Prelude 13. 347
Of more refined humanity, thy breath, 750 Prelude 14. 264
Whether from breath of outward circumstance, 755 Recluse 1. 1. 764
And softly creeping, like a breath of air, 787 Excursion 3. 71
And what, when breath hath ceased, we may become. 789 Excursion 3. 236
—' Blow winds of autumn!—let your chilling breath 790 Excursion 3. 307
When his own breath was silent, chanced to hear 814 Excursion 4. 855
To prize the breath we share with human kind; 832 Excursion 5. 656
With their last breath, from out the smouldering flame, 839 Excursion 6. 70
His last, repentant breath; and closed his eyes, 843 Excursion 6. 364
Than of this breath, which shapes itself in words. 863 Excursion 7. 359
'Tis left untold if here he first drew breath, 871 Excursion 7. 927
Wild pursuivants! until their breath is lost, 880 Excursion 8. 386
Of the same breath are shattered and destroyed. 889 Excursion 9. 343
And yet a breath can do it!" These few words. 891 Excursion 9. 454
The sufferance only of a breath of air!" 891 Excursion 9. 473
More grateful, more harmonious than the breath, K.8. 247 Recluse 1. 1. 407
The idle breath of softest pipe attuned K.8. 247 Recluse 1. 1. 408
The heroic trumpet with the Muse's breath! K.8. 257 Recluse 1. 1. 750

Breathe. Soft bosoms breathe around contagious sighs, 12 Desc. Sk. 105
For creatures doomed to breathe terrestrial air: 22 Desc. Sk. 647
Yet, if the wind breathe soft, the curling waves, 22 Yew-tree 5
Thou wilt have time to breathe and think— Oh, Mercy! 63 Bord. 1405

Breathe—*continued.*

Alive! you heard him breathe? quick, quick— 73 Bord. 2014
All that breathe are thankful debtors 90 Longest Day 7
With this dear holy shepherd-boy breathe a prayer of earnest heart, 91 Norman Boy 30
Our father's spirit seemed in thee to breathe again. 105 Artegal 193
Of Infancy, but still did breathe the air 118 Maternal Grief 15
And cheered; and now together breathe fresh air 119 Maternal Grief 64
Never more to breathe the day: 171 Kitten 54
Enough by her dear side to breathe the air 190 *Lyre! though 16
Shall mothers breathe a like sweet air 224 *'Tis gone 35
Shall rise, and breathe again; 225 Primrose 46
And breathe as in a world where nothing can go wrong. 229 Cuckoo-clock 22
Do Thou, then, breathe those thoughts into my mind 257 *The prayers 9
Cool air I breathe; while the unincumbered Mind, 262 Retirement 12
To breathe in rural peace, to hear the stream 276 Author's Portrait 7
Breathe hopeful air. 285 Nith 18
Was stopped, and could not breathe beneath the load 293 Killicranky 7
And gladsome notes my lips can breathe, 302 Yarrow V. 79
Here, on our native soil, we breathe once more. 306 *Here, on our 1
He only, if such breathe, in strains devout 326 *The Bard 10
Breathe Thou, this day, a vital undulation! 331 Ode: Thanks. 191
Fervent but humble as the lips can breathe 354 Aquap. 102
Who breathe the air he breathed, tread where he trod, 362 *List—'twas 67
Better to breathe at large on this clear height 376 Duddon 1. 11
On gales that breathe too gently to recall 381 Duddon 21. 13
Be loth that we should breathe awhile exempt 382 Duddon 24. 11
Then be *good* Spirits free to breathe a note 423 Ecc. Sonn. 1. 18. 6
Has called him forth to breathe the common air, 423 Ecc. Sonn. 1. 19. 7
Turned to a fearful Thing whose nostrils breathe 439 Ecc. Sonn. 2. 43. 10
Breathe through my soul the blessing of thy grace, 454 *The Sun, that 22
To breathe Elysian peace in upper air. 501 Humanity 76
"Slaves cannot breathe in England"—yet that boast 501 Humanity 83
The social rights of man breathe purer air; 520 Pun. Death 13. 9
If doomed to breathe against his lawful will 528 *Those breathing 77
To breathe and live but for himself alone, 568 Cumb. Beg. 165
And, long as he can wander, let him breathe 568 Cumb. Beg. 172
As long as verse of mine shall breathe the air 585 Ch. Lamb 48
Breathe o'er the failing soul voluptuous dreams; 605 Desc. Sk. Quarto 157
No longer breathe, but all be satisfied. 622 Recluse 1. 1. 82
I cannot miss my way. I breathe again! 632 Prelude 1. 18
To breathe an elevated mood, by form 646 Prelude 2. 305
Of all that breathe?—what in the path of all 668 Prelude 5. 186
For sunshine, and to breathe the fresher air. 696 Prelude 7. 610
Did breathe its sweetness out most sensibly, 714 Prelude 9. 2;6
Be free to breathe in, and the heart of man 717 Prelude 9. 540
Without Whose call this world would cease to breathe, 724 Prelude 10. 421
They first of all that breathe should have awaked 732 Prelude 11. 381
While yet our hearts are young, while yet we breathe 741 Prelude 13. 124
They do not breathe among them: this I speak 744 Prelude 13. 275
The outside of her creatures, and to breathe 744 Prelude 13. 285
Deep—and, aloft ascending, breathe in worlds 755 Recluse 1. 1. 782
Who dwell on earth, yet breathe empyreal air, 804 Excursion 4. 231
To breathe beneath a vault of ignorance? 831 Excursion 5. 588
While in a spot like this we breathe and walk, 836 Excursion 5. 923
Should breathe a word tending to violate 847 Excursion 6. 583
Soothed by the natural spirit which they breathe. 847 Excursion 6. 633
To save the perishing; and, henceforth, I breathe 852 Excursion 6. 923
And breathe the sweet air of futurity; 884 Excursion 9. 25
Though strength decay, to breathe in such estate 885 Excursion 9. 46
To breathe in solitude, above the host 885 Excursion 9. 72
To breathe and to be happy, run and shout 888 Excursion 9. 263
With civil arts, that shall breathe forth their fragrance, 890 Excursion 9. 390
Breathe in the air of fellow-suffering K.8. 246 Recluse 1. 1. 368
Calmly they breathe their own undying life K.8. 249 Recluse 1. 1. 462
To breathe in peace, we shall moreover find K.8. 254 Recluse 1. 1. 644
By all that breathe in Troy, how tired and worn L.2. 318 Frag. Æneid 4. 6

Breathed. *See* **Flower-breathed, Low-breathed, Sweet-breathed.**

Breathed a pale steam around the glaring hill, 2 Ev. Wk. 38
Where breathed the gale that caught Wolfe's happiest sigh, 15 Desc. Sk. 299
We breathed a pestilential air, that made 29 Guilt 283
He breathed for her, and for that merciful pair. 36 Guilt 644
That died the moment the air breathed upon it. 47 Bord. 557
Presumptuous above all that ever breathed, 76 Bord. 2209
As ever breathed:" and that is true; 117 Affl. Marg. 33
Earth breathed in one great presence of the spring; 122 V. and J. 41
Fields, where with cheerful spirits he had breathed 132 Michael 65
Breathed gently from the warm south-west: 156 Oak and Broom 17
When universal nature breathed 191 Seq. Beggars 15
Among the fields she breathed again: 194 Ruth 211
Choicest flowers that ever breathed, 221 Triad 112
But air breathed soft that day, 224 Primrose 26
To sailor's prayer breathed from a darkening sea, 233 Power of Sound 31
O Friend! thy flute has breathed a harmony 252 *The fairest 3
Breathed from eternity; for, as a dart 270 *If these 8
Breathed forth beside the peaceful mountain Stream 275 Rotha Q. 9
Heaven's sapphire pavement, yet breathed well content, 278 *Lo! where she 11
As vapours breathed from dungeons cold 284 Grave of Burns 3
Is breathed upon by Hope's perpetual breath; 308 *These times 11
A dirge devoutly breathed o'er sorrows past; 314 *I dropped 10
Breathed from a soft and lonely instrument, 324 Ode 1814 84
Breathed thy mercy to implore, 336 *Jesu! bless 5

Breathed—*continued.*
Where Mortal never breathed I dare to sit — 350 *Des. Stanzas* 19
Who breathe the air he breathed, tread where he trod, — 362 **List—'twas* 67
If not in vain we breathed the breath — 402 *White Doe* 568
Breathed to a Son forgiven, and blest — 411 *White Doe* 1423
Her arms, or over-deeply breathed, — 415 *White Doe* 1725
We breathed together for a moment's space, — 464 **A point* 12
Breathed the same element; too many wrecks — 466 *St. Bees* 21
Up! up! and drink the spirit breathed — 481 *Expost.* 7
Spontaneous wisdom breathed by health, — 481 *Tables Turned* 19
Truth breathed by cheerfulness. — 481 *Tables Turned* 20
Or need, of counsel breathed through lips divine. — 498 **Enough of climbing* 31
Breathed out these words:—"Here daily do we sit, — 509 *F. Stone* 109
Had breathed a sigh of thanks to God, — 542 *Russ. Fug.* 43
For One who breathed unquiet air — 542 *Russ. Fug.* 91
And words, not breathed in vain, — 544 *Russ. Fug.* 204
My sighs breathed forth in silence,—comfort give! — 562 *Cuck.andNight.*316
A roseate fragrance breathed.—O human life, — 573 *Chiabrera* 2. 13
There never breathed a man who, when his life — 574 *Chiabrera* 4. 1
The mountain top, or breathed the mist — 583 **O for a* 47
That breath'd a death-like peace these woods around, — 603 *Desc. Sk. Quarto* 57
Your presence, when with slackened step we breathed — 644 *Prelude* 2. 134
For its own pleasure, and I breathed with joy. — 645 *Prelude* 2. 188
And the whole year breathed tenderness and love. — 687 *Prelude* 7. 42
Breathed up its smoke, an image of his ghost — 705 *Prelude* 8. 449
What ground I trod on, and what air I breathed. — 719 *Prelude* 10. 65
Her very presence such a sweetness breathed, — 736 *Prelude* 12. 167
No thanks he breathed, he proffered no request; — 759 *Excursion* 1. 214
Breathed immortality, revolving life, — 759 *Excursion* 1. 228
And his whole figure breathed intelligence. — 762 *Excursion* 1. 425
I lived and breathed; most grateful—if to enjoy — 795 *Excursion* 3. 628
There flowed no Gallic blood, nor had I breathed — 796 *Excursion* 3. 742
Lingering behind my comrades, thus I breathed — 822 *Excursion* 5. 14
This file of infants; some that never breathed — 836 *Excursion* 5. 946
Infect the air which he had freely breathed — 844 *Excursion* 6. 382
And breathed its soothing air;—the spirit of hope — 845 *Excursion* 6. 483
Multitudes, who from infancy had breathed — 879 *Excursion* 8. 342
Breathed over them: but suddenly the door — 882 *Excursion* 8. 544
I breathed (for this I better recollect) — K.8. 256 *Recluse* 1.1.705
By flames breathed on her from her own fireside. — K.8. 275 **These vales* 4

Breathes. And breathes in peace the lily of the vale! — 6 *Ev. Wk.* 235
Time softly treads; throughout the landscape breathes — 9 *Ev. Wk.* 361
Breathes o'er the failing soul voluptuous dreams, — 13 *Desc. Sk.* 136
The faintest breath that breathes can move a world; — 65 *Bord.* 1564
Life, which to every one that breathes is full of care." — 140 *Arm. Lady* 18
Sad thoughts, and breathes with easier breath; — 164 **Fair Lady* 34
With aught that breathes the ethereal element, — 213 *Dion* 55
While incense from the altar breathes — 228 *Devot. Incit.* 30
Breathes into him a second breath, — 248 *P. B.* 1074
That breathes on earth the air of paradise. — 256 **Yes! hope* 14
Breathes forth a cloud-like creature of its own, — 282 **While beams* 3
Oh! there is life that breathes not; Powers there are — 290 *Kilchurn* 6
He breathes a subterraneous damp; — 294 *Jedbor.* 27
Than his who breathes, by roof, and floor, and wall, — 308 **There is a bondage* 2
Redoubted Viriathus breathes again; — 320 **They seek* 10
In realms where everlasting freshness breathes!" — 324 *Ode 1814* 52
More sweetly breathes the wind. — 338 **Meek Virgin* 36
And to all living mute memento breathes, — 355 *Aquap.* 164
The woodbine so, with spiral grace, and breathes — 367 *Trajan* 21
No zephyr breathes, no cloud its shadow throws: — 382 *Duddon* 24. 2
While from one pillared chimney breathes — 406 *White Doe* 949
His Country's virtue, fought, and breathes no more; — 426 *Ecc. Sonn.* 1. 32. 10
Defiance breathes with more malignant aim; — 438 *Ecc. Sonn.* 2. 38. 6
And in his prison breathes celestial air. — 440 *Ecc. Sonn.* 2. 45. 8
Mounting while earth her morning incense breathes, — 465 **Pastor and* 11
Enjoys the air it breathes. — 482 *Lines: Spring* 12
And through the very atmosphere she breathes, — 508 *F. Stone* 18
Where shady hamlet, town that breathes — 533 **Blest is* 5
Breathes out from floor or couch, through pallid lips — 541 *Grace Darl.* 90
When aught that breathes had felt a wound; — 583 **O for a* 34
The mighty Minstrel breathes no longer, — 586 *Hogg* 9
That Nature breathes among the hills and groves. — 636 *Prelude* 1. 281
Be hallowed, love that breathes not without awe; — 748 *Prelude* 14. 182
From all that breathes and is, was chastened, stemmed — 750 *Prelude* 14. 295
And the sea breeze as innocently breathes, — 793 *Excursion* 3. 517
Of ignorance or illusion) lives and breathes — 813 *Excursion* 4. 830
The oppressor breathes, their human form divine, — 886 *Excursion* 9. 151
Breathes invitation; easy is the walk — 890 *Excursion* 9. 424

Breath'st. That breath'st with me in sun and air, — 159 **With little* 45

Breathing. *See* **Fiercely-breathing, Incense-breathing, Sweetly-breathing.**
To scent the sweets of Piedmont's breathing rose, — 21 *Desc. Sk.* 595
The breathing pestilence that rose like smoke, — 30 *Guilt* 346
Your natural breathing has been troubled. Nay, — 39 *Bord.* 105
From the stern breathing of the rough sea-wind; — 61 *Bord.* 1296
I am sure I heard something breathing— — 72 *Bord.* 1970
Her sweets, and triumph o'er the breathing rose? — 110 **Look at* 11
Old times, thought I, are breathing there; — 119 *Sailor's Mother* 8
Are mastered by the breathing haze; — 167 *Pilgrim's Dream* 37
By breathing mist; and thine appears to be — 173 *Infant Daughter* 63
Breathing with such suppression of the heart — 185 *Nutting* 22
A Being breathing thoughtful breath, — 186 **She was* 23
And hers shall be the breathing balm, — 187 **Three years* 16
Where will they stop, those breathing Powers, — 228 *Devot. Incit.* 1

Breathing—*continued.*
Happy Associates breathing air remote — 252 **Her only* 8
O'erlooks the torrent breathing showers — 301 *Bran* 121
There's not a breathing of the common wind — 305 *Toussaint* 11
And pure religion breathing household laws. — 307 **O Friend* 14
And horror breathing from the silent ground! — 335 **A wingèd* 14
In beauty clothed, or breathing sweetness — 366 **Ye Trees* 13
Whence half the breathing world received its doom; — 368 *Trajan* 38
"Change me, some God, into that breathing rose!" — 377 *Duddon* 7. 1
Heaven's breathing influence failed not to bestow — 395 *White Doe: Ded.* 29
With air about him breathing sweet, — 401 *White Doe* 429
The fragrance of the breathing flowers — 407 *White Doe* 1025
A thing too bright for breathing man to keep. — 458 *Sea-shore* 20
Breathing, in the light of day, — 502 **Like a* 40
Too soon—thou com'st into this breathing world; — 504 *Warning* 85
And breathing life of flesh, as if already — 510 **Among a* 7
Those breathing Tokens of your kind regard, — 527 **Those breathing* 1
That no one breathing should be left to perish, — 541 *Grace Darl.* 78
He loved the breathing air, — 577 **I come* 22
Or merely silent Nature's breathing life. — 578 *Peele Castle* 28
Pause upon that, and let the breathing frame — 622 *Recluse* 1. 1. 81
With breathing flowers embraced, and fragrant shade. — 624 *Æneid* 52
Whose subtle intercourse with breathing flowers, — 734 *Prelude* 12. 11
By sound diffused, or by the breathing air, — 759 *Excursion* 1. 188
Strengthened and braced, by breathing in content — 760 *Excursion* 1. 305
First, last, and single, in the breathing world, — 777 *Excursion* 2. 363
And there we found him breathing peaceably, — 784 *Excursion* 2. 821
Here are we, in a bright and breathing world. — 789 *Excursion* 3. 237
Not long accustomed to this breathing world; — 826 *Excursion* 5. 262
Breathing fresh air, and treading the green earth; — 878 *Excursion* 8. 280
The breathing creature stood; as beautiful, — 890 *Excursion* 9. 445
The breathing faculty with which thou yield'st — S.3. 433 **The doubt* 41

Breathing-fit. Many a breathing-fit he takes; — 174 *Waggoner* 1. 37

Breathing-place. A fixed, abysmal, gloomy, breathing-place— — 747 *Prelude* 14. 58

Breathings. I marked the breathings of her dragon crest: — 311 **Who rises* 21
Low breathings coming after me, and sounds — 637 *Prelude* 1. 323
Breathings for incommunicable powers; — 651 *Prelude* 3. 187

Breathing-time. Thy scanty breathing-time is portioned out — 172 *Infant Daughter* 17
For breathing-time, is tempted to review — 709 *Prelude* 9. 11
A breathing-time, vacation, or a truce, — 791 *Excursion* 3. 384

Breathing-times. Not in the breathing-times of that poor slave — 454 **Not in the lucid* 5

Breathless. *See* **Half-breathless.**
Breathless he gazed upon her face,—then took — 36 *Guilt* 632
Subdued by breathless harmonies — 112 **How rich* 17
The breathless corse; then peacefully resigned — 123 *V. and J.* 133
Breathless questions followed fast, — 141 *Arm. Lady* 104
With breathless nostrils stretched above the spring. — 202 *Hart-leap* 78
High in the breathless Hall the Minstrel sate, — 203 *Brougham* 1
And breathless calms no longer dreaded, — 216 *Enterprise* 78
Breathless as they, with unabated craving — 220 *Triad* 26
Through many a breathless field of light, — 236 *P. B.* 32
But as an oak in breathless air — 246 *P. B.* 846
Breathless and motionless, the mind — 247 *P. B.* 1017
Breathless with adoration; the broad sun — 258 **It is a* 3
Seems firm as solid crystal, breathless, clear, — 456 **Soft as* 2
To breathless Nature's dark abyss; — 581 **Loud is* 18
Has sunk into a breathless sleep. — 586 *Hogg* 40
Who faint, and beat by summer's breathless ray, — 596 *Ev. Wk. Quarto* 243
The breathless stillness. The succeeding day, — 672 *Prelude* 5. 442
The breathless wilderness of clouds; the clock — 686 *Prelude* 6. 716
And, in the grim and breathless hour of noon, — 782 *Excursion* 2. 706
At breathless eventide at rest — S.3. 438 **My Lord* 21

Breath-like. Came ever and anon a breath-like sound, — 661 *Prelude* 4. 185
Unhappy Nuns, whose common breath's a sigh — 266 **With how* 5

Bred. *See* **Home-bred, Thoroughbred.**
Of virtuous life, by pious parents bred; — 28 *Guilt* 200
As if we two were twins; two songsters bred — 40 *Bord.* 150
I neither know nor care. The insult bred — 47 *Bord.* 553
Bred in house, in grove, and field, — 94 *Westmoreland Girl* 46
—A gentle Maid, whose heart is lowly bred, — 106 *Farewell* 28
A mighty wonder bred among our quiet crew. — 107 *Indolence* 18
Well born, well bred; I sent him forth — 117 *Affl. Marg.* 17
Proud was I that my country bred — 119 *Sailor's Mother* 9
Though with misbelievers bred; but that dark night — 141 *Arm. Lady* 119
What trouble, surely, will be bred; — 156 *Oak and Broom* 26
Short-lived likings may be bred — 163 *Spinning Wheel* 13
You think, those doings must have bred — 178 *Waggoner* 3. 5
And so were better manners bred, — 179 *Waggoner* 3. 108
Where he was born and bred: the churchyard hangs — 183 *Prelude* 5. 392
The wisdom which adversity had bred. — 205 *Brougham* 168
By which such virtue may in me be bred — 257 **The prayers* 10
Soft smiles, by human kindness bred! — 288 *Highland Girl* 35
Are captains such as erst their country bred — 320 **They seek* 5
By antique Fancy trimmed—though lowly, bred — 339 *Schwytz* 1
From flowers 'mid GOLDAU's ruins bred; — 348 **Lulled by* 64
And why shouldst thou?—If rightly trained and bred, — 390 *Highland Hut* 6
Had not thy holy Church her champions bred, — 442 *Ecc. Sonn.* 3. 10. 6
What benefits are missed, what evils bred, — 443 *Ecc. Sonn.* 3. 14. 4
But when a storm, on sea or mountain bred, — 472 *Dunolly Eagle* 2
Of public conflicts trained and bred? — 485 *Poet's Epitaph* 2
Bred in this vale, to which he appertained — 548 **Stranger! this* 22
Vague longing, haply bred by want of power, — 635 *Prelude* 1. 239
Have often stirred the heart of youth, and bred — 654 *Prelude* 3. 340
For I, bred up 'mid Nature's luxuries, — 654 *Prelude* 3. 351
Engrafted far-fetched shapes on feelings bred — 705 *Prelude* 8. 422

Bred—*continued.*
I did not pine like one in cities bred, ... 705 *Prelude* 8. 433
Had bred in me ; but gloomier far, a dim . . . 706 *Prelude* 8. 515
Or in the cultured field, a Man so bred . . . 813 *Excursion* 4. 828
Robust as ever rural labour bred." . . . . . 839 *Excursion* 6. 101
How such consummate elegance was bred . . . 842 *Excursion* 6. 299
Colours as bright on exhalations bred . . . . 847 *Excursion* 6. 596
In forest purlieus ; and the like are bred, . . . 879 *Excursion* 8. 369
These, bred to little pleasure in themselves, . . . 880 *Excursion* 8. 390
To Britons born and bred within the pale . . . 880 *Excursion* 8. 392
Bred also there, I wanted not a scale . . . . K.8. 246 *Recluse* 1.1.349

Breeched. *See* **Blue-breeched.**
And urchins newly breeched—all pass him by : . 567 *Cumb. Beg.* 65

Breed. —Where snakes and lions breed, . . . 327 *Ode 1815* 28
Would breed us thousands brave as they." . . 405 *White Doe* 861
Four dogs, each pair of different breed, . . . 490 *Incident : Dog* 7
The Dog is not of mountain breed ; . . . . 491 *Fidelity* 9
No farther than they breed a second Will more wise.] . . . . 492 *Duty*
The *servum pecus* of a Gallic breed ? . . . . 516 **YoungEngland* 11
And mingle colours, that should breed . . . . 530 *Gleaner* 19
The thought of our past years in me doth breed . 589 *Immortality* 137
I hate that Andrew Jones : he'll breed . . . 621 *Andrew Jones* 1
By help of dreams—can breed such fear and awe 755 *Recluse* 1. 1. 791
In life, in death, what solitude can breed . . . 836 *Excursion* 5. 888
Or, if it breed not, hath not power to cure. . . 836 *Excursion* 5. 890
Bishops, of milder Spanish breed, shall boast . L. 1. 89 *Juvenal* 1. 25

Breeding. First among youths of knightly breeding, One . . . . 71 *Bord.* 1897
And breeding suffer them to be ; . . . . . . 192 *Gipsies* 27

Breeds. 'Tis weariness that breeds these gloomy fancies, ... 40 *Bord.* 145
The common life our nature breeds ; . . . . 158 **In youth* 54
The cruel city breeds. . . . . 239 *P. B.* 300
Which faction breeds? the turmoil where, that passed 349 *Val. Dover* 2
An awe and supernatural horror breeds ; . . . 431 *Ecc. Sonn.* 2. 11. 6
But what her fancy breeds. . . . . 479 *Somnamb.* 72
And all that generous nurture breeds to make . 575 *Chiabrera* 7. 2
Such as a delicate work of humour breeds ; . . 661 *Prelude* 4. 211
Breeds love : yet, suited as it rather is . . . 806 *Excursion* 4. 347
Of the dense air, which town or city breeds . . 838 *Excursion* 6. 22
And, if that ignorance were removed, which breeds 889 *Excursion* 9. 346

Breeze. *See* **Water-breeze.**
In long-drawn vista, rustling in the breeze ; . . 11 *Desc. Sk.* 47
And bays with myrtle fringed, the southern breeze 17 *Desc. Sk.* 367
And every passing breeze will testify. . . . . 21 *Desc. Sk.* 603
Thy three-striped banner fluctuate on the breeze ; 21 *Desc. Sk.* 613
By man and nature ;—if a breeze had blown, . . 68 *Bord.* 1700
Of the soft breeze ruffling the meadow-flowers, . 80 **Loving she* 18
What joy awaits you, when the breeze . . . 106 **I've watched* 7
Is flowing in the breeze. . . . . 110 **Ere with* 16
Bend with the breeze their heads, beside a crystal stream. . . . . 141 *Arm. Lady* 96
Her forehead, like a breeze of Spring ; . . . . 144 **Driven in* 40
The breeze I see is in the tree : . . . . . . 145 *Her Eyes* 39
Making report of an invisible breeze . . . . 148 **A narrow* 23
At every impulse of the moving breeze, . . . 151 **When, to* 103
With sailors longing for a breeze in vain, . . . 154 *Morn. Ex.* 50
There's not a breeze—no breath of air— . . . 155 **A whirl-blast* 14
" 'If breeze or bird to this rough steep . . . 156 *Oak and Broom* 41
The breeze had better been asleep, ... 156 *Oak and Broom* 43
And to her own green bower the breeze . . . 157 *Oak and Broom* 98
That twinkle to the gusty breeze, ... 159 *Green Linnet* 26
To frolic on the breeze. . . . . 170 *Rural Ill.* 12
Comes a tired and sultry breeze . . . . . 173 *Waggoner* 1. 17
And suddenly a ruffling breeze, ... 175 *Waggoner* 1. 184
And yet, even now, a little breeze, perchance . 184 *Airey-force* 8
Yet to be come-at by the breeze : . . . . . 186 **O Nightingale* 14
Fluttering and dancing in the breeze. . . . . 187 **I wandered* 6
The feathers nodded in the breeze, ... 192 *Ruth* 23
And what the creeping breeze that comes . . . 200 *Thorn* 201
While the coarse rushes, to the sweeping breeze, . 215 *Kirkstone* 39
That wakes the breeze, the sparkling lymph . . 217 *Enterprise* 142
Nearer she draws ; a breeze uplifts her veil ; . . 220 *Triad* 43
The vernal breeze invites. . . . . 224 *Primrose* 6
Where oft the venturous heifer drinks the noontide breeze. . . . . 226 *Vernal Ode* 13
They wander with the breeze, they wind . . . 228 *Devot. Incit.* 3
Love them ; and every idle breeze of air . . . 230 *Clouds* 70
Her only pilot the soft breeze, the boat . . . 251 **Her only* 1
Whence I have risen, uplifted on the breeze . . 252 **The fairest* 13
Like to a breeze from heaven. Shall I alone, . 253 **Fond words* 9
But 'tis a chosen soil, where sun and breeze . . 308 **One might* 5
And, if a breeze be straying, ... 311 **Who rises* 7
That breeze she will invite ; . . . . 311 **Who rises* 8
Stirred by the breeze ; they rose, a Nation, true,. 313 *Prophecy* 5
Bright shines the Sun—and not a breeze to shake 332 *Ode : Thanks.* 209
Darkening like water in the breeze, ... 343 *Eclipse* 59
Even such, this day, came wafted on the breeze . 347 *Processions* 41
Of trouble—but the fluttering breeze ; . . . . 348 **Lulled by* 17
And peach and citron, in Spring's mildest breeze . 356 *Aquap.* 218
To that mild breeze with motion and with voice . 356 *Aquap.* 221
A pure poetic Spirit—as the breeze, ... 356 *Aquap.* 234
Anon the breeze became a blast, ... 369 *Eg. Maid* 29
Through hill and valley every breeze . . . . 375 **The Minstrels* 7
Sole listener, Duddon ! to the breeze that played 377 *Duddon* 5. 1
Plenteously yielded to the vagrant breeze. . . 377 *Duddon* 6. 8
Sinks, when the summer breeze hath died, . . 397 *White Doe* 144
Yet Emily is soothed ;—the breeze . . . . . 407 *White Doe* 1020
To wither in the sun and breeze . . . . . 410 *White Doe* 1294
Swept like a breeze the conscious strings, . . . 416 *White Doe* 1837

Breeze—*continued.*
To a soft breeze, in lowly adoration. . . . . 431 *Ecc. Sonn.* 2. 11. 8
But one that leaps to meet the fanning breeze. . 432 *Ecc. Sonn.* 2. 15. 14
Float on the breeze—the heavenliest of all sounds 450 *Ecc. Sonn.* 3. 38. 13
From the warm breeze that bears thee on, alight . 455 *Rydal Mere* 33
This new indifference to breeze or gale, . . . 466 *St. Bees* 11
Which lay in earth expectant, till a breeze . . 466 *St. Bees* 61
Oft have I caught, upon a fitful breeze, . . . 472 *Ossian* 1
By the breeze entered, and wave after wave . . 473 **We saw* 7
I saw thee stagger in the summer breeze, . . . 491 *Tribute : Dog* 18
Though waves, to every breeze, its high-arched roof, 496 **A little* 38
Less quick the stir when tide and breeze . . . 499 **This Lawn* 7
The softest breeze to fairest flowers gives birth : . 516 **Hard task* 12
Sunshine and cloud, whirlwind and breeze, . . 531 †*Float. Isl.* 3
No motion but the moving tide, a breeze, . . . 578 *Peele Castle* 27
Comes on, to whisper hope, the vernal breeze, . 610 *Desc.Sk.Quarto* 443
And the red banner mock the sullen breeze ; . . 615 *Desc.Sk.Quarto* 747
Oh there is blessing in this gentle breeze, . . . 632 *Prelude* 1. 1
Whate'er its mission, the soft breeze can come . 632 *Prelude* 1. 5
A correspondent breeze, that gently moved . . 632 *Prelude* 1. 35
She rocked with every impulse of the breeze. . . 659 *Prelude* 4. 92
With darkness, and before a rippling breeze . . 661 *Prelude* 4. 180
Their faintest whisper to the passing breeze, . . 678 *Prelude* 6. 222
May flow in lasting current. Like a breeze . . 685 *Prelude* 6. 675
Poured out (saluted by that quickening breeze . 687 *Prelude* 7. 2
And pliant harebell, swinging in the breeze . . 722 *Prelude* 10. 277
Hang it with shrubs that twinkle in the breeze, . 749 *Prelude* 14. 254
Our course submitting to the changeful breeze . 772 *Excursion* 2. 84
Or lay its beauty flat before a breeze, ... 787 *Excursion* 3. 66
The first that entered. But no breeze did now . 787 *Excursion* 3. 67
And the sea breeze as innocently breathes, . . 793 *Excursion* 3. 517
The breeze how soft ! Can any thing produced . 798 *Excursion* 3. 881
While the ship glides before a steady breeze. . . 805 *Excursion* 4. 250
Mounts on the breeze the butterfly ; and soars, . 807 *Excursion* 4. 392
Climb every day, those ramparts ; meet the breeze 808 *Excursion* 4. 494
The breeze of nature stirring in his soul, . . . 810 *Excursion* 4. 600
Danced in the breeze, chequering its mossy roof. . 860 *Excursion* 7. 203
And, at the touch of every wandering breeze, . . 864 *Excursion* 7. 480
On all sides open to the fanning breeze, . . . 866 *Excursion* 7. 618
That, on the steady breeze of honour, sailed . . 873 *Excursion* 7. 1015
Of what there is delightful in the breeze, . . . 879 *Excursion* 8. 329
What penetrating power of sun or breeze, . . . 880 *Excursion* 8. 417
Should the sun strike her, and the impartial breeze 882 *Excursion* 8. 513
Her pensive beauty ; from the breeze her sweets. 892 *Excursion* 9. 544
Dying, or dead ! Nor shall the fanning breeze . 892 *Excursion* 9. 552
In mutual stillness ; or, if some faint breeze . . S. 3. 434 **The doubt* 72
Dreadless, as in a kind of fresher breeze . . . K.8. 246 *Recluse* 1.1.369
Delicious as the gentlest breeze that sounds . . K.8. 248 *Recluse* 1.1.414

Breeze-fanned. Within a breeze-fanned rose's breast 582 **O for a* 23

Breezeless. O'er breezeless water, on Locarno's lake, 212 *Dion*
By breezeless air to smoothest polish, yield . . 313 **Clouds, lingering* 3
It was a close, warm, breezeless summer night, . 746 *Prelude* 14. 11

Breeze-like. The breeze-like motion and the self-born carol ; . . . . 88 *H. C.* 4
In soft and breeze-like visitings, ... 399 *White Doe* 332

Breezes. Into a gradual calm the breezes sink, . . 4 *Ev. Wk.* 114
Ye, gentle breezes from the west, ... 154 *Flower Garden* 34
Soon as gentle breezes bring . . . . . . 161 **Pleasures newly* 17
The breezes their own languor lent ; . . . . 193 *Ruth* 136
And when the little breezes make . . . . . 199 *Thorn* 194
Wherever sportive breezes bend . . . . . 227 *Vernal Ode* 69
And, where the feeble breezes glide, ... 242 *P. B.* 534
As the light breezes that with glee . . . . 296 *Highland Boy* 149
Or the soft breezes from the Atlantic sea, . . . 319 *Guernica* 7
Soft breezes fanning your rough brows—the might 350 *Des. Stanzas* 53
Thee gentle breezes waft—or airs that meet . . 363 **List—'twas* 108
Shall a few partial breezes only creep ?— . . . 366 **Fair Land* 11
But breezes played, and sunshine gleamed— . . 385 *Yarrow Rev.* 13
Comes that low sound from breezes rustling o'er . 453 **The Sun, that* 9
That into breezes sink ; impetuous minds . . . 500 *Humanity* 52
As the sun mounts, by sea-born breezes fanned ; . 501 *Humanity* 72
And to the stirring breezes, does he want . . . 547 **Rude is* 28
Molest ; may gentle breezes fan thy brow ; . . 548 **Stay, bold* 8
Internal breezes, sobbings of the place . . . . 644 *Prelude* 2. 122
The fluttering breezes, fountains that run on . . 647 *Prelude* 2. 371
And milder breezes,—melancholy lot ! . . . . 678 *Prelude* 6. 241
Bring straggling breezes of suburban air. . . . 690 *Prelude* 7. 192
Of the green hills ; ye breezes and soft airs, . . 734 *Prelude* 12. 10
Her waters, Air her breezes ; and the sail . . . 876 *Excursion* 8. 112
That flattering breezes blowing thence . . . . S. 3. 431 **The Scottish* 13
That sail on winds, of breezes that delight . . K.8. 237 *Recluse* 1.1. 26
Shadows or breezes, scents or sounds. Nor deem K.8. 249 *Recluse* 1.1. 448

Breezy. 'Mid lawns and shades by breezy rivulets fanned, ... 21 *Desc. Sk.* 576
Bees, wafted on the breezy air, ... 165 *Danish Boy* 17
It was a breezy hour of eve ; . . . . . . 334 **In Bruges* 17
Await my steps when they the breezy height . . 356 *Aquap.* 253
For mild Sorento's breezy waves ; . . . . . . 386 *Yarrow Rev.* 53
To catch the breezy air ; . . . . 482 *Lines : Spring* 18
Towers where red streamers flout the breezy sky . 503 *Warning* 39
And thus, even on the exposed and breezy hill . 539 **Lady ! a* 45
I gazed from Hampstead's breezy heath. . . . 586 *Hogg.* 32
Glanc'd oft upturn'd along the breezy shore, . . 593 *Ev. Wk. Quarto* 102
Safe from your door ye hear at breezy morn, . . 596 *Ev. Wk. Quarto* 233
Here lawns and shades by breezy rivulets fann'd, . 614 *Desc.Sk.Quarto* 686
By cottage-door on breezy mountain-side, . . . 692 *Prelude* 7. 354
The shadows of the breezy elms above . . . 762 *Excursion* 1. 440
I rose ; and, having left the breezy shade, . . 765 *Excursion* 1. 620

Brethren. Ten thousand miles from all his brethren ? 242 *P. B.* 515
And even the prospect of our brethren slain, . . 310 *Anticip.* 12
And O, good Brethren of the cowl, a thing . . 363 **Grieve for* 6

Bright—*continued.*
To wait upon the bright and gracious Muses, . . 573 *Chiabrera* 2. 7
Of wounds, and bright swords flashing in the field, 574 *Chiabrera* 4. 4
To your abodes, bright daisy Flowers ! . . . 579 **Sweet Flower* 25
And her bright dower of clustering charities, . 585 *Ch. Lamb* 74
What though the radiance which was once so bright 590 *Immortality* 179
In youth's wild eye the livelong day was bright, . 592 *Ev. Wk. Quarto* 23
Bright sparks his black and haggard eyeball hurls 594 *Ev. Wk. Quarto* 133
Gives one bright glance, and sinks behind the hill.. 595 *Ev. Wk. Quarto* 174
And, fronting the bright west in stronger lines, . 595 *Ev. Wk. Quarto* 193
—'Tis restless magic all ; at once the bright . . 598 *Ev. Wk. Quarto* 345
Bright as the moon, half hides itself in shade. 604 *Desc. Sk. Quarto* 107
The star of noon that glitters small and bright, . 609 *Desc. Sk. Quarto* 386
Bright stars of ice and azure worlds of snow, . . 612 *Desc. Sk. Quarto* 557
In the bright paths of fair majestic Truth : . . 618 *School Ex.* 12
Let this bright morn and Sandys the song inspire.' 619 *School Ex.* 110
And bright will shine in misery's midnight hour ;. 619 **She wept* 10
What arms the son of bright Aurora wore ;— . 625 *Æneid* 135
Bright as if heaven were ever in its eye, . . . 627 **We gaze* 4
More heavenly bright than when it leads the morn, 627 **The star* 2
Hark to the peals on this bright May-morn ! . . 628 *Installation* 29
And that Presence fair and bright, ... 629 *Installation* 113
Thy Nymphs with more than earthly beauty bright ; 630 [?] **O Moon* 9
Of feudal sway, the bright blue river passed . . 636 *Prelude* 1. 285
Of things forgotten, these same scenes so bright, . 641 *Prelude* 1. 607
Our pastime was, on bright half-holidays, . . . 643 *Prelude* 2. 55
Proud of its own bright fire and sycamore shade. 644 *Prelude* 2. 148
Bright was the summer's noon when quickening steps . . . . 658 *Prelude* 4. 1
The solid mountains shone, bright as the clouds, . 663 *Prelude* 4. 327
More bright than madness or the dreams of wine ; 674 *Prelude* 5. 568
Or could more bright appearances create . . . 676 *Prelude* 6. 91
How bright a face is worn when joy of one . . 680 *Prelude* 6. 348
Hath rolled along, and this bright innocent, . . 692 *Prelude* 7. 378
A bright tradition of the golden age ; . . . . 701 *Prelude* 8. 132
Of ancient Story, thought of each bright spot, . 715 *Prelude* 9. 365
Bright sprinklings of all human excellence, . . 725 *Prelude* 10. 484
That eventide, when under windows bright . . 725 *Prelude* 10. 493
Longing for skill to paint a scene so bright . . 726 *Prelude* 10. 569
In one perpetual progress smooth and bright ?— . 748 *Prelude* 14. 135
Of bright and pleasant sunshine interposed ; . . 756 *Excursion* 1. 8
O then how beautiful, how bright, appeared . . 759 *Excursion* 1. 222
Hung down in heavier tufts ; and that bright weed, 767 *Excursion* 1. 716
Which the bright season favours.—Tabor and pipe 773 *Excursion* 2. 121
And bright, and fertile, furnished in itself . . . 777 *Excursion* 2. 356
Uplifted ; here, serene pavilions bright, . . . 784 *Excursion* 2. 842
With your bright transports fairly may be deemed, 788 *Excursion* 3. 160
Here are we, in a bright and breathing world. . 789 *Excursion* 3. 237
Had sprung, like those bright creatures, from the soil . . . . 790 *Excursion* 3. 251
Of your bright forms and glorious faculties, . . 790 *Excursion* 3. 302
But no—for the serene was also bright ; . . . 792 *Excursion* 3. 429
On the bright form of Her whom once I loved :— 793 *Excursion* 3. 481
Into bright verdure, between fern and gorse, . . 793 *Excursion* 3. 534
Respiring I looked round.—How bright the sun, . 798 *Excursion* 3. 880
Small creature as she is, from earth's bright flowers, 807 *Excursion* 4. 393
Bright apparition, suddenly put forth, ... 808 *Excursion* 4. 462
The nightly hunter, lifting a bright eye . . . 814 *Excursion* 4. 861
All fresh and beautiful, and green and bright, . 830 *Excursion* 5. 546
Replete with vivid promise, bright as spring." . 831 *Excursion* 5. 557
Bright as a sunbeam sleeping till a shower . . 832 *Excursion* 5. 673
By the bright fire, the good Man's form, and face . 834 *Excursion* 5. 779
With personal gifts, and bright instinctive wit, . 843 *Excursion* 6. 305
Colours as bright on exhalations bred . . . . 847 *Excursion* 6. 596
—Bright garland form they for the pensive brow . 855 *Excursion* 6. 1127
Sparry and bright, rough scatterings of the hills. . 856 *Excursion* 6. 1155
Not scantily, bright minutes on the thread . . 862 *Excursion* 7. 307
Of his bright hearth, and from his open door, . 867 *Excursion* 7. 650
" On a bright day—so calm and bright, it seemed 868 *Excursion* 7. 695
Ten hardy Striplings, all in bright attire, . . . 869 *Excursion* 7. 766
Bright was the sun, the sky a cloudless blue— . 871 *Excursion* 7. 876
Victoriously upraised his clear bright eye ; . . 871 *Excursion* 7. 892
Like a bright star, amid the lowly band . . . 872 *Excursion* 7. 954
To linger 'mid the last of those bright clouds . . 873 *Excursion* 7. 1014
He who had seen his own bright order fade, . . 873 *Excursion* 7. 1017
Profusion bright ! and every flower assuming . 881 *Excursion* 8. 471
That charm all eyes. So bright, so fair, appeared 882 *Excursion* 8. 516
That combinations so serene and bright . . . 891 *Excursion* 9. 468
With prodigal communion, the bright hues . . 893 *Excursion* 9. 604
Survive ; all else is swept away.—How bright . 894 *Excursion* 9. 711
That, lodged within thy crystal depths, seem bright, S. 3. 433 **The doubt* 47
On thee, bright Spring, a bashful little one, . . S. 3. 435 **The doubt* 130
Still gleams upon their polish'd plumes—the bright K. 8. 234 **The order'd* 6
Scarcely a wish, but one bright pleasing thought, . K. 8. 237 *Recluse* 1. 1. 16
We entered, bright and solemn was the sky . . K. 8. 241 *Recluse* 1. 1. 171
Mortal though bright, a dying, dying flame. . . K. 8. 248 *Recluse* 1. 1. 439
The bright array of shadowy thoughts from times K. 8. 253 *Recluse* 1. 1. 627
What arms the son of bright Aurora wore, . . L. 2. 123 *Frag. Æneid* 3. 2
Negro princess, ebon bright ! . . . . L. 2. 190 **Queen and* 6
Negress excellently bright ! . . . . L. 2. 190 **Queen and* 12
Sable princess, ebon bright. . . . . L. 2. 190 **Queen and* 18
Brighten. And joy returns, to brighten fortitude. . 318 **In due* 14
Stained and polluted, brighten as they roll, . . 452 *Ecc. Sonn.* 3. 47. 12
All brighten on the bough ; . . . . 502 *Seasons* 12
And thy grieved Spirit brighten strong in faith. . 515 **Men of* 14
May brighten more and more ! True to the mark, 541 *Grace Darl.* 59
When at my feet the ground appeared to brighten, 746 *Prelude* 14. 35
Brightened. The druid-stones a brightened ring unfold ; . . . . 5 *Ev. Wk.* 188
And her face brightened. The old Man was glad, 135 *Michael* 273
Tears brightened by the serenade . . . . . 375 **The Minstrels* 47

Brightened—*continued.*
But by tender fancies brightened. . . . . . 415 *White Doe* 1760
Let fall a brightened tear. . . . . 507 *May* 24
Along the brighten'd gloom reposing deep. . . 607 *Desc. Sk. Quarto* 276
Brightened with joy ; for from within were heard 818 *Excursion* 4. 1138
Was trimmed and brightened by the Matron's care, 860 *Excursion* 7. 171
Are brightened round her. In his native vale . 868 *Excursion* 7. 722
Brightening. Brightening the umbrage of her hair ; . 222 *Triad* 188
Well may'st thou halt—and gaze with brightening eye ! . . . . 250 *Admon.* 1
Thee Vesper ! brightening still, as if the nearer . 281 **What strong* 2
Brightening the archway of revered St. Bees. . . 467 *St. Bees* 99
The cheerful dawn, brightening for me the east ; . 496 **A little* 13
A brightening edge will indicate that soon . . 532 **How beautiful the* 6
Brightening a converse never known to swerve . 583 **With copious* 11
Bright'ning with, tear-breaks the sombrous gill ; . 592 *Ev. Wk. Quarto* 72
Bright'ning the cliffs between where sombrous pine, 594 *Ev. Wk. Quarto* 139
Bright'ning the gloom where thick the forests stoop; 604 *Desc. Sk. Quarto* 129
An image fair, which, brightening in his soul . . 871 *Excursion* 7. 935
Brightens. Brightens with water-breaks the hollow ghyll . . . . 3 *Ev. Wk.* 54
As the Moon brightens round her the clouds of the night, ... 188 *Music* 13
Her countenance brightens—and her eye expands ; 209 *Laod.* 10
Blest be the song that brightens . . . . . 233 *Power of Sound* 49
Brightens her that was so bright ; . . . . . 397 *White Doe* 86
The future brightens on our sight ; . . . . . 583 **O for a* 52
Before the very sun that brightens it, ... 635 *Prelude* 1. 226
Brighter. Through passes yet unreached, a brighter road. . . . . 2 *Ev. Wk.* 26
The housewife there a brighter garden sees, . . 21 *Desc. Sk.* 606
Seems the wide world, far brighter than before ! . 105 *Artegal* 203
Which they are touching ; yea far brighter, even 139 *Widow* 20
But more exalted, with a brighter train : . . . 316 **O'er the* 4
Brighter than brightest loop-hole, in a storm, 323 *Ode 1814* 20
A field or two of brighter green, or plot . . . 379 *Duddon* 14. 4
A brighter crown."—On yon Cistertian wall . . 429 *Ecc. Sonn.* 2. 3. 5
Brighter than eastern skies at daybreak strewn 434 *Ecc. Sonn.* 2. 25. 6
Look only on the Gospel's brighter page: . . . 447 *Ecc. Sonn.* 3. 29. 11
A happier, brighter, purer Heaven than theirs. . 462 **Where lies the truth* 14
And clothes in brighter hues ; . . . . . . 499 *Memory* 12
Cheered with the prospect of a brighter day. . . 520 *Pun. Death* 14. 14
And his bright eyes look brighter, set off by the streak . . . . 569 *Farmer* 7
In brighter rows her table wealth aspires, . . 615 *Desc. Sk. Quarto* 732
And beam'd on Britain's sons a brighter day ; . 618 *School Ex.* 36
Nay brighter shone, by this portentous gloom 709 *Prelude* 8. 657
And with a step or two seemed brighter still ; . 746 *Prelude* 14. 36
And with a brighter eye she looked around . . 766 *Excursion* 1. 688
Those brighter images by books imprest . . 848 *Excursion* 6. 701
Upon the brighter scene. How blest that pair . 888 *Excursion* 9. 256
A brighter joy ; and through such damp and gloom K. 8. 237 *Recluse* 1. 1. 52
Brightest. The very brightest Sunday Autumn saw,. 99 *Brothers* 269
With brightest sunshine round me spread . . . 159 *Green Linnet* 3
Climes which the sun, who sheds the brightest day 211 *Laod.* 107
The brightest star of ages yet to be, ... 220 *Triad* 6
And look, where clothed in brightest green . . 237 *P. B.* 63
The fairest, brightest, hues of ether fade ; . . 252 **The fairest* 1
In brightest sunshine bask ; this nipping air, . 263 **While not* 3
Brighter than brightest loop-hole, in a storm, 323 *Ode 1814* 20
The fairest landscapes and the brightest days— 333 *Ded. Tour* 7
Your glories mingled with the brightest hues . 357 *Aquap.* 294
To rival summer's brightest scarlet flower ; . . 529 *Poor Robin* 10
Its brightest splendour round a leafy wood ; . 532 **Once I* 16
Diamonds dart their brightest lustre . . . . 549 *Hermit's Cell* 1. 15
Enrapt ; but brightest things are wont to draw 726 *Prelude* 10. 528
Shines, in the brightest of ten thousand stars, 750 *Prelude* 14. 273
The brightest jewel of a George's throne. L. 1. 97 *Juvenal* 3. 95
Bright-eyed. Fared this little bright-eyed Orphan . 93 *Westmoreland Girl* 31
All powers that serve the bright-eyed Queen . . 223 *Wishing-gate* 2
In which her bright-eyed beauty is shut up. . . 584 **With copious* 49
The bright-eyed Mariner, and rueful woes . . . 752 *Prelude* 14. 400
Bright-haired. That *would* have loved the bright-haired Boy ! . . . . 342 *Ital. Itin.* 36
Now, while his bright-haired front he bowed, . 373 *Eg. Maid* 307
A bright-haired company of youthful slaves, . . 421 *Ecc. Sonn.* 1. 13. 1
Brightly. To see the sun how brightly it will shine, . 308 **There is a bondage* 10
Unfelt shone brightly round us in our joy. . . 643 *Prelude* 2. 93
" The fire, that burned so brightly to our wih, . 892 *Excursion* 9. 55
The stars shine brightly between clouds at rest, . S. 3. 425 **The rains*
Brightness. Though half a sphere be conscious of their brightness) . . . . v **If thou indeed* 7
With brightness ! leaving her to post along, . . 172 *Infant Daughter* 53
While here sits One whose brightness owes its hues 252 **Her only* 12
A tender hazy brightness ; . . . . 302 *Yarrow V.* 20
Its brightness to recover. . . . . 386 *Yarrow Rev.* 40
Set off her brightness with a pleasing shade. . 440 *Ecc. Sonn.* 3. 1. 4
With sudden brightness, like a Man inspired ; . 493 *Hap. War.* 52
In all her brightness, from the dancing crest . 511 **Who rashly* 5
That, as thy sun in brightness is declining, . 540 **Lady ! a* 78
The soul's pure brightness he beheld . . . 545 *Russ. Fug.* 323
The innocent brightness of a new-born Day . 590 *Immortality* 198
Of a surpassing brightness. At the sight . . 667 *Prelude* 5. 80
She whispered still that brightness would return,. 732 *Prelude* 11. 345
His brightness o'er a tract of sea and land . 794 *Excursion* 3. 542
Her native brightness. As the ample moon, . 817 *Excursion* 4. 1062
With answering brightness in the hearts of all . 828 *Excursion* 5. 416
And that attractive brightness is its own. . . . 832 *Excursion* 5. 678

Britain—*continued.*
Britain put forth her freeborn strength in league, 722 *Prelude* 10. 264
What in those days through Britain was performed 728 *Prelude* 11. 55
Britain opposed the liberties of France. . . . 729 *Prelude* 11. 175
Of Britain circumscribed me ; else, perhaps . . 798 *Excursion* 3. 813
—In Britain, ruled a panic dread of change ; . . 798 *Excursion* 3. 827
Of Britain are resorted to by ships . . . . 876 *Excursion* 8. 134
Of Britain, do invite her to cast off . . . . 889 *Excursion* 9. 377
Britain's. Where be the temples which in Britain's Isle, ... 102 *Artegal* 1
High on that chalky cliff of Britain's Isle, . . 215 *Enterprise* 3
Of Britain's calm felicity and power ! . . . . 219 **This Height* 34
Of Britain's realm, whose leafy crest . . . . 226 *Vernal Ode* 19
Of Britain's acts,—may catch it with rapt ear, . 325 *Ode 1814* 129
Of Britain's acts would sing, ... 330 *Ode : Thanks.* 68
It cannot be that Britain's social frame, . . . 471 **Despond who* 3
In Britain's earliest dawn : . . . . 499 **Departing summer* 33
Should spread on Britain's favoured ground ! . . 534 **Blest is* 72
And beam'd on Britain's sons a brighter day ; . . 618 *School Ex.* 36
Hear Britain's sons rehearse thy praise with joy, . 619 *School Ex.* 101
That Westminster, for Britain's glory, holds . . 842 *Excursion* 6. 264
" The other, born in Britain's southern tract, . 844 *Excursion* 6. 427
In Britain's senate. Fruitless was the attempt : . 845 *Excursion* 6. 448
Of Britain's farthest glens. The Earth has lent . 876 *Excursion* 8. 111
Britannia. With rapture she beheld Britannia smile, 618 *School Ex.* 45
Cease, Britannia, cease to weep ! . . . . . 628 *Installation* 28
Whereon Britannia rests her peaceful fame. . . 629 *Installation* 40
British. A British ship I waked, as from a trance restored." . . . . 30 *Guilt* 306
Nathless, a British record (long concealed . . . 102 *Artegal* 9
The British sceptre, here would I to thee . . . 104 *Artegal* 155
This Lady, dwelling upon British ground, . . . 120 *Emigrant Mother* 5
That British ground commands :—low dusky tracts, 219 **This Height* 5
The chaster coverts of a British hill. . . . . 220 *Triad* 14
Our British Hill is nobler far ; he shrouds . . . 251 **Pelion and* 12
Of waters issue from a British source, ... 272 *Devil's Bridge* 3
Of British freedom, which, to the open sea . . 307 **It is not* 2
But British reason and the British sword. . . . 310 *Invasion* 20
On British ground the Invaders are laid low ; . 310 *Anticip.* 2
And give the treasure to our British tongue ! . . 325 *Ode 1814* 130
" Her course was for the British strand ; . . . 370 *Eg. Maid* 79
Such to this British Isle her christian Fanes, . . 444 *Ecc. Sonn.* 3. 17. 9
The fugitives than to the British strand, . . . 449 *Ecc. Sonn.* 3. 36. 7
On British waters with that look benign ? . . 454 *Sea-side* 35
On ground which British shepherds tread ! . . 457 **Had this* 40
That have no rivals among British bowers ; . . 476 *Eden* 7
At whose behest uprose on British ground . . 477 *Long Meg* 11
A British Painter (eminent for truth . . . . 509 *F. Stone* 99
Think ye your British Ancestors forsook . . . 515 **Men of* 3
Of some old British Chief : 'tis nothing more . . 548 **Stranger ! this* 4
But she who trains the generous British youth . 618 *School Ex.* 11
Will settle on some British theme, some old . . 634 *Prelude* 1. 168
Drawn from the chords of the ancient British harp 857 *Excursion* 7. 11
Are at its centre, British Lawgivers ; . . . . 890 *Excursion* 9. 399
When British floods were worshipped, some faint trace . . . . S. 3. 435 **The doubt* 126
The highest fountain known on British land. . . K. 8. 226 **I will* 61
Seated in a British chair. . . . . L. 2. 190 **Queen and* 3
Briton. A Briton, even in love, should be . . . 110 **Ere with* 19
To the rude Briton, when, in wolf-skin vest . . 265 **Hail, Twilight* 6
A single Briton clothed in wolf-skin vest, . . . 744 *Prelude* 13. 322
A native Briton to these inward chains, . . . 878 *Excursion* 8. 298
Britons. So styled by those fierce Britons, pleased to see . . . . 272 *Lady E. B.* 3
She casts the Britons upon strange Allies, . . . 420 *Ecc. Sonn.* 1. 9. 12
To Britons born and bred within the pale . . . 880 *Excursion* 8. 392
Broach. Still in the Highland Broach is seen, . . 390 *Highland Broach* 18
The silver Broach of massy frame, ... 390 *Highland Broach* 19
Beneath a massier Highland Broach. . . . . 391 *Highland Broach* 48
The hidden silver Broach was left. . . . . . 391 *Highland Broach* 60
Will vanish the last Highland Broach. . . . . 391 *Highland Broach* 78
May render back the Highland Broach. . . . . 391 *Highland Broach* 90
Broached. Butlers have simply broached their Lordships casks, ... L. 1. 98 *Juvenal* 3. 101
Broad. They crush with broad black feet their flowery walk ; . . . . 6 *Ev. Wk.* 243
Dark with bat-haunted ashes stretching broad, . 7 *Ev. Wk.* 263
(For dark and broad the gulf of time between) . 8 *Ev. Wk.* 346
Stretch o'er the pictured mirror broad and blue, . 12 *Desc. Sk.* 94
And the fierce torrent at the flashes broad . . 13 *Desc. Sk.* 181
When, after a broad flash that filled the cave, . 50 *Bord.* 715
Life stretched before me smooth as some broad way 70 *Bord.* 1836
A broad and gilded vane. . . . . 86 *Anecdote* 52
High on a broad unfertile tract of forest-skirted Down, ... 91 *Norman Boy* 1
On wings from broad and steadfast poise let loose by this reply, ... 92 *Poet's Dream* 29
And, while the broad blue wave and sparkling foam 96 *Brothers* 56
Yet all in the broad highway of the world. . . 98 *Brothers* 193
And in the broad highway, I met ; . . . . . 114 *Last of Flock* 6
Along the broad highway he came, ... 114 *Last of Flock* 7
In the broad open eye of the solitary sky, . . 166 *Stray Pleasures* 16
Glittering before him bright and broad ; . . . 177 *Waggoner* 2. 36
For yet it is broad day-light : clouds pass by ; . 208 **It is no* 6
(More fair than heaven's broad causeway paved with stars) . . . . 213 *Dion* 51
On broad Euphrates' palmy shore, ... 215 *Enterprise* 25
The broad blue heavens appeared to glimmer, . 241 *P. B.* 484
Not four yards from the broad highway : . . . 246 *P. B.* 925
Breathless with adoration ; the broad sun . . 258 **It is a* 3

Broad—*continued.*
Come like a giant from a haven broad ; . . . 258 **With Ship* 6
The broad full visage, chest of amplest mould, . 270 *Henry : Portrait* 3
Or where broad waters round him lay : . . . 298 *Brownie's Cell* 12
Of Sanguinetto or broad Thrasymene, ... 361 **For action* 6
When the broad oak drops, a leafless skeleton, . 379 *Duddon* 12. 8
Nor in broad pomp, or courtly state ; . . . . 399 *White Doe* 291
The peacock in the broad ash-tree . . . . . 406 *White Doe* 953
Into broad light, and sends, through regions airy, 476 *Nunnery* 6
Broad, clear, and toned harmoniously, with skill . 508 *F. Stone* 19
Of wrongful acts. Downward it is and broad, . 519 *Pun. Death* 8. 5
Turn a broad front full on his flattering beams : . 539 **Lady ! a* 17
Had placed his staff across the broad smooth stone 566 *Cumb. Beg.* 7
And the broad gulfs I traversed oft and oft. . . 574 *Chiabrera* 4. 17
To meet the world's broad eye, ... 576 *Cenotaph* 3
Ye crush with broad black feet your flow'ry walk ; 596 *Ev. Wk. Quarto* 232
Stretch, o'er their pictur'd mirror, broad and blue, 604 *Desc. Sk. Quarto* 103
The torrent, travers'd by the lustre broad, . . 605 *Desc. Sk. Quarto* 207
Shun the broad way too easily explored, . . . 626 *Rock : Rydal* 2
To the broad ocean and the azure heavens . . 651 *Prelude* 3. 161
Of character, in points of wit as broad, . . . 657 *Prelude* 3. 570
To the broad follies of the licensed world, . . . 670 *Prelude* 5. 312
Who, with a broad highway, have overbridged . 671 *Prelude* 5. 348
Five rivers broad and vast, made rich amends, . 683 *Prelude* 6. 532
Into a lordly river, broad and deep, ... 685 *Prelude* 6. 651
Ere the broad world rang with the maiden's name, 691 *Prelude* 7. 304
Of the broad vale, casting a casual glance, . . 773 *Excursion* 2. 116
By the broad hill, glistened upon our sight . . 773 *Excursion* 2. 127
Upon a broad leaf carried, choicest strings . . 779 *Excursion* 2. 504
A broad oak, stretching forth its leafy arm s . . 825 *Excursion* 5. 227
Was her broad forehead ; like the brow of one . 848 *Excursion* 6. 684
In the broad day, a weeping Magdalene. . . . 850 *Excursion* 6. 814
In the broad day, a rueful Magdalene ! . . . 853 *Excursion* 6. 987
Were working the broad bosom of the lake . . 863 *Excursion* 7. 410
On the broad water's placid breast— . . . . S. 3. 438 **My Lord* 22
Broad-day. Of marvels, broad-day wonders permanent : . . . . 689 *Prelude* 7. 128
Broadening. An edge all flame, the broadening sun appears ; . . . . 5 *Ev. Wk.* 169
It's edge all flame, the broad'ning sun appears ; . 594 *Ev. Wk. Quarto* 152
As on the broadening causeway we advance, . . 690 *Prelude* 7. 199
Broad-spread. And round the broad-spread oak, a glimmering scene, ... 3 *Ev. Wk.* 46
Broidered. The vestments 'broidered with barbaric pride : . . . . 271 *Henry : Portrait* 4
The wounds the broidered Banner showed, . . 412 *White Doe* 1497
With broidered housings. And the lofty Steed— . 872 *Excursion* 7. 946
Broke. Broke only by the slow clock tolling deep, . 9 *Ev. Wk.* 369
For ever broke, the sabbath of her bowers. . . 12 *Desc. Sk.* 76
Each clacking mill, that broke the murmuring streams, ... 22 *Desc. Sk.* 630
The shriek that from the distant battle broke, . 30 *Guilt* 347
Then, with a voice which inward trouble broke . 33 *Guilt* 503
Just as those final words were penned, the sun broke out in power, ... 91 *Poet's Dream* 1
But who shall show, to waking sense, the gleam of light that broke . . . . 92 *Poet's Dream* 33
The old Man's grief broke from him ; to his heart 137 *Michael* 421
Here broke off the dangerous converse : . . . 140 *Arm. Lady* 73
Down from yon cliff a fragment broke ; . . . 156 *Oak and Broom* 35
Broke from the sable orbs of his yet-vivid eyes. . 196 *Resolution* 91
Broke forth in concert flung adown the dells, . . 267 *St. Cath.* 3
Broke from the Matron's strong black eye— . . 294 *Jedbor.* 67
The cries which broke from old and young . . 297 *Highland Boy* 178
Over waves rough and deep, that, when they broke, 354 *Aquap.* 121
Some casual shout that broke the silent air, . . 449 *Ecc. Sonn.* 3. 34. 13
And from the turf a fountain broke, ... 487 *Fountain* 7
Broke threateningly, in sparkles dire . . . . 499 **Departing summer* 41
Endure that silence, and broke out in song, . . 539 **Lady ! a* 31
When, as day broke, the Maid, through misty air, 540 *Grace Darl.* 29
Broke silence, or I heard him in my thought. . 558 *Cuck. and Night.* 90
Chok'd is the pathway, and the pitcher broke. . 596 *Ev. Wk. Quarto* 256
Broke only by th' unvaried torrent's sound, . . 603 *Desc. Sk. Quarto* 58
Broke only by the melancholy sound . . . . 610 *Desc. Sk. Quarto* 434
Shall love, 'till Life has broke her golden bowl, . 615 *Desc. Sk. Quarto* 741
Right to a rough stream's edge, and there broke off ; 683 *Prelude* 6. 569
To rush and disappear. But soon broke forth . 687 *Prelude* 7. 8
Broke forth in armour of resplendent words, . . 695 *Prelude* 7. 539
In the great City, broke like light from far. . . 745 *Prelude* 13. 365
He broke from his contracted bounds, repaired . 774 *Excursion* 2. 215
That he broke faith with them whom he had laid 775 *Excursion* 2. 247
Broke in upon the Speaker with a frank . . . 779 *Excursion* 2. 513
Broke from the happy old Man's reverend lip ; . 787 *Excursion* 3. 76
Into my bosom, whence these words broke forth : 808 *Excursion* 4. 507
Of human kind ! He was it who first broke . . 854 *Excursion* 6. 1068
Divine displeasure, broke the marriage-vow. . . 855 *Excursion* 6. 1093
Thus silence broke :—" Behold a thoughtless Man 862 *Excursion* 7. 299
The Sage broke off. No sooner had he ceased . 890 *Excursion* 9. 417
Broken. *See* **Heart-broken, Sternly-broken.**
Each slip of lawn the broken rocks between . . 5 *Ev. Wk.* 178
Thou wouldst be leaning on a broken reed— . . 40 *Bord.* 164
Is broken, you will hear no more of *him.* . . . 43 *Bord.* 342
And through the broken hawthorn hedge, . . . 83 *Lucy Gray* 47
A broken intercourse ; and, while his eyes . . 118 *Maternal Grief* 58
She says, in faint words by sighs broken, . . . 164 **Fair Lady* 38
Unvisited, where not a broken bough . . . . 185 *Nutting* 17
Be broken down and old : . . . . 194 *Ruth* 231
A broken vow, or bind a true. . . . . . . 223 *Wishing-gate* 47
Which one harsh day has broken. . . . . . 224 **'Tis gone* 24
—Tears had not broken from their source ; . . 227 *Vernal Ode* 129

Broken—*continued.*
Died of a broken heart. 246 P. B. 915
What beast of chase hath broken from the cover? 346 Gemmi 1
Will soon be broken;—a rough course remains, 381 Duddon 20. 7
In vain shall rue the broken intercourse. 383 Duddon 30. 8
Their forms are broken staves; their passions, steeds 438 Ecc. Sonn. 2. 37. 11
And if there be whom broken ties 457 *Had this 41
Broken in fortune, but in mind entire 470 Bala-Sala 1
Stung with remorse for broken vows; 473 Ossian 50
Foundations broken up, the deeps run wild, 504 Warning 65
Broken with all mankind, solicit death. 518 Pun. Death 3. 14
Hence whole day wanderings, broken nightly sleeps 523 Epist. Beaumont 137
That friendship lasts though fellowship is broken! 531 *I know 32
Is broken; yet why grieve? for Time but holds 586 Ch. Lamb 129
Each speck of lawn the broken rocks between; 594 Ev. Wk. Quarto 162
In broken sounds her elder grief demand, 596 Ev. Wk. Quarto 263
That in its broken windings we shall need 646 Prelude 2. 274
The darksome windings of a broken stair, 678 Prelude 6. 213
The broken wall. I looked around, and there, 763 Excursion 1. 459
Of brotherhood is broken: time has been 763 Excursion 1. 487
Had broken their trim border-lines, and straggled 767 Excursion 1. 723
Scribbled with verse: a broken angling-rod 781 Excursion 2. 666
Abruptly broken off. The ruddy boys 883 Excursion 8. 592
Pursued our way, a broken company, 890 Excursion 9. 435
And neither pair be broken? Nay perchance K.8. 244 Recluse 1.1.264
Broken-hearted. Died broken-hearted. 'Tis a common case. 98 Brothers 196
Bronzed. Were bronzed with deepest radiance, stood alone 636 Prelude 1. 296
Brood. Brood o'er the long-parched lands with Nile-like wings! 22 Desc. Sk. 658
The lion roars and gluts his tawny brood 25 Guilt 65
The verminous brood, and cherish what they spare 48 Bord. 587
The mountain raven's youngling brood 84 Shepherd-boys 6
To brood on air than on an earthly stream; 88 H. C. 8
A brood whom no civility could melt, 102 Artegal 15
It may soar with the eagle and brood with the dove, 142 †Lov. and Lik. 50
Waxed wroth, and with four claws, a harpy brood, 255 Detraction 7
An old place, full of many a lovely brood, 260 *How sweet 3
But now upon this thought I cannot brood; 263 *Those words 5
That loves on sullen thoughts to brood! 300 Bran 30
The brood of chaste affection. 302 Yarrow V. 64
Avoid these sights; nor brood o'er Fable's dark abyss! 347 Processions 72
Modest Savona! over all did brood 356 Aquap. 233
The sullen reservoirs whence their bold brood— 382 Duddon 26. 5
To naturalise this tawny Lion brood; 392 Daniel 4
Vouchsafed in gentleness to brood 403 White Doe 668
Yea, offered up this noble Brood, 410 White Doe 1302
Nourish the sufferers then; and mists, that brood 431 Ecc. Sonn. 2. 12. 11
Of sacred truth may enter—till it brood 450 Ecc. Sonn. 3. 38. 7
And over fancied usurpations brood, 505 Warning 115
They heard, and, starting up, the Brood of Night 513 *Said Secrecy 10
Ye brood of Conscience—Spectres! that frequent 518 Pun. Death 6. 1
Fearless of all assaults that would her brood molest. 525 Epist. Beaumont 231
Oh do not Thou too fondly brood, 581 John Words. 68
To brood the nations o'er with Nile-like wings; 617 Desc.Sk.Quarto 805
Behold the parent hen amid her brood, 669 Prelude 5. 246
And straggle from her presence, still a brood, 669 Prelude 5. 248
A brood of gallant creatures, on the deep; 722 Prelude 10. 318
These were the lurking Satyrs, a wild brood 814 Excursion 4. 885
The cackling hen, the tender chicken brood, 834 Excursion 5. 815
Then, o'er that mould, a sanctity shall brood 850 Excursion 6. 804
How fair amid her brood of cottages! 855 Excursion 6. 1108
To guard the royal brood. The sailing glead, 868 Excursion 7. 751
Brooded. I brooded o'er my injuries, deserted 68 Bord. 1699
Has o'er their pillow brooded; 386 Yarrow Rev. 46
While thus he brooded, music sweet 406 White Doe 889
Intensely brooded, even till they acquired 758 Excursion 1. 147
And much she read; and brooded feelingly 854 Excursion 6. 1028
Brooding. When, in the south, the wan noon, brooding still, 2 Ev. Wk. 37
Besides, on griefs so fresh my thoughts were brooding still. 32 Guilt 423
Whate'er the monster brooding in your breast 56 Bord. 1014
Brooding on her eggs reposes 166 Wand. Jew 23
There to the brooding bird her mate 168 Wren's Nest 21
To sit in meekness, like the brooding Dove, 253 *O gentle 3
And spreads in steadfast peace her brooding wing. 254 Wild Duck's Nest 8
Heavenly Guardians, brooding near, 502 *Like a 34
Sits brooding, lives not always to that end, 634 Prelude 1. 141
Brooding above the fierce confederate storm 755 Recluse 1. 1. 831
From brooding clouds; shadows that lay in spots 756 Excursion 1. 6
Broods. *See* **O'er-broods.**
Above yon eastern hill, where darkness broods 8 Ev. Wk. 331
Over his own sweet voice the Stock-dove broods; 195 Resolution 5
The gentleness of heaven broods o'er the Sea: 258 *It is a 5
Broods, visibly portrayed, the mystic Dove, 450 Ecc. Sonn. 3. 39. 13
A tender Spirit broods—the pensive Shade 465 *The cattle 9
That broods and sleeps on his own heart. 485 Poet's Epitaph 52
Broods like the Day, a Master o'er a Slave, 589 Immortality 119
Now o'er the eastern hill, where Darkness broods 599 Ev. Wk. Quarto 399
That feeds upon infinity, that broods 747 Prelude 14. 71
Brook. Beyond, along the vista of the brook, 3 Ev. Wk. 66
Dear Brook, farewell! To-morrow's noon again 3 Ev. Wk. 86
Where the brook brawls along the public road 7 Ev. Wk. 262
In every babbling brook he finds a friend; 11 Desc. Sk. 26
A brook to murmur or a bough to wave, 16 Desc. Sk. 308
No brook to wet his lip or soothe his ear; 24 Guilt 29

Brook—*continued.*
Where wreaths of vapour tracked a winding brook, 34 Guilt 516
When I returned with water from the brook, 59 Bord. 1181
Floats kingcups in the brook—a Hero one 60 Bord. 1235
So from the court I passed, and down the brook, 62 Bord. 1356
Fresh water from the brook, as clear as ever ran; 87 Pet-lamb 42
'Cross the brook its thoughtless dam. 93 Westmoreland Girl 4
The neighbours were alarmed, and to the brook 101 Brothers 378
And, tired with slights his pride no more could brook, 103 Artegal 88
As doth a fly upon a summer brook; 107 Indolence 7
Or lay upon the moss by brook or tree, 108 Indolence 38
When up she winds along the brook 109 Louisa 17
And for us the brook murmured that ran by its side. 116 Repentance 12
To hunt the moon within the brook, 128 Idiot Boy 215
Up the tumultuous brook of Green-head Ghyll, 131 Michael 2
But, courage! for around that boisterous brook 131 Michael 6
Might see and notice not. Beside the brook 131 Michael 16
Near the tumultuous brook of Green-head Ghyll, 136 Michael 322
Beside the boisterous brook of Green-head Ghyll. 138 Michael 482
Were native to the summer.—Up the brook 146 *It was an 17
Of Grecian brook, or Lady of the Mere, 149 *A narrow 37
That overhangs a brook. 168 Wren's Nest 20
As a swoln brook with rugged course, 176 Waggoner 1. 236
Where close fogs hide their parent brook; 180 Waggoner 4. 41
Are steadfast as the rocks; the brook itself, 184 Airey-force 4
And on or in, or near, the brook, espy 190 *Lyre! though 18
And a clear brook with cheerful knell 194 Ruth 203
Which no philosophy can brook! 214 Dion 101
The brook adown the rocky steeps. 215 Kirkstone 76
Hath stirred thee deeply; with its own dear brook, 250 Admon. 3
Or down the tempting maze of Shawford brook— 254 Complete Angler 10
But some (who brook those hackneyed themes full well, 255 Detraction 5
When will she turn, and whither? She will brook 258 *With Ships 12
Brook no continuance of weak-mindedness— 260 *High is 13
Brook! whose society the Poet seeks, 268 *Brook! whose 1
Or groom!—We must run glittering like a brook 307 *O Friend 5
And we can brook the thought that by his hands 319 Spaniard 5
Even yet my heart can scarcely brook, 342 Ital. Itin. 53
Reflected in some crystal brook; 344 *How blest 10
And nobly wilt thou brook the chains 344 *How blest 49
Thick boughs of palm, and willows from the brook, 346 Processions 11
Into a Brook of loud and stately march, 378 Duddon 9. 2
Impetuous thoughts that brook not servile reins. 382 Duddon 26. 14
And Tiber, and each brook and rill 386 Yarrow Rev. 61
That curbs a foaming brook, a Graveyard lies; 387 *Part fenced 2
Ours couch on naked rocks,—will cross a brook 389 Tyndrum 4
Which I myself could scarcely brook. 401 White Doe 494
Where Rylstone brook with Wharf is blended. 414 White Doe 1693
Which ill can brook more rational relief: 423 Ecc. Sonn. 1. 20. 7
Scooped out of living rock, and near a brook 424 Ecc. Sonn. 1. 22. 3
And flung into the brook that travels near; 432 Ecc. Sonn. 2. 17. 4
"As thou these ashes, little Brook! wilt bear 432 Ecc. Sonn. 2. 17. 8
Which Faith has suffered, Heaven could calmly brook. 435 Ecc. Sonn. 2. 29. 8
Early awake, by Siloa's brook, to sing 440 Ecc. Sonn. 2. 46. 5
That so a Church, unforced, uncalled to brook 443 Ecc. Sonn. 3. 13. 6
Gently to brook decline and fatal change; 461 *Queen of 54
Thy brook, and bowers of holly; 478 Somnamb. 29
And the rough bed of many an unbridged brook? 523 Epist. Beaumont 106
Above a murmuring brook. 543 Russ. Fug. 120
And to the brook I ran and got a stone, 560 Cuck.and Night. 217
And flew into a hawthorn by that brook; 562 Cuck.and Night. 287
With his grey hairs he went from the brook and the green; 570 Farmer 46
Where the brook brawls along the painful road, 596 Ev. Wk. Quarto 271
The famous brook, who, soon as he was boxed 659 Prelude 4. 51
Stealing with silent lapse to join the brook 664 Prelude 4. 383
Entered a narrow chasm. The brook and road 684 Prelude 6. 621
And ill could brook, beholding that the best 712 Prelude 9. 213
Of intellect; such sloth I could not brook, 732 Prelude 11. 325
Of sudden admonition—like a brook 732 Prelude 11. 337
Of a clear brook;—beneath an abbey's roof 771 Excursion 2. 7
A napkin, white as foam of that rough brook 781 Excursion 2. 674
Whoe'er hath stood to watch a mountain brook 800 Excursion 3. 969
That he could brook, and glory in;—but when 840 Excursion 6. 127
To the agitation of a brook that runs 849 Excursion 6. 735
May bring; that brook converting as it runs 878 Excursion 8. 257
Fetched by a neighbouring brook.—Across the vale 881 Excursion 8. 453
And where the very monarch of the brook, 882 Excursion 8. 564
To a bold brook that splits for better speed, 883 Excursion 8. 578
Pursued his way toward a brook, whose course K.8. 228 *I will 129
An island in the brook. It was a place K.8. 229 *I will 140
To the green plot of pasture in the brook. K.8. 229 *I will 146
Along the steep that overhung the brook, K.8. 229 *I will 165
Down to the brook he went, and tracked its course K.8. 229 *I will 170
Brook, that hast been my solace days and weeks, K.8. 265 *Brook, that 15
Brooked. A bondage sweetly brooked, a strife 288 Highland Girl 42
Brook's. Our rambles by the swift brook's side 81 †Mother's Return 34
From the brook's margin, wide around, the trees 184 Airey-force 3
Brooks. And all the babbling brooks are liquid gold; 5 Ev. Wk. 189
A Poet, one who loves the brooks 85 Shepherd-boys 84
The little brooks that seem all pastime and all play, 88 Pet-lamb 55
On windy days, in one of those stray brooks, 99 Brothers 260
Sailed through the sky—the brooks ran clear; 191 Seq. Beggars 24
To the caves, and to the brooks, 204 Brougham 65
Where birds and brooks from leafy dells 228 Devot. Incit. 64
So narrow seemed the brooks, the fields so small! 251 *Beloved Vale 11
The azure brooks, where Dian joys to lave 264 *Lady! I 5

Brooks—*continued.*
While your leaves I behold and the brooks they will strew, 364 *Vallomb.* 31
This Valdo brooks not. On the banks of Rhone . 431 *Ecc. Sonn.* 2. 11. 9
He murmurs near the running brooks 485 *Poet's Epitaph* 39
Was felt near murmuring brooks in earliest time ; 502 **The unremitting* 14
I love the Brooks which down their channels fret, 590 *Immortality* 196
The icy brooks, as on we passed, appeared 622 *Recluse* 1. 1. 166
Among the windings hid of mountain brooks. 639 *Prelude* 1. 490
The trees, the mountains shared it, and the brooks, 662 *Prelude* 4. 242
And brooks were like a dream of novelty 672 *Prelude* 5. 429
The wild brooks prattling from invisible haunts ; 700 *Prelude* 8. 67
When up the lonely brooks on rainy days 703 *Prelude* 8. 262
Through the whole compass of the sky ; ye brooks, 734 *Prelude* 12. 18
And now the 'trotting brooks' and whispering trees, 767 *Excursion* 1. 703
The gentle brooks !—Your desolating sway, 790 *Excursion* 3. 311
Even as the multitude of kindred brooks 836 *Excursion* 5. 916
Or the wild brooks ; from which he now returned . 859 *Excursion* 7. 159
Haunting with rod and line the craggy brooks ? . 861 *Excursion* 7. 267
Yet, of the wild brooks ask if he complained ; 864 *Excursion* 7. 488
That paves the brooks, the stationary rocks, 884 *Excursion* 9. 8
To lie beside the lonely mountain brooks, K.8. 224 **I will* 2

Brook-side. We left the willow shade by the brook-side, 39 *Bord.* 104
By the brook-side : it is the abode of One, 44 *Bord.* 380
By the brook-side—'tis gone—and that dark cleft ! 97 *Brothers* 134
And held the pathway down by a brook-side ; 557 *Cuck.and Night.* 60
By a brook-side, we came, a roofless pile, 716 *Prelude* 9. 467
By a brook-side or solitary tarn, 868 *Excursion* 7. 719

Broom. Feeding 'mid purple heath, "green rings," and broom ; 4 *Ev. Wk.* 133
No gipsy cower'd o'er fire of furze or broom ; 26 *Guilt* 140
—'Twas that delightful season when the broom, 147 *Joanna* 38
A Broom out of its feet. 156 *Oak and Broom* 14
The Broom began to doze, 156 *Oak and Broom* 52
The Broom might have pursued 157 *Oak and Broom* 92
The little careless Broom was left 157 *Oak and Broom* 109
Beneath the broom or budding thorn, 239 *P. B.* 259
Passive yet pleased. What ! with this Broom in flower 353 *Aquap.* 26
Who have a broom still ready in your hands 567 *Cumb. Beg.* 69
The Scottish Broom on Bird-nest brae S.3. 431 **The Scottish* 1
Which the poor broom no sooner felt S.3. 431**The Scottish* 19

Broom's. This flowering broom's dear neighbourhood, the light 358 *Aquap.* 369

Brooms. Like cattle through the budded brooms ; 396 *White Doe* 13

Brothel. Of Tavern, Brothel, Gaming-house, and Shop, 710 *Prelude* 9. 54

Brother. He sits a brother at the cottage-meal ; 11 *Desc. Sk.* 36
And I in truth did love him like a brother, 29 *Guilt* 251
I felt thy infant brother in her arms ; 40 *Bord.* 184
Her brother now takes up the note, 81 †*Mother's Return* 25
My sister and my brother ; 83 *We are Seven* 22
My brother John and I. 84 *We are Seven* 56
My brother John was forced to go, 84 *We are Seven* 59
Which to an only brother he has borne 96 *Brothers* 72
If still his Brother lived, or to the file 96 *Brothers* 83
Bearing his brother on his back. I have seen him, 99 *Brothers* 259
'Tis of the elder brother I am speaking : 99 *Brothers* 291
And that he had one Brother— That is but 100 *Brothers* 330
In him was somewhat checked ; and, when his Brother 100 *Brothers* 337
His absent Brother still was at his heart. 100 *Brothers* 348
He sought his brother Leonard.—You are moved ! 101 *Brothers* 353
And, looking at the grave, he said, "My Brother!" 102 *Brothers* 411
And on the vacant throne his worthier Brother placed. 103 *Artegal* 81
"It is the king, my brother !" and, by sound 104 *Artegal* 120
—O Brother ! to my knowledge lost so long, 104 *Artegal* 131
I, Brother ! only should be king in name, 105 *Artegal* 182
Thus was a Brother by a Brother saved ; 105 *Artegal* 234
And her twin Brother, had the parent seen, 118 *Maternal Grief* 39
Your grown-up and your baby brother ; 143 †*Lov. and Lik.* 56
Year followed year, my Brother ! and we two, 151 **When, to* 70
My Brother, and on all which thou hast lost. 151 **When, to* 97
Father, sister, friend, and brother. 157 *Sexton* 8
A Brother of the dancing leaves ; 159 *Green Linnet* 34
All men who know thee call their brother, 162 **Art thou the* 10
Each wave, one and t'other, speeds after his brother ; 167 *Stray Pleasures* 35
Cried out, "Good brother, why so fast ? 176 *Waggoner* 1. 237
And we, as brother should with brother, 179 *Waggoner* 3. 54
And Ghimmer-crag, his tall twin brother, 180 *Waggoner* 4. 21
Of that which went before the brother, 241 *P. B.* 444
Though man for brother man has ceased to feel. 273 **When Philoctetes* 14
Thy elder Brother I would be, 288 *Highland Girl* 60
Nor haply less the Brother whom I marked, 362 **List—'twas* 83
Sir Tristram, dear to thousands as a brother, 373 *Eg. Maid* 290
O Brother ! I revere the choice 375 **The Minstrels* 19
Bear with me, Brother ! quench the thought 376 **The Minstrels* 61
With Strength, her venturous brother ; 386 *Yarrow Rev.* 60
Her recreant Brother—he prevailed 405 *White Doe* 881
Be Brother now to Brother joined ! 406 *White Doe* 918
The injunction by her Brother laid ; 407 *White Doe* 1063
"Your noble brother hath been spared ; 409 *White Doe* 1212
Your brother lives—he lives—is come 411 *White Doe* 1358
To seek her Brother forth she went, 413 *White Doe* 1540
Her youngest Brother brought it home ; 416 *White Doe* 1807
Doth man of brother man a creature make 472 *Dunolly Eagle* 13
Pleased with your triumphs o'er his brother Space, 477 *Steamboats* 12
No brother, no mate has he near him—while I 484 **A plague* 26
Of this the very brother. 486 **We walked* 28

Brother—*continued.*
Brother to brother, *this* is all we can. 490 *Tribute : Dog* 6
Of sorrow ;—feel for all, as brother Men ! 516 **Feel for* 8
What thou askest, noble Brother, 535 *Egremont* 35
Could have *seen* my Brother die ! 535 *Egremont* 54
To his Brother then he came, 536 *Egremont* 98
And unto Pandarus, his own Brother dear, 562 *Troilus* 3
My Brother, too, in loving thee, 579 **Sweet Flower* 5
Have lent his wing, my Brother dear, 580 *John Words.* 7
—Brother and friend, if verse of mine 581 *John Words.* 61
How fast has brother followed brother, 586 *Hogg* 23
From him, a brother at the cottage meal, 602 *Desc. Sk. Quarto* 38
Oft he descends to nurse the brother pair, 612 *Desc.Sk.Quarto* 576
Is come as a brother thy sorrows to share. 621 *Convict* 48
Pursues thy brother—this to thee is known ; 624 *Æneid* 17
In many things my brother, chiefly here 648 *Prelude* 2. 465
I called him Brother, Englishman, and Friend ! 653 *Prelude* 3. 282
Brother to many more. In this mixed sort 653 *Prelude* 3. 321
O Friend ! O Poet ! brother of my soul, 668 *Prelude* 5. 181
From the injustice of our brother men— 772 *Excursion* 2. 74
The brother followed ; and was seen no more ! 795 *Excursion* 3. 649
"Though born a younger brother, need was none 864 *Excursion* 7. 428
To her loved brother and his shy compeer. 890 *Excursion* 9. 431
And one, like them, a brother of our hearts, K.8. 254 *Recluse* 1.1.659

Brotherhood. A work accomplished by the brotherhood 147 *Joanna* 69
Upon that unsubstantial brotherhood 231 *Clouds* 85
A brotherhood of venerable Trees, 292 **Degenerate Douglas* 6
Children of Art, that claim strange brotherhood 392 *Daniel* 5
This fair unrivalled Brotherhood, 410 *White Doe* 1303
Through lawless will the Brotherhood was driven 468 *St. Bees* 146
In objects where no brotherhood exists 647 *Prelude* 2. 385
Lessons of genuine brotherhood, the plain 683 *Prelude* 6. 545
Such as the daring brotherhood of late 691 *Prelude* 7. 294
Of the whole human race one brotherhood. 735 *Prelude* 12. 87
Spread by a brotherhood of lofty elms, 756 *Excursion* 1. 29
Of brotherhood is broken : time has been 763 *Excursion* 1. 487
The bond of brotherhood, when he sees them go, 780 *Excursion* 2. 562
With world-excluding groves, the brotherhood 791 *Excursion* 3. 347
Of the monastic brotherhood, upon rock 791 *Excursion* 3. 393
Of a poor brotherhood who walk the earth 875 *Excursion* 8. 42
The common creature of the brotherhood, K.8. 246 *Recluse* 1.1.353

Brotherly. With brotherly resemblance. Turn your steps 809 *Excursion* 4. 553
Than brotherly forgiveness may attend ; 848 *Excursion* 6. 658

Brother's. And Leonard, chiefly for his Brother's sake, 100 *Brothers* 305
Did place upon his brother's head the crown, 105 *Artegal* 222
In surety for his brother's son, a man 134 *Michael* 211
For she her brother's charge revered, 409 *White Doe* 1196
Yea, by her brother's very name, 409 *White Doe* 1198
But here her Brother's words have failed ; 415 *White Doe* 1785
His Brother's life, for Lands' and Castle's sake ? 535 *Egremont* 48
Asked it by a brother's name, 536 *Egremont* 100
A brother's Child, most tenderly beloved ! 575 *Chiabrera* 8. 5
To comfort me while with a brother's love 770 *Excursion* 1. 923
That pressed upon his brother's house ; for books 864 *Excursion* 7. 439

Brothers. To weep that I am gone. Brothers in arms ! 78 *Bord.* 2325
"Sisters and brothers, little maid, 83 *We are Seven* 13
It seems, these Brothers have not lived to be 99 *Brothers* 285
Two Brothers clomb, and, turning face from face, 276 *Oker Hill* 2
Embraced those Brothers upon earth's wide plain ; 276 *Oker Hill* 11
Untried our Brothers have been loved 401 *White Doe* 471
Suit to his Brothers often made 409 *White Doe* 1235
Partners in faith, and brothers in distress, 437 *Ecc. Sonn.* 2. 37. 6
Brothers in soul ! though distant times 473 *Ossian* 63
Ere the Brothers through the gateway 535 *Egremont* 1
To Palestine the Brothers took their way. 535 *Egremont* 40
Upon equal ground ; that we were brothers all 713 *Prelude* 9. 227
My brothers and myself. There rose a crag, 738 *Prelude* 12. 292
And I and my three brothers, orphans then, 738 *Prelude* 12. 308
Son, husband, brothers—brothers side by side, 780 *Excursion* 2. 580
—Those seven fair brothers variously were moved 867 *Excursion* 7. 657
—Not brothers they in feature or attire, 882 *Excursion* 8. 547
On Deep-dale-head, and Brothers water (named K. 8. 225 **I will* 21
From those two Brothers who were drowned therein) ; K. 8. 225 **I will* 22
All brothers, long endeared by kindred pain, L. 1. 95 *Juvenal* 3. 6

Brothers'. His Brothers' wisdom or their love— 406 *White Doe* 934

Brother-Shepherds. Were brother-shepherds on their native hills. 96 *Brothers* 75

Brough. Rejoiced is Brough, right glad, I deem, 204 *Brougham* 44

Brough'm. We have them at the feast of Brough'm. 204 *Brougham* 39

Brought. Brought from without to inward misery. 25 *Guilt* 75
And nothing to my mind a sweeter pleasure brought. 28 *Guilt* 207
Were not for me, brought up in nothing ill : 32 *Guilt* 422
Through which his Wife, to that kind shelter brought, 36 *Guilt* 642
No kindred sufferer, to his death-place brought 36 *Guilt* 662
But what has brought you hither ? A slight affair, 43 *Bord.* 339
From Palestine, and brought with me a heart, 49 *Bord.* 685
Revealed by lustre brought with it from heaven ; 50 *Bord.* 718
And brought me food. Have I not cause to love her ? 53 *Bord.* 848
I thank you for that hint. He shall be brought 58 *Bord.* 1125
With the glad tidings which this day hath brought ; 66 *Bord.* 1593
But his own crime had brought on him this doom, 69 *Bord.* 1745
—if I had brought him along with me, 72 *Bord.* 1968
till I am brought to a felon's end. 72 *Bord.* 1986
And brought it forth into the light : 85 *Shepherd-boys* 90
"He took thee in his arms, and in pity brought thee home : 87 *Pet-lamb* 37

Brought—*continued.*

" Thou know'st that twice a day I have brought thee in this can — 87 *Pet-lamb* 41
O thou ! whose fancies from afar are brought ; — 88 *H. C.* 1
Had brought upon him ; and we all conjectured — 101 *Brothers* 395
Whom from the borders of the Lake we brought, — 106 *Farewell* 23
Would have brought us more good than a burthen of gold, — 116 *Repentance* 3
The high-born Vaudracour was brought, by years — 121 *V. and J.* 8
Hadst been brought up upon thy Father's knees. — 136 *Michael* 352
Their union brought, will they repay the debt, — 143 **High bliss* 26
A track, that brought us to a slip of lawn, — 149 *M. H.* 6
That instant brought two stripling bees — 157 *Oak and Broom* 99
Night has brought the welcome hour, — 163 *Spinning Wheel* 2
New heavens succeeded, by the dream brought forth : — 168 *Pilgrim's Dream* 59
That is from joyless regions brought ! — 178 *Waggoner* 3. 30
And what the morning brought to light, — 182 *Waggoner* 4. 194
What wealth the show to me had brought : — 187 **I wandered* 18
He brought them from the Cherokees ; — 192 *Ruth* 22
And with him many tales he brought — 192 *Ruth* 44
About its mother's heart, and brought — 199 *Thorn* 140
Should be to public justice brought ; — 200 *Thorn* 222
That brought him up to manhood's prime. — 205 *Brougham* 109
Brought from a pensive though a happy place. — 211 *Laod.* 96
That brought their precious liberty again. — 213 *Dion* 30
Fresh as if Evening brought their natal hour, — 226 *Vernal Ode* 37
And is She brought within the power — 227 *Vernal Ode* 110
Strict passage, through which sighs are brought, — 232 *Power of Sound* 7
To a thick wood he soon is brought — 240 *P. B.* 341
Till brought to a deserted quarry— — 240 *P. B.* 354
It brought full many a sin to light — 245 *P. B.* 759
Together they brought back the Corse. — 249 *P. B.* 1125
Yet to my mind this scanty Stream is brought — 251 **There is a little* 6
At thy meek bidding, shadowy Power ! brought forth ; — 265 **Hail, Twilight* 11
Elates not, brought far nearer the grave's rest, — 278 *Wellington* 10
For all that thou, as if from heaven, hast brought — 281 **Wansfell ! this* 7
Are brought in ships from far. — 296 *Highland Boy* 110
And then, when he was brought to land, — 297 *Highland Boy* 221
Brought low a Power, which from its home — 298 *Brownie's Cell* 35
Hath brought forth no such souls as we had then. — 307 **Great men* 10
That Thou hast brought our warfare to an end, — 328 *Ode 1815* 123
That He has brought our warfare to an end, — 331 *Ode : Thanks.* 181
The glittering crowns and garlands which it brought— — 334 **A wingèd* 4
Brought to this genial climate, when disease — 353 *Aquap.* 58
Has to our generation brought and brings — 357 *Aquap.* 322
Brought to the ark are coming evermore, — 360 **Near Anio's* 10
New love of many a rival image brought — 367 **If with* 2
That brought me down that sunless river, — 370 *Eg. Maid* 104
If thee fond Fancy ever brought — 376 **The Minstrels* 63
More than by smoothest pathway may be brought — 389 *Tyndrum* 7
By wanderers brought from foreign lands — 390 *Highland Broach* 14
And every day brought with it tidings new — 394 **No more* 29
Thus suddenly, and brought so near ? — 404 *White Doe* 790
Involved whate'er by love was brought — 406 *White Doe* 977
To Rylstone he the tidings brought ; — 409 *White Doe* 1205
His own life into danger brought — 411 *White Doe* 1408
A Spearman brought him to the ground. — 412 *White Doe* 1486
Of chance and change, that hath been brought — 413 *White Doe* 1595
Her youngest Brother brought it home ; — 416 *White Doe* 1807
But from our loved Helvellyn's depths was brought, — 480 *Cordelia* 6
The tears into his eyes were brought. — 484 *Simon Lee* 89
So sad a sigh has brought ? " — 486 **We walked* 16
—It is the generous Spirit, who, when brought — 493 *Hap. War.* 3
—What trick of memory to *my* voice hath brought — 496 **A little* 3
Is Death, for one to that condition brought,— — 518 *Pun. Death* 4. 4
By what evil spirit brought ? — 535 *Egremont* 46
Another was on Thursday brought, — 537 *Goody Blake* 111
They brought, each visiting — 544 *Russ. Fug.* 222
She cried, till to the Jewry she was brought, — 555 *Prioress* 147
How from her inmost heart a sigh she brought, — 560 *Cuck.andNight.*207
For birds we are—all here together brought ; — 562 *Cuck.andNight.*273
You see to what end he has brought his grey hairs. — 572 *Avarice* 32
To Arno's side hath brought him, and he charmed — 573 *Chiabrera* 2. 16
That stripped of arms I to my end am brought — 575 *Chiabrera* 6. 11
Here, brought from far, his corse found rest,— — 577 **By playful* 11
Which brought us hither, — 590 *Immortality* 168
But none of those fair Graces brought — 620 *Birth of Love* 18
Among the dust till he had brought — 621 *Andrew Jones* 19
Huge goblets are brought forth ; they crown the wine ; — 625 *Æneid* 98
Continued, brought me to my hermitage. — 633 *Prelude* 1. 107
Desert me not, forthwith shall be brought down — 641 *Prelude* 1. 638
That brought with it a regular desire — 642 *Prelude* 2. 49
That must have fallen upon him had he brought — 656 *Prelude* 3. 486
Our cottage door, and evening soon brought on — 660 *Prelude* 4. 143
Were flown, and autumn brought its annual show — 664 *Prelude* 4. 371
Upon a desert coast, that having brought — 677 *Prelude* 6. 144
In look and air, from that new region brought, — 688 *Prelude* 7. 97
To have, for instance, brought upon the scene — 691 *Prelude* 7. 279
Brought to such spectacle a milder sadness, — 693 *Prelude* 7. 394
Upon his knee, whom he had thither brought — 696 *Prelude* 7. 609
From byre or field the kine were brought ; the sheep — 699 *Prelude* 8. 21
This notwithstanding, being brought more near — 706 *Prelude* 8. 510
That from the press of Paris duly brought — 712 *Prelude* 9. 154
My sorrow ; for I brought with me the faith — 722 *Prelude* 10. 257
Hereafter brought in charge against mankind. — 724 *Prelude* 10. 396
They who with clumsy desperation brought — 726 *Prelude* 10. 583
Brought less encouragement, and unto these — 730 *Prelude* 11. 195

Brought—*continued.*

With all the sorrow that it brought, appeared — 739 *Prelude* 12. 310
Some inward agitations thence are brought, — 739 *Prelude* 12. 332
Vague and unsound ; and having brought the books — 741 *Prelude* 13. 71
When every day brought with it some new sense — 749 *Prelude* 14. 261
And now, O Friend ! this history is brought — 750 *Prelude* 14. 302
On all things which the moving seasons brought — 758 *Excursion* 1. 151
His earnings might supply, and brought away — 760 *Excursion* 1. 246
Or pleased their fancies, with the wares he brought. — 761 *Excursion* 1. 332
Shaggy and grey, had meanings which it brought — 762 *Excursion* 1. 429
And poverty brought on a petted mood — 765 *Excursion* 1. 580
Brought from the cupboard wine and stouter cheer, — 785 *Excursion* 2. 899
With wingèd Messengers ; who daily brought — 811 *Excursion* 4. 639
Promptly received, as prodigally brought, — 812 *Excursion* 4. 722
Power may be trained, and renovation brought — 831 *Excursion* 5. 585
Who, from their lowly mansions hither brought, — 832 *Excursion* 5. 652
A tired way-faring man, once *I* was brought — 833 *Excursion* 5. 734
Brought yesterday from our sequestered dell — 835 *Excursion* 5. 882
Hope from that quarter would, I know, have brought — 853 *Excursion* 6. 1015
" Brought from the woods the honeysuckle twines — 855 *Excursion* 6. 1149
(The hour of life to which he then was brought) — 859 *Excursion* 7. 113
To that complexion brought which prudence trusts in — 881 *Excursion* 8. 505
What renovation had been brought ; and what — 896 *Excursion* 9. 785

Brow. 'Mid groves of clouds that crest the mountain's brow, — 7 *Ev. Wk.* 289
Or, when upon the mountain's silent brow — 18 *Desc. Sk.* 465
Appalling havoc ! but serene his brow, — 21 *Desc. Sk.* 581
And grey-haired men look up with livelier brow,— — 21 *Desc. Sk.* 609
Their brow sublime : in shelter there to bide — 26 *Guilt* 116
Over her brow like dawn of gladness threw ; — 30 *Guilt* 319
Though inward anguish damped the Sailor's brow, — 33 *Guilt* 485
And, if my brow gives back their light, — 112 **What heavenly* 3
In which a love-knot on a lady's brow — 121 *V. and J.* 3
And your brow is free from scorn, — 140 *Arm. Lady* 44
To one or other brow of those twin Peaks — 151 **Forth from* 8
High on the trunk's projecting brow, — 169 *Wren's Nest* 41
Thus leans, with hanging brow and body bent — 169 *Love lies Bleeding* 7
For at the bottom of the brow, — 174 *Waggoner* 1. 52
Under the brow of old Helvellyn— — 176 *Waggoner* 2. 8
Is the light ash ! that, pendent from the brow — 184 *Airey-force* 12
Three leaps have borne him from this lofty brow — 201 *Hart-leap* 55
That wore a threatening brow ; — 215 *Kirkstone* 62
Is it not a brow inviting — 221 *Triad* 111
Her brow hath opened on me—see it there, — 222 *Triad* 187
Ascending from behind the motionless brow — 229 *Clouds* 2
I see the dark-brown curls, the brow, — 232 *Jew. Fam.* 25
With his hands pressed against his brow, — 248 *P. B.* 1089
Aerial Rock—whose solitary brow — 253 **Aerial Rock* 1
That change :—age on thy brow was smoothed—thy cold — 258 **Even so* 6
His visionary brow : a glow-worm lamp, — 260 **Scorn not* 9
Fresh as the star that crowns the brow of morn ; — 265 **There is a pleasure* 11
Invisible ? yet Spring her genial brow — 267 **Desponding Father* 5
With brow in penitential sorrow bent ! — 270 **Though the bold* 14
Take from *her* brow the withering flowers of eve, — 270 **Shame on* 11
And to that brow life's morning wreath restore ; — 270 **Shame on* 12
'Tis said that to the brow of yon fair hill — 276 *Oker Hill* 1
The piercing eye, the thoughtful brow, — 285 *Grave of Burns* 25
That must have followed when his brow — 285 *Nith* 2
Wear rather in thy bonds a cheerful brow : — 305 *Toussaint* 7
Her haughty brow against the coast of France, — 309 *Men of Kent* 3
If a new Temple lift her votive brow — 327 *Ode 1815* 49
Helvellyn's brow severe ? — 344 *Eclipse* 78
On RIGHI's silent brow. — 348 **Lulled by* 66
Had flown with mine to old Helvellyn's brow, — 353 *Aquap.* 62
Descend, and, on the brow of ancient Rome — 357 *Aquap.* 292
Change, with a brow not insolent, though stern. — 358 **Is this* 14
And pallid brow, a melancholy lustre. — 371 *Eg. Maid* 162
Or torrent from the mountain's brow, — 391 *Highland Broach* 84
I helmeted a brow though white, — 410 *White Doe* 1300
In self-defence with warlike brow — 412 *White Doe* 1480
Full oft the unworthy brow of lawless force ; — 418 *Ecc. Sonn.* 1. 1. 12
Screams round the Arch-druid's brow the sea-mew—white — 419 *Ecc. Sonn.* 1. 3. 1
Those flowers of chivalry, to bind the brow — 430 *Ecc. Sonn.* 2. 7. 7
With holiday delight on every brow : — 446 *Ecc. Sonn.* 3. 23. 2
Weep not, meek Bride ! uplift thy timid brow. — 447 *Ecc. Sonn.* 3. 26. 14
When each pale brow to dread hosannas bowed — 450 *Ecc. Sonn.* 3. 40. 3
When darkness creeping o'er thy silver brow — 460 **Queen of* 3
Nemean victor's brow ; less bright was worn, — 464 *Derwent* 10
Still round my shattered brow in beauty wave." — 465 **Thou look'st* 14
A sleeping infant's brow, or wakeful eye — 469 **Why stand* 7
The old Tower's brow yellowed as with the beams — 470 *Bala-Sala* 10
" Shine so, my aged brow, at all hours of the day ! " — 470 *Bala-Sala* 14
The crown of thorns around his bleeding brow — 476 **Tranquillity! the* 8
Her brow was smooth and white : — 487 **We walked* 46
The Conqueror, crowns the Conquered, on this brow — 496 **A little* 5
Around a younger brow ! — 498 **Departing summer* 18
Wherever peace is on the brow, — 506 **While from* 47
A silver line, that runs from brow to crown — 508 *F. Stone* 28
Hooded the open brow that overawed — 513 **Said Secrecy* 5
Of a perpetual dawn from brow and cheek — 525 *Epist. Beaumont* 253
To snatch a sprig from Chaucer's reverend brow)— — 528 **Those breathing* 61
Thus, gifted Friend, but with the placid brow — 529 **Those breathing* 133

Brow—*continued.*
Or when his tiny gems shall deck his brow : . . 530 *Poor Robin* 28
That o'er thy brow are shed ; . . . . . . 530 *Gleaner* 3
Fit for the glimmering brow of Proserpine. . . 532 **Once I* 18
His brow with laurel green ; . . . . . . 543 *Russ. Fug.* 186
Darken the brow of this memorial Stone, . . 546 **The emboweringI*2
Molest ; may gentle breezes fan thy brow ; . . 548 **Stay, bold* 8
Droops, and o'er canopies his regal brow, . . 594 *Ev. Wk. Quarto* 136
She hears, upon the mountain forest's brow, . . 606 *Desc.Sk.Quarto* 225
Or gazing from the mountain's silent brow, . . 612 *Desc.Sk.Quarto* 556
And wilder graces sport around their brow ; . . 615 *Desc.Sk.Quarto* 735
The Despot's laurelled brow ? . . . . . . 628 *Installation* 12
Out of its leafy brow, the more to awe . . . 695 *Prelude* 7. 521
" A cheerful smile unbends the wrinkled brow, . 699 *Prelude* 8. 48
Or as a traveller, who has gained the brow . . 709 *Prelude* 9. 9
In which a love-knot on a lady's brow, . . . 717 *Prelude* 9. 555
Upon the insolent aspiring brow . . . . . 775 *Excursion* 2. 270
He was all fire : no shadow on his brow . . 779 *Excursion* 2. 516
The shade of discontent which on his brow . . 786 *Excursion* 3. 12
With myrtle-wreathed tiara on his brow, . . 811 *Excursion* 4. 675
Its kindly influence, o'er the yielding brow . . 814 *Excursion* 4. 889
Not less than beautiful ; an open brow . . . 834 *Excursion* 5. 780
An English Sovereign's brow ! and to the throne 838 *Excursion* 6. 2
Upon the haughty maiden's brow, 'tis but . . 840 *Excursion* 6. 122
Was her broad forehead ; like the brow of one . 848 *Excursion* 6. 684
—Bright garland form they for the pensive brow 855 *Excursion* 6. 1127
Lay beautiful on Snowdon's sovereign brow, . . 857 *Excursion* 7. 7
Of fire, incensed beneath its hoary brow, . . . 860 *Excursion* 7. 223
Beneath his ample brow, in darkness paired,— . 865 *Excursion* 7. 508
Of his fair eyes, by his capacious brow, . . . 868 *Excursion* 7. 726
—And, surely, he, that spake with kindling brow, 869 *Excursion* 7. 804
Of some stern castle, mouldering on the brow . 876 *Excursion* 8. 103
Whereon our fathers sate. And mark his brow !. 880 *Excursion* 8. 407
Yet mutinously knits his angry brow, ... 888 *Excursion* 9. 316

Browed. *See* **Dusky-browed, Stern-browed.**

Brown. *See* **Dark-brown, Red-brown.**
The rear through iron brown betrays a sullen gleam. 6 *Ev. Wk.* 204
And her brown little-ones around her leads, . . 6 *Ev. Wk.* 225
Here, on the brown wood-cottages they sleep, . 14 *Desc. Sk.* 214
And when a gathering weight of shadows brown . 19 *Desc. Sk.* 470
And what if my poor cheek be brown ? . . . 145 *Her Eyes* 68
Her skin was of Egyptian brown : . . . . . 190 *Beggars* 7
Green, sable, shining yellow, shadowy brown, . 231 **The gentlest Poet* 18
A golden spear to swallow ! and that brown . . 349 *Sky-prosp.* 6
Which a brown morion half-concealed, . . . 404 *White Doe* 747
And clad in homely russet brown ? . . . . . 485 *Poet's Epitaph* 38
Hopeless of further growth, and brown and sere . 521 *Epist. Beaumont* 16
In the brown park, in flocks, the troubl'd deer . 592 *Ev. Wk. Quarto* 63
On the low brown wood-huts delighted sleep . . 607 *Desc.Sk.Quarto* 275
Of that brown ridge, sole outlet of the vale . . 822 *Excursion* 5. 12
To mix the manly brown with silver grey, . . 842 *Excursion* 6. 278

Browner. Spires, rocks, and lawns a browner night o'erspreads ; . . . . 11 *Desc. Sk.* 64

Brownie's. Is warbling near the BROWNIE's Den. . 299 *Brownie's Cell* 90

Brows. Whose brows, the day that she was styled . 162 **Who fancied* 9
And half, by knitting of his brows . . . . . 240 *P. B.* 314
For worthless brows, while in the pensive shade . 254 *Dyer* 8
Intrenched your brows ; ye gloried in each scar : . 283 **Proud were* 3
Or wiped his honourable brows . . . . . . 287 *Sons of Burns* 33
Age ! twine thy brows with fresh spring flowers, . 293 *Jedbor.* 1
The sober Hills thus deck their brows . . . . 302 *Yarrow V.* 71
By more deserving brows.—Yet so ye prop, . . 312 **When, far* 9
They bind the unoffending creature's brows . . 318 **In due* 6
To deck your stern Defenders' modest brows ! . 324 *Ode 1814* 46
Soft breezes fanning your rough brows—the might 350 *Des. Stanzas* 53
When first our infant brows their lustre won ; . 452 *Ecc. Sonn.* 3. 46. 11
The garland withering on their brows ; . . . 473 *Ossian* 49
From that time forth did for his brows disown . 495 *Fact* 20
Of yon wild cave, whose jaggèd brows are fringed . 497 **Enough of climbing* 21
Feelingly their brows incline . . . . . . 502 **Like a* 38
To twine around the Christian's brows, . . . 582 **O for a* 5
And watch, while on your brows the cross ye make, 614 *Desc.Sk.Quarto* 674
So shall that earthly crown thy brows have worn 628 **Deign,Sovereign*15
As calmly, underneath the pleasant brows . . 701 *Prelude* 8. 181
But had not tamed his eye ; that, under brows . 762 *Excursion* 1. 428
Or fierceness, wreathed around their sunburnt brows, 879 *Excursion* 8. 352
Down he sits ; his brows he knits ; . . . . . S. 3. 423 *Tinker* 10

Browsed. Browsed by the side of dashing waterfalls ; 892 *Excursion* 9. 565

Browsing. The White Doe on the Mountain browsing, 415 *White Doe* 1732

Bruce. Young Adam Bruce beside her lay, . . . 287 *Ellen Irwin* 5
The Bruce had been selected ; . . . . . . 287 *Ellen Irwin* 10
If Bruce hath loved sincerely, ... 287 *Ellen Irwin* 15
Rushed forth, and at the heart of Bruce . . . 287 *Ellen Irwin* 27
And Bruce, as soon as he had slain . . . . 287 *Ellen Irwin* 37
By Ellen's side the Bruce is laid ; . . . . . 287 *Ellen Irwin* 53

Bruce's. And, falling into Bruce's arms, . . . 287 *Ellen Irwin* 33

Brugès. Brugès I saw attired with golden light . 333 **Brugès I* 1
In Brugès town is many a street . . . . . 334 **In Brugès* 1

Bruise. And safe without a bruise or wound . . 85 *Shepherd-boys* 68

Bruised. His head was bruised, and there was blood about him—— . . . . 74 *Bord.* 2075

Brun. Less than the painted Magdalene of Le Brun, 710 *Prelude* 9. 77

Bruno's. From Bruno's forest screams the affrighted jay, ... 11 *Desc. Sk.* 67
From Bruno's forest screams the frighted jay, . 603 *Desc. Sk.Quarto* 68
She ceased to speak, but while St. Bruno's pines . 681 *Prelude* 6. 436

Brunswick. That eve, the Star of Brunswick shone . 629 *Installation* 57

Brush. But she, God love her ! feared to brush . 79 **Stay near* 17
Your Minister would brush away . . . . . 214 *Dion* 96
Brush the too happy tear ? . . . . 220 *Triad* 60

Brush—*continued.*
To brush the still breast of a crystal lake. . . . 787 *Excursion* 3. 73
Brush it away, or cloud pass over it ; . . . . 832 *Excursion* 5. 674

Brushed. Brushed by the current of the water-breeze ; . . . . 383 *Duddon* 28. 3
Brushed by the owlet's wing ; . . . . . . 497 *Lycoris* 20

Brushing. Brushing with lucid wands the water's face : . . . . 7 *Ev. Wk.* 302
Made vocal by their brushing wings, ... 164 *Needlecase* 30

Brutal. With brutal laughter and most foul allusion, 59 *Bord.* 1205
Not even in theirs—whose brutal violence . . . 71 *Bord.* 1895
Beneath the brutal sword ?—Her haughty Schools 315 **Alas ! what* 9

Brute. " I'm helping this poor dying brute." . . 242 *P. B.* 490
Calm is the well-deserving brute, ... 247 *P. B.* 936
See the first mighty Hunter leave the brute— . 313 **Go back* 11
Brute rapine, or with gentle lure she tames. . . 429 *Ecc. Sonn.* 2. 2. 6
From both sides ; veteran thunders (the brute test 437 *Ecc. Sonn.* 2. 36. 10
Our varying moods, on human kind or brute, . 501 *Humanity* 98
Not oftentimes, I trust, as we, poor brute ! . . 523 *Epist. Beaumont* 139
Of forms created the most vile and brute, . . 567 *Cumb. Beg.* 75
Whence human kind, and brute ; what natural powers . . . . 625 *Æneid* 124
Chained to its object in brute slavery . . . 820 *Excursion* 4. 1256
Imparted—to brute matter. I rejoice, . . . 877 *Excursion* 8. 204
As a brute mean, without acknowledgment . . 886 *Excursion* 9. 117
The paralytic man, and for the brute— . . . K.8. 250 *Recluse* 1.1.506
In Scripture sanctified—the patient brute, . . K.8. 250 *Recluse* 1.1.507
Human and brute, possessors undisturbed . . K.8. 253 *Recluse* 1.1.622

Brute's. How the poor brute's condition, forced to run 772 *Excursion* 2. 51

Brutes. *See* **Fellow-brutes.**
Only in our relations to the brutes . . . . . 66 *Bord.* 1578
God, who instructs the brutes to scent . . . . 226 *Present.* 73

Brutish. To that abhorrèd den of brutish vice !— . 47 *Bord.* 546
By the deformities of brutish vice : . . . . . 847 *Excursion* 6. 575

Brutus. How Brutus came, by oracles impelled, . 102 *Artegal* 13
To Brutus—that tyrannic power is weak, . . . 721 *Prelude* 10. 200
As Brutus did to Virtue, ' Liberty, ... 797 *Excursion* 3. 776

Bubble. Though a breath made it) like a bubble blown . . . . 250 **Happy the* 3

Bubbled. There were two springs which bubbled side by side, ... 97 *Brothers* 141

Bubbles. Where bubbles burst, and folly's dancing foam . . . . 452 *Ecc. Sonn.* 3. 45. 5
Bubbles gliding under ice, ... 550 *Hermit's Cell* 3. 2
Its dignity ; with gifts he bubbles o'er . . . . 670 *Prelude* 5. 301
And conglobated bubbles undissolved, ... 800 *Excursion* 3. 974

Buccaneer. For both, my honest Buccaneer ! . . S. 3. 441 **The ball* 4

Bucer. Bucer, Erasmus, or Melancthon, read . . 656 *Prelude* 3. 476

Buchanan. How did Buchanan waste the Sage's lore ! L. 1. 96 *Juvenal* 3. 45

Buck. To let slip upon buck or doe. . . . . . 494 *Force of Prayer* 16

Bucket. Does like an empty bucket mount. . . 245 *P. B.* 805

Buckler. A falchion, and a buckler small, . . . 404 *White Doe* 723

Bucks. *See* **Roebucks.**

Bud. *See* **Rosebud.**
Sunshine and shower be with you, bud and bell ! 106 *Farewell* 17
It falls not *here* on bud or bloom. . . . . . 154 *Flower Garden* 18
" When spring came on with bud and bell, . . 155 *Waterfall* 31
Of bud, leaf, blade, and flower—was fashioning . 266 **The stars* 13
Where bud, and bloom, and fruitage, glowed, . 299 *Brownie's Cell* 97
Killing the bud o'er which in vain we grieve. . . 448 *Ecc. Sonn.* 3. 33. 8
Flower and bud together fall ; . . . . . . 628 *Installation* 23

Budded. With songs the budded groves resounding ; 191 *Seq. Beggars* 26
Like cattle through the budded brooms ; . . . 396 *White Doe* 13

Budding. The budding groves seemed eager to urge on 146 **It was an* 9
As budding pines in spring ; . . . . 166 *Danish Boy* 31
The budding flowers, peeped forth the nest . . 169 *Wren's Nest* 43
Among the budding trees, ... 170 *Rural Ill.* 10
With budding, fading, faded flowers . . . . 193 *Ruth* 58
Through fresh green fields, and budding groves among, ... 229 *Cuckoo-clock* 19
Beneath the broom or budding thorn, ... 239 *P. B.* 259
Beneath the budding beeches. . . . . . . 287 *Ellen Irwin* 8
His budding courage to the proof ; and here . . 378 *Duddon* 9. 11
Of winter storms, yet budding cheerfully ; . . 450 *Ecc. Sonn.* 3. 39. 6
The budding twigs spread out their fan, . . . 482 *Lines : Spring* 17
While blossoms and the budding spray . . . 497 *Lycoris* 51
And see the budding leaves the branches throng, 557 *Cuck. and Night.* 27
A blackbird's whistle in a budding grove. . . . 686 *Prelude* 6. 760
The budding rose above the rose full blown. . . 729 *Prelude* 11. 121
And all the earth was budding with these gifts . 750 *Prelude* 14. 263
Those six fair Daughters, budding yet—not one, . 855 *Excursion* 6. 1129
In the bare twigs, each little budding place . . K.8. 252 *Recluse* 1.1. 565

Budding-time. A congregation in its budding-time 652 *Prelude* 3. 219

Buds. Prized above all buds and bells . . . . 161 **Pleasures newly*46
Of treasure sucked from buds and bells, . . . 227 *Vernal Ode* 99
The buds, and freshens the young leaves, . . . 228 *Devot. Incit.* 16
With buds on every bough ! . . . . 291 *Rob Roy* 68
Hopeful and promising with buds and flowers ; . 828 *Excursion* 5. 397
Like blighted buds ; or clouds that mimicked land 843 *Excursion* 6. 315

Buffeted. A cheerful mind,—and buffeted with bond, 98 *Brothers* 214
And buffeted at will by rain and storm. . . . 571 **There is a Flower* 12

Buffoons. Inviting ; with buffoons against buffoons 697 *Prelude* 7. 698

Buffo's. The box resound on Viscount Buffo's ear. L. 1. 95 *Juvenal* 3. 13

Bugle. Hath blown his bugle horn. . . . . . 161 *Binnorie* 20
Must blow to-night his bugle horn. Had I . . 266 **With how* 8

Bugles. The bugles that so joyfully were blown ? . 201 *Hart-leap* 26

Build. Kind pious hands did to the Virgin build . 27 *Guilt* 149
Strong to o'erturn, strong also to build up. . . 77 *Bord.* 2277
We build up the fire, we're snug and warm ; . . 81 †*Address : Child* 33

Build—*continued.*
Of birds that build their nests and sing, . . . 81 †*Mother's Return* 39
And I'll build up a giant with you. . . . . . 86 *Rural Arch.* 24
To build a Sheep-fold ; and, before he heard . . 136 *Michael* 324
Did he repair, to build the Fold of which . . . 138 *Michael* 461
I'll build an Indian bower ; I know . . . 145 *Her Eyes* 55
Thou leav'st the halcyon free her hopes to build . 153 *Morn. Ex.* 33
And the children build their bowers, ... 161 **Pleasures newly* 19
Did never build her nest. . . . . . . 165 *Danish Boy* 15
Or in sequestered lanes they build, ... 168 *Wren's Nest* 25
And build a household fire, and find . . . 193 *Ruth* 77
Build for him, sow for him, and at his call . . 195 *Resolution* 41
" I'll build a pleasure-house upon this spot, . . 201 *Hart-leap* 57
Build up a wild fantastic scene ; . . . . . 244 *P. B.* 682
Swiftly thereon a rainbow arch to build . . . 261 **Fair Prime* 4
"Hell-gates are powerless Phantoms when *we* build." 282 **In my* 14
How Verse may build a princely throne . . . 285 *Grave of Burns* 35
Peculiar ground for hope to build upon. . . . 376 *Duddon* 3. 8
Will build their savage fortunes only there ; . . 421 *Ecc. Sonn.* 1. 11. 12
Eager to build the quiet Fortresses . . . . . 424 *Ecc. Sonn.* 1. 24. 3
Whether they would restore or build—to Thee, . 444 *Ecc. Sonn.* 3. 15. 11
The corner-stone from hands that build to God. . 450 *Ecc. Sonn.* 3. 39. 4
Who thus could build. Be mine, in hours of fear 451 *Ecc. Sonn.* 3. 45.2
Build, at thy choice, or sing, by pool or fount, . 455 *Rydal Mere* 35
And She her happiness can build . . . . . 478 *Somnamb.* 50
Or build thy house upon this grave. . . . . 485 *Poet's Epitaph* 60
To build, within a vale beloved, ... 533 **Blest is* 18
And needful to build up a Poet's praise. . . . 634 *Prelude* 1. 157
The passions that build up our human soul ; . . 638 *Prelude* 1. 407
Bondage, the other to build liberty . . . . 715 *Prelude* 9. 359
Its petty promises, to build a tower . . . . 727 *Prelude* 11. 38
Build social upon personal Liberty, ... 730 *Prelude* 11. 240
Serve to exalt ; they build up greatest things . . 747 *Prelude* 14. 101
And teach the little birds to build their nests . . 749 *Prelude* 14. 255
In what I had to build upon)—this Bride, . . 793 *Excursion* 3. 513
Between them seek the point whereon to build . . 805 *Excursion* 4. 271
For the small wren to build in ;—not in vain, . 807 *Excursion* 4. 389
Let him build systems of his own, and smile . . 810 *Excursion* 4. 605
—So build we up the Being that we are ; . . . 820 *Excursion* 4. 1264
Both ye that shape and build, and ye that force, 831 *Excursion* 5. 612
Builder. A thing of such materials framed, by a builder such as he. . . . . 91 *Norman Boy* 16
That spreads no waste ; a social builder ; one . 227 *Vernal Ode* 106
Musician, gardener, builder, mechanist, . . . 861 *Excursion* 7. 274
Builder's. Where strength has been the Builder's only care ; . . . . 521 *Epist.Beaumont* 23
And from the builder's hand this Stone, . . . 549 **In these* 3
Of mountain turf required the builder's hand . . 834 *Excursion* 5. 772
Save the contentment of the builder's mind ; . . 849 *Excursion* 6. 729
Builders. This, one of those small builders proved . 168 *Wren's Nest* 33
And other little builders who dwell here, . . . 548 **Stranger ! this* 19
Building. In that forsaken building where they sate 28 *Guilt* 197
Of a vast building made of many crags ; . . 101 *Brothers* 365
Our own contrivance, Building without peer ! . 106 *Farewell* 27
He at the building of this Sheep-fold wrought, . 138 *Michael* 471
And yet the building stood, as if sustained . . 646 *Prelude* 2. 280
Of that interminable building reared . . . 647 *Prelude* 2. 383
Of building up a Work that shall endure. . . . 750 *Prelude* 14. 311
Sole building on a mountain's dreary edge, . . 758 *Excursion* 1. 123
A wilderness of building, sinking far . . . 784 *Excursion* 2. 836
Buildings. In sumptuous buildings, vocal in sweet song, 334 **The Spirit* 2
Buildings, albeit rude, that have maintained . . 547 **Rude is* 2
My comrades, leave the crowd, buildings and groves, 650 *Prelude* 3. 92
Builds. Where the eagle builds her aery, . . . 220 *Triad* 39
Builds castles, not of air : . . . . . . 225 *Present.* 21
Of nature trusts the Mind that builds for aye ; . 259 **A volant* 6
That builds, as thy unerring precepts teach, . . 331 *Ode : Thanks.* 173
Who on the good of others builds his own ! . . 433 *Ecc. Sonn.* 2. 19. 14
And One there is who builds immortal lays, . . 441 *Ecc. Sonn.* 3. 4. 6
Unsound as those which Fortune builds— . . 550 *Hermit's Cell* 2. 22
Sits by her fire, and builds her hope in heaven. . 568 *Cumb. Beg.* 161
And dark Oppression builds her thick-ribb'd tow'rs ; 617 *Desc.Sk.Quarto* 795
Builds for herself ; scenes different there are, . . 697 *Prelude* 7. 652
Built. *See* **Earth-built, Frost-built, Ice-built, Love-built, Moss-built, Rock-built, Sky-built, Sod-built, Straw-built, Strong-built, Turf-built, Wood-built.**
I struck my flint, and built up a small fire . . 50 *Bord.* 704
To let a creed, built in the heart of things, . . 59 *Bord.* 1219
Yet, reasoner as he is, his pride has built . . . 63 *Bord.* 1440
And there they built up, without mortar or lime, 86 *Rural Arch.* 5
They built him of stones gathered up as they lay : 86 *Rural Arch.* 7
They built him and christened him all in one day, 86 *Rural Arch.* 8
They went and they built up another. . . . . 86 *Rural Arch.* 18
And in this bush our sparrow built her nest, . . 107 *Farewell* 55
And, at his birth-place, built a chapel floored . 135 *Michael* 269
A last year's nest, conspicuously built . . . 150 **When, to* 21
Built round by those white clouds, enormous clouds, 184 *Night-piece* 21
Had built a bower upon the green, ... 192 *Ruth* 10
And built a house of pleasure in the dell. . . 202 *Hart-leap* 84
Ill-fated Chief ! there are whose hopes are built . 214 *Dion* 102
The stars are mansions built by Nature's hand, . 266 **The stars* 1
(Giants—the same who built in Erin's isle . . 269 *Malham* 4
Built up by soft seducing harmonies ; . . . . 312 **Who rises* 66
Forget thy weakness, upon which is built, . . 321 **Here pause* 13
Built of all precious substances,—so pure . . . 324 *Ode 1814* 70
Of the round world, and built, by laws as strong, 329 *Ode : Thanks.* 48
Was ever built with patient care ; . . . . . 369 *Eg. Maid* 17
For the departed, built with curious pains . . 389 *Breadalb.* 8
The pious Lady built with hope sublime. . . . 393 *Countess' Pillar* 8
And stalking pillars built of fiery sand. . . . 435 *Ecc. Sonn.* 2. 27. 14

Built—*continued.*
Till they have reached the eternal City—built . . 452 *Ecc. Sonn.* 3. 47. 13
A Tower of refuge built for the else forlorn. . . 469 **The feudal* 8
Which they had witnessed, sway the man who built 470 **Did pangs* 3
Built for the air, or wingèd Hippogriff ? . . . 471 **Arran ! a* 5
Within the dell he built a cell, ... 479 *Somnamb.* 147
In the magnific Convent built of yore . . . . 509 *F. Stone* 96
Or Pleasure-house, once destined to be built . . 548 **Stranger ! this* 6
Built at the foot of a huge hill, that they . . . 566 *Cumb. Beg.* 4
Had in high places built her lodge ; though mean 637 *Prelude* 1. 328
Of Nightshade, to St. Mary's honour built, . . 643 *Prelude* 2. 104
In ancient times, and ere the Hall was built . . 644 *Prelude* 2. 145
In this recess, by thoughtful Fancy built, . . . 654 *Prelude* 3. 379
By reason built, or passion, which itself . . . 666 *Prelude* 5. 40
Was that clear synthesis built up aloft . . . 677 *Prelude* 6. 162
Or as a man, who, when his house is built, . . 679 *Prelude* 6. 291
Of airy palaces, and gardens built . . . . . 688 *Prelude* 7. 78
Against all systems built on abstract rights, . . 695 *Prelude* 7. 524
Or palace built by fairies of the rock ; . . . . 705 *Prelude* 8. 418
And built thereon my hopes of good to come. . . 741 *Prelude* 13. 63
Plans without thought, or built on theories . . 741 *Prelude* 13. 70
Ere we built up a pile of better thoughts, . . . 766 *Excursion* 1. 687
" Behold a cabinet for sages built, ... 787 *Excursion* 3. 74
Cannot forget thee here ; where thou hast built, . 802 *Excursion* 4. 41
Built up of life, and food, and means of life ! . . 807 *Excursion* 4. 438
And roofs of temples built by human hands— . . 811 *Excursion* 4. 673
To hopes on knowledge and experience built ; . . 820 *Excursion* 4. 1292
But large and massy ; for duration built ; . . . 824 *Excursion* 5. 145
Is no mechanic structure, built by rule ; . . . 831 *Excursion* 5. 563
And which, once built, retains a steadfast shape . 831 *Excursion* 5. 564
By rude hands built, with rocky knolls in front, . 833 *Excursion* 5. 694
To suit this place ; yet built in no proud scorn . 846 *Excursion* 6. 507
There, and, as seemed, there only. She had built, 853 *Excursion* 6. 1018
Her fond maternal heart had built, a nest . . . 853 *Excursion* 6. 1019
Shows like a mountain built of silver light. . . K.8. 252 *Recluse* 1.1.569
Bulk. That tall Man, a giant in bulk and in height, 189 *Music* 33
Nor wanting, at wide intervals, the bulk . . . 838 *Excursion* 6. 20
Bulky. And this of mine—this bulky creature . . 179 *Waggoner* 3. 73
Bull. The Crab, the Scorpion, and the Bull— . . 236 *P. B.* 36
Bulls. Bulls, pardons, relics, cowls black, white, and grey— . . . . 435 *Ecc. Sonn.* 2. 28. 7
Bulwark. Her bulwark and her tower of strength ! " 178 *Waggoner* 2. 148
In thee a bulwark for the cause of men ; . . . 308 **When I* 10
There is a bulwark in the soul. This knew . . 315 **And is it* 6
Bumming. Bumming, bumming, bumming, . . S. 3. 424 *Tinker* 37
Bunch. Into a ' feathery bunch,' feeds at your hand : 807 *Excursion* 4. 387
Bundle. Her bundle from her lap let fall ; . . . 537 *Goody Blake* 94
Bunker's. Asleep on Bunker's charnel hill afar ; . 596 *Ev. Wk. Quarto* 254
Buonaparté. I grieved for Buonaparté, with a vain 304 **I grieved* 1
Buonaparté's. This is young Buonaparté's natal day, 304 **Festivals have* 2
Buoyant. But ne'er could Fancy bend the buoyant Lark . . . . 153 *Morn. Ex.* 23
Prepared by one who loves the buoyant swell . 254 *Wild Duck's Nest* 6
Her buoyant spirit can prevail . . . . . . 294 *Jedbor.* 58
Companion ! by whose buoyant Spirit cheered, . 352 *H. C. R.* 1
Was this Sea-flower, this buoyant Galley ; . . 369 *Eg. Maid* 38
Else unapproachable, their buoyant way ; . . 380 *Duddon* 16. 11
Light as a buoyant bark from wave to wave, . . 438 *Ecc. Sonn.* 2. 39. 2
Thou buoyant minion of the tropic air ; . . . 511 **Who rashly* 2
A buoyant Spirit, and a heart at ease. . . . . 532 **Once I* 30
And buoyant spirit triumphed over pain ; . . . 574 *Chiabrera* 5. 7
Have been prepared, not with the buoyant spirits 752 *Prelude* 14. 416
Lax, buoyant—less a pastor with his flock . . 774 *Excursion* 2. 183
Buoyantly. For daily bread." " Yes," buoyantly exclaimed . . . . 831 *Excursion* 5. 601
Burden. Dear Master ! gratitude's a heavy burden 38 *Bord.* 30
Would lodge her, and the cherished burden bear . 382 *Duddon* 25. 7
By this sad burden—even that thought, . . . 411 *White Doe* 1409
A toilsome burden up the craggy ways, . . . 702 *Prelude* 8. 227
Burdens. Their burdens do they bear ; . . . . 165 *Danish Boy* 20
Burgh. Or straggling burgh, of ancient charter proud, 875 *Excursion* 8. 101
Burgher. Knight, burgher, yeoman, and esquire, . 404 *White Doe* 707
Of boor or burgher, as they marched along. . . 858 *Excursion* 7. 97
Burghers. Iberian Burghers when the sword they drew . . . . 315 **And is it* 7
Thrice happy, burghers, peasants, warriors old, . 339 *Tell* 6
Of the plain Burghers, who in audience stood . 653 *Prelude* 3. 313
Six simple burghers——To the rope that tied . . L.1. 95 *Juvenal* 3. 9
Burgundy. The vine-clad hills and slopes of Burgundy, 680 *Prelude* 6. 375
Burial. Left without burial ! nay, not dead nor dying, ... 68 *Bord.* 1728
Could have had Christian burial. . . . . . 245 *P. B.* 810
Burial and death : look for them—and descry, . 322 **Humanity, delighting* 36
In Pompeii preserved by her burial in earth ; . . 345 *Stanzas: Simplon* 6
Roof, raiment, bread, or burial : . . . . . 391 *Highland Broach* 58
Burial-day. And, on the burial-day, could scarcely gain . . . . 853 *Excursion* 6. 971
Burial-place. Close to these cloistral steps a burial-place, ... 275 *Gravestone* 11
Is felt, thy Roman burial-place will be . . . 581 **Why should we* 13
And burial-place of passions, and their home . 708 *Prelude* 8. 595
Buried. *See* **Bury'd, Self-buried, Time-buried.**
You have not *buried* anything ? . . . . . . 72 *Bord.* 1919
Lay buried side by side as now they lie, . . . 98 *Brothers* 228
I buried him, poor Youth, and there he lies ! . . 101 *Brothers* 382
Her life and soul were buried. . . . . . . 127 *Idiot Boy* 131
Till a winter's noon-day placed her buried Son . 139 *Widow* 16
By faeries all are buried there, ... 162 *Binnorie* 63
His voice was buried among trees, ... 186 **O Nightingale* 13
Thy corpse shall buried be, ... 195 *Ruth* 255

Burthened. *See* **Guilt-burthened.**
These fields were burthened when they came to me ; 137 Michael 374
Skilful and bold, the horse and burthened *sled* . 523 Epist. Beaumont 110

Burthens. With other burthens than the crop it bore. 98 Brothers 212
Fraught with their burthens ; and a way as smooth 889 Excursion 9. 371
Burthensome. "My life, Heaven knows, hath long been burthensome ; 35 Guilt 586
And burthensome ; and lastly, that poor few . 837 Excursion 5. 967
Bury. To bury this poor Thorn for ever. 197 Thorn 22
And a huge mass, to bury or to hide, 265 *The Shepherd 11
Then sped themselves to bury him full fast ; 555 Prioress 187
Was going then to bury those two books : 667 Prelude 5. 102
Bury'd. The redbreast peace had bury'd it in wood, 605 Desc.Sk.Quarto 169
Bush. *See* **May-bush.**
Hung there, no bush proclaimed to old and poor . 24 Guilt 14
I followed on from brake to bush ; 79 *Stay near 16
And in this bush our sparrow built her nest, 107 Farewell 55
In bush and brake, in black and green ; 128 Idiot Boy 210
Ere a leaf is on a bush, 160 *Pansies, lilies 25
In bush, and tree, and sky. 183 *O blithe 20
" Where there is not a bush or tree, 244 P. B. 708
'Mid its own bush of leafless eglantine— 277 *Why art 13
Whose first-drawn breath from bush and tree . 506 *While from 7
He stood behind a bush of elder, 537 Goody Blake 83
O bush unburnt ! burning in Moses' sight ! 552 Prioress 16
In the next bush that was me fast beside, 558 Cuck. and Night. 97
Good Cuckoo, seek some other bush or brake, 558 Cuck.andNight.112
While every bush and tree, the country through,. 711 Prelude 9. 90
Bushes. While fluttering in the bushes. 159 Green Linnet 40
Among the bushes and trees ; 457 *The sun has 4
Then all is hushed ; the bushes rustle near, 606 Desc.Sk.Quarto 237
Bushy. Of the elder's bushy head ; 397 White Doe 96
Busier. Where hum on busier wing her happy bees; 21 Desc. Sk. 607
And the poor Boy was busier still, with work of anxious heed. 91 Norman Boy 12
Here, as 'mid busier scenes, ground steep and rough, 497 *Enough of climbing 2
While hum with busier joy her happy bees ; 615 Desc.Sk.Quarto 731
Thoughts are not busier in the mind of man . 782 Excursion 2. 723
Was busier with his task—to rid, to plant, 860 Excursion 7. 194
Busies. Busies the eye with images and forms . 707 Prelude 8. 581
Busiest. Is busiest to confer and to bereave ; 269 Gordale 3
Through busiest street and loneliest glen 286 Nith 43
Short leisure even in busiest days ; 376 *The Minstrels 68
Busily. And busily, though yet with fear, untie 34 Guilt 569
Was busily employed as he. 175 Waggoner 1. 151
Their cheerfulness, and busily retrim 420 Ecc. Sonn. 1. 7. 2
Who busily made use of all his might 565 Troilus 165
You might have noticed, busily engaged, 789 Excursion 3. 201
Busily-employed. Among the busily-employed, not more 798 Excursion 3. 839
Business. Yet thither the world's business finds its way 15 Desc. Sk. 246
Asked him in scorn what business there he had ; . 33 Guilt 482
Holla ! No, no, the business must be done.— 43 Bord. 329
I have good business there. I met you at the threshold, 46 Bord. 481
How say you ? in disguise ?— But what's your business 46 Bord. 492
I shall have business with you, Marmaduke ; 66 Bord. 1625
For me, I have business, as you heard, with Oswald, 67 Bord. 1649
With a few drops of blood cut short the business ; 71 Bord. 1868
No, no, my Friend, you may pursue your business— 73 Bord. 2032
Of the world's business to go wild alone : 96 Brothers 106
And find elsewhere his business or delight ; 107 Indolence 11
Yet some did think that he had little business here : 108 Indolence 45
Whose only business was to flow ; 111 A Complaint 4
By chance of business coming within reach 125 V. and J. 288
That no one else may have business near them, . 178 Waggoner 3. 18
When little other business stirred, 182 Waggoner 4. 236
As if life's business were a summer mood ; 195 Resolution 37
Romans for travel girt, for business gowned ; . 275 *While poring 4
The slave of business, time, or care of life, 284 Departure 22
Of the mind's business : these are the degrees 304 *I grieved 12
His business as he likes. Far other show 304 *Festivals have 9
And ordinary business without care ; 308 *One might 7
Of business, care, or pleasure ; or resigned 314 *I dropped 5
Whose only business is to perish !—true 350 Des. Stanzas 23
Time, place, and business, all at his command !— 528 *Those breathing 86
In him it was scarcely a business of art, 570 Farmer 43
To dialogues of business, love, or strife ; 589 Immortality 98
A man of business and expense, and went 649 Prelude 3. 26
Towards human business, to a privileged world . 656 Prelude 3. 520
Her talk, her business, pleased me ; and no less . 661 Prelude 4. 224
Sick of its business, of its pleasures tired, 663 Prelude 4. 356
The business of the day to come, unborn, 697 Prelude 7. 658
Men who, to business of the world untrained, 721 Prelude 10. 197
And all the business of the elements, 739 Prelude 12. 318
Of business roused, or pleasure, ere their time, 773 Excursion 2. 98
Here may I roam at large ;—my business is, 799 Excursion 3. 891
On rural business passing to and fro 881 Excursion 8. 449
Of his own business, and the goings on K. 8. 230 *I will 184
Buskined. With which his genius shook the buskined stage. 547 *Beneath yon 16
Bust. The Bust that speaks and moves its goggling eyes, 698 Prelude 7. 711
Bustard. Save that the bustard, of those regions bleak 26 Guilt 104
Bustle. —Why bustle thus about your door, 126 Idiot Boy 7
What means this bustle, Betty Foy ? 126 Idiot Boy 8

Bustle—*continued.*
The bustle of the mariners 295 Highland Boy 79
And bustle and sluggishness, pleasure and gloom. . 482 Character 4
He had withdrawn from bustle, care, and noise, . 867 Excursion 7. 665
Of needle-work ; no bustle at the fire, 878 Excursion 8. 272
—Now was there bustle in the Vicar's house . 890 Excursion 9. 432
Bustling. Where antique roots its bustling course o'erlook, 3 Ev. Wk. 67
Of feet still bustling round with busy glee, 31 Guilt 392
What bustling—jostling—high and low ! 177 Waggoner 2. 56
Yet tempering, for my sight, its bustling rage 424 Ecc. Sonn. 1. 22. 5
Where antique roots its bustling path o'erlook, 593 Ev. Wk. Quarto 82
And little bustling passions that eclipse, 706 Prelude 8. 500
'Mid the transactions of the bustling crowd ; 810 Excursion 4. 580
Reluctantly amid the bustling crowd ? 878 Excursion 8. 245
Busy. *See* **Over-busy.**
Those busy cares that would allay my pain ; 2 Early Youth 12
How busy all the enormous hive within, 5 Ev. Wk. 160
Of feet still bustling round with busy glee, 31 Guilt 392
And ear still busy on its nightly watch, 32 Guilt 421
For such he is— Your busy fancies, Wilfred, 38 Bord. 25
And know how busy are the tongues of men ; 74 Bord. 2079
Their busy limbs in perfect rest, 82 †Mother's Return 55
The thrush is busy in the wood, 84 Shepherd-boys 25
Spirits busy to do and undo : 86 Rural Arch. 21
Where tufts of herbage tempted each, were busy at their feed, 91 Norman Boy 11
Give to Him prayers, and many thoughts, in thy most busy days ; 93 Poet's Dream 58
Of busy hands and back-and-forward steps, 95 Brothers 25
Then why so busy thou ? 118 †Cottager 10
Is busy at her casement as the swallow 122 V. and J. 82
The vacant city slept ; the busy winds, 123 V. and J. 95
Was busy, looking back into past times. 135 Michael 257
And busy throat whose sink and swell 143 *Driven in 24
That cheats her of too busy cares, 144 *Driven in 35
Meanwhile, a noise was heard, the busy mirth 149 *A narrow 40
When, to the attractions of the busy world 150 *When, to 1
And by the busy streamlet both 168 Wren's Nest 23
And with busy revellings, 171 Kitten 49
By a kitten's busy joy, 171 Kitten 118
The thunder had not been more busy : 177 Waggoner 2. 61
The Showman chooses well his place, 'tis Leicester's busy Square ; 189 Star-gazers 5
On busy days, with thankful nights, be mine. 217 Enterprise 150
What though some busy foes to good, 225 Present. 13
In whom all busy offices unite 227 Vernal Ode 107
Hurrying the busy streets along ? 228 Devot. Incit. 45
Are busy with poor Peter Bell ; 246 P. B. 917
Her eye was busy, while her fingers flew 274 *Wait, prithee 3
Yon busy Little-ones rejoice that soon 280 *Intent on 2
In youth, and 'mid the busy world kept pure . 282 Railway 3
While reapers strove, or busy ploughs 287 Sons of Burns 35
Whence busy life hath fled ; 334 *In Bruges 2
The world forsaken, all its busy cares 363 *The world forsaken 1
No heart had she, no busy brain ; 370 Eg. Maid 57
More lulling than the busy hum of Noon, 381 Duddon 19. 11
For busy thoughts the Stream flowed on 385 Yarrow Rev. 17
Lo ! busy towns spring up, on coasts 391 HighlandBroach 73
And busy with a hand of healing ? 397 White Doe 119
Works busy as the lightning ; but instinct 419 Ecc. Sonn. 1. 6. 2
Though seldom heard by busy human kind)— 432 Ecc. Sonn. 2. 17. 7
Up, down, the busy Thames—rapid as fire 442 Ecc. Sonn. 3. 8. 5
Find solace which a busy world disdains. 444 Ecc. Sonn. 3.17.14
The busy dor-hawk chases the white moth 453 *Calm is the 22
Alas ! too busy Rival of old Tyre, 475 Greenock 9
Hush, hush, the busy Sleeper see ! 479 Somnamb. 104
(Too busy fear !) shall cross its range, 503 Warning 8
By fluttering pinions here and busy bill ; 531 *I know 19
Its busy smoke in social wreaths, 533 *Blest is 6
Heart-soothed, and busy as a wren, 543 Russ. Fug. 117
With face all pale with dread and busy thought, . 554 Prioress 138
The vacant and the busy, maids and youths, . 567 Cumb. Beg. 64
And his fingers as busy as bees in a hive. 570 Farmer 56
And his Grandson's as busy at work by his side. . 572 Avarice 20
Of Childhood, whether busy or at rest, 589 Immortality 141
How busy the enormous hive within, 594 Ev. Wk. Quarto 143
That, barking busy 'mid the glittering rocks, 594 Ev. Wk. Quarto 167
After thy innocent and busy stir 659 Prelude 4. 34
Upon the road, some busy at their work, 659 Prelude 4. 69
Of a too busy world ! Before me flow, 689 Prelude 7. 150
Crowded with Genii busy among works 694 Prelude 7. 456
By pure Imagination : busy Power 705 Prelude 8. 423
And oft amid the " busy hum " I seemed 709 Prelude 8. 680
And busy with an action far advanced. 711 Prelude 9. 95
Was busy knitting in a heartless mood 717 Prelude 9. 515
The general air still busy with the stir 721 Prelude 10. 246
Into one service, busy with one work. 723 Prelude 10. 350
Muttering along the stones, a busy noise 734 Prelude 12. 19
Thoughts over busy in the course they took, 739 Prelude 12. 334
With present objects, and the busy dance . 740 Prelude 13. 30
Busy in solitude and poverty. 760 Excursion 1. 257
Might hear his busy spade, which he would ply, . 764 Excursion 1. 529
So busy, that the things of which he spake 765 Excursion 1. 617
I left her busy with her garden tools ; 766 Excursion 1. 691
Was busy in the distance, shaping things 769 Excursion 1. 881
For he was busy, dealing, from a store 779 Excursion 2. 503
My eyes were busy, and my thoughts no less, 781 Excursion 2. 657
Of my exhausted heart. If busy men 797 Excursion 3. 745
And the weak functions of one busy day, 805 Excursion 4. 284

Call—*continued.*
And, at her call, a waking dream 373 *Eg. Maid* 305
Who from frail earth can call you 374 *Eg. Maid* 385
Duly pronounced with lusty call, 375 **The Minstrels* 17
Call forth the unelaborate sounds, 375 **The Minstrels* 34
Or, at an earlier call, to mark, 375 **The Minstrels* 40
At parent Nature's grateful call, 386 *Yarrow Rev.* 71
This brief this simple wayside Call can slight, 389 *Glencroe* 3
That ancient voice which wont to call 396 *White Doe* 23
That Banner, waiting for the Call, 400 *White Doe* 378
For faithful we must call them, bearing 401 *White Doe* 474
Of Neville, at their Master's call 403 *White Doe* 695
And Dacre to our call replies 408 *White Doe* 1135
And call the Fountain forth by miracle, 418 *Ecc. Sonn.* 1. 2. 7
Increasing multitudes. The potent call 429 *Ecc. Sonn.* 2. 3. 8
And at her call is Wicliffe disinhumed: 432 *Ecc. Sonn.* 2. 17. 2
Who shall complain, or call thee to account? 455 *Rydal Mere* 36
So call thee for heaven's grace through thee made known 459 **Wanderer! that* 13
To call up thoughts that shun the glare of day, 459 **Wanderer! that* 38
Of the pure spring (they call it the "Nun's Well," 465 **The cattle* 7
To call thee so?) or symbol of fierce deeds 472 **The captive* 10
Have sunk, at Nature's call; or strayed 473 *Ossian* 47
I chiefly c ll, the chosen Few, 473 *Ossian* 54
"Roar on, and bring him with thy call; 479 *Somnamb.*.125
Meek, yielding to the occasion's call, 486 **Bright Flower* 21
I call thee: I myself commend 492 *Duty* 50
Or if an unexpected call succeed, 493 *Hap. War.* 55
Reluctant call it was; the rite delayed; 513 *General Fast* 1
As each new Moon obeyed the call of Time, 532 **Once I* 26
Which She is pleased and proud to call her own, 539 **Lady! a* 26
A Maiden gentle, yet, at duty's call, 540 *Grace Darl.* 22
Ye blessèd Creatures, I have heard the call 588 *Immortality* 36
To call from other worlds the wilder'd mind, 598 *Ev. Wk. Quarto* 376
Fearful, beneath, the Water-spirits call, 606 *Desc.Sk.Quarto* 213
But I would call thee beautiful, for mild 622 *Recluse* 1. 1. 114
Call thee, though known but for a few fleet years, 627 **The star* 13
There hung a darkness, call it solitude 638 *Prelude* 1. 394
Call back, O Friend! a moment to thy mind, 653 *Prelude* 3. 309
By birth and call of nature pre-ordained 659 *Prelude* 4. 96
Why call upon a few weak words to say 668 *Prelude* 5. 184
And call of her own natural appetites, 669 *Prelude* 5. 254
Responsive to his call, with quivering peals, 671 *Prelude* 5. 376
Well do I call to mind the very week 672 *Prelude* 5. 426
Philosophy will call you: *then* we feel 673 *Prelude* 5. 526
Philosophy, methinks, at Fancy's call, 703 *Prelude* 8. 249
But something must have felt. Call ye these appearances— 703 *Prelude* 8. 293
Ventured, at some rash Muse's earnest call, 704 *Prelude* 8. 368
For the Man's sake, could feed at Nature's call 706 *Prelude* 8. 456
Came, of themselves, or at her call derived 708 *Prelude* 8. 602
So call it, of a youthful patriot's mind; 716 *Prelude* 9. 499
Grief call it not, 'twas anything but that,— 722 *Prelude* 10. 289
Without Whose call this world would cease to breathe, 724 *Prelude* 10. 421
Not hitherto reflected. Call we this 745 *Prelude* 13. 360
Lamenting the departed, call the groves, 763 *Excursion* 1. 476
They call upon the hills and streams to mourn, 763 *Excursion* 1. 477
Remembrances; or from his tongue call forth 772 *Excursion* 2. 36
So do I call it, though it be the hand 782 *Excursion* 2. 711
That he may call his own, and which depend, 806 *Excursion* 4. 359
Most frequently call forth, and best sustain, 806 *Excursion* 4. 367
By the rough wind unscattered, at whose call 808 *Excursion* 4. 453
Flying, and rainy vapours, call out shapes 809 *Excursion* 4. 522
So call him, for humanity to him 835 *Excursion* 5. 886
(Gain shall I call it?—gain of what?—for whom?) 847 *Excursion* 6. 582
So call her; for not only she bewailed 853 *Excursion* 6. 988
Call to my mind dark hints which I have heard 854 *Excursion* 6. 1075
A Peasant-youth, so call him, for he asked 870 *Excursion* 7. 851
—Call Archimedes from his buried tomb 877 *Excursion* 8. 220
(Or call it comfort, by a humbler name,) 878 *Excursion* 8. 263
Make him more thankful, then to call on verse K.8. 239 *Recluse* 1.1.101
Of memory faithful to the call of love; K.8. 247 *Recluse* 1.1.388
Interpose at envy's call, L. 2. 190 **Queen and* 8

Called. Haply some wretch has eyed, and called thee blessed; 7 *Ev. Wk.* 251
And, whistling, called the wind that hardly curled 31 *Guilt* 356
Such as by Cherith on Elijah called; 62 *Bord.* 1363
With which he called for mercy; and—even so— 68 *Bord.* 1731
You heard!—he called you to him? Of all men 73 *Bord.* 2051
At length I to the boy called out; 82 *Alice Fell* 9
And so without scruple they called him Ralph Jones. 86 *Rural Arch.* 10
Whence by our shepherds it is called THE PILLAR. 101 *Brothers* 368
Thence in our rustic dialect was called 133 *Michael* 168
And, to his office prematurely called, 134 *Michael* 187
Have called the lovely rock, JOANNA'S ROCK." 148 *Joanna* 85
The same admonishment, have called the place 149 **A narrow* 76
If called to choose between the favoured pair, 165 *Parrot* 42
Called the dejected Lingerer *Love lies Bleeding*. 170 **Never enlivened* 27
Thy loneliness: or shall those smiles be called 173 *Infant Daughter* 71
And called on him who must depart 174 *Waggoner* 1. 56
Which called their thoughts another way: 179 *Waggoner* 3. 100
Called for *his* patience and *his* skill;— 182 *Waggoner* 4. 192
From one oblivious winter called 225 *Primrose* 45
She called her babe unborn. 246 *P. B.* 910
A Book came forth of late, called PETER BELL; 254 *Detraction* 1
More urgent called, will stretch his wings at large, 273 **While Anna's* 7
Two Hearts, which in thy presence might be called 290 *Kilchurn* 30
Hath called for thee a second spring; 294 *Jedbor.* 79
Young Vane, and others who called Milton friend. 307 **Great men* 4

Called—*continued.*
He called on Frost's inexorable tooth 321 **Humanity, delighting* 21
Well sang the Bard who called the grave, in strains 389 *Breadalb.* 1
And called the people to the place. 412 *White Doe* 1510
Called the submissive strings to wake 413 *White Doe* 1553
Than heartless misery called them to repel. 420 *Ecc. Sonn.* 1. 9. 14
Has called him forth to breathe the common air, 423 *Ecc. Sonn.* 1. 19. 7
Called forth by wondrous potency 457 **Had this* 26
They called Thee MERRY ENGLAND, in old time; 463 **They called* 1
But who, if he be called upon to face 493 *Hap. War.* 48
The striding-place is called THE STRID, 494 *Force of Prayer* 21
That to an Idol, falsely called "the Wealth 501 *Humanity* 89
Called by the thrifty husbandman a weed; 509 *F. Stone* 61
Called forth by those affections that endear 510 **Among a* 15
The Figure called to mind a beast of prey 523 *Epist. Beaumont* 125
From the pure qualities that called it forth. 539 **Lady! a* 39
Of things which their united power called forth 540 *Grace Darl.* 20
A Tuscan audience: but full soon was called 573 *Chiabrera* 2. 17
Though resolute when duty called 576 *Cenotaph* 2
Yet then, when called ashore, he sought 579 **Sweet Flower* 22
Whose virtues called them forth. That aim is missed; 585 *Ch. Lamb* 43
Lifting the boy to man's estate, had called 585 *Ch. Lamb* 89
Each twilight earlier call'd the Sun to meet, 610 *Desc.Sk.Quarto* 453
Reared Hawkshead's happy roof, and call'd it mine. 619 *School Ex.* 66
That call'd the wanderer home, and home to rest. 619 **She wept* 8
Had dignified, and called to represent 640 *Prelude* 1. 524
Until maturer seasons called them forth 641 *Prelude* 1. 595
I called on both to teach me what they might; 650 *Prelude* 3. 112
Some called it madness—so indeed it was, 651 *Prelude* 3. 146
Of matters which not falsely may be called 651 *Prelude* 3. 169
I called him Brother, Englishman, and Friend! 653 *Prelude* 3. 282
And what may rather have been called to life 658 *Prelude* 3. 612
He left me: I called after him aloud; 667 *Prelude* 5. 133
And evil, overweeningly so called; 670 *Prelude* 5. 281
Of the Enchanter Indolence hath called 677 *Prelude* 6. 181
Than duty called for, or, without regard 677 *Prelude* 6. 184
Imagination—here the Power so called 684 *Prelude* 6. 592
Called forth, at every season, new delights 686 *Prelude* 6. 777
Rose to ideal grandeur, or, called forth 694 *Prelude* 7. 480
I called the pangs of disappointed love, 705 *Prelude* 8. 441
Hath called upon to embody his deep sense 715 *Prelude* 9. 401
On the other side, I called to mind those truths 721 *Prelude* 10. 191
Were called upon to exercise their skill, 729 *Prelude* 11. 139
Even like this maid, before I was called forth 736 *Prelude* 12. 174
A chastisement; and when I called to mind 739 *Prelude* 12. 311
Proves to the most; and called to make good search 742 *Prelude* 13. 174
I called on Darkness—but before the word 744 *Prelude* 13. 327
Sympathies too contracted. Hence, when called 751 *Prelude* 14. 341
Can it be called) which they with blended might 755 *Recluse* 1. 1. 823
Oft as he called those ecstasies to mind, 759 *Excursion* 1. 237
Called out, and sent a blessing after me, 766 *Excursion* 1. 694
Had three times called us to renew our walk, 772 *Excursion* 2. 86
He to the Ministry was duly called; 774 *Excursion* 2. 172
For Nature called my Partner to resign 794 *Excursion* 3. 551
I called on dreams and visions, to disclose 796 *Excursion* 3. 686
Called on the lovely wanderer who bestowed 814 *Excursion* 4. 863
Called me; and, looking down the darksome aisle, 825 *Excursion* 5. 209
In what may now be called a peaceful bed. 868 *Excursion* 7. 694
Of hostile forces; and she called—with voice 869 *Excursion* 7. 760
Called to such office by the peaceful sound 895 *Excursion* 9. 726
As one unknown by others, aptly called K.8. 226 **I will* 53
Are called to try their prowess with his Grace. L.1. 96 *Juvenal* 3. 28

Callest. Shall touch thee to the heart; thou callest this love, 748 *Prelude* 14. 174

Calling. Hears Winter calling all his terrors round, 19 *Desc. Sk.* 490
They bow to, calling the idol, Demonstration. 58 *Bord.* 1158
Had left that calling, tempted to entrust 95 *Brothers* 40
And in his shepherd's calling he was prompt 131 *Michael* 46
Calling a straggler to her side. 232 *Power of Sound* 24
Might work in our high Calling—a bright hope 251 *Appleth.* 6
High is our calling, Friend!—Creative Art 260 **High is* 1
By some of unreflecting mind, as calling 447 *Ecc. Sonn.* 3. 29. 2
Calling to mind this matter when I may, 553 *Prioress* 62
Calling the woodman from his desert cell, 604 *Desc.Sk.Quarto* 143
Like culprits to the bar; calling the mind, 731 *Prelude* 11. 295
Here, calling up to mind what then I saw, 743 *Prelude* 13. 221
His calling laid aside, he lived at ease: 762 *Excursion* 1. 386
Tend what I tended, calling it her own!' 849 *Excursion* 6. 756
Of the poor calling which my youth embraced 873 *Excursion* 7. 1049

Callings. That hung between two callings. May no strife 470 **Did pangs* 11

Calls. Forgetting, calls the wearied to her side; 6 *Ev. Wk.* 229
Upward he looks—"and calls it luxury:" 11 *Desc. Sk.* 24
To his spare meal he calls the passing poor; 11 *Desc. Sk.* 30
Calls forth the woodman from his desert cell, 12 *Desc. Sk.* 124
Of Deep that calls to Deep across the hills, 16 *Desc. Sk.* 355
To guard the Innocent—he calls us "Outlaws;" 38 *Bord.* 63
Idonea, as he calls her; but the Girl 46 *Bord.* 509
the man who calls himself your father; 76 *Bord.* 2219
Such wings as, when our Saviour calls, shall bear us up to heaven." 93 *Poet's Dream* 68
And calls you forth again! 106 **I've watched* 9
And in a moment calls to mind 177 *Waggoner* 2. 29
Calls to the few tired dogs that yet remain: 200 *Hart-leap* 18
On the blood of Clifford calls;— 205 *Brougham* 143
Shouting through one valley calls, 235 *Power of Sound* 205
She calls the poor Ass by his name, 248 *P. B.* 1044
I have no pain that calls for patience, no; 253 **O gentle* 9

Can—*continued.*
What can I do? believe me, gentle Sirs, — 47 *Bord.* 535
What she can urge in his defence; she loves him. — 48 *Bord.* 590
I scarcely can believe it. Myself, I heard — 49 *Bord.* 678
Ere can be known to you how much a Father — 52 *Bord.* 822
Can feel his crimes. I have resigned a privilege; — 53 *Bord.* 875
And most despise the men who best can teach us: — 54 *Bord.* 909
Where Reason has an eye that she can use, — 58 *Bord.* 1119
"'Wherefore I sing, nor can from song refrain, — 556 *Prioress* 212
For he of low hearts can make high, of high — 556 *Cuck. and Night.* 3
He can make low, and unto death bring nigh; — 556 *Cuck. and Night.* 4
And hard hearts he can make them kind and free. — 556 *Cuck. and Night.* 5
He can make sick folk whole and fresh and sound; — 556 *Cuck. and Night.* 7
He can make sick,—bind can he and unbind — 556 *Cuck. and Night.* 9
Foolish men he can make them out of wise;— — 557 *Cuck. and Night.* 12
Loose livers he can make abate their vice, — 557 *Cuck. and Night.* 14
And proud hearts can make tremble in a trice. — 557 *Cuck. and Night.* 15
And, prithee, let us that can sing dwell here; — 558 *Cuck.andNight.*113
And, God of Love, that can right well and may, — 561 *Cuck.andNight.*253
Of that false Bird whom Love can not abide. — 561 *Cuck.andNight.*270
Men said, what may it be, can no one guess — 564 *Troilus* 102
That least of all can aught—that ever owned — 567 *Cumb. Beg.* 80
Or the solicitudes of love can do!) — 568 *Cumb. Beg.* 115
Men who can hear the Decalogue and feel — 568 *Cumb. Beg.* 135
When they can know and feel that they have been, — 568 *Cumb. Beg.* 149
And, long as he can wander, let him breathe — 568 *Cumb. Beg.* 172
Like a magnet, the heart of old Adam can draw; — 570 *Farmer* 78
That keeps not faith, nor yet can point a hope — 573 *Chiabrera* 1. 11
I learned that one poor moment can suffice — 574 *Chiabrera* 4. 23
And that unless above himself he can — 806 *Excursion* 4. 330

Canadian. Say, who, by thinking on Canadian hills, — 15 *Desc. Sk.* 293
Canal. Canal, and Viaduct, and Railway, tell! — 477 *Nunnery* 14
Candidates. There is no end. Such candidates for regard, — 696 *Prelude* 7. 583
Candle. Untouched by his breath see the candle shines bright, — 81 †*Address: Child* 34
Candle-light. It would not pay for candle-light. — 536 *Goody Blake* 28
Candour. Then Tenderness with Candour join'd, — 620 *Birth of Love* 15
Cane. Stumping upon a cane with which he smites, — 693 *Prelude* 7. 426
Canisters. Meantime in canisters is heap'd the bread, — 624 *Æneid* 60
Cankered. Graven on her cankered walls, solemnities — 346 *Processions* 8
Cankerous. (Misdeem it not a cankerous change) may grow — 267 **DespondingFather* 11
Cannon. But here no cannon thunders to the gale; — 384 *Duddon* 33. 1
Bid from on high his lonely cannon sound, — 616 *Desc.Sk.Quarto* 776
With roar of cannon by a furious host. — 719 *Prelude* 10. 54
The sunset cannon. While the orb went down — 723 *Prelude* 10. 325

Cannot. (*Partial list.*) *See* **Can't.**
They cannot mount the hill, by us unseen. — 38 *Bord.* 49
That cannot feel for one, helpless as he is. — 38 *Bord.* 68
There cannot come a day when I shall cease — 39 *Bord.* 88
It cannot be—— What cannot be? Yet that a Father — 42 *Bord.* 268
And would not hear me. No—it cannot be— — 42 *Bord.* 288
Father!—to God himself we cannot give — 47 *Bord.* 543
I cannot leave this paper. Dastard! Come. — 49 *Bord.* 672
Perchance you think so now? I cannot do it: — 53 *Bord.* 889
I care not: fear I have none, and cannot fear—— — 56 *Bord.* 1015
I cannot work thee any woe. — 144 *Her Eyes* 20
"The eye—it cannot choose but see; — 481 *Expost.* 17
He cannot stop his singing by the way. — 554 *Prioress* 106
Such wickedness his judgments cannot spare; — 555 *Prioress* 180
Although I cannot quaver so in vain — 559 *Cuck.andNight.*119
It cannot help itself in its decay; — 571 **There is a Flower* 18
They *cannot* rest, they gambol like young whelps; — K.8. 251 *Recluse* 1.1.548

Canoe. The pointed horns of my canoe; — 236 *P. B.* 17
My gay and beautiful Canoe, — 237 *P. B.* 112
Canonize. Him in their hearts the people canonize; — 426 *Ecc. Sonn.* 1. 32. 11
Canopied. And rudely canopied by leafy boughs, — 172 *Infant Daughter* 20
Canopies. Droops, and o'er canopies his regal brow, — 594 *Ev. Wk. Quarto* 136
Canopy. Under a hoary oak's thin canopy, — 13 *Desc. Sk.* 150
A canopy in some still nook; — 168 *Wren's Nest* 18
Ask, for its pleasure, screen or canopy — 219 *Haunted Tree* 6
A canopy, is smoothed for thy repose!" — 221 *Triad* 79
The lightsome Olive's twinkling canopy— — 361 **List—'twas* 21
Take root again, a boundless canopy, — 384 *Duddon* 31. 8
Whose fondly-overhanging canopy — 440 *Ecc. Sonn.* 3. 1. 3
Or canopy of yet unwithered fern, — 687 *Prelude* 7. 34
Commingled, making up a canopy — 707 *Prelude* 8. 569
Under a shining canopy of state — 784 *Excursion* 2. 863
Under whose shaggy canopy are set — 880 *Excursion* 8. 408

Canst. (*Partial list.*)
Thou that canst shed the bliss of gratitude — 329 *Ode: Thanks.* 2
Canst reach the Prisoner—to his grated cell — 459 **Wanderer! that* 29
That in thy churlishness a cause canst find — 559 *Cuck.andNight.*147
Can't. He can't go wrong go where he will: — S. 3. 424 *Tinker* 28
Canticles. Chime forth unwearied canticles, — 228 *Devot. Incit.* 65
Provoked responses with shrill canticles; — 346 *Processions* 22
Canty. Then at her door the *canty* Dame — 536 *Goody Blake* 39
Canute. While-as Canute the King is rowing by: — 426 *Ecc. Sonn.* 1. 30. 3
—Then Canute, rising from the invaded throne, — 495 *Fact* 9
And Canute (fact more worthy to be known) — 495 *Fact* 19
Canvas. Chequering the canvas roof the sunbeams shone. — 34 *Guilt* 542
Takes down the canvas overhead; — 176 *Waggoner* 1. 273
Against the storm, and canvas spread. — 179 *Waggoner* 3. 82
Canvas-covered. A little yellow, canvas-covered book, — 672 *Prelude* 5. 461
Canvass. Seek other seas, their canvass gleams. — 391 *HighlandBroach* 72
Within that canvass Dwelling, colours, lines, — 548 **Stay, bold* 22

Cap. *See* **Blue-cap, Night-cap, Wishing-cap.**
We should deserve to wear a cap and bells, — 51 *Bord.* 768
And on her head a cap as white as new-fallen snow. — 190 *Beggars* 6
That saw the Corsican his cap and bells — 349 *Boulogne* 7
A student clothed in gown and tasselled cap, — 649 *Prelude* 3. 8
The whip, the cap, and spurs, thy praise attest; — L. 1. 94 *Juvenal* 2. 22
Capability. In every capability of rapture, — 706 *Prelude* 8. 490
Capable. "But thou, though capable of sternest deed, — 210 *Laod.* 55
Capable of clear truth, the one to break — 714 *Prelude* 9. 358
My knowledge, as to make me capable — 750 *Prelude* 14. 310
Ye that are capable of joy be glad! — 796 *Excursion* 3. 729
That spake was capable to lift the soul — 805 *Excursion* 4. 252
Were as a volume, shut, yet capable — 826 *Excursion* 5. 252
Are capable to notice or discern — 830 *Excursion* 5. 498
As only capable to prey on things — 847 *Excursion* 6. 622
The Spirit capable of heaven, assured. — 887 *Excursion* 9. 228
Capacious. Not less capacious than a thousand years. — 172 *Infant Daughter* 12
Joined in one solemn and capacious grove; — 185 *Yew-trees* 15
Of spirit too capacious to require — 214 *Dion* 114
A type of her capacious self and all — 230 *Clouds* 52
For its deliverance—a capacious field — 355 *Aquap.* 162
A gloomy niche, capacious, blank, and cold; — 379 *Duddon* 15. 3
Soft and capacious as a cloudless sky — 508 *F. Stone* 32
Capacious found, or seemed to find, in me — 708 *Prelude* 8. 605
Shall I be silent? O capacious Soul! — 750 *Prelude* 14. 277
In his capacious mind, he loved them all: — 772 *Excursion* 2. 46
Within the depths of his capacious breast, — 800 *Excursion* 3. 971
Capacious and serene. Like power abides — 817 *Excursion* 4. 1070
Yet undiscoloured. A capacious pew — 825 *Excursion* 5. 164
Within these precincts, a capacious bed — 836 *Excursion* 5. 912
Capacious field forth went the Adventurer, there — 843 *Excursion* 6. 311
Capacious and serene; his blameless life, — 854 *Excursion* 6. 1066
Of his fair eyes, by his capacious brow, — 868 *Excursion* 7. 726
On whose capacious surface see outspread — 882 *Excursion* 8. 557
Capacities. And his innate capacities of soul, — 799 *Excursion* 3. 934
The liberal donor of capacities — 870 *Excursion* 7. 826
Capacity. A timorous capacity from prudence, — 635 *Prelude* 1. 241
Capital. Lest, capital pains remitting till ye spare — 518 *Pun. Death* 4. 7
The capital City; what was struggled for, — 720 *Prelude* 10. 128
His capital city!' Thence, along a tract — 869 *Excursion* 7. 794
Capitolian. Is this, ye Gods, the Capitolian Hill? — 358 **Is this* 1
Capped. *See* **Cloud-capped.**
Caprice. Love ebb and flow untroubled by caprice;. — 500 *Humanity* 57
Capricious. Who trembles now at thy capricious mood? — 271 *Henry: Portrait* 9
Caps. With their comely blue aprons, and caps white as snow, — 120 *Childless Father* 7
Capt. *See* **Cloud-capt.**

Captain. Over our much-loved Captain. I have heard — 37 *Bord.* 14
I'd rather see my father's ghost. My Captain, — 56 *Bord.* 1020
Our Captain made a prey to foul device!— — 63 *Bord.* 1418
What if he mean to offer up our Captain — 64 *Bord.* 1456
Ha! my dear Captain. A later meeting, Oswald, — 64 *Bord.* 1470
Against my honour, in the which our Captain — 68 *Bord.* 1691
To dig for water on the spot, the Captain — 68 *Bord.* 1712
Watch over her, I pray—sustain her—— Captain! — 78 *Bord.* 2338
But to each gallant Captain and his crew — 458 *Sea-shore* 25
Nor Miss Taylor, Captain Stamp, — S. 3. 438 **My Lord* 5
Must tell you, Captain, Lord, and Ladies, — S. 3. 438 **My Lord* 25
Captains. Are captains such as erst their country bred — 320 **They seek* 5
And Captains known for worth in arms; — 403 *White Doe* 630
Captivated. To rule and guide his captivated flock. — 695 *Prelude* 7. 572
Captivates. Captivates like passive meekness. — 502 **Like a* 44
Captive. Many a captive hath she rescued, — 94 *Westmoreland Girl* 55
And the fair Captive, who, whene'er she may, — 122 *V. and J.* 81
To behold thy captive state; — 139 *Arm. Lady* 14
The captive promptly coos; — 168 *Turtledove* 6
A captive never wishing to be free. — 253 **O gentle* 4
The captive 'mid damp vaults unsunned, unaired, — 273 **Not the* 5
The captive chieftain, by a tyrant's doom, — 318 **Is there* 2
Captive, whoe'er thou be! — 334 **In Bruges* 30
The captive Bird was gone;—to cliff or moor — 472 **The captive* 1
The emancipated captive through blithe air — 528 **Those breathing* 68
Fair Damsel! o'er my captive mind, — 530 *Gleaner* 22
The Captive shunned all converse proffered there. — 531 **I know* 24
Make him a captive!—for that pent-up din, — 569 *Cumb. Beg.* 180
Which was the captive of another's toil — 637 *Prelude* 1. 320
Or captive led in abject weeds, and jingling — 693 *Prelude* 7. 420
And not a captive pining for his home. — 734 *Prelude* 11. 470
The thankful captive of maternal bonds; — 794 *Excursion* 3. 555
Captive's. On joys that might disgrace the captive's cell, — 13 *Desc. Sk.* 138
Captives. From her whom drooping captives love; — 112 *Lament* 4
With captives chained; and shedding from his car — 464 *Derwent* 12
Accept, mute Captives! thanks and praise; — 527 **The soaring* 53
Captive-wise. My Lady dear, first bound me captive-wise. — 563 *Troilus* 49
Captivity. My husband served in sad captivity — 35 *Guilt* 593
Doomed to a third and last captivity, — 124 *V. and J.* 185
When the captivity of sleep had ceased; — 329 *Ode: Thanks.* 46
Hath witnessed their captivity. — 408 *White Doe* 1125
Weeping captivity, and shuddering fear — 465 **Dear to* 13
I was ill-tutored for captivity; — 654 *Prelude* 3. 356
Captivity by mandate without law — 717 *Prelude* 9. 536
Body and mind in one captivity; — 831 *Excursion* 5. 605
Of her close tasks, and long captivity. — 878 *Excursion* 8. 296
Her captivity to share. — S. 3. 437 **I, whose* 16
Car. Fixed on a smoothly-sliding car. — 177 *Waggoner* 2. 108
Precursors to Aurora's car, — 191 *Beggars* 34

Care—*continued.*
They, with joint care, determined to erect, 845 *Excursion* 6. 496
To sight or mind. Nor less than care divine 850 *Excursion* 6. 770
Their slender means: so, to that parent's care 852 *Excursion* 6. 945
By books unsteadied, by his pastoral care 859 *Excursion* 7. 115
Was trimmed and brightened by the Matron's care, 860 *Excursion* 7. 171
Nor husband's love, nor father's hope or care. 864 *Excursion* 7. 427
He had withdrawn from bustle, care, and noise, 867 *Excursion* 7. 665
Of that foundation in domestic care 872 *Excursion* 7. 964
Faithfully watched, and, by that loving care 876 *Excursion* 8. 149
And female care.—"A blessed lot is yours!" 882 *Excursion* 8. 542
And faithful care of unambitious schools 890 *Excursion* 9. 395
Trust not to partial care a general good; 890 *Excursion* 9. 405
Who hath beheld it, noted it with care, 891 *Excursion* 9. 516
Revive its ashes. What care we for this, 892 *Excursion* 9. 553
On you, the children of my humble care, 895 *Excursion* 9. 739
And sorrow and care blow over him, S. 3. 424 *Tinker* 49
But resolv'd with filial care S. 3. 437 **I, whose* 15
To one who holds it dear; with duteous care K.8.251 *Recluse* 1.1.525
Can make it so, and care of human hands. K.8.251 *Recluse* 1.1.531
And ye as happy under Nature's care, K.8. 251 *Recluse* 1.1.532
No duty that looks further, and no care. K.8. 255 *Recluse* 1.1.668
Earth's petty grievances—its toil and care:— [?] **A sad* 7

Cared. Nor for the moon cared he a tittle, 240 *P. B* 333
And for the stars he cared as little, 240 *P. B.* 334.
In those proud days, he little cared 483 *Simon Lee* 13
He sprang in glee,—for what cared he 494 *Force of Prayer* 29
I neither knew nor cared for; and as such 657 *Prelude* 3. 565
Of this I little saw, cared less for it, 703 *Prelude* 8. 292

Career. The post-boy drove with fierce career, 82 *Alice Fell* 1
Eve renews her calm career; 90 *Longest Day* 10
The wonders of a wild career. 237 *P. B.* 121
That press upon me, crossing the career 350 *Des. Stanzas* 16
A single One, in mid career 414 *White Doe* 1643
The Council closed, the Priest in full career 422 *Ecc. Sonn.* 1. 17. 2
Distinct with signs, through which in set career, 445 *Ecc. Sonn.* 3. 19. 4
Back towards caverned life's first rude career. 489 *Illus. Books* 11

Careful. And chafe her temples, careful hands apply. 34 *Guilt* 571
A careful student he had been 155 *Oak and Broom* 3
Of careful sadness. 158 **In youth* 64
If simple Nature trained by careful Art 281 *Valedict.* 12
With careful hesitation,—then convenes 422 *Ecc. Sonn.* 1. 15. 12
Their work's foundation, gave with careful hand 534 **When in* 11
At early morn the careful housewife, led 615 *Desc.Sk.Quarto* 728
Then wafts him, cherish'd on her careful breast, 624 *Æneid* 49
Was the commodious walk: a careful hand 881 *Excursion* 8. 450
With prompt yet careful hands. This done, we paced 895 *Excursion* 9. 768

Carefully. (Though they had long been carefully observed), 704 *Prelude* 8. 359
Pieces of money carefully enclosed, 766 *Excursion* 1. 670
Before their eyes lay carefully outspread, 869 *Excursion* 7. 785

Careless. In careless mood he looked at me, 86 *Anecdote* 33
As careless as if nothing were, 130 *Idiot Boy* 350
Careless of books, yet having felt the power 131 *Michael* 28
Spread here his careless blossoms, here 156 *Oak and Broom* 69
The little careless Broom was left 157 *Oak and Broom* 109
Like a careless Prodigal; 160 **Pansies, lilies* 30
Careless of thy neighbourhood, 160 **Pansies, lilies* 43
And I will have my careless season 171 *Kitten* 111
With careless air and open mien. 181 *Waggoner* 4. 147
Must vanish, and his careless cheer 204 *Brougham* 93
Which the careless shepherd sleeps on, 222 *Triad* 209
Besprinkled with a careless quire, 233 *Power of Sound* 44
And in a light and careless way, 245 *P. B.* 818
Careless of flowers that in perennial blow 376 *Duddon* 1. 5
And what the little careless innocent 377 *Duddon* 7. 9
So careless and disorderly. 406 *White Doe* 901
If looked at only with a careless eye; 529 *Poor Robin* 12
Yet are by nature careless of the sun 539 **Lady! a* 14
And careless hand his alms upon the ground, 566 *Cumb. Beg.* 27
My careless Little-one, for thee and thine!" 627 **Son of* 14
From street to street with loose and careless mind. 649 *Prelude* 3. 29
Of careless youth, unburdened, unalarmed. 652 *Prelude* 3. 242
With careless ostentation shouldering up 653 *Prelude* 3. 311
Or been regarded with too careless eye, 709 *Prelude* 9. 14
Tranquil almost, and careless as a flower 711 *Prelude* 9. 87
I had but lent a careless ear, assured 730 *Prelude* 11. 191
To careless eyes. And—now convinced at heart 742 *Prelude* 13. 168
My earliest visitations, careless then 748 *Prelude* 14. 141
Extends his careless limbs along the front 756 *Excursion* 1. 10
The careless stillness of a thinking mind 768 *Excursion* 1. 797
The careless wanderer's friend, to him made known 774 *Excursion* 2. 186
Who, entering, round him threw a careless glance 778 *Excursion* 2. 430
Left and forgotten in his careless way, 778 *Excursion* 2. 452
Answered the sick Man with a careless voice— 780 *Excursion* 2. 612
Then, speaking in like careless sort, he said 781 *Excursion* 2. 618
Of insects chirping out their careless lives 789 *Excursion* 3. 246
As books record, and even the careless mind 834 *Excursion* 5. 797
Who holds the land in fee, its careless lord! 866 *Excursion* 7. 575
In a low voice, yet careless who might hear, 892 *Excursion* 9. 549
To shaggy steeps on which the careless goat 892 *Excursion* 9. 564
For his own careless head. S. 3. 423 *Tinker* 22
(Tho' a mere goblet to the careless eye) S. 3. 433 **The doubt* 42

Carelessly. Carelessly watched, sport through the summer day, 377 *Duddon* 5. 12
This was not wanting. Carelessly I roamed 658 *Prelude* 3. 616
Who entered, humming carelessly a tune, 825 *Excursion* 5. 219

Cares. Those busy cares that would allay my pain; 2 *Early Youth* 12
While tender cares and mild domestic loves 6 *Ev. Wk.* 222
"A sailor's wife I knew a widow's cares, 35 *Guilt* 595

Cares—*continued.*
And humble cares, and delicate fears; 79 *Sparrow's Nest* 18
When full of play and childish cares, 117 *Affl. Marg.* 23
To its dull round of ordinary cares; 122 *V. and J.* 52
That cheats her of too busy cares, 144 **Driven in* 35
"Thy father cares not for my breast, 145 *Her Eyes* 61
That did your cares repay. 155 *Waterfall* 30
And if they had care, it has scattered their cares. 167 *Stray Pleasures* 23
Dost thou despise the earth where cares abound? 209 **Ethereal minstrel* 2
Released from life and cares of princely state, 214 *Dion* 120
Whose skill can speed the day with lively cares, 221 *Triad* 62
O, nursed at happy distance from the cares 227 *Vernal Ode* 75
From trivial cares. But, Fancy and the Muse, 252 **Her only* 9
She cares for; let her travel where she may, 258 **Where lies the Land* 6
And nobler cares than listless summer knew. 263 **While not* 14
Gave it while cares were weighing on my heart, 266 **The stars* 10
Though narrow be that old Man's cares, and near, 267 **Though narrow* 1
Unwearied joy, and life without its cares. 268 **Brook! whose* 14
All fitful cares, all transitory zeal! 270 **If these* 12
And in a moment charmed my cares to rest. 279 **Hark! 'tis* 8
Hangs o'er its Parent waking to the cares 282 **While beams* 6
When earthly cares are laid asleep! 288 *Highland Girl* 14
To social cares from jarring passions freed; 334 **The Spirit* 13
While narrow cares their limits overflow. 339 *Tell* 5
Her simple cares to magnify; 344 **How blest* 4
The patriot Mother's weight of anxious cares! 344 **How blest* 52
Than that to which thy cares are gone, 348 **Lulled by* 22
The world forsaken, all its busy cares 363 **The world forsaken* 1
The exultations, pomps, and cares of Rome, 368 *Trajan* 37
They taught me random cares and truant joys, 382 *Duddon* 26. 10
Lulling the year, with all its cares, to rest! 388 *Trosachs* 14
Ye living, tend your holy cares; 397 *White Doe* 69
And stood apart from human cares: 416 *White Doe* 1859
No moment steals; pain narrows not his cares. 425 *Ecc. Sonn.* 1. 26. 10
But of the lights that cherish household cares 426 *Ecc. Sonn.* 1. 31. 4
From finite cares, to rest absorbed in Thee! 454 **The Sun, that* 26
So might it seem, the cares of them that wake; 459 **Wanderer! that* 4
Who gave us nobler loves, and nobler cares— 489 *Pers. Talk* 52
Along a scale of light and life, with cares 500 *Humanity* 29
Cares entangle, sins beset, 503 **Like a* 54
With every hope that mutual cares provide; 519 *Pun. Death* 11. 4
By cares in which simplicity is lost? 528 **Those breathing* 90
Of the world's freezing cares—to generous Youth— 540 *Grace Darl.* 10
After long exercise in social cares 551 **If thou in* 10
To selfishness and cold oblivious cares. 567 *Cumb. Beg.* 95
Found—for all interests, hopes, and tender cares, 585 *Ch. Lamb* 83
And as a swift by tender cares oppress'd 612 *Desc.Sk.Quarto* 572
These cares, and thus she speaks to winged Love: 624 *Æneid* 10
That cares not for his home. All shod with steel, 638 *Prelude* 1. 433
In narrow cares, thy little daily growth 659 *Prelude* 4. 35
Nor selfish with unnecessary cares, 670 *Prelude* 5. 283
Internally from academic cares; 675 *Prelude* 6. 26
His comforts, native occupations, cares, 700 *Prelude* 8. 106
Against the weight of meanness, selfish cares, 703 *Prelude* 8. 319
From whatsoever region of our cares 721 *Prelude* 10. 188
Wilfully to mean cares or low pursuits, 748 *Prelude* 14. 154
Of humble cares and delicate desires, 749 *Prelude* 14. 230
In closelier gathering cares, such as become 750 *Prelude* 14. 290
By mortal cares. Himself no Poet, yet 751 *Prelude* 14. 362
Serene it was, unclouded by the cares 761 *Excursion* 1. 356
From her maternal cares, had taken up 769 *Excursion* 1. 858
Of humble, though, to us, important cares, 795 *Excursion* 3. 610
Its cares and sorrows; he, though taught to own 809 *Excursion* 4. 546
On fickle pleasures, and superfluous cares, 813 *Excursion* 4. 821
Of blessèd angels, pitying human cares. 839 *Excursion* 6. 52
Meanwhile, relinquishing all other cares, 854 *Excursion* 6. 1025
And through the impediment of rural cares, 868 *Excursion* 7. 736
'Mid all his apprehensions, cares, and fears,— 884 *Excursion* 9. 35
All cares forgotten, round its hallowed walls! 895 *Excursion* 9. 728
All her accustomed offices and cares S. 3. 437 **The doubt* 187
Loving what no one cares for but ourselves; K.8. 248 *Recluse* 1.1.429
The joy of fleshly life without its cares. K.8. 265 **Brook, that* 14

Caress. And if the breath of some to no caress 377 *Duddon* 6. 12
Such delicate caress as in the shape S. 3. 434 **The doubt* 77

Caressed. Fair Swan! by all a mother's joys caressed, 7 *Ev. Wk.* 250
Caressed, applauded, upon dainties fed, 165 *Parrot* 45
Which may itself be cherished and caressed 394 **No more* 33
Who comes—with rapture greeted, and caressed 441 *Ecc. Sonn.* 3. 3. 1
And shameless women, treated and caressed; 692 *Prelude* 7. 361

Caresses. Dear caresses given in pity, 94 *Westmoreland Girl* 37
There by caresses from a tremulous hand. 531 **I know* 20
If the caresses of a human voice K.8. 251 *Recluse* 1.1.530

Caressing. Sees them and their caressing; 287 *Ellen Irwin* 23
Caressing him again and yet again. 660 *Prelude* 4. 117

Caring. Happy is he, who, caring not for Pope, 304 **Festivals have* 12
Not caring if the wind did now and then 729 *Prelude* 11. 165

Carl. The Mastiff, ill-conditioned carl! 179 *Waggoner* 3. 101
He was a Carl as wild and rude 239 *P. B.* 273

Carlisle. And merry Carlisle had he been; 239 *P. B.* 217

Carman. She saw the carman bend to scoop the flood 34 *Guilt* 543
The carman wet her lips as well behoved; 34 *Guilt* 546
The boisterous carman, in the miry road, 61 *Bord.* 1334

Carnage. For years the work of carnage did not cease, 25 *Guilt* 55
With such vast hoards of hidden carnage near, 335 **A wingèd* 13
Domestic carnage now filled the whole year 723 *Prelude* 10. 356
Her fields of carnage, and polluted air. 798 *Excursion* 3. 834

Carnation. Of cheek that with carnation vies, 541 *Russ. Fug.* 3

Cause—*continued.*
Doubtless, I should have then made common cause 721 *Prelude* 10. 229
For her great cause record or prophecy . . . 728 *Prelude* 11. 43
As cause was given me afterwards to learn, . . 728 *Prelude* 11. 89
Which, through the later sinkings of this cause, . 732 *Prelude* 11. 355
Promised, now is ; a far more sober cause . . . 733 *Prelude* 11. 387
My deeper feelings, but another cause, ... 736 *Prelude* 12. 123
Or any other cause that hath been named ; . . 737 *Prelude* 12. 197
Nor was time given to ask or learn the cause, 746 *Prelude* 14. 37
You look at me, and you have cause ; to-day 767 *Excursion* 1. 763
The cause of Christ and civil liberty, ... 774 *Excursion* 2. 221
"That righteous cause (such power hath freedom) bound, ... 775 *Excursion* 2. 227
To an exalted pitch (the self-same cause . . . 788 *Excursion* 3. 154
How rapidly the zealots of the cause . . . . 797 *Excursion* 3. 770
So easily deprived ?) but, for that cause, . . . 799 *Excursion* 3. 922
Prime, self-existing cause and end of all . . . 802 *Excursion* 4. 80
To many seemed superfluous—as, no cause . . 805 *Excursion* 4. 265
To see the moment, when the righteous cause 806 *Excursion* 4. 311
The processes of things, and serve the cause . . 820 *Excursion* 4. 1258
Cause should recur, which righteous Heaven avert ! 839 *Excursion* 6. 60
Shall cause to fade, till ages pass away ; . . . 842 *Excursion* 6. 252
And cause for most rare triumph will be thine 844 *Excursion* 6. 436
For his ungrateful cause ; no,—I have heard . . 845 *Excursion* 6. 463
Yet cause was none, whate'er regret might hang . 859 *Excursion* 7. 145
A humble champion of the better cause ; . . . 870 *Excursion* 7. 850
Rejoice !—and ye have special cause for joy. . 889 *Excursion* 9. 368
Gave to triumph Freedom's cause, ... S.3. 442 *Harmodius* 7
Gave to triumph Freedom's cause, ... S.3. 442 *Harmodius* 27
Nor could he guess the cause for which the boy K.8. 229 **I will* 162
Such reasons, and he had less cause to love . K.8. 231 **I will* 211
Had ever more abundant cause to speak . . . K.8. 239 *Recluse* 1. 1. 99
Upon a less incitement than the cause . . . . K.8. 257 *Recluse* 1. 1. 747
Alas ! 'twas other cause than lack of years . . L. 1. 96 *Juvenal* 3. 61

Caused. That, in the undertaking which has caused 37 *Bord.* 6
That, in my zeal, I have caused you so much pain. . . . . 55 *Bord.* 1004
Theirs be the blame who caused the woe, not mine ! 125 *V. and J.* 283
From mischief, caused by spells himself had muttered ; . . . . 370 *Eg. Maid* 68
"Alas ! and I have caused this woe ; . . . . 372 *Eg. Maid* 223
Grief that devouring waves had caused—or guilt . 470 **Did pangs* 2
Caused by the wish, as knows your sapience, . . 562 *Cuck. and Night.* 309
For which, with pain, he caused due obsequies 623 **I find* 4
By false philosophy had caused the woe, . . . 725 *Prelude* 10. 476
Thy bounty caused to flourish deathless flowers, . 802 *Excursion* 4. 53
Or sorrow which his senseless guilt had caused ; . 853 *Excursion* 6. 1007
Have caused her to abate the virgin pride, . . 882 *Excursion* 8. 510

Causeless. O vain and causeless melancholy ! . . 88 *H. C.* 20

Causes. Poor Peter from a thousand causes . . 248 *P. B.* 1034
And murder causes some sad tears to flow, . . 582 *Invoc. Earth* 16
From unknown causes. I was left alone . . . 646 *Prelude* 2. 277
Whence, and from deeper causes, all discourse 711 *Prelude* 9. 118

Causeway. A rude and natural causeway, interposed 148 **A narrow* 2
(More fair than heaven's broad causeway paved with stars) . . . . 213 *Dion* 51
That Causeway with incomparable toil !)— . . 269 *Malham* 5
As on the broadening causeway we advance, . . 690 *Prelude* 7. 199

Caution. With caution, sift the matter artfully. . 42 *Bord.* 293
Caution must not be flung aside ; remember. . . 48 *Bord.* 604
And which, with caution due, may soon be realized." 105 *Artegal* 217
And prudent caution needful to avert . . . . 889 *Excursion* 9. 356
With caution we embarked ; and now the pair . 891 *Excursion* 9. 478

Cautious. Be cautious, my dear Master ! I perceive 37 *Bord.* 21
More cautious as they draw more near ; . . . 297 *Highland Boy* 198
By cautious love supplied . . . . 543 *Russ. Fug.* 152
Though weak his step and cautious, he appeared . 665 *Prelude* 4. 431
And cautious water-fowl, from distant climes, . 869 *Excursion* 7. 754

Cautiously. The horses cautiously pursue . . . 175 *Waggoner* 1. 207
He cautiously surveyed. . . . . 241 *P. B.* 410

Cavalier. Faint sanction given, the Cavalier . . 545 *Russ. Fug.* 341

Cavaliers. A mantle such as Spanish Cavaliers . . 661 *Prelude* 4. 221

Cave. *See* **Sea-cave.**
A cave that opened to the road presented . . . 50 *Bord.* 699
Of many autumns in the cave had piled. . . . 50 *Bord.* 706
When, after a broad flash that filled the cave, . 50 *Bord.* 715
Sometimes he'll hide in the cave of a rock, . . 80 †*Address : Child* 14
Of some old cave, or mossy nook, ... 109 *Louisa* 16
To the dark cave, the goblin's hall ; . . . . 128 *Idiot Boy* 228
Yield him no domestic cave, ... 166 *Wand. Jew* 14
Of yon dim cave; in seeming silence makes . . 184 *Airey-force* 13
Or of some Hermit's cave, where by his fire . . 206 *Tintern* 21
To enter than oracular cave ; . . . . . . 232 *Power of Sound* 6
Piping through cave and battlemented tower ; . 233 *Power of Sound* 69
Comes from the entrance of a cave : . . . . 243 *P. B.* 630
By this dark cave to be distrest . . . . . 243 *P. B.* 648
Sleeping alone within a mossy cave, ... 257 **Methought I* 11
Lady ! I rifled a Parnassian Cave . . . . . 264 **Lady ! I* 1
Not there ; but in dark wood and rocky cave, . 314 **Not 'mid* 5
Into a cave had Merlin fled . . . . 370 *Eg. Maid* 67
Yet is the Prophet calm, nor would the cave . . 392 *Daniel* 11
Far under ground is many a cave, ... 408 *White Doe* 1096
Renews. Through every forest, cave, and den, . 435 *Ecc. Sonn.* 2. 27. 9
Who daily piles up wealth in Mammon's cave— . 454 **Not in the lucid* 6
The elements have heard, and rock and cave replied. 457 **The leaves* 34
And when thy beauty in the shadowy cave . . 460 **Wanderer ! that* 63
That cleaves to rock or pillared cave . . . . 472 *Ossian* 25
The Ghost of Fingal to his tuneful Cave . . . 473 **We saw* 6
"No fountain from its rocky cave . . . . . 487 **We walked* 49
Of yon wild cave, whose jaggèd brows are fringed 497 **Enough of climbing* 21

Cave—*continued.*
Long as the heat shall rage, let that dim cave . 498 **Enough of climbing* 32
Nor wants the dim-lit cave a wreath . . . . 506 **While from* 35
Then, stretcht at ease in some sequestered cave, . 630 [?] **O Moon* 7
Within a rocky cave, its usual home. . . . . 637 *Prelude* 1. 359
While I was seated in a rocky cave . . . . 666 *Prelude* 5. 58
Hid in her vacant interlunar cave." . . . . 691 *Prelude* 7. 284
As the winds fret within the Æolian cave, . . 695 *Prelude* 7. 533
An entrance now into some magic cave . . . 705 *Prelude* 8. 417
Hath passed with torches into some huge cave, . 707 *Prelude* 8. 561
Till the whole cave, so late a senseless mass, . . 707 *Prelude* 8. 580
In wood or echoing cave, for discipline . . . 734 *Prelude* 11. 458
Of some huge cave, whose rocky ceiling casts . . 756 *Excursion* 1. 11
Leapt out together from a rocky cave ; . . . 789 *Excursion* 3. 242
Of lightning startled in a gloomy cave . . . . 796 *Excursion* 3. 708
By echo multiplied from rock or cave, ... 814 *Excursion* 4. 868
Or dwell in chambers of some natural cave ; . . 879 *Excursion* 8. 366
Through Cumbrian wilds, in many a mountain cave, S.3. 426 **Through Cumbrian* 1
As if it were a cave, a multitude . . . . . K.8. 253 *Recluse* 1. 1. 621

Cavendish. Where, Cavendish, *thine* seems nothing but a name ! . . . . 283 **Here, where* 14

Cavern. Was ready with her cavern ; Hammar-scar, 147 *Joanna* 57
To the dim cavern, whence the river . . . . 371 *Eg. Maid* 164
Within some rocky cavern laid, ... 415 *White Doe* 1739
The interlunar cavern of the tomb. . . . . . 596 *Ev. Wk. Quarto* 268
Into a dazzling cavern of romance, ... 694 *Prelude* 7. 455
From the blind cavern whence is faintly heard . 749 *Prelude* 14. 195
Some secret of the mountains, cavern, fall . . 776 *Excursion* 2. 320
And as a cavern is with darkness fill'd, . . . S. 3. 425 **The rains* 3

Caverned. Back towards caverned life's first rude career. . . . . 489 *Illus. Books* 11
And blind recesses of the caverned rocks ; . . . 818 *Excursion* 4. 1172

Cavern's. Into the cavern's mouth he peeps ; . . 243 *P. B.* 638

Caverns. It pierced the caverns of the sluggish North— . . . . 327 *Ode 1815* 20
And in our caverns smooth thy ruffled wings !" . 431 *Ecc. Sonn.* 2. 13. 4
The penal caverns groan . . . . 581 *Invoc. Earth* 10
Caverns there were within my mind which sun . 652 *Prelude* 3. 243
Bare hills and valleys, full of caverns, rocks, . . 708 *Prelude* 8. 635
From rocks, woods, caverns, heaths, and dashing shores ; . . . . 782 *Excursion* 2. 698
Who fled to woods, caverns, and jutting rocks, . 814 *Excursion* 4. 902

Cave's. The dark cave's portal gliding by, . . . 415 *White Doe* 1740

Caves. Of caves and trees:—and when the regular wind 95 *Brothers* 49
Murmuring from Glaramara's inmost caves. . . 185 *Yew-trees* 33
To the caves, and to the brooks, ... 204 *Brougham* 65
And into caves where Faeries sing . . . . . 205 *Brougham* 131
From caves of Indian mountains hoar ! . . . 215 *Enterprise* 27
Of Sherwood's Archer, or in caves of Wallace— . 221 *Triad* 70
And search the fibres of the caves, and they . . 230 *Clouds* 64
Flung back, and, in the sky's blue caves, reborn— 233 *Power of Sound* 36
The caves reply with hollow moan ; . . . . 299 *Cora Linn* 4
Till the caves roar,—and imbecility . . . . 311 **Who rises* 58
Cliffs, woods and caves, her viewless steps resound 315 **Advance—come* 8
Within its awful caves.—From year to year . . 321 **The power* 10
Which from Siberian caves the Monarch freed, . 321 **Humanity, delighting* 28
To sink, and meet them in their fretted caves, . 333 *Fish-women* 7
Tempestuously let loose from central caves ? . . 380 *Duddon* 15. 12
Of tuneful Caves and playful Waterfalls— . . 388 *Loch Etive* 4
Or in the diver's grasp fetched up from caves . 511 **Who rashly* 14
On caves and trees, upon the woods and hills, . 639 *Prelude* 1. 470
Of boyhood, many an hour in caves forlorn, . . 758 *Excursion* 1. 154
Dived into caves, and pierced the matted woods, . 840 *Excursion* 6. 110

Cavities. From the projections, wrinkles, cavities, . 707 *Prelude* 8. 583

Cavity. Aghast within its gloomy cavity . . . 439 *Ecc. Sonn.* 2. 42. 5

Cawing. Whose cawing occupants with joy proclaim 283 **Here, where* 12
Around their ancient grove) with cawing noise . 455 *Rydal Mere* 11
The cawing rooks, and sea-mews from afar, . . 808 *Excursion* 4. 451

Cease. That cease not till night falls, when far and nigh, ... 21 *Desc. Sk.* 618
And cease the acknowledged purpose to withstand ; 22 *Desc. Sk.* 662
For years the work of carnage did not cease, . . 25 *Guilt* 55
The bond of nature, all unkindness cease, . . . 33 *Guilt* 508
There cannot come a day when I shall cease . . 39 *Bord.* 88
Conflict must cease, and, in thy frozen heart, . . 76 *Bord.* 2215
—Here, Lady ! might I cease ; but nay, let *us* before we part . . . . 91 *Norman Boy* 29
But when I cease to look, my hand is on my heart. 110 **'Tis said that some* 20
That murmur once so dear, when will it cease ? . 111 **'Tis said that some* 22
Their labour did not cease ; unless when all . . 132 *Michael* 98
That could not cease to be. Green leaves were here ; 146 **It was an* 30
He did not cease ; but cooed—and cooed ; . . 186 **O Nightingale* 15
Where winds and waters cease to strive— . . . 216 *Enterprise* 72
Glad Hope would almost cease to be . . . . 217 *Enterprise* 158
Nor while sin lasts must effort cease ; . . . . 337 **Oh Life* 8
A Spirit whispered, "Let all wonder cease ; . . 349 *At Dover* 8
Thoughts that would stray from Heaven ? The dream must cease . . . . 363 **Grieve for* 10
Crying with earnestness that might not cease, . . 365 **The Baptist* 13
Nor cease to gaze upon the bold Relief . . . 368 *Trajan* 71
Or cease to please the fickle worshipper ; . . . 380 *Duddon* 18. 4
Their vocal charm ; their sparklings cease to please. 382 *Duddon* 25. 14
If not, O Mortals, better cease to live ! . . . 388 **The pibroch's* 14
But, Harp ! thy murmurs may not cease— . . 399 *White Doe* 330
Can never cease to bear celestial fruit. . . . . 431 *Ecc. Sonn.* 2. 10. 5
Saved by His care who bade the tempest cease ; . 454 *Sea-side* 16

Ceased 123 **Cell**

Cease—*continued.*
If He, through whom alone our conflicts cease, . 455 **Not in the lucid* 27
Yet thy mild aspect does not, cannot, cease . . 460 **Queen of* 35
And straightway cease to aspire, than God disdain 465 **Pastor and* 13
And not alone *harsh* tyranny would cease, . . 500 *Humanity* 58
Mistrust thyself, vain Country! cease to cry, . . 513 *Newspaper* 9
Will take away, may cease to give. . . . . . 532 †*Float. Isl.* 20
For thee she mourns, nor e'er will cease to mourn; 575 *Chiabrera* 7. 8
Beside a sea that could not cease to smile; . . 578 *Peele Castle* 19
Aye, think on that, my heart, and cease to stir, . 622 *Recluse* 1. 1. 80
Cease, Britannia, cease to weep! . . . . . 628 *Installation* 28
Should cease; and open accusation lead . . . 717 *Prelude* 9. 537
Without Whose call this world would cease to breathe, ... 724 *Prelude* 10. 421
The aspiration, nor shall ever cease . . . . 731 *Prelude* 11. 257
And of the poor did many cease to be, . . . 764 *Excursion* 1. 545
In every grove were ringing, 'War shall cease; . 796 *Excursion* 3. 723
Yet cease I not to struggle, and aspire . . . 803 *Excursion* 4. 126
—Yes, you have felt, and may not cease to feel. . 818 *Excursion* 4. 1151
Where he had lived, and could not cease to live, . 843 *Excursion* 6. 369
Extinguished, do not, *therefore*, cease to be. . 865 *Excursion* 7. 520
To both; and, if that partnership must cease, . 888 *Excursion* 9. 272
Then, nor till then, shall persecution cease, . . 894 *Excursion* 9. 649
To finer uses. They for me must cease; . . . S. 3. 433 **The doubt* 21
Is flowing, and will never cease to flow, . . . K. 8. 244 *Recluse* 1. 1. 295
Ceased. The bird, who ceased, with fading light, to thread . . . . 8 *Ev. Wk.* 323
He too was mute: and, ere her weeping ceased, . 30 *Guilt* 311
Have I."—She ceased, and weeping turned away; 32 *Guilt* 447
His anguish, with his heart he ceased to strive; . 35 *Guilt* 618
When Lucy ceased to be; . . . . 109 **She dwelt* 10
The crickets long have ceased their mirth; . . 118 †*Cottager* 7
Here Michael ceased, and to the fields went forth . 135 *Michael* 283
The Mother mourned, nor ceased her tears to flow, 139 *Widow* 15
I ceased the shelter to frequent,—and prized, . 150 **When, to* 41
When files of stateliest plants have ceased to bloom, 169 **Never enlivened* 7
Which Benjamin had ceased to drive: . . . . 182 *Waggoner* 4. 188
That ceased not; on our English land . . . . 191 *Beggars* 15
Ten times and more, I fancied it had ceased; . 218 *Recluse* 1. 1. 217
The lingering world, when time hath ceased to be. 230 *Clouds* 40
Rejoice, as, through that power, it ceased to mourn. 258 **Even so* 14
Though man for brother man has ceased to feel. . 273 **When Philoctetes* 14
—No sooner ceased that peal, than on the verge . 324 *Ode 1814* 82
When the captivity of sleep had ceased; . . . 329 *Ode: Thanks.* 46
For kindnesses that never ceased to flow, . . . 352 *H. C. R.* 7
On knees that ceased from trembling, or intoned . 357 *Aquap.* 302
Bound him, nor, since he raised yon House, have ceased . . . . 362 **List—'twas* 39
Have never ceased to eddy round its base, . . 367 *Trajan* 8
For pleasure hath not ceased to wait . . . . 375 **The Minstrels* 31
For us the stream of fiction ceased to flow, . . 395 *WhiteDoe: Ded.* 25
The Norton ceased not for that sound, . . . 403 *White Doe* 673
Until this storm hath ceased to rave: . . . . 408 *White Doe* 1098
As, when a storm hath ceased, the birds regain . 420 *Ecc. Sonn.* 1. 7. 1
The saintly Youth has ceased to rule, discrowned 436 *Ecc. Sonn.* 2. 33. 1
Men, who have ceased to reverence, soon defy . 438 *Ecc. Sonn.* 2. 41. 1
That union ceased: then, cleaving easy walks . 477 *Nunnery* 9
To righteous Gods when man has ceased to feel, . 500 *Humanity* 2
Ere he had ceased to gaze, perhaps to speak: . 510 *F. Stone* 120
When fire or taper ceased to cheer the room, . . 528 **Those breathing* 54
For us hath such prelusive vigil ceased; . . . 535 **When in* 21
Softening the toils and pains that have not ceased 538 **In desultory* 27
All night the storm had raged, nor ceased, nor paused, ... 540 *Grace Darl.* 28
And when those rites had ceased, the Spot gave birth 547 **Beneath yon* 7
Long time his pulse hath ceased to beat; . . . 578 **I come* 57
A power that never ceased to abide in him, . . 584 *Ch. Lamb* 34
The bird, with fading light who ceas'd to thread . 599 *Ev. Wk. Quarto* 389
Now when the viands were withdrawn, and ceas'd 625 *Æneid* 95
That sang and ceased not; now a Sister Isle . . 643 *Prelude* 2. 59
Had ceased to dazzle, ofttimes did I quit . . . 650 *Prelude* 3. 91
By deluge, now at hand. No sooner ceased . . 667 *Prelude* 5. 98
Ceased, had I left those academic bowers . . . 679 *Prelude* 6. 277
She ceased to speak, but while St. Bruno's pines . 681 *Prelude* 6. 436
Thus have I looked, nor ceased to look, oppressed 696 *Prelude* 7. 630
Put on a milder face; Terror had ceased, . . . 727 *Prelude* 11. 2
And, when that pleasant toil had ceased to please, 742 *Prelude* 13. 137
Ceased from his task; and she with faltering voice 769 *Excursion* 1. 891
The old Man ceased: he saw that I was moved; . 770 *Excursion* 1. 917
He ceased. Ere long the sun declining shot . . 771 *Excursion* 1. 957
And what, when breath hath ceased, we may become. . 789 *Excursion* 3. 236
I ceased, and he resumed.—"Ah! gentle Sir, . 791 *Excursion* 3. 359
So pitiably, that, having ceased to see . . . . 804 *Excursion* 4. 171
Showered miracles, and ceased not to dispense . 811 *Excursion* 4. 658
Ceased, when she learned through what mishap I came, ... 834 *Excursion* 5. 756
That *was* attractive, and hath ceased to be! . . 843 *Excursion* 6. 318
The last hath ceased its solitary knoll. . . . 850 *Excursion* 6. 784
Those visitations, ceased to send her forth; . . 853 *Excursion* 6. 995
The Vicar ceased; and downcast looks made known 854 *Excursion* 6. 1053
With music?' (for he had not ceased to touch . 861 *Excursion* 7. 270
Of Gold-rill side; and, when the hope had ceased 867 *Excursion* 7. 637
When this involuntary strain had ceased, . . . 870 *Excursion* 7. 832
The Pastor ceased.—My venerable Friend . . . 871 *Excursion* 7. 891
When in their land the Almighty's service ceased. 877 *Excursion* 8. 195
Till their short holiday of childhood ceased, . . 878 *Excursion* 8. 281
Encouragement, hath ceased to look that way. . 880 *Excursion* 8. 388
That ceased not when his voice had ceased—as One 883 *Excursion* 8. 598
The Sage broke off. No sooner had he ceased . 890 *Excursion* 9. 417
Even as he sees; but when his voice hath ceased, 891 *Excursion* 8. 466

Ceased—*continued.*
They ceased not to surround us; change of place, 891 *Excursion* 9. 509
They had imbibed, and ceased not to receive. . 893 *Excursion* 9. 606
The rains at length have ceas'd, the winds are still'd, S. 3. 425 **The rains* 1
Issuing when shame hath ceased to check the brawls K. 8. 246 *Recluse* 1. 1. 345
Ceaseless. These, by the pale-blue rocks that ceaseless ring, ... 5. *Ev. Wk.* 166
If some, by ceaseless pains outworn, ... 223 *Wishing-gate* 44
For praise and ceaseless gratulation, poured . . 235 *Power of Sound* 207
This ceaseless play, the genuine life . . . . 499 **This Lawn* 14
Where guilt had urged them on with ceaseless goad, 504 *Warning* 73
We sojourn stunned by Ocean's ceaseless roar; . 521 *Epist. Beaumont* 4
While Hope that ceaseless leans on Pleasure's urn 611 *Desc. Sk. Quarto* 518
Make ceaseless music that composed my thoughts 636 *Prelude* 1. 277
But for the impertinent and ceaseless strife . . 831 *Excursion* 5. 617
In ceaseless pains—and strictest parsimony . . 849 *Excursion* 6. 724
Of traffic glides with ceaseless intercourse, . . 876 *Excursion* 8. 113
Of ceaseless motion, that might scarcely seem . K. 8. 242 *Recluse* 1. 1. 204
Ceases. Are vanished; gladness ceases in the groves, 105 *Artegal* 200
Of beauty never ceases to enrich . . . . . 508 *F. Stone* 7
And love ceases to rebel, ... 550 *Hermit's Cell* 1. 34
With roaring sound, that ceases not to flow, . . 782 *Excursion* 2. 702
Ceasing. *See* **Never-ceasing.**
So looked; not ceasing to pursue . . . . . 112 **How rich* 9
And without ceasing, since it was daylight; . . 561 *Cuck. and Night.* 268
Not ceasing, forth appeared in view a band . . 777 *Excursion* 2. 386
The naked spirit, ceasing to deplore . . . . 820 *Excursion* 4. 1250
Cecilia. So looked Cecilia when she drew . . 112 **How rich* 7
And rapt Cecilia, seraph-haunted Queen . . . 434 *Ecc. Sonn.* 2. 24. 11
Cedar. And followed on, through woods of gloomy cedar, ... 70 *Bord.* 1804
With pine and cedar spreading wide . . . . 407 *White Doe* 992
Emerging from a cedar shade . . . . . . 407 *White Doe* 1000
If but the Cedar thrive that near them stands, . 546 **The embowering* 3
Cedar's. That shook on Lebanon the cedar's top, . 354 *Aquap.* 138
Cedars. Like cedars on the top of Lebanon . . . 870 *Excursion* 7. 846
Ceiling. Down from the ceiling, by the chimney's edge, ... 133 *Michael* 110
The notes are from the floor or ceiling; . . . 143 **Driven in* 21
Swinging from the smoky ceiling! . . . . . 177 *Waggoner* 2. 69
Of some huge cave, whose rocky ceiling casts . . 756 *Excursion* 1. 11
Cellinged. Ceilinged and roofed; that is so fair a thing 254 *Wild Duck's Nest* 4
Celandine. 'Tis the little Celandine. . . . . . 160 **Pansies, lilies* 8
Little, humble Celandine. . . . . 160 **Pansies, lilies* 56
Celandine! and long ago, ... 161 **Pleasures newly* 7
There is a Flower, the lesser Celandine, . . . 571 **There is a Flower* 1
Celebrate. And Time the Shadow;—there to celebrate, 185 *Yew-trees* 28
Unheard by them, their deeds shall celebrate! . 328 *Ode 1815* 86
To celebrate their great deliverance; . . . . 420 *Ecc. Sonn.* 1. 7. 9
A theme for angels, when they celebrate . . . 540 *Grace Darl.* 17
Upon this hour, the bond to celebrate!" . . . 625 *Æneid* 115
The hallowed theme) will rise and celebrate . . 863 *Excursion* 7. 375
Celerities. And to celerities of lawless force; . . 330 *Ode: Thanks.* 118
Celestial. Reflected beams of that celestial light . 118 *Maternal Grief* 17
Spangled with drops of that celestial shower. . . 169 *Love lies Bleeding* 17
Veil of such celestial hue; . . . . 181 *Waggoner* 4. 113
Celestial pity I again implore;— . . . . . 209 *Laod.* 5
Of power ethereal and celestial grace, ... 231 **The gentlest Poet* 37
By the celestial Muses glorified. . . . . . 251 **Pelion and* 8
Beyond the stars, celestial Paradise, ... 284 *Departure* 4
A foil to his celestial cheek! . . . . . . 299 *Brownie's Cell* 100
"Though from my celestial home, ... 323 *Ode 1814* 29
What ye, celestial Maids! have often sung . . 325 *Ode 1814* 128
Thy saintly rapture with celestial aim: . . . 326 *Sobieski* 5
The sacred ENGELBERG, celestial Bands, . . . 338 *Engelberg* 7
Throngs of celestial visages, ... 343 *Eclipse* 58
The turmoil hushed, celestial springs . . . . 371 *Eg. Maid* 145
Celestial Power, as much with love as light? . . 392 **Though joy* 14
The gentle Una, of celestial birth, ... 395 *White Doe: Ded.* 7
Encouraged of celestial power; . . . . . . 416 *White Doe* 1833
Can never cease to bear celestial fruit. . . . 431 *Ecc. Sonn.* 2. 10. 5
Suffused with blushes of celestial hue, . . . 434 *Ecc. Sonn.* 2. 22. 6
Of high with low, celestial with terrene! . . . 434 *Ecc. Sonn.* 2. 25. 14
And in his prison breathes celestial air. . . . 440 *Ecc. Sonn.* 2. 45. 8
And the pure spirit of celestial light . . . . 441 *Ecc. Sonn.* 3. 4. 12
Such hues from their celestial Urn . . . . 458 **Had this* 61
Warmed our sad being with celestial light, . . 476 **Tranquillity! the* 9
Thee, thee my life's celestial sign!) . . . . 497 *Lycoris* 28
Shed round the altar a celestial calm; . . . . 500 *Humanity* 24
Yea, to celestial Choirs, GRACE DARLING's name! 541 *Grace Darl.* 97
Following the Lamb celestial," quoth she, . . 554 *Prioress* 130
I sprinkle thee with soft celestial dews, . . . 582 *Invoc. Earth* 21
Apparelled in celestial light, ... 587 *Immortality* 4
"I look'd obedience: the celestial Fair . . . 619 *School Ex.* 111
For know we not that from celestial spheres, . . 628 **Deign, Sovereign* 25
Celestial, lay unseen the pastoral vales . . . 725 *Prelude* 10. 524
Hope of a flight celestial, will produce . . . 805 *Excursion* 4. 292
Like those celestial messengers beheld . . . . 812 *Excursion* 4. 716
In man's celestial spirit; virtue thus . . . . 817 *Excursion* 4. 1071
Of those celestial splendours; grey the vault— . 895 *Excursion* 9. 760
By powers celestial tossed on land and sea . . K. 8. 281 **Arms and* 4
Celibates. Taught by the hooded Celibates of St. Bees. 467 *St. Bees* 117
Cell. Calls forth the woodman from his desert cell, 12 *Desc. Sk.* 124
On joys that might disgrace the captive's cell, . 13 *Desc. Sk.* 138
And search the affections to their inmost cell; . 19 *Desc. Sk.* 523
In Robin's bosom, as a chosen cell. . . . . 143 **Driven in* 26
In clearer light the moss-built cell . . . . 169 *Wren's Nest* 54
In the impenetrable cell . . . . 171 *Kitten* 96
Cowering beside her rifted cell, ... 175 *Waggoner* 1. 176
—They all were with her in her cell; . . . . 194 *Ruth* 202

Champion—*continued.*

The champion, Jack the Giant-killer : Lo !	691 *Prelude* 7. 280
A humble champion of the better cause ;	870 *Excursion* 7. 850
Of the mild-hearted Champion, save this stone,	872 *Excursion* 7. 966

Champion's. Her Champion's praise recounted ; . 478 *Somnamb.* 56
Through thy champion's faithful heart . . . L. 2. 190 **Queen and* 15

Champions. " Ask not for whom, O Champions true !

	372 *Eg. Maid* 235
Though he, devoutest of all Champions, ere .	373 *Eg. Maid* 273
And with those grey-haired champions stood,	405 *White Doe* 821
Had not thy holy Church her champions bred,	442 *Ecc. Sonn.* 3. 10. 6
From champions of the desperate law . . .	534 **Blest* is 75
Of strenuous champions, in scholastic arts .	839 *Excursion* 6. 57
Two doughty champions ; flaming Jacobite .	845 *Excursion* 6. 458
To cope with stoutest champions of the bowl !	859 *Excursion* 7. 121

Chance. Trusted my life to what chance bounty

yields,	32 *Guilt* 435
By lawless curiosity or chance, ...	36 *Guilt* 663
But for the scene which we by chance have wit-	
nessed.	42 *Bord.* 275
By chance had thither strayed ;	85 *Shepherd-boys* 86
No ill was feared ; till one of them by chance	101 *Brothers* 373
And such chance food as outlaws can obtain, .	103 *Artegal* 101
If any chance to heave a sigh, ...	117 *Affl. Marg.* 73
By chance of business coming within reach .	125 *V. and J.* 288
Me to save from chance of harm	140 *Arm. Lady* 40
By chance retiring from the glare of noon . .	150 **When, to* 46
And one chance look to Thee should turn, .	158 **In youth* 50
As chance would have it, passing by . . .	175 *Waggoner* 1. 130
For, cries the Sailor, " Glorious chance . .	177 *Waggoner* 2. 43
Or note (translucent summer's happiest chance !).	190 **Lyre ! though* 33
Housing, with God's good help, by choice or chance;	196 *Resolution* 104
Were in this place the guests of Chance : . . .	289 *Stepping West.* 5
By choice or chance, did thither come . . .	296 *Highland Boy* 138
Blind Chance, a volunteer ally, ...	391 *Highland Broach* 87
Or chance presented to his eye, ...	406 *White Doe* 979
But quick the turns of chance and change, .	408 *White Doe* 1119
Of chance and change, that hath been brought	413 *White Doe* 1595
(Such have I seen) whom chance of birth . .	414 *White Doe* 1635
Wander the Ministers of God, as chance . .	449 *Ecc. Sonn.* 3. 36. 4
On chance dependent, and the fickle star . .	458 *Sea-shore* 7
Name that first struck by chance my startled ear)	465 **The cattle* 8
Perilous is sweeping change, all chance unsound. .	514 **Blest Statesman* 14
Should sometimes think, where'er they chance to	
spy	530 *Poor Robin* 31
" Such bounty is no gift of chance," . . .	545 *Russ. Fug.* 329
Whom chance may lead to this retreat, . .	550 *Hermit's Cell* 2. 2
A single Glow-worm did I chance to espy ; .	622 **Among all* 6
Even with the chance equipment of that hour,	633 *Prelude* 1. 92
By chance collisions and quaint accidents .	641 *Prelude* 1. 589
Whom chance had stationed in the very room .	653 *Prelude* 3. 294
Saluted the chance comer on the road, . .	656 *Prelude* 3. 472
It chance to wear, is sweetest if the heart . .	660 *Prelude* 4. 148
To land a single volume, saved by chance, .	677 *Prelude* 6. 145
Our comrades gone before. By fortunate chance,	683 *Prelude* 6. 577
Was One, a cripple from his birth, whom chance .	688 *Prelude* 7. 91
Of chance spectators, chiefly dissolute men .	692 *Prelude* 7. 360
And three chance human wanderers, in calm thought	747 *Prelude* 14. 65
Had been a blessèd home, it was my chance .	766 *Excursion* 1. 642
Or, rather say, sate down by very chance, .	776 *Excursion* 2. 308
The sport of Nature, aided by blind Chance .	788 *Excursion* 3. 126
And her blind helper Chance, do *then* suffice .	788 *Excursion* 3. 140
Casts, if he ever chance to enter here, . .	788 *Excursion* 3. 163
This sorry Legend ; which by chance we found	816 *Excursion* 4. 1007
Have been bestowed, through course of common	
chance,	824 *Excursion* 5. 131
Imposes, whensoe'er untoward chance . . .	834 *Excursion* 5. 764
In quarters unobnoxious to such chance, . .	835 *Excursion* 5. 868
And if by chance a stranger, wandering there, .	871 *Excursion* 7. 878
In a deep pool, by happy chance we saw . .	890 *Excursion* 9. 439
And unsought pleasures springing up by chance ;	892 *Excursion* 9. 521

Chance-acquaintance. And, for my chance-acquaintance, ladies bright, ... 488 *Pers. Talk* 5

Chanced. Whose body near our cottage chanced to

lie ;	35 *Guilt* 600
I chanced to see at break of day	82 *Lucy Gray* 3
And gladdened all things ; but, as chanced, within	
that very hour,	91 *Poet's Dream* 2
But, as chanced, a Cottage-maiden . . .	93 *Westmoreland Girl* 9
Of his old cottage,—as it chanced, that day, .	95 *Brothers* 19
Wandering by stealth abroad, he chanced to hear	104 *Artegal* 107
And every man I chanced to see, ...	115 *Last of Flock* 73
That thrifty Pair had lived. For, as it chanced, .	133 *Michael* 131
Were wasted, as I chanced to walk alone .	148 *Joanna* 78
It chanced that I saw standing in a dell . .	202 *Hart-leap* 102
It chanced that by a taper's light	244 *P. B.* 739
Whom in a sunny glade I chanced to see, . .	362 **List—'twas* 76
One summer-day I chanced to see	484 *Simon Lee* 73
But, as it chanced, Sir William having learned	548 **Stranger ! this* 8
It chanc'd that Andrew pass'd that way . . .	621 *Andrew Jones* 21
Upon Winander's spacious breast, it chanced .	664 *Prelude* 4. 373
By the sea-side, perusing, so it chanced, . .	666 *Prelude* 5. 59
Seeking I knew not what, I chanced to cross .	672 *Prelude* 5. 432
From the receding vessel's deck, we chanced .	680 *Prelude* 6. 344
For the abject multitude. And when we chanced	717 *Prelude* 9. 509
And I, as chanced, the foremost of the band ; .	746 *Prelude* 14. 34
As they had chanced to fall. Her infant Babe .	768 *Excursion* 1. 829
Of hidden beauty have I chanced to espy . .	776 *Excursion* 2. 352
When his own breath was silent, chanced to hear	814 *Excursion* 4. 855
As chanced, the portals of the sacred Pile . .	824 *Excursion* 5. 138
And some one, as she entered, having chanced	853 *Excursion* 6. 974
Have been portrayed, I guess not ; but it chanced	865 *Excursion* 7. 540

Chanced—*continued.*

His flock into the vale, but as it chanced, . . .	K.8. 224 **I will* 13

Chance-defilements. Upon thy chance-defilements—
withered twigs . . . . . S.3. 433 **The doubt* 46

Chance-desires. I feel the weight of chance-desires : 492 *Duty* 38

Chance-discovered. On me the chance-discovered
sight . . . . 79 *Sparrow's Nest* 3

Chance-gathered. Share his chance-gathered meal ;
and, finally, ... 569 *Cumb. Beg.* 195

Chancel. Devoutly stretched upon their chancel

floors.	430 *Ecc. Sonn.* 2. 8. 8
In seemly rows ; the chancel only showed . .	824 *Excursion* 5. 156

Chance-mention. May find chance-mention on this
sacred ground)— . . . . 868 *Excursion* 7. 734

Chance-regards. Who walk this favoured ground.

But chance-regards,	828 *Excursion* 5. 417

Chances. Thoughts, chances, sights, or doings, which
we tell . . . . 522 *Epist. Beaumont* 54

Chance-sunbeam. As a chance-sunbeam from his
memory fell . . . . . 528 **Those breathing* 102

Chance-temptation. Of chance-temptation, ere his
journey end, ... 383 *Duddon* 30. 6

Chanceth. But, as it sometimes chanceth, from the
might . . . . 195 *Resolution* 22

Chancing. Chancing to pass this way some six

months gone,	47 *Bord.* 573
But, chancing to espy a path	240 *P. B.* 336
Till, chancing on that lofty ridge to pass . .	784 *Excursion* 2. 811

Change. The spacious landscape change in form and

hue !	4 *Ev. Wk.* 99
" 'Twas a hard change ; an evil time was come ; .	29 *Guilt* 271
Of such rough storm, this happy change to view."	30 *Guilt* 317
To tell the change that Voice within her wrought	35 *Guilt* 622
Father, I would not change that sacred feeling .	40 *Bord.* 139
And will be so through every change of fortune .	50 *Bord.* 721
Than make me change my course. Dear Marma-	
duke,	55 *Bord.* 992
We talked of change, of winter gone, . . .	81 †*Mother's Return* 37
Five minutes past—and, O the change ! . .	82 †*Mother's Return* 53
Why you would change sweet Liswyn farm . .	86 *Anecdote* 43
Wouldst change the course of things in all men's	
sight !	105 *Artegal* 173
Such change in thy estate	105 *Artegal* 215
There is a change—and I am poor ; . . .	111 *A Complaint* 1
—Such change, and at the very door	111 *A Complaint* 17
And range about, disquieted in change, . . .	172 *Infant Daughter* 54
Rich change, and multiplied creation ! . . .	178 *Waggoner* 3. 41
Much witnessing of change and cheer, . . .	192 *Gipsies* 11
He spake of plants that hourly change . . .	193 *Ruth* 55
Nor did he change ; but kept in lofty place . .	205 *Brougham* 167
Nor should the change be mourned, even if the joys	210 *Laod.* 68
Help, under every change of adverse fate. . .	212 *Dion* 17
That Destiny her course should change ; too just	214 *Dion* 115
If still the reckless change we mourn, . . .	224 **'Tis gone* 43
When some great change gives boundless scope .	225 *Present.* 49
Their mansions unsusceptible of change, . .	227 *Vernal Ode* 72
And humours change, are spurned like weeds : .	228 *Devot. Incit.* 49
As if some Protean art the change had wrought, .	230 *Clouds* 75
" Small change it made in Peter's heart . . .	239 *P. B.* 251
Not only stop but turn, and change	243 *P. B.* 657
The mosques and spires change countenance, . .	244 *P. B.* 689
Of outward change, there blooms a deathless flower,	256 **Yes ! hope* 13
That change :—age on thy brow was smoothed—	
thy cold	258 **Even so* 6
Of civil conflict, nor the wrecks of change, . .	262 **Not Love* 2
Of bitter change, and bids the flowers beware ; .	263 **While not* 6
(Misdeem it not a cankerous change) may grow .	267 **Desponding Father* 11
And must he too the ruthless change bemoan	282 *Railway* 6
Change for the worse might please, incursion bold	284 *Departure* 9
That, rough or smooth, is full of change, . .	295 *Highland Boy* 54
Beneath the change ; who heard a claim . . .	299 *Brownie's Cell* 49
Perpetual emptiness ! unceasing change ! . .	307 **Great men* 11
When men change swords for ledgers, and desert .	307 **When I* 3
To fear, to change, to cowardice, and death ? .	308 **These times* 14
But She through many a change of form hath gone,	311 **Who rises* 15
Is this the only change that time can show ? . .	311 **Who rises* 40
The course of things, and change the creed . .	312 **Who rises* 62
Of irksome change, or threats from saddening	
power.	327 *Ode 1815* 16
A silent and unlooked-for change, ...	343 *Eclipse* 10
From mortal change, aught that is born on earth	356 *Aquap.* 230
Change, with a brow not insolent, though stern. .	358 **Is this* 14
In vain ; the sky will change to sunny blue, .	360 *Albano* 7
And temples, doomed to milder change, unfold .	367 *Trajan* 3
No change ;—the fair Izonda he had wooed .	373 *Eg. Maid* 292
Through mortal change and immortality ; . .	374 *Eg. Maid* 346
A Protean change seems wrought while I pursue .	377 *Duddon* 4. 3
" Change me, some God, into that breathing rose !"	377 *Duddon* 7. 1
Shalt change thy temper ; and, with many a shock	381 *Duddon* 20. 11
For thee, O SCOTT ! compelled to change . .	386 *Yarrow Rev.* 49
To mark some change of service. As the swell	387 *Roslin* 3
Survives imagination—to the change . . .	388 **The pibroch's* 12
Of rash change, ominous for the public weal. . .	394 **No more* 30
We by a lamentable change were taught . . .	395 *White Doe: Ded.* 22
But quick the turns of chance and change, . .	408 *White Doe* 1119
Change wide and deep the Land had seen, . .	410 *White Doe* 1262
No ; will not all men deem the change . . .	411 *White Doe* 1401
Of chance and change, that hath been brought .	413 *White Doe* 1595
But now, when such sad change was wrought, .	415 *White Doe* 1770
To Creed or Ritual brings no fatal change. . .	426 *Ecc. Sonn.* 1. 31. 14

Change—*continued.*
For change, to whom the new looks always green! . 436 *Ecc. Sonn.* 2. 33. 3
The soothing recompense, the welcome change. . 454 *Sea-side* 10
Through every change its aspects undergo— . . 455 **Not in the lucid* 23
Is crossed by knowledge, or by dread, of change, 458 *Sea-shore* 18
Gently to brook decline and fatal change ; . . 461 **Queen of* 54
And, spite of change, for me thou keep'st the same 463 **They called* 4
My mind as restless and as apt to change ; . . 470 *†From early* 2
If the whole State must suffer mortal change, . 471 *Tynwald* 13
What change shall happen next to Nunnery Dell ? 477 *Nunnery* 13
Of future change, that point of vision, whence . 477 *Steamboats* 7
But, oh the heavy change !—bereft . . . . 483 *Simon Lee* 25
My hopes no more must change their name, . . 492 *Duty* 39
And if Time leagued with adverse Change . . 503 *Warning* 7
Perilous is sweeping change, all chance unsound. . 514 **Blest Statesman* 14
Portentous change when History can appear . . 514 **Portentous change* 1
Crime might lie better hid. And, should the change 519 *Pun. Death* 8. 9
Whose goodness knows no change, whose love is sure, 519 *Pun. Death* 11. 12
Does in this change exceedingly rejoice ; . . . 520 *Pun. Death* 12. 10
This ever-graceful change, ... 526 **The soaring* 26
And admiration lost, by change of place . . . 527 **Those breathing* 23
But if the change restore his birthright, then, . 527 **Those breathing* 25
In spite of season's change, its own demand. . . 531 **I know* 18
A mournful change, should Reason fail to bring . 533 **Once I* 38
O more than mighty change ! If e'er . . . . 545 *Russ. Fug.* 353
No change can falsify ! . . . . 550 *Hermit's Cell* 5. 16
The old man does not change his course, the boy 566 *Cumb. Beg.* 40
That never art secure from dolorous change ! . 573 *Chiabrera* 2. 14
Calmed in his soul the fear of change and death. . 587 *Crosth.* 18
Might I pursue this theme through every change . 639 *Prelude* 1. 476
Through every change of growth and of decay, . 646 *Prelude* 2. 264
Hence life, and change, and beauty, solitude . . 646 *Prelude* 2. 294
A northern villager. As if the change . . . 649 *Prelude* 3. 35
Yet true it is, that I had made a change . . . 652 *Prelude* 3. 204
Of change, congratulation or regret, ... 662 *Prelude* 4. 240
Superior, and incapable of change, ... 677 *Prelude* 6. 137
By change of accidents, or even, to speak . . . 677 *Prelude* 6. 186
For utterance, to think what easy change . . . 679 *Prelude* 6. 283
And Earth did change her images and forms . . 682 *Prelude* 6. 492
With danger, varying as the seasons change), . . 682 *Prelude* 6. 510
From disappointment, not to find some change . 688 *Prelude* 7. 96
A change of purpose in young Whittington, . . 688 *Prelude* 7. 112
With ominous change, which, night by night, provoked . . . . 695 *Prelude* 7. 535
The elements, and seasons as they change, . . 700 *Prelude* 8. 102
That shift and vanish, change and interchange . 707 *Prelude* 8. 571
Of that great change wandered in perfect faith, . 714 *Prelude* 9. 299
Custom and habit, novelty and change ; . . . 714 *Prelude* 9. 325
Change and subversion from that hour. No shock 722 *Prelude* 10. 268
Is not sequestered—what a change is here ! . . 724 *Prelude* 10. 428
But change of them into their contraries ; . . 730 *Prelude* 11. 180
From ruin and from change, and all the grief . . 770 *Excursion* 1. 950
How shall I trace the change, how bear to tell . 775 *Excursion* 2. 246
And that is joy to him. When change of times . 778 *Excursion* 2. 474
Temptation so prevailing as to change . . . . 781 *Excursion* 2. 616
Went through his usual tasks, a silent change . 785 *Excursion* 2. 893
And change, and emptiness, these freaks of Nature 788 *Excursion* 3. 139
What dignity, what beauty, in this change . . 790 *Excursion* 3. 314
For different lot, or change to higher sphere, . 795 *Excursion* 3. 630
Her cheek to change its colour, was conveyed . . 795 *Excursion* 3. 641
And partner of my loss.—O heavy change ! . . 795 *Excursion* 3. 669
—In Britain, ruled a panic dread of change ; . . 798 *Excursion* 3. 827
Quick change of objects ; and, to laugh alone, . 799 *Excursion* 3. 903
" Possessions vanish, and opinions change, . . 802 *Excursion* 4. 69
Change manifold, for better or for worse : . . . 803 *Excursion* 4. 125
Of time and change disdaining, takes its course . 804 *Excursion* 4. 184
For you should undergo a sudden change ; . . 805 *Excursion* 4. 283
Or solace, varying as the seasons change. . . . 810 *Excursion* 4. 587
Auxiliar to divine. That change shall clothe . . 820 *Excursion* 4. 1249
How vain, thought I, is it by change of place . 822 *Excursion* 5. 20
And, with this change, sharp air and falling leaves, 828 *Excursion* 5. 409
Or, if the change demanded no regret, ... 837 *Excursion* 5. 976
Such universal change as autumn makes . . . 840 *Excursion* 6. 159
With little change of general sentiment, . . . 845 *Excursion* 6. 470
And, by as salutary change, compelled . . . 859 *Excursion* 7. 154
Deploring changes past, or dreading change . . 875 *Excursion* 8. 38
Of this great change I look ; and there behold . 876 *Excursion* 8. 152
What lamentable change, a year—a month— . . 878 *Excursion* 8. 256
And thirst for change ; or habit hath subdued . 878 *Excursion* 8. 294
" Change wide, and deep, and silently performed, 889 *Excursion* 9. 384
They ceased not to surround us ; change of place, 891 *Excursion* 9. 509
Producing change of beauty ever new. . . . . 891 *Excursion* 9. 511
Who saw, of change were conscious—had become 893 *Excursion* 9. 599
Beauty not therefore wanting change to stir . . S. 3. 433 **The doubt* 30

Changed. *See* **Unchanged.**
Back on himself ; but changed into a curse. . . 51 *Bord.* 748
And everlasting hills themselves were changed. . 96 *Brothers* 99
How changed from him who, born to highest place, 103 *Artegal* 94
Be changed, that was so fair to view, ... 145 *Her Eyes* 64
With all its lovely images, was changed . . . 149 **A narrow* 69
Changed countenance, like an object sullied o'er . 173 *Infant Daughter* 62
Seems changed into a pallid spot. . . . . . 173 *Waggoner* 1. 12
Though changed, no doubt, from what I was when first . . . . 206 *Tintern* 66
That love which changed—for wan disease, . . 225 *Primrose* 37
But quickly Peter's mood is changed, ... 240 *P. B.* 346
Oh what a Wreck ! how changed in mien and speech ! . . . . 280 **Oh what* 1
Hung round its top, on wings that changed their hues at will. . . . . 338 *Engelberg* 9

Changed—*continued.*
Of the changed City's long-departed power, . . 355 *Aquap.* 167
Changed, as the pair approached the light, . . 371 *Eg. Maid* 178
Though we were changed and changing ; . . . 386 *Yarrow Rev.* 36
And to green meadows changed the swampy shores ? 468 *St. Bees* 137
Or changed and changing, I not seldom gaze . . 510 *F. Stone* 113
For which, with changèd, pale, and deadly face, . 563 *Troilus* 18
With changèd face, and piteous to behold ; . . 563 *Troilus* 37
Stiff in its members, withered, changed of hue." . 571 **There is a Flower* 19
A drooping daisy changed into a cup . . . . 584 **With copious* 48
On the lone mountain top, their chang'd estate. . 611 *Desc. Sk. Quarto* 489
Resolves that Cupid, chang'd in form and face . 624 *Æneid* 3
Be changed for one whose glory cannot fade. . . 628 **Deign, Sovereign* 16
Had changed their functions ; some, plebeian cards 640 *Prelude* 1. 522
Or circumstance, how far soever changed . . 650 *Prelude* 3. 103
In youth, or *to* be changed in after years. . . 650 *Prelude* 3. 104
Changed also slowly and insensibly. . . . . 652 *Prelude* 3. 206
Changed like a garden in the heat of spring, . . 661 *Prelude* 4. 195
Before us, fast as clouds are changed in heaven. . 682 *Prelude* 6. 493
Though heedless of such honours now, and changed : 711 *Prelude* 9. 142
Changed, and the unbroken dream entangled me 724 *Prelude* 10. 410
That neither passed away nor changed, I gazed . 726 *Prelude* 10. 527
Frenchmen had changed a war of self-defence . 730 *Prelude* 11. 207
With my true self ; for, though bedimmed and changed . . . . 732 *Prelude* 11. 342
Much, as it seemed, I was no further changed . 732 *Prelude* 11. 343
Dies with him, or is changed ; and very soon . . 763 *Excursion* 1. 473
Was changed. As she unlocked the door, she said, 767 *Excursion* 1. 752
And so I waste my time : for I am changed ; . . 768 *Excursion* 1. 767
To flow, when purposes are lightly changed ? . . 773 *Excursion* 2. 151
We shall not sleep, but we shall all be changed ! . 780 *Excursion* 2. 578
The shepherd's grey to martial scarlet changed, . 869 *Excursion* 7. 764
Her temper changed, and bowed to other laws) . 873 *Excursion* 7. 1020
The appearances of things ! From such, how changed . . . . 894 *Excursion* 9. 712
Changed to a crimson flower ; when he, whose pride S. 3. 434 **The doubt* 82
All shall survive—though changed their office, all K.8. 257 *Recluse* 1.1.743

Changeful. Involve their serpent-necks in changeful rings, ... 6 *Ev. Wk.* 246
What more changeful than the sea ? . . . . 222 *Triad* 141
" In vain, through every changeful year, . . . 239 *P. B.* 246
Do serve with all their changeful pageantry ; . . 252 *Picture* 10
O Nature—in thy changeful visions, ... 300 *Bran* 31
For earth through heaven, for heaven, by changeful earth, ... 362 **List—'twas* 47
Life as she is—our changeful Life, ... 386 *Yarrow Rev.* 95
When and wherever, in this changeful world, . . 538 **In desultory* 21
Tracking with silvering path the changeful gale. . 598 *Ev. Wk. Quarto* 344
Yes, I remember when the changeful earth, . . 640 *Prelude* 1. 559
And changeful colours by invisible links . . . 641 *Prelude* 1. 611
Six changeful years have vanished since I first . 687 *Prelude* 7. 1
The changeful language of their countenances . 698 *Prelude* 7. 758
Our course submitting to the changeful breeze . 772 *Excursion* 2. 84
Is the mute company of changeful clouds ; . . 808 *Excursion* 4. 461
Varying its tincture with the changeful light, . . 824 *Excursion* 5. 161
Thus, when in changeful April fields are white . 830 *Excursion* 5. 531
Through all the seasons of the changeful year, . 888 *Excursion* 9. 266

Changes. And yet, some changes must take place among you : . . . . 97 *Brothers* 127
For accidents and changes such as these, . . . 97 *Brothers* 146
On which it stood ; great changes have been wrought 138 *Michael* 478
Through all the changes of the year, ... 182 *Waggoner* 4. 226
All changes of the element, ... 226 *Present.* 74
And, though past pomp no changes can restore, . 272 *Ruins* 13
Who, yielding not to changes Time has made, . 279 **All praise* 3
And the changes it brings had no power to unbind. 364 *Vallomb.* 28
The Princess, passive to all changes : . . . . 371 *Eg. Maid* 182
What harmonious pensive changes . . . . . 397 *White Doe* 79
Changes her means, the Enthusiast as a dupe . 425 *Ecc. Sonn.* 1. 28. 2
Whose virtue changes to a christian Flower . . 445 *Ecc. Sonn.* 3. 20. 3
Turn to minuter changes at our feet ; . . . . 456 **Soft as* 7
Shall find thee through all changes of the year : . 490 *Tribute : Dog* 8
Nought but her changes. Thus, ungrateful Nation ! 505 *Warning* 146
Man changes, but not Thou ! . . . . . . 506 **While from* 24
So changes mortal Life with fleeting years ; . . 533 **Once I* 37
Of shadowy things work endless changes,—there, 674 *Prelude* 5. 599
And yielded to all changes of the scene . . . 694 *Prelude* 7. 474
If you imagine changes slowly wrought, . . . 795 *Excursion* 3. 616
Of social nature changes evermore . . . . . 872 *Excursion* 7. 1000
Deploring changes past, or dreading change . . 875 *Excursion* 8. 38
Or beautifies, like changes undergoes, ... S. 3. 434 **The doubt* 63
Thy changes, which to wiser Spirits seem . . K.8. 301 **And oh* 5

Changing. *See* **Ever-changing.**
Of beauty, by the changing moon adorned, . . 172 *Infant Daughter* 24
Though we were changed and changing ; . . . 386 *Yarrow Rev.* 36
Or changed and changing, I not seldom gaze . . 510 *F. Stone* 113
Lay bedded, changing oftentimes its form . . 685 *Prelude* 6. 706
Faint, but more tranquil, like the changing sun . 699 *Prelude* 8. 51
Opinion ever changing ! I have seen . . . . 818 *Excursion* 4. 1132

Channel. *See* **Slope-channel.**
Whirled adown the rocky channel, ... 93 *Westmoreland Girl* 13
Albeit his deep-worn channel doth immure . . 379 *Duddon* 12. 2
In deep and awful channel runs . . . . . 401 *White Doe* 469
That o'er the channel holds august command, . 470 **Did pangs* 7
Along a channel smooth and deep, ... 499 *Memory* 28
A channel paved by man's officious care. . . . 659 *Prelude* 4. 56
Which in the stony channel of the stream . . . 683 *Prelude* 6. 582
There lies the channel, and original bed, . . . 837 *Excursion* 5. 1004
Down the deep channel of the stream he went, . K.8. 228 **I will* 133

Channelled. Ask of the channelled rivers if they held 864 *Excursion* 7 489

Channels. Channels for tears; no Naiad shouldst thou be,— 268 **Brook ! whose* 9
Like this unheard-of, and their channels wear 392 *Avon* 3
Runs through blind channels of an unknown tongue. 436 *Ecc. Sonn.* 2. 33. 14
Forbear to shape due channels which the Flood 450 *Ecc. Sonn.* 3. 38. 6
The shores and channels, working Nature's will 495 *Fact* 32
I love the Brooks which down their channels fret, 590 *Immortality* 196
Ye long deep channels for the Atlantic's voice, 702 *Prelude* 8. 217
Ran in new channels, leaving old ones dry; 730 *Prelude* 11. 185
Through many channels, ever and anon 883 *Excursion* 8. 580
The shores and channels, working Nature's will S. 3. 427 **My Son* 3
Chant. *See* **Chaunt.**
And we too chant the praise of his good deeds. 54 *Bord.* 907
Leave for one chant;—the dulcet sound 234 *Power of Sound* 134
Thee might thy Minions crown, and chant thy power, 261 **Fair Prime* 7
And let us chant a passing stave, 291 *Rob Roy* 7
—Chant the Deliverer's praise in every tongue! 326 *Sobieski* 11
To chant a love-spell, never intertwined 336 *Staub-bach* 8
To chant, as glides the boat along, 338 *Brientz* 14
To chant, as Angels do above, 338 *Brientz* 16
Moved to the chant of sober litanies. 346 *Processions* 40
Chant in full choir their innocent Te Deum. 367 **If with* 14
Thy cradle decks;—to chant thy birth, thou hast 376 *Duddon* 2. 6
The Torrents chant their praise, inspiring scorn 383 *Duddon* 29. 12
Well pleased that future Bards should chant 386 *Yarrow Rev.* 107
To chant, in strains of heavenly glory, 399 *White Doe* 335
Their nests, or chant a gratulating hymn 420 *Ecc. Sonn.* 1. 7. 3
His voice shall chant, in accents clear, 507 **While from* 61
To chant your praise; nor can approach you now 685 *Prelude* 6. 672
Will chant together." Thereafter, as the shades 687 *Prelude* 7. 31
Would chant, in lonely peace, the spousal verse 755 *Recluse* 1. 1. 810
And the soft woodlark here did never chant 818 *Excursion* 4. 1168
Chanted. *See* **Chaunted.**
Of holy rites chanted in measured round? 11 *Desc. Sk.* 58
This Child, I chanted to myself a lay, 120 *Emigrant Mother* 10
Chanted his pretty songs, when you 155 *Waterfall* 39
Chanted in love that casts out fear 285 *Grave of Burns* 83
For prayer in stillness, or the chanted rite; 430 *Ecc. Sonn.* 2. 6. 8
Am I deceived? Or is their requiem chanted 430 *Ecc. Sonn.* 2. 8. 9
Of self-reproach) have chanted elegies 470 **A youth* 7
And chanted hymns and stiller voice of prayer, 522 *Epist. Beaumont* 73
With hymns resounded, and the chanted rite; 547 **Beneath yon* 6
But chanted by your Orphan Quire 577 **I come* 31
Of the gross fictions chanted in the streets 812 *Excursion* 4. 732
Chanter. Chanter by heaven attracted, whom no bars 154 *Morn. Ex.* 55
Chanting. Chanting with indefatigable bill, 271 **Fame tells* 7
Chanting for patriot heroes the reward 325 *Ode 1814* 116
Chanting her low-voiced hymn, take pride 366 **Ye Trees* 7
While Tweed, best pleased in chanting a blithe strain, 387 *Scott* 6
Chanting in barbarous ears a tuneful prayer— 422 *Ecc. Sonn.* 1. 14. 8
From Monks in Ely chanting service high, 426 *Ecc. Sonn.* 1. 30. 2
Chantry. *See* **Chauntry.**
Pass, pass who will, yon chantry door; 398 *White Doe* 242
Rose, where she touched the strand, the Chantry of St. Bees. 466 *St. Bees* 36
Her chantry blazed with sacrilegious fire, 466 *St. Bees* 58
Chants. *See* **Chaunts.**
The sand-lark chants a joyous song; 84 *Shepherd-boys* 24
While heaven's vast sea of voices chants their praise. 474 **On to* 14
A thrush resorts, and annually chants, 851 *Excursion* 6. 864
Chaos. And on the verge of Chaos hang in fear. 284 *Departure* 12
Bounds calm and clear the chaos still and hoar; 611 *Desc.Sk.Quarto* 503
Havoc and Chaos blast a thousand vales, 615 *Desc.Sk.Quarto* 695
The froward chaos of futurity, 671 *Prelude* 5. 349
I pass them unalarmed. Not Chaos, not 755 *Recluse* 1. 1. 788
Chaotic. "These craggy regions, these chaotic wilds, 807 *Excursion* 4. 427
Chapel. *See* **Mountain-chapel.**
From lonesome chapel at the mountain's feet 4 *Ev. Wk.* 138
A lonesome Chapel stands, deserted now: 73 *Bord.* 2054
The Chapel Oak of Allonville; good Angel, show it me!" 92 *Poet's Dream* 28
Holy as that which long hath crowned the Chapel of this Tree; 93 *Poet's Dream* 60
In which the Parish Chapel stood alone, 95 *Brothers* 27
And, at his birth-place, built a chapel floored 135 *Michael* 269
A little chapel stands alone, 246 *P. B.* 853
And to the chapel far withdrawn, 337 *Cath. Cantons* 11
Where, in her holy chapel, dwells 348 **Lulled by* 5
In Church or Chapel, if my curious quest 356 *Aquap.* 238
A Chapel, like a wild-bird's nest, 396 *White Doe* 27
The long-roofed chapel of King's College lift 649 *Prelude* 3. 4
Ran, ostrich-like, to reach our chapel door 653 *Prelude* 3. 304
A Romish chapel, where the vested priest 726 *Prelude* 10. 559
Of a small chapel, where, in ancient time, 784 *Excursion* 2. 814
To a small Chapel in the vale beyond) 858 *Excursion* 7. 57
And far remote the chapel stood,—remote, 859 *Excursion* 7. 140
Chapel-bell. That Chapel-bell in mercy seemed to guide me, 67 *Bord.* 1651
Chapelry. He turned to this secluded chapelry; 859 *Excursion* 7. 134
In a dependent chapelry that lies 862 *Excursion* 7. 347
Chapel's. I lighted—opened with soft touch the chapel's iron door, 92 *Poet's Dream* 41
Chapels. Far-kenned, her Chapels lurking among trees, 444 *Ecc. Sonn.* 3. 17. 12
Chaplain. Of Chaplain to a military troop 774 *Excursion* 2. 175
Chaplet. Though hasty Fame hath many a chaplet culled 254 *Dyer* 7
A chaplet in contempt of his grey locks. 722 *Prelude* 10. 314
Thy living chaplet of fresh flowers and fern, S. 3. 437 **The doubt* 201
Chaplets. And there receive green chaplets from the hands 324 *Ode 1814* 57
With laurel chaplets crowned. 543 *Russ. Fug.* 192

Char. Nought but the char that for the may-fly leaps, 597 *Ev. Wk. Quarto* 311
Character. And character of gladness, as if Spring 118 *Maternal Grief* 35
Of this late day by character in tree 170 **Never enlivened* 12
Might bow to as their Lord. What character, 231 **The gentlest Poet* 13
A savage character was seen 239 *P. B.* 294
And quieted in character—the strife, 290 *Kilchurn* 41
The genuine mien and character would trace 313 **Go back* 2
That ruled those dances wild in character?— 378 *Duddon* 11. 11
Form spirit and character from holy writ, 430 *Ecc. Sonn.* 2. 9. 11
In character, and depth of feeling, shown 509 *F. Stone* 100
Congenial with thy mind and character, 539 **Lady ! a* 21
More pleasing, and whose character I deem 647 *Prelude* 2. 380
In character, tricked out like aged trees 657 *Prelude* 3. 543
Of character, in points of wit as broad, 657 *Prelude* 3. 570
Of character or life; but at that time, 663 *Prelude* 4. 301
A character of quiet more profound 664 *Prelude* 4. 369
A character more stern. The second night, 685 *Prelude* 6. 691
And every character of form and face: 690 *Prelude* 7. 223
An image, and a character, by books 745 *Prelude* 13. 359
That individual character presents 750 *Prelude* 14. 328
Of dimmer character, he thence attained 758 *Excursion* 1. 144
The ancient rural character, composed 824 *Excursion* 5. 117
A character reflected in himself, 824 *Excursion* 5. 120
Oh! where is now the character of peace, 877 *Excursion* 8. 239
Charactered. So charactered did I maintain a strife 797 *Excursion* 3. 788
Characters. I, like a Runic Priest, in characters 147 *Joanna* 28
I chiselled out in those rude characters 148 *Joanna* 82
So shall the characters of that proud page 325 *Ode 1814* 131
Such deeds to paint, such characters to frame, 359 **Complacent Fictions* 6
The characters of every face, 398 *White Doe* 212
Nor characters of Greek or Roman fame, 419 *Ecc. Sonn.* 1. 5. 11
Impressed upon all forms the characters 639 *Prelude* 1. 471
The threshold, and large golden characters, 644 *Prelude* 2. 150
Characters of the great Apocalypse, 684 *Prelude* 6. 638
Of well-formed characters, with chalk inscribed 690 *Prelude* 7. 206
Manners and characters discriminate, 706 *Prelude* 8. 499
The characters are fresh and visible: 738 *Prelude* 12. 245
Versed in the characters of men; and bound, 875 *Excursion* 8. 62
Charcoal. Coasts, with industrious oar, the charcoal barge. 4 *Ev. Wk.* 127
By silver'd wreaths of quiet charcoal smoke, 599 *Ev. Wk. Quarto* 430
On golden evenings, while the charcoal pile 705 *Prelude* 8. 448
Charcoal-smoke. Of charcoal-smoke, that, o'er the fallen wood, 9 *Ev. Wk.* 363
Charge. O'er life's long deserts with its charge of woe, 13 *Desc. Sk.* 167
This charge of thine, then ill befall thee!—Look, 42 *Bord.* 304
Of sending to his grave our precious Charge: 50 *Bord.* 737
The Shepherds met him with his charge, 85 *Shepherd-boys* 91
Strong as an Eagle with my charge I glided round and round 92 *Poet's Dream* 37
With that sole charge he passed the city-gates, 125 *V. and J.* 244
And Betty's most especial charge, 126 *Idiot Boy* 57
With such a charge in such a spot; 175 *Waggoner* 1. 195
And of his stately Charge, which none 182 *Waggoner* 4. 268
Till oft her guardian Angel, to some charge 273 **While Anna's* 6
Ah! see her helpless Charge! enclosed 294 *Jedbor.* 49
England! all nations in this charge agree: 309 **England ! the* 9
Hast heard the constant Voice its charge repeat, 312 *Clarkson* 6
—Fly, wretched Gauls! ere they the charge renew 322 *Germans* 12
Preserve thy charge with confidence sublime— 368 *Trajan* 36
Sweep to the charge; more high, the Dacian force, 368 *Trajan* 46
Through air, to thee my Charge will I deliver. 370 *Eg. Maid* 108
"Behold to thee my Charge I now deliver! 371 *Eg. Maid* 168
My vehicle shall prove—O precious Charge! 371 *Eg. Maid* 172
Wafting your Charge to soft Parthenope! 387 *Scott* 14
To his high charge, and truly serving God, 387 *Manse* 11
Over the burning wilderness, and charge 392 *Daniel* 7
That charge, impatient Norton sought 405 *White Doe* 807
His parting charge—but ill obeyed— 407 *White Doe* 1064
For she her brother's charge revered, 409 *White Doe* 1196
Bore instantly his Charge away." 411 *White Doe* 1345
As his own charge, had disappeared, 412 *White Doe* 1452
Should that be needed for their sacred Charge; 432 *Ecc. Sonn.* 2. 13. 13
In that blest charge; let us—without offence 461 **Queen of* 44
That, if thy new-born Charge shall tread 503 **Like a* 68
Say first, to whom did we the charge confide, 522 *Epist. Beaumont* 101
For had thy charge been idle flowers, 530 *Gleaner* 21
To me the charge hath given. 545 *Russ. Fug.* 332
Gave to my charge Urbino's numerous flock. 573 *Chiabrera* 3. 7
And purge from Vice's dross my tender charge. 619 *School Ex.* 82
The charge belong'd to her alone) 620 *Birth of Love* 29
Her little charge consign'd. 620 *Birth of Love* 41
He heeded not; but, with his twofold charge 667 *Prelude* 5. 134
Enow there are on earth to take in charge 668 *Prelude* 5. 153
To bring his charge in openness; whereat, 719 *Prelude* 10. 108
The inglorious issue of that charge, and how 720 *Prelude* 10. 114
Hereafter brought in charge against mankind. 724 *Prelude* 10. 396
That could no longer hold its loathsome charge, 725 *Prelude* 10. 479
Filled with vague hopes, he undertook the charge 774 *Excursion* 2. 174
A day of sorrow. I have here a charge"— 779 *Excursion* 2. 528
—But I forget our Charge, as utterly 785 *Excursion* 2. 878
Of mere humanity, present their Charge, 826 *Excursion* 5. 277
To punctual labour in his sacred charge. 859 *Excursion* 7. 149
She reared it, and in speaking of her charge K. 8. 251 *Recluse* 1. 1. 526
Charged. Charged with greetings, benedictions, 141 *Arm. Lady* 123
Charged with a blazon on the field, 143 **Driven in* 8
Believed that earth was charged to quake 246 *P. B.* 843
Charged, and dispersed like foam: but as a flight 320 **Hunger, and* 6
Charged with remembrance of *his* sudden sting, 360 **Long has* 12

Charged—*continued.*
In priestly vest, with holy offerings charged, . . 394 *No more 15
Charged with rich words poured out in thought's defence ; . . . . 441 Ecc. Sonn. 3. 4. 2
Charged as ye are by Christ to feed and keep . . 444 Ecc. Sonn. 3. 16. 4
Charged with these offerings which their fathers bore 448 Ecc. Sonn. 3. 32. 10
Charged with those lays, and others of like mood, 538 *In desultory 15
To me came rarely charged with natural gifts, . 724 Prelude 10 401
With obligation charged, with service taxed, . . 798 Excursion 3. 840
Though beautiful, are both by Nature charged . 800 Excursion 3. 980
Of inward conscience ? with whose service charged 813 Excursion 4. 837
And mellow Autumn, charged with bounteous fruit, 828 Excursion 5. 400
—' Whence do they come ? and with what errand charged ? . . . . 858 Excursion 7. 86
As if their silent company were charged . . . 876 Excursion 8. 162
Reached her with supernatural mandates charged S.3. 436 *The doubt 177
Charger. Upon a Charger gorgeously bedecked . . 872 Excursion 7. 945
Charging. Horse charging horse, 'mid these retired domains ; . . . . 383 Duddon 29. 2
Chariot. That was its wings, its chariot, and its horse, 148 *A narrow 24
" But where attends thy chariot—where ? "— . 371 Eg. Maid 169
Why tarries then thy chariot ? Wherefore stay, 440 Ecc. Sonn. 2. 45. 9
" And has the Sun his flaming chariot driven . 618 School Ex. 1
Even from the blazing chariot of the sun, . . . 814 Excursion 4. 858
Charioteer. What could go wrong with such a Charioteer . . . . 523 Epist. Beaumont 112
Chariots. Now, coaches and chariots ! roar on like a stream ; . . . . 189 Music 41
'Mid coaches and chariots, a waggon of straw, . 570 Farmer 77
May roll in chariots, or provoke the hoofs . . . 773 Excursion 2. 99
Chariot-wheel. The nails of cart or chariot-wheel have left . . . . 567 Cumb. Beg. 56
Charitable. Be heaved of charitable sympathy ; . 20 Desc. Sk. 566
Why should we break Time's charitable seals ? . 449 Ecc. Sonn. 3. 35. 12
And earnestly to charitable care . . . . . 665 Prelude 4. 450
A charitable door. So days and years . . . 860 Excursion 7. 169
Generous and charitable, prompt to serve ; . . 860 Excursion 7. 214
Charities. Kind Nature's charities his steps attend ; 11 Desc. Sk. 25
With all the tender charities of life, ... 19 Desc. Sk. 511
Heavenward ascends with all her charities, . . 467 St. Bees 116
By charities and duties that proceed . . . . 510 *Among a 22
By casual boons and formal charities ; . . . . 516 *Feel for 10
And these inevitable charities, ... 568 Cumb. Beg. 145
And her bright dower of clustering charities, . . 585 Ch. Lamb 74
The charities that soothe, and heal, and bless, . 887 Excursion 9. 239
Charity. And stir the pulse of lazy charity. . . . 39 Bord. 83
He should have used me better !—Charity ! . . 45 Bord. 449
And begged a little aid for charity : . . . . 45 Bord. 473
And temper all our thoughts with charity. . . 149 *A narrow 73
Is to *her* charity no bar, ... 222 Triad 150
Be Charity !—to bid us think, ... 337 Cath. Cantons 17
May this bright flower of Charity display . . . 393 Countess' Pillar 2
" Charity never faileth : " on that creed, . . . 393 Countess' Pillar 6
Pronounces, ne'er abandons Charity. . . . . 429 Ecc. Sonn. 2. 1. 14
We read of faith and purest charity . . . . 441 Ecc. Sonn. 3 5. 5.
Concord and Charity in circles move. . . . . 443 Ecc. Sonn. 3. 14. 14
Thus all things lead to Charity, secured . . . 449 Ecc. Sonn. 3. 37. 1
And Charity extendeth to the dead . . . . 467 St. Bees 65
Fortitude, and that Christian Charity . . . . 478 *Lonsdale ! it 7
Descending to the worm in charity ; . . . . 500 Humanity 32
In a large house of public charity, ... 530 *I know 2
Who means to charity no wrong ; . . . . . 534 *Blest is 88
Past deeds and offices of charity, ... 567 Cumb. Beg. 90
Yet modest hand of charity, ... 577 *By playful 4
Charity, 'mid the multitude of sins . . . . . 584 Ch. Lamb 35
But, speaking more in charity, the dream . . . 730 Prelude 11. 232
Sought daily bread from public charity, . . . 764 Excursion 1. 561
Huts where his charity was blest ; his voice . . 772 Excursion 2. 63
Upon the laws of public charity. . . . . . 783 Excursion 2. 740
Whose charity and goodness were rehearsed . . 825 Excursion 5. 204
Faith, Hope, and Charity—from the visible world 827 Excursion 5. 333
Forgiveness, patience, hope, and charity ! " . . 833 Excursion 5. 727
To charity, and love, that have provided, . . . 836 Excursion 5. 911
From the delights of charity cut off, ... 836 Excursion 5. 939
And human charity, and social love. . . . . 838 Excursion 6. 29
That in a land where charity provides . . . . 844 Excursion 6. 378
From us to infringe the laws of charity. . . . 847 Excursion 6. 590
Of each domestic charity fulfilled, ... 847 Excursion 6. 629
Closed by degrees to charity ; heaven's blessing . 849 Excursion 6. 722
Forbearance, charity in deed and thought, . . 862 Excursion 7. 329
And charity ; nor last nor least for this, . . . 865 Excursion 7. 525
Precludes, and charity beyond the bounds . . K.8. 244 Recluse 1.1.285
Of charity—an overflowing love, ... K.8. 244 Recluse 1.1.286
From men who winnow charity from Faith . . K.8. 325 [?] *The vestal 10
Charity's. For charity's sweet sake alone. . . . 578 *I come 68
Charlemaine. That we approached the Seat of Charlemaine ? . . . . 335 Aix 2
Charles. Do as Charles and I are doing ! . . . . 79 Foresight 2
You and Charles and I will walk ; . . . . . 80 Foresight 28
There's George Fisher, Charles Fleming, and Reginald Shore, ... 86 Rural Arch. 1
Tried in the sea-fights of the second Charles. . . 825 Excursion 5. 187
Charlotte's. Insatiate Charlotte's tears, and Charlotte's smile. . . . . L. 1. 89 Juvenal 1. 23
Charm. The female with a meeker charm succeeds, 6 Ev. Wk. 224
To every charm, and last and chief to you, . . 13 Desc. Sk. 128
To charm the surly house-dog's faithful bark, . 32 Guilt 417
Of inward sadness had its charm ; . . . . . 86 Anecdote 22
By what charm of sight or smell, ... 161 *Pleasures newly 42
A word from me was like a charm ; . . . . 175 Waggoner 1. 132

Charm—*continued.*
Cured the foreboder like a charm ; . . . . . 179 Waggoner 3. 131
That had no need of a remoter charm, ... 206 Tintern 81
Or to repay the potent Charm, ... 221 Triad 100
O the charm that manners draw, ... 222 Triad 154
The Charm is over ; the mute Phantoms gone, . 222 Triad 212
Of coming good ;—the charm is fled ; . . . . 224 *'Tis gone 22
Ungrieved, with charm and spell ; . . . . . 224 *'Tis gone 63
Soft is the music that would charm for ever ; . 262 *Not Love 13
And charm of colours ; *I* applaud those signs . 277 *Haydon ! let 3
Had a musical charm, which the winter of age . 364 Vallomb. 27
Their vocal charm ; their sparklings cease to please. 382 Duddon 25. 14
Add every charm the Universe can show . . . 455 *Not in the lucid 22
The tender charm of poetry and love. . . . . 475 *There ! said 14
This modest charm of not too much, ... 508 May 95
Or seems to charm it, into like repose ; . . . 508 F. Stone 9
Or charm it out of memory ; yea, might fill . . 517 Pun. Death 1. 5
Stopped me at once by charm of what it showed, 524 Epist. Beaumont 172
A charm, *that* thought can not destroy, . . . 530 †Redbreast 7
That, while it only spreads a softening charm . 539 *Lady ! a 42
The ever-varying charm your round displays, . 591 Ev. Wk. Quarto 18
An intellectual charm ; that calm delight . . . 640 Prelude 1. 553
Those recollected hours that have the charm . 641 Prelude 1. 631
The tales that charm away the wakeful night . 673 Prelude 5. 496
With conscious pleasure opened to the charm . 674 Prelude 5. 554
With Poets ever. Mighty is the charm . . . 677 Prelude 6. 158
The charm more superficial that attends . . . 750 Prelude 14. 317
In lines and numbers, and, by charm severe, . . 760 Excursion 1. 254
By melody, and by the charm of verse. . . . 771 Excursion 2. 18
" Such recantation had for me no charm, . . . 797 Excursion 3. 778
Of ornamental interest, and the charm . . . 838 Excursion 6. 27
Yet farther recommended by the charm . . . 843 Excursion 6. 307
By charm of measured words may spread o'er field, 863 Excursion 7. 382
Even to old age, with unabated charm . . . 864 Excursion 7. 443
That charm all eyes. So bright, so fair, appeared 882 Excursion 8. 516
Upstirring but, abstracted by a charm . . . . S.3. 435 *The doubt 99
Though yet the star *some hearts* at court may charm . . . . L.1. 96 Juvenal 3. 37
Charmed. Charmed the tall circle of the enchanted steeps. . . . . 7 Ev. Wk. 304
Rocked the charmed thought in more delightful dreams ; . . . . 22 Desc. Sk. 631
And so may we, with charmèd mind . . . . 164 *Fair Lady 21
And in a moment charmed my cares to rest. . . 279 *Hark ! 'tis 8
'Twas sunlight sheathed and gently charmed, . 343 Eclipse 22
Still as he turns, the charmed spectator sees . . 367 Trajan 15
A part so charmed the pensive soul : . . . . 472 Ossian 4
Of hue and altering shape that charmed all eyes. 527 *Those breathing 20
To Arno's side hath brought him, and he charmed 573 Chiabrera 2. 16
Binding the charmed soul in powerless trance, . 604 Desc. Sk. Quarto 98
Where the charm'd worm of pain shall gnaw no more. . . . . 614 Desc.Sk.Quarto 669
And charm'd to hear his simulating tongue ; . . 624 Æneid 76
That kindles with such glory ! All are charmed, . 694 Prelude 7. 505
Can never utterly be charmed or stilled ; . . . 721 Prelude 10. 204
The constellations—gently was I charmed . . 745 Prelude 13. 342
But never to be charmed to gentleness : . . . 849 Excursion 6. 738
Into our hearts ; and charmed the peaceful flood. 892 Excursion 9. 537
Charmer's. And Love—a charmer's voice, that used to lend, ... 255 *Grief, thou 5
Charming. A charming beverage for you to carouse 53 Bord. 856
And Gaiety the charming office sought ; . . . 620 Birth of Love 16
Of far-off torrents charming the still night, . . 821 Excursion 4. 1322
Charming the air with skill of hand or voice, . . 843 Excursion 6. 356
Charms. Not undelightful are the simplest charms, 5 Ev. Wk. 144
Or heard, while other worlds their charms reveal, 16 Desc. Sk. 342
Had charms for him ; and here he loved to sit, . 23 Yew-tree 25
Charms superior to decay. . . . . 90 Longest Day 64
And not hers only, their peculiar charms . . . 118 Maternal Grief 23
Yes, the sight so stirs and charms . . . . . 171 Kitten 105
Charms of their own ;—then come with me, . . 237 P. B. 87
That, not for Fancy only, pomp hath charms ; . 276 *Chatsworth ! thy 12
The grace of forest charms decayed, ... 302 Yarrow V. 47
Those vernal charms of sight and sound, appeared 356 Aquap. 223
The scimitar, that yields not to the charms . . 427 Ecc. Sonn. 1. 34. 5
O still beloved (for thine, meek Power, are charms 460 *Queen of 17
It charms a feast-day throng of all degrees, . . 467 St Bees 98
The common light ; whose stillness charms the air, 508 F. Stone 8
Charms the tall circle of th' enchanted steeps. . 598 Ev. Wk. Quarto 350
Wooing her varying charms from eve to morn. . 602 Desc. Sk. Quarto 16
Or through her truant pathway's native charms, . 603 Desc. Sk. Quarto 49
Or charms that smile on Tusa's evening stream, . 605 Desc.Sk.Quarto 178
While no Italian arts their charms combine . . 615 Desc.Sk.Quarto 707
Thy charms my only theme ; . . . . . . 626 †Cento 10
Those incidental charms which first attached . . 645 Prelude 2. 198
Amid the fiery furnace. Charms and spells . . 692 Prelude 7. 370
In life or nature of those charms minute . . . 749 Prelude 14. 241
This Dwelling charms me ; often I stop short, . 856 Excursion 6. 1175
To all the charms this Station shows, ... S. 3. 438 *My Lord 24
Charnel. Asleep on Bunker's charnel hill afar ; . . 596 Ev. Wk.Quarto 254
Charnel-house. Beside the well-known charnel-house had then . . . . 704 Prelude 8. 378
Charnwood's. Rugged and high, of Charnwood's forest ground, ... 547 *Beneath yon 2
Charon. Replied, and when the Charon of the flood . . . . 658 Prelude 4. 14
Chart. See, at his feet, some little plan or chart, . 589 Immortality 90
Charter. Had given a charter to irregular hopes. . 680 Prelude 6. 335
By sacred charter, holden for her use. . . . . 856 Excursion 6. 1164
Or straggling burgh, of ancient charter proud, . 875 Excursion 8. 101

Chartered. And let the chartered wind that sweeps the heath . . . . 568 *Cumb. Beg.* 175
Of ancient loyalty, and chartered rights, . . . 714 *Prelude* 9. 324
Charters. Confirmed the charters that were yours before ;— . . . . 309 *Men of Kent* 11
And charters won and guarded by the sword . . 477 **Lowther ! in* 5
Strong by her charters, free because imbound, . 514 **Blest Statesman* 12
His charters and exemptions ; and, perchance . 568 *Cumb. Beg.* 127
Chartreuse. I greet thee, Chartreuse, while I mourn thy doom. . . . . 11 *Desc. Sk.* 53
Beheld the Convent of Chartreuse, and there . . 681 *Prelude* 6. 418
Of the Chartreuse, for worship. Thus was man . 703 *Prelude* 8. 275
Chartreuse'. Ev'n now I sigh at hoary Chartreuse' doom . . . . 603 *Desc. Sk. Quarto* 53
Charybdis. My ship and me Charybdis will devour. 564 *Troilus* 126
Chase. When gentle Spirits urged a sportive chase, 7 *Ev. Wk.* 301
And watch the fearless chamois-hunter chase . . 16 *Desc. Sk.* 305
I could have joined the wanton chase. . . . 81 †*Mother's Return* 52
The royal Elidure, who leads the chase, . . . 104 *Artegal* 114
May the unsullied Goddess of the chase, . . . 104 *Artegal* 150
And he went to the chase with a tear on his cheek. 120 *Childless Father* 20
Associates in that eager chase ; . . . . . . 191 *Seq. Beggars* 33
—This chase it looks not like an earthly chase ; . 201 *Hart-leap* 27
Of panting Wood-nymph, wearied with the chase. 219 *Haunted Tree* 15
That lamentable cry to chase— . . . . . . 243 *P. B.* 659
The northern Wind, to call thee to the chase, . . 266 **With how* 7
To chase for ever, on aerial grounds ! . . . . 267 **Though narrow* 14
In painful struggles. Months each other chase, . 274 *Infant M.* 4
Then rents and factors, rights of chase, . . . 291 *Rob Roy* 69
So have ye seen the fowler chase . . . . . 297 *Highland Boy* 187
And chase this silence from the air, ... 302 *Yarrow V.* 7
To chase mankind, with men in armies packed . 313 **Go back* 12
By just revenge inflamed ? No foot may chase, . 321 **The power* 6
With thoughts which no delights can chase, . . 342 *Ital. Itin.* 32
Which Superstition strove to chase, ... 343 *Eclipse* 5
What beast of chase hath broken from the cover ? 346 *Gemmi* 1
Sun, moon, and stars, and beast of chase or prey ; 380 *Duddon* 16. 13
Withered at eve. From scenes of art which chase 388 *Trosachs* 5
Through park, or chase, or savage wood. . . . 407 *White Doe* 998
Of her most timid touch his sleep would chase, . 461 **Giordano, verily* 7
And often, ere the chase was done, ... 483 *Simon Lee* 19
—Off they fly in earnest chase ; . . . . . 490 *Incident : Dog* 10
Are linked in endless chase ; . . . . 507 *May* 62
Within this whirlpool, they each other chase . . 551 **Behold an* 4
Out of the world this Innocent to chase ; . . . 554 *Prioress* 115
Fair Spirits are abroad ; in sportive chase . . 598 *Ev. Wk. Quarto* 347
Dire clap of hands, distracted chase of feet, . . 614 *Desc.Sk.Quarto* 657
Confederate, imitative of the chase . . . . 638 *Prelude* 1. 435
Of self-forgetfulness. Yes, that heartless chase 663 *Prelude* 4. 297
In chase of him ; whereat I waked in terror, . . 667 *Prelude* 5. 138
Keen hunters in a chase of fourteen weeks, . . 682 *Prelude* 6. 497
Vanished and vanishing in subtle chase, . . . 700 *Prelude* 8. 90
In prosecution of their deadly chase, ... 798 *Excursion* 3. 879
Darkness to chase, and sleep ; and bring the day 803 *Excursion* 4. 115
Chase the wild goat ; and if the bold red deer . 808 *Excursion* 4. 500
Swept in the storm of chase ; as moon and stars . 814 *Excursion* 4. 869
To dread his perseverance in the chase. . . . 868 *Excursion* 7. 746
And solemn chase—from morn to sultry noon . 870 *Excursion* 7. 862
To play on water, or in endless chase . . . . K.8. 237 *Recluse* 1.1. 27
Single at chase among the lonely woods, . . . K.8. 245 *Recluse* 1.1. 324
Or whet his kingly faculties to chase . . . L.1. 94 *Juvenal* 2. 3
Chased. Together chased the butterfly ! . . . . 79 **Stay near* 13
With a vexed people, and the tyrant chased ; . . 103 *Artegal* 80
By which the journeying pair are chased ? . . 244 *P. B.* 702
So these,—and, heard of once again, are chased . 320 **Hunger, and* 8
Both sank and died, the life-veins of the chased . 393 *Hart's-horn* 7
The turf, and thought by thought was chased, . 407 *White Doe* 1075
Have chased far off by righteous victory . . . 427 *Ecc. Sonn.* 1. 33. 7
He taught, till persecution chased him thence, . 431 *Ecc. Sonn.* 2. 11. 10
Chased spectral fears away. . . . . 544 *Russ. Fug.* 216
A shout thrice sent from one who chased . . . 544 *Russ. Fug.* 261
Or chased away, the airy wretchedness . . . 679 *Prelude* 6. 313
'Twas chased away : for, toward the western side 773 *Excursion* 2. 115
Doubt shall be quelled and trouble chased away ; 804 *Excursion* 4. 234
Chaser. *See* **Chamois-chaser.**
And chaser bursting here with one dire smart. . 393 *Hart's-horn* 8
Chases. The busy dor-hawk chases the white moth 453 **Calm is the* 22
Chasing. Chasing those pleasant dreams, the falling leaf . . . . 22 *Desc. Sk.* 632
Or from before it chasing wantonly . . . . 80 **Loving she* 19
Chasing a crimson butterfly ; . . . . . . 191 *Beggars* 22
Ye, too, must fly before a chasing hand, . . . 434 *Ecc. Sonn.* 2. 24. 1
While thou wert chasing the winged butterfly . 465 **Thou look'st* 11
Chasing those long long dreams the falling leaf . 616 *Desc.Sk.Quarto* 768
Chasm. *See* **Gordale-chasm.**
A single chasm, a gulf of gloomy blue, ... 18 *Desc. Sk.* 413
Into a chasm a mighty block . . . . . . 85 *Shepherd-boys* 51
That chasm is much the same— But, surely, yonder— . . . . 97 *Brothers* 137
By chasm or dizzy precipice ; . . . . 216 *Enterprise* 66
From the dread chasm, woods climbing above woods, 272 *Devil's Bridge* 10
Forth flashing out of its own gloomy chasm . . 352 *Aquap.* 15
From this deep chasm, where quivering sunbeams play . . . . 379 *Duddon* 15. 1
The pair have reached that fearful chasm, . . 494 *Force of Prayer* 17
Entered a narrow chasm. The brook and road . 684 *Prelude* 6. 621
I stand—the chasm of sky above my head . . 787 *Excursion* 3. 94
No chasm, no solitude ; from link to link . . 884 *Excursion* 9. 14
Chasms. Or, led where Via Mala's chasms confine . 13 *Desc. Sk.* 162
Into deep chasms troubled by roaring streams ; . 70 *Bord.* 1805
O'er chasms with new-fallen obstacles bestrown, . 431 *Ecc. Sonn.* 2. 12. 12

Chasms—*continued.*
Deep pools, tall trees, black chasms, and dizzy crags, K.8. 256 *Recluse* 1.1. 711
Chasmy. O'er-walk the chasmy torrent's foam-lit bed, 610 *Desc.Sk.Quarto* 464
Chaste. But in chaste hearts, uninfluenced by the power . . . . 256 **Yes ! hope* 12
Chaste Snowdrop, venturous harbinger of Spring, 264 *Snowdrop* 13
The brood of chaste affection. . . . . . . 302 *Yarrow V.* 64
Which the chaste Votaries seek, beyond the grave ; 424 *Ecc. Sonn.* 1. 24. 10
The chaste affections tremble to fulfil . . . . 425 *Ecc. Sonn.* 1. 28. 8
With stainless touch, as chaste as when thy praise 460 **Queen of* 25
Best throve the fire of chaste desire, ... 478 *Somnamb.* 39
In the chaste arms of thy belovèd Love ! . . . 575 *Chiabrera* 7. 13
Sobriety, and order, and chaste love, ... 877 *Excursion* 8. 240
Queen and negress chaste and fair ! . . . . L.2. 190 **Queen and* 1
Chasten. To chasten and subdue. And I have felt 207 *Tintern* 93
Unless they chasten fancies that presume . . . 394 **How profitless* 3
That God will chasten whom he dearly loves. . . 576 **By a* 6
Chastened. With chastened feelings would I pay . 284 *Grave of Burns* 15
From all that breathes and is, was chastened, stemmed . . . . 750 *Prelude* 14. 295
Chastening. While chastening thoughts of sweetest use, bestowed . . . . 11 *Desc. Sk.* 27
And chastening sympathies ! . . . . . . 338 **Meek Virgin* 30
Chastening the fulness of a present bliss, . . . 456 *Rydal Mere* 41
The measure of God's chastening love, ... 577 **By playful* 10
From lowly sympathy and chastening truth : . . 714 *Prelude* 9. 351
Awakening, chastening an intemperate grief, . . 813 *Excursion* 4. 840
Chastens. It chastens only to requite . . . . 338 **Meek Virgin* 33
Chaster. The chaster coverts of a British hill. . . 220 *Triad* 14
Chastise. She kissed him—how could she chastise ? 297 *Highland Boy* 239
Convoked the impious to chastise : . . . . . 405 *White Doe* 838
Chastised. Or be chastised by mortal instruments. 55 *Bord.* 1002
Chastised by self-abasement more profound, . . 513 *General Fast* 10
Chastisement. *See* **Mock-chastisement.**
Reviving, heavier chastisement deserve . . . 327 **Emperors and* 13
But chastisement shall follow peace despised. . . 420 *Ecc. Sonn.* 1. 9. 7
And yet, for chastisement of these regrets, . . 663 *Prelude* 4. 307
Of unintelligible chastisement, ... 724 *Prelude* 10. 455
A chastisement ; and when I called to mind . . 739 *Prelude* 12. 311
Calamity, the chastisement of Heaven, . . . 772 *Excursion* 2. 73
For chastisement, and custody, and bonds, . . 886 *Excursion* 9. 123
Chastity. And Chastity finds many a sheltering bower. 429 *Ecc. Sonn.* 2. 2. 8
This gem of chastity, this emerald, ... 555 *Prioress* 158
Chat. *See* **Stone-chat**
Chatsworth. Chatsworth ! thy stately mansion, and the pride . . . . 275 **Chatsworth ! thy* 1
Chattels. Fields, goods, and far-off chattels we have none : . . . . 106 *Farewell* 13
Lawns, houses, chattels, groves, and fields, . . 214 *Kirkstone* 27
For goods and chattels, or those Infants dear, . 523 *Epist. Beaumont* 113
Chatter. That evermore his teeth they chatter, . 536 *Goody Blake* 3
Chatter, chatter, chatter still ! . . . . . . 536 *Goody Blake* 4
His teeth they chatter, chatter still. . . . . 536 *Goody Blake* 12
His teeth they chatter, chatter still ! . . . . 536 *Goody Blake* 16
His teeth they chatter, chatter still. . . . . 537 *Goody Blake* 126
Chattering. Scarce heard, their chattering lips her shoulder chill, 597 *Ev.Wk. Quarto* 283
The pie, and chattering breaks the night's repose. 606 *Desc.Sk.Quarto* 230
By chattering popinjays ; the inner heart . . . 655 *Prelude* 3. 444
With chattering monkeys dangling from their poles, 697 *Prelude* 7. 694
Chatters. She chatters in her ecstasy. . . . . 81 †*Mother's Return* 24
The magpie chatters with delight ; . . . . . 84 *Shepherd-boys* 5
The Jay makes answer as the Magpie chatters ; . 195 *Resolution* 6
That writhes and chatters in her wiry cage, . . 842 *Excursion* 6. 291
Chatterton. I thought of Chatterton, the marvellous Boy, ... 195 *Resolution* 43
Chaucer. Time-honoured Chaucer speaking through that Lay . . . . 436 *Ecc. Sonn.* 2. 31. 2
I laughed with Chaucer in the hawthorn shade ; . 653 *Prelude* 3. 276
Chaucer's. A Pastor such as Chaucer's verse portrays ; . . . . 380 *Duddon* 18. 12
To snatch a sprig from Chaucer's reverend brow)— 528 **Those breathing* 61
Chaunt. No Nightingale did ever chaunt . . . 289 *Sol. Reap.* 9
Mounts thro' the nearer mist the chaunt of birds, 611 *Desc.Sk.Quarto* 506
Didst chaunt the vision of that Ancient Man, . . 751 *Prelude* 14. 399
Chaunted. Daily with chaunted rites. In such a race 643 *Prelude* 2. 65
That round us chaunted. Well might we be glad, 674 *Prelude* 5. 566
Chauntry. With whip and spur we through the chauntry flew . . . . 643 *Prelude* 2. 116
Chaunts. He chaunts Arcturus,—that fraternal twain 625 *Æneid* 126
Cheap. Fields gaily sown when promises were cheap.— 505 *Warning* 139
Cheap matter offered they to boyish wit, . . . 640 *Prelude* 1. 529
But he was a cheap pleasure to my eyes ; . . . 783 *Excursion* 2. 760
Cheaper. I know no cheaper engine to degrade a man, 58 *Bord.* 1161
Cheaply. No gains too cheaply earned his fancy cloy, 11 *Desc. Sk.* 15
Cheapside. And a river flows on through the vale of Cheapside. . . . . 188 *Poor Susan* 8
Chear. Where silver rocks the savage prospect chear 591 *Ev. Wk. Quarto* 7
Where hardly giv'n the hopeless waste to chear . 608 *Desc.Sk.Quarto* 319
Chear'd. Continual fountains welling chear'd the waste, ... 611 *Desc.Sk.Quarto* 478
Chearfulness. Then did no ebb of chearfulness demand 592 *Ev. Wk. Quarto* 21
Cheat. To cheat the thought she cannot cheer, . 164 *Needlecase* 35
Their soul-subduing looks might cheat . . . . 232 *Jew. Fam.* 35
Can cheat the time ; sending her fancy out . . 273 **While Anna's* 11
Grief of her sting ; nor cheat, where he detains . 389 *Breadalb.* 4
Doubtless shall cheat full oft the heart's desires ; 429 *Ecc. Sonn.* 2. 3. 9
An old resource to cheat a froward time ! . . . 521 *Epist. Beaumont* 35
With curious subtility, from wish to cheat . . 790 *Excursion* 3. 286
To cheat the world, or from herself to hide . . 840 *Excursion* 6. 125

Cheat—*continued.*
To cheat the sadness of a rainy day; . . . . 859 *Excursion* 7. 118
Cheated. That listening sense is pardonably cheated 455 *Rydal Mere* 15
His fancy cheated—that can see . . . . . 533 **Blest is* 42
To ease a father's cheated love he hung . . . 624 *Æneid* 83
Cheats. That cheats her of too busy cares, . . . 144 **Driven in* 35
With garlands, cheats her into happiness; . . . 528 **Those breathing* 99
Check. Check his loud whip and hail us with mild voice, ... 61 *Bord.* 1335
That fastened there, as it would check the current. 73 *Bord.* 2017
Who would check the happy feeling . . . . 90 *Longest Day* 17
And then, as from a sudden check, ... 178 *Waggoner* 2. 127
Check with thy notes the impulse which, betrayed 190 **Lyre! though* 6
Of discontent, and check the birth . . . . . 191 *Seq. Beggars* 18
But whence that sudden check? that fearful start! 213 *Dion* 63
Uprisen, as if to check approaching Night, . . 263 **How clear* 5
Which neither force shall check nor time abate! . 271 *Henry: Portrait* 14
Hangs that day's treasured sword, how firm a check 278 *Wellington* 6
Which spurns the check of salutary bands, . . 307 **It is not* 6
To check this pious haste of erring duty. . . . 372 *Eg. Maid* 246
Nor check, the music of the strings; . . . . . 375 **The Minstrels* 10
Their tents, and check the current of their arms. . 427 *Ecc. Sonn.* 1. 34. 8
He, whose strong arm the Orient could not check, 428 *Ecc. Sonn.* 1. 38. 6
Earth cannot check. O terrible excess . . . 439 *Ecc. Sonn.* 2. 44. 9
Even when they rose to check or to repel . . . 469 **The feudal* 2
"No check, no stay, this Streamlet fears; . . 487 *Fountain* 21
To check the erring, and reprove; . . . . . 492 *Duty* 4
Whatsoever check they bring, ... 503 *Warning* 9
Lo! Streams that April could not check . . . 507 *May* 73
Is to control and check disordered Powers? . . 514 **Who ponders* 14
The little flower her vanity shall check; . . . 807 *Excursion* 4. 425
Conscience to guide and check; and death to be . 887 *Excursion* 9. 224
Communion without check of herbs and flowers . S.3. 435 **The doubt* 104
Issuing when shame hath ceased to check the brawls K.8. 246 *Recluse* 1.1.345
Checked. When crowding cattle, checked by rails that make . . . . 3 *Ev. Wk.* 41
Whether some old Swiss air hath checked her haste, 15 *Desc. Sk.* 268
The stranger till its barking-fit I checked; . . 28 *Guilt* 224
That oft have checked their fury at your bidding. 48 *Bord.* 608
She checked herself in her distress, ... 82 *Alice Fell* 42
In him was somewhat checked; and, when his Brother . . . . 100 *Brothers* 337
Hath checked his foaming courser:—can it be! . 104 *Artegal* 115
Checked her with filial meekness; for no thought 124 *V. and J.* 167
Though timid scruples checked me long; . . . 182 *Waggoner* 4. 200
They checked me—and I left the theme . . . 182 *Waggoner* 4. 201
Here checked by too impetuous haste, ... 228 *Devot. Incit.* 19
Till checked by some necessities severe. . . . 251 *Appleth.* 8
Checked in your course by many a teasing burr; . 268 **Dogmatic Teachers* 5
Checked oft-times in a devious race, ... 285 *Grave of Burns* 74
"All freakishness of mind is checked; . . . . 291 *Rob Roy* 45
Checked in the very act and deed of blood, . . 322 *Germans* 3
That checked the desultory range . . . . . 343 *Eclipse* 11
Of checked ambition, tyranny controlled, . . . 349 *Boulogne* 11
Checked not its rage; unfelt the ground did rock, 361 **When here* 3
—She feels it, and her pangs are checked. . . . 407 *White Doe* 1073
Thus checked, a little while it stayed; . . . . 414 *White Doe* 1648
Till the checked torrent, proudly triumphing, . 418 *Ecc. Sonn.* 1. 1. 7
The Church, whose power hath recently been checked, ... 432 *Ecc. Sonn.* 2. 16. 3
Then be it neither checked nor stayed: . . . 486 *Matthew* 14
And checked him in his leap. . . . . . . 494 *Force of Prayer* 32
Checked, in the moment of its issue, checked . . 539 **Lady! a* 37
Neither checked by the rich nor the needy they roam; . . . . 572 *Avarice* 41
Who checked or turned thy headstrong youth, . 577 **I come* 42
Which checked discussion ere it warmed to strife; 583 **With copious* 14
Hence am I checked: but let me boldly say, . . 669 *Prelude* 5. 264
Checked our unwearied steps. Let this alone . 686 *Prelude* 6. 731
Nor checked by aught of tamer argument, . . 688 *Prelude* 7. 50
Have been preferred, that this fair creature, checked 692 *Prelude* 7. 374
Backwards, nor checked his flight until I saw . 744 *Prelude* 13. 319
Was nothing either seen or heard that checked . 746 *Prelude* 14. 20
By pain of heart—now checked—and now impelled— . . . . 796 *Excursion* 3. 699
Too little checked. An active, ardent mind; . 859 *Excursion* 7. 116
Was reached, the Solitary checked his steps; . . 895 *Excursion* 9. 770
Checking. But a thick umbrage—checking the wild growth . . . . 149 *M. H.* 3
Checking the stream, make a pool smooth and clear 382 *Duddon* 23. 4
Dissension, checking arms that would restrain . 425 *Ecc. Sonn.* 1. 29. 2
Checking the finer spirits that refuse . . . . 773 *Excursion* 2. 150
Checking the sober steed on which he rode, . . 859 *Excursion* 7. 103
Appeared, confusion checking their delight. . . 882 *Excursion* 8. 546
Checks. Strong terror checks the female peasant's sighs, ... 11 *Desc. Sk.* 65
That fosters growth or checks or cheers decay, . 169 **Never enlivened* 2
That, for a brief space, checks the hurrying stream! 220 *Haunted Tree* 40
A sweet confusion checks the Shepherd-lass; . . 378 *Duddon* 10. 3
It neither damps the gay, nor checks the witty. . 475 *Greenock* 8
Checquer. Checquer with paler red the thicket shades. 599 *Ev. Wk. Quarto* 398
Checquer'd. And gives, where woods the checquer'd upland strew, ... 599 *Ev. Wk. Quarto* 405
Cheek. Thy flooded cheek to wet them with its tears; 7 *Ev. Wk.* 276
Still the cold cheek its shuddering tear retains. . 8 *Ev. Wk.* 322
Were hardy, though his cheek seemed worn with care 24 *Guilt* 5
Upon her cheek, to which its youthful hue . . 30 *Guilt* 320
Of me, say that the worm is on my cheek.— . . 35 *Guilt* 590
Even while he printed kisses on the cheek . . 56 *Bord.* 1050
Thy vest is torn, thy cheek is deadly pale; . . 76 *Bord.* 2191

Cheek—*continued.*
Might exalt the loveliest cheek; . . . . . 90 *Longest Day* 24
Still upon his cheek are living . . . . . . 93 *Westmoreland Girl* 35
Tears down his cheek, or solitary smiles . . . 97 *Brothers* 110
He had as white a head and fresh a cheek . . 98 *Brothers* 201
Stolen from his cheek; he drooped, and pined, and pined— . . . . 100 *Brothers* 340
That sparkle on her cheek. . . . . 108 *Louisa* 12
One upright arm sustains the cheek, ... 112 **How rich* 14
And he went to the chase with a tear on his cheek. 120 *Childless Father* 20
Oh, what a kiss was that! my cheek . . . . 121 *Emigrant Mother* 79
A healthy Lad, and carried in his cheek . . . 134 *Michael* 178
While across her virgin cheek pure blushes strayed, 141 *Arm. Lady* 137
And what if my poor cheek be brown? . . . . 145 *Her Eyes* 68
And—with my cheek on one of those green stones 185 *Nutting* 35
With hues of genius on his cheek . . . . . 192 *Ruth* 31
That its fair flowers may from his cheek . . . 220 *Triad* 59
But mark her glowing cheek, her vesture green! . 221 *Triad* 98
Hers is not a cheek shame-stricken, ... 222 *Triad* 163
Tenderest bloom is on her cheek; . . . . . 222 *Triad* 191
The roseate bloom on woman's cheek; . . . 227 *Vernal Ode* 119
"There was a hardness in his cheek, ... 240 *P. B.* 316
Oft have I seen, ere Time had ploughed my cheek, 256 *Decay of Piety* 1
Wan cheek at once was privileged to unfold . . 258 **Even so* 7
Of fretful temper sullies her pure cheek; . . . 274 *Infant M.* 6
When I behold thy blanched unwithered cheek, . 274 **Such age* 6
A foil to his celestial cheek! . . . . . . 299 *Brownie's Cell* 100
Appeared upon his tender cheek) . . . . . 342 *Ital. Itin.* 84
Made to the Twelve, survives: lip, forehead, cheek, 343 *Last Sup.* 10
Shed, on the Slumberer's cold wan cheek . . . 371 *Eg. Maid* 161
Those watery locks, that bloodless cheek! . . . 372 *Eg. Maid* 215
Of colour dawned upon the Damsel's cheek; . . 374 *Eg. Maid* 328
And Neville's cheek grew pale with fear; . . . 404 *White Doe* 792
A few tears down her cheek descend . . . . 415 *White Doe* 1795
Black hair, and vivid eye, and meagre cheek, . 422 *Ecc. Sonn.* 1. 15. 6
Her blushing cheek, love-vows upon her lip, . . 427 *Ecc. Sonn.* 1. 35. 6
Wan cheek, and knees indùrated with prayer, . 433 *Ecc. Sonn.* 2. 19. 3
Goes forth—unveiling timidly a cheek . . . . 434 *Ecc. Sonn.* 2. 22. 5
And many a blooming, many a lovely, cheek . . 446 *Ecc. Sonn.* 3. 23. 7
Though it can wet with tears the hardiest cheek. 460 **Wanderer! that* 62
And still the centre of his cheek . . . . . 483 *Simon Lee* 7
Can draw warmth from the cheek of my Love; . 484 **A plague* 27
Stain her cheek in future years— . . . . . 503 **Like a* 56
Would their lost strength restore and freshen the pale cheek? . . . . 523 *Epist. Beaumont* 117
Of a perpetual dawn from brow and cheek . . 525 *Epist. Beaumont* 253
That cheek—a kindling of the morn, ... 530 *Gleaner* 4
Of cheek that with carnation vies, ... 541 *Russ. Fug.* 3
And cheek embrowned by art; . . . . . . 542 *Russ. Fug.* 78
Of the unfaded rose that still blooms on his cheek. 569 *Farmer* 8
I kissed his cheek before he died; . . . . . 577 **I come* 5
Pale was her hue; yet mortal cheek . . . . 583 **O for a* 31
Her seal, the mortal tear his cheek has wet; . . 613 *Desc. Sk. Quarto* 629
Soon fades her cheek, her blushing beauties fly, . 619 *School Ex.* 97
A visitant that while it fans my cheek . . . . 632 *Prelude* 1. 2
To deck some slighted playmate's homely cheek. 661 *Prelude* 4. 208
Upon the cheek of listening Infancy . . . . 668 *Prelude* 5. 189
He was in limb, in cheek a summer rose . . . 692 *Prelude* 7. 352
Dishevelled, gleaming eyes, and rueful cheek . . 710 *Prelude* 9. 79
Disarmed his voice and fanned his yellow cheek . 712 *Prelude* 9. 157
Time had compressed the freshness of his cheek . 762 *Excursion* 1. 426
Why should a tear be on an old Man's cheek? . 765 *Excursion* 1. 598
Upon his hollow cheek. "How kind," he said, . 779 *Excursion* 2. 525
Her cheek to change its colour, was conveyed . 795 *Excursion* 3. 641
The old Man's cheek; but, at this closing turn . 832 *Excursion* 5. 623
Of undisturbed humanity; a cheek . . . . . 834 *Excursion* 5. 781
Of infancy first blooms upon his cheek; . . . 836 *Excursion* 5. 958
To tinge his cheek; and through his frame it crept 840 *Excursion* 6. 157
—I noted that the Solitary's cheek . . . . . 854 *Excursion* 6. 1062
Within his cheek, as light within a cloud; . . . 866 *Excursion* 7. 554
To his worn cheek; or with uneasy shame . . . 871 *Excursion* 7. 906
Mantle upon his cheek. Is this the form, . . . 879 *Excursion* 8. 315
The beauteous girl, whose cheek was flushed with joy. . . . . 890 *Excursion* 9. 428
Food for sick passion in a minion's cheek, . . . L.1. 96 *Juvenal* 3. 50
Cheeked. *See* **Rosy-cheeked.**
Cheek's. Accordant to the cheek's unquiet glow; . 604 *Desc. Sk. Quarto* 153
Cheeks. On infant cheeks there fresher roses blow; 21 *Desc. Sk.* 608
His cheeks with tears were wet: . . . . . 114 *Last of Flock* 8
Faint colour over both their pallid cheeks, . . 119 *Maternal Grief* 6
By sickness, gaunt and lean, with sunken cheeks . 149 **A narrow* 59
And on he drives with cheeks that burn . . . 240 *P. B.* 347
Like Grecian Artists, give thee human cheeks, . 268 **Brook! whose* 8
Our groans, our blushes, our pale cheeks declare . 319 *Spaniard* 13
How, with empurpled cheeks and pampered eyes, 364 **What aim* 4
How many wan and faded cheeks . . . . . 507 *May* 27
His cheeks were red as ruddy clover; . . . . 536 *Goody Blake* 19
Her infant's cheeks with fresher roses glow, . . 615 *Desc. Sk. Quarto* 734
With cheeks o'erspread by smiles of baleful glow, 617 *Desc. Sk. Quarto* 790
A boy, no better, with his rosy cheeks . . . . 653 *Prelude* 3. 290
The mother; but, upon her cheeks diffused, . . 692 *Prelude* 7. 344
And him who at the trumpet puffs his cheeks, . 697 *Prelude* 7. 702
Cheer. *See* **Chear.**
Till higher mounted, strives in vain to cheer . . 8 *Ev. Wk.* 341
To soothe and cheer the poor man's solitude. . . 13 *Desc. Sk.* 142
Is all we have to cheer our wintry way; . . . 19 *Desc. Sk.* 501
To soothe or cheer, to soften or refine. . . . 21 *Desc. Sk.* 590
But not one dwelling-place his heart to cheer. . 25 *Guilt* 31
The whilst her comrade to her pensive cheer . . 30 *Guilt* 323

Cheer—*continued.*
With joyousness, and with a thoughtful cheer, — 106 *Farewell* 30
For a sunny thought to cheer the Stranger's way, — 141 *Arm. Lady* 125
Wherewith to cheer him in the winter time." — 149 **A narrow* 54
To cheat the thought she cannot cheer, — 164 *Needlecase* 35
That far-off tinkling's drowsy cheer, — 173 *Waggoner* 1. 26
Said cordially, "My Friend, what cheer? — 176 *Waggoner* 1. 248
And gives another lusty cheer; — 176 *Waggoner* 2. 18
And thinking it but sorry cheer — 179 *Waggoner* 3. 62
The jolly bird that learned his cheer — 179 *Waggoner* 3. 120
Their daring wiles, their sportive cheer? — 191 *Seq. Beggars* 12
Much witnessing of change and cheer, — 192 *Gipsies* 11
To see her Master and to cheer— — 204 *Brougham* 53
Must vanish, and his careless cheer — 204 *Brougham* 93
Whether to cheer his coward breast, — 241 *P. B.* 471
To mitigate and cheer its loneliness. — 266 **Even as* 8
Rich are his walks with supernatural cheer; — 267 **Though narrow* 5
Shall guide, his fancy cheer, your way; — 287 *Sons of Burns* 38
Is this a place for mirthful cheer? — 294 *Jedbor.* 23
Smile on his Mother now with bolder cheer. — 294 **Fly, some* 14
And cheer my mind in sorrow. — 302 *Yarrow V.* 88
Nor cheer him; for the illustrious Swede hath done — 305 **The Voice* 9
O dastard whom such foretaste doth not cheer! — 310 **Another year* 9
Is there a power that can sustain and cheer — 318 **Is there* 1
And through all Europe cheer desponding men — 318 **Ah! where* 8
In every nook a lip that it may cheer. — 321 **The power* 14
Found casual vent. She said, "Be of good cheer; — 360 *Albano* 5
And softly touched; but, to his princely cheer — 373 *Eg. Maid* 287
Sad thoughts, avaunt!—partake we their blithe cheer — 381 *Duddon* 23. 1
Then, with mild Una in her sober cheer, — 395 *White Doe: Ded.* 37
With awful cheer a voice of praise; — 397 *White Doe* 157
A sound of military cheer, — 401 *White Doe* 432
Of border tunes was played to cheer — 406 *White Doe* 890
To cheer this sad and pensive time; — 410 *White Doe* 1281
Haunting the spots with lonely cheer — 416 *White Doe* 1879
Even in her own despite, both feed and cheer; — 420 *Ecc. Sonn.* 1. 7. 13
Pours forth his bounty, like the day doth cheer, — 425 *Ecc. Sonn.* 1. 26. 7
As he approaches them, with solemn cheer. — 445 *Ecc. Sonn.* 3. 19. 8
Thou, stately York! and Ye, whose splendours cheer — 451 *Ecc. Sonn.* 3. 42. 13
Touched by accordance of thy placid cheer, — 460 **Wanderer! that* 56
To cheer the long dark hours of vacant night— — 460 **Wanderer! that* 69
To cheer the Itinerant on whom she pours — 463 **Adieu, Rydalian* 12
By hooded Votaresses with saintly cheer; — 465 **The cattle* 11
Of hope, and smiles on you with cheer sublime. — 477 *Steamboats* 14
Art thou a Man of purple cheer? — 485 *Poet's Epitaph* 9
Send through the tarn a lonely cheer; — 491 *Fidelity* 26
To cheer the remnant of his host — 495 *Fact* 27
Nor doth the example fail to cheer — 498 **Departing summer* 13
So, by chequerings of sad cheer, — 502 **Like a* 33
Partakes a livelier cheer; — 507 *May* 22
For time and season, rules that work to cheer— — 515 **Long-favoured* 13
Her work and her work's partners she can cheer, — 523 *Epist. Beaumont* 162
When fire or taper ceased to cheer the room, — 528 **Those breathing* 54
My passing Spirit cheer. — 530 †*Redbreast* 12
Sent forth her peace to cheer. — 544 *Russ. Fug.* 208
Were shaped to cheer dark winter's lonely hours. — 546 **Oft is* 16
His Primer conning with an earnest cheer, — 553 *Prioress* 66
Ah! good sweet Nightingale! for my heart's cheer, — 558 *Cuck. and Night.* 101
Was the boast of the country for excellent cheer; — 569 *Farmer* 14
"The sunshine may not cheer it, nor the dew; — 571 **There is a Flower* 17
But welcome fortitude, and patient cheer, — 579 *Peele Castle* 57
To cheer the wand'ring wretch with hospitable light, — 620 **She wept* 14
Let Bacchus, donor of soul-quick'ning cheer, — 625 *Æneid* 112
To cheer the thoughts of those I love, and mine. — 734 *Prelude* 11. 452
Guide, and support, and cheer me to the end!" — 755 *Recluse* 1. 1. 860
To cheer us both. But long we had not talked — 766 *Excursion* 1. 686
Brought from the cupboard wine and stouter cheer, — 785 *Excursion* 2. 899
Invited, summoned, to partake the cheer — 867 *Excursion* 7. 653
And pure good-will, and hospitable cheer; — 878 *Excursion* 8. 242
Nothing to speed the day, or cheer the mind; — 878 *Excursion* 8. 274
A tributary shed to cheer — S. 3. 425 **No whimsy* 4
And ask no better cheer. — K.8. 262 **Ah! if* 5

Cheered. *See* **Chear'd.**
Continual waters welling cheered the waste, — 17 *Desc. Sk.* 390
Hope cheered my dreams, and to my daily prayers — 35 *Guilt* 597
In spite of all the larks that cheered our path, — 39 *Bord.* 109
With soft illumination cheered the dimness of that place. — 92 *Poet's Dream* 12
Not unvouchsafed—a light that warmed and cheered — 118 *Maternal Grief* 19
And cheered; and now together breathe fresh air — 119 *Maternal Grief* 64
Where by that dream he had been cheered — 168 *Pilgrim's Dream* 71
The mourner is cheered, and the anxious have rest; — 188 *Music* 11
The thoughts with which it then was cheered; — 191 *Seq. Beggars* 28
The Knight hallooed, he cheered and chid them on — 201 *Hart-leap* 21
She looked upon him and was calmed and cheered; — 211 *Load.* 92
That cheered the trellised arbour's privacy, — 221 *Triad* 102
The hoary mountain-heights were cheered, — 224 *Primrose* 27
It cheered mild Spenser, called from Faery-land — 260 **Scorn not* 10
Companion! by whose buoyant Spirit cheered, — 352 *H. C. R.* 1
Failed to reanimate and but feebly cheered — 354 *Aquap.* 97
So cheered, she left that Island bleak, — 371 *Eg. Maid* 157
And o'er wide plains cheered by the lark that trills — 387 *Manse* 5
And rests not thankful? Whether cheered by talk — 389 *Glencroe* 4
This tragic Story cheered us; for it speaks — 395 *White Doe: Ded.* 49
Had, in her solitude, been cheered. — 409 *White Doe* 1199
That calmed her, cheered, and fortified? — 415 *White Doe* 1713

Cheered—*continued.*
Through this still medium, are consoled and cheered; — 476 *Howard* 10
Cheered with the prospect of a brighter day. — 520 *Pun. Death* 14. 14
That through our gipsy travel cheered the way; — 525 *Epist. Beaumont* 271
To launch the boat; and with her blessing cheered, — 541 *Grace Darl.* 48
That greatly cheered his country: to his kin — 575 *Chiabrera* 8. 13
My own voice cheered me, and, far more, the mind's — 633 *Prelude* 1. 55
And nothing cheered our way till first we saw — 649 *Prelude* 3. 3
The assurance which then cheered some heavy thoughts — 687 *Prelude* 7. 13
Cheered with this hope, to Paris I returned, — 719 *Prelude* 10. 48
Then, cheered by short refreshment, sallied forth. — 746 *Prelude* 14. 10
That had not cheered me long—ere, looking round — 765 *Excursion* 1. 622
Baronial court or royal; cheered with gifts — 771 *Excursion* 2. 3
Cheered by the Highland bagpipe, as they marched — 774 *Excursion* 2. 176
Cheered, plainly, and yet serious. What a wreck — 781 *Excursion* 2. 660
For all; and yet how few are warmed or cheered! — 828 *Excursion* 5. 384
That frets, or languishes, be stilled and cheered." — 829 *Excursion* 5. 484
A merry journey, rich in pastime, cheered — 858 *Excursion* 7. 81
Of which adventures, that beguiled and cheered — 859 *Excursion* 7. 108
That dignified and cheered a low estate? — 877 *Excursion* 8. 238
So long unthanked) hast cheered a simple board — S.3. 433 **The doubt* 16

Cheerer. The cheerer Thou of our in-door sadness, — 163 **Art thou the* 30

Cheer'st. Cheer'st the low threshold of the peasant's cell! — 329 *Ode: Thanks.* 7

Cheerful. The sky is veiled, and every cheerful sight: — 15 *Desc. Sk.* 272
The dripping groves resound with cheerful lays, — 34 *Guilt* 519
I comprehend thee—I should be as cheerful — 40 *Bord.* 149
A cheerful mind,—and buffeted with bond, — 98 *Brothers* 214
He talked about him with a cheerful love. — 101 *Brothers* 391
How cheerful, at sunrise, the hill where I stood, — 116 *Repentance* 30
Oh! had he but thy cheerful smiles, — 121 *Emigrant Mother* 49
Fields, where with cheerful spirits he had breathed — 132 *Michael* 65
Nor cheerful, yet with objects and with hopes, — 133 *Michael* 121
Of remedies and of a cheerful hope. — 135 *Michael* 243
As cheerful as a grove in Spring: at length — 136 *Michael* 306
With confident and cheerful thoughts; and now — 138 *Michael* 439
The time was March, a cheerful noon— — 156 *Oak and Broom* 15
Then, cheerful Flower! my spirits play — 158 **In youth* 59
Or the night's darkness, or its cheerful face — 172 *Infant Daughter* 23
Inviting him with cheerful lure: — 174 *Waggoner* 1. 79
From May-time and the cheerful Dawn; — 186 **She was* 8
And a clear brook with cheerful knell — 194 *Ruth* 203
Our cheerful faith, that all which we behold — 207 *Tintern* 133
And cheerful songs, and suns that shine — 217 *Enterprise* 149
A cheerful life is what the Muses love, — 261 **From the dark* 13
Wear rather in thy bonds a cheerful brow: — 305 *Toussaint* 7
In cheerful godliness; and yet thy heart — 307 **Milton! thou* 13
Are cheerful as the rising sun in May. — 308 **These times* 8
All sacred things are covered: cheerful morn — 427 *Ecc. Sonn.* 1. 36. 6
Thinned the rank woods; and for the cheerful grange — 468 *St. Bees* 138
The cheerful dawn, brightening for me the east; — 496 **A little* 13
And golden summer days uniting cheerful hearts. — 524 *Epist. Beaumont* 199
Cheerful alike if bare of flowers as now, — 530 *Poor Robin* 27
Stay, little cheerful Robin! stay, — 530 †*Redbreast* 1
To cheerful intercourse with wood and field, — 538 **In desultory* 40
A bright and cheerful face; — 543 *Russ. Fug.* 130
Green ivy risen from out the cheerful earth — 584 **With copious* 56
Enlivening Hope display'd her cheerful ray, — 618 *School Ex.* 35
Clapp'd her strong wings, and sought the cheerful isle — 618 *School Ex.* 46
Or glancing at each other cheerful looks, — 622 *Recluse* 1. 1. 124
A cheerful confidence in things to come. — 633 *Prelude* 1. 58
"A cheerful smile unbends the wrinkled brow, — 699 *Prelude* 8. 48
And cheerful, but the foremost of the band — 726 *Prelude* 10. 570
Deriving cheerful confidence, shall blend — 748 *Prelude* 14. 145
With cheerful hope, until the second autumn, — 764 *Excursion* 1. 550
Are cheerful; while this multitude of flies — 765 *Excursion* 1. 596
Her cottage, then a cheerful object, wore — 767 *Excursion* 1. 713
Paid cheerful tribute to the moorland house. — 776 *Excursion* 2. 343
Into the presence of the cheerful light— — 779 *Excursion* 2. 489
On the hill-sides, a cheerful quiet scene, — 823 *Excursion* 5. 90
Hopeful and cheerful:—vanished is the pall — 830 *Excursion* 5. 547
The air with cheerful spirit, for thy sake, — 852 *Excursion* 6. 924
And this Survivor, with his cheerful throng — 861 *Excursion* 7. 279
"A Man he seems of cheerful yesterdays — 866 *Excursion* 7. 557
With cheerful heart, an unknown voice of joy, — K.8. 241 *Recluse* 1. 185

Cheerfully. Cheerfully uttered, with demeanour kind, — 197 *Resolution* 135
Of winter storms, yet budding cheerfully; — 450 *Ecc. Sonn.* 3. 39. 6
That owned him; living cheerfully abroad — 688 *Prelude* 7. 74
Cheerfully led to individual ends — 700 *Prelude* 8. 107

Cheerfulness. *See* **Chearfulness.**
Where common cheerfulness would fail; — 294 *Jedbor.* 59
Thy goings—or the cheerfulness — 344 **How blest* 64
Their cheerfulness, and busily retrim — 420 *Ecc. Sonn.* 1. 7. 2
Truth breathed by cheerfulness. — 481 *Tables Turned* 20
Rights equal, laws with cheerfulness obeyed, — 515 *Penn.* 3
See cheerfulness undamped by stealing Time; — 539 **Lady! a* 62
And jollity, fresh cheerfulness, and mirth; — 559 *Cuck. and Night.* 155
To night, unbroken cheerfulness serene. — 633 *Prelude* 1. 113
Where, though the shades with cheerfulness were filled, — 655 *Prelude* 3. 431
Thus gaiety and cheerfulness prevail, — 700 *Prelude* 8. 53
Hence cheerfulness for acts of daily life, — 747 *Prelude* 14. 121
Happy, and quiet in his cheerfulness, — 761 *Excursion* 1. 367
Such easy cheerfulness, a look so mild, — 765 *Excursion* 1. 607
With tender cheerfulness, and with a voice — 766 *Excursion* 1. 695
In peace and meditative cheerfulness; — 819 *Excursion* 4. 1203
Open, and day's pure cheerfulness, but veiled — 822 *Excursion* 5. 5

Cheerfulness—*continued.*
With evening cheerfulness. In powers of mind, . 833 *Excursion* 5. 716
But with a mild and social cheerfulness ; . . . 839 *Excursion* 6. 93
Where health abides, and cheerfulness, and peace.' 841 *Excursion* 6. 175
In grove or pasture ; cheerfulness of soul, . . . 866 *Excursion* 7. 582
Diffusing health and sober cheerfulness, . . . K.8. 249 *Recluse* 1.1.465

Cheerily. Have hailed the morning sun. But cheerily, Father,— . . . . 39 *Bord.* 125
Where cheerily his course he weaves, ... 240 *P. B.* 342
More cheerily ; and town and tower, ... 343 *Eclipse* 64
Full cheerily on convent-bread . . . . . . 398 *White Doe* 219
But Cupid, following cheerily his guide . . . 624 *Æneid* 53

Cheering. *See* **Heart-cheering, Soul-cheering.**
Cheering its naked waste of scattered stone, . . 4 *Ev. Wk.* 94
Her he addressed in words of cheering sound ; . 27 *Guilt* 185
Our little fire sent forth a cheering warmth . . 50 *Bord.* 708
And cheering oft-times their reluctant gloom. 172 *Infant Daughter* 50
Cheering the wakeful tent on Syrian mountains, . 232 *Power of Sound* 19
And cheering oft his peaceful reveries, ... 466 *St. Bees* 44
Is often cheering ; for I neither seem . . . . 634 *Prelude* 1. 149
Cheering my days, and with industrious thought ; 823 *Excursion* 5. 56
And sink, through utter want of cheering light ; . 835 *Excursion* 5. 834

Cheeringly. Abroad, how cheeringly the sunshine lay 682 *Prelude* 6. 479

Cheerless. All, all was cheerless to the horizon's bound ; . . . . 26 *Guilt* 109
A cheerless beverage. How good it was in you . 52 *Bord.* 810
Which she in duty left, sad but not cheerless. 370 *Eg. Maid* 84
And oft a Prisoner in the cheerless place, . . . 521 *Epist. Beaumont* 27
Not cheerless, though forlorn. . . . . . . 580 *John Words.* 20
My thirst I slaked, and, from the cheerless spot . 763 *Excursion* 1. 463
Or a forbidden tract of cheerless view ; . . . 830 *Excursion* 5. 529
Of feeling, which were cheerless and forlorn . . K.8. 248 *Recluse* 1.1.434

Cheerlessness. With more than wintry cheerlessness and gloom . . . . 830 *Excursion* 5. 538

Cheers. Soft as a guiding star that cheers, but cannot burn." . . . . 140 *Arm. Lady* 66
Whose presence cheers the drooping frame . . 164 **Fair Lady* 31
That fosters growth or checks or cheers decay, . 169 **Never enlivened* 2
The feeble motions of thy life, and cheers . . . 173 *Infant Daughter* 70
Her loneliness she cheers : . . . . 195 *Ruth* 243
The night that calms, the day that cheers ; . . 238 *P. B.* 132
And cheers thy melancholy Mate ! . . . . . 294 *Jedbor.* 83
The shouting, and the jolly cheers ; . . . . 295 *Highland Boy* 78
And in fit measure cheers autumnal days. . . . 336 *Rhine* 14
Calls me to pace her honoured Bridge—that cheers 351 *Des. Stanzas* 56
Of dawn, it cheers the lofty spirit most . . . 391 **Though joy* 2
Cheers these Recluses with a steady ray . . . 467 *St. Bees* 84
For thou hadst lived till every thing that cheers . 491 *Tribute : Dog* 13
With process not unlike to that which cheers . . K.8. 249 *Recluse* 1.1.474

Cheese. And their plain home-made cheese. Yet when the meal . . . . 132 *Michael* 102
Of dainties,—oaten bread, curd, cheese, and cream ; 781 *Excursion* 2. 677

Chemic. Urged to close toil with chemic fire ; . . 399 *White Doe* 302

Chequered. *See* **Chequer'd.**
And gives, where woods the chequered upland strew, ... 8 *Ev. Wk.* 337
Oh Life ! without thy chequered scene . . . 337 **Oh Life* 1
As fades the chequer'd bow that paints the sky . 619 *School Ex.* 98
Time a chequered mantle wears— . . . . . 628 *Installation* 25
Chequered the green-grown thatch. And so she lived . . . . 770 *Excursion* 1. 904

Chequering. Chequering the canvas roof the sunbeams shone. . . . . 34 *Guilt* 542
Chequering the ground—from rock, plant, tree, or tower. . . . . 184 *Night-piece* 7
Thou, chequering peaceably the minster's gloom, . 459 **Wanderer! that* 27
Danced in the breeze, chequering its mossy roof. . 860 *Excursion* 7. 203

Chequerings. In the soft chequerings of a sleepy light. 451 *Ecc. Sonn.* 3. 44. 4
So, by chequerings of sad cheer, ... 502 **Like a* 33

Cherish. Who would not cherish dreams so sweet, . 9 *Lines : Boat* 15
The verminous brood, and cherish what they spare 48 *Bord.* 587
If I may dare to cherish hope that gentle eyes will read . . . . 93 *Poet's Dream* 79
Would supplant the weeds, and cherish . . . 94 *Westmoreland Girl* 79
Its presence tempted him to cherish schemes . . 124 *V. and J.* 188
Appears to cherish most that Torrent white, . . 381 *Duddon* 19. 8
But of the lights that cherish household cares . 426 *Ecc. Sonn.* 1. 31. 4
Seek for the good and cherish it—the ill . . 505 *Warning* 161
Uphold us, cherish, and have power to make . 589 *Immortality* 157
Albert, in thy race we cherish . . . . . . 629 *Installation* 95
To keep and cherish ? how shall man unite . . 831 *Excursion* 5. 576
And I as willingly did cherish mine, ... 839 *Excursion* 6. 106
To shelter innocence, and cherish love ; . . . 887 *Excursion* 9. 202
Cherish, and lofty Minds approve the past— . . 896 *Excursion* 9. 795
They [?] to the last my friends did cherish . . K.8. 219 **The snow-tracks* 5

Cherished. *See* **Self-cherished, Time-cherished.**
The spirit sought not then, in cherished sadness, . 2 *Ev. Wk.* 15
Were with him :—his long absence, cherished hopes, 102 *Brothers* 422
And she I cherished turned her wheel . . . . 109 **I travelled* 11
And all those tokens of a cherished sorrow, . . 119 *Maternal Grief* 78
Hopes I cherished—let them go ! . . . . . 140 *Arm. Lady* 58
From the wild sea a cherished Visitant ; . . . 150 **When, to* 55
The cherished tenor of his pace . . . . . . 243 *P. B.* 658
Of which my fancy cherished, ... 301 *Yarrow V.* 2
Though robbed of many a cherished dream, . . 342 *Ital. Itin.* 27
Hath cherished on a healthful soil ; . . . . 344 **How blest* 6
And cannot spare the Thing he cherished : . . 370 *Eg. Maid* 50
Would lodge her, and the cherished burden bear . 382 *Duddon* 25. 7
Which may itself be cherished and caressed . . 394 **No more* 33

Cherished—*continued.*
A cherished Priestess of the new-baptized ! . . 420 *Ecc. Sonn.* 1. 9. 6
Untaught that meekness is the cherished bent . 455 **Not in the lucid* 14
With cherished sullenness of pace . . . . . 490 *Night Thought* 9
Is there a cherished bird (I venture now . . . 528 **Those breathing* 60
And what if he cherished his purse ? 'Twas no more . . . . 572 *Avarice* 27
Or if thy cherished grief have failed to thwart . 576 **By a* 15
Thy cherished fetters to unbind, ... 581 *Invoc. Earth* 6
And thoughts and projects fondly cherished here, 583 **With copious* 37
Can guess the high resolve, the cherish'd pain . 608 *Desc.Sk.Quarto* 360
Then wafts him, cherish'd on her careful breast, . 624 *Æneid* 49
Where Fear sate thus, a cherished visitant, . . 759 *Excursion* 1. 186
Release from fear ; and cherished peaceful days . 791 *Excursion* 3. 364
Your cherished sullenness is forced to bend . . 819 *Excursion* 4. 1191
Culpably cherished, or corrupt relapse . . . . 828 *Excursion* 5. 364
This pleasing fancy (cherished and upheld . . 834 *Excursion* 5. 794
Cherished for him, he suffered to depart, . . . 843 *Excursion* 6. 314
Cherished in shade though peeped at by the sun ; S.3. 437 **The doubt* 202

Cherishes. How little that she cherishes is lost ! . 392 *Bothwell* 14
Which reason cherishes. And thus the soul, . . 567 *Cumb. Beg.* 102
Of Truth that cherishes our daily life ; . . . 635 *Prelude* 1. 230

Cherishing. Or cherishing resentment, or in vain 772 *Excursion* 2. 69
Yet obstinately cherishing itself : . . . . . 796 *Excursion* 3. 677
And cherishing the pang her heart deplored. . . 849 *Excursion* 6. 733
And cherishing with ever-constant love, . . . 885 *Excursion* 9. 112

Cherith. Such as by Cherith on Elijah called ; . . 62 *Bord.* 1363

Cherokees. He brought them from the Cherokees ; 192 *Ruth* 22

Cherry. Dinning from the CHERRY TREE ! . . . 176 *Waggoner* 2. 22
Feasting at the CHERRY TREE ! " . . . . . 177 *Waggoner* 2. 53
The CHERRY TREE shows proof of this ; . . . 177 *Waggoner* 2. 77
Is red as a ripe cherry. . . . . 483 *Simon Lee* 8
Cherry or maple, sate in close array, ... 639 *Prelude* 1. 515

Cherub. It came with sleep and showed the Boy, no cherub, not transformed, ... 92 *Poet's Dream* 15
This sweet-visaged Cherub of Parian stone . . 340 *Fort Fuentes* 2

Cherubim. In wings of Cherubim, ... 526 **The soaring* 36
Between the Cherubim—on the chosen Race . . 811 *Excursion* 4. 657
Of rudely-painted Cherubim. The floor . . . 824 *Excursion* 5. 153
The radiant Cherubim ;—accept the thanks . . 893 *Excursion* 9. 622

Cherub's. A face (no cherub's face more beautiful) 50 *Bord.* 717

Cherubs. Say that the Cherubs carved in stone, . 144 **Driven in* 52

Chest. The swan uplifts his chest, and backward flings . . . . 6 *Ev. Wk.* 218
Till you have marked his heaving chest, . . . 143 **Driven in* 23
It loosens something at my chest ; . . . . . 145 *Her Eyes* 36
His words came feebly, from a feeble chest, . . 196 *Resolution* 92
Across a shady lane ; his chest . . . . . . 247 *P. B.* 983
The broad full visage, chest of amplest mould, . 270 *Henry : Portrait* 3
He swells his lifted chest, and backward flings . 595 *Ev. Wk. Quarto* 201
" *Invisible* " flames forth upon his chest. . . . 691 *Prelude* 7. 287
Stood, propped against a wall, upon his chest . 696 *Prelude* 7. 640
Within a chest imprisoned ; how they came . . 733 *Prelude* 11. 445

Chestnut. Of Como, bosomed deep in chestnut groves. 12 *Desc. Sk.* 78
Halting beneath the chestnut shade . . . . 344 **How blest* 22
Then, not in vain, under these chestnut boughs . 358 *Aquap.* 358
Or some deep chestnut grove, oft have I paused . 537 **In desultory* 2
Of thee, thy chestnut woods, and garden plots . 685 *Prelude* 6. 663

Chestnuts. Yon chestnuts half the latticed boat-house hide, ... 4 *Ev. Wk.* 107

Chestnut-wood. And fruitage gathered from the chestnut-wood, ... 431 *Ecc. Sonn.* 2. 12.10

Chests. The swans that with white chests upreared in pride . . . . 28 *Guilt* 215

Cheviot. I took it for the blaze of Cheviot Beacon : 50 *Bord.* 742
On lofty Cheviot Hills : . . . . 239 *P. B.* 225
Green Eildon-hill and Cheviot . . . . . . 386 *Yarrow Rev.* 50

Chiabrera. Thy gentle Chiabrera !—not a stone, . 356 *Aquap.* 236
By his bereft, his lonely, Chiabrera. . . . . 574 *Chiabrera* 5. 18

Chicken. The cackling hen, the tender chicken brood, 834 *Excursion* 5. 815

Chid. The Knight hallooed, he cheered and chid them on . . . . 201 *Hart-leap* 21

Chidden. Chidden she chides again ; the thrilling touch . . . . 378 *Duddon* 10. 9

Chide. The Fairies are to blame, and you should chide 45 *Bord.* 429
That coo again !—'tis not to chide, ... 168 *Turtledove* 23
And, with a wandering eye that seems to chide, . 220 *Triad* 28
Gently along ; regardless who shall chide . . . 252 **Her only* 6
And, for this feeling's sake, let no one chide . . 393 *Hart's-horn* 13
Nor chide the Muse that stooped to break a spell 525 *Epist. Beaumont* 276
And, as I with the Cuckoo thus 'gan chide, . . 558 *Cuck. and Night.* 96
How she and I did each the other chide, . . . 561 *Cuck. and Night.* 267
There might the love-sick maiden sit, and chide . 607 *Desc.Sk.Quarto* 309
Wouldst thou not chide ? Yet deem not my pains lost : . . . . 717 *Prelude* 9. 564
Heavenward ; and chide the part of me that flags, 803 *Excursion* 4. 127

Chides. Chidden she chides again ; the thrilling touch 378 *Duddon* 10. 9
On, loitering Muse—the swift Stream chides us—on! 379 *Duddon* 12. 1

Chiding. He hears the chiding of the baffled wind, 19 *Desc. Sk.* 489
Secure, the chiding of the baffled wind, . . . 612 *Desc.Sk.Quarto* 579
Might waste their breath in chiding. Under hills— 680 *Prelude* 6. 374

Chidings. Claim for the pilgrim : and, though chidings sharp . . . . 467 *St. Bees* 95

Chief. *See* **Warrior-chief.**
To every charm, and last and chief to you, . . 13 *Desc. Sk.* 128
—Pity that our young Chief will have no part . 37 *Bord.* 4
They chose *him* for their Chief !—what covert part 47 *Bord.* 551
Pleased some favourite chief to follow . . . 181 *Waggoner* 4. 109
A self-devoted chief—by Hector slain." . . . 210 *Load.* 48
Ill-fated Chief ! there are whose hopes are built . 214 *Dion* 102

Chief—*continued.*
O chief of friends ! such feelings I present — 250 **Happy the* 10
He, too, of battle-martyrs chief ! — 341 *San Salv.* 31
And singly thine, O vanquished Chief ! whose corse, — 361 **For action* 9
Behold how fought the Chief whose conquering sword — 368 *Trajan* 29
Still are we present with the imperial Chief, — 368 *Trajan* 70
Meed of some Roman chief—in triumph borne — 464 *Derwent* 11
Peasant and mail-clad Chief with pious awe ; — 467 *St. Bees* 122
Such, haply, to the rugged chief — 473 *Ossian* 75
Yon light shapes forth a Bard, that shade a Chief. — 474 **Ye shadowy* 14
Of some old British Chief : 'tis nothing more — 548 **Stranger ! this* 4
Thy grace above all pleasures first and chief ; — 563 *Troilus* 74
The old grey stones the plaided chief surveys, — 608 *Desc.Sk.Quarto* 359
Then every chief in turn the beverage quaff'd. — 625 *Æneid* 120
At their chief city, in the sight of Heaven. — 681 *Prelude* 6. 390
Imperial, their chief living residence. — 708 *Prelude* 8. 596
Then stationed in the city, were the chief — 711 *Prelude* 9. 126
Such was the state of things. Meanwhile the chief — 712 *Prelude* 9. 181
To love as prime and chief, for there fear ends, — 748 *Prelude* 14. 163
For their own sakes, as mortal life's chief good, — 791 *Excursion* 3. 365
An Indian Chief discharges from his breast — 820 *Excursion* 4. 1278
From youth or maiden, or some honoured chief — 857 *Excursion* 7. 18
And valiant ; but young Oswald, like a chief — 869 *Excursion* 7. 772
Or sent on mission to some northern Chief — 871 *Excursion* 7. 932
No chief, on my troth, — S.3. 440 **Said red-ribboned* 10

Chiefly. Great actions move our admiration, chiefly — 65 *Bord.* 1536
And Leonard, chiefly for his Brother's sake, — 100 *Brothers* 305
Could fashion ; chiefly by that darling bard — 123 *V. and J.* 90
One chiefly, who with voice and look — 144 **Driven in* 75
Fair ferns and flowers, and chiefly that tall fern, — 149 **A narrow* 33
But chiefly from above the board — 204 *Brougham* 21
Encouraged, sanctioned, chiefly for that end ; — 211 *Laod.* 147
But chiefly let one Cottage hear the tale ; — 294 **Fly, some* 4
Shall wander, chiefly let me cull with care — 355 *Aquap.* 199
Thou, chiefly thou, my Sister dear, — 401 *White Doe* 496
But chiefly by that single grave, — 417 *White Doe* 1898
Then chiefly dear, when foes are planted round, — 430 *Ecc. Sonn.* 2. 6. 9
I chiefly call, the chosen Few, — 473 *Ossian* 54
Known chiefly, Aira ! to thy glen, — 478 *Somnamb.* 28
Of reverential awe will chiefly seek — 496 **A little* 40
But chiefly to Smithfield he loves to repair,— — 571 *Farmer* 85
But chiefly Dido, to the coming ill — 624 *Æneid* 79
Those chiefly that first led me to the love — 642 *Prelude* 2. 4
In many things my brother, chiefly here — 648 *Prelude* 2. 465
Found everywhere, but chiefly in the ring — 657 *Prelude* 3. 541
This chiefly, did I note my grey-haired Dame ; — 661 *Prelude* 4. 217
I mused ; upon these chiefly : and at length, — 666 *Prelude* 5. 68
Of travellers, chiefly delegates returning — 681 *Prelude* 6. 388
Of chance spectators, chiefly dissolute men — 692 *Prelude* 7. 360
Among all regions ; chiefly where appear — 698 *Prelude* 7. 743
The latter chiefly ; from the field of Mars — 710 *Prelude* 9. 45
This narrative, my Friend ! hath chiefly told — 735 *Prelude* 12. 44
This efficacious spirit chiefly lurks — 737 *Prelude* 12. 219
I chiefly looked (what need to look beyond ?) — 741 *Prelude* 13. 101
In London chiefly harboured, whence I roamed, — 751 *Prelude* 14. 351
Their passions and their feelings ; chiefly those — 761 *Excursion* 1. 343
In the wild concert—chiefly when the storm — 782 *Excursion* 2. 700

Chiefs. Or fostered, self-supported chiefs,—like those — 320 **They seek* 6
Of Chiefs triumphant after ruthless wars ; — 346 *Processions* 29
Be warned "—His zeal the Chiefs confounded, — 405 *White Doe* 841
I scorn your Chiefs—men who would lead, — 406 *White Doe* 902
That—while at banquet with your Chiefs you sit — 422 *Ecc. Sonn.* 1. 16. 2
Echoed in Heaven, cries out, " Ye Chiefs, abate — 429 *Ecc. Sonn.* 2. 4. 9
Summoned the Chiefs to lay their feuds aside, — 467 *St. Bees* 103
While round a vacant board the chiefs recline, — 625 *Æneid* 97
These titles emperors and chiefs have borne, — 862 *Excursion* 7. 343

Chieftain. Exclaimed the Chieftain—" let me rather see — 213 *Dion* 82
In which some ancient Chieftain finds repose — 262 **Mark the* 8
Wild Chieftain of a savage Clan ! — 292 *Rob Roy* 102
O miserable Chieftain ! where and when — 305 *Toussaint* 5
The captive chieftain, by a tyrant's doom, — 318 **Is there* 2
The war-worn Chieftain quits the world—to hide — 424 *Ecc. Sonn.* 1. 21. 4
Far from the family vault.—A Chieftain one — 844 *Excursion* 6. 413

Chieftain's. But by the Chieftain's look, though at his side — 278 *Wellington* 5

Chieftains. Chieftains and kings in council were detained ; — 211 *Laod.* 119
To London were the Chieftains bent ; — 404 *White Doe* 783
The Chieftains to unfold his thought, — 405 *White Doe* 808
Of chieftains sprung, who stoutly bore — 533 **Blest is* 12

Child. *See* **Bosom-child, Cottage-child, Foster-child, Goatherd-child, Sister-child.**
Fair scenes, erewhile, I taught, a happy child, — 2 *Ev. Wk.* 13
And pray that never child of song — 9 *Collins* 19
With Independence, child of high Disdain. — 15 *Desc. Sk.* 261
Was blest as free—for he was Nature's child. — 18 *Desc. Sk.* 434
A little prattling child, he oft descends, — 19 *Desc. Sk.* 485
And grant that every sceptred child of clay — 22 *Desc. Sk.* 659
And, pointing to a little child that lay — 33 *Guilt* 470
Softly he stroked the child, who lay outstretched — 33 *Guilt* 487
The blessing this a father gives his child ! — 33 *Guilt* 497
Should child of mine e'er wander hither, speak — 35 *Guilt* 589
And thee, my Child ! Believe me, honoured Sire ! — 40 *Bord.* 144
As come, dear Child ! from a far deeper source — 40 *Bord.* 153
Out of thy mind ? My dear, my only, Child ; — 40 *Bord.* 163
My Child, forgetful of the name of Herbert, — 41 *Bord.* 206
May well deceive his Child—What ! leave her thus, — 41 *Bord.* 251
And torture thus the heart of his own Child—— — 42 *Bord.* 270

Child—*continued.*
As I am dear to you, remember, Child ! — 42 *Bord.* 294
A bee came darting, which the Child with joy — 44 *Bord.* 404
Came to my child as by my side he slept, — 44 *Bord.* 412
I parted with the Child. Parted with whom ? — 46 *Bord.* 508
He said to me, that he had seen his Child, — 50 *Bord.* 716
I look at him and tremble like a child. — 51 *Bord.* 786
May love his Child. Thank you, old Man, for this ! — 52 *Bord.* 823
More than ever Parent loved a Child ? — 53 *Bord.* 849
I could forgive him. And should he make the Child — 56 *Bord.* 1044
Of my own child, this Man must die ; my hand, — 57 *Bord.* 1108
My Child, my blessèd Child ! No more of that ; — 63 *Bord.* 1408
Fortitude is the child of Enterprise : — 65 *Bord.* 1535
My Child—my Child—dark—dark—I faint—this wind— — 67 *Bord.* 1657
while he was muttering something about his Child— — 72 *Bord.* 1957
I did not think he had a living Child.— — 74 *Bord.* 2073
How could he call upon his Child !—O Friend ! — 76 *Bord.* 2187
The Child is father of the Man ; — 79 **My heart* 7
" What ails you, child ? "—she sobbed, " Look here ! " — 82 *Alice Fell* 25
" And whither are you going, child, — 82 *Alice Fell* 33
" My child, in Durham do you dwell ? " — 82 *Alice Fell* 41
The solitary child. — 82 *Lucy Gray* 4
And take a lantern, Child, to light — 83 *Lucy Gray* 15
She is a living child ; — 83 *Lucy Gray* 58
——A simple Child, — 83 *We are Seven* 1
And three times to the child I said, — 86 *Anecdote* 47
'Twas little Barbara Lewthwaite, a child of beauty rare ! — 87 *Pet-lamb* 13
O blessèd vision ! happy child ! — 88 *H. C.* 11
With suit that I would speak in verse of that sequestered child — 91 *Norman Boy* 7
The Child, as if the thunder's voice spake with articulate call, — 92 *Poet's Dream* 9
I whispered, " Yet a little while, dear Child ! thou art my own, — 92 *Poet's Dream* 21
The wings they did not flag ; the Child, though grave, was not deprest. — 92 *Poet's Dream* 32
From floor to roof, all round his eyes the Child with wonder cast, — 92 *Poet's Dream* 43
But oh ! that Country-man of thine, whose eye, loved Child, can see — 93 *Poet's Dream* 73
Let me speak of this brave Child — 93 *Westmoreland Girl* 26
Time passed on ; the Child was happy, — 94 *Westmoreland Girl* 41
What then wants the Child to temper, — 94 *Westmoreland Girl* 73
He fed the spindle of his youngest child, — 95 *Brothers* 23
A child is born or christened, a field ploughed, — 97 *Brothers* 158
He was the child of all the dale—he lived — 100 *Brothers* 343
She flung her blameless child, — 103 *Artegal* 38
But One there is, a Child of nature meek, — 103 *Artegal* 45
Thou for our sakes, though Nature's child indeed, — 107 *Farewell* 38
My Child ! they gave thee to another, — 114 *Ind. Wom.* 31
Oh mercy ! like a helpless child. — 114 *Ind. Wom.* 40
My poor forsaken Child, if I — 114 *Ind. Wom.* 65
No tidings of an only child ; — 117 *Affl. Marg.* 9
Departed Child ! I could forget thee once — 118 *Maternal Grief* 1
The Child she mourned had overstepped the pale — 118 *Maternal Grief* 14
Of the survivor's sweetest voice (dear child, — 118 *Maternal Grief* 44
Softened her pangs, and reconciled the child — 118 *Maternal Grief* 55
One Child did it bear, and that Child was his last. — 120 *Childless Father* 12
For sake of a young Child whose home was there. — 120 *Emigrant Mother* 8
This Child, I chanted to myself a lay, — 120 *EmigrantMother* 10
One little hour a child to me ! — 120 *EmigrantMother* 24
My sister's child, who bears my name, — 121 *EmigrantMother* 67
Never was any child more dear ! — 121 *EmigrantMother* 74
Go with the child.—You have been wretched ; yet — 124 *V. and J.* 191
Bounded before him ;—but the unweeting Child — 124 *V. and J.* 208
His father's house, where to the innocent child — 125 *V. and J.* 264
Obsequious service to the precious child, — 125 *V. and J.* 278
An only Child, who had been born to them — 132 *Michael* 87
Than that a child, more than all other gifts — 133 *Michael* 146
Upon the Child, if he disturbed the sheep — 134 *Michael* 174
We have no other Child but thee to lose, — 135 *Michael* 296
Before her eyes, last child of many gone— — 139 *Widow* 17
Yet listen, Child !—I would not preach ; — 142 *†Lov. and Lik.* 2
The fever of that pale-faced Child ; — 144 **Driven in* 38
My beauty, little child, is flown, — 145 *Her Eyes* 66
—Where art thou gone, my own dear child ? — 145 *Her Eyes* 85
Was living, as a child might know, — 155 *Waterfall* 9
Child of the Year ! that round dost run — 158 **In youth* 73
Was it the humour of a child ? — 162 **Who fancied* 7
And this too from the Laureate's Child, — 164 *Needlecase* 13
In which this Child of Spring was reared — 165 *Parrot* 35
And that frail Child of thirsty clay, — 174 *Waggoner* 1. 93
" Thy wife and child are snug and warm, — 179 *Waggoner* 3. 70
This Child I to myself will take ; — 187 **Three years* 4
A slighted child, at her own will — 192 *Ruth* 4
A young and happy Child ! — 195 *Ruth* 252
Even such a happy Child of earth am I ; — 195 *Resolution* 31
Not higher than a two years' child — 197 *Thorn* 5
She was with child, and she was mad ; — 199 *Thorn* 128
Communion with a stirring child ! — 199 *Thorn* 134
For what became of this poor child — 199 *Thorn* 146
Nay—if a child to her was born — 199 *Thorn* 148
Hunt the Mother and the Child. — 204 *Brougham* 60
Save a Mother and her Child ! — 204 *Brougham* 71

Chose—*continued.*
Attractions manifold ;—and this he chose. 761 *Excursion* 1. 337
Of unambitious piety he chose, 824 *Excursion* 5. 111
Chosen. *See* **Love-chosen.**
Bringing thee chosen plants and blossoms blown . 106 *Farewell* 34
Chosen for the Shearer's covert from the sun, . 133 *Michael* 167
In Robin's bosom, as a chosen cell. 143 **Driven in* 26
Preferring studious leisure, I had chosen 150 **When, to* 2
In some nook of chosen ground : 166 *Wand. Jew* 12
From heaven, upon her chosen Favourite !] 212 *Dion*
Shed on the chosen vale a sun-bright day ! 256 *Marriage: Friend* 4
Apart she toils within the chosen ring ; 259 **A volant* 9
As in a dear and chosen banishment, 275 **Chatsworth ! thy* 6
A chosen Tree ; then, eager to fulfil 276 *Oker Hill* 5
The Youth, her chosen lover. 287 *Ellen Irwin* 32
Wild Relique ! beauteous as the chosen spot 299 *Brownie's Cell* 91
They were thy chosen music, Liberty ! 306 **Two Voices* 4
But 'tis a chosen soil, where sun and breeze 308 **One might* 5
From shades, her chosen place of short-lived rest. 311 **Who rises* 38
The chosen sceptre is a withered bough, 321 **Humanity,delighting* 9
Chosen by Rome's legendary Bards, high minds . 356 *Aquap.* 271
Chosen for ornament—stone matched with stone . 378 *Duddon* 9. 5
From chosen comrade turns, or faithful friend— . 383 *Duddon* 30. 7
Memorials chosen to give life 400 *White Doe* 376
And now, upon a chosen plot 404 *White Doe* 762
Beloved of Heaven, Heaven's chosen care, 414 *White Doe* 1666
From wolves your portion of His chosen sheep : . 444 *Ecc. Sonn.* 3. 16. 5
Of God and chosen friends, your troth to plight . 446 *Ecc. Sonn.* 3. 26. 3
Be this the chosen site ; the virgin sod, 450 *Ecc. Sonn.* 3. 39. 1
I chiefly call, the chosen Few, 473 *Ossian* 54
Thus in the chosen spot a tie so strong 531 **I know* 21
The same as they had chosen for the year, 558 *Cuck. and Night.* 79
As with a chosen friend ; nor did he leave 576 *Chiabrera* 9. 12
Well chosen is the spirit that is here ; 579 *Peele Castle* 46
Wouldst thou be gathered to Christ's chosen flock, 626 *Rock : Rydal* 1
This day, when Granta hails her chosen Lord, 629 *Installation* 69
I look about ; and should the chosen guide 632 *Prelude* 1. 16
The road that pointed toward the chosen Vale. 633 *Prelude* 1. 93
Some imperfection in the chosen theme, 636 *Prelude* 1. 262
Proud of his skill, to reach a chosen point . 637 *Prelude* 1. 368
Chosen by the Muses for their Page of State— 653 *Prelude* 3. 279
And phrases pleased me chosen for delight, 674 *Prelude* 5. 557
There, in a clime from widest empire chosen, 700 *Prelude* 8. 82
The plain straight road, for one no better chosen 728 *Prelude* 11. 71
To be his chosen comrade. Many a time, 757 *Excursion* 1. 61
Approach the embowered abode—our chosen seat— 793 *Excursion* 3. 521
Between the Cherubim—on the chosen Race 811 *Excursion* 4. 657
The strain was aptly chosen ; and I could mark . 814 *Excursion* 4. 888
The tiller's hand, a hermit might have chosen, 832 *Excursion* 5. 681
A book, upon whose leaves some chosen plants, . 841 *Excursion* 6. 205
Raised from his seat within the chosen shade, 870 *Excursion* 7. 818
To make that paradise his chosen home 872 *Excursion* 7. 939
Were turned to evils that are new and chosen, 887 *Excursion* 9. 187
The chosen rustic urged a warlike steed S.3. 437 **The doubt* 190
By night, here only ; or in chosen minds K.8. 240 *Recluse* 1.1. 140
They having also chosen this abode ; K.8. 243 *Recluse* 1.1. 253
A chosen one of my regards. See there K.8. 251 *Recluse* 1.1. 523
Christ. That he would turn to Christ our Lord, 372 *Eg. Maid* 226
A Ship to Christ devoted 374 *Eg. Maid* 359
Christ died for—cannot forfeit his high claim . 429 *Ecc. Sonn.* 2. 4. 12
Charged as ye are by Christ to feed and keep 444 *Ecc. Sonn.* 3. 16. 4
To Christ, the Sun of righteousness, espoused. 496 **A little* 48
In which course if Christ our Saviour 535 *Egremont* 27
Hateful to Christ and to His company ; 553 *Prioress* 40
For he so young to Christ did reverence. 553 *Prioress* 64
And praiseth Christ that is our heavenly King, 555 *Prioress* 167
But Jesus Christ, as in the books ye find, 556 *Prioress* 201
The cause of Christ and civil liberty, 774 *Excursion* 2. 221
Christabel. Didst utter of the Lady Christabel ; 752 *Prelude* 14. 401
Christ-cross-row. From infant-conning of the Christ-cross-row, 880 *Excursion* 8. 413
Christen. Here's for your little boy, and when you christen him 46 *Bord.* 520
Christendom. As ever was in Christendom. 130 *Idiot Boy* 431
And sick at heart of strifeful Christendom, 268 **Four fiery* 13
And Christendom respires ; from guilt and shame 326 *Sobieski* 8
To seek the general mart of Christendom ; 425 *Ecc. Sonn.* 1. 25. 4
All Christendom :—they sweep along (was never . 427 *Ecc. Sonn.* 1. 34. 12
The ancient thrones of Christendom are stuff . 428 *Ecc. Sonn.* 1. 39. 11
Age after age to the arch of Christendom 435 *Ecc. Sonn.* 2. 26. 3
For universal Christendom had thrilled 436 *Ecc Sonn.* 2. 31. 10
Christened. They built him and christened him all in one day, 86 *Rural Arch.* 8
A child is born or christened, a field ploughed, 97 *Brothers* 158
Christian. Mohammedan and Christian. But enough ; 37 *Bord.* 19
By Christian disturbers more savage than Turks, 86 *Rural Arch.* 20
How she loved a Christian Slave, and told her pain 139 *Arm. Lady* 5
" Grieved am I, submissive Christian ! 139 *Arm. Lady* 13
Christian meekness smoothed for all the path of life, 142 *Arm. Lady* 149
A Christian psalm for thee. 195 *Ruth* 258
The Christian of his pride : 232 *Jew. Fam.* 36
Could have had Christian burial. 245 *P. B.* 810
But soon, through Christian faith, is grief subdued : 318 **In due* 13
Appeared—to govern Christian pageantries : 346 *Processions* 38
Christian Traditions ! at my Spirit's call 357 *Aquap.* 291
It is, a Christian Fortress, garrisoned 362 **List—'twas* 32
" On Christian service this frail Bark 370 *Eg. Maid* 73
Of Christian rites, in Christian ground to lay her." 372 *Eg. Maid* 240
Though Christian rites be wanting ! From what bank 387 *Roslin* 8

Christian—*continued.*
Do thou, my christian Son, beware 407 *White Doe* 1054
Then, they, for Christian pity's sake, 412 *White Doe* 1520
Of Christian Faith, this savage Island blessed . 418 *Ecc. Sonn.* 1. 2. 4
The virgin sculptured on his Christian shield :— . 421 *Ecc. Sonn.* 1. 10. 7
And Christian monuments, that now must burn . 421 *Ecc. Sonn.* 1. 12. 8
And Christian India, through her widespread clime, 425 *Ecc. Sonn.* 1. 26. 13
From Nazareth—source of Christian piety, 426 *Ecc. Sonn.* 1. 33. 2
Of Christian aspiration, deigned to fill 436 *Ecc. Sonn.* 2. 30. 11
Of Christian unity, and won a meed 444 *Ecc. Sonn.* 3. 15. 7
Such to this British Isle her christian Fanes, 444 *Ecc. Sonn.* 3. 17. 9
Whose virtue changes to a christian Flower 445 *Ecc. Sonn.* 3. 20. 3
And Wisdom, as she holds a Christian place 466 *St. Bees* 30
Where Christian piety's soul-cheering spark 475 **Homeward we* 2
Fortitude, and that Christian Charity 478 **Lonsdale ! it* 7
Where Christian Martyrs stand in hues portrayed, 500 *Humanity* 21
For Christian Faith. But hopeful signs abound ; 520 *Pun. Death* 13. 8
Of holy faith and Christian hope ; 534 **Blest is* 68
Our Christian altar faithful to the east, 535 **When in* 23
'Mong Christian folk, a street where Jews might be, 553 *Prioress* 37
" A little school of Christian people stood 553 *Prioress* 43
A nest of children come of Christian blood, 553 *Prioress* 45
" The Christian folk that through the Jewry went 555 *Prioress* 163
Wherever Christian altars have been raised, 584 *Ch. Lamb* 25
Through his industrious life, and Christian faith . 587 *Crosth.* 17
" Thus, Christian people, God his might hath shown 627 **When Severn's* 3
And Christian meekness hallowing faithful loves. . 635 *Prelude* 1. 185
Deep in the conscience, nor of Christian Hope, 650 *Prelude* 3. 85
Sounding through Christian lands her trumpet, roused 655 *Prelude* 3. 463
By which, on Christian lands, from age to age 828 *Excursion* 5. 377
Which else the Christian virtue might have claimed. 845 *Excursion* 6. 490
The Christian promise with attentive ear ; 866 *Excursion* 7. 578
These tidings, and in Christian temples meet . 894 *Excursion* 9. 653
Christianised. Just God of christianised Humanity, 328 *Ode 1815* 121
Christian's. To twine around the Christian's brows, . 582 **O for a* 5
In earth's dark chambers, with a Christian's hope ! 775 *Excursion* 2. 248
Christians. " Wedded love with loyal Christians, 140 *Arm. Lady* 61
Christmas. The fragments of a Christmas hymn ; 84 *Shepherd-boys* 17
Like happy people round a Christmas fire. 135 *Michael* 303
The laughter of the Christmas hearth 225 *Present.* 43
By Christmas snows, by visitation bleak 256 *Decay of Piety* 5
The Minstrels played their Christmas tune 375 **The Minstrels* 1
And " Merry Christmas " wished to all ! 375 **The Minstrels* 18
Go, seek, when Christmas snows discomfort bring, 448 *Ecc. Sonn.* 3. 33. 9
Christmas-eve. Last Christmas-eve we talked of this, 199 *Thorn* 137
Christmas-tide. To con it all ere Christmas-tide be spent ; 554 *Prioress* 89
Christmas-time. Of these memorials :—One Christmas-time, 738 *Prelude* 12. 287
Christophe. Christophe now is laid asleep L.2. 190 **Queen and* 2
Christopher. Stood Richard, Ambrose, Christopher, 401 *White Doe* 477
Christ's. But for lost Faith and Christ's dear name, 410 *White Doe* 1299
As when, arrayed in Christ's authority, 444 *Ecc. Sonn.* 3. 18. 10
For Christ's dear sake, by human sympathies 468 *St. Bees* 143
The sweetness of Christ's Mother pierced so 554 *Prioress* 104
And Christ's Mother meek and kind 555 *Prioress* 146
Wouldst thou be gathered to Christ's chosen flock, 626 *Rock : Rydal* 1
Into the second ark, Christ's church, with trust 826 *Excursion* 5. 282
Chronicle. To chronicle the time, we all have here . 97 *Brothers* 162
So speaks the Chronicle, and tells of Lear 103 *Artegal* 41
The chronicle were welcome that should call 290 *Kilchurn* 33
An uncouth Chronicle of glorious years. 351 *Des. Stanzas* 58
Of peaceful years ; a chronicle of heaven ;— 578 *Peele Castle* 22
That great emporium, chronicle at once 708 *Prelude* 8. 594
A chronicle that might suffice to show 711 *Prelude* 9. 101
Romance of giants, chronicle of fiends, 759 *Excursion* 1. 180
That in these shows a chronicle survives 787 *Excursion* 3. 89
The ordinary chronicle of birth, 825 *Excursion* 5. 173
Chronicler. To Time, and Man his earth-born chronicler ; 235 *Power of Sound* 210
Forbear to deem the Chronicler unwise, 359 *Plea : Hist.* 1
This lovely chronicler of things 414 *White Doe* 1674
Chronicles. So prayed he :—as our chronicles report, 551 **If thou in* 24
Unnamed among the chronicles of kings, 635 *Prelude* 1. 204
Chuck. Yields, could not chuck his babe beneath the chin, 60 *Bord.* 1243
Church. *See* **Mother-church.**
Leads to her bridge, rude church, and cottaged grounds, 2 *Ev. Wk.* 7
Plucked while the church bells rang their earliest chime. 28 *Guilt* 211
St. Denis, filled with royal tombs, or the Church of Notre Dame ? 92 *Poet's Dream* 24
" Holy as that far seen which crowns the sumptuous Church in Rome 93 *Poet's Dream* 61
Could never keep those boys away from church, . 99 *Brothers* 271
And by the church, and o'er the down, 126 *Idiot Boy* 44
And by the church, and o'er the down, 127 *Idiot Boy* 119
Will holy Church disperse by beams of gospel-light." 141 *Arm. Lady* 120
In a Saxon church survives, 142 *Arm. Lady* 152
And the ancient church was filled with light, 144 **Driven in* 54
We in the church our faith will plight, 193 *Ruth* 104
And, with this other Maid, to church 199 *Thorn* 115
Of their loved Church, on fast or festival 256 *Decay of Piety* 3
The Church, when trusting in divine command 281 *Chris. Words.* 5
Why does this puny Church present to view 335 *Aix* 5
While they the Church engird with motion slow, . 347 *Processions* 56
Within them, church, and town, and hut, and grange, 350 *Des. Stanzas* 40

Church—*continued.*
In Church or Chapel, if my curious quest . . . 356 *Aquap.* 238
And yon resplendent Church are proud to bear. . 360 **Long has* 14
Enter in dance. Of church, or sabbath ties, . . 387 **Part fenced* 5
His church with monumental wreck bestrown ; . 393 *Inglewood* 10
Filling the church with a lofty voice ! . . . . 396 *White Doe* 38
Who dragged Earl Pembroke from Banbury church 399 *White Doe* 252
Who, standing on this old church tower, . . . 399 *White Doe* 297
For holy Church, and the People's right ! " . . 403 *White Doe* 634
For the old and holy Church we mourn, . . . 403 *White Doe* 654
Of novelties in Church and State ; . . . . . 404 *White Doe* 706
—In Rylstone Church her mortal frame . . . 416 *White Doe* 1869
The Church, by mandate shadowing forth the power 427 *Ecc. Sonn.* 1. 36. 2
With like perverseness did the Church abjure . . 428 *Ecc. Sonn.* 2. 1. 5
Witness the Church that oft-times, with effect . 431 *Ecc. Sonn.* 2. 10. 6
Where that pure Church survives, though summer heats . . . . 431 *Ecc. Sonn.* 2. 12. 7
The Church, whose power hath recently been checked, ... 432 *Ecc. Sonn.* 2. 16. 3
Once more the Church is seized with sudden fear, 432 *Ecc. Sonn.* 2. 17. 1
Their Church reformed ! labouring with earnest care . . . . 438 *Ecc. Sonn.* 2. 40. 4
That Church, the unperverted Gospel's seat ; . . 438 *Ecc. Sonn.* 2. 40. 6
Totters the Throne ; the new-born Church is sad, 439 *Ecc. Sonn.* 2. 41. 13
Whether the Church inspire that eloquence, . . 441 *Ecc. Sonn.* 3. 4. 3
Had not thy holy Church her champions bred, . 442 *Ecc. Sonn.* 3. 10. 6
As if a Church, though sprung from heaven, must owe . . . . 443 *Ecc. Sonn.* 3. 11. 11
That so a Church, unforced, uncalled to brook . 443 *Ecc. Sonn.* 3. 13. 6
Fixed on the frame of England's Church their sight, 444 *Ecc. Sonn.* 3. 15. 4
Of England's Church ; stupendous mysteries ! . 445 *Ecc. Sonn.* 3. 19. 6
Dear be the Church that, watching o'er the needs 445 *Ecc. Sonn.* 3. 20. 1
So prays the Church, to consecrate a Vow . . 447 *Ecc. Sonn.* 3. 26. 9
Inspired, the Church sends ministers to kneel . . 447 *Ecc. Sonn.* 3. 28. 5
Forth for His mercy, as the Church ordains, . . 448 *Ecc. Sonn.* 3. 30. 7
To words the Church prescribes aiding the lip . 448 *Ecc. Sonn.* 3. 30. 10
The Church extends her care to thought and deed ; 448 *Ecc. Sonn.* 3. 31. 2
The counter Spirit found in some gay church . . 448 *Ecc. Sonn.* 3. 33. 10
Our Church prepares not, trusting to the might . 450 *Ecc. Sonn.* 3. 40. 7
Types of the spiritual Church which God hath reared ; . . . . 451 *Ecc. Sonn.* 3. 42. 2
Perplex the Church ; but be thou firm,—be true . 465 **Pastor and* 6
Poured from the bosom of thy Church, St. Bees ! 468 *St. Bees* 144
Yet is yon neat trim church a grateful speck . . 474 **How sad* 6
A church in every grove that spreads . . . . 506 *Lab. Hymn* 19
The Mother Church in yon sequestered vale ; . . 534 **When in* 4
As church or abbey furnisheth. . . . . . . 550 *Hermit's Cell* 2. 12
Thy Church and cottages of mountain stone . . 622 *Recluse* 1. 1. 121
St. Mary's Church, the preacher then would cry :— 627 **When Severn's* 2
Let the new Church be worthy of its aim, . . . 627 **When Severn's* 11
For the Church, the State, the Throne ! . . . 629 *Installation* 112
Of the old church, that—though from recent showers . . . . 644 *Prelude* 2. 120
On the plain steeples of our English Church, . . 655 *Prelude* 3. 416
I saw the snow-white church upon her hill . . 658 *Prelude* 4. 21
Saw her go forth to church or other work . . . 661 *Prelude* 4. 218
That self-same village church ; I see her sit . . 671 *Prelude* 5. 399
Of the church clock telling the hours with strokes 685 *Prelude* 6. 693
St. Peter's Church ; or, more aspiring aim, . . 691 *Prelude* 7. 252
As on the pavement of a Gothic church . . . 716 *Prelude* 9. 444
The Scottish Church, both on himself and those . 762 *Excursion* 1. 397
Into the second ark, Christ's church, with trust . 826 *Excursion* 5. 282
Made to the spiritual fabric of her Church ; . . 838 *Excursion* 6. 8
Plagued with uncharitable thoughts the church ; . 845 *Excursion* 6. 467
To fly—but whither ! And this gracious Church, 855 *Excursion* 6. 1105
Altar, and cross, and church of solemn roof, . . 873 *Excursion* 7. 1024
Of vast cathedral or conventual church, . . . 877 *Excursion* 8. 187

Church-aisle. Is raised from the church-aisle, and forward borne . . . . 780 *Excursion* 2. 570

Church-bell. And, oftentimes, hear the church-bell with a sigh, ... 116 *Repentance* 34

Church-clock. "Or of the church-clock and the chimes 487 *Fountain* 13
About the crazy old church-clock, ... 488 *Fountain* 71

Church-clock's. Or when the church-clock's knell profound . . . . 223 *Wishing-gate* 67
Nor does the village Church-clock's iron tone . . 453 **Calm is the* 10

Church-door. He was a parish-boy—at the church-door . . . . 135 *Michael* 259
Of the proud Bearer. To the wide church-door, . 448 *Ecc. Sonn.* 3. 32. 9

Churches. Churches, on whose symbolic beauty gazed 467 *St. Bees* 121
Yet more ; around those Churches, gathered Towns 468 *St. Bees* 127
Courts, cloisters, flocks of churches, gateways, towers : . . . . 649 *Prelude* 3. 33
Her equal rights, her churches and her schools— 880 *Excursion* 8. 430

Church-like. This block—and yon, whose church-like frame . . . . 215 *Kirkstone* 47

Church's. A Saint, the Church's Rock, the mystic Keys . . . . 357 *Aquap.* 309
For the State's guidance, or the Church's weal, . 587 *Crosth.* 8

Church-steeple. She in Grasmere's old church-steeple 94 *Westmoreland Girl* 59

Church-tower. Talk, laughter, and perchance a church-tower knell : . . . . . . 18 *Desc. Sk.* 420
To-night the church-tower bells will ring . . . 113 *Lament* 22
On with your pastime ! till the church-tower bells 233 *Power of Sound* 37
Floats the soft cadence of the church-tower bells ; 332 *Ode : Thanks.* 206
Upon a rising ground a grey church-tower, . . 823 *Excursion* 5. 80
And yet conspicuous, stood the old Church-tower, 892 *Excursion* 9. 575

Churchyard. *See* **Village-churchyard.**
She quits her house and, in the neighbouring Churchyard . . . . 44 *Bord.* 390

Churchyard—*continued.*
And in the Churchyard sod her feet have worn . 44 *Bord.* 394
At midnight, I betook me to the Churchyard : . 47 *Bord.* 574
" Two of us in the church-yard lie, ... 83 *We are Seven* 21
And, in the church-yard cottage, I . . . . . 83 *We are Seven* 23
Two of us in the church-yard lie, ... 84 *We are Seven* 31
Beneath the church-yard tree." . . . . . . 84 *We are Seven* 32
If two are in the church-yard laid, ... 84 *We are Seven* 35
" So in the church-yard she was laid ; . . . . 84 *We are Seven* 53
Why can he tarry *yonder ?*—In our church-yard . 95 *Brothers* 12
That from his cottage to the church-yard led, . 95 *Brothers* 35
He to the solitary church-yard turned ; . . . 96 *Brothers* 80
Unseen by Leonard, at the church-yard gate . . 96 *Brothers* 101
Of this rude church-yard, till the stars appeared . 97 *Brothers* 114
Comes to this church-yard once in eighteen months ; 97 *Brothers* 126
Commend me to these valleys ! Yet your Church-yard . . . . 98 *Brothers* 166
If every English church-yard were like ours ; . . 98 *Brothers* 176
Left in the church-yard wall. That's Walter Ewbank. . . . . 98 *Brothers* 200
And Leonard, when they reached the church-yard gate, ... 102 *Brothers* 409
And here and there a church-yard grave is found 110 **'Tis said that some* 2
The churchyard path to seek : . . . . . . 199 *Thorn* 158
May in Kirkconnell churchyard view . . . . 287 *Ellen Irwin* 51
Than 'mid that wave-washed Churchyard to recline, ... 384 *Duddon* 31. 10
Fast the churchyard fills ;—anon . . . . . 396 *White Doe* 31
Free entrance to the churchyard ground— . . 396 *White Doe* 54
Lie quiet in your churchyard bed ! . . . . . 397 *White Doe* 68
In the Churchyard of the Priory. . . . . . 412 *White Doe* 1523
So to the Churchyard they are bound, ... 413 *White Doe* 1531
The enclosure of this churchyard ground ; . . . 416 *White Doe* 1882
And in the churchyard he must take his bride . 427 *Ecc. Sonn.* 1. 36. 11
Through the still churchyard, each with garland gay, ... 448 *Ecc. Sonn.* 3. 32. 7
At the dim centre of a churchyard yew ; . . . 456 **The leaves* 19
And, to the churchyard come, stopped short . . 486 **We walked* 31
Beside the churchyard yew, ... 487 **We walked* 42
Within this churchyard bound. . . . . . . 623 *G. and S. Green* 24
Where he was born ; the grassy churchyard hangs 671 *Prelude* 5. 392
And through that churchyard when my way has led 671 *Prelude* 5. 394
Lines from the churchyard elegy of Gray. . . 726 *Prelude* 10. 536
Small space of that green churchyard with a light 826 *Excursion* 5. 229
The reverend Pastor toward the churchyard gate 829 *Excursion* 5. 441
Hath gained his noontide height, this churchyard, filled . . . . 830 *Excursion* 5. 534
This Churchyard was. And, whether they had come 845 *Excursion* 6. 476
Green is the Churchyard, beautiful and green, . 847 *Excursion* 6. 605
A long stone-seat, fixed in the Churchyard wall ; . 850 *Excursion* 6. 779
" In that green nook, close by the Churchyard wall, 854 *Excursion* 6. 1080
That, near the quiet churchyard where we sate, . 865 *Excursion* 7. 541

Churl. Of that self-solaced, easy-hearted churl, . 826 *Excursion* 5. 234
Invests the thriving churl, his legs appear, . . 880 *Excursion* 8. 404

Churlish. The churlish gales of penury, that blow . 19 *Desc. Sk.* 504
Or to the churlish elements exposed . . . . 172 *Infant Daughter* 21
Seemed churlish. And behold, both far and near, 356 *Aquap.* 216
Quoth she, to hear this churlish bird thus speak . 560 *Cuck.andNight.*212
The churlish gales, that unremitting blow . . . 613 *Desc.Sk.Quarto* 604
The churlish features of that after-race . . . 814 *Excursion* 4. 901
Are opened. Churlish Winter hath given leave . K.8. 241 *Recluse* 1.1. 189

Churlishness. That in thy churlishness a cause canst find 559 *Cuck.andNight.*147

Chuse. Rather than be disgraced, would chuse to die. 559 *Cuck.andNight.*160

Cicada. Or prayer-bell by the dull cicada drown'd. 603 *Desc. Sk. Quarto* 59

Cincture. (A vest with woollen cincture tied, . . 413 *White Doe* 1607

Cipher. Cipher and syllable ! thine eye . . . . 486 *Matthew* 10

Ciphers. *See* **Cyphers.**

Circean. To wantonness.—Away, Circean revels ! . 441 *Ecc. Sonn.* 3. 3. 9

Circle. In many a whistling circle wheels her flight ; 4 *Ev. Wk.* 91
Charmed the tall circle of the enchanted steeps. . 7 *Ev. Wk.* 304
Dear and more dear the lessening circle grows ; . 19 *Desc. Sk.* 479
What wonders in that circle lie ! . . . . . 142 †*Lov. and Lik.* 12
A dull, contracted circle, yielding light . . . 184 *Night-piece* 5
—There were they all in circle—there . . . . 401 *White Doe* 476
The saint, the scholar, from a circle freed . . . 424 *Ecc. Sonn.* 1. 23. 5
Upon that circle traced from sacred story . . . 445 *Ecc. Sonn.* 3. 19. 9
Apart, to overlook the circle vast— . . . . 477 *Long Meg* 7
Charms the tall circle of th' enchanted steeps. . 598 *Ev. Wk. Quarto* 350
One of a festive circle, I poured out . . . . 653 *Prelude* 3. 298
A centre to the circle which they make ; . . . 669 *Prelude* 5. 252
Into a narrower circle of deep red, ... 762 *Excursion* 1. 427
Widening its circle as the storms advance. . . 775 *Excursion* 2. 262
And the whole circle of the heavens, for him . . 811 *Excursion* 4. 678
In open circle seated round, and hushed . . . 820 *Excursion* 4. 1280
The inevitable circle : better far . . . . . 827 *Excursion* 5. 328
Scattered through half the circle of the sky ; . . 893 *Excursion* 9. 602

Circles. Concord and Charity in circles move. . . 443 *Ecc. Sonn.* 3. 14. 14
(Still marked with green turf circles narrowing . 470 *Tynwald* 2
Small circles of green radiance gleam around. . . 597 *Ev. Wk. Quarto* 278
Small circles glittering idly in the moon, . . . 637 *Prelude* 1. 365
Was figured o'er with circles, lines, or mounds, . 745 *Prelude* 13. 338
In spiral circles mount aloft, and soar . . . . K.8. 234 **The order'd* 2

Circlet. With living snow-drops ? circlet bright ! . 162 **Who fancied* 3

Circlets. Hundreds of curves and circlets, to and fro, 218 *Recluse* 1. 1. 213

Circling. With its dark arms to form a circling bower, 23 *Yew-tree* 11
Went circling, like a multitude of sounds. . . . 146 **It was an* 8
And breaks the mirror of the circling deeps ; . . 597 *Ev. Wk. Quarto* 312
A true reflection of the circling year, ... 828 *Excursion* 5. 394

Circuit. And one day's narrow circuit is to Him . 172 *Infant Daughter* 11

Circuit—*continued.*
A circuit ampler than the lake beneath, . . . 218 *Recluse* I. I. 209
In depth, in height, in circuit, how serene . . . 219 **This Height* 29
Through its wide circuit, that, in deep repose, . 323 *Ode 1814* 17
Within the circuit of those Gothic walls, . . . 328 *Ode 1815* 64
The circuit of this hallowed place. . . . . . 398 *White Doe* 205
And widening circuit of ethereal sky. . . . . 426 *Ecc. Sonn.* I. 29. 14
As when a circuit has been run . . . . . . 479 *Somnamb.* 116
And down the valley, and, a circuit made . . . 644 *Prelude* 2. 129
Once more the circuit of our little lake, . . . 660 *Prelude* 4. 138
Whate'er in this wide circuit we beheld, . . . 683 *Prelude* 6. 541
A whole horizon's circuit, do with power, . . . 690 *Prelude* 7. 242
And the stone abbot, after circuit made . . . 727 *Prelude* 10. 599
In the familiar circuit of my home, ... 743 *Prelude* 13. 223
Within the circuit of this fabric huge, . . . 819 *Excursion* 4. 1177
Majestic circuit, beautiful abyss, ... 822 *Excursion* 5. 9
Within the circuit of this sea-girt isle . . . . 894 *Excursion* 9. 683

Circuitous. Were more circuitous, but not less sure 686 *Prelude* 6. 752

Circulate. To shoot and circulate ; smiles have there been seen ; . . . . 173 *Infant Daughter* 68

Circulates. It circulates, the Soul of all the worlds. 884 *Excursion* 9. 15

Circumambient. Is the recess, the circumambient world . . . . 700 *Prelude* 8. 56
To rest upon their circumambient walls ; . . . 818 *Excursion* 4. 1160

Circumference. Of vast circumference and gloom profound . . . . 184 *Yew-trees* 9
From centre to circumference, unveiled ! . . . 548 **Stay, bold* 11
Eddying within its vast circumference, . . . 788 *Excursion* 3. 147
—Vast the circumference of hope—and ye . . 890 *Excursion* 9. 398

Circumfuse. Of slumber Venus sheds, to circumfuse 624 *Æneid* 47
Or grandeur circumfuse them to no end. . . . 704 *Prelude* 8. 364

Circumfused. Even forms and substances are circumfused . . . . 674 *Prelude* 5. 601

Circumscribe. I would not circumscribe your love : 142 †*Lov. and Lik.* 49
To circumscribe this Shape in fixed repose ; . . 511 **Who rashly* 18

Circumscribed. Formal, and circumscribed in time and space ; . . . . 321 **The power* 2
Of Britain circumscribed me ; else, perhaps . . 798 *Excursion* 3. 813

Circumscribing. And moss-grown alleys, circumscribing shades, ... 497 **Enough of climbing* 14

Circumspect. And circumspect must be our course, and slow, ... 105 *Artegal* 212
Of circumspect humanity ; . . . . 330 *Ode : Thanks.* 74
And, in its movements, circumspect and slow. . 840 *Excursion* 6. 148

Circumspection. And circumspection needful to preserve . . . . 568 *Cumb. Beg.* 129
From circumspection, infinite delay. . . . . 635 *Prelude* I. 242
In circumspection and simplicity, ... 720 *Prelude* 10. 175

Circumstance. There was a circumstance, trifling indeed— . . . . 42 *Bord.* 272
By love, long crossed with adverse circumstance. 278 **Lo ! where she* 8
By shock of circumstance, or lapse of years, . . 510 *F. Stone* 115
Or circumstance, how far soever changed . . . 650 *Prelude* 3. 103
To lean upon extrinsic circumstance . . . . 708 *Prelude* 8. 624
Of one devoted,—one whom circumstance . . . 715 *Prelude* 9. 400
From every object pleasant circumstance . . . 729 *Prelude* 11. 154
When genial circumstance hath favoured them, . 736 *Prelude* 12. 157
Of act and circumstance, and visible form, . . 744 *Prelude* 13. 288
Whether from breath of outward circumstance, . 755 *Recluse* I. I. 764
By circumstance to take unto the height . . . 757 *Excursion* I. 87
But, by the storms of circumstance unshaken, . 802 *Excursion* 4. 71
By circumstance, with intermixture fine . . . 829 *Excursion* 5. 454
The edge of adverse circumstance, and turn . . 835 *Excursion* 5. 859
Of circumstance ; and here the tragic Muse . . 846 *Excursion* 6. 551
Ye wished for act and circumstance, that make . 874 *Excursion* 8. 17
Where circumstance and nature had combined . 887 *Excursion* 9. 201
Lead me, or outward circumstance impels. . . K.8. 233 **Along the* 3

Circumstances. From the clear light of circumstances, flashed . . . . 64 *Bord.* 1495
Of circumstances might to thee have spared . . 679 *Prelude* 6. 284
One guide, the light of circumstances, flashed . 731 *Prelude* 11. 243
'Mid circumstances awful and sublime, . . . 747 *Prelude* 14. 80

Cirque. And cirque and crescent framed by wall . 407 *White Doe* 987

Cistern. Into the dimpling cistern of his heart : 670 *Prelude* 5. 327

Cistern-wheel. Till Death's cold touch her cistern-wheel assail, ... 615 *Desc.Sk.Quarto* 742

Cistertian. *A brighter crown.*"—On yon Cistertian wall 429 *Ecc. Sonn.* 2. 3. 5

Citadel. Salute us ; there stood Indian citadel, . . 262 **Dark and* 6
Shrunk to her citadel ; . . . . 544 *Russ. Fug.* 270
Of temple, palace, citadel, and huge . . . . 784 *Excursion* 2. 858
Of a tall rock, their airy citadel— . . . . . 786 *Excursion* 3. 4

Citadels. And students with their pensive citadels ; 250 **Nuns fret* 3
The citadels of truth ; . . . . 330 *Ode : Thanks.* 108
Citadels dear to studious privacy. . . . . . 529 **Those breathing* 119
Far-heard)—our only citadels. . . . . . . 533 **Blest is* 10

Cities. Whence golden harvests, cities, warlike towers, 102 *Artegal* 21
Fields smiled, and temples rose, and towns and cities grew. . . . . 103 *Artegal* 73
Amid the smoke of cities did you pass . . . . 147 *Joanna* 1
Of towns and cities, I have owed to them, . . 206 *Tintern* 26
My new-planned cities, and unfinished towers. . 211 *Laod.* 132
Heaven grant that other Cities may be gay ! . . 304 **Festivals have* 6
While, to dislodge his game, cities are sacked ! . 313 **Go back* 14
Where towns and cities thick as stars appear, . 327 *Ode 1815* 29
And, drinking towns and cities, still can drink . 328 *Ode 1815* 96
Cities and towns—'tis Thou—the work is Thine !— 328 *Ode 1815* 97
—Wide-wasted regions—cities wrapt in flame— . 330 *Ode : Thanks.* 98
Is this the stream, whose cities, heights, and plains, 335 *Namur* 2
Of midnight,—cities, plains, forests, and mighty streams. . . . . 350 *Des. Stanzas* 18
Where cities fanned by thy brisk airs . . . . 506 **While from* 37

Cities—*continued.*
Can string you names of districts, cities, towns, . 670 *Prelude* 5. 320
Of golden cities ten months' journey deep . . 688 *Prelude* 7. 83
I did not pine like one in cities bred, ... 705 *Prelude* 8. 433
On towns and cities, wallowing in the abyss . . 724 *Prelude* 10. 442
Of cities, where the human heart is sick, . . . 743 *Prelude* 13. 204
Within the walls of cities—may these sounds . . 755 *Recluse* I. I. 833
And turbulence of murmuring cities vast ; . . 787 *Excursion* 3. 104
Thousands of cities, in the desert place . . . 807 *Excursion* 4. 437
Its cities, temples, fields, its awful power, . . 871 *Excursion* 7. 898
In crowded cities, without fear shall live . . . 894 *Excursion* 9. 668
Of cities, 'mid the same eternal flow . . . . K.8. 257 **Shall he* 3

Citizen. "*Good morrow, Citizen !*" a hollow word, . 304 **Jones ! as* 11
In Statesman, Priest, and humble Citizen : . . 441 *Ecc. Sonn.* 3. 5. 6

Citron. Embowered in walnut slopes and citron isles : 13 *Desc. Sk.* 155
And peach and citron, in Spring's mildest breeze . 356 *Aquap.* 218

City. Dismally tolled, that night, the city clock ! . 31 *Guilt* 376
For act and suffering, to the city straight . . . 36 *Guilt* 650
The vacant city slept ; the busy winds, . . . 123 *V. and J.* 95
—So be it ! In the city he remained . . . . 125 *V. and J.* 240
He in the dissolute city gave himself . . . . 138 *Michael* 444
Fresh from the crowded city, to behold . . . 143 **High bliss* 10
Shuddered the walls—the marble city wept— . 214 *Dion* 110
That walled a city with its melody . . . . . 234 *Power of Sound* 130
From the babe's first cry to voice of regal city, . 234 *Power of Sound* 163
In city or in village small, ... 239 *P. B.* 278
The cruel city breeds. . . . . 239 *P. B.* 300
This City now doth, like a garment, wear . . . 269 *Westm. Bridge* 4
She was a maiden City, bright and free ; . . . 305 *Ven. Rep.* 5
Showered equally on city and on field, . . . 316 **O'er the* 6
In the thronged city, from the walks of gain, . . 320 **O'erweening Statesmen* 6
City, and naval stream, suburban grove, . . . 323 *Ode 1814* 9
City and field and flood ;—aloud it cried— . . 323 *Ode 1814* 28
For lo ! the Imperial City stands released . . . 326 *Sobieski* 6
The city one vast temple, dedicate . . . . . 334 **The Spirit* 10
Soon witnessed, and the city of seven hills, . . 353 *Aquap.* 79
Of Commonwealths, each city a starlike seat . . 359 **They—who* 12
Why comes not Francis ?—From the doleful City 411 *White Doe* 1364
Where Tiber's stream the immortal City laves : . 421 *Ecc. Sonn.* I. 13. 4
Till the whole City rings like one vast quire. . . 442 *Ecc. Sonn.* 3. 8. 8
Till they have reached the eternal City—built . 452 *Ecc. Sonn.* 3. 47. 13
We have not passed into a doleful City, . . . 475 *Greenock* 1
Are trivial pomp and city noise, ... 533 **Blest is* 52
From the great City ; never, upon leaves . . . 547 **Rude is* 7
And Nature, while through the great city he hies. 570 *Farmer* 63
From the great city where he first drew breath, . 584 *Ch. Lamb* 3
From the vast city, where I long had pined . . 632 *Prelude* I. 7
Of city smoke, by distance ruralised ; . . . . 633 *Prelude* I. 89
In the great city, 'mid far other scenes ; . . . 648 *Prelude* 2. 452
Of the huge city, on the leaded roof . . . . 679 *Prelude* 6. 267
In a mean city, and among a few, ... 680 *Prelude* 6. 347
At their chief city, in the sight of Heaven. . . 681 *Prelude* 6. 390
To times, when half the city shall break out . . 697 *Prelude* 7. 672
Of what the mighty City is herself, ... 698 *Prelude* 7. 723
Of what in the Great City had been done . . . 708 *Prelude* 8. 626
Of that huge city, oftentimes was seen . . . 709 *Prelude* 8. 666
Whom, in the city, privilege of birth . . . . 711 *Prelude* 9. 115
Then stationed in the city, were the chief . . . 711 *Prelude* 9. 126
Entering the city, here and there a face, . . . 713 *Prelude* 9. 278
The spacious city, and in progress passed . . . 719 *Prelude* 10. 50
To the whole city, "sleep no more." The trance 719 *Prelude* 10. 87
The capital City ; what was struggled for, . . 720 *Prelude* 10. 128
To abide in the great City, where I found . . . 721 *Prelude* 10. 245
And this same city, that did then appear . . . 725 *Prelude* 10. 504
The city of Timoleon ! Righteous Heaven ! . . 732 *Prelude* 11. 379
From the great City, else it must have proved . 741 *Prelude* 13. 114
In the great City, broke like light from far. . . 745 *Prelude* 13. 365
Remote from view of city spire, or sound . . . 758 *Excursion* I. 124
To the great City, an emporium then . . . . 774 *Excursion* 2. 216
Was of a mighty city—boldly say . . . . . 784 *Excursion* 2. 835
Sprung from the desert ? And behold a city . . 799 *Excursion* 3. 884
The obstreperous city ; on the barren seas . . 806 *Excursion* 4. 369
Winding Euphrates, and the city vast . . . . 811 *Excursion* 4. 689
City, and town, and tower,—and sea with ships . 819 *Excursion* 4. 1197
Of the dense air, which town or city breeds . . 838 *Excursion* 6. 22
For knavish purposes ! The city, too, ... 843 *Excursion* 6. 351
His capital city ! ' Thence, along a tract . . . 869 *Excursion* 7. 794
In town and city and sequestered glen, . . . 873 *Excursion* 7. 1023
Nor crowded city can be taxed with aught . . . 880 *Excursion* 8. 422
Toward the beleaguered city, in the might . . S.3. 437 **The doubt* 191
A City where, if indifference to disgust . . . K.8. 253 *Recluse* I. I. 604

City-gates. With that sole charge he passed the city-gates, ... 125 *V. and J.* 244

City's. Of the changed City's long-departed power, 355 *Aquap.* 167
Hence, while the imperial City's din . . . . 376 **The Minstrels* 73
Which met me issuing from the City's walls) . . 687 *Prelude* 7. 3
In that enormous City's turbulent world . . . 700 *Prelude* 8. 71

Civic. When civic renovation . . . . 233 *Power of Sound* 65
And binds her temples with the civic wreath ? . 311 **Who rises* 2
Of peaceful civic virtue : they attest . . . . 316 **Hail, Zaragoza* 7
So may she labour for thy civic halls : . . . . 324 *Ode 1814* 99
That civic strife can turn the happiest hearth . 504 *Warning* 76
Of civic prejudice, the bigotry, ... 716 *Prelude* 9. 498

Civil. Or, since it suits you to be civil, ... 176 *Waggoner* I. 239
Hath stained the robes of civil power with blood, 213 *Dion* 56
Of civil conflict, nor the wrecks of change, . . 262 **Not Love* 2
By civil arts and labours of the pen, ... 389 *Sound of Mull* 10
Ensign of civil power, weapon of war, ... 394 **No more* 12
Of civil slaughter. Yet, while temporal power . 432 *Ecc. Sonn.* 2. 16. 9
The sons who for thy civil rights have bled ! . . 442 *Ecc. Sonn.* 3. 10. 2

Civil—*continued.*
In civil conflict met on Bosworth-field; 546 **The embowering* 18
Of natural rights and civil; and to acts 712 *Prelude* 9. 201
Of civil government, and its wisest forms; 714 *Prelude* 9. 323
Of civil slaughter, was our frequent walk; 716 *Prelude* 9. 433
In arguments of civil polity, 728 *Prelude* 11. 77
The cause of Christ and civil liberty, 774 *Excursion* 2. 221
Of civil action, yielded to a power 798 *Excursion* 3. 825
Of civil polity, and early trained 880 *Excursion* 8. 393
With civil arts, that shall breathe forth their fragrance, 890 *Excursion* 9. 390
The powers of civil polity were given." 890 *Excursion* 9. 415
Civilised. A savage horde among the civilised, 888 *Excursion* 9. 309
Civility. A brood whom no civility could melt, 102 *Artegal* 15
While the fair gardens of civility, 330 *Ode: Thanks.* 109
Among the conquests of civility, 388 **The pibroch's* 11
Of sweet civility, on rustic wilds. 839 *Excursion* 6. 41
Clacking. Each clacking mill, that broke the murmuring streams, 22 *Desc. Sk.* 630
Clad. *See* **Copse-clad, Corn-clad, Fern-clad, Fire-clad, Furze-clad, Grey-clad, Heath-clad, Leaf-clad, Mail-clad, Moss-clad, Snow-clad, Spur-clad, Turf-clad, Vine-clad, Warm-clad.**
And she was wildly clad: 83 *We are Seven* 10
And shepherds clad in the same country grey 96 *Brothers* 64
What shifting pictures—clad in gleams 178 *Waggoner* 3. 36
Are clad in one green hue, and lose themselves 206 *Tintern* 13
And in a white, far-beaming, corselet clad! 213 *Dion* 25
Though clad in colours beautiful and pure, 263 **Those words* 10
And proud she was of heart, when clad 295 *Highland Boy* 31
A shepherd clad in homely grey; 399 *White Doe* 281
And clad in homely russet brown? 485 *Poet's Epitaph* 38
Ill fed she was, and thinly clad; 536 *Goody Blake* 22
Not seldom, clad in radiant vest, 550 *Hermit's Cell* 5. 1
A spirit meek in self-abasement clad. 583 **With copious* 6
Of mitred Prelates, Lords in ermine clad, 688 *Prelude* 7. 108
Of some gigantic warrior clad in mail, 708 *Prelude* 8. 585
In one inseparable glory clad, 725 *Prelude* 10. 519
Of aspect, with aerial softness clad, 773 *Excursion* 2. 95
Is clad with yellow flowers. S.3. 431 **TheScottish* 28
Claim. Confirmed by hoary hairs, belief may claim; 5 *Ev. Wk.* 193
Not ineffectual was that piteous claim: 36 *Guilt* 654
Of war, had I returned to claim my right; 104 *Artegal* 144
Would balance claim with claim, and right with right? 105 *Artegal* 171
Than half his substance. This unlooked-for claim, 134 *Michael* 217
For MARY's humble, SARAH's silent claim, 152 **Forth from* 24
Thou art indeed by many a claim 158 **In youth* 31
One tender claim abate; 223 *Wishing-gate* 15
Such privilege ye claim. 225 *Present.* 6
And, if there be a joy that slights the claim 261 **Fair Prime* 13
Inspired, may in thy leisure claim a part; 269 **If these* 4
Proofs of a higher sovereignty I claim; 270 **Shame on* 10
Which justly it can claim. The Nation hears 271 *George: Death* 12
And claim, among the dead, this awful crown; 275 *Gravestone* 9
If, guarding grossest things from common claim 280 *Plea for Auth.* 6
Some claim upon thee, if I could, 288 *Highland Girl* 57
Beneath the change; who heard a claim 299 *Brownie's Cell* 49
Powers have they left, an impulse, and a claim 316 **It was a* 7
The unfeeling Elements no claim shall raise 322 **By Moscow* 4
Peace that should claim respect from lawless Might. 323 **Now that* 8
With every help that ye from earth and heaven may claim! 327 *Ode 1815* 9
If from a traveller's fortune I might claim 335 *Aix* 9
Before the target stood—to claim 342 *Ital. Itin.* 61
Too much from this frail earth we claim, 348 **Lulled by* 29
Can oft with justice claim. And not disdaining 357 *Aquap.* 288
To greet with instant faith their loftiest claim. 359 **Complacent Fictions* 8
Respect to every Inmate's claim: 375 **The Minstrels* 14
Children of Art, that claim strange brotherhood 392 *Daniel* 5
For great and sacred is the modest claim 392 *Avon* 5
A pure religion, and the claim 400 *White Doe* 387
Such rights did feeble nature claim; 409 *White Doe* 1193
Yet shall it claim our reverence, that to God, 419 *Ecc. Sonn.* 1. 4. 5
Shall, by regenerate life, the promise claim. 423 *Ecc. Sonn.* 1. 17. 14
Christ died for—cannot forfeit his high claim 429 *Ecc. Sonn.* 2. 4. 12
Go forth, great King! claim what thy birth bestows; 432 *Ecc. Sonn.* 2. 15. 6
Claim Heaven's regard like waters that have wet 436 *Ecc. Sonn.* 2. 32. 12
And alien storms with home-bred ferments claim 438 *Ecc. Sonn.* 2. 38. 7
Ere nightfall—truth that well may claim a sigh, 448 *Ecc. Sonn.* 3. 31. 11
Claim for the pilgrim: and, though chidings sharp 467 *St. Bees* 95
In concert with memorial claim 472 *Ossian* 23
There's virtue, the title it surely may claim, 482 *Character* 15
A claim to her disparagement! 497 *Lycoris* 50
Therein a portion claim. 498 **The sylvan* 18
He is come to claim his right: 536 *Egremont* 82
One heart-relieving tear may claim; 577 *Cenotaph* 8
In these lone vales, if aught of faith may claim, 595 *Ev. Wk. Quarto* 175
Are high rewards; but bound they Nature's claim 626 **Son of* 10
Unthought of—this may surely claim a sigh. 627 **We gaze* 8
But now her Spirit hath put forth its claim 627 **When Severn's* 9
These children claim thee for their sire; the breath 627 *Eagle and Dove* 5
Freedom, such as man may claim 628 *Installation* 15
Calmly triumphant; and for humbler claim 682 *Prelude* 6. 461
If love were his sole claim upon their care, 780 *Excursion* 2. 604
May fairly claim, by niggard age enriched 781 *Excursion* 2. 632
A claim that shattered all.—Our blooming girl, 795 *Excursion* 3. 638
Fit recompense of new desert? what claim 805 *Excursion* 4. 281
And mortal ignorance and frailty claim, 847 *Excursion* 6. 587
Full oft procured, yet may they claim respect, 875 *Excursion* 8. 51

Claim—*continued.*
From my own door I shall be free to claim K.8. 250 *Recluse* 1. 1. 519
Forgive me if I add another claim, K.8. 255 *Recluse* 1. 1. 692
What arts had better claim with wrath to warm L. 1. 94 *Juvenal* 2. 5
Of Hercules, though by a dubious claim. L. 2. 120 *Frag. Æneid* 1. 3
Claimed. In stray gifts to be claimed by whoever shall find; 167 *Stray Pleasures* 28
Or herb that claimed peculiar sympathy, 170 **Never enlivened* 13
Who, to spread wide the reverence they claimed 389 *Sound of Mull* 12
If now I ask a grace not claimed 406 *White Doe* 910
How Francis, with the Banner claimed 412 *White Doe* 1451
Claimed by proof upon the Horn: 535 *Egremont* 12
Claimed absolute dominion for the day. 772 *Excursion* 2. 89
The tribute by these various records claimed, 825 *Excursion* 5. 171
Which else the Christian virtue might have claimed. 845 *Excursion* 6. 490
Claiming. (Though claiming high distinction upon earth 837 *Excursion* 5. 980
Claims. And came to—what's your title—eh? your claims 62 *Bord.* 1349
A measure is of Thee, whose claims extend 172 *Infant Daughter* 14
Yet he, not loth, in favour of thy claims 290 *Kilchurn* 16
A Judge, who, as man claims by merit, gives; 317 **Brave Schill* 11
Here pause: the poet claims at least this praise, 321 **Here pause* 1
All States have glorified themselves;—their claims 331 *Ode: Thanks.* 155
Why speak of Roman Pomps? the haughty claims 346 *Processions* 28
Your praise, in meet accordance with your claims 352 *Aquap.* 5
Justice and Peace through Her uphold their claims; 429 *Ecc. Sonn.* 2. 2. 7
And claims from other worlds inspirited 442 *Ecc. Sonn.* 3. 10. 7
Which yet in thy behalf the Poet claims, 459 **Wanderer! that* 8
Ye shadowy Beings, that have rights and claims 473 **Ye shadowy* 1
They urge, "have interwoven claims and rights 519 *Pun. Death* 10. 10
(All claims of duty satisfied;) 579 **Sweet Flower* 54
Through claims of wealth or blood; nor was it least 713 *Prelude* 9. 222
Life, human life, with all its sacred claims 741 *Prelude* 13. 73
His expectations, and announce his claims 826 *Excursion* 5. 271
Clamor. And raise up a radical clamor! S. 3. 431 **If money's* 6
Clamorous. Rejoiced that clamorous spell and magic verse 234 *Power of Sound* 127
A long and clamorous bray! 241 *P. B.* 465
The voice, though clamorous as a horn 247 *P. B.* 941
What need of clamorous bells, or ribands gay, 256 *Marriage: Friend* 1
Of Geneviève. In both her clamorous Halls, 710 *Prelude* 9. 48
Those aberrations—had the clamorous friends 731 *Prelude* 11. 260
In clamorous agitation, round the crest 786 *Excursion* 3. 3
Clamorously. On Bard and Hero clamorously fell. 255 *Detraction* 8
Clamour. Clamour of boys with innocent despites 382 *Duddon* 23. 7
Then shalt thou raise a clamour as do I. 560 *Cuck.andNight.* 185
Clamours. No night-duck clamours for his wilder'd mate, 598 *Ev. Wk. Quarto* 357
Clan. Had been the wildest of his clan, 249 *P. B.* 1132
Wild Chieftain of a savage Clan! 292 *Rob Roy* 102
The faded glories of his Clan! 299 *Brownie's Cell* 60
And feuds, where, clan encountering clan, 391 *Highland Broach* 51
Aroused his clan; and, fighting at their head, 844 *Excursion* 6. 419
Clang. Now, as he plodded on, with sullen clang 25 *Guilt* 76
How did they sparkle to the cymbal's clang! 234 *Power of Sound* 149
The clang of arms is heard, and phantoms glide, 361 **For action* 7
As clear and bold as the trumpet's clang, 629 *Installation* 36
Take flight; while with their clang the air resounds. 808 *Excursion* 4. 459
Clank. The wind is now thy organist;—a clank 387 *Roslin* 1
Clanking. And clanking chains are perfect liberty. 69 *Bord.* 1778
While the jail-mastiff howls at the dull clanking chain, 621 *Convict* 37
Clap. Just as we left the glen a clap of thunder 51 *Bord.* 788
The devils at such sights do clap their hands. 76 *Bord.* 2190
Clap your hands with joy my Hearers, 93 *Westmoreland Girl* 19
With thunder-peals, clap after clap, 175 *Waggoner* 1. 197
Clap, infants, clap your hands! Divine must be 310 *Anticip.* 10
The Swans, in triumph clap their wings; 374 *Eg. Maid* 321
The struggle, clap their wings for victory! 378 *Duddon* 10. 14
Dire clap of hands, distracted chase of feet, 614 *Desc.Sk.Quarto* 657
Clapham. Is John de Clapham, that fierce Esquire, 399 *White Doe* 249
Claphams. The Claphams and Mauleverers stand; 399 *White Doe* 247
Clapped. Rose from the spot;—the Daughter clapped her hands, 74 *Bord.* 2103
"Mine is she," cried the Knight;—again they clapped their pinions. 374 *Eg. Maid* 324
Clapped hands, and shook with glee their matted locks; 513 **Said Secrecy* 11
Clapp'd her strong wings, and sought the cheerful isle, 618 *School Ex.* 46
Clapping. Clapping hands with shout and stare, 171 *Kitten* 35
Over their mirthful triumph clapping hands. 222 *Triad* 173
Claps. Of history, Glory claps her wings, 224 **'Tis gone* 14
Claremont's. A Nation's hopes lie crushed in Claremont's desolate Hall. 628 *Installation* 24
Clarion. On tiptoe reared, he strains his clarion throat, 5 *Ev. Wk.* 152
The cock far off sounded his clarion throat; 30 *Guilt* 329
On tiptoe rear'd he blows his clarion throat, 594 *Ev. Wk. Quarto* 137
Clarions. While clarions prate of kingdoms to be won— 345 **Ambition—following* 3
Clarkson. Clarkson! it was an obstinate hill to climb: 312 *Clarkson* 1
Clarkson's. Shine for Clarkson's pure delight L. 2. 190 **Queen and* 5
Clash. Of turrets, and a clash of swords 372 *Eg. Maid* 203
Clashing. And heeded not the voice of clashing swords, 422 *Ecc. Sonn.* 1. 14. 12
Clasp. The symbol yield; and would undo this clasp, 104 *Artegal* 156
Once having seen her clasp with fond embrace 120 *Emigrant Mother* 9

Clasp—*continued.*
And this poor Thorn they clasp it round . . . 197 Thorn 17
Forth sprang the impassioned Queen her Lord to clasp ; . . . . 210 Laod. 25
Extended, clasp the winds, with mutual moan . 353 Aquap. 45
The clasp that fixed the Roman Gown ; . . . 390 Highland Broach 16
Mere Fibulæ without a robe to clasp ; . . . . 394 *How profitless 12
My Father, do I clasp your knees ; . . . . . 400 White Doe 392
And clasp her Father's knees ;—ah, no ! . . . 407 White Doe 1061
That he might wake to clasp thee in the shade : . 630 [?] *O Moon 13
Clasped. And clasped her to my heart, my heart that ached . . . . 62 Bord. 1361
Clasped the Lamb and kept her hold. . . . . 93 Westmoreland Girl 12
Seen by mine eyes, or clasped in my embrace. . 118 Maternal Grief 7
Fell down and clasped his knees for joy, not uttering word. . . . . 141 Arm. Lady 102
Hands clasped above the crucifix he wore . . . 362 *List—'twas 79
And the realised vision is clasped to my heart. 364 Vallomb. 32
A bead-roll, in his hand a claspèd book, . . . 423 Ecc. Sonn. 1. 21. 2
Of ivy, flourishing and thick, that clasped . . 881 Excursion 8. 480
Clasping. Clasping your infant Daughter to your heart. . . . . 40 Bord. 181
His pleading face, and feel his clasping arms, . . 66 Bord. 1609
Clasping her beauty in my soul's embrace. . . 365 *Rapt above 8
Is clasping mine, it saddens me to think . . . 626 *Son of 2
Clasps. See how her ivy clasps the sacred Ruin, 283 *Here, where 5
She clasps them at that dim-seen roofless stone.— 597 Ev. Wk. Quarto 290
Clasps in her arms, nor weens (O lot unblest !) . 625 Æneid 87
Class. From that soft class of devotees who feel . 48 Bord. 585
In scale and order, class the cabinet . . . 645 Prelude 2. 224
With less delight upon that other class . . . 689 Prelude 7. 127
To every class its station and its office, . . . 806 Excursion 4. 341
And they perhaps err least, the lowly class . . 831 Excursion 5. 593
He was a peasant of the lowest class : . . . . 865 Excursion 7. 550
Classes. The substance classes by some barbarous name, ... 789 Excursion 3. 184
Classic. Ilissus, bending o'er thy classic urn ! . . 213 Dion 43
And, like the Spire that from your classic Hill . 281 Chris. Words. 13
Of him who thus survives by classic art, . . . 368 Trajan 26
May classic Fancy, linking . . . . 386 Yarrow Rev. 54
With all their Arts,—but classic lore glides on . 425 Ecc. Sonn. 1. 25. 13
In classic ages men perceived a soul . . . . 456 *The leaves 26
Now also shall the page of classic lore, . . . 496 *A little 49
The golden precepts of the classic page ; . . . 619 School Ex. 68
But by the trade in classic niceties, ... 676 Prelude 6. 109
Under the weight of classic eloquence, . . . 695 Prelude 7. 542
Ere yet familiar with the classic page, ... 733 Prelude 11. 425
Clatter. Yet still his jaws and teeth they clatter, . 537 Goody Blake 115
He begins to clatter ; . . . . S. 3. 423 Tinker 13
Clatters. The pewter clatters on the wall ; . . . 177 Waggoner 2. 67
Claws. And growls as if he would fix his claws . . 81 †Address : Child 29
Waxed wroth, and with foul claws, a harpy brood, 255 Detraction 7
Clay. And grant that every sceptred child of clay . 22 Desc. Sk. 659
"'Eight weary weeks, through rock and clay, . 156 Oak and Broom 21
And that frail Child of thirsty clay, ... 174 Waggoner 1. 93
My unassisted heart is barren clay, ... 257 *The prayers 3
On "coignes of vantage" hang their nests of clay ; 259 *A volant 3
And honour rest upon the senseless clay. . . . 270 *If these 14
Its glistening dews ; but hallowed is the clay . . 273 *Wild Redbreast 4
To him, and aught that hides his clay . . . . 284 Grave of Burns 17
That less should scorn the abandoned clay ; . . 301 Bran 83
If clay could think and mind were weight, . . 341 Ital. Itin. 15
Lamented youth ! to thy cold clay . . . . . 348 *Lulled by 67
Last lingering look of clay, that tames . . . . 372 Eg. Maid 197
Close to the vital seat of human clay ; . . . . 383 Duddon 28. 10
Beside their moss-grown hut of clay, ... 483 Simon Lee 41
In thee hath tempered so her clay, ... 486 Matthew 2
Who, less insensible than sodden clay . . . . 652 Prelude 3. 215
Earth crouches, the elements are potter's clay, . 673 Prelude 5. 531
By scale exact, in model, wood or clay, . . . 691 Prelude 7. 249
Or wraps an old acquaintance up in clay, . . . 826 Excursion 5. 236
That venerable clay. Meanwhile the best . . 863 Excursion 7. 390
Clean. Engaged, near blazing hearth on clean swept floor, ... S.3. 426 *Through Cumbrian 3
Cleanlier. By clearer taper lit a cleanlier board . 615 Desc.Sk.Quarto 736
Cleanly. Turned to the cleanly supper-board, and there, ... 132 Michael 99
A blazing fire—beside a cleanly hearth . . . . 834 Excursion 5. 769
Cleanse. To soothe and cleanse, not madden and pollute ! . . . . 378 Duddon 8. 14
Could cleanse the Augean stable, by the might . 726 Prelude 10. 585
Cleanse with thy blood my sins, to this incline . K.8. 266 *Rid of 12
Cleansed. Familiarly, yet out of the cleansed heart 362 *List—'twas 50
There stood he, cleansed from the despair . . . 401 White Doe 439
In the cleansed faith for which her martyrs died ; 504 Warning 56
And consecrating element hath cleansed . . . 826 Excursion 5. 280
Of all dishonour, cleansed from mortal stain. . . 893 Excursion 9. 633
Cleansing. *Earlier from cleansing fires, and gains withal* . . . . 429 Ecc. Sonn. 2. 3. 4
Clear. But now the clear bright Moon her zenith gains, ... 8 Ev. Wk. 355
Feeds the clear current of his sympathies. . . . 11 Desc. Sk. 18
On as we journey, in clear view displayed, . . 14 Desc. Sk. 216
Beat round to clear the streets of want and pain. 29 Guilt 274
And clear and open soul, so prized in fearless youth. 32 Guilt 441
No—no—the thing stands clear of mystery ; . . 42 Bord. 261
To-day will clear up all.—You marked a Cottage, 44 Bord. 378
The moon shone clear, the air was still, so still . 47 Bord. 575
From the clear light of circumstances, flashed . 64 Bord. 1495
And burns with a clear and steady light ; . . . 81 †Address : Child 35

Clear—*continued.*
Fresh water from the brook, as clear as ever ran ; 87 Pet-lamb 42
In such clear water, that thy boat . . . . . 88 H. C. 6
Suspended in a stream as clear as sky, ... 88 H. C. 9
"But is that gloom dissolved ? how passing clear 105 Artegal 202
As the clear Moon with modest pride . . . . 112 *What heavenly 5
'Tis eight o'clock,—a clear March night, . . . 126 Idiot Boy 1
So clear, so bright, our fathers said . . . . 142 †Lov. and Lik. 13
It was an April morning : fresh and clear . . 146 *It was an 1
Helvellyn far into the clear blue sky . . . 147 Joanna 61
Warbles by fits his low clear song ; . . . . . 168 Wren's Nest 22
Or by the silent lapse of fountain clear, . . . 170 *Never enlivened 14
But what can all avail to clear him, ... 181 Waggoner 4. 154
The clear Moon, and the glory of the heavens. 184 Night-piece 13
Sailed through the sky—the brooks ran clear ; 191 Seq. Beggars 24
And a clear brook with cheerful knell . . . . 194 Ruth 203
Her looks were calm, her senses clear. . . . 199 Thorn 143
Through half the clear blue sky will go ; . . . 199 Thorn 193
When all the stars shone clear and bright, . . 200 Thorn 239
Solitary, clear, profound, ... 209 *Yes, it 2
Into clear view the cultured fields that streak . 219 *This Height 20
With dread precision, ye made clear . . . . 226 Present. 64
That loads the middle heaven ; and clear and bright 230 Clouds 32
Who from the well-spring of his own clear breast 233 Power of Sound 63
Beneath the clear blue sky he saw . . . . . 240 P. B. 366
Towards the smooth river deep and clear. . . . 241 P. B. 440
More steady looks the moon, and clear, . . . 242 P. B. 493
Yet standing in the clear moonshine ; . . . . 248 P. B. 1097
Lingers beside that Rill, in vision clear. . . . 251 *There is a little 14
Hath shown that nothing human can be clear . 256 Marriage : Friend 12
How clear, how keen, how marvellously bright . 263 *How clear 1
And lo this Work !—a grotto bright and clear . 264 *Lady ! I 10
Yet he repines not, if his thought stand clear, . 265 *There is a pleasure 9
Hurrying and sparkling through the clear blue heaven ; . . . . 266 *With how 12
Clear tops of far-off mountains we descry, . . 268 *Four fiery 4
In festal glee : why not ? For fresh and clear, . 275 *While poring 6
So loud, so clear, my Partner through life's day, . 279 *Hark ! 'tis 11
And clear way made for her triumphal car . . 283 *Proud were 7
Thou wear'st upon thy forehead clear . . . . 288 Highland Girl 32
Then clear the weeds from off his Grave, . . . 291 Rob Roy 6
On Grasmere's clear unruffled breast . . . . 297 Highland Boy 188
And saw, while sea was calm and air was clear, . 306 *Inland, within 2
When morn returns, beneath the clear blue sky, . 322 *Humanity, delighting 37
Solemn effulgence, clear as solar light, ... 324 Ode 1814 78
Of past events ; to whom, in vision clear, . . 326 *The Bard 6
In naked splendour, clear from mist or haze, . 329 Ode : Thanks. 9
Clear shines the glorious sun above ; . . . . 339 *Meek Virgin 39
Another's praise from envy clear. . . . . . 344 *How blest 13
From the clear spring of a plain English heart, . 356 Aquap. 243
Days passed—and Monte Calvo would not clear . 360 Albano 1
To bower as green, from sky to sky as clear, . . 363 *List—'twas 107
Better to breathe at large on this clear height . 376 Duddon 1. 11
With thy clear voice, I caught the fitful sound . 377 Duddon 5. 2
For the clear waters to pursue their race . . . 378 Duddon 9. 7
Checking the stream, make a pool smooth and clear 382 Duddon 23. 4
Rocks, rivers, and smooth lakes more clear than glass 388 Trosachs 8
Substantial motive, reason clear, ... 398 White Doe 201
Of recollections clear and bright ; . . . . . 399 White Doe 317
The hall-clock in the clear moonshine . . . . 406 White Doe 960
That stood'st before my eyes, more clear . . . 407 White Doe 1046
Of duty, seeing with clear sight ; . . . . . 409 White Doe 1219
Around her sees, while air is hushed, a clear . . 426 Ecc. Sonn. 1. 29. 13
In the clear land of vision, but foreseen . . . 436 Ecc. Sonn. 2. 31. 6
Seems firm as solid crystal, breathless, clear, . . 456 *Soft as 2
In vision exquisitely clear, ... 457 *Had this 29
To sit in leafy woods by fountains clear ! . . . 460 *Queen of 16
To glide in open prospect through clear sky. . . 461 *Who but is 8
The cattle crowding round this beverage clear . 465 *The cattle 1
This perilous bay, stands clear of all offence ; . . 469 *The feudal 6
Because the unstained, the clear, the crystalline, . 469 *Why stand 4
On the smooth bottom of this clear bright sea, . 469 *A youth 2
Extracting from clear skies and air serene, . . 475 *Homeward we 10
Clear sight She has of what he was, ... 479 Somnamb. 75
Up ! up ! my Friend, and clear your looks ; . . 481 Tables Turned 3
It breaks, and all is clear : . . . . 491 Fidelity 45
Again unfolded, passage clear shall yield . . . 496 *A little 52
Clear, loud, and lively is the din, ... 498 *Departing summer 10
His voice shall chant, in accents clear, ... 507 *While from 61
Broad, clear, and toned harmoniously, wth skill . 508 F. Stone 19
Then haply, Beaumont ! words in current clear . 522 Epist. Beaumont 56
To Loughrigg-tarn, round clear and bright as heaven, ... 524 Epist. Beaumont 166
Is smooth as clear, save where with dimples small 527 *Those breathing 11
Break forth,—again to walk the clear blue sky. . 532 *How beautiful the 8
And where the wood was clear. . . . . . . 544 Russ. Fug. 264
Yet may I sing, O Alma ! loud and clear. . . . 556 Prioress 204
And in a tomb of precious marble clear . . . 556 Prioress 230
That her clear voice made a loud rioting, . . . 558 Cuck. and Night. 99
Next morning Troilus began to clear . . . . 562 Troilus 1
Singing so well, so goodly, and so clear, . . . 563 Troilus 60
For which, oh, gentle Luna, bright and clear, . . 564 Troilus 137
Bounds calm and clear the chaos still and hoar ; . 611 Desc.Sk.Quarto 503
Now in the clear and open day I feel . . . . 622 Recluse 1. 1. 111
As clear and bold as the trumpet's clang, . . . 629 Installation 36
Shall I take up my home ? and what clear stream 632 Prelude 1. 12
'Twas autumn, and a clear and placid day, . . 633 Prelude 1. 65

Clear—*continued.*
It was a time of rapture ! Clear and loud . . 638 *Prelude* 1. 430
Eastward were sparkling clear, and in the west . 638 *Prelude* 1. 445
Her clear though shallow stream of piety . . . 661 *Prelude* 4. 225
Of the clear flood, from things which there abide 662 *Prelude* 4. 266
Even now appears before the mind's clear eye . 671 *Prelude* 5. 398
Than I beheld loitering on calm clear nights . . 676 *Prelude* 6. 93
Was that clear synthesis built up aloft . . 677 *Prelude* 6. 162
The torrents shooting from the clear blue sky, . 684 *Prelude* 6. 629
Capable of clear truth, the one to break . . . 714 *Prelude* 9. 358
Beneath the trees, clear footing many a mile— . 716 *Prelude* 9. 436
Our dim ancestral Past in vision clear ; . . . 744 *Prelude* 13. 320
I seemed about this time to gain clear sight . . 745 *Prelude* 13. 369
In the clear presence of the full-orbed Moon, . 747 *Prelude* 14. 53
Beside swift-flowing Lowther's current clear. . 753 **Oft, through* 4
No ridges there appeared of clear black mould, . 769 *Excursion* 1. 836
Of a clear brook ;—beneath an abbey's roof . 771 *Excursion* 2. 7
The wandering Herbalist,—who, clear alike . . 788 *Excursion* 3. 161
Dimness o'er this clear luminary crept . . . . 795 *Excursion* 3. 670
Say rather, all his thoughts now flowing clear, . 819 *Excursion* 4. 1222
From a clear fountain flowing, he looks round . 819 *Excursion* 4. 1223
In furnishing clear guidance, a support . . . 820 *Excursion* 4. 1262
Their waters clear or sullied, all are lost . . . 836 *Excursion* 5. 919
He, taking counsel of his own clear thoughts, . . 841 *Excursion* 6. 219
Clear images before your gladdened eyes . . . 848 *Excursion* 6. 652
Or the clear moon. The queen of these gay sports, 851 *Excursion* 6. 838
Victoriously upraised his clear bright eye ; . . 871 *Excursion* 7. 892
Mildly, and with a clear and steady tone. . . . 883 *Excursion* 8. 601
A clear sonorous voice, inaudible . . . . . 885 *Excursion* 9. 89
Thus while my fancy wanders, thou, clear Spring, S. 3. 434 **The doubt* 86
To drink of the clear water, laid himself . . . K.8. 226 **I will* 55
And the clear hills, as high as they ascend . . K.8. 252 *Recluse* 1.1.578
I would stand clear, but yet to me I feel . . . K 8. 255 *Recluse* 1.1.674

Clear-blue. Thy torrents shooting from the clear-blue sky ; . . . . 12 *Desc. Sk.* 113

Cleared. Cleared for a monarch's progress. Priests might spin . . . . 70 *Bord.* 1837
Nor could my heart by second thoughts from heaviness be cleared, ... 91 *Poet's Dream* 5
Abuse hath cleared from vain imaginings ; . . 433 *Ecc. Sonn.* 2. 18. 12
And cleared a way for the first Votaries, . . . 468 *St. Bees* 152
Have cleared a passage for just government, . . 721 *Prelude* 10. 218
The grass is cleared away, and to this hour . . 738 *Prelude* 12. 244
He cleared a passage for me, and the stream . . 751 *Prelude* 14. 368
So, like a fugitive, whose feet have cleared . . 798 *Excursion* 3. 877
Was cleared, I dipped, with arms accordant, oars 891 *Excursion* 9. 489

Clearer. In clearer light the moss-built cell . . . 169 *Wren's Nest* 54
By clearer taper lit a cleanlier board . . . . 615 *Desc.Sk.Quarto* 736
And clearer insight. Thus my days are past . . 635 *Prelude* 1. 237
With clearer knowledge ; with another eye . . 661 *Prelude* 4. 214
The test of such a trial ; clearer far . . . . 740 *Prelude* 13. 57
When, looking back, thou seest, in clearer view . 751 *Prelude* 14. 393
From hollow clefts up to the clearer air . . . 760 *Excursion* 1. 296

Clearest. And clearest insight, amplitude of mind, . 749 *Prelude* 14. 191
In clearest air ascending, showed far off . . . 756 *Excursion* 1. 4
The clearest apprehension of those truths, . . 830 *Excursion* 5. 520

Clearly. With stronger wing, more clearly to discern 358 **Is this* 12
The moon was full and shining clearly, . . . 537 *Goody Blake* 75
Of vanished nations, or more clearly drawn . . 708 *Prelude* 8. 615
I clearly saw that neither these nor aught . . . 725 *Prelude* 10. 474
Too clearly ; feels too vividly ; and longs . . 804 *Excursion* 4. 175

Clearness. In crystal clearness Dian's looking-glass ; 381 *Duddon* 22. 3
Did, in the placid clearness of the night, . . . 798 *Excursion* 3. 859

Clears. And clears Oblivion from reproach, . . . 391 *Highland Broach* 89

Clear-shining. Clear-shining, like a hermit's taper seen 687 *Prelude* 7. 35

Clear-sighted. Clear sighted Honour, and his staid Compeers, ... 329 *Ode : Thanks.* 61

Clear-sounding. Of three clear-sounding and harmonious bells, ... 872 *Excursion* 7. 974

Clear-white. A Doe most beautiful, clear-white, . 414 *White Doe* 1646

Cleave. Thy towns that cleave, like swallows' nests, on high ; . . . . 12 *Desc. Sk.* 114
I still will be your friend, will cleave to you .. . 64 *Bord.* 1499
Cleave to this Stranger : if, upon his entering, . 75 *Bord.* 2159
Now I cleave to the house, and am dull as a snail ; 116 *Repentance* 33
I call thee, and to that cleave fast, ... 159 **With little* 43
That to their object cleave like sleet . . . . 217 *Enterprise* 128
These cleave to it ; from these it cannot roam, . 263 **Those words* 13
Then cleave, O cleave to that which still is left ; . 306 **Two Voices* 10
Which shall not fail, though poor men cleave with pride . . . . 320 **O'erweening Statesmen* 4
Power must resolve to cleave to it through life, . 354 *Aquap.* 116
And to her name my soul shall cleave in sorrow ; " 374 *Eg. Maid* 326
And through this wilderness a passage cleave . . 379 *Duddon* 14. 12
Will cleave to this good cause and me." . . . 400 *White Doe* 411
Espouse thy doom at once, and cleave . . . . 402 *White Doe* 544
And to one purpose cleave, their Being's godlike mate ! . . . . 529 **Those breathing* 132
For very grief of which my heart shall cleave ;— 564 *Troilus* 95
Thy towns, like swallows' nests that cleave on high ; 604 *Desc.Sk.Quarto* 131
Why does their sad remembrance cleave behind ? 613 *Desc.Sk.Quarto* 623
Yet could I only cleave to solitude . . . . . 652 *Prelude* 3. 230
To cleave unto this man ; but when I prayed . 667 *Prelude* 5. 116
How dost thou cleave to the poetic heart, . . . 685 *Prelude* 6. 658
Cleave not so fondly to your moody cell ; . . . 808 *Excursion* 4. 482
Hath said, " Be mild and cleave to gentle things, K.8. 256 *Recluse* 1.1.735

Cleaves. Through which rough Garry cleaves his way, can tell . . . . 15 *Desc. Sk.* 296
And to her mournful habits fondly cleaves. . . 169 **Never enlivened* 6
That downy prow, and softly cleaves . . . . 212 *Dion*
That with moist virtue softly cleaves . . . . 228 *Devot. Incit.* 15

Cleaves—*continued.*
Cleaves the blank air, Life flies : now every day . 270 **If these* 9
Cleaves its glad way, a cry of harvest home . . 322 *Germans* 7
Thy thundering battle-axe as it cleaves the press . 427 *Ecc. Sonn.* 1. 35. 10
What mischief cleaves to unsubdued regret, . . 458 *Sea-shore* 1
That cleaves to rock or pillared cave . . . . 472 *Ossian* 25
Is happy in his vow, and fondly cleaves . . . 586 *Ch. Lamb* 124
Yet to the memory something cleaves at last, . 658 *Prelude* 3. 627
Of some thick wood, her place of covert, cleaves . 891 *Excursion* 9. 493

Cleaveth. Give him a soul that cleaveth unto Thee. 363 **The world forsaken* 14

Cleaving. And white with foam as if with cleaving sleet. . . . . 201 *Hart-leap* 40
Then, by the spade, or cleaving plough, . . . 391 *Highland Broach* 83
Cleaving humbly to his side, ... 397 *White Doe* 129
That union ceased : then, cleaving easy walks . 477 *Nunnery* 9
See them cleaving to the sport ! . . . . . . 490 *Incident : Dog* 26
There, cleaving to the ground, it lies . . . . 580 *John Words.* 55
Cleaving with power inherent and intense, . . 794 *Excursion* 3. 578

Cleft. The deepest cleft the mountain's front displays 8 *Ev. Wk.* 357
With staff in hand across the cleft . . . . . 85 *Shepherd-boys* 56
By the brook-side—'tis gone—and that dark cleft! 97 *Brothers* 134
And, in one hospitable cleft, ... 157 *Oak and Broom* 108
Their birthplace in the rocky cleft . . . . . 221 *Triad* 135
In her dank cleft ;—but be thou curbed, . . . 299 *Brownie's Cell* 74
Thrilling each pearly cleft and sparry grot, . . 333 *Fish-women* 13
Flowers that peep forth from many a cleft and chink, ... 337 *Aar* 6
To Thee, in this aerial cleft, ... 338 **Meek Virgin* 13
A sky-blue stone, within this sunless cleft, . . 378 *Duddon* 11. 2
" Yon cloud with that long purple cleft . . . 486 **We walked* 21

Clefts. From blissful transport some—from clefts of woe . . . . 436 *Ecc. Sonn.* 2. 32. 3
From hollow clefts up to the clearer air . . . 760 *Excursion* 1. 296

Clenched. The Banner clenched ; till, from out the Band, ... 412 *White Doe* 1489

Clerk. Has ended, though no Clerk, with " God be praised ! " . . . . 394 *Countess' Pillar* 14
Frolicked industriously, a simple Clerk . . . 859 *Excursion* 7. 129

Clermont's. The Council-roof and Clermont's towers reply ;— . . . . 427 *Ecc. Sonn.* 1. 33. 11

Cliff. While, near the midway cliff, the silvered kite 3 *Ev. Wk.* 90
The peasant, from yon cliff of fearful edge . . 4 *Ev. Wk.* 130
To see an acre's breadth of that wide cliff . . . 97 *Brothers* 150
Down from yon cliff a fragment broke ; . . . 156 *Oak and Broom* 35
And near the cliff I passed. . . . . 157 *Oak and Broom* 104
In the bosom of the cliff. . . . . 166 *Wand. Jew* 20
High on that chalky cliff of Britain's Isle, . . . 215 *Enterprise* 3
As a selected treasure thy one cliff, ... 355 *Aquap.* 210
Of that high Convent-crested cliff I stood, . . 356 *Aquap.* 232
Flung from yon cliff a shadow large and cold. . 383 *Duddon* 27. 4
Dread cliff of Baruth ! *that* wild wish may sleep, . 466 *St. Bees* 19
And, as a God, light on thy topmost cliff. . . . 471 **Arran ! a* 8
The captive Bird was gone ;—to cliff or moor . 472 **The captive* 1
Not to the clouds, not to the cliff, he flew ; . . 472 *Dunolly Eagle* 1
No cliff so bare but on its steeps . . . . . 507 *May* 43
Threading the painful cragg surmounts the cliff. . 607 *Desc.Sk.Quarto* 298
Save when the startling cliff unfrequent rends : . 609 *Desc.Sk.Quarto* 377
—I see him, up the midway cliff he creeps . . 610 *Desc.Sk.Quarto* 470
Think not, suspended from the cliff on high . . 611 *Desc.Sk.Quarto* 510
My haunt the hollow cliff whose Pine . . . . 626 †*Cento* 11

Cliffed. *See* **White-cliffed.**

Clifford. The villain, Clifford. He hates you, and he knows . . . . 42 *Bord.* 280
Where he can stab you deepest. Clifford never . 42 *Bord.* 281
Of this same Clifford, he became impatient . . 42 *Bord.* 287
A Maiden innocent till ensnared by Clifford, . . 44 *Bord.* 381
I never shall be heard of more. Lord Clifford ? . 47 *Bord.* 534
Lord Clifford—did you see him talk with Herbert ? 47 *Bord.* 537
Her whom the Monster, Clifford, drove to madness. 47 *Bord.* 569
The shattered Castle in which Clifford oft . . . 49 *Bord.* 659
Are brave : Clifford is brave ; and that old Man . 54 *Bord.* 911
But now no longer mine. You know Lord Clifford ; 57 *Bord.* 1103
They say Lord Clifford is a savage man ; . . . 59 *Bord.* 1190
And I loved her, and she loves the Lord Clifford ! 60 *Bord.* 1270
To noble Clifford ; from annoy . . . . . . 180 *Waggoner* 4. 48
A Clifford to his own restored ! . . . . . . 204 *Brougham* 23
Our Clifford was a happy Youth, ... 205 *Brougham* 107
On the blood of Clifford calls ;— . . . . . 205 *Brougham* 143
" The good Lord Clifford " was the name he bore. 205 *Brougham* 172
This Clifford wished for worthier might ; . . . 399 *White Doe* 290

Clifford-moor. Stood by their Sire, on Clifford-moor, 404 *White Doe* 724

Clifford's. As the Lord Clifford's Castle : I have heard . . . . 43 *Bord.* 345
Is brave. To Clifford's arms he would have led . 54 *Bord.* 912
Hath become Clifford's harlot—is *he* living ? . . 55 *Bord.* 977
I'll plant myself before Lord Clifford's Castle, . 60 *Bord.* 1248
And heaviness in Clifford's ear ! . . . . . 204 *Brougham* 103
How, by Heaven's grace, this Clifford's heart was framed : . . . . 205 *Brougham* 158

Cliff's. Under the white cliff's battlemented crown, 349 *At Dover* 3
And carved, on mural cliff's undreaded side, . . 380 *Duddon* 16. 12

Cliffs. That stuns the tremulous cliffs of high Lodore ; 2 *Ev. Wk.* 4
Spotting the northern cliffs with lights between ; . 3 *Ev. Wk.* 40
Blue pomp of lakes, high cliffs and falling floods, 5 *Ev. Wk.* 143
Some, dim between the lofty cliffs descried, . . 5 *Ev. Wk.* 164
'Cross the calm lake's blue shades the cliffs aspire, 5 *Ev. Wk.* 174
Directs his winding dog the cliffs to scale,— . . 5 *Ev. Wk.* 183
Or marks, 'mid opening cliffs, fair dark-eyed maids 12 *Desc. Sk.* 91
Thy cliffs ; the endless waters of thy vales ; . . 12 *Desc. Sk.* 110
The wood-crowned cliffs that o'er the lake recline ; 15 *Desc. Sk.* 278

Clock—*continued.*
The clock is on the stroke of one ; . . . . . 128 *Idiot Boy* 172
—The clock strikes three—a dismal knell ! . . 129 *Idiot Boy* 271
Been mistress also of a clock, ... 176 *Waggoner* 2. 5
Twelve strokes that clock would have been telling 176 *Waggoner* 2. 7
Or clock to toll from ! Many a tempting isle, . 262 **Dark and* 9
Can hear the monitory clock . . . . . . 533 **Blest is* 45
The distant clock forgot, and chilling dew, . 596 *Ev. Wk. Quarto* 273
Or clock, that blind against the wanderer born, . 597 *Ev. Wk. Quarto* 313
The village clock tolled six,—I wheeled about, . 638 *Prelude* 1. 431
Near me hung Trinity's loquacious clock, . . . 650 *Prelude* 3. 53
Of the church clock telling the hours with strokes 685 *Prelude* 6. 693
The breathless wilderness of clouds ; the clock . 686 *Prelude* 6. 716
Of minster clock ! From that bleak tenement . 758 *Excursion* 1. 125
Was silent ; save the solitary clock . . . . 781 *Excursion* 2. 645
Clock's. *See* **Church-clock's.**
Clock-work. The Wax-work, Clock-work, all the marvellous craft . . . . 698 *Prelude* 7. 712
Clod. The encircling turf into a barren clod ; . . 465 **The cattle* 3
Beneath " the random *bield* of clod or stone " . 475 **There ! said* 9
Clog. Can any mortal clog come to her ? . . . 178 *Waggoner* 3. 28
Duty ?—an unwelcome clog ; . . . . . . 549 *Hermit's Cell* 1. 18
Those life-consuming sounds that clog the air, . 569 *Cumb. Beg.* 181
Idleness halting with his weary clog, ... 657 *Prelude* 3. 597
Became a clog to him, whose spirit wished . . 855 *Excursion* 6. 1104
Clogged. Pathway, and lane, and public road, were clogged . . . . 150 **When, to* 6
While thankless thousands are opprest and clogged 835 *Excursion* 5. 830
Cloister. The cloister startles at the gleam of arms. 11 *Desc. Sk.* 60
There ranged through cloister, court, and aisle, . 416 *White Doe* 1813
As in a cloister. Yet the grateful Poor . . . 539 **Lady ! a* 48
As in a cloister. Once—while, in that shade . . 706 *Prelude* 8. 462
Cloistered. In cloistered privacy. But not to dwell 424 *Ecc. Sonn.* 1. 21. 6
If cloistered Avarice scruple not to wrong . . 433 *Ecc. Sonn.* 2. 19. 5
Of cloistered Architects,free their souls to fill . 467 *St. Bees* 119
Pure as the holiest cloist ered nun . . . . 576 *Cenotaph* 4
Cloisters. Courts, cloisters, flocks of churches, gateways, towers : . . . . 649 *Prelude* 3. 33
Went back to Granta's cloisters, not so prompt . 675 *Prelude* 6. 6
Of London, and from cloisters there, thou camest, 679 *Prelude* 6. 279
The floors of those dim cloisters, till that hour, . 682 *Prelude* 6. 476
Cloistral. Of that perennial shade, a cloistral place 150 **When, to* 11
Close to these cloistral steps a burial-place, . . 275 *Gravestone* 11
Of lurking cloistral arch, through trees espied . 335 *Rhine* 9
And, high above that length of cloistral roof, . . 355 *Aquap.* 170
For such a One beset with cloistral snares. . . 363 **The world forsaken* 8
Yet many a Novice of the cloistral shade, . . . 434 *Ecc. Sonn.* 2. 23. 1
League after league, and cloistral avenues, . . 685 *Prelude* 6. 668
Clomb. Most cruelly. As up the steep we clomb, 50 *Bord.* 740
As when he clomb from Rydal Mere ; . . . . 174 *Waggoner* 1. 102
Thou hast clomb aloft, and gazed . . . . . 217 **Inmate of* 2
The strenuous Animal hath clomb . . . . . 244 *P. B.* 696
Those steps I clomb ; the mists before me gave . 257 **Methought I* 9
Two Brothers clomb, and, turning face from face, 276 *Oker Hill* 2
And laughing dares the Adventurer, who hath clomb . . . . 377 *Duddon* 4. 11
And clomb the winding stair that once . . . 386 *Yarrow Rev.* 101
To giddier heights hath clomb the Papal sway. . 427 *Ecc. Sonn.* 1. 35. 14
Was crossed, a bare ridge clomb, upon whose top 658 *Prelude* 4. 3
Have seen us side by side, when, having clomb . 678 *Prelude* 6. 212
When from the Vallais we had turned, and clomb 683 *Prelude* 6. 562
And clomb with eagerness, till anxious fears . . 683 *Prelude* 6. 575
Following our Guide, we clomb the cottage-stairs 781 *Excursion* 2. 647
Had clomb aloft to delve the moorland turf . . 783 *Excursion* 2. 787
Of mere humanity, you clomb those heights ; . . 808 *Excursion* 4. 470
We clomb a green hill's side ; and, as we clomb, . 892 *Excursion* 9. 570
Close. While thick above the rill the branches close, 3 *Ev. Wk.* 57
Close by her mantling wings' embraces prest. . 6 *Ev. Wk.* 231
—At once bewildering mists around him close, . 16 *Desc. Sk.* 328
And, ere his eyes can close upon the day, . . . 16 *Desc. Sk.* 334
While o'er the desert, answering every close, . . 16 *Desc. Sk.* 344
Close on the remnant of their weary way ; . . . 20 *Desc. Sk.* 556
He lays his stiffened limbs,—his eyes begin to close ; . . . . 27 *Guilt* 162
Close by my mother in their native bowers : . . 28 *Guilt* 240
That ragged Dwelling, close beneath a rock . . 44 *Bord.* 379
You will have nobody to close your eyes— . . 72 *Bord.* 1972
His staff had dropped, and close upon the brink . 73 *Bord.* 2062
For once could have thee close to me, ... 114 *Ind. Wom.* 66
Of a close chair, a litter, or sedan, ... 125 *V. and J.* 246
Close to the spot where with his rod and line . . 149 **A narrow* 56
There close the peaceful lives of flowers ? . . . 154 *Flower Garden* 6
Some close behind, some side by side, ... 162 *Binnorie* 45
He'd wish to close them again. . . . . . . 162 **Art thou the* 14
Is close and hot ;—and now and then . . . . 173 *Waggoner* 1. 16
The Vanguard, following close behind, . . . 179 *Waggoner* 3. 68
Where close fogs hide their parent brook ; . . 180 *Waggoner* 4. 41
With a continuous cloud of texture close, . . . 184 *Night-piece* 2
So close, you'd say that they are bent . . . . 197 *Thorn* 18
" And, close beside this aged Thorn, ... 198 *Thorn* 34
Which close beside the Thorn you see, ... 198 *Thorn* 50
Close to the thorn on which Sir Walter leaned . 201 *Hart-leap* 37
Close clings to earth the living rock, ... 224 *Primrose* 19
And close by Peter's side he stands : . . . . 242 *P. B.* 562
—A withered leaf is close behind, ... 244 *P. B.* 703
To a close lane they now are come, ... 244 *P. B.* 711
Close by a brake of flowering furze . . . . . 246 *P. B.* 921
Close to the Ass's feet she fell ; . . . . . . 247 *P. B.* 1013
Close to these cloistral steps a burial-place, . . 275 *Gravestone* 11
For they have learnt to open and to close . . . 320 **They seek* 3

Close—*continued.*
Close at my side ! She bids me fly to greet . . 353 *Aquap.* 27
" The tomb," said Merlin, " may not close . . 372 *Eg. Maid* 241
Close to the vital seat of human clay ; . . . . 383 *Duddon* 28. 10
Urged to close toil with chemic fire ; . . . . 399 *White Doe* 302
That with their joyful shout should close . . . 408 *White Doe* 1146
Close to the summit of this height, ... 416 *White Doe* 1802
Flits and refits along the close arcade ; . . . 453 **Calm is the* 21
The linnet's warble, sinking towards a close, . . 455 *Rydal Mere* 1
From the close confines of a shadowy vale. . . 460 **Queen of* 9
Wafted o'er waves, or creeping through close trees, 466 *St. Bees* 53
Close up those barren leaves ; . . . . . . 482 *Tables Turned* 30
Shut close the door ; press down the latch ; . . 485 *Poet's Epitaph* 33
Of winter rushing in, to close . . . . . . 502 *Seasons* 15
But, O Mother ! by the close . . . . . . 502 **Like a* 13
Falsehood and Treachery, in close council met, . 513 **Said Secrecy* 2
Your gift, ere shutters close— . . . . . . 526 **The soaring* 52
Resounded with deep swell and solemn close, . . 534 **When in* 6
Or gentle Nature close her eyes, ... 544 *Russ. Fug.* 237
In close self-shelter, like a Thing at rest. . . . 571 **There is a Flower* 8
That doth " within itself its sweetness close ; " . . 584 **With copious* 47
Shades of the prison-house begin to close . . . 588 *Immortality* 67
To where, while thick above the branches close, . 592 *Ev. Wk. Quarto* 73
While ere his eyes can close upon the day, . . 609 *Desc.Sk.Quarto* 406
When close and closer they begin to strain, . . 613 *Desc.Sk.Quarto* 610
And Conscience dogging close his bleeding way . 613 *Desc.Sk.Quarto* 640
Close at her side were all the powers, design'd . 618 *School Ex.* 17
Embrace me, then, ye Hills, and close me in, . . 622 *Recluse* 1. 1. 110
Him will I take, and in close covert keep, . . . 624 *Æneid* 31
In a close Box, covert for Justice meet. . . . 626 *Ballot* 8
The star which comes at close of day to shine . 627 **The star* 1
Cherry or maple, sate in close array, ... 639 *Prelude* 1. 515
And close communion. Many are our joys . . 646 *Prelude* 2. 284
Close at my side, an uncouth shape appeared . . 666 *Prelude* 5. 75
The rocks that muttered close upon our ears, . . 684 *Prelude* 6. 630
Dear native Regions, wheresoe'er shall close . . 706 *Prelude* 8. 468
Reality too close and too intense, ... 728 *Prelude* 11. 58
And nothing less), when, finally to close . . . 732 *Prelude* 11. 358
Open ; I would approach them, but they close. . 738 *Prelude* 12. 280
Among the close and overcrowded haunts . . . 743 *Prelude* 13. 203
It was a close, warm, breezeless summer night, . 746 *Prelude* 14. 11
To its appointed close : the discipline . . . . 750 *Prelude* 14. 303
Had reached its close ; but Life is insecure, . . 753 **Oft, through* 10
Not one hour merely, but till evening's close, . . 773 *Excursion* 2. 142
Supplied a boundary less abrupt and close ; . . 776 *Excursion* 2. 336
At the calm close of summer's longest day, . . 782 *Excursion* 2. 718
Of stillness and close privacy, a nook . . . . 793 *Excursion* 3. 471
"Close to his destined habitation, lies . . . . 841 *Excursion* 6. 212
" In that green nook, close by the Churchyard wall, 854 *Excursion* 6. 1080
" These grassy heaps lie amicably close," . . . 857 *Excursion* 7. 31
And, close behind, the comely Matron rode, . . 858 *Excursion* 7. 77
Then, shall the slowly-gathering twilight close . 862 *Excursion* 7. 356
Of her close tasks, and long captivity. . . . . 878 *Excursion* 8. 296
Of Man may rise, as to a welcome close . . . 885 *Excursion* 9. 94
The same should be continued to its close. . . 892 *Excursion* 9. 525
Softens its evening uproar towards a close . . S.3. 437 **The doubt* 195
Th' inevitable close of Dardan power . . . . L.2. 121 *Frag.Æneid* 2.2
Close-attending. From his close-attending cloud, . 181 *Waggoner* 4. 146
Close-clipt. Of close-clipt foliage green and tall, . 407 *White Doe* 988
Close-crowding. Close-crowding round the infant-god; 299 *Brownie's Cell* 98
Closed. Sound of closed gate, across the water borne, 9 *Ev. Wk.* 373
And closed the sparkling eye. . . . . . . 82 †*Mother's Return* 56
There, when they had closed their voyage, . . 141 *Arm. Lady* 99
And casement closed and door made fast, . . . 144 **Driven in* 65
Had closed upon his weary way, ... 167 *Pilgrim's Dream* 2
And, till life's journey closed, the spot . . . 168 *Pilgrim's Dream* 69
Of a closed volume lingering in thy hand . . . 222 *Triad* 184
Here closed the meditative strain ; . . . . . 224 *Primrose* 25
Looked ere his eyes were closed. By him was seen 265 **Hail, Twilight* 9
Uncovered to his grave : 'tis closed,—her loss . 318 **In due* 11
When the soft hand of sleep had closed the latch 323 *Ode 1814* 1
Appended to his bosom, and lips closed . . . 362 **List—'twas* 80
But with closed eyes,—of breath and bloom forsaken. . . . . 371 *Eg. Maid* 138
Self-shaken, as I closed my airy journey. . . . 372 *Eg. Maid* 204
The Council closed, the Priest in full career . . 422 *Ecc. Sonn.* 1. 17. 2
And the sword stopped ; the bleeding wounds were closed ; . . . . 442 *Ecc. Sonn.* 3. 7. 3
Had closed his door before the day was done, . 453 **Calm is the* 17
Then would be closed the restless oblique eye . 500 *Humanity* 49
His ears he closed to listen to the songs . . . 576 *Chiabrera* 9. 16
And the pure vision closed in darkness infinite. . 582 *Invoc. Earth* 36
Has closed the Shepherd-poet's eyes : . . . . 586 *Hogg* 12
His eyes have closed ! And ye, lov'd books, no more . . . . 587 *Crosth.* 3
Last night, while by his dying fire, as clos'd . . 613 *Desc.Sk.Quarto* 596
On the closed eyes of young Endymion fell, . . 630 [?] **O Moon* 12
The cottage threshold where my journey closed. . 658 *Prelude* 4. 26
While listlessly I sate, and, having closed . . . 666 *Prelude* 5. 63
Of strangers, till day closed, we sailed along, . . 681 *Prelude* 6. 385
When, having closed the mighty Shakspeare's page, 694 *Prelude* 7. 484
Closed up each chink, and with fresh bands of straw 770 *Excursion* 1. 903
Closed the preparatory notices . . . . . . 776 *Excursion* 2. 316
Had scarcely closed this high-wrought strain of rapture . . . . 782 *Excursion* 2. 727
Who, for the sake of sterner quiet, closed . . . 791 *Excursion* 3. 354
Here closed the Tenant of that lonely vale . . 801 *Excursion* 4. 1
And guardian of their course, that never closed . 811 *Excursion* 4. 698
To calm the Sufferer when his story closed ; . . 817 *Excursion* 4. 1103
Made the eye blind, and closed the passages . . 818 *Excursion* 4. 1154

Come—*continued.*
And tears of fifteen will come into his eyes. . . 570 *Farmer* 68
I come, ye little noisy Crew, ... 577 **I come* 1
Come streaming down the streaming panes. . . 577 **I come* 19
Of blessedness to come. . . . . 580 *John Words.* 30
I come—thy stains to wash away, ... 581 *Invoc. Earth* 5
The Winds come to me from the fields of sleep, . 588 *Immortality* 28
But trailing clouds of glory do we come . . . 588 *Immortality* 64
And bids her soldier come her woes to share, . . 596 *Ev. Wh. Quarto* 253
Those lips, whose tides of fragrance come, and go, 604 *Desc. Sk. Quarto* 152
For come Diseases on, and Penury's rage, . . . 613 *Desc. Sk. Quarto* 638
Is come as a brother thy sorrows to share. . . 621 *Convict* 48
Would, with its rattling music, come, ... 621 *Andrew Jones* 4
Would, with its rattling music, come, ... 621 *Andrew Jones* 34
On Nature's invitation do I come, ... 621 *Recluse* 1. 1. 71
To question us. "Whence come ye? to what end?" . . . . 622 *Recluse* 1. 1. 167
From such Pandorian gift may come a Pest . . 626 *Ballot* 12
Extend through unambitious years to come, . . 627 **Son of* 13
Whate'er its mission, the soft breeze can come . 632 *Prelude* 1. 5
Come fast upon me: it is shaken off, ... 632 *Prelude* 1. 20
A cheerful confidence in things to come. . . . 633 *Prelude* 1. 58
To passive minds. My seventeenth year was come; . . . . 647 *Prelude* 2. 863
As one far mightier), hither I had come, . . . 650 *Prelude* 3. 87
Come forth, perhaps without one quiet thought. . 652 *Prelude* 3. 255
When Learning, like a stranger come from far, . 655 *Prelude* 3. 462
Whence profit may be drawn in times to come. . 658 *Prelude* 3. 628
Had come among these objects heretofore, . . 662 *Prelude* 4. 250
This heard, I said, in pity, "Come with me." . 665 *Prelude* 4. 426
Be wrenched, or fire come down from far to scorch 666 *Prelude* 5. 31
That all would come to pass of which the voice . 667 *Prelude* 5. 100
Than shaping novelties for times to come, . . 669 *Prelude* 5. 268
May not come near him, nor the little throng . . 670 *Prelude* 5. 303
Nor what it augurs of the life to come; . . . 673 *Prelude* 5. 511
The present, with us in the times to come. . . 678 *Prelude* 6. 243
And sights and sounds that come at intervals, . 689 *Prelude* 7. 173
And of the air, which he had come to seek, . . 696 *Prelude* 7. 617
The business of the day to come, unborn, . . . 697 *Prelude* 7. 658
And in the lapse of many years may come . . 699 *Prelude* 8. 34
His hour being not yet come. Far less had then 704 *Prelude* 8. 356
For worst to them was come; nor would have stirred, ... 711 *Prelude* 9. 136
Of history, the past and that to come! . . . 712 *Prelude* 9. 169
A gift that was come rather late than soon. . . 713 *Prelude* 9. 248
They—who had come elate as eastern hunters . 718 *Prelude* 10. 17
Pressed on me almost like a fear to come. . . . 719 *Prelude* 10. 72
Do come within the reach of humblest eyes; . . 720 *Prelude* 10. 160
Fed on the day of vengeance yet to come. . . 722 *Prelude* 10. 299
Is come Whose harbinger he was; a time . . . 722 *Prelude* 10. 308
Imaginations, sense of woes to come, ... 723 *Prelude* 10. 329
Of their offences, punishment to come; . . . 724 *Prelude* 10. 443
Made manifest. "Come now, ye golden times," . 726 *Prelude* 10. 578
From out the bosom of the night, come ye: . . 726 *Prelude* 10. 581
That wisdom could, in any shape, come near . 728 *Prelude* 11. 45
The man to come, parted, as by a gulph, . . . 735 *Prelude* 12. 59
From Nature doth emotion come, and moods . . 740 *Prelude* 13. 1
And built thereon my hopes of good to come. . 741 *Prelude* 13. 63
Spread over time, past, present, and to come, . 747 *Prelude* 14. 110
Must come, or will by man be sought in vain. . 748 *Prelude* 14. 129
Of their deliverance, surely yet to come. . . 752 *Prelude* 14. 443
—To these emotions, whencesoe'er they come, . 755 *Recluse* 1. 1. 763
Dreaming on things to come; and dost possess . 755 *Recluse* 1. 1. 838
Beheld the stars come out above his head, . . 758 *Excursion* 1. 129
To blend with knowledge of the years to come, . 762 *Excursion* 1. 432
To human life, when he shall come again . . 768 *Excursion* 1. 789
Were now come nearer to her: weeds defaced . 769 *Excursion* 1. 834
Ere Robert come again.' When to the House . 769 *Excursion* 1. 846
And he continued, when worse days were come, . 775 *Excursion* 2. 281
Had vanished, much was come and coming back— 779 *Excursion* 2. 522
Motions of moonlight, all come thither—touch, . 782 *Excursion* 2. 714
And have an answer—thither come, and shape . 782 *Excursion* 2. 715
Been planted, hither come and find a lodge . . 787 *Excursion* 3. 106
From far ye come; and surely with a hope . . 791 *Excursion* 3. 328
(Not to be deemed a stranger, as you come . . 793 *Excursion* 3. 499
—Come, labour, when the worn-out frame requires 802 *Excursion* 4. 57
Perpetual sabbath; come, disease and want; . . 802 *Excursion* 4. 58
Ah! if the time must come, in which my feet . 803 *Excursion* 4. 103
Trust me, that for the instructed, time will come 819 *Excursion* 4. 1235
Till night lies black upon the ground. 'But come, 834 *Excursion* 5. 766
Come,' said the Matron, 'to our poor abode; . . 834 *Excursion* 5. 767
Though loth and slow to come! A battlefield, . 836 *Excursion* 5. 927
This Churchyard was. And, whether they had come 845 *Excursion* 6. 476
O come and hear him! Thou who hast to me . 851 *Excursion* 6. 879
Where injury cannot come:—and here is laid . 854 *Excursion* 6. 1051
—'Whence do they come? and with what errand charged? . . . . 858 *Excursion* 7. 86
Had never come, through space of forty years; . 861 *Excursion* 7. 245
Past or to come; yea, boldly might I say, . . 866 *Excursion* 7. 567
His own appointed hour will come at last; . . 867 *Excursion* 7. 629
To all that come, almost to all that pass; . . . 867 *Excursion* 7. 652
Oft did he say, 'was come to Gold-rill side.' . . 867 *Excursion* 7. 673
Like wild beasts without home! Their hour was come; . . . . 873 *Excursion* 7. 1027
The animating hope that time may come . . . 877 *Excursion* 8. 209
And cannot come. The boy, where'er he turns, . 878 *Excursion* 8. 302
And by the river's margin—whence they come, . 882 *Excursion* 8. 549
The consummation that will come by stealth . . 893 *Excursion* 9. 636
Were left, the other gained.—O ye, who come . 895 *Excursion* 9. 724
Come, gentle Sleep, Death's image tho' thou art, . S. 3. 441 **Come, gentle* 1
Come, share my couch, nor speedily depart; . . S. 3. 441 **Come, gentle* 2

Come—*continued.*
And wherefore, wherefore come they here? . . K. 8. 219 **The snow-tracks* 10
A centre, come from wheresoe'er you will, . . K. 8. 240 *Recluse* 1. 1. 148
Perhaps for many genial days to come, . . . K. 8. 241 *Recluse* 1. 1. 191
Is past we blame it not for having come. . . K. 8. 244 *Recluse* 1. 1. 291
Did we come hither, with romantic hope . . K. 8. 245 *Recluse* 1. 1. 311
Depressed, nor does it fear what is to come, . K. 8. 250 *Recluse* 1. 1. 496
Wild creatures, and of many homes, that come . K. 8. 251 *Recluse* 1. 1. 540
Admonished of the days of love to come . . K. 8. 252 *Recluse* 1. 1. 580
That is to come, the throng of woodland flowers, K. 8. 252 *Recluse* 1. 1. 590
Immortal in the world which is to come. . . K. 8. 255 *Recluse* 1. 1. 691
I come to thee, thou dost my heart renew; . . K. 8. 265 **Brook, that* 3
Whence flows the Latin people, whence have come K. 8. 281 **Arms and* 8
'Tis come, the final hour, ... L. 2. 121 *Frag. Æneid* 2. 1
Hath come! we *have* been Trojans, Ilium *was* . L. 2. 121 *Frag. Æneid* 2. 3

Come-at. Yet to be come-at by the breeze: . . 186 **O Nightingale* 14

Comedy. Rough, bold, as Grecian comedy displayed 691 *Prelude* 7. 289

Comeliness. The comeliness of unenfeebled age. . 860 *Excursion* 7. 208

Comely. Full fifty comely sheep I raised, . . . 115 *Last of Flock* 33
With their comely blue aprons, and caps white as snow, ... 120 *Childless Father* 7
His Helpmate was a comely matron, old— . . 132 *Michael* 79
And saddled his best Steed, a comely grey; . . 200 *Hart-leap* 6
There have I seen a comely bachelor, ... 695 *Prelude* 7. 551
And, close behind, the comely Matron rode, . . 858 *Excursion* 7. 77

Comer. *See* **New-comer.**
Saluted the chance comer on the road, . . . 656 *Prelude* 3. 472

Comers. The comers and the goers face to face, . 689 *Prelude* 7. 156

Comes. Home-felt, and home-created, comes to heal 1 *Early Youth* 8
Blesses the moon that comes with kindly ray, . 11 *Desc. Sk.* 33
Predominates, and darkness comes and goes, . . 13 *Desc. Sk.* 180
Rich steam of sweetest perfume comes and goes. . 16 *Desc. Sk.* 345
Comes on to gladden April with the sight . . 17 *Desc. Sk.* 368
Nearer and nearer comes the trying hour! . . 22 *Desc. Sk.* 641
For a companion—here he comes; our journey . 43 *Bord.* 356
And he is mine for ever—here he comes. . . . 47 *Bord.* 565
ThisBoy—when he comes forth with bloody hands— 54 *Bord.* 938
Whom no one comes to meet, I stood alone;— . 62 *Bord.* 1351
Ha! is it so!—That vagrant Hag!—this comes . 78 *Bord.* 2312
—But see, the evening star comes forth! . . . 81 †*Mother's Return* 45
"Whence comes," said I, "this piteous moan?" 82 *Alice Fell* 18
Comes from the depth of Dungeon Ghyll. . . . 85 *Shepherd-boys* 33
Comes to this church-yard once in eighteen months; 97 *Brothers* 126
Who comes her Sire to seek; . . . . . . 103 *Artegal* 46
Till she comes back again. . . . . 128 *Idiot Boy* 201
As that which comes, or seems to come, from heaven, ... 139 *Widow* 21
Comes from within doors or without! . . . . 143 **Driven in* 17
It comes to cool my babe and me. . . . . . 145 *Her Eyes* 40
That thought comes next—and instantly . . . 159 **With little* 27
The empty house when he comes home; . . . 162 *Binnorie* 40
The bird that comes about our doors . . . . 162 **Art thou the* 14
Comes a tired and sultry breeze . . . . . 173 *Waggoner* 1. 78
A voice that comes from some one near, . . . 176 *Waggoner* 1. 21
With him whatever comes in course, ... 178 *Waggoner* 3. 16
Where no disturbance comes to intrude . . . 180 *Waggoner* 4. 26
Comes to give what help he may, ... 181 *Waggoner* 4. 126
That comes and goes—will sometimes leap . . 182 *Waggoner* 4. 211
And what the creeping breeze that comes . . . 200 *Thorn* 201
He comes to tarry with thee three hours' space; . 209 *Laod.* 23
—Who comes not hither ne'er shall know . . . 215 *Kirkstone* 73
Crowding the quarter whence the sun comes forth 219 **This Height* 11
—She comes!—behold . . . . 220 *Triad* 41
Comes Faith that in auspicious hours . . . . 225 *Present.* 20
Comes from the entrance of a cave: . . . . 243 *P. B.* 630
He knows not how the blood comes there— . . 244 *P. B.* 724
Comes from that tabernacle—List! . . . . 247 *P. B.* 943
He comes, escaped from fields and floods;— . . 249 *P. B.* 1105
No tarrying; where She comes the winds must stir: 258 **With Ships* 13
Their tops, between them comes and goes a sky . 272 **Where holy* 12
Comes not by casting in a formal mould, . . . 277 **A Poet* 13
So sadness comes from out the mould . . . . 284 *Grave of Burns* 5
Music that sorrow comes not near, ... 285 *Grave of Burns* 81
And, when the moment comes, to part . . . . 300 *Bran* 9
He comes like Phœbus through the gates of morn 314 *Hofer* 5
All that I heard comes back upon my ear, . . . 350 *Des. Stanzas* 11
The sea-blast ruffles as the storm comes on, . . 388 *Eagles* 11
And griefs whose aery motion comes not near . 395 *White Doe: Ded.* 35
Comes gliding in with lovely gleam, ... 396 *White Doe* 55
Comes gliding in serene and slow, ... 396 *White Doe* 56
Comes she with a votary's task, ... 397 *White Doe* 108
'Lo, Francis comes,' there were who cried, . . 409 *White Doe* 1229
Why comes not Francis?—From the doleful City 411 *White Doe* 1364
—Why comes not Francis? Thoughts of love . 411 *White Doe* 1372
Why comes he not?—for westward fast . . . 411 *White Doe* 1377
She comes, and in the vale hath heard . . . . 413 *White Doe* 1543
Comes with the people when the bells . . . . 416 *White Doe* 1885
Who comes with functions apostolical? . . . 422 *Ecc. Sonn.* 1. 15. 4
In soft repose he comes. Within his cell, . . . 424 *Ecc. Sonn.* 1. 21. 7
Who comes—with rapture greeted, and caressed . 441 *Ecc. Sonn.* 3. 3. 1
The Hero comes to liberate, not defy; . . . . 442 *Ecc. Sonn.* 3. 9. 10
Its natural echo; but hope comes reborn . . . 448 *Ecc. Sonn.* 3. 31. 12
Comes that low sound from breezes rustling o'er . 453 **The Sun, that* 9
Now when the star of eve comes forth to shine . 454 *Sea-side* 34
For one who comes to watch them and to feed, . 465 **Pastor and* 3
He comes not back; an ampler space . . . . 479 *Somnamb.* 68
Comes to me not; malignant truth, or lie. . . 489 *Pers. Talk* 46
For love, that comes wherever life and sense . 491 *Tribute: Dog* 27
Thither the rainbow comes—the cloud— . . . 491 *Fidelity* 29
The heifer comes in the snow-storm, and here . 547 **Rude is* 15

Comes—*continued.*
For thereof comes all goodness and all worth ; . 559 *Cuck.andNight.*151
Thence worship comes, content and true heart's pleasure, ... 559 *Cuck.andNight.*153
Thence sickness comes, and overwhelming sadness, 560 *Cuck.andNight.*172
When next May comes, if I am not afraid. . . 561 *Cuck.andNight.*235
Duly as Friday comes, though pressed herself . 568 *Cumb. Beg.* 156
Comes in the promise from the Cross, ... 578 **I come* 71
Like these, there comes a mild release ; . . . 580 *John Words.* 47
The Rainbow comes and goes, ... 587 *Immortality* 10
Blesses the Moon that comes with kindest ray . 602 *Desc. Sk. Quarto* 35
On the high summits Darkness comes and goes, . 605 *Desc.Sk.Quarto* 205
—Fierce comes the river down ; the crashing wood 606 *Desc.Sk.Quarto* 211
Comes on, to whisper hope, the vernal breeze, . 610 *Desc.Sk.Quarto* 443
He comes, my dear delight,—and costliest things 624 *Æneid* 29
The star which comes at close of day to shine . 627 **The star* 1
But unto Faith and Loyalty comes aid . . . 628 *Eagle and Dove* 15
It comes, to works of unreproved delight, . . . 673 *Prelude* 5. 493
That comes with night ; the deep solemnity . . 697 *Prelude* 7. 655
Thither he comes with spring-time, there abides . 702 *Prelude* 8. 198
No genuine insight ever comes to her. . . . . 704 *Prelude* 8. 327
Whene'er it comes ! needful in work so long, . . 710 *Prelude* 9. 20
A hymn of triumph : " as the morning comes 726 *Prelude* 10. 580
Who thither comes to find in it his home ? . . 729 *Prelude* 11. 148
Comes o'er my heart : in fancy I behold 733 *Prelude* 11. 430
They had left behind ? So feeling comes in aid . 738 *Prelude* 12. 269
That from thyself it comes, that thou must give, 738 *Prelude* 12. 276
I see by glimpses now ; when age comes on, . . 738 *Prelude* 12. 281
A momentary trance comes over me ; . . . . 768 *Excursion* 1. 784
This notice comes too late.' With joy I saw . . 783 *Excursion* 2. 793
The mountain infant to the sun comes forth, . . 786 *Excursion* 3. 34
Hostility—how dreadful when it comes, . . . 792 *Excursion* 3. 419
A day of solemn ceremonial comes ; . . . . 826 *Excursion* 5. 274
What qualities of mind she bears, who comes, . 832 *Excursion* 5. 640
Whence comes it, then, that yonder we behold . 858 *Excursion* 7. 34
Power that comes forth to quicken and exalt . . 875 *Excursion* 8. 73
He is a slave to whom release comes not, . . . 878 *Excursion* 8. 301
Or locks of wool, announces whence he comes. . 879 *Excursion* 8. 310
And now, my lads, the Election comes . . . S. 3. 431**The Scottish* 25

Comest. *See* **Com'st.**

Comet. Red on his hills his beacon's comet blaze ; . 616 *Desc.Sk.Quarto* 775

Cometh. And the least welfare cometh to their share ; 559 *Cuck.andNight.*144
And cometh from afar : . . . . 588 *Immortality* 61

Comfort. When not a star supplies the comfort of its light ; . . . . 14 *Desc. Sk.* 187
" We lived in peace and comfort ; and were blest 29 *Guilt* 262
Proverbial words of comfort he applied, . . . 32 *Guilt* 458
Comfort by prouder mansions unbestowed . . 34 *Guilt* 525
Kindly the housewife pressed, and they in comfort fed. . . . . 34 *Guilt* 531
" Barred every comfort labour could procure, . 35 *Guilt* 577
Thanks to them, are to us a stream of comfort : . 43 *Bord.* 325
This is true comfort, thanks a thousand times !— 43 *Bord.* 343
Here's what will comfort you. The Saints reward you 44 *Bord.* 408
Though rich in heavenly, poor in earthly, comfort, 49 *Bord.* 686
And we were comforted, and talked of comfort ; . 50 *Bord.* 709
Why so ? a roofless rock had been a comfort, . 52 *Bord.* 814
I come home, and this is my comfort ! . . . 72 *Bord.* 1951
A comfort to each other— That they might . . 99 *Brothers* 286
No peace, no comfort could I find, ... 115 *Last of Flock* 75
Our comfort was near if we ever were crost ; . . 116 *Repentance* 22
But the comfort, the blessings, and wealth that we had, ... 116 *Repentance* 23
All that is left to comfort thee. . . . . . . 117 *Affl. Marg.* 49
What warmth, what comfort would it yield . . 120 *EmigrantMother* 22
To comfort poor old Susan Gale. . . . . . 127 *Idiot Boy* 121
To comfort poor old Susan Gale. . . . . . 129 *Idiot Boy* 276
He was his comfort and his daily hope. . . . 134 *Michael* 206
There is a comfort in the strength of love ; . . 138 *Michael* 448
Comfort have thou of thy merit, ... 160 **Pasies, lilies* 41
To warn, to comfort, and command ; . . . . 186 **She was* 28
Might need for comfort, or for festal mirth ; . . 276 *Filial Piety* 3
Live, and take comfort. Thou hast left behind . 305 *Toussaint* 9
For comfort, being, as I am, opprest, ... 306 **O Friend* 2
To give thee comfort if I may." . . . . . 401 *White Doe* 456
A comfort in the dark abyss. . . . . . . 402 *White Doe* 537
He was their comfort to the last, ... 409 *White Doe* 1220
Of power to comfort or rejoice ; . . . . . 411 *White Doe* 1351
Finds comfort in himself and in his cause ; . . 494 *Hap. War.* 81
And their meaning is, whence can comfort spring 494 *Force of Prayer* 3
Comfort for a faithful mind ; . . . . . . 503 **Like a* 79
And cottage comfort shunned not seemly pride. . 525 *Epist. Beaumont* 249
My sighs breathed forth in silence,—comfort give ! 562 *Cuck.andNight.*316
To comfort him, and make his heart more light ; . 565 *Troilus* 166
He promised comfort ; and the flattering thoughts 575 *Chiabrera* 8. 14
To comfort and to peace. . . . . 580 *John Words.* 50
No star supplies the comfort of it's light, . . 606 *Desc.Sk.Quarto* 216
The Ocean ; not to comfort the oppressed, . . 635 *Prelude* 1. 210
While on I walked, a comfort seemed to touch . 660 *Prelude* 4. 153
In comfort, I entreated that henceforth . . . 665 *Prelude* 4. 454
That were a frequent comfort to my youth. . . 677 *Prelude* 6. 141
And every comfort of that privileged ground, . 688 *Prelude* 7. 55
More firmly ; and a comfort now hath risen . . 752 *Prelude* 14. 424
To human comfort. Stooping down to drink, . 763 *Excursion* 1. 491
In peace and comfort ; and a pretty boy . . . 764 *Excursion* 1. 533
To natural comfort shut our eyes and ears ; . . 765 *Excursion* 1. 602
Stood drinking comfort from the warmer sun, . 765 *Excursion* 1. 621
To give her comfort, and was glad to take . . 766 *Excursion* 1. 684
With the best hope and comfort I could give : . 768 *Excursion* 1. 811
Whose presence gave no comfort, were gone by, . 769 *Excursion* 1. 893

Comfort—*continued.*
To comfort me while with a brother's love . . 770 *Excursion* 1. 923
To draw the line of comfort that divides . . . 772 *Excursion* 2. 72
To comfort ;—but how came ye ?—if yont rack . 779 *Excursion* 2. 532
Of comfort, spread over his pallid face. . . . 785 *Excursion* 2. 886
To seek that comfort which the mind denies ; . 822 *Excursion* 5. 21
My comfort :—would that they were oftener fixed 835 *Excursion* 5. 824
Than their own thoughts to comfort them. Say why 846 *Excursion* 6. 538
A heavenly comfort ; there she recognised . . 853 *Excursion* 6. 1016
Asked comfort of the open air, and found . . . 855 *Excursion* 6. 1100
(Or call it comfort, by a humbler name,) . . . 878 *Excursion* 8. 263
Use, comfort, do this roof endear ; . . . . . S. 3. 425 **No whimsy* 3
He was his comfort and his daily hope. . . . K. 8. 226 **I will* 86

Comforted. And we were comforted, and talked of comfort ; . . . . 50 *Bord.* 709
You understand me—I was comforted ; . . . 69 *Bord.* 1779
—Perplexed, and longing to be comforted, . . 197 *Resolution* 117
From one disburthened so, so comforted, . . . 447 *Ecc. Sonn.* 3. 28. 10

Comforter. A nursling babe her only comforter ; . 13 *Desc. Sk.* 176
A comforter of sorrow ;—there is something . . 48 *Bord.* 635
That I have been his comforter till now ! . . . 50 *Bord.* 720
My faithful true and only Comforter. . . . . 76 *Bord.* 2188
And Care—a comforter that best could suit . . 255 **Grief, thou* 3
Yet, helped by Genius—untired comforter, . . 273 **While Anna's* 9
The Comforter hath found me here, ... 581 **Loud is* 11
And he too hath his comforter. How poor, . . 778 *Excursion* 2. 479
Was now a help to his late comforter, ... 782 *Excursion* 2. 686
A soothing comforter, although forlorn ; . . . 852 *Excursion* 6. 933
As to a spiritual comforter and friend, ... 854 *Excursion* 6. 1030
Guide of our way, mysterious comforter ! . . . 864 *Excursion* 7. 483

Comforters. Dependants, comforters—my wheel, my fire, ... 834 *Excursion* 5. 813

Comfortless. Perplexed and comfortless he gazed around, ... 24 *Guilt* 24
Has been but comfortless ; and yet that place, . 53 *Bord.* 860
A comfortless and hidden well. . . . . . 111 *A Complaint* 12
Report of comfortless despairs, ... 338 **Meek Virgin* 10
And comfortless despairs the soul benumb. . . 427 *Ecc. Sonn.* 1. 36. 14
Which this comfortless oven environ ! . . . . 484 **A plague* 12
Joyless and comfortless. Our days glide on ; . 585 *Ch. Lamb* 71
In the comfortless vault of disease. . . . . . 621 *Convict* 32
The earth was comfortless, and, touched by faint 644 *Prelude* 2. 121
Was comfortless, and her small lot of books, . . 768 *Excursion* 1. 824
Though comfortless !—Not of myself I speak ; . 790 *Excursion* 3. 263
Within myself, not comfortless.—The tenour . . 800 *Excursion* 3. 967

Comforts. it comforts me to think of it. . . . 71 *Bord.* 1913
But delegated Spirits comforts fetch . . . . 280 **Oh what* 7
To travellers, from such comforts as are thine, . 352 *Aquap.* 21
And the Land's humblest comforts. Now her mood 439 *Ecc. Sonn.* 2. 44. 6
With just enough life's comforts to procure, . . 470 †*From early* 10
Who comforts the forlorn ; . . . . 542 *Russ. Fug.* 44
Ye dealt out your plain comforts ? Yet had ye . 639 *Prelude* 1. 505
His comforts, native occupations, cares, . . . 700 *Prelude* 8. 106
Of daily comforts, gladly reconciled . . . . 764 *Excursion* 1. 547

Coming. Dark is the region as with coming night ; . 15 *Desc. Sk.* 273
That he should wait thy coming till the day . . 76 *Bord.* 2231
Coming on with a terrible pother, ... 86 *Rural Arch.* 15
And, coming back with Her who will be ours, . 107 *Farewell* 63
By chance of business coming within reach . . 125 *V. and J.* 288
She's coming from among the trees, ... 130 *Idiot Boy* 364
Coming one knows not how, nor whence, . . . 158 **In youth* 71
Spring is coming, Thou art come ! . . . . . 160 **Pansies, lilies* 40
Now she meets the coming prey, ... 171 *Kitten* 26
And, coming to the Banks of Tone, ... 194 *Ruth* 214
Coming together in life's pilgrimage ; . . . . 196 *Resolution* 67
Cries coming from the mountain head : . . . 199 *Thorn* 160
But at the coming of the milder day . . . . 203 *Hart-leap* 175
Upon her coming wait . . . . 220 *Triad* 44
Of coming good ;—the charm is fled ; . . . . 224 **'Tis gone* 22
Of ages coming, ages gone ; . . . . 227 *Vernal Ode* 94
Then coming from the wayward world, . . . 245 *P. B.* 781
Does joy approach ? they meet the coming tide ; 278 **Life with* 3
So, coming his last help to crave, ... 287 *Ellen Irwin* 45
And, with the coming of the tide, ... 295 *Highland Boy* 66
Of destructive tempests coming, ... 328 *Ode 1815* 73
Brought to the ark are coming evermore, . . . 360 **Near Anio's* 10
Turn from us all the coming woe : . . . . . 408 *White Doe* 1085
As if with prescience of the coming storm, . . 419 *Ecc. Sonn.* 1. 4. 10
Their pearly lustre—coming but to go ; . . . 436 *Ecc. Sonn.* 2. 32. 7
To meet the coming hours of festal mirth, . . 445 *Ecc. Sonn.* 3. 20. 10
Shine on, until ye fade with coming Night !— 451 *Ecc. Sonn.* 3. 44. 8
His coming step has thwarted, ... 479 *Somnamb.* 101
The beauty coming and the beauty gone. . . . 480 **Most sweet* 8
But the whole household, that our coming wait. . 525 *Epist. Beaumont* 235
I might her see again coming to Troy ! . . . 564 *Troilus* 91
The aged Beggar coming, quits her work, . . . 566 *Cumb. Beg.* 35
But chiefly Dido, to the coming ill . . . . 624 *Æneid* 79
Low breathings coming after me, and sounds . . 637 *Prelude* 1. 323
If the night blackened with a coming storm, . . 646 *Prelude* 2. 307
Coming in revelation, did converse . . . . . 647 *Prelude* 2. 393
Upon the basis of the coming time, ... 655 *Prelude* 3. 426
Twilight was coming on, yet through the gloom . 672 *Prelude* 5. 435
Admonished thus, the sweet hour coming on. . . 771 *Excursion* 1. 961
Had vanished, much was come and coming back— 779 *Excursion* 2. 522
" Nor could your coming have been better timed ; 779 *Excursion* 2. 526
By hopes of coming patronage beguiled . . . 859 *Excursion* 7. 130
" O for the coming of that glorious time . . . 888 *Excursion* 9. 293
What is that that's coming ? . . . . . . S. 3. 424 *Tinker* 38
Coming thus to seek my Parent ; . . . . . S. 3. 437 **I, whose* 12
A human voice—a Spirit of coming night, . . K.8.245*Recluse* 1.1.326

Comings-in. To help the small but certain comings-in 860 *Excursion* 7. 166
Command. *See* **Self-command.**
The Crew deceived you? Nay, command yourself. 69 *Bord.* 1764
'Tis his who will command it.—Think of my story— 71 *Bord.* 1873
Thou didst command me to bless all mankind ; 75 *Bord.* 2173
Loth to rule by strict command ; 93 *Westmoreland Girl* 34
With like command of beauty—grant your aid 152 **Forth from* 23
Serving at my heart's command, 160 **Pansies, lilies* 61
He who had once supreme command, 176 *Waggoner* 1. 211
The Waggoner, with prompt command, 176 *Waggoner* 1. 223
Forthwith, obedient to command, 179 *Waggoner* 3. 56
To warn, to comfort, and command ; 186 **She was* 28
Laodamía ! that at Jove's command 209 *Laod.* 21
" Appear !—obey my lyre's command ! 220 *Triad* 15
Whom onset, fiercely urged at Jove's command, 265 **When haughty* 13
Or fortress, reared at Nature's sage command. 266 **The stars* 8
The Church, when trusting in divine command 281 *Chris. Words.* 5
Our pleasure varying at command 286 *Nith* 29
Had thine at their command. 292 *Rob Roy* 112
Less than divine command they spurn ; 300 *Cora Linn* 31
An undisputed symbol of command, 321 **Humanity, delighting* 8
Well obeyed was that command— 323 *Ode 1814* 35
Holding a central station of command, 339 *Schwytz* 10
Wandering, he haunts, at fancy's strong command, 361 **For action* 13
" My books command me to lay bare 372 *Eg. Maid* 247
A voice is with us—a command 399 *White Doe* 334
Embroidered (such her Sire's command) 400 *White Doe* 355
" Might ever son *command* a sire, 401 *White Doe* 450
Proceeding under joint command, 404 *White Doe* 710
Raised, as the Vision gave command, 405 *White Doe* 830
And, with a look of calm command 410 *White Doe* 1331
Was to the harp a strong command, 413 *White Doe* 1552
The shrouded Body to the Soul's command 437 *Ecc. Sonn.* 2. 35. 8
For re-subjecting to divine command 444 *Ecc. Sonn.* 3. 18. 13
Sweet flowers ! at whose inaudible command 445 *Ecc. Sonn.* 3. 22. 11
Who in these Wilds then struggled for command ; 466 *St. Bees* 38
That o'er the channel holds august command, 470 **Did pangs* 7
Then followed Printing with enlarged command 489 *Illus. Books* 3
—Who, if he rise to station of command, 493 *Hap. War.* 35
Or at a doubting Judge's stern command, 500 *Humanity* 3
Not He, whose last faint memory will command 504 *Warning* 53
And Will, whose office, by divine command, 514 **Who ponders* 13
In the weak love of life his least command. 518 *Pun. Death* 4. 14
Bore a light switch, her sceptre of command 523 *Epist. Beaumont* 108
Time, place, and business, all at his command !— 528 **Those breathing* 86
He rose, and straight—as by divine command, 534 **When in* 9
At nature's pure command ; 543 *Russ. Fug.* 116
Their painted couches seek, obedient to command. 624 *Æneid* 72
The minutes fly—till, at the queen's command, 625 *Æneid* 103
Of sharp command and scolding intermixed. 650 *Prelude* 3. 52
In colour so resplendent, with command 667 *Prelude* 5. 91
At full command, to London first I turned, 688 *Prelude* 7. 61
Among new objects serve or give command, 708 *Prelude* 8. 641
He perished fighting, in supreme command, 715 *Prelude* 9. 424
That he had formed, when I, at his command, 726 *Prelude* 10. 551
At thy command, at her command gives way ; 733 *Prelude* 11. 428
At thy command, how awful ! Shall the Soul, 802 *Excursion* 4. 36
Of a command which they have power to break, 807 *Excursion* 4. 379
Do speak, at Heaven's command, to eye and ear, 819 *Excursion* 4. 1205
But He, at whose command the parchèd rock 852 *Excursion* 6. 919
" Meanwhile, at social Industry's command, 876 *Excursion* 8. 117
Nothing to praise, to teach, or to command ! 878 *Excursion* 8. 275
Commander. " Silence ! " the brave Commander cried ; 579 **Sweet Flower* 43
Commanding. He was commanding and entreating, 410 *White Doe* 1256
Of chiming sound, commanding sympathies ; 422 *Ecc. Sonn.* 1. 13. 11
Ere some commanding star dismiss to rest 455 *Rydal Mere* 7
Imploring, or commanding with meet pride, 467 *St. Bees* 102
Had more commanding looks when he was there. 703 *Prelude* 8. 261
Of some commanding eminence, which yet 799 *Excursion* 3. 936
On new-blown heath ; let yon commanding rock 808 *Excursion* 4. 497
'Nay,' said she, with commanding look, a spirit 853 *Excursion* 6. 976
From some commanding eminence had looked 871 *Excursion* 7. 879
Commandments. Mighty were the soul's commandments 141 *Arm. Lady* 87
Commands. That British ground commands :—low dusky tracts, 219 **This Height* 5
While on that isthmus which commands 226 *Present.* 70
No pitying voice commands a halt, 322 **Humanity, delighting* 32
And for the boldest tale belief commands. 338 *Engelberg* 5
By her commands partakes not, in degree, 429 *Ecc. Sonn.* 2. 2. 9
Obedient, as here taught, to thy commands. 447 *Ecc. Sonn.* 3. 26. 8
Noting that in despite of their commands 853 *Excursion* 6. 993
Whose love, whose counsel, whose commands, have made 895 *Excursion* 9. 733
Commemorate. Marched round the altar—to commemorate 346 *Processions* 12
Commemorating. Commemorating genius, talent, skill, 584 **With copious* 61
Commemoration. Commemoration holy that unites 328 *Ode 1815* 66
Commenced. His mournful narrative—commenced in pain, 801 *Excursion* 4. 2
In pain commenced, and ended without peace : 801 *Excursion* 4. 3
Commend. Commend me to the place. If a man should die 61 *Bord.* 1298
Wallace and Wilfred, I commend the Lady, 78 *Bord.* 2333
Commend me to these valleys ! Yet your Churchyard 98 *Brothers* 166

Commend—*continued.*
Commend him, when he's only heard. 143 **Driven in* 29
Whom to this service I commend ; 402 *White Doe* 612
I call thee : I myself commend 492 *Duty* 50
Or does it suit our humour to commend 530 *Poor Robin* 20
This work of thine I blame not, but commend ; 579 *Peele Castle* 43
And doth commend their weakness and disease 841 *Excursion* 6. 182
Commendable. Tremblings withal and commendable fears, 650 *Prelude* 3. 71
Commendation. Unspoiled by commendation and the excess 691 *Prelude* 7. 313
Commendations. With commendations of departed worth ; 847 *Excursion* 6. 627
Commended. Commended him as a poor friendless man, 665 *Prelude* 4. 451
Comment. Meek Nature's evening comment on the shows 349 *Sky-prosp.* 12
Are fostered by the comment and the gibe." 488 *Pers. Talk* 20
Have their authentic comment ; that even these 755 *Recluse* 1. 1. 834
Comments. But vainly comments of a calmer mind 719 *Prelude* 10. 89
Commerce. That holds no commerce with the summer night. 21 *Desc. Sk.* 578
With commerce freighted, or triumphant war. 384 *Duddon* 32. 14
From unimpeded commerce with the Sun, 452 *Ecc. Sonn.* 3. 46. 13
Let us break off all commerce with the Muse : 480 **Most sweet* 10
For commerce of thy nature with herself, 666 *Prelude* 5. 19
Each into commerce with his private thoughts : 746 *Prelude* 14. 18
From a too busy commerce with the heart ! 831 *Excursion* 5. 610
To hold a vacant commerce day by day K.8. 253 *Recluse* 1.1.595
Commination. So shall the fearful words of Commination 447 *Ecc. Sonn.* 3. 29. 13
Commingled. All kinds commingled without fear, 154 *Flower Garden* 8
Commingled—shapes which met me in the way 692 *Prelude* 7. 318
Commingled, making up a canopy 707 *Prelude* 8. 569
Confused, commingled, mutually inflamed, 784 *Excursion* 2. 855
Commingling. These structures rose, commingling old and young, 879 *Excursion* 8. 339
Commingling with the incense that ascends, 885 *Excursion* 9. 42
Commiseration. No word of kind commiseration 241 *P. B.* 452
Feelings of pure commiseration, grief 693 *Prelude* 7. 395
Commissioned. Commissioned by the Band, burst in upon us. 59 *Bord.* 1212
Of riotous men commissioned to expel 681 *Prelude* 6. 425
Like that of angels or commissioned spirits, 690 *Prelude* 7. 243
Commit. I will commit him to this final *Ordeal !*— 62 *Bord.* 1393
Committed. Committed to thy guardianship by Heaven ; 76 *Bord.* 2199
Which few can hold committed to a fight 437 *Ecc. Sonn.* 2. 36. 4
Committed to the silent plains 499 **Departing summer* 32
Committed by forsaken Ellen's hand 851 *Excursion* 6. 891
Commodious. On this commodious Seat ! for much remains 548 **Stay, bold* 2
There in commodious shelter may we rest. 786 *Excursion* 3. 29
Smooth and commodious ; as a stately deck 805 *Excursion* 4. 246
Could find commodious place for every God, 812 *Excursion* 4. 721
Was the commodious walk : a careful hand 881 *Excursion* 8. 450
Common. That common growth of earth, the foodful ear ; 15 *Desc. Sk.* 257
No common soul. In youth by science nursed, 23 *Yew-tree* 13
Of looks where common kindness had no part, 31 *Guilt* 393
At houses, men, and common light, amazed. 31 *Guilt* 401
Answer these questions, from our common knowledge, 38 *Bord.* 39
It is no common thing when one like you 38 *Bord.* 50
Yours is no common life. Self-stationed here, 48 *Bord.* 605
But have they not a world of common ground 60 *Bord.* 1237
Where is our common Friend ? A ghost, methinks— 61 *Bord.* 1301
By the good God, our common Father, doomed !— 62 *Bord.* 1345
Died broken-hearted. 'Tis a common case. 98 *Brothers* 196
Look at the common grass from hour to hour : 107 *Indolence* 23
Within the eddy of a common blast, 122 *V. and J.* 27
And one domestic for their common needs, 125 *V. and J.* 275
And shunning even the light of common day ; 126 *V. and J.* 301
The common air ; hills, which with vigorous step 132 *Michael* 66
Beyond the common life of man, I still 136 *Michael* 365
Of common pleasure : beast and bird, the lamb, 146 **It was an* 25
Than common feelings of fraternal love. 151 **When, to* 75
Nor was it common gratitude 155 *Waterfall* 29
The common life our nature breeds ; 158 **In youth* 54
He whose domain is held in common 175 *Waggoner* 1. 174
This is no common waste, no common gloom ; 203 *Hart-leap* 170
Upon the common weal ; a warrior bold, 227 *Vernal Ode* 102
The common growth of mother-earth 238 *P. B.* 133
Of common sense you're surely sinning ; 238 *P. B.* 197
Unhappy Nuns, whose common breath's a sigh 266 **With how* 5
Well pleased, her foot should print earth's common grass, 278 **Lo ! where she* 12
Which hold, whate'er to common sight appears, 279 **All praise* 13
If, guarding grossest things from common claim 280 *Plea for Auth.* 6
And more than common strength and skill 286 *Sons of Burns* 9
Of common day, so heavenly bright, 288 *Highland Girl* 16
Though but of common neighbourhood. 288 *Highland Girl* 58
All that he holds in common with the stars, 290 *Kilchurn* 19
Where common cheerfulness would fail ; 294 *Jedbor.* 59
There's not a breathing of the common wind 305 *Toussaint* 11
So didst thou travel on life's common way, 307 **Milton ! thou* 12
As to a common centre, tend 338 **Meek Virgin* 14
That gives to common pleasures birth ; 348 **Lulled by* 40
Thy sense from pressure of life's common din ; 349 *At Dover* 10
Turning, for them who pass, the common dust 351 *Des. Stanzas* 78

Companion—*continued.*
Companion of the wise and good, 626 †*Cento* 8
The off and on companion of my walk; 661 *Prelude* 4. 187
With that revered companion. And sometimes— 716 *Prelude* 9. 465
I paced, a dear companion at my side, 725 *Prelude* 10. 497
Companion never lost through many a league— 732 *Prelude* 11. 340
His dear companion wheresoe'er he went 771 *Excursion* 2. 16
To my benign Companion,—" Pity 'tis 781 *Excursion* 2. 619
(The sportive bird's companion in the grove) 799 *Excursion* 3. 948
Of our Companion, gradually diffused; 814 *Excursion* 4. 890
Sprinkled;—be our Companion while we track 819 *Excursion* 4. 1198
His sole companion, and his faithful friend, 872 *Excursion* 7. 947
The dear companion of my lonely walk, K.8. 234 **Witness thou* 2

Companionless. Who, while each stood companionless and eyed 170 **Never enlivened* 22
Though faded, yet entire. Companionless, 664 *Prelude* 4. 399
Companionless your awful solitudes! 702 *Prelude* 8. 222
Or sate companionless; and here the book, 778 *Excursion* 2. 451

Companions. In barn uplighted; and companions boon, 32 *Guilt* 411
With two Companions; one of them, as seemed, 58 *Bord.* 1137
This instant we'll return to our Companions— 66 *Bord.* 1589
Companions for each other: the huge crag 97 *Brothers* 143
With two or three companions, whom their course 101 *Brothers* 359
Were as companions, why should I relate 134 *Michael* 198
Be thy companions, think of me, my Son, 137 *Michael* 406
Companions, fear ye to be left behind, 229 *Clouds* 6
Though simple thy companions were and few; 379 *Duddon* 14. 11
Daunt him—if his Companions, now bedrowsed 392 *Daniel* 12
With Thought and Love companions of our way, 480 **Most sweet* 11
And watch these mute Companions, in the pool, 527 **Those breathing* 42
Or like two birds, companions in mid air, 622 *Recluse* 1. 1. 161
And, from companions in a new abode, 672 *Prelude* 5. 463
With those companions at my side, I watched, 738 *Prelude* 12. 302
My best companions now the driving winds, 766 *Excursion* 1. 702
Your prized companions.—Many are the notes 782 *Excursion* 2. 696
Of gay companions, to the natal roof, 793 *Excursion* 3. 507
Companions daily, often all day long; 794 *Excursion* 3. 585
Companions have I many; many friends, 834 *Excursion* 5. 812
But fond companions, so I guessed, in field, 882 *Excursion* 8. 548
A choice repast—served by our young companions 892 *Excursion* 9. 530
Were as companions, why should I relate K.8. 226 **I will* 78
Faithful companions, yet another year K.8. 243 *Recluse* 1.1.262

Companionship. Companionship with One of crooked ways, 37 *Bord.* 8
Of old companionship, Time counts not minutes 353 *Aquap.* 32
He wont to hold companionship so free, 362 **List—'twas* 60
For her companionship; here dwells soft ease: 382 *Duddon* 25. 10
From whose serene companionship I passed 510 **Among a* 12
Or an *unseen* companionship, a breath, 622 *Recluse* 1. 1. 93
Of long companionship, the artist's hand, 831 *Excursion* 5. 608
Of all companionship, the Sufferer yet 852 *Excursion* 6. 895

Companionships. These delicate companionships are made; 511 **So fair* 11
Might enter in at will. Companionships, 652 *Prelude* 3. 246

Company. She could not, Sir, have failed of company. 43 *Bord.* 327
This have we, but no other company: 61 *Bord.* 1297
From home and company remote and every playful joy, 91 *Norman Boy* 3
He bids his little company advance 104 *Artegal* 112
If but a bird, to keep them company, 108 *Indolence* 70
To have such company so near! 179 *Waggoner* 3. 63
The silent company betray: 180 *Waggoner* 4. 32
In such a jocund company: 187 **I wandered* 16
Her company to Stephen Hill; 198 *Thorn* 107
But lo! the vanished company again 218 *Recluse* 1. 1. 218
Of all his years;—a company 227 *Vernal Ode* 93
Such company I like it not! 237 *P. B.* 40
Should sally forth, to keep thee company, 266 **With how* 11
Muffled in clouds, affords no company 266 **Even as* 7
Of company or friends, and left 295 *Highland Boy* 39
Then do a festal company unite 318 **In due* 8
Upon a princely company below, 324 *Ode 1814* 79
But this swift travel scorns the company 327 *Ode 1815* 15
What sprinklings of blithe company! 396 *White Doe* 10
And float in rueful company! 400 *White Doe* 359
Well-pleased, the armèd Company 402 *White Doe* 601
A bright-haired company of youthful slaves, 421 *Ecc. Sonn.* 1. 13. 1
We stood, a trembling, earnest Company! 445 *Ecc. Sonn.* 3. 22. 4
Who, doomed to go in company with Pain, 493 *Hap. War.* 12
Upon this solemn Company unmoved 510 *F. Stone* 114
Tired of my books, a scanty company! 521 *Epist. Beaumont* 32
With numbers near, alas! no company. 530 **I know* 4
Nor lacking, for fit company, alcove, 547 **Rude is* 12
Hateful to Christ and to His company; 553 *Prioress* 40
The Abbot with his convent's company 555 *Prioress* 186
And take my leave of all such company, 559 *Cuck. and Night.* 138
And seemliness, and faithful company, 559 *Cuck. and Night.* 157
To part from company and take this book 677 *Prelude* 6. 149
The saucy air. In this proud company 681 *Prelude* 6. 394
Presents a company of dancing dogs, 689 *Prelude* 7. 176
A sober company and few, the men 777 *Excursion* 2. 391
As left by the departed company, 781 *Excursion* 2. 644
Is the mute company of changeful clouds; 808 *Excursion* 4. 461
With the ever-welcome company of books; 823 *Excursion* 5. 57
With prospect of the company within, 856 *Excursion* 6. 1177
As if their silent company were charged 876 *Excursion* 8. 162
Pursued our way, a broken company, 890 *Excursion* 9. 435
Making a silent company in death; K.8. 255 *Recluse* 1.1.696

Comparative. Hyperboles of praise comparative; 686 *Prelude* 6. 734

Compare. If nought in loveliness compare 111 **Let other* 7
In snugness may compare. 168 *Wren's Nest* 4
Thee with the welcome Snowdrop I compare; 274 **Such age* 9
Oh! say not so; compare them not; 292 *Rob Roy* 97
Nor art thou wronged, sweet May! when I compare 367 **If with* 4
Rights to compare and duties to discern! 501 *Humanity* 102
With o'erweening complacence our state to compare, 621 *Convict* 46
With these impressions would he still compare 758 *Excursion* 1. 141
In the old World compare, thought I, for power 799 *Excursion* 3. 882
Of that day's prowess! Him might I compare, 883 *Excursion* 8. 576
Compare! thy earthly bed a moment past S.3. 434 **The doubt* 95

Compared. Yet happy thou, poor boy! compared with me, 33 *Guilt* 498
A slavery compared to which the dungeon 69 *Bord.* 1777
Compared with *hers* who long hath lain, 144 **Driven in* 31
May with that issue be compared) 343 *Eclipse* 57
Appears *his* lot, to the small Worm's compared, 366 *Lombardy* 3
Though faint, compared with spear and shield, 478 *Somnamb.* 52
And still be not unblest—compared 534 **Blest is* 65
Such life might not inaptly be compared 654 *Prelude* 3. 332
So different, may rightly be compared), 677 *Prelude* 6. 156
With those of Greece compared and popular Rome, 708 *Prelude* 8. 618
Though filling daily, still was light, compared 709 *Prelude* 8. 685
(If with unworldly ends and aims compared) 712 *Prelude* 9. 203
May with such heinous appetites be compared), 723 *Prelude* 10. 366
My earliest notices; with these compared 741 *Prelude* 13. 104
Compared with ours! who, pacing side by side, 773 *Excursion* 2. 104
How bountiful these elements—compared 790 *Excursion* 3. 318
With this compared, makes a strange spectacle! 836 *Excursion* 5. 929
Dread life of conflict! which I oft compared 849 *Excursion* 6. 734
Smooth task, with *his* compared, whose mind could string, 862 *Excursion* 7. 306
The existing worship; and with those compared, 894 *Excursion* 9. 713

Compares. And Fancy, not less aptly pleased, compares 230 *Clouds* 16
He only judges right who weighs, compares, 429 *Ecc. Sonn.* 2. 1. 12

Comparison. Wild shapes for many a strange comparison! 379 *Duddon* 12. 4
To a comparison of scene with scene, 736 *Prelude* 12. 115
'Tis, by comparison, an easy task 803 *Excursion* 4. 130

Compass. A crucible of mighty compass, felt 15 *Desc. Sk.* 283
Within the compass of a mortal thought, 78 *Bord.* 2300
Though but of compass small, and bare 198 *Thorn* 32
Vast is the compass and the swell of notes: 234 *Power of Sound* 162
Just Heaven, contract the compass of my mind 267 **As the* 9
Into the compass of distinct regard 290 *Kilchurn* 34
In unambitious compass round thee spread. 339 *Schwytz* 8
In narrow compass—narrow as itself: 382 *Duddon* 24. 9
Lodged within compass of the humblest sight, 538 **In desultory* 39
Beyond all compass; spreads, and sends aloft 698 *Prelude* 7. 752
Through the whole compass of the sky; ye brooks, 734 *Prelude* 12. 18
With the whole compass of the universe: 747 *Prelude* 14. 92
That volume—as a compass for the soul— 798 *Excursion* 3. 862
For one day's little compass, has preserved 828 *Excursion* 5. 361
There, or within the compass of her fields, 833 *Excursion* 5. 705
The compass of his argument—began 883 *Excursion* 8. 600
Within the compass of their several shores 889 *Excursion* 9. 347
Of the smooth lake, in compass seen:—far off, 892 *Excursion* 9. 574
—How vast the compass of this theatre, K.8. 252 *Recluse* 1.1.560

Compassed. And darkness and danger had compassed him round, 364 *Vallomb.* 18
That bore it, compassed round by a bold 405 *White Doe* 819
Pleased (though to hardship born, and compassed round 682 *Prelude* 6. 509
Yet—compassed round by mountain solitudes, 748 *Prelude* 14. 139
He fled; but, compassed round by pleasure, sighed 791 *Excursion* 3. 380
Is rank with all unkindness, compassed round 848 *Excursion* 6. 635

Compassing. While, compassing the little mound around, 471 *Tynwald* 5
For compassing the end, else never gained; 504 *Warning* 92

Compassion. In pure compassion she her steps retraced 34 *Guilt* 555
Compassion for me. His influence is great 43 *Bord.* 347
You are a Man—and therefore, if compassion, 48 *Bord.* 626
Work on her nature, and so turn compassion 57 *Bord.* 1061
Compassion!—pity!—pride can do without them; 65 *Bord.* 1553
" Worse than idle is compassion 140 *Arm. Lady* 19
Tempered with awe, and sweetened by compassion 354 *Aquap.* 89
And the tear precious in compassion shed 395 *White Doe: Ded.* 10
Of true compassion greet them. Creed and test 449 *Ecc. Sonn.* 3. 36. 9
But O, restrain compassion, if its course, 517 *Pun. Death* 2. 9
" At thy name though compassion her nature resign, 621 *Convict* 49
While we sate listening with compassion due. 801 *Excursion* 4. 7
A wide compassion which with you I share. 886 *Excursion* 9. 155
Beheld without compassion, yea, with praise! 887 *Excursion* 9. 194

Compassionate. Her feeling, rendered more compassionate; 493 *Hap. War.* 20
He is compassionate; and has no thought, 819 *Excursion* 4. 1228

Compatriot. Revered Compatriot—and to you, kind Sir, 793 *Excursion* 3. 498
" Compatriot, Friend, remote are Garry's hills, 809 *Excursion* 4. 550
Of his compatriot villagers (that hung 857 *Excursion* 7. 19
To his Compatriot, smiling as he spake; 874 *Excursion* 8. 33

Compatriot-protestants. Slain by Compatriot-protestants that draw 442 *Ecc. Sonn.* 3. 7. 10

Compeer. By Palafox, and many a brave compeer, 315 **And is it* 10
And his compeer Aristogiton, known 721 *Prelude* 10. 199
Parted and re-united: his compeer 883 *Excursion* 8. 581
To her loved brother and his shy compeer. 890 *Excursion* 9. 431

Consecrate—*continued.*
Which Sion's Kings did consecrate of old; 576 *Chiabrera* 9. 17
Of thrice ten summers consecrate the board. 613 *Desc.Sk.Quarto* 589
To consecrate, if we have eyes to see, 744 *Prelude* 13. 284
By devious footsteps; regions consecrate 809 *Excursion* 4. 517
This place is consecrate; to Death and Life, 836 *Excursion* 5. 904
From their conjunction; consecrate to faith 836 *Excursion* 5. 906
Consecrated. Mutually consecrated. Poor old Man! 70 *Bord.* 1849
Now, for that consecrated fount 111 *A Complaint* 9
There stood a consecrated Pile; 298 *Brownie's Cell* 16
Of consecrated places, 324 *Ode 1814* 101
As if the streets were consecrated ground, 334 **The Spirit* 9
He kissed the consecrated Maid; 402 *White Doe* 591
But see the consecrated Maid 407 *White Doe* 999
Should on the consecrated breast 410 *White Doe* 1276
Shame if the consecrated Vow be found 445 *Ecc. Sonn.* 3. 21. 13
The consecrated works of Bard and Sage, 666 *Prelude* 5. 42
With that communion. Consecrated be 823 *Excursion* 5. 36
Truth's consecrated residence, the seat 876 *Excursion* 8. 146
Shall we behold them, consecrated friends, K.8. 243 *Recluse* 1. 1. 261
Consecrates. Which, filling, consecrates the human breast. 478 **Lonsdale! it* 8
But for a gift that consecrates the joy? 632 *Prelude* 1. 32
Consecrating. And consecrating element hath cleansed 826 *Excursion* 5. 280
Consecration. Erewhile, by solemn consecration, given 320 **O'erweeningStatesmen* 13
The Priest bestows the appointed consecration; 431 *Ecc. Sonn.* 2. 11. 4
Is now by solemn consecration given 450 *Ecc. Sonn.* 3. 41. 2
The consecration, and the Poet's dream; 578 *Peele Castle* 16
Consent. Until king Elidure, with full consent 105 *Artegal* 219
She gave consent, and Michael was at ease. 136 *Michael* 321
And, following guides whose craft holds no consent 213 *Dion* 54
With one consent the people rejoice, 396 *White Doe* 37
A just memorial; and thine eyes consent 539 **Lady! a* 58
And slaves who will consent to be destroyed— 836 *Excursion* 5. 942
Without his own consent, or knowledge, fixed! 878 *Excursion* 8. 300
If time, with free consent, be yours to give, 896 *Excursion* 9. 782
Consenting. Twice seven consenting years have shed 287 *Highland Girl* 3
To view, and for the mind's consenting eye 355 *Aquap.* 186
Consents. Of the brisk waves, yet here consents to dwell; 254 *Wild Duck's Nest* 7
Consequence. Grow into consequence, till round my mind 730 *Prelude* 11. 220
Is the sure consequence of slow decay. 873 *Excursion* 7. 1040
Consequences. All consequences: work he hath begun 305 **The Voice* 11
Consider. Consider, Johnny's but half-wise; 128 *Idiot Boy* 188
Consign. Shall I this lonely thought consign?— 410 *White Doe* 1291
With vain regrets—the Exile would consign 549 **The massy* 20
Consigned. Domestic Portrait! have to verse consigned 510 *F. Stone* 122
Her little charge consign'd. 620 *Birth of Love* 41
Then, when the body, soon to be consigned 780 *Excursion* 2. 568
Consigns. That lovingly consigns the babe to the arms 836 *Excursion* 5. 951
Consistence. Want due consistence; like a pillar of smoke, 803 *Excursion* 4. 142
Which, ere they gain consistence, by a gust 889 *Excursion* 9. 342
Consistent. So far that, if consistent in their scheme, 518 *Pun. Death* 7. 12
Consistent in self-rule; and heaven revealed 792 *Excursion* 3. 404
Consistory. In consistory, like a diadem 725 *Prelude* 10. 521
Consists. With whose perfection it consists to ordain 514 **Who ponders* 6
Hope, below this, consists not with belief 804 *Excursion* 4. 191
Hope, below this, consists not with belief 804 *Excursion* 4. 194
Consolation. A cup of consolation, filled from Heaven 75 *Bord.* 2146
Dear consolation, kneeling on the turf 119 *Maternal Grief* 71
Of home-felt consolation? 224 *'Tis gone* 36
And seeking consolation from above; 363 **Grieve for* 2
Such consolation, and the excess 402 *White Doe* 524
And hope, and consolation, fall, 534 **Blest is* 92
Fixed on the Cross, that consolation springs, 770 *Excursion* 1. 937
That consolation may descend from far 795 *Excursion* 3. 664
Consolations. Wanted not consolations, nor a creed 724 *Prelude* 10. 440
'Mong other consolations, we may draw 752 *Prelude* 14. 428
Of blessèd consolations in distress; 755 *Recluse* 1. 1. 769
The consolations of a hopeful mind? 789 *Excursion* 3. 228
Consolatory. The Wife, from whose consolatory grave 856 *Excursion* 6. 1189
Console. Rites that console the Spirit, under grief 423 *Ecc. Sonn.* 1. 20. 6
Kindly emotion tending to console 538 **In desultory* 51
Consoled. An aged woman. It consoled him here 125 *V. and J.* 276
Through this still medium, are consoled and cheered; 476 *Howard* 10
To look with bodily eyes, and be consoled." 682 *Prelude* 6. 471
Consonance. Opens a way for life, or consonance 449 *Ecc. Sonn.* 3. 36. 5
Consort. Blessed is and be your consort; 140 *Arm. Lady* 57
"Be taught, O faithful Consort, to control 210 *Laod.* 73
Returned, to seek a Consort upon earth; 220 *Triad* 4
The imperial Consort of the Fairy-king 254 *Wild Duck's Nest* 1
Man, bird, and beast; then, with a consort paired, 388 *Eagles* 6
Welcomes the Consort of a happy Queen. 629 *Installation* 72
And with soft smile, his consort would reprove. 861 *Excursion* 7. 225
Consorted. Consorted, Others, in the power, the faith, 362 **List—'twas* 70
Consorting. Consorting in one mansion unreproved. 663 *Prelude* 4. 343
Conspicuous. Conspicuous to the Nations. Thou, I think, 303 **Fair Star* 6
Yet shall thy name, conspicuous and sublime, 317 **Brave Schill* 6
Conspicuous yet where Oroonoko flows; 380 *Duddon* 16. 3
And doth in more conspicuous torment writhe, 439 *Ecc. Sonn.* 2. 43. 13
Glory of night, conspicuous yet serene, 460 **Queen of* 10
Conspicuous object in a Nation's eye, 494 *Hap. War.* 66
Conspicuous invitation to ascend 683 *Prelude* 6. 572
There, too, conspicuous for stature tall 692 *Prelude* 7. 342

Conspicuous—*continued.*
I glance but at a few conspicuous marks, 695 *Prelude* 7. 573
A blooming Lady—a conspicuous flower, 774 *Excursion* 2. 187
He vanished; but conspicuous to this day 842 *Excursion* 6. 244
As you have seen, bear such conspicuous part 866 *Excursion* 7. 592
Lived in an age conspicuous as our own 873 *Excursion* 7. 1009
The brightness more conspicuous that invests 890 *Excursion* 9. 411
And yet conspicuous, stood the old Church-tower, 892 *Excursion* 9. 575
Conspicuous at the centre of the Lake, K.8. 243 *Recluse* 1. 1. 245
Conspicuously. A last year's nest, conspicuously built 150 **When, to* 21
Empurpled hills, conspicuously renewing 807 *Excursion* 4. 400
Conspiracy. Was hatched among the crew a foul Conspiracy 68 *Bord.* 1690
Conspire. If office help the factious to conspire, 504 *Warning* 105
Conspired. "From that day forward have the Jews conspired 554 *Prioress* 114
Of manliness and freedom) all conspired 662 *Prelude* 4. 286
Constancy. For endless constancy, and placid truth; 122 *V. and J.* 33
In constancy, in fellowship more fair! 437 *Ecc. Sonn.* 2. 34. 14
Unfading constancy? 479 *Somnamb.* 112
Their constancy to prove, 544 *Russ. Fug.* 230
By constancy inviolate, 629 *Installation* 92
O high example, constancy divine! 839 *Excursion* 6. 74
Of his triumphant constancy and love; 851 *Excursion* 6. 885
Constant. *See* **Ever-constant, Over-constant.**
With daily bread, by constant toil supplied. 29 *Guilt* 263
Forgone the home delight of constant truth, 32 *Guilt* 440
Did constant meditation dry my blood; 69 *Bord.* 1773
Constant as a soaring lark, 94 *Westmoreland Girl* 86
And O most constant, yet most fickle Place, 107 *Farewell* 41
And from this constant light, so regular, 133 *Michael* 136
Constant to the fair Armenian, 142 *Arm. Lady* 145
So constant with thy downward eye of love, 153 *Morn. Ex.* 39
Into the service of his constant heart, 169 *Love lies Bleeding* 22
A constant interchange of growth and blight! 212 *Laod.* 174
And this light-hearted Maiden constant is as he. 222 *Triad* 144
The earth is constant to her sphere; 224 *Primrose* 21
Still constant in her worship, still 228 *Devot. Incit.* 68
And constant voice, protest against the wrong. 283 *Railway* 14
She thought of him with constant care, 295 *Highland Boy* 29
Hast heard the constant Voice its charge repeat, 312 *Clarkson* 6
A constant influence, a peculiar grace; 493 *Hap. War.* 47
And said, I am in constant dread I trow, 564 *Troilus* 145
A smooth rock wet with constant springs) was seen 705 *Prelude* 8. 408
With motion constant as his own, I went 710 *Prelude* 9. 39
And constant disposition of his thoughts 761 *Excursion* 1. 363
Through the long year in constant quiet bound, 790 *Excursion* 3. 323
From foul temptations, and by constant care 829 *Excursion* 5. 425
The darksome centre of a constant hope. 842 *Excursion* 6. 249
By choice were spent in constant fellowship; 845 *Excursion* 6. 472
Of constant infelicity,' cut off 846 *Excursion* 6. 533
See him a constant preacher to the poor! 859 *Excursion* 7. 150
And constant as the motion of the day; 862 *Excursion* 7. 325
And placid way of life, and constant love K.8. 243 *Recluse* 1. 1. 250
Bless it then with constant light, L. 2. 190 **Queen and* 11
Constellated. Clustering like constellated eyes 526 **The soaring* 35
Constellations. The constellations—gently was I charmed 745 *Prelude* 13. 342
With answering constellations, under earth, 812 *Excursion* 4. 713
Constitute. To constitute the spiritless shape of Fact, 58 *Bord.* 1157
And, in our dawn of being, constitute 640 *Prelude* 1. 557
Are sister horns that constitute her strength. 740 *Prelude* 13. 4
Me didst thou constitute a priest of thine, 802 *Excursion* 4. 43
Constituting. (Submission constituting strength and power) 802 *Excursion* 4. 98
Constitution. Do, in the constitution of their souls, 818 *Excursion* 4. 1107
Constitutions. The constitutions, powers, and faculties, 806 *Excursion* 4. 338
Constrain. Constrain her heart as quickly to return, 563 *Troilus* 78
Eternity, as men constrain a ghost 796 *Excursion* 3. 688
Their own dire agents, and constrain the good 805 *Excursion* 4. 300
Constrained. Or must we be constrained to think that these Spectators rude, 189 *Star-gazers* 21
But moved by choice; or, if constrained in part, 284 *Departure* 23
I know an aged Man constrained to dwell 530 **I know* 1
As if awakened, summoned, roused, constrained, 650 *Prelude* 3. 105
Lovers of truth, by penury constrained, 656 *Prelude* 3. 475
In vision, yet constrained by natural laws 724 *Prelude* 10. 438
High-titled Powers, am I constrained to ask, 827 *Excursion* 5. 341
Degenerate; who, constrained to wield the sword 839 *Excursion* 6. 62
Constrained forgiveness, and relenting vows, 849 *Excursion* 6. 713
Apart from old temptations, and constrained 859 *Excursion* 7. 148
Constraining. "Fear not a constraining measure! 220 *Triad* 34
Constrains. That stern yet kindly Spirit, who constrains 761 *Excursion* 1. 316
Constraint. As if some dire constraint of pain, or rage 196 *Resolution* 68
For the rich bounties of constraint; 215 *Kirkstone* 58
Ah! wherefore yields it to a foul constraint 438 *Ecc. Sonn.* 2. 38. 12
Like recognitions, but with some constraint 659 *Prelude* 4. 73
Construct. It were a pleasant pastime to construct 58 *Bord.* 1146
"The untutored bird may found, and so construct, 835 *Excursion* 5. 840
Do you, for your own benefit, construct 841 *Excursion* 6. 173
Constructed. *See* **Ill-constructed, Re-constructed.**
Constructed, that sufficed for every end, 849 *Excursion* 6. 728
Construed. Or what their scruples construed to be such— 814 *Excursion* 4. 904
Consul. Consul for life. With worship France proclaims 304 **Festivals have* 4
Consul, or King, can sound himself to know 304 **Festivals have* 13
The Roman Consul doomed his sons to die 517 *Pun. Death* 3. 1
Consult. For her consult the auguries of time, 314 **Not 'mid* 11

Consult—*continued.*
—O prostrate Lands, consult your agonies! . . . 330 *Ode: Thanks.* 126
And, if that fail, consult the Stars . . . . . 370 *Eg. Maid* 113
Consulting. For me, consulting what I feel within . 885 *Excursion* 9. 102
Consume. Life to consume in Manhood's firmest hold; 321 **Humanity, delighting* 22
Silently to consume the heavy clouds; . . . 426 *Ecc. Sonn.* 1. 29. 11
Consume with zeal, in wingèd ecstasies . . . 467 *St. Bees* 88
To consume this crystal Well; . . . . . 550 *Hermit's Cell* 4. 10
Consumed. *See* **Self-consumed.**
Disease consumed thy vitals; War upheaved . . 316 **Hail, Zaragoza* 10
Yea, his dry bones to ashes are consumed . . . 432 *Ecc. Sonn.* 2. 17. 3
His bones are consumed, and his life-blood is dried, 621 *Convict* 21
Was all consumed. A second infant now . . . 764 *Excursion* 1. 556
To aim and purpose, he consumed his days, . . 774 *Excursion* 2. 208
All joy in human nature; was consumed, . . . 776 *Excursion* 2. 297
And, so consumed, she melted from my arms; . 796 *Excursion* 3. 678
A slow disease insensibly consumed . . . . 864 *Excursion* 7. 464
Of all the mighty, withered and consumed! . . 872 *Excursion* 7. 982
Consumes. His drought consumes, his mildew taints with death; . . . . 328 *Ode 1815* 92
Consuming. *See* **Life-consuming.**
Consummate. Rose,—and, to consummate this just intent, ... 105 *Artegal* 221
To guard the fallen, and consummate the event, . 326 **Intrepid sons* 13
That day consummate happiness was mine, . . 660 *Prelude* 4. 140
The wrath consummate and the threat fulfilled; . 724 *Prelude* 10. 446
A habitation, for consummate good, ... 789 *Excursion* 3. 221
How such consummate elegance was bred . . . 842 *Excursion* 6. 299
Praised the consummate harmony serene . . . 882 *Excursion* 8. 538
Consummation. Again that consummation she essayed; . . . . 210 *Laod.* 26
The consummation, the whole ruth . . . . 413 *White Doe* 1549
And consummation of a Poet's mind, ... 750 *Prelude* 14. 304
Of this great consummation:—and, by words . 755 *Recluse* 1. 1. 811
A happy consummation! an accord . . . . 861 *Excursion* 7. 255
The consummation that will come by stealth . . 893 *Excursion* 9. 636
Consumption. On his pale horse shall fell Consumption go. . . . . 617 *Desc. Sk. Quarto* 791
That, for the day's consumption, books may yield 810 *Excursion* 4. 584
Contagious. Soft bosoms breathe around contagious sighs, ... 12 *Desc. Sk.* 105
Contain. These narrow bounds contain our private store . . . . 106 *Farewell* 14
But these, and all that they contain, ... 237 *P. B.* 48
That holds but him, and can contain no more! . 817 *Excursion* 4. 1088
Contained. O'er which they move, wherein they are contained, ... 230 *Clouds* 51
Contains. Contains not such a Monster! For this purpose . . . . 56 *Bord.* 1057
The thing most precious that it now contains: . 75 *Bord.* 2169
Contamination. Without contamination doth she live . . . . 692 *Prelude* 7. 322
Contemplate. When from these forms I turned to contemplate . . . . 70 *Bord.* 1815
That we, who contemplate the turns of life . . 476 *Howard* 9
Heart-swoln, while in your pride ye contemplate . 567 *Cumb. Beg.* 71
Are that which we would contemplate from far. . 830 *Excursion* 5. 491
Contemplated. Of heaven contemplated by Spirits pure . . . . 474 **Hope smiled* 10
Outwardly, inwardly contemplated, ... 706 *Prelude* 8. 486
Contemplated, describe the Mind and Man . . 755 *Recluse* 1. 1. 848
Contemplating. Contemplating in soberness the approach . . . . 668 *Prelude* 5. 157
Contemplating; and who, and what he was— . 755 *Recluse* 1. 1. 849
"And further; by contemplating these Forms . 819 *Excursion* 4. 1230
Contemplating perfection absolute . . . . . K.8. 245 *Recluse* 1.1.307
Contemplation. Of contemplation, the calm port . 190 **Lyre! though* 10
A Soul by contemplation sanctified. . . . . 320 **O'erweening Statesmen* 8
Of contemplation, by no sense of wrong . . . 328 *Ode 1815* 117
For quiet contemplation: . . . . 385 *Yarrow Rev.* 20
Of contemplation almost failed to beat. . . . 654 *Prelude* 3. 331
When Contemplation, like the night-calm felt . . 665 *Prelude* 5. 1
Of contemplation, what intuitive truths, . . . 675 *Prelude* 6. 39
Still higher, men for contemplation framed, . . 743 *Prelude* 13. 267
Detained for contemplation or repose, . . . 757 *Excursion* 1. 42
To happy contemplation soothed his walk; . . 772 *Excursion* 2. 50
—Hail Contemplation! from the stately towers, . 787 *Excursion* 3. 101
Vigils of contemplation; praise; and prayer— . 804 *Excursion* 4. 218
And easy contemplation; gay parterres, . . . 810 *Excursion* 4. 589
Contemplations. Star-guided contemplations move 225 *Present.* 31
To kindred contemplations ministers . . . . 355 *Aquap.* 172
Balanced these contemplations in his mind; . . 714 *Prelude* 9. 330
But contemplations, worthier, nobler far . . . 799 *Excursion* 3. 928
Contemplative. Wide-spreading, steady, calm, contemplative. . . . . 660 *Prelude* 4. 141
For feeling and contemplative regard, ... 696 *Prelude* 7. 624
Contempt. Surely in other thoughts contempt may die. . . . . 20 *Desc. Sk.* 550
Is littleness; that he who feels contempt . . 23 *Yew-tree* 52
More of contempt than hatred; both are flown; . 47 *Bord.* 554
With hard contempt his heart was wrung, . . 241 *P. B.* 454
With morals, trusting, in contempt or fear . . 357 *Aquap.* 334
Unacceptable feelings of contempt, ... 497 **Enough of climbing* 8
I speak, unapprehensive of contempt, ... 648 *Prelude* 2. 455
A chaplet in contempt of his grey locks. . . . 722 *Prelude* 10. 314
An infidel contempt of holy writ . . . . . 775 *Excursion* 2. 249
Made desperate by contempt of men who throve . 776 *Excursion* 2. 300
"Scorn and contempt forbid me to proceed! . . 797 *Excursion* 3. 768

Contempt—*continued.*
By wandering Rhapsodists; and in contempt . 812 *Excursion* 4. 733
Of unbenign aversion or contempt, ... 816 *Excursion* 4. 1014
Until abhorrence and contempt are things . . 819 *Excursion* 4. 1225
The longing, the contempt, the undaunted quest, K.8. 257 *Recluse* 1.1.742
Contemptible. Becomes at last weak and contemptible. . . . . 48 *Bord.* 620
Contemptible as vain. . . . . 495 *Fact* 23
Formal, and odious, and contemptible. . . . 798 *Excursion* 3. 826
Contempts. And those ensuing laughters and contempts, ... 704 *Prelude* 8. 333
Contend. Contend ye with each other? of the sea 229 *Clouds* 8
I cannot for such cause contend; . . . . . 401 *White Doe* 508
For what contend the wise?—for nothing less . 436 *Ecc. Sonn.* 2. 30. 1
Swayed, and thereby enabled to contend . . . 442 *Ecc. Sonn.* 3. 9. 6
And doomed him to contend in faithless courts, . 573 *Chiabrera* 2. 3
There, too, the lusty Wrestlers shall contend: . 773 *Excursion* 2. 146
Nor summoned to contend for virtue's prize, . . 835 *Excursion* 5. 856
Contending. I move at ease; and meet contending themes . . . . 350 *Des. Stanzas* 15
With fancied spots contending; . . . . . 479 *Somnamb.* 85
Ocean and Earth contending for regard. . . . 497 **Enough of climbing* 18
Of oars with oars contending, sails with sails, . . 664 *Prelude* 4. 372
Contending after showers. The mother now . . 692 *Prelude* 7. 365
I love to hear of those, who, not contending . . 835 *Excursion* 5. 855
Contends. While prayer contends with silenced agony, ... 20 *Desc. Sk.* 549
Content. Shine, Poet! in thy place, and be content:— . . . . v **If thou indeed* 3
Shine, Poet! in thy place, and be content. . . v **If thou indeed* 16
At times, while young Content forsook her seat, . 2 *Ev. Wk.* 24
Peace to my parting soul, the fulness of content." 36 *Guilt* 630
I am content—I know that he is guiltless— . . 70 *Bord.* 1847
And, in their happiest moments, not content, . 122 *V. and J.* 24
They lead you on to full content, ... 143 †*Lov. and Lik.* 61
Such calm employments, such entire content. . 143 **High bliss* 12
And, to my soul's content, I find . . . . . 174 *Waggoner* 1. 114
Who that hath seen thy beauty could content . 221 *Triad* 71
But her humility is well content . . . . . 221 *Triad* 115
Peace to embosom and content— . . . . . 223 *Wishing-gate* 28
Wilt smile upon this gift with more than mild content! . . . . 250 **Happy the* 14
And sage content, and placid melancholy; . . 262 **Not Love* 10
Who meekly yields, and is obscured—content . 265 **The Shepherd* 13
With every semblance of entire content; . . . 275 **Chatsworth! thy* 7
Heaven's sapphire pavement, yet breathed well content, ... 278 **Lo! where she* 11
The prize, or be content to see it worn . . . 312 **When, far* 8
In peace of spirit, and sublime content! . . . 324 *Ode 1814* 89
Imagination—ne'er before content, ... 327 *Ode 1815* 1
But with its peaceful majesty content. . . . 355 *Aquap.* 191
There are whose calmer mind it would content . 377 *Duddon* 7. 11
Return, Content! for fondly I pursued, . . . 382 *Duddon* 26. 1
Fair fruit of pleasure and serene content . . 395 *White Doe: Ded.* 31
Content, if foss, and barrow, and the girth . . 421 *Ecc. Sonn.* 1. 11. 13
Disgraced by aught that seems content to sit . 439 *Ecc. Sonn.* 2. 41. 7
Now with her own deep quietness content; . . 439 *Ecc. Sonn.* 2. 44. 3
That ever walk content with Nature's way, . . 456 *Rydal Mere* 38
And that would now content her. . . . . . 479 *Somnamb.* 76
Who, not content that former worth stand fast, . 494 *Hap. War.* 74
In placid beauty and sublime content! . . . 495 *Fact* 37
And aid my verse, content with local bounds . 522 *Epist. Beaumont* 52
For something more than dull content, . . . 526 **The soaring* 7
And, as his tufts of leaves he spreads, content . 529 *Poor Robin* 7
So were both right well content: . . . . . 535 *Egremont* 37
Thence worship comes, content and true heart's pleasure, ... 559 *Cuck. and Night.* 153
Ev'n here Content has fix'd her smiling reign . 608 *Desc. Sk. Quarto* 323
Content upon some simple annual feast, . . . 613 *Desc. Sk. Quarto* 586
Content and not unwilling now to give . . . 633 *Prelude* 1. 59
And now it would content me to yield up . . . 634 *Prelude* 1. 132
If, mingling with the world, I am content . . . 648 *Prelude* 3. 428
Content to observe, to achieve, and to enjoy. . 676 *Prelude* 6. 65
An idler's place; an idler well content . . . . 688 *Prelude* 7. 72
Are generous as the young; and, if content . . 699 *Prelude* 8. 45
Who were content to barter short-lived pangs . 723 *Prelude* 10. 344
Full measure of content; but still I craved . . 741 *Prelude* 13. 110
Strengthened and braced, by breathing in content 760 *Excursion* 1. 305
With this content, that he will live and die . . 776 *Excursion* 2. 313
And with the imagination rest content, . . . 790 *Excursion* 3. 303
And will possess my portion in content! . . . 802 *Excursion* 4. 65
Soul-strengthening patience, and sublime content. 813 *Excursion* 4. 818
Living to God and nature, and content . . . 823 *Excursion* 5. 35
To give assurance of content within; . . . . 828 *Excursion* 5. 413
And with their humble birthright rest content. . 832 *Excursion* 5. 620
Even at the worst, a smooth stream of content, . 833 *Excursion* 5. 712
Distracted in propensity; content . . . . . 843 *Excursion* 6. 370
So placid, so inactive, as content; . . . . . 849 *Excursion* 6. 731
And undertook with dutiful content . . . . 852 *Excursion* 6. 947
Which her poor treasure-house is content to owe, 862 *Excursion* 7. 320
Content with meaner prowess, must have lacked . 866 *Excursion* 7. 609
The wish for liberty to live—content . . . . 888 *Excursion* 9. 278
In placid beauty and entire content. . . . . S.3. 427 **My Son* 8
Lady! to your heart's content; . . . . . S.3. 438 **I, whose* 27
Who finds at last an hour to his content . . . K.8. 254 *Recluse* 1.1.656
Now would you be content with bare release . . L.1. 97 *Juvenal* 3. 69
Contented. *See* **Self-contented.**
Then here contented will I lie! . . . . . . 114 *Ind. Wom.* 19
Could we but have been as contented as they. . 116 *Repentance* 4
I, with my fate contented, will plod on, . . . 160 **Up with me* 30

Contented—*continued.*
Who, contented with each other, 181 *Waggoner* 4. 168
For thy contented Votary. 217 *Enterprise* 137
Of thy contented Votary 227 *Vernal Ode* 83
Each is contented with the other. 236 *P. B.* 25
And hermits are contented with their cells; 250 **Nuns fret* 2
Thus far contented, that for You her verse 333 *Ded. Tour* 13
From the climate of myrtles contented I go. 345 *Stanzas: Simplon* 20
Like this contented, though unknown to Fame: 392 *Avon* 4
Contented if he might enjoy 485 *Poet's Epitaph* 55
Contented and serene; 499 *Memory* 24
Contented, when with bliss ineffable 648 *Prelude* 2. 400
Contented, from the moment that the dawn 682 *Prelude* 6. 512
Even of the dead; contented thence to draw 765 *Excursion* 1. 629
Pleased to have been, contented not to be. 790 *Excursion* 3. 269
The mole contented with her darksome walk 807 *Excursion* 4. 429
O, calm contented days, and peaceful nights! 817 *Excursion* 4. 1050
Contented to partake the quiet meal 859 *Excursion* 7. 160

Contentedly. Contentedly, yet sometimes self-accused, 32 *Guilt* 434
Thou travellest so contentedly, and sleep'st 173 *Infant Daughter* 59
The sweets of earth contentedly resigned, 384 *Duddon* 33. 10

Contentedness. Redundancy of youth's contentedness. 677 *Prelude* 6. 178
To health and joy and pure contentedness; 733 *Prelude* 11. 398
The still contentedness of seventy years. 783 *Excursion* 2. 750
And in what pure contentedness of mind, 864 *Excursion* 7. 475

Contention. Counsel is given; contention they appease 875 *Excursion* 8. 78

Contentious. By false opinion and contentious thought, 737 *Prelude* 12. 211

Contentment. Contentment shares the desolate domain 15 *Desc. Sk.* 260
Contentment, hope, and mother's glee, 121 *EmigrantMother* 87
Such an entire contentment in the air 146 **It was an* 13
To cull contentment upon wildest shores, 284 *Departure* 25
There feeling no contentment, I resolved 798 *Excursion* 3. 831
Save the contentment of the builder's mind; 849 *Excursion* 6. 729
Perfect Contentment, Unity entire. K.8. 240 *Recluse* 1.1.151
Of full contentment, in a little shed K.8. 241 *Recluse* 1. 1.176

Contents. By fits and starts, yet this contents thee not. 379 *Duddon* 14. 8
A readier book of manifold contents, 393 **The Lovers* 13
Upon a volume whose contents he knows 719 *Prelude* 10. 59
Spin in his eyesight, *that* contents him not, 723 *Prelude* 10. 371
Of yielding its contents to eye and ear, 826 *Excursion* 5. 253
And that contents him; bowers that hear no more 828 *Excursion* 5. 406

Contest. Who in the field of contest persevered, 656 *Prelude* 3. 499
Of contest, did opinions every day 730 *Prelude* 11. 219
By ruinous contest, to obtain a seat 845 *Excursion* 6. 447

Contiguous. Of the contiguous torrent, gathering strength 813 *Excursion* 4. 793

Continence. And continence of mind, and sense of right, 715 *Prelude* 9. 388

Continent. In progress from their native continent 673 *Prelude* 5. 537

Continents. When seas and continents shall lie between us— 78 *Bord.* 2306

Contingencies. Contingencies of pomp; and serve to exalt 817 *Excursion* 4. 1061

Continual. Continual waters welling cheered the waste, 17 *Desc. Sk.* 390
Sharp season followed of continual storm 150 **When, to* 4
Continual fountains welling cheard the waste, 611 *Desc.Sk.Quarto* 478
Cold from necessity's continual snow, 613 *Desc.Sk.Quarto* 605

Continually. About the weary moors continually, 197 *Resolution* 130
Before the Lamb singing continually, 554 *Prioress* 133
Continually, like an uneasy place 712 *Prelude* 9. 160
On the dim altar burned continually, 877 *Excursion* 8. 189

Continuance. To a continuance of their fearless sport, 118 *Maternal Grief* 29
Brook no continuance of weak-mindedness— 260 **High is* 13
That no wight his continuance espied. 563 *Troilus* 21

Continuation. Continuation haply of the notes 825 *Excursion* 5. 220

Continue. Long to continue in this world; a world 573 *Chiabrera* 1. 10
And shall continue evermore to make, 735 *Prelude* 12. 86
Spare them, they shall continue to bestow, 838 *Excursion* 6. 36

Continued. *See* **Long-continued.**
She is," continued the detested Slave, 59 *Bord.* 1188
That could withstand it. True," continued he, 59 *Bord.* 1194
The same dead calm, continued many days. 69 *Bord.* 1744
Continued long as life shall last. 288 *Highland Girl* 71
"What boots," continued she, "to mourn? 370 *Eg. Maid* 97
That they dreamt not of dearth;—He continued his rounds, 570 *Farmer* 35
Continued, brought me to my hermitage. 633 *Prelude* 1. 107
How that one Frenchman, through continued force 635 *Prelude* 1. 206
Continued and the loud uproar: at last, 642 *Prelude* 2. 15
Nor otherwise continued to be moved, 708 *Prelude* 8. 591
And to that day continued.—For, the time 741 *Prelude* 13. 106
"I speak," continued he, "of One whose stock 763 *Excursion* 1. 511
And he continued, when worse days were come, 775 *Excursion* 2. 281
The strain continued, spiritual as before; 777 *Excursion* 2. 379
And he continued, glancing on the leaves 778 *Excursion* 2. 469
He thus continued, lifting up his eyes 802 *Excursion* 4. 33
The Sage continued:—"For that other loss, 805 *Excursion* 4. 260
"Much," he continued, with dejected look, 826 *Excursion* 5. 242
Continued, "'tis not in the vital seat 837 *Excursion* 5. 984
Continued yet to vibrate on his ear, 845 *Excursion* 6. 450
From Age," the Priest continued, "turn your thoughts; 867 *Excursion* 7. 633
"Yes," he continued, kindling as he spake, 889 *Excursion* 9. 383
The same should be continued to its close. 892 *Excursion* 9. 525

Continues. Meanwhile the roar continues, till at length, 689 *Prelude* 7. 168
A hardy Girl continues to provide; 856 *Excursion* 6. 1157

Continuing. *See* **Long-continuing.**
And, thus continuing, she said, 119 *Sailor's Mother* 19
Alone, continuing there to muse: the slopes 661 *Prelude* 4. 178
Unnoticed, thus continuing.—"From yon crag 779 *Excursion* 2. 546

Continuity. But had a continuity and substance 69 *Bord.* 1793

Continuous. In this continuous glen, where down a rock 146 **It was an* 21
With a continuous cloud of texture close, 184 *Night-piece* 2
Continuous as the stars that shine 187 **I wandered* 7
By a continuous and acknowledged tie 394 **No more* 5
Or in wide forests of continuous shade, 716 *Prelude* 9. 434
In one continuous stream; a mind sustained 747 *Prelude* 14. 74
Of Life continuous, Being unimpaired; 812 *Excursion* 4. 755
Poured forth with fervour in continuous stream, 820 *Excursion* 4. 1276
Here a huge town, continuous and compact, 876 *Excursion* 8. 120

Contract. Just Heaven, contract the compass of my mind 267 **As the* 9
For steadfast hope the contract to fulfil; 275 *Rotha Q.* 6

Contracted. A dull, contracted circle, yielding light 184 *Night-piece* 5
Was stooping and contracted, and a face, 711 *Prelude* 9. 148
Sympathies too contracted. Hence, when called 751 *Prelude* 14. 341
He broke from his contracted bounds, repaired 774 *Excursion* 2. 215
Too, too contracted are these walls of flesh, 804 *Excursion* 4. 179

Contracting. Years contracting to a moment, 141 *Arm. Lady* 105

Contradict. The future cannot contradict the past: 832 *Excursion* 5. 664

Contradiction. In contradiction; with no skill to part 635 *Prelude* 1. 238
Of contradiction, from some vague desire 828 *Excursion* 5. 363

Contradictions. Stifle the contradictions of their fate, 529 **Those breathing* 131
Sharp contradictions may arise, by doom 792 *Excursion* 3. 447
Yet, mark the contradictions of which Man 797 *Excursion* 3. 806
Of contradictions infinite the slave, 843 *Excursion* 6. 373

Contraries. Of bitter contraries. 225 *Present.* 54
May even by contraries be joined 285 *Grave of Burns* 47
For thereof come all contraries to gladness; 560 *Cuck.andNight.*171
But change of them into their contraries; 730 *Prelude* 11. 180
Into their contraries the petty plagues 835 *Excursion* 5. 860

Contrarieties. Sick, wearied out with contrarieties, 731 *Prelude* 11. 304

Contrast. A contrast and reproach to gross delight, 263 **Those words* 3
Of thy domain, strange contrast do present 275 **Chatsworth! thy* 2
Strange contrast!—verily the world of dreams, 364 **What aim* 9
Even such the contrast that, where'er we move, 439 *Ecc. Sonn.* 2. 44. 1
But o'er the contrast wherefore heave a sigh? 462 **Where lies the truth* 11
In urgent contrast? To diffuse the Word 474 **On to* 4
By power of contrast, made me recognise, 694 *Prelude* 7. 481
Sad contrast! all too often smote his heart 772 *Excursion* 2. 53
And shady groves in studied contrast—each, 810 *Excursion* 4. 591
Over the mountain-sides, in contrast bold 820 *Excursion* 4. 1303
In sober contrast with reality, 826 *Excursion* 5. 249
Of contrast and resemblance. To an oak 829 *Excursion* 5. 455
—This contrast, not unsuitable to life, 831 *Excursion* 5. 552
From unaffected contrast with the gloom 881 *Excursion* 8. 473

Contrasts. Resemblances, or contrasts, that connect, 172 *Infant Daughter* 43
For so many strange contrasts in one human face: 482 *Character* 2
Strange contrasts have we in this world of ours! 509 *F. Stone* 79

Contrite. Softly!—To save the contrite, Jesus bled. 275 *Gravestone* 14
The prayers, the contrite struggle, and the trust 451 *Ecc. Sonn.* 3. 41. 13
And wafts at will the contrite soul to bliss. 519 *Pun. Death* 11. 14
Her tender spirit, and her contrite heart, 854 *Excursion* 6. 1074

Contrition. So grievous is his heart's contrition; 247 *P. B.* 932
A sign he craved, tired slave of vain contrition; 373 *Eg. Maid* 296

Contrivance. Our own contrivance, Building without peer! 106 *Farewell* 27

Contrivances. Towards one, whose bold contrivances and skill, 866 *Excursion* 7. 591

Contrive. But which way shall I lead you?—how contrive, 786 *Excursion* 3. 16

Contrived. Might have been wished for and contrived, to elude 833 *Excursion* 5. 699

Control. *See* **Controul, Self-control.**
Feels not the spirit of the place control, 15 *Desc. Sk.* 291
Where the least things control the greatest, where 65 *Bord.* 1563
To control the froward impulse 94 *Westmoreland Girl* 75
Misgivings, hard to vanquish or control, 112 **O dearer* 5
"Be taught, O faithful Consort, to control 210 *Laod.* 73
'Tis thine the quickening impulse to control, 216 *Enterprise* 100
Too false to guide us or control! 291 *Rob Roy* 26
We know that ye, beneath the stern control 316 **It was a* 10
To live and move exempt from all control 429 *Ecc. Sonn.* 2. 4. 13
I supplicate for thy control; 492 *Duty* 35
Is to control and check disordered Powers? 514 **Who ponders* 14
His mandates, given rash impulse to control 518 *Pun. Death* 7. 10
That Reason *should* control; 543 *Russ. Fug.* 174
I have submitted to a new control: 578 *Peele Castle* 34
By uniform control of after years, 646 *Prelude* 2. 262
Under His great correction and control, 669 *Prelude* 5. 274
Sages who in their prescience would control 671 *Prelude* 5. 355
For due provision to control and guide, 826 *Excursion* 5. 290

Controlled. Of tones and numbers all things are controlled, 235 *Power of Sound* 178
Of checked ambition, tyranny controlled, 349 *Boulogne* 11
Realm there is none that if controlled or sway'd 429 *Ecc. Sonn.* 2. 2. 9
The air controlled, the stars their courses held; 469 **Bold words* 11
Incited it to motion, and controlled. 705 *Prelude* 8. 432
That Love will not submit to be controlled 840 *Excursion* 6. 163

Controlling. *See* **All-controlling, Heart-controlling.**
Of vital principle's controlling law, 357 *Aquap.* 335
Is in controlling Providence, admit 846 *Excursion* 6. 561
Controls. Controls them and subdues, transmutes, bereaves 493 *Hap. War.* 17
Controul. And who but feels a power of strong controul, 608 *Desc.Sk.Quarto* 352
And sway with absolute controul S.3. 439 **Avaunt this* 5
Convened. " With these are many more convened; 238 *P. B.* 161
Of the Devout, as, 'mid your glooms convened 357 *Aquap.* 300
Of every nature, and strange plants convened 690 *Prelude* 7. 231
Plunged—'mid a gay and busy throng convened 870 *Excursion* 7. 868
Which we, thy humble Creatures, here convened, 893 *Excursion* 9. 623
Convenes. With careful hesitation,—then convenes 422 *Ecc. Sonn.* 1. 15. 12
Convenience. For the convenience of unlawful gain, 879 *Excursion* 8. 368
Convenient. To such convenient work as might employ 132 *Michael* 105
Convent. Huge convent domes with pinnacles and towers, 14 *Desc. Sk.* 224
I thought the Convent never would appear; 39 *Bord.* 113
Idonea would have fears for me,—the Convent 43 *Bord.* 352
We'll lead him to the Convent. He shall live, 54 *Bord.* 904
Lady, you'll find your Father at the Convent 58 *Bord.* 1135
I hid my face within a Convent, there 69 *Bord.* 1766
cannot we go to the Convent? 72 *Bord.* 1989
Upon this arm. You led him towards the Convent? 76 *Bord.* 2228
That Convent was Stone-Arthur Castle. Thither 76 *Bord.* 2229
That dooms her to a convent.—Who shall tell, 124 *V. and J.* 222
A convent, even a hermit's cell, 289 *Glen-Al.* 23
A shattered Convent, yet rose proud to have 355 *Aquap.* 212
As we approached the Convent gate, aloft 362 **List—'twas* 84
By panting steers up to this convent gate? 363 **What aim* 3
In the magnific Convent built of yore 509 *F. Stone* 96
Then in a convent went to hide 536 *Egremont* 103
" Eke the whole Convent on the pavement lay, 556 *Prioress* 226
Beheld the Convent of Chartreuse, and there 681 *Prelude* 6. 418
When to a convent in a meadow green, 716 *Prelude* 9. 466
Convent-bread. Full cheerily on convent-bread 398 *White Doe* 219
Convent-crested. Of that high Convent-crested cliff I stood, 356 *Aquap.* 232
Convent-fire. And heard old tales by the convent-fire, 398 *White Doe* 220
Convent-haven. From Tasso's Convent-haven, and retired grave. 353 *Aquap.* 84
Conventicle. Court, theatre, conventicle, or shop, 695 *Prelude* 7. 575
Convent-pile. Where ancient trees this convent-pile enclose, 470 *Bala-Sala* 3
Convent's. Nuns fret not at their convent's narrow room; 250 **Nuns fret* 1
Yet more,—round many a Convent's blazing fire 433 *Ecc. Sonn.* 2. 20. 1
While through the Convent's gate to open view 434 *Ecc. Sonn.* 2. 22. 7
The Abbot with his convent's company 555 *Prioress* 186
Convent-tower. Flung from a Convent-tower, 334 **In Bruges* 6
Conventual. Of vast cathedral or conventual church, 877 *Excursion* 8. 187
Converging. Converging walks, and fountains gay, 407 *White Doe* 989
Conversant. Fervid, yet conversant with holy fear, 326 **The Bard* 3
Must needs be conversant with upward looks, 508 *F. Stone* 34
With which I had been conversant, the mind 650 *Prelude* 3. 95
Are conversant, subservient in their turn 736 *Prelude* 12. 138
Conversation. In conversation between man and man 648 *Prelude* 2. 458
Such conversation, under Attic shades, 715 *Prelude* 9. 408
In thought or conversation, public acts, 717 *Prelude* 9. 543
Frank conversation, made the evening's treat: 834 *Excursion* 5. 776
And in the various conversation bore 882 *Excursion* 8. 528
That made their conversation fresh and fair K.8. 227 **I will* 93
Converse. In converse that ensued she nothing spake; 27 *Guilt* 188
And, through all converse of our later years, 39 *Bord.* 96
Much converse do I find in thee, 79 **Stay near* 3
Here broke off the dangerous converse: 140 *Arm. Lady* 73
Of man converse with immortality? 316 **O'er the* 14
For converse with God, sought through study and prayer. 364 *Vallomb.* 8
In sacred converse gifts with Alfred shares. 425 *Ecc. Sonn.* 1. 26. 14
Converse with Nature in pure sympathy; 511 **So fair* 18
The Captive shunned all converse proffered there. 531 **I know* 24
In earnest converse with belovèd Friends, 549 **The massy* 14
Brightening a converse never known to swerve 583 **With copious* 11
Knowledge and wisdom, gained from converse sweet 584 *Ch. Lamb* 12
From miscellaneous converse, ye were taught 586 *Ch. Lamb* 111
—But, lengthening out the night with converse new, 625 *Æneid* 132
Coming in revelation, did converse 647 *Prelude* 2. 393
From early converse with the works of God 698 *Prelude* 7. 742
Thine be such converse strong and sanative, 733 *Prelude* 11. 396
Converse with men, where if we meet a face 742 *Prelude* 13. 138
To hold fit converse with the spiritual world, 747 *Prelude* 14. 108
Nor in such other converse as is here, 781 *Excursion* 2. 615
Of other converse which mind, soul, and heart, 802 *Excursion* 4. 77
Earth to despise; but, to converse with heaven— 803 *Excursion* 4. 131
Such converse, if directed by a meek, 806 *Excursion* 4. 344
And by his converse crowns a silent day 833 *Excursion* 5. 715
Through lack of converse; no—he must have found 844 *Excursion* 6. 384
In social converse, or by some short space 845 *Excursion* 6. 478
Converse with heaven, nor yet deprest towards earth, 848 *Excursion* 6. 680
For grateful converse: and to these poor men 875 *Excursion* 8. 58
From human converse to frequent alone S.3. 436 **The doubt* 169
And if it was his fortune to converse K.8. 230 **I will* 189
Conversed. I have conversed with more than one who well 138 *Michael* 451

Conversed—*continued.*
With Archimedes also he conversed 576 *Chiabrera* 9. 11
Conversed with promises, had glimmering views 660 *Prelude* 4. 164
There I conversed with majesty and power 708 *Prelude* 8. 631
Before the man with whom he so conversed K.8. 230 **I will* 197
Converses. Through which the ear converses with the heart. 818 *Excursion* 4. 1155
Conversing. Conversing not, knew little in what mould 151 **When, to* 71
Conversing, reading, laughing;—or they sing, 266 **Even as* 13
Conversing as I may, 481 *Expost.* 30
Mute or conversing, single or in pairs. 890 *Excursion* 9. 436
Conversion. Seemed but conversion to a higher creed; 722 *Prelude* 10. 310
Convert. For robes with regal purple tinged; convert 846 *Excursion* 6. 549
Converting. All accidents, converting them to good. 801 *Excursion* 4. 17
May bring; that brook converting as it runs 878 *Excursion* 8. 257
Converts. Around these Converts; and their glories blend, 423 *Ecc. Sonn.* 1. 18. 8
Convex. (Above the convex of the watery globe) 219 **This Height* 19
Convey. Which thou prepar'st, full often, to convey 440 *Ecc. Sonn.* 2. 45. 11
Did Prudence convey, S.3. 440 **Said red-ribboned* 26
Conveyed. Every little leaf conveyed 170 *Kitten* 12
Young Bacchus was conveyed—to lie 299 *Brownie's Cell* 95
Of Egypt, from a rock conveyed 372 *Eg. Maid* 208
Where pity, to the mind conveyed 530 *Gleaner* 13
As once I passed, into my heart conveyed 770 *Excursion* 1. 945
Her cheek to change its colour, was conveyed 795 *Excursion* 3. 641
Convict. Sends the pale Convict to his last retreat 520 *Pun. Death* 13. 3
To the cell where the convict is laid. 620 *Convict* 8
Conviction. For sometimes, in despite of my conviction, 41 *Bord.* 229
Pleasant conviction flashed upon my mind 150 **When, to* 58
It wrought in him conviction strange; 243 *P. B.* 660
With a conviction of the power that waits 654 *Prelude* 3. 388
Preclude conviction, that a spirit strong 720 *Prelude* 10. 165
All feeling of conviction, and, in fine, 731 *Prelude* 11. 303
Convictions. Convictions still more strong than heretofore, 744 *Prelude* 13. 280
Convict's. The convict's summons in the steeple's knell; 234 *Power of Sound* 158
Convinced. Convinced that he, or soon or late, 244 *P. B.* 693
Convinced that there, there only, she can lay 259 **A volant* 7
To careless eyes. And—now convinced at heart 742 *Prelude* 13. 168
And, therefore, not to act—convinced that all 799 *Excursion* 3. 893
That, though immovably convinced, we want 804 *Excursion* 4. 201
In solemn institutions:—men convinced 837 *Excursion* 5. 1001
Convocation. Their place of convocation—there I heard, 723 *Prelude* 10. 322
Convoked. Convoked the impious to chastise: 405 *White Doe* 838
An active partisan, I thus convoked 729 *Prelude* 11. 153
Convolutions. The convolutions of a smooth-lipped shell; 818 *Excursion* 4. 1135
Convolved. Up-coiling and inveterately convolved; 185 *Yew-trees* 18
Convulsed. Convulsed as by a jarring din; 234 *Power of Sound* 102
Convulsions. Into the chilling flood. Convulsions dire 870 *Excursion* 7. 870
Convulsive. That a brief while heaves with convulsive throes— 217 *Enterprise* 115
Conway. And two of us at Conway dwell, 83 *We are Seven* 19
" You say that two at Conway dwell, 84 *We are Seven* 25
Coo. That coo again!—'tis not to chide, 168 *Turtledove* 23
Cooed. He did not cease; but cooed—and cooed; 186 **O Nightingale* 15
Cooing. Perched on an olive branch, and heard her cooing 360 **Near Anio's* 2
Cook. For show; mean handy-work of craftsman, cook, 307 **O Friend* 4
Cooked. Of him who cooked the death of Abel, S.3. 432 **A German* 2
Cool. Lashed the cool water with their restless tails, 3 *Ev. Wk.* 43
The shady porch ne'er offered a cool seat 15 *Desc. Sk.* 244
It comes to cool my babe and me. 145 *Her Eyes* 40
Soft and cool to way-worn feet; 181 *Waggoner* 4. 161
And cool, though in the depth it lies 237 *P. B.* 99
Beside him in the cool recess 238 *P. B.* 159
Cool air I breathe; while the unincumbered Mind, 262 *Retirement* 12
Might cool;—and, as the Genius of the flood 268 **Dogmatic Teachers* 7
In fear that else, when Critics grave and cool 277 **A Poet* 7
As we rest in the cool orange-bower side by side, 345 *Stanzas: Simplon* 27
Thence creeping under sylvan arches cool, 424 *Ecc. Sonn.* 1. 22. 7
Yet cool the space within, and not uncheered 497 **Enough of climbing* 24
As the cool Advocate of foul device; 514 **Portentous change* 2
While musing here I sit in shadow cool, 527 **Those breathing* 41
Hence rustic dinners on the cool green ground, 643 *Prelude* 2. 89
Of cool Lucretilis, where the pipe was heard 701 *Prelude* 8. 182
To him most pleasant who on soft cool moss 756 *Excursion* 1. 9
As cool refreshing water, by the care 757 *Excursion* 1. 70
And cool my temples in the fanning air, 763 *Excursion* 1. 468
When she upheld the cool refreshment drawn 763 *Excursion* 1. 504
And one old moss-grown wall;—a cool recess, 777 *Excursion* 2. 415
Part shaded by cool sycamore, and part 850 *Excursion* 6. 780
Here, resting in cool shelter, we beguiled 882 *Excursion* 8. 520
Coolest. In coolest climes too fugitive, might even here 356 *Aquap.* 226
Cooling. Cooling our heels in this way!—I'll begin 51 *Bord.* 753
I came; and when I felt its cooling shade, 62 *Bord.* 1358
Now cooling, with his passing wing, 144 **Driven in* 39

Cottages—*continued.*
And single cottage and lurking towns, 680 *Prelude* 6. 382
Among the cottages by beds of flowers. 683 *Prelude* 6. 540
A Wanderer then among the cottages, 764 *Excursion* 1. 541
How fair amid her brood of cottages! 855 *Excursion* 6. 1108
Borne by yon clustering cottages, that sprang 872 *Excursion* 7. 968
Cottage-sill. But, stepping o'er the cottage-sill, 247 *P. B.* 999
Cottage-sprinkled. Or from cottage-sprinkled dell, 220 *Triad* 37
Cottage-stairs. Following our Guide, we clomb the cottage-stairs 781 *Excursion* 2. 647
Cottage-threshold. I left our cottage-threshold, sallying forth 185 *Nutting* 5
When through the cottage-threshold we had passed, 786 *Excursion* 3. 7
Cottage-window. Which, in the cottage-window, heretofore 768 *Excursion* 1. 825
Cottage-windows. The cottage-windows through the twilight blazed, 89 *Prelude* 1. 427
Cotter. If ever mortal, King or Cotter, 246 *P. B.* 842
Cotton-flakes. His raiment, whitened o'er with cotton-flakes 878 *Excursion* 8. 309
Couch. Now couch thyself where, heard with fear afar, 16 *Desc. Sk.* 336
To have heard your voice. Your couch, I fear, good Baron, 53 *Bord.* 859
Thy couch the dewy earth, thy roof the forest thorn!" 104 *Artegal* 161
The blooming heath their couch, gazed side by side, 151 **Forth from* 11
Couch the widely-scattered sheep;— 163 *Spinning Wheel* 8
Whose moss-grown root might serve for couch or seat, 167 *Pilgrim's Dream* 11
For oft, when on my couch I lie 187 **I wandered* 19
Give, on this well-known couch, one nuptial kiss 210 *Laod.* 63
A play-ground,—or a couch of rest; 216 *Enterprise* 62
Couch beautiful as e'er for earthly use 219 *Haunted Tree* 10
Where the young lions couch; for so, by leave 269 *Gordale* 6
Couch near their dams, with quiet satisfied; 278 **Life with* 6
Hares couch, and rabbits burrow! 292 *Yarrow Unv.* 14
To couch in this thicket of brambles alone, 340 *Fort Fuentes* 4
When, from the soft couch of her sleeping Lover, 346 *Gemmi* 5
Ours couch on naked rocks,—will cross a brook 389 *Tyndrum* 4
Her sabbath couch has made. 398 *White Doe* 169
Angels hovering round thy couch, 502 **Like a* 51
Blithe Flora from her couch upstarts, 506 **While from* 3
For the dear blessings of a lowly couch, 528 **Those breathing* 84
Till from his couch the wished-for Sun uprose. 534 **When in* 8
Breathes out from floor or couch, through pallid lips 541 *Grace Darl.* 90
When she, whose couch had been the sod, 542 *Russ. Fug.* 41
And couch—all ready to a wish 543 *Russ. Fug.* 147
He makes his summer couch, and here at noon 547 **Rude is* 22
The sharers of her golden couch, was seen 624 *Æneid* 56
From that soft couch I rose not, till the sun 633 *Prelude* 1. 86
Then from his couch he starts; and now his feet 702 *Prelude* 8. 241
The couch his fate had made for him; supine, 718 *Prelude* 9. 575
And on that couch inviting us to rest, 793 *Excursion* 3. 477
Depresses the soul's vigour. Quit your couch— 808 *Excursion* 4. 481
That Belus, nightly to his splendid couch 811 *Excursion* 4. 686
To reconcile his manhood to a couch 817 *Excursion* 4. 1052
A grateful couch was spread for our repose; 821 *Excursion* 4. 1319
Where couch the spotted deer; or raised our eyes 892 *Excursion* 9. 563
Come share my couch, nor speedily depart; S.3. 441 **Come, gentle* 2
Couchant. Still couchant, an inevitable ear, 151 **When, to* 82
Upon the couchant lion's mane! 216 *Enterprise* 35
Mute are all creatures, as this couchant fawn, 360 **Long has* 5
Couchant beside that lonely mound; 398 *White Doe* 203
Couched. The kine are couched upon the dewy grass; 1 *Early Youth* 2
Forth-startled from the fern where she lay couched; 80 **Loving she* 16
Ere thus I have lain couched an hour, 158 **In youth* 42
Couched upon the rocking wave. 166 *Wand. Jew* 16
Couched on a casual bed of moss and leaves, 172 *InfantDaughter* 19
Couched on the bald top of an eminence; 196 *Resolution* 58
Couched in the shadow of Mænalian pines 234 *Power of Sound* 146
Lay couched; on him or his dread bow unbent 273 **WhenPhiloctetes* 3
A nursling couched upon her mother's knee, 274 *Infant M.* 13
The Gordon, couched behind a thorn, 287 *Ellen Irwin* 22
To ruminate, couched on the grassy lea; 349 *Val. Dover* 7
(Couched in their den) with those that roam at large 392 *Daniel* 6
Couched upon the dewy grass, 397 *White Doe* 154
Now couched at ease, though oft this day 407 *White Doe* 1012
The sun is couched, the sea-fowl gone to rest, 454 *Sea-side* 1
The fair Endymion couched on Latmos-hill; 461 **Giordano, verily* 3
At matins froze, and couched at curfew-time, 655 *Prelude* 3. 455
The moon in splendour couched among the leaves 659 *Prelude* 4. 88
Of such a madness, reason did lie couched. 668 *Prelude* 5. 152
Upon my right hand couched a single sheep, 738 *Prelude* 12. 300
Couched in the dewy grass. With such a theme, 750 *Prelude* 14. 275
The appropriate sense, in Latin numbers couched: 846 *Excursion* 6. 514
To whom the appeal couched in its closing words 880 *Excursion* 8. 435
And choice of moss-clad stones, whereon we couched 893 *Excursion* 9. 581
Upon their grassy beds lay couch'd in sleep, S.3. 427 **Through Cumbrian* 13
Couches. And some recline on couches, myrtle-crowned, 275 **While poring* 5
On couches lie, with purple overspread: 624 *Æneid* 59
Their painted couches seek, obedient to command. 624 *Æneid* 72
Couching. That, calmly couching while the nightly dew 380 *Duddon* 17. 8
The lamb is couching by the lion's side, 430 *Ecc. Sonn.* 2. 7. 13
Couching-place. The hare's best couching-place for fearless sleep; 387 **Part fenced* 3
Familiarly, and found a couching-place 767 *Excursion* 1. 747
Couching-time. I left Bethgelert's huts at couching-time, 746 *Prelude* 14. 4
Could. (*Partial list.*)
Of his forlorn appearance, could not fail 39 *Bord.* 81
That staff of yours, I could almost have heart 39 *Bord.* 126
Resound with music, could you see the sun, 40 *Bord.* 147
This Marmaduke—— O could you hear his voice: 40 *Bord.* 165
Dear Father! how *could* I forget and live?— 40 *Bord.* 176
Traitor to both. Oh, could you hear his voice! 41 *Bord.* 210
Could find delight to nurse itself so strangely, 41 *Bord.* 237
It could not be. And yet I now remember 42 *Bord.* 283
She could not, Sir, have failed of company. 43 *Bord.* 327
And need repose. Could you but wait an hour? 43 *Bord.* 360
If I could think one weak or partial feeling—— 48 *Bord.* 630
My heart, could penetrate its inmost core, 48 *Bord.* 632
You could not hear, for the foam beat the rocks 51 *Bord.* 746
Could not come after us—he *must* have perished; 51 *Bord.* 755
I could have dropped asleep upon his breast. 53 *Bord.* 892
I could have quelled the Cowards, but this Stripling 54 *Bord.* 918
Would I could find the old Man and his Daughter. 55 *Bord.* 954
And, by the living God, I could not do it. 55 *Bord.* 990
Else could so strong a mind have ever known 55 *Bord.* 998
I could forgive him. And should he make the Child 56 *Bord.* 1044
To lisp the name of Father—could he look 56 *Bord.* 1052
It ever could be otherwise! Last night, 59 *Bord.* 1180
That could withstand it. True," continued he, 59 *Bord.* 1194
Now I could laugh till my ribs ached. Oh, Fool! 59 *Bord.* 1218
I could fetch lessons out of wiser schools 59 *Bord.* 1221
And you should see how deeply I could reason 59 *Bord.* 1224
That almost I could repine 171 *Kitten* 107
And scarcely could the people that were near 555 *Prioress* 175
He paid what he could with his ill-gotten pelf, 570 *Farmer* 37
Could represent the countenance horrible 574 *Chiabrera* 4. 11
I could have fancied that the mighty Deep 578 *Peele Castle* 11
Couldst. (*Partial list.*)
I knew that thou couldst never have a wish 137 *Michael* 399
Council. Chieftains and kings in council were detained; 211 *Laod.* 119
Of Nature's privy council, as thou art, 389 *Tyndrum* 11
The Council closed, the Priest in full career 422 *Ecc. Sonn.* 1. 17. 2
For Gods in council, whose green vales, retreats 501 *Humanity* 74
Falsehood and Treachery, in close council met, 513 **Said Secrecy* 2
'Mid knots of grooms the council of his state L.1. 94 *Juvenal* 2. 15
Councillors. A synod of his Councillors:—give ear, 422 *Ecc. Sonn.* 1. 15. 13
Council-roof. The Council-roof and Clermont's towers reply;— 427 *Ecc. Sonn.* 1. 33. 11
Councils. The councils of both worlds she stands, 226 *Present.* 71
From councils senseless as intolerant 442 *Ecc. Sonn.* 3. 7. 11
Council-seats. These natural council-seats your acrid blood 268 **DogmaticTeachers* 6
Your council-seats beneath the open sky, 350 *Des. Stanzas* 50
Counsel. I counsel thee by fortitude to seek 211 *Laod.* 141
Who, taking counsel of unbending Truth, 305 **The Voice* 3
"I will not counsel nor exhort, 408 *White Doe* 1102
Or need, of counsel breathed through lips divine. 498 **Enough of climbing* 31
A poor Man's counsel take; 542 *Russ. Fug.* 82
If with that counsel I do e'er comply. 559 *Cuck.andNight.*165
And one thing will I counsel thee also, 561 *Cuck.andNight.*236
This matter asketh counsel good as grave, 562 *Cuck.andNight.*272
Added no farewell to his parting counsel, 726 *Prelude* 10. 538
I looked for counsel as unbending now; 817 *Excursion* 4. 1104
He, taking counsel of his own clear thoughts, 841 *Excursion* 6. 219
Counsel is given; contention they appease 875 *Excursion* 8. 78
Whose love, whose counsel, whose commands, have made 895 *Excursion* 9. 733
Counsellor. A nobler counsellor than my poor heart. 210 *Laod.* 54
Of a shrewd Counsellor, eager to protect 432 *Ecc. Sonn.* 2. 16. 2
Counsellor's. Than the height of a counsellor's bag; 86 *Rural Arch.* 3
Counsellors. Counsellors for the world, of piercing ken; 429 *Ecc. Sonn.* 2. 5. 5
Counsels. Arts yet untried, upon new counsels bent, 624 *Æneid* 2
To those sweet counsels between head and heart 732 *Prelude* 11. 353
Count. And count the stars. That dog of his, you are sure, 51 *Bord.* 754
But some one must be near to count his groans. 75 *Bord.* 2151
What happy moments did I count! 111 *A Complaint* 7
But who shall count the Towers as they recline 625 **The confidence* 6
Counted. Where, hid from me, he counted many years, 71 *Bord.* 1893
And counted them: and oftentimes will start— 267 **Though narrow* 11
Countenance. *See* **Under-countenance.**
'Twas this that put it in my thoughts—that countenance— 54 *Bord.* 925
Idonea's filial countenance was there 55 *Bord.* 986
It is so meek, his countenance so venerable. 57 *Bord.* 1068
His countenance is meek and venerable; 57 *Bord.* 1095
With seeming unconcern and steady countenance. 104 *Artegal* 113
And countenance like a summer's day, 121 *EmigrantMother* 52
And feed his countenance with your own sweet looks, 124 *V. and J.* 202
Yet leafless, showed as if the countenance 146 **It was an* 15
At thy glittering countenance. 161 **Pleasures newly* 16
Changed countenance, like an object sullied o'er 173 *InfantDaughter* 62
A countenance in which did meet 186 **She was* 15
Her countenance brightens—and her eye expands; 209 *Laod.* 10
Shed from thy countenance, as I see thee stand 215 *Enterprise* 2
Fit countenance for the soul of primal truth; 221 *Triad* 139
Whose countenance bore resemblance to the sun, 226 *Vernal Ode* 6
The mosques and spires change countenance, 244 *P. B.* 689
Thy countenance—the still rapture of thy mien— 258 **Even so* 3

Coupled. Ay, we are coupled by a chain of adamant; 70 *Bord.* 1854
Then with the father's name she coupled words . 124 *V. and J.* 165
Of Faith stand coupled for a common flight! . 437 *Ecc. Sonn.* 2. 34. 3
On Patience coupled with such slow endeavour, . 515 **Hard task* 2
Courage. Hope, strength, and courage, social suffering brings, ... 13 *Desc. Sk.* 171
Has given him power to teach: and then for courage . . . . 38 *Bord.* 36
Or own we baby Spirits? Genuine courage . . 57 *Bord.* 1073
Saved by courage that with danger . . . . 93 *Westmoreland Girl* 21
But, courage! for around that boisterous brook . 131 *Michael* 6
Of hardship, skill or courage, joy or fear; . . . 132 *Michael* 69
"Yet you make all courage fruitless, ... 140 *Arm. Lady* 39
"Stranger, 'tis no act of courage . . . . 163 *Hint* 17
Thy matchless courage I bewail no more, . . . 210 *Laod.* 50
That choice lacked courage to bestow! . . . 215 *Kirkstone* 60
Fit aims, with courage to begin, ... 224 **'Tis gone* 47
Of courage you saw little there, ... 239 *P. B.* 303
Of more than martial courage in the breast . 316 **Hail, Zaragoza* 6
The martial courage of a day is vain, . . . 316 **The martial* 1
No courage can repel the dire assault; . . . 322 **Humanity, delighting* 33
Her courage animates the flood; . . . . 344 **How blest* 41
Of virtuous action; all that courage dares, . . 363 **The world forsaken* 4
His budding courage to the proof; and here . . 378 *Duddon* 9. 11
And yet want courage at their need: . . . . 406 *White Doe* 903
The foe from numbers courage drew, . . . 408 *White Doe* 1153
Redoubted King, of courage leonine, . . . 427 *Ecc. Sonn.* 1. 35. 1
That Courage may find something to perform; . 466 *St. Bees* 15
And of the towering courage which past times . 472 **The captive* 11
"But courage, Father! let us out to sea— . . 540 *Grace Darl.* 43
With courage will depart." . . . . . . 542 *Russ. Fug.* 80
This neither is its courage nor its choice, . . . 571 **There is a Flower* 15
To patient courage and unblemished truth, . . 635 *Prelude* 1. 183
Of courage, or integrity, or truth, ... 696 *Prelude* 7. 600
With courage, and new hope risen on our toil. . 710 *Prelude* 9. 18
Courage to them who looked for good by light . 727 *Prelude* 11. 4
One courage seemed to animate them all: . . 775 *Excursion* 2. 232
By courage, to demand from real life . . . 792 *Excursion* 3. 417
As soldiers live by courage; as, by strength . 804 *Excursion* 4. 203
Take courage, and withdraw yourself from ways . 808 *Excursion* 4. 489
The courage that was needful to leap back . . K.8. 229 **I will* 155
An act of courage, and the thing itself . . . K.8. 238 *Recluse* 1. 1. 61
Or sought with courage; enterprize forlorn . . K.8. 256 *Recluse* 1. 1. 717
Courageous. Her humane courageous spirit . . . 94 *Westmoreland Girl* 91
Fixed in the depths of this courageous soil; . . 324 *Ode 1814* 104
That not the less a frank courageous heart . . 574 *Chiabrera* 5. 6
Angelical, keen eye, courageous look, ... 653 *Prelude* 3. 291
Course. *See* **Watercourse.**
And whensoe'er my course shall end, ... 1 *Extract* 4
Where antique roots its bustling course o'erlook, . 3 *Ev. Wk.* 67
The boat her silent course pursues! . . . . 9 *Lines: Boat* 4
With more majestic course the water rolled, . . 22 *Desc. Sk.* 636
With a light heart our course we may renew, . . 22 *Desc. Sk.* 669
Three years a wanderer now my course I bend— 32 *Guilt* 445
And female cries. Their course they thither bent, 33 *Guilt* 467
Wanderers whose course no longer now agrees. . 34 *Guilt* 533
Than make me change my course. Dear Marmaduke, 55 *Bord.* 992
In such a course fit links of sympathy, . . . 78 *Bord.* 2308
With two or three companions, whom their course 101 *Brothers* 359
Wouldst change the course of things in all men's sight! . . . . 105 *Artegal* 173
And circumspect must be our course, and slow, . 105 *Artegal* 212
The way my friends their course did bend, . . 114 *Ind. Wom.* 46
Young as I am, my course is run, ... 114 *Ind. Wom.* 61
The Stream, so ardent in its course before, . . 146 **It was an* 22
While she pursues her course through the dreary sea. . . . . 150 **When, to* 66
"Dost thou presume my course to block? . . 155 *Waterfall* 11
Thy pleasant course,—when day's begun . . 158 **In youth* 74
Hither he his course is bending;— . . . . 174 *Waggoner* 1. 33
As a swoln brook with rugged course, . . . 176 *Waggoner* 1. 236
With him whatever comes in course, ... 178 *Waggoner* 3. 16
Rolled round in earth's diurnal course, . . . 187 **A slumber* 7
The Knight, Sir Walter, died in course of time, . 202 *Hart-leap* 93
But Nature, in due course of time, once more . 203 *Hart-leap* 171
Her statelier Eden's course to guard; . . . 204 *Brougham* 47
In worlds whose course is equable and pure; . . 211 *Laod.* 98
Or ruder weapon which their course might yield, . 212 *Dion* 20
That Destiny her course should change; too just 214 *Dion* 115
Desires whose course in folly ends, ... 223 *Wishing-gate* 41
Their course, or genial showers descend! . . . 227 *Vernal Ode* 70
The golden years maintained a course . . . 228 *Vernal Ode* 131
A mazy course along familiar things, . . . 229 *Cuckoo-clock* 37
Self-cast, as with a desperate course, . . . 234 *Power of Sound* 137
Where cheerily his course he weaves, . . . 240 *P. B.* 342
Why wander from your course so far, . . . 245 *P. B.* 762
He finds no solace in his course; . . . . 246 *P. B.* 882
Heaven-born, the Soul a heavenward course must hold; . . . . 257 **No mortal* 5
Went forth—his course surrendering to the care . 263 *Storm* 3
Checked in your course by many a teasing burr; 268 **Dogmatic Teachers* 5
No public harm that Genius from her course . . 280 *Plea for Auth.* 13
His course was true, ... 286 *Nith* 22
And from the shore their course they take, . . 297 *Highland Boy* 183

Course—*continued.*
A course of lively pleasure; . . . . 302 *Yarrow V.* 78
The course of things, and change the creed . . 312 **Who rises* 62
And, if old judgments keep their sacred course, . 318 **Look now* 12
Of such high course was felt and understood; . 320 **O'erweening Statesmen* 11
The unconquerable Stream his course pursue. . 322 *Germans* 14
Bright be thy course to-day, let not this promise fail! . . . . 329 *Ode: Thanks.* 35
Then give free course to joy and love, ... 339 **Meek Virgin* 40
But from our course why turn—to tread . . 344 **How blest* 66
Rest where thy course was stayed by Power divine! 345 **Ambition—following* 10
How, when their course they through the desert took, ... 346 *Processions* 13
To which sad course, these wrinkled Sons of Time 350 *Des. Stanzas* 24
Nor stagnates, nor precipitates his course, . . 357 *Aquap.* 316
Henceforth a humbler course perplexed and slow; 359 **Those old* 9
And pleasant course; flower after flower has blown, 361 **List—'twas* 11
Thy course and sport around thee softly fan— . 363 **List—'twas* 109
"Her course was for the British strand; . . . 370 *Eg. Maid* 79
To learn thy course; farewell! be prompt and steady." . . . . 370 *Eg. Maid* 114
Fleet was their course, and when they came . . 371 *Eg. Maid* 163
Ere yet our course was graced with social trees . 377 *Duddon* 6. 1
Will soon be broken;—a rough course remains, . 381 *Duddon* 20. 7
Nor have I tracked their course for scanty gains; 382 *Duddon* 26. 9
Her trophies, Fancy crouch; the course of pride . 388 *Loch Etive* 11
To watch thy course when Daylight, fled from earth, ... 391 **Though joy* 3
Still stronger, bends him to his course. . . . 401 *White Doe* 466
To Durham first their course they bear; . . . 404 *White Doe* 711
His solitary course maintain; . . . . . . 409 *White Doe* 1217
A downward course, perverse and strange? . . 411 *White Doe* 1402
And tremblingly her course she bent . . . 413 *White Doe* 1541
And, for delight of him who tracks its course, . 418 *Ecc. Sonn.* 1. 1. 13
Slackens his course—to mark those holy piles . 419 *Ecc. Sonn.* 1. 5. 7
From their known course, or vanish like a dream; 421 *Ecc. Sonn.* 1. 12. 10
In light confirmed while years their course shall run, 431 *Ecc. Sonn.* 2. 10. 13
Ploughs her bold course across the wondering seas; 432 *Ecc. Sonn.* 2. 15. 11
And, if dissevered thence, its course is short. . 442 *Ecc. Sonn.* 3. 10. 14
We, nothing loth a lingering course to measure, . 443 *Ecc. Sonn.* 3. 12. 12
For the brief course that must for me remain; . 454 **The Sun, that* 18
Seen in her course, nor 'mid this quiet heard; . 454 *Sea-side* 21
Learn from thy course, where'er their own be taken, 461 **Queen of* 49
In his lone course the Shepherd oft will pause, . 468 **Ranging the* 2
Measuring thy course, fair Stream! at length I pay 476 *Eden* 9
That searching test thy public course has stood; . 478 **Lonsdale! it* 11
Wild stream of Aira, hold thy course, ... 479 *Somnamb.* 154
And they a blissful course may hold . . . 492 *Duty* 21
Gain a fresh impulse, run a livelier course; . . 503 *Warning* 15
To stop your Leaders in their headstrong course! 505 *Warning* 130
What yet remains of this day's course: . . . 506 *Lab. Hymn* 28
In course of nature under a low roof . . . 510 **Among a* 21
Where'er her course; mysterious Bird! . . . 511 **Who rashly* 25
But O, restrain compassion, if its course, . . . 517 *Pun. Death* 2. 9
The generous course, aspire, and still aspire; . . 529 **Those breathing* 129
Long as the sun his gladsome course renews. . . 534 **When in* 20
In which course if Christ our Saviour . . . 535 *Egremont* 27
To read that they, who mark thy course, behold . 539 **Lady! a* 59
Seven nights her course renewed, ... 542 *Russ. Fug.* 18
"Leave open to my wish the course, ... 545 *Russ. Fug.* 337
And that the sun did take his course not right, . 564 *Troilus* 143
The old man does not change his course, the boy 566 *Cumb. Beg.* 40
Such course he held! Bologna's learned schools 573 *Chiabrera* 2. 9
Returns from her long course:—anon . . . . 579 **Sweet Flower* 30
Flowed in a course of sympathy divine;— . . 583 **With copious* 25
From sign to sign, its steadfast course, . . . 586 *Hogg* 14
His wizard course where hoary Derwent takes 591 *Ev. Wk. Quarto* 3
What perils meet Æneas in his course, ... 624 *Æneid* 15
Your own grief and your friends'—your wandering course; . . . . 625 *Æneid* 141
A smooth free course along the watery gleam, . 626 **The confidence* 12
May'st thou pursue thy course by God approved, 628 **Deign, Sovereign* 11
Upon the river point me out my course? . . . 632 *Prelude* 1. 30
We ran a boisterous course; the year span round 642 *Prelude* 2. 47
Of some small island steered our course with one, 644 *Prelude* 2. 167
Yet Nature, or a happy course of things . . . 653 *Prelude* 3. 327
Judging not ill perhaps, the timid course . . 656 *Prelude* 3. 494
In its late course of even days with all . . . 659 *Prelude* 4. 62
That ran on Sabbath days a fresher course; . . 661 *Prelude* 4. 226
My homeward course led up a long ascent, . . 664 *Prelude* 4. 379
What joy was mine! How often in the course . 673 *Prelude* 5. 480
Yet independent study seemed a course . . . 675 *Prelude* 6. 27
A rigorous student. What a stormy course . . 679 *Prelude* 6. 281
Did this unprecedented course imply . . . . 680 *Prelude* 6. 327
As their forerunners in a glorious course; . . . 681 *Prelude* 6. 405
And, that our future course, all plain to sight, . 683 *Prelude* 6. 584
With some untried adventure, in a course . . 686 *Prelude* 6. 729
Yet, undetermined to what course of life . . . 688 *Prelude* 7. 58
A minuet course; and, winding up his mouth, . 695 *Prelude* 7. 556
His devious course. A glimpse of such sweet life 702 *Prelude* 8. 209
My mortal course, there will I think on you; . . 706 *Prelude* 8. 469
Darkness ere day's mid course, and morning light 709 *Prelude* 8. 661
Turns, and will measure back his course, far back, 709 *Prelude* 9. 5
Through Paris lay my readiest course, and there . 710 *Prelude* 9. 42
Seemed nothing out of nature's certain course, . 713 *Prelude* 9. 247
Of wildest course but treads back his own steps; 719 *Prelude* 10. 79
To turn *all* judgments out of their right course; . 728 *Prelude* 11. 56

Crab. The Crab, the Scorpion, and the Bull— 236 *P. B.* 36
Crabbe. On which with thee, O Crabbe! forth-looking, 586 *Hogg* 31
Crack. Hell opens, and the heavens in vengeance crack 475 **Here on their* 8
And crack the voice in rivalship, the crowd 697 *Prelude* 7. 697
Cracked. And cracked the branches, and strewn them about; 80 †*Address: Child* 23
He neither cracked his whip, nor blew his horn, 201 *Hart-leap* 35
The walls are cracked, sunk is the flowery roof, 390 *Highland Hut* 9
Cradle. Though from the cradle they had lived with Walter, 99 *Brothers* 243
His cradle, as with a woman's gentle hand. 133 *Michael* 158
Rock the cradle of joy, smooth the deathbed of strife. 143 †*Lov. and Lik.* 54
But safe as in a cradle, here 144 *Her Eyes* 17
For infant in the cradle laid. 375 **The Minstrels* 48
Thy cradle decks;—to chant thy birth, thou hast 376 *Duddon* 2. 6
A peaceful cradle given: 582 **O for a* 21
The mother from the cradle of her babe, 723 *Prelude* 10. 359
The snakes about her cradle; that was well, 724 *Prelude* 10. 393
That from the cradle had grown up with me, 729 *Prelude* 11. 170
To rock the cradle of the slumbering babe: 867 *Excursion* 7. 668
To rock the cradle of her peevish babe; 878 *Excursion* 8. 268
Cradled. And haply too the cradled Child, 225 *Present.* 35
Take, cradled Nursling of the mountain, take 377 *Duddon* 4. 1
Cradles. Of such alliance.—From their cradles up, 122 *V. and J.* 19
Craft. And craft of age, seducing reason, first 57 *Bord.* 1081
By which they uphold their craft from age to age: 64 *Bord.* 1492
And, following guides whose craft holds no consent 213 *Dion* 54
No craft this subtle element can bind, 321 **The power* 12
Her sides, the Wizard's craft confounding; 370 *Eg. Maid* 44
Thus is the storm abated by the craft 432 *Ecc. Sonn.* 2. 16. 1
Hast loved the painter's true Promethean craft 508 *F. Stone* 24
The Woodman knew, for such the craft 543 *Russ. Fug.* 105
The dangerous craft of culling term and phrase 676 *Prelude* 6. 110
I do not here allude to subtlest craft, 690 *Prelude* 7. 236
The Wax-work, Clock-work, all the marvellous craft 698 *Prelude* 7. 712
Which craft of delicate Spirits hath composed 755 *Recluse* 1. 1. 797
—Inglorious implements of craft and toil, 831 *Excursion* 5. 611
Craftily. From the confusion, craftily incites 439 *Ecc. Sonn.* 2. 41. 10
Craftsman. For show; mean handy-work of craftsman, cook, 307 **O Friend* 4
Crafty. Was the supremacy of crafty Rome; 435 *Ecc. Sonn.* 2. 26. 2
Poor Robin as a sure and crafty friend, 530 *Poor Robin* 21
Crag. *See* **Ghimmer-crag, Helm-crag, Owlet-Crag, Raven-crag.**
A Man on the peak of the Crag. 86 *Rural Arch.* 6
From the peak of the crag blew the giant away. 86 *Rural Arch.* 16
Then, light-hearted Boys, to the top of the crag; 86 *Rural Arch.* 23
Perched on the forehead of a jutting crag, 95 *Brothers* 6
Companions for each other: the huge crag 97 *Brothers* 143
The high crag cannot work me harm, 145 *Her Eyes* 45
"I saw a crag, a lofty stone 156 *Oak and Broom* 11
Crag, lawn, and wood—with rosy light. 182 *Waggoner* 4. 243
A jutting crag,—and off I ran, 199 *Thorn* 182
The shelter of the crag to gain; 199 *Thorn* 184
Instead of jutting crag I found 199 *Thorn* 186
Or from a rifted crag or ivy tod 456 **The leaves* 20
Appeared the Crag of Ailsa, ne'er did morn 471 *Ailsa Crag* 2
Shouldering the naked crag, oh, at that time 637 *Prelude* 1. 335
The leafless trees and every icy crag 638 *Prelude* 1. 441
Or by its aid leaping from crag to crag, 703 *Prelude* 8. 247
My brothers and myself. There rose a crag, 738 *Prelude* 12. 292
That day so lately past, when from the crag 739 *Prelude* 12. 312
To measure the altitude of some tall crag 760 *Excursion* 1. 274
Trusting ourselves, we wound from crag to crag, 777 *Excursion* 2. 404
Unnoticed, thus continuing.— "From yon crag 779 *Excursion* 2. 546
When ye looked down upon us from the crag, 782 *Excursion* 2. 734
Darken the silver bosom of the crag, 786 *Excursion* 3. 27
O'er the smooth surface of an ample crag, 787 *Excursion* 3. 41
Beginning towards the south, where from Dove Crag K.8. 224 **I will* 19
Leaving St. Sunday's Crag, to Grisdale tarn K.8. 225 **I will* 25
Cragg. Threading the painful cragg surmounts the cliff. 607 *Desc.Sk.Quarto* 298
Craggs. Thro' craggs, and forest glooms, and opening lakes, 591 *Ev. Wk. Quarto* 4
Black drizzling craggs, that beaten by the din, 606 *Desc.Sk.Quarto* 249
Craggy. Roar down many a craggy steep, 166 *Wand. Jew* 2
And up the craggy hill ascending 174 *Waggoner* 1. 35
Old Andes thrusts yon craggy spear 237 *P. B.* 58
To house and home in many a craggy rent 275 **Chatsworth! thy* 3
Through hanging clouds, from craggy height to height, 315 **Advance—come* 11
Lo! in the burning west, the craggy nape 348 *Sky-prosp.* 1
Wafted o'er sullen moss and craggy mound— 377 *Duddon* 5. 3
'Mid woods and wilds, on Nature's craggy throne, 431 *Ecc. Sonn.* 2. 11. 13
And over many a wide hill's craggy crown, 523 *Epist. Beaumont* 104
Sky streaked with purple, grove and craggy *bield*, 524 *Epist. Beaumont* 175
Beneath yon eastern ridge, the craggy bound, 547 **Beneath yon* 1
Yielded by this craggy rent, 550 *Hermit's Cell* 4. 6
Upon the summit of a craggy ridge, 637 *Prelude* 1. 370
When, from behind that craggy steep till then 637 *Prelude* 1. 377
A toilsome burden up the craggy ways, 702 *Prelude* 8. 227
Raised toward those craggy summits, his intent 773 *Excursion* 2. 154
Of craggy fountain; what he hopes for wins, 788 *Excursion* 3. 167
By flowing stream, through wood, or craggy wild, 803 *Excursion* 4. 105
"These craggy regions, these chaotic wilds, 807 *Excursion* 4. 427
Haunting with rod and line the craggy brooks? 861 *Excursion* 7. 267

Craggy—*continued.*
Where nature works in wild and craggy spots, 871 *Excursion* 7. 917
Or founts that gurgle from yon craggy steep, S.3. 433 **The doubt* 11
Crags. On withered briars that o'er the crags recline; 3 *Ev. Wk.* 63
They played like two young ravens on the crags: 99 *Brothers* 278
Of a vast building made of many crags; 101 *Brothers* 365
A narrow girdle of rough stones and crags, 148 **A narrow* 1
Crags, woodlands, waterfalls, and rills; 180 *Waggoner* 4. 53
Gigantic mountains rough with crags; beneath, 219 **This Height* 12
(Above the general roar of woods and crags) 219 *Haunted Tree* 23
Among the rocks and winding crags; 241 *P. B.* 476
Upon its loftiest crags, mine eyes behold 379 *Duddon* 15. 2
Through crags, and smoothing paths beset with danger, 477 *Nunnery* 10
The crags repeat the raven's croak, 491 *Fidelity* 27
Pleased with thy crags, and woody steeps, thy Lake, 622 *Recluse* 1. 1. 118
Among the impervious crags, but having been 660 *Prelude* 4. 98
White Sirius glittering o'er the southern crags, 662 *Prelude* 4. 244
Of naked pools, and common crags that lay 678 *Prelude* 6. 234
Black drizzling crags that spake by the way-side 684 *Prelude* 6. 631
Echoes and waterfalls, and pointed crags 708 *Prelude* 8. 637
Upon the naked pool and dreary crags, 738 *Prelude* 12. 264
The shepherd's lurcher, who, among the crags, 746 *Prelude* 14. 22
And 'mid the hollow depths of naked crags 758 *Excursion* 1. 155
And phantoms from the crags and solid earth 809 *Excursion* 4. 523
O'er stately Edinborough throned on crags? 815 *Excursion* 4. 913
Along the sharp edge of yon lofty crags, 863 *Excursion* 7. 413
(Yon cottage shaded by the woody crags) 864 *Excursion* 7. 467
Huge skeletons of crags which from the coast K.8. 225 **I will* 32
Deep pools, tall trees, black chasms, and dizzy crags, K.8. 256 *Recluse* 1. 1. 711
Cramp. The ethereal eyesight, cramp the wingèd mind! 529 **Those breathing* 136
Would I your flights of *memory* cramp. S. 3. 438 **My Lord* 6
Crams. Crams through the arch, and bellies o'er the ridge? L. 1. 95 *Juvenal* 3. 26
Cranmer. Amid the shuddering throng doth Cranmer stand; 437 *Ecc. Sonn.* 2. 35. 4
Crannies. In the dry crannies of the pendent rocks; 866 *Excursion* 7. 597
Crash. The crash of ruin fitfully resounds; 21 *Desc. Sk.* 580
Last night I heard a crash—'tis true, 156 *Oak and Broom* 27
And dragged to earth both branch and bough, with crash 185 *Nutting* 44
The crash it made in falling! From the wreck 796 *Excursion* 3. 713
Crashes. And somewhere, as he thinks, by crashes 175 *Waggoner* 1. 199
Crashing. —Fierce comes the river down; the crashing wood 606 *Desc.Sk.Quarto* 211
Crave. Here crave an easier lot; 223 *Wishing-gate* 45
Grant me thy love, I crave no other fee! 281 *Valedict.* 14
So, coming his last help to crave, 287 *Ellen Irwin* 45
Then why repine that now in vain I crave 392 *Bothwell* 7
By flames, look up to heaven and crave redress 426 *Ecc. Sonn.* 1. 32. 4
And all who from the law firm safety crave. 517 *Pun. Death* 2. 14
And what beyond this thought we crave 578 **I come* 70
Which then were silent; but crave utterance now. 826 *Excursion* 5. 241
Craved. Nor craved he more to quell his foes, 291 *Rob Roy* 11
A sign he craved, tired slave of vain contrition; 373 *Eg. Maid* 296
Life's rule from passion craved for passion's sake; 455 **Not in the lucid* 13
She welcomed what was given, and craved no more; 736 *Prelude* 12. 158
Full measure of content; but still I craved 741 *Prelude* 13. 110
Nor more would she have craved as due to One 770 *Excursion* 1. 934
He craved a substitute in troubled joy; 855 *Excursion* 6. 1091
But from Him I crav'd no warrant, S. 3. 437 **I, whose* 11
Craven. The craven few who bowed the head 298 *Brownie's Cell* 48
Among her native wilds of Craven; 414 *White Doe* 1618
Craven's. In Craven's dens, on Cumbrian heights; 399 *White Doe* 279
In Craven's Wilds is many a den, 408 *White Doe* 1094
Craves. Where men were monsters. A last grace he craves, 234 *Power of Sound* 133
The immortal Mind craves objects that endure: 263 **Those words* 12
Who, having learnt that name, salvation craves 422 *Ecc. Sonn.* 1. 13. 8
And its possessions, what it has and craves, 747 *Prelude* 14. 68
Craving. Breathless as they, with unabated craving 220 *Triad* 26
Even Joy could tell, Joy craving truce and rest 255 **Grief, thou* 9
Of that licentious craving in the mind 347 *Processions* 65
When craving for the marvellous gives way 673 *Prelude* 5. 540
Far less than craving power; yet knowledge came, 708 *Prelude* 8. 600
Still craving combinations of new forms, 736 *Prelude* 12. 144
For independent happiness; craving peace, 791 *Excursion* 3. 381
Nor rapt, nor craving, but in settled peace, 804 *Excursion* 4. 187
Cravings. These cravings; when the foxglove, one by one, 705 *Prelude* 8. 393
The humbler cravings of the heart; and he 806 *Excursion* 4. 354
Crawl. Of hideous sense, I sank, nor step could crawl: 31 *Guilt* 386
Crawl from beneath our feet we do not ask 66 *Bord.* 1580
He cannot find out in what track he must crawl, 484 **A plague* 13
If he can crawl, he will return again K.8. 228 **I will* 125
Crawled. Like a sea-beast crawled forth, that on a shelf 196 *Resolution* 62
Crawling. For this poor crawling helpless wretch 621 *Andrew Jones* 11
Crawls. That crawls from his secure abode 142 †*Lov. and Lik.* 8
Crazed. Craz'd by the strength of hope at morn he eyes 609 *Desc.Sk.Quarto* 402
On men suspected to be crazed in brain. 660 *Prelude* 4. 130
A gentle dweller in the desert, crazed 667 *Prelude* 5. 145
From my good Host, that being crazed in brain 839 *Excursion* 6. 108
Crazily. And crazily and wearily 115 *Last of Flock* 77
Crazing. Much wondering by what fit of crazing care, 11 *Desc. Sk.* 41
Much wondering what sad stroke of crazing Care 602 *Desc. Sk. Quarto* 43
Crazy. (And one, too, not in crazy plight), 176 *Waggoner* 2. 6
About the crazy old church-clock, 488 *Fountain* 71
Of ragged villages and crazy huts, 655 *Prelude* 3. 465

Crazy—*continued.*
Who shall enumerate the crazy huts — 879 *Excursion* 8. 346
Creaked. No swinging sign-board creaked from cottage elm — 26 *Guilt* 136
Creaking. Trees creaking in the wind (but none are here) — 67 *Bord.* 1662
Blows keenly, it sends forth a creaking sound — 219 *Haunted Tree* 22
Cream. Rich cream, and snow-white eggs fresh from the nest, — 525 *Epist. Beaumont* 242
Refreshment, strawberries and mellow cream. — 644 *Prelude* 2. 160
Of dainties,—oaten bread, curd, cheese, and cream; — 781 *Excursion* 2. 677
Create. And mutual interest failed not to create. — 28 *Guilt* 195
Of eye, and ear,—both what they half create, — 207 *Tintern* 106
May find or there create? — 238 *P. B.* 145
Create, creator and receiver both, — 646 *Prelude* 2. 258
Or could more bright appearances create — 676 *Prelude* 6. 91
Kindred mutations; for themselves create — 747 *Prelude* 14. 94
Earth and the kingdoms of the earth, create— — 845 *Excursion* 6. 487
Receives, or by reflexion can create. — K.8. 250 *Recluse* 1.1.499
Created. *See* **Home-created, New-created, Self-created.**
Yet why repine, created as we are — 231 *Clouds* 92
And others like in fame, created Powers — 357 *Aquap.* 282
How soon—alas! did Man, created pure— — 428 *Ecc. Sonn.* 2. 1. 1
That none, the meanest of created things, — 567 *Cumb. Beg.* 74
Of forms created the most vile and brute, — 567 *Cumb. Beg.* 75
Created out of pure intelligence. — 677 *Prelude* 6. 167
Created for them, catch it, or are caught — 747 *Prelude* 14. 96
Was Man created; but to obey the law — 886 *Excursion* 9. 127
Creates. That both creates and fixes, in despite — 509 *F. Stone* 77
Informs, creates, and thaws the deepest sleep — 661 *Prelude* 4. 167
His eye distinguishes, his soul creates. — 813 *Excursion* 4. 833
And oh! how much, of all that love creates — S.3. 434 **The doubt* 62
Creation. Nor stop but where creation seems to end. — 14 *Desc. Sk.* 233
He who governs the creation, — 90 *Longest Day* 33
My fancy's own creation. — 111 **Yes! thou* 4
Rich change, and multiplied creation! — 178 *Waggoner* 3. 41
Creation of the painter's skill, — 228 *Devot. Incit.* 35
Her delicate creation: — 302 *Yarrow V.* 44
And such a beautiful creation makes — 338 *Engelberg* 3
Their own creation. Such glad welcomings — 431 *Ecc. Sonn.* 2. 13. 8
Creation, as it were, of yesterday— — 510 **Among a* 18
More high, to where creation seems to end, — 607 *Desc.Sk.Quarto* 289
Vexing its own creation. Thanks to both, — 632 *Prelude* 1. 38
Old as creation, drinking in a pure — 640 *Prelude* 1. 563
Creation and divinity itself — 651 *Prelude* 3. 171
And the creation (by no lower name — 755 *Recluse* 1. 1. 822
(As at a first creation and in haste — 809 *Excursion* 4. 526
A new and unforeseen creation rise — 875 *Excursion* 8. 90
Creations. Rich as the mine's most bright creations. — 399 *White Doe* 304
Creations lovely as the work of sleep— — 547 **Rude is* 29
Creations in the mind (and were indeed — K.8. 230 **I will* 194
Creations often), then when he discoursed — K.8. 230 **I will* 195
Creative. High is our calling, Friend!—Creative Art — 260 **High is* 1
In pomp foreseen by her creative eye, — 503 *Warning* 40
My first creative sensibility; — 647 *Prelude* 2. 360
Creative agency. The song would speak — 647 *Prelude* 2. 382
The whole creative powers of man asleep!— — 697 *Prelude* 7. 681
A sensitive being, a *creative* soul. — 737 *Prelude* 12. 207
Creative and enduring, may become — 744 *Prelude* 13. 311
Or by creative feeling overborne, — 758 *Excursion* 1. 158
Obedient to the strong creative power — 763 *Excursion* 1. 480
The moral interests, the creative might, — 798 *Excursion* 3. 823
Creator. Create, creator and receiver both, — 646 *Prelude* 2. 258
Creature. The eye that marks the gliding creature sees — 6 *Ev. Wk.* 220
He seemed the only creature in the wild — 26 *Guilt* 102
Never on earth was gentler creature seen; — 35 *Guilt* 609
The heart of living creature.—My poor Babe — 44 *Bord.* 398
Be worse than death) to that confiding Creature — 53 *Bord.* 897
Thou bring'st, gay creature as thou art! — 79 **Stay near* 7
Even so this happy Creature of herself — 80 **Loving she* 11
Proud creature was she the next day, — 82 *Alice Fell* 59
I heard a voice; it said, "Drink, pretty creature, drink!" — 87 *Pet-lamb* 2
"Drink, pretty creature, drink," she said in such a tone — 87 *Pet-lamb* 11
"It will not, will not rest!—Poor creature, can it be — 88 *Pet-lamb* 49
For never sun on living creature shone — 107 *Indolence* 3
Or like a sinful creature, pale and wan. — 107 *Indolence* 21
For happier soul no living creature has — 108 *Indolence* 30
With mortal creature. An Inhabitant — 125 *V. and J.* 285
With some, the noble Creature never slept; — 139 *Widow* 12
Fit pattern for a human creature, — 142 †*Lov. and Lik.* 26
Thrice happy Creature! in all lands — 144 **Driven in* 58
Sweet silent creature! — 159 **With little* 44
A beautiful creature, — 162 **Art thou the* 25
"Such it is; the aspiring creature — 163 *Hint* 25
Creature none can she decoy — 171 *Kitten* 89
Furnishes to every creature; — 171 *Kitten* 98
The Creature, by the Mastiff's side, — 179 *Waggoner* 3. 59
And this of mine—this bulky creature — 179 *Waggoner* 3. 73
A Creature not too bright or good — 186 **She was* 17
A creature of a "fiery heart":— — 186 **O Nightingale* 2
And yet a boon I gave her, for the creature — 191 *Beggars* 17
Winds the mute Creature without visible Mate — 212 *Dion*
Than fairest spiritual creature of the groves, — 219 *Haunted Tree* 17
That in the living Creature find on earth a place. — 231 **The gentlest Poet* 38
How gaunt the Creature is,—how lean — 241 *P. B.* 449
That earnest Creature turned away, — 243 *P. B.* 599
So with his freight the Creature turns — 244 *P. B.* 671
He sees an unsubstantial creature, — 246 *P. B.* 923

Creature—*continued.*
O gentle Creature! do not use me so, — 253 **O gentle* 13
Breathes forth a cloud-like creature of its own, — 282 **While beams* 3
But, O fair Creature! in the light — 288 *Highland Girl* 15
May human creature leave the shore! — 296 *Highland Boy* 102
The hapless creature which did dwell — 297 *Highland Boy* 193
And stands amidst you now an armèd creature, — 311 **Who rises* 16
But not a living creature could be seen — 323 *Ode 1814* 16
That, while the Creature is sustained, — 341 *San Salv.* 11
Is wheeling hitherward. Thanks, happy Creature, — 361 **List—'twas* 7
And every shape of creature they sustain, — 362 **List—'twas* 53
So like, yet so unlike, a living Creature! — 370 *Eg. Maid* 56
If I with this bright Creature go: — 397 *White Doe* 74
As a common creature might: — 397 *White Doe* 133
While this radiant Creature lies — 397 *White Doe* 153
Bright was the Creature, as in dreams — 398 *White Doe* 192
Which do the gentle Creature wrong. — 398 *White Doe* 216
And even this Creature!" which words saying, — 402 *White Doe* 556
Fair creature, and more white than snow! — 402 *White Doe* 559
The same fair Creature, who hath found — 407 *White Doe* 981
A radiant creature, silver-bright! — 414 *White Doe* 1647
So to her feet the Creature came, — 414 *White Doe* 1653
The saddest thought the Creature brings? — 414 *White Doe* 1679
She saw the Creature once again; — 414 *White Doe* 1698
In which the Creature first was found. — 416 *White Doe* 1804
And prospects of the inferior Creature! — 416 *White Doe* 1831
In that fair Creature whom the fields — 416 *White Doe* 1873
There doth the gentle Creature lie — 417 *White Doe* 1901
The Creature, to the Creature glory give; — 436 *Ecc. Sonn.* 2. 33. 10
Grave Creature!—whether, while the moon shines bright — 456 **The leaves* 14
Doth man of brother man a creature make — 472 *Dunolly Eagle* 13
Such an odd such a kind happy creature as he. — 482 *Character* 20
See that Fly,—a disconsolate creature! perhaps — 484 **A plague* 6
A loving creature she, and brave! — 490 *Incident: Dog* 31
What is the creature doing here? — 491 *Fidelity* 16
As a debt to that frail Creature, — 502 **Like a* 19
How could he think of the live creature—gay — 511 **Who rashly* 3
A creature born of time, that keeps one eye — 519 *Pun. Death* 9. 6
On a green bank a creature stood forlorn — 523 *Epist. Beaumont* 122
That brings to the inward creature no disgrace? — 527 **Those breathing* 24
Of humblest Friends, bright Creature! scorn not one: — 538 **Small service* 2
The fainting creature took the marsh, — 544 *Russ. Fug.* 265
From the most gentle creature nursed in fields — 584 *Ch. Lamb* 23
The heaven-eyed creature sleeps in earth: — 586 *Hogg* 18
Blank misgivings of a Creature — 589 *Immortality* 148
The Poet, gentle creature as he is, — 634 *Prelude* 1. 135
Frail creature as he is, helpless as frail, — 646 *Prelude* 2. 253
With every form of creature, as it looked — 648 *Prelude* 2. 412
Upon thy grave, good creature! While my heart — 659 *Prelude* 4. 31
Are still, the creature trotted on before; — 660 *Prelude* 4. 121
Earth's paramount Creature! not so much for woes — 665 *Prelude* 5. 5
Of the unwieldy creature he bestrode, — 667 *Prelude* 5. 132
Have been preferred, that this fair creature, checked — 692 *Prelude* 7. 374
Meanwhile this creature—spiritual almost — 703 *Prelude* 8. 282
Making man what he is, creature divine, — 724 *Prelude* 10. 424
That almost seems inherent in the creature, — 736 *Prelude* 12. 125
Why is this glorious creature to be found — 741 *Prelude* 13. 87
A human creature, howsoe'er endowed, — 750 *Prelude* 14. 291
And his frail creature Man;—but ye shall hear. — 781 *Excursion* 2. 634
Primeval Nature's child. A creature weak — 799 *Excursion* 3. 919
A creature, squalid, vengeful, and impure; — 800 *Excursion* 3. 953
Small creature as she is, from earth's bright flowers, — 807 *Excursion* 4. 393
The rational creature, left, to feel the weight — 811 *Excursion* 4. 667
Alas! such wisdom bids a creature fly — 817 *Excursion* 4. 1083
To lift the creature toward that eminence — 827 *Excursion* 5. 298
And who shall judge the creature, will forgive. — 828 *Excursion* 5. 368
Perforce? Are we a creature in whom good — 829 *Excursion* 5. 469
What sees he but a creature too perturbed; — 830 *Excursion* 5. 506
The one by which a creature, whom his sins — 837 *Excursion* 5. 988
Been faithless, hear him, though a lowly creature, — 851 *Excursion* 6. 880
Yet is the creature rational, endowed — 866 *Excursion* 7. 576
The breathing creature stood; as beautiful, — 890 *Excursion* 9. 445
Not for the creature only, but for all — K.8. 244 *Recluse* 1.1.287
The common creature of the brotherhood, — K.8. 246 *Recluse* 1.1.353
Creature's. "What thoughts must through the creature's brain have past! — 203 *Hart-leap* 141
Upon the Creature's back, and plied — 241 *P. B.* 398
They bind the unoffending creature's brows — 318 **In due* 6
Upon the happy Creature's face. — 414 *White Doe* 1664
Is in the thankful Creature's power. — 506 *Lab. Hymn* 12
Love for the human creature's absolute self, — 701 *Prelude* 8. 123
Creatures. For creatures doomed to breathe terrestrial air: — 22 *Desc. Sk.* 647
The weakest of God's creatures, stand resolved — 65 *Bord.* 1518
Alone but for a swarm of minute creatures — 68 *Bord.* 1725
Link her with the inferior creatures, — 94 *Westmoreland Girl* 47
If we are creatures of a *winter's* day; — 110 **Look at* 9
Two separate Creatures in their several gifts — 118 *Maternal Grief* 30
Once more, those creatures thus by nature paired, — 143 **High bliss* 23
Say, when the *moving* creatures saw — 154 *Flower Garden* 7
Even as these blissful creatures do I fare; — 195 *Resolution* 32
For the unoffending creatures whom he loves. — 203 *Hart-leap* 168
Hear not we, unthinking Creatures! — 209 **Yes, it* 10
All creatures met in peace, from fierceness free, — 227 *Vernal Ode* 127
Speak, silent creatures.—They are gone, are fled, — 230 *Clouds* 30
Could humanize the creatures of the sea, — 234 *Power of Sound* 132
And trust that spiritual Creatures round us move, — 273 **When Philoctetes* 9

Creatures—*continued.*
“ The creatures see of flood and field, 291 *Rob Roy* 33
“ All kinds, and creatures, stand and fall 291 *Rob Roy* 49
For those offensive creatures shun 299 *Brownie's Cell* 77
Post forward all, like creatures of one kind, 303 **Is it* 5
Mute are all creatures, as this couchant fawn, 360 **Long has* 5
His rank 'mong freeborn creatures that live free, 389 *Eagles* 13
Of the sharp winds;—fair Creatures!—to whom Heaven 395 *White Doe: Ded.* 47
Bold as if men and creatures of the Deep 466 *St. Bees* 20
For all His creatures; and in Him, 498 **The sylvan* 28
Merciful over all his creatures, just 500 *Humanity* 45
But unoffending creatures find release 501 *Humanity* 59
All creatures and all objects, in degree, 501 *Humanity* 103
Creatures—how precious in the Maiden's sight! 540 *Grace Darl.* 38
A waste where creatures bearing human form, 585 *Ch. Lamb* 69
Ye blessèd Creatures, I have heard the call 588 *Immortality* 36
With all his creatures sink—to rise no more. 617 *Desc.Sk.Quarto* 809
For ruminating creatures; a domain 655 *Prelude* 3. 436
Dumb creatures find him tender as a nun, 670 *Prelude* 5. 306
The inferior creatures, beast or bird, attuned 704 *Prelude* 8. 357
A brood of gallant creatures, on the deep; 722 *Prelude* 10. 318
Creatures of one ethereal substance met 725 *Prelude* 10. 520
More perfectly of purer creatures;—yet 735 *Prelude* 12. 69
Towards them and to all creatures. God delights 736 *Prelude* 12. 171
The outside of her creatures, and to breathe 744 *Prelude* 13. 285
And joyous creatures; see that pair, the lamb 748 *Prelude* 14. 172
Had sprung, like those bright creatures, from the soil 790 *Excursion* 3. 251
The tiny creatures strong by social league; 807 *Excursion* 4. 432
Creatures that in communities exist 807 *Excursion* 4. 440
On creatures less intelligent and shrewd. 834 *Excursion* 5. 819
Among her higher creatures born and trained 835 *Excursion* 5. 848
For mortal creatures, conquered and secured. 839 *Excursion* 6. 87
And, verily, the silent creatures made 882 *Excursion* 8. 568
Which we, thy humble Creatures, here convened, 893 *Excursion* 9. 623
Drive one of these poor creatures miles and miles, K.8. 228 **I will* 124
We to the patient creatures carried food K.8. 247 *Recluse* 1.1.398
Wild creatures, and of many homes, that come K.8. 251 *Recluse* 1.1.540
Crecy. Perhaps at earlier Crecy, or Poictiers. 184 *Yew-trees* 8
Credible. Numbers exceeding credible account 347 *Processions* 51
Credit. He does his Master credit. As I live, 45 *Bord.* 459
When You might read, my credit would be gone. 522 *Epist. Beaumont* 88
Like credit to ourselves where less was due, 728 *Prelude* 11. 49
Credulities. Those old credulities, to nature dear, 359 **Those old* 1
Her flight before the bold credulities 468 *St. Bees* 161
Credulous. *See* **Too-credulous.**
In silent rapture, credulous desire 231 *Clouds* 89
Which moonlit elves, far seen by credulous eyes, 387 **Part fenced* 4
Moulding the credulous people to his will. 425 *Ecc. Sonn.* 1. 28. 5
Creed. To let a creed, built in the heart of things, 59 *Bord.* 1219
The faith Heaven strengthens where *he* moulds the Creed. 112 **O dearer* 16
In a sensual creed that trampled 141 *Arm. Lady* 81
Small difference lies between thy creed and mine: 203 *Hart-leap* 162
A Pagan suckled in a creed outworn; 259 **The world is* 10
Or is it but a groundless creed? 289 *Glen-Al.* 18
He sought his moral creed. 291 *Rob Roy* 20
Come ye—whate'er your creed—O waken all, 310 *Invasion* 15
The course of things, and change the creed 312 **Who rises* 62
Be just, be grateful; nor, the oppressor's creed 327 **Emperors and* 12
“ Charity never faileth: ” on that creed, 393 *Countess' Pillar* 6
To Creed or Ritual brings no fatal change. 426 *Ecc. Sonn.* 1. 31. 14
Bowing with reverence to the ancient creed, 444 *Ecc. Sonn.* 3. 15. 3
Of true compassion greet them. Creed and test 449 *Ecc. Sonn.* 3. 36. 9
Wher elies the truth? has Man, in wisdom's creed, 461 **Where lies the truth* 1
Live in the spirit of this creed; 492 *Duty* 23
So taught *their* creed;—nor failed the eastern sky, 534 **When in* 17
Delight and liberty, the simple creed 589 *Immortality* 140
This was her creed, and therefore she was pure 670 *Prelude* 5. 279
And what they do and suffer for their creed; 715 *Prelude* 9. 374
A hope it is, and a desire; a creed 715 *Prelude* 9. 405
Seemed but conversion to a higher creed; 722 *Prelude* 10. 310
Wanted not consolations, nor a creed 724 *Prelude* 10. 440
Hopeful prognostications from a creed, 775 *Excursion* 2. 259
“ Here then we rest; not fearing for our creed 804 *Excursion* 4. 197
Creeds. Decay and languish; or, as creeds 228 *Devot. Incit.* 48
When laws, and creeds, and people all are lost! 421 *Ecc. Sonn.* 1. 12. 14
Dragging all precepts, judgments, maxims, creeds, 731 *Prelude* 11. 294
Religion hailed her creeds by war restored, L.1. 97 *Juvenal* 3. 65
Creek. Near Portland lighthouse in a lonesome creek, 35 *Guilt* 592
Of aught transacted there in bay or creek; 522 *Epist. Beaumont* 80
A creek in the vast sea; for, all degrees 657 *Prelude* 3. 591
And intricate recesses, creek or bay 702 *Prelude* 8. 195
To loiter wilfully within a creek, 717 *Prelude* 9. 562
Our pinnace moves; then, coasting creek and bay, 892 *Excursion* 9. 561
Creeks. Through rocky passes, among flowery creeks, 268 **Brook! whose* 4
The sands of Westmoreland, the creeks and bays 640 *Prelude* 1. 567
O happy Thing! among thy flowery creeks, K.8. 265 **Brook, that* 4
Creep. Soft o'er the surface creep those lustres pale 7 *Ev. Wk.* 295
Creep hushed into the tranquil breast of death. 8 *Ev. Wk.* 354
As up the opposing hills they slowly creep. 12 *Desc. Sk.* 96
There, over rock or sloping pasture creep. 14 *Desc. Sk.* 215
Up from the lake a zigzag path will creep 14 *Desc. Sk.* 236
Or distant herds that pasturing upward creep, 16 *Desc. Sk.* 350
Alas! I creep so slowly. Never fear; 43 *Bord.* 358
The happy man will creep about the fields, 97 *Brothers* 108
Into thy bosom we again shall creep. 107 *Farewell* 64
Up from the eartht hese mosses creep, 197 *Thorn* 16
Takest away, andi nto souls dost creep, 253 **Fond words* 8
To muse, to creep, to halt at will, to gaze— 335 *Rhine* 11

Creep—*continued.*
Shall a few partial breezes only creep?— 366 **Fair Land* 11
No vestige now remains; yet thither creep 387 **Part fenced* 6
The greyhounds to their kennel creep; 406 *White Doe* 952
Creep round its arms through centuries unborn. 450 *Ecc. Sonn.* 3. 40. 14
And now with thankful heart to bed doth creep, 453 **Calm is the* 18
Through which the waters creep, then disappear, 465 **The cattle* 4
Drawn toward the centre whence those sighs creep forth 498 **Enough of climbing* 39
Or mountain rivers, where they creep 499 *Memory* 27
Wants not a healing influence that can creep 501 **The unremitting* 10
When he could creep about, at will, though poor 531 **I know* 5
Creep forth, and through the forest wind 543 *Russ. Fug.* 123
Forbade the weeds to creep o'er its grey line. 549 **The massy* 10
Soft o'er the surface creep the lustres pale 598 *Ev. Wk. Quarto* 343
As up th' opposing hills, with tortoise foot, they creep. 604 *Desc.Sk.Quarto* 105
Nought but the herds that pasturing upward creep, 610 *Desc.Sk.Quarto* 426
That creep along the ground with sinuous trail, 860 *Excursion* 7. 182
May creep (I wish that they would softly creep) 868 *Excursion* 7. 708
Creeping. This mortal stupor which is creeping over me, 51 *Bord.* 777
“ What ails you, that you must come creeping to me!” 116 *Repentance* 20
And what the creeping breeze that comes 200 *Thorn* 201
Now creeping on his hands and knees, 243 *P. B.* 644
Or creeping worm, with sensitive respect. 270 **Though the bold* 8
Thence creeping under sylvan arches cool, 424 *Ecc. Sonn.* 1. 22. 7
Indulging thus at will the creeping feet 424 *Ecc. Sonn.* 1. 23. 2
When darkness creeping o'er thy silver brow 460 **Queen of* 3
Wafted o'er waves, or creeping through close trees, 466 *St. Bees* 53
Warmed by thy influence, creeping things 506 **While from* 27
And spread them with a wider creeping; felt 650 *Prelude* 3. 115
Came creeping over me, when at my side, 666 *Prelude* 5. 74
Beginning timidly, then creeping fast, 707 *Prelude* 8. 579
And softly creeping, like a breath of air, 787 *Excursion* 3. 71
Up from the creeping plant to sovereign Man. 806 *Excursion* 4. 343
In creeping sadness, through oblivious shades 818 *Excursion* 4. 1124
Creeping his gait and cowering, his lip pale, 879 *Excursion* 8. 311
Creeps. That creeps along the bells of the crisp heather. 60 *Bord.* 1264
In flashing leaps and stealthy creeps 190 **Lyre! though* 31
Thence back into the moonlight creeps; 243 *P. B.* 639
He raves, or through some moody passage creeps 476 *Nunnery* 4
And he creeps to the edge of my stove. 484 **A plague* 10
Thy help is with the weed that creeps 507 *May* 41
He softly creeps—'tis Goody Blake; 537 *Goody Blake* 79
This old Man creeps, the villagers in him 567 *Cumb. Beg.* 88
There with his infants man undaunted creeps 607 *Desc.Sk.Quarto* 293
—I see him, up the midway cliff he creeps 610 *Desc.Sk.Quarto* 470
Crept. Or as the wily sailors crept 297 *Highland Boy* 191
Deep in its tomb:—the bramble crept 390 *HighlandBroach* 32
That, in the lapse of ages, hath crept o'er 419 *Ecc. Sonn.* 1. 3. 6
And crept along a ridge of fractured wall, 678 *Prelude* 6. 214
Who crept along fitting her languid gait 717 *Prelude* 9. 511
A heart-felt chilliness crept along my veins. 765 *Excursion* 1. 619
Now faint,—the grass has crept o'er its grey line; 769 *Excursion* 1. 883
Dimness o'er this clear luminary crept 795 *Excursion* 3. 670
To tinge his cheek; and through his frame it crept 840 *Excursion* 6. 157
Crescent. So gleams the crescent moon, that loves 222 *Triad* 189
The crescent moon clove with its glittering prow 270 **Shame on* 4
Against the Moorish crescent. 287 *Ellen Irwin* 40
The Cross shall spread, the Crescent hath waxed dim; 326 *Sobieski* 12
Where unremitting frosts the rocky crescent bleach. 335 *Aix* 14
And cirque and crescent framed by wall 407 *White Doe* 987
The Crescent glitters on the towers of Spain; 427 *Ecc. Sonn.* 1. 34. 3
In his mind's eye thy crescent horns ascend, 460 **Wanderer! that* 71
Who *then*, if Dian's crescent gleamed, 497 *Lycoris* 5
Crescent in simple loveliness serene, 509 *F. Stone* 47
Young, like the Crescent that above me shone, 532 **Once I* 7
Within the crescent of a pleasant bay, 644 *Prelude* 2. 139
Up towards the crescent moon, with grateful heart 814 *Excursion* 4. 862
Crescent-moon. Shaped like the crescent-moon. 236 *P. B.* 5
In shape a very crescent-moon: 236 *P. B.* 7
As is the crescent-moon so bright 236 *P. B.* 29
A Boat twin-sister of the crescent-moon! 237 *P. B.* 80
The Crescent-moon, the Star of Love, 459 **The Crescent* 1
Crescent's. (Who loves the Cross, yet to the Crescent's gleam 336 *Danube* 3
Cresid. Whence Cresid rode, as if in haste she was; 563 *Troilus* 86
Cresida. We must the Palace see of Cresida; 562 *Troilus* 5
That Cresida again thou send me soon. 563 *Troilus* 77
Cresid's. And they right forth to Cresid's Palace went; 562 *Troilus* 10
Heard my own Cresid's laugh; and once at play 563 *Troilus* 51
Cresset. And as a cresset true that darts its length 466 *St. Bees* 41
Cressets. By cressets and love-beacons, intercourse 716 *Prelude* 9. 489
Cressy. In fields that rival Cressy and Poictiers— 432 *Ecc. Sonn.* 2. 16. 6
Crest. A crest of purple tops the warrior's head. 5 *Ev. Wk.* 149
'Mid groves of clouds that crest the mountain's brow, 7 *Ev. Wk.* 289
Yet like a star, with glittering crest, 159 **With little* 37
And made a gallant crest. 192 *Ruth* 24
And, with his dancing crest, 193 *Ruth* 117
Time pressing on with starry crest 223 *Wishing-gate* 70
Of Britain's realm, whose leafy crest 226 *Vernal Ode* 19
—By planting on thy naked head the crest 253 **Aerial Rock* 7
And upward, high as Malvern's cloudy crest; 267 *St. Cath.* 4
Yon grey tower's living crest! 300 *Cora Linn* 24
A crest of blooming heather! 302 *Yarrow V.* 68
Meanwhile, and be to her a glorious crest 303 **Fair Star* 5

Crimson—*continued.*
This undeparting Flower in crimson dyed, 170 *Never enlivened 23
Chasing a crimson butterfly; 191 Beggars 22
Misgiving, while the crimson day 223 Wishing-gate 65
Or in the dust, a crimson stain. 244 P. B. 720
So snugly for that crimson stain, 245 P. B. 803
In crimson stockings, tartan plaid, 295 Highland Boy 32
And lo! with crimson banners proudly streaming, 324 Ode 1814 53
War's favourite playground, are with crimson stains 335 Namur 3
A crimson splendour: lowly is the mast 384 Duddon 33. 3
Behind her hill the Moon, all crimson, rides, 606 Desc.Sk.Quarto 235
And pure as dew bathing their crimson leaves. 773 Excursion 2. 110
Changed to a crimson flower; when he, whose pride S.3. 434 *The doubt 82
Crimson-spotted. Large store of gleaming crimson-spotted trouts; 882 Excursion 8. 558
Cripple. Mark that Cripple who leans on his crutch; like a tower 189 Music 37
A friendless Man, a travelling Cripple! 621 Andrew Jones 10
But the poor Cripple was alone 621 Andrew Jones 14
So with his staff the Cripple wrought 621 Andrew Jones 18
The Cripple in the mid-day heat 621 Andrew Jones 23
And when the Cripple nearer drew, 621 Andrew Jones 27
Was One, a Cripple from his birth, whom chance 688 Prelude 7. 91
A travelling cripple, by the trunk cut short, 690 Prelude 7. 203
On which the cripple, in the quarry maimed, K.8. 250 Recluse 1.1.508
Crippled. Is crippled sore in his narration. 248 P. B. 1035
Or crippled mendicant in soldier's garb, 769 Excursion 1. 889
Crippling. The hour of accident or crippling age, 764 Excursion 1. 555
Crisis. This was the crisis of that strong disease, 731 Prelude 11. 306
Crisp. That creeps along the bells of the crisp heather. 60 Bord. 1264
There to alight upon crisp moss and range, 353 Aquap. 38
Crisp, yellow leaves my bed; the hooting owl 424 Ecc. Sonn. 1. 22. 11
And crisp with frost the stubble land. 537 Goody Blake 76
Critic. Scorn not the Sonnet; Critic, you have frowned, 260 *Scorn not 1
And the small critic wielding his delicate pen, 569 Farmer 3
Criticised. Probed, vexed, and criticised?—Accuse me not 816 Excursion 4. 978
Critics. In fear that else, when Critics grave and cool 277 *A Poet 7
Critics, right honourable Bard, decree S.3.432 *Critics, right 1
Croak. Blithe ravens croak of death; and when the owl 153 Morn. Ex. 7
Two ravens now began to croak 157 Oak and Broom 96
The crags repeat the raven's croak, 491 Fidelity 27
Croaks. Perched on whose top the Danish Raven croaks; 380 Duddon 17. 2
The raven croaks, and fills the upper air K.8. 252 Recluse 1.1.581
Crocodile. There, combats a huge crocodile—agape 348 Sky-prosp. 5
Crocus. The last autumnal crocus, 'twas my joy 636 Prelude 1. 309
Croft. "A little croft we owned—a plot of corn, 28 Guilt 208
The heifer in yon little croft belongs K.8. 251 Recluse 1.1.524
Crofts. A few small crofts of stone-encumbered ground; 835 Excursion 5. 864
Croglin. CROGLIN, the stately Eden's tributary! 476 Nunnery 3
Cromlech. A Druid cromlech!—thus I entertain 788 Excursion 3. 133
Crook. *See* **Nutting-crook.**
He hath thrown aside his crook, 205 Brougham 140
Enough of garlands, of the Arcadian crook, 389 Tyndrum 1
Or staff more harmless than a shepherd's crook, 423 Ecc. Sonn. 1. 21. 3
And he who guides the plough, or wields the crook, 435 Ecc. Sonn. 2. 29. 4
To entwine the crook of eloquence that helped 695 Prelude 7. 570
Thirsting to make the guardian crook of law 728 Prelude 11. 64
And patient spade; praise to the simple crook, 831 Excursion 5. 603
The crook into a sceptre; give the pomp 846 Excursion 6. 550
Crooked. Companionship with One of crooked ways, 37 Bord. 8
To ecstasy; and all the crooked paths 804 Excursion 4. 183
Have ye withdrawn from passion's crooked ways, 827 Excursion 5. 354
Crop. *See* **Stone-crop.**
With other burthens than the crop it bore. 98 Brothers 212
A melancholy crop: 197 Thorn 15
Nor once turns round his head to crop 244 P. B. 714
The herds and flocks are yet abroad to crop 823 Excursion 5. 70
Cropped. And without wrong are cropped the marble tomb to strew. 222 Triad 211
Cropping. Is cropping audibly his later meal: 1 Early Youth 4
Cropping the shrubs of Leming-Lane, 249 P. B. 1128
'Cross. *See* **Across.**
'Cross the calm lake's blue shades the cliffs aspire, 5 Ev. Wk. 174
One I behold who, 'cross the foaming flood, 17 Desc. Sk. 380
I had led him 'cross the torrent, his voice blessed me: 51 Bord. 745
'Cross the brook its thoughtless dam. 93 Westmoreland Girl 4
He 'cross the ocean came. 192 Ruth 30
'Cross the tempestuous torrent; so he stood K.8. 229 *I will 156
Cross. *See* **Death-cross, Red-cross.**
The Cross, by angels planted on the aerial rock. 11 Desc. Sk. 70
That in the shape of man do cross our path 74 Bord. 2084
And he is dead!—that Moor—how shall I cross it? 76 Bord. 2238
"Cross, if you dare, where I shall cross— 85 Shepherd-boys 45
Some limber twigs into a Cross, well-shaped with fingers nice, 91 Norman Boy 19
That Cross he now was fastening there, as the surest power and best 91 Norman Boy 21
That Cross belike he also raised as a standard for the true 91 Norman Boy 25
The Cross, fixed in his soul, may prove an all-sufficing stay. 91 Norman Boy 32
And in His sight the fragile Cross, on thy small hut, will be 93 Poet's Dream 59

Cross—*continued.*
Mix with the day, and cross the hour of rest; 112 *O dearer 6
Nought but the world-redeeming Cross 113 Lament 61
A thousand, if they cross our way. 179 Waggoner 3. 117
The mountain when to cross. 198 Thorn 59
'Mid trivial care and petty cross 224 *'Tis gone 38
The cross upon thy shoulder scored, 247 P. B. 973
Hence am I cross and peevish as a child: 253 *O gentle 10
Swept onwards, did the vision cross your view? 283 *Proud were 10
All vanished;—'twas a heartfelt cross 297 Highland Boy 213
In choral song; and, while the uplifted cross 318 *In due 9
And the red cross on my breast; 323 Ode 1814 32
The Cross shall spread, the Crescent hath waxed dim; 326 Sobieski 12
While the Sun rules, and cross the shades of night— 327 Ode 1815 32
(Who loves the Cross, yet to the Crescent's gleam 336 Danube 3
Hail to the firm unmoving cross, 337 Cath. Cantons 9
The Cross, in calm procession, borne aloft 346 Processions 39
For safety, they of yore enclasped the Cross 357 Aquap. 301
Of purposes which no false thought shall cross, 373 Eg. Maid 263
Ours couch on naked rocks,—will cross a brook 389 Tyndrum 4
Or altar, whence the cross was rent, 397 White Doe 124
The sacred Cross; and figured there 400 White Doe 356
And the sacred Cross on which Jesus died. 403 White Doe 663
In that other day of Neville's Cross? 405 White Doe 828
This Cross in tears: by her, and One 405 White Doe 879
Or let them cross the River Tweed, 408 White Doe 1099
Druids descend, auxiliars of the Cross; 421 Ecc. Sonn. 1. 10. 11
And blest the silver Cross, which ye, instead 422 Ecc. Sonn. 1. 14. 3
The Cross preceding Him who floats in air, 422 Ecc. Sonn. 1. 14. 5
Yet will we not conceal the precious Cross, 450 Ecc. Sonn. 3. 40. 9
Melts, if it cross the threshold; where the wreath 452 Ecc. Sonn. 3. 45. 6
The silent Cross, among the stars shall spread 452 Ecc. Sonn. 3. 45. 11
(Too busy fear!) shall cross its range, 503 Warning 8
There lived, and on the cross His life resigned, 534 *When in 14
In Malta the white symbol of the Cross: 575 Chiabrera 6. 3
Comes in the promise from the Cross, 578 *I come 71
The mountain will we cross." 580 John Words. 60
Beside their sheltering cross of wall, the flock 593 Ev. Wk. Quarto 117
The cross with hideous laughter Demons mock, 603 Desc. Sk. Quarto 70
And watch, while on your brows the cross ye make, 614 Desc.Sk.Quarto 674
A silver cross enchased with Flowers of France 628 Eagle and Dove 11
Seeking I knew not what, I chanced to cross 672 Prelude 5. 432
Of the same isthmus, which our spirits cross 673 Prelude 5. 536
The cross of Jesus stand erect, as if 682 Prelude 6. 484
Sweet coverts did we cross of pastoral life, 682 Prelude 6. 500
Above all height! like an aerial cross 703 Prelude 8. 273
Grieved, and the twilight taper, and the cross 716 Prelude 9. 475
That did but *cross* a lonely road, and now 732 Prelude 11. 338
Fixed on the Cross, that consolation springs, 770 Excursion 1. 937
Some boundary, which his followers may not cross 798 Excursion 3. 878
The cross itself, at whose unconscious feet 827 Excursion 5. 337
In him who bled for man upon the cross; 836 Excursion 5. 907
Altar, and cross, and church of solemn roof, 873 Excursion 7. 1024
Upon the cross, this marvellous advance 895 Excursion 9. 722
Thou good and faithful servant of the Cross." K.8. 325 [?] *The vestal 14
But here's a thought which well our thought may cross L.1. 95 Juvenal 3. 14
Cross-bones. Cross-bones nor skull,—type of our earthly state 98 Brothers 171
Cross-crowned. For bodied forth before my eyes the cross-crowned hut appeared; 91 Poet's Dream 6
Crossed. *See* **Crost.**
Even so the dire phantasma which had crossed 26 Guilt 94
Then pity crossed the path of my resolve: 77 Bord. 2265
And, when I crossed the wild, 82 Lucy Gray 2
And then an open field they crossed: 83 Lucy Gray 49
Was sadly crossed.—Poor Leonard! when we parted, 100 Brothers 321
And wicked fancies crossed my mind; 115 Last of Flock 72
She with her mother crossed the sea; 121 Emigrant Mother 69
Uncharitable crossed his mind, no sense 124 V. and J. 168
And while she crossed the bridge, there came 128 Idiot Boy 212
To Scotland's heaths; or those that crossed the sea 184 Yew-trees 6
Had crossed the Atlantic main. 194 Ruth 168
Had crossed her purpose with some quaint vagary, 222 Triad 171
The mead is crossed—the quarry's mouth 243 P. B. 607
By love, long crossed with adverse circumstance. 278 *Lo! where she 8
And crossed by many a shattered scheme, 342 Ital. Itin. 28
Like spiteful Fiends that vanish, crossed 369 Eg. Maid 34
Full thrice had crossed himself in meek composure. 373 Eg. Maid 276
Crossed ever and anon by plank or arch; 378 Duddon 9. 3
Have helped us: Ure we crossed, and Swale, 402 White Doe 608
Out of his heart, or crossed his thought, 406 White Doe 978
Fair Vision! when it crossed the Maid 415 White Doe 1738
Nor long (that crossed) would Grecian hills detain 427 Ecc. Sonn. 1. 34. 7
Is crossed by knowledge, or by dread, of change, 458 Sea-shore 18
Or crossed by vapoury streaks and clouds that move 459 *Wanderer! that 35
Tempestuous winds her holy errand crossed: 466 St. Bees 33
Crossed by misfortune, or of doubted faith? 508 F. Stone 45
But, if no evil hap his wishes crossed, 531 *I know 26
The billows lengthening, mutually crossed 541 Grace Darl. 54
Till they have crossed the quaking marsh, 543 Russ. Fug. 127
That crossed her way. Now stoops she to entreat 626 Ballot 5
Mine eyes were crossed by butterflies, ears vexed 655 Prelude 3. 443
Was crossed, a bare ridge clomb, upon whose top 658 Prelude 4. 3
In their true dwelling; now is crossed by gleam 662 Prelude 4. 267
Ended in this,—*that we had crossed the Alps.* 684 Prelude 6. 591
We crossed the Brabant armies on the fret 686 Prelude 6. 764

Dam—*continued.*
'Cross the brook its thoughtless dam. — 93 *Westmoreland Girl* 4
That bleat, how tender! of the dam — 232 *Power of Sound* 23
Left in the fabric of a leaky dam — 789 *Excursion* 3. 203

Damage. Who will gladly repair all the damage that's done; — 572 *Avarice* 43

Damaged. In the condition of a damaged seed, — 799 *Excursion* 3. 889

Dame. *See* **Cottage-dame, Step-dame.**
Good Dame, repair to Liddesdale and wait — 46 *Bord.* 516
Him never saw I nor the spot; but from an English Dame, — 91 *Norman Boy* 5
St. Denis, filled with royal tombs, or the Church of Notre Dame? — 92 *Poet's Dream* 24
Where sits the Dame, and wears away — 144 **Driven in* 77
By exhortation of my frugal Dame— — 185 *Nutting* 11
"There sits the Vicar and his Dame; — 238 *P. B.* 166
A poor old Dame will bless them for the boon: — 280 **Intent on* 3
"Thou hast achieved, fair Dame! what none — 371 *Eg. Maid* 153
Was thus accosted by the Dame: — 371 *Eg. Maid* 167
Worn at the breast of some grave Dame — 390 *Highland Broach* 20
So thinks that Dame of haughty air, — 399 *White Doe* 258
Then at her door the *canty* Dame — 536 *Goody Blake* 39
Of those soft starry nights, and that old Dame — 642 *Prelude* 2. 43
To furnish treats more costly than the Dame — 643 *Prelude* 2. 87
From my old Dame, so kind and motherly, — 658 *Prelude* 4. 28
Too full for that reproach. My aged Dame — 659 *Prelude* 4. 64
This chiefly, did I note my grey-haired Dame; — 661 *Prelude* 4. 217
The military Idler, and the Dame, — 690 *Prelude* 7. 209
Solemn or gay: whether some beauteous dame — 693 *Prelude* 7. 413
Hath not completed since our dame, the queen — 783 *Excursion* 2. 775
Dame Nature's pupil of the lowest form, — 789 *Excursion* 3. 198
At any moment may the Dame be found, — 833 *Excursion* 5. 706
The Dame returned. Or ere that glowing pile — 834 *Excursion* 5. 771
For, as reports the dame, whose fire sends up — K.8. 247 *Recluse* 1.1.389

Dames. The Miller with two Dames, on the breast of the Thames! — 166 *Stray Pleasures* 4
The Dames resemble whom we here behold, — 333 *Fish-women* 5
Awe-stricken stood both Knights and Dames — 372 *Eg. Maid* 193
Two poor old Dames, as I have known, — 536 *Goody Blake* 34
All white with flour, the dole of village dames, — 566 *Cumb. Beg.* 9
Nor safe the petticoats of dames that hear — L.1. 95 *Juvenal* 3. 12

Damn. Prime mover in a plot to damn his Victim — 57 *Bord.* 1064
Who damn where they can neither see nor feel, — 64 *Bord.* 1504

Damning. Makes up one damning falsehood. Leave him here — 62 *Bord.* 1398

Damp. Protected from this cold damp air?" — 119 *Sailor's Mother* 16
From damp, and rain, and cold. — 194 *Ruth* 234
To struggle through dark ways; and when a damp — 260 **Scorn not* 11
Sullenly glaring through sepulchral damp, — 266 **Even as* 3
The captive 'mid damp vaults unsunned, unaired, — 273 **Not the* 5
He breathes a subterraneous damp; — 294 *Jedbor.* 27
Fills many a damp obscure recess — 397 *White Doe* 101
And damp those yearnings which had once been mine— — 662 *Prelude* 4. 289
Joined in a cold damp nook, espied a well — 763 *Excursion* 1. 461
With searching damp, and seemingly had lain — 778 *Excursion* 2. 440
A brighter joy; and through such damp and gloom — K.8. 237 *Recluse* 1.1. 52

Damped. *See* **Dew-damped.**
Though inward anguish damped the Sailor's brow, — 33 *Guilt* 485
At large and unrestrained, nor damped too soon — 751 *Prelude* 14. 361
And oak whose roots by noontide dew were damped, — 866 *Excursion* 7. 600

Damps. Alive!—the damps of death were upon him— — 72 *Bord.* 1979
Tho' searching damps and many an envious flaw — 342 *Last Sup.* 1
It neither damps the gay, nor checks the witty. — 475 *Greenock* 8
When sorrow damps it, or, whatever look — 660 *Prelude* 4. 147
Was sapped; and while she slept, the nightly damps — 770 *Excursion* 1. 907
And damps, through all the droughty summer day — 835 *Excursion* 5. 874

Dams. In presence of their heedless dams, — 217 *Enterprise* 139
Couch near their dams, with quiet satisfied; — 278 **Life with* 6

Damsel. "Nay," said I, "more than half to the damsel must belong, — 88 *Pet-lamb* 66
Fairest damsel of the green, — 90 *Longest Day* 70
Her freight, it was a Damsel peerless; — 370 *Eg. Maid* 80
The Damsel, in that trance embound; — 371 *Eg. Maid* 141
Whereon diffused like snow the Damsel lay, — 373 *Eg. Maid* 275
Fair Damsel! o'er my captive mind, — 530 *Gleaner* 22

Damsel's. Of colour dawned upon the Damsel's cheek; — 374 *Eg. Maid* 328

Damsels. *See* **Harvest-damsels.**
A place of love for damsels that are coy. — 201 *Hart-leap* 60
The priests and damsels of Ammonian Jove — 346 *Processions* 21
Certes were self-taught damsels, scattered births — S.3. 436 **The doubt* 153

Dance. While unsuspended wheels the village dance, — 11 *Desc. Sk.* 39
Lip-dewing song, and ringlet-tossing dance; — 13 *Desc. Sk.* 132
Is one of giant stature, who could dance — 111 **'Tis said that some* 46
How they in sprightly dance are worn — 164 **Fair Lady* 5
They dance,—there are three, as jocund as free, — 166 *Stray Pleasures* 17
While they dance on the calm river's breast. — 166 *Stray Pleasures* 18
While they dance, crying, "Long as ye please!" — 167 *Stray Pleasures* 24
They dance not for me, — 167 *Stray Pleasures* 25
That blew us hither!—let him dance, — 177 *Waggoner* 2. 44
'Tis who can dance with greatest vigour— — 177 *Waggoner* 2. 64
They hear—when every dance is done, — 177 *Waggoner* 2. 95
Where rivulets dance their wayward round, — 187 **Three years* 28
Tossing their heads in sprightly dance. — 187 **I wandered* 12
Who quit their fold with dance and shout, — 193 *Ruth* 50
So tripped the Muse, inventress of the dance; — 221 *Triad* 105
Rein the proud steed or through the dance are led; — 273 **While Anna's* 4

Dance—*continued.*
And bid them dance, and bid them sing; — 293 *Jedbor.* 3
But dance! for under Jedborough Tower — 293 *Jedbor.* 8
And she will dance and sing with thee. — 293 *Jedbor.* 12
And heard the billows leap and dance, — 296 *Highland Boy* 93
Knit the blithe dance upon the soft green grass; — 322 **Ye Storms* 9
Amid this dance of objects sadness steals — 335 *Rhine* 1
Nor to her was the dance of soft pleasure unknown: — 340 *Fort Fuentes* 14
Not so that Pair whose youthful spirits dance — 378 *Duddon* 10. 1
Dance, like a Bacchanal, from rock to rock, — 381 *Duddon* 20. 13
Enter in dance. Of church, or sabbath ties, — 387 **Part fenced* 5
In dance, amid a press — 499 **This Lawn* 3
Rash Polity begin her maniac dance, — 504 *Warning* 64
Of song and dance and game; — 506 **While from* 44
To mingle in the rustic dance, — 544 *Russ. Fug.* 247
Lo, yonder saw I mine own Lady dance, — 563 *Troilus* 47
And feast and dance, and public revelry, — 662 *Prelude* 4. 282
Floating in dance, or warbling high in air — 689 *Prelude* 7. 125
On strangers, of all ages; the quick dance — 689 *Prelude* 7. 154
Would leave behind a dance of images, — 700 *Prelude* 8. 114
Tales of the May-pole dance, and wreaths that decked — 701 *Prelude* 8. 151
Looks out, and all the pastures dance with lambs, — 702 *Prelude* 8. 230
For his own fancies, or to dance by the hour, — 703 *Prelude* 8. 286
Of Satyrs in some viewless glade, with dance — 716 *Prelude* 9. 459
With present objects, and the busy dance — 740 *Prelude* 13. 30
Of fine demeanour, and by dance and song, — 843 *Excursion* 6. 308
Permit, like honours, dance and song, are paid — 851 *Excursion* 6. 836
Around whose trunk the maidens dance in May— — 866 *Excursion* 7. 621
Is a perpetual harmony, and dance — K.8. 242 *Recluse* 1.1. 202
And lilies that will dance upon the waves. — K.8. 252 *Recluse* 1.1. 591

Danced. "The suns of twenty summers danced along,— — 28 *Guilt* 226
The waves beside them danced; but they — 187 **I wandered* 13
Had danced his round with Highland lasses; — 239 *P. B.* 223
I've played, I've danced, with my narration; — 245 *P. B.* 791
The waves danced round us as before, — 343 *Eclipse* 14
And sky that danced among those leaves, are still; — 456 **The leaves* 2
Danc'd to the murmuring rill on Lomond's wave, — 630 [?] **O Moon* 2
And, hand in hand, danced round and round the board; — 681 *Prelude* 6. 400
And round and round the board we danced again. — 681 *Prelude* 6. 406
Together danced, Queen of the feast, and King; — 701 *Prelude* 8. 143
Such fate was hers.—The last time Ellen danced, — 851 *Excursion* 6. 849
Danced in the breeze, chequering its mossy roof. — 860 *Excursion* 7. 203

Dancers. The dancers all were gathered round, — 178 *Waggoner* 2. 136
And with the dancers and the minstrel's song — 201 *Hart-leap* 71
And with the dancers and the minstrels' song — 202 *Hart-leap* 91
For dancers in the festive hall — 225 *Present.* 58

Dances. She dances, runs without an aim, — 81 †*Mother's Return* 32
And dances with the daffodils. — 187 **I wandered* 24
That ruled those dances wild in character?— — 378 *Duddon* 11. 11
That dances on the sea. — 487 **We walked* 52
Dances of liberty, and, in late hours — 680 *Prelude* 6. 371
Of darkness, dances in the open air — 680 *Prelude* 6. 372
By dances round its trunk.—And if the sky — 851 *Excursion* 6. 835

Dancing. And send ye dancing to the clouds, like leaves. — 54 *Bord.* 945
And the light dancing of the thoughtless heart; — 65 *Bord.* 1547
Were dancing to the minstrelsy. — 155 **A whirl-blast* 22
And dancing high and dancing low, — 155 *Waterfall* 8
A Brother of the dancing leaves; — 159 *Green Linnet* 34
Gambol like a dancing skiff, — 166 *Wand. Jew* 18
And they're dancing merrily. — 166 *Stray Pleasures* 6
Beheld a dancing—and a glancing; — 180 *Waggoner* 3. 140
A dancing Shape, an Image gay, — 186 **She was* 9
Fluttering and dancing in the breeze. — 187 **I wandered* 6
And, with his dancing crest, — 193 *Ruth* 117
Shot from the dancing Graces, as they move — 233 *Power of Sound* 79
And tracks thee dancing down thy water-breaks; — 268 **Brook! whose* 5
Erewhile within the dancing shell, — 297 *Highland Boy* 194
A gay saloon, with waters dancing — 300 *Bran* 13
The dancing Salii—on the shields of Mars — 346 *Processions* 32
With pleasure dancing through the frame — 348 **Lulled by* 14
Dancing with all their brilliant equipage — 378 *Duddon* 11. 5
Of dancing insects forged upon his breast; — 383 *Duddon* 28. 8
Where bubbles burst, and folly's dancing foam — 452 *Ecc. Sonn.* 3. 45. 5
Tremble on dancing waves and rippling streams — 460 **Queen of* 24
In all her brightness, from the dancing crest — 511 **Who rashly* 5
What is youth?—a dancing billow, — 549 *Hermit's Cell* 1. 29
Dancing and leaping light upon the spray; — 558 *Cuck. and Night.* 77
I sought thy golden vale with dancing flight, — 630 [?] **O Moon* 6
The night in dancing, gaiety, and mirth, — 663 *Prelude* 4. 312
Presents a company of dancing dogs, — 689 *Prelude* 7. 176
A meadow carpet for the dancing hours. — 830 *Excursion* 5. 551
Not like a dancing meteor, but in line — 833 *Excursion* 5. 746
The sportive sea-gull dancing with the waves, — 869 *Excursion* 7. 753
Dancing around her, hinder and disturb — 873 *Excursion* 7. 1035
And dipped my hand in dancing wave — S.3. 438 **My Lord* 15
And happy, dancing down thy water-breaks: — K.8. 265 **Brook, that* 5

Dandelion. Of dandelion seed or thistle's beard, — 148 **A narrow* 18

Dandelion's. That, from the dandelion's naked stalk, — 123 *V. and J.* 137

Dandles. While she dandles the Babe in her arms to the sound. — 189 *Music* 40

Dane. Fierceness and rage; and soon the cruel Dane — 426 *Ecc. Sonn.* 1. 29. 6
This just reproof the prosperous Dane — 495 *Fact* 15

Danger. You start—where are we? Oh, there is no danger; — 52 *Bord.* 837
Saved by courage that with danger — 93 *Westmoreland Girl* 21

Danger—*continued.*
Hoping the danger would be past; 155 *Waterfall* 18
Or for some other danger nigh? 174 *Waggoner* 1. 49
Here is no danger,—none at all! 174 *Waggoner* 1. 70
The danger is so great." 296 *Highland Boy* 90
Who are to judge of danger which they fear, 310 **Another year* 13
And darkness and danger had compassed him round, 364 *Vallomb.* 18
And the waves rose, and sky portended danger. 369 *Eg. Maid* 30
His own life into danger brought 411 *White Doe* 1408
Death, darkness, danger, are our natural lot; 423 *Ecc. Sonn.* 1. 18. 3
And some, too heedless of past danger, court 454 *Sea-side* 17
Through crags, and smoothing paths beset with danger, 477 *Nunnery* 10
Whom neither shape of danger can dismay, 494 *Hap. War.* 72
Ye weave—no danger from without, 526 **The soaring* 15
Though danger, as the Wreck is neared, becomes 541 *Grace Darl.* 62
Where danger roofs the narrow walks of death; 606 *Desc.Sk.Quarto* 246
Unmov'd with each rude form of Danger nigh, 607 *Desc.Sk.Quarto* 260
Whence Danger leans, and pointing ghastly, joys 610 *Desc.Sk.Quarto* 466
Of danger or desire; and thus did make 639 *Prelude* 1. 472
With danger, varying as the seasons change), 682 *Prelude* 6. 510
Above the press and danger of the crowd, 697 *Prelude* 7. 684
But images of danger and distress, 701 *Prelude* 8. 164
Disquiet, danger, and obscurity. 707 *Prelude* 8. 517
Sanctioned, of danger, difficulty, or death. 715 *Prelude* 9. 407
Safe from temptation, and from danger far? 794 *Excursion* 3. 567
Surpassed in strength, I heard of danger, met K.8. 256 *Recluse* 1.1.716
Dangerous. And, not untended, climb the dangerous steep. 16 *Desc. Sk.* 351
No matter—he's a dangerous Man.—That noise!— 43 *Bord.* 350
Here broke off the dangerous converse: 140 *Arm. Lady* 73
Might well be dangerous food 193 *Ruth* 123
Regent of sound, have dangerous Passions trod! 233 *Power of Sound* 82
Driving some vessel toward a dangerous beach— 336 *Staub-bach* 6
And sunshine to a dangerous strife; 400 *White Doe* 377
"To put your love to dangerous proof 542 *Russ. Fug.* 25
A dangerous neighbourhood; 542 *Russ. Fug.* 92
To guide his dangerous tread the taper's gleam. 607 *Desc.Sk.Quarto* 316
Hung dim-discover'd from the dangerous steep, 610 *Desc.Sk.Quarto* 427
The dangerous craft of culling term and phrase 676 *Prelude* 6. 110
From dangerous passions free. Three years had flown 688 *Prelude* 7. 65
Service however dangerous. I revolved, 720 *Prelude* 10. 154
Withal a season dangerous and wild, 722 *Prelude* 10. 311
In kind more dangerous. What had been a pride, 730 *Prelude* 11. 183
Danger's. The noise of danger's in your ears, 236 *P. B.* 13
Darkness before and danger's voice behind; 441 *Ecc. Sonn.* 3. 4. 8
At Danger's bidding, may confront the seas, 466 *St. Bees* 17
Darkness before, and danger's voice behind, 653 *Prelude* 3. 285
Dangers. He landed; and by many dangers scared, 103 *Artegal* 91
Thou to his dangers dost enchain 216 *Enterprise* 64
These hardships ill-sustained, these dangers past, 320 **Hunger, and* 4
When dangers threaten, dangers ever new! 425 *Ecc. Sonn.* 1. 27. 6
Dangle. Here files of ballads dangle from dead walls; 690 *Prelude* 7. 193
Dangled. From any garden scare-crow dangled. 82 *Alice Fell* 28
Dangling. With chattering monkeys dangling from their poles, 697 *Prelude* 7. 694
The faded garlands dangling from its sides. 773 *Excursion* 2. 137
Some in disgrace, hung dangling from the walls. 781 *Excursion* 2. 670
Daniel. Old Daniel his hand to the treasure will slide! 572 *Avarice* 19
Old Daniel begins; he stops short—and his eye, 572 *Avarice* 21
'Twas a path trod by thousands; but Daniel is one 572 *Avarice* 29
And now with old Daniel you see how it fares; 572 *Avarice* 31
Danish. The shadow of a Danish Boy. 165 *Danish Boy* 11
The Danish Boy walks here alone: 165 *Danish Boy* 21
—They hear the Danish Boy, 166 *Danish Boy* 42
The lovely Danish Boy is blest 166 *Danish Boy* 49
Perched on whose top the Danish Raven croaks; 380 *Duddon* 17. 2
The Danish Conqueror, on his royal chair, 495 *Fact* 1
In old time haunted by that Danish Witch, 707 *Prelude* 8. 563
Dank. Or where dank sea-weed lashes Scotland's shores; 21 *Desc. Sk.* 594
In her dank cleft;—but be thou curbed, 299 *Brownie's Cell* 74
Dante. Amid the cypress with which Dante crowned 260 **Scorn not* 8
Dante's. The laurelled Dante's favourite seat. A throne, 365 **Under the* 5
Danube. She of the Danube and the Northern Sea, 313 *Prophecy* 7
Of triumph, how the labouring Danube bore 317 **The martial* 6
Doth DANUBE spring to life! The wandering Stream 336 *Danube* 2
Of wide Hungarian Danube, 'twas my lot 575 *Chiabrera* 6. 7
Eastward, the Danube toward this inland sea, 869 *Excursion* 7. 789
Daphne. Till Daphne, desperate with pursuit 543 *Russ. Fug.* 181
Dappled. —Thy lake that, streaked or dappled, blue or grey, 12 *Desc. Sk.* 119
Oft on the dappled turf at ease 158 **With little* 9
Gleams, streak'd or dappled, hid from morning's ray 604 *Desc.Sk.Quarto* 139
A surface dappled o'er with shadows flung 756 *Excursion* 1. 5
Dappling. Nor stopped, till in the dappling east 542 *Russ. Fug.* 15
Dappling his face. He had not heard the sound 762 *Excursion* 1. 441
Dardan. Th' inevitable close of Dardan power L.2. 121 *Frag. Æneid* 2. 2
Dare. I dare not trust myself with such a thought— 42 *Bord.* 289
You saw, who was it? Nay, I dare not speak; 47 *Bord.* 532
I love her, though I dare not call her daughter. 47 *Bord.* 536
Oft as they dare to follow on your steps. 64 *Bord.* 1501
"Cross, if you dare, where I shall cross— 85 *Shepherd-boys* 45
If I may dare to cherish hope that gentle eyes will read 93 *Poet's Dream* 79

Dare—*continued.*
And I will dare to tell, 109 **Strange fits* 2
What have I? shall I dare to tell? 111 *A Complaint* 11
Do I dare to thank the God, 140 *Arm. Lady* 68
"Nor dare to thrust thy foolish self 155 *Waterfall* 3
I never heard of such as dare 198 *Thorn* 98
For future years. And so I dare to hope, 206 *Tintern* 65
"Whate'er the weak may dread, the wicked dare, 215 *Kirkstone* 85
If to provoke such doom the Impious dare, 217 *Enterprise* 120
By casting on a moment all we dare? 220 *Triad* 31
Yet a rich guerdon waits on minds that dare, 261 **From the dark* 7
Might some aspiring artist dare 301 *Bran* 78
The last that dare to struggle with the Foe. 310 **Another year* 4
Where Mortal never breathed I dare to sit 350 *Des. Stanzas* 19
Dare they confront the lean austerities 364 **What aim* 5
Of the world's hopes, dare to fulfil; awake, 366 **Fair Land* 13
Desperate alternative! what fiend could dare 381 *Duddon* 22. 11
Look down among them, if you dare; 399 *White Doe* 254
If—when they shrink, nor dare oppose 406 *White Doe* 906
Dare to usurp;—thou hast a sword to wield, 432 *Ecc. Sonn.* 2. 15. 8
Of infant passion, scarcely dare to show 436 *Ecc. Sonn.* 2. 32. 6
We only dare to cast a transient glance, 445 *Ecc. Sonn.* 3. 19. 10
The soul of Genius, if he dare to take 455 **Not in the lucid* 12
Effigy of the Vanished—(shall I dare 472 **The captive* 9
But whose rash hand (again I ask) could dare, 511 **Who rashly* 16
With such fell mastery that a man may dare 518 *Pun. Death* 4. 2
God, whom their passions dare defy, 534 **Blest is* 78
Few words they speak, nor dare to slack 543 *Russ. Fug.* 125
Against him dare not any wight say nay; 557 *Cuck. and Night.* 17
Is only fit to die, I dare well say, 559 *Cuck. and Night.* 134
Thy cold doors; but I dare not for this rout; 563 *Troilus* 34
Attend, or dare with minute-steps their way; 610 *Desc.Sk.Quarto* 461
For scanty food the treacherous cliffs to dare. 611 *Desc.Sk.Quarto* 483
And all that Virtue dictates, dare to do; 619 *School Ex.* 84
Up starts some tyrant, Earth and Heaven to dare, 628 *Installation* 9
Her native instincts: let me dare to speak 650 *Prelude* 3. 99
And gracious, almost might I dare to say, 685 *Prelude* 6. 681
Dare I avow that wish was mine to see, 735 *Prelude* 12. 57
Of tender feeling, she might dare repeat 770 *Excursion* 1. 899
And the sole guardian in whose hands we dare 886 *Excursion* 9. 125
Dared. Belovèd! if I dared, so would I call thee— 76 *Bord.* 2214
He had not dared to tell him who he was. 102 *Brothers* 433
Have dared to keep aloof; 168 *Turtledove* 12
A record which I dared to frame, 182 *Waggoner* 4. 199
Could thus have dared the grave to agitate, 275 *Gravestone* 8
To which he only dared to cling; 298 *Brownie's Cell* 46
A lofty Dome, that dared to emulate 324 *Ode 1814* 75
Ne'er could the boldest Eulogist have dared 359 **Complacent Fictions* 5
I gazed with earnestness, and dared no more. 365 **Under the* 10
And smiles, that dared to take their place, 401 *White Doe* 499
To take his life they have not dared; 409 *White Doe* 1213
Would that our scrupulous Sires had dared to leave 448 *Ecc. Sonn.* 3. 33. 1
Good, which they dared not hope for, we have seen; 449 *Ecc. Sonn.* 3. 37. 11
Above thy knowledge as they dared to go, 513 *Newspaper* 13
Under the steel his hand had dared to draw. 517 *Pun. Death* 2. 8
Before her flight she had not dared 544 *Russ. Fug.* 229
Intended, rose in hardihood, and dared 719 *Prelude* 10. 106
Which no one dared to oppose or mitigate. 723 *Prelude* 10. 355
That I have dared to tread this holy ground, 743 *Prelude* 13. 252
Loved fondly, truly, fervently; and dared 840 *Excursion* 6. 119
Foreseen, had dared to couple, even in thought, 875 *Excursion* 8. 39
Dares. The kneeling peasant scarcely dares to gaze; 14 *Desc. Sk.* 201
The bell is left, which no one dares remove; 73 *Bord.* 2055
Who dares report, the tidings to the lord 125 *V. and J.* 223
Yet of their number no one dares to die?' 211 *Laod.* 135
Nor dares to move unpropped upon the staff 277 **A Poet* 2
Which he will break for us he dares to speak, 319 *Spaniard* 9
Of virtuous action; all that courage dares, 363 **The world forsaken* 4
And laughing dares the Adventurer, who hath clomb 377 *Duddon* 4. 11
But now she dares to seek a haven 414 *White Doe* 1617
Lo! Discord at the altar dares to stand 420 *Ecc. Sonn.* 1. 9. 4
The recreant soul, that dares to shun the debt 424 *Ecc. Sonn.* 1. 23. 10
And festive gladness, burns not one that dares 426 *Ecc. Sonn.* 1. 31. 5
Who dares be wedded! Fancies thickly come 427 *Ecc. Sonn.* 1. 36. 12
Far as it dares to follow. Herbs self-sown, 431 *Ecc. Sonn.* 2. 12. 9
Licence and slavish order, dares be free. 450 *Ecc. Sonn.* 3. 37. 14
Their puniest flower-pot-nursling dares 506 **While from* 39
(What, save thyself, none dares through earth and skies) 624 *Æneid* 12
The humblest of this band who dares to hope 744 *Prelude* 13. 306
Daring. The work of Freedom daring to oppose, 18 *Desc. Sk.* 451
With all the daring fictions I have taught her, 44 *Bord.* 368
Mount, daring warbler!—that love-prompted strain 153 *Morn. Ex.* 44
But in man was ne'er such daring 163 *Hint* 5
Their daring wiles, their sportive cheer? 191 *Seq. Beggars* 12
Thy daring in a vapoury bourn, 215 *Kirkstone* 50
The daring thought, forget the name; 231 **The gentlest Poet* 6
Art, daring because souls could feel, 234 *Power of Sound* 122
More daring far than Hippogriff, 238 *P. B.* 154
An outlaw of as daring mood; 291 *Rob Roy* 4
And daring not to feel the majesty of right! 311 **Who rises* 45
Argo—exalted for that daring feat 336 *Danube* 13
Some lofty elm-tree, mounts the daring vine; 367 *Trajan* 20
Ungraciously receives. Too daring choice! 377 *Duddon* 7. 10
That soul of conscientious daring. 401 *White Doe* 475
Hath typified by reach of daring art 452 *Ecc. Sonn.* 3. 45. 9
By their own daring. But the People prayed 513 *General Fast* 5
A little daring would-be waterfall, 524 *Epist. Beaumont* 178

Daring—*continued*
Forgers of daring tales ! we bless you then, . . 673 *Prelude* 5. 524
Offered to notice by less daring pens, ... 673 *Prelude* 5. 543
By such a daring thought, that I might leave . 676 *Prelude* 6. 55
Such as the daring brotherhood of late . . . 691 *Prelude* 7. 294
When those two vessels with their daring freight, 715 *Prelude* 9. 414
Survived, but daring sympathies with power, . . 725 *Prelude* 10. 457
More keen and prouder daring ; yet hath she, . 856 *Excursion* 6. 1161
As that which urged me to a daring feat. . . . K.8. 256 *Recluse* 1.1.710
Mid such bad daring sought a coward's name. . L.1. 96 *Juvenal* 3. 56
Daringly. *See* **All-too-daringly.**
Dark. Of some dark mountain ; or than those which seem . . . . v **If thou indeed* 11
Dark is the ground ; a slumber seems to steal . 1 *Early Youth* 5
Dark with bat-haunted ashes stretching broad, . 7 *Ev. Wk.* 263
On the dark earth the wearied vision fails ; . . 8 *Ev. Wk.* 308
(For dark and broad the gulf of time between) . 8 *Ev. Wk.* 346
And see how dark the backward stream ! . . . 9 *Lines : Boat* 5
Dark is the region as with coming night ; . . . 15 *Desc. Sk.* 273
That dark mysterious gulf ascending, sound . . 18 *Desc. Sk.* 415
With its dark arms to form a circling bower, . . 23 *Yew-tree* 11
'Twas dark and void as ocean's watery realm . . 26 *Guilt* 138
" But ill they suited me—those journeys dark . 32 *Guilt* 415
And *he* had done the deed in the dark wood— . 35 *Guilt* 607
Of some dark deed to which in early life . . . 37 *Bord.* 15
Those eyeballs dark—dark beyond hope of light, . 39 *Bord.* 136
We sate us down. The sky grew dark and darker : 50 *Bord.* 703
'Twas dark—dark as the grave ; yet did I see, . 55 *Bord.* 984
Suffering is permanent, obscure and dark, . . . 65 *Bord.* 1543
My Child—my Child—dark—dark—I faint—this wind— . . . . 67 *Bord.* 1657
By the brook-side—'tis gone—and that dark cleft ! 97 *Brothers* 134
And apprehensions dark and criminal. . . . . 104 *Artegal* 125
Through dark and shapeless fear of things to come, 124 *V. and J.* 182
To the dark cave, the goblin's hall ; . . . . . 128 *Idiot Boy* 228
Though with misbelievers bred ; but that dark night 141 *Arm. Lady* 119
Of the dark firs, a visionary scene ! . . . . 151 **When, to* 93
Hushed the dark earth, fast closing weary eyes, . 167 *Pilgrim's Dream* 27
For still, though all be dark elsewhere, . . . 174 *Waggoner* 1. 80
Stony, and dark, and desolate, ... 176 *Waggoner* 1. 216
And sharp, and bright, along the dark abyss . . 184 *Night-piece* 16
I ask—but all is dark between ! . . . . . 191 *Seq. Beggars* 13
And now, ascending, after one dark hour . . . 192 *Gipsies* 17
'Twas worth your while, though in the dark, . . 199 *Thorn* 157
The last stone-pillar on a dark hill-top. . . . 202 *Hart-leap* 108
And glancing, gleaming, dark or bright, . . . 205 *Brougham* 126
Here, under this dark sycamore, and view . . 205 *Tintern* 10
Informs the cell of Hearing, dark and blind ; . . 232 *Power of Sound* 4
" He had a dark and sidelong walk, ... 240 *P. B.* 306
But through the dark, and through the cold, . . 240 *P. B.* 358
By this dark cave to be distrest . . . . . 243 *P. B.* 648
The chamber walls were dark all round,— . . . 244 *P. B.* 746
Crossing the waters) doubt, and something dark, . 258 **Where lies the Land* 12
And colour life's dark cloud with orient rays. . . 259 **Weak is* 8
To struggle through dark ways ; and when a damp 260 **Scorn not* 11
From the dark chambers of dejection freed, . . 260 **From the dark* 1
Of a dark chamber where the Mighty sleep : . . 262 **Mark the* 11
Dark and more dark the shades of evening fell ; . 262 **Dark and* 1
To summon fancies out of Time's dark cell. . . 275 *Rotha Q.* 14
Dark thoughts !—they came, but not to stay ; . 284 *Grave of Burns* 14
The dewy ground was dark and cold ; . . . . 289 *Stepping West.* 9
That glides the dark hills under ? . . . . . 293 *Yarrow Unv.* 26
Of the world's praise, from dark antiquity . . 307 **It is not* 3
Not there ; but in dark wood and rocky cave, . . 314 **Not 'mid* 5
A meteor wert thou crossing a dark night : . . 317 **Brave Schill* 5
A dungeon dark ! where he must waste the year, . 318 **Is there* 4
Opposed to dark, deep plots of patient skill, . . 330 *Ode : Thanks* 117
That dark unfathomable eye, ... 344 **How blest* 15
Spiry and dark, around their House of prayer, . 347 *Processions* 44
Avoid these sights ; nor brood o'er Fable's dark abyss! 347 *Processions* 72
I saw far off the dark top of a Pine . . . . 358 *Pine : Rome* 1
And, as the Moon, o'er some dark hill ascendant, 369 *Eg. Maid* 8
Snow-muffled winds, and all is dark, ... 375 **The Minstrels* 38
First of his tribe, to this dark dell—who first . 378 *Duddon* 8. 2
A dark plume fetch me from yon blasted yew, . 380 *Duddon* 17. 1
A comfort in the dark abyss. . . . . . . 402 *White Doe* 537
Eyes dark and strong ; and on his head . . . 404 *White Doe* 745
The garden pool's dark surface, stirred . . . 406 *White Doe* 966
Dark is the time—a woeful day ! . . . . . 408 *White Doe* 1079
But dark and dismal is the vault . . . . . 408 *White Doe* 1128
Dark moor, and gleam of pool and stream, . . 409 *White Doe* 1171
A Traitor dark and cowardly ! " . . . . . 412 *White Doe* 1469
The dark cave's portal gliding by, ... 415 *White Doe* 1740
When all the world with midnight gloom was dark.— 432 *Ecc. Sonn.* 2. 14. 5
O'er the dark steeps, or on the horizon line . . 443 *Ecc. Sonn.* 3. 12. 7
Let light and dark duly our thoughts employ ; . 447 *Ecc. Sonn.* 3. 29. 12
To cheer the long dark hours of vacant night— . 460 **Wanderer ! that* 69
And through dark trials still dost thou explore . 460 **Queen of* 27
While a dark storm before my sight . . . . 472 *Ossian* 5
(Kindled from Heaven between the light and dark 475 **Homeward we* 3
With these dark words begins my Tale ; . . . 494 *Force of Prayer* 2
To these dark steps, a little further on ! " . . 496 **A little* 2
Still, as we nearer draw to life's dark goal, . . 497 *Lycoris* 53
Lead, through dark ways by sin and sorrow trod, 504 *Warning* 83
Men of the Western World ! in Fate's dark book 515 **Men of* 1
Bound in a dark abominable pit, ... 515 **Ah why* 4
Think not that Prudence dwells in dark abodes, . 516 **Hard task* 13
Blood would be spilt that in his dark abode . . 519 *Pun. Death* 8. 8
Emblem of those dark corners sometimes found . 524 *Epist. Beaumont* 221

Dark—*continued.*
Never retiring, in thy large dark eyes, ... 525 *Epist. Beaumont* 255
Dark but to every gentle feeling true, ... 525 *Epist. Beaumont* 256
Thy dark Associate ever I discern ; . . . . 532 **Once I* 32
Down to their " dark opprobrious den," . . . 534 **Blest is* 83
Dark is the past to them, and dark . . . . 544 *Russ. Fug.* 233
Your head in this dark lair ! " . . . . . . 545 *Russ. Fug.* 320
Were shaped to cheer dark winter's lonely hours. 546 **Oft is* 16
That ever dark in torment, night by night, . . 564 *Troilus* 122
To breathless Nature's dark abyss ; . . . . 581 **Loud is* 18
That lit the dark slant woods with silvery white ! 593 *Ev. Wk. Quarto* 100
—'Mid the dark steeps repose the shadowy streams, 598 *Ev. Wk. Quarto* 339
On the dark earth the baffl'd vision fails, . . . 598 *Ev. Wk. Quarto* 364
From the dark sylvan roofs the restless spire, . 604 *Desc.Sk.Quarto* 108
Her tawny skin, dark eyes, and glossy locks, . . 605 *Desc.Sk.Quarto* 190
Far o'er the secret water dark with beach, . . 607 *Desc.Sk.Quarto* 288
'Mid the dark pines a little orchard blooms, . . 607 *Desc.Sk.Quarto* 296
To teach the skirt of thy dark cloud to shine ; . 615 *Desc.Sk.Quarto* 708
And dark Oppression builds her thick-ribb'd tow'rs ; . . . . 617 *Desc.Sk.Quarto* 795
In the dark mansions of the bigot's soul, . . . 618 *School Ex.* 34
When from the dark synod, or blood-reeking field, 621 *Convict* 25
O'er the dark steeps, or on the horizon line . . 625 **The confidence* 7
Or sighed for thy sweet presence some dark night, 630 [?] **O Moon* 3
Like harmony in music ; there is a dark . . . 637 *Prelude* 1. 341
When all the ground was dark, and twinkling stars 642 *Prelude* 2. 16
Place also by the side of this dark sense . . . 653 *Prelude* 3. 265
No longer haunting the dark winter night. . . 653 *Prelude* 3. 308
Round the stone table under the dark pine, . . 659 *Prelude* 4. 48
In the dark summit of the waving tree . . . 659 *Prelude* 4. 91
Grew dark with all the shadows on its breast, . 672 *Prelude* 5. 440
Waved their dark tops, not silent as they waved, 681 *Prelude* 6. 437
Sitting within doors between light and dark, . . 687 *Prelude* 7. 20
Tossing in sunshine its dark boughs aloft, . . . 687 *Prelude* 7. 45
And large dark eyes, beside her infant stood . . 692 *Prelude* 7. 343
Without a spirit overcast by dark . . . . . 723 *Prelude* 10. 328
(With shells encrusted, dark with briny weeds) . 726 *Prelude* 10. 557
Tempestuous, dark, and wild, and on the grass . 738 *Prelude* 12. 298
Over the dark abyss, intent to hear . . . . 747 *Prelude* 14. 72
And many a legend, peopling the dark woods, . 758 *Excursion* 1. 165
In the dark hedges. So their days were spent . 764 *Excursion* 1. 532
By this dark hill protected from thy beams ! . . 773 *Excursion* 2. 112
Glitter, with dark recesses interposed, ... 773 *Excursion* 2. 129
In earth's dark chambers, with a Christian's hope ! 775 *Excursion* 2. 248
" To the dark pit ; but he will feel no pain ; . . 779 *Excursion* 2. 510
And reached a small apartment dark and low, . 781 *Excursion* 2. 648
Upon the dark materials of the storm . . . . 784 *Excursion* 2. 847
From me, those dark impervious shades, that hang 790 *Excursion* 3. 296
With dark events. Desirous to divert . . . . 793 *Excursion* 3. 468
From some dark seat of fatal power was urged . 795 *Excursion* 3. 637
This shaded valley leaves ; and leaves the dark . 807 *Excursion* 4. 399
Our dark foundations rest, could he design . . 815 *Excursion* 4. 970
Athwart the concave of the dark blue dome, . . 819 *Excursion* 4. 1179
Primeval forests wrapped thee round with dark . 822 *Excursion* 5. 7
In whose dark vaults my own shall soon be laid, . 827 *Excursion* 5. 346
The natural roof of that dark house in which . . 831 *Excursion* 5. 589
High on the breast of yon dark mountain, dark . 832 *Excursion* 5. 671
Dark on my road the autumnal evening fell, . . 833 *Excursion* 5. 736
Those dark rocks hide it ! ' Entering, I beheld . 834 *Excursion* 5. 768
Of his day's work. ' Three dark mid-winter months 834 *Excursion* 5. 804
To harmony restored.—But yon dark mould . . 841 *Excursion* 6. 196
And the dark sorrows of the line of Thebes ? . . 846 *Excursion* 6. 544
Tall was her stature ; her complexion dark . . 848 *Excursion* 6. 678
Until dark night dismissed her to her bed ! . . 852 *Excursion* 6. 903
Call to my mind dark hints which I have heard . 854 *Excursion* 6. 1075
While the dark shadows of the summer leaves . 860 *Excursion* 7. 202
Which all acknowledged. The dark winter night, 864 *Excursion* 7. 448
Illumination into deep, dark holds, ... 870 *Excursion* 7. 835
Along a hedge of hollies dark and tall, ... 880 *Excursion* 8. 442
And virtue, difficult, abstruse, and dark ; . . . 887 *Excursion* 9. 234
Dark discontent, or loud commotion, each . . . 889 *Excursion* 9. 348
Quiet and dark ; for through the thick-wove trees S.3. 417 **Sweet was* 11
More awful than the chambers of dark earth . . S.3. 436 **The doubt* 178
" Wild wanderers, whither through my dark domain ? " . . . . K.8 241 *Recluse* 1.1.169
How solemn when the sky is dark, and earth . . K.8. 245 *Recluse* 1.1.327
Not dark, nor yet enlightened, but by snow . . K.8. 245 *Recluse* 1.1.328
The dark pines thrusting forth their spiky heads ; K.8. 249 *Recluse* 1.1.480
Dark as a riddle, prove a favourite theme ; . . K.8. 301 **And oh* 6
Dark-blue. From the dark-blue faint silvery threads divide . . . . 9 *Ev. Wk.* 359
Dark-brown. And, towering from the sullen dark-brown mere, ... 8 *Ev. Wk.* 313
I see the dark-brown curls, the brow, ... 232 *Jew. Fam.* 25
In dark-brown bason its wild waves repose, . . 592 *Ev. Wk. Quarto* 74
High towering from the sullen dark-brown mere, . 598 *Ev. Wk. Quarto* 371
Darken. When twilight shades darken the mountain's head. . . . . 255 *S. H.* 6
Darken the brow of this memorial Stone, . . . 546 **The embowering* 12
Darken the silver bosom of the crag, ... 786 *Excursion* 3. 27
And darken, so can deal that they become . . 817 *Excursion* 4. 1060
Darkened. While, from amid the darkened roofs, the spire, ... 12 *Desc. Sk.* 99
Was darkened soon by foul iniquity. . . . . 103 *Artegal* 77
By sorrow darkened and by care disturbed, . . 172 *Infant Daughter* 47
From their high state darkened the Earth with fear, 362 *List—'twas* 64
Till sense in death was darkened, ... 374 *Eg. Maid* 377
But lo ! what sudden cloud has darkened all . . 628 *Installation* 19
Above the darkened hills stood boldly forth . . 895 *Excursion* 9. 764

Day—*continued.*
Truth every day exemplified, no less 848 *Excursion* 6. 669
Till the stars sicken at the day of doom. 850 *Excursion* 6. 805
In the broad day, a weeping Magdalene. 850 *Excursion* 6. 814
In the broad day, a rueful Magdalene ! 853 *Excursion* 6. 987
—The bodily frame wasted from day to day ; 853 *Excursion* 6. 1024
No pleasure in the beauty of the day. 855 *Excursion* 6. 1102
To cheat the sadness of a rainy day ; 859 *Excursion* 7. 118
To rise from timely sleep, and meet the day 859 *Excursion* 7. 155
As seen not seldom on some gusty day, 861 *Excursion* 7. 231
And constant as the motion of the day ; 862 *Excursion* 7. 325
The stormy day, each had its own resource ; 864 *Excursion* 7. 449
With foresight ; hears, too, every sabbath day, 866 *Excursion* 7. 577
Day after day the gladness is diffused 867 *Excursion* 7. 651
Once every day he duteously repaired 867 *Excursion* 7. 667
" On a bright day—so calm and bright, it seemed 868 *Excursion* 7. 695
" One day— a summer's day of annual pomp 870 *Excursion* 7. 861
As that of war, which rests not night or day, 875 *Excursion* 8. 94
Disgorged are now the ministers of day ; 877 *Excursion* 8. 174
Their vigils kept ; where tapers day and night 877 *Excursion* 8. 188
With conscientious reverence, as a day 878 *Excursion* 8. 247
Nothing to speed the day, or cheer the mind ; 878 *Excursion* 8. 274
As abject, as degraded ? At this day, 879 *Excursion* 8. 345
Who, in some placid day of summer, looks 885 *Excursion* 9. 57
They sweep distemper from the busy day, 886 *Excursion* 9. 133
That tens of thousands at this day exist 886 *Excursion* 9. 178
A few short hours of each returning day 888 *Excursion* 9. 259
That, as the day thus far had been enriched 892 *Excursion* 9. 523
And ne'er to fail ? Shall that blest day arrive 894 *Excursion* 9. 666
Exultingly, in view of open day 894 *Excursion* 9. 706
Of yet another summer's day, not loth 895 *Excursion* 9. 777
Day by day he finds his way S.3. 423 *Tinker* 7
Millions of kneeling Hindoos at this day S.3. 435 **The doubt* 122
Yet, having spent a summer's day S.3. 438 **My Lord* 7
I could have lived another day. K.8. 220 **The snow-tracks* 41
Old Michael and his son one day went forth K.8. 224 **I will* 6
The straggler during all the previous day K.8. 224 **I will* 15
That now he might be proud, for he that day K.8. 226 **I will* 59
The glorious sun, and while the light of day K.8. 234 **The order'd* 5
Since that day forth the place to him—*to me* K.8. 237 *Recluse* 1.1. 46
In childhood, here as it abides by day, K.8. 240 *Recluse* 1.1.139
That she should entertain for this one day, K.8. 241 *Recluse* 1.1.190
This day, who drooped, or seemed to droop, so long; K.8. 242 *Recluse* 1.1.196
This day is a thanksgiving, 'tis a day K.8. 243 *Recluse* 1.1.230
Of the whole world. We saw them day by day, K.8. 243 *Recluse* 1.1.243
Which I have felt this day. An awful voice, K.8. 245 *Recluse* 1.1.318
Though slowly opening, opens every day K.8. 249 *Recluse* 1.1.473
To hold a vacant commerce day by day K.8. 253 *Recluse* 1.1.595
Enough to fill the present day with joy, K.8. 254 *Recluse* 1.1.650
To those, who all day long, through a busy life, K.8. 257 **Shall he* 9
And let that heir of Glory's endless day L.1. 94 *Juvenal* 2. 23
Thou that mak's't [? mak'st] a day of night L.2. 190 **Queen and* 17

Day-break. At day-break on a hill they stood 83 *Lucy Gray* 37
Which blow at daybreak, droop ere even-song ; 110 **Look at* 2
His day-break note, a sad vicissitude ! 279 **'Tis he* 3
Union not sad, when sunny daybreak smites 387 **Part fenced* 12
Brighter than eastern skies at daybreak strewn 434 *Ecc. Sonn.* 2. 25. 6
Till this bright Stranger came, fair as day-break, 466 *St. Bees* 40
Came forth—a light, though but as of daybreak, 518 *Pun. Death* 7. 4

Day-deserted. The far-off peasant's day-deserted home ; 605 *Desc.Sk.Quarto* 167

Day-dreams. Dwell fruitless day-dreams, lawless prayer, 223 *Wishing-gate* 8
For day-dreams soft as e'er beguiled 526 **The soaring* 49

Daylight. Where daylight lingers on perpetual snow; 21 *Desc. Sk.* 582
For twenty lives. The daylight dawned, and now— 74 *Bord.* 2100
As soon as 'tis daylight to-morrow, with me 80 †*Address : Child* 20
With daylight Isabel resumed her work ; 135 *Michael* 304
In the world's eye. Her work when daylight failed 139 *Widow* 9
To daylight known deter from that pursuit, 154 *Morn. Ex.* 56
At the corner of Wood Street, when daylight appears, 187 *Poor Susan* 1
When daylight is gone down. 193 *Ruth* 54
Of joyless daylight ; when the fretful stir 206 *Tintern* 52
For yet it is broad day-light : clouds pass by ; 208 **It is no* 6
But in plain daylight :—She, too, at my side, 270 **Shame on* 6
To watch thy course when Daylight, fled from earth, 391 **Though joy* 3
Walked round, affronting the daylight ; 406 *White Doe* 957
Sunward to seek the daylight in its fount, 527 **Those breathing* 38
And without ceasing, since it was daylight ; 561 *Cuck.and Night.* 268
Glad Day-light laughs upon his top of snow, 615 *Desc.Sk.Quarto* 700
Prolonged in summer till the day-light failed : 642 *Prelude* 2. 10
Of daylight, the bare thought of where I was . 694 *Prelude* 7. 453
Inaudible by daylight, blend their notes 818 *Excursion* 4. 1174
Wishes and endless schemes ; by daylight walked 842 *Excursion* 6. 240
And led us to our threshold. Daylight failed K.8. 241 *Recluse* 1.1.173

Daylight's. When the blue daylight's in the skies 198 *Thorn* 72
When the blue daylight's in the sky 198 *Thorn* 83

Day's. *See* **Mid-day's.**
Our heavenly Father granted each day's bread ; 35 *Guilt* 598
This day's event has laid on me the duty 68 *Bord.* 1682
Thy pleasant course,—when day's begun 158 **In youth* 74
And one day's narrow circuit is to Him 172 *Infant Daughter* 11
And each day's shallow grief ; 224 **'Tis gone* 39
While the stars shine, or while day's purple eye 259 **A volant* 10
Day's mutable distinctions.—Ancient Power ! 265 **Hail, Twilight* 4
Hangs that day's treasured sword, how firm a check 278 *Wellington* 6
Lived thankful for day's light, for daily bread, 278 **Lo ! where she* 13

Day's—*continued.*
Say that we come, and come by this day's light ; 294 **Fly, some* 2
By one day's feat, one mighty victory. 326 *Sobieski* 10
The quickening spark of this day's sacrifice ; 329 *Ode : Thanks.* 52
Now all is sun-bright peace. Of that day's shame, 361 **When here* 5
Day's grateful warmth, tho' moist with falling dews. 453 **Calm is the* 2
The heart with each day's care ; 505 **If this* 6
What yet remains if this day's course : 506 *Lab. Hymn* 28
Due to the day's unfinished task ; of pen 508 *F. Stone* 2
With this day's work, in thought and word. 534 **Blest is* 90
Loose-hanging rocks the Day's bless'd eye that hide, 606 *Desc.Sk.Quarto* 255
What radiant fires were drown'd by day's malignant pow'r, 620 **She wept* 12
Defrauding the day's glory, desperate ! 673 *Prelude* 5. 487
Or sees in his day's march ; himself he feels, 703 *Prelude* 8. 251
Darkness ere day's mid course, and morning light 709 *Prelude* 8. 661
Good recompense, I hope, for this day's toil, 774 *Excursion* 2. 158
That, for the day's consumption, books may yield 810 *Excursion* 4. 584
Open, and day's pure cheerfulness, but veiled 822 *Excursion* 5. 5
For one day's little compass, has preserved 828 *Excursion* 5. 361
Of his day's work. 'Three dark mid-winter months 834 *Excursion* 5. 804
From each day's need, out of each day's least gain. 849 *Excursion* 6. 726
Or in dispatch of each day's little growth 878 *Excursion* 8. 270
Of that day's prowess ! Him might I compare, 883 *Excursion* 8. 576
Of one day's pleasure, and all mortal joys ! 892 *Excursion* 9. 555
Partaking this day's pleasure ? From afar K.8. 243 *Recluse* 1.1.240
To every day's demand for daily bread, K.8. 249 *Recluse* 1.1.450

Days. *See* **Birthdays, Feast-days, Sabbath-days.**
To gild the total tablet of his days ; 2 *Ev. Wk.* 30
On lovelier spectacle in faery days ; 7 *Ev. Wk.* 300
Where we, my Friend, to happy days shall rise, 8 *Ev. Wk.* 351
And who, that walks where men of ancient days 15 *Desc. Sk.* 289
Or on the earth strange lines, in former days 26 *Guilt* 112
That happier days we never more must view. 29 *Guilt* 287
And end my days upon the peaceful flood.'— 31 *Guilt* 366
I shall be with them in two days at farthest. 38 *Bord.* 42
'Tis but for a few days—a thought has struck me. 41 *Bord.* 224
What is your meaning ? Two days gone I saw, 42 *Bord.* 276
No more, I pray, of this. Three days at farthest 43 *Bord.* 322
Whom, but some few days past, I saw in Eskdale, 46 *Bord.* 479
And I, no coward in my better days, 61 *Bord.* 1287
Did my pride tame my pride ;—for many days, 68 *Bord.* 1697
The same dead calm, continued many days. 69 *Bord.* 1744
Have I lived many days—my sleep was bound 69 *Bord.* 1791
And I could wish my days to be 79 **My heart* 8
Oh ! pleasant, pleasant were the days, 79 **Stay near* 10
For length of days so much revered, so famous where it stands 92 *Poet's Dream* 35
Give to Him prayers, and many thoughts, in thy most busy days ; 93 *Poet's Dream* 58
'Twas one well known to him in former days, 95 *Brothers* 38
And blew with the same breath through days and weeks, 96 *Brothers* 51
On windy days, in one of those stray brooks, 99 *Brothers* 260
And many, many happy days were his. 100 *Brothers* 346
And summer days, when we were young ; 106 **I've watched* 17
Sweet childish days, that were as long 106 **I've watched* 18
As twenty days are now. 106 **I've watched* 19
In two days more I must have died. 114 *Ind. Wom.* 42
The days are cold, the nights are long, 117 †*Cottager* 1
That occupied his days in solitude 124 *V. and J.* 180
His days he wasted, an imbecile mind ! 126 *V. and J.* 306
His days had not been passed in singleness. 132 *Michael* 78
These two days has been meat and drink to me. 135 *Michael* 275
With a light heart. The Housewife for five days 135 *Michael* 284
Two days, and blessings from thy Father's tongue 136 *Michael* 342
In those old romantic days 141 *Arm. Lady* 86
Nor did aught of future days that kiss belie, 142 *Arm. Lady* 143
While I was seated, now some ten days past, 147 *Joanna* 18
And that fleet messenger of summer days, 153 *Morn. Ex.* 21
That gentle days were nigh ! 155 *Waterfall* 34
If on windy days the Raven 166 *Wand. Jew* 17
Just three days after, passing by 169 *Wren's Nest* 53
In bloodiest battle since the days of Mars ! 180 *Waggoner* 3. 143
Gave to the days a mark and name 182 *Waggoner* 4. 223
The same whom in my schoolboy days 183 **O blithe* 17
One of those heavenly days that cannot die ; 185 *Nutting* 3
" What days and what bright years ! Ah me ! 193 *Ruth* 79
And summer days is gone, 194 *Ruth* 225
Farewell ! and when thy days are told, 195 *Ruth* 253
" And in the summer-time, when days are long, 201 *Hart-leap* 69
And thither, when the summer days were long, 202 *Hart-leap* 89
Hear it, good man, old in days ! 204 *Brougham* 96
(The coarser pleasures of my boyish days, 206 *Tintern* 73
That wretched boon, days lengthened by mistrust. 214 *Dion* 117
On busy days, with thankful nights, be mine. 217 *Enterprise* 150
Thy own heart-stirring days, and be 218 *Young Lady* 5
Were mine in early days ; 225 *Present.* 9
To vanish—fleet as days and months and years, 230 *Clouds* 37
The man who had been four days dead, 243 *P. B.* 578
The Beast four days and nights had past ; 243 *P. B.* 602
And there the Ass four days had been, 243 *P. B.* 604
Thus might *he* paint our lot of mortal days 259 **Weak is* 5
Of glory lavished on our quiet days. 282 **Wansfell ! this* 8
But many days, and many months, 287 *Ellen Irwin* 41
Thus, like the men of earliest days, 301 *Bran* 74
Shine on his soul, reflected from the days 318 **Is there* 13
In the worst moment of these evil days ; 321 **Here pause* 4
Whence bright days of festive beauty ; 323 *Ode 1814* 36

Dead—*continued.*
And oft he groaned aloud, "O God, that I were dead!" 36 *Guilt* 639
Living or dead all things were bodiless, 59 *Bord.* 1215
Delivered to the Judge of all things. Dead! 66 *Bord.* 1587
On a dead sea under a burning sky, 68 *Bord.* 1698
Or mourn him dead. A man by men cast off, 68 *Bord.* 1727
Left without burial! nay, not dead nor dying, 68 *Bord.* 1728
The same dead calm, continued many days. 69 *Bord.* 1744
That drops down dead out of a sky it vexed. 69 *Bord.* 1786
Alive or dead, I'll find him. Alive—perdition! 71 *Bord.* 1881
Dead, dead!— A dismal matter, Sir, for me, 74 *Bord.* 2106
To fear the very worst. My Father is dead; 75 *Bord.* 2121
The dead Man heave a groan, or from his side 75 *Bord.* 2160
Shame! Eldred, shame! The dead have but one face. 75 *Bord.* 2162
And he is dead!—that Moor—how shall I cross it? 76 *Bord.* 2238
Such tales of your dead Father!—God is my judge, 77 *Bord.* 2244
She is not dead. Why!—if I loved this Woman, 77 *Bord.* 2272
And, with a voice at which the dead will quake, 77 *Bord.* 2290
Dead times revive in thee: 79 **Stay near* 6
"But they are dead; those two are dead!" 84 *We are Seven* 65
Nor emblem of our hopes: the dead man's home 98 *Brothers* 172
We talk about the dead by our fire-sides. 98 *Brothers* 179
Living or dead.—When last we heard of him, 100 *Brothers* 316
Dead, and with mangled limbs. The third day after 101 *Brothers* 381
"If Lucy should be dead!" 109 **Strange fits* 28
My fire is dead: it knew no pain; 114 *Ind. Wom.* 11
Yet is it dead, and I remain: 114 *Ind. Wom.* 12
And they are dead, and I will die. 114 *Ind. Wom.* 14
—My fire is dead, and snowy white 114 *Ind. Wom.* 55
Where art thou, worse to me than dead? 116 *Affl. Marg.* 2
Between the living and the dead; 117 *Affl. Marg.* 60
The ancient spirit is not dead; 119 *Sailor's Mother* 7
Sailed on the seas, but he is dead; 119 *Sailor's Mother* 21
I found it when my Son was dead; 119 *Sailor's Mother* 34
"The key I must take, for my Ellen is dead." 120 *Childless Father* 18
The green bough motionless and dead: 127 *Idiot Boy* 79
Where he will stay till he is dead; 128 *Idiot Boy* 224
When clouds gave way at dead of night 144 **Driven in* 53
But still be true till I am dead, 145 *Her Eyes* 58
That skimmed the surface of the dead calm lake, 148 **A narrow* 19
A pittance from the dead unfeeling lake 149 **A narrow* 65
Like a dead Boy he is serene. 166 *Danish Boy* 55
That lies dead and still, 166 *Stray Pleasures* 2
Whether they be alive or dead! 174 *Waggoner* 1. 69
Above Helm-crag—a streak half dead, 175 *Waggoner* 1. 168
"That cannot be," one answered—"she is dead:"— 191 *Beggars* 41
"She has been dead, Sir, many a day."— 191 *Beggars* 43
"O Ruth! I have been worse than dead; 194 *Ruth* 164
Such seemed this Man, not all alive nor dead, 196 *Resolution* 64
And mighty Poets in their misery dead. 197 *Resolution* 116
And if 'twas born alive or dead, 199 *Thorn* 150
Were voices of the dead: 199 *Thorn* 163
But now the Knight beholds him lying dead. 201 *Hart-leap* 32
Revenge, and all ferocious thoughts were dead: 205 *Brougham* 166
Egyptian tombs unlock their dead, 216 *Enterprise* 85
Dead pause abrupt of midnight winds, 225 *Present.* 41
And now among the dead man's hair 242 *P. B.* 574
The man who had been four days dead, 243 *P. B.* 578
Whom seeks he—whom?—the silent dead: 243 *P. B.* 640
A faith that for the dead man's sake, 243 *P. B.* 661
In the dead earth beneath the road, 245 *P. B.* 835
For he is dead—I know it well!" 248 *P. B.* 1027
And that her Husband now lay dead, 248 *P. B.* 1038
Is dead, for ever dead!" 248 *P. B.* 1050
Rise from the dead, erewhile the Cottage-dame 255 *Easter* 3
And claim, among the dead, this awful crown; 275 *Gravestone* 9
Of nature; and, if human hearts be dead, 283 *Railway* 12
Strike pleasure dead, 284 *Grave of Burns* 4
Hath early found among the dead, 285 *Grave of Burns* 68
Yet happy feelings of the dead: 289 *Glen-Al.* 29
Of the dead bodies.—'Twas a day of shame 293 *Killicranky* 8
Utterly dead! yet in the guise 294 *Jedbor.* 53
Renouncing here, as worse than dead, 298 *Brownie's Cell* 47
To dead and living; when her breath 299 *Brownie's Cell* 83
Along thy banks, at dead of night 300 *Cora Linn* 19
As if a dead man spake it! Yet despair 304 **Jones! as* 12
Or is it Tell's great Spirit, from the dead 314 *Hofer* 3
Dead in the sinless time of infancy, 318 **In due* 3
Where all the brave lie dead. But, when of bands 319 *Spaniard* 8
Gone are they, viewless as the buried dead: 320 **Hunger, and* 11
Their monstrous Idol if the dead e'er spake, 325 *Enghien* 7
The living generations with the dead; 328 *Ode 1815* 67
Else we sleep among the dead; 336 **Jesu! bless* 16
That to descendants of the dead it holds 355 *Aquap.* 163
Dead to the world and scorning earth-born joys. 362 **List—'twas* 35
With such fond hope? her very speech is dead; 368 *Trajan* 66
"Mine was she—mine she is, though dead, 374 *Eg. Maid* 325
That thinned the living and disturbed the dead? 378 *Duddon* 8. 8
That, for the living and the dead, demand 389 *Breadalb.* 12
Lie silent in your graves, ye dead! 397 *White Doe* 67
And peace is none, for living or dead! 399 *White Doe* 307
That Francis lives, *he* is not dead?" 409 *White Doe* 1211
A renovation from the dead, 410 *White Doe* 1263
All but the suffering heart was dead 411 *White Doe* 1386
Dead are they, dead!—and I will go, 411 *White Doe* 1433
He should be seized, alive or dead. 412 *White Doe* 1461
Through human hearts, and pleasure dead,— 416 *White Doe* 1843
Dead—but to live again on earth, 416 *White Doe* 1844

Dead—*continued.*
Thy own, if sorrow for thy sin be dead, 447 *Ecc. Sonn.* 3. 29. 7
Of grateful England's overflowing Dead. 452 *Ecc. Sonn.* 3. 45. 14
And Charity extendeth to the dead 467 *St. Bees* 65
Stretched on the dying Mother's lap, lies dead 476 *Howard* 1
From dead men to their kind. 481 *Expost.* 8
His Master's dead,—and no one now 483 *Simon Lee* 29
Men, dogs, and horses, all are dead; 483 *Simon Lee* 31
Then may'st thou think upon the dead. 485 *Poet's Epitaph* 4
"And, Matthew, for thy children dead 488 *Fountain* 61
Both man and woman wept when thou wert dead; 491 *Tribute: Dog* 22
And leave a dead unprofitable name— 494 *Hap. War.* 80
For she knew that her Son was dead. 494 *Force of Prayer* 8
And thinking of my Brethren, dead, dispersed, 510 *F. Stone* 112
Of dear Old England? Think they she is dead, 516 **Young England* 2
Dead to the very name? Presumption fed 516 **Young England* 3
Wife, children, kindred, they were dead and gone; 531 **I know* 25
Her evenings then were dull and dead: 536 *Goody Blake* 45
Stepped One at dead of night, 542 *Russ. Fug.* 10
So long the lost as dead, 545 *Russ. Fug.* 358
Where Reynolds, 'mid our country's noblest dead, 546 **Ye Lime* 7
And also would I that they all were dead, 559 *Cuck. and Night.* 131
So piteously, and with so dead a hue, 563 *Troilus* 41
This to the dead by sacred right belongs; 576 *Chiabrera* 9. 5
Like his till they are dead. 577 **I come* 11
And Ettrick mourns with her their Poet dead. 586 *Hogg* 44
Dead muttering lips, and hair of hungry white, 615 *Desc.Sk.Quarto* 711
Be the dead load of mortal ills forgot, 617 *Desc.Sk.Quarto* 811
Dead to the sense of every finer joy; 618 *School Ex.* 8
The dead, by influx of a living love, 625 *Æneid* 92
And dead still water lay upon my mind 644 *Prelude* 2. 171
Fit reverence for the glorious Dead, the sight 654 *Prelude* 3. 337
At last, the dead man, 'mid that beauteous scene 672 *Prelude* 5. 448
Dead in my eyes, dead as a theatre 674 *Prelude* 5. 551
Here files of ballads dangle from dead walls; 690 *Prelude* 7. 193
On the dead letter, miss the spirit of things; 703 *Prelude* 8. 297
The dead, upon the dying heaped, and gazed 719 *Prelude* 10. 57
When a dead pause ensued, and no one stirred, 719 *Prelude* 10. 109
Cried, "Robespierre is dead!"—nor was a doubt, 726 *Prelude* 10. 573
The noble Living and the noble Dead. 733 *Prelude* 11. 395
Is for both worlds, the living and the dead. 744 *Prelude* 13. 335
In that wild place and at the dead of night, 746 *Prelude* 14. 26
But that it seemed she loved him. She is dead, 763 *Excursion* 1. 507
Even of the dead; contented thence to draw 765 *Excursion* 1. 629
She knew not that he lived; if he were dead, 768 *Excursion* 1. 819
She knew not he was dead. She seemed the same 768 *Excursion* 1. 820
She said, 'I fear it will be dead and gone 769 *Excursion* 1. 845
She told me that her little babe was dead, 769 *Excursion* 1. 856
To private interest dead, and public care. 774 *Excursion* 2. 209
Behold the Man whom he had fancied dead! 779 *Excursion* 2. 497
Swelled in my breast.—'I have been dead,' I cried, 784 *Excursion* 2. 875
If the flowers wither, I am worse than dead! 802 *Excursion* 4. 56
Where soul is dead, and feeling hath no place; 810 *Excursion* 4. 621
But present to the dead; who, so they deemed, 812 *Excursion* 4. 715
In disconnection dead and spiritless; 815 *Excursion* 4. 962
By natural exhalation. With the dead 828 *Excursion* 5. 373
And have the dead around us, take from them 832 *Excursion* 5. 647
To pity dead, the oppressor and the opprest; 836 *Excursion* 5. 940
Dull, to the joy of her own motions dead; 879 *Excursion* 8. 324
Dead—but not sullied or deformed by death, 883 *Excursion* 8. 570
Dying, or dead! Nor shall the fanning breeze 892 *Excursion* 9. 552
As if he would laugh himself dead. S.3. 424 *Tinker* 45
Sunk down, and lay immersed in dead repose S.3. 434 **The doubt* 50
Where, unnumbered with the dead, S.3. 442 *Harmodius* 9
To speak of her dead husband. Is there not K.8. 247 *Recluse* 1.1.401
Far from the living and dead wilderness K.8. 253 *Recluse* 1.1.613
Even he, who yoked the living to the dead, L.1. 88 *Juvenal* 1. 5
Or spend upon the dead the muse's rage? L.1. 94 *Juvenal* 2. 8

Deaden. And the heart is loth to deaden 90 *Longest Day* 39
Nor does that roaring wind deaden his strain 279 **Hark! 'tis* 3
Doth deaden, shocks of tumult, shrieks of crime, 349 *At Dover* 13

Deadened. Drops deadened from a roof so thick with leaves. 49 *Bord.* 676
Repelled the storm and deadened its loud roar. 860 *Excursion* 7. 179

Deadlier. Who in his heart had groaned with deadlier pain 26 *Guilt* 125
As if each blow were deadlier than the last, 33 *Guilt* 474
Strikes through the Traveller's frame with deadlier chill, 267 **As the* 2
And deadlier poisons in the chalice blend. 330 *Ode: Thanks.* 124
Oft worse to bear, or deadlier in effect. 501 *Humanity* 63
To mutual tyranny a deadlier look? 515 **Men of* 8

Deadliest. "Finish the strife by deadliest victory!" 322 **By Moscow* 14
With malice ne'er to deadliest weapon linked, 419 *Ecc. Sonn.* 1. 6. 3
And instruments of deadliest servitude! 420 *Ecc. Sonn.* 1. 8. 14
"Now ruthless Tempest launch thy deadliest dart! 597 *Ev. Wk. Quarto* 291

Deadly. And plants were wholesome, now of deadly taste: 17 *Desc. Sk.* 391
Strange repetition of the deadly wound 33 *Guilt* 491
Her bony visage—gaunt and deadly wan; 34 *Guilt* 561
Thy vest is torn, thy cheek is deadly pale; 76 *Bord.* 2191
Their nearest kin with deadly purpose met) 106 *Artegal* 237
Her thoughts are bent on deadly sin, 129 *Idiot Boy* 293
She thinks no more of deadly sin; 129 *Idiot Boy* 308
Deadly foe both of mouse and rat; 142 †*Lov. and Lik.* 42
About that tight and deadly band 145 *Her Eyes* 37
From touch of *deadly* injury? 192 *Seq. Beggars* 40
Pursue thee with their deadly aim! 214 *Dion* 105
Arm at its blast for deadly wars) 235 *Power of Sound* 214
He launched a deadly javelin! 287 *Ellen Irwin* 28
Another year!—another deadly blow! 310 **Another year* 1

Deadly—_continued._
Sword dropped not, javelin kept its deadly aim.— 361 *When here 4
Who, paying deadly hate in kind . . . . . 403 White Doe 641
Or deadly snare: and He survives to bless . . 470 *A youth 13
For which, with changèd, pale, and deadly face, . 563 Troilus 18
That Hulk which labours in the deadly swell, . 579 Peele Castle 47
Which, as a deadly mischief, and a foul . . . 717 Prelude 9. 551
Or aught of heavier or more deadly weight, . . 737 Prelude 12. 212
In prosecution of their deadly chase, ... 798 Excursion 3. 879
In deadly scorn of superstitious rites, ... 814 Excursion 4. 903
Winning no recompense but deadly hate . . . 870 Excursion 7. 830
Into an instrument of deadly bane . . . . . 878 Excursion 8. 258
The Dalesmen may have aimed the deadly tube, . K.8. 244 Recluse 1.1.266
Of two brave vessels matched in deadly fight, . K.8. 256 Recluse 1.1.722

Deaf. _See_ **Heart-deaf.**
Mocks the dull ear of Time with deaf abortive sound. . . . . 16 Desc. Sk. 315
They are deaf to your murmurs—they care not for you, ... 189 Music 43
Deaf, drooping, that is now his doom: . . . 294 Jedbor. 21
Thy ears were deaf, and feeble were thy knees,— 491 Tribute: Dog 17
Your Master's throne is set."—Deaf was the Sea; 495 Fact 6
Born deaf, and living deaf and dumb. . . . . 577 *I come 40
That, deaf and silent, read'st the eternal deep, 589 Immortality 112
But though not deaf, nor obstinate to find . . 714 Prelude 9. 340

Deafened. With high and spacious rooms, deafened and stunned . . . . 684 Prelude 6. 646

Deafening. With deafening noise,—the benediction fell . . . . 51 Bord. 747
Runs a deafening noise of welcome!— . . . 141 Arm. Lady 129
Deafening the region in his ireful mood. . . . 439 Ecc. Sonn. 2. 43. 14
And, ruining from the cliffs their deafening load . 605 Desc.Sk.Quarto 203
Of colours, lights, and forms; the deafening din; 689 Prelude 7. 155
Amid the deafening tumult, scarcely heard . . 809 Excursion 4. 534

Deal. Then the Muses might deal with me just as they chose, ... 571 Avarice 3
And to such beings temperately deal forth . . 634 Prelude 1. 122
Or round the naked table, snow-white deal, . . 639 Prelude 1. 514
Not more, had been of age to deal about . . . 692 Prelude 7. 338
Deal boldly with substantial things; in truth . 743 Prelude 13. 235
This is the very spirit in which they deal . . . 747 Prelude 14. 91
To deal about his sparkling eloquence, ... 775 Excursion 2. 282
And darken, so can deal that they become . . 817 Excursion 4. 1060
Strange, should He deal herein with nice respects, 887 Excursion 9. 236

Dealers-out. Themselves, the fathers and the dealers-out . . . . 568 Cumb. Beg. 150

Dealing. _See_ **Double-dealing.**
From such rough dealing. Ha! what sound is that? . . . . 67 Bord. 1661
That here has been some wicked dealing; . . . 245 P. B. 812
With friends and kindred dealing. . . . . . 386 Yarrow Rev. 96
The majesty of honest dealing. . . . . . . 472 Ossian 16
Is hospitable dealing, grant my prayer! . . . 625 Æneid 108
In hollow exultation, dealing out . . . . . 686 Prelude 6. 733
For he was busy, dealing, from a store . . . 779 Excursion 2. 503
And honest dealing, and untainted speech, . . 878 Excursion 8. 241

Deals. So with our own the mild Instructor deals, . 449 Ecc. Sonn. 3. 35. 9
Deals with a flower; the keepers of our time, . 671 Prelude 5. 353
Such as an idler deals with in his shame, . . . 673 Prelude 5. 489
And deals it out, their regular nourishment . . 702 Prelude 8. 228
This tale gives proof that Heaven most gently deals 854 Excursion 6. 1072

Dealt. So dealt with him. I have a noble Friend . 71 Bord. 1896
He dealt a sturdy blow. . . . . 241 P. B. 425
Which to the work surpassing skill hath dealt, . 276 Author's Portrait 4
Had found, in ravage widely dealt, ... 298 Brownie's Cell 39
And wanderers of the street, to whom is dealt . 315 *And is it 13
Alms on this stone to be dealt out, _for ever!_ . . 394 Countess' Pillar 9
A State whose generous will through earth is dealt; 450 Ecc. Sonn. 3. 37. 12
Dealt in like sort with feeble human kind . . . 514 *Who ponders 8
Of the silver-rimmed horn whence he dealt his mild ale! . . . . 569 Farmer 16
Ye dealt out your plain comforts? Yet had ye . 639 Prelude 1. 505
A tournament of blows, some hardly dealt . . 657 Prelude 3. 583
In measure only dealt out to himself, ... 674 Prelude 5. 592
And dealt with whatsoever they found there . . 729 Prelude 11. 130
Had dealt with—I will here record in verse; . . 757 Excursion 1. 102
Large measures shall be dealt. Three sabbath-days 808 Excursion 4. 468
Her annual bounty, sparingly dealt forth . . 831 Excursion 5. 614
Unjustly dealt with; but the Maid was gone! . 840 Excursion 6. 136
Both have been fairly dealt with; looking back . 888 Excursion 9. 287
Hath dealt with me as with a turbulent stream, . K.8. 256 Recluse 1.1. 728

Deans. Ye Presidents and Deans, and, till the spirit 655 Prelude 3. 410

Dear. Dear native regions, I foretell, ... 1 Extract 1
On the dear hills where first he rose. . . . . 1 Extract 14
Dear Brook, farewell! To-morrow's noon again . 3 Ev. Wk. 86
Dear is the forest frowning o'er his head, . . . 11 Desc. Sk. 21
And dear the velvet green-sward to his tread: . 11 Desc. Sk. 22
Dear and more dear the lessening circle grows; . 19 Desc. Sk. 479
Be cautious, my dear Master! I perceive . . 37 Bord. 21
Dear Master! gratitude's a heavy burden . . . 38 Bord. 30
Dear Father, you sigh deeply; ever since . . . 39 Bord. 103
As come, dear Child! from a far deeper source . 40 Bord. 153
Out of thy mind? My dear, my only, Child; . 40 Bord. 163
Dear Father! how _could_ I forget and live?— . 40 Bord. 176
Dear Daughter! precious relic of that time— . 40 Bord. 189
As I am dear to you, remember, Child! . . . 42 Bord. 294
That were most dear to me, and some will bear . 49 Bord. 651
And it was you, dear Lady! God be praised, . 50 Bord. 719
Is very dear to you. Oh! but you are young; . 52 Bord. 819
Than make me change my course. Dear Marmaduke, ... 55 Bord. 992

Dear—_continued._
Ha! my dear Captain. A later meeting, Oswald, 64 Bord. 1470
He only spake to me of a dear Daughter, . . . 74 Bord. 2067
Since your dear Mother went away,— . . . . 81 †Mother's Return 2
Things that I know not of belike to thee are dear, 88 Pet-lamb 51
With this dear holy shepherd-boy breathe a prayer of earnest heart, ... 91 Norman Boy 30
I whispered, "Yet a little while, dear Child! thou art my own, ... 92 Poet's Dream 21
Far happier lot, dear Boy, than brings full many to this shrine; . . . . 92 Poet's Dream 54
Dear caresses given in pity, ... 94 Westmoreland Girl 37
We go for One to whom ye will be dear; . . . 106 Farewell 25
Dear Spot! which we have watched with tender heed, ... 106 Farewell 33
And, sooth, these two were each to the other dear: 108 Indolence 66
Those paths so dear to me. . . . . 109 *Strange fits 12
That murmur once so dear, when will it cease? . 111 *'Tis said that some 22
Dear Maid, this truth believe, ... 112 *Yes! thou 6
O dearer far than light and life are dear, . . . 112 *O dearer 1
Dear friends, when ye were gone away. . . . 114 Ind. Wom. 30
But thou, dear Babe, art far away, ... 114 Ind. Wom. 69
As dear as my own children be; . . . . . 115 Last of Flock 82
Of the survivor's sweetest voice (dear child, . . 118 Maternal Grief 44
Dear consolation, kneeling on the turf . . . . 119 Maternal Grief 71
"Dear Babe, thou daughter of another, . . . 120 Emigrant Mother 15
Thy own dear mother's far away, ... 120 Emigrant Mother 19
"My own dear Little-one will sigh, ... 121 Emigrant Mother 45
Dear Baby! I must lay thee down; . . . . 121 Emigrant Mother 59
Never was any child more dear! . . . . . 121 Emigrant Mother 74
And the dear haven where he wished to be . . 122 V. and J. 59
And I have lost my poor dear Boy, ... 129 Idiot Boy 255
"Oh dear, dear Pony! my sweet joy! . . . . 129 Idiot Boy 299
This son of his old age was yet more dear— . . 133 Michael 143
And makes a meeting seem most like a dear farewell. 141 Arm. Lady 132
With hope that we, dear Friends! shall meet again. 143 *High bliss 28
And who but this dear Bird beguiled . . . 144 *Driven in 37
—Where art thou gone, my own dear child? . . 145 Her Eyes 85
For I thy own dear mother am: . . . . . 145 Her Eyes 92
Then, pretty dear, be not afraid: . . . . . 145 Her Eyes 97
And make dear friendships with the streams and groves. . . . . 147 Joanna 8
—Now, by those dear immunities of heart . . 147 Joanna 32
Thus then, each to other dear, ... 157 Sexton 25
Nor be less dear to future men . . . . . . 158 *In youth 78
"Whence strains to love-sick maiden dear, . . 164 Needlecase 33
Is joined through some dear homeborn tie; . . 164 *Glad sight 2
Forcing my way, I came to one dear nook . . 185 Nutting 16
"The stars of midnight shall be dear . . . . 187 *Three years 25
Or gives a thing but small delight that never can be dear? . . . . 189 Star-gazers 14
Enough by her dear side to breathe the air . . 190 *Lyre! though 16
Dear Ruth! more happily set free . . . . . 194 Ruth 176
Him, and his Lady-mother dear! . . . . . 204 Brougham 54
That those dear words should be fulfilled, . . 204 Brougham 81
My dear, dear Friend; and in thy voice I catch . 207 Tintern 116
My dear, dear Sister! and this prayer I make, . 207 Tintern 121
More dear, both for themselves and for thy sake! 207 Tintern 159
Listen, ponder, hold them dear; . . . . . 209 *Yes, it 18
Round the dear Shade she would have clung—'tis vain: . . . . 211 Laod. 152
Or blest procession (to the Immortals dear) . . 213 Dion 29
Dear Child of Nature, let them rail! . . . . 218 Young Lady 1
And the dear voice of harmony, ... 221 Triad 92
Ye did not forfeit one dear right, ... 223 Wishing-gate 14
For modest meanings dear. . . . . 224 *'Tis gone 18
Could from sad regions send him to a dear . . 229 Cuckoo-clock 31
To pencil dear and pen, ... 231 Jew. Fam. 4
At the still hour to Mercy dear, ... 233 Power of Sound 28
Then back to Earth, the dear green Earth:— . 237 P. B. 51
Were a vain notion; but the hope is dear . . . 250 *Happy the 12
Hath stirred thee deeply; with its own dear brook, 250 Admon. 3
In neighbourhood with One to me most dear, . 251 Appleth. 4
Dear Bosom-child we call thee, that dost steep . 253 *Fond words 5
Dear mother of fresh thoughts and joyous health! 254 *A flock 14
Might smile on work, O Lady, once so dear . . 255 S. H. 8
To her indulgent Lord become more dear. . . . 256 Marriage: Friend 14
When thou, dear Sister! wert become Death's Bride: . . . . 258 *Even so 4
Dear Child! dear Girl! that walkest with me here, 258 *It is a 9
Dear God! the very houses seem asleep; . . . 269 Westm. Bridge 13
After her throes, this Stream of name more dear . 275 Rotha Q. 11
As in a dear and chosen banishment, ... 275 *Chatsworth! thy 6
To life thou art, and, in thy truth, how dear! . 277 Author's Portrait 1
Pleased to renounce, does this dear Thrush attune 279 *'Tis he 6
From every object dear to mortal sight, . . . 282 *Wansfell! this 10
Well might such thoughts, dear Sister, throng . 285 Nith 7
With intimations manifold and dear, ... 294 *Fly, some 12
But most of all, his Mother dear, ... 297 Highland Boy 231
In dust, that voice is dear! . . . . 299 Cora Linn 18
From its dear home the Hermit's corse, . . . 301 Bran 59
For my dear Country, many heartfelt sighs, . . 303 *Fair Star 13
With such a dear Companion at my side. . . . 306 *Here, on our 14
Be men who hold its many blessings dear, . . 310 *Another year 11
Ah! that a _Conqueror's_ words should be so dear: 312 *A Roman 11
Dear Liberty! stern Nymph of soul untamed; . 314 *Advance—come 2
And lie cut off from all his heart holds dear: . . 318 *Is there 5
Dear native regions where ye wont to rove 325 Ode 1814 115

Dear—*continued.*
Dear Reliques ! from a pit of vilest mould . . 325 Enghien 1
O Britain ! dearer far than life is dear, . . . 331 Ode : Thanks 139
Dear Fellow-travellers ! think not that the Muse, 333 Ded. Tour 1
The strain seemed doubly dear, ... 334 *In Bruges 14
Though the toil of the way with dear Friends we divide, ... 345 Stanzas: Simplon 25
Had his sunk eye kindled at those dear words . 353 Aquap. 60
To whose dear memories his sepulchral verse . . 356 Aquap. 241
They follow their dear Lord ! Time flows—nor winds, ... 357 Aquap. 315
This flowering broom's dear neighbourhood, the light . . . . 358 Aquap. 369
Those old credulities, to nature dear, ... 359 *Those old 1
Dear as they are to unsuspecting Youth, . . . 359 Plea : Hist. 6
If with old love of you, dear Hills ! I share . . 367 *If with 1
And his dear Daughter on a Knight bestow . 372 Eg. Maid 227
Sir Tristram, dear to thousands as a brother, . . 373 Eg. Maid 290
To dream-light dear while yet unseen, ... 386 Yarrow Rev. 109
Dear to the common sunshine, ... 386 Yarrow Rev. 110
Better to thank a dear and long-past day . . 392 Bothwell 9
All that she suffered for her dear Lord's sake. 395 White Doe : Ded. 40
Of Bolton's dear fraternity ; . . . . 399 White Doe 296
The five dear wounds our Lord did bear ; . . . 400 White Doe 357
Dear Father, hear me when I say . . . . 400 White Doe 383
The name of his only Daughter dear, ... 400 White Doe 401
With a dear Father at their head ! . . . . . 401 White Doe 462
Thou, chiefly thou, my Sister dear, ... 401 White Doe 496
" My all save one, a Daughter dear ! . . . . 403 White Doe 616
Dear daughter of affliction, say . . . . . . 408 White Doe 1080
But for lost Faith and Christ's dear name, . . 410 White Doe 1299
Should bear him to his Sister dear . . . . . 411 White Doe 1373
And now her sainted Mistress dear ? . . . . 414 White Doe 1672
That Presence, dearer and more dear, ... 415 White Doe 1744
For reasons dear and manifold— . . . . . 415 White Doe 1800
A dear look to her lowly Friend ; . . . . . 416 White Doe 1855
Which her dear Mistress once held dear : . . . 416 White Doe 1880
The last dear service of thy passing breath ! . . 424 Ecc. Sonn. 1. 23. 14
The pious ALFRED, King to Justice dear ! . . . 425 Ecc. Sonn. 1. 26. 2
Scooped from the sacred earth where his dear relics lie. . . . . 426 Ecc. Sonn. 1. 32. 14
Then chiefly dear, when foes are planted round, . 430 Ecc. Sonn. 2. 6. 9
Dear to the saints, strives earnestly to eject . . 431 Ecc. Sonn. 2. 10. 7
Spreads high conceits to madding Fancy dear, . 433 Ecc. Sonn. 2. 20. 11
However hardly won or justly dear : . . . . 442 Ecc. Sonn. 3. 10. 12
Dear be the Church that, watching o'er the needs 445 Ecc. Sonn. 3. 20. 1
Isis and Cam, to patient Science dear ! . . . 451 Ecc. Sonn. 3. 42. 14
To king, to peasant, to rough sailor, dear, . . 455 Rydal Mere 29
Which with the dear Betrothèd was to come ; . . 458 Sea-shore 14
With some internal lights to memory dear, . . 460 *Wanderer! that 57
Dear to the Loves, and to the Graces vowed, . . 465 *Dear to 1
For Christ's dear sake, by human sympathies . 468 St. Bees 143
Dear art thou to the light of heaven, ... 480 Somnamb. 158
And thus the dear old Man replied, ... 487 Fountain 19
Two shall be named, pre-eminently dear,— . . 488 Pers. Talk 40
Low in the darksome cell thine own dear lord ? . 489 Spade 18
Yet they to whom thy virtues made thee dear . 490 Tribute : Dog 7
An impulse more profoundly dear . . . . . 498 *The sylvan 11
And to fallen man their innocence is dear. . . 500 Humanity 18
Alfred, dear Babe, thy great Progenitor ! . . . 504 Warning 60
Can such a One, dear Babe ! though glad and proud 504 Warning 78
My Country ! if such warning be held dear, . . 515 *Long-favoured 10
Of dear Old England ? Think they she is dead, . 516 *Young England 2
Dear Mother ! if thou must thy steps retrace, . 516 *Young England 12
From heaviness, oft fly, dear Friend, to thee ; . 521 Epist. Beaumont 11
For goods and chattels, or those Infants dear, . 523 Epist. Beaumont 113
Thus gladdened from our own dear Vale we pass . 524 Epist. Beaumont 164
Take those dear young Ones to a fearless nest ; . 525 *Soon did 2
For the dear blessings of a lowly couch, . . . 528 *Those breathing 84
Citadels dear to studious privacy. . . . . . 529 *Those breathing 119
Thy song would still be dear, ... 530 †Redbreast 10
Dear intercourse was theirs, day after day ; . . 531 *I know 13
You, Foster-father dear, ... 542 Russ. Fug. 70
" Dear child, sweet Mistress, say not so ! . . . 542 Russ. Fug. 75
A thought for your dear sake ; . . . . . . 542 Russ. Fug. 84
Though question followed question, dear . . . 545 Russ. Fug. 343
Yet not the less his Spirit would hold dear . . 547 *Ye Lime 11
If thou in the dear love of some one Friend . . 551 *If thou in 1
To be our guide unto thy Son so dear. . . . 553 Prioress 28
Our blissful Lady, Jesu's Mother dear, ... 553 Prioress 58
Thus saying, ' O dear Child ! I summon thee . . 555 Prioress 194
And, for the worship of His Mother dear, . . . 556 Prioress 203
Weeping and praising Jesu's Mother dear ; . . 556 Prioress 227
And unto Pandarus, his own Brother dear, . . 562 Troilus 3
My Lady dear, first bound me captive-wise. . . 563 Troilus 49
Heard I my most beloved Lady dear, ... 563 Troilus 58
With a soft voice, he of his Lady dear, . . . 564 Troilus 118
When hence did journey my bright Lady dear, . 564 Troilus 135
No—man is dear to man ; the poorest poor . . 568 Cumb. Beg. 147
Leads to the dear Parnassian forest's shade, . . 574 Chiabrera 5. 10
Dear as they were, than that his Flock, . . . 577 *By playful 16
Your hands, dear Little-ones, do all . . . . 577 *I come 9
Round this dear Vale, his native place. . . . 578 *I come 60
But one dear remnant of the night— . . . . 579 *Sweet Flower 48
Have lent his wing, my Brother dear, ... 580 John Words. 7
And hopes as dear as could the heart employ . . 581 *Why should we 5
If things in our remembrance held so dear, . . 583 *With copious 36
To a good Man of most dear memory . . . . 584 Ch. Lamb 1

Dear—*continued.*
To those dear intervals, nor rare nor brief, . . 586 Ch. Lamb 109
And dear the green-sward to his velvet tread ; . 602 Desc. Sk. Quarto 24
And my full heart was swell'd to dear delicious pain. . . . . 619 *She wept 4
Dear was the pause of life, and dear the sigh . 619 *She wept 7
But for the poor dear sake of one . . . . . 621 Andrew Jones 8
Dear Valley, having in thy face a smile . . . 622 Recluse 1. 1. 116
He comes, my dear delight,—and costliest things 624 Æneid 29
A day to future generations dear ! . . . . . 625 Æneid 111
Dear Liberty ! Yet what would it avail . . . 632 Prelude 1. 31
Of humbler industry. But, oh, dear Friend ! . 634 Prelude 1. 134
All over his dear Country ; left the deeds . . . 635 Prelude 1. 216
Habitually dear, and all their forms . . . . 641 Prelude 1. 610
Yet, to this hour, the spot to me is dear . . . 644 Prelude 2. 154
Grew dear to me : already I began . . . . . 644 Prelude 2. 177
Analogous, the moon to me was dear ; . . . . 645 Prelude 2. 191
To thee and thy grey huts, thou one dear Vale ! . 645 Prelude 2. 197
For him, in one dear Presence, there exists . . 645 Prelude 2. 238
Was dear, and hence to finer influxes . . . . 646 Prelude 2. 282
Of pleasant wandering. Happy time ! more dear 647 Prelude 2. 332
So dear, if I should fail with grateful voice . . 648 Prelude 2. 423
At our domestic table : and, dear Friend ! . . 659 Prelude 4. 78
Ah ! need I say, dear Friend ! that to the brim . 663 Prelude 4. 333
Or whatsoever else the heart holds dear ; . . . 668 Prelude 5. 155
When first I learnt, that this dear prize of mine . 672 Prelude 5. 464
With a dear friend, and for the better part . . 674 Prelude 5. 561
Dear to thee also, thy true friend and mine, . . 678 Prelude 6. 200
To whom my worldly interests were dear. . . . 680 Prelude 6. 332
Yet was the theatre my dear delight ; . . . . 693 Prelude 7. 407
Though most at home in this their dear domain, . 696 Prelude 7. 595
Through utter weakness pitiably dear, ... 700 Prelude 8. 61
With that majestic indolence so dear . . . . 703 Prelude 8. 255
As was thy melancholy lot, dear Friend ! . . . 705 Prelude 8. 434
Dear native Regions, wheresoe'er shall close . . 706 Prelude 8. 468
On the dear mountain-tops where first he rose. . 706 Prelude 8. 475
From the best youth in England their dear pride, 722 Prelude 10. 302
I paced, a dear companion at my side, . . . 725 Prelude 10. 497
Pains-taking thoughts, and truth, their dear reward) 732 Prelude 11. 327
On the glad eve of its dear holidays, ... 738 Prelude 12. 288
Oh ! next to one dear state of bliss, vouchsafed . 741 Prelude 13. 120
In my esteem, next to such dear delight, . . . 741 Prelude 13. 129
Or dear voice utter, to complete the man, . . . 749 Prelude 14. 223
This over-sternness ; but for thee, dear Friend ! . 749 Prelude 14. 247
Dear Sister ! was a kind of gentler spring . . . 750 Prelude 14. 265
And dear remembrances, whose presence soothes 755 Recluse 1. 1. 760
His dear companion wheresoe'er he went . . . 771 Excursion 2. 16
Four dear supporters of one senseless weight, . . 780 Excursion 2. 584
If the dear faculty of sight should fail, . . . 803 Excursion 4. 109
Lodged, in a dear appropriated spot, ... 836 Excursion 5. 945
For their dear countrymen, and all mankind. . . 839 Excursion 6. 73
My Infant ! and for that good Mother dear, . . 852 Excursion 6. 925
Dear Youth, by young and old alike beloved, . 868 Excursion 7. 706
The dear memorial footsteps unimpaired . . . 884 Excursion 9. 39
And this dear land, our country, while on earth . 895 Excursion 9. 740
Gracious to all the dear dependencies . . . . S.3. 426 *Through Cumbrian 7
Moved (shall I say ?) like a dear friend who meets S.3. 434 *The doubt 87
To thee, dear Spring, and all-sustaining Heaven ! S.3. 437 *The doubt 206
Dear Harmodius, art thou fled ? . . . . . S.3. 442 Harmodius 10
Let thy name, Harmodius dear . . . . . S.3. 442 Harmodius 21
Dear Aristogiton, live ; . . . . S.3. 442 Harmodius 24
This spot to me must needs be dear, ... K.8. 220 *The snow-tracks 31
Of my dear friends I see the trace. . . . . . K.8. 220 *The snow-tracks 32
The dear companion of my lonely walk . . . K.8. 234 *Witness thou 2
And now 'tis mine, perchance for life, dear Vale, . K.8. 238 Recluse 1.1. 56
And dear Imaginations realized . . . . . . K.8. 239 Recluse 1.1. 108
They were more dear than may be well believed, K.8. 243 Recluse 1.1. 248
To one who holds it dear ; with duteous care . . K.8. 251 Recluse 1.1. 525
Not even the nearest to me and most dear, . . K.8. 255 Recluse 1.1. 688
So welcome, no temptation half so dear . . . K.8. 256 Recluse 1.1. 709
And oh ! dear soother of the pensive breast, . . K.8. 301 *And oh 1

Dearer. Helpless, and loved me dearer than his life. 77 Bord. 2254
O dearer far than light and life are dear, . . . 112 *O dearer 1
Were dearer now ? that from the Boy there came 134 Michael 200
Are dearer than the sun. . . . . 193 Ruth 90
Thou com'st to man's abode the spot grew dearer 281 *What strong 3
But death, becoming death, is dearer far, . . . 326 *Intrepid sons 6
O Britain ! dearer far than life is dear, . . . 331 Ode : Thanks. 139
And dearer still, as now I feel, ... 386 Yarrow Rev. 111
That Presence, dearer and more dear, ... 415 White Doe 1744
No dearer relique, and no better stay, ... 778 Excursion 2. 483
Were dearer now ? that from the Boy there came K.8. 226 *I will 80
Or something dearer still, if reason knows . . . K.8. 234 *Witness thou 4
A dearer thought, or in the heart of love . . . K.8. 234 *Witness thou 5
There be a dearer name. . . . . K.8. 234 *Witness thou 6

Dearest. Far from my dearest Friend, 'tis mine to rove . . . . 2 Ev. Wk. 1
And, balancing the hopes that are the dearest . 66 Bord. 1614
O dearest, dearest boy ! my heart . . . . . 86 Anecdote 57
Then, dearest Maiden, move along these shades . 186 Nutting 54
Had been his dearest joy. . . . . 192 Ruth 36
Of this fair river ; thou my dearest Friend, . . 207 Tintern 115
On you we look, with dearest hope ; . . . . 403 White Doe 651
And no one can tell whither. Dearest Friend ! . 498 *Enough of climbing 45
And dearest helpers, left unthanked, unpraised, . 668 Prelude 5. 169
Are dearest to me now ; for, having scanned, . . 676 Prelude 6. 100
At dearest separation, patriot love . . . . . 713 Prelude 9. 272

Death—*continued.*
And, to his unmolested mansion, death . . . 861 Excursion 7. 244
Had been among them ; all was gentle death, . 861 Excursion 7. 253
Death fell upon him, while reclined he lay . . 861 Excursion 7. 285
Till gentlest death released him. Far from us . 862 Excursion 7. 310
Darkness is banished from the realms of death, . 865 Excursion 7. 529
The waste of death ; and lo ! the giant oak . . 865 Excursion 7. 547
Till nature rested from her work in death. . . 870 Excursion 7. 873
—Life, death, eternity ! momentous themes . . 874 Excursion 8. 10
Dead—but not sullied or deformed by death, . . 883 Excursion 8. 570
And ofttimes Death, avenger of the past, . . . 886 Excursion 9. 124
How with most quiet and most silent death, . . 886 Excursion 9. 149
Conscience to guide and check ; and death to be . 887 Excursion 9. 224
Of harmless Abel's death, by murdering Cain. . S. 3. 432 *Critics, right 4
Of him who cooked the death of Abel, ... S. 3. 432 *A German 2
Thus without death how sweet it is to die. . . S. 3. 441 *Come, gentle 4
More than one thought of death, and his last hour. K.8. 229 *I will 158
One death, and that were mercy given to both. . K.8. 244 Recluse 1.1.268
Making a silent company in death ; . . . . K.8. 255 Recluse 1.1.696
And fighting to the death, but I am pleased . . K.8. 256 Recluse 1.1.723

Death-bed. Thy breast their death-bed, coffined in thine arms ! . . . . 7 Ev. Wk. 278
Rock the cradle of joy, smooth the death-bed of strife. . . . . 143 †Lov. and Lik. 54
And come and make his death-bed near the well. 203 Hart-leap 148
This faithful guide, speaking from his death-bed, 726 Prelude 10. 537

Death-cross. By many a votive death-cross planted near, ... 14 Desc. Sk. 202

Death-cup. This spot—his shadowy death-cup in his hand. . . . . 361 *For action 14

Death-dog. The death-dog, howling loud and long, below ; . . . . 606 Desc.Sk.Quarto 226

Death-doomed. This was the death-doomed Woman heard to say . . . . 849 Excursion 6. 753

Deathful. Whose slippery face derides his deathful tread ! . . . . 609 Desc.Sk.Quarto 393

Death-hour. He would so love it, that in his death-hour . . . . 149 M. H. 21

Deathless. Of outward change, there blooms a deathless flower, ... 256 *Yes ! hope 13
Of virtue crowned with glory's deathless meed : . 327 Ode 1815 36
And tender Goldsmith crowned with deathless praise ! . . . . 380 Duddon 18. 14
For deathless powers to verse belong, ... 499 *Departing summer 25
Oh for a deathless song to meet . . . . . 507 May 11
A deathless spirit. Thou also, man ! hast wrought, 666 Prelude 5. 18
Thy bounty caused to flourish deathless flowers, . 802 Excursion 4. 53

Death-like. *That* Silence, once in deathlike fetters bound, ... 11 Desc. Sk. 56
Where silent Hours their death-like sway extend, 16 Desc. Sk. 311
Mother of Heroes, from thy death-like sleep ! . . 366 *Fair Land 14
That breath'd a death-like peace these woods around, ... 603 Desc. Sk. Quarto 57
Where Silence still her death-like reign extends, . 609 Desc.Sk.Quarto 376
Death-like, of treacherous desertion, felt . . . 724 Prelude 10. 414
Or from its death-like void, with punctual care, . 802 Excursion 4. 88

Death-list. How fast the Marian death-list is unrolled ! . . . . 437 Ecc. Sonn. 2. 34. 1

Death-note. Hark ! the death-note of the year . 113 Lament 64

Death-parted. Death-parted friends, and days too swift in flight, ... 358 Pine : Rome 11

Death-place. No kindred sufferer, to his death-place brought . . . . 36 Guilt 662

Death-proclaiming. A death-proclaiming blast ; . 544 Russ. Fug. 276

Death's. And death's dire aspect daily he surveyed, 25 Guilt 56
Death's minister ; then came his glad release, . 25 Guilt 57
Now are they parted, far as Death's cold hand . 152 *Forth from 16
When thou, dear Sister ! wert become Death's Bride : . . . . 258 *Even so 4
And in Death's arms has long reposed the Friend 525 *Soon did 3
Till Death's cold touch her cistern-wheel assail, . 615 Desc.Sk.Quarto 742
Death's hireling, who scoops out his neighbour's grave, ... 826 Excursion 5. 235
Come, gentle Sleep, Death's image tho' thou art, . S.3. 441 *Come, gentle 1

Death-shriek. Her last death-shriek, distinct among a thousand. . . . . 40 Bord. 187
It was the last death-shriek. . . . . 579 *Sweet Flower 45

Death-sounds. The death-sounds of the Minster-bell : 411 White Doe 1366

Death-watch. Or death-watch : and as readily rejoice, ... 810 Excursion 4. 617

Death-wound. Of his death-wound, when he from innocent air . . . . 169 Lovelies Bleeding 13

Debarred. *See* **Self-debarred.**
And sage Mnemosyne,—full long debarred . . 325 Ode 1814 112
Thus Virtue lives debarred from Virtue's meed ; . 539 *Lady ! a 40
Or rather like a stallèd ox debarred . . . . 669 Prelude 5. 242
Debarred from Nature's living images, ... 675 Prelude 6. 302
Preclude forgiveness, from the praise debarred, . 845 Excursion 6. 489

Debase. The simple dignity no forms debase ; . . 18 Desc. Sk. 443
Seemingly given, debase the general mind ; . . 518 Pun. Death 4. 9
The native dignity no forms debase, ... 611 Desc.Sk.Quarto 530
By artificial lights ; how they debase . . . . 743 Prelude 13. 210
Doth most debase the mind ; the genuine seats . 813 Excursion 4. 776

Debased. Debased and under profanation, made . K.8. 246 Recluse 1.1.342

Debasement. Debasement undergone by body or mind, ... 708 Prelude 8. 646
And from debasement rescued.—By thy grace . 802 Excursion 4. 50

Debasing. *See* **Soul-debasing.**
And their hard service, deemed debasing now, . 761 Excursion 1. 327

Debate. Farewell all wishes, all debate, ... 402 White Doe 540

Debate—*continued.*
That interdicted all debate, ... 407 White Doe 1065
Mistrust and jealousy, despite, debate, . . . 560 Cuck.and Night. 173

Debauchee. Seasoning his wickedness. The Debauchee . . . . 49 Bord. 662

Debonair. Luminous, blithe, and debonair ? . . 370 Eg. Maid 52

Debt. And bore him high through yielding air my debt of love to pay, ... 92 Poet's Dream 19
Of blameless debt. On evil Fortune's spite . . 138 Widow 5
Their union brought, will they repay the debt, . 143 *High bliss 26
All seasons through, another debt, ... 158 *In youth 66
Or flinch from what he deemed his debt : . . . 178 Waggoner 2. 158
Until the debt I owe be paid. . . . . . . 182 Waggoner 4. 215
The well-remembered debt." . . . . 238 P. B. 185
Then pays submissively the appointed debt . . 261 *I watch 8
Is there no debt to pay, no boon to grant ? . . 277 *Why art 4
The mighty debt which nothing can repay ! " . 324 Ode 1814 68
Which ne'er may discharge the magnificent debt ? 345 Stanzas:Simplon 12
The recreant soul, that dares to shun the debt . 424 Ecc. Sonn. 1. 23. 10
As a debt to that frail Creature, ... 502 *Like a 19
We pay a high and holy debt ; . . . . . . 582 *O for a 7
To pay the filial debt, for food to roam, . . . 613 Desc.Sk.Quarto 615
For, not unconscious of the mighty debt . . . 870 Excursion 7. 839

Debtor. Have been fast bound, a begging debtor ;— 239 P. B. 237

Debtors. All that breathe are thankful debtors . 90 Longest Day 7

Debts. Of reason, honourably effaced by debts . . 862 Excursion 7. 319

Decalogue. Men who can hear the Decalogue and feel 568 Cumb. Beg. 135

Decanters. Decanters, glasses, and the blood-red wine. . . . . 644 Prelude 2. 144

Decay. My father's substance fell into decay : . . 28 Guilt 229
Charms superior to decay. . . . . 90 Longest Day 64
That fosters growth or checks or cheers decay, . 169 *Never enlivened 2
That, when time brings on decay, ... 171 Kitten 114
Already hast survived that great decay, . . . 172 Infant Daughter 6
Produced too slowly ever to decay ; . . . . 184 Yew-trees 11
But they have dwindled long by slow decay ; . . 197 Resolution 125
And Nature here were willing to decay. . . . 202 Hart-leap 116
" She leaves these objects to a slow decay, . . 203 Hart-leap 173
Suffer my genial spirits to decay : . . . . . 207 Tintern 113
Shall ne'er submit to cold decay. . . . . . 216 Enterprise 52
Shine subject to decay, ... 226 Vernal Ode 41
Decay and languish ; or, as creeds . . . . 228 Devot. Incit. 48
And in the soul admit of no decay, ... 260 *High is 12
Knits not o'er that discolouring and decay . . 267 *Desponding Father 6
Fall to prevent or beautify decay ; . . . . . 283 *Here, where 6
Impersonated in thy calm decay ! . . . . . 290 Kilchurn 21
Those titles vanish, and that strength decay ; . 305 Ven. Rep. 10
A fond reflection of her own decay, ... 321 *Humanity, delighting 2
Decay submits not. But where'er my steps . . 355 Aquap. 198
And feeble, of themselves, decay ; . . . . . 391 Highland Broach 64
One desolation, one decay ! . . . . 402 White Doe 555
Subdued by outrage and decay, ... 417 White Doe 1906
" Thus fares it still in our decay : . . . . . 487 Fountain 33
Inspire us in our own decay ; . . . . . . 497 Lycoris 52
And dissolution and decay, the warm . . . . 510 *Among a 6
Stript of its frightful powers by slow decay, . . 523 Epist. Beaumont 126
This little Niche, unconscious of decay, . . . 546 *Oft is 8
It cannot help itself in its decay ; . . . . . 571 There is a Flower 18
He suffered not to languish or decay. . . . . 575 Chiabrera 8. 16
The lily of domestic joy decay ; . . . . . . 615 Desc.Sk.Quarto 723
New stores, or rescue from decay the old . . . 633 Prelude 1. 117
Queens gleaming through their splendour's last decay, ... 640 Prelude 1. 533
Through every change of growth and of decay, . 646 Prelude 2. 264
Good might be furthered—in his last decay . . 751 Prelude 14. 358
He had observed the progress and decay . . . 761 Excursion 1. 375
The hut itself abandoned to decay, ... 763 Excursion 1. 509
Sank to decay ; for he was gone, whose hand, . 770 Excursion 1. 901
Of instability, revolt, decay, ... 788 Excursion 3. 138
And sad exclusion through decay of sense ; . . 802 Excursion 4. 59
Doomed to decay, and then expire in dust ! . . 829 Excursion 5. 478
With snares ; tried, tempted, subject to decay. . 830 Excursion 5. 495
The fluctuation and decay of things, ... 837 Excursion 5. 999
Was disappearing by a swift decay, ... 845 Excursion 6. 495
The ghastly face of cold decay put on . . . . 854 Excursion 6. 1036
From vice and premature decay preserved . . . 862 Excursion 7. 300
Her organs and her members, with decay . . . 872 Excursion 7. 1001
Is the sure consequence of slow decay. . . . . 873 Excursion 7. 1040
Its very spring a season of decay ! . . . . . 878 Excursion 8. 291
Though strength decay, to breathe in such estate 885 Excursion 9. 46

Decayed. Felt the loose walls of this decayed Retreat 27 Guilt 173
There *was* he, where of branches rent and withered and decayed, ... 91 Norman Boy 13
The towns in Saturn are decayed, ... 237 P. B. 41
Than noblest objects utterly decayed. . . . . 269 Malham 14
The grace of forest charms decayed, ... 302 Yarrow V. 47
With monuments decayed or overthrown, . . . 360 Alban Hills 3
Of woods decaying, never to be decayed, . . . 684 Prelude 6. 625
Confusion of the judgment, zeal decayed, . . . 734 Prelude 12. 5
That, for support, rests on them ; the decayed . 837 Excursion 5. 966

Decaying. Of thoughts that fail, and a decaying heart ; . . . . 66 Bord. 1631
'Mid those decaying sanctities. . . . . . . 410 White Doe 1295
Round the decaying trunk of human pride, . . 424 Ecc. Sonn. 1. 21. 8
Of woods decaying, never to be decayed, . . . 684 Prelude 6. 625

Decays. From airy words alone, a Pile that ne'er decays. . . . . 547 *Beneath yon 20
While man grows old, and dwindles, and decays ; 812 Excursion 4. 760

Deceit. —And let him nurse his fond deceit, — 9 *Lines : Boat* 13
Deceitfully. Deceitfully goes forth the Morn ; — 550 *Hermit's Cell* 5. 2
Deceive. May well deceive his Child—What ! leave her thus, — 41 *Bord.* 251
I would fain hope that we deceive ourselves : — 44 *Bord.* 375
The world in substance, not deceive by show, — 70 *Bord.* 1829
And here is yours,—or do my eyes deceive me ? — 76 *Bord.* 2226
Or if such faith must needs deceive— — 191 *Seq. Beggars* 31
It is—if sense deceive her not—'tis He ! — 209 *Laod.* 17
I am not sent to scare thee or deceive ; — 210 *Laod.* 39
Is feared as what may most deceive ? — 345 **How blest* 69
A stir of mind too natural to deceive ; — 448 *Ecc. Sonn.* 3. 33. 4
Ah why deceive ourselves ! by no mere fit — 515 **Ah why* 1
Bright colours whether they deceive or no ?— — 530 *Poor Robin* 23
Uplifted ; why deceive ourselves ? in sooth, — 731 *Prelude* 11. 267
And steal away, and for a while deceive — K.8. 245 *Recluse* 1.1.304
Deceived. After his death. I have been much deceived. — 41 *Bord.* 235
Oh heavens ! you've been deceived. Thou art a Woman — 67 *Bord.* 1636
Where ours are baffled. I had been deceived. — 69 *Bord.* 1753
The Crew deceived you ? Nay, command yourself. — 69 *Bord.* 1764
Then, thinking that my fancy had deceived me, — 73 *Bord.* 2046
All deceived, and each deceiver, — 90 *Longest Day* 51
By friends deceived, by foes betrayed, — 113 *Lament* 59
The same weak wish returns, that had before deceived him. — 311 **Who rises* 60
Whom no weak hopes deceived ; whose mind ensued, — 323 **Now that* 6
And confidence deceived. — 338 **Meek Virgin* 12
Am I deceived ? Or is their requiem chanted — 430 *Ecc. Sonn.* 2. 8. 9
Deceived, mistake calamities for wrongs ; — 505 *Warning* 114
Who thus deceived shall lend an eager hand — 514 **Who ponders* 10
By that seducing air deceiv'd, — 620 *Birth of Love* 36
Deserted and deceived, the Spoiler came — 691 *Prelude* 7. 299
Now do I feel how all men are deceived, — 712 *Prelude* 9. 170
Thou gratulatest, willingly deceived— — 734 *Prelude* 11. 468
These occupations oftentimes deceived — 760 *Excursion* 1. 258
Deceiver. A prey to a deceiver ?—no—no—no— — 41 *Bord.* 252
All deceived, and each deceiver, — 90 *Longest Day* 51
Pomp has been a sad deceiver. — L.2. 190 **Queen and* 14
Deceives. My dazzled sight he oft deceives, — 159 *Green Linnet* 33
A simple flower deceives. — 169 *Wren's Nest* 60
Deceiving. *See* **Self-deceiving.**
December. In March, December, and in July, — 536 *Goody Blake* 9
In bleak December, I retraced this way, — 769 *Excursion* 1. 855
December's. That keeps, till June, December's snow ; — 491 *Fidelity* 18
Decency. To an harmonious decency confined : — 334 **The Spirit* 8
Who live a life of virtuous decency, — 568 *Cumb. Beg.* 134
And Decency and Custom starving Truth, — 657 *Prelude* 3. 604
In silence, with a hush of decency ; — 780 *Excursion* 2. 557
Decent. He may give thee decent greeting. — 181 *Waggoner* 4. 137
That field-ward takes her walk with decent steps. — 690 *Prelude* 7. 210
Decent and unreproved. The voice, that greets — 838 *Excursion* 6. 12
Their snow-white curtains hung in decent folds ; — 860 *Excursion* 7. 180
From his wife's Faro-bank a decent rent, — L.1. 97 *Juvenal* 3. 82
Decently. Bare-headed, and all decently attired ! — 777 *Excursion* 2. 392
Deception. Transient deception ! a gay freak — 170 *Rural Ill.* 7
Decide. It shall be done as Wisdom shall decide : — 58 *Bord.* 1129
Deciphered. Not easily deciphered, told of one — 825 *Excursion* 5. 179
Deciphering. Protect us, there deciphering as we may — 498 **Enough of climbing* 33
Decisions. Delivering her decisions from the seat — 792 *Excursion* 3. 412
Decisive. (And fast, from this decisive day, — 406 *White Doe* 908
By violence, at one decisive rent, — 722 *Prelude* 10. 301
Deck. *See* **Quarter-deck.**
The bound of all his vanity, to deck, — 19 *Desc. Sk.* 494
The flowering shrubs that deck our humble door — 106 *Farewell* 11
Or art can fashion, shall you deck our boy, — 124 *V. and J.* 201
On a friendly deck reposing — 141 *Arm. Lady* 97
His short domain upon the vessel's deck, — 150 **When, to* 65
Art pacing thoughtfully the vessel's deck — 151 **When, to* 101
Would deck you many a winter day, — 155 *Waterfall* 49
To deck your slender shape ; — 156 *Oak and Broom* 32
Steals from the deck o'er willing waves, — 234 *Power of Sound* 135
The sober Hills thus deck their brows — 302 *Yarrow V.* 71
To deck your stern Defenders' modest brows ! — 324 *Ode 1814* 46
See what gay wild flowers deck this earth-built Cot, — 390 *Highland Hut* 1
Gives holier invitation than the deck — 447 *Ecc. Sonn.* 3. 30. 2
Paces the deck—no star perhaps in sight, — 460 **Wanderer ! that* 67
Or when his tiny gems shall deck his brow : — 530 *Poor Robin* 28
To deck some slighted playmate's homely cheek. — 661 *Prelude* 4. 208
From the receding vessel's deck, we chanced — 680 *Prelude* 6. 344
No better than a landsman on the deck — 721 *Prelude* 10. 227
O'er paths they used to deck : carnations, once — 767 *Excursion* 1. 724
Bring garlands, bring forth choicest flowers, to deck — 796 *Excursion* 3. 725
Smooth and commodious ; as a stately deck — 805 *Excursion* 4. 246
Why, friend, to deck her supple twigs — S.3. 431 **The Scottish* 7
Decked. *See* **Deckt, Flower-decked.**
With which, though bent on haste, myself I decked ; — 28 *Guilt* 222
The old house-clock is decked with a new face ; — 97 *Brothers* 160
Attends on goodness with dominion decked, — 105 *Artegal* 188
Of boughs, as if for festal purpose decked — 185 *Yew-trees* 24
So richly decked in variegated down, — 231 **The gentlest Poet* 17
If the calm Heaven, now to its zenith decked — 282 **While beams* 11
Remembering, and green Alpine pastures decked — 340 *Ranz* 6
Garden and field all decked with orange bloom, — 356 *Aquap.* 217
With truth, or with each other, decked remains — 389 *Breadalb.* 6
By Nature decked for holiest sacrifice. — 420 *Ecc. Sonn.* 1. 6. 14
Decked as in pride, and with outlandish grace : — 676 *Prelude* 6. 79
Decked with refreshments had this child been placed, — 692 *Prelude* 7. 357

Decked—*continued.*
Tales of the May-pole dance, and wreaths that decked — 701 *Prelude* 8. 151
The unendangered myrtle, decked with flowers, — 793 *Excursion* 3. 523
That sparkling decked the morning grass ; or aught — 843 *Excursion* 6. 317
Decked with autumnal berries, that outshine — 868 *Excursion* 7. 717
Decking. Decking the matron temples of a place — 652 *Prelude* 3. 224
Decks. Even now she decks for me a distant scene, — 8 *Ev. Wk.* 345
That thinly decks his few grey hairs ; — 157 **In youth* 10
Thy cradle decks ;—to chant thy birth, thou hast — 376 *Duddon* 2. 6
Decks, on thy sinuous banks, her thousand thrones, — 464 **Greta, what* 10
Have struck thy sides, too many ghastly decks — 466 *St. Bees* 22
Whose merchants Princes were, whose decks were thrones ; — 475 *Greenock* 10
On regal decks beheld ! yet in the end — 574 *Chiabrera* 4. 22
Where Persecution decks with ghastly smiles — 617 *Desc.Sk.Quarto* 798
Deckt. Well pleased to skim the plain with wild flowers deckt, — 270 **Though the bold* 4
Declaration. To scorn the declaration, — 111 **Yes ! thou* 2
Declare. That name through every age, her hatred to declare. — 103 *Artegal* 40
Our groans, our blushes, our pale cheeks declare — 319 *Spaniard* 13
Feels, and hereafter shall the truth declare, — 327 *Ode 1815* 42
Against all good "—but why declare, — 406 *White Doe* 926
Told, also, how the voiceless heavens declare — 461 **Queen of* 42
And some the hovering clouds, our telegraph, declare. — 522 *Epist. Beaumont* 84
And unto him declare why men sing so ; — 553 *Prioress* 76
Do I declare—in accents which, from truth — 748 *Prelude* 14. 144
—Stoop from those heights, and soberly declare — 813 *Excursion* 4. 774
Of puppetry, that from the lap declare — 826 *Excursion* 5. 270
So to declare the conscience satisfied : — 839 *Excursion* 6. 67
These elements of virtue, that declare — 848 *Excursion* 6. 665
Declared. He journeyed, and forthwith his crime declared : — 36 *Guilt* 651
Sends gladness, by no languid smile declared. — 273 **Not the* 8
The song, than the Arab with calm look declared — 667 *Prelude* 5. 99
Their madness stands declared and visible ; — 726 *Prelude* 10. 587
Declared at large ; and by what exercise — 831 *Excursion* 5. 583
Declares. One with its kindling edge declares that soon — 461 **Who but is* 5
Declares the vital power of social ties — 695 *Prelude* 7. 527
And that most awful scripture which declares — 780 *Excursion* 2. 577
Declares his due, while he makes known his need. — 889 *Excursion* 9. 320
Declination. Such a gradual declination — 90 *Longest Day* 35
Decline. And when thy decline shall come, — 90 *Longest Day* 42
Was in his judgment tempted to decline — 122 *V. and J.* 61
And free from semblance of decline ;— — 226 *Vernal Ode* 36
Oh ! if within me hope should e'er decline, — 258 **Even so* 9
While health, power, glory, from their height decline, — 261 **I watch* 11
And wish the Lord of day his slow decline — 277 **The most* 5
Fade, and participate in man's decline. — 308 **There is a bondage* 14
In the Tower's shadow, of decline and fall — 355 *Aquap.* 180
In conquered Cyprus see thy Bride decline — 427 *Ecc. Sonn.* 1. 35. 5
Confirmed alike in progress and decline. — 431 *Ecc. Sonn.* 2. 10. 14
Gently to brook decline and fatal change ; — 461 **Queen of* 54
When Nature marks the year's decline, — 497 *Lycoris* 29
Through shades that solemnize Life's calm decline, — 627 **The star* 5
And I, without reluctance, could decline — 789 *Excursion* 3. 234
Yet rather would I instantly decline — 810 *Excursion* 4. 613
Right to expect his vigorous decline, — 828 *Excursion* 5. 388
The story that retraced the slow decline — 854 *Excursion* 6. 1059
Of Desolation, aimed : to slow decline — 872 *Excursion* 7. 994
And its devotion gradually decline, — 873 *Excursion* 7. 1018
Declined. Two hours declined towards the west ; a day — 633 *Prelude* 1. 67
Declined their languid heads, wanting support. — 767 *Excursion* 1. 727
Declines. How pleasant, as the sun declines, to view — 4 *Ev. Wk.* 98
Ere hope declines :—their union is beset — 437 *Ecc. Sonn.* 2. 37. 8
How pleasant, as the yellowing sun declines, — 593 *Ev. Wk. Quarto* 97
Declining. That earth can offer to declining man, — 133 *Michael* 147
Declining Manhood learns to note the sly — 378 *Duddon* 9. 12
On our past selves in life's declining day : — 449 *Ecc. Sonn.* 3. 35. 5
A life declining with the golden light — 539 **Lady ! a* 60
That, as thy sun in brightness is declining, — 540 **Lady ! a* 78
(Whene'er the summer sun, declining, smote — 705 *Prelude* 8. 407
He ceased. Ere long the sun declining shot — 771 *Excursion* 1. 957
Decorate. Of hoary Time to decorate ; — 533 **Blest is* 4
Decorated. That to the decorated pillar lead, — 846 *Excursion* 6. 505
Decoration. For festive decoration ; and they said, — 59 *Bord.* 1204
Be there of decoration to beguile — 365 **Under the* 7
For decoration in the Papal time, — 448 *Ecc. Sonn.* 3. 32. 11
With decoration of ideal grace ; — 672 *Prelude* 5. 457
Decoy. Solemnly dedicated—to decoy him !— — 75 *Bord.* 2166
For you and your green twigs decoy — 156 *Oak and Broom* 45
Creature none can she decoy — 171 *Kitten* 89
Decree. Yet in themselves are nothing ! One decree — 306 **Inland, within* 12
Her waves rolled on, respecting his decree — 495 *Fact* 7
From him who judged her lord, a like decree ; — 505 *Warning* 154
Earnest and blind, against the stern decree. — 721 *Prelude* 10. 190
Refuse to echo the sublime decree ? — 890 *Excursion* 9. 404
Time's weary course ! Or if, by thy decree, — 893 *Excursion* 9. 635
Critics, right honourable Bard, decree — S.3. 432 **Critics, right* 1
Decreed. Mark the Almighty Wisdom, which decreed — 57 *Bord.* 1117
And he, whose power restores thee, hath decreed — 210 *Laod.* 57
Though old Bellerophon (so Jove decreed — 260 **From the dark* 5
Unto their martyred Countrymen decreed, — 324 *Ode 1814* 51
They shout aloud—but Heaven decreed — 408 *White Doe* 1145
Decrees. Hastening the stern decrees of Time, — 298 *Brownie's Cell* 34
(While we look round) that Heaven's decrees are just : — 437 *Ecc. Sonn.* 2. 36. 3

Decrees—*continued.*
The Gods revolving the decrees of Fate, . . . 457 *The leaves 31
And, from her vow well weighed in Heaven's decrees, 466 St. Bees 35
But fixing by immutable decrees . . . . . 500 Humanity 47
Are ye prepared to urge, that my decrees . . . 805 Excursion 4. 282
Decrees and resolutions of the Gods ; . . . . 812 Excursion 4. 704
Decrepit. In that decrepit Man so firm a mind. . 197 Resolution 138
That old decrepit Winter—He hath slain . . . 322 *Ye Storms 13
Decried. You have decried the wealth which is your own. . . . . 787 Excursion 3. 79
Dedicate. My EMMA, I will dedicate to thee." . . 146 *It was an 39
The city one vast temple, dedicate . . . . . 334 *The Spirit 10
On Tiber's banks my youth was dedicate . . . 573 Chiabrera 3. 5
Once to Our Lady dedicate, and served . . . 643 Prelude 2. 64
This verse is dedicate to Nature's self, ... 669 Prelude 5. 230
Dedicated. Solemnly dedicated—to decoy him !— . 75 Bord. 2166
A dedicated Spirit. On I walked . . . . . 663 Prelude 4. 337
Dedication. A dedication made, a promise given . 826 Excursion 5. 289
Deduce. Even so deduce the stream of human life 790 Excursion 3. 256
Deduced. Deduced by reason, or to faith revealed. 775 Excursion 2. 240
Dee. A Stream, to mingle with your favourite Dee, 272 Lady E. B. 1
Deed. Such further deed in manhood's name forbade ; 33 Guilt 479
And he had done the deed in the dark wood— . 35 Guilt 607
Out of that deed. My trust, Saviour ! is in thy name ! " . . . . 36 Guilt 657
Of some dark deed to which in early life . . . 37 Bord. 15
For this good deed !—Well, Sirs, this passed away ; 44 Bord. 409
The deed is done—if you will have it so— . . 48 Bord. 641
To look upon the deed. Before we enter . . . 49 Bord. 657
Sigh at the deed ? Hew down a withered tree, . 54 Bord. 928
Begone ! There is some wicked deed in hand : . 55 Bord. 953
Are hushed to sleep, by your own act and deed, . 55 Bord. 956
Shall blessings wait upon a deed of mine. . . . 76 Bord. 2197
A deed that I would shrink from ;—but to endure, 78 Bord. 2301
'Tis done ! The ruthless traitor ! A rash deed !— 78 Bord. 2319
Yet more ;—heart-smitten by the heroic deed, . 105 Artegal 227
And Love is dutiful in thought and deed ; . . 112 *O dearer 14
By word, look, deed, with hope that he might love again. . . . . 139 Arm. Lady 6
And prompt to many a gentle deed : . . . . 143 †Lov. and Lik. 64
Due to that good and pious deed . . . . . 143 *Driven in 9
" But thou, though capable of sternest deed, . . 210 Laod. 55
Mounting from glorious deed to deed . . . . 216 Enterprise 45
In his calm presence ! Him the mighty deed . . 278 Wellington 9
As wise in thought as bold in deed : . . . . 291 Rob Roy 18
Faithfully kept, is as a noble deed ; . . . . 317 *Brave Schill 13
Checked in the very act and deed of blood, . . 322 Germans 3
With second life the deed of Marathon . . . 324 Ode 1814 97
Achieved, this closing deed magnificent, . . . 327 Ode 1815 6
To mutual respect in thought and deed ; . . . 334 *The Spirit 11
Ah, what avails heroic deed ? . . . . . . 342 Ital. Itin. 91
So, from the body of one guilty deed, ... 346 Gemmi 13
More than on written testament or deed, . . . 393 Countess' Pillar 7
The triumph of a desperate deed . . . . . 408 White Doe 1147
Confirmed the deed in peace profound. . . . 410 White Doe 1335
" No choice is left, the deed is mine— . . . . 411 White Doe 1432
Of time, and place, and thought, and deed— . . 415 White Doe 1715
Into main Ocean they, this deed accurst . . . 433 Ecc. Sonn. 2. 17. 11
The Church extends her care to thought and deed ; 448 Ecc. Sonn. 3. 31. 2
What—how ! shall she submit in will and deed . 516 *Young England 9
Take from the horror due to a foul deed, . . . 519 Pun. Death 8. 10
Deed and intent, should turn the Being adrift . 519 Pun. Death 10. 5
The blood cries out on your accursèd deed. . . 554 Prioress 127
To whom a foul deed he had done, ... 621 Andrew Jones 9
Became my prey ; and when the deed was done . 637 Prelude 1. 321
Who make our wish, our power, our thought a deed, 673 Prelude 5. 528
Or the remembrance of a generous deed, . . . 685 Prelude 6. 683
Hard by, soon after that fell deed was wrought, . 737 Prelude 12. 239
Forbearance, charity in deed and thought, . . 862 Excursion 7. 329
Deeds. Have wrought with godlike arm the deeds of praise, ... 15 Desc. Sk. 290
Your justice stamp upon his evil deeds . . . 42 Bord. 266
And we too chant the praise of his good deeds. . 54 Bord. 907
The prey or masters of our own past deeds. . . 65 Bord. 1522
To fit all deeds. Carry him to the Camp !— . . 65 Bord. 1573
Whose good deeds will not stand by their own light ; 74 Bord. 2081
" To wicked deeds I was inclined, ... 115 Last of Flock 71
Bestir them in good deeds. Now, fare thee well— 137 Michael 412
From bloody deeds his thoughts are far ; . . . 166 Danish Boy 51
Haunts the old trunk ; lamenting deeds of which 219 Haunted Tree 29
High deeds, O Germans, are to come from you ! . 313 Prophecy 1
" Be thankful, thou ; for, if unholy deeds . . . 313 *Clouds, lingering 13
With deeds of hope and everlasting praise :— . 318 *Is there 10
For their great deeds, perpetual memory, . . . 325 Ode 1814 147
Unheard by them, their deeds shall celebrate ! . 328 Ode 1815 86
In execution of heroic deeds . . . . 330 Ode : Thanks. 63
Bestowed by Nature, or from man's great deeds . 352 Aquap. 6
In those bold fictions that, by deeds assigned . . 357 Aquap. 280
Such deeds to paint, such characters to frame, . 359 *Complacent Fictions 6
So may all trace and sign of deeds aloof . . . 361 *When here 9
I raise my thoughts, inform my deeds and words, 365 *Rapt above 7
And everlasting deeds to burning words ! . . . 421 Ecc. Sonn. 1. 10. 14
And perished utterly ; but her good deeds . . 466 St. Bees 59
Who taught, and showed by deeds, that gentler chains . . . . 468 St. Bees 140
To call thee so ?) or symbol of fierce deeds . . 472 *The captive 10
Of conscience souls are placed by deeds that lack 475 *Here on their 5
Requires for nobler deeds ; . . . . 479 Somnamb. 69
—I've heard of hearts unkind, kind deeds . . 484 Simon Lee 93

Deeds—*continued.*
For ever, and to noble deeds give birth, . . . 494 Hap. War. 78
By deeds the blackest purpose to lay bare— . . 518 Pun. Death 4. 3
Awaits her now ; but, verily, good deeds . . . 540 Grace Darl. 14
The Czar full oft in words and deeds . . . . 545 Russ. Fug. 333
Past deeds and offices of charity, ... 567 Cumb. Beg. 90
In this cold abstinence from evil deeds, . . . 568 Cumb. Beg. 144
Of meditation on the inhuman deeds . . . . 635 Prelude 1. 207
All over his dear Country ; left the deeds . . 635 Prelude 1. 216
Old heroes and their sufferings and their deeds ; . 712 Prelude 9. 208
We summoned up the honourable deeds . . . 715 Prelude 9. 364
Of Kings, their vices and their better deeds, . . 716 Prelude 9. 494
I might have been entangled among deeds, . . 798 Excursion 3. 814
A race illustrious for heroic deeds, ... 834 Excursion 5. 792
The good man's purposes and deeds ; retrace . . 863 Excursion 7. 376
Father and founder of exalted deeds ; . . . . 870 Excursion 7. 824
To Gods delighting in remorseless deeds ; . . . 894 Excursion 9. 685
Who pushed by thoughtless youth to deeds of shame L.1. 96 Juvenal 3. 55
Deem. Not used to rash conjectures—— If you deem it . . . . 42 Bord. 291
As well indeed it might. And this you deem . 51 Bord. 749
Deem rather that the fervent Youth, who saw . 122 V. and J. 57
Deem that by such fond hope the Youth was swayed, 122 V. and J. 64
Yet not unfit, I deem, for the fireside, . . . 131 Michael 20
To deem that he was old,—in shepherd's phrase, . 132 Michael 83
Nor, I deem, for me unmeet ; . . . . . . 171 Kitten 42
From Indian blood you deem him sprung : . . 192 Ruth 25
Rejoiced is Brough, right glad, I deem, . . . 204 Brougham 44
Who deem that ye from open light . . . . . 225 Present. 2
Nor deem that " light which leads astray . . . 287 Sons of Burns 41
Forbear to deem the Chronicler unwise, . . . 359 Plea : Hist. 1
Nor deem it strange ; the Youth had worn . . 373 Eg. Maid 313
Nor deem that localised Romance . . . . . 386 Yarrow Rev. 89
No ; will not all men deem the change . . . 411 White Doe 1401
Yet do not deem the Autocracy prevailed . . . 429 Ecc. Sonn. 2. 2. 3
Lures not from what they deem the cause of God. 441 Ecc. Sonn. 3. 6. 14
Whose sterner judgments deem that word a snare 463 *They called 7
" Nor less I deem that there are Powers . . . 481 Expost. 21
Nor deem the Poet's hope misplaced, ... 533 *Blest is 41
" From your deportment, Sir ! I deem . . . 544 Russ. Fug. 281
But deem not this Man useless.—Statesmen ! ye . 567 Cumb. Beg. 67
Your talents, power, or wisdom, deem him not . 567 Cumb. Beg. 72
Deem that our puny boundaries are things . . 645 Prelude 2. 218
And deem not profitless those fleeting moods . . 646 Prelude 2. 312
More pleasing, and whose character I deem . . 647 Prelude 2. 380
Yet deem not, Friend ! that human kind with me 704 Prelude 8. 340
Wouldst thou not chide ? Yet deem not my pains lost : . . . . 717 Prelude 9. 564
Thy favour ; trusting that thou wilt not deem . 753 *Oft, through 13
Nor is that fellow-wanderer, so deem I, . . . 788 Excursion 3. 173
I deem not arduous ; but must needs confess . . 803 Excursion 4. 135
Deem not that proof is here of hope withheld . 803 Excursion 4. 169
Subject, you deem, to vital accidents ; . . . . 831 Excursion 5. 566
—Nor deem that his mild presence was a weight . 864 Excursion 7. 438
Shadows or breezes, scents or sounds. Nor deem K.8. 249 Recluse 1.1.448
From self-respecting interests, deem them not . K.8. 249 Recluse 1.1.452
Deemed. Of our weak nature rest not, must be deemed . . . . 119 Maternal Grief 76
Or flinch from what he deemed his debt : . . . 178 Waggoner 2. 158
As if (so Grecian shepherds would have deemed) . 219 Haunted Tree 25
(So faith too fondly deemed) a voice divine . . 319 Guernica 3
Thoughts sadder still, they deemed it best . . 412 White Doe 1517
(As might be deemed) to disciplined intent . . 428 Ecc. Sonn. 1. 37. 6
So deemed the man who fashioned for the sense . 451 Ecc. Sonn. 3. 43. 8
Forth-shadowing, some have deemed, the infinite 477 Long Meg 13
Discourse was deemed Man's noblest attribute, . 489 Illus. Books 1
Their gifts she hails (deemed precious, as they prove 503 Warning 28
And deem'd all merit centred in the sword ; . . 619 School Ex. 54
Or deemed it worth a moment's thought to stir, . 711 Prelude 9. 137
For ill-requited France, by many deemed . . . 733 Prelude 11. 384
Known by whatever name, is falsely deemed . . 742 Prelude 13. 187
He deemed that my pursuits and labours lay . . 751 Prelude 14. 364
That will be deemed no insufficient plea . . . 751 Prelude 14. 390
And their hard service, deemed debasing now, . 761 Excursion 1. 327
Which did not please me, " must be deemed, I fear, 780 Excursion 2. 595
And their arrangement, doubtless must be deemed 788 Excursion 3. 125
With your bright transports fairly may be deemed, 788 Excursion 3. 160
(Not to be deemed a stranger, as you come . . 793 Excursion 3. 499
But present to the dead ; who, so they deemed, . 812 Excursion 4. 715
And such it might be deemed—a sleeping sunbeam ; 832 Excursion 5. 675
" She loved, and fondly deemed herself beloved. . 851 Excursion 6. 844
—Thrice happy, then, the Mother may be deemed, 856 Excursion 6. 1188
That might be deemed forbidding, did not there . 862 Excursion 7. 327
Strange, then, nor less than monstrous, might be deemed . . . . 887 Excursion 9. 229
And new-born waters deemed the happiest source S. 3. 436 *The doubt 165
Deem'st. Nor, as perchance thou rashly deem'st, the Cairn . . . . 548 *Stranger ! this 3
Deeming. Deeming " the evil of the day . . . 339 *Meek Virgin 41
And so they labour, deeming Holy Writ . . . 439 Ecc. Sonn. 2. 41. 6
Deeming our blessèd reason of least use . . . 731 Prelude 11. 308
Deems. He deems their colours shall endure . . 9 Lines : Boat 11
And therefore now she deems it good . . . . 414 White Doe 1702
Above a world that deems itself most wise . . 512 *Who rashly 41
Deep. *See* **Ear-deep, Knee-deep.**
And insects clothe, like dust, the glassy deep : . 4 Ev. Wk. 117
And now the whole wide lake in deep repose . . 4 Ev. Wk. 124
Whose softened image penetrates the deep. . . 5 Ev. Wk. 173
Deep yellow beams the scattered stems illume, . 5 Ev. Wk. 180
Broke only by the slow clock tolling deep, . . 9 Ev. Wk. 369
Or yell, in the deep woods, of lonely hound. . . 9 Ev. Wk. 378

Deep—*continued.*
While from a boat others hung o'er the deep, . . . 672 *Prelude* 5. 446
Of deep and stately vales! A lonely pair . . 680 *Prelude* 6. 384
Of those deep haunts, an aboriginal vale, . . . 683 *Prelude* 6. 519
Into a lordly river, broad and deep, ... 685 *Prelude* 6. 651
Of golden cities ten months' journey deep . . . 688 *Prelude* 7. 83
Advanced in radiance through a deep recess . . 693 *Prelude* 7. 414
That comes with night; the deep solemnity . . 697 *Prelude* 7. 655
With deep devotion, Nature, did I feel, . . . 700 *Prelude* 8. 70
Ye long deep channels for the Atlantic's voice, . 702 *Prelude* 8. 217
By the deep radiance of the setting sun: . . . 703 *Prelude* 8. 270
Hath called upon to embody his deep sense . . 715 *Prelude* 9. 401
Aghast and prayerless. Into a deep wood . . 718 *Prelude* 9. 578
In the great deep; all things have second birth; 719 *Prelude* 10. 83
A brood of gallant creatures, on the deep; . . 722 *Prelude* 10. 318
Great was my transport, deep my gratitude . . 726 *Prelude* 10. 576
Would but have touched the judgment, struck more deep . . . . 730 *Prelude* 11. 187
Ye waves, that out of the great deep steal forth . 734 *Prelude* 12. 21
Deep vale, or anywhere, the home of both, . . 741 *Prelude* 13. 126
With living men—how deep the groans! the voice 744 *Prelude* 13. 332
And so the deep enthusiastic joy, ... 750 *Prelude* 14. 293
Deep—and, aloft ascending, breathe in worlds . 755 *Recluse* I 1. 782
Of greatness; and deep feelings had impressed . 758 *Excursion* 1. 136
Deeply the lesson deep of love which he, . . . 759 *Excursion* 1. 194
Into a narrower circle of deep red, ... 762 *Excursion* 1. 427
Tender and deep in her excess of love; . . . 764 *Excursion* 1. 514
Urn-like it was in shape, deep as an urn; . . . 776 *Excursion* 2. 333
Was heard ascending; mournful, deep, and slow . 777 *Excursion* 2 375
Within how deep a shelter! He had fits, . . . 778 *Excursion* 2. 447
Of privacy is deep enough to hide, ... 778 *Excursion* 2. 472
And, deep within that lonesome valley, stood . 786 *Excursion* 3. 8
Or question deep? what profits all that earth, . 789 *Excursion* 3. 210
To a long voyage on the silent deep! . . . . 798 *Excursion* 3. 846
His bounteous gift! or saw him toward the deep 803 *Excursion* 4. 116
This deep abiding place, before your sight . . 807 *Excursion* 4. 391
In this deep Hollow, like a sullen star . . . . 808 *Excursion* 4. 487
The Sultan hides deep in ancestral tombs. . . . 809 *Excursion* 4. 569
To his small island in the ethereal deep . . . 811 *Excursion* 4. 640
In the deep stillness of a summer even . . . 817 *Excursion* 4. 1063
"Farewell, deep Valley, with thy one rude House, 822 *Excursion* 5. 1
His rank and sacred function. This deep vale . 824 *Excursion* 5. 122
Whereon he sits! Whose deep foundations lie . 838 *Excursion* 6. 3
To the deep shade of those untravelled Wilds; . 845 *Excursion* 6. 455
The practice flow,—if thence, or from a deep . 847 *Excursion* 6. 618
Tho', in this Vale, remembered with deep awe." . 850 *Excursion* 6. 777
Of reconcilement after deep offence— . . . . 854 *Excursion* 6. 1084
And this deep mountain-valley was to him . . 863 *Excursion* 7. 404
Illumination into deep, dark holds, ... 870 *Excursion* 7. 835
Or as a stranger reached this deep recess, . . . 871 *Excursion* 7. 928
Fixed in his soul, so early and so deep; . . . 878 *Excursion* 8. 299
"And tens of thousands suffer wrong as deep. . 879 *Excursion* 8. 336
With bold projections and recesses deep; . . . 881 *Excursion* 8. 462
"Change wide, and deep, and silently performed, 889 *Excursion* 9. 384
In a deep pool, by happy chance we saw . . . 890 *Excursion* 9. 439
A Grecian temple rising from the Deep." . . . 891 *Excursion* 9. 502
That which the heavens displayed, the liquid deep . 893 *Excursion* 9. 607
Alas! how quiet, and how deep! . . . . . K.8. 220 **The snow-tracks* 26
Down the deep channel of the stream he went, . K.8. 228 **I will* 133
Remote and deep, piled round with rocks, where foot K.8. 229 **I will* 141
Of glad emotion and deep quietness; . . . . K.8. 243 *Recluse* 1.1.231
Of winds, this deep Vale,—as it doth in part . . K.8. 247 *Recluse* 1.1.375
Heavenward, so piercing deep the lake below. . K.8. 252 *Recluse* 1.1.579
Than to unite. What sighs more deep than his, . K.8. 253 *Recluse* 1.1.601
And this deep vale its earthly counterpart, . . K.8. 254 *Recluse* 1.1.642
Deep pools, tall trees, black chasms, and dizzy crags, K.8. 256 *Recluse* 1.1.711
From sovereigns deep in pedigree intrenched. . . L.1. 97 *Juvenal* 3. 93

Deep-dale-head. On Deep-dale-head, and Brothers water (named . . . . K.8. 225 **I will* 21

Deep-drawn. My deep-drawn sighs no effort could confine; . . . . 32 *Guilt* 430
Nature reviving, with a deep-drawn sigh . . . 35 *Guilt* 572
More ruefully a deep-drawn shout, ... 241 *P. B.* 479
And turned his eagles back with deep-drawn sighs: 368 *Trajan* 63
To earth attempered and her deep-drawn sighs, . 751 *Prelude* 14. 385

Deep-embattled. And shades of deep-embattled clouds were seen, ... 3 *Ev. Wk.* 39

Deepen. Doth rather deepen than disturb the calm 184 *Airey-force* 6

Deepened. The solitary heifer's deepened low; . . 17 *Desc. Sk.* 360
When the stillness of evening hath deepened its roar; . . . . 345 *Stanzas: Simplon* 4
Lost in the deepen'd darkness, glimmers hoar; . 598 *Ev. Wk. Quarto* 370
Of twilight deepened, going forth, I spied . . . 687 *Prelude* 7. 32
The gloom, that, but a moment past, was deepened 733 *Prelude* 11. 427

Deepening. The soft gloom deepening on the tranquil mind. . . . . 8 *Ev. Wk.* 318
All day the floods a deepening murmur pour: . . 15 *Desc. Sk.* 271
'Twas nothing more than darkness deepening darkness, ... 77 *Bord.* 2285
Light deepening the profoundest sleep of shade. . 272 *Ruins* 8
This hour of deepening darkness here would be . 455 *Rydal Mere* 19
Frowns deepening visibly his native gloom, . . 521 *Epist. Beaumont* 6
Deepening her echoing torrents' awful peal . . 603 *Desc. Sk. Quarto* 76
To soothe regret, though deepening what it soothed, 718 *Prelude* 10. 5

Deepens. Still deepens its unfathomable depth. . 184 *Night-piece* 22
As pensive Evening deepens into night. . . . 274 **Such age* 14
That deepens upon fancy—more and more . . 498 **Enough of climbing* 38
Religion deepens her preventive care; . . . . 520 *Pun. Death* 13. 10
And Nature deepens into Nature's God. . . . S.3. 435 **The doubt* 121

Deeper. And pours a deeper blue to Æther's bound; 8 *Ev. Wk.* 328
Hurtle the clouds in deeper darkness piled, . . 26 *Guilt* 100
As come, dear Child! from a far deeper source . 40 *Bord.* 153
The deeper malady is better hid; . . . . . 56 *Bord.* 1035
In silence deeper far than that of deepest noon! . 173 *Waggoner* 1. 6
Is opened of still deeper pain, ... 180 *Waggoner* 4. 76
With warmer love—oh! with far deeper zeal . 207 *Tintern* 154
From source still deeper, and of higher worth, 216 *Enterprise* 99
Fair Prime of life! arouse the deeper heart; . 261 **Fair Prime* 10
Or, if thy deeper spirit be inclined . . . . 264 **Lady!* I 13
But something deeper far than these: . . . . 289 *Glen-Al.* 26
Faith buried deeper in her own deep breast . . 311 **Who rises* 35
That deeper far it lies . . . . 329 *Ode: Thanks.* 55
A deeper peace than that in deserts found! . . 334 **The Spirit* 14
Smiting with fury; and a deeper dread . . 346 *Processions* 33
Will that, or deeper thoughts, abate . . . 372 *Eg. Maid* 219
And with a deeper peace endued . . . . 415 *White Doe* 1749
Deeper than ocean, in the immensity . . . 456 **Soft as* 4
And impulses of deeper birth . . . . . 485 *Poet's Epitaph* 47
With deeper thankfulness. . . . . 543 *Russ. Fug.* 160
And pouring deeper blue to Æther's bound; . . 599 *Ev. Wk. Quarto* 394
All day the floods a deeper murmur pour, . . 608 *Desc. Sk. Quarto* 333
And hue far deeper than the Tyrian dye; . . 618 *School Ex.* 22
But deeper lies the heart of peace . . . . 623 *G. and S. Green* 21
My deeper pleasures (nay, I had not once, . . 652 *Prelude* 3. 235
And all my deeper passions lay elsewhere. . . 663 *Prelude* 4. 303
Whence, and from deeper causes, all discourse . 711 *Prelude* 9. 118
My deeper feelings, but another cause, . . . 736 *Prelude* 12. 123
Oppose a deeper nature; there, indeed, . . . 743 *Prelude* 13. 201
Still deeper welcome found his pure discourse: . 757 *Excursion* 1. 73
Even at her threshold. Deeper shadows fell . . 767 *Excursion* 1. 748
From sources deeper far than deepest pain, . . 770 *Excursion* 1. 938
One deeper than another, self-condemned . . . 818 *Excursion* 4. 1110
Vales deeper far than these of ours, huge woods, . 869 *Excursion* 7. 802

Deepest. The deepest cleft the mountain's front displays . . . . 8 *Ev. Wk.* 357
Where he can stab you deepest. Clifford never . 42 *Bord.* 281
The deepest grove whose foliage hid . . . . 110 **Look at* 13
In deepest winter; and, from week to week, . . 150 **When, to* 5
In silence deeper far than that of deepest noon! . 173 *Waggoner* 1. 6
Which even in deepest winter testify . . . . 329 *Ode: Thanks.* 11
For deepest sorrows that aspire . . . . . 411 *White Doe* 1352
The deepest dell the mountain's breast displays, . 599 *Ev. Wk. Quarto* 425
Serene he towers, in deepest purple dy'd; . . . 615 *Desc. Sk. Quarto* 699
Were bronzed with deepest radiance, stood alone 636 *Prelude* 1. 296
Informs, creates, and thaws the deepest sleep . 661 *Prelude* 4. 167
The deepest and the best, what keen research, . 675 *Prelude* 6. 40
They had the deepest feeling of the grief. . . 724 *Prelude* 10. 389
Yet in the deepest passion, I bowed low . . . 739 *Prelude* 12. 315
He said, "'Tis now the hour of deepest noon. . 765 *Excursion* 1. 593
From sources deeper far than deepest pain, . . 770 *Excursion* 1. 938

Deep-grooved. The wind might force the deep-grooved harp . . . . 301 *Bran* 99

Deeply. *See* **Over-deeply.**
Dear Father, you sigh deeply; ever since . . . 39 *Bord.* 103
Reverence for life so deeply, that they spare . . 48 *Bord.* 586
As you must needs have deeply felt, it is . . . 48 *Bord.* 615
And you should see how deeply I could reason . 59 *Bord.* 1224
More deeply, taught us that the institutes . . 66 *Bord.* 1575
Of something far more deeply interfused, . . . 207 *Tintern* 96
By none more deeply felt than Thee!" . . . 221 *Triad* 93
Hath stirred thee deeply; with its own dear brook, 250 *Admon.* 3
But once and deeply let me be beguiled. . . . 253 **O gentle* 14
More deeply grieved, for He was gone . . . . 285 *Grave of Burns* 32
Less deeply sad, with these to blend! . . . . 301 *Bran* 104
Deeply embosomed, and your winding shores . . 352 *Aquap.* 2
Full oft, our wish obtained, deeply we sigh; . . 358 **Is this* 9
Had tinged more deeply, as it flowed, ... 412 *White Doe* 1496
Where long and deeply hath been fixed the root . 431 *Ecc. Sonn.* 2. 10. 1
With indignation, deeply moved we grieve, . . 517 *Pun. Death* 2. 3
More deeply read in thy own thoughts; to thee . 645 *Prelude* 2. 211
But in the words of Reason deeply weighed, . . 645 *Prelude* 2. 231
So deeply in my mind, or from excess . . . . 647 *Prelude* 2. 388
Loved deeply all that had been loved before, . . 662 *Prelude* 4. 279
More deeply even than ever: but a swarm . . 662 *Prelude* 4. 280
Almost as deeply seated and as strong . . . 688 *Prelude* 7. 104
I felt most deeply in what world I was, . . . 719 *Prelude* 10. 64
Felt deeply, but not thoroughly understood . . 728 *Prelude* 11. 87
—Yes, in those wanderings deeply did I feel . . 743 *Prelude* 13. 206
More deeply, yet enable me to bear . . . . 752 *Prelude* 14. 423
Deeply the lesson deep of love which he, . . . 759 *Excursion* 1. 194
And presence; and so deeply do I feel . . . 768 *Excursion* 1. 782
And felt, deeply as living man could feel. . . 808 *Excursion* 4. 474
So deeply, that, unsatisfied with aught . . . 819 *Excursion* 4. 1214
Thus deeply drinking-in the soul of things, . . 820 *Excursion* 4. 1265
"He loved," the Vicar answered, "deeply loved, 840 *Excursion* 6. 118
More deeply tinged. Twin might the other be . 882 *Excursion* 8. 553
Deeply, a stranger of our father's house, . . . K.8. 254 *Recluse* 1.1. 654
A baffled conqueror's deeply searching rage, . . L.1. 95 *Juvenal* 3. 4

Deeps. While music, stealing round the glimmering deeps, ... 7 *Ev. Wk.* 303
Tower, bare or sylvan, from the narrow deeps. . 12 *Desc. Sk.* 80
Amid the unfathomable deeps; . . . . . . 227 *Vernal Ode* 58
Foundations broken up, the deeps run wild, . . 504 *Warning* 65
And run in transport to the dimpling deeps; . . 595 *Ev. Wk. Quarto* 198
And breaks the mirror of the circling deeps; . . 597 *Ev. Wk. Quarto* 312
Spotting the steaming deeps, to early mass; . . 604 *Desc. Sk. Quarto* 145

Deep-seated. The love deep-seated in the Saviour's face, ... 342 *Last Sup.* 3

Deep-sunken. But now he half-raises his deep-sunken eye, ... 621 *Convict* 41

Deep-worn. Albeit his deep-worn channel doth immure . . . . 379 *Duddon* 12. 2
Deer. *See* **Fallow-deer, Red-deer.**
In the rough fern-clad park, the herded deer . . 3 *Ev. Wk.* 47
The wounded deer retires to solitude, ... 75 *Bord.* 2152
And drive the flying deer ! . . . . 193 *Ruth* 96
And drive the flying deer. . . . . 193 *Ruth* 102
—Pass onward (even the glancing deer . . . 221 *Triad* 76
And stately forest where the wild deer rove ; . . 323 *Ode 1814* 10
Where stalked the huge deer to his shaggy lair . 376 *Duddon* 2. 11
A troop of deer came sweeping by ; . . . . 414 *White Doe* 1640
For One, among those rushing deer, ... 414 *White Doe* 1642
And wild deer bounded through the forest glade, . 450 *Ecc. Sonn.* 3. 41. 5
Where the slim wild deer roves ; . . . . . 506 **While from* 30
At speed a wounded deer, ... 544 *Russ. Fug.* 262
The desperate deer rushed on, and near . . . 544 *Russ. Fug.* 271
To end life here like this poor deer, . . . 545 *Russ. Fug.* 311
In the brown park, in flocks, the troubl'd deer . 592 *Ev. Wk. Quarto* 63
Chase the wild goat ; and if the bold red deer . 808 *Excursion* 4. 500
Of the live deer, or goat's depending beard,— . 814 *Excursion* 4. 884
Where couch the spotted deer ; or raised our eyes 892 *Excursion* 9. 563
Why do I watch those running deer ? . . . . K.8. 219 **The snow-tracks* 9
Deface. May no rude hand deface it, ... 287 *Ellen Irwin* 55
Defaced. By ignorance defaced, ... 330 *Ode : Thanks.* 110
Of prostrate altars, shrines defaced, ... 416 *White Doe* 1890
Were now come nearer to her : weeds defaced . 769 *Excursion* 1. 834
Defamed. The Mourner, thy true nature was defamed, 464 **Greta, what* 7
Defeat. Mutual the victory, mutual the defeat ! . 393 *Hart's-horn* 9
Defeated. Like an army defeated . . . . . 190 *March* 11
And mortal hopes defeated and o'erthrown . . 212 *Laod.* 165
Effort which, though defeated, had recalled . . 721 *Prelude* 10. 250
And unavengeable, defeated pride, ... 791 *Excursion* 3. 375
Defeating. Defeating, put the Monks to shame, . 301 *Bran* 69
Defeats. A treachery that foils it or defeats ; . . 720 *Prelude* 10. 178
Defect. A whole without dependence or defect, . K.8. 240 *Recluse* 1.1.149
Defects. And learn from thence thy own defects to scan ; . . . . 619 *School Ex.* 86
Heart, soul, and hands,—in mending the defects . 789 *Excursion* 3. 202
Instructs, and prompts her to supply defects . . 875 *Excursion* 8. 56
Excuse and solace for her own defects ; . . . 896 *Excursion* 9. 789
Defence. *See* **Self-defence.**
What she can urge in his defence ; she loves him. 48 *Bord.* 590
And guilt and shame, from which is no defence, . 319 *Biscayan* 13
And sober graces, left her for defence . . . . 333 **Bruges I* 7
What liberty ? if no defence . . . . . . 342 *Ital. Itin.* 92
Hail, ancient Manners ! sure defence, ... 376 **The Minstrels* 55
Like the brave Lion slain in her defence. . . . 395 *White Doe : Ded.* 16
Nor are his Followers loth to seek defence, . . 431 *Ecc. Sonn.* 2. 11. 12
Charged with rich words poured out in thought's defence ; . . . . 441 *Ecc. Sonn.* 3. 4. 2
"Though fierce the assault, and shattered the defence, ... 471 **Despond who* 2
From qualified oppression, whose defence . . . 501 *Humanity* 60
For liberty, would seek from God defence . . . 513 *General Fast* 12
No rampart's stern defence require, ... 533 **Blest is* 7
High Heaven is my defence ; . . . . . . 545 *Russ. Fug.* 302
Was founded a sure safeguard and defence . . 703 *Prelude* 8. 318
Who in attack or in defence were strong . . . 720 *Prelude* 10. 132
And the defence that lies in boundless love . . 801 *Excursion* 4. 23
For her defence, replenished with a band . . . 839 *Excursion* 6. 56
An ill-adjusted turban, for defence . . . . . 879 *Excursion* 8. 351
Defenceless. Defenceless as a wood where tigers roam. 719 *Prelude* 10. 93
Defend. Defend the innocent. Lacy ! we look . 56 *Bord.* 1029
It promised to defend. . . . . 550 *Hermit's Cell* 5. 12
There to defend themselves the winter long. . . K.8. 224 **I will* 11
Defended. *See* **Self-defended.**
From weakness now and pain defended, . . . 157 *Sexton* 15
A hut, by tufted trees defended, ... 414 *White Doe* 1692
Of mossy turf defended from the sun, ... 793 *Excursion* 3. 476
Defended, and appropriate to man's need. . . S.3. 433 **The doubt* 36
Defenders. With these defenders of the Crown, and talked, ... 712 *Prelude* 9. 195
Shall gain defenders zealous and devout . . . 806 *Excursion* 4. 312
Defenders'. To deck your stern Defenders' modest brows ! . . . . 324 *Ode 1814* 46
Defendeth. And he from every blemish them defendeth ; . . . . 560 *Cuck. and Night.* 192
Defending. Assaulting and defending, and the wind, 813 *Excursion* 4. 796
Defends. Him, only him, the shield of Jove defends, 214 *Dion* 123
Darkening the window, ill defends the door . . 521 *Epist. Beaumont* 21
That feeds it and defends ; . . . . 583 **O for a* 45
Defer. To which her judgments reverently defer. . 519 *Pun. Death* 9. 8
Deference. And that respect and deference which a soul . . . . 781 *Excursion* 2. 631
Deferred. *See* **Long-deferred.**
Both gladly now deferred their task ; . . . . 85 *Shepherd-boys* 82
Thy timely mandate, I deferred . . . . . 492 *Duty* 30
Defiance. Drawn in defiance of the Gods, hath laid 214 *Dion* 108
He in jocose defiance showed— . . . . . . 245 *P. B.* 832
That sapped good thoughts, or scared them with defiance. . . . . 369 *Eg. Maid* 24
To God proclaims defiance, ... 374 *Eg. Maid* 357
Defiance breathes with more malignant aim ; . . 438 *Ecc. Sonn.* 2. 38 .6
The shrill defiance of the young crusade . . . 628 *Eagle and Dove* 13
Exulting in defiance, or heart-stung . . . . 718 *Prelude* 10. 34
Deficiencies. For supplying all deficiencies, all wants of the rude nest . . . . 91 *Norman Boy* 22
Deficiency. Prevent omission, help deficiency, . . 445 *Ecc. Sonn.* 3. 21. 11
Deficient. First offered help that the deficient rock S.3. 433 **The doubt* 34
Defied. I should at once be trusted, not defied, . 104 *Artegal* 148

Defied—*continued.*
The future scorned, the past defied ; . . . . 298 *Brownie's Cell* 28
That host, as huge and strong as e'er defied . . 321 **Humanity, delighting* 17
All worse assaults may safely be defied. . . . 383 *Duddon* 27. 14
We Men, who in our morn of youth defied . . . 384 *Duddon* 34. 8
'Tis well, for he the worst defied . . . . . 409 *White Doe* 1231
Ye Thrones that have defied remorse, and cast . 870 *Excursion* 7. 837
Defies. Yet glorious Art the power of Time defies, 368 *Trajan* 67
That scorns temptation ; power defies . . . . 544 *Russ. Fug.* 197
Defile. He, nursed 'mid savage passions that defile 359 **Complacent Fictions* 12
Mounted through every intricate defile, . . . 380 *Duddon* 16. 8
To enervate and defile. . . . . 499 **Departing summer* 30
But I will not defile with dust . . . . . 545 *Russ. Fug.* 293
Defiled. Then into Severn hideously defiled, . . 103 *Artegal* 37
When hunter's arrow first defiled . . . . . 215 *Enterprise* 22
Beneath their feet, detested and defiled. . . . 435 *Ecc. Sonn.* 2. 29. 14
From altars threatened, levelled, or defiled, . . 449 *Ecc. Sonn.* 3. 36. 3
Who first defiled that calm majestic face ? . . L.2. 318 *Frag. Æneid* 4. 9
Defilements. *See* **Chance-defilements.**
Defiles. To kneel, or thrid your intricate defiles, . 451 *Ecc. Sonn.* 3. 42. 5
Define. Shall draw, the limits of the power define, 423 *Ecc. Sonn.* 1. 18. 13
Deformed. Deformed and sullied, patiently gave up 185 *Nutting* 47
Dead—but not sullied or deformed by death, . . 883 *Excursion* 8. 570
Deformities. With the deformities of crowded life, . 704 *Prelude* 8. 332
By the deformities of brutish vice : . . . . 847 *Excursion* 6. 575
Defrauded. Justice had been most cruelly defrauded. 50 *Bord.* 739
O'er the defrauded heart—while sweeping by, . 335 *Rhine* 2
Was soon defrauded, and the banded host . . 633 *Prelude* 1. 97
That spite of the defrauded Kitchen's prayers . L.1. 95 *Juvenal* 3. 16
Defrauding. Defrauding the day's glory, desperate ! 673 *Prelude* 5. 487
Deftly. For, deftly framed within the trunk, the sanctuary showed, ... 92 *Poet's Dream* 45
A pipe on which the wind would deftly play ; . 108 *Indolence* 58
And deftly ambles towards the south. . . . . 243 *P. B.* 610
Deftly prolonged, though grey-haired lookers on . 680 *Prelude* 6. 373
So deftly, and the nicest maiden's locks . . . 851 *Excursion* 6. 841
Deftly-lifted. With deftly-lifted oar ; . . . . 297 *Highland Boy* 190
Defy. Staring to threaten and defy, ... 159 **With little* 26
What if our numbers barely could defy . . . 309 **What if* 1
So did she daunt the Earth, and God defy ! . . 311 **Who rises* 30
Eternal things ; and, if need be, defy . . . . 358 **Is this* 13
Due audience, how for aught but scorn defy . . 365 **The Baptist* 4
Men, who have ceased to reverence, soon defy . 438 *Ecc. Sonn.* 2. 41. 1
The Hero comes to liberate, not defy ; . . . . 442 *Ecc. Sonn.* 3. 9. 10
Since risen from ocean, ocean to defy, ... 471 *Ailsa Crag* 1
God, whom their passions dare defy, ... 534 **Blest is* 78
Degenerate. Degenerate Douglas ! oh, the unworthy Lord ! . . . . 292 **Degenerate Douglas* 1
Shames the degenerate grasp of modern science, . 369 *Eg. Maid* 20
Renounced, abandoned by degenerate Men . . 515 *Penn.* 12
Degenerate ; who, constrained to wield the sword 839 *Excursion* 6. 62
"Two passions, both degenerate, for they both . 849 *Excursion* 6. 706
That one, albeit of these degenerate times, . . 875 *Excursion* 8. 37
Degradation. In truth, the degradation—howsoe'er 737 *Prelude* 12. 193
From sense of degradation, not the less . . . 852 *Excursion* 6. 953
To seek, in degradation of the Kind, ... 896 *Excursion* 9. 788
Degradations. Of woes and degradations hand in hand— . . . . 465 **Dear to* 12
Degrade. I know no cheaper engine to degrade a man, 58 *Bord.* 1161
Degraded. Would seek what the degraded soul . 194 *Ruth* 155
The Roman kilt, degraded to a toy . . . . 388 **The pibroch's* 2
Prove a degraded Race ? and what avails . . . 815 *Excursion* 4. 954
Humbled, but not degraded, may expire. . . . 834 *Excursion* 5. 793
Of Man degraded in his Maker's sight . . . . 847 *Excursion* 6. 574
As abject, as degraded ? At this day, . . . 879 *Excursion* 8. 345
Degree. In *some* degree. Between us stood, I thought, ... 75 *Bord.* 2145
Nurtured, as thy mien bespeaks, in high degree, . 140 *Arm. Lady* 23
Lords, lawyers, statesmen, squires of low degree, . 303 **Is it* 3
In men of low degree, all smooth pretence ! . . 319 **Avaunt all* 2
Horsemen and Foot of each degree, ... 403 *White Doe* 703
In its degree was understood ; . . . . . . 415 *White Doe* 1727
Partakes, in her degree, Heaven's grace ; . . . 416 *White Doe* 1876
By her commands partakes not, in degree, . . 429 *Ecc. Sonn.* 2. 2. 10
From Little down to Least, in due degree, . . 445 *Ecc. Sonn.* 3. 22. 1
Through good and evil thine, in just degree . . 455 **Not in the lucid* 18
Found scarcely anywhere in like degree ! . . . 491 *Tribute : Dog* 26
All creatures and all objects, in degree, . . . 501 *Humanity* 103
At other time, methinks, in like degree. . . . 557 *Cuck. and Night.* 25
In its degree of power, administered . . . . 686 *Prelude* 6. 747
To mention by its name, as in degree, ... 691 *Prelude* 7. 264
And so we all of us in some degree . . . . . 703 *Prelude* 8. 306
That what was in degree the same was likewise . 727 *Prelude* 11. 23
And false conclusions, in degree as gross, . . . 730 *Prelude* 11. 182
Induced, effect, in whatsoe'er degree, . . . 737 *Prelude* 12. 194
Partake of, each in their degree ; 'tis mine . . 740 *Prelude* 13. 12
Laden, for them and all of their degree, . . . 764 *Excursion* 1. 558
To the degree that he desired, beloved. . . . 772 *Excursion* 2. 56
With only such degree of sadness left . . . 804 *Excursion* 4. 235
Kind and degree, among all visible Beings ; . . 806 *Excursion* 4. 337
If tired with systems, each in its degree . . . 810 *Excursion* 4. 603
Far less, than these, yet such, in their degree, . 815 *Excursion* 4. 933
Are they not, still, in some degree, rewards . . 817 *Excursion* 4. 1094
His own firm spirit in degree depressed . . . 862 *Excursion* 7. 297
Such have been, and still are in their degree, . . 875 *Excursion* 8. 65
Shared, though in mild and merciful degree : . . 886 *Excursion* 9. 167
Degree of healing to a wounded spirit, ... 896 *Excursion* 9. 786

Delightful—*continued.*
With which it looked on this delightful day . . 146 *It was an 16
—'Twas that delightful season when the broom, . 147 Joanna 38
That on the banks of this delightful stream . . 207 Tintern 150
Delightful land of verdure, shower and gleam, . 229 Cuckoo-clock 32
In his delightful shell. . . . . 296 Highland Boy 135
To ruminate on that delightful home . . . . 458 Sea-shore 13
Delightful blossoms for the May . . . . 478 Somnamb. 61
" And here, on this delightful day, ... 487 Fountain 25
And the root of this delightful tree . . . . . 495 Force of Prayer 51
Of that delightful fragrance which was once . . 575 Chiabrera 8. 23
Did summon us in his delightful round. . . . 639 Prelude 1. 478
On that delightful time of growing youth . . . 673 Prelude 5. 539
Of two delightful hours we strolled along . . . 674 Prelude 5. 562
And specially delightful unto me . . . . . 677 Prelude 6. 161
With those delightful pathways we advanced, . 685 Prelude 6. 688
Delightful day it is for all who dwell . . . . 699 Prelude 8. 18
That was delightful. Oft in solitude . . . . 714 Prelude 9. 321
In that delightful island which protects . . . 722 Prelude 10. 321
When I began in youth's delightful prime . . . 724 Prelude 10. 416
Of admiration and delightful awe, ... 872 Excursion 7. 950
Of what there is delightful in the breeze, . . . 879 Excursion 8. 329
A Youth, I practised this delightful art ; . . . 891 Excursion 9. 486
This—if delightful hopes, as heretofore, . . . 896 Excursion 9. 793
Delightful Valley, habitation fair ! . . . . . K.8. 245 Recluse 1.1.300
Delighting. *See* **Self-delighting.**
The Rivulet, delighting in its strength, . . . 146 *It was an 2
Humanity, delighting to behold . . . . . 321 *Humanity, delighting 1
To Gods delighting in remorseless deeds ; . . . 894 Excursion 9. 685
Delights. Or rather stay to taste the mild delights . 16 Desc. Sk. 338
And the near heavens impart their own delights. . 19 Desc. Sk. 477
Yet, not the less, in children's hymns and lonely prayer delights. . . . . 93 Poet's Dream 64
Whence all the fixed delights of house and home, . 102 Artegal 23
But now my own delights I make,— . . . . 157 *In youth 5
As joy delights in ; and with wise restraint . . 185 Nutting 23
(For what delights the sense is false and weak) . 257 *No mortal 7
Delights us. Rapine, avarice, expense, . . . 307 *O Friend 9
With thoughts which no delights can chase, . . 342 Ital. Itin. 32
Turned to humbler delights, in which youth might confide, ... 364 Vallomb. 14
Hers in whose sway alone my heart delights, . . 365 *Rapt above 2
While young delights on old encroach, ... 391 Highland Broach 77
Long past, delights and sorrowings ? . . . . 414 White Doe 1675
Lives there a man whose sole delights . . . . 533 *Blest is 51
Oh ! severed, too abruptly, from delights . . . 583 *With copious 26
Return Delights ! with whom my road begun, . . 592 Ev. Wk. Quarto 27
And the near heav'ns their own delights impart. . 612 Desc.Sk.Quarto 561
Delights and exultations of your own. . . . . 639 Prelude 1. 506
That this first transit from the smooth delights . 656 Prelude 3. 517
To seek the same delights, and have one health, . 679 Prelude 6. 258
Called forth, at every season, new delights . . 686 Prelude 6. 777
My own delights do scarcely seem to me . . . 733 Prelude 11. 408
My own delights ; the lordly Alps themselves, . . 733 Prelude 11. 409
But leave we this : enough that my delights . . 736 Prelude 12. 140
Towards them and to all creatures. God delights . 736 Prelude 12. 171
In what the Historian's pen so much delights . . 740 Prelude 13. 42
A course of vain delights and thoughtless guilt, . 794 Excursion 3. 560
As he is known to all. The calm delights . . . 824 Excursion 5. 110
From the delights of charity cut off, ... 836 Excursion 5. 939
Love, knowledge, all my manifold delights . . K.8. 255 Recluse 1.1.697
Delirium. A wild delirium first the infant thrill'd ; . 620 Birth of Love 44
Deliver. Through air, to thee my Charge will I deliver. . . . . 370 Eg. Maid 108
" Behold to thee my Charge I now deliver ! . . 371 Eg. Maid 168
Did I deliver this unfinished Song ; . . . . 582 *To public 2
Her by menace to deliver, ... S.3. 437 *I, whose 14
Deliverance. And he found no deliverance ! The Crew . . . . 69 Bord. 1756
Sad deliverance would it be, and yoked with shame, 140 Arm. Lady 29
In act embodied, my deliverance wrought. . . 211 Laod. 138
Of a deliverance absolute and pure . . . . . 322 *By Moscow 7
His glad deliverance has begun : . . . . . 343 Eclipse 62
For its deliverance—a capacious field . . . . 355 Aquap. 162
To celebrate their great deliverance ; . . . . 420 Ecc. Sonn. 1. 7. 9
Come not to speed the Soul's deliverance ; . . 455 *Not in the lucid 29
And painful struggle and deliverance—prayed . 460 *Queen of 31
And proud deliverance issuing out of pain . . 514 *Who ponders 4
Foretaste deliverance ; but the least perturbed . 541 Grace Darl. 67
Exult in this deliverance wrought through faith . 541 Grace Darl. 85
Preparing your deliverance, ... 545 Russ. Fug. 331
Of their deliverance, surely yet to come. . . . 752 Prelude 14. 443
Till his deliverance, when Mercy made him . . 844 Excursion 6. 374
Delivered. Delivered to the Judge of all things. Dead ! . . . . 66 Bord. 1587
Delivered heart and head ! Let us to Palestine ; 77 Bord. 2282
They sank, delivered o'er . . . . 102 Artegal 6
Brave Schill ! by death delivered, take thy flight 317 *Brave Schill 1
Perchance had flown, delivered by the storm ; . 472 *The captive 2
Came and delivered him, alone he sped . . . 472 Dunolly Eagle 3
Delivered and Deliverer move . . . . . . 545 Russ. Fug. 363
—At length delivered from the rock, ... 579 *Sweet Flower 37
Delivered. No ! the Orator hath yoked . . . 694 Prelude 7. 501
The awful truths delivered thence by tongues . 695 Prelude 7. 547
May be delivered to distress and shame. . . . 851 Excursion 6. 848
Hath here delivered ; words of heartfelt truth, . 873 Excursion 7. 1054
Deliverer. *See* **Lamb-deliv'rer.**
My Deliverer would present . . . . 141 Arm. Lady 112
Looked the beautiful Deliverer . . . . . . 141 Arm. Lady 135
And, as the great Deliverer marches by, . . . 213 Dion 35

Deliverer—*continued.*
Deliverer of the steadfast rocks . . . . . . 341 San Salv. 29
Delivered and Deliverer move . . . . . . 545 Russ. Fug. 363
Deliverer's. —Chant the Deliverer's praise in every tongue ! . . . . 326 Sobieski 11
That landward urged the great Deliverer's sail, . 449 Ecc. Sonn. 3. 37. 3
For a deliverer's glorious task,—and such . . . 715 Prelude 9. 410
Delivering. Delivering her decisions from the seat . 792 Excursion 3. 412
Delivery. Thou offerest up for safe Delivery . . 447 Ecc. Sonn. 3. 27. 7
Dell. Through bare grey dell, high wood, and pastoral cove ; . . . . 2 Ev. Wk. 2
On Zutphen's plain, or on that highland dell, . . 15 Desc. Sk. 295
You will look down into a dell, and there . . . 41 Bord. 217
Now fast up the dell came the noise and the fray, 120 Childless Father 13
Perhaps he's gone along the dell, ... 129 Idiot Boy 305
Nor should I have made mention of this Dell . 131 Michael 14
And to that hollow dell from time to time . . 138 Michael 460
By any who should look beyond the dell . . . 146 *It was an 35
May call it by the name of Emma's Dell. . . 146 *It was an 47
The Torrent down the rocky dell . . . . . 155 Waterfall 52
And in this smooth and open dell . . . . . 165 Danish Boy 5
And in this dell you see . . . . 165 Danish Boy 9
The lovely dell is all his own. . . . . . 165 Danish Boy 22
While in the dell he sings alone . . . . . 166 Danish Boy 43
And wander down yon hawthorn dell, ... 180 Waggoner 4. 16
—Fly also, Muse ! and from the dell . . . . 180 Waggoner 4. 36
Here in this happy dell." . . . . 187 *Three years 36
A basin for that fountain in the dell ! . . . . 201 Hart-leap 62
And built a house of pleasure in the dell. . . . 202 Hart-leap 84
It chanced that I saw standing in a dell . . . 202 Hart-leap 102
Or from cottage-sprinkled dell, ... 220 Triad 37
Around the dell a gleam . . . . 232 Jew. Fam. 46
In the green wood and hollow dell ; . . . . 239 P. B. 242
And there, along the narrow dell, ... 244 P. B. 676
Along this solitary dell, ... 244 P. B. 687
A cottage in a heathy dell ; . . . . 246 P. B. 892
A seemly Cottage in this sunny Dell, ... 251 Appleth. 2
Or Roy, renowned through many a Scottish dell ; 255 Detraction 4
In the low dell 'mid Roslin's faded grove : . . 261 *From the dark 12
Skyward ascending from a woody dell. . . . 262 *Not Love 8
Beside thee in some heathy dell ; . . . . . 288 Highland Girl 50
Would break the silence of this Dell : . . . . 289 Glen-Al. 24
And in the lonely Highland dell . . . . . 297 Highland Boy 246
And what the Dell unwillingly reveals . . . . 335 Rhine 8
First of his tribe, to this dark dell—who first . 378 Duddon 8. 2
High over hill and low adown the dell . . . . 395 White Doe : Ded. 38
O'er path and road, and plain and dell, . . . 409 White Doe 1170
We who were led to-day down a grim dell, . . 475 Greenock 2
What change shall happen next to Nunnery Dell ? 477 Nunnery 13
Beyond her native dell. . . . . 478 Somnamb. 18
And the Stream whirled her down the dell . . 479 Somnamb. 134
Within the dell he built a cell, ... 479 Somnamb. 147
(As records mouldering in the Dell . . . . . 533 *Blest is 15
The deepest dell the mountain's breast displays, . 599 Ev. Wk. Quarto 425
To us who stood low in that hollow dell, . . . 820 Excursion 4. 1300
Of the small Cottage in the lonely Dell . . . 821 Excursion 4. 1318
This, in the lonely dell discoursing, you . . . 831 Excursion 5. 582
Brought yesterday from our sequestered dell . . 835 Excursion 5. 882
To the one cottage in the lonely dell : . . . . 895 Excursion 9. 774
Through some Helvetian dell, when low-hung mists K.8. 249 Recluse 1.1.476
Dells. O'er all its vanished dells, and lawns, and woods ; . . . . 8 Ev. Wk. 332
To other flowers :—to other dells . . . . . 165 Danish Boy 19
Where birds and brooks from leafy dells . . . 228 Devot. Incit. 64
Broke forth in concert flung adown the dells, . . 267 St. Cath. 3
Are heard among the moorland dells, ... 416 White Doe 1886
Glad proclamation make, and heights and dells . 503 Warning 42
Tune in the mountain dells their water lyres. . . 598 Ev. Wk. Quarto 328
Unfathom'd dells and undiscover'd woods ; . . 602 Desc. Sk. Quarto 10
Of pleasure sprinkled over, shady dells . . . 700 Prelude 8. 85
Delphic. " Thou knowest, the Delphic oracle foretold 210 Laod. 43
One who ne'er ventured for a Delphic crown . . 463 *Adieu, Rydalian 5
But with a Delphic life, in sight . . . . . 629 Installation 67
Deluded. Deluded Hope for one short hour . . . 620 Birth of Love 39
For liberty, against deluded men, ... 715 Prelude 9. 426
Deluding. And deluding the unwary . . . . . 549 Hermit's Cell 1. 7
Deluge. Deluge of tender thoughts then rushed amain, ... 33 Guilt 494
Then, when o'er highest hills the Deluge passed ? 380 Duddon 15. 14
And drag their length of deluge train behind. . . 615 Desc.Sk.Quarto 697
By deluge, now at hand. No sooner ceased . . 667 Prelude 5. 98
But burst and spread in deluge through the land. 725 Prelude 10. 480
Who, by the recent deluge stupefied, ... 727 Prelude 11. 36
Deluged. Lands deluged by unbridled floods ; . . 299 Brownie's Cell 64
Delusion. Then shatter the delusion, break it up . 54 Bord. 934
There lack not strange delusion here, ... 398 White Doe 213
Half wishes your delusion were it's own. . . . 614 Desc.Sk.Quarto 679
Delusion bold ! and how can it be wrought ? . . 691 Prelude 7. 285
A shadow, a delusion, ye who pore . . . . . 703 Prelude 8. 296
Thus darkness and delusion round our path . . 830 Excursion 5. 512
Delusion which a moment may destroy ! . . . 887 Excursion 9. 198
Delusions. Men clinging to delusions so insane ? . 728 Prelude 11. 46
Delusive. *To bring, and bear away, delusive hopes,* . 846 Excursion 6. 516
Delve. Had clomb aloft to delve the moorland turf . 783 Excursion 2. 787
Delved. Fetched from Mount Calvary, or haply delved 355 Aquap. 159
Demand. And forced the full-swoln udder to demand, 17 Desc. Sk. 397
Your faculties should grow with the demand ; . 64 Bord. 1498
A generous cause a victim did demand ; . . . 210 Laod. 46
In reverential modesty demand, ... 328 Ode 1815 58
That, for the living and the dead, demand . . 389 Breadalb. 12
The Norton fixed, at this demand, ... 403 White Doe 635

Demand—*continued.*
Her adoration was not your demand, ... 434 *Ecc. Sonn.* 2. 24. 5
So often that demand such sacrifice ; . . . . 493 *Hap. War.* 22
Outstrips the heart's demand ; . . . . . . 499 *Memory* 8
Whose rugged walls may still for years demand . 521 *Epist.Beaumont* 24
In spite of season's change, its own demand, . . 531 **I know* 18
Do my sinful soul demand, ... 535 *Egremont* 28
Go, and demand of him, if there be here . . . 568 *Cumb. Beg.* 143
Then did no ebb of chearfulness demand . . . 592 *Ev. Wk. Quarto* 21
In broken sounds her elder grief demand, . . . 596 *Ev. Wk. Quarto* 263
Then the milk-thistle bad those herds demand . 611 *Desc.Sk.Quarto* 484
Thy Children left unfit, through vain demand . 626 **Son of* 4
And yet the spectacle may well demand . . . 657 *Prelude* 3. 588
To his own eager thoughts. It would demand . 662 *Prelude* 4. 291
" It were a wantonness, and would demand . . 765 *Excursion* 1. 626
By courage, to demand from real life . . . . 792 *Excursion* 3. 417
Enquire of ancient Wisdom ; go, demand . . . 815 *Excursion* 4. 957
' This single act is all that we demand.' . . . 817 *Excursion* 4. 1082
By notice indirect, or blunt demand . . . . 859 *Excursion* 7. 105
Are they—and might demand a seraph's tongue, . 874 *Excursion* 8. 11
To every day's demand for daily bread, . . . K.8. 249 *Recluse* 1.1.450
Demanded. He with grave looks demanded for what cause, ... 147 *Joanna* 26
Or, if the change demanded no regret, ... 837 *Excursion* 5. 976
Demanding. The sanction ; till, demanding formal *proof,* . . . . 731 *Prelude* 11. 301
Demands. When chill night that care demands. . 166 *Wand. Jew* 24
But, though to such demands unused, ... 247 *P. B.* 1019
Demands the service of a mind and heart, . . 260 **High is* 4
Such spectacle demands not tear or sigh. . . . 316 **Hail, Zaragoza* 4
Such food a Tyrant's appetite demands ; . . . 319 *Spaniard* 4
Can spare, and humblest earthly Weal demands, . 357 *Aquap.* 343
Sanctions the forfeiture that Law demands, . . 519 *Pun. Death* 11. 10
But that too much demands still more. You know, 793 *Excursion* 3. 497
Not unamused.—But ridicule demands . . . 799 *Excursion* 3. 902
This hallowed grave demands, where rests in peace 870 *Excursion* 7. 849
Demeanour. So pious in demeanour ! in his look . 60 *Bord.* 1246
Cheerfully uttered, with demeanour kind, . . . 197 *Resolution* 135
Is heard ; to grave demeanour all are bound ; . 283 **Well have* 4
He all the while was in demeanour calm, . . . 665 *Prelude* 4. 440
Of fine demeanour, and by dance and song, . . 843 *Excursion* 6. 308
" Once," and with wild demeanour, as he spake, . 894 *Excursion* 9. 679
Demerits. That my demerits did not sue in vain . 793 *Excursion* 3. 502
Demi-god. No more by step of Demi-god . . . 216 *Enterprise* 44
Demi-gods. And they like Demi-gods are strong . 499 **Departing summer* 26
Democratic. In simple democratic majesty ; . . 350 *Des. Stanzas* 52
Hourly the democratic torrent swells ; . . . . 477 **Lowther ! in* 9
Demolished. At the fond work, demolished with a touch ; . . . . 810 *Excursion* 4. 606
Demon. The Demon of the snow, with angry roar . 16 *Desc. Sk.* 330
Demoniac. Twined round him by demoniac power, 241 *P. B.* 474
Awful as ever stray Demoniac uttered, . . . K.8. 246 *Recluse* 1.1.337
Demons. A viewless flight of laughing Demon's [? Demons] mock . . . . 11 *Desc. Sk.* 69
Black Demons hovering o'er his mitred head, . . 428 *Ecc. Sonn.* 1. 38. 1
Demons and Spirits, many a dolorous groan . . 435 *Ecc. Sonn.* 2. 27. 4
The cross with hideous laughter Demons mock, . 603 *Desc. Sk. Quarto* 70
In wicked pleas, were strong as demons now ; . 723 *Prelude* 10. 334
Howe'er to airy Demons suitable, ... 799 *Excursion* 3. 909
Demonstration. They bow to, calling the idol, Demonstration. . . . . 58 *Bord.* 1158
Demur. Press the point home, or falter and demur, 268 **DogmaticTeachers* 4
But often his mind is compelled to demur, . . 570 *Farmer* 59
Demure. Demure with porringer and plate . . . 127 *Idiot Boy* 129
A nun demure of lowly port ; . . . . . . 158 **With little* 17
A habitation sober and demure . . . . . . 655 *Prelude* 3. 435
Den. To that abhorrèd den of brutish vice !— . . 47 *Bord.* 546
Inheritest the lion's den ; . . . . 117 *Afll. Marg.* 53
The air, as in a lion's den, ... 173 *Waggoner* 1. 15
Nor Anguish strayed from her Tartarean den ; . 227 *Vernal Ode* 130
Is warbling near the BROWNIE'S Den. . . . . 299 *Brownie's Cell* 90
Pillowed in some deep dungeon's earless den ;— . 305 *Toussaint* 4
As springs the lion from his den, ... 331 *Ode : Thanks.* 145
(Couched in their den) with those that roam at large 392 *Daniel* 6
In Craven's Wilds is many a den, ... 408 *White Doe* 1094
And oft-times in the most forbidding den . . . 429 *Ecc. Sonn.* 2. 5. 8
Renews. Through every forest, cave, and den, . 435 *Ecc. Sonn.* 2. 27. 9
To upper air from Mammon's loathsome den. . . 515 *Penn.* 14
And seek the Sufferer in his darkest den, . . . 516 **Feel for* 3
Down to their " dark opprobrious den," . . . 534 **Blest is* 83
She moulds her sight-eluding den . . . . . 543 *Russ. Fug.* 119
The Grotto of Antiparos, or the Den . . . . 707 *Prelude* 8. 562
Denial. *See* **Self-denial.**
I put denial on thy suit, and hence, ... 76 *Bord.* 2234
From Heaven or earth ;—Sir Kaye had like denial. 373 *Eg. Maid* 270
Denial and restraint I prize . . . . 492 *Duty*
Of doubt and bold denial hourly urged . . . 812 *Excursion* 4. 734
Denials. *See* **Self-denials.**
Denied. *See* **Deny'd.**
I see her now, denied to lay her head, ... 7 *Ev. Wk.* 256
Admittance was denied. The young man spake . 125 *V. and J.* 265
A loveliness to living youth denied. . . . . 258 **Even so* 8
Yet one to which is not denied . . . . . . 285 *Grave of Burns* 65
Ditches are graves—funereal rites denied ; . . 427 *Ecc. Sonn.* 1. 36. 10
Heavenly succour, not denied . . . . . . 503 **Like a* 57
Oft to royal hearts denied." . . . . 629 *Installation* 56
It was denied them to acquire, through lack . 757 *Excursion* 1. 82
With a resemblance not to be denied, ... 828 *Excursion* 5. 405
—Nor was his funeral denied the grace . . . 864 *Excursion* 7. 469

Denier. I would not give a denier for the man . . 60 *Bord.* 1241
Denies. To seek that comfort which the mind denies ; 822 *Excursion* 5. 21
Denis. St. Denis, filled with royal tombs, or the Church of Notre Dame ? . . . . . . 92 *Poet's Dream* 24
Denmark. And when the King of Denmark summoned him . . . . 63 *Bord.* 1444
In Denmark he was cast away : . . . . . . 119 *Sailor's Mother* 22
Denote. And whining voice denote them supplicants 879 *Excursion* 8. 360
Denounced. Of reconcilement, then when they denounced, ... 724 *Prelude* 10. 441
Denounces. While he forewarns, denounces, launches forth, ... 695 *Prelude* 7. 523
Dens. Would drive those Scottish Rovers to their dens 50 *Bord.* 729
In Craven's dens, on Cumbrian heights ; . . . 399 *White Doe* 279
Rekindled thus, from dens and savage woods . . 432 *Ecc. Sonn.* 2. 14. 10
Rocks, dens, and groves of foliage taught to melt 700 *Prelude* 8. 88
Dense. In some dense wood or gulf of snow profound, 16 *Desc. Sk.* 314
Of a cloud flat and dense, through which must move 461 **Who but is* 12
Should perish, self-subverted. Black and dense . 471 **Despond who* 8
Hidden from view in dense obscurity. . . . . 532 **How beautiful the* 4
Of the dense air, which town or city breeds . . 838 *Excursion* 6. 22
By the dense air—shot upward to the crown . . 893 *Excursion* 9. 595
Denser. In prospect far above the denser air . . K.8. 234 **The order'd* 3
Denunciation. Bawling, " Denunciation of the Crimes 719 *Prelude* 10. 100
Deny. To them the gentle groups of bliss deny . 19 *Desc. Sk.* 506
He will deny it to the last. He lies . . . . 54 *Bord.* 915
Deny me your support. We have been fooled— . 63 *Bord.* 1426
Nor shall thy foes deny . . . . 105 *Artegal* 191
What though the Granite would deny . . . 301 *Bran* 94
Who tempt their reason to deny . . . . . 534 **Blest is* 77
To us the gentle groups of bliss deny . . . . 613 *Desc.Sk.Quarto* 606
Deny'd. Gazing the tempting shades to them deny'd, 592 *Ev. Wk. Quarto* 57
Deny'd the bread of life the foodful ear, . . . 608 *Desc.Sk.Quarto* 320
Deo. " LAUS DEO." Many a Stranger passing by . 394 *Countess' Pillar* 10
Depart. To think of it. Enough ! you may depart. 47 *Bord.* 542
Float near me ; do not yet depart ! . . . . 79 **Stay near* 5
To bed the children must depart ; . . . . . 81 †*Mother's Return* 46
The clouds pass on ; they from the heavens depart : 110 **'Tis said that some* 17
And Betty will not then depart. . . . . . 127 *Idiot Boy* 96
" He shall depart to-morrow." To this word . 136 *Michael* 317
Abruptly spreading to depart, ... 154 *Flower Garden* 50
And called on him who must depart . . . . 174 *Waggoner* 1. 56
When I depart, for brief is my sojourn— " . . 210 *Laod.* 78
Will not depart when mortal voices bid ; . . . 214 *Dion* 91
When they in pomp depart . . . . 216 *Enterprise* 109
Till we depart intrude not here ;) . . . . . 221 *Triad* 77
Yet how forlorn, should *ye* depart, ... 223 *Wishing-gate* 10
Did never from his lips depart ; . . . . . . 245 *P. B.* 757
Of grateful memory, bid that joy depart. . . . 261 **Fair Prime* 14
Great Nations, how ennobling thoughts depart . 307 **When I* 2
Never may from our souls one truth depart— . 321 **Here pause* 7
But garlands wither ; festal shows depart, . . 324 *Ode 1814* 90
How can I give thee license to depart ? . . . 350 *Des. Stanzas* 4
Some who had early mandates to depart, . . . 381 *Duddon* 21. 4
And she will depart when we are gone ; . . . 398 *White Doe* 189
Can she depart ? can she forego . . . . . 414 *White Doe* 1670
And therefore are ye summoned to depart, . . 434 *Ecc. Sonn.* 2. 24. 7
The living landscapes greet him, and depart ; . . 443 *Ecc. Sonn.* 3. 12. 4
Born only to depart. . . . . 478 *Somnamb.* 63
This picture from nature may seem to depart, . 482 *Character* 17
As my last earnest prayer ere we depart. . . . 535 *Egremont* 24
With courage will depart." . . . . 542 *Russ. Fug.* 80
Was eager to depart, ... 545 *Russ. Fug.* 342
I saw the Bird depart. . . . . 580 *John Words.* 14
But when the great and good depart . . . . 581 **Loud is* 19
Foreboding not how soon he must depart ; . . 582 **To public* 8
Reach after reach, salute us and depart ; . . . 625 **The confidence* 4
The moment to depart. An Englishman, . . . 712 *Prelude* 9. 188
Of grief, depart without occasion given . . . 780 *Excursion* 2. 598
" And what are things eternal ?—powers depart," 802 *Excursion* 4. 66
Depart ; and leave no vestige where they trod. . 812 *Excursion* 4. 762
Cherished for him, he suffered to depart, . . . 843 *Excursion* 6. 314
He should depart, to plant himself anew. . . . 864 *Excursion* 7. 430
Is fled ; we must depart, willing or not ; . . . S.3. 432 **The doubt* 2
Come, share my couch, nor speedily depart ; . . S.3. 441 **Come, gentle* 2
My life would then at once depart. . . . . . K.8. 220 **The snow-tracks* 18

Departed. *See* **Long-departed.**
And memory of departed pleasures, more. . . 2 *Ev. Wk.* 12
When his spirit was departed, ... 94 *Westmoreland Girl* 69
Departed Child ! I could forget thee once . . . 118 *Maternal Grief* 1
Departed with his infant ; and thus reached . . 125 *V. and J.* 263
Their pensive light from a departed sun ! . . . 256 *Decay of Piety* 14
Youthful as Spring.—Shade of departed Power, . 290 *Kilchurn* 31
If life departed be for ever gone, ... 372 *Eg. Maid* 257
Departed ages, shedding where he flew . . . 380 *Duddon* 17. 4
For the departed, built with curious pains . . 389 *Breadalb.* 8
Departed promptly as a Page . . . . . . 408 *White Doe* 1109
Hath not departed, stands forlorn . . . . 506 **While from* 43
She sits, for that departed Mother's sake. . . 509 *F. Stone* 69
The joys of the Departed—what so fair . . . 526 **Soon did* 13
As one of the departed. . . . . 549 **In these* 9
As if but yesterday departed, ... 586 *Hogg* 33
The persons of departed potentates. . . . . 640 *Prelude* 1. 525
The days departed start again to life, ... 699 *Prelude* 8. 49
A history only of departed things, ... 755 *Recluse* 1. 1. 803
Lamenting the departed, call the groves, . . . 763 *Excursion* 1. 476
" He is departed, and finds peace at last ! " . . 777 *Excursion* 2. 384
As left by the departed company, ... 781 *Excursion* 2. 644

Depth—*continued.*
From whose calm centre thou, through height or depth, 787 *Excursion* 3. 108
Where height, or depth, admits not the approach 795 *Excursion* 3. 643
From depth of shaggy covert peeping forth 814 *Excursion* 4. 881
All withered by the depth of shade above. 824 *Excursion* 5. 149
Even by his studied depth of privacy, 844 *Excursion* 6. 397
Not giddy yet aerial, with a depth K.8. 237 *Recluse* 1. 1. 20
Depths. Those fast-receding depths of sable blue 16 *Desc. Sk.* 326
Who knew not to what quiet depths a weight 125 *V. and J.* 225
Love from her depths, and Duty in her might 280 **Intent on* 13
To sound the depths of every Art 301 *Bran* 117
And, through her depths, Saint Mary's Lake 302 *Yarrow V.* 13
Heard from the depths of its aerial bower— 319 *Guernica* 4
Fixed in the depths of this courageous soil; 324 *Ode 1814* 104
Within its depths, and to the shore we came 366 **Fair Land* 6
Be its depths quickened; what thou dost inherit 366 **Fair Land* 12
Came to this hidden pool, whose depths surpass 381 *Duddon* 22. 2
Feels through her lowest depths thy sovereignty; 459 **Wanderer! that* 49
Eyeing the sea's blue depths. Poor Bird! even so 472 *Dunolly Eagle* 12
But from our loved Helvellyn's depths was brought, 480 *Cordelia* 6
Though, in the depths of sunless groves, no more 500 *Humanity* 7
And served in depths where fishes haunt 506 **While from* 31
He rested not; its depths his mind explored; 517 *Pun. Death* 3. 6
Descend and reach, in Yewdale's depths, a plain 525 *Epist. Beaumont* 225
From the pure depths of her humanity! 540 *Grace Darl.* 21
And quiet *now* are the depths of air, 623 *G. and S. Green* 19
Among the depths of time. Yet is it just 668 *Prelude* 5. 197
Who, yet a liveried schoolboy, in the depths 679 *Prelude* 6. 266
And 'mid the hollow depths of naked crags 758 *Excursion* 1. 155
And airy hopes my children.—From the depths 796 *Excursion* 3. 736
Within the depths of its capacious breast, 800 *Excursion* 3. 971
That, lodged within thy crystal depths, seem bright, S.3. 433 **The doubt* 47
Derange. Old laws, and ancient customs to derange, 426 *Ecc. Sonn.* 1. 31. 13
Deranged. Through town and country both deranged 301 *Bran* 107
Dereliction. Of dereliction and dismay, I yet 648 *Prelude* 2. 441
Deride. The altar, to deride the fane, 337 *Cath. Cantons* 4
Derided. How oft from you, derided Powers! 225 *Present.* 19
No recompense, derided; and at length, 841 *Excursion* 6. 224
Derides. Whose slippery face derides his deathful tread! 609 *Desc.Sk.Quarto* 393
Derive. If thou indeed derive thy light from Heaven, v **If thou indeed* 1
In glittering halls—was able to derive 843 *Excursion* 6. 339
Fade,—and the moralising mind derive S.3. 433 **The doubt* 23
Derived. Have I derived from thy sweet power 158 **In youth* 43
Derived from clouds and storms!) the amplest range 219 **This Height* 3
Derived from earth or heaven, 224 **'Tis gone* 27
With attributes from History derived, 357 *Aquap.* 283
Thy confidant! say, whence derived that air 508 *F. Stone* 42
—Not from a source less sacred is derived 509 *F. Stone* 70
Envy and heart-inquietude, derived 574 *Chiabrera* 4. 8
Had been derived the name he bore—a name, 584 *Ch. Lamb* 24
Came, of themselves, or at her call derived 708 *Prelude* 8. 602
Diffused through time and space, with aid derived 708 *Prelude* 8. 611
Derived from academic institutes 713 *Prelude* 9. 224
Derived—find no admission. Then it was— 732 *Prelude* 11. 333
And from the faith derived through Him who bled 895 *Excursion* 9. 721
Derives. Derives its name, reflected as the chime 381 *Duddon* 22. 5
Deriving. Deriving cheerful confidence, shall blend 748 *Prelude* 14. 145
Dernbrook's. By lurking Dernbrook's pathless side, 415 *White Doe* 1711
Derogate. He feels how far the act would derogate 518 *Pun. Death* 5. 10
Derwent. Where Derwent rests, and listens to the roar 2 *Ev. Wk.* 3
Born to be lost in Derwent flowing near; 465 **The cattle* 5
His wizard course where hoary Derwent takes 591 *Ev. Wk. Quarto* 3
O Derwent! winding among grassy holms 636 *Prelude* 1. 275
Down by thy side, O Derwent! murmuring stream, 673 *Prelude* 5. 484
Greta, or Derwent, or some nameless rill, 715 *Prelude* 9. 393
Derwent's. "By Derwent's side my father dwelt—a man 28 *Guilt* 199
Desart. *See* **Desert.**
Whence fragrance scents the water's desart gale, 596 *Ev. Wk. Quarto* 223
No ruder sound your desart haunts invades, 596 *Ev Wk. Quarto* 237
Descant. Recalling now, with descant soft 144 **Driven in* 41
With thankful spirit. The descant, and the wind 538 **In desultory* 10
'Twere idle to descant. My inner judgment 676 *Prelude* 6. 96
Pour forth his meditations, and descant 891 *Excursion* 9. 460
Descend. Descend we now the maddened Reuss our guide; 14 *Desc. Sk.* 197
Five streams of ice amid her cots descend, 20 *Desc. Sk.* 571
On he must pace, perchance till night descend, 24 *Guilt* 17
Through tears have seen him towards that world descend 32 *Guilt* 443
You'd better like we should descend together, 51 *Bord.* 771
Thus rise and thus descend,— 111 **'Tis said that some* 43
Or descend where the ark alighted, 218 **Inmate of* 31
Painted more soft and fair as they descend, 218 *Recluse* 1. 1. 226
Their course, or genial showers descend! 227 *Vernal Ode* 70
Might tempt an angel to descend, 235 *Power of Sound* 167
Descend from this ethereal height; 238 *P. B.* 152
The rising sun, and on the plains descend; 264 *Snowdrop* 6
Forced to descend into his destined tomb— 318 **Is there* 3
Descend on all that issues from our blood. 319 *Biscayan* 14
Descend, and, on the brow of ancient Rome 357 *Aquap.* 292
Ere they descend to nourish root and stalk 390 *Glencroe* 8
Descend on Francis; nor forbear 407 *White Doe* 1051
A few tears down her cheek descend 415 *White Doe* 1795
Druids descend, auxiliars of the Cross; 421 *Ecc. Sonn.* 1. 10. 11
Why do good thoughts, invoked or not, descend, 456 **Soft as* 22

Descend—*continued.*
Descend and reach, in Yewdale's depths, a plain 525 *Epist. Beaumont* 225
Which, though unsued for, fails not to descend 538 **In desultory* 30
So graciously?—that could descend, 582 **O for a* 26
That soften'd from the water-head descend. 597 *Ev. Wk. Quarto* 324
We must descend. A Traveller I am, 652 *Prelude* 3. 195
We must descend, and there should find the road, 683 *Prelude* 6. 581
A weight of ages did at once descend 707 *Prelude* 8. 552
Descend to earth or dwell in highest heaven! 755 *Recluse* 1. 1. 780
Descend, prophetic Spirit! that inspir'st 755 *Recluse* 1. 1. 836
That consolation may descend from far 795 *Excursion* 3. 664
Permitted to descend, and bless mankind. 797 *Excursion* 3. 758
—So we descend: and winding round a rock 823 *Excursion* 5. 77
Ere we descend into these silent vaults, 832 *Excursion* 5. 669
Their place; and genuine piety descend, 889 *Excursion* 9. 361
From whom all gifts descend, all blessings flow!" 895 *Excursion* 9. 754
Descendants. On their Descendants shedding grace— 342 *Ital. Itin.* 73
That to descendants of the dead it holds 355 *Aquap.* 163
To give, in their Descendants, freer vent 515 **Men of* 6
But by our best descendants be unknown, 627 **We gaze* 7
The true descendants of those godly men 814 *Excursion* 4. 897
Descended. *See* **Heaven-descended.**
Descended:—happy are the eyes that meet 423 *Ecc. Sonn.* 1. 19. 9
And I descended. Having reached the house, 785 *Excursion* 2. 881
Of motion, save the water that descended, 787 *Excursion* 3. 69
Whence the bare road descended rapidly 823 *Excursion* 5. 65
May have descended, though I see them here. 834 *Excursion* 5. 789
He had descended from the proud saloon, 843 *Excursion* 6. 329
Descended from Judean heights, to march 870 *Excursion* 7. 812
Descendeth. Looks on, and Grace descendeth from above 445 *Ecc. Sonn.* 3. 20. 7
Descending. Descending, shuts for aye his prison door. 16 *Desc. Sk.* 331
On the descending moon. 109 **Strange fits* 20
The Mother hails in her descending Son 139 *Widow* 40
To this lower world descending, 170 *Kitten* 14
Descending with a graceful flow, 190 *Beggars* 5
And is descending on his embassy; 208 **It is no* 2
Descending slowly, till the two 244 *P. B.* 674
From what huge height, descending? Can such force 272 *Devil's Bridge* 2
Now (for, though Truth descending from above 325 *Ode 1814* 118
Not swans descending with the stealthy tide, 347 *Processions* 60
Till Night, descending upon hill and vale, 363 **List—'twas* 110
Which Angels make, on works of love descending. 371 *Eg. Maid* 150
That seemed from heaven descending, like the flood 380 *Duddon* 19. 3
Aloft ascending, and descending deep, 395 *White Doe: Ded.* 44
To God descending in his power. 405 *White Doe* 834
Of right affections climbing or descending 500 *Humanity* 28
Descending to the worm in charity; 500 *Humanity* 32
Incense-like to Heaven, descending 502 **Like a* 16
When first, descending from the moorlands, 586 *Hogg* 1
Throned in the Sun's descending car 626 †*Cento* 1
Descending from the mountain to make sport 683 *Prelude* 6. 539
Descending slow with something heavenly fraught. 709 *Prelude* 8. 664
Descending, have I faithfully retraced 732 *Prelude* 11. 372
Descending, disembodied, and diffused 787 *Excursion* 3. 40
Descending from the region of the clouds, 809 *Excursion* 4. 528
Descending, there might rest; upon that height 811 *Excursion* 4. 687
And yet again recovered! But descending 819 *Excursion* 4. 1187
Were seen descending:—forth to greet them ran 821 *Excursion* 4. 1309
Without reserve descending upon both. 861 *Excursion* 7. 241
Descending, and supporting his pure heart 871 *Excursion* 7. 900
Descending, we pursued our homeward course, 895 *Excursion* 9. 757
Of vision less and less distinct, descending S.3. 435 **The doubt* 109
The cloud of rooks descending through mid air S.3. 437 **The doubt* 194
Descends. A little prattling child, he oft descends, 19 *Desc. Sk.* 485
Descends along the sloping road; 176 *Waggoner* 1. 263
To humbleness of heart descends 225 *Primrose* 49
Which, at Jove's will, descends on Pelion's top." 312 **When, far* 14
Descends:—beneath this godlike Warrior, see! 314 *Hoter* 12
The Spirit of Caractacus descends 421 *Ecc. Sonn.* 1. 10. 3
While each into himself descends, 580 *John Words.* 22
Oft he descends to nurse the brother pair, 612 *Desc.Sk.Quarto* 576
—Voiceless the stream descends into the gulf 787 *Excursion* 3. 92
Of speculation not unfit, descends; 806 *Excursion* 4. 356
But true humility descends from heaven; 833 *Excursion* 5. 719
Crowned by its antique summer-house—descends, 881 *Excursion* 8. 492
That Man descends into the Vale of years; 885 *Excursion* 9. 49
Descent. Appear; a calm descent of sky conducting 230 *Clouds* 34
(So seemed it) down a strange descent: 299 *Brownie's Cell* 52
Earthward it glided with a swift descent: 323 *Ode 1814* 23
And down the smooth descent 488 *Fountain* 66
So, to a steep and difficult descent 777 *Excursion* 2. 403
Whose sharp descent confounded their array, 865 *Excursion* 7. 544
Describe. An aged Man, and such as you describe. 73 *Bord.* 2050
And with a living pleasure we describe; 488 *Pers. Talk* 16
Contemplated, describe the Mind and Man 755 *Recluse* 1. 1. 848
Described. The Thorn which I described to you, 199 *Thorn* 167
To many living now, have I described K.8. 228 **I will* 108
Descried. *See* **Descry'd, Far-descried.**
Some, dim between the lofty cliffs descried, 5 *Ev. Wk.* 164
That glimmer hoar in eve's last light, descried 12 *Desc. Sk.* 115
To be descried through shady groves. 222 *Triad* 190
A Form not doubtfully descried:— 300 *Cora Linn* 26
And that intrepid Nymph, on Uri's steep descried! 345 **How blest* 78
Bear to the glacier band—those Shapes aloft descried. 347 *Processions* 63
And glistening antlers are descried; 457 **Had this* 31
A plain below stretched seaward, while, descried 475 **There! said* 5

Descried—*continued.*
By whom on this still night descried ? . . . . 479 *Somnamb.* 97
She hath advanced with hope to be descried. . . 524 *Epist. Beaumont* 212
And his crime, through the pains that o'erwhelm him, descried, ... 621 *Convict* 23
Or him have I descried in distant sky, ... 703 *Prelude* 8. 271
Descry. And scarce could any trace of man descry, 24 *Guilt* 25
Clear tops of far-off mountains we descry, . . . 268 **Four fiery* 4
Burial and death : look for them—and descry, . 322 **Humanity, delighting* 36
Pronounced the word,—and the Earls descry, . 402 *White Doe* 600
At least he feels 'tis given him to descry ; . . . 827 *Excursion* 5. 301
Descry'd. *See* **Descried.**
Some, dim between th' aereal cliffs descry'd, . . 594 *Ev. Wk. Quarto* 147
Between the pine's enormous boughs descry'd . 615 *Desc.Sk.Quarto* 698
Desecrate. To desecrate the Fane which heretofore 423 *Ecc. Sonn.* 1. 17. 4
Desecrated. To night, the desecrated floors are worn 359 **They—who* 5
Desert. *See* **Desart.**
Calls forth the woodman from his desert cell, . . 12 *Desc. Sk.* 124
While o'er the desert, answering every close, . . 16 *Desc. Sk.* 344
And nightingales desert the village grove, . . . 21 *Desc. Sk.* 615
A sound of chains along the desert rang ; . . . 25 *Guilt* 77
The pelican and ostrich of the desert, ... 62 *Bord.* 1353
And in this desert ? If never—then the whole . 62 *Bord.* 1396
By envy as a tribute to desert, ... 68 *Bord.* 1686
The moonlight desert, and the moonlight sea : . 70 *Bord.* 1807
Or shake his high desert. . . . . 105 *Artegal* 231
Or thou upon a desert thrown . . . . . . 117 *Affl. Marg.* 52
A desert wilderness will be ! . . . . 129 *Idiot Boy* 331
Whether printing desert sands . . . . . . 141 *Arm. Lady* 92
Vagrant over desert sands, ... 166 *Wand. Jew* 22
Whether, by their own desert, ... 181 *Waggoner* 4. 87
Or caught amid a whirl of desert sands— . . . 216 *Enterprise* 113
At which the desert trembles.—Humming Bee ! . 227 *Vernal Ode* 124
How fearful to the desert wide ! . . . . . 232 *Power of Sound* 22
While the whole world seems adverse to desert. . 260 **High is* 8
When men change swords for ledgers, and desert 307 **When I* 3
And, in the desert places of the earth, ... 325 *Ode 1814* 133
The Arabian desert shapes a willing road . . . 327 *Ode 1815* 25
How, when their course they through the desert took, ... 346 *Processions* 13
'Mid a dry desert ? What is it we hear ? . . . 359 **Those old* 4
Voice of the Desert, fare-thee-well ; sweet Bird ! . 363 **List—'twas* 103
Therefore the Voice spake from the Desert, thence 365 **The Baptist* 9
Utterly to desert, the haunts of men, ... 379 *Duddon* 14. 10
Sea, desert, what do these avail ? . . . . . 413 *White Doe* 1565
Let not your radiant Shapes desert the Land : . 434 *Ecc. Sonn.* 2. 24. 4
Who in the penitential desert met . . . . . 434 *Ecc. Sonn.* 2. 24. 13
As to the sandy desert fountains are, ... 444 *Ecc. Sonn.* 3. 17. 5
If Thought and Love desert us, from that day . 480 **Most sweet* 9
And desert stone-chat, all day long, is heard. . 593 *Ev. Wk. Quarto* 96
Calling the woodman from his desert cell, . . . 604 *Desc.Sk.Quarto* 143
I lov'd, mid thy most desert woods astray, . . 605 *Desc.Sk.Quarto* 164
—She solitary through the desert drear . . . 605 *Desc.Sk.Quarto* 199
—Breaking th' ascending roar of desert floods, . 606 *Desc.Sk.Quarto* 223
Shade above shade the desert pines ascend, . . 607 *Desc.Sk.Quarto* 290
A garden-plot the desert air perfumes, ... 607 *Desc.Sk.Quarto* 295
Flings o'er the desert blood-red streams of fire. . 614 *Desc.Sk.Quarto* 663
Desert me not, forthwith shall be brought down . 641 *Prelude* 1. 638
Would through the desert lead me ; and while yet 667 *Prelude* 5. 83
But was an Arab of the desert too ; . . . . 667 *Prelude* 5. 124
A gentle dweller in the desert, crazed . . . . 667 *Prelude* 5. 145
Upon a desert coast, that having brought . . . 677 *Prelude* 6. 144
By aught, I fear, of genuine desert— . . . . 677 *Prelude* 6. 169
The roving Indian, on his desert sands : . . . 698 *Prelude* 7. 747
And as the desert hath green spots, the sea . . 725 *Prelude* 10. 481
The Desert visible by dismal flames ; . . . . 744 *Prelude* 13. 330
Without desert, what he desired ; weak men, . . 776 *Excursion* 2. 302
Like a ripe date which in the desert falls . . . 780 *Excursion* 2. 605
Above the sandy desert, in the light . . . . 788 *Excursion* 3. 151
Fast anchored in the desert ?—Not alone . . . 791 *Excursion* 3. 372
Sprung from the desert ? And behold a city . . 799 *Excursion* 3. 884
Fit recompense of new desert ? what claim . . 805 *Excursion* 4. 281
Thousands of cities, in the desert place . . . 807 *Excursion* 4. 437
Trust me, pronouncing on your own desert, . . 808 *Excursion* 4. 478
That through the desert rang. Though favoured less, 815 *Excursion* 4. 932
Unlooked-for gladness in the desert place, . . . 852 *Excursion* 6. 922
Amid the untrodden desert, tells his beads, . . 862 *Excursion* 7. 303
Palmyra, central in the desert, fell ; . . . . 877 *Excursion* 8. 218
Deserted. *See* **Day-deserted, Heaven-deserted, Hope-deserted, Long-deserted.**
Leaving to silence the deserted vale ; . . . . 17 *Desc. Sk.* 373
In this deserted Castle—*I repent me.* . . . . 54 *Bord.* 947
I brooded o'er my injuries, deserted . . . . 68 *Bord.* 1699
A lonesome Chapel stands, deserted now : . . . 73 *Bord.* 2054
And we shall howl together. I am deserted . . 74 *Bord.* 2090
Deserted his poor Bride, and Ruth . . . . . 194 *Ruth* 191
Though lonely, a deserted Tower ; . . . . . 204 *Brougham* 37
Till brought to a deserted quarry— . . . . 240 *P. B.* 354
You, whom, though long deserted, he loved best ; 529 **Those breathing* 124
For hope's deserted well why wistful look ? . . 596 *Ev. Wk. Quarto* 255
To silence leaving the deserted vale, ... 610 *Desc.Sk.Quarto* 451
When, for the night deserted, it assumes . . . 664 *Prelude* 4. 368
Deserted and deceived, the Spoiler came . . . 691 *Prelude* 7. 299
Strike the deserted to the heart ; I speak . . . 851 *Excursion* 6. 860
Her own—deserted child !—Once, only once, . . 853 *Excursion* 6. 969
Where is it now ?—Deserted on the beach— . . 892 *Excursion* 9. 551
Desertion. Or blank desertion. No familiar shapes 638 *Prelude* 1. 395
Death-like, of treacherous desertion, felt . . . 724 *Prelude* 10. 414

Desert's. Even in the desert's heart ; but he, returned, ... 25 *Guilt* 66
Deserts. O'er life's long deserts with its charge of woe, 13 *Desc. Sk.* 167
A deeper peace than that in deserts found ! . . 334 **The Spirit* 14
Else it deserts him, surely as he lives. . . . . 354 *Aquap.* 117
Or aught in Syrian deserts left to save . . . . 367 *Trajan* 11
Equal to *his* deserts, who, like the year, . . . 425 *Ecc. Sonn.* 1. 26. 6
Into the deserts of Eternity. . . . . . . 582 *Invoc. Earth* 13
Hast placed me high above my best deserts, . . 653 *Prelude* 3. 318
Unfrequent as in deserts ; at late hours . . . 697 *Prelude* 7. 662
And swallowed up 'mid deserts infinite ! . . . 837 *Excursion* 5. 1007
Deserve. We should deserve to wear a cap and bells, 51 *Bord.* 768
Peace ye deserve ; and may the solid good, . . 143 **High bliss* 4
Reviving, heavier chastisement deserve . . . 327 **Emperors and* 13
Deserve a thought} but little known to fame— . 354 *Aquap.* 94
Deserve they further sacrifice ?— . . . . . 406 *White Doe* 905
They might deserve a good Man's blame ; . . . 409 *White Doe* 1224
Deserve the least return of human thanks ; . . 870 *Excursion* 7. 829
Deserved. Meanwhile the Invaders fared as they deserved : . . . . 724 *Prelude* 10. 390
Or of remembrance even, deserved or not. . . 847 *Excursion* 6. 604
And perseverance their deserved reward. . . . 889 *Excursion* 9. 382
Deservedly. Deservedly have styled.—From his abode 862 *Excursion* 7. 346
Deserves. And felt, if ought on earth deserves a curse, ... 70 *Bord.* 1811
Grieve for her, she deserves no less ; . . . . 370 *Eg. Maid* 55
Deserves the name (this truth the billows preach) 495 *Fact* 13
A name it now deserves, this cowardice, . . . 675 *Prelude* 6. 31
So dreaded, so abhorred. The day deserves . . 725 *Prelude* 10. 513
Aught that deserves respect : for I exist, . . . 800 *Excursion* 3. 966
Deserv'st. More thou deserv'st ; but *this* man gives to man, ... 490 *Tribute : Dog* 5
Deserving. *See* **Well-deserving.**
By more deserving brows.—Yet so ye prop, . . 312 **When, far* 9
Although deserving of all good, ... 581 *John Words.* 69
Deserving notice have escaped regard, ... 709 *Prelude* 9. 13
Design. No pause admitted, no design avowed ! 213 *Dion* 80
He puts the Earthquake on her still design, . . 328 *Ode 1815* 94
This vast design might tempt you to repeat . . 335 *Cologne* 11
The whole design of Scripture history ; . . . 351 *Des. Stanzas* 67
Abrupt—as without preconceived design . . . 394 **No more* 2
Down a swift Stream, thus far, a bold design . . 443 *Ecc. Sonn.* 3. 12. 1
Then noble Sandys, inspir'd with great design, . 619 *School Ex.* 65
Nor by his presence traverse the design. . . . 624 *Æneid* 35
And Hope gay Pilot of the bold design, . . . 625 **The confidence* 2
I read, without design, the opinions, thoughts, . 661 *Prelude* 4. 212
And of design not wholly worn away. . . . . 787 *Excursion* 3. 84
Our dark foundations rest, could he design . . 815 *Excursion* 4. 970
Designed. Much done, and much designed, and more desired,— . . . . 3 *Ev. Wk.* 83
Of flowers were in their hands, as if designed . . 59 *Bord.* 1203
In that deep valley, Michael had designed . . 136 *Michael* 323
Uttered by whom, or how inspired—designed . 336 *Staub-bach* 1
Sickened by injuries, dreading worse designed, . 449 *Ecc. Sonn.* 3. 37. 7
Might seem designed to humble man, when proud 473 **Thanks for* 7
Not to the object specially designed, ... 518 *Pun. Death* 5. 1
Designed to rise in humble privacy, ... 524 *Epist. Beaumont* 190
Close at her side were all the powers, design'd . 618 *School Ex.* 17
Or portraitures for special use designed, . . . 657 *Prelude* 3. 552
The playthings, which her love designed for him, . 670 *Prelude* 5. 338
To hated worth no Tyrant ere design'd . . . L.1. 88 *Juvenal* 1. 3
Designs. What hopes came with him ? what designs were spread . . . . 378 *Duddon* 8. 4
Thoughts without bound, magnificent designs, . 734 *Prelude* 11. 456
Desirable. Whate'er there is desirable and good 740 *Prelude* 13. 36
With aught, as more desirable and fair, . . . 790 *Excursion* 3. 319
Desire. A favoured Being, knowing no desire . 23 *Yew-tree* 16
And restrain the vague desire ? . . . . . . 94 *Westmoreland Girl* 76
The joy of my desire ; . . . . 109 **I travelled* 10
Farewell desire of human aid, ... 113 *Lament* 57
No pleasure now, and no desire. . . . . . 114 *Ind. Wom.* 18
The spirit of enjoyment and desire, ... 146 **It was an* 6
What intenseness of desire . . . . 171 *Kitten* 23
What greater good can heart desire ? . . . . 177 *Waggoner* 2. 71
To his own native greatness to desire . . . . 214 *Dion* 116
Prevail to further our desire, ... 221 *Triad* 87
In silent rapture, credulous desire . . . . . 231 *Clouds* 89
Scattering a ditty each to her desire, ... 233 *Power of Sound* 46
Of timid hope and innocent desire . . . . . 233 *Power of Sound* 78
" These given, what more need I desire . . . 238 *P. B.* 141
Yes ! hope may with my strong desire keep pace, 256 **Yes ! hope* 1
No quest was hers of vague desire, ... 371 *Eg. Maid* 133
Whose current answers to the heart's desire, . . 395 *White Doe : Ded.* 4
For other lore,—by keen desire . . . . . . 399 *White Doe* 301
" Gone are they,—they have their desire ; . . 401 *White Doe* 454
From looks conceiving her desire ; . . . . . 415 *White Doe* 1721
An instant kiss of masterful desire— . . . . 433 *Ecc. Sonn.* 2. 20. 8
And Tyranny is balked of her desire : . . . . 442 *Ecc. Sonn.* 3. 8. 4
Desire we past illusions to recall ? . . . . . 469 **Desire we* 1
In ruin beautiful. When vain desire . . . . 470 *Bala-Sala* 4
Best throve the fire of chaste desire, ... 478 *Somnamb.* 39
Long, barren silence, square with my desire ; . . 488 *Pers. Talk* 10
And in himself possess his own desire ; . . . 493 *Hap. War.* 38
Kindles intense desire for powers withheld . . 496 **A little* 27
The soul's desire—a lay . . . . 507 *May* 12
And what if hence a bold desire should mount . 511 **So fair* 7
And humbler growths as moved with one desire . 529 *Poor Robin* 3
Prevented each desire :— . . . . 542 *Russ. Fug.* 36
Sick are they all for lack of their desire ; . . . 557 *Cuck.and Night.* 33

Desired 211 Desperate

Desire—*continued.*
In loyalty, and worshipful desire, ... 560 *Cuck.andNight.*194
Now mercy, Lord! thou know'st well I desire . 563 *Troilus* 73
In peace eternal; where desire and joy . . 573 *Chiabrera* 1. 5
To throw the "sultry ray" of young Desire; . 604 *Desc.Sk.Quarto* 151
And vain regret and vain desire shall fail; . . 615 *Desc.Sk.Quarto* 743
In these night wanderings, that a strong desire 637 *Prelude* 1. 318
Of danger or desire; and thus did make . . 639 *Prelude* 1. 472
The eagerness of infantine desire? . . . . 642 *Prelude* 2. 26
That brought with it a regular desire . . . 642 *Prelude* 2. 49
Intense desire through meditative peace; . . . 663 *Prelude* 4. 306
Far stronger, now, grew the desire I felt . . 667 *Prelude* 5. 115
Have been possessed by similar desire; . . . 680 *Prelude* 6. 338
Effort, and expectation, and desire, . . . 684 *Prelude* 6. 607
A hope it is, and a desire; a creed . . . . 715 *Prelude* 9. 405
And on the stone were graven by his desire . 726 *Prelude* 10. 535
Did both find, helpers to their hearts' desire, . . 729 *Prelude* 11. 137
In that distraction and intense desire, ... 751 *Prelude* 14. 376
He coloured objects to his own desire . . . 775 *Excursion* 2. 277
Without repining or desire for more, ... 795 *Excursion* 3. 629
As may support longings of pure desire; . . . 804 *Excursion* 4. 236
And daily lose what I desire to keep: . . . . 810 *Excursion* 4. 612
Of contradiction, from some vague desire . . . 828 *Excursion* 5. 363
Love, admiration, fear, desire, and hate, . . . 830 *Excursion* 5. 496
(And Heaven was pleased to accomplish the desire) 845 *Excursion* 6. 501
Her keen desire of knowledge, nor efface . . . 848 *Excursion* 6. 700
Be the desire—too curiously to ask . . . 862 *Excursion* 7. 311
And by desire; we see by the glad light . . . 884 *Excursion* 9. 24
All that luxurious nature could desire, . . . K.8. 237*Recluse* 1. 1. 23
Less timid than desire—but that is passed. . . K.8. 238*Recluse* 1. 1. 70
Without desire in full complacency, ... K.8. 245*Recluse* 1.1.306
Desired. Much done, and much designed, and more desired,— . . . . 3 *Ev. Wk.* 83
And gave me food—and rest, more welcome, more desired. . . . . 31 *Guilt* 405
That gave thee liberty, full long desired, . . . 648 *Prelude* 2. 462
Perhaps than if it had been more desired . . 659 *Prelude* 4. 83
To the degree that he desired, beloved. . . . 772 *Excursion* 2. 56
Without desert, what he desired; weak men, . . 776 *Excursion* 2. 302
Desires. *See* **Chance-desires.**
Shelter and daily bread,—the sum of his desires. . 104 *Artegal* 105
The slave of low desires: . . . . 194 *Ruth* 153
Desires whose course in folly ends, ... 223 *Wishing-gate* 41
Of the dull earth partakes not, nor desires? . . 261 **I heard (alas* 12
Each fashions his desires. . . . . 291 *Rob Roy* 48
But what do his desires avail? . . . . . . 295 *Highland Boy* 81
And for a moment meet the soul's desires! . . 325 *Ode 1814* 126
To her desires, or to her hopes present— . . 327 *Ode 1815* 4
And to desires whose ever waxing horn . . . 330 *Ode: Thanks.* 115
Bend that way her desires. The dew, the storm— 354 *Aquap.* 133
Peace, leisure, freedom, moderate desires; . . 356 *Aquap.* 260
Doubtless shall cheat full oft the heart's desires; 429 *Ecc. Sonn.* 2. 3. 9
Vernal fruitions and desires . . . . . . 507 *May* 61
All vain desires, all lawless wishes quelled, . . 511 **So fair* 19
Kept pace with his desires; . . . . 545 *Russ. Fug.* 346
Of manifold pleasures and many desires: . . . 572 *Avarice* 26
And merciful desires, thy sanctity approve!" . 582 *Invoc. Earth* 34
Devoted, strives in vain her vast desires to fill; . 624 *Æneid* 80
From little enmities and low desires, ... 648 *Prelude* 2. 431
Were waiting with the whole of their desires . 712 *Prelude* 9. 187
His blind desires and steady faculties . . . 714 *Prelude* 9. 357
(If like desires of innocent little ones . . . 723 *Prelude* 10. 365
To God, Who thus corrected my desires; . . . 739 *Prelude* 12. 316
Of humble cares and delicate desires, ... 749 *Prelude* 14. 230
More wise desires, and simpler manners;—nurse . 755 *Recluse* 1. 1. 857
Sublime and comprehensive! Low desires, . . 759 *Excursion* 1. 234
The book that most had tempted his desires . 760 *Excursion* 1. 247
Gay as our spirits, free as our desires; . . . 794 *Excursion* 3. 543
As he desires that they should be, whom winds 799 *Excursion* 3. 887
Her thoughts, her images, her high desires. . . 803 *Excursion* 4. 108
Conceptions equal to the soul's desires; . . . 803 *Excursion* 4. 137
Along the line of limitless desires. . . . . 804 *Excursion* 4. 185
To such desires, and grasped at such delight, . 809 *Excursion* 4. 543
Rests his desires; and hence, in after life, . . 813 *Excursion* 4. 817
Earthly desires; and raise, to loftier heights . 820 *Excursion* 4. 1273
Of one accustomed to desires that feed . . . 820 *Excursion* 4. 1290
Corrupt affections, covetous desires, ... 826 *Excursion* 5. 286
That on the outset wastes its gay desires, . . 829 *Excursion* 5. 433
Had vanished from his prospects and desires; . 840 *Excursion* 6. 137
Ill purposes, and flatter foul desires. . . . 894 *Excursion* 9. 687
Thy prudence, thy experience—thy desires; . . K.8. 238 *Recluse* 1.1. 63
Among wild appetites and blind desires, . . . K.8. 256*Recluse* 1.1.706
Desiring. The help desiring of the pure devout. . 797 *Excursion* 3. 767
Desirous. With dark events. Desirous to divert . 793 *Excursion* 3. 468
Round his domain, desirous not alone . . . . 844 *Excursion* 6. 394
Desist. But they desist not;—and the sacred fire, . 432 *Ecc. Sonn.* 2. 14. 9
Desisted. Desisted, and the quarry and the mound 548 **Stranger! this* 12
And all desisted, save him alone. . . . . 841 *Excursion* 6. 218
Desk. Where at his desk and book he sits, . . . 175 *Waggoner* 1. 172
To the strict labours of the merchant's desk . . 584 *Ch. Lamb* 5
To books, and to the long-forsaken desk, . . . 840 *Excursion* 6. 149
Desolate. Contentment shares the desolate domain 15 *Desc. Sk.* 260
His prey, through tracts abrupt of desolate space, 16 *Desc. Sk.* 306
And desolate, "Here you will find a friend!" . 24 *Guilt* 15
Dried up, despairing, desolate, on board . . . 30 *Guilt* 305
His Victim—haply to this desolate house. . . . 54 *Bord.* 913
Here art thou, then can I be desolate? . . . 76 *Bord.* 2194
Than desolate; for oft-times from the sound . . 118 *Maternal Grief* 43
Stony, and dark, and desolate, ... 176 *Waggoner* 1. 216
When Ruth was left half desolate, ... 192 *Ruth* 1
Farewell, thou desolate Domain! . . . . . 215 *Kirkstone* 77

Desolate—*continued.*
Be left more desolate, more dreary cold . . . 277 **Why art* 11
These desolate remains are trophies high . . . 316 **Hail, Zaragoza* 5
The desolate Slumberer with moss and with leaves. 340 *Fort Fuentes* 12
When with life lengthened out came a desolate time, ... 364 *Vallomb.* 17
Overthrown and desolate! . . . . 397 *White Doe* 82
Thus overwhelmed, and desolate, ... 400 *White Doe* 425
—How desolate is Rylstone-hall! . . . . . 412 *White Doe* 1511
While he struck his desolate harp without hopes or aims. . . . . 474 **Ye shadowy* 8
As blest and as glad, in this desolate gloom, . . 484 **A plague* 28
The skies will weep o'er old men desolate: . . 505 *Warning* 155
Upon her Island desolate; . . . . 544 *Russ. Fug.* 203
The desolate ruins of St. Herbert's Cell. . . . 551 **If thou in* 7
Then said he thus,—O Palace desolate! . . . 563 *Troilus* 22
Where proud Covent-garden, in desolate hours . 570 *Farmer* 73
A Nation's hopes lie crushed in Claremont's desolate Hall. . . . . 628 *Installation* 24
Now, after separation desolate, ... 678 *Prelude* 6. 201
The spot, though fair, was very desolate— . . 767 *Excursion* 1. 740
The longer I remained, more desolate: . . . 767 *Excursion* 1. 741
Before us, mountains stern and desolate; . . . 772 *Excursion* 2. 92
Foretelling aged Winter's desolate sway. . . . 828 *Excursion* 5. 410
Depressed, and desolate of soul, as once . . . . 855 *Excursion* 6. 1131
My Sister, here misplaced and desolate, . . . K.8. 248*Recluse* 1.1.428
Desolated. When desolated countries, towns on fire, 330 *Ode: Thanks.* 103
Before them, in some desolated place, ... 724 *Prelude* 10. 445
Desolating. Of fortune, and the desolating storms . 333 **Bruges I* 9
The gentle brooks!—Your desolating sway, . . 790 *Excursion* 3. 311
And, if the desolating hand of war . . . . . 838 *Excursion* 6. 35
Of desolating anguish for them all! . . . . 867 *Excursion* 7. 676
Desolation. From desolation toward the genial prime; . . . . 274 **Such age* 11
Of Desolation, and to Ruin's scythe . . . . 355 *Aquap.* 197
And Desolation is thy Patron-saint! . . . . 376 *Duddon* 2. 8
One desolation, one decay! . . . . 402 *White Doe* 555
Of utter desolation made . . . . 411 *White Doe* 1428
'Tis done;—despoil and desolation . . . . . 413 *White Doe* 1568
Distress and desolation spread . . . . . . 416 *White Doe* 1842
Can link with desolation. Smooth and green, . 439 *Ecc. Sonn.* 2. 43. 5
Bare steeps, where Desolation stalks, afraid, . . 606 *Desc.Sk.Quarto* 251
A desolation, a simplicity, ... 664 *Prelude* 4. 402
Of Desolation, aimed: to slow decline . . . . 872 *Excursion* 7. 994
Desolations. He sang—"No wintry desolations, . 226 *Vernal Ode* 25
Despair. Until it seemed to bring a joy to my despair. 30 *Guilt* 342
—In deep despair, by frightful wishes stirred, . 31 *Guilt* 381
Too soon I yielded to despair; . . . . . . 114 *Ind. Wom.* 23
While Venus in a passion of despair . . . . 169 *Love lies Bleeding* 15
The heaviest plummet of despair can go— . . 213 *Dion* 62
Into the ambush of despair; . . . . 232 *Power of Sound* 13
Ha! why these sinkings of despair? . . . . 244 *P. B.* 723
As if a dead man spake it! Yet despair . . . 304 **Jones! as* 12
With words of apprehension and despair . . . 308 **These times* 3
Nor must, nor will, nor can, despair of Thee! . 359 **They—who* 14
For maid and mother, when despair . . . 391 *Highland Broach* 53
Her Son, and felt in her despair . . . . . 398 *White Doe* 227
There stood he, cleansed from the despair . . . 401 *White Doe* 439
The self-reliance of despair!'" . . . . . . 407 *White Doe* 1056
This weight of anguish and despair. . . . . 412 *White Doe* 1515
Or wan despair—the ghost of false hope fled . . 514 **Long-favoured* 8
Loving is aye an office of despair, ... 560 *Cuck.andNight.*176
From anguish to despair! . . . . 582 **O for a* 18
At once upon his heart Despair has set . . . 613 *Desc.Sk.Quarto* 628
Despair not of our nature, but retain . . . . 648 *Prelude* 2. 442
There is no grief, no sorrow, no despair, . . . 678 *Prelude* 6. 244
Such ghastly visions had I of despair . . . . 724 *Prelude* 10. 402
Yielded up moral questions in despair. . . . 731 *Prelude* 11. 305
That what we feel of sorrow and despair . . . 770 *Excursion* 1. 949
Love with despair, or grief in agony;— . . . 791 *Excursion* 3. 378
And, least of all, is absolute despair. . . . . 803 *Excursion* 4. 164
Exist; so, none is now for fixed despair; . . . 805 *Excursion* 4. 267
From palpable oppressions of despair." . . . 817 *Excursion* 4. 1077
Battens on spleen, or moulders in despair? . . 830 *Excursion* 5. 510
For languor, or indifference, or despair. . . . K.8. 247*Recluse* 1.1.373
Despaired. To have despaired, have hoped, believed, 117 *Affl. Marg.* 10
Despairing. Dried up, despairing, desolate, on board 30 *Guilt* 305
Snatch'd from her shoulder with despairing moan, 597 *Ev. Wk. Quarto* 289
In the roof'd bridge, at that despairing hour, . . 606 *Desc.Sk.Quarto* 209
Despair's. Soon with despair's whole weight his spirits sink; . . . . 16 *Desc. Sk.* 332
Then with despair's whole weight his spirits sink, 609 *Desc.Sk.Quarto* 404
Despairs. Report of comfortless despairs, . . . 338 **Meek Virgin* 10
And comfortless despairs the soul benumb. . . 427 *Ecc. Sonn.* 1. 36. 14
Despatch. Despatch him! If I pass beneath a rock 78 *Bord.* 2314
Despatched. That will be soon despatched. Did Marmaduke . . . . 43 *Bord.* 340
Desperate. Midway along the hill with desperate speed; . . . . 6 *Ev. Wk.* 197
Or desperate love, bewildered, he came there. . 11 *Desc. Sk.* 42
Restore him, Heaven! The desperate Wretch!—A Flower, ... 61 *Bord.* 1308
Desperate the Maid—the Youth is stained with blood; . . . . 123 *V. and J.* 146
They ran, and with a desperate leap . . . . 162 *Binnorie* 51
A deep, determined, desperate draught! . . . 178 *Waggoner* 2. 156
"For thirteen hours he ran a desperate race; . 203 *Hart-leap* 145
Self-cast, as with a desperate course, ... 234 *Power of Sound* 137
Of fire his desperate self is tethering? . . . . 242 *P. B.* 512
Desperate as thine? Or come the incessant shocks 272 *Devil's Bridge* 6
Whose desperate shock the Carthaginian fled. . 320 **They seek* 8

Destroy—*continued.*
Not scourge, to save the People—not destroy. 515 *Long-favoured 14
A charm, *that* thought can not destroy, 530 †Redbreast 7
Hast thou thy own liege subjects to destroy? 563 Troilus 70
Death conscious that he only could destroy 581 *Why should we 8
Can utterly abolish or destroy! 590 Immortality 164
And here the avalanche of Death destroy 613 Desc.Sk.Quarto 600
Industrious to destroy! With fruitless pains 875 Excursion 8. 95
Delusion which a moment may destroy! 887 Excursion 9. 198
Destroyed. But not destroyed. The proofs—you ought to have seen 69 Bord. 1769
By whom thy Parent was destroyed, Idonea! 75 Bord. 2171
To be destroyed. But worthier still of note 184 Yew-trees 13
The Olympian summit hath destroyed for aye 325 Ode 1814 119
Her peace destroyed! her hopes a wilderness! 439 Ecc. Sonn. 2. 44. 13
By Roman perseverance, are destroyed, 549 *The massy 2
The excess, by which the balance is destroyed. 804 Excursion 4. 178
Destroyed their unoffending commonwealth, 823 Excursion 5. 95
And slaves who will consent to be destroyed— 836 Excursion 5. 942
Hope after hope, encouraged and destroyed. 841 Excursion 6. 229
That shall not die, and cannot be destroyed. 857 Excursion 7. 30
Of the same breath are shattered and destroyed. 889 Excursion 9. 343
Destroyer. This keen Destroyer, in his turn, must fall. 867 Excursion 7. 631
Destroying. *See* **Self-destroying.**
Tyrants who utter the destroying word, 836 Excursion 5. 941
Destroys. And surely as they vanish. Earth destroys 210 Laod. 70
But Death alone their vain regret destroys. 598 Ev. Wk. Quarto 362
And reproduce the troubles he destroys. 846 Excursion 6. 517
Destruction. Regions in destruction steeping,) 227 Vernal Ode 96
When the whirlwind of human destruction is spent, 340 Fort Fuentes 19
Stirs and recedes—destruction to escape! 349 Sky-prosp. 8
Or but forbode destruction, I deplore 440 Ecc. Sonn. 3. 2. 10
Destruction to the children of the earth 667 Prelude 5. 97
Guides to destruction? Is it well to trust 812 Excursion 4. 771
By the destruction of her innocent sons 878 Excursion 8. 286
Now, when destruction is a prime pursuit, 890 Excursion 9. 413
Destructive. Of destructive tempests coming, 328 Ode 1815 73
In his destructive flight on earthly crowns, 460 *Queen of 22
Than her destructive energies, attend 799 Excursion 3. 929
From disregard of time's destructive power, 847 Excursion 6. 621
Desultory. That checked the desultory range 343 Eclipse 11
Of roving tired or desultory war— 444 Ecc. Sonn. 3. 17. 8
In desultory walk through orchard grounds, 537 *In desultory 1
The mid-day hours with desultory talk; 882 Excursion 8. 521
Detached. But with no settled plan. I was detached 675 Prelude 6. 25
To blazon—power and energy detached 740 Prelude 13. 43
Which a detached spectator may regard 799 Excursion 3. 901
Detached from pleasure, to the love of gain 839 Excursion 6. 45
Detaching. With her first growths, detaching by the stroke 788 Excursion 3. 181
Detain. The moving image to detain; 182 Waggoner 4. 233
Assist me to detain 190 *Lyre! though 4
And him no mortal effort can detain: 211 Laod. 154
Welter and flash, a synod might detain 268 *Dogmatic Teachers 12
Nor long this mystery did detain 294 Jedbor. 70
As being all unworthy to detain 320 *O'erweening Statesmen 7
Whose skirts the glowing Mountain thirsted to detain. 338 Engelberg 18
Nor long (that crossed) would Grecian hills detain 427 Ecc. Sonn. 1. 34. 7
'Twere madness—wished we, therefore, to detain, 435 Ecc. Sonn. 2. 28. 4
Detain me from the best of other guides 668 Prelude 5. 168
Detained. Detained them near the gateway of the Castle. 59 Bord. 1201
Chieftains and kings in council were detained; 211 Laod. 119
Some fled; and some their fears detained: 408 White Doe 1159
Should in his childhood be detained for ever! 692 Prelude 7. 376
To humbler matter that detained us oft 717 Prelude 9. 542
Detained us, on what spectacles of woe 734 Prelude 12. 2
Detained for contemplation or repose, 757 Excursion 1. 42
Here would not linger, willingly detained? 787 Excursion 3. 45
Or what detained him, till his closing eyes 791 Excursion 3. 370
And mossy seats, detained us side by side, 794 Excursion 3. 547
A thought of refuge, for a mind detained 878 Excursion 8. 244
Proffered to all, while yet on earth detained. 894 Excursion 9. 657
Detains. Detains me, doubtful of the event; 113 Lament 53
Or rather felt, the entrancement that detains 381 Duddon 20. 2
Grief of her sting; nor cheat, where he detains 389 Breadalb. 4
Of bland entreaty at her court detains; 624 Æneid 20
The matter that detains us now may seem, 694 Prelude 7. 458
Detains; but tempted now to interpose, 814 Excursion 4. 893
Detains him after his accustomed hour 834 Excursion 5. 765
Detect. Avails those modulations to detect, 339 Ranz 2
Cast upwards on thy countenance, to detect 707 Prelude 8. 537
Pleased to detect the dimpling stir of life, S.3. 433 *The doubt 40
Detected. And vowed that she should be detected— 537 Goody Blake 67
Deter. To daylight known deter from that pursuit, 154 Morn. Ex. 56
Though to give timely warning and deter 519 Pun. Death 9. 1
Determinations. In Heaven's determinations, ever just. 795 Excursion 3. 658
Determine. That he the solemn issue would determine. 373 Eg. Maid 312
Doubts, and determine questions, by the rules 792 Excursion 3. 414
Determined. With a determined purpose to resume 96 Brothers 69
A deep, determined, desperate draught! 178 Waggoner 2. 156
No master spirit, no determined road; 307 *Great men 13
Prejudged by foes determined not to spare, 440 Ecc. Sonn. 2. 45. 1
The Wanderer lost in more determined gloom. 461 *Who but is 14
Determined, lies beyond the State's embrace, 519 Pun. Death 8. 2

Determined—*continued.*
To the high altar its determined place; 534 *When in 12
In deep determin'd gloom his subject tides. 598 Ev. Wk. Quarto 338
To brace myself to some determined aim, 633 Prelude 1. 115
Single and of determined bounds; and hence 641 Prelude 1. 641
Determined and unmoved, with steady beams 756 Excursion 1. 7
With no determined object, though upheld 795 Excursion 3. 632
And qualities determined.—Among men 797 Excursion 3. 787
They, with joint care, determined to erect, 845 Excursion 6. 496
A safer, easier, more determined, course. 864 Excursion 7. 490
Determines. Where gold determines between right and wrong. 573 Chiabrera 2. 4
Deterred. *See* **Half-deterred.**
To listen, is prevented or deterred. 885 Excursion 9. 80
Detested. She is," continued the detested Slave, 59 Bord. 1188
Beneath their feet, detested and defiled. 435 Ecc. Sonn. 2. 29. 14
Detraction. In envy or detraction is not heard; 848 Excursion 6. 639
Deum. Chant in full choir their innocent Te Deum. 367 *If with 14
Deva's. On Deva's banks, ye have abode so long; 272 Lady E. B. 12
Devastation. Of devastation; but the hazels rose 185 Nutting 19
Deviate. By Angels guarded, deviate from the line 428 Ecc. Sonn. 2. 1. 2
Deviates. To this conclusion, deviates from the line, 826 Excursion 5. 259
Deviating. Not deviating,—a priest, the like of whom, 839 Excursion 6. 77
Device. This last device must end my work.—Methinks 58 Bord. 1145
Our Captain made a prey to foul device!— 63 Bord. 1418
Nor lacked his calmer hours device or toy 108 Indolence 50
I asked—'twas whispered; The device 162 *Who fancied 13
But mighty Winter the device shall scorn. 321 *Humanity, delighting 12
As the cool Advocate of foul device; 514 *Portentous change 2
Lost wretch, a horrible device enthroned 517 Pun. Death 2. 6
No one knows by what device? 550 Hermit's Cell 3. 4
Not unbecoming, of grotesque device 881 Excursion 8. 476
Devices. Of his devices—buried, lost! 298 Brownie's Cell 14
Conceits, devices, plans, and schemes, K.8. 227 *I will 101
Devil. "The devil take his wisdom!" said 129 Idiot Boy 258
The bane of all that dread the devil! 129 Idiot Boy 336
From life or death, from man or devil; 179 Waggoner 3. 135
No doubt the devil in me wrought; 245 P. B. 813
Devils. The devils at such sights do clap their hands. 76 Bord. 2190
Legions of devils through a key-hole's space. L.1. 94 Juvenal 2. 4
Devious. Opened at once, and stayed my devious feet. 3 Ev. Wk. 56
Checked oft-times in a devious race, 285 Grave of Burns 74
Rebellious, acting in a devious mood; 647 Prelude 2. 364
His devious course. A glimpse of such sweet life 702 Prelude 8. 209
Heard, though unseen,—a devious traveller, 716 Prelude 9. 447
By devious footsteps; regions consecrate 809 Excursion 4. 517
Nor need the windings of his devious course 854 Excursion 6. 1087
Far went these shepherds in their devious quest, K.8. 225 *I will 35
Alone and devious from afar he came; K.8. 236 Recluse 1. 1. 6
Deviously. But *He*—who deviously hath sought 249 P. B. 1101
Devise. Mankind of yore were prompted to devise 346 Processions 6
For he may do all that he will devise; 557 Cuck. and Night. 13
Devised. Is cunningly devised; and, on the back 39 Bord. 80
As I already have in thought devised; 105 Artegal 216
Devised out of a sick man's dream! 300 Bran 26
—Long may these homely Works devised of old, 351 Des. Stanzas 74
And for the outrage which he had devised 548 *Stranger! this 24
Fictions, for ladies of their love, devised 673 Prelude 5. 499
Devised by fancy for the golden age; 790 Excursion 3. 320
Our vital frame, so fearfully devised, 816 Excursion 4. 975
Of trivial occupations well devised, 892 Excursion 9. 520
Devising. "The winds are now devising work for me!" 132 Michael 55
Devoid. And kissed it; seemingly devoid of pain, 125 V. and J. 233
Utterly in himself devoid of guile; 470 *A youth 10
And be not most unfeelingly devoid 889 Excursion 9. 329
Devon. The seignories of Herbert are in Devon; 39 Bord. 84
Devon's. On Devon's leafy shores;—a sheltered hold, 793 Excursion 3. 518
Devoted. *See* **Self-devoted, Soul-devoted.**
We reached the western world, a poor devoted crew. 29 Guilt 297
The cruel Viper!—Poor devoted Maid, 46 Bord. 527
Devoted to the tomb. 300 Cora Linn 42
A Ship to Christ devoted 374 Eg. Maid 359
"Still is he my devoted Knight?" 479 Somnamb. 77
A Voice—devoted to the love whose seeds 538 *In desultory 37
Devoted thus, their spirits did unite 546 *The embowering 7
Devoted, strives in vain her vast desires to fill; 624 Æneid 80
Of earth devoted to eternity!" 681 Prelude 6. 435
Devoted, on the inviolable stream 701 Prelude 8. 179
Of one devoted,—one whom circumstance 715 Prelude 9. 400
Of his devoted worshippers, far-stretched, 811 Excursion 4. 690
Devotedly. Resolves devotedly serene; 543 Russ. Fug. 171
Devotedness. In the devotedness of youthful love, 793 Excursion 3. 505
Devotees. From that soft class of devotees who feel 48 Bord. 585
Thanks to the austere and simple Devotees, 467 St. Bees 70
Devotion. *See* **Self-devotion.**
In mute devotion on the thankful breast! 20 Desc. Sk. 568
To feed my heart's devotion, 112 *Yes! thou 10
With such a strong devotion, that your heart 147 Joanna 5
The triumph of your late devotion! 178 Waggoner 3. 23
Than these, and utter your devotion there 230 Clouds 22
But with one fervour of devotion meek. 256 Decay of Piety 8
That faith which no devotion may renew! 335 Aix 4
Our slack devotion needs them all; 341 San Salv. 15
Which no devotion now respects; 366 *Ye Trees 4
Give to devotion, wheresoe'er awake, 430 Ecc. Sonn. 2. 9. 12
Of meek devotion, which erewhile it gave, 535 *When in 26

Devotion—*continued.*
Which with cold kiss Devotion planted near, . . 606 *Desc.Sk.Quarto* 257
To firm devotion, zeal unquenchable . . . . 635 *Prelude* 1. 184
Hence my obeisance, my devotion hence, . . . 647 *Prelude* 2. 375
In this our deep devotion. Fare thee well ! . 648 *Prelude* 2. 466
With deep devotion, Nature, did I feel, . . . 700 *Prelude* 8. 70
That to devotion willingly would rise, . . . 704 *Prelude* 8. 338
And its devotion gradually decline, ... 873 *Excursion* 7. 1018
Swell his devotion with their voice in storms, . K.8. 253 *Recluse* 1.1.610
And 'tis their due devotion has been paid . . L.1. 89 *Juvenal* 1. 27

Devour. The morning's splendours to devour ; . 327 *Ode* 1815 14
My ship and me Charybdis will devour. . . . 564 *Troilus* 126

Devoured. Devoured like pleasure ere it spreads . 154 *Flower Garden* 15
From fields laid waste, from house and home
    devoured . . . . 426 *Ecc. Sonn.* 1. 32. 3
Were skimmed, devoured, or studiously perused,. 675 *Prelude* 6. 24
Devoured by locusts,—Carra, Gorsas,—add . . 712 *Prelude* 9. 176
Devoured with keenness ere to grove or bank . K.8. 245 *Recluse* 1.1.333

Devouring. Grief that devouring waves had caused
    —or guilt . . . . 470 **Did pangs* 2
In silence, or with keen devouring noise . . 655 *Prelude* 4. 453
And there have read, devouring as I read, . . 673 *Prelude* 5. 486
Flung from the body of devouring fires, . . . 894 *Excursion* 9. 703

Devout. Who more devout enjoyment with us took : 107 *Indolence* 4
Uttered to Heaven in ecstasy devout ! . . . 322 *Germans* 8
He only, if such breathe, in strains devout . 326 **The Bard* 10
But in the bosom, with devout respect . . . 332 *Ode : Thanks.* 221
And with devout solemnities entwined— . . 334 **The Spirit* 4
Of the Devout, as, 'mid your glooms convened . 357 *Aquap.* 300
And melts ; but grief devout that shall endure, . 373 *Eg. Maid* 261
Of the devout, a veil of ecstasy ! . . . . 451 *Ecc. Sonn.* 3. 44. 14
So, with devout humility be it said, ... 724 *Prelude* 10. 447
The help desiring of the pure devout. . . . 797 *Excursion* 3. 767
Shall gain defenders zealous and devout . . 806 *Excursion* 4. 312
Devout above the meaning of your will. . . 818 *Excursion* 4. 1150
With this a salutation as devout, ... 838 *Excursion* 6. 7

Devoutest. Though he, devoutest of all Champions,
    ere . . . . 373 *Eg. Maid* 273

Devoutly. Devoutly, in life's last retreats ! . . 232 *Power of Sound* 16
A dirge devoutly breathed o'er sorrows past ; . 314 **I dropped* 10
(As the crowd press devoutly down the aisle . 332 *Ode : Thanks.* 213
By Hebrew ordinance devoutly kept, . . . 354 *Aquap.* 136
Devoutly stretched upon their chancel floors. . 430 *Ecc. Sonn.* 2. 8. 8
Lady ! devoutly honoured and beloved . . . 628 **Deign, Sovereign* 9
To kneel devoutly in yon reverend Pile, . . 895 *Excursion* 9. 725

Dew. See **Mountain-dew.**
The first whose footsteps print the mountain dew. 22 *Desc. Sk.* 670
Was soft and warm, no dew lay on the grass, . 39 *Bord.* 116
The dew was falling fast, the stars began to blink ; 87 *Pet-lamb* 1
And twice in the day, when the ground is wet with
    dew, ... 87 *Pet-lamb* 43
Ere with cold beads of midnight dew . . . . 109 **Ere with* 1
I've wet my path with tears like dew, . . . 117 *Affl. Marg.* 34
When grass is chill with rain or dew, . . . 156 *Oak and Broom* 85
It fears not rain, nor wind, nor dew ; . . . 166 *Danish Boy* 29
So drooped Adonis, bathed in sanguine dew . 169 *Love lies Bleeding* 12
Nor wanted sun, nor rain, nor dew, ... 194 *Ruth* 200
Scorching blight or noxious dew, ... 226 *Vernal Ode* 26
The lingering dew—there steals along, or stops . 270 **Though the bold* 6
More prompt, more glad, to fall than drops of dew 276 *Author's Portrait* 11
As they from turf yet hoar with sleepy dew . 278 **Life with* 9
ARMINIUS !—all the people quaked like dew . 313 *Prophecy* 4
Of morning dew upon the untrodden meads, . 330 *Ode : Thanks.* 65
That screen the morning dew. . . . . . 343 *Eclipse* 18
Herbs moistened by Virginian dew, ... 348 **Lulled by* 45
Bend that way her desires. The dew, the storm— 354 *Aquap.* 133
The dew whose moisture fell in gentle drops . 354 *Aquap.* 134
Long has the dew been dried on tree and lawn ; . 360 **Long has* 1
Most fair, most welcome, when they drank the dew 361 **List—'twas* 14
That, calmly couching while the nightly dew . 380 *Duddon* 17. 8
Where dew falls not, where rain-drops seem un-
    known ? . . . . 387 *Roslin* 10
And when, ere fall of evening dew, ... 414 *White Doe* 1684
He is retired as noontide dew, ... 485 *Poet's Epitaph* 41
Were tears of light, the dew of gladness. . . 486 *Matthew* 24
With points of morning dew. . . . . . . 487 **We walked* 44
Like harebells bathed in dew, ... 541 *Russ. Fug.* 2
" The sunshine may not cheer it, nor the dew, . 571 **There is a Flower* 17
The distant clock forgot, and chilling dew, . . 596 *Ev. Wk. Quarto* 273
Fall on his shifting hut that gleams mid smoking
    dew ; . . . . 610 *Desc.Sk.Quarto* 455
The thoughts of gratitude shall fall like dew . 658 *Prelude* 4. 30
The whole world over, tight as beads of dew . 670 *Prelude* 5. 321
Her dew is on the flowers. Those were the days 675 *Prelude* 6. 52
And pure as dew bathing their crimson leaves. . 773 *Excursion* 2. 110
Of morning, aided by exhaling dew, ... 773 *Excursion* 2. 135
Upon the mountains gemmed with morning dew . 850 *Excursion* 6. 822
That still unites them, praises, like heaven's dew, . 861 *Excursion* 7. 240
And oak whose roots by noontide dew were damped, 866 *Excursion* 7. 600
A field before them freshened with the dew . . 884 *Excursion* 9. 31

Dew-damped. O'er dew-damped dust our journey
    was begun, ... 522 *Epist.Beaumont* 96

Dew-drop. Thou art a dew-drop, which the morn
    brings forth, ... 88 *H. C.* 27
Protects the lingering dew-drop from the Sun. . 538 **Small service* 4

Dew-drop's. Calm as the dew-drop's, free to rest . 582 **O for a* 22

Dew-drops. To crush the mountain dew-drops—
    soon to melt . . . . 222 *Triad* 202

Dewing. See **Lip-dewing.**

Dews. Fresh gales and dews of life's delicious morn, 20 *Desc. Sk.* 530
When evening dews begin to fall. . . . . 142 †*Lov. and Lik.* 10
And feed on never-sullied dews, ... 154 *Flower Garden* 33
Proud be the rose, with rains and dews . . 158 **In youth* 27
And when, at dusk, by dews opprest . . . . 158 **In youth* 61
But the dews allay the heat, ... 173 *Waggoner* 1. 20
Hoar with the frost-like dews of dawn ; . . . 180 *Waggoner* 4. 39
Of shades, and dews, and silent night ; . . . 186 **O Nightingale* 8
From morn to evening dews. . . . . . . 193 *Ruth* 60
Or blooming thicket moist with morning dews ; . 227 *Vernal Ode* 80
Or moist with dews ; what more unsightly now, . 266 **Desponding Father* 3
Its glistening dews ; but hallowed is the clay . 273 **Wild Redbreast* 4
The flowers in pearly dews their bloom renewing ! 283 **Here, where* 8
Pleased in refreshing dews to steep . . . . 299 *Cora Linn* 10
The dews of morn, or April's tender shower ? . 319 *Guernica* 8
Familiar, as the Morn with pearly dews ? . . 335 *Namur* 4
Reached by the dews of heavenly grace ; . . 390 *Highland Broach* 44
Day's grateful warmth, tho' moist with falling dews. 453 **Calm is the* 2
Soft shades and dews have shed their blended power 456 **The leaves* 4
The Mind's internal heaven shall shed her dews . 480 **Most sweet* 13
And hoary dews are slow to melt. . . . . 536 *Goody Blake* 32
'Mid the dews, in the sunshine of morn,—'mid the
    joy . . . . 569 *Farmer* 9
I sprinkle thee with soft celestial dews, . . . 582 *Invoc. Earth* 21
Whose fragrance, by soft dews and rain unbound, 584 **With copious* 58
Soft gales and dews of life's delicious morn, . . 613 *Desc.Sk.Quarto* 634
Like young Iulus ; but the gentlest dews . . 624 *Æneid* 46
Dews, vapours, and the melody of birds, . . . 663 *Prelude* 4. 331
In the wild turf : the lingering dews of morn . 702 *Prelude* 8. 244
Of dews fast melting on their leafy boughs . . 773 *Excursion* 2. 132
' Gathers, and is preserved ; and feeding dews . 835 *Excursion* 5. 873
Whom Morn awakens, among dews and flowers . 894 *Excursion* 9. 670

Dew-sprinkled. From dew-sprinkled grass to heights
    guarded with snow, ... 345 *Stanzas : Simplon* 18

Dewy. The kine are couched upon the dewy grass ; 1 *Early Youth* 2
The cowslip-gathering in June's dewy prime ; . 28 *Guilt* 214
Thy couch the dewy earth, thy roof the forest
    thorn ! " . . . . 104 *Artegal* 161
Have you espied upon a dewy lawn . . . . 118 *Maternal Grief* 27
Each with the other, on the dewy ground, . . 143 **High bliss* 20
The daisy sleeps upon the dewy lawn, . . . 153 *Morn. Ex.* 25
Dewy night o'ershades the ground ; . . . . 163 *Spinning Wheel* 5
That at my will burns on the dewy lawn, . . 167 *Pilgrim's Dream* 43
Limping o'er the dewy grass, ... 181 *Waggoner* 4. 159
Both with thy nest upon the dewy ground ? . 209 **Ethereal minstrel* 4
In ten thousand dewy rays ; . . . . . . 221 *Triad* 130
The dewy ground was dark and cold ; . . . 289 *Stepping West.* 9
Is more benignant than the dewy eve— . . . 337 *Aar* 10
To sit and muse, fanned by its dewy air . . 367 **If with* 8
Dewy and fresh, till showers again shall fall. . 381 *Duddon* 19. 14
The dewy turf with flowers bestrown ; . . . 397 *White Doe* 139
Couched upon the dewy grass, ... 397 *White Doe* 154
At morning to the dewy field, ... 415 *White Doe* 1748
Wide as the oak extends its dewy gloom, . . 425 *Ecc. Sonn.* 1. 27. 13
Moistened from age to age by dewy eve, . . 450 *Ecc. Sonn.* 3. 39. 2
Observe how dewy Twilight has withdrawn . . 456 **Soft as* 8
Through dewy grass, nor small birds hushed in
    bowers, ... 501 **The unremitting* 4
Like morning's dewy gleams ; . . . . . . 506 **While from* 12
Loving the dewy shade,—a humble band, . . 539 **Lady ! a* 19
Green dewy lights adorn the freshen'd mead, . 607 *Desc.Sk.Quarto* 272
Ye dewy mists the arid rocks o'er-spread . . 609 *Desc.Sk.Quarto* 392
As the soft star of dewy evening tells . . . 619 **She wept* 11
Couched in the dewy grass. With such a theme, 750 *Prelude* 14. 275
Among the dewy grass,—in early spring, . . . 764 *Excursion* 1. 526
Into the dewy clouds. Ambition reigns . . . 807 *Excursion* 4. 394
The dewy grass ; you cannot leave us now, . . 823 *Excursion* 5. 71
The dewy fields ; but ere the Vicar's door . . 895 *Excursion* 9. 769

Diadem. My temples with the Muse's diadem. . 259 *Calvert* 8
Fit to be placed in that pure diadem ; . . . 358 *Aquap.* 357
Planting his favourite silver diadem, ... 496 **A little* 6
In consistory, like a diadem . . . . . . 725 *Prelude* 10. 521
Whose hoary diadem of pendent rocks . . . 788 *Excursion* 3. 145
Lay thy diadem apart, ... L.2. 190 **Queen and* 13

Diadems. Fixed on the front of Eastern diadems, . 331 *Ode : Thanks.* 167

Diagrams. To spots remote, and draw his diagrams 677 *Prelude* 6. 151

Dial. On the green turf, a dial to divide . . . 813 *Excursion* 4. 801
Upon its site, a dial, that might stand . . . 845 *Excursion* 6. 497

Dialect. Thence in our rustic dialect was called . 133 *Michael* 168

Dialogue. Unknown to him, this dialogue ensued. . 97 *Brothers* 120

Dialogues. To dialogues of business, love, or strife ; 589 *Immortality* 98
I held mute dialogues with my Mother's heart, . 646 *Prelude* 2. 268
From earnest dialogues I slipped in thought, . 716 *Prelude* 9. 438
And moving dialogues between this pair, . . K.8. 248 *Recluse* 1.1.419

Dial's. Depicted in the dial's moral round ; . . 2 *Ev. Wk.* 28

Diamond. Strewing the turf's green slope. A
    diamond light . . . . 705 *Prelude* 8. 406
Fabric it seemed of diamond and of gold, . . 784 *Excursion* 2. 839
Before the sailor's eye ; or diamond drops . . 843 *Excursion* 6. 316
Are hung with thousand thousand diamond drops K.8. 252 *Recluse* 1.1.563

Diamonds. Diamonds dart their brightest lustre . 549 *Hermit's Cell* 1. 15
Ironic diamonds,—clubs, hearts, diamonds, spades, 640 *Prelude* 1. 527

Dian. The azure brooks, where Dian joys to lave . 264 **Lady ! I* 5
And Dian gazing on the Shepherd's face . . . 461 **Giordano, verily* 4

Diana's. From Wood-nymph of Diana's throng ? . 344 *How blest* 34
And soon approach Diana's Looking-glass ! . . 524 *Epist. Beaumont* 165

Dian's. In crystal clearness Dian's looking-glass ; . 381 *Duddon* 22. 3
Who *then*, if Dian's crescent gleamed, ... 497 *Lycoris* 5

Diffused—*continued.*
Diffused adown that barrier of steep rock, 787 *Excursion* 3. 70
My soul diffused herself in wide embrace 796 *Excursion* 3. 738
Pure and serene, diffused—to overlook 811 *Excursion* 4. 688
Of our Companion, gradually diffused ; 814 *Excursion* 4. 890
Of pious sentiment diffused afar, 838 *Excursion* 6. 28
Day after day the gladness is diffused 867 *Excursion* 7. 651
Of gravity and elegance, diffused 882 *Excursion* 8. 539
I spake of mischief by the wise diffused 887 *Excursion* 9. 195
On the refulgent spectacle, diffused 893 *Excursion* 9. 611
Diffuses. What Power unseen diffuses far 626 †*Cento* 2
Diffusing. Open it out, diffusing thence a smile 695 *Prelude* 7. 560
Diffusing only those affections wider 729 *Prelude* 11. 169
Where reason yet might hesitate, diffusing 735 *Prelude* 12. 47
Diffusing health and sober cheerfulness, K.8. 249 *Recluse* 1.1.465
Dig. To dig for water on the spot, the Captain 68 *Bord.* 1712
Dig for us ; and present us, in the shape 832 *Excursion* 5. 631
That, like this Labourer, such may dig their way, 842 *Excursion* 6. 259
Dight. When all the fields with freshest green were dight, 226 *Vernal Ode* 2
Maids and Matrons, dight 324 *Ode 1814* 59
And soon again was dight 542 *Russ. Fug.* 50
O house of houses, once so richly dight ! 563 *Troilus* 23
Dignified. Amid their smiles and dimples dignified— 221 *Triad* 138
For "precepts over dignified," 492 *Duty*
Had dignified, and called to represent 640 *Prelude* 1. 524
To many, neither dignified enough 694 *Prelude* 7. 459
More dignified, and stronger in himself ; 799 *Excursion* 3. 923
An air and mien of dignified pursuit ; 839 *Excursion* 6. 40
And dignified by battlements and towers 875 *Excursion* 8. 102
That dignified and cheered a low estate ? 877 *Excursion* 8. 238
Dignify. Of thrice ten summers dignify the board. 19 *Desc. Sk.* 499
To dignify arch looks and laughing eyes ; 80 **Loving she* 3
To dignify the spot that gives thee birth 376 *Duddon* 3. 9
To dignify the humblest state.—Your voice 813 *Excursion* 4. 784
Dignities. The dignities of plain occurrence then 704 *Prelude* 8. 381
Dignity. The simple dignity no forms debase ; 18 *Desc. Sk.* 443
True dignity abides with him alone 23 *Yew-tree* 61
Such strength, a dignity so fair : 119 *Sailor's Mother* 10
Softening their inbred dignity austere— 212 *Dion* 11
And no pride blended with their dignity. 227 *Vernal Ode* 128
How they with dignity may stand ; or fall, 305 **The Voice* 5
To dignity—in thee, O SCHWYTZ ! are seen 339 *Schwytz* 2
For dignity not placed beyond her reach, 357 *Aquap.* 344
Is Roman dignity inviolate ; 368 *Trajan* 50
Their dignity installing 385 *Yarrow Rev.* 10
And even the common dignity of man !— 428 *Ecc. Sonn.* 1. 38. 9
Subsist thy dignity to guard, 472 *Ossian* 22
For not alone by men of dignity 552 *Prioress* 3
The native dignity no forms debase, 611 *Desc.Sk.Quarto* 530
A corresponding dignity within. 654 *Prelude* 3. 382
Honour misplaced, and Dignity astray ; 657 *Prelude* 3. 600
Its dignity ; with gifts he bubbles o'er 670 *Prelude* 5. 301
A dignity, a smoothness, like the works 672 *Prelude* 5. 458
To patriarchal dignity of mind, 682 *Prelude* 6. 506
The meanest thrives the most ; where dignity, 714 *Prelude* 9. 347
True personal dignity, abideth not ; 714 *Prelude* 9. 348
And dignity of individual man, 741 *Prelude* 13. 81
Whence spiritual dignity originates, 745 *Prelude* 13. 373
In the plain presence of his dignity ! 757 *Excursion* 1. 76
For moral dignity, and strength of mind, 775 *Excursion* 2. 287
What dignity, what beauty, in this change 790 *Excursion* 3. 314
" The dignity of life is not impaired 806 *Excursion* 4. 352
In dignity of being we ascend. 812 *Excursion* 4. 765
And learning's solid dignity ; though born 824 *Excursion* 5. 112
An earth-despising dignity of soul ? 831 *Excursion* 5. 578
A natural dignity on humblest rank ; 850 *Excursion* 6. 794
Upon his life an outward dignity 864 *Excursion* 7. 447
With dignity befitting his proud hope ; 879 *Excursion* 8. 318
With motions of true dignity and grace ? K.8. 248 *Recluse* 1.1.411
Dilapidated. Of a dilapidated structure, once 726 *Prelude* 10. 558
Dilate. Those Spectres to dilate 499 *Memory* 14
Dilated. Dilated hang the misty pines on high, 14 *Desc. Sk.* 223
The *west*, that burns like one dilated sun, 15 *Desc. Sk.* 282
Glimmer the dim-lit Alps, dilated, round, 606 *Desc.Sk.Quarto* 217
Dilates. Great joy by horror tam'd dilates his heart, 612 *Desc.Sk.Quarto* 560
Dilating. Where Discord stalks dilating, every hour, 617 *Desc.Sk.Quarto* 800
Dilatory. Though often of such dilatory walk 660 *Prelude* 4. 108
Diligence. Minutely linked with diligence uninspired, 357 *Aquap.* 328
Thy diligence, thy unrelaxing use 424 *Ecc. Sonn.* 1. 23. 12
' Now, certès, I will use my diligence 554 *Prioress* 88
The faith which they by diligence had earned, 839 *Excursion* 6. 71
This baneful diligence :—at early morn 840 *Excursion* 6. 168
Diligent. Has scarcely been more diligent than I ; 134 *Michael* 234
What knowledge can perform, is diligent to learn ; 493 *Hap. War.* 9
Such measured rest the diligent and good S.3. 427 **My Son* 10
Diluvian. Who triumphed o'er diluvian power !—and yet 350 *Des. Stanzas* 21
Diluvian truths, and patriarchal lore. 419 *Ecc. Sonn.* 1. 3. 7
Diluvian records ; or the sighs of Earth 498 **Enough of climbing* 34
Dim. Some, dim between the lofty cliffs descried, 5 *Ev. Wk.* 164
Dim from the twilight water's shaggy side, 12 *Desc. Sk.* 116
Where, 'mid dim towers and woods, her waters gleam. 13 *Desc. Sk.* 157
The green light sparkles ;—the dim bowers recede. 14 *Desc. Sk.* 219
Nor taper glimmered dim from sick man's room ; 26 *Guilt* 142
The gloomy lantern, and the dim blue match, 32 *Guilt* 419
With a dim eye, distracted and amazed ; 34 *Guilt* 563
Filled my dim eyes with tears.—When I returned 49 *Bord.* 684
To stretch her arms, and dim the gladsome light 56 *Bord.* 1046

Dim—*continued.*
By a dim lantern's light I saw that wreaths 59 *Bord.* 1202
In dim relation to imagined Beings. 64 *Bord.* 1455
Through words and things, a dim and perilous way ; 69 *Bord.* 1775
Of day grew dim the Housewife hung a lamp ; 133 *Michael* 114
Lamps of faith, now burning dim, 144 **Driven in* 51
Through a strait passage intricate and dim ? 173 *Infant Daughter* 74
Of yon dim cave, in seeming silence makes 184 *Airey-force* 13
Dim sadness—and blind thoughts, I knew not, nor could name. 195 *Resolution* 28
With many recognitions dim and faint, 206 *Tintern* 59
But neither veil thy head in shadows dim, 215 *Enterprise* 10
A Voice shall finish doubt and dim foreseeing, 235 *Power of Sound* 211
The path grows dim, and dimmer still ; 240 *P. B.* 351
Dim shades—for reliques, upon Lethe's shore, 264 **Lady ! I* 7
In some complaining, dim retreat, 288 *Glen-Al.* 13
An animal delight though dim ! 294 *Jedbor.* 62
The Cross shall spread, the Crescent hath waxed dim ; 326 *Sobieski* 12
Till all is dim, save this bright Stone 337 *Thun* 15
All suffering dim eclipse ! 343 *Eclipse* 54
To the dim cavern, whence the river 371 *Eg. Maid* 164
O'er hill and valley to this dim retreat ! 382 *Duddon* 25. 8
To days of dim antiquity ; 398 *White Doe* 225
Enough ! for see, with dim association 431 *Ecc. Sonn.* 2. 11. 1
At the dim centre of a churchyard yew ; 456 **The leaves* 19
Though brain would swim, and eyes grow dim, 478 *Somnamb.* 57
" My eyes are dim with childish tears, 487 *Fountain* 29
Long as the heat shall rage, let that dim cave 498 **Enough of climbing* 32
Sung as the light of day grows dim : 506 *Lab. Hymn* 4
And Truth, whose eye guilt only can make dim ; 514 **Who ponders* 12
Dim memory keeping of its old intent. 523 *Epist. Beaumont* 128
And now, in twilight dim, 526 **The soaring* 34
Nought I perceived within it dull or dim ; 532 **Once I* 8
Of this fair garden, and its alleys dim, 546 **Oft is* 6
Some, dim between th' aereal cliffs descry'd, 594 *Ev. Wk. Quarto* 147
The cots, those dim religious groves embow'r, 604 *Desc.Sk.Quarto* 124
While mid dim towers and woods her waters gleam : 605 *Desc.Sk.Quarto* 179
Dim dreadful faces thro' the gloom appear, 614 *Desc.Sk.Quarto* 650
Dim were my swimming eyes—my pulse beat slow, 619 **She wept* 3
A foretaste, a dim earnest, of the calm 636 *Prelude* 1. 280
Worked with a dim and undetermined sense 638 *Prelude* 1. 392
Or make their dim abode in distant winds. 646 *Prelude* 2. 310
For solace by dim light of monkish lamps ; 673 *Prelude* 5. 498
The floors of those dim cloisters, till that hour, 682 *Prelude* 6. 476
Had bred in me ; but gloomier far, a dim 706 *Prelude* 8. 515
Remembrances and dim admonishments. 719 *Prelude* 10. 77
Our dim ancestral Past in vision clear ; 744 *Prelude* 13. 319
Went sounding on, a dim and perilous way ! 796 *Excursion* 3. 701
Though inconceivably endowed, too dim 804 *Excursion* 4. 181
Of dim futurity, to Man revealed. 812 *Excursion* 4. 706
In modest panegyric. " These dim lines, 825 *Excursion* 5. 205
—The road is dim, the current unperceived, 851 *Excursion* 6. 845
" So fails, so languishes, grows dim, and dies," 872 *Excursion* 7. 976
On the dim altar burned continually, 877 *Excursion* 8. 189
Two eyes—not dim, but of a healthy stare— 880 *Excursion* 8. 409
Dim-discovered. Hung dim-discover'd from the dangerous steep, 610 *Desc.Sk.Quarto* 427
Dimension. And in dimension, such that thou might'st seem 290 *Kilchurn* 12
Dimensions. A temple framing of dimensions vast, 818 *Excursion* 4. 1161
Dim-eyed. Does the dim-eyed curious Bee, 161 **Pleasures newly* 43
Dim-gleaming. Dim-gleaming among weeds and grass, 417 *White Doe* 1896
Dim-gleaming through imperfect lore, 473 *Ossian* 78
Diminished. Of ether, shining with diminished round, 16 *Desc. Sk.* 320
Wheel pale and silent her diminish'd round, 609 *Desc.Sk.Quarto* 383
Old things repeated with diminished grace ; 829 *Excursion* 5. 436
Faint, and diminished to the gazing eye, 885 *Excursion* 9. 60
Rivall'd by you, hides the diminish'd head. L.1. 88 *Juvenal* 1. 6
Diminishing. Diminishing by distance till it seemed 819 *Excursion* 4. 1185
Diminution. And one night's diminution of her power, 192 *Gipsies* 18
From diminution safe and weakening age ; 812 *Excursion* 4. 759
Diminutive. Not *there* diminutive, but through a scale S.3. 435 **The doubt* 108
Dim-lit. Nor wants the dim-lit cave a wreath 506 **While from* 35
Glimmer the dim-lit Alps, dilated, round, 606 *Desc.Sk.Quarto* 217
Dimly. The horse alone, seen dimly as I pass, 1 *Early Youth* 3
That glimmered like a pine-tree dimly viewed 450 *Ecc. Sonn.* 3. 40. 5
Or dimly seen, 490 *Night Thought* 4
And lurking dimly in their shy retreats, 622 *Recluse* 1. 1. 123
Dimly reflected in a lonely pool. 808 *Excursion* 4. 488
On earth we dimly see, and but in part K.8. 275 **These vales* 5
Dimly-gleaming. And dimly-gleaming Nest,—a hollow crown 254 *Wild Duck's Nest* 10
Dimmed. I wept not then,—but tears have dimmed my sight, 713 *Prelude* 9. 269
Dimmer. The path grows dim, and dimmer still ; 240 *P. B.* 351
The moon uneasy looked and dimmer, 241 *P. B.* 483
Of dimmer character, he thence attained 758 *Excursion* 1. 144
Dimmest. Forth from the grotto's dimmest chamber 371 *Eg. Maid* 176
Dimming. Dimming the stars, and fireworks magical, 689 *Prelude* 7. 123
Dimness. With soft illumination cheered the dimness of that place. 92 *Poet's Dream* 12
That dimness of heart-agony ; 401 *White Doe* 438
—From viewless lamps a ghastly dimness falls, 614 *Desc.Sk.Quarto* 648
Dimness o'er this clear luminary crept 795 *Excursion* 3. 670
Dimple. Stripped of his voice and left to dimple down 659 *Prelude* 4. 54

Dimpled. Every face in the village is dimpled with smiles. 572 *Avarice* 40
Dimples. Amid their smiles and dimples dignified— 221 *Triad* 138
Breaks into dimples small and bright; 406 *White Doe* 968
Is smooth as clear, save where with dimples small 527 **Those breathing* 11
Dimpling. And run in transport to the dimpling deeps; 595 *Ev. Wk. Quarto* 198
Into the dimpling cistern of his heart: 670 *Prelude* 5. 327
Dimpling along in silent majesty, 685 *Prelude* 6. 652
Pleased to detect the dimpling stir of life, S.3. 433 **The doubt* 40
Dim-seen. While trees, dim-seen, in frenzied numbers, tear 263 *Storm* 6
But now are silent as the dim-seen flowers: 453 **Calm is the* 9
She clasps them at that dim-seen roofless stone.— 597 *Ev. Wk. Quarto* 290
Dim-twinkling. The stars dim-twinkling through their forms! 300 *Bran* 4
Din. While Echo dallies with its various din! 5 *Ev. Wk.* 161
May drive at the windows,—we'll laugh at his din; 81 †*Address: Child* 41
He stands, backed by the wall;—he abates not his din; 188 *Music* 25
But oft, in lonely rooms, and 'mid the din 206 *Tintern* 25
Convulsed as by a jarring din; 234 *Power of Sound* 102
—Such din shall trouble them no more. 237 *P. B.* 85
An uproar and a drunken din. 246 *P. B.* 870
Thy sense from pressure of life's common din; 349 *At Dover* 10
And folly, if they with united din 365 **The Baptist* 7
Hence, while the imperial City's din 376 **The Minstrels* 73
A moment ends the fervent din, 396 *White Doe* 43
And din of arms and minstrelsy, 400 *White Doe* 416
The time is ripe. With festive din 403 *White Doe* 621
Clear, loud, and lively is the din, 498 **Departing summer* 10
Make him a captive!—for that pent-up din, 569 *Cumb. Beg.* 180
While Echo dallies with the various din! 594 *Ev. Wk. Quarto* 144
Black drizzling craggs, that beaten by the din, 606 *Desc.Sk.Quarto* 249
And not a voice was idle; with the din 638 *Prelude* 1. 439
With din of instruments and shuffling feet, 663 *Prelude* 4. 313
Of jocund din; and, when a lengthened pause 671 *Prelude* 5. 379
Of colours, lights, and forms; the deafening din; 689 *Prelude* 7. 155
For eyes and ears! what anarchy and din, 697 *Prelude* 7. 686
Rocked high above their heads; anon, the din 716 *Prelude* 9. 456
Heard while the dwelling vibrates to the din 813 *Excursion* 4. 792
With hostile din, and combating in sight 839 *Excursion* 6. 64
To multiply and aggravate the din? 863 *Excursion* 7. 366
Dinas. Abashed, Sir Dinas turned away; 373 *Eg. Maid* 271
Dine. This May-time, every day before thou dine, 561 *Cuck.andNight.*242
Dinner. To cull her dinner from it's garden bed, 615 *Desc.Sk.Quarto* 729
Where once the dinner was prepared with pride; 878 *Excursion* 8. 273
Dinners. Hence rustic dinners on the cool green ground, 643 *Prelude* 2. 89
Dinning. The bag-pipe dinning on the midnight moor 32 *Guilt* 410
Dinning from the CHERRY TREE! 176 *Waggoner* 2. 22
Dint. Ah no, by dint of Magnanimity; 329 *Ode: Thanks.* 58
Diocletian's. Lament! for Diocletian's fiery sword 419 *Ecc. Sonn.* 1. 6. 1
Diomed. What steeds the car of Diomed could boast; 625 *Æneid* 136
Diomede. *What horses there of Diomede, had great* L.2. 123 *Frag. Æneid* 3. 3
Dion. Was princely Dion, in the power 212 *Dion* 5
Long-exiled Dion marching at their head, 213 *Dion* 23
Which Dion learned to measure with sublime delight;— 213 *Dion* 52
The soul of Dion, instantly dissolved. 214 *Dion* 119
Did Dion hold with Plato; ripened thus 715 *Prelude* 9. 409
Dion's. On Dion's virtues, while the lunar beam 212 *Dion* 8
Invoking Dion's tutelary care, 213 *Dion* 40
Dip. Scarcely the hand forbears to dip its palm 469 **Why stand* 9
Peace to the sober matron who shall dip S.3. 435 **The doubt* 135
Dipped. Where'er was dipped the toiling oar, 343 *Eclipse* 13
Till dipp'd his pathway in the river shade; 592 *Ev. Wk. Quarto* 70
I dipped my oars into the silent lake, 637 *Prelude* 1. 374
And I, who at that time was scarcely dipped 714 *Prelude* 9. 331
That ever hermit dipped his maple dish 833 *Excursion* 5. 687
Was cleared, I dipped, with arms accordant, oars 891 *Excursion* 9. 489
And dipped my hand in dancing wave S.3. 438 **My Lord* 15
Dipping. With the next dipping of its slackened oar; 453 **Calm is the* 29
Dire. And death's dire aspect daily he surveyed, 25 *Guilt* 56
Even so the dire phantasma which had crossed 26 *Guilt* 94
She knew not what dire pangs in him such tale could wake. 27 *Guilt* 189
The mine's dire earthquake, and the pallid host 30 *Guilt* 348
A dire suspicion drove us from our shed; 35 *Guilt* 601
How you would be disturbed by this dire news, 59 *Bord.* 1208
Dire poverty assailed; 103 *Artegal* 87
Steeped in dire grief the voice of Philomel; 153 *Morn. Ex.* 20
As if some dire constraint of pain, or rage 196 *Resolution* 68
Small cause of dire effect! for, surely, 246 *P. B.* 841
How toilsome—nay, how dire—it was, by thee 312 *Clarkson* 2
Curses are *his* dire portion, scorn, and hate, 317 **Look now* 10
For whose dire ends tears flow, and blood is spilt, 321 **Here pause* 11
No courage can repel the dire assault; 322 **Humanity,delighting* 33
And the dire flapping of his hoary wing! 322 **Ye Storms* 8
And discipline was passion's dire excess. 330 *Ode: Thanks.* 122
In semblance fresh, as if, with dire affray, 379 *Duddon* 15. 5
And chaser bursting here with one dire smart. 393 *Hart's-horn* 8
The end of that dire Tragedy, 409 *White Doe* 1208
Dire overthrow, and yet how high 416 *White Doe* 1846
Her new-born Babe; dire ending of bright hope! 476 *Howard* 2
Broke threateningly, in sparkles dire 499 **Departing summer* 41
Whence these opprobrious leaves of dire portent? 515 **Men of* 2

Dire—*continued.*
Who reach this dire extremity! 534 **Blest is* 80
In its sweet opening? and what dire mishap 575 *Chiabrera* 7. 6
Dire clap of hands, distracted chase of feet, 614 *Desc.Sk.Quarto* 657.
What dire intrigues disturbed *Cythera's* joy! 620 *Birth of Love* 2
Of dire enchantments faced and overcome 634 *Prelude* 1. 175
Of an event so dire, by signs in earth 668 *Prelude* 5. 158
'Tis true, had gone before this hour, dire work 718 *Prelude* 10. 42
And having thus discerned how dire a thing 741 *Prelude* 13. 76
Strange and uncouth; dire faces, figures dire, 759 *Excursion* 1. 182
Of dire rapacity. There, Man abides, 799 *Excursion* 3. 918
Their own dire agents, and constrain the good 805 *Excursion* 4. 300
Against the dire assaults of papacy 844 *Excursion* 6. 433
Whence dire dependence. What could she perform 849 *Excursion* 6. 717
Of sweetness where dire anguish had been known, 854 *Excursion* 6. 1083
Itself had been unlooked-for; oh! dire stroke 867 *Excursion* 7. 675
Into the chilling flood. Convulsions dire 870 *Excursion* 7. 870
This dire perverseness, cannot choose but ask, 894 *Excursion* 9. 660
Direct. Which heavenward they direct.—Then droop not thou, 261 **From the dark* 10
Would now direct thy notice. Yet in spite 662 *Prelude* 4. 276
We held our way, direct through hamlets, towns, 680 *Prelude* 6. 350
In part by fear to shape a way direct, 709 *Prelude* 9. 3
Communion more direct and intimate 727 *Prelude* 11. 29
Do thou direct it! To the virtuous grant 842 *Excursion* 6. 256
No doubt if you in terms direct had asked K.8. 230 **I will* 178
Directed. *See* **Heaven-directed.**
Now as his choice directed, now as mine; 772 *Excursion* 2. 82
Such converse, if directed by a meek, 806 *Excursion* 4. 344
Again directed to his downcast Friend, 806 *Excursion* 4. 374
Had been directed; and we saw him now 871 *Excursion* 7. 912
Directing. And tendency benign, directing those 673 *Prelude* 5. 494
Directing notice, merely from a wish 893 *Excursion* 9. 586
Directions. But only give some plain directions 142 †*Lov. and Lik.* 3
In opposite directions urged their way 276 *Oker Hill* 7
Questions, directions, warnings and advice, 649 *Prelude* 3. 23
Directly. Directly, but to tender thoughts by means 686 *Prelude* 6. 749
Directress. How much the mild Directress of the plough 876 *Excursion* 8. 131
Directs. Directs his winding dog the cliffs to scale,— 5 *Ev. Wk.* 183
Direful. And direful throes; as if the All-ruling Mind, 514 **Who ponders* 5
Direst. 'Mid direst shocks of mortal accident— 326 **Intrepid sons* 11
Direst of savage beasts, would roam in fear, 585 *Ch. Lamb* 70
Dirge. A dirge devoutly breathed o'er sorrows past; 314 **I dropped* 10
Of exultation hung a dirge 324 *Ode 1814* 83
The funeral dirge;—she sees the knot 413 *White Doe* 1544
The Dirge which for our Master's sake 577 **I come* 27
O for a dirge! But why complain? 582 **O for a* 1
The cadence, as of psalms—a funeral dirge! 777 *Excursion* 2. 376
Some steps when they had thus advanced, the dirge 777 *Excursion* 2. 393
Dirge-like. Stern Winter loves a dirge-like sound. 235 *Power of Sound* 192
Dirges. Hence, prayers are shaped amiss, and dirges sung 423 *Ecc. Sonn.* 1. 20. 8
Disappear. Till, like thyself, I disappear 167 *Pilgrim's Dream* 47
They will not, cannot disappear; 214 *Dion* 99
Clouds at her bidding disappear; 223 *Wishing-gate* 4
That, while ten thousand pleasures disappear, 251 **There is a little* 11
And monuments that soon must disappear: 334 **A winged* 9
The glory of Infant Rome must disappear, 359 **Those old* 5
That shape themselves and disappear 406 *White Doe* 970
Shall disappear, and grateful earth receive 450 *Ecc. Sonn.* 3. 39. 3
Through which the waters creep, then disappear, 465 **The cattle* 4
Shall disappear from both the sister Isles, 474 **On to* 11
Their glory disappear. 581 **Loud is* 16
"Who next will drop and disappear?" 586 *Hogg* 28
Dawns from the east, but dawns to disappear 634 *Prelude* 1. 125
To disappear by a slow gradual death, 635 *Prelude* 1. 194
To rush and disappear. But soon broke forth 687 *Prelude* 7. 8
'Twill be such joy to see them disappear. 729 *Prelude* 11. 152
And what would disappear; prepared to find 741 *Prelude* 13. 65
Of time and conscious nature disappear, 788 *Excursion* 3. 111
They came and go, appeared and disappear, 813 *Excursion* 4. 838
Thy image disappear! The Mountain-ash 868 *Excursion* 7. 714
Disappeared. Has disappeared, and every trace is fled 6 *Ev. Wk.* 209
Was rent with lightning—one hath disappeared; 97 *Brothers* 144
Watching below till he had disappeared 125 *V. and J.* 252
And prematurely disappeared, 154 *Flower Garden* 14
How disappeared He?—ask the newt and toad, 299 *Brownie's Cell* 71
"How disappeared he?" Ask the newt and toad; 391 *Brownie* 1
And scarcely have they disappeared 396 *White Doe* 35
As his own charge, had disappeared, 412 *White Doe* 1452
Had this effulgence disappeared 457 **Had this* 1
Will say, Ye disappeared with England's Glory! 477 **Lowther! in* 14
Had disappeared, or shed a fainter light 747 *Prelude* 14. 52
That he had disappeared—not two months gone. 766 *Excursion* 1. 661
And disappeared. I journeyed back this way, 767 *Excursion* 1. 706
Of that off-sloping outlet, disappeared, 777 *Excursion* 2. 407
Have scarcely disappeared." "This blooming Child," 779 *Excursion* 2. 536
Suddenly then they disappeared · not twice 861 *Excursion* 7. 247
Disappearing. Lingers behind his disappearing wain. 3 *Ev. Wk.* 71
Whole hamlets disappearing as he moves, 617 *Desc.Sk.Quarto* 789
Of childhood, when a disappearing line, 742 *Prelude* 13. 146
Was disappearing by a swift decay, 845 *Excursion* 6. 495
Or disappearing; triumph that proclaims 876 *Excursion* 8. 130
Disappears. Silently disappears, or quickly fades: 349 *Sky-prosp.* 11
That falls and disappears, the house is gone; 872 *Excursion* 7. 958
At once their tender brightness disappears, S.3. 434 **The doubt* 58
Disappoint. You will not disappoint them; and hereafter—— 48 *Bord.* 624

Discourse—*continued.*
Discourse was deemed Man's noblest attribute, . 489 *Illus. Books* 1
But feeling it no longer. Our discourse . . . 665 *Prelude* 4. 445
Whence, and from deeper causes, all discourse . 711 *Prelude* 9. 118
Than human understanding, their discourse . . 713 *Prelude* 9. 260
With him did I discourse about the end . . 714 *Prelude* 9. 322
Fashioned his life ; and many a long discourse, . 715 *Prelude* 9. 421
Still deeper welcome found his pure discourse : . 757 *Excursion* 1. 73
A while on trivial things we held discourse, . 765 *Excursion* 1. 611
Accompanied those strains of apt discourse, . 772 *Excursion* 2. 38
A task it was, I own, to hold discourse . . 783 *Excursion* 2. 758
So, in the imperfect sounds of this discourse, . 795 *Excursion* 3. 604
Impulse and motive to that strong discourse, . 805 *Excursion* 4. 255
"Yes," said the Sage, resuming the discourse . 806 *Excursion* 4. 373
Kindle before us.—Your discourse this day, . 818 *Excursion* 4. 1122
While in this serious mood we held discourse, . 829 *Excursion* 5. 440
A welcome interruption to discourse . . . 829 *Excursion* 5. 464
But, in the quicker turns of the discourse, . 834 *Excursion* 5. 784
Could I discourse ; but as their stay was brief, . 844 *Excursion* 6. 402
In power of mind, and eloquent discourse. . 848 *Excursion* 6. 677
If mild discourse, and manners that conferred . 850 *Excursion* 6. 793
From which the gallant teacher would discourse, . 869 *Excursion* 7. 786
Discourse both wise and pleasant, shrewd remarks K.8. 227 **I will* 90
Old Michael's manners and discourse, and thus . K.8. 228 **I will* 109
Discoursed. Discoursed of natural or moral truth . 865 *Excursion* 7. 512
Discoursed with him . . . . K.8. 230 **I will* 183
Creations often), then when he discoursed . . K.8. 230 **I will* 195
Discoursing. This, in the lonely dell discoursing, you 831 *Excursion* 5. 582
Discoursing on remote imaginations, strong . K.8. 227 **I will* 100
Discover. No screen, no fence could I discover ; . 199 *Thorn* 178
Let the last faint sigh discover . . . . . 550 *Hermit's Cell* 1. 35
Ye would discover, then, a studious work . . 855 *Excursion* 6. 1147
Discovered. *See* **Chance-discovered, Dim-discovered, New-discovered.**
Thou art discovered in a roofless tower, . . . 456 **The leaves* 16
May be discovered what in soul ye are. . . . 477 *Steamboats* 8
A form discover'd at the well-known seat, . . 592 *Ev. Wk. Quarto* 45
Most happy, if, from aught discovered there . 770 *Excursion* 1. 898
The hidden nook discovered to our view . . 787 *Excursion* 3. 51
Discovered or invented ; or set forth, . . . 823 *Excursion* 5. 41
Discovered in their own despite to sense . . 868 *Excursion* 7. 732
Discoverer. Let the bold Discoverer thrid . . 161 **Pleasures newly* 51
The appalled Discoverer with a sigh . . . 491 *Fidelity* 40
Discoverers. "Now, shall our great Discoverers," he exclaimed, 815 *Excursion* 4. 941
Discoveries. Is going from under me ; these strange discoveries— 47 *Bord.* 548
And proud discoveries of the intellect, . . . 255 *S. H.* 13
With such discoveries as his eye can make . 662 *Prelude* 4. 259
His own discoveries ; or to favourite points . 893 *Excursion* 9. 585
Discovering. Discovering traces of the fugitives, . 122 *V. and J.* 77
Discovers. Veins it discovers exquisite and rare, . 250 **Happy the* 7
Discovery. Their liquid world, for bold discovery, . 434 *Ecc. Sonn.* 2. 23. 7
A world, his rich discovery ! But our Swain, . 841 *Excursion* 6. 235
Discreditable. Ye too—whom no discreditable fear . 310 *Invasion* 10
From painful and discreditable shocks . . . 828 *Excursion* 5. 362
Discreet. "No : Let the most discreet of all my train 620 *Birth of Love* 12
Discreetly. Discreetly parted to preserve the peace, 845 *Excursion* 6. 479
Discretion. Have seen her,—her discretion have observed, 691 *Prelude* 7. 310
Discriminate. Manners and characters discriminate, 706 *Prelude* 8. 499
Discriminating. But a discriminating sympathy . 818 *Excursion* 4. 1105
Discrowned. The saintly Youth has ceased to rule, discrowned 436 *Ecc. Sonn.* 2. 33. 1
Discursive. Whether discursive or intuitive ; . . 747 *Prelude* 14. 120
Discuss. Point after point did she discuss ; . . 130 *Idiot Boy* 419
Loch Lomond's beauties to discuss, ... S.3. 438 **My Lord* 12
Discussion. Which checked discussion ere it warmed to strife ; 583 **With copious* 14
Discussions. Of past discussions with this zealous friend 781 *Excursion* 2. 627
Disdain. With Independence, child of high Disdain. 15 *Desc. Sk.* 261
Oh ! give not me that eye of hard disdain . 20 *Desc. Sk.* 545
Into anger or disdain ; . . . . 94 *Westmoreland Girl* 54
He mocked and treated with disdain . . . . 159 *Green Linnet* 38
To some whose minds without disdain . . . . 169 *Wren's Nest* 46
But if such homage thou disdain . . . . 217 *Enterprise* 133
Ere shaken by that mood of stern disdain . . 227 *Vernal Ode* 123
Might scan the narrow province with disdain . 231 **The gentlest Poet* 3
'Tis He whose yester-evening's high disdain . 279 **'Tis he* 1
To share the passion of a just disdain. . . . 283 **Proud were* 14
(Too quick and keen) incited to disdain . . . 328 *Ode 1815* 118
Studious that *He* might not disdain the seat . . 335 *Cologne* 4
It ill befits us to disdain . . . . . . 337 *Cath. Cantons* 3
The Spirit of humanity, disdain . . . . . 394 **No more* 18
Of ease, the narrow Bosphorus will disdain ; . . 427 *Ecc. Sonn.* 1. 34. 6
With hands stretched forth in mollified disdain, . 435 *Ecc. Sonn.* 2. 28. 5
And straightway cease to aspire, than God disdain 465 **Pastor and* 13
—There, did the iron Genius not disdain . . 607 *Desc.Sk.Quarto* 307
Endeared by Custom ; and with high disdain, . . 695 *Prelude* 7. 528
And heard their notions ; nor did they disdain . 712 *Prelude* 9. 196
From the unqualified disdain, that once . . . 792 *Excursion* 3. 410
And, from the impulse of a just disdain, . . . 798 *Excursion* 3. 829
Disdained. He, all superior but his God disdained, . 18 *Desc. Sk.* 435
These humble props disdained not ! O green dales ! 255 *Easter* 10
And nature God disdained not ; Man—whose soul 429 *Ecc. Sonn.* 2. 4. 11
Or, shall I say ?—disdained, the game that lurks 788 *Excursion* 3. 123
Disdainful. The Vicar answered,—"No disdainful pride . . . . 858 *Excursion* 7. 38
Disdainfully. At their false ways disdainfully,—and oft . . . . 860 *Excursion* 7. 221

Disdaining. Can oft with justice claim. And not disdaining . . . . 357 *Aquap.* 288
Of time and change disdaining, takes its course . 804 *Excursion* 4. 184
Disdains. Those raptures duly—Erebus disdains : . 210 *Laod.* 71
Find solace which a busy world disdains. . . . 444 *Ecc. Sonn.* 3. 17. 14
That Fortitude, whose blood disdains to freeze . 466 *St. Bees* 16
Of Beauty, that disdains to climb . . . . . 544 *Russ. Fug.* 195
Disease. Disease and famine, agony and fear, . . 29 *Guilt* 299
A pale-faced Woman, in disease far gone. . . . 34 *Guilt* 545
Like the stifling of disease ; . . . . . . 173 *Waggoner* 1. 19
That love which changed—for wan disease, . . 225 *Primrose* 37
And love of havoc, (for with such disease . . . 292 **Degenerate Douglas* 3
Who from disease and suffering . . . . . . 294 *Jedbor.* 78
Disease consumed thy vitals ; War upheaved . . 316 **Hail, Zaragoza* 10
Brought to this genial climate, when disease . . 353 *Aquap.* 58
Could pierce through a temper that's soft to disease, 482 *Character* 7
Lived I—then yielded to a slow disease. . . . 574 *Chiabrera* 4. 31
In the comfortless vault of disease. . . . . . 621 *Convict* 32
If, when the woodman languished with disease . 705 *Prelude* 8. 438
Lives only by variety of disease. . . . . . 721 *Prelude* 10. 208
This was the crisis of that strong disease, . . 731 *Prelude* 11. 306
Smitten with perilous fever. In disease . . . 764 *Excursion* 1. 552
Perpetual sabbath ; come, disease and want ; . 802 *Excursion* 4. 58
Spread, from disease, whose subtle injury lurks . 830 *Excursion* 5. 513
And doth commend their weakness and disease . 841 *Excursion* 6. 182
For 'tis Heaven's will—that, after a disease . 853 *Excursion* 6. 966
A slow disease insensibly consumed . . . . 864 *Excursion* 7. 464
In spite of vice, and misery, and disease, . . 870 *Excursion* 7. 854
When Calais heard (while Famine and Disease . L.1. 95 *Juvenal* 3. 1
Diseases. For come Diseases on, and Penury's rage, 613 *Desc.Sk.Quarto* 638
Disembodied. Descending, disembodied, and diffused 787 *Excursion* 3. 40
Disenchant. Was it to disenchant, and to undo, . 335 *Aix* 1
Nor could I have been bribed to disenchant . . 705 *Prelude* 8. 419
Disenchanted. When disenchanted from the mood 300 *Bran* 29
Disencumbered. Next, disencumbered of his harp, . 373 *Eg. Maid* 289
And leaves the disencumbered spirit free . . . 456 **Soft as* 18
Ere disencumbered of her mortal chains, . . . 804 *Excursion* 4. 233
Who sits, is disencumbered from the press . . 885 *Excursion* 9. 70
Disencumbering. Of disencumbering thus her fretful wings. . . . . 798 *Excursion* 3. 820
Disentangled. That, disentangled from the shady boughs . . . . 891 *Excursion* 9. 492
Disentangling. Of Prudence, disentangling good and ill . . . . 514 **Blest Statesman* 5
Disesteem. He, who by wilful disesteem of life . 816 *Excursion* 4. 1029
Disgorged. Disgorged are now the ministers of day ; 877 *Excursion* 8. 174
Disgrace. On joys that might disgrace the captive's cell, ... 13 *Desc. Sk.* 138
Clouds of disgrace and envious fortune past ! . . 105 *Artegal* 195
That mimicry should thus disgrace . . . . . 163 *Needlecase* 3
—Let Empires fall ; but ne'er shall Ye disgrace . 350 *Des. Stanzas* 48
That brings to the inward creature no disgrace ? . 527 **Those breathing* 24
And your officious doings bring disgrace . . . 655 *Prelude* 3. 415
To bring disgrace upon their very names ; . . 731 *Prelude* 11. 262
Disgrace, of which, custom and written law, . . 731 *Prelude* 11. 263
Some in disgrace, hung dangling from the walls. . 781 *Excursion* 2. 670
So would I plead for York ; but long disgrace . L.1. 96 *Juvenal* 3. 59
These gashes whence ? This undeserved disgrace ! L.2. 318 *Frag. Æneid* 4. 8
Disgraced. Disgraced by aught that seems content to sit . . . . 439 *Ecc. Sonn.* 2. 41. 7
Rather than be disgraced, would chuse to die. . 559 *Cuck.andNight.*160
Disguise. The black disguise, the warning whistle shrill, ... 32 *Guilt* 420
How say you ? in disguise ?— But what's your business . . . . 46 *Bord.* 492
Tricked out in proud disguise of cast-off weeds . 185 *Nutting* 9
The mutual nod,—the grave disguise . . . . 375 **The Minstrels* 43
And, in disguise, a Milkmaid with her pail . . 521 *Epist. Beaumont* 42
Speech, manners, morals, all without disguise. . 775 *Excursion* 2. 266
Soft, as may seem, but, under that disguise, . . 817 *Excursion* 4. 1053
So, through a simple rustic garb's disguise, . . 868 *Excursion* 7. 735
That inward motion to disguise, he said . . . 874 *Excursion* 8. 32
Disguised. Howe'er disguised in its own majesty, . 23 *Yew-tree* 51
Though at a distance and he was disguised, . . 42 *Bord.* 277
Or fear disguised in simulated scorn. . . . . 70 *Bord.* 1831
Though much disguised by long adversity ! . . 104 *Artegal* 117
There Venus sits disguisèd like a Nun,— . . . 433 *Ecc. Sonn.* 2. 20. 3
To selfishness, disguised in gentle names . . 648 *Prelude* 2. 437
Of luckless rock or prominent stone, disguised . 788 *Excursion* 3. 179
Disgust. To heap disgust upon the worthier Cause : 439 *Ecc. Sonn.* 2. 41. 12
He, in disgust, turned from the neighbouring sea . 470 **Did pangs* 9
Hopes rashly, in disgust as rash recoils ; . . . 830 *Excursion* 5. 509
Haunted him with sensations of disgust . . . 845 *Excursion* 6. 453
I shrink not from the evil with disgust, . . . K.8. 246 *Recluse* 1.1.351
A City where, if indifference to disgust . . K.8. 253 *Recluse* 1.1.604
Disgusted. Disgusted therefore, or appalled, by aims 797 *Excursion* 3. 773
Dish. A maple dish, my furniture should be ; . . 424 *Ecc. Sonn.* 1. 22. 10
Upon a lordly dish ; frank hospitality . . . . 525 *Epist. Beaumont* 247
And hearth was there, and maple dish, . . . 543 *Russ. Fug.* 145
That ever hermit dipped his maple dish . . . 833 *Excursion* 5. 687
Disheartening. In them disheartening doubts and dread ; . . . . 178 *Waggoner* 3. 6
Against disheartening custom, that by Thee . . 445 *Ecc. Sonn.* 3. 21. 6
Dishevelled. Dishevelled, gleaming eyes, and rueful cheek . . . . 710 *Prelude* 9. 79
Dishonour. *See* **State-dishonour.**
Worse is he far, far worse (if foul dishonour . . 53 *Bord.* 896
I die without dishonour. Famished, starved, . 78 *Bord.* 2317

Display—*continued.*
" Thus strives a grateful Country to display . . 324 *Ode 1814* 67
May this bright flower of Charity display . . . 393 *Countess' Pillar* 2
The " trumpery " that acesnds in bare display— 435 *Ecc. Sonn.* 2. 28. 6
" I come to open out, for fresh display, . . . 456 **Soft as* 25
As despot courts their blaze of gems display, . . 615 *Desc.Sk.Quarto* 721
I have endeavoured to display the means . . . 646 *Prelude* 2. 269
Occasion given him to display his skill, . . . 882 *Excursion* 8. 532

Displayed. On as we journey, in clear view displayed, 14 *Desc. Sk.* 216
The image of his glorious Sire displayed, . . . 18 *Desc. Sk.* 440
Moved not ; meanwhile the galaxy displayed . . 123 *V. and J.* 97
I saw, in wondrous perspective displayed, . . 323 *Ode 1814* 5
Been felt, that influence is displayed. . . . . 338 *Brientz* 10
The sky an azure field displayed ; . . . . . 343 *Eclipse* 21
Displayed her richest blossoms among files . . 361 **List—'twas* 17
Triumphs in sun-bright gratitude displayed, . . 367 *Trajan* 17
Be with them openly displayed. . . . . . 405 *White Doe* 802
The testimony there displayed ; . . . . . 410 *White Doe* 1297
In all her quarters temptingly displayed ! . . . 434 *Ecc. Sonn.* 2. 23. 8
In Nature's prodigality displayed . . . . . 508 *F. Stone* 4
Right gladly answering signals we displayed, . . 524 *Epist. Beaumont* 213
Of red Morocco folio saw displayed, ... 547 **Rude is* 8
Enlivening Hope display'd her cheerful ray, . . 618 *School Ex.* 35
Fair to the view is sacred Truth display'd, . . 619 *School Ex.* 71
To see displayed among an eager few, ... 656 *Prelude* 3. 498
Rough, bold, as Grecian comedy displayed . . 691 *Prelude* 7. 289
Triumphantly displayed in records left . . . 759 *Excursion* 1. 174
Such grateful promises his youth displayed : . . 774 *Excursion* 2. 170
Of private life licentiously displayed . . . . 775 *Excursion* 2. 268
And marble monuments were here displayed . . 825 *Excursion* 5. 166
The mansion's self displayed ;—a reverend pile . 881 *Excursion* 8. 461
That which the heavens displayed, the liquid deep 893 *Excursion* 9. 607

Displays. The deepest cleft the mountain's front displays . . . . 8 *Ev. Wk.* 357
Pleased while the sylvan world displays . . . 497 *Lycoris* 33
The ever-varying charm your round displays, . 591 *Ev. Wk. Quarto* 18
The deepest dell the mountain's breast displays, . 599 *Ev. Wk. Quarto* 425
To reverence the volume that displays . . . . 759 *Excursion* 1. 224

Displeased. Displeased that I from lays of love 168 *Turtledove* 11
Than when we soar."—The Other, not displeased, 789 *Excursion* 3. 232

Displeasure. Divine displeasure, broke the marriage-vow. . . . . 855 *Excursion* 6. 1093

Disport. In love's disport employ ; . . . . . 506 **While from* 26

Disporting. By glimpses caught—disporting at their ease, ... 527 **Those breathing* 44
Disporting round your knees ? . . . . . . 542 *Russ. Fug.* 60
Disporting. Nor unmindful was the Boy . . . K.8. 237 *Recluse* 1.1. 31

Dispose. Dispose to judgments temperate as we lay 449 *Ecc. Sonn.* 3. 35. 4
Ah ! let not aught amiss within dispose . . . 816 *Excursion* 4. 1018

Disposed. Disposed some cultured Flowerets (drawn from spots . . . . 280 *Valedict.* 2
Can do for minds disposed to feel its power ! . . 456 **Soft as* 13
Doth find herself insensibly disposed . . . . 567 *Cumb. Beg.* 104
Aptly disposed, had lent its help to raise . . . 778 *Excursion* 2. 435
In avenues disposed ; there, towers begirt . . 784 *Excursion* 2. 843
Instinctively disposed him to retire . . . . 823 *Excursion* 5. 74
By his own hand disposed with nicest care, . . 841 *Excursion* 6. 206
Dejected, and habitually disposed . . . . . 896 *Excursion* 9. 787

Disposer. But Thou, supreme Disposer ! may'st not speed . . . . 312 **Who rises* 61

Disposes. Disposes her, when over-fondly set . . 740 *Prelude* 13. 33

Disposing. *See* **All-disposing.**

Disposition. And constant disposition of his thoughts 761 *Excursion* 1. 363

Dispositions. Such dispositions then were mine unearned . . . . 677 *Prelude* 6. 168

Dispossessed. All, all were dispossessed, save him whose smile . . . . 298 *Brownie's Cell* 41

Dispraise. *See* **Self-dispraise.**
That, fondly seeking in dispraise of man . . . 871 *Excursion* 7. 908

Disproportion. No disproportion in her soul, no strife : . . . . 256 *Marriage : Friend* 10

Disproportioned. Yet, oh ! how disproportioned to the hopes . . . . 873 *Excursion* 7. 1006

Disproves. This one Associate that disproves . . 415 *White Doe* 1789

Disputation. Of disputation, shrunk not, though assailed . . . . 839 *Excursion* 6. 63

Dispute. There, too, ere wiles and politic dispute . 313 **Go back* 9
No sacrifice avert, no power dispute ; . . . . 433 *Ecc. Sonn.* 2. 21. 2
And, sometimes—where the poor man held dispute 772 *Excursion* 2. 65
The field of selfish difference and dispute, . . . 845 *Excursion* 6. 485

Disputed. Who live in these disputed tracts, that own 48 *Bord.* 596

Disputes. Disputes would then relax, like stormy winds . . . . 500 *Humanity* 51
For our disputes, plain pictures. Say what man 832 *Excursion* 5. 638

Disquiet. Unmatchable on earth is their disquiet ! 123 *V. and J.* 147
The most disquiet have and least do thrive ; . . 559 *Cuck.andNight.* 142
Disquiet, danger, and obscurity. . . . . . 707 *Prelude* 8. 517
And, feeding on disquiet, thus disturb . . . 765 *Excursion* 1. 603

Disquieted. Toss it from hand to hand, disquieted ; 7 *Ev. Wk.* 266
And range about, disquieted in change, . . . 172 *Infant Daughter* 54
And all is now disquieted— . . . . 399 *White Doe* 306
And is again disquieted ; . . . . 413 *White Doe* 1536

Disquietude. A habit which disquietude and grief . 101 *Brothers* 394
And thou from all disquietude be free. . . . . 104 *Artegal* 149
Stranger, if such disquietude be thine, ... 551 **Behold an* 7
Affectionate without disquietude, ... 661 *Prelude* 4. 223
'Twas going far to seek disquietude ; . . . . 666 *Prelude* 5. 53
No morbid passions, no disquietude, ... 819 *Excursion* 4. 1211

Disregard. Disregard Thy Suppliants now ! . . 336 **Jesu ! bless* 12
And an habitual disregard of self . . . . . 539 **Lady ! a* 65

Disregard—*continued.*
From disregard of time's destructive power, . . 847 *Excursion* 6. 621

Disregarding. The barriers disregarding that surround 807 *Excursion* 4. 390

Disrepute. Now prose and verse sunk into disrepute 489 *Illus. Books* 6

Disrespect. To poverty, and grief, and disrespect, . 441 *Ecc. Sonn.* 3. 6. 4
In luxury of disrespect . . . . 497 *Lycoris* 24

Dissatisfaction. *See* **Self-dissatisfaction.**

Dissatisfied. Still more and more dissatisfied . . 179 *Waggoner* 3. 103
That doth not slackly go away, as if dissatisfied. . 189 *Star-gazers* 32

Dissect. And dreams that he is happy. We dissect 58 *Bord.* 1166
We murder to dissect. . . . . 481 *Tables Turned* 28

Dissemble. Dissemble ; be that boy in form and face ! 624 *Æneid* 37

Dissension. Dissension, checking arms that would restrain . . . . 425 *Ecc. Sonn.* 1. 29. 2

Dissevered. Wholly dissevered from our present theme ; . . . . 440 *Ecc. Sonn.* 3. 2. 3
And, if dissevered thence, its course is short. . . 442 *Ecc. Sonn.* 3. 10. 14
Dissevered both from all the mysteries . . . 527 **Those breathing* 19
Dissevered, float upon the Lake, ... 531 †*Float. Isl.* 10
For my excuse. Dissevered from mankind, . . 782 *Excursion* 2. 732

Dissipate. Shall dissipate the seas and mountains hoary. . . . . 445 *Ecc. Sonn.* 3. 19. 14

Dissipates. Moves through the vault of heaven, and dissipates the night ; . . . . . . 618 *School Ex.* 40

Dissociation. And blank dissociation from a world S.3. 435 **The doubt* 116

Dissoluble. Might sometimes covet dissoluble chains ; 284 *Departure* 2

Dissolute. Of dissolute tongues, and jealousy, and hate, ... 23 *Yew-tree* 18
He in the dissolute city gave himself . . . . 138 *Michael* 444
Of chance spectators, chiefly dissolute men . . 692 *Prelude* 7. 360
With gaiety and dissolute idleness. . . . . . 710 *Prelude* 9. 66
The Nature of the dissolute ; but thee, . . . 797 *Excursion* 3. 808
To a poor dissolute Son, her only child. . . . 849 *Excursion* 6. 715

Dissolution. To fatal dissolution ; and, I ween, . 102 *Artegal* 7
Thy dissolution brings, that in my soul . . . 118 *Maternal Grief* 3
Of dissolution, melted into air. . . . . . 440 *Ecc. Sonn.* 3. 1. 14
From low to high doth dissolution climb, . . . 449 *Ecc. Sonn.* 3. 34. 1
And dissolution and decay, the warm . . . . 510 **Among a* 6

Dissolve. Dissolve before a twinkling atom !—Oswald, ... 59 *Bord.* 1220
And vanish, though the heavens dissolve, her stay 235 *Power of Sound* 223
Dissolve that beauty, destined to endure, . . . 263 **How clear* 11
Dissolve—and leave to him who gazed a sigh. . 278 **The most* 8
—But, as soft gales dissolve the dreary snow, . 395 *White Doe: Ded.* 27
She sheds her beam, and, lo ! the shades dissolve ; 618 *School Ex.* 48
Shall e'er dissolve the crust wherein his soul . . 880 *Excursion* 8. 418

Dissolved. And every mortal pang dissolved away. . 35 *Guilt* 625
Dissolved the Barons' League, and sent abroad . 56 *Bord.* 1023
" But is that gloom dissolved ? how passing clear 105 *Artegal* 202
Of some unguarded moment that dissolved . . 122 *V. and J.* 55
The snows dissolved, and genial Spring returned . 150 **When, to* 43
The soul of Dion, instantly dissolved. . . . . 214 *Dion* 119
Like vapour, like a towering cloud, dissolved. 352 *Aquap.* 8
Upon frail ties dissolving or dissolved . . . . 510 **Among a* 31
Dissolved, have left him an unshrouded head. . 699 *Prelude* 8. 17
When into air had partially dissolved . . . . 747 *Prelude* 14. 63

Dissolves. And long privation, now dissolves amain, 441 *Ecc. Sonn.* 3. 3. 7
The wizard instantaneously dissolves . . . . 735 *Prelude* 12. 82
Melts, and dissolves, and is no longer seen. . . 803 *Excursion* 4. 145
And, as the heavy cloud of sleep dissolves, . . 826 *Excursion* 5. 266
To speak of him, and instant y dissolves." . . 863 *Excursion* 7. 360

Dissolving. *See* **Snow-dissolving.**
Upon frail ties dissolving or dissolved . . . . 510 **Among a* 31
Mist into air dissolving ! Then a wish, . . . 635 *Prelude* 1. 227

Distained. Shed when the clouds had gathered and distained . . . . 850 *Excursion* 6. 800

Distance. Yet hears her song, " by distance made more sweet," . . . . 6 *Ev. Wk.* 237
Though at a distance and he was disguised, . . 42 *Bord.* 277
Of time and distance, night and day ; . . . . 81 †*Mother's Return* 19
At a short distance from my cottage, stands . . 150 **When, to* 8
That to a dreary distance go— . . . . . . 175 *Waggoner* 1. 202
Its own light to a distance thrown, ... 190 *Beggars* 9
O, nursed at happy distance from the cares . . 227 *Vernal Ode* 75
Frozen by distance ; so, majestic Pile, ... 290 *Kilchurn* 38
At happy distance from earth's groaning field, . 313 **Clouds, lingering* 7
At seemly distance—to advance like Thee ; . . 384 *Duddon* 33. 12
Poured forth, while summer suns at distance shine, 434 *Ecc. Sonn.* 2. 22. 13
And seeming, at a little distance, slow, . . . 439 *Ecc. Sonn.* 2. 43. 6
Are those that are by distance made more sweet ; 488 *Pers. Talk* 26
And now at distance can discern . . . . . 491 *Fidelity* 5
Shame that our laws at distance still protect . . 501 *Humanity* 81
Soon as the herring-shoals at distance shine . . 522 *Epist.Beaumont* 75
To measure height and distance ; lonely task, . 548 **Stay, bold* 16
At distance still the same. Poor Traveller ! . . 567 *Cumb. Beg.* 58
Housed in a dream, at distance from the Kind ! . 579 *Peele Castle* 54
Of city smoke, by distance ruralised ; . . . . 633 *Prelude* 1. 89
When at reluctant distance he hath passed . . 656 *Prelude* 3. 484
The sea lay laughing at a distance ; near, . . . 663 *Prelude* 4. 326
As from a distance ; heard, and saw, and felt, . 686 *Prelude* 6. 768
Ascending, as if distance had the power . . . 699 *Prelude* 8. 3
Removed, and to a distance that was fit : . . . 703 *Prelude* 8. 305
Heaved at safe distance, far retired. I paused, . 726 *Prelude* 10. 568
Ascending at loose distance each from each, . . 746 *Prelude* 14. 33
To finer distance. Mine was at that hour . . 756 *Excursion* 1. 17
Was busy in the distance, shaping things . . . 769 *Excursion* 1. 881
At distance heard, peopled the milder air. . . 771 *Excursion* 1. 964
But, in the majesty of distance, now . . . 772 *Excursion* 2. 93
Forgotten,—at safe distance from ' a world . . 776 *Excursion* 2. 314
At a composing distance from the haunts . . 799 *Excursion* 3. 904
At a safe distance from our native land, . . . 814 *Excursion* 4. 895

Distress—*continued.*
And, weeping loud in this extreme distress, 35 *Guilt* 619
Of our distress—and thou art one of them! 74 *Bord.* 2086
She checked herself in her distress, 82 *Alice Fell* 42
Great God, who feel'st for my distress, 113 *Lament* 54
God cursed me in my sore distress; 115 *Last of Flock* 86
Years to a mother bring distress; 117 *Affl. Marg.* 27
Now first acquainted with distress and grief, 118 *Maternal Grief* 50
No hand to help them in distress; 126 *Idiot Boy* 23
In this distress. He is a prosperous man, 135 *Michael* 249
A twelvemonth's terror and distress!" 176 *Waggoner* 1. 252
Solitude, pain of heart, distress, and poverty. 195 *Resolution* 35
As his distress is sharp, would scorn my theme, 229 *Cuckoo-clock* 28
It only doubled his distress; 244 *P. B.* 707
An Infant, waked by her distress, 248 *P. B.* 1067
Through long-lived pressure of obscure distress, 260 **High is* 10
The embarrassed look of shy distress, 288 *Highland Girl* 30
Repaid thee for that sore distress 294 *Jedbor.* 80
A solid refuge for distress— 329 *Ode: Thanks.* 49
—No more—these lingerings of distress 331 *Ode: Thanks.* 131
If sickness, sorrow, or distress 344 *Eclipse* 80
Of innocence survive to mitigate distress? 344 **How blest* 65
Though pitied, *feel* her own distress; 370 *Eg. Maid* 59
Even so, without distress, doth she 397 *White Doe* 146
Of an unmerited distress; 402 *White Doe* 525
By scattering gleams, through your distress, 409 *White Doe* 1247
Distress and desolation spread 416 *White Doe* 1842
For penitent guilt, and innocent distress. 426 *Ecc. Sonn.* 1. 32. 9
To tell—how, finding in the rash distress 427 *Ecc. Sonn.* 1. 35. 12
Partners in faith, and brothers in distress, 437 *Ecc. Sonn.* 2. 37. 6
The Power that saved him in his strange distress. 470 **A youth* 14
As more exposed to suffering and distress; 493 *Hap. War.* 25
That smoothes foregone distress, the lines 499 *Memory* 9
Attuned to verse that, crowning light Distress 528 **Those breathing* 98
When unforeseen distress spreads far and wide 538 **In desultory* 43
And smiles, fond efforts of distress 543 *Russ. Fug.* 167
A deep distress hath humanised my Soul. 578 *Peele Castle* 36
That the remembrance of foregone distress, 586 *Ch. Lamb* 112
Crouded behind the swain, in mute distress, 592 *Ev. Wk. Quarto* 67
Though no distress be near him but his own 634 *Prelude* 1. 138
And as I looked around, distress and fear 666 *Prelude* 5. 73
Distress of mind ensued upon the sight, 693 *Prelude* 7. 392
But images of danger and distress, 701 *Prelude* 8. 164
Of her distress, was known to have turned her steps 704 *Prelude* 8. 385
Of blessèd consolations in distress; 755 *Recluse* 1. 1. 769
Who, in her worst distress, had ofttimes felt 770 *Excursion* 1. 935
General distress in his particular lot; 772 *Excursion* 2. 68
Not as a refuge from distress or pain, 791 *Excursion* 3. 383
Be left him, trust the freight of his distress 798 *Excursion* 3. 845
Distress and care. What then remains?—To seek 804 *Excursion* 4. 214
That flowing years repealed not: and distress 811 *Excursion* 4. 648
No shelter, for a spirit in distress. 816 *Excursion* 4. 1028
His own peculiar utterance for distress 837 *Excursion* 5. 982
May be delivered to distress and shame. 851 *Excursion* 6. 848
And prayer and thought can bring to worst distress 868 *Excursion* 7. 688
Through which I struggled, not without distress 886 *Excursion* 9. 169
Without distress or fear the shepherd heard K.8. 229 **I will* 174

Distressed. *See* **Distrest.**
Distressed me; from mine eyes escaped no tears; 251 **Beloved Vale* 7
Distressed and harassed, but with mind unbroken: 495 *Fact* 29
Have been distressed to think of what she once 733 *Prelude* 11. 386
Inly distressed or overpowered with awe, 779 *Excursion* 2. 539

Distressful. Of hardship and distressful fear, amid the houseless waste 91 *Norman Boy* 27
Distressful tidings. Long before the time 134 *Michael* 209

Distress-gun. "The vain distress-gun," from a lee-ward shore, 234 *Power of Sound* 159

Distrest. *See* **Distressed.**
Whether for him they are distrest; 181 *Waggoner* 4. 94
To mark its eddying foam-balls prettily distrest 190 **Lyre! though* 27
For this young Bird that is distrest; 204 *Brougham* 98
Is love, though oft to agony distrest, 210 *Laod.* 89
To see how ye are all distrest, 236 *P. B.* 19
By this dark cave to be distrest 243 *P. B.* 648
Wronged, or distrest; 285 *Grave of Burns* 70
Of catholic humanity:—distrest 449 *Ecc. Sonn.* 3. 36. 11
Or blasts the green field and the trees distrest, 571 **There is a Flower* 6
The sick in body, or distrest in mind; 859 *Excursion* 7. 153

Distribution. A skilful distribution of sweet sounds, 757 *Excursion* 1. 68

District. For, born in a poor district, and which yet 712 *Prelude* 9. 215
Of the surrounding district, they might learn 869 *Excursion* 7. 770

Districts. Can string you names of districts, cities, towns, 670 *Prelude* 5. 320
"Yet—in less simple districts, where we see 847 *Excursion* 6. 624

Disturb. That *solitary* man disturb their reign, 19 *Desc. Sk.* 509
Shall not disturb us; further I'll not engage; 51 *Bord.* 775
how could I disturb his last moments? 72 *Bord.* 1939
Their happiness, or to disturb their love. 123 *V. and J.* 111
Concealed from friends who might disturb 169 *Wren's Nest* 61
Doth rather deepen than disturb the calm 184 *Airey-force* 6
Shall e'er prevail against us, or disturb 207 *Tintern* 132
Disturb the liquid music's equipoise. 455 *Rydal Mere* 12
But upon Honour's head disturb the crown, 518 *Pun. Death* 4. 12
That yet disturb not its concealed repose 524 *Epist. Beaumont* 169
No winds disturb; the mirror of whose breast 527 **Those breathing* 10
Disturb its solitude profound. 550 *Hermit's Cell* 2. 8
Disturb the summer dust; he is so still 567 *Cumb. Beg.* 60
And, feeding on disquiet, thus disturb 765 *Excursion* 1. 603
Loth to disturb what Heaven hath hushed in peace. 847 *Excursion* 6. 572
Intrudes, the peaceful concert to disturb 848 *Excursion* 6. 644

Disturb—*continued.*
Dancing around her, hinder and disturb 873 *Excursion* 7. 1035
Or to disturb, so fair a spectacle, 891 *Excursion* 9. 453

Disturbance. *See* **Self-disturbance.**
Where no disturbance comes to intrude 180 *Waggoner* 4. 26
Through no disturbance of my soul, 492 *Duty* 33
In no disturbance of excessive hope, 688 *Prelude* 7. 62

Disturbances. Where the disturbances of space and time— 732 *Prelude* 11. 330
Those revolutions of disturbances 806 *Excursion* 4. 326
Of the revolving world's disturbances 839 *Excursion* 6. 59

Disturbed. A peace enlivened, not disturbed, by wreaths 9 *Ev. Wk.* 362
Inly disturbed, to think that others felt 23 *Yew-tree* 43
How you would be disturbed by this dire news, 59 *Bord.* 1208
And be disturbed, as I am. I have read 62 *Bord.* 1381
—I see I have disturbed you. By no means. 65 *Bord.* 1552
Upon the Child, if he disturbed the sheep 134 *Michael* 174
Was fettered, and the air by storm disturbed, 150 **When, to* 40
By sorrow darkened and by care disturbed, 172 *Infant Daughter* 47
As though his weakness were disturbed by pain: 321 **Humanity, delighting* 6
That thinned the living and disturbed the dead? 378 *Duddon* 8. 8
While, less disturbed than in the narrow Vale 384 *Duddon* 33. 5
Disturbed upon her virgin head; 400 *White Doe* 363
He heard, and it disturbed him not. 401 *White Doe* 434
Which by the visitation was disturbed. 510 *F. Stone* 128
An inmate of these mountains,—if, disturbed 548 **Stranger! this* 27
May she, who once disturbed the seats of bliss 582 *Invoc. Earth* 30
What dire intrigues disturbed *Cythera's* joy! 620 *Birth of Love* 2
I was disturbed at times by prudent thoughts, 650 *Prelude* 3. 77
When so disturbed, whatever palms are won. 656 *Prelude* 3. 502
His countenance, meanwhile, grew more disturbed; 667 *Prelude* 5. 126
Had been erewhile unsettled and disturbed, 795 *Excursion* 3. 654
Sad or disturbed, is ordered by a Being 801 *Excursion* 4. 14
In this sad service, less disturbed than we. 871 *Excursion* 7. 885
Would be disturbed, I fear, with wrathful scorn, 874 *Excursion* 8. 35
This plaintive note disturbed not the repose 892 *Excursion* 9. 559
Disturbed, uneasy in itself as seemed, K.8. 241 *Recluse* 1. 1. 177

Disturbers. By Christian disturbers more savage than Turks, 86 *Rural Arch.* 20

Disturbing. *See* **Street-disturbing.**

Disturbs. No strife disturbs his sister's breast; 81 †*Mother's Return* 17
Disturbs me till the sight is more than I can bear." 111 **'Tis said that some* 44
A presence that disturbs me with the joy 207 *Tintern* 94
Nought wakens or disturbs it's tranquil tides; 597 *Ev. Wk. Quarto* 310

Disunite. Of one who came to disunite their lives 125 *V. and J.* 236

Ditches. Ditches are graves—funereal rites denied; 427 *Ecc. Sonn.* 1. 36. 10

Ditties. Gives plaintive ditties to the heedless wind, 522 *Epist. Beaumont* 47
Their slender ditties when the trees are bare. 881 *Excursion* 8. 483

Ditty. Who, murmuring here a later ditty, 9 *Collins* 14
Scattering a ditty each to her desire, 233 *Power of Sound* 46
These crowded streets resound no plaintive ditty:— 475 *Greenock* 5
Where, tho' her far-off twilight ditty steal, 596 *Ev. Wk. Quarto* 225
A time-beguiling ditty, for delight 851 *Excursion* 6. 867

Diurnal. Rolled round in earth's diurnal course, 187 **A slumber* 7
With visible motion her diurnal round! 639 *Prelude* 1. 460
Her annual, her diurnal, round alike 795 *Excursion* 3. 613

Dive. How they, in bells of crystal, dive— 216 *Enterprise* 71
Or deep into the clouds we dive, 236 *P. B.* 24
Who through the abyss of weakness dive. 330 *Ode: Thanks.* 86
Dive through the stormy surface of the flood 515 **Men of* 10
Dive, at thy choice, or brave the freshening gale! 527 **Those breathing* 36
And they who rather dive than soar, whose pains 815 *Excursion* 4. 951
—Look forth, or each man dive into himself; 830 *Excursion* 5. 505

Dived. Dived into caves, and pierced the matted woods, 840 *Excursion* 6. 110

Diverging. In streaks diverging wide and mounting high; 24 *Guilt* 20
Diverging now (as if his quest had been 776 *Excursion* 2. 319
Now suddenly diverging from the orb 893 *Excursion* 9. 593

Diver's. Or in the diver's grasp fetched up from caves 511 **Who rashly* 14

Divers. So many divers samples from the growth 652 *Prelude* 3. 221

Diverse. Of moral qualities in their diverse aspects; 59 *Bord.* 1226
So diverse in his wilfulness is he. 560 *Cuck. and Night.* 205
Where'er we move, under the diverse shapes 750 *Prelude* 14. 327
Blending their diverse foliage with the green 881 *Excursion* 8. 479

Diversely. True friends though diversely inclined; 285 *Grave of Burns* 43
From kindred features diversely combined, 891 *Excursion* 9. 510

Diversified. Diversified the allurement. Need I fear 691 *Prelude* 7. 263

Diversity. In such diversity of hue 486 *Matthew* 7
On which, with a diversity of pace, 722 *Prelude* 10. 274
Of feeling, and diversity of strength 738 *Prelude* 12. 270

Divert. Or cloud approaching to divert the rays, 329 *Ode: Thanks.* 10
The judgment, and divert the general heart 538 **In desultory* 47
But neither could divert nor soothe my thoughts. 767 *Excursion* 1. 739
With dark events. Desirous to divert 793 *Excursion* 3. 468

Diverted. Young as he is, diverted wish and hope 54 *Bord.* 932
Has been diverted, other lessons taught, 388 *Loch Etive* 12
Swerves not—diverted by a casual law. 442 *Ecc. Sonn.* 3. 9. 8
Neither to be diverted nor withstood 495 *Fact* 42
Those musings or diverted, save that once 746 *Prelude* 14. 21
To be diverted from our present theme, 791 *Excursion* 3. 331
Yet not to be diverted from his aim, 805 *Excursion* 4. 259
Neither to be diverted nor withstood S.3. 427 **My Son* 13

Diverting. With many a most diverting thing, 127 *Idiot Boy* 125
Diverting evil purposes, remorse 813 *Excursion* 4. 839

Divested. Discoloured, then divested. 'Tis affirmed 840 *Excursion* 6. 161
Shall be—divested at the appointed hour 893 *Excursion* 9. 632

Divide. From the dark-blue faint silvery threads divide 9 *Ev. Wk.* 359
He flew to her from whom they would divide him— 123 *V. and J.* 154
Along—and scatter and divide, 180 *Waggoner* 4. 63
Scarce heard; nor word from word could I divide; 197 *Resolution* 108
"One lesson, Shepherd, let us two divide, 203 *Hart-leap* 177
And that inspiring Hill, which "did divide 251 **Pelion and* 4
Though the toil of the way with dear Friends we divide, 345 *Stanzas : Simplon* 25
Did from all other graves divide: 398 *White Doe* 172
'Tis meet that thou with me divide 402 *White Doe* 534
Their purpose—then did he divide, 409 *White Doe* 1238
Ye mingle, or divide. 526 **The soaring* 48
Who love as we do. Speed thee well! divide 678 *Prelude* 6. 247
No other can divide with thee this work: 749 *Prelude* 14. 212
On the green turf, a dial—to divide 813 *Excursion* 4. 801
As shall divide them wholly from the stir 885 *Excursion* 9. 47
And neighbourhood serves rather to divide K.8. 253 *Recluse* I.1.600
Divided. If more divided than a sportive pair 122 *V. and J.* 25
Either to be divided from the place 149 **A narrow* 30
Even with myself divided such delight, 652 *Prelude* 3. 237
Divided from me by one little month, 719 *Prelude* 10. 74
Of such excitement and divided thought 852 *Excursion* 6. 958
Appropriate, and divided from the world K.8. 253 *Recluse* I.1.620
Divides. A long blue bar its ægis orb divides, 5 *Ev. Wk.* 170
Stately, and burning in his pride, divides 595 *Ev. Wk. Quarto* 203
And bottomless, divides the midway tide. 611 *Desc.Sk.Quarto* 499
Divides with me this loved abode, was there, 622 *Recluse* I. 1. 89
To draw the line of comfort that divides 772 *Excursion* 2. 72
That now divides the pair, or rather say, 861 *Excursion* 7. 239
And thus divides and thus relieves the time; 862 *Excursion* 7. 305
Dividing. And still dividing, and dividing still, 815 *Excursion* 4. 963
Dividual. In his dividual being, self-reviewed, 844 *Excursion* 6. 386
Dividually. Dividually.—Here must thou be, O Man! 749 *Prelude* 14. 209
Divine. And I divine the cause. Do not reproach me: 39 *Bord.* 132
Prayer that Grace divine may raise 94 *Westmoreland Girl* 90
Divine, of swearing everlasting truth, 123 *V. and J.* 118
There stood the urchin, as you will divine, 134 *Michael* 188
There is madness about thee, and joy divine 159 **Up with me* 12
Because not of this noisy world, but silent and divine! 189 *Star-gazers* 28
What this imported I could ill divine: 202 *Hart-leap* 105
His death was mourned by sympathy divine. 203 *Hart-leap* 164
Of harmony, with instinct more divine; 209 **Ethereal minstrel* 10
On tables set, as if for rites divine;— 213 *Dion* 34
Shalt show us how divine a thing 218 *Young Lady* 11
Met by the rainbow's form divine, 221 *Triad* 84
Your origin divine. 225 *Present.* 18
To testify of Love and Grace divine. 226 *Vernal Ode* 39
Divine monition Nature yields, 228 *Devot. Incit.* 71
Of divine Love, where Wisdom, Beauty, Truth 234 *Power of Sound* 111
Divine of words quickening insensate things. 252 **Why, Minstrel* 8
And my Soul felt her destiny divine, 256 **No mortal* 3
And let my spirit in that power divine 258 **Even so* 13
Thy nature is not therefore less divine: 258 **It is a* 11
Her functions are they therefore less divine, 270 **Though the bold* 9
But from its *own* divine vitality. 277 **A Poet* 14
Divine communion; both do live and move, 280 **Oh what* 10
The Church, when trusting in divine command 281 *Chris. Words.* 5
Spirit divine through forms of human art: 282 **In my* 7
Less than divine command they spurn; 300 *Cora Linn* 31
Clap, infants, clap your hands! Divine must be 310 *Anticip.* 10
(So faith too fondly deemed) a voice divine 319 *Guernica* 3
Dread King of Kings, vouchsafe a ray divine 323 **Now that* 9
And competent to shed a spark divine 324 *Ode 1814* 106
Of Figures human and divine, 343 *Eclipse* 40
Rest where thy course was stayed by Power divine! 345 **Ambition—following* 10
Albeit lifting human to divine, 357 *Aquap.* 308
Divine affections; and with beast and bird 362 **List—'twas* 54
With justice mark not Thou, O Light divine, 366 **Eternal Lord* 9
And divine Art, that fast to memory clung— 367 **As indignation* 4
So fair, of such divine report 372 *Eg. Maid* 232
From pastoral graves extracting thoughts divine; 384 *Duddon* 31. 11
And her divine employment! 386 *Yarrow Rev.* 42
At the sun's outbreak, as with light divine, 390 *Glencroe* 7
Even to the fountain-head of peace divine." 396 **Action is* 13
Crushed as if by wrath divine? 397 *White Doe* 113
With love divine and gentle light? 405 *White Doe* 871
With hope upon the Will divine." 408 *White Doe* 1091
A more divine and loftier way! 416 *White Doe* 1849
That the firm soul is clothed with fruit divine! 423 *Ecc. Sonn.* 1. 19. 5
He made by wilful breach of law divine. 428 *Ecc. Sonn.* 2. 1. 4
Hailed from aloft those Heirs of truth divine 431 *Ecc. Sonn.* 2. 13. 10
In their afflictions a divine retreat; 438 *Ecc. Sonn.* 2. 40. 7
For re-subjecting to divine command 444 *Ecc. Sonn.* 3. 18. 13
Armour divine, and conquer in your cause! 446 *Ecc. Sonn.* 3. 25. 14
Of simple truth with grace divine imbued; 450 *Ecc. Sonn.* 3. 40. 8
Divine! thou Lincoln, on thy sovereign hill! 451 *Ecc. Sonn.* 3. 42. 12
In filial duty, clothed with love divine, 452 *Ecc. Sonn.* 3. 46. 2
But who *is* innocent? By grace divine, 455 **Not in the lucid* 16
But long as god-like wish, or hope divine, 457 **Had this* 34
Of a young maiden, only not divine. 469 **Why stand* 8
Mechanic laws to agency divine; 473 **Thanks for* 3
A faith more fixed, a rapture more divine 474 **How sad* 13
Or need, of counsel breathed through lips divine. 498 **Enough of climbing* 31

Divine—*continued.*
Ministers of grace divine 502 **Like a* 37
Forgives their interference—Art divine, 509 *F. Stone* 76
Godlike, a humble branch of the divine, 509 *F. Stone* 89
And Will, whose office, by divine command, 514 **Who ponders* 13
So sacred, so informed with light divine, 519 *Pun. Death* 10. 3
Who can divine what impulses from God 527 **Those breathing* 27
The spear, yet gave to works divine 533 **Blest is* 13
He rose, and straight—as by divine command, 534 **When in* 9
In progress, under laws divine, maintained. 538 **In desultory* 55
Favour divine, exalting human love; 540 *Grace Darl.* 5
Of divine tranquillity! 550 *Hermit's Cell* 4. 16
Fall on thy knees and sue for help divine. 551 **Behold an* 8
Thou shouldst have seemed a treasure-house divine 578 *Peele Castle* 21
When such divine communion, which we know, 581 **Why should we* 12
Flowed in a course of sympathy divine;— 583 **With copious* 25
O gift divine of quiet sequestration! 586 *Ch. Lamb* 121
In that divine embrace enchanted lay; 620 *Birth of Love* 6
Nor pass unprais'd the robe and veil divine, 624 *Æneid* 77
But truth divine has sanctified their rage, 628 *Eagle and Dove* 10
On earth to goodness blest by grace divine. 628 **Deign, Sovereign* 8
Cloud-like it mounts, or touched with light divine 665 *Prelude* 5. 7
Shakespeare, or Milton, labourers divine! 668 *Prelude* 5. 165
By that transparent veil with light divine, 674 *Prelude* 5. 602
Through the divine effect of power and love: 706 *Prelude* 8. 491
And grateful memory, as a thing divine. 707 *Prelude* 8. 559
Lo! everything that was indeed divine 709 *Prelude* 8. 655
Of zeal, by an authority Divine 715 *Prelude* 9. 406
And want of hope where evidence divine 720 *Prelude* 10. 162
Making man what he is, creature divine, 724 *Prelude* 10. 424
Divine Comates, by his impious lord 733 *Prelude* 11. 444
O Soul of Nature! that, by laws divine 735 *Prelude* 12. 102
That yet survive, a work, as some divine, 745 *Prelude* 13. 339
From earth to heaven, from human to divine; 747 *Prelude* 14. 118
Actual, divine, and true. To fear and love, 748 *Prelude* 14. 162
Of quality and fabric more divine. 752 *Prelude* 14. 454
The vision and the faculty divine; 757 *Excursion* 1. 79
The divine Milton. Lore of different kind, 760 *Excursion* 1. 250
Shaped his belief, as grace divine inspired, 762 *Excursion* 1. 412
Social and temporal; but in laws divine, 775 *Excursion* 2. 239
From seats of power divine; and hope, or trust, 790 *Excursion* 3. 257
Maintained with faithful care. And you divine 795 *Excursion* 3. 614
Insensibly;—the immortal and divine 795 *Excursion* 3. 671
The particle divine remained unquenched; 802 *Excursion* 4. 51
As if it were a spirit!—How divine, 809 *Excursion* 4. 513
And intuitions moral and divine) 811 *Excursion* 4. 646
But still a high dependence, a divine 815 *Excursion* 4. 928
Auxiliar to divine. That change shall clothe 820 *Excursion* 4. 1249
Of divine love, our intellectual soul." 820 *Excursion* 4. 1274
The other, which the ray divine hath touched, 831 *Excursion* 5. 556
To reason's mandates; and the hopes divine 836 *Excursion* 5. 909
Divine or human; exercised in pain, 837 *Excursion* 5. 1013
O high example, constancy divine! 839 *Excursion* 6. 74
Within the soul, fountains of grace divine; 841 *Excursion* 6. 181
Which a divine philosophy rejects, 846 *Excursion* 6. 559
To sight or mind. Nor less than care divine 850 *Excursion* 6. 770
Is divine mercy. She, who had rebelled, 850 *Excursion* 6. 771
A sun-like beauty, and appeared divine! 854 *Excursion* 6. 1037
Divine displeasure, broke the marriage-vow. 855 *Excursion* 6. 1093
How, likewise, under sufferance divine, 865 *Excursion* 7. 528
The oppressor breathes, their human form divine, 886 *Excursion* 9. 151
Of what in man is human or divine. K.8. 255 *Recluse* I.1.702
Let not thy justice view, O Light Divine, K.8. 266 **Rid of* 9
Divined. Easily may the sequel be divined— 122 *V. and J.* 79
May be divined—perhaps it hath been said:— 800 *Excursion* 3. 964
Divinely. Conqueror, 'mid some sad thoughts, divinely blest! 278 *Wellington* 14
An Apparition more divinely bright! 434 *Ecc. Sonn.* 2. 22. 10
It must not be, if I, divinely taught, K.8. 255 *Recluse* I.1.700
Diviner. Are yet of no diviner origin, v **If thou indeed* 8
An ampler ether, a diviner air, 211 *Laod.* 105
Of a diviner love, will be forgiven— 540 **Lady! a* 81
The first diviner influence of this world, 737 *Prelude* 12. 182
Divinest. —Divinest Object which the uplifted eye 329 *Ode : Thanks.* 27
But Sculpture here, with the divinest scope 476 *Howard* 3
To be the awakener of divinest thoughts, 870 *Excursion* 7. 823
Diving. By diving for it into their own bosoms. 64 *Bord.* 1487
Divinity. For him who to divinity aspired, 213 *Dion* 46
By thy divinity impelled, 216 *Enterprise* 53
Who such divinity to thee imparts 256 **Yes! hope* 8
Of a Divinity, that seemed to smile 371 *Eg. Maid* 131
And calm with fear of God's divinity. 422 *Ecc. Sonn.* 1. 14. 14
With a divinity of colours, drest 511 **Who rashly* 4
Creation and divinity itself 651 *Prelude* 3. 171
Whom I have served, that their DIVINITY 816 *Excursion* 4. 984
Division. Even for the least division of an hour, 257 **Surprised by* 7
The first division of the splendid feast, 625 *Æneid* 96
By the division of her inward self 875 *Excursion* 8. 57
Divisions. In square divisions parcelled out and all 639 *Prelude* 1. 510
Through three divisions of the quartered year 643 *Prelude* 2. 83
Divorce. Who swerves from innocence, who makes divorce 383 *Duddon* 30. 1
Divorced. Divorced from good—a spirit and pulse of good, 567 *Cumb. Beg.* 77
Thrown in, that from humanity divorced 693 *Prelude* 7. 389
Divulged. Of facts divulged, wherein appear 398 *White Doe* 200
Divulged by Truth and magnified by Fame; 691 *Prelude* 7. 293
Dizzy. This little place may well be dizzy! 177 *Waggoner* 2. 63
And all its dizzy raptures. Not for this 206 *Tintern* 85
By chasm or dizzy precipice; 216 *Enterprise* 66
Its dizzy turbulence eludes the eye, 290 *Kilchurn* 37

Dog—*continued.*
The Dog, which still was hovering nigh, . . . 492 *Fidelity* 54
This Dog, had been through three months' space 492 *Fidelity* 56
The Dog had watched about the spot, ... 492 *Fidelity* 60
The Curate's Dog—his long-tried friend, for they, 523 *Epist. Beaumont* 131
Like a sick Lover, then this dog was used . . . 660 *Prelude* 4. 105
Quick as the pantings of the faithful dog, . . 661 *Prelude* 4. 186
No dog attending, by no staff sustained, . . . 664 *Prelude* 4. 400
And breakfasts with his dog. When they have stolen, ... 702 *Prelude* 8. 238.
For manna, take a lesson from the dog . . . 732 *Prelude* 11. 363
And, if a dog passed by, she still would quit . . 769 *Excursion* 1. 878
The fowl domestic, and the household dog— . . 772 *Excursion* 2. 45
Ascended, with his staff and faithful dog ; . . 863 *Excursion* 7. 420
Dogged. What do they here? Listen! What; dogged like thieves! . . . . 56 *Bord.* 1017
I would have dogged him to the jaws of hell— . 78 *Bord.* 2311
Led by Fear's cold wet hand, and dogg'd by Death ; 597 *Ev. Wk. Quarto* 286
Dogging. And Conscience dogging close his bleeding way . . . . 613 *Desc.Sk.Quarto* 640
Dogmatic. Dogmatic Teachers, of the snow-white fur! . . . . 268 **Dogmatic Teachers* 1
Dog's. *See* **House-dog's, Mill-dog's, Sheep-dog's, Watch-dog's.**
Dogs. *See* **Sheep-dogs.**
The bark of dogs, the heifer's tinkling bell, . . 18 *Desc. Sk.* 419
And flung it to the dogs: but I am raised . . 77 *Bord.* 2294
Calls to the few tired dogs that yet remain: . . 200 *Hart-leap* 18
The dogs are stretched among the mountain fern. 201 *Hart-leap* 24
Of barking dogs, and bleatings from strange fear. 382 *Duddon* 23. 8
Men, dogs, and horses, all are dead ; . . . . 483 *Simon Lee* 31
Four dogs, each pair of different breed, . . . 490 *Incident : Dog* 7
Press forward by the teasing dogs unscared. . . 525 *Epist. Beaumont* 238
The bark of dogs, the drowsy tinkling bell, . . 611 *Desc.Sk.Quarto* 508
Presents a company of dancing dogs, ... 689 *Prelude* 7. 176
Doing. *See* **Nothing-doing, Well-doing.**
Suffering not doing ill—fate far more mild. . . 33 *Guilt* 499
Do as Charles and I are doing! . . . . . . 79 *Foresight* 2
What Johnny and his Horse are doing! . . . . 129 *Idiot Boy* 313
What they've been doing all this time, . . . 129 *Idiot Boy* 314
What on the earth is doing. . . . . 237 *P. B.* 120
What would he now? what is he doing? . . . 243 *P. B.* 587
This old Man doing all he could . . . . . 484 *Simon Lee* 74
What is the creature doing here? . . . . . 491 *Fidelity* 16
His fields seemed to know what their Master was doing ; . . . . 569 *Farmer* 18
Not doing in their stead the needful work. . . 653 *Prelude* 3. 328
Though doing wrong and suffering, and full oft . 672 *Prelude* 5. 417
And suffered, and was doing, suffering, still, . . 708 *Prelude* 8. 627
The beauty of his person, doing wrong . . . 711 *Prelude* 9. 145
As we pronounce them, doing them much wrong, K.8. 238 *Recluse* 1. 1. 68
Doings. Rough doings these! as God's my judge, . 176 *Waggoner* 1. 249
You think, those doings must have bred . . . 178 *Waggoner* 3. 5
Till of his doings is no trace, ... 479 *Somnamb.* 71
Thoughts, chances, sights, or doings, which we tell 522 *Epist. Beaumont* 54
And your officious doings bring disgrace . . . 655 *Prelude* 3. 415
How little they, they and their doings, seem, . . 700 *Prelude* 8. 59
Full oft his doings leave me to deplore . . . 866 *Excursion* 7. 595
Dole. All white with flour, the dole of village dames, 566 *Cumb. Beg.* 9
Doleful. You and the story of that doleful night . 40 *Bord.* 177
The north-wind sings a doleful song ; . . . . 117 †*Cottager* 2
Full many a sad and doleful thing: . . . . 144 *Her Eyes* 14
And begged an alms with doleful plea . . . . 191 *Beggars* 14
And there, with many a doleful song . . . . 194 *Ruth* 196
Does she repeat that doleful cry?" . . . . 198 *Thorn* 88
There is a doleful silence in the air. . . . . 200 *Hart-leap* 12
More doleful place did never eye survey ; . . . 202 *Hart-leap* 114
And the long train of doleful pageantry . . . 213 *Dion* 85
Distinctly heard from far—a doleful note! . . . 219 *Haunted Tree* 24
When hark a burst of doleful sound! . . . . 243 *P. B.* 611
And gave his doleful warning. . . . . . . 302 *Yarrow V.* 32
Why comes not Francis?—From the doleful City 411 *White Doe* 1364
We have not passed into a doleful City, . . . 475 *Greenock* 1
Shed on their chains ; and hence that doleful name. 517 *Pun. Death* 1. 14
A doleful bower for penitential song, ... 529 **Those breathing* 115
And them besought to hear her doleful case, . . 561 *Cuck.and Night.* 264
O rest, thou doleful Mother of Mankind!" . . . 581 *Invoc. Earth* 2
Of melancholy space and doleful time, ... 677 *Prelude* 6. 136
The doleful sequel. But our little bark . . . 717 *Prelude* 9. 559
"Noise is there not enough in doleful war, . . 863 *Excursion* 7. 363
Dolorous. This water doth send forth a dolorous groan. . . . . 202 *Hart-leap* 136
Hovering around with dolorous moan! . . . . 243 *P. B.* 650
Demons and Spirits, many a dolorous groan . . 435 *Ecc. Sonn.* 2. 27. 4
That never art secure from dolorous change! . . 573 *Chiabrera* 2. 14
"So ends my dolorous tale, and glad I am . . 785 *Excursion* 2. 896
Dolphin. No dolphin ever was so gay . . . . . 192 *Ruth* 41
Dolphins. And listening dolphins gather round. . 234 *Power of Sound* 136
That sporting dolphins drew. . . . . 296 *Highland Boy* 120
Domain. Contentment shares the desolate domain . 15 *Desc. Sk.* 260
A grand domain to squeak and gibber in. . . . 61 *Bord.* 1304
His short domain upon the vessel's deck, . . . 150 **When, to* 65
Where earth resembles most his own domain! . . 154 *Morn. Ex.* 52
He whose domain is held in common . . . . 175 *Waggoner* 1. 174
Farewell, thou desolate Domain! . . . . . 215 *Kirkstone* 77
Their own domain ;—but ever, while intent . . 218 *Recluse* 1. 1. 210
Garden, and that Domain where kindred, friends, 271 **Where holy* 5
Of thy domain, strange contrast do present . . 275 **Chatsworth! thy* 2

Domain—*continued.*
Parthenope's domain—Virgilian haunt, . . . 356 *Aquap.* 265
Of ocean for her own domain. . . . . . . 397 *White Doe* 66
O'er Rylstone's fair domain have blown ; . . . 413 *White Doe* 1569
In lofty place, or humble Life's domain. . . . 520 *Pun. Death* 14. 8
While Faith aspires to seats in that domain . . 533 **Once I* 41
Shall sojourn in this fair domain ; . . . . . 534 **Blest is* 96
For ruminating creatures ; a domain . . . . 655 *Prelude* 3. 436
A gracious look all over her domain. . . . . 658 *Prelude* 4. 23
Or sunbeam over your domain I passed . . . 685 *Prelude* 6. 676
Though most at home in this their dear domain, . 696 *Prelude* 7. 595
This did I feel, in London's vast domain. . . . 698 *Prelude* 7. 765
I felt his presence in his own domain, ... 703 *Prelude* 8. 257
I ranged at large, through London's wide domain, 710 *Prelude* 9. 24
—There crows the cock, single in his domain: . 776 *Excursion* 2. 344
Said gaily, "This is my domain, my cell, . . . 781 *Excursion* 2. 650
Is heaven's profoundest azure ; no domain . . 787 *Excursion* 3. 95
The Vicar's dwelling, and the whole domain, . . 824 *Excursion* 5. 128
Vanished or hidden ; and the whole domain, . . 830 *Excursion* 5. 549
Around us a domain where you have long . . . 832 *Excursion* 5. 635
"At morn or eve, in your retired domain, . . 839 *Excursion* 6. 95
Round his domain, desirous not alone . . . . 844 *Excursion* 6. 394
Possessed like outskirts of some large domain, . 866 *Excursion* 7. 573
The assured domain of calm simplicity . . . 876 *Excursion* 8. 166
Our ancestors, within the still domain . . . . 877 *Excursion* 8. 186
Around the mansion and its whole domain ; . . 882 *Excursion* 8. 540
"Wild wanderers, whither through my dark domain?" . . . . K.8. 241 *Recluse* 1. 1. 169
Domains. I found how my domains had been usurped, 40 *Bord.* 193
Here, 'mid his own unvexed domains, ... 214 *Kirkstone* 34
Sheriffs, and lairds and their domains, ... 291 *Rob Roy* 70
Horse charging horse, 'mid these retired domains ; 383 *Duddon* 29. 2
But mark how gladly, through their own domains, 429 *Ecc. Sonn.* 2. 4. 6
Should bind the vassal to his lord's domains? . 468 *St. Bees* 141
Alas! how he fumbles about the domains . . . 484 **A plague* 11
Are the domains of tender memory! . . . . 498 **Enough of climbing* 51
To Egremont's Domains and Castle fair. . . . 535 *Egremont* 8
To thee, and those domains of rural peace, . . 700 *Prelude* 8. 73
Upon his rich domains, vineyard and tilth, . . 718 *Prelude* 10. 7
Oft, through thy fair domains, illustrious Peer! . 753 **Oft, through* 1
Dome. Where thousands meet to worship God under a mighty Dome ; . . . . 93 *Poet's Dream* 62
Leading such companion I that gilded dome, . . 140 *Arm. Lady* 41
Grove, isle, with every shape of sky-built dome, . 263 **Those words* 9
All that we see—is dome, or vault, or nest, . . 266 **The stars* 7
Leaving an ancient dome, and towers like these, . 292 **Degenerate Douglas* 7
As active round the hollow dome, ... 300 *Bran* 18
That through the texture of yon azure dome . . 322 *Germans* 6
I saw the banquet spread beneath a Dome of state, 324 *Ode 1814* 74
A lofty Dome, that dared to emulate . . . . 324 *Ode 1814* 75
The Baptistery's dome, and that which swells . 355 *Aquap.* 173
Crowned with St. Peter's everlasting Dome. . . 358 *Pine : Rome* 14
The dome of Florence, pensive and alone, . . . 365 **Under the* 2
Lead to that younger Pile, whose sky-like dome . 452 *Ecc. Sonn.* 3. 45. 8
The silver Tenant of the crystal dome ; . . . 527 **Those breathing* 18
Than the rude embryo of a little Dome . . . 548 **Stranger! this* 5
The gentler manners of the private dome ; . . . 619 *School Ex.* 90
And from Mont Martre southward to the Dome . 710 *Prelude* 9. 47
To heaven:—"How beautiful this dome of sky ; 802 *Excursion* 4. 34
Athwart the concave of the dark blue dome, . . 819 *Excursion* 4. 1179
Supporting gracefully a massy dome . . . . 891 *Excursion* 9. 500
Embowering mountains, and the dome of Heaven K.8. 263 **The Lake* 11
Domes. Huge convent domes with pinnacles and towers, ... 14 *Desc. Sk.* 224
Lucida! from domes of pleasure, ... 220 *Triad* 36
Ships, towers, domes, theatres, and temples lie . 269 *Westm. Bridge* 6
Yet, O ye spires of Oxford! domes and towers! . 270 **Ye sacred* 6
Monastic Domes! following my downward way, . 449 *Ecc. Sonn.* 3. 35. 1
And gorgeous ladies, under splendid domes, . . 689 *Prelude* 7. 124
A sumptuous dream of flowery lawns, with domes 700 *Prelude* 8. 84
With alabaster domes, and silver spires, . . . 784 *Excursion* 2. 840
Domestic. While tender cares and mild domestic loves 6 *Ev. Wk.* 222
Of true domestic loyalty, did e'er . . . . . 124 *V. and J.* 170
And one domestic for their common needs, . . 125 *V. and J.* 275
Of those domestic tales that spake to me . . . 131 *Michael* 22
Yield him no domestic cave, ... 166 *Wand. Jew* 14
Domestic queen, where grandeur is unknown ; . 220 *Triad* 55
Domestic hands the home-bred wool had shorn, . 255 *Easter* 5
Perhaps are seated in domestic ring . . . . 266 **Even as* 11
Seek in domestic oratory small, ... 430 *Ecc. Sonn.* 2. 6. 7
Kennelled and chained. Ye tame domestic fowl, . 472 *Dunolly Eagle* 7
Our own domestic mountain. Thing and thought 480 *Cordelia* 7
Domestic virtue vitally depends, ... 504 *Warning* 75
Domestic Portrait! have to verse consigned . . 510 *F. Stone* 122
A mild domestic pity kept its place, ... 523 *Epist. Beaumont* 145
A zig-zag path from the domestic skiff . . . . 607 *Desc.Sk.Quarto* 297
The little cottage of domestic Joy. . . . . . 613 *Desc.Sk.Quarto* 601
The lily of domestic joy decay : . . . . . . 615 *Desc.Sk.Quarto* 723
To patriotic and domestic love . . . . . . 645 *Prelude* 2. 190
Of peace and quiet and domestic love, ... 648 *Prelude* 2. 438
At our domestic table: and, dear Friend! . . . 659 *Prelude* 4. 78
Wore in old time. Her smooth domestic life, . 661 *Prelude* 4. 222
Shipwreck, or some domestic incident . . . . 691 *Prelude* 7. 292
Domestic manners, customs, gestures, looks, . . 711 *Prelude* 9. 83
Domestic severings, female fortitude . . . . 713 *Prelude* 9. 271
Domestic carnage now filled the whole year . . 723 *Prelude* 10. 356
The fowl domestic, and the household dog— . . 772 *Excursion* 2. 45
Are by domestic pleasure uncaressed . . . . 810 *Excursion* 4. 577

Domestic—*continued.*
And with the blessings of domestic love. 823 *Excursion* 5. 59
Of each domestic charity fulfilled, 847 *Excursion* 6. 629
Is by domestic service unimpaired; 852 *Excursion* 6. 951
Of keen domestic anguish; and beguile 862 *Excursion* 7. 308
Of that foundation in domestic care 872 *Excursion* 7. 964
The old domestic morals of the land, 877 *Excursion* 8. 236
With lip almost as pure.—Domestic bliss 878 *Excursion* 8. 262
Domestic, and in spirit motherly K.8. 251 *Recluse* 1.1.528
Domination. The domination of his glorious themes, 216 *Enterprise* 96
By magic domination, 374 *Eg. Maid* 363
A ghostly Domination, unconfined 428 *Ecc. Sonn.* 1. 39. 4
Yes, to thy domination, Roman See, 429 *Ecc. Sonn.* 2. 2. 12
The domination of the sprightly juice 433 *Ecc. Sonn.* 2. 20. 10
Thy domination; as the whole vast Sea 459 **Wanderer! that* 48
For domination at some riper day; 504 *Warning* 100
That mutual domination which she loves 747 *Prelude* 14. 81
Domine. *Miserere Domine!* 336 **Jesu! bless* 24
Domineer. Amid the burning town the Grecians domineer. L.2. 121 *Frag. Æneid* 2, 6
Domineering. Yet ostentation, domineering, oft 695 *Prelude* 7. 549
A domineering instinct, serves at once 720 *Prelude* 10. 169
And domineering faculties of sense 804 *Excursion* 4. 207
Dominion. Attends on goodness with dominion decked, 105 *Artegal* 188
And this is thy dominion. 159 *Green Linnet* 16
How dreadful the dominion of the impure! 330 *Ode: Thanks.* 92
Were under her dominion placed. 413 *White Doe* 1582
Issues for that dominion overthrown: 435 *Ecc. Sonn.* 2. 27. 5
For thought—dominion vast and absolute 489 *Illus. Books* 4
A like dominion, and the midnight storm 647 *Prelude* 2. 373
Entered thy vast dominion? On the roof 707 *Prelude* 8. 543
Fell under the dominion of a taste 735 *Prelude* 12. 90
In absolute dominion. Gladly here, 736 *Prelude* 12. 131
Nowhere, dominion o'er the enlightened spirit 770 *Excursion* 1. 953
Claimed absolute dominion for the day. 772 *Excursion* 2. 89
Where are your triumphs? your dominion where? 827 *Excursion* 5. 347
And conquests over her dominion gained, 862 *Excursion* 7. 321
Of this dominion over nature gained, 877 *Excursion* 8. 211
A peaceable dominion, wide as earth, 894 *Excursion* 9. 665
Dominions. Or survey their bright dominions 217 **Inmate of* 21
And lo! those Birds, far-famed through Love's dominions, 374 *Eg. Maid* 320
Domo. *See* **Major-domo.**
Doncaster. "At Doncaster, at York, and Leeds, 239 *P. B.* 216
Done. (*Partial list.*) *See* **Ill-done.**
Much done, and much designed, and more desired,— 3 *Ev. Wk.* 83
And when the miserable work was done 25 *Guilt* 71
Of service done with cold formality, 31 *Guilt* 394
Their breakfast done, the pair, though loth, must part; 34 *Guilt* 532
And *he* had done the deed in the dark wood— 35 *Guilt* 607
Holla! No, no, the business must be done.— 43 *Bord.* 329
As I have done, my eyes upon the ground, 45 *Bord.* 433
A lucky woman!—go, you have done good service. 46 *Bord.* 518
What must be done? We will conduct her hither; 48 *Bord.* 593
The deed is done—if you will have it so— 48 *Bord.* 641
I would preserve thee. How may this be done? 49 *Bord.* 653
Touch not a finger—— What then must be done? 53 *Bord.* 877
Away! away!—— Nay, I have done with you: 54 *Bord.* 903
It shall be done as Wisdom shall decide: 58 *Bord.* 1129
And something shall be done which Memory 59 *Bord.* 1173
I will stroll on; you follow when 'tis done. 60 *Bord.* 1259
You have done your duty. I had hopes, which now 64 *Bord.* 1472
'Tis done, and in the after-vacancy 65 *Bord.* 1541
What has befallen you? A stranger has done this, 67 *Bord.* 1671
As I have done. A fresh tide of Crusaders 69 *Bord.* 1771
'Tis Nature's law. What I have done in darkness 71 *Bord.* 1877
I have done him no harm, 71 *Bord.* 1916
If she had never lived I had not done it!— 75 *Bord.* 2155
'Tis done! The ruthless traitor! A rash deed!— 78 *Bord.* 2319
Is out of mind—or done. 84 *Shepherd-boys* 15
As visions still more bright have done, and left no trace behind. 93 *Poet's Dream* 72
Had done so many offices about him, 100 *Brothers* 334
This done, he went on shipboard, and is now 102 *Brothers* 434
When that which has been done no wishes can undo. 104 *Artegal* 169
Think of evening's repose when our labour was done, 116 *Repentance* 27
What must be done? what will betide? 126 *Idiot Boy* 31
Had done him female service, not alone 133 *Michael* 154
As all their Forefathers had done; and, when 136 *Michael* 368
And hope for higher raptures, when life's day is done. 160 **Up with me* 31
They have done as worldlings do, 160 **Pansies, lilies* 54
They hear—when every dance is done, 177 *Waggoner* 2. 95
So said, so done; and masts, sails, yards, 178 *Waggoner* 2. 123
Thus Nature spake—The work was done— 187 **Three years* 37
Which had been done to her. 194 *Ruth* 222
"Some say that here a murder has been done, 203 *Hart-leap* 137
Their indefatigable flight. 'Tis done— 218 *Recluse* 1. 1. 216
And what was boldly promised, truly shall be done. 220 *Triad* 33
A work, one half of which was done 240 *P. B.* 312
As many a wiser man hath done, 240 *P. B.* 338
What may be done with Peter Bell! 245 *P. B.* 785
"Oh, mercy! something must be done, 248 *P. B.* 1058
O, my Belovèd! I have done thee wrong, 279 **Though I* 4
Nor cheer him; for the illustrious Swede hath done 305 **The Voice* 9
Never to rise again!—the work is done. 310 *Anticip.* 5
Suffered or done. When lawless violence 316 **Say, what* 5
The Ark, her melancholy voyage done! 348 *Sky-prosp.* 3

Done—*continued.*
Must, when my part is done, be ready; 370 *Eg. Maid* 110
Thy part is done—thy painful part; 401 *White Doe* 503
—'Twas done: his Sons were with him—all; 408 *White Doe* 1141
For, with God's will, it shall be done!'— 410 *White Doe* 1311
Had closed his door before the day was done. 453 **Calm is the* 17
Now that our morning meal is done, 482 *Sister* 10
And often, ere the chase was done, 483 *Simon Lee* 19
"The will of God be done!" 486 **We walked* 4
Hence, if we wept, it was not done in shame; 491 *Tribute: Dog* 34
Laughs at my pains, and seems to say, "Be done." 525 *Epist. Beaumont* 273
Which done, he bade that they the Jews should bind. 555 *Prioress* 169
And all this shall be done, without a nay, 562 *Cuck.andNight.*281
Vain service! yet not vainly done 579 **Sweet Flower* 57
Whose glorious work is done. 582 **O for a* 6
To whom a foul deed he had done, 621 *Andrew Jones* 9
Became my prey; and when the deed was done 637 *Prelude* 1. 321
As I had done in daily intercourse 654 *Prelude* 3. 353
Fulfilling (could enchantment have done more?) 700 *Prelude* 8. 83
Of what in the Great City had been done 708 *Prelude* 8. 626
Were bent upon undoing what was done: 711 *Prelude* 9. 133
Of ancient Institutions said and done 731 *Prelude* 11. 261
Apart from benefits received or done 810 *Excursion* 4. 579
Had done to her humanity no wrong: 821 *Excursion* 4. 1315
That which is done accords with what is known 826 *Excursion* 5. 256
And, when it is done, away he is gone; S.3. 423 *Tinker* 16
Shall speak of what is done among the fields, K.8. 247 *Recluse* 1.1.404
Done truly there, or felt, of solid good K.8. 247 *Recluse* 1.1.405
For that end only; something must be done. K.8. 255 *Recluse* 1.1.665
Till, at the last, thou hear the voice—"Well done, K.8. 325 [?] **The vestal* 13
Donnerdale. At all the merry pranks of Donnerdale! 379 *Duddon* 13. 14
Donor. Bending low before the Donor, 90 *Longest Day* 75
Let Bacchus, donor of soul-quick'ning cheer, 625 *Æneid* 112
The liberal donor of capacities 870 *Excursion* 7. 826
Donor's. The Donor's farewell blessing, can he dread 438 *Ecc. Sonn.* 2. 39. 7
Dons. He dons his coat of darkness: on the stage 691 *Prelude* 7. 281
Don't. "I only touch—not take—don't fear, S.3. 441 **The ball* 3
Doom. I greet thee, Chartreuse, while I mourn thy doom. 11 *Desc. Sk.* 53
By choice or doom a gipsy wanders here, 13 *Desc. Sk.* 175
"And from your doom," he added, "now I wait, 36 *Guilt* 652
Tut! let them gabble till the day of doom. 55 *Bord.* 963
But his own crime had brought on him this doom, 69 *Bord.* 1745
No more of that; in silence hear my doom: 78 *Bord.* 2339
Hide the knowledge of thy doom. 90 *Longest Day* 44
'He pines,' they'll say, 'it is his doom, 121 *EmigrantMother* 47
Since reason failed want is her threatened doom, 139 *Widow* 32
"Tempt me not, I pray; my doom is 140 *Arm. Lady* 49
If such their harsh untimely doom, 154 *Flower Garden* 17
One after one submitting to their doom, 169 **Never enlivened* 8
Destined, whate'er their earthly doom, 192 *Seq. Beggars* 41
Fitter hope, and nobler doom; 205 *Brougham* 139
"This visage tells thee that my doom is past: 210 *Laod.* 67
If to provoke such doom the Impious dare, 217 *Enterprise* 120
In truth the prison, unto which we doom 250 **Nuns fret* 8
Of Faith and Hope—if thou, by nature's doom, 271 *George: Death* 6
Her doom it is to press a weary bed— 273 **While Anna's* 5
Measuring the periods of his lonely doom, 273 **Not the* 6
Deaf, drooping, that is now his doom: 294 *Jedbor.* 21
For death will be his doom. 296 *Highland Boy* 105
Had fixed, for ever fixed, their doom! 298 *Brownie's Cell* 20
Such doom awaits us. Nay, forbid it Heaven! 316 **O'er the* 9
The captive chieftain, by a tyrant's doom, 318 **Is there* 2
Sad is thy doom, self-solaced dove, 334 **In Bruges* 29
But face like that sweet Boy their mortal doom, 339 *Tell* 21
Prefiguring his own impendent doom, 357 *Aquap.* 311
Whence half the breathing world received its doom; 368 *Trajan* 38
Once more: but, if unchangeable her doom, 372 *Eg. Maid* 256
Untouched memento of her hapless doom! 381 *Duddon* 22. 14
A choice that wears the aspect of a doom; 391 *Brownie* 10
To have no seat for thought were better doom, 394 **How profitless* 6
Espouse thy doom at once, and cleave 402 *White Doe* 544
Here hath a milder doom prevailed; 415 *White Doe* 1786
For Souls whose doom is fixed! The way is smooth 423 *Ecc. Sonn.* 1. 20 9
Of judgment such presumptuous doom repeat!) 437 *Ecc. Sonn.* 2. 35. 3
(By transit not unlike man's frequent doom) 461 **Who but is* 13
A pitiable doom; for respite brief 461 **Wherelies the truth* 2
The cloud is; but brings *that* a day of doom 471 **Despond who* 9
When thousands, by severer doom, 473 *Ossian* 45
And when, subjected to a common doom 474 **On to* 9
Fly where the culprit may, guilt meets a doom; 475 **Here on their* 12
Omen of man's grievous doom! 502 **Like a* 12
And, should a less unnatural doom confide 519 *Pun. Death* 11. 5
Since the primeval doom. Such is the grace 538 **In desultory* 29
And trust in God—to whose eternal doom 574 *Chiabrera* 3. 19
Sad doom, at Sorrow's shrine to kneel, 582 **O for a* 13
If sculptured emblems of our mortal doom 584 **With copious* 54
Ev'n now I sigh at hoary Chartreuse' doom 603 *Desc. Sk. Quarto* 53
The scale of liberty. I read her doom, 730 *Prelude* 11. 211
If man's estate, by doom of Nature yoked 742 *Prelude* 13. 175
How full their joy! Till, pitiable doom! 774 *Excursion* 2. 197
Sharp contradictions may arise, by doom 792 *Excursion* 3. 447
And grief spread wide; but Man escaped the doom 811 *Excursion* 4. 649
—And, as on earth it is the doom of truth 839 *Excursion* 6. 53
Such doom was hers; yet nothing could subdue 848 *Excursion* 6. 699
Till the stars sicken at the day of doom. 850 *Excursion* 6. 805
Of one who died within this vale, by doom 854 *Excursion* 6. 1076

Doom—*continued.*
His sentence to the axe would doom them all. 867 *Excursion* 7. 624
To the vast multitude; whose doom it is 885 *Excursion* 9. 90
Doomed. *See* **Death-doomed, Self-doomed.**
That thou, the slave of slaves, art doomed to pine 21 *Desc. Sk.* 588
For creatures doomed to breathe terrestrial air: 22 *Desc. Sk.* 647
By the good God, our common Father, doomed!— 62 *Bord.* 1345
Doomed to a third and last captivity, 124 *V. and J.* 185
Was doomed to wear out her appointed time, 212 *Laod.* 161
Nor grieves—tho' doomed thro' silent night to bear 216 *Enterprise* 95
Here is my body doomed to tread, this path, 230 *Clouds* 54
Or stubborn spirit doomed to yell 242 *P. B.* 513
Doomed, with their impious Lord, the flying Hart 267 **Though narrow* 13
Doomed as we are our native dust 337 *Cath. Cantons* 1
By godlike insight. To this fate is doomed 357 *Aquap.* 330
And temples, doomed to milder change, unfold 367 *Trajan* 3
Too harshly hath been doomed to taste 396 *White Doe* 19
If she be doomed to inward care, 397 *White Doe* 134
Which, though seemingly doomed in its breast to sustain 398 *White Doe* 238
Are doomed to perish utterly: 402 *White Doe* 533
—But thou, my Sister, doomed to be 402 *White Doe* 566
Which way the tide is doomed to flow. 404 *White Doe* 782
When such good work is doomed to be undone, 431 *Ecc. Sonn.* 2. 10. 10
Though doomed to tread in solitary ways, 441 *Ecc. Sonn.* 3. 4. 7
More hurtful here beset him, doomed though free, 470 **Did pangs* 12
Who, doomed to go in company with Pain, 493 *Hap. War.* 12
Are doomed to flounder on, like wounded whales 516 **As leaves* 13
The Roman Consul doomed his sons to die 517 *Pun. Death* 3. 1
And, the main fear once doomed to banishment, 519 *Pun. Death* 8. 6
If doomed to breathe against his lawful will 528 **Those breathing* 77
Been doomed so long to settle upon earth 569 *Cumb. Beg.* 187
And doomed him to contend in faithless courts, 573 *Chiabrera* 2. 3
And blast of trumpets. He who hath been doomed 574 *Chiabrera* 4. 5
Albeit lifeless then, and doomed to sleep 641 *Prelude* 1. 594
An eye of scorn:—"The lover," said he, "doomed 778 *Excursion* 2. 470
Not doomed to ignorance, though forced to tread, 802 *Excursion* 4. 47
Doomed to decay, and then expire in dust! 829 *Excursion* 5. 478
Is aught so certain as that man is doomed 831 *Excursion* 5. 587
Which hapless Ellen now was doomed to feel: 852 *Excursion* 6. 956
Low things with lofty) I too shall be doomed 873 *Excursion* 7. 1047
Is doom'd a Pincushion to be, S.3. 437 **I, whose* 18
He of the multitude whose eyes are doomed K.8. 252 *Recluse* 1. 1. 594
Dooms. 'Tis that worst principle of ill which dooms 70 *Bord.* 1812
That dooms her to a convent.—Who shall tell, 124 *V. and J.* 222
Door. *See* **Chamber-door, Church-door, Cottage-door, Garden-door, In-door, Next-door, Tavern-door.**
Found by the grassy door of mountain-farms. 5 *Ev. Wk.* 145
Each with its household boat beside the door; 12 *Desc. Sk.* 112
Descending, shuts for aye his prison door. 16 *Desc. Sk.* 331
The pendent grapes glittered above the door;— 24 *Guilt* 16
Nor raised my hand at any door to knock. 31 *Guilt* 373
With panniered asses driven from door to door; 32 *Guilt* 407
While to the door with eager speed they ran, 34 *Guilt* 559
I was compelled to seek my father's door, 35 *Guilt* 579
For I shall never see my father's door again. 35 *Guilt* 585
Thy Mother too!—scarce had I gained the door, 40 *Bord.* 182
Hovering round Herbert's door, a man whose figure 42 *Bord.* 278
Would stoop to skulk about a Cottage door— 42 *Bord.* 282
At Herbert's door. Ay; and if truth were known 46 *Bord.* 480
At Herbert's door—and when he stood beside 47 *Bord.* 539
Her lips for ever moving. At her door 47 *Bord.* 579
And begged our daily bread from door to door. 50 *Bord.* 692
The obstinate bolt of a small iron door 59 *Bord.* 1200
He may knock at the door,—we'll not let him in; 81 †*Address: Child* 40
Beside a human door! 82 *Lucy Gray* 8
A furlong from their door. 83 *Lucy Gray* 40
"Twelve steps or more from my mother's door, 84 *We are Seven* 39
The wide-spread boughs, for view of door, window, and stair that wound 92 *Poet's Dream* 38
I lighted—opened with soft touch the chapel's iron door, 92 *Poet's Dream* 41
The flowering shrubs that deck our humble door 106 *Farewell* 11
A fountain at my fond heart's door, 111 *A Complaint* 3
—Such change, and at the very door 111 *A Complaint* 17
Oh! do not dread thy mother's door; 117 *Affl. Marg.* 38
Filled the funeral basin at Timothy's door; 120 *Childless Father* 10
With a leisurely motion the door of his hut. 120 *Childless Father* 16
Could, by the simple opening of a door, 122 *V. and J.* 47
—Why bustle thus about your door, 126 *Idiot Boy* 7
And while the Mother, at the door, 127 *Idiot Boy* 87
And to the Doctor's door she hies; 128 *Idiot Boy* 243
And now she's at the Doctor's door, 128 *Idiot Boy* 247
Under the large old oak, that near his door 133 *Michael* 165
Were sitting at the door, "Thou must not go: 135 *Michael* 295
That grew beside their door; and the remains 138 *Michael* 480
And feeling sinks as deep! See there the door 138 *Widow* 3
Of sorrow in her heart while through her father's door, 140 *Arm. Lady* 77
And casement closed and door made fast, 144 **Driven in* 65
No door the tenement requires, 168 *Wren's Nest* 5
If he resist that tempting door, 174 *Waggoner* 1. 74
Of open door and shining light. 174 *Waggoner* 1. 98
Had almost reached the festive door, 177 *Waggoner* 2. 26
He draws him to the door—"Come in, 177 *Waggoner* 2. 47
The whip's loud notice from the door, 178 *Waggoner* 3. 3
Pass by her door—'tis seldom shut— 198 *Thorn* 95
And now, as he approached a vassal's door, 200 *Hart-leap* 3
Kind Nature keeps a heavenly door 228 *Devot. Incit.* 58
Even as he passed the door, these words 247 *P. B.* 956

Door—*continued.*
And stopped beside the door. 247 *P. B.* 995
Even thine, though few thy wants!—Roof, window, door, 250 *Admon.* 10
And found the door unbarred. 296 *Highland Boy* 140
Where gazed the peasant from his door, 343 *Eclipse* 29
Or they are offered at the door 375 **The Minstrels* 35
Undressed the pathway leading to the door; 390 *Highland Hut* 10
On road or path, or at the door 390 *Highland Broach* 21
Its impulse took—that sorrow-stricken door, 394 **No more* 21
Pass, pass who will, yon chantry door; 398 *White Doe* 242
And at the mansion's silent door, 402 *White Doe* 590
They met, when they had reached the door, 410 *White Doe* 1322
She arrogates o'er heaven's eternal door, 427 *Ecc. Sonn.* 1. 36. 3
Had closed his door before the day was done, 453 **Calm is the* 17
That stands beside our door. 482 *Sister* 4
Not twenty paces from the door, 483 *Simon Lee* 42
Shut close the door; press down the latch; 485 *Poet's Epitaph* 33
Darkening the window, ill defends the door 521 *Epist. Beaumont* 21
Pace between door and window muttering rhyme, 521 *Epist. Beaumont* 34
With door left open makes a gloomy spot, 524 *Epist. Beaumont* 220
A Redbreast, one that to his cottage door 531 **I know* 7
And any man who passed her door 536 *Goody Blake* 23
Then at her door the *canty* Dame 536 *Goody Blake* 39
The toll-gate, when in summer at her door 566 *Cumb. Beg.* 33
Ere he has passed the door, will turn away, 567 *Cumb. Beg.* 62
Worn out and worthless. While from door to door, 567 *Cumb. Beg.* 87
Who sits at his own door,—and, like the pear 568 *Cumb. Beg.* 117
Of this old Mendicant, and, from her door 568 *Cumb. Beg.* 159
Familiar with him, made an inn of his door: 569 *Farmer* 26
Is a cart-load of turf at an old woman's door? 572 *Avarice* 18
Found by the verdant door of mountain farms. 594 *Ev. Wk. Quarto* 128
Safe from your door ye hear at breezy morn, 596 *Ev. Wk. Quarto* 233
Each with his household boat beside the door, 604 *Desc. Sk. Quarto* 127
There, by the door a hoary-headed sire 605 *Desc. Sk. Quarto* 170
All night the door at every moment ope; 609 *Desc. Sk. Quarto* 409
Ev'n to the summer door his icy tide, 613 *Desc. Sk. Quarto* 599
For thy poor babes that, hurrying from the door, 615 *Desc. Sk. Quarto* 709
And to the door a neater pathway winds, 615 *Desc. Sk. Quarto* 727
Nor rest till they had reached the very door 633 *Prelude* 1. 73
But 'twas a splendid place, the door beset 644 *Prelude* 2. 142
Ran, ostrich-like, to reach our chapel door 653 *Prelude* 3. 304
Our cottage door, and evening soon brought on 660 *Prelude* 4. 143
Like an intruder knocking at the door 660 *Prelude* 4. 157
We reached a cottage. At the door I knocked, 665 *Prelude* 4. 449
The cottage door was speedily unbarred, 665 *Prelude* 4. 461
And lingered near the door a little space, 665 *Prelude* 4. 468
Of Winter that had warbled at my door, 687 *Prelude* 7. 41
Stationed above the door, like guardian saints; 689 *Prelude* 7. 162
Seated, with open door, often and long 705 *Prelude* 8. 411
Lodged only at the sanctuary's door, 728 *Prelude* 11. 91
Rise, from the top of Snowdon. To the door 746 *Prelude* 14. 6
Approach this door but she who dwelt within 763 *Excursion* 1. 498
This lonely Cottage. At the door he stood, 764 *Excursion* 1. 568
Its tender verdure. At the door arrived, 767 *Excursion* 1. 710
Was changed. As she unlocked the door, she said, 767 *Excursion* 1. 752
Stood undisturbed behind the door. And when, 769 *Excursion* 1. 854
And, to my feeling, ere we reached the door, 781 *Excursion* 2. 639
At my own door. The shapes before our eyes 788 *Excursion* 3. 124
Of fury; or, while snow is at the door, 813 *Excursion* 4. 795
Its wasted splendour to repair, the door 834 *Excursion* 5. 773
His door in darkness, nor till dusk returns. 834 *Excursion* 5. 808
Care not for me, he lingers round my door, 834 *Excursion* 5. 821
To the parental door; and with his sighs 844 *Excursion* 6. 381
I well remember, while I passed her door 849 *Excursion* 6. 759
A charitable door. So days and years 860 *Excursion* 7. 169
Of his bright hearth, and from his open door, 867 *Excursion* 7. 650
A fresh band meets them, at the crowded door— 877 *Excursion* 8. 176
Breathed over them: but suddenly the door 882 *Excursion* 8. 544
The dewy fields; but ere the Vicar's door 895 *Excursion* 9. 769
Right before the Farmer's door S.3. 423 *Tinker* 9
From my own door I shall be free to claim K.8. 250 *Recluse* 1. 1. 51
Door-place. He looks, through the open door-place, toward the lake 547 **Rude is* 27
Doors. *See* **Cottage-doors, Out-of-doors.**
Well! they might turn a beggar from their doors, 45 *Bord.* 439
For love of God I must not pass their doors; 46 *Bord.* 524
Shall sun himself before his native doors; 66 *Bord.* 1628
No ease, within doors or without; 115 *Last of Flock* 76
And from their occupations out of doors 132 *Michael* 96
And all the neighbours, as he passed their doors, 137 *Michael* 428
Comes from within doors or without! 143 **Driven in* 17
Who stirs little out of doors, 160 **Pansies, lilies* 38
The bird that comes about our doors 162 **Art thou the* 4
And all is dismal out of doors; 182 *Waggoner* 4. 247
All things that love the sun are out of doors; 195 *Resolution* 8
As of a dweller out of doors; 239 *P. B.* 292
Or He, whose bonds dropped off, whose prison doors 419 *Ecc. Sonn.* 1. 2. 9
Daily to think on old familiar doors, 458 *Sea-shore* 10
To fishers mending nets beside their doors; 522 *Epist. Beaumont* 45
And lonesome watch that out of doors he keeps; 523 *Epist. Beaumont* 138
When lowly doors were shut, 542 *Russ. Fug.* 22
For when he saw her doors fast bolted all, 562 *Troilus* 13
Thy cold doors; but I dare not for this rout; 563 *Troilus* 34
—Before those hermit doors, that never know 607 *Desc. Sk. Quarto* 299
No chair remained before the doors; the bench 642 *Prelude* 2. 11
Before the doors or windows of their cells 656 *Prelude* 3. 477
Sitting within doors between light and dark, 687 *Prelude* 7. 20
And all my young affections out of doors. 688 *Prelude* 7. 76

Doors—*continued.*
The spectacles within doors,—birds and beasts . 690 *Prelude* 7. 230
Aimed at the laggards slumbering within doors ; . 701 *Prelude* 8. 149
By his habitual wanderings out of doors, . . . 762 *Excursion* 1. 404
Her doors to admit this homeless Pensioner . . 783 *Excursion* 2. 744
Lay at the threshold and the inner doors ; . . 860 *Excursion* 7. 185
On all who entered those religious doors. . . 881 *Excursion* 8. 490
Door-way. Porch, door-way, or kirk-pillar ; and of youths, ... 701 *Prelude* 8. 152
Dora. Dora ! sport, as now thou sportest, . . . 90 *Longest Day* 13
Say, Dora ! tell me, by yon placid moon, . . . 165 *Parrot* 41
—O my own Dora, my belovèd child ! . . . . 496 **A little* 11
Dora's. O'er my little Dora's face ; . . . . . 171 *Kitten* 104
Dor-hawk. The buzzing dor-hawk, round and round, is wheeling,— . . . . 173 *Waggoner* 1. 3
The busy dor-hawk chases the white moth . . . 453 **Calm is the* 22
Dorhawk's. Soft as the Dorhawk's to a distant ear, 255 *S. H.* 5
Dormitory. Ere we lie down in our last dormitory ? 281 **What strong* 14
Dormitory's. For dormitory's length laid bare . . 397 *White Doe* 122
Dormouse. Lay passive as a dormouse in mid winter. 69 *Bord.* 1767
Dost. (*Partial list.*)
Stern Lawgiver ! yet thou dost wear . . . . 492 *Duty* 41
"O Thou great God that dost perform Thy laud . 555 *Prioress* 156
Tell me the cause why thou dost sing this hymn, 555 *Prioress* 196
Such uncouth singing verily dost thou make. . . 558 *Cuck.andNight.*115
As thou dost in thy throat, I wot not how. . . 559 *Cuck.andNight.*120
As thou dost mine with longing her to see, . . 563 *Troilus* 79
Dotage. And Love in old folk a great dotage is ; . 559 *Cuck.andNight.*169
Through the lost look of dotage, is cunning and sly : 572 *Avarice* 22
In the last dotage of a dying form. . . . . . K.8. 223 **There is a shapeless* 4
Dotard. Of drowsy, dotard Time ;— . . . . . . 214 *Kirkstone* 32
Dotards. And none look grave but dotards. He may live . . . . 54 *Bord.* 929
Impostors, drivellers, dotards, as the ape . . . 673 *Prelude* 5. 525
Doth. (*Partial list.*)
For my old age, it doth remain with thee . . . 40 *Bord.* 190
Doth prey alike on two distracted Countries, . . 41 *Bord.* 209
That doth concern this Herbert ? You are provoked, ... 46 *Bord.* 498
Which doth play tricks with them that look on it : 54 *Bord.* 924
"She asketh, and she piteously doth pray . . 555 *Prioress* 149
This Provost doth for those bad Jews prepare . 555 *Prioress* 178
"Upon his bier this Innocent doth lie . . . . 555 *Prioress* 184
Before the altar while the Mass doth last : . . 555 *Prioress* 185
Since that thy throat is cut, as it doth seem.' . 555 *Prioress* 197
This unto their rememberance doth bring . . . 557 *Cuck. and Night.* 28
And of that longing heaviness doth come, . . . 557 *Cuck. and Night.* 31
Such shaking doth the fever in me keep . . . 557 *Cuck. and Night.* 41
In which Love's dart its fiery point doth steep. . 557 *Cuck. and Night.* 45
True lovers doth so bitterly annoy, ... 560 *Cuck.andNight.*199
Whereof her hourly bearing proof doth give ; . . 562 *Cuck.andNight.*296
Doth find herself insensibly disposed . . . . 567 *Cumb. Beg.* 104
"It doth not love the shower, nor seek the cold: 571 **There is a Flower* 14
That patience now doth seem a thing of which . 572 *Animal Tran.* 11
I doubt not, when to you it doth impart . . . 818 *Excursion* 4. 1143
Double. Disclose a naked guide-post's double head, 26 *Guilt* 134
I felt a double fever in my veins, ... 68 *Bord.* 1695
"A bowl, a bowl of double measure," . . . . 178 *Waggoner* 2. 145
Lurking in a double shade, ... 180 *Waggoner* 4. 44
His body was bent double, feet and head . . . 196 *Resolution* 66
The double note, as if with living power, . . . 229 *Cuckoo-clock* 10
His double front among Atlantic clouds, . . . 251 **Pelion and* 13
Float double, swan and shadow ! . . . . . 293 *Yarrow Unv.* 44
When thou, uprisen, shalt break thy double yoke, 361 *Alban Hills* 12
Or surely you'll grow double : . . . . . . 481 *Tables Turned* 2
And season's difference—a double tree . . . . 585 *Ch. Lamb* 96
She dreads the treacherous house, the double tongue ; . . . . 624 *Æneid* 7
Doubled. It only doubled his distress ; . . . . 244 *P. B.* 707
And doubled (prospect ever bettering) . . . . S. 3. 438 **My Lord* 9
Double-dealing. Knew not the double-dealing of a smile ; . . . . 470 **A youth* 11
Flattery and double-dealing, strife and wrong. . K.8. 246*Recluse* 1.1.357
Double-faced. Life, like that Roman Jânus, double-faced ; . . . . 775 *Excursion* 2. 251
Doublet. Of stole and doublet, hood and scarf, . 396 *White Doe* 5
Doubling. Doubling and doubling with laborious walk, ... 389 *Glencroe* 1
Doubly. Doubly depressed, setting, and in her wane ? 279 *'*Tis he* 8
The strain seemed doubly dear, ... 334 **In Bruges* 14
Or seek to make assurance doubly sure. . . . 445 *Ecc. Sonn.* 3. 21. 12
Blest are the moments, doubly blest, ... 506 *Lab. Hymn* 13
But doubly pitying Nature loves to show'r . . 602 *Desc. Sk. Quarto* 13
But doubly fortunate my lot ; not here . . . 703 *Prelude* 8. 312
Doubt. The Vagrant must, no doubt, be loitering somewhere . . . . 44 *Bord.* 365
No doubt you have been nobly entertained ? . . 53 *Bord.* 865
Of doubt is unsupportable. Pity, the facts . . 53 *Bord.* 880
How, when the People's mind was racked with doubt, ... 62 *Bord.* 1383
A plain confession, such as leaves no doubt, . . 63 *Bord.* 1420
Of interfering Heaven, I have no doubt, . . . 75 *Bord.* 2129
That he began to doubt ; and even to hope . . 96 *Brothers* 88
Possess a kind of second life : no doubt . . . 98 *Brothers* 185
That would bring down his spirit ; and no doubt, 100 *Brothers* 319
He would himself, no doubt, be happy then . . 100 *Brothers* 327
And so no doubt he perished. When the Youth . 101 *Brothers* 401
No doubt too he the moon had seen ; . . . . 131 *Idiot Boy* 444
Puzzles the listener with a doubt . . . . . 143 **Driven in* 15

Doubt—*continued.*
I have not a doubt but he, ... 161 **Pleasures newly* 9
Nor doubt that something of their spirit swayed . 170 **Never enlivened* 20
It is a doubt with Benjamin . . . . 174 *Waggoner* 1. 68
Though changed, no doubt, from what I was when first . . . . 206 *Tintern* 66
By doubt, propelled thee to the fatal shore ; . . 210 *Laod.* 52
Pure transport undisturbed by doubt or fear . . 213 *Dion* 26
Released from fear and doubt ; . . . . . . 223 *'*Tis gone* 3
A Voice shall finish doubt and dim foreseeing, . 235 *Power of Sound* 211
"No doubt," quoth he, "he is the Master. . . 243 *P. B.* 584
No doubt the devil in me wrought ; . . . . 245 *P. B.* 813
Crossing the waters) doubt, and something dark, . 258 **Where lies the Land* 12
Nor doubt that He marked also for his own . . 275 *Gravestone* 10
His Mother, too, no doubt, above . . . . . 295 *Highland Boy* 26
So that a doubt almost within me springs . . . 309 **When, looking* 8
Nor doubt but He to whom yon Pine-trees nod . 337 *Aar* 12
And its truth who shall doubt ? for his Spirit is here ; . . . . 364 *Vallomb.* 10
With doubt, with fear, and haply with remorse : . 383 *Duddon* 30. 4
The doubt returns against his will : . . . . . 398 *White Doe* 197
Of Brancepeth look in doubt and fear, ... 402 *White Doe* 595
Of the noon-day. Nor doubt that golden cords . 423 *Ecc. Sonn.* 1. 18. 10
Doubt came not, nor regret— . . . . 478 *Somnamb.* 33
Unchecked by pride or scrupulous doubt, . . . 486 **Bright Flower* 18
Of my own wish ; and feel past doubt . . . . 492 *Duty*
Can the pitying spirit doubt . . . . 502 **Like a* 23
He, doubt not, with involuntary dread, . . . 528 **Those breathing* 108
Haply that child in fearful doubt may gaze, . . 609 *Desc.Sk.Quarto* 410
And thou wilt doubt, with me less aptly skilled . 645 *Prelude* 2. 222
Of pain, and doubt, and fear, yet yielding not . 672 *Prelude* 5. 419
While every moment added doubt to doubt, . . 683 *Prelude* 6. 578
And Ossian (doubt not—'tis the naked truth) . 695 *Prelude* 7. 567
Hope takes, or Doubt or Fear is forced to wear, . 710 *Prelude* 9. 61
Then doubt is not, and truth is more than truth,— 715 *Prelude* 9. 404
I added, work of safety : from all doubt . . . 720 *Prelude* 10. 143
Cried, "Robespierre is dead !"—nor was a doubt, 726 *Prelude* 10. 573
And loved the haunts of children ; here, no doubt, 778 *Excursion* 2. 449
From doubt and sorrow, than the senseless grave ?" 789 *Excursion* 3. 224
But in her stead—fear—doubt—and agony !" . 792 *Excursion* 3. 461
I cannot doubt that they whom you deplore . . 804 *Excursion* 4. 188
Doubt shall be quelled and trouble chased away ; 804 *Excursion* 4. 234
Of doubt and bold denial hourly urged . . . 812 *Excursion* 4. 734
I doubt not, when to you it doth impart . . . 818 *Excursion* 4. 1143
Doubt to cast off and weariness ; in trust . . 827 *Excursion* 5. 304
We may not doubt that who can best subject . 830 *Excursion* 5. 517
Such do I mean who, unperplexed by doubt, . . 831 *Excursion* 5. 596
"Doubt can be none," the Pastor said, "for whom 862 *Excursion* 7. 340
No just remembrance, scruple, or wise doubt ? . 873 *Excursion* 7. 1029
Nor less to be deplored. For who can doubt . . 886 *Excursion* 9. 177
The doubt to which a wavering hope had clung . S. 3. 432 **The doubt* 1
No doubt if you in terms direct had asked . . K.8. 230 **I will* 178
Doubted. Crossed by misfortune, or of doubted faith ? . . . . 508 *F. Stone* 45
Nor doubted once but that they both were books, 667 *Prelude* 5. 113
Who doubted not that Providence had times . . 723 *Prelude* 10. 340
Was full ; and had, I doubted not, returned, . . 883 *Excursion* 8. 590
Doubtful. Tell seemingly no doubtful tale ; . . . 110 *Forsaken* 9
Detains me, doubtful of the event ; . . . . 113 *Lament* 53
Or, in no doubtful prospect, let me see . . . 220 *Triad* 5
No glimpse it is, no doubtful gleam ; . . . . 247 *P. B.* 1003
Thy presence turns the scale of doubtful fight, . 328 *Ode 1815* 112
Into the doubtful future. Who would keep . . 354 *Aquap.* 115
Involved a history of no doubtful sense, . . . 359 **Complacent Fictions* 2
To lifted eyelids, and a doubtful shining. . . 374 *Eg. Maid* 336
Till doubtful combat issued in a trance . . . 383 *Duddon* 29. 5
The sacred Structures for less doubtful gains. . 424 *Ecc. Sonn.* 1. 24. 8
That had been offered to his doubtful choice . . 859 *Excursion* 7. 135
Doubtfully. Not doubtfully perceived.—Look homeward now ! . . . . 219 **This Height* 28
Hues doubtfully begun and ended ; . . . . . 231 **The gentlest Poet* 20
A Form not doubtfully descried :— . . . . 300 *Cora Linn* 26
Shapes fairer or less doubtfully discerned . . . 662 *Prelude* 4. 274
Doubting. Gazing, doubting, questioning ; . . . 399 *White Doe* 315
On fireside listeners, doubting what they hear ! . 453 **Calm is the* 15
Or at a doubting Judge's stern command, . . . 500 *Humanity* 3
Though but a doubting hope, that they might serve 585 *Ch. Lamb* 41
Much I rejoiced, not doubting but a guide . . 667 *Prelude* 5. 81
By moonlight, doubting not that day was nigh, . 685 *Prelude* 6. 695
Strong and perturbed, not doubting at that time 721 *Prelude* 10. 210
Doubtless. Doubtless shall cheat full oft the heart's desires ; . . . . 429 *Ecc. Sonn.* 2. 3. 9
In peaceful earth : for, doubtless, he was frank, . 470 **A youth* 9
Attended, doubtless, with a little pride, . . . 659 *Prelude* 4. 74
Doubtless, I should have then made common cause 721 *Prelude* 10. 229
And their arrangement, doubtless must be deemed 788 *Excursion* 3. 125
Wealthier, and doubtless wiser, than before ! . . 789 *Excursion* 3. 189
And, doubtless, sometimes, when the hair was shed 812 *Excursion* 4. 753
Not, doubtless, without help of female taste . . 882 *Excursion* 8. 541
That doubtless wanted not its tender moods, . . K.8. 256*Recluse* 1.1.704
Doubts. Whose natural affection doubts enslave, . 104 *Artegal* 124
On all sides doubts and terrors met her ; . . . 130 *Idiot Boy* 418
In them disheartening doubts and dread ; . . . 178 *Waggoner* 3. 6
His fears, his doubts, may now take flight— . . 181 *Waggoner* 4. 130
Whence doubts that came too late, and wishes vain, 213 *Dion* 58
By doubts and thousand petty fancies crost . . 251 **Beloved Vale* 9
Speak, that my torturing doubts their end may know ! . . . . 277 **Why art* 14

Dragon's—continued.
Even as a dragon's eye that feels the stress . . 266 *Even as 1
Drained. Among the mountains, fens which might be drained : . . . . K.8. 227 *I will 103
What slopes are planted, or what mosses drained ! 522 Epist.Beaumont 68
Dramas. When Art was young ; dramas of living men, ... 691 Prelude 7. 290
Dramatic. That some dramatic tale, endued with shapes . . . . 731 Prelude 11. 283
Drank. No Gothic conqueror ever drank) revealed 102 Artegal 11
This water was perhaps the first he drank . 203 Hart-leap 151
On pictures to gaze where they drank in their hues ; 345 Stanzas: Simplon 7
Most fair, most welcome, when they drank the dew 361 *List—'twas 14
Tells that their turf drank purple from the veins 383 Duddon 29. 3
It seemed as if he drank it up— . . . 486 Matthew 27
Libations, to thy memory drank, till pride . 653 Prelude 3. 299
Ate, drank, and with the fruit and glasses played, 692 Prelude 7. 362
Nor any voice of joy ; his spirit drank . . 759 Excursion 1. 206
Drapery. Though of gorgeous drapery proud, 502 *Like a 28
Of sculptured oak stood here, with drapery lined ; 825 Excursion 5. 165
Draught. A draught of water ? Nay, to see you thus 52 Bord. 800
A minute past, he went to fetch a draught . 52 Bord. 808
Cries Benjamin, " a draught of length ! . . 178 Waggoner 2. 146
A deep, determined, desperate draught ! . . 178 Waggoner 2. 156
—And though to every draught of vital breath, . 226 Vernal Ode 48
And, with that draught, the life-blood : misery, shame, ... 432 Ecc. Sonn. 2. 16. 8
He rais'd the bowl, and took a long deep draught ; 441 Ecc. Sonn. 3. 3. 13
Draughts. I bring the draughts of milk, warm milk it is and new. . . . . 87 Pet-lamb 44
Large draughts of love unhappy Dido drew . 625 Æneid 133
Draw. Much need have ye that time more closely draw . . . . 33 Guilt 507
Should he, by tales which would draw tears from iron, ... 57 Bord. 1060
Were that man, who could draw the line that parts 63 Bord. 1449
" To draw, out of the object of his eyes," . 110 *Look at 20
Draw from my heart the pain away. . . . 145 Her Eyes 34
And music from that pipe could draw . . 192 Ruth 8
Could draw, when we had parted, vain delight, . 211 Laod. 113
O the charm that manners draw, . . . 222 Triad 154
Can draw, and sing his griefs to rest. . . 233 Power of Sound 64
More cautious as they draw more near ; . . 297 Highland Boy 198
Flew high above Atlantic waves, to draw . 388 Eagles 8
" Look, there she is, my Child ! draw near ; . 398 White Doe 178
Shall draw, the limits of the power define, . 423 Ecc. Sonn. 1. 18. 13
" My Oarsmen," quoth the mighty King, " draw near. . . . . 426 Ecc. Sonn. 1. 30. 4
Slain by Compatriot protestants that draw . 442 Ecc. Sonn. 3. 7. 10
Calm as an undercurrent, strong to draw . 442 Ecc. Sonn. 3. 9. 1
Far-distant images draw nigh. . . . 457 *Had this 25
Can draw warmth from the cheek of my Love ; 484 *A plague 2
A Lawyer art thou ?—draw not nigh ! . . 485 Poet's Epitaph 5
Still, as we nearer draw to life's dark goal, . 497 Lycoris 53
And, what ye cannot reach by statute, draw . 516 *Feel for 13
Under the steel his hand had dared to draw. . 517 Pun. Death 2. 8
Which from their own blind hearts they draw ; 534 *Blest is 76
Them therefore with wild horses did he draw, 555 Prioress 182
Nor ever while I live Love's yoke to draw . 559 Cuck.andNight.140
Like a magnet, the heart of old Adam can draw ; 570 Farmer 78
To spots remote, and draw his diagrams . . 677 Prelude 6. 151
To single forms and objects, whence they draw, 696 Prelude 7. 623
The ill-fated pair) in that plain tale will draw 717 Prelude 9. 566
Enrapt ; but brightest things are wont to draw 726 Prelude 10. 528
'Mong other consolations, we may draw . 752 Prelude 14. 428
Even of the dead ; contented thence to draw . 765 Excursion 1. 629
To draw the line of comfort that divides . 772 Excursion 2. 72
On serious minds : then, as the Hindoos draw 790 Excursion 3. 254
Had power to draw him from the world, resolved 871 Excursion 7. 938
Would draw out of his heart the mysteries . K.8. 227 *I will 95
Drawing. While they are drawing the sacred floor . . . . 20 Desc. Sk. 557
The Babe was drawing in its quiet food. . 124 V. and J. 216
And, drawing to his side, to him did say, . 196 Resolution 83
With weary pace is drawing nigh ; . . 249 P. B. 1106
Drawing an ebon car, their hue . . . 371 Eg. Maid 179
While drawing toward the car Sir Gawaine, mailed 373 Eg. Maid 285
And, drawing nigh, with his living eye, . . 479 Somnamb. 120
To both I listened, drawing from them both . 633 Prelude 1. 57
Who, drawing near their final home, and much . 844 Excursion 6. 388
In order, drawing toward their wished-for home. 858 Excursion 7. 71
Drawn. See **Deep-drawn, First-drawn, Long-drawn.**
When round my wrist I felt a cord drawn tight, 55 Bord. 965
Drawn by what peculiar spell, . . . 161 *Pleasures newly 41
But all things else about her drawn . . 186 *She was 7
Drawn in defiance of the Gods, hath laid . 214 Dion 108
Disposed some cultured Flowerets (drawn from spots . . . . 280 Valedict. 2
Drawn almost into frightful neighbourhood. . 306 *Inland, within 4
The solemnising veil was drawn . . . 343 Eclipse 19
That might have drawn down Clio from the skies 359 Plea : Hist. 7
Drawn to his side by look or act of love . 362 *List—'twas 58
Of things not seen, drawn forth from their recess, 436 Ecc. Sonn. 2. 30. 4
Drawn from the wisdom that begins with fear, 454 *The Sun, that 24
Truths whose thick veil Science has drawn aside ? 469 *Desire we 3
For beverage drawn as from a mountain-well. 469 *Why stand 10
Then Arts, which still had drawn a softening grace 476 *Tranquillity ! the 10
Drawn toward the centre whence those sighs creep forth . . . . 498 *Enough of climbing 39

Drawn—continued.
That, drawn from this one hour of rest, . . 506 Lab. Hymn 14
Drawn forth by pressure of his gilded chains, . 528 *Those breathing 101
Drawn from the Sacrifice fulfilled . . 533 *Blest is 27
Drawn from love's purest earthly fount for him 646 Prelude 2. 247
Whence profit may be drawn in times to come. 658 Prelude 3. 628
I mean, O distant Friend ! a story drawn . 691 Prelude 7. 296
Of vanished nations, or more clearly drawn . 708 Prelude 8. 615
My thoughts by slow gradations had been drawn 709 Prelude 8. 677
From their beginnings, inasmuch as drawn . 731 Prelude 11. 289
And lastly, from its progress have we drawn . 749 Prelude 14. 203
When she upheld the cool refreshment drawn . 763 Excursion 1. 504
Drawn towards her native firmament of heaven, . 807 Excursion 4. 396
—Our cogitations this way have been drawn, . 829 Excursion 5. 479
Drawn from her cottage, on that aery height, . 834 Excursion 5. 758
Drawn from his vitals ? Say what meant the woes 846 Excursion 6. 542
Drawn from the chords of the ancient British harp 857 Excursion 7. 11
Drawn by the sunshine—at that hopeful season . 867 Excursion 7. 682
Suffers like loss when drawn out of the soul, . S.3. 434 *The doubt 64
Draws. That lightly draws its breath, . . 83 We are Seven 2
He draws him to the door—" Come in, . . 177 Waggoner 2. 47
Nearer she draws ; a breeze uplifts her veil ; . 220 Triad 43
Points she to aught ?—the bliss draws near, . 223 Wishing-gate 5
And Peter draws him to dry land ; . . 243 P. B. 581
What strong allurement draws, what spirit guides, 281 *What strong 1
The Romanist exults ; fresh hope he draws . 439 Ecc. Sonn. 2. 41. 9
Less humble, draws her lessons, aims, and rules. 468 St. Bees 155
Of all her peaks and ridges. What he draws 468 *Ranging the 6
And, while the mortal mist is gathering, draws . 494 Hap. War. 82
Enraptured Art draws from those sacred springs. 500 Humanity 19
Draws lightning down upon the head . . 550 Hermit's Cell 5. 11
And as on glorious ground he draws his breath, . 612 Desc.Sk.Quarto 536
The learned song from Tyrian hearers draws . 625 Æneid 130
Or draws for minds that are left free to trust . 669 Prelude 5. 276
Which, in his tuneful course, the wind draws forth 782 Excursion 2. 697
From which she draws her meagre sustenance. . 786 Excursion 3. 28
It draws its nourishment imperceptibly— . . 794 Excursion 3. 581
I freely gather ; and my leisure draws . . 856 Excursion 6. 1167
A cabinet stored with gems and pictures—draws . 874 Excursion 8. 23
Dread. In the roofed bridge ; the bridge, in that dread hour, ... 14 Desc. Sk. 184
And oft, when that dread vision hath past by, . 18 Desc. Sk. 461
" Here thou need'st not dread the raven in the sky ; 88 Pet-lamb 57
Oh ! do not dread thy mother's door ; . . 117 Affl. Marg. 38
I dread the rustling of the grass ; . . 117 Affl. Marg. 65
The bane of all that dread the devil ! . . 129 Idiot Boy 336
" Lady ! dread the wish, nor venture . . 140 Arm. Lady 25
And do not dread the waves below, . . 145 Her Eyes 43
" Dread not their taunts, my little Life ; . 145 Her Eyes 71
His whip they do not dread—his voice . . 174 Waggoner 1. 103
Dread pair that, spite of wind and weather, . 175 Waggoner 1. 178
In them disheartening doubts and dread ; . . 178 Waggoner 2. 178
With dread of what will happen next ; . . 179 Waggoner 3. 61
" Whate'er the weak may dread, the wicked dare, 215 Kirkstone 85
Dread Minister of wrath ! . . . . 216 Enterprise 104
For from the summit of BLACK COMB (dread name 218 *This Height 2
Nor dread the depth of meditative eye ; . . 222 Triad 193
Of dread eternity. . . . . . 223 Wishing-gate 72
With dread precision, ye made clear . . 226 Present. 64
From dread of emptiness or dearth. . . 227 Vernal Ode 60
Intricate labyrinth, more dread for thought . 232 Power of Sound 5
Suspicion ripened into dread ; . . . 241 P. B. 421
And straight in sorrow, not in dread, . . 241 P. B. 438
Dread Spirits ! to confound the meek . . 245 P. B. 761
Dread Beings ! and your empire show . . 245 P. B. 774
Had past a sudden shock of dread, . . 248 P. B. 1082
Deep thought, or dread remembrance, had I none. 251 *Beloved Vale 8
Ward of the Law !—dread Shadow of a King ! 271 George : Death 1
From the dread chasm, woods climbing above woods, ... 272 Devil's Bridge 10
Lay couched ; on him or his dread bow unbent . 273 *When Philoctetes 3
Yet—though dread Powers, that work in mystery, spin . . . . 280 *Oh what 2
And Love her towers of dread foundation laid . 282 *In my 10
At this dread moment—even so— . . 285 Grave of Burns 51
And babble of her pastime !—On, dread Power ! . 315 *Advance—come 9
Ah no ! though Nature's dread protection fails, . 315 *And is it 5
Dread trials ! yet encountered and sustained . 316 *Hail, Zaragoza 12
For he it was—dread Winter ! who beset, . 321 *Humanity,delighting 13
Dread King of Kings, vouchsafe a ray divine . 323 *Now that 1
Dread mark of approbation, justly gained ! . 331 Ode : Thanks. 159
Yet a dread local recompense we found ; . 334 *A winged 10
Of God himself from dread pre-eminence— . 340 Ranz 11
Dread hour ! when, upheaved by war's sulphurous blast, ... 340 Fort Fuentes 1
For Tell's dread archery renowned, . . 342 Ital. Itin. 60
Smiting with fury ; and a deeper dread . . 346 Processions 13
From the dread summit of the Queen . . 347 *Lulled by 3
As the dread Voice that speaks from out the sea . 349 At Dover 11
Of mind, that dread heart-freezing discipline, . 362 *List—'twas 44
From hope too distant, not to dread another. . 373 Eg. Maid 294
Of love emboldened, hope with dread entwining, . 374 Eg. Maid 332
Dread swell of sound ! loud as the gusts that lash 379 Duddon 13. 7
Dread arbitress of mutable respect, . . 380 Duddon 18. 2
To what dread Powers He delegates his part . 389 Tyndrum 13
A valiant man, and a name of dread . . 399 White Doe 250
Twelve years had reigned, a Sovereign dread ; 400 White Doe 361
In all its dread emblazonry . . . . 403 White Doe 683
By those dread symbols sanctified . . . 405 White Doe 848

Dread—*continued.*
And with dread signs the nascent Stream invest ? 418 *Ecc. Sonn.* 1. 2. 8
They come—and onward travel without dread, . 422 *Ecc. Sonn.* 1. 14. 7
The Donor's farewell blessing, can he dread . . 438 *Ecc. Sonn.* 2. 39. 7
Of dread Jehovah ; then should wood and waste . 440 *Ecc. Sonn.* 2. 46. 6
Through gloomiest shade ; put on (nor dread its weight) . . . . 446 *Ecc. Sonn.* 3. 25. 13
A crown for Hope !—I dread the boasted lights . 448 *Ecc. Sonn.* 3. 33. 6
When each pale brow to dread hosannas bowed . 450 *Ecc. Sonn.* 3. 40. 3
Dread Power ! whom peace and calmness serve . 458 **Had this* 69
Is crossed by knowledge, or by dread, of change, 458 *Sea-shore* 18
Dread cliff of Baruth ! *that* wild wish may sleep, . 466 *St. Bees* 19
That Tomb, dread centre of all sanctities . . . 467 *St. Bees* 107
No; their dread service nerves the heart it warms, 469 **The feudal* 13
Why keep *we* else the instincts whose dread law . 474 **Ye shadowy* 10
From the dread bosom of the unknown past, . . 477 *Long Meg* 3
He will not dread with Thee a toilsome day— . 489 *Spade* 25
They fail, thy saving arms, dread Power ! around them cast. . . . . 492 *Duty* 16
His arms, as swimmers use, and plunge—dread thought, ... 496 **A little* 30
Presignified by that dread strife . . . . . 503 **Like a* 75
They know the dread requital's source profound ; 520 *Pun. Death* 13. 5
He, doubt not, with involuntary dread, . . . 528 **Those breathing* 108
Nothing has he now to dread. . . . . . . 535 *Egremont* 62
With earnest pains unchecked by dread . . . 543 *Russ. Fug.* 113
With face all pale with dread and busy thought, . 554 *Prioress* 138
And dread of shame that will not do amiss ; . . 559 *Cuck.andNight.* 158
And he for dread did fly away full fast ; . . . 560 *Cuck.andNight.* 219
Dread Lord ! so fearful when provoked, thine ire 563 *Troilus* 71
As one that standeth betwixt hope and dread. . 564 *Troilus* 112
And said, I am in constant dread I trow, . . . 564 *Troilus* 145
O dread reverse ! if aught *be* so, which proves 576 **By a* 5
By whose unpathway'd margin still and dread . 607 *Desc.Sk.Quarto* 285
When the dread peal of swelling torrents fills . 612 *Desc.Sk.Quarto* 552
His last dread pleasure ! watches to the plain— . 613 *Desc.Sk.Quarto* 620
Such apt occasion that I dread a snare. . . 624 *Æneid* 22
How looked Achilles—their dread paramount— . 625 *Æneid* 138
Of him thou lovest ; need I dread from thee . 641 *Prelude* 1. 629
Of awe or tremulous dread, that had given way . 662 *Prelude* 4. 253
To melt away ; and further, the dread awe . . 676 *Prelude* 6. 60
Dread nothing ? From this height I shall not stoop 717 *Prelude* 9. 541
Their dread vibration to this hour prolonged ? . 725 *Prelude* 10. 460
May sort with highest objects, then—dread Power ! 755 *Recluse* 1. 1. 853
Whereon a full-grown man might rest, nor dread . 777 *Excursion* 2. 421
Dread of the persecuting sword, remorse, . . . 791 *Excursion* 3. 373
Of these wild hills. For, lo ! the dread Bastille, . 796 *Excursion* 3. 709
—In Britain, ruled a panic dread of change ; . . 798 *Excursion* 3. 827
Of his perfections ; with habitual dread . . . 801 *Excursion* 4. 24
What more that may not perish ?—Thou, dread source, ... 802 *Excursion* 4. 79
Through sinful choice ; or dread necessity . . 803 *Excursion* 4. 128
And the dread soul within it—should exist . . 816 *Excursion* 4. 976
To see disclosed, by such dread proof, how ill . 826 *Excursion* 5. 255
The internal pangs, are ready ; the dread strife . 846 *Excursion* 6. 555
Dread life of conflict ! which I oft compared . . 849 *Excursion* 6. 734
Or dread was all that had been thought of,—joy . 852 *Excursion* 6. 910
For (blinded by an over-anxious dread . . . 852 *Excursion* 6. 957
That the dread storm is weathered by them both. 867 *Excursion* 7. 647
To dread his perseverance in the chase. . . . 868 *Excursion* 7. 746
Hence a dread arm of floating power, a voice . . 876 *Excursion* 8. 143
At the pretty Maiden's dread . . . . . . S.3. 424 *Tinker* 42

Dreaded. The word, by others dreaded, he can hear 125 *V. and J.* 227
And breathless calms no longer dreaded, . . . 216 *Enterprise* 78
Soon to become more dreaded enemies . . . 420 *Ecc. Sonn.* 1. 9. 13
To be *most* dreaded ? Lawgivers, beware, . . 518 *Pun. Death* 4. 6
Such offering BEAUMONT dreaded and forbade, . 583 **With copious* 5
Sweet honey out of spurned or dreaded weeds. . 669 *Prelude* 5. 278
So dreaded, so abhorred. The day deserves . . 725 *Prelude* 10. 513
Of their most dreaded foe, the strong South-west 833 *Excursion* 5. 702
By others dreaded as the luckless thrall . . . 841 *Excursion* 6. 226

Dreadful. He bore within a breast where dreadful quiet reigned. . . . . 36 *Guilt* 648
Found dreadful provocation : for at night, . . 123 *V. and J.* 125
And Susan has a dreadful night. . . . . . 127 *Idiot Boy* 156
I fear you're in a dreadful way, ... 128 *Idiot Boy* 195
A fierce and dreadful hunter he ; . . . . . 129 *Idiot Boy* 328
And many dreadful fears beset her, ... 130 *Idiot Boy* 413
Large space ('mid dreadful clouds) of purest sky, 264 *Storm* 11
All power was given her in the dreadful trance ; . 313 *Prophecy* 9
Of dreadful sacrifice ; by Russian blood . . . 322 **By Moscow* 2
How dreadful the dominion of the impure ! . . 330 *Ode : Thanks.* 92
The annunciation of the dreadful truth . . . 343 *Last Sup.* 9
And dreadful respite. Thus was Alban tried, . 420 *Ecc. Sonn.* 1. 6. 9
For all things are less dreadful than they seem. . 420 *Ecc. Sonn.* 1. 7. 14
Breaks off the dreadful kiss with angry shriek. . 597 *Ev. Wk. Quarto* 288
Implores the dreadful untried sleep of death. . . 613 *Desc.Sk.Quarto* 643
Dim dreadful faces thro' the gloom appear, . . 614 *Desc.Sk.Quarto* 650
Hostility—how dreadful when it comes, . . . 792 *Excursion* 3. 419
And nurse ' the dreadful appetite of death ? ' . . 810 *Excursion* 4. 602

Dreading. Dreading, tho' wishing, to be near it : . 79 *Sparrow's Nest* 12
This will I here avow, not dreading thy despite." 104 *Artegal* 145
That Rome provides, less dreading from her frown 420 *Ecc. Sonn.* 1. 8. 10
Sickened by injuries, dreading worse designed, . 449 *Ecc. Sonn.* 3. 37. 7
Deploring changes past, or dreading change . . 875 *Excursion* 8. 38

Dreadless. Dreadless, as in a kind of fresher breeze K.8. 246 *Recluse* 1. 1. 369

Dreads. He dreads the presence of a virtuous man 42 *Bord.* 264
That dreads not age, nor suffers from the worm, . 110 **Look at* 23
Flying from something that he dreads than one . 206 *Tintern* 71
Mourn, and lament for him whose spirit dreads . 213 *Dion* 44

Dreads—*continued.*
So blooms this lonely Plant, nor dreads . . . 224 *Primrose* 23
She dreads the treacherous house, the double tongue ; . . . . 624 *Æneid* 7

Dream. To break my dream the vessel reached its bound ; . . . . 31 *Guilt* 367
I've had the saddest dream that ever troubled . 44 *Bord.* 397
But here he is, it must have been a dream. . . 44 *Bord.* 415
Do never dream of. I *have* been what he— . . 54 *Bord.* 937
Worthy the hearing. Fool was I to dream . . 59 *Bord.* 1179
To purposes of reason—not a dream . . . . 69 *Bord.* 1792
And in that dream had left my native land, . . 70 *Bord.* 1840
Almost as vivid as a dream, produced a dream at night ? . . . . 92 *Poet's Dream* 14
Me had the dream equipped with wings, so I took him in my arms, ... 92 *Poet's Dream* 17
Sleep fled, and with it fled the dream—recorded in this book, ... 93 *Poet's Dream* 70
Nor leave untold our happy flight in that adventurous dream. . . . . 93 *Poet's Dream* 76
Alas the dream, to thee, poor Boy ! to thee from whom it flowed, ... 93 *Poet's Dream* 77
Gone like a morning dream, or like a pile . . . 102 *Artegal* 3
'Tis past, that melancholy dream ! . . . . . 109 **I travelled* 5
Ah ! little doth the young-one dream, ... 117 *Affl. Marg.* 22
A dream of that low-warbled hymn . . . . 144 **Driven in* 49
Induced a soft and slumbrous dream, ... 167 *Pilgrim's Dream* 18
A pregnant dream, within whose shadowy bounds 167 *Pilgrim's Dream* 19
New heavens succeeded, by the dream brought forth: 168 *Pilgrim's Dream* 59
Where by that dream he had been cheered 168 *Pilgrim's Dream* 71
Here are twenty souls happy as souls in a dream : 189 *Music* 42
Through dream and vision did she sink, . . . 193 *Ruth* 109
Like one whom I had met with in a dream ; . . 197 *Resolution* 110
Hunt half a day for a forgotten dream. . . . 202 *Hart-leap* 132
As in a dream her own renewing. . . . . . 204 *Brougham* 43
The fetters of a dream opposed to love."— . . 211 *Laod.* 150
'Tis gone—with old belief and dream . . . . 223 **'Tis gone* 1
An echo, or a dream. . . . . 225 *Present.* 42
In sleep, and intermingling with his dream, . . 229 *Cuckoo-clock* 30
Was for belief no dream :—thy skill, Arion ! . . 234 *Power of Sound* 131
Powers that survive but in the faintest dream . 235 *Power of Sound* 171
Of a wild dream, or worse illusion ; . . . . 238 *P. B.* 188
Such place to me is sometimes like a dream . . 260 **How sweet* 10
I heard (alas ! 'twas only in a dream) . . . . 261 **I heard (alas* 1
It is unstable as a dream of night ; . . . . 263 **Those words* 6
The dream, to time and nature's blended powers . 264 **Lady ! the* 6
Warned in a dream, the Wanderer long had sought 267 *St. Cath.* 9
Like something fashioned in a dream ; . . . . 288 *Highland Girl* 12
No soul to dream of. What art Thou, from care 290 *Kilchurn* 9
Yet he had many a restless dream ; . . . . 295 *Highland Boy* 46
Devised out of a sick man's dream ! . . . . 300 *Bran* 26
So faithfully, a waking dream ? . . . . . . 301 *Yarrow V.* 3
To rouse the wicked from their giddy dream— . 330 *Ode : Thanks.* 80
Though robbed of many a cherished dream, . . 342 *Ital. Itin.* 27
Still in the vivid freshness of a dream, . . . 347 *Processions* 46
From ancient Rome downwards through that bright dream . . . . 359 **They—who* 11
Thoughts that would stray from Heaven ? The dream must cease . . . . 363 **Grieve for* 10
And, at her call, a waking dream . . . . . 373 *Eg. Maid* 305
Than toil in needless sleep from dream to dream : 376 *Duddon* 1. 12
Soft and silent as a dream, ... 396 *White Doe* 57
A phantasm like a dream of night ! . . . . . 400 *White Doe* 424
From their known course, or vanish like a dream ; 421 *Ecc. Sonn.* 1. 12. 10
(So might they dream) till victory was achieved, . 423 *Ecc. Sonn.* 1. 17. 7
Thou, too, dost visit oft my midnight dream ; . 440 *Ecc. Sonn.* 3. 2. 6
Of unsubstantial imagery, the dream, ... 456 **The leaves* 10
Or in a dream recalled, whose smoothest range . 458 *Sea-shore* 17
And dream your time away ? . . . . . . 481 *Expost.* 4
And dream my time away." . . . . 481 *Expost.* 32
Like those good Angels whom a dream of night . 500 *Humanity* 33
Woke from the dream, the dreamer to upbraid, . 504 *Warning* 67
By Flatterers carried, mount into a dream . . 505 *Warning* 125
Melting away within him like a dream . . . . 510 *F. Stone* 119
Making of social order a mere dream. . . . . 518 *Pun. Death* 7. 14
Who never caught a noon-tide dream . . . . 533 **Blest is* 55
Forgotten like a dream ! . . . . 544 *Russ. Fug.* 256
And his hearing is touched with the sounds of a dream. . . . . 570 *Farmer* 80
For the Prodigal Son, Joseph's Dream and his sheaves . . . . 571 *Avarice* 11
The consecration, and the Poet's dream ; . . . 578 *Peele Castle* 16
Housed in a dream, at distance from the Kind ! . 579 *Peele Castle* 54
Time's vanities, light fragments of earth's dream— 584 **With copious* 39
The glory and the freshness of a dream. . . . 587 *Immortality* 5
Where is it now, the glory and the dream ? . . 588 *Immortality* 57
Some fragment from his dream of human life, . . 589 *Immortality* 91
" Rocking as in a dream the tedious year ; " . . 592 *Ev. Wk. Quarto* 30
Features which else had vanished like a dream. . 626 **The confidence* 14
Into my heart, and held me like a dream ! . . . 644 *Prelude* 2. 174
For I could dream away my purposes, ... 645 *Prelude* 2. 192
Appeared like something in myself, a dream, . . 647 *Prelude* 2. 351
I was the Dreamer, they the Dream ; I roamed . 649 *Prelude* 3. 30
(If now I yield not to a flattering dream) . . . 654 *Prelude* 3. 372
Sleep seized me, and I passed into a dream. . . 666 *Prelude* 5. 70
(To give it in the language of the dream) . . . 667 *Prelude* 5. 87
Unless it leap upon him in a dream, ... 670 *Prelude* 5. 308
And brooks were like a dream of novelty . . . 672 *Prelude* 5. 429
A sumptuous dream of flowery lawns, with domes 700 *Prelude* 8. 84
Of Fairy, or some dream of actions wrought . . 714 *Prelude* 9. 301
Changed, and the unbroken dream entangled me . 724 *Prelude* 10. 410

Dream—*continued.*
But, speaking more in charity, the dream . . . 730 *Prelude* 11. 232
In the catastrophe (for so they dream, . . . 732 *Prelude* 11. 357
I learnt to dream of Sicily; and lo, . . . 733 *Prelude* 11. 426
Speaking no dream, but things oracular; . . . 743 *Prelude* 13. 253
Into a waking dream, a reverie . . . 745 *Prelude* 13. 343
And Hope full oft fallacious as a dream: . . . 753 **Oft, through* 11
Sank down, as in a dream, among the poor; . . . 764 *Excursion* 1. 544
Appeared an idle dream, that could maintain, . 770 *Excursion* 1. 952
A might of which they dream not. Oh! the curse, 870 *Excursion* 7. 822
Now too, on melancholy's idle dream . . . S.3. 417 **Sweet was* 9
To me the people of a dream; . . . K.8. 220 **The snow-tracks* 20
A dream in which there is no love, . . . K.8. 220 **The snow-tracks* 21
These freaks are worse than any sick man's dream. L.1. 88 *Juvenal* 1. 2
Or looks at Norfolk and can dream of grace? . L.1. 88 *Juvenal* 1. 10

Dreamer. An idolizing dreamer as of yore!— . . 459 **Wanderer! that* 9
Woke from the dream, the dreamer to upbraid, . 504 *Warning* 67
I was the Dreamer, they the Dream; I roamed . 649 *Prelude* 3. 30
Self-taught, as of a dreamer in the woods; . . 762 *Excursion* 1. 410
I am a dreamer among men, indeed . . . 765 *Excursion* 1. 635
An idle dreamer! 'Tis a common tale, . . . 765 *Excursion* 1. 636
Herself, a dreamer of a kindred stock, . . . 791 *Excursion* 3. 339
A dreamer yet more spiritless and dull? . . . 791 *Excursion* 3. 340

Dreamers. We know where we have friends. Ye dreamers, then, . . . 673 *Prelude* 5. 523

Dreaming. Highways of dreaming passion, have too long, . . . 54 *Bord.* 931
Haughtily shake, a dreaming Conqueror!— . . 349 *Boulogne* 8
As that by dreaming Bards to Love assigned, . 428 *Ecc. Sonn.* 1. 39. 5
Dreaming on things to come; and dost possess . 755 *Recluse* 1. 1. 838
Where the wren warbles, while the dreaming man, 756 *Excursion* 1. 13
By waking sense or by the dreaming soul! . . 784 *Excursion* 2. 833
That Fancy, dreaming o'er the map of things, . 789 *Excursion* 3. 218
Who from the anarchy of dreaming sleep, . . . 802 *Excursion* 4. 87
I came not dreaming of unruffled life, . . . K.8. 246 *Recluse* 1.1.347

Dreamless. Till all was tranquil as a dreamless sleep. 639 *Prelude* 1. 463

Dream-light. To dream-light dear while yet unseen, 386 *Yarrow Rev.* 109

Dream-like. Of clouded splendour, on this dream-like sight . . . 151 **When, to* 95
With dream-like smoothness, to Helvellyn's top, . 353 *Aquap.* 37
Group winding after group with dream-like ease; 367 *Trajan* 16
Upon the dream-like issues—the romance . . . 430 *Ecc. Sonn.* 2. 8. 3
(Save some remembrances of dream-like joys . . 790 *Excursion* 3. 273
Dreamlike the blending also of the whole . . . K.8. 252 *Recluse* 1.1.574

Dreams. *See* **Day-dreams.**
Who would not cherish dreams so sweet, . . . 9 *Lines: Boat* 15
Breathes o'er the failing soul voluptuous dreams, 13 *Desc. Sk.* 136
From such romantic dreams, my soul, awake . . 14 *Desc. Sk.* 226
Rocked the charmed thought in more delightful dreams; . . . 22 *Desc. Sk.* 631
Chasing those pleasant dreams, the falling leaf . 22 *Desc. Sk.* 632
Her dwelling in his dreams. By Fancy's aid . . 25 *Guilt* 59
Hope cheered my dreams, and to my daily prayers 35 *Guilt* 597
And dreams that he is happy. We dissect . . 58 *Bord.* 1166
And dreams of things which thou canst neither see nor hear. . . . 88 *Pet-lamb* 52
Our spirits, carrying with them dreams of flowers, 107 *Farewell* 60
In one of those sweet dreams I slept, . . . 109 **Strange fits* 17
The stars, they were among my dreams; . . . 113 *Ind. Wom.* 4
"'Tis gone—like dreams that we forget; . . . 121 *EmigrantMother* 55
With dreams and visionary impulses . . . 148 *Joanna* 71
Of colour bright as feverish dreams! . . . 178 *Waggoner* 3. 37
Or struggle in the net-work of thy dreams! . . 216 *Enterprise* 97
For he hath waking empire, wide as dreams; . . 267 **Though narrow* 3
The treasured dreams of times long past, . . . 293 *Yarrow Unv.* 53
So all his dreams—that inward light . . . 297 *Highland Boy* 211
In his lone Isle, the dreams of night; . . . 299 *Brownie's Cell* 58
Impassioned dreams, that strove to span . . 299 *Brownie's Cell* 59
And hang like dreams around his guilty bed. . . 320 **Hunger, and* 14
Like dreams themselves; and sweetest sound— . 324 *Ode 1814* 91
Of recollections vivid as the dreams . . . 350 *Des. Stanzas* 17
Strange contrast!—verily the world of dreams, . 364 **What aim* 9
What dreams encompassed? Was the intruder nursed . . . 378 *Duddon* 8. 6
Dreams treasured up from early days, . . . 386 *Yarrow Rev.* 79
Memory, like sleep, hath powers which dreams obey, 392 *Bothwell* 12
Dreams, vivid dreams, that are not fugitive; . . 392 *Bothwell* 13
Where anguish, strange as dreams of restless sleep, 395 *White Doe: Ded.* 42
Bright was the Creature, as in dreams . . . 398 *White Doe* 192
And, quitting unsubstantial dreams, . . . 416 *White Doe* 1840
Is natural as dreams to feverish sleep. . . . 420 *Ecc. Sonn.* 1. 9. 3
Would elevate my dreams. A beechen bowl, . . 424 *Ecc. Sonn.* 1. 22. 9
The Might of spiritual sway! his thoughts, his dreams, . . . 425 *Ecc. Sonn.* 1. 28. 10
Of future vanishing like empty dreams) . . . 426 *Ecc. Sonn.* 1. 30. 7
Prelude of night's approach with soothing dreams. 453 **The Sun, that* 4
Survived, 'twas only in my dreams. . . . 458 **Had this* 68
Dreams on the banks, and to the river talks. . . 477 *Nunnery* 12
Dreams, books, are each a world; and books, we know, . . . 488 *Pers. Talk* 33
And passion's feverish dreams. . . . 499 **Departing summer* 24
To regulate the motion of our dreams . . . 502 **The unremitting* 12
To render visible her own soft dreams, . . . 524 *Epist. Beaumont* 186
Heart-breaking tears, and melancholy dreams . 547 **Beneath yon* 14
Breathe o'er the failing soul voluptuous dreams; 605 *Desc.Sk.Quarto* 157
Chasing those long long dreams the falling leaf . 616 *Desc.Sk.Quarto* 768
That flowed along my dreams? For this, didst thou 636 *Prelude* 1. 274

Dreams—*continued.*
By day, and were a trouble to my dreams. . . 638 *Prelude* 1. 400
More bright than madness or the dreams of wine; 674 *Prelude* 5. 568
Lacked not anticipations, tender dreams, . . . 675 *Prelude* 6. 45
In dreams and fictions pensively composed: . . 683 *Prelude* 6. 550
Dreams not unlike to those which once begat . 688 *Prelude* 7. 111
Over still mountains, or appears in dreams; . . 696 *Prelude* 7. 634
Great Spirit as thou art, in endless dreams . . 705 *Prelude* 8. 435
Had been inspired, and walked about in dreams. . 709 *Prelude* 8. 653
And waking thoughts more rich than happiest dreams. . . . 724 *Prelude* 10. 436
They who had fed their childhood upon dreams, . 729 *Prelude* 11. 125
By help of dreams—can breed such fear and awe 755 *Recluse* 1. 1. 791
The liveliness of dreams. Nor did he fail, . . 758 *Excursion* 1. 148
In dreams, in study, and in ardent thought, . . 760 *Excursion* 1. 301
I called on dreams and visions, to disclose . . 796 *Excursion* 3. 686
Where superstition weaves her airy dreams. . . 810 *Excursion* 4. 610
With floating dreams, black and disconsolate, . 817 *Excursion* 4. 1056
Smooth summer dreams, old favours of the place, S.3. 436 **The doubt* 17
As with the varnish, and the gloss of dreams; . K.8. 252 *Recluse* 1.1.573
Dismissing therefore, all Arcadian dreams, . . K.8. 253 *Recluse* 1.1.625

Dreamt. What have I seen, and heard, or dreamt? where am I? where?" . . . 140 *Arm. Lady* 72
They dreamt not of a perishable home . . . 451 *Ecc. Sonn.* 3. 45. 1
That they dreamt not of dearth;—He continued his rounds, . . . 570 *Farmer* 35
But most intensely; never dreamt of aught . . 737 *Prelude* 12. 177

Drear. 'Mid reedy fens wide-spread and marshes drear, . . . 431 *Ecc. Sonn.* 2. 13. 7
—She solitary through the desert drear . . . 605 *Desc.Sk.Quarto* 199

Drearier. The sun on drearier hollow never shone; . 203 *Hart-leap* 158

Dreariest. And winter's dreariest hour. . . . 507 *May* 16

Dreariness. To paint the visionary dreariness . . 738 *Prelude* 12. 256

Dreary. Where'er the dreary roads their bare white lines extend. . . . 24 *Guilt* 18
Of human shelter in that dreary place. . . . 27 *Guilt* 158
Raise on that dreary Waste a monument . . . 78 *Bord.* 2326
Whom, one bleak winter's day, she met upon the dreary Wild. . . . 91 *Norman Boy* 8
While she pursues her course through the dreary sea. 150 **When, to* 66
I have walked through wildernesses dreary, . . 159 **Up with me* 8
Of the dreary season near? . . . 171 *Kitten* 92
That to a dreary distance go— . . . 175 *Waggoner* 1. 202
Thus to the dreary mountain-top . . . 198 *Thorn* 80
The dreary intercourse of daily life, . . . 207 *Tintern* 131
Of mountains and of dreary moors. . . . 239 *P. B.* 295
Over that dull and dreary sound. . . . 246 *P. B.* 875
Of mountains, silent, dreary, motionless: . . . 266 **Even as* 5
Be left more desolate, more dreary cold . . . 277 **Why art* 11
Tinged, we may fancy, in this dreary place . . 277 **Haydon! let* 10
When dreary darkness is discomfited, . . . 314 *Hofer* 6
In dreary billows, wood, and meagre cot, . . . 334 **A wingèd* 8
Not only from the dreary strife . . . 338 **Meek Virgin* 21
Of Lago Mortò, dreary sight and name, . . . 366 **Fair Land* 7
—But, as soft gales dissolve the dreary snow, 395 *White Doe: Ded.* 27
Stood silent under dreary weight,— . . . 400 *White Doe* 421
Then let us leave this dreary place." . . . 411 *White Doe* 1360
On this dreary dull plate of black metal. . . 484 **A plague* 5
That last and dreary living one . . . 623 *G. and S. Green* 31
It was a dreary morning when the wheels . . 649 *Prelude* 3. 1
Followed each other till a dreary moor . . . 658 *Prelude* 4. 2
A dreary mansion, large beyond all need, . . 684 *Prelude* 6. 645
Upon the naked pool and dreary crags, . . . 738 *Prelude* 12. 264
That dreary time,—ere we had been ten days . 738 *Prelude* 12. 306
Lengthening in solitude their dreary line, . . . 744 *Prelude* 13. 317
Sole building on a mountain's dreary edge, . . 758 *Excursion* 1. 123
A steep ascent; and reached a dreary plain, . . 776 *Excursion* 2. 324
An unillumined, blank, and dreary, plain, . . 830 *Excursion* 5. 537
Than this fallen Spirit? in those dreary holds . 843 *Excursion* 6. 342
Her dreary pillow, waited on her needs; . . . 849 *Excursion* 6. 750
'Mid Buxton's dreary heights. In earnest watch, 879 *Excursion* 8. 377

Dregs. Is shaken till the dregs float on the surface; 58 *Bord.* 1163

Drenched. A weight of hostile corses: drenched with gore . . . 317 **The martial* 7
Grain-tinctured, drenched in empyrean light; . 663 *Prelude* 4. 328

Dress. I spied him skulking in his peasant's dress. . 46 *Bord.* 491
To look upon you. In a peasant's dress . . . 47 *Bord.* 531
And graceful in his rustic dress! . . . 86 *Anecdote* 26
Adopt your homely ways, and dress, . . . 288 *Highland Girl* 51
Such is her sovereign mien:—her dress . . . 413 *White Doe* 1606
Put on with speed your woodland dress; . . . 483 *Sister* 14
With speed put on your woodland dress; . . . 483 *Sister* 38
Familiarly, and in his scholar's dress . . . 653 *Prelude* 3. 288
He stood, and in his very dress appeared . . . 664 *Prelude* 4. 401
Extravagance in gesture, mien, and dress, . . 695 *Prelude* 7. 579
I knew from his deportment, mien, and dress, . 779 *Excursion* 2. 498

Dressed. A scare-crow pattern of old age dressed up . . . 693 *Prelude* 7. 423

Dressing-gown. My lordly dressing-gown, I pass it by, 649 *Prelude* 3. 40

Drest. O'er town and tower we fled, and fields in May's fresh verdure drest; . . . 92 *Poet's Dream* 31
A queen in crown of rubies drest; . . . 158 **With little* 21
His beautiful wings in crimson are drest, . . . 163 **Art thou the* 35
With splendid feathers drest; . . . 192 *Ruth* 21
With something of a lofty utterance drest— . . 196 *Resolution* 94
In the gorgeous colours drest . . . 217 **Inmate of* 22
But whether in the semblance drest . . . 222 *Triad* 178
Bright Star! with laughter on her banners, drest 303 **Fair Star* 8
To think that now our life is only drest . . . 306 **O Friend* 3
With nodding plumes, and lightly drest . . . 342 *Ital. Itin.* 57
Must walk the sorrowing mountains, drest . . 390 *HighlandBroach* 39

Drew 235 Drives

Drest—*continued.*
Or leading victims drest for sacrifice. . . . . 394 *No more 16*
Closely embowered and trimly drest; . . . . 396 *White Doe 28*
That our own hands have drest, ... 507 *May 46*
With a divinity of colours, drest . . . . 511 **Who rashly 4*
In bridal garments drest; . . . . 545 *Russ. Fug. 364*
Drew. And now to the sea-coast, with numbers more, we drew. . . . . 29 *Guilt 279*
And from her grateful heart a fresh one drew: . 30 *Guilt 322*
Time, since Man first drew breath, has never moved 65 *Bord. 1531*
He drew it from the troubled pool, ... 85 *Shepherd-boys 89*
With quickening pace my horse drew nigh . . 109 **Strange fits 11*
So looked Cecilia when she drew . . . . 112 **How rich 7*
The fair Joanna drew, as if she wished . . 148 *Joanna 75*
The gentlest breath of resignation drew; . . . 169 *Love lies Bleeding 14*
And drew their sounding bows at Azincour, . . 184 *Yew-trees 7*
And, still as I drew near with gentle pace, . . 196 *Resolution 73*
In courteous speech which forth he slowly drew: 196 *Resolution 86*
And, when at last her time drew near, . . . 199 *Thorn 142*
But, of his scorn repenting soon, he drew . . . 231 **The gentlest Poet 29*
And voice and shell drew forth a tear . . . 234 *Power of Sound 119*
That in high triumph drew the Lord of vines, . 234 *Power of Sound 148*
She rose, and toward the close-shut casement drew, 274 **Wait, prithee 6*
That sportive dolphins drew. . . . . . . 296 *Highland Boy 120*
Iberian Burghers when the sword they drew . . 315 **And is it 7*
Nay—though the hopes that drew, the fears that drove, ... 362 **List—'twas 36*
Became, as nearer to the coast she drew, . . . 369 *Eg. Maid 11*
Such as the heaven-taught skill of Herbert drew; 380 *Duddon 18. 13*
The foe from numbers courage drew, ... 408 *White Doe 1153*
Drew softly near her, and more near— . . . 414 *White Doe 1651*
As one who drew from out Faith's holiest urn . 444 *Ecc. Sonn. 3. 15. 13*
The Queen drew back the wimple that she wore; 465 **Dear to 2*
Drew from the influx of the main, ... 495 *Fact 16*
—Not He, who from her mellowed practice drew 504 *Warning 61*
And as he durst he drew him near and near, . . 553 *Prioress 69*
He drew his scraps and fragments, one by one; . 566 *Cumb. Beg. 10*
Drew Titus from the depth of studious bowers, . 573 *Chiabrera 2. 2*
From the great city where he first drew breath, . 584 *Ch. Lamb 3*
Ye vales and hills whose beauty hither drew . . 587 *Crosth. 1*
And when the Cripple nearer drew, ... 621 *Andrew Jones 27*
In that stern countenance, for our souls thence drew 622 *Recluse 1. 1. 164*
Large draughts of love unhappy Dido drew; . . 625 *Æneid 133*
We from our funds drew largely;—proud to curb, 643 *Prelude 2. 96*
As near and nearer to the spot we drew, . . . 649 *Prelude 3. 13*
Drew to the spot an anxious crowd; some looked 672 *Prelude 5. 444*
More frequently from the same source I drew . 677 *Prelude 6. 129*
More orient in the western cloud, that drew . . 709 *Prelude 8. 662*
As even their pensive influence drew from mine. . 726 *Prelude 10. 530*
To which at intervals the Wanderer drew, . . 757 *Excursion 1. 55*
Drew happier, loftier, more empassioned, thoughts 771 *Excursion 2. 20*
To known restraints; and who most boldly drew 775 *Excursion 2. 258*
"Lo! what is here?" and, stooping down, drew forth . . . . 778 *Excursion 2. 432*
What motive drew, what impulse, I would ask, . 791 *Excursion 3. 367*
At those, which thy soft influence sometimes drew 797 *Excursion 3. 811*
And from their fervent lips drew hymns of praise, 815 *Excursion 4. 931*
We had espied the book, he drew it forth; . . 816 *Excursion 4. 1011*
"Through four months' space the Infant drew its food . . . . 852 *Excursion 6. 939*
'Tis left untold if here he first drew breath, . . 871 *Excursion 7. 927*
On which they stand; as if thereby they drew . 879 *Excursion 8. 355*
Proclaiming boldly that they never drew . . . 880 *Excursion 8. 411*
The quickening spindle drew a trustier line. . . S. 3. 427 **Through Cumbrian 14*

Dried. Dried up, despairing, desolate, on board . 30 *Guilt 305*
Seemed to return, dried the last lingering tear, . 30 *Guilt 321*
Be turned; and streams of truth dried up, even at their source! . . . . 280 *Plea for Auth. 14*
Now that the farewell tear is dried, ... 341 *Ital. Itin. 1*
Long has the dew been dried on tree and lawn; . 360 **Long has 1*
His bones are consumed, and his life-blood is dried, 621 *Convict 21*
That might have dried me up, body and soul. . 669 *Prelude 5. 229*
Drift. One day in silence did we drift at noon . . 68 *Bord. 1705*
Being itself benign. My drift I fear . . . . 670 *Prelude 5. 293*
Drifted. He faltered, drifted to and fro, ... 285 *Nith 5*
The breath of Heaven has drifted them like snow, 310 *Anticip. 3*
Drifted about along the streets and walks, . . 652 *Prelude 3. 250*
Drink. Bread has he none, the snow must be his drink; . . . . 16 *Desc. Sk. 333*
No food was there, no drink, no grass, no shade, . 68 *Bord. 1707*
That never rested—without meat or drink . . 69 *Bord. 1790*
As if he had stooped to drink, and so remained . 73 *Bord. 2064*
I heard a voice; it said, "Drink, pretty creature, drink!" . . . . 87 *Pet-lamb 2*
"Drink, pretty creature, drink," she said in such a tone . . . . 87 *Pet-lamb 11*
These two days has been meat and drink to me. . 135 *Michael 275*
All round this pool both flocks and herds might drink . . . . 149 *M. H. 8*
I drink out of an humbler urn . . . . . . 158 **In youth 51*
Can drink its nurture from the scantiest rill: . . 222 *Triad 148*
Yet some with apprehensive ear shall drink . . 314 **I dropped 9*
And, drinking towns and cities, still can drink . 328 *Ode 1815 96*
And, from the whirlwind of his anger, drink . . 337 *Aar 7*
To wander, and drink inspiration at will. . . 364 *Vallomb. 24*
Your spirit freely let me drink, and live. . . . 449 *Ecc. Sonn. 3. 35. 14*
Up! up! and drink the spirit breathed . . . 481 *Expost. 7*
Our minds shall drink at every pore . . . 483 *Sister 27*
Or drink, with no fastidious lip. . . . . . 497 *Lycoris 44*

Drink—*continued.*
And mix the poison, they themselves must drink. 513 *Newspaper 8*
No bread to feed him, and the snow his drink, . 609 *Desc.Sk.Quarto 405*
Thrice did I drink the visionary power; . . . 646 *Prelude 2. 311*
To drink the waters of some sainted well, . . 701 *Prelude 8. 155*
To which I oft repaired, and thence would drink, 739 *Prelude 12. 325*
To human comfort. Stooping down to drink, . 763 *Excursion 1. 491*
To drink with gratitude the crystal stream . . 817 *Excursion 4. 1044*
Spread on the never-empty board, and drink . . 867 *Excursion 7. 654*
Drink the pure water of its innocent stream . . 878 *Excursion 8. 261*
Unsullied, incorruptible, and drink . . . . 893 *Excursion 9. 629*
To drink of the clear water, laid himself . . K.8. 226 **I will 55*
To drink of the cold well. When in like sort . . K.8. 226 **I will 57*
Drinking. *See* **Water-drinking.**
And, drinking towns and cities, still can drink . 328 *Ode 1815 96*
Old as creation, drinking in a pure . . . . 640 *Prelude 1. 563*
And drinking from the well of homely life. . . 760 *Excursion 1. 307*
Stood drinking comfort from the warmer sun, . 765 *Excursion 1. 621*
Around him, drinking in the impassioned notes . 857 *Excursion 7. 20*
Drinking-in. Thus deeply drinking-in the soul of things, ... 820 *Excursion 4. 1265*
Drinks. Where oft the venturous heifer drinks the noontide breeze. . . . . 226 *Vernal Ode 13*
And drinks up all the pretty rills . . . . . 295 *Highland Boy 59*
Whence the tall window drinks the morning rays; 535 **When in 24*
Drinks in the feelings of his Mother's eye! . . 645 *Prelude 2. 237*
That drinks as if it never could be full. . . . 668 *Prelude 5. 191*
Drip. Wetting, that drip upon the water still; . . 7 *Ev. Wk. 284*
Dripped. The shuddering ivy dripped large drops—yet still . . . . 644 *Prelude 2. 124*
Dripping. The dripping of the oar suspended! . . 9 *Collins 22*
The dripping groves resound with cheerful lays, . 34 *Guilt 519*
Albano's dripping Ilex avenue, ... 360 *Albano 3*
And naked left this dripping Rock, ... 550 *Hermit's Cell 2. 27*
Wan, dull, and glaring, with a dripping fog . . 746 *Prelude 14. 12*
Drive. Would drive those Scottish Rovers to their dens . . . . 50 *Bord. 729*
Or you might drive your head against that wall. . 56 *Bord. 1009*
Drive them down, like men in a battle: . . . 81 †*Address: Child 31*
May drive at the windows,—we'll laugh at his din; 81 †*Address: Child 41*
I heard, I saw the flashes drive, ... 114 *Ind. Wom. 6*
Which Benjamin had ceased to drive: . . . . 182 *Waggoner 4. 188*
Drive as she drives: how fast they wheel away, . 184 *Night-piece 17*
And drive the flying deer! . . . . 193 *Ruth 96*
And drive the flying deer. . . . . 193 *Ruth 102*
His too fond father's car amiss to drive. . . . 564 *Troilus 147*
That drive her as in trouble through the groves; 634 *Prelude 1. 143*
The witless shepherd who persists to drive . . 655 *Prelude 3. 406*
To drive him back, and pound him, like a stray, . 670 *Prelude 5. 335*
To drive their prey enclosed within a ring . . . 718 *Prelude 10. 21*
When from the heights our shepherds drive their flocks . . . . K.8. 224 **I will 8*
Drive one of those poor creatures miles and miles, K.8. 228 **I will 124*
Slap-dash, tail foremost, as his arms shall drive. . L.1. 96 *Juvenal 3. 32*
Drivellers. Impostors, drivellers, dotards, as the ape 673 *Prelude 5. 525*
Driven. *See* **Storm-driven. Tempest-driven.**
Nor Hunger driven the herds from pastures bare, . 17 *Desc. Sk. 394*
Drives, eagle-like, those sons as he was driven; . 19 *Desc. Sk. 515*
Driven by the bomb's incessant thunderstroke . 30 *Guilt 349*
With panniered asses driven from door to door; . 32 *Guilt 407*
Sightless, and from my heritage was driven, . . 52 *Bord. 829*
Has driven him out of harbour? I believe . . 53 *Bord. 867*
Driven out in troops to want and nakedness; . . 56 *Bord. 1032*
(For other impulse let it pass) was driven, . . 71 *Bord. 1863*
In which a Lady driven from France did dwell; . 120 *EmigrantMother 2*
Driven by the autumnal whirlwind to and fro . 123 *V. and J. 140*
Fell on him, so that he was driven at last . . 138 *Michael 446*
Driven in by Autumn's sharpening air . . . 143 **Driven in 1*
For this the passion to excess was driven— . . 211 *Laod. 148*
How rapidly the Child is driven! . . . . . 296 *Highland Boy 157*
Thou from thy Alpine holds at length art driven, 306 **Two Voices 7*
When out of sight the clouds are driven . . . 397 *White Doe 61*
Driven forward like a withered leaf, ... 414 *White Doe 1614*
Along the west; though driven from Aquitaine, . 427 *Ecc. Sonn. 1. 34. 2*
The innocent eyes of youthful Monarchs driven . 436 *Ecc. Sonn. 2. 32. 13*
Unchecked as when by merry Outlaw driven, . . 450 *Ecc. Sonn. 3. 41. 6*
In hours of peace, or when the storm is driven . 452 *Ecc. Sonn. 3. 46. 7*
Through lawless will the Brotherhood was driven . 468 *St. Bees 146*
Where are ye? Driven or venturing to the spot, . 473 **Ye shadowy 3*
When he was driven from coast to coast, . . . 495 *Fact 28*
Driven by strong winds at play among the clouds. 540 **Lady! a 75*
Drives, eagle-like, his sons as he was driven, . . 613 *Desc.Sk.Quarto 619*
"And has the Sun his flaming chariot driven . 618 *School Ex. 1*
To Tyrians, and these exiles driven from Troy; . 625 *Æneid 110*
Of that first Paradise whence man was driven; . 650 *Prelude 3. 109*
That, thither driven from some unsheltered place, 692 *Prelude 7. 326*
Nor such as—when an adverse fate had driven, . 701 *Prelude 8. 136*
At leisure, how the enamoured youth was driven, 717 *Prelude 9. 569*
Left without glory on the field, or driven, . . . 722 *Prelude 10. 287*
Under worst trials, was I driven to think . . . 725 *Prelude 10. 490*
Must that Man have been left, who, hither driven, 778 *Excursion 2. 481*
By soul-engrossing instinct driven along . . . 788 *Excursion 3. 170*
In combination, (wherefore else driven back . . 799 *Excursion 3. 920*
You have been driven far as its opposite, . . . 805 *Excursion 4. 270*
Fly to those harbours, driven by hound and horn 808 *Excursion 4. 501*
The red-deer driven along its native heights . . 870 *Excursion 7. 864*
And oaken leaves that, driven by whirling blasts, S. 3. 433 **The doubt 49*
Old Michael for this purpose had driven down . K.8. 224 **I will 12*
Have driven him twenty miles." . . . . . K.8. 228 **I will 122*
Drives. Drives, eagle-like, those sons as he was driven; . . . . 19 *Desc. Sk. 515*

Drove—*continued.*
The post-boy drove with fierce career, ... 82 *Alice Fell* 1
The chaise drove on ; our journey's end . . . 82 *Alice Fell* 49
Come to him thus, and drove the weary Wight along. . . . . 108 *Indolence* 36
And drove Astræa from the earth. . . . . . 342 *Ital. Itin.* 78
Nay—though the hopes that drew, the fears that drove, ... 362 **List—'twas* 36
Drove from itself, we trust, all frightful gloom. . 391 *Brownie* 14
Where now the ships that drove before the blast, 454 *Sea-side* 11
And thus a day or two drove wearily ; . . . . 564 *Troilus* 110
Drove far away the savage thoughts that roll . 618 *School Ex.* 33
And drove us onward like two ships at sea, . . 622 *Recluse* 1. 1. 160
Onward we drove beneath the Castle ; caught, . 649 *Prelude* 3. 15
And fears for our own safety drove us home. . . 783 *Excursion* 2. 800
Through a long course of later ages, drove, . . 791 *Excursion* 3. 368
Drover. Young Harry was a lusty drover, . . . 536 *Goody Blake* 17
Drown. Lest she should drown herself therein. . 129 *Idiot Boy* 296
To drown herself therein. . . . . 129 *Idiot Boy* 311
Drown the music of a song . . . . 336 **Jesu ! bless* 4
Drown not at once mandate and prophecy ? . . 365 **The Baptist* 8
Drowned. Its way with uproar, till the ruin, drowned 16 *Desc. Sk.* 313
And when that shape, with eyes in sleep half drowned, ... 27 *Guilt* 182
For threatening clouds the moon had drowned ; . 82 *Alice Fell* 2
That Johnny may perhaps be drowned ; . . . 128 *Idiot Boy* 179
Some say she drowned it in the pond, ... 200 *Thorn* 205
In pity to this poor drowned man. . . . . . 243 *P. B.* 595
In which he had been drowned. . . . . . . 248 *P. B.* 1040
Until all voices in one voice are drowned ; . . 312 **A Roman* 5
Her Son in Wharf's abysses drowned, ... 398 *White Doe* 229
Sea—Ship—drowned—Shipwreck—so it came, . 580 *John Words.* 37
Or prayer-bell by the dull cicada drown'd, . . 603 *Desc. Sk. Quarto* 59
In the deep snow the mighty ruin drown'd, . . 609 *Desc.Sk.Quarto* 378
What radiant fires were drown'd by day's malignant pow'r, ... 620 **She wept* 12
Of indignation ; and with shouts that drowned . 796 *Excursion* 3. 712
From those two Brothers who were drowned therein) ; . . . . K.8. 225 **I will* 22
Drowning. With the fleet waters of a drowning world . . . . 667 *Prelude* 5. 137
Drowsèd. *See* **O'er-drowsèd.**
Drowsily. Each in his basket nodding drowsily ; . 858 *Excursion* 7. 74
Drowsiness. His eyes as if in drowsiness half shut, 762 *Excursion* 1. 439
Drowsy. Or to the drowsy crow of midnight cock . 14 *Desc. Sk.* 193
Of drowsy bells, for ever tinkling round ; . . 17 *Desc. Sk.* 357
I lay where, with his drowsy mates, the cock . . 31 *Guilt* 374
Drowsy and weak, and shattered memory ; . . 31 *Guilt* 389
Come, come, for manhood's sake ! These drowsy shiverings, ... 51 *Bord.* 776
That far-off tinkling's drowsy cheer, ... 173 *Waggoner* 1. 26
Of drowsy, dotard Time ;— . . . . 214 *Kirkstone* 32
By a fair Swan on drowsy billows heaved, . . 261 **I heard (alas* 7
Does the hour's drowsy weight his glee restrain ? 279 **'Tis he* 4
His drowsy rings. Look forth !—that Stream behold, ... 452 *Ecc. Sonn.* 3. 47. 5
In drowsy sequence—how unlike the sound . . 453 **Calm is the* 13
Nor unto silent leaves and drowsy flowers,— . . 501 **The unremitting* 5
It's drowsy tinklings on th' attentive hills ; . . 598 *Ev. Wk. Quarto* 354
Followed by drowsy crow of midnight cock. . . 606 *Desc.Sk.Quarto* 228
The bark of dogs, the drowsy tinkling bell, . . 611 *Desc.Sk.Quarto* 508
Drudge. To drudge through a weary life without the help . . . . 888 *Excursion* 9. 307
Drudgery. —An irksome drudgery seems it to plod on, ... 761 *Excursion* 1. 322
Druid. Altars for Druid service fit ; . . . . . 214 *Kirkstone* 13
Where is the Orphean lyre, or Druid harp, . . 230 *Clouds* 60
Or near that mystic Round of Druid frame . . 380 *Duddon* 17. 12
Those forest oaks of Druid memory, ... 450 *Ecc. Sonn.* 3. 39. 7
The Druid stones their lighted fane unfold, . . 594 *Ev. Wk. Quarto* 171
A Druid cromlech !—thus I entertain . . . . 788 *Excursion* 3. 133
Druid-priest. The Druid-priest the hallowed Oak adore ; . . . . 500 *Humanity* 8
Druid's. *See*-**Arch-druid's.**
Druids. Druids descend, auxiliars of the Cross ; . 421 *Ecc. Sonn.* 1. 10. 11
The Druids worshipped, or the antique walls . . 643 *Prelude* 2. 102
Shaped by the Druids, so to represent . . . . 745 *Prelude* 13. 340
Druid-stones. The druid-stones a brightened ring unfold ; . . . . 5 *Ev. Wk.* 188
Drum. *See* **Kettle-drum.**
But soon, with proud parade, the noisy drum . 29 *Guilt* 273
I wish the press-gang or the drum . . . . . 621 *Andrew Jones* 3
And wish'd the press-gang, or the drum . . . 621 *Andrew Jones* 33
Drum's. Scared by the fife and rumbling drum's alarms, ... 21 *Desc. Sk.* 616
Drums. And greet your sons ! drums beat and trumpets blow ! . . . . 310 *Anticip.* 7
Drunk. And, drunk or sober, he may steer them. . 178 *Waggoner* 3. 19
Of death had drunk their punishment, ... 412 *White Doe* 1449
Thy murmurs heard ; and drunk the crystal lymph 812 *Excursion* 4. 750
His son had drunk, the old man said to him . K.8. 226 **I will* 58
Drunken. Betty a drunken pleasure quaffs . . . 130 *Idiot Boy* 380
Drunken Lark ! thou wouldst be loth . . . . 159 **Up with me* 20
An uproar and a drunken din. . . . . . . 246 *P. B.* 870
The language of those drunken joys . . . . 246 *P. B.* 877
Should come in frenzy and in drunken mirth, . 308 **One might* 12
Dry. In a dry nook where fern the floor bestrows . 27 *Guilt* 161
Did constant meditation dry my blood ; . . . 69 *Bord.* 1773
My Father's house, in wet or dry . . . . . 79 *Sparrow's Nest* 8
Save, in a corner, a heap of dry leaves, . . . 80 †*Address : Child* 18
And, when the grass was dry, ... 84 *We are Seven* 54

Dry—*continued.*
One morn we strolled on our dry walk, . . . 85 *Anecdote* 5
Their two books lying both on a dry stone, . . 99 *Brothers* 262
I trust it is,—and never dry : . . . . . . 111 *A Complaint* 14
Of the dry wreck. And, in our vacant mood, . 148 **A narrow* 16
Dry and withered, light and yellow ;— . . . 163 *Hint* 29
This moss-lined shed, green, soft, and dry, . . 165 *Parrot* 29
Of water—never dry, ... 198 *Thorn* 31
The hard dry see-saw of his horrible bray ! . . 241 *P. B.* 480
And Peter draws him to dry land ; . . . . . 243 *P. B.* 581
To Nature's tuneful quire, this rustling dry . . 263 **While not* 10
'Mid a dry desert ? What is it we hear ? . . . 359 **Those old* 4
My feet would rather turn—to some dry nook . 424 *Ecc. Sonn.* 1. 22. 2
Yea, his dry bones to ashes are consumed . . . 432 *Ecc. Sonn.* 2. 17. 3
His legs are thin and dry. . . . . 483 *Simon Lee* 36
And, ere the flowing fount be dry, ... 497 *Lycoris* 42
Of firm dry ground, with healthful grass . . . 543 *Russ. Fug.* 103
Like the dry remnant of a garden-flower . . . 567 *Cumb. Beg.* 85
What's a tempest to him, or the dry parching heats ? 570 *Farmer* 69
The dry leaves stir as with the serpent's walk, . 606 *Desc.Sk.Quarto* 233
With what strange utterance did the loud dry wind 637 *Prelude* 1. 337
Her pleasant habitations, and dry up . . . . 666 *Prelude* 5. 32
Ran in new channels, leaving old ones dry ; . . 730 *Prelude* 11. 185
And they whose hearts are dry as summer dust . 763 *Excursion* 1. 501
The floor was neither dry nor neat, the hearth . 768 *Excursion* 1. 823
Which anger and resentment could not dry. . . 783 *Excursion* 2. 804
In the dry crannies of the pendent rocks ; . . . 866 *Excursion* 7. 597
Palpable to sight as the dry ground, ... S.3. 435 **The doubt* 96
Dryad. Nor leaf-crowned Dryad from a pathless wood, ... 220 *Triad* 10
Oread or Dryad glancing through the shade . . 850 *Excursion* 6. 829
Dryborough. And Dryborough, where with chiming Tweed . . . . 292 *Yarrow Unv.* 19
Drying. Drying their feathers in the sun, at ease ; . 143 **High bliss* 16
Dual. Your *dual* loneliness. The sacred tie . . 586 *Ch. Lamb* 128
Dubious. Furrowing its shallow way with dubious will ; . . . . 251 **There is a little* 5
But so it is, and, in that dubious hour, . . . 673 *Prelude* 5. 512
Resolved the dubious point ; and sentence gave . 772 *Excursion* 2. 78
Of hermit, dubious where to scroop [? scoop] his cell ; . . . . S.3. 433 **The doubt* 18
Of Hercules, though by a dubious claim. . . . L.2. 120 *Frag. Æneid* 1.3
Ducal. The ducal Owner, in his palace-home . . 392 *Daniel* 3
On Gotha's ducal roof, and on . . . . . . 629 *Installation* 59
Duck. *See* **Night-duck.**
Where the duck dabbles 'mid the rustling sedge, . 7 *Ev. Wk.* 281
Duck's. *See* **Wild-duck's.**
Duddon. For Duddon, long-loved Duddon, is my theme ! . . . . 376 *Duddon* 1. 14
Sole listener, Duddon ! to the breeze that played 377 *Duddon* 5. 1
The Bard who walks with Duddon for his guide, . 379 *Duddon* 12. 11
Reckless of angry Duddon sweeping by, . . . 379 *Duddon* 13. 11
These only, Duddon ! with their paths renewed . 379 *Duddon* 14. 7
Hurrying, with lordly Duddon to unite ; . . . 380 *Duddon* 19. 5
Thy waters, Duddon ! 'mid these flowery plains ; 381 *Duddon* 20. 3
Majestic Duddon, over smooth flat sands . . . 384 *Duddon* 32. 7
For, backward, Duddon ! as I cast my eyes, . . 384 *Duddon* 34. 3
Cerulean Duddon from its cloud-fed spring, . . 418 *Ecc. Sonn.* 1. 1. 2
Duddon's. That tunes on Duddon's banks her slender voice. . . . . 377 *Duddon* 7. 14
By Duddon's side ; once more do we unite, . . 381 *Duddon* 21. 6
And what if Duddon's spotless flood receive . . 382 *Duddon* 23. 9
On Duddon's margin, in the sheltering nest ; . . 383 *Duddon* 28. 5
Dudley. They march with Dudley at their head, . 404 *White Doe* 787
Due. Rich guerdons, and to them alone are due. . 22 *Desc. Sk.* 651
Your generous qualities have won due praise, . 48 *Bord.* 621
Your piety would not miss its due reward ; . . 52 *Bord.* 840
Who, in the open air, with due accord . . . . 95 *Brothers* 24
And while he served the Gods with reverence due, 103 *Artegal* 72
And which, with caution due, may soon be realized." . . . . 105 *Artegal* 217
Tears due unto their own. . . . . 113 *Lament* 21
They cried, 'what to the poor is due ?' . . . 115 *Last of Flock* 50
Due requisites a perfect shepherd's staff, . . . 134 *Michael* 183
Due to that good and pious deed . . . . . 143 **Driven in* 9
'My thanks for your discourse are due ; . . . 156 *Oak and Broom* 55
But Nature, in due course of time, once more . 203 *Hart-leap* 171
—Yet tears to human suffering are due ; . . . 212 *Laod.* 164
And in due season send the mandate forth ; . . 216 *Enterprise* 101
And in due time the soft spontaneous shock, . . 229 *Cuckoo-clock* 9
Aerial, upon due migration bound . . . . . 230 *Clouds* 18
And, with due care, ere break of day, ... 249 *P. B.* 1124
On went She, and due north her journey took. . 258 **With Ships* 14
Ah ! show that worthier honours are thy due ; . 261 **Fair Prime* 9
The tribute due . . . . 284 *Grave of Burns* 16
I praise thee, Matron ! and thy due . . . . 294 *Jedbor.* 35
In due observance of an ancient rite, ... 318 **In due* 1
Nor—touched with due abhorrence of *their* guilt . 321 **Here pause* 10
And in due time shall share . . . . 324 *Ode 1814* 49
So many objects to which love is due : . . . 326 **Intrepid sons* 4
That all observance, due to them, be paid . . 328 *Ode 1815* 59
Where haply (kind service to Piety due !) . . . 340 *Fort Fuentes* 9
Due recompense, and safe return . . . . . 342 *Ital. Itin.* 41
Due homage ; nor shall fruitlessly have striven, . 358 *Aquap.* 362
Due audience, how for aught but scorn defy . . 365 **The Baptist* 4
Vain thoughts, and speed ye, with observance due 372 *Eg. Maid* 239
If to Tradition faith be due, ... 390 *HighlandBroach* 1
Less would not at our need be due . . . . . 405 *White Doe* 835
Through saintly habit than from effort due . . 434 *Ecc. Sonn.* 2. 22. 2
From Little down to Least, in due degree, . . 445 *Ecc. Sonn.* 3. 22. 1
And usages, whose due return invites . . . . 448 *Ecc. Sonn.* 3. 33. 3

Dusk—*continued.*
Traceably gliding through the dusk, recall . . 496 **A little* 43
Pleas'd thro' the dusk their breaking smiles to view, 596 *Ev. Wk. Quarto* 274
His door in darkness, nor till dusk returns. . . 834 *Excursion* 5. 808

Dusky. A Glow-worm, in a dusky nook, . . . 167 *Pilgrim's Dream* 15
Like Twilight's, too, her dusky hair ; . . . . 186 **She was* 6
Saw, at a long-drawn gallery's dusky bound, . . 213 *Dion* 66
That British ground commands :—low dusky tracts, 219 **This Height* 5
He burns—transmuted to a dusky fire— . . . 261 **I watch* 7
In thy fresh beauty. There ! that dusky spot . 303 **Fair Star* 9
Nor wanted lurking hamlet, dusky towns, . . . 323 *Ode 1814* 11
Came two mute Swans, whose plumes of dusky white 371 *Eg. Maid* 177
—When soft !—the dusky trees between, . . . 396 *White Doe* 49
And his two pretty pinions of blue dusky gauze . 484 **A plague* 24
The dusky Shape within her arms imbound, . . 532 **Once I* 4
Extended high above a dusky grove. . . . 649 *Prelude* 3. 6
A glow-worm underneath a dusky plume . . . 687 *Prelude* 7. 33
Inglorious, buried in the dusky wood : . . . . 705 *Prelude* 8. 416
A hundred hills their dusky backs upheaved . . 746 *Prelude* 14. 43
Their leafy umbrage, turns the dusky veil . . 817 *Excursion* 4. 1067
Cut off, an island in the dusky waste ; . . . . 832 *Excursion* 5. 677
Behold a dusky spot, a grove of Firs, ... K.8. 247 *Recluse* 1.1.385

Dusky-browed. It gleams on the face, there, of dusky-browed Jack, ... 188 *Music* 15

Dust. And insects clothe, like dust, the glassy deep : 4 *Ev. Wk.* 117
A piece of money glittering through the dust ? . 45 *Bord.* 435
The dust from off its wings. . . . . 79 **Stay near* 18
Woman's birthright into dust. . . . . . . 141 *Arm. Lady* 82
Shone meekly 'mid their native dust, ... 168 *Pilgrim's Dream* 63
" The pleasure-house is dust :—behind, before, . 203 *Hart-leap* 169
The noble Syracusan low in dust ! . . . . . 214 *Dion* 109
O'er hopeless dust, for withered age— . . . . 225 *Primrose* 39
Its ruins to their kindred dust ; . . . . . . 227 *Vernal Ode* 55
Temples are levelled with the dust ; . . . . . 228 *Devot. Incit.* 51
Thy destined bond-slave ? No ! though earth be dust . . . . 235 *Power of Sound* 222
The white dust sleeps upon the lane ; . . . . . 244 *P. B.* 717
Or in the dust, a crimson stain. . . . . . . 244 *P. B.* 720
Thou turn'st the Wheel that slept with dust o'er-spread ; . . . . 255 *S. H.* 3
Dust for oblivion ! To the solid ground . . . 259 **A volant* 5
To level with the dust a noble horde, ... 292 **Degenerate Douglas* 5
In dust, that voice is dear ! . . . . 299 *Cora Linn* 18
More precious than a hermit's dust ; . . . . . 301 *Bran* 91
And, at our feet, amid the silent dust . . . . 315 **The Land* 8
Stoop their proud heads, but not unto the dust— 316 **Say, what* 11
Return us to the dust from which we came ; . . 319 *Spaniard* 3
With his most sacred wealth, heroic dust. . . . 327 *Ode 1815* 56
Shaking the dust and ashes from her head ! . . 331 *Ode : Thanks.* 130
Doomed as we are our native dust . . . . . 337 *Cath. Cantons* 1
Awoke to new life from its ashes and dust ; . . 345 *Stanzas : Simplon* 14
Turning, for them who pass, the common dust . 351 *Des. Stanzas* 78
The grief, the praise, are severed from their dust, 356 *Aquap.* 247
Palace and tower, are crumbled into dust !— . . 379 *Duddon* 12. 10
The sleeping dust, stern Death. How reconcile . 389 *Breadalb.* 5
And ye must raise her from the dust. . . . . 403 *White Doe* 649
Whose arts and honours in the dust are laid . . 421 *Ecc. Sonn.* 1. 11. 8
'Mid clouds enveloped of polemic dust, . . . 437 *Ecc. Sonn.* 2. 36. 7
Are shattered into dust ; and self-exiled . . . 449 *Ecc. Sonn.* 3. 36. 2
The spousal trembling, and the " dust to dust," . 451 *Ecc. Sonn.* 3. 41. 12
A point of life between my Parent's dust, . . . 464 **A point* 1
Into the dust. Erewhile a sterner link . . . 464 **Thou look'st* 5
Near this unprofitable dust . . . . 485 *Poet's Epitaph* 36
Of genius from the dust : . . . . 499 **Departing summer* 57
To the least particle of sentient dust ; . . . . 500 *Humanity* 46
O'er dew-damped dust our journey was begun, . 522 *Epist. Beaumont* 96
But I will not defile with dust . . . . . . 545 *Russ. Fug.* 293
When temples, columns, towers, are laid in dust ; 546 **Oft is* 2
Disturb the summer dust ; he is so still . . . 567 *Cumb. Beg.* 60
Dust are our hopes ;—I, weeping bitterly, . . . 575 *Chiabrera* 7. 15
Taught that the mutual hope was dust, . . . 580 *John Words.* 32
To the cold marble, waits upon thy dust ; . . . 584 **With copious* 43
Fitly to guard the precious dust of him . . . 585 *Ch. Lamb* 42
Inch-thick the dust lay on the ground . . . . 621 *Andrew Jones* 16
Among the dust till he had brought . . . . 621 *Andrew Jones* 19
Dust as we are, the immortal spirit grows . . 637 *Prelude* 1. 340
Of dust, and kindred to the worm ; a Being, . . 706 *Prelude* 8. 488
Where silent zephyrs sported with the dust . . 710 *Prelude* 9. 67
And levity in dungeons, where the dust . . . 724 *Prelude* 10. 408
That gone, we are as dust.—Behold the fields . 748 *Prelude* 14. 170
And they whose hearts are dry as summer dust . 763 *Excursion* 1. 501
From earth the dust of morning, slow to rise ; . 773 *Excursion* 2. 101
Ashes to ashes, dust bequeathed to dust, . . . 780 *Excursion* 2. 569
—Man is of dust : ethereal hopes are his, . . . 803 *Excursion* 4. 140
Even to the dust ; apparently, through weight . 803 *Excursion* 4. 166
Ending in dust ; of upright magistrates, . . . 825 *Excursion* 5. 175
Doomed to decay, and then expire in dust ! . . 829 *Excursion* 5. 478
And look upon the dust of man with awe." . . 832 *Excursion* 5. 657
" Amid the noblest relics, proudest dust, . . . 842 *Excursion* 6. 263
—No more of this, lest I offend his dust : . . 870 *Excursion* 7. 859
In God ; and reverence for the dust of Man." . 873 *Excursion* 7. 1057
Then, following closely with the cloud of dust, . 880 *Excursion* 8. 379
And lays the generations low in dust, . . . 885 *Excursion* 9. 109
Lie down and be forgotten in the dust, . . . K.8. 255 *Recluse* 1.1.694

Dusty. Raised by yon travelling flock, a dusty cloud 4 *Ev. Wk.* 110
Or taught their limbs along the dusty road . . 7 *Ev. Wk.* 254
Through prickly moors or dusty ways must wind ; 160 **Up with me* 27
In dusty sequestration wrapt too long, . . . 435 *Ecc. Sonn.* 2. 29. 2

Dusty—*continued.*
Through hot and dusty ways, or pelting storm, . 761 *Excursion* 1. 323
By cobwebs, stood within a dusty nook ; . . . 781 *Excursion* 2. 668

Duteous. His duteous toil of furrowing the green earth. . . . . 233 *Power of Sound* 52
And guidance have I sought in duteous love . . 520 *Pun. Death* 14. 10
All in one duteous task agree. . . . . . . 531 †*Float. Isl.* 4
While she as duteous as the mother dove . . . 634 *Prelude* 1. 140
To one who holds it dear ; with duteous care . K.8. 251 *Recluse* 1.1.525

Duteously. Bathed duteously her wayworn feet, 542 *Russ. Fug.* 35
Upheld, he duteously pursued the round . . . 863 *Excursion* 7. 418
Once every day he duteously repaired . . . . 867 *Excursion* 7. 667

Duties. The lowliest duties on herself did lay. . 307 **Milton ! thou* 14
All martial duties to fulfil ; . . . . 330 *Ode : Thanks.* 76
And of more arduous duties thence imposed . . 332 *Ode : Thanks.* 236
Than thine hath been, my duties ask ; . . . . 401 *White Doe* 506
Rights to compare and duties to discern ! . . . 501 *Humanity* 102
By charities and duties that proceed . . . . 510 **Among a* 22
Its duties ;—prompt to move, but firm to wait,— 514 **Blest Statesman* 9
Who bends to happier duties, who more wise . . 528 **Those breathing* 87
(Now that their earthly duties were fulfilled) . . 551 **If thou in* 22
For sabbath duties ; yet he was a man . . . 762 *Excursion* 1. 422
The appointed task and duties of the day, . . 773 *Excursion* 2. 148
His round of pastoral duties, is not left . . 813 *Excursion* 4. 805
Their duties from all forms ; and general laws, . 820 *Excursion* 4. 1240
To steal from active duties, and embrace . . . 822 *Excursion* 5. 27
Sheltered, but not to social duties lost, . . . 823 *Excursion* 5. 54
The primal duties shine aloft—like stars ; . . . 887 *Excursion* 9. 238
Thus, duties rising out of good possest . . . 889 *Excursion* 9. 355

Dutiful. I do not see Idonea. Dutiful Girl, . . 43 *Bord.* 337
And Love is dutiful in thought and deed ; . . 112 **O dearer* 14
Of dutiful affection. . . . . 337 *Thun* 8
In faith and hope, and dutiful obedience, . . . 362 **List—'twas* 33
Dutiful Child, her lot how hard ! . . . . . 372 *Eg. Maid* 213
Holy, and ever dutiful—beloved . . . . . 581 **Why should we* 3
Who, with a dutiful and tender hand, ... 836 *Excursion* 5. 944
And undertook with dutiful content . . . . 852 *Excursion* 6. 947

Duty. Unhappy Woman ! Nay, it was my duty . 40 *Bord.* 174
Duty, or love—involve, I feel, my ruin. . . . 47 *Bord.* 550
It now becomes my duty to resume it. . . . 53 *Bord.* 876
Whom he to more than filial love and duty . . 53 *Bord.* 898
Or duty sanctions. We will have ample justice. . 57 *Bord.* 1113
You have done your duty. I had hopes, which now 64 *Bord.* 1472
And if good Angels fail, slack in their duty, . . 65 *Bord.* 1524
To womankind with duty to my Father, . . . 66 *Bord.* 1615
This day's event has laid on me the duty . . . 68 *Bord.* 1682
Duty, like a strict preceptor, ... 90 *Longest Day* 65
'Gainst duty weighed, and faithful love, did seem 106 *Artegal* 238
To slacken in his duty ; and, at length, . . . 138 *Michael* 443
When duty of that day was o'er, ... 182 *Waggoner* 4. 185
Of duty with reluctant will) . . . . 215 *Kirkstone* 56
Nor Duty struggling with afflictions strange— . 262 **Not Love* 3
For health, and time in obvious duty spent. . . 278 **Lo ! where she* 14
Love from her depths, and Duty in her might, . 280 **Intent on* 13
From hope, the paramount *duty* that Heaven lays, . 321 **Here pause* 5
Speak not now of toilsome duty ; . . . . . 323 *Ode 1814* 34
When duty bids you bleed in open war : . . . 326 **Intrepid sons* 7
Your thrones, ye Powers, from duty fear to swerve ! 327 **Emperors and* 11
Where gladness seems a duty—let me guard . . 354 *Aquap.* 103
Which she in duty left, sad but not cheerless. . 370 *Eg. Maid* 84
To check this pious haste of erring duty. . . 372 *Eg. Maid* 246
Fulfil thy pensive duty, ... 386 *Yarrow Rev.* 106
Her duty is to stand and wait ; . . . . . 407 *White Doe* 1069
Of duty, seeing with clear sight ; . . . . . 409 *White Doe* 1219
Of war, but duty summons her away . . . . 427 *Ecc. Sonn.* 1. 35. 11
Prescribed to duty :—woeful forfeiture . . . 428 *Ecc. Sonn.* 2. 1. 3
Move Princes to their duty, peace or war ; . . 429 *Ecc. Sonn.* 2. 5. 7
Deep in your hearts the sense of duty lie ; . . 444 *Ecc. Sonn.* 3. 16. 3
One duty more, last stage of this ascent, . . . 446 *Ecc. Sonn.* 3. 25. 2
In filial duty, clothed with love divine, . . . 452 *Ecc. Sonn.* 3. 46. 2
O Duty ! if that name thou love . . . . . 492 *Duty* 2
Anxious duty hindering, ... 503 *Warning* 10
Was Duty,—Duty calmed his agony. . . . . 517 *Pun. Death* 3. 8
Duty ?—an unwelcome clog ; . . . . 549 *Hermit's Cell* 1. 18
On whom the duty fell (for at that time . . . 575 *Chiabrera* 8. 2
Though resolute when duty called . . . . . 576 *Cenotaph* 2
(All claims of duty satisfied ;) . . . . . . 579 **Sweet Flower* 54
By duty chained. Not seldom did those tasks . 584 *Ch. Lamb* 6
And now by duty urged, I lay this Book . . . 628 **Deign, Sovereign* 17
From the lore of lofty duty ; . . . . . . 629 *Installation* 48
If so he might, to duty and to truth . . . . 642 *Prelude* 2. 25
Of a low pitch—duty and zeal dismissed, . . . 653 *Prelude* 3. 326
Than duty called for, or, without regard . . . 677 *Prelude* 6. 184
To duty, *might* have sprung up of itself . . . 677 *Prelude* 6. 185
His perilous duty, and retire lamenting . . . 720 *Prelude* 10. 118
Of Providence ; and in reverence for duty, . . 750 *Prelude* 14. 298
Duty exists ;—immutably survive, ... 802 *Excursion* 4. 73
The law of duty ; and can therefore move . . 816 *Excursion* 4. 1036
A light of duty shines on every day . . . . 828 *Excursion* 5. 383
An anxious duty ! which the lofty site, . . . 834 *Excursion* 5. 762
Men, whose delight is where their duty leads . 839 *Excursion* 6. 48
No duty that looks further, and no care. . . . K.8. 255 *Recluse* 1.1.668

Duty's. Duty's intrepid liegeman, see, the palm 312 *Clarkson* 9
A Maiden gentle, yet, at duty's call, ... 540 *Grace Darl.* 22

Dwarf. Dwarf panniered steeds, and men, and numerous wains : . . . . 5 *Ev. Wk.* 159
Dwarf Genii, moonlight-loving Fays, ... 164 *Needlecase* 22
Dwarf willows gliding, and by ferny brake. . . 377 *Duddon* 4. 8
That here in dwarf proportions were expressed 657 *Prelude* 3. 580
Up to the dwarf that tops the pinnacle. . . . 882 *Excursion* 8. 560

Dwarfed. Are dwarfed, or magnified ? . . . . 526 **The soaring* 32

Dwarfing. Each weary step, dwarfing the world below, 497 **Enough of climbing* 6
Dwarfs. (Unbashful dwarfs each glittering at his post) . . . . 456 **Soft as* 17
For dwarfs the tallest seem while sailing by, . . 471 *Ailsa Crag* 8
With ample recompense) giants and dwarfs, . . 691 *Prelude* 7. 271
Are here—Albinos, painted Indians, Dwarfs, . . 697 *Prelude* 7. 707
Dwell. But why, ungrateful, dwell on idle pain ? . 2 *Ev. Wk.* 33
While Slavery, forcing the sunk mind to dwell . 13 *Desc. Sk.* 137
'Here will I dwell,' said I, 'my whole life long, . 31 *Guilt* 363
Where now we dwell.—For many years I bore . 41 *Bord.* 202
"My child, in Durham do you dwell ?" . . . 82 *Alice Fell* 41
And two of us at Conway dwell, ... 83 *We are Seven* 19
Dwell near them with my mother." . . . . 83 *We are Seven* 24
"You say that two at Conway dwell, ... 84 *We are Seven* 25
And you, who dwell here, even among these rocks, 97 *Brothers* 128
We leave you here in solitude to dwell . . . . 106 *Farewell* 19
There did they dwell—from earthly labour free, . 108 *Indolence* 68
In which a Lady driven from France did dwell ; . 120 *Emigrant Mother* 2
The babe and mother near me dwell : . . . . 121 *EmigrantMother* 70
Where in forgotten quiet he might dwell, . . . 125 *V. and J.* 269
Betray the Elf that loves to dwell . . . . . 143 **Driven in* 25
And I, and all who dwell by my fireside, . . . 148 *Joanna* 84
Why should we dwell in strife ? . . . . . . 155 *Waterfall* 22
Seven Si.ers that together dwell ; . . . . . 161 *Binnorie* 6
Yet, whate'er enjoyments dwell . . . . . 171 *Kitten* 95
There did she rest ; and dwell alone . . . . 194 *Ruth* 215
And them who dwell among the woods of Ure !" 202 *Hart-leap* 76
Given back to dwell on earth in vernal bloom ? . 210 *Laod.* 82
Dwell fruitless day-dreams, lawless prayer, . . 223 *Wishing-gate* 8
To dwell these rifted rocks between, ... 232 *Jew. Fam.* 11
With Order dwell, in endless youth ? . . . . 234 *Power of Sound* 112
That he is yet where mortals dwell— . . . . 242 *P. B.* 544
That powerful world in which ye dwell, . . . 245 *P. B.* 782
On favoured ground, thy gift, where I might dwell 251 *Appleth.* 3
Of the brisk waves, yet here consents to dwell ; . 254 *Wild Duck's Nest* 7
But where untroubled peace and concord dwell, . 262 **Not Love* 5
Dwell, clothed in radiance, their immortal vest ; . 266 **The stars* 3
Shall dwell together till old Time . . . . . 286 *Nith* 53
O happy pleasure ! here to dwell . . . . . 288 *Highland Girl* 49
The hapless creature which did dwell . . . . 297 *Highland Boy* 193
Will dwell with me—to heighten joy, ... 302 *Yarrow V.* 87
Her sons were bursting forth, to dwell at ease. . 308 **One might* 4
The haughty towers where monarchs dwell ; . . 329 *Ode : Thanks.* 5
And to the heavenly saints in peace who dwell, . 331 *Ode : Thanks.* 184
The undisturbed abodes where Sea-nymphs dwell ! 333 *Fish-women* 14
Where Spirits dwell in undisturbed repose— . . 349 *Sky-prosp.* 10
For them who in the shades of sorrow dwell, . . 354 *Aquap.* 90
And where no flower hath leave to dwell. . . . 397 *White Doe* 99
Where foresters or shepherds dwell, ... 409 *White Doe* 1166
Did holy Paul a while in Britain dwell, . . . 418 *Ecc. Sonn.* 1. 2. 6
In cloistered privacy. But not to dwell . . . 424 *Ecc. Sonn.* 1. 21. 6
When with more hues than in the rainbow dwell . 475 **Homeward we* 8
As from the hive where bees in summer dwell, . 475 *Greenock* 6
And functions dwell in beast and bird that sway . 500 *Humanity* 11
As, at this day, the rudest swains who dwell . . 502 **The unremitting* 15
Where sea-nymphs might be proud to dwell : . . 511 **Who rashly* 15
They roamed through Wastes where now the tented Arabs dwell. . . . . 522 *Epist. Beaumont* 100
No sullen Humours dwell ; . . . . 526 **The soaring* 20
I know an aged Man constrained to dwell . . 530 **I know* 1
And other little builders who dwell here, . . . 548 **Stranger ! this* 19
And, prithee, let us that can sing dwell here ; . 558 *Cuck.and Night.* 113
And here I dwell an outcast from all joy, . . 564 *Troilus* 97
In acts of love to those with whom they dwell, . 568 *Cumb. Beg.* 139
That dwell among the hills where I was born. . 648 *Prelude* 2. 426
Or Angel, if he were to dwell on earth, . . . 662 *Prelude* 4. 237
To earth and human life, the Song might dwell . 673 *Prelude* 5. 538
Delightful day it is for all who dwell . . . 699 *Prelude* 8. 18
Descend to earth or dwell in highest heaven ! . 755 *Recluse* 1. 1. 780
It were your lot to dwell, would soon become . 782 *Excursion* 2. 695
From sleep, and dwell with God in endless love. . 804 *Excursion* 4. 190
Who dwell on earth, yet breathe empyreal air, . 804 *Excursion* 4. 231
With no inferior power. You dwell alone ; . . 809 *Excursion* 4. 558
Where peace and happy consciousness should dwell, 810 *Excursion* 4. 628
In woods, and dwell under impending rocks . . 815 *Excursion* 4. 923
A rural lord might dwell."—"No feudal pomp, . 824 *Excursion* 5. 98
The family who dwell within yon house . . . 832 *Excursion* 5. 643
Gathered this fair report of them who dwell . . 833 *Excursion* 5. 731
Or dwell in chambers of some natural cave ; . . 879 *Excursion* 8. 366
When they, whose choice or lot it is to dwell . . 894 *Excursion* 9. 667
And dwell elsewhere, ... K.8. 230 **I wil* l202
Dweller. As of a dweller out of doors ; . . . . 239 *P. B.* 292
A dweller in that savage place. . . . . . . 492 *Fidelity* 57
A gentle dweller in the desert, crazed . . . . 667 *Prelude* 5. 145
Dwellers. The dwellers in that house where he had lodged . . . . 125 *V. and J.* 249
Of Shepherds, dwellers in the valleys, men . . 131 *Michael* 23
Of vagrant dwellers in the homeless woods, . . 206 *Tintern* 20
Is, for the dwellers upon earth, ... 472 *Ossian* 41
Among the dwellers in the silent fields . . . 540 *Grace Darl.* 1
And make them dwellers in the hearts of men . 634 *Prelude* 1. 164
What stuff the Dwellers in a solitude, ... 781 *Excursion* 2. 622
They who are dwellers in this holy place . . . K.8. 244 *Recluse* 1.1.277
The dwellers of their dwelling. And if this . . K.8. 254 *Recluse* 1.1.648
Dwelleth. To every Jew that dwelleth in that place 555 *Prioress* 150
Dwelling. *See* **Mountain-dwelling.**
Far from all human dwelling : what if here . . 22 *Yew-tree* 2
Her dwelling in his dreams. By Fancy's aid . . 25 *Guilt* 59
That ragged Dwelling, close beneath a rock . . 44 *Bord.* 379
That make the fields their dwelling. If a snake . 66 *Bord.* 1579

Dwelling—*continued.*
No human dwelling ever give me food, . . . 78 *Bord.* 2347
The Sparrow's dwelling, which, hard by . . . 79 *Sparrow's Nest* 7
This Lady, dwelling upon British ground, . . . 120 *Emigrant Mother* 5
My dwelling, and my out-of-doors abode. . . . 146 **It was an* 41
Dwelling retired in our simplicity . . . . . 147 *Joanna* 10
As lowly as the lowliest dwelling, ... 176 *Waggoner* 2. 2
The one only dwelling on earth that she loves. . 188 *Poor Susan* 12
She from her dwelling in the wood . . . . . 194 *Ruth* 236
Whose dwelling is the light of setting suns, . . 207 *Tintern* 97
And is there no one dwelling here, ... 240 *P. B.* 376
Her dwelling was a lonely house, ... 246 *P. B.* 891
Each maiden to her dwelling ! . . . . . . 292 *Yarrow Unv.* 12
Reports of him, his dwelling or his grave ! . . 318 **Ah ! where* 2
Have spared my Dwelling to this hour ; . . . 344 *Eclipse* 81
The dwelling raised,—a veteran Marine. . . . 470 **Did pangs* 8
Beside the torrent dwelling—bound . . . . 479 *Somnamb.* 151
Remote from public road or dwelling, ... 491 *Fidelity* 22
A lowly Dwelling, here to be outspread, . . . 524 *Epist. Beaumont* 191
All day she spun in her poor dwelling : . . . 536 *Goody Blake* 25
The dwelling of this faithful pair . . . . . 542 *Russ. Fug.* 89
Within that canvass Dwelling, colours, lines, . . 548 **Stay, bold* 22
"And must we then part from a dwelling so fair ?" 620 *Convict* 5
When to the Dwelling of my Love I came, . . 622 **Among all* 13
What dwelling shall receive me ? in what vale . 632 *Prelude* 1. 10
On the large island, had this dwelling been . . 644 *Prelude* 2. 146
From human dwelling, or the vernal thrush . . 647 *Prelude* 2. 341
Thee and thy dwelling, and a crowd of things . 659 *Prelude* 4. 41
In their true dwelling ; now is crossed by gleam . 662 *Prelude* 4. 267
That makes her dwelling on the mountain rocks ! 764 *Excursion* 1. 565
And one bare dwelling ; one abode, no more ! . 776 *Excursion* 2. 339
Man's only dwelling, sole appointed seat, . . . 777 *Excursion* 2. 362
To see the Man who owned it, dwelling here, . . 778 *Excursion* 2. 462
Heard while the dwelling vibrates to the din . . 813 *Excursion* 4. 792
The Vicar's dwelling, and the whole domain, . . 824 *Excursion* 5. 128
This Dwelling charms me ; often I stop short, . 856 *Excursion* 6. 1175
And, from his Dwelling, unapproachable, . . . 859 *Excursion* 7. 141
And in his humble dwelling, he appears . . . 862 *Excursion* 7. 337
—But let us hence ! my dwelling is in sight, . . 874 *Excursion* 8. 29
And that smooth slope from which the dwelling rose, ... 881 *Excursion* 8. 468
The dwellers of their dwelling. And if this . . K.8. 254 *Recluse* 1.1.648
Dwelling-house. A farm or dwelling-house within five leagues, ... 51 *Bord.* 767
Dwelling-place. But not one dwelling-place his heart to cheer. . . . . 25 *Guilt* 31
He pointed towards his dwelling-place, entreating 102 *Brothers* 413
My baby and its dwelling-place, ... 121 *EmigrantMother* 40
Thy memory be as a dwelling-place . . . . 207 *Tintern* 141
The Lady to her dwelling-place ; . . . . . 414 *White Doe* 1687
On the Island-rock, her lonely dwelling-place; . 540 *Grace Darl.* 24
For *any* dwelling-place of man . . . . . . 623 *G. and S. Green* 9
My dwelling-place, and lived for ever there . . 644 *Prelude* 2. 127
This little Vale, a dwelling-place of Man, . . . 784 *Excursion* 2. 870
Who, in their noiseless dwelling-place, can hear . 833 *Excursion* 5. 723
So, at his dwelling-place the Priest arrived . . 858 *Excursion* 7. 63
Their Temple, and their glorious dwelling-place. . K.8. 253 *Recluse* 1.1.624
Dwelling's. —This Dwelling's Inmate more than three weeks' space . . . . 521 *Epist.Beaumont* 26
Dwellings. I turned me from the dwellings of my Fathers, ... 52 *Bord.* 843
On verdant hills—with dwellings among trees, . 96 *Brothers* 63
Among the dwellings framed by birds . . . . 168 *Wren's Nest* 1
They were his dwellings night and day,— . . . 239 *P. B.* 243
Our ears, and near the dwellings of mankind ! . 336 *Staub-bach* 3
Hail to the fields—with Dwellings sprinkled o'er, 379 *Duddon* 13. 1
Amid the fretful dwellings of mankind . . . . 636 *Prelude* 1. 279
Or clustered dwellings, where again they raise . 780 *Excursion* 2. 565
Fair dwellings, single, or in social knots ; . . . 823 *Excursion* 5. 88
Who from their dwellings came not forth to join . 871 *Excursion* 7. 884
And pleasant dwellings, to familiar trees . . . S.3. 433 **The doubt* 6
One of thy lowly dwellings is my Home. . . . K.8. 238 *Recluse* 1. 1. 59
Dwells. Cast off by her Betrayer, she dwells alone, 44 *Bord.* 384
He dwells alone . . . . 110 **'Tis said that some* 7
True beauty dwells in deep retreats, ... 111 **Let other* 9
Old Susan, she who dwells alone, ... 126 *Idiot Boy* 19
And She who dwells with me, whom I have loved 148 **There is an* 14
A Genius dwells, that can subdue . . . . . 214 *Kirkstone* 35
Safe through the winter storm in quiet dwells ! . 227 *Vernal Ode* 109
A Matron dwells who, though she bears . . . 293 *Jedbor.* 9
Dwells in the affections and the soul of man . . 315 **O'er the* 2
Who dwells in heaven ! But that aspiring heat . 335 *Cologne* 5
Where everlasting Bounty dwells ?— . . . . 341 *San Salv.* 10
Old Cham, the solar Deity, who dwells . . . 346 *Processions* 25
Where, in her holy chapel, dwells . . . . . 348 **Lulled by* 5
For her companionship ; here dwells soft ease : . 382 *Duddon* 25. 10
The learned Pastor dwells, their watchful Lord. . 444 *Ecc. Sonn.* 3. 18. 4
Where dwells a Sister-child ? And was power given 446 *Ecc. Sonn.* 3. 24. 11
Where light and shade repose, where music dwells 451 *Ecc. Sonn.* 3. 43. 11
He dwells, and hears indignant tempests howl, . 472 *Dunolly Eagle* 6
An old Man dwells, a little man,— . . . . . 483 *Simon Lee* 3
Dwells in the Hall of Ivor ; . . . . 483 *Simon Lee* 30
Think not that Prudence dwells in dark abodes, . 516 **Hard task* 13
Go where at least meek Innocency dwells ; . . 516 **Young England* 13
And moanings, or he dwells (as if the wren . . 516 **Feel for* 5
He dwells in the centre of London's wide Town ; . 569 *Farmer* 5
If, in that country, where he dwells afar, . . . 596 *Ev. Wk. Quarto* 265
That tear proclaims—in thee each virtue dwells, . 619 **She wept* 9
The only daughter of my parents, dwells. . . . 622 *Recluse* 1. 1. 79

Dwells—*continued.*
Where silence dwells if music be not there : . . 685 *Prelude* 6. 669
As in a moment ; yet with Time it dwells, . . 707 *Prelude* 8. 558
On which he dwells, above this frame of things . 752 *Prelude* 14. 450
Among these rugged hills ; where now he dwells, 776 *Excursion* 2. 309
Where no one dwells but the wide-staring owl . 843 *Excursion* 6. 327
And where yet dwells her faithful Partner, left . 855 *Excursion* 6. 1120
Truth justifies herself, and as she dwells . . . K.8. 250 *Recluse* 1.1.500

Dwelt. But where the sower dwelt was nowhere to be found. . . . . 24 *Guilt* 27
"By Derwent's side my father dwelt—a man . 28 *Guilt* 199
She dwelt on a wide moor, ... 82 *Lucy Gray* 6
And, when he dwelt beneath our roof, we found . 100 *Brothers* 349
Within our happy Castle there dwelt One . . . 107 *Indolence* 1
She dwelt among the untrodden ways . . . . 109 **She dwelt* 1
There dwelt we, as happy as birds in their bowers ; 116 *Repentance* 9
The house she dwelt in was a sainted shrine ; . 122 *V. and J.* 44
There dwelt a Shepherd, Michael was his name ; . 131 *Michael* 41
Who dwelt within the limits of the vale, . . 133 *Michael* 138
Dwelt in a tranquil spot. And oftentimes . 150 **When, to* 26
Framed in the schools where Wisdom dwelt retired, 213 *Dion* 49
As if within thee dwelt a glancing mind, . . . 232 *Power of Sound* 2
And there, a saintly Anchoress, she dwelt . . 267 *St. Cath.* 13
Thy soul was like a Star, and dwelt apart ; . . 307 **Milton ! thou* 9
There dwelt the gay, the bountiful, the bold ; . 383 *Duddon* 27. 5
Of years hemmed round, had dwelt, prepared to try 391 *Brownie* 6
Hadst thou, loved Bard ! whose spirit often dwelt 436 *Ecc. Sonn.* 2. 31. 5
But in old times Love dwelt not long . . . . 478 *Somnamb.* 37
On a hill's northern side she dwelt, ... 536 *Goody Blake* 30
Four summer weeks I dwelt in sight of thee : . 578 *Peele Castle* 2
That dwelt among them. Sometimes it befell . 636 *Prelude* 1. 317
Ye lowly cottages wherein we dwelt, ... 639 *Prelude* 1. 499
When all who dwelt within these famous walls . 655 *Prelude* 3. 448
There dwelt, weakened in spirit more and more ; . 718 *Prelude* 9. 580
His Parents, with their numerous offspring, dwelt ; 758 *Excursion* 1. 111
When squire, and priest, and they who round them dwelt . . . . 761 *Excursion* 1. 329
Approach this door but she who dwelt within . 763 *Excursion* 1. 498
Whereon their endless generations dwelt. . . . 790 *Excursion* 3. 252
"In privacy we dwelt, a wedded pair, ... 794 *Excursion* 3. 584
A curious child, who dwelt upon a tract . . . 818 *Excursion* 4. 1133
Have dwelt through ages—Patrons of this Cure. . 824 *Excursion* 5. 126
High on that mountain where they long have dwelt 833 *Excursion* 5. 691
—Beside the cottage in which Ellen dwelt . . 851 *Excursion* 6. 862
Its rocks and woods—the Cottage where she dwelt ; 855 *Excursion* 6. 1119
Of their rude homesteads. Here the Warrior dwelt ; 872 *Excursion* 7. 955
But speaking of the vale in which he dwelt, . . K.8. 230 **I will* 199

Dwindle. To dwindle and to perish one by one, . 635 *Prelude* 1. 195
To dwindle, and give up his majesty, ... 746 *Prelude* 14. 48
That we should pore, and dwindle as we pore, . 815 *Excursion* 4. 960

Dwindled. They dwindled, dwindled, one by one ; . 115 *Last of Flock* 66
"They dwindled, Sir, sad sight to see ! . . . 115 *Last of Flock* 91
But they have dwindled long by slow decay ; . . 197 *Resolution* 125
Lo ! the dwindled woods and meadows ; . . . 217 **Inmate of* 9
A dwindled object, and submits to lie . . . . 219 **This Height* 22
Whose realm had dwindled to one stately room ; . 271 *George : Death* 2
His body, dwindled and awry, ... 483 *Simon Lee* 34

Dwindles. Dwindles the pear on autumn's latest spray, ... 608 *Desc.Sk.Quarto* 321
While man grows old, and dwindles, and decays ; 812 *Excursion* 4. 760

Dwindling. *See* **Ever-dwindling.**

Dye. So deep is their vermilion dye. . . . . . 198 *Thorn* 44
And hue far deeper than the Tyrian dye ; . . . 618 *School Ex.* 22
A flag of *yellow* dye. . . . . S.3.431 **The Scottish* 16
Shame of such dye, but worse remains behind. . L.1. 97 *Juvenal* 3. 80

Dyed. This undeparting Flower in crimson dyed, 170 **Never enlivened* 23
Part from thee without pity dyed in shame : . . 366 **Fair Land* 3
Their Portraitures, their stone-work glimmers, dyed 451 *Ecc. Sonn.* 3. 44. 3
Self-smitten till thy garments reek dyed red . . 514 **Long-favoured* 4
Serene he towers, in deepest purple dy'd ; . . . 615 *Desc.Sk.Quarto* 699

Dyes. So fresh in all its beauteous dyes, . . . 198 *Thorn* 51
The flitting halcyon's vivid dyes ; . . . . . 497 *Lycoris* 14

Dying. *See* **Never-dying.**
And faint the fire a dying heart can yield ! . . 7 *Ev. Wk.* 274
Left without burial ! nay, not dead nor dying, . 68 *Bord.* 1728
no hand to grasp your dying hand—— . . . 72 *Bord.* 1973
As the dying mother witnessed . . . . . . 94 *Westmoreland Girl* 39
I should not feel the pain of dying, ... 114 *Ind. Wom.* 47
My Johnny, till my dying day." . . . . . 128 *Idiot Boy* 236
Soft as the dying throb of the lyre. . . . . 142 †*Lov. and Lik.* 48
The dying Gladiator. So, sad Flower ! . . . 169 *Love lies Bleeding* 9
Till, breaking in upon the dying strain, . . . 175 *Waggoner* 1. 203
"I'm helping this poor dying brute." . . . . 242 *P. B.* 490
A *word*—which to his dying day . . . . . 244 *P. B.* 754
Dying insensibly away . . . . 246 *P. B.* 856
That name—pronounced with a dying fall— . . 400 *White Doe* 400
This dying prayer, and be thou blest !' . . . 410 *White Doe* 1309
For all—all dying in one hour ! . . . . . 411 *White Doe* 1371
Laud, "in the painful art of dying tried, . . 440 *Ecc. Sonn.* 2. 45. 3
Stretched on the dying Mother's lap, lies dead . 476 *Howard* 1
And, dying, from his own embrace, ... 479 *Somnamb.* 143
Methinks that in my dying hour . . . . . 530 †*Redbreast* 9
Hope to the hopeless, to the dying, life— . . 541 *Grace Darl.* 70
See how dying tapers fare ! . . . . 549 *Hermit's Cell* 1. 10
To be our help upon our dying day : . . . . 553 *Prioress* 83
'Thou in thy dying sing this holy lay,' . . . 556 *Prioress* 209
Last night, while by his dying fire, as clos'd . . 613 *Desc.Sk.Quarto* 596
Dying, will cast on you a backward look ; . . . 706 *Prelude* 8. 470
The dead, upon the dying heaped, and gazed . 719 *Prelude* 10. 57
That, from his dying hand, she would accept . . 841 *Excursion* 6. 203

Dying—*continued.*
And functions dying and produced at need,— . 872 *Excursion* 7. 1003
Dying, or dead ! Nor shall the fanning breeze . 892 *Excursion* 9. 552
In the last dotage of a dying form. . . . . . K.8. 223 **There is a shapeless* 4
And, (if a thought of dying, if a thought . . K.8. 236 *Recluse* 1.1.12
Mortal though bright, a dying, dying flame. . . K.8. 248 *Recluse* 1.1.439

Dynasty. Of the Tartarian dynasty composed . 700 *Prelude* 8. 78

E

Each. (*Partial list.*)
No law but what each man makes for himself ; . 48 *Bord.* 597
Three of us—we should keep each other warm : . 51 *Bord.* 773
Each rises as the other falls : and first, . . . 58 *Bord.* 1149
Each in his way ? Troth, I begin to think so. . 60 *Bord.* 1239
In honour of each household name, ... 375 **The Minstrels* 16
Degrees and Orders stood, each under each : . . 471 *Tynwald* 6
Each for her haven ; with her freight of Care, . 471 *Ailsa Crag* 9
And gathered each and all into one place ; . . 561 *Cuck.andNight.* 263
How she and I did each the other chide, . . . 561 *Cuck.andNight.* 267
Of each recalling his peculiar boons, ... 568 *Cumb. Beg.* 126
My neighbour, when with punctual care, each week, 568 *Cumb. Beg.* 155
You would say that each hair of his beard was alive, 570 *Farmer* 55
And each, in his turn, becomes leader or led ; . 572 *Avarice* 38
Himself above each lower thought uplifting, . . 576 *Chiabrera* 9. 15

Eager. While to the door with eager speed they ran, 34 *Guilt* 559
Living a life of eager industry. . . . . . . 133 *Michael* 122
The budding groves seemed eager to urge on . . 146 **It was an* 9
'Tis what can be most prompt and eager ; . . 177 *Waggoner* 2. 65
Eager to repair lost time ; . . . . 181 *Waggoner* 4. 86
With eager eyes the Master pries ; . . . . . 181 *Waggoner* 4. 171
What an eager assembly ! what an empire is this ! 188 *Music* 9
Associates in that eager chase ; . . . . . . 191 *Seq. Beggars* 33
As often as that eager grasp was made. . . . 210 *Laod.* 28
Faint, faint at first ; and then an eager sound . 218 *Recluse* 1. 1. 220
An eager Novice robed in fluttering gown ! . . 270 **Ye sacred* 14
A chosen Tree ; then, eager to fulfil . . . . 276 *Oker Hill* 5
From quick and eager visitings . . . . . . 288 *Highland Girl* 39
"*Lei-gha—Lei-gha*"—with eager shout ; . . . 297 *Highland Boy* 202
Had opened on his eager glance ; . . . . . 348 **Lulled by* 52
The smoking steam-boat eager in pursuit, . . . 388 **The pibroch's* 5
Of horsemen at an eager pace ! . . . . . . 412 *White Doe* 1444
One, the most eager for the prize, ... 412 *White Doe* 1490
Eager to build the quiet Fortresses . . . . . 424 *Ecc. Sonn.* 1. 24. 3
Of a shrewd Counsellor, eager to protect . . . 432 *Ecc. Sonn.* 2. 16. 2
And many chained by vows, with eager glee . . 434 *Ecc. Sonn.* 2. 23. 2
And eager, might be still pursued in vain. . . 469 **Bold words* 7
Yet, spite of all this eager strife, ... 499 **This Lawn* 13
Truths of the heart flock in with eager pace, . . 503 *Warning* 24
Who thus deceived shall lend an eager hand . . 514 **Who ponders* 10
Emblem of thoughts too eager to advance . . . 532 **Once I* 33
Who foiled an Emperor's eager quest ? . . . . 545 *Russ. Fug.* 317
Was eager to depart, ... 545 *Russ. Fug.* 342
Did Francis Beaumont sport, an eager child ; . . 547 **Beneath yon* 10
Like Lightnings eager for th' almighty word, . . 617 *Desc.Sk.Quarto* 802
The Tyrians rushing in, an eager band, . . . 624 *Æneid* 71
With brisk and eager steps ; and came, at length, 633 *Prelude* 1. 61
Eager and never weary we pursued . . . . . 639 *Prelude* 1. 507
And, interrupting oft that eager game, . . . 640 *Prelude* 1. 538
And eager to spur on, the galloping steed ; . . 643 *Prelude* 2. 97
To see displayed among an eager few, ... 656 *Prelude* 3. 498
The limbs of the great world ; its eager strifes . 657 *Prelude* 3. 581
With eager footsteps I advance and reach . . . 658 *Prelude* 4. 25
To his own eager thoughts. It would demand . 662 *Prelude* 4. 291
Was neither slow nor eager ; but, unmoved, . . 664 *Prelude* 4. 418
Or eager, though as gay and undepressed . . . 675 *Prelude* 6. 7
Eager as birds of prey, or as a ship . . . . 682 *Prelude* 6. 498
They made it proudly, eager as a child, . . . 723 *Prelude* 10. 364
That I was led to take an eager part . . . 728 *Prelude* 11. 76
With eager pace, and no less eager thoughts. . . 746 *Prelude* 14. 31
An eager grasp ; and many moments' space— . 779 *Excursion* 2. 519
Then, keen and eager, as a fine-nosed hound . . 788 *Excursion* 3. 169
His looks, tones, gestures, eager eloquence, . . 883 *Excursion* 8. 577
She vanished—eager to impart the scheme . . 890 *Excursion* 9. 430
Dropped the light oar his eager hand had seized. . 891 *Excursion* 9. 481

Eager-hearted. Every dog is eager-hearted, . . 490 *Incident : Dog* 11

Eagerly. My question eagerly did I renew, . . . 197 *Resolution* 118
As eagerly pursued ; the umbrella spread . . . 388 **The pibroch's* 6
Filled with its fray or brawl, how eagerly . . 693 *Prelude* 7. 436
In this secluded glen, and eagerly . . . . . 699 *Prelude* 8. 19
Of Orleans eagerly I turned ; as yet . . . . 719 *Prelude* 10. 95
Feeding the soul, and eagerly imbibed . . . . 757 *Excursion* 1. 69
But eagerly he read, and read again, ... 758 *Excursion* 1. 170
The Wanderer somewhat eagerly exclaimed, . . 847 *Excursion* 6. 580

Eagerness. When, in the eagerness of boyish hope, 185 *Nutting* 4
Oh whither with such eagerness of speed ? . . . 229 *Clouds* 4
Whence, whence, ye Clouds ! this eagerness of speed ? . . . . 230 *Clouds* 29
(As hurry on in eagerness the feet, ... 355 *Aquap.* 176
The eagerness of infantine desire ? . . . . . 642 *Prelude* 2. 26
And clomb with eagerness, till anxious fears . . 683 *Prelude* 6. 575
Laughed as with rival eagerness their hands . . 705 *Prelude* 8. 404
Fair greetings to this shapeless eagerness, . . 710 *Prelude* 9. 19
While yet a child, with a child's eagerness . . 758 *Excursion* 1. 149

Eagle. And slow the insulted eagle wheels away. . 11 *Desc. Sk.* 68
The eagle of the Alps o'ershades her prey. . . 16 *Desc. Sk.* 335
Faint wail of eagle melting into blue . . . . 17 *Desc. Sk.* 358

Eagle—*continued.*
The Eagle lives in Solitude! Even so, 65 *Bord.* 1516
Strong as an Eagle with my charge I glided round and round 92 *Poet's Dream* 37
Watchful as a wheeling eagle, 94 *Westmoreland Girl* 85
Far as in power the eagle doth the worm: 105 *Artegal* 181
It may soar with the eagle and brood with the dove, 142 †*Lov. and Lik.* 50
The eagle, lord of land and sea, 205 *Brougham* 120
The flame-eyed eagle oft wouldst scare 215 *Enterprise* 30
Where the eagle builds her aery, 220 *Triad* 39
Thou too be heard, lone eagle! freed 235 *Power of Sound* 199
The Eagle, he was lord above, 291 *Rob Roy* 59
The eagle worthy of her ancestry? 350 *Des. Stanzas* 47
An Eagle with stretched wings, but beamless eye— 472 **The captive* 7
An Eagle that could neither wail nor soar. 472 **The captive* 8
If unreproved the ambitious eagle mount 527 **Those breathing* 37
And thereat shall the Eagle be our Lord, 562 *Cuck.andNight.*276
The eagle of the Alps o'ershades his prey. 609 *Desc.Sk.Quarto* 407
To see the Eagle ruffled by the Dove 627 *Eagle and Dove* 3
The eagle soars high in the element, 683 *Prelude* 6. 535
When the fresh eagle, in the month of May, 807 *Excursion* 4. 397
As the fierce eagle fastens on the lamb? 849 *Excursion* 6. 748
To the wide-ruling eagle, and his hand 868 *Excursion* 7. 748
Eagle-like. Drives, eagle-like, those sons as he was driven; 19 *Desc. Sk.* 515
And never, eagle-like, beholds again! 19 *Desc. Sk.* 517
Drives, eagle-like, his sons as he was driven, 613 *Desc.Sk.Quarto* 619
Eagle-race. The lordly eagle-race through hostile search 273 **Not the* 9
Eagle's. Glances the wheeling eagle's glorious form! 15 *Desc. Sk.* 276
The soaring eagle's curvèd beak; 227 *Vernal Ode* 120
The lion's sinews, or the eagle's wing; 311 **Who rises* 48
His prominent feature like an eagle's beak; 422 *Ecc. Sonn.* 1. 15. 7
His Eagle's favourite perch, while round him sate 457 **The leaves* 30
Thou near the eagle's nest—within brief sail, 464 *Derwent* 2
Glances the fire-clad eagle's wheeling form; 608 *Desc.Sk.Quarto* 339
The chamois' sinews, and the eagle's wing: 646 *Prelude* 2. 275
That is the eagle's birthplace, or some peak 760 *Excursion* 1. 275
Eagles. Both when he heard the eagles scream, 295 *Highland Boy* 47
And turned his eagles back with deep-drawn sighs: 368 *Trajan* 63
And if those eagles to their ancient hold K.8. 250 *Recluse* 1.1.517
Return, Helvellyn's eagles! with the pair. K.8. 250 *Recluse* 1.1.518
Ear. Say, will my Friend, with unreluctant ear, 2 *Ev. Wk.* 35
Shook the still-twinkling tail and glancing ear; 3 *Ev. Wk.* 48
How sweet its streamlet murmurs in mine ear!) 8 *Ev. Wk.* 350
That common growth of earth, the foodful ear; 15 *Desc. Sk.* 257
Mocks the dull ear of Time with deaf abortive sound. 16 *Desc. Sk.* 315
No brook to wet his lip or soothe his ear; 24 *Guilt* 29
And ear still busy on its nightly watch, 32 *Guilt* 421
Have reached his ear—you have had enemies. 42 *Bord.* 256
With which he taints her ear;—for a plain reason; 42 *Bord.* 263
Imprisoned there, and held it to his ear, 44 *Bord.* 405
That may not be retold to any ear. 59 *Bord.* 1199
I have much to say, but for whose ear?—not thine. 66 *Bord.* 1602
A human voice distinct, struck on my ear. 73 *Bord.* 2048
No human ear shall ever hear me speak; 78 *Bord.* 2346
When, as we hurried on, my ear 82 *Alice Fell* 3
In verse, which to thy ear might come would treat this simple theme, 93 *Poet's Dream* 75
Made, to his ear attentively applied, 108 *Indolence* 57
But in the Lover's ear alone, 109 **Strange fits* 3
That sigh of thine, not meant for human ear, 112 **O dearer* 9
From day to day, to Michael's ear there came 134 *Michael* 208
Never to living ear came sweeter sounds 136 *Michael* 345
Of ancient mountains, or my ear was touched 148 *Joanna* 70
Still couchant, an inevitable ear, 151 **When, to* 82
Urania's self might welcome with pleased ear 154 *Morn. Ex.* 53
"Some, still more delicate of ear, 164 *Needlecase* 25
Plunge, and fling back a spiteful ear, 175 *Waggoner* 1. 127
To her; and she shall lean her ear 187 **Three years* 26
And heaviness in Clifford's ear! 204 *Brougham* 103
Of eye, and ear,—both what they half create, 207 *Tintern* 106
Such rebounds our inward ear 209 **Yes, it* 17
"Come, if the notes thine ear may pierce, 221 *Triad* 89
And was it granted to the simple ear 227 *Vernal Ode* 82
Give ear, O Man! to their appeal, 228 *Devot. Incit.* 23
The mimic notes, striking upon his ear 229 *Cuckoo-clock* 29
To life, to *life* give back thine ear: 234 *Power of Sound* 153
Into the ear of God, their Lord! 235 *Power of Sound* 208
Turns round his long left ear. 241 *P. B.* 415
Turned round his long left ear. 241 *P. B.* 420
A voice to Peter's ear ascends, 247 *P. B.* 939
Hath sought, proclaiming to the ear 249 *P. B.* 1103
Soft as the Dorhawk's to a distant ear, 255 *S. H.* 5
An ample sovereignty of eye and ear. 267 **Though narrow* 4
Whose murmur soothed thy languid Mother's ear 275 *Rotha Q.* 10
Of one deep bliss thine ear hath been bereft: 306 **Two Voices* 9
Haunts, with sad echoes, musing Fancy's ear: 312 **A Roman* 10
Yet some with apprehensive ear shall drink 314 **I dropped* 9
Of Britain's acts,—may catch it with rapt ear, 325 *Ode 1814* 129
Their heavenly Father will incline an ear 332 *Ode: Thanks.* 225
Had fallen upon the ear. 334 **In Bruges* 16
All that I heard comes back upon my ear, 350 *Des. Stanzas* 11
My dull forebodings in a Peasant's ear 360 *Albano* 4
If they received into a conscious ear 363 **List—'twas* 88
My fault, nor hear it with Thy sacred ear; 366 **Eternal Lord* 10
Beats frequent on thy satiate ear, 376 **The Minstrels* 74
And seldom hath ear listened to a tune 381 *Duddon* 19. 10
Satiate are *these;* and stilled to eye and ear; 392 *Daniel* 9

Ear—*continued.*
A synod of his Councillors:—give ear, 422 *Ecc. Sonn.* 1. 15. 13
Silent, but not to high-souled Passion's ear— 431 *Ecc. Sonn.* 2. 13. 6
Come secrets, whispered nightly to his ear; 441 *Ecc. Sonn.* 3. 4. 11
Mine ear has rung, my spirit sunk subdued, 450 *Ecc. Sonn.* 3. 40. 1
And to the soldier's trumpet-wearied ear; 455 *Rydal Mere* 30
Name that first struck by chance my startled ear) 465 **The cattle* 8
With ear not coveting the whole, 472 *Ossian* 3
We cannot bid the ear be still; 481 *Expost.* 18
To which I listen with a ready ear; 488 *Pers. Talk* 39
Must eyes be all in all, the tongue and ear 489 *Illus. Books* 13
Nor shout, nor whistle strikes his ear; 491 *Fidelity* 15
May well afford to mortal ear 498 **The sylvan* 10
And can earthward bend an ear 503 **Like a* 66
Whose boyish ear the voice of her renown 504 *Warning* 57
Nor will he turn his ear aside 506 *Lab. Hymn* 5
Whose silence, for the pleasure of the ear, 508 *F. Stone* 10
The hoary Father in the Stranger's ear 509 *F. Stone* 108
May not avail, nor prayer have for God's ear 519 *Pun. Death* 10. 7
Haunted his ear—he only listening— 528 **Those breathing* 105
The Promise, with uplifted ear; 533 **Blest is* 38
No one's ear had heard the Horn. 535 *Egremont* 68
And friend in the ear of friend, where speech is free 539 **Lady! a* 55
For simple infant hath a ready ear. 553 *Prioress* 60
Which ever to man's ear a passage won. 558 *Cuck. and Night.* 85
Say, will my friend, with soft affection's ear, 592 *Ev. Wk. Quarto* 51
And with strange tinglings sings her fainting ear. 606 *Desc.Sk.Quarto* 238
Deny'd the bread of life the foodful ear, 608 *Desc.Sk.Quarto* 320
When hums the mountain bee in May's glad ear, 610 *Desc.Sk.Quarto* 444
Swing on th' astounded ear it's dull undying roar: 616 *Desc.Sk.Quarto* 779
Blow through my ear! the sky seemed not a sky 637 *Prelude* 1. 338
Most audible, then, when the fleshly ear, 648 *Prelude* 2. 416
That I should hold it to my ear. I did so, 667 *Prelude* 5. 92
Grows tedious even in a young man's ear. 694 *Prelude* 7. 511
Lies to the ear, and lies to every sense— 695 *Prelude* 7. 581
Beat against Albion's shore, since ear of mine 721 *Prelude* 10. 239
I had but lent a careless ear, assured 730 *Prelude* 11. 191
A story destined for thy ear, who now, 732 *Prelude* 11. 375
All ear; but never long without the heart 735 *Prelude* 12. 100
Incessantly to turn his ear and eye 758 *Excursion* 1. 150
We sate together, sighs came on my ear, 768 *Excursion* 1. 802
On the thrilled ear, and flags uprising, yield 773 *Excursion* 2. 119
That on mine ear ticked with a mournful sound.— 781 *Excursion* 2. 646
By each and all of these the pensive ear 786 *Excursion* 3. 5
Like one whose untired ear a murmuring stream 814 *Excursion* 4. 892
Of inland ground, applying to his ear 818 *Excursion* 4. 1134
Is to the ear of Faith; and there are times, 818 *Excursion* 4. 1142
Through which the ear converses with the heart. 818 *Excursion* 4. 1155
Through the calm region, fades upon the ear, 819 *Excursion* 4. 1184
Do speak, at Heaven's command, to eye and ear, 819 *Excursion* 4. 1205
Of yielding its contents to eye and ear, 826 *Excursion* 5. 253
All day the house-clock ticking in mine ear, 834 *Excursion* 5. 814
With her two faculties of eye and ear, 837 *Excursion* 5. 987
Continued yet to vibrate on his ear, 845 *Excursion* 6. 450
Was wasted on the good Man's living ear, 864 *Excursion* 7. 478
Protected, say enlightened, by his ear; 865 *Excursion* 7. 495
The Christian promise with attentive ear; 866 *Excursion* 7. 578
With willingness, to whom the general ear 883 *Excursion* 8. 595
Many and idle, visits not his ear: 885 *Excursion* 9. 75
It mounts to reach the State's parental ear; 889 *Excursion* 9. 327
Instructing simple childhood's ready ear: 890 *Excursion* 9. 396
In like low voice to my particular ear, 891 *Excursion* 9. 458
She pondered murmurs that attuned her ear S.3. 436 **The doubt* 174
The Ball whizz'd by,—it grazed his ear, S.3. 441 **The ball* 1
That Shepherd's voice, it may have reached mine ear K.8. 246 *Recluse* 1.1.341
Had soothed his ear while *they* were hidden: how pleased K.8. 249 *Recluse* 1.1.484
My fault, and keep it from thy sacred ear. K.8. 266 **Rid of* 10
The box resound on Viscount Buffo's ear. L.1. 95 *Juvenal* 3. 13
Ear-deep. No promise. Still, in more than ear-deep seats, 353 *Aquap.* 71
Eared. *See* **Quick-eared.**
Earl. Who dragged Earl Pembroke from Banbury church 399 *White Doe* 252
Earl Pembroke, slain so impiously! 399 *White Doe* 263
Of duke or earl, from scenes of courtly pomp 859 *Excursion* 7. 125
Earldom. Such strength that Earldom held of yore; 403 *White Doe* 697
Earless. Pillowed in some deep dungeon's earless den;— 305 *Toussaint* 4
Earlier. Perhaps at earlier Crecy, or Poictiers. 184 *Yew-trees* 8
Then, or far earlier, let us rove 233 *Power of Sound* 41
Or, at an earlier call, to mark, 375 **The Minstrels* 40
And, earlier still, was heard the hum of bees; 377 *Duddon* 6. 4
Earlier from cleansing fires, and gains withal 429 *Ecc. Sonn.* 2. 3. 4
Were earlier raised, remain to hear 586 *Hogg* 26
Each twilight earlier call'd the Sun to meet, 610 *Desc.Sk.Quarto* 453
With earlier smile the ray of morn to view 610 *Desc.Sk.Quarto* 454
Far earlier, ere one smoke-wreath had risen 647 *Prelude* 2. 340
Than in his earlier season did he love 760 *Excursion* 1. 289
A few days earlier; then would you have seen 781 *Excursion* 2. 621
Ill borne in earlier life; but his was now 783 *Excursion* 2. 749
I read,—how in his manhood's earlier day 825 *Excursion* 5. 190
Earliest. Plucked while the church bells rang their earliest chime. 28 *Guilt* 211
Rome's earliest legion passed! 215 *Kirkstone* 44
Touched by the skylark's earliest note, 222 *Triad* 176
Its earliest green along the lane. 239 *P. B.* 255
As when their earliest flowers of hope were blown, 282 *Railway* 4
Thus, like the men of earliest days, 301 *Bran* 74
Those had given earliest notice, as the lark 432 *Ecc. Sonn.* 2. 14. 1

Earliest—*continued.*
And some, coeval with the earliest blush — 436 *Ecc. Sonn.* 2. 32. 5
Thy glory meets me with the earliest beam — 440 *Ecc. Sonn.* 3. 2. 7
In Britain's earliest dawn: — 499 **Departing summer* 33
Was felt near murmuring brooks in earliest time; — 502 **The unremitting* 14
Heirs from times of earliest record — 535 *Egremont* 9
For which, by earliest glimpse of morning light, — 554 *Prioress* 137
I, who on shipboard lived from earliest youth, — 574 *Chiabrera* 4. 10
At evening, when the earliest stars began — 671 *Prelude* 5. 366
Began to spin, with toil, my earliest songs. — 726 *Prelude* 10. 552
My earliest notices; with these compared — 741 *Prelude* 13. 104
My earliest visitations, careless then — 748 *Prelude* 14. 141
The earliest summoned and the longest spared— — 837 *Excursion* 5. 970
What time the hunter's earliest horn is heard — 850 *Excursion* 6. 830

Earls. Two Earls fast leagued in discontent, — 400 *White Doe* 368
Pronounced the word,—and the Earls descry, — 402 *White Doe* 600
And prayed the Earls in self-defence — 403 *White Doe* 631
" Rise, noble Earls, put forth your might — 403 *White Doe* 633
—Brave Earls! to whose heroic veins — 403 *White Doe* 646
Much injured Earls! by these preferred, — 403 *White Doe* 675
The Earls upon each other gazed, — 404 *White Doe* 791

Early. Along the steaming lake, to early mass. — 13 *Desc. Sk.* 126
Till to his flock the early shepherd goes, — 27 *Guilt* 159
But sickness stopped me in an early stage — 35 *Guilt* 581
Of some dark deed to which in early life — 37 *Bord.* 15
A pledge of endless bliss in acts of early piety, — 93 *Poet's Dream* 74
All that the Priest had said: his early years — 102 *Brothers* 421
While he the issue waits, at early morn — 104 *Artegal* 106
But now we are strangers, go early or late; — 116 *Repentance* 13
Early at evening did it burn—and late, — 133 *Michael* 117
The time of early youth; and there you learned, — 147 *Joanna* 2
But why so early with this prayer?— — 174 *Waggoner* 1. 47
Were mine in early days; — 225 *Present.* 9
Owed many years of early liberty. — 259 *Calvert* 3
At early dawn, or rather when the air — 269 *Gordale* 1
While Anna's peers and early playmates tread, — 273 **While Anna's* 1
Hath early found among the dead, — 285 *Grave of Burns* 68
Out of her early struggles well inspired — 356 *Aquap.* 272
For whom his toil with early day begins. — 366 *Lombardy* 4
Some who had early mandates to depart, — 381 *Duddon* 21. 4
Dreams treasured up from early days, — 386 *Yarrow Rev.* 79
Early awake, by Siloa's brook, to sing — 440 *Ecc. Sonn.* 2. 46. 5
O lost too early for the frequent tear, — 445 *Ecc. Sonn.* 3. 22. 13
The Altar calls; come early under laws — 446 *Ecc. Sonn.* 3. 25. 11
Full early lost, and fruitlessly deplored; — 458 **Had this* 74
From early youth I ploughed the restless Main, — 470 †*From early* 1
Full early to the silent tomb — 473 *Ossian* 46
The voice of praise at early morn, — 506 *Lab. Hymn* 2
For lightsome Fanny had thus early thrown, — 523 *Epist. Beaumont* 157
Not unexpectant that by early day — 524 *Epist. Beaumont* 209
Whom he had early loved. And not in vain — 573 *Chiabrera* 2. 8
Had scarcely flowered: and at this early time, — 575 *Chiabrera* 8. 11
Spotting the steaming deeps to early mass; — 604 *Desc.Sk.Quarto* 145
At early morn the careful housewife, led — 615 *Desc.Sk.Quarto* 728
The terrors, pains, and early miseries, — 637 *Prelude* 1. 345
My story early—not misled, I trust, — 641 *Prelude* 1. 613
Pre-eminent till death. From early days, — 646 *Prelude* 2. 265
Were early;—oft before the hours of school — 647 *Prelude* 2. 330
Obsequious to my steps early and late, — 660 *Prelude* 4. 107
For books and nature at that early age. — 663 *Prelude* 4. 299
Which they partake at pleasure. Early died — 669 *Prelude* 5. 256
Full early trained to worship seemliness, — 670 *Prelude* 5. 298
May books and Nature be their early joy! — 672 *Prelude* 5. 423
Even at that early time, needs must I trust — 679 *Prelude* 6. 309
At early dawn. The monastery bells — 681 *Prelude* 6. 408
Day after day, up early and down late, — 682 *Prelude* 6. 494
From early converse with the works of God — 698 *Prelude* 7. 742
And thus my heart was early introduced — 703 *Prelude* 8. 277
Was guarded from too early intercourse — 704 *Prelude* 8. 331
Thus early took a place pre-eminent; — 704 *Prelude* 8. 341
In which my early feelings had been nursed— — 708 *Prelude* 8. 634
Thus from a very early age, O Friend! — 709 *Prelude* 8. 676
With early morning towards the Palace-walk — 719 *Prelude* 10. 94
Rejoiced through early youth, before the winds — 735 *Prelude* 12. 95
Too forcibly, too early in my life, — 737 *Prelude* 12. 202
Of early love, the loved one at my side, — 738 *Prelude* 12. 262
From moral purpose—early tutored me — 740 *Prelude* 13. 44
Through storm and darkness, early in my mind — 742 *Prelude* 13. 154
Be this ascribed; to early intercourse, — 748 *Prelude* 14. 164
Poured out for all the early tenderness — 749 *Prelude* 14. 234
One whom with thee friendship had early paired; — 750 *Prelude* 14. 267
The written promise! Early had he learned — 759 *Excursion* 1. 223
Among the dewy grass,—in early spring, — 764 *Excursion* 1. 526
We parted.—'Twas the time of early spring; — 766 *Excursion* 1. 690
Who at her bidding early and alone, — 783 *Excursion* 2. 786
Some rare advantages. Your early days — 813 *Excursion* 4. 781
Of gravest import. Early he perceives, — 813 *Excursion* 4. 807
In early youth, among my native hills, — 835 *Excursion* 5. 862
This baneful diligence:—at early morn — 840 *Excursion* 6. 168
From whom, in early childhood, was withdrawn — 863 *Excursion* 7. 401
Fixed in his soul, so early and so deep; — 878 *Excursion* 8. 299
Of civil polity, and early trained — 880 *Excursion* 8. 393
Of this unhappy lot, in early youth — 886 *Excursion* 9. 165
Her pitcher here at early dawn, by me — S. 3. 435 **The doubt* 136

Earn. To earn, by wholesome labour in the field, — 880 *Excursion* 8. 394

Earned. *See* **Well-earned.**
No gains too cheaply earned his fancy cloy, — 11 *Desc. Sk.* 15
Vain hope! for fraud took all that he had earned. — 25 *Guilt* 64

Earned—*continued.*
Yet there the Soul shall enter which hath earned — 211 *Laod.* 109
Was reared and taught; and humbly earned his bread, — 584 *Ch. Lamb* 4
Have fairly earned a victory o'er the weak, — 806 *Excursion* 4. 308
The faith which they by diligence had earned, — 839 *Excursion* 6. 71
Had earned for him sure welcome, and the rights — 859 *Excursion* 7. 122

Earnest. Because they carry in themselves an earnest — 65 *Bord.* 1537
With this dear holy shepherd-boy breathe a prayer of earnest heart, — 91 *Norman Boy* 30
The Boy no answer made by words, but, so earnest was his look, — 93 *Poet's Dream* 69
The other thanked him with an earnest voice; — 102 *Brothers* 415
Unknown to memory, was an earnest given — 122 *V. and J.* 31
With others round them, earnest all and blithe, — 133 *Michael* 171
Such earnest vigils, that belief prevailed — 139 *Widow* 11
Mingling most earnest wishes for the day — 151 **When, to* 108
While Benjamin in earnest mood — 175 *Waggoner* 1. 146
Does, then, a deep and earnest thought the blissful mind employ — 189 *Star-gazers* 25
That earnest Creature turned away, — 243 *P. B.* 599
With earnest feeling I shall pray — 288 *Highland Girl* 22
He sate, and eulogised with earnest pen — 356 *Aquap.* 259
Vain aspiration of an earnest will! — 395 *White Doe: Ded.* 61
And spake in firm and earnest mood. — 406 *White Doe* 896
For Them, and for their Land. The earnest Sire, — 422 *Ecc. Sonn.* 1. 13. 9
Ye holy Men, so earnest in your care, — 423 *Ecc. Sonn.* 1. 20. 13
Their Church reformed! labouring with earnest care — 438 *Ecc. Sonn.* 2. 40. 4
With outstretched hands and earnest speech—in vain! — 442 *Ecc. Sonn.* 3. 8. 10
We stood, a trembling, earnest Company! — 445 *Ecc. Sonn.* 3. 22. 4
—Off they fly in earnest chase; — 490 *Incident: Dog* 10
With no mean earnest of a heritage — 510 **Among a* 9
Such earnest longings and regrets as keen — 528 **Those breathing* 112
As my last earnest prayer ere we depart. — 535 *Egremont* 24
Her earnest tone, and look beaming with faith, — 541 *Grace Darl.* 45
With earnest pains unchecked by dread — 543 *Russ. Fug.* 113
In earnest converse with belovèd Friends, — 549 **The massy* 14
His Primer conning with an earnest cheer, — 553 *Prioress* 66
Those simple lines flowed with an earnest wish, — 585 *Ch. Lamb* 40
Why with such earnest pains dost thou provoke — 589 *Immortality* 127
But speedily an earnest longing rose — 633 *Prelude* 1. 114
A foretaste, a dim earnest, of the calm — 636 *Prelude* 1. 280
Ventured, at some rash Muse's earnest call, — 704 *Prelude* 8. 368
From earnest dialogues I slipped in thought, — 716 *Prelude* 9. 438
Earnest and blind, against the stern decree. — 721 *Prelude* 10. 190
Peeped forth, to give an earnest of the Spring. — 768 *Excursion* 1. 816
My Fellow-traveller, with earnest voice, — 772 *Excursion* 2. 87
Earnest alike, let both from hill to hill — 789 *Excursion* 3. 191
'Mid Buxton's dreary heights. In earnest watch, — 879 *Excursion* 8. 377
And earnest preparation.—Forth we went, — 890 *Excursion* 9. 433

Earnestly. Sometimes, most earnestly, he said, — 194 *Ruth* 163
Dear to the saints, strives earnestly to eject — 431 *Ecc. Sonn.* 2. 10. 7
And earnestly to charitable care — 665 *Prelude* 4. 450

Earnestness. With rival earnestness; far other strife — 280 **Intent on* 5
I gazed with earnestness, and dared no more. — 365 **Under the* 10
Crying with earnestness that might not cease, — 365 **The Baptist* 13
With a look of such earnestness often will stand, — 570 *Farmer* 71
With rival earnestness and kindred glee. — 892 *Excursion* 9. 531

Earning. Look fairly like a lawful earning. — 177 *Waggoner* 2. 40

Earnings. " Take your earnings."—Oh! that I — 535 *Egremont* 53
His earnings might supply, and brought away — 760 *Excursion* 1. 246

Ear-piercing. Crowed with ear-piercing power till then unheard; — 21 *Desc. Sk.* 629

Ears. His ears were never silent; sleep forsook — 36 *Guilt* 635
He is a man, if it should come to his ears — 47 *Bord.* 533
Your words are precious to my ears; go on. — 52 *Bord.* 832
Thou hast left me ears to hear my Daughter's voice, — 53 *Bord.* 852
She gave me eyes, she gave me ears; — 79 *Sparrow's Nest* 17
Seemed to feast with head and ears; and his tail with pleasure shook. — 87 *Pet-lamb* 10
And that green corn all day is rustling in thy ears! — 87 *Pet-lamb* 28
But of this in my ears not a word did he speak; — 120 *Childless Father* 19
That, should he lose his eyes and ears, — 127 *Idiot Boy* 109
And to the road she turns her ears, — 127 *Idiot Boy* 139
The mountain-ponies prick their ears, — 166 *Danish Boy* 41
His ears are by the music thrilled, — 177 *Waggoner* 2. 34
The noise of danger's in your ears, — 236 *P. B.* 13
That overpowered your mortal ears? — 237 *P. B.* 84
Such life is in his limbs and ears; — 242 *P. B.* 567
The like came never to his ears, — 243 *P. B.* 613
Did plainly come to Peter's ears; — 247 *P. B.* 957
Enter through ears and eyesight, with such gleam — 260 **How sweet* 12
By waking ears have sometimes been received — 261 **I heard (alas* 3
Your grandame's ears with pleasure of your noise! — 310 *Anticip.* 9
Our ears, and near the dwellings of mankind! — 336 *Staub-bach* 3
My ears did listen, 'twas enough to gaze; — 338 *Engelberg* 16
Borne by the Muse from rills in shepherds' ears — 368 *Trajan* 23
Shrink from *thy* name, pure Rill, with unpleased ears. — 392 *Avon* 14
Chanting in barbarous ears a tuneful prayer— — 422 *Ecc. Sonn.* 1. 14. 8
In Gallic ears the unadulterate Word, — 431 *Ecc. Sonn.* 2. 12. 4
And prophesy to ears that will not hear. — 438 *Ecc. Sonn.* 2. 40. 14
And he has neither eyes nor ears; — 485 *Poet's Epitaph* 27
For the same sound is in my ears — 487 *Fountain* 31
Thy ears were deaf, and feeble were thy knees,— — 491 *Tribute: Dog* 17
Inviting, at all seasons, ears and eyes — 500 *Humanity* 13
As in a posy, with a few pale ears — 509 *F. Stone* 57
His ears he closed to listen to the songs — 576 *Chiabrera* 9. 16

Earthly—*continued.*
Some vain distinctions, marks of earthly state 824 *Excursion* 5. 157
Whose course of earthly honour was begun 825 *Excursion* 5. 180
Compare ! thy earthly bed a moment past S. 3. 434 **The doubt* 95
These not of earthly texture, and the vault S. 3. 435 **The doubt* 107
And this deep vale its earthly counterpart, K.8. 254 *Recluse* 1. 1. 642
How little dost thou speak of earthly gloom ! [?] **A sad* 12
Earth-nuts. I know the earth-nuts fit for food : 145 *Her Eyes* 96
Earthquake. The mine's dire earthquake, and the pallid host 30 *Guilt* 348
And left as if by earthquake strewn, 214 *Kirkstone* 11
He puts the Earthquake on her still design, 328 *Ode 1815* 94
An earthquake, mingling with the battle's shock, 361 **When here* 2
Volcanic burst, earthquake, and hurricane, 514 **Who ponders* 7
The earthquake is not satisfied at once ; 719 *Prelude* 10. 84
Earthquakes. Like earthquakes, shocks repeated day by day, 712 *Prelude* 9. 179
Earth's. And higher far than lies within earth's bounds : 62 *Bord.* 1373
Earth's noblest penitent ; from bondage freed 105 *Artegal* 229
Rolled round in earth's diurnal course, 187 **A slumber* 7
And withered leaves, from earth's cold breast 217 *Enterprise* 131
The wide earth's storehouse fenced about 217 *Enterprise* 153
" O Lady, worthy of earth's proudest throne ! 220 *Triad* 52
To hear the earth's soft murmuring 237 *P. B.* 74
Or with the Moon conquering earth's misty air, 274 **Such age* 12
Embraced those Brothers upon earth's wide plain ; 276 *Oker Hill* 11
Well pleased, her foot should print earth's common grass, 278 **Lo ! where she* 12
And memory of Earth's bitter leaven, 286 *Nith* 59
Of Earth's first blood, have titles manifold. 307 **It is not* 14
Oh grief that Earth's best hopes rest all with Thee ! 309 **England ! the* 14
At happy distance from earth's groaning field, 313 **Clouds, lingering* 7
Into whose bosom earth's best treasures flow, 327 *Ode 1815* 47
Thou who dost warm Earth's universal mould, 329 *Ode : Thanks.* 31
For they Earth's fairest daughters do excel ; 333 *Fish-women* 10
Heaven upon earth's an empty boast ; 337 **Oh Life* 9
Once more beneath the kind Earth's tranquil light ; 381 *Duddon* 21. 7
Or quietly self-buried in earth's mould, 382 *Duddon* 27. 2
And earth's green grass beneath his feet ; 401 *White Doe* 430
Tired with its daily share of earth's unrest,— 460 **Wanderer ! that* 59
(Earth's lingering love to parting reconciled, 476 *Howard* 7
And earth's precarious days. 498 **The sylvan* 24
Or, bound by oaths, comeforth to tread earth's floor 505 *Warning* 121
Earth's sweetness in thy breath. 507 *May* 40
Time's vanities, light fragments of earth's dream— 584 **With copious* 39
By the first men, earth's first inhabitants, 651 *Prelude* 3. 152
Earth's paramount Creature ! not so much for woes 665 *Prelude* 5. 5
With a due reverence on earth's rightful lord, 704 *Prelude* 8. 335
From earth's materials—waits upon my steps ; 755 *Recluse* 1. 1. 798
In earth's dark chambers, with a Christian's hope ! 775 *Excursion* 2. 248
Upon earth's native energies ; forgetting 792 *Excursion* 3. 423
Small creature as she is, from earth's bright flowers, 807 *Excursion* 4. 393
And the great sun, earth's universal lord ! 808 *Excursion* 4. 465
Earth's melancholy vision through the space 836 *Excursion* 5. 936
But, above all, that mixture of earth's mould 842 *Excursion* 6. 273
Of all-beholding Man, earth's thoughtful lord ; 876 *Excursion* 8. 164
Earth's universal frame shall feel the effect ; 890 *Excursion* 9. 386
Earth's petty grievances—its toil and care :— [?] **A sad* 7
Earth-sullying. Of sad mortality's earth-sullying wing, 263 **How clear* 9
Earth-voice. No ; 'tis the earth-voice of the mighty sea, 453 **The Sun, that* 11
Earthward. Earthward in uncomplaining languishment, 169 *Love lies Bleeding* 8
Earthward it glided with a swift descent : 323 *Ode 1814* 23
Earthward or heavenward, radiant messengers, 500 *Humanity* 36
And can earthward bend an ear 503 **Like a* 66
Shall tottering Age, bent earthward, hear 533 **Blest is* 37
Earthward, as if in opposition set 746 *Prelude* 14. 29
Earthwards. Bent earthwards ; he looks up—the clouds are split 184 *Night-piece* 11
Earthy. Should start out of his earthy, worm-like state, 731 *Prelude* 11. 252
Feebly it tinkles with an earthy sound, 786 *Excursion* 3. 31
Ease. *See* **Heart's-ease.**
How graceful, pride can be, and how majestic, ease. 6 *Ev. Wk.* 221
Brisk toil, alternating with ready ease, 11 *Desc. Sk.* 17
Nor is she more at ease on some *still* night, 14 *Desc. Sk.* 186
Struggled with tears nor could its sorrow ease, 34 *Guilt* 535
I strove to ease my mind, when our two Comrades, 59 *Bord.* 1211
Finds ease because another feels it too. 65 *Bord.* 1556
nothing which might have set you at ease ? 72 *Bord.* 1954
Lay stretched at ease ; but, passing by the place 101 *Brothers* 371
No ease, within doors or without ; 115 *Last of Flock* 76
But Betty is not quite at ease ; 127 *Idiot Boy* 155
" What can I do to ease your pain ? 128 *Idiot Boy* 193
There's nothing that can ease my pain." 128 *Idiot Boy* 198
Poor Betty ! it would ease her pain 129 *Idiot Boy* 269
She gave consent, and Michael was at ease. 136 *Michael* 321
Drying their feathers in the sun, at ease ; 143 **High bliss* 16
For an allotted interval of ease, 150 **When, to* 53
Oft on the dappled turf at ease 158 **With little* 9
Proceeding with a mind at ease ; 176 *Waggoner* 2. 14
Tribute to ease ; and, of its joy secure, 185 *Nutting* 40
If a thief could be here he might pilfer at ease ; 188 *Music* 23
In gaiety and ease. 225 *Present.* 30
He hung,—then floated with angelic ease 226 *Vernal Ode* 10
And then, as if to take his ease, 241 *P. B.* 427
To ease his conscience of its pain. 245 *P. B.* 800

Ease—*continued.*
" Oh ! God be praised—my heart's at ease— 248 *P. B.* 1026
Of this small lute gave ease to Petrarch's wound ; 260 **Scorn not* 4
It is not quiet, is not ease ; 289 *Glen-Al.* 25
Her sons were bursting forth, to dwell at ease. 308 **One might* 4
Hence Forms that glide with swan-like ease along, 334 **The Spirit* 6
And we were gay, our hearts at ease ; 348 **Lulled by* 13
I move at ease ; and meet contending themes 350 *Des. Stanzas* 15
(As if her labour and her ease were twins) 366 *Lombardy* 6
Group winding after group with dream-like ease ; 367 *Trajan* 16
For her companionship ; here dwells soft ease : 382 *Duddon* 25. 10
Win rest, and ease, and peace, with bliss that Angels share. 390 *Glencroe* 14
And live at home in blameless ease ; 400 *White Doe* 395
Now couched at ease, though oft this day 407 *White Doe* 1012
Ease from this noble miser of his time 425 *Ecc. Sonn.* 1. 26. 9
Of ease, the narrow Bosphorus will disdain ; 427 *Ecc. Sonn.* 1. 34. 6
" Woe to you, Prelates ! rioting in ease 433 *Ecc. Sonn.* 2. 18. 1
Floating at ease while nations have effaced 452 *Ecc. Sonn.* 3. 47. 7
Utterance of thanks that we have past with ease, 466 *St. Bees* 26
It is not then when, swept with sportive ease, 467 *St. Bees* 97
Nor dost thou fail, thro' abject love of ease, 468 *St. Bees* 133
Would be rational peace—a philosopher's ease. 482 *Character* 8
Where ravens spread their plumy vans, at ease ! 496 **A little* 32
If Power could live at ease with self-restraint ! 500 *Humanity* 42
Mother ! blest be thy calm ease ; 503 **Like a* 60
Leaves him at ease among grand thoughts : whose eye 514 * *Blest Statesman* 2
Be plighted, not to ease but sullen sloth, 514 **Long-favoured* 7
By glimpses caught—disporting at their ease, 527 **Those breathing* 44
A buoyant Spirit, and a heart at ease. 532 **Once I* 30
This oftentimes, that he might be at ease, 553 *Prioress* 77
For to th' untrue he oft gives ease and joy ; 560 *Cuck.andNight.* 198
May thence remount at ease. The aged Man 566 *Cumb. Beg.* 6
The fields better suited the ease of his soul : 569 *Farmer* 22
For this he did all in the *ease* of his heart. 570 *Farmer* 44
A Picture had it been of lasting ease, 578 *Peele Castle* 25
To ease a father's cheated love he hung 624 *Æneid* 83
Then, stretcht at ease in some sequestered cave, 630 [?] **O Moon* 7
Long months of ease and undisturbed delight 632 *Prelude* 1. 26
A winding passage with majestic ease 680 *Prelude* 6. 379
Or animate an hour of vacant ease. 739 *Prelude* 12. 335
Love cannot be ; nor does it thrive with ease 743 *Prelude* 13. 202
To competence and ease :—to him it offered 761 *Excursion* 1. 336
His calling laid aside, he lived at ease : 762 *Excursion* 1. 386
And they, if blest with health and hearts at ease, 773 *Excursion* 2. 102
We scaled, without a track to ease our steps, 776 *Excursion* 2. 323
Instantly throwing down my limbs at ease 776 *Excursion* 2. 350
Was glad to find her conscience set at ease ; 785 *Excursion* 2. 888
With hearts at ease, and knowledge in our hearts 794 *Excursion* 3. 548
—Truth has her pleasure-grounds, her haunts of ease 810 *Excursion* 4. 588
By ease and leisure ; by the very wealth 835 *Excursion* 5. 831
Helps to internal ease. Of many such 844 *Excursion* 6. 401
For their heart's ease or pleasure. Strains of power 857 *Excursion* 7. 22
A simple curiosity to ease : 859 *Excursion* 7. 107
A festival of unencumbered ease ; 869 *Excursion* 7. 779
And to beguile the lassitude of ease ; S. 3. 426 **Through Cumbrian* 6
Eased. And eased his mind with this reply : 86 *Anecdote* 54
Hath often eased my pensive breast 158 **In youth* 63
Exulting Warbler ! eased a fretted brain, 279 **Hark ! 'tis* 7
Eternal Lord ! eased of a cumbrous load, 366 **Eternal Lord* 1
Then eased his soul at length by praise 374 *Eg. Maid* 341
Thou wilt be eased, and less wilt droop and pine. 561 *Cuck.andNight.* 245
Easedale. High into Easedale, up to Dunmail-Raise, 133 *Michael* 134
Eases. Eases her pain, and helps her prayers. 144 **Driven in* 36
Easier. Sad thoughts, and breathes with easier breath ; 164 **Fair Lady* 34
Here crave an easier lot ; 223 *Wishing-gate* 45
A further, though far easier, task 401 *White Doe* 505
Find easier access to the pious mind, 648 *Prelude* 2. 420
Was easier, the transition more secure, 751 *Prelude* 14. 343
A safer, easier, more determined, course. 864 *Excursion* 7. 490
Or easier links connecting place with place) 876 *Excursion* 8. 108
Easiest. Now, like to things within fate's easiest reach, 471 *Tynwald* 7
Or easiest carried, closed the motley train. 858 *Excursion* 7. 68
Easily. Thou know'st me for a Man not easily moved, 38 *Bord.* 69
Too quickly moved, too easily giving way, 76 *Bord.* 2233
Easily a pious training 94 *Westmoreland Girl* 77
What one short sigh so easily removed ?— 118 *Maternal Grief* 10
Easily may the sequel be divined— 122 *V. and J.* 79
Though the most easily beguiled 224 **'Tis gone* 40
Not easily eluded. 386 *Yarrow Rev.* 48
Shun the broad way too easily explored, 626 *Rock : Rydal* 2
In human language), easily I passed 652 *Prelude* 3. 239
With whom I herded !—(easily, indeed, 671 *Prelude* 5. 408
In which worst losses easily might wear 722 *Prelude* 10. 304
More subtle and less easily explained, 736 *Prelude* 12. 124
The strongest did not easily escape ; 775 *Excursion* 2. 244
So easily deprived ?) but, for that cause, 799 *Excursion* 3. 922
Too easily, despise or overlook 807 *Excursion* 4. 420
Not easily deciphered, told of one 825 *Excursion* 5. 179
The ungentle mind can easily find means 852 *Excursion* 6. 954
East. *See* **North-east.**
And saw the dawn opening the silvery east 30 *Guilt* 313
And they go rambling east and west 84 *Shepherd-boys* 8
In the unrelenting east.—Through all her courts 123 *V. and J.* 94
Watched for tidings from the East, beheld his Lord, 141 *Arm. Lady* 101
From east to west, in ample vest 180 *Waggoner* 4. 55

Echoes—*continued.*
In notes which mountain echoes would take up . S.3. 436 **The doubt* 157
Echoing. Thunders through echoing pines the head-long Aar; 16 *Desc. Sk.* 337
Shouts from the echoing hills with savage joy. 17 *Desc. Sk.* 365
Poured through the echoing hills around, 226 *Vernal Ode* 24
Through Europe, echoing from the newsman's blast, 349 *Val. Dover* 3
How did the cliffs and echoing hills rejoice 467 *St. Bees* 100
Echoing thorough all the green wood wide. 558 *Cuck.andNight.* 100
Deepening her echoing torrents' awful peal 603 *Desc. Sk. Quarto* 76
In wood or echoing cave, for discipline 734 *Prelude* 11. 458
Loud echoing, add your speed to the pursuit; 808 *Excursion* 4. 502
Echo's. Although invisible as Echo's self, 361 **List—'twas* 6
Eclipse. Of hasty anger, rising in the eclipse 124 *V. and J.* 169
All suffering dim eclipse! 343 *Eclipse* 54
Now, faintly darkening with the sun's eclipse, 471 *Ailsa Crag* 5
The paramount ace, a moon in her eclipse, 640 *Prelude* 1. 532
And little bustling passions that eclipse, 706 *Prelude* 8. 500
And subject neither to eclipse nor wane, 802 *Excursion* 4. 72
Eclipsed. Eclipsing or eclipsed, by night or day, 461 **Queen of* 52
Of tides, and when the moon will be eclipsed, 840 *Excursion* 6. 172
In their own arts outdone, their fame eclipsed, 843 *Excursion* 6. 348
Eclipsing. Eclipsing or eclipsed, by night or day, 461 **Queen of* 52
Economic. Avaunt this economic rage! S.3. 439 **Avaunt this* 1
Economists. Economists will tell you that the State 878 *Excursion* 8. 283
Ecstasies. An Angel, and in earthly ecstasies 139 *Widow* 41
Behold him perched in ecstasies, 159 *Green Linnet* 27
When these wild ecstasies shall be matured 207 *Tintern* 138
And for no transient ecstasies! 228 *Devot. Incit.* 39
Consume with zeal, in wingèd ecstasies 467 *St. Bees* 88
Not less than vernal ecstasies, 499 **Departing summer* 23
Oft as he called those ecstasies to mind, 759 *Excursion* 1. 237
Ecstasy. She chatters in her ecstasy. 81 †*Mother's Return* 24
Sharing in the ecstasy; 171 *Kitten* 120
No longer) with what ecstasy upborne 280 *'*Tis he* 11
Uttered to Heaven in ecstasy devout! 322 *Germans* 8
Of the devout, a veil of ecstasy! 451 *Ecc. Sonn.* 3. 44. 14
Of the poetic ecstasy 472 *Ossian* 35
But faith sublimed to ecstasy! 550 *Hermit's Cell* 5. 20
Is stirred to ecstasy, as others are, 674 *Prelude* 5. 590
To ecstasy; and all the crooked paths 804 *Excursion* 4. 183
Ecstatic. With morbid restlessness:—the ecstatic fit 438 *Ecc. Sonn.* 2. 41. 3
Eddies. The crows rushed by in eddies, homeward borne. 25 *Guilt* 40
In silent pools, now in strong eddies chained; 849 *Excursion* 6. 737
Eddy. Within the eddy of a common blast, 122 *V. and J.* 27
Have never ceased to eddy round its base, 367 *Trajan* 8
Eddying. Eddying round and round they sink 170 *Kitten* 9
To mark its eddying foam-bells prettily distrest 190 **Lyre! though* 27
His flight, 'mid eddying pine-tree tops! 213 *Dion* 76
Yon eddying balls of foam, these arrowy gleams 268 **DogmaticTeachers* 10
Of feasts, or scandal, eddying like the wind 522 *Epist. Beaumont* 63
Yet, like to eddying balls of foam 551 **Behold an* 3
While winds are eddying round her, among straws 693 *Prelude* 7. 440
Eddying within its vast circumference, 788 *Excursion* 3. 147
Eddy's. It seemed to suck us in with an eddy's force. 649 *Prelude* 3. 14
Eden. But, for the bowers of Eden lost, 337 **Oh Life* 10
Gales sweet as those that over Eden blew! 434 *Ecc. Sonn.* 2. 24. 14
Eden! till now thy beauty had I viewed 476 *Eden* 1
Of blissful Eden this was neither given, K.8. 239 *Recluse* 1. 1. 105
Eden's. Of Eden's blissful wilderness, 154 *Flower Garden* 4
Her statelier Eden's course to guard; 204 *Brougham* 47
Held with all Kinds in Eden's blissful bowers. 362 **List—'twas* 65
Like sinless snakes in Eden's happy land;— 374 *Eg. Maid* 323
CROGLIN, the stately Eden's tributary! 476 *Nunnery* 3
If Excellence was ever Eden's name? L.1. 88 *Juvenal* 1. 12
Edge. The peasant, from yon cliff of fearful edge 4 *Ev. Wk.* 130
An edge all flame, the broadening sun appears; 5 *Ev. Wk.* 169
By the lake's edge, she rose—to face the noontide heat; 7 *Ev. Wk.* 253
And feeding pike starts from the water's edge, 7 *Ev. Wk.* 282
Near the wood's edge—rest there to-night, I pray you: 67 *Bord.* 1648
Then downwards from the steep hill's edge 83 *Lucy Gray* 45
His flock, along the woodland's edge with relics sprinkled o'er 91 *Norman Boy* 9
Down from the ceiling, by the chimney's edge, 133 *Michael* 110
A heap of stones, which by the streamlet's edge 136 *Michael* 327
When o'er the sea-rock's edge we go; 145 *Her Eyes* 44
Along this mountain's edge, 156 *Oak and Broom* 22
"At noon, when, by the forest's edge 239 *P. B.* 261
Sharpen the keenest edge of present ill,— 267 **As the* 7
Near the bright River's edge. Yet why repine? 335 *Rhine* 10
Forced by intent to take from speech its edge, 353 *Aquap.* 75
Grows from a little edge of light 369 *Eg. Maid* 9
One with its kindling edge declares that soon 461 **Who but is* 5
And he creeps to the edge of my stove. 484 **A plague* 10
A brightening edge will indicate that soon 532 **How beautiful the* 6
It's edge all flame, the broad'ning sun appears; 594 *Ev. Wk. Quarto* 152
To set our minds on edge, and did no more. 656 *Prelude* 3. 539
Standing alone, as from a rampart's edge, 658 *Prelude* 4. 4
Right to a rough stream's edge, and there broke off; 683 *Prelude* 6. 569
Sole building on a mountain's dreary edge, 758 *Excursion* 1. 123
Along the window's edge, profusely grew 767 *Excursion* 1. 718
He who with pocket-hammer smites the edge 788 *Excursion* 3. 178
The edge of adverse circumstance, and turn 835 *Excursion* 5. 859
In blindness all too near the river's edge; 853 *Excursion* 6. 1020

Edge—*continued.*
Along the sharp edge of yon lofty crags, 863 *Excursion* 7. 413
And on the very edge of vacancy 865 *Excursion* 7. 496
Light birch, aloft upon the horizon's edge, 866 *Excursion* 7. 598
And down the vale along the streamlet's edge 890 *Excursion* 9. 434
With prospect underneath of Striding edge, K.8. 225 **I will* 29
Edged. *See* **Sharp-edged.**
This Rock would be if edged around 162 **Who fancied* 2
And wears a frontlet edged with gold. 399 *White Doe* 260
Are edged with golden rays! 479 *Somnamb.* 157
Edged the black clouds, home and to bed we went, 642 *Prelude* 2. 17
Edges. To move along the edges of the hills, 671 *Prelude* 5. 367
Edging. My thoughts become bright like yon edging of Pines 345 *Stanzas: Simplon* 21
Edict. Whether by edict of the one or few; 717 *Prelude* 9. 528
Edifice. To be engrafted on the top of his small edifice. 91 *Norman Boy* 20
An edifice of warlike frame 409 *White Doe* 1167
Rude is this Edifice, and Thou hast seen 547 **Rude is* 1
Of that wide edifice, thy school and home, 679 *Prelude* 6. 268
To the imperial edifice of Blois, 716 *Prelude* 9. 482
—Right toward the sacred Edifice his steps 871 *Excursion* 7. 911
Edifices. Majestic edifices, should not want. 654 *Prelude* 3. 381
Edinborough. O'er stately Edinborough throned on crags? 815 *Excursion* 4. 913
Education. The Power of EDUCATION seemed to rise; 618 *School Ex.* 6
Of education, nor with least delight 698 *Prelude* 7. 739
The name of Education, have to do 742 *Prelude* 13. 171
Educeth. How Providence educeth, from the spring 271 *Henry: Portrait* 12
Edward. Here's a *cozie* warm house for Edward and me. 81 †*Address: Child* 43
"Now, little Edward, say why so: 86 *Anecdote* 37
My little Edward, tell me why."— 86 *Anecdote* 38
"Why, Edward, tell me why?" 86 *Anecdote* 48
Fair Court of Edward! wonder of the world! 430 *Ecc. Sonn.* 2. 7. 9
Of pious Edward kneeling as he knelt 436 *Ecc. Sonn.* 2. 31. 8
Edward will come with you;—and, pray, 483 *Sister* 13
Edward, the flower of chivalry, survey L.1. 94 *Juvenal* 2. 24
Edward's. Now honour'd Edward's less than Bacon's name. 619 *School Ex.* 56
Edwin. Where thoughtful Edwin, tutored in the school 422 *Ecc. Sonn.* 1. 15. 2
E'er. (*Partial list.*) *See* **Ever.**
That either e'er existed is my shame: 47 *Bord.* 555
If with that counsel I do e'er comply. 559 *Cuck.andNight.* 165
For thee she mourns, nor e'er will cease to mourn; 575 *Chiabrera* 7. 8
Efface. Her keen desire of knowledge, nor efface 848 *Excursion* 6. 700
Effaced. Effaced for ever. 286 *Nith* 60
Floating at ease while nations have effaced 452 *Ecc. Sonn.* 3. 47. 7
Of reason, honourably effaced by debts 862 *Excursion* 7. 319
When these particular interests were effaced 893 *Excursion* 9. 589
Effect. It took effect—and yet I baffled it, 75 *Bord.* 2144
So passed the time, till, whether through effect 122 *V. and J.* 54
Small cause of dire effect! for, surely, 246 *P. B.* 841
(Albeit of effect profound) 324 *Ode 1814* 92
Truth's holy lamp, pure source of bright effect, 380 *Duddon* 18. 7
Witness the Church that oft-times, with effect 431 *Ecc. Sonn.* 2. 10. 6
That peace of mind is Virtue's sure effect. 441 *Ecc. Sonn.* 3. 6. 8
With undistracted reverence, the effect 473 **We saw* 11
Oft worse to bear, or deadlier in effect. 501 *Humanity* 63
Forget his feeling: so (if like effect 677 *Prelude* 6. 154
Less often instantaneous in effect; 686 *Prelude* 6. 750
Through the divine effect of power and love; 706 *Prelude* 8. 491
The effect was, still more elevated views 708 *Prelude* 8. 644
Induced, effect, in whatsoe'er degree, 737 *Prelude* 12. 194
Itself, from all malevolent effect 755 *Recluse* 1. 1. 844
By earthly nature had the effect been wrought 784 *Excursion* 2. 846
Which kings might envy!"—Praise to this effect 787 *Excursion* 3. 75
Different effect producing) is for me 788 *Excursion* 3. 155
Again!"—The effect upon the soul was such 807 *Excursion* 4. 405
That this magnificent effect of power, 816 *Excursion* 4. 971
The inward principle that gives effect 831 *Excursion* 5. 572
Gave obvious instance of the sad effect 842 *Excursion* 6. 279
Speaks, less distinctly, to the same effect. 846 *Excursion* 6. 526
Earth's universal frame shall feel the effect; 890 *Excursion* 9. 386
Concealed, nor through effect of some impure S.3. 435 **The doubt* 98
Effects. The worst effects that our condition saw 795 *Excursion* 3. 615
Predominate; whose strong effects are such 806 *Excursion* 4. 328
That, with like burthen of effects most prized 858 *Excursion* 7. 67
Effectual. Their part in this effectual prayer. 415 *White Doe* 1776
Effeminately. Effeminately level down the truth 743 *Prelude* 13. 212
Efficacious. This efficacious spirit chiefly lurks 737 *Prelude* 12. 219
Examples efficacious to refine 875 *Excursion* 8. 66
Efficaciously. More efficaciously than aught that flows 255 **Grief, thou* 6
More efficaciously than realms outspread, 497 **Enough of climbing* 16
Effigies. The Effigies of a valiant Wight 301 *Bran* 46
And shining effigies of brass inlaid. 825 *Excursion* 5. 170
Effigy. The vow performed, in cross-legged effigy, 430 *Ecc. Sonn.* 2. 8. 7
Effigy of the Vanished—(shall I dare 472 **The captive* 9
Effluence. The effluence from yon distant mountain's head, 263 **How clear* 2
To furnish; for this effluence of thyself, 893 *Excursion* 9. 617
Effort. My deep-drawn sighs no effort could confine; 32 *Guilt* 430
"Generous Frank! the just in effort 140 *Arm. Lady* 31
And him no mortal effort can detain: 211 *Laod.* 154
Thankfully took an effort that was meant 231 **The gentlest Poet* 32
Must either win, through effort of his own, 312 **When, far* 7
Nor while sin lasts must effort cease; 337 **Oh Life* 8
With fruitless effort to allay 406 *White Doe* 931

Eminence—*continued.*
Alone upon some jutting eminence, 647 *Prelude* 2. 343
Up to an eminence, and told a tale 651 *Prelude* 3. 168
Relinquishing this lofty eminence 673 *Prelude* 5. 534
In single or in social eminence, 724 *Prelude* 10. 425
Blow keen upon an eminence that gave 729 *Prelude* 11. 166
The beacon crowning the lone eminence, 738 *Prelude* 12. 259
Of water, or some lofty eminence, 776 *Excursion* 2. 321
The eminence whereon her spirit stood, 795 *Excursion* 3. 659
Of some commanding eminence, which yet 799 *Excursion* 3. 936
To lift the creature toward that eminence 827 *Excursion* 5. 298
"Our very first in eminence of years 861 *Excursion* 7. 242
From some commanding eminence had looked 871 *Excursion* 7. 879
As of a final EMINENCE; though bare 885 *Excursion* 9. 52
Eminent. *See* **Pre-eminent.**
A British Painter (eminent for truth 509 *F. Stone* 99
Eminently. *See* **Pre-eminently.** Sweet garden-orchard, eminently fair; 106 *Farewell* 5
Emits. My noble fire emits the joyful ray 365 **Rapt above* 13
Emma. My EMMA, I will dedicate to thee." 146 **It was an* 39
But, faithful Emma! thou with me canst say. 251 **There is a little* 10
The drooping Emma to his breast, 478 *Somnamb.* 44
Yet blest was Emma when she heard 478 *Somnamb.* 55
"Six feet in earth my Emma lay; 487 **We walked* 37
Emma's. Within the sound of Emma's voice, nor know 111 *'Tis said that some* 51
May call it by the name of EMMA'S DELL. 146 **It was an* 47
If Emma's Ghost it were, 479 *Somnamb.* 128
Emmeline. My sister Emmeline and I 79 **Stay near* 12
My sister Emmeline and I 79 *Sparrow's Nest* 9
Emmet. In the cold ground; and to the emmet gives 807 *Excursion* 4. 430
Emont. Of Emont, hitherto unnamed in song, 678 *Prelude* 6. 204
Emont's. And Emont's murmur mingled with the Song.— 203 *Brougham* 2
For one fair House by Emont's side, 204 *Brougham* 51
And shaped these pleasant walks by Emont's side, 489 *Spade* 2
Emotion. Of even the least emotion. Noting this, 125 *V. and J.* 229
The emotion—nay, more fitly were it said— 355 *Aquap.* 152
With tenderness and mild emotion, 371 *Eg. Maid* 140
With prompt emotion, urging them to pass; 378 *Duddon* 10. 2
Sharing the strong emotion of the crowd, 450 *Ecc. Sonn.* 3. 40. 2
To sit without emotion, hope, or aim, 488 *Pers. Talk* 11
Kindly emotion tending to console 538 **In desultory* 51
Alas! such high emotion touched not me. 654 *Prelude* 3. 342
Affecting more emotion than I felt; 710 *Prelude* 9. 73
From Nature doth emotion come, and moods 740 *Prelude* 13. 1
With manifest emotion, and exclaimed; 817 *Excursion* 4. 1079
For me, the emotion scarcely was less strong 854 *Excursion* 6. 1055
Of glad emotion and deep quietness; K.8. 243 *Recluse* 1.1.231
Emotions. I resign my soul's emotions 550 *Hermit's Cell* 4. 3
My Song! those high emotions which thy voice 706 *Prelude* 8. 477
And public persons, and emotions wrought 717 *Prelude* 9. 544
What, then, were my emotions, when in arms 722 *Prelude* 10. 263
Emotions which best foresight need not fear, 748 *Prelude* 14. 122
—To these emotions, whencesoe'er they come, 755 *Recluse* 1. 1. 763
Tender emotions spreading from the heart 871 *Excursion* 7. 905
Their own emotions given to mountain air S.3. 436 **The doubt* 156
Empassioned. *See* **Impassioned.**
Drew happier, loftier, more empassioned, thoughts 771 *Excursion* 2. 20
Empedocles. Philosopher or Bard, Empedocles, 733 *Prelude* 11. 434
Emperor. General or Cham, Sultan or Emperor, 60 *Bord.* 1229
The Emperor sent a pledge as strong 545 *Russ. Fug.* 351
Is summoned in to crown an Emperor— 732 *Prelude* 11. 360
Emperor's. Who foiled an Emperor's eager quest? 545 *Russ. Fug.* 317
Emperors. Emperors and Kings, how oft have temples rung 326 **Emperors and* 1
These titles emperors and chiefs have borne, 862 *Excursion* 7. 343
Princes, and emperors, and the crowns and palms 872 *Excursion* 7. 981
Emphatically. Emphatically such a Being lives, 646 *Prelude* 2. 252
Empire. Man's intellectual empire. We subsist 70 *Bord.* 1856
What an eager assembly! what an empire is this! 188 *Music* 9
Your favourite seat of empire find— 191 *Seq. Beggars* 35
Power, glory, empire, as the world itself, 230 *Clouds* 39
Dread Beings! and your empire show 245 *P. B.* 774
For he hath waking empire, wide as dreams; 267 **Though narrow* 3
Their sovereign empire in a faithful heart. 279 **All praise* 14
Another mighty Empire overthrown! 310 **Another year* 2
Where now the haughty Empire that was spread 368 *Trajan* 65
Relinquished half his empire to the host 392 **Though joy* 8
What further empire would it have? for now 428 *Ecc. Sonn.* 1. 39. 3
Alternate empire in the shades below— 460 **Queen of* 5
Mount toward the empire of the fickle clouds, 497 **Enough of climbing* 5
Perished the Roman Empire: how the friends 635 *Prelude* 1. 190
And feels nor what an empire we inherit 652 *Prelude* 3. 192
An empire, a possession,—ye whom time 673 *Prelude* 5. 529
There, in a clime from widest empire chosen, 700 *Prelude* 8. 82
New pleasure, wider empire for the sight, 736 *Prelude* 12. 145
Empire's. Which stands the universal empire's boast; 105 *Artegal* 189
Empires. When they to future empires have given birth, 325 *Ode 1814* 134
—Let Empires fall; but ne'er shall Ye disgrace 350 *Des. Stanzas* 48
Communities are lost, and Empires die, 547 **Beneath yon* 17
Employ. He would have taught you how you might employ 108 *Indolence* 52
To such convenient work as might employ 132 *Michael* 105
Does, then, a deep and earnest thought the blissful mind employ 189 *Star-gazers* 25
The pleasant season did my heart employ: 195 *Resolution* 19
What robe can Gratitude employ 331 *Ode: Thanks.* 133
The lucid shafts of reason to employ, 436 *Ecc. Sonn.* 2. 31. 13
Let light and dark duly our thoughts employ; 447 *Ecc. Sonn.* 3. 29. 12

Employ—*continued.*
In love's disport employ; 506 **While from* 26
Your silent lives employ 526 **The soaring* 6
And hopes as dear as could the heart employ 581 **Why should we* 5
—No purple prospects now the mind employ 599 *Ev. Wk. Quarto* 379
Thanks to the means which Nature deigned to employ; 637 *Prelude* 1. 351
Supplied our want, we haply might employ 643 *Prelude* 2. 99
Too delicate employ, as would appear, 839 *Excursion* 6. 98
Employed. *See* **Busily-employed.**
Employed in winter's work. Upon the stone 95 *Brothers* 20
Was busily employed as he. 175 *Waggoner* 1. 151
Employed in setting his sword free 301 *Bran* 53
A vulgar hope was yours when ye employed 639 *Prelude* 1. 467
Work like a sea? Not uselessly employed, 639 *Prelude* 1. 475
Reverence was due to a being thus employed; 668 *Prelude* 5. 150
Me, rather, it employed, to note, and keep. 696 *Prelude* 7. 598
Employed, and man's unfolding intellect: 735 *Prelude* 12. 101
Of Poesy thus courteously employed 791 *Excursion* 3. 335
By none, they for the attempt, and pains employed, 792 *Excursion* 3. 408
Swayed by such motives, to such ends employed; 816 *Excursion* 4. 986
Or implement, a passive thing employed 886 *Excursion* 9. 116
Employment. In union with the employment of his heart, 96 *Brothers* 58
Art sole in thy employment: 159 *Green Linnet* 20
That is the worst of his employment: 179 *Waggoner* 3. 128
Employment hazardous and wearisome! 196 *Resolution* 101
And her divine employment! 386 *Yarrow Rev.* 42
Which gave employment to her listless hands— 767 *Excursion* 1. 759
The employment common through these wilds, and gained, 769 *Excursion* 1. 859
Of his employment, with a courteous smile 871 *Excursion* 7. 920
Employments. Such calm employments, such entire content. 143 **High bliss* 12
His old employments, goes to field or wood, 878 *Excursion* 8. 277
Employs. That hut which on the hills so oft employs 19 *Desc. Sk.* 480
The hut which from the hills his eyes employs 612 *Desc.Sk.Quarto* 570
Which Nature studiously employs to thwart 736 *Prelude* 12. 134
Emporium. That great emporium, chronicle at once 708 *Prelude* 8. 594
To the great City, an emporium then 774 *Excursion* 2. 216
Empowers. The other that empowers him to perceive 837 *Excursion* 5. 990
Empress. Empress of Night! are gladdened by thy beams; 459 **Wanderer! that* 24
Emptied. Fresh emptied of spectators. Twice five years 674 *Prelude* 5. 552
Emptiness. From dread of emptiness or dearth. 227 *Vernal Ode* 60
Perpetual emptiness! unceasing change! 307 **Great men* 11
Of Providence, such emptiness at length 309 **When, looking* 9
The child that might have led him; Emptiness 657 *Prelude* 3. 606
Faith given to vanity and emptiness; 712 *Prelude* 9. 172
And change, and emptiness, these freaks of Nature 788 *Excursion* 3. 139
Empty. *See* **Never-empty.**
The empty loom, cold hearth, and silent wheel, 29 *Guilt* 269
Within those empty walls. I too have seen her; 47 *Bord.* 572
Or the empty thing that they would wish to be. 70 *Bord.* 1826
Nothing but silence and empty space; 80 †*Address: Child* 17
Now with her empty can the Maiden turned away: 87 *Pet-lamb* 15
I look—the sky is empty space; 110 *'Tis said that some* 18
The empty house when he comes home; 162 *Binnorie* 40
And empty thy late home, 169 *Wren's Nest* 68
Does like an empty bucket mount. 245 *P. B.* 805
An empty noise of death the battle's roar, 316 **The martial* 2
Heaven upon earth's an empty boast; 337 **Oh Life* 9
With images, and crowns, and empty cars; 346 *Processions* 31
And, for a moment, filled that empty Throne. 365 **Under the* 14
Bare breast I take and an empty hand."— 401 *White Doe* 515
Of future vanishing like empty dreams) 426 *Ecc. Sonn.* 1. 30. 7
An idle form, the Word an empty sound! 445 *Ecc. Sonn.* 3. 21. 14
Is empty of repose. 479 *Somnamb.* 81
When empty terrors overawe; 492 *Duty* 6
On empty air! That name will keep its hold 516 **Young England* 4
O Palace empty and disconsolate! 563 *Troilus* 24
And threshold steps were empty; fast asleep 642 *Prelude* 2. 12
Of loneliness gave way to empty noise 652 *Prelude* 3. 208
Under the pealing organ. Empty thoughts! 653 *Prelude* 3. 315
Moonlight and stars, and empty streets, and sounds 697 *Prelude* 7. 661
That legalised exclusion, empty pomp 717 *Prelude* 9. 526
Spared not the empty throne, and in proud haste 718 *Prelude* 10. 39
I crossed the square (an empty area then!) 719 *Prelude* 10. 55
Stood empty of all shape of life, and silent 807 *Excursion* 4. 409
With empty actions and vain passions stuffed, 835 *Excursion* 5. 851
And the long-privileged house left empty—swept 861 *Excursion* 7. 251
The habitations empty! or perchance 878 *Excursion* 8. 266
Then execration is an empty sound. L. 1. 88 *Juvenal* 1. 14
Empurpled. How, with empurpled cheeks and pampered eyes, 364 **What aim* 4
Empurpled hills, conspicuously renewing 807 *Excursion* 4. 400
Empyreal. Share their empyreal spirits—yea, 178 *Waggoner* 3. 33
Forth towards empyreal Heaven, 332 *Ode: Thanks.* 218
Strains that call forth upon empyreal ground 335 *Cologne* 12
Do thou enjoy the calm empyreal air; 575 *Chiabrera* 8. 20
Of shouting Angels, and the empyreal thrones— 755 *Recluse* 1. 1. 787
Who dwell on earth, yet breathe empyreal air, 804 *Excursion* 4. 231
From thy empyreal throne, the elect of earth 893 *Excursion* 9. 631
Empyrean. Or in the fields of empyrean light. 317 **Brave Schill* 4
Grain-tinctured, drenched in empyrean light; 663 *Prelude* 4. 328
In the empyrean. Underneath that pomp 725 *Prelude* 10. 523
Emulate. A lofty Dome, that dared to emulate 324 *Ode 1814* 75
That would emulate a star. 549 *Hermit's Cell* 1. 12
Emulates. Whose azure depth their colour emulates, 508 *F. Stone* 33

Emulation. Now flush'd as Hebe, Emulation rose; 618 *School Ex.* 20
By generous Emulation taught to rise, . . . 619 *School Ex.* 63
Emulative. Fell on thy tomb; but emulative power 425 *Ecc. Sonn.* 1. 27. 3
Emulous. Stones of all hues, gem emulous of gem, 190 **Lyre! though* 35
So emulous of Macedonian fame, ... 368 *Trajan* 60
Stone lift its forehead emulous of stone . . . 847 *Excursion* 6. 625
En. Round fire-side treason-parties *en famille*? . L.1. 97 *Juvenal* 3. 88
Enable. More deeply, yet enable me to bear . . 752 *Prelude* 14. 423
Enabled. Which have enabled this enormous Culprit 57 *Bord.* 1086
Swayed, and thereby enabled to contend . . . 442 *Ecc. Sonn.* 3. 9. 6
Enabled me to pause for choice, and walk . . 751 *Prelude* 14. 360
Some trace am I enabled to retain . . . . . 796 *Excursion* 3. 703
Is it enabled to maintain its hold . . . . 803 *Excursion* 4. 151
Are each and all enabled to perceive . . . . 887 *Excursion* 9. 219
Enables. When reason that enables him to be . . 724 *Prelude* 10. 427
That penetrates, enables us to mount, ... 737 *Prelude* 12. 217
Enables them to be and to perform. . . . . 875 *Excursion* 8. 53
Enabling. And as it shook, enabling the blind roots 354 *Aquap.* 139
Raised for enabling this penurious stream . . . 789 *Excursion* 3. 204
Enact. "Do Thou my sovereign will enact . . . 291 *Rob Roy* 78
Or Strollers are they, furnished to enact . . . 858 *Excursion* 7. 89
Of all who suffer wrong, and to enact . . . . 873 *Excursion* 7. 1043
To see an English lord enact a fool . . . . . L.1. 97 *Juvenal* 3. 90
Enamelled. *See* **Flower-enamelled.**
Enamoured. And hence the father of the enamoured Youth, ... 122 *V. and J.* 17
Else will the enamoured Monk too surely find . 363 **Grieve for* 12
Turn from the sight, enamoured Muse—we must; 379 *Duddon* 12. 13
Where the enamoured sunny light . . . . . 397 *White Doe* 85
She fastens on the boy enamour'd eyes, . . . 625 *Æneid* 86
At leisure, how the enamoured youth was driven, 717 *Prelude* 9. 569
Enamoured, so the fable runs; but they . . . S.3. 436 **The doubt* 152
Encasing. With honour; which, encasing by the power . . . . 831 *Excursion* 5. 607
Enchain. Thou to his dangers dost enchain . . 216 *Enterprise* 64
And joys of distant home my heart enchain. . . 340 *Ranz* 14
Enchained. What time the fleet at Aulis lay enchained. . . . . 211 *Laod.* 120
Of gospel-truth enchained in harmonies . . . 466 *St. Bees* 52
O'er which enchained by science he had loved . 840 *Excursion* 6. 150
By his malicious wit; then, all enchained . . . 843 *Excursion* 6. 346
Enchanted. Charmed the tall circle of the enchanted steeps. . . . . 7 *Ev. Wk.* 304
Whence lutes and voices down the enchanted woods 12 *Desc. Sk.* 117
A book that is enchanted. . . . . 242 *P. B.* 520
Charms the tall circle of th' enchanted steeps. . 598 *Ev. Wk. Quarto* 350
When fragrant scents beneath th' enchanted tread 610 *Desc. Sk. Quarto* 448
In that divine embrace enchanted lay; . . . 620 *Birth of Love* 6
Enchanter. The sage enchanter Merlin's subtle schemes; . . . . 103 *Artegal* 51
The pleased Enchanter was aware . . . . . 369 *Eg. Maid* 3
Of the Enchanter Indolence hath called . . . 677 *Prelude* 6. 181
Enchanter's. Suddenly raised by some enchanter's power, ... 226 *Vernal Ode* 17
Enchanting. Between thy lofty rocks. Enchanting show . . . . 680 *Prelude* 6. 380
And rustling leaves. Enchanting age and sweet! 693 *Prelude* 7. 441
Enchantment. As by enchantment, an obscure retreat . . . . 3 *Ev. Wk.* 55
Swarmed with enchantment, till his spirit sank, . 122 *V. and J.* 49
'Tis a note of enchantment; what ails her? She sees . . . . 188 *Poor Susan* 5
And unreproved enchantment led us on . . . 639 *Prelude* 1. 487
Fulfilling (could enchantment have done more?) . 700 *Prelude* 8. 83
Enchantments. Of dire enchantments faced and overcome . . . . 634 *Prelude* 1. 175
Enchantress. Nina, the good Enchantress, shed 373 *Eg. Maid* 303
A prime enchantress—to assist the work, . . . 729 *Prelude* 11. 115
What witchcraft, mild enchantress, may with thee S.3. 434 **The doubt* 94
Enchants. Yea, all, that now enchants thee, from the day . . . . 250 *Admon.* 13
Enchased. A silver cross enchased with Flowers of France . . . . 628 *Eagle and Dove* 11
Encincture. Hath reached the encincture of that gloomy sea . . . . 336 *Danube* 8
Shall wound the tender sod. Encincture small, . 451 *Ecc. Sonn.* 3. 41. 9
Encincture's. Though with the Encincture's special sanctity . . . . 824 *Excursion* 5. 159
Encircle. And as his native hills encircle ground . 18 *Desc. Sk.* 449
Lift, and encircle with a cloudy chair, ... 382 *Duddon* 25. 3
Encircled. *See* **Rock-encircled.**
Encircled by familiar faces. . . . . 222 *Triad* 153
Encircling. The encircling laurels, thick with leaves, 375 **The Minstrels* 4
The encircling ground, in native turf arrayed, . 450 *Ecc. Sonn.* 3. 41. 1
The encircling turf into a barren clod; . . . . 465 **The cattle* 3
The encircling region vividly exprest . . . . 524 *Epist. Beaumont* 173
And from encroachment of encircling heath: . . 805 *Excursion* 4. 244
Enclasp. Whose infant arms enclasp the shrine . 366 **Ye Trees* 3
Enclasped. For safety, they of yore enclasped the Cross . . . . 357 *Aquap.* 301
Enclose. A structure stands, which two bare slopes enclose. . . . . 27 *Guilt* 147
Mark the concentred hazels that enclose . . . 262 **Mark the* 1
These venerable mountains now enclose . . . 319 *Biscayan* 8
Half grot, half arbour—proffers to enclose . . 382 *Duddon* 24. 7
Where ancient trees this convent-pile enclose, . 470 *Bala-Sala* 3
Enclosed. Ah! see her helpless Charge! enclosed 294 *Jedbor.* 49
Into my spirit, when I paced, enclosed . . . 355 *Aquap.* 154
How soothed, when in thick bower enclosed, . . 415 *White Doe* 1736
Enclosed when he was stronger; . . . . . 483 *Simon Lee* 46

Enclosed—*continued.*
"With Mother's pity in her breast enclosed . . 555 *Prioress* 142
Enclosed his uncorrupted body sweet.— . . . 556 *Prioress* 231
To drive their prey enclosed within a ring . . 718 *Prelude* 10. 21
Pieces of money carefully enclosed, ... 766 *Excursion* 1. 670
Enclosed between an upright mass of rock . . 777 *Excursion* 2. 414
Each, in its ornamental scroll, enclosed; . . . 824 *Excursion* 5. 151
By which, and under which, we are enclosed . . K.8. 254 *Recluse* 1.1.643
Enclosure. *See* **Inclosure.**
This delicate Enclosure shows . . . . . 154 *Flower Garden* 44
So far from the holy enclosure was cast, . . . 340 *Fort Fuentes* 3
The enclosure of this churchyard ground; . . 416 *White Doe* 1882
That opened from the enclosure of green fields . 779 *Excursion* 2. 495
To have *one* Enclosure where the voice that speaks 848 *Excursion* 6. 638
Busy in that enclosure; while the rill, ... 856 *Excursion* 6. 1170
Enclosures. Through bare enclosures stretches, 'till its line . . . . 858 *Excursion* 7. 44
Encomiums. Of the encomiums by my Friend pronounced . . . . 828 *Excursion* 5. 420
Encompassed. By those huge rocks encompassed round. . . . . 85 *Shepherd-boys* 88
Encompassed me on every side . . . . . . 194 *Ruth* 166
With rocks encompassed round. . . . . . 240 *P. B.* 370
What dreams encompassed? Was the intruder nursed 378 *Duddon* 8. 6
What pleasure once encompassed those sweet names 459 **Wanderer! that* 7
By whom we were encompassed. Taking leave . 681 *Prelude* 6. 414
With rocks encompassed, save that to the south . 776 *Excursion* 2. 334
Encounter. The starts and sallies of our last encounter . . . . 77 *Bord.* 2278
Ay, what shall we encounter next? This issue— 77 *Bord.* 2284
Encounter, and to narrow seas . . . . . 499 **This Lawn* 8
Must he again encounter.—Such a stream . . . 800 *Excursion* 3. 986
Encountered. Hardships for the brave encountered 140 *Arm. Lady* 33
Dread trials! yet encountered and sustained . . 316 **Hail, Zaragoza* 12
By us with hope encountered, be upset;— . . 513 **Said Secrecy* 7
Where spear encountered spear, and sword with sword . . . . 634 *Prelude* 1. 177
And everything encountered or pursued . . . 674 *Prelude* 5. 580
'Tis one encountered here and everywhere; . . 690 *Prelude* 7. 202
On every side encountered; in despite . . . 812 *Excursion* 4. 731
Encountering. And feuds, where, clan encountering clan, ... 391 *Highland Broach* 51
Of that small town encountering thus, they filled, 845 *Excursion* 6. 465
Encounters. Encounters, armed for work of pain and death. . . . . 448 *Ecc. Sonn.* 3. 30. 12
Encouraged. Like a scared Bird encouraged to renew 118 *Maternal Grief* 57
Encouraged, sanctioned, chiefly for that end; . 211 *Laod.* 147
My Song, encouraged by the grace . . . . . 342 *Ital. Itin.* 37
Encouraged of celestial power; . . . . . . 416 *White Doe* 1833
Encouraged and endeared the strain of words . 538 **In desultory* 12
Encouraged by the imperial eye, ... 545 *Russ. Fug.* 373
Encouraged and dismissed, till choice was made . 633 *Prelude* 1. 71
Of freedom which encouraged me to turn . . . 675 *Prelude* 6. 33
Encouraged with a martyr's confidence; . . . 713 *Prelude* 9. 274
Hope after hope, encouraged and destroyed. . . 841 *Excursion* 6. 229
Encouragement. Encouragement to sport or play; 407 *White Doe* 1017
Brought less encouragement, and unto these . . 730 *Prelude* 11. 195
Encouragement, and energy, and will, ... 743 *Prelude* 13. 263
He neither felt encouragement nor hope: . . . 775 *Excursion* 2. 286
And grave encouragement, by song inspired? . 863 *Excursion* 7. 386
Encouragement, hath ceased to look that way. . 880 *Excursion* 8. 388
Encourager. Was with me, my encourager and guide: . . . . 737 *Prelude* 12. 230
Encouraging. A bright, encouraging, example shows; 395 *White Doe: Ded.* 52
In a soft clime encouraging the soil . . . . 793 *Excursion* 3. 519
Encroach. While young delights on old encroach, . 391 *Highland Broach* 77
Encroached. Hence, if dejection has too oft encroached . . . . 394 **No more* 31
Encroaching. Whose shades have never felt the encroaching axe, ... 799 *Excursion* 3. 916
Unsociably sequestered, and encroaching . . . 858 *Excursion* 7. 36
Encroachment. Not so the ethereal vault; encroachment none . . . . 746 *Prelude* 14. 50
And from encroachment of encircling heath; . . 805 *Excursion* 4. 244
Encroachments. And sure encroachments of infirmity, ... 378 *Duddon* 9. 13
Encrust. Till thou with crystal bead-drops didst encrust . . . . S. 3. 434 **The doubt* 53
Encrusted. (With shells encrusted, dark with briny weeds) . . . . 726 *Prelude* 10. 557
Encumbered. *See* **Fleece-encumbered, Stone-encumbered.**
And floors encumbered with rich show . . . 416 *White Doe* 1891
Through a strait passage of encumbered ground, . 786 *Excursion* 3. 36
Encumbrance. Assoiled from all encumbrance of our time, ... 326 **The Bard* 9
Encumbrances. From the encumbrances of mortal life, ... 817 *Excursion* 4. 1074
End. And whensoe'er my course shall end, . . . 1 *Extract* 4
Nor stop but where creation seems to end, . . 14 *Desc. Sk.* 233
And end my days upon the peaceful flood.'— . 31 *Guilt* 366
As if because her tale was at an end, ... 32 *Guilt* 448
Till now I did not think my end had been so near. 35 *Guilt* 576
They placed me—there to end life's pilgrimage, . 35 *Guilt* 583
May my end be! Soon will this voice be dumb: . 35 *Guilt* 588
"O welcome sentence which will end though late," 36 *Guilt* 655
To end her wrongs. But if the blind Man's tale . 38 *Bord.* 72
Would fail you ere our journey's end be reached. 41 *Bord.* 227
Were present, to the end that we might hear . . 48 *Bord.* 589
This last device must end my work.—Methinks . 58 *Bord.* 1145
In which a man may come to his end, whose crimes 61 *Bord.* 1290

End—*continued.*
It shall be for a nobler end—to teach — 65 *Bord.* 1558
I have borne my burthen to its destined end. — 66 *Bord.* 1588
And put an end to his insolence, but my Comrades — 68 *Bord.* 1717
till I am brought to a felon's end. — 72 *Bord.* 1987
Could never, never have an end. — 82 *Alice Fell* 40
The chaise drove on ; our journey's end — 82 *Alice Fell* 49
Nature will either end thee quite ; — 88 *H. C.* 21
Live to such end is what both old and young — 99 *Brothers* 287
He could not come to an unhallowed end ! — 101 *Brothers* 392
Of a steep march : support me to the end. — 112 **O dearer* 12
To see the end of all my gains, — 115 *Last of Flock* 56
Some tidings that my woes may end ; — 117 *Affl. Marg.* 76
To nature for a happy end of all ; — 122 *V. and J.* 63
End happily, as they began ! " These gleams — 124 *V. and J.* 211
And with the owls must end. — 131 *Idiot Boy* 436
If it end in tears and sighs ; — 140 *Arm. Lady* 20
Hope, and a renovation without end. — 173 *Infant Daughter* 65
The loitering journey to its end. — 180 *Waggoner* 4. 10
By this time near their journey's end ; — 180 *Waggoner* 4. 70
To the end that, at your meeting, — 181 *Waggoner* 4. 136
But thereof come in the end despondency and madness. — 196 *Resolution* 49
" The end of man's existence I discerned, — 211 *Laod.* 111
Encouraged, sanctioned, chiefly for that end ; — 211 *Laod.* 147
The throbbing pulse—else troubled without end : — 255 **Grief, thou* 8
Of her own Being is her paramount end ; — 262 *Retirement* 6
Speak, that my torturing doubts their end may know ! — 277 **Why art* 14
Points heavenward, indicate the end and way. — 281 *Chris. Words.* 14
And what to him and his shall be the end ? — 305 **The Voice* 7
It was a *moral* end for which they fought ; — 316 **It was a* 1
That Thou hast brought our warfare to an end, — 328 *Ode 1815* 123
That He has brought our warfare to an end, — 331 *Ode : Thanks.* 181
To bliss unbounded, glory without end. — 366 *Lombardy* 14
Much have my books disclosed, but the end is hidden." — 371 *Eg. Maid* 174
Thinking how fast time runs, life's end how near ! — 378 *Duddon* 9. 14
Of chance-temptation, ere his journey end, — 383 *Duddon* 30. 6
While the Poor gather round, till the end of time — 393 *Countess' Pillar* 1
No more : the end is sudden and abrupt, — 394 **No more* 1
The fatal end of Scotland's King, — 399 *White Doe* 287
Beginning, where the song must end, — 400 *White Doe* 340
These will be faithful to the end ; — 403 *White Doe* 614
The end of that dire Tragedy, — 409 *White Doe* 1208
Oh weak, weak moment ! to what end — 411 *White Doe* 1395
Their labours end ; or they return to lie, — 430 *Ecc. Sonn.* 2. 8. 6
With the wide world's commotions) from its end . — 442 *Ecc. Sonn.* 3. 9. 7
Along a Galaxy that knows no end, — 443 *Ecc. Sonn.* 3. 13. 13
Then gladly would I end my mortal days. — 489 *Pers. Talk* 56
We grieved for thee, and wished thy end were past ; — 491 *Tribute : Dog* 11
Oh, let my weakness have an end ! — 492 *Duty* 52
That shall lack a timely end, — 495 *Force of Prayer* 66
Through heaven-born hope, her end ! — 502 *Seasons* 20
For compassing the end, else never gained ; — 504 *Warning* 92
And love the end, which all through peace must seek. — 518 *Pun. Death* 7. 8
To end life here like this poor deer, — 545 *Russ. Fug.* 311
Free was it, and unbarred at either end. — 553 *Prioress* 42
Down at the farther end, in which there were — 553 *Prioress* 44
And to this end a Homicide they hired, — 554 *Prioress* 116
And soon as she had sung it to the end, — 561 *Cuck.and Night.* 251
To the end that he the Grecian host might see ; — 564 *Troilus* 149
Of the tenth day will come, and end his sorrow. — 565 *Troilus* 168
And happiness, which to the end of time — 567 *Cumb. Beg.* 108
You see to what end he has brought his grey hairs. — 572 *Avarice* 32
Together move in fellowship without end.— — 573 *Chiabrera* 1. 6
On regal decks beheld ! yet in the end — 574 *Chiabrera* 4. 22
That stripped of arms I to my end am brought — 575 *Chiabrera* 6. 11
For this, if other end were none, — 579 **Sweet Flower* 58
Where, from the barren wall's unshelter'd end, — 592 *Ev. Wk. Quarto* 59
More high, to where creation seems to end, — 607 *Desc.Sk.Quarto* 289
To question us. " Whence come ye ? to what end ? " — 622 *Recluse* 1. 1. 167
Sits brooding, lives not always to that end, — 634 *Prelude* 1. 141
Our object and inglorious, yet the end — 637 *Prelude* 1. 329
Am worthy of myself ! Praise to the end ! — 637 *Prelude* 1. 350
One end at least hath been attained ; my mind — 641 *Prelude* 1. 636
Of boldest projects, and a peaceful end — 661 *Prelude* 4. 175
To the end and written spirit of God's works, — 663 *Prelude* 4. 351
From system on to system without end. — 677 *Prelude* 6. 128
Reach after reach, succession without end — 680 *Prelude* 6. 383
Of first, and last, and midst, and without end. — 684 *Prelude* 6. 640
There is no end. Such candidates for regard, — 696 *Prelude* 7. 583
That have no law, no meaning, and no end— — 698 *Prelude* 7. 728
Or grandeur circumfuse them to no end. — 704 *Prelude* 8. 364
The end of life, and everything we know. — 707 *Prelude* 8. 529
With him did I discourse about the end — 714 *Prelude* 9. 322
Or trepidation for the end of things — 720 *Prelude* 10. 144
Their brethren, and her triumphs be in the end — 727 *Prelude* 11. 16
Justice, and make an end of Liberty. — 728 *Prelude* 11. 73
Of all of us,—the place where, in the end, — 729 *Prelude* 11. 143
Our song, and not with these our song must end.— — 734 *Prelude* 12. 8
Yet centring all in love, and in the end — 751 *Prelude* 14. 386
Guide, and support, and cheer me to the end ! " — 755 *Recluse* 1. 1. 860
And for this end had hired a neighbour's boy — 769 *Excursion* 1. 861
As one, and moving to one glorious end. — 774 *Excursion* 2. 222
Far sinking into splendour—without end ! — 784 *Excursion* 2. 838
The *end* of those, who did, by system, rank, — 791 *Excursion* 3. 361
Such was their scheme : and though the wished-for end — 792 *Excursion* 3. 406
And let thy favour, to the end of life, — 802 *Excursion* 4. 61

End—*continued.*
Prime, self-existing cause and end of all — 802 *Excursion* 4. 80
All natures,—to the end that he may find — 806 *Excursion* 4. 334
Or of the end stops short, proposed to all . — 826 *Excursion* 5. 260
That promises to the end a blest old age ! " — 828 *Excursion* 5. 389
And end their journey in the same repose ! — 836 *Excursion* 5. 921
This is the genuine course, the aim, and end — 837 *Excursion* 5. 1008
Constructed, that sufficed for every end, — 849 *Excursion* 6. 728
To end my days ; well pleased was I to see — 860 *Excursion* 7. 199
His triumphs hail, and glorify his end ; — 863 *Excursion* 7. 378
Be satisfied, 'tis well,—the end is gained ; — 874 *Excursion* 8. 7
Of common right or interest in the end ; — 886 *Excursion* 9. 118
Show to the wretched nations for what end — 890 *Excursion* 9. 414
Of effort with the end of Being. — S.3. 439 **Avaunt this* 13
Such power and joy ; but only for this end, — K.8. 237 *Recluse* 1. 1. 38
For that end only ; something must be done. — K.8. 255 *Recluse* 1.1.665

Endangered. Endangered States may yield to terms unjust ; — 316 **Say, what* 10
Maintains the else endangered gift of life ; — 432 *Ecc. Sonn.* 2. 16. 11
Not more endangered than a man whose eye — 865 *Excursion* 7. 497
Of Liberty endangered, and farewell — K.8. 257 *Recluse* 1.1.748

Endear. Where twilight glens endear my Esthwaite's shore, — 2 *Ev. Wk.* 11
Called forth by those affections that endear — 510 **Among a* 15
Her silence to endear ; — 544 *Russ. Fug.* 206
With the green myrtle, to endear the hours — 793 *Excursion* 3. 530
How much they might inspirit and endear, — 806 *Excursion* 4. 371
Use, comfort, do this roof endear ; — S.3. 425 **No whimsy* 3

Endeared. A bosom to the sun endeared ? — 154 *Flower Garden* 16
A name with us endeared to hope, — 164 **Fair Lady* 15
Was to the Pilgrim's soul endeared, — 168 *Pilgrim's Dream* 70
And to my heart are still endeared — 191 *Seq. Beggars* 27
Hence lives He, to his inner self endeared ; — 317 **Call not* 6
Endeared. And who—if not a man as cold — 356 *Aquap.* 269
Illustrated, and mutually endeared. — 362 **List—'twas* 48
Is to my heart of hearts endeared — 375 **The Minstrels* 53
And pain, hath powers to Eternity endeared. — 476 *Howard* 14
And are endeared to simple cottagers)— — 509 *F. Stone* 102
Encouraged and endeared the strain of words — 538 **In desultory* 12
Through life was Owen Lloyd endeared — 577 **By playful* 5
The more endeared. Their several memories here — 653 *Prelude* 3. 269
And placid under-countenance, first endeared ; — 678 *Prelude* 6. 227
Endeared by Custom ; and with high disdain, — 695 *Prelude* 7. 528
That to his memory were most endeared. — 762 *Excursion* 1. 391
And this rude bench, one torturing hope endeared, — 770 *Excursion* 1. 913
Endeared my wanderings ; and the mother's kiss — 794 *Excursion* 3. 582
And loveliness endeared which they removed. — 795 *Excursion* 3. 621
Endeared to him, for this, that, in her state — 825 *Excursion* 5. 196
All brothers, long endeared by kindred pain, — L.1. 95 *Juvenal* 3. 6

Endearing. Endearing title, a responsive chime — 463 **They called* 5
With intermixture of endearing words, — 779 *Excursion* 2. 506
I heard her scatter some endearing words — K.8. 251 *Recluse* 1.1.527

Endears. Endears that Lingerer. And how blest her sway, — 282 **While beams* 9
Like portraiture, from loftier source, endears — 351 *Des. Stanzas* 59
A single Act endears to high and low — 540 *Grace Darl.* 8

Endeavour. Do you observe him, and endeavour — 142 †*Lov. and Lik.* 19
But Heaven has blest a good endeavour ; — 174 *Waggoner* 1. 113
And all have joined in one endeavour — 197 *Thorn* 21
Meek aspirations please her, lone endeavour, — 262 **Not Love* 9
With vain endeavour, — 286 *Nith* 58
To expiate thy sin endeavour : — 370 *Eg. Maid* 98
Of slow endeavour ! or abruptly cast — 379 *Duddon* 15. 10
Blest its humane Memorial's fond endeavour ; — 394 *Countess' Pillar* 12
Be an endeavour that can do — 406 *White Doe* 912
On him and on his high endeavour — 409 *White Doe* 1214
And, if the endeavour prove not vain, — 410 *White Doe* 1289
So vain was his endeavour, — 484 *Simon Lee* 78
By discipline endeavour to grow meek — 500 *Humanity* 53
On Patience coupled with such slow endeavour, — 515 **Hard task* 2
Which neither listlessness, nor mad endeavour, — 589 *Immortality* 161
In this endeavour simply to relate — 659 *Prelude* 4. 79
Could I endeavour to unfold the means — 736 *Prelude* 12. 133
—Endeavour thus to live ; these rules regard ; — 804 *Excursion* 4. 228

Endeavoured. And vainly had endeavoured. — 484 *Simon Lee* 88
Unvisited, endeavoured to retrace — 642 *Prelude* 2. 2
I have endeavoured to display the means — 646 *Prelude* 2. 269
With his brave sword endeavoured to prevent — 844 *Excursion* 6. 420

Endeavouring. Endeavouring, in our English tongue, to trace — 120 *EmigrantMother* 11
Its endeavouring ! " — 163 *Hint* 32

Endeavours. His best endeavours to renew, — 406 *White Doe* 936
In vain endeavours to exterminate, — 432 *Ecc. Sonn.* 2. 14. 7
Whose high endeavours are an inward light — 493 *Hap. War.* 6
The light from past endeavours purely willed — 526 **Soon did* 10
Of high endeavours, daily spreads abroad — 661 *Prelude* 4. 170
With blind endeavours ? Yet, still uppermost, — 760 *Excursion* 1. 263
Of vain endeavours tired ; and by his own, — 798 *Excursion* 3. 868
Which our endeavours have refused to till, — 855 *Excursion* 6. 1138

Ended. It must be ended !— Softly ; do not rouse him ; — 54 *Bord.* 914
For the day that now is ended — 90 *Longest Day* 11
Before it ended in his death, the Youth — 100 *Brothers* 320
It hung ;—and mouldered there. The Priest here ended— — 101 *Brothers* 405
Was ended, Luke (for so the Son was named) — 132 *Michael* 103
The Shepherd ended here ; and Luke stooped down, — 137 *Michael* 418
Begun and ended, in the shady grove, — 150 **When, to* 57
But stately in the main ; and, when he ended, — 197 *Resolution* 136
And all old troubles now are ended.— — 204 *Brougham* 14
Hues doubtfully begun and ended ; — 231 **The gentlest Poet* 20

Ended—*continued.*
And there his sorrow ended 287 *Ellen Irwin* 48
The mournful passion ended 324 *Ode 1814* 88
Has ended, though no Clerk, with "God be praised!" 394 *Countess' Pillar* 14
He ended,—or she heard no more; 402 *White Doe* 588
Or the mute rapture ended in a sigh— 460 **Wanderer! that* 55
The Spirit ended his mysterious rite, 582 *Invoc. Earth* 35
So ended, disappointment could be none, 643 *Prelude* 2. 66
And ended with such mockery. Be wise, 655 *Prelude* 3. 409
Soon ended, and together on we passed 665 *Prelude* 4. 446
Else sooner ended, I have borne in mind 679 *Prelude* 6. 260
Ended in this,—*that we had crossed the Alps.* 684 *Prelude* 6. 591
But, when he ended, there was in his face 765 *Excursion* 1. 606
Was ended, that long anxious day, I learned, 766 *Excursion* 1. 674
And, when she ended, I had little power 766 *Excursion* 1. 683
Ended; and, from the stillness that ensued 777 *Excursion* 2. 394
That it is ended." At these words be turned— 785 *Excursion* 2. 897
In pain commenced, and ended without peace: 801 *Excursion* 4. 3
The Matron ended—nor could I forbear 835 *Excursion* 5. 827
Begun and ended within three days' space, 853 *Excursion* 6. 967
Are ended, and her ears have heard the cry 867 *Excursion* 7. 644
And, when that eulogy was ended, stood 871 *Excursion* 7. 893

Ending. *See* **Never-ending.**
A never never ending song, 84 *Shepherd-boys* 3
Slow to begin, and never ending; 186 **O Nightingale* 18
As if her song could have no ending; 289 *Sol. Reap.* 26
Her new-born Babe; dire ending of bright hope! 476 *Howard* 2
Ending in dust; of upright magistrates, 825 *Excursion* 5. 175

Endless. Even here, amid the sweep of endless woods, 5 *Ev. Wk.* 142
Thy cliffs; the endless waters of thy vales; 12 *Desc. Sk.* 110
Inmate of lonesome Nature's endless year; 26 *Guilt* 121
A pledge of endless bliss in acts of early piety, 93 *Poet's Dream* 74
That come and go with endless play, 108 *Louisa*
For endless constancy, and placid truth; 122 *V. and J.* 33
With other names, an endless string; 127 *Idiot Boy* 160
For endless industry. When day was gone, 132 *Michael* 95
And many an endless, endless lake, 193 *Ruth* 68
She lifts her head for endless spring, 203 *Brougham* 9
In endless union, earth and sea above." 220 *Triad* 23
Your squadrons to an endless flight of birds 230 *Clouds* 17
With Order dwell, in endless youth? 234 *Power of Sound* 112
And hope of endless peace in me grew bold: 257 **No mortal* 4
Before me in my endless way. 289 *Stepping West.* 26
In glory will they sleep and endless sanctity. 310 *Anticip.* 14
And folly cursed with endless memory: 349 *Boulogne* 12
To bowers of endless love! 374 *Eg. Maid* 386
Thy pleased associates:—light as endless May 377 *Duddon* 5. 13
Whose good works formed an endless retinue: 380 *Duddon* 18. 11
Endless history that lies 415 *White Doe* 1716
"The which would endless matrimony make;" 447 *Ecc. Sonn.* 3. 26. 10
Books! 'tis a dull and endless strife: 481 *Tables Turned* 9
And she made answer "ENDLESS SORROW!" 494 *Force of Prayer* 7
Are linked in endless chase; 507 *May* 62
Were endless imitation. 589 *Immortality* 107
To pant slow up the endless Alp of life. 613 *Desc.Sk.Quarto* 593
In common things—the endless store of things, 633 *Prelude* 1. 109
Protracted among endless solitudes; 667 *Prelude* 5. 147
By youthful squires; adventures endless, spun 673 *Prelude* 5. 500
Of shadowy things work endless changes,—there, 674 *Prelude* 5. 599
Her endless streets, a transient visitant: 688 *Prelude* 7. 68
Thou endless stream of men and moving things! 689 *Prelude* 7. 151
Endless, here opening widely out, and there 702 *Prelude* 8. 193
Great Spirit as thou art, in endless dreams 705 *Prelude* 8. 435
Hence endless occupation for the Soul, 747 *Prelude* 14. 119
Faith in life endless, the sustaining thought 749 *Prelude* 14. 204
Whereon their endless generations dwelt. 790 *Excursion* 3. 252
From sleep, and dwell with God in endless love. 804 *Excursion* 4. 190
Of endless agitation. Here you stand, 818 *Excursion* 4. 1147
Through shades and silent rest, to endless joy." 837 *Excursion* 5. 1016
Wishes and endless schemes; by daylight walked 842 *Excursion* 6. 240
To play on water, or in endless chase K.8. 257 *Recluse* 1. 1. 27
And prove with endless puns a monarch's power, L.1. 94 *Juvenal* 2. 2
And let that heir of Glory's endless day L.1. 94 *Juvenal* 2. 23

Endlessly. Their myriads?—endlessly renewed, 227 *Vernal Ode* 66
And all the landscape, endlessly enriched 700 *Prelude* 8. 96
Now disbelieving; endlessly perplexed 731 *Prelude* 11. 298

Endow. A mystery potent human love to endow 447 *Ecc. Sonn.* 3. 26. 12

Endowed. So speaking, and by fervent love endowed 209 *Laod.* 7
The gentlest Poet, with free thoughts endowed, 231 **The gentlest Poet* 1
Further to force their way, endowed its trunk 354 *Aquap.* 140
Bear witness Truth, endowed with holy powers 650 *Prelude* 3. 88
Of forms and colours, passive, yet endowed 685 *Prelude* 6. 679
Endowed with various power to search the soul; 695 *Prelude* 7. 548
Endowed by Nature with her fairest gifts 711 *Prelude* 9. 149
So moulded, joined, abstracted, so endowed 747 *Prelude* 14. 83
A human creature, howsoe'er endowed, 750 *Prelude* 14. 291
By Nature; men endowed with highest gifts, 757 *Excursion* 1. 78
Nor sparingly endowed with worldly wealth, 774 *Excursion* 2. 192
In spot so parsimoniously endowed, 786 *Excursion* 3. 17
Though inconceivably endowed, too dim 804 *Excursion* 4. 181
But by the great Artificer endowed 809 *Excursion* 4. 557
Hence, for this Favourite—lavishly endowed 843 *Excursion* 6. 304
With which the Cure not long had been endowed: 859 *Excursion* 7. 139
Yet is the creature rational, endowed 866 *Excursion* 7. 576
For see the universal Race endowed 887 *Excursion* 9. 208
And in good works; and him, who is endowed 895 *Excursion* 9. 735

Endowment. Alas! the endowment of immortal power 804 *Excursion* 4. 205

Endowments. By their endowments, good or great, that they 733 *Prelude* 11. 439

Endowments—*continued.*
Proud of her own endowments, and rejoiced 736 *Prelude* 12. 146
That by endowments not from me withheld 751 *Prelude* 14. 357

Ends. Which you've collected for the noblest ends, 38 *Bord.* 61
That things will work to ends the slaves o' the world 54 *Bord.* 936
Of love in all its shapes, beginnings, ends; 59 *Bord.* 1225
And there it ends;—if this be not enough 60 *Bord.* 1271
Were there not eyes that see, and for good ends, 69 *Bord.* 1752
Maintained, for peaceful ends beyond our view. 78 *Bord.* 2310
And sometimes, just as listening ends 144 **Driven in* 47
Whose means are fair and spotless as his ends." 214 *Dion* 124
Desires whose course in folly ends, 223 *Wishing-gate* 41
And there the pathway ends. 240 *P. B.* 355
Of goodness, for most gracious ends— 245 *P. B.* 769
—Here ends my Tale: for in a trice 249 *P. B.* 1121
Where holy ground begins, unhallowed ends, 271 **Where holy* 1
To have my ends, maintain my rights, 291 *Rob Roy* 55
For whose dire ends tears flow, and blood is spilt, 321 **Here pause* 11
Sounder and therefore holier than the ends 358 *Aquap.* 351
A moment ends the fervent din, 396 *White Doe* 43
Proofs thickening round her that on public ends 504 *Warning* 74
Power hath been given to please for higher ends 538 **In desultory* 22
By means refined attaining purest ends, 690 *Prelude* 7. 237
Cheerfully led to individual ends 700 *Prelude* 8. 107
(If with unworldly ends and aims compared) 712 *Prelude* 9. 203
By struggling with the crowd for present ends. 714 *Prelude* 9. 339
In France, the men, who, for their desperate ends, 723 *Prelude* 10. 331
To suit my ends; I moved among mankind 729 *Prelude* 11. 155
To the great ends of Liberty and Power. 736 *Prelude* 12. 139
To love as prime and chief, for there fear ends, 748 *Prelude* 14. 163
"So ends my dolorous tale, and glad I am 785 *Excursion* 2. 896
The ends of being would secure, and win 791 *Excursion* 3. 349
Beginning, ends in servitude—still painful, 799 *Excursion* 3. 895
On outward things, with formal inference ends; 810 *Excursion* 4. 623
For less important ends those phantoms move, 813 *Excursion* 4. 842
Swayed by such motives, to such ends employed; 816 *Excursion* 4. 986
Whose ends are gained? Behold an emblem here 892 *Excursion* 9. 554
That satisfies and ends in perfect rest. K.8. 255 *Recluse* 1. 1. 685

Endue. And thought endue thee with all truth— 402 *White Doe* 582
I might endue some airy phantasies 634 *Prelude* 1. 120

Endued. So that it seems a thing endued with sense: 196 *Resolution* 61
But with majestic lowliness endued, 212 *Dion* 14
As noble as the best endued, 342 *Ital. Itin.* 80
And with a deeper peace endued 415 *White Doe* 1749
Through all her nerves with finer sense endued, 437 *Ecc Sonn.* 2. 35. 10
But 'tis endued with power to stay, 457 **Had this* 5
Of *Powers* endued with visible form, instinct 469 **Bold words* 13
—He who, though thus endued as with a sense 493 *Hap. War.* 57
With a congenial function art endued 510 **Among a* 19
That some dramatic tale, endued with shapes 731 *Prelude* 11. 283
With shrinking sensibility endued, 808 *Excursion* 4. 510

Endues. Endues her conscience with external life 519 *Pun. Death* 9. 10

Endurable. 'Twill make a thing endurable, which else 138 *Michael* 449

Endurance. Suffering what no endurance could assuage, 35 *Guilt* 578
Endurance, foresight, strength, and skill; 186 **She was* 26
That vision of endurance and repose. 226 *Vernal Ode* 47
At last, or glorious, by endurance won. 661 *Prelude* 4. 176
And pleasure in endurance. Much she thought, 854 *Excursion* 6. 1027

Endure. He deems their colours shall endure 9 *Lines: Boat* 11
A deed that I would shrink from:—but to endure, 78 *Bord.* 2301
For self-delighting fancy to endure 102 *Artegal* 26
—It looks as if it never could endure 137 *Michael* 379
Even the feeblest may endure: 140 *Arm. Lady* 34
In time's abyss, are privileged to endure 152 **Forth from* 21
A fate that has endured and will endure, 170 **Never enlivened* 25
And he had many hardships to endure: 196 *Resolution* 102
My mansion with its arbour shall endure;— 201 *Hart-leap* 74
"Oh! God, I can endure no more!" 249 *P. B.* 1120
Wreaths that endure affliction's heaviest shower, 259 **Weak is* 13
The immortal Mind craves objects that endure: 263 **Those words* 12
Dissolve that beauty, destined to endure, 263 **How clear* 11
Must perish;—how can they this blight endure? 282 *Railway* 5
Must still have sad or vexing thoughts to endure, 317 **Call not* 11
If this endure, farewell, for us, all good! 319 *Biscayan* 10
We can endure that He should waste our lands, 319 *Spaniard* 1
Ability like splendour to endure: 324 *Ode 1814* 72
As boundless patience only could endure? 330 *Ode: Thanks.* 97
When Sol was destined to endure 343 *Eclipse* 3
Or glory, not a vestige seems to endure, 361 **When here* 6
And melts; but grief devout that shall endure, 373 *Eg. Maid* 261
Bright liquid mansions, fashioned to endure 379 *Duddon* 12. 7
'Tis meet that I endure your scorn; 400 *White Doe* 389
'Mid Heaven-born flowers that shall for aye endure, 428 *Ecc. Sonn.* 2. 1. 7
Not utterly unworthy to endure 435 *Ecc. Sonn.* 2. 26.
And hardships manifold did I endure, 470 †*From early* 7
Through every part in symmetry, to endure, 474 **Hope smiled* 12
As tempted more; more able to endure, 493 *Hap. War.* 24
From all that haughtier kinds endure 526 **The soaring* 43
And ancient ordinance, shall endure, 534 **Blest is* 98
Endure that silence, and broke out in song, 539 **Lady! a* 31
Fate harder still! had he to endure assaults 574 *Chiabrera* 5. 4
Long as these mighty rocks endure,— 581 *John Words.* 67
If but by labour won, and fit to endure 654 *Prelude* 3. 391
To endure this state of meagre vassalage, 673 *Prelude* 5. 518
That shall endure as long as man endures, 682 *Prelude* 6. 467
How far they travel, and how long endure; 715 *Prelude* 9. 375
Of objects that endure; and by this course 740 *Prelude* 13. 32
Of building up a Work that shall endure. 750 *Prelude* 14. 311
Of various tempers; to endure and note 751 *Prelude* 14. 335

Endure—*continued.*
Will give me patience to endure the things . . 768 *Excursion* 1. 775
Should be permitted, ofttimes, to endure . . . 792 *Excursion* 3. 450
For adoration thou endur'st; endure . . . . 802 *Excursion* 4. 94
There shall endure,—existence unexposed . . . 812 *Excursion* 4. 757
They may endure long as the sea surrounds . . 838 *Excursion* 6. 15
And, when I fail, and can endure no more, . . 854 *Excursion* 6. 1047
Nor could endure the weight of his own shame. . 855 *Excursion* 6. 1114
To endure for aye. The Vicar, taking note . . 871 *Excursion* 7. 919
Shall it endure?—Shall enmity and strife, . . 894 *Excursion* 9. 661

Endured. Full long endured in hope of just reward, 25 *Guilt* 50
These fears can never be endured; . . . . . 130 *Idiot Boy* 423
A fate that has endured and will endure, . . . 170 **Never enlivened* 25
Propitious hour! had we, like them, endured . 449 *Ecc. Sonn.* 3. 37. 5
And all that was endured; for, in himself . . 761 *Excursion* 1. 366
But this endured not; his good humour soon . . 764 *Excursion* 1. 578
All night the storm endured: and, soon as help . 784 *Excursion* 2. 805
Inviting penance, fruitlessly endured: . . . . 798 *Excursion* 3. 876
Or soil endured a transfer in the mart . . . . 799 *Excursion* 3. 917
Of aught unworthily conceived, endured . . . 801 *Excursion* 4. 25
The sad privation was by him endured. . . . 864 *Excursion* 7. 476
Much too from war endured till new abodes . . K.8. 281 **Arms and* 6

Endures. But never to be extinct while Earth endures. . . . . 357 *Aquap.* 296
That shall endure as long as man endures, . . 682 *Prelude* 6. 467

Endurest. That thou endurest; heavy though that weight be, ... 665 *Prelude* 5. 6
For adoration thou endur'st; endure . . . . 802 *Excursion* 4. 94

Enduring. *See* **Long-enduring.**
Where, as before, the enduring Ass . . . . . 244 *P. B.* 712
Hence, while we gaze, a more enduring fear! . . 392 *Daniel* 10
Can thy enduring quiet gently raise . . . . 510 **Among a* 28
Now, when the frost was past enduring, . . . 537 *Goody Blake* 57
But with high objects, with enduring things— . 638 *Prelude* 1. 409
Knowledge and increase of enduring joy . . . 674 *Prelude* 5. 593
The soul of Beauty and enduring Life . . . . 698 *Prelude* 7. 767
Creative and enduring, may become . . . . 744 *Prelude* 13. 311
Them the enduring and the transient both . . 747 *Prelude* 14. 100
Keen and enduring, which the mind and heart, . 752 *Prelude* 14. 420
Than with the forest's more enduring growth, . 867 *Excursion* 7. 628

Endymion. The fair Endymion couched on Latmos-hill; . . . . 461 **Giordano, verily* 3
On the closed eyes of young Endymion fell, . . 630 [?] **O Moon* 12

Enemies. And scorn,—against all enemies prepared, 23 *Yew-tree* 19
Have reached his ear—you have had enemies. . 42 *Bord.* 256
Enemies!—of his own coinage. That may be, . 42 *Bord.* 257
Are not the enemies that move my fears. . . . 43 *Bord.* 321
Thy enemies are neither weak nor few; . . . 105 *Artegal* 211
Him and his enemies between! . . . . . . 181 *Waggoner* 4. 115
For perfect triumph o'er your Enemies. . . . 316 **It was a* 14
For Thou art angry with Thine enemies! . . . 328 *Ode 1815* 101
Soon to become more dreaded emenies . . . 420 *Ecc. Sonn.* 1. 9. 13
An emblem yields to friends and enemies . . . 433 *Ecc. Sonn.* 2. 17. 12
Friends, enemies, of all parties, ages, ranks, . . 723 *Prelude* 10. 361

Enemy. Oswald my special enemy, if you . . 63 *Bord.* 1425
Come to me—I'm no enemy: . . . . . . 120 *Emigrant Mother* 28
Or overtake some unknown enemy?— . . . 230 *Clouds* 14
Far—far more abject, is thine Enemy: . . . 309 **England! the* 11
"Thou Enemy, my bane and blight! . . . . 406 *White Doe* 924
Escaped as from an enemy, we turn . . . . 689 *Prelude* 7. 169
Of this new enemy. Tyrants, strong before . . 723 *Prelude* 10. 333
Against an enemy, I panted up . . . . . . 746 *Prelude* 14. 30

Enemy's. And thus they foil their enemy's despite. 437 *Ecc. Sonn.* 2. 34. 8

Energies. Union with those primeval energies . . 357 *Aquap.* 289
Virtues laid low, and mouldering energies. . . 360 *Alban Hills* 8
Her bane, her vital energies recruit. . . . . 431 *Ecc. Sonn.* 2. 10. 8
Upon earth's native energies; forgetting . . . 792 *Excursion* 3. 423
Than her destructive energies, attend . . . . 799 *Excursion* 3. 929
For by superior energies; more strict . . . . 805 *Excursion* 4. 305
An equal among mightiest energies; . . . . 809 *Excursion* 4. 532

Energy. A salient spring of energy; I mounted . 69 *Bord.* 1788
Both hands with rival energy . . . . . . 301 *Bran* 52
The purest stream of patient Energy. . . . . 444 *Ecc. Sonn.* 3. 15. 14
Of those who, in that dauntless energy, . . . 541 *Grace Darl.* 66
A tempest, a redundant energy, ... 632 *Prelude* 1. 37
Of fortitude and energy and love, ... 725 *Prelude* 10. 488
That energy by which he seeks the truth, . . . 740 *Prelude* 13. 8
To blazon—power and energy detached . . . 740 *Prelude* 13. 43
Encouragement, and energy, and will, ... 743 *Prelude* 13. 263
Nor energy, nor fortitude—a calm . . . . . 792 *Excursion* 3. 425
That with majestic energy from earth . . . . 803 *Excursion* 4. 143
Meek to admit; the active energy, ... 831 *Excursion* 5. 574
Life, I repeat, is energy of love . . . . . . 837 *Excursion* 5. 1012
And energy to conquer and repel— . . . . . 848 *Excursion* 6. 664

Enervate. The Pictish cloud darkens the enervate land 420 *Ecc. Sonn.* 1. 9. 8
To enervate and defile. . . . . 499 **Departing summer* 30

Enfeebled. And season favours." To enfeebled Power, ... 896 *Excursion* 9. 783

Enfold. Slow-travelling down the western hills, to enfold . . . . 12 *Desc. Sk.* 121
The mysteries that cups of flowers enfold, . . . 108 *Indolence* 62
Which soon the morning shall enfold, ... 180 *Waggoner* 4. 54
Her subtle essence to enfold, ... 234 *Power of Sound* 118
Through the beloved retreats your arms enfold! . 283 **Proud were* 8
With prompt embrace all beauty to enfold, . . 284 *Departure* 27
'Tis said, fantastic ocean doth enfold . . . . 333 *Fish-women* 1
What Maro loved, shall we enfold? . . . . 499 **Departing summer* 59

Enfolds. Enfolds within its core. The faith be mine, 354 *Aquap.* 106
Enfolds her?—is a rifted tomb . . . . . . 413 *White Doe* 1558

Enforce. Where is the obligation to enforce? . . 732 *Prelude* 11. 317

Enforced. Of fathers, but with patient mind enforced 133 *Michael* 156
Trying their strength, enforced him to start up, . 718 *Prelude* 9. 577
Week after week, the mandate they enforced. . 853 *Excursion* 6. 962

Enfranchised. Forth slips, like an enfranchised slave, 348 **Lulled by* 33

Engage. Shall not disturb us; further I'll not engage; 51 *Bord.* 775
In such peril to engage; . . . . 140 *Arm. Lady* 26
Enraptured,—could he for himself engage . . . 377 *Duddon* 7. 7
Let more substantial themes the pen engage, . . 522 *Epist. Beaumont* 89

Engaged. You might have noticed, busily engaged, 789 *Excursion* 3. 201
Engaged, near blazing hearth on clean swept floor, S.3. 426 **Through Cumbrian* 3

Engagement. With no engagement, in his thoughts, more proud . . . . 859 *Excursion* 7. 156

Engelberg. The sacred ENGELBERG, celestial Bands, 338 *Engelberg* 7

Engender. Engender lightning, whence are falling showers. . . . . 625 *Æneid* 125

Engendered. Engendered between malice and true love, ... 147 *Joanna* 33
Engendered, hangs o'er Eildon's triple height: . 386 *Scott* 3

Engendering. Engendering in the blood of hale fourscore. . . . . 98 *Brothers* 203
Again engendering anguish, ... 311 **Who rises* 59

Engine. But what was made an engine to ensnare thee; . . . . 57 *Bord.* 1100
I know no cheaper engine to degrade a man, . . 58 *Bord.* 1161
While the tubed engine feels the inspiring blast, . 332 *Ode: Thanks.* 216
And the vast engine labouring in the mine, . . 866 *Excursion* 7. 608

Enginery. Wielding her potent enginery to frame . 875 *Excursion* 8. 92

Engines. The engines of her pain, the tools . . . 194 *Ruth* 217
Like engines; when will their presumption learn, 671 *Prelude* 5. 358
Are various engines working, not the same . . 809 *Excursion* 4. 555

Engird. While they the Church engird with motion slow, ... 347 *Processions* 56

Engirding. And visibly engirding Mona's Isle . . 219 **This Height* 16

England. There's never a scholar in England knows. 80 †*Address: Child* 8
Nor, England! did I know till then . . . . 109 **I travelled* 3
From France to sheltering England came; . . 121 *Emigrant Mother* 68
Fame tells of groves—from England far away— . 271 **Fame tells* 1
Like conquest would the Men of England see; . 293 *Killicranky* 13
Beneath thee, that is England; there she lies. . 303 **Fair Star* 10
Of England once again, and hear and see, . . . 306 **Here, on our* 13
England hath need of thee: she is a fen . . . 307 **Milton! thou* 2
England! the time is come when thou shouldst wean . . . . 309 **England! the* 1
England! all nations in this charge agree: . . 309 **England! the* 9
Victorious England! bid the silent Art . . . 324 *Ode 1814* 94
O joy when the girdle of England appears! . . 346 *Stanzas: Simplon* 30
Of England—who in hope her coast had won, . 349 *Boulogne* 3
Darling of England! many a bitter shower . . 425 *Ecc. Sonn.* 1. 27. 2
And scourges England struggling to be free: . . 439 *Ecc. Sonn.* 2. 44. 12
But for what gain? if England soon must sink . 441 *Ecc. Sonn.* 3. 3. 10
The majesty of England interposed . . . . 441 *Ecc. Sonn.* 3. 7. 2
Lavished on *Him*—that England may rebel . . 443 *Ecc. Sonn.* 3. 11. 8
They called Thee MERRY ENGLAND, in old time; . 463 **They called* 1
Forbid it, Heaven!—and MERRY ENGLAND still . 464 **They called* 13
"Slaves cannot breathe in England"—yet that boast . . . . 501 *Humanity* 83
Long-favoured England! be not thou misled . . 514 **Long-favoured* 1
Young ENGLAND—what is then become of Old, . 516 **Young England* 1
Of dear Old England? Think they she is dead, . 516 **Young England* 2
Back again to England steered. . . . . . . 535 *Egremont* 60
Feeling what England lost when Reynolds died. . 547 **Ye Lime* 18
St. George of England! keep a watchful eye . . 626 *Ballot* 9
The Rose of England suffers blight, ... 628 *Installation* 21
Our shores in England,—from those loftiest notes 668 *Prelude* 5. 206
To England I returned, else (though assured . . 721 *Prelude* 10. 225
From the best youth in England their dear pride, 722 *Prelude* 10. 302
Their joy, in England; this, too, at a time. . . 722 *Prelude* 10. 303
—Hail to the State of England! And conjoin . 838 *Excursion* 6. 6
England, the ancient and the free, appeared . . 870 *Excursion* 7. 856
All England through, where nooks and slips of ground . . . . 879 *Excursion* 8. 370
Of merry England, are obstructed less . . . . 886 *Excursion* 9. 175
The unquestionable good—which, England, safe . 889 *Excursion* 9. 331

England's. To Nelson, England's pride and treasure, 178 *Waggoner* 2. 147
In whose collegiate shelter England's Flowers 270 **Ye sacred* 2
On England's bosom; yet well pleased to rest, . 303 **Fair Star* 4
Were England's native growth; and throughout Spain . . . . 319 **Avaunt all* 10
And utter England's name with sadly-plausive voice. . . . . 327 *Ode 1815* 44
England's illustrious sons of long, long ages; . . 328 *Ode 1815* 62
And filled our hearts with grief for England's shame? 349 *Val. Dover* 4
It was the time when England's Queen . . . 400 *White Doe* 360
No loyal rest while England's Crown . . . . 403 *White Doe* 638
For concord's sake and England's good, . . . 409 *White Doe* 1234
England's first Martyr, whom no threats could shake; . . . . 420 *Ecc. Sonn.* 1. 6. 10
For England's shame, O Sister Realm! from wood, 442 *Ecc. Sonn.* 3. 7. 7
Fixed on the frame of England's Church their sight, 444 *Ecc. Sonn.* 3. 15. 4
Of England's Church; stupendous mysteries! . . 445 *Ecc. Sonn.* 3. 19. 6
Is conscious of her want; through England's bounds, ... 450 *Ecc. Sonn.* 3. 38. 10
Of grateful England's overflowing Dead. . . . 452 *Ecc. Sonn.* 3. 45. 14
Will say, Ye disappeared with England's Glory! . 477 **Lowther! in* 14
Rich theme of England's fondest praise, . . . 495 *Fact* 25
"The frost of England's pride will soon be thawed; 513 **Said Secrecy* 4
While England's sceptred Line . . . . . . 629 *Installation* 97
Where England's sovereigns sit in long array, . 689 *Prelude* 7. 137

Enough—*continued.*
Enough that all around is fair, ... 223 Wishing-gate 25
Fair Prime of life! were it enough to gild . . 261 *Fair Prime 1
Is deep enough to exclude the light of love, . . 273 *When Philoctetes 13
Enough of sorrow, wreck, and blight; . . . . 286 Nith 19
Of good things none are good enough:— . . . 291 Rob Roy 86
Enough if in our hearts we know . . . . 293 Yarrow Unv. 47
Have romped enough, my little Boy! . . . . 295 Highland Boy 2
My Country! and 'tis joy enough and pride . . 306 *Here, on our 11
My ears did listen, 'twas enough to gaze; . . 338 Engelberg 16
Enough: my Country's cliffs I can behold, . 349 Boulogne 9
Enough, if something from our hands have power . 384 Duddon 34. 10
Enough of garlands, of the Arcadian crook, . . 389 Tyndrum 1
More than enough; a fault so natural . . . 394 *No more 34
Enough—if eyes, that sought the fountain-head . 419 Ecc. Sonn. 1. 5. 13
Enough! for see, with dim association . . 431 Ecc. Sonn. 2. 11. 1
With just enough life's comforts to procure, . . 470 †From early 10
Enough of Science and of Art; . . . . . . 482 Tables Turned 29
Am I enough beloved." . . . . 487 Fountain 56
—Enough for one soft vernal day, ... 497 Lycoris 9
Enough of climbing toil!—Ambition treads . . 497 *Enough of climbing 1
Enough;—before us lay a painful road, . . . 520 Pun. Death 14. 9
I leave unsearched: enough that memory clings, 525 Epist. Beaumont 265
And coats enough to smother nine. . . . . 536 Goody Blake 8
'Twas well enough, when summer came, . . . 536 Goody Blake 37
Enough to warm her for three days. . . . . 536 Goody Blake 56
Was yet not bold enough to write of Thee. . . 539 *Lady! a 9
Enough of rose-bud lips, and eyes . . . . . 541 Russ. Fug. 1
And, when it likes him, joy enough them sendeth. 560 Cuck. and Night. 195
'Tis sorrow enough on that visage to gaze, . 620 Convict 17
In glory immutable. But peace! enough . . 651 Prelude 3. 121
I play the loiterer: 'tis enough to note . . 657 Prelude 3. 579
Till our joint savings had amassed enough . . 672 Prelude 5. 472
Enough;—the mighty concourse I surveyed . . 690 Prelude 7. 219
Our argument. Enough is said to show . . 693 Prelude 7. 401
To many, neither dignified enough . . . . 694 Prelude 7. 459
Of this I heard, and saw enough to make . . . 701 Prelude 8. 166
Enough of humble arguments; recall, ... 706 Prelude 8. 476
Was not this single confidence enough . . . . 717 Prelude 9. 533
Head after head, and never heads enough . . . 723 Prelude 10. 362
To imitate, not wise enough to avoid; . . . 728 Prelude 11. 69
Enough, 'tis true—could such a plea excuse . 731 Prelude 11. 259
But leave we this: enough that my delights . 736 Prelude 12. 140
Lived long enough, nor in the least survived . . 737 Prelude 12. 181
" My Friend! enough to sorrow you have given, 770 Excursion 1. 932
Of privacy is deep enough to hide, ... 778 Excursion 2. 472
Enough if notions seemed to be high-pitched, . 797 Excursion 3. 786
" Enough is told! Here am I—ye have heard . 800 Excursion 3. 956
Who saw enough for blame and pitying love. . 843 Excursion 6. 362
Enough;—I fear, too much.—One vernal evening, 849 Excursion 6. 757
Be here retraced;—enough that, by mishap . 854 Excursion 6. 1088
That which he had been weak enough to do . . 855 Excursion 6. 1094
" Noise is there not enough in doleful war, . 863 Excursion 7. 363
Pangs are there not enough in hopeless love— . 863 Excursion 7. 367
With no unworthy prospect. But enough; . . 873 Excursion 7. 1050
Enough to fill the present day with joy, . . . K.8. 254 Recluse 1. 1. 650
Enough on these inferiour things. . . . . . L. 1. 96 Juvenal 3. 39

Enow. Enow there are on earth to take in charge . 668 Prelude 5. 153
Enow to stir for these; yea, will I say, . . . 668 Prelude 5. 156

Enquire. Failed in him; and, not venturing to enquire . . . . 96 Brothers 78
Enquire not if the faery race . . . . . . 223 Wishing-gate 19
With our own eyes—I could not but enquire— . 741 Prelude 13. 84
Enquire," said I, " how much of mental power . 741 Prelude 13. 95
Take note of this? When I began to enquire, . 742 Prelude 13. 160
Enquire of ancient Wisdom; go, demand . . . 815 Excursion 4. 957
—Not for a happy land do I enquire, ... 827 Excursion 5. 349
More winningly reserved! If ye enquire . . . 842 Excursion 6. 298

Enquired. *See* **Inquired.**
And what this place might be I then enquired. . 202 Hart-leap 120
That seemed to cling upon me, she enquired . . 766 Excursion 1. 657
We had returned together, she enquired . . . 769 Excursion 1. 847

Enquiries. In these enquiries, with regret I speak, 676 Prelude 6. 118

Enquiring. The maidens eye him with enquiring glance, ... 11 Desc. Sk. 40
Of man's enquiring gaze, but to his hope . . . 226 Vernal Ode 29
Nor to the Child's enquiring mind . . . . . 398 White Doe 206

Enquiry. What boots the enquiry?—Neither friend nor foe . . . . 258 *Where lies the Land 5
Made many a fond enquiry; and when they, . . 769 Excursion 1. 892

Enrapt. Nor is his spirit less enrapt, nor less . 18 Desc. Sk. 423
Here let me gaze enrapt upon that eye, . . . 190 *Lyre! though 8
That one enrapt with gazing on her face . . . 274 Infant M. 8
Stirs not; enrapt I gaze with strange delight, . 349 Val. Dover 10
The enrapt, the beautiful, the young, ... 373 Eg. Maid 310
Enrapt; but brightest things are wont to draw . 726 Prelude 10. 528
Enrapt, as if his inward sense perceived . . . 871 Excursion 7. 894

Enraptured. *See* **All-enraptured.**
With their enraptured vision see— . . . . . 178 Waggoner 3. 34
He with enraptured voice will tell . . . . . 330 Ode: Thanks. 69
Enraptured,—could he for himself engage . . . 377 Duddon 7. 7
Shout which the enraptured multitude astounds! 427 Ecc. Sonn. 1. 33. 10
Enraptured Art draws from those sacred springs . 500 Humanity 19
And when enraptured Dido shall receive . . . 624 Æneid 38

Enrich. Of beauty never ceases to enrich . . . 508 F. Stone 7
Of what this stock hath long produced to enrich . 880 Excursion 8. 396

Enriched. Enriched the earth, or Faery of the woods . . . . 124 V. and J. 207

Enriched—*continued.*
As when their breath enriched Thessalian air. . 210 Laod. 60
Enriched—too transient, were they not renewed . 231 Clouds 87
But are we aught enriched in love and meekness? 281 *What strong 8
Enriched and beautified his studious mind: . . 576 Chiabrera 9. 10
Not so enriched, not so adorned, to thee . . . 585 Ch. Lamb 77
And all the landscape, endlessly enriched . . . 700 Prelude 8. 96
Sought you enriched with everything I prized, . 741 Prelude 13. 118
May fairly claim, by niggard age enriched . . 781 Excursion 2. 632
Lurk in its cells—and thinks himself enriched, . 789 Excursion 3. 188
Enriched by mutual and reflected wealth, . . . 796 Excursion 3. 732
And gradually enriched with things of price, . . 860 Excursion 7. 172
Enriched with knowledge his industrious mind; . 865 Excursion 7. 503
The hoary grandsire felt himself enriched; . . 867 Excursion 7. 660
That, as the day thus far had been enriched . . 892 Excursion 9. 523
But confident, enriched at every glance. . . . K.8. 250 Recluse 1. 1. 497
Our beautiful and quiet home, enriched . . . K.8. 254 Recluse 1. 1. 652

Enriching. Enriching and adorning. Unto thee, . 585 Ch. Lamb 76

Enrobed. The laws to promulgate, enrobed and crowned; . . . . 471 Tynwald 4

Enrolled. Together in immortal books enrolled: . 251 *Pelion and 2
For why—unless for liberty enrolled . . . . 321 *Humanity, delighting 24
Shall live enrolled above the starry spheres. . . 330 Ode: Thanks. 66
Why sleeps the future, as a snake enrolled, . . 452 Ecc. Sonn. 3. 47. 1
To run before him, hath enrolled me yet, . . 496 *A little 8
Among ten thousand innocents, enrolled . . . 810 Excursion 4. 608
The sinless age, by conscience is enrolled, . . 888 Excursion 9. 315

Ensanguined. Hears combats whistling o'er the ensanguined heath: . . . . 345 *Ambition—following 13
O Death! the ensanguined yet triumphant wheels, 440 Ecc. Sonn. 2. 45. 10
Stilled by the ensanguined block of Fotheringay! 465 *Dear to 14

Ensculptured. That yet survive ensculptured on the walls . . . . 394 *No more 7

Enshrine. Than that which in Dodona did enshrine 319 Guernica 2
By love of beauty moved, to enshrine in verse . 358 Aquap. 363

Enshrined. The Spirit of Antiquity—enshrined . 334 *The Spirit 1
Enshrined for ages. Is not then the Art . . . 509 F. Stone 88
Burnt on with ever-strengthening light, enshrined 585 Ch. Lamb 61
And yet a spirit, there for me enshrined . . . 750 Prelude 14. 270
On earth, enshrined within the wandering ark; . 811 Excursion 4. 655

Enshrining. Substance and life to what I feel, enshrining, ... 738 Prelude 12. 284

Enshroud. The gloom that did its loveliness enshroud) 465 *Dear to 8

Enshrouds. Travelling where she from time to time enshrouds . . . . 461 *Who but is 2

Ensign. Ensign of civil power, weapon of war, . . 394 *No more 12
Keep thou this ensign till the day . . . . 400 White Doe 407
They cried, " the Ensign in his hand! . . . 412 White Doe 1465
And under one blest ensign serve the Lord . . 467 St. Bees 104

Ensigns. Spreading her peaceful ensigns, calls the swains . . . . 335 Namur 6
Under the saintly ensigns three, ... 405 White Doe 822
Ensigns of mimic outrage are unfurled. . . . 504 Warning 86

Enslave. Whose natural affection doubts enslave, . 104 Artegal 124
And the one Man that laboured to enslave . . 277 *Haydon! let 7
Let no mean hope your souls enslave; . . . . 287 Sons of Burns 43
Of cold mechanic battle do enslave. . . . . 293 Killicranky 10
Not 'mid the World's vain objects that enslave . 313 *Not 'mid 1
To enslave whole nations on their native soil; . 368 Trajan 59

Enslaved. By gross Utilities enslaved we need . . 358 Aquap. 348
When most enslaved by gross realities! . . . 512 *Who rashly 42

Enslavers. Upon the proud enslavers of mankind! 464 Derwent 14

Ensnare. But what was made an engine to ensnare thee; . . . . 57 Bord. 1100

Ensnared. A Maiden innocent till ensnared by Clifford, ... 44 Bord. 381
Had been ensnared by witchcraft. On the rock . 685 Prelude 6. 709

Ensnares. Of force that daunts, and cunning that ensnares! . . . . 426 Ecc. Sonn. 1. 31. 8

Ensue. She knows that only from high aims ensue . 22 Desc. Sk. 650
Untaught that soon such anguish must ensue, . 29 Guilt 294
And faithful service of his heart in the worst that might ensue . . . . 91 Norman Boy 26
Or from my purpose ruin may ensue. . . . . 105 Artegal 213
Her voice would utter, aught ensue . . . . 222 Triad 157
Should e'er a kindlier time ensue. . . . . . 406 White Doe 937
And kindliest intercourse ensue. . . . . . . 415 White Doe 1729
Whether of truth or virtue, to ensue. . . . . 656 Prelude 3. 530
Victorious, and composure would ensue, . . . 666 Prelude 5. 35

Ensued. In converse that ensued she nothing spake; 27 Guilt 188
Meanwhile discourse ensued of various kind, . . 27 Guilt 193
Unknown to him, this dialogue ensued. . . . 97 Brothers 120
If things ensued that wanted grace, ... 117 Affl. Marg. 19
The perturbation that ensued;—ah, no! . . . 123 V. and J. 145
Whom no weak hopes deceived; whose mind ensued, ... 323 *Now that 6
Came to the proof, nor grieved that there ensued 373 Eg. Maid 291
And then a thoughtful pause ensued: . . . . 403 White Doe 679
Silence ensued. " O Jupiter, whose care . . . 625 Æneid 107
I spare to tell of what ensued, the life . . . . 633 Prelude 1. 108
Ensued a diffidence and modesty, ... 643 Prelude 2. 75
The melancholy slackening that ensued . . . 684 Prelude 6. 617
Distress of mind ensued upon the sight, . . . 693 Prelude 7. 392
When a dead pause ensued, and no one stirred, . 719 Prelude 10. 109
Ended; and, from the stillness that ensued . . 777 Excursion 2. 394
Was greeted, in the silence that ensued, . . . 786 Excursion 3. 6
A pause ensued; and with minuter care . . . 788 Excursion 3. 113
And closer industry. Of what ensued . . . . 840 Excursion 6. 154
His parents laid in earth, no loss ensued . . . 864 Excursion 7. 432
And pure, from further intercourse ensued; . . 896 Excursion 9. 792

Entire—*continued.*
Though faded, yet entire. Companionless, 664 *Prelude* 4. 399
Falls rarely in entire discomfiture 720 *Prelude* 10. 176
To yield entire submission to the law 804 *Excursion* 4. 224
Linked in entire complacence with her choice; 816 *Excursion* 4. 1038
And an entire simplicity of mind 841 *Excursion* 6. 178
Remains entire and indivisible: 889 *Excursion* 9. 345
In placid beauty and entire content. S.3. 427 **My Son* 8
Perfect Contentment, Unity entire. K.8. 240 *Recluse* 1.1.151
Prompt aid, forgiveness speedy and entire. K.8. 266 **Rid of* 14
Entirely. Once, Man entirely free, alone and wild, 18 *Desc. Sk.* 433
Yet may we not entirely overlook 676 *Prelude* 6. 115
Entirely and for ever, and again 737 *Prelude* 12. 205
No longer flourish, he entirely gone, K.8. 248 *Recluse* 1.1.422
Entombed. Where mighty *minds* lie visibly entombed, 654 *Prelude* 3. 339
Near this brave Knight his Father lay entombed; 825 *Excursion* 5. 188
Entombs. Entombs, or forces into light; 391 *HighlandBroach* 86
Entrails. The mountain's entrails offered to his view 841 *Excursion* 6. 232
Entrance. And knock for entrance, in mid holiday. 45 *Bord.* 468
Could not the entrance of this thought forbid: 110 **Look at* 15
Free entrance to this cot has he, 144 **Driven in* 60
Entrance and exit both *yet* free; 144 **Driven in* 61
Comes from the entrance of a cave: 243 *P. B.* 630
With flapping wing for entrance. What a shriek 274 **Wait, prithee* 9
Yet peaceful Arts did entrance gain 390 *HighlandBroach* 11
Free entrance to the churchyard ground— 396 *White Doe* 54
Entrance I gained to that strong-hold. 409 *White Doe* 1252
Finds entrance through yon arch, where way 416 *White Doe* 1887
Find a free entrance to their languid orbs, 569 *Cumb. Beg.* 191
By stealthy entrance of a perilous guest, 625 *Æneid* 93
An entrance now into some magic cave 705 *Prelude* 8. 417
Find entrance;—high or low appeared no trace 787 *Excursion* 3. 68
Did never fail to entrance me, and are now 674 *Prelude* 5. 550
Entranced. He paused, and stood entranced by that still face 373 *Eg. Maid* 299
Attended; then, my spirit was entranced 803 *Excursion* 4. 118
Entrancement. Or rather felt, the entrancement that detains 381 *Duddon* 20. 2
Me hath such strong entrancement overcome, 668 *Prelude* 5. 162
Entreat. Whether the worshippers entreat 331 *Ode: Thanks.* 178
At his approach, and low-bowed necks entreat 423 *Ecc. Sonn.* 1. 19. 11
Ponder the blessing they entreat 530 *Gleaner* 31
For her heart's grief, she will entreat Sebeto 575 *Chiabrera* 7. 10
That crossed her way. Now stoops she to entreat 626 *Ballot* 5
"Have kindly interposed. May I entreat 832 *Excursion* 5. 629
Entreated. In comfort, I entreated that henceforth 665 *Prelude* 4. 454
Entreaties. Profound entreaties, and hand-shaking! 179 *Waggoner* 3. 45
Entreating. He pointed towards his dwelling-place, entreating 102 *Brothers* 413
He was commanding and entreating, 410 *White Doe* 1256
Entreats. Then Benjamin entreats the Man 176 *Waggoner* 1. 253
Such hope, entreats that servants may abound 839 *Excursion* 6. 43
Entreaty. Of bland entreaty at her court detains; 624 *Æneid* 20
At our entreaty: less from want of power 784 *Excursion* 2. 825
Entrenched. *See* **Intrenched.**
Entrenched, say rather peacefully embowered, 622 *Recluse* 1. 1. 76
Entrenchments. Thou, lodged 'mid mountainous entrenchments deep, 339 *Schwytz* 12
Entrust. Had left that calling, tempted to entrust 95 *Brothers* 40
To perilous weakness, and entrust his cause 122 *V. and J.* 62
Grows but to perish, and entrust 227 *Vernal Ode* 54
Entrust the future.—Not for these sad issues 886 *Excursion* 9. 126
Entrusted. *See* **Intrusted.**
Could be entrusted, while the events themselves, 730 *Prelude* 11. 197
Entrusts. Entrusts the imperfect song; 507 **While from* 60
Entry. A narrow, winding, entry opened out 777 *Excursion* 2. 412
Bounded:—triumphant entry this for him! 882 *Excursion* 8. 555
Entwine. A worthier wanting, shall itself entwine 57 *Bord.* 1109
The roses to the porch which they entwine: 250 *Admon.* 12
And now entwine their arms; but ne'er again 276 *Oker Hill* 10
His Mother's neck entwine; 342 *Ital. Itin.* 34
Ye Trees! whose slender roots entwine 366 **Ye Trees* 1
—So, pleased with purple clusters to entwine 367 *Trajan* 19
Strange "weeds" and alpine plants her helm entwine, 608 *Desc.Sk.Quarto* 329
To entwine the crook of eloquence that helped 695 *Prelude* 7. 570
Entwined. His sapling Peter has entwined. 242 *P. B.* 575
Where the main fibres are entwined, 285 *Grave of Burns* 45
That will be welcome, if by you entwined; 324 *Ode 1814* 41
And with devout solemnities entwined— 334 **The Spirit* 4
Of thy soft breath!—Less vivid wreath entwined 464 *Derwent* 9
Entwines. And, fronting the bright west, yon oak entwines 6 *Ev. Wk.* 214
Entwining. Of love emboldened, hope with dread entwining, 374 *Eg. Maid* 332
Enumerate. Who shall enumerate the crazy huts 879 *Excursion* 8. 346
Enveloped. 'Mid clouds enveloped of polemic dust, 437 *Ecc. Sonn.* 2. 36. 7
Enviable. Plain Nature's enviable privilege, 539 **Lady! a* 50
Enviably. That master them. How enviably blest 438 *Ecc. Sonn.* 2. 37. 12
Envied. His envied temples with the Isthmian crown, 312 **When, far* 6
The envied flower beholding, as it lies 377 *Duddon* 7. 3
And envied traveller! When the Boy returned, 688 *Prelude* 7. 93
Admired and envied. Oh! the beating heart, 694 *Prelude* 7. 493
Less to be envied, (you may trace him oft 788 *Excursion* 3. 174
Envies. And envies him that's looking;—what an insight must it be! 189 *Star-gazers* 8
Envious. Clouds of disgrace and envious fortune past! 105 *Artegal* 195
Nor shall the tongue of envious pride 220 *Triad* 19
But clouds and envious darkness hide 300 *Cora Linn* 25
And the whole world, not envious but admiring, 325 *Ode 1814* 137

Envious—*continued.*
Tho' searching damps and many an envious flaw 342 *Last Sup.* 1
Who, gathering up all that Time's envious tooth 359 *Plea: Hist.* 3
Provoked to envious spleen, he cast 369 *Eg. Maid* 25
Hail, Virgin Queen! o'er many an envious bar 438 *Ecc. Sonn.* 2. 38. 1
Yet free from touch of envious discontent, 872 *Excursion* 7. 952
When envious clouds shut out her silver light. [?] **A sad* 14
Environ. Which this comfortless oven environ! 484 **A plague* 12
Envy. Unstained by envy, discontent, and pride; 19 *Desc. Sk.* 493
Might envy, and am now,—but he shall know 54 *Bord.* 939
By envy as a tribute to desert, 68 *Bord.* 1686
Of all this world is solved, well may we envy 69 *Bord.* 1796
They envy not the happy lot, 177 *Waggoner* 2. 99
Another's praise from envy clear. 344 **How blest* 13
Pure minds with sinless envy, than the Abode 387 *Manse* 9
With envy heard in many a distant clime; 463 **They called* 3
Pride where there's no envy, there's so much of joy; 482 *Character* 11
Dishonour, shame, envy importunate, 560 *Cuck.andNight.* 174
With envy, what the Old Man hardly feels. 572 *Animal Tran.* 14
Envy and heart-inquietude, derived 574 *Chiabrera* 4. 8
To fair Aglaia; by what envy moved, 575 *Chiabrera* 7. 4
Forth rushed from Envy sprung and Self-conceit, 626 *Ballot* 1
With envy on thy nameless babe that sleeps, 692 *Prelude* 7. 380
Too weak even for his envy or his hate! 776 *Excursion* 2. 303
Which kings might envy!"—Praise to this effect 787 *Excursion* 3. 75
Place worthier still of envy. May I name, 789 *Excursion* 3. 196
Observe their ways; and, free from envy, find 807 *Excursion* 4. 383
Who rather would not envy, men that feel 847 *Excursion* 6. 616
In envy or distraction is not heard; 848 *Excursion* 6. 639
Which Persian kings might envy; and thy meek S.3. 433 **The doubt* 19
For selfishness, and envy, and revenge, K.8. 246 *Recluse* 1.1. 355
Could aught but envy now his pride rebuke? L.1. 96 *Juvenal* 3. 29
Envying. Not envying Latian shades—if yet they throw 376 *Duddon* 1. 1
Envy's. Shall place thy virtues out of Envy's reach. 478 **Lonsdale! it* 14
Interpose at envy's call, L.2. 190 **Queen and* 8
Enwrapped. Whose impious folds enwrapped even thee; and truth 77 *Bord.* 2260
In fleecy folds voluminous, enwrapped. 784 *Excursion* 2. 860
Enwraps. Like an unfathered vapour that enwraps, 684 *Prelude* 6. 595
Humanity's appointed shroud, enwraps 872 *Excursion* 7. 998
Enwrapt. Enwrapt—and winding, between Alpine trees 347 *Processions* 43
Enwreathed. With Idalian rose enwreathed? 221 *Triad* 114
And what if I enwreathed my own! 302 *Yarrow V.* 69
Enwrought. That eastern Sultan, amid flowers enwrought 219 *Haunted Tree* 12
The echo of the voice enwrought 289 *Stepping West.* 23
Should here be welcome, and in verse enwrought: 466 *St. Bees* 24
And, if with all things not enwrought, 544 *Russ. Fug.* 227
Of lowly thyme, by Nature's skill enwrought 702 *Prelude* 8. 243
Enwrought upon thy mantle; satisfied 707 *Prelude* 8. 534
Ephemeral. Ephemeral monsters, to be seen but once! 719 *Prelude* 10. 46
Ephemeral offspring of the unblushing world; 804 *Excursion* 4. 210
Epicureans. Of soft Epicureans, taught—if they 791 *Excursion* 3. 348
Epitaph. Is neither epitaph nor monument, 95 *Brothers* 13
Who chose his epitaph?—Himself alone 275 *Gravestone* 7
Have killed him, Scorn should write his epitaph. 277 **A Poet* 8
Than fondest epitaph: for, if those fail, 847 *Excursion* 6. 614
Their epitaph, which rain and snow K. 8. 226 **I will* 72
Epitaphs. We have no need of names and epitaphs; 98 *Brothers* 178
Is pictured, or their epitaphs can speak, 355 *Aquap.* 166
And foot-worn epitaphs, and some with small 825 *Excursion* 5. 169
Authentic epitaphs on some of these 832 *Excursion* 5. 651
Epitome. Oh, blank confusion! true epitome 698 *Prelude* 7. 722
Epitomise. Epitomise the life; pronounce, you can, 832 *Excursion* 5. 650
Equable. In worlds whose course is equable and pure; 211 *Laod.* 98
Equal. I would have made us equal once again, 71 *Bord.* 1866
Against an equal host that wore the plaid, 293 *Killicranky* 3
O, that my mind were equal to fulfil 395 *White Doe: Ded.* 59
Equal to *his* deserts, who, like the year, 425 *Ecc. Sonn.* 1. 26. 6
With equal wrath the steps of strong and weak) 434 *Ecc. Sonn.* 2. 22. 4
The truth exploring with an equal mind, 438 *Ecc. Sonn.* 2. 40. 9
Come when it will, is equal to the need: 493 *Hap. War.* 56
Rights equal, laws with cheerfulness obeyed, 515 *Penn.* 3
Hence equal ignorance of both prevails, 516 **As leaves* 11
That all the seasons shared with equal rights;— 583 **With copious* 27
Match'd with an equal number of like age, 624 *Æneid* 67
Upon equal ground; that we were brothers all 713 *Prelude* 9. 227
As best, the government of equal rights 713 *Prelude* 9. 242
Or both, with equal readiness of will, 772 *Excursion* 2. 83
Conceptions equal to the soul's desires; 803 *Excursion* 4. 137
An equal among mightiest energies; 809 *Excursion* 4. 532
Not equal, but sufficient to maintain, 833 *Excursion* 5. 711
In which they find an equal resting-place: 836 *Excursion* 5. 915
Were they not equal to their own support; 874 *Excursion* 8. 12
Her equal rights, her churches and her schools— 880 *Excursion* 8. 430
Gave to Athens equal laws. S. 3. 442 *Harmodius* 8
Gave to Athens equal laws. S. 3. 442 *Harmodius* 28
Equalise. *See* **Equalize.**
Exchanged—to equalise in God's pure sight 682 *Prelude* 6. 455
Equality. Equality by Prudence governèd, 339 *Schwytz* 4
From popular government and equality," 725 *Prelude* 10. 473
A popular equality reigns here, 823 *Excursion* 5. 96
The natural feeling of equality 852 *Excursion* 6. 950
Ponders this true equality, may walk 887 *Excursion* 9. 248
Equalize. *See* **Equalise.**
Ever bestowed to equalize and bless 435 *Ecc. Sonn.* 2. 29. 10
Far as ye may, erect and equalize; 516 **Feel for* 12
To equalize the lofty and the low. 574 *Chiabrera* 4. 24

Escaped—*continued.*
He comes, escaped from fields and floods ;— . . 249 *P. B.* 1105
Distressed me ; from mine eyes escaped no tears ; 251 **Beloved Vale* 7
Bleak Radicofani ! escaped with joy— . . . 352 *Aquap.* 22
Justice, and order. Tremblingly escaped, . . 419 *Ecc. Sonn.* 1. 4. 9
Scattering, like birds escaped the fowler's net, . 437 *Ecc. Sonn.* 2. 37. 1
Whence ye have escaped together, ... 503 **Like a* 76
To none more grateful than to me ; escaped . . 632 *Prelude* 1. 6
This truth escaped me not, and I confess, . . 655 *Prelude* 3. 423
Escaped as from an enemy, we turn . . . . 689 *Prelude* 7. 169
Deserving notice have escaped regard, ... 709 *Prelude* 9. 13
A young enthusiast, who escaped these bonds ; . 736 *Prelude* 12. 152
"In truth the threat escaped me unawares : . . 782 *Excursion* 2. 730
That the poor Sufferer had escaped with life. . . 785 *Excursion* 2. 890
And, like a weary voyager escaped . . . . . 794 *Excursion* 3. 558
Of natural passion, seemingly escaped, . . . 796 *Excursion* 3. 737
And grief spread wide ; but Man escaped the doom 811 *Excursion* 4. 649
Culloden's fatal overthrow. Escaped . . . . 844 *Excursion* 6. 421
The words escaped his lip, with a tender sigh . . 882 *Excursion* 8. 543
After long struggle, had escaped at last— . . . 882 *Excursion* 8. 565
Hath now escaped his memory—but the hour, . K.8. 236 *Recluse* 1. 1. 3
Escapes. My calmest faith escapes not pain ; . . 110 *Forsaken* 12
That through the jealous leaves escapes . . . 342 *Ital. Itin.* 49
What Summer here escapes not, the fierce wave, . 474 **Hope smiled* 3
Hazards and strange escapes, of which the rocks . 701 *Prelude* 8. 170
Escaping. And escaping from that sadness . . . 328 *Ode 1815* 74
And, guilt escaping, passion then might plead . 519 *Pun. Death* 8. 12
Hereafter, not escaping self-reproach, ... 788 *Excursion* 3. 117
Eschews. For every wight eschews thy song to hear, 558 *Cuck.andNight.*114
Escurial. To sanctify the Escurial palace. He— . 509 *F. Stone* 97
Escutcheon. *See* **'Scutcheon.**
Esk. Along the confines of the Esk and Tweed . 38 *Bord.* 62
We, neighbours of the Esk and Tweed : 'tis much 39 *Bord.* 85
Eskdale. Whom, but some few days past, I saw in Eskdale, ... 46 *Bord.* 479
Especial. And Betty's most especial charge, . . 126 *Idiot Boy* 57
So shines that countenance with especial grace . 459 **Wanderer ! that* 50
Of her own thoughts : by some especial care . . 764 *Excursion* 1. 516
Especially. (Especially perceived where nature droops 760 *Excursion* 1. 255
Espied. My hen's rich nest through long grass scarce espied ; . . . . 28 *Guilt* 213
And, looking o'er the hedge, before me I espied . 87 *Pet-lamb* 3
Have you espied upon a dewy lawn . . . . 118 *Maternal Grief* 27
The spring's first rose by you espied, ... 142 †*Lov. and Lik.* 31
I saw, espied its shaded mouth ; . . . . . 169 *Wren's Nest* 55
One after One they take their turn, nor have I one espied . . . . 189 *Star-gazers* 31
At length she learned how he espied . . . . 248 *P. B.* 1036
Of lurking cloistral arch, through trees espied . 335 *Rhine* 9
Espied the uncovered Corse ; the Man . . . . 412 *White Doe* 1507
When she by sudden glimpse espied . . . . 415 *White Doe* 1731
By whom in that lone place espied ? . . . . 479 *Somnamb.* 98
Espied him on his legs sustained, blank, mute, . 523 *Epist. Beaumont* 140
And soon as I a glimpse of day espied, . . . 557 *Cuck. and Night.* 56
That no wight his continuance espied. . . . 563 *Troilus* 21
Advancing, we espied upon the road . . . . 649 *Prelude* 3. 7
And to my wish and to my hope espied . . . 756 *Excursion* 1. 32
Joined in a cold damp nook, espied a well . . 763 *Excursion* 1. 461
Upon the slimy foot-stone I espied . . . . 763 *Excursion* 1. 492
Within her chamber-casement she espied . . . 766 *Excursion* 1. 666
We there espied the object of our search, . . . 784 *Excursion* 2. 817
We had espied the book, he drew it forth ; . . 816 *Excursion* 4. 1011
Had he gone far ere he espied the boy . . . K.8. 229 **I will* 172
Espies. And, looking down, espies . . . . . 85 *Shepherd-boys* 64
Espies—and instantly is ready, ... 181 *Waggoner* 4. 142
Rejoiced when waking she espies . . . . . 297 *Highland Boy* 233
Espies far off a Wreck, amid the surf, ... 540 *Grace Darl.* 30
Espousals. *See* **'Spousals.**
Espouse. She must espouse the everlasting Sea. . 305 *Ven. Rep.* 8
Espouse thy doom at once, and cleave . . . 402 *White Doe* 544
Espoused. O Father !—to the Espoused thy blessing give, ... 446 *Ecc. Sonn.* 3. 26. 6
To Christ, the Sun of righteousness, espoused. . 496 **A little* 48
One only solace—that he had espoused . . . 825 *Excursion* 5. 193
And, having once espoused, would never quit ; . 862 *Excursion* 7. 350
Espy. I started—seeming to espy . . . . . 79 *Sparrow's Nest* 5
About the pendent nest, did thus espy . . . 123 *V. and J.* 84
And on or in, or near, the brook, espy . . . . 190 **Lyre ! though* 18
And soon before me did espy . . . . . 191 *Beggars* 20
Wonder to all who do the same espy, ... 196 *Resolution* 59
This Thorn you on your left espy ; . . . . . 198 *Thorn* 28
Nor Traveller gone from earth the heavens to espy ! 208 **It is no* 3
But, chancing to espy a path . . . . . 240 *P. B.* 336
A goodly Vessel did I then espy . . . . . 258 **With Ships* 5
Flowers we espy beside the torrent growing ; . . 337 *Aar* 5
No faculty yet given me to espy . . . . 532 **Once I* 3
And when he might his time aright espy, . . . 563 *Troilus* 38
A single Glow-worm did I chance to espy ; . . 622 **Among all* 6
Of hidden beauty have I chanced to espy . . . 776 *Excursion* 2. 352
Esquire. *See* **'Squire.**
Is John de Clapham, that fierce Esquire, . . . 399 *White Doe* 249
Knight, burgher, yeoman, and esquire, . . . 404 *White Doe* 707
Essay. Nature by sign or sound made no essay ; . 35 *Guilt* 623
And with his coat did then essay . . . . . 114 *Last of Flock* 13
I gladly would go somewhere to essay . . . . 557 *Cuck. and Night.* 52
Essayed. Again that consummation she essayed ; 210 *Laod.* 26
I, who essayed the nobler Stream to trace . . 418 *Ecc. Sonn.* 1. 1. 5
Urged by his Mother, he essayed to teach . . . 761 *Excursion* 1. 312
Essays. And now the conqueror essays . . . . 174 *Waggoner* 1. 99
Essence. No purer essence, than the one that burns v **If thou indeed* 9

Essence—*continued.*
Her subtle essence to enfold, ... 234 *Power of Sound* 118
Even as one essence of pervading light . . . 750 *Prelude* 14. 272
Essences. Things in their very essences at strife, . 364 **What aim* 11
And essences of things, by which the mind . . 647 *Prelude* 2. 326
Essential. Exhaled, the essential odours climb, . 228 *Devot. Incit.* 8
When, like essential Forms of light, ... 526 **The soaring* 47
Essential and eternal in the heart, ... 761 *Excursion* 1. 344
Establish. *See* **Re-establish.**
Suspiciously, to establish in plain day . . . . 731 *Prelude* 11. 296
Establish sounder titles of esteem . . . . . 791 *Excursion* 3. 342
To establish something of a leader's sway : . . 794 *Excursion* 3. 594
And to establish thankfulness of heart . . . 795 *Excursion* 3. 657
Bound to establish new communities . . . . 889 *Excursion* 9. 379
Established. *See* **'Stablished, Re-established.**
And his is henceforth an established sway— . . 304 **Festivals have* 3
Of periods fixed, and laws established, less . . 469 **Desire we* 13
Established in the land where they abide . . . 568 *Cumb. Beg.* 137
The love established between man and man, . . 585 *Ch. Lamb* 63
Established by the sovereign Intellect, . . . 666 *Prelude* 5. 15
Established seemingly a right to hold . . . . 795 *Excursion* 3. 623
By will or by established ordinance, ... 805 *Excursion* 4. 299
The outward ritual and established forms . . . 827 *Excursion* 5. 310
Embodied and established these high truths . . 837 *Excursion* 5. 1000
In rest established ; and the jarring thoughts . 841 *Excursion* 6. 195
We, whose established and unfailing trust . . 846 *Excursion* 6. 560
Estate. The estate and house were sold ; and all their sheep, ... 100 *Brothers* 301
Such change in thy estate . . . . 105 *Artegal* 215
She begged an alms, like one in poor estate ; . . 119 *Sailor's Mother* 11
Survive her Husband : at her death the estate . 138 *Michael* 474
Poor in estate, of manners base, men of the multitude, ... 189 *Star-gazers* 22
A blest estate when piety sublime . . . . . 255 *Easter* 9
Of him in that forlorn estate ! . . . . . . 294 *Jedbor.* 26
Ye, in your low and undisturbed estate, . . . 332 *Ode : Thanks.* 232
Grave Gentry of estate and name, ... 403 *White Doe* 629
And cumbrous wealth—the shame of your estate ; 433 *Ecc. Sonn.* 2. 18. 2
Flourishing in fair estate. . . . . 535 *Egremont* 76
(Such the immunities of low estate, ... 539 **Lady ! a* 49
Lifting the boy to man's estate, had called . . 585 *Ch. Lamb* 89
On the lone mountain top, their chang'd estate. . 611 *Desc.Sk.Quarto* 489
If man's estate, by doom of Nature yoked . . 742 *Prelude* 13. 175
The estate of man would be indeed forlorn . . 818 *Excursion* 4. 1152
When he had crushed a plentiful estate . . . 845 *Excursion* 6. 446
Whether in soul, in body, or estate ! . . . . 848 *Excursion* 6. 698
That dignified and cheered a low estate ? . . . 877 *Excursion* 8. 238
Though strength decay, to breathe in such estate 885 *Excursion* 9. 46
Where kindred independence of estate . . . K.8. 247*Recluse* 1.1.380
Estates. And left estates and monies to the poor, . 135 *Michael* 268
"Yet, by the good Knight's leave, the two estates 875 *Excursion* 8. 44
Esteem. *See* **Self-esteem.**
A thing of no esteem ; . . . . 106 *Artegal* 239
In just esteem, it rivals ; though no style . . . 365 **Under the* 6
Esteem me, Liege ! if I, whose skill . . . . 372 *Eg. Maid* 244
No sign of hoar Antiquity's esteem . . . . 376 *Duddon* 3. 10
That to a Monk allots, both in the esteem . . 433 *Ecc. Sonn.* 2. 19. 12
In her esteem the thirst that wrought man's fall, . 469 **Desire we* 5
And will not hold in light esteem . . . . . 544 *Russ. Fug.* 283
Shall raise them highest in their own esteem— . 655 *Prelude* 3. 403
And wealth and titles were in less esteem . . . 713 *Prelude* 9. 231
In my esteem, next to such dear delight, . . . 741 *Prelude* 13. 129
Who cannot but possess in your esteem . . . 789 *Excursion* 3. 195
Establish sounder titles of esteem . . . . . 791 *Excursion* 3. 342
Feelings with these accordant ; love, esteem, . . 848 *Excursion* 6. 648
To outlive the kindly use and fair esteem . . . 873 *Excursion* 7. 1048
Esteemed. Esteemed you worthy to conduct the affair . . . . 53 *Bord.* 870
I too exclusively esteemed *that* love, ... 749 *Prelude* 14. 244
Esteeming. Esteeming earthly royalty . . . . 495 *Fact* 22
Esteems. Unto the few whom he esteems his friends 104 *Artegal* 102
Esthwaite. One morning thus, by Esthwaite lake, 481 *Expost.* 13
Esthwaite's. Where twilight glens endear my Esthwaite's shore, ... 2 *Ev. Wk.* 11
When thou hadst quitted Esthwaite's pleasant shore, 150 **When, to* 67
From under Esthwaite's splitting fields of ice . . 640 *Prelude* 1. 539
Make green peninsulas on Esthwaite's Lake : . . 672 *Prelude* 5. 434
The leaves were fading when to Esthwaite's banks 675 *Prelude* 6. 1
Estimate. Above all human estimate ! . . . . 492 *Fidelity* 65
Yet, in the estimate of youth at least, ... 694 *Prelude* 7. 488
Ourselves entail." Such estimate to frame . . 741 *Prelude* 13. 100
Doth, in my estimate of good, appear . . . . 790 *Excursion* 3. 278
Estimating. Misled in estimating words, not only 676 *Prelude* 6. 107
Estranged. From social life estranged ; . . . . 545 *Russ. Fug.* 300
The sea, or trod the earth, to peace estrang'd." . 625 *Æneid* 143
Estuary. Of Leven's ample estuary lay . . . . 725 *Prelude* 10. 515
Etcetera. And all the sad etcetera of the wrong, . 705 *Prelude* 8. 442
Eternal. The sky-roofed temple of the eternal hills ; 18 *Desc. Sk.* 464
Eternal praises on the power that saved her !— . 46 *Bord.* 519
Eternal farewell to unmingled joy . . . . . 65 *Bord.* 1546
Pledge of an eternal band : . . . . 142 *Arm. Lady* 142
Through "heaven's eternal year."—Yet hail to Thee, ... 172 *Infant Daughter* 15
But He hath overleaped the eternal bars ; . . 213 *Dion* 53
The bland composure of eternal youth ! . . . 221 *Triad* 140
And in eternal summer lose . . . . 225 *Primrose* 47
Conforming to the eternal Will, ... 228 *Devot. Incit.* 69
Lodged in the bosom of eternal things ? . . . 231 *Clouds* 94
Such beauty hath the Eternal poured . . . . 232 *Jew. Fam.* 37
Glory to that eternal Peace is paid, ... 256 **Yes ! hope* 7
And doth with his eternal motion make . . . 258 **It is a* 7

Eternity 265 **Eve**

Eternal—*continued.*
It seems the Eternal Soul is clothed in thee . . 268 **Brook ! whose* 11
Thanks to thy virtues, to the eternal youth . . 279 **Though I* 11
And o'er the eternal snows, like Echo, bound ; . . 314 **Advance—come* 5
We know the arduous strife, the eternal laws . . 316 **O'er the* 10
The Eternal looks upon her sword that gleams, . 318 **Ah ! where* 12
Their solemn joy—praising the Eternal Lord . . 332 *Ode : Thanks.* 201
A labour worthy of eternal youth ! . . . . . 343 *Last Sup.* 14
Of God's eternal Word, the Voice of Time . . 349 *At Dover* 12
Eternal things ; and, if need be, defy . . . . 358 **Is this* 13
Eternal Lord ! eased of a cumbrous load, . . . 366 **Eternal Lord* 1
Eternal blessings on the Muse, ... 386 *Yarrow Rev.* 41
For Souls familiar with the eternal Voice ; . . 391 *Brownie* 12
But Daughter of the Eternal Prime ! " . . . 417 *White Doe* 1910
Ancient of days ! that to the eternal Sire, . . 419 *Ecc. Sonn.* 1. 4. 6
Glad HALLE-lujahs to the eternal King ! . . . 422 *Ecc. Sonn.* 1. 13. 14
The Soul's eternal interests to promote : . . . 423 *Ecc. Sonn.* 1. 18. 2
From God's eternal justice. Pitiless . . . . 426 *Ecc. Sonn.* 1. 32. 5
She arrogates o'er heaven's eternal door, . . . 427 *Ecc. Sonn.* 1. 36. 3
Protect them ; and the eternal snow that daunts 431 *Ecc. Sonn.* 2. 12. 13
Nor shall the eternal roll of praise reject . . . 441 *Ecc. Sonn.* 3. 6. 1
Till they have reached the eternal City—built . 452 *Ecc. Sonn.* 3. 47. 13
She in her own would merge the eternal will : . 468 *St. Bees* 159
Intrudes on peace, I pray the eternal Sire . . . 470 *Bala-Sala* 5
Shall gild their passage to eternal rest." . . . 474 **How sad* 14
Blessings be with them—and eternal praise, . . 489 *Pers. Talk* 51
Lest Fancy trifle with eternal laws. . . . . 501 *Humanity* 100
One who would gather from eternal truth, . . 515 **Long-favoured* 12
In peace eternal ; where desire and joy . . . 573 *Chiabrera* 1. 5
And trust in God—to whose eternal doom . . 574 *Chiabrera* 3. 19
That, deaf and silent, read'st the eternal deep, . 589 *Immortality* 112
Haunted for ever by the eternal mind,— . . . 589 *Immortality* 113
Of the eternal Silence : truths that wake, . . . 589 *Immortality* 159
That guides the spirit to eternal day, ... 619 *School Ex.* 106
The living Rock of God's eternal Word. . . . 626 *Rock : Rydal* 4
Essential and eternal in the heart, ... 761 *Excursion* 1. 344
Repose and hope among eternal things— . . . 802 *Excursion* 4. 63
" And what are things eternal ?—powers depart," 802 *Excursion* 4. 66
To glorify the Eternal ! What if these . . . 818 *Excursion* 4. 1165
Of Time's eternal Master, and that peace, . . . 846 *Excursion* 6. 520
" Eternal Spirit ! universal God ! . . . . 893 *Excursion* 9. 614
Vocal thanksgivings to the eternal King ; . . . 895 *Excursion* 9. 732
Live through Heaven's eternal year : . . . . S. 3. 442 *Harmodius* 22
Of cities, 'mid the same eternal flow . . . K.8. 257 **Shall he* 3
Eternal Lord ! and from the world set free, . . K.8. 265 **Rid of* 2
Eternity. Look thou to Eternity ! . . . . . 90 *Longest Day* 48
Of dread eternity. . . . . 223 *Wishing-gate* 72
The appropriate calm of blest eternity. . . . 252 *Picture* 14
Breathed from eternity ; for, as a dart . . . 270 **If these* 8
Bright as the glimpses of eternity, ... 272 **Where holy* 13
That to itself takes all, Eternity. . . . . . 276 *Oker Hill* 14
To the Fountain whence Time and Eternity flow. 365 *Vallomb.* 40
And soul, to mingle with Eternity ! . . . . 384 *Duddon* 33. 14
And pain, hath powers to Eternity endeared. . . 476 *Howard* 14
Fixed on the statutes of Eternity, ... 519 *Pun. Death* 9. 7
For earthly sight. " Eternity and Time," . . 519 *Pun. Death* 10. 9
Here tutored for eternity. . . . . 533 **Blest is* 50
From the rock eternity ! . . . . 550 *Hermit's Cell* 3. 8
Into the deserts of Eternity. . . . . . . 582 *Invoc. Earth* 13
Thou Soul that art the eternity of thought, . . 638 *Prelude* 1. 402
And, from the centre of Eternity . . . . . 651 *Prelude* 3. 119
Of earth devoted to eternity ! " . . . . . 681 *Prelude* 6. 435
The types and symbols of Eternity, ... 684 *Prelude* 6. 639
Boundless, or guide into eternity. . . . . . 742 *Prelude* 13. 151
Of human Being, Eternity, and God. . . . . 749 *Prelude* 14. 205
Of life and death, time and eternity, ... 750 *Prelude* 14. 287
With pain the regions of eternity. . . . . . 774 *Excursion* 2. 205
Lost in unsearchable eternity ! " . . . . . 788 *Excursion* 3. 112
Eternity, as men constrain a ghost . . . . . 796 *Excursion* 3. 688
For time and for eternity ; by faith, ... 801 *Excursion* 4. 21
Far-stretching views into eternity, ... 819 *Excursion* 4. 1189
—Life, death, eternity ! momentous themes . . 874 *Excursion* 8. 10
Time wears the features of Eternity ; . . . . S. 3. 435 **The doubt* 120
Etesian. Of gales Etesian or of tender thoughts. 678 *Prelude* 6. 251
Ether. Of ether, shining with diminished round, . 16 *Desc. Sk.* 320
Of clouds that in cerulean ether blazed ! . . . 102 *Artegal* 4
Of ancient ether was no more, ... 168 *Pilgrim's Dream* 58
An ampler ether, a diviner air, ... 211 *Laod.* 105
And wide as ether her good-will ; . . . . . 222 *Triad* 146
Through seas of ether, where the ruffling sway 231 **The gentlest Poet* 9
Through many a long blue field of ether, . . . 236 *P. B.* 33
The fairest, brightest, hues of ether fade ; . . . 252 **The fairest* 1
Blue ether still surrounds him—yet—and yet ; . 261 **I watch* 4
Forthwith that little cloud, in ether spread . . 265 **The Shepherd* 3
The Moon from cloudless ether sees . . . . 406 *White Doe* 939
To the blue ether and bespangled plain ; . . . 420 *Ecc. Sonn.* 1. 7. 4
Might range the starry ether for a crown . . . 425 *Ecc. Sonn.* 1. 26. 5
Balanced in ether he will never tarry, ... 472 *Dunolly Eagle* 11
Bright, as if through ether steering, ... 549 *Hermit's Cell* 1. 21
Like marble, white, like ether, pure ; . . . . 550 *Hermit's Cell* 2. 14
Carrying through ether, in perpetual round, . . 811 *Excursion* 4. 703
The spotless ether of a maiden life ; . . . . 850 *Excursion* 6. 801
Pure, cloudless, ether ; and the star of eve . . 895 *Excursion* 9. 761
Ethereal. Of the ethereal Orb there came . . . 167 *Pilgrim's Dream* 23
Ethereal minstrel ! pilgrim of the sky ! . . . 209 **Ethereal minstrel* 1
With aught that breathes the ethereal element, . 213 *Dion* 55
Profound of night's ethereal blue ; . . . . . 226 *Vernal Ode* 31
Or racing o'er your blue ethereal field . . . . 229 *Clouds* 7
In listless quiet o'er the ethereal deep . . . . 231 *Clouds* 76
Of power ethereal and celestial grace, ... 231 **The gentlest Poet* 37
Thy functions are ethereal . . . . 232 *Power of Sound* 1

Ethereal—*continued.*
Descend from this ethereal height ; . . . . 238 *P. B.* 152
Or pencil pregnant with ethereal hues,) . . . 260 **High is* 3
The thousand links of that ethereal chain ; . . 268 **Four fiery* 8
Nor wants her eyeball an ethereal glance ; . . 278 **Lo ! where she* 4
Of yon ethereal summits white with snow, . . 329 *Ode : Thanks.* 22
Have marred this Work ; the calm ethereal grace, 342 *Last Sup.* 2
Into the ethereal element . . . . 371 *Eg. Maid* 184
Which God's ethereal storehouses afford : . . . 419 *Ecc. Sonn.* 1. 6. 4
And widening circuit of ethereal sky. . . . . 426 *Ecc. Sonn.* 1. 29. 14
Upwhirled, and flying o'er the ethereal plain . 435 *Ecc. Sonn.* 2. 28. 8
Pierces the ethereal vault ; and ('mid the gleam . 456 **The leaves* 9
If yon ethereal blue . . . . 507 *May* 18
The ethereal eyesight, cramp the wingèd mind ! . 529 **Those breathing* 136
Even the great Newton's own ethereal self, . . 653 *Prelude* 3. 267
Creatures of one ethereal substance met . . . 725 *Prelude* 10. 520
Not so the ethereal vault ; encroachment none . 746 *Prelude* 14. 50
Ethereal natures and the worst of slaves ; . . . 775 *Excursion* 2. 229
Communicates with heaven's ethereal orbs . . 795 *Excursion* 3. 662
—Man is of dust : ethereal hopes are his, . . . 803 *Excursion* 4. 140
By impulse of her own ethereal zeal. . . . . 806 *Excursion* 4. 316
And, over all, in that ethereal vault, ... 808 *Excursion* 4. 460
To his small island in the ethereal deep . . . 811 *Excursion* 4. 640
Through their ethereal texture pierced—ere we, . 893 *Excursion* 9. 598
From all reproach is yon ethereal vault, . . . K.8. 254 *Recluse* 1.1.641
Ether's. For blue Ether's arms, flung round thee, 217 **Inmate of* 7
As if their lustre flowed from ether's purest blue. 525 *Epist. Beaumont* 257
Cerulean ether's pure inhabitants, ... 682 *Prelude* 6. 465
Etive. Yon towering Peaks, " Shepherds of Etive Glen ? " . . . . 389 *Sound of Mull* 14
Etna. Where Etna, over hill and valley, casts . . 732 *Prelude* 11. 377
Etna's. On Etna's side ; and thou, O flowery field 733 *Prelude* 11. 419
On Etna's summit, above earth and sea, . . . 734 *Prelude* 11. 454
Ettrick. The Ettrick Shepherd was my guide. . . 586 *Hogg* 4
And Ettrick mourns with her their Poet dead. . 586 *Hogg* 44
Euclid's. Was " Euclid's Elements ; " and " This," said he, ... 667 *Prelude* 5. 88
Eudemus. Held with Eudemus and Timonides, . 715 *Prelude* 9. 412
Eulogised. He sate, and eulogised with earnest pen 356 *Aquap.* 259
Eulogist. Ne'er could the boldest Eulogist have dared . . . . 359 **Complacent Fictions* 5
Is run, some faithful eulogist may say, . . . 823 *Excursion* 5. 44
Eulogy. With copious eulogy in prose or rhyme . 583 **With copious* 1
And, when that eulogy was ended, stood . . . 871 *Excursion* 7. 893
Euphrates. Winding Euphrates, and the city vast . 811 *Excursion* 4. 689
Euphrates'. On broad Euphrates' palmy shore, . 215 *Enterprise* 25
Euphrosyne. So, truant in waste woods, the blithe Euphrosyne ! . . . . 221 *Triad* 106
Europe. Europe is yet in bonds ; but let that pass, 306 **Here, on our* 9
Europe breaks forth ; then, Shepherds ! shall ye rise . . . . 316 **It was a* 13
And through all Europe cheer desponding men . 318 **Ah ! where* 8
Wide Europe heaves, impatient to be cast, . . 331 *Ode : Thanks.* 149
Europe, a realised romance, ... 348 **Lulled by* 51
Through Europe, echoing from the newsman's blast, ... 349 *Val. Dover* 3
When Europe prostrate lay, the Conqueror's aim, 471 **Despond who* 7
That Europe knows, would echo this appeal ; . . 509 *F. Stone* 94
Indignant Europe cast . . . . 628 *Installation* 4
Let rescued Europe tell the story. . . . . . 628 *Installation* 18
But Europe at that time was thrilled with joy, . 680 *Prelude* 6. 339
Remote from Europe ; from her blasted hopes ; . 798 *Excursion* 3. 833
Europe, through all her habitable bounds, . . 870 *Excursion* 7. 841
Of darkness, stretched o'er guilty Europe, makes 890 *Excursion* 9. 410
European. Survived, and, when the European came 635 *Prelude* 1. 198
Eustace. To the Horn Sir Eustace pointed . . . 535 *Egremont* 3
Which good Sir Eustace sounded, was the last. . 535 *Egremont* 16
With his lance Sir Eustace pointed, ... 535 *Egremont* 17
Months passed on, and no Sir Eustace ! . . . 535 *Egremont* 57
'Tis the breath of good Sir Eustace ! . . . . 536 *Egremont* 81
'Tis Sir Eustace ; if it be . . . . 536 *Egremont* 93
And of Eustace was forgiven : . . . . . . 536 *Egremont* 102
But Sir Eustace, whom good angels . . . . 536 *Egremont* 105
Evanescence. Backward, in rapid evanescence, wheels 335 *Rhine* 5
The evanescence of the Saxon line. . . . . . 426 *Ecc. Sonn.* 1. 31. 2
Evanescent. Bodied forth and evanescent, . . . 550 *Hermit's Cell* 3. 3
Evangelist. " Of which the great Evangelist, Saint John, ... 554 *Prioress* 131
The Evangelist St. John my patron was : . . . 649 *Prelude* 3. 46
Evangelists. Meanwhile the Evangelists, Isaiah, Job, 695 *Prelude* 7. 562
Evans. Said red-ribboned Evans : . . . . . S.3. 440 **Said red-ribboned* 1
Evasive. Mistrusting her evasive skill, ... 168 *Wren's Nest* 38
Eve. *See* **Christmas-eve.**
Or seek at eve the banks of Tusa's stream, . . 13 *Desc. Sk.* 156
Whose long-suspended rights are now on the eve . 78 *Bord.* 2336
Eve renews her calm career ; . . . . . . 90 *Longest Day* 10
His freedom he recovered on the eve . . . . 124 *V. and J.* 186
All summer-long the happy Eve . . . . . 154 *Flower Garden* 19
Of Dawn—or Eve, fair vision of the west, . . . 222 *Triad* 179
From morn to eve, with hallowed rest. . . . 228 *Devot. Incit.* 77
Glimmers with fading light, and shadowy Eve . 269 *Gordale* 2
Take from *her* brow the withering flowers of eve, 270 **Shame on* 11
Morn into noon did pass, noon into eve, . . . 279 **Though I* 7
It was a breezy hour of eve ; . . . . . . 334 **In Bruges* 17
Is more benignant than the dewy eve— . . . 337 *Aar* 10
Years followed years, and when, upon the eve . 353 *Aquap.* 66
Life's temperate Noon, her sober Eve, ... 385 *Yarrow Rev.* 27
Withered at eve. From scenes of art which chase 388 *Trosachs* 5

Everything—*continued.*
Sought you enriched with everything I prized, . 741 *Prelude* 13. 118
In everything that stood most prominent, . . 750 *Prelude* 14. 305
Everywhere. 'Twas Johnny, Johnny, everywhere. . 128 *Idiot Boy* 211
She is uneasy everywhere ; . . . . 130 *Idiot Boy* 390
Love, blessed Love, is everywhere . . . . 168 *Turtledove* 19
That everywhere, before the thoughtful mind, . 364 **What aim* 13
Thus everywhere to truth Tradition clings, . 393 **The Lovers* 7
Bright Flower ! whose home is everywhere, . . 485 **Bright Flower* 1
The shade and light, both there and everywhere, 508 *F. Stone* 17
Found everywhere, but chiefly in the ring . . 657 *Prelude* 3. 541
Here, nowhere, there, and everywhere at once. . 673 *Prelude* 5. 533
Spread like a fragrance everywhere, when spring . 680 *Prelude* 6. 358
'Tis one encountered here and everywhere ; . . 690 *Prelude* 7. 202
Are scattered everywhere, no rarities, . . . 696 *Prelude* 7. 596
When everywhere a vital pulse was felt, . . 706 *Prelude* 8. 480
Are scattered everywhere, taking their date . . 737 *Prelude* 12. 224
To worship, here, and everywhere—as one . . 802 *Excursion* 4. 46
On the stream's bank, and everywhere, appeared 823 *Excursion* 5. 87
But now, when everywhere the summer grass . K.8. 229 **I will* 143
Eve's. And eve's mild hour invites my steps abroad. 3 *Ev. Wk.* 89
Tipt with eve's latest gleam of burning red. . . 6 *Ev. Wk.* 211
That glimmer hoar in eve's last light, descried . 12 *Desc. Sk.* 115
That tips with eve's last gleam his spiry head. . 595 *Ev. Wk. Quarto* 190
Below Eve's listening Star the sheep walk stills . 598 *Ev. Wk. Quarto* 353
Evidence. Did not admit of stronger evidence ; . 53 *Bord.* 881
Uplift his hand—that would be evidence. . . . 75 *Bord.* 2161
Can thus pervert the evidence of joy. . . . . 153 *Morn. Ex.* 12
Bearing the world-acknowledged evidence . . . 355 *Aquap.* 188
History that proves by inward evidence . . . 359 **Complacent Fictions* 3
And to her God restored by evidence . . . . 436 *Ecc. Sonn.* 2. 30. 3
Pursuit and evidence so far must fail, . . . 519 *Pun. Death* 8. 11
Of evidence from monuments, erect, ... 708 *Prelude* 8. 612
And want of hope where evidence divine . . . 720 *Prelude* 10. 162
Her hand upon her object—evidence . . . . 730 *Prelude* 11. 203
On their smooth surface, evidence was none : . 794 *Excursion* 3. 536
What evidence I seek, and vainly seek ; . . . 800 *Excursion* 3. 957
On evidence is not to be ensured . . . . 831 *Excursion* 5. 561
No evidence appears that they who rest . . . 847 *Excursion* 6. 602
Evident. Made evident, as seemed, by blacker guilt, 77 *Bord.* 2259
Evil. "'Twas a hard change ; an evil time was come ; . . . . 29 *Guilt* 271
"For evil tongues made oath how on that day . 35 *Guilt* 604
Your justice stamp upon his evil deeds . . . 42 *Bord.* 266
The wholesome ministry of pain and evil, . . . 48 *Bord.* 619
Through good and evil, obloquy and scorn, . . 64 *Bord.* 1500
A mighty evil for a strong-built mind !— . . . 65 *Bord.* 1511
Surely some evil Spirit abroad to-night . . . 67 *Bord.* 1664
On evil instigation, to make sport . . . . 74 *Bord.* 2085
Evil to any living thing ; but hear me, . . . 75 *Bord.* 2175
Alas ! it was an evil time ; . . . . . . 115 *Last of Flock* 85
And like the very soul of evil, ... 129 *Idiot Boy* 333
To my own family. An evil man . . . . 134 *Michael* 236
That was, and made an evil choice, if he . . 134 *Michael* 237
When thou art gone away, should evil men . . 137 *Michael* 405
To evil courses : ignominy and shame . . . 138 *Michael* 445
Of blameless debt. On evil Fortune's spite . . 138 *Widow* 5
Secure from evil eyes and hands . . . . 169 *Wren's Nest* 63
The evil One is left behind. . . . . . . 174 *Waggoner* 1. 115
Take her at once—for good and evil !" . . . 176 *Waggoner* 1. 240
His heart is up—he fears no evil . . . . 179 *Waggoner* 3. 134
What good or evil have they seen . . . . 191 *Seq. Beggars* 10
But ill he lived, much evil saw, ... 194 *Ruth* 145
"Alas ! when evil men are strong . . . . 204 *Brougham* 87
I said, when evil men are strong, ... 204 *Brougham* 104
With lofty thoughts, that neither evil tongues, . 207 *Tintern* 128
Ye fairies, from all evil keep her ! . . . . 237 *P. B.* 65
His evil spirit up again . . . . 245 *P. B.* 804
All anguish ; Saint that evil thoughts and aims . 253 **Fond words* 7
What mightiness for evil and for good ! . . . 306 **Inland, within* 8
Should perish ; and to evil and to good . . . 307 **It is not* 8
In the worst moment of these evil days ; . . . 321 **Here pause* 4
That soul of Evil—which, from Hell let loose, . 330 *Ode : Thanks.* 95
Deeming "the evil of the day . . . . . 339 **Meek Virgin* 41
Of evil with good Powers . . . . 374 *Eg. Maid* 356
And evil Spirits *may* our walk attend . . . 423 *Ecc. Sonn.* 1. 18. 4
The Apparition ; evil thoughts are stayed . . 423 *Ecc. Sonn.* 1. 19. 10
If good can smooth the way to evil choice, . . 428 *Ecc. Sonn.* 2. 1. 10
Through good and evil thine, in just degree . . 455 **Not in the lucid* 18
Of moral evil and of good, ... 481 *Tables Turned* 23
To evil for a guard against worse ill, . . . 493 *Hap. War.* 30
That looks for evil like a treacherous spy ; . . 500 *Humanity* 50
Is *Death*, when evil against good has fought . 518 *Pun. Death* 4. 1
But, if no evil hap his wishes crossed, . . . 531 **I know* 26
By what evil spirit brought ? . . . . . . 535 *Egremont* 46
Who will do evil, evil shall he bear ; . . . 555 *Prioress* 181
Evil light on her ! she hath done me wrong. . 558 *Cuck. and Night.* 105
In this cold abstinence from evil deeds, . . . 568 *Cumb. Beg.* 144
Through good and evil, help might have, . . . 577 **By playful* 19
"From regions where no evil thing has birth . 581 *Invoc. Earth* 4
Oh evil day ! if I were sullen . . . . . 588 *Immortality* 42
Safe from an evil which these days have laid . 669 *Prelude* 5. 227
And evil, overweeningly so called ; . . . . 670 *Prelude* 5. 281
And we found evil fast as we find good . . . 703 *Prelude* 8. 309
And evil, not as for the mind's delight . . . 707 *Prelude* 8. 521
Predominant in good and evil hearts ; . . . . 709 *Prelude* 8. 670
Of good and evil of the time was shunned . . 711 *Prelude* 9. 119
Where good and evil interchange their names, . 714 *Prelude* 9. 352
With evil expectations ; confidence . . . . 718 *Prelude* 10. 29
Nor the support of good or evil men . . . . 721 *Prelude* 10. 202

Evil—*continued.*
And with such general insight into evil, . . . 728 *Prelude* 11. 93
Of good and evil ; knows not what to fear . . 732 *Prelude* 11. 313
Which, when the spirit of evil reached its height, 735 *Prelude* 12. 42
Evil as one is rashly named by men . . . . 748 *Prelude* 14. 167
The good and evil of our mortal state. . . . 755 *Recluse* 1. 1. 762
Foreboding evil. From his native hills . . . 761 *Excursion* 1. 340
From vain, and, that worse evil, vexing thoughts, 788 *Excursion* 3. 162
Diverting evil purposes, remorse . . . . 813 *Excursion* 4. 839
Bedded for good and evil in a gulf . . . . 826 *Excursion* 5. 295
Preponderates, or evil ? Doth the will . . . 829 *Excursion* 5. 470
The good and evil are our own ; and we . . . 830 *Excursion* 5. 490
Of evil hap and good as oft awaits . . . . 833 *Excursion* 5. 733
And evil, to the just and the unjust ; . . . 836 *Excursion* 5. 914
Of evil inclinations are unknown ; . . . . 848 *Excursion* 6. 641
A simple blessing, or with evil mixed ; . . . 884 *Excursion* 9. 12
And strength in evil ? Hence an after-call . . 886 *Excursion* 9. 122
Impending evil, equally require . . . . . 889 *Excursion* 9. 357
Of good from evil ; as if one extreme . . . 895 *Excursion* 9. 723
I shrink not from the evil with disgust, . . . K.8. 246 *Recluse* 1. 1. 351
And real evil, yet be sweet withal, ... K.8. 247 *Recluse* 1. 1. 406
Evil-minded. Of evil-minded fairies), yet not vain . 641 *Prelude* 1. 591
Evils. What benefits are missed, what evils bred, . 443 *Ecc. Sonn.* 3. 14. 4
Were turned to evils that are new and chosen, . 887 *Excursion* 9. 187
Evil-speaking. From evil-speaking ; rancour, never sought, ... 488 *Pers. Talk* 45
Evince. Evince the want and weakness whence they spring." . . . . 829 *Excursion* 5. 439
Do arts like these a royal mind evince ? . . . L.I. 94 *Juvenal* 2. 11
Evinced. Expression slowly varying, that evinced . 834 *Excursion* 5. 785
Evolves. Their jubilant activity evolves . . . 218 *Recluse* 1. 1. 212
Ewbank. Left in the church-yard wall. That's Walter Ewbank. . . . . 98 *Brothers* 200
That Leonard Ewbank was come home again, . 100 *Brothers* 309
Ewbanks. Had clothed the Ewbanks for a thousand years :—. . . . . 100 *Brothers* 303
Ewe. *See* **Mother-ewe.**
Yet, so it was, an ewe I bought ; . . . . . 115 *Last of Flock* 24
And from this one, this single ewe, ... 115 *Last of Flock* 32
A lamb, a wether, and a ewe ;— . . . . . 115 *Last of Flock* 93
Exact. The mind lay open, to a more exact . . 646 *Prelude* 2. 283
By scale exact, in model, wood or clay, . . . 691 *Prelude* 7. 249
Exacted. Exacted thy return, and our reunion. . 41 *Bord.* 204
Exaction. But not without exaction of a pledge, . 123 *V. and J.* 152
Exacts. While she exacts allegiance, shall admit . 888 *Excursion* 9. 296
Exalt. What high resolves exalt the tenderest thought 15 *Desc. Sk.* 297
Might exalt the loveliest cheek ; . . . . . 90 *Longest Day* 24
The affections, to exalt them or refine ; . . . 172 *Infant Daughter* 35
Quicken the slothful, and exalt the vile !— . . 217 *Enterprise* 156
Doth to the *Soul* exalt it with the chime . . 227 *Vernal Ode* 92
Exalt his still small voice ;—to quell that Host . 322 **By Moscow* 10
Flesh to exalt than prove its nothingness. . . 469 **Desire we* 14
Humbling the body, to exalt the soul ; . . . 510 **Among a* 4
And to exalt the passing hour ; . . . . . 533 **Blest is* 25
Exalt the sense of thoughtful gratitude . . . 538 **In desultory* 53
Exalt thy spirit, hear the voice . . . . . 577 *Cenotaph* 11
To curb, exalt, reform the tender mind : . . . 618 *School Ex.* 18
Far better had it been to exalt the mind . . . 663 *Prelude* 4. 304
Stretched and still stretching far and wide, exalt 698 *Prelude* 7. 746
Serve to exalt ; they build up greatest things . 747 *Prelude* 14. 101
Filling a space, else vacant, to exalt . . . 814 *Excursion* 4. 845
Contingencies of pomp ; and serve to exalt . . 817 *Excursion* 4. 1061
His talents lending to exalt the freaks . . . 843 *Excursion* 6. 343
Power that comes forth to quicken and exalt . . 875 *Excursion* 8. 73
Exaltation. Pregnant with mutual exaltation, . . 178 *Waggoner* 3. 40
For exaltation of her sovereign state. . . . 532 **Once I* 24
And exaltation. Nothing at that time . . . K.8. 256 *Recluse* 1. 1. 708
Exalted. Hues more exalted, "a refinèd Form," . 110 **Look at* 22
"Exalted Star !" the Worm replied, ... 167 *Pilgrim's Dream* 33
Exalted by congenial sway . . . . . . 300 *Bran* 39
But more exalted, with a brighter train : . . . 316 **O'er the* 4
He sits a more exalted Potentate, ... 317 **Call not* 8
Exalted office, worthily sustained ! . . . . 331 *Ode : Thanks.* 160
Argo—exalted for that daring feat . . . . 336 *Danube* 13
The impenetrable heart of that exalted Mount ! . 347 *Processions* 54
Thy fortunes, twice exalted, might provoke . . 360 *Alban Hills* 10
Thy soul, exalted Emily, ... 416 *White Doe* 1866
Upon the exalted hills. He made report . . . 548 **Stay, bold* 20
By their good works exalted, lofty minds, . . 567 *Cumb. Beg.* 106
To thy exalted nature only seem . . . . . 584 **With copious* 38
Full oft the quiet and exalted thoughts . . . 652 *Prelude* 3. 207
As those of books, but more exalted far ; . . . 703 *Prelude* 8. 283
A more exalted nature ; wished that Man . . . 731 *Prelude* 11. 251
And Reason in her most exalted mood. . . . 749 *Prelude* 14. 192
In beauty exalted, as it is itself . . . . . 752 *Prelude* 14. 453
To an exalted pitch (the self-same cause . . . 788 *Excursion* 3. 154
With joy exalted to beatitude ; . . . . . . 803 *Excursion* 4. 119
Could e'er for such exalted confidence . . . 805 *Excursion* 4. 266
Of much exalted good by Heaven vouchsafed . . 813 *Excursion* 4. 783
Of less exalted consciousness, through which . . 830 *Excursion* 5. 524
Father and founder of exalted deeds ; . . . . 870 *Excursion* 7. 824
Are yet exalted, and in soul adore ! . . . . 893 *Excursion* 9. 627
From that exalted station to the plain . . . 895 *Excursion* 9. 756
Exalting. The gift exalting, and with playful smile : 438 *Ecc. Sonn.* 2. 39. 5
Favour divine, exalting human love ; . . . . 540 *Grace Darl.* 5
Exalting tender themes, by just degrees . . . 839 *Excursion* 6. 83
Exalts. Him who thus exalts thy spirit, . . . 140 *Arm. Lady* 69
The blind man's gloom, exalts the veteran's mirth ; 233 *Power of Sound* 50
While the warm hearth exalts the mantling ale, . 379 *Duddon* 13. 12
A virtue which irradiates and exalts . . . . 645 *Prelude* 2. 239
To meekness, and exalts by humble faith ; . . 740 *Prelude* 13. 28

Examination. *See* **Self-examination.**
Examinations. Examinations, when the man was weighed — 650 *Prelude* 3. 69
Examine. Let us examine it. 'Tis a bitter night; — 50 *Bord.* 733
Turned inward,—to examine of what stuff — 796 *Excursion* 3. 696
Examined. Only to be examined, pondered, searched, — 816 *Excursion* 4. 977
Example. May become a blest example — 94 *Westmoreland Girl* 83
Your Father such example gave, — 287 *Sons of Burns* 45
By one example hath set forth to all — 305 **The Voice* 4
A bright, encouraging, example shows; — 395 *White Doe: Ded.* 52
And from example of thy monthly range — 461 **Queen of* 53
Nor doth the example fail to cheer — 498 **Departing summer* 13
Redeemed, according to example given — 721 *Prelude* 10. 220
By the example of his own pure course, — 781 *Excursion* 2. 630
O high example, constancy divine! — 839 *Excursion* 6. 74
For such example. Almost at the root — 863 *Excursion* 7. 395
Examples. By such examples moved to unbought pains, — 424 *Ecc. Sonn.* 1. 24. 1
For those examples, in no age surpassed, — 725 *Prelude* 10. 487
Examples efficacious to refine — 875 *Excursion* 8. 66
Exasperation. Strangely the exasperation of that Land, — 798 *Excursion* 3. 817
Exceed. Temptation here is none to exceed the truth; — 847 *Excursion* 6. 601
Exceeding. Exceeding was the love he bare to him, — 133 *Michael* 151
Of her own exceeding pleasure! — 171 *Kitten* 40
From her exceeding pain. — 199 *Thorn* 130
Numbers exceeding credible account — 347 *Processions* 51
And sorrow bartered for exceeding joy. — 440 *Ecc. Sonn.* 3. 2. 14
That an exceeding love hath dazzled me; — 574 *Chiabrera* 5. 20
That through the time's exceeding fierceness saw — 724 *Prelude* 10. 451
By bodily toil, labour exceeding far — 741 *Prelude* 13. 97
A virtuous household, though exceeding poor! — 758 *Excursion* 1. 112
How goodly, how exceeding fair, how pure — K. 8. 254 *Recluse* 1. 1. 640
Exceedingly. For she was one I loved exceedingly; — 440 *Ecc. Sonn.* 3. 1. 6
Does in this change exceedingly rejoice; — 520 *Pun. Death* 12. 10
Excel. For they Earth's fairest daughters do excel; — 333 *Fish-women* 10
Excellence. Nor less, by excellence of nature, fit — 220 *Triad* 53
Bright sprinklings of all human excellence, — 725 *Prelude* 10. 484
My sense of excellence—of right and wrong: — 740 *Prelude* 13. 58
The excellence, pure function, and best power — 745 *Prelude* 13. 377
Be shown? her glorious excellence—that ranks — 846 *Excursion* 6. 565
In excellence less difficult to reach, — 863 *Excursion* 7. 392
The excellence of moral qualities — 887 *Excursion* 9. 232
If Excellence was ever Eden's name? — L. 1. 88 *Juvenal* 1. 12
Excellent. Was almost terrified. That's excellent!— — 61 *Bord.* 1288
Was the boast of the country for excellent cheer; — 569 *Farmer* 14
O Soul of Nature! excellent and fair! — 735 *Prelude* 12. 93
Excellently. Negress excellently bright! — L. 2. 190 **Queen and* 12
Excelling. —There, though by right the excelling Painter sleep — 547 **Ye Lime* 9
Except. Except for that abatement which is paid — 68 *Bord.* 1685
(Only except some impulses of pride — 795 *Excursion* 3. 631
The torch, the star, the anchor; nor except — 827 *Excursion* 5. 336
Excess. Yet Nature, with excess of grief o'erborne, — 30 *Guilt* 309
And in the excess of amity, — 179 *Waggoner* 3. 49
For this the passion to excess was driven— — 211 *Laod.* 148
And discipline was passion's dire excess. — 330 *Ode: Thanks.* 122
Such consolation, and the excess — 402 *White Doe* 524
By wrong triumphant through its own excess, — 426 *Ecc. Sonn.* 1. 32. 2
Earth cannot check. O terrible excess — 439 *Ecc. Sonn.* 2. 44. 9
To our own prodigal excess — 497 *Lycoris* 25
And joy's excess produced a fear — 545 *Russ. Fug.* 355
In many a thoughtless hour, when, from excess — 645 *Prelude* 2. 186
So deeply in my mind, or from excess — 647 *Prelude* 2. 388
Unspoiled by commendation and the excess — 691 *Prelude* 7. 313
And poverty and labour in excess — 742 *Prelude* 13. 198
Tender and deep in her excess of love; — 764 *Excursion* 1. 514
In that excess which conscience disapproves. — 803 *Excursion* 4. 152
The excess, by which the balance is destroyed. — 804 *Excursion* 4. 178
That is transported to excess; that yearns, — 830 *Excursion* 5. 507
Excesses. For spendthrift feats, excesses of his prime. — 783 *Excursion* 2. 756
Excessive. As in a balance! of excessive hopes, — 650 *Prelude* 3. 70
In no disturbance of excessive hope, — 688 *Prelude* 7. 62
No heat of passion or excessive zeal, — 740 *Prelude* 13. 25
Exchange. Sought by a wise though late exchange, and here — 143 **High bliss* 5
And, after short exchange of village news, — 147 *Joanna* 25
Transformed, and rushing on a bold exchange — 270 **Ye sacred* 9
With Young and Old warm greetings we exchange, — 525 *Epist. Beaumont* 236
Of trivial pleasures was a poor exchange — 663 *Prelude* 4. 298
For rest not needed or exchange of love, — 702 *Prelude* 8. 240
Exchange the shepherd's frock of native grey — 846 *Excursion* 6. 548
For other pastures would exchange the same — K. 8. 230 **I will* 201
Exchanged. Till she exchanged for heaven that happy ground. — 267 *St. Cath.* 14
For summer's heat exchanged, — 545 *Russ. Fug.* 298
Exchanged—to equalise in God's pure sight — 682 *Prelude* 6. 455
A glad congratulation we exchanged — 757 *Excursion* 1. 47
A general greeting was exchanged; and soon — 829 *Excursion* 5. 462
Exchanging. Nor one look more exchanging, grief to still — 276 *Oker Hill* 3
Excitation. Of peace and excitation, finds in her — 740 *Prelude* 13. 6
Excite. The tremulous heart excite; — 506 **While from* 14
Its unsuccessful issue much excite — 722 *Prelude* 10. 256
And those illusions, which excite the scorn — 813 *Excursion* 4. 834
Both knows and loves such objects as excite — 819 *Excursion* 4. 1210
My narratives to subjects that excite — 848 *Excursion* 3. 647
Excited. Never excited by the fumes of wine — 653 *Prelude* 3. 301

Excited—*continued.*
Structures like these the excited spirit mainly — 697 *Prelude* 7. 651
Excitement. Of such excitement and divided thought — 852 *Excursion* 6. 958
Exciting. How, for exciting youth's heroic flame, — 359 **Those old* 13
Exciting self-suspicion strong, — 411 *White Doe* 1410
Exclaim. Despond who will—*I* heard a voice exclaim, — 471 **Despond who* 1
Hard task! exclaim the undisciplined, to lean — 515 **Hard task* 1
And the more faithful were compelled to exclaim, — 797 *Excursion* 3. 775
By him that utters it, exclaim aloud, — 809 *Excursion* 4. 535
To exclaim—' O happy! yielding to the law — 835 *Excursion* 5. 828
The tender age of life, ye would exclaim, — 880 *Excursion* 8. 397
Exclaimed. Then thus exclaimed: " To me, of titles shorn, — 104 *Artegal* 139
" One, are we not?" exclaimed the Maiden—" One, — 124 *V. and J.* 163
" Improvident and reckless," we exclaimed, — 149 **A narrow* 50
Exclaimed an angry Voice, — 155 *Waterfall* 2
Stop," it exclaimed, " and pity me!" — 176 *Waggoner* 1. 220
Exclaimed the Chieftain—" let me rather see — 213 *Dion* 82
Exclaimed the King, " a mockery hateful; — 372 *Eg. Maid* 212
The Muse exclaimed; but Story now must hide — 388 *Loch Etive* 10
Exclaimed he: " righteous Heaven, — 545 *Russ. Fug.* 330
Of will and choice," I bitterly exclaimed, — 732 *Prelude* 11. 310
Impatient to pass on, when I exclaimed, — 778 *Excursion* 2. 431
Exclaimed the Wanderer, " cannot but be his, — 778 *Excursion* 2. 437
Exclaimed my Friend: " here then has been to him — 778 *Excursion* 2. 445
" Those lusty twins," exclaimed our host, " if here — 782 *Excursion* 2. 694
And cloudless sky.—Anon exclaimed our Host, — 786 *Excursion* 3. 10
Sheds,' I exclaimed, ' no sadness upon me, — 790 *Excursion* 3. 312
The Sceptic somewhat haughtily exclaimed: — 812 *Excursion* 4. 767
He with a smile exclaimed:—" 'Tis well you speak — 814 *Excursion* 4. 894
" Now, shall our great Discoverers," he exclaimed, — 815 *Excursion* 4. 941
With manifest emotion, and exclaimed; — 817 *Excursion* 4. 1079
" Yet," with a smile of triumph thus exclaimed — 828 *Excursion* 5. 390
For daily bread." " Yes," buoyantly exclaimed — 831 *Excursion* 5. 601
" Impute it not to impatience, if," exclaimed — 841 *Excursion* 6. 189
Man has his strength," exclaimed the Wanderer, " oh! — 842 *Excursion* 6. 255
Exclaimed the Sceptic, " and the strain of thought — 846 *Excursion* 6. 523
The Wanderer somewhat eagerly exclaimed, — 847 *Excursion* 6. 580
Her child should die; as Ellen now exclaimed, — 853 *Excursion* 6. 968
We followed; and my voice with joy exclaimed: — 870 *Excursion* 7. 820
Exclaimed—" The sagest Antiquarian's eye — 871 *Excursion* 7. 921
The grey-haired Wanderer pensively exclaimed, — 872 *Excursion* 7. 977
The pale Recluse indignantly exclaimed, — 879 *Excursion* 8. 335
And an impassioned majesty, exclaimed— — 888 *Excursion* 9. 292
The Priest in holy transport thus exclaimed: — 893 *Excursion* 9. 613
Exclaims. ' Quell the Scot,' exclaims the Lance— — 205 *Brougham* 144
Exclude. However stern, is powerless to exclude. — 15 *Desc. Sk.* 249
Is deep enough to exclude the light of love, — 273 **When Philoctetes* 13
Nor would the nicest Anchorite exclude — 379 *Duddon* 14. 3
Unsapped by delicate viands; for, exclude — 643 *Prelude* 2. 81
Exclude a power to enjoy the vital beams — 790 *Excursion* 3. 298
To keep his own, but also to exclude — 844 *Excursion* 6. 395
But exclude — K. 8. 231 **I will* 210
Excluded. Sorrow seems here excluded; and that knell, — 475 *Greenock* 7
Excludes. Mild dawn of promise! that excludes — 302 *Yarrow V.* 21
Excluding. *See* **World-excluding.**
Exclusion. That legalised exclusion, empty pomp — 717 *Prelude* 9. 526
And sad exclusion through decay of sense; — 802 *Excursion* 4. 59
Exclusively. I too exclusively esteemed *that* love, — 749 *Prelude* 14. 244
Exclusively with transitory things) — 838 *Excursion* 6. 39
Excursion. Returned from that excursion, soon I bade — 688 *Prelude* 7. 52
Excursions. In one of those excursions (may they ne'er — 746 *Prelude* 14. 1
Excursive. Not treacherous, to the mind's *excursive* power. — 820 *Excursion* 4. 1263
Excuse. *See* **Self-excuse.**
Excuse is needless when with love sincere — 255 *S. H.* 1
To excuse him in his Country's sight? — 411 *White Doe* 1400
Error without excuse upon the side — 714 *Prelude* 9. 341
Enough, 'tis true—could such a plea excuse — 731 *Prelude* 11. 259
For my excuse. Dissevered from mankind, — 782 *Excursion* 2. 732
Excuse and solace for her own defects; — 896 *Excursion* 9. 789
Excuses. Hollow excuses, and triumphant pain; — 213 *Dion* 59
Execration. Then execration is an empty sound. — L. 1. 88 *Juvenal* 1. 14
Execute. Doth all too often harshly execute — 172 *Infant Daughter* 32
Threat has he none to execute; — 242 *P. B.* 487
Execution. Must fall in the execution of his office? — 48 *Bord.* 640
In execution of heroic deeds — 330 *Ode: Thanks.* 63
Executions. To executions, to a street on fire, — 697 *Prelude* 7. 674
Exemplified. Exemplified by mysteries, that were felt — 812 *Excursion* 4. 740
Truth every day exemplified, no less — 848 *Excursion* 6. 669
Exempt. Be loth that we should breathe awhile exempt — 382 *Duddon* 24. 11
To live and move exempt from all control — 429 *Ecc. Sonn.* 2. 4. 13
From all internal injury exempt, — 666 *Prelude* 5. 67
Exemptions. His charters and exemptions; and, perchance, — 568 *Cumb. Beg.* 127
Exercise. Would Michael exercise his heart with looks — 133 *Michael* 172
And exercise of love. — 225 *Present.* 48
Attract us still, and passionate exercise — 445 *Ecc. Sonn.* 3. 19. 2
In face of these doth exercise a power — 493 *Hap. War.* 15
After long exercise in social cares — 551 **If thou in* 10
Of exercise and play, to which the year — 639 *Prelude* 1. 477
The exercise and produce of a toil, — 647 *Prelude* 2. 378
Or covetous of exercise and air; — 649 *Prelude* 3. 10

Experience—*continued.*
Who, with her heart's experience satisfied, 270 *Shame on 7
In whose experience trusting, day by day 352 H. C. R. 2
And sad experience forbade a thought 620 Birth of Love 22
The experience of past ages, as, through help 714 Prelude 9. 335
A time when sage Experience would have snatched 722 Prelude 10. 312
Of rational Experience, for the shoots 727 Prelude 11. 5
And thus, experience proving that no few 728 Prelude 11. 47
That in our best experience he was rich, 761 Excursion 1. 372
Experience daily fixing his regards 813 Excursion 4. 811
To hopes on knowledge and experience built; 820 Excursion 4. 1292
Of your experience to dispel this gloom: 829 Excursion 5. 482
The natural crown that sage Experience wears. 842 Excursion 6. 281
Now, by experience taught, he stands assured, 855 Excursion 6. 1133
Thy prudence, thy experience—thy desires; K.8. 238 Recluse 1. 1. 63
Experienced. He—whose experienced eye can pierce the array 326 *The Bard 5
The great, the experienced, and the wise: 348 *Lulled by 28
Are in the experienced Grandsire's slow to fail; 503 Warning 17
Shrunk, and the mind experienced in herself 663 Prelude 4. 349
Heard as the voice of an experienced friend. 772 Excursion 2. 64
Experienced faith, the reverend Pastor said, 836 Excursion 5. 896
—By these Itinerants, as experienced men, 875 Excursion 8. 77
Experiment. It were a quaint experiment to show 66 Bord. 1623
Expert. He plays the expert ventriloquist; 143 *Driven in 13
Expiate. To expiate thy sin endeavour: 370 Eg. Maid 98
Expiation. An expiation and a sacrifice 64 Bord. 1457
But expiation, will I wander on— 78 Bord. 2350
Expire. Of the new Flame, not suffered to expire. 432 Ecc. Sonn. 2. 14. 14
Where in a mighty crucible expire 608 Desc.Sk.Quarto 346
To expire; yet from the abyss is caught again, 819 Excursion 4. 1186
Doomed to decay, and then expire in dust! 829 Excursion 5. 478
Humbled, but not degraded, may expire. 834 Excursion 5. 793
That privilege, did yet expire too soon, 836 Excursion 5. 948
Expire; and nature's pleasant robe of green, 872 Excursion 7. 997
And cruel wars expire. The way is marked, 894 Excursion 9. 650
Ere time expire, the pageantry that stirs K.8. 253 Recluse 1. 1. 629
Expired. And glad Dundee in "faint huzzas" expired? 16 Desc. Sk. 302
Or here a saint expired. 223 Wishing-gate 24
The heroic Age expired—it slept 390 Highland Broach 31
And gradually expired, and Nature, prized 704 Prelude 8. 346
Walks a lone Monk, when service hath expired, 716 Prelude 9. 445
Thought was not; in enjoyment it expired. 759 Excursion 1. 213
Expires. As the last bleating of the fold expires, 598 Ev. Wk. Quarto 327
Expiring. Where mists, suspended on the expiring gale, 14 Desc. Sk. 210
A sudden joy surprised expiring thought, 35 Guilt 624
While mists, suspended on th' expiring gale, 607 Desc.Sk.Quarto 265
A corpse that lay expiring on the ground, 623 *I find 3
Explain. I will explain the cause. 58 Bord. 1134
Wearing a written paper, to explain 696 Prelude 7. 641
His Schoolmaster supplied; books that explain 760 Excursion 1. 252
Explained. More subtle and less easily explained, 736 Prelude 12. 124
Differ, by mystery not to be explained; 818 Excursion 4. 1108
Explanation. This explanation stilled the alarm, 179 Waggoner 3. 130
Or what need of explanation, 181 Waggoner 4. 155
Of worthier explanation, say at once 789 Excursion 3. 239
Exploding. Exploding upstart Theory, insists 695 Prelude 7. 529
Exploits. Thirsting for some of those exploits that fill 69 Bord. 1782
Of past exploits, nor fondly after more 355 Aquap. 189
Exploratory. To hail the exploratory Bird renewing 360 *Near Anio's 6
Explore. Feelers of love, put forth as if to explore 173 Infant Daughter 72
Less quiet regions to explore, 237 P. B. 107
Her spotless limbs; and ventured to explore 264 *Lady! I 6
And through the human heart explore my way; 314 *Not 'mid 12
And through dark trials still dost thou explore 460 *Queen of 27
O ye, who patiently explore 499 *Departing summer 49
Explore the countless springs of silent good; 515 *Men of 12
From the same beach one ocean to explore 586 Ch. Lamb 103
To explore the destiny of human kind 790 Excursion 3. 284
To explore the world without and world within, 815 Excursion 4. 946
Court the fresh air, explore the heaths and woods; 840 Excursion 6. 169
Explored. Or Sabine vales explored inspire a wish 356 Aquap. 255
Their fugitive Progenitors explored 431 Ecc. Sonn. 2. 12. 5
Then to the new-found World explored their way, 443 Ecc. Sonn. 3. 13. 5
Yields, if with unpresumptuous faith explored, 452 Ecc. Sonn. 3. 47. 3
He rested not; its depths his mind explored; 517 Pun. Death 3. 6
Shun the broad way too easily explored, 626 Rock: Rydal 2
Or scenes renowned for beauty, I explored 677 Prelude 6. 191
As I explored the vast metropolis, 708 Prelude 8. 592
Where Fact with heartless search explored S.3. 439 *Avaunt this 3
Bounds to be leapt, darkness to be explored, K.8. 256 Recluse 1. 1. 740
Explores. Not human nature only, but explores 806 Excursion 4. 333
Exploring. The truth exploring with an equal mind, 438 Ecc. Sonn. 2. 40. 9
Exposed. Or to the churlish elements exposed 172 Infant Daughter 21
Hourly exposed to death, with famine worn, 430 Ecc. Sonn. 2. 6. 11
As more exposed to suffering and distress; 493 Hap. War. 25
Daily exposed, woe that unshrouded lies; 516 *Feel for 2
And thus, even on the exposed and breezy hill 539 *Lady! a 45
That she can cover, left not his exposed 584 Ch. Lamb 36
Exposed on the bare fell, were scattered love, 678 Prelude 6. 235
Exposed, and lifeless as a written book!— 707 Prelude 8. 576
Exposed to eye and hand where'er I turned. 710 Prelude 9. 33
To the injurious elements exposed 778 Excursion 2. 441
A splendid sight, together thus exposed; 883 Excursion 8. 569
Yet was the mind to hinderances exposed, 886 Excursion 9. 168
Expound. That Old Man, studious to expound 398 White Doe 223
Express. I cannot well express the thoughts 246 P. B. 871
Or guilt, that humbly would express 398 White Doe 176

Express—*continued.*
Is homely,—fashioned to express 413 White Doe 1609
With its soft smile the truth express, 507 May 19
Whate'er your forms express, 526 *The soaring 38
That laboureth his language to express, 553 Prioress 33
To express what then I saw; and add the gleam, 578 Peele Castle 14
To bodily sense exhibits, is the express 747 Prelude 14. 88
Express the image of a better time, 755 Recluse 1. 1. 856
Of language shall a feeling heart express 886 Excursion 9. 139
Expressed. *See* **Exprest.**
Nor voice, nor sound, that moment's pain expressed, 30 Guilt 308
True sympathy the Sailor's looks expressed, 32 Guilt 451
That, in his milder moods, he has expressed 43 Bord. 346
My song the workings of her heart expressed. 120 Emigrant Mother 14
Substantially expressed—a place for bell 262 *Dark and 8
Was moved; and in such way expressed 289 Glen-Al. 21
Expressed in every eye we meet 578 *I come 59
And sky, whose beauty and bounty are expressed 650 Prelude 3. 110
That here in dwarf proportions were expressed 657 Prelude 3. 580
Of symmetry and light and bloom, expressed, 711 Prelude 9. 150
Expressed the tumult of their minds, my voice 797 Excursion 3. 751
As he expressed: from out the mountain's heart 807 Excursion 4. 406
Yet is their form and image here expressed 809 Excursion 4. 552
Murmurings, whereby the monitor expressed 818 Excursion 4. 1139
That *ought* to follow faithfully expressed? 828 Excursion 5. 399
O'er hill and vale," the Wanderer thus expressed 876 Excursion 8. 157
Expressing. Expressing, as in mirror, sea and land, 690 Prelude 7. 234
Expressing liveliest thoughts in lively words 743 Prelude 13. 264
Expression. In Nature's face the expression of repose; 272 Lady E. B. 4
His gait, is one expression: every limb, 572 Animal Tran. 4
Expression ever varying! Thus informed, 758 Excursion 1. 162
Expression slowly varying, that evinced 834 Excursion 5. 785
Expressive. Expressive signals of a glorious strife, 324 Ode 1814 105
Exprest. *See* **Expressed.**
The blameless Lady had exprest 400 White Doe 375
The encircling region vividly exprest 524 Epist. Beaumont 173
Exquisite. That exquisite Saint John. 232 Jew. Fam. 24
Veins it discovers exquisite and rare, 250 *Happy the 7
To something purer and more exquisite 274 *Such age 4
And exquisite, that sleep alone bestows 324 Ode 1814 71
On Laura's breast, in exquisite repose; 377 Duddon 7. 4
So exquisite; but *here* do they abide, 509 F. Stone 87
Of rapt irradiation, exquisite. 695 Prelude 7. 561
Of exquisite regard for common things, 750 Prelude 14. 262
Less pure and exquisite, he cannot choose 819 Excursion 4. 1215
By reconcilement exquisite and rare, 850 Excursion 6. 825
Dost tempt me by disclosures exquisite S.3. 434 *The doubt 92
Exquisitely. Thou art so exquisitely wild, 88 H. C. 12
White, radiant, spotless, exquisitely pure, 263 *How clear 12
A thousand times more exquisitely sweet, 438 Ecc. Sonn. 2. 39. 11
In vision exquisitely clear, 457 *Had this 29
With sinuous trunk, boughs exquisitely wreathed, 676 Prelude 6. 77
Was opened; tract more exquisitely fair 700 Prelude 8. 75
A beauty exquisitely wrought, with hair 710 Prelude 9. 78
More grand, more fair, more exquisitely framed 737 Prelude 12. 178
How exquisitely the individual Mind 755 Recluse 1. 1. 816
Is fitted:—and how exquisitely, too— 755 Recluse 1. 1. 819
And even the touch, so exquisitely poured 879 Excursion 8. 325
Extant. Accompanied, still extant, in a wreath 872 Excursion 7. 972
Extend. And, rimy without speck, extend the plains: 8 Ev. Wk. 356
Where silent Hours their death-like sway extend, 16 Desc. Sk. 311
Where'er the dreary roads their bare white lines extend. 24 Guilt 18
A measure is of Thee, whose claims extend 172 Infant Daughter 14
Clouds, lingering yet, extend in solid bars 313 *Clouds, lingering 1
The pyramid extend its monstrous base, 313 *Go back 6
Which should extend thy branches on the ground, 319 Guernica 10
Widens the fatal web, its lines extend, 330 Ode: Thanks. 123
Is one great aim of penalty, extend 519 Pun. Death 9. 2
Long rails into the shallow lake extend; 592 Ev. Wk. Quarto 60
Extend through unambitious years to come, 627 *Son of 13
Of those mutations that extend their sway 755 Recluse 1. 1. 845
For acts of service? Can his love extend 817 Excursion 4. 1095
One spirit seldom failed to extend its sway 845 Excursion 6. 480
Are still permitted to extend their pride, 870 Excursion 7. 845
Extended. His body he extended, 287 Ellen Irwin 47
Extended, clasp the winds, with mutual moan 353 Aquap. 45
Extended and extending to sustain 511 *Who rashly 7
Extended high above a dusky grove. 649 Prelude 3. 6
Extendeth. And Charity extendeth to the dead 467 St. Bees 65
Extending. Extended and extending to sustain 511 *Who rashly 7
Extends. The little Ass his neck extends, 242 P. B. 564
A level plain extends. 244 P. B. 700
Wide as the oak extends its dewy gloom, 425 Ecc. Sonn. 1. 27. 13
The Church extends her care to thought and deed; 448 Ecc. Sonn. 3. 31. 2
Swift as the rising sun his beams extends 503 Warning 26
Where Silence still her death-like reign extends, 609 Desc.Sk.Quarto 376
Extends his careless limbs along the front 756 Excursion 1. 10
Extent. The undisguised extent, of mortal sway! 495 Fact 11
Exterior. Thou, whose exterior semblance doth belie 589 Immortality 108
Exterminate. In vain endeavours to exterminate, 432 Ecc. Sonn. 2. 14. 7
Exterminating. To Thee the exterminating sword is given. 331 Ode: Thanks. 158
External. On fleets and armies, and external wealth: 320 *O'erweening Statesmen 2
To act the God among external things, 347 Processions 66
Endues her conscience with external life 519 Pun. Death 9. 10
Nor am I naked of external things, 634 Prelude 1. 154
Subservient strictly to external things 647 Prelude 2. 367
As they lie hid in all external forms, 651 Prelude 3. 158

External—*continued.*
—Of that external scene which round me lay, . 660 *Prelude* 4. 160
That aught external to the living mind . . . 707 *Prelude* 8. 550
I knew that wound external could not take . . 727 *Prelude* 11. 13
When all the external man is rude in show,— . 743 *Prelude* 13. 228
Of the whole species) to the external World . . 755 *Recluse* 1. 1. 818
The external World is fitted to the Mind ; . . . 755 *Recluse* 1. 1. 821
There, where on few external things his heart . 791 *Excursion* 3. 389
From interference of external force, ... 889 *Excursion* 9. 332
Extinct. But never to be extinct while Earth endures. 357 *Aquap.* 296
Extinct that echoed to the votive strains ; . . 460 **Queen of* 34
The music, and extinct the lay ? . . . . . 473 *Ossian* 44
A younger orphan of a home extinct, ... 622 *Recluse* 1. 1. 78
Whose light of reason is with age extinct ; . . 837 *Excursion* 5. 968
Extinction. That works but by extinction ? On themselves . . . . 886 *Excursion* 9. 143
Extinguish. And they who *should* extinguish, fan the fire— . . . . 504 *Warning* 106
Extinguished. *See* **Half-extinguished.**
Sons haply of extinguished sires, ... 226 *Vernal Ode* 42
Depressed ; and then extinguished : and our state, 261 **I watch* 12
Extinguished in a moment ; total gloom, . . . 548 **Stay, bold* 27
Thou lamp of which extinguished is the light ; . 563 *Troilus* 25
Nor be himself extinguished, but survive, . . . 666 *Prelude* 5. 27
Wert thou extinguished, little would be left . . 670 *Prelude* 5. 330
The light extinguished of her lonely hut, . . . 763 *Excursion* 1. 508
Are not to be extinguished, nor impaired. . . . 849 *Excursion* 6. 705
Extinguished, do not, *therefore*, cease to be. . . 865 *Excursion* 7. 520
Extirpating. Reclaiming and extirpating, perform . 805 *Excursion* 4. 285
Extirpation. But to protect themselves from extirpation ?— . . . . 66 *Bord.* 1584
Extol. Reckless audacity extol, and jeer . . . 514 **Portentous change* 3
Her frenzy only active to extol . . . . . . 723 *Prelude* 10. 353
With wise reluctance ; you would I extol, . . . 831 *Excursion* 5. 615
Extolled. *See* **Self-extolled.**
Extolled, behind Vacuna's crumbling fane. . . 356 *Aquap.* 262
Extorting. While arrowy fire extorting feverish groans, ... 596 *Ev. Wk. Quarto* 245
Extract. Did she extract the food of self-reproach, 118 *Maternal Grief* 46
And luxuries extract from bleakest moors ; . . 284 *Departure* 26
Extracting. From pastoral graves extracting thoughts divine ; . . . . 384 *Duddon* 31. 11
Extracting from clear skies and air serene, . . 475 **Homeward we* 10
Extracts. Extracts from Nature's elemental strife ; 458 *Sea-shore* 22
Extraordinary. They need not extraordinary calls . 747 *Prelude* 14. 104
Extravagance. Extravagance in gesture, mien, and dress, ... 695 *Prelude* 7. 579
Extravagate. In which his youth did first extravagate ; . . . . 673 *Prelude* 5. 503
Extreme. And, weeping loud in this extreme distress, 35 *Guilt* 619
To save thee from the extreme of penury ; . . 40 *Bord.* 158
Nor all asleep—in his extreme old age : . . . 196 *Resolution* 65
That persecution, blind with rage extreme, . . 420 *Ecc. Sonn.* 1. 7. 11
Extreme old age had wasted thee away, . . . 491 *Tribute : Dog* 15
If to the opposite extreme they sank. . . . . 842 *Excursion* 6. 270
Of good from evil ; as if one extreme . . . . 895 *Excursion* 9. 723
That extreme penury is here unknown, . . . K.8. 246 *Recluse* 1.1.363
Extremes. So meet extremes in this mysterious world, ... 65 *Bord.* 1529
The extremes of suffering meet in absolute peace. 76 *Bord.* 2216
The extremes of favoured life, may honour both. 276 **Chatsworth! thy* 14
Shows not a sight incongruous as the extremes . 364 **What aim* 12
In what they see of virtues pushed to extremes, . 425 *Ecc. Sonn.* 1. 28. 13
Firmly between the two extremes to steer ; . . 438 *Ecc. Sonn.* 2. 40. 11
To opposites and fierce extremes her life,— . . 443 *Ecc. Sonn.* 3. 11. 12
If the mind knew no union of extremes, . . . 471 **Arran ! a* 10
Tempers the year's extremes ; . . . . . . 506 **While from* 10
Flattered the young, pleased with extremes, nor least . . . . 730 *Prelude* 11. 233
The two extremes are equally disowned . . . 805 *Excursion* 4. 268
Extremities. Privation's worst extremities, and die 391 *Brownie* 7
Extremity. When in some great extremity breaks out 309 **What if* 11
And justice labours in extremity— . . . . . 321 **Here pause* 12
Who reach this dire extremity ! . . . . . 534 **Blest is* 80
Extrinsic. How Nature by extrinsic passion first . 640 *Prelude* 1. 545
To lean upon extrinsic circumstance . . . . 708 *Prelude* 8. 624
Extrinsic differences, the outward marks . . . 743 *Prelude* 13. 218
Exult. We shall exult, if they who rule the land . 310 **Another year* 10
Tyrants exult to hear of kingdoms won, . . . 327 *Ode 1815* 37
Exult in this deliverance wrought through faith . 541 *Grace Darl.* 85
His proud complacency :—yet do I exult, . . . 877 *Excursion* 8. 199
Casting reserve away, exult to see . . . . . 877 *Excursion* 8. 200
Exultation. Of exultation hung a dirge . . . . 324 *Ode 1814* 83
Of shadowy exultation : not for this, ... 646 *Prelude* 2. 313
And wicked exultation when good men . . . 648 *Prelude* 2. 435
With exultation, at my feet I saw . . . . . 658 *Prelude* 4. 7
Of exultation echoed through the groves ! . . . 674 *Prelude* 5. 578
In hollow exultation, dealing out . . . . . 686 *Prelude* 6. 733
To outrun the rest in exultation, groaned . . . 725 *Prelude* 10. 505
Of exultation, I pursued my way . . . . . 727 *Prelude* 10. 595
In exultation with a living pomp . . . . . 732 *Prelude* 11. 366
Exultations. Thy friends are exultations, agonies, . 305 *Toussaint* 13
The exultations, pomps, and cares of Rome, . . 368 *Trajan* 37
Delights and exultations of your own. . . . . 639 *Prelude* 1. 506
Exulted. Exulted, in the triumph of my soul, . . 722 *Prelude* 10. 285
Exulting. Exulting 'mid the winter of the skies, . 15 *Desc. Sk.* 262
Said Walter then, exulting ; " Here . . . . 85 *Shepherd-boys* 43
As if by that exulting strain . . . . . . 159 *Green Linnet* 37
Exulting, rich beyond the wealth of kings, . . 185 *Nutting* 51
Ah, spare the exulting smile, ... 215 *Enterprise* 7

Exulting—*continued.*
Fame sheds the exulting tear ; . . . . . . 224 *'Tis gone* 15
To an exulting Nation's hope . . . . . . 225 *Present.* 50
Exulting Warbler ! eased a fretted brain, . . . 279 **Hark ! 'tis* 7
Exulting in its imagery ; . . . . 400 *White Doe* 351
The warrant hail, exulting to be free ; . . . . 434 *Ecc. Sonn.* 2. 23. 3
To yon exulting thrush the Muse . . . . . 507 **While from* 59
Proud and exulting like an untired horse . . . 638 *Prelude* 1. 432
By her exulting outside look of youth . . . . 678 *Prelude* 6. 226
We left the Swiss exulting in the fate . . . . 686 *Prelude* 6. 761
Exulting in defiance, or heart-stung . . . . 718 *Prelude* 10. 34
Exultingly. Exultingly, in view of open day . . 894 *Excursion* 9. 706
Exults. The Romanist exults ; fresh hope he draws 439 *Ecc. Sonn.* 2. 41. 9
Exults like him whose javelin from the lair . . 466 *St. Bees* 4
Exults in freedom, can with rapture vouch . . 528 **Those breathing* 83
Eye. In youth's keen eye the livelong day was bright, ... 2 *Ev. Wk.* 17
The eye reposes on a secret bridge, ... 3 *Ev. Wk.* 68
The eye that marks the gliding creature sees . 6 *Ev. Wk.* 220
No favoured eye was e'er allowed to gaze . . . 7 *Ev. Wk.* 299
Moves there a cloud o'er mid-day's flaming eye ? . 11 *Desc. Sk.* 23
The maidens eye him with enquiring glance, . . 11 *Desc. Sk.* 40
How blest, delicious scene ! the eye that greets . 12 *Desc. Sk.* 107
Stretched at his feet, with steadfast upward eye, . 13 *Desc. Sk.* 151
That faded silent from the upward eye . . . 14 *Desc. Sk.* 204
In solemn shapes before the admiring eye . . . 14 *Desc. Sk.* 222
And the last sunbeam fell on Bayard's eye ; . . 16 *Desc. Sk.* 300
The eye sublime, and surly lion-grace : . . . 18 *Desc. Sk.* 444
Oh ! give not me that eye of hard disdain . . 20 *Desc. Sk.* 545
Heart-blessings—outward treasures too which the eye . . . . 21 *Desc. Sk.* 601
Fixing his downcast eye, he many an hour . . 23 *Yew-tree* 30
Till his eye streamed with tears. In this deep vale 23 *Yew-tree* 46
Is in its infancy. The man whose eye . . . . 23 *Yew-tree* 55
Which oft as he looked back had fixed his eye, . 24 *Guilt* 22
The weary eye—which, wheresoe'er it strays, . . 26 *Guilt* 110
With a dim eye, distracted and amazed ; . . . 34 *Guilt* 563
Upon his swinging corse an eye can glance, . . 36 *Guilt* 665
May He whose eye is over all protect you ! . . 38 *Bord.* 43
Like you ; he knows your eye would search his heart, ... 42 *Bord.* 265
Where Reason has an eye that she can use, . . 58 *Bord.* 1119
She hath an eye that sinks into all hearts, . . 61 *Bord.* 1316
Cast round you your mind's eye, and you will learn 65 *Bord.* 1534
And down into the bottom cast his eye, . . . 73 *Bord.* 2016
And closed the sparkling eye. . . . . . . 82 †*Mother's Return* 56
It caught his eye, he saw it plain—'. . . . . 86 *Anecdote* 50
But oh ! that Country-man of thine, whose eye, loved Child, can see . . . . . . 93 *Poet's Dream* 73
Even with the organs of his bodily eye, . . . 96 *Brothers* 60
Upon the moon I fixed my eye, ... 109 **Strange fits* 9
Half hidden from the eye ! . . . . 109 **She dwelt* 6
Daily before the Mother's watchful eye, . . . 118 *Maternal Grief* 22
In the world's eye. Her work when daylight failed 139 *Widow* 9
Oh ! mark the beauty of his eye : . . . . . 142 †*Lov. and Lik.* 11
Tracing the lofty barrier with my eye . . . . 147 *Joanna* 44
He had surveyed it with a finer eye, ... 150 **When, to* 60
And an eye practised like a blind man's touch. . 151 **When, to* 83
So constant with thy downward eye of love, . . 153 *Morn. Ex.* 39
A little Cyclops with one eye . . . . . . 159 **With little* 25
Unless, while with admiring eye . . . . . 164 **Glad sight* 7
In the broad open eye of the solitary sky, . . 166 *Stray Pleasures* 16
Fixed on a Star his upward eye ; . . . . . 167 *Pilgrim's Dream* 12
The hermit has no finer eye . . . . 168 *Wren's Nest* 15
In her upward eye of fire ! . . . . 171 *Kitten* 24
Were her antics played in the eye . . . . . 171 *Kitten* 33
Or an infant's laughing eye . . . . 171 *Kitten* 119
One eye he had, which, bright as ten, ... 178 *Waggoner* 2. 131
Her unsuspecting eye, perchance, ... 180 *Waggoner* 4. 28
His lonesome path, with unobserving eye . . . 184 *Night-piece* 10
And fade, unseen by any human eye ; . . . . 185 *Nutting* 32
And now I see with eye serene . . . . . . 186 **She was* 21
They flash upon that inward eye . . . . . 187 **I wandered* 21
Here let me gaze enrapt upon that eye, . . . 190 **Lyre ! though* 8
As soft almost and deep as her cerulean eye. . . 190 **Lyre ! though* 24
Haughty, as if her eye had seen . . . . . 190 *Beggars* 8
And, in the twinkling of an eye, ... 191 *Beggars* 46
Beside a pool bare to the eye of heaven . . . 196 *Resolution* 54
In my mind's eye I seemed to see him pace . . 197 *Resolution* 129
And cups, the darlings of the eye, ... 198 *Thorn* 43
Her state to any eye was plain ; . . . . . 199 *Thorn* 127
More doleful place did never eye survey ; . . . 202 *Hart-leap* 114
The pair were servants of his eye . . . . . 205 *Brougham* 124
Among the heavens his eye can see . . . . 205 *Brougham* 134
As is a landscape to a blind man's eye : . . . 206 *Tintern* 24
While with an eye made quiet by the power . . 206 *Tintern* 47
Unborrowed from the eye.—That time is past, . 206 *Tintern* 83
Of eye, and ear,—both what they half create, . 207 *Tintern* 106
Or, while the wings aspire, are heart and eye . . 209 **Ethereal minstrel* 3
Her countenance brightens—and her eye expands ; 209 *Laod.* 10
Lords of the visionary eye whose lid, ... 214 *Dion* 92
And the hushed farewell of an eye . . . . . 216 *Enterprise* 48
As was witnessed through thine eye . . . . 218 **Inmate of* 34
And, with a wandering eye that seems to chide, . 220 *Triad* 28
Of an eye where feeling plays . . . . . . 221 *Triad* 129
Nor dread the depth of meditative eye ; . . . 222 *Triad* 193
While trickles from his downcast eye . . . . 223 *Wishing-gate* 53
By this blank wall, from every eye, ... 223 *'Tis gone* 5
Appeared, in presence of the spiritual eye . . . 226 *Vernal Ode* 3
But wandering star and fixed, to mortal eye, . . 226 *Vernal Ode* 34
Sweet flowers ;—what living eye hath viewed . . 227 *Vernal Ode* 65

Eye—*continued.*

Which they are entering, welcome to mine eye . 230 *Clouds* 48
Or made with hope to please that inward eye . 231 **The gentlest Poet* 34
There was a hardness in his eye, ... 240 *P. B.* 317
As ever human eye did view. . . . . . . 240 *P. B.* 365
His shining hazel eye. . . . . 241 *P. B.* 435
Wakes with glazed eye, and feebly sighing— . . 242 *P. B.* 538
His wandering eye is fixed. . . . . . . 242 *P. B.* 550
Whose cunning eye can see the wind, ... 245 *P. B.* 822
Well may'st thou halt—and gaze with brightening eye ! . . . . 250 *Admon.* 1
He who stood visible to Mirza's eye, ... 252 **The fairest* 7
While the stars shine, or while day's purple eye . 259 **A volant* 10
'Mid seas how steadfast ! objects all for the eye . 262 **Dark and* 11
As if the sun were not. He raised his eye . . . 264 *Storm* 9
The moment it has left the virgin's eye, . . . 265 **There is a pleasure* 13
Even as a dragon's eye that feels the stress . . 266 **Even as* 1
An ample sovereignty of eye and ear. . . . . 267 **Though narrow* 4
With the keen threatenings of that fulgent eye, . 271 *Henry : Portrait* 7
Her eye was busy, while her fingers flew . . . 274 **Wait, prithee* 3
Might learn to picture, for the eye of faith, . . 274 *Infant M.* 11
Their hues to sunset. If with raptured eye . . 277 **The most* 3
Or share with me, fond thought ! that inward eye, 279 **All praise* 10
So Fancy, to the musing Poet's eye, ... 282 **While beams* 8
In my mind's eye a Temple, like a cloud . . . 282 **In my* 1
The piercing eye, the thoughtful brow, . . . 285 *Grave of Burns* 25
Its power was felt ; and while my eye . . . . 289 *Stepping West.* 21
Its dizzy turbulence eludes the eye, ... 290 *Kilchurn* 37
He sits, and with a vacant eye ; . . . . . 294 *Jedbor.* 19
Broke from the Matron's strong black eye— . . 294 *Jedbor.* 67
By any human eye. . . . . 296 *Highland Boy* 160
Safe from his step-dame Rhea's eye ; . . . . 299 *Brownie's Cell* 96
All fervour to the sightless eye ; . . . . . 301 *Bran* 95
We read the dictate in the infant's eye ; . . . 315 **The Land* 6
Even to the death :—else wherefore should the eye 316 **O'er the* 13
Hail, Zaragoza ! If with unwet eye . . . . 316 **Hail, Zaragoza* 1
No eye can follow, to a fatal place . . . . 321 **The power* 7
On prosperous tyrants with a dazzled eye ; . . 321 **Here pause* 9
Opening before the sun's triumphant eye— . . 323 *Ode 1814* 21
He—whose experienced eye can pierce the array . 326 **The Bard* 5
—Divinest Object which the uplifted eye . . . 329 *Ode : Thanks.* 27
Shall represent her labouring with an eye . . . 330 *Ode : Thanks.* 73
Who sees, may lift a streaming eye . . . . 330 *Ode : Thanks.* 99
Can hope the general eye thereon would gaze, . 333 *Ded. Tour* 3
What eye can look upon thy shrine . . . . 338 **Meek Virgin* 5
Or feed his eye in paths sun-proof . . . . . 342 *Ital. Itin.* 47
That dark unfathomable eye, ... 344 **How blest* 15
Had his sunk eye kindled at those dear words . 353 *Aquap.* 60
To view, and for the mind's consenting eye . . 355 *Aquap.* 186
Yields to the Stranger's eye. Remembrance holds 355 *Aquap.* 209
Upon the spots with undelighted eye, . . . 356 *Aquap.* 274
In the sun's eye, and in his sister's sight . . . 367 **As indignation* 6
Silent, and to the gazer's eye untrue, ... 377 *Duddon* 4. 6
The KIRK OF ULPHA to the pilgrim's eye . . . 383 *Duddon* 31. 1
Satiate are *these ;* and stilled to eye and ear ; . . 392 *Daniel* 9
And, fastening on those lines an eye tear-glazed, . 394 *Countess' Pillar* 13
His eye could see the hidden spring, ... 399 *White Doe* 285
And, when he waked, his languid eye . . . . 400 *White Doe* 427
But for a glance of his Father's eye, ... 401 *White Doe* 493
His eye upon Northumberland, ... 403 *White Doe* 636
Bold is his aspect ; but his eye . . . . . . 404 *White Doe* 766
A spot of shame to the sun's bright eye, . . . 405 *White Doe* 851
Or chance presented to his eye, ... 406 *White Doe* 979
With an inattentive eye. . . . . 407 *White Doe* 1009
The voice restored, the eye of Truth . . . . 410 *White Doe* 1272
Doth now no hindrance meet his eye, ... 411 *White Doe* 1420
Hath stopped, and fixed her large full eye . . . 414 *White Doe* 1644
His wing who could seem lovelier to man's eye . 421 *Ecc. Sonn.* 1. 13. 6
Black hair, and vivid eye, and meagre cheek, . . 422 *Ecc. Sonn.* 1. 15. 6
How no one can resolve ; but every eye . . . 426 *Ecc. Sonn.* 1. 29. 12
'Tis the most fearful when the people's eye . . 433 *Ecc. Sonn.* 2. 18. 11
That eye (which sees as if fulfilled and done . . 439 *Ecc. Sonn.* 2. 42. 6
To the mind's eye Religion doth present ; . . . 439 *Ecc. Sonn.* 2. 44. 2
Dropped from an Angel's wing. With moistened eye . . . . 441 *Ecc. Sonn.* 3. 5. 4
Shrinks from the verdict of his steadfast eye. . . 442 *Ecc. Sonn.* 3. 9. 14
Striding with shattered crests his eye athwart. . 443 *Ecc. Sonn.* 3. 12. 8
I saw a Mother's eye intensely bent . . . . 446 *Ecc. Sonn.* 3. 24. 1
Pleased with the thanks that in His People's eye 447 *Ecc. Sonn.* 3. 27. 6
Watching, with upward eye, the tall tower grow . 451 *Ecc. Sonn.* 3. 42. 7
Heart-thrilling strains, that cast, before the eye . 451 *Ecc. Sonn.* 3. 44. 13
And motionless ; and, to the gazer's eye, . . . 456 **Soft as* 3
Were wont to stream before mine eye, ... 458 **Had this* 62
Or came and was and is, yet meets the eye . . 458 *Sea-shore* 15
Even till long gazing hath bedimmed his eye, . . 460 **Wanderer! that* 54
In his mind's eye thy crescent horns ascend, . . 460 **Wanderer! that* 71
May sage and simple, catching with one eye . . 461 **Queen of* 47
Will reappear before the uplifted eye . . . . 461 **Who but is* 6
For eye and mind, the present and the past ; . . 463 **Why should the* 12
A sleeping infant's brow, or wakeful eye . . . 469 **Why stand* 7
Self-doomed, to worse inaction, till his eye . . 470 **Did pangs* 13
Off with yon cloud, old Snafell ! that thine eye . 471 *Tynwald* 9
An Eagle with stretched wings, but beamless eye— 472 **The captive* 7
And, drawing nigh, with his living eye, . . . 479 *Somnamb.* 120
" The eye—it cannot choose but see ; . . . . 481 *Expost.* 17
The keenness of that practised eye, ... 485 *Poet's Epitaph* 7
The harvest of a quiet eye . . . . 485 *Poet's Epitaph* 51
Cipher and syllable ! thine eye . . . . . . 486 *Matthew* 10
And fixing still his eye . . . . 486 **We walked* 18

Eye—*continued.*

Oft is she hid from mortal eye . . . . . . 490 *Night Thought* 3
There are who ask not if thine eye . . . . . 492 *Duty* 9
Conspicuous object in a Nation's eye, ... 494 *Hap. War.* 66
And from the look of the Falconer's eye ; . . . 494 *Force of Prayer* 10
Of gentler thought, protracted till thine eye . . 498 **Enough of climbing* 43
Then would be closed the restless oblique eye . 500 *Humanity* 49
In pomp foreseen by her creative eye, ... 503 *Warning* 40
To open a bright eye. . . . . 506 **While from* 40
Fond fancies ! wheresoe'er shall turn thine eye . 511 **So fair* 16
Leaves him at ease among grand thoughts : whose eye . . . . 514 **Blest Statesman* 2
And Truth, whose eye guilt only can make dim ; . 514 **Who ponders* 12
She scans the future with the eye of gods. . . 516 **Hard task* 14
The precept eye for eye, and tooth for tooth, . . 518 *Pun. Death* 7. 3
A creature born of time, that keeps one eye . . 519 *Pun. Death* 9. 6
An eye of fancy only can I cast . . . . 522 *Epist. Beaumont* 69
If looked at only with a careless eye ; . . . . 529 *Poor Robin* 12
But look, and to the watchful eye . . . . . 532 **How beautiful the* 5
That obvious emblem giving to the eye . . . 535 **When in* 25
No one's eye had seen him enter, ... 535 *Egremont* 67
Whose eye reflects it, glistening through a tear . 540 *Grace Darl.* 12
Beneath whose watchful eye the Maiden grew . 541 *Grace Darl.* 93
Encouraged by the imperial eye, ... 545 *Russ. Fug.* 373
To the Traveller's eye it shone : . . . . . 549 *Hermit's Cell* 1. 22
As his own soul. And, when with eye upraised . 551 **If thou in* 16
Weak sinful folk, that God, with pitying eye, . 556 *Prioress* 237
Therewith he cast on Pandarus an eye, . . . 563 *Troilus* 36
The heaven-regarding eye and front sublime . . 567 *Cumb. Beg.* 81
As in the eye of Nature he has lived, ... 569 *Cumb. Beg.* 196
So in the eye of Nature let him die ! . . . . 569 *Cumb. Beg.* 197
Old Daniel begins ; he stops short—and his eye, . 572 *Avarice* 21
A Child whom every eye that looked on loved ; . 576 **Six months* 4
To meet the world's broad eye, ... 576 *Cenotaph* 3
Expressed in every eye we meet . . . . . 578 **I come* 59
Intensely studied with a painter's eye, . . . 583 **With copious* 21
While Friends beheld thee give with eye, voice, mien, ... 583 **With copious* 32
With a keen eye, and overflowing heart : . . . 584 *Ch. Lamb* 14
Thy heritage, thou Eye among the blind, . . . 589 *Immortality* 111
Do take a sober colouring from an eye . . . 590 *Immortality* 201
In youth's wild eye the livelong day was bright, . 592 *Ev. Wk. Quarto* 23
There turns for glad repose the weary eye ; . . 598 *Ev. Wk. Quarto* 366
Loose-hanging rocks the Day's bless'd eye that hide, 606 *Desc. Sk. Quarto* 255
Soon fading " silent " from her upward eye, . . 607 *Desc. Sk. Quarto* 259
The pilgrim's wistful eye hath never stay'd. . . 607 *Desc. Sk. Quarto* 306
He looks below with undelighted eye. . . . . 611 *Desc. Sk. Quarto* 511
Shame follow'd after with reverted eye, . . . 618 *School Ex.* 21
Before the lustre of Religion's eye ; . . . . 618 *School Ex.* 44
Life left my loaded heart, and closing eye ; . . 619 **She wept* 5
But now he half-raises his deep-sunken eye, . . 621 *Convict* 41
Striding, with shattered crests, the eye athwart ? 625 **The confidence* 8
St. George of England ! keep a watchful eye . . 626 *Ballot* 9
Bright as if heaven were ever in its eye, . . . 627 **We gaze* 4
Now dupes me, trusting to an anxious eye . . 635 *Prelude* 1. 247
Even while mine eye hath moved o'er many a league 640 *Prelude* 1. 577
Depicted on the brain, and to the eye . . . . 641 *Prelude* 1. 601
Drinks in the feelings of his Mother's eye ! . . 645 *Prelude* 2. 237
Perceived in things, where, to the unwatchful eye, 646 *Prelude* 2. 300
Grew darker in the presence of my eye : . . . 647 *Prelude* 2. 374
And human knowledge, to the human eye . . 648 *Prelude* 2. 404
Of adoration, with an eye of love. . . . . 648 *Prelude* 2. 414
It was no madness, for the bodily eye . . . . 651 *Prelude* 3. 155
Near or remote, minute or vast ; an eye . . . 651 *Prelude* 3. 159
Angelical, keen eye, courageous look, ... 653 *Prelude* 3. 291
Objects embossed to catch the general eye, . . 657 *Prelude* 3. 551
With clearer knowledge ; with another eye . . 661 *Prelude* 4. 214
With such discoveries as his eye can make . . 662 *Prelude* 4. 259
And in the eye of him who passes me ! " . . . 665 *Prelude* 4. 460
As might appear to the eye of fleeting time, . . 666 *Prelude* 5. 17
A better eye than theirs, most prodigal . . . 671 *Prelude* 5. 361
Even now appears before the mind's clear eye . 671 *Prelude* 5. 398
Possessed me, for my inner eye had seen . . . 672 *Prelude* 5. 453
To have a soulless image on the eye . . . . 683 *Prelude* 6. 526
Walks, and achieves his wonders, from the eye . 691 *Prelude* 7. 282
Of reading them with quick and curious eye ; . 696 *Prelude* 7. 587
But though the picture weary out the eye, . . 698 *Prelude* 7. 731
Of beauty, meets the sun-burnt Arab's eye ; . . 698 *Prelude* 7. 749
Of these vagaries, with an eye so rich . . . . 705 *Prelude* 8. 427
Busies the eye with images and forms . . . . 707 *Prelude* 8. 581
One sense for moral judgments, as one eye . . 709 *Prelude* 8. 671
Or been regarded with too careless eye, . . . 709 *Prelude* 9. 14
Exposed to eye and hand where'er I turned. . . 710 *Prelude* 9. 33
Openly in the eye of earth and heaven, . . . 730 *Prelude* 11. 210
The open eye of Reason. Then I said, . . . 735 *Prelude* 12. 67
I daily waited, now all eye and now . . . . 735 *Prelude* 12. 99
When the bodily eye, in every stage of life . . 736 *Prelude* 12. 128
Her eye was not the mistress of her heart ; . . 736 *Prelude* 12. 153
Again I took the intellectual eye . . . . . 740 *Prelude* 13. 52
Who doth not love to follow with his eye . . . 742 *Prelude* 13. 142
And the eye feeds it not, and cannot feed. . . 743 *Prelude* 13. 205
Both of the object seen, and eye that sees. . . 745 *Prelude* 13. 378
To an attentive eye. For progress meet, . . . 750 *Prelude* 14. 329
With side-long eye looks out upon the scene, . . 756 *Excursion* 1. 15
Incessantly to turn his ear and eye . . . . 758 *Excursion* 1. 150
Or from the power of a peculiar eye, ... 758 *Excursion* 1. 157
And with a superstitious eye of love. . . . . 760 *Excursion* 1. 243
Had watched him with an unrelenting eye. . . 762 *Excursion* 1. 400
But had not tamed his eye ; that, under brows . 762 *Excursion* 1. 428

Eyes—*continued.*

And, like mine eyes that stream with sorrow, blind!" 267 *As the 14
Nor veil, with restless film, his staring eyes. . . 273 *While Anna's 14
Eyes unbedimmed, see bloom that cannot fade, . . 279 *All praise 5
I see its truth with unreluctant eyes ; . . . . 279 *Though I 3
When earth shall vanish from our closing eyes, . 281 *What strong 13
Others look up, and with fixed eyes admire . . 283 *Well have 8
And yet my eyes are filled with tears. . . . . 288 Highland Girl 21
Our Memory, feel that she hath eyes : . . . . 288 Highland Girl 67
The proud heart flashing through the eyes, . . 292 Rob Roy 119
Of little infants, when their eyes . . . . 294 Jedbor. 54
The Child ; when she can trust her eyes, . . . 297 Highland Boy 234
Tears flowed in torrents from her eyes ; . . . 297 Highland Boy 238
Nor have these eyes by greener hills . . . . 302 Yarrow V. 11
Yet still her eyes retained their tropic fire, . . 306 *We had 10
Go back to antique ages, if thine eyes . . . . 313 *Go back 1
With feet, hands, eyes, looks, lips, report your gain ; 322 *Ye Storms 10
Records on which, for pleasure of all eyes, . . 324 Ode 1814 108
The eyes of good men thankfully give heed, . . 327 Ode 1815 34
The ripening corn beneath it. As mine eyes . . 335 Namur 9
When first mine eyes beheld that famous Hill . 338 Engelberg 6
While we look round with favoured eyes, . . . 343 Eclipse 70
When thou didst flit before mine eyes, . . . 344 *How blest 55
That moved in long array before admiring eyes. . 346 Processions 9
The pageant haunts me as it met our eyes ! . . 347 Processions 47
Lessons for every heart, a Bible for all eyes. . . 351 Des. Stanzas 72
To feed his mind with watchful eyes could share . 353 Aquap. 55
Ye Catacombs, give to mine eyes a glimpse . . 357 Aquap. 299
That bloom—those eyes—can they assist to bind 363 *Grieve for 9
How, with empurpled cheeks and pampered eyes, 364 *What aim 4
Thus, if from two fair eyes mine cannot turn, . 365 *Rapt above 9
But with closed eyes,—of breath and bloom forsaken. . . . . 371 Eg. Maid 138
Make to the eyes of men thy features known. . 376 Duddon 3. 4
Whose ruddy children, by the mother's eyes . . 377 Duddon 5. 11
Blushing she eyes the dizzy flood askance ; . . 378 Duddon 10. 4
Upon its loftiest crags, mine eyes behold . . . 379 Duddon 15. 2
For, backward, Duddon ! as I cast my eyes, . . 384 Duddon 34. 3
Which moonlit elves, far seen by credulous eyes, . 387 *Part fenced 4
That thought away, turn, and with watchful eyes 388 Trosachs 6
—But hers are eyes serenely bright, ... 397 White Doe 136
Pensively with downcast eyes. . . . . . . 397 White Doe 155
And his moist eyes were glorified ; . . . . . 400 White Doe 404
Eyes dark and strong ; and on his head . . . 404 White Doe 745
Again he lifts his eyes ; and lo ! . . . . . 404 White Doe 778
Then look at them with open eyes ! . . . . 406 White Doe 904
That stood'st before my eyes, more clear . . . 407 White Doe 1046
Salvation to all eyes that gazed, ... 410 White Doe 1267
Attained a summit whence his eyes . . . . 412 White Doe 1440
A glimmering sense still left, with eyes . . . 412 White Doe 1492
In her silent Follower's eyes ; . . . . . . 415 White Doe 1717
Enough—if eyes, that sought the fountain-head . 419 Ecc. Sonn. 1. 5. 13
Descended :—happy are the eyes that meet . . 423 Ecc. Sonn. 1. 19. 9
Their eyes away in sorrow, others burn . . . 428 Ecc. Sonn. 1. 38. 11
The innocent eyes of youthful Monarchs driven . 436 Ecc. Sonn. 2. 32. 13
Fear hath a hundred eyes that all agree . . . 439 Ecc. Sonn. 2. 42. 1
Stands at the Bar, absolved by female eyes . . 442 Ecc. Sonn. 3. 11. 6
Seem fixed, to eyes that watch them from afar ; . 444 Ecc. Sonn. 3. 17. 4
Which whoso travels in her bosom eyes, . . . 445 Ecc. Sonn. 3. 19. 7
And Heaven is now to gladdened eyes revealing, . 455 *Not in the lucid 21
Yon hazy ridges to their eyes . . . . . . 457 *Had this 43
Looked down with pity upon eyes beguiled . . 465 *The cattle 13
If eyes be still sworn vassals of belief, ... 474 *Ye shadowy 13
Though brain would swim, and eyes grow dim, . 478 Somnamb. 57
Her eyes grew bright with blissful light, . . . 479 Somnamb. 138
Most sweet it is with unuplifted eyes . . . . 480 *Most sweet 1
The tears into his eyes were brought, ... 484 Simon Lee 89
Physician art thou ?—one, all eyes, ... 485 Poet's Epitaph 17
And he has neither eyes nor ears ; . . . . . 485 Poet's Epitaph 27
The tears which came to Matthew's eyes . . . 486 Matthew 23
" My eyes are dim with childish tears, ... 487 Fountain 29
Whose mind is but the mind of his own eyes, . . 488 Pers. Talk 27
Must eyes be all in all, the tongue and ear . . 489 Illus. Books 13
Sheep and cattle eyes with care ; . . . . . 490 Incident : Dog 4
He halts—and searches with his eyes . . . . 491 Fidelity 3
To these glad eyes from bondage freed, again . . 496 *A little 50
Inviting, at all seasons, ears and eyes . . . . 500 Humanity 13
Can its eyes beseech ?—no more . . . . . 502 *Like a 7
And eyes that cannot but be sad . . . . . 507 May 23
The treasure,—what mine eyes behold see thou, . 508 F. Stone 26
The golden harvest grows in ; and those eyes, . 508 F. Stone 31
Stood with eyes fixed upon that masterpiece, . . 509 F. Stone 107
Resplendent Wanderer ! followed with glad eyes . 511 *Who rashly 24
Taught him concealment) hidden from all eyes . 516 *Feel for 6
Softens his heart, till from his eyes outwell . . 520 Pun. Death 12. 8
We started, looked again with anxious eyes, . . 523 Epist. Beaumont 129
Never retiring, in thy large dark eyes, ... 525 Epist. Beaumont 255
By those bright eyes, what weary vigils kept, . 525 Epist. Beaumont 259
Thanks to the moth that spared it for our eyes ; . 526 *Soon did 5
Clustering like constellated eyes . . . . . 526 *The soaring 35
Of hue and altering shape that charmed all eyes. 527 *Those breathing 20
That happy gleam of vernal eyes, ... 530 Gleaner 1
Thither your eyes may turn—the Isle is passed away ; . . . . 532 †Float. Isl. 24
O'er features looked at by discerning eyes, . . 539 *Lady ! a 43
A just memorial ; and thine eyes consent . . 539 *Lady ! a 58
Can scarcely trust his eyes, when he perceives . 541 Grace Darl. 68
Enough of rose-bud lips, and eyes . . . . . 541 Russ. Fug. 1

Eyes—*continued.*

Sleep sealed her eyes, and stole . . . . . . 542 Russ. Fug. 46
Or gentle Nature close her eyes, ... 544 Russ. Fug. 237
In which he sate alone, with unclosed eyes, . . 548 *Stay, bold 28
His eyes from sleep, at the first break of day, . 562 Troilus 2
And in that Temple she with her bright eyes, . 563 Troilus 48
His eyes are turned, and, as he moves along, . . 567 Cumb. Beg. 46
Bow-bent, his eyes for ever on the ground, . . 567 Cumb. Beg. 52
Few are his pleasures : if his eyes have now . . 569 Cumb. Beg. 186
And his bright eyes look brighter, set off by the streak . . . . 569 Farmer 7
You lift up your eyes !—but I guess that you frame 570 Farmer 41
And tears of fifteen will come into his eyes. . . 570 Farmer 68
Rises no mountain to mine eyes unknown ; . . 574 Chiabrera 4. 16
And, should the out-pourings of her eyes suffice not 575 Chiabrera 7. 9
The eyes of all Savona streamed with tears. . . 575 Chiabrera 8. 9
With multitude of purple eyes, ... 580 John Words. 56
And open thy sad eyes upon a milder day. . . 581 Invoc. Earth 7
Has closed the Shepherd-poet's eyes : . . . . 586 Hogg 12
His eyes have closed ! And ye, lov'd books, no more 587 Crosth. 3
With light upon him from his father's eyes ! . . 589 Immortality 89
Fair scenes ! with other eyes, than once, I gaze, . 591 Ev. Wk. Quarto 17
And eyes through tears the mountain's shadeless height ; . . . . 596 Ev. Wk. Quarto 252
Those steadfast eyes, that beating breasts inspire. 604 Desc. Sk. Quarto 150
Her tawny skin, dark eyes, and glossy locks, . . 605 Desc. Sk. Quarto 190
And his red eyes the slinking water hides ; . . 606 Desc. Sk. Quarto 236
And often grasps her sword, and often eyes, . . 608 Desc. Sk. Quarto 327
While burn in his full eyes the glorious tears. . 608 Desc. Sk. Quarto 351
Weak and more weak the issuing current eyes . 609 Desc. Sk. Quarto 396
Craz'd by the strength of hope at morn he eyes . 609 Desc. Sk. Quarto 402
While ere his eyes can close upon the day, . . 609 Desc. Sk. Quarto 406
While flash her upward eyes severe delight. . . 612 Desc. Sk. Quarto 555
The hut which from the hills his eyes employs . 612 Desc. Sk. Quarto 570
Round your pale eyes a wintry lustre wake. . . 614 Desc. Sk. Quarto 675
With pale-blue hands, and eyes that fix'd implore, 615 Desc. Sk. Quarto 710
While thus I mused, methought, before mine eyes, 618 School Ex. 5
Threw back my eyes, return'd, and gazed again. . 618 School Ex. 26
Dim were my swimming eyes—my pulse beat slow, ... 619 *She wept 3
And with steadfast dejection his eyes are intent . 620 Convict 15
Shall gratitude find rest ? Mine eyes did ne'er . 622 Recluse 1. 1. 85
She fastens on the boy enamour'd eyes, . . . 625 Æneid 86
On the closed eyes of young Endymion fell, . . . 630 [?] *O Moon 12
Would overspread my soul, that bodily eyes . . 647 Prelude 2. 349
He passed—nor was I master of my eyes . . . 649 Prelude 3. 11
Mine eyes were crossed by butterflies, ears vexed 655 Prelude 3. 443
Had watched her with fixed eyes while to and fro 659 Prelude 4. 90
The book, had turned my eyes toward the wide sea. 666 Prelude 5. 64
And, looking backwards when he looked, mine eyes 667 Prelude 5. 127
Dead in my eyes, dead as a theatre . . . . 674 Prelude 5. 551
To shut thine eyes, and by internal light . . . 679 Prelude 6. 271
Present before my eyes, have played with times . 679 Prelude 6. 289
That far-famed region, though our eyes had seen, 681 Prelude 6. 422
To look with bodily eyes, and be consoled." . . 682 Prelude 6. 471
Issued, and with uplifted eyes beheld, ... 682 Prelude 6. 482
Before our eyes, we could not choose but read . 683 Prelude 6. 544
Were then the common language of all eyes ; . . 686 Prelude 6. 756
And large dark eyes, beside her infant stood . . 692 Prelude 7. 343
Until the shapes before my eyes became . . . 696 Prelude 7. 632
His steadfast face and sightless eyes, I gazed, . 697 Prelude 7. 648
For eyes and ears ! what anarchy and din, . . 697 Prelude 7. 686
With those that stretch the neck and strain the eyes, ... 697 Prelude 7. 696
The Bust that speaks and moves its goggling eyes, 698 Prelude 7. 711
By mists bewildered, suddenly mine eyes . . . 703 Prelude 8. 264
That men before my inexperienced eyes . . . 703 Prelude 8. 303
From the restraint of over-watchful eyes . . . 704 Prelude 8. 328
Eyes that perceive through minds that can inspire. 708 Prelude 8. 589
And hissing Factionists with ardent eyes, . . . 710 Prelude 9. 59
Dishevelled, gleaming eyes, and rueful cheek . . 710 Prelude 9. 79
Into mine eyes : I do not say I weep— . . . 713 Prelude 9. 268
(How welcome to the weary traveller's eyes !) . 716 Prelude 9. 477
In some sort seeing with my proper eyes . . . 720 Prelude 10. 124
Do come within the reach of humblest eyes ; . . 720 Prelude 10. 160
Or saw, like other men, with bodily eyes, . . . 724 Prelude 10. 444
And in the virtues which mine eyes had seen. . 727 Prelude 11. 12
Though with such awful proof before their eyes . 728 Prelude 11. 66
Who either had not eyes wherewith to see, . . 731 Prelude 11. 269
Thine eyes must see of sorrow in a land, . . . 733 Prelude 11. 388
As it appears to unaccustomed eyes. . . . . 737 Prelude 12. 183
Straining my eyes intensely, as the mist . . . 738 Prelude 12. 303
With our own eyes—I could not but enquire— . 741 Prelude 13. 84
One daily present to my eyes, that crossed . . 742 Prelude 13. 147
To careless eyes. And—now convinced at heart . 742 Prelude 13. 168
To consecrate, if we have eyes to see, ... 744 Prelude 13. 284
That, with believing eyes, where'er I turned, . . 745 Prelude 13. 344
To be transmitted, and to other eyes . . . . 745 Prelude 13. 371
His eyes as if in drowsiness half shut, ... 762 Excursion 1. 439
To natural comfort shut our eyes and ears ; . . 765 Excursion 1. 602
To meet her waking eyes. This tremblingly . . 766 Excursion 1. 668
Her eyelids drooped, her eyes downward were cast ; 768 Excursion 1. 792
The tears stood in her eyes. I left her then . . 768 Excursion 1. 810
That flashed and sparkled from the other's eyes ; 779 Excursion 2. 515
My eyes were busy, and my thoughts no less, . . 781 Excursion 2. 657
As to your eyes and thoughts we must have seemed 782 Excursion 2. 733
But he was a cheap pleasure to my eyes ; . . . 783 Excursion 2. 760
At my own door. The shapes before our eyes . 788 Excursion 3. 124
Or what detained him, till his closing eyes . . 791 Excursion 3. 370
"You never saw, your eyes did never look . . 793 Excursion 3. 480
He thus continued, lifting up his eyes . . . . 802 Excursion 4. 33

Factors. Then rents and factors, rights of chase, . 291 *Rob Roy* 69
Factory. Trusting to crowded factory and mart . 255 *S. H.* 12
Facts. Of doubt is insupportable. Pity, the facts . 53 *Bord.* 880
And hence, so far from wanting facts or dates . 97 *Brothers* 161
Of facts divulged, wherein appear . . . . . 398 *White Doe* 200
Give us, for our abstractions, solid facts ; . . 832 *Excursion* 5. 637
Faculties. For any living thing, hath faculties . . 23 *Yew-tree* 53
Your faculties should grow with the demand ; . 64 *Bord.* 1498
And have faculties to take, ... 172 *Kitten* 124
That virtue and the faculties within . . . 308 **These times* 12
Than many are to range the faculties . . . 645 *Prelude* 2. 223
That through the growing faculties of sense . 646 *Prelude* 2. 256
With growing faculties she doth aspire, . . 646 *Prelude* 2. 319
With faculties still growing, feeling still . . 646 *Prelude* 2. 320
And faculties, whether to work or feel. . . 650 *Prelude* 3. 89
Such was she—not from faculties more strong 670 *Prelude* 5. 288
The guides and wardens of our faculties, . . 671 *Prelude* 5. 354
And seasons serve ; all Faculties to whom 673 *Prelude* 5. 530
Possession of the faculties,—the peace . . . 697 *Prelude* 7. 654
Upon the faculties of man, receive . . . . 713 *Prelude* 9. 240
His blind desires and steady faculties . . . 714 *Prelude* 9. 357
That had stirred up her slackening faculties . 718 *Prelude* 10. 37
To lay the inner faculties asleep. . . . . 736 *Prelude* 12. 147
Accomplished ; minds whose faculties are then 743 *Prelude* 13. 258
Of your bright forms and glorious faculties, . 790 *Excursion* 3. 302
And domineering faculties of sense . . . . 804 *Excursion* 4. 207
The constitutions, powers, and faculties, . . 806 *Excursion* 4. 338
To exercise their untried faculties) . . . . 809 *Excursion* 4. 527
Be of a thousand faculties composed, . . . 816 *Excursion* 4. 988
With her two faculties of eye and ear, . . 837 *Excursion* 5. 987
Upon the earth that faculties, which seem . 865 *Excursion* 7. 519
Had visionary faculties to see . . . . . 894 *Excursion* 9. 699
Or whet his kingly faculties to chase . . . L.1. 94 *Juvenal* 2. 3
Faculty. Who wants the glorious faculty assigned . 259 **Weak is* 6
I listen—but no faculty of mine . . . . 339 *Ranz* 1
No faculty within us which the Soul . . . 357 *Aquap.* 342
And faculty for storm and turbulence, . . . 493 *Hap. War.* 58
No faculty yet given me to espy . . . . 532 **Once I* 3
But when that first poetic faculty . . . . 704 *Prelude* 8. 365
Work for the reasoning faculty enthroned . . 732 *Prelude* 11. 329
Have each his own peculiar faculty, . . . 744 *Prelude* 13. 303
Resemblance of that glorious faculty . . . 747 *Prelude* 14. 89
This faculty hath been the feeding source . . 749 *Prelude* 14. 193
The vision and the faculty divine ; . . . . 757 *Excursion* 1. 79
If the dear faculty of sight should fail, . . 803 *Excursion* 4. 109
—The imaginative faculty was lord . . . 812 *Excursion* 4. 707
" Within the soul a faculty abides, ... 817 *Excursion* 4. 1058
By the inferior Faculty that moulds, . . . 818 *Excursion* 4. 1130
Within the very faculty of sight. . . . . 830 *Excursion* 5. 514
Blest with a kindly faculty to blunt . . . 835 *Excursion* 5. 858
Or turns the godlike faculty of speech . . . 889 *Excursion* 9. 318
The breathing faculty with which thou yield'st S.3. 433 **The doubt* 41
Fade. Ah no ! as fades the vale, they fade away : 8 *Ev. Wk.* 320
Nor rate too high what must so quickly fade, . 110 **Look at* 17
That in Madeira bloom and fade, ... 164 **Fair Lady* 2
And fade, unseen by any human eye ; . . . . 185 *Nutting* 32
She looks, and her heart is in heaven : but they fade, ... 188 *Poor Susan* 13
Which at no season fade, ... 218 *Young Lady* 9
The fairest, brightest, hues of ether fade ; . . 252 **The fairest* 1
Of golden sunset, ere it fade and die. . . . 253 **Aerial Rock* 14
And from our earthly memory fade away. . . 262 **Dark and* 14
Fade and are shed, that from their timely fall . 267 **DespondingFather* 10
Eyes unbedimmed, see bloom that cannot fade, . 279 **All praise* 5
And what if she had seen those glories fade, . 305 *Ven. Rep.* 9
Fade, and participate in man's decline. . . . 308 **There is a bondage* 14
Reflect, in glowing hues that shall not fade, . . 324 *Ode 1814* 95
Of power that perishes, and rights that fade. . 393 *Inglewood* 14
Shine on, until ye fade with coming Night !— 451 *Ecc. Sonn.* 3. 44. 8
Even ere her joys begin to fade ; . . . . . 473 *Ossian* 74
Unfaded, yet prepared to fade, ... 498 **Departing summer* 5
That, might a wish avail, would never fade, . . 500 *Humanity* 22
And learn how sanguine expectations fade . . 504 *Warning* 68
For lilies that must fade, ... 507 *May* 58
And fade into the light of common day. . . . 588 *Immortality* 76
Be changed for one whose glory cannot fade. . . 628 **Deign,Sovereign*16
Should I have seen the light of evening fade . . 679 *Prelude* 6. 307
Fade from remembrance !) through the Northern tracts . . . . 746 *Prelude* 14. 2
Shall cause to fade, till ages pass away ; . . . 842 *Excursion* 6. 252
These ornaments, that fade not with the year, . 856 *Excursion* 6. 1156
He who had seen his own bright order fade, . . 873 *Excursion* 7. 1017
Fade,—and the moralising mind derive . . . S.3. 433 **The doubt* 23
Faded. The lone black fir, forsakes the faded plain ; . 8 *Ev. Wk.* 310
That faded silent from the upward eye . . . 14 *Desc. Sk.* 204
But faded, and stuck o'er with many a patch and shred. . . . . 24 *Guilt* 9
With budding, fading, faded flowers . . . . 193 *Ruth* 58
In the low dell 'mid Roslin's faded grove : . . 261 **From the dark* 12
While not a leaf seems faded ; while the fields, . 263 **While not* 1
The faded glories of his Clan ! . . . . . . 299 *Brownie's Cell* 60
The summer-leaf had faded, passed to Heaven. . 446 *Ecc. Sonn.* 3. 24. 14
How many wan and faded cheeks . . . . . 507 *May* 27
For Her who, ere her summer faded, ... 586 *Hogg* 39
Though faded, yet entire. Companionless, . . 664 *Prelude* 4. 399
The faded garlands dangling from its sides. . 773 *Excursion* 2. 137
Not rustic—dull and faded like himself ! . . . 779 *Excursion* 2. 501
The apparition faded not away, ... 785 *Excursion* 2. 880

Faded—*continued.*
The rainbow smiling on the faded storm ; . . . 808 *Excursion* 4. 463
A faded hatchment hung, and one by time . . 825 *Excursion* 5. 163
Of puzzling out that faded narrative, ... 825 *Excursion* 5. 207
Under a faded sky. No trace remained . . . 895 *Excursion* 9. 759
With wreaths that have not faded to this hour, . S.3. 436 **The doubt* 150
Fades. Ah no ! as fades the vale, they fade away : 8 *Ev. Wk.* 320
Fades like the lustre of an evening cloud ; . . . 20 *Desc. Sk.* 533
In pomp that fades not ; everlasting snows ; . . 272 *Devil's Bridge* 11
Silently disappears, or quickly fades : . . . . 349 *Sky-prosp.* 11
—'Tis past, the visionary splendour fades ; . . 458 **Had this* 79
While rose and poppy, as the glow-worm fades, . 599 *Ev. Wk. Quarto* 397
—Red stream the cottage lights ; the landscape fades, ... 614 *Desc.Sk.Quarto* 688
Soon fades her cheek, her blushing beauties fly, . 619 *School Ex.* 97
As fades the chequer'd bow that paints the sky. . 619 *School Ex.* 98
Through the calm region, fades upon the ear, . 819 *Excursion* 4. 1184
Soon will peep forth the primrose ; ere it fades . K.8. 250*Recluse* 1.1.514
Fading. *See* **Never-fading.**
The bird, who ceased, with fading light, to thread 8 *Ev. Wk.* 323
With budding, fading, faded flowers . . . . 193 *Ruth* 58
Glimmers with fading light, and shadowy Eve 269 *Gordale* 2
Of her memorial halo, fading, fading, ... 357 *Aquap.* 295
Aught of the fading year's inclemency ! . . . 381 *Duddon* 21. 14
The bird, with fading light who ceas'd to thread . 599 *Ev.Wk.Quarto* 389
Soon fading " silent " from her upward eye, . . 607 *Desc.Sk.Quarto* 259
No solemn songstress lull the fading green, . . 616 *Desc.Sk.Quarto* 751
The leaves were fading when to Esthwaite's banks 675 *Prelude* 6. 1
Is fading out of memory, but I see . . . . 692 *Prelude* 7. 366
Then fading with unusual quietness,— . . . 718 *Prelude* 10. 3
" The glory of the times fading away— . . . 776 *Excursion* 2. 293
Winds pipe through fading woods ; but those blithe notes . . . . 851 *Excursion* 6. 859
Faeries. *See* **Fairies.**
By faeries all are buried there, ... 162 *Binnorie* 63
Beholds the faeries in array, ... 180 *Waggoner* 4. 30
And into caves where Faeries sing . . . . 205 *Brougham* 131
Faery. *See* **Fairy.**
On lovelier spectacle in faery days ; . . . . 7 *Ev. Wk.* 300
Thou faery voyager ! that dost float . . . . 88 *H.C.* 5
Enriched the earth, or Faery of the woods . . 124 *V. and J.* 207
That spreads itself, some faery bold . . . . 159 **With little* 31
Had I now the wings of a Faery, ... 159 **Up with me* 10
Help, as if from faery power ; . . . . . . 163 *Spinning Wheel* 4
Sylph or Faery hither tending,— . . . . . 171 *Kitten* 13
An unsubstantial, faery place ; . . . . . . 184 **O blithe* 31
As if she knew that Oberon king of Faery . . . 222 *Triad* 170
Enquire not if the faery race . . . . . . 223 *Wishing-gate* 19
" Or we'll into the realm of Faery, ... 237 *P.B.* 101
Notes could we hear as of a faery shell . . . 395 *WhiteDoe : Ded.* 17
Of faery land, the forest of romance. . . . . 672 *Prelude* 5. 455
Faery-land. *See* **Fairy-land.**
It cheered mild Spenser, called from Faery-land . 260 **Scorn not* 10
Faggot. Came where beneath the trees a faggot blazed ; 31 *Guilt* 403
And, as a faggot sparkles on the hearth, . . . 80 **Loving she* 7
Faggot-band. And snapped a faggot-band ; . . . 83 *Lucy Gray* 22
Fagots. Or bringing fagots from the wood. . . . 126 *Idiot Boy* 36
Fail. He waked her—spake in tone that would not fail, 27 *Guilt* 168
Of his forlorn appearance, could not fail . . . 39 *Bord.* 81
Would fail you ere our journey's end be reached. 41 *Bord.* 227
He that puts his trust in me shall not fail ! " . . 63 *Bord.* 1414
And if good Angels fail, slack in their duty, . . 65 *Bord.* 1524
Of thoughts that fail, and a decaying heart ; . . 66 *Bord.* 1631
Nor will fail the like to render . . . . . . 94 *Westmoreland Girl* 71
As if her very life would fail. . . . . . . 126 *Idiot Boy* 21
No wonder if her senses fail ; . . . . . . 129 *Idiot Boy* 273
By tendency of nature needs must fail. . . . 133 *Michael* 150
Nor did we fail to see within ourselves . . . 149 **A narrow* 71
Nor shall she fail to see . . . . 187 **Three years* 21
But breath and eyesight fail ; and, one by one, . 201 *Hart-leap* 23
" Till the foundations of the mountains fail . . 201 *Hart-leap* 73
Nor let thy genuine impulse fail to beat . . . 217 *Enterprise* 123
Whatever props may fail, ... 224 **'Tis gone* 57
When lights of reason fail. . . . . 226 *Present.* 78
But if perchance your faith should fail, . . . 236 *P. B.* 9
And, ere the light of evening fail, ... 238 *P. B.* 168
And, if thy bounty fail, the forest pants ; . . . 268 **Pure element* 7
Where common cheerfulness would fail ; . . . 294 *Jedbor.* 59
Of near-approaching good that shall not fail : . 294 **Fly, some* 8
Of perilous war her weightiest armies fail, . . . 316 **Say, what* 7
Will fail to illuminate the infant's bier ; . . . 319 *Biscayan* 12
Which shall not fail, though poor men cleave with pride . . . . 320**O'erweening Statesmen* 4
Bright be thy course to-day, let not this promise fail ! . . . . 329 *Ode : Thanks.* 35
And, if that fail, consult the Stars . . . . . 370 *Eg. Maid* 113
Yes, they can make, who fail to find, ... 376 **The Minstrels* 67
Where all his unambitious functions fail. . . . 384 *Duddon* 33. 8
Nor did he fail ere long to hear . . . . . . 401 *White Doe* 431
John with a sword that will not fail, ... 401 *White Doe* 478
Is chilled by death, does mutual service fail ? . 423 *Ecc. Sonn.* 1. 20. 2
Of hardihood with wreaths that shall not fail ?— 430 *Ecc. Sonn.* 2. 7. 8
The solemn promise. Strongest sinews fail, . . 446 *Ecc. Sonn.* 3. 23. 6
Of awful notes, whose concord shall not fail ; . . 449 *Ecc. Sonn.* 3. 34. 3
Nor dost thou fail, thro' abject love of ease, . . 468 *St. Bees* 133
They fail, thy saving arms, dread Power ! around them cast. . . . . 492 *Duty* 16
Nor doth the example fail to cheer . . . . . 498 **Departing summer* 13
Are in the experienced Grandsire's slow to fail ; . 503 *Warning* 17

Fail—*continued.*
Fail to wash out, tears flowing ere thy troth — 514 **Long-favoured* 6
Pursuit and evidence so far must fail, — 519 *Pun. Death* 8. 11
Nor fail to be the harbinger — 530 † *Redbreast* 15
A mournful change, should Reason fail to bring — 533 **Once I* 38
Murder will out; certès it will not fail; — 554 *Prioress* 125
For which upon the tenth night if thou fail — 564 *Troilus* 124
And vain regret and vain desire shall fail; — 615 *Desc.Sk.Quarto* 743
So dear, if I should fail with grateful voice — 648 *Prelude* 2. 423
His being armed with strength that cannot fail. — 661 *Prelude* 4. 171
Did never fail to entrance me, and are now — 674 *Prelude* 5. 550
Each with his humour, could we fail to abound — 683 *Prelude* 6. 549
Nor did the Pulpit's oratory fail — 695 *Prelude* 7. 544
If willing audience fail not, Nature's self, — 732 *Prelude* 11. 350
The liveliness of dreams. Nor did he fail, — 758 *Excursion* 1. 148
If the dear faculty of sight should fail, — 803 *Excursion* 4. 109
That true succession fail of English hearts, — 838 *Excursion* 6. 24
Than fondest epitaph: for, if those fail, — 847 *Excursion* 6. 614
And, when I fail, and can endure no more, — 854 *Excursion* 6. 1047
And they, who were about him, did not fail — 864 *Excursion* 7. 458
Nor fail to note the Man who guides the team." — 865 *Excursion* 7. 549
Fail not to spring from either Parent's eye — 868 *Excursion* 7. 690
And ne'er to fail? Shall that blest day arrive — 894 *Excursion* 9. 666
Began to fail, this sheep by hunger pressed — K.8.229 **I will* 144
Your friend the country-Justice scarce would fail — L.1. 97 *Juvenal* 3. 71

Failed. And mutual interest failed not to create. — 28 *Guilt* 195
What obstacles hath he failed to overcome? — 38 *Bord.* 38
She could not, Sir, have failed of company. — 43 *Bord.* 327
But he had failed through weakness. From his hand — 73 *Bord.* 2061
Failed in him; and, not venturing to enquire — 96 *Brothers* 78
Him, in whose wretched heart ambition failed, — 103 *Artegal* 86
And his heart failed him. "Isabel," said he, — 134 *Michael* 226
In the world's eye. Her work when daylight failed — 139 *Widow* 9
Since reason failed want is her threatened doom, — 139 *Widow* 32
Yet failed to seek the sure relief of prayer, — 263 *Storm* 2
Had failed, would furnish an array — 299 *Brownie's Cell* 69
Of One that 'mid the failing never failed— — 330 *Ode: Thanks.* 71
Hath failed; and now, ye Powers! whose gorgeous wings — 335 *Cologne* 6
The mercy, goodness, have not failed to awe — 342 *Last Sup.* 4
Failed to reanimate and but feebly cheered — 354 *Aquap.* 97
When his touch failed.—Next came Sir Galahad; — 373 *Eg. Maid* 298
Heaven's breathing influence failed not to bestow — 395 *White Doe: Ded.* 29
They are my all"—voice failed him here— — 403 *White Doe* 615
But here her Brother's words have failed; — 415 *White Doe* 1785
What feebler means had failed to give, one aim — 430 *Ecc. Sonn.* 2. 9. 3
Nor failed at even-song. — 495 *Force of Prayer* 60
Months passed in love that failed not to fulfil, — 531 **I know* 17
So taught *their* creed;—nor failed the eastern sky, — 534 **When in* 17
Or if thy cherished grief have failed to thwart — 576 **By a* 15
Nor failed to gild the spires of Bonn, — 629 *Installation* 61
Prolonged in summer till the day-light failed: — 642 *Prelude* 2. 10
Had failed, the mind returned into herself; — 652 *Prelude* 3. 203
Of contemplation almost failed to beat. — 654 *Prelude* 3. 331
Religiously that vow; but firmness failed, — 672 *Prelude* 5. 475
Intruded, for we failed to overtake — 683 *Prelude* 6. 576
Has failed; too slowly moves the promised work. — 687 *Prelude* 7. 15
A monitory sound that never failed,— — 723 *Prelude* 10. 324
Had failed, and every leaf and flower were lost — 764 *Excursion* 1. 531
To love when hope hath failed him—whom no depth — 778 *Excursion* 2. 471
Failed not to greet the merry Mocking-bird; — 799 *Excursion* 3. 946
One spirit seldom failed to extend its sway — 845 *Excursion* 6. 480
I failed not to remind them that they erred; — 853 *Excursion* 6. 997
If his undaunted enterprise had failed — 866 *Excursion* 7. 611
Failed not to notice, inly pleased, and said:— — 874 *Excursion* 8. 4
And led us to our threshold. Daylight failed — K.8. 241 *Recluse* 1.1.173

Faileth. "Charity never faileth:" on that creed, — 393 *Countess' Pillar* 6

Failing. *See* **Never-failing.**
A cloudy substitute for failing gladness. — 2 *Ev. Wk.* 16
Breathes o'er the failing soul voluptuous dreams, — 13 *Desc. Sk.* 136
Failing impartial measure to dispense — 280 *Plea for Auth.* 1
Of One that 'mid the failing never failed— — 330 *Ode: Thanks.* 71
Failing, we finally shall make accord. — 562 *Cuck.andNight.* 280
Breathe o'er the failing soul voluptuous dreams; — 605 *Desc.Sk.Quarto* 157
He asked repose; and, failing oft to win — 760 *Excursion* 1. 293
Not failing, perseverance from their steps — 820 *Excursion* 4. 1245

Failings. Of all his failings, they love best; — 181 *Waggoner* 4. 93
To spare your failings for his sake, — 286 *Sons of Burns* 20

Fails. On the dark earth the wearied vision fails; — 8 *Ev. Wk.* 308
That virtue languishes and pleasure fails, — 21 *Desc. Sk.* 598
A boaster that, when he is tried, fails, and is put to shame? — 189 *Star-gazers* 10
Ah no! though Nature's dread protection fails, — 315 **And is it* 5
For promise fails of Howard's aid; — 408 *White Doe* 1134
Truth fails not; but her outward forms that bear — 449 *Ecc. Sonn.* 3. 34. 7
There's indifference, alike when he fails or succeeds, — 482 *Character* 9
Which, though unsued for, fails not to descend — 538 **In desultory* 30
On the dark earth the baffl'd vision fails, — 598 *Ev. Wk. Quarto* 364
That fails not, in all sorrow my support, — 648 *Prelude* 2. 444
Of stream and headlong flood that seldom fails; — 782 *Excursion* 2. 705
That soonest fails to please, and quickliest turns — 799 *Excursion* 3. 912
Imagination's light when reason's fails, — 812 *Excursion* 4. 772
Her vespers,—Nature fails not to provide — 818 *Excursion* 4. 1169
Thus comprehension fails, and truth is missed; — 830 *Excursion* 5. 511
Herbage that never fails: no grass springs up — 835 *Excursion* 5. 876
"So fails, so languishes, grows dim, and dies," — 872 *Excursion* 7. 976
Play on her streamers, fails she to assume — 882 *Excursion* 8. 514

Failure. Success and failure, could a ground — 337 **Oh Life* 3
The failure, if the Almighty, to this point — 887 *Excursion* 9. 230

Fain. Now she is gone, I fain would call her back. — 43 *Bord.* 328
I would fain hope that we deceive ourselves: — 44 *Bord.* 375

Fain—*continued.*
Then mean I, that I should be wonderous fain — 559 *Cuck.andNight.* 128

Faint. And faint the fire a dying heart can yield! — 7 *Ev. Wk.* 274
From the dark-blue faint silvery threads divide — 9 *Ev. Wk.* 359
And glad Dundee in "faint huzzas" expired? — 16 *Desc. Sk.* 302
Faint wail of eagle melting into blue — 17 *Desc. Sk.* 358
Once did the lightning's faint disastrous gleam — 26 *Guilt* 133
Yet when faint beams of light that ruin showed, — 27 *Guilt* 156
My Child—my Child—dark—dark—I faint—this wind— — 67 *Bord.* 1657
And lifted from the grassy floor, stilling his faint alarms, — 92 *Poet's Dream* 18
Faint colour over both their pallid cheeks, — 119 *Maternal Grief* 62
She says, in faint words by sighs broken, — 164 **Fair Lady* 38
Mixed with a faint yet grating sound — 173 *Waggoner* 1. 27
Faint and somewhat pensively; — 190 **Lyre! though* 20
With many recognitions dim and faint, — 206 *Tintern* 59
Faint I, nor mourn nor murmur; other gifts — 206 *Tintern* 86
Be thankful, even though tired and faint, — 215 *Kirkstone* 57
Faint, faint at first; and then an eager sound — 218 *Recluse* 1. 1. 220
Passed in a moment—and as faint again! — 218 *Recluse* 1. 1. 221
With that faint utterance, which tells — 227 *Vernal Ode* 98
But to recall the truth by some faint trace — 231 **The gentlest Poet* 36
Listening to nun's faint throb of holy fear, — 233 *Power of Sound* 30
Fluttered so faint a heart before;— — 237 *P. B.* 82
Faint recollection seems to tell — 242 *P. B.* 543
By moonlight made more faint and wan; — 244 *P. B.* 722
Faint—far-off—near—deep—solemn and sublime!— — 346 *Gemmi* 12
To sadness not their own, when, with faint smile — 353 *Aquap.* 74
Heard I that voice! and catch it now, though faint, — 361 **List—'twas* 2
Far off and faint, and melting into air, — 361 **List—'twas* 3
The notes whose first faint greeting startled me, — 363 **List—'twas* 89
Seemed from each other a faint warmth to borrow. — 374 *Eg. Maid* 330
Not seldom, when with heat the valleys faint, — 376 *Duddon* 2. 4
Faint—but it reached that sheltered spot; — 401 *White Doe* 433
Yes, she is soothed: an Image faint, — 407 *White Doe* 1033
And yet not faint—a presence bright — 407 *White Doe* 1034
Things that we judge of by a light too faint: — 446 *Ecc. Sonn.* 3. 24. 4
Warbled a while with faint and fainter powers, — 453 **Calm is the* 8
Faint sound, that, for the gayest of the gay, — 453 **Calm is the* 30
Faint types of suffering in thy beamless face. — 460 **Queen of* 38
Where thy deep voice could lull me! Faint the beam — 464 *Derwent* 4
Though faint, compared with spear and shield, — 478 *Somnamb.* 52
Or kettle whispering its faint undersong. — 488 *Pers. Talk* 14
No faint and hesitating trill, — 498 **Departing summer* 7
Not He, whose last faint memory will command — 504 *Warning* 53
Only faint news her mountain-sunbeams yield, — 522 *Epist. Beaumont* 82
With here and there a faint imperfect gleam — 524 *Epist. Beaumont* 181
How faint their portion of his vital beams! — 528 **Those breathing* 57
Faint sanction given, the Cavalier — 545 *Russ. Fug.* 341
Let the last faint sigh discover — 550 *Hermit's Cell* 1. 35
Who faint, and beat by summer's breathless ray, — 596 *Ev. Wk. Quarto* 243
Of boys that bathe remote the faint uproar, — 597 *Ev. Wk. Quarto* 321
The earth was comfortless, and, touched by faint — 644 *Prelude* 2. 121
Faint, but more tranquil, like the changing sun — 699 *Prelude* 8. 51
Faltering and faint, and ignorant of the road: — 738 *Prelude* 12. 247
Now faint,—the grass has crept o'er its grey line; — 769 *Excursion* 1. 883
Shall lack not their enjoyment:—but how faint — 773 *Excursion* 2. 103
Shouteth faint tidings of some gladder place. — 776 *Excursion* 2. 348
They faint not, but advance towards the open grave — 780 *Excursion* 2. 586
The Solitary, with a faint sarcastic smile — 780 *Excursion* 2. 594
By a faint shining from the heart, a gleam — 785 *Excursion* 2. 885
Give back faint echoes from the historian's page; — 795 *Excursion* 3. 603
Faint—and still fainter—as the cry, with which — 819 *Excursion* 4. 1182
In faint reflection of infinitude — 827 *Excursion* 5. 343
Weary and faint, and longs to be released. — 874 *Excursion* 8. 28
Faint, and diminished to the gazing eye, — 885 *Excursion* 9. 60
The faint reflections only of thy face— — 893 *Excursion* 9. 626
Faintly, too faint almost for sight; and some — 895 *Excursion* 9. 763
In mutual stillness; or, if some faint breeze — S. 3. 434 **The doubt* 72
When British floods were worshipped, some faint trace — S. 3. 435 **The doubt* 126

Fainted. She who had fainted with her fear, — 297 *Highland Boy* 232
Fainted with fear. Thrice did he turn his face — K.8. 229 **I will* 153

Fainter. Of fainter gold, a purple gleam betray. — 5 *Ev. Wk.* 177
Awoke a fainter sense of moral grief; — 22 *Desc. Sk.* 633
In fainter howlings told its *rage* was spent: — 27 *Guilt* 192
Warbled a while with faint and fainter powers, — 453 **Calm is the* 8
Awoke a fainter pang of moral grief; — 616 *Desc. Sk.Quarto* 769
Albeit putting forth a fainter light. — 622 **Among all* 12
Had disappeared, or shed a fainter light — 747 *Prelude* 14. 52
Faint—and still fainter—as the cry, with which — 819 *Excursion* 4. 1182

Faintest. The faintest breath that breathes can move a world; — 65 *Bord.* 1564
Powers that survive but in the faintest dream — 235 *Power of Sound* 171
The faintest note to echo which the blast — 440 *Ecc. Sonn.* 2. 46. 2
Sound is there none at which the faintest heart — 456 **The leaves* 6
Something like the faintest breath — 502 **Like a* 41
Their faintest whisper to the passing breeze, — 678 *Prelude* 6. 222

Fainting. Of fainting hopes and backward wills, — 341 *San Salv.* 26
The fainting creature took the marsh, — 544 *Russ. Fug.* 265
And with strange tinglings sings her fainting ear. — 606 *Desc.Sk.Quarto* 238
Support, as heretofore, my fainting steps. — 652 *Prelude* 3. 200

Faintly. Glimmering faintly where it lies; — 175 *Waggoner* 1. 161
Benjamin can faintly hear — 176 *Waggoner* 1. 217
Imaged, though faintly, in the hue — 226 *Vernal Ode* 30
A little hoary line and faintly traced, — 230 *Clouds* 55
The lamp of faith, lost Friend! too faintly burn; — 258 **Even so* 10

Fancy—*continued.*
If thee fond Fancy ever brought 376 **The Minstrels* 63
Shall find such toys of fancy thickly set : 379 *Duddon* 12. 12
Or plague the fancy 'mid the sculptured shows 380 *Duddon* 16. 2
Or if the Fancy, too industrious Elf, 382 *Duddon* 24. 10
Maturer Fancy owes to their rough noise 382 *Duddon* 26. 13
May classic Fancy, linking 386 *Yarrow Rev.* 54
With native Fancy her fresh aid, 386 *Yarrow Rev.* 55
Where Fancy entertains becoming guests ; 388 *Loch Etive* 7
Her trophies, Fancy crouch ; the course of pride 388 *Loch Etive* 11
Or Fancy localises Powers we love. 393 **The Lovers* 8
Free Fancy prized each specious miracle, 395 *White Doe: Ded.* 19
A solemn fancy yet sustains 410 *White Doe* 1282
Nor scorn the aid which Fancy oft doth lend 423 *Ecc. Sonn.* 1. 18. 1
Vows to rapt Fancy humble fealty, 429 *Ecc. Sonn.* 2. 3. 11
Spreads high conceits to madding Fancy dear, 433 *Ecc. Sonn.* 2. 20. 11
(Or was it sleep that with my Fancy played ?) 440 *Ecc. Sonn.* 3. 1. 8
Might here be moved, till Fancy grows so strong 455 *Rydal Mere* 14
And tempting Fancy to ascend, 458 **Had this* 47
How fancy sickens by vague hopes beset ; 458 *Sea-shore* 2
In days when Fancy wrought unchecked by fear 460 **Queen of* 14
And Fancy, unreproved, even yet may trace 460 **Queen of* 37
For inattentive Fancy, like the lime 463 **They called* 8
While in Judea Fancy loves to roam, 467 *St. Bees* 111
From sense, faith, reason, fancy, of the cause, 468 **Ranging the* 7
O Fancy, what an age was *that* for song ! 469 **Bold words* 8
To reinstate wild Fancy, would we hide 469 **Desire we* 2
And fare thee well, to Fancy visible, 475 **Homeward we* 5
If he should speak, by fancy touched, of signs 477 **Lonsdale ! it* 3
Where Fact with Fancy stooped to play ; 478 *Somnamb.* 32
But what her fancy breeds. 479 *Somnamb.* 72
The work of Fancy, or some happy tone 480 **Most sweet* 6
From Fancy following in thy wake, 490 *Night Thought* 15
That deepens upon fancy—more and more 498 **Enough of climbing* 38
Yet, like a tool of Fancy, works 499 *Memory* 13
The reasoning mind, or with the fancy play, 500 *Humanity* 12
Lest Fancy trifle with eternal laws. 501 *Humanity* 100
And Fancy greets them with a fond embrace ; 503 *Warning* 25
Season of fancy and of hope, 508 *May* 89
By the blind Archer-god ; her fancy free : 509 *F. Stone* 50
To whom, by wondering Fancy stirred, 511 **Who rashly* 26
An eye of fancy only can I cast 522 *Epist. Beaumont* 69
For Fancy hath her fits both hot and cold, 522 *Epist. Beaumont* 86
Such name Italian fancy would have given, 524 *Epist. Beaumont* 167
I saw ; and Fancy sped 530 *Gleaner* 6
Whose fancy had a thousand fields to skim ; 532 **Once I* 10
His fancy cheated—that can see 533 **Blest is* 42
Her fancy rode the blast ; 544 *Russ. Fug.* 244
My fancy kindled as I gazed ; 550 *Hermit's Cell* 2. 17
This gives him the fancy of one that is young, 570 *Farmer* 65
Of that arch fancy which would round him play, 583 **With copious* 10
Or Fancy, disciplined by studious art, 587 *Crosth.* 9
Yet my fancy has pierced to his heart, and pourtrays 620 *Convict* 19
If e'er, on wings which active fancy gave, 630 [?] **O Moon* 5
Than Fancy gave assurance of some work 633 *Prelude* 1. 78
In this recess, by thoughtful Fancy built, 654 *Prelude* 3. 379
With playful zest of fancy, did we note 656 *Prelude* 3. 532
Well might sarcastic Fancy then have whispered, 659 *Prelude* 4. 60
He, to my fancy, had become the knight 667 *Prelude* 5. 122
Of Fancy, happy pastures ranged at will, 669 *Prelude* 5. 237
As impotent fancy prompts, by his fireside, 679 *Prelude* 6. 293
And mighty forms, seizing a youthful fancy, 680 *Prelude* 6. 334
With unchecked fancy ever on the stir, 688 *Prelude* 7. 75
Whether the bolt of childhood's Fancy shot 688 *Prelude* 7. 88
The songs of spirits ! Nor had Fancy fed 689 *Prelude* 7. 126
Like one of these, where Fancy might run wild, 702 *Prelude* 8. 187
A wilfulness of fancy and conceit : 704 *Prelude* 8. 373
Tipped with a rain-drop, Fancy loved to seat, 705 *Prelude* 8. 399
That made my fancy restless as itself. 705 *Prelude* 8. 413
Thus wilful Fancy, in no hurtful mood, 705 *Prelude* 8. 421
How Fancy, in a season when she wove 706 *Prelude* 8. 454
Beat high, and filled the fancy with fair forms, 712 *Prelude* 9. 207
Master my fancy while I wandered on 716 *Prelude* 9. 464
The play-fellows of fancy, who had made 729 *Prelude* 11. 126
Comes o'er my heart : in fancy I behold 733 *Prelude* 11. 430
From Fancy, willing to set off her stores 788 *Excursion* 3. 129
That Fancy, dreaming o'er the map of things, 789 *Excursion* 3. 218
Devised by fancy for the golden age ; 790 *Excursion* 3. 320
Above what rules can teach, or fancy feign ; 792 *Excursion* 3. 434
Wherever fancy leads ; by day, by night, 809 *Excursion* 4. 554
Of a quick fancy and an active heart, 810 *Excursion* 4. 583
For studious fancy, his quick hand bestowed 812 *Excursion* 4. 726
Which his poor skill could make, his fancy fetched, 814 *Excursion* 4. 857
Might, with small help from fancy, be transformed 814 *Excursion* 4. 875
This pleasing fancy (cherished and upheld 834 *Excursion* 5. 794
And skill in letters—every fancy shaped 843 *Excursion* 6. 309
Thus did a waking fancy sometimes lose 852 *Excursion* 6. 904
The cloud of fancy and uncouth surmise 858 *Excursion* 7. 84
A fancy pregnant with resource and scheme 859 *Excursion* 7. 117
Fancy, and understanding ; while the voice 865 *Excursion* 7. 511
To which his peaceful fancy oft had turned. 872 *Excursion* 7. 940
And in the lover's fancy ; and to feed 875 *Excursion* 8. 75
And scarcely could you fancy that a gleam 879 *Excursion* 8. 313
And uncouth fancy. From behind the roof 881 *Excursion* 8. 477
Passing, as accident or fancy led, 882 *Excursion* 8. 523
There too did *Fancy* prize the murmuring wheel ; S.3. 426 **Through Cumbrian* 9
The fancy pleased by spectacles unlooked for. S.3. 433 **The doubt* 31

Fancy—*continued.*
Thus while my fancy wanders, thou, clear Spring, S. 3. 434 **The doubt* 86
A fancy in the heart of what might be K.8. 237 *Recluse* 1.1. 17
No where (or is it fancy ?) *can* be found K.8. 240 *Recluse* 1.1.136
Of superstitious fancy, might have seemed K.8. 246 *Recluse* 1.1.336
Fancy's. Her dwelling in his dreams. By Fancy's aid 25 *Guilt* 59
My fancy's own creation. 111 **Yes ! thou* 4
Though entering but as Fancy's Shade. 154 *Flower Garden* 56
For Fancy's errands,—then, from fields half-tilled 261 **Fair Prime* 5
Haunts, with sad echoes, musing Fancy's ear : 312 **A Roman* 10
Wandering, he haunts, at fancy's strong command, 361 **For action* 13
Lurks in it, Memory's Helper, Fancy's Lord, 480 *Cordelia* 13
Even by an innocent fancy's slightest freak 509 *F. Stone* 84
Philosophy, methinks, at Fancy's call, 703 *Prelude* 8. 249
Her works, as they present to Fancy's choice 750 *Prelude* 14. 318
Mad Fancy's favourite vassals ? Does not life 812 *Excursion* 4. 769
Through fancy's heat redounding in the brain, 863 *Excursion* 7. 380
As Fancy's snare for female vanity, S.3. 436 **The doubt* 147
Oft help to make bold fancy's flight more bold ; K.8. 301 **And oh* 8
Fancy-stricken. The fancy-stricken Youth or heart-sick Maid, 170 **Never enlivened* 21
Fane. —The voice of blasphemy the fane alarms, 11 *Desc. Sk.* 59
The pictured fane of Tell suspends his oar ; 15 *Desc. Sk.* 286
That views, undimmed, Einsiedlen's wretched fane. 20 *Desc. Sk.* 546
The altar, to deride the fane, 337 *Cath. Cantons* 4
Extolled, behind Vacuna's crumbling fane. 356 *Aquap.* 262
Even so, in many a re-constructed fane, 420 *Ecc. Sonn.* 1. 7. 5
To desecrate the Fane which heretofore 423 *Ecc. Sonn.* 1. 17. 4
All who, around the hallowed Fane, 534 **Blest is* 95
The Druid stones their lighted fane unfold, 594 *Ev. Wk. Quarto* 171
And Blasphemy the shuddering fane alarms ; 603 *Desc. Sk. Quarto* 61
Round a lone fane the human Genii mourn, 613 *Desc.Sk.Quarto* 646
Of Nightshade, and St. Mary's mouldering fane, 727 *Prelude* 10. 598
Fanes. Vallombre, 'mid her falling fanes, deplores, 12 *Desc. Sk.* 75
Such to this British Isle her christian Fanes, 444 *Ecc. Sonn.* 3. 17. 9
What though the rites be swept away, the fanes 460 **Queen of* 33
Fanned. *See* **Breeze-fanned.**
'Mid lawns and shades by breezy rivulets fanned, 21 *Desc. Sk.* 576
Pinions that fanned the teeming mould 154 *Flower Garden* 3
Fanned by the plausive wings of Love. 233 *Power of Sound* 80
Though by the same zephyr our temples be fanned 345 *Stanzas:Simplon* 26
To sit and muse, fanned by its dewy air 367 **If with* 8
Fanned by the breath of foes. 478 *Somnamb.* 40
As the sun mounts, by sea-born breezes fanned ; 501 *Humanity* 72
Where cities fanned by thy brisk airs 506 **While from* 37
Here lawns and shades by breezy rivulets fann'd, 614 *Desc.Sk.Quarto* 686
Fanned by the breath of angry Providence. 681 *Prelude* 6. 447
Disarmed his voice and fanned his yellow cheek 712 *Prelude* 9. 157
Fanning. Or from high points of rock looked out for fanning gales ; 3 *Ev. Wk.* 44
Soft breezes fanning your rough brows—the might 350 *Des. Stanzas* 53
But one that leaps to meet the fanning breeze. 432 *Ecc. Sonn.* 2. 15. 14
Toss in the fanning wind a humbler plume." 471 **Despond who* 14
And cool my temples in the fanning air, 763 *Excursion* 1. 468
The Zephyrs fanning, as they passed, their wings, 814 *Excursion* 4. 877
On all sides open to the fanning breeze, 866 *Excursion* 7. 618
Fanning his temples under heaven's blue arch. 878 *Excursion* 8. 308
Dying, or dead ! Nor shall the fanning breeze 892 *Excursion* 9. 552
Fanny. For lightsome Fanny had thus early thrown, 523 *Epist. Beaumont* 157
Fans. Of thy renown, from Cambrian mountains, fans 627 *Eagle and Dove* 6
A visitant that while it fans my cheek 632 *Prelude* 1. 2
Fantastic. Mocked me with many a strange fantastic shape !— 39 *Bord.* 112
Build up a wild fantastic scene ; 244 *P. B.* 682
Strange scene, fantastic and uneasy 300 *Bran* 27
'Tis said, fantastic ocean doth enfold 333 *Fish-women* 1
Than aught the sky's fantastic element, 428 *Ecc. Sonn.* 1. 37. 7
When most fantastic, offers to the view. 428 *Ecc. Sonn.* 1. 37. 8
Whose flaccid sails in forms fantastic droop, 604 *Desc.Sk.Quarto* 128
Fantastic pomp of structure without name, 784 *Excursion* 2. 859
From its fantastic birthplace ! And I own, 787 *Excursion* 3. 87
The tedium of fantastic idleness : 829 *Excursion* 5. 430
Than in fantastic conqueror's roving camp, 848 *Excursion* 6. 671
Crowned like the image of fantastic Fear ; 879 *Excursion* 8. 349
Far. Far in the regions of the west, 1 *Extract* 10
Far from my dearest Friend, 'tis mine to rove 2 *Ev. Wk.* 1
A fence far stretched into the shallow lake, 3 *Ev. Wk.* 42
Far in the level forest's central gloom : 5 *Ev. Wk.* 181
And fireless are the valleys far and wide, 7 *Ev. Wk.* 261
Far to the western slopes with hamlets white ; 8 *Ev. Wk.* 336
Her dawn, far lovelier than the moon's own morn, 8 *Ev. Wk.* 340
Where falls the purple morning far and wide 10 *Desc. Sk.* 5
—There be whose lot far otherwise is cast : 13 *Desc. Sk.* 173
Far o'er the water, hung with groves of beech ; 14 *Desc. Sk.* 231
And far and wide the icy summits blaze, 16 *Desc. Sk.* 321
All motions, sounds, and voices, far and nigh, 17 *Desc. Sk.* 362
And hear the rattling thunder far below ; 17 *Desc. Sk.* 377
—Far different life from what Tradition hoar 17 *Desc. Sk.* 386
Far stretched beneath the many-tinted hills, 17 *Desc. Sk.* 407
That cease not till night falls, when far and nigh, 21 *Desc. Sk.* 618
Far from all human dwelling : what if here 22 *Yew-tree* 2
Far lovelier, and his heart could not sustain 23 *Yew-tree* 36
That rang down a bare slope not far remote : 30 *Guilt* 326
The cock far off sounded his clarion throat ; 30 *Guilt* 329
Well met from far with revelry secure 32 *Guilt* 412
Suffering not doing ill—fate far more mild. 33 *Guilt* 499
A pale-faced Woman, in disease far gone. 34 *Guilt* 545
Far as the cottage. "A sad sight is here," 34 *Guilt* 556
As come, dear Child ! from a far deeper source 40 *Bord.* 153

Far—*continued.*

We have thus far adventured, will suffice	40 Bord. 157
So far into your journey ! on my life,	43 Bord. 334
That noise !—would I had gone with her as far	43 Bord. 344
Worse is he far, far worse (if foul dishonour	53 Bord. 896
And higher far than lies within earth's bounds :	62 Bord. 1373
And your support—my hut is not far off.	67 Bord. 1676
Far as the willow-skirted pool,	81 †Mother's Return 35
Went shouting far and wide ;	83 Lucy Gray 34
Far better than the sages' books,	85 Shepherd-boys 85
When my father found thee first in places far away ;	87 Pet-lamb 34
When his light returns from far.	90 Longest Day 56
In which, from burning heat, or tempest driving far and wide,	91 Norman Boy 23
Far happier lot, dear Boy, than brings full many to this shrine ;	92 Poet's Dream 54
" Holy as that far seen which crowns the sumptuous Church in Rome	93 Poet's Dream 61
Far and wide on hill and valley	93 Westmoreland Girl 5
And hence, so far from wanting facts or dates	97 Brothers 161
Have far to travel,—and on these rough paths	98 Brothers 224
And down the Enna, far as Egremont,	100 Brothers 311
Entering, when evening was far spent, the house	101 Brothers 374
And grateful Britain prospered far above	103 Artegal 68
Far as in power the eagle doth the worm :	105 Artegal 181
Seems the wide world, far brighter than before !	105 Artegal 203
Some thought far worse of him, and judged him wrong ;	108 Indolence 33
O dearer far than light and life are dear,	112 *O dearer 1
But thou, dear Babe, art far away,	114 Ind. Wom. 69
Thy own dear mother's far away,	120 Emigrant Mother 19
Far more than I can be to thee.	120 Emigrant Mother 34
And far into the moonlight dale,	127 Idiot Boy 118
And far into the moonlight dale ;	128 Idiot Boy 203
But he is neither far nor near,	129 Idiot Boy 265
That echoes far from hill to hill.	129 Idiot Boy 291
But he is milder far than she,	130 Idiot Boy 395
Father and Son, while far into the night	133 Michael 125
And so far seen, the House itself, by all	133 Michael 137
Far more than we have lost is left us yet.	135 Michael 276
Which they are touching ; yea far brighter, even	139 Widow 20
And she came far from over the main.	144 Her Eyes 4
But nay, my heart is far too glad ;	144 Her Eyes 12
For him that's gone and far away	145 Her Eyes 80
I've sought thy father far and wide.	145 Her Eyes 94
Helvellyn far into the clear blue sky	147 Joanna 61
Our walk was far among the ancient trees :	149 M. H. 1
In some far region, here, while o'er my head,	151 *When, to 102
Now are they parted, far as Death's cold hand	152 *Forth from 16
And whirled, and whirled him far away ;	157 Oak and Broom 107
Of a far superior garden.	157 Sexton 24
Hail to Thee, far above the rest	159 Green Linnet 11
Eyes of some men travel far	160 *Pansies, lilies 9
And Russia far inland ?	162 *Art thou the 8
From bloody deeds his thoughts are far ;	166 Danish Boy 51
But pangs more lasting far *that* Lover knew	169 Love lies Bleeding 19
Far beyond in joy of heart.	171 Kitten 32
Far from human neighbourhood ;	171 Kitten 58
Happier, far happier is thy lot and ours !	172 Infant Daughter 39
In silence deeper far than that of deepest noon !	173 Waggoner 1. 6
Then most of all, then far the most,	182 Waggoner 4. 264
At once far off, and near.	183 *O blithe 8
Scattering fresh flowers ; though happier far, I ween,	191 Beggars 35
An innocent life, yet far astray !	194 Ruth 229
Far from the world I walk, and from all care ;	195 Resolution 33
Or like a man from some far region sent,	197 Resolution 111
And said that, gathering leeches, far and wide	197 Resolution 121
Far less could this with proof be said ;	199 Thorn 151
I will not stop to tell how far he fled,	201 Hart-leap 30
And far and wide the fame thereof did ring.	202 Hart-leap 80
I looked upon the hill both far and near,	202 Hart-leap 113
Of something far more deeply interfused,	207 Tintern 96
With warmer love—oh ! with far deeper zeal	207 Tintern 154
Yet further may relent : for mightier far	210 Laod. 86
And, far beyond thy native East,	216 Enterprise 37
When fields are naked far and wide,	217 Enterprise 130
Where Trent is nursed, far southward ! Cambrian hills	219 *This Height 6
Far into silent regions blue and pale ;—	219 *This Height 15
Distinctly heard from far—a doleful note !	219 Haunted Tree 24
When she is, far from these wild places,	222 Triad 152
Revive unenvied ;—mightier far,	225 Primrose 33
Pervade the lonely ocean far	225 Present. 56
Buried in glory, far beyond the scope	226 Vernal Ode 28
How far off yet a glimpse of morning light,	229 Cuckoo-clock 3
Downcast, or shooting glances far,	232 Jew. Fam. 17
Then, or far earlier, let us rove	233 Power of Sound 41
Far as the woodlands—with the trill to blend	235 Power of Sound 165
More daring far than Hippogriff,	238 P. B. 154
They know not I have been so far ;—	238 P. B. 162
And far as Aberdeen.	239 P. B. 220
He was the wildest far of all ;—	239 P. B. 279
Must spy about him far and near :	240 P. B. 387
All still and silent—far and near !	241 P. B. 412
Among the mountains far away ;	241 P. B. 477
Why wander from your course so far,	245 P. B. 762
By this his heart is lighter far ;	245 P. B. 801
Our British Hill is nobler far ; he shrouds	251 *Pelion and 12
Of limpid water, humbler far than aught	251 *There is a little 2

Far—*continued.*

" Think gentle Lady, of a Harp so far	252 *Why, Minstrel 3
To its sad Lord, far from his native fields ?	252 *Why, Minstrel 14
With Ships the sea was sprinkled far and nigh,	258 *With Ships 1
Save only far as thought and feeling blend	261 Retirement 2
But hardier far, once more I see thee bend	264 Snowdrop 2
Which sends so far its melancholy light,	266 *Even as 10
And, haply, far within the marble belt	269 *Pure element 11
Fame tells of groves—from England far away—	271 *Fame tells 1
Elates not, brought far nearer the grave's rest,	278 Wellington 10
O'er the chilled heart—reflect ; far, far within	280 *Oh what 4
With rival earnestness ; far other strife	280 *Intent on 5
What need of fields in some far clime	286 Nith 49
Far from their noisy haunts retire,	286 Sons of Burns 25
For thee when I am far away :	288 Highland Girl 23
But something deeper far than these :	289 Glen-Al. 26
In a strange Land, and far from home,	289 Stepping West. 4
And, far and near, through vale and hill,	292 Rob Roy 117
Whom mere despite of heart could so far please,	292 *Degenerate Douglas 2
Far higher hills than these of ours !	295 Highland Boy 14
Are brought in ships from far.	296 Highland Boy 110
His father's ship, and had sailed far—	296 Highland Boy 133
She was too happy far.	297 Highland Boy 240
Far distant, when, as legends say,	301 Bran 57
Banners, and happy faces, far and nigh !	304 *Jones ! as 8
His business as he likes. Far other show	304 *Festivals have 9
There is a bondage worse, far worse, to bear	308 *There is a bondage 1
Far—far more abject, is thine Enemy :	309 *England ! the 11
When, far and wide, swift as the beams of morn	312 *When, far 1
Shrink not, though far outnumbered by their Foes,	320 *They seek 2
Springs this indigenous produce far and near ;	321 *The power 11
But fleeter far the pinions of the Wind,	321 *Humanity, delighting 27
But death becoming death, is dearer far,	326 *Intrepid sons 6
That deeper far it lies	329 Ode : Thanks. 55
O Britain ! dearer far than life is dear,	331 Ode : Thanks. 139
Thus far contented, that for You her verse	333 Ded. Tour 13
Thus far pursued (how gloriously !) by Man,	335 Cologne 3
And to the chapel far withdrawn,	337 Cath. Cantons 11
So far from the holy enclosure was cast,	340 Fort Fuentes 3
Cast far or near a murky shroud ;	343 Eclipse 20
I ask in vain—and know far less	344 Eclipse 79
They, too, who send so far a holy gleam	347 Processions 55
Far as St. Maurice, from yon eastern Forks,	350 Des. Stanzas 37
Far more than any heart but mine can know.	352 H. C. R. 9
The simple rapture ;—who that travels far	353 Aquap. 54
For what thus far hath blessed my wanderings, thanks	354 Aquap. 101
More touching far than aught which on the walls	355 Aquap. 165
Seemed churlish. And behold, both far and near,	356 Aquap. 216
I saw far off the dark top of a Pine	358 Pine : Rome 1
Far off and faint, and melting into air,	361 *List—'twas 3
St. Francis, far from Man's resort, to abide	362 *List—'twas 37
Looking far forth from his aerial cell,	362 *List—'twas 85
From far, forgive the wanderings of my thought :	367 *If with 3
Stretched far as earth might own a single lord ;	368 Trajan 30
Like guests that meet, and some from far,	385 Yarrow Rev. 31
Which moonlit elves, far seen by credulous eyes,	387 *Part fenced 4
In sunshine sailing far away,	397 White Doe 64
A further, though far easier, task	401 White Doe 505
He spake bare truth ; for far and near	403 White Doe 625
Saint Cuthbert's Relic—far and near	405 White Doe 831
Unworthier far we are undone—	405 White Doe 880
Far back—far back my mind must go	406 White Doe 887
And southward far, with moor between,	406 White Doe 943
Not distant far, the milk-white Doe—	406 White Doe 972
That, far from human neighbourhood,	407 White Doe 996
Far under ground is many a cave,	408 White Doe 1096
Thus far the Opposer, and repelled	412 White Doe 1455
Possessed the country, far and near ;	412 White Doe 1504
And she *hath* wandered, long and far,	413 White Doe 1611
And thence look round her far and wide,	415 White Doe 1780
Raised far above the law of kind ;	416 White Doe 1878
And far above the mine's most precious ore	426 Ecc. Sonn. 1. 32. 12
Have chased far off by righteous victory	427 Ecc. Sonn. 1. 33. 7
And, in awe-stricken Countries far and nigh	427 Ecc. Sonn. 1. 33. 13
Far as it dares to follow. Herbs self-sown,	431 Ecc. Sonn. 2. 12. 9
Or lonely tapers when from far they fling	441 Ecc. Sonn. 3. 5. 11
Down a swift Stream, thus far, a bold design	443 Ecc. Sonn. 3. 12. 1
'Tis past away ; far other thoughts prevail ;	446 Ecc. Sonn. 3. 23. 3
From roseate hues, far kenned at morn and even,	452 Ecc. Sonn. 3. 46. 6
Such is the prospect far as sight can range,	454 Sea-side 9
Hark to that second larum !—far and wide	457 *The leaves 33
Far as she may, primeval Nature's style.	463 *Why should the 8
With thy stern aspect better far agrees	466 St. Bees 25
But look we now to them whose minds from far	467 St. Bees 109
Strewn far and wide. Think, proud Philosopher !	474 *How sad 8
Where Burns ploughed up the Daisy." Far and wide	475 *There ! said 4
For things far off we toil, while many a good	476 Eden 13
Not far from that fair site whereon	478 Somnamb. 10
Not far from pleasant Ivor-hall,	483 Simon Lee 2
Far from the chimney's merry roar,	486 Matthew 19
And part far from them :—sweetest melodies	488 Pers. Talk 25
Wings have we,—and as far as we can go	488 Pers. Talk 29
Far different we—a froward race,	490 Night Thought 7
Far in the bosom of Helvellyn,	491 Fidelity 21
Nor far had gone before he found	491 Fidelity 38
The umbrageous woods are left—how far beneath !	497 *Enough of climbing 19

Far—*continued.*
And Reason's sway predominates; even so far, 885 *Excursion* 9. 106
But all too fondly followed and too far;— 887 *Excursion* 9. 190
That, as the day thus far had been enriched 892 *Excursion* 9 523
Of the smooth lake, in compass seen:—far off, 892 *Excursion* 9. 574
Be yet far distant, let thy Word prevail, 893 *Excursion* 9. 637
How far those erring notions were reformed; 896 *Excursion* 9. 790
Transmitted far as living memory, S.3. 435 **The doubt* 128
For the reception of far other sounds S.3. 436 **The doubt* 175
Than that brave vessel, though she sailed so far; S.3. 442 **Vasco, whose* 11
And with my friends now far away K.8. 220 **The snow-tracks* 40
Far did they go that morning: with their search K.8. 224 **I will* 18
Far went these shepherds in their devious quest, K.8. 225 **I will* 35
For strangers who have travelled far perhaps, K.8. 226 **I will* 69
Had he gone far ere he espied the boy K.8. 229 **I will* 172
In prospect far above the denser air K.8. 234 **The order'd* 3
A settled residence, or be from far, K.8. 251 *Recluse* 1. 1. 539
That hang aloft in myriads—nay, far less, K.8. 253 *Recluse* 1. 1. 608
Far from the living and dead wilderness K.8. 253 *Recluse* 1. 1. 613
Far-beaming. And in a white, far-beaming, corselet clad! 213 *Dion* 25
Far-darting. And type of man's far-darting reason, therefore 231 *Clouds* 81
Far-descried. Below the white-rimmed bonnet, far-descried. 271 *Henry: Portrait* 8
Far-distant. Tinkled like iron; while far-distant hills 89 *Prelude* 1. 442
Tow'rd some far-distant wood, a Figure quaint, 185 *Nutting* 8
Couldst thou go back into far-distant years, 279 **All praise* 9
While in far-distant lands we roam, 343 *Eclipse* 68
When hope presented some far-distant good, 380 *Duddon* 19. 2
A love-lorn Maid, at some far-distant time, 381 *Duddon* 22. 1
Far-distant images draw nigh, 457 **Had this* 25
Or haply thinking of far-distant friends, 805 *Excursion* 4. 249
From the far-distant quarry's vault returns; 833 *Excursion* 5. 714
Fare. To climb the treacherous cliffs for scanty fare. 17 *Desc. Sk.* 395
You are a lusty Traveller. But how fare you? 43 *Bord.* 335
That Leonard would partake his homely fare: 102 *Brothers* 414
Recovered heart. That evening her best fare 135 *Michael* 301
Bestir them in good deeds. Now, fare thee well— 137 *Michael* 412
And wearily at length should fare; 158 **In youth* 37
That I do not wholly fare 171 *Kitten* 109
I would fare like that or this, 172 *Kitten* 121
Of open house and ready fare. 174 *Waggoner* 1. 82
While thus our jocund Travellers fare, 177 *Waggoner* 2. 101
So forth in dauntless mood they fare, 178 *Waggoner* 3. 20
And now doth fare ill 190 *March* 13
Even as these blissful creatures do I fare; 195 *Resolution* 32
So fare they—the Man serving as her Slave. 366 *Lombardy* 9
Would mirth run round, with generous fare; 409 *White Doe* 1185
Into the secret of to-morrow's fare; 471 *Ailsa Crag* 11
And fare thee well, to Fancy visible, 475 **Homeward we* 5
Goes to learn how all things fare; 490 *Incident: Dog* 2
On thee I look, not sorrowing; fare thee well, 510 *F. Stone* 130
See how dying tapers fare! 549 *Hermit's Cell* 1. 10
Even so fare I; and therefore, I thee pray, 553 *Prioress* 34
As they in order stand, the dainty fare; 624 *Æneid* 64
Our daily meals were frugal, Sabine fare! 643 *Prelude* 2. 78
In this our deep devotion. Fare thee well! 648 *Prelude* 2. 466
The portion gave of coarse but wholesome fare 783 *Excursion* 2. 745
Her Helpmate following. Hospitable fare, 834 *Excursion* 5. 775
"So fare the many; and the thoughtful few, 894 *Excursion* 9. 658
A warning not unwelcome. Fare thee well! S.3. 437 **The doubt* 197
Far-echoed. And Angels carolled these far-echoed verses;— 374 *Eg. Maid* 354
Fared. Fared this little bright-eyed Orphan 93 *Westmoreland Girl* 31
A fellow-mariner; and so had fared 95 *Brothers* 43
—So fared we that bright morning: from the fields, 149 **A narrow* 39
Meanwhile, as thus with him it fared, 194 *Ruth* 187
If we like combatants have fared, 402 *White Doe* 579
They parted.—Well with him it fared 478 *Somnamb.* 46
Thus, and unable to complain, they fared, 528 **Those breathing* 58
It fared that evening. Gently did my soul 660 *Prelude* 4. 150
Meanwhile the Invaders fared as they deserved: 724 *Prelude* 10. 390
Misguided, and misguiding. So I fared, 731 *Prelude* 11. 293
I will proceed. While thus it fared with them, 765 *Excursion* 1. 640
In days of yore how fortunately fared 771 *Excursion* 2. 1
Fares. Thus fares it still with all that takes its birth 102 *Artegal* 31
"How fares Joanna, that wild-hearted Maid! 147 *Joanna* 23
So with the internal mind it fares; and so 357 *Aquap.* 333
And thus she fares, until at last 397 *White Doe* 140
O Man,—if with thy trials thus it fares, 428 *Ecc. Sonn.* 2. 1. 9
"Thus fares it still in our decay: 487 *Fountain* 33
And now with old Daniel you see how it fares; 572 *Avarice* 31
Is human Life; and so the Spirit fares 800 *Excursion* 3. 987
Thus, with the fibres of these thoughts it fares; S.3. 434 **The doubt* 61
Fare-thee-well. Voice of the Desert, fare-thee-well; sweet Bird! 363 **List—'twas* 103
Farewel. —Sweet rill, farewel! To-morrow's noon again, 593 *Ev. Wk. Quarto* 85
Farewel! those forms that, in thy noon-tide shade, 604 *Desc. Sk. Quarto* 148
Farewell. From what I feel at this farewell, 1 *Extract* 2
Dear Brook, farewell! To-morrow's noon again 3 *Ev. Wk.* 86
Now, with religious awe, the farewell light 7 *Ev. Wk.* 287
But now farewell to each and all—adieu 13 *Desc. Sk.* 127
She rose and bade farewell! and, while her heart 34 *Guilt* 534
This last request. You know me, Sire; farewell! 42 *Bord.* 295
Will bring me back—protect him, Saints—farewell! 43 *Bord.* 323
The cloud will soon disperse—farewell—but stay, 49 *Bord.* 647
Has been forgotten. Farewell! Gentle pilgrims, 58 *Bord.* 1140

Farewell—*continued.*
Eternal farewell to unmingled joy 65 *Bord.* 1546
Farewell, thou little Nook of mountain-ground, 106 *Farewell* 1
Farewell!—we leave thee to Heaven's peaceful care, 106 *Farewell* 7
Bright gowan, and marsh-marigold, farewell! 106 *Farewell* 22
Farewell desire of human aid, 113 *Lament* 57
Came forth with wishes and with farewell prayers, 137 *Michael* 429
And makes a meeting seem most like a dear farewell. 141 *Arm. Lady* 132
She left that farewell offering, 154 *Flower Garden* 51
And after farewell to the place, 176 *Waggoner* 1. 274
A brief and unreproved farewell; 180 *Waggoner* 4. 14
By her sweet farewell looks, I longed to aid. 190 **Lyre! though* 7
Farewell! and when thy days are told, 195 *Ruth* 253
Farewell, thou desolate Domain! 215 *Kirkstone* 77
And the hushed farewell of an eye 216 *Enterprise* 48
Shall bid a kind farewell! 224 **'Tis gone* 66
Or quit the stars with a lingering farewell—how 253 **Aerial Rock* 4
Is with me at thy farewell, joyous Bark! 258 **Where lies the Land* 14
Reader, farewell! My last words let them be— 281 *Valedict.* 10
Now, while a farewell gleam of evening light 290 *Kilchurn* 23
If this endure, farewell, for us, all good! 319 *Biscayan* 10
Warbling a farewell to a vernal shower. 329 *Ode: Thanks.* 42
Now that the farewell tear is dried, 341 *Ital. Itin.* 1
Farewell!—but go thy way, no need hast thou 363 **List—'twas* 105
To learn thy course; farewell! be prompt and steady." 370 *Eg. Maid* 114
Farewell the solace of the vagrant reed! 382 *Duddon* 24. 4
Farewell all wishes, all debate, 402 *White Doe* 540
His farewell words; and by the same, 409 *White Doe* 1197
That sullen stroke pronounced farewell 411 *White Doe* 1367
And prayers that would undo her forced farewell; 420 *Ecc. Sonn.* 1. 9. 10
Upon his monstrous urn, the farewell moan 435 *Ecc. Sonn.* 2. 27. 8
The Donor's farewell blessing, can he dread 438 *Ecc. Sonn.* 2. 39. 7
A last farewell, their loved abodes forsook, 443 *Ecc. Sonn.* 3. 13. 3
Farewell! no Minstrels now with harp new-strung 463 **Adieu, Rydalian* 9
Of time) shone like the morning-star, farewell!— 475 **Homeward we* 4
My Song's Inspirer, once again farewell! 510 *F. Stone* 131
The sun's first greeting, his last farewell ray! 511 **Who rashly* 23
Which might have else been on me yet:—FAREWELL. 525 *Epist. Beaumont* 277
Though it should prove a farewell lay 530 †*Redbreast* 3
Yet one word more—one farewell word—a wish 540 **Lady! a* 76
Rejoiced to bid the world farewell, 543 *Russ. Fug.* 157
Out of a farewell yearning—favoured more 549 **The massy* 18
Kept crying, "Farewell!—farewell, Popinjay!" 561 *Cuck. and Night.* 222
Now farewell, quoth she, for I hence must wend; 561 *Cuck. and Night.* 252
Farewell, thou shrine of which the Saint is out! 563 *Troilus* 35
Now farewell, old Adam! when low thou art laid, 571 *Farmer* 89
Take pride in him!—O Passenger, farewell! 576 *Chiabrera* 9. 22
Farewell, farewell the heart that lives alone, 579 *Peele Castle* 53
—When the Sun bids the gorgeous scene farewell, 612 *Desc. Sk. Quarto* 562
Though for brief absence. But farewell! the page 627 **The star* 9
The farewell blessing of the patient man, 665 *Prelude* 4. 466
I bade farewell; and, one among the youth 675 *Prelude* 6. 3
But here I must break off, and bid farewell 686 *Prelude* 6. 727
Farewell for ever to the sheltered seats 688 *Prelude* 7. 53
Still linger, and a farewell lustre sheds 706 *Prelude* 8. 474
Again, and yet again, a farewell look; 718 *Prelude* 10. 9
Added no farewell to his parting counsel, 726 *Prelude* 10. 538
Their farewell benediction, but with hearts 761 *Excursion* 1. 339
To take a farewell of me; for he feared 766 *Excursion* 1. 679
Together casting then a farewell look 771 *Excursion* 1. 967
Took their last farewell of the sun and stars, 791 *Excursion* 3. 371
"Farewell, deep Valley, with thy one rude House, 822 *Excursion* 5. 1
And guardian rocks!—Farewell, attractive seat! 822 *Excursion* 5. 3
Impenetrable shade; once more farewell, 822 *Excursion* 5. 8
In sign of farewell. "Nay," the old Man said, 823 *Excursion* 5. 68
Some farewell words—with one, but one, request; 841 *Excursion* 6. 202
A farewell salutation; and, the like 895 *Excursion* 9. 772
Sky-piercing Hills! must bid farewell to you. S.3. 432 **The doubt* 3
Farewell!—if thy composure be not ours S.3. 437 **The doubt* 199
Then farewell to the Warrior's schemes, farewell K.8. 257 *Recluse* 1. 1. 745
Of Liberty endangered, and farewell K.8. 257 *Recluse* 1. 1. 748
Farewells. In memory of the farewells of that time, 713 *Prelude* 9. 270
Far-famed. Hovered in air above the far-famed Spot. 334 **A wingèd* 5
Ambition—following down this far-famed slope 345 **Ambition—following* 1
For see, Laverna! mark the far-famed Pile, 362 **List—'twas* 29
And lo! those Birds, far-famed through Love's dominions, 374 *Eg. Maid* 320
Not One of us has felt the far-famed sight; 473 **We saw* 2
Of mutability, those far-famed Piles 474 **On to* 10
That far-famed region, though our eyes had seen, 681 *Prelude* 6. 422
If there were not, *then*, in our far-famed Isle, 879 *Excursion* 8. 341
Thro' wrathful Juno's far-famed enmity; K.8. 281 **Arms and* 5
Far-fetched. But surely less so than your far-fetched themes! 268 **Dogmatic Teachers* 14
The far-fetched worm with pleasure would disown 528 **Those breathing* 73
Scattering this far-fetched moisture from my wings, 582 *Invoc. Earth* 23
All out-o'-the-way, far-fetched, perverted things, 698 *Prelude* 7. 714
Engrafted far-fetched shapes on feelings bred. 705 *Prelude* 8. 422
Far-heard. Rang alone the far-heard knell, 94 *Westmoreland Girl* 66
Far-heard)—our only citadels. 533 **Blest is* 10
Faring. *See* **Wayfaring.**
Far-kenned. And stood, far-kenned by mantle furred with ermine, 373 *Eg. Maid* 308
Far-kenned, her Chapels lurking among trees, 444 *Ecc. Sonn.* 3. 17. 12
Far-lifted. Far-lifted towards the unfading sky; 348 **Lulled by* 38

Farm. But town, or farm, or hamlet, none they viewed, ... 30 *Guilt* 330
In grange or farm this Hundred scarcely owns . 46 *Bord.* 522
A farm or dwelling-house within five leagues, . . 51 *Bord.* 767
And so is Liswyn farm. . . . . 86 *Anecdote* 24
Or here at Liswyn farm ?" . . . . 86 *Anecdote* 32
Than here at Liswyn farm." . . . . 86 *Anecdote* 36
Why you would change sweet Liswyn farm . . 86 *Anecdote* 43
"Is Mosgiel Farm ; and that's the very field . . 475 **There ! said* 3
Upon the Sabine farm he loved so well ; . . . 528 **Those breathing* 103
Thus thirty smooth years did he thrive on his farm : 569 *Farmer* 29
Where, on a small hereditary farm, ... 758 *Excursion* 1. 109
To a kind master on a distant farm . . . . 767 *Excursion* 1. 761
Though simply, from their little household farm ; 860 *Excursion* 7. 163
Which to his father's little farm belonged, . . K.8. 228 **I will* 131
Farmer. A Farmer he was ; and his house far and near . . . . 569 *Farmer* 13
Farmer's. Right before the Farmer's door . . . S.3. 423 *Tinker* 9
Blush Pride to see a farmer's wife produce . . L.1. 97 *Juvenal* 3. 96
Farmers. Now think, ye farmers all, I pray, . . 537 *Goody Blake* 127
Farms. *See* **Mountain-farms.**
Threatened by faintly-answering farms remote : . 5 *Ev. Wk.* 153
By lonely farms and secret villages. . . . . . 11 *Desc. Sk.* 49
Of sportive wood run wild : these pastoral farms, 206 *Tintern* 16
To pastoral dales, thin-set with modest farms, . 275 **Chatsworth ! thy* 10
And scattered rural farms of aspect bright ; . . 323 *Ode 1814* 12
Among the farms and solitary huts, ... 567 *Cumb. Beg.* 96
Found by the verdant door of mountain farms. . 594 *Ev. Wk. Quarto* 128
By secret villages and lonely farms, ... 603 *Desc. Sk. Quarto* 50
Those woods and farms and orchards did present, 680 *Prelude* 6. 381
Beautiful region ! o'er thy towns and farms, . . 812 *Excursion* 4. 736
Faro-bank. From his wife's Faro-bank a decent rent, L.1. 97 *Juvenal* 3. 82
Far-off. And peeps the far-off spire, his evening bourn ! . . . . 11 *Desc. Sk.* 20
I told of hills and far-off towns, ... 81 †*Mother's Return* 13
Fields, goods, and far-off chattels we have none : 106 *Farewell* 13
That far-off tinkling's drowsy cheer, ... 173 *Waggoner* 1. 26
Anxious for far-off children, where . . . . 224 **'Tis gone* 34
Clear tops of far-off mountains we descry, . . . 268 **Four fiery* 4
For old, unhappy, far-off things, ... 289 *Sol. Reap.* 19
Faint — far-off — near — deep — solemn and sublime!— . . . . 346 *Gemmi* 12
And hear far-off the mellow horn proclaim . . 349 *Val. Dover* 8
And all the far-off past reveal. . . . . . . 376 **The Minstrels* 72
He takes alone his far-off stand, ... 404 *White Doe* 764
Proud Tiber grieves, and far-off Ganges, blind . 435 *Ecc. Sonn.* 2. 27. 6
Fresh gales to waft them to the far-off port ; . . 454 *Sea-side* 18
And a far-off wind that rushes, ... 457 **The sun has* 6
Fragments of far-off melodies, ... 472 *Ossian* 2
To their own far-off murmurs listening. . . . 499 *Memory* 29
To moulder in a far-off field of Rome ; . . . . 581 **Why should we* 10
Where, tho' her far-off twilight ditty steal, . . 596 *Ev. Wk. Quarto* 225
The far-off minstrels of the haunted hill, . . . 598 *Ev. Wk. Quarto* 326
The far-off peasant's day-deserted home ; . . . 605 *Desc.Sk.Quarto* 167
The naked summit of a far-off hill . . . . . 742 *Prelude* 13. 148
Of far-off torrents charming the still night, . . 821 *Excursion* 4. 1322
Gone forth already to the far-off seat . . . . 834 *Excursion* 5. 803
Far-renowned. A far-renowned alarum ! . . . . 238 *P. B.* 215
Far-seeing. Say, ye far-travelled clouds, far-seeing hills— . . . . 387 *Manse* 1
Far-seen. Red on the hills her beacon's far-seen blaze ; . . . . 22 *Desc. Sk.* 639
Down from the far-seen mount. No blast might kill . . . . 276 *Oker Hill* 8
Steadying, far-seen, a frame of images . . . . 690 *Prelude* 7. 215
Far-sequestered. Or on Cythera's far-sequestered steep, ... 624 *Æneid* 33
Far-shot. Spares thy mild splendour ; still those far-shot beams . . . . 460 **Queen of* 23
Far-stretched. Of far-stretched Meres whose salt flood never rests— . . . . 388 *Loch Etive* 3
Of his devoted worshippers, far-stretched, . . . 811 *Excursion* 4. 690
Far-stretching. Their own far-stretching arms and leafy heads . . . . 220 *Haunted Tree* 38
These pathways, yon far-stretching road ! . . . 286 *Nith* 32
And in far-stretching vales, whose streams . . 391 *HighlandBroach* 71
Of Power's far-stretching hand, ... 543 *Russ. Fug.* 114
From the far-stretching landscape, by the light . 678 *Prelude* 6. 218
Far-stretching views into eternity, ... 819 *Excursion* 4. 1189
Far-surveying. Sublime upon this far-surveying cone, ... 609 *Desc.Sk.Quarto* 367
Farther. No farther than her story needs ; . . . 180 *Waggoner* 4. 8
And be no farther wrought upon : . . . . . 402 *White Doe* 539
No farther than they breed a second Will more wise.] 492 *Duty*
Down at the farther end, in which there were . 553 *Prioress* 44
Who went something farther than others have gone, 572 *Avarice* 30
The Youth, who daily farther from the east . . 588 *Immortality* 71
No farther than the threshold, there I found . . 676 *Prelude* 6. 119
Of her soul's beauty ; farther I was then . . . 693 *Prelude* 7. 397
Would push this censure farther ;—for, if smiles . 791 *Excursion* 3. 333
Into high objects farther than they may, . . . 831 *Excursion* 5. 598
Him, farther off ; the pair, who here are laid ; . 842 *Excursion* 6. 272
Yet farther recommended by the charm . . . 843 *Excursion* 6. 307
Farthest. For me—farthest from earthly port to roam 31 *Guilt* 359
I shall be with them in two days at farthest. . . 38 *Bord.* 42
No more, I pray, of this. Three days at farthest 43 *Bord.* 322
That struck perchance the farthest cone . . . 113 *Lament* 16
As might from India's farthest plain . . . . 190 **Lyre ! though* 2
On farthest Cornwall's rocky shore, ... 238 *P. B.* 209

Farthest—*continued.*
Among the farthest Hebrides. . . . . . . 289 *Sol. Reap.* 16
Yet Adam was far as the farthest from ruin, . . 569 *Farmer* 17
While Freedom's farthest hamlets blessings share, 615 *Desc.Sk.Quarto* 724
Beyond the seas, and to the farthest pole, . . 797 *Excursion* 3. 748
For its own sake ; but farthest from the walk . 797 *Excursion* 3. 801
Of Britain's farthest glens. The Earth has lent . 876 *Excursion* 8. 111
Far-travelled. Say, ye far-travelled clouds, far-seeing hills— . . . . 387 *Manse* 1
And, to far-travelled storms of sea and land, . . 548 **Stay, bold* 5
And once, far-travelled in such mood, beyond . 696 *Prelude* 7. 635
Far-winding. Caught the far-winding barrier Alps among. . . . . 367 **As indignation* 11
Of this far-winding vale, remained as friends . . 844 *Excursion* 6. 409
Fascinate. That fascinate the very Babe in arms, . 460 **Queen of* 18
Fascination. Was under fascination ;—he beheld . 122 *V. and J.* 37
Fascinations. For moonlight fascinations mild, . 526 **The soaring* 51
Fashion. Could fashion ; chiefly by that darling bard 123 *V. and J.* 90
Or art can fashion, shall you deck our boy, . . 124 *V. and J.* 201
Of occupation, not by fashion led, ... 255 *S. H.* 2
In loose fashion tell their joys ; . . . . . . 324 *Ode 1814* 64
The place itself and fashion of the rites. . . . 653 *Prelude* 3. 310
Upon their laws, and fashion of the State. . . 728 *Prelude* 11. 104
Than suit the work we fashion, might set forth . 731 *Prelude* 11. 285
To fashion this ability ; 'tis thine, ... 749 *Prelude* 14. 214
And in their fashion very rioters, ... K.8. 252 *Recluse* 1. 1. 585
Fashioned. Fashioned by the glowing light ; . . 90 *Longest Day* 6
Abounding, but so fashioned that, in all . . . 118 *Maternal Grief* 31
Each other's mind was fashioned ; and at length, 151 **When, to* 72
Was fashioned ; whether by the hand of Art, . . 219 *Haunted Tree* 11
Heroically fashioned——to infuse . . . . . 260 **High is* 6
But it was fashioned and to God was vowed . . 282 **In my* 5
Like something fashioned in a dream ; . . . . 288 *Highland Girl* 12
A garland fashioned of the pure white rose . . 319 *Biscayan* 5
Bright liquid mansions, fashioned to endure . . 379 *Duddon* 12. 7
Or fashioned by the turbulence of waves, . . . 380 *Duddon* 15. 13
A Banner, fashioned to fulfil . . . . . . 400 *White Doe* 352
Is homely,—fashioned to express . . . . . 413 *White Doe* 1609
So deemed the man who fashioned for the sense . 451 *Ecc. Sonn.* 3. 43. 8
Was fashioned for our blissful Lady free ; . . . 553 *Prioress* 81
" ' And is this song fashioned in reverence . . 554 *Prioress* 86
That countenance there fashioned, which, spite of a stain . . . . 569 *Farmer* 11
Some simply fashioned tale, to tell again, . . . 668 *Prelude* 5. 178
Which they have fashioned would confine us down, 671 *Prelude* 5. 357
Fashioned his life ; and many a long discourse, . 715 *Prelude* 9. 421
Its line had first been fashioned by the flock . . 786 *Excursion* 3. 24
Of restoration, fashioned to the steps . . . . 818 *Excursion* 4. 1113
Is fashioned like an ill-constructed tale ; . . . 829 *Excursion* 5. 432
Our system is not fashioned to preclude . . . 847 *Excursion* 6. 567
Guarded and graced, seemed fashioned to unite, . 881 *Excursion* 8. 456
Gods which themselves had fashioned, to promote 894 *Excursion* 9. 686
Fashioning. Of bud, leaf, blade, and flower—was fashioning . . . . 266 **The stars* 13
Fashions. Fashions his neck into a goodly curve ; . 212 *Dion*
Each fashions his desires. . . . . 291 *Rob Roy* 48
Fast. Too little marked how fast they rolled away : 28 *Guilt* 227
Rolled fast along the sky his warm and genial moon. 32 *Guilt* 414
Or we're stuck fast for ever ;—passion, then, . . 58 *Bord.* 1152
The night was wasting fast ; . . . . 72 *Bord.* 1965
The boy then smacked his whip, and fast . . . 82 *Alice Fell* 13
The dew was falling fast, the stars began to blink ; 87 *Pet-lamb* 1
Now fast up the dell came the noise and the fray, 120 *Childless Father* 13
And from the brink she hurries fast, ... 129 *Idiot Boy* 295
And fast she holds her Idiot Boy. . . . . . 130 *Idiot Boy* 376
Thy heart these two weeks has been beating fast . 137 *Michael* 397
Breathless questions followed fast, ... 141 *Arm. Lady* 104
And casement closed and door made fast, . . . 144 **Driven in* 65
Came thundering loud and fast ; . . . . . . 155 *Waterfall* 53
I call thee, and to that cleave fast, ... 159 **With little* 43
To their house and their mill tethered fast : . . 166 *Stray Pleasures* 9
Hushed the dark earth, fast closing weary eyes, . 167 *Pilgrim's Dream* 27
Lets it go as fast, and then . . . . 171 *Kitten* 27
Cried out, " Good brother, why so fast ? . . . 176 *Waggoner* 1. 237
Gained ground upon the Waggon fast, ... 176 *Waggoner* 2. 17
Drive as she drives : how fast they wheel away, . 184 *Night-piece* 17
And oftentimes, when all are fast asleep, . . . 202 *Hart-leap* 135
Of sense were able to return as fast . . . . 210 *Laod.* 69
Fast through the clouds my Boat can sail ; . . . 236 *P. B.* 8
Have been fast bound, a begging debtor ;— . . 239 *P. B.* 237
Some poignant twitches, fast and faster ; . . . 243 *P. B.* 583
Nor ever once did break his fast : . . . . . 243 *P. B.* 605
And fast they fell, a plenteous shower ! . . . 247 *P. B.* 962
And flies their memory fast almost as they ; . . 251 **There is a little* 12
Of their loved Church, on fast or festival . . 256 *Decay of Piety* 3
Some lying fast at anchor in the road, ... 258 **With Ships* 3
And all the stars, fast as the clouds were riven, . 266 **With how* 10
To think that such assurance can stand fast ! . 317 **The martial* 14
But here am I fast bound ; and let it pass, . . 353 *Aquap.* 53
And divine Art, that fast to memory clung—. . 367 **As indignation* 4
Thinking how fast time runs, life's end how near ! 378 *Duddon* 9. 14
Fast the churchyard fills ;—anon . . . . . 396 *White Doe* 31
Two Earls fast leagued in discontent, ... 400 *White Doe* 368
(And fast, from this decisive day, ... 406 *White Doe* 908
Why comes he not ?—for westward fast . . . 411 *White Doe* 1377
How has the Banner clung so fast . . . . . 411 *White Doe* 1415
Her soul doth in itself stand fast, ... 414 *White Doe* 1623
Fast bound for Limbo Lake. And yet not choice 435 *Ecc. Sonn.* 2. 28. 9
How fast the Marian death-list is unrolled ! . . 437 *Ecc. Sonn.* 2. 34. 1
Sees spires fast sinking—up again to start ! . . 443 *Ecc. Sonn.* 3. 12. 5
On the relentless sea that holds him fast . . . 458 *Sea-shore* 6

Father's—*continued.*
Of their undrooping Father's widowhood, 855 Excursion 6. 1128
Her Father's prompt attendant, does for him 856 Excursion 6. 1159
Which, from her Father's honoured hand, herself, 856 Excursion 6. 1184
Nor husband's love, nor father's hope or care. 864 Excursion 7. 427
To wash the fleeces of his Father's flock— 870 Excursion 7. 869
Thus in his Father's sight the Boy grew up; K.8. 226 *I will 84
Which to his father's little farm belonged, K.8. 228 *I will 131
Deeply, a stranger of our father's house, K.8. 254 Recluse 1.1.654
Fathers. But you, Sir, should be kinder. Come hither, Fathers, 45 Bord. 443
I turned me from the dwellings of my Fathers, 52 Bord. 843
Two fathers in one father: and if tears, 99 Brothers 230
Of fathers, but with patient mind enforced 133 Michael 156
May'st bear in mind the life thy Fathers lived, 137 Michael 410
So clear, so bright, our fathers said 142 †Lov. and Lik. 13
The Land we from our fathers had in trust, 315 *The Land 1
As fathers persecute rebellious sons, 321 *Humanity, delighting 19
O'er which his Fathers urged, to ridge and steep 380 Duddon 16. 10
The Fathers urge the People to be still, 442 Ecc. Sonn. 3. 8. 9
And hallowed ground in which their fathers lay; 443 Ecc. Sonn. 3. 13. 4
Fathers! your Virtues, such the power of grace, 443 Ecc. Sonn. 3. 14. 11
Charged with these offerings which their fathers bore 448 Ecc. Sonn. 3. 32. 10
Our fathers glimpses caught of your thin Frames, 474 *Ye shadowy 4
Themselves, the fathers and the dealers-out 568 Cumb. Beg. 150
Whereon our fathers sate. And mark his brow! 880 Excursion 8. 407
And treads the mountains which his fathers trod. K.8. 247 Recluse 1.1.383
Fathom. But who can fathom your intents, 225 Present. 37
And strive to fathom the mysterious laws 468 *Ranging the 3
"Angels may weigh and fathom: they perceive, 829 Excursion 5. 486
Fathoming. As timid eyes might shrink from fathoming. 849 Excursion 6. 740
Fathomless. Your independence in the fathomless Deep! 527 *Those breathing 34
Fathoms. As he were twenty fathoms underground. 61 Bord. 1300
Some twenty fathoms under ground. 245 P. B. 840
All weakness fathoms, can supply all needs: 817 Excursion 4. 1092
Fatter. We might have fed upon a fatter soil 671 Prelude 5. 409
Fault. That you are thus the fault is mine; for the air 39 Bord. 115
'Tis his own fault if he hath got a face 54 Bord. 923
Are terrible, yet ours is not the fault. 69 Bord. 1747
Their way, without mishap or fault; 175 Waggoner 1. 208
Or is it good as others are, and be their eyes in fault? 180 Star-gazers 11
And the fault (if fault it be) 222 Triad 165
That 'tis a fault in Us to have lived and loved 280 Plea for Auth. 11
My fault, nor hear it with Thy sacred ear; 366 *Eternal Lord 10
More than enough; a fault so natural 394 *No more 34
If e'er, through fault of mine, in mutual pain 464 *A point 11
Yet why take refuge in that plea?—the fault, 677 Prelude 6. 188
But no fault of mine, S. 3. 440 *Said red-riboned 5
My fault, and keep it from thy sacred ear. K.8. 266 *Rid of 10
Faultless. Will thank you. Faultless does the Maid appear; 256 Marriage: Friend 9
Faults. For youthful faults ripe virtues shall atone; 105 Artegal 206
And faults of others—gently as he may, 449 Ecc. Sonn. 3. 35. 8
Thy faults, where not already gone 578 *I come 66
A stripling's years may for his faults atone, L.1 96 Juvenal 3. 58
Fauns. While Fauns and Satyrs beat the ground 234 Power of Sound 150
Favorite. *See* **Favourite.**
And his new Favorite. Misery!— I knew 59 Bord. 1207
The bastard gave some favorite stocks of peers L.1. 98 Juvenal 3. 98
Favour. That Oswald finds small favour in our sight, 37 Bord. 12
To take the intruder into favour; 142 †Lov. and Lik. 20
Yet he, not loth, in favour of thy claims 290 Kilchurn 16
The memory of Thy favour, 331 Ode: Thanks. 162
The amplest share of heavenly favour gives; 433 Ecc. Sonn. 2. 19. 11
And by Heaven's favour happily fulfilled; 526 *Soon did 11
Shrinking from each new favour to be shed, 528 *Those breathing 109
With God's favour shall be done." 535 Egremont 36
Favour divine, exalting human love; 540 Grace Darl. 5
Thy favour; trusting that thou wilt not deem 753 *Oft, through 13
Whose gracious favour is the primal source 755 Recluse 1. 1. 854
And let thy favour, to the end of life, 802 Excursion 4. 61
And solitude, that they do favour most, 806 Excursion 4. 366
But for some favour, suited to our need? 885 Excursion 9. 84
Conscious of that abundant favour showered 895 Excursion 9. 738
Favourable. There wait a favourable hour, 405 White Doe 799
Discerns the favourable season, 415 White Doe 1719
Our journey, under favourable skies. 772 Excursion 2. 32
Favoured. *See* **Long-favoured, Tongue-favoured.**
No favoured eye was e'er allowed to gaze 7 Ev. Wk. 299
A favoured Being, knowing no desire 23 Yew-tree 16
To the favoured strawberry-flower. 80 Foresight 26
Kilve, thought I, was a favoured place, 86 Anecdote 23
"Poor Shepherd of the naked Down, a favoured lot is thine, 92 Poet's Dream 53
In truth a favoured plant! 156 Oak and Broom 74
If called to choose between the favoured pair, 165 Parrot 42
With the rude shepherd's favoured glance, 180 Waggoner 4. 29
Into those favoured bowers. 193 Ruth 138
Nor will return—but droop not, favoured Youth; 222 Triad 213
Might stop before this favoured scene, 223 Wishing-gate 58
On favoured ground, thy gift, where I might dwell 251 Appleth. 3
The extremes of favoured life, may honour both. 276 *Chatsworth! thy 14
Wansfell! this Household has a favoured lot, 281 *Wansfell! this 1
More worthy of this favoured Spot; 300 Bran 43

Favoured—*continued.*
That I, or some more favoured Bard, may hear 325 Ode 1814 127
Along the bosom of this favoured Nation, 331 Ode: Thanks. 190
And, if there be a favoured hour 342 Ital. Itin. 69
While we look round with favoured eyes, 343 Eclipse 70
Already gathered in this favoured Land 354 Aquap. 105
Here also, on some favoured height, he would choose 364 Vallomb. 23
So, for the favoured One, the Flower may bloom 372 Eg. Maid 255
Surely, from fairest spots of favoured lands, 455 Rydal Mere 17
In a snug Cove on this our favoured Isle, 470 †From early 11
Should spread on Britain's favoured ground! 534 *Blest is 72
Among the Favoured, favoured not the least) 538 *Lady! a 2
Out of a farewell yearning—favoured more 549 *The massy 18
—And thou! fair favoured region! which my soul 615 Desc.Sk.Quarto 740
Much favoured in my birthplace, and no less 636 Prelude 1. 303
By Nature's gift so favoured. Upon a board 692 Prelude 7. 356
Favoured no less, and more to every sense 700 Prelude 8. 100
Not favoured spots alone, but the whole Earth, 729 Prelude 11. 117
So was I favoured—such my happy lot— 735 Prelude 12. 49
When genial circumstance hath favoured them, 736 Prelude 12. 157
Where is the favoured being who hath held 748 Prelude 14. 133
The measure of themselves, these favoured Beings, 757 Excursion 1. 88
That through the desert rang. Though favoured less, 815 Excursion 4. 932
Where is she imaged? in what favoured clime 828 Excursion 5. 401
Who walk this favoured ground. But chance-regards, 828 Excursion 5. 417
This favoured Land, or sunshine warms her soil. 838 Excursion 6. 16
Corrupted and cast down, on favoured ground, 887 Excursion 9. 200
Thrice favoured Region, the conjecture harsh K.8. 244 Recluse 1.1.270
Favoured by noble privilege like this, K.8. 247 Recluse 1.1.379
Favouring. By favouring Nature and a saintly Mind 274 *Such age 3
And, billow favouring billow, 374 Eg. Maid 381
On favouring nights, she loved to go; 416 White Doe 1812
To social interests, and to favouring Heaven; 450 Ecc. Sonn. 3. 41. 3
Swept by a favouring wind that leaves thought free, 460 *Wanderer! that 66
A needful journey, under favouring skies, 522 Epist. Beaumont 97
Of moon or favouring stars, I could behold 650 Prelude 3. 59
Favourite. *See* **Favorite.**
With one bright bell a favourite heifer's neck; 19 Desc. Sk. 495
Death would be else the favourite friend of woe. 20 Desc. Sk. 539
Which is your favourite, Oswald? That which, while it is 38 Bord. 46
Your favourite saint—no matter—this good day 45 Bord. 430
The meteors make of it a favourite haunt: 148 *There is an 9
Tries his two voices for a favourite strain— 153 Morn. Ex. 8
Art Nature's favourite. 158 *In youth 80
Pleased some favourite chief to follow 181 Waggoner 4. 109
Your favourite seat of empire find— 191 Seq. Beggars 35
And though his favourite seat be feeble woman's breast. 210 Laod. 90
From heaven, upon her chosen Favourite!] 212 Dion
Daughter of Hope! her favourite Child, 215 Enterprise 20
And Thou, thy favourite food to win, 215 Enterprise 29
But thou, O Goddess! in thy favourite Isle 217 Enterprise 151
Bends to the favourite burthen. Moon and stars 230 Clouds 71
A Stream, to mingle with your favourite Dee, 272 Lady E. B. 1
Whence the poor unregarded Favourite, true 274 *Wait, prithee 7
A Foe's most favourite purpose to fulfil: 316 *Say, what 12
War's favourite playground, are with crimson stains 335 Namur 3
The laurelled Dante's favourite seat. A throne, 365 *Under the 5
Clove fondly; to his favourite seat 390 Highland Broach 46
His Eagle's favourite perch, while round him sate 457 *The leaves 30
If Nature, for a favourite child, 486 Matthew 1
Planting his favourite silver diadem, 496 *A little 6
Be hopeful Spring the favourite of the Soul! 497 Lycoris 54
Her Mother's favourite; and the orphan Girl, 509 F. Stone 66
A favourite spot of tournament and war! 548 *Stay, bold 6
To be a Prodigal's Favourite—then, worse truth, 571 *There is a Flower 21
Favourite of all, in this the most of all. 622 Recluse 1. 1. 97
My last and favourite aspiration, mounts 635 Prelude 1. 228
Repeating favourite verses with one voice, 674 Prelude 5. 564
Upon this morning, and my favourite grove, 687 Prelude 7. 44
Blown from their favourite resting-place, or mists 699 Prelude 8. 16
Familiar, and a favourite of the stars: 749 Prelude 14. 252
What wonder, then, if I, whose favourite school 772 Excursion 2. 28
Mad Fancy's favourite vassals? Does not life 812 Excursion 4. 769
Hence, for this Favourite—lavishly endowed 843 Excursion 6. 304
"A favourite boundary to their lengthened walks 845 Excursion 6. 475
Of an old yew, their favourite resting-place. 845 Excursion 6. 493
For her own flowers and favourite herbs, a space, 856 Excursion 6. 1163
As in a favourite son, most beautiful. 870 Excursion 7. 853
Nature (I but repeat your favourite boast) 875 Excursion 8. 59
His own discoveries; or to favourite points 893 Excursion 9. 585
Dark as a riddle, prove a favourite theme; K.8. 301 *And oh 6
Favourites. All kinds alike seemed favourites of Heaven. 377 Duddon 6. 14
Among the favourites whom it pleased me well 659 Prelude 4. 93
Favours. What favours do attend me here, 167 Pilgrim's Dream 46
More humble favours may obtain 217 Enterprise 136
Shed gentle favours: rural works are there, 308 *One might 6
Was free her choicest favours to dispense; 323 Ode 1814 4
So rich to me in favours. For my lot 367 *If with 6
Thy favours may be found; 507 May 44
And, Tyrians, may your choicest favours wait 625 Æneid 114
Which the bright season favours.—Tabor and pipe 773 Excursion 2. 121
Ye need her favours, ye shall find her not; 792 Excursion 3. 460
On every shore whose aspect favours hope 889 Excursion 9. 380
And season favours." To enfeebled Power, 896 Excursion 9. 783
Smooth summer dreams, old favours of the place, S.3. 436 *The doubt 171

Favours—*continued.*
Thanks, and if favours of the heavenly Muse . . K.8. 239 *Recluse* 1.1.100
Fawn. You yet may spy the fawn at play, . . . 83 *Lucy Gray* 9
Did wanton fawn and kid forbear . . . . . 154 *Flower Garden* 11
"She shall be sportive as the fawn . . . . . 187 **Three years* 13
And to the solitary fawn . . . . 217 *Enterprise* 140
Mute are all creatures, as this couchant fawn, . 360 **Long has* 5
As doth the hunted fawn, ... 542 *Russ. Fug.* 14
Light as the silver fawn, a radiant Girl; . . . 881 *Excursion* 8. 493
Fawn's. Light are her sallies as the tripping fawn's 80 **Loving she* 15
Fawns. As lambs or fawns in April clustering lie . 13 *Desc. Sk.* 149
They lie like fawns reposing. . . . . . . 161 *Binnorie* 26
Fays. Dwarf Genii, moonlight-loving Fays, . . . 164 *Needlecase* 22
Fays, Genii of gigantic size! . . . . . . 526 **The soaring* 33
Of fluttering Sylphs, and softly-gliding Fays, . . K.8. 237 *Recluse* 1.1. 33
Fealty. To the oath of fealty, I well remember, . 63 *Bord.* 1445
Stooped down to pay him fealty; . . . . . 205 *Brougham* 121
Unbound by pledge of fealty, ... 403 *White Doe* 704
Vows to rapt Fancy humble fealty, ... 429 *Ecc. Sonn.* 2. 3. 11
Fear. Awed sober Reason till she crouched in fear? 11 *Desc. Sk.* 55
Now couch thyself where, heard with fear afar, . 16 *Desc. Sk.* 336
And Pikes, of darkness named and fear and storms, 19 *Desc. Sk.* 472
Abortive joy, and hope that works in fear; . . . 20 *Desc. Sk.* 548
Be scorn and fear and hope alike forgot . . . 22 *Desc. Sk.* 666
Disease and famine, agony and fear, ... 29 *Guilt* 299
Hope died, and fear itself in agony was lost! . . 30 *Guilt* 351
And busily, though yet with fear, untie . . . 34 *Guilt* 569
That fear is like a cloak which old men huddle . 38 *Bord.* 22
Fear not, I will obey you;—but One so young, . 42 *Bord.* 308
Alas! I creep so slowly. Never fear; . . . . 43 *Bord.* 358
What's this?—I fear, good Woman, ... 46 *Bord.* 489
But how's the day?—I fear, my little Boy, . . 46 *Bord.* 494
Looked at from every point of fear or hope, . . 47 *Bord.* 549
Would lead me to talk fondly. Do not fear; . . 52 *Bord.* 831
To have heard your voice. Your couch, I fear, good Baron, ... 53 *Bord.* 859
I *do* repent me, Sir; I fear the curse . . . . 54 *Bord.* 951
I care not: fear I have none, and cannot fear—— 56 *Bord.* 1015
To fear the virtuous, and reverence misery, . . 61 *Bord.* 1338
Or fear disguised in simulated scorn. . . . . 70 *Bord.* 1831
To fear the very worst. My Father is dead; . . 75 *Bord.* 2121
She looked at it and seemed to fear it; . . . 79 *Sparrow's Nest* 11
For rain and mountain-storms! the like thou need'st not fear, ... 87 *Pet-lamb* 31
Of hardship and distressful fear, amid the houseless waste . . . . 91 *Norman Boy* 27
Bowed meekly in submissive fear, before the Lord of All; . . . . 92 *Poet's Dream* 10
From which the tusky wild boar flies in fear; . 104 *Artegal* 109
Come often to us, fear no wrong; . . . . . 106 **I've watched* 14
And oftentimes, how long I fear to say, . . . 107 *Indolence* 24
Why should I fear to say . . . . 108 *Louisa* 3
Trembling, through my unworthiness, with fear . 112 **O dearer* 3
Of hopelessness and fear. . . . . 113 *Lament* 14
Can I be proud that jealous fear . . . . . 113 *Lament* 48
Alone, I cannot fear to die. . . . . 114 *Ind. Wom.* 20
Then wherefore should I fear to die? . . . . 114 *Ind. Wom.* 60
Shrunk from his Mother's presence, shunned with fear . . . . 118 *Maternal Grief* 51
Were yet with pensive fear and gentle awe . . 118 *Maternal Grief* 59
Through dark and shapeless fear of things to come, 124 *V. and J.* 182
And Susan now begins to fear . . . . . . 128 *Idiot Boy* 177
I fear you're in a dreadful way, ... 128 *Idiot Boy* 195
Of hardship, skill or courage, joy or fear; . . 132 *Michael* 69
And God will strengthen thee: amid all fear . . 137 *Michael* 408
But nothing from their inward selves had they to fear. . . . . 141 *Arm. Lady* 90
He needs not fear the season's rage, ... 144 **Driven in* 67
Then, lovely baby, do not fear! . . . . . 144 *Her Eyes* 15
I pray thee have no fear of me; . . . . . 144 *Her Eyes* 16
"Then do not fear, my boy! for thee . . . . 145 *Her Eyes* 51
To shelter from some object of her fear. . . . 148 *Joanna* 76
Huddling together from two fears—the fear . . 150 **When, to* 31
All kinds commingled without fear, ... 154 *Flower Garden* 8
The Briar quaked—and much I fear . . . . 155 *Waterfall* 55
Is it that they have a fear . . . . 171 *Kitten* 91
I saw you, between rage and fear, ... 175 *Waggoner* 1. 126
And, in fear of some disaster, ... 181 *Waggoner* 4. 125
May meet at noontide; Fear and trembling Hope, 185 *Yew-trees* 26
Of pleasure and of fear; . . . . 192 *Ruth* 45
My former thoughts returned: the fear that kills; 197 *Resolution* 113
Be turned to heaviness and fear. . . . . . 204 *Brougham* 94
"A recreant harp, that sings of fear . . . . 204 *Brougham* 102
Came, and rested without fear; . . . . . . 205 *Brougham* 119
If solitude, or fear, or pain, or grief, ... 207 *Tintern* 143
That calms all fear; "Such grace hath crowned thy prayer, ... 209 *Laod.* 20
Pure transport undisturbed by doubt or fear . . 213 *Dion* 26
"Fear not a constraining measure! . . . . . 220 *Triad* 34
What living man could fear . . . . 220 *Triad* 56
Then why should conscious Spirits fear . . . 223 *Wishing-gate* 37
Released from fear and doubt; . . . . . . 223 **'Tis gone* 3
Retire in fear of shame; . . . . 225 *Present.* 3
Companions, fear ye to be left behind, ... 229 *Clouds* 6
Listening to nun's faint throb of holy fear, . . 233 *Power of Sound* 30
And 'tis, I fear, an age too late) . . . . . 237 *P. B.* 127
What spell so strong as guilty Fear! . . . . 238 *P. B.* 147
To see him was to fear him. . . . . 239 *P. B.* 285
Peter, you need not fear! . . . . 240 *P. B.* 390
Meet Statue for the court of Fear! . . . . . 242 *P. B.* 523
Whom in my fear I love so well; . . . . . 245 *P. B.* 772

Fear—*continued.*
Of night his grief and sorrowful fear— . . . 249 *P. B.* 1104
Of the old Sea some reverential fear, ... 258 **Where lies the Land* 13
Of all things, that at last in fear I shrink, . . . 260 **How sweet* 13
Of high astonishment and pleasing fear. . . . 267 **Though narrow* 8
Her simplest fancies? Should that fear be thine, 270 **Though the bold* 11
In fear that else, when Critics grave and cool . . 277 **A Poet* 7
And on the verge of Chaos hang in fear. . . . 284 *Departure* 12
And both my wishes and my fear . . . . . 284 *Grave of Burns* 11
Chanted in love that casts out fear . . . . . 285 *Grave of Burns* 83
And think, and fear! . . . . 287 *Sons of Burns* 48
For fear and melancholy meet; . . . . . . 288 *Glen-Al.* 14
Yet who would stop, or fear to advance, . . . 289 *Stepping West.* 6
To fear of loss, and hope of gain, ... 294 *Jedbor.* 51
She who had fainted with her fear, ... 297 *Highland Boy* 232
One life, one glory!—I, with many a fear . . . 303 **Fair Star* 12
To fear, to change, to cowardice, and death? . . 308 **These times* 14
Ye too—whom no discreditable fear . . . . 310 *Invasion* 10
Who are to judge of danger which they fear, . . 310 **Another year* 13
By ladies, meek-eyed women without fear; . . . 315 **And is it* 12
In these usurping times of fear and pain? . . 316 **O'er the* 8
Who slighted fear; rejected steadfastly . . . 317 **Call not* 3
A people sunk in apathy and fear. . . . . . 319 *Biscayan* 9
Redeemed, from miserable fear set free . . . 326 *Sobieski* 9
Fervid, yet conversant with holy fear, ... 326 **The Bard* 3
Your thrones, ye Powers, from duty fear to swerve! 327 **Emperors and* 11
And shrill and fierce in accent!—Fear it not: . 333 *Fish-women* 9
Back in astonishment and fear we shrink: . . 336 *Aar* 3
A tender sense of shadowy fear, ... 338 **Meek Virgin* 29
And where the foot with no unmanly fear . . . 350 *Des. Stanzas* 13
Admonished not without some sense of fear, . . 355 *Aquap.* 181
Fear that soon vanishes before the sight . . . 355 *Aquap.* 182
With morals, trusting, in contempt or fear . . 357 *Aquap.* 334
Of flowers the Virgin without fear may own, . . 360 *Albano* 13
From their high state darkened the Earth with fear, 362 **List—'twas* 64
Sacred Religion! "mother of form and fear," . 380 *Duddon* 18. 1
Of barking dogs, and bleatings from strange fear. 382 *Duddon* 23. 8
With doubt, with fear, and haply with remorse: . 383 *Duddon* 30. 4
Hence, while we gaze, a more enduring fear! . . 392 *Daniel* 10
She fears not, wherefore should we fear? . . . 398 *White Doe* 179
Conjecture vague, and idle fear, ... 398 *White Doe* 214
When under cloud of fear he lay, ... 399 *White Doe* 280
Of Brancepeth look in doubt and fear, ... 402 *White Doe* 595
A face to fear and venerate; . . . . . . 404 *White Doe* 744
And Nevile's cheek grew pale with fear; . . . 404 *White Doe* 792
Hath any sway? or pain, or fear? . . . . . 406 *White Doe* 963
Sent upon embassies of fear; . . . . . . 407 *White Doe* 1048
They rose, oh! wherefore should I fear . . . 410 *White Doe* 1316
For at that time bewildering fear . . . . . 412 *White Doe* 1503
Looked round—but saw no cause for fear; . . . 414 *White Doe* 1652
—What now is left for pain or fear? . . . . 415 *White Doe* 1743
Most feelingly instructed 'mid their fear— . . 420 *Ecc. Sonn.* 1. 7. 10
And calm with fear of God's divinity. . . . . 422 *Ecc. Sonn.* 1. 14. 14
To harassed Piety, "Dismiss thy fear, ... 431 *Ecc. Sonn.* 2. 13. 3
Once more the Church is seized with sudden fear, 432 *Ecc. Sonn.* 2. 17. 1
Of pity or fear; and More's gay genius played . 435 *Ecc. Sonn.* 2. 26. 12
Fear hath a hundred eyes that all agree . . . 439 *Ecc. Sonn.* 2. 42. 1
Fear to my Soul, and sadness which might seem . 440 *Ecc. Sonn.* 3. 2. 2
Be lost, through apathy, or scorn, or fear, . . 442 *Ecc. Sonn.* 3. 10. 10
Yes, if the intensities of hope and fear . . . 445 *Ecc. Sonn.* 3. 19. 1
Under the holy fear of God turns pale; . . . 446 *Ecc. Sonn.* 3. 23. 8
Who thus could build. Be mine, in hours of fear 451 *Ecc. Sonn.* 3. 45. 2
That, in rough winter, oft inflicts a fear . . . 453 **Calm is the* 14
Drawn from the wisdom that begins with fear, . 454 **The Sun, that* 24
In days when Fancy wrought unchecked by fear, 460 **Queen of* 14
Weeping captivity, and shuddering fear . . . 465 **Dear to* 13
Nor fear memorial lays, ... 479 *Somnamb.* 155
And now I fear that you expect . . . . . 484 *Simon Lee* 63
The Man had fallen, that place of fear! . . . 491 *Fidelity* 43
And Fear, and Bloodshed, miserable train! . . 493 *Hap. War.* 13
Should fear that pencil's touch! . . . . . 499 *Memory* 20
(Too busy fear!) shall cross its range, ... 503 *Warning* 8
The bashful freed from fear, ... 507 **While from* 54
On wings that fear no glance of God's pure sight, 512 **Who rashly* 38
Till, by repentance stung, they fear to think; . 513 *Newspaper* 5
Betrayed by mockery of holy fear. . . . . . 514 **Portentous change* 8
On Love and Fear, their several powers he blends, 518 *Pun. Death* 5. 7
And, the main fear once doomed to banishment, . 519 *Pun. Death* 8. 6
Then, moved by needless fear of past abuse, . . 520 *Pun. Death* 13. 11
Where Fear is but a transient guest, ... 526 **The soaring* 19
And whither could they dart, if seized with fear? 528 **Those breathing* 52
Scorned, or neglected, fear not such a dearth. . 531 *Octogen.* 8
Without an object, hope, or fear, ... 532 †*Float. Isl.* 23
"Fear not," quickly answered Hubert; . . . 535 *Egremont* 33
And hope and fear mix not in further strife. . . 540 *Grace Darl.* 42
And rapture, with varieties of fear . . . . 541 *Grace Darl.* 64
This, Ina saw; and, pale with fear, ... 544 *Russ. Fug.* 269
And joy's excess produced a fear . . . . . 545 *Russ. Fug.* 355
And fear not lest an idle sound . . . . . . 550 *Hermit's Cell* 2. 6
This rueful sky, this pageantry of fear! . . . 579 *Peele Castle* 48
Labouring for life, in hope and fear, ... 579 **Sweet Flower* 40
Wait the fulfilment of their fear; . . . . . 581 **Loud is* 14
Direst of savage beasts, would roam in fear, . . 585 *Ch. Lamb* 70
And the worse fear of future ill (which oft . . 586 *Ch. Lamb* 113
Calmed in his soul the fear of change and death. . 587 *Crosth.* 18
With bashful fear no cottage children steal . . 602 *Desc. Sk. Quarto* 37
Tam'd "sober Reason" till she crouch'd in fear? 603 *Desc. Sk. Quarto* 56
Spontaneous wanders, hand in hand with Fear. . 605 *Desc.Sk.Quarto* 200
Lo! Fear looks silent down on Uri's lake, . . 607 *Desc.Sk.Quarto* 284

Fear—*continued.*

There hang in fear, when growls the frozen stream, 607 *Desc.Sk.Quarto* 315
Hence shall we turn where, heard with fear afar, . 609 *Desc.Sk.Quarto* 414
Huge Pikes of Darkness named, of Fear and Storms, 612 *Desc.Sk.Quarto* 564
The whole next day, I hoped, and hoped with fear ; 623 **Among all* 17
From fear and grief, and from all need . . . 623 *G. and S. Green* 27
Fostered alike by beauty and by fear : . . . 636 *Prelude* 1. 302
Both pain and fear, until we recognise . . . 638 *Prelude* 1. 413
With triumph and delight, with hope and fear, . 639 *Prelude* 1. 474
By the impressive discipline of fear, . . . 641 *Prelude* 1. 603
More difficult before me ; and I fear . . . 646 *Prelude* 2. 273
The gift is yours ; if in these times of fear . . 648 *Prelude* 2. 432
And poor misguided Shame, and witless Fear, . 657 *Prelude* 3. 598
And as I looked around, distress and fear . . 666 *Prelude* 5. 73
From anxious fear of error or mishap, . . . 670 *Prelude* 5. 280
Being itself benign. My drift I fear . . . 670 *Prelude* 5. 293
And natural or supernatural fear, ... 670 *Prelude* 5. 307
Of pain, and doubt, and fear, yet yielding not . 672 *Prelude* 5. 419
Of terror ; yet no soul-debasing fear, . . . 672 *Prelude* 5. 451
By aught, I fear, of genuine desert— . . . 677 *Prelude* 6. 169
That did not leave us free from personal fear ; 686 *Prelude* 6. 720
In a Child's heart as fear itself) conceived . . 688 *Prelude* 7. 105
Diversified the allurement. Need I fear . . 691 *Prelude* 7. 263
Nothing is listened to. But these, I fear, . . 697 *Prelude* 7. 668
Full of one passion, vengeance, rage, or fear ? 697 *Prelude* 7. 673
From vice and folly, wretchedness and fear ; . 703 *Prelude* 8. 291
In part by fear to shape a way direct, . . . 709 *Prelude* 9. 3
Hope takes, or Doubt or Fear is forced to wear, . 710 *Prelude* 9. 61
Locked up in quiet. For myself, I fear . . 711 *Prelude* 9. 110
No fear had they of bad becoming worse, . . 711 *Prelude* 9. 135
Reading at intervals ; the fear gone by . . 719 *Prelude* 10. 71
Pressed on me almost like a fear to come. . . 719 *Prelude* 10. 72
And innocent victims sinking under fear, . . 724 *Prelude* 10. 404
Tumult was therefore gladness, and the fear . . 724 *Prelude* 10. 434
Of good and evil ; knows not what to fear . . 732 *Prelude* 11. 313
Disjoined me from my comrade ; and, through fear 737 *Prelude* 12. 232
In fear) have walked with quicker step ; but why 742 *Prelude* 13. 159
Emotions which best foresight need not fear, . . 748 *Prelude* 14. 122
Actual, divine, and true. To fear and love, . . 748 *Prelude* 14. 162
To love as prime and chief, for there fear ends, . 748 *Prelude* 14. 163
Did also find its way. Thus fear relaxed . . 750 *Prelude* 14. 282
And melancholy Fear subdued by Faith ; . . . 755 *Recluse* 1. 1. 768
By help of dreams—can breed such fear and awe 755 *Recluse* 1. 1. 791
Where Fear sate thus, a cherished visitant, . . 759 *Excursion* 1. 186
He had imbibed of fear or darker thought . . 762 *Excursion* 1. 407
A strange surprise and fear came to my heart, . 766 *Excursion* 1. 659
The story linger in my heart ; I fear . . . 768 *Excursion* 1. 778
She said, ' I fear it will be dead and gone . . 769 *Excursion* 1. 845
An overweening trust was raised ; and fear . . 775 *Excursion* 2. 241
Hypocrisy, not leagued with fear, but pride. . 775 *Excursion* 2. 253
Confiding thoughts, through love and fear of Him 775 *Excursion* 2. 290
With malady—in part, I fear, provoked . . . 776 *Excursion* 2. 306
Hardened by impious pride !—I did not fear . . 779 *Excursion* 2. 486
Which did not please me, " must be deemed, I fear, 780 *Excursion* 2. 595
Release from fear ; and cherished peaceful days . 791 *Excursion* 3. 364
Stability without regret or fear ; . . . . 791 *Excursion* 3. 386
But in her stead—fear—doubt—and agony ! " 792 *Excursion* 3. 461
But superstitious fear, and abject sloth. . . 800 *Excursion* 3. 955
With hope, and love, and gratitude, and fear ; 811 *Excursion* 4. 660
Fearful ; but resignation tempers fear, . . . 813 *Excursion* 4. 798
With joy, and gratitude, and fear, and love ; . 815 *Excursion* 4. 930
To some unsanctioned fear ? " " If this be so, . 828 *Excursion* 5. 365
Love, admiration, fear, desire, and hate, . . 830 *Excursion* 5. 496
Enough ;—I fear, too much.—One vernal evening, 849 *Excursion* 6. 757
And fear of him who is a righteous judge ; . . 851 *Excursion* 6. 873
For all concerns of fear, or hope, or love, . . 853 *Excursion* 6. 1012
That Father was, and filled with anxious fear, . 855 *Excursion* 6. 1132
Until the Wanderer (whether moved by fear . . 862 *Excursion* 7. 293
Of turbulence, anxiety, and fear— . . . 863 *Excursion* 7. 369
A pride in having, or a fear to lose ; . . . 866 *Excursion* 7. 572
Pity away, soon shall ye quake with *fear !* . . 870 *Excursion* 7. 838
Would be disturbed, I fear, with wrathful scorn, . 874 *Excursion* 8. 35
Crowned like the image of fantastic Fear ; . . 879 *Excursion* 8. 349
" With such foundations laid, avaunt the fear . 889 *Excursion* 9. 363
In crowded cities, without fear shall live . . 894 *Excursion* 9. 668
" I only touch—not take—don't fear, . . . S.3. 441 **The ball* 3
Then wherefore should I fear to die ? . . . K.8. 219 **The snow-tracks* 4
Then wherefore should I fear to die ? . . . K.8. 220 **The snow-tracks* 35
Fainted with fear. Thrice did he turn his face . K.8. 229 **I will* 153
Without distress or fear the shepherd heard . K.8. 229 **I will* 174
Depressed, nor does it fear what is to come, . . K.8. 250 *Recluse* 1.1.496
Where no fear is, and humbler sympathies. . . K.8. 250 *Recluse* 1.1.503
Nor fear, though thou confide in me, a want . . K.8. 256 *Recluse* 1.1.737

Feared. The wet cold ground, he feared, must be his only bed. . . . . 25 *Guilt* 45
All he had feared from man, but roused a train . 25 *Guilt* 85
Feared you to waken him ? he must have been . 55 *Bord.* 960
A sound of laughter, too !—'tis well—I feared . 60 *Bord.* 1260
Who, so he feared, would never see him more ; . 74 *Bord.* 2068
But she, God love her ! feared to brush . . 79 **Stay near* 17
No ill was feared ; till one of them by chance . 101 *Brothers* 373
Flattered and feared, despised yet deified, . . 103 *Artegal* 96
Full twenty times was Peter feared . . . . 238 *P. B.* 204
Such as pursue their feared vagaries . . . 242 *P. B.* 509
Is feared as what may most deceive ? . . . 345 **How blest* 69
Treasures I gained with zeal that neither feared . 352 *H. C. R.* 3
Beheld what I had feared to see, ... 386 *Yarrow Rev.* 77
Where the all-conquering Roman feared to tread. 388 *Loch Etive* 14
For she *had* hoped, had hoped and feared, . . 409 *White Doe* 1192

Feared—*continued.*

Nor feared she in the still moonshine . . . . 416 *White Doe* 1815
Should e'er have felt or feared a wound . . . 534 **Blest is* 74
Too much the heroic Daughter feared . . . . 544 *Russ. Fug.* 231
That ever feared the tempting sun, ... 576 *Cenotaph* 5
To take a farewell of me ; for he feared . . . 766 *Excursion* 1. 679
Father, and king, and judge, adored and feared ! 794 *Excursion* 3. 573
Of passion : whatsoe'er be felt or feared, . . . 816 *Excursion* 4. 1021
That feared, or wholly overlooked the truth, . . K.8. 245 *Recluse* 1.1.310

Fearful. The peasant, from yon cliff of fearful edge 4 *Ev. Wk.* 130
His burning eyes with fearful light illume. . . 13 *Desc. Sk.* 165
You are too fearful ; yet must I confess, . . . 39 *Bord.* 106
I was too fearful—take me for your guide . . . 67 *Bord.* 1675
Has made him fearful, and he'll never be . . . 71 *Bord.* 1901
I've heard of fearful winds and darkness that come there ; . . . . 88 *Pet-lamb* 54
But whence that sudden check ? that fearful start ! 213 *Dion* 63
How fearful to the desert wide ! . . . . . 232 *Power of Sound* 22
Thy forehead as if fearful to offend, ... 264 *Snowdrop* 3
Is gone ; our peace, our fearful innocence, . . 307 **O Friend* 13
Whom hardy Rome was fearful to oppose ; . . 320 **They seek* 7
How fearful were it down through opening waves 333 *Fish-women* 6
Yon petty Steep in truth the fearful Rock, . . 358 **Is this* 2
And speak the word——" Alas ! of fearful things 433 *Ecc. Sonn.* 2. 18. 10
'Tis the most fearful when the people's eye . . . 433 *Ecc. Sonn.* 2. 18. 11
Turned to a fearful Thing whose nostrils breathe . 439 *Ecc. Sonn.* 2. 43. 10
So shall the fearful words of Commination . . 447 *Ecc. Sonn.* 3. 29. 13
Greta, what fearful listening ! when huge stones . 464 **Greta, what* 1
The pair have reached that fearful chasm, . . 494 *Force of Prayer* 17
Dread Lord ! so fearful when provoked, thine ire 563 *Troilus* 71
Fearful, beneath, the Water-spirits call, . . . 606 *Desc.Sk.Quarto* 213
Haply that child in fearful doubt may gaze, . . 609 *Desc.Sk.Quarto* 410
And crouching fearful at the feet of Pow'r, . . 617 *Desc.Sk.Quarto* 801
With will inflexible, those fearful pangs . . . 759 *Excursion* 1. 173
A fearful apprehension from the owl . . . 810 *Excursion* 4. 616
Fearful ; but resignation tempers fear, . . . 813 *Excursion* 4. 798
Hath harassed him toiling through fearful storm, 852 *Excursion* 6. 913

Fearfully. She fearfully caroused. . . . . 194 *Ruth* 198
Our vital frame, so fearfully devised, ... 816 *Excursion* 4. 975
Fearfully low ; nor will your judgment scorn . . 827 *Excursion* 5. 296

Fearing. Not fearing toil, nor length of weary ways, ... 134 *Michael* 196
Yet downcast as a woman fearing blame ; . . . 305 **We had* 4
Not mute, and then retire, fearing no storm ; . . 734 *Prelude* 12. 23
And fearing God ; the very children taught . . 758 *Excursion* 1. 114
" Here then we rest ; not fearing for our creed . 804 *Excursion* 4. 197
Not fearing toil, nor length of weary ways, . . K.8. 226 **I will* 76

Fearless. And watch the fearless chamois-hunter chase . . . . 16 *Desc. Sk.* 305
And clear and open soul, so prized in fearless youth. 32 *Guilt* 441
Thus the fearless Lamb-deliv'rer, ... 94 *Westmoreland Girl* 81
To a continuance of their fearless sport, . . . 118 *Maternal Grief* 29
Voluptuous, fearless of a rival, eyed . . . . 185 *Nutting* 24
For fearless virtue bringeth boundless gain. . . 210 *Laod.* 42
—Within our fearless reach are placed . . . . 216 *Enterprise* 83
And gaily lift its fearless brim . . . . . 296 *Highland Boy* 124
Proud Remnant was he of a fearless Race, . . 298 *Brownie's Cell* 31
With weapons grasped in fearless hands, to assert 315 **The Land* 13
Fearless of plough and scythe ; or darkling wren . 377 *Duddon* 7. 13
Into his coverts, and each fearless link . . . 383 *Duddon* 28. 7
The hare's best couching-place for fearless sleep 387 **Part fenced* 3
And Marmaduke in fearless mail, ... 401 *White Doe* 479
Said fearless Norton to the pair . . . . . 402 *White Doe* 603
My Song, a fearless homager, would attend . . 427 *Ecc. Sonn.* 1. 35. 9
Give to their Faith a fearless resting-place. . . 449 *Ecc. Sonn.* 3. 36. 14
Her temples, fearless for the stately work, . . 496 **A little* 37
Fearless of all assaults that would her brood molest. 525 *Epist. Beaumont* 231
Take those dear young Ones to a fearless nest ; . 525 **Soon did* 2
Fearless (but how obscured !) the golden Power . 527 **Those breathing* 14
'Tis his with fearless step at large to roam . . 609 *Desc.Sk.Quarto* 370
And while the fearless infant smiled, ... 629 *Installation* 43
Whether her fearless visitings, or those . . . 637 *Prelude* 1. 352
Fearless of blame, that hence for future days . . 643 *Prelude* 2. 74
Her new-born infant, fearless as a lamb . . . 692 *Prelude* 7. 325
Show what she was, a high and fearless soul, . . 718 *Prelude* 10. 33
Of blissful gratitude and fearless love ? . . . 735 *Prelude* 12. 56
Fearless of winds and waves. Three several stones 787 *Excursion* 3. 55

Fearlessly. Confirmed of purpose, fearlessly prepared 36 *Guilt* 649
Then Poets fearlessly rehearsed . . . . . . 237 *P. B.* 124
Could fearlessly approach the shade ? . . . . 497 *Lycoris* 8
And then he sang it well and fearlessly, . . . 554 *Prioress* 95
Forth did I go, alone and fearlessly, ... 557 *Cuck.and Night.* 59
Who, mounting fearlessly the rocky heights, . . 856 *Excursion* 6. 1158

Fearlessness. In virgin fearlessness, with step that seemed . . . . 850 *Excursion* 6. 820

Fear's. Led by Fear's cold wet hand, and dogg'd by Death ; . . . . 597 *Ev. Wk. Quarto* 286

Fears. Press the sad kiss, fond mother ! vainly fears. 7 *Ev. Wk.* 275
Not to have learnt to laugh at little fears. . . 43 *Bord.* 316
Are not the enemies that move my fears. . . . 43 *Bord.* 321
Idonea would have fears for me,—the Convent . 43 *Bord.* 352
That well may put some fears into *your* heart. . 52 *Bord.* 813
It is all over then ;—your foolish fears . . . 55 *Bord.* 955
I feel that you will justify. I had fears, . . . 64 *Bord.* 1473
And humble cares, and delicate fears ; . . . . 79 *Sparrow's Nest* 18
I think of thee with many fears . . . . . 88 *H. C.* 13
And yet they leave it short, and fears . . . . 110 *Forsaken* 10
Of fears the prey, of hopes the sport ; . . . . 113 *Lament* 60
Mine wilt thou be, thou hast no fears ; . . . . 120 *EmigrantMother* 37

Feel—*continued.*
From that soft class of devotees who feel . . . 48 *Bord.* 585
Can feel his crimes. I have resigned a privilege ; 53 *Bord.* 875
I feel my error ; shedding human blood . . . 55 *Bord.* 994
You know me, Friends ; I have a heart to feel, . 57 *Bord.* 1111
I feel that you will justify. I had fears, . . 64 *Bord.* 1473
Wherefore press this on me ? Because I feel . . 64 *Bord.* 1484
Who damn where they can neither see nor feel, . 64 *Bord.* 1504
Truth—and I feel it. What ! if you had bid . . 65 *Bord.* 1545
What ! feel remorse, where, if a cat had sneezed, 65 *Bord.* 1565
To God above will make him feel for ours. . . 66 *Bord.* 1596
His pleading face, and feel his clasping arms, . . 66 *Bord.* 1609
It throbs, and you have a heart that does not feel it. 66 *Bord.* 1620
A moment's heaviness they feel, ... 81 †*Mother's Return* 47
I could not feel a pain. . . . . 85 *Anecdote* 16
Learn how she can feel alike . . . . . . 94 *Westmoreland Girl* 50
Among thy mountains did I feel . . . . . 109 **I travelled* 9
I feel I must have died with thee. . . . . 114 *Ind. Wom.* 44
I should not feel the pain of dying, ... 114 *Ind. Wom.* 47
Of natural objects, led me on to feel . . . . 131 *Michael* 30
Thy lips I feel them, baby ! they . . . . . 145 *Her Eyes* 33
I feel thy little fingers prest. . . . . . . 145 *Her Eyes* 38
When the weary fingers feel . . . . . . 163 *Spinning Wheel* 3
Night and day, I feel the trouble . . . . . 166 *Wand. Jew* 27
I feel, but to inspire. . . . . 168 *Turtledove* 24
Whatsoe'er we feel and know . . . . . . 171 *Kitten* 99
Shall feel an overseeing power . . . . . . 187 **Three years* 11
She seemed a thing that could not feel . . . 187 **A slumber* 3
He spake of love, such love as Spirits feel . . 211 *Laod.* 97
The gazers feel ; and, rushing to the plain, . . 213 *Dion* 27
Thou, who canst *think*, as well as feel. . . . 228 *Devot. Incit.* 25
And, if the virtuous feel a pang too sharp, . . 233 *Power of Sound* 91
Art, daring because souls could feel, ... 234 *Power of Sound* 122
I feel I am a man. . . . . 237 *P. B.* 70
How earth and heaven are taught to feel . . . 237 *P. B.* 109
—Let good men feel the soul of nature, . . . 245 *P. B.* 764
I feel that I am all unfit . . . . 245 *P. B.* 789
And now is Peter taught to feel . . . . . 248 *P. B.* 1071
If the whole weight of what we think and feel, . 261 *Retirement* 1
Though man for brother man has ceased to feel. . 273 **When Philoctetes* 14
Too late, I feel, sweet Orphan ! was the day . . 275 *Rotha Q.* 5
And think and feel as once the Poet felt. . . . 276 *Author's Portrait* 8
All seem to feel the spirit of the place, . . . 283 **Well have* 11
Our Memory, feel that she hath eyes : . . . . 288 *Highland Girl* 67
I feel this place was made for her ; . . . . . 288 *Highland Girl* 69
And feel, thou Earth, for this afflicted Race ! . . 306 **We had* 14
And daring not to feel the majesty of right ! . . 311 **Who rises* 45
Shall simply feel and purely meditate— . . . 332 *Ode : Thanks.* 233
Sank in our hearts, we felt as men *should* feel . 334 **A wingèd* 12
And feel, if we would know. . . . . 337 *Cath. Cantons* 18
I feel how in their presence doth abide . . . 365 **Rapt above* 10
Though pitied, *feel* her own distress ; . . . . 370 *Eg. Maid* 59
Both feel, when he renews the wished-for aid : . 378 *Duddon* 10. 10
We feel that we are greater than we know. . . . 384 *Duddon* 34. 14
And dearer still, as now I feel, ... 386 *Yarrow Rev.* 111
They sing a service which they feel : . . . . 396 *White Doe* 39
Though men be, there are angels that can feel . 426 *Ecc. Sonn.* 1. 32. 6
Baronial halls the opprobrious insult feel ; . . 428 *Ecc. Sonn.* 1. 37. 13
Feel not that Conscience never can betray, . . 441 *Ecc. Sonn.* 3. 6. 7
Can do for minds disposed to feel its power ! . . 456 **Soft as* 13
How *could* we feel it ? each the other's blight, . 473 **We saw* 3
Feel with the Mother, think the severed Wife . . 476 *Howard* 11
Our bodies feel, where'er they be, ... 481 *Expost.* 19
Come forth and feel the sun. . . . . 482 *Sister* 12
Of my own wish ; and feel past doubt . . . . 492 *Duty*
I feel the weight of chance-desires : . . . . 492 *Duty* 38
To righteous Gods when man has ceased to feel, . 500 *Humanity* 2
Which ye feel not, happy pair ! . . . . . . 503 *Warning* 4
Nor feel the fulness of that joy reproved ? . . 504 *Warning* 52
Earth, sea, thy presence feel—nor less, . . . 507 *May* 17
Feel for the wrongs to universal ken . . . . 516 **Feel for* 1
Of sorrow ;—feel for all, as brother Men ! . . . 516 **Feel for* 8
Tenderly do we feel by Nature's law . . . . 517 *Pun. Death* 2. 1
Nor is, they feel, its wisdom obsolete— . . . 520 *Pun. Death* 13. 6
From Heaven, and *feel* what they repeat, . . . 530 *Gleaner* 32
All that they think and feel, with tears of joy ; . 539 **Lady ! a* 53
That in my soul I feel the joy of it. . . . . 564 *Troilus* 154
Feel I a wind, that soundeth so like pain ; . . . 565 *Troilus* 160
Make slow to feel, and by sure steps resign . . 567 *Cumb. Beg.* 94
Men who can hear the Decalogue and feel . . . 568 *Cumb. Beg.* 135
When they can know and feel that they have been, 568 *Cumb. Beg.* 149
And when our hearts shall feel a sting . . . . 578 **I come* 53
Even here I feel it, even this Plant . . . . . 580 *John Words.* 48
For ever covetous to feel, ... 582 **O for a* 14
The fulness of your bliss, I feel—I feel it all. . . 588 *Immortality* 41
Feel the gladness of the May ! . . . . . . 590 *Immortality* 178
Yet in my heart of hearts I feel your might ; . . 590 *Immortality* 193
They not the trip of harmless milkmaid feel. . . 596 *Ev. Wk. Quarto* 226
But o'er the sooth'd accordant heart we feel . . 599 *Ev. Wk. Quarto* 381
Now in the clear and open day I feel . . . . 622 *Recluse* 1. 1. 111
Of culture, even to feel or understand . . . . 626 **Son of* 5
And I was taught to feel, perhaps too much, . . 643 *Prelude* 2. 76
Which we behold and feel we are alive ; . . . 645 *Prelude* 2. 181
And faculties, whether to work or feel. . . . 650 *Prelude* 3. 89
I gave a moral life : I saw them feel, ... 651 *Prelude* 3. 129
Where all stand single ; this I feel, and make . . 651 *Prelude* 3. 186
And yet we feel—we cannot choose but feel— . . 666 *Prelude* 5. 21
And humbled down ;—oh ! then we feel, we feel, 673 *Prelude* 5. 522
Philosophy will call you : *then* we feel . . . . 673 *Prelude* 5. 526

Feel—*continued.*
To think, to hope, to worship, and to feel, . . 682 *Prelude* 6. 468
Of these, I feel the imaginative power . . . . 694 *Prelude* 7. 468
Is prompt, or slow, to feel. What say you, then, 697 *Prelude* 7. 671
This did I feel, in London's vast domain. . . . 698 *Prelude* 7. 765
With deep devotion, Nature, did I feel, . . . 700 *Prelude* 8. 70
Power growing under weight : alas ! I feel . . 707 *Prelude* 8. 555
Now do I feel how all men are deceived, . . . 712 *Prelude* 9. 170
A noble aspiration ! *yet* I feel . . . . . . 731 *Prelude* 11. 255
To feel it ;—but return we to our course. . . . 731 *Prelude* 11. 258
I feel for thee, must utter what I feel : . . . 733 *Prelude* 11. 405
On which thy greatness stands ; but this I feel, . 738 *Prelude* 12. 275
Substance and life to what I feel, enshrining, . . 738 *Prelude* 12. 284
—Yes, in those wanderings deeply did I feel . . 743 *Prelude* 13. 206
And cannot choose but feel. The power, which all 747 *Prelude* 14. 86
Have been laid open, needs must make me feel . 752 *Prelude* 14. 422
To feel intensely, cannot but receive. . . . . 759 *Excursion* 1. 196
But in the mountains did he *feel* his faith.. . . 759 *Excursion* 1. 226
And eyed its waters till we seemed to feel . . . 763 *Excursion* 1. 485
Your very soul to see her. Sir, I feel . . . . 768 *Excursion* 1. 777
And presence ; and so deeply do I feel . . . 768 *Excursion* 1. 782
That what we feel of sorrow and despair . . . 770 *Excursion* 1. 949
" To the dark pit ; but he will feel no pain ; . . 779 *Excursion* 2. 510
But, in the process, I began to feel . . . . . 797 *Excursion* 3. 790
Roaming at large, to observe, and not to feel . . 799 *Excursion* 3. 892
They act, or they recede, observe, and feel ; . . 806 *Excursion* 4. 323
And felt, deeply as living man could feel. . . . 808 *Excursion* 4. 474
Shall feel congenial stirrings late and long, . . 809 *Excursion* 4. 544
The rational creature, left, to feel the weight . . 811 *Excursion* 4. 667
—Yes, you have felt, and may not cease to feel. . 818 *Excursion* 4. 1151
No vengeance, and no hatred—needs must feel . . 819 *Excursion* 4. 1212
Or feel, shall tend to quicken and refine ; . . . 820 *Excursion* 4. 1271
Perchance, the heavier woes of guilt ; feel not . . 829 *Excursion* 5. 429
" We see, then, as we feel," the Wanderer thus . 831 *Excursion* 5. 558
" That which we feel we utter ; as we think . . 832 *Excursion* 5. 625
Yet much, I feel, is wanting—else the task . . 832 *Excursion* 5. 660
To feel for those among our fellow-men, . . . 846 *Excursion* 6. 530
Who rather would not envy, men that feel . . 847 *Excursion* 6. 616
I feel, good reasons why we should not leave . . 848 *Excursion* 6. 661
Of what I know, and what we feel within. . . . 851 *Excursion* 6. 861
Which hapless Ellen now was doomed to feel : . 852 *Excursion* 6. 956
Of sorrow and dejection ; but I feel . . . . 855 *Excursion* 6. 1124
" I feel at times a motion of despite . . . . 866 *Excursion* 7. 590
While solitude permits the mind to feel ; . . . 875 *Excursion* 8. 55
For me, consulting what I feel within . . . . 885 *Excursion* 9. 102
Earth's universal frame shall feel the effect ; . . 890 *Excursion* 9. 386
Instilled a confidence—how sweet to feel ! . . S. 3. 427**Through Cumbrian* 11
His folly. Thus (I feel it while I speak), . . . S. 3. 434 **The doubt* 60
So shall our bosoms feel a covert growth . . . S. 3. 437 **The doubt* 203
And feel no wish to be alive, ... K. 8. 220 **The snow-tracks* 24
And not feel motions there ? He thought of clouds K. 8. 237 *Recluse* 1. 1. 25
I would stand clear, but yet to me I feel . . . K. 8. 255 *Recluse* 1. 1. 674
Shall he feel yearning to those lifeless forms, . . K. 8. 257 **Shall he* 7
Feelers. Feelers of love, put forth as if to explore 173 *Infant Daughter* 72
His feelers, methinks, I can see him put forth . 484 **A plague* 18
Feel'st. Great God, who feel'st for my distress, 113 *Lament* 54
Feeling. *See* **Fellow-feeling.**
Father, I would not change that sacred feeling . 40 *Bord.* 139
—These fools of feeling are mere birds of winter 47 *Bord.* 558
If I could think one weak or partial feeling—— 48 *Bord.* 630
He is a puny soul who, feeling pain, ... 65 *Bord.* 1555
Who would check the happy feeling . . . . 90 *Longest Day* 17
And, feeling that the hope is vain, ... 110 *Forsaken* 13
Of meditative feeling ; . . . . 112 **How rich* 18
And, with yet fonder feeling, for the sake . . . 131 *Michael* 37
A pleasurable feeling of blind love, ... 132 *Michael* 76
And feeling sinks as deep ! See there the door . 138 *Widow* 3
" Feeling tunes your voice, fair Princess ! . . . 140 *Arm. Lady* 43
A love for things that have no feeling : . . . 142 †*Lov. and Lik.* 30
He's at your elbow—to your feeling . . . . 143 **Driven in* 20
The very bacon shows its feeling, ... 177 *Waggoner* 2. 68
Was softened into feeling, soothed, and tamed. . 205 *Brougham* 160
An appetite ; a feeling and a love, ... 206 *Tintern* 80
Of an eye where feeling plays . . . . . . 221 *Triad* 129
Happy the feeling from the bosom thrown . . 250 **Happy the* 1
Save only far as thought and feeling blend . . 261 *Retirement* 2
With earnest feeling I shall pray . . . . . 288 *Highland Girl* 22
Recalled some feeling—to set free . . . . . 300 *Bran* 44
Such feeling pressed upon my soul, ... 334 **In Brugès* 33
A feeling sanctified . . . . 334 **In Brugès* 34
Here only serve a feeling to invite . . . . . 349 *Val. Dover* 12
Sustain the heart in feeling . . . . 386 *Yarrow Rev.* 94
In solitude her bitter feeling : . . . . . . 401 *White Doe* 449
Deep feeling, that found utterance loud, . . . 409 *White Doe* 1228
By human feeling, had ordained. . . . . . 410 *White Doe* 1329
The freight of holy feeling which we meet, . . 438 *Ecc. Sonn.* 2. 39. 12
'Tis the still hour of thinking, feeling, loving. . 453 **The Sun, that* 6
Wrecks though they be, announce with feeling . 472 *Ossian* 15
With old poetic feeling, not for this, ... 477 *Steamboats* 2
—It is the hour of feeling. . . . . 483 *Sister* 24
Nor form, nor feeling, great or small ; . . . . 485 *Poet's Epitaph* 30
A chain of heart, a feeling of the mind, . . . 491 *Tribute : Dog* 29
And gave that strength of feeling, great . . . 492 *Fidelity* 64
Her feeling, rendered more compassionate ; . . 493 *Hap. War.* 20
The fount of feeling, if unsought elsewhere, . . 509 *F. Stone* 51
In character, and depth of feeling, shown . . . 509 *F. Stone* 100
Dark but to every gentle feeling true, ... 525 *Epist. Beaumont* 256
And feeling, suited to the place and time . . . 539 **Lady ! a* 5

Feeling—*continued.*
Feeling from limbs with travel spent, ... 542 *Russ. Fug.* 47
Feeling what England lost when Reynolds died. . 547 **Ye Lime* 18
In sooth, I speak from feeling, what though now . 557 *Cuck. andNight.* 36
Most feeling have of sorrow, woe and care, . . 559 *Cuck.andNight.*143
The feeling of my loss will ne'er be old ; . . . 578 *Peele Castle* 39
And he hath feeling of a day . . . . . . 580 *John Words.* 29
A feeling of their strength. The naked trees, . 622 *Recluse* 1. 1. 165
The elements of feeling and of thought, . . . 638 *Prelude* 1. 411
For feeling has to him imparted power . . . 646 *Prelude* 2. 255
With faculties still growing, feeling still . . 646 *Prelude* 2. 320
Were steeped in feeling ; I was only then . . 648 *Prelude* 2. 399
A feeling that I was not for that hour, . . . 650 *Prelude* 3. 81
Or linked them to some feeling : the great mass 651 *Prelude* 3. 130
Of noble feeling, that those spiritual men, . . 653 *Prelude* 3. 266
A pensive feeling ! It spread far and wide ; . . 662 *Prelude* 4. 241
But feeling it no longer. Our discourse . . 665 *Prelude* 4. 445
By love and feeling, and internal thought . . . 667 *Prelude* 5. 146
Forget his feeling : so (if like effect . . . 677 *Prelude* 6. 154
The last night's genial feeling overflowed . . . 687 *Prelude* 7. 43
For feeling and contemplative regard, ... 696 *Prelude* 7. 624
As parts, but with a feeling of the whole. . . 698 *Prelude* 7. 736
Ruled not, and feeling that they ought to rule. . 712 *Prelude* 9. 214
Of virtuous feeling. For myself, I own . . . 722 *Prelude* 10. 253
They had the deepest feeling of the grief. . . . 724 *Prelude* 10. 389
All feeling of conviction, and, in fine, ... 731 *Prelude* 11. 303
They had left behind ? So feeling comes in aid . 738 *Prelude* 12. 269
Of feeling, and diversity of strength . . . 738 *Prelude* 12. 270
With real feeling and just sense ; how vain . . 742 *Prelude* 13. 172
Up to the height of feeling intellect . . . . 749 *Prelude* 14. 226
The feeling pleasures of his loneliness, ... 757 *Excursion* 1. 100
Or by creative feeling overborne, ... 758 *Excursion* 1. 158
And feeling is suppressed) preserve the mind . . 760 *Excursion* 1. 256
And every moral feeling of his soul . . . . . 760 *Excursion* 1. 304
Of tender feeling, she might dare repeat . . . 770 *Excursion* 1. 899
And, to my feeling, ere we reached the door, . . 781 *Excursion* 2. 639
The central feeling of all happiness, ... 791 *Excursion* 3. 382
There feeling no contentment, I resolved . . . 798 *Excursion* 3. 831
Of native feeling, grateful to our minds ; . . . 801 *Excursion* 4. 5
Where soul is dead, and feeling hath no place ; . 810 *Excursion* 4. 621
To sight and feeling, or that in this sort . . . 811 *Excursion* 4. 643
No feeling, which can overcome his love. . . 819 *Excursion* 4. 1229
Of feeling to produce them, without aid . . . 837 *Excursion* 5. 985
Who, with ancestral feeling, can perceive . . . 838 *Excursion* 6. 25
The natural feeling of equality . . . . . . 852 *Excursion* 6. 950
To impress a vivid feeling on the mind . . . 879 *Excursion* 8. 328
Of language shall a feeling heart express . . . 886 *Excursion* 9. 139
For men who in such places, feeling there . . . K.8. 226 **I will* 70
Of feeling, which were cheerless and forlorn . . K.8. 248*Recluse* 1.1.434
Abundance ; and that, feeling as we do . . . K.8. 254*Recluse* 1.1.639

Feelingly. Ye feelingly reprove ; . . . . . . 225 *Present.* 45
Who meet most feelingly the calls of sadness. . 280 **'Tis he* 14
Is known ; by none, perhaps, so feelingly : . . . 312 *Clarkson* 3
Feelingly told by living monuments— . . . . 346 *Processions* 5
How feelingly at home the Sovereign ruled ; . . 368 *Trajan* 32
Most feelingly instructed 'mid their fear— . . 420 *Ecc. Sonn.* 1. 7. 10
Feelingly their brows incline . . . . . . 502 **Like a* 38
Thou against Time so feelingly dost strive. . . 627 **We gaze* 10
Most feelingly, could overthrow my trust . . . 709 *Prelude* 8. 649
Feelingly watched, might teach Man's haughty race 734 *Prelude* 12. 12
Feelingly sweet is stillness after storm, . . . 790 *Excursion* 3. 280
How feelingly religion may be learned . . . . 813 *Excursion* 4. 790
No parent was—feelingly could have told, . . 835 *Excursion* 5. 887
And much she read ; and brooded feelingly . . 854 *Excursion* 6. 1028
And feelingly the Sage shall make report . . . 877 *Excursion* 8. 222

Feeling's. And, for this feeling's sake, let no one chide 393 *Hart's-horn* 13

Feelings. I honour him. Strong feelings to his heart 38 *Bord.* 33
No.—Thoughts and feelings will sink deep, but then 58 *Bord.* 1171
Have human feelings !— Now, for a little more . 61 *Bord.* 1329
Feelings and emanations—things which were . . 134 *Michael* 201
Than common feelings of fraternal love. . . . 151 **When, to* 75
Confound my present feelings with the past, . . 185 *Nutting* 49
" And vital feelings of delight . . . . . . 187 **Three years* 31
The stars had feelings, which they sent . . . 193 *Ruth* 137
With tranquil restoration :—feelings too . . . 206 *Tintern* 30
Thy thoughts and feelings shall not die, . . . 218 *Young Lady* 13
O chief of Friends ! such feelings I present . . 250 **Happy the* 10
With chastened feelings would I pay . . . . 284 *Grave of Burns* 15
Yet happy feelings of the dead : . . . . . 289 *Glen-Al.* 29
And know that noble feelings, manly powers, . . 308 **There is a bondage* 11
By feelings urged that do not vainly seek . . . 329 *Ode : Thanks.* 38
One tribute more : unbidden feelings start . . 350 *Des. Stanzas* 5
Our thoughts have issued, and our feelings flowed, 394 **No more* 23
Unacceptable feelings of contempt, ... 497 **Enough of climbing* 8
While thoughts press on, and feelings overflow, . 503 *Warning* 20
'Mid these more awful feelings, to infuse . . . 534 **When in* 18
Alas, how feebly ! but our feelings rise . . . 583 **With copious* 3
Could private feelings meet for holier rest. . . 587 *Crosth.* 14
The many feelings that oppressed my heart. . . 634 *Prelude* 1. 123
Of obscure feelings representative . . . . . 641 *Prelude* 1. 606
And, from like feelings, humble though intense, . 645 *Prelude* 2. 189
Drinks in the feelings of his Mother's eye ! . . 645 *Prelude* 2. 237
Is moved with feelings of delight, to me . . . 647 *Prelude* 2. 327
Did bind my feelings even as in a chain. . . . 651 *Prelude* 3. 166
Came in reply, translated by our feelings, . . . 684 *Prelude* 6. 590
Mother and child !—These feelings, in themselves 692 *Prelude* 7. 329
Feelings of pure commiseration, grief . . . . 693 *Prelude* 7. 395
Engrafted far-fetched shapes on feelings bred . . 705 *Prelude* 8. 422
In which my early feelings had been nursed— . 708 *Prelude* 8. 634

Feelings—*continued.*
With genial feelings still predominant ; . . . 729 *Prelude* 11. 156
Out of his feelings, to be fixed thenceforth . . 730 *Prelude* 11. 226
My deeper feelings, but another cause, ... 736 *Prelude* 12. 123
Whose variegated feelings were in this . . . . 736 *Prelude* 12. 163
To look with feelings of fraternal love . . . . 740 *Prelude* 13. 45
Became more firm in feelings that had stood . . 740 *Prelude* 13. 56
Accompanied by feelings of delight . . . . . 755 *Recluse* 1. 1. 757
Of greatness ; and deep feelings had impressed . 758 *Excursion* 1. 136
Accumulated feelings pressed his heart . . . 760 *Excursion* 1. 281
Their passions and their feelings ; chiefly those . 761 *Excursion* 1. 343
A kindling eye :—accordant feelings rushed . . 808 *Excursion* 4. 506
His feelings of aversion softened down ; . . . 819 *Excursion* 4. 1219
Of simple manners, feelings unsuppressed . . . 824 *Excursion* 5. 118
These inward feelings, and the aspiring vows . . 827 *Excursion* 5. 312
Feelings with these accordant ; love, esteem, . . 848 *Excursion* 6. 648
All generous feelings flourish and rejoice ; . . . 862 *Excursion* 7. 328
Feelings and emanations, things which were . . K.8. 226 **I will* 81
These feelings, though subservient more than ours K.8. 249*Recluse* 1.1.449

Feels. Yon isle, which feels not even the milkmaid's feet, ... 6 *Ev. Wk.* 236
Feels not the spirit of the place control, . . . 15 *Desc. Sk.* 291
Is littleness ; that he who feels contempt . . . 23 *Yew-tree* 52
Ay, Sir, there's nobody that feels for us. . . . 45 *Bord.* 445
Finds ease because another feels it too. . . . 65 *Bord.* 1556
And feels its life in every limb, ... 83 *We are Seven* 3
Gazing she feels its power beguile . . . . . 164 **Fair Lady* 33
Not undisturbed by the delight it feels, . . . 184 *Night-piece* 24
With sorrow of the meanest thing that feels." . 203 *Hart-leap* 180
The Sage, who feels how blind, how weak . . . 223 *Wishing-gate* 61
He feels the glimmering of the moon ; . . . . 242 *P. B.* 537
He feels what he for human-kind . . . . . 248 *P. B.* 1054
Even as a dragon's eye that feels the stress . . 266 **Even as* 1
Of July suns ; he feels it sweet ; . . . . . 294 *Jedbor.* 61
Feels, and hereafter shall the truth declare, . . 327 *Ode 1815* 42
While the tubed engine feels the inspiring blast, . 332 *Ode : Thanks.* 216
Imagination feels what Reason fears not . . . 356 *Aquap.* 278
—She feels it, and her pangs are checked. . . 407 *White Doe* 1073
Shun will she not, she feels, will bear ;— . . . 414 *White Doe* 1699
His questions urging, feels, in slender ties . . 422 *Ecc. Sonn.* 1. 13. 10
Feels, through the influence of her gentle reign, . 426 *Ecc. Sonn.* 1. 29. 7
And soft Italia feels renewed alarms ; . . . . 427 *Ecc. Sonn.* 1. 34. 4
Who, looking round the fair assemblage, feels . 446 *Ecc. Sonn.* 3. 23. 13
Feels through her lowest depths thy sovereignty ; 459 **Wanderer ! that* 49
If he be one that feels, with skill to part . . . 489 *Spade* 21
The Power least prized is that which thinks and feels. 501 *Humanity* 94
He feels how far the act would derogate . . . 518 *Pun. Death* 5. 10
With envy, what the Old Man hardly feels. . . 572 *Animal Tran.* 14
Acknowledges God's grace, his mercy feels, . . 586 *Ch. Lamb* 119
And who but feels a power of strong controul, . 608 *Desc.Sk.Quarto* 352
Then feels immediately some hollow thought . . 636 *Prelude* 1. 259
And feels not what an empire we inherit . . . 652 *Prelude* 3. 192
Or sees in his day's march ; himself he feels, . . 703 *Prelude* 8. 251
That whoso feels such passion in its strength . . 742 *Prelude* 13. 192
The one that feels, the other that observes. . . 751 *Prelude* 14. 347
Too clearly ; feels too vividly ; and longs . . . 804 *Excursion* 4. 175
Who feels that to exhort is to reproach. . . . 805 *Excursion* 4. 258
Who neither hears, nor feels a wish to hear, . . 810 *Excursion* 4. 581
And guard her fortresses. Who thinks, and feels, 810 *Excursion* 4. 598
At least he feels 'tis given him to descry ; . . . 827 *Excursion* 5. 301
Far livelier than bewildered traveller feels, . . 852 *Excursion* 6. 911

Fees. Who, to that service bound by venial fees, . 467 *St. Bees* 71
To be performed, and paid all holy fees. . . . 623 **I find* 5

Feet. Opened at once, and stayed my devious feet. 3 *Ev. Wk.* 56
From lonesome chapel at the mountain's feet . . 4 *Ev. Wk.* 138
Spur-clad his nervous feet, and firm his tread ; . 5 *Ev. Wk.* 148
Yon isle, which feels not even the milkmaid's feet, 6 *Ev. Wk.* 236
They crush with broad black feet their flowery walk ; . . . . 6 *Ev. Wk.* 243
Stretched at his feet, with steadfast upward eye, 13 *Desc. Sk.* 151
Their thirst they slake :—they wash their toil-worn feet, ... 20 *Desc. Sk.* 561
Pursued his vagrant way, with feet half bare ; . 24 *Guilt* 2
Till on a stone, that sparkled to his feet, . . . 27 *Guilt* 176
Of feet still bustling round with busy glee, . . 31 *Guilt* 392
Her garments, and, to warm her icy feet . . . 34 *Guilt* 570
And in the Churchyard sod her feet have worn . 44 *Bord.* 394
Whirred from among the fern beneath our feet, . 61 *Bord.* 1286
With naked feet walked over burning ploughshares. 62 *Bord.* 1385
Crawl from beneath our feet we do not ask . . 66 *Bord.* 1580
Her feet disperse the powdery snow, ... 83 *Lucy Gray* 27
The print of Lucy's feet. . . . . 83 *Lucy Gray* 44
And now, all eyes and feet, hath gained . . . 85 *Shepherd-boys* 58
The green earth echoed to the feet . . . . . 85 *Anecdote* 17
—As homeward through the lane I went with lazy feet, ... 88 *Pet-lamb* 61
Save six feet of earth where our forefathers lie ! . 116 *Repentance* 36
Your feet must struggle ; in such bold ascent . 131 *Michael* 4
Then old, beside him, lying at his feet. . . . 138 *Michael* 469
His very feet bright as the dazzling snow . . . 139 *Widow* 19
My feet might move without concern or care ; . 150 **When, to* 38
A Broom out of its feet. . . . . 156 *Oak and Broom* 14
From this platform, eight feet square, ... 157 *Sexton* 10
When they lie about our feet : . . . . . . 160 **Pleasures newly* 2
Apparent at his feet. . . . . 167 *Pilgrim's Dream* 16
That with stir of feet and wings . . . . . 171 *Kitten* 46
And, fairly lifted from my feet, ... 179 *Waggoner* 3. 88
There, at Blencathara's rugged feet, ... 180 *Waggoner* 4. 46
Soft and cool to way-worn feet ; . . . . . . 181 *Waggoner* 4. 161
A mantle, to her very feet . . . . 190 *Beggars* 4
And with her feet she from the plashy earth . . 195 *Resolution* 12

Feet—*continued.*
His body was bent double, feet and head . . . 196 *Resolution* 66
He travelled ; stirring thus about his feet . . . 197 *Resolution* 122
At the spectator's feet.—Yon azure ridge, . . 219 **This Height* 23
Their feet among the billows, know . . . . 235 *Power of Sound* 186
Close to the Ass's feet she fell ; . . . . . 247 *P. B.* 1013
A labyrinth, Lady ! which your feet shall rove. . 264 **Lady ! the* 8
Have neither limbs, feet, feathers, joints, nor hairs : 268 **Brook ! whose* 10
Then, pensive Votary ! let thy feet repair . . . 269 *Gordale* 4
Where silver Isis leads my stripling feet ; . . . 270 **Ye sacred* 11
A while he stood upon his feet ; . . . . . 296 *Highland Boy* 151
And, at our feet, amid the silent dust . . . . 315 **The Land* 8
Beneath his haughty feet, like clouds, are laid. . 317 **Look now* 8
With feet, hands, eyes, looks, lips, report your gain ; 322 **Ye Storms* 10
Where, without hurry, noiseless feet . . . . 334 **In Bruges* 3
Pale, ragged, with bare feet and head ; . . . 342 *Ital. Itin.* 88
With golden blossoms opening at the feet . . . 353 *Aquap.* 29
(As hurry on in eagerness the feet, ... 355 *Aquap.* 176
From all her Sanctuaries !—Open for my feet . . 357 *Aquap.* 298
By feet of purse-proud strangers ; they—who have read . . . . 359 **They—who* 6
Their love-songs ; but, where'er my feet might roam, ... 362 **List—'twas* 24
Which her Heaven-guided feet refuse to tread. . 390 *Highland Hut* 8
And earth's green grass beneath his feet ; . . . 401 *White Doe* 430
The wounds of hands and feet and side, . . . 403 *White Doe* 662
And trod the bible beneath their feet. . . . . 404 *White Doe* 714
What, Lady, if their feet were tied ; . . . . 409 *White Doe* 1223
So to her feet the Creature came, ... 414 *White Doe* 1653
In love and pity at her feet ; . . . . . . 416 *White Doe* 1825
My feet would rather turn—to some dry nook . 424 *Ecc. Sonn.* 1. 22. 2
Indulging thus at will the creeping feet . . . 424 *Ecc. Sonn.* 1. 23. 2
At a proud Legate's feet ! The spears that line . 428 *Ecc. Sonn.* 1. 37. 12
Beneath their feet, detested and defiled. . . . 435 *Ecc. Sonn.* 2. 29. 14
His frame is tied ; firm from the naked feet . . 437 *Ecc. Sonn.* 2. 35. 6
Whate'er the path these mortal feet may trace, . 454 **The Sun, that* 21
Turn to minuter changes at our feet ; . . . . 456 **Soft as* 7
" Six feet in earth my Emma lay ; . . . . . 487 **We walked* 37
And gurgled at our feet. . . . . 487 *Fountain* 8
More justly balanced ; partly at their feet, . . 488 *Pers. Talk* 24
With weary feet by all of woman born)— . . . 504 *Warning* 50
Kneel at the feet of Justice, and, for faith . . 518 *Pun. Death* 3. 13
Found at the Widow's feet some sad relief ; . . 523 *Epist. Beaumont* 134
Bathed duteously her wayworn feet, ... 542 *Russ. Fug.* 35
His staff trails with him ; scarcely do his feet . 567 *Cumb. Beg.* 59
No thorns can pierce her tender feet, ... 583 **O for a* 40
The Pansy at my feet . . . . 588 *Immortality* 54
See, at his feet, some little plan or chart, . . . 589 *Immortality* 90
A spot, that angles at the riv'let's feet, . . . 592 *Ev. Wk. Quarto* 46
Alternately relieves their weary feet ; . . . . 595 *Ev. Wk. Quarto* 216
Ye crush with broad black feet your flow'ry walk ; 596 *Ev. Wk. Quarto* 232
Drops at his feet, and stills his droning horn. . 597 *Ev. Wk. Quarto* 314
He opens of his feet the sanguine tides, . . . 609 *Desc.Sk.Quarto* 395
Up the green mountain tracking Summer's feet, . 610 *Desc.Sk.Quarto* 452
Dire clap of hands, distracted chase of feet, . . 614 *Desc.Sk.Quarto* 657
Nor longer naked be your way-worn feet, . . . 614 *Desc.Sk.Quarto* 667
Still have my pilgrim feet unfailing found, . . 615 *Desc.Sk.Quarto* 720
And crouching fearful at the feet of Pow'r, . . 617 *Desc.Sk.Quarto* 801
Standing alone, and at his feet . . . . . . 621 *Andrew Jones* 24
Threatening to lay all Orders at her feet . . . 626 *Ballot* 4
Of a known Vale, whither my feet should turn, . 633 *Prelude* 1. 72
With exultation, at my feet I saw . . . . . 658 *Prelude* 4. 7
In arms, now rosy prattlers at the feet . . . 661 *Prelude* 4. 204
With din of instruments and shuffling feet, . . 663 *Prelude* 4. 313
Kept the same awful steadiness—at his feet . . 664 *Prelude* 4. 407
Who slumbers at her feet,—forgetful, too, . . 671 *Prelude* 5. 402
Then from his couch he starts ; and now his feet 702 *Prelude* 8. 241
Than those few nooks to which my happy feet 737 *Prelude* 12. 179
Beyond the limits that my feet had trod, . . . 742 *Prelude* 13. 149
When at my feet the ground appeared to brighten, 746 *Prelude* 14. 35
Of azure without cloud, and at my feet . . . 746 *Prelude* 14. 41
Beneath our feet, a little lowly vale, ... 776 *Excursion* 2. 328
Conducted hither your most welcome feet, . . 779 *Excursion* 2. 534
Lay low beneath my feet ; 'twas visible— . . 784 *Excursion* 2. 871
Following the guidance of these welcome feet . . 793 *Excursion* 3. 500
Where youth's ambitious feet might move at large ; 794 *Excursion* 3. 539
So, like a fugitive, whose feet have cleared . . 798 *Excursion* 3. 877
Ah ! if the time must come, in which my feet . 803 *Excursion* 4. 103
At the Redeemer's feet ? " In rueful tone, . . 817 *Excursion* 4. 1100
The cross itself, at whose unconscious feet . . 827 *Excursion* 5. 337
Stretched overhead, and at my pensive feet . . 827 *Excursion* 5. 344
Beneath this turf lie mouldering at our feet : . . 832 *Excursion* 5. 653
So hazardous that feet and hands became . . . 833 *Excursion* 5. 738
Upon the earth beneath his feet ; and spake :— . 836 *Excursion* 5. 902
With wrecks, and trod by feet of young and old . 836 *Excursion* 5. 931
Among the humbler Worthies, at our feet . . . 865 *Excursion* 7. 537
Glows at her feet, and all the gloomy rocks . . 868 *Excursion* 7. 721
Measuring the soil beneath their happy feet . . 869 *Excursion* 7. 776
Naked, and coloured like the soil, the feet . . 879 *Excursion* 8. 354
Are scattered at the feet of Man—like flowers. . 887 *Excursion* 9. 240
That our feet are not slow ; . . . . S.3. 440 **Said red-ribboned* 16
Where Achilles swift of feet . . . . S.3. 442 *Harmodius* 13
Sparkle about the feet of wanton boys. . . . K.8. 252 *Recluse* 1.1.559

Feign. Shall feign a sudden illness, and the Girl, 59 *Bord.* 1185
The voiceless Form he chose to feign, ... 159 *Green Linnet* 39
I feign not ; witness that unwelcome shock . . 367 **As indignation* 9
Above what rules can teach, or fancy feign ; . . 792 *Excursion* 3. 434

Feigned. And yet he with no feigned delight . . 194 *Ruth* 157
In Liberty's behalf. Fears, true or feigned, . . 442 *Ecc. Sonn.* 3. 11. 3

Feigned—*continued.*
" Nay, nay, I come with semblance feigned . . 542 *Russ. Fug.* 77
Some with their notes another manner feigned ; . 558 *Cuck. and Night.* 74
There was a time when whatsoe'er is feigned . . 688 *Prelude* 7. 77

Feignings. And transient feignings with plain truth 170 *Rural Ill.* 33

Feigns. A scene more fair than what the Grecian feigns . . . . 20 *Desc. Sk.* 573

Felicities. Quench those felicities whose light I find 267 **As the* 11
Feed it 'mid Nature's old felicities, ... 388 *Trosachs* 7

Felicity. Without another link to my felicity." . 140 *Arm. Lady* 60
Of Britain's calm felicity and power ! . . . . 219 **This Height* 34
Of glory, and felicity, and love, ... 331 *Ode : Thanks.* 137
Through marvellous felicity of skill, ... 357 *Aquap.* 285
Felicity that only can be given . . . . . . 628 **Deign, Sovereign* 7
Felicity, in Grecian song renowned ; . . . . 701 *Prelude* 8. 135
And only reasonable felicity. . . . . 791 *Excursion* 3. 366

Fell. *See* **Cross-fell.**
And the last sunbeam fell on Bayard's eye ; . . 16 *Desc. Sk.* 300
Fell where the blue flood rippled into white ; . . 21 *Desc. Sk.* 627
Down fell in straggling locks his thin grey hair ; . 24 *Guilt* 7
He fell, and without sense or motion lay ; . . . 26 *Guilt* 89
My father's substance fell into decay : . . . . 28 *Guilt* 229
I could not pray :—through tears that fell in showers . . . . 28 *Guilt* 242
Meanwhile the storm fell heavy on the woods ; . 50 *Bord.* 707
With deafening noise,—the benediction fell . . 51 *Bord.* 747
When such a sudden weakness fell upon me, . . 53 *Bord.* 891
Each word of that unhappy letter fell . . . . 66 *Bord.* 1600
Was, I believed, prime Agent. The wind fell ; . 68 *Bord.* 1692
Fell not the wrath of Heaven upon those traitors ? 70 *Bord.* 1800
And said, " My name is Alice Fell ; . . . . 82 *Alice Fell* 43
The little orphan, Alice Fell ! . . . . . . 82 *Alice Fell* 60
His dam had seen him when he fell, ... 85 *Shepherd-boys* 71
Fell, in his hand he must have grasped, we think, 101 *Brothers* 402
Then fell upon thee. Day by day passed on, . . 136 *Michael* 343
Ere the night fell :—with morrow's dawn the Boy 137 *Michael* 425
Fell on him, so that he was driven at last . . . 138 *Michael* 446
Fell down and clasped his knees for joy, not uttering word. . . . . 141 *Arm. Lady* 102
Fell with the weight of drops of lead ;— . . . 175 *Waggoner* 1. 157
The voice of tears that fell unseen ; . . . . 176 *Waggoner* 1. 228
Mount to the ridge of Nathdale Fell ; . . . . 180 *Waggoner* 4. 37
The rain came heavily and fell in floods ; . . . 195 *Resolution* 2
This Beast not unobserved by Nature fell ; . . 203 *Hart-leap* 163
Fell round him in the grove of Academe, . . . 212 *Dion* 10
Panting for glory as he fell ; . . . . 223 *Wishing-gate* 23
The little sprinkling of cold earth that fell . . 234 *Power of Sound* 156
And the blows fell with heavier weight . . . 238 *P. B.* 194
As gently on his side he fell ; . . . . . . 241 *P. B.* 431
Fell at the sight from Peter's tongue ; . . . . 241 *P. B.* 453
And fast they fell, a plenteous shower ! . . . 247 *P. B.* 962
Close to the Ass's feet she fell ; . . . . . 247 *P. B.* 1013
On Bard and Hero clamorously fell. . . . . 255 *Detraction* 8
Fell round the path of Milton, in his hand . . 260 **Scorn not* 12
In wrath) fell headlong from the fields of air, . . 260 **From the dark* 6
Dark and more dark the shades of evening fell ; . 262 **Dark and* 1
Night fell I heard, or seemed to hear, ... 285 *Grave of Burns* 80
Their habitation shook ;—it fell, ... 298 *Brownie's Cell* 23
That day the Tyrant fell: . . . . 300 *Cora Linn* 48
To work against themselves such fell despite : . 308 **One might* 11
And Hope was maddened by the drops that fell . 311 **Who rises* 37
To you who fell, and you whom slaughter spared 326 **Intrepid sons* 12
Though from the same grim turret fell . . . . 334 **In Bruges* 11
And downward by the skirt of Greenside fell, . . 353 *Aquap.* 48
The dew whose moisture fell in gentle drops . . 354 *Aquap.* 134
Sleep fell upon the air, and stilled the ocean: . . 371 *Eg. Maid* 144
Leaf-scattering winds ; and hoar-frost sprinklings fell . . . . 394 **No more* 27
Fell on him, with the sudden thought . . . . 405 *White Doe* 868
Among the wastes of Rylstone Fell, ... 409 *White Doe* 1164
The guardian lance, as Francis fell, ... 412 *White Doe* 1487
Fell on thy tomb ; but emulative power . . . 425 *Ecc. Sonn.* 1. 27. 3
Issues the master Mind, at whose fell swoop . . 425 *Ecc. Sonn.* 1. 28. 7
Fell suddenly upon my Spirit—cast . . . . 477 *Long Meg* 2
Of slumber—shrieking back she fell, ... 479 *Somnamb.* 133
Their first look—blinded as tears fell in showers 517 *Pun. Death* 1. 13
With such fell mastery that a man may dare . . 518 *Pun. Death* 4. 2
As a chance sunbeam from his memory fell . . 528 **Those breathing* 102
If gloom fell on me, swift was my escape ; . . 532 **Once I* 27
And Harry's flesh it fell away ; . . . . . . 537 *Goody Blake* 117
The tangled covert fell. . . . . 544 *Russ. Fug.* 272
Fell the whole Fabric to the ground ; . . . . 550 *Hermit's Cell* 2. 26
He fell again into his sorrows old ; . . . . . 564 *Troilus* 128
Fell on the ground ; and the small mountain birds, 566 *Cumb. Beg.* 19
On whom the duty fell (for at that time . . . 575 *Chiabrera* 8. 2
On his pale horse shall fell Consumption go. . . 617 *Desc.Sk.Quarto* 791
Where Machination her fell soul resigns, . . . 617 *Desc.Sk.Quarto* 796
On the closed eyes of young Endymion fell, . . 630 [?] **O Moon* 12
Oh, with what echoes on the board they fell ! . 640 *Prelude* 1. 526
That fell in ruins round me. Oh, what joy . . 655 *Prelude* 3. 427
No lower than I fell. I did not love, ... 656 *Prelude* 3. 493
Exposed on the bare fell, were scattered love, . 678 *Prelude* 6. 235
Among Tartarian wilds—fell short, far short, . . 688 *Prelude* 7. 84
Fell flatter than a cagèd parrot's note, ... 688 *Prelude* 7. 100
Fell from me in my own despite. But now . . 726 *Prelude* 10. 544
And the errors into which I fell, betrayed . . 731 *Prelude* 11. 287
Fell under the dominion of a taste . . . . . 735 *Prelude* 12. 90
Hard by, soon after that fell deed was wrought, . 737 *Prelude* 12. 239
And on the melancholy beacon, fell . . . . 738 *Prelude* 12. 265
Fell like a flash, and lo ! as I looked up, . . . 746 *Prelude* 14. 39

Felt—*continued.*
If high the transport, great the joy I felt . . . 648 *Prelude* 2. 410
A higher language, say that now I felt . . . . 650 *Prelude* 3. 100
And spread them with a wider creeping ; felt . . 650 *Prelude* 3. 115
Have felt, and every man alive can guess ? . . 659 *Prelude* 4. 45
At least not felt ; and restoration came . . . 660 *Prelude* 4. 156
Nor less do I remember to have felt, ... 662 *Prelude* 4. 231
On what he might himself have seen or felt. . . 665 *Prelude* 4. 439
When Contemplation, like the night-calm felt . 665 *Prelude* 5. 1
Far stronger, now, grew the desire I felt . . . 667 *Prelude* 5. 115
Nor have I pitied him ; but rather felt . . . 668 *Prelude* 5. 149
I saw, or heard, or felt, was but a stream . . . 686 *Prelude* 6. 743
As from a distance ; heard, and saw, and felt, . 686 *Prelude* 6. 768
Since I had felt in heart and soul the shock . . 688 *Prelude* 7. 66
I mused, and thought, and felt, in solitude. . . 694 *Prelude* 7. 485
Yet rich in beauty, beauty that was felt. . . . 701 *Prelude* 8. 163
I felt his presence in his own domain, ... 703 *Prelude* 8. 257
But something must have felt. Call ye these appearances— . . . . 703 *Prelude* 8. 293
When everywhere a vital pulse was felt, . . . 706 *Prelude* 8. 480
The human nature unto which I felt . . . . 708 *Prelude* 8. 608
Affecting more emotion than I felt ; . . . . 710 *Prelude* 9. 73
And felt through every nook of town and field. . 712 *Prelude* 9. 180
I felt most deeply in what world I was, . . . 719 *Prelude* 10. 64
Him who too boldly trusted them, I felt . . . 720 *Prelude* 10. 181
Of her composure, felt that agony, ... 723 *Prelude* 10. 382
Death-like, of treacherous desertion, felt . . . 724 *Prelude* 10. 414
As I advanced, all that I saw or felt . . . . 726 *Prelude* 10. 553
Felt deeply, but not thoroughly understood . . 728 *Prelude* 11. 87
Had felt its power, and mine was both let loose, . 731 *Prelude* 11. 272
Is seen, heard, felt, and caught at every turn, . 732 *Prelude* 11. 339
I felt, observed, and pondered ; did not judge, . 737 *Prelude* 12. 188
To speak, what I myself have known and felt ; . 740 *Prelude* 13. 13
Of human life. I felt that the array . . . . 744 *Prelude* 13. 287
For so it seemed, felt by the starry heavens. . 747 *Prelude* 14. 62
Felt, that the history of a Poet's mind . . . 752 *Prelude* 14. 412
Of earth and sky. But he had felt the power . 759 *Excursion* 1. 191
Nature was at his heart as if he felt, ... 760 *Excursion* 1. 264
No piteous revolutions had he felt, ... 761 *Excursion* 1. 359
Who, in her worst distress, had ofttimes felt . . 770 *Excursion* 1. 935
We sate on that low bench : and now we felt, . 771 *Excursion* 1. 960
Their rights acknowledging he felt for all. . . . 772 *Excursion* 2. 47
He neither felt encouragement nor hope : . . . 775 *Excursion* 2. 286
So much I felt the awfulness of life, ... 780 *Excursion* 2. 555
I saw not, but I felt that it was there. . . . 784 *Excursion* 2. 872
Incalculably distant ; so, I felt . . . . . . 795 *Excursion* 3. 663
I felt : the transformation I perceived, . . . 796 *Excursion* 3. 717
I felt their invitation ; and resumed . . . . 797 *Excursion* 3. 760
Will conscience prey.—Feebly must they have felt 798 *Excursion* 3. 850
Whose shades have never felt the encroaching axe, 799 *Excursion* 3. 916
And felt, deeply as living man could feel. . . . 808 *Excursion* 4. 474
Exemplified by mysteries, that were felt . . . 812 *Excursion* 4. 740
Why ?—for this very reason that they felt. . . 815 *Excursion* 4. 925
Of passion : whatsoe'er be felt or feared, . . . 816 *Excursion* 4. 1021
—Yes, you have felt, and may not cease to feel. . 818 *Excursion* 4. 1151
With such memorials, I have sometimes felt, . . 848 *Excursion* 6. 636
To shake the burthen off ? Ah ! there was felt, . 849 *Excursion* 6. 718
Or less benign than that which I had felt . . 854 *Excursion* 6. 1056
Felt to the centre of that heavenly calm . . . 867 *Excursion* 7. 641
The hoary grandsire felt himself enriched ; . . 867 *Excursion* 7. 660
A not unnatural longing felt, ... S.3. 431 **The Scottish* 5
Which the poor broom no sooner felt . . . . S.3. 431**The Scottish* 19
The tyrant felt their arm sublime. . . . . . S.3. 442 *Harmodius* 20
The illusion strengthening as he gazed, he felt . K.8. 237 *Recluse* 1. 1. 36
Have felt it, not the happy Quires of Spring, . . K.8. 243 *Recluse* 1.1.235
Which I have felt this day. An awful voice, . . K.8. 245 *Recluse* 1.1.318
Done truly there, or felt, of solid good . . . K.8. 247 *Recluse* 1.1.405
That sweeten labour, make it seen and felt . . K.8. 249 *Recluse* 1.1.468
Be privileged to speak as I have felt . . . . K.8. 255 *Recluse* 1.1.701
Female. The female with a meeker charm succeeds, 6 *Ev. Wk.* 224
Strong terror checks the female peasant's sighs, . 11 *Desc. Sk.* 65
And start the astonished shades at female eyes. . 11 *Desc. Sk.* 66
And female cries. Their course they thither bent, 33 *Guilt* 467
Through the pure light of female eyes . . . . 112 **How rich* 20
Had done him female service, not alone . . . 133 *Michael* 154
A female voice :—" Whoe'er you be, ... 176 *Waggoner* 1. 219
To female hands the treasures were resigned ; . 264 **Lady ! I* 9
We had a female Passenger who came . . . . 305 **We had* 1
Of a fair female train— . . . . 324 *Ode 1814* 58
Yet still the female bosom lent, ... 390 *Highland Broach* 41
Of female patience winning firm repose ; . . . 395 *White Doe : Ded.* 50
Stands at the Bar, absolved by female eyes . . 442 *Ecc. Sonn.* 3. 11. 6
Of lofty station, female goodness walks, . . . 539 **Lady ! a* 46
With help from female hands, that proudly strove 546 **Oft is* 14
Twice over with a male and female voice. . . . 650 *Prelude* 3. 56
There, allegoric shapes, female or male, . . . 689 *Prelude* 7. 163
Thrilled by some female vendor's scream, belike . 690 *Prelude* 7. 182
Domestic severings, female fortitude . . . . 713 *Prelude* 9. 271
Rejoicing o'er a female in the midst, ... 716 *Prelude* 9. 460
The female and her garments vexed and tossed . 738 *Prelude* 12. 260
Of female softness shall his life be full, . . . 749 *Prelude* 14. 229
A high-prized plume which female Beauty wears . 840 *Excursion* 6. 123
For in that female infant's name he heard . . 867 *Excursion* 7. 669
Not, doubtless, without help of female taste . . 882 *Excursion* 8. 541
And female care.—" A blessed lot is yours ! " . . 882 *Excursion* 8. 542
Or to Andates, female Power ! who gave . . . 894 *Excursion* 9. 708
As Fancy's snare for female vanity, ... S.3. 436 **The doubt* 147
Females. Of nun-like females, with soft motion, glide ! . . . . 334 **Bruges I* 14
Feminine. Suffused with something of a feminine hue ; . . . . 834 *Excursion* 5. 782
Feminine—*continued.*
With feminine allurement soft and fair, . . . 881 *Excursion* 8. 460
And grace of feminine humanity, ... S.3. 437 **The doubt* 189
Fen. Flings o'er the fen that ponderous knell— . 238 *P. B.* 214
'Tis not a bitttern of the fen ; . . . . . . 243 *P. B.* 617
To barren heath, bleak moor, and quaking fen, . 298 *Brownie's Cell* 1
England hath need of thee : she is a fen . . . 307 **Milton ! thou* 2
Fence. *See* **Hawthorn-fence.**
A fence far stretched into the shallow lake, . . 3 *Ev. Wk.* 42
Where leafy shades fence off the blustering gale, . 6 *Ev. Wk.* 234
Yet, where the guardian fence is wound, . . . 154 *Flower Garden* 25
Of manners, like its viewless fence, ... 154 *Flower Garden* 47
No screen, no fence could I discover ; . . . . 199 *Thorn* 178
From mind and spirit, grudge a short-lived fence. 280 *Plea for Auth.* 8
" Her birth was heathen ; but a fence . . . . 372 *Eg. Maid* 229
Sure guidance, ere a ceremonial fence . . . . 436 *Ecc. Sonn.* 2. 30. 7
Your birthright is a fence . . . . 526 **The soaring* 42
The fence where that aspiring shrub looked out . 763 *Excursion* 1. 452
At evening, from behind the garden fence . . . 764 *Excursion* 1. 528
And well remember, o'er that fence she looked, . 766 *Excursion* 1. 692
A guardian planted to fence off the blast, . . . 866 *Excursion* 7. 613
The stately fence accompanied our steps ; . . . 881 *Excursion* 8. 454
Fenced. By reason fenced from winds that sigh . 190 **Lyre ! though* 11
The wide earth's storehouse fenced about . . . 217 *Enterprise* 153
With green hills fenced, with ocean's murmur lulled ; " . . . . 254 *Dyer* 6
Of things, has fenced this fairest spot on earth. . 284 *Departure* 18
Part fenced by man, part by a rugged steep . . 387 **Part fenced* 1
Wherein were fixed the iron pales that fenced . 696 *Prelude* 7. 606
Fenced round with glittering laurel ; or in that . 832 *Excursion* 5. 644
Fend. *See* **Weather-fend.**
Fended. *See* **Weather-fended.**
Fens. 'Mid reedy fens wide-spread and marshes drear, 431 *Ecc. Sonn.* 2. 13. 7
Among the mountains, fens which might be drained, K.8. 227 **I will* 103
Ferment. Like spectres,—ferment silent and sublime ! . . . . 707 *Prelude* 8. 572
Of universal ferment ; mildest men . . . . 712 *Prelude* 9. 162
For strife and ferment in the minds of men ; . . 873 *Excursion* 7. 1010
Fermentation. The fermentation, and the vernal heat 660 *Prelude* 4. 103
Fermenting. That huge fermenting mass of human-kind . . . . 696 *Prelude* 7. 621
Ferments. And alien storms with home-bred ferments claim . . . . 438 *Ecc. Sonn.* 2. 38. 7
Fermor. Did Fermor live and die. . . . . . 576 *Cenotaph* 6
Fermor's. When FERMOR'S race is run ; . . . . 582 **O for a* 3
Fern. And on these barren rocks, with fern and heath, ... 23 *Yew-tree* 28
In a dry nook where fern the floor bestrows . . 27 *Guilt* 161
Whirred from among the fern beneath our feet, . 61 *Bord.* 1286
Forth-startled from the fern where she lay couched ; 80 **Loving she* 16
Among the fern or in the gorse ; . . . . . 128 *Idiot Boy* 220
Fair ferns and flowers, and chiefly that tall fern, . 149 **A narrow* 33
Like yon TUFT OF FERN ; . . . . 163 *Hint* 24
Through beds of matted fern, and tangled thickets, 185 *Nutting* 15
The dogs are stretched among the mountain fern. 201 *Hart-leap* 24
Winding away between the fern. . . . . . 244 *P. B.* 680
A stirring in a brake of fern ; . . . . . . 491 *Fidelity* 6
With plenteous store of heath and withered fern, 547 **Rude is* 19
Clothed in the sunshine of the withering fern ; . 675 *Prelude* 6. 11
Or canopy of yet unwithered fern, ... 687 *Prelude* 7. 34
Shrouded with willow-flowers and plumy fern. . 763 *Excursion* 1. 462
Into bright verdure, between fern and gorse, . . 793 *Excursion* 3. 534
How often I have marked a plumy fern . . . S.3. 434 **The doubt* 67
Thy living chaplet of fresh flowers and fern, . . S.3. 437 **The doubt* 201
Fern-brake. While 'mid the fern-brake sleeps the doe, 479 *Somnamb.* 91
Fern-clad. In the rough fern-clad park, the herded deer . . . . 3 *Ev. Wk.* 47
Ferns. Fair ferns and flowers, and chiefly that tall fern, ... 149 **A narrow* 33
Fern-thatched. Of fern-thatched hut on heathy moor : 390 *Highland Broach* 22
Ferny. Dwarf willows gliding, and by ferny brake. 377 *Duddon* 4. 8
Ferocious. Sweetly ferocious, round his native walks, 5 *Ev. Wk.* 146
No trace of a ferocious air, ... 166 *Danish Boy* 46
Revenge, and all ferocious thoughts were dead : . 205 *Brougham* 166
Ferocity. Nay, you have had the worst. Ferocity 69 *Bord.* 1784
Lives black with guilt, ferocity it calms. . . . 424 *Ecc. Sonn.* 1. 24. 14
Ferry. Mocking the Man that keeps the ferry ; . . 179 *Waggoner* 3. 123
Ferryman. Or shout that wakes the ferry-man from sleep, ... 9 *Ev. Wk.* 370
For the old Ferryman ; to the shout the rocks . 658 *Prelude* 4. 13
Fertile. With rocks and gloomy woods her fertile fields : . . . . 20 *Desc. Sk.* 570
All that the fertile valley shields ; . . . . . 214 *Kirkstone* 28
Upon this soft and fertile nook ? . . . . . 240 *P. B.* 379
Ye Apennines ! with all your fertile vales . . . 352 *Aquap.* 1
Amid a fertile region green with wood . . . . 392 *Daniel* 1
And aery harvests crown the fertile lea. . . . 429 *Ecc. Sonn.* 2. 3. 14
And bright, and fertile, furnished in itself . . 777 *Excursion* 2. 356
Rivers and fertile plains, and sounding shores,— . 812 *Excursion* 4. 719
This fertile valley ! Not a house but seems . . 828 *Excursion* 5. 412
In fertile pastures—was beheld with eyes . . . 872 *Excursion* 7. 949
These fertile fields, that recompense your pains ; . 895 *Excursion* 9. 744
To wander with us through the fertile vales, . . 895 *Excursion* 9. 778
Fertilise. To fertilise some other ground. . . . 532 †*Float. Isl.* 28
To fertilise the whole Egyptian plain. . . . . 684 *Prelude* 6. 616
Fertilising. A fertilising moisture,' said the Swain, 835 *Excursion* 5. 872
Fervent. Deem rather that the fervent Youth, who saw . . . . 122 *V. and J.* 57
So speaking, and by fervent love endowed . . 209 *Laod.* 7
A fervent, not ungovernable, love. . . . . . 210 *Laod.* 76
Within, a fervent Methodist . . . . . . 247 *P. B.* 944

Fields—*continued.*
They from their fields can see the countenance . 309 *Men of Kent* 6
Were the wide fields, the hamlets heaped with slain. 317 **The martial* 8
Or in the fields of empyrean light. . . . . . 317 **Brave Schill* 4
'Mid fields familiarised to human speech ?— . . 336 *Staub-bach* 4
O'er blooming fields and gushing springs . . . 338 **Meek Virgin* 28
As that of the sweet fields and meadows green . 339 *Schwytz* 7
Twice-glorified fields ! if in sadness I turned . . 345 *Stanzas: Simplon* 15
Ere, from accustomed paths, familiar fields, . . 353 *Aquap.* 33
Ah ! not for emerald fields alone, ... 375 **The Minstrels* 49
O'er twilight fields the autumnal gossamer ? . . 378 *Duddon* 11. 14
Hail to the fields—with Dwellings sprinkled o'er, 379 *Duddon* 13. 1
Announces to the thirsty fields a boon . . . . 381 *Duddon* 19. 13
The sun shines bright ; the fields are gay . . . 396 *White Doe* 3
Of quiet to the neighbouring fields ; . . . . 406 *White Doe* 948
In that fair Creature whom the fields . . . . 416 *White Doe* 1873
Who, as the fields and woods have given them birth, 421 *Ecc. Sonn.* 1. 11. 11
From fields laid waste, from house and home devoured . . . . 426 *Ecc. Sonn.* 1. 32. 3
In fields that rival Cressy and Poictiers— . . . 432 *Ecc. Sonn.* 2. 16. 6
Aid, glorious Martyrs, from your fields of light, . 437 *Ecc. Sonn.* 2. 36. 1
From fields where good men walk, or bowers wherein they rest. . . . . 438 *Ecc. Sonn.* 2. 39. 14
Fields which they love, and paths they daily trod, 441 *Ecc. Sonn.* 3. 6. 10
'Mid fruitful fields that ring with jocund toil, . . 463 **Why should the* 5
Through all the long green fields has spread, . . 481 *Tables Turned* 7
The sylvan slopes with corn-clad fields . . . 498 **The sylvan* 1
Of Worldlings revelling in the fields . . . . 499 **This Lawn* 5
Fields gaily sown when promises were cheap.— . 505 *Warning* 139
From the Vale's peace which all her fields partake, 521 *Epist. Beaumont* 2
You, Muses, books, fields, liberty, and rest ! . . 529 **Those breathing* 125
Whose fancy had a thousand fields to skim ; . . 532 **Once I* 10
To him, their verdure from the fields ; . . . . 533 **Blest is* 58
And to the fields his road would take ; . . . 537 *Goody Blake* 70
Among the dwellers in the silent fields . . . . 540 *Grace Darl.* 1
And bore her toward the fields of France, . . . 544 *Russ. Fug.* 245
Of those belovèd fields she oft . . . . . . 544 *Russ. Fug.* 249
Of fields with rural works, of hill and dale, . . 567 *Cumb. Beg.* 49
Of the fields, he collected that bloom, when a boy ; 569 *Farmer* 10
His fields seemed to know what their Master was doing ; . . . . 569 *Farmer* 18
The fields better suited the ease of his soul : . . 569 *Farmer* 22
He strayed through the fields like an indolent wight, ... 569 *Farmer* 23
He thinks of the fields he so often hath mown, . 571 *Farmer* 83
From the most gentle creature nursed in fields . 584 *Ch. Lamb* 23
Thou wert a scorner of the fields, my Friend, . . 585 *Ch. Lamb* 50
But more in show than truth ; and from the fields, 585 *Ch. Lamb* 51
The Winds come to me from the fields of sleep, . 588 *Immortality* 28
Bosom'd in gloomy woods, her golden fields, . . 614 *Desc.Sk.Quarto* 681
Thy reddening orchards, and thy fields of gold ; . 615 *Desc.Sk.Quarto* 705
Her sons no more in listed fields advance . . . 619 *School Ex.* 57
From the green fields, and from yon azure sky. . 632 *Prelude* 1. 4
Recorded : to the open fields I told . . . . 632 *Prelude* 1. 50
Voluptuously through fields and rural walks, . . 635 *Prelude* 1. 251
The sandy fields, leaping through flowery groves . 636 *Prelude* 1. 293
Of sea or sky, no colours of green fields ; . . . 638 *Prelude* 1. 397
Mine was it in the fields both day and night, . . 638 *Prelude* 1. 423
So beautiful among the pleasant fields . . . . 639 *Prelude* 1. 502
From under Esthwaite's splitting fields of ice . . 640 *Prelude* 1. 539
Of rivers, woods, and fields. The passion yet . 642 *Prelude* 2. 5
And as I paced alone the level fields . . . . 650 *Prelude* 3. 93
And labourers going forth to till the fields. . . 663 *Prelude* 4. 332
One of those open fields, which, shaped like ears, 672 *Prelude* 5. 433
A daily wanderer among woods and fields . . . 674 *Prelude* 5. 587
So reverenced by us both. O'er paths and fields 678 *Prelude* 6. 230
Of peace and self-command. Of rivers, fields, . 679 *Prelude* 6. 264
Spread round my steps like sunshine o'er green fields. . . . . 686 *Prelude* 6. 778
Or daisies swarming through the fields of June. . 696 *Prelude* 7. 593
Among whose happy fields I had grown up . . 725 *Prelude* 10. 525
Not in Utopia,—subterranean fields,— . . . 729 *Prelude* 11. 140
Piping on boughs, or sporting on fresh fields, . . 735 *Prelude* 12. 35
Into the fields, impatient for the sight . . . . 738 *Prelude* 12. 290
Fields with their rural works ; recalled to mind . 741 *Prelude* 13. 103
Sing notes of greeting to strange fields or groves, 742 *Prelude* 13. 135
That gone, we are as dust.—Behold the fields . 748 *Prelude* 14. 170
That is collected among woods and fields, . . . 750 *Prelude* 14. 314
Elysian, Fortunate Fields—like those of old . . 755 *Recluse* 1. 1. 801
Must hear Humanity in fields and groves . . . 755 *Recluse* 1. 1. 829
A lone Enthusiast, and among the fields. . . . 761 *Excursion* 1. 348
Two blighting seasons, when the fields were left . 764 *Excursion* 1. 537
Or wander here and there among the fields. . . 765 *Excursion* 1. 584
About the fields I wander, knowing this . . . 768 *Excursion* 1. 765
Hath been the fields, the roads, and rural lanes, . 772 *Excursion* 2. 29
A quiet treeless nook, with two green fields, . . 776 *Excursion* 2. 337
Though not of want : the little fields, made green 776 *Excursion* 2. 341
That opened from the enclosure of green fields . 779 *Excursion* 2. 495
Her fields of carnage, and polluted air. . . . 798 *Excursion* 3. 834
Which Nature gently gave, in woods and fields ; . 805 *Excursion* 4. 275
" Chaldean Shepherds, ranging trackless fields, . 811 *Excursion* 4. 694
And, all day long, moisten these flowery fields ! ' 812 *Excursion* 4. 752
To range her blooming bowers, and spacious fields, 819 *Excursion* 4. 1194
And its small lot of life-supporting fields, . . . 822 *Excursion* 5. 2
In tournament, upon the fields of France. . . . 825 *Excursion* 5. 184
Thus, when in changeful April fields are white . 830 *Excursion* 5. 531
In the sweet spring that lurks 'mid yon green fields ; 833 *Excursion* 5. 688
There, or within the compass of her fields, . . 833 *Excursion* 5. 705
" When to those shining fields our notice first . 833 *Excursion* 5. 729

Fields—*continued.*
And by what help had gained those distant fields. 834 *Excursion* 5. 757
Of prosperous fortune. On the fields he looked . 842 *Excursion* 6. 238
His flock he slighted : his paternal fields . . . 855 *Excursion* 6. 1103
The cultured fields ; and up the heathy waste, . 858 *Excursion* 7. 47
His fields, or mountains by the heath-cock ranged, 859 *Excursion* 7. 158
Had summer scorched the fields ; not twice had fallen, ... 861 *Excursion* 7. 248
That flashed uncouthly through the woods and fields. . . . . 869 *Excursion* 7. 765
Nor left unstigmatized those fatal fields . . . 869 *Excursion* 7. 798
Its cities, temples, fields, its awful power, . . . 871 *Excursion* 7. 898
And shook their tenants out into the fields, . . 873 *Excursion* 7. 1026
And gaiety of cultivated fields. . . . . . . 879 *Excursion* 8. 374
He may be roused. This Boy the fields produce : 880 *Excursion* 8. 425
The rustic Boy, who walks the fields, untaught ; . 886 *Excursion* 9. 162
Should open while they range the richer fields . 886 *Excursion* 9. 174
The fields of earth with gratitude and hope ; . . 888 *Excursion* 9. 249
Like fields of ice rent by the polar wind, . . . 889 *Excursion* 9. 340
In majesty presiding over fields . . . . . 892 *Excursion* 9. 576
These fertile fields, that recompense your pains ; . 895 *Excursion* 9. 744
The dewy fields ; but ere the Vicar's door . . . 895 *Excursion* 9. 769
On Armath's pleasant fields. And now they came, K.8. 225 **I will* 51
The fields and mountains, not alone for this . . K.8. 230 **I will* 206
His native vale and patrimonial fields . . . . K.8. 231 **I will* 212
Warm woods, and sunny hills, and fresh green fields, K.8. 240 *Recluse* 1. 1. 127
Sent from the mountains or the sheltered fields ; . K.8. 245 *Recluse* 1. 1. 320
Shall speak of what is done among the fields, . . K.8. 247 *Recluse* 1. 1. 404

Field-ward. That field-ward takes her walk with decent steps. . . . . 690 *Prelude* 7. 210

Fiend. Herbert *is* innocent. What fiend could prompt . . . . 71 *Bord.* 1879
Hear me, ye Heavens !—may vengeance haunt the fiend . . . . 75 *Bord.* 2176
Is it a fiend that to a stake . . . . 242 *P. B.* 511
Desperate alternative ! what fiend could dare . 381 *Duddon* 22. 11
To Saint, or Fiend, or to the Godhead whom . . 475 **Here on their* 10
As by the very presence of the Fiend . . . . 843 *Excursion* 6. 349

Fiendish. And fiendish faces, one, two, three, . . 144 *Her Eyes* 23

Fiends. To those infernal fiends ! Now, if the event 64 *Bord.* 1458
An instrument of Fiends. Through me, through me, 76 *Bord.* 2212
Like spiteful Fiends that vanish, crossed . . . 369 *Eg. Maid* 34
By Fiends of aspect more malign ; . . . . . 369 *Eg. Maid* 35
From wandering fiends of air receive a yoke, . . 465 **Pastor and* 12
Fiends in your aspect, yet beneficent . . . . 518 *Pun. Death* 6. 3
Romance of giants, chronicle of fiends, . . . 759 *Excursion* 1. 180

Fierce. And the fierce torrent at the flashes broad . 13 *Desc. Sk.* 181
Snapped fierce to make a morsel of his head : . 44 *Bord.* 414
Of fierce barbarians into Ministers . . . . . 48 *Bord.* 611
That a fierce storm o'ertook us, worn with travel, 50 *Bord.* 697
He bribed me with his gold, and looked so fierce. 77 *Bord.* 2246
The post-boy drove with fierce career, ... 82 *Alice Fell* 1
And while around it storm as fierce seemed troubling earth and air, ... 91 *Poet's Dream* 7
Whose fierce wrath the Girl had braved ; . . . 93 *Westmoreland Girl* 18
And the fierce sharp-toothed pike. . . . . . 94 *Westmoreland Girl* 52
A fierce and dreadful hunter he ; . . . . . 129 *Idiot Boy* 328
Tumultuous harmony and fierce ! . . . . . 186 **O Nightingale* 4
Of the fierce wind, while mid-day lightnings prowl 263 *Storm* 4
So styled by those fierce Britons, pleased to see . 272 *Lady E. B.* 3
Or a fierce impress issues with its foil . . . . 275 **While poring* 11
I shiver, Spirit fierce and bold, ... 284 *Grave of Burns* 1
Thy fierce beginnings, softened and subdued . . 290 *Kilchurn* 40
Of your fierce war, may ken the glittering lance, . 309 *Men of Kent* 7
The fierce Tornado sleeps within Thy courts— . 328 *Ode 1815* 98
Fierce as a flood-gate bursting at midnight . . 330 *Ode : Thanks.* 79
And shrill and fierce in accent !—Fear it not : . 333 *Fish-women* 9
From the fierce aspect of this River, throwing . 336 *Aar* 1
By the fierce waves, a flower in marble graven. . 371 *Eg. Maid* 126
Puts, when the high-swoln Flood runs fierce and wild, ... 378 *Duddon* 9. 10
Could gentleness be scorned by those fierce Men, . 389 *Sound of Mull* 11
Is John de Clapham, that fierce Esquire, . . . 399 *White Doe* 249
With the fierce tempest, while, within the round . 425 *Ecc. Sonn.* 1. 27. 10
No—some fierce Maniac hath usurped her name ; 439 *Ecc. Sonn.* 2. 44. 11
To opposites and fierce extremes her life,— . . 443 *Ecc. Sonn.* 3. 11. 12
'Mid your fierce shock like men afraid to die ? . 469 **The feudal* 12
" Though fierce the assault, and shattered the defence, ... 471 **Despond who* 2
To call thee so ?) or symbol of fierce deeds . . 472 **The captive* 10
What Summer here escapes not, the fierce wave, . 474 **Hope smiled* 3
Of fierce vindictive song. . . . . 499 **Departing summer* 42
In fierce solstitial power, ... 502 *Seasons* 6
When the fierce orbs abate their glare ;— . . . 526 **The soaring* 37
The lightning, the fierce wind, and trampling waves. 579 *Peele Castle* 52
—Fierce comes the river down ; the crashing wood 606 *Desc.Sk.Quarto* 211
Uncertain thro' his fierce uncultur'd soul . . . 612 *Desc.Sk.Quarto* 546
Where fierce the rays of woe collected burn. . . 613 *Desc.Sk.Quarto* 647
Fierce, moody, patient, venturous, modest, shy ; . 672 *Prelude* 5. 415
Bound to the fierce Metropolis. From his throne 718 *Prelude* 10. 11
As fierce a successor ; the tide retreats . . . 719 *Prelude* 10. 81
Brooding above the fierce confederate storm . . 755 *Recluse* 1. 1. 831
By a fierce tempest shaken, soon resumed . . . 840 *Excursion* 6. 145
As the fierce eagle fastens on the lamb ? . . . 849 *Excursion* 6. 748
Stormy and fierce, the Maid of Arc withdrew . . S.3. 436 **The doubt* 168
The reverence by the fierce Anubis lost. . . . L.1. 89 *Juvenal* 1. 26

Fiercely. And fiercely swept the marble floor,— . 213 *Dion* 70
Whom onset, fiercely urged at Jove's command, . 265 **When haughty* 13

Filled—*continued.*
St. Denis, filled with royal tombs, or the Church of Notre Dame? . . . . 92 *Poet's Dream* 24
Between the tropics filled the steady sail, . . . 96 *Brothers* 50
Filled the funeral basin at Timothy's door; . . . 120 *Childless Father* 10
Arabian fiction never filled the world . . . . 122 *V. and J.* 39
A basket, which they filled with pedlar's wares; . 135 *Michael* 262
And the ancient church was filled with light, . . 144 **Driven in* 54
His heart with sudden joy is filled,— . . . . 177 *Waggoner* 2. 33
Was filled with animated toys, ... 191 *Seq. Beggars* 3
And all the air is filled with pleasant noise of waters. 195 *Resolution* 7
Down the long street, rich goblets filled with wine 213 *Dion* 32
Has filled the laughing vales with welcome flowers. 263 **How clear* 14
Than a forsaken bird's-nest filled with snow . . 277 **Why art* 12
And yet my eyes are filled with tears. . . . . 288 *Highland Girl* 21
Yet filled with ardour and on triumph bent . . 326 **Intrepid sons* 10
Had filled the astonished world with such abuse . 330 *Ode; Thanks.* 96
And filled our hearts with grief for England's shame? . . . . 349 *Val. Dover* 4
Life's cup when almost filled with years, like mine. 355 *Aquap.* 204
And, for a moment, filled that empty Throne. . 365 **Under the* 14
My heart, and filled that heart with conflict strong. 367 **As indignation* 14
Tumultuous noises filled the hall; . . . . . 400 *White Doe* 398
Who, having filled a holy place, ... 416 *White Doe* 1875
So vaunt a throng of Followers, filled with pride 425 *Ecc. Sonn.* 1. 28. 12
Filled with mementos, satiate with its part . . 452 *Ecc. Sonn.* 3. 45. 13
Filled with delight three summer morning hours. 525 *Epist. Beaumont* 269
Till she had filled her apron full. . . . . . 537 *Goody Blake* 84
The Goddess then her lap with sweetmeats fill'd . 620 *Birth of Love* 42
From Belus, filled it to the brim with wine; . . 625 *Æneid* 106
Where, though the shades with cheerfulness were filled, ... 655 *Prelude* 3. 431
The peaceful scene oft filled me with surprise . . 661 *Prelude* 4. 194
Space like a heaven filled up with northern lights, 673 *Prelude* 5. 532
Filled all the woods: the cry of unknown birds; . 685 *Prelude* 6. 713
And life and labour seem but one, I filled . . . 688 *Prelude* 7. 71
Filled with its fray or brawl, how eagerly . . . 693 *Prelude* 7. 436
Into a theatre, whose stage was filled . . . . 711 *Prelude* 9. 94
Of passions and opinions, filled the walls . . . 712 *Prelude* 9. 164
Beat high, and filled the fancy with fair forms, . 712 *Prelude* 9. 207
Worthy of liberty, all spirits filled . . . . . 720 *Prelude* 10. 137
Domestic carnage now filled the whole year . . 723 *Prelude* 10. 356
And ignorance filled up from age to age, . . . 725 *Prelude* 10. 478
Of all this glory filled and satisfied. . . . . 737 *Prelude* 12. 190
But, as the mind was filled with inward light, . 757 *Excursion* 1. 95
Had filled with plenty, and possessed in peace, . 764 *Excursion* 1. 567
Amid the uneasy thoughts which filled my mind, . 770 *Excursion* 1. 948
Filled with vague hopes, he undertook the charge 774 *Excursion* 2. 174
The measure of my soul was filled with bliss, . . 803 *Excursion* 4. 120
Judgments, that filled the land from age to age . 811 *Excursion* 4. 659
And filled the illumined groves with ravishment. 814 *Excursion* 4. 860
Bounty and government, that filled their hearts . 815 *Excursion* 4. 929
She with a numerous issue filled his house, . . 825 *Excursion* 5. 198
Hath gained his noontide height, this churchyard, filled . . . . 830 *Excursion* 5. 534
Of that small town encountering thus, they filled, 845 *Excursion* 6. 465
That Father was, and filled with anxious fear, . 855 *Excursion* 6. 1132
And the whole house seems filled with gaiety. . 856 *Excursion* 6. 1187
That filled her plains, that reached her utmost shores, ... 869 *Excursion* 7. 761
And as a cavern is with darkness fill'd, . . . S. 3. 425 **The rains* 3

Fill'st. But thou, how leisurely thou fill'st thy horn 172 *Infant Daughter* 52

Filling. And filling more and more with crystal light 274 **Such age* 13
Filling from morn to night the heroic scene . . 318 **Is there* 9
Filling the soul with sentiments august— . . . 351 *Des. Stanzas* 80
Filling the church with a lofty voice! . . . . 396 *White Doe* 38
Which, filling, consecrates the human breast. . . 478 **Lonsdale! it* 8
Filling from time to time his "humorous stage" 589 *Immortality* 103
Though filling daily, still was light, compared . 709 *Prelude* 8. 685
With tuneful hum is filling all the air; . . . 765 *Excursion* 1. 597
This office filling, yet by native power . . . 774 *Excursion* 2. 178
Filling a space, else vacant, to exalt . . . . 814 *Excursion* 4. 845

Fillip. And send it with a fillip to its grave. . . 60 *Bord.* 1244

Fills. An idle voice the sabbath region fills . . . 16 *Desc. Sk.* 354
A mighty waste of mist the valley fills, . . . 17 *Desc. Sk.* 408
There where the peal of swelling torrents fills . 18 *Desc. Sk.* 463
Is blithe society, who fills the air . . . . . 80 **Loving she* 13
And then my heart with pleasure fills, ... 187 **I wandered* 23
He fills with his power all their hearts to the brim— 188 *Music* 7
That fills my heart with sadness! . . . . . 302 *Yarrow V.* 8
Aught that more surely by its aspect fills . . . 387 *Manse* 8
Fast the churchyard fills;—anon . . . . . . 396 *White Doe* 31
Fills many a damp obscure recess . . . . . 397 *White Doe* 101
That fills the Soul with unavailing ruth. . . . 419 *Ecc. Sonn.* 1. 4. 14
Fills all the hollow of the sky. . . . . . . 457 **The sun has* 9
Hope wanes with her, while lustre fills . . . . 478 *Somnamb.* 64
Earth fills her lap with pleasures of her own; . . 588 *Immortality* 77
Alike, when first the vales the bittern fills, . . 592 *Ev. Wk. Quarto* 25
When the dread peal of swelling torrents fills . . 612 *Desc.Sk.Quarto* 252
Who fills the mother's breast with innocent milk, 669 *Prelude* 5. 272
And streams, whose murmur fills this hollow vale, 836 *Excursion* 5. 917
The raven croaks, and fills the upper air . . . K.8. 252 *Recluse* 1.1.581

Film. Nor veil, with restless film, his staring eyes. . 273 **While Anna's* 14

Filmy. Far as the last gleam of the filmy train . 511 **Who rashly* 6

Final. Must part; the summons came;—our final leave we took. . . . . 28 *Guilt* 234
I will commit him to this final *Ordeal!*— . . . . 62 *Bord.* 1393
Just as those final words were penned, the sun broke out in power, ... 91 *Poet's Dream* 1
A final portion from his father's hand; . . . 123 *V. and J.* 106

Final—*continued.*
Some nook where they had made their final stand, 150 **When, to* 30
When her long life hath reached its final day: . 305 *Ven. Rep.* 12
That Justice seemed to hear her final knell? . . 311 **Who rises* 34
And final retribution,— . . . . 332 *Ode: Thanks.* 241
Is then the final page before me spread, . . . 350 *Des. Stanzas* 1
His acts, his wrongs, his final sacrifice; . . . 351 *Des. Stanzas* 71
And sorrow of this final truth! . . . . . . 413 *White Doe* 1550
That ever looked to heaven for final rest? . . . 430 *Ecc. Sonn.* 2. 9. 8
Nor be unthanked their final lingerings— . . . 431 *Ecc. Sonn.* 2. 13. 5
When we shall sink to final rest. . . . . . 506 *Lab. Hymn* 32
Leaving the final issue in *His* hands . . . . 519 *Pun. Death* 11. 11
The final polish of the Plasterer's hand. . . . 521 *Epist. Beaumont* 25
The State, as if to stamp the final seal . . . . 718 *Prelude* 10. 31
Our final parting; for from that time forth . . 769 *Excursion* 1. 869
Its final home on earth. What traveller—who— 780 *Excursion* 2. 560
Yet, ere that final resting-place be gained, . . 792 *Excursion* 3. 446
Who, drawing near their final home, and much . 844 *Excursion* 6. 388
As of a final Eminence; though bare . . . . 885 *Excursion* 9. 52
'Tis come, the final hour, ... L.2. 121 *Frag. Æneid* 2. 1

Finally. Their eyes, or minds? or, finally, is yon resplendent vault? . . . . 189 *Star-gazers* 12
Where'er I liked; and finally array . . . . . 259 *Calvert* 7
The shock, and finally secure . . . . . . 407 *White Doe* 1071
'Tis, finally, the Man, who, lifted high, ... 494 *Hap. War.* 65
Failing, we finally shall make accord. . . . . 562 *Cuck.and Night.* 280
Share his chance-gathered meal; and, finally, . 569 *Cumb. Beg.* 195
Twine near their loved Permessus.—Finally, . . 576 *Chiabrera* 9. 14
A different worship. Finally, whate'er . . . 686 *Prelude* 6. 742
Did we appeal; and, finally, beheld . . . . 715 *Prelude* 9. 381
And finally, as sum and crown of all, ... 717 *Prelude* 9. 529
And nothing less), when, finally to close . . . 732 *Prelude* 11. 358
Finally, and above all, O Friend! (I speak . . 750 *Prelude* 14. 321
Perpetual, multitudinous! Finally, ... 876 *Excursion* 8. 142

Find. And ever, as we fondly muse, we find . . . 8 *Ev. Wk.* 317
Could find no refuge from distress . . . . . 9 *Collins* 15
Nought round its darling precincts can he find . 18 *Desc. Sk.* 429
And desolate, "Here you will find a friend!" . 24 *Guilt* 15
How glad he was at length to find some trace . 27 *Guilt* 157
In vain to find a friendly face we try, ... 35 *Guilt* 602
Could find delight to nurse itself so strangely, . 41 *Bord.* 237
Let this old Man find at your hands; poor Leader, 42 *Bord.* 302
Expecting still, I knew not how, to find . . . 45 *Bord.* 434
Thee I adore, and find my rest in faith. . . . 53 *Bord.* 854
Would I could find the old Man and his Daughter. 55 *Bord.* 954
Lady, you'll find your Father at the Convent . . 58 *Bord.* 1135
Might in such neighbourhood find seemly use.— . 60 *Bord.* 1253
Such Minds as find amid their fellow-men . . . 63 *Bord.* 1452
Alive or dead, I'll find him. Alive—perdition! . 71 *Bord.* 1881
The wider space the better—we may find . . . 78 *Bord.* 2307
Much converse do I find in thee, ... 79 **Stay near* 3
—Yet seek him,—and what shall you find in the place? . . . . 80 †*Address: Child* 16
You'll find a task for half a year. . . . . . 85 *Shepherd-boys* 44
An orphan could not find his mother's grave: . . 98 *Brothers* 169
And find elsewhere his business or delight; . . 107 *Indolence* 11
The peace which others seek they find; . . . 110 *Forsaken* 1
Find little to perceive. . . . . 112 **Yes! thou* 8
No peace, no comfort could I find, ... 115 *Last of Flock* 75
Oh find me, prosperous or undone! . . . . 116 *Affl. Marg.* 3
I question things and do not find . . . . . 117 *Affl. Marg.* 68
Her sad approach, and stole away to find, . . . 118 *Maternal Grief* 52
I seem to find them all in thee: . . . . . 121 *EmigrantMother* 88
Find place within his bosom.—Once again . . 124 *V. and J.* 171
I thought to find my lost one here, ... 129 *Idiot Boy* 264
And cannot find her Idiot Boy. . . . . . . 130 *Idiot Boy* 361
Who journey thither find themselves alone . . 131 *Michael* 10
Sometimes when he could find a leisure hour . . 138 *Michael* 440
Learning from him to find a reason . . . . 142 †*Lov. and Lik.* 21
We'll find thy father in the wood. . . . . . 145 *Her Eyes* 98
From the next glance she casts, to find . . . 154 *Flower Garden* 22
Lift me, guide me, till I find . . . . . . 159 **Up with me* 6
Enough for him to find . . . . 162 *Binnorie* 39
And find his way to me, ... 162 **Art thou the* 17
Another *Star-of-Bethlehem* find, ... 164 **Fair Lady* 23
Yet they find among the mountains . . . . 166 *Wand. Jew* 3
In stray gifts to be claimed by whoever shall find; 167 *Stray Pleasures* 28
These find, 'mid ivied abbey-walls, ... 168 *Wren's Nest* 17
Find my wisdom in my bliss; . . . . 172 *Kitten* 122
And, to my soul's content, I find . . . . . 174 *Waggoner* 1. 114
You'll find you've much in little here! . . . 178 *Waggoner* 2. 118
Find, within, a blessed harbour! . . . . . 181 *Waggoner* 4. 170
Your favourite seat of empire find— . . . . 191 *Seq. Beggars* 35
Yet as I left I find them here! . . . . . . 192 *Gipsies* 12
And build a household fire, and find . . . . 193 *Ruth* 77
Could never find him more. . . . . 194 *Ruth* 192
Yet still I persevere, and find them where I may." 197 *Resolution* 126
I could have laughed myself to scorn to find . . 197 *Resolution* 137
In truth, you'd find it hard to say . . . . . 197 *Thorn* 2
Where, save the rugged road, we find . . . . 214 *Kirkstone* 5
And I (as all men may find cause, ... 215 *Kirkstone* 53
Up-caught in whirlwinds, nowhere can find rest. . 217 *Enterprise* 132
Where'er the streams a passage find; . . . . 228 *Devot. Incit.* 4
For joy and rest, albeit to find them only . . . 231 *Clouds* 93
That in the living Creature find on earth a place. 231 **ThegentlestPoet* 38
May in life's daily prospect find, ... 238 *P. B.* 144
May find or there create? . . . . 238 *P. B.* 145
But nature ne'er could find the way . . . . 239 *P. B.* 244
"While yet ye may find mercy;—strive . . . 247 *P. B.* 947
From love that cannot find relief. . . . . . 248 *P. B.* 1080

Fire—*continued.*
For, as reports the dame, whose fire sends up . K.8. 247 *Recluse* 1. 1. 389
Fire-clad. Glances the fire-clad eagle's wheeling form; . . . . 608 *Desc. Sk. Quarto* 339
Fireless. And fireless are the valleys far and wide, 7 *Ev. Wk.* 261
Fire-like. Begin to strike him with a fire-like heat, 702 *Prelude* 8. 236
Fires. As one whose brain habitual frenzy fires . 26 *Guilt* 91
Her fires, that like mysterious pulses beat . . . 123 *V. and J.* 98
All alive with the fires 166 *Stray Pleasures* 14
"What if those bright fires . . . . 226 *Vernal Ode* 40
Her own calm fires?—But list! a voice is near; . 313 **Clouds, lingering* 11
That quench, from hut to palace, lamps and fires, 426 *Ecc. Sonn.* 1. 31. 10
Earlier from cleansing fires, and gains withal . . 429 *Ecc. Sonn.* 2. 3. 4
False fires, that others may be lost. . . . 534 **Blest is* 70
Fall fires—but let us perish heart to heart." . 597 *Ev. Wk. Quarto* 292
Refract in rainbow hues the restless fires! . . 609 *Desc. Sk. Quarto* 391
And laugh with merrier blaze her evening fires; . 615 *Desc. Sk. Quarto* 733
The glimmering fires of Virtue to enlarge, . . . 619 *School Ex.* 81
And wakes anew life's glimmering trembling fires, 619 *School Ex.* 100
What radiant fires were drown'd by day's malignant pow'r, ... 620 **She wept* 12
Go forth and prosper; and, ye purging fires, . . 681 *Prelude* 6. 445
O'er which the smoke of unremitting fires . . . 876 *Excursion* 8. 125
Flung from the body of devouring fires, . . . 894 *Excursion* 9. 703
Fireside. For the whole dale, and one for each fire-side— . . . . 97 *Brothers* 164
Yet not unfit, I deem, for the fireside, ... 131 *Michael* 20
Their hands by the fire-side; perhaps to card 132 *Michael* 106
Than when I heard thee by our own fire-side . . 136 *Michael* 346
The living Beings by your own fire-side, . . . 147 *Joanna* 4
And I, and all who dwell by my fireside, . . . 148 *Joanna* 84
Andrew's whole fire-side is there. . . . . . 157 *Sexton* 12
'Mid grove, and by the calm fireside, ... 168 *Turtledove* 21
Thanks; thou hast snapped a fireside Prisoner's chain, ... 279 **Hark! 'tis* 6
Fireside, the heroic wealth of hall and bower, . 307 **Milton! thou* 4
On fireside listeners, doubting what they hear! . 453 **Calm is the* 15
To season my fireside with personal talk,— . . 488 *Pers. Talk* 2
As impotent fancy prompts, by his fireside, . . 679 *Prelude* 6. 293
The pensive moments by this calm fireside, . . 734 *Prelude* 11. 450
Beyond the allowance of our own fireside, . . . 794 *Excursion* 3. 588
Of the fire-side, or of the open field, . . . K.8. 246 *Recluse* 1. 1. 361
That calm fire-side, it is not even in them, . . K.8. 255 *Recluse* 1. 1. 683
By flames breathed on her from her own fireside. K.8. 275 **These vales* 4
Round fire-side treason-parties *en famille?* . L.1. 97 *Juvenal* 3. 88
Fire-sides. We talk about the dead by our fire-sides. 98 *Brothers* 179
Fireworks. Dimming the stars, and fireworks magical, ... 689 *Prelude* 7. 123
Of play-thing fire-works, that on festal nights . K.8. 251 *Recluse* 1. 1. 558
Fir-grove. A stately Fir-grove, whither I was wont 150 **When, to* 9
I love the fir-grove with a perfect love. 151 **When, to* 87
The fir-grove murmurs with a sea-like sound, . . 151 **When, to* 104
Through that aerial fir-grove, could preserve . K.8. 248 *Recluse* 1. 1. 415
Firm. Spur-clad his nervous feet, and firm his tread; 5 *Ev. Wk.* 148
Oswald, the firm foundation of my life 47 *Bord.* 547
You will be firm: but though we well may trust . 48 *Bord.* 602
On its firm margin, even as from a well, . . . 149 *M. H.* 9
The firm protection she bestows; . . . . . 154 *Flower Garden* 46
Erect his port, and firm his going; . . . . 181 *Waggoner* 4. 148
The reason firm, the temperate will, ... 186 **She was* 25
In that decrepit Man so firm a mind. . . . . 197 *Resolution* 138
Enjoins, while firm resolves await . . . . . 224 **'Tis gone* 50
Where nothing was; and firm as some old Tower 226 *Vernal Ode* 18
And let some mood of thine in firm array . . . 233 *Power of Sound* 94
Yet firm his step, and stout his heart; . . . 243 *P. B.* 606
Hangs that day's treasured sword, how firm a check 278 *Wellington* 6
Repose at length, firm friends of human kind! . 313 *Clarkson* 14
In this firm hour Salvation lifts her horn. . . . 326 **Emperors and* 8
Firm as a rock in stationary fight; . . . . 330 *Ode: Thanks.* 77
Hail to the firm unmoving cross, ... 337 *Cath. Cantons* 9
Firm in its pristine majesty hath stood 367 *Trajan* 5
Ere on firm ground the car alighted; . . . . 372 *Eg. Maid* 194
Of female patience winning firm repose; . . . 395 *White Doe: Ded.* 50
And spake in firm and earnest mood. . . . . 406 *White Doe* 896
Watch, and be firm! for soul-subduing vice, . . 420 *Ecc. Sonn.* 1. 8. 1
That the firm soul is clothed with fruit divine! . 423 *Ecc. Sonn.* 1. 19. 5
Firm as the stake to which with iron band . . 437 *Ecc. Sonn.* 2. 35. 5
His frame is tied; firm from the naked feet . . 437 *Ecc. Sonn.* 2. 35. 6
Seems firm as solid crystal, breathless, clear, . 456 **Soft as* 2
Perplex the Church; but be thou firm,—be true 465 **Pastor and* 6
Firm as the towering Headlands of St. Bees. . . 466 *St. Bees* 18
In plunged the Knight!—when on firm ground . 479 *Somnamb.* 136
Yet seek thy firm support, according to their need. 492 *Duty* 24
Its duties;—prompt to move, but firm to wait,— 514 **Blest Statesman* 9
Firm self-denial, manners grave and staid, . . 515 *Penn.* 2
And all who from the law firm safety crave. . . 517 *Pun. Death* 2. 14
Strike not from Law's firm hand that awful rod, . 520 *Pun. Death* 13. 12
Firm and unflinching, as the Lighthouse reared 540 *Grace Darl.* 23
Of firm dry ground, with healthful grass . . 543 *Russ. Fug.* 103
Firm Independence, Bounty's rightful sire; . . 584 *Ch. Lamb* 9
Firm in the sacred paths of moral truth, . . . 619 *School Ex.* 78
With woman's gentleness, yet firm and staid; . 628 **Deign, Sovereign* 14
To firm devotion, zeal unquenchable, ... 635 *Prelude* 1. 184
The balance, and with firm hand weighed myself. 660 *Prelude* 4. 159
To lure my mind from firm habitual quest . . 662 *Prelude* 4. 287
On firm foundations, making social life, . . . 715 *Prelude* 9. 360
Became more firm in feelings that had stood . . 740 *Prelude* 13. 56
Of mine can give it life,) in firm belief . . . 751 *Prelude* 14. 356
Step after step—together, with their firm . . 780 *Excursion* 2. 587
So like the past, and both so firm a pledge . . 792 *Excursion* 2. 455
Affiance in each other; faith more firm . . . 805 *Excursion* 4. 306

Firm—*continued.*
Strong and unbounded to embrace, and firm . . 831 *Excursion* 5. 575
His own firm spirit in degree deprest . . . . 862 *Excursion* 7. 297
Is the firm basis of habitual sense . . . . S.3. 435 **The doubt* 114
Firmament. And soon with crimson fire kindled the firmament. . . . . 30 *Guilt* 315
And in the bosom of the firmament . . . . 230 *Clouds* 50
Approached this glory of the firmament; . . . 265 **The Shepherd* 12
Stand in the spacious firmament of time, . . . 317 **Brave Schill* 7
He keepeth; like the firmament his ways: . . 440 *Ecc. Sonn.* 2. 46. 13
And the firmament benign . . . . 503 **Like a* 62
O'er the blue firmament a radiant white, . . . 709 *Prelude* 8. 663
The Moon hung naked in a firmament . . . . 746 *Prelude* 14. 40
Drawn towards her native firmament of heaven, . 807 *Excursion* 4. 396
As if he wished the firmament of heaven . . . 851 *Excursion* 6. 883
Advance, and in the firmament of heaven . . . 876 *Excursion* 8. 160
Of the blue firmament—aloft, and wide; . . . 893 *Excursion* 9. 596
Firmer. A firmer step than mine. That dismal Moor— . . . . 39 *Bord.* 108
With firmer, holier knot. . . . . 223 *Wishing-gate* 48
What do we gather hence but firmer faith . . . 308 **These times* 9
With firmer soul, yet labour to regain . . . 318 *Biscayan* 2
Hence he will gain a firmer mind, to cope . . . 447 *Ecc. Sonn.* 3. 28. 13
No firmer grasp—a little wild-flower, joined . . 509 *F. Stone* 56
Take firmer hold of us, and words themselves . 673 *Prelude* 5. 544
The heart with firmer grasp! Your snows and streams . . . . 702 *Prelude* 8. 219
Of firmer trust, joint labourers in the work . . 752 *Prelude* 14. 441
Firmest. It would unman the firmest heart to hear. 30 *Guilt* 301
Life to consume in Manhood's firmest hold; . . 321 **Humanity, delighting* 22
Nor lacked she Reason's firmest power; . . . 415 *White Doe* 1777
Self-sacrifice the firmest; generous love, . . . 715 *Prelude* 9. 387
Of safest guidance or of firmest trust— . . . 827 *Excursion* 5. 335
Firmly. he kept them firmly sealed, as if he had been blind. . . . . 72 *Bord.* 2006
Firmly rejects those dazzling flatteries, . . . 359 *Plea: Hist.* 5
Firmly between the two extremes to steer; . . 438 *Ecc. Sonn.* 2. 40. 11
A calm resolve of mind, firmly addressed . . 654 *Prelude* 3. 346
March firmly towards righteousness and peace."— 727 *Prelude* 10. 589
More firmly to old tenets, and, to prove . . . 730 *Prelude* 11. 217
More firmly; and a comfort now hath risen . . 752 *Prelude* 14. 424
Like pillars fixed more firmly, as might seem, . 837 *Excursion* 5. 964
Firmness. Religiously that vow; but firmness failed, ... 672 *Prelude* 5. 475
With firmness, hitherto but slightly touched . . 675 *Prelude* 6. 54
Grant to the wise *his* firmness of resolve!" . . 842 *Excursion* 6. 261
Firs. Beneath those lofty firs, that overtop . . 147 *Joanna* 19
Within this grove of firs! and, on the fork . . 150 **When, to* 19
Of the dark firs, a visionary scene! . . . . 151 **When, to* 93
Where the bare columns of those lofty firs, . . 891 *Excursion* 9. 499
Behold a dusky spot, a grove of Firs, . . . K.8. 247 *Recluse* 1. 1. 385
First. On the dear hills where first he rose. . . 1 *Extract* 14
Alike, when first the bittern's hollow bill . . 2 *Ev. Wk.* 19
Thus Hope, first pouring from her blessed horn . 8 *Ev. Wk.* 339
The boat's first motion—made with dashing oar; 9 *Ev. Wk.* 372
Yes, I must see you when ye first behold . . . 20 *Desc. Sk.* 563
The first whose footsteps print the mountain dew. 22 *Desc. Sk.* 670
First covered, and here taught this aged Tree 23 *Yew-tree* 10
By the moon's sullen lamp she first discerned, . 27 *Guilt* 183
When first I saw him sitting there, alone, . . . 44 *Bord.* 376
But every night at the first stroke of twelve . 44 *Bord.* 389
Lovely as Spring's first rose; a little dog, . . 45 *Bord.* 455
These walls shall witness it—from first to last . 48 *Bord.* 594
Would there perhaps have gathered the first fruits 49 *Bord.* 663
To stay behind!—Hearing at first no answer, . 52 *Bord.* 811
When the tempestuous wind first drove us hither, 53 *Bord.* 861
And craft of age, seducing reason, first . . . 57 *Bord.* 1081
Each rises as the other falls: and first, . . . 58 *Bord.* 1149
But first, how wash our hands of this old Man? . 60 *Bord.* 1254
From the first moment that I loved the Maid; . 61 *Bord.* 1322
Time, since Man first drew breath, has never moved 65 *Bord.* 1531
First among youths of knightly breeding, One . 71 *Bord.* 1897
The first hours of last night were rough with storm: 73 *Bord.* 2043
"The first that died was sister Jane; . . . . 84 *We are Seven* 49
When my father found thee first in places far away; 87 *Pet-lamb* 34
Forth from his eyes, when first the Boy looked down on that huge oak, ' . . . . . . 92 *Poet's Dream* 34
Now first acquainted with distress and grief, . 118 *Maternal Grief* 50
Yea, his first word of greeting was,—"All right . 124 *V. and J.* 56
At the first word that Susan said . . . . 128 *Idiot Boy* 184
Or for the summer shade. It was the first . . 131 *Michael* 21
At the first hearing, for a moment took . . . 134 *Michael* 218
Such was his first resolve; he thought again, . 134 *Michael* 225
First cam'st into the world—as oft befalls . . 136 *Michael* 340
First uttering, without words, a natural tune; . 136 *Michael* 347
The first stone of the Sheep-fold. At the sight . 137 *Michael* 420
The spring's first rose by you espied, ... 142 †*Lov. and Lik.* 31
And taken thy first leave of those green hills . . 151 **When, to* 68
Muttering the verses which I muttered first . . 151 **When, to* 99
Your kind's first seed did bear; . . . . . 156 *Oak and Broom* 42
Since we needs must first have met . . . . 160 **Pansies, lilies* 19
First at sight of thee was glad; . . . . . . 160 **Pleasures newly* 4
Who the first with pointed rays . . . . . 161 **Pleasures newly* 11
Who first, weighed down by scorn, in some lone bower . . . . 169 *Love lies Bleeding* 20
This Flower, that first appeared as summer's guest, 169 **Never enlivened* 4
First at one, and then its fellow, ... 170 *Kitten* 19
And first;—thy sinless progress, through a world 172 *Infant Daughter* 46
Among these hills, from first to last, ... 179 *Waggoner* 3. 79
When first she gleamed upon my sight; . . . 186 **She was* 2

Fitter—*continued.*
Go, carry to some fitter place . . . . . . 485 *Poet's Epitaph* 6
By useful habits, to a fitter soil . . . . . . 862 *Excursion* 7. 301
Fittest. The fittest place? He is growing pitiful. . 51 *Bord.* 750
And fittest to unutterable thought . . . . . . 88 *H. C.* 3
Fitting. Fitting his low voice to the minstrel's harp, 59 *Bord.* 1192
"And now, as fitting is and right, ... 193 *Ruth* 103
And made a fitting song, of words but few, . . 564 *Troilus* 115
Who crept along fitting her languid gait . . . 717 *Prelude* 9. 511
Five. Five streams of ice amid her cots descend, . 20 *Desc. Sk.* 571
A farm or dwelling-house within five leagues, . . 51 *Bord.* 767
Five minutes past—and, O the change! . . . 82 †*Mother's Return* 53
Then ye are only five." . . . . 84 *We are Seven* 36
I have a boy of five years old; . . . . . . 85 *Anecdote* 1
Through five long generations had the heart . . 98 *Brothers* 204
And there is one whom I five years have known; 110 *'Tis said that some* 6
From ten to five, from five to three, ... 115 *Last of Flock* 92
Five years of happiness or more . . . . . 127 *Idiot Boy* 135
In five months' time, should he be seen, . . . 129 *Idiot Boy* 330
From eight o'clock till five. . . . . 131 *Idiot Boy* 446
Two steady roses that were five years old; . . 134 *Michael* 179
With a light heart. The Housewife for five days 135 *Michael* 284
The violets of five seasons re-appear . . . . 185 *Nutting* 31
Not five yards from the mountain path, . . . 198 *Thorn* 27
Five years have past; five summers, with the length 205 *Tintern* 1
Of five long winters! and again I hear . . . 205 *Tintern* 2
Five thousand warriors—O the rapturous day! . 212 *Dion* 18
The five dear wounds our Lord did bear; . . . 400 *White Doe* 357
And I for five centuries right gladly would be . 482 *Character* 19
When full five hundred boats in trim array, . . 522 *Epist. Beaumont* 71
Oh, many a time have I, a five years' child, . . 636 *Prelude* 1. 288
And twice five summers on my mind had stamped 640 *Prelude* 1. 560
I travelled round our little lake, five miles . . 647 *Prelude* 2. 331
Fresh emptied of spectators. Twice five years . 674 *Prelude* 5. 552
Five rivers broad and vast, made rich amends, . 683 *Prelude* 6. 532
His steadfast eye. The planetary Five . . . 811 *Excursion* 4. 699
Five graves, and only five, that rise together . . 858 *Excursion* 7. 35
"At length, when sixty years and five were told, 864 *Excursion* 7. 463
Five-and-thirty. Full five-and-thirty years he lived 483 *Simon Lee* 5
Fix. And growls as if he would fix his claws . . 81 †*Address: Child* 29
Fix thine eyes upon the sea . . . . 90 *Longest Day* 46
And fix on it a steady view, ... 200 *Thorn* 215
Yon cloud, and fix it in that glorious shape; . . 252 *Picture* 2
Would fix itself as smoothly as a cloud, . . . 312 **When, far* 13
To fix in heaven her shape distinct with stars. . 336 *Danube* 14
Relax, to fix and satisfy the mind . . . . . 353 *Aquap.* 25
To fix a wiser sorrow in the heart? . . . . . 467 *St. Bees* 76
He labours good on good to fix, and owes . . . 493 *Hap. War.* 33
Why fix upon his wealth or want a thought? . . 529 *Poor Robin* 16
Fix on a lovely object, nor my mind . . . . 622 *Recluse* 1. 1. 86
Might fix the wavering balance of my mind, . . 641 *Prelude* 1. 622
Reflective acts to fix the moral law . . . . 650 *Prelude* 3. 84
Fix us upon some lofty pinnacle, ... 690 *Prelude* 7. 244
Thither, uncertain on which road to fix . . . 738 *Prelude* 12. 295
—The darts of anguish *fix* not where the seat . 801 *Excursion* 4. 18
From this unstable world, if he could fix . . . 803 *Excursion* 4. 157
Shall fix, in calmer seats of moral strength, . . 820 *Excursion* 4. 1272
To fix her eyes—alas! 'twas hard to bear! . . 853 *Excursion* 6. 964
Upon his sprightly vigour cannot fix . . . . 866 *Excursion* 7. 570
"Then let us rather fix our gladdened thoughts . 888 *Excursion* 9. 255
Fixed. Fixed on the anchor left by Him who saves 14 *Desc. Sk.* 206
Which oft as he looked back had fixed his eye, . 24 *Guilt* 22
Thy curse is fixed; the truth must be laid bare. . 76 *Bord.* 2206
The Cross, fixed in his soul, may prove an all-sufficing stay. . . . . 91 *Norman Boy* 32
Whence all the fixed delights of house and home, 102 *Artegal* 23
"Who, when a crown is fixed upon his head, . . 105 *Artegal* 170
Upon the moon I fixed my eye, ... 109 **Strange fits* 9
Fixed in the spirit; for even here . . . . . 113 *Lament* 47
Stands fixed, her face with joy o'erflows, . . . 127 *Idiot Boy* 88
Restless with fixed to balance, high with low, . 153 *Morn. Ex.* 32
Fixed on a Star his upward eye; . . . . . 167 *Pilgrim's Dream* 12
And fixed an infant's span above . . . . . 169 *Wren's Nest* 42
Fixed on a smoothly-sliding car. . . . . . 177 *Waggoner* 2. 108
"And they had fixed the wedding day, ... 199 *Thorn* 111
In fixed resolves by Reason justified; . . . . 217 *Enterprise* 127
Whose wisdom fixed the scale . . . . 226 *Present.* 75
Some fixed, some wandering with no timid curb; 226 *Vernal Ode* 33
But wandering star and fixed, to mortal eye, . . 226 *Vernal Ode* 34
As if the man had fixed his face, ... 240 *P. B.* 318
His wandering eye is fixed. . . . . 242 *P. B.* 550
Lies fixed for ages on his conscious neck; . . . 278 *Wellington* 4
Lo! where she stands fixed in a saint-like trance, 278 **Lo! where she* 1
Others look up, and with fixed eyes admire . . 283 **Well have* 8
Was fixed upon the glowing Sky, ... 289 *Stepping West.* 22
Had fixed, for ever fixed, their doom! . . . . 298 *Brownie's Cell* 20
Fixed on him an unhallowed name; . . . . . 299 *Brownie's Cell* 54
Fixed, like the Templar of the steep, ... 301 *Bran* 88
Fixed as a star: such glory is thy right. . . . 317 **Brave Schill* 8
Fixed in the depths of this courageous soil; . . 324 *Ode 1814* 104
But He who fixed immoveably the frame . . . 329 *Ode: Thanks.* 47
Fixed on the front of Eastern diadems, . . . 331 *Ode: Thanks.* 167
Conjoined in prospect mutable or fixed . . . 355 *Aquap.* 175
Of Brethren who, here fixed, on Jesu wait . . 364 **What aim* 6
Merlin, as fixed in thought he stood, ... 371 *Eg. Maid* 166
The clasp that fixed the Roman Gown; . . . . 390 *Highland Broach* 16
A world of fixed remembrances . . . . . . 398 *White Doe* 209
The Norton fixed, at this demand, ... 403 *White Doe* 635
He there stands fixed from hour to hour: . . . 404 *White Doe* 769
There hath she fixed it; yet it seems . . . . 413 *White Doe* 1600

Fixed—*continued.*
Hath stopped, and fixed her large full eye . . 414 *White Doe* 1644
For Souls whose doom is fixed! The way is smooth 423 *Ecc. Sonn.* 1. 20. 9
Weeds on whose front the world had fixed her sign. 428 *Ecc. Sonn.* 2. 1. 8
Where long and deeply hath been fixed the root . 431 *Ecc. Sonn.* 2. 10. 1
Fixed on the frame of England's Church their sight, 444 *Ecc. Sonn.* 3. 15. 4
Seem fixed, to eyes that watch them from afar; . 444 *Ecc. Sonn.* 3. 17. 4
Fixed, by her smile, upon some rocky seat; . . 461 **Giordano, verily* 13
A fixed Abode—keep down presageful sighs. . . 465 **Pastor and* 4
Like the fixed Light that crowns yon Headland of St. Bees. . . . . 466 *St. Bees* 45
Of periods fixed, and laws established, less . . 469 **Desire we* 13
For her mute Powers, fixed Forms, or transient Shows. . . . . 471 *Ailsa Crag* 14
A faith more fixed, a rapture more divine . . . 474 **How sad* 13
Stood with eyes fixed upon that masterpiece, . . 509 *F. Stone* 107
To circumscribe this Shape in fixed repose; . . 511 **Who rashly* 18
Be one fixed mind for all; thy rights approve . 515 **Ah why* 10
Fixed on the statutes of Eternity, ... 519 *Pun. Death* 9. 7
I ask what warrant fixed them (like a spell . . 527 **Those breathing* 46
Of witchcraft fixed them) in the crystal cell; . . 527 **Those breathing* 47
On Jesu's Mother fixed was his intent. . . . 554 *Prioress* 99
And scanned them with a fixed and serious look . 566 *Cumb. Beg.* 11
Floating or fixed of polar ice, allow. . . . . 586 *Ch. Lamb* 106
The poet's steps, and fixed him here, on you . 587 *Crosth.* 2
The Moon's fix'd gaze between the opening trees, 596 *Ev. Wk. Quarto* 262
Ev'n here Content has fix'd her smiling reign . . 608 *Desc. Sk. Quarto* 323
With pale-blue hands, and eyes that fix'd implore, 615 *Desc. Sk. Quarto* 710
With pulseless hand, and fix'd unwearied gaze, . 616 *Desc. Sk. Quarto* 786
Fixed on the Suitor; frustrate her request— . . 626 *Ballot* 10
With an unswerving line, I fixed my view . . . 637 *Prelude* 1. 369
Had watched her with fixed eyes while to and fro 659 *Prelude* 4. 90
Hands of angelic powers had fixed it there, . . 682 *Prelude* 6. 485
Now, fixed amid that concourse of mankind . . 688 *Prelude* 7. 69
Wherein were fixed the iron pales that fenced . 696 *Prelude* 7. 606
Shape for mankind, by principles as fixed, . . 698 *Prelude* 7. 754
Out of his feelings, to be fixed thenceforth . . 730 *Prelude* 11. 226
Made visible; as ruled by those fixed laws . . 745 *Prelude* 13. 372
A fixed, abysmal, gloomy, breathing-place— . . 747 *Prelude* 14. 58
He sate, and even in their fixed lineaments, . . 758 *Excursion* 1. 156
Even in their fixed and steady lineaments . . 758 *Excursion* 1. 160
Fixed on the Cross, that consolation springs, . . 770 *Excursion* 1. 937
By weariness of life—he fixed his home, . . . 776 *Excursion* 2. 307
Stood fixed; and fixed resemblances were seen . 784 *Excursion* 2. 864
As the mute insect fixed upon the plant . . . 794 *Excursion* 3. 579
If fixed or wandering star could tidings yield . 796 *Excursion* 3. 692
And the vast hills, in fluctuation fixed . . . . 802 *Excursion* 4. 35
That he, whose fixed despondency had given . . 805 *Excursion* 4. 254
Exist; so, none is now for fixed despair: . . . 805 *Excursion* 4. 267
On fluent operations a fixed shape; . . . . . 812 *Excursion* 4. 727
And, even as these are well and widely fixed, . . 812 *Excursion* 4. 764
For fixed annoyance; and full oft beset . . . 817 *Excursion* 4. 1055
Like the fixed centre of a troubled world. . . . 822 *Excursion* 5. 16
Withdrew, and fixed me in a still retreat; . . . 823 *Excursion* 5. 53
Imbued the altar-window; fixed aloft . . . . 825 *Excursion* 5. 162
Whom the best might of faith, wherever fixed, . 828 *Excursion* 5. 360
Whose root is fixed in stable earth, whose head . 831 *Excursion* 5. 568
And saw the light—now fixed—and shifting now— 833 *Excursion* 5. 745
My comfort:—would that they were oftener fixed 835 *Excursion* 5. 824
Fixed in the centre of a prickly brake, ... 835 *Excursion* 5. 842
Like pillars fixed more firmly, as might seem, . 837 *Excursion* 5. 964
Had fixed his milder loyalty, and placed . . . 844 *Excursion* 6. 428
A long stone-seat, fixed in the Churchyard wall; . 850 *Excursion* 6. 779
Or the necessity that fixed him here; . . . . 859 *Excursion* 7. 147
Fixed at their seat, the centre of the Mere, . . 869 *Excursion* 7. 755
And fixed his home in this sequestered vale. . . 871 *Excursion* 7. 926
Fixed in his soul, so early and so deep; . . . 878 *Excursion* 8. 299
Without his own consent, or knowledge, fixed! . 878 *Excursion* 8. 300
With the same upright form! The sun is fixed, . 887 *Excursion* 9. 209
Fixed, within reach of every human eye; . . . 887 *Excursion* 9. 211
With beverage pure as ever fixed the choice . . S. 3. 433 **The doubt* 17
And will be stirring when our eyes are fixed . . K. 8. 253 *Recluse* 1. 1. 630
He planted, and in Latium fixed his Gods, . . K. 8. 281 **Arms and* 7
Fixedly. Stirred with his staff, and fixedly did look 196 *Resolution* 79
Fixes. That both creates and fixes, in despite . . 509 *F. Stone* 77
Or fixes them; whose least distinguished day . 839 *Excursion* 6. 49
Fixing. Fixing his downcast eye, he many an hour . 23 *Yew-tree* 30
And fixing still his eye . . . . 486 **We walked* 18
But fixing by immutable decrees . . . . . 500 *Humanity* 47
Far happier they who, fixing hope and aim . . 529 **Those breathing* 126
The Wife and Mother pitifully fixing . . . . 798 *Excursion* 3. 854
Experience daily fixing his regards . . . . . 813 *Excursion* 4. 811
Fixing a steady eye, maintain their speed; . . . 880 *Excursion* 8. 384
Fixture. Mute fixture on a stuccoed wall; . . . 300 *Bran* 6
Flaccid. With flaccid threads of ivy, in the still . 497 **Enough of climbing* 22
Whose flaccid sails in forms fantastic droop, . . 604 *Desc. Sk. Quarto* 128
Flag. At remembrance whereof my blood sometimes will flag; . . . . 86 *Rural Arch.* 22
The wings they did not flag; the Child, though grave, was not depressed. . . . . 92 *Poet's Dream* 32
And so, flag flying at mast head, ... 178 *Waggoner* 2. 162
When the proud fleet that bears the red-cross flag 722 *Prelude* 10. 315
For you the hours of labour do not flag; . . . 835 *Excursion* 5. 835
A flag of *yellow* dye. . . . . S. 3. 431 **The Scottish* 16
Flageolet. And merry flageolet; the low of herds, . 18 *Desc. Sk.* 418
His flageolet to liquid notes of love . . . . 702 *Prelude* 8. 200
Flagged. The boyish spirit flagged, and day by day 660 *Prelude* 4. 101
Flagging. Dull, flagging notes that with each other jar?" . . . . 252 **Why, Minstrel* 2

Flags. Tartarean flags are caught at, and unfurled—— . 437 *Ecc. Sonn.* 2. 36. 12
Shall hoist their topmast flags in sign of glee, . 504 *Warning* 45
On the thrilled ear, and flags uprising, yield . 773 *Excursion* 2. 119
Heavenward ; and chide the part of me that flags, . 803 *Excursion* 4. 127
Flag-ship. This was the Flag-ship at the Nile, . 178 *Waggoner* 2. 115
Flail. The measured echo of the distant flail . 22 *Desc. Sk.* 634
Some injury done to sickle, flail, or scythe, . 132 *Michael* 108
Flake. The torch that flames with many a lurid flake, . 213 *Dion* 84
Great is their glee while flake they add to flake . 280 ***Intent on* 4
Flakes. *See* **Cotton-flakes.**
Strong flakes of radiance on the tremulous stream : . 4 *Ev. Wk.* 109
In flakes of light upon the mountain-side, . 10 *Desc. Sk.* 6
That turns its goat's-beard flakes of pea-green moss . 61 *Bord.* 1295
And quick words round him fall like flakes of snow. . 503 *Warning* 21
Flaky. A flaky weight of winter's purest snows ! . 212 *Dion*
Flame. An edge all flame, the broadening sun appears ; . 5 *Ev. Wk.* 169
At once to pillars turned that flame with gold : . 15 *Desc. Sk.* 280
Old Man ! my wrath is as a flame burnt out, . 63 *Bord.* 1402
In secret, like a smothered flame ? . 204 *Brougham* 77
The Highlanders, the slaughter spread like flame ; . 293 *Killicranky* 5
Those new-born Kings she withered like a flame." . 313 *Prophecy* 10
Despoil our temples, and by sword and flame. . 319 *Spaniard* 2
Oh, for a kindling touch from that pure flame . 326 *Sobieski* 1
——There is a radiant though a short-lived flame. . 329 *Ode : Thanks.* 43
——Wide-wasted regions—cities wrapt in flame—— . 330 *Ode : Thanks.* 98
How, for exciting youth's heroic flame, . 359 ***Those old* 13
A greedy flame ; the pompous mass proceeds ; . 431 *Ecc. Sonn.* 2. 11. 3
Of the new Flame, not suffered to expire. . 432 *Ecc. Sonn.* 2. 14. 14
Like Ocean burning with purpureal flame ; . 452 *Ecc. Sonn.* 3. 46. 4
And listen to the flapping of the flame, . 488 *Pers. Talk* 13
He loved, he hoped,—a holy flame . 545 *Russ. Fug.* 325
It's edge all flame, the broad'ning sun appears ; . 594 *Ev. Wk. Quarto* 152
And quench the passions kindling into flame ; . 619 *School Ex.* 80
A flame within them that despises death . 627 *Eagle and Dove* 7
Of single spirits that catch the flame from Heaven, . 715 *Prelude* 9. 368
Who swept from Scotland, in a flame of zeal, . 814 *Excursion* 4. 898
With their last breath, from out the smouldering flame, . 839 *Excursion* 6. 70
Mortal though bright, a dying, dying flame. . K.8. 248 *Recluse* 1.1.439
Flame-eyed. The flame-eyed eagle oft wouldst scare . 215 *Enterprise* 30
And near the flame-eyed eagle sits the dove. . 430 *Ecc. Sonn.* 2. 7. 14
Flames. Lo, from the flames a great and glorious birth ; . 22 *Desc. Sk.* 644
You rushed into the murderous flames, returned . 40 *Bord.* 179
Of towns in flames, fields ravaged, young and old . 56 *Bord.* 1031
Oh ! would that thou hadst perished in the flames ! . 76 *Bord.* 2193
The torch that flames with many a lurid flake, . 213 *Dion* 84
By flames, look up to heaven and crave redress . 426 *Ecc. Sonn.* 1. 32. 4
Lo ! from th' innocuous flames, a lovely birth ! . 616 *Desc.Sk.Quarto* 782
" *Invisible* " flames forth upon his chest. . 691 *Prelude* 7. 287
The Desert visible by dismal flames ; . 744 *Prelude* 13. 330
By flames breathed on her from her own fireside. . K.8. 275 ***These vales* 4
Flameward. Outstretching flameward his upbraided hand . 437 *Ecc. Sonn.* 2. 35. 1
Flaming. Moves there a cloud o'er mid-day's flaming eye ? . 11 *Desc. Sk.* 23
The six-days' Work by flaming Seraphim . 235 *Power of Sound* 203
Michael, and thou, St. George, whose flaming brand . 434 *Ecc. Sonn.* 2. 24. 8
Flaming till thou from Paynim hands release . 467 *St. Bees* 106
" And has the Sun his flaming chariot driven . 618 *School Ex.* 1
Sink, with a retinue of flaming clouds . 803 *Excursion* 4. 117
Two doughty champions ; flaming Jacobite . 845 *Excursion* 6. 458
Flannel. Good duffle grey, and flannel fine ; . 536 *Goody Blake* 6
Flap. When windows flap and chimney roars, . 182 *Waggoner* 4. 246
Flapped. While, flapped with conscious pride, resound his wings ! . 5 *Ev. Wk.* 155
Flapping. With flapping wing for entrance. What a shriek . 274 ***Wait, prithee* 9
And the dire flapping of his hoary wing ! . 322 ***Ye Storms* 8
And listen to the flapping of the flame, . 488 *Pers. Talk* 13
Flaring. Children of the flaring hours ! . 160 ***Pansies, lilies* 50
Flash. And the short thunder, and the flash of arms ; . 21 *Desc. Sk.* 617
For a few swelling phrases, and a flash . 47 *Bord.* 563
When, after a broad flash that filled the cave, . 50 *Bord.* 715
A gentle flash of light that came . 112 *Lament* 3
There came a flash—a startling glare, . 176 *Waggoner* 1. 229
They flash upon that inward eye . 187 ***I wandered* 21
Ere he replied, a flash of mild surprise . 196 *Resolution* 90
As the first flash of beacon light ; . 215 *Enterprise* 9
Up with a sally, and a flash of speed, . 218 *Recluse* 1. 1. 228
Welter and flash, a synod might detain . 268 ***DogmaticTeachers* 12
A flash of something over-bright ! . 294 *Jedbor.* 69
Where golden flash and silver gleam . 526 ***The soaring* 11
Hast thou seen, with flash incessant, . 550 *Hermit's Cell* 3. 1
While flash her upward eyes severe delight. . 612 *Desc.Sk.Quarto* 555
The thought of her was like a flash of light, . 622 *Recluse* 1. 1. 92
Too soon, while yet the very flash and gleam . 682 *Prelude* 6. 502
Goes out, but with a flash that has revealed . 684 *Prelude* 6. 601
Fell like a flash, and lo ! as I looked up, . 746 *Prelude* 14. 39
Even as a thoughtful shepherd by a flash . 796 *Excursion* 3. 707
Flashed. From the clear light of circumstances, flashed . 64 *Bord.* 1495
Air blackened, thunder growled, fire flashed from clouds that hid the sky, . 91 *Poet's Dream* 3
Flashed round him images and hues that wrought . 96 *Brothers* 57
Pleasant conviction flashed upon my mind . 150 ***When, to* 58
That story flashed upon his mind ;—— . 296 *Highland Boy* 142
The barrier Rhine hath flashed, through battle-smoke, . 322 *Germans* 9

Flashed—*continued.*
That flashed upon me from this novel show . 652 *Prelude* 3. 202
His form hath flashed upon me, glorified . 703 *Prelude* 8. 269
One guide, the light of circumstances, flashed . 731 *Prelude* 11. 243
That flashed and sparkled from the other's eyes ; . 779 *Excursion* 2. 515
That flashed uncouthly through the woods and fields. . 869 *Excursion* 7. 765
Flashes. *See* **Sea-flashes.**
And the fierce torrent at the flashes broad . 13 *Desc. Sk.* 181
Fitfully, and in flashes, through his soul, . 18 *Desc. Sk.* 457
Flashes a look of terror upon guilt, . 40 *Bord.* 171
I heard, I saw the flashes drive, . 114 *Ind. Wom.* 6
Close-treading on the silent flashes—— . 175 *Waggoner* 1. 198
Are felt the flashes of his pen ; . 286 *Nith* 44
The vivid flashes of his spoken words. . 584 *Ch. Lamb* 22
In flashes, and with glory not their own. . 674 *Prelude* 5. 605
And with what flashes, as it were, the mind . 693 *Prelude* 7. 437
Of Thirlmere flashes like a warrior's shield . K.8. 225 ***I will* 48
Flashing. Restlessly flashing, seems to mount like fire ; . 12 *Desc. Sk.* 100
In flashing leaps and stealthy creeps . 190 ***Lyre ! though* 31
The proud heart flashing through the eyes, . 292 *Rob Roy* 119
Forth flashing out of its own gloomy chasm . 352 *Aquap.* 15
And temples flashing, bright as polar ice, . 420 *Ecc. Sonn.* 1. 8. 4
And flashing to that Structure's topmost height, . 473 ***Thanks for* 11
Of wounds, and bright swords flashing in the field, . 574 *Chiabrera* 4. 4
Starts like a horse beside the flashing road ; . 605 *Desc.Sk.Quarto* 208
Shakes from behind the clouds his flashing shield. . 608 *Desc.Sk.Quarto* 337
Gleams like the flashing of a shield ;—the earth . 640 *Prelude* 1. 586
Arms flashing, and a military glare . 681 *Prelude* 6. 424
Retained a flashing eye, a burning palm, . 860 *Excursion* 7. 210
Flat. Nought but the *chalets*, flat and bare, on high . 16 *Desc. Sk.* 348
Lo ! where through flat Batavia's willowy groves, . 19 *Desc. Sk.* 520
Majestic Duddon, over smooth flat sands . 384 *Duddon* 32. 7
Of a cloud flat and dense, through which must move . 461 ***Who but is* 12
This straight-lined progress, furrowing a flat lea, . 466 *St. Bees* 12
On a flat and lazy shore. . 549 *Hermit's Cell* 1. 32
Or summer hamlet, flat and bare, on high . 610 *Desc.Sk.Quarto* 428
Upon the smooth flat stones : the Nurse is here, . 690 *Prelude* 7. 207
O'er the flat Common !—With quick step I reached . 766 *Excursion* 1. 646
A fragment, like an altar, flat and smooth : . 787 *Excursion* 3. 60
Or lay its beauty flat before a breeze, . 787 *Excursion* 3. 66
To the flat margin of the Baltic sea, . 889 *Excursion* 9. 337
O'er the flat meadows and indented coast . 892 *Excursion* 9. 573
Flat on the ground, even as a boy might do, . K.8. 226 ***I will* 56
Those small flat stones, which, ranged by traveller's hands . K.8. 226 ***I will* 63
From the flat meadow lonely there. . K.8. 263 ***The Lake* 10
Flat-roofed. To flat-roofed towns, that touch the water's bound, . 12 *Desc. Sk.* 83
Flatter. Will flatter you,—and fool and rake . 286 *Sons of Burns* 21
Fell flatter than a caged parrot's note, . 688 *Prelude* 7. 100
Ill purposes, and flatter foul desires. . 894 *Excursion* 9. 687
Flattered. Nay, but speak out ! He flattered me, and said . 46 *Bord.* 506
Flattered and feared, despised yet deified, . 103 *Artegal* 96
Flattered with promise of escape . 502 *Seasons* 1
The flattered structure glistened, blazed, . 550 *Hermit's Cell* 2. 19
Were flattered, and had trust in human kind : . 723 *Prelude* 10. 388
Flattered the young, pleased with extremes, nor least . 730 *Prelude* 11. 233
Flatterers. By Flatterers carried, mount into a dream . 505 *Warning* 125
Flatteries. Firmly rejects those dazzling flatteries, . 359 *Plea : Hist.* 5
Of the world's flatteries if the brain be full, . 394 ***How profitless* 5
Mingling their glances with grave flatteries . 442 *Ecc. Sonn.* 3. 11. 7
" The babbling flatteries . 542 *Russ. Fug.* 58
Feuds, factions, flatteries, enmity, and guile . 657 *Prelude* 3. 601
Flattering. *See* **Self-flattering.**
Ye flattering eastern lights, once more the hills illume ; . 20 *Desc. Sk.* 529
Not unassisted by the flattering stars, . 216 *Enterprise* 107
Who, while the flattering Zephyrs round them play, . 259 ***A volant* 2
Taught to mistrust her flattering horoscope . 345 ***Ambition—following* 5
Turn a broad front full on his flattering beams : . 539 ***Lady ! a* 17
He promised comfort ; and the flattering thoughts . 575 *Chiabrera* 8. 14
(If now I yield not to a flattering dream) . 654 *Prelude* 3. 372
That framed them ; flattering self-conceit with words, . 743 *Prelude* 13. 216
That flattering breezes blowing thence . S.3. 431 ***The Scottish* 13
Flatters. That flatters us, because it asks not thought ; . 56 *Bord.* 1034
An element that flatters him—to kill, . 528 ***Those breathing* 78
Flattery. Flattery in Ancient Rome's pure-minded style : . 359 ***Complacent Fictions* 10
Of fond sepulchral flattery can beguile . 389 *Breadalb.* 3
At oriental flattery ; . 495 *Fact* 18
Flattery and double-dealing, strife and wrong. . K.8. 246 *Recluse* 1.1.357
Flaunting. Nor flaunting Summer—when he throws . 299 *Brownie's Cell* 85
Flaw. Tho' searching damps and many an envious flaw . 342 *Last. Sup.* 1
Flax. That small, for flax ; and, if one wheel had rest, . 132 *Michael* 84
Fled. Has disappeared, and every trace is fled . 6 *Ev. Wk.* 209
Whither is fled that Power whose frown severe . 11 *Desc. Sk.* 54
Both of the time to come, and time long fled : . 24 *Guilt* 6
He fled, a vagrant since, the murderer's fate to shun. . 25 *Guilt* 72
Now he had fled, and whither none could say, . 35 *Guilt* 606
Hither soon as spring is fled . 80 *Foresight* 27
O'er town and tower we fled, and fields in May's fresh verdure drest ; . 92 *Poet's Dream* 31
Sleep fled, and with it fled the dream—recorded in this book, . 93 *Poet's Dream* 70

Flies—*continued.*
With nerves so steady, that the very flies . . . 62 *Bord.* 1378
From which the tusky wild boar flies in fear ; . 104 *Artegal* 109
Murmur as with the sound of summer flies. . . 133 *Michael* 128
But, though Sir Walter like a falcon flies, . . . 200 *Hart-leap* 11
The Mother o'er the threshold flies, . . . 248 *P. B.* 1083
And flies their memory fast almost as they ; . . 251 **There is a little* 12
Cleaves the blank air, Life flies : now every day . 270 **If these* 9
He hears the word—he flies— . . . . . . 328 *Ode 1815* 99
As on Parnassus rules, when lightning flies, . . 350 *Des. Stanzas* 8
Flies out, and passes on from cold to cold ; . . 422 *Ecc. Sonn.* 1. 16. 6
She seems performing as she flies . . . . . 512 **Who rashly* 31
And happiness that never flies— . . . . 530 *Gleaner* 9
And to the tomb for rescue flies . . . . . 544 *Russ. Fug.* 199
Soon flies the little joy to man allow'd, . . . 613 *Desc.Sk.Quarto* 636
Are cheerful ; while this multitude of flies . . 765 *Excursion* 1. 596
The gilded summer flies to mix and weave . . 807 *Excursion* 4. 446
" *Time flies ; it is his melancholy task* . . 846 *Excursion* 6. 515
Flight. In many a whistling circle wheels her flight ; 4 *Ev. Wk.* 91
Unhurt pursues his lengthened flight, while all . 6 *Ev. Wk.* 198
Force half upon the wave their cumbrous flight. . 6 *Ev. Wk.* 249
A viewless flight of laughing Demon's mock . . 11 *Desc. Sk.* 69
Forced hard against the wind a thick unwieldy flight. . . . . 26 *Guilt* 108
Stay near me—do not take thy flight ! . . . 79 **Stay near* 1
Which the goat cannot climb, takes his sounding flight ; . . . . 80 †*Address : Child* 4
Nor leave untold our happy flight in that adventurous dream. . . . . 93 *Poet's Dream* 76
And blasts of heaven will aid their flight ; . . . 117 *Affl. Marg.* 44
Perpetual flight, unchecked by earthly ties, . . 153 *Morn. Ex.* 35
Some memory that had taken flight ; . . . . 158 **In youth* 46
Hither his flight he would bend ; . . . . . 162 **Art thou the* 16
Sunward now his flight he raises, ... 163 *Hint* 14
Take flight, and thou art free to roam, . . . 169 *Wren's Nest* 66
And higher still—a greedy flight ! . . . . . 178 *Waggoner* 3. 26
Is touched—and all the band take flight. . . . 180 *Waggoner* 4. 35
His fears, his doubts, may now take flight— . . 181 *Waggoner* 4. 130
His flight, 'mid eddying pine-tree tops ! . . . 213 *Dion* 76
With bolder than Icarian flight ? . . . . 216 *Enterprise* 70
Maiden ! now take flight ;—inherit . . . . . 217 **Inmate of* 17
Their indefatigable flight. 'Tis done— . . . 218 *Recluse* 1. 1. 216
Her flight, and take its voice away !— . . . 227 *Vernal Ode* 113
Their subtle flight could satisfy : . . . . . 228 *Devot. Incit.* 10
Sink, to attain a loftier flight ; . . . . . 228 *Devot. Incit.* 29
Of seasons balancing their flight . . . . . 228 *Devot. Incit.* 56
Wouldst thou be taught, when sleep has taken flight, ... 229 *Cuckoo-clock* 1
Your squadrons to an endless flight of birds . . 230 *Clouds* 17
As no unworthy Partner in their flight . . . 231 **The gentlest Poet* 8
With malice—that again takes flight ; . . . . 242 *P. B.* 498
And reason govern that audacious flight . . . 261 **From the dark* 9
Terrestrial, but a surface, by the flight . . . 263 **How clear* 8
O'er Limbo lake with aery flight to steer, . . . 284 *Departure* 11
With such invisible motion speed thy flight, . . 315 **Advance—come* 10
Brave Schill ! by death delivered, take thy flight 317 **Brave Schill* 1
Charged, and dispersed like foam : but as a flight 320 **Hunger, and* 6
The unwearied arrow hath pursued its flight ! . 327 *Ode 1815* 33
Mounts on rapt wing, and with a moment's flight 336 *Danube* 7
Death-parted friends, and days too swift in flight, 358 *Pine : Rome* 11
And stirring interests shunned with desperate flight, 363 **The world forsaken* 2
Then Merlin ! for a rapid flight . . . . . . 370 *Eg. Maid* 107
Startling the flight of timid Yesterday ! . . . 379 *Duddon* 15. 8
For instant flight ; the Sage in yon alcove . . 393 **The Lovers* 4
May guide them in a prudent flight ! " . . . 408 *White Doe* 1118
Their guide in flight—already she . . . . . 408 *White Doe* 1124
He fled,—and, in his flight, could hear . . . . 411 *White Doe* 1365
Slowly the cormorant aims her heavy flight, . . 419 *Ecc. Sonn.* 1. 3. 4
Of Faith stand coupled for a common flight ! . . 437 *Ecc. Sonn.* 2. 34. 3
Some seek with timely flight a foreign strand ; . 437 *Ecc. Sonn.* 2. 37. 2
(After a steady flight on home-bound wings, . . 455 *Rydal Mere* 9
At will, and stay thy migratory flight ; . . . 455 *Rydal Mere* 34
On thy wings opened wide for smoothest flight, . 456 **The leaves* 15
In his destructive flight on earthly crowns, . . 460 **Queen of* 22
Her flight before the bold credulities . . . . 468 *St. Bees* 161
On all that marked the primal flight . . . . 472 *Ossian* 34
Sweet-voiced, nor wishing for a flight . . . . 478 *Somnamb.* 17
Vague sympathies have urged her to take flight : 503 *Warning* 31
Uphold our Spirits urged to kindred flight . . 512 **Who rashly* 37
Blithe hopes and happy musings soon took flight, 523 *Epist. Beaumont* 120
Her flight by vocal wings ; . . . . 526 **The soaring* 4
Cynthia, who puts the *little* stars to flight, . . 532 **Once I* 22
Through long and perilous flight ; . . . . . 542 *Russ. Fug.* 52
Before her flight she had not dared . . . . 544 *Russ. Fug.* 229
Lord of the air, he took his flight ; . . . . . 580 *John Words.* 5
I sought thy golden vale with dancing flight, . . 630 [?] **O Moon* 6
Till he was left an arrow's flight behind. . . . 649 *Prelude* 3. 12
In mind, as when I thence had taken flight . . 675 *Prelude* 6. 8
Outweighed, or put to flight, the set events . . 693 *Prelude* 7. 404
Or spirit that full soon must take her flight. . . 705 *Prelude* 8. 450
Of my associates stood prepared for flight . . . 712 *Prelude* 9. 182
Brave hearts ! to shameful flight. It was a grief,— 722 *Prelude* 10. 288
Backwards, nor checked his flight until I saw . 744 *Prelude* 13. 319
Hope of a flight celestial, will produce . . . . 805 *Excursion* 4. 292
Take flight ; while with their clang the air resounds. 808 *Excursion* 4. 459
The wanderer accompanies her flight . . . . 819 *Excursion* 4. 1183
For its last flight to heaven's security. . . . 853 *Excursion* 6. 1023
Of the lark's flight,—or shaped a rainbow curve, . 868 *Excursion* 7. 743
For those ordained to take their sounding flight . 889 *Excursion* 9. 372

Flight—*continued.*
Gave to thy fame a more illustrious flight . . . S.3. 442 **Vasco, whose* 10
Oft help to make bold fancy's flight more bold ; . K.8. 301 **And oh* 8
Flighted. *See* **Short-flighted.**
Flights. Would I your flights of *memory* cramp. . S.3. 438 **My Lord* 6
Flimsy. This flimsy barrier you have overleaped. . 66 *Bord.* 1585
Flinch. And he belike will flinch or start, . . . 144 **Driven in* 73
Or flinch from what he deemed his debt : . . . 178 *Waggoner* 2. 158
Fling. *See* **Fling't.**
And o'er the whitened wave their shadows fling— 12 *Desc. Sk.* 86
And fling him to the ravens. But his aspect, . 57 *Bord.* 1067
Plunge, and fling back a spiteful ear, ... 175 *Waggoner* 1. 127
I'll fling your carcass like a log . . . . . . 241 *P. B.* 459
Darkness as thick as life o'er life could fling, . . 271 *George : Death* 4
Fling the shadow of thy power, ... 336 **Jesu ! bless* 15
Or lonely tapers when from far they fling . . . 441 *Ecc. Sonn.* 3. 5. 11
To this plain truth, or fling it to the wind ; . . 504 *Warning* 94
How, from his lofty throne, the sun can fling . . 847 *Excursion* 6. 595
Flinging. Flinging round van and rear his ghastly net, ... 321 **Humanity, delighting* 14
Livelier, and flinging out less guarded words . . 731 *Prelude* 11. 284
Flings. The swan uplifts his chest, and backward flings . . . . 6 *Ev. Wk.* 218
Across the gloomy valley flings her light, . . . 8 *Ev. Wk.* 335
Flings o'er the wilderness a stream of fire : . . 20 *Desc. Sk.* 554
Upon his back and body flings . . . . . . 159 *Green Linnet* 30
Flings o'er the fen that ponderous knell— . . 238 *P. B.* 214
Thy very name, O Lady ! flings, ... 338 **Meek Virgin* 27
That Time, unwrinkled grandsire, flings . . . 530 *Gleaner* 15
That flings itself on wild relief . . . . . . 582 **O for a* 11
That flings his shadow in the pictur'd deep. . . 594 *Ev. Wk. Quarto* 156
He swells his lifted chest, and backward flings . 595 *Ev. Wk. Quarto* 201
Above the gloomy valley flings her light, . . . 599 *Ev. Wk. Quarto* 403
Flings o'er the desert blood-red streams of fire. . 614 *Desc.Sk.Quarto* 663
Fling't. To fling't away from you : you make no use 39 *Bord.* 127
Flint. I struck my flint, and built up a small fire . 50 *Bord.* 704
Flinty. As with one voice ; their flinty heart grew soft 513 *General Fast* 6
Flit. Into yon row of willows flit, ... 111 **'Tis said that some* 26
Whether the bird flit here or there, ... 144 **Driven in* 69
Wings let them have, and they might flit . . . 191 *Beggars* 33
When thou didst flit before mine eyes, ... 344 **How blest* 55
Housed near a blazing fire—is seen to flit . . . 422 *Ecc. Sonn.* 1. 16. 3
At wake or fair. And oftentimes do flit . . . 657 *Prelude* 3. 573
To flit from field to rock, from rock to field, . . K.8. 237 *Recluse* 1.1. 39
Flits. Then flits, and from the cottage eaves . . 159 *Green Linnet* 35
Flits and reflits along the close arcade ; . . . 453 **Calm is the* 21
Flitting. Where, till the flitting bird's return, . . 168 *Wren's Nest* 26
Through sunshine flitting from the bough . . . 170 *Rural Ill.* 5
The flitting halcyon's vivid dyes ; . . . . . 497 *Lycoris* 14
Within these groves, where still are flitting by . 584 **With copious* 50
Of flitting pleasures tempt him from his path ; . 670 *Prelude* 5. 304
Float. Long may they float upon this flood serene ; 6 *Ev. Wk.* 232
Now let us, as we float along, ... 9 *Collins* 17
Is shaken till the dregs float on the surface ; . . 58 *Bord.* 1163
Float near me ; do not yet depart ! . . . . 79 **Stay near* 5
Thou faery voyager ! that dost float . . . . 88 *H. C.* 5
On his own time here would he float away, . . 107 *Indolence* 6
Some little pleasure-skiff, that doth on Thames's waters float. . . . . 189 *Star-gazers* 4
But through the clouds I'll never float . . . 236 *P. B.* 3
All that to each is precious, as we float . . . 251 **Her only* 5
Or float with music in the festal barge ; . . . 273 **While Anna's* 3
Would hasten, that such pomp may float on high ? 278 **The most* 6
Or when along thy breast serenely float . . . 281 **Wansfell ! this* 4
Float double, swan and shadow ! . . . . . 293 *Yarrow Unv.* 44
Nor mount the mast, nor row, nor float . . . 295 *Highland Boy* 83
Now, where those harvest-Damsels float . . . 338 *Brientz* 5
And float in rueful company ! . . . . . . 400 *White Doe* 359
Of elevation ; let their odours float . . . . 423 *Ecc. Sonn.* 1. 18. 7
Float on the breeze—the heavenliest of all sounds 450 *Ecc. Sonn.* 3. 38. 13
But all might see it float, obedient to the wind ; . 531 †*Float. Isl.* 8
Dissevered, float upon the Lake, ... 531 †*Float. Isl.* 10
Float with its crest of trees adorned . . . . 531 †*Float. Isl.* 11
Of present sunshine.—Deities that float . . . 790 *Excursion* 3. 299
That he, from wrath redeemed, therein shall float 826 *Excursion* 5. 283
Golden and white, that float upon the waves, . 892 *Excursion* 9. 540
And I shall float upon that stream again. . . . K.8. 244 *Recluse* 1.1.296
Floated. He hung,—then floated with angelic ease 226 *Vernal Ode* 10
Alas ! the bright Ship floated, ... 374 *Eg. Maid* 361
What, if I floated down a pleasant Stream . . K.8. 244 *Recluse* 1.1.292
Floating. Or playing wanton with the floating grass. 6 *Ev. Wk.* 227
By their floating mill, ... 166 *Stray Pleasures* 1
" The floating clouds their state shall lend . . 187 **Three years* 19
Hath fed on pageants floating through the air, . 216 *Enterprise* 93
The white plumes of the floating swan ; . . . 227 *Vernal Ode* 121
Went floating from her, darkening as it went ; . . 265 **The Shepherd* 10
The glittering, floating Pageantry. . . . . 404 *White Doe* 752
Floating through the azure sky. . . . . . 415 *White Doe* 1742
Floating at ease while nations have effaced . . 452 *Ecc. Sonn.* 3. 47. 7
I, of his bold wing floating on the gale, . . . 464 *Derwent* 3
Or floating on the tongues of men, ... 472 *Ossian* 20
As a floating summer cloud, ... 502 **Like a* 27
And, floating there, in pomp serene, ... 579 **Sweet Flower* 19
Floating or fixed of polar ice, allow. . . . . 586 *Ch. Lamb* 106
Up hill or down, or shall some floating thing . . 632 *Prelude* 1. 29
That had been floating loose about for years, . . 634 *Prelude* 1. 121
To a floating island, an amphibious spot . . . 654 *Prelude* 3. 333
Floating in dance, or warbling high in air . . . 689 *Prelude* 7. 125
Though soothing, and the little floating isles . . 800 *Excursion* 3. 979

Flood—*continued.*
And now, its task performed, the flood stands still . S.3. 427 *My Son 6
Of humbler name, whose souls do like the flood . S.3. 427 *My Son 11
Through him her course along the Austral flood . S.3. 442 *Vasco, whose 12
And was borne headlong by the roaring flood. . K.8. 229 *I will 151
But most of all the Birds that haunt the flood . K.8. 241 Recluse 1.1.193
Flooded. Thy flooded cheek to wet them with its tears; . . . . 7 Ev. Wk. 276
Flood-gate. Fierce as a flood-gate bursting at midnight . . . . 330 Ode: Thanks. 79
Floods. Blue pomp of lakes, high cliffs and falling floods, ... 5 Ev. Wk. 143
Steal, and compose the oar-forgotten floods; . . 12 Desc. Sk. 118
All day the floods a deepening murmur pour: . . 15 Desc. Sk. 271
Like sounds of winds and floods; . . . . . 192 Ruth 9
That on those lonesome floods, ... 193 Ruth 111
The rain came heavily and fell in floods; . . . 195 Resolution 2
Or calentured in depth of limpid floods; . . . 216 Enterprise 94
He comes, escaped from fields and floods;— . . 249 P. B. 1105
Such power possess the family of floods . . 272 Devil's Bridge 13
Mountains, and Vales, and Floods, I call on you . 283 *Proud were 13
Lands deluged by unbridled floods; . . . . 299 Brownie's Cell 64
That Mountain floods should thunder as before, . 306 *Two Voices 12
Return, and to her murmuring floods, ... 402 White Doe 561
Through courts, through camps, o'er limitary floods; 432 Ecc. Sonn. 2. 14. 12
The floods are roused, and will not soon be weary; 476 Nunnery 1
—Breaking th' ascending roar of desert floods, . 606 Desc.Sk.Quarto 223
By floods, that, thundering from their dizzy height, 606 Desc.Sk.Quarto 247
All day the floods a deeper murmur pour, . . 608 Desc.Sk.Quarto 333
From these majestic floods, yon shining cliffs, . 682 Prelude 6. 463
When British floods were worshipped, some faint trace . . . . S.3. 435 *The doubt 126
Floor. *See* **Dungeon-floor, Palace-floor, Parlour-floor.**
Green water-rushes overspread the floor; . . . 6 Ev. Wk. 239
While they are drawing toward the sacred floor . 20 Desc. Sk. 557
In a dry nook where fern the floor bestrows . . 27 Guilt 161
While his horse pawed the floor with furious heat; 27 Guilt 175
The floor as he lay shuddering on his bed; . . 36 Guilt 638
And lifted from the grassy floor, stilling his faint alarms, ... 92 Poet's Dream 18
Past softly, leading in the Boy; and while from roof to floor, ... 92 Poet's Dream 42
From floor to roof, all round his eyes the Child with wonder cast, ... 92 Poet's Dream 43
The notes are from the floor or ceiling; . . . 143 *Driven in 21
Of refuge, with an unincumbered floor. . . . 150 *When, to 12
From year to year the spacious floor . . . . 154 *A whirl-blast 9
Along the floor, beneath the shade . . . . . 155 *A whirl-blast 16
Fire raged: and, when the spangled floor . . 168 Pilgrim's Dream 57
That he was lame) across the floor— . . . . 177 Waggoner 2. 104
Upon whose grassless floor of red-brown hue, . . 185 Yew-trees 21
Speak, and the floor thou tread'st on will rejoice. 210 Laod. 34
And fiercely swept the marble floor,— . . . . 213 Dion 70
Than his who breathes, by roof, and floor, and wall, 308 *There is a bondage 2
To the paternal floor; or turn aside, ... 320 *O'erweening States-men 5
To slumber, reclined on the moss-covered floor, . 345 Stanzas: Simplon 2
In Pisa's Campo Santo, the smooth floor . . . 355 Aquap. 155
Mural or level with the trodden floor, ... 356 Aquap. 237
To slumber, reclined on the moss-covered floor!" 364 Vallomb. 2
And through the chink in the fractured floor . . 398 White Doe 243
To kneeling Worshippers no earthly floor . . . 447 Ecc. Sonn. 3. 30. 1
Of art mosaic, in a roofless floor, ... 472 *The captive 6
As if green summer grass were the floor of my room, 484 *A plague 29
Or, bound by oaths, come forth to tread earth's floor 505 Warning 121
Beheld with wonder; whether floor or path . . 540 *Lady! a 72
Breathes out from floor or couch, through pallid lips 541 Grace Darl. 90
The household floor to tread. . . . . . . 545 Russ. Fug. 360
With chips is the carpenter strewing his floor? . 572 Avarice 17
Fresh water rushes strew the verdant floor; . . 596 Ev. Wk. Quarto 228
So to th' untrodden floor, where round him looks 612 Desc.Sk.Quarto 574
From the hard floor reverberated, then . . . 716 Prelude 9. 450
The floor was neither dry nor neat, the hearth . 768 Excursion 1. 823
Whose skill had thronged the floor with a proud show 778 Excursion 2. 424
Had we about us! scattered was the floor, . . 781 Excursion 2. 661
With ostentatious zeal.—Along the floor . . . 821 Excursion 4. 1317
Of rudely-painted Cherubim. The floor . . . 824 Excursion 5. 153
Thronging the walls; and on the floor beneath . 825 Excursion 5. 167
That from the floor of his paternal home . . . 864 Excursion 7. 429
—Just as the Child could totter on the floor, . . 867 Excursion 7. 677
That from the humblest floor ascends to heaven, . 889 Excursion 9. 326
Engaged, near blazing hearth on clean swept floor, S.3. 426 *Through Cumbrian 3
Floored. And, at his birth-place, built a chapel floored 135 Michael 269
In the slope-channel floored with pebbles bright, . 190 *Lyre! though 34
With emerald floored, and with purpureal shell . 254 Wild Duck's Nest 3
Floors. To night, the desecrated floors are worn . 359 *They—who 5
Grew on the floors his sons had trod: . . . . 390 Highland Broach 34
And floors encumbered with rich show . . . 416 White Doe 1891
Or quit with zealous step their knee-worn floors . 424 Ecc. Sonn. 1. 25. 3
Devoutly stretched upon their chancel floors. . 430 Ecc. Sonn. 2. 8. 8
Hearths loved in childhood, and ancestral floors;. 458 Sea-shore 11
Painted on rich men's floors, for one feast-night. . 488 Pers. Talk 8
Though *fettered* slave be none, her floors and soil . 501 Humanity 85
The floors of those dim cloisters, till that hour, . 682 Prelude 6. 476
If Angels traversed their cerulean floors, . . . 796 Excursion 3. 691
Flora. Maternal Flora! show thy face, ... 170 Rural Ill. 13
Blithe Flora from her couch upstarts, ... 506 *While from 3
Florence. The beauty of Florence, the grandeur of Rome . . . . 345 Stanzas: Simplon 9

Florence—*continued.*
The dome of Florence, pensive and alone, . . . 365 *Under the 2
Florid. But tinctured daintily with florid hues, . . 860 Excursion 7. 187
Florizel. Or there where Perdita and Florizel . . 701 Prelude 8. 142
Flounder. Are doomed to flounder on, like wounded whales . . . . 516 *As leaves 13
Flour. All white with flour, the dole of village dames, 566 Cumb. Beg. 9
Flourish. Both roses flourish, red and white: . . 204 Brougham 11
Pelion and Ossa flourish side by side, ... 251 *Pelion and 1
How might he flourish in his pride, ... 291 Rob Roy 67
How canst thou flourish at this blighting hour? . 319 Guernica 5
Sheltered, and flourish in a little grove . . . 568 Cumb. Beg. 121
Thy bounty caused to flourish deathless flowers, . 802 Excursion 4. 53
All generous feelings flourish and rejoice; . . . 862 Excursion 7. 328
No longer flourish, he entirely gone, ... K.8. 248 Recluse 1.1.422
Flourished. Then the milk-thistle flourished through the land, ... 17 Desc. Sk. 396
Who stood and flourished face to face . . . . 298 Brownie's Cell 32
And with their swords flourished as if to fight . 681 Prelude 6. 393
Flourishing. Flourishing in fair estate. . . . . 535 Egremont 76
With flourishing trumpet, came in full-blown state 693 Prelude 7. 417
One might be likened: flourishing appeared, . . 829 Excursion 5. 458
Of ivy, flourishing and thick, that clasped . . 881 Excursion 8. 480
Did plant the grove, now flourishing, while they K.8. 248 Recluse 1.1.421
Flout. Towers where red streamers flout the breezy sky . . . . 503 Warning 39
Flow. Till all our minds for ever flow . . . . 9 Collins 7
In her full lap, he sees such sweet tears flow . . 25 Guilt 62
Thy hours as they flow on are spent, if not in joy in peace. . . . . 92 Poet's Dream 56
Whose only business was to flow; . . . . . 111 A Complaint 4
And flow it did; not taking heed . . . . . 111 A Complaint 5
He makes my tears to flow. . . . . 115 Last of Flock 18
The Mother mourned, nor ceased her tears to flow, 139 Widow 15
The stream will not flow, and the hill will not rise, 188 Poor Susan 15
Descending with a graceful flow, ... 190 Beggars 5
Whence oft invigorating transports flow . . . 215 Kirkstone 59
Flow from your visionary skill, ... 225 Present. 23
Or, where tears flow not, sigh succeeding sigh, . 271 George: Death 10
The tear will start, and let it flow; . . . . 285 Grave of Burns 49
Perhaps the plaintive numbers flow . . . . 289 Sol. Reap. 18
For whose dire ends tears flow, and blood is spilt, 321 *Here pause 11
Our aged Sovereign sits, to the ebb and flow . . 323 *Now that 2
Into whose bosom earth's best treasures flow, . 327 Ode 1815 47
The strain should flow—free Fancy to enthral, . 336 Staub-bach 12
Or whence could virtue flow? . . . . . . 337 *Oh Life 6
Where life and rapture flow in plenitude sublime. 350 Des. Stanzas 27
For kindnesses that never ceased to flow, . . . 352 H. C. R. 7
To the Fountain whence Time and Eternity flow. 365 Vallomb. 40
Pure flow the verse, pure, vigorous, free, and bright, 376 Duddon 1. 13
Flow on for ever, Yarrow Stream! . . . . . 386 Yarrow Rev. 105
Their arts, their customs, ebb and flow; . . . 391 Highland Broach 62
Of Streams to Nature's love, where'er they flow; 392 Avon 6
For us the stream of fiction ceased to flow, . . 395 White Doe: Ded. 25
And how the current was to flow; . . . . . 399 White Doe 286
Which way the tide is doomed to flow. . . . 404 White Doe 782
The precious Current they had taught to flow? . 419 Ecc. Sonn. 1. 2. 14
Flow to the poor, and freedom to the slave; . . 424 Ecc. Sonn. 1. 24. 12
"And shall," the Pontiff asks, "profaneness flow 426 Ecc. Sonn. 1. 33. 1
Not to the golden mean, and quiet flow . . . 443 Ecc. Sonn. 3. 11. 13
Deep in the thankful heart;—yet tears will flow. 448 Ecc. Sonn. 3. 31. 8
Hopes, fears, in never-ending ebb and flow;— . 451 Ecc. Sonn. 3. 41. 11
By its soft music whence the waters flow: . . 453 *Calm is the 26
Such as will promptly flow from every breast, . 458 Sea-shore 29
And flow as now it flows. . . . . 487 Fountain 24
Love ebb and flow untroubled by caprice; . . . 500 Humanity 57
Will flow, and on a welcome page appear . . . 522 Epist. Beaumont 57
See studied kindness flow with easy stream, . . 539 *Lady! a 63
Good, only good, can flow." . . . . 545 Russ. Fug. 340
And live as long as its pure stream shall flow. . 574 Chiabrera 5. 23
Such ebb and flow must ever be, ... 581 *Loud is 23
And murder causes some sad tears to flow, . . 582 Invoc. Earth 16
Aught of these bowers and whence their pleasures flow; . . . . 583 *With copious 35
Teach from the heart the tender tear to flow; . . 619 School Ex. 92
She wept.—Life's purple tide began to flow . . 619 *She wept 1
Of happiness, my blood appeared to flow . . . 645 Prelude 2. 187
To see the river flow with ampler range . . . 656 Prelude 3. 496
May flow in lasting current. Like a breeze . . 685 Prelude 6. 675
Of a too busy world! Before me flow, . . . 689 Prelude 7. 150
And comprehensiveness and memory flow, . . . 698 Prelude 7. 741
To flow, when purposes are lightly changed? . . 773 Excursion 2. 151
With roaring sound, that ceases not to flow, . . 782 Excursion 2. 702
That, like the fabled Lethe, wished to flow . . 818 Excursion 4. 1123
Of ebb and flow, and ever-during power; . . . 818 Excursion 4. 1145
By calculations sage, the ebb and flow . . . 840 Excursion 6. 171
The practice flow,—if thence, or from a deep . . 847 Excursion 6. 618
From whom all gifts descend, all blessings flow!" 895 Excursion 9. 754
Is flowing, and will never cease to flow, . . . K.8. 244 Recluse 1.1.295
Of cities, mid the same eternal flow . . . . K.8. 257 *Shall he 3
Flowed. Then Summer lingered long; and honey flowed . . . . 17 Desc. Sk. 388
And tears which flowed for ills which patience might not heal. . . . . 29 Guilt 270
Alas the dream, to thee, poor Boy! to thee from whom it flowed, ... 93 Poet's Dream 77
The Swale flowed under the grey rocks, . . . 240 P. B. 371
But he flowed quiet and unseen:— . . . . . 240 P. B. 372
As if it from a fountain flowed— . . . . . 244 P. B. 679
And the fresh meads—where flowed, from every nook . . . . 254 Complete Angler 13

Flowed—*continued.*
Tears flowed in torrents from her eyes; 297 *Highland Boy* 238
Hath flowed, "with pomp of waters, unwithstood," 307 **It is not* 4
Blood flowed before thy sight without remorse; 316 **Hail, Zaragoza* 9
Paid simple tribute, such as might have flowed 356 *Aquap.* 242
For busy thoughts the Stream flowed on 385 *Yarrow Rev.* 17
Our thoughts have issued, and our feelings flowed, 394 **No more* 23
Had tinged more deeply, as it flowed, 412 *White Doe* 1496
A flood of tears that flowed apace 414 *White Doe* 1663
As to the one sole fount whence wisdom flowed, 419 *Ecc. Sonn.* 1. 4. 8
The crown of thorns; whose life-blood flowed, the price 420 *Ecc. Sonn.* 1. 8. 8
O wretched Land! whose tears have flowed like fountains; 421 *Ecc. Sonn.* 1. 11. 7
Flowed in thy line through undegenerate veins. 425 *Ecc. Sonn.* 1. 27. 4
From Wisdom's heavenly Father. Hence hath flowed 520 *Pun. Death* 14. 11
As if their lustre flowed from ether's purest blue. 525 *Epist. Beaumont* 257
That haply flowed from me, by fits of silence 538 **In desultory* 13
Flowed from his life what still they hold, 578 **I come* 62
Flowed in a course of sympathy divine;— 583 **With copious* 25
Those simple lines flowed with an earnest wish, 585 *Ch. Lamb* 40
And with rock-honey flow'd the happy land. 611 *Desc.Sk.Quarto* 477
That flowed along my dreams? For this, didst thou, 636 *Prelude* 1. 274
Have since flowed in between us, and, our minds 647 *Prelude* 2. 336
Flowed in upon me, from all sides; fresh day 649 *Prelude* 3. 24
That flowed into a kindred stream; a gale, 686 *Prelude* 6. 744
That flowed awhile with unabating strength, 687 *Prelude* 7. 10
Of a high eastern hill—thus flowed my thoughts 706 *Prelude* 8. 466
Flowed in the bent of Nature. Having now 751 *Prelude* 14. 369
And whence they flowed; and from them he acquired 759 *Excursion* 1. 238
Have flowed as if my body were not such 768 *Excursion* 1. 771
There flowed no Gallic blood, nor had I breathed 796 *Excursion* 3. 742
Among steep hills and woods embosomed, flowed 823 *Excursion* 5. 83
And know we not that from the blind have flowed 865 *Excursion* 7. 534
And answer flowed, the fetters of reserve 882 *Excursion* 8. 525

Flower. *See* **Cuckoo-flower, Garden-flower, Ground-flower, Lily-flower, Meadow-flower, Sea-flower, Strawberry-flower, Wild-flower.**
Or like the beauty in a flower installed, 20 *Desc. Sk.* 534
One flower of hope—oh, pass and leave it there! 20 *Desc. Sk.* 552
Restore him, Heaven! The desperate Wretch!—A Flower, 61 *Bord.* 1308
Look at it—the flower is small, 79 *Foresight* 5
And for that promise spare the flower! 80 *Foresight* 32
In their stead each opening flower. 94 *Westmoreland Girl* 80
Of old tradition, one particular flower 103 *Artegal* 58
While I this flower transplant 103 *Artegal* 62
Self-poised upon that yellow flower; 106 **I've watched* 2
Among the distant mountains, flower and weed, 106 *Farewell* 35
When he came back to us, a withered flower,— 107 *Indolence* 20
Perishing yet more swiftly than the flower, 110 **Look at* 8
From twig or bed an humbler flower, even for your sake!" 139 *Arm. Lady* 12
Flower of an unchristian sod! 140 *Arm. Lady* 70
To note in shrub and tree, in stone and flower, 147 *Joanna* 46
To pluck, some flower or water-weed, too fair 148 **A narrow* 29
Though of both leaf and flower bereft, 155 *Waterfall* 45
Then, cheerful Flower! my spirits play 158 **In youth* 59
Bright *Flower!* for by that name at last, 159 **With little* 41
There's a flower that shall be mine, 160 **Pansies, lilies* 7
Little Flower—I'll make a stir, 160 **Pansies, lilies* 15
Thou, a flower of wiser wits, 161 **Pleasures newly* 37
Who will love my little Flower. 161 **Pleasures newly* 56
From flower to flower let him fly; 163 **Art thou the* 28
This precious Flower, true love's last token. 164 **Fair Lady* 40
A simple flower deceives. 169 *Wren's Nest* 60
When withered is the guardian Flower, 169 *Wren's Nest* 67
Though the red Flower, not prostrate, only droops, 169 *Love lies Bleeding* 2
A flower how rich in sadness! Even thus stoops, 169 *Love lies Bleeding* 5
The dying Gladiator. So, sad Flower! 169 *Love lies Bleeding* 9
His own dejection, downcast Flower! could share 169 *Love lies Bleeding* 23
This Flower, that first appeared as summer's guest, 169 **Never enlivened* 4
This undeparting Flower in crimson dyed, 170 **Never enlivened* 23
Then Nature said, "A lovelier flower 187 **Three years* 2
As with the breath of one sweet flower,— 191 *Seq. Beggars* 16
The red rose is a gladsome flower. 203 *Brougham* 6
Who is the flower of Lancaster! 204 *Brougham* 16
Flower of the winds, beneath her bosom worn— 221 *Triad* 117
Of vision?—o'er this tempting flower 227 *Vernal Ode* 111
Sits blooming like a flower. 238 *P. B.* 160
Of outward change, there blooms a deathless flower, 256 **Yes! hope* 13
'Tis hers to pluck the amaranthine flower 259 **Weak is* 11
Gathering green weeds to mix with poppy flower, 261 **Fair Prime* 6
The flower of sweetest smell is shy and lowly. 262 **Not Love* 14
Lone Flower, hemmed in with snows, and white as they 264 *Snowdrop* 1
Of bud, leaf, blade, and flower—was fashioning 266 **The stars* 13
With shady night. Soft airs, from shrub and flower, 271 **Where holy* 9
Forgets her nature, opening like a flower 274 *Infant M.* 2
By morning shed around a flower half-blown; 277 *Author's Portrait* 12
Because the lovely little flower is free 277 **A Poet* 10
Fresh as the flower, whose modest worth 285 *Grave of Burns* 19
Or tree, or butterfly, or flower, 295 *Highland Boy* 18
Where was it that the famous Flower 302 *Yarrow V.* 25
Perish without reprieve for flower or tree! 330 *Ode: Thanks.* 112

Flower—*continued.*
Passive yet pleased. What! with this Broom in flower 353 *Aquap.* 26
And pleasant course; flower after flower has blown, 361 **List—'twas* 11
Was carved—a Goddess with a Lily flower, 370 *Eg. Maid* 76
By the fierce waves, a flower in marble graven. 371 *Eg. Maid* 126
Than if the Goddess of the flower had spoken: 371 *Eg. Maid* 152
So, for the favoured One, the Flower may bloom 372 *Eg. Maid* 255
The Flower, the Form within it, 374 *Eg. Maid* 367
The envied flower beholding, as it lies 377 *Duddon* 7. 3
Of some sweet Babe—Flower stolen, and coarse Weed left 378 *Duddon* 11. 7
Tree, flower, and green herb, feeding without blame. 392 *Avon* 8
May this bright flower of Charity display 393 *Countess' Pillar* 2
Flower than the loveliest of the vernal prime 393 *Countess' Pillar* 4
And where no flower hath leave to dwell. 397 *White Doe* 99
Of man, our youngest, fairest flower! 401 *White Doe* 483
For him, the sweet half-opened Flower! 411 *White Doe* 1370
Herself most like a stately flower, 414 *White Doe* 1634
What flower in meadow-ground or garden grows 432 *Ecc. Sonn.* 2. 15. 3
Whose virtue changes to a christian Flower 445 *Ecc. Sonn.* 3. 20. 3
On drooping eyelid and the closing flower; 456 **The leaves* 5
Myriads of daisies have shone forth in flower 475 **There! said* 10
And 'tis my faith that every flower 482 *Lines: Spring* 11
Bright Flower! whose home is everywhere, 485 **Bright Flower* 1
Given to no other flower I see 485 **Bright Flower* 7
From flower to flower supported; but to curb 496 **A little* 17
The lowliest flower possesses in its place; 501 *Humanity* 108
Nor add to it a flower! 508 *May* 92
Till they were plucked together; a blue flower 509 *F. Stone* 60
With thy memorial flower, meek Portraiture! 510 **Among a* 11
To rival summer's brightest scarlet flower; 529 *Poor Robin* 10
Your star, your gem, your flower; 542 *Russ. Fug.* 62
There is a Flower, the lesser Celandine, 571 **There is a Flower* 1
But lately, one rough day, this Flower I passed 571 **There is a Flower* 9
O flower of all that springs from gentle blood, 575 *Chiabrera* 7. 1
Sweet Flower! belike one day to have 579 **Sweet Flower* 1
And Thou, sweet Flower, shalt sleep and wake 580 **Sweet Flower* 69
That meets me in this unknown Flower, 580 *John Words.* 16
Meek Flower! To Him I would have said, 580 *John Words.* 52
Of splendour in the grass, of glory in the flower; 590 *Immortality* 182
To me the meanest flower that blows can give 590 *Immortality* 206
Within our hearts, the love whose flower hath blown 627 **We gaze* 3
Whose flower with us will vanish, must survive. 627 **We gaze* 14
The Flower has drooped, the Isle's delight; 628 *Installation* 22
Flower and bud together fall; 628 *Installation* 23
Of Wallace to be found, like a wild flower, 635 *Prelude* 1. 215
Is there a flower, to which he points with hand 645 *Prelude* 2. 245
Hath beautified that flower; already shades 646 *Prelude* 2. 248
To every natural form, rock, fruit, or flower, 651 *Prelude* 3. 127
A flower till it have yielded up its sweets 669 *Prelude* 5. 244
Deals with a flower; the keepers of our time, 671 *Prelude* 5. 353
Tranquil almost, and careless as a flower 711 *Prelude* 9. 87
Had failed, and every leaf and flower were lost 764 *Excursion* 1. 531
When on its sunny bank the primrose flower 768 *Excursion* 1. 815
A blooming Lady—a conspicuous flower, 774 *Excursion* 2. 187
What joy more lasting than a vernal flower?— 792 *Excursion* 3. 439
The little flower her vanity shall check; 807 *Excursion* 4. 425
And not a flower, that droops in the green shade, 842 *Excursion* 6. 297
And the flower drooped; as every eye could see, 853 *Excursion* 6. 1001
Not one of all the band, a full-blown flower. 855 *Excursion* 6. 1130
Of fruit or flower, permission asked or not, 856 *Excursion* 6. 1166
Where, in assemblage with the flower and choice 869 *Excursion* 7. 769
Profusion bright! and every flower assuming 881 *Excursion* 8. 471
In flower and tree, in every pebbly stone 884 *Excursion* 9. 7
Changed to a crimson flower; when he, whose pride S. 3. 434 **The doubt* 82
Imaged in downward show; the flower, the herbs, S. 3. 435 **The doubt* 106
Edward, the flower of chivalry, survey L. 1. 94 *Juvenal* 2. 24

Flower-besprent. In the flower-besprent meadows his genius we trace 364 *Vallomb.* 13

Flower-breathed. Where flower-breathed incense to the skies 228 *Devot. Incit.* 60

Flower-crowned. For victories there won by flower-crowned Spring, 367 **If with* 13

Flower-decked. That—after I had left a flower-decked room 664 *Prelude* 4. 374

Flowered. *See* **Full-flowered.**
Had scarcely flowered: and at this early time, 575 *Chiabrera* 8. 11

Flower-enamelled. While, o'er the flower-enamelled glade, 338 **Meek Virgin* 35
Lingering no more 'mid flower-enamelled lands 384 *Duddon* 32. 2

Floweret. The floweret as it springs, 170 *Rural Ill.* 28
With *one* wild floweret (call it not forlorn) 221 *Triad* 116
To be an unculled floweret of the glen, 377 *Duddon* 7. 12
That ornament, unblamed. The floweret, held 509 *F. Stone* 63
For some rare floweret of the hills, or plant 788 *Excursion* 3. 166
Beholds the gulf beneath.—No floweret blooms 865 *Excursion* 7. 498

Flowerets. When the pretty flowerets die; 80 *Foresight* 22
Than the sweet flowerets of the fields! 113 *Lament* 33
Sacred to flowerets of the hills, 165 *Danish Boy* 3
Disposed some cultured Flowerets (drawn from spots 280 *Valedict.* 2
There berries ripen, flowerets bloom; 532 †*Float. Isl.* 14
Where, haply, crowned with flowerets and green herbs, 786 *Excursion* 3. 33
She, 'mid the humble flowerets of the vale, 848 *Excursion* 6. 687

Flowering. *See* **Fair-flowering, Late-flowering.**
The flowering shrubs that deck our humble door 106 *Farewell* 11
"In April here beneath the flowering thorn 203 *Hart-leap* 153
Close by a brake of flowering furze 246 *P. B.* 921
This flowering broom's dear neighbourhood, the light 358 *Aquap.* 369

Flowers—*continued.*
The unendangered myrtle, decked with flowers, . 793 *Excursion* 3. 523
Bring garlands, bring forth choicest flowers, to deck 796 *Excursion* 3. 725
Thy bounty caused to flourish deathless flowers, . 802 *Excursion* 4. 53
If the flowers wither, I am worse than dead ! . . 802 *Excursion* 4. 56
Small creature as she is, from earth's bright flowers, 807 *Excursion* 4. 393
His stooping body tottered with wreaths of flowers 816 *Excursion* 4. 1001
Hopeful and promising with buds and flowers ; . 828 *Excursion* 5. 397
A Visitor—in quest of herbs and flowers ; . . . 839 *Excursion* 6. 97
A calendar of flowers, plucked as they blow . . 841 *Excursion* 6. 174
And everlasting flowers. These Dalesmen trust . 847 *Excursion* 6. 610
And flowers that prosper in the shade. And when 848 *Excursion* 6. 654
And with the flowers are intermingled stones . . 855 *Excursion* 6. 1154
For her own flowers and favourite herbs, a space, 856 *Excursion* 6. 1163
Their bonnets, I remember, wreathed with flowers, 858 *Excursion* 7. 75
Perish the roses and the flowers of kings, . . . 872 *Excursion* 7. 980
By beds and banks Arcadian of gay flowers . . 881 *Excursion* 8. 469
Are scattered at the feet of Man—like flowers. . 887 *Excursion* 9. 240
(Her flowers were shed) the lily of the vale, . . 892 *Excursion* 9. 542
Whom Morn awakens, among dews and flowers . 894 *Excursion* 9. 670
Is clad with yellow flowers. . . . . S. 3. 431 **The Scottish* 28
Communion without check of herbs and flowers . S. 3. 435 **The doubt* 104
Thy living chaplet of fresh flowers and fern, . . S. 3. 437 **The doubt* 201
And hear the voices of the winds and flowers. . K. 8. 224 **I will* 3
That is to come, the throng of woodland flowers, K. 8. 252 *Recluse* 1. 1. 590
An amaranthine crown of flowers forlorn— . . K. 8. 325 [?] **The vestal* 7

Flowery. They crush with broad black feet their flowery walk ; . . . . 6 *Ev. Wk.* 243
O'er lake and stream, mountain and flowery mead, 151 **Forth from* 5
And Truth would skim the flowery glade, . . . 154 *Flower Garden* 55
And happy in his flowery cove : . . . . . 166 *Danish Boy* 50
The flowery ground is conscious. But no wind . 219 *Haunted Tree* 30
Through rocky passes, among flowery creeks, . . 268 **Brook ! whose* 4
For not a tinge or flowery streak . . . . . 342 *Ital. Itin.* 83
Wide-spreading odours from her flowery wreaths. 367 *Trajan* 22
Thy waters, Duddon ! 'mid these flowery plains ; 381 *Duddon* 20. 3
The walls are cracked, sunk is the flowery roof, . 390 *Highland Hut* 9
That Hill, whose flowery platform seems to rise . 420 *Ecc. Sonn.* 1. 6. 13
But what if One, through grove or flowery mead, 424 *Ecc. Sonn.* 1. 23. 1
That life—the flowery path that winds by stealth— 528 **Those breathing* 91
Hence, when yon mansion and the flowery trim . 546 **Oft is* 5
Ye crush with broad black feet your flow'ry walk ; 596 *Ev. Wk. Quarto* 232
The sandy fields, leaping through flowery groves . 636 *Prelude* 1. 293
Adorning flowery gardens, 'mid vast squares ; . 689 *Prelude* 7. 135
A sumptuous dream of flowery lawns, with domes 700 *Prelude* 8. 84
On Etna's side ; and thou, O flowery field . . 733 *Prelude* 11. 419
Laden from blooming grove or flowery field, . . 733 *Prelude* 11. 446
Placed, among flowery gardens curtained round . 791 *Excursion* 3. 346
And, all day long, moisten these flowery fields !' 812 *Excursion* 4. 752
And, up the flowery lawn as we advance, . . . 881 *Excursion* 8. 497
Upon this flowery slope ; and see—beyond— . 890 *Excursion* 9. 420
Rapaciously we gathered flowery spoils . . . 892 *Excursion* 9. 538
O happy Thing ! among thy flowery creeks, . . K. 8. 265 **Brook, that* 4

Flowing. *See* **Fresh-flowing, Swift-flowing.**
As thy deep waters now are flowing. . . . . 9 *Collins* 8
Follow thou the flowing river . . . . . . 90 *Longest Day* 49
The other, left behind, is flowing still. . . . . 97 *Brothers* 145
Is flowing in the breeze. . . . . 110 **Ere with* 16
The streams with softest sound are flowing, . . 129 *Idiot Boy* 284
The stream is flowing, ... 190 *March* 2
Pure modulations flowing from the heart . . 234 *Power of Sound* 110
While flowing rivers yield a blameless sport, . . 254 *Complete Angler* 1
And all that fetched the flowing rhyme . . . 286 *Nith* 51
And sweet is Yarrow flowing ! . . . . . . 293 *Yarrow Unv.* 34
Time cannot thin thy flowing hair, ... 345 **How blest* 72
Flowing of time and place, and paid to both . 358 *Aquap.* 361
Like the crystal stream now flowing . . . 397 *White Doe* 150
Born to be lost in Derwent flowing near ; . . 465 **The cattle* 5
And, ere the flowing fount be dry, ... 497 *Lycoris* 42
Fail to wash out, tears flowing ere thy troth . 514 **Long-favoured* 6
To the great current flowing underneath ; . . 515 **Men of* 11
I love beside the flowing lake to stray, . . . 595 *Ev. Wk. Quarto* 195
The softly flowing Leine, ... 629 *Installation* 60
And, save the flowing water's peaceful voice, . . 664 *Prelude* 4. 386
We glided forward with the flowing stream. . . 680 *Prelude* 6. 377
With flowing cups elate and happy thoughts . . 681 *Prelude* 6. 398
The rapid river flowing without noise, . . . 681 *Prelude* 6. 410
He traced an ebbing and a flowing mind, . . . 758 *Excursion* 1. 161
Or flowing from the universal face . . . . . 759 *Excursion* 1. 190
By flowing stream, through wood, or craggy wild 803 *Excursion* 4. 105
That flowing years repealed not : and distress . 811 *Excursion* 4. 648
Upon the flowing stream, a thought arose . . 812 *Excursion* 4. 754
Say rather, all his thoughts now flowing clear, . 819 *Excursion* 4. 1222
From a clear fountain flowing, he looks round . 819 *Excursion* 4. 1223
Is flowing, and will never cease to flow, . . . K. 8. 244 *Recluse* 1. 1. 295
Pure and unsullied, flowing from the heart . . K. 8. 248 *Recluse* 1. 1. 410

Flown. More of contempt than hatred ; both are flown ; . . . . 47 *Bord.* 554
Joy will be flown in its mortality ; . . . . . 107 *Farewell* 51
My beauty, little child, is flown, ... 145 *Her Eyes* 66
To me hath often flown, ... 156 *Oak and Broom* 82
It is no Spirit who from heaven hath flown, . . 208 **It is no* 1
And back he falls, as if his life were flown ! . . 242 *P. B.* 530
His sudden fit of joy is flown,— . . . . . 243 *P. B.* 588
Is ancient Piety for ever flown ? . . . . . 256 *Decay of Piety* 11
When truth, when sense, when liberty were flown, 303 **Is it* 12
Angels she sees—that might from heaven have flown, ... 343 *Eclipse* 45
When youth had flown did hope still bless . . 344 **How blest* 63

Flown—*continued.*
Had flown with mine to old Helvellyn's brow, . 353 *Aquap.* 62
The mind, depressed by thought of greatness flown. 365 **Under the* 8
By apter pencil, from the light had flown. . . 368 *Trajan* 40
Without restraint. How swiftly have they flown, 378 *Duddon* 9. 8
'Tis flown—the Vision, and the sense . . . . 407 *White Doe* 1042
Perchance had flown, delivered by the storm ; . 472 **The captive* 2
And virtue, flown, come back ; . . . . . . 505 **If this* 4
But time, irrevocable time, is flown, ... 524 *Epist. Beaumont* 200
But tells a plain tale of the days that are flown. . 572 *Avarice* 24
Were flown, and autumn brought its annual show 664 *Prelude* 4. 371
At thought of raptures now for ever flown ; . . 673 *Prelude* 5. 546
From dangerous passions free. Three years had flown . . . . 688 *Prelude* 7. 65
" Those fervent raptures are for ever flown ; . . 803 *Excursion* 4. 123
Let grandeur tell thee whither now is flown . . L. 1. 97 *Juvenal* 3. 94

Flows. While from his heart the appropriate lesson flows, ... 33 *Guilt* 512
The stream that flows out of the lake, ... 162 *Binnorie* 56
And a river flows on through the vale of Cheapside. 188 *Poor Susan* 8
Back flows the willing current of my Song : . . 217 *Enterprise* 119
More efficaciously than aught that flows . . 255 **Grief, thou* 6
Along the Vale of Meditation flows ; . . . 272 *Lady E. B.* 2
Yet why ?—a silvery current flows . . . . 302 *Yarrow V.* 9
They follow their dear Lord ! Time flows—nor winds, ... 357 *Aquap.* 315
Conspicuous yet where Oroonoko flows ; . . . 380 *Duddon* 16. 3
The tear in answer flows ; . . . . . . 479 *Somnamb.* 78
In flows the joyous year. . . . . . . 507 **While from* 56
But He beholds the light, and whence it flows, . 588 *Immortality* 69
Issuing, however feebly, nowhere flows . . 804 *Excursion* 4. 220
As merciless proscription ebbs and flows. . . 848 *Excursion* 6. 674
Flows on in solitude. But, when the gloom . . 856 *Excursion* 6. 1173
Now pointing this way, and now that.—'Here flows,' 869 *Excursion* 7. 787
Whence flows the Latin people, whence have come K. 8. 281 **Arms and* 8

Fluctuate. Thy three-striped banner fluctuate on the breeze ; . . . . 21 *Desc. Sk.* 613

Fluctuating. Nor less to guide the fluctuating youth 619 *School Ex.* 77
And passions hold a fluctuating seat : . . . . 802 *Excursion* 4. 70

Fluctuation. And the vast hills, in fluctuation fixed 802 *Excursion* 4. 35
The fluctuation and decay of things, ... 837 *Excursion* 5. 999

Fluctuations. And various fluctuations in the breast ; 841 *Excursion* 6. 209

Fluent. For way and guide, a fluent receptacle . 720 *Prelude* 10. 170
On fluent operations a fixed shape ; . . . . 812 *Excursion* 4. 727

Flung. Caution must not be flung aside ; remember, 48 *Bord.* 604
And flung it to the dogs : but I am raised . . 77 *Bord.* 2294
She flung her blameless child, ... 103 *Artegal* 38
From out the lowly hedge-rows flung ; . . . . 180 *Waggoner* 4. 78
For what one moment flung aside, ... 191 *Seq. Beggars* 8
For blue Ether's arms, flung round thee, . . . 217 **Inmate of* 7
Flung from off the purple pinions . . . . 217 **Inmate of* 23
Or, flung from swinging censer, shrouds . . . 228 *Devot. Incit.* 32
Flung back, and, in the sky's blue caves, reborn— 233 *Power of Sound* 36
Broke forth in concert flung adown the dells, . . 267 *St. Cath.* 3
Which, spurning God, had flung away remorse— 330 *Ode : Thanks.* 119
Inviting words—perchance already flung . . . 332 *Ode : Thanks.* 212
Flung from a Convent-tower, ... 334 **In Bruges* 6
Fancy hath flung for me an airy bridge . . . 350 *Des. Stanzas* 28
Their foliage ; ashes flung their arms around ; . 377 *Duddon* 5. 7
Flung from yon cliff a shadow large and cold. . 383 *Duddon* 27. 4
And flung into the brook that travels near ; . . 432 *Ecc. Sonn.* 2. 17. 4
Flung back from distant climes a streaming fire, . 453 **The Sun, that* 2
Flung from her to the stream. . . . . . 479 *Somnamb.* 108
With shadows flung from leaves—to strive . . 499 **This Lawn* 2
Flung by labouring Nature forth . . . . . 502 **Like a* 5
In recklessness flung out to overturn . . . 538 **In desultory* 46
That from his ardent countenance are flung, . . 624 *Æneid* 75
To industry, by glistenings flung on rocks, . . 682 *Prelude* 6. 515
Flung from the setting sun, as they reposed . . 706 *Prelude* 8. 464
A surface dappled o'er with shadows flung . . 756 *Excursion* 1. 5
Flung from the body of devouring fires, . . . 894 *Excursion* 9. 703

Flurried. By this time is not quite so flurried : . 127 *Idiot Boy* 128

Flurry. Though Betty's in a mighty flurry, . . 126 *Idiot Boy* 68

Flush. —Would I had ne'er renounced it !" A slight flush . . . . 832 *Excursion* 5. 621

Flushed. Now flush'd as Hebe, Emulation rose ; . 618 *School Ex.* 20
The beauteous girl, whose cheek was flushed with joy. . . . . 890 *Excursion* 9. 428

Flushes. *See* **Joy-flushes.**

Flute. Or thrown away ; but with a flute . . . 195 *Ruth* 242
This flute, made of a hemlock stalk, ... 195 *Ruth* 244
O Friend ! thy flute has breathed a harmony . . 252 **The fairest* 3
Whose breath would labour at the flute in vain, . 521 *Epist. Beaumont* 29
He marches with his flute, his book, and sword, . 611 *Desc. Sk. Quarto* 533
And rowed off gently, while he blew his flute . . 644 *Prelude* 2. 169

Flutter. There ! where the flutter of his wings . . 159 *Green Linnet* 29
They try all frolic motions ; flutter, plunge, . . K. 8. 251 *Recluse* 1. 1. 550

Fluttered. Fluttered, perched, into a round . . 171 *Kitten* 70
Fluttered so faint a heart before ;— . . . . 237 *P. B.* 82
How fluttered then thy anxious heart for me, . 445 *Ecc. Sonn.* 3. 22. 8
A Guardian Angel fluttered . . . . . . 628 *Installation* 31

Flutterer. Then peck or perch, fond Flutterer ! nor forbear . . . . 273 **Wild Redbreast* 13

Fluttering. Fluttering its pinions, almost within reach, ... 122 *V. and J.* 83
While fluttering o'er this gay Recess, ... 154 *Flower Garden* 2
While fluttering in the bushes. . . . . . 159 *Green Linnet* 40
Fluttering and dancing in the breeze. . . . . 187 **I wandered* 6
To hunt their fluttering game o'er rock and level green. . . . . 191 *Beggars* 36

Fluttering—*continued.*
An eager Novice robed in fluttering gown! . . . 270 **Ye sacred* 14
Of trouble—but the fluttering breeze; . . . . 348 **Lulled by* 17
Ah! if their fluttering hearts should stir too much, 378 *Duddon* 10. 11
Safe from the wintry tempest. Fluttering, . . 422 *Ecc. Sonn.* 1. 16. 4
By fluttering pinions here and busy bill; . . . 531 **I know* 19
With new-fledged hope still fluttering in his breast:— . . . . 589 *Immortality* 142
The fluttering breezes, fountains that run on . . 647 *Prelude* 2. 371
The fluttering nerves composed; the beating heart 841 *Excursion* 6. 194
Of fluttering Sylphs, and softly-gliding Fays, . . K.8. 237 *Recluse* 1. 1. 33
Flutterings. *Her* wingless flutterings, ... 170 *Rural Ill.* 26
Flutters. Whose heart still flutters, though his wings forbear . . . . 440 *Ecc. Sonn.* 2. 45. 5
That flutters on the bough, lighter than he; . . 842 *Excursion* 6. 296
Fly. *See* **May-fly.**
And, hovering, round it often did a raven fly. . 25 *Guilt* 81
Of kitten, bird, or summer fly; . . . . . . 81 †*Mother's Return* 22
For Allonville, o'er down and dale, away then did we fly; . . . . 92 *Poet's Dream* 30
As doth a fly upon a summer brook; . . . . 107 *Indolence* 7
If to a rock from rains he fly, ... 158 **In youth* 33
Up to thee would I fly. . . . . 159 **Up with me* 11
Away they fly to left, to right— . . . . . 161 *Binnorie* 29
Away the seven fair Campbells fly, ... 162 *Binnorie* 34
From flower to flower let him fly; . . . . . 163 **Art thou the* 28
And fly about in the air together! . . . . . 163 **Art thou the* 34
—Fly also, Muse! and from the dell . . . . 180 *Waggoner* 4. 36
Give her wings that she may fly, ... 204 *Brougham* 57
Open, ye thickets! let her fly, ... 221 *Triad* 119
A Fly, that up and down himself doth shove . . 253 **O gentle* 6
Yes, there was One;—for One, asunder fly . . 268 **Four fiery* 7
Fly, some kind Harbinger, to Grasmere-dale! . . 294 **Fly, some* 1
Fly upon swiftest wing round field and height, . 294 **Fly, some* 3
—Fly, wretched Gauls! ere they the charge renew 322 *Germans* 12
—Fly, ministers of Fame, ... 327 *Ode 1815* 8
Close at my side! She bids me fly to greet . . 353 *Aquap.* 27
Ye, too, must fly before a chasing hand, . . . 434 *Ecc. Sonn.* 2. 24. 1
There, should vain thoughts outspread their wings and fly . . . . 445 *Ecc. Sonn.* 3. 20. 9
That he might fly, where no one could pursue, . 471 **Arran! a* 6
Fly where the culprit may, guilt meets a doom; . 475 **Here on their* 12
See that Fly,—a disconsolate creature! perhaps . 484 **A plague* 6
But when the clouds asunder fly . . . . . 490 *Night Thought* 5
—Off they fly in earnest chase; . . . . . 490 *Incident: Dog* 10
Or, from long stress of real injuries fly . . . 505 *Warning* 117
Yet on presumptuous wing as far would fly . . 513 *Newspaper* 12
From heaviness, oft fly, dear Friend, to thee; . 521 *Epist. Beaumont* 11
A fly may settle, or a blossom fall. . . . . . 527 **Those breathing* 12
And he for dread did fly away full fast; . . . 560 *Cuck. and Night.* 219
Small as a bird the chamois-chaser fly. . . . 609 *Desc. Sk. Quarto* 369
Science with joy saw Superstition fly . . . . 618 *School Ex.* 43
Soon fades her cheek, her blushing beauties fly, . 619 *School Ex.* 97
The minutes fly—till, at the queen's command, . 625 *Æneid* 103
To fly, for safeguard, to some foreign shore, . . 798 *Excursion* 3. 832
Fly to those harbours, driven by hound and horn 808 *Excursion* 4. 501
Alas! such wisdom bids a creature fly . . . . 817 *Excursion* 4. 1083
To fly—but whither! And this gracious Church, 855 *Excursion* 6. 1105
Flying. Flying till vision can no more pursue! . . 16 *Desc. Sk.* 327
—Alas! in every clime a flying ray . . . . 19 *Desc. Sk.* 500
O wind, that o'er my head art flying . . . . 114 *Ind. Wom.* 45
And so, flag flying at mast head, ... 178 *Waggoner* 2. 162
Nor what ye are flying, nor what ye pursue! . . 189 *Music* 44
And drive the flying deer! . . . . 193 *Ruth* 96
And drive the flying deer. . . . . 193 *Ruth* 102
Flying from something that he dreads than one . 206 *Tintern* 71
There's something in a flying horse, ... 236 *P. B.* 1
To the flying moments, and is seen no more. . . 261 **I watch* 9
Doomed, with their impious Lord, the flying Hart 267 **Though narrow* 13
And birds, high flying in the element, ... 312 **A Roman* 7
But, flying through the heights around, . . . 342 *Ital. Itin.* 65
Or, free as air, with flying inquest viewed . . 382 *Duddon* 26. 4
(And flying shall behold again) . . . . . . 405 *White Doe* 816
Upwhirled, and flying o'er the ethereal plain . . 435 *Ecc. Sonn.* 2. 28. 8
Friends strike at friends—the flying shall pursue— 437 *Ecc. Sonn.* 2. 36. 13
And by a train of flying clouds bemocked; . . . 454 *Sea-side* 13
With flying haste, I might have sent, ... 457 **Had this* 2
Before a flying season's rash pretence . . . . 471 **Despond who* 5
And mists that spread the flying shroud; . . . 491 *Fidelity* 30
And flying fleet behind his orb to view . . . 609 *Desc. Sk. Quarto* 388
Through bursts of sunshine and through flying showers, ... 622 *Recluse* 1. 1. 154
Of active days urged on by flying hours,— . . . 632 *Prelude* 1. 42
Flying, found shelter in the Fortunate Isles, . . 635 *Prelude* 1. 192
That fled, and, flying still before me, gleamed . 638 *Prelude* 1. 451
And unaimed prattle flying up and down; . . . 663 *Prelude* 4. 315
Flying or seeking, could yet bring with him . . 778 *Excursion* 2. 482
Of flying sunbeams, or to the outward form . . 794 *Excursion* 3. 577
Flying, and rainy vapours, call out shapes . . 809 *Excursion* 4. 522
One voice—the solitary raven, flying . . . . 819 *Excursion* 4. 1178
Could have transferred him to the flying clouds, . 829 *Excursion* 5. 449
Foam. *See* **Torrent-foam.**
Save where, with sparkling foam, a small cascade 3 *Ev. Wk.* 64
You could not hear, for the foam beat the rocks . 51 *Bord.* 746
Which with their foam could cover it at will. . . 69 *Bord.* 1742
And, while the broad blue wave and sparkling foam . . . . 96 *Brothers* 56
That, all bespattered with his foam, ... 155 *Waterfall* 7
For ever; and I saw the sparkling foam, . . . 185 *Nutting* 34
And white with foam as if with cleaving sleet. . 201 *Hart-leap* 40
His force on Caspian foam to try; . . . . . 213 *Dion* 72

Foam—*continued.*
Bespattered with the salt sea foam; . . . . 239 *P. B.* 232
Yon eddying balls of foam, these arrowy gleams . 268 **Dogmatic Teachers* 10
Charged, and dispersed like foam: but as a flight 320 **Hunger, and* 6
Dashed their white foam against the palace walls 354 *Aquap.* 122
Robed instantly in garb of snow-white foam; . . 377 *Duddon* 4. 10
(A spotless Youngling white as foam) . . . . 416 *White Doe* 1806
As Menai's foam; and toward the mystic ring . 419 *Ecc. Sonn.* 1. 3. 2
Purer than foam on central ocean tost; . . . 434 *Ecc. Sonn.* 2. 25. 5
Where bubbles burst, and folly's dancing foam . 452 *Ecc. Sonn.* 3. 45. 5
Or, tossed about along a waste of foam, . . . 458 *Sea-shore* 12
Yet, like to eddying balls of foam . . . . . 551 **Behold an* 3
Illumes with sparkling foam the twilight shade. . 593 *Ev. Wk. Quarto* 80
A napkin, white as foam of that rough brook . . 781 *Excursion* 2. 674
And, on its glassy surface, specks of foam, . . 800 *Excursion* 3. 973
Foam-balls. To mark its eddying foam-balls prettily distrest . . . . 190 **Lyre! though* 27
Foamed. And met a man who foamed with anger vehement. . . . . 33 *Guilt* 468
Foaming. One I behold who, 'cross the foaming flood, ... 17 *Desc. Sk.* 380
Hath checked his foaming courser:—can it be! . 104 *Artegal* 115
Within the vortex of a foaming flood, ... 123 *V. and J.* 143
What tankards foaming from the tap! . . . . 177 *Waggoner* 2. 58
Is lifted of a foaming surge— . . . . . . 242 *P. B.* 559
Yon foaming flood seems motionless as ice; . . 290 *Kilchurn* 36
And hollow vale which foaming torrents fill . . 314 **Not 'mid* 6
That curbs a foaming brook, a Graveyard lies; . 387 **Part fenced* 2
Along its foaming bed. . . . . 479 *Somnamb.* 135
Of foaming torrents.—From thy orisons . . . 496 **A little* 20
Foam-lit. O'er-walk the chasmy torrent's foam-lit bed, ... 610 *Desc. Sk. Quarto* 464
Foamy. In foamy breaks the rill, with merry song, 4 *Ev. Wk.* 136
In foamy agitation; . . . . 385 *Yarrow Rev.* 18
Gurgling in foamy water-break, ... 508 *May* 75
Fodder. The fodder of his herds in winter snows. . 610 *Desc. Sk. Quarto* 473
Foe. Deadly foe both of mouse and rat; . . . 142 †*Lov. and Lik.* 42
"But should suspense permit the Foe to cry, . . 211 *Laod.* 133
Am pleased by fits to have thee for my foe, . . 253 **O gentle* 11
What boots the enquiry?—Neither friend nor foe 258 **Where lies the Land* 5
Against the threatening foe your trustiest shields." 263 **While not* 8
Of battle and the routed foe . . . . . . 299 *Brownie's Cell* 68
The last that dare to struggle with the Foe. . . 310 **Another year* 4
Its even tenor, and the foe was quelled, . . . 325 *Ode 1814* 143
None bleed, and none lie prostrate but the foe; . 368 *Trajan* 48
The friend shrinks back—the foe recoils . . . 408 *White Doe* 1149
The foe from numbers courage drew, ... 408 *White Doe* 1153
As bravely as the foe was keenly sought. . . . 458 *Sea-shore* 24
"The Serpent, Satan, our first foe, that hath . 554 *Prioress* 107
Her stormy foe at last . . . . 628 *Installation* 5
Whether affliction be the foe, or guilt! . . . 792 *Excursion* 3. 420
Of their most dreaded foe, the strong South-west 833 *Excursion* 5. 702
How my eyes watched the foe, ... S.3. 440 **Said red-ribboned* 14
Foeman's. Where now?—Their sword is at the Foeman's heart! . . . . 320 **Hunger, and* 12
Foes. With few in arms, innumerable foes, . . . 18 *Desc. Sk.* 452
—But foes are gathering—Liberty must raise . 22 *Desc. Sk.* 638
Else can ye hope but with such numerous foes . 33 *Guilt* 510
Nor shall thy foes deny . . . . 105 *Artegal* 191
By friends deceived, by foes betrayed, ... 113 *Lament* 59
Foes might hang upon their path, snakes rustle near, ... 141 *Arm. Lady* 89
What though some busy foes to good, ... 225 *Present.* 13
Nor craved he more to quell his foes, ... 291 *Rob Roy* 11
And her Foes find a like inglorious grave. . . 293 *Killicranky* 14
Threatened her foes,—or, pompously at rest, . . 311 **Who rises* 26
A Foe's most favourite purpose to fulfil: . . . 316 **Say, what* 12
Yet, yet, Biscayans! we must meet our Foes . . 318 *Biscayan* 1
Shrink not, though far outnumbered by their Foes, 320 **They seek* 2
Hath plucked such foes, like weeds, from out the land; . . . . 383 *Duddon* 27. 11
In open field their gathering foes, ... 406 *White Doe* 907
Which struck with terror friends and foes! . . . 408 *White Doe* 1148
How they have scourged old foes, perfidious friends: . . . . 421 *Ecc. Sonn.* 1. 10. 2
Then chiefly dear, when foes are planted round, . 430 *Ecc. Sonn.* 2. 6. 9
Conquer the Gallic lily which thy foes . . . . 432 *Ecc. Sonn.* 2. 15. 7
Prejudged by foes determined not to spare, . . 440 *Ecc. Sonn.* 2. 45. 1
Fanned by the breath of foes. . . . . . . 478 *Somnamb.* 40
Their veteran foes mock as an idle noise; . . . 628 *Eagle and Dove* 14
With foreign foes mustered for instant war. . . 712 *Prelude* 9. 185
Meets foes irreconcilable, and at best . . . . 721 *Prelude* 10. 207
And thus, on every side beset with foes, . . . 723 *Prelude* 10. 335
Life from the young Republic; that new foes . . 727 *Prelude* 11. 14
In *all*; in most with superadded foes, ... 804 *Excursion* 4. 208
To be perpetually attacked by foes . . . . . 839 *Excursion* 6. 54
Of aspirations that *have* been, of foes . . . . K.8. 256 *Recluse* 1. 1. 738
Fog. In size a giant, stalking through thick fog, . 703 *Prelude* 8. 266
Wan, dull, and glaring, with a dripping fog . . 746 *Prelude* 14. 12
Foggy. A foggy day in winter time) . . . . . 119 *Sailor's Mother* 2
Fogs. Where close fogs hide their parent brook; . 180 *Waggoner* 4. 41
Foil. Or a fierce impress issues with its foil . . 275 **While poring* 11
A foil to his celestial cheek! . . . . 299 *Brownie's Cell* 100
And thus they foil their enemy's despite. . . . 437 *Ecc. Sonn.* 2. 34. 8
With a bad world, and foil the Tempter's arts. . 447 *Ecc. Sonn.* 3. 28. 14
Foil to a Jewel rich in light . . . . 478 *Somnamb.* 14
Or tenderness, which there, set off by foil, . . 696 *Prelude* 7. 601
That task would foil;" then, letting fall his voice 871 *Excursion* 7. 922

Follower 326 Fondly

Followed—*continued.*
I followed, till he made a sudden stand : . . . 779 *Excursion* 2. 493
More might have followed—but my honoured Friend . . . . 779 *Excursion* 2. 512
Strains followed of acknowledgment addressed . 794 *Excursion* 3. 568
The brother followed ; and was seen no more ! . 795 *Excursion* 3. 649
" What followed cannot be reviewed in thought ; 796 *Excursion* 3. 680
A pause of silence followed ; then, with voice . 801 *Excursion* 4. 8
This answer followed.—" You have turned my thoughts . . . . 815 *Excursion* 4. 919
Withdrew ; and straight we followed,—to a spot . 825 *Excursion* 5. 225
We followed ; and my voice with joy exclaimed : 870 *Excursion* 7. 820
His steps had followed, fleetest of the fleet, . . 870 *Excursion* 7. 863
No longer led or followed by the Sons ; . . . 878 *Excursion* 8. 278
—We followed, taking as he led, a path . . . 880 *Excursion* 8. 441
But all too fondly followed and too far ;— . . 887 *Excursion* 9. 190
Follower. He had no follower, dog, nor man, nor boy : 201 *Hart-leap* 34
From youth a zealous follower of the Art . . . 547 **Ye Lime* 15
A punctual follower on the stroke of nine, . . 676 *Prelude* 6. 71
Was left without a follower to discharge . . . 720 *Prelude* 10. 117
Far less a common follower of the world, . . . 751 *Prelude* 14. 363
Follower's. In her silent Follower's eyes ; . . 415 *White Doe* 1717
Followers. Dismiss thy followers ;—let them calmly wait . . . . 105 *Artegal* 214
Where be the noisy followers of the game . . . 349 *Val. Dover* 1
His Followers gathering in from Tees, ... 403 *White Doe* 691
Against the Followers of the incarnate Lord . . 420 *Ecc. Sonn.* 1. 6. 5
So vaunt a throng of Followers, filled with pride . 425 *Ecc. Sonn.* 1. 28. 12
Nor are his Followers loth to seek defence, . . 431 *Ecc. Sonn.* 2. 11. 12
" My faithful followers, lo ! the tide is spent . . 495 *Fact* 30
And followers of Sertorius, out of Spain . . . 635 *Prelude* 1. 191
Some boundary, which his followers may not cross 798 *Excursion* 3. 878
Followers'. As to be likened in his Followers' minds 362 **List—'twas* 62
Following. But, heedless of the following gloom, . 9 *Lines : Boat* 10
The wain pursued its way ; and following near . 34 *Guilt* 554
Following his fancies by the hour, to bring . . 97 *Brothers* 109
The VANGUARD, following close behind, . . . 179 *Waggoner* 3. 68
Following after in full sail ! . . . . 181 *Waggoner* 4. 166
Following his plough, along the mountain-side : . 196 *Resolution* 46
(Each hero following his peculiar bent) . . . 211 *Laod.* 116
And, following guides whose craft holds no consent 213 *Dion* 54
That served my turn, when following still . . . 246 *P. B.* 863
Was joy, in following joy, as keen . . . . . 344 **How blest* 61
Ambition—following down this far-famed slope . 345 **Ambition—following* 1
Following the margin of a bay, ... 371 *Eg. Maid* 135
Of famed Persepolis ; each following each, . . 394 **No more* 9
He, following wheresoe'er he might, ... 404 *White Doe* 757
Monastic Domes ! following my downward way, . 449 *Ecc. Sonn.* 3. 35. 1
From Fancy following in thy wake, ... 490 *Night Thought* 15
All are following at full speed, ... 490 *Incident : Dog* 22
O'er rocks and stones, following the Dog . . . 491 *Fidelity* 36
Following the Lamb celestial," quoth she, . . . 554 *Prioress* 130
Remained behind ; the ship the following day . 623 **I find* 10
But Cupid, following cheerily his guide . . . 624 *Æneid* 53
Following a band of muleteers, we reached . . 683 *Prelude* 6. 564
Following the tide that slackens by degrees, . . 690 *Prelude* 7. 190
On the green turf following the vested Priest, . . 780 *Excursion* 2. 583
Following our Guide, we clomb the cottage-stairs 781 *Excursion* 2. 647
Through the dull mist, I following—when a step, 784 *Excursion* 2. 829
Following the guidance of these welcome feet . . 793 *Excursion* 3. 500
Following the rugged road, by sledge or wheel . 823 *Excursion* 5. 61
Her Helpmate following. Hospitable fare, . . 834 *Excursion* 5. 775
Then, following closely with the cloud of dust, . 880 *Excursion* 8. 379
Following its fortunes like the beasts or trees . . 887 *Excursion* 9. 181
Follows. And set him free. What follows ? I have learned . . . . 54 *Bord.* 935
SUMMER ebbs ;—each day that follows . . . 90 *Longest Day* 29
That follows the thought—We've no land in the vale, ... 116 *Repentance* 35
Remember she follows the law of her kind, . . . 142 †*Lov. and Lik.* 43
When sunshine follows shower, the breast can thrill 273 **Not the* 2
A soothing spirit follows in the way . . . . 283 **Here, where* 3
That follows—yet more awful than that awful sound ! . . . . 350 *Des. Stanzas* 45
That follows—striking on some kindred chord . 448 *Ecc. Sonn.* 3. 31. 7
Folly. O too industrious folly ! . . . . . . 88 *H. C.* 19
Upbraided his distempered folly. . . . . . 180 *Waggoner* 4. 82
Slaves of folly, love, or strife— . . . . . . 209 **Yes, it* 11
Wages of folly—baits of crime, ... 214 *Kirkstone* 29
Desires whose course in folly ends, ... 223 *Wishing-gate* 41
Forsook his crimes, renounced his folly, . . . 249 *P. B.* 1133
And wandering seem but folly,— . . . . . 293 *Yarrow Unv.* 58
And folly cursed with endless memory : . . . 349 *Boulogne* 12
The shouts of folly, and the groans of sin." . . 349 *At Dover* 14
And folly, if they with united din . . . . . 365 **The Baptist* 7
O weakness of the Great ! O folly of the Wise ! . 368 *Trajan* 64
With freaks of graceful folly,— . . . . . . 385 *Yarrow Rev.* 26
He served in folly. Woden falls, and Thor . . 423 *Ecc. Sonn.* 1. 17. 5
That all but love is folly ; . . . . 478 *Somnamb.* 31
When novel trusts by folly are betrayed,— . . 504 *Warning* 69
Be Folly and False-seeming free to affect . . . 655 *Prelude* 3. 401
When Folly from the frown of fleeting Time . . 663 *Prelude* 4. 348
Looked out for admiration. Folly, vice, . . . 695 *Prelude* 7. 578
From vice and folly, wretchedness and fear ; . . 703 *Prelude* 8. 291
Of vice and folly thrust upon my view, . . . 706 *Prelude* 8. 497
The dupe of folly, or the slave of crime." . . 732 *Prelude* 11. 320
Presumption, folly, madness, in the men . . . 741 *Prelude* 13. 66
Of strife and folly, though it be a treat . . . 799 *Excursion* 3. 905
Produced, when thoughtless Folly hath usurped . 842 *Excursion* 6. 280
His folly. Thus (I feel it while I speak), . . . S.3. 434 **The doubt* 60

Folly—*continued.*
As rich in folly as the past in crime. . . . . L.1. 94 *Juvenal* 2. 10
Folly's. Where bubbles burst, and folly's dancing foam . . . . 452 *Ecc. Sonn.* 3. 45. 5
Folly's own hyperbole. . . . . S.3. 438 **My Lord* 28
Fond. Press the sad kiss, fond mother ! vainly fears 7 *Ev. Wk.* 275
—And let him nurse his fond deceit, ... 9 *Lines : Boat* 13
And *there* are those fond thoughts which Solitude, 15 *Desc. Sk.* 248
Then, settling into fond discourse, ... 81 †*Mother's Return* 29
Some fond regrets to entertain ; . . . . . . 85 *Anecdote* 14
With a more fond, familiar, tenderness ; . . . 99 *Brothers* 246
What fond and wayward thoughts will slide . . 109 **Strange fits* 25
I grieved, fond Youth ! that thou shouldst sue . 109 **Ere with* 3
A fountain at my fond heart's door, ... 111 *A Complaint* 3
Of my fond heart, hath made me poor. . . . 111 *A Complaint* 18
As now it is, seems to her own fond heart . . . 119 *Maternal Grief* 80
Once having seen her clasp with fond embrace . 120 *Emigrant Mother* 9
And petty quarrels, had grown fond again ; . . 122 *V. and J.* 22
Deem that by such fond hope the Youth was swayed, ... 122 *V. and J.* 64
Fond Youth ! that mournful solace now must pass 124 *V. and J.* 218
Fond lovers ! yet not quite hob nob, ... 129 *Idiot Boy* 289
Fond spirit that blindly works in the blood of all— 133 *Michael* 145
Of fond correction and reproof bestowed . . . 133 *Michael* 173
Begone, thou fond presumptuous Elf," . . . 155 *Waterfall* 1
And many a fond and idle name . . . . . 158 **With little* 13
To peace, or fond regret. . . . . 164 **Fair Lady* 16
That those fond Idlers most are pleased . . . 170 *Rural Ill.* 35
Fond thoughts about a father's love : . . . . 193 *Ruth* 86
At their own fond belief. . . . . 224 **'Tis gone* 42
Fond words have oft been spoken to thee, Sleep ! 253 **Fond words* 1
Then peck or perch, fond Flutterer ! nor forbear . 273 **Wild Redbreast* 13
Or blight that fond memorial ;—the trees grew, . 276 *Oker Hill* 9
Or share with me, fond thought ! that inward eye, 279 **All praise* 10
To fond imagination, ... 302 *Yarrow V.* 42
A fond reflection of her own decay, ... 321 **Humanity,delighting* 2
Seat Sandal, a fond suitor of the clouds, . . . 353 *Aquap.* 36
Fond wish that was granted at last, and the Flood, 364 *Vallomb.* 3
With such fond hope ? her very speech is dead ; . 368 *Trajan* 66
If thee fond Fancy ever brought . . . . . 376 **The Minstrels* 63
Of fond sepulchral flattery can beguile . . . 389 *Breadalb.* 3
Blest its humane Memorial's fond endeavour ; . 394 *Countess' Pillar* 12
Our fond regrets tenacious in their grasp ? . . 394 **How profitless* 10
And fond unclouded memory. . . . . . . 414 *White Doe* 1657
The fond heart proffered it—the servile heart ; . 434 *Ecc. Sonn.* 2. 24. 6
Of thy fond hopes hereafter walk inclined . . 447 *Ecc. Sonn.* 3. 27. 9
To the heart's fond belief ; though some there are 463 **They called* 6
And FANCY greets them with a fond embrace ; . 503 *Warning* 25
A prisoner of fond fears ; . . . . 507 *May* 36
Fond fancies ! wheresoe'er shall turn thine eye . 511 **So fair* 16
The parting moment and its fond regret. . . . 531 **I know* 16
And smiles, fond efforts of distress . . . . 543 *Russ. Fug.* 167
His too fond father's car amiss to drive. . . . 564 *Troilus* 147
Small cause there is for that fond wish of ours . 573 *Chiabrera* 1. 9
Of fond regret be still thy choice, ... 577 *Cenotaph* 10
Planted with such fond hope the tree ; . . . . 577 **By playful* 14
Fond healing, like a mother's kiss. . . . . 578 **I come* 56
Such, in the fond illusion of my heart, ... 578 *Peele Castle* 29
No fond hand left to staunch th' unclosing vein, . 613 *Desc.Sk.Quarto* 611
Some fond hearts to COMPLIANCE seem'd inclin'd ; 620 *Birth of Love* 20
With many a fond embrace, while joy runs high, 624 *Æneid* 40
Gaz'd on thy lovely Nymphs with fond delight, . 630 [?] **O Moon* 8
With fond and feeble tongue a tedious tale. . . 641 *Prelude* 1. 619
That maniac's fond anxiety, and go . . . . 668 *Prelude* 5. 160
And fond conceit of sadness, with the sound . . 680 *Prelude* 6. 367
Through fond ambition of that hour, I strove . 685 *Prelude* 6. 671
Of what my fond simplicity believed . . . . 688 *Prelude* 7. 85
Doth with the fond remains of his last power . . 706 *Prelude* 8. 473
For sacrifice, and struggling with fond mirth . . 724 *Prelude* 10. 407
Made many a fond enquiry ; and when they, . . 769 *Excursion* 1. 892
At the fond work, demolished with a touch ; . . 810 *Excursion* 4. 606
Yet so it pleased a fond, a vain, old Man, . . 816 *Excursion* 4. 1004
Of his fond partner, silent in the nest. . . . 851 *Excursion* 6. 868
The fond affection. She no more could bear . . 852 *Excursion* 6. 942
Her fond maternal heart had built, a nest . . 853 *Excursion* 6. 1019
(Said the good Vicar with a fond half-smile) . . 866 *Excursion* 7. 589
But fond companions, so I guessed, in field, . . 882 *Excursion* 8. 548
Fond looks on colours three or four . . . . S.3. 431 **The Scottish* 23
Seat-Sandal, a fond lover of the clouds ; . . . K.8. 225 **I will* 27
In fond obedience to her private thoughts . . K.8. 247 *Recluse* 1.1.400
Fonder. And, with yet fonder feeling, for the sake 131 *Michael* 37
Fondest. Gilding that cottage with her fondest ray, 8 *Ev. Wk.* 347
And in her fondest love— . . . . 223 *Wishing-gate* 27
Rich theme of England's fondest praise, . . . 495 *Fact* 25
Than fondest epitaph : for, if those fail, . . . 847 *Excursion* 6. 614
Fondling. And, fondling, licked his face, then on a sudden . . . . 44 *Bord.* 413
Is there a brilliant fondling of the cage, . . . 528 **Those breathing* 62
Fondly. *See* **Over-fondly.**
A lingering light he fondly throws . . . . . 1 *Extract* 13
And ever, as we fondly muse, we find . . . . 8 *Ev. Wk.* 317
Where, so they fondly think, the worm shall gnaw no more. . . . . 20 *Desc. Sk.* 558
And hope returned, and pleasure fondly made . 25 *Guilt* 58
Would lead me to talk fondly. Do not fear ; . . 52 *Bord.* 831
With not unfrequent rapture fondly hailed. . . 118 *Maternal Grief* 26
Which old folk, fondly pleased to trim . . . 144 **Driven in* 50
Fondly settle upon Thee . . . . 161 **Pleasures newly* 45
Love *stoops* as fondly as he soars." . . . . . 164 *Needlecase* 40
And to her mournful habits fondly cleaves. . . 169 **Never enlivened* 6

Fondly—*continued.*
On thee too fondly did my memory hang, . . . 211 *Laod.* 129
As fondly he believes.—Upon the side . . . . 212 *Laod.* 167
And fondly licks his hands. . . . . 242 *P. B.* 565
Nor be unthanked, unless I fondly err. . . . 281 *Valedict.* 8
Is fondly lingering on thy shattered front, . . 290 *Kilchurn* 24
Thus, after he had fondly braved . . . . . 297 *Highland Boy* 241
(So faith too fondly deemed) a voice divine . . 319 *Guernica* 3
Of past exploits, nor fondly after more . . . 355 *Aquap.* 189
Return, Content ! for fondly I pursued, . . . 382 *Duddon* 26. 1
Clove fondly ; to his favourite seat . . . . 390 *Highland Broach* 46
Language, and letters ;—these, though fondly viewed . . . . 420 *Ecc. Sonn.* 1. 8. 12
From false assumption rose, and fondly hailed . 429 *Ecc. Sonn.* 2. 2. 1
" Thou look'st upon me, and dost fondly think, . 464 **Thou look'st* 1
Was fondly seized by Sculpture, to restore . . 476 **Tranquillity ! the* 6
And fondly strives her struggling friend to save. . 490 *Incident : Dog* 32
Was fondly grafted with a virtuous aim, . . . 515 *Penn.* 11
Fondly embosomed in the tranquil flood, . . . 524 *Epist. Beaumont* 188
How fondly will the woods embrace . . . . 533 **Blest is* 21
" The blossom you so fondly praised . . . . 542 *Russ. Fug.* 65
Oh do not Thou too fondly brood, ... 581 *John Words.* 68
And thoughts and projects fondly cherished here, 583 **With copious* 37
Is happy in his vow, and fondly cleaves . . . 586 *Ch. Lamb* 124
Must keep to all, as fondly all believe, ... 656 *Prelude* 3. 482
But imitations, fondly made in plain . . . . 690 *Prelude* 7. 238
Or father fondly gazed upon with pride. . . . 692 *Prelude* 7. 341
Each fondly reared on his own pedestal, . . . 695 *Prelude* 7. 577
When they were silent : far more fondly now . 760 *Excursion* 1. 288
Fondly, though with an interest more mild, . . 770 *Excursion* 1. 926
Cleave not so fondly to your moody cell ; . . . 808 *Excursion* 4. 482
Fondly to prize the silence which he kept, . . 839 *Excursion* 6. 105
Loved fondly, truly, fervently ; and dared . . 840 *Excursion* 6. 119
" She loved, and fondly deemed herself beloved. . 851 *Excursion* 6. 844
That, fondly seeking in dispraise of man . . . 871 *Excursion* 7. 908
Upon unwritten story fondly traced . . . . 872 *Excursion* 7. 942
Do we revert so fondly to the walks . . . . 884 *Excursion* 9. 37
But all too fondly followed and too far ;— . . 887 *Excursion* 9. 190
Why does this inward lustre fondly seek, . . . K.8. 255 *Recluse* 1.1.677
Fondly-anxious. A fondly-anxious Mother strove . 407 *White Doe* 1030
Fondly-lingering. As evening's fondly-lingering rays, 348 **Lulled by* 65
Fondly-overhanging. Whose fondly-overhanging canopy . . . . 440 *Ecc. Sonn.* 3. 1. 3
Fondness. With fondness on those sweet Nestorian strains. . . . . 573 *Chiabrera* 2. 11
His friends had in their fondness entertained, . 575 *Chiabrera* 8. 15
But fondness, and a kind of radiant joy . . . 714 *Prelude* 9. 315
As vanity and fondness for applause, ... 775 *Excursion* 2. 225
Font. When at the sacred font for thee I stood ; . 274 *Rotha Q.* 2
On the baptismal font ; his pallid face . . . 825 *Excursion* 5. 212
At the baptismal font. And when the pure . . 826 *Excursion* 5. 279
Fontarabbia. Fontarabbia can tell . . . . . S.3. 440 **Said red-ribboned* 13
Food. Fresh food ; for only then, when memory . 1 *Early Youth* 10
Food for his beasts in time of winter snows. . . 17 *Desc. Sk.* 385
To greet the traveller needing food and rest ; . . 21 *Desc. Sk.* 610
And with the food of pride sustained his soul . . 23 *Yew-tree* 23
Bears not to those he loves their needful food. . 25 *Guilt* 67
And near a thousand tables pined and wanted food. 31 *Guilt* 369
And gave me food—and rest, more welcome, more desired. . . . . 31 *Guilt* 405
He'd not have robbed the raven of its food. . . 35 *Guilt* 610
Supplied my helplessness with food and raiment, 41 *Bord.* 200
She eats her food which every day the peasants . 44 *Bord.* 386
And brought me food. Have I not cause to love her ? . . . . 53 *Bord.* 848
The scrip that held his food, and I forgot . . . 67 *Bord.* 1643
No food was there, no drink, no grass, no shade, . 68 *Bord.* 1707
I had been nourished by the sickly food . . . 70 *Bord.* 1821
No human dwelling ever give me food, . . . 78 *Bord.* 2347
In search of their own food ; . . . . . . 84 *Shepherd-boys* 9
And wanted neither food, nor clothes, nor love : . 100 *Brothers* 345
And such chance food as outlaws can obtain, . . 103 *Artegal* 101
For clothes, for warmth, for food, and fire ; . . 114 *Ind. Wom.* 16
And he has stolen away my food. . . . . . 114 *Ind. Wom.* 58
And they were healthy with their food ; . . . 115 *Last of Flock* 53
Did she extract the food of self-reproach, . . 118 *Maternal Grief* 46
The Babe was drawing in its quiet food. . . . 124 *V. and J.* 216
I know the earth-nuts fit for food : . . . . 145 *Her Eyes* 96
For human nature's daily food ; . . . . . 186 **She was* 18
Might well be dangerous food . . . . . . 193 *Ruth* 123
If she is prest by want of food, ... 194 *Ruth* 235
That in this moment there is life and food . . 206 *Tintern* 64
And Thou, thy favourite food to win, ... 215 *Enterprise* 29
Disparaging Man's gifts, and proper food. . . . 263 **Those words* 8
Of that Man's mind—what can it be ? what food 304 **I grieved* 3
Thy heart from its emasculating food ; . . . . 309 **England ! the* 2
Such food a Tyrant's appetite demands ; . . . 319 *Spaniard* 4
The wind with terror while they roar for food. . 392 *Daniel* 8
And food cut off by sacerdotal ire, ... 419 *Ecc. Sonn.* 1. 4. 3
Brings to thy food, mysterious Sacrament ! . . . 446 *Ecc. Sonn.* 3. 25. 3
Wanting accustomed food, must pass from earth, 531 *Octogen.* 4
Food, shelter, safety, there they find ; . . . . 532 †*Float. Isl.* 13
He sat, and ate his food in solitude : . . . . 566 *Cumb. Beg.* 15
For scanty food the treacherous cliffs to dare. . 611 *Desc.Sk.Quarto* 483
To pay the filial debt, for food to roam, . . . 613 *Desc.Sk.Quarto* 615
Food for the hungry ears of little ones, . . . 668 *Prelude* 5. 211
She scratches, ransacks up the earth for food, . 669 *Prelude* 5. 255
As innocent instincts, and as innocent food ; . . 669 *Prelude* 5. 275
And *they must* have their food. Our childhood sits, 673 *Prelude* 5. 507

Food—*continued.*
Although of food and clothing destitute, . . . 677 *Prelude* 6. 147
These were our food ; and such a summer's night 686 *Prelude* 6. 723
And, when she at her table gave me food, . . 768 *Excursion* 1. 793
Built up of life, and food, and means of life ! . . 807 *Excursion* 4. 438
Food not unwholesome ; earth and air correct . 810 *Excursion* 4. 585
Ill-sheltered, and oft wanting fire and food ; . . 815 *Excursion* 4. 924
" Through four months' space the Infant drew its food . . . . 852 *Excursion* 6. 939
To rear for food, for shelter, and delight ; . . . 860 *Excursion* 7. 195
Its most apparent home. The food of hope . . 884 *Excursion* 9. 20
Their summons, and are gathering round for food, K.8. 245 *Recluse* 1.1.332
We to the patient creatures carried food . . . K.8. 247 *Recluse* 1. 1.398
Food for sick passion in a minion's cheek, . . L. 1. 96 *Juvenal* 3. 50
Foodful. That common growth of earth, the foodful ear ; . . . . 15 *Desc. Sk.* 257
Deny'd the bread of life the foodful ear, . . . 608 *Desc.Sk.Quarto* 320
Their town, and foodful region for support . . 811 *Excursion* 4. 692
Fool. The little fool is loth to stay behind. . . . 42 *Bord.* 305
Three good round years, for playing the fool here 51 *Bord.* 769
Worthy the hearing. Fool was I to dream . . 59 *Bord.* 1179
Now I could laugh till my ribs ached. Oh, Fool ! 59 *Bord.* 1218
And say no name was mine—and so, poor fool, . 77 *Bord.* 2275
A Fool and Coward blended to my wish ! . . . 78 *Bord.* 2318
Write fool upon his forehead.—Planted thus . . 97 *Brothers* 112
And I have lived to be a fool at last . . . . 134 *Michael* 235
Will flatter you,—and fool and rake . . . . 286 *Sons of Burns* 21
Has seduced the poor fool from his winter retreat, 484 **A plague* 9
Ah, fool ! quoth she, wist thou not what it is ? . 559 *Cuck.andNight.* 126
What fool, besotted as we are by names, . . . L. 1. 96 *Juvenal* 3. 43
To see an English lord enact a fool . . . . L. 1. 97 *Juvenal* 3. 90
Fooled. Deny me your support. We have been fooled— . . . . 63 *Bord.* 1426
Foolish. The cold blast struck me. 'Twas a foolish question. . . . . 52 *Bord.* 838
It is all over then ;—your foolish fears . . . 55 *Bord.* 955
" Nor dare to thrust thy foolish self . . . . 155 *Waterfall* 3
Wise, foolish, weak, or strong. . . . . . . 156 *Oak and Broom* 60
Which foolish birds are caught with. Can, I ask, 463 **They called* 9
A foolish strife ; they see . . . . 487 *Fountain* 42
Foolish men he can make them out of wise ;— . 557 *Cuck. and Night.* 12
For thou hast many a foolish and quaint cry :— . 559 *Cuck.andNight.* 123
With all its foolish pomp. The garden lay . . 644 *Prelude* 2. 155
That foolish men opposed them. To a strain . . 728 *Prelude* 11. 52
There let it lie—how foolish are such thoughts ! . 763 *Excursion* 1. 496
Foolishly. He tamed, who foolishly aspires ; . . 291 *Rob Roy* 46
Foolishness. True symbol of hope's foolishness, whose strong . . . . 639 *Prelude* 1. 486
But foolishness and madness in parade, . . . 696 *Prelude* 7. 594
Fools. —These fools of feeling are mere birds of winter . . . . 47 *Bord.* 558
To occupy—both fools, or wise alike, ... 60 *Bord.* 1238
It is the toy of fools, and little fit . . . . 65 *Bord.* 1548
Nor aught that troubles us, the fools of Nature. . 370 *Eg. Maid* 60
Foot. More pleased, my foot the hidden margin roves 12 *Desc. Sk.* 77
Winds neither road nor path for foot to tread : . 14 *Desc. Sk.* 229
I used to sing it.—Listen !—what foot is there ? . 60 *Bord.* 1268
There again ! 'Tis my husband's foot. Good Eldred . . . . 71 *Bord.* 1899
Now there's a grave—your foot is half upon it,— . 98 *Brothers* 194
He had the lightest foot in Ennerdale : . . . . 98 *Brothers* 219
That venturous foot could reach, to one or both . 99 *Brothers* 275
They found him at the foot of that same rock . 101 *Brothers* 380
Equipped from head to foot in iron mail. . . . 111 **'Tis said that some* 47
The foot of horse, the voice of man ; . . . . 129 *Idiot Boy* 283
With one foot in the grave. This only Son, . . 132 *Michael* 90
In that habitual restlessness of foot . . . . 150 **When, to* 63
There never foot had been ; . . . . 162 *Binnorie* 50
Just half a foot in height. . . . . 198 *Thorn* 37
Softly she treads, as if her foot were loth . . . 222 *Triad* 201
Work, shall we call it, of the shepherd's foot . . 230 *Clouds* 56
Where human foot did never stray ; . . . . 237 *P. B.* 97
That every foot might fall with heavier tread, . 275 *Gravestone* 12
Well pleased, her foot should print earth's common grass, ... 278 **Lo ! where she* 12
By just revenge inflamed ? No foot may chase, . 321 **The power* 6
And where the foot with no unmanly fear . . 350 *Des. Stanzas* 13
Or grass-grown spaces, where the heaviest foot . 355 *Aquap.* 194
Horsemen and Foot of each degree, ... 403 *White Doe* 703
On foot they girt their Father round ; . . . . 404 *White Doe* 726
Levelled with earth this foot of mine may tread." 428 *Ecc. Sonn.* 1. 38. 4
Sighed on the wing as her foot pressed the strand, 465 **Dear to* 10
His spindles sink under him, foot, leg, and thigh ! 484 **A plague* 21
E'er tripped with foot so free ; . . . . . . 487 **We walked* 50
From trace of human foot or hand. . . . . 491 *Fidelity* 24
Where never foot doth tread." . . . . . . 542 *Russ. Fug.* 88
Built at the foot of a huge hill, that they . . . 566 *Cumb. Beg.* 4
As up th' opposing hills, with tortoise foot, they creep. . . . . 604 *Desc.Sk.Quarto* 105
Votary (in vast cathedral, where no foot . . . 664 *Prelude* 4. 362
When foot hath crushed them. He through the events . . . . 714 *Prelude* 9. 298
Of vehicles and travellers, horse and foot, . . 726 *Prelude* 10. 564
Right at the foot of that moist precipice, . . . 787 *Excursion* 3. 53
Which foot of boldest stranger would attempt, . 822 *Excursion* 5. 13
And yet the very sound of that kind foot . . . 849 *Excursion* 6. 751
A stirring foot, a head which beat at nights . . 860 *Excursion* 7. 211
Or foot, or lip, in summer's warmth—perceived. . 879 *Excursion* 8. 332
—Not shaped by simple wearing of the foot . . 881 *Excursion* 8. 448
Unsettled by a wanton blow from foot . . . K.8. 226 **I will* 67

Foot—*continued.*
Remote and deep, piled round with rocks, where foot — K. 8. 229 **I will* 141
Football. The inglorious football mounted to the pitch — 868 *Excursion* 7. 742
Foot-bound. Foot-bound uplooking at this lovely tree — 676 *Prelude* 6. 86
Footed. *See* **Light-footed.**
Footfall. Their peace, perhaps, our lightest footfall marred; — 527 **Those breathing* 50
Footing. And fragrance in thy footing treads; — 492 *Duty* 46
Beneath the trees, clear footing many a mile— — 716 *Prelude* 9. 436
Footmarks. They tracked the footmarks small; — 83 *Lucy Gray* 46
Those footmarks, one by one, — 83 *Lucy Gray* 54
Is of the very footmarks unbereft — 378 *Duddon* 11. 3
Their foot-marks do not trouble me, — K. 8. 219 **The snow-tracks* 2
Foot-path. The foot-path faintly marked, the horse-track wild, — 876 *Excursion* 8. 105
Footstep. And, wheresoe'er the stealing footstep tends, — 271 **Where holy* 4
Footsteps. O'er Gallia's wastes of corn my footsteps led; — 11 *Desc. Sk.* 45
The first whose footsteps print the mountain dew. — 22 *Desc. Sk.* 670
Nor any friendly sound his footsteps led; — 26 *Guilt* 132
But ere ten yards were gone her footsteps did she stay. — 87 *Pet-lamb* 16
By random footsteps to be prest, — 154 *Flower Garden* 32
Whose footsteps superstitiously avoid — 219 *Haunted Tree* 20
From these wild rocks thy footsteps I will guide — 222 *Triad* 216
Along the shade with footsteps true — 244 *P. B.* 673
That in thy holy footsteps I may tread; — 257 **The prayers* 11
Methought I saw the footsteps of a throne — 257 **Methought I* 1
Wandering with timid footsteps oft betrayed, — 272 *Ruins* 2
The footsteps of a quick retreat; — 406 *White Doe* 891
In thy footsteps, and be led — 503 **Like a* 69
Or not far off. Where'er my footsteps turned, — 622 *Recluse* 1. 1. 90
With eager footsteps I advance and reach — 658 *Prelude* 4. 25
With slackened footsteps I advanced, and soon — 757 *Excursion* 1. 46
By devious footsteps; regions consecrate — 809 *Excursion* 4. 577
The dear memorial footsteps unimpaired — 884 *Excursion* 9. 39
His haste, for hasty had his footsteps been — K.8. 236 *Recluse* 1.1.9
Foot-stone. Here's neither head nor foot-stone, plate of brass, — 98 *Brothers* 170
Upon the slimy foot-stone I espied — 763 *Excursion* 1. 492
Footstool. But a mere footstool to yon sovereign Lord, — 290 *Kilchurn* 13
Foot-travellers. Of this glad throng, foot-travellers side by side, — 681 *Prelude* 6. 415
Foot-way. There was a foot-way all along the fields — 97 *Brothers* 133
And, while I paced along the foot-way path, — 766 *Excursion* 1. 693
Foot-worn. And foot-worn epitaphs, and some with small — 825 *Excursion* 5. 169
For, *omitted.*
Forage. No bold *bird* gone forth to forage — 163 *Hint* 19
Forager. A cunning forager — 227 *Vernal Ode* 105
Foraging. And simple Pleasure foraging for Death; — 657 *Prelude* 3. 599
Foray. Back to our post, and strip the Scottish Foray — 37 *Bord.* 2
Forbad. Whose waves the Orphean lyre forbad to meet — 336 *Danube* 9
Forbad her all communion with her own: — 853 *Excursion* 6. 961
Forbade. Such further deed in manhood's name forbade; — 33 *Guilt* 479
Forbade the weeds to creep o'er its grey line. — 549 **The massy* 10
Such offering Beaumont dreaded and forbade, — 583 **With copious* 5
And sad experience forbade a thought — 620 *Birth of Love* 22
When spells forbade the voyager to land, — 735 *Prelude* 12. 53
Forbear. Did wanton fawn and kid forbear — 154 *Flower Garden* 11
If such thy meaning, O forbear, — 168 *Turtledove* 17
Forbear to covet a Repeater's stroke, — 229 *Cuckoo-clock* 5
But covet not the Abode;—forbear to sigh, — 250 *Admon.* 5
Then peck or perch, fond Flutterer! nor forbear — 273 **Wild Redbreast* 13
Forbear:—to Thee— — 328 *Ode 1815* 114
Forbear to deem the Chronicler unwise, — 359 *Plea: Hist.* 1
Descend on Francis; nor forbear — 407 *White Doe* 1051
Whose heart still flutters, though his wings forbear — 440 *Ecc. Sonn.* 2. 45. 5
Forbear to shape due channels which the Flood — 450 *Ecc. Sonn.* 3. 38. 6
To bear, and to forbear! — 505 **If this* 8
The motions that it graces—and forbear — 511 **Who rashly* 8
Penned these sad lines, nor can forbear to pray — 575 *Chiabrera* 7. 16
Nor could I, while we journeyed thus, forbear — 665 *Prelude* 4. 435
"Your impious work forbear: perish what may, — 681 *Prelude* 6. 433
I could not, ever and anon, forbear — 782 *Excursion* 2. 691
The Matron ended—nor could I forbear — 835 *Excursion* 5. 827
Forbearance. On such forbearance as the deep may show; — 153 *Morn. Ex.* 34
Yea, both for souls who God's forbearance try, — 229 *Cuckoo-clock* 43
Forbearance and self-sacrifice; — 402 *White Doe* 578
Perpetual lessons of forbearance yield; — 501 *Humanity* 106
Lie in forbearance, strength in standing still? — 505 *Warning* 150
In slight of that forbearance and reserve — 847 *Excursion* 6. 585
Forbearance, charity in deed and thought, — 862 *Excursion* 7. 329
And lived by his forbearance. From the coast — 869 *Excursion* 7. 757
And mercy, and forbearance. Nay—not these, — K.8. 244 *Recluse* 1.1.283
Forbearances. To leisure, to forbearances sedate; — 334 **The Spirit* 12
Forbears. Scarcely the hand forbears to dip its palm — 469 **Why stand* 9
Which he forbears again to look upon; — 480 **Most sweet* 4
Forbid. Nay, you abuse my friendship! Heaven forbid!— — 42 *Bord.* 271
With aspect so inviting. Why forbid me — 55 *Bord.* 970

Forbid—*continued.*
Heaven forbid that I should lift my hand — 71 *Bord.* 1911
Which now thou tak'st upon thee. God forbid — 74 *Bord.* 2113
Nay, God forbid!—You recollect I mentioned — 101 *Brothers* 393
Could not the entrance of this thought forbid: — 110 **Look at* 15
With, "God forbid it should be true!" — 128 *Idiot Boy* 183
"Oh God forbid!" poor Susan cries. — 128 *Idiot Boy* 191
Such doom awaits us. Nay, forbid it Heaven! — 316 **O'er the* 9
Forbid it, Heaven!—and Merry England still — 464 **They called* 13
And what may now forbid — 494 *Force of Prayer* 26
Forbid a moment's rest; — 499 **This Lawn* 9
They must forbid the State to inflict a pain, — 518 *Pun. Death* 7. 13
"Scorn and contempt forbid me to proceed! — 797 *Excursion* 3. 768
Who would forbid them, if their presence serve, — 813 *Excursion* 4. 843
On humble life, forbid the judging mind — 828 *Excursion* 5. 421
Forbidden. And thou forbidden to appear? — 284 *Grave of Burns* 8
Her way into forbidden ground; — 407 *White Doe* 982
You not forbidden to recline — 408 *White Doe* 1090
Along forbidden ways; — 544 *Russ. Fug.* 196
And by sullen weeds forbidden — 549 *Hermit's Cell* 1. 27
Or a forbidden tract of cheerless view; — 830 *Excursion* 5. 529
Forbidding. Some jealous and forbidding cell, — 397 *White Doe* 97
And oft-times in the most forbidding den — 429 *Ecc. Sonn.* 2. 5. 8
In which the meagre, stale, forbidding ways — 729 *Prelude* 11. 110
Had almost a forbidding nakedness; — 781 *Excursion* 2. 640
Wholly untraced a more forbidding way. — 848 *Excursion* 6. 662
Rough and forbidding were the choicest roads — 858 *Excursion* 7. 59
That might be deemed forbidding, did not there — 862 *Excursion* 7. 327
In aspect and forbidding, yet a point — 885 *Excursion* 9. 53
A dull forbidding blast, — S.3. 431 **The Scottish* 18
Their looks forbidding, read and disobey, — K.8. 256 *Recluse* 1.1.713
Forbids. —That smile forbids the thought; for on thy face — 173 *Infant Daughter* 66
Forbode. *See* **Forebode.**
If, as needs he must forbode, — 181 *Waggoner* 4. 128
Or but forbode destruction, I deplore — 440 *Ecc. Sonn.* 3. 2. 10
Forbore. And with untired humility forbore — 500 *Humanity* 39
Force. *See* **Aira-force.**
Force half upon the wave their cumbrous flight. — 6 *Ev. Wk.* 249
Half raised, for well his arm might lose its force — 27 *Guilt* 179
And homefelt force of sympathy sincere, — 34 *Guilt* 551
Burst on the mountains with hell-rousing force. — 51 *Bord.* 789
His Sheriffs with fit force to reinstate — 56 *Bord.* 1024
As if to force his sympathy. — 81 *†Mother's Return* 28
I look for ghosts; but none will force — 117 *Affl. Marg.* 57
Which thunders down with headlong force, — 130 *Idiot Boy* 348
She darts, as with a torrent's force, — 130 *Idiot Boy* 374
In one impression, by connecting force — 147 *Joanna* 49
As with the force of billows shattered; — 175 *Waggoner* 1. 189
To the utmost of his force! — 181 *Waggoner* 4. 101
No motion has she now, no force; — 187 **A slumber* 5
"Ah wherefore?—Did not Hercules by force — 210 *Laod.* 79
His force on Caspian foam to try; — 213 *Dion* 72
The lagging shower, and force coy Phœbus out, — 221 *Triad* 83
And with like force, if need there be, — 245 *P. B.* 778
Was the aim frustrated by force or guile, — 269 *Malham* 1
And force their passage to the salt-sea tides! — 269 *Gordale* 14
Which neither force shall check nor time abate! — 271 *Henry: Portrait* 14
From what huge height, descending? Can such force — 272 *Devil's Bridge* 2
The Monks of Fountain's thronged to force — 301 *Bran* 58
The wind might force the deep-grooved harp — 301 *Bran* 99
No guile seduced, no force could violate; — 305 *Ven. Rep.* 6
The ground beneath thee with volcanic force: — 316 **Hail, Zaragoza* 11
O joyless power that stands by lawless force! — 317 **Look now* 9
And to celerities of lawless force; — 330 *Ode: Thanks.* 118
Further to force their way, endowed its trunk — 354 *Aquap.* 140
But who is He—the Conquerer? Would he force — 361 **For action* 11
Sweep to the charge; more high, the Dacian force, — 368 *Trajan* 46
And oft-times he—who, yielding to the force — 383 *Duddon* 30. 5
Where haughty Force had striven in vain; — 390 *Highland Broach* 12
That down the steep hills force their way, — 396 *White Doe* 12
To noble Percy; and a force — 401 *White Doe* 465
A Soul, by force of sorrows high, — 402 *White Doe* 585
He spake—"would stem, or quell, a force — 405 *White Doe* 855
Through force of natural piety; — 409 *White Doe* 1232
Of vengeful military force, — 411 *White Doe* 1383
Full oft the unworthy brow of lawless force; — 418 *Ecc. Sonn.* 1. 1. 12
Of force that daunts, and cunning that ensnares! — 426 *Ecc. Sonn.* 1. 31. 8
But who would force the Soul tilts with a straw — 442 *Ecc. Sonn.* 3. 7. 13
What force had severed. Thence they fetched the seed — 444 *Ecc. Sonn.* 3. 15. 6
That gallops away with such fury and force — 484 **A plague* 4
By objects, which might force the soul to abate — 493 *Hap. War.* 19
And strangled by a merciless force; — 494 *Force of Prayer* 34
Stings to the quick, and, with resistless force, — 519 *Pun. Death* 12. 3
I knew the force; and hence the rough sea's pride — 574 *Chiabrera* 4. 19
More than theatric force to Shakspeare's scene;— — 583 **With copious* 33
How Juno's hate with unrelenting force — 624 *Æneid* 16
From Heaven, gigantic force to beardless boys. — 628 *Eagle and Dove* 16
How that one Frenchman, through continued force — 635 *Prelude* 1. 206
So frequently repeated, and by force — 641 *Prelude* 1. 605
It seemed to suck us in with an eddy's force. — 649 *Prelude* 3. 14
Did also often mitigate the force — 716 *Prelude* 9. 497
And seemed with difficult steps to force her way — 738 *Prelude* 12. 252
And force of native inclination made — 774 *Excursion* 2. 179
Will force upon his notice; undeterred — 781 *Excursion* 2. 629
With their united force, have left undone? — 805 *Excursion* 4. 287
Both ye that shape and build, and ye that force, — 831 *Excursion* 5. 612
Hastily smitten by a fever's force; — 841 *Excursion* 6. 198
This vestige, neither force of beating rain, — 842 *Excursion* 6. 250

Force—*continued.*
The Stuart, landing to resume, by force 844 Excursion 6. 417
Save at worst need, from bold impetuous force, 873 Excursion 7. 1031
Measuring the force of those gigantic powers 877 Excursion 8. 205
"Then," said the Solitary, "by what force 886 Excursion 9. 138
From interference of external force, 889 Excursion 9. 332
And as these lofty barriers break the force K.8. 247 Recluse 1.1.374
Forced. And forced the full-swoln udder to demand, 17 Desc. Sk. 397
He to an armèd fleet was forced away 25 Guilt 51
Forced hard against the wind a thick unwieldy flight. 26 Guilt 108
Had heard of one who, forced from storms to shroud, 27 Guilt 172
My brother John was forced to go, 84 We are Seven 59
While I am forced to watch and weep, 113 Lament 27
And forced unworthy stripes to bear, 175 Waggoner 1. 122
The Lady's words, when forced away 204 Brougham 82
How he, long forced in humble walks to go, 205 Brougham 159
Forced from that voice so lately tuned to a strain 274 *Wait, prithee 10
That, having forced its way from birth to birth, 311 *Who rises 19
Forced to descend into his destined tomb— 318 *Is there 3
Than ever forced unpitied hearts to bleed. 327 *Emperors and 14
Forced by intent to take from speech its edge, 353 Aquap. 75
I repose, nor am forced from sweet fancy to part, 364 Vallomb. 30
And prayers that would undo her forced farewell; 420 Ecc. Sonn. 1. 9. 10
Like a gaunt shaggy Porter forced to wait 523 Epist. Beaumont 152
And forced to live on alms, this old Man fed 531 *I know 6
You, Lady, forced to wear 545 Russ. Fug. 318
Nor Hunger forc'd the herds from pastures bare 611 Desc. Sk. Quarto 482
The father forc'd by Powers that only deign 613 Desc. Sk. Quarto 616
Forc'd from my native mountains bleak and bare; 615 Desc. Sk. Quarto 714
Forced labour, and more frequently forced hopes; 652 Prelude 3. 210
Nor all the misery forced upon my sight, 708 Prelude 8. 647
Hope takes, or Doubt or Fear is forced to wear, 710 Prelude 9. 61
Forced by the gracious providence of Heaven,— 721 Prelude 10. 224
Forced from the street-disturbing newsman's horn, 728 Prelude 11. 42
How the poor brute's condition, forced to run 772 Excursion 2. 51
Not doomed to ignorance, though forced to tread, 802 Excursion 4. 47
Your cherished sullenness is forced to bend 819 Excursion 4. 1191
And notice forced upon incurious ears; 828 Excursion 5. 418
Was forced to rend away its only hope; 840 Excursion 6. 130
Before his temples, prematurely forced 842 Excursion 6. 277
Was forced to vent his wisdom with a sigh 845 Excursion 6. 444
Into a wild disorder; or be forced 888 Excursion 9. 306
And forced to join in less obnoxious shapes 889 Excursion 9. 341
Such pleasure now is mine, albeit forced, K.8. 250 Recluse 1.1.491
Forces. Experience forces—then adieu! 237 P. B. 115
Entombs, or forces into light; 391 Highland Broach 86
Of hostile forces; and she called—with voice 869 Excursion 7. 760
Forcibly. Too forcibly, too early in my life, 737 Prelude 12. 202
Forcing. While Slavery, forcing the sunk mind to dwell 13 Desc. Sk. 137
Hard passage forcing on, with head 179 Waggoner 3. 81
Forcing my way, I came to one dear nook 185 Nutting 16
Fords. At home, go staggering through the slippery fords, 99 Brothers 258
And from his fords and shallows, sent a voice 636 Prelude 1. 273
Forebode. *See* **Forbode.**
Forebode not any severing of our loves! 590 Immortality 192
As from these intimations I forebode, 778 Excursion 2. 465
Foreboder. Cured the foreboder like a charm; 179 Waggoner 3. 131
Forebodes. Forebodes mishap or seems but to complain; 153 Morn. Ex. 10
Foreboding. Meekly, with foreboding thought, 400 White Doe 347
Foreboding not how soon he must depart; 582 *To public 8
Foreboding evil. From his native hills 761 Excursion 1. 340
Forebodings. My dull forebodings in a Peasant's ear 360 Albano 4
Forefathers. Of Walter's forefathers o'erflowed the bounds 98 Brothers 205
Save six feet of earth where our forefathers lie! 116 Repentance 36
As all their Forefathers had done; and, when 136 Michael 368
Their forefathers; lo! sects are formed, and split 438 Ecc. Sonn. 2. 41. 2
Hath overpowered his forefathers, and soon 799 Excursion 3. 926
Forefathers, who, to guard against the shocks, 837 Excursion 5. 998
Forefend. Sweet heaven forefend! his was a lawful right; 108 Indolence 46
Forego. Thou wouldst forego the neighbouring Rhine, 231 Jew. Fam. 5
Loose Idless to forego her wily mask. 382 Duddon 24. 14
Can she depart? can she forego 414 White Doe 1670
Their altars they forego, their homes they quit, 441 Ecc. Sonn. 3. 6. 9
Warned thee these upper regions to forego, 460 *Queen of 4
Thought that should teach the zealot to forego 516 *As leaves 5
Unwilling to forego, confess, submit, 673 Prelude 5. 519
Foregoing. —Such grateful haunts foregoing, if I oft 755 Recluse 1. 1. 825
Foregone. Pleasing remembrance of a thought foregone; 258 Methought I 13
That smoothes foregone distress, the lines 499 Memory 9
That the remembrance of foregone distress, 586 Ch. Lamb 112
Forehead. Perched on the forehead of a jutting crag, 95 Brothers 6
Write fool upon his forehead.—Planted thus 97 Brothers 112
Profound his forehead was, though not severe; 108 Indolence 44
Her forehead, like a breeze of Spring; 144 *Driven in 40
The forehead of a pollard oak, 168 Wren's Nest 35
A studious forehead to incline 231 Jew. Fam. 7
"His forehead wrinkled was and furred; 240 P. B. 311
Into two ample horns his forehead wide," 251 *Pelion and 5
Lift up that grey-haired forehead, and rejoice 255 Detraction 13
Thy forehead as if fearful to offend, 264 Snowdrop 3
Luxuriant wreaths around thy forehead hoar; 272 Ruins 12
Thou wear'st upon thy forehead clear 288 Highland Girl 32
And on my True-love's forehead plant 302 Yarrow V. 67
Made to the Twelve, survives: lip, forehead, cheek, 343 Last Sup. 10

Forehead—*continued.*
Seated alone, with forehead sky-ward raised, 362 *List—'twas 78
Its shining forehead through the peaceful rent 383 Duddon 31. 3
Your love of Him upon whose forehead sate 420 Ecc. Sonn. 1. 8. 7
His sides, or wreathe with mist his forehead high: 471 Ailsa Crag 4
To bow his forehead in the courts of kings, 574 Chiabrera 4. 6
The rapt One, of the godlike forehead, 586 Hogg 17
Stern was her forehead, but a smile serene 618 School Ex. 15
In silence as before. With forehead bent 746 Prelude 14. 28
The sun-burnt forehead of the weeping child— 779 Excursion 2. 530
Stone lift its forehead emulous of stone 847 Excursion 6. 625
Was her broad forehead; like the brow of one 848 Excursion 6. 684
And on whose forehead inaccessible 866 Excursion 7. 601
And seen the Simplon's forehead hoary, S. 3. 438 *My Lord 19
Forehead's. How rich that forehead's calm expanse! 112 *How rich 1
Foreheads. Go—and with foreheads meekly bowed 332 Ode: Thanks. 228
And antique towers nodded their foreheads high, 529 *Those breathing 118
And such as lift their foreheads over-prized, 530 Poor Robin 30
Foreign. If justice ruled the breast of foreign kings, 104 Artegal 142
With marble, which he sent from foreign lands. 135 Michael 270
The arithmetic of babes, must foreign hordes, 309 *What if 2
Which, heard in foreign lands, the Swiss affect 339 Ranz 3
By wanderers brought from foreign lands 390 Highland Broach 14
Some seek with timely flight a foreign strand; 437 Ecc. Sonn. 2. 37. 2
O sad it is, in sight of foreign shores, 458 Sea-shore 9
Bold settlers on some foreign shore, 577 *I come 46
He knows the policies of foreign lands; 670 Prelude 5. 319
On thy departure to a foreign land 687 Prelude 7. 14
With foreign foes mustered for instant war. 712 Prelude 9. 185
To fly, for safeguard, to some foreign shore, 798 Excursion 3. 832
From that disastrous rout, to foreign shores 844 Excursion 6. 422
Whose country groan'd under a foreign scourge? S.3. 436 *The doubt 173
Foreknowledge. Thou hast foreknowledge that such task is thine; 173 Infant Daughter 58
Foreland. Or foreland, on a new-discovered coast; 149 *A narrow 79
Foremost. *See* **Head-foremost.**
Last and foremost, every horse 181 Waggoner 4. 100
The foremost prow in pressing to the strand,— 211 Laod. 125
But Thou art foremost in the field:—there stand: 331 Ode: Thanks. 153
Not seldom foremost in the way; 402 White Doe 572
Foremost in freedom, noblest of mankind? 505 Warning 143
Are now my theme; and, foremost of the scenes, 692 Prelude 7. 334
And cheerful, but the foremost of the band 726 Prelude 10. 570
And I, as chanced, the foremost of the band; 746 Prelude 14. 34
Foremost in my affections, had fallen back 749 Prelude 14. 258
He, with the foremost whose impatience hailed 844 Excursion 6. 416
Slap-dash, tail foremost, as his arms shall drive. L.1. 96 Juvenal 3. 32
Forenoon. —How lovely robed in forenoon light and shade, 355 Aquap. 205
Foreran. Foreran the expected Power, 506 *While from 6
Forerunner. Last forerunner of "Good night!" 90 Longest Day 28
Forerunners. With thy Forerunners that through many a year 538 *In desultory 18
As their forerunners in a glorious course; 681 Prelude 6. 405
Forerunning. To vice and guilt, forerunning wretchedness, 706 Prelude 8. 511
Foresaw. In calmness made, and sees what he foresaw; 493 Hap. War. 54
Foresee. Measured by all that, trembling, we foresee, 110 *Look at 5
Which, they foresee, must soon alight 181 Waggoner 4. 91
Foreseeing. A Voice shall finish doubt and dim foreseeing, 235 Power of Sound 211
Foreseen. In the clear land of vision, but foreseen 436 Ecc. Sonn. 2. 31. 6
In pomp foreseen by her creative eye, 503 Warning 40
Foreseen, had dared to couple, even in thought, 875 Excursion 8. 39
Foresees. Who sees, foresees; who cannot judge amiss, 519 Pun. Death 11. 13
Foreshown. But not to them had Providence foreshown 443 Ecc. Sonn. 3. 14. 3
Foresight. Full oft our human foresight I deplore; 112 *O dearer 2
In foresight, or in love. 169 Wren's Nest 72
Silence and Foresight; Death the Skeleton 185 Yew-trees 27
Endurance, foresight, strength, and skill; 186 *She was 26
If foresight could have rent the veil 348 *Lulled by 19
The day pass lightly on, when foresight sleeps, 656 Prelude 3. 506
Emotions which best foresight need not fear, 748 Prelude 14. 122
Her foresight, and intelligence that makes 807 Excursion 4. 431
By foresight, or remembrance, undisturbed! 827 Excursion 5. 330
With foresight; hears, too, every sabbath day, 866 Excursion 7. 577
Forest. The latest lingerer of the forest train, 8 Ev. Wk. 309
Dear is the forest frowning o'er his head, 11 Desc. Sk. 21
From Bruno's forest screams the affrighted jay, 11 Desc. Sk. 67
Among the forest glades, while jocund June 32 Guilt 413
To Calaterium's forest he repaired. 103 Artegal 93
Thy couch the dewy earth, thy roof the forest thorn!" 104 Artegal 161
Deep in a forest, with leave given, at the age 125 V. and J. 272
Of his retirement, to the forest lodge 125 V. and J. 289
Beneath her sway, a simple forest cry 153 Morn. Ex. 5
No more than in some forest wild; 154 Flower Garden 28
In field or forest with nice care, 168 Wren's Nest 2
Nor mute the forest hum of noon; 235 Power of Sound 198
And, if thy bounty fail, the forest pants; 268 *Pure element 7
Or into trackless forest set 298 Brownie's Cell 3
The grace of forest charms decayed, 302 Yarrow V. 47
And stately forest where the wild deer rove; 323 Ode 1814 10
Darkens the sun, hath bade the forest sink, 328 Ode 1815 95
He quakes not like the timid forest game, 339 Tell 24
Sate watching in a forest shed, 342 Ital. Itin. 87
The forest to embolden; 385 Yarrow Rev. 14
On airy upland, and by forest rills, 387 Manse 4

Forest—*continued.*
The forest huge of ancient Caledon . . . . . 392 *Inglewood* 1
Whether she be of forest bowers, ... 397 *White Doe* 75
Hill-top, and flood, and forest green, ... 406 *White Doe* 944
What mighty forest in its gloom . . . . 413 *White Doe* 1557
Support, and whom the forest shields ; . . . 416 *White Doe* 1874
Renews. Through every forest, cave, and den, . 435 *Ecc. Sonn.* 2. 27. 9
Those forest oaks of Druid memory, ... 450 *Ecc. Sonn.* 3. 39. 7
And wild deer bounded through the forest glade, 450 *Ecc. Sonn.* 3. 41. 5
Deep in a forest, thy secure abode, ... 456 **The leaves* 21
The forest thorough ! . . . . 485 **Bright Flower* 8
And ripening fruits and forest leaves . . . . 502 *Seasons* 11
And wander forth, in forest glades . . . . . 506 **While from* 19
Or, Pilgrim-like, on forest moss reclined, . . . 522 *Epist. Beaumont* 46
But wide around lay forest ground . . . . . 542 *Russ. Fug.* 93
Creep forth, and through the forest wind . . . 543 *Russ. Fug.* 123
Rugged and high, of Charnwood's forest ground, . 547 **Beneath yon* 2
Thro' craggs, and forest glooms, and opening lakes, 591 *Ev. Wk. Quarto* 4
I hear, while in the forest depth he sees, . . . 596 *Ev. Wk. Quarto* 261
From Bruno's forest screams the frighted jay, . 603 *Desc. Sk. Quarto* 68
A giant moan along the forest swells . . . . 605 *Desc. Sk. Quarto* 201
And Sabra in the forest with St. George ! . . . 670 *Prelude* 5. 344
Of faery land, the forest of romance. . . . . 672 *Prelude* 5. 455
Through a thick forest. Silence touched me here 687 *Prelude* 7. 36
Of thick entangled forest, like the moon . . . 693 *Prelude* 7. 415
Of the Hercynian forest. Yet, hail to you . . 702 *Prelude* 8. 215
Through field or forest with the maid we love, . 741 *Prelude* 13. 123
The shady forest of its green attire,— . . . . 790 *Excursion* 3. 309
The hermit to his cell in forest wide ; . . . . 791 *Excursion* 3. 369
Or forest, fetched the enormous axle-tree . . . 866 *Excursion* 7. 606
In forest purlieus ; and the like are bred, . . . 879 *Excursion* 8. 369
Forest and field, and hill and dale appear, . . 885 *Excursion* 9. 61
War's tincture, 'mid the forest green and still, . S.3. 436 **The doubt* 184
Than to the forest hermit are the leaves . . . K.8. 253 *Recluse* 1. 1. 607
Forestall. (Not to forestall such knowledge as may be 774 *Excursion* 2. 161
Forest-brake. As from a forest-brake . . . . 331 *Ode : Thanks.* 146
Foresters. Like foresters in leaf-green vest, . . . 342 *Ital. Itin.* 58
Where foresters or shepherds dwell, ... 409 *White Doe* 1166
Forest-fruit. Forest-fruit with social hands ; . . 141 *Arm. Lady* 94
Forest-glade. Or let their wishes loose, in forest-glade, ... 311 **Who rises* 49
Forest-glooms. Yet, when above the forest-glooms 544 *Russ. Fug.* 241
Forest-ground. Wild tracts of forest-ground, and scattered groves, ... 891 *Excursion* 9. 505
Forest-lawn. Have roused her from her sleep : and forest-lawn, ... 314 **Advance—come* 7
Forest's. Far in the level forest's central gloom : . 5 *Ev. Wk.* 181
And now, emerging from the forest's gloom, . . 11 *Desc. Sk.* 52
Listens, or quakes while from the forest's gulf . 14 *Desc. Sk.* 194
" At noon, when, by the forest's edge . . . . 239 *P. B.* 261
And penetrates the forest's inmost shades ; . . 459 **Wanderer ! that* 26
Leads to the dear Parnassian forest's shade, . . 574 *Chiabrera* 5. 10
She hears, upon the mountain forest's brow, . . 606 *Desc. Sk. Quarto* 225
Than with the forest's more enduring growth, . 867 *Excursion* 7. 628
Forests. There, all unshaded, blazing forests throw 12 *Desc. Sk.* 101
How tunefully the forests ring ! . . . . . 237 *P. B.* 73
(Thanks to high God) forests of such remain : . 319 **Avaunt all* 11
Of midnight,—cities, plains, forests, and mighty streams. . . . . 350 *Des. Stanzas* 18
Those mighty forests, once the bison's screen, . 376 *Duddon* 2. 10
The matted forests of Ontario's shore . . . . 379 *Duddon* 13. 8
And back to the forests again ! . . . . . . 485 **A plague* 35
Through woods and spacious forests,—to behold . 496 **A little* 34
Bright'ning the gloom where thick the forests stoop ; . . . . 604 *Desc. Sk. Quarto* 129
These forests unapproachable by death, . . . 682 *Prelude* 6. 466
Or in wide forests of continuous shade, . . . 716 *Prelude* 9. 434
The width of those huge forests, unto me . . . 716 *Prelude* 9. 462
Primeval forests wrapped thee round with dark . 822 *Excursion* 5. 7
Like trees in forests,—spread through spacious tracts, ... 876 *Excursion* 8. 124
Mines opened, forests planted, and rocks split, . K.8. 227 **I will* 104
Forest-side. Upon the forest-side in Grasmere Vale 131 *Michael* 40
Above the Rotha, by the forest-side. . . . . 147 *Joanna* 31
Forest-skirted. High on a broad unfertile tract of forest-skirted Down, ... 91 *Norman Boy* 1
Forest-tree. And so the grandeur of the Forest-tree 277 **A Poet* 12
Forest-trees. Even to the inferior Kinds ; whom forest-trees . . . . 395 *White Doe: Ded.* 45
Foreswore. Her *wished-for* yellow she foreswore, . S.3. 431 **The Scottish* 21
Foretaste. The simply-meek foretaste the springs . 225 *Present.* 53
His icy scimitar, a foretaste yields . . . . . 263 **While not* 5
O dastard whom such foretaste doth not cheer ! . 310 **Another year* 9
(Foretaste of winter) on the moorland heights ; . 394 **No more* 28
Foretaste deliverance ; but the least perturbed . 541 *Grace Darl.* 67
A foretaste, a dim earnest, of the calm . . . 636 *Prelude* 1, 280
Of greedy foretaste, from the secret stand . . 872 *Excursion* 7. 993
Insensibly the foretaste of this parting . . . S.3. 433 **The doubt* 13
Foretasted. Foretasted, immortality conceived . . 887 *Excursion* 9. 225
Foretell. Dear native regions, I foretell, ... 1 *Extract* 1
And, leaving it to others to foretell, ... 840 *Excursion* 6. 170
Foretelling. Foretelling and proclaiming, ere thou leave . . . . 363 **List—'twas* 99
Foretelling aged Winter's desolate sway. . . . 828 *Excursion* 5. 410
Foretells. Protracted, and the twilight storm foretells, ... 605 *Desc. Sk. Quarto* 202
Forethought. Without uneasy forethought of the pain, ... 680 *Prelude* 6. 330
Foretold. Should be as Lennox has foretold, then swear, ... 64 *Bord.* 1459
" Thou knowest, the Delphic oracle foretold . . 210 *Laod.* 43

Foretold—*continued.*
Transfigured, from this kindling hath foretold . 437 *Ecc. Sonn.* 2. 34. 5
Her happier destiny foretold :— . . . . . 629 *Installation* 44
An Ode, in passion uttered, which foretold . . 667 *Prelude* 5. 96
Foretold, and added prayer to prophecy ; . . . 797 *Excursion* 3. 765
Foretrace. By paths no human wisdom can foretrace ! . . . . 505 *Warning* 133
Forewarning. And no forewarning gives ; . . . 88 *H. C.* 31
He knew not one forewarning pain ; . . . . 248 *P. B.* 1048
Had given forewarning, and that he himself . . 667 *Prelude* 5. 101
Forewarns. While he forewarns, denounces, launches forth, ... 695 *Prelude* 7. 523
Forfeit. That wretched life of thine shall be the forfeit. . . . . 54 *Bord.* 950
Ye did not forfeit one dear right, ... 223 *Wishing-gate* 14
Christ died for—cannot forfeit his high claim . . 429 *Ecc. Sonn.* 2. 4. 12
That woman ne'er should forfeit, keep *thy* vow ; . 529 **Those breathing* 134
To works that ne'er shall forfeit their renown, . 587 *Crosth.* 5
Forfeited. Have forfeited their ancient English dower . . . . 307 **Milton ! thou* 5
Are forfeited ; but infamy doth kill. . . . . 316 **Say, what* 14
From his own sight—this gone, he forfeited . . 776 *Excursion* 2. 296
Forfeiting. Is reached, where, forfeiting his bright attire, ... 261 **I watch* 6
Forfeiture. Was summoned to discharge the forfeiture, ... 134 *Michael* 215
Prescribed to duty :—woeful forfeiture . . . 428 *Ecc. Sonn.* 2. 1. 3
Sanctions the forfeiture that Law demands, . . 519 *Pun. Death* 11. 10
Too oft by wilful forfeiture, have lost . . . . 800 *Excursion* 3. 961
Thrives by the forfeiture—unfeeling thought, . . 878 *Excursion* 8. 284
Forgat. To worship aye, and he forgat it not ; . . 553 *Prioress* 59
Forgave. He had been sore misused ; but he forgave . . . . 74 *Bord.* 2070
Forge. Still tempering, from the unguilty forge . 298 *Brownie's Cell* 29
Forged. Of dancing insects forged upon his breast ; 383 *Duddon.* 28. 8
Forgers. Forgers of daring tales ! we bless you then, 673 *Prelude* 5. 524
Forge's. The distant forge's swinging thump profound ; . . . . 9 *Ev. Wk.* 377
Forget. Would he forget those, Beings to whose minds . . . . 23 *Yew-tree* 39
Can I forget our freaks at shearing time ! . . . 28 *Guilt* 212
Thus much to speak ; but think not I forget— . 40 *Bord.* 175
Dear Father ! how *could* I forget and live ?— . 40 *Bord.* 176
Departed Child ! I could forget thee once . . 118 *Maternal Grief* 1
" 'Tis gone—like dreams that we forget ; . . . 121 *Emigrant Mother* 55
What will be left to us !—But I forget . . . 137 *Michael* 402
—Therefore, unwilling to forget that day, . . . 149 **A narrow* 74
Nor did the battered Tar forget, ... 178 *Waggoner* 2. 157
Of past existence—wilt thou then forget . . . 207 *Tintern* 149
Of holier love. Nor wilt thou then forget . . 207 *Tintern* 155
Or, to forget their madness and their woes, . . 217 *Enterprise* 117
The daring thought, forget the name ; . . . . 231 **The gentlest Poet* 6
No wonder if you quite forget . . . . . . 237 *P. B.* 119
But how could I forget thee ? Through what power, ... 257 **Surprised by* 6
We should forget them ; they are of the sky, . . 262 **Dark and* 13
Nor will I then thy modest grace forget, . . . 264 *Snowdrop* 12
Behold, already they forget to shine, ... 278 **The most* 7
That will forget thee ; thou hast great allies ; . 305 *Toussaint* 12
Forget thy weakness, upon which is built, . . . 321 **Here pause* 13
Who can forget thy prowess, never more . . . 331 *Ode : Thanks.* 142
Nor shall forget the Maiden coy . . . . . 342 *Ital. Itin.* 35
Sink, and forget their nature—*now* expands . . 384 *Duddon* 32. 6
Will we forget that, as the fowl can keep . . . 390 *Glencroe* 10
The hawk forget his perch ; the hound . . . 402 *White Doe* 552
Imposed on human kind, must first forget . . 424 *Ecc. Sonn.* 1. 23. 11
By dauntless Luther freed, could they forget . . 437 *Ecc. Sonn.* 2. 37. 4
Ungrateful Country, if thou e'er forget . . . 442 *Ecc. Sonn.* 3. 10. 1
Teaching us to forget them or forgive. . . . 449 *Ecc. Sonn.* 3. 35. 10
Of prayer and praise forget their rosaries, . . . 467 *St. Bees* 89
And Bards, who hailed thee, may forget . . . 507 *May* 3
Forget the glories he hath known, ... 588 *Immortality* 83
Can I forget you, being as you were . . . . 639 *Prelude* 1. 501
In which ye stood ? or can I here forget . . . 639 *Prelude* 1. 503
Can beat never will I forget thy name. . . . 659 *Prelude* 4. 32
Forget his feeling : so (if like effect . . . . 677 *Prelude* 6. 154
Of a long exile. Nor could I forget, ... 679 *Prelude* 6. 274
—But I forget our Charge, as utterly . . . . 785 *Excursion* 2. 878
My lips, that may forget thee in the crowd, . . 802 *Excursion* 4. 40
Cannot forget thee here ; where thou hast built, . 802 *Excursion* 4. 41
Shall it forget that its most noble use, ... 820 *Excursion* 4. 1260
On a kind parent willing to forget . . . . . 852 *Excursion* 6. 944
Nor so the Valley shall forget her loss. . . . 868 *Excursion* 7. 705
Think not, that, pitying him, I could forget . . 886 *Excursion* 9. 161
That rapturous moment never shall I forget . . 893 *Excursion* 9. 588
Forget'st. Meek lustre, nor forget'st the humble Vale ; . . . . 329 *Ode : Thanks.* 30
Forgetful. In open air forgetful would I sit . . . 32 *Guilt* 431
My Child, forgetful of the name of Herbert, . . 41 *Bord.* 206
Forgetful of the body they sustained.— . . . 149 **A narrow* 62
The high-souled virtues which forgetful earth . 540 *Grace Darl.* 18
On her green hill, forgetful of this Boy . . . 671 *Prelude* 5. 401
Who slumbers at her feet,—forgetful, too, . . 671 *Prelude* 5. 402
Forgetfully. Forgetfully ; uncalled upon to pay . 777 *Excursion* 2. 367
Forgetfulness. *See* **Self-forgetfulness.**
In the entire forgetfulness of pain. . . . . . 65 *Bord.* 1551
Beguiled into forgetfulness of care . . . . . 508 *F. Stone* 1
Not in entire forgetfulness, ... 588 *Immortality* 62

Forgetfulness—*continued.*
Promised soft peace and sweet forgetfulness. 719 *Prelude* 10. 90
In soft forgetfulness the livelong hours, 752 *Prelude* 14. 403
Inviting sleep and soft forgetfulness. 821 *Excursion* 4. 1324
Doth, by a rapture of forgetfulness, 845 *Excursion* 6. 488
To save themselves from blank forgetfulness!" 877 *Excursion* 8. 230
By such forgetfulness the soul becomes, K.8. 244 *Recluse* 1.1.297
Forget-me-not. A new *Forget-me-not.* 164 **Fair Lady* 24
Forgets. That rose, and now forgets to rise, 112 **How rich* 16
Forgets her nature, opening like a flower 274 *Infant M.* 2
Above her head and so forgets her vows— 522 *Epist. Beaumont* 49
Forgets, unweary'd watching every side, 595 *Ev. Wk. Quarto* 214
One precious gain, that he forgets himself. 670 *Prelude* 5. 346
Hears, and forgets his purpose;—furnished thus, 810 *Excursion* 4. 573
Who here forgets her errand, nothing loth S.3. 436 **The doubt* 142
Forgetting. *See* **Self-forgetting.**
Forgetting, calls the wearied to her side; 6 *Ev. Wk.* 229
Forgetting in thy care 109 **Ere with* 10
Alive to all things and forgetting all. 146 **It was an* 19
Iona's Saints, forgetting not past days, 474 **On to* 12
Our birth is but a sleep and a forgetting: 588 *Immortality* 58
Upon earth's native energies; forgetting 792 *Excursion* 3. 423
Forgive. I neither ask nor wish—forgive me, but forgive!" 35 *Guilt* 621
(Reader, forgive the intolerable thought) 36 *Guilt* 659
I never can forgive it: but how steadily 39 *Bord.* 110
You must forgive me. Ay, and if you think 45 *Bord.* 428
You will forgive me—— If I ever knew 48 *Bord.* 631
You will forgive me, but my heart runs over. 52 *Bord.* 833
Heavens! my good Friend! Forgive me, gracious Sir!— 54 *Bord.* 943
I could forgive him. And should he make the Child 56 *Bord.* 1044
Forgive me.—Oswald knows it all—he knows, 66 *Bord.* 1599
Oh let me be forgiven! I *do* forgive thee. 66 *Bord.* 1618
I pity, can forgive, you; but those wretches— 70 *Bord.* 1832
Forgive me!—Saints forgive me. Had I thought 76 *Bord.* 2241
Forgive me, Sir: before I spoke to you, 101 *Brothers* 354
Nor to my wishes lost;—forgive the wrong, 104 *Artegal* 133
Had been no sorrow. I forgive him;—but 134 *Michael* 240
Another Master. Heaven forgive me, Luke, 137 *Michael* 380
Forgive me then; for I had been 182 *Waggoner* 4. 216
Thou found'st—and I forgive thee—here thou art— 210 *Laod.* 53
From its own country, and forgive the strings." 252 **Why, Minstrel* 4
Just God, forgive! 286 *Nith* 66
Forgive me if the phrase be strong;— 291 *Rob Roy* 14
Forgive, illustrious Country! these deep sighs, 360 *Alban Hills* 1
From far, forgive the wanderings of my thought: 367 **If with* 3
Thickens, the pastoral River will forgive 382 *Duddon* 23. 11
Teaching us to forget them or forgive. 449 *Ecc. Sonn.* 3. 35. 10
Ye will forgive the weakness of that hour, 653 *Prelude* 3. 319
Genius of Burke! forgive the pen seduced 694 *Prelude* 7. 512
Forgive them;—never—never did my steps 763 *Excursion* 1. 497
Of sun or moon.—Forgive me, if I say 788 *Excursion* 3. 152
And who shall judge the creature, will forgive. 828 *Excursion* 5. 368
Forgive me if I venture to suspect 880 *Excursion* 8. 400
Recal my song the ungenerous thought; forgive, K.8. 244 *Recluse* 1.1.269
Forgive me if I add another claim, K.8. 255 *Recluse* 1.1.692
Forgiven. Yes, be it so;—repent and be forgiven— 63 *Bord.* 1415
Oh let me be forgiven! I *do* forgive thee. 66 *Bord.* 1618
no harm, but—it will be forgiven me; 71 *Bord.* 1917
And, if thou hast forgiven me, let me hope, 76 *Bord.* 2200
And adding, with a hope to be forgiven, 102 *Brothers* 431
This Minstrel lead, his sins forgiven; 286 *Nith* 56
May hope to be forgiven. 341 *San Salv.* 18
"Then be we, each and all, forgiven! 401 *White Doe* 495
Breathed to a Son forgiven, and blest 411 *White Doe* 1423
To gratitude, to injuries forgiven— 436 *Ecc. Sonn.* 2. 32. 11
And thou, in lovers' hearts forgiven, 480 *Somnamb.* 161
And be forgiven. 490 *Night Thought* 18
And of Eustace was forgiven: 536 *Egremont* 102
Of a diviner love, will be forgiven— 540 **Lady! a* 81
Of righteousness, of sins forgiven, 577 **By playful* 21
Of arts and letters—but be that forgiven)— 671 *Prelude* 5. 410
And harsh unkindnesses are all forgiven, 850 *Excursion* 6. 776
Forgiveness. Of that old Man's forgiveness on thy heart, 77 *Bord.* 2297
All past forgiveness it repealed; 181 *Waggoner* 4. 180
Forgiveness from God's mercy-seat; 331 *Ode: Thanks.* 179
Help, and forgiveness speedy and entire. 366 **Eternal Lord* 14
For prompt forgiveness will not sue in vain. 394 **No more* 36
Made confession, asked forgiveness, 536 *Egremont* 99
Entire forgiveness!—But if thou art one 548 **Stranger! this* 25
Forgiveness, patience, hope, and charity!" 833 *Excursion* 5. 727
Preclude forgiveness, from the praise debarred, 845 *Excursion* 6. 489
Than brotherly forgiveness may attend; 848 *Excursion* 6. 658
Constrained forgiveness, and relenting vows, 849 *Excursion* 6. 713
Of mutual pity and forgiveness, sweet 851 *Excursion* 6. 877
He could not find forgiveness in himself; 855 *Excursion* 6. 1113
Prompt aid, forgiveness speedy and entire. K.8. 266 **Rid of* 14
Forgives. Forgives their interference—Art divine, 509 *F. Stone* 76
Forgoes. Their watch-dog ne'er his angry bark forgoes, 15 *Desc. Sk.* 242
Forgone. Forgone the home delight of constant truth, 32 *Guilt* 440
Forgot. Be scorn and fear and hope alike forgot 22 *Desc. Sk.* 666
I too forgot the heavings of my breast. 30 *Guilt* 338
The scrip that held his food, and I forgot 67 *Bord.* 1643
Have you forgot your own troubles 72 *Bord.* 1976
"Rest, little young One, rest; thou hast forgot the day 87 *Pet-lamb* 33

Forgot—*continued.*
He quite forgot his holly whip, 127 *Idiot Boy* 84
She quite forgot to send the Doctor, 129 *Idiot Boy* 275
And he hath now forgot his Wife, 177 *Waggoner* 2. 85
Of sense despised, a world forgot, 301 *Bran* 63
We forgot Thee, do not Thou 336 **Jesu! bless* 11
In conflict; whose rough winds forgot their jars 336 *Danube* 10
(So beautiful is Clyde) forgot to mourn 392 *Bothwell* 2
"Have you forgot"—and here she smiled— 542 *Russ. Fug.* 57
The distant clock forgot, and chilling dew, 596 *Ev. Wk. Quarto* 273
Save in the land where all things are forgot, 614 *Desc.Sk.Quarto* 677
Be the dead load of mortal ills forgot, 617 *Desc.Sk.Quarto* 811
Forgot the beverage—and pin'd away. 620 *Birth of Love* 8
Forgot her functions, and slept undisturbed. 648 *Prelude* 2. 418
With our own inner being are forgot. 656 *Prelude* 3. 508
Forgot, at seasons, whence they had their being; 723 *Prelude* 10. 376
Forgot that such a sound was ever heard 723 *Prelude* 10. 377
And I at once forgot I was a Stranger. 772 *Excursion* 2. 61
I then forgot him:—there I stood and gazed: 785 *Excursion* 2. 879
And, like an ardent hunter, I forgot, 788 *Excursion* 3. 122
Its humble destination were forgot— 866 *Excursion* 7. 615
At sight of this seclusion, he forgot K.8. 236 *Recluse* 1. 1. 8
Forgotten. *See* **Oar-forgotten.**
Forgotten? have my warnings passed so quickly 40 *Bord.* 162
Has been forgotten. Farewell! Gentle pilgrims, 58 *Bord.* 1140
Plague on my memory, him I had forgotten. 60 *Bord.* 1256
He had forgotten. He had lost his path, 96 *Brothers* 91
The marvellous current of forgotten things; 102 *Artegal* 12
Where in forgotten quiet he might dwell, 125 *V. and J.* 269
Would surely be forgotten. But at length 136 *Michael* 320
His flock had need. 'Tis not forgotten yet 138 *Michael* 462
To words of a forgotten tongue 166 *Danish Boy* 36
Hath quite forgotten her—or may be 177 *Waggoner* 2. 86
Hunt half a day for a forgotten dream. 202 *Hart-leap* 132
Relic of Kings! Wreck of forgotten wars, 272 *Ruins* 9
And this forgotten Taper to the last 391 *Brownie* 13
Scorned or forgotten, Thou canst testify, 442 *Ecc. Sonn.* 3. 7. 6
God's bounty, soon forgotten; or indeed, 462 **Where lies the truth* 5
For thy worst rage, forgotten. Oft as Spring 464 **Greta, what* 9
Nor be it e'er forgotten how by skill 467 *St. Bees* 118
Forgotten like a dream! 544 *Russ. Fug.* 256
All effort seems forgotten; one to whom 572 *Animal Tran.* 9
That would not be forgotten, and are here 632 *Prelude* 1. 49
And is forgotten; even then I felt 640 *Prelude* 1. 585
Of things forgotten, these same scenes so bright, 641 *Prelude* 1. 607
Were utterly forgotten, and what I saw 647 *Prelude* 2. 350
Be not forgotten, that I still retained 647 *Prelude* 2. 359
As if I had forgotten her; but no, 709 *Prelude* 8. 682
A hundred other names, forgotten now, 712 *Prelude* 9. 177
To notice old forgotten principles, 722 *Prelude* 10. 251
Or, seeing, had forgotten! A strong shock 731 *Prelude* 11. 270
Being over and forgotten, on we wound 746 *Prelude* 14. 27
Could never be forgotten! In his heart, 759 *Excursion* 1. 185
Familiar with forgotten years, that shows 760 *Excursion* 1. 276
And she forgotten in the quiet grave. 763 *Excursion* 1. 510
Passed from my mind like a forgotten sound. 765 *Excursion* 1. 610
Forgotten,—at safe distance from 'a world 776 *Excursion* 2. 314
Left and forgotten in his careless way, 778 *Excursion* 2. 452
By snatches, and lets fall, to be forgotten; 820 *Excursion* 4. 1285
All cares forgotten, round its hallowed walls! 895 *Excursion* 9. 728
Lie down and be forgotten in the dust, K.8. 255 *Recluse* 1.1.694
Fork. Within this grove of firs! and, on the fork 150 **When, to* 19
Oft as I pass along the fork 214 *Kirkstone* 3
In the deep fork of Amerdale; 415 *White Doe* 1707
Forkèd. Concealed among the forkèd hills— 403 *White Doe* 693
The forkèd weapon of the skies can send 870 *Excursion* 7. 834
Forks. Far as St. Maurice, from yon eastern Forks, 350 *Des. Stanzas* 37
Forlorn. But sought in vain; for now, all wild, forlorn, 25 *Guilt* 43
Here paused she, of all present thought forlorn, 30 *Guilt* 307
Of his forlorn appearance, could not fail 39 *Bord.* 81
And most forlorn, should bribe a Mother, pressed 56 *Bord.* 1039
Sent forth a cry forlorn, 85 *Shepherd-boys* 75
While thou art roving, wretched and forlorn, 104 *Artegal* 160
The most forlorn—one life of that bright star, 172 *Infant Daughter* 4
So kind and so forlorn! 194 *Ruth* 162
A wretched thing forlorn. 197 *Thorn* 9
"Oh! it was a time forlorn 204 *Brougham* 55
And from the infernal Gods, 'mid shades forlorn 209 *Laod.* 3
With *one* wild floweret (call it not forlorn) 221 *Triad* 116
Yet how forlorn, should *ye* depart, 223 *Wishing-gate* 10
Upon them not forlorn, 232 *Jew. Fam.* 38
She drooped and pined like one forlorn; 246 *P. B.* 907
Save one, one only, when I stood forlorn, 257 **Surprised by* 11
Have glimpses that would make me less forlorn; 259 **The world is* 12
To mimic Time's forlorn humanities. 262 **Mark the* 14
She is not what she seems, a forlorn wretch, 280 **Oh what* 6
Ne'er can the way be irksome or forlorn 284 *Departure* 31
And its forlorn Hic jacet! 287 *Ellen Irwin* 56
Of him in that forlorn estate! 294 *Jedbor.* 26
On the forlorn unfortunate, 296 *Highland Boy* 17
Returned to animate an age forlorn? 314 *Hofer* 4
These emblems suit the helpless and forlorn, 321 **Humanity, delighting* 11
To his forlorn condition! let thy grace 323 **Now that* 10
Appear to sight still more forlorn. 366 **Ye Trees* 18
In the blank earth, neglected and forlorn, 383 *Duddon* 29. 10
Soon, like a lingering star forlorn 391 *Highland Broach* 75
Under an arch of that forlorn abode; 391 *Brownie* 4
And there stood bravely, though forlorn. 412 *White Doe* 1479

Forlorn—*continued.*
And she is thoroughly forlorn : 414 *White Doe* 1622
Forlorn, but not disconsolate : 416 *White Doe* 1820
How sad would be their durance, if forlorn 430 *Ecc. Sonn.* 2. 6. 13
The forlorn traveller, or sailor wrecked 467 *St. Bees* 92
A Tower of refuge built for the else forlorn. 469 **The feudal* 8
When first I saw that family forlorn. 477 *Long Meg* 4
To Beings else forlorn and blind ! 481 *Expost.* 6
The kindness that would make him less forlorn ; 501 *Humanity* 66
Hath not departed, stands forlorn 506 **While from* 43
On a green bank a creature stood forlorn 523 *Epist. Beaumont* 122
A soul so pitiably forlorn, 534 **Blest is* 61
Where by the Castle-gate it hung forlorn. 535 *Egremont* 80
Who comforts the forlorn ; 542 *Russ. Fug.* 44
The ivied Ruins of forlorn GRACE DIEU ; 547 **Beneath yon* 4
Not one word have I now, I am so forlorn,— 560 *Cuck.and Night.*209
Not cheerless, though forlorn. 580 *John Words.* 20
Who plods o'er hills and vales his road forlorn, 602 *Desc. Sk. Quarto* 15
Is Friendship's emblem, whether the forlorn 627 **The star* 3
All the green summer, to forlorn cascades 639 *Prelude* 1. 489
When, in forlorn and naked chambers cooped 655 *Prelude* 3. 450
Abject, depressed, forlorn, disconsolate. 666 *Prelude* 5. 28
Led through the lanes in forlorn servitude ; 669 *Prelude* 5. 241
Weep, and the river sides are all forlorn. 670 *Prelude* 5. 340
Winds thwarting winds, bewildered and forlorn, 684 *Prelude* 6. 628
Hearing, I be not downcast or forlorn !— 755 *Recluse* 1. 1. 835
Of boyhood, many an hour in caves forlorn, 758 *Excursion* 1. 154
And chambers of transgression, now forlorn. 817 *Excursion* 4. 1049
The estate of man would be indeed forlorn 818 *Excursion* 4. 1152
A soothing comforter, although forlorn ; 852 *Excursion* 6. 933
No pleasure-house forlorn ; S.3. 425 **No whimsy* 2
Alas that one beloved, forlorn, K.8. 220 **The snow-tracks* 36
Of feeling, which were cheerless and forlorn K.8. 248*Recluse* 1.1.434
Or sought with courage ; enterprize forlorn K.8. 256*Recluse* 1.1.717
An amaranthine crown of flowers forlorn— K.8. 325 [?]**The vestal* 7

Forlornest. Meek Infant ! among all forlornest things 172 *Infant Daughter* 2

Form. The spacious landscape change in form and hue ! 4 *Ev. Wk.* 99
The form appears of one that spurs his steed 6 *Ev. Wk.* 196
Long grass and willows form the woven wall, 6 *Ev. Wk.* 240
Weak roof a cowering form two babes to shield, 7 *Ev. Wk.* 273
The half-seen form of Twilight roams astray 7 *Ev. Wk.* 292
Unmoved with each rude form of peril nigh ; 14 *Desc. Sk.* 205
Glances the wheeling eagle's glorious form ! 15 *Desc. Sk.* 276
With its dark arms to form a circling bower, 23 *Yew-tree* 11
Within that fabric of mysterious form 26 *Guilt* 127
They hung not :—no one on *his* form or face 36 *Guilt* 660
No tree, nor jutting eminence, nor form 68 *Bord.* 1708
Hues more exalted, " a refinèd Form," 110 **Look at* 22
Of antique form ; this large, for spinning wool ; 132 *Michael* 83
Then think of her beautiful gliding form, 142 †*Lov. and Lik.* 45
The voiceless Form he chose to feign, 159 *Green Linnet* 39
Yet seems a form of flesh and blood ; 165 *Danish Boy* 24
—There doth she ken the awful form 180 *Waggoner* 4. 18
To form, an undissolving cloud ; 181 *Waggoner* 4. 105
Of form and aspect too magnificent 184 *Yew-trees* 12
Grace that shall mould the Maiden's form 187 **Three years* 23
Shall rear her form to stately height, 187 **Three years* 32
But unsubstantial Form eludes her grasp 210 *Laod.* 27
On thy reclining form with more delight 220 *Haunted Tree* 35
Met by the rainbow's form divine, 221 *Triad* 84
The form and rich habiliments of One 226 *Vernal Ode* 5
" My little vagrant Form of light, 237 *P. B.* 111
Disordering colour, form, and stature ! 245 *P. B.* 763
His very self in form and feature, 246 *P. B.* 924
Ideal Form, the universal mould. 257 **No mortal* 8
Like a Form sculptured on a monument 273 **When Philoctetes* 2
But what are Gordon's form and face, 287 *Ellen Irwin* 17
A Form not doubtfully descried :— 300 *Cora Linn* 26
But She through many a change of form hath gone, 311 **Who rises* 15
Issued, to sudden view, a glorious Form ! 323 *Ode 1814* 22
The graceful form of milk-white Steed, 341 *Ital. Itin.* 9
The form and motion of a stream to take ; 351 *Des. Stanzas* 62
Of battle meets him in authentic form ! 368 *Trajan* 44
The Flower, the Form within it, 374 *Eg. Maid* 367
The sun in heaven !—but now, to form a shade 377 *Duddon* 5. 5
Sacred Religion ! " mother of form and fear," 380 *Duddon* 18. 1
The Form remains, the Function never dies ; 384 *Duddon* 34. 6
In the beautiful form of this innocent Doe : 398 *White Doe* 237
That Form beneath the spreading tree, 401 *White Doe* 444
Glimmers through many a superstitious form 419 *Ecc. Sonn.* 1. 4. 13
Form spirit and character from holy writ, 430 *Ecc. Sonn.* 2. 9. 11
The bright corporeal presence—form and face— 440 *Ecc. Sonn.* 3. 1. 9
An idle form, the Word an empty sound ! 445 *Ecc. Sonn.* 3. 21. 14
A Form as bright, as beautiful a moon, 461 **Who but is* 7
Of *Powers* endued with visible form, instinct 469 **Bold words* 13
Nor form, nor feeling, great or small ; 485 *Poet's Epitaph* 30
Long as we gazed upon the form and face, 523 *Epist. Beaumont* 144
What mortal form, what earthly face 530 *Gleaner* 17
A nymph-like liberty, in nymph-like form, 540 **Lady ! a* 71
Diffused through form and face, 543 *Russ. Fug.* 170
And recognised it, though an altered form, 571 **There is a Flower* 10
Thy Form was sleeping on a glassy sea. 578 *Peele Castle* 4
A waste where creatures bearing human form, 585 *Ch. Lamb* 69
A form discover'd at the well-known seat, 592 *Ev. Wk. Quarto* 45

Form—*continued.*
A desperate form appears, that spurs his steed, 595 *Ev. Wk. Quarto* 179
Proud of the varying arch and moveless form of snow. 595 *Ev. Wk. Quarto* 206
And bidding paler shades her form conceal, 603 *Desc.Sk.Quarto* 77
Unmov'd with each rude form of Danger nigh, 607 *Desc.Sk.Quarto* 260
Glances the fire-clad eagle's wheeling form ; 608 *Desc.Sk.Quarto* 339
Strong poison not a form of steel can brave 613 *Desc.Sk.Quarto* 630
Resolves that Cupid, chang'd in form and face 624 *Æneid* 3
Dissemble ; be that boy in form and face ! 624 *Æneid* 37
In that bold form and impress high 629 *Installation* 84
To breathe an elevated mood, by form 646 *Prelude* 2. 305
With every form of creature, as it looked 648 *Prelude* 2. 412
To every natural form, rock, fruit, or flower, 651 *Prelude* 3. 127
Or some uneasy thought ; yet still his form 664 *Prelude* 4. 406
Lay bedded, changing oftentimes its form 685 *Prelude* 6. 706
And every character of form and face : 690 *Prelude* 7. 223
In twain, yet leaving the same outward form. 693 *Prelude* 7. 391
His form hath flashed upon me, glorified 703 *Prelude* 8. 269
Of human nature ; hence the human form 703 *Prelude* 8. 279
Far more of an imaginative form 703 *Prelude* 8. 284
A form and body ; all things were to me 711 *Prelude* 9. 105
Of kindred permanence, unchanged in form 740 *Prelude* 13. 37
Of act and circumstance, and visible form, 744 *Prelude* 13. 288
In sense conducting to ideal form, 747 *Prelude* 14. 76
That ever was put forth in personal form— 755 *Recluse* 1. 1. 785
The spectacle : sensation, soul, and form, 759 *Excursion* 1. 207
In bodily form.—But without further bidding 765 *Excursion* 1. 639
Dame Nature's pupil of the lowest form, 789 *Excursion* 3. 198
On the bright form of Her whom once I loved :— 793 *Excursion* 3. 481
Of flying sunbeams, or to the outward form 794 *Excursion* 3. 577
Yet is their form and image here expressed 809 *Excursion* 4. 552
The semblance bearing of a sculptured form 825 *Excursion* 5. 215
By the bright fire, the good Man's form, and face 834 *Excursion* 5. 779
The Solitary answered : " Such a Form 839 *Excursion* 6. 102
Fictions in form, but in their substance truths, 846 *Excursion* 6. 545
The form, port, motions, of this Cottage-girl 850 *Excursion* 6. 826
—Bright garland form they for the pensive brow 855 *Excursion* 6. 1127
Pan or Apollo, veiled in human form : 868 *Excursion* 7. 730
Whose uncouth form was grafted on the wall, 871 *Excursion* 7. 914
Mantle upon his cheek. Is this the form, 879 *Excursion* 8. 315
The finer lineaments of form and face ; 881 *Excursion* 8. 504
" To every Form of being is assigned," 884 *Excursion* 9. 1
The oppressor breathes, their human form divine, 886 *Excursion* 9. 151
With the same upright form ! The sun is fixed, 887 *Excursion* 9. 209
In the last dotage of a dying form. K.8. 223 **There is a shapeless* 4
And to whatever else of outward form K.8. 245*Recluse* 1.1.301

Formal. Imprisoned 'mid the formal props 214 *Kirkstone* 23
Comes not by casting in a formal mould, 277 **A Poet* 13
Formal, and circumscribed in time and space ; 321 **The power* 2
Boastful Idolatress of formal skill 468 *St. Bees* 158
Once on the top of Tynwald's formal mound 470 *Tynwald* 1
And formal fellowship of petty things ! 497 **Enough of climbing* 11
By casual boons and formal charities ; 516 **Feel for* 10
The formal World relaxes her cold chain 520 *Pun. Death* 14. 1
To thee, unblinded by these formal arts, 645 *Prelude* 2. 220
Whatever formal gait of discipline 655 *Prelude* 3. 402
From formal gardens of the lady Sorrow, 683 *Prelude* 6. 555
Did I frequent the formal haunts of men, 711 *Prelude* 9. 114
The sanction ; till, demanding formal *proof*, 731 *Prelude* 11. 301
Formal, and odious, and contemptible. 798 *Excursion* 3. 826
On outward things, with formal inference ends ; 810 *Excursion* 4. 623

Formalities. How little those formalities, to which 742 *Prelude* 13. 169

Formality. Of service done with cold formality, 31 *Guilt* 394

Formalized. Subdued, composed, and formalized by art, 467 *St. Bees* 75

Formed. *See* **Full-formed, Half-formed, Well-formed.**
And formed itself upon the paper 244 *P. B.* 749
Its blossoms shrivelled, and its fruit, if formed, 266 **DespondingFather* 4
Whose good works formed an endless retinue : 380 *Duddon* 18. 11
Their forefathers ; lo ! sects are formed, and split 438 *Ecc. Sonn.* 2. 41. 2
Was formed between the solitary pair, 531 **I know* 22
Nor had, in truth, the scheme been formed by me 680 *Prelude* 6. 329
We rose at signal given, and formed a ring 681 *Prelude* 6. 399
How quickly mighty Nations have been formed, 715 *Prelude* 9. 376
That he had formed, when I, at his command, 726 *Prelude* 10. 551
Already formed upon the village-green. 773 *Excursion* 2. 125
A thriving covert ! And when wishes, formed 860 *Excursion* 7. 196

Former. Or on the earth strange lines, in former days 26 *Guilt* 112
My thoughts on former pleasures ran ; 85 *Anecdote* 9
'Twas one well known to him in former days, 95 *Brothers* 38
Back to his former cause of mourning, 179 *Waggoner* 3. 111
My former thoughts returned : the fear that kills ; 197 *Resolution* 113
Which in my former rhyme I have rehearsed. 202 *Hart-leap* 122
The language of my former heart, and read 207 *Tintern* 117
My former pleasures in the shooting lights 207 *Tintern* 118
In worse than former helplessness—and lie 311 **Who rises* 57
Who, not content that former worth stand fast, 494 *Hap. War.* 74
Invigorating thoughts from former years ; 641 *Prelude* 1. 621
Wanting,—the tragedies of former times, 701 *Prelude* 8. 169
In former days, when—spurring from the Vale 727 *Prelude* 10. 597
From all the sources of her former strength ; 735 *Prelude* 12. 80
Came to a bottom, where in former times 737 *Prelude* 12. 235
Of former loves and interests. Then my soul 796 *Excursion* 3. 695

Formidable. Of formidable size had chiselled out 147 *Joanna* 29
And formidable length of plashy lane, 876 *Excursion* 8. 106

Forming. Abode with me ; a forming hand, at times 647 *Prelude* 2. 363

Forms. The simple dignity no forms debase ; 18 *Desc. Sk.* 443

Forms—*continued.*

Uplift in quiet their illumined forms, ... 19 *Desc. Sk.* 473
If Thou be one whose heart the holy forms . . 23 *Yew-tree* 48
What mighty objects do impress their forms . . 70 *Bord.* 1809
When from these forms I turned to contemplate . 70 *Bord.* 1815
Saw mountains; saw the forms of sheep that grazed 96 *Brothers* 62
By laws to which all Forms submit . . . 112 **Yes! thou* 11
Over material forms that mastered reason. . . 139 *Widow* 27
The beauteous forms of nature wrought, . . . 193 *Ruth* 134
For passions linked to forms so fair . . . 193 *Ruth* 142
The Hermit sits alone. These beauteous forms, . 206 *Tintern* 22
Their colours and their forms, were then to me . 206 *Tintern* 79
Shall be a mansion for all lovely forms. . . . 207 *Tintern* 140
Their own fair forms, upon the glimmering plain, 218 *Recluse* 1. 1. 225
Around angelic Forms, the still . . . . . . 228 *Devot. Incit.* 34
And solemn rites and awful forms . . . . . 228 *Devot. Incit.* 52
The shadowy forms of mountains bare, . . . 237 *P. B.* 103
By lovely forms, and silent weather, ... 239 *P. B.* 287
Owe to a troubled element their forms, . . . 277 **The most* 2
With glorious forms in numberless array, . . . 282 **While beams* 12
Spirit divine through forms of human art : . . 282 **In my* 7
Such Forms as from their covert peep . . . 288 *Highland Girl* 13
The stars dim-twinkling through their forms ! . 300 *Bran* 4
Of stateliest architecture, where the Forms . . 334 **Bruges I* 13
Hence Forms that glide with swan-like ease along, 334 **The Spirit* 6
Than the fair Forms, that in long order glide, . 347 *Processions* 62
From that which *is* and actuates, by forms, . . 357 *Aquap.* 326
In Forms that must perish, frail objects of sense ; 364 *Vallomb.* 34
And sculptured Forms of Warriors brave : . . 417 *White Doe* 1897
Root there, and not in forms, her holiness ;— . 436 *Ecc. Sonn.* 2. 30. 5
Their forms are broken staves ; their passions, steeds . . . . 438 *Ecc. Sonn.* 2. 37. 11
Truth fails not ; but her outward forms that bear 449 *Ecc. Sonn.* 3. 34. 7
For her mute Powers, fixed Forms, or transient Shows. . . . . 471 *Ailsa Crag* 14
Mis-shapes the beauteous forms of things :— . . 481 *Tables Turned* 27
No joyless forms shall regulate . . . . . 483 *Sister* 17
These all wear out of me, like Forms with chalk . 488 *Pers. Talk* 7
Whate'er your forms express, ... 526 **The soaring* 38
When, like essential Forms of light, ... 526 **The soaring* 47
Of forms created the most vile and brute, . . 567 *Cumb. Beg.* 75
Whose flaccid sails in forms fantastic droop, . 604 *Desc.Sk.Quarto* 128
Farewel ! those forms that, in thy noon-tide shade, 604 *Desc.Sk.Quarto* 148
Where solitary forms illumin'd stray . . . 607 *Desc.Sk.Quarto* 273
The native dignity no forms debase, . . . 611 *Desc.Sk.Quarto* 530
Mixed with auxiliar Rocks, three hundred Forms ; 612 *Desc.Sk.Quarto* 539
Lift, all serene, their still, illumin'd forms, . . 612 *Desc.Sk.Quarto* 565
No shadowy forms entice the soul aside, . . . 619 *School Ex.* 51
Forms, images, nor numerous other aids . . 634 *Prelude* 1. 155
But huge and mighty forms, that do not live . . 638 *Prelude* 1. 398
That givest to forms and images a breath . . 638 *Prelude* 1. 403
Impressed upon all forms the characters . . . 639 *Prelude* 1. 471
Peopled the mind with forms sublime or fair, . 640 *Prelude* 1. 546
Habitually dear, and all their forms . . . 641 *Prelude* 1. 610
Of visionary things, those lovely forms . . . 641 *Prelude* 1. 632
For calmer pleasures, when the winning forms . 642 *Prelude* 2. 50
As they lie hid in all external forms, . . . 651 *Prelude* 3. 158
Of sedentary peace. Those lovely forms . . . 654 *Prelude* 3. 359
A universe of Nature's fairest forms . . . 658 *Prelude* 4. 9
And glancing forms, and tapers glittering, . . 663 *Prelude* 4. 314
Even forms and substances are circumfused . . 674 *Prelude* 5. 601
Of human forms with superhuman powers, . . 676 *Prelude* 6. 92
Not heedlessly, the laws, and watched the forms . 676 *Prelude* 6. 101
Among the schoolmen, and Platonic forms . . 679 *Prelude* 6. 298
And mighty forms, seizing a youthful fancy, . . 680 *Prelude* 6. 334
And Earth did change her images and forms . . 682 *Prelude* 6. 492
Of forms and colours, passive, yet endowed . . 685 *Prelude* 6. 679
On outward forms—did we in presence stand . . 686 *Prelude* 6. 738
Of colours, lights, and forms ; the deafening din ; 689 *Prelude* 7. 155
Here, too, were " forms and pressures of the time," 691 *Prelude* 7. 288
I was returning, when, with sundry forms . . 691 *Prelude* 7. 317
To single forms and objects, whence they draw, . 696 *Prelude* 7. 623
To majesty. Like virtue have the forms . . . 698 *Prelude* 7. 756
Man suffering among awful Powers and Forms ; . 701 *Prelude* 8. 165
Subordinate to her, her visible forms . . . 704 *Prelude* 8. 351
And lovely region, I had forms distinct . . . 705 *Prelude* 8. 429
With vulgar men about me, trivial forms . . . 707 *Prelude* 8. 545
Of shapes and forms and tendencies to shape . . 707 *Prelude* 8. 570
Busies the eye with images and forms . . . 707 *Prelude* 8. 581
Beat high, and filled the fancy with fair forms, . 712 *Prelude* 9. 207
Of civil government, and its wisest forms ; . . 714 *Prelude* 9. 323
Still craving combinations of new forms, . . . 736 *Prelude* 12. 144
What passion makes them ; that meanwhile the forms . . . . 744 *Prelude* 13. 290
Upon the vulgar forms of present things, . . . 745 *Prelude* 13. 356
In presence of sublime or beautiful forms, . . 748 *Prelude* 14. 165
Surpassing the most fair ideal Forms . . . 755 *Recluse* 1. 1. 796
All his remembrances, thoughts, shapes, and forms ; 758 *Excursion* 1. 142
With long and ghostly shanks—forms which once seen . . . . 759 *Excursion* 1. 184
Her forms, and with the spirit of her forms, . . 760 *Excursion* 1. 268
That, 'mid the simpler forms of rural life, . . 761 *Excursion* 1. 345
The forms of things with an unworthy eye ? . . 770 *Excursion* 1. 940
In vision—forms uncouth of mightiest power . . 784 *Excursion* 2. 868
Upon these uncouth Forms a slight regard . . 788 *Excursion* 3. 164
Of your bright forms and glorious faculties, . . 790 *Excursion* 3. 302
Of institutions, and the forms of things ; . . 796 *Excursion* 3. 739
For our support, the measures and the forms, . 802 *Excursion* 4. 74
The forms of Nature, and enlarge her powers ? . 814 *Excursion* 4. 846
Who, in this spirit, communes with the Forms . 819 *Excursion* 4. 1208
" And further ; by contemplating these Forms . 819 *Excursion* 4. 1230

Forms—*continued.*

Their duties from all forms ; and general laws, . 820 *Excursion* 4. 1240
The outward ritual and established forms . . . 827 *Excursion* 5. 310
And by her beautiful array of forms . . . . 841 *Excursion* 6. 186
Whence alteration in the forms of things, . . 873 *Excursion* 7. 1011
Could do them wrong. The universal forms . . 874 *Excursion* 8. 14
Blocks out the forms of nature, preconsumes . . 878 *Excursion* 8. 288
His mind gives back the various forms of things, 891 *Excursion* 9. 463
Innumerable multitude of forms . . . . . 893 *Excursion* 9. 601
Lively and beautiful, in rural forms, ... K.8. 227 **I will* 92
Shall he feel yearning to those lifeless forms, . . K.8. 257 **Shall he* 7

Forsake. And hear his prayer that I would not forsake him . . . . 66 *Bord.* 1610
And say'st, when we forsake thee, " Let them go ! " 107 *Farewell* 45
If his sweet boy he could forsake, ... 145 *Her Eyes* 75
Nor those bright sunbeams to forsake the day ; . 252 *Picture* 4
Thou dost forsake thy subterranean haunts, . . 268 **Pure element* 2
Even to this hour,—yet, some shall now forsake . 325 *Enghien* 6
The young horse must forsake his manger, . . 402 *White Doe* 550
And for the faith ; nor shall his name forsake . 420 *Ecc. Sonn.* 1. 6. 12
Her seat upon Olympus, doth forsake . . . 521 *Epist.Beaumont* 39
Be not dismayed, I will not thee forsake ! ' . . 556 *Prioress* 218
Loth to forsake the spot, and still more loth . . 791 *Excursion* 3. 330
For those, who, yet untempted to forsake . . 878 *Excursion* 8. 259

Forsaken. *See* **Long-forsaken.**
In that forsaken building where they sate . . 28 *Guilt* 197
He was forsaken ? There is a power in sounds : . 68 *Bord.* 1732
My poor forsaken Child, if I . . . . . 114 *Ind. Wom.* 65
To this forsaken covert, there I found . . . 150 **When, to* 47
Than a forsaken bird's-nest filled with snow . . 277 **Why art* 12
Places forsaken now, though loving still . . . 353 *Aquap.* 50
The world forsaken, all its busy cares . . . 363 **The world forsaken* 1
But with closed eyes,—of breath and bloom forsaken. . . . . 371 *Eg. Maid* 138
Or musing sits forsaken halls among. . . . 463**Adieu, Rydalian* 14
Forsaken " in the shade ! . . . . 507 *May* 60
Thou 'lt be as others that forsaken are ; . . . 560 *Cuck.and Night.*184
Never forsaken, that, by acting well, . . . 707 *Prelude* 8. 527
From that forsaken spring ; and no one came . 763 *Excursion* 1. 505
Committed by forsaken Ellen's hand . . . 851 *Excursion* 6. 891

Forsakes. The lone black fir, forsakes the faded plain ; 8 *Ev. Wk.* 310

Forsaking. Erelong, forsaking all her natural haunts, S.3. 436 **The doubt* 186

Forsook. At times, while young Content forsook her seat, ... 2 *Ev. Wk.* 24
His ears were never silent ; sleep forsook . . 36 *Guilt* 635
Johnny perhaps his horse forsook, ... 128 *Idiot Boy* 214
Forsook his crimes, renounced his folly, . . . 249 *P. B.* 1133
Guided by signs which ne'er the sky forsook, . . 346 *Processions* 14
A last farewell, their loved abodes forsook, . . 443 *Ecc. Sonn.* 3. 13. 3
Think ye your British Ancestors forsook . . . 515 **Men of* 3
Forsook their homes, and, errant in the quest . 655 *Prelude* 3. 466
Ere I forsook the crowded solitude, ... 710 *Prelude* 9. 29

Forsooth. A tiny tenement, forsooth, and frail, as needs must be . . . . 91 *Norman Boy* 15
And said, Forsooth, my friend, do I thank thee, . 561 *Cuck.and Night.*227

Forswear. Their aims I utterly forswear ; . . . 401 *White Doe* 509

Forsworn. Sinks smilingly forsworn. . . . . 550 *Hermit's Cell* 5. 4
Like a cowled monk who hath forsworn the world , 735 *Prelude* 12. 78

Fort. Near the sea-side I reached a ruined fort ; . 31 *Guilt* 382
The impregnable and awe-inspiring fort . . . 190 **Lyre! though* 9
Smooth space of turf which from the guardian fort 356 *Aquap.* 224

Forth. (*Partial list.*)
Come forth, and here retire in purple shade ; . . 4 *Ev. Wk.* 103
Calls forth the woodman from his desert cell, . . 12 *Desc. Sk.* 124
From that day forth no place to him could be . 25 *Guilt* 73
Our little fire sent forth a cheering warmth . . 50 *Bord.* 708
This Boy—when he comes forth with bloody hands— 54 *Bord.* 938
Young as I am, I might go forth a teacher, . . 59 *Bord.* 1223
Even such a Man my fancy bodied forth . . . 61 *Bord.* 1321
Send forth such noises—and that weary bell ! . 67 *Bord.* 1663
But standing, walking, stretching forth his arms, 68 *Bord.* 1729
Might lead to good—I saw it and burst forth, . 69 *Bord.* 1781
Sent forth a cry forlorn, ... 85 *Shepherd-boys* 75
And brought it forth into the light : . . . . 85 *Shepherd-boys* 90
Just half a week after, the wind sallied forth, . 86 *Rural Arch.* 13
Thou art a dew-drop, which the morn brings forth 88 *H. C.* 27
For bodied forth before my eyes the cross-crowned hut appeared ; . . . . 91 *Poet's Dream* 6
The pointed steeple peering forth from the centre of the shade. . . . . 92 *Poet's Dream* 40
He had gone forth among the new-dropped lambs, 101 *Brothers* 358
And calls you forth again ! . . . . 106 **I've watched* 9
Stole forth, unsettled by the shock ; . . . . 113 *Lament* 67
Well born, well bred ; I sent him forth . . . 117 *Affl. Marg.* 17
From this time forth he never shared a smile . 125 *V. and J.* 284
Did she bring forth, and all together sat . . 135 *Michael* 302
And the tall Steep of Silver-how, sent forth . . 147 *Joanna* 58
Forth from a jutting ridge, around whose base . 151 **Forth from* 1
At break of day I ventured forth, ... 157 *Oak and Broom* 103
Pours forth his song in gushes ; . . . . . 159 *Green Linnet* 36
No bold *bird* gone forth to forage . . . . 163 *Hint* 19
New heavens succeeded, by the dream brought forth : . . . . 168 *Pilgrim's Dream* 59
The budding flowers, peeped forth the nest . . 169 *Wren's Nest* 43
Feelers of love, put forth as if to explore . . 173 *Infant Daughter* 72
So forth in dauntless mood they fare, . . . 178 *Waggoner* 3. 20
Each peering forth to meet the other :— . . . 180 *Waggoner* 4. 22
Who from Keswick has pricked forth, . . . 181 *Waggoner* 4. 123
I left our cottage-threshold, sallying forth . . 185 *Nutting* 5
Advancing, forth she stretched her hand . . . 191 *Beggars* 13

Fortune—*continued.*
For Fortune on me never deigned to smile ; 470 †*From early* 8
Broken in fortune, but in mind entire 470 *Bala-Sala* 1
By fortune crushed, or tamed by grief ; 473 *Ossian* 76
But Fortune, who had long been used to sport 529 **Those breathing* 120
Unsound as those which Fortune builds— 550 *Hermit's Cell* 2. 22
Me did a kindlier fortune then invite 574 *Chiabrera* 3. 13
It was my fortune scarcely to have seen, 713 *Prelude* 9. 218
A happier fortune than to wither there : 722 *Prelude* 10. 281
Where Fortune led :—and Fortune, who oft proves 774 *Excursion* 2. 185
That fortune did not guide you to this house 781 *Excursion* 2. 620
Not placed by fortune within easy reach 794 *Excursion* 3. 586
Of prosperous fortune. On the fields he looked 842 *Excursion* 6. 238
His suit to Fortune ; and she smiled again 843 *Excursion* 6. 333
And if it was his fortune to converse K.8. 230 **I will* 189
"What happy fortune were it here to live ! K.8. 236 *Recluse* 1. 1. 11
Fortune's. Of blameless debt. On evil Fortune's spite 138 *Widow* 5
The worst of Fortune's malice, wert Thou near, 220 *Triad* 57
Not Fortune's slave is Man : our state 224 **'Tis gone* 49
Survive, and Fortune's utmost anger try ; 265 **When haughty* 5
Is Fortune's frail dependant ; yet there lives 317 **Brave Schill* 10
In Fortune's rhetoric. Daughter of the Rock, 345 **Ambition—following* 9
Appears, and none of modern Fortune's care ; 376 *Duddon* 3. 11
Thousands though rich in Fortune's grace 490 *Night Thought* 8
Thrust out abruptly into Fortune's way 656 *Prelude* 3. 525
Heaved from the heart in fortune's bitterness, 845 *Excursion* 6. 445
Fortunes. Do you tell fortunes ? Oh Sir, you are like the rest. 45 *Bord.* 437
But in Man's fortunes. Hence a thousand tales 170 **Never enlivened* 18
Set, like his fortunes ; but not set for aye 277 **Haydon ! let* 12
Thy fortunes, twice exalted, might provoke 360 *Alban Hills* 10
Will build their savage fortunes only there ; 421 *Ecc. Sonn.* 1. 11. 12
Follow the fortunes which they may not share. 467 *St. Bees* 110
With this green isle my fortunes, come not where 495 *Fact* 5
My fortunes hid, my countenance 545 *Russ. Fug.* 287
From house and home, the courtly band whose fortunes 701 *Prelude* 8. 137
Following its fortunes like the beasts or trees 887 *Excursion* 9. 181
Fortune-telling. Belong they to the foretune-telling [*sic*] tribe 858 *Excursion* 7. 87
Forty. Till I was forty years of age, not more 137 *Michael* 375
There are forty feeding like one ! 190 *March* 10
Had never come, through space of forty years ; 861 *Excursion* 7. 245
Forward. *See* **Back-and-forward, Forwards.**
With forward neck the closing gate to press— 3 *Ev. Wk.* 52
That long has leaned forward, leans hour after hour !— 189 *Music* 38
Thy genius forward like a wingèd steed. 260 **From the dark* 4
Post forward all, like creatures of one kind, 303 **Is it* 5
'Tis well ! from this day forward we shall know 310 **Another year* 5
Presumptuous Book ! too forward to be read, 350 *Des. Stanzas* 3
So forward with a steady will 412 *White Doe* 1436
Driven forward like a withered leaf, 414 *White Doe* 1614
Than his who sees, borne forward by the Rhine, 443 *Ecc. Sonn.* 3. 12. 3
And mildness, and spirit both forward and coy. 482 *Character* 12
Looks forward, persevering to the last, 494 *Hap. War.* 75
Press forward by the teasing dogs unscared. 525 *Epist. Beaumont* 238
He started forward, with a shout, 537 *Goody Blake* 87
Will guide me in my forward path ; 542 *Russ. Fug.* 71
"From that day forward have the Jews conspired 554 *Prioress* 114
When hurrying forward till the slack'ning stream 626 **The confidence* 10
We glided forward with the flowing stream. 680 *Prelude* 6. 377
Press forward, in all colours, on the sight ; 690 *Prelude* 7. 195
Have I gone forward with the crowd, and said 696 *Prelude* 7. 627
To forward reason's else too scrupulous march. 708 *Prelude* 8. 643
Which then was going forward in her name ! 729 *Prelude* 11. 116
And, having shown in study forward zeal, 774 *Excursion* 2. 171
Is raised from the church-aisle, and forward borne 780 *Excursion* 2. 570
Of forward youth—that scruples not to solve 792 *Excursion* 3. 413
Saddening the heart. Go forward, and look back ; 830 *Excursion* 5. 539
The stream, that bears thee forward, prove not,'soon 844 *Excursion* 6. 438
—Can hope look forward to a manhood raised 879 *Excursion* 8. 333
A willing, nay, at times, a forward part ; 882 *Excursion* 8. 529
The sheep sprang forward to the further shore, K.8. 229 **I will* 150
Forwarding. Faithful alike in forwarding a day 752 *Prelude* 14. 440
Forward-looking. Brings hope with it, and forward-looking thoughts, 133 *Michael* 148
A man of hope and forward-looking mind 861 *Excursion* 7. 276
Forwardness. The forwardness of soul which looks that way K.8. 257 *Recluse* 1. 1. 746
Forwards. Then have I darted forwards to let loose 660 *Prelude* 4. 115
Foss. Content, if foss, and barrow, and the girth 421 *Ecc. Sonn.* 1. 11. 13
Fossils. With books, maps, fossils, withered plants and flowers, 781 *Excursion* 2. 663
Foster-child. To make her Foster-child, her Inmate Man, 588 *Immortality* 82
—At length the parents of the foster-child, 853 *Excursion* 6. 992
Fostered. Or fostered, self-supported chiefs,—like those 320 **They seek* 6
The fostered hyacinths spread their purple bloom. 425 *Ecc. Sonn.* 1. 27. 14
Received, and fostered in her iron breast : 441 *Ecc. Sonn.* 3. 3. 4
Are fostered by the comment and the gibe." 488 *Pers. Talk* 20
Proscribed the spirit fostered by that rule, 518 *Pun. Death* 7. 6
Fostered alike by beauty and by fear : 636 *Prelude* 1. 302
Or pleasure sown, or fostered thus, may be 668 *Prelude* 5. 194
Thus are they born, thus fostered, thus maintained ; 837 *Excursion* 5. 996
Foster-father. You, Foster-father dear, 542 *Russ. Fug.* 70
Fostering. Of intellectual power, fostering love, 735 *Prelude* 12. 45

Fostering—*continued.*
O fostering Nature ! I rejected—smiled 797 *Excursion* 3. 809
The Poet, fostering for his native land 839 *Excursion* 6. 42
—What kindly warmth from touch of fostering hand, 880 *Excursion* 8. 416
Foster-mother. Prompt offering to thy Foster-mother, Earth ! 376 *Duddon* 3. 14
Foster-mother's. Her Foster-mother's hut. 542 *Russ. Fug.* 24
A Foster-mother's office. 'Tis, perchance, 852 *Excursion* 6. 948
Foster-parents. The Foster-parents sate ; 545 *Russ. Fug.* 372
Fosters. That fosters growth or checks or cheers decay, 169 **Never enlivened* 2
That fosters peace, and gentleness recalls ; 339 *Tell* 15
Fotheringay. Stilled by the ensanguined block of Fotheringay ! 465 **Dear to* 14
Fought. But he, bold Knight as ever fought, 161 *Binnorie* 7
Among the Indians he had fought, 192 *Ruth* 43
And fought with rage incessant 287 *Ellen Irwin* 39
And stars that in their courses fought ; 299 *Brownie's Cell* 62
Sons of the brave who fought at Marathon, 312 **When, far* 10
It was a *moral* end for which they fought ; 316 **It was a* 1
By hands of men, humble as brave, who fought 355 *Aquap.* 161
Behold how fought the Chief whose conquering sword 368 *Trajan* 29
His Country's virtue, fought, and breathes no more ; 426 *Ecc. Sonn.* 1. 32. 10
And welcome glory won in battles fought 458 *Sea-shore* 23
Is *Death*, when evil against good has fought 518 *Pun. Death* 4. 1
Side by side they fought (the Lucies 535 *Egremont* 41
The cause they fought for in their earthly home, 627 *Eagle and Dove* 2
Fought, as if conscious of the blazonry 634 *Prelude* 1. 178
How Wallace fought for Scotland ; left the name 635 *Prelude* 1. 214
And would have fought, even to the death, to attest 728 *Prelude* 11. 81
Have fought and perished for Helvetia's rights— 869 *Excursion* 7. 807
Fought'st. Thou fought'st against him ; but hast vainly striven : 306 **Two Voices* 6
Foul. Worse is he far, far worse (if foul dishonour 53 *Bord.* 896
Has marked out this foul Wretch as one whose crimes 55 *Bord.* 1000
Of foul pollution—— The whole visible world 56 *Bord.* 1056
With brutal laughter and most foul allusion, 59 *Bord.* 1205
Our Captain made a prey to foul device !— 63 *Bord.* 1418
Was hatched among the crew a foul Conspiracy 68 *Bord.* 1690
When, whether it blew foul or fair, they two 96 *Brothers* 74
Was darkened soon by foul iniquity. 103 *Artegal* 77
Through foul and fair our task fulfilling ; 179 *Waggoner* 3. 95
"Ay," said the Tar, "through fair and foul— 179 *Waggoner* 3. 97
Waxed wroth, and with foul claws, a harpy brood, 255 *Detraction* 7
Her sabbath morning, foul or fair." 398 *White Doe* 191
Ah ! wherefore yields it to a foul constraint 438 *Ecc. Sonn.* 2. 38. 12
As the cool Advocate of foul device ; 514 **Portentous change* 2
Take from the horror due to a foul deed, 519 *Pun. Death* 8. 10
There are ninety good seasons of fair and foul weather 572 *Avarice* 15
By night or day, blow foul or fair, 577 **I come* 12
To whom a foul deed he had done, 621 *Andrew Jones* 9
Which, as a deadly mischief, and a foul 717 *Prelude* 9. 551
From foul temptations, and by constant care 829 *Excursion* 5. 425
Ill purposes, and flatter foul desires. 894 *Excursion* 9. 687
Foulest. Not to be jeopardised through foulest crime : 519 *Pun. Death* 10. 11
Found. *See* **New-found.**
Alas ! the idle tale of man is found 2 *Ev. Wk.* 27
Found by the grassy door of mountain-farms. 5 *Ev. Wk.* 145
Where from distress a refuge might be found, 10 *Desc. Sk.* 2
Still have I found, where Tyranny prevails, 21 *Desc. Sk.* 597
—Yet hast thou found that Freedom spreads her power 21 *Desc. Sk.* 620
But where the sower dwelt was nowhere to be found. 24 *Guilt* 27
And well it was that of the corse there found 27 *Guilt* 187
That I, at last, a resting-place had found ; 31 *Guilt* 362
At once the griding iron passage found ; 33 *Guilt* 493
Till one was found by stroke of violence dead, 35 *Guilt* 599
Who might have found a nothing-doing hour 39 *Bord.* 120
I found how my domains had been usurped, 40 *Bord.* 193
You are found at last, thanks to the vagrant Troop 56 *Bord.* 1018
Tell where you found us. At some future time 58 *Bord.* 1133
I found in you the kindest of Protectors ; 60 *Bord.* 1281
It might have found its way into my heart, 68 *Bord.* 1701
And he found no deliverance ! The Crew 69 *Bord.* 1756
Twin sisters both of Ignorance, I found 70 *Bord.* 1835
So guided, distant a few steps, I found 73 *Bord.* 2049
Hast thou pursued the monster ? I have found him.— 76 *Bord.* 2192
And there a little Girl I found, 82 *Alice Fell* 19
And there the helpless lamb he found 85 *Shepherd-boys* 87
When my father found thee first in places far away ; 87 *Pet-lamb* 34
Another grave was added.—He had found 96 *Brothers* 84
And, when he dwelt beneath our roof, we found 100 *Brothers* 349
On their return, they found that he was gone. 101 *Brothers* 372
They found him at the foot of that same rock 101 *Brothers* 380
Yes, long before he died, he found that time 101 *Brothers* 388
Hath found you out among the trees, 106 **I've watched* 8
The loveliest spot that man hath ever found, 106 *Farewell* 6
And here and there a church-yard grave is found 110 **'Tis said that some* 2
I found it when my Son was dead ; 119 *Sailor's Mother* 34
To a poor neighbouring cottage ; as I found, 120 *Emigrant Mother* 7
Found means to hurry her away by night, 122 *V. and J.* 70

Found—*continued.*

Found dreadful provocation: for at night, 123 *V. and J.* 125
Repaired, but only found the matron there, 125 *V. and J.* 290
Or lost, perhaps, and never found; 128 *Idiot Boy* 180
Which, going by from year to year, had found, 133 *Michael* 119
Went up to London, found a master there, 135 *Michael* 264
From base to summit; such delight I found 147 *Joanna* 45
To hasten, for I found, beneath the roof 150 **When, to* 10
To this forsaken covert, there I found 150 **When, to* 47
Since the day I found thee out, 160 **Pansies, lilies* 14
Pleasures newly found are sweet 160 **Pleasures newly* 1
In a moment lost and found, 173 *Waggoner* 1. 28
Whatever in those climes he found 193 *Ruth* 127
Instead of jutting crag I found 199 *Thorn* 186
Four roods of sheer ascent) Sir Walter found 201 *Hart-leap* 50
Love had he found in huts where poor men lie; 205 *Brougham* 161
Will now so readily be found 224 *'Tis gone* 32
Or found on earth a name; 232 *Jew. Fam.* 12
As sages taught, where faith was found to merit 235 *Power of Sound* 179
These silent raptures found no place; 239 *P. B.* 272
Which Peter in those noises found;— 246 *P. B.* 872
Some willing neighbour must be found. 248 *P. B.* 1060
Should find brief solace there, as I have found. 250 **Nuns fret* 14
He found the longest summer day too short, 254 *Complete Angler* 8
A volant Tribe of Bards on earth are found, 259 **A volant* 1
How in thy pensive glooms our hearts found rest. 282 **Wansfell! this* 14
Hath early found among the dead, 285 *Grave of Burns* 68
And found the door unbarred. 296 *Highland Boy* 140
To such apartments as they found; 298 *Brownie's Cell* 8
Had found, in ravage widely dealt, 298 *Brownie's Cell* 39
Still hint that quiet best is found, 301 *Bran* 66
With joy in Kent's green vales; but never found 306 **Here, on our* 7
Thus in your books the record shall be found, 313 *Prophecy* 2
It found no barrier on the ridge 327 *Ode 1815* 21
With medicable wounds, or found their graves 328 *Ode 1815* 81
A deeper peace than that in deserts found! 334 **The Spirit* 14
Yet a dread local recompense we found; 334 **A wingèd* 10
For magnanimity be found; 337 **Oh Life* 4
And nothing in our hearts we found 348 **Lulled by* 41
Found casual vent. She said, "Be of good cheer; 360 *Albano* 5
And here once again a kind shelter be found. 364 *Vallomb.* 20
Landing, she found not what she sought, 371 *Eg. Maid* 123
How he was found, cold as an icicle, 391 *Brownie* 3
And through yon gateway, where is found, 396 *White Doe* 52
From Rylstone she hath found her way 398 *White Doe* 186
Why thus the milk-white Doe is found 398 *White Doe* 202
Of God had in her heart found place— 398 *White Doe* 232
He found his way to a postern-gate; 400 *White Doe* 426
And fervent words a passage found. 401 *White Doe* 460
The same fair Creature, who hath found 407 *White Doe* 981
Where she had found a grateful seat 407 *White Doe* 1058
Deep feeling, that found utterance loud, 409 *White Doe* 1228
Of that same Temple have found rest: 410 *White Doe* 1277
A habitation she had found, 414 *White Doe* 1689
In which the Creature first was found. 416 *White Doe* 1804
And every sabbath here is found; 416 *White Doe* 1884
Of a HOLY RIVER, on whose banks are found 418 *Ecc. Sonn.* 1. 1. 10
Shame if the consecrated Vow be found 445 *Ecc. Sonn.* 3. 21. 13
The counter Spirit found in some gay church 448 *Ecc. Sonn.* 3. 33. 10
And the wild storm hath somewhere found a nest; 454 *Sea-side* 2
Oh may this work have found its last retreat 461 **Giordano, verily* 9
Yet I at last a resting-place have found, 470 †*From early* 9
The power is merged, the pomp a grave has found. 471 *Tynwald* 8
Him found we not: but, climbing a tall tower, 472 **The captive* 4
In language thou may'st yet be found, 472 *Ossian* 18
In hermits' weeds repose he found, 479 *Somnamb.* 149
For precious tremblings in your bosom found! 480 *Cordelia* 14
Found scarcely anywhere in like degree! 491 *Tribute: Dog* 26
Nor far had gone before he found 491 *Fidelity* 38
Thy favours may be found; 507 *May* 44
Will not be found. Her right hand, as it lies 509 *F. Stone* 52
Knowing, things rashly sought are rarely found; 514 **Blest Statesman* 10
Found at the Widow's feet some sad relief; 523 *Epist. Beaumont* 134
Emblem of those dark corners sometimes found 524 *Epist. Beaumont* 221
An easy seat this worn-out Labourer found 531 **I know* 10
Its place no longer to be found; 532 †*Float. Isl.* 26
Might tell what intercourse she found, 544 *Russ. Fug.* 205
Within a little time, as hath been found, 556 *Cuck. and Night.* 6
Yet for all that, the truth is found elsewhere; 559 *Cuck.andNight.* 167
A cause he found into the Town to go, 562 *Troilus* 9
In which they found their kindred with a world 568 *Cumb. Beg.* 115
And his Permessus found on Lebanon. 576 *Chiabrera* 9. 18
Here, brought from far, his corse found rest,— 577 **By playful* 11
And there they found him at her side; 579 **Sweet Flower* 55
That is not to be found. 580 *John Words.* 24
The Comforter hath found me here, 581 **Loud is* 11
Yet have we found how slowly genuine grief 584 **With copious* 44
Found—for all interests, hopes, and tender cares, 585 *Ch. Lamb* 83
Found by the verdant door of mountain farms. 594 *Ev. Wk. Quarto* 128
Still have my pilgrim feet unfailing found, 615 *Desc.Sk.Quarto* 720
Found still beneath her smile, and only there. 615 *Desc.Sk.Quarto* 725
Just at the time; and there he found 621 *Andrew Jones* 22
That travelling in strange countries once he found 623 **I find* 2
True to the King of Kings is found; 629 *Installation* 98
Found all about me in one neighbourhood— 633 *Prelude* 1. 111
Are found in plenteous store, but nowhere such 634 *Prelude* 1. 159
Flying, found shelter in the Fortunate Isles, 635 *Prelude* 1. 192
Of Wallace to be found, like a wild flower, 635 *Prelude* 1. 215

Found—*continued.*

One summer evening (led by her) I found 637 *Prelude* 1. 357
Which, wrought upon instinctively, had found 654 *Prelude* 3. 361
Found everywhere, but chiefly in the ring 657 *Prelude* 3. 541
Were wanting here, I took what might be found 657 *Prelude* 3. 566
Within our garden, found himself at once, 659 *Prelude* 4. 52
A freshness also found I at this time 661 *Prelude* 4. 191
Wherever man is found? The trickling tear 668 *Prelude* 5. 188
A heart that found benignity and hope, 670 *Prelude* 5. 292
Of words in tuneful order, found them sweet 674 *Prelude* 5. 555
No farther than the threshold, there I found 676 *Prelude* 6. 119
And found benevolence and blessedness 680 *Prelude* 6. 357
Although well pleased to be where they were found, 696 *Prelude* 7. 584
And we found evil fast as we find good 703 *Prelude* 8. 309
In our first years, or think that it is found, 703 *Prelude* 8. 310
Where no sufficient pleasure could be found. 704 *Prelude* 8. 383
Capacious found, or seemed to find, in me 708 *Prelude* 8. 605
Here then my young imagination found 708 *Prelude* 8. 639
Of orders and degrees, I nothing found 712 *Prelude* 9. 210
That would be found in all recorded time, 715 *Prelude* 9. 366
Be found no more, that we should see the earth 717 *Prelude* 9. 522
To abide in the great City, where I found 721 *Prelude* 10. 245
Not in my single self alone I found, 722 *Prelude* 10. 266
For those that bade them fall. They found their joy, 723 *Prelude* 10. 363
Distempered, till they found, in every blast 727 *Prelude* 11. 41
And dealt with whatsoever they found there 729 *Prelude* 11. 130
Now was it that *both* found, the meek and lofty 729 *Prelude* 11. 136
Found ready welcome. Tempting region *that* 730 *Prelude* 11. 228
Glorying, I found a counterpoise in her, 735 *Prelude* 12. 41
Thus moderated, thus composed, I found 740 *Prelude* 13. 48
Why is this glorious creature to be found 741 *Prelude* 13. 87
I prized such walks still more, for there I found 742 *Prelude* 13. 179
As found among the best of those who live— 743 *Prelude* 13. 242
Men may be found of other mould than these, 743 *Prelude* 13. 261
Murmuring of him who, joyous hap, was found, 752 *Prelude* 14. 404
And found a kind of home or harbour there. 757 *Excursion* 1. 56
Still deeper welcome found his pure discourse: 757 *Excursion* 1. 73
Have somewhere found relief." He, at the word, 762 *Excursion* 1. 450
He found the little he had stored, to meet 764 *Excursion* 1. 554
But we have known that there is often found 765 *Excursion* 1. 632
In mournful thoughts, and always might be found, 765 *Excursion* 1. 633
She opened—found no writing, but beheld 766 *Excursion* 1. 669
I found that she was absent. In the shade, 767 *Excursion* 1. 711
Familiarly, and found a couching-place 767 *Excursion* 1. 747
I found her sad and drooping: she had learned 768 *Excursion* 1. 817
From week to week,) I found to be a work 778 *Excursion* 2. 442
Must by the cottage-children have been found: 778 *Excursion* 2. 453
"That I came hither; neither have I found 781 *Excursion* 2. 613
We sallied forth together; found the tools 783 *Excursion* 2. 795
And there we found him breathing peaceably, 784 *Excursion* 2. 821
I found its rescued inmate safely lodged, 785 *Excursion* 2. 882
A tall and shining holly, that had found 787 *Excursion* 3. 62
Only by records in myself not found. 796 *Excursion* 3. 705
Or even found pleasure, in such vagrant course, 797 *Excursion* 3. 800
I found him not. There, in his stead, appeared 800 *Excursion* 3. 952
This sorry Legend; which by chance we found 816 *Excursion* 4. 1007
Of levity no refuge can be found, 816 *Excursion* 4. 1027
Its most illustrious province, must be found 820 *Excursion* 4. 1261
And rightful government subverted, found 825 *Excursion* 5. 192
At any moment may the Dame be found, 833 *Excursion* 5. 706
"The untutored bird may found, and so construct, 835 *Excursion* 5. 840
Then, Pity could have scarcely found on earth 840 *Excursion* 6. 131
Passed on, while still his lonely efforts found 841 *Excursion* 6. 223
Through lack of converse; no—he must have found 844 *Excursion* 6. 384
In lonely reading found a meek resource: 852 *Excursion* 6. 896
Asked comfort of the open air, and found 855 *Excursion* 6. 1100
They found the cottage, their allotted home; 859 *Excursion* 7. 137
Such on the breast of darksome heaths are found; 879 *Excursion* 8. 362
Motive to sadder grief, as we have found; 888 *Excursion* 9. 251
Have also these, but *no* where else is found, K.8. 240 *Recluse* 1.1.135
No where (or is it fancy?) *can* be found K.8. 240 *Recluse* 1.1.136
Here as it found its way into my heart K.8. 240 *Recluse* 1.1.138
And found us faithful through the gloom, and heard K.8. 241 *Recluse* 1.1.183
Half-seen or wholly, lost and found again, K.8. 250 *Recluse* 1.1.488

Foundation. Oswald, the firm foundation of my life 47 *Bord.* 547
And Love her towers of dread foundation laid 282 **In my* 10
But the foundation of our nature shakes, 330 *Ode: Thanks.* 101
Doth seldom on a right foundation rest, 493 *Hap. War.* 32
Their work's foundation, gave with careful hand 534 **When in* 11
From their foundation, strangers to the presence 682 *Prelude* 6. 477
Here, the foundation of his future years! 749 *Prelude* 14. 220
Of that foundation in domestic care 872 *Excursion* 7. 964

Foundations. "Till the foundations of the mountains fall 201 *Hart-leap* 73
Secure foundations. As the year runs round, 259 **A volant* 8
Vain earth! false world! Foundations must be laid 269 *Malham* 10
Foundations broken up, the deeps run wild, 504 *Warning* 65
Though worlds to their foundations reel 629 *Installation* 93
Their sure foundations in the heart of man, 668 *Prelude* 5. 199
On firm foundations, making social life, 715 *Prelude* 9. 360
So the foundations of his mind were laid. 758 *Excursion* 1. 132
Our dark foundations rest, could he design 815 *Excursion* 4. 970
Whereon he sits! Whose deep foundations lie 838 *Excursion* 6. 3
On such foundations?" "Hope is none for him!" 879 *Excursion* 8. 334
"With such foundations laid, avaunt the fear 889 *Excursion* 9. 363

Founded. Was founded a sure safeguard and defence 703 *Prelude* 8. 318
Founded in truth; by blood of Martyrdom 838 *Excursion* 6. 9

Founder. Founder amid fanatic storms. 228 *Devot. Incit.* 53

Founder—continued.
Father and founder of exalted deeds ; . . . 870 *Excursion* 7. 824
Founder's. Here, in the Founder's Spirit sought . 629 *Installation* 82
Found'st. Thou found'st—and I forgive thee—here thou art— . . . . . 210 *Laod.* 53
Foundress. Margaret, the saintly Foundress, take thy place ; . . . . . 276 *Author's Portrait* 2
Foundrous. And many a foundrous pit surrounded ! 179 *Waggoner* 3. 92
Fount. Now, for that consecrated fount . . . 111 *A Complaint* 9
Of the wild impulse. From a fount of life . . 230 *Clouds* 45
Issuing or issued from a wintry fount ; . . . 347 *Processions* 53
Of his Bandusian fount ; or I invoke . . . 356 *Aquap.* 257
As to the one sole fount whence wisdom flowed, . 419 *Ecc. Sonn.* 1. 4. 8
Build, at thy choice, or sing, by pool or fount, . 455 *Rydal Mere* 35
In progress toward the fount of Love,—the throne 469 **Desire we* 11
And, ere the flowing fount be dry, ... 497 *Lycoris* 42
The fount of feeling, if unsought elsewhere, . . 509 *F. Stone* 51
Of all that issues from his glorious fount ! . . 511 **So fair* 9
Sunward to seek the daylight in its fount, . . 527 **Those breathing* 38
Drawn from love's purest earthly fount for him . 646 *Prelude* 2. 247
Poured from his fount of Abyssinian clouds . . 684 *Prelude* 6. 615
Fount of my country's destiny and the world's ; . 708 *Prelude* 8. 593
Their holy Ganges from a skyey fount, . . . 790 *Excursion* 3. 255
His thirst from rill or gushing fount, and thanked 814 *Excursion* 4. 872
A tardy apprehension. From a fount . . . 834 *Excursion* 5. 786
Which from the unapparent fount of glory . . 893 *Excursion* 9. 605
Who with their Hippocrene and grottoed fount . S.3. 436 **The doubt* 161
Fountain. At the same poisonous fountain ! 'Twas an island . . . . . 69 *Bord.* 1740
A heart, the fountain of sweet tears ; . . . 79 *Sparrow's Nest* 19
A fountain at my fond heart's door, ... 111 *A Complaint* 3
Or by the silent lapse of fountain clear, . . . 170 **Never enlivened* 14
Down to the very fountain where he lies. . . . 201 *Hart-leap* 56
A basin for that fountain in the dell ; . . . 201 *Hart-leap* 62
And, near the fountain, flowers of stature tall . 202 *Hart-leap* 85
You see the stones, the fountain, and the stream ; 202 *Hart-leap* 130
Lulled by the fountain in the summer-tide ; . . 203 *Hart-leap* 150
Till trees, and stones, and fountain, all are gone," 203 *Hart-leap* 160
Nile trembles at his fountain head ; . . . . 216 *Enterprise* 86
As if it from a fountain flowed— . . . . 244 *P. B.* 679
From the Castalian fountain of the heart, . . 252 **Why, Minstrel* 6
Now, on the margin of some spotless fountain, . 325 *Ode 1814* 123
To the Fountain whence Time and Eternity flow. 365 *Vallomb.* 40
Light from the fountain of the setting sun. . . 388 *Eagles* 9
And call the Fountain forth by miracle, . . . 418 *Ecc. Sonn.* 1. 2. 7
Fountain of Grace, whose Son for sinners died. . 446 *Ecc. Sonn.* 3. 25. 8
Of ritual honours to this Fountain paid . . . 465 **The cattle* 10
Or fountain in a noon-day grove ; . . . . 485 *Poet's Epitaph* 42
" No fountain from its rocky cave . . . . 487 **We walked* 49
And from the turf a fountain broke, ... 487 *Fountain* 7
Informs the fountain in the human breast . . 510 *F. Stone* 127
Each from his fountain of self-sacrifice ! . . . 516 **Feel for* 14
Or fountain, listen to the grave reports . . . 634 *Prelude* 1. 174
Came from yon fountain ? " Thou, my Friend ! art one . . . . . 645 *Prelude* 2. 210
As generous as a fountain ; selfishness . . . 670 *Prelude* 5. 302
For spring or fountain, which the traveller finds, 702 *Prelude* 8. 207
Who from the Fountain of Thy grace dost fill . 724 *Prelude* 10. 422
Or, if that fountain be in truth no more, . . . 734 *Prelude* 11. 466
As at a fountain ; and on winter nights, . . . 739 *Prelude* 12. 326
Of craggy fountain ; what he hopes for wins, . 788 *Excursion* 3. 167
A stream, which, from the fountain of the heart, 804 *Excursion* 4. 219
From a clear fountain flowing, he looks round . 819 *Excursion* 4. 1223
The Fountain of the Fairies. What to her . . S.3. 436 **The doubt* 170
Of the benignant fountain, while she stood . . S.3. 436 **The doubt* 180
The fountain of the mists. The father stooped . K.8. 226 **I will* 54
The highest fountain known on British land. . . K.8. 226 **I will* 61
Fountain-head. Whence, as a current from its fountain-head, ... 394 **No more* 22
Even to the fountain-head of peace divine." . . 396 **Action is* 13
Enough—if eyes, that sought the fountain-head . 419 *Ecc. Sonn.* 1. 5. 13
Such Milton, to the fountain-head . . . . 473 *Ossian* 81
As the sole spring and fountain-head of tears, . 837 *Excursion* 5. 981
Fountain-light. Are yet the fountain-light of all our day, ... 589 *Immortality* 155
Fountain's. The Monks of Fountain's thronged to force . . . . . 301 *Bran* 58
Beside this fountain's brink. . . . . . 487 *Fountain* 28
Or shady fountain's, while among the leaves . . 643 *Prelude* 2. 91
Fountains. The fountains reared for them amid the waste ! . . . . . 20 *Desc. Sk.* 560
Though the torrents from their fountains . . . 166 *Wand. Jew* 1
There's life in the fountains ; . . . . . 190 *March* 17
By spouts and fountains wild— . . . . 195 *Ruth* 249
The paths which we had trod—these fountains, flowers ; . . . . . 211 *Laod.* 131
Thine are all the choral fountains . . . . 217 **Inmate of* 25
From Hebrew fountains sprung ; . . . . 232 *Jew. Fam.* 44
The headlong streams and fountains . . . . 232 *Power of Sound* 17
Why leap the fountains from their cells . . . 341 *San Salv.* 9
Cliffs, fountains, rivers, seasons, times— . . . 341 *San Salv.* 13
Her sparkling fountains, and her mouldering tombs ; 353 *Aquap.* 80
Round the moist marge of Persian fountains cling ; 376 *Duddon* 1. 6
Converging walks, and fountains gay, . . . 407 *White Doe* 989
O wretched Land ! whose tears have flowed like fountains ; . . . . . 421 *Ecc. Sonn.* 1. 11. 7
Who near his fountains sought obscure repose, . 431 *Ecc. Sonn.* 2. 13. 11
As to the sandy desert fountains are, . . . 444 *Ecc. Sonn.* 3. 17. 5
To sit in leafy woods by fountains clear ! . . 460 **Queen of* 16
And let, for them, thy fountains utter strange . 471 *Tynwald* 11

Fountains—continued.
From shadowy fountains of the Infinite, . . . 476 **Tranquillity ! the* 11
And O, ye Fountains, Meadows, Hills, and Groves, 590 *Immortality* 191
Continual fountains welling chear'd the waste, . 611 *Desc. Sk. Quarto* 478
The fountains rear'd for you amid the waste ! . 614 *Desc. Sk. Quarto* 671
The fluttering breezes, fountains that run on . . 647 *Prelude* 2. 371
Sprang out of fountains, there abounding most, . 701 *Prelude* 8. 125
Within the soul, fountains of grace divine ; . . 841 *Excursion* 6. 181
Those little fountains, sparkling in the sun, . . K.8. 251 *Recluse* 1.1.553
Fountains and spouts, yet somewhat in the guise K.8. 251 *Recluse* 1.1.557
Fountain-side. We rose up from the fountain-side ; 488 *Fountain* 65
Founts. Streaming from founts above the starry sky, 229 *Cuckoo-clock* 39
To transports from the secondary founts . . . 358 *Aquap.* 360
Or founts that gurgle from yon craggy steep, . . S.3. 433 **The doubt* 11
Four. See **Eighty-four.**
While our four travellers homeward wend ; . . 131 *Idiot Boy* 433
If there be but three or four . . . . . 161 **Pleasures newly* 55
Now she works with three or four, ... 171 *Kitten* 29
Are those fraternal Four of Borrowdale, . . . 185 *Yew-trees* 14
Four roods of sheer ascent) Sir Walter found . 201 *Hart-leap* 50
And one, not four yards distant, near a well. . 202 *Hart-leap* 104
On which four thousand years have gazed ! . . 214 *Kirkstone* 20
The man who had been four days dead, . . . 243 *P. B.* 578
The Beast four days and nights had past ; . . 243 *P. B.* 602
And there the Ass four days had been, . . . 243 *P. B.* 604
Not four yards from the broad highway : . . . 246 *P. B.* 925
Four fiery steeds impatient of the rein . . . 268 **Four fiery*
Four dogs, each pair of different breed, . . . 490 *Incident : Dog* 7
All the four are in the race : . . . . . 490 *Incident : Dog* 12
Four summer weeks I dwelt in sight of thee : . 578 *Peele Castle* 2
That there were four large volumes, laden all . 672 *Prelude* 5. 466
Four years and thirty, told this very week, . . 675 *Prelude* 6. 48
Four rapid years had scarcely then been told . 693 *Prelude* 7. 382
From the four quarters of the winds to do . . 720 *Prelude* 10. 140
Appeared a roofless Hut ; four naked walls . . 756 *Excursion* 1. 30
Four dear supporters of one senseless weight, . 780 *Excursion* 2. 584
To the four quarters of the winds, proclaims. . 837 *Excursion* 5. 993
" Through four months' space the Infant drew its food . . . . . 852 *Excursion* 6. 939
Fond looks on colours three or four . . . . S.3. 431 **The Scottish* 23
Four-and-twenty. Of four-and-twenty summers he withdrew ; . . . . . 125 *V. and J.* 273
Four-legged. I'll answer for it that our four-legged friend . . . . . 51 *Bord.* 774
Fourscore. Engendering in the blood of hale fourscore. . . . . . 98 *Brothers* 203
Fourteen. These fourteen years, by strong indentures : . . . . . 129 *Idiot Boy* 338
Keen hunters in a chase of fourteen weeks, . . 682 *Prelude* 6. 497
Fourth. The fourth part of a mile, I ween, . . 296 *Highland Boy* 158
Fowl. See **Sea-fowl, Water-fowl.**
Say not you *love* a roasted fowl, ... 142 †*Lov. and Lik.* 5
Tu-whit—Tu-whoo ! the unsuspecting fowl . . 153 *Morn. Ex.* 9
How cattle pine, and droop the shivering fowl, . 229 *Cuckoo-clock* 14
Will we forget that, as the fowl can keep . . 390 *Glencroe* 10
Like hungry fowl to the feeder's hand . . . 403 *White Doe* 623
My night-watch : nor should e'er the crested fowl 424 *Ecc. Sonn.* 1. 22. 12
Kennelled and chained. Ye tame domestic fowl, 472 *Dunolly Eagle* 7
And mountains, ranging like a fowl of the air, . 654 *Prelude* 3. 355
The fowl domestic, and the household dog— . 772 *Excursion* 2. 45
Unfelt among the sedentary fowl . . . . 808 *Excursion* 4. 456
Of a young fowl beneath one mother hatched, . 843 *Excursion* 6. 367
Nor wanted timely treat of fish or fowl . . . 860 *Excursion* 7. 164
Fowler. So have ye seen the fowler chase . . 297 *Highland Boy* 187
Fowler's. Scattering, like birds escaped the fowler's net, ... 437 *Ecc. Sonn.* 2. 37. 1
That never fowler's gun, nor shaft . . . . 543 *Russ. Fug.* 107
As scattered birds troop to the fowler's lure, . 675 *Prelude* 6. 5
Fowles. When in the woods the little Fowles . S.3.424 *Tinker* 23
Fowls. Alas ! the fowls of heaven have wings, . 117 *Affl. Marg.* 43
The clouds and fowls of the air thy way pursue ! . 379 *Duddon* 14. 14
Fox. Nor can it be a barking fox, ... 243 *P. B.* 618
The owl of evening and the woodland fox . . 433 *Ecc. Sonn.* 2. 21. 9
A cry as of a dog or fox ; . . . . . 491 *Fidelity* 2
Low barks the fox : by Havoc rouz'd the bear; . 606 *Desc.Sk.Quarto* 231
To hunt the badger and unearth the fox . . . 660 *Prelude* 4. 97
The indefatigable fox had learned . . . . 868 *Excursion* 7. 745
Foxglove. Where scarce the foxglove peeps, or thistle's beard ; . . . . . 4 *Ev. Wk.* 96
I put a slip of foxglove in his hand, ... 44 *Bord.* 401
Will murmur by the hour in foxglove bells : . . 250 **Nuns fret* 7
Where scarce the foxglove peeps, and thistle's beard, ... 593 *Ev. Wk. Quarto* 95
These cravings ; when the foxglove, one by one, . 705 *Prelude* 8. 393
Fox's. We call stag-horn, or fox's tail, . . . 84 *Shepherd-boys* 19
Foy. What means this bustle, Betty Foy ? . . 126 *Idiot Boy* 8
And, by the moonlight, Betty Foy . . . . 126 *Idiot Boy* 38
"Oh Sir ! you know I'm Betty Foy, . . . 129 *Idiot Boy* 254
Where is she, where is Betty Foy ? . . . . 130 *Idiot Boy* 358
Then calm your terrors, Betty Foy ! . . . . 130 *Idiot Boy* 363
Why stand you thus, good Betty Foy ? . . . 130 *Idiot Boy* 368
She knows not, happy Betty Foy ! . . . . 130 *Idiot Boy* 393
Fractions. Into those jarring fractions.—Let thy scope . . . . . 515 **Ah why* 9
Fractured. With fractured summit, no indifferent sight . . . . . 352 *Aquap.* 20
From fractured arch and mouldering wall— . . 366 *Ye Trees* 14
And through the chink in the fractured floor . 398 *White Doe* 243
By fractured cell, or tomb, or vault, . . . 417 *White Doe* 1894
Stands yet a mouldering pile with fractured arch, 643 *Prelude* 2. 105
And crept along a ridge of fractured wall, . . 678 *Prelude* 6. 214

Free—*continued.*
And now, when free to move with lighter pace. . 772 *Excursion* 2. 27
And she was in youth's prime. How free their love, 774 *Excursion* 2. 196
The mind is full—and free from pain their pastime." 789 *Excursion* 3. 193
That in more genial times, when I was free . . 790 *Excursion* 3. 283
Gay as our spirits, free as our desires ; . . . 794 *Excursion* 3. 543
Free as the sun, and lonely as the sun, . . . 799 *Excursion* 3. 941
I, speaking now from such disorder free, . . . 804 *Excursion* 4. 186
Observe their ways ; and, free from envy, find . 807 *Excursion* 4. 383
And trivial ostentation—is left free . . . . 813 *Excursion* 4. 822
" But how begin ? and whence ?—' The Mind is free— . . . . 817 *Excursion* 4. 1080
While, free as air, o'er printless sands we march, . 819 *Excursion* 4. 1200
By choice, and conscious that the Will is free, . 820 *Excursion* 4. 1267
From all injurious servitude was free. . . . . 820 *Excursion* 4. 1297
The very multitude are free to range, ... 830 *Excursion* 5. 525
Nor shall the elements be free to hurt . . . . 838 *Excursion* 6. 32
Humiliation, when no longer free. . . . . . 840 *Excursion* 6. 126
In place from outward molestation free, . . . 844 *Excursion* 6. 400
Their life's appointed prison ; not more free . . 846 *Excursion* 6. 535
A heaving surface, almost wholly free . . . 847 *Excursion* 6. 607
Thoughts, which the rich are free from, came and crossed . . . . 852 *Excursion* 6. 941
From trepidation and repining free. . . . . 866 *Excursion* 7. 583
England, the ancient and the free, appeared . . 870 *Excursion* 7. 856
Yet free from touch of envious discontent, . . 872 *Excursion* 7. 952
That, far as kindly Nature hath free scope . . 885 *Excursion* 9. 105
A servile band among the lordly free ! . . . . 888 *Excursion* 9. 310
Free from obstruction ; and the boat advanced . 891 *Excursion* 9. 490
If time, with free consent, be yours to give, . . 896 *Excursion* 9. 782
And more than once been free at Luss . . . S.3. 438 **My Lord* 11
From my own door I shall be free to claim . . K.8. 250 *Recluse* 1.1.519
Eternal Lord ! and from the world set free, . . K.8. 265 **Rid of* 2
Were Kings a free born work, a people's choice. . L.1. 96 *Juvenal* 3. 41
Freebooter. Had given her love to a wild Freebooter, 41 *Bord.* 207
Freebooters. Buzz, buzz, ye black and winged freebooters ; . . . . 73 *Bord.* 2022
Free-born. Resolving (this a free-born Nation can) 310 *Invasion* 17
The free-born Soul—that World whose vaunted skill . . . . 313 **Not 'mid* 2
The freeborn mind enthralling, ... 385 *Yarrow Rev.* 22
His rank 'mong freeborn creatures that live free, . 389 *Eagles* 13
Britain put forth her freeborn strength in league, . 722 *Prelude* 10. 264
The freeborn Swiss to leave his narrow vales, . 761 *Excursion* 1. 318
Freed. From which I have freed myself—but 'tis my wish . . . . 64 *Bord.* 1474
It hung, nor could at once be freed ; . . . . 82 *Alice Fell* 30
Earth's noblest penitent ; from bondage freed . 105 *Artegal* 229
And of this Stranger speak by whom her lord was freed. . . . . 141 *Arm. Lady* 108
The Worldling, pining to be freed . . . . . 223 *Wishing-gate* 55
And, with a spirit freed from discontent, . . . 231 **The gentlest Poet* 31
Thou too be heard, lone eagle ! freed . . . . 235 *Power of Sound* 199
From the dark chambers of dejection freed, . . 260 **From the dark* 1
But from that bondage when her thoughts were freed . . . . 274 **Wait, prithee* 5
Hers is a holy Being, freed from Sin. . . . . 280 **Oh what* 5
Which from Siberian caves the Monarch freed, . . 321 **Humanity, delighting* 28
Of popular reason, long mistrusted, freed . . . 327 **Emperors and* 10
Lo, Justice triumphs ! Earth is freed ! . . . 327 *Ode 1815* 18
To social cares from jarring passions freed ; . . 334 **The Spirit* 13
Had freed his Realm, he plighted word . . . 372 *Eg. Maid* 225
Nor from mishap be freed. . . . . 374 *Eg. Maid* 370
Body and mind, from molestation freed, . . . 382 *Duddon* 24. 8
And be at once from peril freed ! " . . . . 408 *White Doe* 1100
The saint, the scholar, from a circle freed . . . 424 *Ecc. Sonn.* 1. 23. 5
When thy great soul was freed from mortal chains, 425 *Ecc. Sonn.* 1. 27. 1
More safely rests, dies happier, is freed . . . . 429 *Ecc. Sonn.* 2. 3. 3
Than that the Soul, freed from the bonds of Sense, 436 *Ecc. Sonn.* 2. 30. 2
By dauntless Luther freed, could they forget . . 437 *Ecc. Sonn.* 2. 37. 4
Were they who, when their Country had been freed, 444 *Ecc. Sonn.* 3. 15. 2
Nor quits the Body when the Soul is freed, . . 448 *Ecc. Sonn.* 3. 31. 3
To these glad eyes from bondage freed, again . 496 **A little* 50
The bashful freed from fear, ... 507 **While from* 54
When the third summer freed us from restraint, . 680 *Prelude* 6. 322
A single step, that freed me from the skirts . . 784 *Excursion* 2. 830
And who among them but an Exile, freed . . . 798 *Excursion* 3. 837
This he is freed from, and from thousand notes . 885 *Excursion* 9. 76
Freedom. Shy as the jealous chamois, Freedom flies, 15 *Desc. Sk.* 263
The work of Freedom daring to oppose, . . . 18 *Desc. Sk.* 451
Hail Freedom ! whether it was mine to stray, . 21 *Desc. Sk.* 591
—Yet hast thou found that Freedom spreads her power . . . . 21 *Desc. Sk.* 620
Whose natural element was freedom—— Stop— 70 *Bord.* 1819
Seems, if such freedom may be used with you, . 98 *Brothers* 167
His freedom he recovered on the eve . . . . 124 *V. and J.* 186
Nor could the voice of Freedom, which through France . . . . 126 *V. and J.* 302
In thoughtless freedom, bold. . . . . . . 192 *Ruth* 6
That voice of Freedom, in its power . . . . 233 *Power of Sound* 71
Hence, if in freedom I have loved the truth ; . . 259 *Calvert* 9
Of Patriots scoop their freedom out, with hand . 272 *Devil's Bridge* 5
In freedom, mountain-turf and river's marge ; . 273 **While Anna's* 2
Down to its root, and, in that freedom, bold ; . 277 **A Poet* 11
Yet still with Nature's freedom at the heart ;— . 284 *Departure* 24
The freedom of a Mountaineer : . . . . . 288 *Highland Girl* 33
Books, leisure, perfect freedom, and the talk . . 304 **I grieved* 10
And give us manners, virtue, freedom, power. . 307 **Milton ! thou* 8
Of British freedom, which, to the open sea . . 307 **It is not* 2
Our ancient freedom : else 'twere worse than vain 318 *Biscayan* 3

Freedom—*continued.*
Or hide, at will,—for freedom combating . . . 321 **The power* 5
Thy name, O SCHWYTZ, in happy freedom keep ! 339 *Schwytz* 14
Peace, leisure, freedom, moderate desires ; . . 356 *Aquap.* 260
Of freedom, with mind grasping the whole theme 359 **They—who* 10
Whose souls take pride in freedom, virtue, fame, 366 **Fair Land* 2
Flow to the poor, and freedom to the slave ; . . 424 *Ecc. Sonn.* 1. 24. 12
Shouting to Freedom, " Plant thy banners here ! " 431 *Ecc. Sonn.* 2. 13. 2
In freedom. Men they were who could not bend ; 443 *Ecc. Sonn.* 3. 13. 9
There's freedom, and sometimes a diffident stare . 482 *Character* 13
I, loving freedom, and untried ; . . . . . 492 *Duty* 25
Me this unchartered freedom tires ; . . . . 492 *Duty* 37
Foremost in freedom, noblest of mankind ? . . 505 *Warning* 143
If freedom, set, will rise again, ... 505 **If this* 3
True freedom where for ages they have lain . . 515 **Ah why* 3
For the least boon that freedom can bestow ? . 528 **Those breathing* 80
Exults in freedom, can with rapture vouch . . 528 **Those breathing* 83
Of heaven-born freedom on thy being's height, . 589 *Immortality* 126
Where Freedom oft, with Victory and Death, . 612 *Desc.Sk.Quarto* 537
Freedom, such as man may claim . . . . . 628 *Installation* 15
Of manliness and freedom) all conspired . . . 662 *Prelude* 4. 286
Of freedom which encouraged me to turn . . . 675 *Prelude* 6. 33
As hitherto, in freedom I may speak, ... 698 *Prelude* 7. 762
On works of love or freedom, or revolved . . . 714 *Prelude* 9. 317
Nor could the voice of Freedom, which through France . . . . 718 *Prelude* 9. 581
From this last spot of earth, where Freedom now 733 *Prelude* 11. 400
Preserved, enlarged, this freedom in himself ? . 748 *Prelude* 14. 131
My Heart in genuine freedom :—all pure thoughts 755 *Recluse* 1. 1. 858
" That righteous cause (such power hath freedom) bound, ... 775 *Excursion* 2. 227
Old freedom was old servitude, and they . . . 775 *Excursion* 2. 256
Her share in the pure freedom of that life, . . 794 *Excursion* 3. 552
And stand in freedom loosened from this world, . 803 *Excursion* 4. 134
Hail to the crown by Freedom shaped—to gird . 838 *Excursion* 6. 1
Freedom and hope ; but keen, withal, and shrewd. 866 *Excursion* 7. 561
This is the freedom of the universe ; . . . . 884 *Excursion* 9. 16
Imagination, freedom in the will ; . . . . . 887 *Excursion* 9. 223
On Albion's noble Race in freedom born, . . . 890 *Excursion* 9. 393
Of holy freedom, by redeeming love . . . . 894 *Excursion* 9. 656
His tongue, and give it the wind's freedom ; then, K.8. 227 **I will* 99
Freedom's. (Freedom's impregnable redoubt, . . 217 *Enterprise* 152
While Freedom's farthest hamlets blessings share, 615 *Desc.Sk.Quarto* 724
Oh give, great God, to Freedom's waves to ride . 617 *Desc.Sk.Quarto* 792
Waged in Freedom's holy cause, ... 628 *Installation* 14
Gave to triumph Freedom's cause, ... S.3. 442 *Harmodius* 7
Gave to triumph Freedom's cause, ... S.3. 442 *Harmodius* 27
Freely. Which here was freely given ? . . . . 224 **'Tis gone* 30
Yes, freely let our hearts expand, ... 286 *Nith* 25
Freely as in youth's season bland, ... 286 *Nith* 26
Your spirit freely let me drink, and live. . . . 449 *Ecc. Sonn.* 3. 35. 14
Shunned and not tolerated, freely lived . . . 712 *Prelude* 9. 194
We took, and let this freely be confessed, . . . 714 *Prelude* 9. 343
I yet was standing, freely to respire, ... 763 *Excursion* 1. 467
Infect the air which he had freely breathed . . 844 *Excursion* 6. 382
I freely gather ; and my leisure draws . . . . 856 *Excursion* 6. 1167
Freeman. And make himself a freeman of this spot 548 **Stranger ! this* 10
A freeman, wedded to his life of hope . . . . 703 *Prelude* 8. 253
A freeman, therefore, sound and unimpaired ; . K.8. 246 *Recluse* 1.1.362
Freer. To give, in their Descendants, freer vent . 515 **Men of* 6
And freer pace ; but more, far more, I grieved . 656 *Prelude* 3. 497
Frees. By heaven inspired ; that frees from chains the soul, ... 748 *Prelude* 14. 184
Freeze. To freeze the blood I have no ready arts : . 202 *Hart-leap* 98
Keen was the air, but could not freeze, . . . 375 **The Minstrels* 9
That Fortitude, whose blood disdains to freeze . 466 *St. Bees* 16
Freezes. Between life and death his blood freezes and thaws ; . . . . 484 **A plague* 23
Freezing. *See* **Heart-freezing.**
Which now with freezing thoughts did all her powers assail ; . . . . 27 *Guilt* 171
" If Care with freezing years should come, . . 293 *Yarrow Unv.* 57
Of the world's freezing cares—to generous Youth— 540 *Grace Darl.* 10
Freight. Fears either for himself or freight ; . . 178 *Waggoner* 3. 9
The summit of a cumbrous freight, ... 182 *Waggoner* 4. 255
Spurning her freight with indignation ! . . . 238 *P. B.* 172
So with his freight the Creature turns . . . . 244 *P. B.* 671
Therefore the wise pray for thee, though the freight 309 **England ! the* 12
The vast Pacific gladdens with the freight— . . 327 *Ode 1815* 23
And Shakspeare at his side—a freight, . . . 341 *Ital. Itin.* 14
Her freight, it was a Damsel peerless ; . . . . 370 *Eg. Maid* 80
" Though this unhappy freight I bear ; . . . 412 *White Doe* 1471
The freight of holy feeling which we meet, . . 438 *Ecc. Sonn.* 2. 39. 12
Each for her haven ; with her freight of Care, . 471 *Ailsa Crag* 9
In calms is conscious, finding for his freight . . 473 **Thanks for* 13
And is happy as if the rich freight were his own. . 571 *Farmer* 84
Full soon thy Soul shall have her earthly freight, 589 *Immortality* 130
I looked and looked, self-questioned what this freight . . . . 667 *Prelude* 5. 84
With freight of slippers piled beneath his arm ! . 690 *Prelude* 7. 218
But with its universal freight the tide . . . . 692 *Prelude* 7. 377
Its freight of public news, the fever came, . . 712 *Prelude* 9. 155
When those two vessels with their daring freight, 715 *Prelude* 9. 414
I, with my freight of winter raiment, saw . . . 764 *Excursion* 1. 542
And with their freight homeward the shepherds moved . . . . 784 *Excursion* 2. 828
Be left him, trust the freight of his distress . . 798 *Excursion* 3. 845
Two ruddy children hung, a well-poised freight, . 858 *Excursion* 7. 73
A team of horses, with a ponderous freight . . 865 *Excursion* 7. 542
A lone pedestrian with a scanty freight, . . . 875 *Excursion* 8. 98
And, on the freight of merry passengers . . . 880 *Excursion* 8. 383

Freight—*continued.*
With its rich freight; their number he proclaims; 882 *Excursion* 8. 562
Freighted. With commerce freighted, or triumphant war. 384 *Duddon* 32. 14
Thoughtfully freighted with a various store; 522 *Epist. Beaumont* 94
Freighted from every climate of the world 876 *Excursion* 8. 135
Freights. Freights every day from a new world of hope. 774 *Excursion* 2. 218
French. Here lay the French—and *thus* came we!" 178 *Waggoner* 2. 134
In the French tongue, a Novel of Voltaire, 778 *Excursion* 2. 443
Frenchman. How that one Frenchman, through continued force 635 *Prelude* 1. 206
The Frenchman and the Spaniard; from remote 690 *Prelude* 7. 225
Frenchmen. Frenchmen had changed a war of self-defence 730 *Prelude* 11. 207
Frenzied. While trees, dim-seen, in frenzied numbers, tear 263 *Storm* 6
26 *Guilt* 91
Frenzy. As one whose brain habitual frenzy fires
The chains of frenzy, or entice a smile 232 *Power of Sound* 12
Should come in frenzy and in drunken mirth, 308 **One might* 12
Else shall your blood-stained hands in frenzy reap 505 *Warning* 138
Lest alien frenzy seize thee, waxing wroth, 514 **Long-favoured* 3
Her frenzy only active to extol 723 *Prelude* 10. 353
Frenzy-stricken. To fiercer mood the frenzy-stricken brain, 459 **Wanderer! that* 42
Frequent. Yet frequent transports mitigate the gloom: 139 *Widow* 33
With frequent showers of snow. Upon a hill, 150 **When, to* 7
I ceased the shelter to frequent,—and prized, 150 **When, to* 41
And frequent sharer of their calm delight 151 **Forth from* 13
Doth yet frequent the hill of storms, 300 *Bran* 3
Beats frequent on thy satiate ear, 376 **The Minstrels* 74
O lost too early for the frequent tear, 445 *Ecc. Sonn.* 3. 22. 13
(By transit not unlike man's frequent doom) 461 **Who but is* 13
Ye brood of Conscience—Spectres! that frequent 518 *Pun. Death* 6. 1
Shall he frequent these precincts; locked no more 549 **The massy* 13
What noble pomp and frequent have not I 574 *Chiabrera* 4. 21
And frequent sights of what is to be borne! 579 *Peele Castle* 58
Did I by night frequent the College groves 676 *Prelude* 6. 67
That were a frequent comfort to my youth. 677 *Prelude* 6. 141
Myself from frequent perils; nor were tales 701 *Prelude* 8. 168
Not seeking frequent intercourse with men, 710 *Prelude* 9. 26
Did I frequent the formal haunts of men, 711 *Prelude* 9. 114
Of civil slaughter, was our frequent walk; 716 *Prelude* 9. 433
Religious, 'mid those frequent monuments 716 *Prelude* 9. 493
Bent as he moves, and needing frequent rest; 761 *Excursion* 1. 325
Such is the summer pilgrim's frequent wish; 773 *Excursion* 2. 113
—Such the too frequent tenour of his boast 843 *Excursion* 6. 359
From human converse to frequent alone S.3. 436 **The doubt* 169
From tasks too frequent, or beyond its power K.8. 246 *Recluse* 1.1.372
Frequented. *See* **Half-frequented.**
Be your frequented watch-tower; roll the stone 808 *Excursion* 4. 498
Frequented, and beset with howling winds. 859 *Excursion* 7. 144
Frequently. So frequently repeated, and by force 641 *Prelude* 1. 605
Forced labour, and more frequently forced hopes; 652 *Prelude* 3. 210
More frequently from the same source I drew 677 *Prelude* 6. 129
Most frequently call forth, and best sustain, 806 *Excursion* 4. 367
Fresh. Fresh food; for only then, when memory 1 *Early Youth* 10
Fresh gales and dews of life's delicious morn, 20 *Desc. Sk.* 530
And from her grateful heart a fresh one drew: 30 *Guilt* 322
Besides, on griefs so fresh my thoughts were brooding still. 32 *Guilt* 423
Thy absence, till old age and fresh infirmities 41 *Bord.* 203
As I have done. A fresh tide of Crusaders 69 *Bord.* 1771
His face is fair and fresh to see; 85 *Anecdote* 2
Fresh water from the brook, as clear as ever ran; 87 *Pet-lamb* 42
Fresh flowers blow as flowers have blown, 90 *Longest Day* 38
O'er town and tower we fled, and fields in May's fresh verdure drest; 92 *Poet's Dream* 31
He had as white a head and fresh a cheek 98 *Brothers* 201
Fresh as a rose in June, 109 **Strange fits* 6
And cheered; and now together breathe fresh air 119 *Maternal Grief* 64
Fresh sprigs of green box-wood, not six months before, 120 *Childless Father* 9
And likings fresh and innocent, 143 †*Lov. and Lik.* 62
Fresh from the crowded city, to behold 143 **High bliss* 10
It was an April morning: fresh and clear 146 **It was an* 1
A small Cascade fresh swoln with snows 155 *Waterfall* 5
My branches are so fresh and gay 156 *Oak and Broom* 78
Fresh blows the wind, a western wind, 161 *Binnorie* 12
But in the storm 'tis fresh and blue 166 *Danish Boy* 30
Fresh as the bloom upon his face. 166 *Danish Boy* 33
Transfigured through that fresh abode 168 *Pilgrim's Dream* 61
Scattering fresh flowers; though happier far, I ween, 191 *Beggars* 35
More fresh, more bright, than princes wear; 191 *Seq. Beggars* 7
Fresh as a banner bright, unfurled 194 *Ruth* 170
There is a fresh and lovely sight, 198 *Thorn* 35
So fresh in all its beauteous dyes, 198 *Thorn* 51
Fresh beauty through the vale. 224 **'Tis gone* 60
Fresh as if Evening brought their natal hour, 226 *Vernal Ode* 37
Through fresh green fields, and budding groves among, 229 *Cuckoo-clock* 19
Dear mother of fresh thoughts and joyous health! 254 *A flock* 14
And the fresh meads—where flowed, from every nook 254 *Complete Angler* 13
Put on fresh raiment—till that hour unworn: 255 *Easter* 4
Fresh as a lark mounting at break of day, 258 **Where lies the Land* 2
Fresh as the star that crowns the brow of morn; 265 **There is a pleasure* 11
In festal glee: why not? For fresh and clear, 275 **While poring* 6

Fresh—*continued.*
Fresh as the flower, whose modest worth 285 *Grave of Burns* 19
Age! twine thy brows with fresh spring flowers, 293 *Jedbor.* 1
In thy fresh beauty. There! that dusky spot 303 **Fair Star* 9
Fresh risen, and beautiful within!—there meet 327 *Ode 1815* 53
Fresh from the beauty and the bliss 334 **In Bruges* 39
Hues ever fresh, in rocky fortress blowing: 337 *Aar* 8
Bright sunbeams—the fresh verdure of this lawn 352 *Aquap.* 16
Mild—as the verdure, fresh—the sunshine, bright— 356 *Aquap.* 235
To be for ever fresh and young, 370 *Eg. Maid* 46
In semblance fresh, as if, with dire affray, 379 *Duddon* 15. 5
Dewy and fresh, till showers again shall fall. 381 *Duddon* 19. 14
With native Fancy her fresh aid, 386 *Yarrow Rev.* 55
And fresh with rivers, well did it become 392 *Daniel* 2
Receiving, willingly or not, fresh strength 394 **No more* 24
And there, by fresh hopes beautified, 401 *White Doe* 481
Heard near fresh streams; and thousands, who rejoice 423 *Ecc. Sonn.* 1. 17. 12
The Romanist exults; fresh hope he draws 439 *Ecc. Sonn.* 2. 41. 9
Green with fresh holly, every pew a perch 448 *Ecc. Sonn.* 3. 33. 11
And the fresh air of incense-breathing morn 450 *Ecc. Sonn.* 3. 40. 12
Fresh gales to waft them to the far-off port; 454 *Sea-side* 18
As a fresh morning for new harmony; 455 *Rydal Mere* 20
"I come to open out, for fresh display, 456 **Soft as* 25
Children of Summer! Ye fresh Flowers that brave 474 **Hope smiled* 2
Brings fresh into my mind 486 **We walked* 22
And the most ancient heavens, through Thee, are fresh and strong. 492 *Duty* 48
Gain a fresh impulse, run a livelier course; 503 *Warning* 15
In thy fresh wreaths, than they for praise 508 *May* 87
The appropriate Picture, fresh from Titian's hand, 509 *F. Stone* 105
In faith, which fresh offences, were he cast 520 *Pun. Death* 12. 13
No tales of Runagates fresh landed, whence 522 *Epist. Beaumont* 61
Rich cream, and snow-white eggs fresh from the nest, 525 *Epist. Beaumont* 242
To the fresh waters of a living Well— 527 **Those breathing* 8
The vocal raptures of fresh poesy, 549 **The massy* 12
He can make sick folk whole and fresh and sound; 556 *Cuck. and Night.* 7
There sate I down among the fair fresh flowers, 558 *Cuck. and Night.* 66
And jollity, fresh cheerfulness, and mirth; 559 *Cuck. and Night.* 155
Go look on the fresh daisy; then say I, 561 *Cuck. and Night.* 243
Fresh flowers; while the sun shines warm, 588 *Immortality* 48
Fresh water rushes strew the verdant floor; 596 *Ev. Wk. Quarto* 228
Fresh with lustre all their own. 629 *Installation* 52
Flowed in upon me, from all sides; fresh day 649 *Prelude* 3. 24
With prompt rebound seemed fresh as heretofore. 650 *Prelude* 3. 97
Than as they were a badge glossy and fresh 662 *Prelude* 4. 285
Too learned, or too good; but wanton, fresh, 671 *Prelude* 5. 412
Fresh emptied of spectators. Twice five years 674 *Prelude* 5. 552
Share with us thy fresh spirits, whether gift 678 *Prelude* 6. 250
Or Indian cabins over the fresh lawns 683 *Prelude* 6. 522
Fresh from a toilette of two hours, ascend 695 *Prelude* 7. 552
In a pure stream of words fresh from the heart: 706 *Prelude* 8. 467
Keeping such fresh remembrance of the day, 707 *Prelude* 8. 540
Fresh as the morning star. Elate we looked 715 *Prelude* 9. 385
Do of itself blow fresh, and make the vanes 723 *Prelude* 10. 370
Piping on boughs, or sporting on fresh fields, 735 *Prelude* 12. 35
The characters are fresh and visible: 738 *Prelude* 12. 245
Closed up each chink, and with fresh bands of straw 770 *Excursion* 1. 903
"Fresh blew the wind, when o'er the Atlantic Main 798 *Excursion* 3. 835
Fresh, youthful, and aspiring! What are these 799 *Excursion* 3. 885
When the fresh eagle, in the month of May, 807 *Excursion* 4. 397
Fresh in the strength and majesty of age, 829 *Excursion* 5. 457
All fresh and beautiful, and green and bright, 830 *Excursion* 5. 546
So green, so fresh, so plentiful, as mine!' 835 *Excursion* 5. 877
Court the fresh air, explore the heaths and woods; 840 *Excursion* 6. 169
Of the fresh shower, but of poor Ellen's tears 850 *Excursion* 6. 816
Of winter cannot thin; the fresh air lodged 865 *Excursion* 7. 553
A fresh band meets them, at the crowded door— 877 *Excursion* 8. 176
Breathing fresh air, and treading the green earth; 878 *Excursion* 8. 280
Fresh power to commune with the invisible world, 885 *Excursion* 9. 86
The vernal field infuses fresh delight 887 *Excursion* 9. 213
In fresh abodes—their labour to renew; 889 *Excursion* 9. 374
Thy living chaplet of fresh flowers and fern, S.3. 437 **The doubt* 201
That made their conversation fresh and fair K.8. 227 **I will* 93
Warm woods, and sunny hills, and fresh green fields, K.8. 240 *Recluse* 1.1.127
Fresh as the freshest field, scoop'd out, and green K.8. 263 **The Lake* 6
Fresh-cloven. And ground fresh-cloven by the plough 228 *Devot. Incit.* 62
Freshen. Would their lost strength restore and freshen the pale cheek? 523 *Epist. Beaumont* 117
Freshened. Of low-hung vapour: on the freshened mead 14 *Desc. Sk.* 218
My leaves you freshened and bedewed; 155 *Waterfall* 28
Green dewy lights adorn the freshen'd mead, 607 *Desc. Sk. Quarto* 272
A field before them freshened with the dew 884 *Excursion* 9. 31
Freshening. Freshening the wilderness with shades and springs. 13 *Desc. Sk.* 172
A freshening lustre mellow 481 *Tables Turned* 6
A quickening hope, a freshening glee, 506 **While from* 5
Dive, at thy choice, or brave the freshening gale! 527 **Those breathing* 36
Freshening the waste of sand with shades and springs. 605 *Desc. Sk. Quarto* 198
Freshens. The buds, and freshens the young leaves, 228 *Devot. Incit.* 16
Fresher. On infant cheeks there fresher roses blow; 21 *Desc. Sk.* 608
With gleams of fresher, purer, light; 338 **Meek Virgin* 34
Her infant's cheeks with fresher roses glow, 615 *Desc. Sk. Quarto* 734
The chamber hearth with fresher boughs is spread, 615 *Desc. Sk. Quarto* 738
That ran on Sabbath days a fresher course; 661 *Prelude* 4. 226
For sunshine, and to breathe the fresher air. 696 *Prelude* 7. 610
Dreadless, as in a kind of fresher breeze K.8. 246 *Recluse* 1.1.369
Freshest. When all the fields with freshest green were dight, 226 *Vernal Ode* 2

Freshest—continued.
Fresh as the freshest field, scoop'd out, and green K.8. 263 *The Lake 6
Fresh-flowing. When thankfulness were best?—Fresh-flowing tears, 271 George: Death 9
Freshness. The freshness, the everlasting youth, 301 Bran 113
In realms where everlasting freshness breathes!" 324 Ode 1814 52
Still in the vivid freshness of a dream, 347 Processions 46
Of brilliant moss, instinct with freshness rare; 376 Duddon 3. 13
The freshness of the valleys; let his blood 568 Cumb. Beg. 173
The glory and the freshness of a dream. 587 Immortality 5
A freshness in those objects of her love, 654 Prelude 3. 362
Those walks in all their freshness now came back 660 Prelude 4. 136
A freshness also found I at this time 661 Prelude 4. 191
Time had compressed the freshness of his cheek 762 Excursion 1. 426
Fresh-smitten. Fresh-smitten by the morning ray, 158 *In youth 57
Fret. And who would grieve and fret, if, welcome come 97 Brothers 123
Why are you in this mighty fret? 126 Idiot Boy 9
Yes, let my master fume and fret, 174 Waggoner 1. 116
The Newsman is stopped, though he stops on the fret; 188 Music 19
Nuns fret not at their convent's narrow room; 250 *Nuns fret 1
As false to expectation. Nor fret thou 267 *DespondingFather 7
That—whatever griefs may fret, 503 *Like a 53
I love the Brooks which down their channels fret, 590 Immortality 196
We crossed the Brabant armies on the fret 686 Prelude 6. 764
As the winds fret within the Æolian cave, 695 Prelude 7. 533
Or fret and labour on the Plain below. 885 Excursion 9. 92
Fret, burn, and struggle, and in soul am there; K.8. 256 Recluse 1.1.725
Fretful. Of joyless daylight; when the fretful stir 206 Tintern 52
Upon a fretful rivulet, now above, 253 *O gentle 7
Of fretful temper sullies her pure cheek; 274 Infant M. 6
On Vaga's breast the fretful waves, 296 Highland Boy 122
And, though the passions of man's fretful race 367 Trajan 7
Pure as the morning, fretful, boisterous, keen, 382 Duddon 26. 6
Amid the fretful dwellings of mankind 636 Prelude 1. 279
Of disencumbering thus her fretful wings. 798 Excursion 3. 820
Frets. Now but in wantonness she frets, 165 Parrot 23
Where the whirlpool frets and raves 336 *Jesu! bless 21
She burns, she frets—by Juno's rancour stung; 624 Æneid 8
That frets, or languishes, be stilled and cheered." 829 Excursion 5. 484
Fretted. Exulting Warbler! eased a fretted brain, 279 *Hark! 'tis 7
As if the fretted roof were riven. 332 Ode: Thanks. 219
To sink, and meet them in their fretted caves, 333 Fish-women 7
"Rich robes are fretted by the moth; 372 Eg. Maid 217
Fretted by sallies of his mother's kisses, 588 Immortality 88
And if, at times, they fretted with the yoke, 845 Excursion 6. 473
But fretted, vexed, and wrought upon, almost 849 Excursion 6. 745
The cornice, richly fretted, of grey stone; 881 Excursion 8. 467
Fretting. Fretting the fever round the languid heart, 31 Guilt 395
Fretting and whitening, keener and more keen; 439 Ecc. Sonn. 2. 43. 8
Fret-work. And through each window's open fret-work looked 355 Aquap. 157
Of fret-work imagery laid low; 416 White Doe 1892
Friar. While Bacchus, clothed in semblance of a Friar, 433 Ecc. Sonn. 2. 20. 4
Friar's. I had as lief turn to the Friar's school 45 Bord. 467
Friars. Or given upon report by pilgrim friars, 688 Prelude 7. 82
Friday. Duly as Friday comes, though pressed herself 568 Cumb. Beg. 156
Friend. See **Sailor-friend.**
Far from my dearest Friend, 'tis mine to rove 2 Ev. Wk. 1
Say, will my Friend, with unreluctant ear, 2 Ev. Wk. 35
Where we, my Friend, to happy days shall rise, 8 Ev. Wk. 351
In every babbling brook he finds a friend; 11 Desc. Sk. 26
Death would be else the favourite friend of woe. 20 Desc. Sk. 539
To-night, my Friend, within this humble cot 22 Desc. Sk. 665
And desolate, "Here you will find a friend!" 24 Guilt 15
My father! gone was every friend of thine: 32 Guilt 425
Oh! tell me whither—for no earthly friend 32 Guilt 446
Into the court, my Friend, and perch yourself 44 Bord. 370
To be the friend and father of the oppressed 48 Bord. 634
And see your Friend again. The good old Man 50 Bord. 695
I'll answer for it that our four-legged friend 51 Bord. 774
I do not hear the voice of my friend Oswald. 52 Bord. 807
Herbert!—confusion! Here it is, my Friend, 53 Bord. 855
Heavens! my good Friend! Forgive me, gracious Sir!— 54 Bord. 943
His most familiar Friend. There was a letter 58 Bord. 1138
So saintly and so pure!——Harkee, my Friend, 60 Bord. 1247
Where is our common Friend? A ghost, me-thinks— 61 Bord. 1301
I am your friend. What need of this assurance 64 Bord. 1478
I still will be your friend, will cleave to you 64 Bord. 1499
Now would you? and for ever?— My young Friend, 65 Bord. 1520
You are my Father's Friend. Alas, you know not, 66 Bord. 1604
Murdered! alas! speak—speak, I am your friend: 67 Bord. 1668
So dealt with him. I have a noble Friend 71 Bord. 1896
I have no friend; 72 Bord. 1966
No, no, my Friend, you may pursue your business— 73 Bord. 2032
How could he call upon his Child!—O Friend! 76 Bord. 2187
As if she had lost her only friend 82 Alice Fell 51
Stranger to me and yet my friend, a simple notice came, 91 Norman Boy 6
Ay, there, indeed, your memory is a friend 97 Brothers 138
Is a true friend to sorrow; and, unless 101 Brothers 389
Me, unapproached by any friend, 113 Lament 19
I followed him, and said, "My friend, 115 Last of Flock 15
I have no other earthly friend! 117 Affl. Marg. 77
Another kinsman—he will be our friend 135 Michael 248

Friend—continued.
"Hie thee to the Countess, friend! return with speed, 141 Arm. Lady 107
Most soothing was it for a welcome Friend, 143 *High bliss 9
—Now whether (said I to our cordial Friend, 147 Joanna 66
My Friend, Myself, and She who then received 149 *A narrow 75
Father, sister, friend, and brother. 157 Sexton 8
Thou art!—a friend at hand, to scare 158 *In youth 39
—If the Butterfly knew but his friend, 162 *Art thou the 15
He is the friend of our summer gladness: 163 *Art thou the 31
Said cordially, "My Friend, what cheer? 176 Waggoner 1. 248
We want your streamers, friend, you know; 179 Waggoner 3. 76
Accept, O Friend, for praise or blame, 182 Waggoner 4. 197
Of this fair river; thou my dearest Friend, 207 Tintern 115
My dear, dear Friend; and in thy voice I catch 207 Tintern 116
Where thou, a Wife and Friend, shalt see 218 Young Lady 4
And there my good friend, Stephen Otter; 238 P. B. 167
O Friend! thy flute has breathed a harmony 252 *The fairest 3
Grief, thou hast lost an ever-ready friend 255 *Grief, thou 1
The lamp of faith, lost Friend! too faintly burn; 258 *Even so 10
What boots the enquiry?—Neither friend nor foe 258 *Where lies the Land 5
High is our calling, Friend!—Creative Art 260 *High is 1
With action, were as nothing, patriot Friend! 261 Retirement 3
Yet art thou welcome, welcome as a friend 264 Snowdrop 7
To Him who is our lord and friend! 294 Jedbor. 77
And was his friend; and gave him joy 295 Highland Boy 24
O Friend! I know not which way I must look 306 *O Friend 1
Young Vane, and others who called Milton friend. 307 *Great men 4
Repose at length, firm friend of human kind! 313 Clarkson 14
Well judged the Friend who placed it there 337 Thun 5
Nor wish for earthly friend. 338 *Meek Virgin 18
This tribute from a casual Friend 348 *Lulled by 75
To this bright land, Hope was for him no friend, 353 Aquap. 69
From chosen comrade turns, or faithful friend— 383 Duddon 30. 7
With some loved friend, or by the unseen hawk 389 Glencroe 5
With her, and with her sylvan Friend; 400 White Doe 341
The Friend, who stood before her sight, 400 White Doe 342
Upon no help of outward friend; 402 White Doe 543
Who, 'mong those thousands, friend hath none, 404 White Doe 755
The friend shrinks back—the foe recoils 408 White Doe 1149
For this her last and living Friend. 415 White Doe 1796
A dear look to her lowly Friend; 416 White Doe 1855
Self-offered victim, for his friend he died, 420 Ecc. Sonn. 1. 6. 11
Of those Enthusiasts a subservient friend, 427 Ecc. Sonn. 1. 35. 13
That bid me hail thee as the Sailor's Friend; 459 *Wanderer! that 12
And thou art still, O Moon, that Sailor's Friend! 460 *Wanderer! that 72
To me my good friend Matthew spake, 481 Expost. 15
Up! up! my Friend, and quit your books; 481 Tables Turned 1
Up! up! my Friend, and clear your looks; 481 Tables Turned 3
We from to-day, my Friend, will date 483 Sister 19
"My days, my Friend, are almost gone, 487 Fountain 53
And fondly strives her struggling friend to save. 490 Incident: Dog 32
Of Him to be our friend! 495 Force of Prayer 68
And no one can tell whither. Dearest Friend! 498 *Enough of climbing 45
From heaviness, oft fly, dear Friend, to thee; 521 Epist. Beaumont 11
The Curate's Dog—his long-tried friend, for they, 523 Epist. Beaumont 131
To our kind Friend high on the sunny hill— 524 Epist. Beaumont 216
And in Death's arms has long reposed the Friend 525 *Soon did 3
Thus, gifted Friend, but with the placid brow 529 *Those breathing 133
Poor Robin as a sure and crafty friend, 530 Poor Robin 21
Witness how oft upon my noble Friend 539 *Lady! a 27
And friend in the ear of friend, where speech is free 539 *Lady! a 55
Fletcher's Associate, Jonson's Friend beloved. 546 *The embowering 21
If thou in the dear love of some one Friend 551 *If thou in 1
Far from St. Cuthbert his belovèd Friend, 551 *If thou in 26
And said, Forsooth, my friend, do I thank thee, 561 Cuck. and Night. 227
Youth amiable; O friend so true of soul 575 Chiabrera 7. 3
As with a chosen friend; nor did he leave 576 Chiabrera 9. 12
Our common Friend and Father sent. 577 *I come 4
Then, Beaumont, Friend! who would have been the Friend, 579 Peele Castle 41
—Brother and friend, if verse of mine 581 John Words. 61
Thou wert a scorner of the fields, my Friend, 585 Ch. Lamb 50
With thine, O silent and invisible Friend! 586 Ch. Lamb 108
Say, will my friend, with soft affection's ear, 592 Ev. Wk. Quarto 51
Where we, my friend, to golden days shall rise, 599 Ev. Wk. Quarto 419
And so, my Friend, good-day to you." 621 Andrew Jones 30
But that the precious love this friend hath sown 627 *We gaze 2
Thus far, O Friend! did I, not used to make 632 Prelude 1. 46
Of humbler industry. But, oh, dear Friend! 634 Prelude 1. 134
Nor will it seem to thee, O Friend! so prompt 641 Prelude 1. 617
This labour will be welcome, honoured Friend! 641 Prelude 1. 646
Thus far, O Friend! have we, though leaving much 642 Prelude 2. 1
And to my Friend who knows me I may add, 643 Prelude 2. 73
Came from yon fountain?" Thou, my Friend! art one 645 Prelude 2. 210
For this, that one was by my side, a Friend, 647 Prelude 2. 333
And purest passion. Thou, my Friend! wert reared 648 Prelude 2. 451
And here, O Friend! have I retraced my life 651 Prelude 3. 167
To follow, and if thou, my honoured Friend! 652 Prelude 3. 198
I called him Brother, Englishman, and Friend! 653 Prelude 3. 282
Call back, O Friend! a moment to thy mind, 653 Prelude 3. 309
And thou, O Friend! who in thy ample mind 653 Prelude 3. 317
Thus in submissive idleness, my Friend! 658 Prelude 3. 629
At our domestic table: and, dear Friend! 659 Prelude 4. 78

Friendless 344 Friends

Friend—*continued.*
To watch me, an attendant and a friend, . . . 660 *Prelude* 4. 106
Than these to which the Tale, indulgent Friend ! 662 *Prelude* 4. 275
Ah ! need I say, dear Friend ! that to the brim 663 *Prelude* 4. 333
Had fallen in presence of a studious friend, . . 666 *Prelude* 5. 51
O Friend ! O Poet ! brother of my soul, . . . 668 *Prelude* 5. 181
Where had we been, we two, belovèd Friend ! . 669 *Prelude* 5. 233
With a dear friend, and for the better part . . 674 *Prelude* 5. 561
Risen on mid noon ; blest with the presence, Friend ! . . . . 678 *Prelude* 6. 198
Dear to thee also, thy true friend and mine, . . 678 *Prelude* 6. 200
O Friend ! we had not seen thee at that time, . 678 *Prelude* 6. 237
And groves I speak to thee, my Friend ! to thee, 679 *Prelude* 6. 265
A youthful friend, he too a mountaineer, . . . 680 *Prelude* 6. 323
That thou, O Friend ! the trouble or the calm 682 *Prelude* 6. 473
Oh, most belovèd Friend ! a glorious time, . . 686 *Prelude* 6. 754
Before last primrose-time. Belovèd Friend ! . . 687 *Prelude* 7. 12
I mean, O distant Friend ! a story drawn . . 691 *Prelude* 7. 296
Yet deem not, Friend ! that human kind with me 704 *Prelude* 8. 340
As was thy melancholy lot, dear Friend ! . . . 705 *Prelude* 8. 434
Thus from a very early age, O Friend ! . . . 709 *Prelude* 8. 676
In his first outset ; so have we, my Friend ! . . 709 *Prelude* 9. 7
And individual worth. And hence, O Friend ! . 713 *Prelude* 9. 243
Or such retirement, Friend ! as we have known . 715 *Prelude* 9. 391
Though like ambition, such was he, O Friend ! 715 *Prelude* 9. 418
Of solitude, and at the sight my friend . . . 717 *Prelude* 9. 516
Told by my Patriot friend, of sad events, . . . 717 *Prelude* 9. 548
Useless, and even, beloved Friend ! a soul . . 721 *Prelude* 10. 235
And gave it vent in her last words. O Friend ! . 723 *Prelude* 10. 383
Most melancholy at that time, O Friend ! . . 724 *Prelude* 10. 397
O Friend ! few happier moments have been mine 725 *Prelude* 10. 511
Searched to its heart. Share with me, Friend ! the wish . . . . 731 *Prelude* 11. 282
Sets like an Opera phantom. Thus, O Friend ! . 732 *Prelude* 11. 370
And thou, O Friend ! wilt be refreshed. There is 733 *Prelude* 11. 393
When thinking on my own beloved friend, . . 733 *Prelude* 11. 442
This narrative, my Friend ! hath chiefly told 735 *Prelude* 12. 44
His best and purest friend ; from her receives 740 *Prelude* 13. 7
We almost meet a friend, on naked heaths . . 742 *Prelude* 13. 139
And so shall stand for ever. Dearest Friend ! . 744 *Prelude* 13. 299
From monumental hints : and thou, O Friend ! . 745 *Prelude* 13. 352
Of Cambria ranging with a youthful friend, . . 746 *Prelude* 14. 3
This over-sternness ; but for thee, dear Friend ! . 749 *Prelude* 14. 247
And now, O Friend ! this history is brought . . 750 *Prelude* 14. 302
Finally, and above all, O Friend ! (I speak . . 750 *Prelude* 14. 321
O Friend ! The termination of my course . . 751 *Prelude* 14. 374
Is all uncertain : but, beloved Friend ! . . . 751 *Prelude* 14. 392
It will be known, by thee at least, my Friend ! . 752 *Prelude* 14. 411
The Friend I sought ; a Man of reverend age, . 756 *Excursion* 1. 33
Things which you cannot see : we die, my Friend, 763 *Excursion* 1. 470
A sore heart-wasting ! I have heard, my Friend, 769 *Excursion* 1. 875
Fast rooted at her heart : and here, my Friend,— 770 *Excursion* 1. 914
" My Friend ! enough to sorrow you have given, 770 *Excursion* 1. 932
Heard as the voice of an experienced friend. . . 772 *Excursion* 2. 64
The careless wanderer's friend, to him made known 774 *Excursion* 2. 186
Recovering, to my Friend I said, " You spake, . 777 *Excursion* 2. 395
Exclaimed my Friend : " here then has been to him 778 *Excursion* 2. 445
This sad memorial of their hapless friend ! " . . 778 *Excursion* 2. 456
My venerable Friend, as forth we stepped . . 779 *Excursion* 2. 488
More might have followed—but my honoured Friend . . . . 779 *Excursion* 2. 512
Of past discussions with this zealous friend . . 781 *Excursion* 2. 627
And pleased I looked upon my grey-haired Friend, 781 *Excursion* 2. 658
Was wholly ignorant that my ancient Friend— . 783 *Excursion* 2. 785
My grey-haired Friend said courteously—" Nay, nay, ... 785 *Excursion* 2. 901
And, to remove those doubts, mygrey-haired Friend 786 *Excursion* 3. 21
A sound unknown to you ; else, honoured Friend ! 793 *Excursion* 3. 483
Again directed to his downcast Friend, . . . 806 *Excursion* 4. 374
" Compatriot, Friend, remote are Garry's hills, 809 *Excursion* 4. 550
Restored it to its owner. " Gentle Friend," . . 816 *Excursion* 4. 1015
With whisper soft my venerable Friend . . . 825 *Excursion* 5. 208
My ancient Friend and I together took . . . 826 *Excursion* 5. 231
Like this our honoured Friend ; and thence acquire 828 *Excursion* 5. 387
Of the encomiums by my Friend pronounced . . 828 *Excursion* 5. 420
Of native cordiality, our Friend . . . . . 829 *Excursion* 5. 443
As to a spiritual comforter and friend, . . . 854 *Excursion* 6. 1030
—Much did she suffer : but, if any friend, . . 854 *Excursion* 6. 1042
When seated near my venerable Friend, . . . 854 *Excursion* 6. 1057
That might have touched the sick heart of his Friend . . . . 862 *Excursion* 7. 295
The fellow-labourer and friend of him . . . . 864 *Excursion* 7. 436
The Pastor ceased.—My venerable Friend . . . 871 *Excursion* 7. 891
His sole companion, and his faithful friend, . . 872 *Excursion* 7. 947
For she hath recognised her honoured friend, . . 881 *Excursion* 8. 494
My grey-haired Friend was moved ; his vivid eye 883 *Excursion* 8. 588
Why, friend, to deck her supple twigs . . . S.3. 431 **The Scottish* 7
Moved (shall I say ?) like a dear friend who meets S.3. 432 **The doubt* 87
My hope, my joy, my sister, and my friend, . . K.8. 234**Witness thou* 3
For some one, serves as a familiar friend. . . . K.8. 248*Recluse* 1.1.444
Your friend the country-Justice scarce would fail L.1. 97 *Juvenal* 3. 71
Friendless. Nor friendless he, the prisoner of the mine, ... 233 *Power of Sound* 62
And friendless, by their own sad choice ! . . . 473 *Ossian* 52
A friendless Man, a travelling Cripple ! . . . 621 *Andrew Jones* 10
Commended him as a poor friendless man, . . 665 *Prelude* 4. 451
When he, a friendless and a drooping boy, . . 688 *Prelude* 7. 113
Friendly. From gulf of parting clouds one friendly beam, ... 26 *Guilt* 131
Nor any friendly sound his footsteps led ; . . . 26 *Guilt* 132
Yet, to relieve her heart, in friendly style . . . 32 *Guilt* 457

Friendly—*continued.*
In vain to find a friendly face we try, ... 35 *Guilt* 602
A friendly shelter, and we entered in. . . . . 50 *Bord.* 700
Hath been so friendly to industrious hours ; . . 107 *Farewell* 58
With him there often walked in friendly guise, . 108 *Indolence* 37
Accomplished under friendly shade of night. . . 123 *V. and J.* 86
On a friendly deck reposing . . . . . . 141 *Arm. Lady* 97
" ' From me this friendly warning take '— . . 156 *Oak and Broom* 51
Which with such friendly voice will call ; . . . 174 *Waggoner* 1. 75
Our treat shall be a friendly bowl ! " . . . . 177 *Waggoner* 2. 46
On friendly terms with this Machine : . . . . 182 *Waggoner* 4. 217
So shall he touch at length a friendly strand, . 234 *Power of Sound* 142
Well have you played your friendly part ; . . 237 *P. B.* 113
Friendly ; as here to my repose hath been . . 358 *Aquap.* 368
From new incitements friendly to our task, . . 382 *Duddon* 24. 12
Yet in the Temple they a friendly niche . . 387 *Roslin* 11
And to Religion's self no friendly will, . . . 442 *Ecc. Sonn.* 3. 8. 13
Of Patron, famous school or friendly nook, . . 655 *Prelude* 3. 467
Friendly to studious or to festive hours ; . . . 659 *Prelude* 4. 49
A spirit friendly to the Poet's task, . . . 687 *Prelude* 7. 48
A power to virtue friendly ; were 't not so, . . 765 *Excursion* 1. 634
For one hostility, in friendly league, . . . 775 *Excursion* 2. 228
How Nature hems you in with friendly arms ! . 786 *Excursion* 3. 14
Thought I—some friendly covert must be near. . 833 *Excursion* 5. 749
Or, in the garden, under friendly veil . . . 852 *Excursion* 6. 900
And, by some friendly finger's help upstayed . . 867 *Excursion* 7. 678
As if some friendly Genius had ordained . . 892 *Excursion* 9. 522
Friendly the weight of leisure to remove, . . . S.3 426 **Through Cumbrian* 5
A friendly covert. " And they knew it well," . K.8. 247*Recluse* 1.1.396
Friends. Is hushed, am I at rest. My Friends ! restrain . . . . 2 *Early Youth* 11
The friends whom she had left but a few minutes past. . . . . 34 *Guilt* 558
Give me your hand ; where are you, Friends ? and tell me . . . . 52 *Bord.* 804
Ay, what is it you mean ? Harkee, my Friends ;— 56 *Bord.* 1037
By heaven, his words are reason ! Yes, my Friends, ... 57 *Bord.* 1094
You know me, Friends ; I have a heart to feel, . 57 *Bord.* 1111
Who are we, Friends ? Do we not live on ground 57 *Bord.* 1114
My Friends, his heart shall have as many wounds 64 *Bord.* 1460
Unto the few whom he esteems his friends . . 104 *Artegal* 102
That friends, by death disjoined, may meet no more ! . . . . 112 **O dearer* 4
By friends deceived, by foes betrayed, . . . 113 *Lament* 59
My friends, I did not follow you ! . . . . . 114 *Ind. Wom.* 28
Dear friends, when ye were gone away. . . . 114 *Ind. Wom.* 30
The way my friends their course did bend, . . 114 *Ind. Wom.* 46
Too soon, my friends, ye went away ; . . . . 114 *Ind. Wom.* 49
She spies her Friends, she shouts a greeting ; . . 130 *Idiot Boy* 429
You love your sister and your friends, . . . 143 †*Lov. and Lik.* 57
With hope that we, dear Friends ! shall meet again. 143 **High bliss* 28
Good friends he has to take his part ; . . . . 144 **Driven in* 74
And there myself and two beloved Friends, . . 148 **A narrow* 6
My last year's friends together. . . . . . 159 *Green Linnet* 8
Concealed from friends who might disturb . . 169 *Wren's Nest* 61
I'll set, my friends, to do you honour, . . . 178 *Waggoner* 2. 121
While friends and kindred all approved . . . 198 *Thorn* 109
Yet lacks not friends for simple glee, . . . 205 *Brougham* 116
The woods, my Friends, are round you roaring, . 236 *P. B.* 11
Resume, my Friends ! within the shade . . . 238 *P. B.* 183
Are not unused to trouble friends . . . . . 245 *P. B.* 768
O chief of Friends ! such feelings I present . . 250 **Happy the* 10
Garden, and that Domain where kindred, friends, 271 **Where holy* 5
And friends too rarely prop the languid head. . 273 **While Anna's* 8
Neighbours we were, and loving friends . . . 285 *Grave of Burns* 41
True friends though diversely inclined ; . . . 285 *Grave of Burns* 43
Or keep his friends from harm. . . . . . 291 *Rob Roy* 12
Of company or friends, and left . . . . . 295 *Highland Boy* 39
Thy friends are exultations, agonies, ... 305 *Toussaint* 13
Though the toil of the way with dear Friends we divide, ... 345 *Stanzas : Simplon* 25
Death-parted friends, and days too swift in flight, 358 *Pine : Rome* 11
With friends and kindred tenderly beloved ; . . 381 *Duddon* 21. 3
With friends and kindred dealing. . . . . . 386 *Yarrow Rev.* 96
And choice of studious friends had he . . . 399 *White Doe* 295
Which struck with terror friends and foes ! . . 408 *White Doe* 1148
How they have scourged old foes, perfidious friends : 421 *Ecc. Sonn.* 1. 10. 2
An emblem yields to friends and enemies . . . 433 *Ecc. Sonn.* 2. 17. 12
Of saintly Friends the " murtherer's chain partake, 437 *Ecc. Sonn.* 2. 34. 11
Friends strike at friends—the flying shall pursue— 437 *Ecc. Sonn.* 2. 36. 13
Who, with sad hearts, of friends and country took 443 *Ecc. Sonn.* 3. 13. 2
Of God and chosen friends, your troth to plight . 446 *Ecc. Sonn.* 3. 26. 3
Of health, strength, friends, and kindred, see ! . 483 *Simon Lee* 26
With friends to greet thee, or without, . . . 486 **Bright Flower* 19
A pair of friends, though I was young, . . . 487 *Fountain* 3
Of friends, who live within an easy walk, . . 488 *Pers. Talk* 3
Upon that law as on the best of friends ; . . . 493 *Hap. War.* 28
Are friends and patrons of humanity. . . . . 501 *Humanity* 104
She shoots the tidings forth to distant friends ; . 503 *Warning* 27
Though poor and destitute of friends thou art, . 531 *Octogen.* 9
Of humblest Friends, bright Creature ! scorn not one : . . . . 538 **Small service* 2
In earnest converse with belovèd Friends, . . 549 **The massy* 14
Weep not, belovèd Friends ! nor let the air . . 573 *Chiabrera* 1. 1
From intricate cabals of treacherous friends. . 574 *Chiabrera* 4. 9
His friends had in their fondness entertained, . 575 *Chiabrera* 8. 15
For that last thought of parting Friends . . . 580 *John Words.* 23
While Friends beheld thee give with eye, voice, mien, ... 583 **With copious* 32

Friends—*continued.*
Perished the Roman Empire: how the friends . 635 *Prelude* 1. 190
And be ye happy! Yet, my Friends! I know . 642 *Prelude* 2. 41
Some friends I had, acquaintances who there . . 649 *Prelude* 3. 19
Seemed friends, poor simple schoolboys, now hung round . . . . 649 *Prelude* 3. 20
We know where we have friends. Ye dreamers, then, ... 673 *Prelude* 5. 523
Of hardy disobedience towards friends . . . 675 *Prelude* 6. 28
With these blithe friends our voyage we renewed 681 *Prelude* 6. 407
From kindred, friends, and playmates, to partake 701 *Prelude* 8. 122
Friends, enemies, of all parties, ages, ranks, . . 723 *Prelude* 10. 361
Those aberrations—had the clamorous friends . 731 *Prelude* 11. 260
We were tried Friends: amid a pleasant vale, . 757 *Excursion* 1. 52
Attentive audience. But, oh! gentle Friends, . 794 *Excursion* 3. 600
Or haply thinking of far-distant friends, . . . 805 *Excursion* 4. 249
Of knightly race, nor wanting powerful friends. . 824 *Excursion* 5. 113
Companions have I many; many friends, . . 834 *Excursion* 5. 812
Of friends or kindred, whom the angry sea . 836 *Excursion* 5. 933
By mastery:—and the good Man lacked not friends 840 *Excursion* 6. 164
Of this far-winding vale, remained as friends . . 844 *Excursion* 6. 409
Abandoning and all his showy friends, . . . 859 *Excursion* 7. 132
Of long-past banquetings with high-born friends: 860 *Excursion* 7. 218
Of friends and kindred bore him from his home . 864 *Excursion* 7. 466
The sober sympathies of long-tried friend . . 875 *Excursion* 8. 76
The snow-tracks of my friends I see, ... K.8. 219 **The snow-tracks* 1
They [?] to the last my friends did cherish . . K.8 219 **The snow-tracks* 5
My friends, you live, and yet you seem . . . K.8. 220 **The snow-tracks* 19
And yet, my friends, you live and move. . . . K.8. 220 **The snow-tracks* 22
Of my dear friends I see the trace. . . . . K.8. 220 **The snow-tracks* 32
You saw me, friends, you laid me here, . . . K.8. 220 **The snow-tracks* 33
And with my friends now far away . . . . K.8. 220 **The snow-tracks* 40
Shall we behold them, consecrated friends, . . K.8. 243 *Recluse* 1.1.261
Friends shall I have at dawn, blackbird and thrush K.8. 250 *Recluse* 1.1.515
Thy kindred and thy friends such travail borne. . L.2. 318 *Frag. Æneid* 4. 5

Friends'. Your own grief and your friends'—your wandering course; . . . . 625 *Æneid* 141

Friendship. Nay, you abuse my friendship! Heaven forbid!— . . . . 42 *Bord.* 271
In friendship she to me would often tell. . . . 120 *Emigrant Mother* 4
In ours, the Vale of Friendship, let *this* spot . 272 *Lady E. B.* 10
In friendship—strive—for his sake go— . . . 408 *White Doe* 1084
In friendship; rival hunters they, ... 409 *White Doe* 1203
That friendship lasts though fellowship is broken! 531 **I know* 32
Might any common friendship shame, ... 544 *Russ. Fug.* 219
What is friendship?—do not trust her, . . . 549 *Hermit's Cell* 1. 13
For all that friendship, all that love can do, . . 749 *Prelude* 14. 221
One whom with thee friendship had early paired; 750 *Prelude* 14. 267
Friendship betrayed, affection unreturned, . . 791 *Excursion* 3. 377
His natural wings!—To friendship let him turn . 817 *Excursion* 4. 1085

Friendship's. Self-hidden praise, and Friendship's private tear: . . . . 547 **Ye Lime* 12
Is Friendship's emblem, whether the forlorn . . 627 **The star* 3
With virtuous friendship's soul-sustaining aid, . 823 *Excursion* 5. 58

Friendships. Friendships that will not break, and love that cannot roam. . . . . 102 *Artegal* 24
And make dear friendships with the streams and groves. . . . . 147 *Joanna* 8
Friendships, acquaintances, were welcome all. . 652 *Prelude* 3. 247

Frieze. But ye, bright Flowers, on frieze and architrave . . . . 474 **Hope smiled* 7

Frighted. From Bruno's forest screams the frighted jay, ... 603 *Desc. Sk. Quarto* 68

Frighten. A noise at midnight does *so* frighten me. 71 *Bord.* 1890

Frightful. —In deep despair, by frightful wishes stirred, ... 31 *Guilt* 381
Within that black and frightful rent. . . . . 85 *Shepherd-boys* 66
Oh! it was a frightful current . . . . . . 93 *Westmoreland Girl* 17
He gives a loud and frightful shriek, ... 242 *P. B.* 529
Drawn almost into frightful neighbourhood. . . 306 **Inland, within* 4
Drove from itself, we trust, all frightful gloom. . 391 *Brownie* 14
Stript of its frightful powers by slow decay, . . 523 *Epist. Beaumont* 126
Were frightful to behold, but had you then . . K.8. 230 **I will* 182
From frightful storms into a quiet road. . . . K.8. 266 **Rid of* 4

Fringe. Will fringe the lettered stone; and herbs spring forth, ... 584 **With copious* 57

Fringed. And bays with myrtle fringed, the southern breeze . . . . 17 *Desc. Sk.* 367
Thy temples fringed with locks of gleaming white, 274 **Such age* 7
Of yon wild cave, whose jaggèd brows are fringed 497 **Enough of climbing* 21
With birch-trees fringed; my hand shall guide the helm, ... 891 *Excursion* 9. 496
Of the fair Isle with birch-trees fringed—and there, 892 *Excursion* 9. 528

Fringes. Where the road it fringes, sweet, . . . 181 *Waggoner* 4. 160

Frisking. Frisking, bleating merriment, ... 171 *Kitten* 77

Frith. The frith that glittered like a warrior's shield, 105 *Artegal* 198

Frivolous. And a most frivolous people. Him I mean . . . . 816 *Excursion* 4. 1005

Fro. Of horsemen-shadows moving to and fro; . 6 *Ev. Wk.* 201
The face of traveller passing to and fro,) . . . 15 *Desc. Sk.* 239

Fro—*continued.*
Walks to and fro—watchings at every hour; . . 122 *V. and J.* 80
Driven by the autumnal whirlwind to and fro . 123 *V. and J.* 140
A length of open space, where to and fro . . . 150 **When, to* 37
Moved to and fro, for his delight. . . . . . 205 *Brougham* 127
Like Auster whirling to and fro, ... 213 *Dion* 71
Hundreds of curves and circlets, to and fro, . . 218 *Recluse* 1. 1. 213
Ever waving to and fro, ... 235 *Power of Sound* 189
Shoot to and fro through heart and reins, . . 244 *P. B.* 734
He faltered, drifted to and fro, ... 285 *Nith* 5
Begin to follow to and fro . . . . . . 294 *Jedbor.* 55
The pageant glancing to and fro; . . . . . 404 *White Doe* 779
Upon the height walks to and fro; . . . . 409 *White Doe* 1189
On the great waters toiling to and fro, . . . 459 **Wanderer! that* 32
And now precede thee, winding to and fro, . . 496 **A little* 24
Glance to and fro, like aery Sprites . . . . 499 **This Lawn* 11
Of that same Bard—repeated to and fro . . . 549 **The massy* 7
This little Child, as he came to and fro, . . . 554 *Prioress* 101
And up and down there went, and to and fro, . 564 *Troilus* 87
Whose state, like pine-trees, waving to and fro, . 594 *Ev. Wk. Quarto* 135
Of horsemen shadows winding to and fro; . . 595 *Ev. Wk. Quarto* 184
Had watched her with fixed eyes while to and fro 659 *Prelude* 4. 90
There, to and fro, she paced through many a day . 769 *Excursion* 1. 884
Which to and fro the mariner is used . . . . 805 *Excursion* 4. 247
In set rotation passing to and fro, ... 812 *Excursion* 4. 710
Pace to and fro, from morn till eventide, . . . 831 *Excursion* 5. 599
Of never-varying motion, to and fro. . . . . 833 *Excursion* 5. 747
That, through her inland regions, to and fro . . 876 *Excursion* 8. 140
On rural business passing to and fro . . . . 881 *Excursion* 8. 449
Rides to and fro: I know them and their ways. . K.8. 250 *Recluse* 1.1.509

Frock. there are stains in that frock . . . . . 71 *Bord.* 1904
Exchange the shepherd's frock of native grey . 846 *Excursion* 6. 548
Beneath a cumbrous frock, that to the knees . . 880 *Excursion* 8. 403

Frog. A frog leaps out from bordering grass, . . 142 †*Lov. and Lik.* 17

Frolic. To frolic on the breeze. . . . . . . 170 *Rural Ill.* 12
And implements of frolic mirth; . . . . . 191 *Seq. Beggars* 4
She who incites the frolic lambs . . . . . 217 *Enterprise* 138
Nor interrupts her frolic graces . . . . . . 222 *Triad* 151
On the soft west-wind and his frolic peers; . . 264 *Snowdrop* 11
The kitten frolic, like a gamesome sprite, . . . 294 **Fly, some* 6
Heroes before your time, in frolic fancy bold! . 339 *Tell* 9
The frolic Loves, who, from yon high rock, see . 378 *Duddon* 10. 13
And Lamb, the frolic and the gentle, ... 586 *Hogg* 19
They try all frolic motions; flutter, plunge, . . K.8. 251 *Recluse* 1.1.550

Frolicked. Frolicked industriously, a simple Clerk 859 *Excursion* 7. 129

Frolics. Poor Matthew, all his frolics o'er, . . . 486 *Matthew* 17

From, *omitted.*

Front. The deepest cleft the mountain's front displays . . . . 8 *Ev. Wk.* 357
The pastoral mountains front you, face to face. . 131 *Michael* 5
And, when we came in front of that tall rock . 147 *Joanna* 42
A Rock there is whose homely front . . . . 224 *Primrose* 1
High as the imperial front of man; . . . . 227 *Vernal Ode* 118
His double front among Atlantic clouds, . . . 251 **Pelion and* 13
And the fair front of many a happy Home; . . 268 **Four fiery* 10
Yes, I will forth, bold Bird! and front the blast, 279 **Hark! 'tis* 9
Is fondly lingering on thy shattered front, . . 290 *Kilchurn* 24
One loud cascade in front, and lo! . . . . . 300 *Bran* 15
The shattered front of Newark's Towers, . . . 302 *Yarrow V.* 55
Fixed on the front of Eastern diadems, . . . 331 *Ode: Thanks.* 167
A type of age in man, upon its front . . . . 355 *Aquap.* 187
Now, while his bright-haired front he bowed, . . 373 *Eg. Maid* 307
And fishes front, unmoved, the torrent's sweep,— 390 *Glencroe* 12
Its perilous front in mists and clouds? . . . 413 *White Doe* 1563
Or smooth his front, our world is in his hand! . 428 *Ecc. Sonn.* 1. 39. 14
Weeds on whose front the world had fixed her sign. 428 *Ecc. Sonn.* 2. 1. 8
Battering the Temple's front, its long-drawn nave 474 **Hope smiled* 5
A lofty precipice in front, ... 491 *Fidelity* 19
The front in self-defence. . . . . 496 *Lycoris* 4
Lifting her front with modest grace . . . . 533 **Blest is* 23
Turn a broad front full on his flattering beams: . 539 **Lady! a* 17
The front with such nice care . . . . . . 543 *Russ. Fug.* 138
The heaven-regarding eye and front sublime . . 567 *Cumb. Beg.* 81
Glorious as e'er I had beheld—in front, . . . 663 *Prelude* 4. 325
But on the front of his reproof confessed . . . 666 *Prelude* 5. 54
Of that magnificent region. On the front . . 686 *Prelude* 6. 739
Presumptuous cloud, on whose black front was written . . . . 718 *Prelude* 10. 13
His front against the blast, and runs amain, . . 723 *Prelude* 10. 373
Extends his careless limbs along the front . . 756 *Excursion* 1. 10
By rude hands built, with rocky knolls in front, . 833 *Excursion* 5. 694
On the green turf, with his imperial front . . . 890 *Excursion* 9. 443

Fronted. As the wain fronted her,—wherein lay one, 34 *Guilt* 544
That, fronted with a most imposing word, . . 690 *Prelude* 7. 197
Of glory, fronted multitudes in arms. . . . . K.8. 256 *Recluse* 1.1.720

Frontier. To meet the war upon her frontier bounds. 713 *Prelude* 9. 266

Fronting. And, fronting the bright west, yon oak entwines . . . . 6 *Ev. Wk.* 214
And, fronting the bright west in stronger lines, . 595 *Ev. Wk. Quarto* 193
Fronting our cottage. Oft beside the hearth . . 705 *Prelude* 8. 410
Fronting the window of that little cell, . . . 782 *Excursion* 2. 690
Fronting the noontide sun. We paused to admire 881 *Excursion* 8. 464

Frontlet. And wears a frontlet edged with gold. . 399 *White Doe* 260

Fronts. It fronts all quarters, and looks round . . 409 *White Doe* 1169
Here, fronts of houses, like a title-page, . . . 689 *Prelude* 7. 160
With battlements that on their restless fronts . 784 *Excursion* 2. 844
Or posy, girding round the several fronts . . . 872 *Excursion* 7. 973

Frost. *See* **Hoar-frost.**
The Frost hath wrought both night and day, . . 156 *Oak and Broom* 23
And when the Frost is in the sky, ... 156 *Oak and Broom* 77
Or nipping frost remind thee trees are bare, . . 229 *Cuckoo-clock* 13

Frost—*continued.*
Or as the weakest things, if frost . . . . . 246 *P. B.* 848
'Mid frost and snow, the instinctive joys of song, 263 **While not* 13
Of Pharaoh, said to Famine, Snow, and Frost, . 322 **By Moscow* 13
Indúrated by frost. . . . . 343 *Eclipse* 42
Thy handmaid Frost with spangled tissue quaint 376 *Duddon* 2. 5
From wind, or frost, or vapours wet— . . . 409 *White Doe* 1176
Are glued to his sides by the frost. . . . . . 484 **A plague* 25
Thinly by a one night's frost ; . . . . . 490 *Incident : Dog* 18
" The frost of England's pride will soon be thawed ; 513 **Said Secrecy* 4
Now, when the frost was past enduring, . . . 537 *Goody Blake* 57
And there, at night, in frost and snow, . . . 537 *Goody Blake* 71
And crisp with frost the stubble land. . . . 537 *Goody Blake* 76
But frost had reared the gorgeous Pile . . . 550 *Hermit's Cell* 2. 21
Like frost he thought his heart was icy cold ; . 563 *Troilus* 17
Heavy as frost, and deep almost as life ! . . . 589 *Immortality* 132
In breaking up a long-continued frost, . . . 632 *Prelude* 1. 40
Frost, and the breath of frosty wind, had snapped 636 *Prelude* 1. 308
Incessant rain was falling, or the frost . . . . 640 *Prelude* 1. 536
Powdered like rimy trees, when frost is keen. . 649 *Prelude* 3. 39
At the first nipping of October frost, ... 770 *Excursion* 1. 902
Until her house by frost, and thaw, and rain, . 770 *Excursion* 1. 906
Impends ; the frost will gather round my heart ; 802 *Excursion* 4. 55
Nor the vicissitudes of frost and thaw . . . 842 *Excursion* 6. 251
By seasonable frost of age ; nor died . . . . 842 *Excursion* 6. 276
Frost-built. —Of cloudless suns no more ye frost-built spires . . . . 609 *Desc.Sk.Quarto* 390
Frosting. Frosting with hoary light the pearly ground, ... 599 *Ev. Wk. Quarto* 393
Frost-like. Hoar with the frost-like dews of dawn ; 180 *Waggoner* 4. 39
Frost's. He called on Frost's inexorable tooth . . 321 **Humanity, delighting* 21
Frosts. While with a hoary light she frosts the ground, ... 8 *Ev. Wk.* 327
Where the frosts of winter lie. . . . . . . 90 *Longest Day* 32
Where unremitting frosts the rocky crescent bleach. 335 *Aix* 14
Frosty. Through the calm and frosty air . . . 170 *Kitten* 7
Or frosty air is keen and still, ... 198 *Thorn* 74
Or frosty air is keen and still, ... 198 *Thorn* 85
Insight as keen as frosty star . . . . . 222 *Triad* 149
Nor less, the stillness of these frosty plains, . . 329 *Ode : Thanks.* 20
The longest date do melt like frosty rime, . . 449 *Ecc. Sonn.* 3. 34. 8
In frosty moonlight glistening ; . . . . . 499 *Memory* 26
Struggle with frosty air and winter snows ; . . 568 *Cumb. Beg.* 174
The frosty wind, as if to make amends . . . 622 *Recluse* 1. 1. 158
Frost, and the breath of frosty wind, had snapped 636 *Prelude* 1. 308
And in the frosty season, when the sun . . 638 *Prelude* 1. 425
Beneath a frosty moon. The hemisphere . . . 676 *Prelude* 6. 87
To the Twelfth Night, beneath the frosty stars . 851 *Excursion* 6. 837
That gave them nourishment. When frosty winds 881 *Excursion* 8. 445
Froward. To control the froward impulse . . . 94 *Westmoreland Girl* 75
Her froward mood, and softliest reprehend ; . . 255 **Grief, thou* 4
O froward Fancy ! 'mid a scene . . . . . 299 *Brownie's Cell* 75
Not froward to thy sovereign will . . . . . 372 *Eg. Maid* 243
Far different we—a froward race, ... 490 *Night Thought* 7
An old resource to cheat a froward time ! . . . 521 *Epist.Beaumont* 35
The froward chaos of futurity, ... 671 *Prelude* 5. 349
Some—say at once a froward multitude— . . 695 *Prelude* 7. 531
" If, with the froward will and grovelling soul . 806 *Excursion* 4. 375
Frowardness. To which her frowardness must needs submit. . . . . 862 *Excursion* 7. 322
Frown. Whither is fled that Power whose frown severe . . . . 11 *Desc. Sk.* 54
Yet not for this will sober reason frown . . . 22 *Desc. Sk.* 648
Sometimes frowns, or seems to frown ; . . . 90 *Longest Day* 66
Though some may frown and make a stir, . . 144 **Driven in* 71
Saints would not grieve nor guardian angels frown 354 *Aquap.* 118
That Rome provides, less dreading from her frown 420 *Ecc. Sonn.* 1. 8. 10
And awes like night with mercy-tempered frown. 425 *Ecc. Sonn.* 1. 26. 8
Of giant yews that frown on Rydale's mere ; . . 591 *Ev. Wk. Quarto* 8
Where now is fled that Power whose frown severe 603 *Desc. Sk. Quarto* 55
When Folly from the frown of fleeting Time . . 663 *Prelude* 4. 348
Frowned. Jove frowned in heaven : the conscious Parcæ threw . . . . 210 *Laod.* 65
Scorn not the Sonnet ; Critic, you have frowned, 260 **Scorn not* 1
Frowning. Dear is the forest frowning o'er his head, 11 *Desc. Sk.* 21
Frowns. Sometimes frowns, or seems to frown ; . 90 *Longest Day* 66
Frowns are on every Muse's face, ... 163 *Needlecase* 1
Of rock that frowns, and stream that roars, . . 300 *Bran* 38
O still beloved, once worshipped ! Time, that frowns 460 **Queen of* 21
Safe from the feudal Castle's haughty frowns ; . 468 *St. Bees* 128
Frowns deepening visibly his native gloom, . . 521 *Epist. Beaumont* 6
Froze. At matins froze, and couched at curfew-time, 655 *Prelude* 3. 455
Frozen. *See* **Long-frozen.**
Their frozen arms her neck no more can fold ; . 7 *Ev. Wk.* 272
Nor Winter yet his frozen stores had piled, . . 17 *Desc. Sk.* 392
Conflict must cease, and, in thy frozen heart, . 76 *Bord.* 2215
How motionless !—not frozen seas . . . . . 106 **I've watched* 5
What if through the frozen centre . . . . . 166 *Wand. Jew* 9
Go with thee to the frozen zone ; . . . . . 233 *Power of Sound* 26
Frozen by distance ; so, majestic Pile, . . . 290 *Kilchurn* 38
Of Andes—frozen gulfs became its bridge— . . 327 *Ode 1815* 22
Was frozen at its marvellous source ; . . . . 586 *Hogg* 16
There hang in fear, when growls the frozen stream, 607 *Desc.Sk.Quarto* 315
Strewn on the frozen snow. And when the spring 702 *Prelude* 8. 229
" Calm as a frozen lake when ruthless winds . . 795 *Excursion* 3. 650
To the bare rock, on frozen Caucasus ; . . . 846 *Excursion* 6. 540
Frugal. Intense, and frugal, apt for all affairs, . 131 *Michael* 45
By exhortation of my frugal Dame— . . . 185 *Nutting* 11
That I, if frugal and severe, might stray . . . 259 *Calvert* 6

Frugal—*continued.*
Our daily meals were frugal, Sabine fare ! . . 643 *Prelude* 2. 78
Frugal as there was need, and, though self-willed, 688 *Prelude* 7. 64
Frugal, affectionate, sober, and withal . . . 764 *Excursion* 1. 522
And on a frugal plan without more words. . . L.1. 95 *Juvenal* 3. 24
Fruit. *See* **First-fruit, Forest-fruit.**
Daisies leave no fruit behind . . . . . . 80 *Foresight* 21
But when the fruit, so often praised . . . . 142 †*Lov. and Lik.* 35
Its blossoms shrivelled, and its fruit, if formed, . 266 **DespondingFather* 4
Has sown as yields, we trust, the fruit of fame . 278 *Wellington* 12
Or strip the bough whose mellow fruit bestrews . 335 *Namur* 8
No breach of promise in the fruit ? . . . . 344 **How blest* 60
Those seeds of expectation which the fruit . . 354 *Aquap.* 104
Of orange-trees bedecked with glowing fruit . . 361 **List—'twas* 18
Than a soft record, that, whatever fruit . . . 378 *Duddon* 8. 11
The target mouldering like ungathered fruit ; . 388 **The pibroch's* 4
A timely promise of unlooked-for fruit, . . . 395 *White Doe: Ded.* 30
Fair fruit of pleasure and serene content . . . 395 *White Doe: Ded.* 31
That the firm soul is clothed with fruit divine ! . 423 *Ecc. Sonn.* 1. 19. 5
Can never cease to bear celestial fruit. . . . 431 *Ecc. Sonn.* 2. 10. 5
The gadding bramble hang her purple fruit ; . . 433 *Ecc. Sonn.* 2. 21. 6
Whose fruit around the sun-burnt Native falls . 444 *Ecc. Sonn.* 3. 17. 7
Yield timely fruit of peace and love and joy. . . 447 *Ecc. Sonn.* 3. 29. 14
The season) sprinklings of ripe strawberry fruit. . 529 *Poor Robin* 14
Is come to bitter fruit ; . . . . 542 *Russ. Fug.* 66
O'er ripe fruit, seasonably gathered, ... 586 *Hogg* 35
With invitations, suppers, wine and fruit, . . 649 *Prelude* 3. 43
To every natural form, rock, fruit, or flower, . . 651 *Prelude* 3. 127
Ate, drank, and with the fruit and glasses played, 692 *Prelude* 7. 362
Stripped as I am of all the golden fruit . . . 793 *Excursion* 3. 488
Rashly, to fall once more ; and that false fruit, . 805 *Excursion* 4. 290
When wisdom shows her seasonable fruit, . . 816 *Excursion* 4. 1041
And mellow Autumn, charged with bounteous fruit, 828 *Excursion* 5. 400
Of fruit or flower, permission asked or not, . . 856 *Excursion* 6. 1166
Fruitage. Where bud, and bloom, and fruitage, glowed, ... 299 *Brownie's Cell* 97
And fruitage gathered from the chestnut-wood, . 431 *Ecc. Sonn.* 2. 12. 10
And goodly fruitage with the mother-spray ; . . 435 *Ecc. Sonn.* 2. 28. 3
To greet the flowers and fruitage of a land, . . 501 *Humanity* 71
On fruitage gathered from the tree of life ; . . 820 *Excursion* 4. 1291
Fruitful. Or as a fruitful palm-tree towering high . 383 *Duddon* 31. 5
And may it prove a fruitful meeting ! . . . . 414 *White Doe* 1668
'Mid fruitful fields that ring with jocund toil, . 463 **Why should the* 5
The theme is fruitful ; nor can sorrow find . . L.1. 97 *Juvenal* 3. 79
Fruitfulness. If child-like fruitfulness in passing joy, 651 *Prelude* 3. 147
Fruitions. Vernal fruitions and desires . . . . 507 *May* 61
Fruit-laden. Let not flowers, or boughs fruit-laden, 90 *Longest Day* 43
Fruitless. " Yet you make all courage fruitless, . 140 *Arm. Lady* 39
Vows have I made by fruitless hope inspired ; . 209 *Laod.* 2
Dwell fruitless day-dreams, lawless prayer, . . 223 *Wishing-gate* 8
Him hath he sought with fruitless pains, . . . 243 *P. B.* 642
But 'tis a fruitless task to paint for me, . . . 279 **All praise* 2
Would keep, perhaps with many a fruitless tear, . 310 *Invasion* 11
And sorrow that to fruitless sorrow clung ! . . 326 **Emperors and* 6
Such fruitless questions may not long beguile . 380 *Duddon* 16. 1
And sorrow of his fruitless prayer. . . . . 401 *White Doe* 440
With fruitless effort to allay . . . . . . 406 *White Doe* 931
And fruitless wishes eat the heart away, . . . 458 *Sea-shore* 4
'Twill be no fruitless moment. I was born . . 573 *Chiabrera* 3. 3
Pay fruitless worship to humanity, ... 722 *Prelude* 10. 259
And fruitless indignation ; galled by pride ; . . 776 *Excursion* 2. 299
Fruitless as those of aery alchemists, ... 832 *Excursion* 5. 633
In Britain's senate. Fruitless was the attempt : . 845 *Excursion* 6. 448
Industrious to destroy ! With fruitless pains . 875 *Excursion* 8. 95
Fruitlessly. Unfolding, did not fruitlessly exhort . 254 *Complete Angler* 4
Due homage ; nor shall fruitlessly have striven, . 358 *Aquap.* 362
Full early lost, and fruitlessly deplored ; . . . 458 **Had this* 74
Inviting penance, fruitlessly endured : . . . 798 *Excursion* 3. 876
—This sacred right is fruitlessly announced, . . 889 *Excursion* 9. 321
Fruits. Would there perhaps have gathered the first fruits . . . . 49 *Bord.* 663
Yet we mark it not ;—fruits redden, ... 90 *Longest Day* 37
Which at this season, with their unripe fruits, . 206 *Tintern* 12
He looks on festal ground with fruits bestrown ; . 213 *Dion* 36
The wild-wood fruits to gather, ... 302 *Yarrow V.* 66
And earth with all her pleasant fruits and flowers 308 **There is a bondage* 13
Sing ye, with blossoms crowned, and fruits, and flowers, ... 322 **Ye Storms* 6
Wherever fruits are gathered, and where'er . . 327 *Ode 1815* 30
And ripening fruits and forest leaves . . . . 502 *Seasons* 11
Of snow and hoar-frost, spreads her fruits and her flowers, ... 570 *Farmer* 74
For permanent possession, better fruits, . . . 656 *Prelude* 3. 529
May try this modern system by its fruits, . . 670 *Prelude* 5. 295
Fruits of her father's orchard are her wares, . . 699 *Prelude* 8. 40
Culled the best fruits of Time's uncounted hours, 701 *Prelude* 8. 140
Our table, small parade of garden fruits, . . . 782 *Excursion* 2. 683
Spread true religion and her genuine fruits) . . 839 *Excursion* 6. 80
The fruits of earth though space of twice ten years, 841 *Excursion* 6. 231
Fruit-tree. Beneath these fruit-tree boughs that shed 159 *Green Linnet* 1
Frustrate. Fixed on the Suitor ; frustrate her request— . . . . 626 *Ballot* 10
And frustrate all the rest ! Believe it not : . . 887 *Excursion* 9. 237
Frustrated. Was the aim frustrated by force or guile, 269 *Malham* 1
Frustrates. It frustrates its own purpose, and recalls S.3. 434 **The doubt* 90
Fuel. That sadness finds its fuel. Hitherto, . . 666 *Prelude* 5. 11
For winter fuel—to his noontide meal . . . . 783 *Excursion* 2. 788
Fuentes. Fuentes once harboured the good and the brave, ... 340 *Fort Fuentes* 13

Fugitive. But small and fugitive our gain . . . 143 **Driven in* 30
The lovely Fugitive : . . . . 190 **Lyre! though* 5
In coolest climes too fugitive, might even here . 356 *Aquap.* 226
Frank are the sports, the stains are fugitive. . . 382 *Duddon* 23. 14
Dreams, vivid dreams, that are not fugitive ; . . 392 *Bothwell* 13
Whose aim is pleasure light and fugitive : . . 395 *White Doe: Ded.* 58
Their fugitive Progenitors explored . . . . 431 *Ecc. Sonn.* 2. 12. 5
Nor shorten the sweet life, too fugitive, . . . 501 *Humanity* 109
And wherefore fugitive or on what pretence ; . . 522 *Epist. Beaumont* 62
But hung upon the Fugitive, ... 542 *Russ. Fug.* 31
To the lorn Fugitive . . . . 545 *Russ. Fug.* 350
What was so fugitive ! . . . . 589 *Immortality* 136
Keen as a Truant or a Fugitive, ... 633 *Prelude* 1. 90
Erminia, fugitive as fair as she. . . . . . 716 *Prelude* 9. 453
So, like a fugitive, whose feet have cleared . . 798 *Excursion* 3. 877
A fugitive of fate. Long time was he . . . . K.8. 281 **Arms and* 3
Fugitives. Discovering traces of the fugitives, . . 122 *V. and J.* 77
Judge both Fugitives with knowledge : . . . 141 *Arm. Lady* 85
The fugitives than to the British strand, . . . 449 *Ecc. Sonn.* 3. 36. 7
Fulfil. Hath falsely trained—shall he fulfil his purpose ? . . . . 53 *Bord.* 899
Her wishes to fulfil. . . . . 168 *Wren's Nest* 40
Leave of our fate thy wishes to fulfil ; . . . . 251 *Appleth.* 11
For steadfast hope the contract to fulfil ; . . . 275 *Rotha Q.* 6
A chosen Tree ; then, eager to fulfil . . . . 276 *Oker Hill* 5
A Foe's most favourite purpose to fulfil : . . . 316 **Say, what* 12
And all the Nations labour to fulfil . . . . 329 *Ode 1815* 127
All martial duties to fulfil ; . . . . 330 *Ode : Thanks.* 76
Of the world's hopes, dare to fulfil ; awake, . . 366 **Fair Land* 13
So high, a rival purpose to fulfil ; . . . . . 377 *Duddon* 4. 12
Fulfil thy pensive duty, ... 386 *Yarrow Rev.* 106
O, that my mind were equal to fulfil . . . . 395 *White Doe: Ded.* 59
A Banner, fashioned to fulfil . . . . . . 400 *White Doe* 352
The chaste affections tremble to fulfil . . . . 425 *Ecc. Sonn.* 1. 28. 8
Resolute, at all hazards, to fulfil . . . . . 514 **Blest Statesman* 8
Months passed in love that failed not to fulfil, . . 531 **I know* 17
While truth and love their purposes fulfil, . . . 584 **With copious* 60
Of prophecy, accoutred to fulfil . . . . . S.3. 437 **The doubt* 192
Fulfilled. It was a spot where, ancient vows fulfilled, 27 *Guilt* 148
My Office is fulfilled—the Man is now . . . 66 *Bord.* 1586
That those dear words should be fulfilled, . . . 204 *Brougham* 81
And, if the word had been fulfilled, ... 292 *Rob Roy* 93
More than fulfilled, as gay Campania's shores . . 353 *Aquap.* 78
Behold the prophecy fulfilled, ... 415 *White Doe* 1783
Fulfilled, and she sustains her part ! . . . . 415 *White Doe* 1784
But all shall be fulfilled ;—the Julian spear . . 419 *Ecc. Sonn.* 1. 3. 10
That eye (which sees as if fulfilled and done . . 439 *Ecc. Sonn.* 2. 42. 6
Their wrongs, since they fulfilled their destiny ? . 474 **On to* 8
Advancing Summer, Nature's law fulfilled, . . . 523 *Epist. Beaumont* 154
And by Heaven's favour happily fulfilled ; . . . 526 **Soon did* 11
Drawn from the Sacrifice fulfilled, ... 533 **Blest is* 27
Go forth upon a mission best fulfilled . . . . 538 **In desultory* 20
(Now that their earthly duties were fulfilled) . . 551 **If thou in* 22
The wrath consummate and the threat fulfilled ; . 724 *Prelude* 10. 446
But speedily the promise was fulfilled ; . . . . 781 *Excursion* 2. 671
Of each domestic charity fulfilled, ... 847 *Excursion* 6. 629
Than the old hereditary wish fulfilled ; . . . . 888 *Excursion* 9. 277
Fulfilled, the hope accomplished ; and thy praise . 894 *Excursion* 9. 677
Which had been sighed for, ancient thought fulfilled . . . . K.8. 239 *Recluse* 1.1.107
And common, yet all worthy if fulfilled . . . K.8. 255 *Recluse* 1.1.670
Fulfilling. She, fulfilling her sire's office, . . . 94 *Westmoreland Girl* 65
Through foul and fair our task fulfilling ; . . . 179 *Waggoner* 3. 95
In peace fulfilling. . . . . 486 **Bright Flower* 24
Fulfilling (could enchantment have done more ?) . 700 *Prelude* 8. 83
My vow fulfilling, do I here present, ... 812 *Excursion* 4. 747
Fulfilment. Fulfilment ; but, we trust, her upward track . . . . 360 *Albano* 11
Fulfilment of a Father's prayer . . . . . 411 *White Doe* 1422
And, in fulfilment of God's mercy, lodged . . . 541 *Grace Darl.* 82
Fulfilment of his own request ;— . . . . . 577 **By playful* 12
Wait the fulfilment of their fear ; . . . . . 581 **Loud is* 14
Fulgent. Then issued Vesper from the fulgent west, 192 *Gipsies* 14
She cast away, and showed her fulgent head . . 265 **The Shepherd* 5
With the keen threatenings of that fulgent eye, . 271 *Henry : Portrait* 7
From childhood. On the fulgent spectacle, . . 725 *Prelude* 10. 526
Full. *See* **Brim-full.**
Full oft the father, when his sons have grown . 19 *Desc. Sk.* 512
He saw and passed a stately inn, full sure . 24 *Guilt* 11
Full long endured in hope of just reward, . . . 25 *Guilt* 50
In her full lap, he sees such sweet tears flow . . 25 *Guilt* 62
From her full eyes their watery load released. . 30 *Guilt* 310
Who at full speed swept by us where the wood . 50 *Bord.* 735
Rushing along in the full tide of play, ... 61 *Bord.* 1332
Our quiet home all full in view, ... 85 *Anecdote* 6
Far happier lot, dear Boy, than brings full many to this shrine ; . . . . 92 *Poet's Dream* 54
Another grave,—near which a full half-hour . . 96 *Brothers* 85
Full soon this generous purpose thou may'st rue, 104 *Artegal* 168
Until king Elidure, with full consent . . . . 105 *Artegal* 219
I've watched you now a full half-hour, ... 106 **I've watched* 1
Full many a time, upon a stormy night, . . . 107 *Indolence* 13
Oft could we see him driving full in view . . . 107 *Indolence* 15
Full oft our human foresight I deplore ; . . . 112 **O dearer* 2
My very moments are too full . . . . . . 113 *Lament* 13
A healthy man, a man full grown, ... 114 *Last of Flock* 3
Of sheep I numbered a full score, ... 115 *Last of Flock* 29
Full fifty comely sheep I raised, ... 115 *Last of Flock* 33
When full of play and childish cares, ... 117 *Affl. Marg.* 23

Full—*continued.*
And tottering spirit. And full oft the Boy, . . 118 *Maternal Grief* 49
To their full hearts the universe seemed hung . 123 *V. and J.* 100
Stirred nowhere without weapons, that full soon . 123 *V. and J.* 124
Full speedily resounded, public hope, ... 126 *V. and J.* 303
His heart it was so full of glee . . . . . . 127 *Idiot Boy* 82
That, till full fifty yards were gone, ... 127 *Idiot Boy* 83
And thence full many a sound she hears, . . . 127 *Idiot Boy* 140
And now all full in view she sees . . . . . 130 *Idiot Boy* 365
Though younger than himself full twenty years. . 132 *Michael* 80
But soon as Luke, full ten years old, could stand . 134 *Michael* 194
To-morrow thou wilt leave me : with full heart . 136 *Michael* 332
Wrote loving letters, full of wondrous news, . . 138 *Michael* 433
The length of full seven years, from time to time, 138 *Michael* 470
Life, which to every one that breathes is full of care." . . . . 140 *Arm. Lady* 18
They lead you on to full content, ... 143 †*Lov. and Lik.* 61
Full many a sad and doleful thing : . . . . . 144 *Her Eyes* 14
Of me and of the storm. Full many an hour . . 150 **When, to* 32
Full oft is pleased a wayward dart to throw ; . . 153 *Morn. Ex.* 2
As full of gladness and as free of heaven, . . . 160 **Up with me* 29
In such a heedless peace. Alas ! full soon . . 173 *Infant Daughter* 60
Full proof of this the Country gained ; . . . . 175 *Waggoner* 1. 120
Full often make you stretch and strain, . . . 175 *Waggoner* 1. 142
And near that lurid light, full well . . . . . 175 *Waggoner* 1. 170
And you shall see her in full trim : . . . . 178 *Waggoner* 2. 120
Wheeled her back in full apparel ; . . . . . 178 *Waggoner* 2. 161
Following after in full sail ! . . . . . . 181 *Waggoner* 4. 166
Full soon that better mind was gone : . . . . 194 *Ruth* 181
" Full twenty years are past and gone . . . . 198 *Thorn* 104
" They say, full six months after this, . . . 199 *Thorn* 122
A wind full ten times over. . . . . 199 *Thorn* 180
And, for full fifty yards around, ... 200 *Thorn* 227
And this I know, full many a time, ... 200 *Thorn* 236
Is full of blessings. Therefore let the moon . . 207 *Tintern* 134
Of warblers in full concert strong . . . . . 221 *Triad* 81
Full surely, when with such proud gifts of life . 231 **ThegentlestPoet* 24
A stream as if from one full heart. . . . . 233 *Power of Sound* 48
Great Jove is full of stately bowers ; . . . . 237 *P. B.* 47
Full nine of them or more ! . . . . 238 *P. B.* 180
Full twenty times was Peter feared . . . . 238 *P. B.* 204
When the full moon was shining bright . . . 240 *P. B.* 324
Full suddenly the Ass doth rise ! . . . . . 242 *P. B.* 560
Though he has been, full thirty years, . . . 243 *P. B.* 614
It brought full many a sin to light . . . . 245 *P. B.* 759
Beneath the full moon shining bright, ... 247 *P. B.* 1012
Of his full bosom, gladsome Piety ! . . . . 254 *Complete Angler* 14
But some (who brook those hackneyed themes full well, ... 255 *Detraction* 5
An old place, full of many a lovely brood, . . 260 **How sweet* 3
The broad full visage, chest of amplest mould, . 270 *Henry : Portrait* 3
Full soon the Aspirant of the plough, ... 285 *Grave of Burns* 27
That, rough or smooth, is full of change, . . . 295 *Highland Boy* 54
Full sure they were a happy band, ... 297 *Highland Boy* 222
Roused though it be full often to a mood . . . 307 **It is not* 5
O'erweening Statesmen have full long relied . . 320 **O'erweeningStatesmen* 1
And sage Mnemosyne,—full long debarred . . 325 *Ode 1814* 112
Stern GEMMI listens to as full a cry, ... 346 *Gemmi* 2
Walk in the light of day, pertain full surely . . 357 *Aquap.* 324
Full oft, our wish obtained, deeply we sigh ; . . 358 **Is this* 9
And ye—full often spurned as weeds— . . . 366 **Ye Trees* 12
Chant in full choir their innocent Te Deum. . . 367 **If with* 14
To a full orb, this Pinnace bright . . . . . 369 *Eg. Maid* 10
Full thrice had crossed himself in meek composure. 373 *Eg. Maid* 276
Though public care full often tills . . . . . 375 **The Minstrels* 22
Anguish, and death : full oft where innocent blood 392 *Avon* 10
Of the world's flatteries if the brain be full, . . 394 **How profitless* 5
What would they there ?—full fifty years . . . 396 *White Doe* 17
Turn towards the spot where, full in view, . . 398 *White Doe* 167
Full cheerily on convent-bread . . . . . . 398 *White Doe* 219
Rode full of years to Flodden-field, ... 399 *White Doe* 284
Harp ! we have been full long beguiled . . . 399 *White Doe* 324
Full soon to be uplifted high, ... 400 *White Doe* 358
Full sixteen thousand fair to see ; " . . . . 404 *White Doe* 717
And where full many a brave tree stood, . . . 413 *White Doe* 1587
Hath stopped, and fixed her large full eye . . 414 *White Doe* 1644
Full oft the unworthy brow of lawless force ; . . 418 *Ecc. Sonn.* 1. 1. 12
The Council closed, the Priest in full career . . 422 *Ecc. Sonn.* 1. 17. 2
And if full oft the Sanctuary save . . . . . 424 *Ecc. Sonn.* 1. 24. 13
Doubtless shall cheat full oft the heart's desires ; 429 *Ecc. Sonn.* 2. 3. 9
Like ships before whose keels, full long embayed . 434 *Ecc. Sonn.* 2. 23. 4
Which thou prepar'st, full often, to convey . . 440 *Ecc. Sonn.* 2. 45. 11
And soon, full soon, the lonely Sexton's spade . 450 *Ecc. Sonn.* 3. 41. 8
With a full heart ; " our thoughts are *heard* in heaven ! " . . . . 454 *Sea-side* 39
When the East kindles with the full moon's light ; 455 *Rydal Mere* 23
Full early lost, and fruitlessly deplored ; . . . 458 **Had this* 74
Full early to the silent tomb . . . . . . 473 *Ossian* 46
Full happy season, when was known, ... 478 *Somnamb.* 25
She warbled from full heart ; . . . . . . 478 *Somnamb.* 60
And attention full ten times as much as there needs ; 482 *Character* 10
Full five-and-thirty years he lived . . . . . 483 *Simon Lee* 5
Here stretch thy body at full length ; . . . . 485 *Poet's Epitaph* 59
Full thirty years behind. . . . . 486 **We walked* 24
All are following at full speed, ... 490 *Incident : Dog* 22
In the full might they hitherto have shown, . . 518 *Pun. Death* 6. 12
Far higher, else full surely shalt thou err. . . . 519 *Pun. Death* 9. 4
When full five hundred boats in trim array, . . 522 *Epist. Beaumont* 71
And lilies face the March-winds in full blow, . . 529 *Poor Robin* 2
The moon was full and shining clearly, . . . 537 *Goody Blake* 75

Full—*continued.*
Till she had filled her apron full. . . . . . . 537 Goody Blake 84
Turn a broad front full on his flattering beams : . 539 *Lady ! a 17
The Czar full oft in words and deeds . . . . 545 Russ. Fug. 333
And of that famous Youth, full soon removed . 546 *The embowering 19
Full many a glimpse (but sparingly bestowed . 548 *Stay, bold 18
Full oft, when storms the welkin rend, . . . 550 Hermit's Cell 5. 10
Full merrily then would he sing and cry, . . . 554 Prioress 102
Then sped themselves to bury him full fast ; . . 555 Prioress 187
And he gave up the ghost full peacefully ; . . 556 Prioress 221
And some did sing all out with the full throat. . 558 Cuck. and Night. 75
Full little joy have I now of thy cry. . . . . 558 Cuck. and Night. 95
He may full soon go with an old man's hair. . . 560 Cuck.andNight.180
Within this court full seldom Truth avails, . . 560 Cuck.andNight.204
And he for dread did fly away full fast ; . . . 560 Cuck.andNight.219
And then did she begin this song full high, . . 561 Cuck.andNight.249
Then spake one Bird, and full assent all gave ; . 562 Cuck.andNight.271
For love of God, full piteously did say, . . . 562 Troilus 4
I yonder saw her eke full blissfully ; . . . . 563 Troilus 52
And to himself full oft he said, alas ! . . . . 564 Troilus 88
Full ten times a day takes his heart by surprise. . 570 Farmer 64
A Tuscan audience : but full soon was called . . 573 Chiabrera 2. 17
In odious litigation ; and full long, ... 574 Chiabrera 5. 3
And full of hope day followed day . . . . . 579 *Sweet Flower 15
Full soon in sorrow did I weep, ... 580 John Words. 31
Full soon thy Soul shall have her earthly freight, 589 Immortality 130
While burn in his full eyes the glorious tears. . 608 Desc.Sk.Quarto 351
And my full heart was swell'd to dear delicious pain. 619 *She wept 4
Though peaceful, full of gladness. Thou art pleased, 622 Recluse 1. 1. 117
But from this awful burthen I full soon . . . 635 Prelude 1. 234
Then passionately loved ; with heart how full . 647 Prelude 2. 334
That gave thee liberty, full long desired, . . . 648 Prelude 2. 462
My spirit was up, my thoughts were full of hope ; 649 Prelude 3. 18
Full oft the quiet and exalted thoughts . . . 652 Prelude 3. 207
Their smooth enthralment ;" but the heart was full, ... 659 Prelude 4. 63
Too full for that reproach. My aged Dame . . 659 Prelude 4. 64
My heart was full ; I made no vows, but vows . 663 Prelude 4. 334
Still in his grasp, before me, full in view, . . . 667 Prelude 5. 135
Full often, taking from the world of sleep . . 667 Prelude 5. 141
That drinks as if it never could be full. . . . 668 Prelude 5. 191
Full early trained to worship seemliness, . . . 670 Prelude 5. 298
In childhood, ere he was full twelve years old. . 671 Prelude 5. 390
Though doing wrong and suffering, and full oft . 672 Prelude 5. 417
And, though full oft the objects of our love . 674 Prelude 5. 569
At full command, to London first I turned, . . 688 Prelude 7. 61
Was more than full ; amid my sobs and tears . 694 Prelude 7. 471
Full of one passion, vengeance, rage, or fear ? . 697 Prelude 7. 673
Or spirit that full soon must take her flight. . . 705 Prelude 8. 450
Bare hills and valleys, full of caverns, rocks, . 708 Prelude 8. 635
Full speedily resounded, public hope, ... 718 Prelude 9. 582
After the lapse of full eight years, those words, . 726 Prelude 10. 541
The budding rose above the rose full blown. . . 729 Prelude 11. 121
Full measure of content ; but still I craved . . 741 Prelude 13. 110
In balmy spring-time full of rising flowers . . 748 Prelude 14. 171
Of female softness shall his life be full, . . . 749 Prelude 14. 229
And Hope full oft fallacious as a dream : . . . 753 *Oft, through 11
Full often wished he that the winds might rage . 760 Excursion 1. 287
Untunes full oft the pleasures of the day ; . . 773 Excursion 2. 149
How full their joy ! Till, pitiable doom ! . . 774 Excursion 2. 197
Upon a bed of heath ;—full many a spot . . . 776 Excursion 2. 351
For full in view, approaching through a gate . . 779 Excursion 2. 494
Full seventy winters hath he lived, and mark ! . 780 Excursion 2. 600
Our housewife knew full well what she possessed ! 783 Excursion 2. 763
Lying full three parts buried among tufts . . . 784 Excursion 2. 818
The mind is full—and free from pain their pastime." . . . . 789 Excursion 3. 193
Full on that tender-hearted Man he turned . . 793 Excursion 3. 478
Give birth, full often, to unguarded words ; . . 793 Excursion 3. 494
Use them, full oft, as pioneers to ruin, . . . 812 Excursion 4. 770
For fixed annoyance ; and full oft beset . . . 817 Excursion 4. 1055
Full well I recollect. We often crossed . . . 839 Excursion 6. 103
She bore a secret burthen ; and full soon . . . 851 Excursion 6. 851
That wears a look so full of peace and hope . . 855 Excursion 6. 1106
(Full eight years past) the solitary prop . . . 855 Excursion 6. 1121
Full oft his doings leave me to deplore . . . 866 Excursion 7. 595
Full blest he was, 'Another Margaret Green,' . 867 Excursion 7. 672
These, and the name and title at full length,— . 872 Excursion 7. 970
Full oft procured, yet may they claim respect, . 875 Excursion 8. 51
Then, in full many a region, once like this . . 876 Excursion 8. 165
And that full trim of inexperienced hope . . . 882 Excursion 8. 511
Was full ; and had, I doubted not, returned, . . 883 Excursion 8. 590
From the full river in the vale below, ... 885 Excursion 9. 68
And full assemblage of a barbarous host ; . . . 894 Excursion 9. 707
For, though in whispers speaking, the full heart . 895 Excursion 9. 751
With *yellow* in full blow. . . . . S.3. 431 *The Scottish 8
But soon as Luke, full ten years old, could stand K.8.226 *I will 74
And thickets full of songsters, and the voice . . K.8. 240 Recluse 1.1.129
Of full contentment, in a little shed . . . . K.8. 241 Recluse 1.1.176
Without desire in full complacency, ... K.8. 245 Recluse 1.1.306
Tearless, yet full of grief. —How heavenly fair . [?] *A sad 2

Full-assurèd. And full-assurèd trust, joy without measure, ... 559 Cuck.andNight.154

Full-blown. All about with full-blown flowers, . . 161 *Pleasures newly 21
With flourishing trumpet, came in full-blown state 693 Prelude 7. 417
Not one of all the band, a full-blown flower. . . 855 Excursion 6. 1130

Full-flowered. Full-flowered, and visible on every steep, ... 147 Joanna 39

Full-formed. Full-formed, like Venus rising from the sea ; . . . . 660 Prelude 4. 114
Full-formed, that take, with small internal help, . 697 Prelude 7. 653

Full-grown. A young lamb's heart among the full-grown flocks. . . . . 88 H. C. 24
But these are all the graves of full-grown men ! . 100 Brothers 341
" Ne'er in the breast of full-grown Poet . . . 237 P. B. 81
That from the shore a full-grown man might wade, 548 *Stranger ! this 9
Whereon a full-grown man might rest, nor dread 777 Excursion 2. 421

Full-orbed. The full-orbed Moon, slow-climbing, doth appear . . . . 426 Ecc. Sonn. 1. 29. 10
In the clear presence of the full-orbed Moon, . . 747 Prelude 14. 53

Full-swoln. And forced the full-swoln udder to demand, ... 17 Desc. Sk. 397

Fully. Till fully passed and gone was the ninth night ; . . . . 565 Troilus 163

Fulminations. Of truth) are met by fulminations new— . . . . 437 Ecc. Sonn. 2. 36. 11

Fulness. Peace to my parting soul, the fulness of content." . . . . 36 Guilt 630
I bless her in the fulness of my joy ! . . . . 62 Bord. 1376
In the whole fulness of its bloom, affords . . . 219 Haunted Tree 9
Chastening the fulness of a present bliss, . . . 456 Rydal Mere 41
Nor feel the fulness of that joy reproved ? . . 504 Warning 52
The fulness of your bliss, I feel—I feel it all. 588 Immortality 41
Have fulness in herself ; even so with me . . . 660 Prelude 4. 149
By Siddons trod in the fulness of her power. . . 693 Prelude 7. 406
Though somewhat past the fulness of his prime, . 829 Excursion 5. 459
Will cover him, in the fulness of his strength, . 841 Excursion 6. 197

Fumbles. Alas ! how he fumbles about the domains 484 *A plague 11

Fume. Yes, let my master fume and fret, . . . 174 Waggoner 1. 116
And fume the household deities with store . . 624 Æneid 65

Fumes. Never excited by the fumes of wine . . 653 Prelude 3. 301
That virtue, like the fumes and vapoury clouds . 863 Excursion 7. 379

Fuming. From all the fuming vanities of Earth ! . 349 Sky-prosp. 14

Fun. Amid their own delight and fun, ... 177 Waggoner 2. 94
Of one tired out with fun and madness ; . . . 486 Matthew 22
The Tinker lives in fun, ... S.3. 424 Tinker 47

Function. Each lighter function slumbering in the brain, ... 268 *Dogmatic Teachers 9
Thy function was to heal and to restore, . . . 378 Duddon 8. 13
The Form remains, the Function never dies ; . . 384 Duddon 34. 6
Thy function apostolical . . . . 486 *Bright Flower 23
But some their function have disclaimed, . . . 499 *Departing summer 28
With a congenial function art endued . . . . 510 *Among a 19
Locks every function up in blank reserve, . . . 635 Prelude 1. 246
And function, or, through strict vicissitude . . 740 Prelude 13. 38
The excellence, pure function, and best power . 745 Prelude 13. 377
One function, above all, of such a mind . . . 747 Prelude 14. 78
" His sacred function was at length renounced ; . 775 Excursion 2. 263
His rank and sacred function. This deep vale . 824 Excursion 5. 122
" A Priest he was by function ; but his course . 859 Excursion 7. 111
But a glad function natural to man. . . . . K.8. 249 Recluse 1.1.470

Functions. With all fine functions that afford delight— . . . . 227 Vernal Ode 108
Thy functions are ethereal, ... 232 Power of Sound 1
Her functions are they therefore less divine, . . 270 *Though the bold 9
Where all his unambitious functions fail. . . . 384 Duddon 33. 8
Who comes with functions apostolical ? . . . 422 Ecc. Sonn. 1. 15. 4
To humbler functions, awful Power ! . . . . 492 Duty 49
And functions dwell in beast and bird that sway . 500 Humanity 11
That, for the functions of an ancient State— . . 514 *Blest Statesman 11
From even the humblest functions of the State ; . 518 Pun. Death 5. 11
Had changed their functions ; some, plebeian cards 640 Prelude 1. 522
Forgot her functions, and slept undisturbed. . . 648 Prelude 2. 418
Instinct with vital functions, but a block . . 703 Prelude 8. 299
Hath dropped all functions by the gods bestowed, 732 Prelude 11. 368
The varied functions and high attributes . . . 798 Excursion 3. 824
And the weak functions of one busy day, . . . 805 Excursion 4. 284
The outward functions of intelligent man ; . . 826 Excursion 5. 268
And functions dying and produced at need,— . . 872 Excursion 7. 1003
Performs its functions ; rarely competent . . . 879 Excursion 8. 327
The god-like functions of the Soul. . . . . S.3. 439 *Avaunt this 6

Funds. We from our funds drew largely ;—proud to curb, ... 643 Prelude 2. 96

Funeral. For whom at morning tolled the funeral bell ; . . . . 15 Desc. Sk. 241
They cannot be remembered ? Scarce a funeral . 97 Brothers 125
Filled the funeral basin at Timothy's door ; . . 120 Childless Father 10
'Tis worse than any funeral bell ; . . . . . 179 Waggoner 3. 113
For thee a funeral bell shall ring, ... 195 Ruth 256
Her annual funeral. . . . . 224 Primrose 24
As at an innocent funeral. . . . . 401 White Doe 468
The funeral dirge ;—she sees the knot . . . . 413 White Doe 1544
For us who here in funeral strain . . . . . 578 *I come 49
A mourning or a funeral ; . . . . 589 Immortality 94
The land as with a funeral pall ? . . . . . 628 Installation 20
The cadence, as of psalms—a funeral dirge ! . . 777 Excursion 2. 376
Ye could not miss the funeral train—they yet . 779 Excursion 2. 535
The funeral train, the Shepherd and his Mate . 821 Excursion 4. 1308
She reached the house, last of the funeral train ; . 853 Excursion 6. 973
—Nor was his funeral denied the grace . . . 864 Excursion 7. 469
A soldier's honours. At his funeral hour . . 871 Excursion 7. 875

Funereal. Ditches are graves—funereal rites denied ; 427 Ecc. Sonn. 1. 36. 10
And sober posies of funereal flowers, ... 683 Prelude 6. 553

Fur. A regal vest of fur he wears, ... 166 Danish Boy 27
Dogmatic Teachers, of the snow-white fur ! . . 268 *Dogmatic Teachers 1

Furies. Which they behold, whom vengeful Furies haunt ; . . . . 213 Dion 86
The vengeful Furies. *Beautiful* regards . . . 798 Excursion 3. 852

Furious. While his horse pawed the floor with furious heat ; . . . . 27 Guilt 175

Futurity—*continued.*
Which in her breast Futurity concealed; . . . 346 *Processions* 3
As a loved substance, their futurity: . . . . 449 *Ecc. Sonn.* 3. 37. 10
With golden prospect for futurity, ... 463 **Why should the* 13
Alas! with most, who weigh futurity . . . . 516 **As leaves* 9
The froward chaos of futurity, ... 671 *Prelude* 5. 349
Prospect so large into futurity; . . . . . 729 *Prelude* 11. 167
Of dim futurity, to Man revealed. . . . . 812 *Excursion* 4. 706
The vapoury phantoms of futurity? . . . . 817 *Excursion* 4. 1057
Futurity was thought, in ancient times, . . . 865 *Excursion* 7. 532
And breathe the sweet air of futurity; . . . . 884 *Excursion* 9. 25
Transfer not to futurity a work . . . . . 890 *Excursion* 9. 406

Fy. *See* **Fie.**
That word was hasty. Fy! no more of it. . . 38 *Bord.* 29

G

Gabble. Tut! let them gabble till the day of doom. 55 *Bord.* 963
Gabriel's. For overhead are sweeping Gabriel's Hounds . . . . 267 **Though narrow* 12
Gadding. The gadding bramble hang her purple fruit; . . . . 433 *Ecc. Sonn.* 2. 21. 6
Gads. Now gads the wild vine o'er the pathless ascent:— . . . . 340 *Fort Fuentes* 17
Gaelic. In Gaelic, or the English tongue, . . . 297 *Highland Boy* 179
Gage. Thanks and praises, each a gage . . . . 141 *Arm. Lady* 124
Gaiety. In thoughtless gaiety I coursed the plain, . 2 *Ev. Wk.* 21
Sweeter even than gaiety? . . . . 171 *Kitten* 94
Laughter-loving gaiety, ... 222 *Triad* 167
In gaiety and ease. . . . . 225 *Present.* 30
To win the palm of gaiety and wit; . . . . 528 **Those breathing* 107
And Gaiety the charming office sought; . . . 620 *Birth of Love* 16
The night in dancing, gaiety, and mirth, . . . 663 *Prelude* 4. 312
Thus gaiety and cheerfulness prevail, ... 700 *Prelude* 8. 53
With gaiety and dissolute idleness. . . . . 710 *Prelude* 9. 66
Gay, and affecting graceful gaiety; . . . . 774 *Excursion* 2. 182
The wreck of gaiety! But soon revived . . . 843 *Excursion* 6. 331
And the whole house seems filled with gaiety. . 856 *Excursion* 6. 1187
Of Nature's impress,—gaiety and health, . . . 866 *Excursion* 7. 560
And gaiety of cultivated fields. . . . . . . 879 *Excursion* 8. 374
Gaily. How gaily murmur and how sweetly taste . 20 *Desc. Sk.* 559
And downward Image gaily vying . . . . . 190 **Lyre! though* 21
And gaily lift its fearless brim . . . . . . 296 *Highland Boy* 124
Borne gaily o'er the sea, ... 334 **In Bruges* 38
We gaily passed,—till Nature wrought . . . 343 *Eclipse* 9
Fields gaily sown when promises were cheap.— . 505 *Warning* 139
Said gaily, "This is my domain, my cell, . . 781 *Excursion* 2. 650
Gain. Stooping his gait, but not as if to gain . . 24 *Guilt* 3
Than he who, tempest-driven, thy shelter now would gain? . . . . 26 *Guilt* 126
We had no hope, and no relief could gain: . . 29 *Guilt* 272
To gain the torrent's brink. It seems an age . 52 *Bord.* 802
He who will gain his Seignory when Idonea . . 55 *Bord.* 976
This beech is standing by, its covert thou canst gain; . . . . 87 *Pet-lamb* 30
Hopeless of honour and of gain, ... 117 *Affl. Marg.* 37
Though at my bosom nursed; this woeful gain . 118 *Maternal Grief* 2
The certainty of honourable gain; . . . . . 132 *Michael* 73
And see so little gain from threescore years. . 137 *Michael* 373
But small and fugitive our gain . . . . . 143 **Driven in* 30
The Man was using his best skill to gain . . . 149 **A narrow* 64
Seem to meet with little gain, seem less happy than before: . . . . 189 *Star-gazers* 30
The shelter of the crag to gain; . . . . . 199 *Thorn* 184
For fearless virtue bringeth boundless gain. . . 210 *Laod.* 42
And from affectionate observance gain . . . 212 *Dion* 16
Weighing the mischief with the promised gain, . 283 **Proud were* 12
To fear of loss, and hope of gain, ... 294 *Jedbor.* 51
Fed his first hopes? what knowledge could *he* gain? 304 **I grieved* 4
In the thronged city, from the walks of gain, . 320 **O'erweening Statesmen* 6
With feet, hands, eyes, looks, lips, report your gain; . . . . 322 **Ye Storms* 10
What could they gain but shadows of redress? . 330 *Ode: Thanks.* 120
Have striven by purity to gain . . . . . 343 *Eclipse* 47
Yet peaceful Arts did entrance gain . . . . 390 *Highland Broach* 11
To win some look of love, or gain . . . . 407 *White Doe* 1016
Nor liberty nor rest could gain: . . . . . 411 *White Doe* 1407
But for what gain? if England soon must sink . 441 *Ecc. Sonn.* 3. 3. 10
Hence he will gain a firmer mind, to cope . . . 447 *Ecc. Sonn.* 3. 28. 13
Intent, and sedulous of abject gain, ... 450 *Ecc. Sonn.* 3. 38. 4
What boots the gain if Nature should lose more? 466 *St. Bees* 29
That no adventurer's bark had power to gain . . 468 **Bold words* 3
In hope at length a competence to gain; . . . 470 †*From early* 4
Turns his necessity to glorious gain; . . . . 493 *Hap. War.* 14
Till we by perseverance gain the top . . . . 496 **A little* 25
Gain a fresh impulse, run a livelier course; . . 503 *Warning* 15
Nor gain, from past or future, skill . . . . 505 **If this* 7
An awful balancing of loss and gain, ... 514 **Who ponders* 2
His utterance finds; and, conscious of the gain, . 520 *Pun. Death* 14. 3
Whate'er the difference, boundless is the gain. . 527 **Those breathing* 26
Shades of past bliss, or phantoms that, to gain . 533 **Once I* 35
By a great Lord, for gain and usury, ... 553 *Prioress* 39
That whatsoever point they gain, they yet . . 646 *Prelude* 2. 321
One precious gain, that he forgets himself. . . 670 *Prelude* 5. 346
I seemed about this time to gain clear sight . . 745 *Prelude* 13. 369
Heights which the soul is competent to gain. . . 803 *Excursion* 4. 139
Shall gain defenders zealous and devout . . . 806 *Excursion* 4. 312

Gain—*continued.*
Through each vicissitude of loss and gain, . . 816 *Excursion* 4. 1037
Knowledge, for us, is difficult to gain— . . . 830 *Excursion* 5. 492
Is difficult to gain, and hard to keep— . . . 830 *Excursion* 5. 493
And act in that obedience, he shall gain . . . 830 *Excursion* 5. 519
And, through Heaven's blessing, thus we gain the bread . . . . 834 *Excursion* 5. 809
Detached from pleasure, to the love of gain . 839 *Excursion* 6. 45
"Wish could be ours that you, for such poor gain, 847 *Excursion* 6. 581
(Gain shall I call it?—gain of what?—for whom?) 847 *Excursion* 6. 582
From each day's need, out of each day's least gain. 849 *Excursion* 6. 726
And, on the burial-day, could scarcely gain . . 853 *Excursion* 6. 971
"Happy," rejoined the Wanderer, "they who gain 875 *Excursion* 8. 82
To Gain, the master-idol of the realm, . . . 877 *Excursion* 8. 184
For the convenience of unlawful gain, ... 879 *Excursion* 8. 368
Which, ere they gain consistence, by a gust . . 889 *Excursion* 9. 342
Working through love, such conquest shall it gain, 894 *Excursion* 9. 673
Which Age, with many a slow stoop, strove to gain; . . . . S.3. 417 **Sweet was* 5
A mighty gain, that Labour here preserves . . K.8. 246 *Recluse* 1.1.359
Gained. But now the sun has gained his western road, ... 3 *Ev. Wk.* 88
Another high on that green ledge;—he gained . 17 *Desc. Sk.* 382
Well may we wonder he has gained such power . 37 *Bord.* 13
Thy Mother too!—scarce had I gained the door, . 40 *Bord.* 182
Would be most welcome. Yon white hawthorn gained, ... 41 *Bord.* 216
With proper speed our quarters may be gained . 50 *Bord.* 743
And now, all eyes and feet, hath gained . . . 85 *Shepherd-boys* 58
Was pardon gained, and liberty procured; . . 123 *V. and J.* 151
What can be gained?" At this the old Man paused, ... 135 *Michael* 255
Appeared, and spiritual presence gained a power . 139 *Widow* 26
And so have gained the top of the hill; . . . 174 *Waggoner* 1. 41
Full proof of this the Country gained; . . . 175 *Waggoner* 1. 120
Gained ground upon the Waggon fast, . . . 176 *Waggoner* 2. 17
And in this way he gained an honest maintenance. 196 *Resolution* 105
And ever, when such stature they had gained . 212 *Laod.* 171
What spirit-stirring power it gained . . . . 224 *'*Tis gone* 10
When little could be gained from that rich dower 262 **Dark and* 3
No mightier work had gained the plausive smile . 269 *Malham* 8
Have gained a sanction from thy falling tears; . 270 **If these* 6
And so hath gained at length a prosperous height, 317 **Look now* 6
Though they have gained a worthier meed, . . 324 *Ode 1814* 48
Dread mark of approbation, justly gained! . . 331 *Ode: Thanks.* 159
Treasures I gained with zeal that neither feared . 352 *H. C. R.* 3
The gallant Youth, who may have gained, . . 385 *Yarrow Rev.* 1
Who, that has gained at length the wished-for Height, ... 389 *Glencroe* 2
Entrance I gained to that strong-hold. . . . 409 *White Doe* 1252
The troop of horse have gained the height . . 412 *White Doe* 1462
Not sought, because too near, is never gained. . 476 *Eden* 14
He gained whate'er a regal mind might ask, . . 498 **Enough of climbing* 30
For compassing the end, else never gained; . . 504 *Warning* 92
The last year's cup whose Ram or Heifer gained, 522 *Epist. Beaumont* 67
His wish was gained: a little time . . . . 579 **Sweet Flower* 11
Knowledge and wisdom, gained from converse sweet 584 *Ch. Lamb* 12
But we, by different roads, at length have gained 648 *Prelude* 2. 453
'Tis true, some casual knowledge might be gained 663 *Prelude* 4. 300
Who knows what thus may have been gained, both then . . . . 675 *Prelude* 6. 36
Or as a traveller, who has gained the brow . . 709 *Prelude* 9. 9
The most despotic of our senses, gained . . . 736 *Prelude* 12. 129
Scout-like, and gained the summit; 'twas a day . 738 *Prelude* 12. 297
Is lodged, and how increased; and having gained 741 *Prelude* 13. 79
Whate'er was wanting, something had I gained, . 750 *Prelude* 14. 331
Gained merited respect in simpler times; . . . 761 *Excursion* 1. 328
The employment common through these wilds, and gained, ... 769 *Excursion* 1. 859
And, from the dazzling conquests daily gained . 775 *Excursion* 2. 233
Yet, ere that final resting-place be gained, . . 792 *Excursion* 3. 446
There imaged: or when, having gained the top . 799 *Excursion* 3. 935
Lies within reach, and one day shall be gained." . 827 *Excursion* 5. 308
Hath gained his noontide height, this churchyard, filled . . . . 830 *Excursion* 5. 534
And by what help had gained those distant fields. 834 *Excursion* 5. 757
A very hero till his point was gained, ... 842 *Excursion* 6. 236
Those troubles had appeased, he sought and gained, 844 *Excursion* 6. 424
Wretched at home, he gained no peace abroad; . 855 *Excursion* 6. 1098
And conquests over her dominion gained, . . . 862 *Excursion* 7. 321
Be satisfied, 'tis well,—the end is gained; . . 874 *Excursion* 8. 7
Of this dominion over nature gained, ... 877 *Excursion* 8. 211
Whose ends are gained? Behold an emblem here 892 *Excursion* 9. 554
Were left, the other gained.—O ye, who come . 895 *Excursion* 9. 724
Yet is it something gained, it is in truth . . . K.8. 246 *Recluse* 1.1.358
Already have I gained. The inward frame . . K.8. 249 *Recluse* 1.1.472
Gainful. He had repaired to ply a gainful trade: . 29 *Guilt* 254
Gaining. To the Mind's gaining that prophetic sense 477 *Steamboats* 6
"So prayed, more gaining than he asked, the Bard— . . . . 755 *Recluse* 1. 1. 777
The growth of intellect, yet gaining more, . . 760 *Excursion* 1. 303
Gains. But now the clear bright Moon her zenith gains, ... 8 *Ev. Wk.* 355
No gains too cheaply earned his fancy cloy, . . 11 *Desc. Sk.* 15
To see the end of all my gains, ... 115 *Last of Flock* 56
Till the waggon gains the top; . . . . . . 181 *Waggoner* 4. 139
Innumerable gains; yet we, who now . . . . 357 *Aquap.* 323
Nor have I tracked their course for scanty gains; 382 *Duddon* 26. 9
The sacred Structures for less doubtful gains. . 424 *Ecc. Sonn.* 1. 24. 8
Earlier from cleansing fires, and gains withal . . 429 *Ecc. Sonn.* 2. 3. 4.

Gains—*continued.*
The Other gains a confidence as bold; . . . 437 *Ecc. Sonn.* 2. 34. 7
Great gains are mine; for thus I live remote . . 488 *Pers. Talk* 44
Of labourer plodding for his daily gains, . . . 546 **Oft is* 12
But they as well as I have gains;— . . . . 580 *John Words.* 45
For gains, and who that sees her would not buy? 699 *Prelude* 8. 39
And seal up all the gains of France, a Pope . . 732 *Prelude* 11. 359
The Housewife, tempted by such slender gains . 783 *Excursion* 2. 741
Gainsaid. But Nature might not be gainsaid; . . 182 *Waggoner* 4. 206
Gainsay. Such bold report I venture to gainsay: . 271 **Fame tells* 5
Yet will not heaven disown nor earth gainsay . 331 *Ode: Thanks.* 176
'Gainst. (*Partial list.*) *See* **Against.**
Which genius did not hallow; 'gainst the taint . 23 *Yew-tree* 17
'Gainst all that in *his* heart, or theirs perhaps, said nay. . . . . 25 *Guilt* 54
'Gainst him who raised it,—his last work on earth: 276 *Filial Piety* 7
Gait. Stooping his gait, but not as if to gain . . 24 *Guilt* 3
And like a Roman matron's was her mien and gait. 119 *Sailor's Mother* 6
His richest splendour—when his veering gait . . 220 *Triad* 48
And long and slouching was his gait; . . . . 240 *P. B.* 307
His gait, is one expression: every limb, . . . 572 *Animal Tran.* 4
Whatever formal gait of discipline . . . . 655 *Prelude* 3. 402
My voice, composed my gait, and, with the air . 660 *Prelude* 4. 126
Who crept along fitting her languid gait . . . 717 *Prelude* 9. 511
Active and nervous was his gait; his limbs . . 762 *Excursion* 1. 424
Creeping his gait and cowering, his lip pale, . . 879 *Excursion* 8. 311
Galahad. When his touch failed.—Next came Sir Galahad; . . . . 373 *Eg. Maid* 298
Sir Galahad! a treasure, that God giveth, . . 374 *Eg. Maid* 344
Galaxy. Moved not; meanwhile the galaxy displayed . . . . 123 *V. and J.* 97
Along a Galaxy that knows no end, ... 443 *Ecc. Sonn.* 3. 13. 13
Alas for thee, bright Galaxy of Isles, ... 501 *Humanity* 69
Each in the other's blaze, a galaxy . . . . 706 *Prelude* 8. 484
Gale. Where leafy shades fence off the blustering gale, ... 6 *Ev. Wk.* 234
And like a torrent roars the headstrong gale; . 7 *Ev. Wk.* 270
Tracking the motions of the fitful gale. . . . 7 *Ev. Wk.* 296
Where mists, suspended on the expiring gale, . 14 *Desc. Sk.* 210
Approaching, and upbraid the tardy gale; . . 15 *Desc. Sk.* 251
Where breathed the gale that caught Wolfe's happiest sigh, ... 15 *Desc. Sk.* 299
Waves the ripe harvest in the autumnal gale; . 21 *Desc. Sk.* 587
And orange gale that o'er Lugano blows; . . . 21 *Desc. Sk.* 596
And stir not in the gale. . . . . 111 **'Tis said that some* 40
For her good neighbour Susan Gale, ... 126 *Idiot Boy* 18
There's none to help poor Susan Gale; . . . 126 *Idiot Boy* 30
Or she will die, old Susan Gale. . . . . . 126 *Idiot Boy* 46
Away she hies to Susan Gale: . . . . . . 127 *Idiot Boy* 102
To comfort poor old Susan Gale. . . . . . 127 *Idiot Boy* 121
To comfort poor old Susan Gale. . . . . . 129 *Idiot Boy* 276
Who is it, but old Susan Gale? . . . . . 130 *Idiot Boy* 411
Where oft the stormy winter gale . . . . . 197 *Thorn* 24
As pure a sunshine and as soft a gale . . . . 220 *Triad* 45
What seek ye, or what shun ye? of the gale . . 229 *Clouds* 5
You need a strong and stormy gale . . . . 240 *P. B.* 373
Thou Victim of the stormy gale; . . . . . 348 **Lulled by* 23
A sea of foliage, tossing with the gale, ... 350 *Des. Stanzas* 35
Turn into port; and, reckless of the gale, . . . 379 *Duddon* 13. 10
But here no cannon thunders to the gale; . . . 384 *Duddon* 33. 1
What heartfelt fragrance mingles with the gale . 430 *Ecc. Sonn.* 2. 7. 4
By THEM who blessed the soft and happy gale . 449 *Ecc. Sonn.* 3. 37. 2
I, of his bold wing floating on the gale, . . . 464 *Derwent* 3
When a soft summer gale at evening parts . . 465 **Dear to* 7
This new indifference to breeze or gale, . . . 466 *St. Bees* 11
To him who catches on the gale . . . . . 478 *Somnamb.* 7
Dive, at thy choice, or brave the freshening gale! 527 **Those breathing* 36
Whence fragrance scents the water's desart gale, . 596 *Ev. Wk. Quarto* 223
And roars between the hills the torrent gale, . . 597 *Ev. Wk. Quarto* 280
Tracking with silvering path the changeful gale. . 598 *Ev. Wk. Quarto* 344
He tastes the meanest note that swells the gale; . 602 *Desc. Sk. Quarto* 20
While mists, suspended on th' expiring gale, . . 607 *Desc. Sk. Quarto* 265
That flowed into a kindred stream; a gale, . . 686 *Prelude* 6. 744
Or nowhere; days unruffled by the gale . . . 777 *Excursion* 2. 365
Gales. Or from high points of rock looked out for fanning gales; . . . . 3 *Ev. Wk.* 44
The churlish gales of penury, that blow . . . 19 *Desc. Sk.* 504
Fresh gales and dews of life's delicious morn, . . 20 *Desc. Sk.* 530
With breakers roaring to the gales . . . . . 217 *Enterprise* 154
And the wind loves them; and the gentle gales— 230 *Clouds* 66
Rise, GILLIES, rise: the gales of youth shall bear . 260 **From the dark* 3
To rouse the dawn, soft gales shall speed thy wing, 274 **Not the* 13
With warmer suns and softer gales, ... 295 *Highland Boy* 74
In Zaragoza, naked to the gales . . . . . 315 **And is it* 8
On gales that breathe too gently to recall . . . 381 *Duddon* 21. 13
—But, as soft gales dissolve the dreary snow, . 395 *White Doe: Ded.* 27
Gales sweet as those that over Eden blew! . . 434 *Ecc. Sonn.* 2. 24. 14
In thoughtful moments, wafted by the gales . . 438 *Ecc. Sonn.* 2. 39. 13
Fresh gales to waft them to the far-off port; . . 454 *Sea-side* 18
—Thy fragrant gales and lute-resounding streams, 605 *Desc. Sk. Quarto* 156
The churlish gales, that unremitting blow . . 613 *Desc. Sk. Quarto* 604
Soft gales and dews of life's delicious morn, . . 613 *Desc. Sk. Quarto* 634
Of gales Etesian or of tender thoughts. . . . 678 *Prelude* 6. 251
Galesus. Of delicate Galesus; and no less . . . 701 *Prelude* 8. 175
Galilee. Beneath some shady palm of Galilee. . . 274 *Infant M.* 14
Gall. But whence this gall, this lengthened face of woe? . . . . L.1. 96 *Juvenal* 3. 51
Galla. "There's Galla Water, Leader Haughs, . . 292 *Yarrow Unv.* 17
Gallant. *See* **Top-gallant.**
The gallant ship is borne; . . . . 161 *Binnorie* 17

Gallant—*continued.*
A gallant stately Man-of-war, ... 177 *Waggoner* 2. 107
And made a gallant crest. . . . . 192 *Ruth* 24
"And, gallant Stag! to make thy praises known, 201 *Hart-leap* 65
To join that gallant ship of war, ... 296 *Highland Boy* 134
Did from the Norman win a gallant wreath; . . 309 *Men of Kent* 10
Like gallant Falkland, by the Monarch's side, . . 310 *Invasion* 3
The gallant Youth, who may have gained, . . 385 *Yarrow Rev.* 1
All followed him, a gallant band! . . . . . 400 *White Doe* 413
And overpowered that gallant few. . . . . 408 *White Doe* 1154
But to each gallant Captain and his crew . . . 458 *Sea-shore* 25
Or art thou one of gallant pride, ... 485 *Poet's Epitaph* 13
n gallant soldiership, and posting on . . . . 713 *Prelude* 9. 265
A brood of gallant creatures, on the deep; . . 722 *Prelude* 10. 318
And praised the gallant bearing, of a Knight . . 825 *Excursion* 5. 186
From which the gallant teacher would discourse, 869 *Excursion* 7. 786
Gallantry. A passion and a gallantry, like that . 714 *Prelude* 9. 311
Galled. Galled by their monarch's chain. The times were big . . . . 695 *Prelude* 7. 534
And fruitless indignation; galled by pride; . . 776 *Excursion* 2. 299
Galleries. Through shattered galleries, 'mid roofless halls, ... 272 *Ruins* 1
Gallery. And Whispering Gallery of St. Paul's; the tombs . . . . 689 *Prelude* 7. 130
For you a stately gallery maintain . . . . . 809 *Excursion* 4. 561
Gallery's. Saw, at a long-drawn gallery's dusky bound, 213 *Dion* 66
Galley. Was this Sea-flower, this buoyant Galley; . 369 *Eg. Maid* 38
So richly was this Galley laden, ... 370 *Eg. Maid* 62
Gallia's. O'er Gallia's wastes of corn my footsteps led; . . . . 11 *Desc. Sk.* 45
O'er Gallia's wastes of corn dejected led, . . . 602 *Desc. Sk. Quarto* 47
Gallic. Why cast ye back upon the Gallic shore, . 349 *Boulogne* 1
In Gallic ears the unadulterate Word, ... 431 *Ecc. Sonn.* 2. 12. 4
Conquer the Gallic lily which thy foes . . . . 432 *Ecc. Sonn.* 2. 15. 7
The *servum pecus* of a Gallic breed? . . . . 516 **Young England* 11
"From Gallic parents sprung, ... 545 *Russ. Fug.* 314
There flowed no Gallic blood, nor had I breathed 796 *Excursion* 3. 742
The air of France, not less than Gallic zeal . . 797 *Excursion* 3. 743
Gallop. And so will gallop on for aye, ... 129 *Idiot Boy* 335
Urged o'er the wilderness in sportive gallop. . . 371 *Eg. Maid* 120
To gallop through the country in blind zeal . . 652 *Prelude* 3. 252
Galloped. That as they galloped made the echoes roar; . . . . 200 *Hart-leap* 14
Galloping. He's galloping away, away, ... 129 *Idiot Boy* 334
And eager to spur on, the galloping steed; . . 643 *Prelude* 2. 97
Gallops. That gallops away with such fury and force 484 **A plague* 4
Gallows. The gallows would one day of him be glad;— . . . . 33 *Guilt* 484
Is it a gallows there portrayed? . . . . . . 242 *P. B.* 503
Gambol. Gambol like a dancing skiff, ... 166 *Wand. Jew* 18
To gambol with Life's falling Leaf. . . . . 172 *Kitten* 128
Or gambol—each with his shadow at his side, . 278 **Life with* 7
They *cannot* rest, they gambol like young whelps; K.8. 251 *Recluse* 1. 1. 548
Gambols. In boyish gambols;—I was lost . . . 237 *P. B.* 68
And where the rugged colts their gambols played, 450 *Ecc. Sonn.* 3. 41. 4
Game. The game is up!— If it be needful, Sir, . 73 *Bord.* 2030
As is the humour of the game, ... 158 **With little* 15
To hunt their fluttering game o'er rock and level green. . . . . 191 *Beggars* 36
Of life's uneasy game the stake, ... 214 *Kirkstone* 30
Six thousand veterans practised in war's game, . 293 *Killicranky* 1
While, to dislodge his game, cities are sacked! . 313 **Go back* 14
He quakes not like the timid forest game, . . . 339 *Tell* 24
Where be the noisy followers of the game . . . 349 *Val. Dover* 1
And a last game of mazy hoverings . . . . 455 *Rydal Mere* 10
Of song and dance and game; . . . . . . 506 **While from* 44
Across the marsh, the game in view, ... 544 *Russ. Fug.* 273
War is passion's basest game . . . . . . 628 *Installation* 7
And, interrupting oft that eager game, . . . 640 *Prelude* 1. 538
Or, shall I say?—disdained, the game that lurks 788 *Excursion* 3. 123
(Not as an intellectual game pursued . . . . 790 *Excursion* 3. 285
Games. Who from ignoble games and revelry . . 211 *Laod.* 112
Her approbation, and with pomps and games. . 304 **Festivals have* 5
And to the people at the Isthmian Games . . 312 **A Roman* 2
The feast of Neptune—and the Cereal Games, . . 346 *Processions* 30
To practise games and archery: . . . . . . 409 *White Doe* 1179
Plays, in the many games of life, that one . . 494 *Hap. War.* 70
We hissed along the polished ice in games . . 638 *Prelude* 1. 434
A round of tumult. Duly were our games . . 642 *Prelude* 2. 9
And sports and games (too grateful in themselves, 662 *Prelude* 4. 283
Hands apt for all ingenious arts and games; . . 859 *Excursion* 7. 119
Gamesome. They run up stairs in gamesome race; 81 †*Mother's Return* 50
Noisy he was, and gamesome as a boy; . . . 108 *Indolence* 47
The kitten frolic, like a gamesome sprite, . . . 294 **Fly, some* 6
Of gamesome Deities; or Pan himself, ... 814 *Excursion* 4. 886
Gaming-house. Of Tavern, Brothel, Gaming-house, and Shop, ... 710 *Prelude* 9. 54
'Gan. *See* **Began.**
And, as the Child 'gan to the school to pace, . . 554 *Prioress* 118
The *Alma Redemptoris* 'gan to sing . . . . 555 *Prioress* 161
And, as I with the Cuckoo thus 'gan chide, . . 558 *Cuck. and Night.* 96
Well nigh for sorrow down he 'gan to fall. . . 562 *Troilus* 14
Therewith when this true Lover 'gan behold, . . 562 *Troilus* 15
Without word uttered, forth he 'gan to pace; . . 563 *Troilus* 19
And yonder once she unto me 'gan say— . . . 563 *Troilus* 53
As ye have heard; such life 'gan he to lead . . 564 *Troilus* 111
That absent was, 'gan sing as ye may hear. . . 564 *Troilus* 119
Gang. *See* **Press-gang.**
Ganges. Oftener than Ganges or the Nile; a thought 251 **There is a little* 7
Proud Tiber grieves, and far-off Ganges, blind . 435 *Ecc. Sonn.* 2. 27. 6
Their holy Ganges from a skyey fount, . . . 790 *Excursion* 3. 255

Gave—*continued.*
Those steps I climb; the mists before me gave . 257 *Methought I* 9
Of this small lute gave ease to Petrarch's wound; 260 **Scorn not* 4
I gave this paradise for winter hours, ... 264 **Lady! the* 7
Gave it while cares were weighing on my heart, . 266 **The stars* 10
Yet He whose heart in childhood gave her troth . 275 **Chatsworth! thy* 9
Your Father such example gave, ... 287 *Sons of Burns* 45
Heaven gave Rob Roy a dauntless heart . . 291 *Rob Roy* 9
Who on that day the word of onset gave! . . . 293 *Killicranky* 12
And was his friend; and gave him joy . . . 295 *Highland Boy* 24
And gave his doleful warning. . . . . . . 302 *Yarrow V.* 32
Gave specious colouring to aim and act, . . . 313 **Go back* 10
She gave, if Faith might tread the beaten ways . 322 **By Moscow* 8
Haste, Virgins, haste!—the flowers which summer gave . . . . 323 *Ode 1814* 37
Which to unequal laws gave birth, ... 342 *Ital. Itin.* 77
In keen pursuit—and gave, where'er she flew, . 346 *Gemmi* 7
That gave the Roman his triumphal shells; . . 349 *Boulogne* 6
And shrubs, whose pleasant looks gave proof how kind . . . . 356 *Aquap.* 214
And very names of those who gave them birth . 356 *Aquap.* 276
That gave them being, vanish to a sound. . . 361 **When here* 14
Embellishing the ground that gave them birth . 361 **List—'twas* 12
Gave back a rich and dazzling sheen, ... 375 **The Minstrels* 5
As thy own Yarrow gave to me . . . . 386 *Yarrow Rev.* 75
Who gave their wishes open vent; . . . . 400 *White Doe* 369
Raised, as the Vision gave command, . . . 405 *White Doe* 830
That passion, prudently gave way; . . . . 406 *White Doe* 932
"Your Father gave me cordial greeting; . . . 410 *White Doe* 1253
Were mine the trusty staff that Jewel gave . 438 *Ecc. Sonn.* 2. 39. 3
Which that sweet season gave, ... 486 **We walked* 30
Who gave us nobler loves, and nobler cares— . 489 *Pers. Talk* 52
He knows, who gave that love sublime; . . . 492 *Fidelity* 63
And gave that strength of feeling, great . . . 492 *Fidelity* 64
Gave, in the field of Luz, to Jacob's sight . 500 *Humanity* 34
Gave him first the wished-for part . . . 503 **Like a* 72
The spear, yet gave to works divine . . . . 533 **Blest is* 13
Their work's foundation, gave with careful hand . 534 **When in* 11
Of meek devotion, which erewhile it gave, . . 535 **When in* 26
That gave them birth:—months passed, and still this hand, ... 539 **Lady! a* 6
And the fifth morning gave him sight . . . . 545 *Russ. Fug.* 347
Soon gratitude gave way to love . . . . . 545 *Russ. Fug.* 361
And when those rites had ceased, the Spot gave birth . . . . 547 **Beneath yon* 7
Gave to her thought, that in a little space . . 555 *Prioress* 153
And he gave up the ghost full peacefully; . . 556 *Prioress* 221
Then spake one Bird, and full assent all gave; . 562 *Cuck. and Night.* 271
He gave them the best that he had; or, to say . 569 *Farmer* 27
Gave to my charge Urbino's numerous flock. . . 573 *Chiabrera* 3. 7
And if in him meekness at times gave way, . . 584 *Ch. Lamb* 27
A timely utterance gave that thought relief, . . 588 *Immortality* 23
And gave, in handfuls gave, the treacherous store: 620 *Birth of Love* 43
I gave a fervent welcome to the sight, . . . 622 **Among all* 7
And gave to Bitias, urging the prompt lord; . . 625 *Æneid* 118
If e'er, on wings which active fancy gave, . . 630 [?] **O Moon* 5
Than Fancy gave assurance of some work . . 633 *Prelude* 1. 78
Gave out to meadow-grounds and hills a loud . 640 *Prelude* 1. 541
That gave thee liberty, full long desired, . . . 648 *Prelude* 2. 462
I gave a moral life: I saw them feel, . . . 651 *Prelude* 3. 129
Of loneliness gave way to empty noise . . . 652 *Prelude* 3. 208
Gave treacherous sanction to that over-love . . 675 *Prelude* 6. 32
And gave it vent in her last words. O Friend! . 723 *Prelude* 10. 383
Blow keen upon an eminence that gave . . . 729 *Prelude* 11. 166
Gave way to overpressure from the times . . . 735 *Prelude* 12. 51
Gave intermitting prospect of the copse . . . 738 *Prelude* 12. 304
And gave the Mind that apprehensive power . . 758 *Excursion* 1. 167
A daughter's welcome gave me, and I loved her . 763 *Excursion* 1. 499
Which gave employment to her listless hands— . 767 *Excursion* 1. 759
And, when she at her table gave me food, . . 768 *Excursion* 1. 793
"Ere my departure, to her care I gave, . . . 768 *Excursion* 1. 804
Whose presence gave no comfort, were gone by, . 769 *Excursion* 1. 893
Resolved the dubious point; and sentence gave . 772 *Excursion* 2. 78
The portion gave of coarse but wholesome fare . 783 *Excursion* 2. 745
His countenance gave notice that my zeal . . 791 *Excursion* 3. 357
Gave modest intimation to the mind . . . . 793 *Excursion* 3. 528
That happiness; and use and habit gave . . . 795 *Excursion* 3. 624
Which Nature gently gave, in woods and fields; . 805 *Excursion* 4. 275
"Such timely warning," said the Wanderer, "gave 805 *Excursion* 4. 295
Gave obvious instance of the sad effect . . . 842 *Excursion* 6. 279
True to their choice; and gave their bones in trust 844 *Excursion* 6. 410
To no perverse suspicion he gave way, . . . 864 *Excursion* 7. 456
That gave them nourishment. When frosty winds 881 *Excursion* 8. 445
The Valley, opening out her bosom, gave . . 892 *Excursion* 9. 571
Or to Andates, female Power! who gave . . . 894 *Excursion* 9. 708
Entering the cell gave restlessness to one, . . S.3. 434 **The doubt* 73
Gave to thy fame a more illustrious flight . . S.3. 442 **Vasco, whose* 10
Gave to triumph Freedom's cause, ... S.3. 442 *Harmodius* 7
Gave to Athens equal laws. . . . . S.3. 442 *Harmodius* 8
Gave to triumph Freedom's cause, ... S.3. 442 *Harmodius* 27
Gave to Athens equal laws. . . . . S.3. 442 *Harmodius* 28
The bastard gave some favorite [? favourite] stocks of peers . . . . L.1. 98 *Juvenal* 3. 98

Gavel. From the Great Gavel, down by Leeza's banks, 100 *Brothers* 310

Gawaine. While drawing toward the car Sir Gawaine, mailed . . . . 373 *Eg. Maid* 285

Gawds. Of heady schemes jostling each other, gawds, ... 662 *Prelude* 4. 281

Gay. Gay lark of hope, thy silent song resume! . 20 *Desc. Sk.* 528
Thou bring'st, gay creature as thou art! . . . 79 **Stay near* 7

Gay—*continued.*
Rapid and gay, as if the earth were air, . . . 95 *Brothers* 3
Perused him with a gay complacency. . . . 96 *Brothers* 103
The sky, the gay green field, ... 105 *Artegal* 199
Limbs stout as thine, and lips as gay, . . . 121 *Emigrant Mother* 50
And left, the couple neither gay perhaps . . . 133 *Michael* 120
Now laugh and be gay, to the woods away! . . 145 *Her Eyes* 99
While fluttering o'er this gay Recess, ... 154 *Flower Garden* 2
My branches are so fresh and gay . . . . 156 *Oak and Broom* 78
When thou art up, alert and gay . . . . . 158 **In youth* 58
"Gay Sylphs this miniature will court, . . . 164 *Needlecase* 29
Transient deception! a gay freak . . . . . 170 *Rural Ill.* 7
The Sailor, Man by nature gay, ... 177 *Waggoner* 2. 83
Whose party-coloured garments gay . . . . 180 *Waggoner* 4. 31
A dancing Shape, an Image gay, ... 186 **She was* 9
A poet could not but be gay, ... 187 **I wandered* 15
Pleased with herself, nor sad, nor gay; . . . 192 *Ruth* 16
No dolphin ever was so gay . . . . 192 *Ruth* 41
This Stripling, sportive, gay, and bold, . . . 193 *Ruth* 116
And she was blithe and gay, ... 198 *Thorn* 108
Are confident and gay; . . . . 223 *Wishing-gate* 3
The sunny vale looked gay; . . . . . . 224 *Primrose* 28
My gay and beautiful Canoe, ... 237 *P. B.* 112
What need of clamorous bells, or ribands gay, . 256 *Marriage: Friend* 1
The Sonnet glittered a gay myrtle leaf . . . 260 **Scorn not* 7
A gay society with faces bright, ... 266 **Even as* 12
Calm expectations, leaving to the gay . . . . 278 **The most* 12
So the bright faces of the young and gay . . . 281 *Chris. Words.* 9
And, on the mouldered walls, how bright, how gay, 283 **Here, where* 7
Its second twilight, and looks gay; . . . . 294 *Jedbor.* 46
And bonnet with a feather gay, ... 295 *Highland Boy* 33
Alone, and innocent, and gay! . . . . . . 296 *Highland Boy* 172
A gay saloon, with waters dancing . . . . . 300 *Bran* 13
Heaven grant that other Cities may be gay! . . 304 **Festivals have* 6
A white-robed Negro, like a lady gay, ... 305 **We had* 3
Was fit for some gay throng; . . . . . . 334 **In Bruges* 10
From the smooth breast of gay Winandermere? . 344 *Eclipse* 75
Gay vision under sullen skies, ... 344 **How blest* 56
And we were gay, our hearts at ease; . . . . 348 **Lulled by* 13
More than fulfilled, as gay Campania's shores . 353 *Aquap.* 78
Gay June would scorn us. But when bleak winds roar . . . . 379 *Duddon* 13. 5
There dwelt the gay, the bountiful, the bold; . . 383 *Duddon* 27. 5
See what gay wild flowers deck this earth-built Cot, 390 *Highland Hut* 1
(Even with the young, the hopeful, or the gay) . 394 **No more* 35
In trellised shed with clustering roses gay, . . 395 *White Doe: Ded.* 1
The sun shines bright; the fields are gay . . . 396 *White Doe* 3
Converging walks, and fountains gay, ... 407 *White Doe* 989
Of pity or fear; and More's gay genius played . 435 *Ecc. Sonn.* 2. 26. 12
Through the still churchyard, each with garland gay, ... 448 *Ecc. Sonn.* 3. 32. 7
The counter Spirit found in some gay church . . 448 *Ecc. Sonn.* 3. 33. 10
Faint sound, that, for the gayest of the gay, . . 453 **Calm is the* 30
And make the serious happier than the gay? . . 459 **Wanderer! that* 39
It neither damps the gay, nor checks the witty. . 475 *Greenock* 8
And if the harp pleased his gay youth, it rings . 503 *Warning* 18
Queen art thou still for each gay plant . . . 506 **While from* 29
(Her Father told her so) in youth's gay dawn . . 509 *F. Stone* 65
In her own dawn—a dawn less gay and bright, . 509 *F. Stone* 67
How could he think of the live creature—gay . . 511 **Who rashly* 3
With nets and sails outspread and streamers gay, 522 *Epist. Beaumont* 72
Mid the gay prattle of those infant tongues, . . 523 *Epist. Beaumont* 158
More could my pen report of grave or gay . . 525 *Epist. Beaumont* 270
Poor Robin is yet flowerless; but how gay . . 529 *Poor Robin* 5
Such happy privilege hath life's gay Prime, . . 532 **Once I* 28
Would sit, as any linnet, gay. . . . . . 536 *Goody Blake* 40
They pruned themselves, and made themselves right gay, ... 558 *Cuck. and Night.* 76
At Woodstock, on the meadow green and gay. . 562 *Cuck. and Night.* 285
Ye Striplings, light of heart and gay, ... 577 **I come* 45
Oh true of heart, of spirit gay, ... 578 **I come* 65
And all the earth is gay; . . . . 588 *Immortality* 29
And soft, and gay, and beautiful thou art, . . 622 *Recluse* 1. 1. 115
And Hope gay Pilot of the bold design, . . . 625 **The confidence* 2
Of gay confusion still be uppermost, ... 658 *Prelude* 3. 625
Magnificent, and beautiful, and gay. . . . . 658 *Prelude* 4. 11
The transformation wrought by gay attire. . . 659 *Prelude* 4. 76
A parti-coloured show of grave and gay, . . . 663 *Prelude* 4. 340
Or eager, though as gay and undepressed . . . 675 *Prelude* 6. 7
Like bees they swarmed, gaudy and gay as bees; 681 *Prelude* 6. 391
Among the wretched and the falsely gay, . . . 692 *Prelude* 7. 368
Solemn or gay: whether some beauteous dame . 693 *Prelude* 7. 413
Than the gay Corin of the groves, who lives . . 703 *Prelude* 8. 285
With scoffers, seeking light and gay revenge . . 732 *Prelude* 11. 322
That gay assemblage. Round them and above, . 773 *Excursion* 2. 128
Gay, and affecting graceful gaiety; . . . . . 774 *Excursion* 2. 182
Vilest hypocrisy—the laughing, gay . . . . 775 *Excursion* 2. 252
Choose, with the gay Athenian, a conceit . . . 789 *Excursion* 3. 248
From mild to angry, and from sad to gay, . . . 790 *Excursion* 3. 315
Of gay companions, to the natal roof, ... 793 *Excursion* 3. 507
Gay as our spirits, free as our desires; . . . 794 *Excursion* 3. 543
Of gay or tragic pictures. You have seen, . . 809 *Excursion* 4. 562
And easy contemplation; gay parterres, . . . 810 *Excursion* 4. 589
A gay or pensive tenderness prevailed, . . . 812 *Excursion* 4. 743
"How gay the habitations that bedeck . . . 828 *Excursion* 5. 411
That on the outset wastes its gay desires, . . 829 *Excursion* 5. 433
Gay, volatile, ingenious, quick to learn, . . . 842 *Excursion* 6. 282
Sincerely wretched hearts, or falsely gay. . . . 843 *Excursion* 6. 358
Or the clear moon. The queen of these gay sports, 851 *Excursion* 6. 838

Gay—*continued.*
Mild Man! he is not gay, but they are gay; 856 *Excursion* 6. 1186
With a gay confidence and seemly pride; 869 *Excursion* 7. 775
Plunged—'mid a gay and busy throng convened 870 *Excursion* 7. 868
Shadowy, yet gay and lightsome as it stood 881 *Excursion* 8. 463
By beds and banks Arcadian of gay flowers 881 *Excursion* 8. 469
Of the gay mind, as ofttimes splenetic youth K.8. 237 *Recluse* 1.1.53
Ah! if I were a lady gay K.8. 262 **Ah! if* 1

Gayest. Wreathed round with yellow flowers the gayest of the land. 191 *Beggars* 24
Faint sound, that, for the gayest of the gay, 453 **Calm is the* 30

Gaze. No favoured eye was e'er allowed to gaze 7 *Ev. Wk.* 299
The kneeling peasant scarcely dares to gaze; 14 *Desc. Sk.* 201
And, lifting up his head, he then would gaze 23 *Yew-tree* 33
Thou seest,—and he would gaze till it became 23 *Yew-tree* 35
Could gaze, as on a show by idlers sought; 36 *Guilt* 661
Over the vessel's side, and gaze and gaze; 96 *Brothers* 55
The while on thee they gaze in simple truth, 110 **Look at* 21
And while I gaze upon the spectacle 151 **When, to* 94
We gaze, we also learn to love. 164 **Glad sight* 8
Here let me gaze enrapt upon that eye, 190 **Lyre! though* 8
Where no procrastinating gaze 216 *Enterprise* 49
Of man's enquiring gaze, but to his hope 226 *Vernal Ode* 29
From age to age, and did not, while we gaze 231 *Clouds* 88
Well may'st thou halt—and gaze with brightening eye! 250 *Admon.* 1
She loves to gaze upon a crystal river— 262 **Not Love* 11
Gaze on the moon by parting clouds revealed. 268 **Four fiery* 14
Living with liberty on thee to gaze, 281 **Wansfell! this* 2
The traveller, at this day, will stop and gaze 292 **Degenerate Douglas* 10
That an accursed thing it is to gaze 321 **Here pause* 8
On men who gaze heart-smitten by the view, 322 *Germans* 10
Dazzling the vision that presumes to gaze. 329 *Ode: Thanks.* 13
Can hope the general eye thereon would gaze, 333 *Ded. Tour* 3
To muse, to creep, to halt at will, to gaze— 335 *Rhine* 11
Upon some knee-worn cell to gaze: 337 *Cath. Cantons* 8
My ears did listen, 'twas enough to gaze; 338 *Engelberg* 16
On pictures to gaze where they drank in their hues; 345 *Stanzas: Simplon* 7
Stirs not; enrapt I gaze with strange delight, 349 *Val. Dover* 10
Nor cease to gaze upon the bold Relief 368 *Trajan* 71
In silence did King Arthur gaze 374 *Eg. Maid* 337
Hence, while we gaze, a more enduring fear! 392 *Daniel* 10
With unparticipated gaze; 404 *White Doe* 754
In vain, upon the growing Rill may gaze. 419 *Ecc. Sonn.* 1. 5. 14
But, rooted here, I stand and gaze 458 **Had this* 50
Its ripeness to the feeding gaze; 497 *Lycoris* 34
As in a map, before the adventurer's gaze— 497 **Enough of climbing* 17
I gaze upon a Portrait whose mild gleam 508 *F. Stone* 6
Or changed and changing, I not seldom gaze 510 *F. Stone* 113
Ere he had ceased to gaze, perhaps to speak: 510 *F. Stone* 120
Hides half their beauty from the common gaze; 539 **Lady! a* 44
Fair scenes! with other eyes, than once, I gaze, 591 *Ev. Wk. Quarto* 17
And long, with wistful gaze, his walk survey'd 592 *Ev. Wk. Quarto* 69
—With backward gaze, lock'd joints, and step of pain, 596 *Ev. Wk. Quarto* 247
The Moon's fix'd gaze between the opening trees, 596 *Ev. Wk. Quarto* 262
With hollow ringing ears and darkening gaze, 603 *Desc. Sk. Quarto* 97
On Zutphen's plain; or where with soften'd gaze 608 *Desc.Sk.Quarto* 358
Haply that child in fearful doubt may gaze, 609 *Desc.Sk.Quarto* 410
With pulseless hand, and fix'd unwearied gaze, 616 *Desc.Sk.Quarto* 786
'Tis sorrow enough on that visage to gaze, 620 *Convict* 17
They look with wonder on the gifts—they gaze 624 *Æneid* 73
We gaze—nor grieve to think that we must die, 627 **We gaze* 1
Standing to gaze upon her while she hung 645 *Prelude* 2. 193
Wert used to lie and gaze upon the clouds 679 *Prelude* 6. 269
Sit in the shade together, while they gaze, 699 *Prelude* 8. 47
But stirring to the spirit. Who could gaze K.8. 237 *Recluse* 1. 1. 24

Gazed. Think not the peasant from aloft has gazed 18 *Desc. Sk.* 421
Perplexed and comfortless he gazed around, 24 *Guilt* 24
We gazed with terror on their gloomy sleep, 29 *Guilt* 293
Dismissed, again on open day I gazed, 31 *Guilt* 400
No pity asking, on the group she gazed 34 *Guilt* 562
Breathless he gazed upon her face,—then took 36 *Guilt* 632
He had remained; but, as he gazed, there grew 96 *Brothers* 86
He gazed rejoicing, and again he gazed, 104 *Artegal* 118
Would that mine eyes had never gazed 113 *Lament* 31
I gazed and gazed, and to myself I said, 146 **It was an* 37
—When I had gazed perhaps two minutes' space, 147 *Joanna* 51
And took no note of the hour while thence they gazed, 151 **Forth from* 10
The blooming heath their couch, gazed side by side, 151 **Forth from* 11
I gazed—and gazed—but little thought 187 **I wandered* 17
Of him who gazes, or has gazed? a grave and steady joy, 189 *Star-gazers* 26
But gazed upon the spoil with silent joy. 201 *Hart-leap* 36
And gazed and gazed upon that darling spot. 201 *Hart-leap* 48
And, while I gazed, there came to me a thought 208 **It is no* 12
On which four thousand years have gazed! 214 *Kirkstone* 20
Thou hast clomb aloft, and gazed 217 **Inmate of* 2
On which they gazed themselves away. 239 *P. B.* 270
I gazed—and, self-accused while gazing, sighed 254 *WildDuck'sNest* 13
Dissolve—and leave to him who gazed a sigh. 278 **The most* 8
This Work, I now have gazed on it so long 279 **Though I* 2
Trembling I gazed, but heard a voice—it said, 282 **In my* 13
Where gazed the peasant from his door, 343 *Eclipse* 29
I stood, and gazed upon a marble stone, 365 **Under the* 4
I gazed with earnestness, and dared no more. 365 **Under the* 10
Sage Merlin gazed with admiration: 369 *Eg. Maid* 14
When first I gazed upon her; 386 *Yarrow Rev.* 76

Gazed—*continued.*
The Earls upon each other gazed, 404 *White Doe* 791
Salvation to all eyes that gazed, 410 *White Doe* 1267
But while I gazed in tender reverie 440 *Ecc. Sonn.* 3. 1. 7
Churches, on whose symbolic beauty gazed 467 *St. Bees* 121
Long as we gazed upon the form and face, 523 *Epist. Beaumont* 144
A mighty One upon me gazed; 542 *Russ. Fug.* 67
My fancy kindled as I gazed; 550 *Hermit's Cell* 2. 17
And, while I gazed, with sudden shock 550 *Hermit's Cell* 2. 25
I gazed from Hampstead's breezy heath. 586 *Hogg* 32
Gaz'd by his sister-wives, the monarch stalks; 594 *Ev. Wk. Quarto* 130
I gazed upon the visionary train, 618 *School Ex.* 25
Threw back my eyes, return'd, and gazed again. 618 *School Ex.* 26
Gaz'd on thy lovely Nymphs with fond delight, 630 [?] **O Moon* 8
I gazed with growing love, a higher power 633 *Prelude* 1. 77
Or father fondly gazed upon with pride. 692 *Prelude* 7. 341
His steadfast face and sightless eyes, I gazed, 697 *Prelude* 7. 648
Upon this restless lustre have I gazed, 705 *Prelude* 8. 412
The dead, upon the dying heaped, and gazed 719 *Prelude* 10. 57
That neither passed away nor changed, I gazed 726 *Prelude* 10. 527
Who, from her sovereign elevation, gazed 747 *Prelude* 14. 54
He gazed upon that mighty orb of song, 760 *Excursion* 1. 249
I then forgot him:—there I stood and gazed: 785 *Excursion* 2. 879
To One on whose mild radiance many gazed 793 *Excursion* 3. 503
She gazed as on a pure and spotless gift 852 *Excursion* 6. 908
He gazed, with admiration unsuppressed, 882 *Excursion* 8. 534
The Lady whispered, while we stood and gazed 891 *Excursion* 9. 455
We gazed, in silence hushed, with eyes intent 893 *Excursion* 9. 610
The illusion strengthening as he gazed, he felt K.8. 237 *Recluse* 1. 1.36

Gazer's. Silent, and to the gazer's eye untrue, 377 *Duddon* 4. 6
And motionless; and, to the gazer's eye, 456 **Soft as* 3

Gazers. The gazers feel; and, rushing to the plain, 213 *Dion* 27

Gazes. Of him who gazes, or has gazed? a grave and steady joy, 189 *Star-gazers* 26
Who never gazes but to beautify; 339 *Tell* 12

Gazing. While I am gazing. 158 **With little* 16
Gazing she feels its power beguile 164 **Fair Lady* 33
So he, beneath the gazing moon!— 246 *P. B.* 850
I gazed—and, self-accused while gazing, sighed 254 *WildDuck'sNest* 13
That one enrapt with gazing on her face 274 *Infant M.* 8
And, gazing, saw that Rose, which from the prime 381 *Duddon* 22. 4
Gazing, doubting, questioning; 399 *White Doe* 315
Even till long gazing hath bedimmed his eye, 460 **Wanderer! that* 54
And Dian gazing on the Shepherd's face 461 **Giordano, verily* 4
Why stand we gazing on the sparkling Brine, 469 **Why stand* 1
Gazing and take into his mind and heart, 473 **We saw* 10
Gazing the tempting shades to them deny'd, 592 *Ev. Wk. Quarto* 57
Or gazing from the mountain's silent brow, 612 *Desc.Sk.Quarto* 556
Insatiable looks, and gazing burns. 624 *Æneid* 82
There linger, listening, gazing, with delight 748 *Prelude* 14. 179
Faint, and diminished to the gazing eye, 885 *Excursion* 9. 60
Gazing intensely, the translucent lymph S.3. 436 **The doubt* 181

Gear. Of Peasants in their homely gear; 403 *White Doe* 627

Gehol's. Or Gehol's matchless gardens, for delight 700 *Prelude* 8. 77

Gem. A gem that glitters while it lives, 88 *H. C.* 30
Bright gem instinct with music, vocal spark; 153 *Morn. Ex.* 29
Stones of all hues, gem emulous of gem, 190 **Lyre! though* 35
Though small his kingdom as a spark or gem, 425 *Ecc. Sonn.* 1. 26. 11
Whether in gem, in water, or in sky, 469 **Why stand* 6
To make this Gem their own, 478 *Somnamb.* 20
Your star, your gem, your flower; 542 *Russ. Fug.* 62
This gem of chastity, this emerald, 555 *Prioress* 158

Gem-like. Whate'er it strikes with gem-like hues! 457 **Had this* 28

Gemmed. Upon the mountains gemmed with morning dew, 850 *Excursion* 6. 822

Gemmi. Stern GEMMI listens to as full a cry, 346 *Gemmi* 2

Gems. The beetle panoplied in gems and gold, 108 *Indolence* 60
Lives inexhaustibly in precious gems, 331 *Ode: Thanks.* 166
Or when his tiny gems shall deck his brow: 530 *Poor Robin* 28
As despot courts their blaze of gems display, 615 *Desc.Sk.Quarto* 721
Bore stars—illumination of all gems! 784 *Excursion* 2. 845
And orient gems, which, for a day of need, 809 *Excursion* 4. 568
A cabinet stored with gems and pictures—draws 874 *Excursion* 8. 23

General. The general sorrows of the human race: 19 *Desc. Sk.* 503
General or Cham, Sultan or Emperor, 60 *Bord.* 1229
But still, where general choice is good, 168 *Wren's Nest* 29
Nor doth the general voice abstain from prayer, 213 *Dion* 39
(Above the general roar of woods and crags) 219 *Haunted Tree* 23
And by the general reverence God is praised: 283 **Well have* 12
Deep in the general heart of men 286 *Nith* 47
And in the general joy of heart 297 *Highland Boy* 226
And spreads her arms, as if the general air 311 **Who rises* 11
To the general sense of men by chains confined 314 **I dropped* 4
Can hope the general eye thereon would gaze, 333 *Ded. Tour* 3
Else more and more the general mind will droop, 357 *Aquap.* 340
And boldly urged a general plea, 400 *White Doe* 370
From Heaven a *general* blessing; timely rains 424 *Ecc. Sonn.* 1. 24. 5
To seek the general mart of Christendom; 425 *Ecc. Sonn.* 1. 25. 4
And taught the general voice to prophesy 433 *Ecc. Sonn.* 2. 18. 13
Seemingly given, debase the general mind; 518 *Pun. Death* 4. 9
The judgment, and divert the general heart 538 **In desultory* 47
Nor general Truths, which are themselves a sort 634 *Prelude* 1. 151
With general tendency, but, for the most, 647 *Prelude* 2. 366
Objects embossed to catch the general eye, 657 *Prelude* 3. 551
The general air still busy with the stir 721 *Prelude* 10. 246
And with such general insight into evil, 728 *Prelude* 11. 93
Which, to the blind restraints of general laws 731 *Prelude* 11. 241
To certain general notions, for the sake 743 *Prelude* 13. 213
General distress in his particular lot; 772 *Excursion* 2. 68
None! 'tis the general plaint of human kind 792 *Excursion* 3. 440

General—*continued.*
Yet, through this weakness of the general heart, 803 Excursion 4. 150
Less, as might seem, for general guardianship 807 Excursion 4. 441
Their duties from all forms; and general laws, 820 Excursion 4. 1240
—Yet, in its general tenor, your complaint 828 Excursion 5. 369
Do tend their flocks) partake man's general lot 829 Excursion 5. 427
A general greeting was exchanged; and soon 829 Excursion 5. 462
" Yet for the general purposes of faith 830 Excursion 5. 515
With little change of general sentiment, 845 Excursion 6. 470
And general humility in death? 847 Excursion 6. 619
From trivial themes to general argument 882 Excursion 8. 522
With willingness, to whom the general ear 883 Excursion 8. 595
Trust not to partial care a general good; 890 Excursion 9. 405
The general aspect of the scene; but each 893 Excursion 9. 583
Would More or Henry boast the general voice? L.1. 96 Juvenal 3. 42
Generate. To generate, to preserve, and to restore; 841 Excursion 6. 185
Generation. Has to our generation brought and brings 357 Aquap. 322
And wither, every human generation 516 *As leaves 2
'Vain-glorious Generation! what new powers 805 Excursion 4. 278
Restless, and restless generation, powers 872 Excursion 7. 1002
Which we, a generation self-extolled, 877 Excursion 8. 197
Generations. Through five long generations had the heart 98 Brothers 204
That, while the generations of mankind 152 *Forth from 19
Fleet as the generations of mankind, 230 Clouds 38
The living generations with the dead; 328 Ode 1815 67
As generations come and go, 391 Highland Broach 61
Where happy generations lie, 533 *Blest is 49
A day to future generations dear! 625 Æneid 111
Of generations of illustrious men, 652 Prelude 3. 260
And with the generations of mankind 747 Prelude 14. 109
Whereon their endless generations dwelt. 790 Excursion 3. 252
Supports the generations, multiplies 807 Excursion 4. 433
And countless generations of mankind 812 Excursion 4. 761
The generations of mankind have knelt 827 Excursion 5. 338
A child of hope? Do generations press 829 Excursion 5. 466
On generations, without progress made? 829 Excursion 5. 467
The generations are prepared; the pangs, 846 Excursion 6. 554
And lays the generations low in dust, 885 Excursion 9. 109
Generous. Your generous qualities have won due praise, 48 Bord. 621
But, intermingled with the generous seed, 102 Artegal 29
Full soon this generous purpose thou may'st rue, 104 Artegal 168
Immoveable by generous sighs, 109 *Ere with 5
They parted; and the generous Vaudracour 123 V. and J. 102
" Generous Frank! the just in effort 140 Arm. Lady 31
Which, with a generous shout, the crowd did ratify. 142 Arm. Lady 144
By generous pride within the breast; 174 Waggoner 1. 107
A generous cause a victim did demand; 210 Laod. 46
The mind's least generous wish a mendicant 277 *Why art 7
Be independent, generous, brave; 287 Sons of Burns 44
Said generous Rob, " What need of books? 291 Rob Roy 21
Laugh with the generous household heartily 379 Duddon 13. 13
Say, rather, with that generous sympathy 393 Hart's-horn 11
Would mirth run round, with generous fare; 409 White Doe 1185
A State whose generous will through earth is dealt; 450 Ecc. Sonn. 3. 37. 12
—It is the generous Spirit, who, when brought 493 Hap. War. 3
If generous Loyalty must stand in awe 504 Warning 101
The generous course, aspire, and still aspire; 529 *Those breathing 129
Of the world's freezing cares—to generous Youth— 540 Grace Darl. 10
All caught the infection—as generous as he. 569 Farmer 20
And all that generous nurture breeds to make 575 Chiabrera 7. 2
But she who trains the generous British youth 618 School Ex. 11
By generous Emulation taught to rise, 619 School Ex. 63
Him now the generous Dido by soft chains 624 Æneid 19
Passions unworthy of youth's generous heart 656 Prelude 3. 500
As generous as a fountain; selfishness 670 Prelude 5. 302
Or the remembrance of a generous deed, 685 Prelude 6. 683
Are generous as the young; and, if content 699 Prelude 8. 45
Though under skies less generous, less serene: 702 Prelude 8. 188
Self-sacrifice the firmest; generous love, 715 Prelude 9. 387
A generous spirit, and a body strong 859 Excursion 7. 120
Generous and charitable, prompt to serve; 860 Excursion 7. 214
All generous feelings flourish and rejoice; 862 Excursion 7. 328
This generous Youth, too negligent of self, 870 Excursion 7. 867
A panegyric from your generous tongue! 875 Excursion 8. 83
The generous inclination, the just rule, 887 Excursion 9. 241
Genève. Of Eau de Zurich, Lac Genève, S.3 438 *My Lord 16
Geneviève. Of Geneviève. In both her clamorous Halls, 710 Prelude 9. 48
Genial. Rolled fast along the sky his warm and genial moon. 32 Guilt 414
The snows dissolved, and genial Spring returned 150 *When, to 43
A happy, genial influence, 158 *In youth 70
They met me in a genial hour, 191 Seq. Beggars 14
To genial faith, still rich in genial good; 195 Resolution 39
Suffer my genial spirits to decay: 207 Tintern 113
Their course, or genial showers descend! 227 Vernal Ode 70
Through all vicissitudes, till genial Spring 263 *How clear 13
Invisible? yet Spring her genial brow 267 *Desponding Father 5
From desolation toward the genial prime; 274 *Such age 11
The genial spot had *ever* shown 348 *Lulled by 10
Brought to this genial climate, when disease 353 Aquap. 58
Those images of genial beauty, oft 355 Aquap. 200
A genial hearth, a hospitable board, 444 Ecc. Sonn. 3. 18. 1
Strains offered only to the genial Spring. 449 Ecc. Sonn. 3. 33. 14
Hence have I genial seasons, hence have I 489 Pers. Talk 47
Upon the genial sense of youth 492 Duty 12

Genial—*continued.*
Should praise thee, genial Power! 507 May 14
To rural incidents, whose genial powers 525 Epist. Beaumont 268
To his own genial instincts; and was heard 537 *In desultory 5
Old am I, and to genial pleasure slow; 557 Cuck. and Night. 37
Hath been revived, and if this genial mood 641 Prelude 1. 637
The last night's genial feeling overflowed 687 Prelude 7. 43
The Swede, the Russian; from the genial south, 690 Prelude 7. 224
My journey, and beneath a genial sun, 725 Prelude 10. 516
With genial feelings still predominant; 729 Prelude 11. 156
Prophetic sympathies of genial faith: 735 Prelude 12. 48
When genial circumstance hath favoured them, 736 Prelude 12. 157
Of genial thought in childhood, and in spite 749 Prelude 14. 239
Ministering to our need. In genial mood, 782 Excursion 2. 688
Beside a fire whose genial warmth seemed met 785 Excursion 2. 884
That in more genial times, when I was free 790 Excursion 3. 283
For every genial power of heaven and earth, 888 Excursion 9. 265
Perhaps for many genial days to come, K.8. 241 Recluse 1. 1. 191
With a strange sound of genial harmony; K.8. 252 Recluse 1. 1. 582
Genii. The native Genii walk the mountain green? 16 Desc. Sk. 341
Dwarf Genii, moonlight-loving Fays, 164 Needlecase 22
Ye Genii! to his covert speed; 458 *Had this 57
Fays, Genii of gigantic size! 526 *The soaring 33
Aw'd, while below the Genii hold their state. 598 Ev. Wk. Quarto 358
Round a lone fane the human Genii mourn, 613 Desc. Sk. Quarto 646
By Genii of romance; or hath in grave 688 Prelude 7. 79
Crowded with Genii busy among works 694 Prelude 7. 456
Genii, and winged Angels that are Lords K.8. 237 Recluse 1. 1. 34
Genius. The " parting Genius " sighs with hollow breath 12 Desc. Sk. 71
Which genius did not hallow; 'gainst the taint 23 Yew-tree 17
When the wings of genius rise, 163 Hint 2
With hues of genius on his cheek 192 Ruth 31
His genius and his moral frame 194 Ruth 151
Of Plato's genius, from its lofty sphere, 212 Dion 9
A Genius dwells, that can subdue 214 Kirkstone 35
The local Genius ne'er befriends 223 Wishing-gate 40
Genius of Raphael! if thy wings 231 Jew. Fam. 1
Such strains of rapture as the Genius played 252 *The fairest 5
Bard of the Fleece, whose skilful genius made 254 Dyer 1
Thy genius forward like a wingèd steed. 260 *From the dark 4
Might cool;—and, as the Genius of the flood 268 *Dogmatic Teachers 7
Yet, helped by Genius—untired comforter, 273 *While Anna's 9
No public harm that Genius from her course 280 Plea for Auth. 13
He sang, his genius " glinted " forth, 285 Grave of Burns 20
There seek the genius of your Sire, 286 Sons of Burns 29
The local Genius hurries me aloft, 353 Aquap. 34
His milder Genius (thanks to the good God 362 *List—'twas 42
In the flower-besprent meadows his genius we trace 364 Vallomb. 13
And ne'er did Genius slight them, as they go, 392 Avon 7
Of pity or fear; and More's gay genius played 435 Ecc. Sonn. 2. 26. 12
Thy heart! what hopes inspired thy genius, skilled, 436 Ecc. Sonn. 2. 31. 11
The soul of Genius, if he dare to take 455 *Not in the lucid 12
Alas! the Genius of our age, from Schools 468 St. Bees 154
Whose lofty genius could survive 473 Ossian 57
Of genius from the dust: 499 *Departing summer 57
Then Genius, shunning fellowship with Pride, 500 Humanity 55
Sighed for, in heart and genius, overcome 528 *Those breathing 93
With which his genius shook the buskined stage. 547 *Beneath yon 16
The Genius of plenty preserved him from harm: 569 Farmer 30
O now that the genius of Bewick were mine, 571 Avarice 1
And his pure native genius, lead him back 573 Chiabrera 2. 6
Commemorating genius, talent, skill, 584 *With copious 61
So genius triumphed over seeming wrong, 584 Ch. Lamb 15
—There, did the iron Genius not disdain 607 Desc. Sk. Quarto 307
Yet more; the tyrant Genius, still at strife 613 Desc. Sk. Quarto 608
What Genius smiles on yonder flood? 626 †Cento 4
The glory of my youth. Of genius, power, 651 Prelude 3. 170
Genius of Burke! forgive the pen seduced 694 Prelude 7. 512
Whose genius spangled o'er a gloomy theme 695 Prelude 7. 565
Entered, with Shakspeare's genius, the wild woods 701 Prelude 8. 138
Or genius, under Nature, under God, 703 Prelude 8. 259
Hence Genius, born to thrive by interchange 740 Prelude 13. 5
And that the Genius of the Poet hence 744 Prelude 13. 295
" Yes," said the Priest, " the Genius of our hills— 844 Excursion 6. 392
His genius mounted to the plains of heaven. 865 Excursion 7. 506
In him revealed a scholar's genius shone; 868 Excursion 7. 737
As if some friendly Genius had ordained 892 Excursion 9. 522
Genoa. Of Genoa the superb—should there be led 354 Aquap. 123
Gentiles. The Apostle of the Gentiles; both prepared 357 Aquap. 312
Gentiless. All gentiless and honour thence come forth; 559 Cuck. and Night. 152
In winning words, since through her gentiless, 562 Cuck. and Night. 300
Gentle. When gentle Spirits urged a sportive chase, 7 Ev. Wk. 301
To them the gentle groups of bliss deny 19 Desc. Sk. 506
And in such wise to rack her gentle heart 41 Bord. 241
God bless and thank you both, my gentle Masters. 46 Bord. 526
What can I do? believe me, gentle Sirs, 47 Bord. 535
As beautiful, and gentle and benign, 57 Bord. 1105
Has been forgotten. Farewell! Gentle pilgrims, 58 Bord. 1140
Soon would her gentle voice make peace between us. 61 Bord. 1318
We must be gentle. Leave him to my care. 73 Bord. 2035
If I may dare to cherish hope that gentle eyes will read 93 Poet's Dream 79
He laid his implements with gentle care, 95 Brothers 33
Now, gentle Muses, your assistance grant, 103 Artegal 61
—A gentle Maid, whose heart is lowly bred, 106 Farewell 28
Great wonder to our gentle tribe it was 108 Indolence 28

Ghost—*continued.*
Returning, like a ghost unlaid, 182 *Waggoner* 4. 214
By ruder fancy, that a troubled ghost 219 *Haunted Tree* 28
Uprises like a ghost ! 243 *P. B.* 580
No ghost more softly ever trod ; 247 *P. B.* 987
But this wild Ruin is no ghost 298 *Brownie's Cell* 13
A ghost, by glimpses, may present 301 *Bran* 80
In the grey sky hath left his lingering Ghost, 392 **Though joy* 4
The feudal Warrior-chief, a Ghost unlaid, 393 *Inglewood* 11
Here wanders like a gliding ghost, 416 *White Doe* 1883
Along the plain of Sarum, by the ghost 419 *Ecc. Sonn.* 1. 5. 4
In him who at the ghost of guilt doth start. 423 *Ecc. Sonn.* 1. 20. 12
By sound, or ghost of sound, in mazy strife ; 451 *Ecc. Sonn.* 3. 44. 12
The Ghost of Fingal to his tuneful Cave 473 **We saw* 6
A wandering Ghost, so thinks the Knight, 479 *Somnamb.* 100
If Emma's Ghost it were, 479 *Somnamb.* 128
Or wan despair—the ghost of false hope fled 514 **Long-favoured* 8
Which some have named her Predecessor's ghost. 532 **Once I* 6
And he gave up the ghost full peacefully ; 556 *Prioress* 221
Soon after, this man's Ghost unto him came 623 **I find* 6
Simonides, admonished by the ghost, 623 **I find* 9
A dismal look ; the yew-tree had its ghost, 704 *Prelude* 8. 379
Breathed up its smoke, an image of his ghost 705 *Prelude* 8. 449
Eternity, as men constrain a ghost 796 *Excursion* 3. 688
He came, the ghost of beauty and of health, 843 *Excursion* 6. 330
Is haunted—by what ghost ? a gentle spirit K.8. 247 *Recluse* 1. 1. 387
Ghost-like. The ghost-like image of a cloud ? 242 *P. B.* 502
Spots where a word, ghost-like, survives to show 389 *Sound of Mull* 5
Ghostliness. Had bodied forth the ghostliness of things 681 *Prelude* 6. 428
Ghostly. With unrejoicing berries—ghostly Shapes 185 *Yew-trees* 25
Pray in ghostly agonies. 204 *Brougham* 68
The ghostly word, thus plainly seen, 245 *P. B.* 756
A thousand ghostly fears, and haunting thoughts, proceed ! 346 *Gemmi* 14
By ghostly power :—but Time's unsparing hand 383 *Duddon* 27. 10
A ghostly Domination, unconfined 428 *Ecc. Sonn.* 1. 39. 4
But from the ghostly tenants of the wind, 435 *Ecc. Sonn.* 2. 27. 3
And they could hear *his* ghostly song who trod 474 **Ye shadowy* 6
The ghostly language of the ancient earth, 646 *Prelude* 2. 309
His ghostly figure moving at my side ; 665 *Prelude* 4. 434
The ghostly semblance of a hooded monk, 708 *Prelude* 8. 586
With long and ghostly shanks—forms which once seen 759 *Excursion* 1. 184
Ghosts. I look for ghosts ; but none will force 117 *Affl. Marg.* 57
Among the ghosts his own undoing ; 128 *Idiot Boy* 230
We shall be meeting ghosts to-night ! " 179 *Waggoner* 3. 115
Apart from happy Ghosts, that gather flowers 212 *Laod.* 162
Into the land where ghosts and phantoms be ; 279 **All praise* 7
Unhappy ghosts in troops by moonlight seen ; 361 **For action* 8
Thronged yesterday by airy ghosts ; 391 *HighlandBroach* 74
Than ghosts are fabled to appear 407 *White Doe* 1047
In long succession, pre-existing ghosts 547 **Rude is* 9
Of Wallace, like a family of Ghosts, 635 *Prelude* 1. 217
Ghyll. *See* **Dungeon-Ghyll, Gill.**
Brightens with water-breaks the hollow ghyll 3 *Ev. Wk.* 54
Up the tumultuous brook of Green-head Ghyll, 131 *Michael* 2
Near the tumultuous brook of Green-head Ghyll, 136 *Michael* 322
Beside the boisterous brook of Green-head Ghyll. 138 *Michael* 482
Giant. Even if thou saw'st the giant wicker rear 26 *Guilt* 122
Spares not the worm. The giant and the worm— 57 *Bord.* 1079
From the peak of the crag blew the giant away. 86 *Rural Arch.* 16
And I'll build up a giant with you. 86 *Rural Arch.* 24
Is one of giant stature, who could dance 111 *'Tis said that some 46
This Oak, a giant and a sage, 156 *Oak and Broom* 19
That tall Man, a giant in bulk and in height, 189 *Music* 33
Come like a giant from a haven broad ; 258 **With Ships* 6
His giant body o'er the steep rock's brink, 336 *Aar* 2
Of giant yews that frown on Rydale's mere ; 591 *Ev. Wk. Quarto* 8
Beyond the mountain's giant reach that hides 598 *Ev. Wk. Quarto* 337
A giant moan along the forest swells 605 *Desc.Sk.Quarto* 201
—Bursts from the troubl'd Larch's giant boughs 606 *Desc.Sk.Quarto* 229
In size a giant, stalking through thick fog, 703 *Prelude* 8. 266
Oh ! wrap him in your shades, ye giant woods 733 *Prelude* 11. 418
Of those that crowd the giant wicker thrills 744 *Prelude* 13. 333
The waste of death ; and lo ! the giant oak 865 *Excursion* 7. 547
Giant-killer. Of Jack the Giant-killer, Robin Hood, 670 *Prelude* 5. 343
The champion, Jack the Giant-killer : Lo ! 691 *Prelude* 7. 280
Giant-mother. Speak, Giant-mother ! tell it to the Morn 477 *Long Meg* 8
Giant-quelling. The giant-quelling bolts of Jove, I flee, 624 *Æneid* 13
Giant's. The giant's strength ; and, at the voice of Justice, 57 *Bord.* 1078
Giants. And Albion's giants quelled, 102 *Artegal* 14
When giants scooped from out the rocky ground, 269 *Malham* 2
(Giants—the same who built in Erin's isle 269 *Malham* 4
Of Westminster ; the Giants of Guildhall ; 689 *Prelude* 7. 131
With ample recompense; giants and dwarfs, 691 *Prelude* 7. 271
Giants, Ventriloquists, the Invisible Girl, 698 *Prelude* 7. 710
Romance of giants, chronicle of fiends, 759 *Excursion* 1. 180
Giant-size. Advertisements, of giant-size, from high 690 *Prelude* 7. 194
Gibber. A grand domain to squeak and gibber in. 61 *Bord.* 1304
Gibbet. He looked, and saw upon a gibbet high 25 *Guilt* 78
Gibbet-mast. The gibbet-mast had mouldered down, the bones 737 *Prelude* 12. 237
Gibe. Are fostered by the comment and the gibe." 488 *Pers. Talk* 20
Gibraltar. From high Gibraltar to Siberian plains, 509 *F. Stone* 92
Giddier. To giddier heights hath clomb the Papal sway. 427 *Ecc. Sonn.* 1. 35. 1
Giddiness. Which, in the giddiness of self-applause, 358 *Aquap.* 352
Giddy. No meadows thrown between, the giddy steeps 12 *Desc. Sk.* 79
Where is he that giddy Sprite, 171 *Kitten* 63
To rouse the wicked from their giddy dream— 330 *Ode : Thanks.* 80
Of giddy Bacchanals belong ? 344 **How blest* 36
Or, to the giddy top of self-esteem 505 *Warning* 124
Are prompt attendants, 'mid that giddy bliss 640 *Prelude* 1. 583
With giddy motion. But the time approached 642 *Prelude* 2. 48
And giddy prospect of the raving stream, 684 *Prelude* 6. 633
Giddy and restless ; ever and anon 842 *Excursion* 6. 241
Into the lists of giddy enterprise— 842 *Excursion* 6. 286
To run the giddy round of vain delight, 885 *Excursion* 9. 91
Not giddy yet aerial, with a depth K.8. 237 *Recluse* 1. 1. 20
Gideon. And Gideon blew the trumpet, soul-inflamed, 870 *Excursion* 7. 815
Gift. The same that tempted me to loathe the gift.— 54 *Bord.* 921
Softened till it becomes a gift of mercy. 61 *Bord.* 1340
Grew, by strength the gift of love, 93 *Westmoreland Girl* 22
Nor can the winds restore his simple gift. 103 *Artegal* 44
I but repay a gift which I myself 136 *Michael* 363
As sure as I've the gift of sight, 179 *Waggoner* 3. 114
The gift of this adventurous song ; 182 *Waggoner* 4. 198
To them I may have owed another gift, 206 *Tintern* 36
Accept the gift, behold him face to face ! " 209 *Laod.* 24
The bosom-weight, your stubborn gift, 225 *Present.* 25
The Gift to king Amphion 234 *Power of Sound* 129
Wilt smile upon this gift with more than mild content ! 250 **Happy the* 14
On favoured ground, thy gift, where I might dwell 251 *Appleth.* 3
A soothing recompense, his gift, is thine ! 272 *Ruins* 14
That every gift of noble origin 308 **These times* 10
A gift of that which is not to be given 312 **A Roman* 13
The gift of immortality ; 345 **How blest* 75
Were but the Gift a meet Return to thee 352 *H. C. R.* 6
Or gift to be presented at the throne 394 **No more* 13
There let at least the gift be laid, 410 *White Doe* 1296
And welcome, as a gift of grace, 414 *White Doe* 1678
Thou wretched Outcast, from the gift of fire 419 *Ecc. Sonn.* 1. 4. 2
Maintains the else endangered gift of life ; 432 *Ecc. Sonn.* 2. 16. 11
The gift exalting, and with playful smile : 438 *Ecc. Sonn.* 2. 39. 5
A portion of the gift is won ; 457 **Had this* 38
Shall *now* by such a gift with joy be moved, 504 *Warning* 51
Of an immortal spirit, is a gift 519 *Pun. Death* 10. 2
Your gift, ere shutters close— 526 **The soaring* 52
" Such bounty is no gift of chance," 545 *Russ. Fug.* 329
But benefits, his gift, we trace— 578 **I come* 58
O gift divine of quiet sequestration ! 586 *Ch. Lamb* 121
From such Pandorian gift may come a Pest 626 *Ballot* 12
But for a gift that consecrates the joy ? 632 *Prelude* 1. 32
To lack that first great gift, the vital soul, 634 *Prelude* 1. 150
The gift is yours ; if in these times of fear 648 *Prelude* 2. 432
The blessing of my life ; the gift is yours, 648 *Prelude* 2. 445
A gift then first bestowed. The varied banks 678 *Prelude* 6. 203
Share with us thy fresh spirits, whether gift 678 *Prelude* 6. 250
By Nature's gift so favoured. Upon a board 692 *Prelude* 7. 356
A gift that was come rather late than soon. 713 *Prelude* 9. 248
The gift which God has placed within his power, 714 *Prelude* 9. 356
The gift of tongues might fall, and power arrive 720 *Prelude* 10. 139
Yea, never thought of judging ; with the gift 737 *Prelude* 12. 189
Of calmness equally are Nature's gift : 740 *Prelude* 13. 2
A gift, to use a term which they would use, 742 *Prelude* 13. 188
Heaven's gift, a sense that fits him to perceive 744 *Prelude* 13. 304
The last and later portions of this gift 752 *Prelude* 14. 415
A gift of genuine insight ; that my Song 755 *Recluse* 1. 1. 841
A precious gift ; for, as he grew in years, 758 *Excursion* 1. 140
Of red ripe currants ; gift by which he strove, 779 *Excursion* 2. 505
His bounteous gift ! or saw him toward the deep 803 *Excursion* 4. 116
No—they sank into me, the bounteous gift 820 *Excursion* 4. 1286
To those who need the gift. But, after all, 831 *Excursion* 5. 586
And that best gift of heaven hath fallen on them ; 833 *Excursion* 5. 720
She gazed as on a pure and spotless gift 852 *Excursion* 6. 908
His Daughter, and that late and high-prized gift, 861 *Excursion* 7. 261
The precious gift of hearing. He grew up 863 *Excursion* 7. 402
" The Father—him at this unlooked-for gift 867 *Excursion* 7. 648
That in the steeple hang, his pious gift." 872 *Excursion* 7. 975
Seems but a fleeting sunbeam's gift, whose peace 891 *Excursion* 9. 472
The gift of winds, and whom the winds again K.8. 251 *Recluse* 1. 1. 541
With zeal, acknowledgment that with the gift K.8. 255 *Recluse* 1. 1. 671
Gifted. *See* **Soul-gifted.**
Gifted to purge the vapoury atmosphere 380 *Duddon* 18. 8
Thus, gifted Friend, but with the placid brow 529 **Those breathing* 133
Why, gifted with such powers to send abroad 666 *Prelude* 5. 48
Gifts. With these our latest gifts of tender thought ; 106 *Farewell* 20
Hast taken gifts which thou dost little need. 107 *Farewell* 40
And fortune with her gifts and lies. 117 *Affl. Marg.* 42
Two separate Creatures in their several gifts 118 *Maternal Grief* 30
Its natural gifts for purposes of rest, 123 *V. and J.* 139
Than that a child, more than all other gifts 133 *Michael* 146
In stray gifts to be claimed by whoever shall find ; 167 *Stray Pleasures* 28
Faint I, nor mourn nor murmur ; other gifts 206 *Tintern* 86
His gifts imperfect :—Spectre though I be, 210 *Laod.* 38
Full surely, with such proud gifts of life 231 **The gentlest Poet* 24
Disparaging Man's gifts, and proper food. 263 **Those words* 8
Sweet Fancy ! other gifts must I receive ; 270 **Shame on* 9
And so, His gifts and promises between, 278 **Life with* 13
Gifts which, for wonder or delight, 296 *Highland Boy* 109
Such gifts had those seafaring men 296 *Highland Boy* 111
Such simple gifts prepare, 324 *Ode 1814* 47

Gifts—*continued.*
Thy gifts, magnificent Region, ever young . . 367 **As indignation* 5
In sacred converse gifts with Alfred shares. . . 425 *Ecc. Sonn.* 1. 26. 14
Were not some gifts withheld by jealous hands, . 455 *Rydal Mere* 18
A peaceful spot where Nature's gifts abound ; . 470 †*From early* 12
What witchery, for pure gifts of inward seeing, . 480 *Cordelia* 12
Their gifts she hails (deemed precious, as they prove 503 *Warning* 28
Thy gifts, thy beauty scorn ; . . . . . . 507 *May* 4
And shall the Verse not tell of lighter gifts . . 540 **Lady ! a* 67
Present the maddening gifts, and kindle heat . 624 *Æneid* 5
Achates, with the gifts to Carthage hied ; . . . 624 *Æneid* 54
They look with wonder on the gifts—they gaze . 624 *Æneid* 73
She views the gifts ; upon the child then turns . 624 *Æneid* 81
Those lofty hopes awhile, for present gifts . . 634 *Prelude* 1. 133
Its dignity ; with gifts he bubbles o'er . . 670 *Prelude* 5. 301
Where I was reared ; in Nature's primitive gifts . 700 *Prelude* 8. 99
Endowed by Nature with her fairest gifts . . . 711 *Prelude* 9. 149
To me came rarely charged with natural gifts, . 724 *Prelude* 10. 401
And all the earth was budding with these gifts . 750 *Prelude* 14. 263
By Nature ; men endowed with highest gifts, . 757 *Excursion* 1. 78
Baronial court or royal ; cheered with gifts . 771 *Excursion* 2. 3
" For this fair Bride, most rich in gifts of mind, . 774 *Excursion* 2. 191
On you have been conferred ? what gifts, withheld 805 *Excursion* 4. 279
But is that bounty absolute ?—His gifts, . . . 817 *Excursion* 4. 1093
Powers not unjustly likened to those gifts . . 835 *Excursion* 5. 844
With personal gifts, and bright instinctive wit, . 843 *Excursion* 6. 305
Fall to the ground ; whose gifts of nature lie . . 862 *Excursion* 7. 317
Thy gifts were utterly withheld from him . . 864 *Excursion* 7. 486
Gifts nobler are vouchsafed alike to all ; . . . 887 *Excursion* 9. 221
From whom all gifts descend, all blessings flow ! " 895 *Excursion* 9. 754
On objects unaccustomed to the gifts K.8. 248*Recluse* 1.1.433
Gigantic. Left by gigantic arms—at length surveys 26 *Guilt* 113
Gigantic mountains rough with crags ; beneath, . 219 **This Height* 12
Science advances with gigantic strides ; . . . 281 **What strong* 7
Among the interior Alps, gigantic crew, . . . 350 *Des. Stanzas* 20
Fays, Genii of gigantic size ! . . . . . 526 **The soaring* 33
Swell more gigantic on the steadfast sight ; . . 606 *Desc.Sk.Quarto* 248
From Heaven, gigantic force to beardless boys. . 628 *Eagle and Dove* 16
Of some gigantic warrior clad in mail, . . . 708 *Prelude* 8. 585
And majesty with this gigantic stream, . . . 799 *Excursion* 3. 883
Measuring the force of those gigantic powers . . 877 *Excursion* 8. 205
Gild. To gild the total tablet of his days ; . . . 2 *Ev. Wk.* 30
Fair Prime of life ! were it enough to gild . . 261 **Fair Prime* 1
Shall gild their passage to eternal rest." . . . 474 **How sad* 14
Nor failed to gild the spires of Bonn, ... 629 *Installation* 61
Gilded. A broad and gilded vane. . . . . . 86 *Anecdote* 52
Leading such companion I that gilded dome, . . 140 *Arm. Lady* 41
Within her gilded cage confined . . . . . 165 *Parrot* 1
And the green, gilded snake, without troubling the calm . . . . 340 *Fort Fuentes* 7
And the green lizard and the gilded newt . . . 433 *Ecc. Sonn.* 2. 21. 7
And gilded flocks appear. . . . . 457 **Had this* 32
Drawn forth by pressure of his gilded chains, . . 528 **Those breathing* 101
The gilded turf arrays in richer green . . . . 594 *Ev. Wk. Quarto* 161
From gilded rafters many a blazing light . . . 625 *Æneid* 101
And gilded sympathies, the willow wreath, . . 683 *Prelude* 6. 552
And the horse under him—in gilded pomp . . 689 *Prelude* 7. 134
More solid than the gilded clouds of heaven ? . . 792 *Excursion* 3. 438
The gilded summer flies to mix and weave . . 807 *Excursion* 4. 446
Gilding. Gilding that cottage with her fondest ray, 8 *Ev. Wk.* 347
The very gilding, lamps and painted scrolls, . . 693 *Prelude* 7. 408
Gilds. Sapped by the very beam that gilds. . . 550 *Hermit's Cell* 2. 24
Giles. And from long banishment recall Saint Giles, 815 *Excursion* 4. 911
Gilfred. We've weathered out together. My poor Gilfred ! . . . . 46 *Bord.* 513
Gill. *See* **Ghyll.**
What is't that ails young Harry Gill ? . . . . 536 *Goody Blake* 2
'Tis all the same with Harry Gill ; . . . . . 536 *Goody Blake* 10
'Tis all the same with Harry Gill ; . . . . . 536 *Goody Blake* 14
To seek the hedge of Harry Gill. . . . . . 537 *Goody Blake* 64
She's at the hedge of Harry Gill ! . . . . . 537 *Goody Blake* 80
Alas ! that day for Harry Gill ! . . . . . 537 *Goody Blake* 108
" Poor Harry Gill is very cold." . . . . . 537 *Goody Blake* 124
Of Goody Blake and Harry Gill ! . . . . . 537 *Goody Blake* 128
Bright'ning with water-breaks the sombrous gill ; . 592 *Ev. Wk. Quarto* 72
Gillies. Rise, GILLIES, rise : the gales of youth shall bear . . . . 260 **From the dark* 3
Gilt. *See* **Sun-gilt.**
And now the van is guilt with evening's beam, . 595 *Ev. Wk. Quarto* 185
Giordano. Giordano, verily thy Pencil's skill . . 401 **Giordano, verily* 1
Gipsy. *See* **Gypsey.**
By choice or doom a gipsy wanders here, . . . 13 *Desc. Sk.* 175
No gipsy cower'd o'er fire of furze or broom ; . . 26 *Guilt* 140
That through our gipsy travel cheered the way ; . 525*Epist.Beaumont* 271
—But, like the vagrants of the gipsy tribe, . . 880 *Excursion* 8. 389
Gipsy-faces. That on their Gipsy-faces falls, . . 192 *Gipsies* 7
Gipsy-fire. A gipsy-fire we kindled on the shore . 892 *Excursion* 9. 527
Gipsy-folk. And joined the wandering gipsy-folk. . 128 *Idiot Boy* 226
Gird. Hail to the crown by Freedom shaped—to gird 838 *Excursion* 6. 1
Girded. Of time and nature, girded by a zone . . 813 *Excursion* 4. 824
Girding. Or posy, girding round the several fronts 872 *Excursion* 7. 973
Girdle. A narrow girdle of rough stones and crags, 148 **A narrow* 1
O joy when the girdle of England appears ! . . 346 *Stanzas:Simplon* 30
And thus, with girdle round his waist, ... 404 *White Doe* 749
Girds. With orb and cycle girds the starry throng. 429 *Ecc. Sonn.* 2. 5. 14
Girl. *See* **Cottage-Girl.**
I do not see Idonea. Dutiful Girl, ... 43 *Bord.* 337
I cast a look upon the Girl, and felt . . . . 45 *Bord.* 476
Idonea, as he calls her ; but the Girl . . . . 46 *Bord.* 509
The blind Man—at the silent Girl he looked . . 47 *Bord.* 540

Girl—*continued.*
To make a bed for me !—My Girl will weep . . 52 *Bord.* 817
Shall feign a sudden illness, and the Girl, . . . 59 *Bord.* 1185
And there a little Girl I found, ... 82 *Alice Fell* 19
Sat the poor girl, and forth did send . . . . 82 *Alice Fell* 38
I met a little cottage Girl : . . . . 83 *We are Seven* 5
Whose fierce wrath the Girl had braved ; . . . 93 *Westmoreland Girl* 18
Yes, the wild Girl of the mountains . . . . 94 *Westmoreland Girl* 61
Such union, in the lovely Girl maintained . . . 118 *Maternal Grief* 38
The Girl, in rock and plain, ... 187 **Three years* 9
A sweet and playful Highland girl, ... 246 *P. B.* 888
The Highland girl—it is no other ; . . . . . 246 *P. B.* 927
Forthwith a little Girl appeared. . . . . . 247 *P. B.* 1000
Dear Child ! dear Girl ! that walkest with me here, 258 **It is a* 9
Like a bold Girl, who plays her agile pranks . 260 **How sweet* 6
Sweet Highland Girl, a very shower . . . . 287 *Highland Girl* 1
Sweet Highland Girl ! from thee to part ; . . 288 *Highland Girl* 73
The HELVETIAN Girl—who daily braves, . . . 344 **How blest* 29
" Sweet HIGHLAND Girl ! a very shower . . . 344 **How blest* 53
A blooming Girl, whose hair was wet . . . . 487 **We walked* 43
Her Mother's favourite ; and the orphan Girl, . 509 *F. Stone* 66
When, yet a slender Girl, she often led, . . . 523 *Epist. Beaumont* 109
His slender manacles ; or romping girl . . . 693 *Prelude* 7. 421
Giants, Ventriloquists, the Invisible Girl, . . . 698 *Prelude* 7. 710
One day to meet a hunger-bitten girl, ... 717 *Prelude* 9. 510
Its sustenance, while the girl with pallid hands . 717 *Prelude* 9. 514
A girl, who bore a pitcher on her head, . . . 738 *Prelude* 12. 251
So, with more ardour than an unripe girl . . . 781 *Excursion* 2. 654
A claim that shattered all.—Our blooming girl, . 795 *Excursion* 3. 638
A hardy Girl continues to provide ; . . . . 856 *Excursion* 6. 1157
Health and good wishes to his new-born girl, . . 867 *Excursion* 7. 655
Light as the silver fawn, a radiant Girl ; . . . 881 *Excursion* 8. 493
To that fair girl who from the garden-mount . . 882 *Excursion* 8. 554
—But to what object shall the lovely Girl . . 883 *Excursion* 8. 584
The beauteous girl, whose cheek was flushed with joy. . . . . 890 *Excursion* 9. 428
The lovely Girl supplied—a simple song, . . . 892 *Excursion* 9. 534
Feeding on sunshine—to the blushing girl . . . S.3. 435 **The doubt* 141
Girlish. Yet something of a girlish child-like gloss . 693 *Prelude* 7. 446
Girls. " Seven boys and girls are we ; . . . . 84 *We are Seven* 30
The girls on the hills made a holiday show. . . 120 *Childless Father* 8
Of reapers, men and women, boys and girls. . . 149 **A narrow* 41
He told of girls—a happy rout ! . . . . . 193 *Ruth* 49
Weary of barking at him. Boys and girls, . . 567 *Cumb. Beg.* 63
And growing girls whose beauty, filched away . 661 *Prelude* 4. 206
Equestrians, tumblers, women, girls, and boys, . 697 *Prelude* 7. 704
Mother and little children, boys and girls, . . 877 *Excursion* 8. 181
Girt. *See* **Sea-girt, Well-girt.**
Girt round with a bare ring of mossy wall, . . 95 *Brothers* 28
Romans for travel girt, for business gowned ; . . 275 **While poring* 4
On foot they girt their Father round ; . . . . 404 *White Doe* 726
The mountain-side. The mist soon girt us round, 746 *Prelude* 14. 15
That girt her waist, spinning the long-drawn thread 769 *Excursion* 1. 886
A labourer, with moral virtue girt, ... 862 *Excursion* 7. 338
Girth. Content, if foss, and barrow, and the girth . 421 *Ecc. Sonn.* 1. 11. 13
Give. To which the sage would give a prouder name. 10 *Desc. Sk.* 14
Oh ! give not me that eye of hard disdain . . 20 *Desc. Sk.* 545
In an impartial balance, give thine aid . . . 22 *Desc. Sk.* 653
For all this world can give. Nay, be composed : 40 *Bord.* 140
Will give me quiet lodging. You have a boy, good Host, ... 43 *Bord.* 353
When I had none to give him ; whereupon . 44 *Bord.* 400
Shall give me half. What's this ?—I fear, good Woman, ... 46 *Bord.* 489
Father !—to God himself we cannot give . . . 47 *Bord.* 543
'Tis a wild night. I'd give my cloak and bonnet 50 *Bord.* 725
Give me your hand ; where are you, Friends ? and tell me . . . . 52 *Bord.* 804
And spake to you, why did you give no answer ? 55 *Bord.* 959
Give me your sword—nay, here are stones and fragments, ... 56 *Bord.* 1007
When he should give her up, a Woman grown, . 56 *Bord.* 1054
I would not give a denier for the man . . . . 60 *Bord.* 1241
To give it back again ! What mean your words ? 67 *Bord.* 1644
That waking life had never power to give. . . 69 *Bord.* 1794
Give not to them a thought. From Palestine . 70 *Bord.* 1801
Give me a reason why the wisest thing . . . 75 *Bord.* 2149
No human dwelling ever give me food, ... 78 *Bord.* 2347
In search of nothing that this earth can give, . . 78 *Bord.* 2349
Did not virtue give the meanest . . . . . 90 *Longest Day* 63
Give to Him prayers, and many thoughts, in thy most busy days ; . . . . 93 *Poet's Dream* 58
But they to me no joy can give, ... 114 *Ind. Wom.* 17
'Do this : how can we give to you,' . . . . 115 *Last of Flock* 49
He clove to her who could not give him peace— . 123 *V. and J.* 155
He seems, I think, the rein to give ; . . . . 130 *Idiot Boy* 353
(His very words I give to you,) . . . . . . 131 *Idiot Boy* 449
To give their bodies to the family mould. . . . 137 *Michael* 370
But only give some plain directions . . . . 142 †*Lov. and Lik.* 3
I give to thee, for praise or blame, ... 158 **With little* 14
No like remembrances can give, ... 164 **Fair Lady* 10
Comes to give what help he may, ... 181 *Waggoner* 4. 126
He may give thee decent greeting. . . . . . 181 *Waggoner* 4. 137
Such thoughts to Lucy I will give . . . . . 187 **Three years* 34
New objects did new pleasure give, ... 194 *Ruth* 184
Religious men, who give to God and man their dues. . . . . 196 *Resolution* 98
To give me human strength, by apt admonishment. 197 *Resolution* 112

Givest—continued.

And Thou, wild Stream, that giv'st the honoured name . . . . 539 *Lady! a 23
That givest to forms and images a breath . 638 Prelude 1. 403

Giveth. Sir Galahad! a treasure, that God giveth, 374 Eg. Maid 344

Giving. See Alms-giving.

Too quickly moved, too easily giving way, . 76 Bord. 2233
By giving him, for both our sakes, an hour of holiday. . . . . 92 Poet's Dream 20
Giving to her sound for sound! . . . 209 *Yes, it 4
Nor giving heed to aught that passed the while, 365 *Under the 3
Giving to Memory help when she would weave 448 Ecc. Sonn. 3. 33. 5
That obvious emblem giving to the eye . 535 *When in 25
Giving him always hope, that she the morrow 565 Troilus 167
Marshal the banquet, giving with due grace . 624 Æneid 69
To more than infant softness, giving me . 636 Prelude 1. 278
Accomplished, giving thus unto events . 711 Prelude 9. 104
Was never much my habit—giving way . 736 Prelude 12. 114
And, to the silent language giving voice, . 825 Excursion 5. 189
Of giving welcome to the first of May . 851 Excursion 6. 834
And giving back, and shedding each on each, 893 Excursion 9. 603
Joy giving voice to fervent gratitude. . 895 Excursion 9. 742
And giving to the moments as they pass . K.8. 249 Recluse 1.1.466

Glacier. The glacier Pillars join in solemn guise 347 Processions 49
Bear to the glacier band—those Shapes aloft descried. . . . . 347 Processions 63

Glad. And glad Dundee in "faint huzzas" expired? 16 Desc. Sk. 302
In that glad moment will for you a sigh . 20 Desc. Sk. 565
In that glad moment when your hands are prest . 20 Desc. Sk. 567
Death's minister; then came his glad release, . 25 Guilt 57
How glad he was at length to find some trace . 27 Guilt 157
The gallows would one day of him be glad;— 33 Guilt 484
'Twill glad her heart to see her father's signature. 49 Bord. 669
How glad I am to hear your voice! I know not 60 Bord. 1279
With the glad tidings which this day hath brought; 66 Bord. 1593
—Her beauty made me glad. . . . 83 We are Seven 12
Should come, 'twould needs be a glad day for him; 100 Brothers 326
Of glad or willing service to thy share would fall." 105 Artegal 185
And Skiddaw is glad with the cry of the hounds." 120 Childless Father 4
And Betty listens, glad to hear it. . . 127 Idiot Boy 101
The little Pony glad may be, . . . 130 Idiot Boy 394
And her face brightened. The old Man was glad, 135 Michael 273
But Isabel was glad when Sunday came . 135 Michael 288
But nay, my heart is far too glad; . . 144 Her Eyes 12
Sent forth such sallies of glad sound, that all . 146 *It was an 23
Fancy, who leads the pastimes of the glad, . 153 Morn. Ex. 1
First at sight of thee was glad; . . . 160 *Pleasures newly 4
Glad sight wherever new with old . . 164 *Glad sight 1
The echoes make a glad reply.— . . 180 Waggoner 4. 6
I am glad for him, blind as he is!—all the while 188 Music 31
"How glad is Skipton at this hour" . . 204 Brougham 36
How glad Pendragon—though the sleep . 204 Brougham 40
Rejoiced is Brough, right glad, I deem, . 204 Brougham 44
Glad were the vales, and every cottage-hearth; 205 Brougham 169
And their glad animal movements all gone by) 206 Tintern 74
Glad Hope would almost cease to be . 217 Enterprise 158
Glad moment is it when the throng . . 221 Triad 80
Wherever strikes the sun's glad ray; . . 227 Vernal Ode 67
And the glad Muse at liberty to note . 251 *Her only 4
Glad thought for every season! but the Spring 266 *The stars 9
More prompt, more glad, to fall than drops of dew 276 Author's Portrait 11
Glad acclamation by which air was rent! . 312 *A Roman 6
Cleaves its glad way, a cry of harvest home . 322 Germans 7
Now that all hearts are glad, all faces bright, 323 *Now that 1
His glad deliverance has begun . . 343 Eclipse 62
Of my own Fairfield. The glad greeting given, 353 Aquap. 30
Verse to glad notes prophetic of the hour . 361 Alban Hills 11
To carry thy glad tidings over heights . 363 *List—'twas 101
The royal Guinever looked passing glad . 373 Eg. Maid 297
Glad meetings, tender partings, that upstay . 383 Duddon 28. 11
And glad acknowledgment, of lawful sway. . 383 Duddon 29. 14
Glad tidings to Iona's shore, . . . 390 Highland Broach 4
Fit offering of glad victory! . . . 410 White Doe 1279
And all the hills were glad to bear . . 415 White Doe 1775
Glad HALLE-lujahs to the eternal King! . 422 Ecc. Sonn. 1. 13. 14
Their own creation. Such glad welcomings . 431 Ecc. Sonn. 2. 13. 8
Glad music! yet there be that, worn with pain . 447 Ecc. Sonn. 3. 28. 2
Glad, through a perfect love, a faith sincere . 454 *The Sun, that 23
Glad to expand; and, for a season, free . 454 *The Sun, that 25
Spreading his little palms in his glad Mother's sight) . . . . 460 *Queen of 20
Seats of glad instinct and love's carolling, . 464 *Greta, what 11
As blest and as glad, in this desolate gloom, . 484 *A plague 28
And often, glad no more, . . . 487 Fountain 46
We have been glad of yore. . . . 487 Fountain 48
It came, and we were glad; yet tears were shed; 491 Tribute: Dog 21
Glad Hearts! without reproach or blot; . 492 Duty 13
To these glad eyes from bondage freed, again . 496 *A little 50
Glad proclamation make, and heights and dells . 503 Warning 42
Can such a One, dear Babe! though glad and proud . . . . 504 Warning 78
The inmost heart of man if glad . . 507 May 21
Resplendent Wanderer! followed with glad eyes 511 *Who rashly 24
Right glad was he when he beheld her: . 537 Goody Blake 81
And glad, in sooth, was I when he was gone. . 560 Cuck.andNight.220
I shall be glad if all the world be true. . 564 Troilus 133
Glad am I, glad that it is past; . . 580 John Words. 42
Glad from their airy baskets hang and sing. . 594 Ev. Wk. Quarto 150
There turns for glad repose the weary eye; . 598 Ev. Wk. Quarto 366
When hums the mountain bee in May's glad ear, 610 Desc.Sk.Quarto 444
Glad Day-light laughs upon his top of snow, . 615 Desc.Sk.Quarto 700

Glad—continued.

But salutation taking its glad way . . 628 *Deign, Sovereign 3
Glad welcome had I, with some tears, perhaps, . 658 Prelude 4. 27
Of those glad respites, though a soft west wind . 673 Prelude 5. 481
That round us chaunted. Well might we be glad, 674 Prelude 5. 566
Of this glad throng, foot-travellers side by side, . 681 Prelude 6. 415
A glad preamble to this Verse: I sang . 687 Prelude 7. 4
And vein of water, glad to be rolled on . 720 Prelude 10. 172
Had plucked up mercy by the roots, were glad 723 Prelude 10. 332
Of the glad times when first I traversed France . 725 Prelude 16. 288
I see thee linger a glad votary, . . 734 Prelude 11. 469
On the glad eve of its dear holidays, . . 738 Prelude 12. 288
A glad congratulation we exchanged . 757 Excursion 1. 47
To give her comfort, and was glad to take . 766 Excursion 1. 684
Was glad to find her conscience set at ease; . 785 Excursion 2. 888
And not less glad, for sake of her good name, . 785 Excursion 2. 889
"So ends my dolorous tale, and glad I am . 785 Excursion 2. 896
Ye that are capable of joy be glad! . . 796 Excursion 3. 729
Opened, and she re-entered with glad looks, . 834 Excursion 5. 774
To intercept the sun's glad beams—may ne'er . 838 Excursion 6. 23
That he was glad to lose) slunk from the world . 845 Excursion 6. 454
And by desire; we see by the glad light . 884 Excursion 9. 24
A like glad impulse; and so moves the man . 884 Excursion 9. 34
But why be so glad on . . . . S.3. 440 *Said red-ribboned 29
Of glad emotion and deep quietness; . K.8. 243 Recluse 1.1.231
But a glad function natural to man. . K.8. 249 Recluse 1.1.470

Gladden. Comes on to gladden April with the sight 17 Desc. Sk. 368
Like thine, shall gladden, as in seasons past, . 279 *Hark! 'tis 13
That all the Alps may gladden in thy might, . 315 *Advance—come 13
To gladden or to grieve, he hath like skill; . 557 Cuck. and Night. 19

Gladdened. And gladdened all things; but, as chanced, within that very hour, . 91 Poet's Dream 20
And Heaven is now to gladdened eyes revealing, . 455 *Not in the lucid 21
Empress of Night! are gladdened by thy beams; . 459 *Wanderer! that 24
Thus gladdened from our own dear Vale we pass . 524 Epist. Beaumont 164
Were gladdened by the Sage's voice, and hung . 573 Chiabrera 2. 10
From gladdened Elbe to startled Tiber heard. . 629 Installation 104
Gladdened me more than if I had been led . 694 Prelude 7. 454
Clear images before your gladdened eyes . 848 Excursion 6. 652
"Then let us rather fix our gladdened thoughts . 888 Excursion 9. 255

Gladdening. Gladdening the people's heart from shore to shore; . . . 105 Artegal 205
Than pleasure only; gladdening to prepare . 538 *In desultory 23
And meet the gladdening pilgrims on their way. . 614 Desc.Sk.Quarto 665

Gladdens. It gladdens me, O worthy, short-lived, Youth! . . . . 260 Calvert 13
The vast Pacific gladdens with the freight— . 327 Ode 1815 23

Gladder. Shouteth faint tidings of some gladder place. . . . . 776 Excursion 2. 348

Gladdest. The gladdest of the gladsome band, . 177 Waggoner 2. 93

Glade. See Forest-glade, Garden-glade.

Rest near your little plots of wheaten glade; . 13 Desc. Sk. 130
Of lambs that bounded through the glade, . 85 Anecdote 18
This glade of water and this one green field. . 149 M. H. 14
And Truth would skim the flowery glade, . 154 Flower Garden 55
In earth and heaven, in glade and bower, . 187 *Three years 10
A home in every glade? . . . 193 Ruth 78
What wouldst thou more? In sunny glade, . 222 Triad 197
Resounding from the woody glade: . . 247 P. B. 940
Softly resounded through this rocky glade; . 252 *The fairest 4
How sweet the prospect of yon watery glade, . 335 Namur 11
While, o'er the flower-enamelled glade, . 338 *Meek Virgin 35
Jubilant outcry! rock and glade . . 344 *How blest 37
Whom in a sunny glade I chanced to see, . 362 *List—'twas 76
Lingering in a woody glade . . . 407 White Doe 1005
And wild deer bounded through the forest glade, . 450 Ecc. Sonn. 3. 41. 5
Rest, near their little plots of wheaten glade; . 604 Desc.Sk.Quarto 149
Winding it's dark-green wood and emerald glade, . 607 Desc.Sk.Quarto 269
Through upper air to an Italian glade, . 624 Æneid 50
Of Satyrs in some viewless glade, with dance . 716 Prelude 9. 459

Glades. Tend the small harvest of their garden glades; . . . . 12 Desc. Sk. 92
Among the forest glades, while jocund June . 32 Guilt 413
And penetrates the glades. . . . 457 *Had this 24
And wander forth, in forest glades . . 506 *While from 19
And labyrinthine walks, her sunny glades: . 810 Excursion 4. 590
Glades we behold, and into thickets peep, . 892 Excursion 9. 562

Gladiator. The dying Gladiator. So, sad Flower! 169 Love lies Bleeding 9

Gladliest. Where what we gladliest would believe 345 *How blest 68

Gladly. "That, Father! will I gladly do: . 83 Lucy Gray 17
Both gladly now deferred their task; . 85 Shepherd-boys 82
Do thou look gladly on the sight; . . 112 *What heavenly 4
"Susan, I'd gladly stay with you. . . 128 Idiot Boy 186
Yon minarets, would gladly leave for his worst home." . . . 140 Arm. Lady 42
That you will gladly listen to discourse . 147 Joanna 14
Under my cottage-roof, had gladly come . 150 *When, to 54
The harmony thy notes most gladly make . 154 Morn. Ex. 51
And gladly Nature's love partake . . 157 *In youth 7
Right gladly had the horses stirred, . . 178 Waggoner 3. 1
But would you gladly view the spot, . 198 Thorn 91
Would gladly vanish from a Stranger's sight; . 221 Triad 122
Enlightened Teacher, gladly from thy hand . 281 Chris. Words. 1
I gladly commune with the mind and heart . 368 Trajan 25
With mute obeisance gladly paid . . 398 White Doe 166
But mark how gladly, through their own domains, 429 Ecc. Sonn. 2. 4. 6
Approach, come gladly, ye prepared, in sight . 446 Ecc. Sonn. 3. 26. 2
Yet oh! how gladly would the air be stirred . 454 Sea-side 22
And I for five centuries right gladly would be . 482 Character 19

Glass—*continued.*	
Faith may be given, we see as in a glass	828 *Excursion* 5. 393
Glassed. Glassed in a greenhouse, or a parlour shrub	711 *Prelude* 9. 88
The other, glassed in thy unruffled breast,	S.3. 434 **The doubt* 74
Glasses. Glasses he had, that little things display,	108 *Indolence* 59
Decanters, glasses, and the blood-red wine.	644 *Prelude* 2. 144
Ate, drank, and with the fruit and glasses played,	692 *Prelude* 7. 362
Glassy. And insects clothe, like dust, the glassy deep:	4 *Ev. Wk.* 117
Vividly pictured in some glassy pool,	220 *Haunted Tree* 39
And then—upon the glassy flood	242 *P. B.* 549
And showed the Bark upon the glassy flood	252 *Picture* 7
Loitering in glassy pool:	508 *May* 76
Yet might your glassy prison seem	526 **The soaring* 9
Removed in kindness from their glassy Cell	527 **Those breathing* 7
Thy Form was sleeping on a glassy sea.	578 *Peele Castle* 4
Upon the glassy plain; and oftentimes,	639 *Prelude* 1. 452
Through a whole month of calm and glassy days	722 *Prelude* 10. 320
And, on its glassy surface, specks of foam,	800 *Excursion* 3. 973
Along the level of the glassy flood,	891 *Excursion* 9. 508
Yet not at rest, upon the glassy lake.	K.8. 251 *Recluse* 1. 1. 547
Glastonbury. Proud Glastonbury can no more refuse	433 *Ecc. Sonn.* 2. 21. 10
Glazed. *See* **Tear-glazed.**	
Wakes with glazed eye, and feebly sighing—	242 *P. B.* 538
Glead. To guard the royal brood. The sailing glead,	868 *Excursion* 7. 751
Gleam. Be given, not one memorial gleam,	1 *Extract* 12
Of fainter gold, a purple gleam betray.	5 *Ev. Wk.* 177
The rear through iron brown betrays a sullen gleam.	6 *Ev. Wk.* 204
Tipt with eve's latest gleam of burning red.	6 *Ev. Wk.* 211
And still, perhaps, with faithless gleam,	9 *Lines: Boat* 7
The cloister startles at the gleam of arms.	11 *Desc. Sk.* 60
Where, 'mid dim towers and woods, her waters gleam.	13 *Desc. Sk.* 157
Once did the lightning's faint disastrous gleam	26 *Guilt* 133
Sight which, tho' lost at once, a gleam of pleasure shed.	26 *Guilt* 135
Which high and higher mounts with silver gleam:	33 *Guilt* 463
But who shall show, to waking sense, the gleam of light that broke	92 *Poet's Dream* 33
And yet the soul-awakening gleam,	113 *Lament* 15
And one green island, gleam between the stems	151 **When, to* 92
And that bright gleam which thence will fall	174 *Waggoner* 1. 77
Untouched;—in spite of many a gleam	182 *Waggoner* 4. 202
At length a pleasant instantaneous gleam	184 *Night-piece* 8
—Of flowers that with one scarlet gleam	193 *Ruth* 64
Delightful land of verdure, shower and gleam,	229 *Cuckoo-clock* 32
Around the dell a gleam	232 *Jew. Fam.* 46
And rocks that spread a hoary gleam,	240 *P. B.* 392
No glimpse it is, no doubtful gleam;	247 *P. B.* 1003
Which for the loss of that moist gleam atone	250 **Happy the* 8
Rise, then, ye votive Towers! and catch a gleam	253 **Aerial Rock* 13
Enter through ears and eyesight, with such gleam	260 **How sweet* 12
O'er which her pinions shed a silver gleam.	261 **I heard (alas* 8
Thus did the waters gleam, the mountains lower,	265 **Hail, Twilight* 5
And prompt to welcome every gleam	285 *Nith* 15
Now, while a farewell gleam of evening light	290 *Kilchurn* 23
In motion rapid as the lightning's gleam;	330 *Ode: Thanks.* 78
(Who loves the Cross, yet to the Crescent's gleam	336 *Danube* 3
They, too, who send so far a holy gleam	347 *Processions* 55
Yet thou thyself hast round thee shed a gleam	376 *Duddon* 3. 12
Comes gliding in with lovely gleam,	396 *White Doe* 55
Dark moor, and gleam of pool and stream,	409 *White Doe* 1171
And, ever and anon, how bright a gleam	430 *Ecc. Sonn.* 2. 7. 2
That slackens, and spreads wide a watery gleam,	443 *Ecc. Sonn.* 3. 12. 11
Pierces the ethereal vault; and ('mid the gleam	456 **The leaves* 9
Than doth this silent spectacle—the gleam—	457 **Had this* 19
Of human life when first allowed to gleam	464 *Derwent* 5
I gaze upon a Portrait whose mild gleam	508 *F. Stone* 6
Far as the last gleam of the filmy train	511 **Who rashly* 6
With here and there a faint imperfect gleam	524 *Epist. Beaumont* 181
Where golden flash and silver gleam	526 **The soaring* 11
That happy gleam of vernal eyes	530 *Gleaner* 1
To express what then I saw; and add the gleam,	578 *Peele Castle* 14
Whither is fled the visionary gleam?	588 *Immortality* 56
That tips with eve's last gleam his spiry head.	595 *Ev. Wk. Quarto* 190
Small circles of green radiance gleam around.	597 *Ev. Wk. Quarto* 278
Thence red from different heights with restless gleam	598 *Ev. Wk. Quarto* 373
While mid dim towers and woods her waters gleam:	605 *Desc. Sk. Quarto* 179
To guide his dangerous tread the taper's gleam.	607 *Desc. Sk. Quarto* 316
Gleam war's discordant habits thro' the trees,	615 *Desc. Sk. Quarto* 746
A smooth free course along the watery gleam,	626 **The confidence* 12
At the first gleam of dawn-light, when the Vale,	647 *Prelude* 2. 344
In their true dwelling; now is crossed by gleam	662 *Prelude* 4. 267
The spirit of pleasure, and youth's golden gleam.	678 *Prelude* 6. 236
Too soon, while yet the very flash and gleam	682 *Prelude* 6. 502
Is no where touched by one memorial gleam)	706 *Prelude* 8. 472
A spirit of pleasure and youth's golden gleam:	738 *Prelude* 12. 266
By a faint shining from the heart, a gleam	785 *Excursion* 2. 885
The lingering gleam of their departed lives	847 *Excursion* 6. 611
By his ingenuous beauty, by the gleam	868 *Excursion* 7. 725
And scarcely could you fancy that a gleam	879 *Excursion* 8. 313
With sight of now and then a straggling gleam	K.8. 225 **I will* 50
Gleamed. Gleamed like a vision of delight.	79 *Sparrow's Nest* 4
When first she gleamed upon my sight;	186 **She was* 2
But breezes played, and sunshine gleamed—	385 *Yarrow Rev.* 13
Who *then*, if Dian's crescent gleamed,	497 *Lycoris* 5
That fled, and, flying still before me, gleamed	638 *Prelude* 1. 451
Gleaming. *See* **Dim-gleaming, Dimly-gleaming, Mildly-gleaming.**	
Gleaming—*continued.*	
With pearl or gleaming agate vies	165 *Parrot* 7
And glancing, gleaming, dark or bright,	205 *Brougham* 126
Gleaming like a silver shield!	217 **Inmate of* 16
Tempt the smooth water, or the gleaming ice,	218 *Recluse* 1. 1. 223
Waves high, embellished by a gleaming shower!	226 *Vernal Ode* 20
Thy temples fringed with locks of gleaming white,	274 **Such age* 7
And upright weapons innocently gleaming,	324 *Ode 1814* 54
Was seated in her gleaming shallop,	371 *Eg. Maid* 116
The tribulation—and the gleaming blades—	421 *Ecc. Sonn.* 1. 12. 2
Traversed by gleaming ships, looked up to thee	460 **Queen of* 7
With gleaming lights more gracefully adorn	471 *Ailsa Crag* 3
Queens gleaming through their splendour's last decay,	640 *Prelude* 1. 533
Of colours, lurking, gleaming up and down	657 *Prelude* 3. 561
Lake, islands, promontories, gleaming bays,	658 *Prelude* 4. 8
Cased in the gleaming mail the monarch wore,	689 *Prelude* 7. 139
Gleaming through colouring of other times,	706 *Prelude* 8. 507
Dishevelled, gleaming eyes, and rueful cheek	710 *Prelude* 9. 79
Large store of gleaming crimson-spotted trouts;	882 *Excursion* 8. 558
Abstract those gleaming relics, and uplift them,	S.3. 434 **The doubt* 56
Gleams. Gleams that upon the lake's still bosom fall;	7 *Ev. Wk.* 294
The hills, while gleams below the azure tide;	9 *Ev. Wk.* 360
'Mid smoking woods gleams hid from morning's ray	12 *Desc. Sk.* 120
In sleep I heard the northern gleams;	113 *Ind. Wom.* 3
End happily, as they began!" These gleams	124 *V. and J.* 211
Soft darkness o'er its latest gleams is stealing;	173 *Waggoner* 1. 2
What shifting pictures—clad in gleams	178 *Waggoner* 3. 36
It gleams on the face, there, of dusky-browed Jack,	188 *Music* 15
And now, with gleams of half-extinguished thought,	206 *Tintern* 58
Thy voice, nor catch from thy wild eyes these gleams	207 *Tintern* 148
And fields invested with purpureal gleams;	211 *Laod.* 106
So gleams the crescent moon, that loves	222 *Triad* 189
With vital sounds and monitory gleams	267 **Though narrow* 7
Yon eddying balls of foam, these arrowy gleams	268 **Dogmatic Teachers* 10
Gleams from a world in which the saints repose.	282 **While beams* 14
Gleams on the grass-crowned top of yon tall Tower,	283 **Here, where* 11
The Eternal looks upon her sword that gleams,	318 **Ah! where* 12
With gleams of fresher, purer, light;	338 **Meek Virgin* 34
With gleams that owed not to the sun their birth,	371 *Eg. Maid* 148
Seek other seas, their canvass gleams.	391 *Highland Broach* 72
By scattering gleams, through your distress,	409 *White Doe* 1247
That face, which cannot lose the gleams,	413 *White Doe* 1602
Lose utterly the tender gleams,	413 *White Doe* 1603
That tears burst forth amain. Did gleams appear?	446 *Ecc. Sonn.* 3. 24. 9
Whose blaze is now subdued to tender gleams,	453 **The Sun, that* 3
For, if a vestige of those gleams	458 **Had this* 67
If neither soothing to the worm that gleams	501 **The unremitting* 3
Like morning's dewy gleams;	506 **While from* 12
Gleams 'mid the peace of this deep dale	508 *May* 83
Gleams by the richest jewel unsurpast;	527 **Those breathing* 16
As touch'd with dawning moonlight's hoary gleams,	598 *Ev. Wk. Quarto* 340
Gleams, streak'd or dappled, hid from morning's ray	604 *Desc. Sk. Quarto* 139
Fall on his shifting hut that gleams mid smoking dew;	610 *Desc. Sk. Quarto* 455
Gleams like the flashing of a shield;—the earth	640 *Prelude* 1. 586
Lighted by gleams of mooonlight from the sea	644 *Prelude* 2. 136
A grove, with gleams of water through the trees	644 *Prelude* 2. 158
(Ah! surely not without attendant gleams	682 *Prelude* 6. 513
And on these spots with many gleams I looked	716 *Prelude* 9. 500
With distant prospect among gleams of sky	725 *Prelude* 10. 517
The gleams of his slow-varying countenance,	864 *Excursion* 7. 461
Scarce peeps the curious star, till solemn gleams	S.3. 417 **Sweet was* 12
Still gleams upon their polish'd plumes—the bright	K.8. 234 **The order'd* 6
Swarms with sensation, as with gleams of sunshine,	K.8. 249 *Recluse* 1. 1. 447
Gleamy. And antique castles seen through gleamy showers.	14 *Desc. Sk.* 225
Glean. His simple truths did Andrew glean	155 *Oak and Broom* 1
Gleaned. Nearer ourselves. Such often might be gleaned	741 *Prelude* 13. 113
Glee. Of feet still bustling round with busy glee,	31 *Guilt* 392
The eldest heard with steady glee;	81 †*Mother's Return* 6
And echoes back his sister's glee;	81 †*Mother's Return* 26
Contentment, hope, and mother's glee,	121 *Emigrant Mother* 87
His heart it was so full of glee	127 *Idiot Boy* 82
And all those leaves, in festive glee,	155 **A whirl-blast* 21
By social glee inspired;	165 *Parrot* 26
Yet mine is their glee!	167 *Stray Pleasures* 26
It is a fiddle in its glee	176 *Waggoner* 2. 21
Then, in the turbulence of glee,	179 *Waggoner* 3. 48
Of serious faith, and inward glee;	186 **O Nightingale* 19
That wild with glee across the lawn	187 **Three years* 14
Out-did the sparkling waves in glee:	187 **I wandered* 14
Yet lacks not friends for simple glee,	205 *Brougham* 116
How vivid, yet how delicate, her glee!	221 *Triad* 104
A greeting give of measured glee;	233 *Power of Sound* 38
In festal glee: why not? For fresh and clear,	275 **While poring* 6
Does the hour's drowsy weight his glee restrain?	279 **'Tis he* 4
Great is their glee while flake they add to flake	280 **Intent on* 4
Lives in the light of youthful glee,	293 *Jedbor.* 11
As the light breezes that with glee	296 *Highland Boy* 149
There came a Tyrant, and with holy glee	306 **Two Voices* 5
Unfolds a willing breast) with infant glee	336 *Danube* 4
Had often heard the sound of glee	409 *White Doe* 1177
And many chained by vows, with eager glee	434 *Ecc. Sonn.* 2. 23. 2
To sight so shallow, with a bather's glee,	469 **A youth* 3
And hill and valley rang with glee	483 *Simon Lee* 10
The grey-haired man of glee:	487 *Fountain* 20

Glee—*continued.*
Sound sense, and love itself, and mirth and glee . 488 *Pers. Talk* 19
He sprang in glee,—for what cared he . . . . 494 *Force of Prayer* 29
Shall hoist their topmost flags in sign of glee, . . 504 *Warning* 45
A quickening hope, a freshening glee, ... 506 *While from 5
Clapped hands, and shook with glee their matted locks; . . . . 513 *Said Secrecy 11
Not far we travelled ere a shout of glee, . . . 524 *Epist. Beaumont* 203
But bold Hubert lives in glee: . . . . . . 535 *Egremont* 69
Or happy blunder triumphed, bursts of glee . . 644 *Prelude* 2. 163
With amity and glee; we bore a name . . . 681 *Prelude* 6. 402
Inviting us in glee to sit and eat. . . . . . 781 *Excursion* 2. 673
With undiminished glee, in hoary age. . . . . 859 *Excursion* 7. 110
The sound of titled names, and talked in glee 860 *Excursion* 7. 217
With rival earnestness and kindred glee. . . . 892 *Excursion* 9. 531
As one or other takes the fit of glee, ... K.8. 251 *Recluse* 1.1.556
His desperate course of tumult and of glee. . . K.8. 256 *Recluse* 1.1.732

Glen. Just as we left the glen a clap of thunder 51 *Bord.* 788
He leaned upon the bridge that spans the glen, 73 *Bord.* 2015
In this continuous glen, where down a rock . . 146 **It was an* 21
As through the glen it rambles, ... 162 *Binnorie* 57
Ruffles the bosom of this leafy glen. . . . . 184 *Airey-force* 2
And grey-haired Wilfred of the glen . . . . 199 *Thorn* 138
Might bear thee to this glen, ... 231 *Jew. Fam.* 2
Nor wild-cat in a woody glen! . . . . . . 243 *P. B.* 620
Heed not, wild Rover once through heath and glen, 255 *Detraction* 9
Through busiest street and loneliest glen . . . 286 *Nith* 43
Sleeps Ossian, in the NARROW GLEN; . . . . 288 *Glen-Al.* 2
Spread round that haven in the glen; . . . . 296 *Highland Boy* 112
Or depth of labyrinthine glen; . . . . . . 298 *Brownie's Cell* 2
To be an unculled floweret of the glen, . . . 377 *Duddon* 7. 12
Scattered all Britain over, through deep glen, . 387 *Manse* 3
Yon towering Peaks, "Shepherds of Etive Glen?" 389 *Sound of Mull* 14
Speak from the woody glen! . . . . 478 *Somnamb.* 4
Known chiefly, Aira! to thy glen, ... 478 *Somnamb.* 28
In this secluded glen, and eagerly . . . . . 699 *Prelude* 8. 19
Him, as we entered from the open glen, . . . 789 *Excursion* 3. 200
The streams far distant of your native glen; . . 809 *Excursion* 4. 551
—Adown the path that from the glen had led . 821 *Excursion* 4. 1307
In town and city and sequestered glen, . . . 873 *Excursion* 7. 1023

Glencoign. And by Glenridding-screes, and low Glencoign, ... 353 *Aquap.* 49

Glenderamakin's. To Glenderamakin's lofty springs; 204 *Brougham* 92

Glendoveers. This the Sun's Bird, whom Glendoveers might own . . . . 231 **The gentlest Poet* 7

Glenridding-screes. And by Glenridding-screes, and low Glencoign, ... 353 *Aquap.* 49

Glens. Where twilight glens endear my Esthwaite's shore, ... 2 *Ev. Wk.* 11
Or lurk in woody sunless glens profound, . . . 12 *Desc. Sk.* 84
"This Land of Rainbows spanning glens whose walls, ... 388 *Loch Etive* 1
To roam at large among unpeopled glens . . . 809 *Excursion* 4. 515
Of Britain's farthest glens. The Earth has lent . 876 *Excursion* 8. 111

Glide. Glide gently, thus for ever glide, ... 9 *Collins* 1
O glide, fair stream! for ever so, ... 9 *Collins* 5
Through Nature's vale his homely pleasures glide, 19 *Desc. Sk.* 492
Yes, as I roamed where Loiret's waters glide . . 21 *Desc. Sk.* 624
Where two fair swans together glide. . . . . 81 †*Mother's Return* 36
And now they smoothly glide along, ... 174 *Waggoner* 1. 43
Bright volumes of vapour through Lothbury glide, 188 *Poor Susan* 7
How soaring Mortals glide between . . . . 216 *Enterprise* 68
Learned from the tuneful spheres that glide . . 220 *Triad* 22
And, where the feeble breezes glide, ... 242 *P. B.* 534
If the heavens smile, and leave us free to glide, . 252 **Her only* 7
Pace the long avenue, or glide adown . . . . 270 **Ye sacred* 12
Of the wild Peak; where new-born waters glide . 275 **Chatsworth! thy* 4
Of nun-like females, with soft motion, glide! . . 334 **Bruges I* 14
Hence Forms that glide with swan-like ease along, 334 **The Spirit* 6
Than the fair Forms, that in long order glide, . 347 *Processions* 62
The clang of arms is heard, and phantoms glide, . 361 **For action* 7
Still glides the Stream, and shall for ever glide; . 384 *Duddon* 34. 5
How subtly glide its finest threads along! . . 429 *Ecc. Sonn.* 2. 5. 11
To glide in open prospect through clear sky. . . 461 **Who but is* 8
Of the green sheep-track did we glide; . . . 488 *Fountain* 67
Such gentle mists as glide, ... 508 *May* 78
For mutual pleasure glide; . . . . 526 **The soaring* 30
Softly as morning vapours glide . . . . . 534 **Blest is* 85
Joyless and comfortless. Our days glide on; . . 585 *Ch. Lamb* 71
I saw the Stream of Yarrow glide . . . . . 586 *Hogg* 2
A patriot of the world, how could I glide . . . 721 *Prelude* 10. 242

Glided. Strong as an Eagle with my charge I glided round and round . . . . 92 *Poet's Dream* 37
And, like a shadow, glided out of view. . . . 126 *V. and J.* 297
Earthward it glided with a swift descent: . . . 323 *Ode 1814* 23
While Cam's ideal current glided by, ... 529 **Those breathing* 117
We glided forward with the flowing stream. . . 680 *Prelude* 6. 377

Glides. Slow glides the sail along the illumined shore, 12 *Desc. Sk.* 103
That glides the dark hills under? . . . . . 293 *Yarrow Unv.* 26
To chant, as glides the boat along, ... 338 *Brientz* 14
Still glides the Stream, and shall for ever glide; . 384 *Duddon* 34. 5
The river glides, the woods before me wave; . . 392 *Bothwell* 6
And glides o'er the earth like an angel of light. . 398 *White Doe* 241
With all their Arts,—but classic lore glides on . 425 *Ecc. Sonn.* 1. 25. 13
Softly she glides, another home to seek. . . . 434 *Ecc. Sonn.* 2. 22. 8
By sleepless prudence ruled, glides slowly on; . 438 *Ecc. Sonn.* 2. 38. 9
In white arrayed, glides on the Maid . . . . 479 *Somnamb.* 93
And sail that glides the well-known alders by. . 592 *Ev. Wk. Quarto* 48
Or beats the gladsome air; o'er all that glides . 648 *Prelude* 2. 407

Glides—*continued.*
A second-sight procession, such as glides . . . 696 *Prelude* 7. 633
With length of shade so thick, that whoso glides . 706 *Prelude* 8. 460
While the ship glides before a steady breeze. . . 805 *Excursion* 4. 250
Of traffic glides with ceaseless intercourse, . . 876 *Excursion* 8. 113
Light as a sunbeam glides along the hills . . . 890 *Excursion* 9. 429

Glideth. The river glideth at his own sweet will: . 269 *Westm. Bridge* 12

Gliding. *See* **Softly-gliding.**
The eye that marks the gliding creature sees . . 6 *Ev. Wk.* 220
By pointing to the gliding moon on high. . . . 7 *Ev. Wk.* 259
Then think of her beautiful gliding form, . . . 142 †*Lov. and Lik.* 45
And pendent rocks, where'er, in gliding state, . 212 *Dion*
Will mingle with her lustres gliding . . . . 237 *P. B.* 93
He spake; and gliding into view . . . . . 371 *Eg. Maid* 175
Dwarf willows gliding, and by ferny brake. . . 377 *Duddon* 4. 8
Gliding in silence with unfettered sweep! . . . 384 *Duddon* 32. 8
Nor wants the holy Abbot's gliding Shade . . 393 *Inglewood* 9
Comes gliding in with lovely gleam, ... 396 *White Doe* 55
Comes gliding in serene and slow, ... 396 *White Doe* 56
The dark cave's portal gliding by, ... 415 *White Doe* 1740
Here wanders like a gliding ghost, ... 416 *White Doe* 1883
Traceably gliding through the dusk, recall . . 496 **A little* 43
From his smoothly gliding wings. . . . . . 530 *Gleaner* 16
Bubbles gliding under ice, ... 550 *Hermit's Cell* 3. 2
When by the gliding Loire I paused, and cast . 718 *Prelude* 10. 6
The ship went gliding with her thoughtless crew; 798 *Excursion* 3. 836
Or through the groves gliding like morning mist . 810 *Excursion* 4. 637
Gliding apace, with shadows in their train, . . 814 *Excursion* 4. 874
Her rivers populous with gliding life; . . . . 819 *Excursion* 4. 1199

Glimmer. That glimmer hoar in eve's last light, descried . . . . 12 *Desc. Sk.* 115
The broad blue heavens appeared to glimmer, . 241 *P. B.* 484
Glimmer the dim-lit Alps, dilated, round, . . . 606 *Desc.Sk.Quarto* 217

Glimmered. Nor taper glimmered dim from sick man's room; . . . . 26 *Guilt* 142
Glimmered our dear-loved home, alas! no longer ours! . . . . 28 *Guilt* 243
By light of lamp and precious stones, that glimmered here, there glowed, ... 92 *Poet's Dream* 46
That glimmered like a pine-tree dimly viewed . 450 *Ecc. Sonn.* 3. 40. 5

Glimmering. And round the broad-spread oak, a glimmering scene, ... 3 *Ev. Wk.* 46
While music, stealing round the glimmering deeps, 7 *Ev. Wk.* 303
His glimmering eyes that peep and doze! . . . 128 *Idiot Boy* 250
Glimmering faintly where it lies; . . . . . 175 *Waggoner* 1. 161
Glimmering through the twilight pale; . . . . 180 *Waggoner* 4. 20
Their own fair forms upon the glimmering plain, . 218 *Recluse* 1. 1. 225
He feels the glimmering of the moon; . . . . . 242 *P. B.* 537
Is but a glimmering spoke in the swift wheel . . 270 **If these* 10
Save haply for some feeble glimmering . . . 271 *George: Death* 5
O'er intervenient waste, through glimmering haze, 352 *Aquap.* 18
A glimmering sense still left, with eyes . . . 412 *White Doe* 1492
And left thee but a glimmering of the day; . . 491 *Tribute: Dog* 16
Fit for the glimmering brow of Proserpine. . . 532 **Once I* 18
Beside the glimmering fire, ... 542 *Russ. Fug.* 34
And round the humming elm, a glimmering scene! 592 *Ev. Wk. Quarto* 62
The glimmering fires of Virtue to enlarge, . . . 619 *School Ex.* 81
And wakes anew life's glimmering trembling fires, 619 *School Ex.* 100
I pause; and at length, through the glimmering grate, ... 620 *Convict* 11
Conversed with promises, had glimmering views . 660 *Prelude* 4. 164
Beneath the trees or by the glimmering lake, . . 671 *Prelude* 5. 369

Glimmerings. And did not want glimmerings of quiet hope. . . . . 62 *Bord.* 1355
Shadows and sunny glimmerings, ... 159 *Green Linnet* 31

Glimmers. Lost in the thickened darkness, glimmers hoar; . . . . 8 *Ev. Wk.* 312
Glimmers with fading light, and shadowy Eve . 269 *Gordale* 2
Glimmers through many a superstitious form . 419 *Ecc. Sonn.* 1. 4. 13
Their Portraitures, their stone-work glimmers, dyed 451 *Ecc. Sonn.* 3. 44. 3
Lost in the deepen'd darkness, glimmers hoar; . 598 *Ev. Wk. Quarto* 370
Glimmers before my sight through thankful tears, 627 **The star* 10

Glimpse. Though but a glimpse, it sent me to my prayers. . . . . 55 *Bord.* 973
I've had a glimpse of you—*avast!* . . . . . 176 *Waggoner* 1. 238
His soul with but a *glimpse* of heavenly day? . 221 *Triad* 72
We were not mocked with glimpse and shadow then, 228 *Vernal Ode* 133
How far off yet a glimpse of morning light, . . 229 *Cuckoo-clock* 3
A glimpse of sudden joy was his, ... 244 *P. B.* 729
No glimpse it is, no doubtful gleam; . . . . 247 *P. B.* 1003
Ye Catacombs, give to mine eyes a glimpse . . 357 *Aquap.* 299
When she by sudden glimpse espied . . . . 415 *White Doe* 1731
This glimpse of glory, why renewed? . . . . 458 **Had this* 65
A glimpse I caught of that Abode, by Thee . . 524 *Epist. Beaumont* 189
Full many a glimpse (but sparingly bestowed . . 548 **Stay, bold* 18
For which, by earliest glimpse of morning light, . 554 *Prioress* 137
As soon as I a glimpse of day espied, ... 557 *Cuck.and Night.* 56
While crossing Magdalene Bridge, a glimpse of Cam; 649 *Prelude* 3. 16
In the old wall, an unexpected glimpse . . . 694 *Prelude* 7. 452
Yea, when a glimpse of those imperial bowers . 700 *Prelude* 8. 111
His devious course. A glimpse of such sweet life 702 *Prelude* 8. 209

Glimpses. And, caught by glimpses now—now missed, ... 143 **Driven in* 14
Have glimpses that would make me less forlorn; . 259 **The world is* 12
Bright as the glimpses of eternity, ... 272 **Where holy* 13
A ghost, by glimpses, may present . . . . . 301 *Bran* 80
Nor less attractive when by glimpses seen . . . 460 **Queen of* 11
Our fathers glimpses caught of your thin Frames, 474 **Ye shadowy* 4
By glimpses only, and confess with shame . . 476 *Eden* 2
By glimpses caught—disporting at their ease, . 527 **Those breathing* 44

Glimpses—*continued.*
Glimpses of retribution, terrible, 724 *Prelude* 10. 452
I see by glimpses now; when age comes on, 738 *Prelude* 12. 281
Glinted. He sang, his genius "glinted" forth, 285 *Grave of Burns* 20
Glisten. Glisten with a livelier ray: 233 *Power of Sound* 61
Glistened. The flattered structure glistened, blazed, 550 *Hermit's Cell.* 2. 19
By the broad hill, glistened upon our sight 773 *Excursion* 2. 127
Glistened with tenderness; his mind, I knew, 883 *Excursion* 8. 589
Glistening. On the tall peaks the glistening sunbeams play, 22 *Desc. Sk.* 668
Nor Sea-nymph glistening from her coral bower; 220 *Triad* 11
With all their fragrance, all their glistening, 222 *Triad* 205
Glistening with unparticipated ray, 267 **As the* 4
Its glistening dews; but hallowed is the clay 273 **Wild Redbreast* 4
Her glistening tresses bound, yet light and free 381 *Duddon* 21. 11
And glistening antlers are descried; 457 **Had this* 31
In frosty moonlight glistening; 499 *Memory* 26
Whose eye reflects it, glistening through a tear 540 *Grace Darl.* 12
Glistening along the low and woody dale; 876 *Excursion* 8. 114
Glistenings. And the glistenings—heavenly fair! 217 **Inmate of* 12
To industry, by glistenings flung on rocks, 682 *Prelude* 6. 515
Glistens. Loves, as it glistens on the silent rocks; 700 *Prelude* 8. 64
Glistered. The barrows glistered bright with drops of rain, 30 *Guilt* 327
Glistering. Upstarts a glistering snake, 331 *Ode: Thanks.* 147
Or rather thou appear'st a glistering snake, 377 *Duddon* 4. 5
Glitter. Toy with the sun and glitter from afar. 11 *Desc. Sk.* 51
Glitter the stars above, and all is black below. 21 *Desc. Sk.* 583
Vainly glitter hill and plain, 171 *Kitten* 85
The lake doth glitter, 190 *March* 4
Glitter, with dark recesses interposed, 773 *Excursion* 2. 129
Glitter—but undisturbing, undisturbed; 876 *Excursion* 8. 161
The nobler badge shall glitter on *his arm.* L. I. 96 *Juvenal* 3. 38
Glittered. The pendent grapes glittered above the door;— 24 *Guilt* 16
Its stony surface glittered like a shield; 68 *Bord.* 1723
The frith that glittered like a warrior's shield, 105 *Artegal* 198
Glittered at evening like a starry sky; 107 *Farewell* 54
And *That* which glittered from afar; 167 *Pilgrim's Dream* 21
The Sonnet glittered a gay myrtle leaf 260 **Scorn not* 7
And glittered on the Rhine. 629 *Installation* 62
Of that sharp rising, glittered to the moon 664 *Prelude* 4. 381
A liquid pool that glittered in the sun, 776 *Excursion* 2. 338
And no vain mirror glittered upon the walls, 860 *Excursion* 7. 176
Glittering. *See* **Thickly-glittering.**
'Mid thy soft glooms the glittering steel unsheath; 3 *Ev. Wk.* 75
The dog, loud barking, 'mid the glittering rocks, 5 *Ev. Wk.* 184
Thy glittering steeples, whence the matin bell 12 *Desc. Sk.* 123
Eastward, in long perspective glittering, shine 15 *Desc. Sk.* 277
In the calm sunshine slept the glittering main; 30 *Guilt* 336
A piece of money glittering through the dust? 45 *Bord.* 435
Or through the glittering vapours dart 84 *Shepherd-boys* 10
Upon the house-top, glittering bright, 86 *Anecdote* 51
While, from the twin cards toothed with glittering wire, 95 *Brothers* 22
Through a thin veil of glittering haze was seen 149 **A narrow* 45
Glittering and twinkling near yon rosy cloud; 153 *Morn. Ex.* 28
I see thee glittering from afar— 159 **With little* 33
Yet like a star, with glittering crest, 159 **With little* 37
At thy glittering countenance. 161 **Pleasures newly* 16
Glittering before him bright and broad; 177 *Waggoner* 2. 36
Now lost amid a glittering steam: 180 *Waggoner* 4. 68
Raises a mist; that, glittering in the sun, 195 *Resolution* 13
'Tis Hesperus—there he stands with glittering crown, 208 **It is no* 4
Stretched on the block the glittering axe recoils; 252 **Why, Minstrel* 10
(So might he seem) of all the glittering quire! 261 **I watch* 3
If so he might, yon mountain's glittering head— 263 **How clear* 7
All bright and glittering in the smokeless air. 269 *Westm. Bridge* 8
The crescent moon clove with its glittering prow 270 **Shame on* 4
Or groom!—We must run glittering like a brook 307 **O Friend* 5
Of your fierce war, may ken the glittering lance, 309 *Men of Kent* 7
The glittering crowns and garlands which it brought— 334 **A wingèd* 4
Then, glittering like a star, she joins the festal band. 344 **How blest* 26
Glittering before the Thunderer's sight, 375 **The Minstrels* 52
A glittering ship, that hath the plain 397 *White Doe* 65
The glittering, floating Pageantry. 404 *White Doe* 752
With glittering finger points at nine. 406 *White Doe* 961
Her Spires, her Steeple-towers with glittering vanes 444 *Ecc. Sonn.* 3. 17. 11
(Unbashful dwarfs each glittering at his post) 456 **Soft as* 17
That these two words of glittering gold 486 *Matthew* 31
With hair of glittering grey; 486 **We walked* 6
Your motions, glittering Elves! 526 **The soaring* 14
Buried beneath the glittering Lake, 532 †*Float Isl.* 25
Of Moscow's glittering spires. 545 *Russ. Fug.* 348
And loved you glittering in your bowers, 579 **Sweet Flower* 27
That, barking busy 'mid the glittering rocks, 594 *Ev. Wk. Quarto* 167
The glittering waves reflect the dazzling blaze; 618 *School Ex.* 42
The glittering Bears,—the Pleiads fraught with rain; 625 *Æneid* 127
Small circles glittering idly in the moon, 637 *Prelude* 1. 365
White Sirius glittering o'er the southern crags, 662 *Prelude* 4. 244
And glancing forms, and tapers glittering, 663 *Prelude* 4. 314
A bed of glittering light: I asked the cause: 667 *Prelude* 5. 129
By glittering verse; but further, doth receive, 674 *Prelude* 5. 591
Society became my glittering bride, 796 *Excursion* 3. 735
To sight restored, and glittering in the sun. 823 *Excursion* 5. 86
Fenced round with glittering laurel; or in that 832 *Excursion* 5. 644
In glittering halls—was able to derive 843 *Excursion* 6. 339
And, like a serpent, shows his glittering back 869 *Excursion* 7. 791

Glittering—*continued.*
A glittering spectacle; but every face 871 *Excursion* 7. 881
Of vapour glittering in the morning sun. 876 *Excursion* 8. 127
His spade and hoe, mattock and glittering scythe, 880 *Excursion* 8. 426
The glittering rabble housed to . . . and swear L. I. 97 *Juvenal* 3. 83
Glitters. To him the day-star glitters small and bright, 16 *Desc. Sk.* 323
A gem that glitters while it lives, 88 *H. C.* 30
The Crescent glitters on the towers of Spain; 427 *Ecc. Sonn.* 1. 34. 3
The star of noon that glitters small and bright, 609 *Desc.Sk.Quarto* 386
Globe. (Above the convex of the watery globe) 219 **This Height* 19
Gloom. Far in the level forest's central gloom: 5 *Ev. Wk.* 181
The soft gloom deepening on the tranquil mind. 8 *Ev. Wk.* 318
Yet still the tender, vacant gloom remains; 8 *Ev. Wk.* 321
But, heedless of the following gloom, 9 *Lines: Boat* 10
And now, emerging from the forest's gloom, 11 *Desc. Sk.* 52
The sylvan cabin's lute-enlivened gloom. 13 *Desc. Sk.* 134
From the bright wave, in solemn gloom, retire 13 *Desc. Sk.* 158
Hang o'er the abyss, whose else impervious gloom 13 *Desc. Sk.* 164
Then sets. In total gloom the Vagrant sighs, 14 *Desc. Sk.* 190
While ghastly faces through the gloom appear, 20 *Desc. Sk.* 547
Roaring with storms beneath night's starless gloom; 26 *Guilt* 139
Has held infernal orgies—with the gloom, 49 *Bord.* 660
"But is that gloom dissolved? how passing clear 105 *Artegal* 202
Yet frequent transports mitigate the gloom: 139 *Widow* 33
And so, when night with grateful gloom had fallen, 143 **High bliss* 17
To show her taper in the gloom, 167 *Pilgrim's Dream* 29
And cheering oft-times their reluctant gloom. 172 *Infant Daughter* 50
Hung round and overhung with gloom; 175 *Waggoner* 1. 165
Of massy gloom and radiance bold. 180 *Waggoner* 4. 56
Of vast circumference and gloom profound 184 *Yew-trees* 9
This is no common waste, no common gloom; 203 *Hart-leap* 170
The blind man's gloom, exalts the veteran's mirth; 233 *Power of Sound* 50
Though given to sadness and to gloom, 244 *P. B.* 737
Upon that roof, amid embowering gloom, 262 **Mark the* 6
Becoming thoughts, I trust, of solemn gloom 264 **Lady! the* 10
Whose universe was gloom immersed in gloom, 271 *George: Death* 3
Or thrid the shadowy gloom, 300 *Cora Linn* 39
In gloom on wings with confidence outspread 354 *Aquap.* 87
Drove from itself, we trust, all frightful gloom. 391 *Brownie* 14
What mighty forest in its gloom 413 *White Doe* 1557
And, with this silent gloom agreeing, 413 *White Doe* 1579
Not sunless gloom or unenlightened, 415 *White Doe* 1759
Wide as the oak extends its dewy gloom, 425 *Ecc. Sonn.* 1. 27. 13
Thus often, when thick gloom the east o'ershrouds, 426 *Ecc. Sonn.* 1. 29. 9
When all the world with midnight gloom was dark.— 432 *Ecc. Sonn.* 2. 14. 5
Thou, chequering peaceably the minster's gloom, 459 **Wanderer! that* 27
The Wanderer lost in more determined gloom. 461 **Who but is* 14
The gloom that did its loveliness enshroud) 465 **Dear to* 8
By which the clouds, arrayed in light or gloom, 468 **Ranging the* 4
Her Temples rose, 'mid pagan gloom; but why, 474 **On to* 6
And bustle and sluggishness, pleasure and gloom. 482 *Character* 4
As blest and as glad, in this desolate gloom, 484 **A plague* 28
Whose saintly radiance mitigates the gloom 496 **A little* 46
Frowns deepening visibly his native gloom, 521 *Epist. Beaumont* 6
They wore away the night in starless gloom; 528 **Those breathing* 55
If gloom fell on me, swift was my escape; 532 **Once I* 27
His face was gloom, his heart was sorrow, 537 *Goody Blake* 107
Extinguished in a moment; total gloom, 548 **Stay, bold* 27
But if the pensive gloom 577 *Cenotaph* 9
—Ah me! all light is mute amid the gloom, 596 *Ev. Wk. Quarto* 267
In deep determin'd gloom his subject tides. 598 *Ev. Wk. Quarto* 338
With bordering lines of intervening gloom, 598 *Ev. Wk. Quarto* 342
Weeping beneath his chill of mountain gloom. 603 *Desc. Sk. Quarto* 54
The bosom'd cabin's lyre-enliven'd gloom; 604 *Desc.Sk.Quarto* 101
Bright'ning the gloom where thick the forests stoop; 604 *Desc.Sk.Quarto* 129
Bend o'er th' abyss?—the else impervious gloom 605 *Desc.Sk.Quarto* 186
By the deep quiet gloom appall'd, she sighs, 606 *Desc.Sk.Quarto* 221
While in soft gloom the scattering bowers recede, 607 *Desc.Sk.Quarto* 271
Along the brighten'd gloom reposing deep. 607 *Desc.Sk.Quarto* 276
Dim dreadful faces thro' the gloom appear, 614 *Desc.Sk.Quarto* 650
The cottage windows blazed through twilight gloom, 638 *Prelude* 1. 427
So sweetly 'mid the gloom the invisible bird 644 *Prelude* 2. 125
'Mid gloom and tumult, but no less 'mid fair 647 *Prelude* 2. 323
Twilight was coming on, yet through the gloom 672 *Prelude* 5. 435
A treasured and luxurious gloom of choice 677 *Prelude* 6. 176
Nay brighter shone, by this portentous gloom 709 *Prelude* 8. 657
The gloom, that, but a moment past, was deepened 733 *Prelude* 11. 427
Thither I came, and there, amid the gloom 756 *Excursion* 1. 28
And whose soft gloom, and boundless depth, might tempt 787 *Excursion* 3. 99
Or in the gloom of twilight hum their joy? 808 *Excursion* 4. 448
Lost in a gloom of uninspired research; 810 *Excursion* 4. 626
Or pierce the gloom of her majestic woods; 819 *Excursion* 4. 1201
Of your experience to dispel this gloom: 829 *Excursion* 5. 482
With more than wintry cheerlessness and gloom 830 *Excursion* 5. 538
And night succeeded with unusual gloom, 833 *Excursion* 5. 737
High in the gloom appeared, too high, methought, 833 *Excursion* 5. 740
That round his mansion cast a sober gloom, 844 *Excursion* 6. 441
Flows on in solitude. But, when the gloom 856 *Excursion* 6. 1173
Easy and bold, that penetrate the gloom 876 *Excursion* 8. 110
From unaffected contrast with the gloom 881 *Excursion* 8. 473
To gloom imperishable. So (if truths S. 3. 435 **The doubt* 110
A brighter joy; and through such damp and gloom K. 8. 237 *Recluse* 1. 1. 52
And found us faithful through the gloom, and heard K. 8. 241 *Recluse* 1. 1. 183
These vales were saddened with no common gloom K. 8. 275 **These vales* 1
How little dost thou spare of earthly gloom! [?] **A sad* 12
Gloomier. Had bred in me; but gloomier far, a dim 706 *Prelude* 8. 515
Gloomiest. Through gloomiest shade; put on (nor dread its weight) 446 *Ecc. Sonn* 3. 25. 13

Glooms. *See* **Forest-glooms.**
'Mid thy soft glooms the glittering steel unsheath ; 3 *Ev. Wk.* 75
Clouds and utter glooms ! . . . . 163 *Hint* 12
Pale twilight's lingering glooms,—and in the sun . 278 **Life with* 5
How in thy pensive glooms our hearts found rest. 282 **Wansfell ! this* 14
Of the Devout, as, 'mid your glooms convened . 357 *Aquap.* 300
Thro' craggs, and forest glooms, and opening lakes, 591 *Ev. Wk. Quarto* 4
Gloomy. Inverted shrubs, and moss of gloomy green, 3 *Ev. Wk.* 59
Like Una shining on her gloomy way, ... 7 *Ev. Wk.* 291
Across the gloomy valley flings her light, . . . 8 *Ev. Wk.* 335
A single chasm, a gulf of gloomy blue, ... 18 *Desc. Sk.* 413
With rocks and gloomy woods her fertile fields : . 20 *Desc. Sk.* 570
In solitude.—Stranger ! these gloomy boughs . 23 *Yew-tree* 24
We gazed with terror on their gloomy sleep, . . 29 *Guilt* 293
The gloomy lantern, and the dim blue match, . 32 *Guilt* 419
'Tis weariness that breeds these gloomy fancies, . 40 *Bord.* 145
And followed on, through woods of gloomy cedar, 70 *Bord.* 1804
The Vicar from his gloomy house hard by . . . 147 *Joanna* 21
To *seek* for thoughts of a gloomy cast, ... 177 *Waggoner* 2. 74
The mountain, and the deep and gloomy wood. . 206 *Tintern* 78
Buried together in yon gloomy mass . . . . 230 *Clouds* 31
Luminous or gloomy, welcome to the vale . . 230 *Clouds* 47
Into a gloomy grove of beech, ... 244 *P. B.* 672
Behind, all gloomy to behold ; . . . . . . 289 *Stepping West.* 10
Hail, orient Conqueror of gloomy Night ! . . . 329 *Ode : Thanks.* 1
Hath reached the encincture of that gloomy sea . 336 *Danube* 8
Forth flashing out of its own gloomy chasm . . 352 *Aquap.* 15
A gloomy NICHE, capacious, blank, and cold ; . . 379 *Duddon* 15. 3
Now some gloomy nook partakes . . . . . 397 *White Doe* 91
Aghast within its gloomy cavity . . . . . 439 *Ecc. Sonn.* 2. 42. 5
Though cold as winter, gloomy as the grave, . . 501 *Humanity* 77
With door left open makes a gloomy spot, . . 524 *Epist. Beaumont* 220
Above the gloomy valley flings her light, . . . 599 *Ev. Wk. Quarto* 403
A gulf of gloomy blue, that opens wide . . . 611 *Desc.Sk.Quarto* 498
Bosom'd in gloomy woods, her golden fields, . . 614 *Desc.Sk.Quarto* 681
No jarring monks, to gloomy cell confined, . . 619 *School Ex.* 49
Waves o'er the gloomy stream ; . . . . . 626 †*Cento* 12
Beneath the gloomy hills homeward I went . . 638 *Prelude* 1. 421
Deep, gloomy were they, and severe ; the scatterings . . . . 662 *Prelude* 4. 252
In silence through a wood gloomy and still. . . 665 *Prelude* 4. 447
Were fellow-travellers in this gloomy strait, . . 684 *Prelude* 6. 622
Gloomy as coffins, and unsightly lanes . . . . 689 *Prelude* 7. 181
Whose genius spangled o'er a gloomy theme . . 695 *Prelude* 7. 565
Rouse him ; but, hidden in those gloomy shades, 718 *Prelude* 9. 584
A fixed, abysmal, gloomy, breathing-place— . . 747 *Prelude* 14. 58
Of lightning startled in a gloomy cave . . . . 796 *Excursion* 3. 708
Of day-spring, in the gloomy east, revealed, . . 852 *Excursion* 6. 915
Glows at her feet, and all the gloomy rocks . . 868 *Excursion* 7. 721
Amid impending rocks and gloomy woods— . . 894 *Excursion* 9. 691
His light high up among the gloomy rocks, . . K.8. 225 **I will* 49
Gloried. Intrenched your brows ; ye gloried in each scar : . . . . 283 **Proud were* 3
Of him who gloried in its nodding plume. . . . 394 **How profitless* 8
What Horace gloried to behold, ... 499 **Departing summer* 58
Loving the sports which once he gloried in. . . 809 *Excursion* 4. 549
Glories. Have we not seen the glories of the spring 105 *Artegal* 196
She glories in a train . . . . 109 **Ere with* 6
How he glories, when he sees . . . . . . 157 *Sexton* 18
With thy acknowledged glories ;—No ! . . . 167 *Pilgrim's Dream* 44
Among the glories of a happier age." . . . 222 *Triad* 186
The faded glories of his Clan ! . . . . . 299 *Brownie's Cell* 60
And what if she had seen those glories fade, . . 305 *Ven. Rep.* 9
Your glories mingled with the brightest hues . . 357 *Aquap.* 294
Around these Converts ; and their glories blend, . 423 *Ecc. Sonn.* 1. 18. 8
Those watery glories, on the stormy brine . . . 434 *Ecc. Sonn.* 2. 22. 12
Glories of evening, as ye there are seen . . . 459 **The Crescent* 2
Forget the glories he hath known, ... 588 *Immortality* 83
Turn where I might, was opening out its glories, . 686 *Prelude* 6. 775
Glorified. *See* **Self-glorified, Twice-glorified.**
Glorified by heavenly light, ... 141 *Arm. Lady* 134
By the celestial Muses glorified. . . . . . . 251 **Pelion and* 8
All States have glorified themselves ;—their claims 331 *Ode : Thanks.* 155
Did waft him to Sion, the glorified hill, . . . 364 *Vallomb.* 22
And his moist eyes were glorified ; . . . . . 400 *White Doe* 404
And glorified Ascension ? Warriors, go, . . . 427 *Ecc. Sonn.* 1. 33. 4
Woman ! above all women glorified, ... 434 *Ecc. Sonn.* 2. 25. 3
Are glorified while this once-mitred pair . . . 437 *Ecc. Sonn.* 2. 34. 10
Was glorified, and took its place, above . . . 466 *St. Bees* 56
His form hath flashed upon me, glorified . . . 703 *Prelude* 8. 269
But vast in size, in substance glorified ; . . . 784 *Excursion* 2. 866
Are glorified ; or, if they sleep, shall wake . . 804 *Excursion* 4. 189
Meek Saint ! through patience glorified on earth ! 854 *Excursion* 6. 1034
Glorifies. And glorifies the truant youth of Vannes. 627 *Eagle and Dove* 8
Glorify. Doth glorify its humble birth . . . . 285 *Grave of Burns* 23
And glorify for us the west, ... 506 *Lab. Hymn* 31
Upon the breast Thy name do glorify. . . . 552 *Prioress* 7
To glorify the Eternal ! What if these . . . 818 *Excursion* 4. 1165
His triumphs hail, and glorify his end ; . . . 863 *Excursion* 7. 378
Glorious. *See* **Vain-glorious.**
Glances the wheeling eagle's glorious form ! . . 15 *Desc. Sk.* 276
The image of his glorious Sire displayed, . . . 18 *Desc. Sk.* 440
Lo, from the flames a great and glorious birth ; . 22 *Desc. Sk.* 644
How glorious to this orchard-ground ! . . . . 162 **Who fancied* 4
For, cries the Sailor, " Glorious chance . . . 177 *Waggoner* 2. 43
Was beautiful to see—a weed of glorious feature. 191 *Beggars* 18
The glorious path in which he trod. . . . . 192 *Gipsies* 16
" Before me shone a glorious world— . . . . 194 *Ruth* 169
" This morning gives us promise of a glorious day." 196 *Resolution* 84

Glorious—*continued.*
Which he had mounted on that glorious day. . 200 *Hart-leap* 8
Stood his dumb partner in this glorious feat ; . 201 *Hart-leap* 38
A privacy of glorious light is thine ; . . . . 209 **Ethereal minstrel* 8
Prepared themselves for glorious enterprise . . 211 *Laod.* 117
Upon the ruins of thy glorious name ; . . . . 214 *Dion* 103
Mounting from glorious deed to deed . . . . 216 *Enterprise* 45
The domination of his glorious themes, . . . 216 *Enterprise* 96
Truth shows a glorious face, ... 226 *Present.* 69
Yon cloud, and fix it in that glorious shape ; . . 252 *Picture* 2
With each recurrence of this glorious morn . . 255 *Easter* 1
Who wants the glorious faculty assigned . . 259 **Weak is* 6
The stream-like windings of that glorious street— 270 **Ye sacred* 13
With glorious forms in numberless array, . . . 282 **While beams* 12
Meanwhile, and be to her a glorious crest . . 303 **Fair Star* 5
Which all his glorious ancestors approve : . . . 305 **The Voice* 13
Issued, to sudden view, a glorious Form ! . . . 323 *Ode 1814* 22
Expressive signals of a glorious strife, . . . 324 *Ode 1814* 105
Clear shines the glorious sun above ; . . . . 339 **Meek Virgin* 39
An uncouth Chronicle of glorious years. . . . 351 *Des. Stanzas* 58
The glorious temple—did alike proceed . . . 354 *Aquap.* 142
Yet glorious Art the power of Time defies, . . 368 *Trajan* 67
More glorious, with spread sail and streaming pendant. . . . . 369 *Eg. Maid* 12
Most glorious sunset ! and a ray . . . . . 416 *White Doe* 1871
Fit haunt of shapes whose glorious equipage . . 424 *Ecc. Sonn.* 1. 22. 8
The Race of Alfred covet glorious pains . . . 425 *Ecc. Sonn.* 1. 27. 5
Yet came prepared as glorious lights to shine, . 432 *Ecc. Sonn.* 2. 13. 12
Aid, glorious Martyrs, from your fields of light, . 437 *Ecc. Sonn.* 2. 36. 1
By men and angels blest, the glorious light ? . . 438 *Ecc. Sonn.* 2. 38. 14
And magnify the glorious name of God, . . . 446 *Ecc. Sonn.* 3. 25. 7
And glorious Work of fine intelligence ! . . . 451 *Ecc. Sonn.* 3. 43. 5
Present a glorious scale, ... 457 **Had this* 44
The glorious work of time and providence, . . 471 **Despond who* 4
Turns his necessity to glorious gain ; . . . . 493 *Hap. War.* 14
To heights more glorious still, and into shades . 496 **A little* 53
To saintly bosoms !—Glorious is the blending . 500 *Humanity* 27
Came, in that service, to a glorious work, . . . 509 *F. Stone* 103
Of all that issues from his glorious fount ! . . 511 **So fair* 9
Millions from glorious aims. Our chains to sever . 516 **Hard task* 6
To serve the glorious Henry, King of France, . 574 *Chiabrera* 3. 14
Whose glorious work is done. . . . . . . 582 **O for a* 6
The sunshine is a glorious birth ; . . . . . 587 *Immortality* 16
Thou little Child, yet glorious in the might . . 589 *Immortality* 125
While burn in his full eyes the glorious tears. . 608 *Desc.Sk.Quarto* 351
And as on glorious ground he draws his breath, . 612 *Desc.Sk.Quarto* 536
Pierced by thy spear in glorious victory. . . . 626 *Ballot* 14
That the shield bore, so glorious was the strife ; . 634 *Prelude* 1. 179
And wasted down by glorious death that race . 635 *Prelude* 1. 201
Fit reverence for the glorious Dead, the sight . 654 *Prelude* 3. 337
From their first childhood : in that glorious time 655 *Prelude* 3. 461
At last, or glorious, by endurance won. . . . 661 *Prelude* 4. 176
Glorious as e'er I had beheld—in front, . . . 663 *Prelude* 4. 325
As their forerunners in a glorious course ; . . . 681 *Prelude* 6. 405
Oh, most belovèd Friend ! a glorious time, . . 686 *Prelude* 6. 754
For a deliverer's glorious task,—and such . . . 715 *Prelude* 9. 410
The glorious renovation would proceed. . . . 727 *Prelude* 10. 593
How glorious ! in self-knowledge and self-rule, . 730 *Prelude* 11. 236
In glorious apparition, Powers on whom . . . 735 *Prelude* 12. 98
Why is this glorious creature to be found . . . 741 *Prelude* 13. 87
Resemblance of that glorious faculty . . . . 747 *Prelude* 14. 89
Communing with the glorious universe. . . . 760 *Excursion* 1. 286
A glorious opening, the unlooked-for dawn, . . 774 *Excursion* 2. 212
As one, and moving to one glorious end. . . . 774 *Excursion* 2. 222
Of your bright forms and glorious faculties, . . 790 *Excursion* 3. 302
Glorious ! because the shadow of thy might. . . 803 *Excursion* 4. 101
Crowning the glorious hills of paradise ; . . . 810 *Excursion* 4. 636
Into a substance glorious as her own, ... 817 *Excursion* 4. 1068
The glorious habit by which sense is made . . 820 *Excursion* 4. 1247
Be shown ? her glorious excellence—that ranks . 846 *Excursion* 6. 565
Roused me, her voice ; it said, ' That glorious star 849 *Excursion* 6. 763
Such and so glorious did this Youth appear ; . . 868 *Excursion* 7. 723
" O for the coming of that glorious time . . . 888 *Excursion* 9. 293
Her glorious destiny. Begin even now, . . . 890 *Excursion* 9. 408
(For so they fancied) glorious victory. . . . . 894 *Excursion* 9. 709
The glorious sun, and while the light of day . . K.8. 234 **The order'd* 5
Their Temple, and their glorious dwelling-place. . K.8. 253 *Recluse* 1. 1. 624
Gloriously. A Man so gloriously attended ! . . 177 *Waggoner* 2. 112
Thus far pursued (how gloriously !) by Man, . . 335 *Cologne* 3
Glory. *See* **Vain-glory.**
Rejoicing in the glory of her rays : . . . . 16 *Desc. Sk.* 322
—Waft her to glory, wingèd Powers, ... 112 **How rich* 3
Her chamber-window did surpass in glory . . . 122 *V. and J.* 45
Of Johnny's wit, and Johnny's glory. . . . . 127 *Idiot Boy* 126
—Thus answered Johnny in his glory, ... 131 *Idiot Boy* 452
Her own angelic glory seems begun. . . . . 139 *Widow* 42
Primroses will have their glory ; . . . . . 160 **Pansies, lilies* 4
Vain is the glory of the sky, ... 164 **Glad sight* 5
The second glory of the Heavens ?—Thou hast ; . 172 *Infant Daughter* 5
But what is time ? What outward glory ? Neither 172 *Infant Daughter* 13
Benjamin, this outward glory . . . . . 181 *Waggoner* 4. 121
The clear Moon, and the glory of the heavens. . 184 *Night-piece* 13
The moon, the glory of the sun, ... 192 *Ruth* 34
Of Him who walked in glory and in joy . . . 196 *Resolution* 45
The glory of their loyalty. . . . . . . 204 *Brougham* 35
Like a glory from afar, ... 205 *Brougham* 155
Panting for glory as he fell ; . . . . . . 223 *Wishing-gate* 23
Of history, Glory claps her wings, ... 224 **'Tis gone* 14
New glory o'er the mountain's head, ... 224 **'Tis gone* 59
Buried in glory, far beyond the scope . . . . 226 *Vernal Ode* 28
The glory of the sun's bright head— . . . . 228 *Devot. Incit.* 67

Goad. Their panniered train a group of potters goad, 4 *Ev. Wk.* 128
We need an inward sting to goad us on. 70 *Bord.* 1859
Where guilt had urged them on with ceaseless goad, 504 *Warning* 73
To sinners whom their sins oppress and goad. K.8. 266 **Rid of* 8
Goaded. The goaded land waxed mad; the crimes of few 723 *Prelude* 10. 336
Let loose and goaded. After what hath been 731 *Prelude* 11. 273
Goadings. But like the innocent bird, hath goadings on 634 *Prelude* 1. 142
Goal. The goal is reached. My Master shall become 73 *Bord.* 2038
Never nearer to the goal; 166 *Wand. Jew* 26
They shrunk, insane ambition's barren goal— 321 **Humanity, delighting* 16
Still, as we nearer draw to life's dark goal, 497 *Lycoris* 53
Of our small market village, was the goal 642 *Prelude* 2. 35
Goat. Which the goat cannot climb, takes his sounding flight; 80 †*Address: Child* 4
Chase the wild goat; and if the bold red deer 808 *Excursion* 4. 500
To shaggy steeps on which the careless goat 892 *Excursion* 9. 564
Goatherd. Of rich Clitumnus; and the goat-herd lived 701 *Prelude* 8. 180
Because the goatherd, blessed man! had lips 733 *Prelude* 11. 448
Goatherd-child. —Oh might he tempt that Goatherd-child 342 *Ital. Itin.* 51
Goat's. Of the live deer, or goat's depending beard,— 814 *Excursion* 4. 884
Goats. Served, tending a few sheep and goats, a ragged Norman Boy. 91 *Norman Boy* 4
Apart, beside his silent goats, 342 *Ital. Itin.* 86
Goat's-beard. That turns its goat's-beard flakes of pea-green moss 61 *Bord.* 1295
Goblet. (Tho' a mere goblet to the careless eye) S.3. 433 **The doubt* 42
Goblets. No goblets shall, for thee, be crowned with flowers, 3 *Ev. Wk.* 76
Down the long street, rich goblets filled with wine 213 *Dion* 32
And goblets crown the proud festivity, 624 *Æneid* 41
Huge goblets are brought forth; they crown the wine; 625 *Æneid* 98
Goblin. It is no goblin, 'tis no ghost, 130 *Idiot Boy* 369
Goblin's. To the dark cave, the goblin's hall; 128 *Idiot Boy* 228
God. *See* **Archer-god, Demi-god, Infant-god.**
Sure, nature's God that spot to man had given 10 *Desc. Sk.* 4
Of angry Nature to avenge her God. 17 *Desc. Sk.* 402
He, all superior but his God disdained, 18 *Desc. Sk.* 435
He holds with God himself communion high, 18 *Desc. Sk.* 462
Great God! by whom the strifes of men are weighed 22 *Desc. Sk.* 652
Bidding me trust in God, he stood and prayed;— 28 *Guilt* 241
Fervently cried the housewife—"God be praised, 34 *Guilt* 565
The God in heaven my prayers for you will hear; 35 *Guilt* 575
And oft he groaned aloud, "O God, that I were dead!" 36 *Guilt* 639
'Twere wrong to trouble you. God speed you both. 41 *Bord.* 222
That's all—God save you, Sir. Ha! as I live, 43 *Bord.* 332
At which I half accused the God in Heaven.— 45 *Bord.* 427
For love of God I must not pass their doors; 46 *Bord.* 524
God bless and thank you both, my gentle Masters. 46 *Bord.* 526
Father!—to God himself we cannot give 47 *Bord.* 543
And it was you, dear Lady! God be praised, 50 *Bord.* 719
Yes, yes. I will not murmur, merciful God! 53 *Bord.* 850
And, by the living God, I could not do it. 55 *Bord.* 990
By the good God, our common Father, doomed!— 62 *Bord.* 1345
I bless her with sad spirit,—when of God, 62 *Bord.* 1375
Here will I leave him—here—All-seeing God! 62 *Bord.* 1391
God and that staff are now thy only guides. 63 *Bord.* 1416
That often, when the name of God is uttered, 63 *Bord.* 1438
To God above will make him feel for ours. 66 *Bord.* 1596
These stifling blasts—God help me! Better this bare rock, 67 *Bord.* 1658
Then God be thanked—— 72 *Bord.* 1922
God knows what was in my heart, 72 *Bord.* 1960
We are betrayed! His Daughter!—God have mercy! 72 *Bord.* 2009
Passing before him, such as God will not 73 *Bord.* 2027
Which now thou tak'st upon thee. God forbid 74 *Bord.* 2113
All die in solitude. Mysterious God, 75 *Bord.* 2154
If e'er he entereth the house of God, 76 *Bord.* 2181
Such tales of your dead Father!—God is my judge, 77 *Bord.* 2244
But she, God love her! feared to brush 79 **Stay near* 17
God has given a kindlier power 80 *Foresight* 25
Till God released her of her pain; 84 *We are Seven* 51
"Then offer up thy heart to God in thankfulness and praise, 93 *Poet's Dream* 57
Where thousands meet to worship God under a mighty Dome; 93 *Poet's Dream* 62
"God for His service needeth not proud work of human skill; 93 *Poet's Dream* 65
God only knows, but to the very last 98 *Brothers* 218
That God who made the great book of the world 99 *Brothers* 266
Nay, God forbid!—You recollect I mentioned 101 *Brothers* 393
Great God, who feel'st for my distress, 113 *Lament* 54
God cursed me in my sore distress; 115 *Last of Flock* 86
Assist me, God, their boundaries to know, 118 *Maternal Grief* 12
And now, God help me for my little wit! 119 *Sailor's Mother* 35
With, "God forbid it should be true!" 128 *Idiot Boy* 183
"Oh God forbid!" poor Susan cries. 128 *Idiot Boy* 191
That God poor Susan's life would spare, 128 *Idiot Boy* 200
I toiled and toiled; God blessed me in my work, 137 *Michael* 377
And God will strengthen thee: amid all fear 137 *Michael* 408
Do I dare to thank the God, 140 *Arm. Lady* 68
And countless blessings which God sends: 143 †*Lov. and Lik.* 58

God—*continued.*
And long shall be so yet—God willing!" 179 *Waggoner* 3. 96
"Yon owl!—pray God that all be well! 179 *Waggoner* 3. 112
Thou sing'st as if the God of wine 186 **O Nightingale* 5
Outshining like a visible God 192 *Gipsies* 15
God help thee, Ruth!—Such pains she had, 194 *Ruth* 193
Religious men, who give to God and man their dues. 196 *Resolution* 98
"God," said I, "be my help and stay secure; 197 *Resolution* 139
God loves the Child; and God hath willed 204 *Brougham* 80
For of God,—of God they are. 209 **Yes, it* 20
And a God leads him, wingèd Mercury! 209 *Laod.* 18
Some God or Hero, from the Olympian clime 220 *Triad* 3
And God upholds them all: 224 *Primrose* 22
God, who instructs the brutes to scent 226 *Present.* 73
Of worshippers kneeling to their up-risen God? 230 *Clouds* 28
In old time worshipped as the god of verse, 231 *Clouds* 82
And blackening clouds in thunder speak of God, 233 *Power of Sound* 84
Into the ear of God, their Lord! 235 *Power of Sound* 208
"Oh! God be praised—my heart's at ease— 248 *P. B.* 1026
"Oh! God, I can endure no more!" 249 *P. B.* 1120
In sight of Heaven, then, wherefore hath God made 256 **Yes! hope* 4
God being with thee when we know it not. 258 **It is a* 14
It moves us not.—Great God! I'd rather be 259 **The world is* 9
Dear God! the very houses seem asleep; 269 *Westm. Bridge* 13
To thy heart's wish, thy labour blest by God! 281 *Chris. Words.* 8
But it was fashioned and to God was vowed 282 **In my* 5
And by the general reverence God is praised: 283 **Well have* 12
Just God, forgive! 286 *Nith* 66
God shield thee to thy latest years! 288 *Highland Girl* 19
All that the God of Nature hath conferred, 290 *Kilchurn* 18
For God took pity on the Boy, 295 *Highland Boy* 23
Of that great Water give God thanks, 297 *Highland Boy* 224
That God might suitably be praised. 298 *Brownie's Cell* 10
Even so doth God protect us if we be 306 **Inland, within* 9
Sound, healthy, children of the God of heaven, 308 **These times* 7
Seems at the heart of all things. But, great God! 309 **When, looking* 10
Of a just God for liberty and right. 309 **What if* 14
So did she daunt the Earth, and God defy! 311 **Who rises* 30
And God and Nature say that it is just. 315 **The Land* 4
And piety towards God. Such men of old 319 **Avaunt all* 9
(Thanks to high God) forests of such remain: 319 **Avaunt all* 11
Their God, and placed their trust in human pride! 321 **Humanity, delighting* 18
Ye slight not life—to God and Nature true; 326 **Intrepid sons* 5
He conquering through God, and God by him." 326 *Sobieski* 14
Nor will the God of peace and love 328 *Ode 1815* 87
And magnify Thy name, Almighty God! 328 *Ode 1815* 105
Tremendous God of battles, Lord of Hosts! 328 *Ode 1815* 113
Just God of christianised Humanity, 328 *Ode 1815* 121
That bind thee to the path which God ordains 329 *Ode: Thanks.* 17
For that Almighty God to whom we owe, 330 *Ode: Thanks.* 90
Which, spurning God, had flung away remorse— 330 *Ode: Thanks.* 119
Awake! the majesty of God revere! 332 *Ode: Thanks.* 227
Their heads in sign of worship, Nature's God, 337 *Aar* 13
Of God himself from dread pre-eminence— 340 *Ranz* 11
His God may be adored. 341 *San Salv.* 12
They round his altar bore the hornèd God, 346 *Processions* 24
To act the God among external things, 347 *Processions* 66
His milder Genius (thanks to the good God 362 **List—'twas* 42
For converse with God, sought through study and prayer. 364 *Vallomb.* 8
Light which to God is both the way and guide; 365 **Rapt above* 11
God reigns above, and Spirits strong 370 *Eg. Maid* 81
Of God, and Heaven's pure Queen—the blissful Mary. 374 *Eg. Maid* 342
Sir Galahad! a treasure, that God giveth, 374 *Eg. Maid* 344
To God proclaims defiance, 374 *Eg. Maid* 357
"Change me, some God, into that breathing rose!" 377 *Duddon* 7. 1
To his high charge, and truly serving God, 387 *Manse* 11
With no one near save the omnipresent God. 391 *Brownie* 8
Man placed him here, and God, he knows, can save. 392 *Daniel* 14
Has ended, though no Clerk, with "God be praised!" 394 *Countess' Pillar* 14
For what survives of house where God 397 *White Doe* 114
Of God had in her heart found place— 398 *White Doe* 232
To God or man; such innocence, 402 *White Doe* 523
Of God, and fill thy destined place: 402 *White Doe* 584
Trusting himself to the earth, and God. 404 *White Doe* 731
To God descending in his power. 405 *White Doe* 834
The invisible God, and take for guide 407 *White Doe* 1040
"Yes—God is rich in mercy," said 411 *White Doe* 1354
Their sabbath music—"God us ayde!" 415 *White Doe* 1762
With vocal music, "God us ayde;" 415 *White Doe* 1774
By sorrow lifted towards her God; 416 *White Doe* 1851
Rose to the God from whom it came! 416 *White Doe* 1868
Yet shall it claim our reverence, that to God, 419 *Ecc. Sonn.* 1. 4. 5
Drops, and the God himself is seen no more. 423 *Ecc. Sonn.* 1. 17. 8
Servants of God! who not a thought will share 423 *Ecc. Sonn.* 1. 19. 2
"God willeth it," the whole assembly cry; 427 *Ecc. Sonn.* 1. 33. 9
"God willeth it," from hill to hill rebounds, 427 *Ecc. Sonn.* 1. 33. 12
And nature God disdained not; Man—whose soul 429 *Ecc. Sonn.* 2. 4. 11
Yet will yourselves to God no service pay; 433 *Ecc. Sonn.* 2. 18. 6
Of God and man, place higher than to him 433 *Ecc. Sonn.* 2. 19. 13
And to her God restored by evidence 436 *Ecc. Sonn.* 2. 30. 3
One (like those prophets whom God sent of old) 437 *Ecc. Sonn.* 2. 34. 4
(O God of mercy, may no earthly Seat 437 *Ecc. Sonn.* 2. 35. 2
The peace of God within his single breast! 438 *Ecc. Sonn.* 2. 37. 14
Despised by that stern God to whom they raise 440 *Ecc. Sonn.* 2. 46. 11
Lures not from what they deem the cause of God. 441 *Ecc. Sonn.* 3. 6. 14
Father! to God himself we cannot give 445 *Ecc. Sonn.* 3. 21. 1
Under the holy fear of God turns pale; 446 *Ecc. Sonn.* 3. 23. 8

God—*continued.*
And magnify the glorious name of God, 446 *Ecc. Sonn.* 3. 25. 7
Of God and chosen friends, your troth to plight 446 *Ecc. Sonn.* 3. 26. 3
Suppliants! the God to whom your cause ye trust 448 *Ecc. Sonn.* 3. 30. 13
Wander the Ministers of God, as chance 449 *Ecc. Sonn.* 3. 36. 4
The corner-stone from hands that build to God. 450 *Ecc. Sonn.* 3. 39. 4
Types of the spiritual Church which God hath reared; 451 *Ecc. Sonn.* 3. 42. 2
Glory to God! and to the Power who came 452 *Ecc. Sonn.* 3. 46. 1
May silent thanks at least to God be given 454 *Sea-side* 38
To sue the God; but, haunting your green shade 463 **Adieu, Rydalian* 6
And straightway cease to aspire, than God disdain 465 **Pastor and* 13
With love of God, throughout the Land were raised 467 *St. Bees* 120
The thoughtful Monks, intent their God to please, 468 *St. Bees* 142
And, as a God, light on thy topmost cliff. 471 **Arran! a* 8
The inviolable God, that tames the proud! 477 *Long Meg* 14
Union significant of God adored, 477 **Lowther! in* 4
And will maintain, if God his help afford. 477 **Lowther! in* 8
Yet, God is my witness, thou small helpless Thing! 484 **A plague* 31
Himself his world, and his own God; 485 *Poet's Epitaph* 28
"The will of God be done!" 486 **We walked* 4
Are given by God, in thee was most intense; 491 *Tribute: Dog* 28
Stern Daughter of the Voice of God! 492 *Duty* 1
If but to God we turn, and ask 495 *Force of Prayer* 67
Too late—or, should the providence of God 504 *Warning* 82
Up to the throne of God is borne 506 *Lab. Hymn* 1
Upon the service of our God! 506 *Lab. Hymn* 16
Through which yon house of God 508 *May* 82
One above all, a Monk who waits on God 509 *F. Stone* 95
Thanks given to God for daily bread, and here 509 *F. Stone* 110
The Bird of God! whose blessed will 512 **Who rashly* 30
Their spirit mounted, crying, "God us aid!" 513 *General Fast* 8
For liberty, would seek from God defence 513 *General Fast* 12
Works not the righteousness of God? Oh bend, 514 **Portentous change* 10
The heart with joy and gratitude to God 517 *Pun. Death* 1. 6
Neither of God nor man, and only saw, 517 *Pun. Death* 2. 5
Oh, speed the blessed hour, Almighty God! 520 *Pun. Death* 13. 14
Who can divine what impulses from God 527 **Those breathing* 27
God, whom their passions dare defy, 534 **Blest is* 78
To kneel together, and adore their God! 534 **Blest is* 100
To God that is the judge of all. 537 *Goody Blake* 96
"God! who art never out of hearing, 537 *Goody Blake* 99
Had breathed a sigh of thanks to God, 542 *Russ. Fug.* 43
The God in heaven;—attend, be just; 545 *Russ. Fug.* 295
Unto Thee, mysterious God! 550 *Hermit's Cell* 4. 4
Gracious God, the pure oblation 550 *Hermit's Cell.* 4. 15
But by the mouths of children, gracious God! 552 *Prioress* 5
Know, that the honour of high God may spread, 554 *Prioress* 126
"O Thou great God that dost perform Thy laud 555 *Prioress* 156
Where'er he be, God grant us him to meet! 556 *Prioress* 232
Weak sinful folk, that God, with pitying eye, 556 *Prioress* 237
The God of Love—*ah, benedicite!* 556 *Cuck. and Night.* 1
Now, God, quoth I, that died upon the rood, 558 *Cuck. and Night.* 93
For who is loth the God of Love to obey, 559 *Cuck.andNight.*133
The God of Love afflict thee with all teen, 560 *Cuck.andNight.*187
Now, God of Love! thou help me in some wise, 560 *Cuck.andNight.*214
Unto the God of Love I make a vow, 561 *Cuck.andNight.*229
And, God of Love, that can right well and may, 561 *Cuck.andNight.*253
I pray to God with her always to be, 561 *Cuck.andNight.*257
For love of God, full piteously did say, 562 *Troilus* 4
O blissful God of Love! then thus he cried, 563 *Troilus* 64
O would the blissful God now for his joy, 564 *Troilus* 90
For love of God, run fast above thy sphere; 564 *Troilus* 138
Without offence to God cast out of view; 567 *Cumb. Beg.* 84
And trust in God—to whose eternal doom 574 *Chiabrera* 3. 19
That God will chasten whom he dearly loves. 576 **By a* 6
That Man, who is from God sent forth, 581 **Loud is* 21
Doth yet again to God return?— 581 **Loud is* 22
The God upon whose mercy they are thrown. 584 **With copious* 64
Through God, is raised a spirit and soul of love 585 *Ch. Lamb* 66
From God, who is our home: 588 *Immortality* 65
Oh give, great God, to Freedom's waves to ride 617 *Desc.Sk.Quarto* 792
The God of day, in all the pomp of light, 618 *School Ex.* 39
Think all, he is the God of young delight." 620 *Birth of Love* 14
—Oh if such silence be not thanks to God 622 *Recluse* 1. 1. 83
Hence, ere some hostile God can intervene, 624 *Æneid* 23
How great a God, incumbent o'er her breast, 625 *Æneid* 88
What God in whispers from the wood 626 †*Cento* 5
"Thus, Christian people, God his might hath shown 627 **When Severn's* 3
May'st thou pursue thy course by God approved, 628 **Deign, Sovereign* 11
With God and Nature communing, removed 648 *Prelude* 2. 430
And to the God who sees into the heart. 651 *Prelude* 3. 143
But spare the House of God. Was ever known 655 *Prelude* 3. 405
Naked, as in the presence of her God. 660 *Prelude* 4. 152
He said, "My trust is in the God of Heaven, 665 *Prelude* 4. 459
The other that was a god, yea many gods, 667 *Prelude* 5. 106
Than Nature's self, which is the breath of God, 669 *Prelude* 5. 221
And hath the name of, God. Transcendent peace 677 *Prelude* 6. 139
When God, the giver of all joy, is thanked 685 *Prelude* 6. 685
From early converse with the works of God 698 *Prelude* 7. 742
Of Pan, Invisible God, thrilling the rocks 701 *Prelude* 8. 183
Or genius, under Nature, under God, 703 *Prelude* 8. 259
And ye adore! But blessèd be the God 703 *Prelude* 8. 301
On the pure bliss, and takes her rest with God. 709 *Prelude* 8. 675
The gift which God has placed within his power, 714 *Prelude* 9. 356
And made of that their God, the hopes of men 723 *Prelude* 10. 343
Towards them and to all creatures. God delights 736 *Prelude* 12. 171
To God, Who thus corrected my desires; 739 *Prelude* 12. 316
In gratitude to God, Who feeds our hearts 744 *Prelude* 13. 276

God—*continued.*
Of human Being, Eternity, and God. 749 *Prelude* 14. 205
And fearing God; the very children taught 758 *Excursion* 1. 114
Of visitation from the living God, 759 *Excursion* 1. 212
Was their best hope, next to the God in heaven. 764 *Excursion* 1. 534
More easy; and I hope,' said she, 'that God 768 *Excursion* 1. 774
In death thy faithfulness?"—"God rest his soul!" 777 *Excursion* 2. 382
In what she most doth value, love of God 781 *Excursion* 2. 633
Faith absolute in God, including hope, 801 *Excursion* 4. 22
From sleep, and dwell with God in endless love. 804 *Excursion* 4. 190
Of God; and Angels to his sight appeared 810 *Excursion* 4. 635
Single and one, the omnipresent God, 811 *Excursion* 4. 652
A sensitive existence, and a God, 811 *Excursion* 4. 679
Could find commodious place for every God, 812 *Excursion* 4. 721
The simple shepherd's awe-inspiring God!" 814 *Excursion* 4. 887
Peace in ourselves, and union with our God. 818 *Excursion* 4. 1116
Living to God and nature, and content 823 *Excursion* 5. 35
But, blessing God and praising him, bequeathed 839 *Excursion* 6. 69
More holy in the sight of God or Man; 850 *Excursion* 6. 803
Though pitied among men, absolved by God, 855 *Excursion* 6. 1112
That God, who takes away, yet takes not half 855 *Excursion* 6. 1134
In God; and reverence for the dust of Man." 873 *Excursion* 7. 1057
Watching to God. Religious men were they; 877 *Excursion* 8. 191
"Eternal Spirit! universal God! 893 *Excursion* 9. 614
"Whence but from thee, the true and only God, 895 *Excursion* 9. 720
The fair Narcissus, by some pitying God S.3. 434 **The doubt* 81
And Nature deepens into Nature's God. S.3. 435 **The doubt* 121
And admirations that were there, of God K.8. 227 **I will* 96
One household under God for high and low, K.8. 253*Recluse* 1.1.618

Goddard. Oh GODDARD!—what art thou?—a name— 348 **Lulled by* 25

Goddess. May the unsullied Goddess of the chase, 104 *Artegal* 150
—Bold Goddess! range our Youth among; 217 *Enterprise* 122
But thou, O Goddess! in thy favourite Isle 217 *Enterprise* 151
To flesh and blood; no Goddess from above, 252 **Her only* 13
The power of Merlin, Goddess! this should be: 266 **With how* 9
By the blind Goddess,—ruthless, undismayed; 317 **Look now* 5
A wingèd Goddess—clothed in vesture wrought 334 **A wingèd* 1
Was carved—a Goddess with a Lily flower, 370 *Eg. Maid* 76
Than if the Goddess of the flower had spoken: 371 *Eg. Maid* 152
When lo! the heavenly goddess thus began, 618 *School Ex.* 27
On the wild Goddess of VOLUPTUOUS JOY. 620 *Birth of Love* 23
The Goddess then her lap with sweetmeats fill'd 620 *Birth of Love* 42
When Wisdom, like the Goddess from Jove's brain, 695 *Prelude* 7. 538
And hence, a beaming Goddess with her Nymphs, 814 *Excursion* 4. 865

Godfather. I'll be his Godfather. Oh Sir, you are merry with me. 46 *Bord.* 521

Godhead. A Godhead, like the universal PAN; 315 **O'er the* 3
To Saint, or Fiend, or to the Godhead whom 475 **Here on their* 10
With godhead, and, by reason and by will, 706 *Prelude* 8. 493
To trust in; that the godhead which is ours 721 *Prelude* 10. 203

Godhead's. The Godhead's most benignant grace; 492 *Duty* 42
And throttled with an infant godhead's might 724 *Prelude* 10. 392

Godless. The sport of factious Hate or godless Zeal. 629 *Installation* 94

Godlike. Have wrought with godlike arm the deeds of praise, 15 *Desc. Sk.* 290
And Reason's godlike Power be proud to own. 173 *Infant Daughter* 78
Descends:—beneath this godlike Warrior, see! 314 *Hofer* 12
For privilege redeemed of godlike sway) 325 *Ode 1814* 122
By godlike insight. To this fate is doomed 357 *Aquap.* 330
But long as god-like wish, or hope divine, 457 **Had this* 34
Godlike, a humble branch of the divine, 509 *F. Stone* 89
And to one purpose cleave, their Being's godlike mate! 529 **Those breathing* 132
The rapt One, of the godlike forehead, 586 *Hogg* 17
That lives who hath not known his god-like hours, 651 *Prelude* 3. 191
How the immortal soul with God-like power 661 *Prelude* 4. 166
Or turns the godlike faculty of speech 889 *Excursion* 9. 318
The god-like functions of the Soul. S.3. 439 **Avaunt this* 6

Godliness. In cheerful godliness; and yet thy heart 307 **Milton! thou* 13

Godly. The godly book was in his hand— 244 *P. B.* 751
The true descendants of those godly men 814 *Excursion* 4. 897

God's. Of God's parental mercies—with Idonea 60 *Bord.* 1267
The weakest of God's creatures, stand resolved 65 *Bord.* 1518
And in the open sunshine of God's love 134 *Michael* 229
Rough doings these! as God's my judge, 176 *Waggoner* 1. 249
Housing, with God's good help, by choice or chance; 196 *Resolution* 104
Is God's redeeming love; 225 *Primrose* 36
Yea, both for souls who God's forbearance try, 229 *Cuckoo-clock* 43
Not with God's bounty, Nature's love, to vie, 231 **The gentlest Poet* 33
Why to God's goodness cannot We be true, 278 **Life with* 12
At God's appointed hour to them who tread 278 **Lo! where she* 10
'Tis God's appointment who must sway, 291 *Rob Roy* 51
Forgiveness from God's mercy-seat; 331 *Ode: Thanks.* 179
A portion of God's peace. 337 **Oh Life* 12
Of God's eternal Word, the Voice of Time 349 *At Dover* 12
In sackcloth, and God's anger deprecate 364 **What aim* 7
Yea, trusting in God's holy aid, 401 *White Doe* 488
For, with God's will, it shall be done!'— 410 *White Doe* 1311
Which God's ethereal storehouses afford: 419 *Ecc. Sonn.* 1. 6. 4
DE-IRIANS—he would save them from God's IRE; 422 *Ecc. Sonn.* 1. 13. 12
And calm with fear of God's divinity. 422 *Ecc. Sonn.* 1. 14. 14
From God's eternal justice. Pitiless 426 *Ecc. Sonn.* 1. 32. 5
Aliens, is God's good winter for their haunts. 431 *Ecc. Sonn.* 2. 12. 14
That pardon, from God's throne, may set its seal 447 *Ecc. Sonn.* 3. 28. 8
God's goodness—measuring bounty as it may; 456 *Rydal Mere* 39
God's glory; and acknowledging thy share 461 **Queen of* 43
God's bounty, soon forgotten; or indeed, 462 **Where lies the truth* 5
—Thou soul of God's best earthly mould! 486 *Matthew* 29
On wings that fear no glance of God's pure sight, 512 **Who rashly* 38
May not avail, nor prayer have for God's ear. 519 *Pun. Death* 10. 7

God's—*continued.*
With God's favour shall be done." . . . . . 535 *Egremont* 36
And, in fulfilment of God's mercy, lodged . . 541 *Grace Darl.* 82
The measure of God's chastening love, . . . 577 **By playful* 10
Acknowledges God's grace, his mercy feels, . . 586 *Ch. Lamb* 119
The living Rock of God's eternal Word. . . . 626 *Rock : Rydal* 4
Under God's restraining laws. . . . . . . 628 *Installation* 16
To the end and written spirit of God's works, . 663 *Prelude* 4. 351
Exchanged—to equalise in God's pure sight . . 682 *Prelude* 6. 455
To presences of God's mysterious power . . . 713 *Prelude* 9. 234
Stern self-respect, a reverence for God's word, . 758 *Excursion* 1. 115
In God's good love, and seek his help by prayer. . 768 *Excursion* 1. 808
As God's most intimate presence in the soul, . . 804 *Excursion* 4. 226
One of God's simple children that yet know not . 851 *Excursion* 6. 881
And must be, with God's will, a happy band. . K.8. 254 *Recluse* 1. 1. 663

Gods. *See* **Demi-gods.**
For his paternal Gods, the Trojan raised ? . . 102 *Artegal* 2
And while he served the Gods with reverence due, 103 *Artegal* 72
And from the infernal Gods, 'mid shades forlorn . 209 *Laod.* 3
Not to appal me have the gods bestowed . . . 210 *Laod.* 35
Rebellious passion : for the Gods approve . . 210 *Laod.* 74
" The Gods to us are merciful—and they . . . 210 *Laod.* 85
By the just Gods whom no weak pity moved, . . 212 *Laod.* 160
Ye Gods, thought He, that servile Implement . 214 *Dion* 94
Drawn in defiance of the Gods, hath laid . . . 214 *Dion* 108
Angels and gods ! We struggle with our fate, . 261 **I watch* 10
To appease the Gods ; or public thanks to yield ; 346 *Processions* 1
Is this, ye Gods, the Capitolian Hill ? . . . . 358 **Is this* 1
A Pontiff, Trajan *here* the Gods implores, . . 368 *Trajan* 41
Their Gods of wood and stone ; and, at the sound 436 *Ecc. Sonn.* 2. 33. 5
The Gods revolving the decrees of Fate, . . . 457 **The leaves* 31
To righteous Gods when man has ceased to feel, . 500 *Humanity* 2
For Gods in council, whose green vales, retreats . 501 *Humanity* 74
She scans the future with the eye of gods. . . 516 **Hard task* 14
The bay ; and conquerors thanked the Gods, . . 543 *Russ. Fug.* 191
The other that was a god, yea many gods, . . 667 *Prelude* 5. 106
Hath dropped all functions by the gods bestowed, 732 *Prelude* 11. 368
Of heroes ; or, in reverence to the gods, . . . 734 *Prelude* 11. 459
Decrees and resolutions of the Gods ; . . . . 812 *Excursion* 4. 704
They fortified with reverence for the Gods ; . . 815 *Excursion* 4. 939
Tell in their idle songs of wandering gods, . . 868 *Excursion* 7. 729
To Gods delighting in remorseless deeds ; . . . 894 *Excursion* 9. 685
Gods which themselves had fashioned, to promote 894 *Excursion* 9. 686
He planted, and in Latium fixed his Gods, . K.8. 281 **Arms and* 7

Goers. The comers and the goers face to face, . . 689 *Prelude* 7. 156

Goes. Predominates, and darkness comes and goes, 13 *Desc. Sk.* 180
Rich steam of sweetest perfume comes and goes. . 16 *Desc. Sk.* 345
Falls on the valleys as the sun goes down ; . . 19 *Desc. Sk.* 471
When downward to his winter hut he goes, . . 19 *Desc. Sk.* 478
Till to his flock the early shepherd goes, . . . 27 *Guilt* 159
And One so fair, it goes against my heart . . . 43 *Bord.* 309
How goes the night. 'Tis hard to measure time . 52 *Bord.* 805
But how he will come, and whither he goes, . . 80 †*Address : Child* 7
How quietly her Johnny goes. . . . . . . 127 *Idiot Boy* 91
As on he goes beneath the moon. . . . . . 127 *Idiot Boy* 106
So, through the moonlight lane she goes, . . . 128 *Idiot Boy* 202
Away she goes up hill and down, ... 130 *Idiot Boy* 427
And with them goes the guardian pair. . . . 178 *Waggoner* 3. 21
And with him goes his Sailor-friend, ... 180 *Waggoner* 4. 69
That comes and goes—will sometimes leap . . 182 *Waggoner* 4. 211
This wretched Woman thither goes ; . . . . . 198 *Thorn* 68
The spot to which she goes ; . . . . 198 *Thorn* 92
" But that she goes to this old Thorn, ... 199 *Thorn* 166
Up goes my Boat among the stars . . . . 236 *P. B.* 31
Up goes my little Boat so bright ! . . . . . 236 *P. B.* 35
And up the stony lane he goes ; . . . . . 247 *P. B.* 986
Away goes Rachel weeping loud ;— . . . . 248 *P. B.* 1066
Their tops, between them comes and goes a sky . 272 **Where holy* 12
Of Jesus goes before, the child is borne . . . 318 **In due* 10
Of the whole world's good wishes with him goes ; 387 *Scott* 9
Whither it goes. Even such, that transient Thing, 422 *Ecc. Sonn.* 1. 16. 8
Goes forth—unveiling timidly a cheek . . . . 434 *Ecc. Sonn.* 2. 22. 5
That ere the Sun goes down their childhood sets. . 446 *Ecc. Sonn.* 3. 23. 14
In many an hour when judgment goes astray. . 467 *St. Bees* 85
How merrily it goes ! . . . . 487 *Fountain* 22
Goes to learn how all things fare ; . . . . . 490 *Incident : Dog* 2
Deceitfully goes forth the Morn ; . . . . . 550 *Hermit's Cell* 5. 2
For he's not like an Old Man that leisurely goes . 570 *Farmer* 57
The Rainbow comes and goes, ... 587 *Immortality* 10
On the high summits Darkness comes and goes, . 605 *Desc.Sk.Quarto* 205
Goes out, but with a flash that has revealed . . 684 *Prelude* 6. 601
" Alas ! before to-morrow's sun goes down . . 840 *Excursion* 6. 113
His old employments, goes to field or wood, . . 878 *Excursion* 8. 277
To have about him, which way e'er he goes, . . K.8. 250 *Recluse* 1.1.485

Goest. " But if thou goest, I follow— " " Peace ! " he said,— . . . 211 *Laod.* 91
Thou goest before in thy benignity, ... 552 *Prioress* 26

Goeth. *Ave Marie*, as he goeth by the way. . . 553 *Prioress* 56
She goeth, as she were half out of her mind, . . 555 *Prioress* 143

Goggling. The Bust that speaks and moves its goggling eyes, ... 698 *Prelude* 7. 711

Going. And are you going then ? Come, come, Idonea, ... 42 *Bord.* 296
Is going from under me ; these strange discoveries— 47 *Bord.* 548
How now, what mean you ? Truly, I was going . 51 *Bord.* 765
And whither were you going ? Learn, young Man,— . . . . 61 *Bord.* 1337
" And whither are you going, child, ... 82 *Alice Fell* 33
And now that Johnny is just going, ... 126 *Idiot Boy* 67
" What can I do ? " says Betty, going, . . . 128 *Idiot Boy* 192

Going—*continued.*
Which, going by from year to year, had found, . 133 *Michael* 119
Nor whither going. . . . . 158 **In youth* 72
Of the sun going down to his rest, ... 166 *Stray Pleasures* 15
That side by side we still are going ! . . . . 175 *Waggoner* 1. 145
Erect his port, and firm his going ; . . . . 181 *Waggoner* 4. 148
Joy have I had ; and going hence . . . . . 288 *Highland Girl* 64
Of his last going from Tweed-side, thought turned, 353 *Aquap.* 67
The day is placid in its going, ... 397 *White Doe* 148
" On good service we are going . . . . . 535 *Egremont* 25
And labourers going forth to till the fields. . . 663 *Prelude* 4. 332
'Twas going far to seek disquietude ; . . . . 666 *Prelude* 5. 53
Was going then to bury those two books : . . . 667 *Prelude* 5. 102
Of twilight deepened, going forth, I spied . . . 687 *Prelude* 7. 32
Which then was going forward in her name ! . . 729 *Prelude* 11. 116
Of soldiers, going to a distant land. . . . . 766 *Excursion* 1. 677
And while the work is going on . . . . . S.3. 423 *Tinker* 14

Going-out. (Still to the very going-out of youth) 749 *Prelude* 14. 243

Goings. Thy goings—or the cheerfulness . . . 344 **How blest* 64
In all my goings, in the new and old . . . . 622 *Recluse* 1. 1. 95
To watch their goings, whatsoever track . . . 702 *Prelude* 8. 233
Of his own business, and the goings on . . K.8. 230 **I will* 184

Gold. Of fainter gold, a purple gleam betray. . . 5 *Ev. Wk.* 177
And all the babbling brooks are liquid gold ; . . 5 *Ev. Wk.* 189
In robes of azure, fleecy-white, and gold. . . 8 *Ev. Wk.* 330
Its green-tinged margin in a blaze of gold ; . . 12 *Desc. Sk.* 122
At once to pillars turned that flame with gold : . 15 *Desc. Sk.* 280
'Tis morn : with gold the verdant mountain glows ; 17 *Desc. Sk.* 405
Those holy turrets tipped with evening gold, . . 20 *Desc. Sk.* 564
And ripening foliage shone with richer gold. . . 22 *Desc. Sk.* 637
He bribed me with his gold, and looked so fierce. 77 *Bord.* 2246
The beetle panoplied in gems and gold, . . . 108 *Indolence* 60
Would have brought us more good than a burthen of gold, ... 116 *Repentance* 3
Before his eyes, to price above all gold ; . . . 122 *V. and J.* 43
Your Pony's worth his weight in gold : . . . 130 *Idiot Boy* 362
Along the copses runs in veins of gold. . . . 147 *Joanna* 40
" ' The butterfly, all green and gold, ... 156 *Oak and Broom* 81
A silver shield with boss of gold, ... 159 **With little* 30
Radiant all over with unburnished gold ; . . . 227 *Vernal Ode* 103
Now, for your shame, a Power, the Thirst of Gold, ... 283 **Proud were* 4
The student's bower for gold, some fears unnamed 308 **When I* 4
Her arts, her strength, her iron, and her gold. . 320 **Avaunt all* 14
Of servile opportunity to gold ; . . . . . . 351 *Des. Stanzas* 79
And the material finest gold ; . . . . . . 390 *Highland Broach* 24
And wears a frontlet edged with gold. . . . . 399 *White Doe* 260
In vermeil colours and in gold . . . . . . 400 *White Doe* 348
Came Barons bold, with store of gold, ... 478 *Somnamb.* 21
That these two words of glittering gold . . . 486 *Matthew* 31
Through Moscow's gates, with gold unbarred, . . 542 *Russ. Fug.* 9
Where gold determines between right and wrong. 573 *Chiabrera* 2. 4
Only by gold. And now a simple stone . . . 574 *Chiabrera* 5. 16
Where tipp'd with gold the mountain-summits glow'd. . . . . 592 *Ev. Wk. Quarto* 36
Their moveless boughs and leaves like threads of gold ; . . . . 593 *Ev. Wk. Quarto* 104
Here half a village shines, in gold array'd, . . 604 *Desc.Sk.Quarto* 106
Those turrets tipp'd by hope with morning gold. . 614 *Desc.Sk.Quarto* 673
Thy reddening orchards, and thy fields of gold ; . 615 *Desc.Sk.Quarto* 705
And glowed the sun-gilt groves in richer gold : . 616 *Desc.Sk.Quarto* 773
Where, throned in gold, immortal Science reigns ; 619 *School Ex.* 70
Through that state arras woven with silk and gold ; 657 *Prelude* 3. 562
Not like a temple rich with pomp and gold, . . 743 *Prelude* 13. 229
Silver and gold. ' I shuddered at the sight,' . . 766 *Excursion* 1. 671
Of gold, the Maypole shines ; as if the rays . . 773 *Excursion* 2. 134
Fabric it seemed of diamond and of gold, . . . 784 *Excursion* 2. 839
Than that accumulated store of gold . . . . 809 *Excursion* 4. 567
Of virgin ore, that gold which we, by pains . . 832 *Excursion* 5. 632

Goldau's. From flowers 'mid GOLDAU'S ruins bred ; 348 **Lulled by* 64

Golden. And breaks the spreading of its golden tides ; 5 *Ev. Wk.* 171
He views the sun uplift his golden fire, . . . 11 *Desc. Sk.* 31
In golden light ; half hides itself in shade : . . 12 *Desc. Sk.* 98
Rich golden verdure on the lake below. . . . 12 *Desc. Sk.* 102
" St. Ouen's golden Shrine ? Or choose what else would please thee most . . . . 92 *Poet's Dream* 25
Whence golden harvests, cities, warlike towers, . 102 *Artegal* 21
Rent, weeping over him, her golden hair . . . 169 *LoveliesBleeding* 16
That golden time again. . . . . 184 **O blithe* 28
A host, of golden daffodils ; . . . . 187 **I wandered* 4
Rested a golden harp ;—he touched the strings ; . 226 *Vernal Ode* 22
The golden years maintained a course . . . . 228 *Vernal Ode* 131
Of golden sunset, ere it fade and die. . . . . 253 **Aerial Rock* 14
Of golden leaves inlaid with silver down, . . . 254 *WildDuck's Nest* 11
Bruges I saw attired with golden light . . . 333 **Bruges I* 1
When the first Ship sailed for the Golden Fleece— 336 *Danube* 12
Touched by his golden finger. . . . . . . 337 *Thun* 16
The genuine features of the golden mean ; . . 339 *Schwytz* 3
To prophesy a golden lot ; . . . . 342 *Ital. Itin.* 40
What present bliss !—what golden views ! . . . 348 **Lulled by* 53
A golden spear to swallow ! and that brown . . 349 *Sky-prosp.* 6
With golden blossoms opening at the feet . . . 353 *Aquap.* 29
Nor is least pleased, we trust, when golden beams, 354 *Aquap.* 111
As golden locks of birch, that rise and fall . . 381 *Duddon* 21. 12
Transparence through the golden. . . . . . 385 *Yarrow Rev.* 16
If from a golden perch of aspen spray . . . . 388 *Trosachs* 10
In great Eliza's golden time. . . . . . . 396 *White Doe* 42
Of the noon-day. Nor doubt that golden cords . 423 *Ecc. Sonn.* 1. 18. 10
Like sunny mist ;—at length the golden hair, . . 440 *Ecc. Sonn.* 3. 1. 11
Not to the golden mean, and quiet flow . . . 443 *Ecc. Sonn.* 3. 11. 13
And near the golden sceptre grasped by Jove, . 457 **The leaves* 29

Gone—*continued.*
But hark the word !—the ship is gone ;— 579 *Sweet Flower 29
The meek, the brave, the good, was gone ; 580 John Words. 38
With which she speaks when storms are gone, 581 *Loud is 2
Gone from this world of earth, air, sea, and sky, 583 *With copious 19
Thou too art gone before ; but why, 586 Hogg 34
Both of them speak of something that is gone : 588 Immortality 53
Gone was the old grey stone, and in its place 642 Prelude 2. 38
But—though the rhymes were gone that once inscribed 644 Prelude 2. 149
With all its pleasant promises, was gone 661 Prelude 4. 207
Our comrades gone before. By fortunate chance, 683 Prelude 6. 577
Have I gone forward with the crowd, and said 696 Prelude 7. 627
Of that gone by, locked up, as in the grave ; 697 Prelude 7. 659
Till, every effort, every motion gone, 707 Prelude 8. 574
And, in despite of all that had gone by, 708 Prelude 8. 629
'Tis true, had gone before this hour, dire work 718 Prelude 10. 42
Reading at intervals ; the fear gone by 719 Prelude 10. 71
Should to the breast of Nature have gone back, 721 Prelude 10. 232
To me the grief confined, that thou art gone 733 Prelude 11. 399
A lonely wanderer art gone, by pain 733 Prelude 11. 402
And iron case were gone ; but on the turf, 737 Prelude 12. 238
Else never canst receive. The days gone by 738 Prelude 12. 277
That gone, we are as dust.—Behold the fields 748 Prelude 14. 170
That he had disappeared—not two months gone. 766 Excursion 1. 661
She said, ' I fear it will be dead and gone 769 Excursion 1. 845
Whose presence gave no comfort, were gone by, 769 Excursion 1. 893
Sank to decay ; for he was gone, whose hand, 770 Excursion 1. 901
From his own sight—this gone, he forfeited 776 Excursion 2. 296
And he is gone ! " The book, which in my hand 778 Excursion 2. 438
Are gone, or stealing from us ; this, I hope, 780 Excursion 2. 552
If from my poor retirement ye had gone 788 Excursion 3. 118
To Youth or Maiden gone before their time, 825 Excursion 5. 202
Gone forth already to the far-off seat 834 Excursion 5. 803
Unjustly dealt with ; but the Maid was gone ! 840 Excursion 6. 136
Sole Mistress of this house, when I am gone ? 849 Excursion 6. 755
" ' All gone, all vanished ! he deprived and bare, 861 Excursion 7. 263
That falls and disappears, the house is gone ; 872 Excursion 7. 958
Aught of romantic interest, it is gone. 875 Excursion 8. 85
Is gone for ever ; and this organic frame, 879 Excursion 8. 322
An uncouth feat exhibit, and are gone 880 Excursion 8. 380
And, when it is done, away he is gone ; S.3. 432 Tinker 16
Are gone, what summer loiterer will regard, S.3. 433 *The doubt 38
Yet as thou still when we are gone wilt keep S.3. 437 *The doubt 200
Had he gone far ere he espied the boy K.8. 229 *I will 172
He well remembers, though the year be gone. K.8. 236 Recluse 1. 1. 5
And parted them ; or haply both are gone K.8. 244 Recluse 1.1.267
And now am landed, and the motion gone, K.8. 244 Recluse 1.1.293
No longer flourish, he entirely gone, K.8. 248 Recluse 1.1.422

Good. Of happy wisdom, meditating good, 3 Ev. Wk. 81
And afterwards, by my good father taught, 28 Guilt 204
Near his own home !—but he was mild and good ; 35 Guilt 608
In this good service. Rather let us grieve 37 Bord. 5
From whose perverted soul can come no good 37 Bord. 9
And be at rest. Oh, Sir ! Peace, my good Wilfred ; 38 Bord. 40
Soon after, the good Abbot of St. Cuthbert's 41 Bord. 199
Good morrow, Strangers ! If you want a Guide, 41 Bord. 213
Good Host, such tendance as you would expect 42 Bord. 300
With Henry, our good King ;—the Baron might 43 Bord. 348
Will give me quiet lodging. You have a boy, good Host, 43 Bord. 353
For this good deed !—Well, Sirs, this passed away ; 44 Bord. 409
And put your head, good Woman, under cover. 45 Bord. 417
Your favourite saint—no matter—this good day 45 Bord. 430
This woman is a prater. Pray, good Lady ! 45 Bord. 436
I owe him no ill will, but in good sooth 45 Bord. 458
I think, good Woman, you are the very person 45 Bord. 478
I have good business there. I met you at the threshold, 46 Bord. 481
But 'tis all over now. That good old Lady 46 Bord. 486
Shall give me half. What's this ?—I fear, good Woman, 46 Bord. 489
Good Dame, repair to Liddesdale and wait 46 Bord. 516
A lucky woman !—go, you have done good service. 46 Bord. 518
A dog that does not know me.—These good Folks,— 46 Bord. 523
Nay, be not terrified—it does me good 47 Bord. 530
And see your Friend again. The good old Man 50 Bord. 695
Three good round years, for playing the fool here 51 Bord. 769
A cheerless beverage. How good it was in you 52 Bord. 810
And do good service, though she knew it not. 52 Bord. 842
To have heard your voice. Your couch, I fear, good Baron, 53 Bord. 859
And we too chant the praise of his good deeds. 54 Bord. 907
Heavens ! my good Friend ! Forgive me, gracious Sir !— 54 Bord. 943
Strews twenty acres of good meadow-ground 60 Bord. 1230
Good Baron, have you ever practised tillage ? 60 Bord. 1277
By the good God, our common Father, doomed !— 62 Bord. 1345
To whom I owe the best of all the good 62 Bord. 1371
Through good and evil, obloquy and scorn, 64 Bord. 1500
And if good Angels fail, slack in their duty, 65 Bord. 1524
A license to destroy him : our good governors 66 Bord. 1581
His good works will be balm and life to him. 67 Bord. 1632
Were there not eyes that see, and for good ends, 69 Bord. 1752
Might lead to good—I saw it and burst forth, 69 Bord. 1781
Holla ! to bed, good Folks, within ! O save us ! 71 Bord. 1884
There again ! 'Tis my husband's foot. Good Eldred 71 Bord. 1899
The man he was. I will retire ;—good night ! 71 Bord. 1902
Have you, good Peasant, seen a blind old Man ? 73 Bord. 2041
Whose good deeds will not stand by their own light ; 74 Bord. 2081

Good—*continued.*
To travel half a mile alone.—Good Lady ! 76 Bord. 2240
James stopped with no good will : 85 Shepherd-boys 42
Last forerunner of " Good night ! " 90 Longest Day 28
The Chapel Oak of Allonville ; good Angel, show it me ! " 92 Poet's Dream 28
The good Man might have communed with himself, 97 Brothers 115
They loved this good old Man ?—They did—and truly : 99 Brothers 240
Hanging in the open air—but, O good Sir ! 100 Brothers 314
He poured rewards and honours on the good ; 103 Artegal 70
For me—it never did me good. 115 Last of Flock 54
Would have brought us more good than a burthen of gold, 116 Repentance 3
Good, good art thou :—alas ! to me 120 Emigrant Mother 33
How cold it is ! but thou art good ; 121 Emigrant Mother 80
Good Betty, put him down again ; 126 Idiot Boy 13
For her good neighbour Susan Gale, 126 Idiot Boy 18
Her Pony, that is mild and good ; 126 Idiot Boy 33
But Betty, poor good woman ! she, 127 Idiot Boy 132
Good Susan tell me, and I'll stay ; 128 Idiot Boy 194
" Nay, Betty, go ! good Betty, go ! 128 Idiot Boy 197
The Pony he is mild and good, 129 Idiot Boy 303
Why stand you thus, good Betty Foy ? 130 Idiot Boy 368
And when by Heaven's good grace the boy grew up 134 Michael 177
Were younger ;—but this hope is a good hope. 135 Michael 278
Of our two histories ; 'twill do thee good 136 Michael 337
A kind and a good Father : and herein 136 Michael 362
If I judge ill for thee, but it seems good 137 Michael 381
Nay, Boy, be of good hope ;—we both may live 137 Michael 388
Bestir them in good deeds. Now, fare thee well— 137 Michael 412
A good report did from their Kinsman come, 138 Michael 431
No good but by the way that leads to bliss 139 Widow 30
Innocent, and meek, and good, 141 Arm. Lady 118
Peace ye deserve ; and may the solid good, 143 *High bliss 4
Due to that good and pious deed 143 *Driven in 9
Good friends he has to take his part ; 144 *Driven in 74
It came at once to do me good ; 144 Her Eyes 26
That may respect the good old age 154 Flower Garden 53
Attained a good old age. 156 Oak and Broom 70
But 'tis good enough for thee. 160 *Pansies, lilies 48
Can this be the bird, to man so good, 162 *Art thou the 20
But still, where general choice is good, 168 Wren's Nest 29
Offered a greeting of good ale 174 Waggoner 1. 54
He knows it to his cost, good Man ! 174 Waggoner 1. 87
But Heaven has blest a good endeavour ; 174 Waggoner 1. 113
Cried out, " Good brother, why so fast ? 176 Waggoner 1. 237
Take her at once—for good and evil ! " 176 Waggoner 1. 240
That make the good, tow'rds which he's yearning, 177 Waggoner 2. 39
What greater good can heart desire ? 177 Waggoner 2. 71
On both sides, Benjamin the good, 181 Waggoner 4. 182
Which robbed us of good Benjamin ;— 182 Waggoner 4. 267
A Creature not too bright or good 186 *She was 17
Or is it good as others are, and be their eyes in fault ? 189 Star-gazers 11
Is nothing of that radiant pomp so good as we have here ? 189 Star-gazers 13
What good or evil have they seen 191 Seq. Beggars 10
To genial faith, still rich in genial good ; 195 Resolution 39
Housing, with God's good help, by choice or chance ; 196 Resolution 104
No life is good, no pleasure long. 204 Brougham 88
Hear it, good man, old in days ! 204 Brougham 96
No life is good, no pleasure long, 204 Brougham 105
" The good Lord Clifford " was the name he bore. 205 Brougham 172
On that best portion of a good man's life, 206 Tintern 33
Wert kind as resolute, and good as brave ; 210 Laod. 56
Unjustly shed, though for the public good. 213 Dion 57
Thy lot, O Man, is good, thy portion fair ! " 215 Kirkstone 86
Of coming good ;—the charm is fled ; 224 *'Tis gone 22
What though some busy foes to good, 225 Present. 13
And there my good friend, Stephen Otter ; 238 P. B. 167
And made the good man round him look. 244 P. B. 745
Perplexed the good man's gentle soul. 244 P. B. 755
—Let good men feel the soul of nature, 245 P. B. 764
Ye waited then on my good pleasure ; 245 P. B. 793
But many good and pious thoughts 246 P. B. 896
And this good Man, whom Heaven requite, 248 P. B. 1064
" When shall I be as good as thou ? 248 P. B. 1098
A heart but half as good as thine ! " 248 P. B. 1100
Became a good and honest man. 249 P. B. 1135
Not negligent the style ;—the matter ?—good 254 Detraction 2
Of good and pious works Thou art the seed, 257 *The prayers 5
If there be aught of pure, or good, or great, 259 Calvert 10
And hath bestowed on thee a safer good ; 268 *Brook ! whose 13
Of lawless will, unlooked-for streams of good, 271 Henry : Portrait 13
Of good and fair, 285 Nith 16
Through twilight shades of good and ill 286 Sons of Burns 7
And Scotland has a thief as good, 291 Rob Roy 3
" For why ?—because the good old rule 291 Rob Roy 37
Of good things none are good enough :— 291 Rob Roy 86
Of near-approaching good that shall not fail : 294 *Fly, some 8
For, if good Angels love to wait 296 Highland Boy 173
" *Good morrow, Citizen !* " a hollow word, 304 *Jones ! as 11
The Governor who must be wise and good, 304 *I grieved 6
What mightiness for evil and for good ! 306 *Inland, within 8
The homely beauty of the good old cause 307 *O Friend 12
Should perish ; and to evil and to good 307 *It is not 8
Aught good were destined, thou wouldst step between. 309 *England ! the 8
Is man as good as man, none low, none high ?— 309 *What if 8
And thou henceforth wilt have a good man's calm, 313 Clarkson 12
Of moral prudence, sought through good and ill ; 315 *Alas ! what 2

Good-day 377 Gossamer

Good—*continued.*
All accidents, converting them to good. . . . 801 *Excursion* 4. 17
Their own dire agents, and constrain the good . 805 *Excursion* 4. 300
The vacillating, inconsistent good. . . . . . 806 *Excursion* 4. 309
Of much exalted good by Heaven vouchsafed . 813 *Excursion* 4. 783
To good Saint Fillan and to fair Saint Anne ; . . 815 *Excursion* 4. 910
They looked ; were humbly thankful for the good 815 *Excursion* 4. 936
At once, all traces from the good Man's heart . 816 *Excursion* 4. 1013
Who, when such good can be obtained, would strive 817 *Excursion* 4. 1051
And seeks for good ; and finds the good he seeks : 819 *Excursion* 4. 1224
Of order and of good. Whate'er we see, . . 820 *Excursion* 4. 1270
Sweet to himself, was exercised in good . . . 823 *Excursion* 5. 47
Adorns, in which the good Man's ancestors . . 824 *Excursion* 5. 125
Bedded for good and evil in a gulf . . . . . 826 *Excursion* 5. 295
Of a good shepherd tended, as themselves . . . 829 *Excursion* 5. 426
Perforce ? Are we a creature in whom good . . 829 *Excursion* 5. 469
Our inquest turns.—Accord, good Sir ! the light . 829 *Excursion* 5. 481
The good and evil are our own ; and we . . . 830 *Excursion* 5. 490
This is the good man's not unfrequent pang ! . . 831 *Excursion* 5. 592
Not for gross good alone which ye produce, . . 831 *Excursion* 5. 616
Of evil hap and good as oft awaits . . . . . 833 *Excursion* 5. 733
By the bright fire, the good Man's form, and face 834 *Excursion* 5. 779
Miss not the humbler good at which they aim, . 835 *Excursion* 5. 857
And receptacle, open to the good . . . . . 836 *Excursion* 5. 913
From my good Host, that being crazed in brain . 839 *Excursion* 6. 108
By mastery :—and the good Man lacked not friends 840 *Excursion* 6. 164
With neither element of good or ill ; . . . . 843 *Excursion* 6. 371
I feel, good reasons why we should not leave . . 848 *Excursion* 6. 661
And reason that in man is wise and good, . . . 851 *Excursion* 6. 872
My Infant ! and for that good Mother dear, . . 852 *Excursion* 6. 925
For her soul's good ? Nor was that office vain. . 854 *Excursion* 6. 1041
Their grave migration, the good pair would tell, . 859 *Excursion* 7. 109
This portraiture is sketched. The great, the good, 862 *Excursion* 7. 341
That lowly, great, good Man. A simple stone . 862 *Excursion* 7. 352
The good man's purposes and deeds ; retrace . . 863 *Excursion* 7. 376
Was wasted on the good Man's living ear, . . . 864 *Excursion* 7. 478
(Said the good Vicar with a fond half-smile) . . 866 *Excursion* 7. 589
Health and good wishes to his new-born girl, . . 867 *Excursion* 7. 655
—"The peaceable remains of this good Knight . 874 *Excursion* 8. 34
"Yet, by the good Knight's leave, the two estates 875 *Excursion* 8. 44
And Heaven's good providence, preserved from taint ! . . . . 876 *Excursion* 8. 150
This ardent sally pleased the mild good Man, . . 880 *Excursion* 8. 434
Beyond itself, communicating good, ... 884 *Excursion* 9. 11
That good and wise ever will be allowed, . . . 885 *Excursion* 9. 45
Perverted thus, but weakness in all good, . . . 886 *Excursion* 9. 121
A bondage lurking under shape of good,— . . 887 *Excursion* 9. 188
Kind wishes, and good actions, and pure thoughts— 887 *Excursion* 9. 242
The unquestionable good—which, England, safe . 889 *Excursion* 9. 331
Thus, duties rising out of good possest . . . . 889 *Excursion* 9. 355
Trust not to partial care a general good ; . . . 890 *Excursion* 9. 405
And persevere in good, that they shall rise, . . 893 *Excursion* 9. 645
—Father of good ! this prayer in bounty grant, . 894 *Excursion* 9. 647
Of good from evil ; as if one extreme . . . . 895 *Excursion* 9. 723
And in good works ; and him, who is endowed . 895 *Excursion* 9. 735
And whether aught, of tendency as good . . . 896 *Excursion* 9. 791
Right good ale he bowses ; . . . . S.3. 423 *Tinker* 15
Such measured rest the diligent and good . . . S.3. 427 **My Son* 10
Nor to you, good Lady Vane, ... S.3. 438 **My Lord* 3
Camoëns, he the accomplished and the good, . . S.3. 442 **Vasco,whose* 9
And to the last were good and kind, ... K.8. 219 **The snow-tracks* 6
Nor could be given, possession of the good . . K.8. 239 *Recluse* 1.1.106
To regulate my hopes. Pleased with the good, . K.8. 246 *Recluse* 1.1.350
Done truly there, or felt, of solid good . . . . K.8. 247 *Recluse* 1.1.405
When good Jemima perished in her bloom ; . . K.8. 275 **These vales* 2
Thou good and faithful servant of the Cross." K.8. 325[?] **The vestal* 14
Good honest souls !—if right my judgment lies . L.1. 95 *Juvenal* 3. 20
Good-day. And so, my Friend, good-day to you." . 621 *Andrew Jones* 30
Good-fellow. Some Robin Good-fellow were there, 155 **A whirl-blast* 20
Goodly. With goodly arts and usages refined ; . . 102 *Artegal* 20
Fashions his neck into a goodly curve ; . . . 212 *Dion*
A goodly Vessel did I then espy . . . . . 258 **With Ships* 5
Oh, 'tis a goodly Ordinance,—the sight, . . . 331 *Ode : Thanks.* 194
A goodly Knight that hath no peer that liveth !" 374 *Eg. Maid* 348
I bring with me a goodly train ; . . . . . 402 *White Doe* 606
Was with this goodly Personage ; . . . . . 404 *White Doe* 738
For pleasure made, a goodly spot, ... 407 *White Doe* 984
And goodly fruitage with the mother-spray ; . . 435 *Ecc. Sonn.* 2. 28. 3
Of ancient honour ; whence that goodly state 477 **Lowther ! in* 6
Singing so well, so goodly, and so clear, . . . 563 *Troilus* 60
That Ship was goodly to be seen, ... 579 **Sweet Flower* 20
It was a goodly prospect : for, in sooth, . . . 652 *Prelude* 3. 226
When wedded to this goodly universe . . . . 755 *Recluse* 1. 1. 806
This goodly Matron, shining in the beams . . . 882 *Excursion* 8. 517
How goodly, how exceeding fair, how pure . K.8. 254 *Recluse* 1.1.640
Good-natured. "Good-natured lounging," and behold a map . . . . 677 *Prelude* 6. 182
Goodness. "Who never tasted grace, and goodness ne'er had felt." . . . . 102 *Artegal* 16
Attends on goodness with dominion decked, . . 105 *Artegal* 188
"Princess, at this burst of goodness, ... 140 *Arm. Lady* 37
Whose goodness, sinking deep, would reconcile 221 *Triad* 67
Of goodness, for most gracious ends— . . . . 245 *P. B.* 769
Of providential goodness ever nigh ! . . . . 264 *Storm* 14
For grace and goodness lost, thy murmurs melt 269 **Pure clement* 13
Why to God's goodness cannot We be true, . . 278 **Life with* 12
Of all thy goodness, never melancholy ; . . . 279 **Though I* 12
The mercy, goodness, have not failed to awe . . 342 *Last Sup.* 4
God's goodness—measuring bounty as it may ; . 456 *Rydal Mere* 39

Goodness—*continued.*
Whose goodness knows no change, whose love is sure, ... 519 *Pun. Death* 11. 12
Of lofty station, female goodness walks, . . . 539 **Lady ! a* 46
Thy goodness is set forth ; they when they lie . 552 *Prioress* 6
Of goodness, next her Son, our soul's best boot. . 552 *Prioress* 14
"Lady ! thy goodness, thy magnificence, . . . 552 *Prioress* 22
For thereof comes all goodness and all worth ; . 559 *Cuck.and Night.* 151
Illumined ! root of beauty and goodnesse, . . 562 *Cuck.and Night.* 314
To virtue and true goodness. Some there are, . 567 *Cumb. Beg.* 105
On earth to goodness blest by grace divine. . . 628 **Deign,Sovereign* 8
Fetching her goodness rather from times past, . 669 *Prelude* 5. 267
As virtue is, or goodness ; sweet as love, . . . 685 *Prelude* 6. 682
By loneliness, and goodness, and kind works, . 762 *Excursion* 1. 405
Her goodness, that, not seldom, in my walks . . 768 *Excursion* 1. 783
Whose charity and goodness were rehearsed . . 825 *Excursion* 5. 204
Goodnesse. *See* **Goodness.**
Goods. Fields, goods, and far-off chattels we have none : . . . . 106 *Farewell* 13
For goods and chattels, or those Infants dear, . 523 *Epist. Beaumont* 113
With store of household goods, in panniers slung . 858 *Excursion* 7. 64
Good-will. The Horses have worked with right good-will, ... 174 *Waggoner* 1. 40
Gave with a maiden's true good-will . . . . 198 *Thorn* 106
And wide as ether her good-will ; . . . . . 222 *Triad* 146
Nay, we would simply praise the free good-will . 530 *Poor Robin* 24
Smiles of good-will from faces that he knew . 772 *Excursion* 2. 57
—Those transports, with staid looks of pure good-will, ... 860 *Excursion* 7. 224
And pure good-will, and hospitable cheer ; . . 878 *Excursion* 8. 242
Their healing offices a pure goodwill . . . K.8. 244 *Recluse* 1.1.284
Goody. Old Goody Blake was old and poor ; . . 536 *Goody Blake* 21
'Twas a hard time for Goody Blake. . . . . 536 *Goody Blake* 44
Than an old hedge to Goody Blake ? . . . . 537 *Goody Blake* 60
This trespass of old Goody Blake ; . . . . . 537 *Goody Blake* 66
He watched to seize old Goody Blake. . . . . 537 *Goody Blake* 72
He softly creeps—'tis Goody Blake ; . . . . 537 *Goody Blake* 79
Stick after stick did Goody pull : . . . . . 537 *Goody Blake* 82
And sprang upon poor Goody Blake. . . . . 537 *Goody Blake* 88
Then Goody, who had nothing said, ... 537 *Goody Blake* 93
Thus on her knees did Goody pray ; . . . . 537 *Goody Blake* 102
Of Goody Blake and Harry Gill ! . . . . . 537 *Goody Blake* 128
Gooseberry. The gooseberry trees that shot in long lank slips, ... 763 *Excursion* 1. 456
Gorbonian. Than wise Gorbonian ruled not in his day ; 103 *Artegal* 67
Gorbonian's. Gorbonian's first-born son, your rightful king restored !" . . . . 105 *Artegal* 225
Gordale-chasm. To Gordale-chasm, terrific as the lair 269 *Gordale* 5
Gordon. And Gordon, fairest of them all, . . . 287 *Ellen Irwin* 11
That Gordon loves as dearly. . . . . . . 287 *Ellen Irwin* 16
The Gordon, couched behind a thorn, ... 287 *Ellen Irwin* 22
Proud Gordon, maddened by the thoughts . . 287 *Ellen Irwin* 25
The Gordon, sailed away to Spain ; . . . . 287 *Ellen Irwin* 38
Gordon's. But what are Gordon's form and face, . 287 *Ellen Irwin* 17
Gore. The grove, and stained the turf with gore ; . 215 *Enterprise* 23
A weight of hostile corses : drenched with gore . 317 **The martial* 7
The rivers stained so oft with human gore, . . 582 *Invoc. Earth* 26
Gored. Of sacred home ;—with pomp are others gored . . . . 420 *Ecc. Sonn.* 1. 6. 8
When the tyrant's heart they gor'd . . . . S.3. 442 *Harmodius* 5
Ye the tyrant's bosom gor'd, ... S.3. 442 *Harmodius* 26
Gorge. They stem the current of that perilous gorge, 541 *Grace Darl.* 60
Gorgeous. Anon, appears a brave, a gorgeous show 6 *Ev. Wk.* 200
And all the gorgeous sights which fairies do behold. 108 *Indolence* 63
Fair trees and gorgeous flowers ; . . . . . 193 *Ruth* 135
In the gorgeous colours drest . . . . . . 217 **Inmate of* 22
The softest Nursling of a gorgeous palace . . . 221 *Triad* 68
Fair as a gorgeous Fabric of the east . . . . 226 *Vernal Ode* 16
Owns not a sylvan bower ; or gorgeous cell . . 254 *Wild Duck's Nest* 2
Once did She hold the gorgeous east in fee ; . . 304 *Ven. Rep.* 1
Hath failed ; and now, ye Powers ! whose gorgeous wings . . . . 335 *Cologne* 6
Though of gorgeous drapery proud, ... 502 **Like a* 28
And gorgeous insects copied with nice care . . 511 **Who rashly* 11
But frost had reared the gorgeous Pile . . . . 550 *Hermit's Cell* 2. 21
Anon, in order mounts a gorgeous show . . . 595 *Ev. Wk. Quarto* 183
—When the Sun bids the gorgeous scene farewell, 612 *Desc.Sk.Quarto* 562
Of thee, thy learning, gorgeous eloquence, . . 679 *Prelude* 6. 295
And gorgeous ladies, under splendid domes, . . 689 *Prelude* 7. 124
Whether for gorgeous tournament addressed, . . 689 *Prelude* 7. 140
And gorgeous as the colours side by side . . . 700 *Prelude* 8. 93
And afterwards, when through the gorgeous Alps 737 *Prelude* 12. 191
And gorgeous insect hovering in the air, . . . 772 *Excursion* 2. 44
Gorgeously. Upon a Charger gorgeously bedecked . 872 *Excursion* 7. 945
Gorsas. Devoured by locusts,—Carra, Gorsas,—add 712 *Prelude* 9. 176
Gorse. Among the fern or in the gorse ; . . . 128 *Idiot Boy* 220
Into bright verdure, between fern and gorse, . . 793 *Excursion* 3. 534
Goslar. Of Goslar, once imperial, I renewed . . 702 *Prelude* 8. 211
Goslings. The goslings green, the ass's colt, . . 81 †*Mother's Return* 43
Gospel. When this low Pile a Gospel Teacher knew, 380 *Duddon* 18. 10
In the blest soil of gospel truth, the Tree, . . . 431 *Ecc. Sonn.* 2. 10. 2
Gospel-light. Will holy Church disperse by beams of gospel-light." . . . . 141 *Arm. Lady* 120
Gospel's. That Church, the unperverted Gospel's seat ; 438 *Ecc. Sonn.* 2. 40. 6
Look only on the Gospel's brighter page : . . 447 *Ecc. Sonn.* 3. 29. 11
Gospel-truth. But Gospel-truth is potent to allay . 426 *Ecc. Sonn.* 1. 29. 5
Of gospel-truth enchained in harmonies . . . 466 *St. Bees* 52
Gossamer. Whose framework is of gossamer, . . 164 *Needlecase* 27
O'er twilight fields the autumnal gossamer ? . . 378 *Duddon* 11. 14
Upon a gossamer thread ; he sifts, he weighs ; . 670 *Prelude* 5. 322

Grace—*continued.*
Rest, shielded by our Lady's grace, 542 *Russ. Fug.* 85
That monumental grace 543 *Russ. Fug.* 172
The ivied Ruins of forlorn Grace Dieu ; 547 **Beneath yon* 4
To closer fellowship with ideal grace. 547 **Rude is* 4
They all said—Nay ; but Jesu of His grace 555 *Prioress* 152
My Lady first me took unto her grace. 563 *Troilus* 63
Thy grace above all pleasures first and chief ; 563 *Troilus* 74
And pray that in his faithful breast the grace 576 **By a* 21
He would have loved thy modest grace, 580 *John Words.* 51
Rapt in the grace of undismantled age, 583 **With copious* 28
Acknowledges God's grace, his mercy feels, 586 *Ch. Lamb* 119
Obsequious Grace the winding swan pursue. 595 *Ev. Wk. Quarto* 200
Marshal the banquet, giving with due grace 624 *Æneid* 69
On earth to goodness blest by grace divine. 628 **Deign, Sovereign* 8
Who deigns to grace our festal rite, 629 *Installation* 115
Put on a lowly and a touching grace 653 *Prelude* 3. 272
And spot in which she lived, and through a grace 670 *Prelude* 5. 290
With decoration of ideal grace ; 672 *Prelude* 5. 457
Decked as in pride, and with outlandish grace : 676 *Prelude* 6. 79
Mine, through heaven's grace and inborn aptitudes. 677 *Prelude* 6. 170
And carriage, marked by unexampled grace. 691 *Prelude* 7. 308
And beauty, and inevitable grace. 700 *Prelude* 8. 110
Of grace and honour, power and worthiness. 703 *Prelude* 8. 281
Occasional, an accidental grace, 704 *Prelude* 8. 355
Who from the Fountain of Thy grace dost fill 724 *Prelude* 10. 422
Salutes the being at his birth, where grace 742 *Prelude* 13. 196
My soul, too reckless of mild grace, had stood 749 *Prelude* 14. 248
Far more : for Nature's secondary grace 750 *Prelude* 14. 315
(Should Providence such grace to us vouchsafe) 752 *Prelude* 14. 442
Shaped his belief, as grace divine inspired, 762 *Excursion* 1. 412
And from debasement rescued.—By thy grace 802 *Excursion* 4. 50
Grace, be their composition what it may, 808 *Excursion* 4. 492
To hearts that own not him ? Will showers of grace, 817 *Excursion* 4. 1096
Old things repeated with diminished grace ; 829 *Excursion* 5. 436
Shares with her species, nature's grace sometimes 835 *Excursion* 5. 846
Or, through illuminating grace, received, 839 *Excursion* 6. 72
Within the soul, fountains of grace divine ; 841 *Excursion* 6. 181
With its appropriate grace, yet rather seeking 848 *Excursion* 6. 689
Like Indian mats, that with appropriate grace 860 *Excursion* 7. 184
Upon its Master's frame, a wintry grace ; 860 *Excursion* 7. 207
—Nor was his funeral denied the grace 864 *Excursion* 7. 469
Holy and blest ? and where the winning grace 878 *Excursion* 8. 249
Yet with the grace of one who in the world 882 *Excursion* 8. 530
Do, by the almighty Ruler's grace, partake 885 *Excursion* 9. 110
Almighty Lord, thy further grace impart ! 894 *Excursion* 9. 675
From the live rock with grace inimitable S.3. 434 **The doubt* 68
And grace of feminine humanity, S.3. 437 **The doubt* 189
So stinted in the measure of their grace K.8. 238 *Recluse* 1. 1. 67
The boon is absolute ; surpassing grace K.8. 239 *Recluse* 1. 1. 103
Magnificent. Behold, how with a grace K.8. 242 *Recluse* 1. 1. 203
With motions of true dignity and grace ? K.8. 248 *Recluse* 1. 1. 411
On much repentance Grace will be bestow'd. K.8. 266 **Rid of* 5
Benign, meek, . . ., offers grace K.8. 266 **Rid of* 7
Or looks at Norfolk and can dream of grace ? L.1. 88 *Juvenal* 1. 10
Are called to try their prowess with his Grace. L.1. 96 *Juvenal* 3. 28
His Grace and his protection win the prize. L.1. 96 *Juvenal* 3. 34
Shall stick new splendour on his gartered Grace. L.1. 97 *Juvenal* 3. 78
And see the blue beyond.—Type of that grace [?] **A sad* 9

Graced. *See* **Ill-graced.**
Beautiful in yourselves, and richly graced 152 **Forth from* 22
More than in humbler times graced human story ; 281 **What strong* 10
Within my reach ; of knowledge graced 285 *Grave of Burns* 56
As nobly graced by Sculpture's patient toil ; 324 *Ode 1814* 102
By Poesy irradiate, and yet graced, 357 *Aquap.* 284
Ere yet our course was graced with social trees 377 *Duddon* 6. 1
Whether she graced a royal chair, 390 *Highland Broach* 26
So graced the sunshine of that day. 404 *White Doe* 736
Graced the Refectory : and there, while both 509 *F. Stone* 106
Clothed with impassive majesty, and graced 510 **Among a* 8
Antique, and Cottage with verandah graced, 547 **Rude is* 11
Graced with redundant hair, Iopas sings 625 *Æneid* 121
Yet richly graced with honours of her own, 691 *Prelude* 7. 266
And one, moreover, little graced with power 720 *Prelude* 10. 149
Graced mutually by difference of sex, 794 *Excursion* 3. 591
On sturdy horses graced with jingling bells, 858 *Excursion* 7. 65
And graced with shining weapons, weekly marched, 869 *Excursion* 7. 767
Are graced with some resemblance. Errant those, 875 *Excursion* 8. 45
Guarded and graced, seemed fashioned to unite, 881 *Excursion* 8. 456
For high—yet not for low ; for proudly graced— 887 *Excursion* 9. 244

Graceful. *See* **Ever-graceful.**
Where, mixed with graceful birch, the sombrous pine 5 *Ev. Wk.* 156
How graceful, pride can be, and how majestic, ease. 6 *Ev. Wk.* 221
Leaps with a bound of graceful hardihood ; 17 *Desc. Sk.* 381
And graceful in his rustic dress ! 86 *Anecdote* 26
Descending with a graceful flow, 190 *Beggars* 5
Smooth, graceful, tender, or sublime— 300 *Bran* 33
The graceful form of milk-white Steed, 341 *Ital. Itin.* 9
With freaks of graceful folly,— 385 *Yarrow Rev.* 26
Less scanty measure of those graceful rites 448 *Ecc. Sonn.* 3. 33. 2
His graceful manners, and the temperate ray 583 **With copious* 9
Graceful support ; his countenance as he stood 757 *Excursion* 1. 43
Gay, and affecting graceful gaiety ; 774 *Excursion* 2. 182
As skill and graceful nature might suggest 793 *Excursion* 3. 465
Withal so graceful in his gentleness, 834 *Excursion* 5. 791
Was graceful, when it pleased him, smooth and still 842 *Excursion* 6. 292
Cordially greeted. Graceful was her port : 881 *Excursion* 8. 501
Unite the graceful qualities of both, 883 *Excursion* 8. 586
Abruptly here, but with a graceful air, 890 *Excursion* 9. 416

Gracefully. Gracefully up the gnarled trunk ; nor left we unsurveyed 92 *Poet's Dream* 39
With gleaming lights more gracefully adorn 471 *Ailsa Crag* 3
So gracefully ; even then when it appeared 677 *Prelude* 6. 163
How gracefully that slender shrub looks forth 787 *Excursion* 3. 86
In some abstraction ;—gracefully he stood, 825 *Excursion* 5. 214
Less gracefully were braided ;—but this praise, 851 *Excursion* 6. 842
Supporting gracefully a massy dome 891 *Excursion* 9. 500

Grace's. His Grace's waterman in open race L.1. 96 *Juvenal* 3. 27

Graces. From which her graces and her honours sprung : 122 *V. and J.* 16
Come, like the Graces, hand in hand ! 220 *Triad* 16
Nor interrupts her frolic graces 222 *Triad* 151
Shot from the dancing Graces, as they move 233 *Power of Sound* 79
Of human life : a Stripling's graces blow, 267 **Desponding Father* 9
And sober graces, left her for defence 333 **Bruges I* 7
As humanising graces, are but parts 420 *Ecc. Sonn.* 1. 8. 13
Dear to the Loves, and to the Graces vowed, 465 **Dear to* 1
The motions that it graces—and forbear 511 **Who rashly* 8
And wilder graces sport around their brow ; 615 *Desc.Sk.Quarto* 735
But none of those fair Graces brought 620 *Birth of Love* 18
These lighter graces ; and the rural ways 701 *Prelude* 8. 159
His graces unrevealed and unproclaimed. 757 *Excursion* 1. 94
Approach their reverend graces, unopposed ; 838 *Excursion* 6. 31
With spiritual graces, like a glory, crowned." 862 *Excursion* 7. 339
By all the graces with which nature's hand 868 *Excursion* 7. 727

Gracing. Gracing his doctrine with authority 820 *Excursion* 4. 1288

Gracious. Heavens ! my good Friend ! Forgive me, gracious Sir !— 54 *Bord.* 943
That, in the gracious opening of thy reign, 105 *Artegal* 192
Oh, gracious Heaven, in pity make her thine ! 139 *Widow* 28
" Gracious Allah ! by such title 140 *Arm. Lady* 67
Of goodness, for most gracious ends— 245 *P. B.* 769
Be gracious as the music and the bloom 264 **Lady ! the* 13
Gracious to service hallowed by its aim ;— 332 *Ode : Thanks.* 226
Now, surely, hath that gracious aid 338 *Brientz* 9
From the same gracious will, were both an offspring 354 *Aquap.* 143
By unsought means for gracious purposes ; 362 **List—'twas* 46
A gracious welcome shall be thine, 386 *Yarrow Rev.* 73
And irremoveable) gracious openings lie, 396 **Action is* 8
It is, thinks he, the gracious Fairy, 399 *White Doe* 267
A just and gracious Queen have we, 400 *White Doe* 386
Beamed from that gracious countenance ; 416 *White Doe* 1828
A gracious smile, that seems to say— 417 *White Doe* 1908
Offenders, dost put off the gracious look, 454 **The Sun, that* 14
His gracious help, or give what we abuse. 455 **Not in the lucid* 31
Gracious God, the pure oblation 550 *Hermit's Cell* 4. 15
I bent before Thy gracious throne, 550 *Hermit's Cell* 5. 17
But by the mouths of children, gracious God ! 552 *Prioress* 5
But nature is gracious, necessity kind, 570 *Farmer* 51
To wait upon the bright and gracious Muses, 573 *Chiabrera* 2. 7
A gracious look all over her domain. 658 *Prelude* 4. 23
How gracious, how benign, is Solitude ; 663 *Prelude* 4. 357
A gracious spirit o'er this earth presides, 673 *Prelude* 5. 491
And gracious, almost might I dare to say, 685 *Prelude* 6. 681
Made *him* more gracious, and his nature then 714 *Prelude* 9. 295
Forced by the gracious providence of Heaven,— 721 *Prelude* 10. 224
Whose gracious favour is the primal source 755 *Recluse* 1. 1. 854
With gracious smile, deliberately pleased, 758 *Excursion* 1. 106
Advanced to greet him. With a gracious mien 829 *Excursion* 5. 444
To fly—but whither ! And this gracious Church, 855 *Excursion* 6. 1105
A woman of soft speech and gracious smile, 858 *Excursion* 7. 78
But Heaven was gracious ; yet a little while, 861 *Excursion* 7. 278
To stop, and yield our gracious Teacher thanks 873 *Excursion* 7. 1052
Gracious to all the dear dependencies S.3. 426 **Through Cumbrian* 7

Graciously. And there so graciously did me behold, 563 *Troilus* 55
So graciously ?—that could descend, 582 **O for a* 26
And graciously composed, but that, no less, 744 *Prelude* 13. 282

Graciousness. Until that natural graciousness of mind 735 *Prelude* 12. 50

Gradation. Needles for strings in apt gradation ! 163 *Needlecase* 6
By a more just gradation did lead on 656 *Prelude* 3. 527
Raising, through just gradation, savage life 875 *Excursion* 8. 70

Gradations. My thoughts by slow gradations had been drawn 709 *Prelude* 8. 677

Gradual. Into a gradual calm the breezes sink, 4 *Ev. Wk.* 114
Such a gradual declination 90 *Longest Day* 35
With gradual stealth the lateral windows hide 451 *Ecc. Sonn.* 3. 44. 2
Wanderer by spring with gradual progress led, 455 *Rydal Mere* 27
And gradual progress ?—Twilight leads to day, 516 **Hard task* 9
Lost gradual o'er the heights in pomp they go, 595 *Ev. Wk. Quarto* 187
To disappear by a slow gradual death, 635 *Prelude* 1. 194
By nature's gradual processes be taught ; 805 *Excursion* 4. 288

Gradually. To what he saw, he gradually returned, 118 *Maternal Grief* 56
But, gradually a calmer look bestowing, 337 *Aar* 4
To thy own conscience gradually renewed ; 515 **Ah why* 11
Were tempered ; thus was gradually produced 643 *Prelude* 2. 71
And gradually expired, and Nature, prized 704 *Prelude* 8. 346
Proved tedious, and I gradually withdrew 711 *Prelude* 9. 121
Of our Companion, gradually diffused ; 814 *Excursion* 4. 890
By slow degrees, were gradually regained ; 841 *Excursion* 6. 193
Of these opponents gradually was wrought, 845 *Excursion* 6. 469
Began in honour, gradually obtained 849 *Excursion* 6. 707
And gradually enriched with things of price, 860 *Excursion* 7. 172
And its devotion gradually decline, 873 *Excursion* 7. 1018

Grafted. He left this moral grafted on his Fate ; 214 *Dion* 121
That grafted, on so fair a spot, 224 **'Tis gone* 20
Was fondly grafted with a virtuous aim, 515 *Penn.* 11
Whose uncouth form was grafted on the wall, 871 *Excursion* 7. 914

Grasped—*continued.*
Which he had grasped unknowingly, 401 *White Doe* 436
Had blindly grasped in that strong trance, 401 *White Doe* 437
Which he had grasped in that strong trance ; 401 *White Doe* 517
And near the golden sceptre grasped by Jove, 457 **The leaves* 29
At this he grasped my hand, and said, 488 *Fountain* 63
Of hopeful preparation, grasped his staff ; 771 *Excursion* 1. 966
To such desires, and grasped at such delight, 809 *Excursion* 4. 543
Herewith he grasped the Solitary's hand, 816 *Excursion* 4. 1016

Grasping. A slender volume grasping in thy hand— 215 *Enterprise* 4
Grasping a hawthorn branch in hand, 243 *P. B.* 636
Of freedom, with mind grasping the whole theme 359 **They—who* 10
To the stern embrace of that grasping hour. 411 *White Doe* 1431
Grasping his twofold treasure.—Lance in rest, 667 *Prelude* 5. 120
When they are grasping with their greatest strength, 744 *Prelude* 13. 274

Grasps. And grasps by fits her sword, and often eyes ; 15 *Desc. Sk.* 264
Each grasps an oar, and struggling on they go— 541 *Grace Darl.* 51
And often grasps her sword, and often eyes, 608 *Desc.Sk.Quarto* 327
That finds and cannot fasten down ; that grasps 827 *Excursion* 5. 323
And is rejoiced, and loses while it grasps ; 827 *Excursion* 5. 324

Grass. *See* **Spear-grass.**
The kine are couched upon the dewy grass ; 1 *Early Youth* 2
Or playing wanton with the floating grass, 6 *Ev. Wk.* 227
Long grass and willows form the woven wall, 6 *Ev. Wk.* 240
And downward thence a knot of grass he throws, 17 *Desc. Sk.* 384
Or whistling thro' thin grass along the unfurrowed plain. 25 *Guilt* 36
My hen's rich nest through long grass scarce espied ; 28 *Guilt* 213
Was soft and warm, no dew lay on the grass, 39 *Bord.* 116
No food was there, no drink, no grass, no shade, 68 *Bord.* 1707
And, when the grass was dry, 84 *We are Seven* 54
Beneath a rock, upon the grass, 84 *Shepherd-boys* 12
With one knee on the grass did the little Maiden kneel, 87 *Pet-lamb* 7
Thy plot of grass is soft, and green as grass can be ; 87 *Pet-lamb* 23
This grass is tender grass ; these flowers they have no peers ; 87 *Pet-lamb* 27
Look at the common grass from hour to hour : 107 *Indolence* 23
Long blades of grass, plucked round him as he lay, 108 *Indolence* 56
I dread the rustling of the grass ; 117 *Affl. Marg.* 65
Here's grass to play with, here are flowers ; 121 *EmigrantMother* 89
The grass you almost hear it growing, 129 *Idiot Boy* 285
A frog leaps out from bordering grass, 142 †*Lov. and Lik.* 17
When grass is chill with rain or dew, 156 *Oak and Broom* 85
Green is the grass for beast to graze, 176 *Waggoner* 1. 270
Limping o'er the dewy grass, 181 *Waggoner* 4. 159
While I am lying on the grass 183 **O blithe* 5
The grass is bright with rain-drops ;—on the moors 195 *Resolution* 10
The grass—it shook upon the ground ! 200 *Thorn* 228
" Here on the grass perhaps asleep he sank, 203 *Hart-leap* 149
" Now, here is neither grass nor pleasant shade ; 203 *Hart-leap* 157
Light as the wind along the grass. 204 *Brougham* 75
Where'er the tender grass was leading 239 *P. B.* 254
Does no one live near this green grass ? 240 *P. B.* 380
Is Peter driving through the grass— 240 *P. B.* 382
Leaving the body on the grass. 243 *P. B.* 600
A bramble-leaf or blade of grass. 244 *P. B.* 715
Well pleased, her foot should print earth's common grass, 278 **Lo ! where she* 12
For one hour's perfect bliss, to tread the grass 306 **Here, on our* 12
Knit the blithe dance upon the soft green grass ; 322 **Ye Storms* 9
From dew-sprinkled grass to heights guarded with snow, 345 *Stanzas : Simplon* 18
That Life is but a tale of morning grass 388 *Trosachs* 4
Couched upon the dewy grass, 397 *White Doe* 154
And earth's green grass beneath his feet ; 401 *White Doe* 430
Dim-gleaming among weeds and grass, 417 *White Doe* 1896
Man is as grass that springeth up at morn, 448 *Ecc. Sonn.* 3. 31. 9
And grass in the green field. 482 *Sister* 8
As if green summer grass were the floor of my room, 484 **A plague* 29
And on that morning, through the grass, 486 **We walked* 9
Is in the grass beneath, that grows 499 **This Lawn* 16
Through dewy grass, nor small birds hushed in bowers, 501 **The unremitting* 4
Of firm dry ground, with healthful grass 543 *Russ. Fug.* 103
Strung on slender blades of grass ; 549 *Hermit's Cell* 1. 2
May one blade of grass spring up over thy head ; 571 *Farmer* 90
Of splendour in the grass, of glory in the flower ; 590 *Immortality* 182
Thence down the steep a pile of grass he throws 610 *Desc.Sk.Quarto* 472
With silver clouds, and sunshine on the grass, 633 *Prelude* 1. 68
Above the raven's nest, by knots of grass 637 *Prelude* 1. 331
Ground where the grass had yielded to the steps 652 *Prelude* 3. 259
And lay till now neglected in the grass. 665 *Prelude* 4. 430
From touch of growing grass, that may not taste 669 *Prelude* 5. 243
Catching from tufts of grass and harebell flowers 678 *Prelude* 6. 221
To bend as doth a slender blade of grass 705 *Prelude* 8. 398
The grass is cleared away, and to this hour 738 *Prelude* 12. 244
Tempestuous, dark, and wild, and on the grass 738 *Prelude* 12. 298
Couched in the dewy grass. With such a theme, 750 *Prelude* 14. 275
Among the dewy grass,—in early spring, 764 *Excursion* 1. 526
Was yellow ; and the soft and bladed grass, 767 *Excursion* 1. 708
The hardened soil, and knots of withered grass : 769 *Excursion* 1. 835
Now faint,—the grass has crept o'er its grey line ; 769 *Excursion* 1. 883
On the soft grass through half a summer's day, 814 *Excursion* 4. 852
The dewy grass ; you cannot leave us now, 823 *Excursion* 5. 71
Herbage that never fails : no grass springs up 835 *Excursion* 5. 876
That sparkling decked the morning grass ; or aught 843 *Excursion* 6. 317
For noontide solace on the summer grass, 861 *Excursion* 7. 286
Stretched on the grass, or seated in the shade, 869 *Excursion* 7. 783
He spied the sheep upon a plot of grass, K.8. 229 **I will* 139
But now, when everywhere the summer grass K.8. 229 **I will* 143

Grass—*continued.*
Of grass or corn, over and through and through, K.8. 237 *Recluse* 1. 1.29

Grass-crowned. Gleams on the grass-crowned top of yon tall Tower, 283 **Here, where* 11
The grass-crowned headland that conceals the shore ? 453 **The Sun, that* 10

Grass-green. Now stretched beneath his grass-green mound 577 **I come* 20

Grass-grown. His grave grass-grown. 285 *Grave of Burns* 60
The grass-grown pavement tread. 334 **In Bruges* 4
Or grass-grown spaces, where the heaviest foot 355 *Aquap.* 194

Grasshoppers. With golden grasshoppers, in sign that they 790 *Excursion* 3. 250

Grassless. Upon whose grassless floor of red-brown hue, 185 *Yew-trees* 21

Grass-plot. A spacious grass-plot ; there, in silence, sate 696 *Prelude* 7. 607

Grassy. Found by the grassy door of mountain-farms. 5 *Ev. Wk.* 145
And lifted from the grassy floor, stilling his faint alarms, 92 *Poet's Dream* 18
And, scouring toward him o'er the grassy plain, 104 *Artegal* 110
Upon bough or grassy blade) 171 *Kitten* 48
Had left imprinted on the grassy ground. 201 *Hart-leap* 52
To ruminate, couched on the grassy lea ; 349 *Val. Dover* 7
I choose to saunter o'er the grassy plain, 383 *Duddon* 30. 12
O'er Fingal's hearth ; the grassy sod 390 *Highland Broach* 33
Beside the ridge of a grassy grave 397 *White Doe* 141
Alone, beside that grassy heap ! 399 *White Doe* 311
He stands upon the grassy sod, 404 *White Doe* 730
The grassy rock-encircled Pound 416 *White Doe* 1803
Hath slept since noon-tide on the grassy ground, 458 **Had this* 56
Beneath the trees, or on a grassy bank 569 *Cumb. Beg.* 193
The grassy seat beneath their casement shade 607 *Desc.Sk.Quarto* 305
O Derwent ! winding among grassy holms 636 *Prelude* 1. 275
Where he was born ; the grassy churchyard hangs 671 *Prelude* 5. 392
Or grassy bottom, all, with little hills— 807 *Excursion* 4. 435
" These grassy heaps lie amicably close," 857 *Excursion* 7. 31
Or range the grassy lawn in vacancy ; 888 *Excursion* 9. 262
A twofold image ; on a grassy bank 890 *Excursion* 9. 440
While from the grassy mountain's open side 893 *Excursion* 9. 609
Upon their grassy beds lay couch'd in sleep, S.3. 427 **ThroughCumbrian* 13

Grate. 'Twas through an iron grate. 334 **In Bruges* 24
I pause ; and at length, through the glimmering grate, 620 *Convict* 11

Grated. Canst reach the Prisoner—to his grated cell 459 **Wanderer ! that* 29

Grateful. And from her grateful heart a fresh one drew : 30 *Guilt* 322
And grateful Britain prospered far above 103 *Artegal* 68
And so, when night with grateful gloom had fallen, 143 **High bliss* 17
Hath this conception, grateful to behold, 173 *InfantDaughter* 61
My Soul was grateful for delight 215 *Kirkstone* 61
By soft reflection—grateful to the sky, 219 *Haunted Tree* 4
The voice of grateful memory 224 *'*Tis gone* 65
Shall Fancy pay to thee a grateful vow ? 253 **Aerial Rock* 5
A grateful few, shall love thy modest Lay, 254 *Dyer* 11
Of grateful memory, bid that joy depart. 261 **Fair Prime* 14
We rather think, with grateful mind sedate, 271 *Henry : Portrait* 11
Our sires set forth their grateful praise : 301 *Bran* 75
" Thus strives a grateful Country to display 324 *Ode 1814* 67
Be just, be grateful ; nor, the oppressor's creed 327 **Emperors and* 12
A grateful coolness round that crystal Spring, 376 *Duddon* 1. 2
At parent Nature's grateful call, 386 *Yarrow Rev.* 71
Where she had found a grateful seat 407 *White Doe* 1058
Mild, and grateful, melancholy : 415 *White Doe* 1758
All hail, sage Lady, whom a grateful Isle 438 *Ecc. Sonn.* 2. 38. 3
Shall disappear, and grateful earth receive 450 *Ecc. Sonn.* 3. 39. 3
Of grateful England's overflowing Dead. 452 *Ecc. Sonn.* 3. 45. 14
Day's grateful warmth, tho' moist with falling dews. 453 **Calm is the* 2
With grateful thoughts, doth now thy rising hail 460 **Queen of* 8
Yet is yon neat trim church a grateful speck 474 **How sad* 6
Of water-breaks, with grateful heart could tell. 502 **Theunremitting* 17
Are grateful and rejoice ! 507 *May* 8
The cause of grateful reason to sustain ; 520 *Pun. Death* 14. 5
Grateful to Thee, while service pure, 534 **Blest is* 97
As in a cloister. Yet the grateful Poor 539 **Lady ! a* 48
He conned the new-born Lay with grateful heart— 582 **To public* 7
To none more grateful than to me ; escaped 632 *Prelude* 1. 6
And every boyish sport, less grateful else 642 *Prelude* 2. 53
So dear, if I should fail with grateful voice 648 *Prelude* 2. 423
Grateful for that admonishment, I hushed 660 *Prelude* 4. 125
And sports and games (too grateful in themselves, 662 *Prelude* 4. 283
Yet in themselves less grateful, I believe, 662 *Prelude* 4. 284
And grateful memory, as a thing divine. 707 *Prelude* 8. 559
—Such grateful haunts foregoing, if I oft 755 *Recluse* 1. 1. 825
Under a shade as grateful I should find 756 *Excursion* 1. 19
To every grateful sound of earth and air ; 773 *Excursion* 2. 107
Such grateful promises his youth displayed : 774 *Excursion* 2. 170
I lived and breathed ; most grateful—if to enjoy 795 *Excursion* 3. 628
Most grateful, if in such wise to enjoy 795 *Excursion* 3. 634
Of native feeling, grateful to our minds ; 801 *Excursion* 4. 5
To meditative spleen a grateful feast. 808 *Excursion* 4. 477
A grateful recollection must supply 813 *Excursion* 4. 782
Up towards the crescent moon, with grateful heart 814 *Excursion* 4. 862
Roaming, or resting under grateful shade 819 *Excursion* 4. 1202
A grateful couch was spread for our repose ; 821 *Excursion* 4. 1319
A grateful coolness fell, that seemed to strike 824 *Excursion* 5. 141
Grateful to sight, refreshing to the soul, 830 *Excursion* 5. 528
Would be most grateful. True indeed it is 832 *Excursion* 5. 661
Whose grateful owner can attest these truths, 855 *Excursion* 6. 1140

Grateful—*continued.*
For grateful converse: and to these poor men . 875 *Excursion* 8. 58
Is here—how grateful this impervious screen! . 881 *Excursion* 8. 447
As beautiful—as grateful to the mind. . . . 883 *Excursion* 8. 583
A grateful tribute to all-ruling Heaven. . . . 890 *Excursion* 9. 391
Their place I took—and for a grateful office . . 891 *Excursion* 9. 483
Of grateful recollections, tribute due . . . . S.3. 437 **The doubt* 204
Grateful is Sleep; my life in stone bound fast . S.3. 441 **Grateful is sleep; my* 1
More grateful still: while wrong and shame shall last, ... S.3. 441 **Grateful is sleep; my* 2
Grateful is Sleep, more grateful still to be . . S.3. 441 **Grateful is sleep, more* 1
More grateful, more harmonious than the breath, K.8. 247 *Recluse* 1. 1. 407

Grating. From ringing team apart and grating wain— . . . . 12 *Desc. Sk.* 82
Mixed with a faint yet grating sound . . . . 173 *Waggoner* 1. 27
Nor harsh nor grating, though of ample power . 207 *Tintern* 92
To ringing team unknown and grating wain, . . 603 *Desc.Sk.Quarto* 85

Gratis. Stand back, and you shall see her gratis! . 177 *Waggoner* 2. 114

Gratitude. And gratitude to ministers of vice, . . 57 *Bord.* 1062
Had strength to teach;—and therefore gratitude 64 *Bord.* 1482
Of his own rights restored, his gratitude . . . 66 *Bord.* 1595
his gratitude may reward us. . . . . 72 *Bord.* 1995
Shrine, Altar, Image, Offerings hung in sign of gratitude; . . . . 92 *Poet's Dream* 47
Nor was it common gratitude . . . . . . 155 *Waterfall* 29
Of gratitude, beneath Italian skies, ... 326 *Sobieski* 3
Thou that canst shed the bliss of gratitude . . 329 *Ode: Thanks.* 2
What robe can Gratitude employ . . . . . 331 *Ode: Thanks.* 133
With lip and heart to tell their gratitude . . . 331 *Ode: Thanks.* 199
Her modest gratitude. . . . . 348 **Lulled by* 60
When gratitude, though disciplined to look . . 354 *Aquap.* 108
Triumphs in sun-bright gratitude displayed, . . 367 *Trajan* 17
Their holy rites with vocal gratitude: . . . . 420 *Ecc. Sonn.* 1. 7. 7
To gratitude, to injuries forgiven— . . . . 436 *Ecc. Sonn.* 2. 32. 11
Nay, rather speak with gratitude; . . . . . 458 **Had this* 66
Whose heart with gratitude to thee inclines, . . 477 **Lonsdale! it* 2
Alas! the gratitude of men . . . . 484 *Simon Lee* 95
His look of pitiable gratitude! . . . . . . 501 *Humanity* 68
A song of gratitude and praise. . . . . . . 506 *Lab. Hymn* 8
The heart with joy and gratitude to God . . . 517 *Pun. Death* 1. 6
Exalt the sense of thoughtful gratitude . . . 538 **In desultory* 53
Fitly attuned to all that gratitude . . . . . 541 *Grace Darl.* 89
Soon gratitude gave way to love . . . . . 545 *Russ. Fug.* 361
And in its depth of gratitude is still. . . . . 586 *Ch. Lamb* 120
Do thou, if gratitude inspire thy breast, . . . 619 *School Ex.* 107
Shall gratitude find rest? Mine eyes did ne'er 622 *Recluse* 1. 1. 85
And gratitude grew dizzy in a brain . . . . 653 *Prelude* 3. 300
The thoughts of gratitude shall fall like dew . . 658 *Prelude* 4. 30
And gratitude, and perfect joy of heart— . . . 660 *Prelude* 4. 135
In gratitude, and for the sake of truth, . . . 669 *Prelude* 5. 265
With spiteful gratitude the baffled League, . . 718 *Prelude* 10. 36
Hath neither gratitude, nor faith, nor love, . . 721 *Prelude* 10. 201
Great was my transport, deep my gratitude . . 726 *Prelude* 10. 576
Of blissful gratitude and fearless love? . . . 735 *Prelude* 12. 56
Are piety, her life is gratitude. . . . . . 736 *Prelude* 12. 173
By gratitude, and confidence in truth. . . . . 740 *Prelude* 13. 15
In gratitude to God, Who feeds our hearts . . 744 *Prelude* 13. 276
Of high respect and gratitude sincere. . . . 753 **Oft, through* 8
Lowly; for he was meek in gratitude, ... 759 *Excursion* 1. 236
With gratitude, and reverential thoughts. . . . 762 *Excursion* 1. 402
Be proof of gratitude for what we have; . . . 795 *Excursion* 3. 635
While, overcome with speechless gratitude, . . 795 *Excursion* 3. 666
With hope, and love, and gratitude, and fear; . 811 *Excursion* 4. 660
With joy, and gratitude, and fear, and love; . . 815 *Excursion* 4. 930
To drink with gratitude the crystal stream . . 817 *Excursion* 4. 1044
Acknowledgments of gratitude sincere . . . . 823 *Excursion* 5. 49
Quaffed in his gratitude immoderate cups; . . 842 *Excursion* 6. 242
Of amity and gratitude." "Thus sanctioned," . . 848 *Excursion* 6. 645
Heart-sorrow rendered sweet by gratitude. . . . 864 *Excursion* 7. 471
Whom he, in gratitude, let loose to range . . . 872 *Excursion* 7. 948
But why no softening thought of gratitude, . . 873 *Excursion* 7. 1028
The fields of earth with gratitude and hope; . . 888 *Excursion* 9. 249
Of gratitude to Providence, will grant . . . . 889 *Excursion* 9. 330
The common course of human gratitude!" . . . 892 *Excursion* 9. 558
Joy giving voice to fervent gratitude. . . . . 895 *Excursion* 9. 742

Gratitude's. Dear Master! gratitude's a heavy burden . . . . 38 *Bord.* 30

Gratuitous. Are a gratuitous emblazonry . . . . 654 *Prelude* 3. 399

Gratulant. All gratulant, if rightly understood. . . 751 *Prelude* 14. 387

Gratulate. Springs from the ground the morn to gratulate; . . . . 432 *Ecc. Sonn.* 2. 14. 2

Gratulatest. Thou gratulatest, willingly deceived— 734 *Prelude* 11. 468

Gratulating. But hark! a gratulating voice, . . . 297 *Highland Boy* 216
Their nests, or chant a gratulating hymn . . . 420 *Ecc. Sonn.* 1. 7. 3

Gratulation. For praise and ceaseless gratulation, poured . . . . 235 *Power of Sound* 207
In thankful joy and gratulation pure. . . . . 317 **Call not* 14
With gratulation thoroughly benign! . . . . . 324 *Ode 1814* 110
A gratulation from that vagrant Voice . . . . 362 **List—'twas* 27

Grave. Bows his young head with sorrow to the grave. . . . . 20 *Desc. Sk.* 527
If the sad grave of human ignorance bear . . . 20 *Desc. Sk.* 551
Thrice happy! that for him the grave could hide 29 *Guilt* 268
I ne'er had heart to separate—my grave, . . . 40 *Bord.* 143
Blind as the grave, but, as you oft have told me, . 40 *Bord.* 180
She paces round and round an Infant's grave, . 44 *Bord.* 393
He has been two years in his grave. Enough. . 46 *Bord.* 514
Of sending to his grave our precious Charge: . . 50 *Bord.* 737
And none look grave but dotards. He may live . 54 *Bord.* 929

Grave—*continued.*
'Twas dark—dark as the grave; yet did I see, . 55 *Bord.* 984
And send it with a fillip to its grave. . . . . 60 *Bord.* 1244
I shall be in my grave. . . . . 72 *Bord.* 1974
Together round her grave we played, ... 84 *We are Seven* 55
Yet by some grave thoughts attended . . . . 90 *Longest Day* 9
The wings they did not flag; the Child, though grave, was not deprest. . . . . . 92 *Poet's Dream* 32
Another grave was added.—He had found . . 96 *Brothers* 84
Another grave,—near which a full half-hour . . 96 *Brothers* 85
That it was not another grave; but one . . . 96 *Brothers* 90
But that the Stranger, who had left the grave, . 97 *Brothers* 116
An orphan could not find his mother's grave: . 98 *Brothers* 169
Now there's a grave—your foot is half upon it,— 98 *Brothers* 194
And went into his grave before his time. . . . 98 *Brothers* 216
Ay—you may turn that way—it is a grave . . 99 *Brothers* 238
And that then *is* his grave!— Before his death 101 *Brothers* 383
And, looking at the grave, he said, "My Brother!" 102 *Brothers* 411
But she is in her grave, and, oh, ... 109 **She dwelt* 11
And here and there a church-yard grave is found . 110 **'Tis said that some* 2
Three years had Barbara in her grave been laid . 110 **'Tis said that some* 11
Or, if the grave be now thy bed, ... 116 *Affl. Marg.* 4
In walks whose boundary is the lost One's grave, 119 *Maternal Grief* 68
With one foot in the grave. This only Son, . . 132 *Michael* 90
That I could not lie quiet in my grave. . . . 134 *Michael* 232
And bear thy memory with me to the grave." . 137 *Michael* 417
He with grave looks demanded for what cause, . 147 *Joanna* 26
Lashed out of life, not quiet in the grave. . . 153 *Morn. Ex.* 18
Let one grave hold the Loved and Lover! . . 157 *Sexton* 32
The mountains against heaven's grave weight . 173 *Waggoner* 1. 13
Of him who gazes, or has gazed? a grave and steady joy, ... 189 *Star-gazers* 26
Such as grave Livers do in Scotland use, . . . 196 *Resolution* 97
Is like an infant's grave in size, ... 198 *Thorn* 52
An infant's grave was half so fair. . . . . . 198 *Thorn* 55
So like an infant's grave in size, ... 198 *Thorn* 61
The hillock like an infant's grave, ... 198 *Thorn* 93
Echoes from beyond the grave, ... 209 **Yes, it* 15
Thou shouldst elude the malice of the grave: . 210 *Laod.* 58
Shall lead thee to thy grave. . . . . . . 218 *Young Lady* 18
The grave shall open, quench the stars. . . . 235 *Power of Sound* 216
Well may you tremble and look grave! . . . 243 *P. B.* 627
A lovely Beauty in a summer grave! . . . . 258 **Methought I* 14
Her thoughts less deep, or void of grave intent 270 **Though the bold* 10
Waft fragrant greetings to each silent grave; . 272 **Where holy* 10
Could thus have dared the grave to agitate, . . 275 *Gravestone* 8
In fear that else, when Critics grave and cool . 277 **A Poet* 7
Under the grave of things; Hope had her spire . 282 **In my* 11
Is heard; to grave demeanour all are bound; . 283 **Well have* 4
And silent grave. . . . . 285 *Grave of Burns* 30
His grave grass-grown. . . . . 285 *Grave of Burns* 60
Over the grave of Burns we hung . . . . . 285 *Nith* 9
I sought the untimely grave of Burns; . . . 286 *Sons of Burns* 2
But be admonished by his grave, ... 287 *Sons of Burns* 47
Heart-broken, upon Ellen's grave . . . . . 287 *Ellen Irwin* 46
The grave of lovely Ellen: . . . . 287 *Ellen Irwin* 52
More like a grave reality: . . . . 288 *Highland Girl* 54
Is of the grave; and of austere . . . . . . 289 *Glen-Al.* 28
Then clear the weeds from off his Grave, . . . 291 *Rob Roy* 6
Here standing by thy grave. . . . . . . 292 *Rob Roy* 100
And her Foes find a like inglorious grave. . . 293 *Killicranky* 14
Reports of him, his dwelling or his grave! . . 318 **Ah! where* 2
Uncovered to his grave: 'tis closed,—her loss . 318 **In due* 11
Oh, bear the infant covered to his grave! . . 319 *Biscayan* 7
Haste, Virgins, haste; and you, ye Matrons grave, 324 *Ode 1814* 42
By aught redeemed out of the hollow grave: . . 325 *Enghien* 9
Calm is the grave, and calmer none . . . . 348 **Lulled by* 21
A most untimely grave to strew, ... 348 **Lulled by* 46
From Tasso's Convent-haven, and retired grave. . 353 *Aquap.* 84
Has spared of sound and grave realities, . . . 359 *Plea: Hist.* 4
Transfigured, sinks into a hopeless grave; . . 366 *Lombardy* 12
Grave Merlin (and belike the more . . . . 369 *Eg. Maid* 21
The mutual nod,—the grave disguise . . . . 375 **The Minstrels* 43
Grave thoughts ruled wide on that sweet day, . . 385 *Yarrow Rev.* 9
Well sang the Bard who called the grave, in strains 389 *Breadalb.* 1
Worn at the breast of some grave Dame . . . 390 *Highland Broach* 20
Beside the ridge of a grassy grave . . . . . 397 *White Doe* 141
And to his grave will go with scars, ... 398 *White Doe* 221
Grave Gentry of estate and name, ... 403 *White Doe* 629
In the cold grave hath long been laid: . . . . 405 *White Doe* 884
Where they might lie as in the grave, ... 408 *White Doe* 1097
In holy ground a grave would make; . . . . 412 *White Doe* 1521
The grave where Francis must be laid. . . . 412 *White Doe* 1525
She reached the grave, and with her breast . . 413 *White Doe* 1547
But chiefly by that single grave, ... 417 *White Doe* 1898
Which the chaste Votaries seek, beyond the grave; 424 *Ecc. Sonn.* 1. 24. 10
Of its grave echoes, swells a choral strain . . 433 *Ecc. Sonn.* 2. 20. 13
(Grave this within thy heart!) if spiritual things . 442 *Ecc. Sonn.* 3. 10. 9
Mingling their glances with grave flatteries . . 442 *Ecc. Sonn.* 3. 11. 7
Where is thy Sting?—O Grave, where is thy Victory?" . . . . 448 *Ecc. Sonn.* 3. 31. 14
Grave Creature!—whether, while the moon shines bright . . . . 456 **The leaves* 14
Is hidden, buried in its monthly grave; . . . 460 **Wanderer! that* 64
Make thy young thoughts acquainted with the grave; . . . . 465 **Thou look'st* 10
The power is merged, the pomp a grave has found. 471 *Tynwald* 8
This grave no cushion is for thee. . . . . . 485 *Poet's Epitaph* 12
Upon his mother's grave? . . . . 485 *Poet's Epitaph* 20

Grave—*continued.*	
Or build thy house upon this grave.	485 Poet's Epitaph 60
Beside my daughter's grave.	486 *We walked 32
" And, turning from her grave, I met,	487 *We walked 41
Matthew is in his grave, yet now,	487 *We walked 57
This Oak points out thy grave ; the silent tree	491 Tribute : Dog 9
Was in her husband's grave !	495 Force of Prayer 52
Though cold as winter, gloomy as the grave,	501 Humanity 77
To his grave touch with no unready strings,	503 Warning 19
Among a grave fraternity of Monks,	510 *Among a 1
Into a shameful grave. Among thy youth,	514 *Long-favoured 9
Firm self-denial, manners grave and staid,	515 Penn. 2
Blameless—with them that shuddered o'er his grave,	517 Pun. Death 2. 13
More could my pen report of grave or gay	525 Epist.Beaumont270
Triumphant o'er the darkness of the grave.	535 *When in 28
This matter asketh counsel good as grave,	562 Cuck.and Night.272
And I hope that thy grave, wheresoever it be,	571 Farmer 91
To the perpetual silence of the grave.	573 Chiabrera 2. 18
Admonished, from his silent grave,	577 *By playful 20
Shining upon thy happy grave.	578 *I come 72
A place upon thy Poet's grave,	579 *Sweet Flower 2
And bore him to the grave.	579 *Sweet Flower 56
Upon his senseless grave.	580 *Sweet Flower 70
As snowdrop on an infant's grave,	583 *O for a 43
As from a cloud of some grave sympathy,	584 Ch. Lamb 20
And from the mountains, to thy rural grave	585 Ch. Lamb 52
In darkness lost, the darkness of the grave ;	589 Immortality 117
[To whom the grave	589 Immortality 121
Bows his young hairs with sorrow to the grave.	613 Desc.Sk.Quarto 631
Whose grave may here be seen.	623 G. and S. Green 4
Look gently on this grave ;	623 G. and S. Green 18
O darkness of the grave ! how deep,	623 G. and S. Green 29
When thou wert hidden in thy monthly grave ;	630 [?] *O Moon 4
Or fountain, listen to the grave reports	634 Prelude 1. 174
Unprofitably travelling toward the grave,	636 Prelude 1. 267
And through the meadows homeward went, in grave	638 Prelude 1. 389
Gowns grave, or gaudy, doctors, students, streets,	649 Prelude 3. 32
Of the grave Elders, men unscoured, grotesque	657 Prelude 3. 542
Upon thy grave, good creature ! While my heart	659 Prelude 4. 31
A parti-coloured show of grave and gay,	663 Prelude 4. 340
Mute, looking at the grave in which he lies !	671 Prelude 5. 397
By Genii of romance ; or hath in grave	688 Prelude 7. 79
Now mute, for ever mute in the cold grave.	695 Prelude 7. 518
Of that gone by, locked up, as in the grave ;	697 Prelude 7. 659
To the cold grave in which her husband slept,	704 Prelude 8. 386
To help him to his grave ? Meanwhile the man,	705 Prelude 8. 443
Grave Teacher, stern Preceptress ! for at times	707 Prelude 8. 530
Followed his body to the grave. The event,	739 Prelude 12. 309
For my grave looks, too thoughtful for my years.	757 Excursion 1. 59
And go to the grave, unthought of. Strongest minds	757 Excursion 1. 91
Pure livers were they all, austere and grave,	758 Excursion 1. 113
Human, or such as lie beyond the grave.	762 Excursion 1. 433
And she forgotten in the quiet grave.	763 Excursion 1. 510
To hold communion with the grave, and face	774 Excursion 2. 204
These words :—" Shall in the grave thy love be known,	777 Excursion 2. 381
As if disconsolate.—" They to the grave	779 Excursion 2. 508
At any grave or solemn spectacle,	779 Excursion 2. 538
They faint not, but advance towards the open grave	780 Excursion 2. 586
From doubt and sorrow, than the senseless grave ?"	789 Excursion 3. 224
Why should not grave Philosophy be styled,	791 Excursion 3. 338
To appear and answer ; to the grave I spake	796 Excursion 3. 689
In the sublime attractions of the grave."	804 Excursion 4. 238
As bonds, on grave philosopher imposed	812 Excursion 4. 741
And they had hopes that overstepped the Grave.	815 Excursion 4. 940
Before his time into a quiet grave,	821 Excursion 4. 1314
Grave doctors strenuous for the mother-church,	825 Excursion 5. 176
Death's hireling, who scoops out his neighbour's grave,	826 Excursion 5. 235
Of what it holds could speak, and every grave	826 Excursion 5. 251
A grave proficient in amusive feats	826 Excursion 5. 269
Grave, and in truth too often sad.—" Is Man	829 Excursion 5. 465
Upon the southern side of every grave	830 Excursion 5. 543
That open grave is destined." " Died he then	840 Excursion 6. 115
With resignation sink into the grave ;	850 Excursion 6. 774
The sheltering hillock is the Mother's grave.	850 Excursion 6. 792
There, by her innocent Baby's precious grave,	850 Excursion 6. 811
" You see the Infant's Grave ; and to this spot,	853 Excursion 6. 983
And from her grave.—Behold—upon that ridge,	855 Excursion 6. 1116
The Wife, from whose consolatory grave	856 Excursion 6. 1189
Their grave migration, the good pair would tell,	859 Excursion 7. 109
And grave encouragement, by song inspired ?	863 Excursion 7. 386
To the profounder stillness of the grave.	864 Excursion 7. 468
Murmurs, not idly, o'er his peaceful grave.	864 Excursion 7. 481
A grave assemblage, seated while they shear	866 Excursion 7. 619
Let down into the hollow of that grave,	868 Excursion 7. 699
Moved towards the grave ;—instinctively his steps	870 Excursion 7. 819
This hallowed grave demands, where rests in peace	870 Excursion 7. 849
Through the still air, the closing of the Grave ;	871 Excursion 7. 888
Upon the grave of vanished Syracuse,	877 Excursion 8. 221
Gravedona. Of Gravedona with this hope ; but soon	685 Prelude 6. 700
Gravel. With pure cerulean gravel, from the heights	881 Excursion 8. 452
Gravelled. A gravelled pathway treading,	337 Thun 2
Gravely. Gravely to ponder—judging between good	707 Prelude 8. 520
Of Pompey's pillar ; that I gravely style	788 Excursion 3. 131
Graven. Prayer, text, or symbol, graven upon the stone ;	275 Gravestone 2
These find I graven on my heart :	291 Rob Roy 31
Graven on her cankered walls, solemnities	346 Processions 8
By the fierce waves, a flower in marble graven.	371 Eg. Maid 126
Graven on the tomb we struggle against Time,	583 *With copious 2

Graven—*continued.*	
And on the stone were graven by his desire	726 Prelude 10. 535
With tender pleasure of the verses graven	726 Prelude 10. 546
Sepulchral stones appeared, with emblems graven	825 Excursion 5. 168
Graver. Spake of heroic arts in graver mood	211 Laod. 101
Or like those hymns that soothe with graver sound	454 Sea-side 29
Grave's. Elates not, brought far nearer the grave's rest,	278 Wellington 10
Graves. The trees were silent as the graves beneath them.	47 Bord. 576
" Their graves are green, they may be seen,"	84 We are Seven 37
And a few natural graves." To Jane, his wife,	95 Brothers 15
Or half these graves ? For eight-score winters past,	98 Brothers 187
Beneath yon ridge, the last of those three graves ?	98 Brothers 198
You said his kindred all were in their graves,	100 Brothers 329
But these are all the graves of full-grown men !	100 Brothers 341
Years after we are gone and in our graves,	146 *It was an 45
With medicable wounds, or found their graves	328 Ode 1815 81
From pastoral graves extracting thoughts divine ;	384 Duddon 31. 11
Lie silent in your graves, ye dead !	397 White Doe 67
Did from all other graves divide :	398 White Doe 172
Ditches are graves—funereal rites denied ;	427 Ecc. Sonn. 1. 36. 10
And to those graves looking habitually	464 *A point 3
And on your turf-clad graves ! "	507 May 56
Old humourists, who have been long in their graves,	657 Prelude 3. 575
Or sleeping nameless in their scattered graves,	668 Prelude 5. 215
Of all her silent neighbourhood of graves,	671 Prelude 5. 403
To seek the ground where, 'mid a throng of graves,	726 Prelude 10. 533
Beyond these humble graves, of grievous crimes	847 Excursion 6. 570
Five graves, and only five, that rise together	858 Excursion 7. 35
That family (whose graves you there behold)	861 Excursion 7. 289
Gravest. For whom the gravest thought of what they miss,	456 Rydal Mere 40
At gravest heads, by enmity to France	727 Prelude 11. 40
Of gravest import. Early he perceives,	813 Excursion 4. 807
Grave-yard. That curbs a foaming brook, a Grave-yard lies ;	387 *Part fenced 2
Into its graveyard will ere long be borne	862 Excursion 7. 351
Gravitation. The gravitation and the filial bond	645 Prelude 2. 243
Gravity. Of gravity and elegance, diffused	882 Excursion 8. 539
Gray. Oft I had heard of Lucy Gray :	82 Lucy Gray 1
But the sweet face of Lucy Gray	83 Lucy Gray 11
That you may see sweet Lucy Gray	83 Lucy Gray 59
Lines from the churchyard elegy of Gray.	726 Prelude 10. 536
Graze. Of scattered herds, that in the meadow graze,	34 Guilt 521
Green is the grass for beast to graze,	176 Waggoner 1. 270
Than this, to graze the herb in thoughtless peace,	827 Excursion 5. 329
Grazed. Saw mountains ; saw the forms of sheep that grazed	96 Brothers 62
As fine a flock as ever grazed !	115 Last of Flock 34
And planted where thy hoofs the turf have grazed.	201 Hart-leap 68
Our horses grazed. To more than inland peace,	643 Prelude 2. 108
The Ball whizz'd by,—it grazed his ear,	S.3. 441 *The ball 1
To watch the spreading lawns with cattle grazed,	K.8. 249 Recluse 1.1.481
Grazing. The cattle are grazing,	190 March 8
Great. See **Over-great.**	
Lo, from the flames a great and glorious birth ;	22 Desc. Sk. 644
Great God ! by whom the strifes of men are weighed	22 Desc. Sk. 652
Compassion for me. His influence is great	43 Bord. 347
Yes, to my sorrow—under the great oak	47 Bord. 538
Appeal was made to the great Judge : the Accused	62 Bord. 1384
Great actions move our admiration, chiefly	65 Bord. 1536
A thing so great to perish self-consumed.	70 Bord. 1813
That he has been there, and made a great rout,	80 †Address : Child 22
To the top of Great How did it please them to climb :	86 Rural Arch. 4
That God who made the great book of the world	99 Brothers 266
From the Great Gavel, down by Leeza's banks,	100 Brothers 310
Great wonder to our gentle tribe it was	108 Indolence 28
Great God, who feel'st for my distress,	113 Lament 54
Earth breathed in one great presence of the spring ;	122 V. and J. 41
In great and small, in round and square,	128 Idiot Boy 208
On which it stood ; great changes have been wrought	138 Michael 478
Is rendered vain as love for great.	154 Flower Garden 24
Will reach both great and small ;	156 Oak and Broom 62
Of things that in the great world be,	158 *With little 2
I'm as great as they, I trow,	160 *Pansies, lilies 13
With great enterprise ;	163 Hint 4
Already hast survived that great decay,	172 Infant Daughter 6
But as to the great Lodge ! you might as well	202 Hart-leap 131
On this great throng, this bright array !	204 Brougham 18
A taste of this great pleasure, viewing	204 Brougham 42
Restore him to my sight—great Jove, restore ! "	209 Laod. 6
" Great Jove, Laodamía ! doth not leave	210 Laod. 37
And, as the great Deliverer marches by,	213 Dion 35
But over his great tides	222 Triad 142
When some great change gives boundless scope	225 Present. 49
Great Jove is full of stately bowers ;	237 P. B. 47
What was the great Parnassus' self to Thee,	251 *Pelion and 10
It moves us not.—Great God ! I'd rather be	259 *The world is 9
If there be aught of pure, or good, or great,	259 Calvert 10
Great is the glory, for the strife is hard !	260 *High is 14
Observe the faithful flowers ! if small to great	265 *When haughty 9
Great is their glee while flake they add to flake	280 *Intent on 4
The great Sea-water finds its way	295 Highland Boy 57
The danger is so great."	296 Highland Boy 90
Of that great Water give God thanks,	297 Highland Boy 224
Of that which once was great is passed away.	305 Ven. Rep. 14
To that great King : shall hail the crownèd Youth	305 *The Voice 2
That will forget thee ; thou hast great allies ;	305 Toussaint 12

Greet—*continued.*
Shall greet that symbol crowning the low Pile : . 450 *Ecc. Sonn.* 3. 40. 11
A face of love which he in love would greet, . . 461 **Giordano, verily* 12
May sometimes greet the strolling minstrel's harp, 467 *St. Bees* 96
With friends to greet thee, or without, . . . 486 **Bright Flower* 19
To greet the flowers and fruitage of a land, . . 501 *Humanity* 71
—Now with joy's tearful kiss each other greet, . 614 *Desc.Sk.Quarto* 666
And the PRINCE whom we greet . . . . . 629 *Installation* 107
Failed not to greet the merry Mocking-bird ; . . 799 *Excursion* 3. 946
Were seen descending :—forth to greet them ran . 821 *Excursion* 4. 1309
Advanced to greet him. With a gracious mien . 829 *Excursion* 5. 444
Then will a vernal prospect greet your eye, . . 830 *Excursion* 5. 545
Not with more transport did Columbus greet . . 841 *Excursion* 6. 234

Greeted. Who comes—with rapture greeted, and caressed . . . . 441 *Ecc. Sonn.* 3. 3. 1
Where wood or stream by thee was never greeted. 455 *Rydal Mere* 16
Enticing valleys, greeted them and left . . 682 *Prelude* 6. 501
That greeted me on entering, I could hear . . 719 *Prelude* 10. 98
Greeted us all day long ; we took our seats . . 772 *Excursion* 2. 58
Was greeted, in the silence that ensued, . . . 786 *Excursion* 3. 6
Cordially greeted. Graceful was her port : . . 881 *Excursion* 8. 501
No longer greeted—to the tottering sire, . . . S.3. 435 **The doubt* 137
Then to be greeted by the scattered huts, . . . K.8. 249 *Recluse* 1.1.482

Greet'st. Thou greet'st the traveller in the lane ; . 158 **In youth* 18

Greeting. Spare me awhile that greeting. It may be 64 *Bord.* 1507
That silent greeting from above ; . . . . 112 *Lament* 2
Yea, his first word of greeting was,—" All right . 124 *V. and J.* 156
She spies her Friends, she shouts a greeting ; . . 130 *Idiot Boy* 429
Pleased at his greeting thee again ; . . . . . 158 **In youth* 19
Offered a greeting of good ale . . . . . 174 *Waggoner* 1. 54
A welcome greeting he can hear ;— . . . . 176 *Waggoner* 2. 20
When they the wished-for greeting heard, . . . 178 *Waggoner* 3. 2
He may give thee decent greeting. . . . . . 181 *Waggoner* 4. 137
Fair greeting doth she send to all . . . . . 204 *Brougham* 19
A greeting give of measured glee ; . . . . . 233 *Power of Sound* 38
I liked the greeting ; 'twas a sound . . . . 289 *Stepping West.* 13
Or does the greeting to a rout . . . . . 344 **How blest* 35
Of my own Fairfield. The glad greeting given, . 353 *Aquap.* 30
For this unthought-of greeting ! While allured . 361 **List—'twas* 8
The notes whose first faint greeting startled me, . 363 **List—'twas* 89
In that announcement, greeting seemed to mock . 367 **As indignation* 12
On Nina, as she passed, with hopeful greeting. . 371 *Eg. Maid* 132
The greeting given, the music played, ... 375 **The Minstrels* 15
Shines in the greeting of the sun's first ray . . 390 *Highland Hut* 3
Approached, and, greeting her, thus spake ; . . 408 *White Doe* 1077
" Your Father gave me cordial greeting ; . . . 410 *White Doe* 1253
This was for you a precious greeting ; . . . . 414 *White Doe* 1667
With natural smiles of greeting. Bells are dumb ; 427 *Ecc. Sonn.* 1. 36. 9
Such greeting heard, away with sighs . . . . 507 *May* 57
The sun's first greeting, his last farewell ray ! . 511 **Who rashly* 23
Oft-times from Alpine *chalets* sends a greeting. . 524 *Epist. Beaumont* 206
Without a cordial greeting. Thence with speed . 658 *Prelude* 4. 17
To give and take a greeting that might save . . 660 *Prelude* 4. 128
Sing notes of greeting to strange fields or groves, 742 *Prelude* 13. 135
Then given it greeting as it rose once more . . 749 *Prelude* 14. 200
And ere our lively greeting into peace . . . . 762 *Excursion* 1. 447
And cordial greeting.—Vivid was the light . . 779 *Excursion* 2. 514
The thunder's greeting. Nor have nature's laws . 782 *Excursion* 2. 708
A general greeting was exchanged ; and soon . . 829 *Excursion* 5. 462
Of joyful greeting were on him bestowed, . . . 843 *Excursion* 6. 320
And he returned our greeting with a smile. . . 866 *Excursion* 7. 555
The greeting " peace be with you " unto them, . K.8. 244 *Recluse* 1.1.281

Greetings. And, after greetings interchanged, and given . . . . 97 *Brothers* 118
Charged with greetings, benedictions, ... 141 *Arm. Lady* 123
Fifty greetings in a day. . . . . 160 **Pansies, lilies* 24
Nor greetings where no kindness is, nor all . . 207 *Tintern* 130
Waft fragrant greetings to each silent grave ; . . 272 **Where holy* 10
Two solitary greetings have I heard, ... 304 **Jones! as* 10
With Young and Old warm greetings we exchange, 525 *Epist. Beaumont* 236
Unceremonious greetings interchanged . . . . 659 *Prelude* 4. 70
Fair greetings to this shapeless eagerness, . . . 710 *Prelude* 9. 19

Greets. How blest, delicious scene ! the eye that greets 12 *Desc. Sk.* 107
" No Spectre greets me,—no vain Shadow this ; . 210 *Laod.* 61
Peace greets us ;—rambling on without an aim . 349 *Val. Dover* 5
There greets an Embassy from Indian shores ; . 368 *Trajan* 42
Witness yon Pile that greets us from St. Bees. . 467 *St. Bees* 126
And FANCY greets them with a fond embrace ; . 503 *Warning* 25
Decent and unreproved. The voice, that greets . 838 *Excursion* 6. 12
And greets it with thanksgiving. 'Till this hour,' 852 *Excursion* 6. 916

Gregory. Than they appear to holy Gregory ; . . 421 *Ecc. Sonn.* 1. 13. 7

Grenville's. These seven long years to Grenville's onion head. . . . . L.1. 89 *Juvenal* 1. 28

Greta. With murmuring Greta for her guide. . . 180 *Waggoner* 4. 17
Greta, what fearful listening ! when huge stones . 464 *Greta, what* 1
Greta, or Derwent, or some nameless rill, . . . 715 *Prelude* 9. 393

Grew. The gathering clouds grew red with stormy fire, ... 24 *Guilt* 19
Who soon grew weary of her ; but, alas ! . . . 44 *Bord.* 382
And suddenly grew black, as he would die. . . 44 *Bord.* 406
We sate us down. The sky grew dark and darker : 50 *Bord.* 703
Her very heart, her grief grew strong ; . . . . 82 *Alice Fell* 47
—The sweetest thing that ever grew . . . . 82 *Lucy Gray* 7
Grew, by strength the gift of love, ... 93 *Westmoreland Girl* 22
He had remained ; but, as he gazed, there grew . 96 *Brothers* 86
Grew many a poisonous weed ; . . . . . . 102 *Artegal* 30
Fields smiled, and temples rose, and towns and cities grew. . . . . 103 *Artegal* 73

Grew—*continued.*
" Year after year my stock it grew ; . . . . 115 *Last of Flock* 31
And, as her mind grew worse and worse, . . . 130 *Idiot Boy* 415
Her body—it grew better. . . . . 130 *Idiot Boy* 416
Her body still grew better. . . . . 130 *Idiot Boy* 421
Of day grew dim the Housewife hung a lamp ; . 133 *Michael* 114
And when by Heaven's good grace the boy grew up 134 *Michael* 177
Thus in his Father's sight the Boy grew up : . . 134 *Michael* 204
Beyond the seas ; where he grew wondrous rich, . 135 *Michael* 267
That grew beside their door ; and the remains . 138 *Michael* 480
On which it grew, or to be left alone . . . . 149 **A narrow* 31
Hither repaired.—A single beech-tree grew . . 150 **When, to* 18
Three years she grew in sun and shower, . . . 187 **Three years* 1
She grew to woman's height. . . . . . . 192 *Ruth* 18
A knot of spiry trees for ages grew . . . . . 212 *Laod.* 169
Yet earth grew calm while angels mused ? . . 222 *Triad* 200
But, in its helplessness, grew mild . . . . 247 *P. B.* 968
And hope of endless peace in me grew bold : . . 257 **No mortal* 4
Or blight that fond memorial ;—the trees grew, . 276 *Oker Hill* 9
Thou com'st to man's abode the spot grew dearer 281 **What strong* 3
And virtue grew. . . . . 286 *Nith* 24
Burst, when repose grew wearisome ; . . . . 298 *Brownie's Cell* 36
Grew on the floors his sons had trod : . . . . 390 *Highland Broach* 34
As that unhallowed Banner grew . . . . . 401 *White Doe* 501
And Neville's cheek grew pale with fear ; . . . 404 *White Doe* 792
Remaining still distinct grew thin and rare, . . 440 *Ecc. Sonn.* 3. 1. 10
Trembled the groves, the stars grew pale, . . . 499 **Departing summer* 34
Of hope that grew by stealth, ... 507 *May* 26
As with one voice ; their flinty heart grew soft . 513 *General Fast* 6
Beneath whose watchful eye the Maiden grew . 541 *Grace Darl.* 93
Had noted well the stars, all flowers that grew . 622 **Among all* 2
Fair seed-time had my soul, and I grew up . . 636 *Prelude* 1. 301
Grew dear to me : already I began . . . . . 644 *Prelude* 2. 177
Grew weaker, and I hasten on to tell . . . . 645 *Prelude* 2. 200
Grew darker in the presence of my eye : . . . 647 *Prelude* 2. 374
And gratitude grew dizzy in a brain . . . . 653 *Prelude* 3. 300
Far stronger, now, grew the desire I felt . . . 667 *Prelude* 5. 115
His countenance, meanwhile, grew more disturbed ; 667 *Prelude* 5. 126
Grew dark with all the shadows on its breast, . 672 *Prelude* 5. 440
Grew there ; an ash which Winter for himself . 676 *Prelude* 6. 78
Nothing was safe : the elder-tree that grew . . 704 *Prelude* 8. 377
Nor wanted such half-insight as grew wild . . 711 *Prelude* 9. 98
From her first ground expelled, grew proud once more. . . . . 731 *Prelude* 11. 246
Whence grew that genuine knowledge, fraught with peace, ... 732 *Prelude* 11. 354
As I grew up, it was my best delight . . . . 757 *Excursion* 1. 60
A precious gift ; for, as he grew in years, . . . 758 *Excursion* 1. 140
With whom from childhood he grew up, had held 762 *Excursion* 1. 398
Along the window's edge, profusely grew . . . 767 *Excursion* 1. 718
Wherefore, when humbled Liberty grew weak, . 775 *Excursion* 2. 275
The hand grew slack in alms-giving, the heart . 849 *Excursion* 6. 721
They stayed not long.—The blameless Infant grew ; 852 *Excursion* 6. 930
The precious gift of hearing. He grew up . . 863 *Excursion* 7. 402
Thus in his Father's sight the Boy grew up ; . . K.8. 226 **I will* 84
Said she, " for thither as the trees grew up, . . K.8. 247 *Recluse* 1.1.397

Grey. *See* **Old-grey.**
Through bare grey dell, high wood, and pastoral cove ; . . . . 2 *Ev. Wk.* 2
Half grey, half shagged with ivy to its ridge ; . . 3 *Ev. Wk.* 69
By lichens grey, and scanty moss, o'ergrown ; . . 4 *Ev. Wk.* 95
From his grey re-appearing tower shall soon . . 8 *Ev. Wk.* 325
—Thy lake that, streaked or dappled, blue or grey, 12 *Desc. Sk.* 119
Down fell in straggling locks his thin grey hair ; . 24 *Guilt* 7
In his grey hairs !— I love the Father in thee. . 57 *Bord.* 1110
" And let it be of duffil grey, ... 82 *Alice Fell* 57
And shepherds clad in the same country grey . 96 *Brothers* 64
A noticeable Man with large grey eyes, . . . 108 *Indolence* 39
—Of coats and of jackets grey, scarlet, and green, 120 *Childless Father* 5
That thinly decks his few grey hairs ; . . . . 157 **In youth* 10
Even while I speak, their skirts of grey . . . 180 *Waggoner* 4. 59
The oldest man he seemed that ever wore grey hairs. 196 *Resolution* 56
Upon a long grey staff of shaven wood : . . . . 196 *Resolution* 72
It looks so old and grey. . . . . 197 *Thorn* 4
The pond—and Thorn, so old and grey ; . . . 198 *Thorn* 94
And saddled his best Steed, a comely grey ; . . 200 *Hart-leap* 6
The trees were grey, with neither arms nor head ; 202 *Hart-leap* 109
Nor leave thee, when grey hairs are nigh, . . . 218 *Young Lady* 14
Through the grey clouds ; the Alps are here, . . 237 *P. B.* 59
Where blue and grey, and tender green, . . . 240 *P. B.* 363
The Swale flowed under the grey rocks, . . . 240 *P. B.* 371
Yon old grey Stone, protected from the ray . . 262 **Mark the* 2
And thou, grey Stone, the pensive likeness keep . 262 **Mark the* 10
Which the Muse warms ; and I, whose head is grey, 273 **Wild Redbreast* 5
Rotha, my Spiritual Child ! this head was grey . 274 *Rotha Q.* 1
And these grey rocks ; that household lawn ; . . 288 *Highland Girl* 5
Yon grey tower's living crest ! . . . . . . 300 *Cora Linn* 24
Through the grey west ; and lo ! these waters, steeled . . . . 313 **Clouds, lingering* 2
With its grey rocks clustering in pensive shade— 335 *Namur* 12
Strewn with grey rocks, and on the horizon's verge, 352 *Aquap.* 17
' Mid sheltering pines, this Cottage rude and grey ; 377 *Duddon* 5. 10
A concave free from shrubs and mosses grey ; . 379 *Duddon* 15. 4
In the grey sky hath left his lingering Ghost, . . 392 **Though joy* 4
A shepherd clad in homely grey ; . . . . . 399 *White Doe* 281
Bulls, pardons, relics, cowls black, white, and grey— 435 *Ecc. Sonn.* 2. 28. 7
Of old grey stone, and high-born name . . . 472 *Ossian* 24
Were at that time, as now, in colour grey. . . 474 **Here on their* 3
" Why, William, on that old grey stone, . . . 481 *Expost.* 1
I sit upon this old grey stone, ... 481 *Expost.* 31

Greybeard 388 Grief

Grey—*continued.*
With hair of glittering grey ; 486 *We walked 6
Of sea and land, with yon grey towers that still 517 Pun. Death 1. 2
As well we knew, together had grown grey. 523 Epist. Beaumont 132
Ere on its banks the few grey cabins rose 524 Epist. Beaumont 168
Good duffle grey, and flannel fine ; 536 Goody Blake 6
Forbade the weeds to creep o'er its grey line. 549 *The massy 10
Beat his grey locks against his withered face. 568 Cumb. Beg. 176
His staff is a sceptre—his grey hairs a crown ; 569 Farmer 6
With his grey hairs he went from the brook and the green ; 570 Farmer 46
And, in my spleen, I smiled that it was grey. 571 *There is a Flower 20
You see to what end he has brought his grey hairs. 572 Avarice 32
Mourn, Shepherd, near thy old grey stone ; 577 *I come 33
—Thy lake, mid smoking woods, that blue and grey 604 Desc.Sk.Quarto 138
The old grey stones the plaided chief surveys, 608 Desc.Sk.Quarto 359
Whence the scared Owl on pinions grey 626 †Cento 13
Was nothing but the stars and the grey sky. 637 Prelude 1. 372
Gone was the old grey stone, and in its place 642 Prelude 2. 38
Of the old grey stone, from her scant board, supplied. 643 Prelude 2. 88
To thee and thy grey huts, thou one dear Vale ! 645 Prelude 2. 197
On some grey rock—its birthplace—so had I 722 Prelude 10. 278
A chaplet in contempt of his grey locks. 722 Prelude 10. 314
Shaggy and grey, had meanings which it brought 762 Excursion 1. 429
Now faint,—the grass has crept o'er its grey line ; 769 Excursion 1. 883
Upon a rising ground a grey church-tower, 823 Excursion 5. 80
Halts the individual, ere his hairs be grey, 829 Excursion 5. 468
To mix the manly brown with silver grey, 842 Excursion 6. 278
Exchange the shepherd's frock of native grey 846 Excursion 6. 548
In the grey cottage by the murmuring stream 848 Excursion 6. 670
Grey locks profusely round his temples hung 865 Excursion 7. 551
The shepherd's grey to martial scarlet changed, 869 Excursion 7. 764
The cornice, richly fretted, of grey stone ; 881 Excursion 8. 467
Of those celestial splendours ; grey the vault— 895 Excursion 9. 760
Through tall green silent woods and ruins grey. S.3. 417 *Sweet was 14
By the grey moss, but not a single stone K.8. 226 *I will 66
Yon curling smoke from the grey cot below, K.8. 247 Recluse 1.1.390
A liking for the small grey horse that bears K.8. 250 Recluse 1.1.505
Greybeard. A blind old Greybeard and accosted him, 45 Bord. 447
For this old venerable Grey-beard—faith 54 Bord. 922
For not misleading us. That subtle Grey-beard— 56 Bord. 1019
Grey-clad. Tho' now, where erst the grey-clad peasant stray'd, 615 Desc.Sk.Quarto 714
Grey-haired. And grey-haired men look up with livelier brow,— 21 Desc. Sk. 609
And stern looks on the man her grey-haired Comrade cast. 33 Guilt 477
Swiftly went that grey-haired Servant, 141 Arm. Lady 121
And grey-haired Wilfred of the glen 199 Thorn 138
Lift up that grey-haired forehead, and rejoice 255 Detraction 13
And grey-haired sires, on staffs supported, 324 Ode 1814 65
And with those grey-haired champions stood, 405 White Doe 821
That grey-haired Man of gentle blood, 409 White Doe 1201
A grey-haired, pensive, thankful Refugee ; 470 Bala-Sala 7
The grey-haired man of glee : 487 Fountain 20
This chiefly, did I note my grey-haired Dame ; 661 Prelude 4. 217
Deftly prolonged, though grey-haired lookers on 680 Prelude 6. 373
And pleased I looked upon my grey-haired Friend, 781 Excursion 2. 658
My grey-haired Friend said courteously—" Nay, nay, 785 Excursion 2. 901
And, to remove those doubts, my grey-haired Friend 786 Excursion 3. 21
" Is this," the grey-haired Wanderer mildly said, 789 Excursion 3. 225
The grey-haired Wanderer steadfastly replied, 802 Excursion 4. 67
" Much was I pleased," the grey-haired Wanderer said, 833 Excursion 5. 728
Of rustic loneliness : that grey-haired Orphan— 835 Excursion 5. 885
More pleased than sad, the grey-haired Wanderer sate ; 854 Excursion 6. 1064
The grey-haired Wanderer pensively exclaimed, 872 Excursion 7. 977
My grey-haired Friend was moved ; his vivid eye 883 Excursion 8. 588
Grey-headed. A seaman, a grey-headed Mariner. 102 Brothers 435
" Grey-headed Shepherd, thou hast spoken well ; 203 Hart-leap 161
For the grey-headed Sire has a daughter at home, 572 Avarice 42
Like harshness,—that the old grey-headed Sire, 861 Excursion 7. 258
Greyhound. Breaks—and the greyhound, Dart, is overhead ! 490 Incident : Dog 24
And holds a greyhound in a leash, 494 Force of Prayer 15
But the greyhound in the leash hung back, 494 Force of Prayer 31
Greyhounds. The greyhounds to their kennel creep ; 406 White Doe 952
Griding. At once the griding iron passage found ; 33 Guilt 493
Grief. That grief for which the senses still supply 1 Early Youth 9
Though grief and pain may come to-morrow ? 9 Lines : Boat 16
But in the milder grief of pity. 9 Collins 16
Yet, when oppress by sickness, grief, or care 20 Desc. Sk. 536
Awoke a fainter sense of moral grief ; 22 Desc. Sk. 633
What tears of bitter grief, till then unknown, 29 Guilt 255
He well could love in grief ; his faith he kept ; 29 Guilt 260
Yet Nature, with excess of grief o'erborne, 30 Guilt 309
More with delight than grief—I heard a voice 62 Bord. 1362
Sob after sob, as if her grief 82 Alice Fell 39
Her very heart, her grief grew strong ; 82 Alice Fell 47
Of Alice and her grief I told ; 82 Alice Fell 54
And Grief, uneasy lover ! never rest 88 H. C. 17
Sympathy that soothed his grief, 94 Westmoreland Girl 38
A habit which disquietude and grief 101 Brothers 394
Grief—*continued.*
Of universal grief bedewed his honoured bier. 105 Artegal 233
My pride was tamed, and in our grief 115 Last of Flock 43
Think not of me with grief and pain : 117 Affl. Marg. 39
They pity me, and not my grief. 117 Affl. Marg. 74
Now first acquainted with distress and grief, 118 Maternal Grief 50
Of pious faith the vanities of grief ; 119 Maternal Grief 73
Carried about her for a secret grief 122 V. and J. 67
The old Man's grief broke from him ; to his heart 137 Michael 421
Steeped in dire grief the voice of Philomel ; 153 Morn. Ex. 20
What grief is mine you see, 155 Waterfall 42
Spite of care, and spite of grief, 172 Kitten 127
If solitude, or fear, or pain, or grief, 207 Tintern 143
Each grief, through meekness, settling into rest. 222 Triad 182
And each day's shallow grief ; 224 *'Tis gone 39
As if he were his grief renewing ; 243 P. B. 590
In agony of silent grief— 248 P. B. 1077
Of night his grief and sorrowful fear— 249 P. B. 1104
Grief, thou hast lost an ever-ready friend 255 *Grief, thou 1
With it Camöens soothed an exile's grief ; 260 *Scorn not 6
Why should we bend in grief, to sorrow cling, 271 George : Death 8
Nor one look more exchanging, grief to still 276 Oker Hill 3
Can pomp and show allay one heart-born grief ? 280 *Intent on 9
In social grief— 285 Nith 10
And an unthinking grief ! The tenderest mood 304 *I grieved 2
Oh grief that Earth's best hopes rest all with Thee ! 309 *England ! the 14
But soon, through Christian faith, is grief subdued : 318 *In due 13
Whom grief hath spared—who sheds no tear 344 *How blest 11
As grief can be in grief's pursuit ? 344 *How blest 62
And filled our hearts with grief for England's shame ? 349 Val. Dover 4
With all who want not skill to couple grief 356 Aquap. 245
The grief, the praise, are severed from their dust, 356 Aquap. 247
As indignation mastered grief, my tongue 367 *As indignation 1
Ill sight ! but grief may vanish ere the morrow." 372 Eg. Maid 210
Not with a grief that, like a vapour, rises 373 Eg. Maid 260
And melts ; but grief devout that shall endure, 373 Eg. Maid 261
Her grief with, as she might !—But, where, oh ! where 378 Duddon 11. 9
Grief of her sting ; nor cheat, where he detains 389 Breadalb. 4
To the grief of her soul that doth come and go, 398 White Doe 236
O'er pain and grief a triumph pure. 407 White Doe 1072
Rushed in ; and—while, O grief to tell ! 412 White Doe 1491
Hath roamed in trouble and in grief, 414 White Doe 1613
Rites that console the Spirit, under grief 423 Ecc. Sonn. 1. 20. 6
To poverty, and grief, and disrespect, 441 Ecc. Sonn. 3. 6. 4
A care more anxious, or a heavier grief ? 461 *Where lies the truth 3
Did pangs of grief for lenient time too keen, 470 *Did pangs 1
Grief that devouring waves had caused—or guilt 470 *Did pangs 2
Pleasure, or Grief, and Toil that seldom looks 471 Ailsa Crag 10
By fortune crushed, or tamed by grief ; 473 Ossian 76
And a patience to her grief. 495 Force of Prayer 64
The Master died, his drooping servant's grief 523 Epist. Beaumont 133
Admiring, loving, and with grief and pride 547 *Ye Lime 17
Well hast thou wreaked on me by pain and grief ; 563 Troilus 72
For very grief of which my heart shall cleave ;— 564 Troilus 95
For her heart's grief, she will entreat Sebeto 575 Chiabrera 7. 10
Not without heavy grief of heart did He 575 Chiabrera 8. 1
Or if thy cherished grief have failed to thwart 576 *By a 15
Ill-worthy, Beaumont ! were the grief 582 *O for a 10
Yet have we found how slowly genuine grief 584 *With copious 44
With sharper grief is Yarrow smitten, 586 Hogg 43
To me alone there came a thought of grief : 588 Immortality 22
No more shall grief of mine the season wrong ; 588 Immortality 26
In broken sounds her elder grief demand, 596 Ev. Wk. Quarto 263
Labour, and Pain, and Grief, and joyless Age, 613 Desc.Sk.Quarto 639
Awoke a fainter pang of moral grief ; 616 Desc.Sk.Quarto 769
But if grief, self-consumed, in oblivion would doze, 621 Convict 29
From fear and grief, and from all need 623 G. and S. Green 27
Your own grief and your friends'—your wandering course ; 625 Æneid 141
Or grief—the inheritance of humankind. 628 *Deign, Sovereign 24
There is no grief, no sorrow, no despair, 678 Prelude 6. 244
Such grief for thee would be the weakest thought 679 Prelude 6. 317
Feelings of pure commiseration, grief 693 Prelude 7. 395
Brave hearts ! to shameful flight. It was a grief,— 722 Prelude 10. 288
Grief call it not, 'twas anything but that,— 722 Prelude 10. 289
They had the deepest feeling of the grief. 724 Prelude 10. 389
Of ancient heroes. If I suffered grief 733 Prelude 11. 383
To me the grief confined, that thou art gone 733 Prelude 11. 399
That doth not yield a solace to my grief : 733 Prelude 11. 436
But, under pressure of a private grief, 752 Prelude 14. 419
No wild varieties of joy and grief. 761 Excursion 1. 360
With fervent love, and with a face of grief 766 Excursion 1. 655
Had from its mother caught the trick of grief, 768 Excursion 1. 830
More plainly still, that poverty and grief 769 Excursion 1. 833
I blessed her in the impotence of grief. 770 Excursion 1. 924
From ruin and from change, and all the grief 770 Excursion 1. 950
Sickness, or accident, or grief, or pain. 777 Excursion 2. 369
In silent grief their unuplifted heads, 780 Excursion 2. 575
Of grief, depart without occasion given 780 Excursion 2. 598
Love with despair, or grief in agony ;— 791 Excursion 3. 378
Into a gulf obscure of silent grief, 795 Excursion 3. 675
If grief be something hallowed and ordained, 803 Excursion 4. 148
And grief spread wide ; but Man escaped the doom 811 Excursion 4. 649
Awakening, chastening an intemperate grief, 813 Excursion 4. 840
Of pain and grief ? " the Solitary asked, 840 Excursion 6. 116
Of unexpected promise, where a grief 852 Excursion 6. 909
Is sure, that through remorse and grief he died ; 855 Excursion 6. 1111

Grief—*continued.*
Of many tears, virtuous and thoughtful grief ; 864 *Excursion* 7. 470
By virtue.—He, sighing with pensive grief, 877 *Excursion* 8. 227
Motive to sadder grief, as we have found ; 888 *Excursion* 9. 251
Tearless, yet full of grief. —How heavenly fair [?] **A sad* 2
Grief's. As grief can be in grief's pursuit ? 344 **How blest* 62
Griefs. Besides, on griefs so fresh my thoughts were brooding still. 32 *Guilt* 423
The big and lesser griefs with which she mourned 120 *Emigrant Mother* 3
So lively a remembrance of their griefs, 125 *V. and J.* 287
Can draw, and sing his griefs to rest. 233 *Power of Sound* 64
Griefs to allay which Reason cannot heal ; 273 **WhenPhiloctetes* 10
And griefs whose aery motion comes not near 395 *White Doe : Ded.* 35
That—whatever griefs may fret, 503 **Like a* 53
So spake the mild Jeronymite, his griefs 510 *F. Stone* 118
And sympathy with man's substantial griefs— 538 **In desultory* 41
From whence to Thebes came griefs in multitude. 563 *Troilus* 84
His joys, his griefs, have vanished like a cloud 587 *Crosth.* 15
—Without one hope her written griefs to blot, 614 *Desc.Sk.Quarto* 676
And oft-times hast thou made my griefs thine own. 624 *Æneid* 18
Of unsunned griefs, too many and too keen, 861 *Excursion* 7. 281
Griesly. *See* **Grisly.**
Look down, and see a griesly sight ; 398 *White Doe* 244
And in that griesly object recognise 523 *Epist. Beaumont* 130
Grievance. A standing grievance, an indigenous vice 887 *Excursion* 9. 185
Grievances. A hoard of grievances unsealed ; 181 *Waggoner* 4. 179
Earth's petty grievances—its toil and care :— [?] **A sad* 7
Grieve. In this good service. Rather let us grieve 37 *Bord.* 5
Nay, but I grieve that we should part. This Stranger, 38 *Bord.* 24
Now, on my life, I grieve for you. The misery 53 *Bord.* 879
A thought that's worth a thousand worlds ! I grieve 55 *Bord.* 1003
And who would grieve and fret, if, welcome come 97 *Brothers* 123
Then do not weep and grieve for me ; 114 *Ind. Wom.* 43
Whate'er befell she could not grieve or pine ; 139 *Widow* 24
Nor e'er, with ruffled fancy, grieve, 154 *Flower Garden* 21
Then grieve not, jolly team ! though tough 175 *Waggoner* 1. 138
And more would grieve, but that it turns 286 *Sons of Burns* 5
Men are we, and must grieve when even the Shade 305 *Ven. Rep.* 13
Saints would not grieve nor guardian angels frown 354 *Aquap.* 118
Grieve for the Man who hither came bereft, 363 **Grieve for* 1
Nor grieve the less that skill to him was left 363 **Grieve for* 3
Grieve for her, she deserves no less ; 370 *Eg. Maid* 55
Killing the bud o'er which in vain we grieve. 448 *Ecc. Sonn.* 3. 33. 8
Why grieve for these, though past away 473 *Ossian* 43
Grieve for the land on whose wild woods his name 515 *Penn.* 10
With indignation, deeply moved we grieve, 517 *Pun. Death* 2. 3
To gladden or to grieve, he hath like skill ; 557 *Cuck. and Night.* 19
And grieve, and know that I must grieve, 580 *John Words.* 19
And let him grieve who cannot choose but grieve 585 *Ch. Lamb* 72
Is broken ; yet why grieve ? for Time but holds 586 *Ch. Lamb* 129
We will grieve not, rather find 590 *Immortality* 183
We gaze—nor grieve to think that we must die, 627 **We gaze* 1
I grieve not ; happy is the gownèd youth, 656 *Prelude* 3. 491
Even then I sometimes grieve for thee, O Man, 665 *Prelude* 5. 4
Yet did I grieve, nor only grieved, but thought 720 *Prelude* 10. 146
Of this same life, compelling us to grieve 792 *Excursion* 3. 448
I grieve that, in your presence, from my tongue 793 *Excursion* 3. 495
With you I grieve, when on the darker side 876 *Excursion* 8. 151
I grieve not," to the Pastor here he turned, 888 *Excursion* 9. 273
I should not grieve with thee to play ; K.8. 262 **Ah ! if* 2
Grieved. He had a Guide, a Shepherd's boy ; but grieved 49 *Bord.* 688
I grieved, fond Youth ! that thou shouldst sue 109 **Ere with* 3
And, grieved for their brief date, confess that ours, 110 **Look at* 3
" Grieved am I, submissive Christian ! 139 *Arm. Lady* 13
Nor grieved if thou be set at nought : 158 **In youth* 21
'Tis gone ! (so seemed it) and we grieved 169 *Wren's Nest* 51
Am grieved for that unhappy sin 182 *Waggoner* 4. 266
More deeply grieved, for He was gone 285 *Grave of Burns* 32
I grieved for Buonaparté, with a vain 304 **I grieved* 1
Yet were the thoughtful grieved ; and still that voice 312 **A Roman* 9
Came to the proof, nor grieved that there ensued 373 *Eg. Maid* 291
Can she be grieved for quire or shrine, 397 *White Doe* 112
Am grieved this backward march to see 406 *White Doe* 900
To a grieved heart the notes are benisons. 464 **Greta, what* 14
And much it grieved my heart to think 482 *Lines : Spring* 7
We grieved for thee, and wished thy end were past ; 491 *Tribute : Dog* 11
Nor grieved to see (himself not unbeguiled)— 504 *Warning* 66
And thy grieved Spirit brighten strong in faith. 515 **Men of* 14
And freer pace ; but more, far more, I grieved 656 *Prelude* 3. 497
Meanwhile old grandame earth is grieved to find 670 *Prelude* 5. 337
Unveiled the summit of Mont Blanc, and grieved 683 *Prelude* 6. 525
Loth to believe what we so grieved to hear, 684 *Prelude* 6. 586
Grieved, and the twilight taper, and the cross 716 *Prelude* 9. 475
Yet did I grieve, nor only grieved, but thought 720 *Prelude* 10. 146
Which I behold at home.' It would have grieved 768 *Excursion* 1. 776
For whom she suffered. Yes, it would have grieved 768 *Excursion* 1. 790
Grieved shall I be—less for my sake than yours, 778 *Excursion* 2. 466
With courteous voice thus spake— " I should have grieved 788 *Excursion* 3. 116
Nor would I bend to it ; who should have grieved 797 *Excursion* 3. 779
And gentle ' Nature grieved, that one should die ; ' 837 *Excursion* 5. 975
The grieved one whom it meant to send away, S.3. 434 **The doubt* 91
Grieves. Nor grieves—tho' doomed thro' silent night to bear 216 *Enterprise* 95
Proud Tiber grieves, and far-off Ganges, blind 435 *Ecc. Sonn.* 2. 27. 6
For whom, belike, the old Man grieves still more 540 *Grace Darl.* 39
This only grieves me, for it seems a wrong, 575 *Chiabrera* 6. 10

Grieves—*continued.*
' It grieves me you have waited here so long, 767 *Excursion* 1. 753
Grieving. Grieving for sin, and penitential tears 850 *Excursion* 6. 799
And for the injustice grieving, that hath made 888 *Excursion* 9. 253
Grievous. His love was such a grievous pain. 110 *'*Tis said that some* 5
A grievous penalty, but little less 134 *Michael* 216
And took it in most grievous part ; 246 *P. B.* 912
So grievous is his heart's contrition ; 247 *P. B.* 932
To my most grievous loss !—That thought's return 257 **Surprised by* 9
Omen of man's grievous doom ! 502 **Like a* 12
Into a grievous sore of self-tormenting earth. 504 *Warning* 77
He lets them perish through that grievous ill. 560 *Cuck.and Night.* 200
Acknowledging, and grievous self-reproach, 804 *Excursion* 4. 200
Beyond these humble graves, of grievous crimes 847 *Excursion* 6. 570
Grievously. Yet was I grievously provoked to think 38 *Bord.* 70
And oh, how grievously I rue, 114 *Ind. Wom.* 26
Grim. Disclosing the grim head of a late murdered corse. 27 *Guilt* 180
The Doctor, looking somewhat grim, 129 *Idiot Boy* 259
The ridges of grim war ; and at their head 320 **They seek* 4
Though from the same grim turret fell 334 **In Bruges* 11
We who were led to-day down a grim dell, 475 *Greenock* 2
While,day by day,grim neighbour ! hugeBlack Comb 521 *Epist. Beaumont* 5
Hath seen in grim array amid their Storms 612 *Desc.Sk.Quarto* 538
And growing still in stature the grim shape 637 *Prelude* 1. 381
And, in the grim and breathless hour of noon, 782 *Excursion* 2. 706
And visage grim and sooty, S.3. 424 *Tinker* 36
Grimace. But what of this ! the laugh, the grin, grimace, 693 *Prelude* 7. 430
To see the arch grimace of Marquis Scrub, L.1. 95 *Juvenal* 3. 11
Grimacing. Grimacing, writhing, screaming,—him who grinds 697 *Prelude* 7. 699
Grin. But what of this ! the laugh, the grin, grimace, 693 *Prelude* 7. 430
Grinding. Grinding through rough and smooth our way ; 179 *Waggoner* 3. 94
Grinds. Grimacing, writhing, screaming,—him who grinds 697 *Prelude* 7. 699
Grinned. The Ass turned round his head and *grinned.* 245 *P. B.* 825
Grinning. And, grinning in his turn, his teeth 245 *P. B.* 831
Gripe. Caught in the gripe of death, with such brief time 795 *Excursion* 3. 639
Griped. To anger, by the malady that griped 849 *Excursion* 6. 746
Grisdale. Leaving St. Sunday's Crag, to Grisdale tarn K.8. 225 **I will* 25
Grisdale's. And Grisdale's houseless vale, along the brink K.8. 225 **I will* 30
Grisly. *See* **Griesly.**
A grisly idol hewn in stone ? 242 *P. B.* 506
In grisly folds and strictures serpentine ; 424 *Ecc. Sonn.* 1. 21. 12
Grison. The Grison gypsey here her tent has plac'd, 605 *Desc.Sk.Quarto* 188
Groan. His battered head, a groan the Sailor fetched 33 *Guilt* 489
A human groan. Ha ! what is here ? Poor Man— 67 *Bord.* 1667
The dead Man heave a groan, or from his side 75 *Bord.* 2160
Perhaps some dungeon hears thee groan, 117 *Affl. Marg.* 50
Nor did he utter groan or sigh, 155 *Waterfall* 17
And with the last deep groan his breath had fetched 201 *Hart-leap* 43
This water doth send forth a dolorous groan. 202 *Hart-leap* 136
Groan thou with our victory ! 205 *Brougham* 149
He gave a groan, and then another, 241 *P. B.* 443
He sees a motion—hears a groan ; 242 *P. B.* 527
" Thou art our king, O Death ! to thee we groan." 257 **Methought I* 8
Demons and Spirits, many a dolorous groan 435 *Ecc. Sonn.* 2. 27. 4
Groan underneath a weight of slavish toil, 501 *Humanity* 86
The penal caverns groan 581 *Invoc. Earth* 10
Tearing their bleeding ties leaves Age to groan 613 *Desc.Sk.Quarto* 612
As makes the nations groan. This active course 761 *Excursion* 1. 381
Groaned. Who in his heart had groaned with deadlier pain 26 *Guilt* 125
And oft he groaned aloud, " O God, that I were dead ! " 36 *Guilt* 639
Groaned the poor Beast—alas ! in vain ; 238 *P. B.* 192
On proud temptations, till the victim groaned 517 *Pun. Death* 2. 7
To outrun the rest in exultation, groaned 725 *Prelude* 10. 505
Whose country groan'd under a foreign scourge ? S.3. 436 **The doubt* 173
Groaning. Bent o'er the groaning flood that sweeps away his tears. 11 *Desc. Sk.* 62
At happy distance from earth's groaning field, 313 **Clouds, lingering* 7
And swells the groaning torrent with his tears. 603 *Desc. Sk. Quarto* 67
The groaning nations ; when the impious rule, 805 *Excursion* 4. 298
Or shall the groaning Spirit cast her load 817 *Excursion* 4. 1099
Groans. And groans that rage of racking famine spoke ; 30 *Guilt* 344
And groans which, as they said, might make a dead man start. 31 *Guilt* 396
But some one must be near to count his groans. 75 *Bord.* 2151
Poor Susan moans, poor Susan groans ; 127 *Idiot Boy* 142
Poor Susan moans, poor Susan groans ; 127 *Idiot Boy* 147
He gave three miserable groans ; 241 *P. B.* 447
Our groans, our blushes, our pale cheeks declare 319 *Spaniard* 13
What groans ! what shrieks ! what quietness in death ! 345 **Ambition—following* 14
The shouts of folly, and the groans of sin." 349 *At Dover* 14
Combat, while darkness aggravates the groans : 464 **Greta, what* 4
While arrowy fire extorting feverish groans, 596 *Ev. Wk. Quarto* 245
With living men—how deep the groans ! the voice 744 *Prelude* 13. 332
Though aided by wild winds, the groans and shrieks 894 *Excursion* 9. 696
Grongar. Long as the thrush shall pipe on Grongar Hill ! 254 *Dyer* 14
Groom. *See* **Shepherd-groom.**
I have a palfrey and a groom : the lad 43 *Bord.* 311
Knight, squire, and yeoman, page and groom : 204 *Brougham* 38

Groom—*continued.*
Or groom !—We must run glittering like a brook 307 *O Friend 5
Served as stable-boy, errand-boy, porter, and groom ; 570 Farmer 50
And at your will what in a groom were base L.1. 97 Juvenal 3. 77
Grooms. *See* **Shepherd-grooms.**
Of lasses and of shepherd grooms, 396 White Doe 11
With chaises, grooms, and liveries, and within 644 Prelude 2. 143
Mid knots of grooms the council of his state L.1. 94 Juvenal 2. 15
Grooved. *See* **Deep-grooved.**
Groping. Scarcely, by groping, had I reached the Spot, 55 Bord. 964
And Benjamin is groping near them, 175 Waggoner 1. 192
Gross. A contrast and reproach to gross delight, 263 *Those words 3
Which the gross world no sense hath to perceive, 290 Kilchurn 8
By gross Utilities enslaved we need 358 Aquap. 348
The gross materials of this world present 428 Ecc. Sonn. 1. 37. 2
When most enslaved by gross realities ! 512 *Who rashly 42
And false conclusions, in degree as gross, 730 Prelude 11. 182
For the gross spirit of mankind,—the one 799 Excursion 3. 911
Of the gross fictions chanted in the streets 812 Excursion 4. 732
Not for gross good alone which ye produce, 831 Excursion 5. 616
With the gross aims and body-bending toil 875 Excursion 8. 41
But, while the gross and visible frame of things 885 Excursion 9. 63
Grosser. That aids or supersedes our grosser sight, 226 Vernal Ode 4
When Music deigned within this grosser sphere 234 Power of Sound 117
Grossest. If, guarding grossest things from common claim 280 Plea for Auth. 6
Grossly. And grossly that man errs, who should suppose 132 Michael 62
Yet were I grossly destitute of all 648 Prelude 2. 421
Grot. *See* **Shell-grot.**
In Nysa's isle, the embellished grot ; 299 Brownie's Cell 92
So had they rushed into the grot 301 Bran 62
Like some Nymph-haunted grot beneath the roaring sea. 324 Ode 1814 81
Thrilling each pearly cleft and sparry grot, 333 Fish-women 13
And in the hallowed grot. 341 San Salv. 24
Then was, within the famed Egerian Grot 367 *If with 7
Half grot, half arbour—proffers to enclose 382 Duddon 24. 7
In every cell of Fingal's mystic Grot, 473 *Ye shadowy 2
As Numa loved ; when, in the Egerian grot, 498 *Enough of climbing 28
[Grote.] Hurrah for —— [Grote], hugging his Ballot-box ! 513 *Said Secrecy 14
Grotesque. Withered, grotesque, immeasurably old, 333 Fish-women 8
Of the grave Elders, men unscoured, grotesque 657 Prelude 3. 542
With gentle whisper. Withered boughs grotesque, 814 Excursion 4. 879
Not unbecoming, of grotesque device 881 Excursion 8. 476
Grots. Grots, pebbles, roots of trees, and fancies more, 662 Prelude 4. 262
Grotto. Beside a grotto of their own, 161 Binnorie 23
And lo this Work !—a grotto bright and clear 264 *Lady ! I 10
Quick to the secret grotto they retire 619 School Ex. 61
The Grotto of Antiparos, or the Den 707 Prelude 8. 562
Grottoed. Who with their Hippocrene and grottoed fount S.3. 436 *The doubt 161
Grotto's. Forth from the grotto's dimmest chamber 371 Eg. Maid 176
Ground. *See* **Background, Cottage-ground, Forest-ground, Meadow-ground, Mountain-ground, Orchard-ground, Playground, Pleasure-ground, Tillage-ground, Underground, Vantage-ground.**
Dark is the ground ; a slumber seems to steal 1 Early Youth 5
While with a hoary light she frosts the ground, 8 Ev. Wk. 327
Were there, below, a spot of holy ground 10 Desc. Sk. 1
And as his native hills encircle ground 18 Desc. Sk. 449
The wet cold ground, he feared, must be his only bed. 25 Guilt 45
And half upon the ground, with strange affright, 26 Guilt 107
And, from the perilous ground dislodged, through storm 26 Guilt 129
The ground I for my bed have often used : 32 Guilt 437
Stretched on the ground, began a piteous tale ; 33 Guilt 471
As if he saw—there and upon that ground— 33 Guilt 490
About this ground ; she hath a tongue well skilled, 44 Bord. 366
As I have done, my eyes upon the ground, 45 Bord. 433
A few leagues hence we shall have open ground, 49 Bord. 655
From the unpretending ground we mortals tread ;— 54 Bord. 933
Who are we, Friends ? Do we not live on ground 57 Bord. 1114
But have they not a world of common ground 60 Bord. 1237
an old Man lying stretched upon the ground— 72 Bord. 1924
I let him sink again to the ground. 72 Bord. 1936
Withered on the ground must lie ; 79 Foresight 20
Forthwith alighting on the ground, 82 Alice Fell 17
And there upon the ground I sit, 84 We are Seven 43
" And when the ground was white with snow, 84 We are Seven 57
Said Walter, leaping from the ground, 85 Shepherd-boys 34
And twice in the day, when the ground is wet with dew, 87 Pet-lamb 43
Of his own voice confirmed, he leaps upon the ground. 104 Artegal 121
In the cold north's unhallowed ground, 110 *'Tis said that some 3
But such a one, on English ground, 114 Last of Flock 5
This Lady, dwelling upon British ground, 120 Emigrant Mother 5
Their cottage on a plot of rising ground 133 Michael 132
Is gone—the ploughshare has been through the ground 138 Michael 477
" Princess fair, I till the ground, but may not take 139 Arm. Lady 11
On the ground the weeping Countess 142 Arm. Lady 139

Ground—*continued.*
Each with the other, on the dewy ground, 143 *High bliss 20
At such small elevation from the ground 150 *When, to 22
Dewy night o'ershades the ground ; 163 Spinning Wheel 5
In some nook of chosen ground : 166 Wand. Jew 12
Hung—head pointing towards the ground— 171 Kitten 69
That from out the rocky ground 171 Kitten 83
Now he leaves the lower ground, 174 Waggoner 1. 34
Gained ground upon the Waggon fast, 176 Waggoner 2. 17
Chequering the ground—from rock, plant, tree, or tower. 184 Night-piece 7
To drag it to the ground ; 197 Thorn 20
A Woman seated on the ground. 199 Thorn 187
The grass—it shook upon the ground ! 200 Thorn 228
To drag it to the ground ; 200 Thorn 235
Had left imprinted on the grassy ground. 201 Hart-leap 52
Some ground not mine ; and, strong her strength above, 208 *It is no 15
Both with thy nest upon the dewy ground ? 209 *Ethereal minstrel 4
He looks on festal ground with fruits bestrown ; 213 Dion 36
That British ground commands :—low dusky tracts, 219 *This Height 5
The flowery ground is conscious. But no wind 219 Haunted Tree 30
The infection of the ground partakes, 223 Wishing-gate 34
Blest is that ground, where, o'er the springs 224 *'Tis gone 13
Up from their native ground they rise 228 Devot. Incit. 5
And ground fresh-cloven by the plough 228 Devot. Incit. 62
While Fauns and Satyrs beat the ground 234 Power of Sound 150
A little field of meadow ground ; 240 P. B. 367
Some twenty fathoms under ground. 245 P. B. 840
The Woman rises from the ground— 248 P. B. 1057
Within the Sonnet's scanty plot of ground ; 250 *Nuns fret 11
On favoured ground, thy gift, where I might dwell 251 Appleth. 3
But all the steps and ground about were strown 257 *Methought I 4
Dust for oblivion ! To the solid ground 259 *A volant 5
Till she exchanged for heaven that happy ground. 267 St. Cath. 14
Whirled us o'er sunless ground beneath a sky 268 *Four fiery 2
When giants scooped from out the rocky ground, 269 Malham 2
Where holy ground begins, unhallowed ends, 271 *Where holy 1
Vouchsafed no sparrow falleth to the ground ? 273 *Wild Redbreast 10
While poring Antiquarians search the ground 275 *While poring 1
On ground yet strewn with their last battle's wreck ; 278 Wellington 2
Is then no nook of English ground secure 282 Railway 1
Well have yon Railway Labourers to THIS ground 283 *Well have 1
The dewy ground was dark and cold ; 289 Stepping West. 9
But the ground lay within that ring 298 Brownie's Cell 45
Even by the *Living*, under ground ; 301 Bran 67
Of Terror, bear us to the ground, and tie 309 *What if 5
On British ground the Invaders are laid low ; 310 Anticip. 2
A Roman Master stands on Grecian ground, 312 *A Roman 1
Advance—come forth from thy Tyrolean ground, 314 *Advance—come 1
The ground beneath thee with volcanic force : 316 *Hail, Zaragoza 11
Which should extend thy branches on the ground, 319 Guernica 10
As if the streets were consecrated ground, 334 *The Spirit 9
And horror breathing from the silent ground ! 335 *A wingèd 14
Strains that call forth upon empyreal ground 335 Cologne 12
Success and failure, could a ground 337 *Oh Life 3
Sung from that heavenly ground in middle air, 338 Engelberg 12
The Helvetian Mountaineers, on ground 342 Ital. Itin. 59
But heath-bells from thy native ground, 345 *How blest 71
And murmur sweet songs on the ground of their birth ! 345 Stanzas:Simplon 8
We parted upon solemn ground 348 *Lulled by 37
Such ground I from my very heart enjoy ! 349 Boulogne 14
In heart as dull in brain—while pacing ground 356 Aquap. 270
Checked not its rage ; unfelt the ground did rock, 361 *When here 3
Or warning serve, thus let them all, on ground 361 *When here 13
Embellishing the ground that gave them birth 361 *List—'twas 12
Meet on the solid ground of waking life. 364 *What aim 14
And, while she raised her from the ground, 371 Eg. Maid 142
Ere on firm ground the car alighted ; 372 Eg. Maid 194
Of Christian rites, in Christian ground to lay her." 372 Eg. Maid 240
The ground where we were born and reared ! 375 *The Minstrels 54
Peculiar ground for hope to build upon. 376 Duddon 3. 8
Free entrance to the churchyard ground— 396 White Doe 54
Which two spears' length of level ground 398 White Doe 171
Be parted from his ancient ground : 402 White Doe 553
And so will keep the appointed ground 404 White Doe 727
Of rising ground, yon heathy spot ! 404 White Doe 763
While ground was left for hope ; unblamed 406 White Doe 911
Her way into forbidden ground ; 407 White Doe 982
Far under ground is many a cave, 408 White Doe 1096
High on a point of rugged ground 409 White Doe 1163
A Spearman brought him to the ground. 412 White Doe 1486
In holy ground a grave would make ; 412 White Doe 1521
Of kindred for him in that ground : 413 White Doe 1530
Upon the ground received the rest,— 413 White Doe 1548
That nook where, on paternal ground, 414 White Doe 1688
All now was trouble-haunted ground ; 414 White Doe 1701
The enclosure of this churchyard ground ; 416 White Doe 1882
As oft, 'mid some green plot of open ground, 425 Ecc. Sonn. 1. 27. 12
Deplorable his lot who tills the ground, 429 Ecc. Sonn. 2. 4. 1
Springs from the ground the morn to gratulate ; 432 Ecc. Sonn. 2. 14. 2
Rejoicing did they cast upon the ground 436 Ecc. Sonn. 2. 33. 4
And hallowed ground in which their fathers lay ; 443 Ecc. Sonn. 3. 13. 4
The encircling ground, in native turf arrayed, 450 Ecc. Sonn. 3. 41. 1
On ground which British shepherds tread ! 457 *Had this 40
Hath slept since noon-tide on the grassy ground, 458 *Had this 56
At whose behest uprose on British ground 477 Long Meg 11
And holier seems the ground 478 Somnamb. 6
In plunged the Knight !—when on firm ground 479 Somnamb. 136
To pace the ground, if path be there or none, 480 *Most sweet 2

Grove—*continued.*
There are to whom the garden, grove, and field, . 501 *Humanity* 105
A church in every grove that spreads . . . . 506 *Lab. Hymn* 19
The choristers in every grove had stilled ; . . . 523 *Epist. Beaumont* 155
Sky streaked with purple, grove and craggy *bield*, 524 *Epist. Beaumont* 175
Or some deep chestnut grove, oft have I paused . 537 **In desultory* 2
A laurel in the grove. . . . . 543 *Russ. Fug.* 184
Tall were the flowers, the grove a lofty cover, . 557 *Cuck. and Night.* 64
Sheltered, and flourish in a little grove . . . 568 *Cumb. Beg.* 121
That neighbourhood of grove and field . . . 580 **Sweet Flower* 64
There was a time when meadow, grove, and stream, 587 *Immortality* 1
Emerging slow from Academus' grove . . . . 618 *School Ex.* 13
Shall be my harbour ? underneath what grove . 632 *Prelude* 1. 11
And in the sheltered and the sheltering grove . 633 *Prelude* 1. 69
Save when, amid the stately grove of oaks, . . 633 *Prelude* 1. 82
A grove, with gleams of water through the trees . 644 *Prelude* 2. 158
Extended high above a dusky grove. . . . . 649 *Prelude* 3. 6
Its own protection ; a primeval grove, ... 655 *Prelude* 3. 430
A blackbird's whistle in a budding grove. . . . 686 *Prelude* 6. 760
Upon this morning, and my favourite grove, . . 687 *Prelude* 7. 44
The younger brethren of the grove. But some— 695 *Prelude* 7. 522
Maturer years. A grove there is whose boughs . 706 *Prelude* 8. 458
Laden from blooming grove or flowery field, . . 733 *Prelude* 11. 446
Palace or grove, even so could I unsoul . . 735 *Prelude* 12. 83
While in a grove I walk, whose lofty trees, . . 739 *Prelude* 12. 329
Upon that open moorland stood a grove, . . . 756 *Excursion* 1. 26
And, crowned with garlands in the summer grove, 792 *Excursion* 3. 444
'That all the grove and all the day was ours.' . 794 *Excursion* 3. 549
In every grove were ringing, 'War shall cease ; . 796 *Excursion* 3. 723
(The sportive bird's companion in the grove) . . 799 *Excursion* 3. 948
With grove and field and garden interspersed ; . 811 *Excursion* 4. 691
And armèd warrior ; and in every grove . . 812 *Excursion* 4. 742
Across the lawn and through the darksome grove, 814 *Excursion* 4. 866
Rising behind a thick and lofty grove, . . . 817 *Excursion* 4. 1064
Island or grove, that hides a blessed few . . . 827 *Excursion* 5. 350
And to the grove that holds it. She beguiles . . 833 *Excursion* 5. 708
In the fair body of a leafy grove . . . . . 840 *Excursion* 6. 160
Could field or grove, could any spot of earth, . 850 *Excursion* 6. 807
In grove or pasture ; cheerfulness of soul, . . . 866 *Excursion* 7. 582
No eye can overlook, when 'mid a grove . . . 868 *Excursion* 7. 715
When grove was felled, and altar was cast down, 870 *Excursion* 7. 814
Devoured with keenness ere to grove or bank . K.8. 245 *Recluse* 1.1.333
Behold a dusky spot, a grove of Firs, ... K.8. 247 *Recluse* 1.1.385
That seems still smaller than it is. This grove . K.8. 247 *Recluse* 1.1.386
Did plant the grove, now flourishing, while they . K.8. 248 *Recluse* 1.1.421
Upon one tree, while all the distant grove . . . K.8. 252 *Recluse* 1.1.567
Grovelled. Who neither grovelled nor aspired : . . 298 *Brownie's Cell* 26
Groveller. And let the groveller sip his stagnant pool, 277 **A Poet* 6
Grovelling. Or grovelling thought, to seek a refuge here ; . . . . 451 *Ecc. Sonn.* 3. 45. 3
Perish the grovelling few, who, prest between . 516 **Hard task* 4
The grovelling mind, the erring to recall, . . . 519 *Pun. Death* 9. 13
" If, with the froward will and grovelling soul . 806 *Excursion* 4. 375
Grovels. With him who grovels, self-debarred . . 534 **Blest is* 66
Groves. *See* **Palm-groves.**
'Mid groves of clouds that crest the mountain's brow, ... 7 *Ev. Wk.* 289
Of Como, bosomed deep in chestnut groves. . . 12 *Desc. Sk.* 78
Far o'er the water, hung with groves of beech ; . 14 *Desc. Sk.* 231
Lo ! where through flat Batavia's willowy groves, 19 *Desc. Sk.* 520
That babbled on through groves and meadows green ; . . . . 34 *Guilt* 517
The dripping groves resound with cheerful lays, . 34 *Guilt* 519
Are vanished ; gladness ceases in the groves, . . 105 *Artegal* 200
The budding groves seemed eager to urge on . . 146 **It was an* 9
And make dear friendships with the streams and groves. . . . . 147 *Joanna* 8
Now sleeping in these peaceful groves. . . . . 186 **O Nightingale* 10
With songs the budded groves resounding ; . . . 191 *Seq. Beggars* 26
That is in the green leaves among the groves, . 203 *Hart-leap* 166
The Boy must part from Mosedale's groves, . . 204 *Brougham* 89
'Mid groves and copses. Once again I see . . 206 *Tintern* 14
Mourn, hills and groves of Attica ! and mourn . 213 *Dion* 42
Lawns, houses, chattels, groves, and fields, . . 214 *Kirkstone* 27
Pours forth in shady groves, shall plead for me ; . 217 *Enterprise* 146
Than fairest spiritual creature of the groves, . . 219 *Haunted Tree* 17
To be descried through shady groves. . . . . 222 *Triad* 190
Through fresh green fields, and budding groves among, ... 229 *Cuckoo-clock* 19
With groves that never were imagined, lay . . 262 **Dark and* 10
Gardens and groves ! your presence overpowers . 270 **Ye sacred* 7
Fame tells of groves—from England far away— . 271 **Fame tells* 1
Groves that inspire the Nightingale to trill . . 271 **Fame tells* 2
Rich groves of lofty stature, ... 302 *Yarrow V.* 50
And, rising from those lofty groves, ... 302 *Yarrow V.* 53
In Yarrow's groves were centred ; . . . . . 386 *Yarrow Rev.* 98
Of Swains reposing myrtle groves among ! . . 389 *Tyndrum* 3
And, ranging through the wasted groves, . . . 415 *White Doe* 1753
Trembled the groves, the stars grew pale, . . . 499 **Departing summer* 34
Though, in the depths of sunless groves, no more 500 *Humanity* 7
Their own mysterious groves. . . . . . . 506 **While from* 32
High-born Augusta ! Witness, Towers and Groves ! 539 **Lady ! a* 22
These groves have heard the Other's pensive strains ; 546 **The embowering* 6
Within these groves, where still are flitting by . 584 **With copious* 50
Through groves that had begun to shed . . . 586 *Hogg* 6
And O, ye Fountains, Meadows, Hills, and Groves, 590 *Immortality* 191
Where rocks and groves the power of waters shakes 602 *Desc. Sk. Quarto* 11
The cots, those dim religious groves embow'r, . 604 *Desc.Sk.Quarto* 124

Groves—*continued.*
Or where thick sails illume Batavia's groves ; . . 613 *Desc.Sk.Quarto* 625
And glowed the sun-gilt groves in richer gold : . 616 *Desc.Sk.Quarto* 773
No more, along thy vales and viny groves, . . 617 *Desc.Sk.Quarto* 788
'Mid groves Idalian, lull'd to gentle sleep, . . . 624 *Æneid* 32
That drive her as in trouble through the groves ; 634 *Prelude* 1. 143
Within the groves of Chivalry, I pipe . . . . 634 *Prelude* 1. 171
That Nature breathes among the hills and groves. 636 *Prelude* 1. 281
The sandy fields, leaping through flowery groves . 636 *Prelude* 1. 293
My comrades, leave the crowd, buildings and groves, 650 *Prelude* 3. 92
Should spread from heart to heart ; and stately groves, ... 654 *Prelude* 3. 380
Of exultation echoed through the groves ! . . . 674 *Prelude* 5. 578
Did I by night frequent the College groves . . 676 *Prelude* 6. 67
And groves I speak to thee, my Friend ! to thee, 679 *Prelude* 6. 265
Upon the open lawns ! Vallombre's groves . . 682 *Prelude* 6. 480
Of your green groves, and wilderness of lamps . 689 *Prelude* 7. 122
Rocks, dens, and groves of foliage taught to melt 700 *Prelude* 8. 88
Of level pasture, islanded with groves . . . . 702 *Prelude* 8. 191
Than the gay Corin of the groves, who lives . . 703 *Prelude* 8. 285
Oh, sweet it is, in academic groves, ... 715 *Prelude* 9. 390
And you, ye groves, whose ministry it is . . . 734 *Prelude* 12. 24
Sing notes of greeting to strange fields or groves, 742 *Prelude* 13. 135
An hourly neighbour. Paradise, and groves . . 755 *Recluse* 1. 1. 800
Must hear Humanity in fields and groves . . . 755 *Recluse* 1. 1. 829
Lamenting the departed, call the groves, . . . 763 *Excursion* 1. 476
From academic groves, that have for thee . . 787 *Excursion* 3. 105
With world-excluding groves, the brotherhood . 791 *Excursion* 3. 347
I left not uninvoked ; and, in still groves, . . 797 *Excursion* 3. 753
And shady groves in studied contrast—each, . . 810 *Excursion* 4. 591
Or through the groves gliding like morning mist . 810 *Excursion* 4. 637
And filled the illumined groves with ravishment. . 814 *Excursion* 4. 860
As if, amid these peaceful hills and groves, . . 837 *Excursion* 5. 973
Amid the groves, under the shadowy hills, . . 846 *Excursion* 6. 553
Wild tracts of forest-ground, and scattered groves, 891 *Excursion* 9. 505
Grow. Where Souls are self-defended, free to grow 57 *Bord.* 1115
Your faculties should grow with the demand ; . . 64 *Bord.* 1498
So be it when I shall grow old, ... 79 **My heart* 5
Was known as well as to the flowers that grow there. 99 *Brothers* 276
If e'er he should grow rich, he would return, . . 100 *Brothers* 323
Ere it wither and grow pale." . . . . . . 139 *Arm. Lady* 10
Rise up, and grow to wondrous height. . . . 173 *Waggoner* 1. 14
An Orpheus ! an Orpheus ! yes, Faith may grow bold, ... 188 *Music* 1
(Misdeem it not a cankerous change) may grow . 267 **DespondingFather* 11
For I, methinks, till I grow old, ... 288 *Highland Girl* 74
True Power doth grow on ; and her rights are these. . . . . 304 **I grieved* 14
Who, gathering true pleasures wherever they grow, 365 *Vallomb.* 38
Watching, with upward eye, the tall tower grow . 451 *Ecc. Sonn.* 3. 42. 7
So, like the Mountain, may we grow more bright 452 *Ecc. Sonn.* 3. 46. 12
Though brain would swim, and eyes grow dim, . 478 *Somnamb.* 57
Or surely you'll grow double : . . . . . . 481 *Tables Turned* 2
Our pastime and our happiness will grow. . . . 488 *Pers. Talk* 36
By discipline endeavour to grow meek . . . . 500 *Humanity* 53
As leaves are to the tree whereon they grow . . 516 **As leaves* 1
Grow weary of attending on a track . . . . 694 *Prelude* 7. 504
And wise men, willing to grow wiser, caught, . . 695 *Prelude* 7. 516
But, for such purpose, flowers no longer grow : . 701 *Prelude* 8. 157
If from the affliction somewhere do not grow . 725 *Prelude* 10. 466
Grow into consequence, till round my mind . . 730 *Prelude* 11. 220
As we grow up, such thraldom of that sense . . 736 *Prelude* 12. 150
Grow larger in the darkness ; all alone . . . 758 *Excursion* 1. 128
And grow with thought. Beside yon spring I stood, 763 *Excursion* 1. 484
Growing. The fittest place ? He is growing pitiful. 51 *Bord.* 750
For daily with my growing store . . . . . 115 *Last of Flock* 83
And Susan's growing worse and worse, ... 128 *Idiot Boy* 167
The grass you almost hear it growing, ... 129 *Idiot Boy* 285
Housed near the growing Primrose-tuft . . . 169 *Wren's Nest* 71
Was growing inwardly more strong ; . . . . 175 *Waggoner* 1. 149
Power in my breast, wings growing in my mind, . 284 *Departure* 14
But we will leave it growing. . . . . . . 293 *Yarrow Unv.* 36
From beauty infinitely growing . . . . . . 301 *Bran* 115
Flowers we espy beside the torrent growing ; . . 337 *Aar* 5
Vague minds, while men are growing out of boys ; 382 *Duddon* 26. 12
In vain, upon the growing Rill may gaze. . . 419 *Ecc. Sonn.* 1. 5. 14
Or sacred wonder, growing with the power . . 510 **Among a* 25
Upon the growing Boy, ... 588 *Immortality* 68
I gazed with growing love, a higher power . . 633 *Prelude* 1. 77
And growing still in stature the grim shape . . 637 *Prelude* 1. 381
That through the growing faculties of sense . . 646 *Prelude* 2. 256
With growing faculties she doth aspire, . . . 646 *Prelude* 2. 319
With faculties still growing, feeling still . . 646 *Prelude* 2. 320
And growing girls whose beauty, filched away . 661 *Prelude* 4. 206
From touch of growing grass, that may not taste 669 *Prelude* 5. 243
On that delightful time of growing youth . . . 673 *Prelude* 5. 539
Power growing under weight : alas ! I feel . . 707 *Prelude* 8. 555
Under a growing weight of vulgar sense, . . . 748 *Prelude* 14. 159
Such was the Boy—but for the growing Youth . 759 *Excursion* 1. 197
And yet a growing prospect in the main. . . . K.8. 250 *Recluse* 1.1.490
Growl. The thunder had begun to growl— . . . 175 *Waggoner* 1. 152
He heard the monitory growl ; . . . . . . 178 *Waggoner* 2. 154
What must he do but growl and snarl, ... 179 *Waggoner* 3. 102
Insidiously, untimely thunders growl ; . . . . 263 *Storm* 5
Growled. Air blackened, thunder growled, fire flashed from clouds that hid the sky, . 91 *Poet's Dream* 3
Growling. Quits, growling, the white bones that strew his lair ; . . . . 606 *Desc.Sk.Quarto* 232
Growls. And growls as if he would fix his claws . 81 †*Address : Child* 29
There hang in fear, when growls the frozen stream, 607 *Desc.Sk.Quarto* 315

Grown. *See* **Full-grown, Grass-grown, Green-grown, Moss-grown, Woman-grown.**
Full oft the father, when his sons have grown — 19 *Desc. Sk.* 512
When he should give her up, a Woman grown, — 56 *Bord.* 1054
A healthy man, a man full grown, — 114 *Last of Flock* 3
And petty quarrels, had grown fond again ; — 122 *V. and J.* 22
Out of its head an Oak had grown, — 156 *Oak and Broom* 13
Reclining on this moss grown bar, — 223 *Wishing-gate* 32
Whate'er thy fate, those features have not grown — 276 *Author's Portrait* 9
On the remorseless hearts of men grown old — 325 *Enghien* 4
The struggling Rill insensibly is grown — 378 *Duddon* 9. 1
You with my Father have grown old — 408 *White Doe* 1083
Who with her Father had grown old — 409 *White Doe* 1202
Adieu, Rydalian Laurels ! that have grown — 463 **Adieu, Rydalian* 1
And I, grown old, but in a happier land, — 510 *F. Stone* 121
As well we knew, together had grown grey. — 523 *Epist. Beaumont* 132
Among whose happy fields I had grown up — 725 *Prelude* 10. 525
That from the cradle had grown up with me, — 729 *Prelude* 11. 170
That it had sprung self-raised from earth, or grown — 855 *Excursion* 6. 1144
Or rather seemed to have grown into the side — 871 *Excursion* 7. 915

Grown-up. Your grown-up and your baby brother ; — 143 †*Lov. and Lik.* 56

Grows. Dear and more dear the lessening circle grows ; — 19 *Desc. Sk.* 479
From human care, or grows upon the breast of earth. — 102 *Artegal* 32
My long-frozen heart grows warm ! " — 140 *Arm. Lady* 38
Her bosom heaves and spreads, her stature grows ; — 209 *Laod.* 11
Grows but to perish, and entrust — 227 *Vernal Ode* 54
The path grows dim, and dimmer still ; — 240 *P. B.* 351
The cry grows weak—and weaker still ; — 244 *P. B.* 669
Are seldom free to touch the moss that grows — 262 **Mark the* 5
Grows from a little edge of light — 369 *Eg. Maid* 9
Grows sad as night—no seemly garb is worn, — 427 *Ecc. Sonn* 1. 36. 7
What flower in meadow-ground or garden grows — 432 *Ecc. Sonn.* 2. 15. 3
Grows green, and is cut down and withereth — 448 *Ecc. Sonn.* 3. 31. 10
No perfect cure grows on that bounded field. — 455 **Not in the lucid* 25
Might here be moved, till Fancy grows so strong — 455 *Rydal Mere* 14
Is in the grass beneath, that grows — 499 **This Lawn* 16
Sung as the light of day grows dim : — 506 *Lab. Hymn* 4
The golden harvest grows in ; and those eyes, — 508 *F. Stone* 31
Of bliss that grows without a care, — 530 *Gleaner* 8
Whence oft great sickness grows of heart and home ; — 557 *Cuck. and Night.* 32
" It grows upon its native bed — 580 *John Words.* 53
Still blackens and grows on his view. — 621 *Convict* 24
Dust as we are, the immortal spirit grows — 637 *Prelude* 1. 340
Knowing that he grows wiser every day — 670 *Prelude* 5. 324
Grows tedious even in a young man's ear. — 694 *Prelude* 7. 511
While man grows old, and dwindles, and decays ; — 812 *Excursion* 4. 760
" So fails, so languishes, grows dim, and dies," — 872 *Excursion* 7. 976
How pleased he is where thin and thinner grows — K.8. 249 *Recluse* 1.1.478

Growth. That common growth of earth, the foodful ear ; — 15 *Desc. Sk.* 257
Of scarcely seven years' growth, beneath the Elm — 39 *Bord.* 90
Which, while I listened, seemed like the wild growth — 146 **It was an* 28
But a thick umbrage—checking the wild growth — 149 *M. H.* 3
That fosters growth or checks or cheers decay, — 169 **Never enlivened* 2
Had aught of sylvan growth been there), — 175 *Waggoner* 1. 186
Huge trunks ! and each particular trunk a growth — 185 *Yew-trees* 16
A constant interchange of growth and blight ! — 212 *Laod.* 174
Welcomed wisely ; though a growth — 222 *Triad* 208
And life be one perpetual growth — 224 **'Tis gone* 53
The common growth of mother-earth — 238 *P. B.* 133
May learn, if judgment strengthen with his growth, — 275 **Chatsworth! thy* 11
Were England's native growth ; and throughout Spain — 319 **Avaunt all* 10
And a perpetual growth secure — 373 *Eg. Maid* 262
Yet, while they strangle, a fair growth they bring, — 424 *Ecc. Sonn.* 1. 21. 13
Whence thickly-sprouting growth of poisonous weeds ; — 438 *Ecc. Sonn.* 2. 37. 10
A Growth from sinful Nature's bed of weeds !— — 445 *Ecc. Sonn.* 3. 20. 4
Which a fine skill, of Indian growth, has wrought — 480 *Cordelia* 3
While, as one kindly growth retires, — 507 *May* 63
By monstrous theories of alien growth, — 514 **Long-favoured* 2
And simple honesty a common growth— — 515 *Penn.* 5
Hopeless of further growth, and brown and sere — 521 *Epist. Beaumont* 16
To expectations spreading with wild growth, — 532 **Once I* 11
And be not slow a stately growth to rear — 546 **Ye Lime* 3
Through every change of growth and of decay, — 646 *Prelude* 2. 264
And, worst of all, a treasonable growth — 652 *Prelude* 3. 211
So many divers samples from the growth — 652 *Prelude* 3. 221
Peasant and king ; when boys and youths, the growth — 655 *Prelude* 3. 464
In narrow cares, thy little daily growth — 659 *Prelude* 4. 35
For this unnatural growth the trainer blame, — 670 *Prelude* 5. 328
For whom it registers the birth, and marks the growth, — 679 *Prelude* 6. 261
Could through my understanding's natural growth — 730 *Prelude* 11. 200
Of vulgar nature ; that its growth requires — 742 *Prelude* 13. 189
Nourished Imagination in her growth, — 758 *Excursion* 1. 166
The growth of intellect, yet gaining more, — 760 *Excursion* 1. 303
By blast of trumpet ? ' Plenteous was the growth — 858 *Excursion* 7. 94
Than with the forest's more enduring growth, — 867 *Excursion* 7. 628
Or in dispatch of each day's little growth — 878 *Excursion* 8. 270
Or wearing, (shall we say ?) in that white growth — 879 *Excursion* 8. 350
To the prevention of all healthful growth — 889 *Excursion* 9. 365
So shall our bosoms feel a covert growth — S.3. 437 **The doubt* 203

Growths. For the still growths that prosper here ? — 154 *Flower Garden* 10
To be confounded with live growths, — 170 *Rural Ill.* 21
And humbler growths as moved with one desire — 529 *Poor Robin* 3

Growths—*continued.*
Have stopped, as some believe, the kindliest growths. — 692 *Prelude* 7. 372
With her first growths, detaching by the stroke — 788 *Excursion* 3. 181
To beautify with nature's fairest growths — 860 *Excursion* 7. 205

Grudge. The sky owes somebody a grudge ! — 176 *Waggoner* 1. 250
From mind and spirit, grudge a short-lived fence. — 280 *Plea for Auth.* 8
On the bare coast ; nor do they grudge the boon — 467 *St. Bees* 93
Know, if thou grudge not to prolong thy rest, — 548 **Stay, bold* 12

Grumbling. And, grumbling, he went back to bed ! — 129 *Idiot Boy* 261

Guard. With this " the blessings he enjoys to guard." — 18 *Desc. Sk.* 448
To guard the Innocent—he calls us " Outlaws ; " — 38 *Bord.* 63
You know, Sir, I have been too long your guard — 43 *Bord.* 315
To stand upon our guard, and with our swords — 56 *Bord.* 1028
They guard, with wingèd baby-faces. — 144 **Driven in* 57
His best resolves) be on his guard ? — 174 *Waggoner* 1. 62
Her statelier Eden's course to guard ; — 204 *Brougham* 47
Intent to guard St. Robert's cell ; — 301 *Bran* 55
And guard the way of life from all offence — 316 **Say, what* 4
To guard the fallen, and consummate the event, — 326 **Intrepid sons* 13
The treasures they enjoy to guard ! " — 342 *Ital. Itin.* 68
O Ye, who guard and grace my home — 343 *Eclipse* 67
And piety shall guard the Stone — 348 **Lulled by* 69
Where gladness seems a duty—let me guard — 354 *Aquap.* 103
And ye that guard them, Mountains old ! — 376 **The Minstrels* 60
From a bold headland, their loved aery's guard, — 388 *Eagles* 7
Verse that would guard thy memory, Hart's-horn Tree ! — 393 *Hart's-horn* 14
To guard the Standard which he bore. — 404 *White Doe* 725
Pass from their Master, sojourned here to guard — 419 *Ecc. Sonn.* 1. 2. 13
The sword from Bangor's walls, and guard the store — 421 *Ecc. Sonn.* 1. 12. 6
Subsist thy dignity to guard, — 472 *Ossian* 22
To evil for a guard against worse ill, — 493 *Hap. War.* 30
But lo ! where darkness seems to guard the mouth — 497 **Enough of climbing* 20
Whom, then, shall meekness guard ? What saving skill — 505 *Warning* 149
Their wings to guard the unconscious Innocent— — 518 *Pun. Death* 6. 5
Whom such high beauty could not guard — 542 *Russ. Fug.* 11
Fitly to guard the precious dust of him — 585 *Ch. Lamb* 42
And guard her fortresses. Who thinks, and feels, — 810 *Excursion* 4. 598
That the thorns wound her not ; they only guard. — 835 *Excursion* 5. 843
Forefathers, who, to guard against the shocks, — 837 *Excursion* 5. 998
To guard the royal brood. The sailing glead, — 868 *Excursion* 7. 751

Guarded. *See* **Nicely-guarded.**
Even so, by faithful Nature guarded, here — 18 *Desc. Sk.* 441
There, safely guarded by the woods behind, — 19 *Desc. Sk.* 488
And guarded in their tranquil state of life, — 143 **High bliss* 24
Guarded by lone San Salvador ; — 341 *San Salv.* 3
From dew-sprinkled grass to heights guarded with snow, — 345 *Stanzas : Simplon* 18
By Angels guarded, deviate from the line — 428 *Ecc. Sonn.* 2. 1. 2
And charters won and guarded by the sword — 477 **Lowther ! in* 5
There set, and guarded well ; — 478 *Somnamb.* 15
As when it guarded holy Cuthbert's cell. — 540 *Grace Darl.* 27
Ev'n so, by vestal Nature guarded, here — 611 *Desc.Sk.Quarto* 528
Was guarded from too early intercourse — 704 *Prelude* 8. 331
Guarded within the bosom of Thy will. — 724 *Prelude* 10. 432
Livelier, and flinging out less guarded words — 731 *Prelude* 11. 284
The unguarded taper where the guarded faints ? — 813 *Excursion* 4. 773
Now simply guarded by the sober powers — 815 *Excursion* 4. 917
Lies guarded by its neighbour ; the small heap — 850 *Excursion* 6. 790
Guarded and graced, seemed fashioned to unite, — 881 *Excursion* 8. 456

Guardian. And belike a guardian angel — 93 *Westmoreland Girl* 23
I was their natural guardian ; and 'tis just — 104 *Artegal* 136
Yet, where the guardian fence is wound, — 154 *Flower Garden* 25
When withered is the guardian Flower, — 169 *Wren's Nest* 67
And with them goes the guardian pair. — 178 *Waggoner* 3. 21
The guide, the guardian of my heart, and soul — 207 *Tintern* 110
Wrest from the guardian Monster of the tomb — 210 *Laod.* 80
The lovely Cottage in the guardian nook — 250 *Admon.* 2
Till oft her guardian Angel, to some charge — 273 **While Anna's* 6
That still invests the guardian Pass, — 300 *Cora Linn* 40
I, the Guardian of this Land, — 323 *Ode1814* 33
And be the guardian spaces — 324 *Ode 1814* 100
Majestic Berne, high on her guardian steep, — 339 *Schwytz* 9
Saints would not grieve nor guardian angels frown — 354 *Aquap.* 118
Smooth space of turf which from the guardian fort — 356 *Aquap.* 224
Was on his right, from that guardian hand — 403 *White Doe* 657
The guardian lance, as Francis fell, — 412 *White Doe* 1487
Infinity's embrace ; whose guardian crest, — 452 *Ecc. Sonn.* 3. 45. 10
A guardian Spirit sent from pitying Heaven, — 541 *Grace Darl.* 73
And oft, as either Guardian came, — 544 *Russ. Fug.* 217
A Guardian Angel fluttered — 628 *Installation* 31
Stationed above the door, like guardian saints ; — 689 *Prelude* 7. 162
Thirsting to make the guardian crook of law — 728 *Prelude* 11. 64
Rule and restraint—my guardian—shall I say — 794 *Excursion* 3. 564
And guardian of their course, that never closed — 811 *Excursion* 4. 698
And guardian rocks !—Farewell, attractive seat ! — 822 *Excursion* 5. 3
From some staid guardian of the public peace, — 859 *Excursion* 7. 102
A guardian planted to fence off the blast, — 866 *Excursion* 7. 613
And the sole guardian in whose hands we dare — 886 *Excursion* 9. 125
In tasks which guardian Angels might approve, — S.3. 426 **Through Cumbrian* 4

Guardians. Guardians of Biscay's ancient liberty. — 319 *Guernica* 14
Whose Guardians bent the knee to Jove and Mars : — 380 *Duddon* 17. 11
Who teach the intrepid guardians of the place— — 430 *Ecc. Sonn.* 2. 6. 10
Heavenly Guardians, brooding near, — 502 **Like a* 34
Are guardians of their own tranquillity. — 806 *Excursion* 4. 322

Guardianship. Committed to thy guardianship by Heaven; — 76 *Bord.* 2199
Ground-flowers, beneath your guardianship, self-sown. — 463 **Adieu, Rydalian* 8
Your guardianship; I take it to my heart; — 622 *Recluse* 1. 1. 112
Less, as might seem, for general guardianship — 807 *Excursion* 4. 441
In his own valley's rocky guardianship. — 829 *Excursion* 5. 451
To ensure for it respectful guardianship. — 846 *Excursion* 6. 509

Guarding. If, guarding grossest things from common claim — 280 *Plea for Auth.* 6

Guards. Thine arm from peril guards the coasts — 328 *Ode 1815* 110
That guards the Temple night and day; — 343 *Eclipse* 44
That guards the lowliest of the poor. — 375 **The Minstrels* 36
She guards thee, ruthless Power! who would not spare — 376 *Duddon* 2. 9
Guards the sacred heart of youth, — 629 *Installation* 75
Of courtiers, banners, and a length of guards; — 693 *Prelude* 7. 419
With Guards and Uhlans run along the Rhine, — L.1. 97 *Juvenal* 3. 64

Guendolen. By Guendolen against her faithless lord; — 103 *Artegal* 34

Guerdon. Yet a rich guerdon waits on minds that dare, — 261 **From the dark* 7
The guerdon of the steadiest aim. — 342 *Ital. Itin.* 62
For their high guerdon not in vain have panted! — 430 *Ecc. Sonn.* 2. 8. 14
For which I ask for guerdon but one boon, — 563 *Troilus* 76

Guerdons. Rich guerdons, and to them alone are due. — 22 *Desc. Sk.* 651

Guernica. Oak of Guernica! Tree of holier power — 319 *Guernica* 1

Guess. To pull the cord. I guess he must have heard it; — 73 *Bord.* 2058
He knows it not, he cannot guess: — 117 *Affl. Marg.* 26
For what she ails they cannot guess. — 126 *Idiot Boy* 26
But yet I guess that now and then — 127 *Idiot Boy* 137
Joanna! and I guess, since you have been — 147 *Joanna* 12
Nor seldom, if I rightly guess, while Thou, — 151 **When, to* 98
He was a lovely Youth! I guess — 192 *Ruth* 37
Nor can he guess how lightly leaps — 215 *Kirkstone* 75
The tear whose source I could not guess, — 225 *Present.* 7
Advancing, you might guess an hour, — 543 *Russ. Fug.* 137
So that, I guess, the linnet and the thrush, — 548 **Stranger! this* 18
Men said, what may it be, can no one guess — 564 *Troilus* 102
You lift up your eyes!—but I guess that you frame — 570 *Farmer* 41
And you guess that the more then his body must stir. — 570 *Farmer* 60
Can guess the high resolve, the cherish'd pain — 608 *Desc.Sk.Quarto* 360
Have felt, and every man alive can guess? — 659 *Prelude* 4. 45
I guess not what this tells of Being past, — 673 *Prelude* 5. 510
I guess that, welcome to your lonely hearth, — 807 *Excursion* 4. 385
Awhile they stood in conference, and I guess — 829 *Excursion* 5. 446
Have been portrayed, I guess not; but it chanced — 865 *Excursion* 7. 540
Nor could he guess the cause for which the boy — K.8. 229 **I will* 162
Their safe retreat. We knew them well, I guess. — K.8. 243 *Recluse* 1.1.246

Guessed. You have guessed right. The trees renew their murmur: — 53 *Bord.* 868
And thus, from what I heard and knew, or guessed, — 120 *Emigrant Mother* 13
And there's a riddle to be guessed, — 143 **Driven in* 22
I've guessed, when I've been sitting in the sun, — 203 *Hart-leap* 139
And no one could have guessed his aim,— — 247 *P. B.* 993
But fond companions, so I guessed, in field, — 882 *Excursion* 8. 548

Guesses. And guesses their intent. — 297 *Highland Boy* 200

Guessing. A stranger passed; and, guessing whom I sought, — 767 *Excursion* 1. 732

Guest. *See* **Fellow-guest.**
Housed for the night, or but a half-hour's guest. — 21 *Desc. Sk.* 611
I thought of times when Pain might be thy guest, — 88 *H. C.* 15
But enters as a looked-for guest, — 143 **Driven in* 5
One have I marked, the happiest guest — 159 *Green Linnet* 9
This Flower, that first appeared as summer's guest, — 169 **Never enlivened* 4
"Avaunt, inexplicable Guest!—avaunt," — 213 *Dion* 81
Like an unbidden guest. Though day by day — 264 *Snowdrop* 4
The peaceful guest advancing from afar. — 327 *Ode 1815* 51
The humid precipice, and seize the guest — 381 *Duddon* 22. 9
Lonsdale! it were unworthy of a Guest, — 477 **Lonsdale! it* 1
And there was Sorrow's guest; — 479 *Somnamb.* 148
Then welcome, above all, the Guest — 497 *Lycoris* 45
With a new visitant, an infant guest— — 503 *Warning* 38
And every man sit down as Plenty's Guest! — 505 *Warning* 128
Where Fear is but a transient guest, — 526 **The soaring* 19
And there, 'mid many a noble guest, — 545 *Russ. Fug.* 371
By stealthy entrance of a perilous guest, — 625 *Æneid* 93
"But nay—the fatal wiles, O guest, recount, — 625 *Æneid* 139
I only, like an uninvited guest — 722 *Prelude* 10. 297

Guests. That nod to welcome transient guests; — 154 *Flower Garden* 40
Were in this place the guests of Chance: — 289 *Stepping West.* 5
Like guests that meet, and some from far, — 385 *Yarrow Rev.* 31
Where Fancy entertains becoming guests; — 388 *Loch Etive* 7
Guests welcome almost as the angels were — 681 *Prelude* 6. 396
In condescension among rural guests. — 859 *Excursion* 7. 127
His guests, and make them jocund. They are pleased, — K.8. 241 *Recluse* 1.1.192

Guidance. From the true guidance of humanity, — 361 **When here* 10
Meanwhile, for further guidance, look — 370 *Eg. Maid* 111
Emboldened by thy guidance, holy Star, — 392 **Though joy* 9
Sure guidance, ere a ceremonial fence — 436 *Ecc. Sonn.* 2. 30. 7
Unto thy guidance from this hour; — 492 *Duty* 51
And guidance have I sought in duteous love — 520 *Pun. Death* 14. 10
For the State's guidance, or the Church's weal, — 587 *Crosth.* 8
But for her guidance—one who was to *act*, — 707 *Prelude* 8. 522
Thy guidance, or a greater Muse, if such — 755 *Recluse* 1. 1. 779
Following the guidance of these welcome feet — 793 *Excursion* 3. 500
Its guidance; but the infallible support — 798 *Excursion* 3. 864
In furnishing clear guidance, a support — 820 *Excursion* 4. 1262
Of safest guidance or of firmest trust— — 827 *Excursion* 5. 335
On what, for guidance in the way that leads — 835 *Excursion* 5. 825

Guide. Descend we now, the maddened Reuss our guide; — 14 *Desc. Sk.* 197
Good morrow, Strangers! If you want a Guide, — 41 *Bord.* 213
I'll point him out;—a Maiden is his guide, — 45 *Bord.* 454
He had a Guide, a Shepherd's boy; but grieved — 49 *Bord.* 688
And said, with tears, that he would be our guide: — 62 *Bord.* 1367
I had a better guide—that innocent Babe— — 62 *Bord.* 1368
And was his guide; if once, why not again, — 62 *Bord.* 1395
That Chapel-bell in mercy seemed to guide me, — 67 *Bord.* 1651
I was too fearful—take me for your guide — 67 *Bord.* 1675
The best and kindest!—but where is he? guide me, — 73 *Bord.* 2052
The Spectre of that innocent Man, my guide. — 78 *Bord.* 2345
To serve them for a guide. — 83 *Lucy Gray* 36
Mother's care no more her guide, — 93 *Westmoreland Girl* 30
But neither Doctor nor his Guide — 128 *Idiot Boy* 173
There's neither Doctor nor his Guide. — 128 *Idiot Boy* 221
To guide your speech and your affections. — 142 †*Lov. and Lik.* 4
Our heavenward guide is holy love, — 143 †*Lov. and Lik.* 67
And I will always be thy guide, — 145 *Her Eyes* 53
Lift me, guide me, till I find — 159 **Up with me* 6
Lift me, guide me, high and high — 159 **Up with me* 14
He paces on, a trusty Guide,— — 174 *Waggoner* 1. 31
In part, the offences of their guide) — 178 *Waggoner* 3. 11
With murmuring Greta for her guide. — 180 *Waggoner* 4. 17
It lingered on;—guide after guide — 182 *Waggoner* 4. 189
With tools for ready wit to guide; — 191 *Seq. Beggars* 5
The guide, the guardian of my heart, and soul — 207 *Tintern* 110
"Protesiláus, lo! thy guide is gone!" — 210 *Laod.* 31
When thou shalt be my guide: — 215 *Kirkstone* 52
Who, with a sunbeam for her guide, — 215 *Kirkstone* 81
From these wild rocks thy footsteps I will guide — 222 *Triad* 216
If like ambition be *their* guide. — 228 *Devot. Incit.* 12
He left a trusty guide for one — 240 *P. B.* 339
Is reached; but there the trusty guide — 243 *P. B.* 608
Yet Nature seems to them a heavenly guide. — 278 **Life with* 2
By Thee to guide thy Pupils on the road — 281 *Chris. Words.* 3
Shall guide, his fancy cheer, your way; — 287 *Sons of Burns* 38
Too false to guide us or control! — 291 *Rob Roy* 26
Without a better guide. — 295 *Highland Boy* 40
Guide our Bark among the waves; — 336 **Jesu! bless* 19
Heaven prosper thee, be hope thy guide! — 341 *Ital. Itin.* 2
Hope be thy guide, adventurous Boy; — 341 *Ital. Itin.* 3
Hope be thy guide, adventurous Boy; — 341 *Ital. Itin.* 17
To her purblind guide Expediency; and so — 357 *Aquap.* 336
Light which to God is both the way and guide; — 365 **Rapt above* 11
The Bard who walks with Duddon for his guide, — 379 *Duddon* 12. 11
I thought of Thee, my partner and my guide, — 384 *Duddon* 34. 1
And guide the Bard, ambitious to be One — 389 *Tyndrum* 10
The invisible God, and take for guide — 407 *White Doe* 1040
May guide them in a prudent flight!" — 408 *White Doe* 1118
Their guide in flight—already she — 408 *White Doe* 1124
Blest Pilgrims, surely, as they took for guide — 443 *Ecc. Sonn.* 3. 13. 10
Who cast not off the acknowledged guide, — 473 *Ossian* 55
But he finds neither guide-post nor guide. — 484 **A plague* 20
Who art a light to guide, a rod — 492 *Duty* 3
Yet being to myself a guide, — 492 *Duty* 27
Let me, thy happy guide, now point thy way, — 496 **A little* 23
By that other Guide, whose light — 503 **Like a* 70
And to your wrath cry out, "Be thou our guide;" — 505 *Warning* 120
Guide, from thy love's abundant source, — 506 *Lab. Hymn* 27
Who promptly undertook the Wain to guide — 522 *Epist. Beaumont* 102
Will guide me in my forward path; — 542 *Russ. Fug.* 71
To be our guide unto thy Son so dear. — 553 *Prioress* 28
Guide thou my song which I of thee shall say. — 553 *Prioress* 35
And up to yonder hill was I her guide; — 564 *Troilus* 92
With thy bright beams to guide me but one hour, — 564 *Troilus* 125
Could hear to guide them in their choice — 577 **By playful* 18
Thou drooping sick Man, bless the Guide — 577 **I come* 41
To govern and to guide: — 579 **Sweet Flower* 10
The Ettrick Shepherd was my guide. — 586 *Hogg* 4
To guide his dangerous tread the taper's gleam. — 607 *Desc.Sk.Quarto* 316
"Here Penury oft from misery's mount will guide — 613 *Desc.Sk.Quarto* 598
Secure she walks, Philosophy her guide. — 619 *School Ex.* 52
Nor less to guide the fluctuating youth — 619 *School Ex.* 77
But Cupid, following cheerily his guide — 624 *Æneid* 53
Guide hither, O sweet Moon, the maid I love so well. — 630 [?] **O Moon* 15
I look about; and should the chosen guide — 632 *Prelude* 1. 16
Much I rejoiced, not doubting but a guide — 667 *Prelude* 5. 81
Ships he can guide across the pathless sea, — 670 *Prelude* 5. 316
Their noon-tide meal. Hastily rose our guide, — 683 *Prelude* 6. 566
To rule and guide his captivated flock. — 695 *Prelude* 7. 572
Those slender cords, to guide the unconscious Boy — 706 *Prelude* 8. 455
For way and guide, a fluent receptacle — 720 *Prelude* 10. 170
This faithful guide, speaking from his death-bed, — 726 *Prelude* 10. 537
Wading beneath the conduct of their guide — 726 *Prelude* 10. 565
Guide faithful as is needed—I began — 728 *Prelude* 11. 98
One guide, the light of circumstances, flashed — 731 *Prelude* 11. 243
Was with me, my encourager and guide: — 737 *Prelude* 12. 230
Which, while I looked all round for my lost guide, — 738 *Prelude* 12. 257
Boundless, or guide into eternity. — 742 *Prelude* 13. 151
The adventurous stranger's steps, a trusty guide; — 746 *Prelude* 14. 9
Guide, and support, and cheer me to the end!" — 755 *Recluse* 1. 1. 860
Looked on this guide with reverential love? — 772 *Excursion* 2. 30
I could not choose but beckon to my Guide, — 778 *Excursion* 2. 429
That fortune did not guide you to this house — 781 *Excursion* 2. 620
Following our Guide, we clomb the cottage-stairs — 781 *Excursion* 2. 647
Said—"Shall we take this pathway for our guide?— — 786 *Excursion* 3. 22
Is still the sport! Here Nature was my guide, — 797 *Excursion* 3. 807
Looked on the polar star, as on a guide — 811 *Excursion* 4. 697

Guide—*continued.*
That meditation and research may guide 823 *Excursion* 5. 39
For due provision to control and guide, 826 *Excursion* 5. 290
Or paced the ground—to guide her Husband home, 834 *Excursion* 5. 760
Guide of our way, mysterious comforter ! 864 *Excursion* 7. 483
Conscience to guide and check ; and death to be 887 *Excursion* 9. 224
With birch-trees fringed ; my hand shall guide the helm, 891 *Excursion* 9. 496
The guide appointed, and the ransom paid. 894 *Excursion* 9. 651
A stranger long ; nor will the blind man's guide, K.8. 250 *Recluse* 1.1.512
Guided. *See* **Heaven-guided, Star-guided.**
So guided, distant a few steps, I found 73 *Bord.* 2049
Guided by signs which ne'er the sky forsook, 346 *Processions* 14
To Prowess guided by her insight keen 468 *St. Bees* 156
By a blest Husband guided, Mary came 576 **By a* 1
Walked proudly at my side : she guided me ; 659 *Prelude* 4. 65
When thou wert thither guided. From the heart 679 *Prelude* 6. 278
The plough he guided, and the scythe he swayed ; 863 *Excursion* 7. 421
Guide-post. He's at the guide-post—he turns right ; 127 *Idiot Boy* 94
But he finds neither guide-post nor guide. 484 **A plague* 20
Guide-post's. Disclose a naked guide-post's double head, 26 *Guilt* 134
Guides. Lies on your way ; accept us as your Guides. 43 *Bord.* 357
Thou wilt have many guides if thou art innocent ; 63 *Bord.* 1409
God and that staff are now thy only guides. 63 *Bord.* 1416
We were his guides. I on that night resolved 76 *Bord.* 2230
('Tis Fancy guides me willing to be led, 169 *Love lies Bleeding* 10
And, following guides whose craft holds no consent 213 *Dion* 54
By higher, sometimes humbler, guides, 226 *Present.* 77
What strong allurement draws, what spirit guides, 281 **What strong* 1
He guides the Pestilence—the cloud 328 *Ode 1815* 89
That He who guides and governs all, approves 354 *Aquap.* 107
Spirit in him pre-eminent, who guides, 368 *Trajan* 51
That guides them through a stormy night. 404 *White Doe* 761
Hope guides the young ; but when the old must pass 434 *Ecc. Sonn.* 2. 23. 9
And he who guides the plough, or wields the crook, 435 *Ecc. Sonn.* 2. 29. 4
That guides the spirit to eternal day, 619 *School Ex.* 106
Detain me from the best of other guides 668 *Prelude* 5. 168
The guides and wardens of our faculties, 671 *Prelude* 5. 354
Beginning to mistrust their boastful guides, 695 *Prelude* 7. 515
Guides to destruction ? Is it well to trust 812 *Excursion* 4. 771
" You have known lights and guides better than these. 816 *Excursion* 4. 1017
Guides better than mine eyes—until a light 833 *Excursion* 5. 739
Nor fail to note the Man who guides the team." 865 *Excursion* 7. 549
Guid'st. Guid'st the pale Mourner to the lost one's tomb ; 459 **Wanderer ! that* 28
Guiding. May in its progress see thy guiding hand, 22 *Desc. Sk.* 661
Soft as a guiding star that cheers, but cannot burn." 140 *Arm. Lady* 66
And guiding, like the Patmos Saint, 299 *Brownie's Cell* 56
A guiding ray ; or seen—like stars on high, 441 *Ecc. Sonn.* 3. 5. 12
Guiding the mariner through troubled seas, 466 *St. Bees* 43
" *A little onward lend thy guiding hand* 496 **A little* 1
Guiding, from cell to cell and room to room, 509 *F. Stone* 98
Of sun or guiding star. 623 *G. and S. Green* 28
The time (our guiding object from the first) 750 *Prelude* 14. 307
That earthly Providence, whose guiding love 794 *Excursion* 3. 565
In perfect wisdom, guiding mightiest power, 804 *Excursion* 4. 195
I turn, and reach at last the guiding light ; 834 *Excursion* 5. 751
In this blind world the guiding vein of hope ; 842 *Excursion* 6. 258
Guild-hall. Of Westminster ; the Giants of Guild-hall ; 689 *Prelude* 7. 131
Guile. Was the aim frustrated by force or guile, 269 *Malham* 1
No guile seduced, no force could violate ; 305 *Ven. Rep.* 6
Utterly in himself devoid of guile ; 470 **A youth* 10
To undermine with secret guile, 550 *Hermit's Cell* 2. 23
Feuds, factions, flatteries, enmity, and guile 657 *Prelude* 3. 601
Falsehood and guile, be left to sow their seed ; 894 *Excursion* 9. 662
Guileless. Of wind or wave—a meek and guileless Maiden. 370 *Eg. Maid* 66
There, too, behold the lamb and guileless dove 500 *Humanity* 25
Guilt. Alas ! that human guilt provoked the rod 17 *Desc. Sk.* 401
Flashes a look of terror upon guilt, 40 *Bord.* 171
His guilt a thousand-fold. 'Tis most perplexing : 48 *Bord.* 592
The truth shall be laid open, his guilt proved 48 *Bord.* 600
Of this mock Father's guilt. The Baron Herbert 49 *Bord.* 664
This is a time, said he, when guilt may shudder ; 51 *Bord.* 790
Thou too art deep in guilt. We have indeed 55 *Bord.* 996
Been most presumptuous. There *is* guilt in this, 55 *Bord.* 997
Lost Man ! if thou have any close-pent guilt 61 *Bord.* 1305
His guilt was marked—these things could never be 69 *Bord.* 1751
The guilt—have touched it—felt it at your heart— 69 *Bord.* 1770
Proof after proof was pressed upon me ; guilt 77 *Bord.* 2258
Made evident, as seemed, by blacker guilt, 77 *Bord.* 2259
Who, through the portal of one moment's guilt, 214 *Dion* 104
O care ! O guilt !—O vales and plains, 214 *Kirkstone* 33
And when, impatient of her guilt and woes, 316 **It was a* 12
And guilt and shame, from which is no defence, 319 *Biscayan* 13
Nor—touched with due abhorrence of *their* guilt 321 **Here pause* 10
And Christendom respires ; from guilt and shame 326 *Sobieski* 8
No more—the guilt is banished, 330 *Ode : Thanks.* 127
And, with the guilt, the shame is fled ; 330 *Ode : Thanks.* 128
And, with the guilt and shame, the Woe hath vanished, 330 *Ode : Thanks.* 129
Or guilt, that humbly would express 398 *White Doe* 176
In him who at the ghost of guilt doth start. 423 *Ecc. Sonn.* 1. 20. 12
Lives black with guilt, ferocity it calms. 424 *Ecc. Sonn.* 1. 24. 14
For penitent guilt, and innocent distress. 426 *Ecc. Sonn.* 1. 32. 8
Guilt unrepented, pardon unimplored. 447 *Ecc. Sonn.* 3. 29. 8
The living Waters, less and less by guilt 452 *Ecc. Sonn.* 3. 47. 11
Grief that devouring waves had caused—or guilt 470 **Did pangs* 2
Fly where the culprit may, guilt meets a doom : 475 **Here on their* 12

Guilt—*continued.*
Where guilt had urged them on with ceaseless goad, 504 *Warning* 73
And Truth, whose eye guilt only can make dim ; 514 **Who ponders* 12
And, guilt escaping, passion then might plead 519 *Pun. Death* 8. 12
Of yet more heinous guilt, with fiercer pride. 519 *Pun. Death* 11. 8
By spectral shapes of guilt, or to the ground, 523 *Epist. Beaumont* 150
To vice and guilt, forerunning wretchedness, 706 *Prelude* 8. 511
Of human nature. Neither vice nor guilt, 708 *Prelude* 8. 645
Far was I, far as angels are from guilt. 720 *Prelude* 10. 145
But a terrific reservoir of guilt 725 *Prelude* 10. 477
Long time have human ignorance and guilt 734 *Prelude* 12. 1
Whether affliction be the foe, or guilt ! 792 *Excursion* 3. 420
A course of vain delights and thoughtless guilt, 794 *Excursion* 3. 560
From error, disappointment—nay, from guilt ; 817 *Excursion* 4. 1075
Through manifold degrees of guilt and shame ; 818 *Excursion* 4. 1111
Perchance, the heavier woes of guilt ; feel not 829 *Excursion* 5. 429
Or sorrow which his senseless guilt had caused ; 853 *Excursion* 6. 1007
Such triumph over sin and guilt achieve ? 894 *Excursion* 9. 674
Guilt-burthened. And the guilt-burthened soul is no longer opprest. 188 *Music* 12
Guiltiest. Heaven grants even to the guiltiest mind 110 *Forsaken* 3
Guiltless. I am content—I know that he is guiltless— 70 *Bord.* 1847
That both are guiltless, without spot or stain, 70 *Bord.* 1848
From the submissive necks of guiltless men 252 **Why, Minstrel* 9
Guilty. Who has been guilty of some horrid crime. 73 *Bord.* 2029
Who, casting as I thought a guilty Person 76 *Bord.* 2210
O guilty Father—would that death 199 *Thorn* 131
What spell so strong as guilty Fear ! 238 *P. B.* 147
And grandeur crouches like a guilty thing, 265 **When haughty* 2
And hang like dreams around his guilty bed. 320 **Hunger, and* 14
So, from the body of one guilty deed, 346 *Gemmi* 13
Did tremble like a guilty Thing surprised : 589 *Immortality* 151
(With shame I speak it) to her guilty bowers 843 *Excursion* 6. 352
Of darkness, stretched o'er guilty Europe, makes 890 *Excursion* 9. 410
Guinever. The royal Guinever looked passing glad 373 *Eg. Maid* 297
Guise. With him there often walked in friendly guise, 108 *Indolence* 37
When this in modest guise was said, 167 *Pilgrim's Dream* 49
Utterly dead ! yet in the guise 294 *Jedbor.* 53
The glacier Pillars join in solemn guise 347 *Processions* 49
Yet sometimes in more humble guise 404 *White Doe* 770
Through peopled Vales ; yet something in the guise 522 *Epist. Beaumont* 98
And pocketed the relic, in the guise 710 *Prelude* 9. 70
Both while he trod the earth in humblest guise 772 *Excursion* 2. 25
Where, in the guise of mountaineers, we lay, 821 *Excursion* 4. 1320
Of nave and aisle, in unpretending guise, 824 *Excursion* 5. 154
To place those hillocks in that lonely guise. 858 *Excursion* 7. 41
With which the parlour-floor, in simplest guise 860 *Excursion* 7. 190
Fountains and spouts, yet somewhat in the guise K.8. 251 *Recluse* 1.1.557
Such sorrow is more lovely in its guise [?] **A sad* 4
Gules. Marshal forth-with a pair of oars in gules. L.1. 96 *Juvenal* 3. 36
Gulf. *See* **Gulph.**
Toil, small as pygmies in the gulf profound ; 5 *Ev. Wk.* 163
(For dark and broad the gulf of time between) 8 *Ev. Wk.* 346
Listens, or quakes while from the forest's gulf 14 *Desc. Sk.* 194
In some dense wood or gulf of snowy profound, 16 *Desc. Sk.* 314
A single chasm, a gulf of gloomy blue, 18 *Desc. Sk.* 413
That dark mysterious gulf ascending, sound 18 *Desc. Sk.* 415
From gulf of parting clouds one friendly beam, 26 *Guilt* 131
" Some mighty gulf of separation passed, 31 *Guilt* 352
The gulf is deep below ; 85 *Shepherd-boys* 53
Into the gulf profound. 85 *Shepherd-boys* 70
Toward the mighty gulf of things, 90 *Longest Day* 58
Ridge, and gulf, and distant ocean 217 **Inmate of* 15
Down to that hidden gulf from which they rose 230 *Clouds* 36
These mighty barriers, and the gulf between ; 265 **Hail, Twilight* 12
Into a gulf which all distinction levels— 441 *Ecc. Sonn.* 3. 3. 11
Bishops and Priests, think what a gulf profound 444 *Ecc. Sonn.* 3. 16. 12
Or gulf of mystery, which thou alone, 469 **Desire we* 9
—Vex'd by the darkness, from the piny gulf 606 *Desc.Sk.Quarto* 239
A gulf of gloomy blue, that opens wide 611 *Desc.Sk.Quarto* 498
Loud thro' that midway gulf ascending, sound 611 *Desc.Sk.Quarto* 504
—Voiceless the stream descends into the gulf 787 *Excursion* 3. 92
Into a gulf obscure of silent grief, 795 *Excursion* 3. 675
The unfathomable gulf, where all is still ! " 800 *Excursion* 3. 991
Bedded for good and evil in a gulf 826 *Excursion* 5. 295
Beholds the gulf beneath.—No floweret blooms 865 *Excursion* 7. 498
Gulfs. Of Andes—frozen gulfs became its bridge— 327 *Ode 1815* 22
Bays, gulfs, and ocean's Indian width, shall be, 527 **Those breathing* 39
And the broad gulfs I traversed oft and oft. 574 *Chiabrera* 4. 17
Gulfy. The gulfy coast of Norway iron-bound ; 454 *Sea-side* 30
Gull. *See* **Sea-gull.**
Gulph. The man to come, parted, as by a gulph, 735 *Prelude* 12. 59
Gun. *See* **Distress-gun.**
That never fowler's gun, nor shaft 543 *Russ. Fug.* 107
Gunpowder. Plying with gunpowder their trade, 245 *P. B.* 839
Coursing a train of gunpowder—it went, 442 *Ecc. Sonn.* 3. 8. 6
Gun's. *See* **Rifle-gun's.**
Guns. Of ships to ships and guns to guns ; 178 *Waggoner* 2. 141
Gurdy. *See* **Hurdy-gurdy.**
Gurgle. Or founts that gurgle from yon craggy steep, S. 3. 433 **The doubt* 11
Gurgled. And gurgled at our feet. 487 *Fountain* 8
Gurgling. And gurgling rills, assist her in the work 497 **Enough of climbing* 15
Gurgling in foamy water-break, 508 *May* 75
Gush. Oh, what a gush of tenderness was mine ! 358 *Pine : Rome* 8
The tears of man in various measure gush 436 *Ecc. Sonn.* 2. 32. 1
With the gush of earthly love, 502 **Like a* 18
Gushes. Pours forth his song in gushes ; 159 *Green Linnet* 36
And a sound of water that gushes, 457 **The sun has* 7
Gushing. A gushing from his heart, that took away 101 *Brothers* 407

Gushing—*continued.*
—Behold !—as with a gushing impulse heaves . 212 *Dion*
O'er blooming fields and gushing springs . . . 338 **Meek Virgin* 28
Fed in the Libyan waste by gushing wells, . . 346 *Processions* 20
Yet is there cause for gushing tears ; . . . . 370 *Eg. Maid* 61
And, by her gushing thoughts subdued, . . . 414 *White Doe* 1661
When gushing, copious as a thunder-shower, . . 439 *Ecc. Sonn.* 2. 42. 13
His thirst from rill or gushing fount, and thanked 814 *Excursion* 4. 872
Gust. No sport of every random gust, ... 492 *Duty* 26
Which, ere they gain consistence, by a gust . . 889 *Excursion* 9. 342
Sprang like a gust of wind : [and with a heart . K.8. 228 **I will* 119
Gustavus. Withering the Oppressor : how Gustavus sought . . . . 635 *Prelude* 1. 212
Gusts. Dread swell of sound ! loud as the gusts that lash . . . . 379 *Duddon* 13. 7
By gusts of vernal storm, attuned his song . . 537 **In desultory* 4
Gusty. That twinkle to the gusty breeze, . . . 159 *Green Linnet* 26
Or, from the meadows sent on gusty days, . . . 639 *Prelude* 1. 496
As seen not seldom on some gusty day, . . . 861 *Excursion* 7. 231
Gypsey. *See* **Gipsy.**
The Grison gypsey here her tent has plac'd, . . 605 *Desc.Sk.Quarto* 188

H

Ha. That's all—God save you, Sir. Ha ! as I live, 43 *Bord.* 332
My hands are numb. Ha ! ha ! 'tis nipping cold. 50 *Bord.* 727
This bitter night. Ha ! Oswald ! ten bright crosses 53 *Bord.* 857
These fifteen years—*Ha ! speak*—what Thing art thou ? . . . . 54 *Bord.* 942
Ha ! ha !— As 'twill be but a moment's work, 60 *Bord.* 1258
Ha ! what is here ? and carved by her own hand ! 63 *Bord.* 1412
Ha ! my dear Captain. A later meeting, Oswald, 64 *Bord.* 1470
From such rough dealing. Ha ! what sound is that ? 67 *Bord.* 1661
A human groan. Ha ! what is here ? Poor Man— 67 *Bord.* 1667
Ha ! is it so !—That vagrant Hag !—this comes . 78 *Bord.* 2312
Ha ! why these sinkings of despair ? . . . . 244 *P. B.* 723
Ha ! what a ghastly sight for man to see ; . . 331 *Ode : Thanks.* 183
"Ha," quoth I, "pretty prisoner, are you there !" 659 *Prelude* 4. 59
Habiliments. The form and rich habiliments of One 226 *Vernal Ode* 5
These rude habiliments, and rest . . . . . 545 *Russ. Fug.* 319
But with more shame, for my habiliments, . . 659 *Prelude* 4. 75
Habit. A habit which disquietude and grief . . 101 *Brothers* 394
A Mountaineer by habit, would resound . . . 352 *Aquap.* 4
And habit of his vow. That ancient Man— . . 362 **List—'twas* 82
Through saintly habit than from effort due . . 434 *Ecc. Sonn.* 2. 22. 2
But habit rules the unreflecting herd, . . . 435 *Ecc. Sonn.* 2. 28. 10
To acts of love ; and habit does the work . . 567 *Cumb. Beg.* 100
And, whether from this habit rooted now . . 647 *Prelude* 2. 387
Nor did by habit of her thoughts mistrust . . 669 *Prelude* 5. 270
Simplicity in habit, truth in speech, . . . 672 *Prelude* 5. 421
Custom and habit, novelty and change ; . . . 714 *Prelude* 9. 325
Power had reverted : habit, custom, law, . . . 727 *Prelude* 11. 32
Was never much my habit—giving way . . . 736 *Prelude* 12. 114
For this to last : I shook the habit off . . . 737 *Prelude* 12. 204
That happiness ; and use and habit gave . . 795 *Excursion* 3. 624
The glorious habit by which sense is made . . 820 *Excursion* 4. 1247
Far nearer, in the habit of her soul, . . . 861 *Excursion* 7. 228
And thirst for change ; or habit hath subdued . 878 *Excursion* 8. 294
Habitable. Her habitable shores, but now appears 219 **This Height* 21
Europe, through all her habitable bounds, . . 870 *Excursion* 7. 841
Even till the smallest habitable rock, ... 890 *Excursion* 9. 387
Habitation. No habitation can be seen ; but they . 131 *Michael* 9
A habitation in this peaceful Vale, ... 150 **When, to* 3
Though habitation none appear, ... 215 *Kirkstone* 65
A habitation marvellously planned, ... 266 **The stars* 5
Their habitation shook ;—it fell, ... 298 *Brownie's Cell* 23
While, in their ancient habitation . . . . 413 *White Doe* 1573
A habitation she had found, ... 414 *White Doe* 1689
Or human habitation rose . . . . 533 **Blest is* 29
A habitation sober and demure . . . . . 655 *Prelude* 3. 435
A habitation, for consummate good, ... 789 *Excursion* 3. 221
For human habitation ; but I longed . . . 833 *Excursion* 5. 741
His habitation will be here : for him . . . 840 *Excursion* 6. 114
"Close to his destined habitation, lies . . . 841 *Excursion* 6. 212
Where not a habitation stood before, . . . 876 *Excursion* 8. 122
Delightful Valley, habitation fair ! . . . . K.8. 245 *Recluse* 1.1.300
Habitations. Affect my native habitations ; . . 226 *Vernal Ode* 27
Her pleasant habitations, and dry up . . . 666 *Prelude* 5. 32
"How gay the habitations that bedeck . . . 828 *Excursion* 5. 411
The habitations, and the ways of men, . . . 833 *Excursion* 5. 685
The rudest habitations. Ye might think . . . 855 *Excursion* 6. 1143
The habitations empty ! or perchance . . . 878 *Excursion* 8. 266
And habitations seemingly preserved . . . 892 *Excursion* 9. 577
Habits. And to her mournful habits fondly cleaves. 169 **Never enlivened* 6
Gleam war's discordant habits thro' the trees, . 615 *Desc.Sk.Quarto* 746
His habits were first sown, even as a seed ? . . 645 *Prelude* 2. 207
Of inconsiderate habits and sedate, . . . 663 *Prelude* 4. 342
Imperfect, with these habits must be joined . . 677 *Prelude* 6. 172
My calmer habits, and more steady voice, . . 679 *Prelude* 6. 311
To rules and habits, whereby much was done, . 795 *Excursion* 3. 608
By useful habits, to a fitter soil . . . . 862 *Excursion* 7. 301
Be rooted out, and virtuous habits take . . . 889 *Excursion* 9. 360
Habitual. As one whose brain habitual frenzy fires 26 *Guilt* 91
In that habitual restlessness of foot . . . 150 **When, to* 63
By the habitual light of memory see . . . 279 **All praise* 4
And the habitual murmur that atones . . . 464 **Greta, what* 8
And an habitual disregard of self . . . . 539 **Lady ! a* 65
Instead of common and habitual sight . . . 567 *Cumb. Beg.* 48
To live beneath your more habitual sway. . . 590 *Immortality* 195

Habitual—*continued.*
To my own passions and habitual thoughts ; . . 635 *Prelude* 1. 223
To lure my mind from firm habitual quest . . 662 *Prelude* 4. 287
In my habitual thoughts ; the scale of love, . . 709 *Prelude* 8. 684
And an habitual piety, maintained . . . . 758 *Excursion* 1. 116
By his habitual wanderings out of doors, . . . 762 *Excursion* 1. 404
Of his perfections ; with habitual dread . . . 801 *Excursion* 4. 24
Wrinkled and furrowed with habitual thought . 848 *Excursion* 6. 683
For those cold humours of habitual spleen . . 871 *Excursion* 7. 907
Is the firm basis of habitual sense . . . . S.3. 435 **The doubt* 114
Habitually. And to those graves looking habitually 464 **A point* 3
Habitually dear, and all their forms . . . . 641 *Prelude* 1. 610
Of Whom they are, habitually infused . . . 747 *Prelude* 14. 115
Admitted more habitually a mild . . . . . 750 *Prelude* 14. 288
Dejected, and habitually disposed . . . . 896 *Excursion* 9. 787
Hack. For Lubbock vote—no legislative hack . L.3. 27 **For Lubbock* 1
Hackneyed. But some (who brook those hackneyed themes full well, ... 255 *Detraction* 5
(A theme for boys, too hackneyed for their sires,) 721 *Prelude* 10. 193
Had, *omitted.*
Hadst. (*Partial list.*)
Oh ! would that thou hadst perished in the flames ! 76 *Bord.* 2193
Hadst been brought up upon thy Father's knees. 136 *Michael* 352
Not idly.—Hadst thou been of Indian birth, . . 172 *Infant Daughter* 18
Hadst this to boast of ; thou didst love . . . 292 *Rob Roy* 103
Thou hadst a voice whose sound was like the sea : 307 **Milton ! thou* 10
Hag. Ha ! is it so !—That vagrant Hag !—this comes . . . . 78 *Bord.* 2312
Haggard. Bright sparks his black and haggard eye-ball hurls . . . . 594 *Ev. Wk. Quarto* 133
Haggis. A German Haggis from receipt . . . S.3. 432 **A German* 1
Hail. Hail Freedom ! whether it was mine to stray, 21 *Desc. Sk.* 591
Check his loud whip and hail us with mild voice, 61 *Bord.* 1335
I witness'd, and now hail your victory. . . . 64 *Bord.* 1506
Hail, blest above all kinds !—Supremely skilled . 153 *Morn. Ex.* 31
Hail to Thee, far above the rest . . . . . 159 *Green Linnet* 11
Through "heaven's eternal year."—Yet hail to Thee, ... 172 *Infant Daughter* 15
—Or I would hail thee when some high-wrought page 222 *Triad* 183
When I step forth to hail the morning light ; . . 253 **Aerial Rock* 3
Hail, Twilight, sovereign of one peaceful hour ! . 265 **Hail, Twilight* 1
To that great King : shall hail the crownèd Youth 305 **The Voice* 2
Hail, Zaragoza ! If with unwet eye . . . . 316 **Hail, Zaragoza* 1
Methinks that we shall hail thee, Champion brave, 318 **Ah ! where* 6
The triumph hail, which from their peaceful clime 326 **The Bard* 13
Hail, orient Conqueror of gloomy Night ! . . . 329 *Ode : Thanks.* 1
Once more, heart-cheering Sun, I bid thee hail ! . 329 *Ode : Thanks.* 34
Hail to the firm unmoving cross, ... 337 *Cath. Cantons* 9
Honour to word-preserving Arts, and hail . . 356 *Aquap.* 250
To hail the exploratory Bird renewing . . . 360 **Near Anio's* 6
Hail, ancient Manners ! sure defence, . . . 376 **The Minstrels* 55
Hail, Usages of pristine mould, ... 376 **The Minstrels* 59
All hail, ye mountains ! hail, thou morning light ! 376 *Duddon* 1. 10
Hail to the fields—with Dwellings sprinkled o'er, 379 *Duddon* 13. 1
Hail countless Temples ! that so well befit . . 430 *Ecc. Sonn.* 2. 9. 9
The warrant hail, exulting to be free ; . . . 434 *Ecc. Sonn.* 2. 23. 3
Hail, Virgin Queen ! o'er many an envious bar . 438 *Ecc. Sonn.* 2. 38. 1
All hail, sage Lady, whom a grateful Isle . . 438 *Ecc. Sonn.* 2. 38. 3
And lays as prompt would hail the dawn of Night : 455 *Rydal Mere* 21
Hail to the virtues which that perilous life . . 458 *Sea-shore* 21
That bid me hail thee as the SAILOR'S FRIEND ; . 459 **Wanderer ! that* 12
With grateful thoughts, doth now thy rising hail 460 **Queen of* 8
Hail, Bards of mightier grasp ! on you . . . 473 *Ossian* 53
Whence the blithe hail ? behold a Peasant stand 524 *Epist. Beaumont* 207
Once I could hail (howe'er serene the sky) . . 532 **Once I* 1
And hospitably did they give us hail, ... 681 *Prelude* 6. 404
Hail to the mighty projects of the time ! . . 681 *Prelude* 6. 443
Of the Hercynian forest. Yet, hail to you . . 702 *Prelude* 8. 215
Gladly the highest promises, and hail, . . . 713 *Prelude* 9. 241
—Hail Contemplation ! from the stately towers, . 787 *Excursion* 3. 101
Hail to the crown by Freedom shaped—to gird . 838 *Excursion* 6. 1
—Hail to the State of England ! And conjoin . 838 *Excursion* 6. 6
His triumphs hail, and glorify his end ; . . . 863 *Excursion* 7. 378
Words cannot say, how beautiful. Then hail, . K.8. 244 *Recluse* 1.1.298
Hail to the visible Presence, hail to thee, . . K.8. 245 *Recluse* 1.1.299
Hailed. Have hailed the morning sun. But cheerily, Father,— . . . . 39 *Bord.* 125
Hailed us as if he had been sent from heaven, . 62 *Bord.* 1366
With not unfrequent rapture fondly hailed. . . 118 *Maternal Grief* 26
Those brilliant strangers, hailed with joy . . . 170 *Rural Ill.* 9
Or were ye rightlier hailed, when first mine eyes . 229 *Clouds* 11
Whose light I hailed when first it shone, . . . 285 *Grave of Burns* 33
Her love ye hailed—her wrath have felt ! . . . 311 **Who rises* 14
Whom he had hailed with joy, and cried, . . . 369 *Eg. Maid* 27
The sight was hailed with loud acclaim . . . 400 *White Doe* 415
From false assumption rose, and fondly hailed . 429 *Ecc. Sonn.* 2. 2. 1
Hailed from aloft those Heirs of truth divine . 431 *Ecc. Sonn.* 2. 13. 10
Her landing hailed, how touchingly she bowed ! . 465 **Dear to* 4
And Bards, who hailed thee, may forget . . . 507 *May* 3
He hath hailed it re-appearing— . . . . . 549 *Hermit's Cell* 1. 23
Was like a volume to me ; some were hailed . . 659 *Prelude* 4. 68
And hailed him. Slowly from his resting-place . 664 *Prelude* 4. 412
(The thronèd Lady whom erewhile we hailed) . 671 *Prelude* 5. 400
As if awaked from sleep, the Nations hailed . . 686 *Prelude* 6. 757
At length I hailed him, seeing that his hat . . 762 *Excursion* 1. 444
And let the light mechanic tool be hailed . . . 831 *Excursion* 5. 606
He, with the foremost whose impatience hailed . 844 *Excursion* 6. 416
Religion hailed her creeds by war restored, . . L.1. 97 *Juvenal* 3. 65
Hailing. As if a new-made heaven were hailing a new earth ! . . . . 22 *Desc. Sk.* 645

Hand—*continued.*

Hand—*continued.*

Happiest 403 Happy

Happier—*continued.*
Is still a happier man, who, for those heights . . 806 *Excursion* 4. 355
The spots where such abide ! But happier still . 823 *Excursion* 5. 37
Who happier for the moment—who more blithe . 843 *Excursion* 6. 341
For work of happier issue, to the side . . . 869 *Excursion* 7. 809
Resumed the manners of his happier days ; . . 882 *Excursion* 8. 527
On me can Time no happier state bestow . . . S.3. 441 **Grateful is sleep ; my* 3

Happiest. Where breathed the gale that caught Wolfe's happiest sigh, ... 15 *Desc. Sk.* 299
The happiest lovers Arcady might boast, . . . 110 **Look at* 14
He knew it not) and from his happiest looks, . . 118 *Maternal Grief* 45
And, in their happiest moments, not content, . . 122 *V. and J.* 24
The happiest bird that sprang out of the Ark ! . 153 *Morn. Ex.* 30
One have I marked, the happiest guest . . 159 *Green Linnet* 9
Though wrought in Vulcan's happiest mood, . . 163 *Needlecase* 11
Our Travellers are the happiest pair ; . . . . 177 *Waggoner* 2. 79
Or note (translucent summer's happiest chance !) 190 **Lyre ! though* 33
When happiest Fancy has inspired the strains, . 265 **There is a pleasure* 5
A landscape more august than happiest skill . . 323 *Ode 1814* 6
Or, at a touch, produced by happiest transformation. . . . . 369 *Eg. Maid* 18
Was happiest, proudest, of them all ! . . . . 409 *White Doe* 1187
The wisest, happiest, of our kind are they . . . 456 *Rydal Mere* 37
Hath here portrayed with Nature's happiest grace 461 **Giordano, verily* 2
That civic strife can turn the happiest hearth 504 *Warning* 76
The happiest for your home ; . . . . . . 507 *May* 52
Within the happiest breast on earthly ground. . 524 *Epist. Beaumont* 222
This sad belief, the happiest that is left . . . 531 *Octogen.* 6
The happiest of the band ! . . . . 544 *Russ. Fug.* 248
Portrayed with happiest pencil, not untrue . . 583 **With copious* 23
In happiness to the happiest upon earth. . . . 672 *Prelude* 5. 420
Their fairest, softest, happiest influence. . . . 686 *Prelude* 6. 726
And waking thoughts more rich than happiest dreams. . . . . 724 *Prelude* 10. 436
For his delight—the happiest he of all ! " . . . 789 *Excursion* 3. 206
" Far happiest," answered the desponding Man, . 789 *Excursion* 3. 207
Caught in their fairest, happiest, attitude ! . . 891 *Excursion* 9. 464
And seemingly her happiest, look so fair . . . S.3. 434 **The doubt* 89
And new-born waters deemed the happiest source S.3. 436 **The doubt* 165
Happiest of happy though I be, like them . . K.8. 242 *Recluse* 1.1.198
Happiest-looking. Among the happiest-looking homes of men . . . . 387 *Manse* 2
Happily. Measures not crimes like his. *We* rank not, happily, ... 48 *Bord.* 583
End happily, as they began ! " These gleams . 124 *V. and J.* 211
Dear Ruth ! more happily set free . . . . . 194 *Ruth* 176
Was wanting ;—and most happily till now. . 362 **List—'twas* 28
And by Heaven's favour happily fulfilled ; . . 526 **Soon did* 11
Now happily apprenticed.—'I perceive . . . 767 *Excursion* 1. 762
Was from his Parents happily concealed ; . . . 843 *Excursion* 6. 361
And small birds singing happily to mates . . . 851 *Excursion* 6. 857
Happily spared, a little Gothic niche . . . 881 *Excursion* 8. 486
Happiness. Alive to independent happiness, . . 18 *Desc. Sk.* 424
With so much happiness to spare, ... 85 *Anecdote* 15
Such happiness as I have known to-day. . . . 111 **'Tis said that some* 52
Their happiness, or to disturb their love. . . . 123 *V. and J.* 111
Of future happiness. " You shall return, . . . 124 *V. and J.* 189
Five years of happiness or more . . . . . 127 *Idiot Boy* 135
With sudden happiness beyond all hope. . . . 185 *Nutting* 29
All happiness her own. . . . . 223 *Wishing-gate* 36
For nought but what thy happiness could spare. . 277 **Why art* 8
The strife of happiness and pain, ... 294 *Jedbor.* 52
Of inward happiness. We are selfish men ; . . 307 **Milton ! thou* 6
A great man's happiness ; thy zeal shall find . 313 *Clarkson* 13
All pride ; by which all happiness is blighted. . 372 *Eg. Maid* 198
A happy hour with holier happiness. . . . . 395 *White Doe: Ded.* 56
Of a redeeming happiness. . . . . 409 *White Doe* 1248
Sigh for the obscurities of happiness. . . . . 458 *Sea-shore* 33
And She her happiness can build . . . . 478 *Somnamb.* 50
Our pastime and our happiness will grow. . . 488 *Pers. Talk* 36
Thou monument of peaceful happiness ! . . . 489 *Spade* 24
Nor thought of tender happiness betray ; . . . 494 *Hap. War.* 73
Of too familiar happiness. . . . . 497 *Lycoris* 26
Long-vanished happiness refines, ... 499 *Memory* 11
With garlands, cheats her into happiness ; . . 528 **Thosebreathing* 99
And happiness that never flies— . . . . 530 *Gleaner* 9
Will sometimes in the happiness of love . . . 551 **If thou in* 3
And happiness, which to the end of time . . . 567 *Cumb. Beg.* 108
Of happiness and hope, a youthful Bride. . . . 576 **By a* 4
Such happiness, wherever it be known, . . . 579 *Peele Castle* 55
And settling into gentler happiness. . . . . 633 *Prelude* 1. 64
Nor saw a band in happiness and joy . . . . 639 *Prelude* 1. 481
By pleasure and repeated happiness, ... 641 *Prelude* 1. 604
Of happiness, my blood appeared to flow . . . 645 *Prelude* 2. 187
In youth, but oh ! what happiness to live . . 646 *Prelude* 2. 285
If ever happiness hath lodged with man, . . . 660 *Prelude* 4. 139
That day consummate happiness was mine, . . 660 *Prelude* 4. 140
Might love in individual happiness. . . . . . 662 *Prelude* 4. 238
In happiness to the happiest upon earth. . . . 672 *Prelude* 5. 420
Of present happiness, while future years . . . 675 *Prelude* 6. 44
One happiness. Throughout this narrative, . . 679 *Prelude* 6. 259
Their happiness or misery, depends . . . . 728 *Prelude* 11. 103
To happiness unthought of ? The inert . . . 729 *Prelude* 11. 123
We find our happiness, or not at all ! . . . . 729 *Prelude* 11. 144
Maintained for me a secret happiness. . . . . 735 *Prelude* 12. 43
And through a perfect happiness of soul, . . . 736 *Prelude* 12. 162
Nothing but happiness, in some lone nook, . . 741 *Prelude* 13. 125

Happiness—*continued.*
To thee, in memory of that happiness, ... 752 *Prelude* 14. 410
Rich in true happiness if allowed to be . . . 752 *Prelude* 14. 439
Might live on earth a life of happiness. . . . 764 *Excursion* 1. 519
And walked along my road in happiness." . . 770 *Excursion* 1. 956
That showed like happiness. But, in despite . . 775 *Excursion* 2. 284
For independent happiness ; craving peace, . . 791 *Excursion* 3. 381
The central feeling of all happiness, ... 791 *Excursion* 3. 382
Enlivened happiness with joy o'erflowing, . . 792 *Excursion* 3. 430
Life's genuine inspiration, happiness . . . . 792 *Excursion* 3. 433
That happiness ; and use and habit gave . . . 795 *Excursion* 3. 624
Which I had trod in happiness and peace, . . 797 *Excursion* 3. 802
We have, or hope, of happiness and joy, . . . 803 *Excursion* 4. 133
Embosomed happiness, and placid love ; . . . 828 *Excursion* 5. 414
' Joy be their lot, and happiness,' he cried, . 840 *Excursion* 6. 141
It was no momentary happiness . . . . 848 *Excursion* 6. 637
A happiness that ebbed not, but remained . . 867 *Excursion* 7. 661
Their virtue, service, happiness, and state . . 872 *Excursion* 7. 996
All praise, all safety, and all happiness, . . . 877 *Excursion* 8. 215
And pleasure sobered down to happiness ! . . S.3. 436 **The doubt* 144
Thy glory and thy happiness be there. . . . K.8. 256 *Recluse* 1.1.736
Happy. Fair scenes, erewhile, I taught, a happy child, ... 2 *Ev. Wk.* 13
Of happy wisdom, meditating good, ... 3 *Ev. Wk.* 81
Where we, my Friend, to happy days shall rise, . 8 *Ev. Wk.* 351
Where hum on busier wing her happy bees ; . . 21 *Desc. Sk.* 607
The happy husband flies, his arms to throw . . 25 *Guilt* 60
And knew not why. My happy father died, . . 29 *Guilt* 266
Thrice happy ! that for him the grave could hide . . . . 29 *Guilt* 268
Of such rough storm, this happy change to view." 30 *Guilt* 317
Yet happy thou, poor boy ! compared with me, . 33 *Guilt* 498
When I had been most happy. Pardon me . . 39 *Bord.* 98
He shall reveal himself. Happy are we, . . . 48 *Bord.* 595
And dreams that he is happy. We dissect . . 58 *Bord.* 1166
One happy thought has passed across my mind. . 61 *Bord.* 1326
This is a happy day. My Father soon . . . 66 *Bord.* 1627
Even so this happy Creature of herself . . . 80 **Loving she* 11
To-morrow is the happy day. . . . . . 81 †*Mother's Return* 4
And thus, as happy as the day, ... 84 *Shepherd-boys* 21
O blessèd vision ! happy child ! . . . . . 88 *H. C.* 11
Who would check the happy feeling . . . . 90 *Longest Day* 17
Nor leave untold our happy flight in that adventurous dream. . . . . 93 *Poet's Dream* 76
Time passed on ; the Child was happy, . . . 94 *Westmoreland Girl* 41
In all his hardships, since that happy time . . 96 *Brothers* 73
The happy man will creep about the fields, . . 97 *Brothers* 108
He would himself, no doubt, be happy then . . 100 *Brothers* 327
As any that should meet him— Happy ! Sir— . 100 *Brothers* 328
And many, many happy days were his. . . . 100 *Brothers* 346
You say that he saw many happy years ? . . . 101 *Brothers* 384
This vale, where he had been so happy, seemed . 102 *Brothers* 425
O, happy Britain ! region all too fair . . . 102 *Artegal* 25
O happy Garden ! whose seclusion deep . . . 107 *Farewell* 57
Within our happy Castle there dwelt One . . . 107 *Indolence* 1
As happy spirits as were ever seen ; . . . . 108 *Indolence* 69
What happy moments did I count ! . . . . 111 *A Complaint* 7
Of happy millions lulled in sleep ; . . . . 113 *Lament* 26
With happy heart I then would die, ... 114 *Ind. Wom.* 67
And my last thought would happy be ; . . . 114 *Ind. Wom.* 68
There dwelt we, as happy as birds in their bowers ; 116 *Repentance* 9
O happy time of youthful lovers (thus . . . 121 *V. and J.* 1
A man too happy for mortality ! . . . . . 122 *V. and J.* 53
To nature for a happy end of all ; . . . . 122 *V. and J.* 63
Oh ! happy, happy, happy John. . . . . 127 *Idiot Boy* 86
That happy time all past and gone, ... 128 *Idiot Boy* 163
She's happy here, is happy there, ... 130 *Idiot Boy* 389
She knows not, happy Betty Foy ! . . . . . 130 *Idiot Boy* 393
Like happy people round a Christmas fire. . . 135 *Michael* 303
That is for him a happy school, ... 142 †*Lov. and Lik.* 24
Even, as your happy presence to my mind . . 143 **High bliss* 25
Thrice happy Creature ! in all lands . . . 144 **Driven in* 58
And I am happy when I sing . . . . . 144 *Her Eyes* 13
Then happy lie ; for blest am I ; . . . . . 145 *Her Eyes* 49
That they, with whom you once were happy, talk 147 *Joanna* 16
The happy idleness of that sweet morn, . . . 149 **A narrow* 68
A second time, in Grasmere's happy Vale. . . 151 **When, to* 110
All summer-long the happy Eve . . . . . 154 *Flower Garden* 19
Once lived a happy life ! . . . . 155 *Waterfall* 24
A happy Eglantine ! " . . . . 155 *Waterfall* 50
My father many a happy year . . . . . . 156 *Oak and Broom* 68
A happy, genial influence, ... 158 **In youth* 70
Happy, happy Liver, ... 160 **Up with me* 22
Wouldst thou be happy in thy nest, ... 163 **Art thou the* 37
And happy in his flowery cove : . . . . . 166 *Danish Boy* 50
They are happy, for that is their right ! . . . 167 *Stray Pleasures* 36
And all the happy Souls that rode . . . . . 168 *Pilgrim's Dream* 60
Over happy to be proud, ... 171 *Kitten* 38
For soon, of all the happy there, ... 177 *Waggoner* 2. 78
They envy not the happy lot, ... 177 *Waggoner* 2. 99
Here in this happy dell." . . . . . . 187 **Three years* 36
Here are twenty souls happy as souls in a dream : 189 *Music* 42
And is as happy in his night, for the heavens are blue and fair ; . . . . 189 *Star-gazers* 6
Seem to meet with little gain, seem less happy than before : . . . . 189 *Star-gazers* 30
That they, so happy and so fair . . . . . 191 *Seq. Beggars* 37
He told of girls—a happy rout ! . . . . . 193 *Ruth* 49
That to sweet Ruth that happy day . . . . 193 *Ruth* 107
A young and happy Child ! . . . . 195 *Ruth* 252

Happy—*continued.*
Or heard them not, as happy as a boy : . . . 195 Resolution 18
Even such a happy Child of earth am I ; . . . 195 Resolution 31
The horse and horseman are a happy pair ; . . 200 Hart-leap 10
And now, too happy for repose or rest, . . . 201 Hart-leap 45
They both are happy at this hour, ... 204 Brougham 48
Our Clifford was a happy Youth, ... 205 Brougham 107
Happy day, and mighty hour, ... 205 Brougham 150
Brought from a pensive though a happy place. . 211 Laod. 96
Apart from happy Ghosts, that gather flowers . 212 Laod. 162
Brush the too happy tear ? . . . . 220 Triad 60
Her happy spirit as a bird is free, ... 221 Triad 125
And one of the bright Three become thy happy Bride. . . . . 222 Triad 218
It was in sooth a happy thought . . . . 224 *'Tis gone 19
O, nursed at happy distance from the cares . . 227 Vernal Ode 75
Will make thee happy, happy as a child ; . . . 229 Cuckoo-clock 20
Happy milk-maids, one by one . . . . . . 233 Power of Sound 45
Around those happy fields we span . . . . . 237 P. B. 67
The soul of happy sound was spread, ... 239 P. B. 257
A happy respite ! but at length . . . . . 242 P. B. 536
Happy the feeling from the bosom thrown . . 250 *Happy the 1
Happy the thought best likened to a stone . . 250 *Happy the 5
Sit blithe and happy ; bees that soar for bloom, . 250 *Nuns fret 5
The immortal Spirit of one happy day . . . . 251 *There is a little 13
Happy Associates breathing air remote . . . 252 *Her only 8
Till she exchanged for heaven that happy ground. 267 St. Cath. 14
And the fair front of many a happy Home ; . . 268 *Four fiery 10
Shall look more bright—the happy, happier still ; 281 Chris. Words. 10
Such happy fields, abodes so calm as thine ; . . 284 Departure 20
O happy pleasure ! here to dwell . . . . . 288 Highland Girl 49
Yet happy feelings of the dead : . . . . . 289 Glen-Al. 29
Full sure they were a happy band, ... 297 Highland Boy 222
She was too happy far. . . . . 297 Highland Boy 240
The haunts of happy Lovers, ... 302 Yarrow V. 34
Banners, and happy faces, far and nigh ! . . . 304 *Jones ! as 8
Happy is he, who, caring not for Pope, . . . 304 *Festivals have 12
At happy distance from earth's groaning field, . 313 *Clouds,lingering 7
Happy occasions oft by self-mistrust . . . 316 *Say, what 13
With happy garlands of the pure white rose : . . 318 *In due 7
Thrice happy, burghers, peasants, warriors old, . 339 Tell 6
Thy name, O SCHWYTZ, in happy freedom keep ! . 339 Schwytz 14
To COMO's steeps—his happy bourne ! . . . 342 Ital. Itin. 42
Of love in the heart made more happy by tears ? 346 Stanzas : Simplon 32
These records take, and happy should I be . . 352 H. C. R. 5
Is wheeling hitherward. Thanks, happy Creature, 361 *List—'twas 7
Like sinless snakes in Eden's happy land ;— . . 374 Eg. Maid 323
Be happy and unenvied, thou who art . . . . 374 Eg. Maid 347
We made a day of happy hours, ... 385 Yarrow Rev. 23
Our happy days recalling. . . . . 385 Yarrow Rev. 24
Untouched, unbreathed upon. Thrice happy quest, 388 Trosachs 9
Belike less happy.—Stand no more aloof ! . . 390 Highland Hut 14
A happy hour with holier happiness. . . . . 395 White Doe: Ded. 56
Most happy in the shy recess . . . . . . 399 White Doe 293
And thou, (O happy thought this day !) . . . 402 White Doe 571
Happy as others of her kind, ... 407 White Doe 995
How proud and happy they ! the crowd . . . 409 White Doe 1180
Together died, a happy death !— . . . . . 410 White Doe 1339
Upon the happy Creature's face. . . . . . 414 White Doe 1664
Was happy that she lived to greet . . . . . 416 White Doe 1823
How happy in its turn to meet . . . . . . 416 White Doe 1826
Descended :—happy are the eyes that meet . . 423 Ecc. Sonn. 1. 19. 9
Most happy, re-assembled in a land . . . . 437 Ecc. Sonn. 2. 37. 3
Belovèd Mother ! Thou whose happy hand . . 445 Ecc. Sonn. 3. 22. 9
Happy the crew who this have felt, and pour . . 448 Ecc. Sonn. 3. 30. 6
By THEM who blessed the soft and happy gale . 449 Ecc. Sonn. 3. 37. 2
When ye would shelter in a happy home, . . . 463 *Adieu, Rydalian 3
A happy people won for thee that name . . . 463 *They called 2
The concert, for the happy, then may vie . . . 464 *Greta, what 12
Have passed away ; less happy than the One . . 475 *There ! said 12
Full happy season, when was known, ... 478 Somnamb. 25
The work of Fancy, or some happy tone . . . 480 *Most sweet 6
Such an odd such a kind happy creature as he. . 482 Character 20
Thou happy Soul ! and can it be . . . . . 486 Matthew 30
She seemed as happy as a wave . . . . . 487 *We walked 51
A happy youth, and their old age . . . . . 487 Fountain 43
Upon these happy plains ; . . . . 487 Fountain 60
Sails with her happy destiny ; . . . . . . 490 Night Thought 2
And happy will our nature be, ... 492 Duty 18
Who is the happy Warrior ? Who is he . . . 493 Hap. War. 1
Is happy as a Lover ; and attired . . . . . 493 Hap. War. 51
This is the happy Warrior ; this is He . . . . 494 Hap. War. 84
Let me, thy happy guide, now point thy way, . . 496 *A little 23
We two have known such happy hours together . 498 *Enough of climbing 46
Which ye feel not, happy pair ! . . . . . . 503 Warning 4
How happy at all seasons, could like aim . . . 512 *Who rashly 36
This People, once so happy, so renowned . . . 513 General Fast 11
Blithe hopes and happy musings soon took flight, 523 Epist. Beaumont 120
That happy gleam of vernal eyes, ... 530 Gleaner 1
Such happy privilege hath life's gay Prime, . . 532 *Once I 28
Where happy generations lie, ... 533 *Blest is 49
And happy were I, if the Czar . . . . . 545 Russ. Fug. 309
Hast been so happy that thou know'st what thoughts . . . . 551 *If thou in 2
And is happy as if the rich freight were his own. . 571 Farmer 84
Shining upon thy happy grave. . . . . . . 578 *I come 72
In more than happy mood . . . . 579 *Sweet Flower 24
Yet for one happy issue :—and I look . . . . 582 *To public 3

Happy—*continued.*
Is happy in his vow, and fondly cleaves . . . 586 Ch. Lamb 124
Shout round me, let me hear thy shouts, thou happy Shepherd-boy ! . . . . 588 Immortality 35
Than when, erewhile, I taught, " a happy child," 591 Ev. Wk. Quarto 19
And with rock-honey flow'd the happy land. . . 611 Desc.Sk.Quarto 477
For ye have reach'd at last the happy shore, . . 614 Desc.Sk.Quarto 668
While hum with busier joy her happy bees ; . . 615 Desc.Sk.Quarto 731
Reared Hawkshead's happy roof, and call'd it mine. 619 School Ex. 66
Take pleasure in the midst of happy thoughts, . 622 Recluse 1. 1. 87
Doth make the happy happier. This have we . 627 *The star 6
Welcomes the Consort of a happy Queen. . . . 629 Installation 72
I heeded not their summons : happy time . . 638 Prelude 1. 428
And be ye happy ! Yet, my Friends ! I know . 642 Prelude 2. 41
Or happy blunder triumphed, bursts of glee . . 644 Prelude 2. 163
Of pleasant wandering. Happy time ! more dear 647 Prelude 2. 332
So many happy youths, so wide and fair . . . 652 Prelude 3. 218
Yet Nature, or a happy course of things . . . 653 Prelude 3. 327
I grieve not ; happy is the gownèd youth, . . 656 Prelude 3. 491
Of Fancy, happy pastures ranged at will, . . . 669 Prelude 5. 237
Or conning more, as happy as the birds . . . 674 Prelude 5. 565
With flowing cups elate and happy thoughts . . 681 Prelude 6. 398
A happy time that was ; triumphant looks . . 686 Prelude 6. 755
When storms are raging. Happy are they both— 692 Prelude 7. 328
Happy, and now most thankful that my walk . 704 Prelude 8. 330
O, happy time of youthful lovers, (thus . . . 717 Prelude 9. 553
With happy faces and with garlands hung, . . 725 Prelude 10. 494
Among whose happy fields I had grown up . . 725 Prelude 10. 525
In temperament, withal a happy man, ... 731 Prelude 11. 276
Her seas yet smiling, her once happy vales ; . . 733 Prelude 11. 431
So was I favoured—such my happy lot— . . . 735 Prelude 12. 49
Than those few nooks to which my happy feet . 737 Prelude 12. 179
From her that happy stillness of the mind . . 740 Prelude 13. 9
Thou in bewitching words, with happy heart, . 751 Prelude 14. 398
Or by the silent looks of happy things, . . . 759 Excursion 1. 189
Happy, and quiet in his cheerfulness, ... 761 Excursion 1. 367
This happy Land was stricken to the heart ! . . 764 Excursion 1. 540
That seemed the very sound of happy thoughts. . 766 Excursion 1. 696
Most happy, if, from aught discovered there . . 770 Excursion 1. 898
To happy contemplation soothed his walk ; . . 772 Excursion 2. 50
A happy service ; for he was sincere . . . . 775 Excursion 2. 224
Broke from the happy old Man's reverend lip ; . 787 Excursion 3. 76
A course of days composing happy months, . . 792 Excursion 3. 453
And they as happy years ; the present still . . 792 Excursion 3. 454
" O happy time ! still happier was at hand ; . . 794 Excursion 3. 550
The twain within our happy cottage born, . . 794 Excursion 3. 589
Our happy life's only remaining stay— . . . 795 Excursion 3. 648
Shall then be yours among the happy few . . . 804 Excursion 4. 230
' Happy is he who lives to understand, . . . 806 Excursion 4. 332
Where peace and happy consciousness should dwell, 810 Excursion 4. 628
Where on the labours of the happy throng . . 819 Excursion 4. 1195
For my own peaceful lot and happy choice ; . . 823 Excursion 5. 51
" As 'mid some happy valley of the Alps," . . 823 Excursion 5. 92
Said I, " once happy, ere tyrannic power, . . . 823 Excursion 5. 93
—Not for a happy land do I enquire, ... 827 Excursion 5. 349
To exclaim—' O happy ! yielding to the law . . 835 Excursion 5. 828
Of happy instinct which the woodland bird . . 835 Excursion 5. 845
In happy infancy. He could not pine . . . . 844 Excursion 6. 383
Happy as they. With spirit-saddening power . 851 Excursion 6. 858
See daily in that happy family. . . . . . 855 Excursion 6. 1126
—Thrice happy, then, the Mother may be deemed, 856 Excursion 6. 1188
A happy consummation ! an accord . . . . 861 Excursion 7. 255
Measuring the soil beneath their happy feet . . 869 Excursion 7. 776
" Happy," rejoined the Wanderer, " they who gain 875 Excursion 8. 82
" And yet, O happy Pastor of a flock . . . . 876 Excursion 8. 148
Hangs on the old Man with a happy look, . . . 881 Excursion 8. 498
Their happy year spins round. The youth obeys 884 Excursion 9. 33
To breathe and to be happy, run and shout . . 888 Excursion 9. 263
The happy Island where ye think and act ; . . 890 Excursion 9. 412
In a deep pool, by happy chance we saw . . . 890 Excursion 9. 439
Be happy in himself ?—The law of faith . . . 894 Excursion 9. 672
Was raised again : and to a happy few, . . . 895 Excursion 9. 718
Who leads a happy life . . . . S.3. 423 Tinker 1
Than their too happy minstrelsy,—a voice . . S.3. 436 *The doubt 176
" What happy fortune were it here to live ! . . K. 8. 236 Recluse 1. 1. 11
Was that same young and happy being) became . K. 8. 237 Recluse 1. 1. 48
Made for itself ; and happy in itself, ... K. 8. 240 Recluse 1. 1. 150
The sunbeam said, " Be happy." When this Vale K. 8. 241 Recluse 1. 1. 170
Happiest of happy though I be, like them . . K. 8. 242 Recluse 1. 1. 198
Have felt it, not the happy Quires of Spring, . . K. 8. 243 Recluse 1. 1. 235
Which in this happy region they behold ! . . . K. 8. 244 Recluse 1. 1. 289
He, happy man ! is master of the field, . . . K. 8. 247 Recluse 1. 1. 382
Herein less happy than the Traveller . . . . K. 8. 250 Recluse 1. 1. 492
She being herself a Mother, happy Beast . . . K. 8. 251 Recluse 1. 1. 529
And ye as happy under Nature's care, ... K. 8. 251 Recluse 1. 1. 532
And must be, with God's will, a happy band. . . K. 8. 254 Recluse 1. 1. 663
O happy Thing ! among thy flowery creeks, . . K. 8. 265 *Brook, that 4
And happy, dancing down thy water-breaks : . K. 8. 265 *Brook, that 5
Though very happy are not very wise . . . . L. 1. 95 Juvenal 3. 21
Yet happy they who in life's later scene . . . L. 1. 96 Juvenal 3. 53

Harangue. Here closed the Sage that eloquent harangue, ... 820 Excursion 4. 1275

Haranguers. To Hawkers and Haranguers, hubbub wild ! . . . . 710 Prelude 9. 58

Harangues. Lo ! he harangues his cohorts—*there* the storm . . . . 368 Trajan 43
Poured forth harangues, how sadly out of place !— 695 Prelude 7. 550

Harass. Fancy, intent to harass and annoy, . . 153 Morn. Ex. 11
Harass the mind and strip from off the bowers 538 *In desultory 35

Harassed. To harassed Piety, " Dismiss thy fear, 431 Ecc. Sonn. 2. 13. 3
Distressed and harassed, but with mind unbroken : 495 Fact 29

Harassed—*continued.*
I have been harassed with the toil of verse, . . 660 *Prelude* 4. 111
Hath harassed him toiling through fearful storm, 852 *Excursion* 6. 913
Harassing. Harassing both; until he sank and pressed . . . . 718 *Prelude* 9. 574
Harbinger. To the harbinger of night. . . . . 90 *Longest Day* 8
Is but a harbinger of death : . . . . . . 164 **Fair Lady* 36
Chaste Snowdrop, venturous harbinger of Spring, 264 *Snowdrop* 13
Fly, some kind Harbinger, to Grasmere-dale ! . 294 **Fly, some* 1
Nor fail to be the harbinger . . . . . . 530 †*Redbreast* 15
Is come Whose harbinger he was ; a time . . 722 *Prelude* 10. 308
Harbour. Has driven him out of harbour ? I believe 53 *Bord.* 867
For the sun is in his harbour, ... 90 *Longest Day* 3
Find, within, a blessed harbour ! . . . . . 181 *Waggoner* 4. 170
A harbour and a hold ; . . . . 218 *Young Lady* 3
Suns that through blood their western harbour sought, ... 299 *Brownie's Cell* 61
Rocks in its harbour, lodging peaceably. . . . 489 *Pers. Talk* 50
Shall be my harbour ? underneath what grove . 632 *Prelude* 1. 11
Some inner meanings which might harbour there. 707 *Prelude* 8. 538
And found a kind of home or harbour there. . . 757 *Excursion* 1. 56
The huge round chimneys, harbour of delight . 881 *Excursion* 8. 481
And make a stormy harbour for the winds. . . K.8. 225 **I will* 34
Harboured. Harboured where none can be misled, 285 *Grave of Burns* 69
FUENTES once harboured the good and the brave, 340 *Fort Fuentes* 13
And harboured ships, whose pride is on the sea, . 504 *Warning* 44
That ever harboured in the breast of man. . 679 *Prelude* 6. 318
In London chiefly harboured, whence I roamed, . 751 *Prelude* 14. 351
That harboured them,—the souls retaining yet . 814 *Excursion* 4. 900
Harbourless. Lest virtue should be harbourless, . 545 *Russ. Fug.* 307
Harbours. Harbours a self-contented Wren, . . 165 *Parrot* 30
Once hung, a Poet harbours now, ... 174 *Waggoner* 1. 59
Fair Pilgrim ! harbours she a sense . . . . 397 *White Doe* 110
There harbours ; whether we be young or old, . 684 *Prelude* 6. 603
Fly to those harbours, driven by hound and horn 808 *Excursion* 4. 501
Hard. Oh ! give not me that eye of hard disdain . 20 *Desc. Sk.* 545
Hath told ; for, landing after labour hard, . . 25 *Guilt* 49
Forced hard against the wind a thick unwieldy flight. . . . . 26 *Guilt* 108
" 'Twas a hard change ; an evil time was come ; . 29 *Guilt* 271
" Bad is the world, and hard is the world's law . 33 *Guilt* 505
I have been waiting in the wood hard by . . . 43 *Bord.* 355
Beat hard upon my head—and yet I saw . . . 45 *Bord.* 424
How goes the night. 'Tis hard to measure time . 52 *Bord.* 805
Of misery that was not—— Troth, 'tis hard— . 56 *Bord.* 1048
The storm beats hard—Mercy for poor or rich, . 71 *Bord.* 1882
Hard by a Man I met, who, from plain proofs . 75 *Bord.* 2128
Start not !—Here is another face hard by ; . . 77 *Bord.* 2288
The Sparrow's dwelling, which, hard by . . . 79 *Sparrow's Nest* 7
Night and day thou art safe,—our cottage is hard by. . . . . 88 *Pet-lamb* 58
Misgivings, hard to vanquish or control, . . . 112 **O dearer* 5
Hard labour in a time of need ! . . . . . 115 *Last of Flock* 42
Our lot is a hard lot ; the sun himself . . . . 134 *Michael* 233
The Vicar from his gloomy house hard by . . 147 *Joanna* 21
Turns to a little tent hard by : . . . . . 176 *Waggoner* 1. 265
Hard passage forcing on, with head . . . . 179 *Waggoner* 3. 81
In truth, you'd find it hard to say . . . . 197 *Thorn* 2
With hard contempt his heart was wrung, . . 241 *P. B.* 454
The hard dry see-saw of his horrible bray ! . . 241 *P. B.* 480
Great is the glory, for the strife is hard ! . . 260 **High is* 14
Bent by a load of Mulberry leaves !—most hard . 366 *Lombardy* 2
Dutiful Child, her lot how hard ! . . . . . 372 *Eg. Maid* 213
Or with bravado insolent and hard, ... 504 *Warning* 103
Hard task ! exclaim the undisciplined, to lean . 515 **Hard task* 1
(Suspect not, Anna, that their fate is hard ; . . 527 **Those breathing* 2
With a hard bed and scanty nourishment, . . 529 *Poor Robin* 8
'Twas a hard time for Goody Blake. . . . . 536 *Goody Blake* 44
The pang was hard to bear ; . . . . . . 544 *Russ. Fug.* 226
Of hard ascent before thou reach the top . . . 548 **Stay, bold* 3
Where he was cast into a pit hard by. . . . 555 *Prioress* 155
And hard hearts he can make them kind and free. 556 *Cuck. and Night.* 5
How hard, alas ! to bear, I only know. . . . 557 *Cuck. and Night.* 40
But straightway to a wood that was hard by, . 557 *Cuck. and Night.* 58
Toils long and hard.—The warrior will report . 574 *Chiabrera* 4. 3
May cling ;—hard fate ! which haply need not be 626 **Son of* 7
Hard task, vain hope, to analyse the mind, . . 645 *Prelude* 2. 228
Roar, and the rain beat hard ; where I so oft . 659 *Prelude* 4. 86
Of study and hard thought ; there, there, it is . 665 *Prelude* 5. 10
Behold, turned upwards, a face hard and strong . 690 *Prelude* 7. 200
Are falling hard, with people yet astir, . . . 697 *Prelude* 7. 664
And hazard, and hard labour interchanged . . 703 *Prelude* 8. 254
From the hard floor reverberated, then . . . 716 *Prelude* 9. 450
Seems hard to shun. And yet I knew a maid, . 736 *Prelude* 12. 151
Hard by, soon after that fell deed was wrought, . 737 *Prelude* 12. 239
If virtue be indeed so hard to rear, ... 742 *Prelude* 13. 177
And their hard service, deemed debasing now, . 761 *Excursion* 1. 327
Is difficult to gain, and hard to keep— . . . 830 *Excursion* 5. 493
To fix her eyes—alas ! 'twas hard to bear ! . . 853 *Excursion* 6. 964
Hard to be won, and only by a few ; . . . . 887 *Excursion* 9. 235
Hard to believe, yet could they well discern . . K.8. 225 **I will* 41
Hardened. The Pharaohs of the earth, the men of hardened heart ! . . . . 216 *Enterprise* 106
Yon reverend hawthorns, hardened to the rod . 450 *Ecc. Sonn.* 3. 39. 5
The hardened soil, and knots of withered grass : . 769 *Excursion* 1. 835
Hardened by impious pride !—I did not fear . . 779 *Excursion* 2. 486
Hardening. Hardening a heart that loathes or slights 533 **Blest is* 53
Harder. Fate harder still ! had he to endure assaults 574 *Chiabrera* 5. 4
Led by Philosophers. With harder fate, . . . 715 *Prelude* 9. 417
Hardest. He has the very hardest heart on earth ; 45 *Bord.* 466
And airy bonds are hardest to disown ; . . . 435 *Ecc. Sonn.* 2. 28. 11

Hardest—*continued.*
Making your hardest task your best delight, . . 444 *Ecc. Sonn.* 3. 16. 7
Hard-hearted. Speak. Speak ! He is a most hard-hearted Man. . . . . 46 *Bord.* 501
With a hard-hearted ignorance ; your struggles . 64 *Bord.* 1505
Hardier. But hardier far, once more I see thee bend 264 *Snowdrop* 2
Hardiest. For all she taught of hardiest and of best, 441 *Ecc. Sonn.* 3. 3. 5
Though it can wet with tears the hardiest cheek. 460 **Wanderer ! that* 62
Hardihood. Leaps with a bound of graceful hardihood ; . . . . 17 *Desc. Sk.* 381
Lavished in fight with desperate hardihood ; . . 322 **By Moscow* 3
Of hardihood with wreaths that shall not fail ?— 430 *Ecc. Sonn.* 2. 7. 8
Intended, rose in hardihood, and dared . . . 719 *Prelude* 10. 106
Hardily. Which at the Cuckoo hardily I cast, . . 560 *Cuck.and Night.* 218
Hardiment. Now is the time to prove your hardiment ! . . . . 309 *Men of Kent* 4
Hardiness. Who did on thee the hardiness bestow 562 *Cuck.and Night.* 293
Hardknot's. Slept amid that lone Camp on Hardknot's height, ... 380 *Duddon* 17. 10
Hardly. There, waves that, hardly weltering, die away, ... 4 *Ev. Wk.* 122
Now hardly heard, beguiles my homeward way. . 9 *Ev. Wk.* 366
And, whistling, called the wind that hardly curled 31 *Guilt* 356
The Doctor's self could hardly spare : . . . 128 *Idiot Boy* 238
She hardly can sustain her fears ; . . . . . 130 *Idiot Boy* 359
You hardly can perceive his joy. . . . . . 130 *Idiot Boy* 396
The owls have hardly sung their last, ... 131 *Idiot Boy* 432
Is hardly worse beset than mine, ... 179 *Waggoner* 3. 86
These hedge-rows, hardly hedge-rows, little lines . 206 *Tintern* 15
Sinks, hardly conscious of the influence— . . 227 *Vernal Ode* 89
The conquests lost that were so hardly won :— . 431 *Ecc. Sonn.* 2. 10. 11
However hardly won or justly dear : . . . . 442 *Ecc. Sonn.* 3. 10. 12
Alas ! 'twas hardly worth the telling, ... 536 *Goody Blake* 27
'Tis a look which at this time is hardly his own, . 572 *Avarice* 23
With envy, what the Old Man hardly feels. . . 572 *Animal Tran.* 14
Some, hardly heard their chissel's clinking sound, 594 *Ev. Wk. Quarto* 145
Where hardly giv'n the hopeless waste to chear . 608 *Desc.Sk.Quarto* 319
Beyond his native valley hardly stray, . . . 611 *Desc.Sk.Quarto* 515
But hardly less industrious ; with shrill notes . 650 *Prelude* 3. 51
A tournament of blows, some hardly dealt . . 657 *Prelude* 3. 583
A tale of silent suffering, hardly clothed . . . 765 *Excursion* 1. 638
I knew not how, and hardly whence they came. . 768 *Excursion* 1. 803
Such as is sometimes seen, and hardly seen, . . 787 *Excursion* 3. 72
Hardly-paining. Till our small share of hardly-paining sighs . . . . 8 *Ev. Wk.* 352
Hardness. " There was a hardness in his cheek, . 240 *P. B.* 316
There was a hardness in his eye, ... 240 *P. B.* 317
The hardness of that sallow face. . . . . . 485 *Poet's Epitaph* 8
Hardship. Of hardship and distressful fear, amid the houseless waste . . . . 91 *Norman Boy* 27
Of hardship, skill or courage, joy or fear ; . . 132 *Michael* 69
What hardship had it been to wait an hour ? . . 303 **Is it* 13
Pleased (though to hardship born, and compassed round . . . . 682 *Prelude* 6. 509
With needless services, from hardship free. . . 762 *Excursion* 1. 385
From risk and hardship, inwardly retrace . . 794 *Excursion* 3. 559
And hardship undergone in various climes, . . 882 *Excursion* 8. 509
Hardships. In all his hardships, since that happy time . . . . 96 *Brothers* 73
Hardships for the brave encountered . . . . 140 *Arm. Lady* 33
And he had many hardships to endure : . . . 196 *Resolution* 102
These hardships ill-sustained, these dangers past, 320 **Hunger, and* 4
And hardships manifold did I endure, ... 470 †*From early* 7
To turn from present hardships to the past, . . 665 *Prelude* 4. 436
And how through hardships manifold and long . 727 *Prelude* 10. 592
The hardships of that season : many rich . . . 764 *Excursion* 1. 543
Hardy. Were hardy, though his cheek seemed worn with care . . . . 24 *Guilt* 5
" Or, if you thirst with hardy zeal . . . . 237 *P. B.* 106
Whom hardy Rome was fearful to oppose ; . . 320 **They seek* 7
Of hardy laurel and wild holly boughs— . . . 324 *Ode 1814* 45
So stout and hardy were the band . . . . 375 **The Minstrels* 11
Teach what *they* learn ? Up, hardy Mountaineer ! 389 *Tyndrum* 9
To sap your hardy virtue, and abate . . . . 420 *Ecc. Sonn.* 1. 8. 6
Enlivened, braced, by hardy luxuries, ... 527 **Those breathing* 45
Half-and-half idlers, hardy recusants, . . . 650 *Prelude* 3. 67
Of hardy disobedience towards friends . . . . 675 *Prelude* 6. 28
Bound to the distant Alps. A hardy slight . . 680 *Prelude* 6. 326
In hardy independence, to stand up . . . . 751 *Prelude* 14. 333
Hardy and grand, a weather-beaten oak, . . . 829 *Excursion* 5. 456
A hardy Girl continues to provide ; . . . . 856 *Excursion* 6. 1157
Ten hardy Striplings, all in bright attire, . . 869 *Excursion* 7. 766
The rudiments of war ; ten—hardy, strong, . . 869 *Excursion* 7. 771
Hare.
Hurrying the timid hare through rustling corn ; . 9 *Ev. Wk.* 374
The hare upon the green ; . . . . 83 *Lucy Gray* 10
The hare has just started from Hamilton's grounds, 120 *Childless Father* 3
While hare and leveret, seen at play, ... 154 *Flower Garden* 41
The hare is running races in her mirth ; . . . 195 *Resolution* 11
I saw the hare that raced about with joy ; . . 195 *Resolution* 16
And I bethought me of the playful hare : . . . 195 *Resolution* 30
Sad were our lot : no hunter of the hare . . . 466 *St. Bees* 3
See a hare before him started ! . . . . . 490 *Incident : Dog* 9
And the hare whom they pursue, ... 490 *Incident : Dog* 13
But the nimble Hare hath trusted . . . . . 490 *Incident : Dog* 19
Hurrying the feeding hare thro' rustling corn ; . 600 *Ev. Wk. Quarto* 442
The pack loud chiming, and the hunted hare. . 638 *Prelude* 1. 437
Harebell. Catching from tufts of grass and harebell flowers . . . . 678 *Prelude* 6. 221
And pliant harebell, swinging in the breeze . . . 722 *Prelude* 10. 277
Harebells. Like harebells bathed in dew, . . . 541 *Russ. Fug.* 2

Haunts—*continued.*
He fled, to shun the haunts of human kind ; 718 *Prelude* 9. 579
Among the close and overcrowded haunts . 743 *Prelude* 13. 203
—Such grateful haunts foregoing, if I oft 755 *Recluse* 1. 1. 825
An intellectual ruler in the haunts 774 *Excursion* 2. 180
And loved the haunts of children ; here, no doubt, 778 *Excursion* 2. 449
At a composing distance from the haunts 799 *Excursion* 3. 904
Loved haunts like these ; the unimprisoned Mind 803 *Excursion* 4. 106
—Truth has her pleasure-grounds, her haunts of ease 810 *Excursion* 4. 588
And the owl's prey ; from these bare haunts, to which 843 *Excursion* 6. 328
Erelong, forsaking all her natural haunts, S.3. 436 **The doubt* 186

Have, *omitted.*

Haven. *See* **Convent-haven.**
And the dear haven where he wished to be 122 *V. and J.* 59
Not the less she loves her haven 166 *Wand. Jew* 19
Yet still I ask, what haven is her mark ? 258 **Where lies the Land* 9
Come like a giant from a haven broad ; 258 **With Ships* 6
Spread round that haven in the glen ; 296 *Highland Boy* 112
That Isle without a house or haven ; 371 *Eg. Maid* 122
But now she dares to seek a haven 414 *White Doe* 1617
The precious Tomb, their haven of salvation. 427 *Ecc. Sonn.* 1. 34. 14
Or in the haven rest, or sheltering bay, 454 *Sea-side* 37
Each for her haven ; with her freight of Care, 471 *Ailsa Crag* 9
The haven of her hope she won, 542 *Russ. Fug.* 23
Death is the quiet haven of us all. 574 *Chiabrera* 4. 27
With which she left her haven—not for this, 882 *Excursion* 8. 512

Having. Of having left a thing like her alive ! 78 *Bord.* 2313
And, having seen that lovely Maid, 108 *Louisa* 2
Once having seen her clasp with fond embrace 120 *Emigrant Mother* 9
Careless of books, yet having felt the power 131 *Michael* 28
He, having made a pause, the same discourse renewed. 197 *Resolution* 133
And having rights in all that we behold. 284 *Departure* 28
That, having forced its way from birth to birth, 311 **Who rises* 19
Who having left the Cemetery stands 355 *Aquap.* 179
(Life's three first seasons having passed away) 394 **No more* 26
Who, having filled a holy place, 416 *White Doe* 1875
Storm-driven ; who, having seen the cup of woe 419 *Ecc. Sonn.* 1. 2. 12
Or, having known the splendours of success, 458 *Sea-shore* 32
Where one poor Plane-tree, having as it might 521 *Epist. Beaumont* 14
But, as it chanced, Sir William having learned 548 **Stranger ! this* 8
Which having been must ever be ; 590 *Immortality* 186
Dear Valley, having in thy face a smile 622 *Recluse* 1. 1. 116
That having 'mid my native hills given loose 655 *Prelude* 3. 424
And having almost in my mind put off 657 *Prelude* 3. 576
Among the impervious crags, but having been 660 *Prelude* 4. 98
While listlessly I sate, and, having closed 666 *Prelude* 5. 63
Having a perfect faith in all that passed. 667 *Prelude* 5. 114
Are dearest to me *now ;* for, having scanned, 676 *Prelude* 6. 100
Upon a desert coast, that having brought 677 *Prelude* 6. 144
Have seen us side by side, when, having clomb 678 *Prelude* 6. 212
When, having closed the mighty Shakspeare's page, 694 *Prelude* 7. 484
When, having thridded the long labyrinth 707 *Prelude* 8. 541
And public news ; but having never seen 711 *Prelude* 9. 100
Should see the people having a strong hand 717 *Prelude* 9. 530
Vague and unsound ; and having brought the books 741 *Prelude* 13. 71
And having thus discerned how dire a thing 741 *Prelude* 13. 76
Is lodged, and how increased : and having gained 741 *Prelude* 13. 79
Imagination having been our theme, 749 *Prelude* 14. 206
Flowed in the bent of Nature. Having now 751 *Prelude* 14. 369
For having given the story of myself, 751 *Prelude* 14. 391
Nor having e'er, as life advanced, been led 757 *Excursion* 1. 86
And I descended. Having reached the house, 785 *Excursion* 2. 881
Who, having o'er the past no power, would live 798 *Excursion* 3. 873
There imaged : or when, having gained the top 799 *Excursion* 3. 935
Rises ; but, having reached the thinner air, 803 *Excursion* 4. 144
So pitiably, that, having ceased to see 804 *Excursion* 4. 171
If, having walked with Nature threescore years, 816 *Excursion* 4. 980
And some one, as she entered, having chanced 853 *Excursion* 6. 974
And, having once espoused, would never quit ; 862 *Excursion* 7. 350
A pride in having, or a fear to lose ; 866 *Excursion* 7. 572
Yet, having spent a summer's day S.3. 438 **My Lord* 7
They having also chosen this abode ; K.8. 243 *Recluse* 1.1.253
Is past we blame it not for having come. K.8. 244 *Recluse* 1.1.291

Havoc. Appalling havoc ! but serene his brow, 21 *Desc. Sk.* 581
Here, where, of havoc tired and rash undoing, 283 **Here, where* 1
And love of havoc, (for with such disease 292 **Degenerate Douglas* 3
From further havoc, but repent in vain,— 504 *Warning* 71
To social havoc. Is not Conscience ours, 514 **Who ponders* 11
Unpitied havoc ! Victims unlamented ! 582 *Invoc. Earth* 14
Low barks the fox ; by Havoc rouz'd the bear, 606 *Desc.Sk.Quarto* 231
Havoc and Chaos blast a thousand vales, 615 *Desc.Sk.Quarto* 695
Look up for sign of havoc, Fire and Sword, 617 *Desc.Sk.Quarto* 803
In works of havoc ; taking from these vales, 866 *Excursion* 7. 593

Hawes. As I from Hawes to Richmond did repair, 202 *Hart-leap* 101

Hawk. *See* **Dor-hawk.**
As yon Hawk exhibits, pairing 163 *Hint* 6
With some loved friend, or by the unseen hawk 389 *Glencroe* 5
The hawk forget his perch ; the hound 402 *White Doe* 552
Through crystal water, smoothly as a hawk, 891 *Excursion* 9. 491

Hawker's. Of hawker's wares—books, pictures, combs, and pins— 699 *Prelude* 8. 29

Hawkers. To Hawkers and Haranguers, hubbub wild ! 710 *Prelude* 9. 58
Shrill voices from the hawkers in the throng, 719 *Prelude* 10. 99

Hawkshead's. Reared Hawkshead's happy roof, and call'd it mine. 619 *School Ex.* 66

Hawthorn. Would be most welcome. Yon white hawthorn gained, 41 *Bord.* 216
Of green leaves on the hawthorn spray, 81 †*Mother's Return* 38
And through the broken hawthorn hedge, 83 *Lucy Gray* 47
And wander down yon hawthorn dell, 180 *Waggoner* 4. 16
Grasping a hawthorn branch in hand, 243 *P. B.* 636
And wild rose tip-toe upon hawthorn stocks, 260 **How sweet* 5
It lacked not old remains of hawthorn bowers, 377 *Duddon* 6. 2
The White Doe, in the hawthorn brake ; 405 *White Doe* 877
Untouched the hawthorn bough, 506 **While from* 22
And flew into a hawthorn by that brook ; 562 *Cuck.andNight.* 287
I laughed with Chaucer in the hawthorn shade ; 653 *Prelude* 3. 276
Of a thick hawthorn, I could mark him well, 664 *Prelude* 4. 390
Upon my left a blasted hawthorn stood ; 738 *Prelude* 12. 301
Beneath yon hawthorn, planted by myself 854 *Excursion* 6. 1081

Hawthorn-fence. That cuts along the hawthorn-fence ; 239 *P. B.* 302

Hawthorn-roof. To the bare life beneath the hawthorn-roof 221 *Triad* 69

Hawthorns. Yon reverend hawthorns, hardened to the rod 450 *Ecc. Sonn.* 3. 39. 5
Where from sea-blasts the hawthorns lean, 536 *Goody Blake* 31
Caught by the hawthorns from the loaded wain, S.3. 417 **Sweet was* 4

Hawthorn-tree. While thy tired lute hangs on the hawthorn-tree, 227 *Vernal Ode* 87

Hay. Thrusts his hands in a waggon, and smells at the hay ; 570 *Farmer* 82
Turning with quiet touch the valley's hay, 607 *Desc.Sk.Quarto* 274
Shagged with wild pale green tufts of fragrant hay, S.3. 417 **Sweet was* 3

Haycock. The maiden spread the haycock in the sun, 683 *Prelude* 6. 537
'Mid a green hay-cock in a sunny field. 784 *Excursion* 2. 823

Haycocks. With haycocks studded, striped with yellowing grain— 525 *Epist. Beaumont* 226

Haydon. Haydon ! let worthier judges praise the skill 277 **Haydon ! let* 1

Hay-field. Springing afresh, had o'er the hay-field spread 767 *Excursion* 1. 709

Hay-makers. Of hay-makers, beneath the burning sun 783 *Excursion* 2. 767

Haymarket. Up the Haymarket hill he oft whistles his way, 570 *Farmer* 81

Hay-stack. And underneath the hay-stack warm, 144 *Her Eyes* 7

Hayti's. Hayti's shining queen was made L.2. 190 **Queen and* 9

Hazard. Armed to repel them ? Every hazard faced 541 *Grace Darl.* 76
Hazard or toil ; among the sands was seen 575 *Chiabrera* 6. 5
And hazard, and hard labour interchanged 703 *Prelude* 8. 254
Without some hazard to the finer sense ; 751 *Prelude* 14. 367

Hazardous. Employment hazardous and wearisome ! 196 *Resolution* 101
So hazardous that feet and hands became 833 *Excursion* 5. 738

Hazards. Resolute, at all hazards, to fulfil 514 **Blest Statesman* 8
Hazards and strange escapes, of which the rocks 701 *Prelude* 8. 170

Haze. Through a haze of human nature, 141 *Arm. Lady* 133
Through a thin veil of glittering haze was seen 149 **A narrow* 45
Are mastered by the breathing haze ; 167 *Pilgrim's Dream* 37
In naked splendour, clear from mist or haze, 329 *Ode : Thanks.* 9
O'er intervenient waste, through glimmering haze, 352 *Aquap.* 18
Hidden by clouds, and oft bedimmed by haze, 849 *Excursion* 6. 704

Hazel. Amid yon tuft of hazel trees, 159 *Green Linnet* 25
His shining hazel eye. 241 *P. B.* 435
The woods of autumn, and their hazel bowers 639 *Prelude* 1. 484
Around me from among the hazel leaves, 661 *Prelude* 4. 183

Hazels. Of devastation ; but the hazels rose 185 *Nutting* 19
Of hazels, and the green and mossy bower, 185 *Nutting* 46
Mark the concentred hazels that enclose 262 **Mark the* 1

Hazy. In hazy straits the clouds between, 173 *Waggoner* 1. 10
A tender hazy brightness ; 302 *Yarrow V.* 20
Yon hazy ridges to their eyes 457 **Had this* 43

He, *omitted.*

Head. *See* **Deep-dale-head, Fountain-head, Green-head, Orrest-head, Water-head.**
A crest of purple tops the warrior's head. 5 *Ev. Wk.* 149
Of splendour—save the beacon's spiry head 6 *Ev. Wk.* 210
I see her now, denied to lay her head, 7 *Ev. Wk.* 256
Dear is the forest frowning o'er his head, 11 *Desc. Sk.* 21
Her files of road-elms, high above my head 11 *Desc. Sk.* 46
Above a melancholy mountain's head, 14 *Desc. Sk.* 189
Stoops her sick head, and shuts her weary eyes ; 14 *Desc. Sk.* 191
Bows his young head with sorrow to the grave. 20 *Desc. Sk.* 527
And, lifting up his head, he then would gaze 23 *Yew-tree* 33
Or hovel from the storm to shield his head, 25 *Guilt* 42
And the sharp wind his head he oft hath bared ; 25 *Guilt* 47
Disclose a naked guide-post's double head, 26 *Guilt* 134
From one who mourned in sleep, he raised his head, 27 *Guilt* 164
Disclosing the grim head of a late murdered corse. 27 *Guilt* 180
His battered head, a groan the Sailor fetched 33 *Guilt* 489
She strove, and not in vain, her head to rear ; 35 *Guilt* 573
Snapped fierce to make a morsel of his head : 44 *Bord.* 414
And put your head, good Woman, under cover. 45 *Bord.* 417
Beat hard upon my head—and yet I saw 45 *Bord.* 424
Over your head twice twenty years must roll, 52 *Bord.* 820
Beheld a star twinkling above my head, 55 *Bord.* 989
Or you might drive your head against that wall. 56 *Bord.* 1009
Was to be yielded up. Now, by the head 57 *Bord.* 1107
Though it were tottering over a man's head, 67 *Bord.* 1659
I hid my head within a Convent, there. 69 *Bord.* 1766
for his head was cut ; 72 *Bord.* 1944
Ay, and his head was bare ; 72 *Bord.* 1984
His head was bruised, and there was blood about him—— 74 *Bord.* 2075
The roof, self-moved, unsettling o'er his head ; 76 *Bord.* 2182
Delivered heart and head ! Let us to Palestine ; 77 *Bord.* 2282

Head—*continued.*

That clustered round her head. 83 *We are Seven* 8
At this my boy hung down his head, 86 *Anecdote* 45
His head he raised—there was in sight, 86 *Anecdote* 49
Seemed to feast with head and ears; and his tail with pleasure shook. 87 *Pet-lamb* 10
The innocent Boy, else shelterless, his lonely head must hide. 91 *Norman Boy* 24
Here's neither head nor foot-stone, plate of brass, 98 *Brothers* 170
He had as white a head and fresh a cheek 98 *Brothers* 201
"Who, when a crown is fixed upon his head, 105 *Artegal* 170
Did place upon his brother's head the crown, 105 *Artegal* 222
Into a Lover's head! 109 **Strange fits* 26
Equipped from head to foot in iron mail. 111 **'Tis said that some* 47
Ere the tired head of Scotland's Queen 113 *Lament* 69
O wind, that o'er my head art flying 114 *Ind. Wom.* 45
And hide my head where wild beasts roam. 115 *Last of Flock* 80
Too heavily upon the lily's head, 124 *V. and J.* 193
His head upon one breast, while from the other 124 *V. and J.* 215
Both with his head and with his hand, 126 *Idiot Boy* 63
For joy his head and heels are idle, 127 *Idiot Boy* 75
The Moon that shines above his head 127 *Idiot Boy* 80
A thought is come into her head: 129 *Idiot Boy* 302
Perhaps, with head and heels on fire, 129 *Idiot Boy* 332
And now is at the Pony's head,— 130 *Idiot Boy* 383
And gently turned the Pony's head 130 *Idiot Boy* 400
He wears a jewel in his head! 142 †*Lov. and Lik.* 14
With languid limbs and patient head 144 **Driven in* 32
Her eyes are wild, her head is bare, 144 *Her Eyes* 1
And in my head a dull, dull pain; 144 *Her Eyes* 22
And Kirkstone tossed it from his misty head. 147 *Joanna* 65
He stood alone; whereat he turned his head 149 **A narrow* 57
In some far region, here, while o'er my head 151 **When, to* 102
Not lifting yet the head that evening bowed; 153 *Morn. Ex.* 26
Out of its head an Oak had grown, 156 *Oak and Broom* 13
Look up! and think, above your head 156 *Oak and Broom* 25
And o'er your head, as you may see, 156 *Oak and Broom* 39
Doth in thy crimson head delight 157 **In youth* 15
Her head impearling, 157 **In youth* 28
Their snow-white blossoms on my head, 159 *Green Linnet* 2
Upon its head this coronet? 162 **Who fancied* 6
Hung—head pointing towards the ground— 171 *Kitten* 69
He shrugs his shoulders, shakes his head, 174 *Waggoner* 1. 66
But soon large rain-drops on his head 175 *Waggoner* 1. 156
A rending o'er his head begins the fray again. 175 *Waggoner* 1. 204
And so, flag flying at mast head, 178 *Waggoner* 2. 162
Hard passage forcing on, with head 179 *Waggoner* 3. 81
Salutes the Mastiff on the head; 179 *Waggoner* 3. 107
Upon *his* head, whom, in despite 181 *Waggoner* 4. 92
A wound upon the Mastiff's head, 181 *Waggoner* 4. 174
Asunder,—and above his head he sees 184 *Night-piece* 12
And on her head a cap as white as new-fallen snow. 190 *Beggars* 6
I looked reproof—they saw—but neither hung his head. 191 *Beggars* 42
High as a cloud, high over head! 193 *Ruth* 62
His body was bent double, feet and head 196 *Resolution* 66
Cries coming from the mountain head: 199 *Thorn* 160
The trees were grey, with neither arms nor head; 202 *Hart-leap* 109
She lifts her head for endless spring, 203 *Brougham* 9
First shall head the flock of war!" 205 *Brougham* 156
Long-exiled Dion marching at their head, 213 *Dion* 23
But neither veil thy head in shadows dim, 215 *Enterprise* 10
Nile trembles at his fountain head: 216 *Enterprise* 86
But the ringlets of that head 221 *Triad* 107
New glory o'er the mountain's head, 224 **'Tis gone* 59
The foliaged head in cloud-like majesty, 227 *Vernal Ode* 62
The glory of the sun's bright head— 228 *Devot. Incit.* 67
Was heart or head the better. 239 *P. B.* 240
By pleasure running in his head, 240 *P. B.* 329
When, turning round his head, he sees 240 *P. B.* 384
Of the green meadow hangs his head 240 *P. B.* 394
His head is with a halter bound; 241 *P. B.* 396
He turned the eye-ball in his head 241 *P. B.* 439
He lifts his head, he sees his staff; 242 *P. B.* 541
His head upon his elbow propped, 242 *P. B.* 546
So toward the stream his head he bent, 242 *P. B.* 553
Vengeance upon his head will fall, 243 *P. B.* 663
Nor once turns round his head to crop 244 *P. B.* 714
Where he had struck the Ass's head; 244 *P. B.* 727
The Ass turned round his head and *grinned*. 245 *P. B.* 825
He turns aside his head, he pauses; 248 *P. B.* 1033
And on the pillow lays her burning head. 248 *P. B.* 1085
He lifts his head—and sees the Ass 248 *P. B.* 1096
Yet sacred is to me this Mountain's head, 252 **The fairest* 12
—By planting on thy naked head the crest 253 **Aerial Rock* 7
Of cold neglect she leaves thy head ungraced, 254 *Dyer* 9
When twilight shades darken the mountain's head. 255 *S. H.* 6
When she stands cresting the Clown's head, and mocks 260 **How sweet* 8
The effluence from yon distant mountain's head, 263 **How clear* 2
If so he might, yon mountain's glittering head— 263 **How clear* 7
She cast away, and showed her fulgent head 265 **The Shepherd* 5
Which the Muse warms; and I, whose head is grey, 273 **Wild Redbreast* 5
And friends too rarely prop the languid head. 273 **While Anna's* 8
And head that droops because the soul is meek, 274 **Such age* 8
Rotha, my Spiritual Child! this head was grey 274 *Rotha Q.* 1
And, for the stone upon his head, 287 *Ellen Irwin* 54
Their utmost bounty on thy head: 287 *Highland Girl* 4
Jane hangs her head upon my breast, 295 *Highland Boy* 3
What sin would be upon her head 296 *Highland Boy* 87
And bore it on his head. 296 *Highland Boy* 145

Head—*continued.*

The craven few who bowed the head 298 *Brownie's Cell* 48
And let no Slave his head incline, 300 *Cora Linn* 43
Head, harp, and body, split asunder, 300 *Bran* 11
Within thy hearing, or thy head be now 305 *Toussaint* 3
If Kingship bowed its head to Commonwealth— 310 *Invasion* 9
Your feeble spirits! Greece her head hath bowed, 312 **When, far* 11
Yet mark his modest state! upon his head, 314 *Hofer* 7
The ridges of grim war; and at their head 320 **They seek* 4
Shaking the dust and ashes from her head! 331 *Ode: Thanks.* 130
Each slumbering on some mountain's head), 338 *Brientz* 8
Whose head the ruddy apple tops, while he 339 *Tell* 22
Might well be styled this noble body's HEAD; 339 *Schwytz* 11
Or on thy head to poise a show 341 *Ital. Itin.* 7
Pale, ragged, with bare feet and head; 342 *Ital. Itin.* 88
And on the mountain's head. 343 *Eclipse* 30
Of Corybantian cymbals, while the head 346 *Processions* 35
From the Pier's head, musing, and with increase 349 *At Dover* 1
Break forth at thought of laying down his head, 359 **They—who* 2
His head from mist; and, as the wind sobbed through 360 *Albano* 2
He heard a voice, and saw, with half-raised head, 370 *Eg. Maid* 71
To weather-fend the Celtic herdsman's head— 388 **The pibroch's* 7
That make the Patriot-spirit bow her head 388 *Loch Etive* 13
Of the elder's bushy head; 397 *White Doe* 96
Nor spares to stoop her head, and taste 397 *White Doe* 138
And smote off his head on the stones of the porch! 399 *White Doe* 253
Disturbed upon her virgin head; 400 *White Doe* 363
The hairs are white upon your head; 400 *White Doe* 382
Her head upon her lap, concealing 401 *White Doe* 448
With a dear Father at their head! 401 *White Doe* 462
Eyes dark and strong; and on his head 404 *White Doe* 745
They march with Dudley at their head, 404 *White Doe* 787
—So speaking, he his reverend head 405 *White Doe* 862
Too oft, alas! by her whose head 405 *White Doe* 883
But Emily hath raised her head, 413 *White Doe* 1535
To hide her poor afflicted head? 413 *White Doe* 1556
There did she rest, with head reclined, 414 *White Doe* 1633
And laid its head upon her knee, 414 *White Doe* 1654
Black Demons hovering o'er his mitred head, 428 *Ecc. Sonn.* 1. 38. 1
To stoop her head before these desperate shocks— 433 *Ecc. Sonn.* 2. 21. 12
To the bare head. The victory is complete; 437 *Ecc. Sonn.* 2. 35. 7
For thus equipped, and bearing on his head 438 *Ecc. Sonn.* 2. 39. 6
How, like a Roman, Sidney bowed his head, 442 *Ecc. Sonn.* 3. 10. 3
While on each head his lawn-robed servant lays 446 *Ecc. Sonn.* 3. 23. 9
Unsheathed in wrath to strike the offender's head, 447 *Ecc. Sonn.* 3. 29. 6
That, carried sceptre-like, o'ertops the head 448 *Ecc. Sonn.* 3. 32. 8
Her head, and nothing loth her Majesty 461 **Who but is* 3
Above his head uplifted in vain prayer 475 **Here on their* 9
Of luminous faith, heavenward hath raised that head 476 *Howard* 4
The sun, above the mountain's head, 481 *Tables Turned* 5
"A basket on her head she bare; 487 **We walked* 45
Whom they must follow; on whose head must fall, 493 *Hap. War.* 43
Fall, rosy garlands, from my head! 498 **Departing summer* 16
His head in sunbeams or a bowery cloud, 503 *Warning* 35
In cunning patience, from the head that wears it. 505 *Warning* 110
Drops on the mouldering turret's head, 507 *May* 55
Of motion they renounce, and with the head 508 *F. Stone* 37
For ever.—The Spirit of Alfred, at the head 516 **Young England* 6
But upon Honour's head disturb the crown, 518 *Pun. Death* 4. 12
Above her head and so forgets her vows— 522 *Epist. Beaumont* 49
From the peat-yielding Moss on Gowdar's head. 523 *Epist. Beaumont* 111
Like a small Hamlet, with its bashful head 524 *Epist. Beaumont* 192
By the world's Ruler, on his honoured head! 528 **Those breathing* 110
They rise, or rest the weary head, 530 *Gleaner* 30
Where, ever and anon, her head she shrouds 532 **How beautiful the* 3
And at the head of their Array 535 *Egremont* 39
His melancholy head, and there he died. 536 *Egremont* 104
The cold, cold moon above her head, 537 *Goody Blake* 101
Now rests her weary head. 542 *Russ. Fug.* 40
Above his antlered head; 544 *Russ. Fug.* 268
Your head in this dark lair!" 545 *Russ. Fug.* 320
From a palsy-shaken head. 549 *Hermit's Cell* 1. 16
Draws lightning down upon the head 550 *Hermit's Cell* 5. 11
Another time he took into his head, 564 *Troilus* 106
That overhangs his head from the green wall, 568 *Cumb. Beg.* 118
Then let him pass, a blessing on his head! 568 *Cumb. Beg.* 162
—Then let him pass, a blessing on his head! 568 *Cumb. Beg.* 171
May one blade of grass spring up over thy head; 571 *Farmer* 90
Its mellow lustre round thy honoured head; 583 **With copious* 31
My head hath its coronal, 588 *Immortality* 40
A crest of purple tops his warrior head. 594 *Ev. Wk. Quarto* 132
That tips with eve's last gleam his spiry head. 595 *Ev. Wk. Quarto* 190
Soon shall the Light'ning hold before thy head 597 *Ev. Wk. Quarto* 297
Her road elms rustling thin above my head, 602 *Desc. Sk. Quarto* 48
"Here," cried a swain, whose venerable head 613 *Desc. Sk. Quarto* 594
And quietness pillow his head. 621 *Convict* 28
The Trojans too (Æneas at their head), 624 *Æneid* 58
Licence to hide at intervals her head 626 *Ballot* 6
Were shining o'er my head. I was alone, 636 *Prelude* 1. 315
Upreared its head. I struck and struck again, 637 *Prelude* 1. 380
We schemed and puzzled, head opposed to head 639 *Prelude* 1. 512
Bowing her head before her sister Faith 650 *Prelude* 3. 86
The head turns round and cannot right itself; 658 *Prelude* 3. 623
I turned my head to look if he were there; 661 *Prelude* 4. 189

Head—*continued.*
And made of it a pillow for her head. 661 *Prelude* 4. 230
Whose transient pleasure mounted to the head, 663 *Prelude* 4. 318
In measured gesture lifted to his head 664 *Prelude* 4. 414
Or, not less pleased, lay on some turret's head, 678 *Prelude* 6. 220
Boyle, Shakspeare, Newton, or the attractive head 689 *Prelude* 7. 166
Upon his head; with basket at his breast 690 *Prelude* 7. 216
Dissolved, have left him an unshrouded head. 699 *Prelude* 8. 17
Erelong, the massy roof above his head, 707 *Prelude* 8. 566
Head after head, and never heads enough 723 *Prelude* 10. 362
But said to me, " My head will soon lie low;" 726 *Prelude* 10. 539
To those sweet counsels between head and heart 732 *Prelude* 11. 353
A girl, who bore a pitcher on her head, 738 *Prelude* 12. 251
Beheld the stars come out above his head, 758 *Excursion* 1. 129
And, while, beside him, with uncovered head, 763 *Excursion* 1. 466
A little while; then turned her head away 766 *Excursion* 1. 649
Her head from off her pillow, to look forth, 766 *Excursion* 1. 664
The faithful servant, who must hide his head 778 *Excursion* 2. 476
I stand—the chasm of sky above my head 787 *Excursion* 3. 94
Pouring above his head its radiance down 799 *Excursion* 3. 942
Whose root is fixed in stable earth, whose head 831 *Excursion* 5. 568
The head and mighty paramount of truths,— 839 *Excursion* 6. 85
Aroused his clan; and, fighting at their head, 844 *Excursion* 6. 419
And saturnine; her head not raised to hold 848 *Excursion* 6. 679
It hung its head in mortal languishment. 853 *Excursion* 6. 1002
A stirring foot, a head which beat at nights 860 *Excursion* 7. 211
Of yet unfaded trees she lifts her head 868 *Excursion* 7. 716
Heels over head, like tumblers on a stage. 880 *Excursion* 8. 381
Unheard, the savage nations bowed the head 894 *Excursion* 9. 684
For his own careless head. S.3. 423 *Tinker* 22
The Tinker shakes his head, S.3. 424 *Tinker* 43
Rivall'd by you, hides the diminish'd head. L.1. 88 *Juvenal* 1. 6
These seven long years to Grenville's onion head. L.1. 89 *Juvenal* 1. 28

Headed. *See* **Bare-headed, Grey-headed, Heavy-headed, Hoary-headed, Many-headed.**
I have seen traces of it. Once he headed 63 *Bord.* 1442
Or adverse tides and currents headed, 216 *Enterprise* 77

Head-foremost. Head-foremost, through the driving rain, 199 *Thorn* 183
Head-foremost down the river!" 241 *P. B.* 460
Head-foremost from the river's bed 243 *P. B.* 579

Headland. On headland, or in hollow bay;— 239 *P. B.* 234
From a bold headland, their loved aery's guard, 388 *Eagles* 7
The grass-crowned headland that conceals the shore? 453 **The Sun, that* 10
For some rare plant, yon Headland of St. Bees. 466 *St. Bees* 9
Like the fixed Light that crowns yon Headland of St. Bees. 466 *St. Bees* 45
Of some bold headland, he beheld the sun 759 *Excursion* 1. 199

Headlands. The towering headlands, crowned with mist, 235 *Power of Sound* 185
Firm as the towering Headlands of St. Bees. 466 *St. Bees* 18
As millions thus shall do, the Headlands of St. Bees. 466 *St. Bees* 27
Moors, mountains, headlands, and ye hollow vales, 702 *Prelude* 8. 216
In headlands, tongues, and promontory shapes, 746 *Prelude* 14. 46

Headless. The headless martyrs of the Covenant, 442 *Ecc. Sonn.* 3. 7. 9
Of sapience in thy aspect, headless Owl! 456 **The leaves* 27

Headlong. Shot, down the headlong path darts with his sledge; 4 *Ev. Wk.* 131
Attend, at every stretch, his headlong fall. 6 *Ev. Wk.* 199
Thunders through echoing pines the headlong Aar; 16 *Desc. Sk.* 337
Had walked, and from the summit had fallen headlong: 101 *Brothers* 400
Headlong yon waterfall must come, 111 *'Tis said that some* 34
And from the headlong streams. 112 **What heavenly* 8
Which thunders down with headlong force, 130 *Idiot Boy* 348
I'll hurl thee headlong with the rock 155 *Waterfall* 13
Cast headlong to the pit! 167 *Pilgrim's Dream* 56
The headlong streams and fountains 232 *Power of Sound* 17
In wrath) fell headlong from the fields of air, 260 **From the dark* 6
Shot, down the headlong pathway darts his sledge; 593 *Ev. Wk. Quarto* 112
Dashed headlong, and rejected by the storm. 639 *Prelude* 1. 498
Of stream and headlong flood that seldom fails; 782 *Excursion* 2. 705
And was borne headlong by the roaring flood. K.8. 229 **I will* 151

Heads. Cloud-piercing pine-trees nod their troubled heads, 11 *Desc. Sk.* 63
"The pains and plagues that on our heads came down, 29 *Guilt* 298
But 'twas an angry night, and o'er our heads 50 *Bord.* 710
Whose heads are shelterless in such a night! 71 *Bord.* 1883
Bend with the breeze their heads, beside a crystal stream. 141 *Arm. Lady* 96
On the heads of towering hills. 166 *Wand. Jew* 8
Tossing their heads in sprightly dance. 187 **I wandered* 12
Their heads never raising; 190 *March* 9
Their own far-stretching arms and leafy heads 220 *Haunted Tree* 38
Poising your splendours high above the heads 230 *Clouds* 27
Thrilling the unweaponed crowd with plumeless heads?— 233 *Power of Sound* 75
Shame on you, feeble Heads, to slavery prone! 303 **Is it* 14
Stoop their proud heads, but not unto the dust— 316 **Say, what* 11
The aspiring heads of future things appear, 326 **The Bard* 7
We bow our heads before Thee, and we laud 328 *Ode 1815* 104
Above whose heads the tide so long hath rolled, 333 *Fish-women* 4
Their heads in sign of worship, Nature's God, 337 *Aar* 13
From sorrow, like the sky above our heads. 353 *Aquap.* 65
Higher to lift their lofty heads, impelled 354 *Aquap.* 145
And all the people bow their heads, like reeds 431 *Ecc. Sonn.* 2. 11. 7
Their meek heads to the nipping air, 503 *Warning* 3
Its living roof above our heads. 506 *Lab. Hymn* 20

Heads—*continued.*
Nod the cloud-piercing pines their troubl'd heads, 603 *Desc. Sk. Quarto* 62
Those immaterial agents bowed their heads 677 *Prelude* 6. 125
Of that great kingdom, rustled o'er our heads, 680 *Prelude* 6. 362
With heads; the midway region, and above, 697 *Prelude* 7. 691
Rocked high above their heads; anon, the din 716 *Prelude* 9. 456
Head after head, and never heads enough 723 *Prelude* 10. 362
At gravest heads, by enmity to France 727 *Prelude* 11. 40
Bend the complying heads of lordly pines, 734 *Prelude* 12. 16
Through want of better knowledge in the heads 743 *Prelude* 13. 215
Carved uncouth figures on the heads of sticks— 764 *Excursion* 1. 571
Declined their languid heads, wanting support. 767 *Excursion* 1. 727
In silent grief their unuplifted heads, 780 *Excursion* 2. 575
Each also crowned with wingèd heads—a pair 824 *Excursion* 5. 152
Woods waving in the wind their lofty heads, 895 *Excursion* 9. 746
The dark pines thrusting forth their spiky heads; K.8. 249 *Recluse* 1.1.480

Headstrong. And like a torrent roars the headstrong gale; 7 *Ev. Wk.* 270
Man's headstrong violence and Time's fleetness, 366 **Ye Trees* 16
Too perfectly his headstrong will: 400 *White Doe* 353
The headstrong current of their fate: 407 *White Doe* 1068
Of headstrong will! Can this be Piety? 439 *Ecc. Sonn.* 2. 44. 10
To stop your Leaders in their headstrong course! 505 *Warning* 130
Who checked or turned thy headstrong youth, 577 **I come* 42

Heady. Of heady schemes jostling each other, gawds, 662 *Prelude* 4. 281

Heal. Home-felt, and home-created, comes to heal 1 *Early Youth* 8
And tears which flowed for ills which patience might not heal. 29 *Guilt* 270
Strong to destroy, is also strong to heal— 38 *Bord.* 47
By wounds that may not heal. 113 *Lament* 28
No fears to beat away—no strife to heal— 211 *Laod.* 99
Who shun the mischief which they cannot heal. 262 *Retirement* 8
So timely Grace the immortal wing may heal, 270 **If these* 13
Griefs to allay which Reason cannot heal; 273 **When Philoctetes* 10
Thy function was to heal and to restore, 378 *Duddon* 8. 13
For wounds that death alone has power to heal, 426 *Ecc. Sonn.* 1. 32. 7
Old Wharf might heal her sorrow. 494 *Force of Prayer* 44
Striving to hide, what nought could heal, the wounds 730 *Prelude* 11. 215
The charities that soothe, and heal, and bless, 887 *Excursion* 9. 239

Healed. The Wanderer, "I infer that he was healed 841 *Excursion* 6. 190

Healing. Should be thy portion, with what healing thoughts 207 *Tintern* 144
All trust abandoned in the healing might 363 **The world forsaken* 3
And busy with a hand of healing? 397 *White Doe* 119
For healing and composure.—But as least 459 **Wanderer! that* 46
Wants not a healing influence that can creep 501 **The unremitting* 10
Into Bethesda's pool, with healing virtue 510 *F. Stone* 126
Or soothe it with a healing power 533 **Blest is* 26
Fond healing, like a mother's kiss. 578 **I come* 56
Soft on his wounded heart her healing pow'r, 602 *Desc. Sk. Quarto* 14
And steadiness, and healing and repose 742 *Prelude* 13. 181
The sting of self-reproach, with healing words. 854 *Excursion* 6. 1033
Degree of healing to a wounded spirit, 896 *Excursion* 9. 786
Their healing offices a pure goodwill K.8. 244 *Recluse* 1.1.284

Heals. The Saint or Patriot to the world that heals 440 *Ecc. Sonn.* 2. 45. 13
And knows not when he hurts and when he heals; 560 *Cuck. and Night.* 203

Health. To taint the health which ye infuse; 225 *Present.* 16
Dear mother of fresh thoughts and joyous health! 254 **A flock* 14
While health, power, glory, from their height decline, 261 **I watch* 11
For health, and time in obvious duty spent. 278 **Lo! where she* 14
Ill health of body; and had pined 294 *Jedbor.* 74
Think that a State would live in sounder health 310 *Invasion* 8
But from *within* proceeds a Nation's health; 320 **O'erweening Statesmen* 3
May Health return to mellow Age, 386 *Yarrow Rev.* 59
Spontaneous wisdom breathed by health, 481 *Tables Turned* 19
Of health, strength, friends, and kindred, see! 483 *Simon Lee* 26
Health, meekness, ardour, quietness secure, 489 *Spade* 9
Of Nations," sacrifice a People's health, 501 *Humanity* 90
Have kindled into health! 507 *May* 28
Which Horace needed for his spirit's health; 528 **Those breathing* 92
Trained to health and artless beauty; 629 *Installation* 46
Health and the quiet of a healthful mind 648 *Prelude* 2. 467
Of health, and hope, and beauty, all at once 652 *Prelude* 3. 220
Far art thou wandered now in search of health 678 *Prelude* 6. 240
To seek the same delights, and have one health, 679 *Prelude* 6. 258
These vain regrets; health suffers in thee, else 679 *Prelude* 6. 316
To health and joy and pure contentedness; 733 *Prelude* 11. 398
Restored to us in renovated health; 752 *Prelude* 14. 426
—Vigorous in health, of hopeful spirits, undamped 762 *Excursion* 1. 392
And they, if blest with health and hearts at ease, 773 *Excursion* 2. 102
"Oh! what a joy it were, in vigorous health, 808 *Excursion* 4. 508
Fleeting as health or beauty, and unsound? 829 *Excursion* 5. 473
Where health abides, and cheerfulness, and peace.' 841 *Excursion* 6. 175
He came, the ghost of beauty and of health, 843 *Excursion* 6. 330
While she was yet in prime of health and strength, 849 *Excursion* 6. 758
There blossoms, strong in health, and will be soon 855 *Excursion* 6. 1152
Of Nature's impress,—gaiety and health, 866 *Excursion* 7. 560
Health and good wishes to his new-born girl, 867 *Excursion* 7. 655
We look for health from seeds that have been sown 886 *Excursion* 9. 141
Possessed of health, and strength, and peace of mind; 887 *Excursion* 9. 204
The tribute of enjoyment, knowledge, health, 888 *Excursion* 9. 269
Diffusing health and sober cheerfulness, K.8. 249 *Recluse* 1.1.465
That keeps in health the insatiable mind; K.8. 254 *Recluse* 1.1.637

Healthful. Hath cherished on a healthful soil; 344 **How blest* 6
Of firm dry ground, with healthful grass 543 *Russ. Fug.* 103

Hear—*continued.*
Can hear the monitory clock — 533 *Blest is 45
Hear, then, and neglect me not! — 535 Egremont 21
Hear the challenge with delight. — 536 Egremont 84
The *Alma Redemptoris* did he hear; — 553 Prioress 68
For now when they may hear the small birds' song, — 557 Cuck. and Night. 26
That it was good to hear the Nightingale, — 557 Cuck. and Night. 49
If I perchance a Nightingale might hear, — 557 Cuck. and Night. 53
But hear you now a wondrous thing, I pray; — 558 Cuck.and Night. 106
For every wight eschews thy song to hear, — 558 Cuck.and Night. 114
Quoth she, to hear this churlish bird thus speak — 560 Cuck.and Night. 212
And tnem besought to hear her doleful case, — 561 Cuck.and Night. 264
That in my soul methinks I yet do hear — 563 Troilus 61
That absent was, 'gan sing as ye may hear. — 564 Troilus 119
Men who can hear the Decalogue and feel — 568 Cumb. Beg. 135
Will hear the wind sigh through the leaves of a tree. — 571 Farmer 92
To hear the sanguinary trumpet sounded. — 575 Chiabrera 6. 8
Exalt thy spirit, hear the voice — 577 Cenotaph 11
Could hear to guide them in their choice — 577 *By playful 18
Could hear the wind and mark the showers — 577 *I come 18
Were earlier raised, remain to hear — 586 Hogg 26
I hear the Echoes through the mountains throng, — 588 Immortality 27
Shout round me, let me hear thy shouts, thou happy Shepherd-boy! — 588 Immortality 35
I hear, I hear, with joy I hear! — 588 Immortality 50
And hear the mighty waters rolling evermore. — 590 Immortality 171
Staying his silent waves, to hear the roar — 591 Ev. Wk. Quarto 5
Safe from your door ye hear at breezy morn, — 596 Ev. Wk. Quarto 233
I hear, while in the forest depth he sees, — 596 Ev. Wk. Quarto 261
Hear Britain's sons rehearse thy praise with joy, — 619 School Ex. 101
Hear, and assist;—the father's mandate calls — 624 Æneid 27
And charm'd to hear his simulating tongue; — 624 Æneid 76
To hear such music. Through the walls we flew — 644 Prelude 2. 128
I heard it then, and seem to hear it now— — 681 Prelude 6. 432
Loth to believe what we so grieved to hear, — 684 Prelude 6. 586
Sit, see, and hear, unthankful, uninspired? — 695 Prelude 7. 543
All summer, and at sunrise ye may hear — 702 Prelude 8. 199
Of some great trial, and we hear the voice — 715 Prelude 9. 399
Until I seemed to hear a voice that cried, — 719 Prelude 10. 86
That greeted me on entering, I could hear — 719 Prelude 10. 98
And never hear the sound of their own names. — 730 Prelude 11. 231
I hear thee tell how bees with honey fed — 733 Prelude 11. 443
To hear of, for the glory that redounds — 743 Prelude 13. 248
Over the dark abyss, intent to hear — 747 Prelude 14. 72
That men, least sensitive, see, hear, perceive, — 747 Prelude 14. 85
Where art thou? Hear I not a voice from thee — 751 Prelude 14. 378
Which 'tis reproach to hear? Anon I rose — 751 Prelude 14. 379
Must hear Humanity in fields and groves — 755 Recluse 1. 1. 829
Might hear his busy spade, which he would ply, — 764 Excursion 1. 529
That any heart had ached to hear her, begged — 769 Excursion 1. 866
And his frail creature Man;—but ye shall hear. — 781 Excursion 2. 634
Depressed I hear, how faithless is the voice — 795 Excursion 3. 605
Did ye not hear that conquest is abjured? — 796 Excursion 3. 724
Who neither hears, nor feels a wish to hear, — 810 Excursion 4. 581
To this would rather bend than see and hear — 810 Excursion 4. 619
When his own breath was silent, chanced to hear — 814 Excursion 4. 855
He only knows by name; and, if he hear, — 819 Excursion 4. 1226
Or plant a tree. And did you hear his voice? — 826 Excursion 5. 238
And that contents him; bowers that hear no more — 828 Excursion 5. 406
Who, in their noiseless dwelling-place, can hear — 833 Excursion 5. 723
I love to hear of those, who, not contending — 835 Excursion 5. 855
O come and hear him! Thou who hast to me — 851 Excursion 6. 879
Been faithless, hear him, though a lowly creature, — 851 Excursion 6. 880
A century shall hear his name pronounced, — 862 Excursion 7. 354
Oft as they hear of sorrow like their own, — 868 Excursion 7. 691
That many, sweet to hear of in soft verse, — 880 Excursion 8. 401
Of her own native vigour; thence can hear — 884 Excursion 9. 40
And hear the mighty stream of tendency — 885 Excursion 9. 87
Beaten by lonely billows, hear the songs — 890 Excursion 9. 388
"I love to hear that eloquent old Man — 891 Excursion 9. 459
In a low voice, yet careless who might hear. — 892 Excursion 9. 549
Throughout all lands: let every nation hear — 893 Excursion 9. 641
They hear my lips present their sacrifice, — 895 Excursion 9. 749
I, whose pretty Voice you hear, — S.3. 437 *I, whose 1
And wished, at least, to hear the blarney — S.3. 438 *My Lord 13
Prevail, 'tis best to neither hear nor see. — S.3. 441 *Grateful is sleep, more 3
And hear the voices of the winds and flowers. — K.8. 224 *I will 3
He seemed to hear a voice, which was again — K.8. 229 *I will 166
Till, at the last, thou hear the voice—" Well done, — K.8. 325 [?]*The vestal 13
Nor safe the petticoats of dames that hear — L. 1. 95 Juvenal 3. 12

Heard. *See* **Far-heard.**
Was heard, or woodcocks roamed the moonlight hill. — 2 Ev. Wk. 20
And restless stone-chat, all day long, is heard. — 4 Ev. Wk. 97
And *blasted* quarry thunders, heard remote! — 4 Ev. Wk. 141
Heard by calm lakes, as peeps the folding star, — 7 Ev. Wk. 280
Now hardly heard, beguiles my homeward way. — 9 Ev. Wk. 366
And its last echo can be heard no more. — 15 Desc. Sk. 253
Now couch thyself where, heard with fear afar, — 16 Desc. Sk. 336
Or heard, while other worlds their charms reveal, — 16 Desc. Sk. 342
Or rumbling, heard remote, of falling snow. — 17 Desc. Sk. 361
And heard with heart unmoved, with soul unraised: — 18 Desc. Sk. 422
Through rustling aspens heard from side to side, — 21 Desc. Sk. 625
For of that ruin she had heard a tale — 27 Guilt 170
Had heard of one who, forced from storms to shroud, — 27 Guilt 172
Ravage for which no knell was heard. We prayed — 29 Guilt 284
I heard my neighbours in their beds complain — 31 Guilt 390
They paused, and heard a hoarser voice blaspheme, — 33 Guilt 466

Heard—*continued.*
The Soldier's Widow heard and stood aghast; — 33 Guilt 476
They saw and heard, and, winding with the road — 34 Guilt 523
Over our much-loved Captain. I have heard — 37 Bord. 14
And I had heard the like before: in sooth — 38 Bord. 78
That instant rushed between us, and I heard — 40 Bord. 186
I am perplexed. What hast thou heard or seen? — 42 Bord. 260
As the Lord Clifford's Castle: I have heard — 43 Bord. 345
Have heard my suit, and urged my plea at Court. — 43 Bord. 349
Ten years; and no one ever heard her voice; — 44 Bord. 388
I never shall be heard of more. Lord Clifford? — 47 Bord. 534
I scarcely can believe it. Myself, I heard — 49 Bord. 678
To have heard your voice. Your couch, I fear, good Baron, — 53 Bord. 859
And never heard a sound so terrible. — 53 Bord. 888
You have not heard that Henry has at last — 56 Bord. 1022
Of which I heard them speak, but that I fancy — 58 Bord. 1139
Stood silent as we passed them! I have heard — 61 Bord. 1333
More with delight than grief—I heard a voice — 62 Bord. 1362
He heard a voice—a shepherd-lad came to him — 62 Bord. 1394
For me, I have business, as you heard, with Oswald, — 67 Bord. 1649
Of every tongue—as you are now. You've heard — 68 Bord. 1688
No more was heard of? I had been betrayed. — 69 Bord. 1755
I am sure I heard something breathing— — 72 Bord. 1969
Alive! you heard him breathe? quick, quick— — 73 Bord. 2014
As is heard often after stormy nights. — 73 Bord. 2020
I heard—— You heard him, where? when heard him? As you know, — 73 Bord. 2042
Returning late, I heard a moaning sound; — 73 Bord. 2045
You heard!—he called you to him? Of all men — 73 Bord. 2051
To pull the cord. I guess he must have heard it; — 73 Bord. 2058
And then I heard a shriek so terrible — 74 Bord. 2104
And words that tell these things be heard in vain? — 77 Bord. 2271
The eldest heard with steady glee; — 81 †Mother's Return 6
I heard the sound,—and more and more; — 82 Alice Fell 6
And still I heard it as before. — 82 Alice Fell 8
Nor aught else like it, could be heard. — 82 Alice Fell 12
Oft I had heard of Lucy Gray: — 82 Lucy Gray 1
I heard a voice; it said, "Drink, pretty creature, drink!" — 87 Pet-lamb 2
I've heard of fearful winds and darkness that come there; — 88 Pet-lamb 54
"Hither the Afflicted come, as thou hast heard thy Mother say, — 92 Poet's Dream 49
What mournful sighs have here been heard, and, when the voice was stopt — 92 Poet's Dream 51
Oft in the piping shrouds had Leonard heard — 95 Brothers 47
With what I've witnessed, and with what I've heard, — 98 Brothers 188
If there were one among us who had heard — 100 Brothers 308
Living or dead.—When last we heard of him, — 100 Brothers 316
In sleep I heard the northern gleams; — 113 Ind. Wom. 3
I heard, I saw the flashes drive, — 114 Ind. Wom. 6
Heard by his mother unawares! — 117 Affl. Marg. 25
She answered, soon as she the question heard, — 119 Sailor's Mother 17
And thus, from what I heard and knew, or guessed, — 120 EmigrantMother 13
Who heard the heart-felt music of his suit — 121 V. and J. 13
And of the lark's note heard before its time, — 123 V. and J. 92
(The like was never heard of yet) — 126 Idiot Boy 40
And never will be heard of more. — 128 Idiot Boy 216
What you have heard, what you have seen: — 131 Idiot Boy 440
Now Johnny all night long had heard — 131 Idiot Boy 442
When others heeded not, He heard the South — 132 Michael 50
Two evenings after he had heard the news, — 134 Michael 227
Heard him, how he was troubled in his sleep: — 135 Michael 291
To build a Sheep-fold; and, before he heard — 136 Michael 324
Than when I heard thee by our own fireside — 136 Michael 346
Years after he had heard this heavy news. — 138 Michael 453
You have heard "a Spanish Lady — 139 Arm. Lady 1
What have I seen, and heard, or dreamt? where am I? where?" — 140 Arm. Lady 72
Commend him, when he's only heard. — 143 *Driven in 29
Which I till then had heard appeared the voice — 146 *It was an 24
A noise of laughter; southern Loughrigg heard, — 147 Joanna 59
Meanwhile, a noise was heard, the busy mirth — 149 *A narrow 40
Is heard the spirit of a toil-worn slave, — 153 Morn. Ex. 17
Last night I heard a crash—'tis true, — 156 Oak and Broom 27
Ambitious to be seen or heard, — 165 Parrot 27
In clouds above, the lark is heard, — 165 Danish Boy 12
Is all that can be heard — 173 Waggoner 1. 5
He heard not, too intent of soul; — 175 Waggoner 1. 153
Gave the word—the horses heard — 177 Waggoner 2. 50
As if it heard the fiddle's call, — 177 Waggoner 2. 66
You might have heard a nibbling mouse; — 178 Waggoner 2. 138
He heard the monitory growl; — 178 Waggoner 2. 154
Heard—and in opposition quaffed — 178 Waggoner 2. 155
When they the wished-for greeting heard, — 178 Waggoner 3. 2
And little other sound was heard; — 182 Waggoner 4. 237
O blithe New-comer! I have heard, — 183 *O blithe 1
I heard the murmur and the murmuring sound, — 185 Nutting 38
I heard a Stock-dove sing or say — 186 *O Nightingale 11
Poor Susan has passed by the spot, and has heard — 188 Poor Susan 3
Was aught ever heard like his fiddle and him? — 188 Music 8
I heard the woods and distant waters roar; — 195 Resolution 17
Or heard them not, as happy as a boy: — 195 Resolution 18
I heard the sky-lark warbling in the sky; — 195 Resolution 29
Scarce heard; nor word from word could I divide; — 197 Resolution 108
I never heard of such as dare — 198 Thorn 98
For many a time and oft were heard — 199 Thorn 159
And others, I've heard many swear, — 199 Thorn 162
Ere I had heard of Martha's name, — 199 Thorn 173

Heart—*continued.*

Has a kind heart; but his imprisonment — 71 *Bord.* 1900
God knows what was in my heart, — 72 *Bord.* 1961
let us take heart; this Man may be rich; — 72 *Bord.* 1994
My heart was willing, Sir, but I am one — 74 *Bord.* 2080
With such a purpose in thine heart as mine was. — 74 *Bord.* 2115
My voice was silent, but my heart hath joined thee. — 76 *Bord.* 2185
All nature curses me, and in my heart — 76 *Bord.* 2205
Conflict must cease, and, in thy frozen heart, — 76 *Bord.* 2215
—But hear me. For *one* question, I have a heart — 77 *Bord.* 2255
Delivered heart and head! Let us to Palestine; — 77 *Bord.* 2282
Who with bare hands would have plucked out thy heart — 77 *Bord.* 2293
Of that old Man's forgiveness on thy heart, — 77 *Bord.* 2297
My heart leaps up when I behold — 79 **My heart* 1
A solemn image to my heart, — 79 **Stay near* 8
Such heart was in her, being then — 79 *Sparrow's Nest* 13
A heart, the fountain of sweet tears; — 79 *Sparrow's Nest* 19
A sadness at the heart: — 81 †*Mother's Return* 48
As if her innocent heart would break; — 82 *Alice Fell* 23
Her very heart, her grief grew strong; — 82 *Alice Fell* 47
In very wantonness of heart. — 84 *Shepherd-boys* 11
Again!—his heart within him dies— — 85 *Shepherd-boys* 61
The Boy recovered heart, and told — 85 *Shepherd-boys* 80
O dearest, dearest boy! my heart — 86 *Anecdote* 57
That I almost received her heart into my own. — 87 *Pet-lamb* 12
"What is it thou wouldst seek? What is wanting to thy heart? — 87 *Pet-lamb* 25
That 'tis thy mother's heart which is working so in thee? — 88 *Pet-lamb* 50
That I almost received her heart into my own." — 88 *Pet-lamb* 68
A young lamb's heart among the full-grown flocks. — 88 *H. C.* 24
And the heart is loth to deaden — 90 *Longest Day* 39
And faithful service of his heart in the worst that might ensue — 91 *Norman Boy* 26
With this dear holy shepherd-boy breathe a prayer of earnest heart, — 91 *Norman Boy* 30
Nor could my heart by second thoughts from heaviness be cleared, — 91 *Poet's Dream* 5
But the poor ragged Thing whose ways my human heart had warmed. — 92 *Poet's Dream* 16
"Then offer up thy heart to God in thankfulness and praise, — 93 *Poet's Dream* 57
For her tender heart beloved. — 94 *Westmoreland Girl* 44
Among the mountains, and he in his heart — 95 *Brothers* 45
In union with the employment of his heart, — 96 *Brothers* 58
When Leonard had approached his home, his heart — 96 *Brothers* 77
Sent to his heart! he lifted up his eyes, — 96 *Brothers* 95
Through five long generations had the heart — 98 *Brothers* 204
They left to him the family heart, and land — 98 *Brothers* 211
Are aught of what makes up a mother's heart, — 99 *Brothers* 233
His absent Brother still was at his heart. — 100 *Brothers* 348
A gushing from his heart, that took away — 101 *Brothers* 407
That it was from the weakness of his heart — 102 *Brothers* 432
Him, in whose wretched heart ambition failed, — 103 *Artegal* 86
Thus Elidure, by words, relieved his struggling heart. — 104 *Artegal* 129
Gladdening the people's heart from shore to shore; — 105 *Artegal* 205
—A gentle Maid, whose heart is lowly bred, — 106 *Farewell* 28
And wish, as if my heart would burst. — 110 *Forsaken* 7
But when I cease to look, my hand is on my heart. — 110 *'*Tis said that some* 20
Your sound my heart of rest bereaves, — 111 *'*Tis said that some* 23
It robs my heart of peace. — 111 *'*Tis said that some* 24
Of my fond heart, hath made me poor. — 111 *A Complaint* 18
Till heart with heart in concord beats, — 111 **Let other* 11
Through my very heart they shine; — 112 **What heavenly* 2
With happy heart I then would die, — 114 *Ind. Wom.* 67
Like blood-drops from my heart they dropped. — 115 *Last of Flock* 64
Those several qualities of heart and mind — 118 *Maternal Grief* 20
As now it is, seems to her own fond heart — 119 *Maternal Grief* 80
My song the workings of her heart expressed. — 120 *EmigrantMother* 14
And sure a mother's heart is mine: — 120 *EmigrantMother* 18
To my poor heart, if thou wouldst be — 120 *EmigrantMother* 23
Yet does my yearning heart to thee — 121 *EmigrantMother* 71
My heart again is in its place! — 121 *EmigrantMother* 84
He suffered—breaking down in heart and mind! — 124 *V. and J.* 184
Shall by his beauty win his grandsire's heart, — 124 *V. and J.* 209
Was a dependant on the obdurate heart — 125 *V. and J.* 235
His heart it was so full of glee — 127 *Idiot Boy* 82
What hopes it sends to Betty's heart! — 127 *Idiot Boy* 93
And Betty's drooping at the heart, — 128 *Idiot Boy* 162
A thought with which her heart is sore— — 128 *Idiot Boy* 213
If she had heart to knock again; — 129 *Idiot Boy* 270
On man, the heart of man, and human life. — 131 *Michael* 33
An old man, stout of heart, and strong of limb. — 131 *Michael* 42
Amid the heart of many thousand mists, — 132 *Michael* 59
Whose heart was in her house: two wheels she had — 132 *Michael* 82
Have loved his Helpmate; but to Michael's heart — 133 *Michael* 142
His heart and his heart's joy! For oftentimes — 133 *Michael* 152
Would Michael exercise his heart with looks — 133 *Michael* 172
And that the old Man's heart seemed born again? — 134 *Michael* 203
And his heart failed him. "Isabel," said he, — 134 *Michael* 226
With a light heart. The Housewife for five days — 135 *Michael* 284
Recovered heart. That evening her best fare — 135 *Michael* 301
A prouder heart than Luke's. When Isabel — 136 *Michael* 315
To-morrow thou wilt leave me: with full heart — 136 *Michael* 332
Luke had a manly heart; but at these words — 136 *Michael* 357

Heart—*continued.*

Thy heart these two weeks has been beating fast — 137 *Michael* 397
The old Man's grief broke from him; to his heart — 137 *Michael* 421
Would overset the brain, or break the heart: — 138 *Michael* 450
The pity which was then in every heart — 138 *Michael* 463
Her children from her inmost heart bewept. — 139 *Widow* 14
My long-frozen heart grows warm!" — 140 *Arm. Lady* 38
Our faith hath been,—O would that eyes could see the heart!" — 140 *Arm. Lady* 48
Body, heart, and soul in union, — 140 *Arm. Lady* 63
Of sorrow in her heart while through her father's door, — 140 *Arm. Lady* 77
Of her who in my heart still holds her ancient place. — 141 *Arm. Lady* 114
For every tender sacrifice her heart had made. — 141 *Arm. Lady* 138
For a light heart in a dull season. — 142 †*Lov. and Lik.* 22
Nor blush if o'er your heart be stealing — 142 †*Lov. and Lik.* 29
With images about her heart, — 144 **Driven in* 79
But nay, my heart is far too glad; — 144 *Her Eyes* 12
Draw from my heart the pain away. — 145 *Her Eyes* 34
I roamed in the confusion of my heart, — 146 **It was an* 18
With such a strong devotion, that your heart — 147 *Joanna* 5
—Now, by those dear immunities of heart — 147 *Joanna* 32
Of their own beauty, imaged in the heart. — 147 *Joanna* 50
A heart more wakeful; and had worn the track — 150 **When, to* 61
Of the vast sea didst bring a watchful heart — 151 **When, to* 81
With thankful heart, to either Eminence — 151 **Forth from* 14
Memento for some docile heart; — 154 *Flower Garden* 52
My heart with terrors? Am I not — 156 *Oak and Broom* 73
"Her voice was blithe, her heart was light; — 157 *Oak and Broom* 91
By the heart of Man, his tears, — 157 *Sexton* 21
My heart with gladness, and a share — 159 **With little* 47
And to-day my heart is weary; — 159 **Up with me* 9
February last, my heart — 160 **Pleasures newly* 3
Blithe of heart, from week to week; — 161 **Pleasures newly* 33
Your portraits still may reach the heart — 164 **Fair Lady* 11
Proceeding, made the heart rejoice — 168 *Pilgrim's Dream* 66
Had heart or voice for me. — 168 *Turtledove* 16
Into the service of his constant heart, — 169 *Love lies Bleeding* 22
Far beyond in joy of heart. — 171 *Kitten* 32
Light of heart and light of limb; — 171 *Kitten* 74
Of the silent heart which Nature — 171 *Kitten* 97
Of naked instinct, wound about the heart. — 172 *Infant Daughter* 38
To leave it with a jovial heart; — 174 *Waggoner* 1. 57
And with proud cause my heart is light: — 174 *Waggoner* 1. 111
Which now ye climb with heart and hope, — 175 *Waggoner* 1. 125
His heart with sudden joy is filled,— — 177 *Waggoner* 2. 33
What greater good can heart desire? — 177 *Waggoner* 2. 71
His heart is up—he fears no evil — 179 *Waggoner* 3. 134
As if his heart by notes were stung. — 180 *Waggoner* 4. 77
But a shy spirit in my heart, — 182 *Waggoner* 4. 210
Breathing with such suppression of the heart — 185 *Nutting* 22
The heart luxuriates with indifferent things, — 185 *Nutting* 41
In gentleness of heart; with gentle hand — 186 *Nutting* 55
A creature of a "fiery heart":— — 186 **O Nightingale* 2
And then my heart with pleasure fills, — 187 **I wandered* 23
She looks, and her heart is in heaven: but they fade, — 188 *Poor Susan* 13
A humbler bliss would satisfy my heart. — 190 **Lyre! though* 14
Yet *they*, so blithe of heart, seemed fit — 191 *Beggars* 31
And to my heart are still endeared — 191 *Seq. Beggars* 27
Around the heart such tender ties, — 193 *Ruth* 88
The workings of his heart. — 193 *Ruth* 132
Whose heart with so much nature played? — 194 *Ruth* 161
The pleasant season did my heart employ: — 195 *Resolution* 19
Solitude, pain of heart, distress, and poverty. — 195 *Resolution* 35
About its mother's heart, and brought — 199 *Thorn* 140
Bear me to the heart of France, — 205 *Brougham* 145
How, by Heaven's grace, this Clifford's heart was framed: — 205 *Brougham* 158
Felt in the blood, and felt along the heart; — 206 *Tintern* 28
Have hung upon the beatings of my heart— — 206 *Tintern* 54
The guide, the guardian of my heart, and soul — 207 *Tintern* 110
The language of my former heart, and read — 207 *Tintern* 117
The heart that loved her; 'tis her privilege, — 207 *Tintern* 123
Or, while the wings aspire, are heart and eye — 209 **Ethereal minstrel* 3
A nobler counsellor than my poor heart. — 210 *Laod.* 54
As, through the abysses of a joyless heart, — 213 *Dion* 61
The Pharaohs of the earth, the men of hardened heart! — 216 *Enterprise* 106
And in its silence even, no heart is proof; — 221 *Triad* 66
Call to the heart for inward listening— — 222 *Triad* 206
Ye superstitions of the *heart*, — 223 *Wishing-gate* 11
That truth informing mind and heart, — 224 *'*Tis gone* 61
To humbleness of heart descends — 225 *Primrose* 49
With fancy, I obey my heart, — 225 *Present.* 11
Free for a sabbath of the heart: — 228 *Devot. Incit.* 75
Into thy heart; and fancies, running wild — 229 *Cuckoo-clock* 18
And whispers for the heart, their slave; — 232 *Power of Sound* 8
A stream as if from one full heart. — 233 *Power of Sound* 48
Pure modulations flowing from the heart — 234 *Power of Sound* 110
I've left my heart at home. — 237 *P. B.* 55
Fluttered so faint a heart before;— — 237 *P. B.* 82
As kindly take what from my heart — 237 *P. B.* 114
With sympathetic heart may stray, — 238 *P. B.* 139
Was heart or head the better. — 239 *P. B.* 240
Into the heart of Peter Bell. — 239 *P. B.* 245
"Small change it made in Peter's heart — 239 *P. B.* 251
Into his heart; be never felt — 239 *P. B.* 264
"Though Nature could not touch his heart — 239 *P. B.* 286
With hard contempt his heart was wrung, — 241 *P. B.* 454
This outcry, on the heart of Peter, — 241 *P. B.* 466

Hearts—*continued.*
A metropolitan temple in the hearts 755 *Recluse* 1. 1. 839
Their farewell benediction, but with hearts 761 *Excursion* 1. 339
And they whose hearts are dry as summer dust 763 *Excursion* 1. 501
From natural wisdom turn our hearts away; 765 *Excursion* 1. 601
Severe reproof, if we were men whose hearts 765 *Excursion* 1. 627
And they, if blest with health and hearts at ease, 773 *Excursion* 2. 102
A language not unwelcome to sick hearts 782 *Excursion* 2. 716
With hearts at ease, and knowledge in our hearts 794 *Excursion* 3. 548
Beyond the tenderness of human hearts: 804 *Excursion* 4. 193
Bounty and government, that filled their hearts 815 *Excursion* 4. 929
To hearts that own not him? Will showers of grace, 817 *Excursion* 4. 1096
With answering brightness in the hearts of all 828 *Excursion* 5. 416
That true succession fail of English hearts, 838 *Excursion* 6. 24
Sincerely wretched hearts, or falsely gay. 843 *Excursion* 6. 358
Upon our hearts, not wholly lost, I grant, 846 *Excursion* 6. 528
A sunbeam introducing among hearts 848 *Excursion* 6. 650
To keep two hearts together, that began 851 *Excursion* 6. 875
Yet shall not thy remembrance leave our hearts, 868 *Excursion* 7. 713
A sight that kindled pleasure in all hearts 868 *Excursion* 7. 724
Those blooming Boys, whose hearts are almost sick 884 *Excursion* 9. 29
They cannot lean, nor turn to their own hearts 886 *Excursion* 9. 144
Into all hearts. Throughout the world of sense, 887 *Excursion* 9. 214
Sent from the jocund hearts of those two Boys, 891 *Excursion* 9. 475
Into our hearts; and charmed the peaceful flood. 892 *Excursion* 9. 537
Inspire the serious song, and gentle Hearts 896 *Excursion* 9. 794
Will seek us also, sisters of our hearts, K.8. 254 *Recluse* 1.1.658
And one, like them, a brother of our hearts, K.8. 254 *Recluse* 1.1.659
Though yet the star *some hearts* at court may charm L.1. 96 *Juvenal* 3. 37
I grant that not in parents' hearts alone L.1. 96 *Juvenal* 3. 57
Hearts'. Did both find, helpers to their hearts' desire, 729 *Prelude* 11. 137
Heart's-ease. A *Heart's-ease* will perhaps be there, 164 **Fair Lady* 19
Heart-sick. To loathsome vaults, where heart-sick anguish tossed, 30 *Guilt* 350
The fancy-stricken Youth or heart-sick Maid, 170 **Never enlivened* 21
Attempts which still the heart-sick Maid 407 *White Doe* 1018
Turned into blood before her heart-sick eye. S.3. 436 **The doubt* 185
Heart-smitten. Yet more;—heart-smitten by the heroic deed, 105 *Artegal* 227
On men who gaze heart-smitten by the view, 322 *Germans* 10
He sued:—heart-smitten by the wrong, 545 *Russ. Fug.* 349
Heartsome. "Ye heartsome Choristers, ye and I will be 687 *Prelude* 7. 29
Heart-soothed. Heart-soothed, and busy as a wren, 543 *Russ. Fug.* 117
Heart-sorrow. Heart-sorrow rendered sweet by gratitude. 864 *Excursion* 7. 471
Heart-stirring. Thy own heart-stirring days, and be 218 *Young Lady* 5
Heart-stirring music! hourly heard that name; 867 *Excursion* 7. 671
Heart-stricken. Heart-stricken by stern destiny of yore 476 **Tranquillity! the* 3
Heart-stung. Exulting in defiance, or heart-stung 718 *Prelude* 10. 34
Heart-swoln. Heart-swoln, while in your pride ye contemplate 567 *Cumb. Beg.* 71
Heart-thrilling. Heart-thrilling strains, that cast, before the eye 451 *Ecc. Sonn.* 3. 44. 13
Heart-touched. Not loth, and listening Little-ones, heart-touched, their fancies feed. 93 *Poet's Dream* 80
Heart-touched, and haply not without a tear. 426 *Ecc. Sonn.* 1. 30. 8
Heart-wasting. A sore heart-wasting! I have heard, my Friend, 769 *Excursion* 1. 875
Hearty. Gave me a hearty welcome; they had laid 69 *Bord.* 1757
Thus, after two hours' hearty stay, 178 *Waggoner* 2. 165
Heat. By the lake's edge, she rose—to face the noontide heat; 7 *Ev. Wk.* 253
To pilgrims overcome by summer's heat. 15 *Desc. Sk.* 245
High and more high in summer's heat they go, 17 *Desc. Sk.* 376
While his horse pawed the floor with furious heat; 27 *Guilt* 175
In which, from burning heat, or tempest driving far and wide, 91 *Norman Boy* 23
But the dews allay the heat, 173 *Waggoner* 1. 20
Her face from summer's noontide heat 190 *Beggars* 2
Nor heat, at Tam o'Shanter's name, their blood) 255 *Detraction* 6
Through summer heat and winter snow: 291 *Rob Roy* 58
She strikes upon him with the heat 294 *Jedbor.* 60
Hunger, and sultry heat, and nipping blast 320 **Hunger, and* 1
Who dwells in heaven! But that aspiring heat 335 *Cologne* 5
May well suffice, till noon-tide's sultry heat 352 *Aquap.* 24
Not seldom, when with heat the valleys faint, 376 *Duddon* 2. 4
And, sorrow for him! the dull treacherous heat 484 **A plague* 8
And, through the heat of conflict, keeps the law 493 *Hap. War.* 53
Long as the heat shall rage, let that dim cave 498 **Enough of climbing* 32
For *that* from turbulence and heat 498 **The sylvan* 13
Through summer heat, autumnal cold, 507 *May* 15
Nor heat, nor cold, nor weary ways, 533 **Blest is* 32
For summer's heat exchanged, 545 *Russ. Fug.* 298
The Cripple in the mid-day heat 621 *Andrew Jones* 23
Present the maddening gifts, and kindle heat 624 *Æneid* 5
The fermentation, and the vernal heat 660 *Prelude* 4. 103
Changed like a garden in the heat of spring, 661 *Prelude* 4. 195
Given out while mid-day heat oppressed the plains. 678 *Prelude* 6. 223
They give it welcome. Long ere heat of noon, 699 *Prelude* 8. 20
Begin to strike him with a fire-like heat, 702 *Prelude* 8. 236
And through the nation spread a novel heat 722 *Prelude* 10. 252
Their temper, strained them more; and thus, in heat 730 *Prelude* 11. 218
No heat of passion or excessive zeal, 740 *Prelude* 13. 25
With my accustomed load; in heat and cold, 766 *Excursion* 1. 698
Through fancy's heat redounding in the brain, 863 *Excursion* 7. 380
Might overarch thee, from pernicious heat S.3. 433 **The doubt* 35
Of winter, nor from summer's sultry heat) K.8. 247 *Recluse* 1.1.395

Heath. *See* **Mountain-heath.**
Feeding 'mid purple heath, "green rings," and broom; 4 *Ev. Wk.* 133
And on these barren rocks, with fern and heath, 23 *Yew-tree* 28
We might have made a kindly bed of heath, 39 *Bord.* 122
Upon its aëry summit crowned with heath, 101 *Brothers* 369
On the soft heath,—and, waiting for his comrades, 101 *Brothers* 397
The blooming heath their couch, gazed side by side, 151 **Forth from* 11
This heath, this calm, and quiet scene; 187 **Three years* 40
Spreads o'er this tuft of heath, which now, attired 219 *Haunted Tree* 8
Preferr'st a garland culled from purple heath, 227 *Vernal Ode* 79
The like on heath, in lonely wood; 245 *P. B.* 827
Heed not, wild Rover once through heath and glen, 255 *Detraction* 9
To barren heath, bleak moor, and quaking fen, 298 *Brownie's Cell* 1
Quickens, as now, the withered heath;— 299 *Brownie's Cell* 84
Hears combats whistling o'er the ensanguined heath: 345 **Ambition—following* 13
This scrap of land he from the heath 483 *Simon Lee* 45
Cloud-piercing peak, and trackless heath, 506 **While from* 33
With plenteous store of heath and withered fern, 547 **Rude is* 19
Blew softly o'er the russet heath, 550 *Hermit's Cell* 2. 10
And let the chartered wind that sweeps the heath 568 *Cumb. Beg.* 175
I gazed from Hampstead's breezy heath. 586 *Hogg* 32
All blind she wilders o'er the lightless heath, 597 *Ev. Wk. Quarto* 285
Upon a bed of heath;—full many a spot 776 *Excursion* 2. 351
And from encroachment of encircling heath: 805 *Excursion* 4. 244
On new-blown heath; let yon commanding rock 808 *Excursion* 4. 497
Stretched upon fragrant heath, and lulled by sound 821 *Excursion* 4. 1321
Of Margaret, sinking on the lonely heath 854 *Excursion* 6. 1060
Soft heath this elevated spot supplied, 892 *Excursion* 9. 580
Heath-bells. But heath-bells from thy native ground, 345 **How blest* 71
Heath-besprinkled. Or heath-besprinkled copse might yield, 167 *Pilgrim's Dream* 7
Heath-clad. On the bleak sides of Cumbria's heath-clad moors, 21 *Desc. Sk.* 593
Winds our deep Vale, two heath-clad Rocks ascend 151 **Forth from* 2
Was one small opening, where a heath-clad ridge 776 *Excursion* 2. 335
Heath-cock. His fields, or mountains by the heath-cock ranged, 859 *Excursion* 7. 158
Heathen. To suffer pains with heathen scorn and hate 357 *Aquap.* 313
Though on her prow a sign of heathen power 370 *Eg. Maid* 75
"Her birth was heathen; but a fence 372 *Eg. Maid* 229
Of sorrow, still maintains a heathen rule, 422 *Ecc. Sonn.* 1. 15. 3
Like those the Heathen served; and mass is sung; 436 *Ecc. Sonn.* 2. 33. 12
In heathen schools of philosophic lore; 476 **Tranquillity! the* 2
Heather. That creeps along the bells of the crisp heather. 60 *Bord.* 1264
Or on wild heather. 285 *Grave of Burns* 54
A crest of blooming heather! 302 *Yarrow V.* 68
Heath-plant. Of heath-plant, under and above him strewn, 784 *Excursion* 2. 819
Heaths. To Scotland's heaths; or those that crossed the sea 184 *Yew-trees* 6
We almost meet a friend, on naked heaths 742 *Prelude* 13. 139
From rocks, woods, caverns, heaths, and dashing shores; 782 *Excursion* 2. 698
On thinly-peopled mountains and wild heaths, 813 *Excursion* 4. 844
Court the fresh air, explore the heaths and woods; 840 *Excursion* 6. 169
Such on the breast of darksome heaths are found; 879 *Excursion* 8. 362
Heathy. A cottage in a heathy dell; 246 *P. B.* 892
Beside thee in some heathy dell; 288 *Highland Girl* 50
Of fern-thatched hut on heathy moor: 390 *Highland Broach* 22
Of rising ground, yon heathy spot! 404 *White Doe* 763
Of the mute train, behind the heathy top 777 *Excursion* 2. 406
The cultured fields; and up the heathy waste, 858 *Excursion* 7. 47
Heat-oppressed. I rose while yet the cattle, heat-oppressed, 383 *Duddon* 28. 1
Heats. Where that pure Church survives, though summer heats 431 *Ecc. Sonn.* 2. 12. 7
What's a tempest to him, or the dry parching heats? 570 *Farmer* 69
Upward it winds, as if, in summer heats, 786 *Excursion* 3. 23
Heave. The dead Man heave a groan, or from his side 75 *Bord.* 2160
If any chance to heave a sigh, 117 *Affl. Marg.* 73
To Heaven;—who never saw, may heave a sigh; 330 *Ode: Thanks.* 100
Quivered and seemed almost to heave, 334 **In Bruges* 19
How subtly works man's weakness, sighs may heave 363 **The world forsaken* 7
But o'er the contrast wherefore heave a sigh? 462 **Where lies the truth* 11
For worst offenders: though the heart will heave 517 *Pun. Death* 2. 2
May heave a gentle sigh for him, 549 **In these* 8
Should frail survivors heave a sigh? 586 *Hogg* 36
Heaved. *See* **Up-heaved.**
Be heaved of charitable sympathy; 20 *Desc. Sk.* 566
And for the Subject of my Verse I heaved a pensive sigh. 91 *Poet's Dream* 4
And sylvan places heaved a pensive sigh; 214 *Dion* 111
His lank sides heaved, his limbs they stirred; 241 *P. B.* 442
By a fair Swan on drowsy billows heaved, 261 **I heard (alas* 7
Heaved less for thy bright plains and hills bestrown 360 *Alban Hills* 2
Is overturned; the mace, in battle heaved 423 *Ecc. Sonn.* 1. 17. 6
Heaved over ruin with stability 474 **On to* 3
The sighs which Matthew heaved were sighs 486 *Matthew* 21
Beside that hearth what sighs may have been heaved 525 *Epist. Beaumont* 260
At such an hour I heav'd the human sigh, 615 *Desc. Sk. Quarto* 702
In ancient story versed, whose breast had heaved 695 *Prelude* 7. 541
Heaved at safe distance, far retired. I paused, 726 *Prelude* 10. 568
To his own covert; as a billow, heaved 823 *Excursion* 5. 75
Heaved from the heart in fortune's bitterness, 845 *Excursion* 6. 445
Heaven. If thou indeed derive thy light from Heaven, v **If thou indeed* 1

Heaven—*continued.*

Through earth and heaven to bind and to unbind !— 428 *Ecc. Sonn.* 1. 39. 8
Echoed in Heaven, cries out, " Ye Chiefs, abate . 429 *Ecc. Sonn.* 2. 4. 9
By voices never mute when Heaven unties . . 430 *Ecc. Sonn.* 2. 8. 10
That ever looked to Heaven for final rest ? . . 430 *Ecc. Sonn.* 2. 9. 8
All promises vouchsafed by Heaven will shine . 431 *Ecc. Sonn.* 2. 10. 12
And Heaven will crown the right."—The mitred Sire 432 *Ecc. Sonn.* 2. 15. 9
To Heaven ; for, either lost in vanities . . . 433 *Ecc. Sonn.* 2. 18. 8
Supremacy from Heaven transmitted pure, . . 435 *Ecc. Sonn.* 2. 26. 5
Which Faith has suffered, Heaven could calmly brook. . . . . 435 *Ecc. Sonn.* 2. 29. 8
If thou hast fallen, and righteous Heaven restore 440 *Ecc. Sonn.* 3. 2. 12
What came from heaven to heaven by nature clings, 442 *Ecc. Sonn.* 3. 10. 13
As if a Church, though sprung from heaven, must owe . . . . 443 *Ecc. Sonn.* 3. 11. 11
Of praise from Heaven. To Thee, O saintly WHITE, 444 *Ecc. Sonn.* 3. 15. 8
What perfect glory ye in Heaven shall reap !— . 444 *Ecc. Sonn.* 3. 16. 8
With what man hopes from Heaven, yet fears from Earth. . . . . 445 *Ecc. Sonn.* 3. 20. 14
The summer-leaf had faded, passed to Heaven. . 446 *Ecc. Sonn.* 3. 24. 14
In Heaven, have lifted up their hearts to laud . 446 *Ecc. Sonn.* 3. 25. 6
To social interests, and to favouring Heaven ; . 450 *Ecc. Sonn.* 3. 41. 3
Give all thou canst ; high Heaven rejects the lore 451 *Ecc. Sonn.* 3. 43. 6
Earth prompts—Heaven urges ; let us seek the light, ... 452 *Ecc. Sonn.* 3. 46. 9
With a full heart ; " our thoughts are *heard* in heaven ! " . . . . 454 *Sea-side* 39
And Heaven is now to gladdened eyes revealing, . 455 **Not in the lucid* 21
Warbled, for heaven above and earth below, . . 457 **Had this* 14
A happier, brighter, purer Heaven than theirs. . 462 **Where lies the truth* 14
Forbid it, Heaven !—and MERRY ENGLAND still . 464 **They called* 13
Nor felt a wish that heaven would show . . . 472 *Ossian* 9
And, measuring heaven by earth, would overrule 473 **Thanks for* 4
Of heaven contemplated by Spirits pure . . . 474 **Hope smiled* 10
(Kindled from Heaven between the light and dark 475 **Homeward we* 3
Dear art thou to the light of heaven, ... 480 *Somnamb.* 158
The Mind's internal heaven shall shed her dews . 480 **Most sweet* 13
If this belief from heaven be sent, ... 482 *Lines : Spring* 21
Yet wants heaven knows what to be worthy the name. . . . . 482 *Character* 16
Led, Heaven knows how ! to this poor sod : . . 485 *Poet's Epitaph* 26
Nothing ? Heaven keep us from a lower stage ! . 489 *Illus. Books* 14
Bright ship of heaven ! . . . . 490 *Night Thought* 16
Some awful moment to which Heaven has joined 493 *Hap. War.* 49
Whose everlasting laws, sea, earth, and heaven obey." . . . . 495 *Fact* 14
Until they reach the bounds by Heaven assigned." 495 *Fact* 43
Of heaven, when Venus held the reins ! . . . 497 *Lycoris* 18
Or tax high Heaven with prodigality ?) . . . 501 **The unremitting* 9
Incense-like to Heaven, descending . . . . 502 **Like a* 16
Look up to Heaven ! the industrious Sun . . . 506 *Lab. Hymn* 21
On earth, will be revived, we trust, in heaven. . 510 **Among a* 32
A holy name—the Bird of Heaven ! . . . . 511 **Who rashly* 28
Tears of salvation. Welcome death ! while Heaven 520 *Pun. Death* 12. 9
To Loughrigg tarn, round clear and bright as heaven, ... 524 *Epist. Beaumont* 166
Of heaven in pity visiting the place. . . . . 525 *Epist. Beaumont* 263
Are Ye to heaven allied, ... 526 **The soaring* 46
How just, how bountiful, the hand of Heaven. . 530 *Poor Robin* 36
From Heaven, and *feel* what they repeat, . . . 530 *Gleaner* 32
One to whom Heaven assigns that mournful part 531 *Octogen.* 11
Heaven prosper it ! may peace, and love, . . . 534 **Blest is* 91
And by all the saints in heaven ; . . . . . 536 *Egremont* 101
And benedictions not unheard in heaven : . . . 539 **Lady ! a* 54
Save in the rolls of heaven, where hers may live . 540 *Grace Darl.* 16
A guardian Spirit sent from pitying Heaven, . . 541 *Grace Darl.* 73
Have unto Heaven and You been paid : . . . 542 *Russ. Fug.* 55
And Heaven doth to her virtue grant . . . . 543 *Russ. Fug.* 149
More mild doth Heaven ordain . . . . . . 544 *Russ. Fug.* 202
The God in heaven ;—attend, be just ; . . . 545 *Russ. Fug.* 295
High Heaven is my defence ; . . . . . . 545 *Russ. Fug.* 302
Exclaimed he : " righteous Heaven, ... 545 *Russ. Fug.* 330
To heaven he knelt before the crucifix, . . . 551 **If thou in* 17
Sits by her fire, and builds her hope in heaven. . 568 *Cumb. Beg.* 161
The good which the benignant law of Heaven . 568 *Cumb. Beg.* 167
And troubles that were each a step to Heaven : . 576 **By a* 8
For peace on earth and bliss in heaven. . . . 577 **By playful* 22
Of peaceful years ; a chronicle of heaven ;— . . 578 *Peele Castle* 22
But Heaven is now, blest Child, thy Spirit's home : 581 **Why should we* 11
Which good men take with them from earth to heaven. . . . . 582 **To public* 10
Till it exhales to Heaven. . . . . 582 **O for a* 24
To an unforgiving judgment from just Heaven. . 584 *Ch. Lamb* 37
And feeding daily on the hope of heaven, . . . 586 *Ch. Lamb* 123
From Skiddaw's top ; but he to heaven was vowed 587 *Crosth.* 16
Heaven lies about us in our infancy ! . . . . 588 *Immortality* 66
As sent from heav'n the raven of the skies, . . 609 *Desc.Sk.Quarto* 403
From his bare nest amid the storms of heaven . 613 *Desc.Sk.Quarto* 618
Two hundred times around the ring of heaven, . 618 *School Ex.* 2
Moves through the vault of heaven, and dissipates the night ; . . . . 618 *School Ex.* 40
To roam from heaven to heaven, from pole to pole, 619 *School Ex.* 74
Look up to heaven, and bless his darling boy. . 619 *School Ex.* 102
Bright as if heaven were ever in its eye, . . . 627 **We gaze* 4
And Heaven still lacked its due, though piety . 627 **When Severn's* 7
From Heaven, gigantic force to beardless boys. . 628 *Eagle and Dov* 16
Queen, Wife and Mother ! may All-judging Heaven 628 **Deign, Sovereign* 5
For thirst of power that Heaven disowns, . . . 628 *Installation* 1
Up starts some tyrant, Earth and Heaven to dare, 628 *Installation* 9

Heaven—*continued.*

For I, methought, while the sweet breath of heaven 632 *Prelude* 1. 33
We were a noisy crew ; the sun in heaven . . 639 *Prelude* 1. 479
With scoffs and taunts, like Vulcan out of heaven : 640 *Prelude* 1. 531
Communing in this sort through earth and heaven 648 *Prelude* 2. 411
By the proud name she bears—the name of Heaven. 650 *Prelude* 3. 111
Sweet Spenser, moving through his clouded heaven 653 *Prelude* 3. 280
The stars of Heaven, now seen in their old haunts— 662 *Prelude* 4. 243
He said, " My trust is in the God of Heaven, . . 665 *Prelude* 4. 459
Upon the speaking face of earth and heaven . . 666 *Prelude* 5. 13
Or heaven made manifest, that I could share . . 668 *Prelude* 5. 159
Its woods, and that uncertain heaven, received . 671 *Prelude* 5. 387
Space like a heaven filled up with northern lights, 673 *Prelude* 5. 532
Moving in heaven ; or, of that pleasure tired, . 679 *Prelude* 6. 270
At their chief city, in the sight of Heaven. . . 681 *Prelude* 6. 390
Before us, fast as clouds are changed in heaven. . 682 *Prelude* 6. 493
Locarno ! spreading out in width like Heaven, . 685 *Prelude* 6. 657
Before us, while she still was high in heaven ;— . 686 *Prelude* 6. 722
Duly to reach the point marked out by Heaven. . 686 *Prelude* 6. 753
Nor least, Heaven bless him ! the renowned Lord Mayor : . . . . 688 *Prelude* 7. 110
Here placed to be the inheritor of heaven, . . 704 *Prelude* 8. 336
Arguments sent from Heaven to prove the cause . 713 *Prelude* 9. 283
Of single spirits that catch the flame from Heaven, 715 *Prelude* 9. 368
One body, spreading wide as clouds in heaven. . 715 *Prelude* 9. 379
Is fairer than the fairest star in Heaven ! . . . 717 *Prelude* 9. 556
One nature, as there is one sun in heaven ; . . 720 *Prelude* 10. 158
Forced by the gracious providence of Heaven,— . 721 *Prelude* 10. 224
From hell came sanctified like airs from heaven. . 723 *Prelude* 10. 338
To which the silver wands of saints in Heaven . 725 *Prelude* 10. 485
But to be young was very Heaven ! O times, . 728 *Prelude* 11. 109
Or some secreted island, Heaven knows where ! . 729 *Prelude* 11. 141
Openly in the eye of earth and heaven, . . . 730 *Prelude* 11. 210
That once looked up in faith, as if to Heaven . . 732 *Prelude* 11. 362
The city of Timoleon ! Righteous Heaven ! . . 732 *Prelude* 11. 379
Prevailed among the powers of heaven and earth, 733 *Prelude* 11. 438
Or boldly seeking pleasure nearer heaven . . . 735 *Prelude* 12. 36
From earth to heaven, from human to divine ; . 747 *Prelude* 14. 118
By heaven inspired ; that frees from chains the soul, 748 *Prelude* 14. 184
Descend to earth or dwell in highest heaven ! . 755 *Recluse* 1. 1. 780
To which the heaven of heavens is but a veil. . 755 *Recluse* 1. 1. 783
His triangles—they were the stars of heaven, . . 760 *Excursion* 1. 272
Was their best hope, next to the God in heaven. . 764 *Excursion* 1. 534
With half a harvest. It pleased Heaven to add . 764 *Excursion* 1. 538
Calamity, the chastisement of Heaven, . . . 772 *Excursion* 2. 73
From regions opposite as heaven and hell. . . 775 *Excursion* 2. 231
Heaven bless them, and their inconsiderate work ! 778 *Excursion* 2. 454
His body is at rest, his soul in heaven." . . . 779 *Excursion* 2. 511
Beside our roads and pathways, though, thank Heaven ! . . . . 788 *Excursion* 3. 176
'*His body is at rest, his soul in heaven.*' . . . 789 *Excursion* 3. 229
Consistent in self-rule ; and heaven revealed . . 792 *Excursion* 3. 404
More solid than the gilded clouds of heaven ? . . 792 *Excursion* 3. 438
That walk the earth—Father of heaven and earth, 794 *Excursion* 3. 572
Confusion infinite of heaven and earth, . . . 796 *Excursion* 3. 721
To heaven :—" How beautiful this dome of sky ; 802 *Excursion* 4. 34
Father of heaven and earth ! and I am rich, . . 802 *Excursion* 4. 64
Earth to despise ; but, to converse with heaven— 803 *Excursion* 4. 131
Drawn towards her native firmament of heaven, . 807 *Excursion* 4. 396
Nor let the hallowed powers, that shed from heaven 808 *Excursion* 4. 483
Or cloud of darkness, localised in heaven ; . . 811 *Excursion* 4. 654
Of much exalted good by Heaven vouchsafed . 813 *Excursion* 4. 783
Glance rapidly along the clouded heaven, . . . 814 *Excursion* 4. 870
Oh ! there is laughter at their work in heaven ! . 815 *Excursion* 4. 956
Even like an altar lit by fire from heaven, . . 818 *Excursion* 4. 1121
And Heaven is weary, of the hollow words . . 828 *Excursion* 5. 379
But true humility descends from heaven ; . . . 833 *Excursion* 5. 719
And that best gift of heaven hath fallen on them ; 833 *Excursion* 5. 720
To heaven, I know, by my Redeemer taught.' . 835 *Excursion* 5. 826
To the pure heaven, he cast them down again . 836 *Excursion* 5. 901
Have rendered prone, can upward look to heaven ; 837 *Excursion* 5. 989
And spires whose " silent finger points to heaven ; " 838 *Excursion* 6. 19
Cause should recur, which righteous Heaven avert ! 839 *Excursion* 6. 60
A thing most sacred in the eye of Heaven ; . . 841 *Excursion* 6. 179
Which wafts that prayer to heaven, is due to all, 842 *Excursion* 6. 267
(And Heaven was pleased to accomplish the desire) 845 *Excursion* 6. 501
Loth to disturb what Heaven hath hushed in peace. 847 *Excursion* 6. 572
Converse with heaven, nor yet deprest towards earth, ... 848 *Excursion* 6. 680
As if he wished the firmament of heaven . . . 851 *Excursion* 6. 883
As ever raised to heaven a streaming eye ! . . 853 *Excursion* 6. 991
This tale gives proof that Heaven most gently deals 854 *Excursion* 6. 1072
But Heaven was gracious ; yet a little while, . . 861 *Excursion* 7. 278
The memory of the just survives in heaven : . . 863 *Excursion* 7. 388
Whose sacred influence, spread through earth and heaven, ... 864 *Excursion* 7. 484
His genius mounted to the plains of heaven. . . 865 *Excursion* 7. 506
Nor will, I trust, the Majesty of Heaven . . . 866 *Excursion* 7. 579
Advance, and in the firmament of heaven . . . 876 *Excursion* 8. 160
Of azure heaven, the unenduring clouds, . . . 884 *Excursion* 9. 6
Of every country under heaven. My thoughts . 887 *Excursion* 9. 186
And the infinite magnificence of heaven . . . 887 *Excursion* 9. 210
The Spirit capable of heaven, assured. . . . . 887 *Excursion* 9. 228
To heaven as lightly from the cottage-hearth . . 887 *Excursion* 9. 246
For every genial power of heaven and earth, . . 888 *Excursion* 9. 265
With what Heaven grants, and die—in peace of mind, ... 888 *Excursion* 9. 279
That from the humblest floor ascends to heaven, . 889 *Excursion* 9. 326
A grateful tribute to all-ruling Heaven. . . . 890 *Excursion* 9. 391
Of those who fill thy courts in highest heaven, . 893 *Excursion* 9. 621
To have a nearer view of thee, in heaven. . . . 894 *Excursion* 9. 646

Heavens—*continued.*
The clouds pass on; they from the heavens depart: 110 *'*Tis said that some* 17
In the mid heavens, is never half so fair . . . 148 **There is an* 11
Up and down the heavens they go, ... 160 **Pansies, lilies* 11
New heavens succeeded, by the dream brought forth: . . . . 168 *Pilgrim's Dream* 59
The second glory of the Heavens?—Thou hast; . 172 *Infant Daughter* 5
Do for thee what the finger of the heavens . . 172 *Infant Daughter* 31
The clear Moon, and the glory of the heavens. . 184 *Night-piece* 13
And is as happy in his night, for the heavens are blue and fair; . . . . 189 *Star-gazers* 6
Among the heavens his eye can see . . . . 205 *Brougham* 134
Nor Traveller gone from earth the heavens to espy! 208 **It is no* 3
The heavens, whose aspect makes our minds as still 235 *Power of Sound* 181
And vanish, though the heavens dissolve, her stay 235 *Power of Sound* 223
The broad blue heavens appeared to glimmer, . 241 *P. B.* 484
If the heavens smile, and leave us free to glide, . 252 **Her only* 7
As the beginning of the heavens and earth! . . 265 **Hail, Twilight* 14
To mock the Outcast—O ye Heavens, be kind! . 306 **We had* 13
Pure as the naked heavens, majestic, free, . . 307 **Milton! thou* 11
How long shall vengeance sleep? Ye patient Heavens, how long? . . . . . . 311 **Who rises* 41
Till, with the heavens and earth, thou pass away! 329 *Ode: Thanks.* 19
On Earth, who works in the heaven of heavens, alone. . . . . 389 *Tyndrum* 14
Told, also, how the voiceless heavens declare . . 461 **Queen of* 42
Hell opens, and the heavens in vengeance crack . 475 **Here on their* 8
And the most ancient heavens, through Thee, are fresh and strong. . . . . 492 *Duty* 48
The heavens have felt it too. . . . . . . 507 *May* 20
Of every cloud which in the heavens might stir . 574 *Chiabrera* 4. 18
The Heavens are thronged with martyrs that have risen . . . . 581 *Invoc. Earth* 8
Look round her when the heavens are bare, . . 587 *Immortality* 13
The heavens laugh with you in your jubilee; . . 588 *Immortality* 38
And the near heav'ns their own delights impart. . 612 *Desc.Sk.Quarto* 561
To the broad ocean and the azure heavens . . 651 *Prelude* 3. 161
O Heavens! how awful is the might of souls, . 651 *Prelude* 3. 177
The unfettered clouds and region of the Heavens, 684 *Prelude* 6. 634
The blended calmness of the heavens and earth, . 697 *Prelude* 7. 660
Triumphant, winning from the invaded heavens . 734 *Prelude* 11. 455
Theirs is the language of the heavens, the power, 744 *Prelude* 13. 271
Their knowledge of the heavens, and image forth 745 *Prelude* 13. 341
For so it seemed, felt by the starry heavens. . . 747 *Prelude* 14. 62
I have protracted, in the unwearied heavens . . 751 *Prelude* 14. 383
To which the heaven of heavens is but a veil. . 755 *Recluse* 1. 1. 783
Imploringly;—looked up, and asked the Heavens, 796 *Excursion* 3. 690
The mild assemblage of the starry heavens; . . 808 *Excursion* 4. 464
And the whole circle of the heavens, for him . 811 *Excursion* 4. 678
Aught by these perishable heavens disclosed . . 850 *Excursion* 6. 769
Undaunted, toward the imperishable heavens, . 885 *Excursion* 9. 43
That which the heavens displayed, the liquid deep 893 *Excursion* 8. 607
Heavens! who sees majesty in George's face? . L.1. 88 *Juvenal* 1. 9

Heaven-sanctioned. Now, from Heaven-sanctioned victory, Peace is sprung; . . . . . 326 **Emperors and* 7

Heaven-taught. Impelled by thirst of all but Heaven-taught skill. . . . . 358 **Is this* 8
Such as the heaven-taught skill of Herbert drew; 380 *Duddon* 18. 13
That moral sweeten by a heaven-taught lay, . . 388 *Trosachs* 13

Heavenward. Our heavenward guide is holy love, 143 †*Lov. and Lik.* 67
With faith, the Suppliant heavenward lifts her hands; . . . . 209 *Laod.* 8
Of heaven-ward enterprise. . . . . 224 *'*Tis gone* 54
Heaven-born, the Soul a heavenward course must hold; . . . . 257 **No mortal* 5
Which heavenward they direct.—Then droop not thou, ... 261 **From the dark* 10
Points heavenward, indicate the end and way. . 281 *Chris. Words.* 14
In the pines pointing heavenward her beauty austere; . . . . 364 *Vallomb.* 12
On those bright steps that heavenward raise . . 458 **Had this* 51
Heavenward ascends with all her charities, . . 467 *St. Bees* 116
Of luminous faith, heavenward hath raised that head . . . . 476 *Howard* 4
Earthward or heavenward, radiant messengers, . 500 *Humanity* 36
Heavenward; and chide the part of me that flags, 803 *Excursion* 4. 127
Heavenward, so piercing deep the lake below. . K.8. 252 *Recluse* 1.1.579

Heaves. His bosom heaves, his Spirit towers amain, 18 *Desc. Sk.* 459
Her bosom heaves and spreads, her stature grows; 209 *Laod.* 11
—Behold!—as with a gushing impulse heaves . 212 *Dion*
That a brief while heaves with convulsive throes— 217 *Enterprise* 115
Wide Europe heaves, impatient to be cast, . . 331 *Ode: Thanks.* 149
But Ocean under magic heaves, ... 370 *Eg. Maid* 49

Heavier. Heavier than work, raised it: within that hut . . . . 39 *Bord.* 121
The heavier substance of a leaf-clad bough, . . 123 *V. and J.* 142
And the blows fell with heavier weight . . . 238 *P. B.* 194
On the crushed heart a heavier burthen lay. . . 267 **As the* 8
That every foot might fall with heavier tread, . 275 *Gravestone* 12
Reviving, heavier chastisement deserve . . . 327 **Emperors and* 13
A care more anxious, or a heavier grief? . . . 461 **Where lies the truth* 3
Month falls on month with heavier weight, . . 479 *Somnamb.* 79
Thou wilt provoke a heavier penalty. . . . . 513 *Newspaper* 14
Against far heavier ill, the pestilence . . . . 513 *General Fast* 13
Or aught of heavier or more deadly weight, . . 737 *Prelude* 12. 212
Hung down in heavier tufts; and that bright weed, 767 *Excursion* 1. 716
Perchance, the heavier woes of guilt; feel not . 829 *Excursion* 5. 429
Heavier, as his offence was heavier far. . . . 854 *Excursion* 6. 1077

Heaviest. The heaviest storms not longest last; . 110 *Forsaken* 2

Heaviest—*continued.*
Nor by the heaviest rain-drops more deprest, . . 169 **Never enlivened* 3
The heaviest plummet of despair can go— . . 213 *Dion* 62
Wreaths that endure affliction's heaviest shower, 259 **Weak is* 13
—Woe to them all! but heaviest woe and shame 313 *Prophecy* 11
Whose heaviest sin it is to look . . . . . . 344 **How blest* 8
Or grass-grown spaces, where the heaviest foot . 355 *Aquap.* 194
Methinks that I could trip o'er heaviest soil, . . 438 *Ecc. Sonn.* 2. 39. 1
That, under heaviest sorrow earth can bring, . . 725 *Prelude* 10. 465

Heavily. Pressing as heavily as it doth on mine. . 78 *Bord.* 2298
Ye travel heavily and slow; . . . . 114 *Ind. Wom.* 50
Too heavily upon the lily's head, ... 124 *V. and J.* 193
The rain came heavily and fell in floods; . . . 195 *Resolution* 2

Heaviness. A moment's heaviness they feel, . . 81 †*Mother's Return* 47
Nor could my heart by second thoughts from heaviness be cleared, ... 91 *Poet's Dream* 5
Be turned to heaviness and fear. . . . . . 204 *Brougham* 94
And heaviness in Clifford's ear! . . . . . 204 *Brougham* 103
And the Lady prayed in heaviness . . . . . 495 *Force of Prayer* 61
From heaviness, oft fly, dear Friend, to thee; . 521 *Epist. Beaumont* 11
And of that longing heaviness doth come, . . . 557 *Cuck. and Night.* 31
Why Troilus hath all this heaviness? . . . . 564 *Troilus* 103

Heaving. Till you have marked his heaving chest, 143 **Driven in* 23
Only a heaving of the deep survives, ... 454 *Sea-side* 4
So that the very heaving of his breath . . . . 523 *Epist. Beaumont* 142
Or lily heaving with the wave . . . . . . 583 **O for a* 44
Went heaving through the water like a swan; . 637 *Prelude* 1. 376
No heaving of the heart. While by the fire . 768 *Excursion* 1. 801
A heaving surface, almost wholly free . . . . 847 *Excursion* 6. 607
Said I, "like surges heaving in the wind . . . 858 *Excursion* 7. 32

Heavings. I too forgot the heavings of my breast. . 30 *Guilt* 338

Heavy. Dear Master! gratitude's a heavy burden . 38 *Bord.* 30
Meanwhile the storm fell heavy on the woods; . 50 *Bord.* 707
Heavy his low-hung lip did oft appear, . . . 108 *Indolence* 42
Years after he had heard this heavy news. . . 138 *Michael* 453
Heavy and wan, all whitened by the Moon, . . 184 *Night-piece* 3
And hung with heavy tufts of moss, ... 197 *Thorn* 14
With heavy tufts of moss that strive . . . . 200 *Thorn* 234
In which the heavy and the weary weight . . 206 *Tintern* 39
Heavy is woe;—and joy, for human-kind, . . 259 **Weak is* 3
That she had borne a heavy yoke, ... 294 *Jedbor.* 72
To him, a heavy, bitter loss, ... 297 *Highland Boy* 214
Of thy offences be a heavy weight: . . . . . 309 **England! the* 13
Through heavy swamp, or over snow-clad height— 320 **Hunger, and* 3
When snow lies heavy upon the land." . . . 403 *White Doe* 624
Slowly the cormorant aims her heavy flight . . 419 *Ecc. Sonn.* 1. 3. 4
Ye heavy laden!" such the inviting voice . . . 423 *Ecc. Sonn.* 1. 17. 11
Silently to consume the heavy clouds; . . . . 426 *Ecc. Sonn.* 1. 29. 11
And like a Star (that, from a heavy cloud . . . 465 **Dear to* 5
But, oh the heavy change!—bereft . . . . 483 *Simon Lee* 25
"But we are pressed by heavy laws; . . . . 487 *Fountain* 45
And all the heavy or light vassalage . . . . 501 *Humanity* 96
And pine-trees made a heavy shade . . . . 542 *Russ. Fug.* 95
Is of my Lady's sighs heavy and sore; . . . . 565 *Troilus* 157
Not without heavy grief of heart did He . . . 575 *Chiabrera* 8. 1
Importunate and heavy load! . . . . 581 **Loud is* 10
Heavy as frost, and deep almost as life! . . . 589 *Immortality* 132
—Heavy, and dull, and cloudy is the night, . . 606 *Desc.Sk.Quarto* 215
The heavy weight of many a weary day . . . 632 *Prelude* 1. 22
That thou endurest; heavy though that weight be, 665 *Prelude* 5. 6
The assurance which then cheered some heavy thoughts . . . . 687 *Prelude* 7. 13
A vagrant Merchant under a heavy load . . . 761 *Excursion* 1. 324
And partner of my loss.—O heavy change! . . 795 *Excursion* 3. 669
And, as the heavy cloud of sleep dissolves, . . 826 *Excursion* 5. 266
Was no access for wain, heavy or light. . . . 858 *Excursion* 7. 62
Thick storm, and heavy, which for three hours' space . . . . K.8. 228 **I will* 136
In times of heavy snow." She then began . . K.8. 247 *Recluse* 1.1.399
Rid of a vexing and a heavy load, ... K.8. 265 **Rid of* 1

Heavy-headed. But still the heavy-headed Thing . 241 *P. B.* 404

Hebe. Now flush'd as Hebe, Emulation rose; . . 618 *School Ex.* 20

Hebrew. From Hebrew fountains sprung; . . . 232 *Jew. Fam.* 44
By Hebrew ordinance devoutly kept, ... 354 *Aquap.* 136
O Hebrew people!' said he in his wrath, . . 554 *Prioress* 109
Such as by Hebrew Prophets were beheld . . 784 *Excursion* 2. 867
—With promises the Hebrew Scriptures teem: . 797 *Excursion* 3. 759

Hebrews. The Hebrews thus, carrying in joyful state 346 *Processions* 10

Hebrides. Among the farthest Hebrides. . . . 289 *Sol. Reap.* 16

Hector. A self-devoted chief—by Hector slain." . 210 *Laod.* 48
Of Priam ask'd, of Hector,—o'er and o'er— . . 625 *Æneid* 134
Of Hector asked if [of] Priam o'er and o'er, . L.2. 123 *Frag. Æneid* 3. 1
Where hast thou tarried, Hector? from what coast L.2. 318 *Frag. Æneid* 4. 3

He'd. He'd not have robbed the raven of its food. 35 *Guilt* 610
He'd wish to close them again. . . . . . 162 **Art thou the* 14
He'd drag as well what he is dragging; . . . 179 *Waggoner* 3. 53

Hedge. Silent the hedge or steamy rivulet's bed, . 8 *Ev. Wk.* 324
Hedge in the life of every pest and plague . . 66 *Bord.* 1582
And through the broken hawthorn hedge, . . 83 *Lucy Gray* 47
And, looking o'er the hedge, before me I espied . 87 *Pet-lamb* 3
When I walk by the hedge on a bright summer's day, 116 *Repentance* 17
Intent on gathering wool from hedge and brake . 280 **Intent on* 1
Than an old hedge to Goody Blake? . . . . 537 *Goody Blake* 60
To seek the hedge of Harry Gill, ... 537 *Goody Blake* 64
She's at the hedge of Harry Gill! . . . . . 537 *Goody Blake* 80
Silent the hedge or steaming rivulet's bed, . . 599 *Ev. Wk. Quarto* 390
Along a hedge of hollies dark and tall, . . . 880 *Excursion* 8. 442

Hedgehog. Or track the hedgehog to his hole. . . 142 †*Lov. and Lik.* 52

Hedgehog—*continued.*
Had to his joy unearthed a hedgehog, teased — 746 *Prelude* 14. 23
Hedge-row. Nor hedge-row screen invites my steps abroad; — 521 *Epist. Beaumont* 13
Its hinder part concealed by hedge-row thorn. — 523 *Epist. Beaumont* 124
The little hedgerow birds, — 572 *Animal Tran.* 1
Flowers out of any hedge-row to compose — 722 *Prelude* 10. 313
Hedge-rows. To willowy hedge-rows, and to emerald meads; — 2 *Ev. Wk.* 6
From out the lowly hedge-rows flung; — 180 *Waggoner* 4. 78
These hedge-rows, hardly hedge-rows, little lines — 206 *Tintern* 15
Stretched under wayside hedge-rows, ballad tunes, — 668 *Prelude* 5. 210
Where two tall hedge-rows of thick alder boughs — 763 *Excursion* 1. 460
That peck along the hedge-rows, or the kite — 764 *Excursion* 1. 564
At noon, the bank and hedgerows all the way — S.3. 417 **Sweet was* 2
Hedges. Between the hedges as they go, — 244 *P. B.* 716
In the dark hedges. So their days were spent — 764 *Excursion* 1. 532
Heed. And the poor Boy was busier still, with work of anxious heed. — 91 *Norman Boy* 12
Dear Spot! which we have watched with tender heed, — 106 *Farewell* 33
And flow it did; not taking heed — 111 *A Complaint* 5
Heed not tho' none should call thee fair; — 111 **Let other* 5
Of moon or stars he takes no heed; — 130 *Idiot Boy* 354
Never heed them; I aver — 160 **Pansies, lilies* 35
Methinks you take small heed! — 161 *Binnorie* 31
Love him, who for himself will take no heed at all? — 195 *Resolution* 42
Heed not, wild Rover once through heath and glen, — 255 *Detraction* 9
Heed not such onset! nay, if praise of men — 255 *Detraction* 11
Heed not the pillage of man's ancient heart. — 255 *S. H.* 14
Forth to her Dove, and took no further heed. — 274 **Wait, prithee* 2
On wrongs, which Nature scarcely seems to heed: — 292 **Degenerate Douglas* 11
And to the attendant promise will give heed— — 314 **I dropped* 11
The eyes of good men thankfully give heed, — 327 *Ode 1815* 34
Nor giving heed to aught that passed the while, — 365 **Under the* 3
More promptly rises, walks with stricter heed, — 429 *Ecc. Sonn.* 2. 3. 2
And wake him with such gentle heed — 458 **Had this* 58
Is he ungrateful, and doth little heed — 461 **Where lies the truth* 4
She hath crost, and without heed — 490 *Incident: Dog* 21
Less than they heed a breath of wanton air. — 495 *Fact* 8
While yet the solemn heed the State hath given — 520 *Pun. Death.* 12. 11
I of a token thought which Lovers heed; — 557 *Cuck. and Night.* 47
And for that cause Osee I cry; take heed! — 559 *Cuck.and Night.* 135
He took no heed; but in his brawny arms — 696 *Prelude* 7. 612
Heeded. When others heeded not, He heard the South — 132 *Michael* 50
And heeded not the voice of clashing swords, — 422 *Ecc. Sonn.* 1. 14. 12
Upheld by warnings heeded not too late — 529 **Those breathing* 130
I heeded not their summons: happy time — 638 *Prelude* 1. 428
He heeded not; but, with his twofold charge — 667 *Prelude* 5. 134
And heeded not: you lingered, you perceived — 808 *Excursion* 4. 473
Heedeth. Nor heedeth Man's perverseness; Spring returns,— — 734 *Prelude* 12. 32
Heedfully. Maintained his place; or heedfully pursued — 783 *Excursion* 2. 768
Heeding. On the green herb, and nothing heeding, — 406 *White Doe* 974
Heedless. The shining glow-worm; or, in heedless play, — 7 *Ev. Wk.* 265
But, heedless of the following gloom, — 9 *Lines: Boat* 10
To say that you are heedless of the past: — 98 *Brothers* 168
Thou, too heedless, art the Warden — 157 *Sexton* 23
In such a heedless peace. Alas! full soon — 173 *Infant Daughter* 60
In presence of their heedless dams, — 217 *Enterprise* 139
Is preaching to no heedless flock! — 247 *P. B.* 945
Ever too heedless, as I now perceive: — 279 **Though I* 6
Heedless of Alpine torrents thundering — 376 *Duddon* 1. 7
And some, too heedless of past danger, court — 454 *Sea-side* 17
The shrill-voiced thrush is heedless, and again — 455 *Rydal Mere* 3
Gives plaintive ditties to the heedless wind, — 522 *Epist.Beaumont* 47
No longer, scattering to the heedless winds — 549 **The massy* 11
Heedless how Pliny, musing here, survey'd — 604 *Desc.Sk.Quarto* 116
Though heedless of such honours now, and changed: — 711 *Prelude* 9. 142
Heedless how far; and, in such piteous sort — 769 *Excursion* 1. 865
More than the heedless impress that belongs — 787 *Excursion* 3. 81
And, heedless even of listeners; warbled out — S.3. 436 **The doubt* 155
Heedlessly. Not heedlessly, the laws, and watched the forms — 676 *Prelude* 6. 101
Heeds. The homely sympathy that heeds — 158 **In youth* 53
Who heeds not beauty, love, or song, — 169 *Wren's Nest* 50
But the sage Muse the revel heeds — 180 *Waggoner* 4. 7
Who knows not pomp, who heeds not pelf; — 344 **How blest* 7
Ye, too, wild Flowers! that no one heeds, — 366 **Ye Trees* 11
Unchecked he hurries on;—nor heeds — 411 *White Doe* 1380
Heels. Cooling our heels in this way!—I'll begin — 51 *Bord.* 753
For joy his head and heels are idle, — 127 *Idiot Boy* 75
Perhaps, with head and heels on fire, — 129 *Idiot Boy* 332
With ready heels his shaggy side; — 241 *P. B.* 399
Have I, reclining back upon my heels, — 639 *Prelude* 1. 457
Heels over head, like tumblers on a stage. — 880 *Excursion* 8. 381
Heifer. I had been out in search of a stray heifer; — 73 *Bord.* 2044
"There's neither dog nor heifer, horse nor sheep, — 202 *Hart-leap* 133
Where oft the venturous heifer drinks the noontide breeze. — 226 *Vernal Ode* 13
The last year's cup whose Ram or Heifer gained, — 522 *Epist.Beaumont* 67
The heifer comes in the snow-storm, and here — 547 **Rude is* 15
Stringed like a poor man's heifer at its feed, — 669 *Prelude* 5. 240

Heifer—*continued.*
The heifer lows, uneasy at the voice — 699 *Prelude* 8. 23
The heifer in yon little croft belongs — K.8. 251 *Recluse* 1.1.524
Heifer's. The solitary heifer's deepened low; — 17 *Desc. Sk.* 360
The bark of dogs the heifer's tinkling bell, — 18 *Desc. Sk.* 419
With one bright bell a favourite heifer's neck; — 19 *Desc. Sk.* 495
Unto a heifer's motion, by a cord — 717 *Prelude* 9. 512
Height. And plods through some wide realm o'er vale and height, — 10 *Desc. Sk.* 11
—'Tis his, while wandering on from height to height, — 16 *Desc. Sk.* 316
Of green isles widening on each snow-clad height; — 17 *Desc. Sk.* 369
They sport beneath that mountain's matchless height — 21 *Desc. Sk.* 577
Join twenty tapers of unequal height — 65 *Bord.* 1512
Already I've been punished to the height — 67 *Bord.* 1638
Through wood, and through vale; and o'er rocky height, — 80 †*Address: Child* 3
Than the height of a counsellor's bag; — 86 *Rural Arch.* 3
Of occupation led from height to height — 101 *Brothers* 360
His voice came to us from the neighbouring height: — 107 *Indolence* 14
How beautiful when up a lofty height — 138 *Widow* 1
Above us, and so distant in its height, — 148 **There is an* 6
Rising to no ambitious height; yet both, — 151 **Forth from* 4
Rise up, and grow to wondrous height. — 173 *Waggoner* 1. 14
Save that above a single height — 175 *Waggoner* 1. 166
Still mounting to a higher height; — 178 *Waggoner* 3. 25
See, perched upon the naked height — 182 *Waggoner* 4. 254
Shall rear her form to stately height, — 187 **Three years* 32
That tall Man, a giant in bulk and in height, — 189 *Music* 33
She had a tall man's height or more; — 190 *Beggars* 1
She grew to woman's height. — 192 *Ruth* 18
Just half a foot in height. — 198 *Thorn* 37
I climbed the mountain's height:— — 199 *Thorn* 174
This Height a ministering Angel might select: — 218 **This Height* 1
In depth, in height, in circuit, how serene — 219 **This Height* 29
Swift as a Thracian Nymph o'er field and height! — 221 *Triad* 120
In strains that from their solemn height — 228 *Devot. Incit.* 28
Children, thus post ye over vale and height — 229 *Clouds* 9
Descend from this ethereal height; — 238 *P. B.* 152
The staff was raised to loftier height, — 238 *P. B.* 193
While health, power, glory, from their height decline, — 261 **I watch* 11
Rejoicing, from her loftiest height she drops — 270 **Though the bold* 3
From what huge height, descending? Can such force — 272 *Devil's Bridge* 2
Fly upon swiftest wing round field and height, — 294 **Fly, some* 3
Through hanging clouds, from craggy height to height, — 315 **Advance—come* 11
And so hath gained at length a prosperous height, — 317 **Look now* 6
Him from that height shall Heaven precipitate — 318 **Look now* 13
Through heavy swamp, or over snow-clad height— — 320 **Hunger, and* 3
Than fairest Star, upon the height — 338 **Meek Virgin* 2
The starry zone of sovereign height— — 343 *Eclipse* 52
That lifts the spirit to a calmer height, — 349 *Val. Dover* 13
Await my steps when they the breezy height — 356 *Aquap.* 253
To virtue consecrate, stoop ye from your height — 357 *Aquap.* 290
(Then first apparent from the Pincian Height) — 358 *Pine: Rome* 13
Here also, on some favoured height, he would choose — 364 *Vallomb.* 23
Better to breathe at large on this clear height — 376 *Duddon* 1. 11
Slept amid that lone Camp on Hardknot's height, — 380 *Duddon* 17. 10
Of yon pure waters, from their aery height — 380 *Duddon* 19. 4
Engendered, hangs o'er Eildon's triple height: — 386 *Scott* 3
Of music reached its height, and even when sank — 387 *Roslin* 4
Who, that has gained at length the wished-for Height, — 389 *Glencroe* 2
Of seventy years, to loftier height; — 404 *White Doe* 742
Upon the turf-clad height he lies — 404 *White Doe* 771
Upon the height walks to and fro; — 409 *White Doe* 1189
Then on this height the Maid had sought, — 409 *White Doe* 1206
With Emily, on the Watch-tower height, — 411 *White Doe* 1348
The troop of horse have gained the height — 412 *White Doe* 1461
Close to the summit of this height, — 416 *White Doe* 1802
From the collegiate pomps on Windsor's height — 430 *Ecc. Sonn.* 2. 6. 4
Or, crowning, star-like, each some sovereign height, — 457 **Had this* 13
Was yielding, on a mountain height — 472 *Ossian* 6
And flashing to that Structure's topmost height, — 473 **Thanks for* 11
All round, in hollow or on height; — 491 *Fidelity* 14
Attained a stature twice a tall man's height, — 521 *Epist. Beaumont* 15
To measure height and distance; lonely task, — 548 **Stay, bold* 16
Survive upon the tall mast's height; — 579 **Sweet Flower* 47
Of heaven-born freedom on thy being's height, — 589 *Immortality* 126
And eyes through tears the mountain's shadeless height; — 596 *Ev. Wk. Quarto* 252
By floods, that, thundering from their dizzy height, — 606 *Desc.Sk.Quarto* 247
The woods, and distant Skiddaw's lofty height, — 636 *Prelude* 1. 295
Beset me, and to height unusual rose, — 666 *Prelude* 5. 62
At a slow pace. The immeasurable height — 684 *Prelude* 6. 624
Above all height! like an aerial cross — 703 *Prelude* 8. 273
Strives, from that height, with one and yet one more — 709 *Prelude* 9. 15
Dread nothing? From this height I shall not stoop — 717 *Prelude* 9. 541
Which, when the spirit of evil reached its height, — 735 *Prelude* 12. 42
Up to the height of feeling intellect — 749 *Prelude* 14. 226
By circumstance to take unto the height — 757 *Excursion* 1. 87
To meet for worship on that central height)— — 784 *Excursion* 2. 816
From whose calm centre thou, through height or depth, — 787 *Excursion* 3. 108
Where height, or depth, admits not the approach — 795 *Excursion* 3. 643
Descending, there might rest; upon that height — 811 *Excursion* 4. 687
That speculative height *we* may not reach. — 830 *Excursion* 5. 489
Hath gained his noontide height, this churchyard, filled — 830 *Excursion* 5. 534

Height—*continued.*
—Stoop from your height, ye proud, and copy these! — 833 *Excursion* 5. 722
Drawn from her cottage, on that aery height, — 834 *Excursion* 5. 758
The voice of Deity, on height and plain, — 837 *Excursion* 5. 991
Ascending! For on that superior height — 885 *Excursion* 9. 69
On height or bottom did they see, in flocks — K.8. 225 **I will* 39
Of vale below, a height of hills above. — K.8. 237 *Recluse* 1. 1. 21

Heighten. Methinks 'twould heighten joy, to overleap — 284 *Departure* 5
Will dwell with me—to heighten joy, — 302 *Yarrow V.* 87

Heightened. With wonder heightened, or sublimed by awe— — 689 *Prelude* 7. 153
Of speech as wild as ever heightened mirth. — K.8. 301 **And oh* 10

Height's. When, through this Height's inverted arch, — 215 *Kirkstone* 43

Heights. *See* **Mountain-heights, Rydal-heights.**
Of pensive Underwalden's pastoral heights. — 16 *Desc. Sk.* 339
That came to him, and left him, on the heights. — 132 *Michael* 60
Against the mountain blasts; and to the heights, — 134 *Michael* 195
Up to the heights, and in among the storms, — 137 *Michael* 393
Like stars, at various heights; — 224 *Primrose* 4
To pause at last on more aspiring heights — 230 *Clouds* 21
To Her from heights that Reason may not win. — 280 **Oh what* 8
Or where 'mid "lonely heights and hows," — 287 *Sons of Burns* 31
Lost on the aerial heights of the Crusades! — 290 *Kilchurn* 43
Alone upon Loch Veol's heights, — 292 *Rob Roy* 115
The vapours linger round the Heights, — 302 *Yarrow V.* 81
Thou, who upon those snow-clad Heights hast poured — 329 *Ode: Thanks.* 29
Is this the stream, whose cities, heights, and plains, — 335 *Namur* 2
But, flying through the heights around, — 342 *Ital. Itin.* 65
From dew-sprinkled grass to heights guarded with snow, — 345 *Stanzas: Simplon* 18
Of sounds as rang the heights of Latmos over, — 346 *Gemmi* 4
Among these sterile heights of Apennine, — 362 **List—'twas* 38
To carry thy glad tidings over heights — 363 **List—'twas* 101
I mingle with the blest on those pure heights — 365 **Rapt above* 3
On cloud-sequestered heights, that see and hear — 389 *Tyndrum* 12
(Foretaste of winter) on the moorland heights; — 394 **No more* 28
In Craven's dens, on Cumbrian heights; — 399 *White Doe* 279
Now seek upon the heights of Time the source — 418 *Ecc. Sonn.* 1. 1. 9
To giddier heights hath clomb the Papal sway. — 427 *Ecc. Sonn.* 1. 35. 14
Ranging the heights of Scawfell or Black-comb, — 468 **Ranging the* 1
To heights more glorious still, and into shades — 496 **A little* 53
Glad proclamation make, and heights and dells — 503 *Warning* 42
Those heights (like Phœbus when his golden locks — 521 *Epist. Beaumont* 40
The massy Ways, carried across these heights — 549 **The massy* 1
Lost gradual o'er the heights in pomp they go, — 595 *Ev. Wk. Quarto* 187
Thence red from different heights with restless gleam — 598 *Ev. Wk. Quarto* 373
And emerald isles to spot the heights appear, — 610 *Desc.Sk.Quarto* 445
Wensley's rich Vale and Sedbergh's naked heights. — 622 *Recluse* 1. 1. 157
—Why suns in winter, shunning heaven's steep heights — 625 *Æneid* 128
To range the open heights where woodcocks run — 636 *Prelude* 1. 311
With those crystalline rivers, solemn heights, — 654 *Prelude* 3. 354
And heights meanwhile were slowly overspread — 661 *Prelude* 4. 179
Without repining from the coves and heights — 675 *Prelude* 6. 10
Rests his substantial orb;—between those heights — 782 *Excursion* 2. 719
Returned not, and now, haply, on the heights — 783 *Excursion* 2. 789
As our enjoyments, boundless.—From those heights — 794 *Excursion* 3. 544
Heights which the soul is competent to gain. — 803 *Excursion* 4. 139
Is still a happier man, who, for those heights — 806 *Excursion* 4. 355
Of mere humanity, you clomb those heights; — 808 *Excursion* 4. 470
Sounds which the wandering shepherd from these heights — 809 *Excursion* 4. 572
Tidings of joy and love.—From those pure heights — 811 *Excursion* 4. 641
To loftiest heights ascending, from their tops, — 811 *Excursion* 4. 674
—Stoop from those heights, and soberly declare — 813 *Excursion* 4. 774
Sends inspiration from the shadowy heights, — 818 *Excursion* 4. 1171
From these imaginative heights, that yield — 819 *Excursion* 4. 1188
Earthly desires; and raise, to loftier heights — 820 *Excursion* 4. 1273
Who, mounting fearlessly the rocky heights, — 856 *Excursion* 6. 1158
Descended from Judean heights, to march — 870 *Excursion* 7. 812
The red-deer driven along its native heights — 870 *Excursion* 7. 864
'Mid Buxton's dreary heights. In earnest watch, — 879 *Excursion* 8. 377
With pure cerulean gravel, from the heights — 881 *Excursion* 8. 452
To Taranis erected on the heights — 894 *Excursion* 9. 704
When from the heights our shepherds drive their flocks — K.8. 224 **I will* 8
Against the mountain blasts, and to the heights — K.8. 226 **I will* 75
Of this fair Vale, and o'er its spacious heights — K.8. 248 *Recluse* 1. 1. 431

Heinous. Thou seest me what I am. It was most heinous, — 75 *Bord.* 2124
Of yet more heinous guilt, with fiercer pride. — 519 *Pun. Death* 11. 8
May with such heinous appetites be compared), — 723 *Prelude* 10. 366

Heir. And taught that pain is pleasure's natural heir, — 20 *Desc. Sk.* 537
Remains without an Heir, the bait — 403 *White Doe* 639
The infant Heir of Mowbray's blood— — 405 *White Doe* 823
From Childbirth's perilous throes. And should the Heir — 447 *Ecc. Sonn.* 3. 27. 8
And all the long year through the heir — 485 **Bright Flower* 3
Save He who came as rightful Heir — 535 *Egremont* 7
Fam'd Pygmalion's Son and Heir, — S.3. 437 **I, whose* 6
And let that heir of Glory's endless day — L.1. 94 *Juvenal* 2. 23

Heirloom. What poor abodes the heirloom hide, — 391 *Highland Broach* 65
An *heir-loom* in his cottage wilt Thou be:— — 490 *Spade* 30

Heirs. Hailed from aloft those Heirs of truth divine — 431 *Ecc.Sonn.* 2. 13. 10
The Poets, who on earth have made us heirs — 489 *Pers. Talk* 53
Heirs from times of earliest record — 535 *Egremont* 9

Heirs—*continued.*
And through ages, heirs of heirs, — 536 *Egremont* 110
Twin labourers and heirs of the same hopes; — 666 *Prelude* 5. 44
Inmates, and heirs of our united love; — 794 *Excursion* 3. 590
Such as theboy you painted, lineal heirs — 886 *Excursion* 9. 179

Held. *See* **Upheld, Withheld.**
Imprisoned there, and held it to his ear, — 44 *Bord.* 405
Has held infernal orgies—with the gloom, — 49 *Bord.* 660
While in my lap I held my little Babe — 62 *Bord.* 1360
The scrip that held his food, and I forgot — 67 *Bord.* 1643
And held such intermitted talk — 85 *Anecdote* 7
While still I held him by the arm, — 86 *Anecdote* 34
That now I should restore what hath been held in trust." — 104 *Artegal* 137
He whose domain is held in common — 175 *Waggoner* 1. 174
Held that the unborn infant wrought — 199 *Thorn* 139
He raised her up; and while he held — 248 *P. B.* 1021
The house that held this prize; and, led — 296 *Highland Boy* 137
Which Milton held.—In every thing we are sprung — 307 **It is not* 13
Which hath been held aloft before men's sight — 312 **Who rises* 63
Nor wanted, when their fortitude had held — 325 *Ode 1814* 142
Ne'er saw a race who held, by right of birth, — 325 **Intrepid sons* 3
Held with all Kinds in Eden's blissful bowers. — 362 **List—'twas* 65
Held; but in radiant progress toward the Deep — 384 *Duddon* 32. 4
Such strength that Earldom held of yore; — 403 *White Doe* 697
And strength of Reason; held above — 414 *White Doe* 1625
Which her dear Mistress once held dear: — 416 *White Doe* 1880
He, who had held the Soldan at his beck, — 428 *Ecc. Sonn.* 1. 38. 7
The air controlled, the stars their courses held; — 469 **Bold words* 11
Of heaven, when Venus held the reins! — 497 *Lycoris* 18
That ornament, unblamed. The floweret, held — 509 *F. Stone* 63
My Country! if such warning be held dear, — 515 **Long-favoured* 10
Who of right had held the Lordship — 535 *Egremont* 11
And by the arm he held her fast, — 537 *Goody Blake* 90
While Harry held her by the arm— — 537 *Goody Blake* 98
Was held with costly state; — 545 *Russ. Fug.* 370
This cruel Jew him seized, and held him fast — 554 *Prioress* 119
And held the pathway down by a brookside; — 557 *Cuck. and Night.* 60
Is gone who held us both in sovereignty. — 563 *Troilus* 28
Such course he held! Bologna's learned schools — 573 *Chiabrera* 2. 9
If things in our remembrance held so dear, — 583 **With copious* 36
So prized, and things inward and outward held — 586 *Ch. Lamb* 117
I held unconscious intercourse with beauty — 640 *Prelude* 1. 562
Into my heart, and held me like a dream! — 644 *Prelude* 2. 174
I held mute dialogues with my Mother's heart, — 646 *Prelude* 2. 268
Whether held forth in Nature or in Man, — 663 *Prelude* 4. 352
The one that held acquaintance with the stars, — 667 *Prelude* 5. 103
When I have held a volume in my hand, — 668 *Prelude* 5. 163
We held our way, direct through hamlets, towns, — 680 *Prelude* 6. 350
That from the torrent's further brink held forth — 683 *Prelude* 6. 571
And thought of London—held me by a chain — 688 *Prelude* 7. 86
He held the child, and, bending over it, — 696 *Prelude* 7. 615
And rules, that they held something up to view — 713 *Prelude* 9. 225
Held with Eudemus and Timonides, — 715 *Prelude* 9. 412
Prompt as the voice, held forth a printed speech, — 719 *Prelude* 10. 102
Such strength in *me* as often held my mind — 736 *Prelude* 12. 130
Where is the favoured being who hath held — 748 *Prelude* 14. 133
With whom from childhood he grew up, had held — 762 *Excursion* 1. 398
A while on trivial things we held discourse, — 765 *Excursion* 1. 611
And, sometimes—where the poor man held dispute — 772 *Excursion* 2. 65
While in this serious mood we held discourse, — 829 *Excursion* 5. 440
That held her spirit, in its own despite, — 849 *Excursion* 6. 711
Ask of the channelled rivers if they held — 864 *Excursion* 7. 489
Of nicest workmanship; that once had held — 881 *Excursion* 8. 487
Surrounded us; and, as we held our way — 891 *Excursion* 9. 507

Helena. A St. Helena next—in shape and hue, — 471 **Arran! a* 2

Hell. I would have dogged him to the jaws of hell— — 78 *Bord.* 2311
Hell to the lyre bowed low; the upper arch — 234 *Power of Sound* 126
That soul of Evil—which, from Hell let loose, — 330 *Ode: Thanks.* 95
For deep as hell itself, the avenging draught — 432 *Ecc. Sonn.* 2. 16. 8
Hell opens, and the heavens in vengeance crack — 475 **Here on their* 8
By some too boldly named "the Jaws of Hell:" — 475 *Greenock* 3
From hell came sanctified like airs from heaven. — 723 *Prelude* 10. 338
From regions opposite as heaven and hell. — 775 *Excursion* 2. 231

He'll. Has made him fearful, and he'll never be — 71 *Bord.* 1901
Sometimes he'll hide in the cave of a rock, — 80 †*Address: Child* 14
Cries Betty, "he'll be back again; — 127 *Idiot Boy* 144
The almanack he'll follow must be new. — L.3. 27 **For Lubbock* 4

Hellespont. Of Hellespont (such faith was entertained) — 212 *Laod.* 168

Hell-gates. "Hell-gates are powerless Phantoms when *we* build." — 282 **In my* 14

Hellish. Some scoffed at him with hellish mockery, — 68 *Bord.* 1736

Hell-rousing. Burst on the mountains with hell-rousing force. — 51 *Bord.* 789

Hell's. Rouse hell's own aid, and wrap thy fields in fire: — 22 *Desc. Sk.* 643
Rouze Hell's own aid, and wrap thy hills in fire. — 616 *Desc.Sk.Quarto* 781

Helm. *See* **State-helm.**
On my helm the dragon crest, — 323 *Ode 1814* 31
Strange "weeds" and alpine plants her helm entwine, — 608 *Desc.Sk.Quarto* 329
With birch-trees fringed; my hand shall guide the helm, — 891 *Excursion* 9. 496

Helm-crag. That ancient Woman seated on Helm-crag — 147 *Joanna* 56
Above Helm-crag—a streak half dead, — 175 *Waggoner* 1. 168
Still sit upon Helm-crag together! — 175 *Waggoner* 1. 179

Helmet. His helmet has a vernal grace, — 166 *Danish Boy* 32
Like this old helmet, or the eyeless skull — 394 **How profitless* 7

Helmeted. I helmeted a brow though white, — 410 *White Doe* 1300

Helmet-like. Helmet-like themselves will fasten . 166 *Wand. Jew* 7
Helmets. And nod their helmets, smitten by the wing 265 **When haughty* 7
Help. Help from the staff he bore; for mien and air 24 *Guilt* 4
"No help I sought; in sorrow turned adrift, . . 31 *Guilt* 370
Unsought for was the help that did my life recall. 31 *Guilt* 387
Small help; and, after marriage such as mine, . 32 *Guilt* 427
Of Time's sure help to calm and reconcile, . . 32 *Guilt* 454
These stifling blasts—God help me! Better this bare rock, ... 67 *Bord.* 1658
Not one of which could help him while alive, . . 68 *Bord.* 1726
let us return, I can help you. . . . . . . 72 *Bord.* 1930
To do with others; help me to my Father— . . 75 *Bord.* 2132
You, Sir, could help me to the history . . . 98 *Brothers* 186
Help us to tell Her tales of years gone by, . . 107 *Farewell* 49
Said, "Pride shall help me in my wrong: . . 117 *Affl. Marg.* 31
And now, God help me for my little wit! . . 119 *Sailor's Mother* 35
"—I cannot help it; ill intent 121 *EmigrantMother*75
I think, to help me if they could. 121 *EmigrantMother*82
No hand to help them in distress; . . . . 126 *Idiot Boy* 23
There's none to help poor Susan Gale; . . . 126 *Idiot Boy* 30
What speedy help her Boy will bring, ... 127 *Idiot Boy* 124
Something between a hindrance and a help; . . 134 *Michael* 189
And with his kinsman's help and his own thrift . 135 *Michael* 251
Look up—and help a hand that longs to set thee free." . . . . 140 *Arm. Lady* 24
Ever beheld. Up-led with mutual help, . . . 151 **Forth from* 7
Help, as if from faery power; . . . . . . 163 *Spinning Wheel* 4
Through help of honest Benjamin; . . . . . 176 *Waggoner* 1. 244
Comes to give what help he may, ... 181 *Waggoner* 4. 126
God help thee, Ruth!—Such pains she had, . . 194 *Ruth* 193
Housing, with God's good help, by choice or chance; 196 *Resolution* 104
"God," said I, "be my help and stay secure; . 197 *Resolution* 139
Help, under every change of adverse fate. . . 212 *Dion* 17
Is man, though loth such help to *seek*, . . . 223 *Wishing-gate* 62
And those that seek his help, and for his mercy sigh. 229 *Cuckoo-clock* 44
Will help to bring the body home." . . . . 248 *P. B.* 1065
Help by his labour to maintain . . . . . . 249 *P. B.* 1129
So, coming his last help to crave, ... 287 *Ellen Irwin* 45
We'll show that we can help to frame . . . 291 *Rob Roy* 87
Till not a wreck of help or hope remained, . . 316 **Hail, Zaragoza* 13
With every help that ye from earth and heaven may claim! . . . . 327 *Ode 1815* 9
O for the help of Angels to complete . . . . 335 *Cologne* 1
Knowledge no help; Imagination shaped . . . 353 *Aquap.* 70
That would yield him fit help while prefiguring that Place . . . . 364 *Vallomb.* 15
So well, that by its help and through His grace . 365 **Rapt above* 6
Help, and forgiveness speedy and entire. . . . 366 **Eternal Lord* 14
"My Art shall help to tame her pride—" . . 369 *Eg. Maid* 28
She sues for help with piteous utterance! . . . 378 *Duddon* 10. 8
Superior? Help to virtue does she give? . . 388 **The pibroch's* 13
Upon no help of outward friend; . . . . . 402 *White Doe* 543
Or by his mantle's help to find . . . . . 404 *White Doe* 774
My Father! I would help to find . . . . . 406 *White Doe* 914
Help did she give at need, and joined . . . 416 *White Doe* 1862
Is he who can, by help of grace, enthrone . . 438 *Ecc. Sonn.* 2. 37. 13
Prevent omission, help deficiency, ... 445 *Ecc. Sonn.* 3. 21. 11
Giving to Memory help when she would weave . 448 *Ecc. Sonn.* 3. 33. 5
His gracious help, or give what we abuse. . . 455 **Not in the lucid* 31
Their way, with thy pure help, to heart and mind; 459 **Wanderer! that* 18
And will maintain, if God his help afford. . . 477 **Lowther! in* 8
If office help the factious to conspire, ... 504 *Warning* 105
Help with thy grace, through life's short day, . 506 *Lab. Hymn* 29
Thy help is with the weed that creeps . . . 507 *May* 41
A bounteous help in days of yore, ... 533 **Blest is* 14
With help from female hands, that proudly strove 546 **Oft is* 14
Vitruvius of our village had no help . . . . 547 **Rude is* 6
Fall on thy knees and sue for help divine. . . 551 **Behold an* 8
Help me to tell it in thy reverence! . . . . 552 *Prioress* 21
To be our help upon our dying day: . . . . 553 *Prioress* 83
Now, God of Love! thou help me in some wise, . 560 *Cuck.andNight.*214
It cannot help itself in its decay; . . . . . 571 **There is a Flower* 18
Through good and evil, help might have, . . . 577 **By playful* 19
With mutual help, and sailing—to their league . 586 *Ch. Lamb* 104
And could not stoop—no help was nigh. . . . 621 *Andrew Jones* 15
And help life onward in its noblest aim. . . . 628 **Deign, Sovereign* 28
Help at his need in Dalecarlia's mines: . . . 635 *Prelude* 1. 213
But ask for timely furtherance and help . . . 665 *Prelude* 4. 456
Such help; the ever-living universe, ... 686 *Prelude* 6. 774
From blended colours also borrowing help, . . 691 *Prelude* 7. 250
Full-formed, that take, with small internal help, . 697 *Prelude* 7. 653
For once, the Muse's help will we implore, . . 697 *Prelude* 7. 682
Of myriads and boon nature's lavish help; . . 700 *Prelude* 8. 81
Insensibly, each with the other's help. . . . . 700 *Prelude* 8. 120
First communed with him by their help. And thus 703 *Prelude* 8. 317
To help him to his grave? Meanwhile the man, . 705 *Prelude* 8. 443
To travel independent of her help, ... 709 *Prelude* 8. 681
The experience of past ages, as, through help . 714 *Prelude* 9. 335
For France, what without help she could not do, 720 *Prelude* 10. 141
By help of dreams—can breed such fear and awe 755 *Recluse* 1. 1. 791
In God's good love, and seek his help by prayer. . 768 *Excursion* 1. 808
To give her needful help. That very time . . 769 *Excursion* 1. 862
Aptly disposed, had lent its help to raise . . . 778 *Excursion* 2. 435
Was now a help to his late comforter, ... 782 *Excursion* 2. 686
All night the storm endured: and, soon as help . 784 *Excursion* 2. 805
And by her help ye are my prisoners still. . . 786 *Excursion* 3. 15
The help desiring of the pure devout. . . . . 797 *Excursion* 3. 767
Might, with small help from fancy, be transformed 814 *Excursion* 4. 875
Your further help? The mine of real life . . 832 *Excursion* 5. 630

Help—*continued.*
And by what help had gained those distant fields. 834 *Excursion* 5. 757
By the last lingering help of the open sky . . 852 *Excursion* 6. 902
To help the small but certain comings-in . . . 860 *Excursion* 7. 166
Time, which had thus afforded willing help . . 860 *Excursion* 7. 204
May cover him; and by its help, perchance, . . 862 *Excursion* 7. 353
And, by some friendly finger's help upstayed . . 867 *Excursion* 7. 678
Benevolence is mild; nor borrows help, . . . 873 *Excursion* 7. 1030
Not, doubtless, without help of female taste. . . 882 *Excursion* 8. 541
To drudge through a weary life without the help 888 *Excursion* 9. 307
And with that help the wonder shall be seen . . 894 *Excursion* 9. 676
To help it and adorn. . . . . S.3. 425 **No whimsy* 6
First offered help that the deficient rock . . S.3. 433 **The doubt* 34
Wins help from something greater than herself— S.3. 435 **The doubt* 113
Can give us inward help, can purify, ... K.8. 245 *Recluse* 1.1.302
Oft help to make bold fancy's flight more bold; . K.8. 301 **And oh* 8
Helped. Had helped thee to a Valentine; . . . 186 **O Nightingale* 6
Earth helped him with the cry of blood: . . . 204 *Brougham* 27
Yet, helped by Genius—untired comforter, . . 273 **While Anna's* 9
Have helped us: Ure we crossed, and Swale, . . 402 *White Doe* 608
To entwine the crook of eloquence that helped . 695 *Prelude* 7. 570
Upon that meagre soil, helped out by talk . . 711 *Prelude* 9. 99
Of strange or tragic accident, hath helped . . 858 *Excursion* 7. 40
As Tom, but when he helped her to her horse . L.1. 98 *Juvenal* 3. 103
Helper. Lurks in it, Memory's Helper, Fancy's Lord, 480 *Cordelia* 13
His helper and not theirs, laid stronger hold . . 717 *Prelude* 9. 506
Of their own helper have been swept away; . . 726 *Prelude* 10. 586
Power to thyself; no Helper hast thou here; . 749 *Prelude* 14. 210
And her blind helper Chance, do *then* suffice . 788 *Excursion* 3. 140
Helpers. Where once his airy helpers schemed and planned . . . . 435 *Ecc. Sonn.* 2. 27. 12
Spare, too, the human helpers! Do they stir . 469 **The feudal* 11
Subordinate helpers of the living mind: . . . 634 *Prelude* 1. 153
And dearest helpers, left unthanked, unpraised, . 668 *Prelude* 5. 169
Did both find, helpers to their hearts' desire, . . 729 *Prelude* 11. 137
Helpful. And helpful to his utmost power: and there . . . . 783 *Excursion* 2. 762
Helping. "I'm helping this poor dying brute." . . 242 *P. B.* 490
The noble-minded Mother's helping hand . . 541 *Grace Darl.* 47
The Mother left alone,—no helping hand . . . 878 *Excursion* 8. 267
Helpless. Like fate; was hurried off, a helpless prey, 25 *Guilt* 53
That cannot feel for one, helpless as he is. . . 38 *Bord.* 68
Woman, thou hast a helpless Infant—keep . . 54 *Bord.* 948
Were there a Man who, being weak and helpless . 56 *Bord.* 1038
And helpless innocence—do they protect . . 57 *Bord.* 1084
Helpless and harmless as a babe: a Man . . . 75 *Bord.* 2164
Helpless, and loved me dearer than his life. . . 77 *Bord.* 2254
And there the helpless lamb he found . . . 85 *Shepherd-boys* 87
Oh mercy! like a helpless child. . . . . . 114 *Ind. Wom.* 40
A dull helpless thing, ... 163 *Hint* 28
Even now—to solemnise thy helpless state, . . 172 *Infant Daughter* 40
And helpless almost as the blind, ... 247 *P. B.* 1020
Ah! see her helpless Charge! enclosed . . . 294 *Jedbor.* 49
These emblems suit the helpless and forlorn, . . 321 **Humanity, delighting* 11
Yet not alone, nor helpless to repel . . . . 441 *Ecc. Sonn.* 3. 4. 9
Yet, God is my witness, thou small helpless Thing! 484 **A plague* 31
He is helpless and alone: . . . . 536 *Egremont* 86
So helpless in appearance, that for him . . . 566 *Cumb. Beg.* 25
His father helpless as the babe he rocks, . . . 612 *Desc.Sk.Quarto* 575
For this poor crawling helpless wretch . . . . 621 *Andrew Jones* 11
Frail creature as he is, helpless as frail, . . . 646 *Prelude* 2. 253
Unutterably helpless, and a look . . . . . 766 *Excursion* 1. 656
And to this helpless infant. I have slept . . . 768 *Excursion* 1. 769
Of sickness, accident, and helpless age. . . . 834 *Excursion* 5. 811
Of many helpless Children. I begin . . . . 855 *Excursion* 6. 1122
Helplessness. Supplied my helplessness with food and raiment, ... 41 *Bord.* 200
In helplessness, when innocence is with them. . 51 *Bord.* 792
Here do I stand, alone, to helplessness, . . . 62 *Bord.* 1344
But, in its helplessness, grew mild . . . . . 247 *P. B.* 968
In worse than former helplessness—and lie . . 311 **Who rises* 57
Lies the Babe, in helplessness . . . . . . 502 **Like a* 3
Helpmate. His Helpmate was a comely matron, old— 132 *Michael* 79
Have loved his Helpmate; but to Michael's heart 133 *Michael* 142
My helpmate in the woods to be, ... 193 *Ruth* 92
Man and his help-mate in fast wedlock joined . 585 *Ch. Lamb* 65
When her life's Helpmate on a sick-bed lay, . . 764 *Excursion* 1. 551
Her Helpmate following. Hospitable fare, . . 834 *Excursion* 5. 775
Helpmate's. My helpmate's face by light of day. He quits . . . . 834 *Excursion* 5. 807
Helps. Eases her pain, and helps her prayers. . . 144 **Driven in* 36
While, borrowing helps where'er he may, . . 178 *Waggoner* 2. 139
Those helps rejected, they, whose minds perceive 363 **The world forsaken* 6
Helps to restore and spread a Pagan sway: . . 426 *Ecc. Sonn.* 1. 29. 4
'Tis well—but what are helps of time and place, . 456 **Soft as* 20
She helps to make a Holy-land at home: . . . 467 *St. Bees* 112
Helps him to meet the last Tribunal's voice . . 520 *Pun. Death* 12. 12
Those helps for his occasions ever near . . . 804 *Excursion* 4. 215
These helps solicit; and a steadfast seat . . . 804 *Excursion* 4. 229
Helps to internal ease. Of many such . . . 844 *Excursion* 6. 401
Helvellyn. Helvellyn far into the clear blue sky . 147 *Joanna* 61
Under the brow of old Helvellyn— . . . . 176 *Waggoner* 2. 8
From the watch-towers of Helvellyn; . . . . 217 **Inmate of* 3
Then, when old Helvellyn won thee . . . . 218 **Inmate of* 35
Far in the bosom of Helvellyn, ... 491 *Fidelity* 21
By Sidney, where, in sight of our Helvellyn, . . 678 *Prelude* 6. 208
What sounds are those, Helvellyn, that are heard 699 *Prelude* 8. 1
Helvellyn, in the silence of his rest, ... 699 *Prelude* 8. 14
And old Helvellyn, conscious of the stir . . . 700 *Prelude* 8. 68

Helvellyn—*continued.*
Thence up Helvellyn, a superior mount, . . . K.8. 225 **I will* 28
Of old Helvellyn spread their arms abroad . . K.8. 225 **I will* 33
Helvellyn's. Upon Helvellyn's side : . . . . 110 **'Tis saidthat some* 8
Helvellyn's brow severe ? . . . . 344 *Eclipse* 78
With dream-like smoothness, to Helvellyn's top, . 353 *Aquap.* 37
Had flown with mine to old Helvellyn's brow, . 353 *Aquap.* 62
But from our loved Helvellyn's depths was brought, 480 *Cordelia* 6
So to Helvellyn s eastern side they went, . . . K.8. 225 **I will* 46
In cyphers on Helvellyn's highest ridge, . . . K.8. 226 **I will* 64
Return, Helvellyn's eagles ! with the pair . . K.8. 250 *Recluse* 1.1.518
Helvetian. The Helvetian Mountaineers, on ground 342 *Ital. Itin.* 59
The Helvetian Girl—who daily braves, . . . 344 **How blest* 29
The breath of an Helvetian Maid. . . . . . 344 **How blest* 39
These simple efforts of Helvetian skill, . . . 351 *Des. Stanzas* 75
Through some Helvetian dell, when low-hung mists K.8. 249 *Recluse* 1.1.476
Helvetia's. Have fought and perished for Helvetia's rights— . . . . 869 *Excursion* 7. 807
Hem. In some a hideous one--hem ! shall I stop ? . 58 *Bord.* 1170
My kerchief there I hem ; . . . . 84 *We are Seven* 42
They hem him round—" Behold the proof," . . 412 *White Doe* 1464
Hemisphere. Beneath a frosty moon. The hemisphere . . . . 676 *Prelude* 6. 87
Hemlock. This flute, made of a hemlock stalk, . . 195 *Ruth* 244
Hemmed. Lone Flower, hemmed in with snows, and white as they . . . . 264 *Snowdrop* 1
Of years hemmed round,had dwelt, prepared to try 391 *Brownie* 6
Hemp. By spinning hemp , a pittance for herself ; . 769 *Excursion* 1. 860
Of the warm summer, from a belt of hemp . . 769 *Excursion* 1. 885
Hems. How Nature hems you in with friendly arms ! 786 *Excursion* 3. 14
Hen. Behold the parent hen amid her brood, . . 669 *Prelude* 5. 246
The cackling hen, the tender chicken brood, . . 834 *Excursion* 5. 815
Hence. The loitering traveller hence, at evening, sees 12 *Desc. Sk.* 89
But let us hence ; for fair Locarno smiles . . 13 *Desc. Sk.* 154
A few leagues hence we shall have open ground, . 49 *Bord.* 655
I put denial on thy suit, and hence, ... 76 *Bord.* 2234
And hence, so far from wanting facts or dates . 97 *Brothers* 161
Hence, and how soon ! that war of vengeance waged . . . . 103 *Artegal* 33
And hence the father of the enamoured Youth, . 122 *V. and J.* 17
And hence this Tale, while I was yet a Boy . . 131 *Michael* 27
Hence had he learned the meaning of all winds, . 131 *Michael* 48
—And hence, long afterwards, when eighteen moons 148 *Joanna* 77
But in Man's fortunes. Hence a thousand tales . 170 **Never enlivened* 18
Ourselves, no prison is : and hence for me, . . 250 **Nuns fret* 9
Hence am I cross and peevish as a child : . . 253 **O gentle* 10
Hence, if in freedom I have loved the truth ; . . 259 *Calvert* 9
In Heaven ; hence no one blushes for thy name, . 278 *Wellington* 13
Joy have I had ; and going hence . . . . . 288 *Highland Girl* 64
Hence all who love their country, love . . . 299 *Cora Linn* 13
What do we gather hence but firmer faith . . 308 **These times* 9
Hence lives He, to his inner self endeared ; . . 317 **Call not* 6
And hence, wherever virtue is revered, . . . 317 **Call not* 7
Hence hath your prowess quelled that impious crew. 326 **Intrepid sons* 8
Hence Forms that glide with swan-like ease along, 334 **The Spirit* 6
Hence motions, even amid the vulgar throng, . 334 **The Spirit* 7
And hence, O Virgin Mother mild ! . . . . 338 **Meek Virgin* 19
When the Being of Beings shall summon her hence. 364 *Vallomb.* 36
Hence, while the imperial City's din . . . . 376 **The Minstrels* 73
Hence, while we gaze, a more enduring fear ! . 392 *Daniel* 10
Hence, if dejection has too oft encroached . . 394 **No more* 31
Hence not for them unfitted who would bless . 395 *White Doe: Ded.* 55
And hence when he, with spear and shield, . . 399 *White Doe* 283
Hence, prayers are shaped amiss, and dirges sung 423 *Ecc. Sonn.* 1. 20. 8
Hence, with the spiritual sovereignty transferred . 435 *Ecc. Sonn.* 2. 28. 12
Hence he will gain a firmer mind, to cope . . 447 *Ecc. Sonn.* 3. 28. 13
Hence, while in you each sad regret . . . . 473 *Ossian* 67
Hence have I genial seasons, hence have I . . 489 *Pers. Talk* 47
Hence, if we wept, it was not done in shame ; . 491 *Tribute : Dog* 34
And what if hence a bold desire should mount . 511 **So fair* 7
Hence equal ignorance of both prevails, . . . 516 **As leaves* 11
Shed on their chains ; and hence that doleful name. 517 *Pun. Death.* 1. 14
Hence thoughtful Mercy, Mercy sage and pure, . 519 *Pun. Death* 11. 9
From Wisdom's heavenly Father. Hence hath flowed . . . . 520 *Pun Death* 14. 11
Hence whole day wanderings, broken nightly sleeps 523 *Epist. Beaumont* 137
Hence, when yon mansion and the flowery trim . 546 **Oft is* 5
Hence, on my patrimonial grounds, have I . . 547 **Ye Lime* 13
Sweet is the holiness of youth : and hence, . . 553 *Prioress* 61
Hence hast thou stayed a little while too long ; . 558 *Cuck.and Night.*102
Now farewell, quoth she, for I hence must wend ; 561 *Cuck.and Night.*252
From hence my hope and solace forth did pass. . 564 *Troilus* 89
When hence did journey my bright Lady dear, . 564 *Troilus* 135
I knew the force ; and hence the rough sea's pride 574 *Chiebrera* 4. 19
Hence in a season of calm weather . . . . 590 *Immortality* 165
The viewless lingerer hence, at evening, sees . 603 *Desc. Sk. Quarto* 92
Hence shall we seek where fair Locarno smiles 605 *Desc.Sk.Quarto* 176
Hence shall we turn where, heard with fear afar, 609 *Desc.Sk.Quarto* 414
And *hence* I say, that Andrew's boys . . . . 621 *Andrew Jones* 31
Hence, ere some hostile God can intervene, . . 624 *Æneid* 23
That issuing hence may steal into thy mind . . 628 **Deign,Sovereign*22
Single and of determined bounds ; and hence . 641 *Prelude* 1. 641
Fearless of blame, that hence for future days . . 643 *Prelude* 2. 74
Of vigorous hunger—hence corporeal strength . 643 *Prelude* 2. 80
Hence rustic dinners on the cool green ground, . 643 *Prelude* 2. 89
Was dear, and hence to finer influxes . . . . 646 *Prelude* 2. 282
Hence life, and change, and beauty, solitude . . 646 *Prelude* 2. 294
No difference is, and hence, from the same source, 646 *Prelude* 2. 301
Hence my obeisance, my devotion hence, . . . 647 *Prelude* 2. 375

Hence—*continued.*
And hence my transport. Nor should this, perchance, ... 647 *Prelude* 2. 376
Hence am I checked : but let me boldly say, . 669 *Prelude* 5. 264
Of human nature ; hence the human form . . 703 *Prelude* 8. 279
Like independent natures. Hence the place . . 708 *Prelude* 8. 632
But hence to my more permanent abode . . . 711 *Prelude* 9. 81
And individual worth. And hence, O Friend ! . 713 *Prelude* 9. 243
With Nature,—hence, ofttimes, with reason too— 727 *Prelude* 11. 30
Hence could I see how Babel-like their task, . . 727 *Prelude* 11. 35
And hence a blow that, in maturer age, . . . 730 *Prelude* 11. 186
Hence Genius, born to thrive by interchange . . 740 *Prelude* 13. 5
And that the Genius of the Poet hence . . . 744 *Prelude* 13. 295
For they are Powers ; and hence the highest bliss 747 *Prelude* 14. 113
Hence endless occupation for the Soul, . . . 747 *Prelude* 14. 119
Hence cheerfulness for acts of daily life, . . . 747 *Prelude* 14. 121
Hence, amid ills that vex and wrongs that crush . 748 *Prelude* 14. 124
Sympathies too contracted. Hence, when called . 751 *Prelude* 14. 341
And was ; and hence this Song, which like a lark 751 *Prelude* 14. 382
With those whom he saw suffer. Hence it came . 761 *Excursion* 1. 371
For hence, minutely, in his various rounds, . . 761 *Excursion* 1. 374
Have parted hence ; and still that length of road, 770 *Excursion* 1. 912
Stole by degrees upon his mind ; and hence . . 775 *Excursion* 2. 250
But let us hence, that we may learn the truth : . 777 *Excursion* 2. 399
" That poor Man taken hence to-day," replied . 780 *Excursion* 2. 593
And hence, this upright shaft of unhewn stone, . 788 *Excursion* 3. 128
Of better entertainment :—let us hence ! " . . 791 *Excursion* 3. 329
Rests his desires ; and hence, in after life, . . 813 *Excursion* 4. 817
And hence, a beaming Goddess with her Nymphs, 814 *Excursion* 4. 865
Hence, for this Favourite—lavishly endowed . . 843 *Excursion* 6. 304
—But let us hence ! my dwelling is in sight, . . 874 *Excursion* 8. 29
—Hence is the wide sea peopled,—hence the shores 876 *Excursion* 8. 133
With the world's choicest produce. Hence that sum . . . . 876 *Excursion* 8. 136
Hence a dread arm of floating power, a voice . 876 *Excursion* 8. 143
And strength in evil ? Hence an after-call . . 886 *Excursion* 9. 122
Among us,—hence the more do we require . . 889 *Excursion* 9. 352
Hence deified as sisters they were bound . . . S.3. 436 **The doubt* 159
Hence, while on your toilet, She . . . . . S.3. 437 **I, whose* 17
That take it with them hence, where'er they go. . K.8. 240 *Recluse* 1.1.141
But ye who make our manners laws, and hence . L.1. 97 *Juvenal* 3. 75
Hence we behold the bay that bears the name . L.2. 120 *Frag. Æneid* 1. 1

Henceforth. Stranger ! henceforth be warned ; and know that pride, ... 23 *Yew-tree* 50
Henceforth it shall be said that bad men only . 54 *Bord.* 910
Henceforth, then, will I never in camp or field . 55 *Bord.* 979
Henceforth new prospects open on your path ; . 64 *Bord.* 1497
Thy office, thy ambition, be henceforth . . 78 *Bord.* 2303
And his is henceforth an established sway— . . 304 **Festivals have* 3
One of a Nation who, henceforth, must wear . . 308 **There is a bondage* 5
And thou henceforth wilt have a good man's calm, 313 *Clarkson* 12
Thy law, and live henceforth in peace, in pure good will. . . . . 329 *Ode 1815* 128
Henceforth a humbler course perplexed and slow ; 359 **Those old* 9
Henceforth bestride ;—triumphantly . . . . 404 *White Doe* 729
Henceforth, as on the bosom of a stream . . . 443 *Ecc. Sonn.* 3. 12. 10
In comfort, I entreated that henceforth . . . 665 *Prelude* 4. 454
Relaxing in their hold, henceforth I lived . . 675 *Prelude* 6. 21
A thought to human welfare,—that, henceforth . 717 *Prelude* 9. 535
Henceforth in whatsoever nook he may, . . . 778 *Excursion* 2. 477
Henceforth, whate'er is wanting to yourselves . 796 *Excursion* 3. 730
To save the perishing ; and, henceforth, I breathe 852 *Excursion* 6. 923
Henge. *See* **Stone-henge.**
Henry. With Henry, our good King ;—the Baron might . . . . 43 *Bord.* 348
You have not heard that Henry has at last . . 56 *Bord.* 1022
Saw we not Henry scourged at Becket's Shrine ? 428 *Ecc. Sonn.* 1. 37. 9
To serve the glorious Henry, King of France, . 574 *Chiabrera* 3. 14
Of the eighth Henry, when he crossed the seas . 825 *Excursion* 5. 182
Would More or Henry boast the general voice ? . L.1. 96 *Juvenal* 3. 42
Henry's. Go, modern Prince, at Henry's tomb proclaim . . . . L.1. 94 *Juvenal* 2. 19
Hen's. My hen's rich nest through long grass scarce espied ; . . . . 28 *Guilt* 213
Her, *omitted.*
Herald. Herald of a mighty band, ... 160 **Pansies, lilies* 59
Heraldic. But ill according. An heraldic shield, . 824 *Excursion* 5. 160
Herald's. Assembled, He, by a herald's voice, proclaims . . . . 312 **A Roman* 3
Heralds. Now, Norfolk set thy heralds to their tools, L.1. 96 *Juvenal* 3. 35
Herb. No sparkling rivulet spread the verdant herb ? 22 *Yew-tree* 3
Or herb that claimed peculiar sympathy, . . . 170 **Never enlivened* 13
Tree, flower, and green herb, feeding without blame. 392 *Avon* 8
On the green herb, and nothing heeding, . . . 406 *White Doe* 974
Than this, to graze the herb in thoughtless peace, 827 *Excursion* 5. 329
In hope to find some virtuous herb of power . . 840 *Excursion* 6. 111
Herbage. Usurping where the fairest herbage smiled : 17 *Desc. Sk.* 393
Where tufts of herbage tempted each, were busy at their feed, ... 91 *Norman Boy* 11
As e'er, on herbage covering earthly mould, . . 220 *Triad* 46
And give the timid herbage leave to shoot, . . 395 *White Doe: Ded.* 28
Upon a bed of herbage green, ... 407 *White Doe* 1004
Take the live herbage from the mead, and strip . 790 *Excursion* 3. 308
Herbage that never fails : no grass springs up . 835 *Excursion* 5. 876
Herbalist. The wandering Herbalist,—who, clear alike 788 *Excursion* 3. 161
Herbert. The Baron Herbert perish in the waves . 38 *Bord.* 76
The seignories of Herbert are in Devon ; . . . 39 *Bord.* 84
And leading Herbert. We must let them pass— 39 *Bord.* 101
My Child, forgetful of the name of Herbert; . . 41 *Bord.* 206

Herbert—*continued.*
The Baron Herbert. Mercy, the Baron Herbert! 43 *Bord.* 333
'Tis Herbert and no other! 'Tis a feast to see him, 45 *Bord.* 460
With Herbert or his Daughter? Daughter! truly— . . . . 46 *Bord.* 493
That doth concern this Herbert? You are provoked, ... 46 *Bord.* 498
Lord Clifford—did you see him talk with Herbert? 47 *Bord.* 537
Of this mock Father's guilt. The Baron Herbert 49 *Bord.* 664
The Baron Herbert, who, as was supposed, . . 49 *Bord.* 681
Herbert!—confusion! Here it is, my Friend, . 53 *Bord.* 855
Herbert! since you will have it, Baron Herbert; 55 *Bord.* 975
Herbert is *innocent*. You do but echo . . . 71 *Bord.* 1874
Herbert *is* innocent. What fiend could prompt . 71 *Bord.* 1879
"Herbert. . . . . 76 *Bord.* 2223
Such as the heaven-taught skill of Herbert drew; 380 *Duddon* 18. 13
Herbert's. Hovering round Herbert's door, a man whose figure . . . . 42 *Bord.* 278
At Herbert's door. Ay; and if truth were known 46 *Bord.* 480
Yours, Woman! are you Herbert's wife? . . . 46 *Bord.* 510
At Herbert's door—and when he stood beside . 47 *Bord.* 539
The desolate ruins of St. Herbert's Cell. . . . 551 **If thou in* 7
Herbs. Where flowers and herbs unite, and haply some weeds be, ... 103 *Artegal* 64
Green herbs, bright flowers, and berry-bearing plants, ... 268 **Pure element* 3
Where herbs look up, and opening flowers are seen; 278 **Life with* 11
Of herbs and lowly flowers, ... 311 **Who rises* 51
Herbs moistened by Virginian dew, ... 348 **Lulled by* 45
Clinging to its steep sides a thousand herbs . . 355 *Aquap.* 213
Now that their snows must melt, their herbs and flowers . . . . 363 **List—'twas* 95
Came those live herbs? by what hand were they sown . . . . 387 *Roslin* 9
Far as it dares to follow. Herbs self-sown, . . 431 *Ecc. Sonn.* 2. 12. 9
Will fringe the lettered stone; and herbs spring forth, ... 584 **With copious* 57
Of weedless herbs a healthier prospect sees, . . 615 *Desc.Sk.Quarto* 730
Strewing in peace life's humblest ground with herbs, 750 *Prelude* 14. 300
No winter greenness; of her herbs and flowers, . 769 *Excursion* 1. 837
Where, haply, crowned with flowerets and green herbs, ... 786 *Excursion* 3. 33
A Visitor—in quest of herbs and flowers; . . . 839 *Excursion* 6. 97
For her own flowers and favourite herbs, a space, 856 *Excursion* 6. 1163
To me as precious as my own!—Green herbs . . 868 *Excursion* 7. 707
Communion without check of herbs and flowers . S.3. 435 **The doubt* 104
Imaged in downward show; the flower, the herbs, S.3. 435 **The doubt* 106
Herculanean. The wreck of Herculanean lore, . . 499 **Departing summer* 50
Herculean. The Herculean Commonwealth had put forth her arms, ... 724 *Prelude* 10. 391
Hercules. "Ah wherefore?—Did not Hercules by force . . . . 210 *Laod.* 79
Whom the Dog Hercules pursued—his part . . 393 *Hart's-horn* 5
Of Hercules, though by a dubious claim. . . . L.2. 120 *Frag. Æneid* 1. 3
Hercynian. Of the Hercynian forest. Yet, hail to you . . . . 702 *Prelude* 8. 215
Herd. *See* **Goatherd.**
Where huge rocks tremble to the bellowing herd. 17 *Desc. Sk.* 379
On which the herd is feeding: . . . . . . 302 *Yarrow V.* 28
If not a straggler from the herd . . . . . 366 **Ye Trees* 5
But habit rules the unreflecting herd, ... 435 *Ecc. Sonn.* 2. 28. 10
That sigh and shudder to the lowing herd. . . 610 *Desc.Sk.Quarto* 469
Smooth life had herdsman, and his snow-white herd 701 *Prelude* 8. 177
Is for Society's unreasoning herd . . . . . 720 *Prelude* 10. 168
How the calm pleasures of the pasturing herd . 772 *Excursion* 2. 49
Herd-boy. Nor herd-boy of the wood. . . . . 165 *Danish Boy* 26
Herded. In the rough fern-clad park, the herded deer 3 *Ev. Wk.* 47
With whom I herded!—(easily, indeed, . . . 671 *Prelude* 5. 408
Herds. Or distant herds that pasturing upward creep, 16 *Desc. Sk.* 350
When shouts and lowing herds the valley fill, . . 17 *Desc. Sk.* 370
Nor Hunger driven the herds from pastures bare, . 17 *Desc. Sk.* 394
And merry flageolet; the low of herds, . . . 18 *Desc. Sk.* 418
Of scattered herds, that in the meadow graze, . 34 *Guilt* 521
All round this pool both flocks and herds might drink . . . . 149 *M. H.* 8
Give, herds and flocks, your voices to the wind! . 315 **The Land* 11
We mark majestic herds of cattle, free . . . . 349 *Val. Dover* 6
Herds range along the mountain side; . . . . 457 **Had this* 30
When stood the shorten'd herds amid the tide, . 592 *Ev. Wk. Quarto* 58
Nought but the herds that pasturing upward creep, 610 *Desc.Sk.Quarto* 426
Bless'd with his herds, as in the patriarch's age, . 610 *Desc.Sk.Quarto* 456
The fodder of his herds in winter snows. . . . 610 *Desc.Sk.Quarto* 473
Nor Hunger forc'd the herds from pastures bare . 611 *Desc.Sk.Quarto* 482
Then the milk-thistle bad those herds demand . 611 *Desc.Sk.Quarto* 484
And talking voices, and the low of herds, . . 611 *Desc.Sk.Quarto* 507
The herds and flocks are yet abroad to crop . . 823 *Excursion* 5. 70
And mountains not less green, and flocks, and herds, K.8. 240 *Recluse* 1.1.128
Herdsman. No traveller, peasant, herdsman? Not a soul: . . . . 61 *Bord.* 1293
Of thoughtful Herdsman when he strays . . . 292 *Rob Roy* 114
Smooth life had herdsman, and his snow-white herd 701 *Prelude* 8. 177
A Herdsman on the lonely mountain-tops, . . 759 *Excursion* 1. 219
—In that fair clime, the lonely herdsman, stretched 814 *Excursion* 4. 851
Herdsman-like. Stretched, herdsman-like, as if to bask . . . . 404 *White Doe* 772
Herdsman's. Or some stone-basin which the herdsman's hand . . . . 149 *M. H.* 10
Through the green vales and through the herdsman's bower— . . . . 315 **Advance—come* 12

Herdsman's—*continued.*
To weather-fend the Celtic herdsman's head— . 388 **The pibroch's* 7
The poor, the lonely, herdsman's joy and pride. . 475 *Greenock* 14
Herdsmen. Shepherds and herdsmen.—Like a whirlwind came . . . . 293 *Killicranky* 4
Among the herdsmen of the Alps, have wrought . 315 **Alas! what* 12
Here, *omitted.*
Hereafter. You will not disappoint them; and hereafter—— . . . . 48 *Bord.* 624
Hereafter you will thank me for this service. . . 75 *Bord.* 2127
As I requested; and hereafter, Luke, ... 137 *Michael* 404
Than will hereafter move them, if they make . 280 **Intent on* 6
Feels, and hereafter shall the truth declare, . . 327 *Ode 1815* 42
Of thy fond hopes hereafter walk inclined . . 447 *Ecc. Sonn.* 3. 27. 9
(Save only one, hereafter to be named) . . 711 *Prelude* 9. 132
Hereafter brought in charge against mankind. . 724 *Prelude* 10. 396
And, lastly, as hereafter will be shown, . . . 732 *Prelude* 11. 349
Hereafter, not escaping self-reproach, . . . 788 *Excursion* 3. 117
Hereby. Nor can I not believe but that hereby 488 *Pers. Talk* 43
Hereditary. He from his old hereditary nook . . 28 *Guilt* 233
She saw the hereditary bowers, ... 544 *Russ. Fug.* 253
Where, on a small hereditary farm, ... 758 *Excursion* 1. 109
Than the old hereditary wish fulfilled; . . . 888 *Excursion* 9. 277
Herein. A kind and a good Father: and herein . 136 *Michael* 362
Strange, should He deal herein with nice respects, 887 *Excursion* 9. 236
Herein less happy than the Traveller . . . . K.8. 250 *Recluse* 1.1.492
Here's. Here's what will comfort you. The Saints reward you . . . . 44 *Bord.* 408
Here's for your little boy, and when you christen him . . . . 46 *Bord.* 520
Here's a *cozie* warm house for Edward and me. . 81 †*Address: Child* 43
Here's neither head nor foot-stone, plate of brass, 98 *Brothers* 170
Here's grass to play with, here are flowers; . . 121 *EmigrantMother* 89
But here's a thought which well our mirth may cross L.1. 95 *Juvenal* 3. 14
Heresies. That heresies should strike (if truth be scanned . . . . 420 *Ecc. Sonn.* 1. 9. 1
Heretofore. Had heretofore, in humble trust, . . 168 *Pilgrim'sDream* 62
But such he had been heretofore— . . . . . 176 *Waggoner* 1. 256
A strength unthought of heretofore! . . . . 294 *Jedbor.* 42
Sink (if thou must) as heretofore, ... 341 *San Salv.* 4
Of ignorance thou might'st witness heretofore. . 378 *Duddon* 8. 12
Of him who heretofore did bear . . . . . . 405 *White Doe* 806
To desecrate the Fane which heretofore . . . 423 *Ecc. Sonn.* 1. 17. 4
With prompt rebound seemed fresh as heretofore. 650 *Prelude* 3. 97
Support, as heretofore, my fainting steps. . . . 652 *Prelude* 3. 200
Had come among these objects heretofore, . . 662 *Prelude* 4. 250
Has heretofore made known; that bursting forth 706 *Prelude* 8. 478
And ranged, with ardour heretofore unfelt, . . 719 *Prelude* 10. 49
Resistance strong as heretofore, I thought . . 727 *Prelude* 11. 22
Not with less interest than heretofore, . . . 741 *Prelude* 13. 85
Convictions still more strong than heretofore, . 744 *Prelude* 13. 280
Which, in the cottage-window, heretofore . . . 768 *Excursion* 1. 825
When, heretofore, I placed before your sight . . 886 *Excursion* 9. 156
This—if delightful hopes, as heretofore, . . . 896 *Excursion* 9. 793
Herewith. Herewith he grasped the Solitary's hand, 816 *Excursion* 4. 1016
Heritage. Sightless, and from my heritage was driven, ... 52 *Bord.* 829
It is my pleasant heritage; . . . . 156 *Oak and Broom* 67
Appointed by man's common heritage, . . . 354 *Aquap.* 92
With no mean earnest of a heritage . . . . 510 **Among a* 9
Thy heritage, thou Eye among the blind, . . . 589 *Immortality* 111
Rights that transcend the loftiest heritage . . 826 *Excursion* 5. 276
Hermes. Mild Hermes spake—and touched her with his wand . . . . 209 *Laod.* 19
Aloud she shrieked! for Hermes re-appears! . . 211 *Laod.* 151
Hermit. —A Hermit with his family around! . . 13 *Desc. Sk.* 153
The hermit has no finer eye . . . . . . 168 *Wren's Nest* 15
The Hermit sits alone. These beauteous forms, . 206 *Tintern* 22
No hermit with his beads and glass? . . . . 240 *P. B.* 377
Or haply there some pious hermit chose . . . 272 *Lady E. B.* 5
The Hermit saw the Angel spread his wings . . 393 **The Lovers* 3
Though here the Hermit numbered his last day . 551 **If thou in* 25
The hermit, exercised in prayer and praise, . . 586 *Ch. Lamb* 122
Long may ye roam these hermit waves that sleep, 595 *Ev. Wk. Quarto* 219
—Before those hermit doors, that never know . 607 *Desc.Sk.Quarto* 299
With an appropriate human centre—hermit, . . 664 *Prelude* 4. 360
Some Hermit, from his cell forth-strayed, might pace . . . . 716 *Prelude* 9. 442
You have regaled us as a hermit ought; . . . 785 *Excursion* 2. 902
The hermit to his cell in forest wide; . . . 791 *Excursion* 3. 369
The tiller's hand, a hermit might have chosen, . 832 *Excursion* 5. 68
That ever hermit dipped his maple dish . . . 833 *Excursion* 5. 687
Transplanted ere too late.—The hermit, lodged . 862 *Excursion* 7. 302
Of hermit, dubious where to scroop [? scoop] his cell; . . . . S.3. 433 **The doubt* 18
Than to the forest hermit are the leaves . . . K.8. 253 *Recluse* 1.1.607
Hermitage. A hermitage has furnished fit relief . 78 *Bord.* 2340
Methinks that to some vacant hermitage . . . 424 *Ecc. Sonn.* 1. 22. 1
Green-house, shell-grot, and moss-lined hermitage. 547 **Rude is* 13
Continued, brought me to my hermitage. . . . 633 *Prelude* 1. 107
My hermitage, my cabin, what you will—. . . 781 *Excursion* 2. 651
Hermitess. Proof that the hermitess still lives, . . 165 *Parrot* 39
Hermit's. Or of some Hermit's cave, where by his fire 206 *Tintern* 21
Above the hermit's long-forsaken cell!" . . . 220 *Triad* 40
A convent, even a hermit's cell, ... 289 *Glen-Al.* 23
From its dear home the Hermit's corse, . . . 301 *Bran* 59
More precious than a hermit's dust; . . . . 301 *Bran* 91
Clear-shining, like a hermit's taper seen . . . 687 *Prelude* 7. 35
Or haply shrouded in a hermit's cell. . . . . 771 *Excursion* 2. 11
Hermits. And hermits are contented with their cells; 250 **Nuns fret* 2
Hermits'. In hermits' weeds repose he found . . 479 *Somnamb.* 149

Herself—*continued.*
She being herself a Mother, happy Beast . . . K.8. 251 *Recluse* 1.1.529
Never did Rome herself so set at naught . . . L.1. 88 *Juvenal* 1. 7
He's. (*Partial list.*)
No matter—he's a dangerous Man.—That noise !— 43 *Bord.* 350
That he's left, for a bed, to beggars or thieves ! . 80 †*Address : Child* 19
He's idle all for very joy. . . . . 127 *Idiot Boy* 76
He's at the guide-post—he turns right ; . . . 127 *Idiot Boy* 94
He's not so wise as some folks be : " . . . 129 *Idiot Boy* 257
Perhaps he's turned himself about, ... 129 *Idiot Boy* 322
He's at your elbow—to your feeling . . . . 143 **Driven in* 20
That make the good, tow'rds which he's yearning, 177 *Waggoner* 2. 39
What matter ! he's caught—and his time runs to waste ; . . . . 188 *Music* 18
He's the terror of boys in the midst of their noise. S.3. 424 *Tinker* 31
He's got his red ribbon . . . . S.3. 440 **Said red-ribboned* 31
Hesitate. Where reason yet might hesitate, diffusing 735 *Prelude* 12. 47
Hesitating. But smiles—the hesitating shaft to free ; 339 *Tell* 25
He touched with hesitating hand— . . . . 374 *Eg. Maid* 319
No faint and hesitating trill, ... 498 **Departing summer* 7
And told of lapse and hesitating choice, . . . 748 *Prelude* 14. 137
Hesitation. With careful hesitation,—then convenes 422 *Ecc. Sonn.* 1. 15. 12
Hesperus. 'Tis Hesperus—there he stands with glittering crown, ... 208 **It is no* 4
Hew. Sigh at the deed ? Hew down a withered tree, 54 *Bord.* 928
Oswald, what say you to it ? Hew him down, . 57 *Bord.* 1066
Then let him hew with patient stroke . . . . 301 *Bran* 84
" Young Hew of Lincoln ! in like sort laid low . 556 *Prioress* 233
Hewn. *See* **Rock-hewn, Rough-hewn.**
Mockery—or model roughly hewn, ... 214 *Kirkstone* 10
A grisly idol hewn in stone ? . . . . . . 242 *P. B.* 506
Will stand though to the centre hewn ; . . . 246 *P. B.* 847
By beautiful conceptions, thou hast hewn . . . 548 **Stranger ! this* 28
And let thy path be hewn out of the Rock, . . 626 *Rock : Rydal* 3
Was but a block hewn from a mighty quarry— . 672 *Prelude* 5. 465
Hey-day. Who in the hey-day of astonishment . 147 *Joanna* 67
Hic. And its forlorn Hic jacet ! . . . . . . 287 *Ellen Irwin* 56
Hid. 'Mid smoking woods gleams hid from morning's ray . . . . 12 *Desc. Sk.* 120
A cowering shape half hid in curling smoke ! . . 13 *Desc. Sk.* 178
At length, though hid in clouds, the moon arose ; 27 *Guilt* 145
The deeper malady is better hid ; . . . . . 56 *Bord.* 1035
I hid my head within a Convent, there . . . 69 *Bord.* 1766
Hid in the earth, or there can be no harvest ; . 71 *Bord.* 1876
Where, hid from me, he counted many years, . 71 *Bord.* 1893
Air blackened, thunder growled, fire flashed from clouds that hid the sky, ... 91 *Poet's Dream* 3
The deepest grove whose foliage hid . . . . 110 **Look at* 13
With those bright beams yet hid it not, must steer 359 **Those old* 8
Unburied, lay hid under heaps of slain : . . . 361 **For action* 10
Oft is she hid from mortal eye . . . . . . 490 *Night Thought* 3
Crime might lie better hid. And, should the change 519 *Pun. Death* 8. 9
Half hid in native trees. Alas 'tis not, . . . 524 *Epist. Beaumont* 193
My fortunes hid, my countenance . . . . . 545 *Russ. Fug.* 287
Gleams, streak'd or dappled, hid from morning's ray 604 *Desc.Sk.Quarto* 139
'Tis storm ; and hid in mist from hour to hour . 608 *Desc.Sk.Quarto* 332
Among the windings hid of mountain brooks. . 639 *Prelude* 1. 490
As they lie hid in all external forms, ... 651 *Prelude* 3. 158
Hid in her vacant interlunar cave." . . . . 691 *Prelude* 7. 284
Whose wonders in a covered wain lie hid. . . . 699 *Prelude* 8. 36
Hidden. *See* **Self-hidden.**
More pleased, my foot the hidden margin roves . 12 *Desc. Sk.* 77
The house is hidden by the shade. Old Man, . 41 *Bord.* 219
Are hidden in her eyes. . . . . 108 *Louisa*
Half hidden from the eye ! . . . . 109 **She dwelt* 6
A comfortless and hidden well. . . . . . . 111 *A Complaint* 12
Or hidden only by the concave depth . . . . 122 *V. and J.* 28
And made a hidden valley of their own. . . . 131 *Michael* 8
Of that tall rock, as from a hidden world, . . 229 *Clouds* 3
Down to that hidden gulf from which they rose . 230 *Clouds* 36
With such vast hoards of hidden carnage near, . 335 **A wingèd* 13
Much have my books disclosed, but the end is hidden." . . . . 371 *Eg. Maid* 174
Came to this hidden pool, whose depths surpass . 381 *Duddon* 22. 2
The hidden silver Broach was left. . . . . . 391 *HighlandBroach* 60
A song of Nature's hidden powers ; . . . . 399 *White Doe* 271
His eye could see the hidden spring, ... 399 *White Doe* 285
The stifled sigh, the hidden tear, ... 401 *White Doe* 498
Up to another cottage, hidden . . . . . . 414 *White Doe* 1706
Perversely curious, then, for hidden ill . . . 449 *Ecc. Sonn.* 3. 35. 11
Is hidden, buried in its monthly grave ; . . . 460 **Wanderer ! that* 64
Taught him concealment) hidden from all eyes . 516 **Feel for* 6
Hidden from view in dense obscurity. . . . . 532 **How beautiful the* 4
And must be hidden from his wrath : . . . . 542 *Russ. Fug.* 69
Stand yet, but, Stranger ! hidden from thy view, 547 **Beneath yon* 3
Or hidden under ground, like sleeping worms. . 549 **The massy* 3
Such is Joy—as quickly hidden, ... 549 *Hermit's Cell* 1. 25
That might from him be hidden ; not a track . 574 *Chiabrera* 5. 11
Hidden was Grasmere Vale from sight, . . . 580 *John Words.* 25
Whose shades protect the hidden wave serene ; . 595 *Ev. Wk. Quarto* 222
Her Voice was like a hidden Bird that sang, . . 622 *Recluse* 1. 1. 91
When thou wert hidden in thy monthly grave ; . 630 [?] **O Moon* 4
And, hidden in the cloud of years, became . . 635 *Prelude* 1. 188
It lies far hidden from the reach of words. . . 651 *Prelude* 3. 184
Where still it works, though hidden from all search 668 *Prelude* 5. 196
Dumb yearnings, hidden appetites, are ours, . . 673 *Prelude* 5. 506
Pried into Yorkshire dales, or hidden tracts . . 678 *Prelude* 6. 194

Hidden—*continued.*
Rouse him ; but, hidden in those gloomy shades, 718 *Prelude* 9. 584
Was hidden from my view, and he remained . . 757 *Excursion* 1. 44
Of hidden beauty have I chanced to espy . . . 776 *Excursion* 2. 352
Were hidden, and black vapours coursed their sides ; 783 *Excursion* 2. 783
The hidden nook discovered to our view . . . 787 *Excursion* 3. 51
Hidden from all men's view. To our attempt . 793 *Excursion* 3. 474
Here traceable, there hidden—there again . . 823 *Excursion* 5. 85
Winds far in reaches hidden from our sight, . . 824 *Excursion* 5. 123
Vanished or hidden ; and the whole domain, . . 830 *Excursion* 5. 549
That they whom death has hidden from our sight 832 *Excursion* 5. 662
Hidden by clouds, and oft bedimmed by haze, . 849 *Excursion* 6. 704
By which the road is hidden, also hides . . . 858 *Excursion* 7. 51
And so, not wholly hidden from men's sight, . . 868 *Excursion* 7. 738
Had soothed his ear while *they* were hidden : how pleased . . . . K.8. 249 *Recluse* 1.1.484
Hide. Shall hide me, wooing long thy wildwood strain ; . . . . 3 *Ev. Wk.* 87
Yon chestnuts half the latticed boat-house hide, . 4 *Ev. Wk.* 107
—When low-hung clouds each star of summer hide, 7 *Ev. Wk.* 260
Thrice happy ! that for him the grave could hide 29 *Guilt* 268
Sometimes he'll hide in the cave of a rock, . . 80 †*Address : Child* 14
Hide the knowledge of thy doom. . . . . . 90 *Longest Day* 44
The innocent Boy, else shelterless, his lonely head must hide. . . . . 91 *Norman Boy* 24
As if he wished himself to hide : . . . . . 114 *Last of Flock* 12
And hide my head where wild beasts roam. . . 115 *Last of Flock* 80
Of modest kindness, that would hide . . . . 154 *Flower Garden* 45
For this they know (and let it hide, ... 178 *Waggoner* 3. 10
Where close fogs hide their parent brook ; . . 180 *Waggoner* 4. 41
Alas ! what boots it ?—who can hide, . . . 181 *Waggoner* 4. 116
The liquid veil that seeks not to hide them. . . 190 **Lyre ! though* 37
What could she seek ?—or wish to hide ? . . . 199 *Thorn* 126
Aspiring Road ! that lov'st to hide . . . . 215 *Kirkstone* 49
Asks of the clouds what occupants they hide :— . 220 *Triad* 29
Of skill, upon the sounding hide . . . . . 241 *P. B.* 424
And a huge mass, to bury or to hide, ... 265 **The Shepherd* 11
But clouds and envious darkness hide . . . . 300 *Cora Linn* 25
Or hide, at will,—for freedom combating . . . 321 **The power* 5
Of future war. Advance not—spare to hide, . . 334 **Bruges I* 10
Did sullen mists hide lake and skies . . . . 343 *Eclipse* 71
In aught that ye would grace or hide— . . . 366 **Ye Trees* 8
Upon her yet, earth hide her beauty ; . . . . 372 *Eg. Maid* 242
The Muse exclaimed ; but Story now must hide . 388 *Loch Etive* 10
What poor abodes the heirloom hide, ... 391 *HighlandBroach* 65
To hide her poor afflicted head ? . . . . . 413 *White Doe* 1556
Temple and Altar sink, to hide their shame . . 423 *Ecc. Sonn.* 1. 17. 9
The war-worn Chieftain quits the world—to hide 424 *Ecc. Sonn.* 1. 21. 4
To hide himself, but only magnifies ; . . . . 439 *Ecc. Sonn.* 2. 43. 12
With gradual stealth the lateral windows hide . 451 *Ecc. Sonn.* 3. 44. 2
Of the strange sight, nor hide his theory . . . 468 **Ranging the* 11
Mists rose to hide the Land—that search, though long . . . . 469 **Bold words* 6
To reinstate wild Fancy, would we hide . . . 469 **Desire we* 2
No dull oblivious nook shall hide thy fate. . . 489 *Spade* 28
Then in a convent went to hide . . . . . . 536 *Egremont* 103
To hide what they betray ! . . . . 543 *Russ. Fug.* 168
You would in mystery hide ; . . . . 545 *Russ. Fug.* 292
The Cuckoo—'tis not well that I should hide . . 561 *Cuck.andNight.* 266
Loose-hanging rocks the Day's bless'd eye that hide, 606 *Desc.Sk.Quarto* 255
Licence to hide at intervals her head . . . . 626 *Ballot* 6
Striving to hide, what nought could heal, the wounds . . . . 730 *Prelude* 11. 215
Of privacy is deep enough to hide, ... 778 *Excursion* 2. 472
The faithful servant, who must hide his head . . 778 *Excursion* 2. 476
That with interpositions, which would hide . . 817 *Excursion* 4. 1059
Those dark rocks hide it ! ' Entering, I beheld . 834 *Excursion* 5. 768
To cheat the world, or from herself to hide . . 840 *Excursion* 6. 125
Liberal and undistinguishing, should hide . . . 887 *Excursion* 9. 231
Hide-and-seek. Thou dost play at hide-and-seek ; . 161 **Pleasures newly* 34
Hideous. Of hideous sense, I sank, nor step could crawl : . . . . 31 *Guilt* 386
The truth is hideous, but how stifle it ? . . . 56 *Bord.* 1006
In some a hideous one—hem ! shall I stop ? . . 58 *Bord.* 1170
A hideous plot, against the soul of man : . . . 75 *Bord.* 2143
And hideous aspect, stalking round and round ! . 213 *Dion* 68
What hideous warfare hath been waged, . . . 224 *Primrose* 7
A spectacle more hideous —yet . . . . . . 245 *P. B.* 829
Shall worthily rehearse the hideous rout, . . . 326 **The Bard* 12
Scattered on all sides by the hideous jars . . . 346 *Processions* 34
In hideous usages, and rights accursed, . . . 378 *Duddon* 8. 7
Whom Obloquy pursues with hideous bark : . . 432 *Ecc. Sonn.* 2. 14. 8
The cross with hideous laughter Demons mock, . 603 *Desc. Sk. Quarto* 70
Of a ship struggling with a hideous storm) . . 721 *Prelude* 10. 228
Hideously. Then into Severn hideously defiled, . 103 *Artegal* 37
Hides. Scarce hides a shadow from her searching rays ; . . . . 9 *Ev. Wk.* 358
In golden light ; half hides itself in shade : . . 12 *Desc. Sk.* 98
This hides not from the moral Muse . . . . 225 *Present.* 17
Recumbent : Him thou may'st behold, who hides 269 *Gordale* 10
Night after night ? True is it Nature hides . . 281 **What strong* 4
To him, and aught that hides his clay . . . . 284 *Grave of Burns* 17
In his own storms he hides himself from sight. . 521 *Epist. Beaumont* 9
Hides half their beauty from the common gaze ; . 539 **Lady ! a* 44
Beyond the mountain's giant reach that hides . 598 *Ev. Wk. Quarto* 337
Bright as the moon, half hides itself in shade. . 604 *Desc.Sk.Quarto* 107
And his red eyes the slinking water hides ; . . 606 *Desc.Sk.Quarto* 236
That hides her, like the mighty flood of Nile . . 684 *Prelude* 6. 614
Snug as a child that hides itself in sport . . . 784 *Excursion* 2. 822
The Sultan hides deep in ancestral tombs. . . 809 *Excursion* 4. 569
Island or grove, that hides a blessed few . . . 827 *Excursion* 5. 350

Hides—*continued.*
By which the road is hidden, also hides . . . 858 *Excursion* 7. 51
Rivall'd by you, hides the diminish'd head. . . L.I. 88 *Juvenal* I. 6
Hiding. Among the stars, the stars now hiding, . 237 *P. B.* 94
Hiding their fiery clouds, their rocks, and snows ; 605 *Desc.Sk.Quarto* 206
Hiding the face of earth for leagues—and there, . 876 *Excursion* 8. 121
Hiding-place. To seek a hiding-place beyond the seas. 138 *Michael* 447
Follow each other to their hiding-place . . . 152 **Forth from* 20
The promised hiding-place ; . . . . 543 *Russ. Fug.* 132
But to return out of its hiding-place . . . . 719 *Prelude* 10. 82
Or the least penetrable hiding-place . . . . 829 *Excursion* 5. 450
Hiding-places. From hiding-places ten years deep ; 182 *Waggoner* 4. 212
Of life : the hiding-places of man's power . . . 738 *Prelude* 12. 279
Hie. The Troop will be impatient ; let us hie . . 37 *Bord.* I
" Hie thee to the Countess, friend ! return with speed, ... 141 *Arm. Lady* 107
And thus in joyous mood they hie . . . . . 396 *White Doe* 15
Back therefore will they hie to seize . . . . 405 *White Doe* 797
Hied. Then up the steep ascent they hied, . . . 85 *Shepherd-boys* 95
Achates, with the gifts to Carthage hied ; . . . 624 *Æneid* 54
Hieroglyphic. Vanity's hieroglyphic ; a choice trope 345 **Ambition—following* 8
That Sisterhood, in hieroglyphic round . . . 477 *Long Meg* 12
Hies. Away she hies to Susan Gale : . . . . . 127 *Idiot Boy* 102
Then off she hies ; but with a prayer, ... 128 *Idiot Boy* 199
And to the Doctor's door she hies ; . . . . . 128 *Idiot Boy* 243
Then up along the town she hies, ... 129 *Idiot Boy* 272
And up the cottage stairs she hies, ... 248 *P. B.* 1084
But down the irriguous valley hies, ... 338 **Meek Virgin* 26
And Nature, while through the great city he hies, 570 *Farmer* 63
Smoke round him, as from hill to hill he hies, . 702 *Prelude* 8. 245
High. *See* **Roof-high, Star-high.**
Through bare grey dell, high wood, and pastoral cove ; . . . . 2 *Ev. Wk.* 2
Or from high points of rock looked out for fanning gales ; . . . . 3 *Ev. Wk.* 44
Beholds, of all from her high powers required, . 3 *Ev. Wk.* 82
Blue pomp of lakes, high cliffs and falling floods, 5 *Ev. Wk.* 143
By pointing to the gliding moon on high. . . . 7 *Ev. Wk.* 259
Her files of road-elms, high above my head . . 11 *Desc. Sk.* 46
Thy towns that cleave, like swallows' nests, on high ; 12 *Desc. Sk.* 114
Dilated hang the misty pines on high, ... 14 *Desc. Sk.* 223
With Independence, child of high Disdain. . . 15 *Desc. Sk.* 261
What high resolves exalt the tenderest thought . 15 *Desc. Sk.* 297
Nought but the *chalets*, flat and bare, on high . 16 *Desc. Sk.* 348
High and more high in summer's heat they go, . 17 *Desc. Sk.* 376
Another high on that green ledge ;—he gained . 17 *Desc. Sk.* 382
More high, the snowy peaks with hues of rose. . 17 *Desc. Sk.* 406
He holds with God himself communion high, . . 18 *Desc. Sk.* 462
She knows that only from high aims ensue . . 22 *Desc. Sk.* 650
In streaks diverging wide and mounting high ; . 24 *Guilt* 20
He looked, and saw upon a gibbet high . . . 25 *Guilt* 78
Ran mountains high before the howling blast, . 29 *Guilt* 291
Which high and higher mounts with silver gleam : 33 *Guilt* 463
His voice with indignation rising high . . . . 33 *Guilt* 478
Is a reflux from on high, ... 90 *Longest Day* 30
High on a broad unfertile tract of forest-skirted Down, ... 91 *Norman Boy* I
And bore him high through yielding air my debt of love to pay, ... 92 *Poet's Dream* 19
Or shake his high desert. . . . . 105 *Artegal* 231
Nor rate too high what must so quickly fade, . 110 **Look at* 17
Born all too high, by wedlock raised . . . . 113 *Lament* 29
In high and low, above, below, ... 128 *Idiot Boy* 207
Now is she high upon the down, ... 128 *Idiot Boy* 217
And now she's high upon the down, ... 129 *Idiot Boy* 277
The cliffs and peaks so high that are, ... 129 *Idiot Boy* 319
High into Easedale, up to Dunmail-Raise, . . 133 *Michael* 134
Nurtured, as thy mien bespeaks, in high degree, . 140 *Arm. Lady* 23
" High bliss is only for a higher state," . . . 143 **High bliss* I
The high crag cannot work me harm, ... 145 *Her Eyes* 45
Along the public way, this Peak, so high . . . 148 **There is an* 5
Restless with fixed to balance, high with low, . 153 *Morn. Ex.* 32
Where leafless oaks towered high above, . . . 154 **A whirl-blast* 5
And dancing high and dancing low, ... 155 *Waterfall* 8
Of pleasure high and turbulent, ... 157 **In youth* 3
Lift me, guide me, high and high . . . . . 159 **Up with me* 14
I have seen thee, high and low, ... 160 **Pansies, lilies* 20
Pass high above those fragrant bells . . . . 165 *Danish Boy* 18
High on the trunk's projecting brow, ... 169 *Wren's Nest* 41
—Yes, without me, up hills so high . . . . 175 *Waggoner* I. 136
What bustling—jostling—high and low ! . . . 177 *Waggoner* 2. 56
While to the music, from on high, ... 180 *Waggoner* 4. 5
That floats on high o'er vales and hills, . . . 187 **I wandered* 2
High as a cloud, high over head ! . . . . . 193 *Ruth* 62
The wind, the tempest roaring high, ... 193 *Ruth* 121
Pure hopes of high intent : . . . . 193 *Ruth* 141
As high as we have mounted in delight . . . 195 *Resolution* 24
" High on a mountain's highest ridge, ... 197 *Thorn* 23
When she was on the mountain high, ... 200 *Thorn* 237
High in the breathless Hall the Minstrel sate, . 203 *Brougham* I
High on that chalky cliff of Britain's Isle, . . 215 *Enterprise* 3
Yet still the bosom beating high, ... 216 *Enterprise* 47
High as the level of the mountain tops, . . . 218 *Recluse* I. I. 208
High is her aim as heaven above, ... 222 *Triad* 145
This prescience from on high, ... 225 *Primrose* 50
Waves high, embellished by a gleaming shower ! . 226 *Vernal Ode* 20
Mysteriously remote and high ; . . . . . . 227 *Vernal Ode* 117
High as the imperial front of man ; . . . . 227 *Vernal Ode* 118
Poising your splendours high above the heads . 230 *Clouds* 27
That in high triumph drew the Lord of vines, . 234 *Power of Sound* 148

High—*continued.*
High o'er the red-haired race of Mars, ... 237 *P. B.* 38
He lay beneath the branches high, ... 239 *P. B.* 262
Hath left him high in preparation,— . . . . 244 *P. B.* 692
For such high argument. . . . . 245 *P. B.* 790
High as the highest Peak of Furness-fells, . . 250 **Nuns fret* 6
Might work in our high Calling—a bright hope 251 *Appleth.* 6
In his still haunt on Bagdad's summit high ; . . 252 **The fairest* 6
Her tackling rich, and of apparel high. . . . 258 **With Ships* 8
High is our calling, Friend !—Creative Art . . 260 **High is* I
Or of high gladness you shall hither bring ; . . 264 **Lady ! the* 11
Where art thou ? Thou so often seen on high 266 **With how* 3
And upward, high as Malvern's cloudy crest ; . 267 *St. Cath.* 4
Of high astonishment and pleasing fear. . . . 267 **Though narrow* 8
The World, sole-standing high on the bare hill— 277 **Haydon ! let* 8
Would hasten, that such pomp may float on high ? 278 **The most* 6
'Tis He whose yester-evening's high disdain . . 279 **'Tis he* I
While beams of orient light shoot wide and high, 282 **While beams* I
To keep, so high in air, its strength and grace : . 283 **Well have* 10
High lodged the *Warrior*, like a bird of prey ; . 298 *Brownie's Cell* 11
(High Servant of paternal Love) 299 *Brownie's Cell* 94
Plain living and high thinking are no more : . . 307 **O Friend* 11
Is man as good as man, none low, none high ?— . 309 **What if* 8
And birds, high flying in the element, ... 312 **A Roman* 7
High deeds, O Germans, are to come from you ! . 313 *Prophecy* I
For his field-pastime high and absolute, . . . 313 **Go back* 13
High sacrifice, and labour without pause, . . . 316 **O'er the* 12
These desolate remains are trophies high . . . 316 **Hail, Zaragoza* 5
Like his own lightning, over mountains high, . . 318 **Ah ! where* 13
Patience and temperance with this high reserve, . 319 **Avaunt all* 6
(Thanks to high God) forests of such remain : . 319 **Avaunt all* 11
Of such high course was felt and understood ; . 320 **O'erweeningStatesmen* 11
Midway on some high hill, while father Time . . 322 **Ye Storms* 3
Of Providence. But now did the Most High . . 322 **By Moscow* 9
Those high achievements ; even as she arrayed 324 *Ode 1814* 96
By Works of spirit high and passion pure ! . . 325 *Ode 1814* 149
High on the shore of silver Thames—to greet . . 327 *Ode 1815* 50
On this high DAY of THANKS, before the Throne of Grace ! . . . . 332 *Ode : Thanks* 244
And when that calm Spectatress from on high . 339 *Tell* 10
Majestic BERNE, high on her guardian steep, . . 339 *Schwytz* 9
High on her speculative tower . . . . . . 343 *Eclipse* I
Beats with a fancy running high, ... 344 **How blest* 3
High poised—or as the wren that sings . . . 348 **Lulled by* 58
O'er high and low, and if requiring rest, . . . 354 *Aquap.* 99
And, high above that length of cloistral roof, . 355 *Aquap.* 170
Of that high Convent-crested cliff I stood, . . 356 *Aquap.* 232
Chosen by Rome's legendary Bards, high minds . 356 *Aquap.* 271
With something more propitious to high aims . 357 *Aquap.* 286
That bound it to its native earth—poised high . 358 *Pine : Rome* 3
From that depression raised, to mount on high . 358 **Is this* 11
And enter, with prompt aid from the Most High, 361 *Alban Hills* 13
High on the brink of that precipitous rock, . . 362 **List—'twas* 30
From their high state darkened the Earth with fear, 362 **List—'twas* 64
Near that Cell—yon sequestered Retreat high in air— . . . . 364 *Vallomb.* 6
Sweep to the charge ; more high, the Dacian force, 368 *Trajan* 46
To hoof and finger mailed ;—yet, high or low, . 368 *Trajan* 47
Top-gallant high, rebounding and rebounding ! . 370 *Eg. Maid* 48
Sailed " (hear me, Merlin !) " under high protection, ... 370 *Eg. Maid* 74
For some high day of long-expected pleasure. . 372 *Eg. Maid* 192
Here must a high attest be given, ... 372 *Eg. Maid* 249
A harvest of high hopes and noble enterprises." 373 *Eg. Maid* 264
And high expectancy, no sign was granted. . . 373 *Eg. Maid* 288
Deep was the awe, the rapture high, ... 374 *Eg. Maid* 331
So high, a rival purpose to fulfil ; . . . . . 377 *Duddon* 4. 12
The frolic Loves, who, from yon high rock, see 378 *Duddon* 10. 13
Tossing her frantic thyrsus wide and high ! . . 381 *Duddon* 20. 14
Of April, smiling high in upper air ? . . . . 381 *Duddon* 22. 10
Of power usurped ; with proclamation high, . . 383 *Duddon* 29. 13
Or as a fruitful palm-tree towering high . . . 383 *Duddon* 31. 5
To his high charge, and truly serving God, . . 387 *Manse* 11
And of old honours, too, and passions high : . . 388 **The pibroch's* 9
Flew high above Atlantic waves, to draw . . . 388 *Eagles* 8
High was the trophy hung with pitiless pride ; . 393 *Hart's-horn* 10
Too high, or idle agitations lull ! . . . . . 394 **How profitless* 4
High over hill and low adown the dell . . . 395 *White Doe : Ded.* 38
To mass or some high festival ; . . . . . 396 *White Doe* 24
The spectacle, is mounting high . . . . . 398 *White Doe* 224
Harsh thoughts with her high mood agree— . . 399 *White Doe* 261
Full soon to be uplifted high, ... 400 *White Doe* 358
A Soul, by force of sorrows high, ... 402 *White Doe* 585
The watchmen from their station high . . . 402 *White Doe* 599
Who saw the Banner reared on high . . . . 403 *White Doe* 682
At need, he stood, advancing high . . . . 404 *White Doe* 751
For, with a high and valiant name, ... 404 *White Doe* 793
Beneath yon cypress spiring high, ... 407 *White Doe* 991
High on a point of rugged ground . . . . . 409 *White Doe* 1163
On him and on his high endeavour . . . . . 409 *White Doe* 1214
I would myself have hung it high, ... 410 *White Doe* 1278
—High transport did the Father shed . . . . 410 *White Doe* 1336
Go high, no transport ever higher. . . . . . 411 *White Doe* 1353
Which was to teem with high communion, . . 414 *White Doe* 1681
White as whitest cloud on high . . . . . . 415 *White Doe* 1741
Dire overthrow, and yet how high . . . . . 416 *White Doe* 1846
Uplifting toward high Heaven her fiery brand, . 420 *Ecc. Sonn.* I. 9. 5
For instant victory. But Heaven's high will . 421 *Ecc. Sonn.* I. 11. 3
Of Ignorance, that ran so rough and high . . 422 *Ecc. Sonn.* I. 14. 11
From Monks in Ely chanting service high, . . 426 *Ecc. Sonn.* I. 30. 2

High—*continued.*
Christ died for—cannot forfeit his high claim 429 *Ecc. Sonn.* 2. 4. 12
For their high guerdon not in vain have panted ! 430 *Ecc. Sonn.* 2. 8. 14
Pinions of high and higher sweep, and make 430 *Ecc. Sonn.* 2. 9. 13
Of victory mounts high, and blood is quaffed 432 *Ecc. Sonn.* 2. 16. 5
Pours out his choicest beverage high and higher 433 *Ecc. Sonn.* 2. 20. 5
Spreads high conceits to madding Fancy dear, 433 *Ecc. Sonn.* 2. 20. 11
She whose high pomp displaced, as story tells, 434 *Ecc. Sonn.* 2. 21. 13
Of high with low, celestial with terrene ! 434 *Ecc. Sonn.* 2. 25. 14
Of the Most High. Again do they invoke 436 *Ecc. Sonn.* 2. 33. 9
A guiding ray ; or seen—like stars on high, 441 *Ecc. Sonn.* 3. 5. 12
Against her ancient virtue. HIGH and Low, 443 *Ecc. Sonn.* 3. 11. 9
(As yours above all offices is high) 444 *Ecc. Sonn.* 3. 16. 2
As the high service pledges now, now pleads. 445 *Ecc. Sonn.* 3. 20. 8
Woman ! the Power who left His throne on high, 447 *Ecc. Sonn.* 3. 27. 1
From low to high doth dissolution climb, 449 *Ecc. Sonn.* 3. 34. 1
And sink from high to low, along a scale 449 *Ecc. Sonn.* 3. 34. 2
Give all thou canst ; high Heaven rejects the lore 451 *Ecc. Sonn.* 3. 43. 6
That, while the sun rode high, was lost beneath their dazzling sheen. 456 **Soft as* 11
Who but is pleased to watch the moon on high 461 **Who but is* 1
No,—let this Age, high as she may, instal 469 **Desire we* 4
His sides, or wreathe with mist his forehead high : 471 *Ailsa Crag* 4
And Knights of high renown ; 478 *Somnamb.* 22
And high her blushes mounted ; 478 *Somnamb.* 58
Whose life combines the best of high and low, 489 *Spade* 7
High will he hang thee up, well pleased to adorn 490 *Spade* 31
Whose high endeavours are an inward light 493 *Hap. War.* 6
'Tis, finally, the Man, who lifted high, 494 *Hap. War.* 65
Is ranging high and low ; 494 *Force of Prayer* 14
Up to the sovereign seat of the Most High ; 500 *Humanity* 31
Or tax high Heaven with prodigality ?) 501 *The unremitting* 9
Less fair is summer riding high 502 *Seasons* 5
From high Gibraltar to Siberian plains, 509 *F. Stone* 92
High as the Sun, that he could take account 511 **So fair* 8
With patient care. What tho' assaults run high, 514 **Blest Statesman* 6
Bend, ye Perverse ! to judgments from on High, 514 **Portentous change* 11
This high repute, with bounteous Nature's aid, 515 *Penn.* 6
A theme for praise and admiration high. 517 *Pun. Death* 3. 4
Each takes in this high matter, all may move 520 *Pun. Death* 14. 13
On high, a kerchief waving in her hand ! 524 *Epist. Beaumont* 208
To our kind Friend high on the sunny hill— 524 *Epist. Beaumont* 216
While, high and low, and all about, 526 **The soaring* 13
And antique towers nodded their foreheads high, 529 **Those breathing* 118
How beautiful the Queen of Night, on high 532 **How beautiful the* 1
For Him upon whose high behests 533 **Blest is* 19
To the high altar its determined place ; 534 **When in* 12
That symbol of the day-spring from on high, 535 **When in* 27
A single Act endears to high and low 540 *Grace Darl.* 8
Whom such high beauty could not guard 542 *Russ. Fug.* 11
So high their hearts would beat ; 544 *Russ. Fug.* 220
High as the pitch of their swift plumes 544 *Russ. Fug.* 243
High Heaven is my defence ; 545 *Russ. Fug.* 302
Great was their bliss, the honour high 545 *Russ. Fug.* 375
Rugged and high, of Charnwood's forest ground, 547 **Beneath yon* 2
O *Alma Redemptoris !* high and low : 554 *Prioress* 103
Know, that the honour of high God may spread, 554 *Prioress* 126
For he of low hearts can make high, of high 556 *Cuck. and Night.* 3
And then did she begin this song full high, 561 *Cuck.andNight.*249
Behold a high injunction suddenly 573 *Chiabrera* 2. 15
And in his hands I saw a high reward 574 *Chiabrera* 3. 15
But not on high, where madness is resented, 582 *Invoc. Earth* 15
We pay a high and holy debt ; 582 **O for a* 7
His spirit, but the recompense was high ; 584 *Ch. Lamb* 8
Otherwise wrought the will of the Most High ; 585 *Ch. Lamb* 100
High instincts before which our mortal Nature 589 *Immortality* 150
By pointing to a shooting star on high : 596 *Ev. Wk. Quarto* 260
If peep between the clouds a star on high, 598 *Ev. Wk. Quarto* 365
High towering from the sullen dark-brown mere, 598 *Ev. Wk. Quarto* 371
Thy towns, like swallows' nests that cleave on high ; 604 *Desc.Sk.Quarto* 131
On the high summits Darkness comes and goes, 605 *Desc.Sk.Quarto* 205
More high, to where creation seems to end, 607 *Desc.Sk.Quarto* 289
Can guess the high resolve, the cherish'd pain 608 *Desc.Sk.Quarto* 360
Or summer hamlet, flat and bare, on high 610 *Desc.Sk.Quarto* 428
Think not, suspended from the cliff on high 611 *Desc.Sk.Quarto* 510
Bid from on high his lonely cannon sound, 616 *Desc.Sk.Quarto* 776
With many a fond embrace, while joy runs high, 624 *Æneid* 40
Are high rewards ; but bound they Nature's claim 626 **Son of* 10
In that bold form and impress high 629 *Installation* 84
Abstruse, nor wanting punctual service high, 632 *Prelude* 1. 44
Had in high places built her lodge ; though mean 637 *Prelude* 1. 328
But with high objects, with enduring things— 638 *Prelude* 1. 409
The paper kite high among fleecy clouds 639 *Prelude* 1. 494
If high the transport, great the joy I felt 648 *Prelude* 2. 410
Extended high above a dusky grove. 649 *Prelude* 3. 6
Hast placed me high above my best deserts, 653 *Prelude* 3. 318
Alas ! such high emotion touched not me. 654 *Prelude* 3. 342
To minister to works of high attempt— 654 *Prelude* 3. 385
A hundred times when, roving high and low, 660 *Prelude* 4. 110
Of high endeavours, daily spreads abroad 661 *Prelude* 4. 170
And their high privilege of lasting life, 666 *Prelude* 5. 66
Upon a dromedary, mounted high, 666 *Prelude* 5. 76
The eagle soars high in the element, 683 *Prelude* 6. 535
With high and spacious rooms, deafened and stunned 684 *Prelude* 6. 646
From high, the sullen water far beneath, 685 *Prelude* 6. 704
Before us, while she still was high in heaven ;— 686 *Prelude* 6. 722

High—*continued.*
Floating in dance, or warbling high in air 689 *Prelude* 7. 125
Advertisements, of giant-size, from high 690 *Prelude* 7. 194
Of Tivoli ; and, high upon that steep, 691 *Prelude* 7. 255
Endeared by Custom ; and with high disdain, 695 *Prelude* 7. 528
And them the silent rocks, which now from high 700 *Prelude* 8. 65
Of a high eastern hill—thus flowed my thoughts 706 *Prelude* 8. 466
My Song ! those high emotions which thy voice 706 *Prelude* 8. 477
Beat high, and filled the fancy with fair forms, 712 *Prelude* 9. 207
Rocked high above their heads ; anon, the din 716 *Prelude* 9. 456
High on the topmost pinnacle, a sign. 716 *Prelude* 9. 476
Show what she was, a high and fearless soul, 718 *Prelude* 10. 33
High was my room and lonely, near the roof 719 *Prelude* 10. 66
Therefore to serve was high beatitude ; 724 *Prelude* 10. 433
The town of Arras, whence with promise high 725 *Prelude* 10. 498
When high, more high, and lifts us up when fallen. 737 *Prelude* 12. 218
How oft high service is performed within, 743 *Prelude* 13. 227
Of high respect and gratitude sincere. 753 **Oft, through* 8
Accomplish :—this is our high argument. 755 *Recluse* 1. 824
'Twas summer, and the sun had mounted high : 756 *Excursion* 1. 1
The high and tender Muses shall accept 757 *Excursion* 1. 105
In such access of mind, in such high hour 759 *Excursion* 1. 211
Those weeds, and the high spear-grass on that wall, 770 *Excursion* 1. 943
A lowly vale, and yet uplifted high 776 *Excursion* 2. 329
Rides high ; then all the upper air they fill 782 *Excursion* 2. 701
And blazing terrace upon terrace, high 784 *Excursion* 2. 841
Find entrance ;—high or low appeared no trace 787 *Excursion* 3. 68
To lift thee high above the misty air 787 *Excursion* 3. 103
Or Syria's marble ruins towering high 788 *Excursion* 3. 150
Ah ! what avails imagination high 789 *Excursion* 3. 209
The varied functions and high attributes 798 *Excursion* 3. 824
Appeared, of high pretensions—unreproved 799 *Excursion* 3. 898
Her thoughts, her images, her high desires. 803 *Excursion* 4. 108
Carried so high, that every thought, which looked 805 *Excursion* 4. 263
But still a high dependence, a divine 815 *Excursion* 4. 928
Are all renounced ; high as the thought of man 826 *Excursion* 5. 287
Into high objects farther than they may, 831 *Excursion* 5. 598
High on the breast of yon dark mountain, dark 832 *Excursion* 5. 671
High on that mountain where they long have dwelt 833 *Excursion* 5. 691
High in the gloom appeared, too high, methought, 833 *Excursion* 5. 740
From high to low, ascent from low to high, 834 *Excursion* 5. 796
(Though claiming high distinction upon earth 837 *Excursion* 5. 980
Embodied and established these high truths 837 *Excursion* 5. 1000
O high example, constancy divine ! 839 *Excursion* 6. 74
High in these mountains, that allured a band 841 *Excursion* 6. 215
From his youth up, and high as manhood's noon, 859 *Excursion* 7. 112
" With these high comrades he had revelled long, 859 *Excursion* 7. 128
Save through a gap high in the hills, an opening 859 *Excursion* 7. 142
On those high peaks, the first autumnal snow, 861 *Excursion* 7. 249
Not for reproof, but high and warm delight, 863 *Excursion* 7. 385
But towering high the roof above, as if 866 *Excursion* 7. 614
Fraternities and orders—heaping high 872 *Excursion* 7. 989
Those arts, and high inventions, if unpropped 877 *Excursion* 8. 226
High peaks, that bound the vale where now we are. 885 *Excursion* 9. 59
For high—yet not for low ; for proudly graced— 887 *Excursion* 9. 244
The high behest, and every heart obey ; 893 *Excursion* 9. 642
That puzzled high and low, S.3. 431 **The Scottish* 4
Sprung from high Jove, of sage Mnemosyne S.3. 436 **The doubt* 151
His light high up among the gloomy rocks, K.8. 225 **I will* 49
To that high spring which bears no human name, K.8. 225 **I will* 52
From high to low, from low to high, yet still K.8. 237 *Recluse* 1. 1. 43
Within the bound of this high concave ; here K.8. 237 *Recluse* 1. 1. 44
That ranging o'er the high and houseless ground K.8. 247 *Recluse* 1.1.393
And the clear hills, as high as they ascend K.8. 252 *Recluse* 1.1.578
One household under God for high and low, K.8. 253 *Recluse* 1.1.618

High-arched. Though waves, to every breeze, its high-arched roof, 496 **A little* 38

High-born. The high-born Vaudracour was brought, by years 121 *V. and J.* 8
Of old grey stone, and high-born name 472 *Ossian* 24
High-born Augusta ! Witness, Towers and Groves ! 539 **Lady ! a* 22
Of long-past banquetings with high-born friends : 860 *Excursion* 7. 218

High-climbing. High-climbing rock, low sunless dale, 413 *White Doe* 1564

Higher. Till higher mounted, strives in vain to cheer 8 *Ev. Wk.* 341
Which high and higher mounts with silver gleam 33 *Guilt* 463
And higher far than lies within earth's bounds : 62 *Bord.* 1373
Or art thou of still higher birth ? 112 *Lament* 5
Still higher—to be cast thus low ! 113 *Lament* 30
But affections higher, holier, 141 *Arm. Lady* 79
" High bliss is only for a higher state," 143 **High bliss* 1
And hope for higher raptures, when life's day is done. 160 **Up with me* 31
Still mounting to a higher height ; 178 *Waggoner* 3. 25
And higher still—a greedy flight ! 178 *Waggoner* 3. 26
Not higher than a two years' child 197 *Thorn* 5
No object higher than my knee. 199 *Thorn* 176
Nor yet for higher sympathy. 205 *Brougham* 117
Seeking a higher object. Love was given, 211 *Laod.* 146
From source still deeper, and of higher worth, 216 *Enterprise* 99
By higher, sometimes humbler, guides, 226 *Present.* 77
Of higher mood, which now I meditate ;— 259 *Calvert* 12
Proofs of a higher sovereignty I claim ; 270 **Shame on* 10
Star-high, and pointing still to something higher ; 282 **In my* 12
And yet a higher joy partake : 294 *Jedbor.* 44
Far higher hills than these of ours ! 295 *Highland Boy* 14
Higher to lift their lofty heads, impelled 354 *Aquap.* 145
And higher still, above the bower 406 *White Doe* 958
Go high, no transport ever higher. 411 *White Doe* 1353
Pinions of high and higher sweep, and make 430 *Ecc. Sonn.* 2. 9. 13
Of God and man, place higher than to him 433 *Ecc. Sonn.* 2. 19. 13
Pours out his choicest beverage high and higher 433 *Ecc. Sonn.* 2. 20. 5
And even a title higher still, 512 **Who rashly* 29

Himself—*continued.*
Nor be himself extinguished, but survive, 666 *Prelude* 5. 27
One precious gain, that he forgets himself. 670 *Prelude* 5. 346
Man free, man working for himself, with choice 700 *Prelude* 8. 104
Lord of himself, in undisturbed delight— 731 *Prelude* 11. 254
Perfect him, made imperfect in himself, 749 *Prelude* 14. 224
By mortal cares. Himself no Poet, yet 751 *Prelude* 14. 362
And reverence for himself; and, last and best, 775 *Excursion* 2. 289
And in serene possession of himself, 785 *Excursion* 2. 883
More dignified, and stronger in himself; 799 *Excursion* 3. 923
Answering the question which himself had asked, 802 *Excursion* 4. 68
And that unless above himself he can 806 *Excursion* 4. 330
Erect himself, how poor a thing is man!' 806 *Excursion* 4. 331
Within himself, a measure and a rule, 813 *Excursion* 4. 808
Of gamesome Deities; or Pan himself, 814 *Excursion* 4. 886
—Look forth, or each man dive into himself; 830 *Excursion* 5. 505
One with himself, and one with them that sleep." 844 *Excursion* 6. 375
The harp or viol which himself had framed, 861 *Excursion* 7. 271
As if he would laugh himself dead. S.3. 424 *Tinker* 45
To drink of the clear water, laid himself K.8. 226 **I will* 55
Brimful of glory said within himself, K.8. 228 **I will* 120
Hind. The Ass, uplifting a hind hoof, 179 *Waggoner* 3. 106
And hart and hind and hunter with his spear 268 **Pure element* 8
Behold," she said, "a striken Hind 544 *Russ. Fug.* 279
Hinder. And no one hinder their intent, 412 *White Doe* 1519
Its hinder part concealed by hedge-row thorn. 523 *Epist. Beaumont* 124
Dancing around her, hinder and disturb 873 *Excursion* 7. 1035
Hindered. My words too long have hindered." Undeterred, 836 *Excursion* 5. 892
Hindering. Anxious duty hindering, 503 *Warning* 10
Hinders. What hinders, then, that ye should be 163 **Art thou the* 32
He spoils thy sport, and hinders mine: 179 *Waggoner* 3. 51
Hindoos. Temples like those among the Hindoos, 244 *P. B.* 683
On serious minds: then, as the Hindoos draw 790 *Excursion* 3. 254
Millions of kneeling Hindoos at this day S.3. 435 **The doubt* 122
Hindrance. Something between a hindrance and a help; 134 *Michael* 189
At last, of hindrance and obscurity, 265 **There is a pleasure* 10
Doth now no hindrance meet his eye, 411 *White Doe* 1420
Or hindrance raised by sordid purposes, 468 *St. Bees* 134
Will be a hindrance to the voice 533 **Blest is* 33
And part through outward hindrance. But I heard, 687 *Prelude* 7. 18
Hindrances. Were only hindrances that stood between 146 **It was an* 11
And hindrances with which they stand beset. 835 *Excursion* 5. 861
Yet was the mind to hinderances [*sic*] exposed, 886 *Excursion* 9. 168
Hinge. And hinge of all our learnings and our loves: 669 *Prelude* 5. 258
Hint. Pile of Stone-henge! so proud to hint yet keep 26 *Guilt* 118
I thank you for that hint. He shall be brought 58 *Bord.* 1125
She prefaced half a hint of this 128 *Idiot Boy* 182
Nor hint of man; if stone or rock 214 *Kirkstone* 7
Still hint that quiet best is found, 301 *Bran* 66
The Soul transported sees, from hint of thine, 345 **Ambition—following* 11
But not a hint from under-ground, no sign 532 **Once I* 17
Under a sheltering tree."—Upon this hint 890 *Excursion* 9. 426
To give a hint of whips and the cart's tail, L.1. 97 *Juvenal* 3. 72
Hinted. Already hinted at, of other mould— 714 *Prelude* 9. 289
Hinting. Then (what is too true) without hinting a word, 570 *Farmer* 39
Hints. Yet hints at peace to be o'erthrown, 344 **How blest* 18
Hints to the thrush 'tis time for their repose; 455 *Rydal Mere* 2
From monumental hints: and thou, O Friend! 745 *Prelude* 13. 352
As nicest observation furnished hints 812 *Excursion* 4. 725
Call to my mind dark hints which I have heard 854 *Excursion* 6. 1075
Hippocrene. Mounts to pellucid Hippocrene, but he 574 *Chiabrera* 5. 12
Who with their Hippocrene and grottoed fount S.3. 436 **The doubt* 161
Hippogriff. More daring far than Hippogriff, 238 *P. B.* 154
Built for the air, or wingèd Hippogriff? 471 **Arran! a* 5
Hips. Rich store of scarlet hips is mine, 155 *Waterfall* 47
Hire. Receiving from his Father hire of praise; 134 *Michael* 191
Of the mid harvest, when the labourer's hire 149 **A narrow* 52
Hired. And to this end a Homicide they hired, 554 *Prioress* 116
And for this end had hired a neighbour's boy 769 *Excursion* 1. 861
Or could perform; a zealous actor, hired 842 *Excursion* 6. 284
Hired minstrel of voluptuous blandishment; 843 *Excursion* 6. 355
Hireling. Death's hireling, who scoops out his neighbour's grave, 826 *Excursion* 5. 235
His, *omitted.*
Hissed. We hissed along the polished ice in games 638 *Prelude* 1. 434
Hissing. And hissing Factionists with ardent eyes, 710 *Prelude* 9. 59
Historian. Historian of my infancy! 79 **Stay near* 4
While thus from theme to theme the Historian passed, 857 *Excursion* 7. 1
Historian's. Almost indifferent, even the historian's tale 712 *Prelude* 9. 204
In what the Historian's pen so much delights 740 *Prelude* 13. 42
Give back faint echoes from the historian's page; 795 *Excursion* 3. 603
Historians. Yours was a stranger's judgment: for historians, 97 *Brothers* 165
By Poets loathed; from which Historians shrink! 441 *Ecc. Sonn.* 3. 3. 14
Historic. Historic figures round the shaft embost 367 *Trajan* 13
Whether he traced historic truth, with zeal 587 *Crosth.* 7
Song of the muses, sage historic tale, 864 *Excursion* 7. 450
Histories. Of our two histories; 'twill do thee good 136 *Michael* 337
History. The history of a poet's evening hear? 2 *Ev. Wk.* 36
You, Sir, could help me to the history 98 *Brothers* 186
Therefore, although it be a history 131 *Michael* 34
Thine infant history, on the minds of those 172 *Infant Daughter* 27
Of history, Glory claps her wings, 224 **'Tis gone* 14

History—*continued*
The whole design of Scripture history; 351 *Des. Stanzas* 67
With attributes from History derived, 357 *Aquap.* 283
Of History, stript naked as a rock 359 **Those old* 3
Involved a history of no doubtful sense, 359 **Complacent Fictions* 2
History that proves by inward evidence 359 **Complacent Fictions* 3
Were only History licensed to take note 393 **The Lovers* 9
Could tell a tragic history 398 *White Doe* 199
Endless history that lies 415 *White Doe* 1716
Its history of two hundred years. 486 *Matthew* 8
Looks round, to learn the history. 491 *Fidelity* 41
Portentous change when History can appear 514 **Portentous change* 1
Men thence a book might make, a history; 563 *Troilus* 67
Run through the history and birth of each 645 *Prelude* 2. 226
A Poet's history, may I leave untold 659 *Prelude* 4. 80
His history, the veteran, in reply, 664 *Prelude* 4. 417
The famous history of the errant knight 666 *Prelude* 5. 60
Authentic history been set forth of Rome, 688 *Prelude* 7. 80
'Tis true, the history of our native land, 708 *Prelude* 8. 617
Of history, the past and that to come! 712 *Prelude* 9. 169
From tragic fictions or true history, 719 *Prelude* 10. 76
To my own history. It hath been told 728 *Prelude* 11. 75
And now, O Friend! this history is brought 750 *Prelude* 14. 302
Felt, that the history of a Poet's mind 752 *Prelude* 14. 412
That in this meditative history 752 *Prelude* 14. 421
A history only of departed things, 755 *Recluse* 1. 1. 803
The history of many a winter storm, 760 *Excursion* 1. 278
The history of many families; 761 *Excursion* 1. 377
But History, time's slavish scribe, will tell 797 *Excursion* 3. 769
Some portion of its human history K.8. 248 *Recluse* 1. 1. 416
The dupe of history—that "old almanack"; L.3. 27 **For Lubbock* 2
History's. Art's noblest relics, history's rich bequests, 354 *Aquap.* 96
Hit. Might in this pageant be supposed to hit 657 *Prelude* 3. 585
How where on random topics as they hit K.8. 301 **And oh* 3
Hither. Should child of mine e'er wander hither, speak 35 *Guilt* 589
But what has brought you hither? A slight affair, 43 *Bord.* 339
But you, Sir, should be kinder. Come hither, Fathers, 45 *Bord.* 443
What must be done? We will conduct her hither; 48 *Bord.* 593
Let us begone and bring her hither;—here 48 *Bord.* 599
And yet it is not.—Let us lead him hither. 48 *Bord.* 637
When the tempestuous wind first drove us hither, 53 *Bord.* 861
It would have come to this!—What brings you hither? speak! 77 *Bord.* 2242
Hither soon as spring is fled 80 *Foresight* 27
"Hither the Afflicted come, as thou hast heard thy Mother say, 92 *Poet's Dream* 49
Upon the hither side: and once I said, 99 *Brothers* 263
And of this moment; hither turn thy thoughts, 137 *Michael* 407
Hither repaired.—A single beech-tree grew 150 **When, to* 18
And hither throngs of birds resort; 154 *Flower Garden* 37
Hither his flight he would bend; 162 **Art thou the* 16
Sylph or Faery hither tending,— 170 *Kitten* 13
Hither he his course is bending;— 174 *Waggoner* 1. 33
That blew us hither!—let him dance, 177 *Waggoner* 2. 44
The Lass with her barrow wheels hither her store;— 188 *Music* 22
I will come hither with my Paramour; 201 *Hart-leap* 70
Can this be He who hither came 204 *Brougham* 76
A worshipper of Nature, hither came 207 *Tintern* 152
—Who comes not hither ne'er shall know 215 *Kirkstone* 73
And hither is he come at last, 243 *P. B.* 646
Or of high gladness you shall hither bring; 264 **Lady! the* 11
Hither, like yon ancient Tower 336 **Jesu! bless* 13
Grieve for the Man who hither came bereft, 363 **Grieve for* 1
Wafted her hither, interpose 372 *Eg. Maid* 245
She was before she hither came; 402 *White Doe* 563
And oft her steps had hither steered, 409 *White Doe* 1194
—Come hither in thy hour of strength; 485 *Poet's Epitaph* 57
And hither is young Romilly come, 494 *Force of Prayer* 25
Hither come thou back straightway, 535 *Egremont* 29
And hither does one Poet sometimes row 547 **Rude is* 17
And hither home I came when it was eve; 564 *Troilus* 96
That every gentle Spirit hither led 575 *Chiabrera* 7. 17
Ye vales and hills whose beauty hither drew 587 *Crosth.* 1
Which brought us hither, 590 *Immortality* 168
Guide hither, O sweet Moon, the maid I love so well. 630 [?] **O Moon* 15
As one far mightier), hither I had come, 650 *Prelude* 3. 87
The other to make music; hither, too, 699 *Prelude* 8. 27
Must that Man have been left, who, hither driven, 778 *Excursion* 2. 481
Conducted hither your most welcome feet, 779 *Excursion* 2. 534
"That I came hither; neither have I found 781 *Excursion* 2. 613
Been planted, hither come and find a lodge 787 *Excursion* 3. 106
Hither, in prime of manhood, he withdrew 824 *Excursion* 5. 114
Your walk conduct you hither, ere the sun 830 *Excursion* 5. 533
Who, from their lowly mansions hither brought, 832 *Excursion* 5. 652
Hither she came; here stood, and sometimes knelt 853 *Excursion* 6. 986
When hither came its last Inhabitant. 858 *Excursion* 7. 58
Did we come hither, with romantic hope K.8. 245 *Recluse* 1. 1. 311
Hitherto. Of reckless mastery, hitherto unknown. 435 *Ecc. Sonn.* 2. 28. 14
In the full might they hitherto have shown, 518 *Pun. Death* 6. 12
To utter waste. Hitherto I had stood 656 *Prelude* 3. 510
For objects hitherto the absolute wealth 662 *Prelude* 4. 234
That sadness finds its fuel. Hitherto, 666 *Prelude* 5. 11
With firmness, hitherto but slightly touched 675 *Prelude* 6. 54
Of Emont, hitherto unnamed in song, 678 *Prelude* 6. 204
As hitherto, in freedom I may speak, 698 *Prelude* 7. 762

Holds—*continued.*
As thence she holds her way to Palestine. — 427 *Ecc. Sonn.* 1. 35. 8
(Nor idlest that !) which holds communion — 439 *Ecc. Sonn.* 2. 42. 3
On the relentless sea that holds him fast — 458 *Sea-shore* 6
And Wisdom, as she holds a Christian place — 466 *St. Bees* 30
Who thinks that priestly cunning holds the keys — 467 *St. Bees* 80
That o'er the channel holds august command, — 470 **Did pangs* 7
Some ragged child holds up for sale a store — 474 **How sad* 2
But that enormous barrier holds it fast. — 491 *Fidelity* 33
And holds a greyhound in a leash, — 494 *Force of Prayer* 15
Upon her lap reposing, holds—but mark — 509 *F. Stone* 54
They daunt not him who holds his ministry, — 514 **Blest Statesman* 7
Against time present, passion holds the scales : — 516 **As leaves* 10
Is broken ; yet why grieve ? for Time but holds — 586 *Ch. Lamb* 129
Yea, all the adamantine holds of truth — 666 *Prelude* 5. 39
Or whatsoever else the heart holds dear ; — 668 *Prelude* 5. 155
Holds up before the mind intoxicate — 740 *Prelude* 13. 29
Which my life holds, he readily may conceive — 800 *Excursion* 3. 968
That holds but him, and can contain no more ! — 817 *Excursion* 4. 1088
Of what it holds could speak, and every grave — 826 *Excursion* 5. 251
And ponderous loom—resounding while it holds — 831 *Excursion* 5. 604
And to the grove that holds it. She beguiles — 833 *Excursion* 5. 708
That Westminster, for Britain's glory, holds — 842 *Excursion* 6. 264
Than this fallen Spirit ? in those dreary holds — 843 *Excursion* 6. 342
Who holds the land in fee, its careless lord ! — 866 *Excursion* 7. 575
That sycamore, which annually holds — 866 *Excursion* 7. 616
Illumination into deep, dark holds, — 870 *Excursion* 7. 835
Between his hands he holds a smooth blue stone, — 882 *Excursion* 8. 556
To one who holds it dear ; with duteous care — K.8. 251 *Recluse* 1.1.525

Hole. *See* **Loop-hole.**
Or track the hedgehog to his hole. — 142 *†Lov. and Lik.* 52

Hole's. *See* **Key-hole's.**

Holes. *See* **Loop-holes.**

Holiday. Though seeking only holiday delight ; — 10 *Desc. Sk.* 12
And knock for entrance, in mid holiday. — 45 *Bord.* 468
By giving him, for both our sakes, an hour of holiday. — 92 *Poet's Dream* 20
His arms have a perpetual holiday ; — 96 *Brothers* 107
The girls on the hills made a holiday show. — 120 *Childless Father* 8
Her long and vacant holiday ; — 144 **Driven in* 78
It roused the Vale to holiday. — 294 *Jedbor.* 34
With holiday delight on every brow : — 446 *Ecc. Sonn.* 3. 23. 2
On a spring holiday. — 486 **We walked* 8
Doth every Beast keep holiday ;— — 588 *Immortality* 33
Of all things, and deliberate holiday. — 636 *Prelude* 1. 254
To every scheme of holiday delight — 642 *Prelude* 2. 52
Of innocence, and holiday repose ; — 661 *Prelude* 4. 173
Kept holiday, a never-ending show, — 674 *Prelude* 5. 582
Partly from voluntary holiday, — 687 *Prelude* 7. 17
The inner spirit keeping holiday, — 869 *Excursion* 7. 780
Till their short holiday of childhood ceased, — 878 *Excursion* 8. 281
Relieves the tedious holiday of age— — S.3. 435 **The doubt* 139
One of a golden summer holiday, — K.8. 236 *Recluse* 1. 1. 4

Holidays. *See* **Half-holidays.**
From the half-yearly holidays returned, — 643 *Prelude* 2. 85
The holidays returned me, there to find — 672 *Prelude* 5. 478
On the glad eve of its dear holidays, — 738 *Prelude* 12. 288
On holidays, we rambled through the woods : — 757 *Excursion* 1. 62

Holier. A holier name ; and, under such a mask, — 47 *Bord.* 544
But affections higher, holier, — 141 *Arm. Lady* 79
Of holier love. Nor wilt thou then forget — 207 *Tintern* 155
With firmer, holier knot. — 223 *Wishing-gate* 48
Oak of Guernica ! Tree of holier power — 319 *Guernica* 1
He knows that from a holier altar came — 329 *Ode : Thanks.* 51
Sounder and therefore holier than the ends — 358 *Aquap.* 351
A happy hour with holier happiness. — 395 *White Doe: Ded.* 56
A holier name ! then lightly do not bear — 445 *Ecc. Sonn.* 3. 21. 2
Gives holier invitation than the deck — 447 *Ecc. Sonn.* 3. 30. 2
And holier seems the ground — 478 *Somnamb.* 6
Kindlier issues, holier rest, — 503 **Like a* 80
The holier deprecation, given in trust — 584 **With copious* 42
Could private feelings meet for holier rest. — 587 *Crosth.* 14
Where science, leagued with holier truth, — 629 *Installation* 74
To which thou may'st resort for holier peace,— — 787 *Excursion* 3. 107
And, with a holier love inspired, I looked — 795 *Excursion* 3. 667

Holiest. By virtue's holiest Powers attended. — 9 *Collins* 24
Awe in his breast with holiest love unites, — 19 *Desc. Sk.* 476
Of law and holiest sympathy, — 113 *Lament* 52
Joy, as her holiest language, shall adopt ; — 173 *Infant Daughter* 77
Of that holiest of Bards, and the name for my mind — 364 *Vallomb.* 26
By Nature decked for holiest sacrifice. — 420 *Ecc. Sonn.* 1. 6. 14
As one who drew from out Faith's holiest urn — 444 *Ecc. Sonn.* 3. 15. 13
To aught of highest, holiest, influence— — 461 **Queen of* 45
Pure as the holiest cloistered nun — 576 *Cenotaph* 4
In holiest mood. Urania, I shall need — 755 *Recluse* 1. 1. 778
And holiest love ; as earth, sea, air, with light, — 803 *Excursion* 4. 121
The highest, holiest, raptures of the lyre ; — 865 *Excursion* 7. 535

Holiness. How beautiful is holiness !—what wonder if the sight, — 92 *Poet's Dream* 13
The holiness within ; — 232 *Jew. Fam.* 28
Silence, and holiness, and innocence, — 365 **The Baptist* 11
Root there, and not in forms, her holiness ;— — 436 *Ecc. Sonn.* 2. 30. 5
" Sweet is the holiness of Youth "—so felt — 436 *Ecc. Sonn.* 2. 31. 1
Sweet is the holiness of youth : and hence, — 553 *Prioress* 61
In holiness and truth." " You cannot blame," — 826 *Excursion* 5. 292
In beauty of holiness, with ordered pomp, — 838 *Excursion* 6. 11
To them whose holiness on earth shall make — 887 *Excursion* 9. 227
A blended holiness of earth and sky, — K.8. 240 *Recluse* 1.1.144

Holla. Hoila ! No, no, the business must be done.— — 43 *Bord.* 329
Where is she—holla ! You are Idonea's Mother ?— — 46 *Bord.* 529
Holla ! to bed, good Folks, within ! O save us ! — 71 *Bord.* 1884

Hollies. Of tallest hollies, tall and green ; — 154 **A whirl-blast* 7
By those embowering hollies made, — 155 **A whirl-blast* 17
Along a hedge of hollies dark and tall, — 880 *Excursion* 8. 442

Hollow. Alike, when first the bittern's hollow bill — 2 *Ev. Wk.* 19
Brightens with water-breaks the hollow ghyll — 3 *Ev. Wk.* 54
The " parting Genius " sighs with hollow breath — 12 *Desc. Sk.* 71
A hollow ring ; they say it is knee-deep—— — 44 *Bord.* 395
Among these rocks, and every hollow place — 99 *Brothers* 274
And to that hollow dell from time to time — 138 *Michael* 460
Through hollow snows and rivers wide. — 145 *Her Eyes* 54
And over hill and hollow, — 162 *Binnorie* 35
Wait—and you shall see how hollow — 163 *Hint* 31
Swept through the Hollow long and bare : — 175 *Waggoner* 1. 187
Came up the hollow :—him did I accost, — 202 *Hart-leap* 119
The sun on drearier hollow never shone ; — 203 *Hart-leap* 158
Hollow excuses, and triumphant pain ; — 213 *Dion* 59
On headland, or in hollow bay ;— — 239 *P. B.* 234
In the green wood and hollow dell ; — 239 *P. B.* 242
And dimly gleaming Nest,—a hollow crown — 254 *Wild Duck's Nest* 10
That bliss awaits her which the ungenial Hollow — 261 **I heard (alas* 11
The caves reply with hollow moan ; — 299 *Cora Linn* 4
As active round the hollow dome, — 300 *Bran* 18
" *Good morrow, Citizen !* " a hollow word, — 304 **Jones ! as* 11
Inland, within a hollow vale, I stood ; — 306 **Inland, within* 1
Seem vain and hollow ; I find nothing great : — 309 **When, looking* 6
And hollow vale which foaming torrents fill — 314 **Not mid* 6
By aught redeemed out of the hollow grave : — 325 *Enghien* 9
But fill the hollow vale with joy ! — 376 **The Minstrels* 78
Through " Nature's hollow arch " that voice resounds. — 427 *Ecc. Sonn.* 1. 33. 14
Or, in the hollow surge, at anchor rocked — 454 *Sea-side* 14
Fills all the hollow of the sky. — 457 **The sun has* 9
The hollow vale from steep to steep, — 457 **Had this* 23
All round, in hollow or on height ; — 491 *Fidelity* 14
Rests on a hollow plea of recompense ; — 501 *Humanity* 61
Through the quick turns of many a hollow nook, — 523 *Epist. Beaumont* 105
While, in a hollow nook, — 543 *Russ. Fug.* 118
Deposit in the hollow of this tomb — 575 *Chiabrera* 8. 4
With hollow ringing ears and darkening gaze, — 603 *Desc.Sk.Quarto* 97
Unnumber'd streams with hollow roar profound. — 611 *Desc.Sk.Quarto* 505
My haunt the hollow cliff whose Pine — 626 *†Cento* 11
Then feels immediately some hollow thought — 636 *Prelude* 1. 259
Hollow as ever vexed the tranquil air ; — 655 *Prelude* 3. 414
In hollow exultation, dealing out — 686 *Prelude* 6. 733
Moors, mountains, headlands, and ye hollow vales, — 702 *Prelude* 8. 216
And 'mid the hollow depths of naked crags — 758 *Excursion* 1. 155
The listless hours, while in the hollow vale, — 760 *Excursion* 1. 259
Hollow and green, he lay on the green turf — 760 *Excursion* 1. 260
From hollow clefts up to the clearer air — 760 *Excursion* 1. 296
Upon his hollow cheek. " How kind," he said, — 779 *Excursion* 2. 525
In this deep Hollow, like a sullen star — 808 *Excursion* 4. 487
The planets in the hollow of their hand ; — 815 *Excursion* 4. 950
To us who stood low in that hollow dell, — 820 *Excursion* 4. 1300
And Heaven is weary, of the hollow words — 828 *Excursion* 5. 379
And streams, whose murmur fills this hollow vale, — 836 *Excursion* 5. 917
When, in the hollow of some shadowy vale, — 857 *Excursion* 7. 5
Let down into the hollow of that grave, — 868 *Excursion* 7. 699
Down looking on that hollow, where the pool — K.8. 225 **I will* 47

Hollow-blustering. Pipe wild along the hollow-blustering coast, — 608 *Desc.Sk.Quarto* 335

Hollowed. That seems by Nature hollowed out to be — 781 *Excursion* 2. 623
From the beginning, hollowed out and scooped — 837 *Excursion* 5. 1005

Hollow-parting. Soon follow'd by his hollow-parting oar, — 600 *Ev. Wk. Quarto* 439

Hollows. While coves and secret hollows, through aray — 5 *Ev. Wk.* 176
Tending to the darksome hollows — 90 *Longest Day* 31
The coves and secret hollows thro' a ray — 594 *Ev. Wk. Quarto* 159
And starting from the hollows of the earth — 809 *Excursion* 4. 529

Holly. He quite forgot his holly whip, — 127 *Idiot Boy* 84
The yew, the holly, and the bright green thorn, — 146 **It was an* 32
Near the green holly, — 158 **In youth* 36
With holly spray, — 285 *Nith* 4
Of hardy laurel and wild holly boughs— — 324 *Ode 1814* 45
Among the rocks and holly bowers. — 399 *White Doe* 273
Green with fresh holly, every pew a perch — 448 *Ecc. Sonn.* 3. 33. 11
Thy brook, and bowers of holly ; — 478 *Somnamb.* 29
And to a holly bower ; — 479 *Somnamb.* 96
As if they from the holly tree — 479 *Somnamb.* 106
A tall and shining holly, that had found — 787 *Excursion* 3. 62
Those native plants, the holly and the yew, — 793 *Excursion* 3. 527

Holly-bough. For Johnny has his holly-bough, — 126 *Idiot Boy* 49

Holly-sprinkled. 'Mid clustering isles, and holly-sprinkled steeps ; — 2 *Ev. Wk.* 10

Holms. Theirs be these holms untrodden, still, and green, — 6 *Ev. Wk.* 233
" Oh ! green," said I, " are Yarrow's holms, — 293 *Yarrow Unv.* 33
The bonny holms of Yarrow ! " — 293 *Yarrow Unv.* 64
These fairy holms untrodden, still, and green, — 595 *Ev. Wk. Quarto* 221
O Derwent ! winding among grassy holms — 636 *Prelude* 1. 275

Holy. Were there, below, a spot of holy ground — 10 *Desc. Sk.* 1
Of holy rites chanted in measured round ? — 11 *Desc. Sk.* 58
Awful the light, and holy is the air. — 18 *Desc. Sk.* 456
Those holy turrets tipped with evening gold, — 20 *Desc. Sk.* 564
If Thou be one whose heart the holy forms — 23 *Yew-tree* 48
When from the Holy Land I had returned — 52 *Bord.* 828
St. Cuthbert speed you on your holy errand. — 58 *Bord.* 1141
I fancy when you left the Holy Land, — 62 *Bord.* 1348
With this dear holy shepherd-boy breathe a prayer of earnest heart, — 91 *Norman Boy* 30

Holy—_continued._

What shall it be ? a mirthful throng ? or that holy place and calm 92 _Poet's Dream_ 23
Holy as that which long hath crowned the Chapel of this Tree ; 93 _Poet's Dream_ 60
" Holy as that far-seen which crowns the sumptuous Church in Rome 93 _Poet's Dream_ 61
Will holy Church disperse by beams of gospel-light." 141 _Arm. Lady_ 120
Our heavenward guide is holy love, 143 †_Lov. and Lik._ 67
Or holy festal pomps adorn, 164 _*Fair Lady_ 7
In strains of rapture pure and holy 180 _Waggoner_ 4. 81
Salute those strangers as a holy train 213 _Dion_ 28
She who inspires that strain of joyance holy 217 _Enterprise_ 144
Listening to nun's faint throb of holy fear, 233 _Power of Sound_ 30
A holy sense pervades his mind ; 248 _P. B._ 1053
That man's heart is a holy thing ; 248 _P. B._ 1072
That in thy holy footsteps I may tread ; 257 _*The prayers_ 11
The holy time is quiet as a Nun 258 _*It is a_ 2
To holy musing, it may enter here. 264 _*Lady ! I_ 14
Where holy ground begins, unhallowed ends, 271 _*Where holy_ 1
More beautiful, as being a thing more holy : 279 _*Though I_ 10
Hers is a holy Being, freed from Sin. 280 _*Oh what_ 5
A softness still and holy ; 302 _Yarrow V._ 46
There came a Tyrant, and with holy glee 306 _*Two Voices_ 5
Fervid, yet conversant with holy fear, 326 _*The Bard_ 3
Commemoration holy that unites 328 _Ode 1815_ 66
The Holy One will hear ! 332 _Ode : Thanks._ 230
A holy Structure to the Almighty's praise. 338 _Engelberg_ 14
So far from the holy enclosure was cast, 340 _Fort Fuentes_ 3
A holy sadness shared. 343 _Eclipse_ 60
They, too, who send so far a holy gleam 347 _Processions_ 55
Where, in her holy chapel, dwells 348 _*Lulled by_ 5
The beautiful, the brave, the holy, and the just ! 351 _Des. Stanzas_ 81
Oft for a holy warning may it serve, 360 _*Long has_ 11
Of holy Angels round her hovered : 372 _Eg. Maid_ 230
Truth's holy lamp, pure source of bright effect, 380 _Duddon_ 18. 7
The holy and the tender. 386 _Yarrow Rev._ 80
Emboldened by thy guidance, holy Star, 392 _*Though joy_ 9
Holy as princely, who that looks on thee 392 _*Though joy_ 10
Nor wants the holy Abbot's gliding Shade 393 _Inglewood_ 9
In priestly vest, with holy offerings charged, 394 _*No more_ 15
Trooping to that summons holy. 396 _White Doe_ 8
Recites the holy liturgy, 396 _White Doe_ 46
Ye living, tend your holy cares ; 397 _White Doe_ 69
But say, among these holy places, 397 _White Doe_ 106
Is spotless, and holy, and gentle, and bright ; 398 _White Doe_ 240
He glanced a look of holy pride, 400 _White Doe_ 403
Yea, trusting in God's holy aid, 401 _White Doe_ 488
For holy Church, and the People's right ! " 403 _White Doe_ 634
For the old and holy Church we mourn, 403 _White Doe_ 654
While she the holy work pursued." 403 _White Doe_ 669
When the Prior of Durham with holy hand 405 _White Doe_ 829
In holy ground a grave would make ; 412 _White Doe_ 1521
And psalms they sing—a holy sound 413 _White Doe_ 1533
To the subjection of a holy, 413 _White Doe_ 1596
With a soft spring-day of holy, 415 _White Doe_ 1757
May on these holy bells be seen, 415 _White Doe_ 1765
Who, having filled a holy place, 416 _White Doe_ 1875
Of a HOLY RIVER, on whose banks are found 418 _Ecc. Sonn._ 1. 1. 10
Did holy Paul a while in Britain dwell, 418 _Ecc. Sonn._ 1. 2. 6
Slackens his course—to mark those holy piles 419 _Ecc. Sonn._ 1. 5. 7
Their holy rites with vocal gratitude : 420 _Ecc. Sonn._ 1. 7. 7
Than they appear to holy Gregory ; 421 _Ecc. Sonn._ 1. 13. 7
Ye holy Men, so earnest in your care, 423 _Ecc. Sonn._ 1. 20. 13
A gentler life spreads round the holy spires ; 429 _Ecc. Sonn._ 2. 3. 12
Form spirit and character from holy writ, 430 _Ecc. Sonn._ 2. 9. 11
The freight of holy feeling which we meet, 438 _Ecc. Sonn._ 2. 39. 12
Holy and heavenly Spirits as they are, 438 _Ecc. Sonn._ 2. 40. 1
And so they labour, deeming Holy Writ 439 _Ecc. Sonn._ 2. 41. 6
Their suppliant hands ; but holy is the feast 440 _Ecc. Sonn._ 2. 46. 12
Had not thy holy Church her champions bred, 442 _Ecc. Sonn._ 3. 10. 6
Under the holy fear of God turns pale ; 446 _Ecc. Sonn._ 3. 23. 8
Once ye were holy, ye are holy still ; 449 _Ecc. Sonn._ 3. 35. 13
May-garlands, there let the holy altar stand 450 _Ecc. Sonn._ 3. 39. 11
Strains suitable to both.—Such holy rite, 457 _*Had this_ 15
Tempestuous winds her holy errand crossed : 466 _St. Bees_ 33
If such be Nature's holy plan, 482 _Lines : Spring_ 22
Lie open ; and the book of Holy Writ, 496 _*A little_ 51
This, this is holy ;—while I hear 498 _*The sylvan_ 19
Alternate ; carrying holy thoughts and prayers 500 _Humanity_ 30
Affections pure and holy in their source 503 _Warning_ 14
From holy offerings at noontide. 506 _Lah. Hymn_ 6
A holy name—the Bird of Heaven ! 511 _*Who rashly_ 28
Betrayed by mockery of holy fear. 514 _*Portentous change_ 8
Of holy faith and Christian hope ; 534 _*Blest is_ 68
As when it guarded holy Cuthbert's cell. 540 _Grace Darl._ 27
The Holy Virgin gives to me 542 _Russ. Fug._ 83
He loved, he hoped,—a holy flame 545 _Russ. Fug._ 325
And things of holy use unhallowed lie ; 547 _*Beneath yon_ 18
Those holy Men both died in the same hour. 551 _*If thou in_ 27
And, when they holy water on him cast, 555 _Prioress_ 188
" This Abbot, for he was a holy man, 555 _Prioress_ 191
In virtue of the holy Trinity 555 _Prioress_ 195
' Thou in thy dying sing this holy lay,' 556 _Prioress_ 209
" This holy Monk, this Abbot—him mean I, 556 _Prioress_ 219
Of Love, and of his holy services ; 560 _Cuck.andNight._ 213
Holy, and ever dutiful—beloved 581 _*Why should we_ 3
We pay a high and holy debt ; 582 _*O for_ 7
Mourn rather for that holy Spirit, 586 _Hogg_ 37
His children's children join'd the holy sound, 605 _Desc.Sk.Quarto_ 174

Holy—_continued._

To be performed, and paid all holy fees. 623 _*I find_ 5
Their badge, attests the holy fight they wage. 628 _Eagle and Dove_ 12
Waged in Freedom's holy cause, 628 _Installation_ 14
Such hope was mine, for holy services. 633 _Prelude_ 1. 54
A holy scene !—Along the smooth green turf 643 _Prelude_ 2. 107
Oft in these moments such a holy calm 647 _Prelude_ 2. 348
Bear witness Truth, endowed with holy powers 650 _Prelude_ 3. 88
In meditations holy and sublime, 693 _Prelude_ 7. 445
With zeal expanding in Truth's holy light, 720 _Prelude_ 10. 138
And holy passion overcame me first, 724 _Prelude_ 10. 418
That I have dared to tread this holy ground, 743 _Prelude_ 13. 252
Our hearts—if here the words of Holy Writ 748 _Prelude_ 14. 125
In love and holy passion, shall find these 755 _Recluse_ 1. 1. 807
An infidel contempt of holy writ 775 _Excursion_ 2. 249
This scarcely spoken, and those holy strains 777 _Excursion_ 2. 385
Their holy Ganges from a skyey fount, 790 _Excursion_ 3. 255
The priest announces from his holy seat : 792 _Excursion_ 3. 443
To the dishonour of his holy name. 801 _Excursion_ 4. 27
Which reason promises, and holy writ 803 _Excursion_ 4. 160
On the first motion of a holy thought ; 804 _Excursion_ 4. 217
A holy tenderness pervade his frame. 819 _Excursion_ 4. 1220
Or rather, as we stand on holy earth, 832 _Excursion_ 5. 646
Administration of the holy rite 836 _Excursion_ 5. 950
The faith partaking of those holy times, 837 _Excursion_ 5. 1011
What in those holy structures ye possess 838 _Excursion_ 6. 26
Before me stood that day ; on holy ground 839 _Excursion_ 6. 81
The visible quiet of this holy ground, 845 _Excursion_ 6. 482
More holy in the sight of God or Man ; 850 _Excursion_ 6. 803
For holy Nature might not thus be crossed, 853 _Excursion_ 6. 998
All that her holy customs recommend, 862 _Excursion_ 7. 332
Science severe, or word of holy Writ 864 _Excursion_ 7. 451
Holy and blest ? and where the winning grace 878 _Excursion_ 8. 249
The Priest in holy transport thus exclaimed : 893 _Excursion_ 9. 613
As it is written in thy holy book, 893 _Excursion_ 9. 640
Of holy freedom, by redeeming love 894 _Excursion_ 9. 656
They who are dwellers in this holy place K.8. 244 _Recluse_ 1.1.277
And hangs her garland on the Holy Rood. K.8. 325 [?] _*The vestal_ 8
Let not " Willy's " holy shade L.2.190 _*Queen and_ 7
That lit _Her_ holy features, from whose womb [?] _*A sad_ 10

Holy-land. She helps to make a Holy-land at home : 467 _St. Bees_ 112
Holy-thistle. A _Holy-thistle_ here we meet 164 _*Fair Lady_ 27
Homage. Act of soul-devoted homage, 142 _Arm. Lady_ 141
And what pure homage _then_ did wait 212 _Dion_ 7
But if such homage thou disdain 217 _Enterprise_ 133
Its homage offered up in purity. 222 _Triad_ 196
To pay thee homage ; and with these are joined, 290 _Kilchurn_ 28
Due homage ; nor shall fruitlessly have striven, 358 _Aquap._ 362
Instinctive homage pay ; 506 _*While from_ 34
A homage frankly offered up, like that 654 _Prelude_ 3. 377
Upon their knees, and daily homage pay 866 _Excursion_ 7. 585
Homager My Song, a fearless homager, would attend 427 _Ecc. Sonn._ 1. 35. 9
Home. _See_ **Cottage-home, Palace-home.**
Yon isle conceals their home, their hut-like bower ; 6 _Ev. Wk._ 238
Who at the call of summer quits his home, 10 _Desc. Sk._ 10
By silent cottage-doors, the peasant's home 13 _Desc. Sk._ 143
His home approaching, but in such a mood 25 _Guilt_ 68
Glimmered our dear-loved home, alas ! no longer ours ! 28 _Guilt_ 243
And in a quiet home once more my father slept. 29 _Guilt_ 261
The silent sea. From the sweet thoughts of home 31 _Guilt_ 357
Forgone the home delight of constant truth, 32 _Guilt_ 440
Near his own home !—but he was mild and good ; 35 _Guilt_ 608
To take thee to her home—and for myself, 40 _Bord._ 198
But that was a vain hope. You have struck home, 71 _Bord._ 1867
I come home, and this is my comfort ! 72 _Bord._ 1951
The home and sheltered bed, 79 _Sparrow's Nest_ 6
Let him seek his own home wherever it be ; 81 †_Address : Child_ 42
Our quiet home all full in view, 85 _Anecdote_ 6
Our pleasant home when spring began, 85 _Anecdote_ 11
" He took thee in his arms, and in pity brought thee home : 87 _Pet-lamb_ 37
From home and company remote and every playful joy, 91 _Norman Boy_ 3
To his paternal home he is returned, 96 _Brothers_ 68
When Leonard had approached his home, his heart 96 _Brothers_ 77
Nor emblem of our hopes : the dead man's home 98 _Brothers_ 172
At home, go staggering through the slippery fords, 99 _Brothers_ 258
That Leonard Ewbank was come home again, 100 _Brothers_ 309
Which at that time was James's home, there learned 101 _Brothers_ 375
Whence all the fixed delights of house and home, 102 _Artegal_ 23
Thus often would he leave our peaceful home, 107 _Indolence_ 10
They throve, and we at home did thrive : 115 _Last of Flock_ 36
And oft was moved to flee from home, 115 _Last of Flock_ 79
For sake of a young Child whose home was there. 120 _Emigrant Mother_ 8
And I have left a babe at home : 120 _Emigrant Mother_ 26
And, when once more my home I see, 121 _Emigrant Mother_ 94
Come home again, nor stop at all,— 126 _Idiot Boy_ 59
Come home again, whate'er befall, 126 _Idiot Boy_ 60
And in his pocket bring it home. 129 _Idiot Boy_ 321
For, while they all were travelling home, 131 _Idiot Boy_ 437
The Son and Father were come home, even then, 132 _Michael_ 97
Yon minarets, would gladly leave for his worst home." 140 _Arm. Lady_ 42
Brisk Robin seeks a kindlier home : 143 _*Driven in_ 3
——Soon did the spot become my other home, 146 _*It was an_ 40
Of nature and of love had made their home 150 _*When, to_ 24
In an unhappy home. 155 _Waterfall_ 10
This spot is my paternal home, 156 _Oak and Broom_ 66
Joys to spy thee near her home ; 160 _*Pansies, lilies_ 39

Homely-featured 443 Honoured

Homely—*continued.*
And all the homely in their homely works, . . 714 *Prelude* 9. 308
There are among the walks of homely life . . . 743 *Prelude* 13. 266
And drinking from the well of homely life. . . 760 *Excursion* 1. 307
Her homely tale with such familiar power, . . 765 *Excursion* 1. 615
Led toward the Cottage. Homely was the spot ; 781 *Excursion* 2. 638
Homely-featured. A tavern stood ; no homely-featured house, ... 644 *Prelude* 2. 140
Home-made. And their plain home-made cheese. Yet when the meal . . . . . . 132 *Michael* 102
Homer. From Homer the great Thunderer, from the voice . . . . 668 *Prelude* 5. 202
Homes. And homeless near a thousand homes I stood, ... 31 *Guilt* 368
A wood is felled :—and then for our own homes ! 97 *Brothers* 157
If he had one, the Youth had twenty homes. . . 101 *Brothers* 386
With but a step between their several homes, . 122 *V. and J.* 20
Among the happiest-looking homes of men . . 387 *Manse* 2
Their altars they forego, their homes they quit, . 441 *Ecc. Sonn.* 3. 6. 9
Forsook their homes, and, errant in the quest . 655 *Prelude* 3. 466
While all things else are gathering to their homes, 876 *Excursion* 8. 159
And thence let loose, to seek their pleasant homes 888 *Excursion* 9. 261
Wild creatures, and of many homes, that come . K.8. 251 *Recluse* 1.1.540
Homesick. " Was ever such a homesick Loon, . . 237 *P. B.* 77
Homespun. And a fair carpet, woven of homespun wool . . . . 860 *Excursion* 7. 186
Homestalls. Into the homestalls, ere they send them back . . . . K.8. 224 **I will* 10
Homestead. So to the homestead, where the grandsire tends . . . . 19 *Desc. Sk.* 484
Oh ! the poor tenant of that ragged homestead, . 47 *Bord.* 568
Walks, pools, and arbours, homestead, hall— . 402 *White Doe* 548
This Homestead, placed where nothing could be seen, ... 470 **Did pangs* 4
His flock, and thither from the homestead bears . 702 *Prelude* 8. 226
Homesteads. And to the nearest homesteads ran . 412 *White Doe* 1509
Of pastoral homesteads, had been long inlaid. . 860 *Excursion* 7. 191
Of their rude homesteads. Here the Warrior dwelt ; 872 *Excursion* 7. 955
Homeward. Now hardly heard, beguiles my homeward way. . . . . 9 *Ev. Wk.* 366
The crows rushed by in eddies, homeward borne. 25 *Guilt* 40
They wept—and, turning homeward, cried, . . 83 *Lucy Gray* 41
—As homeward through the lane I went with lazy feet, ... 88 *Pet-lamb* 61
While our four travellers homeward wend ; . . 131 *Idiot Boy* 433
At evening in his homeward walk . . . . . 195 *Ruth* 245
Not doubtfully perceived.—Look homeward now ! 219 **This Height* 28
Homeward in their rugged Boat, ... 338 *Brientz* 6
Homeward or schoolward, ape what ye behold ; . 339 *Tell* 8
Each step hath its value while homeward we move ;— . . . . 346 *Stanzas : Simplon* 29
Homeward we turn. Isle of Columba's Cell, . . 475 **Homeward we* 1
As they went homeward taught him privily . . 554 *Prioress* 94
Homeward and schoolward whensoe'er he went, . 554 *Prioress* 98
And through the meadows homeward went, in grave 638 *Prelude* 1. 389
Beneath the gloomy hills homeward I went . . 638 *Prelude* 1. 421
And homeward led my steps. Magnificent . . 663 *Prelude* 4. 323
My homeward course led up a long ascent, . . 664 *Prelude* 4. 379
Now homeward through the thickening hubbub, where . . . . 690 *Prelude* 7. 211
And with their freight homeward the shepherds moved . . . . 784 *Excursion* 2. 828
On homeward voyage,—what if wind and wave, . 882 *Excursion* 8. 508
Descending, we pursued our homeward course, . 895 *Excursion* 9. 757
So saying, homeward, down the hill the boy . . K.8. 228 **I will* 118
Homewards. We scampered homewards. Oh, ye rocks and streams, ... 644 *Prelude* 2. 131
Homicide. And to this end a Homicide they hired, 554 *Prioress* 116
Honest. The Soldier's Widow learned with honest pain . . . . 34 *Guilt* 550
Twelve honest men, plain men, would set us right ; 53 *Bord.* 882
And, for the honest folk within, ... 174 *Waggoner* 1. 67
Through help of honest Benjamin ; . . . . 176 *Waggoner* 1. 244
Who can or will !—my honest soul, ... 177 *Waggoner* 2, 45
And in this way he gained an honest maintenance. 196 *Resolution* 105
It was to lead an honest life ; . . . . . . 246 *P. B.* 902
Became a good and honest man. . . . . . 249 *P. B.* 1135
For honest men delight will take . . . . 286 *Sons of Burns* 19
The majesty of honest dealing. . . . . . . 472 *Ossian* 16
' Is it an honest thing ? Shall this be so ? . . 554 *Prioress* 110
Severely honest, break no plighted trust, . . . 619 *School Ex.* 87
And honest dunces—of important days, . . . 650 *Prelude* 3. 68
Of an enthusiast ; yet, in honest truth, . . . 710 *Prelude* 9. 71
Some, tired of honest service ; these, outdone, . 797 *Excursion* 3. 772
This honest sheep-dog's countenance I read ; . . 834 *Excursion* 5. 817
Than honest maintenance, by irksome toil . . 875 *Excursion* 8. 50
And honest dealing, and untainted speech, . . 878 *Excursion* 8. 241
For honest worth one poet's trade is, ... S.3. 438 **My Lord* 26
For both, my honest Buccaneer ! . . . . . S.3. 441 **The ball* 4
Good honest souls !—if right my judgment lies L.1. 95 *Juvenal* 3. 20
Honestly. And Peter honestly might say, . . . 243 *P. B.* 612
Honesty. We two will live in honesty. . . . . 145 *Her Eyes* 74
And simple honesty a common growth— . . . . 515 *Penn.* 5
Honey. *See* **Rock-honey.**
Then Summer lingered long ; and honey flowed . 17 *Desc. Sk.* 388
That sucks from mountain-heath her honey fee, . 503 *Warning* 33
With amber honey from the mountain's breast ; . 525 *Epist. Beaumont* 243
For his hive had so long been replenished with honey, ... 570 *Farmer* 34
Sweet honey out of spurned or dreaded weeds. . 669 *Prelude* 5. 278

Honey—*continued.*
I hear thee tell how bees with honey fed . . . 733 *Prelude* 11. 443
Honeysuckle. The honeysuckle, crowding round the porch, ... 767 *Excursion* 1. 715
" Brought from the woods the honeysuckle twines 855 *Excursion* 6. 1149
Honied. His seat beneath the honied sycamore 28 *Guilt* 219
That spreads, in gentle pomp, its honied shade. . 829 *Excursion* 5. 461
Honour. I honour him. Strong feelings to his heart 38 *Bord.* 33
Against my honour, in the which our Captain . 68 *Bord.* 1691
And ensures those palms of honour . . . . 90 *Longest Day* 73
Hopeless of honour and of gain, ... 117 *Affl. Marg.* 37
Honour ascends among the humblest poor, . . 138 *Widow* 2
Such honour could not merit. . . . . . . 163 *Needlecase* 12
In honour of their Queen. . . . . 170 *Rural Ill.* 18
I'll set, my friends, to do you honour, ... 178 *Waggoner* 2. 121
And honour rest upon the senseless clay. . . . 270 **If these* 14
The extremes of favoured life, may honour both. 276 **Chatsworth ! thy* 14
In honour of that Hero brave ! . . . . . 291 *Rob Roy* 8
And honour which they do not understand. . . 310 **Another year* 14
Say, what is Honour ?—'Tis the finest sense . . 316 **Say, what* 1
Honour is hopeful elevation,—whence . . . . 316 **Say, what* 8
Honour that knows the path and will not swerve ; 319 **Avaunt all* 7
For its own honour, on man's suffering heart. . 321 **Here pause* 6
Clear-sighted Honour, and his staid Compeers, . 329 *Ode : Thanks.* 61
Honour to word-preserving Arts, and hail . . 356 *Aquap.* 250
In honour of each household name, ... 375 **The Minstrels* 16
Such looks of love and honour . . . . . 386 *Yarrow Rev.* 74
From honour misconceived, or fancied wrong, . 389 *Sound of Mull* 7
All ancient honour in the realm. . . . . . 403 *White Doe* 645
Yet fetched from Paradise that honour came, . 476 *Eden* 5
Of ancient honour ; whence that goodly state . 477 **Lowther ! in* 6
Thou art a tool of honour in my hands ; . . . 489 *Spade* 3
To honour thee, sweet May ! . . . . . . 506 **While from* 36
Our schemes ; the faith and honour, never yet . 513 **Said Secrecy* 6
Lived with honour on his lands. . . . . . 536 *Egremont* 108
And honour want a home ; . . . . 545 *Russ. Fug.* 308
Great was their bliss, the honour high . . . 545 *Russ. Fug.* 375
For she herself is honour, and the root . . . 552 *Prioress* 13
Know, that the honour of high God may spread, 554 *Prioress* 126
And eke His Mother, honour of Mankind : . . 555 *Prioress* 168
In honour of that blissful Maiden free, . . . 556 *Prioress* 213
Began to honour May with all their powers. . . 558 *Cuck. and Night.* 70
All gentiless and honour thence come forth ; . . 559 *Cuck. and Night.* 152
Of Nightshade, to St. Mary's honour built, . . 643 *Prelude* 2. 104
With honour and importance : in a world . . 649 *Prelude* 3. 21
Honour misplaced, and Dignity astray ; . . . 657 *Prelude* 3. 600
Responded ; " Honour to the patriot's zeal ! . . 681 *Prelude* 6. 441
Of grace and honour, power and worthiness. . . 703 *Prelude* 8. 281
In honour, as in one community, ... 713 *Prelude* 9. 228
In honour to their honour : zeal, which yet . . 713 *Prelude* 9. 254
For patrimonial honour set apart, ... 714 *Prelude* 9. 327
A work of honour ; think not that to this . . 720 *Prelude* 10. 142
Honour which could not else have been, a faith, . 725 *Prelude* 10. 467
Through times of honour and through times of shame . . . . 732 *Prelude* 11. 371
Replete with honour ; sounds in unison . . . 742 *Prelude* 13. 184
Honour and shame, looking to right and left, . 751 *Prelude* 14. 338
Honour my little cell with some few tears . . 783 *Excursion* 2. 803
Than did to her due honour, and to me . . . 793 *Excursion* 3. 511
Shall with one heart honour their common kind. 796 *Excursion* 3. 733
Whose course of earthly honour was begun . . 825 *Excursion* 5. 180
With honour ; which, encasing by the power . . 831 *Excursion* 5. 607
Began in honour, gradually obtained . . . . 849 *Excursion* 6. 707
Honour assumed or given : and him, the Wonderful, 862 *Excursion* 7. 344
That, on the steady breeze of honour, sailed . . 873 *Excursion* 7. 1015
Love what I see, and honour humankind. . . K.8. 248 *Recluse* 1.1.426
Must honour still to Lonsdale's tail be bound ? . L.1. 88 *Juvenal* 1. 13
My Lord can muster (all but honour spent) . . L.1. 97 *Juvenal* 3. 81
Honourable. In honourable wedlock with his Love, 122 *V. and J.* 60
The certainty of honourable gain ; . . . . 132 *Michael* 73
Or wiped his honourable brows . . . . . 287 *Sons of Burns* 33
And meekness tempering honourable pride ; . . 430 *Ecc. Sonn.* 2. 7. 12
On honourable terms, or else retire, ... 493 *Hap. War.* 37
To honourable Men of various worth : . . . . 547 **Beneath yon* 8
To honourable toil. Yet should these hopes . . 641 *Prelude* 1. 625
We summoned up the honourable deeds . . . 715 *Prelude* 9. 364
For ancient worth and honourable things, . . . 872 *Excursion* 7. 960
Critics, right honourable Bard, decree . . . S.3. 432 **Critics, right* 1
Honourably. Of reason, honourably effaced by debts 862 *Excursion* 7. 319
Honoured. *See* **Time-honoured.**
And thee, my Child ! Believe me, honoured Sire ! 40 *Bord.* 144
Of universal grief bedewed his honoured bier. 105 *Artegal* 233
Could I withhold thy honoured name,—and now 151 **When, to* 86
The Shepherd-lord was honoured more and more ; 205 *Brougham* 170
And should these slacken, honoured Beaumont ! still . . . . 251 *Appleth.* 9
Or save this honoured Land from every Lord . 310 *Invasion* 19
Some bird (like our own honoured redbreast) may strew . . . . 340 *Fort Fuentes* 11
Calls me to pace her honoured Bridge—that cheers 351 *Des. Stanzas* 56
From honoured Instruments that round him wait ; 368 *Trajan* 54
From Sages justly honoured by mankind ; . . 435 *Ecc. Sonn.* 2. 27. 2
And, therefore, shalt thou be an honoured name ! 491 *Tribute : Dog* 36
By the world's Ruler, on his honoured head ! . . 528 **Those breathing* 110
And Thou, wild Stream, that giv'st the honoured name . . . . 539 **Lady ! a* 23
Honoured with costliest sepulture. . . . . 550 *Hermit's Cell* 2. 16
Where'er Permessus bears an honoured name, . 574 *Chiabrera* 5. 22
Its mellow lustre round thy honoured head ; . . 583 **With copious* 31
Who walks, where honour'd men of ancient days 608 *Desc. Sk. Quarto* 354

Honoured—*continued.*
Now honour'd Edward's less than Bacon's name. 619 *School Ex.* 56
A Book time-cherished and an honoured name 626 **Son of* 9
Lady ! devoutly honoured and beloved 628 **Deign, Sovereign* 9
This labour will be welcome, honoured Friend ! 641 *Prelude* 1. 646
To follow, and if thou, my honoured Friend ! 652 *Prelude* 3. 198
Honoured by Milton's name. O temperate Bard ! 653 *Prelude* 3. 295
Honoured with little less than filial love. 659 *Prelude* 4. 39
My honoured Mother, she who was the heart 669 *Prelude* 5. 257
And knowledge, rightly honoured with that name— 672 *Prelude* 5. 424
Honoured in France, the name of Englishmen, 681 *Prelude* 6. 403
With like persuasion honoured, we maintained : 715 *Prelude* 9. 422
An honoured teacher of my youth was laid, 726 *Prelude* 10. 534
Of note belonging to that honoured isle, 733 *Prelude* 11. 433
Beloved and honoured—far as he was known. 757 *Excursion* 1. 97
Yet not the noblest of that honoured Race 771 *Excursion* 2. 19
More might have followed—but my honoured Friend 779 *Excursion* 2. 512
A sound unknown to you ; else, honoured Friend ! 793 *Excursion* 3. 483
Like this our honoured Friend ; and thence acquire 828 *Excursion* 5. 387
But honoured once, those features and that mien 834 *Excursion* 5. 788
Which, from her Father's honoured hand, herself, 856 *Excursion* 6. 1184
From youth or maiden, or some honoured chief 857 *Excursion* 7. 18
For she hath recognised her honoured friend, 881 *Excursion* 8. 494
Honouring. Honouring the hope of noble ancestry. 504 *Warning* 46
Honour's. But upon Honour's head disturb the crown, 518 *Pun. Death* 4. 12
Not that I may increase her honour's dower, 552 *Prioress* 12
Honours. He poured rewards and honours on the good ; 103 *Artegal* 70
From which her graces and her honours sprung : 122 *V. and J.* 16
Mindless of its just honours ; with this key 260 **Scorn not* 2
Ah ! show that worthier honours are thy due ; 261 **Fair Prime* 9
Thine are the honours of the lofty waste ; 376 *Duddon* 2. 3
And of old honours, too, and passions high ; 388 **The pibroch's* 9
Whose arts and honours in the dust are laid 421 *Ecc. Sonn.* 1. 11. 8
Of wealth and power and honours, long for rest ; 458 *Sea-shore* 31
Of ritual honours to this Fountain paid 465 **The cattle* 10
For wealth, or honours, or for worldly state ; 493 *Hap. War.* 42
Yet no sepulchral honours to her Son 574 *Chiabrera* 5. 14
Their honours, and should, once for all, pronounce 669 *Prelude* 5. 217
And all the tradesman's honours overhead : 689 *Prelude* 7. 159
Yet richly graced with honours of her own, 691 *Prelude* 7. 266
Though heedless of such honours now, and changed : 711 *Prelude* 9. 142
Her titles and her honours ; now believing, 731 *Prelude* 11. 297
Proceed thy honours. I am lost, but see 738 *Prelude* 12. 273
Permit, like honours, dance and song, are paid 851 *Excursion* 6. 836
A soldier's honours. At his funeral hour 871 *Excursion* 7. 875
Thy ancient honours when shalt thou resume ? L.I. 94 *Juvenal* 2. 17
Hood. As aught that song records of Robin Hood ; 255 *Detraction* 3
Ye wrangling Schoolmen, of the scarlet hood ! 268 **Dogmatic Teachers* 2
A famous man is Robin Hood, 290 *Rob Roy* 1
Of stole and doublet, hood and scarf, 396 *White Doc* 5
A hood of mountain-wool undyed) 413 *White Doe* 1608
Of Jack the Giant-killer, Robin Hood, 670 *Prelude* 5. 343
Hooded. In hooded mantle, limping o'er the plain, 321 **Humanity, delighting* 5
From a long train—in hooded vestments fair 347 *Processions* 42
That many hooded Cenobites there are, 429 *Ecc. Sonn.* 2. 5. 2
By hooded Votaresses with saintly cheer ; 465 **The cattle* 11
Taught by the hooded Celibates of St. Bees. 467 *St. Bees* 117
Hooded the open brow that overawed 513 **Said Secrecy* 5
The ghostly semblance of a hooded monk, 708 *Prelude* 8. 586
Hoof. The echoed hoof nearing the distant shore, 9 *Ev. Wk.* 371
My horse moved on ; hoof after hoof 109 **Strange fits* 21
The Ass, uplifting a hind hoof, 179 *Waggoner* 3. 106
What feats an Ass's hoof can do ! 181 *Waggoner* 4. 176
To hoof and finger mailed ;—yet, high or low, 368 *Trajan* 47
And echo'd hoof approaching the far shore ; 600 *Ev. Wk. Quarto* 440
Hoof-marks. Three several hoof-marks which the hunted Beast 201 *Hart-leap* 51
Hoofs. And planted where thy hoofs the turf have grazed. 201 *Hart-leap* 68
Sets down his hoofs inaudibly, 247 *P. B.* 989
As if with felt his hoofs were shod. 247 *P. B.* 990
Wheels and the tread of hoofs are heard no more ; 453 **Calm is the* 27
To slake their thirst, with reckless hoofs have trod 465 **The cattle* 2
We beat with thundering hoofs the level sand. 644 *Prelude* 2. 137
With speed and echoes loud of trampling hoofs 716 *Prelude* 9. 449
We beat with thundering hoofs the level sand. 727 *Prelude* 10. 603
May roll in chariots, or provoke the hoofs 773 *Excursion* 2. 99
Hook. At this the Father raised his hook, 83 *Lucy Gray* 21
Hooker. To youthful HOOKER, in familiar style 438 *Ecc. Sonn.* 2. 39. 4
Hooker's. And Hooker's voice the spectacle approves ! 448 *Ecc. Sonn.* 3. 32. 14
Hoop. And at the *Hoop* alighted, famous Inn. 649 *Prelude* 3. 17
Hooped. With his own hand a sapling, which he hooped 134 *Michael* 181
Hoot. The owlets hoot, the owlets curr, 127 *Idiot Boy* 104
Hooted. The owls have hooted all night long, 131 *Idiot Boy* 434
Hooting. Crisp, yellow leaves my bed ; the hooting owl 424 *Ecc. Sonn.* 1. 22. 11
Hootings. Blew mimic hootings to the silent owls, 671 *Prelude* 5. 373
Hop. The withered leaves all skip and hop ; 155 **A whirl-blast* 13
And let the redbreast hop from stone to stone. 549 **Stranger ! this* 35
Hope. And hope itself was all I knew of pain ; 2 *Ev. Wk.* 22
Hope with reflection blends her social rays 2 *Ev. Wk.* 29
Thus Hope, first pouring from her blessed horn 8 *Ev. Wk.* 339
A hope, that prudence could not then approve, 11 *Desc. Sk.* 43
Hope, strength, and courage, social suffering brings, 13 *Desc. Sk.* 171

Hope—*continued.*
While Hope, reclining upon Pleasure's urn, 18 *Desc. Sk.* 431
Gay lark of hope, they silent song resume ! 20 *Desc. Sk.* 528
Abortive joy, and hope that works in fear ; 20 *Desc. Sk.* 548
One flower of hope—oh, pass and leave it there ! 20 *Desc. Sk.* 552
Upon that promise, nor the hope disown ; 22 *Desc. Sk.* 649
Be scorn and fear and hope alike forgot 22 *Desc. Sk.* 666
Full long endured in hope of just reward, 25 *Guilt* 50
And hope returned, and pleasure fondly made 25 *Guilt* 58
Vain hope ! for fraud took all that he had earned. 25 *Guilt* 64
For never could I hope to meet with such another. 29 *Guilt* 252
We had no hope, and no relief could gain : 29 *Guilt* 272
Tempered fit words of hope ; and the lark warbled near. 30 *Guilt* 324
Hope died, and fear itself in agony was lost ! 30 *Guilt* 351
And from all hope I was for ever hurled. 31 *Guilt* 358
Else can ye hope but with such numerous foes 33 *Guilt* 510
Hope cheered my dreams, and to my daily prayers 35 *Guilt* 597
Those eyeballs dark—dark beyond hope of light, 39 *Bord.* 136
I would fain hope that we deceive ourselves : 44 *Bord.* 375
Looked at from every point of fear or hope, 47 *Bord.* 549
I hope you are refreshed.—I have just written 49 *Bord.* 666
I hope Idonea is well housed. That horseman, 50 *Bord.* 734
Young as he is, diverted wish and hope 54 *Bord.* 932
And did not want glimmerings of quiet hope. 62 *Bord.* 1355
But that was a vain hope. You have struck home, 71 *Bord.* 1867
the hope that we might shelter and restore him. 72 *Bord.* 1925
And, if thou hast forgiven me, let me hope, 76 *Bord.* 2200
With witless hope to bring her near !— 81 †*Mother's Return* 10
If I may dare to cherish hope that gentle eyes will read 93 *Poet's Dream* 79
That he began to doubt ; and even to hope 96 *Brothers* 88
Which will bear looking at. These boys—I hope 99 *Brothers* 239
And adding, with a hope to be forgiven, 102 *Brothers* 431
And, feeling that the hope is vain, 110 *Forsaken* 13
Contentment, hope, and mother's glee, 121 *EmigrantMother* 87
Deem that by such fond hope the Youth was swayed, 122 *V. and J.* 64
Full speedily resounded, public hope, 126 *V. and J.* 303
Poor Betty now has lost all hope, 129 *Idiot Boy* 292
Brings hope with it, and forward-looking thoughts, 133 *Michael* 148
He was his comfort and his daily hope. 134 *Michael* 206
More hope out of his life than he supposed 134 *Michael* 219
Of remedies and of a cheerful hope. 135 *Michael* 243
Were younger ;—but this hope is a good hope. 135 *Michael* 278
Nay, Boy, be of good hope ;—we both may live 137 *Michael* 388
By word, look, deed, with hope that he might love again. 139 *Arm. Lady* 6
With hope that we, dear Friends ! shall meet again. 143 **High bliss* 28
With all the ministers of hope 154 *Flower Garden* 35
And hope for higher raptures, when life's day is done. 160 **Up with me* 31
A name with us endeared to hope, 164 **Fair Lady* 15
Hope, and a renovation without end. 173 *Infant Daughter* 6 5
And hope—the OLIVE-BOUGH and DOVE ; 174 *Waggoner* 1. 86
Which now ye climb with heart and hope, 175 *Waggoner* 1. 125
And thou wert still a hope, a love ; 184 **O blithe* 23
May meet at noontide ; Fear and trembling Hope, 185 *Yew-trees* 26
When, in the eagerness of boyish hope, 185 *Nutting* 4
With sudden happiness beyond all hope. 185 *Nutting* 29
No hope, no wish remained, not one,— 194 *Ruth* 182
And hope that is unwilling to be fed ; 197 *Resolution* 114
Fitter hope, and nobler doom ; 205 *Brougham* 139
For future years. And so I dare to hope, 206 *Tintern* 65
Vows have I made by fruitless hope inspired ; 209 *Laod.* 2
Hope, pointing to the cultured plain, 215 *Kirkstone* 78
Daughter of Hope ! her favourite Child, 215 *Enterprise* 20
Glad Hope would almost cease to be 217 *Enterprise* 158
Come with each anxious hope subdued 222 *Triad* 180
Hope rules a land for ever green : 223 *Wishing-gate* 1
To hearts so oft by hope betrayed ; 224 **'Tis gone* 28
Our vernal tendencies to hope, 225 *Primrose* 35
To an exulting Nation's hope 225 *Present.* 50
Of man's enquiring gaze, but to his hope 226 *Vernal Ode* 29
Nourish the hope that memory lacks not power 231 *Clouds* 90
Or made with hope to please that inward eye 231 **The gentlest Poet* 34
And to their hope the distant shrine 233 *Power of Sound* 60
Of timid hope and innocent desire 233 *Power of Sound* 78
A mother's hope is hers ;—but soon 246 *P. B.* 906
Sweet tears of hope and tenderness ! 247 *P. B.* 961
Were a vain notion ; but the hope is dear. 250 **Happy the* 12
Might work in our high Calling—a bright hope 251 *Appleth.* 6
With keen-eyed Hope, with Memory, at her side, 251 **Her only* 3
Yes ! hope may with my strong desire keep pace, 256 **Yes ! hope* 1
His hope is treacherous only whose love dies 256 **Yes ! hope* 10
And hope of endless peace in me grew bold : 257 **No mortal* 4
Oh ! if within me hope should e'er decline, 258 **Even so* 9
Remembrance persecutes, and Hope betrays ; 259 **Weak is* 2
To hope—in Parents, sinful above all. 267 **Desponding Father* 14
Of Faith and Hope—if thou, by nature's doom, 271 *George : Death* 6
For steadfast hope the contract to fulfil ; 275 *Rotha Q.* 6
Under the grave of things ; Hope had her spire 282 **In my* 11
As when their earliest flowers of hope were blown, 282 *Railway* 4
Let no mean hope your souls enslave ; 287 *Sons of Burns* 43
To fear of loss, and hope of gain, 294 *Jedbor.* 51
Blessings be on you both ! one hope, one lot, 303 **Fair Star* 11
The destiny of Man, and live in hope. 304 **Festivals have* 14
Meek, destitute, as seemed, of hope or aim 305 **We had* 5
And Hope was maddened by the drops that fell 311 **Who rises* 37
And neither hope nor steadfast promise yield 316 **O'er the* 7

Horrid. Who has been guilty of some horrid crime. — 73 *Bord.* 2029
With all the chambers in its horrid towers, — 796 *Excursion* 3. 710
Horror. Cold stony horror all her senses bound. — 27 *Guilt* 184
With horror is this world) am unto thee — 75 *Bord.* 2168
And horror breathing from the silent ground! — 335 **A wingèd* 14
To vacancy, and horror strong: — 411 *White Doe* 1388
An awe and supernatural horror breeds; — 431 *Ecc. Sonn.* 2. 11. 6
Take from the horror due to a foul deed, — 519 *Pun. Death* 8. 10
Great joy by horror tam'd dilates his heart, — 612 *Desc.Sk.Quarto* 560
By horror of their impious rites, preserved; — 870 *Excursion* 7. 844
Horror-led. Where Horror-led his sea of ice assails, — 615 *Desc.Sk.Quarto* 694
Horror-striking. Of monstrous crime!—that horror-striking blade, — 214 *Dion* 107
Horse. *See* **Mountain-horse, Sea-horse, War-horse.**
The horse alone, seen dimly as I pass, — 1 *Early Youth* 3
Starts, like a horse, beside the glaring road— — 13 *Desc. Sk.* 182
While his horse pawed the floor with furious heat; — 27 *Guilt* 175
Struck, and still struck again, the troubled horse: — 27 *Guilt* 177
A cart and horse beside the rivulet stood; — 34 *Guilt* 541
We kill a worn-out horse, and who but women — 54 *Bord.* 927
With quickening pace my horse drew nigh — 109 **Strange fits* 11
My horse moved on; hoof after hoof — 109 **Strange fits* 21
The horse, and the horn, and the hark! hark away! — 120 *Childless Father* 14
But then he is a horse that thinks! — 127 *Idiot Boy* 112
There's neither horse nor man abroad, — 128 *Idiot Boy* 175
Johnny perhaps his horse forsook, — 128 *Idiot Boy* 214
There's neither Johnny nor his Horse — 128 *Idiot Boy* 219
The foot of horse, the voice of man; — 129 *Idiot Boy* 283
What Johnny and his Horse are doing! — 129 *Idiot Boy* 313
Sits upright on a feeding horse? — 130 *Idiot Boy* 351
Unto his horse—there feeding free, — 130 *Idiot Boy* 352
She almost has o'erturned the Horse, — 130 *Idiot Boy* 375
That was its wings, its chariot, and its horse, — 148 **A narrow* 24
No, not a horse of all the eight, — 178 *Waggoner* 3. 7
Last and foremost, every horse — 181 *Waggoner* 4. 100
"Bring forth another horse!" he cried aloud. — 200 *Hart-leap* 4
"Another horse!"—That shout the vassal heard — 200 *Hart-leap* 5
The horse and horseman are a happy pair; — 200 *Hart-leap* 10
But horse and man are vanished, one and all; — 200 *Hart-leap* 15
And, pulling now the rein my horse to stop, — 202 *Hart-leap* 106
"There's neither dog nor heifer, horse nor sheep, — 202 *Hart-leap* 133
A proud One docile as a managed horse; — 234 *Power of Sound* 139
There's something in a flying horse, — 236 *P.B.* 1
Ask him to lend his horse to-night, — 248 *P. B.* 1063
Arrived a neighbour with his horse; — 249 *P. B.* 1122
Unharnessed, naked, troops of Moorish horse — 368 *Trajan* 45
Horse charging horse, 'mid these retired domains; — 383 *Duddon* 29. 2
The young horse must forsake his manger, — 402 *White Doe* 550
And horse and harness followed—see — 402 *White Doe* 609
Ten times their number, man and horse; — 405 *White Doe* 856
The troop of horse have gained the height — 412 *White Doe* 1462
Could leave both man and horse behind; — 483 *Simon Lee* 18
And the tongs and the poker, instead of that horse — 484 **A plague* 3
Skilful and bold, the horse and burthened *sled* — 523 *Epist. Beaumont* 110
But still, when he has given his horse the rein, — 566 *Cumb. Beg.* 30
Starts like a horse beside the flashing road; — 605 *Desc.Sk.Quarto* 208
On his pale horse shall fell Consumption go. — 617 *Desc.Sk.Quarto* 791
And from my Horse I leapt; great joy had I. — 622 **Among all* 8
Proud and exulting like an untired horse — 638 *Prelude* 1. 432
And the horse under him—in gilded pomp — 689 *Prelude* 7. 134
The Horse of knowledge, and the learned Pig, — 697 *Prelude* 7. 708
The horse is taught his manage, and no star — 719 *Prelude* 10. 78
Of vehicles and travellers, horse and foot, — 726 *Prelude* 10. 564
I led my horse, and, stumbling on, at length — 737 *Prelude* 12. 234
A liking for the small grey horse that bears — K.8. 250 *Recluse* 1.1.505
As Tom, but when he helped her to her horse — L.1. 98 *Juvenal* 3. 103
Horseback. And why on horseback have you set — 126 *Idiot Boy* 10
Horsed. Mailed and horsed, with lance and sword, — 205 *Brougham* 152
All horsed and harnessed with him to ride,— — 400 *White Doe* 418
Horseman. I hope Idonea is well housed. That horseman, — 50 *Bord.* 734
The horse and horseman are a happy pair; — 200 *Hart-leap* 10
The sauntering Horseman throws not with a slack — 566 *Cumb. Beg.* 26
Some Horseman who was passing by, — 621 *Andrew Jones* 12
And when a stranger horseman came, the latch — 769 *Excursion* 1. 896
Horseman-ghost. All silent as a horseman-ghost, — 129 *Idiot Boy* 325
Horsemanship. And all his skill in horsemanship: — 127 *Idiot Boy* 85
Of senseless horsemanship, or on the breast — 652 *Prelude* 3. 253
Horsemen. Horsemen and Foot of each degree, — 403 *White Doe* 703
Of horsemen at an eager pace! — 412 *White Doe* 1444
Proudly the Horsemen bore away — 412 *White Doe* 1499
Of horsemen shadows winding to and fro; — 595 *Ev. Wk. Quarto* 184
Horsemen-shadows. Of horsemen-shadows moving to and fro; — 6 *Ev. Wk.* 201
Horsemen-travellers. The horsemen-travellers ride. — 194 *Ruth* 240
Horse's. The hound, the horse's tread, and mellow horn; — 6 *Ev. Wk.* 245
His face unto his horse's tail, — 129 *Idiot Boy* 323
Horses. When horses in the sunburnt intake stood, — 3 *Ev. Wk.* 49
He stopped his horses at the word, — 82 *Alice Fell* 10
The horses scampered through the rain; — 82 *Alice Fell* 14
The Horses have worked with right good-will, — 174 *Waggoner* 1. 40
Here am I—with my horses yet! — 174 *Waggoner* 1. 117
The horses are dismayed, nor know — 175 *Waggoner* 1. 190
The horses cautiously pursue — 175 *Waggoner* 1. 207
Summons his horses to a stand. — 176 *Waggoner* 1. 224
Gave the word—the horses heard — 177 *Waggoner* 2. 50
Right gladly had the horses stirred, — 178 *Waggoner* 3. 1
The horses made a quiet stand; — 179 *Waggoner* 3. 57
But the horses stretch and pull — 180 *Waggoner* 4. 84

Horses—*continued.*
With trampling horses and refulgent cars— — 216 *Enterprise* 110
Of pompous horses; whom vain titles please; — 433 *Ecc. Sonn.* 2. 18. 4
Men, dogs, and horses, all are dead; — 483 *Simon Lee* 31
Them therefore with wild horses did he draw, — 555 *Prioress* 182
Who lead their horses down the steep rough road — 566 *Cumb. Beg.* 5
When horses in the wall-girt intake stood, — 592 *Ev. Wk. Quarto* 65
Our horses grazed. To more than inland peace, — 643 *Prelude* 2. 108
On sturdy horses graced with jingling bells, — 858 *Excursion* 7. 65
A team of horses, with a ponderous freight — 865 *Excursion* 7. 542
What horses there of Diomede, had great — L.2. 123 *Frag. Æneid* 3. 3
Horse-track. The foot-path faintly marked, the horse-track wild, — 876 *Excursion* 8. 105
Hosannas. Hosannas pealing down the long-drawn aisle, — 232 *Power of Sound* 14
When each pale brow to dread hosannas bowed — 450 *Ecc. Sonn.* 3. 40. 3
Hose. In splendid garb, with hose of silk, and hair — 649 *Prelude* 3. 38
Hospitable. And under every hospitable tree — 125 *V. and J.* 257
Nurtured by hospitable hands: — 144 **Driven in* 59
And, in one hospitable cleft, — 157 *Oak and Broom* 108
A genial hearth, a hospitable board, — 444 *Ecc. Sonn.* 3. 18. 1
Nor do they need, our hospitable care, — 527 **Those breathing* 6
And whiter is the hospitable bed. — 615 *Desc.Sk.Quarto* 739
To cheer the wand'ring wretch with hospitable light. — 620 **She wept* 14
Is hospitable dealing, grant my prayer! — 625 *Æneid* 108
He went about his hospitable task. — 781 *Excursion* 2. 656
A hospitable chink, and stood upright, — 787 *Excursion* 3. 63
Her Helpmate following. Hospitable fare, — 834 *Excursion* 5. 775
Theirs was a hospitable board, and theirs — 860 *Excursion* 7. 168
And pure good-will, and hospitable cheer; — 878 *Excursion* 8. 242
Hospitably. And hospitably did they give us hail, — 681 *Prelude* 6. 404
Hospital. "Borne to a hospital, I lay with brain — 31 *Guilt* 388
Humbly in a religious hospital; — 771 *Excursion* 2. 9
Hospitalities. Junonian hospitalities prepare — 624 *Æneid* 21
Hospitality. Lord of thy house and hospitality; — 88 *H. C.* 16
The hospitality—the alms (alas! — 434 *Ecc. Sonn.* 2. 23. 11
Upon a lordly dish; frank hospitality — 525 *Epist. Beaumont* 247
Of hospitality and peaceful rest. — 716 *Prelude* 9. 478
Hospitals. Our hospitals, too, — S.3. 440 **Said red-ribboned* 17
Host. Host of his welcome inn, the noon-tide bower, — 11 *Desc. Sk.* 29
The mine's dire earthquake, and the pallid host — 30 *Guilt* 348
Good Host, such tendance as you would expect — 42 *Bord.* 300
Sir Host! by all the love you bear to courtesy, — 42 *Bord.* 306
Will give me quiet lodging. You have a boy, good Host, — 43 *Bord.* 353
And I gave money to the host, — 82 *Alice Fell* 55
Unless our Landlord be your host to-night, — 98 *Brothers* 223
For it was painted by the Host; — 174 *Waggoner* 1. 90
A host, of golden daffodils; — 187 **I wandered* 4
Army of Clouds! ye wingèd Host in troops — 229 *Clouds* 1
Against an equal host that wore the plaid, — 293 *Killicranky* 3
But half their host is buried:—rock on rock — 314 *Hofer* 11
That host, when from the regions of the Pole — 321 **Humanity, delighting* 15
That host, as huge and strong as e'er defied — 321 **Humanity, delighting* 17
That Host, which rendered all your bounties vain! — 322 **Ye Storms* 14
Exalt his still small voice;—to quell that Host — 322 **By Moscow* 10
And there alights 'mid that aerial host — 343 *Eclipse* 39
Relinquished half his empire to the host — 392 **Though joy* 8
"They mustered their host at Wetherby, — 404 *White Doe* 716
Can such a mighty host be raised — 404 *White Doe* 789
While through the Host, from man to man, — 405 *White Doe* 803
Of mitred Thurston—what a Host — 405 *White Doe* 814
Back through the melancholy Host — 405 *White Doe* 843
The Host that followed Urien as he strode — 421 *Ecc. Sonn.* 1. 10. 9
The *unarmed* Host who by their prayers would turn — 421 *Ecc. Sonn.* 1. 12. 5
So huge a host!)—to tear from the Unbeliever — 427 *Ecc. Sonn.* 1. 34. 13
And, while the HOST is raised, its elevation — 431 *Ecc. Sonn.* 2. 11. 5
Meek eve shuts up the whole usurping host — 456 **Soft as* 16
To cheer the remnant of his host — 495 *Fact* 27
Casting weak words amid a host of thoughts — 541 *Grace Darl.* 75
To the end that he the Grecian host might see; — 564 *Troilus* 149
Among the leaders of the Grecian host — 625 *Æneid* 137
Was soon defrauded, and the banded host — 633 *Prelude* 1. 97
There, darkness makes abode, and all the host — 674 *Prelude* 5. 598
Of those emancipated, a blithe host — 681 *Prelude* 6. 387
The King had fallen, and that invading host— — 718 *Prelude* 10. 12
With roar of cannon by a furious host. — 719 *Prelude* 10. 54
The host of insects gathering round my face, — 756 *Excursion* 1. 24
Which was no sooner entered than our Host — 781 *Excursion* 2. 649
A feast before us, and a courteous Host — 781 *Excursion* 2. 672
"Those lusty twins," exclaimed our host, "if here — 782 *Excursion* 2. 694
Now let us forth into the sun!"—Our Host — 785 *Excursion* 2. 903
And cloudless sky.—Anon exclaimed our Host, — 786 *Excursion* 3. 10
Here did our pensive Host put forth his hand — 823 *Excursion* 5. 67
A morning salutation with my Host, — 834 *Excursion* 5. 802
From my good Host, that being crazed in brain — 839 *Excursion* 6. 108
Necessity, the stationary host — 843 *Excursion* 6. 325
To breathe in solitude, above the host — 885 *Excursion* 9. 72
And full assemblage of a barbarous host; — 894 *Excursion* 9. 707
Or is the painted staffs [? staff's] avenging host — L.1. 97 *Juvenal* 3. 85
Hostel. Hath need of rest; the sight of Hut or Hostel — 41 *Bord.* 215
Follow me to the Hostel. Marmaduke, — 66 *Bord.* 1626
Hostess. Kind Hostess! Handmaid also of the feast, — 525 *Epist. Beaumont* 250

Hour—*continued.*
Oh, speed the blessed hour, Almighty God! 520 *Pun. Death* 13. 14
What wonder at this hour of stillness deep, 524 *Epist. Beaumont* 183
Methinks that in my dying hour 530 †*Redbreast* 9
And to exalt the passing hour; 533 **Blest is* 25
Each at the appointed hour 535 *Egremont* 13
And at an hour which nobody could name. 535 *Egremont* 64
So—at an hour yet distant for *their* sakes 540 **Lady! a* 79
In many a cloudless hour! 542 *Russ. Fug.* 64
Advancing, you might guess an hour, 543 *Russ. Fug.* 137
The triumph of that hour. 545 *Russ. Fug.* 368
At any hour he chose, the prudent Knight 548 **Stranger! this* 11
Those holy Men both died in the same hour. 551 **If thou in* 27
And shall be beaten three times in an hour, 554 *Prioress* 91
And in the hour when I my death did meet 556 *Prioress* 207
With thy bright beams to guide me but one hour, 564 *Troilus* 125
Of threescore years, and to thy latest hour, 585 *Ch. Lamb* 60
Though nothing can bring back the hour 590 *Immortality* 181
In the roof'd bridge, at that despairing hour, 606 *Desc.Sk.Quarto* 209
'Tis storm; and hid in mist from hour to hour 608 *Desc.Sk.Quarto* 332
At such an hour there are who love to stray, 614 *Desc.Sk.Quarto* 664
At such an hour I heav'd the human sigh, 615 *Desc.Sk.Quarto* 702
Receives at supper hour her tempting hoard; 615 *Desc.Sk.Quarto* 737
Where Discord stalks dilating, every hour, 617 *Desc.Sk.Quarto* 800
The wretch, the short-lived vision of an hour; 619 *School Ex.* 96
And bright will shine in misery's midnight hour; 619 **She wept* 10
Deluded Hope for one short hour 620 *Birth of Love* 39
Upon this hour, the bond to celebrate!" 625 *Æneid* 115
Even with the chance equipment of that hour, 633 *Prelude* 1. 92
Baffled and plagued by a mind that every hour 636 *Prelude* 1. 257
—Unfading recollections! at this hour 639 *Prelude* 1. 491
Yet, to this hour, the spot to me is dear 644 *Prelude* 2. 154
In many a thoughtless hour, when, from excess 645 *Prelude* 2. 186
Who knows the individual hour in which 645 *Prelude* 2. 206
When every hour brings palpable access 646 *Prelude* 2. 286
A feeling that I was not for that hour, 650 *Prelude* 3. 81
Before that hour, or since. Then, forth I ran 653 *Prelude* 3. 302
Ye will forgive the weakness of that hour, 653 *Prelude* 3. 319
A sober hour, not winning or serene, 660 *Prelude* 4. 144
The memory of one particular hour 663 *Prelude* 4. 308
To a late hour), and spirits overwrought 664 *Prelude* 4. 376
A long half hour together I have stood 671 *Prelude* 5. 396
But so it is, and, in that dubious hour, 673 *Prelude* 5. 512
The floors of those dim cloisters, till that hour, 682 *Prelude* 6. 476
Did sweeten many a meditative hour. 683 *Prelude* 6. 556
Through fond ambition of that hour, I strove 685 *Prelude* 6. 671
Like an uneasy snake. From hour to hour 685 *Prelude* 6. 707
After the hour of sunset yester-even, 687 *Prelude* 7. 19
For his own fancies, or to dance by the hour, 703 *Prelude* 8. 286
His hour being not yet come. Far less had then 704 *Prelude* 8. 356
Unhealthy and vexatious. With the hour, 712 *Prelude* 9. 153
In his own body. 'Twas in truth an hour 712 *Prelude* 9. 161
'Tis true, had gone before this hour, dire work 718 *Prelude* 10. 42
Change and subversion from that hour. No shock 722 *Prelude* 10. 268
The illustrious wife of Roland, in the hour 723 *Prelude* 10. 381
Of those atrocities, the hour of sleep 724 *Prelude* 10. 400
Their dread vibration to this hour prolonged? 725 *Prelude* 10. 460
Said matins at the hour that suited those 726 *Prelude* 10. 560
In a calm hour to kiss the pebbly shore, 734 *Prelude* 12. 22
The grass is cleared away, and to this hour 738 *Prelude* 12. 244
Or animate an hour of vacant ease. 739 *Prelude* 12. 335
Thus might we wear a midnight hour away, 746 *Prelude* 14. 32
Heard over earth and sea, and, in that hour, 747 *Prelude* 14. 61
—I, long before the blissful hour arrives, 755 *Recluse* 1. 1. 809
To finer distance. Mine was at that hour 756 *Excursion* 1. 17
Of boyhood, many an hour in caves forlorn, 758 *Excursion* 1. 154
Whose echo rings through Scotland to this hour! 759 *Excursion* 1. 176
In such access of mind, in such high hour 759 *Excursion* 1. 211
The hour of accident or crippling age, 764 *Excursion* 1. 555
He said, "'Tis now the hour of deepest noon. 765 *Excursion* 1. 593
This hour when all things which are not at rest 765 *Excursion* 1. 595
And dragged them to the earth. Ere this an hour 767 *Excursion* 1. 730
Admonished thus, the sweet hour coming on. 771 *Excursion* 1. 961
Not one hour merely, but till evening's close, 773 *Excursion* 2. 142
You will receive, before the hour of noon, 774 *Excursion* 2. 157
This simple Child will mourn his one short hour, 780 *Excursion* 2. 601
And, in the grim and breathless hour of noon, 782 *Excursion* 2. 706
Thought I, if master of a vacant hour, 787 *Excursion* 3. 44
Hopeless, and still more hopeless every hour; 797 *Excursion* 3. 789
And invitation every hour renewed, 806 *Excursion* 4. 377
With the loud streams: and often, at the hour 819 *Excursion* 4. 1175
We must not part at this inviting hour." 823 *Excursion* 5. 72
Until the expected hour at which her Mate 833 *Excursion* 5. 713
Detains him after his accustomed hour 834 *Excursion* 5. 765
In the transition of that bitter hour! 840 *Excursion* 6. 133
In the prime hour of sweetest scents and airs. 850 *Excursion* 6. 823
And greets it with thanksgiving. 'Till this hour,' 852 *Excursion* 6. 916
(The hour of life to which he then was brought) 859 *Excursion* 7. 113
His own appointed hour will come at last; 867 *Excursion* 7. 629
"Oft have I marked him, at some leisure hour, 869 *Excursion* 7. 782
A soldier's honours. At his funeral hour 871 *Excursion* 7. 875
Like wild beasts without home! Their hour was come; 873 *Excursion* 7. 1027
And at the appointed hour a bell is heard, 877 *Excursion* 8. 170
To-morrow—nay perchance this very hour 884 *Excursion* 9. 27
Shall be—divested at the appointed hour 893 *Excursion* 9. 632
Might almost think, at this affecting hour, 895 *Excursion* 9. 716
With wreaths that have not faded to this hour, S.3. 436 **The doubt* 150
More than one thought of death, and his last hour. K.8. 229 **I will* 158
Hath now escaped his memory—but the hour, K.8. 236 *Recluse* 1. 1. 3

Hour—*continued.*
Who finds at last an hour to his content K.8. 254 *Recluse* 1. 1. 656
Yea to this hour I cannot read a tale K.8. 256 *Recluse* 1. 1. 721
So patient Senates quibble by the hour L.1. 94 *Juvenal* 2. 1
'Tis come, the final hour, L.2. 121 *Frag. Æneid* 2. 1

Hourly. He spake of plants that hourly change 193 *Ruth* 55
Man holds with week-day man in the hourly walk 304 **I grieved* 11
That hourly speaks within us? 386 *Yarrow Rev.* 88
Hourly exposed to death, with famine worn, 430 *Ecc. Sonn.* 2. 6. 11
Hourly the democratic torrent swells; 477 **Lowther! in* 9
Retirement then might hourly look 499 *Memory* 21
Whereof her hourly bearing proof doth give; 562 *Cuck.and Night.* 296
We had been followed, hourly watched, and noosed, 669 *Prelude* 5. 238
Of conquest over sense, hourly achieved 682 *Prelude* 6. 458
An hourly neighbour. Paradise, and groves 755 *Recluse* 1. 1. 800
Of doubt and bold denial hourly urged 812 *Excursion* 4. 734
Heart-stirring music! hourly heard that name; 867 *Excursion* 7. 671

Hour's. *See* **Half-hour's.**
Does the hour's drowsy weight his glee restrain? 279 **'Tis he* 4
For one hour's perfect bliss, to tread the grass 306 **Here, on our* 12
'Twas but a short hour's walk, ere veering round 658 *Prelude* 4. 20

Hours. *See* **Summer-hours.**
Where silent Hours their death-like sway extend, 16 *Desc. Sk.* 311
Whole hours, with idle arms in moping sorrow knit. 32 *Guilt* 432
How would you like to travel on whole hours 45 *Bord.* 432
About your own; but for these two hours past 61 *Bord.* 1284
She weeps, she weeps—*my* brain shall burn for hours 66 *Bord.* 1612
The first hours of last night were rough with storm: 73 *Bord.* 2043
In joy I met thee, but a few hours past; 75 *Bord.* 2133
Thy hours as they flow on are spent, if not in joy in peace. 92 *Poet's Dream* 56
Along the cloudless Main, he, in those hours 96 *Brothers* 53
Hath been so friendly to industrious hours; 107 *Farewell* 58
Here on his hours he hung as on a book, 107 *Indolence* 5
Nor lacked his calmer hours device or toy. 108 *Indolence* 50
To store up kindred hours for me, thy face 111 **'Tis said that some* 49
And intercourse with mortal hours 112 **How rich* 5
Surviving comrade of uncounted hours, 133 *Michael* 118
Making the cottage through the silent hours 133 *Michael* 127
Nor Her who thinking of me there counts widowed hours." 140 *Arm. Lady* 54
Nor from this vestige of thy musing hours 151 **When, to* 85
Did only softly-stealing hours 154 *Flower Garden* 5
And in the sultry summer hours 155 *Waterfall* 35
Children of the flaring hours! 160 **Pansies, lilies* 50
Hours of perfect gladsomeness. 171 *Kitten* 116
Of visionary hours. 183 **O blithe* 12
—Twelve hours, twelve bounteous hours are gone, while I 192 *Gipsies* 9
Yet sometimes milder hours she knew, 194 *Ruth* 199
"For thirteen hours he ran a desperate race; 203 *Hart-leap* 145
In hours of weariness, sensations sweet, 206 *Tintern* 27
The hours are past—too brief had they been years; 211 *Laod.* 153
Comes Faith that in auspicious hours 225 *Present.* 20
But a few hours ago, had been 246 *P. B.* 879
The winds that will be howling at all hours, 259 **The world is* 6
I gave this paradise for winter hours, 264 **Lady! the* 7
Expand, enjoying through their vernal hours 270 **Ye sacred* 3
And call a train of laughing Hours; 293 *Jedbor.* 2
—Hours, Days, and Months, *have* borne them in the sight 327 *Ode 1815* 11
Lone vigils through the hours of sleep, 338 **Meek Virgin* 4
Reflected through the mists of age, from hours 354 *Aquap.* 112
We made a day of happy hours, 385 *Yarrow Rev.* 23
Of the good Priest: who, faithful through all hours 387 *Manse* 10
For joy its sunny hours were free to give 392 *Bothwell* 10
'Tis a work for sabbath hours 397 *White Doe* 73
Telling melancholy hours! 402 *White Doe* 596
Revived a memory of those hours 407 *White Doe* 1026
To meet the coming hours of festal mirth, 445 *Ecc. Sonn.* 3. 20. 10
Who thus could build. Be mine, in hours of fear 451 *Ecc. Sonn.* 3. 45. 2
In hours of peace, or when the storm is driven 452 *Ecc. Sonn.* 3. 46. 7
To cheer the long dark hours of vacant night— 460 **Wanderer! that* 69
Depress the hours. Up, Spirit of the storm! 466 *St. Bees* 14
"Shine so, my aged brow, at all hours of the day!" 470 *Bala-Sala* 14
Unhurt, the assault of Time with all his hours, 474 **Hope smiled* 13
To trouble hours that winged their way, 478 *Somnamb.* 34
On woman's quiet hours; 478 *Somnamb.* 51
We two have known such happy hours together 498 **Enough of climbing* 46
That serves the steadfast hours, 499 **This Lawn* 15
Nought equals when the hours are winged with crime) 505 *Warning* 152
Though these dull hours (mine is it, or their shame?) 521 *Epist.Beaumont* 36
Filled with delight three summer morning hours. 525 *Epist. Beaumont* 269
Let easy mirth his social hours inspire, 528 **Those breathing* 96
The sweet illusion might have hung, for hours. 530 *Gleaner* 25
For seasons and for hours. 541 *Russ. Fug.* 8
Were shaped to cheer dark winter's lonely hours. 546 **Oft is* 16
I should have died, yea many hours ago; 556 *Prioress* 200
Where proud Covent-garden, in desolate hours 570 *Farmer* 73
Here did he sit confined for hours; 577 **I come* 16
He then would steal at leisure hours 579 **Sweet Flower* 26
And when the precious hours of leisure came, 584 *Ch. Lamb* 11
Of active days urged on by flying hours,— 632 *Prelude* 1. 42
Two hours declined towards the west; a day 633 *Prelude* 1. 67
And ask no record of the hours, resigned 635 *Prelude* 1. 252

House—continued.

Home to her mother's house. The Youth was fled ;   853 *Excursion 6.* 1005
With the neglected house to which she clung.   854 *Excursion 6.* 1061
And the whole house seems filled with gaiety.   856 *Excursion 6.* 1187
Passed on ;—the inside of that rugged house .   860 *Excursion 7.* 170
And the long-privileged house left empty—swept   861 *Excursion 7.* 251
That pressed upon his brother's house ; for books   864 *Excursion 7.* 439
That falls and disappears, the house is gone ; .   872 *Excursion 7.* 958
And old religious house—pile after pile ; .   873 *Excursion 7.* 1025
In token that the House was evermore   877 *Excursion 8.* 190
The Pastor's mansion with the house of prayer.   881 *Excursion 8.* 458
—Now was there bustle in the Vicar's house .   890 *Excursion 9.* 432
Of house and field,—to plenty, peace, and love.   S.3.426 **Through Cumbrian* 8

Deeply, a stranger of our father's house, . . .   K.8. 254 *Recluse* 1.1.654
House-affairs. Pertaining to her house-affairs, appeared   768 *Excursion* 1. 796
House-clock. The old house-clock is decked with a new face ;   97 *Brothers* 160
All day the house-clock ticking in mine ear, . .   834 *Excursion 5.* 814
Housed. *See* **Pent-housed.**
Housed for the night, or but a half-hour's guest..   21 *Desc. Sk.* 611
I hope Idonea is well housed. That horseman.   50 *Bord.* 734
Housed near the growing Primrose-tuft   169 *Wren's Nest* 71
Will, among us warm-clad and warmly housed, .   172 *Infant Daughter* 30
Are impatient to be housed :   181 *Waggoner 4.* 96
And in a prison housed ; .   194 *Ruth* 195
Housed near a blazing fire—is seen to flit .   422 *Ecc. Sonn.* 1. 16. 3
That when his fate had housed him 'mid a throng   531 **I know* 23
But she, poor Woman ! housed alone.   536 *Goody Blake* 36
Housed, in a dream, at distance from the Kind !   579 *Peele Castle* 54
The glittering rabble housed to . . . and swear   L.1. 97 *Juvenal* 3. 83
House-dog. Our watchful house-dog, that would tease and tire   28 *Guilt* 223
The cricket chirped, the house-dog dozed, .   542 *Russ. Fug.* 37
House-dog's. To charm the surly house-dog's faithful o'er,   32 *Guilt* 417
Household. Each with its household boat beside the door ;   12 *Desc. Sk.* 112
Made all their household. I may truly say, . .   132 *Michael* 93
While in this sort the simple household lived .   134 *Michael* 207
Of your fair household, Father-knight,   161 *Binnorie* 30
Her household motions light and free, .   186 **She was* 13
And build a household fire, and find   193 *Ruth* 77
Save from the trickling household rill ;   247 *P. B.* 998
To household virtues. Venerable Art,   255 *S. H.* 9
But, long as cock shall crow from household perch   274 **Not the* 12
Unrecognised through many a household tear   276 *Author's Portrait* 10
Wansfell ! this Household has a favoured lot, .   281 **Wansfell ! this* 1
And these grey rocks ; that household lawn ; .   288 *Highland Girl* 5
And pure religion breathing household laws.   307 **O Friend* 14
On the tired household of corporeal sense, .   323 *Ode 1814* 2
In honour of each household name,   375 **The Minstrels* 16
Laugh with the generous household heartily .   379 *Duddon* 13. 13
But of the lights that cherish household cares .   426 *Ecc. Sonn.* 1. 31. 4
For summer wandering quit their household bowers ;   463 **Adieu, Rydalian*

The household hearts that were his own ; . .   487 *Fountain* 51
Old household thoughts, in which thou hadst thy share ;   491 *Tribute : Dog* 24
A household small and sensitive,—whose love,   510 **Among a* 29
But the whole household, that our coming wait. .   525 *Epist. Beaumont* 235

All are daunted, all the household   536 *Egremont* 91
The household floor to tread.   545 *Russ. Fug.* 360
Of his own Household : nor, while from his bed .   547 **Rude is* 26
Each with his household boat beside the door,   604 *Desc.Sk.Quarto* 127
And fume the household deities with store   624 *Æneid* 65
A stripling, scarcely of the household then .   680 *Prelude 6.* 766
Familiarly, a household term, like those, .   694 *Prelude 7.* 496
A virtuous household, though exceeding poor !   758 *Excursion* 1. 112
The fowl domestic, and the household dog—   772 *Excursion* 2. 45
That skill in this or other household work, .   856 *Excursion 6.* 1183
With store of household goods, in panniers slung.   858 *Excursion 7.* 64
Though simply, from their little household farm ;   860 *Excursion 7.* 163
Among the mountain coves. Yon household fir,.   866 *Excursion 7.* 612
The household lost their pride and soul's delight.   868 *Excursion 7.* 686
Of household occupation ; no nice arts .   878 *Excursion 8.* 271
Round which the Shepherd and his household sate   K.8. 228 **I will* 111
Of winter's household, they keep festival .   K.8. 241 *Recluse* 1.1.195
One household under God for high and low, .   K.8. 253 *Recluse* 1.1.618
Housekeeping. Smooth housekeeping within, and all without   649 *Prelude 3.* 44
Houseless. Besoiled with mire, and let the houseless snail   61 *Bord.* 1311
Of hardship and distressful fear, amid the houseless waste   91 *Norman Boy* 27
Of vagrant dwellers in the houseless woods, .   206 *Tintern* 20
A mute procession on the houseless road ; .   780 *Excursion* 2. 563
And Grisdale's houseless vale, along the brink   K.8. 225 **I will* 30
That ranging o'er the high and houseless ground .   K.8. 247 *Recluse* 1.1.393
Houses. *See* **Baby-houses.**
At houses, men, and common light, amazed. .   31 *Guilt* 401
Lawns, houses, chattels, groves, and fields, .   214 *Kirkstone* 27
Where'er a knot of houses lay .   239 *P. B.* 233
Dear God ! the very houses seem asleep ; .   269 *Westm. Bridge* 13
Fair houses, baths, and banquets delicate, .   420 *Ecc. Sonn.* 1. 8. 3
O house of houses, once so richly dight ! .   563 *Troilus* 23
O, of all houses once the crowned boast ! .   563 *Troilus* 29
Here, fronts of houses, like a title-page, .   689 *Prelude 7.* 160
Of houses, pavement, streets, of men and things,—   707 *Prelude 8.* 546

Houses—continued.

Of peaceful houses with unquiet sounds. . .   712 *Prelude 9.* 165
Among the lonely houses : .   S.3. 423 *Tinker* 8
House-top. The Sparrow so on the house-top, and I,   65 *Bord.* 1517
Upon the house-top, glittering bright,   86 *Anecdote* 51
Housewife. The housewife there a brighter garden sees,   21 *Desc. Sk.* 606
Kindly the housewife pressed, and they in comfort fed.   34 *Guilt* 531
Fervently cried the housewife—" God be praised,   34 *Guilt* 565
Of day grew dim the Housewife hung a lamp ; .   133 *Michael* 114
The Housewife plied her own peculiar work, .   133 *Michael* 126
With a light heart. The Housewife for five days   135 *Michael* 284
The Housewife answered, talking much of things   136 *Michael* 318
Which, as the Housewife phrased it, were throughout   138 *Michael* 434
At early morn the careful housewife, led .   615 *Desc.Sk.Quarto* 728
The Housewife, tempted by such slender gains .   783 *Excursion 2.* 741
Our housewife knew full well what she possessed !   783 *Excursion 2.* 763
Great show of joy the housewife made, and truly   785 *Excursion 2.* 887
Housewife's. Wool for the Housewife's spindle, or repair   132 *Michael* 107
" Those pleasing works the Housewife's skill produced :   860 *Excursion 7.* 192
Housing. Housing, with God's good help, by choice or chance :   196 *Resolution* 104
Housings. With broidered housings. And the lofty Steed—   872 *Excursion 7.* 946
Hovel. Or hovel from the storm to shield his head,   25 *Guilt* 42
Hovels. In tattered garb, from hovels where abides   843 *Excursion 6.* 324
And tottering hovels, whence do issue forth   879 *Excursion 8.* 347
Hover. Yet seeming still to hover ;   159 *Green Linnet* 28
Yet shall my blessing hover o'er thee still, .   275 *Rotha Q.* 7
Yield to the lure of vain regret, and hover .   354 *Aquap.* 86
Hovered. Hovered in air above the far-famed Spot.   334 **A wingèd* 5
Of holy Angels round her hovered :   372 *Eg. Maid* 230
When Inspiration hovered o'er this ground, .   546 **The embowering* 16
Hovered above our destiny on earth : .   826 *Excursion 5.* 247
Hovering. Or hovering over wastes too bleak to rear   15 *Desc. Sk.* 256
And, hovering, round it often did a raven fly.   25 *Guilt* 81
Hovering round Herbert's door, a man whose figure   42 *Bord.* 278
Of sea-fowl, conscious both that they are hovering   122 *V. and J.* 26
Sweet thoughts of angels hovering nigh, .   144 **Driven in* 43
Hovering until the petals stay   227 *Vernal Ode* 112
While hovering o'er the moonlight vale.   235 *Power of Sound* 168
Hovering around with dolorous moan !   243 *P. B.* 650
Swift insects shine, thy hovering pursuivants :   268 **Pure element* 6
Thy hovering Shade, O venerable Bede ! .   424 *Ecc. Sonn.* 1. 23. 4
Black Demons hovering o'er his mitred head,.   428 *Ecc. Sonn.* 1. 38. 1
The Dog, which still was hovering nigh, .   492 *Fidelity* 54
Angels hovering round thy couch, .   502 **Like a* 51
In act, as hovering Angels when they spread .   518 *Pun. Death* 6. 4
And some the hovering clouds, our telegraph, declare. .   522 *Epist.Beaumont* 84
And gorgeous insect hovering in the air, .   772 *Excursion* 2. 44
Hovering above these inland solitudes, .   808 *Excursion* 4. 452
Hoverings. And a last game of mazy hoverings   455 *Rydal Mere* 10
Hovers. Transported, my soothed spirit hovers o'er   585 *Ch. Lamb* 53
How. (*Partial list.*) *See* **Silver-how.**
True ; and, remembering how the Band have proved   37 *Bord.* 11
How wilt thou stand alone ? Is he not strong ? .   40 *Bord.* 160
Dear Father ! how could I forget and live ?— .   40 *Bord.* 176
I found how my domains had been usurped, .   40 *Bord.* 193
And the blind Man was told how you had rescued   42 *Bord.* 285
It struck upon my heart I know not how. .   44 *Bord.* 377
Than twenty armies. How ? The old blind Man,   51 *Bord.* 760
But how, what say you, Oswald ? Stab him, were it   57 *Bord.* 1069
Idonea ! How ! what ? your Idonea ? .   57 *Bord.* 1102
Person, and place—the where, the when, the how,   58 *Bord.* 1155
How you would be disturbed by this dire news, .   59 *Bord.* 1208
To the top of GREAT HOW did it please them to climb :   86 *Rural Arch.* 4
With how sad steps, O Moon, thou climb'st the sky,   266 **With how* 1
" How silently, and with how wan a face ! " .   266 **With how* 2
Its murmur how soft ! as it falls down the steep,   364 *Vallomb.* 5
" O Lord, our Lord ! how wondrously," (quoth she)   552 *Prioress* 1
How mighty and how great a Lord is he ! .   556 *Cuck. and Night.* 2
How among them it was a common tale, .   557 *Cuck.and Night.* 48
How she and I did each the other chide, .   561 *Cuck.and Night.* 267
How shut was every window of the place, .   562 *Troilus* 16
How fleeting and how frail is human life ! .   575 *Chiabrera* 6. 16
Howard's. From Naworth come ; and Howard's aid   405 *White Doe* 801
For promise fails of Howard's aid ; .   408 *White Doe* 1134
Howe'er. *See* **However.**
Howe'er disguised in its own majesty, .   23 *Yew-tree* 51
Howe'er magnificent or fair, .   227 *Vernal Ode* 53
On hearts howe'er insensible or rude ; .   329 *Ode : Thanks.* 3
Howe'er momentous in itself it be, .   518 *Pun. Death* 5. 2
To thousands, share not Thou ; howe'er bereft,   531 *Octogen.* 7
Once I could hail (howe'er serene the sky)   532 **Once I* 1
Which man is born to—sink, howe'er depressed, .   567 *Cumb. Beg.* 82
Howe'er attractive, Fellow voyager ! .   717 *Prelude 9.* 563
Howe'er to airy Demons suitable. .   799 *Excursion 3.* 909
That the procession of our fate, howe'er .   801 *Excursion 4.* 13
" An active Principle :—howe'er removed .   884 *Excursion 9.* 3
However. (*Partial list.*) *See* **Howe'er.**
However stern, is powerless to exclude. .   15 *Desc. Sk.* 249
Me and all worldly harms and wrongs however keen."   35 *Guilt* 612

However—*continued.*
However trivial, if you thence be taught 147 *Joanna* 15
Nor will I praise a cloud, however bright, 263 **Those words* 7
However hardly won or justly dear: 442 *Ecc. Sonn.* 3. 10.12
However bright and fair. 507 *May* 72
On any earthly hope, however pure! 581 *John Words.* 70
However proud and strong. 583 **O for a* 36
However multitudinous, to move 698 *Prelude* 7. 760
Service however dangerous. I revolved, 720 *Prelude* 10. 154
Thus wrongfully of verse, however rude, 745 *Prelude* 13. 363
However destitute, be left to droop 888 *Excursion* 9. 304
However gently, toward the vulgar air, S.3. 434 **The doubt* 57
Howl. And at long intervals the mill-dog's howl; 9 *Ev. Wk.* 376
And he shall howl and I will laugh, a medley 60 *Bord.* 1250
And we shall howl together. I am deserted 74 *Bord.* 2090
Nor leaping torrents when they howl 145 *Her Eyes* 46
List, Cuckoo—Cuckoo!—oft tho' tempests howl, 229 *Cuckoo-clock* 12
And shivering wolves, surprised with darkness, howl 264 *Storm* 8
He dwells, and hears indignant tempests howl, 472 *Dunolly Eagle* 6
That howl so dismally for him who treads 702 *Prelude* 8. 221
Howl from the north, what kindly warmth, methought, 881 *Excursion* 8. 446
Howling. Ran mountains high before the howling blast, 29 *Guilt* 291
To keep at bay the howling blast, 144 **Driven in* 66
The winds that will be howling at all hours, 259 **The world is* 6
The death-dog, howling loud and long, below; 606 *Desc.Sk.Quarto* 226
Howling in troops ong the Bothnic Main. 640 *Prelude* 1. 543
Frequented, and beset with howling winds. 859 *Excursion* 7. 144
Howlings. In fainter howlings told its *rage* was spent: 27 *Guilt* 192
Howls. Howls near and nearer yet the famished wolf. 14 *Desc. Sk.* 195
It is a dismal night—how the wind howls! 69 *Bord.* 1765
Ascending, nearer howls the famish'd wolf, 606 *Desc.Sk.Quarto* 240
While the jail-mastiff howls at the dull clanking chain, 621 *Convict* 37
How's. But how's the day?—I fear, my little Boy, 46 *Bord.* 494
Hows. Or where 'mid "lonely heights and hows," 287 *Sons of Burns* 31
Howsoe'er. *See* **Howsoever.**
Nor shall your presence, howsoe'er it mar 477 *Steamboats* 4
In truth, the degradation—howsoe'er 737 *Prelude* 12. 193
May have sustained, that, howsoe'er misled, 748 *Prelude* 14. 149
A human creature, howsoe'er endowed, 750 *Prelude* 14. 291
Which bears the name of action, howsoe'er 799 *Excursion* 3. 894
Howsoever. *See* **Howsoe'er.**
Howsoever mean it be, 160 **Pansies, lilies* 47
And howsoever; were it otherwise, 703 *Prelude* 8. 308
Hubbub. Now homeward through the thickening hubbub, where 690 *Prelude* 7. 211
To Hawkers and Haranguers, hubbub wild! 710 *Prelude* 9. 58
Hubert. And to Hubert thus said he, 535 *Egremont* 18
Hubert, if alive that day; 535 *Egremont* 30
"Fear not," quickly answered Hubert; 535 *Egremont* 33
"Sir!" the Ruffians said to Hubert, 535 *Egremont* 49
Pale and trembling Hubert stood. 535 *Egremont* 52
To his Castle Hubert sped; 535 *Egremont* 61
But bold Hubert lives in glee: 536 *Egremont* 69
Hubert! though the blast be blown 536 *Egremont* 85
Speak!—astounded Hubert cannot; 536 *Egremont* 89
Thus Hubert thought in his dismay, 536 *Egremont* 95
Huckster's. And watched her table with its huckster's wares 642 *Prelude* 2. 45
Huddle. That fear is like a cloak which old men huddle 38 *Bord.* 22
Huddling. Then, while I wandered where the huddling rill 3 *Ev. Wk.* 53
Huddling together from two fears—the fear 150 **When, to* 31
—Then Quiet led me up the huddling rill, 592 *Ev. Wk. Quarto* 71
Hue. The spacious landscape change in form and hue! 4 *Ev. Wk.* 99
To the green corn of summer, autumn's hue. 8 *Ev. Wk.* 338
Upon her cheek, to which its youthful hue 30 *Guilt* 320
'Tis all thine own!—and if its hue 145 *Her Eyes* 63
Veil of such celestial hue; 181 *Waggoner* 4. 113
Hurrying the pallid hue away 181 *Waggoner* 4. 152
Upon whose grassless floor of red-brown hue, 185 *Yew-trees* 21
Are clad in one green hue, and lose themselves 206 *Tintern* 13
Upon those roseate lips a Stygian hue. 210 *Laod.* 66
That flowers themselves, whate'er their hue, 222 *Triad* 204
Imaged, though faintly, in the hue 226 *Vernal Ode* 30
A scene of soft and lovely hue! 240 *P. B.* 362
As lightly, though of altered hue, 343 *Eclipse* 15
Like moonshine—but the hue was green; 343 *Eclipse* 26
Heard them, unchecked by aught of saddening hue, 367 **If with* 12
Drawing an ebon car, their hue 371 *Eg. Maid* 179
Suffused with blushes of celestial hue, 434 *Ecc. Sonn.* 2. 22. 6
A St. Helena next—in shape and hue, 471 **Arran! a* 2
In such diversity of hue 486 *Matthew* 7
Unscared by thronging fancies of strange hue 523 *Epist. Beaumont* 146
Of hue and altering shape that charmed all eyes. 527 **Those breathing* 20
And veins of violet hue; 541 *Russ. Fug.* 4
So piteously, and with so dead a hue, 563 *Troilus* 41
Stiff in its members, withered, changed of hue." 571 **There is a Flower* 19
Pale was her hue; yet mortal cheek 583 **O for a* 31
And hue far deeper than the Tyrian dye; 618 *School Ex.* 22
Varying their composition and their hue, 750 *Prelude* 14. 326
A golden hue, delicate as their own 782 *Excursion* 2. 680
Suffused with something of a feminine hue; 834 *Excursion* 5. 782

Hue—*continued.*
A more than natural vividness of hue 881 *Excursion* 8. 472
From land and water; lilies of each hue— 892 *Excursion* 9. 539
Hue-and-cry. As ever hue-and-cry pursued, 239 *P. B.* 274
Hues. Before us, tinged with evening hues, 9 *Lines: Boat* 2
More high, the snowy peaks with hues of rose. 17 *Desc. Sk.* 406
Flashed round him images and hues that wrought 96 *Brothers* 57
Hues more exalted, "a refinèd Form," 110 **Look at* 22
The steps of June; as if their various hues 146 **It was an* 10
That intermixture of delicious hues, 147 *Joanna* 47
Her plumy mantle's living hues, 165 *Parrot* 9
Stones of all hues, gem emulous of gem, 190 **Lyre! though* 35
With hues of genius on his cheek 192 *Ruth* 31
Of intermingling hues; 193 *Ruth* 57
Hues doubtfully begun and ended; 231 **The gentlest Poet* 20
While here sits One whose brightness owes its hues 252 **Her only* 12
The fairest, brightest, hues of ether fade; 252 **The fairest* 1
Or pencil pregnant with ethereal hues,) 260 **High is* 3
As if its hues were of the passing year, 275 **While poring* 7
Their hues to sunset. If with raptured eye 277 **The most* 3
Reflect, in glowing hues that shall not fade, 324 *Ode 1814* 95
As on a mirror that gives back the hues 333 *Ded. Tour* 4
O gentle Power of darkness! these mild hues; 334 **Bruges I* 11
Hues ever fresh, in rocky fortress blowing: 337 *Aar* 8
Hung round its top, on wings that changed their hues at will. 338 *Engelberg* 9
On pictures to gaze where they drank in their hues; 345 *Stanzas: Simplon* 7
Your glories mingled with the brightest hues 357 *Aquap.* 294
'Mid evening hues, along the horizon line, 358 *Pine: Rome* 4
Reddened the fiery hues, and shot 385 *Yarrow Rev.* 15
From roseate hues, far kenned at morn and even, 452 *Ecc. Sonn.* 3. 46. 6
Whate'er it strikes with gem-like hues! 457 **Had this* 28
Such hues from their celestial Urn 458 **Had this* 61
When with more hues than in the rainbow dwell 475 **Homeward we* 8
And clothes in brighter hues; 499 *Memory* 12
Where Christian Martyrs stand in hues portrayed, 500 *Humanity* 21
Refract in rainbow hues the restless fires! 609 *Desc.Sk. Quarto* 391
This wily interchange of snaky hues, 657 *Prelude* 3. 563
Into each other their obsequious hues, 700 *Prelude* 8. 89
Might tend to wean him. Therefore with her hues, 760 *Excursion* 1. 267
Varies its rainbow hues. But vainly thus, 760 *Excursion* 1. 298
But tinctured daintily with florid hues, 860 *Excursion* 7. 187
How pure his spirit! in what vivid hues 891 *Excursion* 9. 462
With prodigal communion, the bright hues 893 *Excursion* 9. 604
Hug. They hug the infant in my arms, 81 †*Mother's Return* 27
Huge. Huge convent domes with pinnacles and towers, 14 *Desc. Sk.* 224
Where huge rocks tremble to the bellowing herd. 17 *Desc. Sk.* 379
And vacant, a huge waste around him spread; 25 *Guilt* 44
Right in the slates, and with a huge rattle 81 †*Address: Child* 30
By those huge rocks encompassed round. 85 *Shepherd-boys* 88
Forth from his eyes, when first the Boy looked down on that huge oak, 92 *Poet's Dream* 34
Companions for each other: the huge crag 97 *Brothers* 143
With huge and black projection overbrowed 133 *Michael* 112
And your huge burthen, safe from harm, 175 *Waggoner* 1. 134
Majestically huge and slow: 182 *Waggoner* 4. 229
Huge trunks! and each particular trunk a growth 185 *Yew-trees* 16
With a huge wallet o'er my shoulders slung, 185 *Nutting* 6
As a huge stone is sometimes seen to lie 196 *Resolution* 57
There's something in a huge balloon; 236 *P. B.* 2
So huge hath been my wickedness!" 244 *P. B.* 710
And a huge mass, to bury or to hide, 265 **The Shepherd* 11
Huge Ocean shows, within his yellow strand, 266 **The stars* 4
From what huge height, descending? Can such force 272 *Devil's Bridge* 2
Huge Criffel's hoary top ascends 285 *Grave of Burns* 39
Huge Cruachan, (a thing that meaner hills 290 *Kilchurn* 14
That host, as huge and strong as e'er defied 321 **Humanity, delighting* 17
That Roland clove with huge two-handed sway, 335 *Aix* 12
There, combats a huge crocodile—agape 348 *Sky-prosp.* 5
Forth from the towers of that huge Pile, wherein 365 **The Baptist* 2
Breasts the sea-flashes, and huge waves 370 *Eg. Maid* 47
Where stalked the huge deer to his shaggy lair 376 *Duddon* 2. 11
The forest huge of ancient Caledon 392 *Inglewood* 1
To his huge trunk, or, with more subtle art, 393 *Hart's-horn* 2
So huge a host!)—to tear from the Unbeliever 427 *Ecc. Sonn.* 1. 34. 13
Greta, what fearful listening! when huge stones 464 **Greta, what* 1
It was a cove, a huge recess, 491 *Fidelity* 17
While, day by day, grim neighbour! huge Black Comb 521 *Epist. Beaumont* 5
Of this huge Eminence,—from blackness named, 548 **Stay, bold* 4
Built at the foot of a huge hill, that they 566 *Cumb. Beg.* 4
From huge Pelorus to the Atlantic pillars, 574 *Chiabrera* 4. 15
And this huge Castle, standing here sublime, 579 *Peele Castle* 49
Huge Pikes of Darkness named, of Fear and Storms, 612 *Desc.Sk.Quarto* 564
Huge goblets are brought forth; they crown the wine; 625 *Æneid* 98
The horizon's bound, a huge peak, black and huge, 637 *Prelude* 1. 378
But huge and mighty forms, that do not live 638 *Prelude* 1. 398
Of the huge city, on the leaded roof 679 *Prelude* 6. 267
Of the huge town's first presence, and had paced 688 *Prelude* 7. 67
With letters huge inscribed from top to toe, 689 *Prelude* 7. 161
That huge fermenting mass of human-kind 696 *Prelude* 7. 621
Is thronged with staring pictures and huge scrolls, 697 *Prelude* 7. 692
Hath passed with torches into some huge cave, 707 *Prelude* 8. 561
Of that huge city, oftentimes was seen 709 *Prelude* 8. 666
The Arcades I traversed, in the Palace huge 710 *Prelude* 9. 52
The width of those huge forests, unto me 716 *Prelude* 9. 462

Huge—*continued.*
Of some huge cave, whose rocky ceiling casts . 756 *Excursion* 1. 11
With a tumultuous waste of huge hill tops . . 776 *Excursion* 2. 325
To glance an upward look on two huge Peaks, . 782 *Excursion* 2. 692
Of temple, palace, citadel, and huge . 784 *Excursion* 2. 858
Not less than that huge Pile (from some abyss . 788 *Excursion* 3. 143
Of some huge hill, expectant, I beheld . . . . 803 *Excursion* 4. 113
From yon huge breast of rock, a voice sent forth 807 *Excursion* 4. 403
Within the circuit of this fabric huge, ... 819 *Excursion* 4. 1177
Who trembled, trunk and limbs, like some huge oak 840 *Excursion* 6. 144
On Cader Idris, or huge Penmanmaur) . . . 857 *Excursion* 7. 8
Vales deeper far than these of ours, huge woods, . 869 *Excursion* 7. 802
Here a huge town, continuous and compact, . . 876 *Excursion* 8. 120
Breaks from a many-windowed fabric huge ; . . 877 *Excursion* 8. 169
The huge round chimneys, harbour of delight . 881 *Excursion* 8. 481
By rocks impassable and mountains huge. . . 892 *Excursion* 9. 579
Huge skeletons of crags which from the coast K.8. 225 **I will* 32
Hugging. Hurrah for —— [Grote], hugging his Ballot-box ! . . . . 513 **Said Secrecy* 14
Huguenots. The blood of Huguenots through Paris streamed. . . . . 439 *Ecc. Sonn.* 2. 42.14
Hulk. The unluckiest hulk that stems the brine . 179 *Waggoner* 3. 85
That Hulk which labours in the deadly swell, . 579 *Peele Castle* 47
Hum. Where hum on busier wing her happy bees ; 21 *Desc. Sk.* 607
Nor mute the forest hum of noon ; . . . . 235 *Power of Sound* 198
Save insect-swarms that hum in air afloat, . . 360 **Long has* 6
And, earlier still, was heard the hum of bees ; . 377 *Duddon* 6. 4
More lulling than the busy hum of Noon, . . . 381 *Duddon* 19. 11
Though blind, thy tunes in sadness hum ; . . . 577 **I come* 38
While hum with busier joy her happy bees ; . . 615 *Desc.Sk.Quarto* 731
And heard, the pausing village hum between, . 616 *Desc.Sk.Quarto* 750
And oft amid the "busy hum" I seemed . . . 709 *Prelude* 8. 680
With tuneful hum is filling all the air ; . . . 765 *Excursion* 1. 597
Or in the gloom of twilight hum their joy ? . . 808 *Excursion* 4. 448
A not unfrequent pastime from the hum . . . 856 *Excursion* 6. 1168
Human. *See* **Half-human.**
Entire affection for all human kind. . . . . 3 *Ev. Wk.* 85
(For sighs will ever trouble human breath) . . 8 *Ev. Wk.* 353
Sole human tenant of the piny waste, ... 13 *Desc. Sk.* 174
Touched by the beggar's moan of human woes ; . 15 *Desc. Sk.* 243
Alas ! that human guilt provoked the rod . . 17 *Desc. Sk.* 401
The general sorrows of the human race : . . . 19 *Desc. Sk.* 503
If the sad grave of human ignorance bear . . . 20 *Desc. Sk.* 551
Far from all human dwelling : what if here . . 22 *Yew-tree* 2
The world, and human life, appeared a scene . . 23 *Yew-tree* 41
A human body that in irons swang, ... 25 *Guilt* 79
But there no human being could remain, . . . 27 *Guilt* 152
Of human shelter in that dreary place. . . . 27 *Guilt* 158
I feel my error ; shedding human blood . . . 55 *Bord.* 994
Have human feelings !— Now, for a little more . 61 *Bord.* 1329
He recks not human law ; and I have noticed . 63 *Bord.* 1437
Deep, deep and vast, vast beyond human thought, 64 *Bord.* 1466
Banished from human intercourse, exist . . . 66 *Bord.* 1577
Can scarcely be the work of human hands. . . 67 *Bord.* 1653
A human groan. Ha ! what is here ? Poor Man— 67 *Bord.* 1667
A human voice distinct, struck on my ear. . . 73 *Bord.* 2048
It rings, as if a human hand were there . . . 73 *Bord.* 2057
And thus we meet again ; one human stay . . 75 *Bord.* 2134
No human ear shall ever hear me speak ; . . . 78 *Bord.* 2346
No human dwelling ever give me food, . . . 78 *Bord.* 2347
Beside a human door . . . . 82 *Lucy Gray* 8
To the life of human kind. . . . . 90 *Longest Day* 36
But the poor ragged Thing whose ways my human heart had warmed. . . . . 92 *Poet's Dream* 16
For twofold hallowing—Nature's care, and work of human hands ? . . . . 92 *Poet's Dream* 36
"God for His service needeth not proud work of human skill ; . . . . 93 *Poet's Dream* 65
From human care, or grows upon the breast of earth. . . . . 102 *Artegal* 32
If human Life do pass away, ... 110 **Look at* 7
Full oft our human foresight I deplore ; . . . 112 **O dearer* 2
That sigh of thine, not meant for human ear, . . 112 **O dearer* 9
Farewell desire of human aid, ... 113 *Lament* 57
Should abrogate his human privilege . . . . 123 *V. and J.* 117
On man, the heart of man, and human life. . . 131 *Michael* 33
Through a haze of human nature, ... 141 *Arm. Lady* 133
Fit pattern for a human creature, ... 142 †*Lov. and Lik.* 26
On human nature's second infancy. . . . . 144 **Driven in* 81
Unfolding prospects fair as human eyes . . . 151 **Forth from* 6
Almost as thought itself, of human ken. . . . 165 *Parrot* 32
Far from human neighbourhood ; . . . . . 171 *Kitten* 58
From whom the Race of human kind proceed, . 172 *Infant Daughter* 9
And fade, unseen by any human eye ; . . . . 185 *Nutting* 32
For human nature's daily food ; . . . . . 186 **She was* 18
I had no human fears : . . . . 187 **A slumber* 2
Or is it that, when human Souls a journey long have had . . . . 189 *Star-gazers* 19
Of human Beings, in the self-same spot ! . . . 192 *Gipsies* 2
Was more than human life. . . . . 193 *Ruth* 108
A more than human weight upon his frame had cast. 196 *Resolution* 70
To give me human strength, by apt admonishment. 197 *Resolution* 112
Such sight was never seen by human eyes : . . 201 *Hart-leap* 54
And even the motion of our human blood . . . 206 *Tintern* 44
—Yet tears to human suffering are due ; . . . 212 *Laod.* 164
No appanage of human kind, ... 214 *Kirkstone* 6
To rocks, fields, woods. Nor doth our human sense 219 *Haunted Tree* 5
How poor, were human life ! . . . . . . 223 *Wishing-gate* 12
Nightly, on human kind . . . . 226 *Vernal Ode* 46
Where human foot did never stray ; . . . . 237 *P. B.* 97
As ever human eye did view. . . . . . . 240 *P. B.* 365

Human—*continued.*
From human thoughts and purposes, ... 246 *P. B.* 857
Never before to human sight betrayed. . . . 252 **The fairest* 8
That saw the Saviour in his human frame . . . 255 *Easter* 2
Hath shown that nothing human can be clear . 256 *Marriage : Friend* 12
Of human life : a Stripling's graces blow, . . . 267 **DespondingFather* 9
When human touch (as monkish books attest) . 267 *St. Cath.* 1
Like Grecian Artists, give thee human cheeks, . 268 **Brook ! whose* 8
Is given to triumph and all human pride . . 278 *Wellington* 7
More than in humbler times graced human story ; 281 **What strong* 10
Spirit divine through forms of human art : . . 282 **In my* 7
Of nature ; and, if human hearts be dead, . 283 *Railway* 12
I bless thee with a human heart ; . . . . . 288 *Highland Girl* 18
Soft smiles, by human kindness bred ! . . . . 288 *Highland Girl* 35
A human sweetness with the thought . . . . 289 *Stepping West.* 24
May human creature leave the shore ! . . . . 296 *Highland Boy* 102
By any human eye. . . . . 296 *Highland Boy* 160
To human weal and woe. . . . . 300 *Cora Linn* 36
Repose at length, firm friend of human kind ! . 313 *Clarkson* 14
And through the human heart explore my way ; . 314 **Not 'mid* 12
Of *justice* which the human mind can frame, . . 316 **Say, what* 2
Of pitying human nature ? Once again . . . 318 **Ah ! where* 5
Their God, and placed their trust in human pride ! 321 **Humanity, delighting* 18
That can belong to human story ! . . . . . 330 *Ode : Thanks.* 84
'Mid fields familiarised to human speech ?— . . 336 *Staub-bach* 4
And pine, of human hope bereft, ... 338 **Meek Virgin* 17
When the whirlwind of human destruction is spent, 340 *Fort Fuentes* 19
But ne'er to human rage ! . . . . 341 *San Salv.* 6
Of Figures human and divine, ... 343 *Eclipse* 40
Of *kindred* human hands ! . . . . 348 **Lulled by* 48
That I—so near the term to human life . . . 354 *Aquap.* 91
Albeit lifting human to divine, ... 357 *Aquap.* 308
Close to the vital seat of human clay ; . . . 383 *Duddon* 28. 10
Still shy of human neighbourhood ; . . . . 398 *White Doe* 175
That, far from human neighbourhood, ... 407 *White Doe* 996
By human feeling, had ordained. . . . . . 410 *White Doe* 1329
Appears a joyless human Being, ... 413 *White Doe* 1580
Who with a power like human reason . . . . 415 *White Doe* 1718
Through human hearts, and pleasure dead,— . . 416 *White Doe* 1843
And stood apart from human cares : . . . . 416 *White Doe* 1859
The human Soul ; not utterly unknown . . . 422 *Ecc. Sonn.* 1. 16. 9
For Power that travels with the human heart : . 423 *Ecc. Sonn.* 1. 20. 10
Round the decaying trunk of human pride, . . 424 *Ecc. Sonn.* 1. 21. 8
Imposed on human kind, must first forget . . 424 *Ecc. Sonn.* 1. 23. 11
Though seldom heard by busy human kind)— . . 432 *Ecc. Sonn.* 2. 17. 7
To human kind ; though peace be on his tongue, . 444 *Ecc. Sonn.* 3. 18. 7
A mystery potent human love to endow . . . 447 *Ecc. Sonn.* 3. 26. 12
That made His human tabernacle shine . . . 452 *Ecc. Sonn.* 3. 46. 3
To human life's unsettled atmosphere ; . . . 459 **Wanderer ! that* 2
Which thou canst touch in every human heart, . 459 **Wanderer ! that* 45
Of human life when first allowed to gleam . . 464 *Derwent* 5
For Christ's dear sake, by human sympathies . 468 *St. Bees* 143
Spare, too, the human helpers ! Do they stir . 469 **The feudal* 11
Ye lingered among human kind, ... 473 *Ossian* 69
Has deigned to work as if with human Art ! . . 473 **We saw* 14
Which, filling, consecrates the human breast. . 478 **Lonsdale ! it* 8
The human soul that through me ran ; . . . 482 *Lines : Spring* 6
For so many strange contrasts in one human face : 482 *Character* 2
From trace of human foot or hand. . . . . 491 *Fidelity* 24
A human skeleton on the ground ; . . . . . 491 *Fidelity* 39
Above all human estimate ! . . . . 492 *Fidelity* 65
Which is our human nature's highest dower ; . . 493 *Hap. War.* 16
Great issues, good or bad for human kind, . . 493 *Hap. War.* 50
There how the Original of human art, ... 496 **A little* 35
The anxieties of human love, ... 498 **The sylvan* 23
Our varying moods, on human kind or brute, . 501 *Humanity* 98
Into the human breast, and mix with sleep . . 501 **Theunremitting* 11
By paths no human wisdom can foretrace ! . . 505 *Warning* 133
Informs the fountain in the human breast . . 510 *F. Stone* 127
Would through the clouds break forth on human sight ! . . . . 511 **So fair* 15
Dealt in like sort with feeble human kind . . . 514 **Who ponders* 8
And wither, every human generation . . . . 516 **As leaves* 2
Might soothe in human breasts the sense of ill, . 517 *Pun. Death* 1. 4
A single human life have wrongly taken, . . . 517 *Pun. Death* 3. 10
Type of a sunny human breast . . . . . 526 **The soaring* 17
Or human habitation rose . . . . 533 **Blest is* 29
Are sown in every human breast, to beauty . . 538 **In desultory* 38
Favour divine, exalting human love ; . . . . 540 *Grace Darl.* 5
Behold an emblem of our human mind . . . 551 **Behold an* 1
Wherewith to satisfy the human soul ? . . . 568 *Cumb. Beg.* 146
That we have all of us one human heart. . . . 568 *Cumb. Beg.* 153
Gives the last human interest to his heart. . . 569 *Cumb. Beg.* 178
A roseate fragrance breathed.—O human life, . 573 *Chiabrera* 2. 13
How fleeting and how frail is human life ! . . 575 *Chiabrera* 6. 16
The rivers stained so oft with human gore, . . 582 *Invoc. Earth* 26
A waste where creatures bearing human form, . 585 *Ch. Lamb* 69
Wide were his aims, yet in no human breast . . 587 *Crosth.* 13
Some fragment from his dream of human life, . 589 *Immortality* 91
Out of human suffering ; . . . . 590 *Immortality* 188
Thanks to the human heart by which we live, . 590 *Immortality* 204
Ye ne'er, like hapless human wanderers, throw . 596 *Ev. Wk. Quarto* 239
So vanish those fair Shadows, human joys, . . 598 *Ev. Wk. Quarto* 361
And, bending, water'd with the human tear, . . 606 *Desc.Sk.Quarto* 258
But human vices have provok'd the rod . . . 611 *Desc.Sk.Quarto* 486
Round a lone fane the human Genii mourn, . . 613 *Desc.Sk.Quarto* 646
At such an hour I heav'd the human sigh, . . 615 *Desc.Sk.Quarto* 702
Whence human kind, and brute; what natural powers 625 *Æneid* 124

Hung—*continued*.
With spade and mattock o'er his shoulder hung ;   825 *Excursion* 5. 222
Turned towards the planet Jupiter that hung   849 *Excursion* 6. 761
It hung its head in mortal languishment. . .   853 *Excursion* 6. 1002
Of his compatriot villagers (that hung . .   857 *Excursion* 7. 19
Two ruddy children hung, a well-poised freight,   858 *Excursion* 7. 73
Their snow-white curtains hung in decent folds ; .   860 *Excursion* 7. 180
She was a soft attendant cloud, that hung . .   861 *Excursion* 7. 234
Grey locks profusely round his temples hung . .   865 *Excursion* 7. 551
Hung in his rustic hall. One ivied arch . .   872 *Excursion* 7. 962
Are hung with thousand thousand diamond drops   K.8. 252 *Recluse* 1.1.563
Hungarian. Of wide Hungarian Danube, 'twas my lot . . . .   575 *Chiabrera* 6. 7
Hunger. And cold and hunger are his least of woes ;   16 *Desc. Sk.* 329
Nor Hunger driven the herds from pastures bare, .   17 *Desc. Sk.* 394
At morn my sick heart hunger scarcely stung, .   31 *Guilt* 377
From cold, from hunger, penury, and death ; . .   62 *Bord.* 1370
To cold and hunger !—Pain is of the heart, .   62 *Bord.* 1399
but I think his malady was cold and hunger. .   72 *Bord.* 1945
Hunger, and sultry heat, and nipping blast .   320 **Hunger, and* 1
Outstretched and listless, were by hunger roused :   392 *Daniel* 13
And, for hunger and thirst and such troublesome calls, ...   571 *Avarice* 7
Nor Hunger forc'd the herds from pastures bare .   611 *Desc.Sk.Quarto* 482
Of vigorous hunger—hence corporeal strength .   643 *Prelude* 2. 80
And miserable hunger. Much, too much, .   886 *Excursion* 9. 164
Began to fail, this sheep by hunger pressed .   K.8. 229 **I will* 144
Hunger-bitten. One day to meet a hunger-bitten girl,   717 *Prelude* 9. 510
Hungering. Me and his children hungering in his view ; . . . .   29 *Guilt* 276
Hunger's. And cold and hunger's abject wretchedness, ...   K.8. 246 *Recluse* 1.1.364
Hungry. The lame, the hungry, will be welcome there. . . . .   66 *Bord.* 1629
Save one *wee*, hungry, nibbling mouse, .   118 †*Cottager* 9
The weary have life, and the hungry have bliss ;   188 *Music* 10
Thy hungry barkings to the hymn . .   235 *Power of Sound* 201
Like hungry fowl to the feeder's hand . .   403 *White Doe* 623
There are the naked clothed, the hungry fed ;   467 *St. Bees* 64
Dead muttering lips, and hair of hungry white, .   615 *Desc.Sk.Quarto* 711
Food for the hungry ears of little ones, .   668 *Prelude* 5. 211
Hunt. A most strange faintness,—will you hunt me out . . . .   52 *Bord.* 799
Yes, you are right, we need not hunt for motives :   63 *Bord.* 1435
To hunt the waterfalls. . . . . .   109 *Louisa* 18
To hunt the moon within the brook, . .   128 *Idiot Boy* 215
To hunt their fluttering game o'er rock and level green. . . . . . .   191 *Beggars* 36
Hunt half a day for a forgotten dream. .   202 *Hart-leap* 132
Hunt the Mother and the Child. . . .   204 *Brougham* 60
They hunt through the streets with deliberate tread,   572 *Avarice* 37
To hunt the badger and unearth the fox .   660 *Prelude* 4. 97
I did not hunt after, nor greatly prize, .   696 *Prelude* 7. 585
Hunted. Three several hoof-marks which the hunted Beast . . . . . .   201 *Hart-leap* 51
The palmy antlers of a hunted Hart, .   393 *Hart's-horn* 4
As doth the hunted fawn, ...   542 *Russ. Fug.* 14
And on I hunted him from tree to tree, .   561 *Cuck.andNight.*224
The pack loud chiming, and the hunted hare. .   638 *Prelude* 1. 437
The grounds'which we have hunted through before."   K.8. 228 **I will* 117
Hunter. *See* Chamois-hunter.
A very hunter did I rush . . . .   79 **Stay near* 14
Behold the hunter train ! . . . .   104 *Artegal* 111
A fierce and dreadful hunter he ; . . .   129 *Idiot Boy* 328
A fisher or a hunter there, . . .   193 *Ruth* 74
And hart and hind and hunter with his spear .   268 **Pure element* 8
See the first mighty Hunter leave the brute—   313 **Go back* 11
Like Echo, when the hunter train at dawn .   314 **Advance—come* 6
Was pierced by whizzing shaft of hunter keen !   376 *Duddon* 2. 14
Sad were our lot : no hunter of the hare .   466 *St. Bees* 3
The Hunter followed fast, ...   544 *Russ. Fug.* 274
And, like an ardent hunter, I forgot, . .   788 *Excursion* 3. 122
The nightly hunter, lifting a bright eye .   814 *Excursion* 4. 861
Hunter-Indian. America, the Hunter-Indian ; Moors,   690 *Prelude* 7. 226
Hunter's. When hunter's arrow first defiled .   215 *Enterprise* 22
Light as a hunter's of the field ; . . .   404 *White Doe* 748
His staff protending like a hunter's spear, .   702 *Prelude* 8. 246
What time the hunter's earliest horn is heard .   850 *Excursion* 6. 830
Hunters. In friendship ; rival hunters they, .   409 *White Doe* 1203
Seized it, as hunters seize their prey, .   412 *White Doe* 1494
Keen hunters in a chase of fourteen weeks, .   682 *Prelude* 6. 497
They—who had come elate as eastern hunters   718 *Prelude* 10. 17
Hunting. What kind of plunder he was hunting now ;   33 *Guilt* 483
And now, perhaps, is hunting sheep, . .   129 *Idiot Boy* 327
Huntress. A sylvan huntress at my side, .   193 *Ruth* 95
Hunts. Hunts, where his master points, the intercepted flocks. . . . .   5 *Ev. Wk.* 185
Hunts, where he points, the intercepted flocks ;   594 *Ev. Wk. Quarto* 168
Huntsman. A running huntsman merry ; .   483 *Simon Lee* 6
Hurdy-gurdy. The hurdy-gurdy, at the fiddle weaves,   697 *Prelude* 7. 700
Hurl. I'll hurl thee headlong with the rock . .   155 *Waterfall* 13
Hurled. And from all hope I was for ever hurled. .   31 *Guilt* 358
Transmute him to a wretch from quiet hurled—   234 *Power of Sound* 101
When madding Power her bolts had hurled, .   298 *Brownie's Cell* 22
Not hurled precipitous from steep to steep ; .   384 *Duddon* 32. 1
Hurled down a mountain-cove from stage to stage,   424 *Ecc. Sonn.* 1. 22. 4
Than to allay. Anathemas are hurled .   437 *Ecc. Sonn.* 2. 36. 9
Of France a boastful Tryant hurled his threats ;   869 *Excursion* 7. 758
Hurls. Bright sparks his black and rolling eyeball hurls   5 *Ev. Wk.* 150
Rides forth, an armèd man, and hurls a spear .   422 *Ecc. Sonn.* 1. 17. 3
Bright sparks his black and haggard eye-ball hurls   594 *Ev. Wk. Quarto* 133

Hurly-burly. And with a *hurly-burly* now . . .   126 *Idiot Boy* 50
Hurrah. Hurrah for —— [Grote], hugging his Ballot-box ! . . . . .   513 **Said Secrecy* 14
Hurricane. Grant that by this unsparing hurricane   435 *Ecc. Sonn.* 2. 28. 1
Volcanic burst, earthquake, and hurricane, .   514 **Who ponders* 7
For the spent hurricane the air provides . .   719 *Prelude* 10. 80
Hurried. Like fate ; was hurried off, a helpless prey,   25 *Guilt* 53
I hurried on, when straight a second moan, .   73 *Bord.* 2047
I hurried back with her.—Oh save me, Sir, .   74 *Bord.* 2096
When, as we hurried on, my ear . . .   82 *Alice Fell* 3
So have we hurried on with troubled pleasure : .   443 *Ecc. Sonn.* 3. 12. 9
Hurried and hurrying, volatile and loud. .   473 **We saw* 4
To share his enterprise, he hurried on .   667 *Prelude* 5. 117
Was soon dislodged. Downwards we hurried fast,   684 *Prelude* 6. 619
Hurries. And from the brink she hurries fast, .   129 *Idiot Boy* 295
Then hurries back the road it came— .   295 *Highland Boy* 61
The local Genius hurries me aloft, . .   353 *Aquap.* 34
Unchecked he hurries on ;—nor heeds .   411 *White Doe* 1380
And hurries on ; or from the fragments picks .   789 *Excursion* 3. 185
Hurry. Found means to hurry her away by night,   122 *V. and J.* 70
And seems no longer in a hurry. . .   126 *Idiot Boy* 71
Doth hurry to the lawn ; . . . .   217 *Enterprise* 143
Where, without hurry, noiseless feet . .   334 **In Bruges* 3
(As hurry on in eagerness the feet, . .   355 *Aquap.* 176
That, if it could, would hurry past ; . .   491 *Fidelity* 32
Hurrying. Hurrying the timid hare through rustling corn ; . . . . . .   9 *Ev. Wk.* 374
Hurrying the pallid hue away . . .   181 *Waggoner* 4. 152
That, for a brief space, checks the hurrying stream !   220 *Haunted Tree* 40
Hurrying the busy streets along ? . . .   228 *Devot. Incit.* 45
Hurrying and sparkling through the clear blue heaven ; . . . . . .   266 **With how* 12
On the swift flood is hurrying down, . .   296 *Highland Boy* 99
Of mortals, hurrying like a sudden shower .   327 *Ode 1815* 12
Hurrying, with lordly Duddon to unite ; .   380 *Duddon* 19. 5
Thoughts press, and time is hurrying on '—   410 *White Doe* 1258
Hurried and hurrying, volatile and loud. .   473 **We saw* 4
Hurrying the feeding hare thro' rustling corn ; .   600 *Ev. Wk. Quarto* 442
For thy poor babes that, hurrying from the door,   615 *Desc.Sk.Quarto* 709
When hurrying forward till the slack'ning stream   626 **The confidence* 10
Been parted by the hurrying world, and droop,   663 *Prelude* 4. 355
Went hurrying o'er the illimitable waste, .   667 *Prelude* 5. 136
Boons inexhaustible ? Who, hurrying on .   S.3. 433 **The doubt* 43
Hurt. If he is hurt in life or limb "— . .   128 *Idiot Boy* 190
Nor shall the elements be free to hurt .   838 *Excursion* 6. 32
Hurtful. More hurtful here beset him, doomed though free, ...   470 **Did pangs* 12
From every hurtful blast, ...   502 *Seasons* 2
Thus wilful Fancy, in no hurtful mood, .   705 *Prelude* 8. 421
Hurtle. Hurtle the clouds in deeper darkness piled,   26 *Guilt* 100
Hurtless. That came with soft alarm, like hurtless light . . . . . .   637 *Prelude* 1. 353
Hurts. And knows not when he hurts and when he heals ; 560 *Cuck.andNight.*203
Husband. The happy husband flies, his arms to throw . . . . . .   25 *Guilt* 60
Husband and children ! one by one, by sword .   30 *Guilt* 303
And kindred of dead husband are at best . .   32 *Guilt* 426
My husband served in sad captivity . .   35 *Guilt* 593
My husband lurked about the neighbourhood ; .   35 *Guilt* 605
Yet still, while over her the husband bent, .   36 *Guilt* 627
Wife, Sir ! his wife—not I ; my husband, Sir, .   46 *Bord.* 511
What can this mean ? Alas, for my poor husband !— . . . . . .   71 *Bord.* 1885
Hush ! They are gone. On such a night my husband, ...   71 *Bord.* 1891
Survive her Husband : at her death the estate .   138 *Michael* 474
" It is my Husband," softly said . . .   176 *Waggoner* 1. 241
A husband and a wife." . . . .   193 *Ruth* 105
Thy Husband walks the paths of upper air : .   209 *Laod.* 22
And that her Husband now lay dead, . .   248 *P. B.* 1038
His present blessings, and to husband up . .   568 *Cumb. Beg.* 130
By a blest Husband guided, Mary came .   576 **By a* 1
Did wife and husband roam ; . . .   623 *G. and S. Green* 6
The husband to the wife. . . . .   623 *G. and S. Green* 16
With the most common ; husband, father ; learned,   703 *Prelude* 8. 289
To the cold grave in which her husband slept, .   704 *Prelude* 8. 386
If I had seen her husband. As she spake .   766 *Excursion* 1. 658
From one who by my husband had been sent   766 *Excursion* 1. 675
No tidings of her husband ; if he lived, .   768 *Excursion* 1. 818
Son, husband, brothers—brothers side by side, .   780 *Excursion* 2. 580
Her husband enter—from a distant vale. .   783 *Excursion* 2. 794
Or paced the ground—to guide her Husband home,   834 *Excursion* 5. 760
Were planted by her husband and herself, .   K.8. 247 *Recluse* 1.1.392
To speak of her dead husband. Is there not .   K.8. 247 *Recluse* 1.1.401
Husbanded. Which for that service had been husbanded, ...   185 *Nutting* 10
But husbanded through many a long campaign. .   640 *Prelude* 1. 520
Husbanding. Husbanding that which they possess within, ...   757 *Excursion* 1. 90
Husbandman. Called by the thrifty husbandman a weed ; . . . . . .   509 *F. Stone* 61
Of the industrious husbandman, diffused .   757 *Excursion* 1. 71
Husbandry. For husbandry or tillage ; . .   483 *Simon Lee* 14
By husbandry of many thrifty years, . .   776 *Excursion* 2. 342
Husband's. My husband's arms now only served to strain . . . . . .   29 *Guilt* 275
My husband's loving kindness stood between .   35 *Guilt* 611
There again ! 'Tis my husband's foot. Good Eldred . . . . . .   71 *Bord.* 1899
And Betty's husband's at the wood, . .   126 *Idiot Boy* 27

I

Icy—*continued.*
Blithe Autumn's purple crown, and Winter's icy mail! . . . . 350 *Des. Stanzas* 36
Rest not in hope want's icy chain to thaw . . 516 **Feel for* 9
And icy cold he turned away. . . . . . . 537 *Goody Blake* 104
Like frost he thought his heart was icy cold; . . 563 *Troilus* 17
While far and wide the icy summits blaze . . 609 *Desc.Sk.Quarto* 384
And tempt the icy valley yawning deep, . . . 610 *Desc.Sk.Quarto* 463
Ev'n to the summer door his icy tide, . . . 613 *Desc.Sk.Quarto* 599
The icy brooks, as on we passed, appeared . . 622 *Recluse* 1. 1. 166
The leafless trees and every icy crag . . . . 638 *Prelude* 1. 441
I'd. (*Partial list.*) *See* **I.**
I'd wager on his life for twenty years. . . . . 41 *Bord.* 246
'Tis a wild night. I'd give my cloak and bonnet 50 *Bord.* 725
I'd rather see my father's ghost. My Captain, . 56 *Bord.* 1020
And said, "At Kilve I'd rather be . . . . . 86 *Anecdote* 35
"Susan, I'd gladly stay with you. . . . . . 128 *Idiot Boy* 186
Till my ribs ached I'd laugh at you! . . . . 236 *P. B.* 20
It moves us not.—Great God! I'd rather be . . 259 **The world is* 9
For I'd take my last leave both of verse and of prose. . . . . 571 *Avarice* 4
Idalian. With Idalian rose enwreathed? . . . 221 *Triad* 114
'Mid groves Idalian, lull'd to gentle sleep, . . . 624 *Æneid* 32
Through upper air to an Idalian glade, . . . 624 *Æneid* 50
Ida's. Shall with Mount Ida's triple lustre fill . 220 *Triad* 13
Idea. Communed with that Idea face to face: . . 476 **Tranquillity! the* 12
The idea, or abstraction of the kind. . . . . 706 *Prelude* 8. 502
By a sublime *idea*, whencesoe'er . . . . . 709 *Prelude* 8. 673
Ideal. Intent to trace the ideal path of right . . 213 *Dion* 50
Features to old ideal grace allied, ... 221 *Triad* 137
And others of your kind, ideal crew! . . . . 252 **Her only* 11
Ideal Form, the universal mould. . . . . . 257 **No mortal* 8
Destroy the ideal Power within, 'twere done . . 358 **Is this* 6
Pleased rather with some soft ideal scene, . . . 480 **Most sweet* 5
While Cam's ideal current glided by, ... 529 **Those breathing* 117
To closer fellowship with ideal grace. . . . . 547 **Rude is* 4
With decoration of ideal grace; . . . . . 672 *Prelude* 5. 457
Of wild ideal pageantry, shaped out . . . . 679 *Prelude* 6. 299
Rose to ideal grandeur, or, called forth . . . 694 *Prelude* 7. 480
In sense conducting to ideal form, ... 747 *Prelude* 14. 76
Surpassing the most fair ideal Forms . . . . 755 *Recluse* 1. 1. 796
To vindicate the ideal rights . . . . . . S. 3. 439 **Avaunt this* 10
Idealising. To Spirit; for the idealising Soul . . S. 3. 435 **The doubt* 119
Identity. To one identity, by differences . . . 698 *Prelude* 7. 727
Idiot. Him whom you love, your Idiot Boy? . . 126 *Idiot Boy* 11
Him whom she loves, her Idiot Boy. . . . . 126 *Idiot Boy* 41
On which her Idiot Boy must ride, ... 126 *Idiot Boy* 70
Oh! then for the poor Idiot Boy! . . . . . 127 *Idiot Boy* 73
The silence of her Idiot Boy, ... 127 *Idiot Boy* 92
Oh carry back my Idiot Boy! . . . . . . 129 *Idiot Boy* 300
And cannot find her Idiot Boy. . . . . . . 130 *Idiot Boy* 361
Him whom she loves, her Idiot Boy. . . . . 130 *Idiot Boy* 366
He whom you love, your Idiot Boy. . . . . 130 *Idiot Boy* 371
And fast she holds her Idiot Boy. . . . . . 130 *Idiot Boy* 376
To hear again her Idiot Boy. . . . . . . 130 *Idiot Boy* 381
Him whom she loves, her Idiot Boy; . . . . 130 *Idiot Boy* 388
Idiot's. The mouldy vaults of the dull idiot's brain, 234 *Power of Sound* 100
Idle. Alas! the idle tale of man is found . . . 2 *Ev. Wk.* 27
But why, ungrateful, dwell on idle pain? . . . 2 *Ev. Wk.* 33
An idle voice the sabbath region fills . . . . 16 *Desc. Sk.* 354
Whole hours, with idle arms in moping sorrow knit. 32 *Guilt* 432
All thoughts whose idle composition lives . . . 65 *Bord.* 1550
Those idle Shepherd-boys upbraid, ... 85 *Shepherd-boys* 98
These tears—and my poor idle tongue. . . . 121 *Emigrant Mother* 78
For joy his head and heels are idle, ... 127 *Idiot Boy* 75
He's idle all for very joy. . . . . . . 127 *Idiot Boy* 76
"A little idle sauntering Thing!" . . . . 127 *Idiot Boy* 159
"Worse than idle is compassion . . . . . 140 *Arm. Lady* 19
To whom I sometimes in our idle talk . . . . 146 **It was an* 43
And many a fond and idle name . . . . . 158 **With little* 13
Love them; and every idle breeze of air . . . 230 *Clouds* 70
Among the Ruins, but no idle talk . . . . . 283 **Well have* 3
Too high, or idle agitations lull! . . . . . 394 **How profitless* 4
Conjecture vague, and idle fear, ... 398 *White Doe* 214
Whence idle fears, and needless pain, ... 408 *White Doe* 1121
An idle form, the Word an empty sound! . . . 445 *Ecc. Sonn.* 3. 21. 14
I live and sing my idle songs . . . . . . 487 *Fountain* 59
For had thy charge been idle flowers, ... 530 *Gleaner* 21
And fear not lest an idle sound . . . . . 550 *Hermit's Cell* 2. 6
Of idle computation. In the sun, ... 566 *Cumb. Beg.* 12
Alas! what idle words; but take . . . . . 577 **I come* 26
For him lost flowers their idle sweets exhale; . . 602 *Desc. Sk. Quarto* 19
"Poor victim! no idle intruder has stood . . . 621 *Convict* 45
Their veteran foes mock as an idle noise; . . . 628 *Eagle and Dove* 14
And not a voice was idle; with the din . . . 638 *Prelude* 1. 439
Not in a mystical and idle sense, ... 645 *Prelude* 2. 230
Transient and idle, lacked not intervals . . . 663 *Prelude* 4. 347
'Twere idle to descant. My inner judgment . . 676 *Prelude* 6. 96
An idle dreamer! 'Tis a common tale, . . . 765 *Excursion* 1. 636
Are like an idle matter. Still she sighed, . . . 768 *Excursion* 1. 799
Of sorrow. Yet I saw the idle loom . . . . 769 *Excursion* 1. 851
Appeared an idle dream, that could maintain, . 770 *Excursion* 1. 952
And idle spirits:—there the sun himself, . . . 782 *Excursion* 2. 717
Than the loose pendant—to the idle wind . . . 798 *Excursion* 3. 841
Tell in their idle songs of wandering gods, . . 868 *Excursion* 7. 729
Many and idle, visits not his ear: . . . . . 885 *Excursion* 9. 75
Idle,—but no delay, no harm, no loss; . . . . 888 *Excursion* 9. 264
Now too, on melancholy's idle dream . . . . S. 3. 417 **Sweet was* 9
The idle breath of softest pipe attuned . . . K. 8. 247 *Recluse* 1. 1. 408

Idleness. In very idleness. . . . . 86 *Ancedote* 28
But, for that moping Son of Idleness, ... 95 *Brothers* 11
The happy idleness of that sweet morn, . . . 149 **A narrow* 68
Or Idleness in tatters mendicant . . . . . 336 *Staub-bach* 11
We'll give to idleness. . . . . 483 *Sister* 16
We'll give to idleness. . . . . 483 *Sister* 40
Of strenuous idleness; . . . . 499 **This Lawn* 6
Was social, and loved idleness and joy. . . . 652 *Prelude* 3. 233
Idleness halting with his weary clog, ... 657 *Prelude* 3. 597
Thus in submissive idleness, my Friend! . . . 658 *Prelude* 3. 629
Spent in a round of strenuous idleness— . . . 664 *Prelude* 4. 378
With gaiety and dissolute idleness. . . . . . 710 *Prelude* 9. 66
In pensive idleness. What could he do, . . . 760 *Excursion* 1. 261
The tedium of fantastic idleness: . . . . . 829 *Excursion* 5. 430
Idler. Hath been an idler in the land; . . . . 485 *Poet's Epitaph* 54
Such as an idler deals with in his shame, . . . 673 *Prelude* 5. 489
An idler's place; an idler well content . . . 688 *Prelude* 7. 72
The military Idler, and the Dame, ... 690 *Prelude* 7. 209
An Idler among academic bowers, ... 706 *Prelude* 8. 503
Which he, a soldier, in his idler day . . . . 714 *Prelude* 9. 312
Idler's. An idler's place; an idler well content . 688 *Prelude* 7. 72
Idlers. Could gaze, as on a show by idlers sought; 36 *Guilt* 661
That those fond Idlers most are pleased . . . 170 *Rural Ill.* 35
Half-and-half idlers, hardy recusants, ... 650 *Prelude* 3. 67
Idlers perchance they were,—but in *his* sight; . 878 *Excursion* 8. 279
Idless. Loose Idless to forego her wily mask. . . 382 *Duddon* 24. 14
Idlest. (Nor idlest that!) which holds communion . 439 *Ecc. Sonn.* 2. 42. 3
Idly. If this be idly spoken. See, they come, . . 39 *Bord.* 99
Not idly.—Hadst thou been of Indian birth, . . 172 *Infant Daughter* 18
Nor pity idly born, ... 334 **In Bruges* 26
My heart is idly stirred, ... 487 *Fountain* 30
More than the feeblest wind that idly blows. . . 524 *Epist. Beaumont* 170
Small circles glittering idly in the moon, . . . 637 *Prelude* 1. 365
Erewhile my verse played idly with the flowers . 707 *Prelude* 8. 533
And senseless rocks; nor idly; for they speak, . 763 *Excursion* 1. 478
Then, not less idly, sought, through every nook . 764 *Excursion* 1. 572
How idly, how perversely, life's whole course, . 826 *Excursion* 5. 258
Murmurs, not idly, o'er his peaceful grave. . . 864 *Excursion* 7. 481
Idol. *See* **Master-idol.**
They bow to, calling the idol, Demonstration. . 58 *Bord.* 1158
A grisly idol hewn in stone? . . . . . . 242 *P. B.* 506
Pastime their idol, give their day of life . . . 280 **Intent on* 7
Their monstrous Idol if the dead e'er spake, . . 325 *Enghien* 7
An Idol at her prow. . . . . 374 *Eg. Maid* 362
That to an Idol, falsely called "the Wealth . . 501 *Humanity* 89
(The idol weak as the idolater), ... 657 *Prelude* 3. 603
Is worshipped in that idol proudly named . . . 741 *Prelude* 13. 77
Idolater. Born of Conceit, Power's blind Idolater; 514 **Portentous change* 6
(The idol weak as the idolater), ... 657 *Prelude* 3. 603
Idolatress. Boastful Idolatress of formal skill . . 468 *St. Bees* 158
Idolatrously. Metal or stone, idolatrously served. . 812 *Excursion* 4. 728
Idolatry. Reviving obsolete idolatry, ... 147 *Joanna* 27
Which old idolatry abused. . . . . 301 *Bran* 93
This is idolatry; and these we adore: . . . . 307 **O Friend* 10
Ah! if the old idolatry be spurned, ... 434 *Ecc. Sonn.* 2. 24. 3
A bigot to a new idolatry— . . . . 735 *Prelude* 12. 77
This age fall back to old idolatry, ... 752 *Prelude* 14. 434
Against idolatry with warlike mind, ... 815 *Excursion* 4. 921
And strong in hatred of idolatry." . . . . . 870 *Excursion* 7. 816
Of that idolatry, through monkish rites . . . S. 3. 435 **The doubt* 127
Idolizing. An idolizing dreamer as of yore!— . . 459 **Wanderer! that* 9
Idols. Of those terrific Idols some received . . 894 *Excursion* 9. 692
Idonea. 'Twas my delight to sit and hear Idonea . 39 *Bord.* 92
Two Travellers! The woman is Idonea. . . 39 *Bord.* 100
On this green bank. Idonea, you are silent, . . 39 *Bord.* 131
Idonea, we must part. Be not alarmed— . . 41 *Bord.* 223
And are you going then? Come, come, Idonea, . 42 *Bord.* 296
When you are by my side. Idonea, wolves . . 43 *Bord.* 320
I do not see Idonea. Dutiful Girl, ... 43 *Bord.* 337
Idonea would have fears for me,—the Convent . 43 *Bord.* 352
Idonea, as he calls her; but the Girl . . . 46 *Bord.* 509
I thought I saw the skeleton of Idonea. . . . 47 *Bord.* 581
While feeding on their bodies. Would that Idonea 48 *Bord.* 588
I hope Idonea is well housed. That horseman, . 50 *Bord.* 734
But after that? The features of Idonea . . . 55 *Bord.* 967
He who will gain his Seignory when Idonea . . 55 *Bord.* 976
But yet I trust, Idonea, thou art safe. . . . . 57 *Bord.* 1101
Idonea! How! what? your Idonea? *Mine;* . 57 *Bord.* 1102
Of God's parental mercies—with Idonea . . . 60 *Bord.* 1267
I interrupt you? Think not so. Idonea, . . 66 *Bord.* 1597
But for Idonea!—I have cause to think . . . 67 *Bord.* 1677
By whom thy Parent was destroyed, Idonea! . 75 *Bord.* 2171
Idonea! thy blind Father on the Ordeal . . . 77 *Bord.* 2267
Idonea's. Where is she—holla! You are Idonea's Mother?— . . . . 46 *Bord.* 529
You thought his voice the echo of Idonea's. . . 53 *Bord.* 887
Idonea's filial countenance was there . . . . 55 *Bord.* 986
Idris. On Cader Idris, or huge Penmanmaur) . . 857 *Excursion* 7. 8
If, *omitted.*
Ignoble. Who from ignoble games and revelry . . 211 *Laod.* 112
By hands of no ignoble birth, ... 403 *White Doe* 666
Was not ignoble. Oh! when I have hung . . 637 *Prelude* 1. 330
Can aught be more ignoble than the man . . 735 *Prelude* 12. 71
And on the back of more ignoble beast; . . . 858 *Excursion* 7. 66
Ignominious. By violent and ignominious death. . 318 **Look now* 14
Ignominy. To evil courses: ignominy and shame . 138 *Michael* 445
As the tide ebbs, to ignominy and shame . . . 752 *Prelude* 14. 436
Ignorance. If the sad grave of human ignorance bear 20 *Desc. Sk.* 551
With a hard-hearted ignorance; your struggles . 64 *Bord.* 1505

Ignorance—*continued.*
Twin sisters both of Ignorance, I found . . . 70 *Bord* 1835
By ignorance defaced, ... 330 *Ode : Thanks.* 110
Of ignorance thou might'st witness heretofore, . 378 *Duddon* 8. 12
Aimed at the White Man's ignorance the while, . 380 *Duddon* 16. 5
Of Ignorance, that ran so rough and high . . 422 *Ecc. Sonn.* 1. 14. 11
Blest in their pious ignorance, though weak . . 468 **Ranging the* 13
Hence equal ignorance of both prevails, . . . 516 **As leaves* 11
With Indian awe and wonder, ignorance pleased . 677 *Prelude* 6. 121
One spirit over ignorance and vice . . . . . 709 *Prelude* 8. 669
And ignorance in the labouring multitude. . . 714 *Prelude* 9. 328
Through ignorance and false teaching, sadder proof 721 *Prelude* 10. 215
And ignorance filled up from age to age, . . . 725 *Prelude* 10. 478
Long time have human ignorance and guilt . . 734 *Prelude* 12. 1
With toil, be therefore yoked with ignorance ; . 742 *Prelude* 13. 176
And by his nature's, ignorance, dismayed ! . . 798 *Excursion* 3. 869
Not doomed to ignorance, though forced to tread, 802 *Excursion* 4. 47
From unreflecting ignorance preserved, . . . 802 *Excursion* 4. 49
Of a most rustic ignorance, and take . . . . 810 *Excursion* 4. 615
Of ignorance (or illusion) lives and breathes . . 813 *Excursion* 4. 830
To breathe beneath a vault of ignorance ? . . 831 *Excursion* 5. 588
And mortal ignorance and frailty claim, . . . 847 *Excursion* 6. 587
The slave of ignorance, and oft of want, . . . 886 *Excursion* 9. 163
By indigence, their ignorance is not less, . . . 886 *Excursion* 9. 176
And, if that ignorance were removed, which breeds 889 *Excursion* 9. 346
Let Ignorance o'er the monster swarms preside, . L.1. 88 *Juvenal* 1. 19
Ignorant. Why am I ignorant of the same . . . 116 *Affl. Marg.* 5
But worse, more ignorant in love and hate, . . 309 **England ! the* 10
And Victory sickens, ignorant where to rest ! . . 437 *Ecc. Sonn.* 2. 36. 14
That I was ignorant, had been falsely taught, . 709 *Prelude* 8. 651
When Robespierre, not ignorant for what mark . 719 *Prelude* 10. 104
Faltering and faint, and ignorant of the road : . 738 *Prelude* 12. 247
Not ignorant was the Youth that still no few . . 761 *Excursion* 1. 333
Was wholly ignorant that my ancient Friend— . 783 *Excursion* 2. 785
Wide, sluggish, blank, and ignorant, and strange— 880 *Excursion* 8. 410
Ilex. Albano's dripping Ilex avenue, ... 360 *Albano* 3
Of Ilex, or, if better suited to the hour, . . . 361 **List—'twas* 20
Ilissus. Ilissus, bending o'er thy classic urn ! . . 213 *Dion* 43
Ilium. Hath come ! we *have* been Trojans, Ilium *was* L.2. 121 *Frag. Æneid* 2. 3
Ilium's. That Ilium's walls were subject to their view, ... 212 *Laod.* 172
Ill. He hoped, to calm her mind ; but ill he sped, . 27 *Guilt* 169
"But ill they suited me—those journeys dark . 32 *Guilt* 415
Were not for me, brought up in nothing ill : . . 32 *Guilt* 422
Suffering not doing ill—fate far more mild. . . 33 *Guilt* 499
(I wot not what ill tongue has wronged him with you) . . . . 40 *Bord.* 167
This charge of thine, then ill befall thee !—Look, 42 *Bord.* 304
I owe him no ill will, but in good sooth . . . 45 *Bord.* 458
Ill names, can render no ill services, ... 65 *Bord.* 1527
Ill can I bear that look—Plead for me, Oswald ! . 66 *Bord.* 1603
'Tis that worst principle of ill which dooms . . 70 *Bord.* 1812
that my ill stars have kept me abroad to-night . 72 *Bord.* 1949
Ill fitted to sustain unkindly shocks, ... 88 *H. C.* 28
No ill was feared ; till one of them by chance . 101 *Brothers* 373
What ill was on him, what he had to do, . . . 107 *Indolence* 17
I thought he knew some ill of me : . . . . . 115 *Last of Flock* 74
From that ill thought ; and, being blind, . . . 117 *Affl. Marg.* 30
"—I cannot help it ; ill intent . . . . . . 121 *EmigrantMother* 75
"If Susan had not been so ill, ... 128 *Idiot Boy* 234
If I judge ill for thee, but it seems good . . . 137 *Michael* 381
——Ill suits the road with one in haste ; but we . 148 **A narrow* 10
Ill befall the yellow flowers, ... 160 **Pansies, lilies* 49
Thy quiet with no ill intent, ... 169 *Wren's Nest* 62
On working out an ill intent ? . . . . 181 *Waggoner* 4. 118
And now doth fare ill . . . . 190 *March* 13
But ill he lived, much evil saw, ... 194 *Ruth* 145
Nor ever taxed them with the ill . . . . . 194 *Ruth* 221
What this imported I could ill divine : . . . . 202 *Hart-leap* 105
That privilege by virtue.—"Ill," said he, . . . 211 *Laod.* 110
Sharpen the keenest edge of present ill,— . . . 267 **As the* 7
Through twilight shades of good and ill . . . 286 *Sons of Burns* 7
Ill health of body ; and had pined . . . . . 294 *Jedbor.* 74
Of moral prudence, sought through good and ill ; 315 **Alas ! what* 2
It ill befits us to disdain . . . . 337 *Cath. Cantons* 3
That ill supports the luscious fig ; . . . . . 342 *Ital. Itin.* 46
If with his vows this object ill agree ; . . . . 363 **The world forsaken* 10
Spake bitter words ; words that did ill agree . . 367 **As indignation* 2
Ill sight ! but grief may vanish ere the morrow." 372 *Eg. Maid* 210
Would ill suffice for persons and events : . . . 393 **The Lovers* 11
He serves the Muses erringly and ill, ... 395 *White Doe: Ded.*57
Ill tears she wept ; I saw them fall, ... 405 *White Doe* 874
His parting charge—but ill obeyed— . . . . 407 *White Doe* 1064
Which ill can brook more rational relief : . . . 423 *Ecc. Sonn.* 1. 20. 7
And turn the instruments of good to ill, . . . 425 *Ecc. Sonn.* 1. 28. 4
Into the pensive heart ill fortified, ... 427 *Ecc. Sonn.* 1. 36. 13
And ill requited by this heartfelt sigh ! . . . 445 *Ecc. Sonn.* 3. 22. 14
Perversely curious, then, for hidden ill . . . . 449 *Ecc. Sonn.* 3. 35. 11
Which I could ill confine ; . . . . 487 **We walked* 54
To evil for a guard against worse ill, ... 493 *Hap. War.* 30
Seek for the good and cherish it—the ill . . . 505 *Warning* 161
Against far heavier ill, the pestilence . . . . 513 *General Fast* 13
Of Prudence, disentangling good and ill . . . 514 **Blest Statesman* 5
Joy based on sorrow, good with ill combined, . 514 **Who ponders* 3
Might soothe in human breasts the sense of ill, . 517 *Pun. Death* 1. 4
Darkening the window, ill defends the door . . 521 *Epist. Beaumont* 21
Stricken by this ill assurance, ... 535 *Egremont* 51
Ill fed she was, and thinly clad ; . . . . . . 536 *Goody Blake* 2
What may your ill intentions you avail ? . . . 554 *Prioress* 124

Ill—*continued.*
And who was then ill satisfied but I ? . . . . 558 *Cuck.and Night.* 92
Fie, quoth she, on thy name, Bird ill beseen ! . 560 *Cuck.andNight.* 186
He lets them perish through that grievous ill. . 560 *Cuck.andNight.* 200
Would ill suffice : for Plato's lore sublime, . . 576 *Chiabrera* 9. 8
With learnèd ears may ill agree, ... 577 **I come* 30
From ill we meet or good we miss, ... 578 **I come* 54
And the worse fear of future ill (which oft . . 586 *Ch. Lamb* 113
But chiefly Dido, to the coming ill . . . . . 624 *Æneid* 79
But ill sustained, and almost (so it seemed) . . 637 *Prelude* 1. 333
Judging not ill perhaps, the timid course . . . 656 *Prelude* 3. 494
Of good or ill report ; or those with whom . . 656 *Prelude* 3. 535
With an astonishment but ill suppressed, . . . 665 *Prelude* 4. 433
From things well-matched or ill, and words for things, ... 679 *Prelude* 6. 300
To human-kind, and to the good and ill . . . 709 *Prelude* 8. 678
And ill could brook, beholding that the best . . 712 *Prelude* 9. 213
The man who had an ill surmise of him . . . 719 *Prelude* 10. 107
That voice, ill requiem ! seldom heard by me . 723 *Prelude* 10. 327
And fellowships of men, and see ill sights . . . 755 *Recluse* 1. 1. 827
This, in itself not ill, would yet have been . . 783 *Excursion* 2. 748
Ill borne in earlier life ; but his was now . . . 783 *Excursion* 2. 749
Where knowledge, ill begun in cold remark . . 810 *Excursion* 4. 622
But ill according. An heraldic shield, ... 824 *Excursion* 5. 160
To see disclosed, by such dread proof, how ill . 826 *Excursion* 5. 255
With neither element of good or ill ; . . . . 843 *Excursion* 6. 371
As with her office would but ill accord) . . . 853 *Excursion* 6. 959
Ill purposes, and flatter foul desires. . . . . 894 *Excursion* 9. 687
(Ill home for bird so gentle), they looked down . K.8. 225 **I will* 20
Ill neighbourhood—pity that this should be— . K.8. 246 *Recluse* 1.1.356
I'll. (*Partial list.*) *See* **I.**
But I'll be even with him—here again . . . . 45 *Bord.* 451
Against this venerable Man ? I'll tell you : . . 45 *Bord.* 465
Well then, says I—I'll out with it ; at which . . 45 *Bord.* 475
And long as I can stir I'll dog him.—Yesterday, . 46 *Bord.* 483
I'll answer for it that our four-legged friend . . 51 *Bord.* 774
Shall not disturb us ; further I'll not engage ; . 51 *Bord.* 775
I'll lead you to the spot. . . . . 72 *Bord.* 2013
And I'll build up a giant with you. . . . . . 86 *Rural Arch.* 24
Then I'll yoke thee to my cart like a pony in the plough ; . . . . 88 *Pet-lamb* 46
I'll follow you across the snow ; . . . . . 114 *Ind. Wom.* 51
I'll look upon your tents again. . . . . . . 114 *Ind. Wom.* 54
I'll call thee by my darling's name ; . . . . 121 *EmigrantMother* 90
I'll tell him many tales of Thee." . . . . . 121 *EmigrantMother* 95
Good Susan tell me, and I'll stay ; . . . . . 128 *Idiot Boy* 194
I'll to the wood."—The word scarce said, . . . 130 *Idiot Boy* 424
I'll build an Indian bower ; I know . . . . 145 *Her Eyes* 55
"I'll teach my boy the sweetest things : . . . 145 *Her Eyes* 81
I'll teach him how the owlet sings. . . . . . 145 *Her Eyes* 82
I'll hurl thee headlong with the rock . . . . 155 *Waterfall* 13
Little Flower—I'll make a stir, ... 160 **Pansies, lilies* 15
I'll think of the Leech-gatherer on the lonely moor !" 197 *Resolution* 140
"I'll build a pleasure-house upon this spot, . . 201 *Hart-leap* 57
But through the clouds I'll never float . . . . 236 *P. B.* 3
I'll fling your carcass like a log . . . . . . 241 *P. B.* 459
I'll be a son to thee !" . . . . 488 *Fountain* 62
By Jove I'll be in, ... S.3. 431 **If money's* 5
By her side I'll take my place, ... S.3. 437 **I, whose* 19
Ill-adjusted. An ill-adjusted turban, for defence 879 *Excursion* 8. 351
Ill-advised. Of ill-advised Ambition and of Pride K.8. 255 *Recluse* 1.1.673
Ill-conditioned. The Mastiff, ill-conditioned carl ! . 179 *Waggoner* 3. 101
Ill-constructed. Is fashioned like an ill-constructed tale ; . . . . 829 *Excursion* 5. 432
Ill-done. Impatiently, ill-done, or left undone, . . 801 *Excursion* 4. 26
Ill-fated. Ill-fated Ruth, in hallowed mould . . 195 *Ruth* 254
Ill-fated Chief ! there are whose hopes are built . 214 *Dion* 102
When this ill-fated Traveller died, ... 492 *Fidelity* 59
Ill-fated Vessel !—ghastly shock ! . . . . . 579 **Sweet Flower* 36
The ill-fated pair) in that plain tale will draw . 717 *Prelude* 9. 566
Ill-gotten. He paid what he could with his ill-gotten pelf, ... 570 *Farmer* 37
Ill-governed. Ill-governed passions, ranklings of despite, ... 804 *Excursion* 4. 212
Ill-graced. Thus (where the intrusive Pile, ill-graced 301 *Bran* 119
Illimitable. Roaming the illimitable waters round ; 31 *Guilt* 364
Went hurrying o'er the illimitable waste, . . . 667 *Prelude* 5. 136
Ill-judging. Oh, ill-judging sire of an innocent son 116 *Repentance* 25
Ill-matched. With ill-matched aims the Architect who planned— . . . . 451 *Ecc. Sonn.* 3. 43. 2
There, 'mid a peal of ill-matched sounds and cries, 719 *Prelude* 10. 97
Illness. Shall feign a sudden illness, and the Girl, . 59 *Bord.* 1185
"A sudden illness seized her in the strength . . 849 *Excursion* 6. 741
Ill-omening. The censures, and ill-omening of those 680 *Prelude* 6. 331
Ill-requited. Ill-requited upon earth ; . . . . 160 **Pansies, lilies* 58
For ill-requited France, by many deemed . . . 733 *Prelude* 11. 384
From ill-requited labour turned adrift . . . . 764 *Excursion* 1. 560
Ills. And tears which flowed for ills which patience might not heal. . . . . 29 *Guilt* 270
Cold, pain, and labour, and all fleshly ills ; . . 197 *Resolution* 115
And meekly bear the ills which bear I must : . . 464 **A point* 8
But who (though neither reckoning ills assigned . 504 *Warning* 47
Be wanting that sometimes, where fancied ills . 538 **In desultory* 34
Be the dead load of mortal ills forgot, ... 617 *Desc.Sk.Quarto* 811
Some tempting island, could but know the ills . 656 *Prelude* 3. 485
Hence, amid ills that vex and wrongs that crush . 748 *Prelude* 14. 124
Ill-sheltered. Ill-sheltered, and oft wanting fire and food ; . . . . 815 *Excursion* 4. 924
Ill-sorted. (Like those ill-sorted unions, work supposed 641 *Prelude* 1. 590
Ill-sustained. These hardships ill-sustained, these dangers past, ... 320 **Hunger, and* 4

Ill-timed. This humble tribute as ill-timed or vain. 465 *Pastor and 14
Ill-tutored. I was ill-tutored for captivity; . . . 654 Prelude 3. 356
Illume. Bright beams the lonely mountain-horse illume . . . . 4 Ev. Wk. 132
Deep yellow beams the scatter'd stems illume, . 5 Ev. Wk. 180
Where sparkling eyes and breaking smiles illume . 13 Desc. Sk. 133
His burning eyes with fearful light illume. . 13 Desc. Sk. 165
Ye flattering eastern lights, once more the hills illume! . . . . 20 Desc. Sk. 529
Deep yellow beams the scatter'd boles illume, . 594 Ev.Wk.Quarto 163
Long streaks of fairy light the wave illume . . 598 Ev. Wk.Quarto 341
Or where thick sails illume Batavia's groves;. . 613 Desc.Sk.Quarto 625
Fair smiling lights the purpled hills illume! . . 613 Desc.Sk.Quarto 633
Illumed. An aspect tenderly illumed, ... 498 *Departing summer 2
Illumes. Illumes with sparkling foam the twilight shade. . . . . 593 Ev. Wk. Quarto 80
Illuminate. Gently illuminate a sober scene:— 14 Desc. Sk. 213
Will fail to illuminate the infant's bier; . . . 319 Biscayan 12
To illuminate the abyss of ages past, ... 735 Prelude 12. 63
Illuminating. Or, through illuminating grace, received, ... 839 Excursion 6. 72
Illumination. See **Soul-illumination.**
With soft illumination cheered the dimness of that place. . . . . 92 Poet's Dream 12
Of all illumination,—may my Life . . . . . 755 Recluse 1. 1. 855
Bore stars—illumination of all gems! . . . . 784 Excursion 2. 845
Illumination into deep, dark holds, ... 870 Excursion 7. 835
Illumine. To illumine Playford hall, ... L.2. 190 *Queen and 10
Illumined. See **Moon-illumined, Self-illumined.**
Slow glides the sail along the illumined shore, . 12 Desc. Sk. 103
Uplift in quiet their illumined forms, ... 19 Desc. Sk. 473
While thus illumined, tells of painful strife . . 278 *Lo! where she 6
Inly illumined by Heaven's pitying love; . . . 280 *Oh what 12
Illumined! root of beauty and goodnesse, . . 562 Cuck.and Night. 314
Palace illumined with the sun of bliss; . . . 563 Troilus 30
Where solitary forms illumin'd stray . . . . 607 Desc.Sk.Quarto 273
Lift, all serene, their still, illumin'd forms, . 612 Desc.Sk.Quarto 565
And filled the illumined groves with ravishment. . 814 Excursion 4. 860
And, as they issue from the illumined pile, . . 877 Excursion 8. 175
Illumines. Illumines, from within, the leafy shade; 3 Ev. Wk. 65
Illusion. Sustained by delicate illusion? . . . 143 *Driven in 19
Of a wild dream, or worse illusion; . . . . 238 P. B. 188
Mounts, in this fine illusion, toward the skies: . 368 Trajan 69
The sweet illusion might have hung, for hours. . 530 Gleaner 25
Such, in the fond illusion of my heart, ... 578 Peele Castle 29
Who shared at first the illusion; but was soon . 805 Excursion 4. 273
Of ignorance or illusion) lives and breathes . . 813 Excursion 4. 830
"Of such illusion do we here incur; . . . . 847 Excursion 6. 600
The illusion strengthening as he gazed, he felt . K.8. 237 Recluse 1.1. 36
Illusions. Of these illusions, or they please no more. 270 *Shame on 14
Desire we past illusions to recall? . . . . . 469 *Desire we 1
And those illusions, which excite the scorn . . 813 Excursion 4. 834
Illusive. Not such the World's illusive shows; . 170 Rural Ill. 25
Illusive cataracts! of their terrors . . . . . 300 Bran 19
By impulse sent from such illusive power,— . . 827 Excursion 5. 322
Who dictates and inspires illusive feats, . . . 843 Excursion 6. 350
Illustrate. To illustrate Nature's book of rudiments— 657 Prelude 3. 554
Illustrated. Illustrated with never-dying verse, . 356 Aquap. 266
Illustrated, and mutually endeared. . . . . 362 *List—'twas 48
Illustrated with inborn courtesy; . . . . . 539 *Lady! a 64
Illustrations. Apt illustrations of the moral world, 750 Prelude 14. 319
Illustrious. Nor cheer him; for the illustrious Swede hath done . . . . 305 *The Voice 9
England's illustrious sons of long, long ages; . 328 Ode 1815 62
Forgive, illustrious Country! these deep sighs, . 360 Alban Hills 1
POZZOBONNELLI his illustrious house; . . . . 575 Chiabrera 8. 7
Of generations of illustrious men, ... 652 Prelude 3. 260
To a poor scholar!"—when illustrious men, . . 656 Prelude 3. 474
The illustrious wife of Roland, in the hour . . 723 Prelude 10. 381
Oft, through thy fair domains, illustrious Peer! . 753 *Oft, through 1
Its most illustrious province, must be found . . 820 Excursion 4. 1261
A race illustrious for heroic deeds, ... 834 Excursion 5. 792
Gave to thy fame a more illustrious flight . . . S.3. 442 *Vasco, whose 10
Ill-worthy. Ill-worthy, Beaumont! were the grief 582 *O for a 10
I'm. (Partial list.) See **I.**
I'm fatherless and motherless. . . . . . . 82 Alice Fell 44
Come to me—I'm no enemy: . . . . 120 Emigrant Mother 28
"I'm here, what is't you want with me?" . . 129 Idiot Boy 253
"Oh Sir! you know I'm Betty Foy, ... 129 Idiot Boy 254
I'm as great as they, I trow, ... 160 *Pansies, lilies 13
"I'm helping this poor dying brute." . . . . 242 P. B. 490
Image. Whose softened image penetrates the deep. 5 Ev. Wk. 173
The image of a poet's heart, ... 9 Collins 11
By cells upon whose image, while he prays, . . 14 Desc. Sk. 200
The image of his glorious Sire displayed, . . 18 Desc. Sk. 440
On the mute Image and the troubled walls. . . 20 Desc. Sk. 544
An image of this old Man still was present, . . 39 Bord. 97
Do recognise some image of themselves, . . . 70 Bord. 1824
A solemn image to my heart, ... 79 *Stay near 8
Image that, flying still before me, gleamed . . 89 Prelude 1. 451
Shrine, Altar, Image, Offerings hung in sign of gratitude; . . . . 92 Poet's Dream 47
Its image would survive among his thoughts: . . 149 M. H. 22
Thou sink'st, the image of thy rest . . . . . 158 *In youth 62
The moving image to detain; . . . . . . 182 Waggoner 4. 233
A dancing Shape, an Image gay, ... 186 *She was 9
And downward Image gaily vying . . . . . 190 *Lyre! though 21
To show them a fair image; 'tis themselves, . . 218 Recluse 1. 1. 224
An image, too, of that sweet Boy, ... 232 Jew. Fam. 13

Image—continued.
The ghost-like image of a cloud? . . . . . 242 P. B. 502
The very image framing of a Tomb, ... 262 *Mark the 7
Proud thoughts that Image overawes, ... 286 Nith 37
There where you see his Image stand . . . . 301 Bran 70
An image that hath perished! . . . . . . 301 Yarrow V. 4
Thy genuine image, Yarrow! . . . . 302 Yarrow V. 86
New love of many a rival image brought . . . 367 *If with 2
A venerable image yields . . . . 406 White Doe 947
Yes, she is soothed: an Image faint, ... 407 White Doe 1033
Might seem a saintly Image from its shrine . . 423 Ecc. Sonn. 1. 19. 8
Thy Image falls to earth. Yet some, I ween, . 434 Ecc. Sonn. 2. 25. 9
Oft with his musings doth thy image blend, . . 460 *Wanderer! that 70
The image of its perfect bow. . . . . . . 472 Ossian 10
That not an image of the past . . . . . . 499 Memory 19
Who rashly strove thy Image to portray? . . 511 *Who rashly 1
And eke, when he the image did behold . . 553 Prioress 53
Whene'er I looked, thy Image still was there; . 578 Peele Castle 7
By cells whose image, trembling as he prays, . 606 Desc.Sk.Quarto 253
An image of her soul is kept alive, ... 627 *We gaze 12
Or image unprofaned; and I would stand, . . 646 Prelude 2. 306
Some lovely Image in the song rose up . . . 660 Prelude 4. 113
Of his own image, by a sunbeam now, . . . 662 Prelude 4. 268
How potent a mere image of her sway; . . . 664 Prelude 4. 358
Who through that bodily image hath diffused, . 666 Prelude 5. 16
Some element to stamp her image on . . . . 666 Prelude 5. 46
To have a soulless image on the eye . . . . 683 Prelude 6. 526
On which a dull red image of the moon . . . 685 Prelude 6. 705
That we must tread—thy image rose again, . . 692 Prelude 7. 319
Or waxen image which yourselves have made, . 703 Prelude 8. 300
Breathed up its smoke, an image of his ghost . 705 Prelude 8. 449
For lingering yet an image in my mind . . . 725 Prelude 10. 509
For me that image of pure gladsomeness . . . 733 Prelude 11. 412
And image of right reason; that matures . . 740 Prelude 13. 22
The thought, the image, and the silent joy: . . 744 Prelude 13. 272
Their knowledge of the heavens, and image forth 745 Prelude 13. 341
An image, and a character, by books . . . . 745 Prelude 13. 359
Through every image and through every thought, 747 Prelude 14. 116
Express the image of a better time, ... 755 Recluse 1. 1. 856
So still an image of tranquillity, ... 770 Excursion 1. 946
We have an image of the pristine earth, . . . 777 Excursion 2. 360
Or, if a different image be recalled . . . . 789 Excursion 3. 244
Saw a seductive image of herself. . . . . . 797 Excursion 3. 805
And his most perfect image in the world. . . . 804 Excursion 4. 227
Yet is their form and image here expressed . . 809 Excursion 4. 552
Altar and image, and the inclusive walls . . 811 Excursion 4. 672
Shrine, altar, image, and the massy piles . . . 814 Excursion 4. 899
Show to his eye an image of the pangs . . . 850 Excursion 6. 808
Thy image disappear! The Mountain-ash . . 868 Excursion 7. 714
An image fair, which, brightening in his soul . . 871 Excursion 7. 935
Who, in the bodily image, in the mind, . . . 872 Excursion 7. 986
Crowned like the image of fantastic Fear; . . 879 Excursion 8. 349
Like image of solemnity, conjoined . . . . . 881 Excursion 8. 459
The sculptured image of some patron-saint, . . 881 Excursion 8. 488
A twofold image; on a grassy bank . . . . 890 Excursion 9. 440
Come, gentle Sleep, Death's image tho' thou art, . S.3. 441 *Come, gentle 1
That parts the image from reality; . . . . . K.8. 252 Recluse 1.1.577
Imaged. Of their own beauty, imaged in the heart. 147 Joanna 50
Of all that is most beauteous—imaged there . . 211 Laod. 103
Imaged, though faintly, in the hue . . . . . 226 Vernal Ode 30
There imaged: or when, having gained the top . 799 Excursion 3. 935
Where is she imaged? in what favoured clime . 828 Excursion 5. 401
Imaged in downward show; the flower, the herbs, S.3. 435 *The doubt 106
Imagery. Where earth and heaven do make one imagery; . . . . 88 H. C. 10
His music, and to view his imagery: . . . . 108 Indolence 65
Of still or moving imagery— . . . . 228 Devot. Incit. 41
With those rich stores of Nature's imagery, . . 367 *As indignation 3
Exulting in its imagery; . . . . 400 White Doe 351
Raised toward that Imagery once more: . . . 405 White Doe 863
Of fret-work imagery laid low; . . . . . . 416 White Doe 1892
Of unsubstantial imagery, the dream, ... 456 *The leaves 10
From all its spirit-moving imagery, ... 583 *With copious 20
With all its intervenient imagery, ... 656 Prelude 3. 522
With all its solemn imagery, its rocks, . . . 671 Prelude 5. 386
Fair trains of imagery before me rise, ... 755 Recluse 1. 1. 756
Behold the universal imagery . . . . . . K.8. 252 Recluse 1.1.571
Images. For images of other worlds are there; . 18 Desc. Sk. 455
The many-coloured images imprest . . . . . 80 *Loving she 20
Flashed round him images and hues that wrought 96 Brothers 57
With images about her heart, ... 144 *Driven in 79
With all its lovely images, was changed . . . 149 *A narrow 69
And Images of voice—to hound and horn . . . 233 Power of Sound 34
Of Images in seemly row; . . . . 341 Ital. Itin. 8
With images, and crowns, and empty cars; . . 346 Processions 31
Those images of genial beauty, oft . . . . . 355 Aquap. 200
Her peace from images to pain allied. . . . 361 *For action 4
Who, 'mid a world of images imprest . . . . 381 Duddon 19. 6
These outward images of fate, ... 413 White Doe 1592
Far-distant images draw nigh, ... 457 *Had this 25
Sweet images! which, wheresoe'er he be, . . . 494 Hap. War. 61
More terrible images there. . . . . 620 Convict 20
Forms, images, nor numerous other aids . . . 634 Prelude 1. 155
Remained, no pleasant images of trees, . . . 638 Prelude 1. 396
That givest to forms and images a breath . . 638 Prelude 1. 403
Belfry, and images, and living trees; . . . . 643 Prelude 2. 106
As aught by wooden images performed . . . 657 Prelude 3. 571
For, images, and sentiments, and words, . . . 674 Prelude 5. 579
With images, and haunted by herself, ... 677 Prelude 6. 160
Debarred from Nature's living images, . . . 679 Prelude 6. 302
And Earth did change her images and forms . . 682 Prelude 6. 492

Images—*continued.*
Steadying, far-seen, a frame of images . . . . 690 *Prelude* 7. 215
Would leave behind a dance of images, . . . 700 *Prelude* 8. 114
But images of danger and distress, ... 701 *Prelude* 8. 164
Busies the eye with images and forms . . . . 707 *Prelude* 8. 581
And find a thousand bounteous images . . . 734 *Prelude* 11. 451
An active power to fasten images . . . . . 758 *Excursion* 1. 145
Her thoughts, her images, her high desires. . . 803 *Excursion* 4. 108
From some affecting images and thoughts, . . 826 *Excursion* 5. 240
Clear images before your gladdened eyes . . . 848 *Excursion* 6. 652
Those brighter images by books imprest . . . 848 *Excursion* 6. 701
Of memory, images and precious thoughts, . . . 857 *Excursion* 7. 29
With images attendant on the sound ; . . . . 862 *Excursion* 7. 355
Of moral prudence, clothed in images . . . . K.8. 227 **I will* 91
Imagination. Of young imagination have kept pure, 23 *Yew-tree* 49
Imagination needs must stir ; . . . . . . 112 **Yes ! thou* 5
Of rapt imagination sped her march . . . . 234 *Power of Sound* 124
Imagination is that sacred power, ... 259 **Weak is* 9
Imagination lofty and refined : . . . . . 259 **Weak is* 10
To fond imagination, ... 302 *Yarrow V.* 42
Imagination—ne'er before content, ... 327 *Ode 1815* 1
Knowledge no help ; Imagination shaped . . . 353 *Aquap.* 70
Imagination feels what Reason fears not . . . 356 *Aquap.* 278
Of a baptized imagination, prompt . . . . . 362 **List—'twas* 71
Survives imagination—to the change . . . . 388 **The pibroch's* 12
Known to the moral world, Imagination, . . . 427 *Ecc. Sonn.* 1. 34. 10
Intensely —from Imagination take . . . . . 508 *F. Stone* 25
Imagination works with bolder hope . . . . 520 *Pun. Death* 14. 4
In this new life. Imagination slept, ... 652 *Prelude* 3. 257
Imagination—here the Power so called . . . 684 *Prelude* 6. 592
Imagination restless ; nor was free . . . . . 701 *Prelude* 8. 167
Of plain Imagination and severe, ... 704 *Prelude* 8. 366
By pure Imagination : busy Power . . . . . 705 *Prelude* 8. 423
Here then my young imagination found . . . 708 *Prelude* 8. 639
Imagination, potent to inflame . . . . . . 716 *Prelude* 9. 495
Of pure imagination, and of love ; . . . . . 740 *Prelude* 13. 50
On my imagination since the morn . . . . . 742 *Prelude* 13. 145
Which on thy young imagination, trained . . . 745 *Prelude* 13. 364
Without Imagination, which, in truth, ... 749 *Prelude* 14. 189
Imagination having been our theme, ... 749 *Prelude* 14. 206
Nourished Imagination in her growth, ... 758 *Excursion* 1. 166
Ah ! what avails imagination high . . . . . 789 *Excursion* 3. 209
And with the imagination rest content, ... 790 *Excursion* 3. 303
Imagination—not permitted here . . . . . 813 *Excursion* 4. 819
Of pure imagination ;—above all, ... 836 *Excursion* 5. 910
That to the imagination may be given . . . . 865 *Excursion* 7. 526
Imagination, freedom in the will ; . . . . . 887 *Excursion* 9. 223
Imagination's. Imagination's light when reason's fails, ... 812 *Excursion* 4. 772
Shall be Imagination's Lord, ... S.3. 439 **Avaunt this* 4
Imaginations. Those bold imaginations in due time 689 *Prelude* 7. 142
Imaginations, sense of woes to come, ... 723 *Prelude* 10. 329
Discoursing on remote imaginations, strong . . K.8. 227 **I will* 100
And dear Imaginations realized . . . . . . K.8. 239 *Recluse* 1.1.108
Imaginative. To the still lake) the imaginative Bird 456 **The leaves* 12
Imaginative Faith ! canst overleap, ... 469 **Desire we* 10
Of that imaginative impulse sent . . . . . 682 *Prelude* 6. 462
Of these, I feel the imaginative power . . . . 694 *Prelude* 7. 468
Far more of an imaginative form . . . . . . 703 *Prelude* 8. 284
Visitings of imaginative power . . . . . . 737 *Prelude* 12. 203
—The imaginative faculty was lord . . . . . 812 *Excursion* 4. 707
Which the imaginative Will upholds . . . . 818 *Excursion* 4. 1128
From these imaginative heights, that yield . . 819 *Excursion* 4. 1188
Thanks to his pure imaginative soul . . . . 854 *Excursion* 6. 1065
Imagine. Imagine (but ye Saints ! who can ?) . 373 *Eg. Maid* 277
And of himself did he imagine oft, ... 564 *Troilus* 99
If you imagine changes slowly wrought, . . . 795 *Excursion* 3. 616
Imagined. The Patriot nymph starts at imagined sounds, ... 15 *Desc. Sk.* 266
In dim relation to imagined Beings. . . . . 64 *Bord.* 1455
And, looking round, imagined that he saw . . 96 *Brothers* 96
With groves that never were imagined, lay . . 262 **Dark and* 10
A better will ; and, in the imagined view . . 447 *Ecc. Sonn.* 3. 27. 13
Part seen, imagined part ! . . . . 508 *May* 96
Imaginings. With thy best imaginings ; . . . 90 *Longest Day* 60
Abuse hath cleared from vain imaginings ; . . . 433 *Ecc. Sonn.* 2. 18. 12
Imbecile. His days he wasted, an imbecile mind ! 126 *V. and J.* 306
His days he wasted,—an imbecile mind. . . . 718 *Prelude* 9. 585
Imbecility. Till the caves roar,—and imbecility 311 **Who rises* 58
Of shameful imbecility uprisen, ... 715 *Prelude* 9. 384
Imbibe. From which it did itself imbibe a ray . . 861 *Excursion* 7. 236
Imbibed. Which I from thee imbibed: and 'tis most true 749 *Prelude* 14. 235
Feeding the soul, and eagerly imbibed . . . . 757 *Excursion* 1. 69
He had imbibed of fear or darker thought . . 762 *Excursion* 1. 407
Butter that had imbibed from meadow-flowers . 782 *Excursion* 2. 679
They had imbibed, and ceased not to receive. . 893 *Excursion* 9. 606
Imbound. *See* **Embound.**
Spirit of Ossian ! if imbound . . . . . . 472 *Ossian* 17
Strong by her charters, free because imbound, . 514 **Blest Statesman* 12
The dusky Shape within her arms imbound, . . 532 **Once I* 4
Imbue. Imbue your prison-bars with solemn sheen, 451 *Ecc. Sonn.* 3. 44. 7
Imbued. And this too-long-polluted land imbued . 102 *Artegal* 19
Of simple truth with grace divine imbued ; . . 450 *Ecc. Sonn.* 3. 40. 8
Imbued the altar-window ; fixed aloft . . . . 825 *Excursion* 5. 162
Imbues. Outshine the splendour that imbues . . 165 *Parrot* 11
Of beamy radiance, that imbues . . . . . . 457 **Had this* 27
Imitable. Of imitable lineament, ... 301 *Bran* 81
Imitate. And this for one who cannot imitate . . 105 *Artegal* 174
Of Truth and Beauty, strives to imitate, . . . 463 **Why should the* 7
Could imitate for indolent survey, ... 511 **Who rashly* 19
To imitate, not wise enough to avoid ; . . . . 728 *Prelude* 11. 69

Imitate—*continued.*
Of sombre foliage, seem to imitate . . . . . 891 *Excursion* 9. 501
Imitation. Were endless imitation. . . . . . 589 *Immortality* 107
Imitations. But imitations, fondly made in plain . 690 *Prelude* 7. 238
Imitative. To Beardless Boys—an imitative race, . 516 **Young England* 10
Confederate, imitative of the chase . . . . . 638 *Prelude* 1. 435
Immaterial. Those immaterial agents bowed their heads . . . . 677 *Prelude* 6. 125
Immaturity. Of immaturity, and—in the teeth . 721 *Prelude* 10. 216
Immeasurable. " Peaceful as this immeasurable plain 30 *Guilt* 334
By an immeasurable stream . . . . 247 *P. B.* 979
At a slow pace. The immeasurable height . . 684 *Prelude* 6. 624
Immeasurably. Immeasurably distant ; and the vault, 184 *Night-piece* 20
Withered, grotesque, immeasurably old, . . . 333 *Fish-women* 8
Immediate. Submits to recognise; the immediate law, 64 *Bord.* 1494
A rapture often, and immediate love . . . . 704 *Prelude* 8. 353
The immediate proof of principles no more . . 730 *Prelude* 11. 196
Immediately. What thoughts immediately were ours, nor how . . . . 149 **A narrow* 67
Immediately he came, not tarrying, ... 555 *Prioress* 166
Then feels immediately some hollow thought . . 636 *Prelude* 1. 259
And with a shepherd's joy. Immediately . . K.8. 229 **I will* 149
Immemorial. By immemorial privilege allowed ; . 824 *Excursion* 5. 158
Immense. Objects immense portrayed in miniature, 379 *Duddon* 12. 3
Of white-robed Scholars only—this immense . . 451 *Ecc. Sonn.* 3. 43. 4
Were lost, bewildered among woods immense, . 685 *Prelude* 6. 701
And no one seems to want his share.—Immense . 700 *Prelude* 8. 55
Mine was unable to attain. Immense . . . . 795 *Excursion* 3. 660
And, from the plain, with toil immense, upreared 811 *Excursion* 4. 684
Immensity. In undisturbed immensity . . . . 244 *P. B.* 699
Deeper than ocean, in the immensity . . . . 456 **Soft as* 4
Thy Soul's immensity ; . . . . 589 *Immortality* 190
Immersed. Whose universe was gloom immersed in gloom, ... 271 *George : Death* 3
Sunk down, and lay immersed in dead repose . S.3. 434 **The doubt* 50
Imminent. More imminent. Not unseen do they approach ; . . . . 541 *Grace Darl.* 63
Immoderate. Immoderate wishes, pining discontent, 804 *Excursion* 4. 213
Quaffed in his gratitude immoderate cups ; . . 842 *Excursion* 6. 242
Or with immoderate pain. I look for Man, . . K.8. 246 *Recluse* 1.1.352
Immortal. And then, for our immortal part ! *we* want 98 *Brothers* 180
Immortal as the love that gave it being. . . . 119 *Maternal Grief* 81
For mercy and immortal bloom ? . . . . . . 192 *Seq. Beggars* 42
Together in immortal books enrolled : . . . . 251 **Pelion and* 2
The immortal Spirit of one happy day . . . . 251 **There is a little* 13
If aught be in them of immortal seed, ... 261 **From the dark* 8
Yon slowly-sinking star—immortal Sire . . . 261 **I watch* 2
Mount, tuneful Bird, and join the immortal quires ! 261 **I heard (alas* 13
The immortal Mind craves objects that endure : . 263 **Those words* 12
And so the bright immortal Theban band, . . 265 **When haughty* 12
Dwell, clothed in radiance, their immortal vest ; . 266 **The stars* 3
So timely Grace the immortal wing may heal, . 270 **If these* 13
Immortal Fabrics, rising to the sound . . . . 335 *Cologne* 13
Of joy immortal and of pure affection. . . . 370 *Eg. Maid* 78
Avon—a precious, an immortal name ! . . . 392 *Avon* 1
A spring-tide of immortal green : . . . . . 410 *White Doe* 1264
Immortal amaranth and palms abound. . . . 418 *Ecc. Sonn.* 1. 1. 14
Where Tiber's stream the immortal City laves : . 421 *Ecc. Sonn.* 1. 13. 4
Truth, their immortal Una ? Babylon, . . . 425 *Ecc. Sonn.* 1. 25. 9
And One there is who builds immortal lays, . . 441 *Ecc. Sonn.* 3. 4. 6
And with immortal Spirits blend ! . . . . . 458 **Had this* 48
As if through an immortal day . . . . . . 478 *Somnamb.* 35
But our immortal Spirits may. . . . . . . 506 *Lab. Hymn* 24
Of an immortal spirit, is a gift . . . . . . 519 *Pun. Death* 10. 2
And would that some immortal Voice—a Voice . 541 *Grace Darl.* 88
A garland of immortal boughs . . . . . . 582 **O for a* 4
Adding immortal labours of his own— . . . . 587 *Crosth.* 6
Our Souls have sight of that immortal sea . . 590 *Immortality* 167
Where, throned in gold, immortal Science reigns ; 619 *School Ex.* 70
Recesses in man's heart, immortal verse . . . 635 *Prelude* 1. 232
Dust as we are, the immortal spirit grows . . . 637 *Prelude* 1. 340
How the immortal soul with God-like power . . 661 *Prelude* 4. 166
It gives, to think that our immortal being . . 666 *Prelude* 5. 23
Poor earthly casket of immortal verse, . . . 668 *Prelude* 5. 164
The very being of the immortal soul. . . . . 730 *Prelude* 11. 222
Or season's difference ; the immortal Soul . . 792 *Excursion* 3. 403
Insensibly ;—the immortal and divine . . . . 795 *Excursion* 3. 671
Alas ! the endowment of immortal power . . . 804 *Excursion* 4. 205
Immortal life, in never-fading worlds, ... 839 *Excursion* 6. 86
And wisdom married to immortal verse ? " . . 865 *Excursion* 7. 536
And their immortal soul, may waste away." . . 886 *Excursion* 9. 152
Immortal in the world which is to come. . . . K.8. 255 *Recluse* 1.1.691
Immortality. In their immortality ; . . . . . 205 *Brougham* 125
Of man converse with immortality ? . . . . . 316 **O'er the* 14
The gift of immortality ; . . . . 345 **How blest* 75
Through mortal change and immortality ; . . . 374 *Eg. Maid* 346
That they were born for immortality. . . . . 451 *Ecc. Sonn.* 3. 43. 14
In visible quest of immortality, ... 509 *F. Stone* 90
Thou, over whom thy Immortality . . . . . 589 *Immortality* 118
Breathed immortality, revolving life, ... 759 *Excursion* 1. 228
Of immortality, in Nature's course, ... 812 *Excursion* 4. 739
That life is love and immortality, ... 837 *Excursion* 5. 1002
Announcing immortality and joy . . . . . . 864 *Excursion* 7. 452
Foretasted, immortality conceived . . . . . 887 *Excursion* 9. 225
By all,—a blissful immortality, ... 887 *Excursion* 9. 226
Immortalize. Anxious an aery name to immortalize. 313 **Go back* 8
Immortals. She suffered, as Immortals sometimes do; 169 *Love lies Bleeding* 1
Or blest procession (to the Immortals dear) . . 213 *Dion* 29
Immovably. *See* **Immoveably.**
Upon herself resting immovably. . . . . . 574 *Chiabrera* 3. 12
That, though immovably convinced, we want . 804 *Excursion* 4. 201

Imperial—*continued.*
Right at the imperial station's western base, 219 **This Height* 13
High as the imperial front of man; 227 *Vernal Ode* 118
Of an imperial Castle, which the plough 253 **Aerial Rock* 8
The imperial Consort of the Fairy-king 254 *Wild Duck's Nest* 1
The imperial Stature, the colossal stride, 270 *Henry: Portrait* 1
Redeemed to baffle that imperial Slave, 318 **Ah! where* 7
For lo! the Imperial City stands released 326 *Sobieski* 6
Still are we present with the imperial Chief, 368 *Trajan* 70
Hence, while the imperial City's din 376 **The Minstrels* 73
Aloft, the imperial Bird of Rome invokes 380 *Duddon* 17. 3
Neglecting in imperial state 413 *White Doe* 1591
And the vain splendours of Imperial Rome?— 528 **Those breathing* 95
Encouraged by the imperial eye, 545 *Russ. Fug.* 373
And that imperial palace whence he came. 588 *Immortality* 84
Yea, when a glimpse of those imperial bowers 700 *Prelude* 8. 111
Of Goslar, once imperial, I renewed 702 *Prelude* 8. 211
Imperial, their chief living residence. 708 *Prelude* 8. 596
To the imperial edifice of Blois, 716 *Prelude* 9. 482
Towered like the imperial thistle, not unfurnished 848 *Excursion* 6. 688
And best protection, this imperial Realm, 888 *Excursion* 9. 295
On the green turf, with his imperial front 890 *Excursion* 9. 443
Imperious. Imperious at all times, his temper rose; 68 *Bord.* 1715
Would, with imperious admonition, then 172 *Infant Daughter* 25
Imperious passion in a heart set free:— 363 **The world forsaken* 12
A less imperious sympathy is due, 458 *Sea-shore* 26
Of his imperious love, 543 *Russ. Fug.* 182
Imperiously. Reminded less imperiously of thee;— 868 *Excursion* 7. 710
Imperishable. And let imperishable Columns rise 324 *Ode 1814* 103
Do no imperishable record find 540 *Grace Darl.* 15
Through knowledge spreading and imperishable, 715 *Prelude* 9. 361
Of pure, imperishable, blessedness, 803 *Excursion* 4. 159
By man's imperishable spirit, quelled. 865 *Excursion* 7. 530
Undaunted, toward the imperishable heavens, 885 *Excursion* 9. 43
Imperishable majesty streamed forth 893 *Excursion* 9. 630
To gloom imperishable. So (if truths S.3. 435 **The doubt* 110
Imperishably. Transferred to bowers imperishably green, 381 *Duddon* 20. 5
Remained imperishably interwoven 585 *Ch. Lamb* 93
Impersonated. Impersonated in thy calm decay! 290 *Kilchurn* 21
As well they might, the impersonated thought, 706 *Prelude* 8. 501
Impertinent. But for the impertinent and ceaseless strife 831 *Excursion* 5. 617
Impervious. The weary hills, impervious, blackening near; 8 *Ev. Wk.* 342
Hang o'er the abyss, whose else impervious gloom 13 *Desc. Sk.* 164
Impervious, and storm-proof. 168 *Wren's Nest* 8
Impervious to the tide of war: 390 *Highland Broach* 10
From sea to sea, impervious to the sun 442 *Ecc. Sonn.* 3. 9. 3
Impervious to the wind. 542 *Russ. Fug.* 96
Bend o'er th' abyss?—the else impervious gloom 605 *Desc.Sk.Quarto* 186
Among the impervious crags, but having been 660 *Prelude* 4. 98
From me, those dark impervious shades, that hang 790 *Excursion* 3. 296
Is here—how grateful this impervious screen! 881 *Excursion* 8. 447
Impetuous. And such impetuous blood. 193 *Ruth* 126
Here checked by too impetuous haste, 228 *Devot. Incit.* 19
Beheld in your impetuous march the likeness 229 *Clouds* 12
Impetuous motion to the Stars above her. 346 *Gemmi* 8
Impetuous thoughts that brook not servile reins. 382 *Duddon* 26. 14
Such is the impetuous spirit that pervades 421 *Ecc. Sonn.* 1. 12. 3
That into breezes sink; impetuous minds 500 *Humanity* 52
Pull at her rein like an impetuous courser; 639 *Prelude* 1. 495
(So willed the Muse) a less impetuous stream, 687 *Prelude* 7. 9
Of soul impetuous, and the bashful maid 836 *Excursion* 5. 960
Save at worst need, from bold impetuous force, 873 *Excursion* 7. 1031
Impiety. This precious leaf, with harsh impiety. 250 *Admon.* 8
Through their impiety—my inmost soul 720 *Prelude* 10. 133
From ribaldry, impiety, or wrath K.8. 246 *Recluse* 1. 1. 344
Impious. Whose impious folds enwrapped even thee; and truth 77 *Bord.* 2260
If to provoke such doom the Impious dare, 217 *Enterprise* 120
An impious oath confirmed the threat— 241 *P. B.* 461
Doomed, with their impious Lord, the flying Hart 267 **Though narrow* 13
Hence hath your prowess quelled that impious crew. 326 **Intrepid sons* 8
With impious thanksgiving, the Almighty's scorn! 326 **Emperors and* 2
Which, in our time, the impious have disclosed; 332 *Ode: Thanks.* 235
Convoked the impious to chastise: 405 *White Doe* 838
"Your impious work forbear: perish what may, 681 *Prelude* 6. 433
Would have abashed those impious crests—have quelled 721 *Prelude* 10. 212
Divine Comates, by his impious lord 733 *Prelude* 11. 444
Hardened by impious pride!—I did not fear 779 *Excursion* 2. 486
The groaning nations; when the impious rule, 805 *Excursion* 4. 298
An impious warfare with the very life 815 *Excursion* 4. 967
By horror of their impious rites, preserved; 870 *Excursion* 7. 844
To impious use—by process indirect 889 *Excursion* 9. 319
Impiously. Earl Pembroke, slain so impiously! 399 *White Doe* 263
Of revolution, impiously unbound! 513 *General Fast* 14
Implanted. Implanted like a Fortress, as in truth 362 **List—'twas* 31
Implement. Or other implement of house or field. 132 *Michael* 109
Yet, Showman, where can lie the cause? Shall thy Implement have blame, 189 *Star-gazers* 9
Ye Gods, thought He, that servile Implement 214 *Dion* 94
Whose seeds are shed, or as an implement 567 *Cumb. Beg.* 86
Or implement, a passive thing employed 886 *Excursion* 9. 116
Implements. He laid his implements with gentle care, 95 *Brothers* 33
Life turned the meanest of her implements, 122 *V. and J.* 42
These base implements to wield; 140 *Arm. Lady* 50
And implements of frolic mirth; 191 *Seq. Beggars* 4

Implements—*continued.*
And tyranny, and implements of death; 724 *Prelude* 10. 403
To implements of ordinary use, 784 *Excursion* 2. 865
—Inglorious implements of craft and toil, 831 *Excursion* 5. 611
Of intellectual implements and tools; 888 *Excursion* 9. 308
Implore. Celestial pity I again implore;— 209 *Laod.* 5
Even then we may perhaps in vain implore 251 *Appleth.* 10
Breathed thy mercy to implore, 336 **Jesu! bless* 5
Do neither promise ask nor grace implore 360 **Near Anio's* 13
Solemn thanksgiving. Nor will *they* implore 448 *Ecc. Sonn.* 3. 30. 8
Than the hands are free to implore: 502 **Like a* 8
Widow, or wife, implore on tremulous knee, 505 *Warning* 153
Upon the act a blessing I implore, 582 *Invoc. Earth* 24
With pale-blue hands, and eyes that fix'd implore, 615 *Desc.Sk.Quarto* 710
For once, the Muse's help will we implore, 697 *Prelude* 7. 682
Implored. Revered among the nations. I implored 798 *Excursion* 3. 863
Wasting that love the nymphs implored in vain. S.3. 434 **The doubt* 85
Implores. A Pontiff, Trajan *here* the Gods implores, 368 *Trajan* 41
Conjures, implores, and labours all he can 444 *Ecc. Sonn.* 3. 18. 12
Implores the dreadful untried sleep of Death. 613 *Desc.Sk.Quarto* 643
Imploring. Imploring, or commanding with meet pride, 467 *St. Bees* 102
Imploringly. Imploringly;—looked up, and asked the Heavens 796 *Excursion* 3. 690
Imply. Did this unprecedented course imply 680 *Prelude* 6. 327
More near akin to those than names imply,— 694 *Prelude* 7. 489
Such acquiescence neither doth imply, 790 *Excursion* 3. 264
Import. Of sleep took import terrible;— 299 *Brownie's Cell* 66
Whose import then we had not learned, we rose 685 *Prelude* 6. 694
Of gravest import. Early he perceives, 813 *Excursion* 4. 807
Of kindred import, pleased and satisfied— 845 *Excursion* 6. 443
Of harsher import than the curfew-knoll 877 *Excursion* 8. 171
Importance. *See* **Self-importance.**
With honour and importance: in a world 649 *Prelude* 3. 21
Knowing too well the importance of his theme, 665 *Prelude* 4. 444
Important. Long undecided lay th' important choice, 620 *Birth of Love* 24
And honest dunces—of important days, 650 *Prelude* 3. 68
Of humble, though, to us, important cares, 795 *Excursion* 3. 610
For less important ends those phantoms move, 813 *Excursion* 4. 842
Importation. By importation of unlooked-for arts, 875 *Excursion* 8. 68
Imported. What this imported I could ill divine: 202 *Hart-leap* 105
Imports. Whatever imports from the world of death 662 *Prelude* 4. 249
Importunate. Dishonour, shame, envy importunate, 560 *Cuck.and Night.* 174
Importunate and heavy load! 581 **Loud is* 10
Albeit long after the importunate bell 653 *Prelude* 3. 306
Impose. The Priest replied—"An office you impose 832 *Excursion* 5. 658
To impose severe restraints and laws unjust, 852 *Excursion* 6. 955
Imposed. And of more arduous duties thence imposed 332 *Ode: Thanks.* 236
Imposed on human kind, must first forget 424 *Ecc. Sonn.* 1. 23. 11
On human nature from above imposed. 803 *Excursion* 4. 129
As bonds, on grave philosopher imposed 812 *Excursion* 4. 741
To be no arbitrary weight imposed, K.8. 249 *Recluse* 1. 1. 496
Imposes. Imposes, whensoe'er untoward chance 834 *Excursion* 5. 764
Imposing. *That*, fronted with a most imposing word, 690 *Prelude* 7. 197
Impossible. Impossible! The man had never wronged me. 69 *Bord.* 1749
That 'tis a thing impossible to frame 803 *Excursion* 4. 136
On which 'tis not impossible to sit 885 *Excursion* 9. 54
Impostor. *See* **Arch-impostor.**
Impostors. Impostors, drivellers, dotards, as the ape 673 *Prelude* 5. 525
Impotence. And weakness crowned with the impotence of death!— 77 *Bord.* 2286
Or half-insensate impotence of mind, 705 *Prelude* 8. 388
I blessed her in the impotence of grief. 770 *Excursion* 1. 924
Impotent. Impotent wish! which reason would despise 471 **Arran! a* 9
And impotent to bear! 582 **O for a* 15
As impotent fancy prompts, by his fireside, 679 *Prelude* 6. 293
Were impotent to make my hopes put on 713 *Prelude* 9. 252
Incongruous, impotent, and blank.—But, oh! 827 *Excursion* 5. 317
Impracticable. —To wet the peak's impracticable sides 609 *Desc.Sk.Quarto* 394
Impregnable. The impregnable and awe-inspiring fort 190 **Lyre! though* 9
(Freedom's impregnable redoubt, 217 *Enterprise* 152
Impregnable of Liberty and Peace. 876 *Excursion* 8. 147
Impregnate. To impregnate and to elevate the mind. 641 *Prelude* 1. 596
Impregnations. Was thronged with impregnations like the Wilds 708 *Prelude* 8. 633
Impress. What mighty objects do impress their forms 70 *Bord.* 1809
That on a wild secluded scene impress 205 *Tintern* 6
The mind that is within us, so impress 207 *Tintern* 126
For lasting impress, by the Lord 247 *P. B.* 974
Or a fierce impress issues with its foil 275 **While poring* 11
Which of themselves our minds impress; 481 *Expost.* 22
Must needs impress a transitory thought 568 *Cumb. Beg.* 124
In that bold form and impress high 629 *Installation* 84
More than the heedless impress that belongs 787 *Excursion* 3. 81
Of Nature's impress,—gaiety and health, 866 *Excursion* 7. 560
To impress a vivid feeling on the mind 879 *Excursion* 8. 328
Impressed. *See* **Imprest.**
He had so often climbed; which had impressed 132 *Michael* 67
The old mythologists, more impressed than we 170 **Never enlivened* 11
Which tiny Elves impressed;—on that smooth stage 378 *Duddon* 11. 4
Impressed on the white road,—in the same line, 567 *Cumb. Beg.* 57
Impressed upon all forms the characters 639 *Prelude* 1. 471
Nor profitless, if haply they impressed 641 *Prelude* 1. 592
Most potent when impressed upon the mind 664 *Prelude* 4. 539

Impressed—*continued*.
Of greatness ; and deep feelings had impressed . 758 *Excursion* 1. 136
Impresses. Seemed trivial, and the impresses without 655 *Prelude* 3. 445
Impression. In one impression, by connecting force 147 *Joanna* 49
Impressions. Be those impressions which incline the heart . . . . 354 *Aquap.* 131
By sensible impressions not enthralled, . . . 747 *Prelude* 14. 106
With these impressions would he still compare . 758 *Excursion* 1. 141
Impressive. Yet, at this impressive season, . . . 90 *Longest Day* 21
By the impressive discipline of fear, . . . 641 *Prelude* 1. 603
Imprest. Is now, by beams of dawning light imprest, 30 *Guilt* 335
The many-coloured images imprest . . . . . 80 **Loving she* 20
Who, 'mid a world of images imprest . . . . 381 *Duddon* 19. 6
On thy Abode harmoniously imprest, ... 478 **Lonsdale! it* 4
Those brighter images by books imprest . . . 848 *Excursion* 6. 701
Imprint. To imprint a kiss that lacked not power to spread . . . . 119 *Maternal Grief* 61
That had not been too timid to imprint . . . 539 **Lady! a* 7
Imprinted. Had left imprinted on the grassy ground. 201 *Hart-leap* 52
Imprisoned. Imprisoned there, and held it to his ear, 44 *Bord.* 405
And every day the imprisoned lake . . . . 110 **Ere with* 15
Imprisoned by hot sunshine lie . . . . . . 158 **In youth* 35
Imprisoned 'mid the formal props . . . . . 214 *Kirkstone* 23
Within a chest imprisoned ; how they came . . 733 *Prelude* 11. 445
Imprisonment. Has a kind heart ; but his imprisonment . . . . 71 *Bord.* 1900
Improve. In framing models to improve the scheme 791 *Excursion* 3. 336
Improvidence. And, through improvidence or want of love . . . . 872 *Excursion* 7. 959
Improvident. "Improvident and reckless," we exclaimed, ... 149 **A narrow* 50
Impudence. Of cunning and of impudence. . . . 239 *P. B.* 305
Impulse. By one soft impulse saved from vacancy. 22 *Yew-tree* 7
(For other impulse let it pass) was driven, . . 71 *Bord.* 1863
To control the froward impulse . . . . . . 94 *Westmoreland Girl* 75
At every impulse of the moving breeze, . . . 151 **When, to* 103
Both law and impulse : and with me . . . . 187 **Three years* 8
Check with thy notes the impulse which, betrayed 190 **Lyre! though* 6
A kindred impulse, seemed allied . . . . . 193 *Ruth* 130
—Behold !—as with a gushing impulse heaves 212 *Dion*
'Tis thine the quickening impulse to control, . . 216 *Enterprise* 100.
Nor let thy genuine impulse fail to beat . . . 217 *Enterprise* 123
Thy impulse is the life of Fame ; . . . . . 217 *Enterprise* 157
Of the wild impulse. From a fount of life . . 230 *Clouds* 45
Gave the first impulse to the Poet's song ; . . 231 **ThegentlestPoet* 28
And, taking impulse from the sword, ... 298 *Brownie's Cell* 37
Powers have they left, an impulse, and a claim . 316 **It was a* 7
More of ennobling impulse from the past, . . . 358 *Aquap.* 349
Its impulse took—that sorrow-stricken door, . . 394 **No more* 21
Some with ungovernable impulse rush ; . . . 436 *Ecc. Sonn.* 2. 32. 4
With quickening impulse answered their mute pleas, 466 *St. Bees* 62
One impulse from a vernal wood . . . . . 481 *Tables Turned* 21
A counter impulse let me take . . . . . . 490 *Night Thought* 17
An impulse more profoundly dear . . . . . 498 **The sylvan* 11
Gain a fresh impulse, run a livelier course ; . . 503 *Warning* 15
His mandates, given rash impulse to control . . 518 *Pun. Death* 7. 10
From paramount impulse not to be withstood, . 635 *Prelude* 1. 240
She rocked with every impulse of the breeze. . . 659 *Prelude* 4. 92
Of that imaginative impulse sent . . . . . 682 *Prelude* 6. 462
With impulse, motive, right and wrong, the ground 731 *Prelude* 11. 299
But by their quickening impulse made more prompt 747 *Prelude* 14. 107
Or from the Soul—an impulse to herself— . . 755 *Recluse* 1. 1. 765
Of impulse or allurement, for the Soul . . . 789 *Excursion* 3. 212
What motive drew, what impulse, I would ask, . 791 *Excursion* 3. 367
And, from the impulse of a just disdain, . . . 798 *Excursion* 3. 829
Impulse and motive to that strong discourse, . . 805 *Excursion* 4. 255
By impulse of her own ethereal zeal. . . . . 806 *Excursion* 4. 316
Impulse and utterance. The whispering air . . 818 *Excursion* 4. 1170
By impulse sent from such illusive power,— . . 827 *Excursion* 5. 322
Upon this impulse, to the theme—erewhile . . 883 *Excursion* 8. 591
A like glad impulse ; and so moves the man . . 884 *Excursion* 9. 34
Mount with a thoughtless impulse, and wheel there, K.8. 242*Recluse*1.1.200
Impulses. With dreams and visionary impulses . 148 *Joanna* 71
Whate'er they bring of impulses sublime. . . . 362 **List—'twas* 73
And impulses of deeper birth . . . . . . 485 *Poet's Epitaph* 47
Who can divine what impulses from God . . . 527 **Those breathing* 27
(Only except some impulses of pride . . . . 795 *Excursion* 3. 631
With impulses that scarcely were by these . . K.8. 256*Recluse*1.1.715
Impure. Wild beasts, or uncouth savages impure ! 102 *Artegal* 28
How dreadful the dominion of the impure ! . . 330 *Ode : Thanks.* 92
Erewhile, with rites impure. . . . . 343 *Eclipse* 6
Impure conceits discharging from a heart . . . 779 *Excursion* 2. 485
A creature, squalid, vengeful, and impure ; . . 800 *Excursion* 3. 953
Concealed, nor through effect of some impure . S.3. 435 **The doubt* 98
Impute. "Impute it not to impatience, if," exclaimed . . . . 841 *Excursion* 6. 189
In, *omitted*.
Ina. And Ina looked for her abode, ... 543 *Russ. Fug.* 131
This, Ina saw ; and, pale with fear, ... 544 *Russ. Fug.* 269
Inaccessible. From us to inaccessible worlds, to regions . . . . 795 *Excursion* 3. 642
And on whose forehead inaccessible . . . . 866 *Excursion* 7. 601
Power inaccessible to human thought, ... 893 *Excursion* 9. 615
Inaction. Self-doomed, to worse inaction, till his eye 470 **Did pangs* 13
Inactive. So placid, so inactive, as content ; . . 849 *Excursion* 6. 731
Inanimate. Inanimate large as the body of man, . 68 *Bord.* 1709
That age, when not by *laws* inanimate, . . . 469 **Bolds words* 9
Where living things, and things inanimate, . . 819 *Excursion* 4. 1204
Dull and inanimate, no more shall hang . . . 820 *Excursion* 4. 1255
Inapt. Inapt conjecture ! Childhood here, a moon 509 *F. Stone* 46
Inaptitude. Remissness and inaptitude of mind, . 736 *Prelude* 12. 108
Inaptly. Such life might not inaptly be compared . 654 *Prelude* 3. 332
And not inaptly so, for love it is, ... 748 *Prelude* 14. 175
Inaptness. Impatience through inaptness to perceive 772 *Excursion* 2. 67
Inarticulate. Your inarticulate notes with the voice of words ! . . . . 235 *Power of Sound* 196
With inarticulate language. For, the Man— . . 819 *Excursion* 4. 1207
Inasmuch. From their beginnings,inasmuch as drawn 731 *Prelude* 11. 289
Inattentive. With an inattentive eye. . . . . 407 *White Doe* 1009
For inattentive Fancy, like the lime . . . . 463 **They called* 8
To the inattentive children of the world : . . 805 *Excursion* 4. 277
Inaudible. Of streams inaudible by day ; . . . 406 *White Doe* 965
Sweet flowers ! at whose inaudible command . 445 *Ecc. Sonn.* 3. 22. 11
Inaudible—was transient ; I had known . . . 737 *Prelude* 12. 201
Inaudible by daylight, blend their notes . . . 818 *Excursion* 4. 1174
A clear sonorous voice, inaudible . . . . . 885 *Excursion* 9. 89
Inaudibly. Sets down his hoofs inaudibly, . . . 247 *P. B.* 989
Inborn. But most the Bard is true to inborn right, 528 **Those breathing* 81
Illustrated with inborn courtesy ; . . . . . 539 **Lady! a* 64
Mine, through heaven's grace and inborn aptitudes. 677 *Prelude* 6. 170
Inbred. Softening their inbred dignity austere— 212 *Dion* 11
Incalculably. Incalculably distant ; so, I felt . . 795 *Excursion* 3. 663
Incapable. Superior, and incapable of change, . . 677 *Prelude* 6. 137
Incapable although they be of rest, ... K.8. 252*Recluse* 1.1.584
Incapacity. Is of such incapacity, methinks, . . 803 *Excursion* 4. 162
Incarnate. Against the Followers of the incarnate Lord . . . . 420 *Ecc. Sonn.* 1. 6. 5
But Thou art true, incarnate Lord, ... 550 *Hermit's Cell* 5. 13
Incarnation. The incarnation of the spirits that move . . . . 694 *Prelude* 7. 478
Incense. While incense from the altar breathes . 228 *Devot. Incit.* 30
Where flower-breathed incense to the skies . . 228 *Devot. Incit.* 60
For this refreshing incense from the West !—. . 327 *Ode 1815* 27
The tapers burn ; the odorous incense feeds . . 431 *Ecc. Sonn.* 2. 11. 2
While clouds of incense mounting veiled the rood, 450 *Ecc. Sonn.* 3. 40. 4
Mounting while earth her morning incense breathes, 465 **Pastor and* 11
Of odorous incense ; while a hundred more . 624 *Æneid* 66
With music, incense, festival, and flowers ! . . 674 *Prelude* 5. 583
Reject the incense offered up by him, ... 866 *Excursion* 7. 580
Commingling with the incense that ascends, . . 885 *Excursion* 9. 42
Incense-bearing. Did incense-bearing altars rise, . 216 *Enterprise* 40
Incense-breathing. And the fresh air of incense-breathing morn . . . . 450 *Ecc. Sonn.* 3. 40. 12
Incensed. Till, not incensed though put to proof, . 179 *Waggoner* 3. 105
Of fire, incensed beneath its hoary brow. . . . 860 *Excursion* 7. 223
Incense-like. Incense-like to Heaven, descending . 502 **Like a* 16
Incessant. Swoln with incessant rains from hour to hour, ... 15 *Desc. Sk.* 270
Rock to incessant neighings shrill and loud, . . 27 *Guilt* 174
Driven by the bomb's incessant thunder-stroke . 30 *Guilt* 349
Desperate as thine ? Or come the incessant shocks 272 *Devil's Bridge* 6
And fought with rage incessant . . . . . . 287 *Ellen Irwin* 39
Where ruthless mortals wage incessant wars. . . 313 **Clouds, lingering* 8
The incessant Rovers of the northern main, . . 425 *Ecc. Sonn.* 1. 29. 3
Hast thou seen, with flash incessant, ... 550 *Hermit's Cell* 3. 1
Incessant rain was falling, or the frost . . . 640 *Prelude* 1. 536
Incessantly. Renewed—renewed incessantly— . . 526 **The soaring* 27
Incessantly conflicting, thrills the frames . . 541 *Grace Darl.* 65
Where Pleasure whirls about incessantly, . . . 688 *Prelude* 7. 70
Incessantly to turn his ear and eye . . . . . 758 *Excursion* 1. 150
Inch. *See* **Half-inch.**
An inch, till I am answered. Know you aught . 46 *Bord.* 497
Before he shall go with an inch of the land !" . 116 *Repentance* 8
Set every inch of sail upon her." . . . . . 178 *Waggoner* 2. 122
Not an inch of his body is free from delight ; . . 189 *Music* 34
From his poor inch or two of daisied sod ? . . 527 **Those breathing* 29
Inch-thick. Inch-thick the dust lay on the ground 621 *Andrew Jones* 16
Incident. Would issue, let one incident make known. 683 *Prelude* 6. 561
Shipwreck, or some domestic incident . . . . 691 *Prelude* 7. 292
Incidental. Those incidental charms which first attached . . . . 645 *Prelude* 2. 198
Incidents. So many incidents upon his mind . . 132 *Michael* 68
To rural incidents, whose genial powers . . . 525 *Epist. Beaumont* 268
How casual incidents of real life, ... 693 *Prelude* 7. 402
Of manners and familiar incidents, ... 708 *Prelude* 8. 621
Incite. Which showers of blood seem rather to incite 437 *Ecc. Sonn.* 2. 36. 8
Incited. And seems, as more incited, still more blest. 279 **Hark! tis* 5
(Too quick and keen) incited to disdain . . . 328 *Ode 1815* 118
Incited it to motion, and controlled. . . . . 705 *Prelude* 8. 432
And straight, incited by a curious mind . . . 774 *Excursion* 2. 173
Perhaps incited rather, by these shocks, . . . 836 *Excursion* 5. 893
Incitement. Is seized with strong incitement to push forth . . . . 496 **A little* 29
Upon a less incitement than the cause K.8. 257*Recluse* 1.1.747
Incitements. Incitements of a battle-day, . . . 233 *Power of Sound* 74
From new incitements friendly to our task, . . 382 *Duddon* 24. 12
Incites. She who incites the frolic lambs . . . 217 *Enterprise* 138
From the confusion, craftily incites . . . . 439 *Ecc.Sonn.* 2. 41. 10
Inclemency. Aught of the fading year's inclemency ! 381 *Duddon* 21. 14
Inclement. But, through the inclement and the perilous days . . . . 758 *Excursion* 1. 120
Inclination. Partake its inclination towards earth . 508 *F. Stone* 38
And inclination mainly, and the mere . . . . 677 *Prelude* 6. 177
And force of native inclination made . . . . 774 *Excursion* 2. 179
The generous inclination, the just rule, . . . 887 *Excursion* 9. 241
Inclinations. Of evil inclinations are unknown ; . 848 *Excursion* 6. 641
Incline. With little kindness would to me incline. . 32 *Guilt* 428
For not an eyelid could to sleep incline . . . 154 *Morn. Ex.* 59
A studious forehead to incline . . . . . . 231 *Jew. Fam.* 7
And let no Slave his head incline, ... 300 *Cora Linn* 43

Incline—*continued.*
Their heavenly Father will incline an ear . . . 332 *Ode: Thanks.* 225
Be those impressions which incline the heart . . 354 *Aquap.* 131
Wash with Thy blood my sins; thereto incline . 366 **Eternal Lord* 12
Which way soe'er our fate incline, ... 403 *White Doe* 613
Feelingly their brows incline . . . . . . 502 **Like a* 38
Are occupied; and the Soul, that would incline . 885 *Excursion* 9. 79
Cleanse with thy blood my sins, to this incline . K.8. 266 **Rid of* 12
Inclined. When next inclined to sleep, take my advice . . . . 44 *Bord.* 416
Inclined to both by reason of his age, ... 99 *Brothers* 245
"To wicked deeds I was inclined, ... 115 *Last of Flock* 71
Or, if thy deeper spirit be inclined . . . . . 264 **Lady! I* 13
True friends though diversely inclined; . . . 285 *Grave of Burns* 43
And marvel not that antique Faith inclined . . 347 *Processions* 68
Of thy fond hopes hereafter walk inclined . . . 447 *Ecc. Sonn.* 3. 27. 9
Some fond hearts to COMPLIANCE seem'd inclin'd; 620 *Birth of Love* 20
It happen'd that, to sleep inclin'd, ... 620 *Birth of Love* 38
Would have inclined each to abate his zeal . . 845 *Excursion* 6. 462
—Still less, far less, am I inclined to treat . . 847 *Excursion* 6. 573
This way and that the {vulgar / many} are inclined, . L.2. 318 *Frag. Æneid* 4. 1
Inclines. Whose heart with gratitude to thee inclines, ... 477 **Lonsdale! it* 2
Inclosure. *See* **Enclosure.**
Wake where they waked, range that inclosure old, 653 *Prelude* 3. 263
Includest. Which thou includest, as the sea her waves: . . . . 802 *Excursion* 4. 93
Including. Faith absolute in God, including hope, . 801 *Excursion* 4. 22
She smiles, including in her wide embrace . . . 819 *Excursion* 4. 1196
Inclusive. Altar and image, and the inclusive walls 811 *Excursion* 4. 672
Incommunicable. An incommunicable rivalship . 78 *Bord.* 2309
An incommunicable sleep. . . . . 117 *Affl. Marg.* 56
Breathings for incommunicable powers; . . . 651 *Prelude* 3. 187
Incomparable. That Causeway with incomparable toil!)— . . . . 269 *Malham* 5
Incompetence. And therefore no incompetence of mine . . . . 874 *Excursion* 8. 13
Through sad incompetence of human speech, . . 684 *Prelude* 6. 593
Incomplete. Things incomplete and purposes betrayed . . . . 269 *Malham* 12
A straggling volume, torn and incomplete, . . 759 *Excursion* 1. 178
Were incomplete) a relique of old times . . . 881 *Excursion* 8. 485
Inconceivably. Though inconceivably endowed, too dim . . . . 804 *Excursion* 4. 181
Incongruous. Shows not a sight incongruous as the extremes . . . . 364 **What aim* 12
Incongruous, impotent, and blank.—But, oh! . 827 *Excursion* 5. 317
Incongruously. Trusting that not incongruously I blend . . . . 873 *Excursion* 7. 1046
Inconsiderate. Of inconsiderate habits and sedate, 663 *Prelude* 4. 342
Heaven bless them, and their inconsiderate work! 778 *Excursion* 2. 454
Inconsistent. The vacillating, inconsistent good. . 806 *Excursion* 4. 309
Inconstant. Inconstant glancing, mounts like springing fire, ... 604 *Desc. Sk. Quarto* 109
With an inconstant and unmellowed light; . . 861 *Excursion* 7. 233
By the inconstant nature we inherit . . . S.3. 433 **The doubt* 25
Incontinence. Than that most strange incontinence in crime; . . . . 63 *Bord.* 1431
Incorporate. Are seen incorporate with the living rock— . . . . 871 *Excursion* 7. 918
Of many into one incorporate. . . . . . . K.8. 253 *Recluse* 1. 1. 616
Incorporated. Yea, with her own incorporated, by power . . . . 817 *Excursion* 4. 1069
Incorruptible. Unsullied, incorruptible, and drink . 893 *Excursion* 9. 629
Increase. Your pains shall ever with your years increase?"— . . . . 33 *Guilt* 511
From the Pier's head, musing, and with increase . 349 *At Dover* 1
Thy way for increase punctual as of yore, . . . 460 **Queen of* 28
Not that I may increase her honour's dower, . . 552 *Prioress* 12
Knowledge and increase of enduring joy . . . 674 *Prelude* 5. 593
At every moment—and, with strength, increase . 813 *Excursion* 4. 794
With *silent* increase: summers, winters—past, . 866 *Excursion* 7. 566
How quick, how vast an increase! From the germ 876 *Excursion* 8. 118
The limbs increase; but liberty of mind . . . 879 *Excursion* 8. 321
In sickness, and for increase in a power . . . 886 *Excursion* 9. 142
Of increase and the mandate from above . . . 889 *Excursion* 9. 367
Increased. And every year increased my store. . 115 *Last of Flock* 30
With rolling years thy strength increased; . . 216 *Enterprise* 36
Is lodged, and how increased; and having gained 741 *Prelude* 13. 79
Increaseth. By moments thus increaseth in my face, 565 *Troilus* 156
Increasing. And still I loved thee with increasing love. . . . . 136 *Michael* 344
While, with increasing agitation, ... 176 *Waggoner* 1. 225
With increasing vigour climb, ... 181 *Waggoner* 4. 85
Increasing multitudes. The potent call . . . 429 *Ecc. Sonn.* 2. 3. 8
With still increasing weight; he was o'erpowered 760 *Excursion* 1. 282
Incumbencies. Incumbencies more awful, visitings 650 *Prelude* 3. 116
Incumbent. Past, future, shrinking up beneath the incumbent Now; . . . . 504 *Warning* 96
How great a God, incumbent o'er her breast, . . 625 *Æneid* 88
Incumbent o'er the surface of past time . . . 662 *Prelude* 4. 272
The incumbent mystery of sense and soul, . . 750 *Prelude* 14. 286
Incumbrances. On throwing off incumbrances, to seek . . . . 740 *Prelude* 13. 34
Incur. "Of such illusion do we here incur; . . 847 *Excursion* 6. 600
Incurious. With no incurious eye; and books are yours, ... 809 *Excursion* 4. 564
And notice forced upon incurious ears; . . . 828 *Excursion* 5. 418
Incurred. May grant at leisure; without risk incurred . . . . 889 *Excursion* 9. 333
Incursion. Change for the worse might please, incursion bold . . . . 284 *Departure* 9
Indebted. Shone mutually indebted, or half lost . 706 *Prelude* 8. 483
Indecent. While oaths and laughter and indecent speech . . . . 692 *Prelude* 7. 363
Indecision. The indecision on their part whose aim 720 *Prelude* 10. 130
Indecisive. Of indecisive judgments, that impaired 652 *Prelude* 3. 212
Indeed. (*Partial list.*)
If thou indeed derive thy light from Heaven, . . v **If thou indeed* 1
"It was indeed a miserable hour . . . . . 28 *Guilt* 235
There was a circumstance, trifling indeed— . . 42 *Bord.* 272
Here justice has indeed a field of triumph. . . 48 *Bord.* 598
Indeed we meant no harm; we lodge sometimes . 54 *Bord.* 946
Has met unkindness; so indeed he told me, . . 74 *Bord.* 2118
A miserable rag indeed! . . . . 82 *Alice Fell* 32
Ay, there, indeed, your memory is a friend . . 97 *Brothers* 138
And, little Butterfly! indeed . . . . . . 106 **I've watched* 3
Thou for our sakes, though Nature's child indeed, 107 *Farewell* 38
(At random and imperfectly indeed) . . . . 131 *Michael* 32
By a memorial name, uncouth indeed . . . . 149 **A narrow* 77
Our life were life indeed, with thee . . . . 193 *Ruth* 80
The prayers I make will then be sweet indeed 257 **The prayers* 1
Does then the Bard sleep here indeed? . . . 289 *Glen-Al.* 17
That was indeed a parting! oh, ... 580 *John Words.* 41
Perpetual benediction: not indeed . . . . 589 *Immortality* 138
It was indeed for all of us—for me . . . . 638 *Prelude* 1. 429
Some called it madness—so indeed it was, . . 651 *Prelude* 3. 146
Great and benign, indeed, must be the power . . 668 *Prelude* 5. 166
Lo! everything that was indeed divine . . . 709 *Prelude* 8. 655
If virtue be indeed so hard to rear, ... 742 *Prelude* 13. 177
I am a dreamer among men, indeed . . . . 765 *Excursion* 1. 635
The estate of man would be indeed forlorn . . 818 *Excursion* 4. 1152
Creations in the mind (and were indeed . . . K.8. 230 **I will* 194
Dispensed indeed to other solitudes, ... K.8. 247 *Recluse* 1. 1. 378
Indefatigable. Their indefatigable flight. 'Tis done— . . . . 218 *Recluse* 1. 1. 216
Chanting with indefatigable bill, ... 271 **Fame tells* 7
Seeking with indefatigable quest . . . . . 512 **Who rashly* 40
The indefatigable fox had learned . . . . . 868 *Excursion* 7. 745
Indefinite. With an indefinite terror and dismay, . 706 *Prelude* 8. 513
Indented. Along the indented shore; when suddenly, 149 **A narrow* 44
"And all along the indented coast, ... 239 *P. B.* 231
O'er the flat meadows and indented coast . . . 892 *Excursion* 9. 573
Indentures. These fourteen years, by strong indentures: . . . . 129 *Idiot Boy* 338
Independence. With Independence, child of high Disdain. . . . . 15 *Desc. Sk.* 261
This independence upon oar and sail, ... 466 *St. Bees* 10
Your independence in the fathomless Deep! . . 527 **Those breathing* 34
Firm Independence, Bounty's rightful sire; . . 584 *Ch. Lamb* 9
Of independence and stern liberty. . . . . . 635 *Prelude* 1. 220
A quiet independence of the heart; . . . . 643 *Prelude* 2. 72
In hardy independence, to stand up . . . . 751 *Prelude* 14. 333
His independence, when along the side . . . 799 *Excursion* 3. 930
Where kindred independence of estate . . . . K.8. 247 *Recluse* 1. 1. 380
Independent. Alive to independent happiness, . . 18 *Desc. Sk.* 424
Upon an independent Intellect, ... 64 *Bord.* 1496
All independent of the leafy spring. . . . . 153 *Morn. Ex.* 48
Be independent, generous, brave; . . . . . 287 *Sons of Burns* 44
That, burning independent of the mind, . . . 306 **We had* 11
Or fragrance independent of the wind. . . . . 622 *Recluse* 1. 1. 94
As of a single independent thing. . . . . . 645 *Prelude* 2. 227
What independent solaces were mine, ... 650 *Prelude* 3. 101
And independent musings pleased me so . . . 652 *Prelude* 3. 228
Yet independent study seemed a course . . . 675 *Prelude* 6. 27
In verity, an independent world, ... 677 *Prelude* 6. 166
And the independent spirit of pure youth . . . 686 *Prelude* 6. 776
Like independent natures. Hence the place . . 708 *Prelude* 8. 632
To travel independent of her help, ... 709 *Prelude* 8. 681
Upon an independent intellect. . . . . . . 731 *Prelude* 11. 244
For independent happiness; craving peace, . . 791 *Excursion* 3. 381
By the pure bond of independent love, . . . 864 *Excursion* 7. 434
Index. The marble index of a mind for ever . . 650 *Prelude* 3. 62
To me became an index of delight, ... 703 *Prelude* 8. 280
India. If for Greece, Egypt, India, Africa, . . . 309 **England! the* 7
And Christian India, through her widespread clime, 425 *Ecc. Sonn.* 1. 26. 13
Indian. *See* **Hunter-Indian.**
Acquired by traffic 'mid the Indian Isles, . . . 96 *Brothers* 67
And she will prize this Bower, this Indian shed, . 106 *Farewell* 26
And, like a naked Indian, slept himself away. . 107 *Indolence* 27
I'll build an Indian bower; I know . . . . 145 *Her Eyes* 55
Like an Indian conjurer; . . . . 171 *Kitten* 30
Not idly.—Hadst thou been of Indian birth, . . 172 *Infant Daughter* 18
From Indian blood you deem him sprung: . . 192 *Ruth* 25
Their pleasant Indian town, ... 193 *Ruth* 51
From caves of Indian mountains hoar! . . . 215 *Enterprise* 27
The naked Indian of the wild, ... 225 *Present.* 34
Salute us; there stood Indian citadel, ... 262 **Dark and* 6
Among the Indian isles, where lay . . . . . 296 *Highland Boy* 132
There greets an Embassy from Indian shores; . 368 *Trajan* 42
There would the Indian answer with a smile . . 380 *Duddon* 16. 4
Or the Indian tree whose branches, downward bent, 383 *Duddon* 31. 7
Answers with more than Indian fortitude, . . 437 *Ecc. Sonn.* 2. 35. 9
Which a fine skill, of Indian growth, has wrought 480 *Cordelia* 3
Bays, gulfs, and ocean's Indian width, shall be, . 527 **Those breathing* 39
Of those who conquered first the Indian Isles, . 635 *Prelude* 1. 208
On Indian plains, and from my mother's hut . . 636 *Prelude* 1. 298
With Indian awe and wonder, ignorance pleased . 677 *Prelude* 6. 121
Or Indian cabins over the fresh lawns . . . . 683 *Prelude* 6. 522
Of Indian corn tended by dark-eyed maids; . . 685 *Prelude* 6. 664
The roving Indian, on his desert sands: . . . 698 *Prelude* 7. 747

Infants—*continued.*
Clap, infants, clap your hands! Divine must be 310 *Anticip.* 10
Infants in arms, and ye, that as ye go 339 *Tell* 7
For goods and chattels, or those Infants dear, 523 *Epist. Beaumont* 113
There with his infants man undaunted creeps 607 *Desc.Sk.Quarto* 293
As tender infants are: and yet how great! 700 *Prelude* 8. 62
This file of infants; some that never breathed 836 *Excursion* 5. 946
Infect. Infect the thoughts; the languor of the frame 808 *Excursion* 4. 480
Infect the air which he had freely breathed 844 *Excursion* 6. 382
Infected. I, too, infected by their mood, 81 †*Mother's Return* 51
Infection. The infection of the ground partakes, 223 *Wishing-gate* 34
All caught the infection—as generous as he. 569 *Farmer* 20
Although a strong infection of the age, 736 *Prelude* 12. 113
Infections. And like the soft infections of the heart, 863 *Excursion* 7. 381
Infelicity. Of constant infelicity,' cut off 846 *Excursion* 6. 533
Infer. The Wanderer, "I infer that he was healed 841 *Excursion* 6. 190
Inference. On outward things, with formal inference ends; 810 *Excursion* 4. 623
Inferior. Link her with the inferior creatures, 94 *Westmoreland Girl* 47
Inferior to angelical, they prolong 218 *Recluse* 1. 1. 205
And thirst for no inferior zeal, 228 *Devot. Incit.* 24
Even to the inferior Kinds; whom forest-trees 395 *White Doe: Ded.* 45
And prospects of the inferior Creature! 416 *White Doe* 1831
My surplice, through the inferior throng I clove 653 *Prelude* 3. 312
The inferior creatures, beast or bird, attuned 704 *Prelude* 8. 357
Was there, nor loss; only the inferior stars 747 *Prelude* 14. 51
Among the inferior kinds; not merely those 806 *Excursion* 4. 358
With no inferior power. You dwell alone; 809 *Excursion* 4. 558
By the inferior Faculty that moulds, 818 *Excursion* 4. 1130
Was wanting; but inferior lights appeared 895 *Excursion* 9. 762
Inferiour. Enough on these inferiour things. L.1. 96 *Juvenal* 3. 39
Infernal. Has held infernal orgies—with the gloom, 49 *Bord.* 660
To those infernal fiends! Now, if the event 64 *Bord.* 1458
And from the infernal Gods, 'mid shades forlorn 209 *Laod.* 3
Barbarian and infernal,—a phantasma, 697 *Prelude* 7. 687
Infidel. An infidel contempt of holy writ 775 *Excursion* 2. 249
Infinite. With love and longings infinite. 117 *Affl. Marg.* 63
A revelation infinite it seems; 219 **This Height* 32
Dependence infinite, proportion just; 327 *Ode 1815* 54
And with an infinite pain the spirit aches, 330 *Ode: Thanks.* 102
From your infinite marvels, the sadness was just. 345 *Stanzas: Simplon* 16
Of bounty infinite. Between Powers that aim 354 *Aquap.* 144
Yet through that darkness (infinite though it seem 396 **Action is* 7
Merciless act of sorrow infinite! 439 *Ecc. Sonn.* 2. 42. 11
But infinite its grasp of weal and woe! 451 *Ecc. Sonn.* 3. 41. 10
Infinite Power. The pillared vestibule, 473 **Thanks for* 5
From shadowy fountains of the Infinite, 476 **Tranquillity! the* 11
Forth-shadowing, some have deemed, the infinite 477 *Long Meg* 13
Which nothing less than Infinite Power could give. 501 *Humanity* 110
Infinite Power, perfect Intelligence. 519 *Pun. Death* 10. 14
And the pure vision closed in darkness infinite. 582 *Invoc. Earth* 36
From circumspection, infinite delay. 635 *Prelude* 1. 242
Above the rest raised infinite ascents 724 *Prelude* 10. 426
And greatness still revolving; infinite: 759 *Excursion* 1. 229
Seemed infinite; and there his spirit shaped 759 *Excursion* 1. 231
Confusion infinite of heaven and earth, 796 *Excursion* 3. 721
Of infinite benevolence and power; 801 *Excursion* 4. 15
Even to thy Being's infinite majesty! 802 *Excursion* 4. 99
In mercy, carried infinite degrees 804 *Excursion* 4. 192
Of infinite Being, twinkling restlessly! 816 *Excursion* 4. 994
And swallowed up 'mid deserts infinite! 837 *Excursion* 5. 1007
Of contradictions infinite the slave, 843 *Excursion* 6. 373
And the infinite magnificence of heaven 887 *Excursion* 9. 210
Infinitely. From beauty infinitely growing 301 *Bran* 115
The universe is infinitely wide; 469 **Desire we* 6
Infinitude. Is with infinitude, and only there; 684 *Prelude* 6. 605
In faint reflection of infinitude 827 *Excursion* 5. 343
Infinity. And shares the nature of infinity. 65 *Bord.* 1544
That feeds upon infinity, that broods 747 *Prelude* 14. 71
Infinity's. Infinity's embrace; whose guardian crest, 452 *Ecc. Sonn.* 3. 45. 10
Infirm. Thought infirm ne'er came between them, 141 *Arm. Lady* 91
Mild Offspring of infirm humanity, 172 *Infant Daughter* 2
—Infirm ejaculation! from the tongue 311 **Who rises* 42
Or our infirm affections Nature pleads, 721 *Prelude* 10. 189
Infirm, dependent, and now destitute? 796 *Excursion* 3. 685
Thus pitiably infirm; then, he who made, 828 *Excursion* 5. 367
Is too infirm to reach. But, waiving this, 830 *Excursion* 5. 522
Infirmities. Thy absence, till old age and fresh infirmities 41 *Bord.* 203
The infant lamb? and shall the infirmities, 57 *Bord.* 1085
The infirmities of mortal love; 414 *White Doe* 1626
We learn to tolerate the infirmities 449 *Ecc. Sonn.* 3. 35. 7
Infirmities of nature, time, and place, 730 *Prelude* 11. 239
Infirmity. With tales of weakness and infirmity! 41 *Bord.* 245
And hauntings from the infirmity of love, 99 *Brothers* 232
Be one of much infirmity; 174 *Waggoner* 1. 51
A last infirmity betrays, 216 *Enterprise* 50
And sure encroachments of infirmity, 378 *Duddon* 9. 13
By an infirmity of love for days 641 *Prelude* 1. 614
To our infirmity. No officious slave 645 *Prelude* 2. 215
Which through the lapse of their infirmity 657 *Prelude* 3. 544
In all the tatters of infirmity 693 *Prelude* 7. 424
From this infirmity of mortal kind 803 *Excursion* 4. 146
Of all infirmity, and tending all. 818 *Excursion* 4. 1114
To the infirmity of mortal sense 893 *Excursion* 9. 618
Infirmly. Infirmly grasped within a palsied hand. 321 **Humanity, delighting* 10
Inflame. Would I, by previous wiles, inflame the queen 624 *Æneid* 24
Imagination, potent to inflame 716 *Prelude* 9. 495
Inflamed. *See* **Soul-inflamed.**
Inflamed by thee, the blooming Boy 216 *Enterprise* 59
By just revenge inflamed? No foot may chase, 321 **The power* 6
Inflamed by sense of wrong; 499 *Departing summer* 39
Inflamed by passion, blind with prejudice, 713 *Prelude* 9. 250
I scorned indifference; but, inflamed with thirst 731 *Prelude* 11. 248
Of madding passions mutually inflamed; 755 *Recluse* 1. 1. 828
Confused, commingled, mutually inflamed, 784 *Excursion* 2. 855
To overweening faith; and is inflamed, 792 *Excursion* 3. 416
All that inflamed thy infant heart, the love, K.8. 257 *Recluse* 1. 1. 741
Inflexible. With will inflexible, those fearful pangs 759 *Excursion* 1. 173
Inflict. That he has power to inflict what we lack strength to bear. 319 *Spaniard* 14
And to inflict shame's salutary stings 325 *Enghien* 3
They must forbid the State to inflict a pain, 518 *Pun. Death* 7. 13
Inflicted. He had himself inflicted. Through his brain 33 *Guilt* 492
Inflicted;—blessèd Men, for so to Heaven 357 *Aquap.* 314
For wounds inflicted, nor what toil relieved 525 *Epist. Beaumont* 261
Inflicted upon confidence so pure. K.8. 244 *Recluse* 1. 1. 272
Inflicts. Inflicts his tender wound. 215 *Kirkstone* 72
Pains which the World inflicts can she requite? 280 **Intent on* 10
That, in rough winter, oft inflicts a fear 453 **Calm is the* 14
And then betrays; accuses and inflicts 827 *Excursion* 5. 326
Influence. Compassion for me. His influence is great 43 *Bord.* 347
For him, by private influence with the Court, 123 *V. and J.* 150
A happy, genial influence, 158 **In youth* 70
Through your sweet influence, and the care 191 *Seq. Beggars* 38
As have no slight or trivial influence 206 *Tintern* 32
Shed kindly influence on the place, 223 *Wishing-gate* 20
Sinks, hardly conscious of the influence— 227 *Vernal Ode* 89
To a voluptuous influence 233 *Power of Sound* 87
From harp or lute, kind influence to compose 255 **Grief, thou* 7
For more than Fancy to the influence bends 262 **Mark the* 12
(Like influence never may my soul reject), 282 **While beams* 10
Been felt, that influence is displayed. 338 *Brientz* 10
Yield to the Music's touching influence; 340 *Ranz* 13
Aid, with congenial influence, to uphold 351 *Des. Stanzas* 76
Influence, at least among a scattered few, 358 *Aquap.* 366
Thro' Time and Nature's influence, purify 361 **When here* 11
Heaven's breathing influence failed not to bestow 395 *White Doe: Ded.* 29
Of that beguiling influence; 407 *White Doe* 1043
Feels, through the influence of her gentle reign, 426 *Ecc. Sonn.* 1. 29. 7
The time's and season's influence disown; 453 **Calm is the* 11
A kindly influence whereof few will speak, 460 **Wanderer! that* 61
To aught of highest, holiest, influence— 461 **Queen of* 45
Of their bad influence, and their good receives: 493 *Hap. War.* 18
A constant influence, a peculiar grace; 493 *Hap. War.* 47
Wants not a healing influence that can creep 501 **The unremitting* 10
Warmed by thy influence, creeping things 506 **While from* 27
Through its meek influence, from above, 534 **Blest is* 93
Luna by night, with heavenly influence 562 *Cuck.and Night.* 313
Without whose blissful influence Paradise 585 *Ch. Lamb* 67
To the mild influence of the finer arts; 613 *School Ex.* 60
Mild influence; nor left in me one wish 639 *Prelude* 1. 103
To the sky's influence in a kindred mood 651 *Prelude* 3. 137
Would with an influence benign have soothed, 679 *Prelude* 6. 312
Their fairest, softest, happiest influence. 686 *Prelude* 6. 726
No longer a mute influence of the soul, 704 *Prelude* 8. 367
As even their pensive influence drew from mine. 726 *Prelude* 10. 530
To the reanimating influence lost 733 *Prelude* 11. 389
The wondrous influence of power gently used, 734 *Prelude* 12. 15
The first diviner influence of this world, 737 *Prelude* 12. 182
For, spite of thy sweet influence and the touch 749 *Prelude* 14. 237
Thy kindred influence to my heart of hearts 750 *Prelude* 14. 281
Shedding benignant influence, and secure, 755 *Recluse* 1. 1. 843
In all things that from her sweet influence 760 *Excursion* 1. 266
With gladsome influence could re-animate 773 *Excursion* 2. 136
At those, which thy soft influence sometimes drew 797 *Excursion* 3. 811
More obviously the self-same influence rules 808 *Excursion* 4. 449
For influence undefined a personal shape; 811 *Excursion* 4. 683
Its kindly influence, o'er the yielding brow 814 *Excursion* 4. 889
Shedding sweet influence from above; or pure 841 *Excursion* 6. 187
If, then, their blended influence be not lost 846 *Excursion* 6. 527
Whose sacred influence, spread through earth and heaven, 864 *Excursion* 7. 484
Is salutary, or an influence sweet, 887 *Excursion* 9. 218
That power, that influence, by impartial law. 887 *Excursion* 9. 220
Vouchsafe sweet influence, while her Poet speaks 892 *Excursion* 9. 519
Influences. Ye kindred local influences that still, 356 *Aquap.* 251
Influx. Drew from the influx of the main, 495 *Fact* 16
By stealthy influx of the timid day 497 **Enough of climbing* 26
The dead, by influx of a living love, 625 *Æneid* 92
To the still influx of the morning light 822 *Excursion* 5. 4
And, with a sudden influx overpowered K.8. 236 *Recluse* 1. 1. 7
Influxes. Was dear, and hence to finer influxes 646 *Prelude* 2. 282
Sought or unsought, and influxes of power 708 *Prelude* 8. 601
Inform. From joy to joy: for she can so inform 207 *Tintern* 125
I raise my thoughts, inform my deeds and words, 365 **Rapt above* 7
The rudiments of letters, and inform 888 *Excursion* 9. 301
Informed. Informed, were resolute to do his will, 436 *Ecc. Sonn.* 2. 30. 13
Patriots informed with Apostolic light 444 *Ecc. Sonn.* 3. 15. 1
So sacred, so informed with light divine, 519 *Pun. Death* 10. 3
Inform'd his pen, or wisdom of the heart, 587 *Crosth.* 10
Informed with such a spirit as might be 655 *Prelude* 3. 429

Intention 482 Interminglin

Intent—*continued.*
And hear you shouting forth your brave intent. . 309 *Men of Kent* 8
Intent each lurking frailty to disclaim, . . . 316 **Say, what* 3
And, ere a thought could ask on what intent . 323 *Ode 1814* 25
In working out a pure intent; . . . . . . 328 *Ode 1815* 107
Even these, without intent of theirs, ... 338 **Meek Virgin* 9
Forced by intent to take from speech its edge, . 353 *Aquap.* 75
Unblamed—if the Soul be intent on the day . . 364 *Vallomb.* 35
My seat, while I give way to such intent;. . 376 *Duddon* 3. 2
Nor can it be with good intent: . . . . . 399 *White Doe* 257
Between him and the pure intent . . . . . 401 *White Doe* 519
But what avails the bold intent? . . . . . 404 *White Doe* 784
One with profane and harsh intent . . . . . 410 *White Doe* 1323
And no one hinder their intent, ... 412 *White Doe* 1519
(As might be deemed) to disciplined intent . . 428 *Ecc. Sonn.* 1. 37. 6
With mind intent upon the King of Glory, . . 445 *Ecc. Sonn.* 3. 19. 12
Intent, and sedulous of abject gain, ... 450 *Ecc. Sonn.* 3. 38. 4
The thoughtful Monks, intent their God to please, 468 *St. Bees* 142
What means the Spectre? Why intent . . . 479 *Somnamb.* 109
Nor he, nor minister of his—intent . . . . . 496 **A little* 7
Or, like the warbling lark intent to shroud . . 503 *Warning* 34
Curling with unconfirmed intent, ... 508 *May* 79
Deed and intent, should turn the Being adrift . 519 *Pun. Death* 10. 5
Dim memory keeping of its old intent. . . . 523 *Epist. Beaumont* 128
Came ministers of peace, intent to rear . . . 534 **When in* 3
Rivals in effort; and, alike intent . . . . . 541 *Grace Darl.* 52
And offices humane, intent to adore . . . . 551 **If thou in* 11
On Jesu's Mother fixed was his intent.. . . . 554 *Prioress* 99
And had good knowing both of their intent . . 558 *Cuck.and Night.*109
For mine intent it neither is to die, ... 559 *Cuck.and Night.*139
And judgment there be given; or that intent . 562 *Cuck.and Night.*279
And therewithal to cover his intent . . . . 562 *Troilus* 8
Intent upon thy way, pause, though in haste! . 573 *Chiabrera* 3. 2
Time still intent on his insidious part, ... 576 **By a* 16
And with steadfast dejection his eyes are intent . 620 *Convict* 15
Intent on little but substantial needs, ... 701 *Prelude* 8. 162
This was their undisguised intent, and they . . 712 *Prelude* 9. 186
Diffused around him, while he was intent . . . 714 *Prelude* 9. 316
Rajahs and Omrahs in his train, intent . . . 718 *Prelude* 10. 20
When most intent on making of herself . . . 729 *Prelude* 11. 114
I summoned my best skill, and toiled, intent . 731 *Prelude* 11. 279
Over the dark abyss, intent to hear . . . . 747 *Prelude* 14. 72
Or elevates the Mind, intent to weigh . . . . 755 *Recluse* 1. 1. 761
Raised toward those craggy summits, his intent . 773 *Excursion* 2. 154
On these and kindred thoughts intent I lay . . 777 *Excursion* 2. 370
Departs, intent upon his onward quest!— . . 788 *Excursion* 3. 172
Too nearly, or intent to reinforce . . . . . 862 *Excursion* 7. 296
Intent upon a monumental stone, ... 871 *Excursion* 7. 913
We gazed, in silence hushed, with eyes intent . 893 *Excursion* 9. 610
By one, sole keeper of his own intent, ... K.8.256*Recluse* 1.1.718
Intention. Pious beyond the intention of your thought; . . . . 818 *Excursion* 4. 1149
Intentions. What may your ill intentions you avail? 554 *Prioress* 124
Intents. But who can fathom your intents, . . . 225 *Present.* 37
And that the past might have its true intents . 346 *Processions* 4
Intercept. To intercept the sun's glad beams—may ne'er . . . . 838 *Excursion* 6. 23
Intercepted. Hunts, where his master points, the intercepted flocks. . . . . 5 *Ev. Wk.* 185
Hunts, where he points, the intercepted flocks; . 594 *Ev. Wk. Quarto* 168
Fair prospect, intercepted less and less, . . . 892 *Excursion* 9. 572
Intercessions. Are intercessions of the fervent tongue 423 *Ecc. Sonn.* 1. 20. 4
Her intercessions made for the soul's rest . . . 467 *St. Bees* 66
Interchange. With restless interchange at once the bright . . . . 7 *Ev. Wk.* 297
A constant interchange of growth and blight! . 212 *Laod.* 174
Life, Death, in amicable interchange;— . . . 350 *Des. Stanzas* 43
By interchange of knowledge and delight. . . . 546 **The embowering* 8
This wily interchange of snaky hues, ... 657 *Prelude* 3. 563
That shift and vanish, change and interchange . 707 *Prelude* 8. 571
Where good and evil interchange their names, . 714 *Prelude* 9. 352
To ruminate, with interchange of talk, . . . 715 *Prelude* 9. 394
Hence Genius, born to thrive by interchange . . 740 *Prelude* 13. 5
A balance, an ennobling interchange . . . . 745 *Prelude* 13. 375
I yet had risen too late to interchange . . . . 834 *Excursion* 5. 801
An interchange of soft or solemn tunes, . . . 857 *Excursion* 7. 15
Whole hours with but small interchange of speech, K.8. 227 **I will* 88
Interchangeable. With interchangeable supremacy, 747 *Prelude* 14. 84
Interchanged. And, after greetings interchanged, and given . . . . 97 *Brothers* 118
By affectations interchanged, ... 301 *Bran* 108
And wisdom and the pledges interchanged . . 656 *Prelude* 3. 507
Unceremonious greetings interchanged . . . . 659 *Prelude* 4. 70
And hazard, and hard labour interchanged . . 703 *Prelude* 8. 254
Intercourse. Banished from human intercourse, exist 66 *Bord.* 1577
And intercourse with mortal hours . . . . . 112 **How rich* 5
That there was ever intercourse . . . . . 117 *Aff. Marg.* 59
A broken intercourse; and, while his eyes . . 118 *Maternal Grief* 58
The dreary intercourse of daily life, ... 207 *Tintern* 131
But on all proffered intercourse did lay . . . 306 **We had* 7
In vain shall rue the broken intercourse. . . . 383 *Duddon* 30. 8
And kindliest intercourse ensue. . . . . . 415 *White Doe* 1729
Studious of that pure intercourse begun . . . 452 *Ecc. Sonn.* 3. 46. 10
Thou a mysterious intercourse dost hold, . . . 475 **Homeward we* 9
Dear intercourse was theirs, day after day; . . 531 **I know* 13
To cheerful intercourse with wood and field, . . 538 **In desultory* 40
Might tell what intercourse she found, ... 544 *Russ. Fug.* 205
In solitude, such intercourse was mine; . . . 638 *Prelude* 1. 422
I held unconscious intercourse with beauty . . 640 *Prelude* 1. 562
Objects through widest intercourse of sense. . . 645 *Prelude* 2. 240

Intercourse—*continued*
In which, a Babe, by intercourse of touch . . . 646 *Prelude* 2. 267
As I had done in daily intercourse . . . . . 654 *Prelude* 3. 353
As her prime teacher, intercourse with man . . 666 *Prelude* 5. 14
Was guarded from too early intercourse . . . 704 *Prelude* 8. 331
Not seeking frequent intercourse with men, . . 710 *Prelude* 9. 26
By cressets and love-beacons, intercourse . . . 716 *Prelude* 9. 489
As books and common intercourse with life . . 728 *Prelude* 11. 95
Maintained for me a saving intercourse . . . 732 *Prelude* 11. 341
Whose subtle intercourse with breathing flowers,. 734 *Prelude* 12. 11
Of ordinary intercourse, our minds . . . . . 737 *Prelude* 12. 214
Beneath them, summoned to such intercourse: . 744 *Prelude* 13. 270
Be this ascribed; to early intercourse,. . . . 748 *Prelude* 14. 164
Such intercourse was his, and in this sort . . . 759 *Excursion* 1. 220
Such intercourse I witnessed, while we roved, . 772 *Excursion* 2. 81
Of various intercourse, nor wishing aught . . . 794 *Excursion* 3. 587
(And that is intercourse, and union, too,) . . . 795 *Excursion* 3. 665
A step, or link, for intercourse with thee. . . . 803 *Excursion* 4. 102
Of worldly intercourse between man and man, . 862 *Excursion* 7. 336
Rude intercourse; apt agents to expel, . . . 875 *Excursion* 8. 67
Of traffic glides with ceaseless intercourse, . . 876 *Excursion* 8. 113
And pure, from further intercourse ensued; . . 896 *Excursion* 9. 792
For loftier intercourse. The Muses, crowned . . S.3. 436**The doubt* 149
All intercourse of knowledge or of love . . . K.8. 251*Recluse* 1.1.535
Interdict. Hang like an interdict upon her hopes. . 636 *Prelude* 1. 260
Interdicted. That interdicted all debate, . . . 407 *White Doe* 1065
Interest. And mutual interest failed not to create. 28 *Guilt* 195
Interest, and mortgages; at last he sank, . . . 98 *Brothers* 215
By thought supplied, nor any interest . . . . 206 *Tintern* 82
In selfish interest perverts the will, ... 313 **Not 'mid* 3
Gives the last human interest to his heart. . . 569 *Cumb. Beg.* 178
Without a vital interest. At that time, . . . 711 *Prelude* 9. 107
Not with less interest than heretofore, ... 741 *Prelude* 13. 85
Fondly, though with an interest more mild, . . 770 *Excursion* 1. 926
To private interest dead, and pubiic care. . . . 774 *Excursion* 2. 209
Of transitory interest, and peeps round . . . 788 *Excursion* 3. 165
Of ornamental interest, and the charm . . . 838 *Excursion* 6. 27
Of livelier interest to his hopes and fears, . . . 869 *Excursion* 7. 795
By ties of daily interest, to maintain . . . . 875 *Excursion* 8. 63
Aught of romantic interest, it is gone. . . . . 875 *Excursion* 8. 85
Of common right or interest in the end; . . . 886 *Excursion* 9. 118
For social interest such as I have shared. . . . S.3. 435 **The doubt* 134
Interests. And stirring interests shunned with desperate flight, ... 363 **The world forsaken* 2
The Soul's eternal interests to promote: . . . 423 *Ecc. Sonn.* 1. 18. 2
How widely spread the interests of our theme. . 443 *Ecc. Sonn.* 3. 12. 14
To social interests, and to favouring Heaven; . 450 *Ecc. Sonn.* 3. 41. 3
And nearer interests culled from the opening stage 522 *Epist. Beaumont* 90
Found—for all interests, hopes, and tender cares, 585 *Ch. Lamb* 83
Whose tone bespake reviving interests . . . 665 *Prelude* 4. 464
To whom my worldly interests were dear. . . . 680 *Prelude* 6. 332
And ordinary interests of man, ... 700 *Prelude* 8. 117
Of nations and their passing interests, ... 712 *Prelude* 9. 202
Mild interests and gentlest sympathies. . . . 749 *Prelude* 14. 231
Amid conflicting interests, and the shock . . . 751 *Prelude* 14. 334
And precious interests? Smoothly did our life . 795 *Excursion* 3. 611
Of former loves and interests. Then my soul . 796 *Excursion* 3. 695
The moral interests, the creative might, . . . 798 *Excursion* 3. 823
Of the world's interests—such a one hath need . 810 *Excursion* 4. 582
And twice ten thousand interests, do yet prize . 816 *Excursion* 4. 989
And pleasant interests—for the sequel leaving . 829 *Excursion* 5. 435
When these particular interests were effaced . . 893 *Excursion* 9. 589
From self-respecting interests, deem them not . K.8. 249*Recluse* 1.1.452
Interference. If, when that interference hath relieved him, ... 311 **Who rises* 55
Forgives their interference—Art divine, . . . 509 *F. Stone* 76
By timely interference: and therewith . . . 633 *Prelude* 1. 118
From interference of external force, ... 889 *Excursion* 9. 332
Interfering. Of interfering Heaven, I have no doubt, 75 *Bord.* 2129
Interfused. Of something far more deeply interfused, 207 *Tintern* 96
Regrets, vexations, lassitudes interfused . . . 637 *Prelude* 1. 346
Along his infant veins are interfused . . . . 645 *Prelude* 2. 242
Interior. Among the interior Alps, gigantic crew, . 350 *Des. Stanzas* 20
Interlaced. Bounding through branches interlaced, 544 *Russ. Fug.* 263
Interlacing. What solemn, vacant, interlacing, . . 179 *Waggoner* 3. 46
Interlards. He names them all; and interlards . 178 *Waggoner* 2. 124
Interlunar. The interlunar cavern of the tomb. . 596 *Ev. Wk. Quarto* 268
Hid in her vacant interlunar cave." . . . . 691 *Prelude* 7. 284
Intermeddler. Some intermeddler still is on the watch . . . . 670 *Prelude* 5. 334
Leaving the intermeddler to upbraid . . . . S.3. 434 **The doubt* 59
Intermeddlers. Of intermeddlers, steady purposes . 723 *Prelude* 10. 347
Intermeddling. Or barren intermeddling subtleties, 736 *Prelude* 12. 155
Intermediate. A little space of intermediate time . 688 *Prelude* 7. 60
Of nature's intermediate hours of rest, ... 697 *Prelude* 7. 656
Interminable. Between interminable tracts of pine, 20 *Desc. Sk.* 541
Th' interminable sea of sable blue. . . . . . 609 *Desc. Sk. Quarto* 389
Of that interminable building reared . . . . 647 *Prelude* 2. 383
Intermingled. But, intermingled with the generous seed, ... 102 *Artegal* 29
Some intermingled notes that plead . . . . 243 *P. B.* 654
An intermingled pomp of vale and hill, . . . 323 *Ode 1814* 8
By intermingled work of house and field . . . 833 *Excursion* 5. 709
And with the flowers are intermingled stones . . 855 *Excursion* 6. 1154
Intermingles. That intermingles with those works of man . . . . 744 *Prelude* 13. 292
Intermingling. Of intermingling hues; . . . . 193 *Ruth* 57
In sleep, and intermingling with his dream, . . 229 *Cuckoo-clock* 30
With intermingling motions soft and still, . . . 338 *Engelberg* 8
Nor falls that intermingling shade . . . . 338 **Meek Virgin* 31

Intricate—*continued.*
Upwards and downwards, progress intricate 218 *Recluse* 1. 1. 214
Intricate labyrinth, more dread for thought 232 *Power of Sound* 5
Mounted through every intricate defile, 380 *Duddon* 16. 8
To kneel, or thrid your intricate defiles, 451 *Ecc. Sonn.* 3. 42. 5
From intricate cabals of treacherous friends. 574 *Chiabrera* 4. 9
And, through the turnings intricate of verse, 674 *Prelude* 5. 603
And intricate recesses, creek or bay 702 *Prelude* 8. 195
Turned and returned with intricate delay. 709 *Prelude* 9. 8
Along this intricate and difficult path, 750 *Prelude* 14. 330
Thy motions, intricate and manifold, K.8. 301 **And oh* 7
Intricately. By naked rafters intricately crossed, 824 *Excursion* 5. 147
Intrigue. And all unfit for tumult or intrigue, 720 *Prelude* 10. 151
Intrigues. What dire intrigues disturbed *Cythera's* joy! 620 *Birth of Love* 2
Introduced. And thus my heart was early introduced 703 *Prelude* 8. 277
Or introduced at this more quiet time. 787 *Excursion* 3. 49
Introducing. A sunbeam introducing among hearts 848 *Excursion* 6. 650
Introverted. His introverted spirit; and bestowed 864 *Excursion* 7. 446
Intrude. Where no disturbance comes to intrude 180 *Waggoner* 4. 26
Till we depart intrude not here;) 221 *Triad* 77
This day we purposed to intrude."—" I did so, 777 *Excursion* 2. 398
Of mortal separation, could intrude K.8. 236 *Recluse* 1. 1. 13
Intruded. Intruded, for we failed to overtake 683 *Prelude* 6. 576
Intruder. To take the intruder into favour; 142 †*Lov. and Lik.* 20
What dreams encompassed? Was the intruder nursed 378 *Duddon* 8. 6
" Poor victim! no idle intruder has stood 621 *Convict* 45
Like an intruder knocking at the door 660 *Prelude* 4. 157
Intruder ne'er beheld, he thence surveys 799 *Excursion* 3. 937
Each other's path; but, as the Intruder seemed 839 *Excursion* 6. 104
Intruders. Intruders—who would tear from Nature's book 250 *Admon.* 7
Intrudes. Intrudes on peace, I pray the eternal Sire 470 *Bala-Sala* 5
Intrudes, the peaceful concert to disturb 848 *Excursion* 6. 644
Intruding. The silent trees, and saw the intruding sky.— 186 *Nutting* 53
Intrusion. From all intrusion free; 543 *Russ. Fug.* 110
Who, but for this intrusion, would have lived, 887 *Excursion* 9. 203
From all intrusion of the restless world 892 *Excursion* 9. 578
Intrusive. Thus (where the intrusive Pile, ill-graced 301 *Bran* 119
That with intrusive restlessness beats off 635 *Prelude* 1. 248
Intrusted. If aught (intrusted to the pen 472 *Ossian* 19
When I was first intrusted to the care 672 *Prelude* 5. 427
Intrusted safely each to his pursuit, 789 *Excursion* 3. 190
Intuition. This intuition led me to confound 727 *Prelude* 11. 18
A passionate intuition; whence the Soul, 820 *Excursion* 4. 1295
Intuitions. And intuitions moral and divine) 811 *Excursion* 4. 646
Intuitive. Of contemplation, what intuitive truths, 675 *Prelude* 6. 39
Whether discursive or intuitive; 747 *Prelude* 14. 120
Inundation. Triumphant.—Inundation wide and deep, 380 *Duddon* 16. 9
Inurned. Thou fortunate Region! whose Greatness inurned 345 *Stanzas: Simplon* 13
Invaded. —Then Canute, rising from the invaded throne, 495 *Fact* 9
Triumphant, winning from the invaded heavens 734 *Prelude* 11. 455
Invaders. On British ground the Invaders are laid low; 310 *Anticip.* 2
Meanwhile the Invaders fared as they deserved: 724 *Prelude* 10. 390
Invades. Invades a Realm, so pressed that in the scale 316 **Say, what* 6
No ruder sound your desart haunts invades, 596 *Ev. Wk. Quarto* 237
Invading. For, when my prowess from invading Neighbours 372 *Eg. Maid* 224
The King had fallen, and that invading host— 718 *Prelude* 10. 12
Invasive. Your patriot sons, to stem invasive war, 283 **Proud were* 2
Invent. But Cytherea, studious to invent 624 *Æneid* 1
Sometimes it suits me better to invent 635 *Prelude* 1. 221
Invented. Discovered or invented; or set forth, 823 *Excursion* 5. 41
Invention. Or stray invention. 158 **In youth* 48
Inventions. Thus to torment her with *inventions!*—death—— 41 *Bord.* 238
And certes not in vain; he had inventions rare. 108 *Indolence* 54
When Art's abused inventions were unknown; 256 *Easter* 12
Those arts, and high inventions, if unpropped 877 *Excursion* 8. 226
To those inventions of corrupted man 894 *Excursion* 9. 689
Inventive. The old inventive Poets, had they seen, 381 *Duddon* 20. 1
To their inventive humour, by stern looks, 859 *Excursion* 7. 100
Is past for ever.—An inventive Age 875 *Excursion* 8. 87
Inventress. So tripped the Muse, inventress of the dance; 221 *Triad* 105
Invents. By all that mind invents or hand prepares; 221 *Triad* 64
Inverness. " And he had been at Inverness; 239 *P. B.* 221
Inversion. Inversion strange! that, unto One who lives 433 *Ecc. Sonn.* 2. 19. 9
Inversneyd. Near the rough Falls of Inversneyd! 344 **How blest* 58
Inverted. Inverted shrubs, and moss of gloomy green, 3 *Ev. Wk.* 59
Vanish inverted hill, and shadowy wood, 212 *Dion*
When, through this Height's inverted arch, 215 *Kirkstone* 43
Meets him, among the inverted trees. 242 *P. B.* 500
Seems, 'mid inverted mountains, not unheard. 456 **The leaves* 13
Inverted shrubs, and moss of darkest green, 593 *Ev. Wk. Quarto* 75
At peace inverted your lithe necks ye lave, 596 *Ev. Wk. Quarto* 235
Inverted trees, rocks, clouds, and azure sky; 800 *Excursion* 3. 972
Inverted, all its sun-bright features touched K.8. 252 *Recluse* 1. 1. 572
Invest. And with dread signs the nascent Stream invest? 418 *Ecc. Sonn.* 1. 2. 8
With which communities of men invest 827 *Excursion* 5. 311
Invested. And fields invested with purpureal gleams; 211 *Laod.* 106
Invested moorland waste, and naked pool, 738 *Prelude* 12. 258
Invests. That still invests the guardian Pass, 300 *Cora Linn* 40
Yes, something of the grandeur which invests 742 *Prelude* 13. 152
Invests the thriving churl, his legs appear, 880 *Excursion* 8. 404
The brightness more conspicuous that invests 890 *Excursion* 9. 411
Inveterately. Up-coiling, and inveterately convolved; 185 *Yew-trees* 18
Widely—inveterately usurped upon, 797 *Excursion* 3. 794
Invidious. Slowly surmounting some invidious hill, 282 **In my* 2
Invigorated. Of waters, with invigorated peal 885 *Excursion* 9. 67
Invigorates. That, while it binds, invigorates and supports. 813 *Excursion* 4. 825
Invigorating. Whence oft invigorating transports flow 215 *Kirkstone* 59
Invigorating thoughts from former years; 641 *Prelude* 1. 621
Invincible. Armoury of the invincible Knights of old: 307 **It is not* 10
Or like the invincible Rock itself that braves, 540 *Grace Darl.* 25
A Champion steadfast and invincible, 573 *Chiabrera* 2. 20
Inviolable. The inviolable God, that tames the proud! 477 *Long Meg* 14
Devoted, on the inviolable stream 701 *Prelude* 8. 179
Inviolate. Maintains inviolate its slightest vow! 270 **Shame on* 8
Inviolate, whate'er the cottage hearth 276 *Filial Piety* 2
Is Roman dignity inviolate; 368 *Trajan* 50
By constancy inviolate, 629 *Installation* 92
To privileged regions and inviolate, 690 *Prelude* 7. 186
Retained its purity inviolate, 709 *Prelude* 8. 656
Inviolate retirement, subject there 755 *Recluse* 1. 1. 773
Oh long may it remain inviolate, K.8. 249 *Recluse* 1. 1. 464
Invisible. And the invisible sympathy 144 **Driven in* 44
Making report of an invisible breeze 148 **A narrow* 23
Each invisible and mute, 170 *Kitten* 15
No bird, but an invisible thing, 183 **O blithe* 15
The invisible world with thee hath sympathised; 211 *Laod.* 143
Invisible, the long procession moves 230 *Clouds* 46
Serve Thee, invisible Spirit, with untired powers; 232 *Power of Sound* 18
Invisible, unlooked-for, minister 264 *Storm* 13
Invisible? yet Spring her genial brow 267 **Desponding Father* 5
With light reflected from the invisible sun 277 **Haydon! let* 11
With such invisible motion speed thy flight, 315 **Advance—come* 10
Although invisible as Echo's self, 361 **List—'twas* 6
And that soft rustling of invisible wings 371 *Eg. Maid* 149
The invisible God, and take for guide 407 *White Doe* 1040
To adore the Invisible, and Him alone. 431 *Ecc. Sonn.* 2. 11. 11
Of things invisible to mortal sight." 441 *Ecc. Sonn.* 3. 4. 14
And, from invisible worlds at need laid bare, 475 **Here on their* 13
Audible tears, from some invisible source 498 **Enough of climbing* 37
Became invisible: for all around 548 **Stay, bold* 24
With thine, O silent and invisible Friend! 586 *Ch. Lamb* 108
And changeful colours by invisible links 641 *Prelude* 1. 611
So sweetly 'mid the gloom the invisible bird 644 *Prelude* 2. 125
Invisible, yet liveth to the heart; 648 *Prelude* 2. 405
Of Fortunatus, and the invisible coat 670 *Prelude* 5. 342
The invisible world, doth greatness make abode, 684 *Prelude* 6. 602
" *Invisible* " flames forth upon his chest. 691 *Prelude* 7. 287
And only not invisible, again 695 *Prelude* 7. 559
Giants, Ventriloquists, the Invisible Girl, 698 *Prelude* 7. 710
The wild brooks prattling from invisible haunts; 700 *Prelude* 8. 67
Of Pan, Invisible God, thrilling the rocks 701 *Prelude* 8. 183
As by some tie invisible, oaths professed 714 *Prelude* 9. 305
Do read the invisible soul; by men adroit 743 *Prelude* 13. 256
And its invisible counterpart, adorned 812 *Excursion* 4. 712
Authentic tidings of invisible things; 818 *Excursion* 4. 1144
He had become invisible,—a pomp 820 *Excursion* 4. 1301
The moving waters, and the invisible air. 884 *Excursion* 9. 9
Fresh power to commune with the invisible world, 885 *Excursion* 9. 86
For Time's invisible tooth to prey upon, S.3. 434 **The doubt* 51
The boundary lost, the line invisible K.8. 252 *Recluse* 1. 1. 576
Invisibly. Lengthening invisibly its weary line 96 *Brothers* 52
And o'er the heart of man: invisibly 673 *Prelude* 5. 492
Are nourished and invisibly repaired; 737 *Prelude* 12. 215
Invitation. To France be words of invitation sent! 309 *Men of Kent* 5
Gives holier invitation than the deck 447 *Ecc. Sonn.* 3. 30. 2
On Nature's invitation do I come, 621 *Recluse* 1. 1. 71
Conspicuous invitation to ascend 683 *Prelude* 6. 572
Was like an invitation into space 742 *Prelude* 13. 150
I felt their invitation; and resumed 797 *Excursion* 3. 760
And invitation every hour renewed, 806 *Excursion* 4. 377
With invitation urgently renewed. 880 *Excursion* 8. 440
Breathes invitation; easy is the walk 890 *Excursion* 9. 424
Invitations. With invitations, suppers, wine and fruit, 649 *Prelude* 3. 43
Invite. That breeze she will invite; 311 **Who rises* 8
Here only serve a feeling to invite 349 *Val. Dover* 12
Wherever they invite Thee, 386 *Yarrow Rev.* 70
O for those motions only that invite 473 **We saw* 5
Me did a kindlier fortune then invite 574 *Chiabrera* 3. 13
Invite us; shall we quit our road, and join 773 *Excursion* 2. 139
Of Britain, do invite her to cast off 889 *Excursion* 9. 377
Invited. To Niphates' top invited, 218 **Inmate of* 29
Approach;—and, thus invited, crown with rest 219 *Haunted Tree* 18
Invited, forth they peeped so fair to view, 377 *Duddon* 6. 13
By cordial love invited. 385 *Yarrow Rev.* 32
Invited, often would he leave his home 762 *Excursion* 1. 389
Invited, summoned, to partake the cheer 867 *Excursion* 7. 653
" If ye, by whom invited I began 874 *Excursion* 8. 5
Of jutting rock invited us to land. 892 *Excursion* 9. 568
Invites. And eve's mild hour invites my steps abroad. 3 *Ev. Wk.* 89
The vernal breeze invites. 224 *Primrose* 6
And usages, whose due return invites 448 *Ecc. Sonn.* 3. 33. 3

Invites—*continued.*
Of faith invites. More welcome to no land 449 *Ecc. Sonn.* 3. 36. 6
The Star of Bethlehem from its sphere invites 467 *St. Bees* 113
Nor hedge-row screen invites my steps abroad; 521 *Epist. Beaumont* 13
Inviting. With aspect so inviting. Why forbid me 55 *Bord.* 970
Inviting him with cheerful lure: 174 *Waggoner* 1. 79
Is it not a brow inviting 221 *Triad* 111
Inviting words—perchance already flung 332 *Ode: Thanks.* 212
The greenest bowers, the most inviting ways, 333 *Ded. Tour* 6
Ye heavy laden!" such the inviting voice 423 *Ecc. Sonn.* 1. 17. 11
The Sabbath bells renew the inviting peal; 447 *Ecc. Sonn.* 3. 28. 1
Inviting, at all seasons, ears and eyes 500 *Humanity* 13
Inviting shades of opportune recess, 676 *Prelude* 6. 74
Inviting; with buffoons against buffoons 697 *Prelude* 7. 698
Inviting us in glee to sit and eat. 781 *Excursion* 2. 673
Ere with inviting smile the Wanderer said: 782 *Excursion* 2. 728
And on that couch inviting us to rest, 793 *Excursion* 3. 477
Was most inviting to a troubled mind; 797 *Excursion* 3. 803
Inviting penance, fruitlessly endured: 798 *Excursion* 3. 876
Inviting sleep and soft forgetfulness. 821 *Excursion* 4. 1324
We must not part at this inviting hour." 823 *Excursion* 5. 72
Invocations. In these their invocations, with a voice 763 *Excursion* 1. 479
Invoke. Invoke we those bright Beings one by one; 220 *Triad* 32
Of his Bandusian fount; or I invoke 356 *Aquap.* 257
Of the Most High. Again do they invoke 436 *Ecc. Sonn.* 2. 33. 9
Invoked. Why do good thoughts, invoked or not, descend, 456 **Soft as* 22
When from afar invoked by anxious love? 733 *Prelude* 11. 423
With lifted hands invoked, and songs of praise: 811 *Excursion* 4. 680
Invokes. Aloft, the imperial Bird of Rome invokes 380 *Duddon* 17. 3
Invoking. Invoking Dion's tutelary care, 213 *Dion* 40
With scorn, invoking a vindictive ban 428 *Ecc. Sonn.* 1. 38. 12
Involuntary. With gladness and involuntary songs. 80 **Loving she* 14
He, doubt not, with involuntary dread, 528 **Those breathing* 108
When this involuntary strain had ceased, 870 *Excursion* 7. 832
Involve. Involve their serpent-necks in changeful rings, 6 *Ev. Wk.* 246
Duty, or love—involve, I feel, my ruin. 47 *Bord.* 550
The shades of night no more the soul involve, 618 *School Ex.* 47
Involved. *See* **Self-involved.**
The shepherd, all involved in wreaths of fire, 4 *Ev. Wk.* 112
Involved and restless all—a scene 178 *Waggoner* 3. 39
So were the hopeless troubles, that involved 214 *Dion* 118
Involved a history of no doubtful sense 359 **Complacent Fictions* 2
And their necks play, involved in rings, 374 *Eg. Maid* 322
Involved whate'er by love was brought 406 *White Doe* 977
With an untoward fate was long involved 574 *Chiabrera* 5. 2
The purer elements of truth involved 760 *Excursion* 1. 253
Involving. *See* **All-involving.**
Inward. Who, in the silent hour of inward thought, 23 *Yew-tree* 62
Brought from without to inward misery. 25 *Guilt* 75
Though inward anguish damped the Sailor's brow, 33 *Guilt* 485
Then, with a voice which inward trouble broke 33 *Guilt* 503
We need an inward sting to goad us on. 70 *Bord.* 1859
Of inward sadness had its charm; 86 *Anecdote* 22
Are of inward peace secure: 140 *Arm. Lady* 32
But nothing from their inward selves had they to fear. 141 *Arm. Lady* 90
Who, to his inward thoughts confined, 176 *Waggoner* 2. 25
Of serious faith, and inward glee; 186 **O Nightingale* 19
They flash upon that inward eye 187 **I wandered* 21
Such rebounds our inward ear 209 **Yes, it* 17
Call to the heart for inward listening— 222 *Triad* 206
Or made with hope to please that inward eye 231 **The gentlest Poet* 34
Was playing with some inward bait. 240 *P. B.* 310
Or share with me, fond thought! that inward eye, 279 **All praise* 10
Some inward trouble suddenly 294 *Jedbor.* 66
So all his dreams—that inward light 297 *Highland Boy* 211
Of inward happiness. We are selfish men; 307 **Milton! thou* 6
History that proves by inward evidence 359 **Complacent Fictions* 3
How wide a space can part from inward peace 363 **Grieve for* 13
Our inward prospect over, 386 *Yarrow Rev.* 38
If she be doomed to inward care, 397 *White Doe* 134
And carrying inward a serene 413 *White Doe* 1593
To the sole temple of the inward mind; 441 *Ecc. Sonn.* 3. 4. 5
As men the dictate of whose inward sense 441 *Ecc. Sonn.* 3. 6. 12
What witchery, for pure gifts of inward seeing, 480 *Cordelia* 12
Whose high endeavours are an inward light 493 *Hap. War.* 6
That brings to the inward creature no disgrace? 527 **Those breathing* 24
Mute offerings, tribute from an inward sense 539 **Lady! a* 28
So prized, and things inward and outward held 586 *Ch. Lamb* 117
Of pity cast from inward tenderness 646 *Prelude* 2. 249
That I beheld respired with inward meaning. 651 *Prelude* 3. 132
Remembered less; but I had inward hopes 660 *Prelude* 4. 162
Should the whole frame of earth by inward throes 666 *Prelude* 5. 30
Who, looking inward, have observed the ties 694 *Prelude* 7. 461
Of inward consciousness, and hope that laid 730 *Prelude* 11. 202
Some inward agitations thence are brought, 739 *Prelude* 12. 332
Turned inward; or at my request would sing 757 *Excursion* 1. 66
But, as the mind was filled with inward light, 757 *Excursion* 1. 95
Inward and outward; humble, yet sublime: 792 *Excursion* 3. 399
Turned inward,—to examine of what stuff 796 *Excursion* 3. 696
And inward self-disparagement affords 808 *Excursion* 4. 476
Or, if the mind turn inward, she recoils 810 *Excursion* 4. 624
Of inward conscience? with whose service charged 813 *Excursion* 4. 837
These inward feelings, and the aspiring vows 827 *Excursion* 5. 312
The inward principle that gives effect 831 *Excursion* 5. 572
Stung by his inward thoughts, and by the smiles 855 *Excursion* 6. 1096

Inward—*continued.*
Of open projects, and his inward hoard 861 *Excursion* 7. 280
Enrapt, as if his inward sense perceived 871 *Excursion* 7. 894
That inward motion to disguise, he said 874 *Excursion* 8. 32
By the division of her inward self 875 *Excursion* 8. 57
A native Briton to these inward chains, 878 *Excursion* 8. 298
As inward motions of the wandering thought K.8. 233 **Along the* 2
Can give us inward help, can purify, K.8. 245 *Recluse* 1.1.302
Already have I gained. The inward frame K.8. 249 *Recluse* 1.1.472
Why does this inward lustre fondly seek, K.8. 255 *Recluse* 1.1.677
Inwardly. Was growing inwardly more strong; 175 *Waggoner* 1. 149
Methought, was yielding inwardly, 401 *White Doe* 491
Her sanction inwardly she bore, 416 *White Doe* 1858
And inwardly sustained by silent prayer, 541 *Grace Darl.* 49
Yet, being inwardly unstained, 542 *Russ. Fug.* 79
To a meek spirit suffering inwardly. 691 *Prelude* 7. 315
Outwardly, inwardly contemplated, 706 *Prelude* 8. 486
Compelled to look, and inwardly oppressed 734 *Prelude* 12. 3
Of discontent, and inwardly opprest 776 *Excursion* 2. 305
He outwardly, and inwardly perhaps, 780 *Excursion* 2. 589
From risk and hardship, inwardly retrace 794 *Excursion* 3. 559
Iona. On to Iona!—What can she afford 474 **On to* 1
Iona's. Glad tidings to Iona's shore, 390 *Highland Broach* 4
Which yet survive on bleak Iona's coast. 419 *Ecc. Sonn.* 1. 5. 8
Iona's Saints, forgetting not past days, 474 **On to* 12
Iopas. Graced with redundant hair, Iopas sings 625 *Æneid* 121
Ire. Rejoice, brave Land, though pride's perverted ire 22 *Desc. Sk.* 642
"Bard! moderate your ire; 164 *Needlecase* 18
And food cut off by sacerdotal ire, 419 *Ecc. Sonn.* 1. 4. 3
De-irians—he would save them from God's Ire; 422 *Ecc. Sonn.* 1. 13.12
Dread Lord! so fearful when provoked, thine ire 563 *Troilus* 71
Yet, yet rejoice, tho' Pride's perverted ire 616 *Desc.Sk.Quarto* 780
Ireful. Deafening the region in his ireful mood. 439 *Ecc. Sonn.* 2.43.14
Irians. *See* **De-irians.**
Iris. Not Iris, issuing from her cloudy shrine, 434 *Ecc. Sonn.* 2. 22. 9
Irksome. To banish listlessness and irksome care; 108 *Indolence* 51
Ne'er can the way be irksome or forlorn 284 *Departure* 31
Of irksome change, or threats from saddening power. 327 *Ode 1815* 16
—An irksome drudgery seems it to plod on, 761 *Excursion* 1. 322
Irksome sensations; but by love of truth 790 *Excursion* 3. 287
No more to open on that irksome world 843 *Excursion* 6. 365
Than honest maintenance, by irksome toil 875 *Excursion* 8. 50
Iron. The rear through iron brown betrays a sullen gleam. 6 *Ev. Wk.* 204
At once the griding iron passage found; 33 *Guilt* 493
His fate was pitied. Him in iron case 36 *Guilt* 658
Should he, by tales which would draw tears from iron, 57 *Bord.* 1060
Like red-hot iron burnt into my heart. 59 *Bord.* 1183
The obstinate bolt of a small iron door 59 *Bord.* 1200
I lighted—opened with soft touch the chapel's iron door, 92 *Poet's Dream* 41
Equipped from head to foot in iron mail. 111 **'Tis said that some* 47
With iron, making it throughout in all 134 *Michael* 182
Tugging at the iron chain, 181 *Waggoner* 4. 98
Would have pulled up an iron ring; 241 *P. B.* 403
He will be turned to iron soon, 242 *P. B.* 522
Through all his iron frame was felt 247 *P. B.* 964
Of vain conceit, an iron scourge! 298 *Brownie's Cell* 30
Her arts, her strength, her iron, and her gold. 320 **Avaunt all* 14
'Twas through an iron grate. 334 **In Bruges* 24
When of an iron age they told, 342 *Ital. Itin.* 76
The Monks relax or break these iron chains; 429 *Ecc. Sonn.* 2. 4. 7
Firm as the stake to which with iron band 437 *Ecc. Sonn.* 2. 35. 5
Received, and fostered in her iron breast: 441 *Ecc. Sonn.* 3. 3. 4
Nor does the village Church-clock's iron tone 453 **Calm is the* 10
And now on the brink of the iron. 484 **A plague* 15
And feudal rapine clothed with iron mail, 534 **When in* 2
—There, did the iron Genius not disdain 607 *Desc.Sk.Quarto* 307
Tinkled like iron; while far distant hills 638 *Prelude* 1. 442
Wherein were fixed the iron pales that fenced 696 *Prelude* 7. 606
A murderer had been hung in iron chains. 737 *Prelude* 12. 236
And iron case were gone; but on the turf, 737 *Prelude* 12. 238
"But all was quieted by iron bonds 798 *Excursion* 3. 821
An iron knell! with echoes from afar 819 *Excursion* 4. 1181
What would it bring?—an iron age, S.3. 439 **Avaunt this* 2
Iron-bound. The gulfy coast of Norway iron-bound; 454 *Sea-side* 30
Ironic. Ironic diamonds,—clubs, hearts, diamonds, spades, 640 *Prelude* 1. 527
Iron-pointed. An iron-pointed staff lay at his side. 756 *Excursion* 1. 37
Irons. A human body that in irons swang, 25 *Guilt* 79
Sounding with grappling irons and long poles. 672 *Prelude* 5. 447
Irradiate. By Poesy irradiate, and yet graced, 357 *Aquap.* 284
Irradiates. A virtue which irradiates and exalts 645 *Prelude* 2. 239
Irradiation. Of rapt irradiation, exquisite. 695 *Prelude* 7. 561
Irrational. Though yet irrational of soul, to grasp 826 *Excursion* 5. 264
Irreconcilable. Meets foes irreconcilable, and at best 721 *Prelude* 10. 207
Irregular. Irregular in sight or sound 193 *Ruth* 128
Had given a charter to irregular hopes. 680 *Prelude* 6. 335
Traversed but by a few irregular paths, 834 *Excursion* 5. 763
Had been irregular, I might say, wild; 859 *Excursion* 7. 114
Irregularly. Abodes of men irregularly massed 876 *Excursion* 8. 123
Irreligious. How still! no irreligious sound or sight 16 *Desc. Sk.* 352
Irremoveable. And irremoveable) gracious openings lie, 396 **Action is* 8
Irresistible. Of being, smites with irresistible pain, 234 *Power of Sound* 98
With touches irresistible. 243 *P. B.* 655
Aloud, with fervour irresistible 687 *Prelude* 7. 5
Great, universal, irresistible. 727 *Prelude* 11. 17

Irreverence. In daily sight of this irreverence, . . 655 *Prelude* 3. 419
Irrevocable. Upon the irrevocable past, . . . 223 *Wishing-gate* 50
But time, irrevocable time, is flown, ... 524 *Epist. Beaumont* 200
Irriguous. But down the irriguous valley hies, . . 338 **Meek Virgin* 26
Irthing. Sir Alfred Irthing, with appropriate words 872 *Excursion* 7. 971
Irwin. Fair Ellen Irwin, when she sate . . . . 287 *Ellen Irwin* 1
Is. (*Partial list.*) *See* **Is't.**
In Heaven; for, 'mid the wreck of IS and WAS, . 269 *Malham* 11
Isabel. And his heart failed him. "Isabel," said he, 134 *Michael* 226
Our Luke shall leave us, Isabel; the land 135 *Michael* 244
And Isabel sat silent, for her mind . . 135 *Michael* 256
Passed quickly through the mind of Isabel, . . 135 *Michael* 272
And thus resumed:—"Well, Isabel! this scheme 135 *Michael* 274
But Isabel was glad when Sunday came . . 135 *Michael* 288
And Isabel, when she had told her fears, . . 135 *Michael* 300
With daylight Isabel resumed her work; . . 135 *Michael* 304
The letter was read over; Isabel . . . 136 *Michael* 312
A prouder heart than Luke's. When Isabel . . 136 *Michael* 315
Three years, or little more, did Isabel . . . 138 *Michael* 473
Learnt, Isabel, from thy society, ... 627 **The star* 7
Isaiah. Meanwhile the Evangelists, Isaiah, Job, . 695 *Prelude* 7. 562
Isis. Where silver Isis leads my stripling feet; . 270 **Ye sacred* 11
Isis and Cam, to patient Science dear! . . . 451 *Ecc. Sonn.* 3. 42. 14
Island. Where peace to Grasmere's lonely island leads, ... 2 *Ev. Wk.* 5
That haunt some barren island of the north, . . 47 *Bord.* 559
At the same poisonous fountain! 'Twas an island . . . . 69 *Bord.* 1740
And one green island, gleam between the stems . 151 **When, to* 92
In some green island of the western main. . . 320 **They seek* 14
So cheered, she left that Island bleak, . . . 371 *Eg. Maid* 157
Some island which the wild waves beat— . . 413 *White Doe* 1560
Of Christian Faith, this savage Island blessed . 418 *Ecc. Sonn.* 1. 2. 4
This little Island may survive; . . . . . 532 †*Float. Isl.* 18
A single Island rose . . . . 543 *Russ. Fug.* 102
Upon her Island desolate; . . . . . . 544 *Russ. Fug.* 203
And toward the Island fled, ... 544 *Russ. Fug.* 266
Its one green Island and its winding shores; . . 622 *Recluse* 1. 1. 119
And through the astonished Island swept in storm, 626 *Ballot* 3
And a joyful cry through the Island rang, . . 629 *Installation* 35
Was now an Island musical with birds . . . 643 *Prelude* 2. 58
And now a third small Island, where survived . 643 *Prelude* 2. 62
On the large island, had this dwelling been . . 644 *Prelude* 2. 146
Of some small island steered our course with one, 644 *Prelude* 2. 167
To a floating island, an amphibious spot . . 654 *Prelude* 3. 333
Some tempting island, could but know the ills . 656 *Prelude* 3. 485
In that delightful island which protects . . . 722 *Prelude* 10. 321
And rocky island near, a fragment stood . . . 726 *Prelude* 10. 555
Or some secreted island, Heaven knows where! . 729 *Prelude* 11. 141
To his small island in the ethereal deep . . . 811 *Excursion* 4. 640
Island or grove, that hides a blessed few . . . 827 *Excursion* 5. 350
Cut off, an island in the dusky waste; . . . 832 *Excursion* 5. 677
The happy Island where ye think and act; . . 890 *Excursion* 9. 412
An island in the brook. It was a place . . . K.8. 229 **I will* 140
He leapt upon the island, with proud heart, . . K.8. 229 **I will* 148
A prisoner on the island, not without . . . K.8. 229 **I will* 157
From shore to island, and from isle to shore, . . K.8. 237 *Recluse* 1. 1. 40
Islanded. Of level pasture, islanded with groves . 702 *Prelude* 8. 191
Islander. Of either sea, an Islander by birth, . . 352 *Aquap.* 3
Islanders. Eastern Islanders have given . . . 511 **Who rashly* 27
Islanders 'mid a stormy mountain sea, . . . 782 *Excursion* 2. 735
Island-rock. On the Island-rock, her lonely dwelling-place; . . . . 540 *Grace Darl.* 24
Island's. Stage above stage) would sit this Island's King, ... 470 *Tynwald* 3
Islands. With hanging islands of resplendent furze: 146 **It was an* 33
Seven little Islands, green and bare, . . . 162 *Binnorie* 60
Of islands, that together lie . . . . . 193 *Ruth* 70
Nor the green Islands, nor the shining Seas; . . 252 **The fairest* 11
With heroes, 'mid the islands of the Blest, . . 317 **Brave Schill* 3
The Pride of the Islands, VICTORIA THE QUEEN! 629 *Installation* 116
Lake, islands, promontories, gleaming bays, . . 658 *Prelude* 4. 8
That in the Tropic Islands he had served, . . 664 *Prelude* 4. 422
And islands of Winander!—many a time . . . 671 *Prelude* 5. 365
Small islands scattered amid stormy waves, . . 725 *Prelude* 10. 482
In the islands of the blest, ... S.3. 442 *Harmodius* 12
Rocky or green, that do like islands rise . . K.8. 263 **The Lake* 9
Isle. Yon isle, which feels not even the milkmaid's feet, ... 6 *Ev. Wk.* 236
Yon isle conceals their home, their hut-like bower; 6 *Ev. Wk.* 238
Where be the temples which in Britain's Isle, . 102 *Artegal* 1
To the small wooden isle where, their work to beguile, ... 166 *Stray Pleasures* 10
High on that chalky cliff of Britain's Isle, . . 215 *Enterprise* 3
But thou, O Goddess! in thy favourite Isle . . 217 *Enterprise* 151
And visibly engirding Mona's Isle . . . . 219 **This Height* 16
Is a sweet Isle, of isles the Queen; . . . 237 *P. B.* 64
Or clock to toll from! Many a tempting isle, . 262 **Dark and* 9
Grove, isle, with every shape of sky-built dome, . 263 **Those words* 9
(Giants—the same who built in Erin's isle . . 269 *Malham* 4
When Philoctetes in the Lemnian isle . . . 273 **When Philoctetes* 1
That, in our native isle, and every land, . . 281 *Chris. Words.* 4
Within this little lonely isle . . . . . 298 *Brownie's Cell* 15
Shot lightning through this lonely Isle! . . . 298 *Brownie's Cell* 42
In his lone Isle, the dreams of night; . . . 299 *Brownie's Cell* 58
In Nysa's isle, the embellished grot; . . . 299 *Brownie's Cell* 92
Own—that the progeny of this fair Isle . . . 325 *Ode 1814* 139
In the proud Isle of liberty! . . . . . 342 *Ital. Itin.* 30
From the bleak isle where she is laid, . . . 370 *Eg. Maid* 99
That Isle without a house or haven; . . . . 371 *Eg. Maid* 122

Isle—*continued.*
Nor lacks this sea-girt Isle a timely share . . . 432 *Ecc. Sonn.* 2. 14. 13
All hail, sage Lady, whom a grateful Isle . . 438 *Ecc. Sonn.* 2. 38. 3
Such to this British Isle her christian Fanes, . . 444 *Ecc. Sonn.* 3. 17. 9
Why should the Enthusiast, journeying through this Isle, ... 463 **Why should the* 1
In a snug Cove on this our favoured Isle, . . . 470 †*From early* 11
Nor let one billow of our heaven-blest Isle . . 471 **Despond who* 13
Homeward we turn. Isle of Columba's Cell, . . 475 **Homeward we* 1
With this green isle my fortunes, come not where 495 *Fact* 5
What shall I treat of? News from Mona's Isle? . 522 *Epist. Beaumont* 59
Thither your eyes may turn—the Isle is passed away; . . . . 532 †*Float. Isl.* 24
Blest is this Isle—our native Land; . . . . 533 **Blest is* 1
And reached the lonely Isle. . . . . . 543 *Russ. Fug.* 128
Among the birch-trees of this rocky isle. . . . 548 **Stranger! this* 7
Along the beach of this small isle and thought . . 551 **If thou in* 20
Clapp'd her strong wings, and sought the cheerful isle, ... 618 *School Ex.* 46
That sang and ceased not; now a Sister Isle . . 643 *Prelude* 2. 59
Of note belonging to that honoured isle, . . . 733 *Prelude* 11. 433
With hostile purposes the blessèd Isle, . . . 876 *Excursion* 8. 145
If there were not, *then*, in our far-famed Isle, . . 879 *Excursion* 8. 341
—"Observe," the Vicar said, "yon rocky isle . . 891 *Excursion* 9. 495
Of the fair Isle with birch-trees fringed—and there, 892 *Excursion* 9. 528
Within the circuit of this sea-girt isle . . . 894 *Excursion* 9. 683
From shore to island, and from isle to shore, . . K.8. 237 *Recluse* 1. 1. 40
Isle's. The Flower has drooped, the Isle's delight; 628 *Installation* 22
Isles. 'Mid clustering isles, and holly-sprinkled steeps; 2 *Ev. Wk.* 10
Embowered in walnut slopes and citron isles: . 13 *Desc. Sk.* 155
Of green isles widening on each snow-clad height; 17 *Desc. Sk.* 369
Acquired by traffic 'mid the Indian Isles, . . . 96 *Brothers* 67
Or ruling Bandit's wife among the Grecian isles. . 190 *Beggars* 12
Is a sweet Isle, of isles the Queen; . . . . 237 *P. B.* 64
Among the Indian isles, where lay . . . . 296 *Highland Boy* 132
And where the boatman of the Western Isles . . 419 *Ecc. Sonn.* 1. 5. 6
Shall disappear from both the sister Isles, . . 474 **On to* 11
Alas for thee, bright Galaxy of Isles, . . . 501 *Humanity* 69
Beating on one of those disastrous isles— . . 540 *Grace Darl.* 31
And winds between thine isles the vocal barge. . 605 *Desc.Sk.Quarto* 161
And emerald isles to spot the heights appear, . 610 *Desc.Sk.Quarto* 445
Flying, found shelter in the Fortunate Isles, . . 635 *Prelude* 1. 192
Of those who conquered first the Indian Isles, . 635 *Prelude* 1 208
Though soothing, and the little floating isles . . 800 *Excursion* 3. 979
Bespotted—with innumerable isles: . . . . 869 *Excursion* 7. 792
Meantime the sovereignty of these fair Isles . . 889 *Excursion* 9. 344
Islet. Upon a rocky islet, side by side, . . . 143 **High bliss* 15
Issue. The issue to the justice of the cause, . . 48 *Bord.* 603
To abide the issue of my act, alone. . . . . 65 *Bord.* 1519
With the disastrous issue of last night, . . . 76 *Bord.* 2235
Ay, what shall we encounter next? This issue— 77 *Bord.* 2284
While he the issue waits, at early morn . . . 104 *Artegal* 106
And she expects the issue in repose. . . . 209 *Laod.* 12
Knit every thought the impending issue needs, . 233 *Power of Sound* 95
Of waters issue from a British source, . . . 272 *Devil's Bridge* 3
May with that issue be compared) . . . . 343 *Eclipse* 57
Just at the point of issue, where it fears . . 351 *Des. Stanzas* 61
That he the solemn issue would determine. . . 373 *Eg. Maid* 312
And for this issue been prepared; . . . . 402 *White Doe* 580
At length, the issue of a prayer . . . . 406 *White Doe* 927
Disastrous issue!—he had said . . . . . 408 *White Doe* 1130
False in the issue, that yon seeming space . . 461 **Who but is* 10
Leaving the final issue in *His* hands . . . 519 *Pun. Death* 11. 11
Checked, in the moment of its issue, checked . . 539 **Lady! a* 37
Yet for one happy issue;—and I look . . . 582 **To public* 3
Would issue, let one incident make known. . . 683 *Prelude* 6. 561
The inglorious issue of that charge, and how . 720 *Prelude* 10. 114
Its unsuccessful issue much excite . . . . 722 *Prelude* 10. 256
The solemn voice appeared to issue, startling . 807 *Excursion* 4. 407
May issue thence, recruited for the tasks . . 810 *Excursion* 4. 595
When issue forth the first pale stars, is heard, . 819 *Excursion* 4. 1176
She with a numerous issue filled his house, . . 825 *Excursion* 5. 198
Shall pass uncensured; though the issue prove, . 827 *Excursion* 5. 315
For work of happier issue, to the side . . . 869 *Excursion* 7. 809
And, as they issue from the illumined pile, . . 877 *Excursion* 8. 175
And tottering hovels, whence do issue forth . . 879 *Excursion* 8. 347
Issued. Then issued Vesper from the fulgent west, . 192 *Gipsies* 14
Issued, to sudden view, a glorious Form! . . . 323 *Ode 1814* 22
Issuing or issued from a wintry fount; . . . 347 *Processions* 53
Issued into the salt-sea flood, ... 371 *Eg. Maid* 165
Till doubtful combat issued in a trance . . . 383 *Duddon* 29. 5
Our thoughts have issued, and our feelings flowed, 394 **No more* 23
Issued forth with old and young, ... 535 *Egremont* 2
Issued low muttered sounds, as if of pain . . 664 *Prelude* 4. 405
Issued, and with uplifted eyes beheld, . . . 682 *Prelude* 6. 482
Issued, on delegation to sustain . . . . 725 *Prelude* 10. 499
Then, as we issued from that covert nook, . . 802 *Excursion* 4. 32
Hath issued any portion of the joy . . . . K.8. 245 *Recluse* 1.1.317
Issued the blest Redeemer of our race— . . . [?] **A sad* 11
Issues. Issues from his radiant shroud, . . . 181 *Waggoner* 4. 145
Or a fierce impress issues with its foil . . . 275 **While poring* 11
Descend on all that issues from our blood. . . 319 *Biscayan* 14
Issues, revealed in no presumptuous vision, . . 357 *Aquap.* 307
Perturbed she issues. She will go! . . . . 407 *White Doe* 1059
Issues the master Mind, at whose fell swoop . . 425 *Ecc. Sonn.* 1. 28. 7
Upon the dream-like issues—the romance . . 430 *Ecc. Sonn.* 2. 8. 3
Issues for that dominion overthrown: . . . . 435 *Ecc. Sonn.* 2. 27. 5
Great issues, good or bad for human kind, . . 493 *Hap. War.* 50
For kindly issues—as through every clime . . 502 **The unremitting* 13
Kindlier issues, holier rest, ... 503 **Like a* 80
Of all that issues from his glorious fount! . . 511 **So fair* 9

Issues—*continued.*
And their disastrous issues. What availed, 735 *Prelude* 12. 52
To most strange issues. I have lived to mark 875 *Excursion* 8. 89
Entrust the future.—Not for these sad issues 886 *Excursion* 9. 126
Except these mighty issues: from the pains 890 *Excursion* 9. 394

Issuing. *See* **Forth-issuing.**
Thence issuing often with unwieldy stalk, 6 *Ev. Wk.* 242
Issuing from her cloudy shrine;— 221 *Triad* 85
Issuing or issued from a wintry fount; 347 *Processions* 53
And murmur issuing from yon pendent flood, 358 *Aquap.* 370
Not Iris, issuing from her cloudy shrine, 434 *Ecc. Sonn.* 2. 22. 9
And proud deliverance issuing out of pain 514 **Who ponders* 4
Issuing in pomp, shall come to judge mankind. 534 **When in* 16
Thence issuing oft, unwieldly as ye stalk, 596 *Ev. Wk. Quarto* 231
Weak and more weak the issuing current eyes 609 *Desc. Sk. Quarto* 396
That issuing hence may steal into thy mind 628 **Deign, Sovereign* 22
Which met me issuing from the City's walls) 687 *Prelude* 7. 3
By annual custom, issuing forth in troops, 701 *Prelude* 8. 154
Its voices issuing forth to silent light 747 *Prelude* 14. 73
When, from the blind mist issuing, I beheld 796 *Excursion* 3. 719
Issuing, however feebly, nowhere flows 804 *Excursion* 4. 220
From out their substance issuing, maintain 835 *Excursion* 5. 875
Issuing when shame hath ceased to check the brawls K.8. 246 *Recluse* 1. 1. 345

Is't. *See* **Is.**
Rest, little young One, rest; what is't that aileth thee? 87 *Pet-lamb* 24
"I'm here, what is't you want with me?" 129 *Idiot Boy* 253

Isthmian. And to the people at the Isthmian Games 312 **A Roman* 2
And of that joy which shook the Isthmian Field, 312 **When, far* 3
His envied temples with the Isthmian crown, 312 **When, far* 6

Isthmus. Stand like an isthmus 'twixt two stormy seas 48 *Bord.* 607
While on that isthmus which commands 226 *Present.* 70
Of the same isthmus, which our spirits cross 673 *Prelude* 5. 536

It, *omitted.*

Italia. Italia! on the surface of thy spirit, 366 **Fair Land* 9
And soft Italia feels renewed alarms; 427 *Ecc. Sonn.* 1. 34. 4

Italian. And droop, while no Italian arts are thine, 21 *Desc. Sk.* 589
Of gratitude, beneath Italian skies, 326 *Sobieski* 3
What though the Italian pencil wrought not here, 339 *Tell* 1
Afloat beneath Italian skies, 343 *Eclipse* 7
Such, haply, yon ITALIAN Maid, 344 **How blest* 20
This thy last haunt beneath Italian skies 363 **List—'twas* 100
For thee, O great Italian nation, split 515 **Ah why* 8
Such name Italian fancy would have given, 524 *Epist. Beaumont* 167
While no Italian arts their charms combine 615 *Desc. Sk. Quarto* 707
The Italian, as he thrids his way with care, 690 *Prelude* 7. 214

Italy. Of rival glory; they—fallen Italy— 359 **They—who* 13
And all that Greece and Italy have sung 389 *Tyndrum* 2
Mourn, Italy, the loss of him who stood 573 *Chiabrera* 2. 19

Iterated. The iterated summons loud, 228 *Devot. Incit.* 42

Iteration. And in thy iteration, "WHIP POOR WILL!" 153 *Morn. Ex.* 16
Whose sedulous iteration thrilled with joy 363 **List—'twas* 90
This mournful iteration? For though Time, 496 **A little* 4
Which in that iteration recognise K.8. 245 *Recluse* 1. 1. 331

Itinerant. To cheer the Itinerant on whom she pours 463 **Adieu, Rydalian* 12
Prouder itinerant, mountebank, or he 699 *Prelude* 8. 35
Of an itinerant vehicle I sate, 707 *Prelude* 8. 544
Itinerant in this labour, he had passed 761 *Excursion* 1. 349
Than this obscure Itinerant had skill 771 *Excursion* 2. 22

Itinerants. —By these Itinerants, as experienced men, 875 *Excursion* 8. 77

It's. (*Partial list.*)
It's edge all flame, the broad'ning sun appears; 594 *Ev. Wk. Quarto* 152
Nought wakens or disturbs it's tranquil tides; 597 *Ev. Wk. Quarto* 310
And Silence loves it's purple roof of vines. 603 *Desc. Sk. Quarto* 91

Its, *omitted.*

Itself. (*Partial list.*)
And hope itself was all I knew of pain; 2 *Ev. Wk.* 22
In golden light; half hides itself in shade: 12 *Desc. Sk.* 98
Itself all trembling at the torrent's power. 14 *Desc. Sk.* 185
Hope died, and fear itself in agony was lost! 30 *Guilt* 351
Is bold, and would relieve itself by praise. 64 *Bord.* 1483
The pleasure which there is in life itself. 132 *Michael* 77
Beneath the branches—of itself had made 149 *M. H.* 5
That spreads itself, some faery bold 159 **With little* 31
Almost as thought itself, of human ken. 165 *Parrot* 32
And the maternal sympathy itself, 172 *Infant Daughter* 36
Are steadfast as the rocks; the brook itself, 184 *Airey-force* 4
Of rock or sand reposeth, there to sun itself; 196 *Resolution* 63
Which might not burn itself to rest. 199 *Thorn* 121
Power, glory, empire, as the world itself, 230 *Clouds* 39
Which ever strives in vain itself to satisfy, 231 **The gentlest Poet* 35
And formed itself upon the paper 244 *P. B.* 749
Fairer than life itself, in this sweet Book, 254 *Complete Angler* 11
That to itself takes all, Eternity. 276 *Oker Hill* 14
That winds into itself for sweet return. 284 *Departure* 32
And for the law itself we fight 291 *Rob Roy* 27
Would fix itself as smoothly as a cloud, 312 **When, far* 13
And beauty unimpaired. Grand in itself, 355 *Aquap.* 184
In narrow compass—narrow as itself: 382 *Duddon* 24. 9
Drove from itself, we trust, all frightful gloom. 391 *Brownie* 14
Which may itself be cherished and caressed 394 **No more* 33
Exhaust itself and sink to rest; 406 *White Doe* 917
Her soul doth in itself stand fast, 414 *White Doe* 1623
For deep as hell itself, the avenging draught 432 *Ecc. Sonn.* 2. 16. 8
That nothing of itself will come, 481 *Expost.* 27
Above a world that deems itself most wise 512 **Who rashly* 41
The blameless cause lay in the Theme itself. 539 **Lady! a* 11
It cannot help itself in its decay; 571 **There is a Flower* 18

Itself—*continued.*
That flings itself on wild relief 582 **O for a* 11
That doth "within itself its sweetness close;" 584 **With copious* 47
With life itself. Thus, 'mid a shifting world, 585 *Ch. Lamb* 94
Laid safely by itself, beneath a Tree. 622 **Among all* 16
The pent-up air, struggling to free itself, 640 *Prelude* 1. 540
Wearied itself out of the memory, 641 *Prelude* 1. 598
Beneath the wave, yea, in the wave itself, 648 *Prelude* 2. 408
Creation and divinity itself 651 *Prelude* 3. 171
The place itself and fashion of the rites. 653 *Prelude* 3. 310
Itself a living part of a live whole, 657 *Prelude* 3. 590
The head turns round and cannot right itself; 658 *Prelude* 3. 623
And talking to itself when all things else 660 *Prelude* 4. 120
Unpeaceful in itself. A single tree 676 *Prelude* 6. 76
That made my fancy restless as itself. 705 *Prelude* 8. 413
A spirit thoroughly faithful to itself, 720 *Prelude* 10. 167
Do of itself blow fresh, and make the vanes 723 *Prelude* 10. 370
Among the bowers of Paradise itself) 729 *Prelude* 11. 120
And, lastly, utter loss of hope itself 734 *Prelude* 12. 6
What in itself it is, and would become. 747 *Prelude* 14. 69
Snug as a child that hides itself in sport 784 *Excursion* 2. 822
Yet obstinately cherishing itself: 796 *Excursion* 3. 677
Of a poor lamb—left somewhere to itself, 807 *Excursion* 4. 411
Even such a shell the universe itself 818 *Excursion* 4. 1141
The cross itself, at whose unconscious feet 827 *Excursion* 5. 337
Than of this breath, which shapes itself in words 863 *Excursion* 7. 359
That whirls (how slow itself!) ten thousand spindles: 866 *Excursion* 7. 607
How insecure, how baseless in itself, 877 *Excursion* 8. 223
The infant Being in itself, and makes 878 *Excursion* 8. 290
Country, society, and time itself, 885 *Excursion* 9. 107
Scorning love-whispers shrinks from love itself S.3. 436 **The doubt* 146
An act of courage, and the thing itself K.8. 238 *Recluse* 1. 1. 61
Made for itself; and happy in itself, K.8. 240 *Recluse* 1. 1. 150
Disturbed, uneasy in itself as seemed, K.8. 241 *Recluse* 1. 1. 177
In answering to itself; or like a hound K.8. 245 *Recluse* 1. 1. 323
Strange question, yet it answers not itself. K.8. 255 *Recluse* 1. 1. 681
Than joy itself—for underneath it lies [?] **A sad* 5

Iulus. Like young Iulus; but the gentlest dews 624 *Æneid* 46
Upon Iulus, dazzled with the rays 624 *Æneid* 74

I've. (*Partial list.*) *See* **I.**
I've had the saddest dream that ever troubled 44 *Bord.* 397
Oh, Sir, I've been a wicked Woman. 46 *Bord.* 505
Woman, I've lent my body to the service 74 *Bord.* 2112
—Some little I've seen of blind boisterous works 86 *Rural Arch.* 19
I've heard of fearful winds and darkness that come there; 88 *Pet-lamb* 54
With what I've witnessed, and with what I've heard, 98 *Brothers* 188
I've watched you now a full half-hour, 106 **I've watched* 1
I've wet my path with tears like dew, 117 *Affl. Marg.* 34
I've none, my pretty Innocent! 121 *Emigrant Mother* 76
I've sought thy father far and wide. 145 *Her Eyes* 94
I've had a glimpse of you—*avast!* 176 *Waggoner* 1. 238
"I've heard, the moss is spotted red 200 *Thorn* 210
I've left my heart at home. 237 *P. B.* 55
I've heard of one, a gentle Soul, 244 *P. B.* 736
I've played, I've danced, with my narration; 245 *P. B.* 791
—I've heard of hearts unkind, kind deeds 484 *Simon Lee* 93

Ivied. These find, 'mid ivied abbey-walls, 168 *Wren's Nest* 17
To ivied castles and to moonlight skies, 273 **While Anna's* 12
The ivied Ruins of forlorn GRACE DIEU; 547 **Beneath yon* 4
Whose place of rest is near yon ivied porch. 864 *Excursion* 7. 487
Hung in his rustic hall. One ivied arch 872 *Excursion* 7. 962

Ivor. Dwells in the Hall of Ivor; 483 *Simon Lee* 30

Ivor-hall. Not far from pleasant Ivor-hall, 483 *Simon Lee* 2

Ivy. Half grey, half shagged with ivy to its ridge; 3 *Ev. Wk.* 69
And castles all with ivy green! 244 *P. B.* 685
With greenest ivy overgrown, 246 *P. B.* 854
And tufted with an ivy grove; 246 *P. B.* 855
See how her ivy clasps the sacred Ruin, 283 **Here, where* 5
Beneath the arch with ivy bound, 396 *White Doe* 53
Of stone, and ivy, and the spread 397 *White Doe* 95
Like ivy, round some ancient elm, they twine 424 *Ecc. Sonn.* 1. 21. 11
Or from a rifted crag or ivy tod 456 **The leaves* 20
With flaccid threads of ivy, in the still 497 **Enough of climbing* 22
Green ivy risen from out the cheerful earth 584 **With copious* 56
The shuddering ivy dripped large drops—yet still 644 *Prelude* 2. 124
With clustering ivy, and the lightsome twigs 676 *Prelude* 6. 82
In clustering curls, like ivy, which the bite 865 *Excursion* 7. 552
Of ivy, flourishing and thick, that clasped 881 *Excursion* 8. 480

Izonda. No change:—the fair Izonda he had wooed 373 *Eg. Maid* 292

J

Jacet. And its forlorn Hic jacet! 287 *Ellen Irwin* 56

Jack. It gleams on the face, there, of dusky-browed Jack, 188 *Music* 15
Of Jack the Giant-killer, Robin Hood, 670 *Prelude* 5. 343
The champion, Jack the Giant-killer: Lo! 691 *Prelude* 7. 280

Jackets. —Of coats and of jackets grey, scarlet, and green, 120 *Childless Father* 5

Jacobins. The National Synod and the Jacobins, 710 *Prelude* 9. 49

Jacobite. Two doughty champions: flaming Jacobite 845 *Excursion* 6. 458

Jacob's. Gave, in the field of Luz, to Jacob's sight 500 *Humanity* 34

Jagged. And mineral crown, beside his jagged urn, 269 *Gordale* 9

Jagged—*continued.*
Of yon wild cave, whose jaggèd brows are fringed 497 **Enough of climbing* 21

Jail-mastiff. While the jail-mastiff howls at the dull clanking chain, 621 *Convict* 37
James. James stopped with no good will: 85 *Shepherd-boys* 42
Leonard and James! I warrant, every corner 99 *Brothers* 273
But Leonard— Then James still is left among you! 99 *Brothers* 290
James, though not sickly, yet was delicate; 100 *Brothers* 332
Could pause between a Raleigh and a James? L.I. 96 *Juvenal* 3. 44
James's. Which at that time was James's home, there learned 101 *Brothers* 375
Jane. "The first that died was sister Jane; 84 *We are Seven* 49
And a few natural graves." To Jane, his wife, 95 *Brothers* 15
Seven widowed years without my Jane, 157 *Sexton* 30
Jane hangs her head upon my breast, 295 *Highland Boy* 3
January. Will come wth loads of January snow, 97 *Brothers* 152
Janus. Life, like that Roman Janus, double-faced; 775 *Excursion* 2. 251
Jar. Dull, flagging notes that with each other jar?" 252 **Why, Minstrel* 2
But stop! these theoretic fancies jar 790 *Excursion* 3. 253
Jarred. On their quick sense our sweetest music jarred; 527 **Those breathing* 51
Jarring. Convulsed as by a jarring din; 234 *Power of Sound* 102
To social cares from jarring passions freed; 334 **The Spirit* 13
Into those jarring fractions.—Let thy scope 515 **Ah why* 9
No jarring monks, to gloomy cell confined, 619 *School Ex.* 49
In rest established; and the jarring thoughts 841 *Excursion* 6. 195
With resignation; and no jarring tone 848 *Excursion* 6. 643
With all remembrance of a jarring world, K.8. 254 *Recluse* 1.1.632
Jars. In conflict; whose rough winds forgot their jars 336 *Danube* 10
Scattered on all sides by the hideous jars 346 *Processions* 34
Jasmine. There, to the porch, belike wth jasmine bound 21 *Desc. Sk.* 604
As climbing jasmine, pure— 583 **O for a* 42
Javelin. He launched a deadly javelin! 287 *Ellen Irwin* 28
Sword dropped not, javelin kept its deadly aim.— 361 **When here* 4
Exults like him whose javelin from the lair 466 *St. Bees* 4
Jaws. I would have dogged him to the jaws of hell— 78 *Bord.* 2311
By some too boldly named "the Jaws of Hell:" 475 *Greenock* 3
Yet still his jaws and teeth they clatter, 537 *Goody Blake* 115
Jay. From Bruno's forest screams the affrighted jay, 11 *Desc. Sk.* 67
The Jay makes answer as the Magpie chatters; 195 *Resolution* 6
From Bruno's forest screams the frighted jay, 603 *Desc.Sk.Quarto* 68
Jealous. Shy as the jealous chamois, Freedom flies, 15 *Desc. Sk.* 263
Till she, in jealous fury unassuaged, 103 *Artegal* 35
Can I be proud that jealous fear 113 *Lament* 48
And though the jealous turf refuse 154 *Flower Garden* 31
Or jealous Nature ruling in her stead; 339 *Schwytz* 5
That through the jealous leaves escapes 342 *Ital. Itin.* 49
Some jealous and forbidding cell, 397 *White Doe* 97
These jealous Ministers of law aspire, 419 *Ecc. Sonn.* 1. 4. 7
Were not some gifts withheld by jealous hands, 455 *Rydal Mere* 18
At our approach, a jealous watch-dog's bark, 525 *Epist. Beaumont* 233
Of slighted love, and scorn, and jealous rage, 547 **Beneath yon* 15
Jealous that Hope had been preferr'd 620 *Birth of Love* 30
Purloined, in times less jealous than our own, 879 *Excursion* 8. 371
Jealousies. Small jealousies, and triumphs good or bad— 650 *Prelude* 3. 72
Jealousy. Of dissolute tongues, and jealousy, and hate, 23 *Yew-tree* 18
And jealousy, and quivering strife, 498 **The sylvan* 17
Mistrust and jealousy, despite, debate, 560 *Cuck.andNight.* 173
Uneasiness, or pain, or jealousy: 643 *Prelude* 2. 67
Had no presumption, no such jealousy, 669 *Prelude* 5. 269
But shrunk with apprehensive jealousy 748 *Prelude* 14. 155
Jedborough. But dance! for under Jedborough Tower 293 *Jedbor.* 8
He is as mute as Jedborough Tower: 294 *Jedbor.* 29
Jeer. Reckless audacity extol, and jeer 514 **Portentous change* 3
Jehovah. His Father served Jehovah; but how win 365 **The Baptist* 3
Of dread Jehovah; then should wood and waste 440 *Ecc. Sonn.* 2. 46. 6
Jehovah—with his thunder, and the choir 755 *Recluse* 1. 1. 786
—Jehovah—shapeless Power above all Powers, 811 *Excursion* 4. 651
"Once, while the Name, Jehovah, was a sound 894 *Excursion* 9. 682
Jemima. When good Jemima perished in her bloom; K.8. 275 **These vales* 2
Jemima's. Wild Redbreast! hadst thou at Jemima's lip 272 **Wild Redbreast* 1
Jeopardised. Not to be jeopardised through foulest crime: 519 *Pun. Death* 10. 11
Jeopardy. I saw you in that jeopardy: 175 *Waggoner* 1. 131
From battle and from jeopardy, 192 *Ruth* 29
Shield us in our jeopardy! 336 **Jesu! bless* 18
Given and received in mutual jeopardy, 381 *Duddon* 20. 12
Jericho. Down to the earth the walls of Jericho, 346 *Processions* 17
Jerk. Then Peter gave a sudden jerk, 241 *P. B.* 401
A jerk that from a dungeon-floor 241 *P. B.* 402
Jeronymite. So spake the mild Jeronymite, his griefs 510 *F. Stone* 118
Jerusalem. And proud Jerusalem! 232 *Jew. Fam.* 48
Entering the proud Jerusalem, 247 *P. B.* 978
Of the Jerusalem below, her sin 365 **The Baptist* 6
Of Alfred boasts remote Jerusalem, 425 *Ecc. Sonn.* 1. 26. 12
Jest. By music, prank, and laughter-stirring jest; 858 *Excursion* 7. 82
Jesu. Jesu! bless our slender Boat, 336 **Jesu! bless* 1
Of Brethren who, here fixed, on Jesu wait 364 **What aim* 6
The Maid to Jesu hearkened, 374 *Eg. Maid* 375
Jesu! of Thee, and the white Lily-flower 552 *Prioress* 9
They all said—Nay; but Jesu of His grace 555 *Prioress* 152
Jesu's. She steeped, but not for Jesu's sake, 405 *White Doe* 878

Jesu's—*continued.*
At Jesu's bidding. We rejoice, "O Death, 448 *Ecc. Sonn.* 3. 31. 13
Of Jesu's Mother, as he had been told, 553 *Prioress* 54
Our blissful Lady, Jesu's Mother dear, 553 *Prioress* 58
Of Jesu's Mother?' said this Innocent; 554 *Prioress* 87
On Jesu's Mother fixed was his intent. 554 *Prioress* 99
"'This well of mercy, Jesu's Mother sweet, 556 *Prioress* 205
Weeping and praising Jesu's Mother dear; 556 *Prioress* 227
Jesus. When Jesus humbly deigned to ride, 247 *P. B.* 977
Softly!—To save the contrite, Jesus bled. 275 *Gravestone* 14
Of Jesus goes before, the child is borne 318 **In due* 10
And the sacred Cross on which Jesus died. 403 *White Doe* 663
The tidings come of Jesus crucified; 419 *Ecc. Sonn.* 1. 3. 12
But Jesus Christ, as in the books ye find, 556 *Prioress* 201
Of Jesus from her tomb! 577 *Cenotaph* 12
The cross of Jesus stand erect, as if 682 *Prelude* 6. 484
Of Jesus, and his everlasting care. 836 *Excursion* 5. 952
Jet. Like beads of glossy jet her eyes; 165 *Parrot* 5
Jew. This cruel Jew him seized, and held him fast 554 *Prioress* 119
To every Jew that dwelleth in that place 555 *Prioress* 150
The Jew; the stately and slow-moving Turk, 690 *Prelude* 7. 217
Jewel. He wears a jewel in his head! 142 †*Lov. and Lik.* 14
Were mine the trusty staff that Jewel gave 438 *Ecc. Sonn.* 2. 39. 3
Foil to a Jewel rich in light 478 *Somnamb.* 14
Gleams by the richest jewel unsurpast; 527 **Those breathing* 16
The brightest jewel of a George's throne. L.I. 97 *Juvenal* 3. 95
Jewish. Yet am I with the Jewish Child, 232 *Jew. Fam.* 23
That roars along the bed of Jewish song, 668 *Prelude* 5. 203
Jewry. "Through all the Jewry (this before said I) 554 *Prioress* 100
She cried, till to the Jewry she was brought, 555 *Prioress* 147
"The Christian folk that through the Jewry went 555 *Prioress* 163
Jew's. His wasp's nest in Jew's heart, upswelled—'O woe, 554 *Prioress* 108
Jews. 'Mong Christian folk, a street where Jews might be, 553 *Prioress* 37
"From that day forward have the Jews conspired 554 *Prioress* 114
And him among the accursèd Jews she sought. 555 *Prioress* 148
Which done, he bade that they the Jews should bind. 555 *Prioress* 169
This Provost doth for those bad Jews prepare 555 *Prioress* 178
By cursèd Jews—thing well and widely known, 556 *Prioress* 234
Jews'. In the Jews' street, and there he last was seen. 554 *Prioress* 141
Jingling. Made a sweet jingling in our youthful ears; 681 *Prelude* 6. 409
Or captive led in abject weeds, and jingling 693 *Prelude* 7. 420
On sturdy horses graced with jingling bells, 858 *Excursion* 7. 65
Joanna. Joanna! and I guess, since you have been 147 *Joanna* 12
"How fares Joanna, that wild-hearted Maid! 147 *Joanna* 23
At break of day, Joanna and myself. 147 *Joanna* 37
Joanna, looking in my eyes, beheld 147 *Joanna* 52
The fair Joanna drew, as if she wished 148 *Joanna* 75
Joanna's. Joanna's name deep in the living stone:— 148 *Joanna* 83
Have called the lovely rock, Joanna's Rock." 148 *Joanna* 85
Job. Meanwhile the Evangelists, Isaiah, Job, 695 *Prelude* 7. 562
Jockey's. There hang thy trophies; bid the jockey's vest, L.I. 94 *Juvenal* 2. 21
Jocose. He in jocose defiance showed— 245 *P. B.* 832
Jocund. Among the forest glades, while jocund June 32 *Guilt* 413
The Youth made answer with a jocund voice; 135 *Michael* 299
They dance,—there are three, as jocund as free, 166 *Stray Pleasures* 17
Matter for a jocund thought, 172 *Kitten* 126
While thus our jocund Travellers fare, 177 *Waggoner* 2. 101
In such a jocund company: 187 **I wandered* 16
She jocund as it was of yore, 294 *Jedbor.* 30
'Mid fruitful fields that ring with jocund toil, 463 **Why should the* 5
And jocund smiles, and toward the lowly Grange 525 *Epist. Beaumont* 237
On her I looked whom jocund Fairies love, 532 **Once I* 21
Of jocund din; and, when a lengthened pause 671 *Prelude* 5. 379
By the warm sunshine, and the jocund voice 789 *Excursion* 3. 245
Among the jocund reapers. For himself, 863 *Excursion* 7. 423
Whether regarded as a jocund time, 888 *Excursion* 9. 284
Sent from the jocund hearts of those two Boys, 891 *Excursion* 9. 475
His guests, and make them jocund. They are pleased, K.8. 241 *Recluse* 1.1.192
John. My brother John and I. 84 *We are Seven* 56
My brother John was forced to go, 84 *We are Seven* 59
Oh! happy, happy, happy John. 127 *Idiot Boy* 86
Of "Matthew, Mark, and Luke, and John, 144 **Driven in* 45
That exquisite Saint John. 232 *Jew. Fam.* 24
Is John de Clapham, that fierce Esquire, 399 *White Doe* 249
John with a sword that will not fail, 401 *White Doe* 478
Lo! John self-stripped of his insignia:—crown, 428 *Ecc. Sonn.* 1. 37. 10
"Of which the great Evangelist, Saint John, 554 *Prioress* 131
He who had been our living John 580 *John Words.* 39
The Evangelist St. John my patron was: 649 *Prelude* 3. 46
Johnny. For Johnny has his holly-bough, 126 *Idiot Boy* 49
Was, "Johnny! Johnny! mind that you 126 *Idiot Boy* 58
My Johnny, do, I pray you, do." 126 *Idiot Boy* 61
To this did Johnny answer make, 126 *Idiot Boy* 62
And now that Johnny is just going, 126 *Idiot Boy* 67
How quietly her Johnny goes. 127 *Idiot Boy* 91
And Johnny makes the noise he loves, 127 *Idiot Boy* 100
Now, though he knows poor Johnny well, 127 *Idiot Boy* 114
And Johnny is not yet in sight: 127 *Idiot Boy* 153
On Johnny vile reflections cast: 127 *Idiot Boy* 158
That Johnny may perhaps be drowned; 128 *Idiot Boy* 179
In tree and tower was Johnny seen, 128 *Idiot Boy* 209
'Twas Johnny, Johnny, everywhere. 128 *Idiot Boy* 211
Johnny perhaps his horse forsook, 128 *Idiot Boy* 214
There's neither Johnny nor his Horse 128 *Idiot Boy* 219
My Johnny, till my dying day." 128 *Idiot Boy* 236

Joy—*continued.*
Pride where there's no envy, there's so much of joy ; 482 *Character* 11
Which seems a sense of joy to yield 482 *Sister* 6
Of joy and sorrow ; 485 **Bright Flower* 4
We wear a face of joy, because 487 *Fountain* 47
And joy its own security. 492 *Duty* 20
Shall *now* by such a gift with joy be moved, 504 *Warning* 51
Nor feel the fulness of that joy reproved ? 504 *Warning* 52
If this great world of joy and pain 505 **If this* 1
Awake to silent joy : 506 **While from* 28
Joy based on sorrow, good with ill combined, 514 **Who ponders* 3
Then shall a Veteran's heart be thrilled with joy, 515 **Long-favoured* 11
The heart with joy and gratitude to God 517 *Pun. Death* 1. 6
Though haply less than joy. 526 **The soaring* 8
A place where joy is known, 526 **The soaring* 10
While not one joy of ours by them was shared. 528 **Those breathing* 59
O joy for her ! whene'er in winter 536 *Goody Blake* 49
All that they think and feel, with tears of joy ; 539 **Lady ! a* 53
When joy had passed away, 543 *Russ. Fug.* 166
The joy in that retreat 544 *Russ. Fug.* 218
Fair sights, and visions of romantic joy ! 547 **Rude is* 30
Joy ?—a moon by fits reflected 549 *Hermit's Cell* 1. 19
Such is Joy—as quickly hidden, 549 *Hermit's Cell* 1. 25
To joy, or be it to some mourning ; never 557 *Cuck. and Night.* 24
Full little joy have I now of thy cry. 558 *Cuck. and Night.* 95
And full-assurèd trust, joy without measure, 559 *Cuck.andNight.*154
And, when it likes him, joy enough them sendeth. 560 *Cuck.andNight.*195
For to th' untrue he oft gives ease and joy ; 560 *Cuck.andNight.*198
Send unto thee as mickle joy this day, 561 *Cuck.andNight.*254
And joy of love to send her evermore ; 561 *Cuck.andNight.*258
Since I am wholly at Thy will ? what joy 563 *Troilus* 69
O would the blissful God now for his joy, 564 *Troilus* 90
And here I dwell an outcast from all joy, 564 *Troilus* 97
That in my soul I feel the joy of it. 564 *Troilus* 154
'Mid the dews, in the sunshine of morn,—'mid the joy 569 *Farmer* 9
In peace eternal ; where desire and joy 573 *Chiabrera* 1. 5
Thou one blind Sailor, rich in joy 577 **I come* 37
From day to day with never-ceasing joy, 581 **Why should we* 4
Unweeting that to him the joy was given 582 **To public* 9
His moiety in trust, till Joy shall lead 586 *Ch. Lamb* 130
Thou Child of Joy, 588 *Immortality* 34
I hear, I hear, with joy I hear ! 588 *Immortality* 50
He sees it in his joy ; 588 *Immortality* 70
And with new joy and pride 589 *Immortality* 101
O joy ! that in our embers 589 *Immortality* 133
Nor all that is at enmity with joy, 590 *Immortality* 163
Sad tides of joy from Melancholy's hand ; 592 *Ev. Wk. Quarto* 22
Glowing in golden sunset tints of joy, 599 *Ev. Wk. Quarto* 380
Blows not a Zephyr but it whispers joy ; 602 *Desc. Sk. Quarto* 18
Light up of tranquil joy a sober scene ; 607 *Desc.Sk.Quarto* 268
—No vulgar joy is his, at even tide 611 *Desc.Sk.Quarto* 512
Great joy by horror tam'd dilates his heart, 612 *Desc.Sk.Quarto* 560
The little cottage of domestic Joy. 613 *Desc.Sk.Quarto* 601
Soon flies the little joy to man allow'd, 613 *Desc.Sk.Quarto* 636
The lily of domestic joy decay ; 615 *Desc.Sk.Quarto* 723
While hum with busier joy her happy bees ; 615 *Desc.Sk.Quarto* 731
Dead to the sense of every finer joy ; 618 *School Ex.* 8
Science with joy saw Superstition fly 618 *School Ex.* 43
Hear Britain's sons rehearse thy praise with joy, 619 *School Ex.* 101
What dire intrigues disturbed *Cythera's* joy ! 620 *Birth of Love* 2
On the wild Goddess of Voluptuous Joy. 620 *Birth of Love* 23
While the joy that precedes the calm season of rest 620 *Convict* 3
And from my Horse I leapt ; great joy had I. 622 **Among all* 8
Oh ! joy it was for her, and joy for me ! 623 **Among all* 20
With many a fond embrace, while joy runs high, 624 *Æneid* 40
Productive day be this of lasting joy 625 *Æneid* 109
Doth seem half-conscious of the joy it brings 632 *Prelude* 1. 3
But for a gift that consecrates the joy ? 632 *Prelude* 1. 32
A present joy the matter of a song, 632 *Prelude* 1. 47
The last autumnal crocus, 'twas my joy 636 *Prelude* 1. 309
Nor saw a band in happiness and joy 639 *Prelude* 1. 481
The bond of union between life and joy. 640 *Prelude* 1. 558
Thus oft amid those fits of vulgar joy 640 *Prelude* 1. 581
—And if the vulgar joy by its own weight 641 *Prelude* 1. 597
The scenes which were a witness of that joy 641 *Prelude* 1. 599
Unfelt shone brightly round us in our joy. 643 *Prelude* 2. 93
For its own pleasure, and I breathed with joy. 645 *Prelude* 2. 188
Sublimer joy ; for I would walk alone, 646 *Prelude* 2. 302
If high the transport, great the joy I felt 648 *Prelude* 2. 410
A never-failing principle of joy 648 *Prelude* 2. 450
If child-like fruitfulness in passing joy, 651 *Prelude* 3. 147
Was social, and loved idleness and joy. 652 *Prelude* 3. 233
That fell in ruins round me. Oh, what joy 655 *Prelude* 3. 427
What joy was mine to see thee once again, 659 *Prelude* 4. 40
My hand upon his back with stormy joy, 660 *Prelude* 4. 116
And gratitude, and perfect joy of heart— 660 *Prelude* 4. 135
May books and Nature be their early joy ! 672 *Prelude* 5. 423
What joy was mine ! How often in the course 673 *Prelude* 5. 480
Knowledge and increase of enduring joy 674 *Prelude* 5. 593
Between these sundry wanderings with a joy 678 *Prelude* 6. 196
Receive it daily as a joy of ours ; 678 *Prelude* 6. 249
But Europe at that time was thrilled wth joy, 680 *Prelude* 6. 339
How bright a face is worn when joy of one 680 *Prelude* 6. 348
Is joy for tens of millions. Southward thence 680 *Prelude* 6. 349
Some vapoured in the unruliness of joy, 681 *Prelude* 6. 392
When God, the giver of all joy, is thanked 685 *Prelude* 6. 685
I wanted not that joy, I did not need 686 *Prelude* 6. 773
For her own sake, became my joy, even then— 704 *Prelude* 8. 347
But fondness, and a kind of radiant joy 714 *Prelude* 9. 315
Their joy, in England ; this, too, at a time 722 *Prelude* 10. 303

Joy—*continued.*
For those that bade them fall. They found their joy, 723 *Prelude* 10. 363
Might point with rapturous joy. Yet not the less, 725 *Prelude* 10. 486
O pleasant exercise of hope and joy ! 728 *Prelude* 11. 105
'Twill be such joy to see them disappear. 729 *Prelude* 11. 152
To health and joy and pure contentedness ; 733 *Prelude* 11. 398
The thought, the image, and the silent joy : 744 *Prelude* 13. 272
Had to his joy unearthed a hedgehog, teased 746 *Prelude* 14. 23
With the adverse principles of pain and joy— 748 *Prelude* 14. 166
Else is not thine at all. But joy to him, 749 *Prelude* 14. 218
Oh, joy to him who here hath sown, hath laid 749 *Prelude* 14. 219
And so the deep enthusiastic joy, 750 *Prelude* 14. 293
Of joy in widest commonalty spread ; 755 *Recluse* 1. 1. 771
Rest, and be welcomed there to livelier joy. 756 *Excursion* 1. 20
Nor any voice of joy ; his spirit drank 759 *Excursion* 1. 206
No wild varieties of joy and grief. 761 *Excursion* 1. 360
Not speaking much, pleased rather with the joy 764 *Excursion* 1. 515
He tossed them with a false unnatural joy : 765 *Excursion* 1. 587
As if she had been shedding tears of joy. 766 *Excursion* 1. 689
How full their joy ! Till, pitiable doom ! 774 *Excursion* 2. 197
That promised everlasting joy to France ! 774 *Excursion* 2. 213
All joy in human nature ; was consumed, 776 *Excursion* 2. 297
And that is joy to him. When change of times 778 *Excursion* 2. 474
This notice comes too late.' With joy I saw 783 *Excursion* 2. 793
Great show of joy the housewife made, and truly 785 *Excursion* 2. 887
Of admiration, and all sense of joy ? " 791 *Excursion* 3. 356
Enlivened happiness with joy o'erflowing, 792 *Excursion* 3. 430
With joy, and—oh ! that memory should survive 792 *Excursion* 3. 431
What joy more lasting than a vernal flower ?— 792 *Excursion* 3. 439
That the prosperities of love and joy 792 *Excursion* 3. 449
Blameless, so intimate with love and joy 796 *Excursion* 3. 682
Ye that are capable of joy be glad ! 796 *Excursion* 3. 729
With joy exalted to beatitude ; 803 *Excursion* 4. 119
We have, or hope, of happiness and joy, 803 *Excursion* 4. 133
Or in the gloom of twilight hum their joy ? 808 *Excursion* 4. 448
" Oh ! what a joy it were, in vigorous health, 808 *Excursion* 4. 508
Their way before them—what a joy to roam 809 *Excursion* 4. 531
Tidings of joy and love.—From those pure heights 811 *Excursion* 4. 641
With joy, and gratitude, and fear, and love ; 815 *Excursion* 4. 930
Brightened with joy ; for from within were heard 818 *Excursion* 4. 1138
The joy of that pure principle of love 819 *Excursion* 4. 1213
In fellow-natures and a kindred joy. 819 *Excursion* 4. 1217
Of human suffering, or of human joy. 820 *Excursion* 4. 1238
Was he received, and mutual joy prevailed. 829 *Excursion* 5. 445
Cold, sullen, blank, from hope and joy shut out ; 831 *Excursion* 5. 555
Floats on the tossing waves. With joy sincere 831 *Excursion* 5. 569
Joy to myself ! but to the heart of her 834 *Excursion* 5. 752
Through shades and silent rest, to endless joy." 837 *Excursion* 5. 1016
' Joy be their lot, and happiness,' he cried, 840 *Excursion* 6. 141
And truly might be said to die of joy ! 842 *Excursion* 6. 243
Or dread was all that had been thought of,—joy 852 *Excursion* 6. 910
He craved a substitute in troubled joy ; 855 *Excursion* 6. 1091
Announcing immortality and joy 864 *Excursion* 7. 452
And so acknowledged with a tremulous joy 867 *Excursion* 7. 640
We followed ; and my voice with joy exclaimed : 870 *Excursion* 7. 820
With patriotic confidence and joy. 871 *Excursion* 7. 901
When joy of war and pride of chivalry 871 *Excursion* 7. 936
Sublime from present purity and joy ! 879 *Excursion* 8. 320
Dull, to the joy of her own motions dead ; 879 *Excursion* 8. 324
Even as she shares the pride and joy of both. 883 *Excursion* 8. 587
Rejoice !—and ye have special cause for joy. 889 *Excursion* 9. 368
The beauteous girl, whose cheek was flushed with joy, 890 *Excursion* 9. 428
To impart a joy, imperfect while unshared. 893 *Excursion* 9. 587
Be sung with transport and unceasing joy. 894 *Excursion* 9. 678
Joy giving voice to fervent gratitude. 895 *Excursion* 9. 742
And with a shepherd's joy. Immediately K.8. 229 **I will* 149
Through joy and sorrow ; if my lot be joy K.8. 233 **Along the* 6
My hope, my joy, my sister, and my friend, K.8. 234**Witness thou* 3
Such power and joy ; but only for this end, K.8. 237 *Recluse* 1.1.38
Of pure affections, shedding upon joy K.8. 237 *Recluse* 1. 1.51
A brighter joy ; and through such damp and gloom K.8. 237 *Recluse* 1. 1.52
To aid him, and in Song resound his joy. K.8. 239 *Recluse* 1.1.102
With cheerful heart, an unknown voice of joy, K.8. 241 *Recluse* 1.1.185
Hath issued any portion of the joy K.8. 245 *Recluse* 1.1.317
Joy spreads, and sorrow spreads ; and this whole Vale, K.8. 248 *Recluse* 1.1.445
Associates in the joy of purest minds, K.8. 249 *Recluse* 1.1.460
Active as lambs, and overcome with joy. K.8. 251 *Recluse* 1.1.549
Enough to fill the present day with joy, K.8. 254 *Recluse* 1.1.650
These mountains will rejoice with open joy. K.8. 254 *Recluse* 1.1.661
His strength, and had his triumph and his joy, K.8. 256 *Recluse* 1.1.731
The joy of fleshly life without its cares. K.8. 265 **Brook, that* 14
Joy be poured, and thou the giver, L.2. 190 **Queen and* 16
Than joy itself—for underneath it lies [?] **A sad* 5
Joyance. She who inspires that strain of joyance holy 217 *Enterprise* 144
Joyed. We act as if we joyed in the sad tune 505 *Warning* 144
O Moon ! if e'er I joyed when thy soft light 630 [?] **O Moon* 1
Joy-flushes. But her blushes are joy-flushes ; 222 *Triad* 164
Joyful. These joyful tidings from no lips but mine. 50 *Bord.* 724
May fill your breast with joyful pride ; 142 †*Lov. and Lik.* 32
(Never had living man such joyful lot !) 201 *Hart-leap* 46
And they such joyful tidings were, 247 *P. B.* 958
He conquering, as in joyful Heaven is sung, 326 *Sobieski* 13
Joyful annunciation !—it went forth— 327 *Ode 1815* 19
The Hebrews thus, carrying in joyful state 346 *Processions* 10
My noble fire emits the joyful ray 365 **Rapt above* 13
This Banner raised with joyful pride, 405 *White Doe* 846
That with their joyful shout should close 408 *White Doe* 1146
Who were so joyful at the light of day, 558 *Cuck. and Night.* 69

Joyful—*continued.*
But we will see it, joyful tide ! . . . . . . 580 *John Words.* 58
And a joyful cry through the Island rang, . . 629 *Installation* 35
—' Be joyful all ye nations ; in all lands, . . . 796 *Excursion* 3. 728
Would o'er the bosom of a joyful land . . . 839 *Excursion* 6. 79
Of joyful greeting were on him bestowed, . . . 843 *Excursion* 6. 320
Stands in our valley, named THE JOYFUL TREE ; . 851 *Excursion* 6. 832
Among her equals, round THE JOYFUL TREE, . 851 *Excursion* 6. 850
The fleece-encumbered flock—the JOYFUL ELM, . 866 *Excursion* 7. 620
So joyful in its motions, is become . . . . . 879 *Excursion* 8. 323
More joyful if it be with sorrow sooth'd. . . . K.8. 233 **Along the* 7
Joyfully. The bugles that so joyfully were blown ? 201 *Hart-leap* 26
Of speculation, joyfully outspread, ... 826 *Excursion* 5. 246
Joyless. And joyless sylvan sport, ... 104 *Artegal* 159
—Back to the joyless Ocean thou art gone ; . . 151 **When, to* 84
Though strong, is, in the main, a joyless tie . . 172 *Infant Daughter* 37
That is from joyless regions brought ! . . . . 178 *Waggoner* 3. 30
Of joyless daylight ; when the fretful stir . . 206 *Tintern* 52
As, through the abysses of a joyless heart, . . 213 *Dion* 61
Yet, round the body of that joyless Thing . . 266 **Even as* 9
O joyless power that stands by lawless force ! . 317 **Look now* 9
Appears a joyless human Being, ... 413 *White Doe* 1580
No joyless forms shall regulate . . . . . 483 *Sister* 17
Joyless and comfortless. Our days glide on ; . 585 *Ch. Lamb* 71
Labour, and Pain, and Grief, and joyless Age, . 613 *Desc.Sk.Quarto* 639
Be joyless as the blind ? Ambitious spirits— . 815 *Excursion* 4. 947
Joyous. The sand-lark chants a joyous song ; . . 84 *Shepherd-boys* 24
The day would be a joyous festival ; . . . . 100 *Brothers* 312
Joyous as morning, ... 159 **Up with me* 16
Of a joyous train ensuing, ... 160 **Pansies, lilies* 60
Off to some other play the joyous Vagrants flew ! 191 *Beggars* 48
Dear mother of fresh thoughts and joyous health ! 254 **A flock* 14
Is with me at thy farewell, joyous Bark ! . . . 258 **Where lies the Land* 14
Or, like the nightingale, her joyous vein . . . 279 *'*Tis he* 5
The joyous Woman is the Mate . . . . . 294 *Jedbor.* 25
And thus in joyous mood they hie . . . . 396 *White Doe* 15
Smooth passions, smooth discourse, and joyous thought : . . . . 489 *Pers. Talk* 48
In flows the joyous year. . . . . 507 **While from* 56
Now, while the birds thus sing a joyous song, . 588 *Immortality* 19
Then sing, ye Birds, sing, sing a joyous song ! . 590 *Immortality* 172
Joyous, nor scared at its own liberty, ... 632 *Prelude* 1. 15
Even in this joyous time I sometimes felt . . 644 *Prelude* 2. 133
And joyous loves, that hallow innocent days . . 679 *Prelude* 6. 263
In wantonness of heart, a joyous band . . . 727 *Prelude* 10. 600
And joyous creatures ; see that pair, the lamb . 748 *Prelude* 14. 172
Murmuring of him who, joyous hap, was found, . 752 *Prelude* 14. 404
That timely light, to share his joyous sport : . 814 *Excursion* 4. 864
From cups replenished by his joyous hand. . . 867 *Excursion* 7. 656
Of joyous comrades. Soon as the reedy marge . 891 *Excursion* 9. 488
Them leaving to their joyous hours I pass, . . K.8. 252 *Recluse* 1.1.588
Joyously. Like stars in heaven, and joyously it showed ; . . . . 258 **With Ships* 2
Joyousness. With joyousness, and with a thoughtful cheer, ... 106 *Farewell* 30
By no untimely joyousness ; . . . . . . 294 *Jedbor.* 81
Joy's. Joy's second spring and Hope's long-treasured smile, ... 32 *Guilt* 455
And joy's excess produced a fear . . . . . 545 *Russ. Fug.* 355
—Now with joy's tearful kiss each other greet, . 614 *Desc.Sk.Quarto* 666
Joys. Fair Swan ! by all a mother's joys caressed, . 7 *Ev. Wk.* 250
On joys that might disgrace the captive's cell, . 13 *Desc. Sk.* 138
Joys only given to uncorrupted hearts. . . . 17 *Desc. Sk.* 404
His thoughts, the central point of all his joys. . 19 *Desc. Sk.* 481
When long familiar joys are all resigned, . . . 19 *Desc. Sk.* 518
And other joys my fancy to allure— . . . . 32 *Guilt* 409
Joys to spy thee near her home ; . . . . . 160 **Pansies, lilies* 39
Had for their joys a killing power. . . . . . 180 *Waggoner* 4. 74
And all its aching joys are now no more, . . . 206 *Tintern* 84
Nor should the change be mourned, even if the joys 210 *Laod.* 68
And on the joys we shared in mortal life,— . . 211 *Laod.* 130
Whose joys, from all but memory swept away, . 229 *Cuckoo-clock* 25
The language of those drunken joys . . . . 246 *P. B.* 877
'Mid frost and snow, the instinctive joys of song, 263 **While not* 13
The azure brooks, where Dian joys to lave . . 264 **Lady! I* 5
So joys, remembered without wish or will, . . 267 **As the* 6
Ah ! that a *boon* could shed such rapturous joys ! 312 **A Roman* 12
In loose fashion tell their joys ; . . . . . . 324 *Ode 1814* 64
And joys of distant home my heart enchain. . . 340 *Ranz* 14
Dead to the world and scorning earth-born joys. . 362 **List—'twas* 35
And smothered joys into new being start. . . . 381 *Duddon* 21. 8
Such wrong ; nor need *we* blame the licensed joys, 382 *Duddon* 23. 12
They taught me random cares and truant joys, . 382 *Duddon* 26. 10
Even ere her joys begin to fade ; . . . . . 473 *Ossian* 74
If loves and joys, while up they sprung, . . . 507 *May* 69
Of unexperienced joys that might have been ; . 524 *Epist. Beaumont* 197
The joys of the Departed—what so fair . . . 526 **Soon did* 13
While I salute my joys, thoughts sad or stern ; . 533 **Once I* 34
Where joys are perfect—neither wax nor wane. . 533 **Once I* 42
Both his new sorrow and his joys of old, . . . 563 *Troilus* 40
His joys, his griefs, have vanished like a cloud . 587 *Crosth.* 15
Thanks to its tenderness, its joys, and fears, . . 590 *Immortality* 205
To shew her yet some joys to me remain, . . . 592 *Ev. Wk. Quarto* 50
So vanish those fair Shadows, human joys, . . 598 *Ev.Wk.Quarto* 361
Whence Danger leans, and pointing ghastly, joys 610 *Desc.Sk.Quarto* 466
So oft, the central point of all his joys. . . . 612 *Desc.Sk.Quarto* 571
When the poor heart has all its joys resign'd, . 613 *Desc.Sk.Quarto* 622
How other pleasures have been mine, and joys . 640 *Prelude* 1. 548
And close communion. Many are our joys . . 646 *Prelude* 2. 284

Joys—*continued.*
And of old men who have survived their joys— . 668 *Prelude* 5. 212
Above all joys, that seemed another morn . . 678 *Prelude* 6. 197
With human kindnesses and simple joys. . . . 741 *Prelude* 13. 119
(Save some remembrances of dream-like joys . . 790 *Excursion* 3. 273
Of one day's pleasure, and all mortal joys ! . . 892 *Excursion* 9. 555
Joy-smitten. And yonder with joy-smitten heart have I . . . . 563 *Troilus* 50
Jubilant. Their jubilant activity evolves . . . 218 *Recluse* 1. 1. 212
With thunderous voice ? Or are ye jubilant, . 230 *Clouds* 23
Jubilant outcry ! rock and glade . . . . . 344 **How blest* 37
Jubilate. With *jubilate* from the choirs of spring ! . 387 **Part fenced* 14
Jubilee. Keep jubilee, and, more than all, . . . 84 *Shepherd-boys* 29
O fancy—what a jubilee ! . . . . 178 *Waggoner* 3. 35
The heavens laugh with you in your jubilee ; . . 588 *Immortality* 38
Judea. While in Judea Fancy loves to roam, . . 467 *St. Bees* 111
Judean. Descended from Judean heights, to march 870 *Excursion* 7. 812
Judge. Appeal was made to the great Judge : the Accused . . . . 62 *Bord.* 1384
Delivered to the Judge of all things. Dead ! . 66 *Bord.* 1587
Such tales of your dead Father !—God is my judge, 77 *Bord.* 2244
If I judge ill for thee, but it seems good . . . 137 *Michael* 381
Through Death,—so judging we should judge amiss. 139 *Widow* 31
Judge both Fugitives with knowledge : . . . 141 *Arm. Lady* 85
Rough doings these ! as God's my judge, . . . 176 *Waggoner* 1. 249
Now should you say I judge amiss, ... 177 *Waggoner* 2. 76
Presentiments ! they judge not right . . . . 225 *Present.* 1
Judge thou of law and fact ! . . . . . . 291 *Rob Roy* 80
Who are to judge of danger which they fear, . . 310 **Another year* 13
A Judge, who, as man claims by merit, gives ; . 317 **Brave Schill* 11
Father and Judge of all, with fervent tongue, . 328 *Ode 1815* 115
On Sarnen's Mount, there judge of fit and right, . 350 *Des. Stanzas* 51
Things that we judge of by a light too faint : . 446 *Ecc. Sonn.* 3. 24.
Who sees, foresees ; who cannot judge amiss, . 519 *Pun. Death* 11. 13
Issuing in pomp, shall come to judge mankind. . 534 **When in* 16
To God that is the judge of all. . . . . . 537 *Goody Blake* 96
Bear with Him—judge *Him* gently who makes known . . . . 576 **By a* 19
Thy virtues *He* must judge, and He alone, . . 584 **With copious* 63
I was a better judge of thoughts than words, . . 676 *Prelude* 6. 106
Before the ermined judge, or that great stage . 694 *Prelude* 7. 491
Was prayed to as a judge ; but these were past, . 719 *Prelude* 10. 44
Of a village steeple, as I do, can judge, . . . 722 *Prelude* 10. 292
I felt, observed, and pondered ; did not judge, . 737 *Prelude* 12. 188
Witness and judge ; and I remember well . . 745 *Prelude* 13. 367
To him appeal was made as to a judge ; . . . 772 *Excursion* 2. 75
Father, and king, and judge, adored and feared ! 794 *Excursion* 3. 573
Whether to act, judge, suffer, or enjoy. . . . 799 *Excursion* 3. 924
You judge unthankfully : distempered nerves . 808 *Excursion* 4. 479
And who shall judge the creature, will forgive. . 828 *Excursion* 5. 368
Or to record ; we judge, but cannot be . . . 830 *Excursion* 5. 499
And fear of him who is a righteous judge ; . . 851 *Excursion* 6. 873
Judged. I judged you most unkindly. But this Youth, 101 *Brothers* 355
Some thought far worse of him, and judged him wrong ; . . . . 108 *Indolence* 33
Well judged the Friend who placed it there . . 337 *Thun* 5
Shall ye, by Poets even, be judged amiss ! . . 477 *Steamboats* 3
From him who judged her lord, a like decree ; . 505 *Warning* 154
And by frail man most equitably judged. . . . 832 *Excursion* 5. 649
Self judged, can with such discipline dispense, . L.1. 97 *Juvenal* 3. 76
Judge's. Or at a doubting Judge's stern command, 500 *Humanity* 3
Judges. I am not of the world's presumptuous judges, ... 64 *Bord.* 1503
Haydon ! let worthier judges praise the skill . . 277 **Haydon ! let* 1
He only judges right who weighs, compares, . . 429 *Ecc. Sonn.* 2. 1. 12
All accidents, and judges were of all. . . . 812 *Excursion* 4. 717
Indifferent judges. 'Spite of proudest boast, . 830 *Excursion* 5. 500
Judging. *See* **All-judging, Ill-judging.**
Through Death,—so judging we should judge amiss. 139 *Widow* 31
Judging not ill perhaps, the timid course . . . 656 *Prelude* 3. 494
Gravely to ponder—judging between good . . 707 *Prelude* 8. 520
Yea, never thought of judging ; with the gift . 737 *Prelude* 12. 189
On humble life, forbid the judging mind . . . 828 *Excursion* 5. 421
Judgment. *See* **Rash-judgment.**
And yet, in plumbing the abyss for judgment, . 51 *Bord.* 782
And therefore leave thee to a righteous judgment. 63 *Bord.* 1407
Upon Heaven's righteous judgment, did become . 76 *Bord.* 2211
some signal judgment has befallen the man . . 76 *Bord.* 2218
Yours was a stranger's judgment : for historians, 97 *Brothers* 165
Was in his judgment tempted to decline . . . 122 *V. and J.* 61
Ere judgment prompted from within . . . . 224 *'*Tis gone* 46
A juster judgment from a calmer view ; . . . 231 **The gentlest Poet* 30
" Weak is the will of Man, his judgment blind ; . 259 **Weak is* 1
May learn, if judgment strengthen with his growth, 275 **Chatsworth! thy* 11
His judgment with benignant ray . . . . . 287 *Sons of Burns* 37
Of judgment such presumptuous doom repeat !) . 437 *Ecc. Sonn.* 2. 35. 3
In many an hour when judgment goes astray. . 467 *St. Bees* 85
Survive not Judgment that requires his own ? . 518 *Pun. Death* 6. 14
The judgment, and divert the general heart . . 538 **In desultory* 47
And judgment there be given ; or that intent . 562 *Cuck.and Night.* 279
A judgment too harsh of the sin and the shame ; . 570 *Farmer* 42
To an unforgiving judgment from just Heaven. . 584 *Ch. Lamb* 37
'Twere idle to descant. My inner judgment . . 676 *Prelude* 6. 96
Into the turmoil, bore a sounder judgment . . 714 *Prelude* 9. 332
Would but have touched the judgment, struck more deep . . . . 730 *Prelude* 11. 187
Confusion of the judgment, zeal decayed, . . . 734 *Prelude* 12. 5
Of sitting thus in judgment interrupt . . . . 736 *Prelude* 12. 122
A partial judgment—and yet why ? for *then* . . 745 *Prelude* 13. 361
Yet happier in my judgment, even than you . . 788 *Excursion* 3. 159
For to my judgment such they then appeared, . 790 *Excursion* 3. 291

Kept—*continued.*
By those bright eyes, what weary vigils kept, . 525 *Epist. Beaumont* 259
What recompense is kept in store or left . . . 530 *Poor Robin* 33
And hope that kept with me her plighted troth. . 532 **Once I* 12
Kept pace with his desires ; . . . . 545 *Russ. Fug.* 346
Kept crying, "Farewell !—farewell, Popinjay !" 561 *Cuck.andNight.*222
That hath kept watch o'er man's mortality ; . . 590 *Immortality* 202
An image of her soul is kept alive, ... 627 **We gaze* 12
Kept the same awful steadiness—at his feet . . 664 *Prelude* 4. 407
Kept holiday, a never-ending show, ... 674 *Prelude* 5. 582
With unextinguished taper I kept watch, . . . 719 *Prelude* 10. 70
Kept sacred to restorative delight, ... 733 *Prelude* 11. 422
And liberty of nature ; there he kept . . . . 761 *Excursion* 1. 353
Fondly to prize the silence which he kept, . . 839 *Excursion* 6. 105
And by the unclosed coffin kept her seat . . . 853 *Excursion* 6. 979
And still his harsher passions kept their hold— . 860 *Excursion* 7. 215
Their vigils kept ; where tapers day and night . 877 *Excursion* 8. 188
Where now the beauty of the sabbath kept . . 878 *Excursion* 8. 246
Kerchief. My kerchief there I hem ; . . . . . 84 *We are Seven* 42
On high, a kerchief waving in her hand ! . . . 524 *Epist. Beaumont* 208
A kerchief sprinkled with his master's blood, . . 778 *Excursion* 2. 478
'Kerchief-plots. Sticking 'kerchief-plots of mould . 161 **Pleasures newly* 20
Keswick. Who from Keswick has pricked forth, . 181 *Waggoner* 4. 123
Kettle. Let me have the song of the kettle ; . . 484 **A plague* 2
Or kettle whispering its faint undersong. . . . 488 *Pers. Talk* 14
Kettle-drum. Rattles the salt-box, thumps the kettle-drum, ... 697 *Prelude* 7. 701
Key. A Woman rules my prison's key ; . . . . 113 *Lament* 50
"The key I must take, for my Ellen is dead." 120 *Childless Father* 18
Mindless of its just honours ; with this key . . 260 **Scorn not* 2
A pen—to register ; a key— . . . . . . 499 *Memory* 1
Key-hole's. Legions of devils through a key-hole's space. . . . . L.I. 94 *Juvenal* 2. 4
Keys. A Saint, the Church's Rock, the mystic Keys 357 *Aquap.* 309
Who thinks that priestly cunning holds the keys . 467 *St. Bees* 80
The mighty tumults of the House of Keys ; . . 522 *Epist.Beaumont* 66
To stern Plantagenet resigned her keys) . . . L.I. 95 *Juvenal* 3. 2
Keystone. Aerial keystone haughtily secure ; . . 435 *Ecc. Sonn.* 2. 26. 4
Kid. No kid with piteous outcry thrill thy bowers ; 3 *Ev. Wk.* 77
Did wanton fawn and kid forbear . . . . . 154 *Flower Garden* 11
Kidney. A true knight of his kidney. . . . . S.3. 440 **Said red-rib boned* 8
Kilda. Remote St. Kilda, lone and loved sea-mark 475 **Homeward we* 6
Kill. We kill a worn-out horse, and who but women 54 *Bord.* 927
That kill the bloom before its time ; . . . . 113 *Lament* 40
But kill a new-born infant thus, ... 200 *Thorn* 212
Down from the far-seen mount. No blast might kill . . . . 276 *Oker Hill* 8
Are forfeited ; but infamy doth kill. . . . . 316 **Say, what* 14
Our pride misleads, our timid likings kill. . . . 351 *Des. Stanzas* 73
Here did not kill, but nourished, Piety. . . . 355 *Aquap.* 169
To kill for merry feast their venison. . . . . 393 *Inglewood* 8
An element that flatters him—to kill, ... 528 **Those breathing* 78
Killarney. Of the sly boatmen of Killarney, . . S.3. 438 **My Lord* 14
Killed. He struck me ; and that instant had I killed him, ... 68 *Bord.* 1716
Have killed him, Scorn should write his epitaph. . 277 **A Poet* 8
Killer. *See* **Giant-killer.**
Killicranky. Tried men, at Killicranky were arrayed 293 *Killicranky* 2
Killing. *See* **Heart-killing.**
Had for their joys a killing power. . . . . . 180 *Waggoner* 4. 74
Killing the bud o'er which in vain we grieve. . . 448 *Ecc. Sonn.* 3. 33. 8
Kills. My former thoughts returned : the fear that kills ; . . . . 197 *Resolution* 113
That kills the soul : love betters what is best, . 257 **No mortal* 13
Kiln. No labourer watched his red kiln glaring bright, 26 *Guilt* 141
Kilt. The Roman kilt, degraded to a toy . . . 388 **The pibroch's* 2
Kilve. Kilve, thought I, was a favoured place, . . 86 *Anecdote* 23
And said, "At Kilve I'd rather be . . . . . 86 *Anecdote* 35
For Kilve by the green sea." . . . . . . 86 *Anecdote* 44
"At Kilve there was no weather-cock ; . . . 86 *Anecdote* 55
Kilve's. I thought of Kilve's delightful shore, . . 85 *Anecdote* 10
"On Kilve's smooth shore, by the green sea, . . 86 *Anecdote* 31
Kin. Their nearest kin with deadly purpose met) . 106 *Artegal* 237
That greatly cheered his country : to his kin . . 575 *Chiabrera* 8. 13
Kind. *See* **Ever-kind, Human-kind.**
Entire affection for all human kind. . . . . 3 *Ev. Wk.* 85
Kind Nature's charities his steps attend ; . . . 11 *Desc. Sk.* 25
Kind pious hands did to the Virgin build . . . 27 *Guilt* 149
But soon his voice and words of kind intent . . 27 *Guilt* 190
Meanwhile discourse ensued of various kind, . . 27 *Guilt* 193
What kind of plunder he was hunting now ; . . 33 *Guilt* 483
Through which his Wife, to that kind shelter brought, ... 36 *Guilt* 642
Of thy kind Patroness, which to receive . . . 40 *Bord.* 156
Which to our kind is natural as life, ... 48 *Bord.* 627
Has a kind heart ; but his imprisonment . . . 71 *Bord.* 1900
Violets, a barren kind, ... 79 *Foresight* 19
To the life of human kind. . . . . 90 *Longest Day* 36
Possess a kind of second life : no doubt . . . 98 *Brothers* 185
And rooted out the intolerable kind ; . . . . 102 *Artegal* 18
Kind Nature's gentlest boon ! . . . . . . 109 **Strange fits* 18
Kind mother have I been, as kind . . . . . 117 *Affl. Marg.* 32
O gentle Muses ! is this kind ? . . . . . . 130 *Idiot Boy* 342
Service beyond all others of its kind. . . . . 133 *Michael* 116
With kind assurances that he would do . . . 136 *Michael* 308
A kind and a good Father : and herein . . . 136 *Michael* 362
"Yes, kind Lady ! otherwise man could not bear 140 *Arm. Lady* 17
Remember she follows the law of her kind, . . 142 †*Lov. and Lik.* 43

Kind—*continued.*
Yet we, who are transgressors in this kind, . . 147 *Joanna* 9
But hearing thee, or others of thy kind, . . . 160 **Up with me* 28
For us be fair and kind !" . . . . 162 *Binnorie* 42
A Parrot of that famous kind . . . . . . 165 *Parrot* 3
Thus a rich loving-kindness, redundantly kind, . 167 *Stray Pleasures* 29
That to the Kind by special grace . . . . . 168 *Wren's Nest* 11
From whom the Race of human kind proceed, . 172 *Infant Daughter* 9
We make a kind of handsome show ! . . . . 179 *Waggoner* 3. 78
Kind Spirits ! may we not believe . . . . . 191 *Seq. Beggars* 36
So kind and so forlorn ! . . . . 194 *Ruth* 162
Cheerfully uttered, with demeanour kind, . . . 197 *Resolution* 135
Blanch, Swift, and Music, noblest of their kind, . 201 *Hart-leap* 19
Wert kind as resolute, and good as brave ; . . 210 *Laod.* 56
No appanage of human kind, ... 214 *Kirkstone* 6
Shall bid a kind farewell ! . . . . 224 **'Tis gone* 66
Nightly, on human kind . . . . 226 *Vernal Ode* 46
Kind Nature keeps a heavenly door . . . . 228 *Devot. Incit.* 58
No word of kind commiseration . . . . . 241 *P. B.* 452
Kind Listeners, that around me sit, ... 245 *P. B.* 788
And others of your kind, ideal crew ! . . . . 252 **Her only* 11
From harp or lute, kind influence to compose . 255 **Grief, thou* 7
Torn from the Poor ! yet shall kind Heaven protect 255 *S. H.* 10
Kind Nature's various wealth was all your own ; . 256 *Easter* 13
So kind is simple Nature, fairly tried ! . . . . 275 **Chatsworth ! thy* 8
Each kind in several beds of one parterre ; . . 281 *Valedict.* 4
Seen birds of tempest-loving kind— . . . . 288 *Highland Girl* 45
A kind of *heavenly* destiny : . . . . 289 *Stepping West.* 12
They stir us up against our kind ; . . . . . 291 *Rob Roy* 23
Fly, some kind Harbinger, to Grasmere-dale ! . 294 **Fly, some* 1
Post forward all, like creatures of one kind, . . 303 **Is it* 5
To mock the Outcast—O ye Heavens, be kind ! . 306 **We had* 13
Repose at length, firm friend of human kind ! . 313 *Clarkson* 14
Affections which, if put to proof, are kind ; . . 319 **Avaunt all* 8
And sent him forth, with squadrons of his kind, . 321 **Humanity,delighting* 29
Where haply (kind service to Piety due !) . . . 340 *Fort Fuentes* 9
And shrubs, whose pleasant looks gave proof how kind . . . . 356 *Aquap.* 214
And here once again a kind shelter be found. . . 364 *Vallomb.* 20
Once more beneath the kind Earth's tranquil light ; 381 *Duddon* 21. 7
Meek, patient, kind, and, were its trials fewer, . 390 *Highland Hut* 13
On kind occasions I may wait, ... 401 *White Doe* 513
Who, paying deadly hate in kind . . . . . 403 *White Doe* 641
Happy as others of her kind, ... 407 *White Doe* 995
Hath separated from its kind, ... 414 *White Doe* 1636
Raised far above the law of kind ; . . . . . 416 *White Doe* 1878
Imposed on human kind, must first forget . . 424 *Ecc. Sonn.* 1. 23. 11
Though seldom heard by busy human kind)— . . 432 *Ecc. Sonn.* 2. 17. 7
To human kind ; though peace be on his tongue, . 444 *Ecc. Sonn.* 3. 18. 7
The wisest, happiest, of our kind are they . . . 456 *Rydal Mere* 37
Ye lingered among human kind, ... 473 *Ossian* 69
From dead men to their kind. . . . . . . 481 *Expost.* 8
Such an odd such a kind happy creature as he. . 482 *Character* 20
—I've heard of hearts unkind, kind deeds . . . 484 *Simon Lee* 93
Not only to us Men, but to thy Kind : . . . . 491 *Tribute : Dog* 31
Great issues, good or bad for human kind, . . 493 *Hap. War.* 50
Our varying moods, on human kind or brute, . . 501 *Humanity* 98
Dealt in like sort with feeble human kind . . . 514 **Who ponders* 8
His Spirit, when most severe, is oft most kind ; . 518 *Pun. Death* 5. 5
To our kind Friend high on the sunny hill— . . 524 *Epist. Beaumont* 216
Kind Hostess ! Handmaid also of the feast, . . 525 *Epist. Beaumont* 250
Those breathing Tokens of your kind regard, . . 527 **Those breathing* 1
Of a kind mistress, fairest of the land, ... 528 **Those breathing* 65
And ever on Christ's Mother meek and kind . . 555 *Prioress* 146
Said this young Child, 'and by the law of kind . 556 *Prioress* 199
And hard hearts he can make them kind and free. 556 *Cuck. and Night.* 5
To every wight that gentle is of kind. 559 *Cuck.andNight.*150
Of some small blessings ; have been kind to such 568 *Cumb. Beg.* 151
—Such pleasure is to one kind Being known, . . 568 *Cumb. Beg.* 154
But nature is gracious, necessity kind, ... 570 *Farmer* 51
Housed in a dream, at distance from the Kind ! . 579 *Peele Castle* 54
That innocence belongs not to our kind, . . . 584 *Ch. Lamb* 33
Yearnings she hath in her own natural kind, . . 588 *Immortality* 78
Whence human kind, and brute ; what natural powers . . . . 625 *Æneid* 124
Bids every thought be kind ? . . . . 626 †*Cento* 6
Nor wanted we rich pastime of this kind, . . . 657 *Prelude* 3. 540
From my old Dame, so kind and motherly, . . 658 *Prelude* 4. 28
Through every clime, the heart of human kind. . 667 *Prelude* 5. 109
Was, for the purposes of kind, a man . . . . 703 *Prelude* 8. 288
With an advantage furnished by that kind . . 704 *Prelude* 8. 324
Yet deem not, Friend ! that human kind with me 704 *Prelude* 8. 340
The idea, or abstraction of the kind. . . . . 706 *Prelude* 8. 502
But fondness, and a kind of radiant joy . . . 714 *Prelude* 9. 315
He fled, to shun the haunts of human kind ; . . 718 *Prelude* 9. 579
Sorrow for human kind, and pain of heart. . . 723 *Prelude* 10. 330
Were flattered, and had trust in human kind : . 723 *Prelude* 10. 388
Of promise, nor belying the kind hope . . . . 726 *Prelude* 10. 550
In kind more dangerous. What had been a pride, 730 *Prelude* 11. 183
Oft, as my thoughts were turned to human kind, 731 *Prelude* 11. 247
Therefrom to human kind, and what we are. . . 743 *Prelude* 13. 249
Dear Sister ! was a kind of gentler spring . . . 750 *Prelude* 14. 265
And found a kind of home or harbour there. . . 757 *Excursion* 1. 56
The divine Milton. Lore of different kind, . . 760 *Excursion* 1. 250
By loneliness, and goodness, and kind works, . . 762 *Excursion* 1. 405
To a kind master on a distant farm . . . . . 767 *Excursion* 1. 761
Upon his hollow cheek. "How kind," he said, . 779 *Excursion* 2. 525
To explore the destiny of human kind . . . . 790 *Excursion* 3. 284

Kind—*continued*.

None ! 'tis the general plaint of human kind . .	792 *Excursion* 3. 440
Revered Compatriot—and to you, kind Sir, . .	793 *Excursion* 3. 498
Shall with one heart honour their common kind.'	796 *Excursion* 3. 733
From this infirmity of mortal kind	803 *Excursion* 4. 146
Beyond the temporal destiny of the Kind, . .	805 *Excursion* 4. 264
Kind and degree, among all visible Beings ; .	806 *Excursion* 4. 337
To me some portion of a kind regard ; . . .	824 *Excursion* 5. 107
To prize the breath we share with human kind ;	832 *Excursion* 5. 656
(The same kind Matron whom your tongue hath praised)	834 *Excursion* 5. 754
Save when the sabbath brings its kind release,	834 *Excursion* 5. 806
Society were touched with kind concern, . .	837 *Excursion* 5. 974
Though marvellous in its kind. A place there is .	841 *Excursion* 6. 214
Though from another sprung, different in kind : .	843 *Excursion* 6. 368
Depositories faithful and more kind . . .	847 *Excursion* 6. 613
And yet the very sound of that kind foot . .	849 *Excursion* 6. 751
And nature that is kind in woman's breast, .	851 *Excursion* 6. 871
On a kind parent willing to forget	852 *Excursion* 6. 944
Of human kind ! He was it who first broke .	854 *Excursion* 6. 1068
And propagate its kind, far as he may ? . . .	863 *Excursion* 7. 373
Though of the kind which beasts and birds present	866 *Excursion* 7. 581
Kind nature's various wealth is all their own. .	875 *Excursion* 8. 61
To whom kind Nature, therefore, may afford .	885 *Excursion* 9. 99
Arts, in themselves beneficent and kind, . .	887 *Excursion* 9. 189
Kind wishes, and good actions, and pure thoughts—	887 *Excursion* 9. 242
And the kind never perish ? Is the hope .	894 *Excursion* 9. 663
To seek, in degradation of the Kind, . . .	896 *Excursion* 9. 788
And to the last were good and kind, . . .	K.8. 219 **The snow tracks* 6
Dreadless, as in a kind of fresher breeze . .	K.8. 246 *Recluse* 1.1.369
By Nature's kind and ever-present aid . .	K.8. 249 *Recluse* 1.1.455
That parts the individual from his kind, . .	K.8. 251 *Recluse* 1.1.536
And shall we think that Nature is less kind .	K.8. 257 **Shall he* 8

Kinder.   When Fortune might put on a kinder look ;   28 *Guilt* 231

But you, Sir, should be kinder. Come hither, Fathers, ...	45 *Bord.* 443
Upon the mountain-tops no kinder could have been.	87 *Pet-lamb* 40
And in the kinder spirit ; placable, . . .	729 *Prelude* 11. 158

Kindest.   I found in you the kindest of Protectors ;   60 *Bord.* 1281

The best and kindest !—but where is he ? guide me,	73 *Bord.* 2052
Blesses the Moon that comes with kindest ray	602 *Desc. Sk. Quarto* 35

Kindle.   To kindle or restrain. . . . . . 187 **Three years* 12

And kindle sportive wit—	222 *Triad* 168
Permit his heart to kindle, and to embrace . .	323 **Now that* 12
Will live, and spread, and kindle : even such minds	567 *Cumb. Beg.* 109
Present the maddening gifts, and kindle heat . .	624 *Æneid* 5
Kindle before us.—Your discourse this day, .	818 *Excursion* 4. 1122
For then her heart shall kindle ; her dull eye,	820 *Excursion* 4. 1254

Kindled.   *See* **Newly-kindled**.

And soon with crimson fire kindled the firmament.	30 *Guilt* 315
A fire was kindled in her breast, ...	199 *Thorn* 120
That kindled recollections	324 *Ode 1814* 85
And oft my soul hath kindled at the same, .	329 *Ode : Thanks.* 45
Had his sunk eye kindled at those dear words .	353 *Aquap.* 60
(Kindled from Heaven between the light and dark	475 **Homeward we* 3
Have kindled into health !	507 *May* 28
Kindled 'mid rapturous tears ;	545 *Russ. Fug.* 326
My fancy kindled as I gazed ;	550 *Hermit's Cell* 2. 17
Ne'er kindled with a livelier streak . . .	583 **O for a* 32
Along my veins I kindled with the stir, . .	660 *Prelude* 4. 102
Kindled and burnt among the sapless twigs .	797 *Excursion* 3. 744
A sight that kindled pleasure in all hearts . .	868 *Excursion* 7. 724
A gipsy-fire we kindled on the shore . . .	892 *Excursion* 9. 527

Kindles.   When the East kindles with the full moon's light ; . . . . 455 *Rydal Mere* 23

Kindles intense desire for powers withheld . .	496 **A little* 27
Or, shipwrecked, kindles on the coast . . .	534 **Blest is* 69
That kindles with such glory ! All are charmed,	694 *Prelude* 7. 505

Kindlier.   God has given a kindlier power . . . 80 *Foresight* 25

Brisk Robin seeks a kindlier home : . . .	143 **Driven in* 3
For me, who under kindlier laws belong . .	263 **While not* 9
Should e'er a kindlier time ensue.	406 *White Doe* 937
Kindlier issues, holier rest, ...	503 **Like a* 80
Me did a kindlier fortune then invite . . .	574 *Chiabrera* 3. 13
A man of kindlier nature. The rough sports .	762 *Excursion* 1. 415
" A kindlier passion opened on her soul . .	852 *Excursion* 6. 906

Kindliest.   And pines the unripened pear in summer's kindliest ray ; . . . . . . 15 *Desc. Sk.* 259

Roused by this kindliest of May-showers, . .	228 *Devot. Incit.* 13
And kindliest intercourse ensue.	415 *White Doe* 1729
May Nature's kindliest powers sustain the Tree,	546 **The embowering* 9
Have stopped, as some believe, the kindliest growths.	692 *Prelude* 7. 372
In fits of kindliest apprehensiveness, . .	708 *Prelude* 8. 603

Kindliness.   Wasting its kindliness on stocks and stones, ... 185 *Nutting* 42

That noticeable kindliness of heart	701 *Prelude* 8. 124
From nature's kindliness received a frame . .	839 *Excursion* 6. 100
Unprofitable kindliness, bestowed . . .	K.8. 248 *Recluse* 1.1.432

Kindling.   Merciful protectress, kindling . . . 94 *Westmoreland Girl* 53

Beware of kindling hopes for me unmeet ! .	104 *Artegal* 165
Oh, for a kindling touch from that pure flame .	326 *Sobieski* 1
And, kindling at their lustre, if I burn, . .	365 **Rapt above* 12
Transfigured, from this kindling hath foretold	437 *Ecc. Sonn.* 2. 34. 5
One with its kindling edge declares that soon .	461 **Who but is* 5
Thou be that, kindling with a poet's soul, .	508 *F. Stone* 23
If thou be lovelier than the kindling East, .	525 *Epist. Beaumont* 251
That cheek—a kindling of the morn, ...	530 *Gleaner* 4

Kindling—*continued*.

And quench the passions kindling into flame ;	619 *School Ex.* 80
Was kindling, not unseen, from humble copse .	663 *Prelude* 4. 321
A kindling eye :—accordant feelings rushed . .	808 *Excursion* 4. 506
In the green trees ; and, kindling on all sides .	817 *Excursion* 4. 1066
—And, surely, he, that spake with kindling brow,	869 *Excursion* 7. 804
" Yes," he continued, kindling as he spake, . .	889 *Excursion* 9. 383

Kindlings.   And kindlings like the morning—presage sure . . . . 666 *Prelude* 5. 36

Kindly.   Blesses the moon that comes with kindly ray, ... 11 *Desc. Sk.* 33

Kindly the housewife pressed, and they in comfort fed.	34 *Guilt* 531
We might have made a kindly bed of heath, . .	39 *Bord.* 122
Kindly have you protected me to-night, . .	52 *Bord.* 825
Kindly, unassuming Spirit !	160 **Pansies, lilies* 42
Which the kindly wool supplies, ...	163 *Spinning Wheel* 16
Shed kindly influence on the place, ...	223 *Wishing-gate* 20
As kindly take what from my heart . . .	237 *P. B.* 114
And profit by those kindly rays	376 **The Minstrels* 70
Came fraught with kindly sympathies. . . .	407 *White Doe* 1021
A kindly influence whereof few will speak, .	460 **Wanderer ! that* 61
And you must kindly take it :	484 *Simon Lee* 70
For kindly issues—as through every clime .	502 **The unremitting* 13
Sunk into a kindly sleep.	503 *Warning* 5
While, as one kindly growth retires, . . .	507 *May* 63
Kindly emotion tending to console . . .	538 **In desultory* 51
What avails the kindly shelter	550 *Hermit's Cell* 4. 5
The kindly mood in hearts which lapse of years, .	567 *Cumb. Beg.* 92
His father views that good, that kindly star ; .	596 *Ev. Wk. Quarto* 266
Be present ; kindly Juno be thou near ! . .	625 *Æneid* 113
The stern yet kindly Spirit, who constrains .	761 *Excursion* 1. 316
See, rooted in the earth, her kindly bed, . .	793 *Excursion* 3. 522
Its kindly influence, o'er the yielding brow .	814 *Excursion* 4. 889
But we are kindly welcomed—promptly served .	821 *Excursion* 4. 1316
" Have kindly interposed. May I entreat .	832 *Excursion* 5. 629
Blest with a kindly faculty to blunt . . .	835 *Excursion* 5. 858
That yields such kindly product. He, whose bed	835 *Excursion* 5. 880
How long, and by what kindly outward aids, .	864 *Excursion* 7. 474
To outlive the kindly use and fair esteem . .	873 *Excursion* 7. 1048
—What kindly warmth from touch of fostering hand, ...	880 *Excursion* 8. 416
Howl from the north, what kindly warmth, me- thought, ...	881 *Excursion* 8. 446
That, far as kindly Nature hath free scope .	885 *Excursion* 9. 105
Then let both be kindly treated, ...	S.3. 438 **I, whose* 23

Kindness.   *See* **Loving-kindness**.

Of looks where common kindness had no part,	31 *Guilt* 393
With little kindness would to me incline. . .	32 *Guilt* 428
My husband's loving kindness stood between .	35 *Guilt* 611
Making all kindness registered and known ; .	107 *Farewell* 37
Of modest kindness, that would hide . . .	154 *Flower Garden* 45
And then, what kindness in their hearts ! . .	178 *Waggoner* 3. 43
Of kindness and of love. Nor less, I trust, .	206 *Tintern* 35
Nor greetings where no kindness is, nor all .	207 *Tintern* 130
Soft smiles, by human kindness bred ! . .	288 *Highland Girl* 35
The kindness that would make him less forlorn ; .	501 *Humanity* 66
Removed in kindness from their glassy Cell .	527 **Those breathing* 7
See studied kindness flow with easy stream, .	539 **Lady ! a* 63
As needed kindness, for this single cause, . .	568 *Cumb. Beg.* 152
With stinted kindness. In November days, .	638 *Prelude* 1. 416

Kindnesses.   For kindnesses that never ceased to flow, ... 352 *H. C. R.* 7

With human kindnesses and simple joys. . . 741 *Prelude* 13. 119

Kindred.   Of kindred loveliness : then he would sigh,   23 *Yew-tree* 42

And kindred of dead husband are at best . .	32 *Guilt* 426
No kindred sufferer, to his death-place brought .	36 *Guilt* 662
Among its kindred cobwebs. I had been, . .	70 *Bord.* 1839
Heaven bless you when you are among your kindred !	99 *Brothers* 237
You said his kindred all were in their graves, .	100 *Brothers* 329
To store up kindred hours for me, thy face . .	111 **'Tis said that some* 49
As they did love. Ye kindred Pinnacles— . .	152 **Forth from* 18
With kindred gladness :	158 **In youth* 60
He turned, and watched with kindred look . .	167 *Pilgrim's Dream* 14
A kindred impulse, seemed allied	193 *Ruth* 130
While friends and kindred all approved . .	198 *Thorn* 109
True to the kindred points of Heaven and Home !	209 **Ethereal minstrel* 12
Its ruins to their kindred dust ;	227 *Vernal Ode* 55
Garden, and that Domain where kindred, friends,	271 **Where holy* 5
The Virgin, as she shone with kindred light ; .	274 *Infant M.* 12
When kindred thoughts and yearnings bear . .	286 *Nith* 62
What He—who, mid the kindred throng . . .	300 *Bran* 1
Your kindred Deities, Ye live and move, . .	325 *Ode 1814* 120
Of *kindred* human hands !	348 **Lulled by* 48
That work of kindred frame, which spans the lake	351 *Des. Stanzas* 60
To kindred contemplations ministers . .	355 *Aquap.* 172
Ye kindred local influences that still, . .	356 *Aquap.* 251
With friends and kindred tenderly beloved ; .	381 *Duddon* 21. 3
With friends and kindred dealing.	386 *Yarrow Rev.* 96
For kindred Power departing from their sight ; .	386 *Scott* 5
From kindred sources ; while around us sighed .	394 **No more* 25
Of kindred for him in that ground	413 *White Doe* 1530
Sang in this Presence kindred themes ; . . .	416 *White Doe* 1841
Of kindred agitations for thy sake ; . . .	440 *Ecc. Sonn.* 3. 2. 5
Each linked to each for kindred services ; . .	444 *Ecc. Sonn.* 3. 17. 10
That follows—striking on some kindred chord .	448 *Ecc. Sonn.* 3. 31. 7
In kindred quiet I repose my trust. . . .	464 **A point* 4
Of health, strength, friends, and kindred, see ! .	483 *Simon Lee* 26

Kindred—*continued.*
His kindred laid in earth, 487 *Fountain* 50
If kindred humours e'er would make 490 *Night Thought* 13
Which, haply, kindred souls may prize 499 **Departing summer* 22
Uphold our Spirits urged to kindred flight 512 **Who rashly* 37
Moved by the touch of kindred sympathies. 526 **Soon did* 7
Wife, children, kindred, they were dead and gone; 531 **I know* 25
Thee kindred aspirations moved 533 **Blest is* 17
Than kindred wishes mated suitably 549 **The massy* 19
In which they found their kindred with a world 568 *Cumb. Beg.* 115
Of their own kindred;—all behold in him 568 *Cumb. Beg.* 122
Their kindred, and the children of their blood. 568 *Cumb. Beg.* 140
From nearest kindred, Vernon her new name; 576 **By a* 2
No conscious memory of a kindred sight, 640 *Prelude* 1. 574
That they are kindred to our purer mind 646 *Prelude* 2. 314
To the sky's influence in a kindred mood 651 *Prelude* 3. 137
Spangled with kindred multitudes of stars, 651 *Prelude* 3. 162
Of these and other kindred notices 658 *Prelude* 3. 609
To kindred hauntings. Whereupon I told, 666 *Prelude* 5. 56
With kindred matter, 'twas to me, in truth, 672 *Prelude* 5. 467
And kindred, proud rebellion and unkind. 675 *Prelude* 6. 29
From star to star, from kindred sphere to sphere, 677 *Prelude* 6. 127
That flowed into a kindred stream; a gale, 686 *Prelude* 6. 744
From kindred, friends, and playmates, to partake 701 *Prelude* 8. 122
Of dust, and kindred to the worm; a Being, 706 *Prelude* 8. 488
Which they were wont to be. Through kindred scenes, 733 *Prelude* 11. 413
All these were kindred spectacles and sounds 739 *Prelude* 12. 324
Of kindred permanence, unchanged in form 740 *Prelude* 13. 37
Kindred mutations; for themselves create 747 *Prelude* 14. 94
Of kindred hands that opened out the springs 749 *Prelude* 14. 238
Thy kindred influence to my heart of hearts 750 *Prelude* 14. 281
More tranquil, yet perhaps of kindred birth, 763 *Excursion* 1. 482
On these and kindred thoughts intent I lay 777 *Excursion* 2. 370
Herself, a dreamer of a kindred stock, 791 *Excursion* 3. 339
But seek for objects of a kindred love 819 *Excursion* 4. 1216
In fellow-natures and a kindred joy. 819 *Excursion* 4. 1217
Even as the multitude of kindred brooks 836 *Excursion* 5. 916
Of friends or kindred, whom the angry sea 836 *Excursion* 5. 933
Of kindred mould.—Such haply here are laid?" 844 *Excursion* 6. 391
Of kindred import, pleased and satisfied— 845 *Excursion* 6. 443
Of friends and kindred bore him from his home 864 *Excursion* 7. 466
Our thoughts unite in kindred quietness! 868 *Excursion* 7. 704
Or kindred, gathered round him. As a tree 872 *Excursion* 7. 957
From kindred features diversely combined, 891 *Excursion* 9. 510
With rival earnestness and kindred glee. 892 *Excursion* 9. 531
Where kindred independence of estate K.8.247 *Recluse* 1.1.380
All brothers, long endeared by kindred pain, L.1. 95 *Juvenal* 3. 6
Thy kindred and thy friends such travail borne L.2. 318 *Frag. Æneid* 4. 5

Kind's. Your kind's first seed did bear; 156 *Oak and Broom* 42

Kinds. Performed all kinds of labour for his sheep, 138 *Michael* 458
Hail, blest above all kinds!—Supremely skilled 153 *Morn. Ex.* 31
All kinds commingled without fear, 154 *Flower Garden* 8
And among the Kinds that keep 171 *Kitten* 59
"All kinds, and creatures, stand and fall 291 *Rob Roy* 49
In a sweet fellowship with kinds beloved, 361 **List—'twas* 15
Held with all Kinds in Eden's blissful bowers. 362 **List—'twas* 65
All kinds alike seemed favourites of Heaven. 377 *Duddon* 6. 14
Even to the inferior Kinds; whom forest-trees 395 *White Doe: Ded.* 45
From all that haughtier kinds endure 526 **The soaring* 43
A noble instinct; in all kinds the same, 528 **Those breathing* 75
All kinds of pleasure mix'd with sorrowing; 557 *Cuck. and Night.* 29
Among the inferior kinds; not merely those 806 *Excursion* 4. 358
The feathered kinds; the fieldfare's pensive flock, 808 *Excursion* 4. 450

Kine. The kine are couched upon the dewy grass; 1 *Early Youth* 2
Nor sheep nor kine were near; the lamb was all alone, 87 *Pet-lamb* 5
Looking down on the kine, and our treasure of sheep 116 *Repentance* 31
"Let beeves and home-bred kine partake 293 *Yarrow Unv.* 41
(So fame reports) and die,—his sweet-breathed kine 340 *Ranz* 5
From byre or field the kine were brought; the sheep 699 *Prelude* 8. 21
Her garden, from the pasture fetched her kine; 783 *Excursion* 2. 765
To tend the sheep and kine. K.8. 262 **Ah! if* 10

King. *See* **Fairy-king, Shepherd-king.**
With Henry, our good King;—the Baron might 43 *Bord.* 348
You take it as it merits—— One a King, 60 *Bord.* 1228
And when the King of Denmark summoned him 63 *Bord.* 1444
A KING more worthy of respect and love 103 *Artegal* 66
From that wild region where the crownless king 103 *Artegal* 98
"It is the king, my brother!" and, by sound 104 *Artegal* 120
He reign, thou still must be his king, and sovereign lord; 105 *Artegal* 177
I, Brother! only should be king in name, 105 *Artegal* 182
Until king Elidure, with full consent 105 *Artegal* 219
Gorbonian's first-born son, your rightful king restored!" 105 *Artegal* 225
Heaped over brave King Dunmail's bones, 176 *Waggoner* 1. 210
Last king of rocky Cumberland; 176 *Waggoner* 1. 212
As if she knew that Oberon king of Faery 222 *Triad* 170
The GIFT to king Amphion 234 *Power of Sound* 129
If ever mortal, King or Cotter, 246 *P. B.* 842
"Thou art our king, O Death! to thee we groan." 257 **Methought I* 8
'Mid those surrounding Worthies, haughty King, 271 *Henry: Portrait* 10
Ward of the Law!—dread shadow of a King! 271 *George: Death* 1
Consul, or King, can sound himself to know 304 **Festivals have* 13
To that great King: shall hail the crownèd Youth 305 **The Voice* 2
Ye Storms, resound the praises of your King! 322 **Ye Storms* 1
Dread King of Kings, vouchsafe a ray divine 323 **Now that* 9
Said Merlin: "Mighty King, fair Lords, 372 *Eg. Maid* 199

King—*continued.*
Exclaimed the King, "a mockery hateful; 372 *Eg. Maid* 212
"So be it," said the King;—"anon, 373 *Eg. Maid* 265
Though King or Knight the most renowned in story. 373 *Eg. Maid* 318
In silence did King Arthur gaze 374 *Eg. Maid* 337
King Arthur led the Egyptian Maid, 374 *Eg. Maid* 353
Than sceptred king or laurelled conqueror knows, 387 *Scott* 11
Of the Great King; and others, as they go 394 **No more* 14
The fatal end of Scotland's King, 399 *White Doe* 287
Glad HALLE-lujahs to the eternal King! 422 *Ecc. Sonn.* 1. 13. 14
"Man's life is like a Sparrow, mighty King! 422 *Ecc. Sonn.* 1. 16. 1
The pious ALFRED, King to Justice dear! 425 *Ecc. Sonn.* 1. 26. 2
While-as Canùte the King is rowing by: 426 *Ecc. Sonn.* 1. 30. 3
"My Oarsmen," quoth the mighty King, "draw near, 426 *Ecc. Sonn.* 1. 30. 4
Redoubted King, of courage leonine, 427 *Ecc. Sonn.* 1. 35. 1
Go forth, great King! claim what thy birth bestows; 432 *Ecc. Sonn.* 2. 15. 6
Transcendent Boon! noblest that earthly King 435 *Ecc. Sonn.* 2. 29. 9
King, child, and seraph, blended in the mien 436 *Ecc. Sonn.* 2. 31. 7
Weep with the good, beholding King and Priest 440 *Ecc. Sonn.* 2. 46. 10
With mind intent upon the King of Glory, 445 *Ecc. Sonn.* 3. 19. 12
Martyr, or King, or sainted Eremite, 451 *Ecc. Sonn.* 3. 44. 5
To king, to peasant, to rough sailor, dear, 455 *Rydal Mere* 29
Stage above stage) would sit this Island's King, 470 *Tynwald* 3
He had insulted—Peasant, King, or Thane? 475 **Here on their* 11
He only is a King, and he alone 495 *Fact* 12
And praiseth Christ that is our heavenly King, 55 *Prioress* 167
To serve the glorious Henry, King of France, 574 *Chiabrera* 3. 14
True to the King of Kings is found; 629 *Installation* 98
Peasant and king; when boys and youths, the growth 655 *Prelude* 3. 464
The King, and the King's Palace, and, not last, 688 *Prelude* 7. 109
Opening the clouds; or sovereign king, announced 693 *Prelude* 7. 416
Together danced, Queen of the feast, and King; 701 *Prelude* 8. 143
The King had fallen, and that invading host— 718 *Prelude* 10. 12
To a new transition, when the King was crushed, 718 *Prelude* 10. 38
Father, and king, and judge, adored and feared! 794 *Excursion* 3. 573
The shepherd of his flock; or, as a king 824 *Excursion* 5. 102
To king and people true. A brazen plate, 825 *Excursion* 5. 178
Vocal thanksgivings to the eternal King; 895 *Excursion* 9. 732
Thou, thou art king, and sole proprietor. K.8. 263 **The Lake* 4
The first of genuine kings, a king for use, L.1. 97 *Juvenal* 3. 97

Kingcups. Floats kingcups in the brook—a Hero one 60 *Bord.* 1235
Pansies, lilies, kingcups, daisies, 160 **Pansies, lilies* 1

Kingdom. Suppliant for aid his kingdom to regain; 103 *Artegal* 83
To me a kingdom! spare the bitter scorn: 104 *Artegal* 141
Dawns on a kingdom, and for needful haste 233 *Power of Sound* 66
Though small his kingdom as a spark or gem, 425 *Ecc. Sonn.* 1. 26. 11
With frantic love—his kingdom to regain? 441 *Ecc. Sonn.* 3. 3. 2
Of that great kingdom, rustled o'er our heads, 680 *Prelude* 6. 362
Whose kingdom is, where time and space are not. 802 *Excursion* 4. 76

Kingdom's. Whose votive burthen is—"OUR KINGDOM'S HERE!" 433 *Ecc. Sonn.* 2. 20. 14

Kingdoms. What kingdoms overthrown, 224 *Primrose* 8
Thou, on thy rock reclined, though kingdoms melt 276 *Author's Portrait* 5
Kingdoms shall shift about, like clouds, 292 *Rob Roy* 91
Armies or kingdoms. We have heard a strain 317 **The martial* 5
Of states and kingdoms, to their joy or woe, 323 **Now that* 3
Tyrants exult to hear of kingdoms won, 327 *Ode 1815* 37
While clarions prate of kingdoms to be won— 345 **Ambition—following* 3
For fifty kingdoms by my sword recovered. 372 *Eg. Maid* 234
Which States and Kingdoms utter when they talk 828 *Excursion* 5. 380
Earth and the kingdoms of the earth, create— 845 *Excursion* 6. 487

Kingly. Temptation; and whose kingly name and state 317 **Call not* 4
Or whet his kingly faculties to chase L.1. 94 *Juvenal* 2. 3

King's. The long-roofed chapel of King's College lift 649 *Prelude* 3. 4
The King, and the King's Palace, and, not last, 688 *Prelude* 7. 109

Kings. If justice ruled the breast of foreign kings, 104 *Artegal* 142
Exulting, rich beyond the wealth of kings, 185 *Nutting* 51
Chieftains and kings in council were detained; 211 *Laod.* 119
The shades of palaces and kings! 237 *P. B.* 105
Relic of Kings! Wreck of forgotten wars, 272 *Ruins* 9
"I, too, will have my kings that take 292 *Rob Roy* 89
Those new-born Kings she withered like a flame." 313 *Prophecy* 10
Dread King of Kings, vouchsafe a ray divine 323 **Now that* 9
Uprisen—to lodge among ancestral kings; 325 *Enghien* 2
Emperors and Kings, how oft have temples rung 326 **Emperors and* 1
Kings, warriors, high-souled poets, saint-like sages, 328 *Ode 1815* 61
Long lines of mighty Kings—look forth, my Soul! 452 *Ecc. Sonn.* 3. 47. 9
By labours that have touched the hearts of kings, 509 *F. Stone* 101
To bow his forehead in the courts of kings, 574 *Chiabrera* 4. 6
Which Sion's Kings did consecrate of old; 576 *Chiabrera* 9. 17
True to the King of Kings is found; 629 *Installation* 98
Unnamed among the chronicles of kings, 635 *Prelude* 1. 204
Land-warriors, kings, or admirals of the sea, 689 *Prelude* 7. 165
Of Romorentin, home of ancient kings, 716 *Prelude* 9. 481
Of Kings, their vices and their better deeds, 716 *Prelude* 9. 494
Hath summoned kings to scaffolds, do but give 778 *Excursion* 2. 475
Which kings might envy!"—Praise to this effect 787 *Excursion* 3. 75
The new succession, as a line of kings 844 *Excursion* 6. 431
Perish the roses and the flowers of kings, 872 *Excursion* 7. 980
Which Persian kings might envy; and thy meek S.3. 433 **The doubt* 19
Ye Kings, in wisdom, sense, and power supreme, L.1. 88 *Juvenal* 1. 1
A single word on Kings, and sons of Kings, L.1. 96 *Juvenal* 3. 40
Were Kings a free born work, a people's choice. L.1. 96 *Juvenal* 3. 41
The first of genuine kings, a king for use, L.1. 97 *Juvenal* 3. 97

Kingship. If Kingship bowed its head to Commonwealth— 310 *Invasion* 9

Knell—*continued.*
The time is come that rings the knell . . . . 402 *White Doe* 528
To Ambrose that! and then a knell . . . . 411 *White Doe* 1369
For she returns not.—Awed by her own knell, . 420 *Ecc. Sonn.* 1. 9. 11
Sorrow seems here excluded; and that knell, . 475 *Greenock* 7
Pleased when the sullen winds resound the knell . 497 *Lycoris* 35
Where torrents roar, or hear the tinkling knell . 502 **The unremitting* 16
An iron knell! with echoes from afar . . . . 819 *Excursion* 4. 1181
To hearths when first they darkened at the knell: K.8. 246 *Recluse* 1.1.340

Knelt. Knelt and kissed the Stranger's hand; . . 142 *Arm. Lady* 140
Go, faithful Portrait! and where long hath knelt 276 *Author's Portrait* 1
I to my Father knelt and prayed; . . . . . 401 *White Doe* 489
Of pious Edward kneeling as he knelt . . . . 436 *Ecc. Sonn.* 2. 31. 8
Upon a Maiden trembling as she knelt; . . . 446 *Ecc. Sonn.* 3. 24. 2
Even to this Rite? For thus *She* knelt, and, ere 446 *Ecc. Sonn.* 3. 24. 13
She knelt in prayer—the waves their wrath appease; 466 *St. Bees* 34
They knelt in prayer, or sang to blissful Mary. . 477 *Nunnery* 8
To heaven he knelt before the crucifix, . . . 551 **If thou in* 17
Yea, by the very mourners who had knelt . . 780 *Excursion* 2. 573
The generations of mankind have knelt . . . 827 *Excursion* 5. 338
Hither she came; here stood, and sometimes knelt 853 *Excursion* 6. 986

Knew. And hope itself was all I knew of pain; . 2 *Ev. Wk.* 22
She knew not what dire pangs in him such tale could wake. . . . . 27 *Guilt* 189
And knew not why. My happy father died, . . 29 *Guilt* 266
For our departure; wished and wished—nor knew, 29 *Guilt* 285
"A sailor's wife I knew a widow's cares, . . . 35 *Guilt* 595
The Sailor knew too well. That wickedness . . 35 *Guilt* 614
Upon the midland Sea. You knew his bearing . 37 *Bord.* 17
Oh, Sir, you would not talk thus, if you knew . 45 *Bord.* 418
Expecting still, I knew not how, to find . . . 45 *Bord.* 434
You will forgive me—— If I ever knew . . . 48 *Bord.* 631
And do good service, though she knew it not. . 52 *Bord.* 842
There's witchery in 't. I never knew a maid . . 59 *Bord.* 1193
And his new Favorite. Misery!— I knew . . 59 *Bord.* 1207
Feed on her leaves. You knew her well—ay, there, 61 *Bord.* 1312
Old Man! you were a very Lynx, you knew . . 61 *Bord.* 1313
No mate, no comrade Lucy knew; . . . . 82 *Lucy Gray* 5
Wayward, yet by all who knew her . . . . 94 *Westmoreland Girl* 43
That, as he knew in what particular spot . . . 96 *Brothers* 81
My fire is dead: it knew no pain; . . . . . 114 *Ind. Wom.* 11
I thought he knew some ill of me: . . . . 115 *Last of Flock* 74
Weeping for him when no one knew. . . . . 117 *Affl. Marg.* 35
He knew it not) and from his happiest looks, . 118 *Maternal Grief* 45
And thus, from what I heard and knew, or guessed, 120 *EmigrantMother* 13
Who knew not to what quiet depths a weight . 125 *V. and J.* 225
Before I knew thy face.—Heaven bless thee, Boy! 137 *Michael* 396
I knew that thou couldst never have a wish . . 137 *Michael* 399
That knew not of his wants. I will not say . . 149 **A narrow* 66
Conversing not, knew little in what mould . . 151 **When, to* 71
—If the Butterfly knew but his friend, . . . 162 **Art thou the* 15
But pangs more lasting far *that* Lover knew . . 169 *LoveliesBleeding* 19
By which we knew them when they came. . . 182 *Waggoner* 4. 224
Such woes, I knew, could never be; . . . . 191 *Beggars* 16
Yet sometimes milder hours she knew, . . . 194 *Ruth* 199
Dim sadness—and blind thoughts, I knew not, nor could name. . . . . 195 *Resolution* 28
No mortal ever knew; . . . . 199 *Thorn* 147
He knew the rocks which Angels haunt . . . 205 *Brougham* 128
As if she knew that Oberon king of Faery . . 222 *Triad* 170
And well he knew the spire of Sarum; . . . 238 *P. B.* 212
He knew not one forewarning pain; . . . . 248 *P. B.* 1048
Some veering up and down, one knew not why. . 258 **With Ships* 4
And nobler cares than listless summer knew. . . 263 **While not* 14
Nor aught of mutual joy or sorrow knew . . . 276 *Oker Hill* 12
He knew and prized them all. . . . . . . 296 *Highland Boy* 115
And this the little blind Boy knew; . . . . 296 *Highland Boy* 126
They knew how genuine glory was put on; . . 307 **Great men* 6
There is a bulwark in the soul. This knew . . 315 **And is it* 6
We journeyed; all we knew of care— . . . . 348 **Lulled by* 15
When this low Pile a Gospel Teacher knew, . . 380 *Duddon* 18. 10
Are calm; they knew each other's worth, . . . 410 *White Doe* 1320
And spread as if ye knew that days might come . 463 **Adieu, Rydalian* 2
Knew not the double-dealing of a smile; . . . 470 **A youth* 11
If the mind knew no union of extremes, . . . 471 **Arran! a* 10
And, by your mien and bearing, knew your names; 474 **Ye shadowy* 5
Soul-shattered was the Knight, nor knew . . . 479 *Somnamb.* 127
When life was sweet, I knew not why, . . . 481 *Expost.* 14
For she knew that her Son was dead. . . . . 494 *Force of Prayer* 8
She knew it by the Falconer's words, ... 494 *Force of Prayer* 9
As well we knew, together had grown grey. . . 523 *Epist. Beaumont* 132
That haunted us in spite of what we knew. . . 523 *Epist. Beaumont* 147
Loosed from its hold; how, no one knew, . . 531 †*Float. Isl.* 7
As every man who knew her says, ... 536 *Goody Blake* 54
The Woodman knew, for such the craft . . . 543 *Russ. Fug.* 105
"This Latin knew he nothing what it said, . . 553 *Prioress* 72
I knew the force; and hence the rough sea's pride 574 *Chiabrera* 4. 19
A Glow-worm, never one, and this I knew. . . 622 **Among all* 4
More than we wished we knew the blessing then . 643 *Prelude* 2. 79
Midway between the hills, as if she knew . . . 645 *Prelude* 2. 194
I neither knew nor cared for; and as such . . 657 *Prelude* 3. 565
The worth I knew of powers that I possessed, . 663 *Prelude* 4. 344
There was a Boy: ye knew him well, ye cliffs . 671 *Prelude* 5. 364
Seeking I knew not what, I chanced to cross . . 672 *Prelude* 5. 432
To die at home, was haply as I knew, ... 705 *Prelude* 8. 445
I knew that wound external could not take . . 727 *Prelude* 11. 13
Seems hard to shun. And yet I knew a maid, . 736 *Prelude* 12. 151
Though yet he knew not how, a wasting power . 760 *Excursion* 1. 265

Knew—*continued.*
And their place knew them not. Meanwhile, abridged . . . . 764 *Excursion* 1. 546
Said Margaret, 'for I knew it was his hand . . 766 *Excursion* 1. 672
I knew not how, and hardly whence they came. . 768 *Excursion* 1. 803
She knew not that he lived; if he were dead, . 768 *Excursion* 1. 819
She knew not he was dead. She seemed the same 768 *Excursion* 1. 820
Smiles of good-will from faces that he knew . . 772 *Excursion* 2. 57
I knew from his deportment, mien, and dress, . 779 *Excursion* 2. 498
Our housewife knew full well what she possessed! 783 *Excursion* 2. 763
I knew a Scottish Peasant who possessed . . . 835 *Excursion* 5. 863
Glistened with tenderness; his mind, I knew, . 883 *Excursion* 8. 589
Before the boy knew well what he had seen . . K.8. 229 **I will* 147
Their safe retreat. We knew them well, I guess . K.8. 243 *Recluse* 1.1.246
That the whole Valley knew them; but to us . K.8. 243 *Recluse* 1.1.247
A friendly covert. "And they knew it well," . K.8. 247 *Recluse* 1.1.396

Knife. That had no mirth in them; or with his knife 764 *Excursion* 1. 570

Knight. *See* **Father-knight.**
Where a cross-legged Knight lies sculptured . . 142 *Arm. Lady* 153
But he, bold Knight as ever fought, ... 161 *Binnorie* 7
The Knight had ridden down from Wensley Moor 200 *Hart-leap* 1
The Knight hallooed, he cheered and chid them on 201 *Hart-leap* 21
But now the Knight beholds him lying dead. . . 201 *Hart-leap* 32
—Soon did the Knight perform what he had said; 202 *Hart-leap* 79
The Knight, Sir Walter, died in course of time, . 202 *Hart-leap* 93
Knight, squire, and yeoman, page and groom: . 204 *Brougham* 38
This wretched Knight did vainly seek . . . . 287 *Ellen Irwin* 43
I once beheld, a Templar Knight; . . . . 301 *Bran* 47
But a bold Knight, the selfish aim . . . . . 301 *Bran* 68
And his dear Daughter on a Knight bestow . . 372 *Eg. Maid* 227
Though King or Knight the most renowned in story. 373 *Eg. Maid* 318
"Mine is she," cried the Knight;—again they clapped their pinions. . . . . . . 374 *Eg. Maid* 324
A goodly Knight that hath no peer that liveth!" 374 *Eg. Maid* 348
To seek her Knight went wandering o'er the earth. 395 *White Doe: Ded.* 8
Knight, burgher, yeoman, and esquire, . . . 404 *White Doe* 707
That, like the Red-cross Knight, they urge their way, ... 425 *Ecc. Sonn.* 1. 25. 7
Down to the humbler altar, which the Knight . 430 *Ecc. Sonn.* 2. 6. 5
A knight of proof in love's behoof, ... 478 *Somnamb.* 48
"Still is he my devoted Knight?" . . . . 479 *Somnamb.* 77
A wandering Ghost, so thinks the Knight, . . 479 *Somnamb.* 100
Soul-shattered was the Knight, nor knew . . 479 *Somnamb.* 127
In plunged the Knight!—when on firm ground . 479 *Somnamb.* 136
At any hour he chose, the prudent Knight . . 548 **Stranger! this* 11
For old Sir William was a gentle Knight, . . . 548 **Stranger! this* 21
In uncouth race, and left the cross-legged knight, 643 *Prelude* 2. 117
The famous history of the errant knight . . . 666 *Prelude* 5. 60
He, to my fancy, had become the knight . . . 667 *Prelude* 5. 122
Whose tale Cervantes tells; yet not the knight, . 667 *Prelude* 5. 123
Practised to commune with her royal knight . . 716 *Prelude* 9. 488
Now meeting on his road an armed knight, . . 771 *Excursion* 2. 5
And praised the gallant bearing, of a Knight . 825 *Excursion* 5. 186
Near this brave Knight his Father lay entombed; 825 *Excursion* 5. 188
That, in Eliza's golden days, a Knight . . . 871 *Excursion* 7. 924
The Knight arrived, with spear and shield, and borne 872 *Excursion* 7. 944
The spear and shield are vanished, which the Knight . . . . 872 *Excursion* 7. 961
"The courteous Knight, whose bones are here interred, ... 873 *Excursion* 7. 1008
"Even," said the Wanderer, "as that courteous Knight, ... 873 *Excursion* 7. 1041
A true knight of his kidney. . . . . . . S.3. 440 **Said red-ribboned* 8

Knightly. First among youths of knightly breeding, One . . . . 71 *Bord.* 1897
The feats of Arthur and his knightly peers; . . 103 *Artegal* 52
Of knightly race, nor wanting powerful friends. . 824 *Excursion* 5. 113

Knight's. Suspended over a knight's tomb, who lay 705 *Prelude* 8. 415
"Yet, by the good Knight's leave, the two estates 875 *Excursion* 8. 44

Knights. And soothed war-wearied knights in raftered hall. . . . . 221 *Triad* 103
From many knights and many squires . . . 287 *Ellen Irwin* 9
Armoury of the invincible Knights of old: . . 307 **It is not* 10
Soon will the Knights of Arthur's Table . . . 370 *Eg. Maid* 86
Awe-stricken stood both Knights and Dames . . 372 *Eg. Maid* 193
Thy Knights must touch the cold hand of the Virgin; . . . . 372 *Eg. Maid* 254
Knights each in order as ye stand . . . . . 373 *Eg. Maid* 267
That overcame some not ungenerous Knights; . 373 *Eg. Maid* 280
Proud tomb is none; but rudely-sculptured knights, 387 **Part fenced* 9
Seven hundred Knights, Retainers all . . . . 403 *White Doe* 694
And Knights of high renown; . . . . . . 478 *Somnamb.* 22
Amid reposing knights by a river side . . . . 634 *Prelude* 1. 173
Sometimes methought I saw a pair of knights . 716 *Prelude* 9. 454

Knit. Whole hours, with idle arms in moping sorrow knit. . . . . 32 *Guilt* 432
"My stockings there I often knit, ... 84 *We are Seven* 41
His soul was knit to this his native soil. . . . 100 *Brothers* 298
Knit every thought the impending issue needs, . 233 *Power of Sound* 95
Knit the blithe dance upon the soft green grass; 322 **Ye Storms* 9
That they may knit together, and therewith . . 868 *Excursion* 7. 703

Knits. Knits not o'er that discolouring and decay . 267 **DespondingFather* 6
Yet mutinously knits his angry brow, ... 888 *Excursion* 9. 316
Down he sits; his brows he knits; . . . . S.3. 423 *Tinker* 10

Knitting. And half, by knitting of his brows . . 240 *P. B.* 314
Was busy knitting in a heartless mood . . . 717 *Prelude* 9. 515

Knock. Nor raised my hand at any door to knock. 31 *Guilt* 373
And knock for entrance, in mid holiday. . . . 45 *Bord.* 468
He may knock at the door,—we'll not let him in; 81 †*Address: Child* 40

Knock—*continued.*
If she had heart to knock again ; 129 *Idiot Boy* 270
Knock-down. To shout with transport o'er a knock-down blow, L.1. 94 *Juvenal* 2. 14
Knocked. Knocked here—and knocked there, pounds still adding to pounds. 570 *Farmer* 36
We reached a cottage. At the door I knocked, 665 *Prelude* 4. 449
Knocker. She lifts the knocker, rap, rap, rap ; 128 *Idiot Boy* 248
Knocking. Like an intruder knocking at the door 660 *Prelude* 4. 157
Knocks. Joy at the heart of Peter knocks ; 241 *P. B.* 468
Upon the lid he knocks. 245 *P. B.* 820
Knoll. *See* **Curfew-knoll, Knell.**
Halting together on a rocky knoll, 823 *Excursion* 5. 64
The last hath ceased its solitary knoll. 850 *Excursion* 6. 784
Knolls. By rude hands built, with rocky knolls in front, 833 *Excursion* 5. 694
Knot. *See* **Love-knot.**
And downward thence a knot of grass he throws, 17 *Desc. Sk.* 384
Yet are they here the same unbroken knot 192 *Gipsies* 1
A knot of spiry trees for ages grew 212 *Laod.* 169
With firmer, holier knot. 223 *Wishing-gate* 48
Where'er a knot of houses lay 239 *P. B.* 233
The funeral dirge ;—she sees the knot 413 *White Doe* 1544
To where a scanty knot of verdure peeps, 610 *Desc.Sk.Quarto* 471
Of merriment a party-coloured knot, 773 *Excursion* 2. 124
Of melted hoar-frost, every tiny knot K.8.252*Recluse* 1.1.564
Knots. Where they bloomed singly, or in scattered knots,) 280 *Valedict.* 3
Above the raven's nest, by knots of grass 637 *Prelude* 1. 331
In knots, or pairs, or single. Not a look 710 *Prelude* 9. 60
The hardened soil, and knots of withered grass : 769 *Excursion* 1. 835
Fair dwellings, single, or in social knots ; 823 *Excursion* 5. 88
Mid knots of grooms the council of his state L.1. 94 *Juvenal* 2. 15
Knotted. It is a mass of knotted joints, 197 *Thorn* 8
And what is Penance with her knotted thong ; 433 *Ecc. Sonn.* 2. 19. 1
Know. May know that Poet's sorrows more. 9 *Collins* 20
—Before those thresholds (never can they know 15 *Desc. Sk.* 238
We still confide in more than we can know ; 20 *Desc. Sk.* 538
Stranger ! henceforth be warned ; and know that pride, 23 *Yew-tree* 50
As if thenceforth nor pain nor trouble she could know. 25 *Guilt* 63
You know that you have saved his life. I know it. 38 *Bord.* 27
Besides, I know not what strange prejudice 38 *Bord.* 59
Alas ! you do not know him. He is one 40 *Bord.* 166
This last request. You know me, Sire ; farewell ! 42 *Bord.* 295
You know, Sir, I have been too long your guard 43 *Bord.* 315
It struck upon my heart I know not how. 44 *Bord.* 377
An inch, till I am answered. Know you aught 46 *Bord.* 497
And I will tell you all !—You know not, Sir, 46 *Bord.* 503
A dog that does not know me.—These good Folks,— 46 *Bord.* 523
I neither know nor care. The insult bred 47 *Bord.* 553
A notice for your Daughter, that she may know 49 *Bord.* 667
Might envy, and am now,—but he shall know 54 *Bord.* 939
Mine ; But now no longer mine. You know Lord Clifford ; 57 *Bord.* 1103
You know me, Friends ; I have a heart to feel, 57 *Bord.* 1111
I know no cheaper engine to degrade a man, 58 *Bord.* 1161
You know we left him sitting—see him yonder. 60 *Bord.* 1257
How glad I am to hear your voice ! I know not 60 *Bord.* 1279
My Daughter does not know how weak I am ; 62 *Bord.* 1342
I know the need that all men have of mercy, 63 *Bord.* 1406
Knowing what otherwise we know too well, 63 *Bord.* 1421
I know him well ; there needs no other motive 63 *Bord.* 1430
I would be left alone. I know your motives ! 64 *Bord.* 1502
And what if you should never know them more !— 65 *Bord.* 1554
You are my Father's Friend. Alas, you know not, 66 *Bord.* 1604
This is most strange !—I know not what it was, 67 *Bord.* 1633
I know not what I said—all may be well. 67 *Bord.* 1645
I know not how he perished ; but the calm, 69 *Bord.* 1743
I am content—I know that he is guiltless— 70 *Bord.* 1847
Must be cast off.—Know then that I was urged, 71 *Bord.* 1862
I am belated, and you must know the cause— 71 *Bord.* 1907
Eldred, I know that ours is the only house 72 *Bord.* 1992
I heard—— You heard him, where ? when heard him ? As you know, 73 *Bord.* 2042
And know how busy are the tongues of men ; 74 *Bord.* 2079
Mercy ! I said I know not what—oh pity me— 77 *Bord.* 2247
Coward I have been ; know, there lies not now, 78 *Bord.* 2299
All last summer, as well you know, 80 †*Address : Child* 26
What should it know of death ? 83 *We are Seven* 4
" I cannot tell, I do not know."— 86 *Anecdote* 39
Things that I know not of belike to thee are dear, 88 *Pet-lamb* 51
Which then it had ! Nay, Sir, for aught I know, 97 *Brothers* 136
A pretty flock, and which, for aught I know, 100 *Brothers* 302
But thou—I know not how inspired, how led— 105 *Artegal* 172
" But, not to overlook what thou may'st know, 105 *Artegal* 210
I know not if you sleep or feed. 106 **I've watched* 4
Who, being loved, in love no bounds dost know, 107 *Farewell* 44
She lived unknown, and few could know 109 **She dwelt* 9
Nor, England ! did I know till then 109 **I travelled* 3
I only pray to know the worst ; 110 *Forsaken* 6
I know not what I trace ; 110 *'*Tis said that some* 19
Within the sound of Emma's voice, nor know 111 *'*Tis said that some* 51
I cannot lift my limbs to know 114 *Ind. Wom.* 63
Assist me, God, their boundaries to know, 118 *Maternal Grief* 12
I weep—I know they do thee wrong, 121 *EmigrantMother* 77
Of suffering or of peace, I know not which : 125 *V. and J.* 282
" Oh Sir ! you know I'm Betty Foy, 129 *Idiot Boy* 254

Know—*continued.*
You know him—him you often see ; 129 *Idiot Boy* 256
" What, Woman ! should I know of him ? " 129 *Idiot Boy* 260
On things thou canst not know of.—— After thou 136 *Michael* 339
Lack any pleasure which a boy can know." 136 *Michael* 356
To thee I know too much I owe ; 144 *Her Eyes* 19
I'll build an Indian bower ; I know 145 *Her Eyes* 55
I know the poisons of the shade ; 145 *Her Eyes* 95
I know the earth-nuts fit for food : 145 *Her Eyes* 96
The travellers know it not, and 'twill remain 149 *M. H.* 16
Alone I tread this path ;—for aught I know, 151 **When, to* 105
Was living, as a child might know, 155 *Waterfall* 9
I know, and I have known it long ; 156 *Oak and Broom* 57
'Twas a face I did not know ; 160 **Pansies, lilies* 22
Praise of which I nothing know. 161 **Pleasures newly* 8
All men who know thee call their brother, 162 **Art thou the* 10
Whatsoe'er we feel and know 171 *Kitten* 99
Who does not know the famous SWAN ? 174 *Waggoner* 1. 88
The horses are dismayed, nor know 175 *Waggoner* 1. 190
For this they know (and let it hide, 178 *Waggoner* 3. 10
We want your streamers, friend, you know ; 179 *Waggoner* 3. 76
I know that Wanton's noisy station, 179 *Waggoner* 3. 118
I know him and his occupation ; 179 *Waggoner* 3. 119
And all the while," said he, " to know 193 *Ruth* 82
" More know I not, I wish I did, 199 *Thorn* 144
As all the country know, 199 *Thorn* 196
And this I know, full many a time, 200 *Thorn* 236
And he perhaps, for aught we know, was born 203 *Hart-leap* 155
Alas ! the impassioned minstrel did not know 205 *Brougham* 157
Answers, and we know not whence ; 209 **Yes, it* 14
Swift, toward the realms that know not earthly day, 211 *Laod.* 155
—Who comes not hither ne'er shall know 215 *Kirkstone* 73
And know—that, even for him who shuns the day 229 *Cuckoo-clock* 23
Know—that, for him whose waking thoughts, severe 229 *Cuckoo-clock* 27
Their feet among the billows, know 235 *Power of Sound* 186
" I know the secrets of a land 237 *P. B.* 96
They know not I have been so far ;— 238 *P. B.* 162
Yet, potent Spirits ! well I know, 245 *P. B.* 766
For well did Peter know the sound ; 246 *P. B.* 876
For he is dead—I know it well ! " 248 *P. B.* 1027
God being with thee when we know it not. 258 **It is a* 14
Which only Poets know ;—'twas rightly said ; 265 **There is a pleasure* 2
Speak, that my torturing doubts their end may know ! 277 **Why art* 14
Thee, neither know I, nor thy peers ; 288 *Highland Girl* 20
Might crush, nor know that it had suffered harm ;) 290 *Kilchurn* 15
Enough if in our hearts we know 293 *Yarrow Unv.* 47
Because, my Darlings, ye must know 295 *Highland Boy* 12
Of which we nothing know. 295 *Highland Boy* 25
Ye soon shall know how this befell) 296 *Highland Boy* 97
Thee neither do they know nor us 300 *Bran* 35
But that I know, where'er I go, 302 *Yarrow V.* 85
Consul, or King, can sound himself to know 304 **Festivals have* 13
O Friend ! I know not which way I must look 306 **O Friend* 1
And know that noble feelings, manly powers, 308 **There is a bondage* 11
'Tis well ! from this day forward we shall know 310 **Another year* 5
We know the arduous strife, the eternal laws 316 **O'er the* 10
We know that ye, beneath the stern control 316 **It was a* 10
And feel, if we would know. 337 *Cath. Cantons* 18
" What know we of the Blest above 338 *Brientz* 1
I ask in vain—and know far less 344 *Eclipse* 79
Whose turf may never know the care 348 **Lulled by* 47
Far more than any heart but mine can know. 352 *H. C. R.* 9
Know them no more. If Truth, who veiled her face 359 **Those old* 7
Severe research, that in our hearts we know 359 **Those old* 12
We feel that we are greater than we know. 384 *Duddon* 34. 14
(We know not whence) ministers for a bell 387 *Roslin* 2
And know that it is Emily ? 401 *White Doe* 445
But whence it came we know not, nor behold 422 *Ecc. Sonn.* 1. 16. 7
For aught the wisest know or comprehend ; 423 *Ecc. Sonn.* 1. 18. 5
Ye have no skill to teach, or if ye know 433 *Ecc. Sonn.* 2. 18. 9
Will listen, and ye know that He is just. 448 *Ecc. Sonn.* 3. 30. 14
Blest Rite for him who hears in faith, " I know 448 *Ecc. Sonn.* 3. 31. 5
A stream is heard—I see it not, but know 453 **Calm is the* 25
Of shame scarcely seeming to know that she's there, 482 *Character* 14
Dreams, books, are each a world ; and books, we know, 488 *Pers. Talk* 33
Rare master has it been thy lot to know ; 489 *Spade* 5
Who do thy work, and know it not : 492 *Duty* 14
Nor know we anything so fair 492 *Duty* 43
For if than other rash ones more thou know, 513 *Newspaper* 11
And some, we know, when they by wilful act 517 *Pun. Death* 3. 9
They know the dread requital's source profound ; 520 *Pun. Death* 13.
I know an aged Man constrained to dwell 530 **I know* 1
Know, if thou grudge not to prolong thy rest, 548 **Stay, bold* 12
For he too tender was of age to know ; 553 *Prioress* 73
If there is more in this, I know it not ; 553 *Prioress* 84
Know, that the honour of high God may spread, 554 *Prioress* 126
That never fleshly woman they did know. 554 *Prioress* 134
How hard, alas ! to bear, I only know. 557 *Cuck. and Night.* 40
Well did they know that service all by rote, 558 *Cuck. and Night.* 71
Unlearned Book and rude, as well I know, 562 *Cuck.andNight.* 291
Then know I well that she would not sojourn. 563 *Troilus* 80
When they can know and feel that they have been, 568 *Cumb. Beg.* 149
His fields seemed to know what their Master was doing ; 569 *Farmer* 18
If more of my condition ye would know, 574 *Chiabrera* 4. 28
This, which I know I speak with mind serene. 578 *Peele Castle* 40

Know—*continued.*
And grieve, and know that I must grieve, . . 580 *John Words.* 19
When such divine communion, which we know, . 581 **Why should we* 12
If thou hast heard me—if thy Spirit know . . 583 **With copious* 34
But yet I know, where'er I go, ... 587 *Immortality* 17
—Before those hermit doors, that never know . 607 *Desc.Sk.Quarto* 299
That he may neither know what hope is mine, . 624 *Æneid* 34
For know we not that from celestial spheres, . . 628 **Deign, Sovereign* 25
To understand myself, nor thou to know . . . 641 *Prelude* 1. 627
And be ye happy ! Yet, my Friends ! I know . 642 *Prelude* 2. 41
On every side fall off, we know not how, . . . 648 *Prelude* 2. 436
Let others that know more speak as they know. . 650 *Prelude* 3. 73
Some tempting island, could but know the ills . 656 *Prelude* 3. 485
Who care not, know not, think not what they do. 673 *Prelude* 5. 495
We know where we have friends. Ye dreamers, then, ... 673 *Prelude* 5. 523
This label seemed of the utmost we can know, . 696 *Prelude* 7. 645
As, more than anything we know, instinct . 706 *Prelude* 8. 492
The end of life, and everything we know. . . . 707 *Prelude* 8. 529
That flesh can know is theirs—the consciousness 747 *Prelude* 14. 114
Who know not what they speak. By love subsists 748 *Prelude* 14. 168
Find solace—knowing what we have learnt to know, 752 *Prelude* 14. 438
But know we not that he, who intermits . . . 773 *Excursion* 2. 147
—But why this tedious record ?—Age, we know, . 791 *Excursion* 3. 325
But that too much demands still more. You know, 793 *Excursion* 3. 497
Adore, and worship, when you know it not ; . . 818 *Excursion* 4. 1148
To heaven, I know, by my Redeemer taught.' . 835 *Excursion* 5. 826
" And blest are they who sleep ; and we that know, 836 *Excursion* 5. 922
Of what I know, and what we feel within. . 851 *Excursion* 6. 861
One of God's simple children that yet know not . 851 *Excursion* 6. 881
Hope from that quarter would, I know, have brought 853 *Excursion* 6. 1015
But you, Sir, know that in a neighbouring vale . 862 *Excursion* 7. 315
And know we not that from the blind have flowed 865 *Excursion* 7. 534
The more we know ; and yet is reverenced least, 884 *Excursion* 9. 18
To know what they must do ; their wisdom is . 886 *Excursion* 9. 145
They know if I be silent, morn or even : . . . 895 *Excursion* 9. 750
What longing would ye know ? . . . . . . S.3. 431 **The Scottish* 6
You know where my poor bones shall be, . . . K.8. 220 **The snow-tracks* 34
Of pleasure which I know that I shall give . . K.8. 228 * *I will* 107
" I know where I shall find him, though the storm K.8. 228 **I will* 121
For ye must know] that though the storm . . K.8. 228 **I will* 123
Rides to and fro : I know them and their ways. . K.8. 250*Recluse* 1.1.509
We know, yet faith sustains the sorrowing heart ; K.8. 275 **These vales* 6

Knowest.
Thou know'st me for a Man not easily moved, . 38 *Bord.* 69
And, as thou know'st, gave me that humble Cot . 41 *Bord.* 201
" Thou know'st that twice a day I have brought thee in this can . . . . 87 *Pet-lamb* 41
Thou know'st the pillow of my breast ; . . . 120 *EmigrantMother* 32
That passes over it. We have, thou know'st, . 135 *Michael* 247
As well thou knowest, in us the old and young . 136 *Michael* 354
Will say't, who know'st both land and sea, . . 179 *Waggoner* 3. 84
" Thou knowest, the Delphic oracle foretold . . 210 *Laod.* 43
Hast been so happy that thou know'st what thoughts . . . . 551 **If thou in* 2
Now mercy, Lord ! thou know'st well I desire . 563 *Troilus* 73

Knoweth. For His own service ; knoweth, loveth us, 744 *Prelude* 13. 277

Knowing. A favoured Being, knowing no desire . 23 *Yew-tree* 16
To serve me so, and knowing that he owes . . 46 *Bord.* 484
Knowing what otherwise we know too well, . . 63 *Bord.* 1421
" Trust, angry Bard ! a knowing Sprite, . . . 164 *Needlecase* 37
Not knowing that he had befriended . . . 177 *Waggoner* 2. 111
Knowing what cause there is for shame, . . . 181 *Waggoner* 4. 88
Knowing that Nature never did betray . . . 207 *Tintern* 122
Knowing my heart's best treasure was no more ; . 257 **Surprised by* 12
Knowing, things rashly sought are rarely found ; 514 **Blest Statesman* 10
And had good knowing both of their intent, . . 558 *Cuck.andNight.*109
And seldom knowing that he sees, some straw, . 567 *Cumb. Beg.* 54
Seeking the visible world, nor knowing why. . . 646 *Prelude* 2. 278
Knowing too well the importance of his theme, . 665 *Prelude* 4. 444
Knowing that he grows wiser every day . . . 670 *Prelude* 5. 324
Strangers, not knowing each the other's name. . 689 *Prelude* 7. 118
Find solace—knowing what we have learnt to know, 752 *Prelude* 14. 438
About the fields I wander, knowing this . . . 768 *Excursion* 1. 765
' Knowing the heart of man is set to be . . . 806 *Excursion* 4. 324
At this, not knowing why—as often-times . . K.8. 229 **I will* 168

Knowingly. Did knowingly conform itself ; there came . . . . 704 *Prelude* 8. 371

Knowledge. *See* **Self-knowledge.**
Instructed that true knowledge leads to love ; . 23 *Yew-tree* 60
Answer these questions, from our common knowledge, ... 38 *Bord.* 39
Of living without knowledge that you live : . . 71 *Bord.* 1871
Hide the knowledge of thy doom. . . . . . 90 *Longest Day* 44
—O Brother ! to my knowledge lost so long, . . 104 *Artegal* 131
Judge both Fugitives with knowledge : . . . 141 *Arm. Lady* 85
This knowledge, from an Angel's voice . . . 168 *Pilgrim's Dream* 65
I speak with knowledge,—by that Voice beguiled, 229 *Cuckoo-clock* 16
Within my reach ; of knowledge graced . . . 285 *Grave of Burns* 56
Fed his first hopes ? what knowledge could *he* gain ? 304 **I grieved* 4
Of knowledge ; that whole myriads should unite . 308 **One might* 10
Or to solicit knowledge of events, ... 346 *Processions* 2
Knowledge no help ; Imagination shaped . . . 353 *Aquap.* 70
From Knowledge !—If the Muse, whom I have served . . . . 358 *Aquap.* 355
So pure, so fraught with knowledge and delight, . 362 **List—'twas* 61
And knowledge has a narrow range ; . . . . 408 *White Doe* 1120
Is crossed by knowledge, or by dread, of change, 458 *Sea-shore* 18
What knowledge can perform, is diligent to learn ; 493 *Hap. War.* 9

Knowledge—*continued.*
" Knowledge will save me from the threatened woe." 513 *Newspaper* 10
Above thy knowledge as they dared to go, . . 513 *Newspaper* 13
The light of Knowledge, and the warmth of Love. 515 **Ah why* 14
By interchange of knowledge and delight. . . . 546 **The embowering* 8
" My knowledge is so weak, O blissful Queen ! . 553 *Prioress* 29
After my knowledge I have loved alwày ; . . . 556 *Prioress* 206
Have knowledge, I thee pray, what this may be ? 559 *Cuck.andNight.*125
Knowledge and wisdom, gained from converse sweet 584 *Ch. Lamb* 12
With better knowledge how the heart was framed 641 *Prelude* 1. 628
Of knowledge, when all knowledge is delight, . . 646 *Prelude* 2. 287
And human knowledge, to the human eye . . 648 *Prelude* 2. 404
On knowledge, when sincerely sought and prized . 654 *Prelude* 3. 389
With clearer knowledge ; with another eye . . 661 *Prelude* 4. 214
Of pleasure won, and knowledge not withheld, . 662 *Prelude* 4. 277
'Tis true, some casual knowledge might be gained 663 *Prelude* 4. 300
And knowledge, rightly honoured with that name— 672 *Prelude* 5. 424
Knowledge not purchased by the loss of power ! . 672 *Prelude* 5. 425
Knowledge and increase of enduring joy . . . 674 *Prelude* 5. 593
Of Nature, in that knowledge I possessed . . . 676 *Prelude* 6. 102
Moves the great spirit of human knowledge, spare 681 *Prelude* 6. 450
The Horse of knowledge, and the learned Pig, . 697 *Prelude* 7. 708
Are led to knowledge, wheresoever led, . . . 703 *Prelude* 8. 307
Receives no knowledge that can bring forth good, 704 *Prelude* 8. 326
Without the light of knowledge. Where the harm, 705 *Prelude* 8. 437
Have pleased me, seeking knowledge at that time 708 *Prelude* 8. 599
Far less than craving power ; yet knowledge came, 708 *Prelude* 8. 600
With needful knowledge, had abruptly passed . 711 *Prelude* 9. 93
Through knowledge spreading and imperishable, . 715 *Prelude* 9. 361
Whence grew that genuine knowledge, fraught with peace, ... 732 *Prelude* 11. 354
Profoundest knowledge to what point, and how, . 737 *Prelude* 12. 221
Long time in search of knowledge did I range . 740 *Prelude* 13. 16
Knowledge was given accordingly ; my trust . . 740 *Prelude* 13. 55
A more judicious knowledge of the worth . . . 741 *Prelude* 13. 80
Knowledge that step by step might lead me on . 742 *Prelude* 13. 132
Through want of better knowledge in the heads . 743 *Prelude* 13. 215
Where knowledge leads me : it shall be my pride 743 *Prelude* 13. 251
Their knowledge of the heavens, and image forth 745 *Prelude* 13. 341
My knowledge, as to make me capable 750 *Prelude* 14. 310
By knowledge gathered up from day to day ; . . 762 *Excursion* 1. 395
To blend with knowledge of the years to come, . 762 *Excursion* 1. 432
(Not to forestall such knowledge as may be . . 774 *Excursion* 2. 161
" For I have knowledge that you do not shrink . 779 *Excursion* 2. 490
Some recompense of knowledge or delight ? " . 786 *Excursion* 3. 19
With hearts at ease, and knowledge in our hearts 794 *Excursion* 3. 548
For knowledge is delight ; and such delight . . 806 *Excursion* 4. 346
May we behold ; their knowledge register ; . . 807 *Excursion* 4. 382
Where knowledge, ill begun in cold remark . . 810 *Excursion* 4. 622
This knowledge ample recompense affords . . 813 *Excursion* 4. 814
To hopes on knowledge and experience built ; . 820 *Excursion* 4. 1292
—Knowledge, methinks, in these disordered times, 823 *Excursion* 5. 29
Knowledge, for us, is difficult to gain— . . . 830 *Excursion* 5. 492
Be genuine knowledge, bear we then in mind . . 847 *Excursion* 6. 594
Her keen desire of knowledge, nor efface . . 848 *Excursion* 6. 700
His knowledge, wisdom, love of truth, and love . 854 *Excursion* 6. 1067
Enriched with knowledge his industrious mind ; . 865 *Excursion* 7. 503
That, in his presence, humbler knowledge stood . 865 *Excursion* 7. 514
Without his own consent, or knowledge, fixed ! . 878 *Excursion* 8. 300
The tribute of enjoyment, knowledge, health, . 888 *Excursion* 9. 269
When, prizing knowledge as her noblest wealth . 888 *Excursion* 9. 294
With scantiest knowledge, master of all truth . 895 *Excursion* 9. 736
Not *thus* can Knowledge elevate . . . . . S.3. 439 **Avaunt this* 7
All intercourse of knowledge or of love . . . K.8.251*Recluse* 1.1.535
That we shall have for knowledge and for love . K.8.254*Recluse* 1.1.638
Love, knowledge, all my manifold delights . . K.8.255*Recluse* 1.1.697

Known. *See* **Well-known.**
In thy loved presence known, and only there ; . 21 *Desc. Sk.* 600
The red-breast, known for years, which at my casement pecked. . . . . 28 *Guilt* 225
He must have felt it then, known what it was, . 41 *Bord.* 240
At Herbert's door. Ay ; and if truth were known 46 *Bord.* 480
Be known unto you, you will love this Woman, . 48 *Bord.* 628
Ere can be known to you how much a Father . 52 *Bord.* 822
Else could so strong a mind have ever known . 55 *Bord.* 998
Hopes that she so long hath known. . . . . 90 *Longest Day* 40
'Twas one well known to him in former days, . 95 *Brothers* 38
Through fields which once had been well known to him : . . . . 96 *Brothers* 93
Was known as well as to the flowers that grow there. 99 *Brothers* 276
Making all kindness registered and known ; . . 107 *Farewell* 37
Strange fits of passion have I known : . . . . 109 **Strange fits* 1
And there is one whom I five years have known ; 110 **'Tis said that some* 6
Such happiness as I have known to-day. . . . 111 **'Tis said that some* 52
In his known haunts of joy where'er he might, . 118 *Maternal Grief* 53
Than ever fortune hath been known to do) . . 121 *V. and J.* 7
None will reproach you, for our truth is known ; . 124 *V. and J.* 197
And looked, as mothers ne'er were known to look, 125 *V. and J.* 260
" Make it known that my Companion . . . . 141 *Arm. Lady* 115
To daylight known deter from that pursuit, . . 154 *Morn. Ex.* 56
I know, and I have known it long ; . . . . 156 *Oak and Broom* 57
Is known, and by as strong a spell . . . . . 174 *Waggoner* 1. 84
A temper known to those who, after long . . . 185 *Nutting* 27
Nor better life was known ; . . . . 194 *Ruth* 147
And she is known to every star, ... 198 *Thorn* 69
" And, gallant Stag ! to make thy praises known, 201 *Hart-leap* 65
That what we are, and have been, may be known ; 203 *Hart-leap* 174
To thee, by varying titles known . . . . . 216 *Enterprise* 38
To me was never known. . . . . 240 *P. B.* 330

Known—*continued.*
An infant that has known no sin. . . . . . 247 *P. B.* 970
I see the places where they once were known, . 256 *Decay of Piety* 9
And to the Boy they all were known— . . . 296 *Highland Boy* 114
As he had ever known. . . . . 297 *Highland Boy* 215
Men known, and men unknown, sick, lame, and blind, ... 303 **Is it* 4
—Have we not known—and live we not to tell— 311 **Who rises* 33
"'Tis known," cried they, "that he, who would adorn . . . . 312 **When, far* 5
Is known; by none, perhaps, so feelingly: . . 312 *Clarkson* 3
Made known the spot where piety should raise . 338 *Engelberg* 13
Deserve a thought) but little known to fame— . 354 *Aquap.* 94
From century on to century, must have known . 355 *Aquap.* 151
Her conquests, in the world of sense made known. 357 *Aquap.* 332
Lo! by a destiny well known . . . . . . 372 *Eg. Maid* 205
Make to the eyes of men thy features known. . 376 *Duddon* 3. 4
And Captains known for worth in arms; . . . 403 *White Doe* 630
My wish is known, and I have done: . . . . 410 *White Doe* 1307
But that Heaven's purpose might be known . . 411 *White Doe* 1419
From their known course, or vanish like a dream; 421 *Ecc. Sonn.* 1. 12. 10
Known to the moral world, Imagination, . . . 427 *Ecc. Sonn.* 1. 34. 10
The noblest drops to admiration known, . . . 436 *Ecc. Sonn.* 2. 32. 10
Or, having known the splendours of success, . . 458 *Sea-shore* 32
So call thee for heaven's grace through thee made known . . . . 459 **Wanderer! that* 13
Makes known, when thou no longer canst be seen, 475 **Homeward we* 13
Full happy season, when was known, ... 478 *Somnamb.* 25
Known chiefly, Aira! to thy glen, ... 478 *Somnamb.* 28
And Canute (fact more worthy to be known) . . 495 *Fact* 19
We two have known such happy hours together . 498 **Enough of climbing* 46
Known but to this *one* release— . . . . . 502 **Like a* 22
Oft-times makes its bounty known . . . . . 502 **Like a* 31
And what if thou, sweet May, hast known . . . 507 *May* 65
That to this mountain-daisy's self were known . 511 **So fair* 4
A place where joy is known, ... 526 **The soaring* 10
Two poor old Dames, as I have known, . . . 536 *Goody Blake* 34
Known unto few but prized as far as known, . 540 *Grace Darl.* 7
Perchance may still survive. And be it known . 546 **Oft is* 9
By cursèd Jews—thing well and widely known, . 556 *Prioress* 234
Him from my childhood have I known; and then 566 *Cumb. Beg.* 22
—Such pleasure is to one kind Being known, . . 568 *Cumb. Beg.* 154
Bear with Him—judge *Him* gently who makes known . . . . 576 **By a* 19
Such happiness, wherever it be known, . . . 579 *Peele Castle* 55
Have power to make thy virtues known, . . . 581 *John Words.* 62
Brightening a converse never known to swerve . 583 **With copious* 11
That could not lie concealed where Thou wert known; . . . . 584 **With copious* 62
Forget the glories he hath known, ... 588 *Immortality* 83
Pursues thy brother—this to thee is known; . . 624 *Æneid* 17
Call thee, though known but for a few fleet years, 627 **The star* 13
Of a known Vale, whither my feet should turn, . 633 *Prelude* 1. 72
That lives who hath not known his godlike hours, 651 *Prelude* 3. 191
But spare the House of God. Was ever known . 655 *Prelude* 3. 405
And known authority of office served . . . . 656 *Prelude* 3. 538
Strength came where weakness was not known to be, 660 *Prelude* 4. 155
A narrow Vale where each was known to all, . . 661 *Prelude* 4. 199
And of the men that framed them, whether known, 668 *Prelude* 5. 214
This model of a child is never known . . . . 670 *Prelude* 5. 299
Would issue, let one incident make known. . . 683 *Prelude* 6. 561
Of her distress, was known to have turned her steps 704 *Prelude* 8. 385
Has heretofore made known; that bursting forth 706 *Prelude* 8. 478
Or such retirement, Friend! as we have known . 715 *Prelude* 9. 391
"I, Robespierre, accuse thee!" Well is known . 720 *Prelude* 10. 113
In all their comprehensive bearings known . . 721 *Prelude* 10. 195
Lived in the shade; and to Harmodius known . 721 *Prelude* 10. 198
And his compeer Aristogiton, known . . . . 721 *Prelude* 10. 199
Given to my moral nature had I known . . . 722 *Prelude* 10. 269
Could they have known her, would have loved; methought . . . . 736 *Prelude* 12. 166
Inaudible—was transient; I had known . . . 737 *Prelude* 12. 201
To speak, what I myself have known and felt; . 740 *Prelude* 13. 13
Known by whatever name, is falsely deemed . . 742 *Prelude* 13. 187
What was not understood, though known to be; . 751 *Prelude* 14. 336
It will be known, by thee at least, my Friend! . 752 *Prelude* 14. 411
Beloved and honoured—far as he was known. . 757 *Excursion* 1. 97
With strictness scarcely known on English ground. 758 *Excursion* 1. 117
Whom I had known and loved. He had rehearsed 765 *Excursion* 1. 614
But we have known that there is often found . 765 *Excursion* 1. 632
The careless wanderer's friend, to him made known 774 *Excursion* 2. 186
To known restraints; and who most boldly drew 775 *Excursion* 2. 258
These words;—"*Shall in the grave thy love be known*, 777 *Excursion* 2. 381
And all known places and familiar sights . . . 793 *Excursion* 3. 508
Known and familiar, which the vaulted sky . . 798 *Excursion* 3. 858
With the same pensive office; and make known . 800 *Excursion* 3. 981
"You have known lights and guides better than these. . . . . 816 *Excursion* 4. 1017
As he is known to all. The calm delights . . . 824 *Excursion* 5. 110
That which is done accords with what is known . 826 *Excursion* 5. 256
His soul is pent! How little can be known— . 831 *Excursion* 5. 590
Your instances; for they are both best known, . 832 *Excursion* 5. 648
The Vicar ceased; and downcast looks made known 854 *Excursion* 6. 1053
Of sweetness where dire anguish had been known, 854 *Excursion* 6. 1083
The individual known and understood; . . . . 874 *Excursion* 8. 18
Pitied, and, where they are not known, despised. 875 *Excursion* 8. 43
Of life, and hope, and action. And 'tis known . 886 *Excursion* 9. 128
Declares his due, while he makes known his need. 889 *Excursion* 9. 320
Not seldom over anxious to make known . . . 893 *Excursion* 9. 584
And wild-flowers known as well as if our hands . S.3. 433 **The doubt* 7

Known—*continued.*
Is known to all beneath the polar star, . . . S.3. 442 **Vasco, whose* 13
The highest fountain known on British land. . . K.8. 226 **I will* 61

Knows. He knows but from its shade the present hour. . . . . 2 *Ev. Wk.* 32
She knows that only from high aims ensue . . 22 *Desc. Sk.* 650
"My life, Heaven knows, hath long been burthensome; . . . . 35 *Guilt* 586
Like you; he knows your eye would search his heart, ... 42 *Bord.* 265
The villain, Clifford. He hates you, and he knows 42 *Bord.* 280
Forgive me.—Oswald knows it all—he knows, . 66 *Bord.* 1599
God knows what was in my heart, ... 72 *Bord.* 1960
Perhaps you are his son? The All-seeing knows, 74 *Bord.* 2072
Summer knows but little of them: . . . . . 79 *Foresight* 18
There's never a scholar in England knows. . . 80 †*Address: Child* 8
God only knows, but to the very last . . . . 98 *Brothers* 218
He knows it not, he cannot guess: . . . . . 117 *Affl. Marg.* 26
Shouts from nobody knows where; . . . . . 126 *Idiot Boy* 4
Now, though he knows poor Johnny well, . . . 127 *Idiot Boy* 114
She knows not, happy Betty Foy! . . . . . 130 *Idiot Boy* 393
Both you and he, Heaven knows how soon! . . 156 *Oak and Broom* 49
Coming one knows not how, nor whence, . . . 158 **In youth* 71
He knows it to his cost, good Man! . . . . 174 *Waggoner* 1. 87
It knows how ye were vexed and strained, . . 175 *Waggoner* 1. 121
I stagger onward—heaven knows how; . . . . 179 *Waggoner* 3. 89
For the true reason no one knows: . . . . . 198 *Thorn* 90
Earth knows, is all unworthy to survey. . . . 211 *Laod.* 108
He knows not how the blood comes there— . . 244 *P. B.* 724
He sees the blood, knows what it is,— . . . 244 *P. B.* 728
Where he sits down, he knows not how, . . . 248 *P. B.* 1088
And knows she not, singing as he inspires, . . 261 **I heard (alas* 10
Honour that knows the path and will not swerve; 319 **Avaunt all* 7
He knows that from a holier altar came . . . 329 *Ode: Thanks.* 51
Knows that the source is nobler whence doth rise 329 *Ode: Thanks.* 53
Who knows not pomp, who heeds not pelf; . . 344 **How blest* 7
No one knows how; nor seldom is put forth . . 357 *Aquap.* 319
Than sceptred king or laurelled conqueror knows, 387 *Scott* 11
Man placed him here, and God, he knows, can save. 392 *Daniel* 14
Along a Galaxy that knows no end, ... 443 *Ecc. Sonn.* 3. 13. 13
Who knows not *that?*—yet would this delicate age 447 *Ecc. Sonn.* 3. 29. 10
The Sailor knows; he best, whose lot is cast . . 458 *Sea-shore* 5
Yet wants heaven knows what to be worthy the name. . . . . 482 *Character* 16
Led, Heaven knows how! to this poor sod: . . 485 *Poet's Epitaph* 26
Knows from instinct what to do; . . . . . 490 *Incident: Dog* 14
He knows, who gave that love sublime; . . . 492 *Fidelity* 63
To virtue every triumph that he knows: . . . 493 *Hap. War.* 34
In scarcely conscious fingers, was, she knows, . 509 *F. Stone* 64
That Europe knows, would echo this appeal; . . 509 *F. Stone* 94
Knows that this prophecy is not too bold. . . 516 **Young England* 8
Whose goodness knows no change, whose love is sure, ... 519 *Pun. Death* 11. 12
How beautiful!—Yet none knows why . . . 526 **The soaring* 25
No one knows by what device? . . . . . . 550 *Hermit's Cell* 3. 4
And knows not when he hurts and when he heals; 560 *Cuck.andNight.* 203
Caused by the wish, as knows your sapience, . . 562 *Cuck.andNight.* 309
About work that he knows, in a track that he knows; . . . . 570 *Farmer* 58
This child but half knows it, and that not at all. . 572 *Avarice* 36
Had traced its windings.—This Savona knows, . 574 *Chiabrera* 5. 13
And to my Friend who knows me I may add, . 643 *Prelude* 2. 73
Who knows the individual hour in which . . . 645 *Prelude* 2. 206
And wavering motions sent he knows not whence, 662 *Prelude* 4. 269
He knows the policies of foreign lands; . . . 670 *Prelude* 5. 319
Who knows what thus may have been gained, both then . . . . 675 *Prelude* 6. 36
Upon a volume whose contents he knows . . . 719 *Prelude* 10. 59
Or some secreted island, Heaven knows where! . 729 *Prelude* 11. 141
Of good and evil; knows not what to fear . . 732 *Prelude* 11. 313
He knows not wherefore;—but the boy to-day, . 779 *Excursion* 2. 540
On nature's wants, he knows how few they are, . 813 *Excursion* 4. 812
Both knows and loves such objects as excite . . 819 *Excursion* 4. 1210
He only knows by name; and, if he hear, . . 819 *Excursion* 4. 1226
'He who afflicts me knows what I can bear; . . 854 *Excursion* 6. 1046
Spirit that knows no insulated spot, ... 884 *Excursion* 9. 13
I, not insensible, Heaven knows, ... S.3. 438 **My Lord* 23
Hernani knows well . . . . S.3. 440 **Said red-ribboned* 15
Or something dearer still, if reason knows . . K.8. 234 **Witness thou* 4
The vestal priestess of a sisterhood who knows . K.8. 325 [?] **The vestal* 1

Kremlin. The Kremlin and its haughty towers . 544 *Russ. Fug.* 255

L

La. And, kneeling, supplication make to our Lady de la Paix; . . . . 92 *Poet's Dream* 50
Label. This label seemed of the utmost we can know, 696 *Prelude* 7. 645
Laboratory. Its silent laboratory! Words should say . . . . S.3. 434 **The doubt* 65
Laborious. Alas! what boots the long laborious quest . . . . 315 **Alas! what* 1
Doubling and doubling with laborious walk, . . 389 *Glencroe* 1
To most laborious service, though to them . . 869 *Excursion* 7. 778
Labour. Hath told; for, landing after labour hard, 25 *Guilt* 49

Labour—*continued.*
“ Barred every comfort labour could procure, 35 *Guilt* 577
They please Him best who labour most to do in peace His will: 93 *Poet's Dream* 66
There did they dwell—from earthly labour free, 108 *Indolence* 68
Hard labour in a time of need! 115 *Last of Flock* 42
Think of evening's repose when our labour was done, 116 *Repentance* 27
At labour in the harvest field: 120 *EmigrantMother* 20
Their labour did not cease; unless when all 132 *Michael* 98
Performed all kinds of labour for his sheep, 138 *Michael* 458
Too weak to labour in the harvest field, 149 **A narrow* 63
Ply the pleasant labour, ply! 163 *Spinning Wheel* 9
A mournful labour, while to her is given 173 *Infant Daughter* 64
Cold, pain, and labour, and all fleshly ills; 197 *Resolution* 115
But should she labour night and day, 214 *Dion* 98
My further labour might prevent! 245 *P. B.* 787
Help by his labour to maintain 249 *P. B.* 1129
To thy heart's wish, thy labour blest by God! 281 *Chris. Words.* 8
High sacrifice, and labour without pause, 316 **O'er the* 12
With firmer soul, yet labour to regain 318 *Biscayan* 2
To labour, and to prayer, to nature, and to heaven. 320 **O'erweeningStatesmen* 14
So may she labour for thy civic halls: 324 *Ode 1814* 99
And all the Nations labour to fulfil 329 *Ode 1815* 127
To highest Heaven—the labour of the Soul; 331 *Ode: Thanks.* 172
And to the enormous labour left his name, 335 *Aix* 13
A labour worthy of eternal youth! 343 *Last Sup.* 14
Whom Labour, never urged to toil, 344 **How blest* 5
Labour their proper greatness to subdue; 350 *Des. Stanzas* 25
Labour accomplishes, or patience bears— 363 **The world forsaken* 5
(As if her labour and her ease were twins). 366 *Lombardy* 6
And so they labour, deeming Holy Writ 439 *Ecc. Sonn.* 2. 41. 6
Must Man, with labour born, awake to sorrow 462 **Where lies the truth* 6
From labour could not wean them, 483 *Simon Lee* 54
Of sleepless Labour, 'mid whose dizzy wheels 501 *Humanity* 93
Against all barriers which his labour meets 520 *Pun. Death* 14. 7
Whose breath would labour at the flute in vain, 521 *Epist.Beaumont* 29
The bold good Man his labour sped 543 *Russ Fug.* 115
Labour, and Pain, and Grief, and joyless Age, 613 *Desc.Sk.Quarto* 639
This labour will be welcome, honoured Friend! 641 *Prelude* 1. 646
Forced labour, and more frequently forced hopes; 652 *Prelude* 3. 210
If but by labour won, and fit to endure 654 *Prelude* 3. 391
Spare diet, patient labour, and plain weeds. 655 *Prelude* 3. 457
And here was Labour, his own bondslave; Hope, 657 *Prelude* 3. 595
And life and labour seem but one, I filled 688 *Prelude* 7. 71
Must labour, whence the strongest are not free. 698 *Prelude* 7. 730
And hazard, and hard labour interchanged 703 *Prelude* 8. 254
By bodily toil, labour exceeding far 741 *Prelude* 13. 97
And poverty and labour in excess 742 *Prelude* 13. 198
Of our long labour: we have traced the stream 749 *Prelude* 14. 194
The mood in which this labour was begun, 751 *Prelude* 14. 373
And I, associate with such labour, steeped 752 *Prelude* 14. 402
Is labour not unworthy of regard: 752 *Prelude* 14. 413
Be not this labour useless. If such theme 755 *Recluse* 1. 1. 852
Itinerant in this labour, he had passed 761 *Excursion* 1. 349
From ill-requited labour turned adrift 764 *Excursion* 1. 560
He was her vassal of all labour, tilled 783 *Excursion* 2. 764
—Come, labour, when the worn-out frame requires 802 *Excursion* 4. 57
Their labour, covered, as a lake with waves; 807 *Excursion* 4. 436
For you the hours of labour do not flag; 835 *Excursion* 5. 835
Robust as ever rural labour bred.” 839 *Excursion* 6. 101
To punctual labour in his sacred charge. 859 *Excursion* 7. 149
Like Youths released from labour, and yet bound 869 *Excursion* 7. 777
Bound by his vow to labour for redress 873 *Excursion* 7. 1042
To earn, by wholesome labour in the field, 880 *Excursion* 8. 394
Or fret and labour on the Plain below. 885 *Excursion* 9. 92
To labour for them; bringing each in turn 888 *Excursion* 9. 268
In fresh abodes—their labour to renew; 889 *Excursion* 9. 374
Said, “ Father, 'tis lost labour; with your leave K.8. 228 **I will* 115
A mighty gain, that Labour here preserves K.8. 246 *Recluse* 1.1.359
That sweeten labour, make it seen and felt K.8. 249 *Recluse* 1.1.468

Laboured. And seldom needs a laboured roof; 168 *Wren's Nest* 6
As laboured minstrelsies through ages wear! 235 *Power of Sound* 174
And the one Man that laboured to enslave 277 **Haydon! let* 7
That not in vain they laboured to secure, 325 *Ode 1814* 146
Well did I watch, much laboured, nor had power 573 *Chiabrera* 3. 8
Zealously laboured to cut off my heart 735 *Prelude* 12. 79
And all the laboured novelties at best 829 *Excursion* 5. 437

Labourer. *See* **Fellow-labourer.**
Some labourer, thought he, may perchance be near; 25 *Guilt* 32
No labourer watched his red kiln glaring bright, 26 *Guilt* 141
Or the stooping labourer, 502 **Like a* 30
An easy seat this worn-out Labourer found 531 **I know* 10
Of labourer plodding for his daily gains, 546 **Oft is* 12
A geographic Labourer pitched his tent, 548 **Stay, bold* 14
So, like a home-bound labourer, I pursued 633 *Prelude* 1. 101
The labourer, and the old man who had sate 642 *Prelude* 2. 13
A sightless labourer, whistles at his work— 813 *Excursion* 4. 797
That, like this Labourer, such may dig their way, 842 *Excursion* 6. 259
A labourer, with moral virtue girt, 862 *Excursion* 7. 338

Labourer's. Of the mid harvest, when the labourer's hire 149 **A narrow* 52

Labourers. *See* **Fellow-labourers.**
Well have yon Railway Labourers to THIS ground 283 **Well have* 1
And labourers going forth to till the fields. 663 *Prelude* 4. 332
Twin labourers and heirs of the same hopes; 666 *Prelude* 5. 44
Shakespeare, or Milton, labourers divine! 668 *Prelude* 5. 165
Of firmer trust, joint labourers in the work 752 *Prelude* 14. 441

Laboureth. That laboureth his language to express, 553 *Prioress* 33

Labouring. Or rouse and agitate his labouring soul? 15 *Desc. Sk.* 292
Alas! the thing she told with labouring breath 35 *Guilt* 613
Labouring for her waxen cells, 161 **Pleasures newly* 44
They are labouring to avert 181 *Waggoner* 4. 89
Of triumph, how the labouring Danube bore 317 **The martial* 6
Shall represent her labouring with an eye 330 *Ode: Thanks.* 73
Lo! while I speak, the labouring Sun 343 *Eclipse* 61
Their Church reformed! labouring with earnest care 438 *Ecc. Sonn.* 2. 40. 4
Labouring as ever in your Master's sight, 444 *Ecc. Sonn.* 3. 16. 6
Albeit labouring for a scanty band 451 *Ecc. Sonn.* 3. 43. 3
The labouring and the resting few; 489 *Spade* 8
Flung by labouring Nature forth 502 **Like a* 5
Lost above all, ye labouring multitude! 505 *Warning* 112
Labouring for life, in hope and fear, 579 **Sweet Flower* 40
Felt only there, oppress his labouring soul, 608 *Desc.Sk.Quarto* 353
The labouring time of autumn, winter, spring, 658 *Prelude* 3. 630
And ignorance in the labouring multitude. 714 *Prelude* 9. 328
Labouring, a brain confounded, and a sense, 724 *Prelude* 10. 413
Murmured the labouring bee. When stormy winds 863 *Excursion* 7. 409
And the vast engine labouring in the mine, 866 *Excursion* 7. 608

Labour's. And wounds and weakness oft his labour's sole remains. 459 **Wanderer! that* 22
Prepared for never-resting Labour's eyes 877 *Excursion* 8. 168

Labours. Warm from the labours of benevolence 23 *Yew-tree* 40
The labours of my hand are still your joy; 67 *Bord.* 1640
And justice labours in extremity—. 321 **Here pause* 12
Whom I should choose for love and matchless labours. 372 *Eg. Maid* 228
By civil arts and labours of the pen, 389 *Sound of Mull* 10
Their labours end; or they return to lie, 430 *Ecc. Sonn.* 2. 8. 6
Conjures, implores, and labours all he can 444 *Ecc. Sonn.* 3. 18. 12
He labours good on good to fix, and owes 493 *Hap. War.* 33
The labours of the plough, 502 *Seasons* 10
By labours that have touched the hearts of kings, 509 *F. Stone* 101
That Hulk which labours in the deadly swell, 579 *Peele Castle* 47
To the strict labours of the merchant's desk 584 *Ch. Lamb* 5
Adding immortal labours of his own— 587 *Crosth.* 6
The labours of the Sun, the lunar wanderings; 625 *Æneid* 123
Of College labours, of the Lecturer's room 650 *Prelude* 3. 64
He deemed that my pursuits and labours lay 751 *Prelude* 14. 364
Where on the labours of the happy throng 819 *Excursion* 4. 1195
Of rural labours; the steep mountain-side 863 *Excursion* 7. 419
From out the labours of a peaceful Land 875 *Excursion* 8. 91
My future labours may not leave untold. 896 *Excursion* 9. 796

Labyrinth. Intricate labyrinth, more dread for thought 232 *Power of Sound* 5
A labyrinth, Lady! which your feet shall rove. 264 **Lady! the* 8
When, having thridded the long labyrinth 707 *Prelude* 8. 541

Labyrinthine. Or depth of labyrinthine glen; 298 *Brownie's Cell* 2
And labyrinthine walks, her sunny glades 810 *Excursion* 4. 590

Labyrinths. Conducted through those labyrinths, unawares, 690 *Prelude* 7. 185
Through what perplexing labyrinths, abrupt 800 *Excursion* 3. 982

Lac. Of Eau de Zurich, Lac Genève, S.3. 438 **My Lord* 16

Laced. And of the streaks that laced the severing clouds 123 *V. and J.* 93

Lacerated. The meek, benign, and lacerated face, 366 **Eternal Lord* 6

Lack. Thou wilt lack the only symbol 90 *Longest Day* 71
Lack any pleasure which a boy can know.” 136 *Michael* 356
“ These nether precincts do not lack 237 *P. B.* 86
Who hath no lack of wit mercurial; 245 *P. B.* 807
That he has power to inflict what we lack strength to bear. 319 *Spaniard* 14
Shall lack not power the “meeting soul to pierce!” 333 *Ded. Tour* 14
But not in scorn:—the Matron's Faith may lack 360 *Albano* 9
There lack not strange delusion here, 398 *White Doe* 213
Of conscience souls are placed by deeds that lack 475 **Here on their* 5
That shall lack a timely end, 495 *Force of Prayer* 66
But leave it thence to drop for lack of use: 520 *Pun. Death* 13. 13
Of waistcoats Harry has no lack, 536 *Goody Blake* 5
Dispel the Father's doubts: nor do they lack 541 *Grace Darl.* 46
Sick are they all for lack of their desire; 557 *Cuck. and Night.* 33
To lack that first great gift, the vital soul, 634 *Prelude* 1. 150
The lack of beard.—The weeks went roundly on, 649 *Prelude* 3. 42
Not that I slighted books,—that were to lack 654 *Prelude* 3. 364
By moonshine through mere lack of taper light. 656 *Prelude* 3. 478
It was denied them to acquire, through lack 757 *Excursion* 1. 82
Shall lack not their enjoyment:—but how faint 773 *Excursion* 2. 103
Our origin, what matters it? In lack 789 *Excursion* 3. 238
Lack virtue to receive; what I myself, 800 *Excursion* 3. 960
Of anguish unrelieved, and lack of power 803 *Excursion* 4. 167
That neither she nor Silence lack the power 816 *Excursion* 4. 1033
Through lack of converse; no—he must have found 844 *Excursion* 6. 384
Alas! 'twas other cause than lack of years L.I. 96 *Juvenal* 3. 61

Lacked. The hut stood finished by his pains, nor seemingly lacked aught 91 *Norman Boy* 17
Nor lacked his calmer hours device or toy 108 *Indolence* 50
To imprint a kiss that lacked not power to spread 119 *Maternal Grief* 61
That choice lacked courage to bestow! 215 *Kirkstone* 60
Into this world in days when story lacked 359 **Those old* 11
It lacked not old remains of hawthorn bowers, 377 *Duddon* 6. 2
One small possession lacked not power, 391 *HighlandBroach* 55
Nor lacked she Reason's firmest power; 415 *White Doe* 1777
But we, we lacked not music of our own, 523 *Epist. Beaumont* 156
And Heaven still lacked its due, though piety 627 **When Severn's* 7
Once more made trial of her strength, nor lacked 633 *Prelude* 1. 95
Transient and idle, lacked not intervals 663 *Prelude* 4. 347
Lacked not anticipations, tender dreams, 675 *Prelude* 6. 45
Which lacked not voice to welcome me in turn: 742 *Prelude* 13. 136

Laid—*continued.*
Thy curse is fixed; the truth must be laid bare. . 76 *Bord.* 2206
Those bright blue eggs together laid! . . . . 79 *Sparrow's Nest* 2
If two are in the church-yard laid, ... 84 *We are Seven* 35
"So in the church-yard she was laid; . . . . 84 *We are Seven* 53
When his corse is laid in earth. . . . . . 94 *Westmoreland Girl* 72
He laid his implements with gentle care, . . . 95 *Brothers* 33
His family were laid, he thence might learn . . 96 *Brothers* 82
Three years had Barbara in her grave been laid . 110 *'Tis said that some* 11
Laid him with timid care upon his knees, . . . 125 *V. and J.* 259
Of the garden-gate his hand was laid, he shrunk— 126 *V. and J.* 296
Those fields, those hills—what could they less? had laid . . . . 132 *Michael* 74
And, as his Father had requested, laid . . . . 137 *Michael* 419
So when the rain is over, the storm laid, . . . 143 **High bliss* 13
Where three thousand skulls are laid; . . . . 157 *Sexton* 6
The Seven are laid, and in the shade . . . . 161 *Binnorie* 25
All have laid their mirth aside. . . . . . . 171 *Kitten* 62
And all Seat-Sandal was laid bare! . . . . 176 *Waggoner* 1. 230
Laid down his whip—and served no more.— . . 182 *Waggoner* 4. 186
And, ages after he was laid in earth, ... 205 *Brougham* 171
Almost suspended, we are laid asleep . . . . 206 *Tintern* 45
Drawn in defiance of the Gods, hath laid . . . 214 *Dion* 108
Blest times when mystery is laid bare, . . . 226 *Present.* 68
"There is some plot against me laid;" . . . 241 *P. B.* 407
He on his knees hath laid him down, ... 243 *P. B.* 589
Here roving wild, he laid him down to rest . . 265 **Hail, Twilight* 7
Vain earth! false world! Foundations must be laid . . . . 269 *Malham* 10
Of Destiny, upon these wounds hath laid . . . 272 *Ruins* 5
And Love her towers of dread foundation laid . 282 **In my* 10
Where Burns is laid. . . . . 284 *Grave of Burns* 6
Where Man is laid, ... 285 *Grave of Burns* 76
By Ellen's side the Bruce is laid; . . . . . 287 *Ellen Irwin* 53
When earthly cares are laid asleep! . . . . 288 *Highland Girl* 14
Have rightfully been laid at last . . . . . 288 *Glen-Al.* 8
Lord of the vale! to Heroes laid . . . . . 299 *Cora Linn* 17
Whose vernal coverts winter hath laid bare. . . 304 **Jones! as* 14
On British ground the Invaders are laid low; . 310 *Anticip.* 2
That we must stand unpropped, or be laid low. . 310 **Another year* 8
Beneath his haughty feet, like clouds, are laid. . 317 **Look now* 8
And bloodshed, longed in quiet to be laid . . 320 **They seek* 13
Where their serene progenitors are laid; . . . 328 *Ode 1815* 60
By violence laid waste, ... 330 *Ode: Thanks.* 111
Upon a Sister's shoulder laid,— . . . . . 338 *Brientz* 13
And as in slumber laid,— . . . . 343 *Eclipse* 24
Virtues laid low, and mouldering energies. . . 360 *Alban Hills* 8
From the bleak isle where she is laid, ... 370 *Eg. Maid* 99
For infant in the cradle laid. . . . . . . 375 **The Minstrels* 48
For dormitory's length laid bare . . . . . 397 *White Doe* 122
The Lady's work;—but now laid low; . . . . 398 *White Doe* 235
And would have laid his purpose by, ... 401 *White Doe* 492
In the cold grave hath long been laid: . . . 405 *White Doe* 884
Beneath the cypress-spire is laid; . . . . . 407 *White Doe* 1002
The injunction by her Brother laid; . . . . 407 *White Doe* 1063
Be left, is no restriction laid; . . . . . . 408 *White Doe* 1089
Where Norton and his sons are laid! . . . . 408 *White Doe* 1129
"And so in Prison were they laid— . . . . 409 *White Doe* 1244
There let at least the gift be laid, ... 410 *White Doe* 1296
And life in death laid the heart bare?— . . . 411 *White Doe* 1425
The grave where Francis must be laid. . . . 412 *White Doe* 1525
And laid its head upon her knee, ... 414 *White Doe* 1654
Within some rocky cavern laid, ... 415 *White Doe* 1739
Of fret-work imagery laid low; . . . . . . 416 *White Doe* 1892
Whose arts and honours in the dust are laid . . 421 *Ecc. Sonn.* 1. 11. 8
From fields laid waste, from house and home devoured . . . . 426 *Ecc. Sonn.* 1. 32. 3
These sons of Amalek, or laid them low!"— . . 427 *Ecc. Sonn.* 1. 33. 8
Sceptre and mantle, sword and ring, laid down . 428 *Ecc. Sonn.* 1. 37. 11
Of Justice armed, and Pride to be laid low. . . 433 *Ecc. Sonn.* 2. 18. 14
And soothe the heart confession hath laid bare— 447 *Ecc. Sonn.* 3. 28. 7
The mortal weight cast off to be laid low. . . 448 *Ecc. Sonn.* 3. 31. 4
A tell-tale motion! soon will it be laid, . . . 454 *Sea-side* 5
Of Science laid them open to mankind— . . . 461 **Queen of* 41
Forth from their cells; their ancient House laid low 468 *St. Bees* 147
Bewailing his sad fate, when he was laid . . . 470 **A youth* 8
And, from invisible worlds at need laid bare, . . 475 **Here on their* 13
His kindred laid in earth, ... 487 *Fountain* 50
Who shall inherit Thee when death has laid . . 489 *Spade* 17
And willingly have laid thee here at last: . . . 491 *Tribute: Dog* 12
Depressed the melancholy Cowley, laid . . . 528 **Those breathing* 113
Laid one by one, or scattered on the ground. . . 531 **I know* 12
When temples, columns, towers, are laid in dust; 546 **Oft is* 2
In the last sanctity of fame is laid. . . . . . 546 **Ye Lime* 8
Methought she laid a grain upon my tongue. . . 556 *Prioress* 211
"Young Hew of Lincoln! in like sort laid low . 556 *Prioress* 233
Now farewell, old Adam! when low thou art laid, 571 *Farmer* 89
And, when beneath this stone the Corse was laid, 575 *Chiabrera* 8. 8
Here laid in mortal darkness, wouldst prefer . . 576 *Chiabrera* 9. 3
Two Babes were laid in earth before she died; . 576 **By a* 9
The bodily frame. That beauty is laid low . . 581 **Why should we* 9
That said, "Let praise be mute where I am laid;" 584 **With copious* 41
The skiffs with naked masts at anchor laid, . . 593 *Ev. Wk. Quarto* 105
Laid snares to make the babe her own. . . . 620 *Birth of Love* 31
To the cell where the convict is laid. . . . . 620 *Convict* 8
Laid safely by itself, beneath a Tree. . . . . 622 **Among all* 16
Where he on soft *amaracus* is laid, ... 624 *Æneid* 51
The thankfulness with which I laid me down . . 659 *Prelude* 4. 81

Laid—*continued.*
Safe from an evil which these days have laid . . 669 *Prelude* 5. 227
His helper and not theirs, laid stronger hold . . 717 *Prelude* 9. 506
Was laid with tears. Then suddenly the scene . 724 *Prelude* 10. 409
An honoured teacher of my youth was laid, . . 726 *Prelude* 10. 534
Of inward consciousness, and hope that laid . . 730 *Prelude* 11. 202
Oh, joy to him who here hath sown, hath laid . 749 *Prelude* 14. 219
Have been laid open, needs must make me feel . 752 *Prelude* 14. 422
So the foundations of his mind were laid. . . . 758 *Excursion* 1. 132
His calling laid aside, he lived at ease: . . . 762 *Excursion* 1. 386
By sorrow laid asleep; or borne away, . . . 768 *Excursion* 1. 786
That he broke faith with them whom he had laid 775 *Excursion* 2. 247
That laid their country waste. No need to speak 825 *Excursion* 5. 200
In whose dark vaults my own shall soon be laid, . 827 *Excursion* 5. 346
These that in trembling hope are laid apart; . . 836 *Excursion* 5. 953
That basis laid, those principles of faith . . . 839 *Excursion* 6. 88
Wherever laid, who living fell below . . . . 842 *Excursion* 6. 268
Him, farther off; the pair, who here are laid; . 842 *Excursion* 6. 272
Of kindred mould.—Such haply here are laid?". . 844 *Excursion* 6. 391
As now it shines, when we are laid in earth . . 849 *Excursion* 6. 765
Where injury cannot come:—and here is laid . . 854 *Excursion* 6. 1051
Where, Sir, I pray you, where are laid the bones . 854 *Excursion* 6. 1078
Laid open through the blazing window:—there . 856 *Excursion* 6. 1178
His parents laid in earth, no loss ensued . . . 864 *Excursion* 7. 432
To be laid open, and they prophesied. . . . . 865 *Excursion* 7. 533
That object is laid open to the view . . . . 887 *Excursion* 9. 216
"With such foundations laid, avaunt the fear . 889 *Excursion* 9. 363
You saw me, friends, you laid me here, . . . K.8. 220 **The snow-tracks* 33
To drink of the clear water, laid himself . . . K.8. 226 **I will* 55
Between ourselves! The noble laid aside), . . L.1. 97 *Juvenal* 3. 68
Christophe now is laid asleep . . . . . . L.2. 190 **Queen and* 2

Lain. Three lovely babes had lain upon my breast; 29 *Guilt* 264
That, as the day was warm, he had lain down . 101 *Brothers* 396
Compared with *hers* who long hath lain, . . . 144 **Driven in* 31
Ere thus I have lain couched an hour, . . . 158 **In youth* 42
When Ruth three seasons thus had lain, . . . 194 *Ruth* 205
And he had lain beside his asses . . . . . 239 *P. B.* 224
And sickness, listen where they long have lain, . 447 *Ecc. Sonn.* 3. 28. 3
True freedom where for ages they have lain . . 515 **Ah why* 3
I might have lain concealed, ... 545 *Russ. Fug.* 286
Had lain awake on summer nights to watch . . 659 *Prelude* 4. 87
For a whole day together, have I lain . . . . 673 *Prelude* 5. 483
Of the Carrousel, where so late had lain . . . 719 *Prelude* 10. 56
With searching damp, and seemingly had lain . 778 *Excursion* 2. 440

Lair. To Gordale-chasm, terrific as the lair . . 269 *Gordale* 5
Where stalked the huge deer to his shaggy lair . 376 *Duddon* 2. 11
Exults like him whose javelin from the lair . . 466 *St. Bees* 4
Your head in this dark lair!" . . . . . . 545 *Russ. Fug.* 320
Quits, growling, the white bones that strew his lair; 606 *Desc.Sk.Quarto* 232
And thought that, in the blind and awful lair . 668 *Prelude* 5. 151

Laird. In which the Scottish Laird had long possessed . . . . 845 *Excursion* 6. 456

Lairds. Sheriffs, and lairds and their domains, . . 291 *Rob Roy* 70

Lake. *See* **Lac, Lago.**
A fence far stretched into the shallow lake, . . 3 *Ev. Wk.* 42
And now the whole wide lake in deep repose . . 4 *Ev. Wk.* 124
'Tis pleasant near the tranquil lake to stray . . 6 *Ev. Wk.* 216
Rich golden verdure on the lake below. . . . 12 *Desc. Sk.* 102
—Thy lake that, streaked or dappled, blue or grey, 12 *Desc. Sk.* 119
Along the steaming lake, to early mass. . . . 13 *Desc. Sk.* 126
To sterner pleasure, where, by Uri's lake, . . . 14 *Desc. Sk.* 227
Up from the lake a zigzag path will creep . . . 14 *Desc. Sk.* 236
The wood-crowned cliffs that o'er the lake recline; 15 *Desc. Sk.* 278
Upon the bosom of a placid lake. . . . . . 80 **Loving she* 21
Only in the lake below. . . . . 93 *Westmoreland Girl* 16
Some hastened; some ran to the lake: ere noon . 101 *Brothers* 379
Whom from the borders of the Lake we brought, 106 *Farewell* 23
And every day the imprisoned lake . . . . 110 **Ere with* 15
And westward to the village near the lake; . . 133 *Michael* 135
That skimmed the surface of the dead calm lake, 148 **A narrow* 19
Angling beside the margin of the lake. . . . . 149 **A narrow* 49
A pittance from the dead unfeeling lake . . . 149 **A narrow* 65
Of Silver-how, and Grasmere's peaceful lake . . 151 **When, to* 91
O'er lake and stream, mountain and flowery mead, 151 **Forth from* 5
A lake was near; the shore was steep; . . . 162 *Binnorie* 49
The stream that flows out of the lake, ... 162 *Binnorie* 56
And, while they coast the silent lake, ... 178 *Waggoner* 3. 31
Earth, spangled sky, and lake serene, ... 178 *Waggoner* 3. 38
Beside the lake, beneath the trees, ... 187 **I wandered* 5
The lake doth glitter, ... 190 *March* 4
And many an endless, endless lake, ... 193 *Ruth* 68
O'er breezeless water, on Locarno's lake, . . . 212 *Dion*
A circuit ampler than the lake beneath, . . . 218 *Recluse* 1. 1. 209
Upon the lake below, ... 224 **'Tis gone* 9
The rocks, and quivering trees, and billowy lake, 230 *Clouds* 63
Wafted adown the wind from lake or stream; . 261 **I heard (alas* 4
The lake below reflects it not; the sky . . . 266 **Even as* 6
O'er Limbo lake with aery flight to steer, . . . 284 *Departure* 11
A murmur near the silent lake; . . . . . . 288 *Highland Girl* 8
The lake, the bay, the waterfall; . . . . . 288 *Highland Girl* 77
Was walking by her native lake: . . . . . . 289 *Stepping West.* 18
Whose mountains, torrents, lake, and woods, unite 290 *Kilchurn* 27
The swan on still St. Mary's Lake . . . . . 293 *Yarrow Unv.* 43
Beside a lake their cottage stood, ... 295 *Highland Boy* 51
For to this lake, by night and day, ... 295 *Highland Boy* 56
And swiftly down the running lake. . . . . . 297 *Highland Boy* 184
By Uri's lake, where Tell . . . . 300 *Cora Linn* 45
And, through her depths, Saint Mary's Lake . . 302 *Yarrow V.* 13
Was like a lake, or river bright and fair, . . . 306 **Inland, within* 6

Lark—*continued.*
And was; and hence this Song, which like a lark . . . 751 *Prelude* 14. 382
Rise with the lark! your matins shall obtain . 808 *Excursion* 4. 491
Lark's. And of the lark's note heard before its time, 123 *V. and J.* 92
Near the lark's nest, and in their natural hour . 475 **There! said* 11
Of the lark's flight,—or shaped a rainbow curve, . 868 *Excursion* 7. 743
Larks. In spite of all the larks that cheered our path, 39 *Bord.* 109
When Flowers rejoice and Larks with rival speed 462 **Where lies the truth* 7

Larum. *See* **Alarum.**
And ring a sharp 'larum;—but, if you should look, 80 †*Address: Child* 10
Who loudest rang his pulpit 'larum bell, . . . 442 *Ecc. Sonn.* 3. 11. 5
Hark to that second larum!—far and wide . . 457 **The leaves* 33
Larum-bell. His larum-bell from village-tow'r to tow'r . 616 *Desc.Sk.Quarto* 778
Lascars. Malays, Lascars, the Tartar, the Chinese, . 690 *Prelude* 7. 227
Lash. Dread swell of sound! loud as the gusts that lash . . . . 379 *Duddon* 13. 7
Lashed. Lashed the cool water with their restless tails, 3 *Ev. Wk.* 43
Lashed out of life, not quiet in the grave. . . . 153 *Morn. Ex.* 18
Lashes. Or where dank sea-weed lashes Scotland's shores; . . . . 21 *Desc. Sk.* 594
Lass. *See* **Shepherd-lass.**
The Lass with her barrow wheels hither her store;— 188 *Music* 22
Yon solitary Highland Lass! . . . . . . 289 *Sol. Reap.* 2
A blooming Lass—who in her better hand . . 523 *Epist. Beaumont* 107
Some sweet lass of the valley, looking out . . 699 *Prelude* 8. 38
Lasses. Had danced his round with Highland lasses; 239 *P. B.* 223
Of lasses and of shepherd grooms, ... 396 *White Doe* 11
Lassitude. And to beguile the lassitude of ease; . S.3.426 **Through Cumbrian* 6
Lassitudes. Regrets, vexations, lassitudes interfused 637 *Prelude* 1. 346
Last. Till the last banner of their long array . . 6 *Ev. Wk.* 208
Last evening sight, the cottage smoke, no more, . 8 *Ev. Wk.* 311
That glimmer hoar in eve's last light, descried 12 *Desc. Sk.* 115
To every charm, and last and chief to you, . . 13 *Desc. Sk.* 128
And its last echo, can be heard no more. . . 15 *Desc. Sk.* 253
And the last sunbeam fell on Bayard's eye; . . 16 *Desc. Sk.* 300
Last, let us turn to Chamouny that shields . . 20 *Desc. Sk.* 569
When, from the last hill-top, my sire surveyed, . 28 *Guilt* 236
What tender vows our last sad kiss delayed! . 29 *Guilt* 256
The parting signal streamed—at last the land withdrew. . . . . 29 *Guilt* 288
Seemed to return, dried the last lingering tear, . 30 *Guilt* 321
That I, at last, a resting-place had found; . . 31 *Guilt* 362
As if each blow were deadlier than the last, . 33 *Guilt* 474
With her last words, unable to suppress . . . 35 *Guilt* 617
Her last death-shriek, distinct among a thousand. 40 *Bord.* 187
This last request. You know me, Sire; farewell! 42 *Bord.* 295
But yesterday was worse than all; at last . . 45 *Bord.* 471
These walls shall witness it—from first to last . 48 *Bord.* 594
Becomes at last weak and contemptible. . . . 48 *Bord.* 620
He will deny it to the last. He lies . . . 54 *Bord.* 915
You are found at last, thanks to the vagrant Troop 56 *Bord.* 1018
You have not heard that Henry has at last . . 56 *Bord.* 1022
This last device must end my work.—Methinks . 58 *Bord.* 1145
It ever could be otherwise! Last night, . . . 59 *Bord.* 1180
Here to impart the tale, of which, last night, . . 59 *Bord.* 1210
Last night, when moved to lift the avenging steel, 59 *Bord.* 1213
Wherein I have offended you;—last night . . 60 *Bord.* 1280
His tool, the wandering Beggar, made last night 63 *Bord.* 1419
how could I disturb his last moments? . . . . 72 *Bord.* 1939
The first hours of last night were rough with storm: 73 *Bord.* 2043
With the disastrous issue of last night, . . . 76 *Bord.* 2235
The starts and sallies of our last encounter . . 77 *Bord.* 2278
All last summer, as well you know, ... 80 †*Address: Child* 26
Last forerunner of "Good night!" . . . . . 90 *Longest Day* 28
Of last night's snow, beneath a sky threatening the fall of more, ... 91 *Norman Boy* 10
Pleasure on pleasure crowded in, each livelier than the last. . . . . 92 *Poet's Dream* 44
Many a long look of wonder: and at last, . . 95 *Brothers* 30
Which he himself had worn. And now, at last, . 96 *Brothers* 65
—They were the last of all their race: and now, . 96 *Brothers* 76
Beneath yon ridge, the last of those three graves? 98 *Brothers* 198
Interest, and mortgages; at last he sank, . . 98 *Brothers* 215
God only knows, but to the very last . . . 98 *Brothers* 218
Living or dead.—When last we heard of him, . 100 *Brothers* 316
How did he die at last? One sweet May-morning, 101 *Brothers* 356
And thine too is the last green field . . . . 109 **I travelled* 15
The heaviest storms not longest last; . . . . 110 *Forsaken* 2
And my last thought would happy be; . . . . 114 *Ind. Wom.* 68
He is the last of all my flock. . . . . . . 115 *Last of Flock* 20
Reckless of what might come at last . . . . 115 *Last of Flock* 69
And then at last from three to two; . . . . 115 *Last of Flock* 94
It is the last of all my flock." . . . . . . 116 *Last of Flock* 100
When last he sailed, he left the bird behind; . . 119 *Sailor's Mother* 29
One Child did it bear, and that Child was his last. 120 *ChildlessFather* 12
That last, that sweetest smile of his? . . . . 121 *EmigrantMother* 64
Doomed to a third and last captivity, ... 124 *V. and J.* 185
For the last time, attendant by the side . . . 125 *V. and J.* 245
But of his father begged, a last request, . . . 125 *V. and J.* 267
The Tale I follow to its last recess . . . . . 125 *V. and J.* 281
The last of all her thoughts would be . . . . 129 *Idiot Boy* 310
The owls have hardly sung their last, ... 131 *Idiot Boy* 432
And I have lived to be a fool at last . . . . 134 *Michael* 235
By Michael's side, she through the last two nights 135 *Michael* 290
Befall thee, I shall love thee to the last, . . . 137 *Michael* 416
Fell on him, so that he was driven at last . . 138 *Michael* 446

Last—*continued.*
Before her eyes, last child of many gone— . . 139 *Widow* 17
Each word greedier than the last; . . . . . 141 *Arm. Lady* 106
The last that parleys with the setting sun; . . 148 **There is an* 2
A last year's nest, conspicuously built . . . . 150 **When, to* 21
To the last point of vision, and beyond, . . . 153 *Morn. Ex.* 43
But, seeing no relief, at last . . . . . . 155 *Waterfall* 19
Those accents were his last. . . . . . . 155 *Waterfall* 56
Last night I heard a crash—'tis true, ... 156 *Oak and Broom* 27
Bright *Flower!* for by that name at last, . . . 159 **With little* 41
My last year's friends together. . . . . . 159 *Green Linnet* 8
February last, my heart . . . . 160 **Pleasures newly* 3
This precious Flower, true love's last token. . . 164 **Fair Lady* 40
The last stone of a lonely hut; . . . . . 165 *Danish Boy* 8
Proved last year's leaves, pushed from the spray 170 *Rural Ill.* 11
Last king of rocky Cumberland; . . . . . . 176 *Waggoner* 1. 212
If such the bright amends at last. . . . . 177 *Waggoner* 2. 75
Among these hills, from first to last, ... 179 *Waggoner* 3. 79
Last and foremost, every horse . . . . . . 181 *Waggoner* 4. 100
Says nothing—till at last he spies . . . . 181 *Waggoner* 4. 173
Last Christmas-eve we talked of this, ... 199 *Thorn* 137
And, when at last her time drew near, . . . 199 *Thorn* 142
And with the last deep groan his breath had fetched 201 *Hart-leap* 43
The last stone-pillar on a dark hill-top. . . . 202 *Hart-leap* 108
Are but three bounds—and look, Sir, at this last— 203 *Hart-leap* 143
The red rose is revived at last; . . . . . 203 *Brougham* 8
The last she to her Babe did say: . . . . . 204 *Brougham* 83
A last infirmity betrays, ... 216 *Enterprise* 50
Unbosom their last mysteries. . . . . . . 216 *Enterprise* 88
"Last of the Three, though eldest born, . . . 222 *Triad* 174
To pause at last on more aspiring heights . . . 230 *Clouds* 21
Devoutly, in life's last retreats! . . . . . 232 *Power of Sound* 16
Where men were monsters. A last grace he craves, 234 *Power of Sound* 133
We've reached at last the promised Tale;) . . 240 *P. B.* 322
In his last sleep securely bound! . . . . . 242 *P. B.* 552
And hither is he come at last, ... 243 *P. B.* 646
And now at last it dies away. . . . . . . 244 *P. B.* 670
Still last to come where thou art wanted most! . 253 **Fond words* 14
Even thus last night, and two nights more, I lay 253 **A flock* 9
Of all things, that at last in fear I shrink, . . 260 **How sweet* 13
At last, of hindrance and obscurity, ... 265 **There is a pleasure* 10
'Gainst him who raised it,—his last work on earth: 276 *Filial Piety* 7
On ground yet strewn with their last battle's wreck; 278 *Wellington* 2
Feed to the last on pleasures ever new? . . . 278 **Life with* 14
Love pitying innocence, not long to last, . . . 280 **Oh what* 13
Reader, farewell! My last words let them be— . 281 *Valedict.* 10
Ere we lie down in our last dormitory? . . . 281 **What strong* 14
So, coming his last help to crave, ... 287 *Ellen Irwin* 45
Continued long as life shall last. . . . . . 288 *Highland Girl* 71
Have rightfully been laid at last . . . . . 288 *Glen-Al.* 8
That Ossian, last of all his race! . . . . . 289 *Glen-Al.* 31
With them no strife can last; they live . . . 291 *Rob Roy* 35
As long as earth shall last. . . . . 295 *Highland Boy* 65
That he is safe at last. . . . . 297 *Highland Boy* 220
The last that dare to struggle with the Foe. . . 310 **Another year* 4
The roving Spanish Bands are reached at last, . 320 **Hunger, and* 5
Recall a Sister's last embrace, ... 342 *Ital. Itin.* 33
Of his last going from Tweed-side, thought turned, 353 *Aquap.* 67
Though even to their last syllable the Lays . . 356 *Aquap.* 275
This thy last haunt beneath Italian skies . . . 363 **List—'twas* 100
Fond wish that was granted at last, and the Flood, 364 *Vallomb.* 3
Thy present birth-morn with thy last, so fair, . 367 **If with* 5
For in that face they saw the last . . . . . 372 *Eg. Maid* 196
Last lingering look of clay, that tames . . . 372 *Eg. Maid* 197
By the "last Minstrel," (not the last!) . . . 386 *Yarrow Rev.* 103
Vexed is he, and screams loud. The last I saw . 388 *Eagles* 4
Still pity to this last retreat . . . . . . 390 *Highland Broach* 45
Will vanish the last Highland Broach. . . . 391 *Highland Broach* 78
And this forgotten Taper to the last . . . . 391 *Brownie* 13
On her last thorn the nightly moon has shone; . 393 *Inglewood* 4
Each desperately sustaining, till at last . . . 393 *Hart's-horn* 6
Their last embrace; beside those crystal springs . 393 **The Lovers* 2
Troubling the last holds of ambitious Rome, . . 394 **How profitless* 2
And thus she fares, until at last . . . . . 397 *White Doe* 140
It is the last, the parting song; . . . . . 397 *White Doe* 158
And last, the Doe herself is gone. . . . . . 399 *White Doe* 323
Her last companion in a dearth . . . . . . 400 *White Doe* 344
The last leaf on a blasted tree; . . . . . . 402 *White Doe* 567
Stung with sharp thoughts; and, ere the last . . 406 *White Doe* 893
His last words in the yew-tree shade, ... 406 *White Doe* 976
He was their comfort to the last, ... 409 *White Doe* 1220
Even to the last—one effort more . . . . . 410 *White Doe* 1284
My Son, the last wish of my heart. . . . . 410 *White Doe* 1287
Is that the Sufferer's last retreat? . . . . . 413 *White Doe* 1561
For this her last and living Friend. . . . . 415 *White Doe* 1796
Where Francis slept in his last abode. . . . . 416 *White Doe* 1818
The last dear service of thy passing breath! . . 424 *Ecc. Sonn.* 1. 23. 14
Last night, without a voice, that Vision spake . 440 *Ecc. Sonn.* 3. 2. 1
A last farewell, their loved abodes forsook, . . 443 *Ecc. Sonn.* 3. 13. 3
One duty more, last stage of this ascent, . . . 446 *Ecc. Sonn.* 3. 25. 2
As a last token of man's toilsome day! . . . 453 **Calm is the* 32
And a last game of mazy hoverings . . . . 455 *Rydal Mere* 10
Oh may this work have found its last retreat . 461 **Giordano, verily* 9
If that be reverenced which ought to last. . . 463 **Why should the* 14
Yet I at last a resting-place have found, . . . 470 †*From early* 9
Though smiling on the last hill-top! . . . . 473 *Ossian* 72
Smiting, as if each moment were their last. . . 474 **Hope smiled* 6
Which you last April made!" . . . . . . 487 *Fountain* 16
His rustic chimney with the last of Thee! . . 490 *Spade* 32
And willingly have laid thee here at last: . . 491 *Tribute: Dog* 12

Laura's. On Laura's breast, in exquisite repose ; . 377 *Duddon* 7. 4
Laureat. Those laureat wreaths ungathered which the Nymphs . . . . 576 *Chiabrera* 9. 13
Laureate. No Laureate offering of elaborate art ; . 628 **Deign, Sovereign* 2
Laureate's. And this too from the Laureate's Child, 164 *Needlecase* 13
Laurel. Then, like a hero crowned with laurel, . . 178 *Waggoner* 2. 159
With leaves of laurel stuck about ; . . . . . 191 *Beggars* 26
And to her sister Clio's laurel wreath, ... 227 *Vernal Ode* 78
Of hardy laurel and wild holly boughs— . . . 324 *Ode 1814* 45
A laurel in the grove. . . . . 543 *Russ. Fug.* 184
His brow with laurel green ; . . . . . . 543 *Russ. Fug.* 186
With laurel chaplets crowned. . . . . . . 543 *Russ. Fug.* 192
With laurel planted upon hoary hairs, ... 816 *Excursion* 4. 998
Fenced round with glittering laurel ; or in that . 832 *Excursion* 5. 644
Laurelled. The laurelled Dante's favourite seat. A throne, ... 365 **Under the* 5
Then sceptred king or laurelled conqueror knows, 387 *Scott* 11
And laurelled armies, not to be withstood— . . 450 *Ecc. Sonn.* 3. 38. 2
The Despot's laurelled brow ? . . . . . 628 *Installation* 12
Laurels. The encircling laurels, thick with leaves, . 375 **The Minstrels* 4
Sweet pastoral flowers, and laurels that have crowned . . . . 418 *Ecc. Sonn.* 1. 1. 11
Adieu, Rydalian Laurels ! that have grown . . 463 **Adieu, Rydalian* 1
Laurels to some, a night-shade wreath to thee, . S.3. 432 **Critics, right* 2
Laurel-shaded. And, by the Poet's laurel-shaded tomb, ... 356 *Aquap.* 267
Laus. "Laus Deo." Many a Stranger passing by 394 *Countess' Pillar* 10
Lave. The azure brooks, where Dian joys to lave . 264 **Lady ! I* 5
A sea-green river, proud to lave, ... 348 **Lulled by* 34
At piece inverted your lithe necks ye lave, . . 596 *Ev. Wk. Quarto* 235
Laverna. Fior see, Laverna ! mark the far-famed Pile, ... 362 **List—'twas* 29
Laves. Behold, how wantonly she laves . . . 370 *Eg. Maid* 43
Where Tiber's stream the immortal City laves : . 421 *Ecc. Sonn.* 1. 13. 4
Lavish. Bold, and lavish of thyself ; . . . . 160 **Pansies, lilies* 18
Such (but O lavish Nature ! why . . . . . 344 **How blest* 14
Of myriads and boon nature's lavish help ; . . 700 *Prelude* 8. 81
Her lavish pomp, and ripe magnificence ? . . . 828 *Excursion* 5. 402
Lo ! Smiling Nature's lavish hand . . . . . S.3.431 **The Scottish* 31
Lavished. Of glory lavished on our quiet days. . . 282 **Wansfell ! this* 8
Lavished in fight with desperate hardihood ; . . 322 **By Moscow* 3
Lavished on *Him*—that England may rebel . . 443 *Ecc. Sonn.* 3. 11. 8
You lavished on me when a child . . . . . 542 *Russ. Fug.* 59
Lavishing. With bright jonquils, their odours lavishing . . . . 264 *Snowdrop* 10
Lavishly. Hence, for this Favourite—lavishly endowed . . . . 843 *Excursion* 6. 304
Had lavishly arrayed him. As old bards . . . 868 *Excursion* 7. 728
Law. *See* **Sword-law.**
Confessed no law but what his reason taught, . 18 *Desc. Sk.* 437
"Bad is the world, and hard is the world's law . 33 *Guilt* 505
But the pretended Father—— Earthly law . 47 *Bord.* 582
No law but what each man makes for himself ; . 48 *Bord.* 597
Shall it be law to stab the petty robber . . . 53 *Bord.* 894
He recks not human law ; and I have noticed . 63 *Bord.* 1437
You have obeyed the only law that sense . . . 64 *Bord.* 1493
Submits to recognise ; the immediate law, . . . 64 *Bord.* 1494
'Tis Nature's law. What I have done in darkness 71 *Bord.* 1877
Of law and holiest sympathy, ... 113 *Lament* 52
His person to the law, was lodged in prison, . . 123 *V. and J.* 134
Remember she follows the law of her kind, . . 142 †*Lov. and Lik.* 43
Prevailed a like indulgent law . . . . . 154 *Flower Garden* 9
Both law and impulse : and with me . . . . 187 **Three years* 8
With men to whom no better law . . . . . 194 *Ruth* 146
Nature, from thy genuine law ! . . . . . 222 *Triad* 155
Trust in that sovereign law can spread . . . 224 **'Tis gone* 58
Ward of the Law !—dread Shadow of a King ! . 271 *George : Death* 1
Law but a servile dupe of false pretence, . . . 280 *Plea for Auth.* 5
"We have a passion—make a law, ... 291 *Rob Roy* 25
And for the law itself we fight . . . . . 291 *Rob Roy* 27
Judge thou of law and fact ! . . . . . . 291 *Rob Roy* 80
And law was from necessity received. . . . . 316 **Hail, Zaragoza* 14
Thy law, and live henceforth in peace, in pure good will. . . . . 329 *Ode 1815* 128
Of disobedience to the primal law. . . . . 343 *Last Sup.* 8
Of vital principle's controlling law, ... 357 *Aquap.* 335
Dishonoured Rock and Ruin ! that, by law . . 388 *Eagles* 1
And all the assembly own a law . . . . . 399 *White Doe* 320
Raised far above the law of kind ; . . . . . 416 *White Doe* 1878
These jealous Ministers of law aspire, ... 419 *Ecc. Sonn.* 1. 4. 7
He made by wilful breach of law divine. . . . 428 *Ecc. Sonn.* 2. 1. 4
Swerves not—diverted by a casual law. . . . 442 *Ecc. Sonn.* 3. 9. 8
Why keep *we* else the instincts whose dread law . 474 **Ye shadowy* 10
A soul of love, love's intellectual law :— . . . 491 *Tribute : Dog* 33
Thou, who art victory and law . . . . . . 492 *Duty* 5
—'Tis he whose law is reason ; who depends . . 493 *Hap. War.* 27
Upon that law as on the best of friends ; . . . 493 *Hap. War.* 28
And, through the heat of conflict, keeps the law . 493 *Hap. War.* 53
Of subtle Treason, in his mask of law, . . . 504 *Warning* 102
Learn to be just, just through impartial law ; . 516 **Feel for* 11
Tenderly do we feel by Nature's law . . . . 517 *Pun. Death* 2. 1
And all who from the law firm safety crave. . . 517 *Pun. Death* 2. 14
Patience *his* law, long-suffering *his* school, . . 518 *Pun. Death* 7. 7
Sanctions the forfeiture that Law demands, . . 519 *Pun. Death* 11. 10
Advancing Summer, Nature's law fulfilled, . . 523 *Epist. Beaumont* 154
From champions of the desperate law . . . . 534 **Blest is* 75
And after that he hung them by the law. . . . 555 *Prioress* 183
Said this young Child, 'and by the law of kind . 556 *Prioress* 199
Ay, quoth the Cuckoo, that is a quaint law, . . 559 *Cuck.and Night.* 136
A burthen of the earth ! 'Tis Nature's law . . 567 *Cumb. Beg.* 73

Law—*continued.*
No self-reproach ; who of the moral law . . . 568 *Cumb. Beg.* 136
The good which the benignant law of Heaven . 568 *Cumb. Beg.* 167
Spurn Reason's law and humour Passion's rage ; . 618 *School Ex.* 10
Reflective acts to fix the moral law . . . . 650 *Prelude* 3. 84
That have no law, no meaning, and no end— . 698 *Prelude* 7. 728
To reason well of polity or law, ... 712 *Prelude* 9. 199
Is law for all, and of that barren pride . . . 717 *Prelude* 9. 503
Captivity by mandate without law . . . . 717 *Prelude* 9. 536
Nature's rebellion against monstrous law ; . . 717 *Prelude* 9. 571
Power had reverted : habit, custom, law, . . 727 *Prelude* 11. 32
Thirsting to make the guardian crook of law . 728 *Prelude* 11. 64
Of custom, law, and statute, took at once . . 729 *Prelude* 11. 111
Disgrace, of which, custom and written law, . . 731 *Prelude* 11. 263
And, to acknowledged law rebellious, still, . . 732 *Prelude* 11. 318
To Conscience only, and the law supreme . . 755 *Recluse* 1. 1. 774
For calm subjection to acknowledged law ; . . 790 *Excursion* 3. 268
Subsisting under nature's steadfast law. . . 791 *Excursion* 3. 391
The appointed seat of equitable law . . . . 796 *Excursion* 3. 715
Remorseless, and submissive to no law . . . 800 *Excursion* 3. 954
To yield entire submission to the law . . . 804 *Excursion* 4. 224
Prevents me not from owning, that the law, . . 805 *Excursion* 4. 303
The law that governs each ; and where begins 806 *Excursion* 4. 335
The law of duty ; and can therefore move . . 816 *Excursion* 4. 1036
Acknowledge reason's law ? A living power . . 829 *Excursion* 5. 471
The will to reason's law, can strictliest live . . 830 *Excursion* 5. 518
To exclaim—' O happy ! yielding to the law . . 835 *Excursion* 5. 828
Whose steps are equity, whose seat is law. . . 838 *Excursion* 6. 5
And by this law the mighty whole subsists : . . 872 *Excursion* 7. 1004
By sword and lance the law of gentleness, . . 873 *Excursion* 7. 1044
Upon the moral law. Egyptian Thebes, . . . 877 *Excursion* 8. 216
Of sottish vice or desperate breach of law, . . 880 *Excursion* 8. 423
Was Man created ; but to obey the law . . . 886 *Excursion* 9. 127
That power, that influence, by impartial law. . 887 *Excursion* 9. 220
Through mutual injury ! Rather in the law . . 889 *Excursion* 9. 366
The sting of human nature. Spread the law, . 893 *Excursion* 9. 639
Be happy in himself ?—The law of faith . . . 894 *Excursion* 9. 672
Relinquishing, but treasuring every law . . . S.3. 437 **The doubt* 188
Unless resolved in mercy to the law . . . . L.1. 95 *Juvenal* 3. 22
Lawful. Sweet heaven forefend ! his was a lawful right ; . . . . 108 *Indolence* 46
Look fairly like a lawful earning. . . . . . 177 *Waggoner* 2. 40
His board with lawful joy, and bear . . . . 193 *Ruth* 113
Its lawful sway. . . . . 286 *Sons of Burns* 12
And glad acknowledgment, of lawful sway. . . 383 *Duddon* 29. 14
Her lawful offspring in Man's art ; and Time, . 477 *Steamboats* 11
If doomed to breathe against his lawful will . . 528 **Those breathing* 77
Lawgiver. Stern Lawgiver ! yet thou dost wear . 492 *Duty* 41
By the almighty Lawgiver pronounced . . . 878 *Excursion* 8. 248
Lawgivers. Those lofty-minded Lawgivers shall meet, 319 *Guernica* 12
To be *most* dreaded ? Lawgivers, beware, . . 518 *Pun. Death* 4. 6
By ancient lawgivers. In this frame of mind, . 721 *Prelude* 10. 221
Are at its centre, British Lawgivers ; . . . . 890 *Excursion* 9. 399
Lawless. By lawless curiosity or chance, . . . 36 *Guilt* 663
As lawless as before. . . . . 194 *Ruth* 186
Dwell fruitless day-dreams, lawless prayer, . . 223 *Wishing-gate* 8
"Of all that lead a lawless life, ... 239 *P. B.* 276
Of all that love their lawless lives, ... 239 *P. B.* 277
Of lawless will, unlooked-for streams of good, . 271 *Henry : Portrait* 13
And, sterenuous to protect from lawless harms . 276 **Chatsworth ! thy* 13
Suffered or done. When lawless violence . . 316 **Say, what* 5
O joyless power that stands by lawless force ! . 317 **Look now* 9
Peace that should claim respect from lawless Might. 323 **Now that* 8
And to celerities of lawless force ; . . . . . 330 *Ode : Thanks.* 118
Full oft the unworthy brow of lawless force ; . . 418 *Ecc. Sonn.* 1. 1. 12
These spreading towns a cloak for lawless will ? . 464 **They called* 12
Through lawless will the Brotherhood was driven 468 *St. Bees* 146
All vain desires, all lawless wishes quelled, . . 511 **So fair* 19
I spurned his lawless suit, ... 542 *Russ. Fug.* 68
Retain his lawless will, ... 545 *Russ. Fug.* 310
Lawn. *See* **Forest-lawn.**
Of bright obscurity, hill, lawn, and wood ; . . 4 *Ev. Wk.* 101
Each slip of lawn the broken rocks between . 5 *Ev. Wk.* 178
Have you espied upon a dewy lawn . . . 118 *Maternal Grief* 27
I see him sporting on the sunny lawn ; . . . 124 *V. and J.* 204
A track, that brought us to a slip of lawn, . . 149 *M. H.* 6
The daisy sleeps upon the dewy lawn, ... 153 *Morn. Ex.* 25
That at my will burns on the dewy lawn, . . . 167 *Pilgrim's Dream* 43
Thence look thou forth o'er wood and lawn . . 180 *Waggoner* 4. 38
Crag, lawn, and wood—with rosy light. . . . 182 *Waggoner* 4. 243
That wild with glee across the lawn . . . 187 **Three years* 14
Doth hurry to the lawn ; . . . . 217 *Enterprise* 143
Which by their aid re-clothe the naked lawn . . 230 *Clouds* 67
And these grey rocks ; that household lawn ; . . 288 *Highland Girl* 5
I love, where spreads the village lawn, . . . 337 *Cath. Cantons* 7
Porlezza's verdant lawn. . . . . 343 *Eclipse* 36
Bright sunbeams—the fresh verdure of this lawn 352 *Aquap.* 16
Long has the dew been dried on tree and lawn ; . 360 **Long has* 1
The crowd of daisies from the shaven lawn, . . 456 **Soft as* 9
Thy nymph-like step swift-bounding o'er the lawn, 496 **A little* 18
In youth we love the darksome lawn . . . . 497 *Lycoris* 19
This Lawn, a carpet all alive . . . . . . 499 **This Lawn* 1
For May is on the lawn. . . . . 506 **While from* 4
If, mixed with what appeared of rock, lawn, wood, 524 *Epist. Beaumont* 187
Till to a lawn I came all white and green, . . 557 *Cuck.and Night.* 61
Each speck of lawn the broken rocks between ; . 594 *Ev. Wk. Quarto* 162
How fair it's lawn and silvery woods appear ! . 599 *Ev. Wk. Quarto* 417
Shut up in lesser lakes or beds of lawn . . . 702 *Prelude* 8. 194
Across the lawn and through the darksome grove, 814 *Excursion* 4. 866
And, up the flowery lawn as we advance, . . . 881 *Excursion* 8. 497

Lawn—*continued.*
Or range the grassy lawn in vacancy ; 888 *Excursion* 9. 262
Lawn-robed. While on each head his lawn-robed servant lays 446 *Ecc. Sonn.* 3. 23. 9
Lawns. O'er all its vanished dells, and lawns, and woods ; 8 *Ev. Wk.* 332
How fair its lawns and sheltering woods appear ! 8 *Ev. Wk.* 349
Spires, rocks, and lawns a browner night o'erspreads ; 11 *Desc. Sk.* 64
'Mid lawns and shades by breezy rivulets fanned, 21 *Desc. Sk.* 576
Nor through their sunny lawns have strayed ? 164 **Fair Lady* 4
Lawns, houses, chattels, groves, and fields, 214 *Kirkstone* 27
With lawns and beds of flowers, and shades 407 *White Doe* 985
Calm huts, and lawns between, and sylvan slopes. 607 *Desc.Sk.Quarto* 264
Of cabins, woods, and lawns a pleasant shore 611 *Desc.Sk.Quarto* 502
Here lawns and shades by breezy rivulets fann'd, 614 *Desc.Sk.Quarto* 686
Upon the open lawns ! Vallombre's groves 682 *Prelude* 6. 480
Or Indian cabins over the fresh lawns 683 *Prelude* 6. 522
A sumptuous dream of flowery lawns, with domes 700 *Prelude* 8. 84
To watch the spreading lawns with cattle grazed, K.8. 249 *Recluse* 1.1.481
Law's. Speaking through Law's dispassionate voice the State 519 *Pun. Death* 9. 9
Strike not from Law's firm hand that awful rod, 520 *Pun. Death* 13. 12
Laws. Of actions, and their laws and tendencies. 60 *Bord.* 1227
Laws, but we ask not whence those laws have come ; 70 *Bord.* 1858
By laws to which all Forms submit 112 **Yes ! thou* 11
To solve the mystery, not in Nature's laws 170 **Never enlivened* 17
But through dependence on the sacred laws 213 *Dion* 48
For me, who under kindlier laws belong 263 **While not* 9
Spake laws to *them*, and said that by the soul 306 **Inland, within* 13
And pure religion breathing household laws. 307 **O Friend* 14
We know the arduous strife, the eternal laws 316 **O'er the* 10
Of them who in Thy laws delight : 328 *Ode 1815* 111
Of the round world, and built, by laws as strong, 329 *Ode : Thanks.* 48
Which to unequal laws gave birth, 342 *Ital. Itin.* 77
Where they survive, of wholesome laws ; 376 **The Minstrels* 56
When laws, and creeds, and people all are lost ! 421 *Ecc. Sonn.* 1. 12. 14
Old laws, and ancient customs to derange, 426 *Ecc. Sonn.* 1. 31. 13
And sift her laws—much wondering that the wrong, 435 *Ecc. Sonn.* 2. 29. 7
The Altar calls ; come early under laws 446 *Ecc. Sonn.* 3. 25. 11
And strive to fathom the mysterious laws 468 **Ranging the* 3
That age, when not by *laws* inanimate, 469 **Bold words* 9
Of periods fixed, and laws established, less 469 **Desire we* 13
The laws to promulgate, enrobed and crowned ; 471 *Tynwald* 4
Mechanic laws to agency divine ; 473 **Thanks for* 3
Some silent laws our hearts will make, 483 *Sister* 29
" But we are pressed by heavy laws ; 487 *Fountain* 45
Whose everlasting laws, sea, earth, and heaven obey." 495 *Fact* 14
Shame that our laws at distance still protect 501 *Humanity* 81
Lest Fancy trifle with eternal laws. 501 *Humanity* 100
Laws that lay under Heaven's perpetual ban 514 **Portentous change* 12
By laws immutable. But woe for him 514 **Who ponders* 9
Rights equal, laws with cheerfulness obeyed, 515 *Penn.* 3
In progress, under laws divine, maintained. 538 **In desultory* 55
Which is against the reverence of our laws !' 554 *Prioress* 113
Under God's restraining laws. 628 *Installation* 16
And left their usages, their arts and laws, 635 *Prelude* 1. 193
Not heedlessly, the laws, and watched the forms 676 *Prelude* 6. 101
To Nature's laws, and by what process led, 677 *Prelude* 6. 124
To note the laws and progress of belief ; 691 *Prelude* 7. 276
Of Institutes and Laws, hallowed by time ; 695 *Prelude* 7. 526
With arts and laws so tempered, that their lives 701 *Prelude* 8. 130
In framing their own laws ; whence better days 717 *Prelude* 9. 531
In vision, yet constrained by natural laws 724 *Prelude* 10. 438
Upon their laws, and fashion of the State. 728 *Prelude* 11. 104
Which, to the blind restraints of general laws 731 *Prelude* 11. 241
O Soul of Nature ! that, by laws divine 735 *Prelude* 12. 102
Her processes by steadfast laws ; gives birth 740 *Prelude* 13. 23
Made visible ; as ruled by those fixed laws 745 *Prelude* 13. 372
Of science, and among her simplest laws, 760 *Excursion* 1. 271
The peace required, he scanned the laws of light 760 *Excursion* 1. 294
Social and temporal ; but in laws divine, 775 *Excursion* 2. 239
The thunder's greeting. Nor have nature's laws 782 *Excursion* 2. 708
Upon the laws of public charity. 783 *Excursion* 2. 740
Of the pure intellect, that stand as laws 802 *Excursion* 4. 97
Their duties from all forms ; and general laws, 820 *Excursion* 4. 1240
From us to infringe the laws of charity. 847 *Excursion* 6. 590
To impose severe restraints and laws unjust, 852 *Excursion* 6. 955
Her temper changed, and bowed to other laws) 873 *Excursion* 7. 1020
Laws overturned ; and territory split, 889 *Excursion* 9. 339
Gave to Athens equal laws. S.3. 442 *Harmodius* 8
Gave to Athens equal laws. S.3. 442 *Harmodius* 28
But ye who make our manners laws, and hence L.1. 97 *Juvenal* 3. 75
Lawyer. If there's a lawyer in the land, the knave 46 *Bord.* 488
A Lawyer art thou ?—draw not nigh ! 485 *Poet's Epitaph* 5
Lawyers. Lords, lawyers, statesmen, squires of low degree, 303 **Is it* 3
Where from their airy lodges studious lawyers 690 *Prelude* 7. 187
I mean the brawls of lawyers in their courts 694 *Prelude* 7. 490
Lax. Lax, buoyant—less a pastor with his flock 774 *Excursion* 2. 183
Laxity. A laxity that could not but impair 518 *Pun. Death* 6. 7
Lay. *See* **After-lay, Waylay.**
I see her now, denied to lay her head, 7 *Ev. Wk.* 256
Oft has she taught them on her lap to lay 7 *Ev. Wk.* 264
He fell, and without sense or motion lay ; 26 *Guilt* 89
The unburied dead that lay in festering heaps, 30 *Guilt* 345
I lay where, with his drowsy mates, the cock 31 *Guilt* 374
" Borne to a hospital, I lay with brain 31 *Guilt* 388

Lay—*continued.*
Of that perpetual weight which on her spirit lay. 32 *Guilt* 450
And, pointing to a little child that lay 33 *Guilt* 470
Softly he stroked the child, who lay outstretched 33 *Guilt* 487
As the wain fronted her,—wherein lay one, 34 *Guilt* 544
Borne gently to a bed, in death she lay ; 36 *Guilt* 626
The floor as he lay shuddering on his bed ; 36 *Guilt* 638
Was soft and warm, no dew lay on the grass, 39 *Bord.* 116
We lay becalmed week after week, until 68 *Bord.* 1693
Lay passive as a dormouse in mid winter. 69 *Bord.* 1767
I will assist you to lay hands upon him. 73 *Bord.* 2031
Forth-startled from the fern where she lay couched ; 80 **Loving she* 16
In bed she moaning lay, 84 *We are Seven* 50
They built him of stones gathered up as they lay : 86 *Rural Arch.* 7
Lay buried side by side as now they lie, 98 *Brothers* 228
And lay his bones among us. If that day 100 *Brothers* 325
Lay stretched at ease ; but, passing by the place 101 *Brothers* 371
Lay in concealment with his scanty train, 103 *Artegal* 99
Retired in that sunshiny shade he lay ; 107 *Indolence* 26
Or lay upon the moss by brook or tree, 108 *Indolence* 38
Long blades of grass, plucked round him as he lay, 108 *Indolence* 56
For strong and without pain I lay, 114 *Ind. Wom.* 29
This Child, I chanted to myself a lay, 120 *Emigrant Mother* 10
Dear Baby ! I must lay thee down ; 121 *Emigrant Mother* 59
But whatsoe'er of such rare treasure lay 122 *V. and J.* 34
To lay his hands upon a star, 129 *Idiot Boy* 320
Long time lay Susan lost in thought ; 130 *Idiot Boy* 412
Scared them, while they lay still beneath the shears. 134 *Michael* 176
To stop her in her work : for, when she lay 135 *Michael* 289
Lay thrown together, ready for the work. 136 *Michael* 328
It is a work for me. But, lay one stone— 137 *Michael* 386
Here, lay it for me, Luke, with thine own hands. 137 *Michael* 387
My purposes. Lay now the corner-stone, 137 *Michael* 403
Of whom I sing this rustic lay, 174 *Waggoner* 1. 94
Here lay the French—and *thus* came we !" 178 *Waggoner* 2. 134
Where he lay, watchful as a dragon, 178 *Waggoner* 2. 151
—Said Benjamin, " This whip shall lay 179 *Waggoner* 3. 116
Lay round me, scattered like a flock of sheep— 185 *Nutting* 37
Among thy branches safe he lay, 204 *Brougham* 99
What time the fleet at Aulis lay enchained. 211 *Laod.* 120
And on the palace-floor a lifeless corse She lay. 211 *Laod.* 157
Who that hath loved thee, but would lay 221 *Triad* 73
Like morning mist : and, where it lay, 225 *Present.* 28
Where'er a knot of houses lay 239 *P. B.* 233
He lay beneath the branches high, 239 *P. B.* 262
Massy and black, before him lay ; 240 *P. B.* 357
And, while he lay like one that mourned, 241 *P. B.* 433
With legs stretched out and stiff he lay :— 241 *P. B.* 451
The meagre beast lay still as death ; 241 *P. B.* 456
Whereat from the earth on which he lay 241 *P. B.* 462
And that her Husband now lay dead, 248 *P. B.* 1038
Even thus last night, and two nights more, I lay 253 **A flock* 9
A grateful few, shall love thy modest Lay, 254 *Dyer* 11
Getting and spending, we lay waste our powers : 259 **The world is* 2
Convinced that there, there only, she can lay 259 **A volant* 7
With groves that never were imagined, lay 262 **Dark and* 10
On the crushed heart a heavier burthen lay. 267 **As the* 8
Elsewhere unmatched, her ever-varying lay ; 271 **Fame tells* 4
Lay couched ; on him or his dread bow unbent 273 **When Philoctetes* 3
Embodied in the music of this Lay, 275 *Rotha Q.* 8
Thrilled by loose snatches of the social Lay. 279 **Hark ! 'tis* 14
Of each sweet Lay. 286 *Nith* 30
But ne'er to a seductive lay 287 *Sons of Burns* 39
Young Adam Bruce beside her lay, 287 *Ellen Irwin* 5
Of travelling through the world that lay 289 *Stepping West.* 25
Or is it some more humble lay, 289 *Sol. Reap.* 21
Among the Indian isles, where lay 296 *Highland Boy* 132
Or where broad waters round him lay : 298 *Brownie's Cell* 12
But the ground lay within that ring 298 *Brownie's Cell* 45
Of Spirits, and the undying Lay, 300 *Bran* 40
Of Yarrow Vale lay bleeding ? 302 *Yarrow V.* 26
Delicious is the Lay that sings 302 *Yarrow V.* 33
But on all proffered intercourse did lay 306 **We had* 7
The lowliest duties on herself did lay. 307 **Milton ! thou* 14
Lay hushed ; till—through a portal in the sky 323 *Ode 1814* 19
It tinged the Julian steeps—it lay, 343 *Eclipse* 31
That treasures, yet untouched, may grace some future Lay. 351 *Des. Stanzas* 90
To lay a new world open. Nor less prized 354 *Aquap.* 130
Unburied, lay hid under heaps of slain : 361 **For action* 10
Of Christian rites, in Christian ground to lay her." 372 *Eg. Maid* 240
" My books command me to lay bare 372 *Eg. Maid* 247
Whereon diffused like snow the Damsel lay, 373 *Eg. Maid* 275
That moral sweeten by a heaven-taught lay, 388 *Trosachs* 13
The Sage's theory ? the Poet's lay ?— 394 **How profitless* 11
Did we together read in Spenser's Lay 395 *White Doe : Ded.* 5
When under cloud of fear he lay, 399 *White Doe* 280
And lay it on Saint Mary's shrine ; 410 *White Doe* 1293
Will lay the Relic on the shrine." 411 *White Doe* 1435
Unclosed the noble Francis lay— 412 *White Doe* 1493
The Standard ; and where Francis lay 412 *White Doe* 1500
Her mute Companion as it lay 416 *White Doe* 1824
Time-honoured Chaucer speaking through that Lay 436 *Ecc. Sonn.* 2. 31. 2
And hallowed ground in which their fathers lay ; 443 *Ecc. Sonn.* 3. 13. 4
Of annual joy one tributary lay ; 448 *Ecc. Sonn.* 3. 32. 3
Dispose to judgments temperate as we lay 449 *Ecc. Sonn.* 3. 35. 4
Which lay in earth expectant, till a breeze 466 *St. Bees* 61
Summoned the Chiefs to lay their feuds aside, 467 *St. Bees* 103
When Europe prostrate lay, the Conqueror's aim, 471 **Despond who* 7
The music, and extinct the lay ? 473 *Ossian* 44
Earth, till the flesh lay on him like a load, 474 **Ye shadowy* 7

Lay—*continued.*
Or when a bold heroic lay 478 *Somnamb.* 59
The rescued Maiden lay, 479 *Somnamb.* 137
Of inspiration on the humblest lay. 480 **Most sweet* 14
Welcome !—but lay thy sword aside, 485 *Poet's Epitaph* 15
“ Six feet in earth my Emma lay ; 487 **We walked* 37
We lay beneath a spreading oak, 487 *Fountain* 5
In silence Matthew lay, and eyed 487 *Fountain* 17
How oft, a vigorous man, I lay 487 *Fountain* 27
Lay on the moral will a withering ban ? 501 *Humanity* 80
And have renewed the tributary Lay. 503 *Warning* 23
The soul's desire—a lay 507 *May* 12
Laws that lay under Heaven's perpetual ban 514 **Portentous change* 12
By deeds the blackest purpose to lay bare— 518 *Pun. Death* 4. 3
Enough ;—before us lay a painful road, 520 *Pun. Death* 14. 9
Is the string touched in prelude to a lay 529 *Poor Robin* 17
Though it should prove a farewell lay 530 †*Redbreast* 3
The blameless cause lay in the Theme itself. 539 **Lady ! a* 11
But wide around lay forest ground 542 *Russ. Fug.* 93
As if, beneath, some hero lay, 550 *Hermit's Cell* 2. 15
There, where with mangled throat he lay upright, 555 *Prioress* 160
His Mother swooning by the body lay : 555 *Prioress* 174
‘ Thou in thy dying sing this holy lay,’ 556 *Prioress* 209
And still he lay as if he had been bound. 556 *Prioress* 225
“ Eke the whole Convent on the pavement lay, 556 *Prioress* 226
And as I lay, the Cuckoo, bird unholy, 558 *Cuck. and Night.* 89
As long as in that swooning-fit I lay, 558 *Cuck.and Night.*107
While that stout Ship at anchor lay 579 **Sweet Flower* 16
He lay in slumber quietly ; 579 **Sweet Flower* 51
He conned the new-born Lay with grateful heart— 582 **To public* 7
Shall stain this votive lay ; 582 **O for a* 9
In that divine embrace enchanted lay ; 620 *Birth of Love* 6
Long undecided lay th' important choice, 620 *Birth of Love* 24
Inch-thick the dust lay on the ground 621 *Andrew Jones* 16
Upon a leaf the Glow-worm did I lay, 622 **Among all* 9
A corpse that lay expiring on the ground, 623 **I find* 3
Who sang in ancient Greece his loving lay, 623 **I find* 13
Threatening to lay all Orders at her feet 626 *Ballot* 4
My simplest Lay that to their memory 626 **Son of* 6
Deign, Sovereign Mistress ! to accept a lay, 628 **Deign, Sovereign* 1
And now by duty urged, I lay this Book 628 **Deign,Sovereign* 17
Reading or thinking ; either to lay up 633 *Prelude* 1. 116
With all its foolish pomp. The garden lay 644 *Prelude* 2. 155
And dead still water lay upon my mind 644 *Prelude* 2. 171
But for this cause, that I had seen him lay 645 *Prelude* 2. 183
The mind lay open, to a more exact 646 *Prelude* 2. 283
Yet slumbering, lay in utter solitude. 647 *Prelude* 2. 345
Lay bedded in a quickening soul, and all 651 *Prelude* 3. 131
—Of that external scene which round me lay, 660 *Prelude* 4. 160
That time can lay upon her ; how on earth 661 *Prelude* 4. 168
And all my deeper passions lay elsewhere. 663 *Prelude* 4. 303
The sea lay laughing at a distance ; near, 663 *Prelude* 4. 326
His shadow lay, and moved not. From self-blame 664 *Prelude* 4. 408
And lay till now neglected in the grass. 665 *Prelude* 4. 430
That here, in memory of all books which lay 668 *Prelude* 5. 198
A covenant that each should lay aside 672 *Prelude* 5. 470
Or, not less pleased, lay on some turret's head, 678 *Prelude* 6. 220
Of naked pools, and common crags that lay 678 *Prelude* 6. 234
Abroad, how cheeringly the sunshine lay 682 *Prelude* 6. 479
Lay a few steps, and then along its banks ; 683 *Prelude* 6. 583
Lay bedded, changing oftentimes its form 685 *Prelude* 6. 706
On Como's Lake, and all that round it lay, 686 *Prelude* 6. 725
Gathered the purple cups that round them lay, 705 *Prelude* 8. 405
Suspended over a knight's tomb, who lay 705 *Prelude* 8. 415
With that in which *her* mighty objects lay. 709 *Prelude* 8. 686
Through Paris lay my readiest course, and there 710 *Prelude* 9. 42
Distinction open lay to all that came, 713 *Prelude* 9. 230
In part lay here, that unto me the events 713 *Prelude* 9. 246
The prison where the unhappy Monarch lay, 719 *Prelude* 10. 51
Of Leven's ample estuary lay 725 *Prelude* 10. 515
Celestial, lay unseen the pastoral vales 725 *Prelude* 10. 524
Lay spotted with a variegated crowd 726 *Prelude* 10. 563
To lay the inner faculties asleep. 736 *Prelude* 12. 147
A naked pool that lay beneath the hills, 738 *Prelude* 12. 249
Upon the billowy ocean, as it lay 747 *Prelude* 14. 55
He deemed that my pursuits and labours lay 751 *Prelude* 14. 364
From brooding clouds ; shadows that lay in spots 756 *Excursion* 1. 6
An iron-pointed staff lay at his side. 756 *Excursion* 1. 37
So vividly great objects that they lay 758 *Excursion* 1. 137
And ocean's liquid mass, in gladness lay 759 *Excursion* 1. 202
Hollow and green, he lay on the green turf 760 *Excursion* 1. 260
His heart lay open ; and, by nature tuned 761 *Excursion* 1. 362
Screened from the sun. Supine the Wanderer lay, 762 *Excursion* 1. 438
When her life's Helpmate on a sick-bed lay, 764 *Excursion* 1. 551
Lay scattered here and there, open or shut, 768 *Excursion* 1. 828
Of a young apple-tree, lay at its root ; 769 *Excursion* 1. 841
On these and kindred thoughts intent I lay 777 *Excursion* 2. 370
Into a platform—that lay, sheepfold-wise, 777 *Excursion* 2. 413
Lay intermixed with scraps of paper, some 781 *Excursion* 2. 665
Lay at the mercy of this raging storm. 783 *Excursion* 2. 790
Lay shrouded in impenetrable mist ; 784 *Excursion* 2. 809
Lay low beneath my feet ; 'twas visible— 784 *Excursion* 2. 871
A mass of rock, resembling, as it lay 787 *Excursion* 3. 52
Or lay its beauty flat before a breeze, 787 *Excursion* 3. 66
But, there, lay open to our daily haunt, 794 *Excursion* 3. 537
Where mild enthusiasts tuned a pensive lay 797 *Excursion* 3. 754
Where, in the guise of mountaineers, we lay, 821 *Excursion* 4. 1320
And towards a crystal Mere, that lay beyond 823 *Excursion* 5. 82
Near this brave Knight his Father lay entombed ; 825 *Excursion* 5. 188
Masses of every shape and size, that lay 835 *Excursion* 5. 865

Lay—*continued.*
How on her bed of death the Matron lay, 849 *Excursion* 6. 743
By her offence to lay a twofold weight 852 *Excursion* 6. 943
The words he uttered, and the scene that lay 857 *Excursion* 7. 2
Lay beautiful on Snowdon's sovereign brow, 857 *Excursion* 7. 7
Lay at the threshold and the inner doors ; 860 *Excursion* 7. 185
Death fell upon him, while reclined he lay 861 *Excursion* 7. 285
Before their eyes lay carefully outspread, 869 *Excursion* 7. 785
The hasty rivulet where it lay becalmed 890 *Excursion* 9. 438
Sunk down, and lay immersed in dead repose S.3. 434 **The doubt* 50
Layeth. For Him who lifteth up and layeth low ; 330 *Ode : Thanks.* 89
Laying. Break forth at thought of laying down his head, 359 **They—who* 2
Layman. Where priest and layman with the vigilance 449 *Ecc. Sonn.* 3. 36. 8
Layman's. The unshackled layman's natural liberty ; 775 *Excursion* 2. 265
Lays. He lays his stiffened limbs,—his eyes begin to close ; 27 *Guilt* 162
The dripping groves resound with cheerful lays, 34 *Guilt* 519
And lays it to his heart—. I pray you speak ! 67 *Bord.* 1670
What wonder ? at her bidding, ancient lays 153 *Morn. Ex.* 19
Lays it by, at will resumes ! 163 *Hint* 10
And suit their slender lays. 164 *Needlecase* 24
Displeased that I from lays of love 168 *Turtledove* 11
And on the pillow lays her burning head. 248 *P. B.* 1085
In my past verse ; or shall be, in the lays 259 *Calvert* 11
From hope, the paramount *duty* that Heaven lays, 321 **Here pause* 5
To You presenting these memorial Lays, 333 *Ded. Tour* 2
The very Angels whose authentic lays, 338 *Engelberg* 11
Though even to their last syllable the Lays 356 *Aquap.* 275
And this poor verse, and worthier lays, 391 *Highland Broach* 81
Was the beginning ; yet the several Lays 394 **No more* 3
In quietness she lays her down ; 397 *White Doe* 142
Nor Taliesin's unforgotten lays, 419 *Ecc. Sonn.* 1. 5. 10
And One there is who builds immortal lays, 441 *Ecc. Sonn.* 3. 4. 6
While on each head his lawn-robed servant lays 446 *Ecc. Sonn.* 3. 23. 9
Soft in its temper as those vesper lays 454 *Sea-side* 24
And lays as prompt would hail the dawn of Night : 455 *Rydal Mere* 21
Was sung by Virgin-choirs in festal lays ; 460 **Queen of* 26
Nor fear memorial lays, 479 *Somnamb.* 155
Of truth and pure delight by heavenly lays ! 489 *Pers. Talk* 54
Their harvest of sweet lays. 498 **Departing summer* 12
Charged with those lays, and others of like mood, 538 **In desultory* 15
Some future Poet meditate his lays ; 546 **The embowering* 14
A work completed to our hands, that lays, 697 *Prelude* 7. 679
Upon the board he lays the sky-blue stone 882 *Excursion* 8. 561
And lays the generations low in dust, 885 *Excursion* 9. 109
Lazily. Read lazily in trivial books, went forth 652 *Prelude* 3. 251
Lazy. And steals into the shade the lazy oar ; 12 *Desc. Sk.* 104
Or by the lazy Seine, the exile roves ; 19 *Desc. Sk.* 521
And stir the pulse of lazy charity. 39 *Bord.* 83
—As homeward through the lane I went with lazy feet, 88 *Pet-lamb* 61
Made the warm earth his lazy bed. 239 *P. B.* 260
On a flat and lazy shore. 549 *Hermit's Cell* 1. 32
Lo ! by the lazy Seine the exile roves, 613 *Desc.Sk.Quarto* 624
Insidiously stretched out its lazy length, 860 *Excursion* 7. 175
Le. Less than the painted Magdalene of Le Brun, 710 *Prelude* 9. 77
Lea. All over the wide lea ; 109 **Strange fits* 10
Of Him who slept upon the open lea : 168 *Pilgrim's Dream* 67
So might I, standing on this pleasant lea, 259 **The world is* 11
To ruminate, couched on the grassy lea ; 349 *Val. Dover* 7
And aery harvests crown the fertile lea. 429 *Ecc. Sonn.* 2. 3. 14
This straight-lined progress, furrowing a flat lea, 466 *St. Bees* 12
And turnips, and corn-land, and meadow, and lea, 569 *Farmer* 19
Lead. His burning eyelids stretched and stiff as lead ; 36 *Guilt* 636
And he must lead me back. You are most lucky ; 43 *Bord.* 354
Most willingly !—Come, let me lead you in, 43 *Bord.* 361
To lead a Spirit, spotless as the blessed, 47 *Bord.* 545
And yet it is not.—Let us lead him hither. 48 *Bord.* 637
Would lead me to talk fondly. Do not fear ; 52 *Bord.* 831
We'll lead him to the Convent. He shall live, 54 *Bord.* 904
Might lead to good—I saw it and burst forth, 69 *Bord.* 1781
I'll lead you to the spot. 72 *Bord.* 2013
I'll lead you to his Daughter ; but 'twere best 74 *Bord.* 2108
For the boy loved the life which we lead here ; 100 *Brothers* 296
And love the blessed life that we lead here. 106 *Farewell* 32
They lead you on to full content, 143 †*Lov. and Lik.* 61
Dost lead the revels of the May ; 159 *Green Linnet* 15
Fell with the weight of drops of lead ;— 175 *Waggoner* 1. 157
To lead those ancient Amazonian files ; 190 *Beggars* 11
In which the affections gently lead us on,— 206 *Tintern* 42
Through all the years of this our life, to lead 207 *Tintern* 124
As thou from clime to clime didst lead ; 216 *Enterprise* 46
Shall lead thee to thy grave. 218 *Young Lady* 18
Will to composure lead—or make thee blithe as bird in bower. 229 *Cuckoo-clock* 11
But lead sick Fancy to a harp 233 *Power of Sound* 89
Did Nature lead him as before ; 239 *P. B.* 247
“ Of all that lead a lawless life, 239 *P. B.* 276
It was to lead an honest life ; 246 *P. B.* 902
No man can find it : Father ! Thou must lead. 257 **The prayers* 8
May lead the thoughts, thus struggling used to stand 265 **When haughty* 10
This Minstrel lead, his sins forgiven ; 286 *Nith* 56
With such a sky to lead him on ? 289 *Stepping West.* 8
Didst first lead forth that enterprise sublime, 312 *Clarkson* 5
Whose factions lead astray the wise and brave— 314 **Not 'mid* 4
And lead us on to that transcendent rest 315 **Alas ! what* 4
I scorn your Chiefs—men who would lead, 406 *White Doe* 902
To lead the prisoners to their fate. 410 *White Doe* 1315

Lead—*continued.*
To lead in memorable triumph home — 425 *Ecc. Sonn.* 1. 25. 8
Lead unmolested lives, and die of age. — 433 *Ecc. Sonn.* 2. 21. 8
Thus all things lead to Charity, secured — 449 *Ecc. Sonn.* 3. 37. 1
Instinct—to rouse the heart and lead the will — 451 *Ecc. Sonn.* 3. 42. 9
Lead to that younger Pile, whose sky-like dome — 452 *Ecc. Sonn.* 3. 45. 8
Lead, through dark ways by sin and sorrow trod, — 504 *Warning* 83
These mists, and lead you to a safer place, — 505 *Warning* 132
Whom chance may lead to this retreat, — 550 *Hermit's Cell* 2. 2
Who do not think in love their life to lead; — 559 *Cuck.andNight.*132
As ye have heard; such life 'gan he to lead — 564 *Troilus* 111
Who lead their horses down the steep rough road — 566 *Cumb. Beg.* 5
And his pure native genius, lead him back — 573 *Chiabrera* 2. 6
His hand:—it dropped like lead. — 577 **I come* 8
His moiety in trust, till Joy shall lead — 586 *Ch. Lamb* 130
Or desperate Love could lead a wanderer there. — 602 *Desc. Sk. Quarto* 44
To lead the mind to those Elysian plains — 619 *School Ex.* 69
By a more just gradation did lead on — 656 *Prelude* 3. 527
Would through the desert lead me; and while yet — 667 *Prelude* 5. 83
Rises to lead him toward a better clime, — 670 *Prelude* 5. 333
Whose evening shadows lead him to repose. — 682 *Prelude* 6. 516
Beginning, lead his voice through many a maze — 695 *Prelude* 7. 555
Should cease; and open accusation lead — 717 *Prelude* 9. 537
Knowledge that step by step might lead me on — 742 *Prelude* 13. 132
But which way shall I lead you?—how contrive, — 786 *Excursion* 3. 16
May'st penetrate, wherever truth shall lead; — 787 *Excursion* 3. 109
That to the decorated pillar lead, — 846 *Excursion* 6. 505
That in itself may terminate, or lead — 888 *Excursion* 9. 285
Lead me, or outward circumstance impels. — K.8. 233 **Along the* 3
Would lead me, I should whisper to myself; — K.8. 244*Recluse* 1.1.276
Leaded. Of the huge city, on the leaded roof — 679 *Prelude* 6. 267
Leader. To our confiding, open-hearted, Leader. — 37 *Bord.* 10
Let this old Man find at your hands; poor Leader, — 42 *Bord.* 302
When my old Leader slipped into the flood — 52 *Bord.* 834
And hark! the Leader of the band — 161 *Binnorie* 19
"There's Galla Water, Leader Haughs, — 292 *Yarrow Unv.* 17
With that great Leader vies, who, sick of strife — 320 **They seek* 12
I thanked the Leader of my onward way. — 383 *Duddon* 28. 14
For me, thy natural leader, once again — 496 **A little* 14
And each, in his turn, becomes leader or led; — 572 *Avarice* 38
Leader's. To establish something of a leader's sway; — 794 *Excursion* 3. 594
Leaders. To stop your Leaders in their headstrong course! — 505 *Warning* 130
Among the leaders of the Grecian host — 625 *Æneid* 137
Leaders'. Upon his Leaders' bells and manes, — 174 *Waggoner* 1. 78
Leading. And leading Herbert. We must let them pass— — 39 *Bord.* 101
Past softly, leading in the Boy; and while from roof to floor, — 92 *Poet's Dream* 42
Leading such companion I that gilded dome, — 140 *Arm. Lady* 41
A leading from above, a something given, — 196 *Resolution* 51
Where'er the tender grass was leading — 239 *P. B.* 254
Visibly leading on the thunder's harmonies. — 350 *Des. Stanzas* 9
Of Nature leading back to life; — 374 *Eg. Maid* 340
Undressed the pathway leading to the door; — 390 *Highland Hut* 10
Or leading victims drest for sacrifice. — 394 **No more* 16
Upon their leading mothers hung— — 398 *White Doe* 165
Leading sometimes an inexperienced child — 783 *Excursion* 2. 770
Track leading into track; how marked, how worn — 793 *Excursion* 3. 533
For recreation, leading into each: — 810 *Excursion* 4. 592
Leads. Where peace to Grasmere's lonely island leads, — 2 *Ev. Wk.* 5
Leads to her bridge, rude church, and cottaged grounds, — 2 *Ev. Wk.* 7
And her brown little-ones around her leads, — 6 *Ev. Wk.* 225
The pathway leads, as round the steeps it twines; — 12 *Desc. Sk.* 87
Move, as the verdure leads, from stage to stage; — 17 *Desc. Sk.* 375
Instructed that true knowledge leads to love; — 23 *Yew-tree* 60
The royal Elidure, who leads the chase, — 104 *Artegal* 114
No good but by the way that leads to bliss — 139 *Widow* 30
Fancy, who leads the pastimes of the glad, — 153 *Morn. Ex.* 1
And a God leads him, wingèd Mercury! — 209 *Laod.* 18
Who leads them on?—The anxious people see — 213 *Dion* 22
"Him only pleasure leads, and peace attends, — 214 *Dion* 122
Where silver Isis leads my stripling feet; — 270 **Ye sacred* 11
Nor deem that "light which leads astray — 287 *Sons of Burns* 41
The path that leads them to the grove, — 302 *Yarrow V.* 35
Leads through space of open day, — 397 *White Doe* 84
Reckless of what impels or leads, — 411 *White Doe* 1379
—'Tis Sir George Bowes who leads the Band: — 412 *White Doe* 1446
That animate my way where'er it leads! — 472 **The captive* 14
That leads her to the torrent's side — 479 *Somnamb.* 95
And gradual progress?—Twilight leads to day, — 516 **Hard task* 9
All leads to gentleness. — 526 **The soaring* 40
Leads to the dear Parnassian forest's shade, — 574 *Chiabrera* 5. 10
Her babe's small cry, that leads him to his prey. — 606 *Desc.Sk.Quarto* 242
Cries out, and leads her Spectres to their prey, — 613 *Desc.Sk.Quarto* 641
More heavenly bright than when it leads the morn, — 627 **The star* 2
Higher and higher, him his office leads — 702 *Prelude* 8. 232
Leads, though by sinuous ways, if here I show — 706 *Prelude* 8. 453
Toil, say I, for it leads to thoughts abstruse— — 715 *Prelude* 9. 397
Where knowledge leads me: it shall be my pride — 743 *Prelude* 13. 251
Wherever Nature leads; that he hath stood — 744 *Prelude* 13. 297
Apart from all that leads to wealth, or even — 751 *Prelude* 14. 365
Or rise as venerable Nature leads, — 757 *Excursion* 1. 104
No more shall stray where meditation leads, — 803 *Excursion* 4. 104
For any passion of the soul that leads — 804 *Excursion* 4. 182
Wherever fancy leads; by day, by night, — 809 *Excursion* 4. 554
On what, for guidance in the way that leads — 835 *Excursion* 5. 825
Men, whose delight is where their duty leads — 839 *Excursion* 6. 48
Receiving, took the slender path that leads — 895 *Excursion* 9. 773

Leads—*continued.*
Who leads a happy life — S.3. 423 *Tinker* 1
With Hope, who would not follow where she leads? — K.8. 250*Recluse* 1.1.501
Some nursling of the mountains, which she leads. — K.8. 256*Recluse* 1.1.729
Leaf. *See* **Bramble-leaf, Summer-leaf, Vine-leaf.**
Chasing those pleasant dreams, the falling leaf — 22 *Desc. Sk.* 632
A leaf had fallen, the thing had never been — 65 *Bord.* 1566
Feather, or leaf, or weed, or withered bough, — 148 **A narrow* 14
Though of both leaf and flower bereft, — 155 *Waterfall* 45
Ere a leaf is on a bush, — 160 **Pansies, lilies* 25
Each leaf, that and this, his neighbour will kiss; — 167 *Stray Pleasures* 34
Though silent as a leaf before, — 168 *Turtledove* 5
Every little leaf conveyed — 170 *Kitten* 12
To gambol with Life's falling Leaf. — 172 *Kitten* 128
—A withered leaf is close behind, — 244 *P. B.* 703
This precious leaf, with harsh impiety. — 250 *Admon.* 8
The Sonnet glittered a gay myrtle leaf. — 260 **Scorn not* 7
While not a leaf seems faded; while the fields, — 263 **While not* 1
Of bud, leaf, blade, and flower—was fashioning — 266 **The stars* 13
The dullest leaf in this thick wood — 299 *Cora Linn* 2
The last leaf on a blasted tree; — 402 *White Doe* 567
Driven forward like a withered leaf, — 414 *White Doe* 1614
Me, conscious that my leaf is sere, — 498 **Departing summer* 14
No meaner leaf was seen; — 543 *Russ. Fug.* 188
Some scattered leaf, or marks which, in one track, — 567 *Cumb. Beg.* 55
Chasing those long long dreams the falling leaf — 616 *Desc.Sk.Quarto* 768
Upon a leaf the Glow-worm did I lay, — 622 **Among all* 9
Which, from a tree, a stone, a withered leaf, — 651 *Prelude* 3. 160
Had failed, and every leaf and flower were lost — 764 *Excursion* 1. 531
Upon a broad leaf carried, choicest strings — 779 *Excursion* 2. 504
But that some leaf of your regard should hang — 793 *Excursion* 3. 492
As the unbreathing air, when not a leaf — 820 *Excursion* 4. 1281
Anchors her placid beauty. Not a leaf, — 842 *Excursion* 6. 295
Leaf-clad. The heavier substance of a leaf-clad bough, — 123 *V. and J.* 142
Leaf-crowned. Nor leaf-crowned Dryad from a pathless wood, — 220 *Triad* 10
Leaf-green. Like foresters in leaf-green vest, — 342 *Ital. Itin.* 58
Leafless. Among the branches of the leafless trees; — v **If thou indeed* 13
Yet leafless, showed as if the countenance — 146 **It was an* 15
Where leafless oaks towered high above, — 154 **A whirl-blast* 5
'Mid its own bush of leafless eglantine— — 277 **Why art* 13
When the broad oak drops, a leafless skeleton, — 379 *Duddon* 12. 8
A self-surviving leafless oak — 414 *White Doe* 1630
The leafless trees and every icy crag — 638 *Prelude* 1. 441
Or currants, hanging from their leafless stems, — 763 *Excursion* 1. 457
Like leafless underboughs, in some thick wood, — 824 *Excursion* 5. 148
Leaf-scattering. Leaf-scattering winds; and hoar-frost sprinklings fell — 394 **No more* 27
Leafy. Illumines from within, the leafy shade; — 3 *Ev. Wk.* 65
Where leafy shades fence off the blustering gale, — 6 *Ev. Wk.* 234
The leafy wood, or sleeps in quiet lakes. — 10 *Desc. Sk.* 8
Behold, within the leafy shade, — 79 *Sparrow's Nest* 1
Each within its leafy bower; — 80 *Foresight* 31
Let us quit the leafy arbour, — 90 *Longest Day* 1
And wild notes warbled among leafy bowers; — 107 *Farewell* 61
All independent of the leafy spring. — 153 *Morn. Ex.* 48
The leafy antlers sprout; — 168 *Wren's Nest* 36
And rudely canopied by leafy boughs, — 172 *Infant Daughter* 20
And snug as birds in leafy arbour, — 181 *Waggoner* 4. 169
Ruffles the bosom of this leafy glen. — 184 *Airey-force* 2
A leafy shelter from the sun and wind. — 202 *Hart-leap* 88
Their own far-stretching arms and leafy heads — 220 *Haunted Tree* 38
Of Britain's realm, whose leafy crest — 226 *Vernal Ode* 19
Where birds and brooks from leafy dells — 228 *Devot. Incit.* 64
On the bare rock, or through a leafy bower — 265 **Hail, Twilight* 8
To this small spot, his leafy shade; — 298 *Brownie's Cell* 44
The leafy grove that covers: — 302 *Yarrow V.* 36
Of birds, in leafy bower, — 329 *Ode: Thanks.* 41
They lodged in leafy tents and cabins low; — 346 *Processions* 15
The warbling wren shall find a leafy cage; — 433 *Ecc. Sonn.* 2. 21. 5.
To sit in leafy woods by fountains clear! — 460 **Queen of* 16
"The blackbird amid leafy trees, — 487 *Fountain* 37
That calls from yonder leafy shade — 498 **Departing summer* 4
How delicate the leafy veil — 508 *May* 81
(Among reflected boughs of leafy trees) — 527 **Those breathing* 43
Its brightest splendour round a leafy wood; — 532 **Once I* 16
Want store of leafy *arbours* where the light — 652 *Prelude* 3. 245
There small birds warble from the leafy trees, — 683 *Prelude* 6. 534
Out of its leafy brow, the more to awe — 695 *Prelude* 7. 521
Of dews fast melting on their leafy boughs — 773 *Excursion* 2. 132
On Devon's leafy shores;—a sheltered hold, — 793 *Excursion* 3. 518
Their leafy umbrage, turns the dusky veil — 817 *Excursion* 4. 1067
A broad oak, stretching forth its leafy arms — 825 *Excursion* 5. 227
In the fair body of a leafy grove — 840 *Excursion* 6. 160
Of leafy spray, concealed the stems and roots — 881 *Excursion* 8. 444
League. We must not part,—I have measured many a league — 42 *Bord.* 297
Dissolved the Barons' League, and sent abroad — 56 *Bord.* 1023
That rose a brief league distant from the town, — 125 *V. and J.* 248
His banner in accursed league with France, — 313 *Prophecy* 13
With mutual help, and sailing—to their league — 586 *Ch. Lamb* 104
Even while mine eye hath moved o'er many a league — 640 *Prelude* 1. 577
With what, and how great might ye are in league, — 673 *Prelude* 5. 527
Where elms for many and many a league in files — 680 *Prelude* 6. 360
League after league, and cloistral avenues, — 685 *Prelude* 6. 668
With spiteful gratitude the baffled League, — 718 *Prelude* 10. 36
Britain put forth her freeborn strength in league, — 722 *Prelude* 10. 264

Leave—*continued.*

And leave his body here, it were all one . . . 61 *Bord.* 1299
Here will I leave him—here—All-seeing God! . 62 *Bord.* 1391
Makes up one damning falsehood. Leave him here 62 *Bord.* 1398
And therefore leave thee to a righteous judgment. 63 *Bord.* 1407
That she is innocent. Leave that thought awhile 67 *Bord.* 1678
That we should leave him there, alive!—we did so. 68 *Bord.* 1720
We must be gentle. Leave him to my care. . . 73 *Bord.* 2035
Of provocation. Leave me, with the weight . . 77 *Bord.* 2296
In Heaven, and Mercy gives me leave to die. . . 78 *Bord.* 2353
Daisies leave no fruit behind . . . . 80 *Foresight* 21
Nor leave untold our happy flight in that adventurous dream. . . . . 93 *Poet's Dream* 76
Leave that thought; and here be uttered . . . 94 *Westmoreland Girl* 89
'Tis one of those who needs must leave the path . 96 *Brothers* 105
Farewell!—we leave thee to Heaven's peaceful care, ... 106 *Farewell* 7
We leave you here in solitude to dwell . . . . . 106 *Farewell* 19
Thus often would he leave our peaceful home, . 107 *Indolence* 10
And yet they leave it short, and fears . . . . 110 *Forsaken* 10
Deep in a forest, with leave given, at the age . . 125 *V. and J.* 272
What do, and what to leave undone, ... 126 *Idiot Boy* 55
And can ye thus unfriended leave me; . . . . 130 *Idiot Boy* 345
Our Luke shall leave us, Isabel; the land . . . 135 *Michael* 244
For if thou leave thy Father he will die." . . . 135 *Michael* 298
To-morrow thou wilt leave me: with full heart . 136 *Michael* 332
To leave me, Luke: thou hast been bound to me 137 *Michael* 400
Yon minarets, would gladly leave for his worst home." . . . . 140 *Arm. Lady* 42
Handmaid's privilege would leave my purpose free, 140 *Arm. Lady* 59
And taken thy first leave of those green hills . . 151 **When, to* 68
Love him, or leave him alone! . . . . . . 163 **Art thou the* 39
To leave it with a jovial heart; . . . . . . 174 *Waggoner* 1. 57
And leave Blencathara's rugged coves, . . . 204 *Brougham* 90
Leave to the nightingale her shady wood; . . . 209 **Ethereal minstrel* 7
"Great Jove, Laodamía! doth not leave . . . 210 *Laod.* 37
Nor leave thee, when grey hairs are nigh, . . . 218 *Young Lady* 14
That every day should leave some part . . . 228 *Devot. Incit.* 74
They leave, and speed on nightly embassy . . 229 *Cuckoo-clock* 41
Leave for one chant;—the dulcet sound . . . 234 *Power of Sound* 134
Leave of our fate thy wishes to fulfil. . . . . 251 *Appleth.* 11
If the heavens smile, and leave us free to glide, . 252 **Her only* 7
Where the young lions couch; for so, by leave . 269 *Gordale* 6
Dissolve—and leave to him who gazed a sigh. . 278 **The most* 8
But we will leave it growing. . . . . . . 293 *Yarrow Unv.* 36
Whate'er you do, leave this undone; . . . . 296 *Highland Boy* 89
May human creature leave the shore! . . . . 296 *Highland Boy* 102
And leave me to myself!" . . . . 297 *Highland Boy* 205
And leave the figurative Man— . . . . . . 301 *Bran* 86
See the first mighty Hunter leave the Brute— . 313 **Go back* 11
Could I leave them unseen, and not yield to regret? 345 *Stanzas: Simplon* 10
Foretelling and proclaiming, ere thou leave . . 363 **List—'twas* 99
And, if thou canst, leave them without regret! . 379 *Duddon* 12. 14
Thee hath some awful Spirit impelled to leave, . 379 *Duddon* 14. 9
And leave thy Tweed and Tiviot . . . . . 386 *Yarrow Rev.* 52
And give the timid herbage leave to shoot, . . 395 *White Doe: Ded.* 28
And where no flower hath leave to dwell. . . . 397 *White Doe* 99
Then let us leave this dreary place." . . . . 411 *White Doe* 1360
To leave.—Unwooed, yet unforbidden, . . . 414 *White Doe* 1704
Would that our scrupulous Sires had dared to leave 448 *Ecc. Sonn.* 3. 33. 1
Could leave both man and horse behind; . . . 483 *Simon Lee* 18
And leave a dead unprofitable name— . . . 494 *Hap. War.* 80
But leave it thence to drop for lack of use: . . 520 *Pun. Death* 13. 13
I leave unsearched: enough that memory clings, 525 *Epist. Beaumont* 265
"Leave open to my wish the course, ... 545 *Russ. Fug.* 337
By old Sir William and his quarry, leave . . . 549 **Stranger! this* 32
And take my leave of all such company, . . . 559 *Cuck.and Night.* 138
Thus takes the Nightingale her leave of me; . . 561 *Cuck.and Night.* 256
She thankèd them; and then her leave she took, 562 *Cuck.and Night.* 286
Alas, and there I took of her my leave; . . . 564 *Troilus* 93
For I'd take my last leave both of verse and of prose. . . . . 571 *Avarice* 4
As with a chosen friend; nor did he leave . . 576 *Chiabrera* 9. 12
My comrades, leave the crowd, buildings and groves, ... 650 *Prelude* 3. 92
A Poet's history, may I leave untold . . . . 659 *Prelude* 4. 80
That portion of my story I shall leave . . . . 668 *Prelude* 5. 192
Leave let me take to place before her sight . . 670 *Prelude* 5. 296
That cannot take long leave of pleasant thoughts. 675 *Prelude* 6. 19
By such a daring thought, that I might leave . 676 *Prelude* 6. 55
And not to leave the story of that time . . 677 *Prelude* 6. 171
By whom we were encompassed. Taking leave . 681 *Prelude* 6. 414
That did not leave us free from personal fear; . 686 *Prelude* 6. 720
Would leave behind a dance of images, . . . 700 *Prelude* 8. 114
But leave we this: enough that my delights . 736 *Prelude* 12. 140
The freeborn Swiss to leave his narrow vales, . 761 *Excursion* 1. 318
Invited, often would he leave his home . . . 762 *Excursion* 1. 389
And he would leave his work—and to the town . 765 *Excursion* 1. 582
That passing shows of Being leave behind, . . 770 *Excursion* 1. 951
This wanting, he would leave the sight of men, . 780 *Excursion* 2. 603
We signified a wish to leave that place . . . 793 *Excursion* 3. 470
Leave this unknit Republic to the scourge . . 799 *Excursion* 3. 914
But leave me unabated trust in thee— . . . 802 *Excursion* 4. 60
Depart; and leave no vestige where they trod. . 812 *Excursion* 4. 762
The dewy grass; you cannot leave us now, . . 823 *Excursion* 5. 71
Sate down; and to her office, with leave asked, . 834 *Excursion* 5. 770
I feel, good reasons why we should not leave . . 848 *Excursion* 6. 661
Full oft his doings leave me to deplore . . . 866 *Excursion* 7. 595

Leave—*continued.*

Yet shall not thy remembrance leave our hearts, . 868 *Excursion* 7. 713
"Yet, by the good Knight's leave, the two estates 875 *Excursion* 8. 44
Nor must I leave untouched (the picture else . . 881 *Excursion* 8. 484
Wishful to leave an opening for my choice, . . 891 *Excursion* 9. 480
My future labours may not leave untold. . . . 896 *Excursion* 9. 796
Said, "Father, 'tis lost labour; with your leave . K.8. 228 **I will* 115
Are opened. Churlish Winter hath given leave . K.8. 241 *Recluse* 1. 1. 189

Leaved. *See* **Green-leaved.**

Leaven. And memory of Earth's bitter leaven, . . 286 *Nith* 59

Leaves. Its darkening boughs and leaves in stronger lines; . . . . 6 *Ev. Wk.* 215
Drops deadened from a roof so thick with leaves. 49 *Bord.* 676
With rotten boughs and leaves, such as the winds 50 *Bord.* 705
And send ye dancing to the clouds, like leaves. . 54 *Bord.* 945
Feed on her leaves. You knew her well—ay, there, 61 *Bord.* 1312
A plain confession, such as leaves no doubt, . . 63 *Bord.* 1420
Save, in a corner, a heap of dry leaves, . . . 80 †*Address: Child* 18
Of green leaves on the hawthorn spray, . . . 81 †*Mother's Return* 38
"O! what a weight is in these shades! Ye leaves, 111 **'Tis said that some* 21
Oft leaves a saving moisture at its root. . . . 124 *V. and J.* 194
The leaves that make the softest bed: . . . . 145 *Her Eyes* 56
That could not cease to be. Green leaves were here; . . . . 146 **It was an* 30
Of copse and thicket, leaves the eastern shore . 148 **A narrow* 4
With withered leaves is covered o'er, ... 154 **A whirl-blast* 10
The withered leaves all skip and hop; . . . . 155 **A whirl-blast* 13
The leaves in myriads jump and spring, ... 155 **A whirl-blast* 18
And all those leaves, in festive glee, ... 155 **A whirl-blast* 21
My leaves you freshened and bedewed; . . . . 155 *Waterfall* 28
I sheltered you with leaves and flowers; . . . . 155 *Waterfall* 36
And in my leaves—now shed and gone, . . . 155 *Waterfall* 37
A Brother of the dancing leaves; . . . . . 159 *Green Linnet* 34
Covered with leaves the little children, . . . 162 **Art thou the* 22
The largest of her upright leaves; . . . . . 169 *Wren's Nest* 58
Preserves her beauty 'mid autumnal leaves, . . 169 **Never enlivened* 5
Proved last year's leaves, pushed from the spray . 170 *Rural Ill.* 11
Sporting with the leaves that fall, ... 170 *Kitten* 4
Withered leaves—one—two—and three— . . 170 *Kitten* 5
Couched on a casual bed of moss and leaves, . . 172 *Infant Daughter* 19
Now he leaves the lower ground, ... 174 *Waggoner* 1. 34
Drooped with its withered leaves, ungracious sign 185 *Nutting* 18
Perhaps it was a bower beneath whose leaves . 185 *Nutting* 30
With leaves of laurel stuck about; . . . . . 191 *Beggars* 26
The vernal leaves—she loved them still; . . . 194 *Ruth* 220
No leaves it has, no prickly points; . . . . 197 *Thorn* 7
While yet the summer leaves were green, . . . 199 *Thorn* 123
That is in the green leaves among the groves, . . 203 *Hart-leap* 166
"She leaves these objects to a slow decay, . . 203 *Hart-leap* 173
He leaves behind a moon-illumined wake: . . . 212 *Dion*
And withered leaves, from earth's cold breast . 217 *Enterprise* 131
Or under leaves of thickest shade, ... 222 *Triad* 198
The buds, and freshens the young leaves, . . . 228 *Devot. Incit.* 16
Darkling, among the boughs and leaves. . . . 240 *P. B.* 345
The very leaves they follow me— . . . . . 244 *P. B.* 709
"Blood drops—leaves rustle—yet," quoth he, . 245 *P. B.* 808
Of golden leaves inlaid with silver down, . . . 254 *Wild Duck's Nest* 11
Of cold neglect she leaves thy head ungraced, . 254 *Dyer* 9
Through leaves yet green, and yon crystalline sky, 263 **While not* 11
Thy green leaves rustle or thy torrents roar. . . 331 *Ode: Thanks.* 144
The desolate Slumberer with moss and with leaves. 340 *Fort Fuentes* 12
That through the jealous leaves escapes . . . 342 *Ital. Itin.* 49
While your leaves I behold and the brooks they will strew, ... 364 *Vallomb.* 31
Bent by a load of Mulberry leaves!—most hard . 366 *Lombardy* 2
The storm has stripped her of her leaves; . . . 370 *Eg. Maid* 53
With backward curve, the leaves revealed . . 371 *Eg. Maid* 129
The encircling laurels, thick with leaves, . . . 375 **The Minstrels* 4
In gentle bosoms, while sere leaves . . . . 385 *Yarrow Rev.* 11
Crisp, yellow leaves my bed; the hooting owl . 424 *Ecc. Sonn.* 1. 22. 11
Nor leaves her Speech one word to aid the sigh . 425 *Ecc. Sonn.* 1. 25. 11
Green leaves with yellow mixed are torn away, . 435 *Ecc. Sonn.* 2. 28. 2
And leaves the disencumbered spirit free . . . 456 **Soft as* 18
The leaves that rustled on this oak-crowned hill, . 456 **The leaves* 1
And sky that danced among those leaves, are still; 456 **The leaves* 2
Swept by a favouring wind that leaves thought free, 460 **Wanderer! that* 66
Close up those barren leaves; . . . . . . 482 *Tables Turned* 30
Than what it leaves behind. . . . . 487 *Fountain* 36
With shadows flung from leaves—to strive . . 499 **This Lawn* 2
Nor unto silent leaves and drowsy flowers,— . . 501 **The unremitting* 5
And ripening fruits and forest leaves . . . . 502 *Seasons* 11
His Mother leaves him free to taste . . . . 507 *May* 39
Leaves him at ease among grand thoughts: whose eye . . . . 514 **Blest Statesman* 2
Whence these opprobrious leaves of dire portent? 515 **Men of* 2
As leaves are to the tree whereon they grow . . 516 **As leaves* 1
And, as his tufts of leaves he spreads, content 529 *Poor Robin* 7
Trilled by the redbreast, when autumnal leaves 539 **Lady! a* 34
Of summer, in the season of sere leaves; . . . 539 **Lady! a* 61
The leaves of any pleasant tree . . . . . . 543 *Russ. Fug.* 179
From the great City; never, upon leaves . . . 547 **Rude is* 7
And see the budding leaves the branches throng, . 557 *Cuck. and Night.* 27
Him even the slow-paced waggon leaves behind. . 567 *Cumb. Beg.* 66
Will hear the wind sigh through the leaves of a tree. 571 *Farmer* 92
That shook the leaves in myriads as it passed;— 583 **With copious* 18
Their golden leaves upon the pathways, . . . 586 *Hogg* 7
Their moveless boughs and leaves like threads of gold; . . . . 593 *Ev. Wk. Quarto* 104
The dry leaves stir as with the serpent's walk, . 606 *Desc.Sk.Quarto* 233

Led—*continued.*
Alert to follow as the Pastor led, 892 *Excursion* 9. 569
And led us to our threshold. Daylight failed K.8. 241 *Recluse* 1.1.173
Ledbury. Nor was applied nor could be, Ledbury bells 267 *St. Cath.* 2
Ledge. Another high on that green ledge;—he gained 17 *Desc. Sk.* 382
Backed also by a ledge of rock, whose crest 833 *Excursion* 5. 695
Ledgers. When men change swords for ledgers, and desert 307 **When I* 3
Lee. To his loved pastime given by sedgy Lee, 254 *Complete Angler* 9
The halloo of Simon Lee. 483 *Simon Lee* 12
"You're overtasked, good Simon Lee, 484 *Simon Lee* 81
Leeches. To gather leeches, being old and poor: 196 *Resolution* 100
And said that, gathering leeches, far and wide 197 *Resolution* 121
Leech-gatherer. I'll think of the Leech-gatherer on the lonely moor!" 197 *Resolution* 140
Leeds. "At Doncaster, at York, and Leeds, 239 *P. B.* 216
Leeward. "The vain distress-gun," from a leeward shore, 234 *Power of Sound* 159
Leeza's. From the Great Gavel, down by Leeza's banks, 100 *Brothers* 310
Left. Left vacant for the day, I loved to roam. 13 *Desc. Sk.* 144
Fixed on the anchor left by Him who saves 14 *Desc. Sk.* 206
Left his mind still as a deep evening stream. 26 *Guilt* 96
Left by gigantic arms—at length surveys 26 *Guilt* 113
She left him there; for, clustering round his knees, 34 *Guilt* 536
The friends whom she had left but a few minutes past. 34 *Guilt* 558
We left the willow shade by the brookside, 39 *Bord.* 104
As if my heart would burst; and so I left him. 45 *Bord.* 477
Has left a power of riches; and I say it, 46 *Bord.* 487
They think it is to feed them. I have left him 47 *Bord.* 561
Before her face. The rest be left to me. 48 *Bord.* 601
Just as we left the glen a clap of thunder 51 *Bord.* 788
Since that Man left me.—No, I am not lost. 52 *Bord.* 803
Thou hast left me ears to hear my Daughter's voice, 53 *Bord.* 852
Within the Vault, a spear's length to the left. 54 *Bord.* 916
As I have told you: He left us yesterday 58 *Bord.* 1136
You know we left him sitting—see him yonder. 60 *Bord.* 1257
I did not think that aught was left in me 61 *Bord.* 1324
I fancy when you left the Holy Land, 62 *Bord.* 1348
I would be left alone. I know your motives! 64 *Bord.* 1502
And in that miserable place we left him, 68 *Bord.* 1724
Left without burial! nay, not dead nor dying, 68 *Bord.* 1728
We marched to Syria: oft I left the Camp, 70 *Bord.* 1802
And in that dream had left my native land, 70 *Bord.* 1840
You are no richer than when you left me? 72 *Bord.* 1920
And you left him alive? 72 *Bord.* 1978
The bell is left, which no one dares remove; 73 *Bord.* 2055
I left him. I believe that there are phantoms, 74 *Bord.* 2083
Is left me still in thee. Nay, shake not so. 75 *Bord.* 2135
Left to the mercy of that savage Man! 76 *Bord.* 2186
Of the bleak Waste—left him—and so he died! 77 *Bord.* 2268
Of having left a thing like her alive! 78 *Bord.* 2313
That he's left, for a bed, to beggars or thieves! 80 †*Address: Child* 19
Have left the mother and the nest; 84 *Shepherd-boys* 7
Gracefully up the gnarled trunk; nor left we unsurveyed 92 *Poet's Dream* 39
As visions still more bright have done, and left no trace behind. 93 *Poet's Dream* 72
Left among her native mountains 93 *Westmoreland Girl* 27
Had left that calling, tempted to entrust 95 *Brothers* 40
But that the Stranger, who had left the grave, 97 *Brothers* 116
The other, left behind, is flowing still. 97 *Brothers* 145
Left in the church-yard wall. That 's Walter Ewbank. 98 *Brothers* 200
They left to him the family heart, and land 98 *Brothers* 211
But Leonard— Then James still is left among you! 99 *Brothers* 290
Was gone to sea, and he was left alone, 100 *Brothers* 338
The power of speech. Both left the spot in silence; 101 *Brothers* 408
No vestige then was left that such had ever been. 102 *Artegal* 8
For ever left alone am I; 114 *Ind. Wom.* 59
Till thirty were not left alive 115 *Last of Flock* 65
All that is left to comfort thee. 117 *Affl. Marg.* 49
Death in a moment parted them, and left 118 *Maternal Grief* 41
When last he sailed, he left the bird behind; 119 *Sailor's Mother* 29
Had left it, to be watched and fed, 119 *Sailor's Mother* 32
And I have left a babe at home: 120 *Emigrant Mother* 26
Alas! before I left the spot, 121 *Emigrant Mother* 39
A portion of the tale may well be left 124 *V. and J.* 176
Of that same town, in which the pair had left 125 *V. and J.* 286
How turn to left, and how to right. 126 *Idiot Boy* 56
In Johnny's left hand you may see 127 *Idiot Boy* 78
That came to him, and left him, on the heights. 132 *Michael* 60
And left, the couple neither gay perhaps 133 *Michael* 120
Though nought was left undone which staff, or voice, 134 *Michael* 192
And left estates and monies to the poor, 135 *Michael* 268
Far more than we have lost is left us yet. 135 *Michael* 276
What will be left to us!—But I forget 137 *Michael* 402
And left the work unfinished when he died. 138 *Michael* 472
In all the neighbourhood:—yet the oak is left 138 *Michael* 479
Of One, a Widow, left beneath a weight 138 *Widow* 4
On which it grew, or to be left alone 149 **A narrow* 31
She left that farewell offering, 154 *Flower Garden* 51
Some ornaments to me are left— 155 *Waterfall* 46
The little careless Broom was left 157 *Oak and Broom* 109
Away they fly to left, to right— 161 *Binnorie* 29
The evil One is left behind. 174 *Waggoner* 1. 115
They checked me—and I left the theme 182 *Waggoner* 4. 201

Left—*continued.*
Is left to muse upon the solemn scene. 184 *Night-piece* 26
I left our cottage-threshold, sallying forth 185 *Nutting* 5
She died, and left to me 187 **Three years* 39
I left her, and pursued my way; 191 *Beggars* 19
Yet as I left I find them here! 192 *Gipsies* 12
When Ruth was left half desolate, 192 *Ruth* 1
This Thorn you on your left espy; 198 *Thorn* 28
And to the left, three yards beyond, 198 *Thorn* 29
A rout this morning left Sir Walter's Hall, 200 *Hart-leap* 13
Sir Walter and the Hart are left alone. 201 *Hart-leap* 28
Had left imprinted on the grassy ground. 201 *Hart-leap* 52
Then home he went, and left the Hart stone-dead, 202 *Hart-leap* 77
He left this moral grafted on his Fate; 214 *Dion* 121
And left as if by earthquake strewn, 214 *Kirkstone* 11
That, as we left the plain, before our sight 219 **This Height* 17
O'er timid waters that have scarcely left 221 *Triad* 134
If here a warrior left a spell, 223 *Wishing-gate* 22
Companions, fear ye to be left behind, 229 *Clouds* 6
With faithful memory left of things 231 *Jew. Fam.* 3
I've left my heart at home. 237 *P. B.* 55
He left a trusty guide for one 240 *P. B.* 339
Turns round his long left ear. 241 *P. B.* 415
Turned round his long left ear. 241 *P. B.* 420
We left our Hero in a trance, 242 *P. B.* 531
Hath left him high in preparation,— 244 *P. B.* 692
—The light had left the lonely taper, 244 *P. B.* 748
And left her mother at sixteen, 246 *P. B.* 894
The moment it has left the virgin's eye, 265 **There is a pleasure* 13
Be left more desolate, more dreary cold 277 **Why art* 11
Man left this Structure to become Time's prey, 283 **Here, where* 2
Of company or friends, and left 295 *Highland Boy* 39
That region left, the vale unfolds 302 *Yarrow V.* 49
Live, and take comfort. Thou hast left behind 305 *Toussaint* 9
Then cleave, O cleave to that which still is left; 306 **Two Voices* 10
Nothing is left which I can venerate; 309 **When, looking* 7
Left single, in bold parley, ye, of yore, 309 *Men of Kent* 9
And left them lying in the silent sun, 310 *Anticip.* 4
And We are left, or shall be left, alone; 310 **Another year* 3
Powers have they left, an impulse, and a claim 316 **It was a* 7
That curbed the baser passions, and left free 329 *Ode: Thanks.* 59
And sober graces, left her for defence 333 **Bruges I* 7
And to the enormous labour left his name, 335 *Aix* 13
He left his Transatlantic home: 348 **Lulled by* 50
Which hath not left the spot unknown 348 **Lulled by* 70
Nor further outlet left to mind or heart? 350 *Des. Stanzas* 2
Who having left the Cemetery stands 355 *Aquap.* 179
But restless Fancy left that olive grove 360 **Near Anio's* 5
Nor grieve the less that skill to him was left 363 **Grieve for* 3
Or aught in Syrian deserts left to save 367 *Trajan* 11
Which she in duty left, sad but not cheerless. 370 *Eg. Maid* 84
So cheered, she left that Island bleak, 371 *Eg. Maid* 157
Of some sweet Babe—Flower stolen, and coarse Weed left 378 *Duddon* 11. 7
And each tumultuous working left behind 384 *Duddon* 33. 11
Long left without a warder, 385 *Yarrow Rev.* 6
The hidden silver Broach was left. 391 *Highland Broach* 60
In the grey sky hath left his lingering Ghost, 392 **Though joy* 4
And she is left alone in heaven; 397 *White Doe* 62
Nor left him at his later day. 399 *White Doe* 282
"For thee, for thee, is left the sense 402 *White Doe* 521
Whom I have left, Love's mildest birth, 403 *White Doe* 617
While ground was left for hope; unblamed 406 *White Doe* 911
Be left, is no restriction laid; 408 *White Doe* 1089
And left—but be the rest unsaid, 410 *White Doe* 1305
"No choice is left, the deed is mine— 411 *White Doe* 1432
A glimmering sense still left, with eyes 412 *White Doe* 1492
There was he left alone, unwept, 412 *White Doe* 1501
—What now is left for pain or fear? 415 *White Doe* 1743
Hath yet this faithful Partner left; 415 *White Doe* 1788
When, left in solitude, erewhile 416 *White Doe* 1838
Back to the Land those Pilgrims left of yore, 443 *Ecc. Sonn.* 3. 14. 8
Woman! the Power who left His throne on high, 447 *Ecc. Sonn.* 3. 27. 1
Throughout the Country they have left, our shores 449 *Ecc. Sonn.* 3. 36. 13
Be left as silent as the mountain-tops, 455 *Rydal Mere* 6
To her I left, shall prove 479 *Somnamb.* 114
Old Simon to the world is left '. 483 *Simon Lee* 27
Hath oftener left me mourning. 484 *Simon Lee* 96
A day like this which I have left 486 **We walked* 23
And left thee but a glimmering of the day; 491 *Tribute: Dog* 16
Or left unthought-of in obscurity,— 494 *Hap. War.* 67
The umbrageous woods are left—how far beneath! 497 **Enough of climbing* 19
Across the slender wrist of the left arm 509 *F. Stone* 53
Thinking of past and gone, with what is left 509 *F. Stone* 81
Nor ever was; I sighed, and left the spot 524 *Epist. Beaumont* 194
With door left open makes a gloomy spot, 524 *Epist. Beaumont* 220
Rich prospect left behind of stream and vale, 524 *Epist. Beaumont* 223
What recompense is kept in store or left 530 *Poor Robin* 33
One living Stay was left, and on that one 531 **I know* 27
This sad belief, the happiest that is left 531 *Octogen.* 6
Still shall be left some corner of the heart 531 *Octogen.* 13
May have a living House still left in thee!" 535 *Egremont* 32
She left her fire, or left her bed, 537 *Goody Blake* 63
Left, 'mid the Records of this Book inscribed, 538 **Lady! a* 3
That no one breathing should be left to perish, 541 *Grace Darl.* 78
For I have left my Father's roof, 542 *Russ. Fug.* 27

Leg. *See* **Mid-leg.**

His spindles sink under him, foot, leg, and thigh !   484 *A plague* 21

Legalised. That legalised exclusion, empty pomp   717 *Prelude* 9. 526

Legalized. These legalized oppressions ! Man— whose name   429 *Ecc. Sonn.* 2. 4. 10

Legate's. At a proud Legate's feet ! The spears that line   428 *Ecc. Sonn.* I. 37. 12

Legberthwaite. The Magog of Legberthwaite dale.   86 *Rural Arch.* 12

Legend. Inscriptive legend which I ween   415 *White Doe* 1764

That legend and her Grandsire's name ;	415 *White Doe* 1766
And many a legend, peopling the dark woods,	758 *Excursion* 1. 165
This sorry Legend ; which by chance we found	816 *Excursion* 4. 1007
Winds an inscriptive legend."—At these words	846 *Excursion* 6. 512

Legendary. Chosen by Rome's legendary Bards, high minds   356 *Aquap.* 271

Legends. Far distant, when, as legends say,   301 *Bran* 57

In Araby, romances ; legends penned   673 *Prelude* 5. 497

Legged. *See* **Cross-legged, Four-legged.**

Legion. Rome's earliest legion passed !   215 *Kirkstone* 44

Legions. Whole legions sink—and, in one instant, find   322 *Humanity, delighting* 35

' My legions in Spain   S.3. 440 *Said red-ribboned* 2

Legions of devils through a key-hole's space.   L.1. 94 *Juvenal* 2. 4

Legislative. Of this recess, their legislative hall,   K.8. 253 *Recluse* 1.1.623

| Their legislative licence to withdraw | L.1. 95 *Juvenal* 3. 23 |
| For Lubbock vote—no legislative hack | L.3. 27 *For Lubbock* 1 |

Legislator's. Is the wise Legislator's view confined.   518 *Pun. Death* 5. 4

Legs. But when the Pony moved his legs,   127 *Idiot Boy* 72

And, while the Pony moves his legs,	127 *Idiot Boy* 77
By catching at their legs, or with his shouts	134 *Michael* 175
And wasted limbs, his legs so long and lean	149 *A narrow* 60
On two poor legs, toward my stone-table .	238 *P. B.* 174
With legs stretched out and stiff he lay :—	241 *P. B.* 451
With legs that move not, if they can,	294 *Jedbor.* 17
His legs are thin and dry.	483 *Simon Lee* 36
Espied him on his legs sustained, blank, mute,	523 *Epist. Beaumont* 140
And there, with small wealth but his legs and his hands,	570 *Farmer* 47
Invests the thriving churl, his legs appear,	880 *Excursion* 8. 404

Leicester's. The Showman chooses well his place, 'tis Leicester's busy Square?   189 *Star-gazers* 5

Lei-gha. " Lei-gha—Lei-gha "—he then cried out,   297 *Highland Boy* 201

" Lei-gha—Lei-gha "—with eager shout ;   297 *Highland Boy* 202

Leine. The softly flowing Leine,   629 *Installation* 60

Leisure. That on the noon-day bank of leisure lie.   19 *Desc. Sk.* 507

Stopped short,—and thence, at leisure, limb by limb	96 *Brothers* 102
Sometimes when he could find a leisure hour	138 *Michael* 440
Preferring studious leisure, I had chosen	150 *When, to* 2
Of hearts at leisure.	158 *In youth* 56
He thus pursues his thoughts at leisure.	174 *Waggoner* I. 109
She bends) at leisure may be seen	221 *Triad* 136
Inspired, may in thy leisure claim a part ;	269 *If these* 4
Books, leisure, perfect freedom, and the talk	304 *I grieved* 10
To leisure, to forbearances sedate ;	334 *The Spirit* 12
Lulling the leisure of that high-perched town,	352 *Aquap.* 12
Peace, leisure, freedom, moderate desires ;	356 *Aquap.* 260
Short leisure even in busiest days ;	376 *The Minstrels* 68
How sweet were leisure ! could it yield no more	384 *Duddon* 31. 9
May gather up our thoughts, and mark at leisure	443 *Ecc. Sonn.* 3. 12. 13
Nor leisure unto thee more worth to give ;	562 *Cuck.and Night.* 303
He then would steal at leisure hours,	579 *Sweet Flower* 26
And when the precious hours of leisure came,	584 *Ch. Lamb* 11
Think calmly on the past, and mark at leisure	626 *The confidence* 13
Days of sweet leisure, taxed with patient thought	632 *Prelude* 1. 43
When in our pinnace we returned at leisure	644 *Prelude* 2. 165
At leisure, thence, through tracts of thin resort,	689 *Prelude* 7. 172

Lie—*continued.*
Where mighty *minds* lie visibly entombed, 654 *Prelude* 3. 339
Of such a madness, reason did lie couched. 668 *Prelude* 5. 152
Wert used to lie and gaze upon the clouds 679 *Prelude* 6. 269
Lie melancholy among weary bones. 684 *Prelude* 6. 648
Whose wonders in a covered wain lie hid. 699 *Prelude* 8. 36
Lie in the arbitrement of those who ruled 720 *Prelude* 10. 127
To mingle, I beheld the vessels lie, 722 *Prelude* 10. 317
The first was service paid to things which lie 724 *Prelude* 10. 431
But said to me, " My head will soon lie low ; " 726 *Prelude* 10. 539
Human, or such as lie beyond the grave. 762 *Excursion* 1. 433
There let it lie—how foolish are such thoughts ! 763 *Excursion* 1. 496
—In rugged arms how softly does it lie, 777 *Excursion* 2. 358
And where they lie, how answered and appeased. 813 *Excursion* 4. 813
Beneath this turf lie mouldering at our feet : 832 *Excursion* 5. 653
Here to lie down in lasting quiet, he, 835 *Excursion* 5. 883
Whereon he sits ! Whose deep foundations lie 838 *Excursion* 6. 3
That, undivided, their remains should lie. 845 *Excursion* 6. 502
" These grassy heaps lie amicably close," 857 *Excursion* 7. 31
Fall to the ground ; whose gifts of nature lie 862 *Excursion* 7. 317
How sweet thus living without life to lie, S.3. 441 **Come, gentle* 3
Should lie beneath the cold starlight ! K.8. 220 **The snow-tracks* 37
That lie together, some in heaps, and some K.8. 223 **There is a shapeless* 2
To lie beside the lonely mountain brooks, K.8. 224 **I will* 2
Lie loose on the bare turf, some half-o'ergrown K.8. 226 **I will* 65
Lie down and be forgotten in the dust, K.8. 255 *Recluse* 1.1.694
Right gladly would I lie awake K.8. 262 **Ah ! if* 3
Lief. I had as lief turn to the Friar's school 45 *Bord.* 467
Liege. A loyal band to follow their liege Lord 329 *Ode : Thanks.* 60
Esteem me, Liege ! if I, whose skill 372 *Eg. Maid* 244
Hast thou thy own liege subjects to destroy ? 563 *Troilus* 70
And written lore, acknowledged my liege lord, 654 *Prelude* 3. 376
Liegeman. Duty's intrepid liegeman, see, the palm 312 *Clarkson* 9
Lieges. Thy feathered Lieges bill and wings 506 **While from* 25
Lies. Then, when he lies, out-stretched, at even-tide 18 *Desc. Sk.* 425
Lies on your way ; accept us as your Guides. 43 *Bord.* 357
He will deny it to the last. He lies 54 *Bord.* 915
And higher far than lies within earth's bounds : 62 *Bord.* 1373
Coward I have been ; know, there lies not now, 78 *Bord.* 2299
And he lies by her side." 84 *We are Seven* 60
We'll take another : who is he that lies 98 *Brothers* 197
I buried him, poor Youth, and there he lies ! 101 *Brothers* 382
And one across the bosom lies— 112 **How rich* 15
And here it lies upon my arm, 116 *Last of Flock* 97
And fortune with her gifts and lies. 117 *Affl. Marg.* 42
Old Susan lies a-bed in pain, 126 *Idiot Boy* 24
Where a cross-legged Knight lies sculptured 142 *Arm. Lady* 153
Blessing the bed she lies upon ? " 144 **Driven in* 46
Lies with her infant lamb ; I see 156 *Oak and Broom* 87
Simon's sickly daughter lies, 157 *Sexton* 14
That lies dead and still, 166 *Stray Pleasures* 2
You call it, " Love lies bleeding,"—so you may, 169 *Love lies Bleeding* 1
Called the dejected Lingerer *Love lies Bleeding.* 170 **Never enlivened* 27
Glimmering faintly where it lies ; 175 *Waggoner* 1. 161
The little Babe lies buried there, 200 *Thorn* 230
Down to the very fountain where he lies. 201 *Hart-leap* 56
Small difference lies between thy creed and mine : 203 *Hart-leap* 162
And cool, though in the depth it lies 237 *P. B.* 99
That overwhelmed and prostrate lies, 242 *P. B.* 557
Where lies the Land to which yon Ship must go ? 258 **Where lies the Land* 1
Of him who lies beneath. Most wretched one, 275 *Gravestone* 6
Lies fixed for ages on his conscious neck ; 278 *Wellington* 4
Even for the tenants of the zone that lies 284 *Departure* 3
Lies gathered to his Father's side, 285 *Grave of Burns* 63
Lies buried in this lonely place. 289 *Glen-Al.* 32
Beneath thee, that is England ; there she lies. 303 **Fair Star* 10
That deeper far it lies 329 *Ode : Thanks.* 55
A verdant path before us lies ; 339 **Meek Virgin* 38
In lowliness—a mid-way tract there lies 355 *Aquap.* 148
For all that tottering stands or prostrate lies, 360 *Alban Hills* 4
Here, where the Princess lies, begin the trial ; 373 *Eg. Maid* 266
On infant bosoms lonely Nature lies. 377 *Duddon* 5. 14
The envied flower beholding, as it lies 377 *Duddon* 7. 3
That curbs a foaming brook, a Graveyard lies ; 387 **Part fenced* 2
While this radiant Creature lies 397 *White Doe* 153
When snow lies heavy upon the land." 403 *White Doe* 624
Upon the turf-clad height he lies 404 *White Doe* 771
Endless history that lies 415 *White Doe* 1716
Lies open on the sabbath day ; 416 *White Doe* 1888
Of lofty thoughts, the way before us lies 445 *Ecc. Sonn.* 3. 19. 3
Where lies the truth ? has Man, in wisdom's creed, 461 **Where lies the truth* 1
Beneath stern mountains many a soft vale lies, 472 **Arran ! a* 13
Stretched on the dying Mother's lap, lies dead 476 *Howard* 1
While a fair region round the traveller lies 480 **Most sweet* 3
Children are blest, and powerful ; their world lies 488 *Pers. Talk* 23
Lies the Babe, in helplessness 502 **Like a* 3
Will not be found. Her right hand, as it lies 509 *F. Stone* 52
Daily exposed, woe that unshrouded lies ; 516 **Feel for* 2
Determined, lies beyond the State's embrace, 519 *Pun. Death* 8. 2
Instinct with light whose sweetest promise lies, 525 *Epist. Beaumont* 254
From all that lies within the scope 534 **Blest is* 67
" Deep he lies in Jordan flood." 535 *Egremont* 50
Or set, to him where now he lies, 577 **I come* 24
There, cleaving to the ground, it lies 580 *John Words.* 55
This Stone is sacred. Here he lies apart 584 *Ch. Lamb* 2
'Mid mouldering ruins low he lies ; 586 *Hogg* 10

Lies—*continued.*
Heaven lies about us in our infancy ! 588 *Immortality* 66
See, where 'mid work of his own hand he lies, 588 *Immortality* 87
But deeper lies the heart of peace 623 *G. and S. Green* 21
The road lies plain before me ;—'tis a theme 641 *Prelude* 1. 640
It lies far hidden from the reach of words. 651 *Prelude* 3. 184
Mute, looking at the grave in which he lies ! 671 *Prelude* 5. 397
That lies before us, needful to be told. 688 *Prelude* 7. 51
Another lies at length, beside a range 690 *Prelude* 7. 205
Lies to the ear, and lies to every sense— 695 *Prelude* 7. 581
Than he lies down upon some shining rock, 702 *Prelude* 8. 237
In those vast regions where his service lies, 703 *Prelude* 8. 252
He thus imparted :— " In a spot that lies 773 *Excursion* 2. 155
And the defence that lies in boundless love 801 *Excursion* 4. 23
And over-constant yearning ;—there—there lies 804 *Excursion* 4. 177
Within whose silent chambers treasure lies 809 *Excursion* 4. 565
Lies open : we have heard from you a voice 818 *Excursion* 4. 1118
" Rites which attest that Man by nature lies 826 *Excursion* 5. 294
Lies within reach, and one day shall be gained." 827 *Excursion* 5. 308
Seek from the torturing crucible. There lies 832 *Excursion* 5. 634
Till night lies black upon the ground. 'But come, 834 *Excursion* 5. 766
There lies the channel, and original bed, 837 *Excursion* 5. 1004
" Close to his destined habitation, lies 841 *Excursion* 6. 212
Lies guarded by its neighbour ; the small heap 850 *Excursion* 6. 790
In a dependent chapelry that lies 862 *Excursion* 7. 347
Of what lies here confines us to degrees 863 *Excursion* 7. 391
A plain blue stone, a gentle Dalesman lies, 863 *Excursion* 7. 400
That lies beyond life's ordinary bounds, 866 *Excursion* 7. 569
And she lies conscious, in a blissful rest, 867 *Excursion* 7. 646
If consciousness could reach him where he lies 875 *Excursion* 8. 36
To the lake's margin, where a boat lies moored 890 *Excursion* 9. 425
Good honest souls !—if right my judgment lies L.1. 95 *Juvenal* 3. 20
Than joy itself—for underneath it lies [?] **A sad* 5
Liest. Thou liest in Abraham's bosom all the year ; 258 **It is a* 12
Heaven's blessing be upon thee where thou liest 659 *Prelude* 4. 33
Lieu. In lieu of wandering, as we did, through vales 669 *Prelude* 5. 235
Life. *See* **Country-life.**
Along the mystic streams of Life and Death. 12 *Desc. Sk.* 72
Thro' worlds where Life, and Voice, and Motion sleep ; 16 *Desc. Sk.* 310
—Far different life from what Tradition hoar 17 *Desc. Sk.* 386
With all the tender charities of life, 19 *Desc. Sk.* 511
An emblem of his own unfruitful life : 23 *Yew-tree* 32
The world, and human life, appeared a scene 23 *Yew-tree* 41
Of virtuous life, by pious parents bred ; 28 *Guilt* 200
' Here will I dwell,' said I, ' my whole life long, 31 *Guilt* 363
Unsought for was the help that did my life recall. 31 *Guilt* 387
But life of happier sort set forth to me, 32 *Guilt* 408
Trusted my life to what chance bounty yields, 32 *Guilt* 435
' My life, Heaven knows, hath long been burthensome ; 35 *Guilt* 586
Of some dark deed to which in early life 37 *Bord.* 15
You know that you have saved his life. I know it. 38 *Bord.* 27
I'd wager on his life for twenty years. 41 *Bord.* 246
So far into your journey ! on my life, 43 *Bord.* 334
What life is this of ours, how sleep will master 45 *Bord.* 419
Your life is at my mercy. Do not harm me, 46 *Bord.* 502
Oswald, the firm foundation of my life 47 *Bord.* 547
Reverence for life so deeply, that they spare 48 *Bord.* 586
Yours is no common life. Self-stationed here, 48 *Bord.* 605
Which to our kind is natural as life, 48 *Bord.* 627
Now, on my life, I grieve for you. The misery 53 *Bord.* 879
Must needs step in, and save my life. The look 54 *Bord.* 919
That wretched life of thine shall be the forfeit. 54 *Bord.* 950
Tottering upon the very verge of life, 57 *Bord.* 1071
Which haunts this Oswald. Power is life to him 63 *Bord.* 1432
Hedge in the life of every pest and plague 66 *Bord.* 1582
His good works will be balm and life to him. 67 *Bord.* 1632
That smile hath life in it ! This road is perilous ; 67 *Bord.* 1646
Nor any living thing whose lot of life 68 *Bord.* 1710
That was no life for me—I was o'erthrown, 69 *Bord.* 1768
That waking life had never power to give. 69 *Bord.* 1794
Life stretched before me smooth as some broad way 70 *Bord.* 1836
He did not seem to wish for life : 72 *Bord.* 1931
Helpless, and loved me dearer than his life. 77 *Bord.* 2254
Yet loathing life—till anger is appeased 78 *Bord.* 2352
So was it when my life began ; 79 **My heart* 3
And feels its life in every limb, 83 *We are Seven* 3
Whose life and limbs the flood had spared ; 85 *Shepherd-boys* 94
Slips in a moment out of life. 88 *H. C.* 33
To the life of human kind. 90 *Longest Day* 36
A profitable life : some glance along, 95 *Brothers* 2
The life he had lived there ; both for the sake 96 *Brothers* 70
You live, Sir, in these dales, a quiet life : 97 *Brothers* 121
Possess a kind of second life : no doubt 98 *Brothers* 185
For the boy loved the life which we lead here ; 100 *Brothers* 296
Supporting life by water from the spring, 103 *Artegal* 100
Awaits on virtuous life, and ever most 105 *Artegal* 187
And love the blessed life that we lead here. 106 *Farewell* 32
If human Life do pass away, 110 **Look at* 7
O dearer far than light and life are dear, 112 **O dearer* 1
To bind a lingering life in chains : 113 *Lament* 44
If they have any life or no. 114 *Ind. Wom.* 64
Death, life, and sleep, reality and thought, 118 *Maternal Grief* 11
By ready nature for a life of love, 122 *V. and J.* 32
Life turned the meanest of her implements, 122 *V. and J.* 42
As if her very life would fail. 126 *Idiot Boy* 21
Yet, for his life, he cannot tell 127 *Idiot Boy* 115
Her life and soul were buried. 127 *Idiot Boy* 131
If he is hurt in life or limb "— 128 *Idiot Boy* 190
That God poor Susan's life would spare, 128 *Idiot Boy* 200

Life—*continued.*
Nor shorten the sweet life, too fugitive, 501 Humanity 109
With hoary Winter, and Life touch, 502 Seasons 19
Then, amid the storms of life 503 *Like a 74
Upon the events of home as life proceeds, 503 Warning 13
And shunning nought, their own peculiar life 508 F. Stone 36
And breathing life of flesh, as if already 510 *Among a 7
A single human life have wrongly taken, 517 Pun. Death 3. 10
In the weak love of life his least command. 518 Pun. Death 4. 14
The last alternative of Life or Death. 518 Pun. Death 5. 14
Endues her conscience with external life 519 Pun. Death 9. 10
Our bodily life, some plead, that life the shrine 519 Pun. Death 10. 1
Ah, think how one compelled for life to abide 519 Pun. Death 11. 1
Raised by remembrances of misused life, 526 *Soon did 9
Above all grandeur, a pure life uncrossed 528 *Those breathing 89
That life—the flowery path that winds by stealth— 528 *Those breathing 91
So changes mortal Life with fleeting years; 533 *Once I 37
There lived, and on the cross His life resigned, 534 *When in 14
Life to risk by sea and land, 535 Egremont 26
His Brother's life, for Lands' and Castle's sake? 535 Egremont 48
Of private life their natural pleasantness, 538 *In desultory 36
A life declining with the golden light 539 *Lady! a 60
Hope to the hopeless, to the dying, life— 541 Grace Darl. 70
When life would be a blot. 544 Russ. Fug. 200
From social life estranged; 545 Russ. Fug. 300
To end life here like this poor deer, 545 Russ. Fug. 311
Such is life; and death a shadow 550 Hermit's Cell 3. 7
Would my Life present to Thee, 550 Hermit's Cell 4. 14
Who do not think in love their life to lead; 559 Cuck.and Night. 132
"For term of life Love shall have hold of me"— 562 Cuck.and Night. 289
As ye have heard; such life 'gan he to lead 564 Troilus 111
A life and soul, to every mode of being 567 Cumb. Beg. 78
Who live a life of virtuous decency, 568 Cumb. Beg. 134
Long for some moments in a weary life 568 Cumb. Beg. 148
Has hung around him: and, while life is his, 568 Cumb. Beg. 168
That his life hath received, to the last will remain. 569 Farmer 12
For me with sighs be troubled. Not from life 573 Chiabrera 1. 2
Have I been taken; this is genuine life 573 Chiabrera 1. 3
And this alone—the life which now I live 573 Chiabrera 1. 4
A roseate fragrance breathed.—O human life, 573 Chiabrera 2. 13
There never breathed a man who, when his life 574 Chiabrera 4. 1
Was closing, might not of that life relate 574 Chiabrera 4. 2
We sail the sea of life—a *Calm* One finds, 574 Chiabrera 4. 25
How fleeting and how frail is human life! 575 Chiabrera 6. 16
Alas! the twentieth April of his life 575 Chiabrera 8. 10
But truly did *He* live his life. Urbino, 576 Chiabrera 9. 21
"I AM THE WAY, THE TRUTH, AND THE LIFE." 577 Cenotaph 13
Through life was OWEN LLOYD endeared 577 *By playful 5
Flowed from his life what still they hold, 578 *I come 62
Or merely silent Nature's breathing life. 578 Peele Castle 28
And free for life, these hills to climb, 579 *Sweet Flower 13
Labouring for life, in hope and fear, 579 *Sweet Flower 40
Upon a way of life unmeet 580 *Sweet Flower 60
Of hopeful life,—by battle's whirlwind blown 582 Invoc. Earth 12
Whose life was, like the violet, sweet, 583 *O for a 41
That sense, the bland philosophy of life, 583 *With copious 13
Many and strange, that hung about his life; 584 Ch. Lamb 29
With life itself. Thus, 'mid a shifting world, 585 Ch. Lamb 94
Such were they—such thro' life they *might* have been 585 Ch. Lamb 98
Our haughty life is crowned with darkness, 586 Hogg 29
Through his industrious life, and Christian faith 587 Crosth. 17
Some fragment from his dream of human life, 589 Immortality 91
That Life brings with her in her equipage; 589 Immortality 105
Heavy as frost, and deep almost as life! 589 Immortality 132
When Life rear'd laughing up her morning sun; 592 Ev. Wk. Quarto 28
Nought else of man or life remains behind 598 Ev.Wk.Quarto 375
Deny'd the bread of life the foodful ear, 608 Desc.Sk.Quarto 320
Thro' worlds where Life and Sound, and Motion sleep, 609 Desc.Sk.Quarto 375
Far different life to what tradition hoar 610 Desc.Sk.Quarto 474
To pant slow up the endless Alp of life. 613 Desc.Sk.Quarto 593
Shall love, 'till Life has broke her golden bowl, 615 Desc.Sk.Quarto 741
If e'er they smooth'd the rugged walks of life, 619 School Ex. 104
Life left my loaded heart, and closing eye; 619 *She wept 5
Dear was the pause of life, and dear the sigh 619 *She wept 7
A body without life— 623 G. and S. Green 14
And help life onward in its noblest aim. 628 *Deign, Sovereign 28
But with a Delphic life, in sight 629 Installation 67
Who threw the Saxon shield o'er Luther's life 629 Installation 100
With any promises of human life), 632 Prelude 1. 25
I spare to tell of what ensued, the life 633 Prelude 1. 108
Came hopes still higher, that with outward life 634 Prelude 1. 119
Of Truth that cherishes our daily life; 635 Prelude 1. 230
With life and nature—purifying thus 638 Prelude 1. 410
The bond of union between life and joy. 640 Prelude 1. 558
And sweet sensations that throw back our life, 641 Prelude 1. 633
Through later years the story of my life. 641 Prelude 1. 639
And surety of our earthly life, a light 645 Prelude 2. 180
Poetic spirit of our human life, 646 Prelude 2. 261
Hence life, and change, and beauty, solitude 646 Prelude 2. 294
And intellectual life; but that the soul, 646 Prelude 2. 315
In the great social principle of life 647 Prelude 2. 389
The blessing of my life; the gift is yours, 648 Prelude 2. 445
I gave a moral life: I saw them feel, 651 Prelude 3. 129
And here, O Friend! have I retraced my life 651 Prelude 3. 167
In this new life. Imagination slept, 652 Prelude 3. 257
With the accustomed garb of daily life) 653 Prelude 3. 271
Such life might not inaptly be compared 654 Prelude 3. 332
Led in abstemiousness a studious life; 655 Prelude 3. 449
In my own mind remote from social life, 656 Prelude 3. 511

Life—*continued.*
Among the conflicts of substantial life; 656 Prelude 3. 526
The surfaces of artificial life 657 Prelude 3. 559
Of texture midway between life and books. 657 Prelude 3. 578
And what may rather have been called to life 658 Prelude 3. 612
And more than eighty, of untroubled life, 659 Prelude 4. 37
"An emblem here behold of thy own life; 659 Prelude 4. 61
How life pervades the undecaying mind; 660 Prelude 4. 165
In human Life, the daily life of those 661 Prelude 4. 192
Wore in old time. Her smooth domestic life, 661 Prelude 4. 222
Of character or life; but at that time, 663 Prelude 4. 301
Things that aspire to unconquerable life; 666 Prelude 5. 20
Of day returning and of life revived. 666 Prelude 5. 37
And their high privilege of lasting life, 666 Prelude 5. 66
In the simplicities of opening life 669 Prelude 5. 277
Nor what it augurs of the life to come; 673 Prelude 5. 511
To earth and human life, the Song might dwell 673 Prelude 5. 538
Of human life. What wonder, then, if sounds 674 Prelude 5. 577
And the simplicities of cottage life 675 Prelude 6. 2
And some remain, hopes for my future life. 675 Prelude 6. 47
Supreme Existence, the surpassing life 677 Prelude 6. 134
Of my collegiate life—far less intense 677 Prelude 6. 183
Of my collegiate life I still have had 679 Prelude 6. 287
Compelled to be a life unto herself, 679 Prelude 6. 303
Murmured the sister streams of Life and Death, 681 Prelude 6. 439
Sweet coverts did we cross of pastoral life, 682 Prelude 6. 500
Of social life, I looked upon these things 686 Prelude 6. 767
Yet, undetermined to what course of life 688 Prelude 7. 58
And life and labour seem but one, I filled 688 Prelude 7. 71
Or life or death upon the battle-field. 689 Prelude 7. 141
Of life, and life-like mockery beneath, 690 Prelude 7. 246
And recent things yet warm with life; a sea-fight, 691 Prelude 7. 291
I heard, and for the first time in my life, 693 Prelude 7. 384
How casual incidents of real life, 693 Prelude 7. 402
That bind the perishable hours of life 694 Prelude 7. 462
When the great tide of human life stands still; 697 Prelude 7. 657
Its currents; magnifies its shoals of life 698 Prelude 7. 751
The soul of Beauty and enduring Life 698 Prelude 7. 767
The days departed start again to life, 699 Prelude 8. 49
Were the unluxuriant produce of a life 701 Prelude 8. 161
Smooth life had flock and shepherd in old time, 701 Prelude 8. 173
Smooth life had herdsman, and his snow-white herd 701 Prelude 8. 177
His devious course. A glimpse of such sweet life 702 Prelude 8. 209
A freeman, wedded to his life of hope 703 Prelude 8. 253
Alone, that something of a better life 703 Prelude 8. 313
With the deformities of crowded life, 704 Prelude 8. 332
Among the simple shapes of human life 704 Prelude 8. 372
Of life and glory. In the midst stood Man, 706 Prelude 8. 485
Of present, actual, superficial life, 706 Prelude 8. 506
I trembled,—thought, at times, of human life 706 Prelude 8. 512
The end of life, and everything we know. 707 Prelude 8. 529
Stript of their harmonising soul, the life 708 Prelude 8. 620
Of human life: Nature had led me on; 709 Prelude 8. 679
And all the attire of ordinary life, 711 Prelude 9. 84
The soil of common life, was, at that time, 712 Prelude 9. 166
Of books and common life, it makes sure way 714 Prelude 9. 336
Of royal courts, and that voluptuous life 714 Prelude 9. 345
On firm foundations, making social life, 715 Prelude 9. 360
Fashioned his life; and many a long discourse, 715 Prelude 9. 421
That Liberty, and Life, and Death would soon 720 Prelude 10. 125
Of life and death, in majesty severe 721 Prelude 10. 185
And all the accidents of life were pressed 723 Prelude 10. 349
The veins that branch through every frame of life, 724 Prelude 10. 423
Life from the young Republic; that new foes 727 Prelude 11. 14
As books and common intercourse with life 728 Prelude 11. 95
They clung, as if they were its life, nay more, 730 Prelude 11. 221
To anatomise the frame of social life; 731 Prelude 11. 280
(Too well I loved, in that my spring of life, 732 Prelude 11. 326
With an impassioned life, what feeble ones 735 Prelude 12. 104
When the bodily eye, in every stage of life 736 Prelude 12. 128
By her benign simplicity of life, 736 Prelude 12. 161
Are piety, her life is gratitude. 736 Prelude 12. 173
Too forcibly, too early in my life, 737 Prelude 12. 202
Among those passages of life that give 737 Prelude 12. 220
Of life: the hiding-places of man's power 738 Prelude 12. 279
Substance and life to what I feel, enshrining, 738 Prelude 12. 284
The field of human life, in heart and mind 740 Prelude 13. 17
In man, and in the frame of social life, 740 Prelude 13. 35
Of life and death, revolving. Above all 740 Prelude 13. 39
Life, human life, with all its sacred claims 741 Prelude 13. 73
There are among the walks of homely life 743 Prelude 13. 266
Of human life. I felt that the array 744 Prelude 13. 287
To rouse them; in a world of life they live, 747 Prelude 14. 105
Hence cheerfulness for acts of daily life, 747 Prelude 14. 121
Oh! who is he that hath his whole life long 748 Prelude 14. 130
Revolving with the accidents of life, 748 Prelude 14. 148
For that which moves with light and life informed, 748 Prelude 14. 161
The works of man and face of human life; 749 Prelude 14. 202
Faith in life endless, the sustaining thought 749 Prelude 14. 204
Of female softness shall his life be full, 749 Prelude 14. 229
In life or nature of those charms minute 749 Prelude 14. 241
Of life and death, time and eternity, 750 Prelude 14. 287
In life among the passions of mankind, 750 Prelude 14. 325
I led an undomestic wanderer's life, 751 Prelude 14. 350
Of mine can give it life,) in firm belief 751 Prelude 14. 356
I said unto the life which I had lived, 751 Prelude 14. 377
Whether to me shall be allotted life, 751 Prelude 14. 388
And, with life, power to accomplish aught of worth, 751 Prelude 14. 389
Oh! yet a few short years of useful life, 752 Prelude 14. 430
Had reached its close; but Life is insecure, 753 *Oft, through 10
"On Man, on Nature, and on Human Life, 755 Recluse 1. 1. 754

Life's—*continued.*
Of natural beauty and life's daily rounds, . . 522 *Epist. Beaumont* 53
Life's book for Thee may lie unclosed, till age . 529 **Those breathing* 139
Life's daily tasks with them to share . . . . 530 *Gleaner* 28
Such happy privilege hath life's gay Prime, . . 532 **Once I* 28
Nor in life's vigorous season did I shun . . 575 *Chiabrera* 6. 4
The Soul that rises with us, our life's Star, . . 588 *Immortality* 59
Soft gales and dews of life's delicious morn, . . 613 *Desc.Sk.Quarto* 634
And wakes anew life's glimmering trembling fires, 619 *School Ex.* 100
She wept.—Life's purple tide began to flow . . 619 **She wept* 1
Through shades that solemnize Life's calm decline,. 627 **The star* 5
Of life's sweet season—could have seen unmoved 652 *Prelude* 3. 222
Bending beneath our life's mysterious weight . 672 *Prelude* 5. 418
Life's morning radiance hath not left the hills, . 675 *Prelude* 6. 51
Leaves far behind life's treacherous vanities, . . 682 *Prelude* 6. 453
For present good in life's familiar face, . . . 741 *Prelude* 13. 62
The bliss of walking daily in life's prime . . . 741 *Prelude* 13. 122
That in life's every-day appearances . . . . 745 *Prelude* 13. 368
Strewing in peace life's humblest ground with herbs, 750 *Prelude* 14. 300
When her life's Helpmate on a sick-bed lay, . . 764 *Excursion* 1. 551
For their own sakes, as mortal life's chief good, . 791 *Excursion* 3. 365
Life's genuine inspiration, happiness . . . . 792 *Excursion* 3. 433
Our happy life's only remaining stay— . . . 795 *Excursion* 3. 648
Upon life's surface. What, though in my veins . 796 *Excursion* 3. 741
" Life's autumn past, I stand on winter's verge ; . 810 *Excursion* 4. 611
Frail life's possessions, that even they whose fate 822 *Excursion* 5. 24
How idly, how perversely, life's whole course, . 826 *Excursion* 5. 258
Their life's appointed prison ; not more free . . 846 *Excursion* 6. 535
Of life's autumnal season.—Shall I tell . . . 849 *Excursion* 6. 742
For a life's stay (slender it was, but sure) . . . 859 *Excursion* 7. 133
That lies beyond life's ordinary bounds, . . . 866 *Excursion* 7. 569
Yet happy they who in life's later scene . . . L.1. 96 *Juvenal* 3. 53

Life-supporting. And its small lot of life-supporting fields, ... 822 *Excursion* 5. 2

Life-threatening. Before the point of the life-threatening spear . . . . 718 *Prelude* 10. 23

Life-veins. Both sank and died, the life-veins of the chased . . . . 393 *Hart's-horn* 7

Lift. Nor morsel to my mouth that day did lift, . 31 *Guilt* 372
Last night, when moved to lift the avenging steel, 59 *Bord.* 1213
Heaven forbid that I should lift my hand . . 71 *Bord.* 1911
Oh ! lift me up and carry me to the place. . . 72 *Bord.* 2010
Shall lift his country's fame above the polar star ! 103 *Artegal* 56
I cannot lift my limbs to know . . . . . . 114 *Ind. Wom.* 63
Lift me, guide me, till I find . . . . . . 159 **Up with me* 6
Lift me, guide me, high and high . . . . . 159 **Up with me* 14
Lift men from their native stations, ... 163 *Hint* 23
That no philosophy can lift, ... 225 *Present.* 26
Lift up that grey-haired forehead, and rejoice . 255 *Detraction* 13
And gaily lift its fearless brim . . . . . . 296 *Highland Boy* 124
If a new Temple lift her votive brow . . . . 327 *Ode 1815* 49
Who sees, may lift a streaming eye . . . . 330 *Ode : Thanks.* 99
Higher to lift their lofty heads, impelled . . . 354 *Aquap.* 145
Once more did gentle Nina lift . . . . . . 371 *Eg. Maid* 181
Lift, and encircle with a cloudy chair, ... 382 *Duddon* 25. 3
Lift up your hearts, ye Mourners ! for the might . 387 *Scott* 8
Spare it, ye waves, and lift the mariner, . . . 469 **The feudal* 9
A voice—that world whose veil no hand can lift . 519 *Pun. Death* 10. 8
And such as lift their foreheads over-prized, . . 530 *Poor Robin* 30
You lift up your eyes !—but I guess that you frame 570 *Farmer* 41
And skyward lift, like one that prays, his hand, . 596 *Ev. Wk. Quarto* 264
Lift, all serene, their still, illumin'd forms, . . 612 *Desc.Sk.Quarto* 565
Nor seldom did I lift our cottage latch . . . 647 *Prelude* 2. 339
The long-roofed chapel of King's College lift . . 649 *Prelude* 3. 4
Would lift, and in his face look wistfully : . . 769 *Excursion* 1. 897
To lift thee high above the misty air . . . . 787 *Excursion* 3. 103
That spake was capable to lift the soul . . . 805 *Excursion* 4. 252
To lift the creature toward that eminence . . 827 *Excursion* 5. 298
Stone lift its forehead emulous of stone . . . 847 *Excursion* 6. 625
With admiration would he lift his eyes . . . 868 *Excursion* 7. 747
They lift the animal being, do themselves . . K.8. 249 *Recluse* 1.1.454

Lifted. *See* **Deftly-lifted, Far-lifted.**
Or hang on tip-toe at the lifted latch. . . . . 32 *Guilt* 418
And lifted from the grassy floor, stilling his faint alarms, ... 92 *Poet's Dream* 18
Sent to his heart ! he lifted up his eyes, . . . 96 *Brothers* 95
As the Priest lifted up the latch, turned round,— 102 *Brothers* 410
" Lifted in magnanimity above . . . . . 105 *Artegal* 178
And never lifted up a single stone. . . . . . 138 *Michael* 466
And, fairly lifted from my feet, ... 179 *Waggoner* 3. 88
Strikes upon his lifted face, ... 181 *Waggoner* 4. 151
Anon his lifted eyes . . . . 213 *Dion* 65
A veil is lifted—can she slight . . . . . . 215 *Kirkstone* 63
Is lifted of a foaming surge— . . . . . . 242 *P. B.* 559
Shouts rise, and storms of sound from lifted trumpets blow ! . . . . 346 *Processions* 18
To lifted eyelids, and a doubtful shining. . . . 374 *Eg. Maid* 336
By sorrow lifted towards her God ; . . . . 416 *White Doe* 1851
In Heaven, have lifted up their hearts to laud . 446 *Ecc. Sonn.* 3. 25. 6
'Tis, finally, the Man, who, lifted high, . . . 494 *Hap. War.* 65
And lifted up this Martyr from the bier, . . . 556 *Prioress* 229
He swells his lifted chest, and backward flings . 595 *Ev. Wk. Quarto* 201
In measured gesture lifted to his head . . . 664 *Prelude* 4. 414
Lifted above the ground by airy fancies, . . . 674 *Prelude* 5. 567
Lifted, in union with the purest, best, ... 748 *Prelude* 14. 185
The threshold, lifted with light hand the latch : . 766 *Excursion* 1. 647
In that one moment when the corse is lifted . . 780 *Excursion* 2. 556
" So was he lifted gently from the ground, . . 784 *Excursion* 2. 827
The Solitary lifted toward the hills . . . . 808 *Excursion* 4. 505
With lifted hands invoked, and songs of praise : . 811 *Excursion* 4. 680

Lifted—*continued.*
He paused—and having lifted up his eyes . . 836 *Excursion* 5. 900
Of ancient minster lifted above the cloud . . . 838 *Excursion* 6. 21
We sojourn, have I lifted up my soul, ... 895 *Excursion* 9. 741
They see the offering of my lifted hands, . . . 895 *Excursion* 9. 748

Lifteth. For Him who lifteth up and layeth low ; . 330 *Ode : Thanks.* 89

Lifting. And, lifting up his head, he then would gaze 23 *Yew-tree* 33
Said she, lifting up her veil ; . . . . . . 139 *Arm. Lady* 8
Not lifting yet the head that evening bowed ; . 153 *Morn. Ex.* 26
Thus, in their stations, lifting tow'rd the sky . . 227 *Vernal Ode* 61
Albeit lifting human to divine, ... 357 *Aquap.* 308
Lifting them up, the worship to confound . . 436 *Ecc. Sonn.* 2. 33. 8
Lifting her front with modest grace . . . . 533 **Blest is* 23
Lifting the boy to man's estate, had called . . 585 *Ch. Lamb* 89
He thus continued, lifting up his eyes . . . 802 *Excursion* 4. 33
The nightly hunter, lifting a bright eye . . . 814 *Excursion* 4. 861
And admiration ; lifting up a veil, ... 848 *Excursion* 6. 649

Lifts. No answer—hush—lost wretch, he lifts his hand . . . . 67 *Bord.* 1669
She lifts the knocker, rap, rap, rap ; . . . . 128 *Idiot Boy* 248
She lifts her head for endless spring, ... 203 *Brougham* 9
With faith, the Suppliant heavenward lifts her hands ; . . . . 209 *Laod.* 8
For the tired slave, Song lifts the languid oar, . 233 *Power of Sound* 53
He lifts his head, he sees his staff ; . . . . . 242 *P. B.* 541
He lifts his head—and sees the Ass . . . . 248 *P. B.* 1096
In this firm hour Salvation lifts her horn. . . . 326 **Emperors and* 8
That lifts the spirit to a calmer height, . . . 349 *Val. Dover* 13
Again he lifts his eyes ; and lo ! . . . . . 404 *White Doe* 778
He from the pulpit lifts his awful hand ; . . . 444 *Ecc. Sonn.* 3. 18. 11
And lifts the latch for him that he may pass. . . 566 *Cumb. Beg.* 36
That lifts up the veil of our nature in thee. . . 572 *Avarice* 48
She lifts in silence up her lovely face ; . . . . 599 *Ev. Wk. Quarto* 402
Or moonlight Upland lifts her hoary breast ; . . 602 *Desc. Sk. Quarto* 8
When high, more high, and lifts us up when fallen. 737 *Prelude* 12. 218
Of yet unfaded trees she lifts her head . . . 868 *Excursion* 7. 716
And lifts his wilful hand on mischief bent, . . 889 *Excursion* 9. 317

Light. *See* **Candle-light, Dawn-light, Daylight, Dream-light, Fountain-light, Gospel-light, Master-light, Star-light, Taper-light.**
If thou indeed derive thy light from Heaven, . v **If thou indeed* 1
Then, to the measure of that heaven-born light, . v **If thou indeed* 2
Then, to the measure of the light vouchsafed, . v **If thou indeed* 15
A lingering light he fondly throws . . . . . 1 *Extract* 13
Soften their glare before the mellow light ; . . 4 *Ev. Wk.* 105
With thousand thousand twinkling points of light ; 4 *Ev. Wk.* 121
Shines in the light with more than earthly green : 5 *Ev. Wk.* 179
When up the hills, as now, retired the light, . . 5 *Ev. Wk.* 194
Green unmolested light upon their mossy bed. . 7 *Ev. Wk.* 268
Now, with religious awe, the farewell light . . 7 *Ev. Wk.* 287
Wins on the shade, the shade upon the light. . . 7 *Ev. Wk.* 298
The bird, who ceased, with fading light, to thread 8 *Ev. Wk.* 323
While with a hoary light she frosts the ground, . 8 *Ev. Wk.* 327
Across the gloomy valley flings her light, . . . 8 *Ev. Wk.* 335
In flakes of light upon the mountain-side ; . . 10 *Desc. Sk.* 6
To light him shaken by his rugged way. . . . 11 *Desc. Sk.* 34
In golden light ; half hides itself in shade : . . 12 *Desc. Sk.* 98
That glimmer hoar in eve's last light, descried . 12 *Desc. Sk.* 115
His burning eyes with fearful light illume. . . 13 *Desc. Sk.* 165
When not a star supplies the comfort of its light ; 14 *Desc. Sk.* 187
The green light sparkles ;—the dim bowers recede. 14 *Desc. Sk.* 219
But what a sudden burst of overpowering light ! 15 *Desc. Sk.* 274
To see a planet's pomp and steady light . . . 16 *Desc. Sk.* 317
Awful the light, and holy is the air. . . . . 18 *Desc. Sk.* 456
By an uncertain light revealed, that falls . . . 20 *Desc. Sk.* 543
When from October clouds a milder light . . . 21 *Desc. Sk.* 626
With a light heart our course we may renew, . . 22 *Desc. Sk.* 669
Shy tenant, seeing by the uncertain light . . . 26 *Guilt* 105
Along the waste no line of mournful light . . . 27 *Guilt* 143
Yet when faint beams of light that ruin showed, . 27 *Guilt* 156
The moon a wan dead light around her shed. . . 27 *Guilt* 167
Is now, by beams of dawning light imprest, . . 30 *Guilt* 335
At houses, men, and common light, amazed. . . 31 *Guilt* 401
Those eyeballs dark—dark beyond hope of light, 39 *Bord.* 136
Even as I do ; but I should loathe the light, . . 48 *Bord.* 629
To stretch her arms, and dim the gladsome light . 56 *Bord.* 1046
By a dim lantern's light I saw that wreaths . . 59 *Bord.* 1202
Light up this beacon. You shall be obeyed. . . 64 *Bord.* 1465
From the clear light of circumstances, flashed . 64 *Bord.* 1495
And light them joined, and you will see the less . 65 *Bord.* 1513
And the light dancing of the thoughtless heart ; . 65 *Bord.* 1547
Light to thy path, warmth to thy blood !—Together . . . . 70 *Bord.* 1852
by the light of the moon I saw the stains of blood 72 *Bord.* 1932
Whose good deeds will not stand by their own light ; 74 *Bord.* 2081
As light itself—be there withheld from Her . . 78 *Bord.* 2329
Light are her sallies as the tripping fawn's . . 80 **Loving she* 15
And burns with a clear and steady light ; . . . 81 †*Address : Child* 35
And take a lantern, Child, to light . . . . . 83 *Lucy Gray* 15
When it is light and fair, ... 84 *We are Seven* 46
And brought it forth into the light : . . . . 85 *Shepherd-boys* 90
Fashioned by the glowing light ; . . . . . 90 *Longest Day* 6
On this platform, light and free ; . . . . . 90 *Longest Day* 14
When his light returns from far. . . . . . 90 *Longest Day* 56
But who shall show, to waking sense, the gleam of light that broke . . . . 92 *Poet's Dream* 33
By light of lamp and precious stones, that glimmered here, there glowed, ... 92 *Poet's Dream* 46
Of Arthur,—who, to upper light restored, . . 103 *Artegal* 53
Through the pure light of female eyes . . . . 112 **How rich* 20
And, if my brow gives back their light, . . . 112 **What heavenly* 3

Light—*continued.*
—Ah ! that such beauty, varying in the light . 891 *Excursion* 9. 512
Attained his western bound ; but rays of light— 893 *Excursion* 9. 592
With a light soul to cover him ; . . . . . S.3. 424 *Tinker* 48
His light high up among the gloomy rocks, . . K.8. 225 **I will* 49
Light to the sun and music to the wind ; . . . K.8. 226 **I will* 82
—The light was famous in the neighbourhood . K.8. 228 **I will* 112
The glorious sun, and while the light of day . . K.8. 234 **The order'd* 5
Mistakes for sorrow darting beams of light . . K.8. 238 *Recluse* 1. 1. 54
Shows like a mountain built of silver light. . . K.8. 252 *Recluse* 1.1.569
Let not thy justice view, O Light Divine, . . . K.8. 266 **Rid of* 9
Bless it then with constant light, ... L.2. 190 **Queen and* 11
When envious clouds shut out her silver light. . [?] **A sad* 14
Lighted. I lighted—opened with soft touch the chapel's iron door, ... 92 *Poet's Dream* 41
The Druid stones their lighted fane unfold, . . 594 *Ev. Wk. Quarto* 171
Like lighted tempests troubled transports roll ; . 612 *Desc.Sk.Quarto* 547
Lighted by gleams of moonlight from the sea . 644 *Prelude* 2. 136
(Whose in-door pastime, lighted up, survived . 664 *Prelude* 4. 375
Lightened. But they will soon be lightened. Ay, look up— . . . . 65 *Bord.* 1533
Is lightened :—that serene and blessed mood, 206 *Tintern* 41
And lightened o'er the pallid countenance. . . 383 *Duddon* 29. 8
Lightens. Unscorned the peasant's whistling breath, that lightens . . . . 233 *Power of Sound* 51
Lighter. By this his heart is lighter far ; . . . 245 *P. B.* 801
Each lighter function slumbering in the brain, . 268 **DogmaticTeachers* 9
And shall the Verse not tell of lighter gifts . . 540 **Lady ! a* 67
These lighter graces ; and the rural ways . . 701 *Prelude* 8. 159
And now, when free to move with lighter pace. . 772 *Excursion* 2. 27
That flutters on the bough, lighter than he ; . . 842 *Excursion* 6. 296
Of all the lighter ornaments attached . . . 878 *Excursion* 8. 250
Lightest. He had the lightest foot in Ennerdale : . 98 *Brothers* 219
Their smoothest paths, to wear their lightest chains ? 265 **There is a pleasure* 4
And, with cloud-streaks lightest and loftiest, share 511 **Who rashly* 22
Their peace, perhaps, our lightest footfall marred ; 527 **Those breathing* 50
Light-footed. Now, risen ere the light-footed Chamois retires . . . . 345 *Stanzas : Simplon* 17
Light-hearted. Then, light-hearted Boys, to the top of the crag ; . . . . 86 *Rural Arch.* 23
And this light-hearted Maiden constant is as he. . 222 *Triad* 144
Lighthouse. Near Portland lighthouse in a lonesome creek, ... 35 *Guilt* 592
Firm and unflinching, as the Lighthouse reared . 540 *Grace Darl.* 23
Within the sheltering Lighthouse.—Shout, ye Waves ! . . . . 541 *Grace Darl.* 83
Of lighthouse, beaten by Atlantic waves ; . . . 664 *Prelude* 4. 365
Lightless. All blind she wilders o'er the lightless heath, ... 597 *Ev. Wk. Quarto* 285
Lightly. Dashed o'er the rough rock, lightly leaps along ; . . . . 4 *Ev. Wk.* 137
That lightly draws its breath, ... 83 *We are Seven* 2
Nor can he guess how lightly leaps . . . . 215 *Kirkstone* 75
With nodding plumes, and lightly drest . . . 342 *Ital. Itin.* 57
As lightly, though of altered hue, ... 343 *Eclipse* 15
" Lightly for both the bosom's lord did sit . . 435 *Ecc. Sonn.* 2. 26. 9
A holier name ! then lightly do not bear . . . 445 *Ecc. Sonn.* 3. 21. 2
Who would not lightly violate the grace . . . 501 *Humanity* 107
Light words, that were more lightly heard . . 542 *Russ. Fug.* 63
Even more than when I tripped lightly as they ; . 590 *Immortality* 197
Dash'd down the rough rock, lightly leaps along ; 593 *Ev. Wk. Quarto* 120
Unmoved. I could not always lightly pass . . 652 *Prelude* 3. 261
The day pass lightly on, when foresight sleeps, . 656 *Prelude* 3. 506
A passing word erewhile did lightly touch . . 679 *Prelude* 6. 319
Lightly equipped, and but a few brief looks . . 680 *Prelude* 6. 342
Were its admonishments, nor lightly heard . . 695 *Prelude* 7. 546
Misery not lightly passed, but sometimes scanned 708 *Prelude* 8. 648
I loved whate'er I saw : nor lightly loved, . . 737 *Prelude* 12. 176
Matter not lightly to be heard by those . . . 743 *Prelude* 13. 254
One while he would speak lightly of his babes, . 765 *Excursion* 1. 585
To flow, when purposes are lightly changed ? . 773 *Excursion* 2. 151
Have fallen more lightly, if it had not fallen . . 779 *Excursion* 2. 544
I treat the matter lightly, but, alas ! . . . . 783 *Excursion* 2. 780
Perchance too lightly occupied, or lulled . . . 807 *Excursion* 4. 419
To some, too lightly minded, might appear . . 830 *Excursion* 5. 550
Softly and lightly from a passing cloud, . . . 861 *Excursion* 7. 284
To heaven as lightly from the cottage-hearth . . 887 *Excursion* 9. 246
Lightness. To awe the lightness of humanity. . . 498 **Enough of climbing* 40
Lightning. When lightning among clouds and mountain-snows . . . . 13 *Desc. Sk.* 179
Was rent with lightning—one hath disappeared ; 97 *Brothers* 144
Faithful, though swift as lightning, the meek dove ; 153 *Morn. Ex.* 37
A corner-stone by lightning cut, ... 165 *Danish Boy* 7
And through his brain like lightning pass. . . 244 *P. B.* 735
Shot lightning through this lonely Isle ! . . . 298 *Brownie's Cell* 42
Like his own lightning, over mountains high, . . 318 **Ah ! where* 13
As on Parnassus rules, when lightning flies, . . 350 *Des. Stanzas* 8
Works busy as the lightning ; but instinct . . 419 *Ecc. Sonn.* 1. 6. 2
Draws lightning down upon the head . . . 550 *Hermit's Cell* 5. 11
The lightning, the fierce wind, and trampling waves. . . . . 579 *Peele Castle* 52
And as round mountain-tops the lightning plays, 584 *Ch. Lamb* 18
Soon shall the Light'ning hold before thy head 597 *Ev. Wk. Quarto* 297
Engender lightning, whence are falling showers. . 625 *Æneid* 125
But will the Lightning glance aside to spare . . 628 *Installation* 11
Of lightning startled in a gloomy cave . . . 796 *Excursion* 3. 708
Lightning's. Once did the lightning's faint disastrous gleam . . . . 26 *Guilt* 133

Lightning's—*continued.*
In motion rapid as the lightning's gleam ; . . . 330 *Ode : Thanks.* 78
Lightnings. Ye lightnings, hear his voice !—they cannot hear, ... 103 *Artegal* 43
And all degrees of beauty. O ye Lightnings ! . 231 *Clouds* 78
Of the fierce wind, while mid-day lightnings prowl 263 *Storm* 4
Like Lightnings eager for th' almighty word, . . 617 *Desc.Sk.Quarto* 802
Lights. *See* **Taper-lights.**
Spotting the northern cliffs with lights between ; 3 *Ev. Wk.* 40
Slant watery lights, from parting clouds, apace . 4 *Ev. Wk.* 92
—The lights are vanished from the watery plains : 8 *Ev. Wk.* 305
And track the yellow lights from steep to steep, 12 *Desc. Sk.* 95
Ye flattering eastern lights, once more the hills illume ! . . . . 20 *Desc. Sk.* 529
Of purple lights and ever-vernal plains ; . . . 20 *Desc. Sk.* 574
My former pleasures in the shooting lights . . 207 *Tintern* 118
When lights of reason fail. . . . . 226 *Present.* 78
But of the lights that cherish household cares . 426 *Ecc. Sonn.* 1. 31. 4
Yet came prepared as glorious lights to shine, . 432 *Ecc. Sonn.* 2. 13. 12
With evening lights, advance in long array . . 448 *Ecc. Sonn.* 3. 32. 6
A crown for Hope !—I dread the boasted lights . 448 *Ecc. Sonn.* 3. 33. 6
With some internal lights to memory dear, . . 460 **Wanderer ! that* 57
With gleaming lights more gracefully adorn . . 471 *Ailsa Crag* 3
The medley less when boreal Lights . . . . 499 **This Lawn* 10
The sentence rule by mercy's heaven-born lights." 519 *Pun. Death* 10. 12
Slow lights upon the lake's still bosom fall, . . 598 *Ev. Wk. Quarto* 336
Small cottage lights across the water stream, . 598 *Ev. Wk. Quarto* 374
Green dewy lights adorn the freshen'd mead. . . 607 *Desc.Sk.Quarto* 272
Fair smiling lights the purpled hills illume ! . . 613 *Desc.Sk.Quarto* 633
Of purple lights and even vernal plains. . . 614 *Desc.Sk.Quarto* 685
—Red stream the cottage lights ; the landscape fades, ... 614 *Desc.Sk.Quarto* 688
Space like a heaven filled up with northern lights, 673 *Prelude* 5. 532
Of colours, lights, and forms ; the deafening din ; 689 *Prelude* 7. 155
And roaring waters, and in lights and shades . . 735 *Prelude* 12. 96
By artificial lights ; how they debase . . . . 743 *Prelude* 13. 210
" You have known lights and guides better than these. . . . . 816 *Excursion* 4. 1017
Than those resplendent lights, his rich bequest ; . 821 *Excursion* 4. 1305
Was wanting ; but inferior lights appeared . . 895 *Excursion* 9. 762
Lightsome. " Blithe souls and lightsome hearts have we . . . . 177 *Waggoner* 2. 52
The lightsome Olive's twinkling canopy— . . 361 **List—'twas* 21
For lightsome Fanny had thus early thrown, . . 523 *Epist. Beaumont* 157
The long, warm, lightsome summer-day, . . . 536 *Goody Blake* 38
In lightsome mood—such privilege has youth . 675 *Prelude* 6. 18
With clustering ivy, and the lightsome twigs . . 676 *Prelude* 6. 82
To wisdom ; or, as lightsome as a bird . . . 742 *Prelude* 13. 133
Shadowy, yet gay and lightsome as it stood . . 881 *Excursion* 8. 463
Like. (*Partial list.*) *See* **Babel-like, Bird-like, Breath-like, Breeze-like, Child-like, Church-like, Cloud-like, Death-like, Dirge-like, Dream-like, Eagle-like, Fire-like, Flower-like, Frost-like, Gem-like, Ghost-like, Godlike, Helmet-like, Herdsman-like, Hut-like, Incense-like, Lance-like, Life-like, Nile-like, Nun-like, Nymph-like, Ostrich-like, Phantom-like, Pilgrim-like, Rock-like, Saint-like, Sceptre-like, Scout-like, Sea-like, Serpent-like, Sky-like, Star-like, Stealth-like, Stream-like, Sun-like, Swan-like, Urn-like, Worm-like, Wren-like.**
Like an untended watch-fire, on the ridge . . v **If thou indeed* 10
Humbly to hang, like twinkling winter lamps, . v **If thou indeed* 12
And insects clothe, like dust, the glassy deep : 4 *Ev. Wk.* 117
Is hushed, and like a burnished mirror glows, . 4 *Ev. Wk.* 125
And like a torrent roars the headstrong gale ; . 7 *Ev. Wk.* 270
Like Una shining on her gloomy way, ... 7 *Ev. Wk.* 291
Like a black wall, the mountain-steeps appear. . 8 *Ev. Wk.* 314
Air listens, like the sleeping water, still, . . 9 *Ev. Wk.* 367
Or sink, with heart alive like Memnon's lyre ; . 11 *Desc. Sk.* 32
Restlessly flashing, seems to mount like fire : . . 12 *Desc. Sk.* 100
Thy towns that cleave, like swallows' nests, on high ; . . . . 12 *Desc. Sk.* 114
Starts, like a horse, beside the glaring road— . 13 *Desc. Sk.* 182
The *west*, that burns like one dilated sun, . . 15 *Desc. Sk.* 282
And, like the Patriarchs in their simple age, . . 17 *Desc. Sk.* 374
That like to leaning masts of stranded ships appear. 18 *Desc. Sk.* 412
Like sun-lit tempests, troubled transports roll ; . 18 *Desc. Sk.* 458
Tinged like an angel's smile all rosy red— . . 19 *Desc. Sk.* 475
Or like the beauty in a flower installed, . . . 20 *Desc. Sk.* 534
Like fate ; was hurried off, a helpless prey, . . 25 *Guilt* 53
Recovering heart, like answer did she make ; . . 27 *Guilt* 186
We two had sung, like gladsome birds in May ; . 28 *Guilt* 247
And I in truth did love him like a brother, . . 29 *Guilt* 251
Like one revived, upon his neck I wept ; . . . 29 *Guilt* 258
Over her brow like dawn of gladness threw ; . . 30 *Guilt* 319
The breathing pestilence that rose like smoke, . 30 *Guilt* 346
That fear is like a cloak which old men huddle 38 *Bord.* 22
And I had heard the like before : in sooth . . 38 *Bord.* 78
How would you like to travel on whole hours . 45 *Bord.* 432
Well !—he has often spurned me like a toad, . . 45 *Bord.* 470
Stand like an isthmus 'twixt two stormy seas 48 *Bord.* 607
Which looks like a transition in my soul, . . . 48 *Bord.* 636
You said you did not like his looks—that he . . 51 *Bord.* 757
You'd better like we should descend together, . 51 *Bord.* 771
I look at him and tremble like a child. . . . 51 *Bord.* 786
And send ye dancing to the clouds, like leaves, . 54 *Bord.* 945
Like mountain oaks rocked by the stormy wind. . 57 *Bord.* 1116
Like red-hot iron burnt into my heart. . . . 59 *Bord.* 1183

Lips—*continued.*
Upon the lips of men in hall or bower; 863 *Excursion* 7. 384
When from the Wanderer's lips these words had fallen, 877 *Excursion* 8. 231
By savage Nature? Shrivelled are their lips; 879 *Excursion* 8. 353
They hear my lips present their sacrifice, 895 *Excursion* 9. 749
For baffled lips and disappointed arms S.3. 434 **The doubt* 79
No benediction from the stranger's lips, K.8. 244 *Recluse* I. I. 279
As gathered from the Matron's lips, and tell K.8. 248 *Recluse* I. I. 417

Liquid. And all the babbling brooks are liquid gold; 5 *Ev. Wk.* 189
While Grasmere smoothed her liquid plain 182 *Waggoner* 4. 232
The liquid veil that seeks not to hide them. 190 **Lyre! though* 37
A liquid concert matchless by nice Art, 233 *Power of Sound* 47
Their voices into liquid music swell, 333 *Fish-women* 12
Nor turns, nor winds, as doth the liquid flood; 351 *Des. Stanzas* 83
Bright liquid mansions, fashioned to endure 379 *Duddon* 12. 74
The still repose, the liquid lapse serene, 381 *Duddon* 20. 4
Their liquid world, for bold discovery, 434 *Ecc. Sonn.* 2. 23. 7
Disturb the liquid music's equipoise. 455 *Rydal Mere* 12
Temptation centres in the liquid Calm; 469 **Why stand* 11
And smooths her liquid breast—to show 497 *Lycoris* 15
His flageolet to liquid notes of love 702 *Prelude* 8. 200
And ocean's liquid mass, in gladness lay 759 *Excursion* 1. 202
A liquid pool that glittered in the sun, 776 *Excursion* 2. 338
Or lapse of liquid element—by hand, 879 *Excursion* 8. 331
That which the heavens displayed, the liquid deep 893 *Excursion* 9. 607

Lisp. To lisp, he made me kneel beside my bed, 28 *Guilt* 202
To lisp the name of Father—could he look 56 *Bord.* 1052

Lisping. Even in the time of lisping infancy; 668 *Prelude* 5. 170
This sacred right, the lisping babe proclaims 888 *Excursion* 9. 311

Lisps. Who tripping lisps a merry song 507 *May* 33
To Infancy, that lisps her praise—to Age 540 *Grace Darl.* 11

List. *See* **Death-list.**
When list! he hears a piteous moan— 85 *Shepherd-boys* 60
Into the list of things that cannot be! 124 *V. and J.* 219
List to those shriller notes!—*that* march 215 *Kirkstone* 41
List, Cuckoo—Cuckoo!—oft tho' tempests howl, 229 *Cuckoo-clock* 12
Comes from that tabernacle—List! 247 *P. B.* 943
Her own calm fires?—But list! a voice is near; 313 **Clouds, lingering* 11
But list! the avalanche—the hush profound 350 *Des. Stanzas* 44
List—'twas the Cuckoo.—O with what delight 361 **List—'twas* 1
But, from the arms of silence—list! O list! 451 *Ecc. Sonn.* 3. 44. 9
List, ye who pass by Lyulph's Tower 478 *Somnamb.* 1
But list!—though winter storms be nigh, 498 **The sylvan* 25
List, the winds of March are blowing; 503 *Warning* 1
And through this street who list might ride and wend; 553 *Prioress* 41
There list at midnight till is heard no more, 607 *Desc.Sk.Quarto* 313
Low sunk beneath the horizon!—List!—I heard, 807 *Excursion* 4. 402
From the thronged hive, and settle where they list 889 *Excursion* 9. 373

Listed. Her sons no more in listed fields advance 619 *School Ex.* 57

Listen. What do they here? Listen! What; dogged like thieves! 56 *Bord.* 1017
But listen, for my peace—— Why, I *believe* you. 59 *Bord.* 1175
I used to sing it.—Listen!—what foot is there? 60 *Bord.* 1268
Listen yet awhile;—with patience 94 *Westmoreland Girl* 57
Why did ye listen to my prayer? 114 *Ind. Wom.* 24
Yet listen, Child!—I would not preach; 142 †*Lov. and Lik.* 2
That you will gladly listen to discourse 147 *Joanna* 14
Delighted much to listen to those sounds, 149 **A narrow* 42
If you listen, all is still, 171 *Kitten* 81
Listen! you can scarcely hear! 174 *Waggoner* 1. 32
And I can listen to thee yet; 184 **O blithe* 25
And listen, till I do beget 184 **O blithe* 27
To lie, and listen to the mountain flood 185 *Yew-trees* 32
Listen, ponder, hold them dear; 209 **Yes, it* 19
Listen to their songs!—or halt, 217 **Inmate of* 28
To lie and listen—till o'er-drowsèd sense 227 *Vernal Ode* 88
Did listen with a faith sincere 237 *P. B.* 122
Listen! the mighty Being is awake, 258 **It is a* 6
O listen! for the Vale profound 289 *Sol. Reap.* 7
That you can listen quietly: 295 *Highland Boy* 7
And look and listen—gathering, whence I may, 314 **Not 'mid* 13
My ears did listen, 'twas enough to gaze; 338 *Engelberg* 16
I listen—but no faculty of mine 339 *Ranz* 1
To listen to ANIO's precipitous flood, 345 *Stanzas: Simplon* 3
That lulled me asleep, bids me listen once more. 364 *Vallomb.* 4
Upon her records, listen to her song, 435 *Ecc. Sonn.* 2. 29. 6
And sickness, listen where they long have lain, 447 *Ecc. Sonn.* 3. 28. 3
In sadness listen. With maternal zeal 447 *Ecc. Sonn.* 3. 28. 4
Will listen, and ye know that He is just. 448 *Ecc. Sonn.* 3. 30. 14
And listen to the flapping of the flame, 488 *Pers. Talk* 13
To which I listen with a ready ear; 488 *Pers. Talk* 39
Now listen to my fears! 542 *Russ. Fug.* 56
His ears he closed to listen to the songs 576 *Chiabrera* 9. 16
Or fountain, listen to the grave reports 634 *Prelude* 1. 174
Listen who would, be wrought upon who might, 843 *Excursion* 6. 357
Should listen, and give back to him the voice 851 *Excursion* 6. 884
To listen, is prevented or deterred. 885 *Excursion* 9. 80

Listened. His children's children listened to the sound; 13 *Desc. Sk.* 152
He listened too; did you not say he listened? 73 *Bord.* 2018
And listened to the wind; and, as before, 138 *Michael* 457
Which, while I listened, seemed like the wild growth 146 **It was an* 28
I listened, nor aught else could hear; 155 *Waterfall* 54
I listened to; that Cry 183 **O blithe* 18
To rapture! Mabel listened at the side 267 *St. Cath.* 6
I listened, motionless and still; 289 *Sol. Reap.* 29
I dropped my pen; and listened to the Wind 314 **I dropped* 1

Listened—*continued.*
And who but listened?—till was paid 375 **The Minstrels* 13
And seldom hath ear listened to a tune 381 *Duddon* 19. 10
I stood, looked, listened, and with Thee, 385 *Yarrow Rev.* 7
To both I listened, drawing from them both 633 *Prelude* 1. 57
Pored, watched, expected, listened, spread my thoughts 650 *Prelude* 3. 114
Nothing is listened to. But these, I fear, 697 *Prelude* 7. 668
I stared and listened, with a stranger's ears, 710 *Prelude* 9. 57
So that worst tempests might be listened to. 725 *Prelude* 10. 463
The perturbation; listened to the plea; 772 *Excursion* 2. 77
We listened, looking down upon the hut, 777 *Excursion* 2. 377
Listened intensely; and his countenance soon 818 *Excursion* 4. 1137
That each had listened with his inmost heart. 854 *Excursion* 6. 1054
A wandering Youth, I listened with delight 857 *Excursion* 7. 9
Listened with readier patience than to strain 883 *Excursion* 8. 596

Listener. Puzzles the listener with a doubt 143 **Driven in* 15
Sole listener, Duddon! to the breeze that played 377 *Duddon* 5. 1
Indulgent listener was he to the tongue 762 *Excursion* 1. 417

Listener's. Sweet poison spreads along the listener's veins, 19 *Desc. Sk.* 524

Listeners. Kind Listeners, that around me sit, 245 *P. B.* 788
From all the listeners that stood round, 403 *White Doe* 671
On fireside listeners, doubting what they hear! 453 **Calm is the* 15
In death; though Listeners shudder all around. 520 *Pun. Death* 13. 4
Listeners who not unwillingly admit 538 **In desultory* 50
And, heedless even of listeners, warbled out S.3. 436 **The doubt* 155

Listening. Listening in vain. He has a tender heart! 51 *Bord.* 764
Not loth, and listening Little-ones, heart-touched, their fancies feed. 93 *Poet's Dream* 80
And sometimes, just as listening ends 144 **Driven in* 47
And, while we both were listening, to my side 148 *Joanna* 74
Call to the heart for inward listening— 222 *Triad* 206
Listening to nun's faint throb of holy fear, 233 *Power of Sound* 30
And listening dolphins gather round. 234 *Power of Sound* 136
The listening Ass conjectures well; 243 *P. B.* 652
Listening, and listening long, in rapturous mood, 271 **Fame tells* 13
With breath suspended, like a listening scout. 322 *Germans* 4
While she sate listening in the shade, 415 *White Doe* 1773
Listening within his Temple see his sword 447 *Ecc. Sonn.* 3. 29. 5
That listening sense is pardonably cheated 455 *Rydal Mere* 15
Greta, what fearful listening! when huge stones 464 **Greta, what* 1
Love listening while the Lesbian Maid 499 **Departing summer* 46
To their own far-off murmurs listening. 499 *Memory* 29
For needful listening, pledge is here, 503 **Like a* 67
And tired of listening to the boisterous sea— 521 *Epist.Beaumont* 33
Haunted his ear—he only listening— 528 **Those breathing* 105
Is listening quietly. 581 **Loud is* 8
Below Eve's listening Star the sheep walk stills 598 *Ev. Wk. Quarto* 353
List'ning th' aëreal music of the hill, 600 *Ev. Wk. Quarto* 436
Beneath some rock, listening to notes that are 646 *Prelude* 2. 308
Upon the cheek of listening Infancy 668 *Prelude* 5. 189
Listening, a gentle shock of mild surprise 671 *Prelude* 5. 382
And listening only to the gladsome sounds 671 *Prelude* 5. 404
Smote me, and, listening, I in whispers said, 687 *Prelude* 7. 28
And mocks the prompter's listening. Marvellous things 688 *Prelude* 7. 102
There linger, listening, gazing, with delight 748 *Prelude* 14. 179
And listening Time reward with sacred praise. 758 *Excursion* 1. 107
That we beheld; and lend the listening sense 773 *Excursion* 2. 106
While we sate listening with compassion due. 801 *Excursion* 4. 7
While, listening, he had paced the noiseless turf, 814 *Excursion* 4. 891
And patient listening, thanks accept from me. 874 *Excursion* 8. 9

Listens. Where Derwent rests, and listens to the roar 2 *Ev. Wk.* 3
Air listens, like the sleeping water, still, 9 *Ev. Wk.* 367
Listens, or quakes while from the forest's gulf 14 *Desc. Sk.* 194
At midnight listens till his parting oar, 15 *Desc. Sk.* 252
He listens, puzzled, sore perplexed, 81 †*Mother's Return* 15
And Betty listens, glad to hear it. 127 *Idiot Boy* 101
She listens, but she cannot hear 129 *Idiot Boy* 282
He listens—not a sound is heard 247 *P. B.* 997
Stern GEMMI listens to as full a cry, 346 *Gemmi* 2
He listens (all past conquests and all schemes 426 *Ecc. Sonn.* 1. 30. 6
Or listens to its play among the boughs 522 *Epist. Beaumont* 48

Listless. There, bending o'er the stream, the listless swain 3 *Ev. Wk.* 70
In listless quiet o'er the ethereal deep 231 *Clouds* 76
And nobler cares than listless summer knew. 263 **While not* 14
Outstretched and listless, were by hunger roused: 392 *Daniel* 13
To shun the memory of a listless life 470 **Did pangs* 10
The listless hours, while in the hollow vale, 760 *Excursion* 1. 259
Which gave employment to her listless hands— 767 *Excursion* 1. 759
Beguiling harmlessly the listless hours. 788 *Excursion* 3. 136

Listlessly. While listlessly I sate, and, having closed 666 *Prelude* 5. 63

Listlessness. To banish listlessness and irksome care; 108 *Indolence* 51
Which neither listlessness, nor mad endeavour, 589 *Immortality* 161
In listlessness from vain perplexity, 636 *Prelude* 1. 266

Lists. That such a Boy where'er he lists shall go 554 *Prioress* 111
Into the lists of giddy enterprise— 842 *Excursion* 6. 286

Liswyn. And so is Liswyn farm. 86 *Anecdote* 24
Or here at Liswyn farm?" 86 *Anecdote* 32
Than here at Liswyn farm." 86 *Anecdote* 36
Why you would change sweet Liswyn farm 86 *Anecdote* 43

Lit. *See* **Dim-lit, Foam-lit, Heaven-lit, Moonlit, Sun-lit.**
(But where no fire was ever lit, 214 *Kirkstone* 14
Lit by that evening lamp which loved to shed 583 **With copious* 30
That lit the dark slant woods with silvery white! 593 *Ev. Wk. Quarto* 100

Little—*continued.*
For you, in presence of this little band . . . 895 Excursion 9. 729
His little rake with cunning sidelong look, . . S.3. 417 *Sweet was 7
When in the woods the little Fowles . . . S.3. 424 Tinker 23
The little cottage that is near, ... S.3. 425 *No whimsy 5
On thee, bright Spring, a bashful little one, . S.3. 435 *The doubt 130
Which to his father's little farm belonged, . . K.8. 228 *I will 131
Of full contentment, in a little shed . . . K.8. 241 Recluse 1.1.176
Differing but little from the Man elsewhere, . . K.8. 246 Recluse 1.1.354
Sprinkles these little pastures but the same . . K.8. 248 Recluse 1.1.442
Their little boons of animating thought . . K.8. 249 Recluse 1.1.467
The heifer in yon little croft belongs . . . K.8. 251 Recluse 1.1.524
Those little fountains, sparkling in the sun, . . K.8. 251 Recluse 1.1.553
In the bare twigs, each little budding place . . K.8. 252 Recluse 1.1.565
Some little feeble stars, but all is thine, . . K.8. 263 *The Lake 3
The multitude of little rocky hills, ... K.8. 263 *The Lake 8
How little dost thou speak of earthly gloom ! . [?] *A sad 12
As little as the unblemish'd Queen of Night, . [?] *A sad 13
Littleness. Is littleness ; that he who feels contempt 23 Yew-tree 52
There littleness was not ; the least of things . . 759 Excursion 1. 230
With the perverse attempt, while littleness . 815 Excursion 4. 965
Little-one. This Little-one—it cuts me to the heart— 45 Bord. 438
But you were then a tottering Little-one— . . 50 Bord. 702
" My own dear Little-one will sigh, ... 121 Emigrant Mother 45
Who with him ?—even the senseless Little-one. . 125 V. and J. 243
My careless Little-one, for thee and thine ! " . . 627 *Son of 14
Are bearing him, my Little-one," he said, . . 779 Excursion 2. 509
That feeds him ; and the tottering little-one . . 836 Excursion 5. 956
While she was yet a little-one, had learned. . . 856 Excursion 6. 1185
Yet this departed Little-one, too long . . . . 868 Excursion 7. 692
A Little-one, subjected to the arts . . . . . 886 Excursion 9. 157
While yet an innocent little-one, with a heart . K.8. 256 Recluse 1.1.703
Little-ones. And her brown little-ones around her leads, ... 6 Ev. Wk. 225
A month, sweet Little-ones, is past . . . . 81 †Mother's Return 1
Not loth, and listening Little-ones, heart-touched, their fancies feed. . . . . 93 Poet's Dream 80
To all the Little-ones on sinful earth . . . 118 Maternal Grief 18
Yon busy Little-ones rejoice that soon . . . 280 *Intent on 2
And yours, my buried Little-ones ! am I ; . . 464 *A point 2
Ye little-ones ! Earth shudders at your fate, . 505 Warning 156
Your hands, dear Little-ones, do all . . . . 577 *I come 9
Liturgy. Recites the holy liturgy, ... 396 White Doe 46
Live. Here will I live, of all but heaven disowned, 31 Guilt 365
Nor could we live together those poor boys and I ; 35 Guilt 603
He cried—" Do pity me ! That thou shouldst live 35 Guilt 620
Dear Father ! how *could* I forget and live ?— . 40 Bord. 176
That's all—God save you, Sir. Ha ! as I live, . 43 Bord. 332
He does his Master credit. As I live, ... 45 Bord. 459
Who live in these disputed tracts, that own . . 48 Bord. 596
We'll lead him to the Convent. He shall live, . 54 Bord. 904
And none look grave but dotards. He may live . 54 Bord. 929
Who are we, Friends ? Do we not live on ground 57 Bord. 1114
It cannot live with thought ; think on, think on, 65 Bord. 1561
That I should ever live to see this moment ! . . 66 Bord. 1598
Of living without knowledge that you live : . . 71 Bord. 1871
For this most cruel murder : let him live . . 75 Bord. 2177
A Man by pain and thought compelled to live, . 78 Bord. 2351
So let us strive to live, and to our Spirits will be given . . . . 93 Poet's Dream 67
" These Tourists, heaven preserve us ! needs must live . . . . 95 Brothers 1
You live, Sir, in these dales, a quiet life : . . . 97 Brothers 121
Live to such end is what both old and young . 99 Brothers 287
To live in peace upon his father's land, . . . 100 Brothers 324
A place in which he could not bear to live : . . 102 Brothers 426
When I was well, I wished to live, ... 114 Ind. Wom. 15
Where they may live, with no one to behold . . 123 V. and J. 110
And should he live a thousand years, ... 127 Idiot Boy 110
—'Tis Johnny ! Johnny ! as I live. . . . . 130 Idiot Boy 356
I wished that thou shouldst live the life they lived, 137 Michael 371
Nay, Boy, be of good hope ;—we both may live . 137 Michael 388
You *live* each moment of your day ; . . . . 143 †Lov. and Lik. 60
But thou wilt live with me in love ; . . . . 145 Her Eyes 67
We two will live in honesty. . . . . . . 145 Her Eyes 74
And there, my babe, we'll live for aye." . . . 145 Her Eyes 100
To live for many a day." . . . . 157 Oak and Broom 110
And should I live through sun and rain . . . 157 Sexton 29
Let them live upon their praises ; . . . . . 160 *Pansies, lilies 2
And there for gentle pleasure live ; . . . . 164 *Fair Lady 12
To be confounded with live growths, ... 170 Rural Ill. 21
While she and I together live . . . . . . 187 *Three years 35
Lyre ! though such power do in thy magic live . 190 *Lyre ! though 1
She seemed to live ; her thoughts her own ; . . 192 Ruth 14
To live at liberty. . . . . 194 Ruth 174
And once again he wished to live . . . . . 194 Ruth 185
" How is it that you live, and what is it you do ? " 197 Resolution 119
Is of the clime in which we live ; . . . . . 215 Kirkstone 68
That not by bread alone we live, ... 228 Devot. Incit. 72
Predestined here to live. . . . . 232 Jew. Fam. 16
Does no one live near this green grass ? . . . 240 P. B. 380
Shall live the name of Walton : Sage benign ! . 254 Complete Angler 2
Among the lonely mountains.—Live, ye trees ! . 262 *Mark the 9
To live and die, the peace of heaven his aim ; . 272 Lady E. B. 6
Thy Art be Nature ; the live current quaff, . . 277 *A Poet 5
Divine communion ; both do live and move, . . 280 *Oh what 10
With all that live ?— . . . . 286 Nith 64
With them no strife can last ; they live . . . 291 Rob Roy 35
And, had it been thy lot to live . . . . . 292 Rob Roy 105
To live in peace on shore. . . . . 297 Highland Boy 245
Wisdom doth live with children round her knees : 304 *I grieved 9

Live—*continued.*
The destiny of Man, and live in hope. . . . . 304 *Festivals have 14
Live, and take comfort. Thou hast left behind . 305 Toussaint 9
Think that a State would live in sounder health . 310 Invasion 8
But the live scales of a portentous nature ; . . 311 *Who rises 18
—Have we not known—and live we not to tell— 311 *Who rises 33
Your kindred Deities, *Ye* live and move, . . . 325 Ode 1814 120
Thy law, and live henceforth in peace, in pure good will. . . . . 329 Ode 1815 128
Shall live enrolled above the starry spheres. . . 330 Ode : Thanks. 66
On the great flood were spared to live and move. 360 *Near Anio's 8
Stringent as flesh can tolerate and live ; . . . 362 *List—'twas 41
To be ; by Faith, not sight, his soul must live ; . 363 *Grieve for 11
To live, and act, and serve the future hour ; . . 384 Duddon 34. 11
Came those live herbs ? by what hand were they sown . . . . 387 Roslin 9
If not, O Mortals, better cease to live ! . . . 388 *The pibroch's 14
His rank 'mong freeborn creatures that live free, 389 Eagles 13
Verily so to live was an awful choice— . . . 391 Brownie 9
Yet in this moral Strain a power may live, . . 395 White Doe Ded. 62
And live at home in blameless ease ; . . . . 400 White Doe 395
" Plant it,—by this we live or die." . . . . 403 White Doe 672
To live and die in a shady bower, ... 414 White Doe 1637
Dead—but to live again on earth, ... 416 White Doe 1844
To live and move exempt from all control . . 429 Ecc. Sonn. 2. 4. 13
What joy to live, what blessedness to die ! . . 441 Ecc. Sonn. 3. 5. 8
That mutually assisted they may live . . . . 446 Ecc. Sonn. 3. 26. 7
Your spirit freely let me drink, and live. . . . 449 Ecc. Sonn. 3. 35. 14
I live and sing my idle songs . . . . . . 487 Fountain 59
Of friends, who live within an easy walk, . . . 488 Pers. Talk 3
Great gains are mine ; for thus I live remote . . 488 Pers. Talk 44
Live in the spirit of this creed ; . . . . . 492 Duty 23
And in the light of truth thy Bondman let me live ! 493 Duty 56
When the live chords Alcæus smote, ... 499 *Departing summer 38
If Power could live at ease with self-restraint ! . 500 Humanity 42
Would that the little Flowers were born to live, . 511 *So fair 2
How could he think of the live creature—gay . 511 *Who rashly 3
Into strange woods, where he at large may live . 528 *Those breathing 69
And forced to live on alms, this old Man fed . . 531 *I know 6
There insects live their lives, and die ; . . . . 532 †Float. Isl. 15
Will often live in one small cottage ; . . . . 536 Goody Blake 35
That, live as long as live he may, ... 537 Goody Blake 119
Save in the rolls of heaven, where hers may live . 540 Grace Darl. 16
Nor ever while I live Love's yoke to draw. . . 559 Cuck.and Night. 140
Now say—in such belief I'll live and die ; . . 559 Cuck.and Night. 162
Yet if I live it shall amended be, ... 561 Cuck.and Night. 234
And live and die I will in thy belief ; . . . . 563 Troilus 75
Will live, and spread, and kindle : even such minds 567 Cumb. Beg. 109
The prosperous and unthinking, they who live . 568 Cumb. Beg. 120
Who live a life of virtuous decency, ... 568 Cumb. Beg. 134
To breathe and live but for himself alone, . . 568 Cumb. Beg. 165
Long yet may'st thou live ! for a teacher we see . 572 Avarice 47
And this alone—the life which now I live . . . 573 Chiabrera 1. 4
And live as long as its pure stream shall flow. . 574 Chiabrera 5. 23
But truly did *He* live his life. Urbino, . . . 576 Chiabrera 9. 21
Did Fermor live and die. . . . . 576 Cenotaph 6
Is something that doth live, ... 589 Immortality 134
To live beneath your more habitual sway. . . 590 Immortality 195
Thanks to the human heart by which we live, . 590 Immortality 204
Now living, or to live in future years. . . . . 634 Prelude 1. 165
Of zeal and just ambition, than to live . . . 636 Prelude 1. 256
But huge and mighty forms, that do not live . . 638 Prelude 1. 398
In youth, but oh ! what happiness to live . . 646 Prelude 2. 285
We live as if those hours had never been. . . 647 Prelude 2. 338
That mocks the recreant age *we* live in, then . 654 Prelude 3. 400
Itself a living part of a live whole, ... 657 Prelude 3. 590
Man, if he do but live within the light . . . 661 Prelude 4. 169
All things are put to question ; he must live . . 670 Prelude 5. 323
Or else not live at all, and seeing too . . . 670 Prelude 5. 325
Of these will live till man shall be no more. . . 673 Prelude 5. 505
The time of trial, ere we learn to live . . . 67 Prelude 5. 516
Without contamination doth she live . . . . 6 2 Prelude 7. 322
How could the innocent heart bear up and live ! . 703 Prelude 8. 311
Month after month. Obscurely did I live, . . 710 Prelude 9. 25
And genuine virtue they possess who live . . . 741 Prelude 13. 96
Must live within the very light and air . . . 742 Prelude 13. 193
As found among the best of those who live— . . 743 Prelude 13. 242
To rouse them ; in a world of life they live, . . 747 Prelude 14. 105
The name of Calvert—it shall live, if words . . 751 Prelude 14. 355
All but a scattered few, live out their time, . . 757 Excursion 1. 89
His animal being ; in them did he live, . . . 759 Excursion 1. 209
And by them did he live ; they were his life. . 759 Excursion 1. 210
That live in darkness. From his intellect . . 760 Excursion 1. 291
—And surely never did there live on earth . . 762 Excursion 1. 414
Might live on earth a life of happiness. . . . 764 Excursion 1. 519
She had no wish to live, that she must die . . 769 Excursion 1. 850
With this content, that he will live and die . . 776 Excursion 2. 313
Oh ! blest are they who live and die like these, . 780 Excursion 2. 591
' And now I live ! Oh ! wherefore *do* I live ? ' . 784 Excursion 2. 876
Take the live herbage from the mead, and strip . 790 Excursion 3. 308
Who, having o'er the past no power, would live . 798 Excursion 3. 873
As soldiers live by courage ; as, by strength . . 804 Excursion 4. 203
—Endeavour thus to live ; these rules regard ; . 804 Excursion 4. 228
You walk, you live, you speculate alone ; . . . 809 Excursion 4. 559
" We live by Admiration, Hope, and Love ; . . 812 Excursion 4. 763
Of the live deer, or goat's depending beard,— . 814 Excursion 4. 884
The will to reason's law, can strictliest live . . 830 Excursion 5. 518
Where he had lived, and could not cease to live, . 843 Excursion 6. 369
" There live who yet remember here to have seen 845 Excursion 6. 491
Its birthplace ; none whose figure did not live . 865 Excursion 7. 501

Live—*continued.*

We perish also; for we live by hope 884 *Excursion* 9. 23
And so we live, or else we have no life. 884 *Excursion* 9. 26
The wish for liberty to live—content 888 *Excursion* 9. 278
In crowded cities, without fear shall live 894 *Excursion* 9. 668
From the live rock with grace inimitable S.3. 434 **The doubt* 68
Live through Heaven's eternal year: S.3. 442 *Harmodius* 22
Dear Aristogiton, live; S.3. 442 *Harmodius* 24
The things that live, the things that move? K.8. 219 **The snow-tracks* 12
I do not live for what I see. K.8. 219 **The snow-tracks* 14
My friends, you live, and yet you seem K.8. 220 **The snow-tracks* 19
And yet, my friends, you live and move. K.8. 220 **The snow-tracks* 22
When I could live without a pain, K.8. 220 **The snow-tracks* 23
" What happy fortune were it here to live! K.8. 236 *Recluse* 1. 1. 11
(For I who live to register the truth K.8. 237 *Recluse* 1. 1. 47
Shall live,—it is not in their power to die." K.8. 257 *Recluse* 1. 1. 744

Lived. *See* **Long-lived, Short-lived.**

" We lived in peace and comfort; and were blest 29 *Guilt* 262
Bring to her hut; and so the Wretch has lived 44 *Bord.* 387
Have I lived many days—my sleep was bound 69 *Bord.* 1791
If she had never lived I had not done it!— 75 *Bord.* 2155
The life he had lived there; both for the sake 96 *Brothers* 70
If still his Brother lived, or to the file 96 *Brothers* 83
Yet not while Walter lived:—for, though their parents 98 *Brothers* 227
Though from the cradle they had lived with Walter, 99 *Brothers* 243
It seems, these Brothers have not lived to be 99 *Brothers* 285
He was the child of all the dale—he lived 100 *Brothers* 343
She lived unknown, and few could know 109 **She dwelt* 9
As one that lived ungrateful for the stay 118 *Maternal Grief* 47
The visitor retired. Thus lived the Youth 126 *V. and J.* 299
So lived he till his eightieth year was past. 132 *Michael* 61
That thrifty Pair had lived. For, as it chanced, 133 *Michael* 131
While in this sort the simple household lived 134 *Michael* 207
Have we all lived; yet, if these fields of ours 134 *Michael* 230
And I have lived to be a fool at last 134 *Michael* 235
Both of them sleep together: here they lived, 136 *Michael* 367
I wished that thou shouldst live the life they lived, 137 *Michael* 371
May'st bear in mind the life thy Fathers lived, 137 *Michael* 410
Once lived a happy life! 155 *Waterfall* 24
But ill he lived, much evil saw, 194 *Ruth* 145
My whole life I have lived in pleasant thought, 195 *Resolution* 36
By Voices how men lived of old. 205 *Brougham* 133
That men have lived for whom, 226 *Present.* 63
For she had learned how Peter lived, 246 *P. B.* 911
Lived thankful for day's light, for daily bread, 278 **Lo! where she* 13
That 'tis a fault in Us to have lived and loved 280 *Plea for Auth.* 11
And thus among these rocks he lived, 291 *Rob Roy* 57
He from his birth had lived. 295 *Highland Boy* 15
Thus lived he by Loch Leven's side 296 *Highland Boy* 91
How loud! yet lived in peace with shame. 299 *Brownie's Cell* 50
In One who lived unknown a shepherd's life 320 **They seek* 9
Was happy that she lived to greet 416 *White Doe* 1823
And none had lived before you!" 481 *Expost.* 12
Full five-and-thirty years he lived 483 *Simon Lee* 5
For thou hadst lived till every thing that cheers 491 *Tribute: Dog* 13
Yet still he lived in pining discontent, 523 *Epist. Beaumont* 135
There lived, and on the cross His life resigned, 534 **When in* 14
Lived with honour on his lands. 536 *Egremont* 108
As in the eye of Nature he has lived, 569 *Cumb. Beg.* 196
I, who on shipboard lived from earliest youth, 574 *Chiabrera* 4. 10
Lived I—then yielded to a slow disease. 574 *Chiabrera* 4. 31
So lived I, and repined not at such fate: 575 *Chiabrera* 6. 9
If he had lived, of Him whom I deplore, 579 *Peele Castle* 42
O, he was good, if e'er a good Man lived! 584 *Ch. Lamb* 38
From week to week, from month to month, we lived 642 *Prelude* 2. 8
A little weekly stipend, and we lived 643 *Prelude* 2. 82
My dwelling-place, and lived for ever there 644 *Prelude* 2. 127
With my own modest pleasures, and have lived 648 *Prelude* 2. 429
I made it, for it only lived to me, 651 *Prelude* 3. 142
Of those who lived distinguished by the badge 656 *Prelude* 3. 534
A d spot in which she lived, and through a grace 670 *Prelude* 5. 290
Re. xing in their hold, henceforth I lived 675 *Prelude* 6. 21
Baffle.l my understanding: how men lived 688 *Prelude* 7. 116
Mary! may now have lived till he could look 692 *Prelude* 7. 379
Of rich Clitumnus; and the goat-herd lived 701 *Prelude* 8. 180
Shunned and not tolerated, freely lived 712 *Prelude* 9. 194
Than this lived never, nor a more benign, 714 *Prelude* 9. 293
Lived not to see, nor what we now behold, 716 *Prelude* 9. 429
Lived in the shade; and to Harmodius known 721 *Prelude* 10. 198
Lived long enough, nor in the least survived 737 *Prelude* 12. 181
I said unto the life which I had lived, 751 *Prelude* 14. 377
This Vision; when and where, and how he lived;— 755 *Recluse* 1. 1. 851
So not without distinction had he lived, 757 *Excursion* 1. 96
His calling laid aside, he lived at ease: 762 *Excursion* 1. 386
Thus had he lived a long and innocent life. 762 *Excursion* 1. 396
Could they have lived as do the little birds 764 *Excursion* 1. 563
No tidings of her husband; if he lived, 768 *Excursion* 1. 818
She knew not that he lived; if he were dead, 768 *Excursion* 1. 819
Chequered the green-grown thatch. And so she lived 770 *Excursion* 1. 904
Than a soldier among soldiers—lived and roamed 774 *Excursion* 2. 184
So lived he; so he might have died. But now, 774 *Excursion* 2. 210
Full seventy winters hath he lived, and mark! 780 *Excursion* 2. 600
Relinquished, lived dependent for his bread 783 *Excursion* 2. 739

Lived—*continued.*

I lived and breathed; most grateful—if to enjoy 795 *Excursion* 3. 628
Recalls! *He* lived not till his locks were nipped 842 *Excursion* 6. 275
Where he had lived, and could not cease to live, 843 *Excursion* 6. 369
That they have lived for harsher servitude, 848 *Excursion* 6. 697
And lived by his forbearance. From the coast 869 *Excursion* 7. 757
Lived in an age conspicuous as our own 873 *Excursion* 7. 1009
To most strange issues. I have lived to mark 875 *Excursion* 8. 89
Air unimprisoned, and had lived at large; 879 *Excursion* 8. 343
Who, but for this intrusion, would have lived, 887 *Excursion* 9. 203
Thus would have lived, or never have been born. 887 *Excursion* 9. 205
I could have lived another day. K.8. 220 **The snow-tracks* 41
That from his very childhood he had lived K.8. 230 **I will* 207
Than others have, for Michael had liv'd on K.8. 231 **I will* 213
And lived so long in quiet, side by side. K.8. 243 *Recluse* 1. 1. 260

Livelier. And grey-haired men look up with livelier brow,— 21 *Desc. Sk.* 609
Pleasure on pleasure crowded in, each livelier than the last. 92 *Poet's Dream* 44
No livelier love in such a place could be: 108 *Indolence* 67
Stirred him up to livelier wrath; 181 *Waggoner* 4. 133
Glisten with a livelier ray: 233 *Power of Sound* 61
A livelier sisterly resemblance show 347 *Processions* 61
Have we pursued, with livelier stir of heart 443 *Ecc. Sonn.* 3. 12. 2
Gain a fresh impulse, run a livelier course; 503 *Warning* 15
Partakes a livelier cheer; 507 *May* 22
Impelled to livelier pace. But now, my Book! 538 **In desultory* 14
Ne'er kindled with a livelier streak 583 **O for a* 32
With livelier hope a region wider far. 679 *Prelude* 6. 321
Crush out a livelier fragrance from the flowers 702 *Prelude* 8. 242
Livelier, and flinging out less guarded words 731 *Prelude* 11. 284
Rest, and be welcomed there to livelier joy. 756 *Excursion* 1. 20
Far livelier than bewildered traveller feels, 852 *Excursion* 6. 911
Of livelier interest to his hopes and fears, 869 *Excursion* 7. 795

Liveliest. Liveliest of the vernal train 161 **Pleasures newly* 39
Never enlivened with the liveliest ray 169 **Never enlivened* 1
All colours,—and the liveliest streak 299 *Brownie's Cell* 99
The fairest, softest, liveliest of them all! 381 *Duddon* 19. 9
Source of their liveliest hope, and tenderest prayer!— 438 *Ecc. Sonn.* 2. 40. 8
With liveliest peals of birth-day harmony: 464 **Greta, what* 13
With which, more zealous than the liveliest bird 523 *Epist. Beaumont* 160
Expressing liveliest thoughts in lively words 743 *Prelude* 13. 264
Than any liveliest sight of yesterday, 751 *Prelude* 14. 394

Liveliness. A more than sunny liveliness. 397 *White Doe* 105
More than inherent liveliness and power. 696 *Prelude* 7. 625
Yet, with a revelation's liveliness, 721 *Prelude* 10. 194
The liveliness of dreams. Nor did he fail, 758 *Excursion* 1. 148

Livelong. In youth's keen eye the livelong day was bright, 2 *Ev. Wk.* 17
And, passing thus the live-long day, 192 *Ruth* 17
Throughout the live-long day, 507 **While from* 62
In youth's wild eye the livelong day was bright, 592 *Ev. Wk. Quarto* 23
In soft forgetfulness the livelong hours, 752 *Prelude* 14. 403

Lively. So lively a remembrance of their griefs, 125 *V. and J.* 287
Whose skill can speed the day with lively cares, 221 *Triad* 62
Prompt, lively, self-sufficing, yet so meek 274 *Infant M.* 7
A course of lively pleasure; 302 *Yarrow V.* 78
The lively beauty of the leopard shows? 432 *Ecc. Sonn.* 2. 15. 2
Clear, loud, and lively is the din, 498 **Departing summer* 10
Shoot forth with lively power at Spring's return; 546 **Ye Lime* 2
Which we will now resume with lively hope, 687 *Prelude* 7. 49
Were roused, and lively natures rapt away! 729 *Prelude* 11. 124
Expressing liveliest thoughts in lively words 743 *Prelude* 13. 264
And ere our lively greeting into peace 762 *Excursion* 1. 447
Upon my naked branches:—lively thoughts 793 *Excursion* 3. 493
" The lively Grecian, in a land of hills, 812 *Excursion* 4. 718
Lively and beautiful, in rural forms, K.8. 227 **I will* 92
Thy lively spirits to partake, K.8. 262 **Ah! if* 4

Liver. Happy, happy Liver, 160 **Up with me* 22

Liveried. In liveried poverty. 483 *Simon Lee* 28
Noise that brings forth no liveried Page of state, 525 *Epist. Beaumont* 234
Who, yet a liveried schoolboy, in the depths 679 *Prelude* 6. 266

Liveries. With chaises, grooms, and liveries, and within 644 *Prelude* 2. 143

Livers. Such as grave Livers do in Scotland use, 196 *Resolution* 97
Loose livers he can make abate their vice, 557 *Cuck. and Night.* 14
Pure livers were they all, austere and grave, 758 *Excursion* 1. 113

Lives. That lives but in the torpid acquiescence 64 *Bord.* 1489
The Eagle lives in Solitude! Even so, 65 *Bord.* 1516
All thoughts whose idle composition lives 65 *Bord.* 1550
Who lives but to protect the weak or injured. 71 *Bord.* 1898
Without the strength to rise. Well, well, he lives, 73 *Bord.* 2065
For twenty lives. The daylight dawned, and now— 74 *Bord.* 2100
A gem that glitters while it lives, 88 *H. C.* 30
Of one who came to disunite their lives 125 *V. and J.* 236
There close the peaceful lives of flowers? 154 *Flower Garden* 6
Proof that the hermitess still lives, 165 *Parrot* 39
Of all that love their lawless lives, 239 *P. B.* 277
Lives in the light of youthful glee, 293 *Jedbor.* 11
Is Fortune's frail dependant; yet there lives 317 **Brave Schill* 10
Hence lives He, to his inner self endeared; 317 **Call not* 6
Lives inexhaustibly in precious gems, 331 *Ode: Thanks.* 166
Else it deserts him, surely as he lives. 354 *Aquap.* 117
Even as if bent on perishing. There lives 357 *Aquap.* 341
That Francis lives, *he* is not dead?" 409 *White Doe* 1211
Your brother lives—he lives—is come 411 *White Doe* 1358

Lives—*continued.*
Lives black with guilt, ferocity it calms. . . . 424 *Ecc. Sonn.* 1. 24. 14
" *Here Man more purely lives, less oft doth fall,* . 429 *Ecc. Sonn.* 2. 3. 1
Inversion strange ! that, unto One who lives . . 433 *Ecc. Sonn.* 2. 19. 9
Lead unmolested lives, and die of age. . . . 433 *Ecc. Sonn.* 2. 21. 8
Was shaped that traced the lives of these good men, 441 *Ecc. Sonn.* 3. 5. 3
Who framed the Ordinance by your lives disowned ! 444 *Ecc. Sonn.* 3. 16. 14
And lives there one, of all that come and go . . 459 **Wanderer ! that* 31
Lives with him, near the waterfall, ... 483 *Simon Lee* 39
And consecrate our lives to truth and love. . . 496 **A little* 57
There lives Who can provide . . . . . . 498 **The sylvan* 27
O ! that our lives, which flee so fast, ... 499 *Memory* 17
Your silent lives employ . . . . . . 526 **The soaring* 6
There insects live their lives, and die ; . . . . 532 †*Float. Isl.* 15
Lives there a man whose sole delights . . . . 533 **Blest is* 51
But bold Hubert lives in glee : . . . . . . 535 *Egremont* 69
Thus Virtue lives debarred from Virtue's meed ; . 539 **Lady ! a* 40
Farewell, farewell the heart that lives alone, . . 579 *Peele Castle* 53
Timidly uttered, for she *lives*, the meek, . . . 585 *Ch. Lamb* 80
Which we are toiling all our lives to find, . . . 589 *Immortality* 116
Sits brooding, lives not always to that end, . . 634 *Prelude* 1. 141
Emphatically such a Being lives, ... 646 *Prelude* 2. 252
All finite motions overruling, lives . . . . . 651 *Prelude* 3. 120
That lives who hath not known his godlike hours, 651 *Prelude* 3. 191
Maiden of Buttermere ! She lives in peace . . 692 *Prelude* 7. 320
With arts and laws so tempered, that their lives . 701 *Prelude* 8. 130
Than the gay Corin of the groves, who lives . . 703 *Prelude* 8. 285
Lives only by variety of disease. . . . . 721 *Prelude* 10. 208
From sight of One who lives secluded there, . . 774 *Excursion* 2. 159
Of insects chirping out their careless lives . . 789 *Excursion* 3. 246
" Happy is he who lives to understand, . . . 806 *Excursion* 4. 332
Of ignorance or illusion) lives and breathes . . 813 *Excursion* 4. 830
And, like the water-lily, lives and thrives, . . 831 *Excursion* 5. 567
She lives another's wishes to complete,— . . 840 *Excursion* 6. 140
The lingering gleam of their departed lives . . 847 *Excursion* 6. 611
Reading, where'er we turn, of innocent lives, . . 847 *Excursion* 6. 628
The Tinker lives in fun, ... S.3. 424 *Tinker* 47
Scrub lives a genuine Marquess above stairs, . . L.1. 95 *Juvenal* 3. 17

Liv'st. Thou liv'st with less ambitious aim, . . 158 **In youth* 29

Liveth. A goodly Knight that hath no peer that liveth ! " . . . . 374 *Eg. Maid* 348
That my Redeemer liveth,"—hears each word . 448 *Ecc. Sonn.* 3. 31. 6
Invisible, yet liveth to the heart ; . . . . . 648 *Prelude* 2. 405

Living. *See* **Ever-living, Plain-living.**
—Did Sabine grace adorn my living line, . . . 3 *Ev. Wk.* 72
For any living thing, hath faculties . . . . 23 *Yew-tree* 53
Rolled at his back along the living plain ; . . . 25 *Guilt* 88
For sacrifice its throngs of living men, . . . 26 *Guilt* 123
The heart of living creature.—My poor Babe . . 44 *Bord.* 398
Hath become Clifford's harlot—is *he* living ? . . 55 *Bord.* 977
And, by the living God, I could not do it. . . 55 *Bord.* 990
Living or dead all things were bodiless, . . . 59 *Bord.* 1215
What there is not another living man . . . 64 *Bord.* 1481
Nor any living thing whose lot of life . . . 68 *Bord.* 1710
Of living without knowledge that you live : . . 71 *Bord.* 1871
I did not think he had a living Child.— . . . 74 *Bord.* 2073
Oh, had you seen him living !— I (so filled . . 75 *Bord.* 2167
Evil to any living thing ; but hear me, . . . 75 *Bord.* 2175
She is a living child ; . . . . 83 *Lucy Gray* 58
Still upon his cheek are living . . . . . 93 *Westmoreland Girl* 35
Living or dead.—When last we heard of him, . 100 *Brothers* 316
For never sun on living creature shone . . . 107 *Indolence* 3
For happier soul no living creature has . . . 108 *Indolence* 30
Of murmuring, sparkling, living love, . . . 111 *A Complaint* 10
Between the living and the dead ; . . . . . 117 *Affl. Marg.* 60
To living thing—not even to her.—Behold ! . . 125 *V. and J.* 293
Living a life of eager industry. . . . . . 133 *Michael* 122
Thus living on through such a length of years, . 133 *Michael* 140
Never to living ear came sweeter sounds . . . 136 *Michael* 345
And hopes and wishes, from all living things . . 146 **It was an* 7
The living Beings by your own fire-side, . . . 147 *Joanna* 4
Joanna's name deep in the living stone :— . . 148 *Joanna* 83
Was living, as a child might know, ... 155 *Waterfall* 9
With living snow-drops ? circlet bright ! . . . 162 **Who fancied* 3
A living lord of melody ! . . . . 164 *Needlecase* 14
Her plumy mantle's living hues, ... 165 *Parrot* 9
Of the countless living things, ... 171 *Kitten* 45
Spreads with such a living grace . . . . . 171 *Kitten* 103
A living almanack had we ; . . . . 182 *Waggoner* 4. 220
This solitary Tree ! a living thing . . . . . 184 *Yew-trees* 10
With its upright living tree . . . . . . 190 **Lyre ! though* 22
Some plainly living voices were ; . . . . . 199 *Thorn* 161
(Never had living man such joyful lot !) . . . 201 *Hart-leap* 46
A cup of stone received the living well ; . . . 202 *Hart-leap* 82
In body, and become a living soul : . . . . 206 *Tintern* 46
And the round ocean and the living air, . . . 207 *Tintern* 98
An Army now, and now a living hill . . . . 217 *Enterprise* 114
What living man could fear . . . . . . 220 *Triad.* 56
Close clings to earth the living rock, ... 224 *Primrose* 19
Sweet flowers ;—what living eye hath viewed . 227 *Vernal Ode* 65
And armed with living spear for mortal fight ; . 227 *Vernal Ode* 104
The double note, as if with living power, . . . 229 *Cuckoo-clock* 10
That in the living Creature find on earth a place. 231 **The gentlest Poet* 38
Doth here preserve a living light, ... 232 *Jew. Fam.* 43
Within a living Boat to sit, ... 237 *P.B.* 78
He sees the Ass—and nothing living . . . . 249 *P. B.* 1107
That work a living landscape fair and bright ; . 254 *Dyer* 2
A loveliness to living youth denied. . . . . 258 **Even so* 8
Living with liberty on thee to gaze, ... 281 **Wansfell ! this* 2
For, were the bold Man living *now*, ... 291 *Rob Roy* 66

Living—*continued.*
To dead and living ; when her breath . . . . 299 *Brownie's Cell* 83
Yon grey tower's living crest ! . . . . . . 300 *Cora Linn* 24
But sculptured out of living stone, ... 301 *Bran* 50
Even by the *Living*, under ground ; . . . . 301 *Bran* 67
Plain living and high thinking are no more : . . 307 **O Friend* 11
Milton ! thou should'st be living at this hour : . 307 **Milton ! thou* 1
But not a living creature could be seen . . . 323 *Ode 1814* 16
To warn the living ; if truth were ever told . . 325 *Enghien* 8
The living generations with the dead ; . . . . 328 *Ode 1815* 67
Of living Nature ; no—though free to choose . . 333 *Ded. Tour* 5
Feelingly told by living monuments— . . . . 346 *Processions* 5
Still, with those white-robed Shapes—a living Stream, 347 *Processions* 48
And to all living mute memento breathes, . . . 355 *Aquap.* 164
But when I learned the Tree was living there, . . 358 *Pine : Rome* 6
In what alone is ours, the living Now. . . . . 360 **Near Anio's* 14
So like, yet so unlike, a living Creature ! . . . 370 *Eg. Maid* 56
That thinned the living and disturbed the dead ? 378 *Duddon* 8. 8
That, for the living and the dead, demand . . 389 *Breadalb.* 12
Where is no living thing to be seen ; . . . . 396 *White Doe* 51
Ye living, tend your holy cares ; . . . . . 397 *White Doe* 69
That doth the living stars repel, ... 397 *White Doe* 98
And peace is none, for living or dead ! . . . . 399 *White Doe* 307
For this her last and living Friend. . . . . 415 *White Doe* 1796
Scooped out of living rock, and near a brook . . 424 *Ecc. Sonn.* 1. 22. 3
The living landscapes greet him, and depart ; . 443 *Ecc. Sonn.* 3. 12. 4
And mount, at every step, with living wiles . . 451 *Ecc. Sonn.* 3. 42. 8
The living Waters, less and less by guilt . . . 452 *Ecc. Sonn.* 3. 47. 11
Says to the Living, profit while ye may ! . . . 467 *St. Bees* 78
And, drawing nigh, with his living eye, . . . 479 *Somnamb.* 120
Our living calendar : . . . . 483 *Sister* 18
—First learn to love one living man ; . . . . 485 *Poet's Epitaph* 3
And with a living pleasure we describe ; . . . 488 *Pers. Talk* 16
Upon a living staff, with borrowed sight. . . . 496 **A little* 10
To mind the living presences of nuns ; . . . . 496 **A little* 44
Its living roof above our heads. . . . . . 506 *Lab. Hymn* 20
To the fresh waters of a living Well— . . . . 527 **Those breathing* 8
Spread, tiny nautilus, the living sail ; . . . . 527 **Those breathing* 35
One living Stay was left, and on that one . . . 531 **I know* 27
Where Love for living Thing can find a place. . 531 *Octogen.* 14
No one upon living ground, ... 535 *Egremont* 6
May have a living House still left in thee ! " . . 535 *Egremont* 32
Living man, it must be he ! . . . . . . 536 *Egremont* 94
That it was scooped within the living stone,— . 546 **Oft is* 10
That any living heart should sleepy be . . . 557 *Cuck. and Night.* 44
Born deaf, and living deaf and dumb. . . . . 577 **I come* 40
He who had been our living John . . . . . 580 *John Words.* 39
Rush down the living rocks with whirlwind sound. 612 *Desc.Sk.Quarto* 581
After that living night— . . . . 623 *G. and S. Green* 30
That last and dreary living one . . . . . . 623 *G. and S. Green* 31
The dead, by influx of a living love, ... 625 *Æneid* 92
We saw the living Landscapes of the Rhine, . . 625 **The confidence* 3
The living Rock of God's eternal Word. . . . 626 *Rock : Rydal* 4
The trumpet of the Living Word . . . . . 629 *Installation* 102
Subordinate helpers of the living mind : . . . 634 *Prelude* 1. 153
Now living, or to live in future years. . . . 634 *Prelude* 1. 165
And measured motion like a living thing, . . . 638 *Prelude* 1. 384
Like living men, moved slowly through the mind 638 *Prelude* 1. 399
Belfry, and images, and living trees ; . . . . 643 *Prelude* 2. 106
And yet more often living with thyself, . . . 648 *Prelude* 2. 469
And pleasant flowers. The thirst of living praise, 654 *Prelude* 3. 336
Itself a living part of a live whole, ... 657 *Prelude* 3. 590
No living thing appeared in earth or air, . . . 664 *Prelude* 4. 385
Yet would the living Presence still subsist . . 666 *Prelude* 5. 34
A substance, fancied him a living man, . . . 667 *Prelude* 5. 144
Of living nature, which could thus so long . . 668 *Prelude* 5. 167
With living Nature hath been intimate, . . . 674 *Prelude* 5. 588
From languages that want the living voice . . 676 *Prelude* 6. 111
Debarred from Nature's living images, . . . 679 *Prelude* 6. 302
That had usurped upon a living thought . . . 683 *Prelude* 6. 527
That owned him ; living cheerfully abroad . . 688 *Prelude* 7. 74
And now I looked upon the living scene ; . . . 689 *Prelude* 7. 144
Others of wider scope, where living men, . . . 691 *Prelude* 7. 261
Of living Mortal covert, " as the moon . . . 691 *Prelude* 7. 283
When Art was young ; dramas of living men, . . 691 *Prelude* 7. 290
Of these, and of the living shapes they wear, . . 696 *Prelude* 7. 582
Living amid the same perpetual whirl . . . . 698 *Prelude* 7. 725
That aught external to the living mind . . . 707 *Prelude* 8. 550
Imperial, their chief living residence. . . . . 708 *Prelude* 8. 596
A living confirmation of the whole . . . . . 715 *Prelude* 9. 382
In exultation with a living pomp . . . . . 732 *Prelude* 11. 366
The noble Living and the noble Dead. . . . . 733 *Prelude* 11. 395
With living men—how deep the groans ! the voice 744 *Prelude* 13. 332
Is for both worlds, the living and the dead. . . 744 *Prelude* 13. 335
—Beauty—a living Presence of the earth, . . 755 *Recluse* 1. 1. 795
Of visitation from the living God, ... 759 *Excursion* 1. 212
Of a living ocean ; or, to sink engulfed, . . . 790 *Excursion* 3. 260
Of living man, though longing to pursue. . . . 795 *Excursion* 3. 644
Of amity, whose living threads should stretch . 797 *Excursion* 3. 747
Upon a living and rejoicing world ! . . . . 799 *Excursion* 3. 943
And felt, deeply as living man could feel. . . 808 *Excursion* 4. 474
Removed from all approach of living sight . . 812 *Excursion* 4. 714
Where living things, and things inanimate, . . 819 *Excursion* 4. 1204
Living to God and nature, and content . . . 823 *Excursion* 5. 35
In their repose, the living in their mirth, . . 828 *Excursion* 5. 374
Acknowledge reason's law ? A living power . . 829 *Excursion* 5. 471
One picture from the living. You behold, . . . 832 *Excursion* 5. 670
If living now, could otherwise report . . . . 835 *Excursion* 5. 884
Wherever laid, who living fell below . . . . 842 *Excursion* 6. 268
Out of the living rock, to be adorned . . . . 855 *Excursion* 6. 1145
Was wasted on the good Man's living ear, . . . 864 *Excursion* 7. 478

Lofty—*continued.*
Spread by a brotherhood of lofty elms, 756 *Excursion* 1. 29
And when these lofty elms once more appeared 766 *Excursion* 1. 644
A linnet warbled from those lofty elms, 771 *Excursion* 1. 962
Of water, or some lofty eminence, 776 *Excursion* 2. 321
And well those lofty brethren bear their part 782 *Excursion* 2. 699
Till, chancing on that lofty ridge to pass 784 *Excursion* 2. 811
Lofty, and steep, and naked as a tower. 787 *Excursion* 3. 42
By natural piety; nor a lofty mind, 790 *Excursion* 3. 266
That are not lofty as her rights; aspiring 806 *Excursion* 4. 315
Rising behind a thick and lofty grove, 817 *Excursion* 4. 1064
In some calm season, when these lofty rocks 818 *Excursion* 4. 1158
The lofty sight [? site], by nature framed to tempt 832 *Excursion* 5. 679
An anxious duty! which the lofty site, 834 *Excursion* 5. 762
To lofty raised; and to the highest, last; 839 *Excursion* 6. 84
How, from his lofty throne, the sun can fling 847 *Excursion* 6. 595
Along the sharp edge of yon lofty crags, 863 *Excursion* 7. 413
Throughout the lofty range of these rough hills, 865 *Excursion* 7. 499
With broidered housings. And the lofty Steed— 872 *Excursion* 7. 946
Low things with lofty) I too shall be doomed 873 *Excursion* 7. 1047
Or, in its progress, on the lofty side 876 *Excursion* 8. 115
A lofty stature undepressed by time, 881 *Excursion* 8. 502
Where the bare columns of those lofty firs, 891 *Excursion* 9. 499
Woods waving in the wind their lofty heads, 895 *Excursion* 9. 746
Cherish, and lofty Minds approve the past— 896 *Excursion* 9. 795
And as these lofty barriers break the force K.8. 247 *Recluse* 1.1.374
The Alban Sites and walls of lofty Rome. K.8. 281 **Arms and* 9

Lofty-minded. Those lofty-minded Lawgivers shall meet, 319 *Guernica* 12

Log. I'll fling your carcass like a log 241 *P. B.* 459

Logic. Which spake perpetual logic to my soul, 651 *Prelude* 3. 164
What memory and what logic! till the strain 694 *Prelude* 7. 509
And Truth had blest the logic of his sword. L.1. 97 *Juvenal* 3. 66

Logician. And Peter is a deep logician 245 *P. B.* 806

Loire. Washed by the current of the stately Loire. 710 *Prelude* 9. 41
Upon the borders of the unhappy Loire, 715 *Prelude* 9. 425
Along that very Loire, with festal mirth 716 *Prelude* 9. 431
When by the gliding Loire I paused, and cast 718 *Prelude* 10. 6

Loiret's. Yes, as I roamed where Loiret's waters glide 21 *Desc. Sk.* 624

Loiter. Or let me loiter, soothed with what is given, 356 *Aquap.* 263
Oft does the White Doe loiter there, 399 *White Doe* 255
To blush for me. Thou, loiter not nor halt 575 *Chiabrera* 6. 14
To loiter wilfully within a creek, 717 *Prelude* 9. 562

Loitered. "The roads I paced, I loitered through the fields; 32 *Guilt* 433
I loitered long ere I began: 245 *P. B.* 792
Unchecked, or loitered 'mid her sylvan combs, 751 *Prelude* 14. 397

Loiterer. The loiterer, not unnoticed by his comrades, 101 *Brothers* 370
Both to allure the casual Loiterer, 281 *Valedict.* 5
I play the loiterer: 'tis enough to note 657 *Prelude* 3. 579
Are gone, what summer loiterer will regard, S.3. 433 **The doubt* 38

Loiterers. Some other loiterers beguiling. 9 *Lines: Boat* 8

Loitering. The loitering traveller hence, at evening, sees 12 *Desc. Sk.* 89
The Vagrant must, no doubt, be loitering somewhere 44 *Bord.* 365
The loitering journey to its end. 180 *Waggoner* 4. 10
Thou hast been loitering on the road! 181 *Waggoner* 4. 129
On, loitering Muse—the swift Stream chides us—on! 379 *Duddon* 12. 1
Loitering in glassy pool: 508 *May* 76
A pleasant loitering journey, through three days 633 *Prelude* 1. 106
Than I beheld loitering on calm clear nights 676 *Prelude* 6. 93
Loitering, I watched the golden beams of light 706 *Prelude* 8. 463
Alone, with loitering step, and upward eye 849 *Excursion* 6. 760

Lomond's. And by Loch Lomond's braes. 292 *Rob Roy* 116
Danc'd to the murmuring rill on Lomond's wave, 630 [?] **O Moon* 2
Loch Lomond's beauties to discuss, S.3. 438 **My Lord* 12

London. Went up to London, found a master there, 135 *Michael* 264
Whether for London bound—to trill 341 *Ital. Itin.* 5
To London were the Chieftains bent: 404 *White Doe* 783
In London, "and masquerading," 457 **The sun has* 11
To London—a sad emigration I ween— 570 *Farmer* 45
Like London with its own black wreath, 586 *Hogg* 30
Of London, and from cloisters there, thou camest, 679 *Prelude* 6. 279
At full command, to London first I turned, 688 *Prelude* 7. 61
And thought of London—held me by a chain 688 *Prelude* 7. 86
Summoned from school to London; fortunate 688 *Prelude* 7. 92
The very shrillest of all London cries, 690 *Prelude* 7. 183
London, to thee I willingly return. 707 *Prelude* 8. 532
In London chiefly harboured, whence I roamed, 751 *Prelude* 14. 351

London's. He dwells in the centre of London's wide Town; 569 *Farmer* 5
This did I feel, in London's vast domain. 698 *Prelude* 7. 765
I ranged at large, through London's wide domain, 710 *Prelude* 9. 24

Lone. The lone black fir, forsakes the faded plain; 8 *Ev. Wk.* 310
Thy open beauties, or thy lone retreats; 12 *Desc. Sk.* 108
Such tale of this lone mansion she had learned, 27 *Guilt* 181
Reposing on a lone sick-bed; 144 *Driven in* 33
Who first, weighed down by scorn, in some lone bower 169 *Love lies Bleeding* 20
Toll from thy loftiest perch, lone bell-bird, toll! 233 *Power of Sound* 27
Thou too be heard, lone eagle! freed 235 *Power of Sound* 199
Meek aspirations please her, lone endeavour, 262 **Not Love* 9
Lone Flower, hemmed in with snows, and white as they 264 *Snowdrop* 1
To the lone shepherd on the hills disclose 282 **While beams* 13
In his lone Isle, the dreams of night; 299 *Brownie's Cell* 58
Lone vigils through the hours of sleep, 338 **Meek Virgin* 4
Guarded by lone San Salvador; 341 *San Salv.* 3
Than a lone obelisk, 'mid Nubian sands, 367 *Trajan* 10

Lone—*continued.*
Slept amid that lone Camp on Hardknot's height, 380 *Duddon* 17. 10
Like a lone criminal whose life is spared. 388 *Eagles* 3
Where he is perched, from yon lone Tower 406 *White Doe* 959
Lone Sufferer! will not she believe 414 *White Doe* 1676
In his lone course the Shepherd oft will pause, 468 **Ranging the* 2
Still is he seen, in lone sublimity, 471 *Ailsa Crag* 6
An abbey in its lone recess, 472 *Ossian* 13
Remote St. Kilda, lone and loved sea-mark 475 **Homeward we* 6
By whom in that lone place espied? 479 *Somnamb.* 98
When the lone shepherd sees the morning spread 508 *F. Stone* 21
And to the lone Recluse, whate'er 544 *Russ. Fug.* 221
In these lone vales, if aught of faith may claim, 595 *Ev. Wk. Quarto* 175
On the lone mountain top, their chang'd estate. 611 *Desc.Sk.Quarto* 489
Round a lone fane the human Genii mourn, 613 *Desc.Sk.Quarto* 646
And down the lone vale sails away 626 †*Cento* 15
Like a lone shepherd on a promontory 656 *Prelude* 3. 513
Walks a lone Monk, when service hath expired, 716 *Prelude* 9. 445
The beacon crowning the lone eminence, 738 *Prelude* 12. 259
Nothing but happiness, in some lone nook, 741 *Prelude* 13. 125
A lone Enthusiast, and among the fields, 761 *Excursion* 1. 348
From this lone valley, to a central spot 869 *Excursion* 7. 768
A lone pedestrian with a scanty freight, 875 *Excursion* 8. 98
Musing, the lone spot with my soul agrees S.3. 417 **Sweet was* 10

Loneliest. (It is the loneliest place of all these hills) 97 *Brothers* 140
The loneliest place we have among the clouds. 148 **There is an* 13
Through busiest street and loneliest glen 286 *Nith* 43

Loneliness. Thy loneliness: or shall those smiles be called 173 *Infant Daughter* 71
Her loneliness she cheers: 195 *Ruth* 243
To mitigate and cheer its loneliness. 266 **Even as* 8
A penitential loneliness. 398 *White Doe* 177
Your *dual* loneliness. The sacred tie 586 *Ch. Lamb* 128
Of loneliness gave way to empty noise 652 *Prelude* 3. 208
The feeling pleasures of his loneliness, 757 *Excursion* 1. 100
By loneliness, and goodness, and kind works, 762 *Excursion* 1. 405
The loneliness of this sublime retreat!" 806 *Excursion* 4. 372
Of rustic loneliness: that grey-haired Orphan— 835 *Excursion* 5. 885
From year to year in loneliness of soul; 863 *Excursion* 7. 403
She withering in her loneliness. Be this K.8. 248 *Recluse* 1.1.423

Lonely. Where peace to Grasmere's lonely island leads, 2 *Ev. Wk.* 5
Bright beams the lonely mountain-horse illume 4 *Ev. Wk.* 132
Or yell, in the deep woods, of lonely hound. 9 *Ev. Wk.* 378
By lonely farms and secret villages. 11 *Desc. Sk.* 49
From age to age, throughout his lonely bounds 21 *Desc. Sk.* 579
With shrill winds whistling round my lonely way, 21 *Desc. Sk.* 592
Nay, Traveller! rest. This lonely Yew-tree stands 22 *Yew-tree* 1
So lonely, but that thence might come a pang 25 *Guilt* 74
From lamp of lonely toll-gate streamed athwart the night. 27 *Guilt* 144
A lonely Spital, the belated swain 27 *Guilt* 150
Only were told there stood a lonely cot 30 *Guilt* 331
In these my lonely wanderings I perceived 70 *Bord.* 1808
The innocent Boy, else shelterless, his lonely head must hide. 91 *Norman Boy* 24
Yet, not the less, in children's hymns and lonely prayer delights. 93 *Poet's Dream* 64
Once in a lonely hamlet I sojourned 120 *Emigrant Mother* 1
He lengthens out his lonely shout, 126 *Idiot Boy* 5
That lonely union, privacy so deep, 143 **High bliss* 11
Hath to this lonely Summit given my Name. 148 **There is an* 17
By myself a lonely pleasure, 161 **Pleasures newly* 26
While in her lonely bower she tries 164 *Needlecase* 34
The last stone of a lonely hut; 165 *Danish Boy* 8
I wandered lonely as a cloud 187 **I wandered* 1
Yet it befell that, in this lonely place, 196 *Resolution* 52
While he was talking thus, the lonely place, 197 *Resolution* 127
I'll think of the Leech-gatherer on the lonely moor!" 197 *Resolution* 140
Though lonely, a deserted Tower; 204 *Brougham* 37
Though each is but a lonely Tower:— 204 *Brougham* 49
The sleep that is among the lonely hills. 205 *Brougham* 164
But oft, in lonely rooms, and 'mid the din 206 *Tintern* 25
Of the deep rivers, and the lonely streams, 206 *Tintern* 69
Who, for thy service trained in lonely woods, 216 *Enterprise* 92
Of nature, and the lonely elements. 221 *Triad* 96
So blooms this lonely Plant, nor dreads 224 *Primrose* 23
Pervade the lonely ocean far 225 *Present.* 56
—The light had left the lonely taper, 244 *P. B.* 748
The like on heath, in lonely wood; 245 *P. B.* 827
Her dwelling was a lonely house, 246 *P. B.* 891
Till to a lonely house he came, 247 *P. B.* 994
Faith in the whispers of the lonely Muse, 260 **High is* 7
Among the lonely mountains.—Live, ye trees! 262 **Mark the* 9
Produced as lonely Nature or the strife 269 **If these* 2
Measuring the periods of his lonely doom, 273 **Not the* 6
Or where 'mid "lonely heights and hows," 287 *Sons of Burns* 31
Hath led me to this lonely place. 288 *Highland Girl* 63
Whose Fancy in this lonely Spot 289 *Glen-Al.* 20
Lies buried in this lonely place. 289 *Glen-Al.* 32
And in the lonely Highland dell 297 *Highland Boy* 246
Within this little lonely isle 298 *Brownie's Cell* 15
Shot lightning through this lonely Isle! 298 *Brownie's Cell* 42
And, even to sadness, lonely and serene, 323 *Ode 1814* 18
Breathed from a soft and lonely instrument, 324 *Ode 1814* 84
That lurks by lonely ways! 337 *Cath. Cantons* 12
Where our Milton was wont lonely vigils to keep 364 *Vallomb.* 7
She spied the lonely Cast-away, 371 *Eg. Maid* 136
On infant bosoms lonely Nature lies. 377 *Duddon* 5. 14
The lonely Primrose yet renews its bloom, 381 *Duddon* 22. 13
But love, as Nature loves, the lonely Poor 390 *Highland Hut* 11

Long-deserted. Hallows once more the long-deserted Quire — 283 *Well have 6
Long-drawn. In long-drawn vista, rustling in the breeze; — 11 Desc. Sk. 47
Saw, at a long-drawn gallery's dusky bound, — 213 Dion 66
Hosannas pealing down the long-drawn aisle, — 232 Power of Sound 14
Sees long-drawn files, concentric rings — 343 Eclipse 49
Of long-drawn rampart, witness what they were. — 421 Ecc. Sonn. 1. 11. 14
Battering the Temple's front, its long-drawn nave — 474 *Hope smiled 5
That girt her waist, spinning the long-drawn thread — 769 Excursion 1. 886
Up through the trenches of the long-drawn vales — 808 Excursion 4. 454
Longed. Still longed for, never seen. — 184 *O blithe 24
By her sweet farewell looks, I longed to aid. — 190 *Lyre! though 7
And bloodshed, longed in quiet to be laid — 320 *They seek 13
Vallombrosa! I longed in thy shadiest wood — 345 Stanzas: Simplon 1
" Vallombrosa—I longed in thy shadiest wood — 364 Vallomb. 1
She longed to ravish;—shall she plunge, or climb — 381 Duddon 22. 8
And can reap nothing better,—child-like longed — 728 Prelude 11. 68
For human habitation; but I longed — 833 Excursion 5. 741
Had swept away; and now her Spirit longed — 853 Excursion 6. 1022
Long-enduring. Tough moss, and long-enduring mountain-plants, — 860 Excursion 7. 181
Longer. Glimmered our dear-loved home, alas! no longer ours! — 28 Guilt 243
Wanderers whose course no longer now agrees. — 34 Guilt 533
But now no longer mine. You know Lord Clifford; — 57 Bord. 1103
A little longer stay in sight! — 79 *Stay near 2
That, afterwards, a little longer, — 114 Ind. Wom. 27
Are withered; thou no longer canst be mine, — 124 V. and J. 159
—That pillow is no longer to be thine, — 124 V. and J. 217
And seems no longer in a hurry. — 126 Idiot Boy 71
And the guilt-burthened soul is no longer opprest. — 188 Music 12
And breathless calms no longer dreaded, — 216 Enterprise 78
In hearts no longer young; — 217 Enterprise 124
No longer) with what ecstasy upborne — 280 *'Tis he 11
Plead with the sovereign Sun for longer stay — 356 Aquap. 227
Shall they no longer bloom upon the stock — 359 *Those old 2
The Lily floats no longer!—She hath perished. — 370 Eg. Maid 54
No longer: ye, whom to the saving rite — 446 Ecc. Sonn. 3. 25. 10
Air slumbers—wave with wave no longer strives, — 454 Sea-side 3
Makes known, when thou no longer canst be seen, — 475 *Homeward we 13
Which he can till no longer? — 483 Simon Lee 48
Before the Stone of Power no longer stand— — 500 Humanity 4
And, though no longer upon rapine bent, — 523 Epist. Beaumont 127
Those silent Inmates now no longer share, — 527 *Those breathing 5
If love exist no longer, it must die,— — 531 Octogen. 3
Its place no longer to be found; — 532 *Float. Isl. 26
No longer, scattering to the heedless winds — 549 *The massy 11
No longer would I in my bed abide, — 557 Cuck. and Night. 57
By this mishap no longer be dismayed, — 561 Cuck.andNight.232
The day is more, and longer every night — 564 Troilus 141
By longer way than he was wont to go; — 564 Troilus 144
The mighty Minstrel breathes no longer, — 586 Hogg 9
Nor longer naked be your way-worn feet, — 614 Desc.Sk.Quarto 667
No longer steel their indurated hearts — 619 School Ex. 59
That the weight can no longer be borne, — 621 Convict 34
No longer breathe, but all be satisfied. — 622 Recluse 1. 1. 82
Oft when the dazzling show no longer new — 650 Prelude 3. 90
No longer haunting the dark winter night. — 653 Prelude 3. 308
Some skill, and longer time than may be spared, — 662 Prelude 4. 292
But feeling it no longer. Our discourse — 665 Prelude 4. 445
But, for such purpose, flowers no longer grow: — 701 Prelude 8. 157
No longer a mute influence of the soul, — 704 Prelude 8. 367
That could no longer hold its loathsome charge, — 725 Prelude 10. 479
No longer keep their ground, by faith maintained — 730 Prelude 11. 201
The longer I remained, more desolate: — 767 Excursion 1. 741
No longer in subjection to the past, — 798 Excursion 3. 874
Melts, and dissolves, and is no longer seen. — 803 Excursion 4. 145
Humiliation, when no longer free. — 840 Excursion 6. 126
For all that can no longer feed themselves, — 844 Excursion 6. 379
A plant no longer wild; the cultured rose — 855 Excursion 6. 1151
No longer led or followed by the Sons; — 878 Excursion 8. 278
Of that which is no longer needed, see — 892 Excursion 9. 557
No longer greeted—to the tottering sire, — S.3. 435 *The doubt 137
No longer flourish, he entirely gone, — K.8. 248 Recluse 1.1.422
Longest. Is the longest of the year. — 90 Longest Day 12
Take thy bliss, while longest, shortest, — 90 Longest Day 15
Even in the longest day of midsummer— — 98 Brothers 23
The heaviest storms not longest last; — 110 Forsaken 2
He found the longest summer day too short, — 254 Complete Angler 8
And longest life is but a day; — 291 Rob Roy 54
The longest date do melt like frosty rime, — 449 Ecc. Sonn. 3. 34. 8
At the calm close of summer's longest day, — 782 Excursion 2. 718
The earliest summoned and the longest spared— — 837 Excursion 5. 970
To swell thee into voice; nor longest drought — S.3. 433 *The doubt 28
Long-exiled. Long-exiled Dion marching at their head, — 213 Dion 23
Long-expected. For some high day of long-expected pleasure. — 372 Eg. Maid 192
Long-expecting. A voice, from long-expecting thousands sent, — 442 Ecc. Sonn. 3. 8. 1
Long-favoured. Long-favoured England! be not thou misled — 514 *Long-favoured 1
Long-forsaken. Above the hermit's long-forsaken cell!" — 220 Triad 40
To books, and to the long-forsaken desk, — 840 Excursion 6. 149
Long-frozen. My long-frozen heart grows warm!" — 140 Arm. Lady 38
Longing. The longing look alone on you. — 1 Extract 8
He towards his native country cast a longing look. — 103 Artegal 89
With sailors longing for a breeze in vain, — 154 Morn. Ex. 50

Longing—*continued.*
—Perplexed, and longing to be comforted, — 197 Resolution 117
Is the longing of the Shield— — 205 Brougham 146
Longing for his Beloved—who makes — 223 Wishing-gate 35
Ye who are longing to be rid — 234 Power of Sound 154
And longing of sweet thoughts that ever long. — 557 Cuck. and Night. 30
And of that longing heaviness doth come, — 557 Cuck. and Night. 3
As thou dost mine with longing her to see, — 563 Troilus 79
But speedily an earnest longing rose — 633 Prelude 1. 114
Vague longing, haply bred by want of power, — 635 Prelude 1. 239
Longing for skill to paint a scene so bright — 726 Prelude 10. 569
Of other longing, I pursued what seemed — 731 Prelude 11. 250
The longing for confirmed tranquillity, — 792 Excursion 3. 398
Of living man, though longing to pursue. — 795 Excursion 3. 644
And daily longing that the same were reached, — 844 Excursion 6. 389
A not unnatural longing felt, — S.3. 431 *The Scottish 5
What longing would ye know? — S.3. 431 *The Scottish 6
The longing, the contempt, the undaunted quest, — K.8. 257 Recluse 1.1.742
Longings. With love and longings infinite. — 117 Affl. Marg. 63
Such earnest longings and regrets as keen — 528 *Those breathing 112
With few wise longings and but little love, — 658 Prelude 3. 626
As may support longings of pure desire; — 804 Excursion 4. 236
And by ambitious longings undisturbed; — 839 Excursion 6. 47
Long-linked. Hear ye that Whistle? As her long-linked Train — 283 *Proud were 9
Long-lived. Through long-lived pressure of obscure distress, — 260 *High is 10
That long-lived servitude must last for ever. — 515 *Hard task 3
Under a long-lived storm of great events— — 732 Prelude 11. 374
But as the remnant of the long-lived tree — 845 Excursion 6. 494
Long-lost. Thy long-lost praise thou shalt regain; — 158 *In youth 77
'Mid that soft air, those long-lost bowers, — 530 Gleaner 24
Long-loved. For Duddon, long-loved Duddon, is my theme! — 376 Duddon 1. 14
Long-parched. Brood o'er the long-parched lands with Nile-like wings! — 22 Desc. Sk. 658
Long-past. Better to thank a dear and long-past day — 392 Bothwell 9
Of long-past times, nor obsolete in ours. — 846 Excursion 6. 547
Vivid remembrance of those long-past hours; — 857 Excursion 7. 4
Of long-past banquetings with high-born friends: — 860 Excursion 7. 218
Long-polluted. *See* **Too-long-polluted.**
Long-practised. With combinations of long-practised art — 320 *Hunger, and 9
Long-privileged. And the long-privileged house left empty—swept — 861 Excursion 7. 251
Long-protected. The long-protected to assume the part — 585 Ch. Lamb 90
Long-reverenced. Long-reverenced titles cast away as weeds; — 889 Excursion 9. 338
Long-roofed. This long-roofed Vista penetrate—but see, — 351 Des. Stanzas 65
The long-roofed chapel of King's College lift — 649 Prelude 3. 4
Longs. Look up—and help a hand that longs to set thee free." — 140 Arm. Lady 24
He longs to press her to his heart, — 248 P. B. 1079
Too clearly; feels too vividly; and longs — 804 Excursion 4. 175
Weary and faint, and longs to be released. — 874 Excursion 8. 28
Long-suffering. Patience *his* law, long-suffering *his* school, — 518 Pun. Death 7. 7
Long-suspended. Whose long-suspended rights are now on the eve — 78 Bord. 2336
A long-suspended office in the House — 797 Excursion 3. 761
Long-treasured. Joy's second spring and Hope's long-treasured smile, — 32 Guilt 455
Long-tried. The Curate's Dog—his long-tried friend, for they, — 523 Epist. Beaumont 131
The sober sympathies of long-tried friends. — 875 Excursion 8. 76
Long-vanished. Long-vanished happiness refines, — 499 Memory 11
Long-wished. Com'st thou long-wished for? After thousands lost, — L.2. 318 Frag. Æneid 4. 4
Lonsdale. Lonsdale! it were unworthy of a Guest, — 477 *Lonsdale! it 1
Before thee, Lonsdale, and this Work present, — 753 *Oft, through 6
Lonsdale's. Must honour still to Lonsdale's tail be bound? — L.1. 88 Juvenal 1. 13
Loo. And to the combat, Loo or Whist, led on — 639 Prelude 1. 516
Look. The longing look alone on you. — 1 Extract 8
And he can look beyond the sun, and view — 16 Desc. Sk. 325
To glance a look upon the well-matched pair; — 19 Desc. Sk. 486
And grey-haired men look up with livelier brow,— — 21 Desc. Sk. 609
Is ever on himself doth look on one, — 23 Yew-tree 56
When Fortune might put on a kinder look; — 28 Guilt 231
Forthwith the pair passed on; and down they look — 33 Guilt 514
A look was in her face which seemed to say, — 36 Guilt 628
When on his own he cast a rueful look. — 36 Guilt 634
And look upon the pleasant face of Nature—— — 40 Bord. 148
Flashes a look of terror upon guilt, — 40 Bord. 171
You will look down into a dell, and there — 41 Bord. 217
This charge of thine, then ill befall thee!—Look, — 42 Bord. 304
A look of mine would send him scouring back, — 43 Bord. 318
This they can do, and look upon my face— — 45 Bord. 442
With look as sad as he were dumb; the cur, — 45 Bord. 457
I cast a look upon the Girl, and felt — 45 Bord. 476
To look upon you. In a peasant's dress — 47 Bord. 531
With such a look—it makes me tremble, Sir, — 47 Bord. 541
But vigorous Spirits look for something more — 48 Bord. 622
By showing that you look beyond the instant. — 49 Bord. 654
To look upon the deed. Before we enter — 49 Bord. 657
I look at him and tremble like a child. — 51 Bord. 786
You say he was asleep,—look at this arm, — 52 Bord. 796
Must needs step in, and save my life. The look — 54 Bord. 919

Look—*continued.*

Which doth play tricks with them that look on it : 54 *Bord.* 924
And none look grave but dotards. He may live . 54 *Bord.* 929
To share your triumph ? Yes, her very look, . 55 *Bord.* 971
Defend the innocent. Lacy ! we look . . . . 56 *Bord.* 1029
To lisp the name of Father—could he look . . 56 *Bord.* 1052
But softly ! we must look a little nearer. . . . 58 *Bord.* 1132
So pious in demeanour ! in his look . . . . 60 *Bord.* 1246
But they will soon be lightened. Ay, look up— . 65 *Bord.* 1533
Ill can I bear that look—Plead for me, Oswald ! . 66 *Bord.* 1603
to look up at this roof in storm or fair . . . . 72 *Bord.* 1947
Ay, come to me and weep. Yes, Varlet, look, . 76 *Bord.* 2189
Look at it—the flower is small, ... 79 *Foresight* 5
As, if you look up, you plainly may see ; . . . 80 †*Address : Child* 6
And ring a sharp 'larum ;—but, if you should look, 80 †*Address : Child* 10
"What ails you, child?"—she sobbed, "Look here!" 82 *Alice Fell* 25
" Alas, the mountain-tops that look so green and fair ! . . . . 88 *Pet-lamb* 53
For she looked with such a look, and she spake with such a tone, ... 88 *Pet-lamb* 67
Look thou to Eternity ! . . . . 90 *Longest Day* 48
The Boy no answer made by words, but, so earnest was his look, ... 93 *Poet's Dream* 69
Will look and scribble, scribble on and look, . . 95 *Brothers* 8
Many a long look of wonder : and at last, . . . 95 *Brothers* 30
He towards his native country cast a longing look. 103 *Artegal* 89
To them who look not daily on thy face ; . . . 107 *Farewell* 43
Look at the common grass from hour to hour : . 107 *Indolence* 23
Look at the fate of summer flowers, ... 110 **Look at* 1
I look—the sky is empty space ; . . . . . 110 *'*Tis said that some* 18
But when I cease to look, my hand is on my heart. 110 *'*Tis said that some* 20
Do thou look gladly on the sight ; . . . . . 112 **What heavenly* 4
On me how strangely did he look ! . . . . . 114 *Ind. Wom.* 34
I'll look upon your tents again. . . . . . . 114 *Ind. Wom.* 54
I look at the fields, but I cannot go in ! . . . 116 *Repentence* 16
I look for ghosts ; but none will force . . . . 117 *Affl. Marg.* 57
Thou hast, I think, a look of ours, ... 121 *Emigrant Mother* 91
And looked, as mothers ne'er were known to look, 125 *V. and J.* 260
To look his trouble in the face, it seemed . . . 134 *Michael* 222
I look upon thee, for thou art the same . . . 136 *Michael* 333
But 'tis a long time to look back, my Son, . . 137 *Michael* 372
By word, look, deed, with hope that he might love again. . . . . 139 *Arm. Lady* 6
Look up—and help a hand that longs to set thee free." . . . . 140 *Arm. Lady* 24
" Humble love in me would look for no return, . 140 *Arm. Lady* 65
One chiefly, who with voice and look . . . . 144 **Driven in* 75
Alas ! Alas ! that look so wild, ... 145 *Her Eyes* 87
By any who should look beyond the dell . . . 146 **It was an* 35
Who look upon the hills with tenderness, . . . 147 *Joanna* 7
Look up ! and think, above your head . . . 156 *Oak and Broom* 25
That you might look at me and say, ... 156 *Oak and Broom* 79
Look but at the gardener's pride— . . . . 157 *Sexton* 17
He needs but look about, and there . . . . 158 **In youth* 38
And one chance look to Thee should turn, . . . 158 **In youth* 50
Still as we look with nicer care, ... 164 **Fair Lady* 17
He turned, and watched with kindred look . . 167 *Pilgrim's Dream* 14
Take root (so seems it) and look up . . . . 170 *Rural Ill.* 17
That way look, my Infant, lo ! . . . . . . 170 *Kitten* 1
If you look to vale or hill, ... 171 *Kitten* 80
Look fairly like a lawful earning. . . . . . 177 *Waggoner* 2. 40
But, pretty Maid, if you look near, ... 178 *Waggoner* 2. 117
Thence look thou forth o'er wood and lawn . . 180 *Waggoner* 4. 38
Across yon meadowy bottom look, ... 180 *Waggoner* 4. 40
Which made me look a thousand ways . . . 183 **O blithe* 19
Stirred with his staff, and fixedly did look . . 196 *Resolution* 79
Whene'er you look on it, 'tis plain . . . . . 200 *Thorn* 219
Are but three bounds—and look, Sir, at this last— 203 *Hart-leap* 143
To look on nature, not as in the hour . . . . 207 *Tintern* 89
What doth she look on ?—whom doth she behold ? 209 *Laod.* 14
Whence angry perturbations,—and that look . . 214 *Dion* 100
Not doubtfully perceived.—Look homeward now ! 219 **This Height* 28
Is mute ; and, in his silence, would look down, . 220 *Haunted Tree* 33
That opening—but a look ye cast . . . . . 224 *'*Tis gone* 8
And from aloft look down into a cove . . . . 233 *Power of Sound* 43
Look up—and you shall see me soon ! . . . . 236 *P. B.* 10
And look, where clothed in brightest green . . 237 *P. B.* 63
And does no little cottage look . . . . . . 240 *P. B.* 378
A look more tender than severe ; . . . . . 241 *P. B.* 436
'Twas but one mild, reproachful look, ... 241 *P. B.* 437
He looks, he cannot choose but look ; . . . . 242 *P. B.* 518
Well may you tremble and look grave ! . . . . 243 *P. B.* 627
And look at Peter Bell ! . . . . 244 *P. B.* 690
And made the good man round him look. . . . 244 *P. B.* 745
A piercing look the Widow cast . . . . . . 248 *P. B.* 1041
As many do, repining while they look ; . . . . 250 *Admon.* 6
Old Skiddaw will look down upon the Spot . . 251 *Appleth.* 13
Angels of love, look down upon the place ; . . 256 *Marriage : Friend* 3
Yet I pursued her with a Lover's look ; . . . 258 **With Ships* 10
Nor one look more exchanging, grief to still . . 276 *Oker Hill* 3
But by the Chieftain's look, though at his side . 278 *Wellington* 5
Where herbs look up, and opening flowers are seen ; 278 **Life with* 11
Shall look more bright—the happy, happier still ; 281 *Chris. Words.* 10
Others look up, and with fixed eyes admire . . 283 **Well have* 8
Perchance without one look behind me cast, . . 284 *Departure* 16
The embarrassed look of shy distress, ... 288 *Highland Girl* 30
Look at him—look again ! for he . . . . . 294 *Jedbor.* 15
To look on thee—delight to rove . . . . . 299 *Cora Linn* 14
O Friend ! I know not which way I must look . 306 **O Friend* 1

Look—*continued.*

And calls a look of love into her face, ... 311 **Who rises* 10
And look and listen—gathering, whence I may, . 314 **Not 'mid* 13
Look now on that Adventurer who hath paid . 317 **Look now* 1
Burial and death : look for them—and descry, . 322 **Humanity, delighting* 36
Look round, and by their smiling seem to say, . 324 *Ode 1814* 66
But, gradually a calmer look bestowing, . . . 337 *Aar* 4
Whate'er we look on, at our side . . . . 337 *Cath. Cantons* 16
What eye can look upon thy shrine . . . 338 **Meek Virgin* 5
To share his wanderings ! him whose look . . 342 *Ital. Itin.* 52
While we look round with favoured eyes, . . 343 *Eclipse* 70
Whose heaviest sin it is to look . . . . . 344 **How blest* 8
Trembling, I look upon the secret springs . . 347 *Processions* 64
Given with a voice and by a look returned . . 353 *Aquap.* 31
When gratitude, though disciplined to look . . 354 *Aquap.* 108
To localise heroic acts— could look . . . . 356 *Aquap.* 273
Look like a cloud—a slender stem the tie . . 358 *Pine : Rome* 2
Drawn to his side by look or act of love . . 362 **List—'twas* 58
An altered look upon the advancing Stranger . 369 *Eg. Maid* 26
Meanwhile, for further guidance, look . . . . 370 *Eg. Maid* 111
Last lingering look of clay, that tames . . . 372 *Eg. Maid* 197
Moments, to cast a look behind, ... 376 **The Minstrels* 69
As this we look on. Distant Mountains hear, . 382 *Duddon* 23. 5
Swoln with chill rains, nor ever cast a look . . 389 *Tyndrum* 5
Look again, and they all are gone ; . . . . . 396 *White Doe* 32
" Look, there she is, my Child ! draw near ; . 398 *White Doe* 178
Look down, and see a griesly sight ; . . . . 398 *White Doe* 244
Look down among them, if you dare ; . . . . 399 *White Doe* 254
But look again at the radiant Doe ! . . . . 399 *White Doe* 309
He glanced a look of holy pride, ... 400 *White Doe* 403
But look not for me when I am gone, ... 402 *White Doe* 538
Of Brancepeth look in doubt and fear, ... 402 *White Doe* 595
On you we look, with dearest hope ; . . . . 403 *White Doe* 651
Then look at them with open eyes ! . . . . 406 *White Doe* 904
To win some look of love, or gain . . . . . 407 *White Doe* 1016
And, with a look of calm command . . . . 410 *White Doe* 1331
Though without one uplifted look, ... 411 *White Doe* 1362
A look of pure benignity, ... 414 *White Doe* 1656
The pleading look the Lady viewed, ... 414 *White Doe* 1660
From look, deportment, voice, or mien, . . . 415 *White Doe* 1722
And thence look round her far and wide, . . . 415 *White Doe* 1780
To look upon Saint Mary's shrine ; . . . . . 416 *White Doe* 1816
A dear look to her lowly Friend ; . . . . . 416 *White Doe* 1855
By flames, look up to heaven and crave redress . 426 *Ecc. Sonn.* 1. 32. 4
With understanding spirit now may look . . . 435 *Ecc. Sonn.* 2. 29. 5
(While we look round) that Heaven's decrees are just : . . . . 437 *Ecc. Sonn.* 2. 36. 3
Is to the sky while we look up in love ; . . . 444 *Ecc. Sonn.* 3. 17. 2
Look only on the Gospel's brighter page : . . . 447 *Ecc. Sonn.* 3. 29. 11
His drowsy rings. Look forth !—that Stream behold, ... 452 *Ecc. Sonn.* 3. 47. 5
Long lines of mighty Kings—look forth, my Soul ! 452 *Ecc. Sonn.* 3. 47. 9
Look for the stars, you'll say that there are none ; 453 **Calm is the* 3
Look up a second time, and, one by one, . . . 453 **Calm is the* 4
Look round ;—of all the clouds not one is moving ; 453 **The Sun, that* 5
Offenders, dost put off the gracious look, . . . 454 **The Sun, that* 14
On British waters with that look benign ? . . 454 *Sea-side* 35
Among the speechless clouds, a look . . . . 457 **Had this* 3
Come forth, ye drooping old men, look abroad, . 458 **Had this* 53
A look of thine the wilderness pervades, . . . 459 **Wanderer ! that* 25
" To look on tempests, and be never shaken ; " . 461 **Queen of* 50
But look we now to them whose minds from far . 467 *St. Bees* 109
Look to thy plumage and thy life !—The roe, . 472 *Dunolly Eagle* 9
Which he forbears again to look upon ; . . . 480 **Most sweet* 4
" You look round on your Mother Earth, . . . 481 *Expost.* 9
And from the look of the Falconer's eye ; . . . 494 *Force of Prayer* 10
The gentlest look of spring ; . . . . . . 498 **Departing summer* 3
Retirement then might hourly look . . . . 499 *Memory* 21
His look of pitiable gratitude ! . . . . . . 501 *Humanity* 68
She may look for serene weather ; . . . . . 503 **Like a* 77
Look up to Heaven ! the industrious Sun . . . 506 *Lab. Hymn* 21
Thou and thy train are proud to look, ... 507 *May* 47
Upon the mountains. Look at her, whoe'er . . 508 *F. Stone* 22
That posture, and the look of filial love . . 509 *F. Stone* 80
On thee I look, not sorrowing ; fare thee well, . 510 *F. Stone* 130
To mutual tyranny a deadlier look ? . . . . 515 **Men of* 8
Their first look—blinded as tears fell in showers . 517 *Pun. Death* 1. 13
Were tempting all astir to look aloft or climb ; . 524 *Epist. Beaumont* 218
To every act, word, thought, and look of love, . 529 **Those breathing* 138
But look, and to the watchful eye . . . . . 532 **How beautiful the* 5
Her earnest tone, and look beaming with faith, . 541 *Grace Darl.* 45
No second look she cast, ... 542 *Russ. Fug.* 30
Go look on the fresh daisy ; then say I, . . . 561 *Cuck.andNight.* 243
And scanned them with a fixed and serious look . 566 *Cumb. Beg.* 11
Watches the aged Beggar with a look . . . . 566 *Cumb. Beg.* 31
In look and motion, that the cottage curs, . . 567 *Cumb. Beg.* 61
And his bright eyes look brighter, set off by the streak . . . . 569 *Farmer* 7
With a look of such earnestness often will stand, . 570 *Farmer* 71
Poor winter look fine in such strange masquerade. 570 *Farmer* 76
Through the lost look of dotage, is cunning and sly : 572 *Avarice* 22
'Tis a look which at this time is hardly his own, . 572 *Avarice* 23
His look and bending figure, all bespeak . . . 572 *Animal Tran.* 5
I love to see the look with which it braves, . . 579 *Peele Castle* 50
Yet for one happy issue ;—and I look . . . . 582 **To public* 3
Such look the Oppressor might confound, . . . 583 **O for a* 35
Look round her when the heavens are bare, . . 587 *Immortality* 13

Looked—*continued.*
And, looking backwards when he looked, mine eyes 667 *Prelude* 5. 127
Drew to the spot an anxious crowd; some looked 672 *Prelude* 5. 444
Not without trembling, we in safety looked . . 678 *Prelude* 6. 215
Of social life, I looked upon these things . . . 686 *Prelude* 6. 767
And now I looked upon the living scene; . . . 689 *Prelude* 7. 144
Romantic almost, looked at through a space, . . 693 *Prelude* 7. 442
Not to be looked at by the common sun. . . . 694 *Prelude* 7. 457
Looked out for admiration. Folly, vice, . . . 695 *Prelude* 7. 578
Of those who passed, and me who looked at him, 696 *Prelude* 7. 611
Thus have I looked, nor ceased to look, oppressed 696 *Prelude* 7. 630
And manners which my childhood looked upon . 701 *Prelude* 8. 160
Of most to move in, but that first I looked . . 703 *Prelude* 8. 315
I looked for something that I could not find, . . 710 *Prelude* 9. 72
Looked thitherward. One, reckoning by years, . 711 *Prelude* 9. 139
Fresh as the morning star. Elate we looked . . 715 *Prelude* 9. 385
And on these spots with many gleams I looked . 716 *Prelude* 9. 500
Courage to them who looked for good by light . 727 *Prelude* 11. 4
That once looked up in faith, as if to Heaven . 732 *Prelude* 11. 362
And everything she looked on, should have had . 736 *Prelude* 12. 169
Which, while I looked all round for my lost guide, 738 *Prelude* 12. 257
I looked in such anxiety of hope; . . . . . 739 *Prelude* 12. 313
I chiefly looked (what need to look beyond?) . 741 *Prelude* 13. 101
Fell like a flash, and lo! as I looked up, . . . 746 *Prelude* 14. 39
That stared upon each other!—I looked round, . 756 *Excursion* 1. 31
Rise up, and bathe the world in light! He looked— 759 *Excursion* 1. 200
The fence where that aspiring shrub looked out . 763 *Excursion* 1. 452
The broken wall. I looked around, and there, . 763 *Excursion* 1. 459
But, when I entered, Margaret looked at me . . 766 *Excursion* 1. 648
And with a brighter eye she looked around . . 766 *Excursion* 1. 688
And well remember, o'er that fence she looked, . 766 *Excursion* 1. 692
So calm and still, and looked so beautiful . . . 770 *Excursion* 1. 947
Looked on this guide with reverential love? . . 772 *Excursion* 2. 30
We had looked down upon it. All within, . . 781 *Excursion* 2. 643
And pleased I looked upon my grey-haired Friend, 781 *Excursion* 2. 658
When ye looked down upon us from the crag, . 782 *Excursion* 2. 734
But through all quarters looked for him in vain. . 783 *Excursion* 2. 797
So saying, round he looked, as if perplexed; . . 786 *Excursion* 3. 20
And, with a holier love inspired, I looked . . . 795 *Excursion* 3. 667
Imploringly;—looked up, and asked the Heavens 796 *Excursion* 3. 690
Respiring I looked round.—How bright the sun, . 798 *Excursion* 3. 880
Carried so high, that every thought, which looked 805 *Excursion* 4. 263
Looked on the polar star, as on a guide . . . 811 *Excursion* 4. 697
They looked; were humbly thankful for the good 815 *Excursion* 4. 936
I looked for counsel as unbending now; . . . 817 *Excursion* 4. 1104
—For me, I looked upon the pair, well pleased: . 829 *Excursion* 5. 452
Even as the same is looked at, or approached. . 830 *Excursion* 5. 530
I looked with steadiness as sailors look . . . 833 *Excursion* 5. 743
Of prosperous fortune. On the fields he looked . 842 *Excursion* 6. 238
From some commanding eminence had looked . 871 *Excursion* 7. 879
(Ill home for bird so gentle), they looked down . K.8. 225 **I will* 20
At this the boy looked round him, and his heart . K.8. 229 **I will* 152
And looked at him as with a poet's eye. . . . K.8. 230 **I will* 198
The station whence he looked was soft and green, K.8. 237 *Recluse* 1. 1.19
That must be looked for here, paternal sway, . . K.8. 253 *Recluse* 1.1.617
Looked-for. But enters as a looked-for guest, . . 143 **Driven in* 5
Lookers. Deftly prolonged, though grey-haired lookers on . . . . 680 *Prelude* 6. 373
Lookers-on. Of Lookers-on how pleased and proud! 409 *White Doe* 1181
The pride and pleasure of all lookers-on . . . 692 *Prelude* 7. 348
Look'st. "Thou look'st upon me, and dost fondly think, ... 464 **Thou look'st* 1
Looking. *See* **Back-looking, Backward-looking, Down-looking, Forth-looking, Forward-looking, Further-looking, Happiest-looking, Onward-looking.**
Rooted I stood; for, looking at the woman, . . 47 *Bord.* 580
And, looking down, espies . . . . 85 *Shepherd-boys* 64
And, looking o'er the hedge, before me I espied . 87 *Pet-lamb* 3
And, looking round, imagined that he saw . . 96 *Brothers* 96
Which will bear looking at. These boys—I hope 99 *Brothers* 239
As I remember, looking round these rocks . . . 99 *Brothers* 264
And, looking at the grave, he said, "My Brother!" 102 *Brothers* 411
Looking down on the kine, and our treasure of sheep . . . . 116 *Repentance* 31
The Doctor, looking somewhat grim, ... 129 *Idiot Boy* 259
Was busy, looking back into past times. . . . 135 *Michael* 257
Joanna, looking in my eyes, beheld . . . . 147 *Joanna* 52
And envies him that's looking;—what an insight must it be! . . . . 189 *Star-gazers* 8
The Shepherd, looking eastward, softly said, . . 265 **The Shepherd* 1
When, looking on the present face of things, . . 309 **When, looking* 1
Looking far forth from his aerial cell, ... 362 **List—'twas* 85
'Tis night: in silence looking down, ... 406 *White Doe* 938
Who, looking round the fair assemblage, feels . 446 *Ecc. Sonn.* 3. 23. 13
And to those graves looking habitually . . . 464 **A point* 3
The mountains looking on. . . . . 498 **The sylvan* 6
Thus looking out did Harry stand: . . . . 537 *Goody Blake* 74
Where I was looking on, a babe in arms, . . . 636 *Prelude* 1. 276
And from my pillow, looking forth by light . . 650 *Prelude* 3. 58
And often looking round was moved to smiles . 661 *Prelude* 4. 210
And, looking backwards when he looked, mine eyes 667 *Prelude* 5. 127
Mute, looking at the grave in which he lies! . . 671 *Prelude* 5. 397
Who, looking inward, have observed the ties . . 694 *Prelude* 7. 461
Some sweet lass of the valley, looking out . . 699 *Prelude* 8. 38
With looking on, some ancient wedded pair . . 699 *Prelude* 8. 46
Honour and shame, looking to right and left, . . 751 *Prelude* 14. 338
When, looking back, thou seest, in clearer view . 751 *Prelude* 14. 393
And, looking up to those enormous elms, . . . 765 *Excursion* 1. 592
That had not cheered me long—ere, looking round 765 *Excursion* 1. 622
And, looking round me, now I first observed . . 767 *Excursion* 1. 742

Looking—*continued.*
We listened, looking down upon the hut, . . . 777 *Excursion* 2. 377
Called me; and, looking down the darksome aisle, 825 *Excursion* 5. 209
Around him looking; "Where shall I begin? . 836 *Excursion* 5. 897
Weeping and looking, looking on and weeping, . 853 *Excursion* 6. 980
Or of the blessèd Virgin, looking down . . . 881 *Excursion* 8. 489
Both have been fairly dealt with; looking back . 888 *Excursion* 9. 287
Than, looking forth, the gentle Lady said, . . 890 *Excursion* 9. 418
I, thus boldly looking at you, ... S.3. 437 **I, whose* 4
Down lookng on that hollow, where the pool . . K.8. 225 **I will* 47
Looking-glass. In crystal clearness Dian's looking-glass; . . . . 381 *Duddon* 22. 3
And soon approach Diana's Looking-glass! . . 524 *Epist. Beaumont* 165

Looks. Upward he looks—"and calls it luxury:" 11 *Desc. Sk.* 24
His humble looks no shy restraint impart; . . 11 *Desc. Sk.* 37
Of looks where common kindness had no part, . 31 *Guilt* 393
True sympathy the Sailor's looks expressed, . . 32 *Guilt* 451
His looks—for pondering he was mute the while. 32 *Guilt* 452
And stern looks on the man her grey-haired Comrade cast. . . . . 33 *Guilt* 477
The stranger's looks and tears of wrath beguiled . 33 *Guilt* 500
Have power to yield? perhaps he looks elsewhere.— 42 *Bord.* 259
Which looks like a transition in my soul, . . . 48 *Bord.* 636
You said you did not like his looks—that he . 51 *Bord.* 757
I bore her in my arms; her looks won pity; . . 53 *Bord.* 846
Of infant playfulness with piteous looks . . . 56 *Bord.* 1047
Of what he says, and looks, and does, and is, . . 62 *Bord.* 1397
And innocence, embodied in his looks, . . . 77 *Bord.* 2261
To dignify arch looks and laughing eyes; . . . 80 **Loving she* 3
And never looks behind; . . . . 83 *Lucy Gray* 62
It looks just like the rest; and yet that man . . 98 *Brothers* 195
"But, if my looks did with my words agree, . . 104 *Artegal* 147
That Nature prompts them to display, their looks, 118 *Maternal Grief* 32
He knew it not) and from his happiest looks, . . 118 *Maternal Grief* 45
An infant's face and looks are thine . . . . 120 *EmigrantMother* 17
Thy looks, thy cunning, and thy wiles, . . . 121 *EmigrantMother* 51
And feed his countenance with your own sweet looks, ... 124 *V. and J.* 202
She stops, she stands, she looks about; . . . 129 *Idiot Boy* 267
She looks again—her arms are up— . . . . 130 *Idiot Boy* 372
Would Michael exercise his heart with looks . . 133 *Michael* 172
Or looks, or threatening gestures, could perform. . 134 *Michael* 193
—It looks as if it never could endure . . . . 137 *Michael* 379
What wicked looks are those I see? . . . . 145 *Her Eyes* 86
He with grave looks demanded for what cause, . 147 *Joanna* 26
That eastward looks, I there stopped short—and stood . . . . 147 *Joanna* 43
It seems that all looks wondrous cold; . . . 174 *Waggoner* 1. 65
Looks in and out, and through and through; . 181 *Waggoner* 4. 172
Bent earthwards; he looks up—the clouds are split 184 *Night-piece* 11
Nor uninformed with Phantasy, and looks . . 185 *Yew-trees* 19
She looks, and her heart is in heaven: but they fade, ... 188 *Poor Susan* 13
By her sweet farewell looks, I longed to aid. . . 190 **Lyre! though* 7
She looks as if at them—but they . . . . . 192 *Gipsies* 20
'There is a Thorn—it looks so old, ... 197 *Thorn* 1
It looks so old and grey. . . . . 197 *Thorn* 4
Her looks were calm, her senses clear. . . . . 199 *Thorn* 143
And that it looks at you; . . . . 200 *Thorn* 218
The baby looks at you again. . . . . . . 200 *Thorn* 220
—This chase it looks not like an earthly chase; . 201 *Hart-leap* 27
To the clouds of heaven she looks; . . . . . 204 *Brougham* 66
He looks on festal ground with fruits bestrown; . 213 *Dion* 36
Looks to the earth, and to the vacant air; . . 220 *Triad* 27
Loves his own glory in their looks, and showers . 231 *Clouds* 84
Their soul-subduing looks might cheat . . . . 232 *Jew. Fam.* 35
Beneath his looks so bare and bold, ... 240 *P. B.* 308
More steady looks the moon, and clear, . . . 242 *P. B.* 493
He looks, he cannot choose but look; . . . . 242 *P. B.* 518
He looks, he ponders, looks again; . . . . . 242 *P. B.* 526
Sky-ward he looks—to rock and wood— . . . 242 *P. B.* 548
The Ass looks on—and to his work . . . . . 242 *P. B.* 571
He pulls—and looks—and pulls again; . . . 243 *P. B.* 576
The meagre shadow that looks on— . . . . 243 *P. B.* 586
Thy looks, thy gestures, all present . . . . 294 *Jedbor.* 39
Its second twilight, and looks gay; . . . . 294 *Jedbor.* 46
The Eternal looks upon her sword that gleams, . 318 **Ah! where* 12
Looks on delighted—meet in festal ring, . . . 322 **Ye Storms* 4
With feet, hands, eyes, looks, lips, report your gain; 322 **Ye Storms* 10
Looks down—the bright and solitary Moon, . . 339 *Tell* 11
Am free to rove where Nature's loveliest looks, . 354 *Aquap.* 95
And shrubs, whose pleasant looks gave proof how kind . . . . 356 *Aquap.* 214
Looks up in all places, for joy or for rest, . . . 365 *Vallomb.* 39
Such looks of love and honour . . . . . 386 *Yarrow Rev.* 74
Holy as princely, who that looks on thee . . 392 **Though joy* 10
"This meeting, noble Lords! looks fair, . . . 402 *White Doe* 605
Who with mild looks and language mild . . . 407 *White Doe* 1036
It fronts all quarters, and looks round . . . 409 *White Doe* 1169
From looks conceiving her desire; . . . . . 415 *White Doe* 1721
Looks down upon her with a smile, ... 417 *White Doe* 1907
For change, to whom the new looks always green! 436 *Ecc. Sonn.* 2. 33. 3
Looks on, and Grace descendeth from above . . 445 *Ecc. Sonn.* 3. 20. 7
That to the Almighty Father looks through all. . 451 *Ecc. Sonn.* 3. 41. 14
Pleasure, or Grief, and Toil that seldom looks . 471 *Ailsa Crag* 10
Up! up! my Friend, and clear your looks; . . 481 *Tables Turned* 3
But who is He, with modest looks, ... 485 *Poet's Epitaph* 37
Looks round, to learn the history. . . . . . 491 *Fidelity* 41
Looks forward, persevering to the last, . . . 494 *Hap. War.* 75
That looks for evil like a treacherous spy; . . 500 *Humanity* 50

Lot—*continued.*
And milder breezes,—melancholy lot ! 678 *Prelude* 6. 241
But doubly fortunate my lot ; not here 703 *Prelude* 8. 312
As was thy melancholy lot, dear Friend ! 705 *Prelude* 8. 434
So was I favoured—such my happy lot— 735 *Prelude* 12. 49
Far other lot, yet with good hope that soon 756 *Excursion* 1. 18
Was comfortless, and her small lot of books, 768 *Excursion* 1. 824
General distress in his particular lot ; 772 *Excursion* 2. 68
It were your lot to dwell, would soon become 782 *Excursion* 2. 695
For different lot, or change to higher sphere, 795 *Excursion* 3. 630
"A piteous lot it were to flee from Man— 810 *Excursion* 4. 575
And its small lot of life-supporting fields, 822 *Excursion* 5. 2
For my own peaceful lot and happy choice ; 823 *Excursion* 5. 51
Do tend their flocks) partake man's general lot 829 *Excursion* 5. 427
'Joy be their lot, and happiness,' he cried, 840 *Excursion* 6. 141
'His lot and hers, as misery must be mine !' 840 *Excursion* 6. 142
Which did to him assign a pensive lot— 873 *Excursion* 7. 1013
The lot is wretched, the condition sad, 878 *Excursion* 8. 292
And female care.—"A blessed lot is yours !" 882 *Excursion* 8. 542
Of this unhappy lot, in early youth 886 *Excursion* 9. 165
We both have witnessed, lot which I myself 886 *Excursion* 9. 166
Blest in their several and their common lot ! 888 *Excursion* 9. 258
When they, whose choice or lot it is to dwell 894 *Excursion* 9. 667
Through joy and sorrow ; if my lot be joy K.8. 233 **Along the* 6
The lot of others, never could be his. K.8. 237 *Recluse* 1. 1. 18

Loth. Their breakfast done, the pair, though loth, must part ; 34 *Guilt* 532
Though loth to be a burthen on his age. 35 *Guilt* 580
The little fool is loth to stay behind. 42 *Bord.* 305
And the heart is loth to deaden 90 *Longest Day* 39
Not loth, and listening Little-ones, heart-touched, their fancies feed. 93 *Poet's Dream* 80
Loth to rule by strict command ; 93 *Westmoreland Girl* 34
Loth to restrain the moving interview, 104 *Artegal* 126
At length their time was come, they were not loth 137 *Michael* 369
I was not loth to be so catechised, 147 *Joanna* 34
The redbreast near me hopped ; nor was I loth 150 **When, to* 15
Drunken Lark ! thou wouldst be loth 159 **Up with me* 20
Not loth to furnish weapons for the bands 184 *Yew-trees* 4
Softly she treads, as if her foot were loth 222 *Triad* 201
Is man, though loth such help to *seek*, 223 *Wishing-gate* 62
There also is the Muse not loth to range, 262 **Not Love* 6
Not loth to thank each moment for its boon 278 **The most* 9
Then, why should I be loth to stir ? 288 *Highland Girl* 68
Nor am I loth, though pleased at heart, 288 *Highland Girl* 72
Yet he, not loth, in favour of thy claims 290 *Kilchurn* 16
Should we be loth to stir from home, 293 *Yarrow Unv.* 59
Be loth that we should breathe awhile exempt 382 *Duddon* 24. 11
—Not loth the sleepy lance to wield, 403 *White Doe* 700
Nor are his Followers loth to seek defence, 431 *Ecc. Sonn.* 2. 11. 12
We, nothing loth a lingering course to measure, 443 *Ecc. Sonn.* 3. 12. 12
Not loth we quit the newly-hallowed sward 451 *Ecc. Sonn.* 3. 42. 3
Lingering—and wandering on as loth to die ; 451 *Ecc. Sonn.* 3. 43. 12
Calm is the fragrant air, and loth to lose 453 **Calm is the* 1
Her head, and nothing loth her Majesty 461 **Who but is* 3
Departing sunbeams, loth to stop, 473 *Ossian* 71
Loth should I be to use it : passing sweet 498 **Enough of climbing* 50
For who is loth the God of Love to obey, 559 *Cuck.andNight.* 133
Harsh judgments, if the song be loth to quit 641 *Prelude* 1. 630
Quitted, not loth, the mild magnificence 675 *Prelude* 6. 12
Loth to believe what we so grieved to hear, 684 *Prelude* 6. 586
—Nor was he loth to enter ragged huts, 772 *Excursion* 2. 62
These festive matins ?"—He replied, "Not loth 773 *Excursion* 2. 140
I interposed, though loth to speak, and said, 780 *Excursion* 2. 607
Loth to forsake the spot, and still more loth 791 *Excursion* 3. 330
Though loth and slow to come ! A battlefield, 836 *Excursion* 5. 927
Loth to disturb what Heaven hath hushed in peace. 847 *Excursion* 6. 572
Was loth to assault the majesty he loved : 868 *Excursion* 7. 749
Of yet another summer's day, not loth 895 *Excursion* 9. 777

Lothbury. Bright volumes of vapour through Lothbury glide, 188 *Poor Susan* 7

Lotus. But a carved Lotus cast upon the beach 371 *Eg. Maid* 125

Loud. The dog, loud barking, 'mid the glittering rocks, 5 *Ev. Wk.* 184
Where with loud voice the power of water shakes 10 *Desc. Sk.* 7
Rock to incessant neighings shrill and loud, 27 *Guilt* 174
And, weeping loud in this extreme distress, 35 *Guilt* 619
Check his loud whip and hail us with mild voice, 61 *Bord.* 1335
And laughed so loud it seemed that the smooth sea 68 *Bord.* 1737
But loud and bitterly she wept, 82 *Alice Fell* 22
And carols loud and strong. 84 *Shepherd-boys* 26
The people answered with a loud acclaim : 105 *Artegal* 226
Thou Thrush, that singest loud —and loud and free, 111 *'*Tis said that some* 25
As loud as any mill, or near it ; 127 *Idiot Boy* 98
From the loud waterfall. 130 *Idiot Boy* 401
That there was a loud uproar in the hills. 148 *Joanna* 73
Came thundering loud and fast ; 155 *Waterfall* 53
With menace proud, and insult loud, 162 *Binnorie* 36
The whip's loud notice from the door, 178 *Waggoner* 3. 3
Hangs a Thrush that sings loud, it has sung for three years : 187 *Poor Susan* 2
He sways them with harmony merry and loud ; 188 *Music* 6
That heareth not the loud winds when they call ; 196 *Resolution* 76
Loud voice the Land has uttered forth, 204 *Brougham* 30
The iterated summons loud, 228 *Devot. Incit.* 42
And whistling loud may yet be heard, 240 *P. B.* 343
He gives a loud and frightful shriek, 242 *P. B.* 529
And Peter, wont to whistle loud 243 *P. B.* 623

Loud—*continued.*
Away goes Rachel weeping loud ;— 248 *P. B.* 1066
Sobs loud, he sobs even like a child, 249 *P. B.* 1119
So loud, so clear, my Partner through life's day, 279 **Hark ! 'tis* 11
Faith had her arch—her arch, when winds blow loud, 282 **In my* 8
How loud ! yet lived in peace with shame. 290 *Brownie's Cell* 50
One loud cascade in front, and lo ! 300 *Bran* 15
And loud and long of Winter's triumph sing ! 322 **Ye Storms* 5
Loud its threatenings—let them not 336 **Jesu ! bless* 3
Loud was the rifle-gun's report— 342 *Ital. Itin.* 63
Into a Brook of loud and stately march, 378 *Duddon* 9. 2
Dread swell of sound ! loud as the gusts that lash 379 *Duddon* 13. 7
Vexed is he, and screams loud. The last I saw 388 *Eagles* 4
The bells ring loud with gladsome power ; 396 *White Doe* 2
The sight was hailed with loud acclaim 400 *White Doe* 415
Deep feeling, that found utterance loud, 409 *White Doe* 1228
Merry and loud and safe from prying search, 449 *Ecc. Sonn.* 3. 33. 13
Hurried and hurrying, volatile and loud. 473 **We saw* 4
Clear, loud, and lively is the din, 498 **Departing summer* 10
So loud, that with his voice the place did ring. 555 *Prioress* 162
Yet may I sing, O *Alma !* loud and clear. 556 *Prioress* 204
Some, singing loud, as if they had complained ; 558 *Cuck.and Night.* 73
That her clear voice made a loud rioting, 558 *Cuck.and Night.* 99
For love of thee, as loud as I may cry ; 561 *Cuck.andNight.* 248
The Sheep-boy whistled loud, and lo ! 580 *John Words.* 1
Loud is the Vale ! the Voice is up 581 **Loud is* 1
Loud is the Vale ;—this inland Depth 581 **Loud is* 5
The death-dog, howling loud and long, below ; 606 *Desc.Sk.Quarto* 226
Loud thro' that midway gulf ascending, sound 611 *Desc.Sk.Quarto* 504
Dropp'd loud at once, Oppression shriek'd, and flew. 612 *Desc.Sk.Quarto* 541
While loud and dull ascends the weeping cry, 614 *Desc.Sk.Quarto* 658
Rang loud through the meadow and wood. 620 *Convict* 4
Loud shouts,—the Trojans echo the applause. 625 *Æneid* 131
With what strange utterance did the loud dry wind 637 *Prelude* 1. 337
It was a time of rapture ! Clear and loud 638 *Prelude* 1. 430
The pack loud chiming, and the hunted hare. 638 *Prelude* 1. 437
Gave out to meadow-grounds and hills a loud 640 *Prelude* 1. 541
Continued and the loud uproar : at last, 642 *Prelude* 2. 15
A loud prophetic blast of harmony ; 667 *Prelude* 5. 95
And long halloos and screams, and echoes loud, 671 *Prelude* 5. 377
All hearts were open, every tongue was loud 681 *Prelude* 6. 401
Still as a sheltered place when winds blow loud ! 689 *Prelude* 7. 171
With speed and echoes loud of trampling hoofs 716 *Prelude* 9. 449
That 'mid the loud distractions of the world 720 *Prelude* 10. 182
Near the loud waterfall ; or her who sate 752 *Prelude* 14. 406
A thrush sang loud, and other melodies, 771 *Excursion* 1. 963
Into a loud and white-robed waterfall, 787 *Excursion* 3. 48
Loud echoing, add your speed to the pursuit ; 808 *Excursion* 4. 502
With the loud streams : and often, at the hour 819 *Excursion* 4. 1175
Repelled the storm and deadened its loud roar. 860 *Excursion* 7. 179
All unsubstantialized,—how loud the voice 885 *Excursion* 9. 66
Dark discontent, or loud commotion, each 889 *Excursion* 9. 348

Loud-chiming. The pack loud-chiming, and the hunted hare. 89 *Prelude* 1. 437

Louder. And louder torrents stun the noon-tide hill, 17 *Desc. Sk.* 371
Louder and louder did he shout, 81 †*Mother's Return* 9
Those louder cries give notice that the Bird, 361 **List—'twas* 5
Of calmer lakes and louder streams ; and you, 675 *Prelude* 6. 13
To laughter multiplied in louder peals 843 *Excursion* 6. 345

Loudest. We loudest in the faithful north : 204 *Brougham* 31
Who loudest rang his pulpit 'larum bell, 442 *Ecc. Sonn.* 3. 11. 5
Nor hear the loudest surges of St. Bees. 467 *St. Bees* 90
Such dismal service, that the loudest voice 894 *Excursion* 9. 693

Loudly. And never heart so loudly panted ; 242 *P. B.* 517
So loudly, that I with that song awoke. 562 *Cuck.andNight.* 290
Prate somewhat loudly of the whereabout 693 *Prelude* 7. 428

Loud-throated. Child of loud-throated War ! the mountain Stream 290 *Kilchurn* 1

Loughrigg. A noise of laughter ; southern Loughrigg heard, 147 *Joanna* 59

Loughrigg-tarn. To Loughrigg-tarn, round clear and bright as heaven, 524 *Epist. Beaumont* 166

Louisa. I met Louisa in the shade, 108 *Louisa* 1

Lounging. "Good-natured lounging," and behold a map 677 *Prelude* 6. 182

Louvet. Louvet walked single through the avenue, 720 *Prelude* 10. 111

Love. *See* **Lady-love, Over-love, Self-love, True-love.**
I love to mark the quarry's moving trains, 5 *Ev. Wk.* 158
Or desperate love, bewildered, he came there. 11 *Desc. Sk.* 42
That clung to Nature with a truant's love, 11 *Desc. Sk.* 44
Awe in his breast with holiest love unites, 19 *Desc. Sk.* 476
Though martial songs have banished songs of love, 21 *Desc. Sk.* 614
What if the bee love not these barren boughs ? 22 *Yew-tree* 4
Instructed that true knowledge leads to love ; 23 *Yew-tree* 60
Though he had little cause to love the abode 27 *Guilt* 154
And I in truth did love him like a brother, 29 *Guilt* 251
He well could love in grief ; his faith he kept ; 29 *Guilt* 260
About their love, as if to keep it warm. 38 *Bord.* 23
Yourself, you do not love him. I do more, 38 *Bord.* 32
To love him. I remember, when a Boy 39 *Bord.* 89
And that was the beginning of my love. 39 *Bord.* 95
All gentleness and love. His face bespeaks 40 *Bord.* 168
Had given her love to a wild Freebooter, 41 *Bord.* 207
But sure he loves the Maiden, and never love 41 *Bord.* 236
Should in his love admit no rivalship, 42 *Bord.* 269
Sir Host ! by all the love you bear to courtesy, 42 *Bord.* 306
For love of God I must not pass their doors ; 46 *Bord.* 524
Now I *do* love thee. I am thunderstruck. 46 *Bord.* 528
I love her, though I dare not call her daughter. 47 *Bord.* 536

Loves—*continued.*
And why she duly loves to pace — 398 *White Doe* 204
Received the memory of old loves, — 415 *White Doe* 1754
His words remains for her, and loves. — 415 *White Doe* 1790
Loves most what Emily loved most— — 416 *White Doe* 1881
Dear to the Loves, and to the Graces vowed, — 465 **Dear to* 1
While in Judea Fancy loves to roam, — 467 *St. Bees* 111
He dearly loves their voices ! — 483 *Simon Lee* 24
Who gave us nobler loves, and nobler cares— — 489 *Pers. Talk* 52
If loves and joys, while up they sprung, — 507 *May* 69
Loves it, while there in solitary peace — 509 *F. Stone* 68
How cold the quarter that the wind best loves, — 521 *Epist. Beaumont* 19
The beetle loves his unpretending track, — 528 **Those breathing* 71
That still he loves the Bird, and still must love ; — 531 **I know* 31
But chiefly to Smithfield he loves to repair,— — 571 *Farmer* 85
That God will chasten whom he dearly loves. — 576 **By a* 6
Forebode not any severing of our loves ! — 590 *Immortality* 192
But doubly pitying Nature loves to show'r — 602 *Desc. Sk. Quarto* 13
I said not this, because he loves — 621 *Andrew Jones* 6
And Christian meekness hallowing faithful loves. — 635 *Prelude* 1. 185
Their wives, their children, and their virgin loves, — 668 *Prelude* 5. 154
And hinge of all our learnings and our loves : — 669 *Prelude* 5. 258
And joyous loves, that hallow innocent days — 679 *Prelude* 6. 263
The Bachelor, that loves to sun himself, — 690 *Prelude* 7. 208
Confession of man's weakness and his loves. — 690 *Prelude* 7. 239
Loves, as it glistens on the silent rocks ; — 700 *Prelude* 8. 64
Was now a shame ; my likings and my loves — 730 *Prelude* 11. 184
That mutual domination which she loves — 747 *Prelude* 14. 81
Of former loves and interests. Then my soul — 796 *Excursion* 3. 695
Whom, for the very sake of love, he loves. — 806 *Excursion* 4. 364
Both knows and loves such objects as excite — 819 *Excursion* 4. 1210
And wisdom loves.—But when a stately ship — 882 *Excursion* 8. 506
That loves the ground, and from the sun withholds — 892 *Excursion* 9. 543
It loves us now, this Vale so beautiful — K.8. 241 *Recluse* 1.1.179
Nor let me pass unheeded other loves — K.8. 250 *Recluse* 1.1.502

Love-sick. "Whence strains to love-sick maiden dear, — 164 *Needlecase* 33
The love-sick Stripling fancifully sighs, — 377 *Duddon* 7. 2
There might the love-sick maiden sit, and chide — 607 *Desc.Sk.Quarto* 309

Love-songs. Their love-songs ; but, where'er my feet might roam, — 362 **List—'twas* 24

Love-spell. To chant a love-spell, never intertwined — 336 *Staub-bach* 8

Lovest. Thy secrets, thou that lov'st to stand and hear — 26 *Guilt* 119
Aspiring Road ! that lov'st to hide — 215 *Kirkstone* 49
Who lov'st with Night and Silence to partake, — 459 **Wanderer ! that* 3
Of him thou lovest ; need I dread from thee — 641 *Prelude* 1. 629

Love-tale. Of that shy songstress, whose love-tale — 235 *Power of Sound* 166

Loveth. For His own service ; knoweth, loveth us, — 744 *Prelude* 13. 277

Love-vows. Her blushing cheek, love-vows upon her lip, — 427 *Ecc. Sonn.* 1. 35. 6

Love-whispers. Scorning love-whispers shrinks from love itself — S.3. 436 **The doubt* 146

Loving. *See* **Cloud-loving, Earth-loving, Laughter-loving, Moonlight-loving, Tempest-loving.**
My husband's loving kindness stood between — 35 *Guilt* 611
And in her ample heart loving even me— — 57 *Bord.* 1106
Loving she is, and tractable, though wild ; — 80 **Loving she* 1
Wrote loving letters, full of wondrous news, — 138 *Michael* 433
Your most loving father's rage : — 140 *Arm. Lady* 28
Who, loving most, should wiseliest love, their only strife. — 142 *Arm. Lady* 150
Loving and liking are the solace of life, — 142 †*Lov. and Lik.* 53
In loving words he talks to him, — 249 *P. B.* 1113
Love cannot have than that in loving thee — 256 **Yes ! hope* 6
Neighbours we were, and loving friends — 285 *Grave of Burns* 41
Places forsaken now, though loving still — 353 *Aquap.* 50
Some true Partakers of his loving spirit — 362 **List—'twas* 68
Beneath a loving old Man's view. — 401 *White Doe* 502
'Tis the still hour of thinking, feeling, loving. — 453 **The Sun, that* 6
A loving creature she, and brave ! — 490 *Incident : Dog* 31
I, loving freedom, and untried ; — 492 *Duty* 25
Loving the dewy shade,—a humble band, — 539 **Lady ! a* 19
Admiring, loving, and with grief and pride — 547 **Ye Lime* 17
Loving is aye an office of despair, — 560 *Cuck.and Night.* 176
My Brother, too, in loving thee, — 579 **Sweet Flower* 5
Who sang in ancient Greece his loving lay, — 623 **I find* 13
Loving the sports which once he gloried in. — 809 *Excursion* 4. 549
Faithfully watched, and, by that loving care — 876 *Excursion* 8. 149
Loving what no one cares for but ourselves ; — K.8. 248 *Recluse* 1.1.429
Unheard-of days, though loving peaceful thoughts. — K.8. 257 *Recluse* 1.1.752

Loving-kindness. Thus a rich loving-kindness, redundantly kind, — 167 *Stray Pleasures* 29
And loving-kindness ever bright : — 413 *White Doe* 1605

Lovingly. Lie down in peace, and lovingly. — 397 *White Doe* 147
That lovingly consigns the babe to the arms — 836 *Excursion* 5. 951
Which in his soul he lovingly embraced, — 862 *Excursion* 7. 349

Low. The solitary heifer's deepened low ; — 17 *Desc. Sk.* 360
And merry flageolet ; the low of herds, — 18 *Desc. Sk.* 418
Fitting his low voice to the minstrel's harp, — 59 *Bord.* 1192
Small and low, though fair as any : — 79 *Foresight* 6
Bending low before the Donor, — 90 *Longest Day* 75
Still higher—to be cast thus low ! — 113 *Lament* 30
In high and low, above, below, — 128 *Idiot Boy* 207
Restless with fixed to balance, high with low, — 153 *Morn. Ex.* 32
And dancing high and dancing low, — 155 *Waterfall* 8
I have seen thee, high and low, — 160 **Pansies, lilies* 20
I spake, when whispered a low voice, — 164 *Needlecase* 17
Warbles by fits his low clear song ; — 168 *Wren's Nest* 22
What bustling—jostling—high and low ! — 177 *Waggoner* 2. 56
Hung low, begin to rise and spread ; — 180 *Waggoner* 4. 58

Low—*continued.*
The slave of low desires : — 194 *Ruth* 153
In our dejection do we sink as low ; — 195 *Resolution* 25
And oft his cogitations sink as low — 213 *Dion* 60
The noble Syracusan low in dust ! — 214 *Dion* 109
That British ground commands :—low dusky tracts, — 219 **This Height* 5
Hell to the lyre bowed low ; the upper arch — 234 *Power of Sound* 126
Where deep and low the hamlets lie — 239 *P. B.* 228
From this low threshold daily meets my sight ; — 253 **Aerial Rock* 2
As this low structure, for the tasks of Spring — 254 *Wild Duck's Nest* 5
In the low dell 'mid Roslin's faded grove : — 261 **From the dark* 12
Slept, with the obscurest, in the low — 285 *Grave of Burns* 29
Should life be dull, and spirits low, — 293 *Yarrow Unv.* 61
Brought low a Power, which from its home — 298 *Brownie's Cell* 35
Lords, lawyers, statesmen, squires of low degree, — 303 **Is it* 3
Is man as good as man, none low, none high ?— — 309 **What if* 8
On British ground the Invaders are laid low ; — 310 *Anticip.* 2
That we must stand unpropped, or be laid low. — 310 **Another year* 8
In men of low degree, all smooth pretence ! — 319 **Avaunt all* 2
Cheer'st the low threshold of the peasant's cell ! — 329 *Ode : Thanks.* 7
For Him who lifteth up and layeth low ; — 330 *Ode : Thanks.* 89
Ye, in your low and undisturbed estate, — 332 *Ode : Thanks.* 232
They lodged in leafy tents and cabins low ; — 346 *Processions* 15
And by Glenridding-screes, and low Glencoign, — 353 *Aquap.* 49
O'er high and low, and if requiring rest, — 354 *Aquap.* 99
And liberate our hearts from low pursuits. — 358 *Aquap.* 347
Stops not at this low point, nor wants the lure — 360 *Albano* 12
Virtues laid low, and mouldering energies. — 360 *Alban Hills* 8
To hoof and finger mailed ;—yet, high or low, — 368 *Trajan* 47
When this low Pile a Gospel Teacher knew, — 380 *Duddon* 18. 10
Whence that low voice ?—A whisper from the heart, — 381 *Duddon* 21. 1
High over hill and low adown the dell — 395 *White Doe: Ded.* 38
Again the Mother whispered low, — 398 *White Doe* 184
The Lady's work ;—but now laid low ; — 398 *White Doe* 235
High-climbing rock, low sunless dale, — 413 *White Doe* 1564
Of fret-work imagery laid low ; — 416 *White Doe* 1892
These sons of Amalek, or laid them low !"— — 427 *Ecc. Sonn.* 1. 33. 8
Sits there in sober truth—to raise the low, — 428 *Ecc. Sonn.* 1. 39. 6
Of Justice armed, and Pride to be laid low. — 433 *Ecc. Sonn.* 2. 18. 14
Of high with low, celestial with terrene ! — 434 *Ecc. Sonn.* 2. 25. 14
Against her ancient virtue. High and Low, — 443 *Ecc. Sonn.* 3. 11. 9
With low soft murmur, like a distant bee, — 445 *Ecc. Sonn.* 3. 22. 5
The mortal weight cast off to be laid low. — 448 *Ecc. Sonn.* 3. 31. 4
From low to high doth dissolution climb, — 449 *Ecc. Sonn.* 3. 34. 1
And sink from high to low, along a scale — 449 *Ecc. Sonn.* 3. 34. 2
Shall greet that symbol crowning the low Pile : — 450 *Ecc. Sonn.* 3. 40. 11
Comes that low sound from breezes rustling o'er — 453 **The Sun, that* 9
Wanderer ! that stoop'st so low, and com'st so near — 459 **Wanderer ! that* 1
Forth from their cells ; their ancient House laid low — 468 *St. Bees* 147
Towards a low roof with green trees half concealed, — 475 **There ! said* 2
Which with the lofty sanctifies the low. — 488 *Pers. Talk* 32
Whose life combines the best of high and low, — 489 *Spade* 7
Low in the darksome cell thine own dear lord ? — 489 *Spade* 18
Is ranging high and low ; — 494 *Force of Prayer* 14
In course of nature under a low roof — 510 **Among a* 21
They thus would rise, must low and lower sink — 513 *Newspaper* 4
While, high and low, and all about, — 526 **The soaring* 13
(Such the immunities of low estate, — 539 **Lady ! a* 49
A single Act endears to high and low — 540 *Grace Darl.* 8
O *Alma Redemptoris !* high and low : — 554 *Prioress* 103
"Young Hew of Lincoln ! in like sort laid low — 556 *Prioress* 233
For he of low hearts can make high, of high — 556 *Cuck. and Night.* 3
He can make low, and unto death bring nigh ; — 556 *Cuck. and Night.* 4
On a low structure of rude masonry — 566 *Cumb. Beg.* 3
So low as to be scorned without a sin ; — 567 *Cumb. Beg.* 83
Now farewell, old Adam ! when low thou art laid, — 571 *Farmer* 89
To equalize the lofty and the low. — 574 *Chiabrera* 4. 24
The bodily frame. That beauty is laid low — 581 **Why should we* 9
'Mid mouldering ruins low he lies ; — 586 *Hogg* 10
Low bending o'er the colour'd water, fold — 593 *Ev. Wk. Quarto* 103
Stays it's low murmur in th' unbreathing vale ; — 598 *Ev. Wk. Quarto* 356
Low barks the fox : by Havoc rouz'd the bear, — 606 *Desc.Sk.Quarto* 231
On the low brown wood-huts delighted sleep — 607 *Desc.Sk.Quarto* 275
And talking voices, and the low of herds, — 611 *Desc.Sk.Quarto* 507
Worse than the Dragon that bowed low his crest, — 626 *Ballot* 13
Low breathings coming after me, and sounds — 637 *Prelude* 1. 323
From little enmities and low desires, — 648 *Prelude* 2. 431
Of a low pitch—duty and zeal dismissed, — 653 *Prelude* 3. 326
A hundred times when, roving high and low, — 660 *Prelude* 4. 110
Issued low muttered sounds, as if of pain — 664 *Prelude* 4. 405
Down to the low and wren-like warblings, made — 668 *Prelude* 5. 207
Upon a corner-stone of that low wall, — 696 *Prelude* 7. 605
That prove to what low depth had struck the roots, — 717 *Prelude* 9. 549
But said to me, "My head will soon lie low ;" — 726 *Prelude* 10. 539
(Itself like a sea rock) the low remains — 726 *Prelude* 10. 556
Of low ambition or distempered love ?" — 735 *Prelude* 12. 74
Yet in the deepest passion, I bowed low — 739 *Prelude* 12. 315
Wilfully to mean cares or low pursuits, — 748 *Prelude* 14. 154
To penetrate the lofty and the low ; — 750 *Prelude* 14. 271
Sublime and comprehensive ! Low desires, — 759 *Excursion* 1. 234
Low thoughts had there no place ; yet was his heart — 759 *Excursion* 1. 235
She did not look at me. Her voice was low, — 768 *Excursion* 1. 794
From that low bench, rising instinctively — 770 *Excursion* 1. 918
We sate on that low bench : and now we felt, — 771 *Excursion* 1. 960
And reached a small apartment dark and low, — 781 *Excursion* 2. 648
Lay low beneath my feet ; 'twas visible— — 784 *Excursion* 2. 871
Find entrance ;—high or low appeared no trace — 787 *Excursion* 3. 68
To a low cottage in a sunny bay, — 793 *Excursion* 3. 515

Lustre—*continued.*
The torrent, travers'd by the lustre broad, 605 *Desc.Sk.Quarto* 207
Round your pale eyes a wintry lustre wake. 614 *Desc.Sk.Quarto* 675
Wide o'er the main a trembling lustre plays, 618 *School Ex.* 41
Before the lustre of Religion's eye ; 618 *School Ex.* 44
Fresh with lustre all their own. 629 *Installation* 52
Upon this restless lustre have I gazed, 705 *Prelude* 8. 412
Still linger, and a farewell lustre sheds 706 *Prelude* 8. 474
Shines with some portion of that heavenly lustre 839 *Excursion* 6. 50
Of pleasing lustre.—But no more of this ; 861 *Excursion* 7. 237
A golden lustre slept upon the hills ; 871 *Excursion* 7. 877
In twinkling lustre, ere the boat attained 895 *Excursion* 9. 765
Whose lustre we alone participate, K.8. 248 *Recluse* 1. 1. 437
Why does this inward lustre fondly seek, K.8. 255 *Recluse* 1. 1. 677
Lustres. Soft o'er the surface creep those lustres pale 7 *Ev. Wk.* 295
To where afar rich orange lustres glow 13 *Desc. Sk.* 160
Will mingle with her lustres gliding 237 *P. B.* 93
Who scattereth lustres o'er noon-day, 506 **While from* 11
Soft o'er the surface creep the lustres pale 598 *Ev. Wk.Quarto* 343
From play-house lustres thrown without reserve 692 *Prelude* 7. 346
Lusty. You are a lusty Traveller. But how fare you ? 43 *Bord.* 335
—" Shame on me, Sir ! this lusty Lamb, 115 *Last of Flock* 17
—This lusty Lamb of all my store 115 *Last of Flock* 37
And gives another lusty cheer ; 176 *Waggoner* 2. 18
With what ?—a Ship of lusty size ; 177 *Waggoner* 2. 106
Duly pronounced with lusty call, 375 **The Minstrels* 17
The youngest, then a lusty boy, 416 *White Doe* 1808
Proceeds from infancy to lusty youth ; 432 *Ecc. Sonn.* 2. 16. 12
Young Harry was a lusty drover, 536 *Goody Blake* 17
And scattered many a lusty splinter 536 *Goody Blake* 51
I heard the lusty Nightingale so sing, 558 *Cuck. and Night.* 98
Of lusty vigour, more than infantine 692 *Prelude* 7. 351
There, too, the lusty Wrestlers shall contend : 773 *Excursion* 2. 146
" Those lusty twins," exclaimed our host, " if here 782 *Excursion* 2. 694
But, green in age and lusty as he is, 867 *Excursion* 7. 625
—Seven lusty Sons sate daily round the board 867 *Excursion* 7. 636
Flew open, and a pair of lusty Boys 882 *Excursion* 8. 545
Lute. She bears the stringèd lute of old romance, 221 *Triad* 101
While thy tired lute hangs on the hawthorn-tree, 227 *Vernal Ode* 87
From harp or lute, kind influence to compose 255 **Grief, thou* 7
Of this small lute gave ease to Petrarch's wound ; 260 **Scorn not* 4
Her own Æolian lute. 499 **Departing summer* 48
To the low-warbled breath of twilight lute, 615 *Desc.Sk.Quarto* 749
Of passion ; was obedient as a lute 651 *Prelude* 3. 138
A beardless Youth, who touched a golden lute, 814 *Excursion* 4. 859
Of music, lute or harp, a long delight 883 *Excursion* 8. 597
Lute-enlivened. The sylvan cabin's lute-enlivened gloom. 13 *Desc. Sk.* 134
Lute-resounding. —Thy fragrant gales and lute-resounding streams, 605 *Desc.Sk.Quarto* 156
Lutes. Whence lutes and voices down the enchanted woods 12 *Desc. Sk.* 117
Have lutes (believe my words) 164 *Needlecase* 26
And wild-wood mountain lutes of saddest swell. 611 *Desc.Sk.Quarto* 509
Luther. By dauntless Luther freed, could they forget 437 *Ecc. Sonn.* 2. 37. 4
Lutherian. With punctual care, Lutherian harmonies. 454 *Sea-side* 32
Luther's. Who threw the Saxon shield o'er Luther's life 629 *Installation* 100
Luxuriant. An arch thrown back between luxuriant wings 212 *Dion*
Luxuriant wreaths around thy forehead hoar ; 272 *Ruins* 12
To a luxuriant bounty !—As our steps 793 *Excursion* 3. 520
Luxuriate. The notes luxuriate, every stone is kissed 451 *Ecc. Sonn.* 3. 44. 11
Luxuriates. The heart luxuriates with indifferent things, 185 *Nutting* 41
Luxuries. And luxuries extract from bleakest moors ; 284 *Departure* 26
'Mid a trim garden's summer luxuries, 466 *St. Bees* 7
Enlivened, braced, by hardy luxuries, 527 **Those breathing* 45
For I, bred up 'mid Nature's luxuries, 654 *Prelude* 3. 351
Yet still in me with those soft luxuries 683 *Prelude* 6. 557
Luxurious. Vain pleasures of luxurious life, 301 *Bran* 105
A treasured and luxurious gloom of choice 677 *Prelude* 6. 176
With less regret for its luxurious pomp, 710 *Prelude* 9. 30
The wealthy, the luxurious, by the stress 773 *Excursion* 2. 97
All that luxurious nature could desire, K.8. 237 *Recluse* 1. 1. 23
Luxury. Upward he looks—" and calls it luxury : " 11 *Desc. Sk.* 24
To feed the tender luxury, 348 **Lulled by* 77
Heart-killing luxury, on your steps await. 420 *Ecc. Sonn.* 1. 8. 2
In luxury of disrespect 497 *Lycoris* 24
Days undefiled by luxury or sloth, 515 *Penn.* 1
The day, in luxury my limbs repos'd, 613 *Desc. Sk. Quarto* 597
There is a luxury in self-dispraise ; 808 *Excursion* 4. 475
Luz. Gave, in the field of Luz, to Jacob's sight 500 *Humanity* 34
Lybia. Of Lybia ; and not seldom, on the banks 575 *Chiabrera* 6. 6
Lycoris. Lycoris (if such name befit 497 *Lycoris* 27
Lycoris ! life requires an *art*. 497 *Lycoris* 39
Lydian. Even She whose Lydian airs inspire 233 *Power of Sound* 76
Lying. old Man lying stretched upon the ground— 72 *Bord.* 1924
Their two books lying both on a dry stone, 99 *Brothers* 262
Then old, beside him, lying at his feet. 138 *Michael* 469
While I am lying on the grass 183 **O blithe* 5
Shade upon the sunshine lying 190 **Lyre ! though* 19
But now the Knight beholds him lying dead. 201 *Hart-leap* 32
Upon his side the Hart was lying stretched : 201 *Hart-leap* 41
To sink, perhaps, where he is lying, 242 *P. B.* 539
Some lying fast at anchor in the road, 258 **With Ships* 3
And all that mighty heart is lying still ! 269 *Westm. Bridge* 14
From rapture, lying softly on her breast ! 278 **Lo ! where she* 3

Lying—*continued.*
Both lying right before us ; 292 *Yarrow Unv.* 18
And left them lying in the silent sun, 310 *Anticip.* 4
A folded paper, lying as if placed 766 *Excursion* 1. 667
Lying full three parts buried among tufts 784 *Excursion* 2. 818
With mounds transversely lying side by side 830 *Excursion* 5. 535
Lying insensible to human praise, 865 *Excursion* 7. 538
Lymph. That wakes the breeze, the sparkling lymph 217 *Enterprise* 142
Thy murmurs heard ; and drunk the crystal lymph 812 *Excursion* 4. 750
Gazing intensely, the translucent lymph S.3. 436 **The doubt* 181
Lynx. Old Man ! you were a very Lynx, you knew 61 *Bord.* 1313
Lyre. Or sink, with heart alive like Memnon's lyre ; 11 *Desc. Sk.* 32
Soft as the dying throb of the lyre. 142 †*Lov. and Lik.* 48
In presence of the lyre. 164 *Needlecase* 20
Though 'mid the stars the Lyre shine bright, 164 *Needlecase* 39
Love animates my lyre— 168 *Turtledove* 22
Sung to the plaintive lyre in Grecian vales. 170 **Never enlivened* 19
Lyre ! though such power do in thy magic live 190 **Lyre ! though* 1
So may the thrillings of the lyre 221 *Triad* 86
Where is the Orphean lyre, or Druid harp, 230 *Clouds* 60
Hell to the lyre bowed low ; the upper arch 234 *Power of Sound* 126
Whose waves the Orphean lyre forbad to meet 336 *Danube* 9
And taught her faithful servants how the lyre 359 *Plea : Hist.* 13
As a true man, who long had served the lyre, 365 **Under the* 9
Musæus, stationed with his lyre 472 *Ossian* 39
Woe ! woe to Tyrants ! from the lyre 499 *Departing summer* 40
Hush, feeble lyre ! weak words refuse 507 **While from* 57
And fiction animate his sportive lyre, 528 **Those breathing* 97
Touch'd with his wither'd hand an aged lyre ; 605 *Desc.Sk.Quarto* 171
To court majestic truth, or wake the golden lyre ; 619 *School Ex.* 62
Awake, awake ! and snatch the slumbering lyre, 619 *School Ex.* 109
Thoughtfully fitted to the Orphean lyre ; 635 *Prelude* 1. 233
The poet fits it to his pensive lyre. 792 *Excursion* 3. 445
The highest, holiest, raptures of the lyre ; 865 *Excursion* 7. 535
Of inspiration for the conscious lyre. S.3. 436 **The doubt* 166
Lyre-enliven'd. The bosom'd cabin's lyre-enliven'd gloom ; 604 *Desc.Sk.Quarto* 101
Lyre's. " Appear !—obey my lyre's command ! 220 *Triad* 15
Lyres. Strike audibly the noblest of your lyres, 325 *Ode 1814* 125
Tune in the mountain dells their water lyres. 598 *Ev. Wk.Quarto* 328
Lyulph's. List, ye who pass by Lyulph's Tower 478 *Somnamb.* 1

M

Mabel. To rapture ! Mabel listened at the side 267 *St. Cath.* 6
Mace. Had swayed the royal mace, 103 *Artegal* 95
Is overturned ; the mace, in battle heaved 423 *Ecc. Sonn.* 1. 17. 6
Plebeian hands the . . . mace have wrenched L.1. 97 *Juvenal* 3. 92
Macedonian. So emulous of Macedonian fame, 368 *Trajan* 60
Machination. Where Machination her fell soul resigns, 617 *Desc.Sk.Quarto* 796
Machine. On friendly terms with this Machine : 182 *Waggoner* 4. 217
The very pulse of the machine ; 186 **She was* 22
Matter and Spirit are as one Machine ; 468 *St. Bees* 157
Is ever urging on the vast machine 501 *Humanity* 92
And, turned into a gewgaw, a machine, 732 *Prelude* 11. 369
The senseless member of a vast machine, 886 *Excursion* 9. 159
Machinery. Such small machinery as she turned 195 *Ruth* 250
Mad. *See* **Half-mad.**
" You shall be baffled in your mad intent 123 *V. and J.* 120
" Sweet babe ! they say that I am mad, 144 *Her Eyes* 11
If thou art mad, my pretty lad, 145 *Her Eyes* 89
That she in half a year was mad, 194 *Ruth* 194
She was with child, and she was mad ; 199 *Thorn* 128
The overweening, personates the mad— 439 *Ecc. Sonn.* 2. 41. 11
For thou art worse than mad a thousand fold ; 560 *Cuck.and Night.* 188
Which neither listlessness, nor mad endeavour, 589 *Immortality* 161
Her bed, his mountains mad Ambition piles ; 617 *Desc.Sk.Quarto* 799
Mad at their sports like withered leaves in winds ; 672 *Prelude* 5. 416
The goaded land waxed mad ; the crimes of few 723 *Prelude* 10. 336
Mad Fancy's favourite vassals ? Does not life 812 *Excursion* 4. 769
Madden. To soothe and cleanse, not madden and pollute ! 378 *Duddon* 8. 14
Maddened. Descend we now, the maddened Reuss our guide ; 14 *Desc. Sk.* 197
Proud Gordon, maddened by the thoughts 287 *Ellen Irwin* 25
And Hope was maddened by the drops that fell 311 **Who rises* 37
Break from the maddened nations at the sight 873 *Excursion* 7. 1038
Maddening. Present the maddening gifts, and kindle heat 624 *Æneid* 5
Prosperity subverted, maddening want, 791 *Excursion* 3. 376
Madding. When madding Power her bolts had hurled, 298 *Brownie's Cell* 22
Spreads high conceits to madding Fancy dear, 433 *Ecc. Sonn.* 2. 20. 11
(What time a State with madding faction reels) 440 *Ecc. Sonn.* 2. 45. 12
The madding factions might be tranquillised, 727 *Prelude* 10. 591
Of madding passions mutually inflamed ; 755 *Recluse* 1. 1. 828
Made. *See* **Half-made, Home-made, New-made.**
Yet hears her song, " by distance made more sweet," 6 *Ev. Wk.* 237
The boat's first motion—made with dashing oar ; 9 *Ev. Wk.* 372
No voice made answer, he could only hear 25 *Guilt* 34
And hope returned, and pleasure fondly made 25 *Guilt* 58
To lisp, he made me kneel beside my bed, 28 *Guilt* 202
That on his marriage day sweet music made ! 28 *Guilt* 238
We breathed a pestilential air, that made 29 *Guilt* 283
The peasant, wild in passion, made reply 33 *Guilt* 480

Made—*continued.*

" For evil tongues made oath how on that day . 35 *Guilt* 604
Nature by sign or sound made no essay ; . . . 35 *Guilt* 623
We might have made a kindly bed of heath, . . 39 *Bord.* 122
Has made amends. Thanks to you both ; but, Oh Sir ! . . . . 45 *Bord.* 431
This news ! it made my heart leap up with joy. . 49 *Bord.* 677
The thunder rolled in peals that would have made 50 *Bord.* 711
Made quiet as he is. Why came you down ? . . 55 *Bord.* 957
Made weakness a protection, and obscured . . 57 *Bord.* 1082
But what was made an engine to ensnare thee ; . 57 *Bord.* 1100
Then plain it is as day that eyes were made . . 60 *Bord.* 1273
Our Captain made a prey to foul device !— . . 63 *Bord.* 1418
His tool, the wandering Beggar, made last night . 63 *Bord.* 1419
'Twas a strange answer that he made ; he said, . 63 *Bord.* 1446
I have no cases by me ready made . . . . . 65 *Bord.* 1572
I would have made us equal once again, . . . 71 *Bord.* 1866
Has made him fearful, and he'll never be . . . 71 *Bord.* 1901
A shadow of myself—made by myself. . . . . 73 *Bord.* 2039
My conscience made me wish to be struck blind ; 77 *Bord.* 2250
Made evident, as seemed, by blacker guilt, . . 77 *Bord.* 2259
Who, through most wicked arts, was made an orphan . . . . 78 *Bord.* 2330
That he has been there, and made a great rout, . 80 †*Address : Child* 22
—Her beauty made me glad. . . . . . . 83 *We are Seven* 12
Hath fallen, and made a bridge of rock : . . . 85 *Shepherd-boys* 52
Made answer to that plaintive sound. . . . . 85 *Shepherd-boys* 77
He blushed with shame, nor made reply ; . . . 86 *Anecdote* 46
Nor kept by Nature for herself, nor made by man his own, ... 91 *Norman Boy* 2
For covert from the keen north wind, his hands a hut had made. . . . . 91 *Norman Boy* 14
The Boy no answer made by words, but, so earnest was his look, ... 93 *Poet's Dream* 69
As if they had been made that they might be . 97 *Brothers* 142
That God who made the great book of the world 99 *Brothers* 266
Of a vast building made of many crags ; . . . 101 *Brothers* 365
A startling outcry made by hound and horn, . . 104 *Artegal* 108
Where apple-trees in blossom made a bower, . . 107 *Indolence* 25
Made, to his ear attentively applied, ... 108 *Indolence* 57
When thus his moan he made : . . . . . . 110 **'Tis said that some* 12
Of my fond heart, hath made me poor. . . . 111 *A Complaint* 18
Be pleased that nature made thee fit . . . . 112 **Yes ! thou* 9
The girls on the hills made a holiday show. . . 120 *Childless Father* 8
Sate yesterday, and made a nest . . . . . 120 *EmigrantMother* 30
Was made to seize him by three armèd men, . . 123 *V. and J.* 127
The Doctor, he has made him wait ; . . . . 128 *Idiot Boy* 165
Made answer, like a traveller bold, ... 131 *Idiot Boy* 448
And made a hidden valley of their own. . . . 131 *Michael* 8
Nor should I have made mention of this Dell . . 131 *Michael* 14
Made all their household. I may truly say, . . 132 *Michael* 93
That was, and made an evil choice, if he . . . 134 *Michael* 237
They made a gathering for him, shillings, pence, . 135 *Michael* 260
The Youth made answer with a jocund voice ; . . 135 *Michael* 299
For every tender sacrifice her heart had made. . 141 *Arm. Lady* 138
Where He that made them blesses their repose.— 143 **High bliss* 21
But he, poor man ! is wretched made ; . . . 145 *Her Eyes* 78
Vied with this waterfall, and made a song . . 146 **It was an* 27
Beneath the branches—of itself had made . . 149 *M. H.* 5
The spot was made by Nature for herself ; . . 149 *M. H.* 15
Of nature and of love had made their home . . 150 **When, to* 24
Some nook where they had made their final stand, 150 **When, to* 30
By those embowering hollies made, ... 155 **A whirl-blast* 17
In a field of battle made, ... 157 *Sexton* 5
By bird or beast made vocal, sought a cause . . 170 **Never enlivened* 16
From the motions that are made, ... 170 *Kitten* 11
Made such wanton spoil and rout, ... 171 *Kitten* 67
The horses made a quiet stand ; . . . . . 179 *Waggoner* 3. 57
This new arrangement made, the Wain . . . 179 *Waggoner* 3. 64
By trees and lingering twilight made ! . . . . 180 *Waggoner* 4. 45
Which made me look a thousand ways . . . 183 **O blithe* 19
And she had made a pipe of straw, ... 192 *Ruth* 7
And made a gallant crest. . . . . 192 *Ruth* 24
Made of wild words, her cup of wrong . . . . 194 *Ruth* 197
This flute, made of a hemlock stalk, ... 195 *Ruth* 244
He, having made a pause, the same discourse renewed. . . . . 197 *Resolution* 133
That as they galloped made the echoes roar ; . . 200 *Hart-leap* 14
And a small arbour, made for rural joy ; . . . 201 *Hart-leap* 58
Made merriment within that pleasant bower. . . 202 *Hart-leap* 92
While with an eye made quiet by the power . . 206 *Tintern* 47
Vows have I made by fruitless hope inspired ; . 209 *Laod.* 2
As often as that eager grasp was made. . . . 210 *Laod.* 28
A Woman may be made. . . . . 218 *Young Lady* 12
Oft, startled and made wise . . . . . . 225 *Present.* 51
With dread precision, ye made clear . . . . 226 *Present.* 64
Or made with hope to please that inward eye . 231 **The gentlest Poet* 34
" Small change it made in Peter's heart . . . 239 *P. B.* 251
Made the warm earth his lazy bed. . . . . 239 *P. B.* 260
By moonlight made more faint and wan ; . . . 244 *P. B.* 722
And made the good man round him look. . . . 244 *P. B.* 745
'Twas by a troop of miners made, ... 245 *P. B.* 838
Though a breath made it) like a bubble blown . 250 **Happy the* 3
I surely not a man ungently made, ... 253 **Fond words* 10
Bard of the Fleece, whose skilful genius made . 254 *Dyer* 1
In sight of Heaven, then, wherefore hath God made 256 **Yes ! hope* 4
For a sick heart made weary of this life . . . 278 **Lo ! where she* 7
Who, yielding not to changes Time has made, . 279 **All praise* 3
And clear way made for her triumphal car . . 283 **Proud were* 7

Made—*continued.*

To see how things are made and managed there. . 284 *Departure* 8
I feel this place was made for her ; . . . . . 288 *Highland Girl* 69
Made blithe with plough and harrow : . . . . 293 *Yarrow Unv.* 22
For none made sweeter melody . . . . . . 295 *Highland Boy* 44
With sound the least that can be made, . . . 297 *Highland Boy* 196
No right had he but what he made . . . . . 298 *Brownie's Cell* 43
As ever made a maniac dizzy, ... 300 *Bran* 28
No sign of answer made by word or face : . . . 306 **We had* 9
Had blasted France, and made of it a land . . 308 **One might* 2
Hath followed wheresoe'er a way was made . . 317 **Look now* 4
Upon the internal conquests made by each, . . 331 *Ode : Thanks.* 174
A harp that tuneful prelude made . . . . . 334 **In Bruges* 7
Made known the spot where piety should raise . 338 *Engelberg* 13
Made to the Twelve, survives : lip, forehead, cheek, 343 *Last Sup.* 10
Of love in the heart made more happy by tears ? 346 *Stanzas : Simplon* 32
But by reflexion made so, which do best . . . 355 *Aquap.* 202
Her conquests, in the world of sense made known. 357 *Aquap.* 332
That made us) over those severe restraints . . 362 **List—'twas* 43
With Him who made the Work that Work accords 365 **Rapt above* 5
For whom the sea was made unnavigable. . . . 370 *Eg. Maid* 90
We made a day of happy hours, ... 385 *Yarrow Rev.* 23
Unsanctifies our tears—made sport . . . . 386 *Yarrow Rev.* 91
Her sabbath couch has made. . . . . . . 398 *White Doe* 169
For pleasure made, a goodly spot, ... 407 *White Doe* 984
Upon that hostile castle made ;— . . . . . 408 *White Doe* 1127
Suit to his Brothers often made . . . . . 409 *White Doe* 1235
This Banner (for such vow I made) . . . . 410 *White Doe* 1275
He felt—and made a sudden stand. . . . . 411 *White Doe* 1392
What hath he done ? what promise made ? . . 411 *White Doe* 1394
Of utter desolation made . . . . 411 *White Doe* 1428
Made halt—but hark ! a noise behind . . . . 412 *White Doe* 1443
Apart, some little space, was made . . . . . 412 *White Doe* 1524
A little thoughtful pause it made ; . . . . . 414 *White Doe* 1649
And vows, that bind the will, in silence made. . 423 *Ecc. Sonn.* 1. 19. 14
He made by wilful breach of law divine. . . . 428 *Ecc. Sonn.* 2. 1. 4
In polar ice, propitious winds have made . . . 434 *Ecc. Sonn.* 2. 23. 5
And some a bold unerring answer made : . . . 445 *Ecc. Sonn.* 3. 22. 7
For as, by discipline of Time made wise, . . . 449 *Ecc. Sonn.* 3. 35. 6
That made His human tabernacle shine . . . 452 *Ecc. Sonn.* 3. 46. 3
So call thee for heaven's grace through thee made known . . . . 459 **Wanderer ! that* 13
Fair Land ! by Time's parental love made free, . 463 **Why should the* 9
Her intercessions made for the soul's rest . . . 467 *St. Bees* 66
Made room where wolf and boar were used to range ? 468 *St. Bees* 139
That made the worlds, the sovereign Architect, . 473 **We saw* 13
For many a voyage made in her swift bark, . . 475 **Homeward we* 7
And thus I made reply : . . . . 481 *Expost.* 16
What man has made of man. . . . . . . 482 *Lines : Spring* 8
But the least motion which they made, . . . 482 *Lines : Spring* 15
What man has made of man ? . . . . . . 482 *Lines : Spring* 24
Which for himself he had not made. . . . . 486 *Matthew* 16
To me he made reply : . . . . 486 **We walked* 20
Which you last April made ! " . . . . . . 487 *Fountain* 16
Are those that are by distance made more sweet ; . 488 *Pers. Talk* 26
The Poets, who on earth have made us heirs . . 489 *Pers. Talk* 53
Yet they to whom thy virtues made thee dear . 490 *Tribute : Dog* 7
Give unto me, made lowly wise, ... 493 *Duty* 53
In calmness made, and sees what he foresaw ; . 493 *Hap. War.* 54
And she made answer " ENDLESS SORROW ! " . . 494 *Force of Prayer* 7
The Future made to play so false a part, . . . 505 *Warning* 141
These delicate companionships are made ; . . . 511 **So fair* 11
This humble offering made by Truth to Love, . 525 *Epist. Beaumont* 275
Made confession, asked forgiveness, ... 536 *Egremont* 99
The winds at night had made a rout ; . . . . 536 *Goody Blake* 50
And made her poor old bones to ache, ... 537 *Goody Blake* 58
And pine-trees made a heavy shade . . . . 542 *Russ. Fug.* 95
Upon the exalted hills. He made report . . . 548 **Stay, bold* 20
Is not a Ruin spared or made by time, . . . 548 **Stranger ! this* 2
Nor the vows which she has made ; . . . . 549 *Hermit's Cell* 1. 14
They pruned themselves, and made themselves right gay, ... 558 *Cuck. and Night.* 76
That her clear voice made a loud rioting, . . . 558 *Cuck. and Night.* 99
And made a fitting song, of words but few, . . 564 *Troilus* 115
Who busily made use of all his might . . . . 565 *Troilus* 165
Familiar with him, made an inn of his door : . . 569 *Farmer* 26
Old Adam will smile at the pains that have made 570 *Farmer* 75
Made not, as thousands do, a vulgar sleep ; . . 576 *Chiabrera* 9. 20
Such Picture would I at that time have made : . 578 *Peele Castle* 30
The May had then made all things green ; . . 579 **Sweet Flower* 18
That made the calmest, fairest spot of earth, . . 621 *Recluse* 1. 1. 73
And oft-times hast thou made my griefs thine own. . . . . 624 *Æneid* 18
Not mine, and such as were not made for me. . 632 *Prelude* 1. 23
Encouraged and dismissed, till choice was made . 633 *Prelude* 1. 71
Once more made trial of her strength, nor lacked 633 *Prelude* 1. 95
Made one long bathing of a summer's day ; . . 636 *Prelude* 1. 290
When vapours rolling down the valley made . . 638 *Prelude* 1. 417
And made me love them, may I here omit . . 640 *Prelude* 1. 547
Sang to herself, that there I could have made . 644 *Prelude* 2. 126
And down the valley, and, a circuit made . . . 644 *Prelude* 2. 129
Made all the mountains ring. But, ere nightfall, 644 *Prelude* 2. 164
That we perceive, and not that we have made. . 645 *Prelude* 2. 219
Society made sweet as solitude . . . . . . 646 *Prelude* 2. 296
Right underneath, the College kitchens made . . 649 *Prelude* 3. 49
I made it, for it only lived to me, ... 651 *Prelude* 3. 142
Yet true it is, that I had made a change . . . 652 *Prelude* 3. 204
Have made me pay to science and to arts . . . 654 *Prelude* 3. 375

Magnificent—*continued.*
Rise, and to-morrow greet magnificent Rome. 358 *Aquap.* 372
Thy gifts, magnificent Region, ever young 367 **As indignation* 5
Magnificent, and beautiful, and gay. 658 *Prelude* 4. 11
And homeward led my steps. Magnificent 663 *Prelude* 4. 323
Of that magnificent region. On the front 686 *Prelude* 6. 739
Magnificent, by which they are embraced : 700 *Prelude* 8. 57
Thoughts without bound, magnificent designs, 734 *Prelude* 11. 456
That this magnificent effect of power, 816 *Excursion* 4. 971
Thence look for these magnificent results ! 890 *Excursion* 9. 397
Magnificent. Behold, how with a grace K.8. 242 *Recluse* 1.1.203
Magnified. Well worthy to be magnified are they 443 *Ecc. Sonn.* 3. 13. 1
Are dwarfed, or magnified ? 526 **The soaring* 32
Led by the stream, ere noon-day magnified 685 *Prelude* 6. 650
Divulged by Truth and magnified by Fame ; 691 *Prelude* 7. 293
When copious rains have magnified the stream 787 *Excursion* 3. 47
Magnifies. To hide himself, but only magnifies ; 439 *Ecc. Sonn.* 2. 43. 12
—Oh ! 'tis the *heart* that magnifies this life, 497 **Enough of climbing* 12
And by that thinning magnifies the great, 532 **Once I* 23
Its currents ; magnifies its shoals of life 698 *Prelude* 7. 751
Sets forth and magnifies herself ; thus feeds 817 *Excursion* 4. 1072
Magnify. Mists that distort and magnify, 215 *Kirkstone* 38
And vapours magnify and spread 228 *Devot. Incit.* 66
Unite, to magnify the Ever-living, 235 *Power of Sound* 195
And magnify Thy name, Almighty God ! 328 *Ode 1815* 105
Her simple cares to magnify ; 344 **How blest* 4
And magnify the glorious name of God, 446 *Ecc. Sonn.* 3. 25. 7
Magnitude. The stars pre-eminent in magnitude, v **If thou indeed* 4
With magnitude and strength fit to uphold 354 *Aquap.* 141
Through every magnitude distinguishable, 706 *Prelude* 8. 482
Magnolia. He told of the magnolia, spread 193 *Ruth* 61
Magog. The Magog of Legberthwaite dale. 86 *Rural Arch.* 12
Magpie. The magpie chatters with delight ; 84 *Shepherd-boys* 5
The Jay makes answer as the Magpie chatters ; 195 *Resolution* 6
Magpies. If two auspicious magpies crossed my way ;— 810 *Excursion* 4. 618
Maid. *See* **Milk-maid, Mother-maid.**
'Tis plain he loves the Maid, and what he said 41 *Bord.* 231
The cruel Viper !— Poor devoted Maid, 46 *Bord.* 527
There's witchery in 't. I never knew a maid 59 *Bord.* 1193
From the first moment that I loved the Maid ; 61 *Bord.* 1322
" Sisters and brothers, little maid, 83 *We are Seven* 13
Sweet Maid, how this may be." 84 *We are Seven* 28
Then did the little Maid reply, 84 *We are Seven* 29
" You run about, my little Maid, 84 *We are Seven* 33
The little Maid replied, 84 *We are Seven* 38
The little Maid would have her will, 84 *We are Seven* 68
Thus, thought I, to her lamb that little Maid might sing : 87 *Pet-lamb* 20
She might prove our Maid of Arc. 94 *Westmoreland Girl* 88
—A gentle Maid, whose heart is lowly bred, 106 *Farewell* 28
And, having seen that lovely Maid, 108 *Louisa* 2
A Maid whom there were none to praise 109 **She dwelt* 3
O be thou wise as they, soul-gifted Maid ! 110 **Look at* 16
Dear Maid, this truth believe, 112 **Yes ! thou* 6
Was the Youth's birth-place. There he wooed a Maid 121 *V. and J.* 12
The threatened shame, the parents of the Maid 122 *V. and J.* 69
Upon the altar, to the Maid he loved. 123 *V. and J.* 119
Desperate the Maid—the Youth is stained with blood ; 123 *V. and J.* 146
By the unbending Parents of the Maid, 125 *V. and J.* 238
If she, a timid Maid, hath put such boldness on. 141 *Arm. Lady* 84
" How fares Joanna, that wild-hearted Maid ! 147 *Joanna* 23
Or rather of some gentle maid, 162 **Who fancied* 8
The fancy-stricken Youth or heart-sick Maid, 170 **Never enlivened* 21
But, pretty Maid, if you look near, 178 *Waggoner* 2. 117
Recall the not unwilling Maid, 190 **Lyre ! though* 3
Such tales as told to any maid 192 *Ruth* 46
What could he less than love a Maid 194 *Ruth* 160
But Stephen to another Maid 199 *Thorn* 113
And, with this other Maid, to church 199 *Thorn* 115
Maid and Mother undefiled, 204 *Brougham* 70
Will thank you. Faultless does the Maid appear ; 256 *Marriage: Friend* 9
Was lovely as a Grecian maid 287 *Ellen Irwin* 3
For, high-souled Maid, what sorrow would it be 306 **Two Voices* 11
Shall tend, with his own dark-eyed Maid, 342 *Ital. Itin.* 44
How blest the Maid whose heart—yet free 344 **How blest* 1
Such, haply, yon ITALIAN Maid, 344 **How blest* 20
The breath of an Helvetian Maid. 344 **How blest* 39
Fetched by our art, the Egyptian Maid 370 *Eg. Maid* 100
This is the wished-for Bride, the Maid 372 *Eg. Maid* 207
King Arthur led the Egyptian Maid, 374 *Eg. Maid* 353
The Maid to Jesu hearkened, 374 *Eg. Maid* 375
A love-lorn Maid, at some far-distant time, 381 *Duddon* 22. 1
For maid and mother, when despair 391 *Highland Broach* 53
And a solitary Maid ; 400 *White Doe* 339
For She it was—this Maid, who wrought 400 *White Doe* 346
This to himself—and to the Maid, 401 *White Doe* 452
He kissed the consecrated Maid ; 402 *White Doe* 591
A Maid o'er whom the blessed Dove 403 *White Doe* 667
When Francis, uttering to the Maid 406 *White Doe* 975
But see the consecrated Maid 407 *White Doe* 999
Attempts which still the heart-sick Maid 407 *White Doe* 1018
Then on this height the Maid had sought, 409 *White Doe* 1206
Oh hear me, hear me, gentle Maid, 409 *White Doe* 1245
The old Man to the silent Maid, 411 *White Doe* 1355
Fair Vision ! when it crossed the Maid 415 *White Doe* 1738

Maid—*continued.*
Maid of the blasted family, 416 *White Doe* 1867
I saw the figure of a lovely Maid 440 *Ecc. Sonn.* 3. 1. 1
Such to the tender-hearted maid 473 *Ossian* 73
In white arrayed, glides on the Maid 479 *Somnamb.* 93
Or boding Shade, or if the Maid 479 *Somnamb.* 129
Love listening while the Lesbian Maid 499 **Departing summer* 46
When, as day broke, the Maid, through misty air, 540 *Grace Darl.* 29
Came forth the Maid—" In me 544 *Russ. Fug.* 278
" Are you the Maid," the Stranger cried, 545 *Russ. Fug.* 313
Which did Thee bear, and is a Maid for aye, 552 *Prioress* 10
" O Mother Maid ! O Maid and Mother free ! 552 *Prioress* 15
For slaughtered Youth or love-lorn Maid ! 586 *Hogg* 42
Soft as the gentle kiss of amorous maid 630 [?] **O Moon* 11
Guide hither, O sweet Moon, the maid I love so well. 630 [?] **O Moon* 15
Another maid there was, who also shed 678 *Prelude* 6. 224
From our own ground,—the Maid of Buttermere,— 691 *Prelude* 7. 297
Each with his maid, before the sun was up, 701 *Prelude* 8. 153
Upon her palfrey, or that gentle maid 716 *Prelude* 8. 452
Seems hard to shun. And yet I knew a maid, 736 *Prelude* 12. 151
Even like this maid, before I was called forth 736 *Prelude* 12. 174
Through field or forest with the maid we love, 741 *Prelude* 13. 123
Of soul impetuous, and the bashful maid 836 *Excursion* 5. 960
Unjustly dealt with ; but the Maid was gone ! 840 *Excursion* 6. 136
Silly Maid as ever was ! S.3. 424 *Tinker* 39
Stormy and fierce, the Maid of Arc withdrew S.3. 436 **The doubt* 168
Maiden. *See* **Cottage-maiden.**
There doth the maiden watch her lover's sail 15 *Desc. Sk.* 250
But sure he loves the Maiden, and never love 41 *Bord.* 236
A maiden from the ruffian violence 42 *Bord.* 286
Pity the Maiden did not wait a while ; 43 *Bord.* 326
A Maiden innocent till ensnared by Clifford, 44 *Bord.* 381
I'll point him out ;—a Maiden is his guide, 45 *Bord.* 454
He is the Man to whom the Maiden—pure 57 *Bord.* 1104
A snow-white mountain-lamb with a Maiden at its side. 87 *Pet-lamb* 4
With one knee on the grass did the little Maiden kneel, 87 *Pet-lamb* 7
Now with her empty can the Maiden turned away : 87 *Pet-lamb* 15
Be thou wiser, youthful Maiden ! 90 *Longest Day* 41
" One, are we not ? " exclaimed the Maiden—" One, 124 *V. and J.* 163
Or sprightly maiden, of Love's court, 158 **With little* 18
" Whence strains to love-sick maiden dear, 164 *Needlecase* 33
Then, dearest Maiden, move along these shades 186 *Nutting* 54
Had wooed the Maiden, day and night 194 *Ruth* 158
Maiden ! now take flight ;—inherit 217 **Inmate of* 17
And this light-hearted Maiden constant is as he. 222 *Triad* 144
Whate'er the theme, the Maiden sang 289 *Sol. Reap.* 25
Each maiden to her dwelling ! 292 *Yarrow Unv.* 12
She was a maiden City, bright and free ; 305 *Ven. Rep.* 5
From the Maiden at my side ; 334 **In Bruges* 36
Nor shall forget the Maiden coy 342 *Ital. Itin.* 35
Of wind or wave—a meek and guileless Maiden. 370 *Eg. Maid* 66
Thy fatal work, O Maiden, innocent as good ! 412 *White Doe* 1498
Of mother's love with maiden purity, 434 *Ecc. Sonn.* 2. 25. 13
Upon a Maiden trembling as she knelt ; 446 *Ecc. Sonn.* 3. 24. 2
To sound the crystal depth of maiden rights ; 467 *St. Bees* 114
Of a young maiden, only not divine. 469 **Why stand* 8
The rescued Maiden lay, 479 *Somnamb.* 137
A Maiden gentle, yet, at duty's call, 540 *Grace Darl.* 22
Beneath whose watchful eye the Maiden grew 541 *Grace Darl.* 93
In honour of that blissful Maiden free, 556 *Prioress* 213
Like a maiden of twenty he trembles and sighs, 570 *Farmer* 67
There might the love-sick maiden sit, and chide 607 *Desc. Sk. Quarto* 309
The maiden spread the haycock in the sun, 683 *Prelude* 6. 537
Maiden of Buttermere ! She lives in peace 692 *Prelude* 7. 320
The maiden from the bosom of her love, 723 *Prelude* 10. 358
To Youth or Maiden gone before their time, 825 *Excursion* 5. 202
The spotless ether of a maiden life ; 850 *Excursion* 6. 801
From youth or maiden, or some honoured chief 857 *Excursion* 7. 18
When the market Maiden, S.3. 424 *Tinker* 32
Maidenly. And maidenly shamefacedness : 288 *Highland Girl* 31
Maiden-queen. As pleased as if the same had been a Maiden-queen. 108 *Indolence* 72
Maiden's. Grace that shall mould the Maiden's form 187 **Three years* 23
Gave with a maiden's true good-will 198 *Thorn* 106
Where, for the love-lorn maiden's wound, 224 **'Tis gone* 31
While the Monks prayed in Maiden's Bower 405 *White Doe* 833
In glory for this Maiden's sake, 413 *White Doe* 1554
Creatures—how precious in the Maiden's sight ! 540 *Grace Darl.* 38
To the Maiden's filial heart. 545 *Russ. Fug.* 344
Within the Maiden's breast ; 545 *Russ. Fug.* 362
Ere the broad world rang with the maiden's name, 691 *Prelude* 7. 304
Upon the haughty maiden's brow, 'tis but 840 *Excursion* 6. 122
So deftly, and the nicest maiden's locks 851 *Excursion* 6. 841
At the pretty Maiden's dread S.3. 424 *Tinker* 42
Maidens. The maidens eye him with enquiring glance, 11 *Desc. Sk.* 40
Ye lovely maidens that in noontide shade 13 *Desc. Sk.* 129
Man and Maidens wheel, 167 *Stray Pleasures* 19
The rustic Maidens, every hand 338 *Brientz* 12
Sons, mothers, maidens withering on the stalk, 488 *Pers. Talk* 6
Around whose trunk the maidens dance in May— 866 *Excursion* 7. 621
Among the rocks below. Men, maidens, youths, 877 *Excursion* 8. 180
Maid's. Quick was the little Maid's reply, 84 *We are Seven* 63
Their steps he followed to the Maid's retreat. 122 *V. and J.* 78
Maids. *See* **Milk-maids.**
Or marks, 'mid opening cliffs, fair dark-eyed maids 12 *Desc. Sk.* 91

Maids—*continued.*
Aloft upon the elm-tree. Pretty Maids, — 44 *Bord.* 371
Maids at the wheel, the weaver at his loom, — 250 **Nuns fret* 4
Maids and Matrons, dight — 324 *Ode 1814* 59
What ye, celestial Maids! have often sung — 325 *Ode 1814* 128
Time was, blest Power! when youths and maids — 506 **While from* 17
The vacant and the busy, maids and youths, — 567 *Cumb. Beg.* 64
'Tho' now no more thy maids their voices suit — 615 *Desc.Sk.Quarto* 748
Of maids and youths, old men, and matrons staid, — 663 *Prelude* 4. 310
Frank-hearted maids of rocky Cumberland, — 675 *Prelude* 6. 14
Of Indian corn tended by dark-eyed maids; — 685 *Prelude* 6. 664
Of maids at sunrise bringing in from far — 701 *Prelude* 8. 146
Mail. Equipped from head to foot in iron mail. — 111 *'*Tis said that some* 47
Thou cloth'st the wicked in their dazzling mail, — 328 *Ode 1815* 108
Blithe Autumn's purple crown, and Winter's icy mail! — 350 *Des. Stanzas* 36
And Marmaduke in fearless mail, — 401 *White Doe* 479
And feudal rapine clothed with iron mail, — 534 **When in* 2
Cased in the gleaming mail the monarch wore, — 689 *Prelude* 7. 139
Of some gigantic warrior clad in mail, — 708 *Prelude* 8. 585
Mail-clad. Peasant and mail-clad Chief with pious awe; — 467 *St. Bees* 122
Mailed. A mailèd angel on a battle-day; — 108 *Indolence* 61
Mailed and horsed, with lance and sword, — 205 *Brougham* 152
To hoof and finger mailed;—yet, high or low, — 368 *Trajan* 47
While drawing toward the car Sir Gawaine, mailed — 373 *Eg. Maid* 285
Maimed. Maimed, mangled by inhuman men; — 117 *Affl. Marg.* 51
By Heaven afforded to uphold her maimed — 118 *Maternal Grief* 48
Maimed, spiritless; and, in their weakness strong, — 713 *Prelude* 9. 261
On which the cripple, in the quarry maimed, — K.8. 250 *Recluse* 1.1.508
Main. In the calm sunshine slept the glittering main; — 30 *Guilt* 336
Along the cloudless Main, he, in those hours — 96 *Brothers* 53
And she came far from over the main. — 144 *Her Eyes* 4
Though strong, is, in the main, a joyless tie — 172 *Infant Daughter* 37
Tugging all with might and main, — 181 *Waggoner* 4. 99
Had crossed the Atlantic main. — 194 *Ruth* 168
But stately in the main; and, when he ended, — 197 *Resolution* 136
Main ocean, breaking audibly, and stretched — 219 **This Height* 14
Where the main fibres are entwined, — 285 *Grave of Burns* 45
In some green island of the western main. — 320 **They seek* 14
Whisper it to the billows of the main, — 322 **Ye Storms* 11
Down the main avenue my sight can range: — 350 *Des. Stanzas* 38
The main flood roughened into hill and valley. — 369 *Eg. Maid* 42
The incessant Rovers of the northern main, — 425 *Ecc. Sonn.* 1. 29. 3
Into main Ocean they, this deed accurst — 433 *Ecc. Sonn.* 2. 17. 11
But liberty, and triumphs on the Main, — 450 *Ecc. Sonn.* 3. 38. 1
For, suddenly up-conjured from the Main, — 469 **Bold words* 5
From early youth I ploughed the restless Main, — 470 †*From early* 1
Not in the mines beyond the western main, — 480 *Cordelia* 1
Drew from the influx of the main, — 495 *Fact* 16
And, the main fear once doomed to banishment, — 519 *Pun. Death* 8. 6
Wide o'er the main a trembling lustre plays, — 618 *School Ex.* 41
Some variegated story, in the main — 635 *Prelude* 1. 224
Howling in troops along the Bothnic Main. — 640 *Prelude* 1. 543
With hand however weak, but in the main — 651 *Prelude* 3. 183
Were, in the main, of mood less tender: strong, — 662 *Prelude* 4. 251
Led me to these by paths that, in the main, — 686 *Prelude* 6. 751
Whence the main organs of the public power — 711 *Prelude* 9. 102
In the main outline, such it might be said — 729 *Prelude* 11. 173
Into the main Atlantic, that appeared — 746 *Prelude* 14. 47
My haunt, and the main region of my song. — 755 *Recluse* 1. 1. 794
Sought in the Atlantic Main—why should they be — 755 *Recluse* 1. 1. 802
" Fresh blew the wind, when o'er the Atlantic Main — 798 *Excursion* 3. 835
Of these privations, richer in the main!— — 835 *Excursion* 5. 829
With an ascent and progress in the main; — 872 *Excursion* 7. 1005
And yet a growing prospect in the main. — K.8. 250 *Recluse* 1.1.490
Mainly. And inclination mainly, and the mere — 677 *Prelude* 6. 177
Structures like these the excited spirit mainly — 697 *Prelude* 7. 651
Is mainly to the pleasure of the mind — 744 *Prelude* 13. 289
Are they not mainly outward ministers — 813 *Excursion* 4. 836
Maintain. —Yet some maintain that to this day — 83 *Lucy Gray* 57
Have stiffened them, maintain their post; — 246 *P. B.* 849
Help by his labour to maintain — 249 *P. B.* 1129
To have my ends, maintain my rights, — 291 *Rob Roy* 55
His solitary course maintain; — 409 *White Doe* 1217
Such conflict long did he maintain, — 411 *White Doe* 1406
Let me a compensating faith maintain; — 459 **Wanderer! that* 43
And will maintain, if God his help afford. — 477 **Lowther! in* 8
Thanks to the Powers that yet maintain their sway, — 503 *Warning* 22
Did, like a pestilence, maintain its hold — 635 *Prelude* 1. 200
Which do both give it being and maintain — 745 *Prelude* 13. 374
Appeared an idle dream, that could maintain, — 770 *Excursion* 1. 952
So charactered did I maintain a strife — 797 *Excursion* 3. 788
Is it enabled to maintain its hold — 803 *Excursion* 4. 151
For you a stately gallery maintain — 809 *Excursion* 4. 561
Not equal, but sufficient to maintain, — 833 *Excursion* 5. 711
From out their substance issuing, maintain — 835 *Excursion* 5. 875
By ties of daily interest, to maintain — 875 *Excursion* 8. 63
Fixing a steady eye, maintain their speed; — 880 *Excursion* 8. 384
Maintained. Maintained, for peaceful ends beyond our view. — 78 *Bord.* 2310
Such union, in the lovely Girl maintained — 118 *Maternal Grief* 38
The golden years maintained a course — 228 *Vernal Ode* 131
In progress, under laws divine, maintained. — 538 **In desultory* 55
Buildings, albeit rude, that have maintained — 547 **Rude is* 2
Maintained even by the very name and thought — 676 *Prelude* 6. 58
With like persuasion honoured, we maintained: — 715 *Prelude* 9. 422
No longer keep their ground, by faith maintained — 730 *Prelude* 11. 201
Maintained for me a saving intercourse — 732 *Prelude* 11. 341

Maintained—*continued.*
Maintained for me a secret happiness. — 735 *Prelude* 12. 43
And an habitual piety, maintained — 758 *Excursion* 1. 116
And, from the pulpit, zealously maintained — 774 *Excursion* 2. 220
Maintained his place; or heedfully pursued — 783 *Excursion* 2. 768
Maintained with faithful care. And you divine — 795 *Excursion* 3. 614
Communications spiritually maintained, — 811 *Excursion* 4. 645
Thus are they born, thus fostered, thus maintained; — 837 *Excursion* 5. 996
Maintains. Maintains a deep and reverential care — 203 *Hart-leap* 167
Maintains inviolate its slightest vow! — 270 **Shame on* 8
Of sorrow, still maintains a heathen rule, — 422 *Ecc. Sonn.* 1. 15. 3
Maintains the else endangered gift of life; — 432 *Ecc. Sonn.* 2. 16. 11
The heart that first had roused him. Youth maintains, — 727 *Prelude* 11. 27
For all the children whom her soil maintains — 888 *Excursion* 9. 300
Maintenance. And in this way he gained an honest maintenance. — 196 *Resolution* 105
About my future worldly maintenance, — 650 *Prelude* 3. 79
A necessary maintenance insures, — 751 *Prelude* 14. 366
To yield him no unworthy maintenance. — 761 *Excursion* 1. 311
Than honest maintenance, by irksome toil — 875 *Excursion* 8. 50
Maize. The towering maize, and prop the twig — 342 *Ital. Itin.* 45
Majestic. How graceful, pride can be, and how majestic, ease. — 6 *Ev. Wk.* 221
With more majestic course the water rolled, — 22 *Desc. Sk.* 636
Majestic in her person, tall and straight; — 119 *Sailor's Mother* 5
Calm pleasures there abide—majestic pains. — 210 *Laod.* 72
But with majestic lowliness endued, — 212 *Dion* 14
Frozen by distance; so, majestic Pile, — 290 *Kilchurn* 38
Pure as the naked heavens, majestic, free, — 307 **Milton! thou* 11
Majestic Berne, high on her guardian steep, — 339 *Schwytz* 9
We mark majestic herds of cattle, free, — 349 *Val. Dover* 6
Majestic Duddon, over smooth flat sands — 384 *Duddon* 32. 7
Lowther! in thy majestic Pile are seen — 477 **Lowther! in* 1
A more majestic tide the water roll'd — 616 *Desc.Sk.Quarto* 777
In the bright paths of fair majestic Truth: — 618 *School Ex.* 12
To court majestic truth, or wake the golden lyre; — 619 *School Ex.* 62
Are haunted by majestic Powers, — 629 *Installation* 79
So beautiful, so majestic in themselves, — 641 *Prelude* 1. 608
Majestic edifices, should not want — 654 *Prelude* 3. 381
A winding passage with majestic ease — 680 *Prelude* 6. 379
From these majestic floods, yon shining cliffs, — 682 *Prelude* 6. 463
With that majestic indolence so dear — 703 *Prelude* 8. 255
Of a majestic intellect, its acts — 747 *Prelude* 14. 67
That with majestic energy from earth — 803 *Excursion* 4. 143
Or pierce the gloom of her majestic woods; — 819 *Excursion* 4. 1201
Majestic circuit, beautiful abyss, — 822 *Excursion* 5. 9
A like majestic frame of mind in those — K.8. 245 *Recluse* 1.1.314
Who first defiled that calm majestic face? — L.2. 318 *Frag. Æneid* 4.9
Majestically. Majestically huge and slow: — 182 *Waggoner* 4. 229
Majesties. Thy visionary majesties of light, — 282 **Wansfell! this* 13
Majesty. In Nature's pristine majesty outspread, — 14 *Desc. Sk.* 228
Howe'er disguised in its own majesty, — 23 *Yew-tree* 51
The majesty of Him who rules the world. — 48 *Bord.* 617
We'll not insult thy majesty by time, — 58 *Bord.* 1154
No, no, this cannot be;—men thirst for power and majesty! — 189 *Star-gazers* 24
[Fair is the Swan, whose majesty, prevailing — 212 *Dion*
To confess their majesty! — 218 **Inmate of* 36
To take thee in thy majesty away? — 221 *Triad* 75
When it reveals, in evening majesty, — 226 *Vernal Ode* 7
The foliaged head in cloud-like majesty, — 227 *Vernal Ode* 62
And all his majesty— — 231 *Jew. Fam.* 6
Queen both for beauty and for majesty. — 266 **With how* 14
A sight so touching in its majesty: — 269 *Westm. Bridge* 3
To the memorial majesty of Time — 290 *Kilchurn* 20
In France, before the new-born Majesty. — 303 **Is it* 7
And daring not to feel the majesty of right! — 311 **Who rises* 45
Thy power and majesty, — 329 *Ode: Thanks.* 12
Awake! the majesty of God revere! — 332 *Ode: Thanks.* 227
In simple democratic majesty; — 350 *Des. Stanzas* 52
But with its peaceful majesty content. — 355 *Aquap.* 191
Supplanted the whole majesty of Rome — 358 *Pine: Rome* 12
To vindicate the majesty of truth. — 359 *Plea: Hist.* 8
Firm in its pristine majesty hath stood — 367 *Trajan* 5
His power, his beauty, and his majesty. — 389 *Eagles* 14
The majesty of England interposed — 441 *Ecc. Sonn.* 3. 7. 2
Her head, and nothing loth her Majesty — 461 **Who but is* 3
The majesty of honest dealing. — 472 *Ossian* 16
Clothed with impassive majesty, and graced — 510 **Among a* 8
If she, self-shorn of Majesty, ordain — 518 *Pun. Death* 5. 12
In heavenly majesty she seem'd to move. — 618 *School Ex.* 14
In all the majesty of light array'd, — 619 *School Ex.* 72
Before thy Majesty, in humble trust — 628 **Deign, Sovereign* 18
Dimpling along in silent majesty, — 685 *Prelude* 6. 652
Keen ridicule; the majesty proclaims — 695 *Prelude* 7. 525
To majesty. Like virtue have the forms — 698 *Prelude* 7. 756
There I conversed with majesty and power — 708 *Prelude* 8. 631
Of life and death, in majesty severe — 721 *Prelude* 10. 185
Long mouldered, of barbaric majesty. — 744 *Prelude* 13. 326
To dwindle, and give up his majesty, — 746 *Prelude* 14. 48
But, in the majesty of distance, now — 772 *Excursion* 2. 93
And majesty with this gigantic stream, — 799 *Excursion* 3. 883
Even to thy Being's infinite majesty! — 802 *Excursion* 4. 99
To avenge their own insulted majesty. — 816 *Excursion* 4. 1034
On which, now fallen, erewhile in majesty — 827 *Excursion* 5. 299
Fresh in the strength and majesty of age, — 829 *Excursion* 5. 457
The majesty of both, shall pray for both; — 838 *Excursion* 6. 13
Nor will, I trust, the Majesty of Heaven — 866 *Excursion* 7. 579
Was loth to assault the majesty he loved: — 868 *Excursion* 7. 749

Majesty—*continued.*
And an impassioned majesty, exclaimed— 888 *Excursion* 9. 292
In majesty presiding over fields 892 *Excursion* 9. 576
Imperishable majesty streamed forth 893 *Excursion* 9. 630
Of majesty, and beauty, and repose, K.8.240 *Recluse* 1.1.143
Love, perfect love ; of so much majesty K.8.245 *Recluse* 1.1.313
And silent majesty ; the birch-tree woods K.8.252 *Recluse* 1.1.562
Heavens ! who sees majesty in George's face ? L.1. 88 *Juvenal* 1. 9
Major-domo. And bowed to many a major-domo S.3. 438 **My Lord* 17
Make. When crowding cattle, checked by rails that make 3 *Ev. Wk.* 41
Recovering heart, like answer did she make ; 27 *Guilt* 186
And groans which, as they said, might make a dead man start. 31 *Guilt* 396
To make the proud and vain his tributaries, 39 *Bord.* 82
To fling't away from you : you make no use 39 *Bord.* 127
To make it what thou wilt. Thou hast been told, 40 *Bord.* 191
Snapped fierce to make a morsel of his head : 44 *Bord.* 414
To make a bed for me !—My Girl will weep 52 *Bord.* 817
And no return have I to make but prayers ; 52 *Bord.* 826
Than make me change my course. Dear Marmaduke, 55 *Bord.* 992
I could forgive him. And should he make the Child 56 *Bord.* 1044
And make the spotless spirit of filial love 57 *Bord.* 1063
Her bonds and chains, which make the mighty feeble. 57 *Bord.* 1091
To make mankind merry for evermore, 60 *Bord.* 1272
Soon would her gentle voice make peace between us. 61 *Bord.* 1318
Between my breast-plate and my skin than make 63 *Bord.* 1424
That make the fields their dwelling. If a snake 66 *Bord.* 1579
To God above will make him feel for ours. 66 *Bord.* 1596
I should make wondrous revolution here ; 66 *Bord.* 1622
But let us make the attempt. 72 *Bord.* 1998
On evil instigation, to make sport 74 *Bord.* 2085
By lowly nature reared, as if to make her 78 *Bord.* 2334
Make your bed, or make your bower ; 79 *Foresight* 14
Who of thy words dost make a mock apparel, 88 *H. C.* 2
Where earth and heaven do make one imagery ; 88 *H. C.* 10
And, kneeling, supplication make to our Lady de la Paix ; 92 *Poet's Dream* 50
Your years make up one peaceful family ; 97 *Brothers* 122
But do not make her love the less. 117 *Affl. Marg.* 28
To this did Johnny answer make, 126 *Idiot Boy* 62
Make subterraneous music, like the noise 132 *Michael* 51
Make ready Luke's best garments, of the best 135 *Michael* 279
'Twill make a thing endurable, which else 138 *Michael* 449
She wasted no complaint, but strove to make 138 *Widow* 6
Oh, gracious Heaven, in pity make her thine ! 139 *Widow* 28
" Yet you make all courage fruitless, 140 *Arm. Lady* 39
Make one being of a pair." 140 *Arm. Lady* 64
" Make it known that my Companion 141 *Arm. Lady* 115
Though some may frown and make a stir, 144 **Driven in* 71
The leaves that make the softest bed : 145 *Her Eyes* 56
And make dear friendships with the streams and groves. 147 *Joanna* 8
The meteors make of it a favourite haunt : 148 **There is an* 9
The harmony thy notes most gladly make 154 *Morn. Ex.* 51
The love they to each other make, 156 *Oak and Broom* 88
But now my own delights I make,— 157 **In youth* 5
Make all one band of paramours, 159 *Green Linnet* 18
Little Flower—I'll make a stir, 160 **Pansies, lilies* 15
They themselves make the reel, 167 *Stray Pleasures* 20
Full often make you stretch and strain, 175 *Waggoner* 1. 142
That make the good, tow'rds which he's yearning, 177 *Waggoner* 2. 39
And, if they had a prayer to make, 178 *Waggoner* 3. 14
We make a kind of handsome show ! 179 *Waggoner* 3. 78
Where a tribe of them make merry, 179 *Waggoner* 3. 122
The echoes make a glad reply.— 180 *Waggoner* 4. 6
She shall be mine, and I will make 187 **Three years* 5
A gentle answer did the old Man make, 196 *Resolution* 85
And when the little breezes make 199 *Thorn* 194
And they who do make mention of the same, 201 *Hart-leap* 63
" And, gallant Stag ! to make thy praises known, 201 *Hart-leap* 65
We will make merry in that pleasant bower. 201 *Hart-leap* 72
And come and make his death-bed near the well. 203 *Hart-leap* 148
My dear, dear Sister ! and this prayer I make, 207 *Tintern* 121
The coronal that coiling vipers make ; 213 *Dion* 83
Will to composure lead—or make thee blithe as bird in bower. 229 *Cuckoo-clock* 11
Will make thee happy, happy as a child ; 229 *Cuckoo-clock* 20
And make no better use of it ; 237 *P. B.* 79
Together make as sweet a scene 240 *P. B.* 364
That make, with curses not a few, 246 *P. B.* 869
" Make haste—my little Rachel—do, 248 *P. B.* 1061
The prayers I make will then be sweet indeed 257 **The prayers* 1
And doth with his eternal motion make 258 **It is a* 7
Have glimpses that would make me less forlorn ; 259 **The world is* 12
Make sadder transits o'er thought's optic glass 269 *Malham* 13
Could scarcely make more placid, heaven more bright) 274 *Infant M.* 10
Than will hereafter move them, if they make 280 **Intent on* 6
And of your Father's name will make 286 *Sons of Burns* 23
This fall of water that doth make 288 *Highland Girl* 7
" We have a passion—make a law, 291 *Rob Roy* 25
If not, make merry in despite 293 *Jedbor.* 6
A sight to make a stranger sigh ! 294 *Jedbor.* 20
And, like Montrose, make Loyalty your pride— 310 *Invasion* 4
Make merry, wives ! ye little children, stun 310 *Anticip.* 8
" Make straight a highway for the Lord—repent ! " 365 **The Baptist* 14
Which Angels make, on works of love descending. 371 *Eg. Maid* 150
Yes, they can make, who fail to find, 376 **The Minstrels* 67
Make to the eyes of men thy features known. 376 *Duddon* 3. 4

Make—*continued.*
The curves, a loosely-scattered chain doth make ; 377 *Duddon* 4. 4
Checking the stream, make a pool smooth and clear 382 *Duddon* 23. 4
That make the Patriot-spirit bow her head 388 *Loch Etive* 13
But you, at least, may make report 408 *White Doe* 1104
In holy ground a grave would make ; 412 *White Doe* 1521
Pinions of high and higher sweep, and make 430 *Ecc. Sonn.* 2. 9. 13
Or seek to make assurance doubly sure. 445 *Ecc. Sonn.* 3. 21. 12
" The which would endless matrimony make ; " 447 *Ecc. Sonn.* 3. 26. 10
To courses fit to make a mother rue 447 *Ecc. Sonn.* 3. 27. 10
And make the serious happier than the gay ? 459 **Wanderer ! that* 39
Make thy young thoughts acquainted with the grave ; 465 **Thou look'st* 10
She helps to make a Holy-land at home : 467 *St. Bees* 112
Doth man of brother man a creature make 472 *Dunolly Eagle* 13
To make this Gem their own, 478 *Somnamb.* 20
Make haste, your morning task resign ; 482 *Sister* 11
Some silent laws our hearts will make, 483 *Sister* 29
Perhaps a tale you'll make it. 484 *Simon Lee* 72
For Matthew a request I make 486 *Matthew* 15
If kindred humours e'er would make 490 *Night Thought* 13
To mix with hymns that Spirits make and hear ; 500 *Humanity* 17
The kindness that would make him less forlorn ; 501 *Humanity* 66
Stone-walls a prisoner make, but not a slave. 501 *Humanity* 78
Glad proclamation make, and heights and dells 503 *Warning* 42
Storms make in rising, valued in the moon 505 *Warning* 145
Offspring of soul-bewitching Art, make me 508 *F. Stone* 41
And Truth, whose eye guilt only can make dim ; 514 **Who ponders* 12
Learn to make Time the father of wise Hope ; 515 **Ah why* 12
Here as elsewhere, to notices that make 525 *Epist. Beaumont* 266
To make a fair recess more fair ; 533 **Blest is* 24
And make himself a freeman of this spot 548 **Stranger ! this* 10
Rains, that make each rill a torrent, 550 *Hermit's Cell* 4. 11
Make the heart sink, then wilt thou reverence 551 **If thou in* 4
For he of low hearts can make high, of high 556 *Cuck. and Night.* 3
He can make low, and unto death bring nigh ; 556 *Cuck. and Night.* 4
And hard hearts he can make them kind and free. 556 *Cuck. and Night.* 5
He can make sick folk whole and fresh and sound ; 556 *Cuck. and Night.* 7
He can make sick,—bind can he and unbind 556 *Cuck. and Night.* 9
Foolish men he can make them out of wise ;— 557 *Cuck. and Night.* 12
Loose livers he can make abate their vice, 557 *Cuck. and Night.* 14
And proud hearts can make tremble in a trice. 557 *Cuck. and Night.* 15
Such uncouth singing verily dost thou make. 558 *Cuck. and Night.* 115
Unto the God of Love I make a vow, 561 *Cuck. and Night.* 229
Failing, we finally shall make accord. 562 *Cuck. and Night.* 280
Men thence a book might make, a history ; 563 *Troilus* 67
Somewhat his woeful heart to make more light ; 564 *Troilus* 116
To comfort him, and make his heart more light 565 *Troilus* 166
Make slow to feel, and by sure steps resign 567 *Cumb. Beg.* 94
Make him a captive !—for that pent-up din, 569 *Cumb. Beg.* 180
And all that generous nurture breeds to make 575 *Chiabrera* 7. 2
And yours, love prompted me to make. 577 **I come* 28
Will make a touching melody. 577 **I come* 32
The birds shall sing and ocean make 580 **Sweet Flower* 67
Have power to make thy virtues known, 581 *John Words.* 62
Ye to each other make ; I see 588 *Immortality* 37
To make her Foster-child, her Inmate Man, 588 *Immortality* 82
Uphold us, cherish, and have power to make 589 *Immortality* 157
And watch, while on your brows the cross ye make, 614 *Desc. Sk. Quarto* 674
Laid snares to make the babe her own. 620 *Birth of Love* 31
The frosty wind, as if to make amends 622 *Recluse* 1. 1. 158
Doth make the happy happier. This have we 627 **The star* 6
Thus far, O Friend ! did I, not used to make 632 *Prelude* 1. 46
Make rigorous inquisition, the report 634 *Prelude* 1. 148
And make them dwellers in the hearts of men 634 *Prelude* 1. 164
Make ceaseless music that composed my thoughts 636 *Prelude* 1. 277
Of danger or desire ; and thus did make 639 *Prelude* 1. 472
And almost make remotest infancy 641 *Prelude* 1. 634
Or make their dim abode in distant winds. 646 *Prelude* 2. 310
Those human sentiments that make this earth 648 *Prelude* 2. 422
Where all stand single ; this I feel, and make 651 *Prelude* 3. 186
With such discoveries as his eye can make 662 *Prelude* 4. 259
Impediments that make his task more sweet ; 662 *Prelude* 4. 270
Make a strange back-ground. From his lips, ere long, 664 *Prelude* 4. 404
A centre to the circle which they make ; 669 *Prelude* 5. 252
To manage books, and things, and make them act 671 *Prelude* 5. 351
Make green peninsulas on Esthwaite's Lake : 672 *Prelude* 5. 434
To make this book our own. Through several months, 672 *Prelude* 5. 473
Who make our wish, our power, our thought a deed, 673 *Prelude* 5. 528
Descending from the mountain to make sport 683 *Prelude* 6. 539
Would issue, let one incident make known. 683 *Prelude* 6. 561
The invisible world, doth greatness make abode, 684 *Prelude* 6. 602
As if to make the strong wind visible, 687 *Prelude* 7. 46
To make the sounds more audible ? What crowd 699 *Prelude* 8. 4
The other to make music ; hither, too, 699 *Prelude* 8. 27
Of this I heard, and saw enough to make 701 *Prelude* 8. 166
Last look, to make the best amends he may : 709 *Prelude* 9. 16
Were impotent to make my hopes put on 713 *Prelude* 9. 252
Do of itself blow fresh, and make the vanes 723 *Prelude* 10. 370
Thirsting to make the guardian crook of law 728 *Prelude* 11. 64
Justice, and make an end of Liberty. 728 *Prelude* 11. 73
And shall continue evermore to make, 735 *Prelude* 12. 86
And their impassioned sounds, which well might make 737 *Prelude* 12. 199
Proves to the most ; and called to make good search 742 *Prelude* 13. 174
My knowledge, as to make me capable 750 *Prelude* 14. 310
Have been laid open, needs must make me feel 752 *Prelude* 14. 422
Her temper had been framed, as if to make 764 *Excursion* 1. 517

Mankind 583 Man's

Manifold—*continued.*
A readier book of manifold contents, ... 393 *The Lovers 13
Of colours manifold and bright . . . . . 406 White Doe 956
For reasons dear and manifold— . . . . . 415 White Doe 1800
And hardships manifold did I endure, ... 470 †From early 7
For many a one hath virtues manifold, . . . 560 Cuck.and Night. 189
Of manifold pleasures and many desires : . . . 572 Avarice 26
From manifold distinctions, difference . . . . 646 Prelude 2. 299
And how through hardships manifold and long . 727 Prelude 10. 592
Attractions manifold ;—and this he chose. . . 761 Excursion 1. 337
Change manifold, for better or for worse : . . 803 Excursion 4. 125
For manifold privations ; he refers . . . . . 813 Excursion 4. 815
Through manifold degrees of guilt and shame ; . 818 Excursion 4. 1111
So manifold and various are the ways . . . . 818 Excursion 4. 1112
And bleatings manifold of mountain sheep, . . K.8. 245 Recluse 1.1.330
Love, knowledge, all my manifold delights . . K.8. 255 Recluse 1.1.697
Thy motions, intricate and manifold, ... K.8. 301 *And oh 7
Mankind. To make mankind merry for evermore, . 60 Bord. 1272
Thou didst command me to bless all mankind ; . 75 Bord. 2173
That, while the generations of mankind . . . 152 *Forth from 19
Fleet as the generations of mankind, ... 230 Clouds 38
"There was a time when all mankind . . . . 237 P. B. 121
Becoming that mankind should learn . . . . 291 Rob Roy 82
To chase mankind, with men in armies packed . 313 *Go back 12
Our virtue, and to vindicate mankind. . . . . 315 *The Land 14
More for mankind at this unhappy day . . . 315 *Alas ! what 13
Against the life of virtue in mankind ; . . . . 330 Ode : Thanks. 106
Our ears, and near the dwellings of mankind ! . 336 Staub-bach 3
Mankind of yore were prompted to devise . . 346 Processions 6
Announcing, One was born mankind to free ; . . 351 Des. Stanzas 70
From Sages justly honoured by mankind ; . . 435 Ecc. Sonn. 2. 27. 2
Of Science laid them open to mankind— . . . 461 *Queen of 41
Upon the proud enslavers of mankind ! . . . 464 Derwent 14
Foremost in freedom, noblest of mankind ? . . 505 Warning 143
Broken with all mankind, solicit death. . . . 518 Pun. Death 3. 14
Issuing in pomp, shall come to judge mankind. . 534 *When in 16
And eke His Mother, honour of Mankind : . . 555 Prioress 168
O rest, thou doleful Mother of Mankind !" . . 581 Invoc. Earth 2
"False Parent of Mankind ! . . . . 582 Invoc. Earth 19
By reverence for the rights of all mankind. . . 587 Crosth. 12
Amid the fretful dwellings of mankind . . . 636 Prelude 1. 279
Of all mankind, who covets not at times . . . 642 Prelude 2. 23
Be many, and a blessing to mankind. . . . . 648 Prelude 2. 471
But all the meditations of mankind, ... 666 Prelude 5. 38
And universal reason of mankind, ... 683 Prelude 6. 546
Now, fixed amid that concourse of mankind . . 688 Prelude 7. 69
Shape for mankind, by principles as fixed, . . 698 Prelude 7. 754
Among mankind he was in service bound,. . . 714 Prelude 9. 304
To all mankind. But, these things set apart, . 717 Prelude 9. 532
Hereafter brought in charge against mankind. . 724 Prelude 10. 396
To suit my ends ; I moved among mankind . . 729 Prelude 11. 155
This sorrowful reverse for all mankind. . . . 733 Prelude 11. 404
With most delight the passions of mankind, . . 742 Prelude 13. 164
May boldly take his way among mankind . . . 744 Prelude 13. 296
And with the generations of mankind . . . . 747 Prelude 14. 109
In life among the passions of mankind, . . . 750 Prelude 14. 325
For my excuse. Dissevered from mankind, . . 782 Excursion 2. 732
And these were the first parents of mankind : . 789 Excursion 3. 243
Permitted to descend, and bless mankind. . . 797 Excursion 3. 758
For the gross spirit of mankind,—the one . . . 799 Excursion 3. 911
By which mankind now suffers, is most just. . . 805 Excursion 4. 304
That spirit only can redeem mankind ; . . . 806 Excursion 4. 317
And countless generations of mankind . . . . 812 Excursion 4. 761
That shines for him, and shines for all mankind. . 813 Excursion 4. 810
The generations of mankind have knelt . . . 827 Excursion 5. 338
And from the private struggles of mankind . . 835 Excursion 5. 852
For their dear countrymen, and all mankind. . . 839 Excursion 6. 73
Manliness. Of manliness and freedom) all conspired 662 Prelude 4. 286
Manly. Luke had a manly heart ; but at these words 136 Michael 357
And know that noble feelings, manly powers, . . 308 *There is a bondage 11
But manly sovereignty its hold retains ; . . . 425 Ecc. Sonn. 1. 27. 8
Of rational and manly sympathy. . . . . . 455 *Not in the lucid 19
Of manly virtues, mildly bright, ... 503 *Like a 71
But each of manly sex, a docile page, ... 624 Æneid 68
To mix the manly brown with silver grey, . . 842 Excursion 6. 278
Whether through manly instinct to conceal . . 871 Excursion 7. 904
Manna. Like showers of manna, if they come at all : 493 Hap. War. 44
For manna, take a lesson from the dog . . . 732 Prelude 11. 363
Manner. This was the manner in which Vaudracour 125 V. and J. 262
This, and the manner, and the voice, ... 179 Waggoner 3. 132
Some with their notes another manner feigned ; . 558 Cuck.and Night. 74
Do I perceive her manner, and her look, . . . 768 Excursion 1. 781
In manner of a bird that takes delight . . . . K.8. 245 Recluse 1.1.322
State in humbler manner keep . . . . . . L.2. 190 *Queen and 4
Manners. Of manners, like its viewless fence, . . 154 Flower Garden 47
And so were better manners bred, ... 179 Waggoner 3. 108
Poor in estate, of manners base, men of the multitude, ... 189 Star-gazers 22
O the charm that manners draw, ... 222 Triad 154
And give us manners, virtue, freedom, power. . 307 *Milton ! thou 8
Hail, ancient Manners ! sure defence, ... 376 *The Minstrels 55
All speak of manners withering to the root, . . 388 *The pibroch's 8
A land where gentle manners ruled . . . . . 390 Highland Broach 7
Of good, o'er manners arts and arms, diffused : . 429 Ecc. Sonn. 2. 2. 11
Firm self-denial, manners grave and staid, . . 515 Penn. 2
From thy mild manners quietly exhaled. . . . 575 Chiabrera 8. 24
His graceful manners, and the temperate ray . . 583 *With copious 9
The gentler manners of the private dome ; . . 619 School Ex. 90
Time, place, and manners do I seek, and these . 634 Prelude 1. 158
(How could we less ?) the manners and the ways . 656 Prelude 3. 533

Manners—*continued.*
And manners finely wrought, the delicate race . 657 Prelude 3. 560
Of manners put to school I took small note, . . 663 Prelude 4. 302
And manners which my childhood looked upon . 701 Prelude 8. 160
Coarse manners, vulgar passions, that beat in . 704 Prelude 8. 320
Manners and characters discriminate, ... 706 Prelude 8. 499
Of manners and familiar incidents, ... 708 Prelude 8. 621
Domestic manners, customs, gestures, looks, . . 711 Prelude 9. 83
By manners studied and elaborate ; . . . . 742 Prelude 13. 191
More wise desires, and simpler manners ;—nurse . 755 Recluse 1. 1. 857
Their manners, their enjoyments, and pursuits, . 761 Excursion 1. 342
Speech, manners, morals, all without disguise. . 775 Excursion 2. 266
Of simple manners, feelings unsuppressed . . . 824 Excursion 5. 118
Two sets of manners could the Youth put on ; . 842 Excursion 6. 289
And unaffecting manners might at once . . . 847 Excursion 6. 578
If mild discourse, and manners that conferred . 850 Excursion 6. 793
His gentle manners : and his peaceful smiles, . . 864 Excursion 7. 460
Conciliatory manners and smooth speech ; . . 875 Excursion 8. 64
Her simple manners, and the stable worth . . 877 Excursion 8. 237
Resumed the manners of his happier days ; . . 882 Excursion 8. 527
Old Michael's manners and discourse, and thus . K.8. 228 *I will 109
Untainted manners ; born among the hills, . . K.8. 246 Recluse 1.1.348
But ye who make our manners laws, and hence . L.1. 97 Juvenal 3. 75
Man-of-war. A gallant stately Man-of-war, . . 177 Waggoner 2. 107
Manorial. And one a turreted manorial hall . . 824 Excursion 5. 124
Man's.
To soothe and cheer the poor man's solitude. . . 13 Desc. Sk. 142
Nor taper glimmered dim from sick man's room ; 26 Guilt 142
More of man's thoughts and ways than his experience 38 Bord. 35
To end her wrongs. But if the blind Man's tale . 38 Bord. 72
To bear a part in this Man's punishment, . . . 49 Bord. 649
Of this Man's crimes beyond the reach of thought ? 51 Bord. 781
This man's the property of him who best . . . 53 Bord. 874
As if the blind Man's dog were pulling at it. . . 55 Bord. 966
The least of which would beat out a man's brains ; 56 Bord. 1008
Though it were tottering over a man's head, . . 67 Bord. 1659
Man's intellectual empire. We subsist . . . 70 Bord. 1856
Of that old Man's forgiveness on thy heart, . . 77 Bord. 2297
Nor emblem of our hopes : the dead man's home 98 Brothers 172
And that the old Man's heart seemed born again ? 134 Michael 203
The old Man's grief broke from him ; to his heart . 137 Michael 421
Ran with a young man's speed ; and yet the voice 146 *It was an 3
And an eye practised like a blind man's touch. . 151 *When, to 83
Becomes an echo of man's misery. . . . . . 153 Morn. Ex. 6
Not shunning man's abode, though shy, . . . 165 Parrot 31
But in Man's fortunes. Hence a thousand tales . 170 *Never enlivened 18
'Twere worth a wise man's while to try . . . 177 Waggoner 2. 72
She had a tall man's height or more ; . . . . 190 Beggars 1
The old Man's shape, and speech—all troubled me : 197 Resolution 128
For shelter, and a poor man's bread ! . . . . 204 Brougham 79
As is a landscape to a blind man's eye : . . . 206 Tintern 24
On that best portion of a good man's life, . . . 206 Tintern 33
"The end of man's existence I discerned, . . . 211 Laod. 111
Display august of man's inheritance, ... 219 *This Height 33
Of man's enquiring gaze, but to his hope . . . 226 Vernal Ode 29
And type of man's far-darting reason, therefore . 231 Clouds 81
The blind man's gloom, exalts the veteran's mirth ; 233 Power of Sound 50
O Silence ! are Man's noisy years . . . . . 235 Power of Sound 217
And now among the dead man's hair . . . . 242 P. B. 574
A faith that for the dead man's sake, ... 243 P. B. 661
Perplexed the good man's gentle soul. . . . . 244 P. B. 755
Thought Peter, 'tis the poor man's home. . . . 247 P. B. 996
That man's heart is a holy thing ; . . . . . 248 P. B. 1072
Heed not the pillage of man's ancient heart. . . 255 S. H. 14
Disparaging Man's gifts, and proper food. . . . 263 *Those words 8
Though narrow be that old Man's cares, and near, 267 *Though narrow 1
In man's perturbèd soul thy sway benign ; . . . 269 *Pure element 10
That cry can reach ; and to the sick man's room 273 *Not the 7
Thou com'st to man's abode the spot grew dearer 281 *What strong 3
For thou wert still the poor man's stay, . . . 292 Rob Roy 109
The poor man's heart, the poor man's hand ; . . 292 Rob Roy 110
Devised out of a sick man's dream ! . . . . . 300 Bran 26
Of that Man's mind—what can it be ? what food 304 *I grieved 3
And love, and man's unconquerable mind. . . . 305 Toussaint 14
Fade, and participate in man's decline. . . . 308 *There is a bondage 14
And thou henceforth wilt have a good man's calm, 313 Clarkson 12
A great man's happiness ; thy zeal shall find . . 313 Clarkson 13
For its own honour, on man's suffering heart. . 321 *Here pause 6
As were performed in man's heroic prime ; . . 325 Ode 1814 141
Bestowed by Nature, or from man's great deeds . 352 Aquap. 6
Appointed by man's common heritage, ... 354 Aquap. 92
St. Francis, far from Man's resort, to abide . . 362 *List—'twas 37
How subtly works man's weakness, sighs may heave 363 *The world forsaken 7
Man's headstrong violence and Time's fleetness, . 366 *Ye Trees 16
And, though the passions of man's fretful race . 367 Trajan 7
Who ne'er embittered any good man's chalice. . 370 Eg. Maid 96
Whether the rich man's sumptuous gate . . . 375 *The Minstrels 33
Aimed at the White Man's ignorance the while, . 380 Duddon 16. 5
Beneath a loving old Man's view. . . . . . 401 White Doe 502
"An old man's privilege, I take : . . . . . 408 White Doe 1078
They might deserve a good Man's blame ; . . . 409 White Doe 1224
His wing who could seem lovelier to man's eye . 421 Ecc. Sonn. 1. 13. 6
"Man's life is like a Sparrow, mighty King ! . . 422 Ecc. Sonn. 1. 16. 1
And prayer, man's rational prerogative, . . . 436 Ecc. Sonn. 2. 33. 13
But theirs the wise man's ordinary lot, . . . 438 Ecc. Sonn. 2. 40. 12
As a last token of man's toilsome day ! . . . 453 *Calm is the 32
(By transit not unlike man's frequent doom) . . 461 *Who but is 13
In man's intelligence sublimed by grace ? . . . 466 St. Bees 31
In her esteem the thirst that wrought man's fall, 469 *Desire we 5

Man's—*continued.*
Her lawful offspring in Man's art; and Time, . 477 *Steamboats* 11
Discourse was deemed Man's noblest attribute, . 489 *Illus. Books* 1
Omen of man's grievous doom! . . . . . 502 **Like a* 12
Man's feverish passions, His pure light of love, 505 *Warning* 135
An altar is in each man's cot, ... 506 *Lab. Hymn* 18
The bad man's restless walk, and haunt his bed— 518 *Pun. Death* 6. 2
If for deliberate shedder of man's blood . . . 518 *Pun. Death* 6. 13
Attained a stature twice a tall man's height, . . 521 *Epist.Beaumont* 15
And sympathy with man's substantial griefs— 538 **In desultory* 41
A poor Man's counsel take; . . . . . . 542 *Russ. Fug.* 82
Which ever to man's ear a passage won. . . . 558 *Cuck. and Night.* 85
He may full soon go with an old man's hair. . . 560 *Cuck.andNight.*180
Within the old Man's hat; nor quits him so, . . 566 *Cumb. Beg.* 29
Lifting the boy to man's estate, had called . . 585 *Ch. Lamb* 89
That hath kept watch o'er man's mortality; . . 590 *Immortality* 202
Bloom'd with the snow-drops of Man's narrow bed, 613 *Desc.Sk.Quarto* 595
Soon after, this man's Ghost unto him came . . 623 **I find* 6
Recesses in man's heart, immortal verse . . . 635 *Prelude* 1. 232
A channel paved by man's officious care. . . . 659 *Prelude* 4. 56
A span above man's common measure, tall, . . 664 *Prelude* 4. 392
Stringed like a poor man's heifer at its feed, . . 669 *Prelude* 5. 240
Confession of man's weakness and his loves. . . 690 *Prelude* 7. 239
Grows tedious even in a young man's ear. . . . 694 *Prelude* 7. 511
For the Man's sake, could feed at Nature's call . 706 *Prelude* 8. 456
Feelingly watched, might teach Man's haughty race 734 *Prelude* 12. 12
Nor heedeth Man's perverseness; Spring returns,— 734 *Prelude* 12. 32
Employed, and man's unfolding intellect: . . . 735 *Prelude* 12. 101
Of life: the hiding-places of man's power . . . 738 *Prelude* 12. 279
If man's estate, by doom of Nature yoked . . 742 *Prelude* 13. 175
Moreover, each man's Mind is to herself . . . 745 *Prelude* 13. 366
Of garrulous age; nor did the sick man's tale, . 762 *Excursion* 1. 418
Why should a tear be on an old Man's cheek? . 765 *Excursion* 1. 598
An ordinary sorrow of man's life, ... 765 *Excursion* 1. 637
Man's only dwelling, sole appointed seat, . . . 777 *Excursion* 2. 362
By this, the book was in the old Man's hand; . 778 *Excursion* 2. 468
'Inhuman!'—said I, 'was an old Man's life . 783 *Excursion* 2. 791
Broke from the happy old Man's reverend lip; . 787 *Excursion* 3. 76
Of Man's existence, and recast the world, . . . 791 *Excursion* 3. 337
As the prime object of a wise man's aim, . . . 791 *Excursion* 3. 362
At once, all traces from the good Man's heart . 816 *Excursion* 4. 1013
In man's celestial spirit; virtue thus . . . . 817 *Excursion* 4. 1071
Adorns, in which the good Man's ancestors . . 824 *Excursion* 5. 125
And man's substantial life. If this mute earth . 826 *Excursion* 5. 250
In man's autumnal season is set forth . . . . 828 *Excursion* 5. 404
Do tend their flocks) partake man's general lot . 829 *Excursion* 5. 427
This is the wise man's sigh; how far we err— . 831 *Excursion* 5. 591
This is the good man's not unfrequent pang! . 831 *Excursion* 5. 592
The old Man's cheek; but, at this closing turn . 832 *Excursion* 5. 623
By the bright fire, the good Man's form, and face 834 *Excursion* 5. 779
For Man's affections—else betrayed and lost, . . 837 *Excursion* 5. 1006
The good man's purposes and deeds; retrace . . 863 *Excursion* 7. 376
Was wasted on the good Man's living ear, . . . 864 *Excursion* 7. 478
By man's imperishable spirit, quelled. . . . . 865 *Excursion* 7. 530
"This qualified respect, the old Man's due, . . 866 *Excursion* 7. 587
How art thou blighted for the poor Man's heart! 878 *Excursion* 8. 264
Defended, and appropriate to man's need. . . S.3. 433 **The doubt* 36
And that the old man's heart seem'd born again? K.8. 226 **I will* 83
A stranger long; nor will the blind man's guide, . K.8. 250*Recluse* 1.1.512
From year to year, not shunning Man's abode, . K.8. 251*Recluse* 1.1.538
These freaks are worse than any sick man's dream. L.1. 88 *Juvenal* 1. 2

Mansion. Such tale of this lone mansion she had learned, ... 27 *Guilt* 181
Straight from her osier mansion near . . . . 168 *Turtledove* 3
My mansion with its arbour shall endure;— . . 201 *Hart-leap* 74
These were the bower; and here a mansion stood, 202 *Hart-leap* 127
Shall be a mansion for all lovely forms, . . . 207 *Tintern* 140
Chatsworth! thy stately mansion, and the pride . 275 **Chatsworth! thy* 1
This Mansion and these pleasant bowers, . . . 402 *White Doe* 547
The lordly Mansion of its pride . . . . . . 413 *White Doe* 1575
To the neat mansion, where, his flock among, . 444 *Ecc. Sonn.* 3. 18. 3
From her religious Mansion of St. Bees. . . . 466 *St. Bees* 54
Hence, when yon mansion and the flowery trim . 546 **Oft is* 5
Of thy trim Mansion destined soon to blaze . . 548 **Stranger! this* 30
Consorting in one mansion unreproved. . . . 663 *Prelude* 4. 343
As in a mansion like their proper home, . . . 674 *Prelude* 5. 600
A mansion visited (as fame reports) . . . . 678 *Prelude* 6. 207
As toward the sacred mansion we advanced, . . 681 *Prelude* 6. 423
A dreary mansion, large beyond all need, . . . 684 *Prelude* 6. 645
Of a large mansion or hotel, a lodge . . . . 719 *Prelude* 10. 67
That round his mansion cast a sober gloom, . . 844 *Excursion* 6. 441
And, to his unmolested mansion, death . . . 861 *Excursion* 7. 244
They saw a mansion at his bidding rise, . . . 872 *Excursion* 7. 953
And, in that mansion, children of his own, . . 872 *Excursion* 7. 956
The Pastor's mansion with the house of prayer. . 881 *Excursion* 8. 458
Around the mansion and its whole domain; . . 882 *Excursion* 8. 540
One family, and one mansion; to themselves . . K.8. 253*Recluse* 1.1.619

Mansion's. And at the mansion's silent door, . . 402 *White Doe* 590
The mansion's self displayed;—a reverend pile . 881 *Excursion* 8. 461

Mansions. Comfort by prouder mansions unbestowed 34 *Guilt* 525
Their mansions unsusceptible of change, . . . 227 *Vernal Ode* 72
The stars are mansions built by Nature's hand, . . 266 **The stars* 1
From your first mansions, exiled all too long . . 325 *Ode 1814* 113
Bright liquid mansions, fashioned to endure . . 379 *Duddon* 12. 7
In the dark mansions of the bigot's soul, . . . 618 *School Ex.* 34
And from the mansions where our youth was taught. 814 *Excursion* 4. 896
Who, from their lowly mansions hither brought, . 832 *Excursion* 5. 652

Mantle. Thy royal mantle worn: . . . . . 104 *Artegal* 135
A mantle, to her very feet . . . . 190 *Beggars* 4
In hooded mantle, limping o'er the plain, . . . 321 **Humanity, delighting* 5

Mantle—*continued.*
When winter the grove of its mantle bereaves, . . 340 *Fort Fuentes* 10
And stood, far-kenned by mantle furred with ermine, ... 373 *Eg. Maid* 308
That very mantle on a day of glory, ... 373 *Eg. Maid* 314
Sceptre and mantle, sword and ring, laid down . 428 *Ecc. Sonn.* 1. 37. 11
Time a chequered mantle wears— . . . . . 628 *Installation* 25
A mantle such as Spanish Cavaliers . . . . 661 *Prelude* 4. 221
Enwrought upon thy mantle; satisfied . . . 707 *Prelude* 8. 534
Mantle upon his cheek. Is this the form, . . . 879 *Excursion* 8. 315

Mantled. And mantled o'er with aboriginal turf . 847 *Excursion* 6. 609

Mantle's. Her plumy mantle's living hues, . . . 165 *Parrot* 9
Or by his mantle's help to find . . . . . . 404 *White Doe* 774
Time, in his mantle's sunniest fold . . . . . 629 *Installation* 41

Mantles. As sound—blithe race! whose mantles were bedecked . . . . 790 *Excursion* 3. 249

Mantling. Close by her mantling wings' embraces prest. . . . . 6 *Ev. Wk.* 231
Mantling in the tiny square. . . . . 161 **Pleasures newly* 24
Behold! the mantling spirit of reserve . . . 212 *Dion*
The mantling triumphs of a day too blest. . . 255 **Grief, thou* 14
While the warm hearth exalts the mantling ale, . 379 *Duddon* 13. 12

Manx-harvest. For the old Manx-harvest to the Deep repair, ... 522 *Epist.Beaumont* 74

Many. In many a whistling circle wheels her flight; 4 *Ev. Wk.* 91
By many a votive death-cross planted near, . . 14 *Desc. Sk.* 202
For many a marvellous victory renowned, . . 18 *Desc. Sk.* 450
What marvel then if many a Wanderer sigh, . . 21 *Desc. Sk.* 584
Fixing his downcast eye, he many an hour . . 23 *Yew-tree* 30
But faded, and stuck o'er with many a patch and shred. . . . . 24 *Guilt* 9
A Sailor he, who many a wretched hour . . . 25 *Guilt* 48
'Mid the green mountains many a thoughtless song 28 *Guilt* 246
And many perished in the whirlwind's sweep. . 29 *Guilt* 292
And, after many interruptions short . . . . 31 *Guilt* 385
Of many things which never troubled me— . . 31 *Guilt* 391
Mocked me with many a strange fantastic shape!— 39 *Bord.* 112
Where now we dwell.—For many years I bore . 41 *Bord.* 202
We must not part,—I have measured many a league 42 *Bord.* 297
Was of Kirkoswald—many a snowy winter . . 46 *Bord.* 512
Nor be its witness? I had many hopes . . . 49 *Bord.* 650
Of many autumns in the cave had piled. . . . 50 *Bord.* 706
I would have given, not many minutes gone, . . 53 *Bord.* 858
So you bethought you of the many ways . . . 61 *Bord.* 1289
Thou wilt have many guides if thou art innocent; 63 *Bord.* 1409
My Friends, his heart shall have as many wounds 64 *Bord.* 1460
Did my pride tame my pride;—for many days, . 68 *Bord.* 1697
The same dead calm, continued many days. . . 69 *Bord.* 1744
Have I lived many days—my sleep was bound . 69 *Bord.* 1791
Where, hid from me, he counted many years, . 71 *Bord.* 1893
Many there be whose eyes will not want cause . 78 *Bord.* 2324
We must spare them—here are many: . . . 79 *Foresight* 4
Pull as many as you can. . . . . 79 *Foresight* 10
As many will be blowing here. . . . . . . 80 *Foresight* 24
As if the wind blew many ways, ... 82 *Alice Fell* 5
With many a wanton stroke . . . . 83 *Lucy Gray* 26
And many a hill did Lucy climb: . . . . . 83 *Lucy Gray* 31
Her hair was thick with many a curl . . . . 83 *We are Seven* 7
How many may you be?" . . . . 83 *We are Seven* 14
"How many? Seven in all," she said, . . . 83 *We are Seven* 15
"How many are you, then," said I, ... 84 *We are Seven* 61
Many flocks were on the hills, but thou wert owned by none, ... 87 *Pet-lamb* 35
I think of thee with many fears . . . . . 88 *H. C.* 13
Through the bounds which many a star . . . 90 *Longest Day* 54
Far happier lot, dear Boy, than brings full many to this shrine; . . . . 92 *Poet's Dream* 54
Give to Him prayers, and many thoughts, in thy most busy days; . . . . 93 *Poet's Dream* 58
Many a captive hath she rescued, ... 94 *Westmoreland Girl* 55
Many a long look of wonder: and at last, . . . 95 *Brothers* 30
Of many darling pleasures, and the love . . . 96 *Brothers* 71
(For many years ago I passed this road) . . . 97 *Brothers* 132
As many of their betters—and for Leonard! . . 99 *Brothers* 280
Had done so many offices about him, ... 100 *Brothers* 334
And many, many happy days were his. . . . 100 *Brothers* 346
Of a vast building made of many crags; . . . 101 *Brothers* 365
You say that he saw many happy years? . . . 101 *Brothers* 384
Grew many a poisonous weed; . . . . . . 102 *Artegal* 30
In many a court, and many a warrior's tent, . . 103 *Artegal* 84
He landed; and by many dangers scared, . . 103 *Artegal* 91
Full many a time, upon a stormy night, . . . 107 *Indolence* 13
Yourself; and many did to him repair,— . . 108 *Indolence* 53
For I had many things to say. . . . . . . 114 *Ind. Wom.* 50
And I may say, that many a time . . . . . 115 *Last of Flock* 67
"I had a Son, who many a day . . . . . 119 *Sailor's Mother* 20
He kept it: many voyages . . . . 119 *Sailor's Mother* 27
I'll tell him many tales of Thee." . . . . . 121 *EmigrantMother* 95
So many bars between his present state . . . 122 *V. and J.* 58
With many a most diverting thing, ... 127 *Idiot Boy* 125
And thence full many a sound she hears, . . . 127 *Idiot Boy* 140
And many dreadful fears beset her, ... 130 *Idiot Boy* 413
Amid the heart of many thousand mists, . . . 132 *Michael* 59
So many incidents upon his mind . . . . . 132 *Michael* 68
With two brave sheep-dogs tried in many a storm, 132 *Michael* 91
Who, out of many, chose the trusty boy . . . 135 *Michael* 265
These thoughts, and many others of like sort, . 135 *Michael* 271
With many tasks that were resigned to thee: . 137 *Michael* 392
With many hopes; it should be so—yes—yes— . 137 *Michael* 398
So, many months passed on: and once again . . 138 *Michael* 437

Mass—*continued.*
Before the altar while the Mass doth last : . . . 555 *Prioress* 185
Spotting the steaming deeps, to early mass ; . . 604 *Desc.Sk.Quarto* 145
And of some other Being. A rude mass . . . 642 *Prelude* 2. 33
Or linked them to some feeling : the great mass . 651 *Prelude* 3. 130
Between the show, and many-headed mass . . 693 *Prelude* 7. 434
That huge fermenting mass of human-kind . . 696 *Prelude* 7. 621
Till the whole cave, so late a senseless mass, . . 707 *Prelude* 8. 580
And ocean's liquid mass, in gladness lay . . 759 *Excursion* 1. 202
Enclosed between an upright mass of rock . . 777 *Excursion* 2. 414
A mass of rock, resembling, as it lay . . . . 787 *Excursion* 3. 52
Massacre. Of massacre, in which the senseless sword 719 *Prelude* 10. 43
Massacres. I thought of those September massacres, 719 *Prelude* 10. 73
Massed. Abodes of men irregularly massed . . . 876 *Excursion* 8. 123
Masses. The solace beads and masses yield, . . 478 *Somnamb.* 53
Masses of every shape and size, that lay . . 835 *Excursion* 5. 865
Massier. Beneath a massier Highland Broach. . . 391 *Highland Broach* 48
Massy. Of massy gloom and radiance bold.. . . 180 *Waggoner* 4. 56
Massy and black, before him lay ; . . . . . 240 *P. B.* 357
And massy grove, so near yon blazing town, . . 349 *Sky-prosp.* 7
Is that embattled House, whose massy Keep . . 382 *Duddon* 27. 3
The silver Broach of massy frame, ... 390 *Highland Broach* 19
Speak Thou, whose massy strength and stature scorn . . . . 477 *Long Meg* 5
The massy Ways, carried across these heights . 549 **The massy* 1
Erelong, the massy roof above his head, . . . 707 *Prelude* 8. 566
Shrine, altar, image, and the massy piles . . . 814 *Excursion* 4. 899
But large and massy ; for duration built ; . . . 824 *Excursion* 5. 145
Stretched on his bier—that massy timber wain ; . 865 *Excursion* 7. 548
Rose the slim ash and massy sycamore, . . . 881 *Excursion* 8. 478
Supporting gracefully a massy dome . . . . 891 *Excursion* 9. 500
Mast. *See* **Gibbet-mast.**
A thought resigned with pain, when from the mast 31 *Guilt* 354
And so, flag flying at mast head, ... 178 *Waggoner* 2. 162
Long is it as a barber's pole, or mast of little boat, 189 *Star-gazers* 3
Nor mount the mast, nor row, nor float . . . 295 *Highland Boy* 83
A crimson splendour : lowly is the mast . . . 384 *Duddon* 33. 3
By the strong sunbeams smitten. Like a mast . 773 *Excursion* 2. 133
Upon the tall mast streaming. But, ye Powers . 798 *Excursion* 3. 842
Her strong knee-timbers, and the mast that bears 866 *Excursion* 7. 604
Master. *See* **Task-master.**
Hunts, where his master points, the intercepted flocks. . . . . 5 *Ev. Wk.* 185
And lustily the master carved the bread, . . . 34 *Guilt* 530
Be cautious, my dear Master ! I perceive . . 37 *Bord.* 21
Dear Master ! gratitude's a heavy burden . . 38 *Bord.* 30
What life is this of ours, how sleep will master . 45 *Bord.* 419
He does his Master credit. As I live, ... 45 *Bord.* 459
You are now in truth my Master ; you have taught me . . . . 64 *Bord.* 1480
Of a tyrannic Master whom they loathed. . . . 69 *Bord.* 1759
The goal is reached. My Master shall become 73 *Bord.* 2038
There will be need of preparation. Master ! . . 74 *Bord.* 2110
Of which I have been proud. O my poor Master ! 78 *Bord.* 2321
"O Master ! we are seven." . . . . . . 84 *We are Seven* 64
For that her Master never uttered word . . 125 *V. and J.* 292
Went up to London, found a master there, . . 135 *Michael* 264
Another Master. Heaven forgive me, Luke, . . 137 *Michael* 380
Yes, let my master fume and fret, ... 174 *Waggoner* 1. 116
Cannot shield thee from thy Master, ... 181 *Waggoner* 4. 122
For the Master sees, alas ! . . . . 181 *Waggoner* 4. 157
With eager eyes the Master pries ; . . . . . 181 *Waggoner* 4. 171
O Master ! it has been a cruel leap. . . . . 203 *Hart-leap* 144
To see her Master and to cheer— . . . . . 204 *Brougham* 53
And a true master of the glowing strain, . . . 231 **The gentlest Poet* 2
Sweeps his harp, the Master rides ; . . . . 234 *Power of Sound* 141
"No doubt," quoth he, "he is the Master . . 243 *P. B.* 584
No master spirit, no determined road ; . . . 307 **Great men* 13
A Roman Master stands on Grecian ground, . . 312 **A Roman* 1
The Master of whose humble board . . . . 414 *White Doe* 1690
Pass from their Master, sojourned here to guard . 419 *Ecc. Sonn.* 1. 2. 13
Issues the master Mind, at whose fell swoop . . 425 *Ecc. Sonn.* 1. 28. 7
To each new Master, like a steer or hound, . . 429 *Ecc. Sonn.* 2. 4. 4
That master them. How enviably blest . . . 438 *Ecc. Sonn.* 2. 37. 12
Rare master has it been thy lot to know ; . . . 489 *Spade* 5
On his morning rounds the Master . . . . 490 *Incident : Dog* 1
Strong as could then be borne. A Master meek . 518 *Pun. Death* 7. 5
The Master died, his drooping servant's grief . . 523 *Epist. Beaumont* 133
With such a master would I never be ; . . . 560 *Cuck.and Night.* 201
His fields seemed to know what their Master was doing; . . . . 569 *Farmer* 18
Broods like the Day, a Master o'er a Slave, . . 589 *Immortality* 119
He passed—nor was I master of my eyes . . 649 *Prelude* 3. 11
The trunk and every master branch were green . 676 *Prelude* 6. 81
Of a new master ; bleat the flocks aloud. . . 699 *Prelude* 8. 24
As of a lord and master, or a power, . . . 703 *Prelude* 8. 258
Master my fancy while I wandered on . . . . 716 *Prelude* 9. 464
The mind is lord and master—outward sense . 737 *Prelude* 12. 222
To a kind master on a distant farm . . . 767 *Excursion* 1. 761
Thought I, if master of a vacant hour, . . . 787 *Excursion* 3. 44
"What other yearning was the master tie . . 791 *Excursion* 3. 392
Or late, a perilous master. He—who oft, . . 844 *Excursion* 6. 439
Of Time's eternal Master, and that peace, . . 846 *Excursion* 6. 520
By some accomplished Master, while he sate . . 857 *Excursion* 7. 12
In vain, if he were master of their fate ; . . . 867 *Excursion* 7. 623
With scantiest knowledge, master of all truth . 895 *Excursion* 9. 736
He, happy man ! is master of the field, . . . K.8. 247 *Recluse* 1.1.382
Master-bias. Is yet a Soul whose master-bias leans 494 *Hap. War.* 59
Master-current. The master-current of her brain . 194 *Ruth* 212
Mastered. Over material forms that mastered reason. 139 *Widow* 27

Mastered—*continued.*
Are mastered by the breathing haze ; . . . . 167 *Pilgrim's Dream* 37
As indignation mastered grief, my tongue . . . 367 **As indignation* 1
But both will soon be mastered, and the copse . 455 *Rydal Mere* 5
And difficulty mastered, with resolve . . . 541 *Grace Darl.* 77
His temper was quite mastered by the times, . . 711 *Prelude* 9. 143
Masterful. An instant kiss of masterful desire— . 433 *Ecc. Sonn.* 2. 20. 8
Master-idol. To Gain, the master-idol of the realm, 877 *Excursion* 8. 184
Master-light. Are yet a master-light of all our seeing ; 589 *Immortality* 156
Master-pamphlets. With care, the master-pamphlets of the day ; . . . . 711 *Prelude* 9. 97
Masterpiece. A pretty prospect this, a masterpiece 60 *Bord.* 1275
Stood with eyes fixed upon that masterpiece, . . 509 *F. Stone* 107
Master's. Let the Steed glory while his Master's hand 278 *Wellington* 3
His master's hands in sign of bliss, ... 297 *Highland Boy* 229
Of Neville, at their Master's call . . . . . 403 *White Doe* 695
Labouring as ever in your Master's sight, . . . 444 *Ecc. Sonn.* 3. 16. 6
Now near his master's house in open view . . 472 *Dunolly Eagle* 5
His Master's dead,—and no one now . . . . 483 *Simon Lee* 29
Or by his master's side : . . . . 492 *Fidelity* 61
Your Master's throne is set."—Deaf was the Sea ; 495 *Fact* 6
The Dirge which for our Master's sake . . . . 577 **I come* 27
A kerchief sprinkled with his master's blood, . . 778 *Excursion* 2. 478
Meanwhile the unsedentary Master's hand . . 860 *Excursion* 7. 193
Upon its Master's frame, a wintry grace ; . . . 860 *Excursion* 7. 207
Masters. *See* **Posture-masters.**
God bless and thank you both, my gentle Masters. 46 *Bord.* 526
I now perceive we do mistake our masters, . . 54 *Bord.* 908
Of the world's masters, with the musty rules . . 64 *Bord.* 1491
The prey or masters of our own past deeds. . . 65 *Bord.* 1522
Proclaim it, let your Masters hear . . . . . 402 *White Doe* 597
Nor were we ever masters of our wish. . . . . 672 *Prelude* 5. 476
Among the unthinking masters of the earth . . 761 *Excursion* 1. 380
Mastery. 'Tis vain to strive for mastery. . . . . 175 *Waggoner* 1. 137
Of reckless mastery, hitherto unknown. . . . 435 *Ecc. Sonn.* 2. 28. 14
With such fell mastery that a man may dare . . 518 *Pun. Death* 4. 2
And, with a resolute mastery shaking off . . . 730 *Prelude* 11. 238
By its inevitable mastery, ... 747 *Prelude* 14. 97
By mastery :—and the good Man lacked not friends 840 *Excursion* 6. 164
An intellectual mastery exercised . . . . . 877 *Excursion* 8. 201
Till perfect mastery crown the pains at last. . . 880 *Excursion* 8. 415
Mastiff. *See* **Jail-mastiff.**
A surly mastiff kennels at the gate, ... 60 *Bord.* 1249
The mastiff, from beneath the waggon, . . . 178 *Waggoner* 2. 150
The Mastiff wondering, and perplext . . . . 179 *Waggoner* 3. 60
The Mastiff, ill-conditioned carl ! . . . . . 179 *Waggoner* 3. 101
Salutes the Mastiff on the head ; . . . . . 179 *Waggoner* 3. 107
Mastiff's. The Creature, by the Mastiff's side, . . 179 *Waggoner* 3. 59
By his noble Mastiff's side, ... 181 *Waggoner* 4. 163
A wound upon the Mastiff's head, ... 181 *Waggoner* 4. 174
Mast's. Survive upon the tall mast's height ; . . 579 **Sweet Flower* 47
Masts. That like to leaning masts of stranded ships appear. . . . . 18 *Desc. Sk.* 412
So said, so done ; and masts, sails, yards, . . . 178 *Waggoner* 2. 123
The skiffs with naked masts at anchor laid, . . 593 *Ev.Wk.Quarto* 105
Like leaning masts of stranded ships appear . . 611 *Desc.Sk.Quarto* 500
Match. The gloomy lantern, and the dim blue match, 32 *Guilt* 419
To match the spark of local fire, ... 167 *Pilgrim's Dream* 42
And I will mate and match him blissfully. . . 220 *Triad* 7
Better, if Reason's triumphs match with these, . 468 *St. Bees* 160
"Now, Matthew !" said I, "let us match . . 487 *Fountain* 9
Matched. *See* **Ill-matched, Well-matched.**
For matched with these shall policy prove vain, . 320 **Avaunt all* 13
Chosen for ornament—stone matched with stone . 378 *Duddon* 9. 5
Match'd with an equal number of like age, . . 624 *Æneid* 67
Is matched unequally with custom, time, . . . 804 *Excursion* 4. 206
Of two brave vessels matched in deadly fight, . K.8. 256 *Recluse* 1.1.722
Matchless. They sport beneath that mountain's matchless height . . . . 21 *Desc. Sk.* 577
Stood single, and, from matchless depth of shade, 133 *Michael* 166
Thy matchless courage I bewail no more, . . . 210 *Laod.* 50
O matchless perfidy ! portentous lust . . . . 214 *Dion* 106
A liquid concert matchless by nice Art, . . . 233 *Power of Sound* 47
See ! there she is, the matchless Earth ! . . . 237 *P. B.* 56
With matchless beams. . . . . ; 285 *Grave of Burns* 24
Thy matchless worth to all posterity. . . . . 316 **Hail, Zaragoza* 8
Whom I should choose for love and matchless labours. . . . . 372 *Eg. Maid* 228
The day when he achieved that matchless feat, . 373 *Eg. Maid* 315
I see a matchless blazonry unfurled . . . . 430 *Ecc. Sonn.* 2. 7. 10
Or Gehol's matchless gardens, for delight . . 700 *Prelude* 8. 77
They are matchless in story ; . . . . . . S.3. 440 **Said red-ribboned* 18

Mate. *See* **Co-mate, Helpmate.**
No mate, no comrade Lucy knew ; . . . . . 82 *Lucy Gray* 5
And, sooth to say, an apter Mate . . . . . 165 *Parrot* 13
There to the brooding bird her mate . . . . 168 *Wren's Nest* 21
Thee and thy mate and sister of the sky. . . . 172 *Infant Daughter* 45
Her Father took another Mate ; . . . . . 192 *Ruth* 2
Among the shepherd-grooms no mate . . . . 205 *Brougham* 114
Winds the mute Creature without visible Mate . 212 *Dion*
And I will mate and match him blissfully. . . 220 *Triad* 7
Am all unfit to be your mate. . . . . . . 237 *P. B.* 130
The joyous Woman is the Mate . . . . . . 294 *Jedbor.* 25
And cheers thy melancholy Mate ! . . . . . 294 *Jedbor.* 83
And, when she took unto herself a Mate, . . . 305 *Ven. Rep.* 7
No brother, no mate has he near him—while I . 484 **A plague* 26
Thee his loved servant, his inspiring mate ! . . 489 *Spade* 26
And to one purpose cleave, their Being's godlike mate ! . . . . 529 **Those breathing* 132
If long time from thy mate thou be, or far, . . 560 *Cuck.and Night.* 183

Me—*continued.*

The Spirit of Nature was upon me there; . . . 698 *Prelude* 7. 766
And Shepherds were the men that pleased me first; 701 *Prelude* 8. 128
His form hath flashed upon me, glorified . . . 703 *Prelude* 8. 269
To me became an index of delight, ... 703 *Prelude* 8. 280
Won from me those minute obeisances . . . 704 *Prelude* 8. 360
'Twas now for me a burnished silver shield . . 705 *Prelude* 8. 414
With vulgar men about me, trivial forms . . . 707 *Prelude* 8. 545
All that took place within me came and went . 707 *Prelude* 8. 557
Have pleased me, seeking knowledge at that time 708 *Prelude* 8. 599
Had never much delighted me. And less . . . 708 *Prelude* 8. 622
Weighed with me, could support the test of thought; 708 *Prelude* 8. 628
Of human life: Nature had led me on; . . . 709 *Prelude* 8. 679
France lured me forth; the realm that I had crossed 710 *Prelude* 9. 34
The wish to bring me over to their cause. . . . 712 *Prelude* 9. 197
That would have pleased me in more quiet times; 719 *Prelude* 10. 68
Pressed on me almost like a fear to come. . . . 719 *Prelude* 10. 72
Divided from me by one little month, ... 719 *Prelude* 10. 74
Erewhile my tuneful haunt? It pleased me more 721 *Prelude* 10. 244
My sorrow; for I brought with me the faith . . 722 *Prelude* 10. 257
That voice, ill requiem! seldom heard by me . . 723 *Prelude* 10. 327
To me came rarely charged with natural gifts, . 724 *Prelude* 10. 401
Changed, and the unbroken dream entangled me . 724 *Prelude* 10. 410
And holy passion overcame me first, ... 724 *Prelude* 10. 418
On me uplifted from the vantage-ground . . . 724 *Prelude* 10. 449
To mock me under such a strange reverse. . . 725 *Prelude* 10. 510
Fell from me in my own despite. But now . . 726 *Prelude* 10. 544
Would have loved me, as one not destitute . . 726 *Prelude* 10. 549
Yet, in me, confidence was unimpaired; . . . 727 *Prelude* 11. 7
To daunt me; in the People was my trust, . . 727 *Prelude* 11. 11
This intuition led me to confound . . . . . 727 *Prelude* 11. 18
To me, what an inheritance, new-fallen, . . . 729 *Prelude* 11. 146
That from the cradle had grown up with me, . . 729 *Prelude* 11. 170
This threw me first out of the pale of love; . . 729 *Prelude* 11. 176
Searched to its heart. Share with me, Friend! the wish . . . . 731 *Prelude* 11. 282
Maintained for me a saving intercourse . . . 732 *Prelude* 11. 341
She, in the midst of all, preserved me still . . 732 *Prelude* 11. 346
A Poet, made me seek beneath that name, . . 732 *Prelude* 11. 347
Assisted, led me back through opening day . . 732 *Prelude* 11. 352
Hath still upheld me, and upholds me now . . 732 *Prelude* 11. 356
To me the grief confined, that thou art gone . . 733 *Prelude* 11. 399
My own delights do scarcely seem to me . . . 733 *Prelude* 11. 408
What ye have done for me. The morning shines, 734 *Prelude* 12. 31
Maintained for me a secret happiness. . . . . 735 *Prelude* 12. 43
Trust the elevation which had made me one . . 735 *Prelude* 12. 61
Such strength in *me* as often held my mind . . 736 *Prelude* 12. 130
Roaming, I carried with me the same heart: . . 737 *Prelude* 12. 192
Disjoined me from my comrade; and, through fear 737 *Prelude* 12. 232
Return upon me almost from the dawn . . . 738 *Prelude* 12. 278
From moral purpose—early tutored me . . . 740 *Prelude* 13. 44
Ambitious projects, pleased me less; I sought . 741 *Prelude* 13. 61
And the world's tumult unto me could yield, . . 741 *Prelude* 13. 108
To me a heart-depressing wilderness; . . . . 741 *Prelude* 13. 115
Knowledge that step by step might lead me on . 742 *Prelude* 13. 132
Which lacked not voice to welcome me in turn: . 742 *Prelude* 13. 136
If future years mature me for the task, . . . 743 *Prelude* 13. 233
Where knowledge leads me: it shall be my pride 743 *Prelude* 13. 251
Rejoiced with them and me in those sweet sounds. 745 *Prelude* 13. 349
And yet a spirit, there for me enshrined . . . 750 *Prelude* 14. 270
My knowledge, as to make me capable . . . 750 *Prelude* 14. 310
That by endowments not from me withheld . . 751 *Prelude* 14. 357
Enabled me to pause for choice, and walk . . 751 *Prelude* 14. 360
He cleared a passage for me, and the stream . . 751 *Prelude* 14. 368
Whether to me shall be allotted life, ... 751 *Prelude* 14. 388
Have been laid open, needs must make me feel . 752 *Prelude* 14. 422
More deeply, yet enable me to bear . . . . 752 *Prelude* 14. 423
Fair trains of imagery before me rise, ... 755 *Recluse* 1. 1. 756
I sing:—'fit audience let me find though few!' . 755 *Recluse* 1. 1. 776
Pitches her tents before me as I move, . . . 755 *Recluse* 1. 1. 799
Of mighty Poets: upon me bestow . . . . 755 *Recluse* 1. 1. 840
Be with me;—so shall thy unfailing love . . . 755 *Recluse* 1. 1. 859
Guide, and support, and cheer me to the end!" . 755 *Recluse* 1. 1. 860
He by appointment waited for me here, . . . 757 *Excursion* 1. 50
He loved me; from a swarm of rosy boys . . 757 *Excursion* 1. 57
Singled out me, as he in sport would say, . . . 757 *Excursion* 1. 58
We sate—we walked; he pleased me with report 757 *Excursion* 1. 63
That sometimes his religion seemed to me . . 762 *Excursion* 1. 409
"Me," said I, "most doth it surprise, to find . 778 *Excursion* 2. 457
—For me, I looked upon the pair, well pleased: . 829 *Excursion* 5. 452
For me, the emotion scarcely was less strong . . 854 *Excursion* 6. 1055
The clouded moon, and calls me forth to stray . S.3. 417 **Sweet was* 13
Hath ruled my steps, and seals me to thy side, . S.3. 433 **The doubt* 14
To finer uses. They for me must cease; . . . S.3. 433 **The doubt* 21
Dost tempt me by disclosures exquisite . . . S.3. 434 **The doubt* 92
That your praise appears to me . . . . . . S.3. 438 **My Lord* 27
Lead me, or outward circumstance impels. . . K.8. 233 **Along the* 3
Since that day forth the place to him—*to me* . . K.8.237 *Recluse* 1.1. 46
Have been to me more bountiful than hope, . . K.8.238 *Recluse* 1.1. 69
To me hath been vouchsafed; among the bowers K.8.239 *Recluse* 1.1.104
Not upon me alone hath been bestowed, . . . K.8.243 *Recluse* 1.1.232
Me rich in many onward-looking thoughts, . . K.8.243 *Recluse* 1.1.233
Would lead me, I should whisper to myself; . . K.8.244 *Recluse* 1.1.276
Nor let me pass unheeded other loves . . . K.8.250 *Recluse* 1.1.502
To rouse me, and a hundred warblers more; . . K.8.250 *Recluse* 1.1.516
I would stand clear, but yet to me I feel . . . K.8.255 *Recluse* 1.1.674
Why do they teach me whom I thus revere? . . K.8.255 *Recluse* 1.1.680
Not even the nearest to me and most dear, . . K.8.255 *Recluse* 1.1.688
Forgive me if I add another claim, ... K.8.255 *Recluse* 1.1.692
All buried with me without monument . . . K.8.255 *Recluse* 1.1.698
As that which urged me to a daring feat. . . . K.8.256 *Recluse* 1.1.710

Me—*continued.*

But me hath Nature tamed, and bade to seek . K.8.256 *Recluse* 1.1.726
Hath dealt with me as with a turbulent stream, . K.8.256 *Recluse* 1.1.728
And Moore and Partridge stare me in the face. . L.1. 96 *Juvenal* 3. 60

Mead. Of low-hung vapour: on the freshened mead 14 *Desc. Sk.* 218
O'er lake and stream, mountain and flowery mead, 151 **Forth from* 5
Nor hushed be service from the lowing mead, . 235 *Power of Sound* 197
The mead is crossed—the quarry's mouth . . . 243 *P. B.* 607
For the blood-thirsty mead of Odin's riotous Hall. 359 **Complacent Fictions* 14
Mid-noon is past;—upon the sultry mead . . . 382 *Duddon* 24. 1
But what if One, through grove or flowery mead, 424 *Ecc. Sonn.* 1. 23. 1
Green dewy lights adorn the freshen'd mead, . . 607 *Desc.Sk.Quarto* 272
Take the live herbage from the mead, and strip . 790 *Excursion* 3. 308

Meadow. Of scattered herds, that in the meadow graze, ... 34 *Guilt* 521
The lambs that in the meadow go. . . . . . 81 †*Mother's Return* 44
A little field of meadow ground; . . . . . 240 *P. B.* 367
But field or meadow name it not; . . . . . 240 *P. B.* 368
Of the green meadow hangs his head . . . . 240 *P. B.* 394
A sweeter meadow ne'er was seen, ... 243 *P. B.* 603
The sweets of Burn-mill meadow; . . . . . 293 *Yarrow Unv.* 42
And down the meadow ranging, ... 386 *Yarrow Rev.* 34
Or in the meadow wandered wide! . . . . . 415 *White Doe* 1733
Such are thoughts!—A wind-swept meadow . . 550 *Hermit's Cell* 3. 5
At Woodstock, on the meadow green and gay. . 562 *Cuck.andNight.*285
And turnips, and corn-land, and meadow, and lea, 569 *Farmer* 19
There was a time when meadow, grove, and stream, 587 *Immortality* 1
Rang loud through the meadow and wood. . . 620 *Convict* 4
When to a convent in a meadow green, . . . 716 *Prelude* 9. 466
A meadow carpet for the dancing hours. . . . 830 *Excursion* 5. 551
From the flat meadow lonely there. . . . . K.8. 263 **The Lake* 10

Meadow-flower. How does the Meadow-flower its bloom unfold? . . . . 277 **A Poet* 9

Meadow-flowers. Of the soft breeze ruffling the meadow-flowers, ... 80 **Loving she* 18
Butter that had imbibed from meadow-flowers . 782 *Excursion* 2. 679
Of meadow-flowers into a tuft of wood, . . . K.8.237 *Recluse* 1.1.42

Meadow-ground. Strews twenty acres of good meadow-ground . . . . 60 *Bord.* 1230
Once more the little meadow-ground . . . . 241 *P. B.* 408
The Ass in that small meadow-ground; . . . . 248 *P. B.* 1037
Of bells;—those boys who in yon meadow-ground 306 **Here, on our* 3
From the smooth meadow-ground, serene and still! 335 *Namur* 14
What flower in meadow-ground or garden grows . 432 *Ecc. Sonn.* 2. 15. 3
Green meadow-ground, and many-coloured woods, 718 *Prelude* 10. 8
Through a parched meadow-ground, in time of drought. . . . . 757 *Excursion* 1. 72

Meadow-grounds. Gave out to meadow-grounds and hills a loud . . . . 640 *Prelude* 1. 541

Meadow's. No tree was there, no meadow's pleasant green, ... 24 *Guilt* 28

Meadows. No meadows thrown between, the giddy steeps . . . . 12 *Desc. Sk.* 79
That babbled on through groves and meadows green; . . . . 34 *Guilt* 517
A lover of the meadows and the woods, . . . 207 *Tintern* 103
Smoothly skims the meadows wide; . . . . 215 *Kirkstone* 82
Lo! the dwindled woods and meadows; . . . 217 **Inmate of* 9
From rocky steep and rock-bestudded meadows . 233 *Power of Sound* 35
If, while through the meadows green . . . . 336 **Jesu! bless* 9
As that of the sweet fields and meadows green . 339 *Schwytz* 7
In the flower-besprent meadows his genius we trace 364 *Vallomb.* 13
And to green meadows changed the swampy shores? 468 *St. Bees* 137
And O, ye Fountains, Meadows, Hills, and Groves, 590 *Immortality* 191
And through the meadows homeward went, in grave 638 *Prelude* 1. 389
Or, from the meadows sent on gusty days, . . 639 *Prelude* 1. 496
And in the meadows and the lower grounds . . 663 *Prelude* 4. 329
See trees, and meadows, and thy native stream, . 679 *Prelude* 6. 272
To the green meadows of another vale. . . . 823 *Excursion* 5. 66
O'er the flat meadows and indented coast . . . 892 *Excursion* 9. 573
Through the meadows, over stiles, ... S.3. 423 *Tinker* 5
Through quiet meadows, after he has learnt . K.8. 256 *Recluse* 1.1.730

Meadowy. Across yon meadowy bottom look, . . 180 *Waggoner* 4. 40

Meads. To willowy hedge-rows, and to emerald meads; . . . . 2 *Ev. Wk.* 6
And the fresh meads—where flowed, from every nook . . . . 254 *Complete Angler* 13
Of morning dew upon the untrodden meads, . . 330 *Ode: Thanks.* 65

Meagre. The meagre beast lay still as death; . . 241 *P. B.* 456
The meagre shadow that looks on— . . . . 243 *P. B.* 586
To these few meagre Vales confined; . . . . 291 *Rob Roy* 74
In dreary billows, wood, and meagre cot, . . . 334 **A wingèd* 8
Of things gone by, her meagre monuments . . 393 **The Lovers* 10
Black hair, and vivid eye, and meagre cheek, . . 422 *Ecc. Sonn.* 1. 15. 6
Stiff, lank, and upright; a more meagre man . . 664 *Prelude* 4. 393
To endure this state of meagre vassalage, . . . 673 *Prelude* 5. 518
Through meagre lines and colours, and the press . 698 *Prelude* 7. 769
Upon that meagre soil, helped out by talk . . 711 *Prelude* 9. 99
In which the meagre, stale, forbidding ways . . 729 *Prelude* 11. 110
Pampering myself with meagre novelties . . . 736 *Prelude* 12. 117
A meagre person, tall, and in a garb . . . . 779 *Excursion* 2. 500
From which she draws her meagre sustenance. . 786 *Excursion* 3. 28

Meal. *See* **Cottage-meal.**
Is cropping audibly his later meal: . . . . 1 *Early Youth* 4
To his spare meal he calls the passing poor; . . 11 *Desc. Sk.* 30
When threatened war reduced the children's meal: 29 *Guilt* 267
While to that mountain-lamb she gave its evening meal. . . . . 87 *Pet-lamb* 8
And their plain home-made cheese. Yet when the meal . . . . 132 *Michael* 102

Meanwhile—*continued.*

And heard meanwhile the Psalmist's mournful plaint,	780 *Excursion* 2. 576
Dazzling the soul. Meanwhile, prophetic harps .	796 *Excursion* 3. 722
Else imperceptible. Meanwhile, is heard . .	800 *Excursion* 3. 977
Meanwhile, the heart within the heart, the seat	810 *Excursion* 4. 627
Meanwhile, relinquishing all other cares, . .	854 *Excursion* 6. 1025
Meanwhile the unsedentary Master's hand . .	860 *Excursion* 7. 193
That venerable clay. Meanwhile the best .	863 *Excursion* 7. 390
"Meanwhile, at social Industry's command, .	876 *Excursion* 8. 117
Prying through every nook. Meanwhile the rain	K.8. 228 * *I will* 134
They blend therewith congenially : meanwhile,	K.8. 249 *Recluse* 1.1.461

Measure. Then, to the measure of that heaven-born

light, ...	v * *If thou indeed* 2
Then, to the measure of the light vouchsafed, .	v * *If thou indeed* 15
There an old man an olden measure scanned .	13 *Desc. Sk.* 147
How goes the night. 'Tis hard to measure time .	52 *Bord.* 805
Might stretch beyond the measure of one moon. .	68 *Bord.* 1711
Often have I sighed to measure	161 * *Pleasures newly* 25
Their ability to measure	163 *Hint* 3
A measure is of Thee, whose claims extend .	172 *Infant Daughter* 14
Their efforts and their time they measure . .	174 *Waggoner* 1. 106
" A bowl, a bowl of double measure," . . .	178 *Waggoner* 2. 145
Which Dion learned to measure with sublime delight ;—	213 *Dion* 52
"Fear not a constraining measure !	220 *Triad* 34
O bounty without measure ! while the grace .	229 *Cuckoo-clock* 34
All worlds, all natures, mood and measure keep	235 *Power of Sound* 206
Pour out indulgence still, in measure . . .	245 *P. B.* 794
Failing impartial measure to dispense . . .	280 *Plea for Auth.* 1
While to the measure of his might	291 *Rob Roy* 47
Accordant to the measure.	302 *Yarrow V.* 80
I measure back the steps which I have trod ; .	309 * *When, looking* 11
Up to the measure of accorded might, . . .	311 * *Who rises* 44
Blest, above measure blest, ...	329 *Ode 1815* 125
The measure, simple truth to tell, . . .	334 * *In Bruges* 9
And in fit measure cheers autumnal days. .	336 *Rhine* 14
Instructs the Swans their way to measure ; .	372 *Eg. Maid* 188
The tears of man in various measure gush .	436 *Ecc. Sonn.* 2. 32. 1
We, nothing loth a lingering course to measure,	443 *Ecc. Sonn.* 3. 12. 12
Less scanty measure of those graceful rites .	448 *Ecc. Sonn.* 3. 33. 2
One measure, Orpheus ! of thy verse ; . .	472 *Ossian* 38
Their thoughts I cannot measure	482 *Lines : Spring* 14
We'll frame the measure of our souls : . . .	483 *Sister* 35
(For who what is shall measure by what seems .	501 * *The unremitting* 7
At will, your power the measure of your troth !—	515 *Penn.* 8
To measure height and distance ; lonely task, .	548 * *Stay, bold* 16
And full-assured trust, joy without measure, .	559 *Cuck.and Night.*154
The measure of God's chastening love, . .	577 * *By playful* 10
With pensive step to measure my slow way, .	605 *Desc.Sk.Quarto* 165
Spread like a spacious Mere, we there could measure	626 * *The confidence* 11
A span above man's common measure, tall, .	664 *Prelude* 4. 392
In measure only dealt out to himself, . . .	674 *Prelude* 5. 592
Turns, and will measure back his course, far back,	709 *Prelude* 9. 5
Full measure of content ; but still I craved .	741 *Prelude* 13. 110
The measure of themselves, these favoured Beings,	757 *Excursion* 1. 88
To measure the altitude of some tall crag .	760 *Excursion* 1. 274
The measure of my soul was filled with bliss, .	803 *Excursion* 4. 120
Within himself, a measure and a rule, . . .	813 *Excursion* 4. 808
To fill the total measure of his soul ! . . .	867 *Excursion* 7. 662
Yet to the measure of thy promises . . .	S.3. 435 * *The doubt* 131
So stinted in the measure of their grace . .	K.8. 238 *Recluse* 1.1. 67
Up to their highest measure, yea and more. .	K.8. 239 *Recluse* 1.1.109

Measured. *See* **Well-measured.**

Of holy rites chanted in measured round ? . .	11 *Desc. Sk.* 58
The measured echo of the distant flail . . .	22 *Desc. Sk.* 634
We must not part,—I have measured many a league	42 *Bord.* 297
If Nature to her tongue could measured numbers bring, ...	87 *Pet-lamb* 19
Measured by what we are and ought to be, . .	110 * *Look at* 4
Measured by all that, trembling, we foresee, . .	110 * *Look at* 5
Choice word and measured phrase, above the reach	196 *Resolution* 95
A greeting give of measured glee ;	233 *Power of Sound* 38
That, when his age was measured with his aim, .	368 *Trajan* 61
Such measured rest the sedulous and good .	495 *Fact* 39
For the poor Many, measured out by rules .	501 *Humanity* 87
Nor has the rolling year twice measured, . .	586 *Hogg* 13
Pour forth that day my soul in measured strains .	632 *Prelude* 1. 48
And measured motion like a living thing, . .	638 *Prelude* 1. 384
In measured gesture lifted to his head . . .	664 *Prelude* 4. 414
And measured passions of the stage, albeit .	693 *Prelude* 7. 405
To measured admiration, or to aught . . .	737 *Prelude* 12. 186
By charm of measured words may spread o'er field,	863 *Excursion* 7. 382
Where there are no measured miles, . . .	S.3. 423 *Tinker* 6
Such measured rest the diligent and good . .	S.3. 427 * *My Son* 10

Measures. O'er the curled waters Alpine measures

swell, ...	19 *Desc. Sk.* 522
Measures not crimes like his. We rank not, happily,	48 *Bord.* 583
In prompt obedience to spontaneous measures .	331 *Ode : Thanks.* 136
Heaven-prompted Nature, measures and erects .	496 * *A little* 36
Soft o'er the waters mournful measures swell, .	613 *Desc.Sk.Quarto* 626
And measures of the Government, though both .	727 *Prelude* 11. 9
For our support, the measures and the forms, .	802 *Excursion* 4. 74
Large measures shall be dealt. Three sabbath-days	808 *Excursion* 4. 468

Measuring. That haunts the Sailor, measuring o'er

and o'er	150 * *When, to* 64
Measuring the periods of his lonely doom, . .	273 * *Not the* 6
Her fate there measuring ;—all is stilled,— .	415 *White Doe* 1781
God's goodness—measuring bounty as it may ; .	456 *Rydal Mere* 39
And, measuring heaven by earth, would overrule	473 * *Thanks for* 4

Measuring—*continued.*

Measuring thy course, fair Stream ! at length I pay	476 *Eden* 9
Soon as the measuring of life's little span . .	478 * *Lonsdale ! it* 13
Even so ; but measuring not by finite sense .	519 *Pun. Death* 10. 13
Measuring our steps in quiet, we pursued . .	681 *Prelude* 6. 416
Measuring through all degrees, until the scale .	787 *Excursion* 3. 110
Measuring the soil beneath their happy feet .	869 *Excursion* 7. 776
Measuring the force of those gigantic powers .	877 *Excursion* 8. 205

Meat. That never rested—without meat or drink .

	69 *Bord.* 1790
These two days has been meat and drink to me. .	135 *Michael* 275

Mechanic. Of cold mechanic battle do enslave. .

	293 *Killicranky* 10
Mechanic laws to agency divine ;	473 * *Thanks for* 3
Or more mechanic artist represent	691 *Prelude* 7. 248
And tufts of mountain moss. Mechanic tools .	781 *Excursion* 2. 664
Is no mechanic structure, built by rule ; . .	831 *Excursion* 5. 563
And let the light mechanic tool be hailed . .	831 *Excursion* 5. 606

Mechanist. Now, though a Mechanist, whose skill .

	369 *Eg. Maid* 19
Musician, gardener, builder, mechanist, . .	861 *Excursion* 7. 274

Medal. Oft is the medal faithful to its trust . . 546 * *Oft is* 1

Meddle. Which they can hear who meddle not with crime, ... 449 *Ecc. Sonn.* 3. 34. 5

Meddling. Not injured more by touch of meddling

hands	367 *Trajan* 9
Our meddling intellect	481 *Tables Turned* 26

Medea's. Medea's spells dispersed the weight of years 210 *Laod.* 83

Medicable. With medicable wounds, or found their graves . . . . 328 *Ode 1815* 81

Medicine. Yea, hath it ? use, quoth she, this medicine ; 561 *Cuck.andNight.*241

Meditate. Of higher mood, which now I meditate ;— 259 *Calvert* 12

Shall simply feel and purely meditate— . .	332 *Ode : Thanks.* 233
To meditate upon his own appointed tasks, .	354 *Aquap.* 124
Some future Poet meditate his lays ; . . .	546 * *The embowering* 14
And meditate on everlasting things, . . .	551 * *If thou in* 13
With its own struggles, did I meditate . . .	677 *Prelude* 6. 122
To meditate with ardour on the rule . . .	728 *Prelude* 11. 99
Where I could meditate in peace, and cull .	742 *Prelude* 13. 131
There could I meditate on follies past ; . .	794 *Excursion* 3. 557

Meditated. From meditated blight . . . . 542 *Russ. Fug.* 12

Is meditated action ; robbed of this . . . 884 *Excursion* 9. 21

Meditating. Of happy wisdom, meditating good, . 3 *Ev. Wk.* 81

Meditation. *See* **After-meditation.**

To solitary meditation :—now	47 *Bord.* 562
Did constant meditation dry my blood ; . .	69 *Bord.* 1773
Along the VALE OF MEDITATION flows ; . .	272 *Lady E. B.* 2
Of meditation, slipping in between . . .	480 * *Most sweet* 7
Of meditation that attempts to weigh, . .	510 * *Among a* 26
Of meditation on the inhuman deeds . . .	635 *Prelude* 1. 207
And ardent meditation. Later years . . .	693 *Prelude* 7. 393
From those sad scenes when meditation turned, .	709 *Prelude* 8. 654
In sylvan meditation undisturbed ; . . .	716 *Prelude* 9. 443
To meditation in that quietness :— . . .	792 *Excursion* 3. 405
No more shall stray where meditation leads, .	803 *Excursion* 4. 104
That meditation and research may guide . .	823 *Excursion* 5. 39
Yet, in that meditation, will he find . . .	888 *Excursion* 9. 250
For meditation, nor inopportune . . .	S.3. 435 * *The doubt* 133

Meditations. His meditations thus pursued, . 175 *Waggoner* 1. 147

Accordant meditations, which in times . .	358 *Aquap.* 364
Our meditations, give we to a day . . .	448 *Ecc. Sonn.* 3. 32. 2
Of all my meditations, and in this . . .	622 *Recluse* 1. 1. 96
With meditations passionate from deep . .	635 *Prelude* 1. 231
But all the meditations of mankind, . . .	666 *Prelude* 5. 38
Sweet meditations, the still overflow . .	675 *Prelude* 6. 43
In meditations holy and sublime, . . .	693 *Prelude* 7. 445
Those meditations of the soul that feed .	873 *Excursion* 7. 1036
Pour forth his meditations, and descant .	891 *Excursion* 9. 460

Meditative. Of meditative feeling ; . . . 112 * *How rich* 18

Nor dread the depth of meditative eye ; . .	222 *Triad* 193
Here closed the meditative strain ; . . .	224 *Primrose* 25
Bedewed with meditative tears	473 *Ossian* 61
And meditative, authors of delight . . .	567 *Cumb. Beg.* 107
Intense desire through meditative peace ;— .	663 *Prelude* 4. 306
Through faith and meditative reason, resting .	682 *Prelude* 6. 459
Did sweeten many a meditative hour. . .	683 *Prelude* 6. 556
A meditative, oft a suffering, man— . .	748 *Prelude* 14. 143
That in this meditative history	752 *Prelude* 14. 421
That steal upon the meditative mind, . .	763 *Excursion* 1. 483
Whose meditative sympathies repose . .	770 *Excursion* 1. 954
To meditative spleen a grateful feast. . .	808 *Excursion* 4. 477
In peace and meditative cheerfulness ; . .	819 *Excursion* 4. 1203

Medium. Through this still medium, are consoled

and cheered	476 *Howard* 10

Medley. And he shall howl and I will laugh, a medley 60 *Bord.* 1250

But, in its stead, a medley air	239 *P. B.* 304
In this quaint medley, that might seem . .	300 *Bran* 25
The medley less when boreal Lights . . .	499 * *This Lawn* 10
A medley of all tempers, I had passed . .	663 *Prelude* 4. 311

Meed. Though they have gained a worthier meed . 324 *Ode 1814* 48

Of virtue crowned with glory's deathless meed : .	327 *Ode 1815* 36
Nor such fine skill as did the meed bestow .	339 *Tell* 2
Of Christian unity, and won a meed . . .	444 *Ecc. Sonn.* 3. 15. 7
Meed of some Roman chief—in triumph borne .	464 *Derwent* 11
Thus Virtue lives debarred from Virtue's meed ; .	539 * *Lady ! a* 40

Meek. *See* **Simply-meek.**

But, if I have not meekly suffered, meek . .	35 *Guilt* 587
It is so meek, his countenance so venerable. .	57 *Bord.* 1068
His countenance is meek and venerable ; . .	57 *Bord.* 1095
And such a Man—so meek and unoffending— .	75 *Bord.* 2163
Was meek and patient, feeble, old and blind, .	77 *Bord.* 2253
But One there is, a Child of nature meek, . .	103 *Artegal* 45
That gave it birth : in service meek . . .	112 * *How rich* 13

Meek—*continued.*
Peace settles where the intellect is meek, . . . 112 **O dearer* 13
Meek as a lamb the Pony moves, ... 127 *Idiot Boy* 99
Innocent, and meek, and good, ... 141 *Arm. Lady* 118
Faithful, though swift as lightning, the meek dove ; 153 *Morn. Ex.* 37
Of thy meek nature ! . . . . 159 **With little* 48
Alas ! that meek that tender smile . . . . 164 **Fair Lady* 35
Meek Infant ! among all forlornest things . . 172 *Infant Daughter* 3
With the meek comrade at his side ! . . . . 179 *Waggoner* 3. 104
Humbling that lily-stem, thy sceptre meek, . . 220 *Triad* 58
Dread Spirits ! to confound the meek . . . . 245 *P. B.* 761
'Tis said, meek Beast ! that, through Heaven's grace, ... 247 *P. B.* 971
Meek, nobly versed in simple discipline— . . . 254 *Complete Angler* 7
Yet pure and powerful minds, hearts meek and still, ... 254 *Dyer* 10
But with one fervour of devotion meek. . . . 256 *Decay of Piety* 8
Meek aspirations please her, lone endeavour, . . 262 **Not Love* 9
At thy meek bidding, shadowy Power ! brought forth ; . . . . 265 **Hail, Twilight* 11
Prompt, lively, self-sufficing, yet so meek . . . 274 *Infant M.* 7
And head that droops because the soul is meek, . 274 **Such age* 8
But one meek streamlet, only one : . . . . 288 *Glen-Al.* 4
Meek loveliness is round thee spread, ... 302 *Yarrow V.* 45
Thoughts motherly, and meek as womanhood. . 304 **I grieved* 8
Meek, destitute, as seemed, of hope or aim . . 305 **We had* 5
O murdered Prince ! meek, loyal, pious, brave ! . 325 *Enghien* 10
The Bard—whose soul is meek as dawning day, . 326 **The Bard* 1
Meek lustre, nor forget'st the humble Vale ; . . 329 *Ode : Thanks.* 30
Meek Virgin Mother, more benign . . . . . 338 **Meek Virgin* 1
Associate with the simply meek, ... 341 *San Salv.* 22
Meek Nature's evening comment on the shows . . 349 *Sky-prosp.* 12
In one meek smile, beneath a peasant's shed, . . 359 **They—who* 7
The meek, benign, and lacerated face, ... 366 **Eternal Lord* 6
Of wind or wave—a meek and guileless Maiden. . 370 *Eg. Maid* 66
Full thrice had crossed himself in meek composure. 373 *Eg. Maid* 276
Meek, patient, kind, and, were its trials fewer, . 390 *Highland Hut* 13
Ere the meek Saint, Columba, bore . . . . 390 *Highland Broach* 3
Meek as that emblem of her lowly heart . . . 395 *White Doe: Ded.* 13
Meek filial smiles, upon thy face, ... 401 *White Doe* 500
Of gentleness and meek delight, ... 413 *White Doe* 1604
And oftentimes the Lady meek . . . . . . 415 *White Doe* 1767
Haughty the Bard: can these meek doctrines blight . . . . 419 *Ecc. Sonn.* 1. 3. 8
The lovely Nun (submissive, but more meek . . 434 *Ecc. Sonn.* 2. 22. 1
In meek and simple infancy, what joy . . . 436 *Ecc. Sonn.* 2. 31. 9
Around meek Walton's heavenly memory. . . . 441 *Ecc. Sonn.* 3. 5. 14
Though meek and patient as a sheathed sword ; . 444 *Ecc. Sonn.* 3. 18. 5
Weep not, meek Bride ! uplift thy timid brow. . 447 *Ecc. Sonn.* 3. 26. 14
Whispering how meek and gentle he *can* be ! . . 453 **The Sun, that* 12
Meek eve shuts up the whole usurping host . . 456 **Soft as* 16
Gentle awakenings, visitations meek ; . . . . 460 **Wanderer ! that* 60
O still beloved (for thine, meek Power, are charms 460 **Queen of* 17
Meek, patient, steadfast, and with loftier scope, . 461 **Queen of* 55
Such thy meek outset, with a crown, though frail, 464 *Derwent* 7
That satisfies the simple and the meek, . . . 468 **Ranging the* 12
Meek, yielding to the occasion's call, ... 486 **Bright Flower* 21
By discipline endeavour to grow meek . . . . 500 *Humanity* 53
Their meek heads to the nipping air, ... 503 *Warning* 3
With thy memorial flower, meek Portraiture ! . . 510 **Among a* 11
Go where at least meek Innocency dwells ; . . 516 **Young England* 13
Strong as could then be borne. A Master meek . 518 *Pun. Death* 7. 5
Through its meek influence, from above, . . . 534 **Blest is* 93
Of meek devotion, which erewhile it gave, . . 535 **When in* 26
Though young so wise, though meek so resolute— 541 *Grace Darl.* 95
Meek Catherine had her own reward ; . . . . 545 *Russ. Fug.* 365
And ever on Christ's Mother meek and kind . . 555 *Prioress* 146
She came, though meek of soul, in seemly pride . 576 **By a* 3
A meek man and a brave ! . . . . 580 **Sweet Flower* 66
The meek, the brave, the good, was gone . . . 580 *John Words.* 38
Meek Flower ! To Him I would have said, . . 580 *John Words.* 52
A spirit meek in self-abasement clad. . . . . 583 **With copious* 6
Timidly uttered, for she *lives*, the meek, . . . 585 *Ch. Lamb* 80
Followed as of good omen, and meek Worth . . 658 *Prelude* 3. 607
So near to us, that meek confiding heart, . . . 678 *Prelude* 6. 229
To a meek spirit suffering inwardly. . . . . 691 *Prelude* 7. 315
Meek though enthusiastic. Injuries . . . . 714 *Prelude* 9. 294
Whereof he was a part : yet this was meek . . 714 *Prelude* 9. 319
The meek, the lowly, patient child of toil, . . 717 *Prelude* 9. 524
Now was it that *both* found, the meek and lofty . 729 *Prelude* 11. 136
Meek men, whose very souls perhaps would sink . 744 *Prelude* 13. 269
All meek and silent, save that through a rift— . 747 *Prelude* 14. 56
And, the meek worm that feeds her lonely lamp . 750 *Prelude* 14. 274
Lowly ; for he was meek in gratitude, ... 759 *Excursion* 1. 236
For the meek Sufferer. Why then should we read 770 *Excursion* 1. 939
Of his old age ; and yet less calm and meek, . . 783 *Excursion* 2. 752
Winningly meek or venerably calm, ... 783 *Excursion* 2. 753
Young, modest, meek, and beautiful, I led . . 793 *Excursion* 3. 514
Such converse, if directed by a meek, ... 806 *Excursion* 4. 344
Of meek repentance, wafting wallflower scents . 817 *Excursion* 4. 1047
Meek to admit ; the active energy, ... 831 *Excursion* 5. 574
In lonely reading found a meek resource : . . . 852 *Excursion* 6. 896
Meek Saint ! through patience glorified on earth ! 854 *Excursion* 6. 1034
When the meek Partner of his age, his Son, . . 861 *Excursion* 7. 260
Yet not for meek of heart. The smoke ascends . 887 *Excursion* 9. 245
Which Persian kings might envy ; and thy meek . S.3. 433 **The doubt* 19
Meek and neglected thing, of no renown ! . . . K.8. 250 *Recluse* 1.1.513
Benign, meek, . . ., offers grace . . . . . . K.8. 266 **Rid of* 7
6 *Ev. Wk.* 224

Meeker. The female with a meeker charm succeeds, As of a different caste. A meeker man . . . 714 *Prelude* 9. 292
Meekest. The meekest Child on this blessed earth. 403 *White Doe* 618

Meek-eyed. By ladies, meek-eyed women without fear ; . . . . 315 **And is it* 12
Meek-hearted. Woman-grown, meek-hearted, sage, 94 *Westmoreland Girl* 82

Meekly. But, if I have not meekly suffered, meek . 35 *Guilt* 587
Bowed meekly in submissive fear, before the Lord of All ; . . . . 92 *Poet's Dream* 10
Shone meekly 'mid their native dust, ... 168 *Pilgrim's Dream* 63
Thy transports moderate ; and meekly mourn . 210 *Laod.* 77
Who meekly yields, and is obscured—content . 265 **The Shepherd* 13
Go—and with foreheads meekly bowed . . . 332 *Ode : Thanks.* 228
Did meekly bear the pang unmerited ; . . . 395 *White Doe: Ded.* 12
Meekly, with foreboding thought, ... 400 *White Doe* 347
And meekly bear the ills which bear I must : . . 464 **A point* 8
Beseech her meekly with all lowliness, . . . 562 *Cuck.and Night.* 305
And sufferings meekly borne—I, for my part, . 847 *Excursion* 6. 630
Meekly-bending. In me, a meekly-bending spirit soothed . . . . 790 *Excursion* 3. 265
Meekness. A deep and simple meekness : and that Soul, ... 40 *Bord.* 169
Checked her with filial meekness ; for no thought 124 *V. and J.* 167
Christian meekness smoothed for all the path of life, 142 *Arm. Lady* 149
Each grief, through meekness, settling into rest. . 222 *Triad* 182
To sit in meekness, like the brooding Dove, . . 253 **O gentle* 3
But are we aught enriched in love and meekness ? 281 **What strong* 8
But in magnanimous meekness. France, 'tis strange, ... 307 **Great men* 9
And meekness tempering honourable pride ; . . 430 *Ecc. Sonn.* 2. 7. 12
Untaught that meekness is the cherished bent 455 **Not in the lucid* 14
Health, meekness, ardour, quietness secure, . . 489 *Spade* 9
Captivates like passive meekness. . . . . . 502 **Like a* 44
Whom, then, shall meekness guard ? What saving skill . . . . 505 *Warning* 149
Hallowed to meekness and to innocence ; . . . 584 *Ch. Lamb* 26
And if in him meekness at times gave way, . . 584 *Ch. Lamb* 27
And Christian meekness hallowing faithful loves. 635 *Prelude* 1. 185
Of modest meekness, simple-mindedness, . . . 670 *Prelude* 5. 291
To meekness, and exalts by humble faith ; . . 740 *Prelude* 13. 28
Was into meekness softened and subdued ; . . 850 *Excursion* 6. 772

Meet. Now meet we other pilgrims ere the day 20 *Desc. Sk.* 555
Rushing and racing came to meet me at the water-side ! . . . . 28 *Guilt* 216
For never could I hope to meet with such another. 29 *Guilt* 252
We soon shall meet again. If thou neglect . . 42 *Bord.* 303
Whom no one comes to meet, I stood alone ;— . 62 *Bord.* 1351
So meet extremes in this mysterious world, . . 65 *Bord.* 1529
That thou shouldst ever meet a like occasion . 74 *Bord.* 2114
You should prepare to meet him. I have nothing 75 *Bord.* 2131
And thus we meet again ; one human stay . . 75 *Bord.* 2134
The extremes of suffering meet in absolute peace. 76 *Bord.* 2216
" In heaven we all shall meet ; " . . . . . 83 *Lucy Gray* 42
Where thousands meet to worship God under a mighty Dome ; . . . . 93 *Poet's Dream* 62
To hear, to meet them !—From their house the school . . . . 99 *Brothers* 251
As any that should meet him— Happy ! Sir— . 100 *Brothers* 328
That friends, by death disjoined, may meet no more ! 112 **O dearer* 4
With hope that we, dear Friends ! shall meet again. 143 **High bliss* 28
Is slow to meet the sympathies of them . . . 147 *Joanna* 6
When we, and others whom we love, shall meet . 151 **When, to* 109
We meet thee, like a pleasant thought, . . . 158 **In youth* 23
A *Holy-thistle* here we meet . . . . 164 **Fair Lady* 27
Each peering forth to meet the other :— . . . 180 *Waggoner* 4. 22
May meet at noontide ; Fear and trembling Hope, 185 *Yew-trees* 26
A countenance in which did meet . . . . . 186 **She was* 15
Near the stately Pantheon you'll meet with the same . . . . 188 *Music* 3
Seem to meet with little gain, seem less happy than before : . . . . 189 *Star-gazers* 30
" Once I could meet with them on every side ; . 197 *Resolution* 124
Of a wide army pressing on to meet . . . . 230 *Clouds* 13
Then starts the sluggard, pleased to meet . . . 233 *Power of Sound* 70
Meet Statue for the court of Fear ! . . . . 242 *P. B.* 523
This very night will meet his fate— . . . . 244 *P. B.* 694
The first you meet with—bid him come, . . . 248 *P. B.* 1062
Does joy approach ? they meet the coming tide ; 278 **Life with* 3
Who meet most feelingly the calls of sadness. . 280 **'Tis he* 14
With service meet ; . . . . 286 *Sons of Burns* 28
And, starting up to meet the same, ... 287 *Ellen Irwin* 30
For fear and melancholy meet ; . . . . . 288 *Glen-Al.* 14
To meet the wintry season. . . . . 302 *Yarrow V.* 72
Yet, yet, Biscayans ! we must meet our Foes 318 *Biscayan* 1
Those lofty-minded Lawgivers shall meet, . . 319 *Guernica* 12
Looks on delighted—meet in festal ring, . . . 322 **Ye Storms* 4
And for a moment meet the soul's desires ! . . 325 *Ode 1814* 126
Fresh risen, and beautiful within !—there meet 327 *Ode 1815* 53
To sink, and meet them in their fretted caves, . 333 *Fish-women* 7
But faintly picture, 'twere an office meet . . 335 *Cologne* 8
Whose waves the Orphean lyre forbad to meet . 336 *Danube* 9
I move at ease ; and meet contending themes . 350 *Des. Stanzas* 15
For my enjoyment meet in vision strange ; . . 350 *Des. Stanzas* 41
Were but the Gift a meet Return to thee . . . 352 *H. C. R.* 6
Your praise, in meet accordance with your claims 352 *Aquap.* 5
To meet the shade of Horace by the side . . . 356 *Aquap.* 256
Thee gentle breezes waft—or airs that meet . . 363 **List—'twas* 108
Meet on the solid ground of waking life. . . . 364 **What aim* 14
That we, who part in love, shall meet again. . . 383 *Duddon* 30. 14
Like guests that meet, and some from far, . . 385 *Yarrow Rev.* 31
Did meet us with unaltered face, ... 386 *Yarrow Rev.* 35
His sky-born warblings—does aught meet your ken 387 *Manse* 6
To meet such need as might befall— . . . . 391 *Highland Broach* 57

Memory's 599 Men

Memory—*continued.*
Revived a memory of those hours . . . . . 407 *White Doe* 1026
Sustained by memory of the past . . . . . 414 *White Doe* 1624
And fond unclouded memory. . . . . . . 414 *White Doe* 1657
Received the memory of old loves, ... 415 *White Doe* 1754
And bears a memory and a mind . . . . . 416 *White Doe* 1877
Around meek Walton's heavenly memory. . . 441 *Ecc. Sonn.* 3. 5. 14
Giving to Memory help when she would weave 448 *Ecc. Sonn.* 3. 33. 5
Those forest oaks of Druid memory, ... 450 *Ecc. Sonn.* 3. 39. 7
Never but in the world of memory ; . . . . 458 *Sea-shore* 16
With some internal lights to memory dear, . . 460 **Wanderer! that* 57
Sickened, or died) in pious memory kept : . . 467 *St. Bees* 69
To shun the memory of a listless life . . . . 470 **Did pangs* 10
Does little on his memory rest, ... 485 **Bright Flower* 11
—What trick of memory to *my* voice hath brought 496 **A little* 3
Are the domains of tender memory ! . . . . 498 **Enough of climbing* 51
Are well assigned to Memory . . . . . . 499 *Memory* 3
Not He, whose last faint memory will command . 504 *Warning* 53
All who revere the memory of Penn . . . . 515 *Penn.* 9
Or charm it out of memory ; yea, might fill . 517 *Pun. Death* 1. 5
Dim memory keeping of its old intent. . . . 523 *Epist. Beaumont* 128
I leave unsearched : enough that memory clings, 525 *Epist. Beaumont* 265
As a chance-sunbeam from his memory fell . . 528 **Those breathing* 102
No successors ; and, lodged in memory, . . . 531 *Octogen.* 2
For thy better memory. . . . . 535 *Egremont* 20
Raised this frail tribute to his memory ; . . . 547 **Ye Lime* 14
When I the process have in memory, ... 563 *Troilus* 65
With a thousand soft pictures his memory will teem, 570 *Farmer* 79
No—he was One whose memory ought to spread 574 *Chiabrera* 5. 21
An everlasting spring ! in memory . . . . . 575 *Chiabrera* 8. 22
May touches of his memory bring . . . . . 578 **I come* 55
From memory, prolong their stay . . . . . 578 **I come* 67
To a good Man of most dear memory . . . . 584 *Ch. Lamb* 1
Of memory, or see the light of love. . . . . 585 *Ch. Lamb* 49
While, Memory at my side, I wander here, . . 592 *Ev. Wk. Quarto* 43
If, while a half-slumber his memory bedims, . . 621 *Convict* 35
My simplest Lay that to their memory . . . 626 **Son of* 6
Will pass so soon from human memory ; . . . 627 **We gaze* 5
May soothe thy memory of the chains of Rome. . 627 *Eagle and Dove* 4
No picture of mere memory ever looked . . . 633 *Prelude* 1. 75
No conscious memory of a kindred sight, . . . 640 *Prelude* 1. 574
Wearied itself out of the memory, ... 641 *Prelude* 1. 598
Disowned by memory—ere the breath of spring . 641 *Prelude* 1. 615
But is not each a memory to himself ?— . . . 651 *Prelude* 3. 188
Libations, to thy memory drank, till pride . . 653 *Prelude* 3. 299
Thy memory languidly revolved, the heart . . 653 *Prelude* 3. 329
Yet to the memory something cleaves at last, . 658 *Prelude* 3. 627
The memory of one particular hour . . . . 663 *Prelude* 4. 308
That here, in memory of all books which lay . 668 *Prelude* 5. 198
Bask in the sunshine of the memory ; . . . . 685 *Prelude* 6. 659
Which yet survive in memory, appears . . . 692 *Prelude* 7. 335
Is fading out of memory, but I see . . . . 692 *Prelude* 7. 366
By which the world of memory and thought . . 694 *Prelude* 7. 464
What memory and what logic ! till the strain . 694 *Prelude* 7. 509
In memory, those individual sights . . . . 696 *Prelude* 7. 599
And comprehensiveness and memory flow, . . 698 *Prelude* 7. 741
And grateful memory, as a thing divine. . . . 707 *Prelude* 8. 559
In memory of the farewells of that time, . . . 713 *Prelude* 9. 270
Or personal memory of his own worst wrongs, . 718 *Prelude* 9. 583
Of memory, to virtue lost and hope, ... 733 *Prelude* 11. 390
To thee, in memory of that happiness, . . . 752 *Prelude* 14. 410
That to his memory were most endeared. . . . 762 *Excursion* 1. 391
The life where hope and memory are as one ; . . 792 *Excursion* 3. 400
With joy, and—oh ! that memory should survive 792 *Excursion* 3. 431
These acts of mind, and memory, and heart, . . 794 *Excursion* 3. 574
For, like a plague, will memory break out ; . . 798 *Excursion* 3. 847
Crowned was he, if my memory do not err, . . 816 *Excursion* 4. 997
That shall survive his name and memory. . . 823 *Excursion* 5. 48
And it is named, in memory of the event, . . 842 *Excursion* 6. 253
Upon her memory, faithfully as stars . . . . 848 *Excursion* 6. 702
In memory and for warning, and in sign . . . 854 *Excursion* 6. 1082
Of memory, images and precious thoughts, . . 857 *Excursion* 7. 29
The memory of the just survives in heaven : . . 863 *Excursion* 7. 388
Their monuments and their memory. The vast Frame . . . . 872 *Excursion* 7. 999
Transmitted far as living memory, ... S.3. 435 **The doubt* 128
Would I your flights of *memory* cramp. . . . S.3. 438 **My Lord* 6
Hath now escaped his memory—but the hour, . K.8. 236 *Recluse* 1. 1. 3
Of memory faithful to the call of love ; . . . K.8. 247 *Recluse* 1.1.388
Memory's. To memory's shadowy moonshine ! . 386 *Yarrow Rev.* 112
Lurks in it, Memory's Helper, Fancy's Lord, . . 480 *Cordelia* 13
Memphis. That would lament her ;—Memphis, Tyre, are gone . . . . 425 *Ecc. Sonn.* 1. 25. 12
Men. *See* **Countrymen, Fellow-men.**
Dwarf panniered steeds, and men, and numerous wains : . . . . 5 *Ev. Wk.* 159
Where beasts and men together o'er the plain . 13 *Desc. Sk.* 169
And who, that walks where men of ancient days . 15 *Desc. Sk.* 289
And grey-haired men look up with livelier brow,— 21 *Desc. Sk.* 609
Great God ! by whom the strifes of men are weighed . . . . 22 *Desc. Sk.* 652
For sacrifice its throngs of living men, . . . 26 *Guilt* 123
To join those miserable men he flew, . . . 29 *Guilt* 278
At houses, men, and common light, amazed. . . 31 *Guilt* 401
That fear is like a cloak which old men huddle . 38 *Bord.* 22
Of peace and order. Aged men with tears . . 48 *Bord.* 612
Men who are little given to sift and weigh— . . 49 *Bord.* 645

Men—*continued.*
Twelve honest men, plain men, would set us right ; 53 *Bord.* 882
And most despise the men who best can teach us : 54 *Bord.* 909
Henceforth it shall be said that bad men only . 54 *Bord.* 910
Shall be proclaimed : brave Men, they all shall hear it. . . . . 55 *Bord.* 981
And old, and blind—— Blind, say you ? Are we Men, ... 57 *Bord.* 1072
And Men alone are Umpires. To the Camp . . 58 *Bord.* 1120
About your Daughter ! Troops of armed men, . 61 *Bord.* 1330
In Story, what men now alive have witnessed, . 62 *Bord.* 1382
I know the need that all men have of mercy, . 63 *Bord.* 1406
We wonder at ourselves like men betrayed : . . 65 *Bord.* 1542
Hear me, ye Men upon the cliffs, if such . . . 67 *Bord.* 1654
Or mourn him dead. A man by men cast off, . 68 *Bord.* 1727
That we are praised, only as men in us . . . 70 *Bord.* 1823
Was off for ever ; and the men, from whom . . 70 *Bord.* 1842
You heard !—he called you to him ? Of all men . 73 *Bord.* 2051
And know how busy are the tongues of men ; . 74 *Bord.* 2079
Of this too much. Men are there, millions, Oswald, 77 *Bord.* 2292
A little Prattler among men. . . . . . . 79 *Sparrow's Nest* 14
Drive them down, like men in a battle : . . . 81 †*Address : Child* 31
But these are all the graves of full-grown men ! . 100 *Brothers* 341
Discord in hearts of men till they have braved . 105 *Artegal* 236
I travelled among unknown men, ... 109 **I travelled* 1
Maimed, mangled by inhuman men ; . . . . 117 *Affl. Marg.* 51
Was made to seize him by three armèd men, . . 123 *V. and J.* 127
Of Shepherds, dwellers in the valleys, men . . 131 *Michael* 23
And watchful more than ordinary men. . . . 131 *Michael* 47
When thou art gone away, should evil men . . 137 *Michael* 405
Of reapers, men and women, boys and girls. . . 149 **A narrow* 41
Nor be less dear to future men . . . . . 158 **In youth* 78
Eyes of some men travel far . . . . . . 160 **Pansies, lilies* 9
Men that keep a mighty rout ! . . . . . . 160 **Pansies, lilies* 12
Poets, vain men in their mood ! . . . . . 160 **Pansies, lilies* 33
All men who know thee call their brother, . . 162 **Art thou the* 10
The darling of children and men ? . . . . . 162 **Art thou the* 11
Lift men from their native stations, ... 163 *Hint* 23
Burned like a fire among his men ; . . . . . 178 *Waggoner* 2. 132
Men, women, heartless with the cold ; . . . . 182 *Waggoner* 4. 259
Poor in estate, of manners base, men of the multitude, ... 189 *Star-gazers* 22
No, no, this cannot be ;—men thirst for power and majesty ! . . . . 189 *Star-gazers* 24
Men, women, children, yea the frame . . . . 192 *Gipsies* 3
With men to whom no better law . . . . . 194 *Ruth* 146
And all the ways of men, so vain and melancholy. 195 *Resolution* 21
Of ordinary men ; a stately speech ; . . . . 196 *Resolution* 96
Religious men, who give to God and man their dues. 196 *Resolution* 98
"Alas ! when evil men are strong . . . . . 204 *Brougham* 87
I said, when evil men are strong, ... 204 *Brougham* 104
By Voices how men lived of old. . . . . . 205 *Brougham* 133
And, if that men report him right, ... 205 *Brougham* 136
Love had he found in huts where poor men lie ; . 205 *Brougham* 161
Rash judgments, nor the sneers of selfish men, . 207 *Tintern* 129
And I (as all men may find cause, ... 215 *Kirkstone* 53
The Pharaohs of the earth, the men of hardened heart ! . . . . 216 *Enterprise* 106
The reasoning Sons of Men, ... 225 *Primrose* 44
That men have lived for whom, ... 226 *Present.* 63
Bright Seraphs mixed familiarly with men ; . . 228 *Vernal Ode* 134
Whether men sow or reap the fields, ... 228 *Devot. Incit.* 70
Where men were monsters. A last grace he craves, 234 *Power of Sound* 133
—Let good men feel the soul of nature, . . . 245 *P. B.* 764
From men of pensive virtue go, ... 245 *P. B.* 773
As men who with their purpose play, ... 245 *P. B.* 819
Like planet-stricken men of yore, ... 246 *P. B.* 883
That ever among Men or Naiads sought . . . 251 **There is a little* 3
From the submissive necks of guiltless men . . 252 **Why, Minstrel* 9
Heed not such onset ! nay, if praise of men . . 255 *Detraction* 11
In all men, sinful is it to be slow . . . . . 267 **DespondingFather* 13
Takes fire :—The men that have been reappear ; . 275 **While poring* 3
While thus these simple-hearted men are moved ? 283 **Well have* 14
Deep in the general heart of men . . . . . 286 *Nith* 47
For honest men delight will take . . . . . 286 *Sons of Burns* 19
Remote from men, Thou dost not need . . . 288 *Highland Girl* 29
In this still place, remote from men, ... 288 *Glen-Al.* 1
Tried men, at Killicranky were arrayed . . . 293 *Killicranky* 2
Like conquest would the Men of England see ; . 293 *Killicranky* 13
Such gifts had those seafaring men . . . . 296 *Highland Boy* 111
World-wearied Men withdrew of yore ; . . . 298 *Brownie's Cell* 5
Thus, like the men of earliest days, ... 301 *Bran* 74
Among men who do not love her, linger here. . 303 **Fair Star* 14
Men known, and men unknown, sick, lame, and blind, ... 303 **Is it* 4
'Tis ever thus. Ye men of prostrate mind, . . 303 **Is it* 8
Men are we, and must grieve when even the Shade 305 *Ven. Rep.* 13
Toussaint, the most unhappy man of men ! . . 305 *Toussaint* 1
Of inward happiness. We are selfish men ; . . 307 **Milton! thou* 6
Great men have been among us ; hands that penned 307 **Great men* 1
But equally a want of books and men ! . . . 307 **Great men* 14
When men change swords for ledgers, and desert . 307 **When I* 3
In thee a bulwark for the cause of men ; . . . 308 **When I* 10
Unfit for men ; and that in one great band . . 308 **One might* 3
Even rich men, brave by nature, taint the air . 308 **These times* 2
Men unto whom sufficient for the day . . . . 308 **These times* 5
I see one man, of men the meanest too ! . . . 309 **When, looking* 2
Vanguard of Liberty, ye men of Kent, . . . 309 *Men of Kent* 1
Ye men of Kent, 'tis victory or death ! . . . 309 *Men of Kent* 14
Come forth, ye old men, now in peaceful show . 310 *Anticip.* 6

Men—*continued.*
With which communities of men invest . . . 827 Excursion 5. 311
The habitations, and the ways of men, . . . 833 Excursion 5. 685
Cannot but notice among men and things) 834 Excursion 5. 798
In solemn institutions:—men convinced . . . 837 Excursion 5. 1001
Upon the thronged abodes of busy men . . . 838 Excursion 6. 37
Men, whose delight is where their duty leads . . 839 Excursion 6. 48
Tremendous truths! familiar to the men . . 846 Excursion 6. 546
Who rather would not envy, men that feel . . 847 Excursion 6. 616
Though pitied among men, absolved by God, . . 855 Excursion 6. 1112
Upon the lips of men in hall or bower; . . . 863 Excursion 7. 384
To the assembled spirits of just men . . . 864 Excursion 7. 453
Unto the men who see not as we see . . . 865 Excursion 7. 531
Less, as might seem, in rivalship with men . . 867 Excursion 7. 627
For strife and ferment in the minds of men; . . 873 Excursion 7. 1010
For grateful converse: and to these poor men 875 Excursion 8. 58
Versed in the characters of men; and bound, 875 Excursion 8. 62
—By these Itinerants, as experienced men, . . 875 Excursion 8. 77
Abodes of men irregularly massed . . . 876 Excursion 8. 123
Among the rocks below. Men, maidens, youths, 877 Excursion 8. 180
Watching to God. Religious men were they; . 877 Excursion 8. 191
Men of all lands shall exercise the same . . 877 Excursion 8. 212
For men who in such places, feeling there . . K.8. 226 *I will 70
This small abiding-place of many men, . . K.8. 240 Recluse 1.1.146
Strangers to me, and all men, or at least . . K.8. 251 Recluse 1.1.533
Yield not, to scorn, or sorrow, living men . . K.8. 253 Recluse 1.1.605
From men who winnow charity from Faith . . K.8. 325 [?] *The vestal 10

Menace. With menace proud, and insult loud, . . 162 Binnorie 36
Her by menace to deliver, ... S.3. 437 *I, whose 14
Menaced. Unhurt by violence, from menaced taint 438 Ecc. Sonn. 2. 38. 10
Menai's. As Menai's foam; and toward the mystic ring . . . . 419 Ecc. Sonn. 1. 3. 2
Mendicant. Were undisputed! Like a mendicant, 62 Bord. 1350
The mind's least generous wish a mendicant . . 277 *Why art 7
Or Idleness in tatters mendicant . . . 336 Staub-bach 11
Of this old Mendicant, and, from her door . . 568 Cumb. Beg. 159
Or crippled mendicant in soldier's garb, . . . 769 Excursion 1. 889
Mending. To fishers mending nets beside their doors; 522 Epist. Beaumont 45
Heart, soul, and hands,—in mending the defects . 789 Excursion 3. 202
Men's. Wouldst change the course of things in all men's sight! . . . . 105 Artegal 173
Those wild men's vices he received, ... 194 Ruth 149
Which hath been held aloft before men's sight . 312 *Who rises 63
And took a place in all men's sight; . . . . 410 White Doe 1301
Wrought in men's minds, like miracles achieved; 466 St. Bees 47
Nor aught that makes men's promises a blank, . 470 *A youth 12
Painted on rich men's floors, for one feast-night. . 488 Pers. Talk 8
And when he was removed from all men's sight, . 564 Troilus 117
Was given to old opinions; all men's minds . . 731 Prelude 11. 271
Hidden from all men's view. To our attempt . 793 Excursion 3. 474
That poor men's children, they, and they alone, . 813 Excursion 4. 786
And so, not wholly hidden from men's sight, . . 868 Excursion 7. 738
Present themselves at once to all men's view: . 874 Excursion 8. 16
Mental. Thy mental vision further and ascend . . 519 Pun. Death 9. 3
Enquire," said I, "how much of mental power 741 Prelude 13. 95
Mention. *See* **Chance-mention.**
Nor should I have made mention of this Dell . . 131 Michael 14
Nor will I mention by what death he died; . . 201 Hart-leap 31
And they who do make mention of the same, . 201 Hart-leap 63
Why mention other thoughts unmeet . . . 399 White Doe 312
To mention by its name, as in degree, ... 691 Prelude 7. 264
Told what best merits mention, further pains . 751 Prelude 14. 370
Survives, for worthy mention, of a pair . . 844 Excursion 6. 405
May I not mention—that, within those walls, . 854 Excursion 6. 1038
Mentioned. Nay, God forbid!—You recollect I mentioned . . . . 101 Brothers 393
Be mentioned as a parting word, that not . . 686 Prelude 6. 732
Merchandise. To go and overlook his merchandise . 135 Michael 266
Merchant. A vagrant Merchant under a heavy load 761 Excursion 1. 324
Merchant's. To the strict labours of the merchant's desk . . . . 584 Ch. Lamb 5
Merchants. Whence they, like richly-laden merchants, come . . . . 425 Ecc. Sonn. 1. 25. 5
Whose merchants Princes were, whose decks were thrones; . . . . 475 Greenock 10
Mercies. Of God's parental mercies—with Idonea . 60 Bord. 1267
Upon the mercies of the earth. . . . . . . 502 *Like a 6
The tender mercies of the dismal wind . . . 718 Prelude 10. 14
Merciful. He breathed for her, and for that merciful pair. . . . . 36 Guilt 644
Yes, yes. I will not murmur, merciful God! . 53 Bord. 850
For a like trial, but more merciful. . . . . . 62 Bord. 1387
Merciful protectress, kindling . . . . . 94 Westmoreland Girl 53
"The Gods to us are merciful—and they . . . 210 Laod. 85
Stroke merciful and welcome would that be . . 319 Guernica 9
Merciful over all his creatures, just . . . 500 Humanity 45
And merciful desires, thy sanctity approve!" 582 Invoc. Earth 34
Shared, though in mild and merciful degree: . . 886 Excursion 9. 167
To victims, which the merciful can see . . . 887 Excursion 9. 191
Mercifully. And, to the sinner, mercifully bent; . 464 *A point 6
Will mercifully take me to himself.' . . . . 854 Excursion 6. 1048
Merciless. And merciless ravage: and the shady nook 185 Nutting 45
Merciless act of sorrow infinite! . . . . 439 Ecc. Sonn. 2. 42. 11
The strong were merciless, without hope the weak; 466 St. Bees 39
And strangled by a merciless force; . . . 494 Force of Prayer 34
As merciless proscription ebbs and flows. . . . 848 Excursion 6. 674
Mercurial. Who hath no lack of wit mercurial; . 245 P. B. 807
Mercuries. Those radiant Mercuries, that seemed to move . . . . 811 Excursion 4. 702

Mercury. And a God leads him, wingèd Mercury! 209 Laod. 18
Swift Mercury resounds with mirth, ... 237 P. B. 46
Mercy. That we the mercy of the waves should rue: 29 Guilt 296
The Baron Herbert. Mercy, the Baron Herbert! 43 Bord. 333
Your life is at my mercy. Do not harm me, . . 46 Bord. 502
The worm was in her—— Mercy! Sir, what mean you? . . . . 61 Bord. 1314
Softened till it becomes a gift of mercy. . . . 61 Bord. 1340
Thou wilt have time to breathe and think—— Oh, Mercy! . . . . 63 Bord. 1405
I know the need that all men have of mercy, . . 63 Bord. 1406
I hung this belt. Mercy of Heaven! What ails you! . . . . 67 Bord. 1642
That Chapel-bell in mercy seemed to guide me, . 67 Bord. 1651
With which he called for mercy; and—even so— 68 Bord. 1731
The storm beats hard—Mercy for poor or rich, . 71 Bord. 1882
We are betrayed! His Daughter!—God have mercy! . . . . 72 Bord. 2009
Left to the mercy of that savage Man! . . . 76 Bord. 2186
Mercy! I said I know not what—oh pity me— . 77 Bord. 2247
In Heaven, and Mercy gives me leave to die. . . 78 Bord. 2353
"O mercy!" to myself I cried, ... 109 *Strange fits 27
Oh mercy! like a helpless child. . . . . . 114 Ind. Wom. 40
For mercy and immortal bloom? . . . . . 192 Seq. Beggars 42
And those that seek his help, and for his mercy sigh. 229 Cuckoo-clock 44
At the still hour to Mercy dear, ... 233 Power of Sound 28
Mercy from her twilight throne . . . . . . 233 Power of Sound 29
"While yet ye may find mercy;—strive . . . 247 P. B. 947
"Oh, mercy! something must be done, . . . 248 P. B. 1058
Sweet Mercy! to the gates of Heaven . . . . 286 Nith 55
Upon his inner soul in mercy shine; . . . . 323 *Now that 11
Breathed thy mercy to implore, ... 336 *Jesu! bless 5
Mercy has placed within our reach . . . . 337 *Oh Life 11
The mercy, goodness, have not failed to awe . . 342 Last Sup. 4
Father of Mercy! rectify his view, ... 363 *The world forsaken 9
Thy veil in mercy o'er the records, hung . . . 389 Sound of Mull 2
But in the mould of mercy all is cast . . . . 391 Brownie 11
"Yes—God is rich in mercy," said . . . . 411 White Doe 1354
Mercy and Love have met thee on thy road, . . 419 Ecc. Sonn. 1. 4. 1
While Mercy, uttering, through their voice, a sound 429 Ecc. Sonn. 2. 4. 8
(O God of mercy, may no earthly Seat . . . 437 Ecc. Sonn. 2. 35. 2
Hear also of that name, and mercy cast . . . 440 Ecc. Sonn. 2. 46. 7
Forth for His mercy, as the Church ordains, . . 448 Ecc. Sonn. 3. 30. 7
By confidence supplied and mercy shown, . . 459 *Wanderer! that 14
Still on her sons the beams of mercy shine; . . 474 *How sad 10
Hence thoughtful Mercy, Mercy sage and pure, . 519 Pun. Death 11. 9
And, in fulfilment of God's mercy, lodged . . 541 Grace Darl. 82
And mercy am I thrown; . . . . 543 Russ. Fug. 162
"'This well of mercy, Jesu's Mother sweet, . . 556 Prioress 205
In mercy would His mercy multiply . . . . 556 Prioress 238
Now mercy, Lord! thou know'st well I desire 563 Troilus 73
Faith bore her up through pains in mercy given, . 576 *By a 7
O blessèd Lord! whose mercy then removed . . 576 *Six months 3
His might, nor less his mercy, as behoved— . 581 *Why should we 7
The God upon whose mercy they are thrown. . 584 *With copious 64
Acknowledges God's grace, his mercy feels, . . 586 Ch. Lamb 119
War is mercy, glory, fame, ... 628 Installation 13
Had plucked up mercy by the roots, were glad 723 Prelude 10. 332
Lay at the mercy of this raging storm. . . . 783 Excursion 2. 790
In mercy, carried infinite degrees . . . . 804 Excursion 4. 192
Till his deliverance, when Mercy made him . . 844 Excursion 6. 374
Let judgment here in mercy be pronounced; . . 847 Excursion 6. 591
Is divine mercy. She, who had rebelled, . . . 850 Excursion 6. 771
In mercy grant it, to thy wretched sons. . . . 894 Excursion 9. 648
One death, and that were mercy given to both. . K.8. 244 Recluse 1.1.268
And mercy, and forbearance. Nay—not these. . K.8. 244 Recluse 1.1.283
Sister of Mercy, bravely hast thou won . . . K.8. 325 [?] *The vestal 9
Unless resolved in mercy to the law . . . . L.1. 95 Juvenal 3. 22
Mercy's. For mercy's sake, is nobody in sight? . 61 Bord. 1292
The sentence rule by mercy's heaven-born lights." 519 Pun. Death 10. 12
Mercy-seat. Forgiveness from God's mercy-seat; . 331 Ode: Thanks. 179
Mercy-tempered. And awes like night with mercy-tempered frown. . . . . 425 Ecc. Sonn. 1. 26. 8
Mere. *See* **Thurston-mere.**
And, towering from the sullen dark-brown mere, 8 Ev. Wk. 313
—These fools of feeling are mere birds of winter . 47 Bord. 558
Of Grecian brook, or Lady of the Mere, . . . 149 *A narrow 37
Along the banks of Rydal Mere . . . . . 174 Waggoner 1. 30
As when he clomb from Rydal Mere; . . . . 174 Waggoner 1. 102
Mere Mortals, bodied forth in vision still, . . . 220 Triad 12
Mere slave of them who never for thee prayed, . 253 *Fond words 13
But a mere footstool to yon sovereign Lord, . . 290 Kilchurn 13
Whom mere despite of heart could so far please, . 292 *Degenerate Douglas 2
Mere Fibulæ without a robe to clasp; . . . . 394 *How profitless 12
A pleasant music floats along the Mere, . . . 426 Ecc. Sonn. 1. 30. 1
Soft as a cloud is yon blue Ridge—the Mere . . 456 *Soft as 1
Blank ocean and mere sky, support that mood . 488 Pers. Talk 31
Ah why deceive ourselves! by no mere fit . . 515 *Ah why 1
Making of social order a mere dream. . . . . 518 Pun. Death 7. 14
Of giant yews that frown on Rydale's mere; . . 591 Ev. Wk. Quarto 8
High towering from the sullen dark-brown mere, 598 Ev. Wk. Quarto 371
Spread like a spacious Mere, we there could measure 626 *The confidence 11
No picture of mere memory ever looked . . . 633 Prelude 1. 75
By moonshine through mere lack of taper light. . . 656 Prelude 3. 478
How potent a mere image of her sway; . . . 664 Prelude 4. 358
Not more than a mere plaything, or a toy . . 677 Prelude 6. 164
And inclination mainly, and the mere . . . 677 Prelude 6. 177
Herself were nothing, a mere pensioner . . . 686 Prelude 6. 737

Midst—*continued.*
Rejoicing o'er a female in the midst, — 716 *Prelude* 9. 460
Into the midst of turbulent events; — 725 *Prelude* 10. 462
Bearing a coffin in the midst, with which — 777 *Excursion* 2. 388
A book, that, in the midst of stones and moss — 778 *Excursion* 2. 433
Right in the midst, where interspace appeared — 784 *Excursion* 2. 861
He's the terror of boys in the midst of their noise. — S.3. 424 *Tinker* 31
To find, in midst of so much loveliness, — K.8. 245 *Recluse* 1. 1. 312
And waters in the midst, a Second Heaven. — K.8. 263 **The Lake* 12

Midsummer. Even in the longest day of midsummer— — 98 *Brothers* 225
When, in the warmth of midsummer, the wheat — 767 *Excursion* 1. 707
Spare, burning sun of midsummer, these sods, — 868 *Excursion* 7. 702

Midway. While, near the midway cliff, the silvered kite — 3 *Ev. Wk.* 90
Midway along the hill with desperate speed; — 6 *Ev. Wk.* 197
And midway on the waste ere night had fallen — 39 *Bord.* 117
It had been caught mid-way; and there for years — 101 *Brothers* 404
Midway on some high hill, while father Time — 322 **Ye Storms* 3
In lowliness—a mid-way tract there lies — 355 *Aquap.* 148
And midway in the unsafe morass, — 543 *Russ. Fug.* 101
Along the midway cliffs with violent speed; — 595 *Ev. Wk. Quarto* 180
—I see him, up the midway cliff he creeps — 610 *Desc. Sk. Quarto* 470
And bottomless, divides the midway tide. — 611 *Desc. Sk. Quarto* 499
Loud thro' that midway gulf ascending, sound — 611 *Desc. Sk. Quarto* 504
Of native rock, left midway in the square — 642 *Prelude* 2. 34
Midway on long Winander's eastern shore, — 644 *Prelude* 2. 138
Midway between the hills, as if she knew — 645 *Prelude* 2. 194
Within a world, a midway residence — 656 *Prelude* 3. 521
Of texture midway between life and books. — 657 *Prelude* 3. 578
With heads; the midway region, and above, — 697 *Prelude* 7. 691

Mid-winter. Of his day's work. 'Three dark mid-winter months — 834 *Excursion* 5. 804

Mien. Help from the staff he bore; for mien and air — 24 *Guilt* 4
And like a Roman matron's was her mien and gait. — 119 *Sailor's Mother* 6
Nurtured, as thy mien bespeaks, in high degree, — 140 *Arm. Lady* 23
Others, too, of lofty mien; — 160 **Pansies, lilies* 53
For calm and gentle is his mien; — 166 *Danish Boy* 54
With careless air and open mien. — 181 *Waggoner* 4. 147
Such garb with such a noble mien; — 205 *Brougham* 113
In his deportment, shape, and mien, appeared — 211 *Laod.* 94
And there (while, with sedater mien, — 221 *Triad* 133
In his whole figure and his mien — 239 *P. B.* 293
Modest her mien; and she, whose thoughts keep pace — 256 *Marriage: Friend* 7
Thy countenance—the still rapture of thy mien— — 258 **Even so* 3
Oh what a Wreck! how changed in mien and speech! — 280 **Oh what* 1
For never saw I mien, or face, — 288 *Highland Girl* 24
What joy to read the promise of her mien! — 311 **Who rises* 3
The genuine mien and character would trace — 313 **Go back* 2
His actions witness, venerate his mien, — 368 *Trajan* 27
Rough as the past; where Thou, of placid mien, — 381 *Duddon* 20. 8
In stately mien to sovereign Thames allied — 384 *Duddon* 32. 12
Such is her sovereign mien:—her dress — 413 *White Doe* 1606
From look, deportment, voice, or mien, — 415 *White Doe* 1722
King, child, and seraph, blended in the mien — 436 *Ecc. Sonn.* 2. 31. 7
When I shall scorn thy voice or mock thy mien! — 456 **The leaves* 25
And, by your mien and bearing, knew your names; — 474 **Ye shadowy* 5
With the baronial castle's sterner mien; — 477 **Lowther! in* 3
How bright her mien! — 490 *Night Thought* 6
That quietly restores the natural mien — 505 *Warning* 136
And in her face and mien — 545 *Russ. Fug.* 322
While Friends beheld thee give with eye, voice, mien, — 583 **With copious* 32
'Soften'd the terrors of her awful mien.' — 618 *School Ex.* 16
The blushing mien and downcast look; — 620 *Birth of Love* 33
And mien of one whose thoughts are free, advanced — 660 *Prelude* 4. 127
His mien and person, nor was free, in sooth, — 688 *Prelude* 7. 95
With admiration of her modest mien — 691 *Prelude* 7. 307
Save when realities of act and mien, — 694 *Prelude* 7. 477
Extravagance in gesture, mien, and dress, — 695 *Prelude* 7. 579
The old Man rose, and, with a sprightly mien — 771 *Excursion* 1. 965
I knew from his deportment, mien, and dress, — 779 *Excursion* 2. 498
At aught, however fair, that bore the mien — 797 *Excursion* 3. 780
With some impatience in his mien, he spake: — 817 *Excursion* 4. 1101
Standing before us:—"Did you note the mien — 826 *Excursion* 5. 233
Advanced to greet him. With a gracious mien — 829 *Excursion* 5. 444
But honoured once, those features and that mien — 834 *Excursion* 5. 788
An air and mien of dignified pursuit; — 839 *Excursion* 6. 40
For one, who, though of drooping mien, had yet — 839 *Excursion* 6. 99
And with a lady's mien.—From far they came, — 858 *Excursion* 7. 79
Are all vivacious as his mien and looks." — 866 *Excursion* 7. 563
Figure and mien, complexion and attire, — 879 *Excursion* 8. 358
But O, the animation in the mien — 883 *Excursion* 8. 572

Might. (*Partial list.*)
Might tempt me to a smile; but what of him? — 38 *Bord.* 26
Might want no cover, and rapacity — 38 *Bord.* 66
Who might have found a nothing-doing hour — 39 *Bord.* 120
We might have made a kindly bed of heath, — 39 *Bord.* 122
With Henry, our good King;—the Baron might — 43 *Bord.* 348
Well! they might turn a beggar from their doors, — 45 *Bord.* 439
And he seemed angry. Angry! well he might; — 46 *Bord.* 482
He in the preference, modest Youth, might take, — 47 *Bord.* 552
Were present, to the end that we might hear — 48 *Bord.* 589
As well indeed it might. And this you deem — 51 *Bord.* 749
Might envy, and am now,—but he shall know — 54 *Bord.* 939
Or you might drive your head against that wall. — 56 *Bord.* 1009
Of every country might be present. There — 58 *Bord.* 1127
Young as I am, I might go forth a teacher, — 59 *Bord.* 1223
The dismal conflict, and the might — 178 *Waggoner* 2. 143
Tugging all with might and main, — 181 *Waggoner* 4. 99
But, as it sometimes chanceth, from the might — 195 *Resolution* 22

Might—*continued.*
St. George was for us, and the might — 204 *Brougham* 28
His tongue could whisper words of might. — 205 *Brougham* 137
Submissive to the might of verse — 221 *Triad* 91
When magic lore abjured its might, — 223 *Wishing-gate* 13
The might of magic lore!" — 237 *P. B.* 110
If aught on earth have heavenly might, — 238 *P. B.* 149
Or whence the might of this strange sound? — 241 *P. B.* 482
To love the Lord with all your might; — 247 *P. B.* 948
Love from her depths, and Duty in her might, — 280 **Intent on* 13
While to the measure of his might — 291 *Rob Roy* 47
Up to the measure of accorded might, — 311 **Who rises* 44
That all the Alps may gladden in thy might, — 315 **Advance—come* 13
Round which the elements of worldly might — 317 **Look now* 7
With new-born hope. Unbounded is the might — 318 **Ah! where* 9
Peace that should claim respect from lawless Might. — 323 **Now that* 8
Of warnings—from the unprecedented might, — 332 *Ode: Thanks.* 234
Soft breezes fanning your rough brows—the might — 350 *Des. Stanzas* 53
All trust abandoned in the healing might — 363 **The world forsaken* 3
Lift up your hearts, ye Mourners! for the might — 387 *Scott* 8
Or whirlwind, reckless what his might — 391 *Highland Broach* 85
This Clifford wished for worthier might; — 399 *White Doe* 290
"Rise, noble Earls, put forth your might — 403 *White Doe* 633
This by their own unaided might, — 405 *White Doe* 857
Not vainly struggled in the might — 409 *White Doe* 1218
The Might of spiritual sway! his thoughts, his dreams, — 425 *Ecc. Sonn.* 1. 28. 10
See Latimer and Ridley in the might — 437 *Ecc. Sonn.* 2. 34. 2
That shows, ev'n on its better side, the might — 437 *Ecc. Sonn.* 2. 36. 5
Our Church prepares not, trusting to the might — 450 *Ecc. Sonn.* 3. 40. 7
Oh! might my name be numbered among theirs, — 489 *Pers. Talk* 55
In the full might they hitherto have shown, — 518 *Pun. Death* 6. 12
And shattered, and re-gathering their might; — 541 *Grace Darl.* 55
Upon thy heart, whence, through that glory's might, — 552 *Prioress* 19
'Mong Christian folk, a street where Jews might be, — 553 *Prioress* 37
And through this street who list might ride and wend; — 553 *Prioress* 41
This oftentimes, that he might be at ease, — 553 *Prioress* 77
By mouths of Innocents, lo! here Thy might; — 555 *Prioress* 157
To tell his might my wit may not suffice; — 557 *Cuck. and Night.* 11
But most his might he sheds on the eve of May. — 557 *Cuck. and Night.* 20
If I perchance a Nightingale might hear, — 557 *Cuck. and Night.* 53
And when he might his time aright espy, — 563 *Troilus* 38
That every wight might on his sorrow rue. — 563 *Troilus* 42
Men thence a book might make, a history; — 563 *Troilus* 67
I might her see again coming to Troy! — 564 *Troilus* 91
The occasion of his woe, as best he might; — 564 *Troilus* 114
To the end that he the Grecian host might see; — 564 *Troilus* 149
Who busily made use of all his might — 565 *Troilus* 165
And something, it might be, reserved for himself: — 570 *Farmer* 38
You might think he'd twelve reapers at work in the Strand. — 570 *Farmer* 72
Age might but take the things Youth needed not! — 571 **There is a Flower* 24
Then the Muses might deal with me just as they chose, — 571 *Avarice* 3
Was closing, might not of that life relate — 574 *Chiabrera* 4. 2
Of every cloud which in the heavens might stir — 574 *Chiabrera* 4. 18
That might from him be hidden; not a track — 574 *Chiabrera* 5. 11
His might, nor less his mercy, as behoved— — 581 **Why should we* 7
Thou little Child, yet glorious in the might — 589 *Immortality* 125
Yet in my heart of hearts I feel your might; — 590 *Immortality* 193
"Thus, Christian people, God his might hath shown — 627 **When Severn's* 3
O Heavens! how awful is the might of souls, — 651 *Prelude* 3. 177
With what, and how great might ye are in league, — 673 *Prelude* 5. 527
As with the might of waters; an apt type — 696 *Prelude* 7. 644
And throttled with an infant godhead's might — 724 *Prelude* 10. 392
Could cleanse the Augean stable, by the might — 726 *Prelude* 10. 585
Can it be called) which they with blended might — 755 *Recluse* 1. 1. 823
The unbounded might of prayer; and learned, with soul — 770 *Excursion* 1. 936
The moral interests, the creative might, — 798 *Excursion* 3. 823
Glorious! because the shadow of thy might, — 803 *Excursion* 4. 101
In thunder down the mountains; with all your might — 808 *Excursion* 4. 499
Whom the best might of faith, wherever fixed, — 828 *Excursion* 5. 360
How could the might, that lurks within her, then — 846 *Excursion* 6. 564
A might of which they dream not. Oh! the curse, — 870 *Excursion* 7. 822
But Human-kind rejoices in the might — 873 *Excursion* 7. 1033
When, strengthened, yet not dazzled, by the might — 877 *Excursion* 8. 210
Toward the beleaguered city, in the might — S.3. 437 **The doubt* 191

Might'st. (*Partial list.*)
Yet might'st thou seem, proud privilege! to sing — 153 *Morn. Ex.* 47
And in dimension, such that thou might'st seem — 290 *Kilchurn* 12
Of ignorance thou might'st witness heretofore, — 378 *Duddon* 8. 12
Might'st hold, on earth, communion undisturbed; — 802 *Excursion* 4. 86

Mightier. Yet further may relent: for mightier far — 210 *Laod.* 86
And where the mightier Waters burst — 215 *Enterprise* 26
Pure as herself—(song lacks not mightier power) — 220 *Triad* 9
Revive unenvied;—mightier far, — 225 *Primrose* 33
No mightier work had gained the plausive smile — 269 *Malham* 8
Hail, Bards of mightier grasp! on you — 473 *Ossian* 53
As one far mightier), hither I had come, — 650 *Prelude* 3. 87
But wrought with mightier arm than now prevails. — 787 *Excursion* 3. 91
To benefit and bless, through mightier power:— — 811 *Excursion* 4. 670
A mightier river, winds from realm to realm; — 869 *Excursion* 7. 790

Mightiest. The silver moon with all her vales, and hills of mightiest fame, — 189 *Star-gazers* 15
And now, in preference to the mightiest names, — 331 *Ode: Thanks.* 157
Where mightiest rivers into powerless sleep — 384 *Duddon* 32. 5

Mightiest—*continued.*
Then blame not those who, by the mightiest lever . 427 *Ecc. Sonn.* 1. 34. 9
And mightiest billows ever have confessed . . 459 **Wanderer! that* 47
In vision—forms uncouth of mightiest power . . 784 *Excursion* 2. 868
In perfect wisdom guiding mightiest power, . . 804 *Excursion* 4. 195
An equal among mightiest energies ; . . . . 809 *Excursion* 4. 532
True ; as the mightiest ; upon thee sequestered . S.3. 435 **The doubt* 132
Mightiness. What mightiness for evil and for good ! 306 **Inland, within* 8
Mighty. Move on—a mighty caravan of pain : . . 13 *Desc. Sk.* 170
A crucible of mighty compass, felt . . . . . 15 *Desc. Sk.* 283
A mighty waste of mist the valley fills, . . . 17 *Desc. Sk.* 408
Over the mighty stream now spreading wide : . 22 *Desc. Sk.* 655
" Some mighty gulf of separation passed, . . . 31 *Guilt* 352
What an odd moaning that is !— Mighty odd . 51 *Bord.* 751
Her bonds and chains, which make the mighty feeble. . . . . 57 *Bord.* 1091
A mighty evil for a strong-built mind !— . . . 65 *Bord.* 1511
What mighty objects do impress their forms . . 70 *Bord.* 1809
Availed against the mighty ; never more . . . 76 *Bord.* 2196
Into a chasm a mighty block . . . . . . 85 *Shepherd-boys* 51
Toward the mighty gulf of things, ... 90 *Longest Day* 58
Where thousands meet to worship God under a mighty Dome ; . . . . 93 *Poet's Dream* 62
A mighty wonder bred among our quiet crew. . 107 *Indolence* 18
Why are you in this mighty fret ? . . . . . 126 *Idiot Boy* 9
Though Betty's in a mighty flurry, ... 126 *Idiot Boy* 68
And struck him with a mighty stroke, . . . 157 *Oak and Broom* 106
Men that keep a mighty rout ! . . . . . . 160 **Pansies, lilies* 12
Herald of a mighty band, ... 160 **Pansies, lilies* 59
And mighty Fairfield, with a chime . . . . 182 *Waggoner* 4. 234
Behold the mighty Moon ! this way . . . . 192 *Gipsies* 19
And mighty Poets in their misery dead. . . . 197 *Resolution* 116
Happy day, and mighty hour, ... 205 *Brougham* 150
From this green earth ; of all the mighty world . 207 *Tintern* 105
That Ocean is a mighty harmonist ; . . . . 235 *Power of Sound* 187
Listen ! the mighty Being is awake, ... 258 **It is a* 6
Of a dark chamber where the Mighty sleep : . . 262 **Mark the* 11
And all the mighty ravishment of spring. . . . 264 **Lady ! the* 14
These mighty barriers, and the gulf between ; . 265 **Hail, Twilight* 12
And all that mighty heart is lying still ! . . . 269 *Westm. Bridge* 14
In his calm presence ! Him the mighty deed . 278 *Wellington* 9
But one of mighty size, and strange ; . . . . 295 *Highland Boy* 53
Whether of mighty towns, or vales . . . . . 295 *Highland Boy* 73
Down to the mighty Sea. . . . . 296 *Highland Boy* 100
One of the mountains ; each a mighty Voice : . 306 **Two Voices* 2
With mighty Nations for his underlings, . . . 309 **When, looking* 4
Shout, for a mighty Victory is won ! . . . . 310 *Anticip.* 1
Another mighty Empire overthrown ! . . . . 310 **Another year* 2
Whether the mighty beam, in scorn upheld, . . 311 **Who rises* 25
True to herself—the mighty Germany, ... 313 *Prophecy* 6
See the first mighty Hunter leave the brute— . 313 **Go back* 11
Here, mighty Nature ! in this school sublime . 314 **Not 'mid* 9
Else how, when mighty Thrones were put to shame, 316 **It was a* 2
Yet see (the mighty tumult overpast) . . . . 317 **The martial* 9
But mighty Winter the device shall scorn. . . 321 **Humanity, delighting* 12
The mighty debt which nothing can repay ! " . 324 *Ode 1814* 68
Support their mighty theme from age to age ; . 325 *Ode 1814* 132
By one day's feat, one mighty victory. . . . 326 *Sobieski* 10
And slaves are pleased to learn that mighty feats are done ; . . . . 327 *Ode 1815* 38
And well might it beseem that mighty Town . . 327 *Ode 1815* 46
Did mighty Tell repair of old— . . . . . 341 *San Salv.* 27
Where, from a deep lake's mighty urn, . . . 348 **Lulled by* 32
Of midnight,—cities, plains, forests, and mighty streams. . . . . 350 *Des. Stanzas* 18
But in his breast the mighty Poet bore . . . 365 **Under the* 11
Said Merlin : " Mighty King, fair Lords, . . . 372 *Eg. Maid* 199
Those mighty forests, once the bison's screen, . 376 *Duddon* 2. 10
While we, the brave, the mighty, and the wise, . . 384 *Duddon* 34. 7
Yea, what were mighty Nature's self ? . . . . 386 *Yarrow Rev.* 85
Where shields of mighty heroes hung, ... 390 *HighlandBroach* 29
Can such a mighty host be raised . . . . 404 *White Doe* 789
What mighty forest in its gloom . . . . . 413 *White Doe* 1557
The mighty sorrow hath been borne, ... 414 *White Doe* 1621
" Man's life is like a Sparrow, mighty King ! . . 422 *Ecc. Sonn.* 1. 16. 1
Of your own mighty instruments beware ! . . 423 *Ecc. Sonn.* 1. 20. 14
" My Oarsmen," quoth the mighty King, " draw near, ... 426 *Ecc. Sonn.* 1. 30. 4
Long lines of mighty Kings—look forth, my Soul ! 452 *Ecc. Sonn.* 3. 47. 9
No ; 'tis the earth-voice of the mighty sea, . . 453 **The Sun, that* 11
(Thy Paramount, mighty Nature ! and Time's Lord) . . . . 474 **On to* 5
" Think you, 'mid all this mighty sum . . . 481 *Expost.* 25
Is to the Being of a mighty nation, ... 516 **As leaves* 3
The mighty tumults of the House of Keys ; . . 522 *Epist. Beaumont* 66
A mighty One upon me gazed ; . . . . . . 542 *Russ. Fug.* 67
O more than mighty change ! If e'er . . . 545 *Russ. Fug.* 353
To tell abroad thy mighty worthiness, ... 553 *Prioress* 30
" There was in Asia, in a mighty town, . . . 553 *Prioress* 36
How mighty and how great a Lord is he ! . . . 556 *Cuck. and Night.* 2
For Love, and it hath done me mighty woe. . . 561 *Cuck.andNight.* 240
I could have fancied that the mighty Deep . . 578 *Peele Castle* 11
Long as these mighty rocks endure,— . . . . 581 *John Words.* 67
A mighty unison of streams ! . . . . . . 581 **Loud is* 3
The mighty Minstrel breathes no longer, . . . 586 *Hogg* 9
Mighty Prophet ! Seer blest ! . . . . . . 589 *Immortality* 114
And hear the mighty waters rolling evermore. . 590 *Immortality* 171
Where in a mighty crucible expire . . . . . 608 *Desc.Sk.Quarto* 346
In the deep snow the mighty ruin drown'd, . . 609 *Desc.Sk.Quarto* 378
My care, if the arm of the mighty were mine, . 621 *Convict* 51

Mighty—*continued.*
But huge and mighty forms, that do not live . . 638 *Prelude* 1. 398
And mighty depth of waters. Wonder not . . 648 *Prelude* 2. 409
Where mighty *minds* lie visibly entombed, . . 654 *Prelude* 3. 339
These mighty workmen of our later age, . . . 671 *Prelude* 5. 347
Was but a block hewn from a mighty quarry— . 672 *Prelude* 5. 465
Of mighty Poets. Visionary power . . . . 674 *Prelude* 5. 595
Of mighty names was softened down and seemed 676 *Prelude* 6. 61
With Poets ever. Mighty is the charm . . . 677 *Prelude* 6. 158
And mighty forms, seizing a youthful fancy, . . 680 *Prelude* 6. 334
Hail to the mighty projects of the time ! . . . 681 *Prelude* 6. 443
A motionless array of mighty waves, ... 683 *Prelude* 6. 531
That hides her, like the mighty flood of Nile . . 684 *Prelude* 6. 614
Enough ;—the mighty concourse I surveyed . . 690 *Prelude* 7. 219
When, having closed the mighty Shakspeare's page, 694 *Prelude* 7. 484
Of what the mighty City is herself, ... 698 *Prelude* 7. 723
(Beyond that mighty wall, not fabulous, . . . 700 *Prelude* 8. 79
Should have such mighty sway ! yet so it was), . 707 *Prelude* 8. 551
With that in which *her* mighty objects lay. . . 709 *Prelude* 8. 686
How quickly mighty Nations have been formed, . 715 *Prelude* 9. 376
For mighty were the auxiliars which then stood . 728 *Prelude* 11. 106
How are the mighty prostrated ! They first, . 732 *Prelude* 11. 380
Had never been when throes of mighty Nations . 741 *Prelude* 13. 107
Connected in a mighty scheme of truth, . . . 744 *Prelude* 13. 302
Shaken by arms of mighty bone, in strength, . . 744 *Prelude* 13. 325
Of mighty Poets : upon me bestow . . . . 755 *Recluse* 1. 1. 840
He gazed upon that mighty orb of song, . . . 760 *Excursion* 1. 249
In mighty current ; theirs, too, is the song . . 782 *Excursion* 2. 704
Was of a mighty city—boldly say . . . . . 784 *Excursion* 2. 835
Through all the mighty commonwealth of things ; 806 *Excursion* 4. 342
Of mighty Nature, if 'twas ever meant . . . 815 *Excursion* 4. 958
Stirs in the mighty woods.—So did he speak : . 820 *Excursion* 4. 1282
The head and mighty paramount of truths,— . 839 *Excursion* 6. 85
On which the sons of mighty Germany . . . 869 *Excursion* 7. 799
For, not unconscious of the mighty debt . . . 870 *Excursion* 7. 839
Of all the mighty, withered and consumed ! . . 872 *Excursion* 7. 982
And by this law the mighty whole subsists : . . 872 *Excursion* 7. 1004
And hear the mighty stream of tendency . . . 885 *Excursion* 9. 87
Expect these mighty issues : from the pains . . 890 *Excursion* 9. 394
The Vale is by a mighty sound possess'd. . . . S.3. 425 **The rains* 4
One of a mighty multitude, whose way . . . K.8. 242 *Recluse* 1.1.201
A mighty gain, that Labour here preserves . . K.8. 246 *Recluse* 1.1.359
A moon among her stars, a mighty vale, . . . K.8. 263 **The Lake* 5
Migration. Aerial, upon due migration bound . . 230 *Clouds* 18
Of our migration.—Ere the welcome dawn . . 522 *Epist. Beaumont* 91
Migration strange for a stripling of the hills, . . 649 *Prelude* 3. 34
Their grave migration, the good pair would tell, . 859 *Excursion* 7. 109
Migratory. At will, and stay thy migratory flight ; 455 *Rydal Mere* 34
Milan's. Hath past to Milan's loftiest spire, . . 343 *Eclipse* 38
Mild. And eve's mild hour invites my steps abroad. 3 *Ev. Wk.* 89
While tender cares and mild domestic loves . . 6 *Ev. Wk.* 222
Shedding, through paly loop-holes mild and small, 7 *Ev. Wk.* 293
Or rather stay to taste the mild delights . . . 16 *Desc. Sk.* 338
Suffering not doing ill—fate far more mild. . . 33 *Guilt* 499
Near his own home !—but he was mild and good ; 35 *Guilt* 608
Check his loud whip and hail us with mild voice, 61 *Bord.* 1335
Her Pony, that is mild and good ; . . . . . 126 *Idiot Boy* 33
Even he, of cattle the most mild, ... 128 *Idiot Boy* 240
The Pony he is mild and good, ... 129 *Idiot Boy* 303
Mild Offspring of infirm humanity, ... 172 *Infant Daughter* 2
The praises of mild Benjamin. . . . . . . 174 *Waggoner* 1. 45
Ere he replied, a flash of mild surprise . . . . 196 *Resolution* 90
Blissful Mary, Mother mild, ... 204 *Brougham* 69
Mild Hermes spake—and touched her with his wand 209 *Laod.* 19
Of a too-anxious world, mild pastoral Muse ! . . 227 *Vernal Ode* 76
'Twas but one mild, reproachful look, ... 241 *P. B.* 436
But, in its helplessness, grew mild . . . . . 247 *P. B.* 968
Wilt smile upon this gift with more than mild content ! . . . . 250 **Happy the* 14
It cheered mild Spenser, called from Faery-land . 260 **Scorn not* 10
Mild dawn of promise ! that excludes . . . . 302 *Yarrow V.* 21
And ye mild Seasons—in a sunny clime, . . . 322 **Ye Storms* 2
O gentle Power of darkness ! these mild hues ; . 334 **Bruges I* 11
And hence, O Virgin Mother mild ! . . . . . 338 **Meek Virgin* 19
The sky was blue, the air was mild ; . . . . 348 **Lulled by* 7
To mild, to lowly, and to seeming weak, . . . 354 *Aquap.* 132
To that mild breeze with motion and with voice . 356 *Aquap.* 221
Mild—as the verdure, fresh—the sunshine, bright— 356 *Aquap.* 235
With tenderness and mild emotion, ... 371 *Eg.Maid* 140
For mild Sorento's breezy waves ; . . . . . 386 *Yarrow Rev.* 53
Then, with mild Una in her sober cheer, . . . 395 *White Doe:Ded.* 37
Who with mild looks and language mild . . . 407 *White Doe* 1036
Mild, and grateful, melancholy : . . . . . . 415 *White Doe* 1758
The recognition ! the mild glance . . . . . 416 *White Doe* 1827
May not the less, through Heaven's mild countenance, ... 420 *Ecc. Sonn.* 1. 7. 12
Oh could we copy their mild virtues, then . . 441 *Ecc. Sonn.* 3. 5. 7
From his mild advent till his countenance . . 445 *Ecc. Sonn.* 3. 19. 13
So with our own the mild Instructor deals, . . 449 *Ecc. Sonn.* 3. 35. 9
Stealthy withdrawings, interminglings mild . . 454 *Sea-side* 7
Spares thy mild splendour ; still those far-shot beams . . . . 460 **Queen of* 23
Yet thy mild aspect does not, cannot, cease . . 460 **Queen of* 35
Albeit oft the Virgin-mother mild . . . . . 465 **The cattle* 12
It is the first mild day of March : . . . . . 482 *Sister* 1
Or mild concerns of ordinary life, ... 493 *Hap. War.* 46
I gaze upon a Portrait whose mild gleam . . . 508 *F. Stone* 6
So spake the mild Jeronymite, his griefs . . . 510 *F. Stone* 118
A mild domestic pity kept its place, ... 523 *Epist. Beaumont* 145
For moonlight fascinations mild, ... 526 **The soaring* 51

Mild—*continued.*
Not soon does aught to which mild fancies cling . 527 **Those breathing* 3
The way, mild Lady ! that hath led . . . . 534 **Blest is* 82
More mild doth Heaven ordain . . . . . . 544 *Russ. Fug.* 202
The mild necessity of use compels . . . . . 567 *Cumb. Beg.* 99
That first mild touch of sympathy and thought, . 568 *Cumb. Beg.* 114
Of the silver-rimmed horn whence he dealt his mild ale ! . . . . 569 *Farmer* 16
Long patience hath such mild composure given, . 572 *Animal Tran.* 10
From thy mild manners quietly exhaled. . . . 575 *Chiabrera* 8. 24
Like these, there comes a mild release ; . . . 580 *John Words.* 47
Thence, from three paly loopholes mild and small, . 598 *Ev. Wk. Quarto* 335
To the mild influence of the finer arts ; . . . 619 *School Ex.* 60
But I would call thee beautiful, for mild . . . 622 *Recluse* 1. 1. 114
" Infancy, by Wisdom mild, ... 629 *Installation* 45
Mild influence ; nor left in me one wish . . . 633 *Prelude* 1. 103
A stately air of mild indifference, ... 664 *Prelude* 4. 420
Listening, a gentle shock of mild surprise . . . 671 *Prelude* 5. 382
Quitted, not loth, the mild magnificence . . . 675 *Prelude* 6. 12
Had fitted their own thoughts, schemers more mild, 729 *Prelude* 11. 134
Mild interests and gentlest sympathies. . . . 749 *Prelude* 14. 231
My soul, too reckless of mild grace, had stood 749 *Prelude* 14. 248
Admitted more habitually a mild . . . . 750 *Prelude* 14. 288
Such easy cheerfulness, a look so mild, . . . 765 *Excursion* 1. 607
Fondly, though with an interest more mild, . . 770 *Excursion* 1. 926
Mild, inoffensive, ready in *his* way, ... 783 *Excursion* 2. 761
From mild to angry, and from sad to gay, . . 790 *Excursion* 3. 315
To One on whose mild radiance many gazed . . 793 *Excursion* 3. 503
And mild paternal sway. The potent shock . . 796 *Excursion* 3. 716
Where mild enthusiasts tuned a pensive lay . . 797 *Excursion* 3. 754
The mild assemblage of the starry heavens ; . . 808 *Excursion* 4. 464
That her mild nature can be terrible ; . . . . 816 *Excursion* 4. 1032
Approached ; and, with a mild respectful air . . 829 *Excursion* 5. 442
" Our nature," said the Priest, in mild reply, . . 829 *Excursion* 5. 485
Eyes beaming courtesy and mild regard ; . . . 834 *Excursion* 5. 783
But with a mild and social cheerfulness ; . . . 839 *Excursion* 6. 93
If mild discourse, and manners that conferred . 850 *Excursion* 6. 793
Mild Man ! he is not gay, but they are gay ; . . 856 *Excursion* 6. 1186
—Nor deem that his mild presence was a weight . 864 *Excursion* 7. 438
Which the mild sunbeam hath not power to pierce. 870 *Excursion* 7. 836
Benevolence is mild ; nor borrows help, . . . 873 *Excursion* 7. 1030
How much the mild Directress of the plough . . 876 *Excursion* 8. 131
This ardent sally pleased the mild good Man, . . 880 *Excursion* 8. 434
Shared, though in mild and merciful degree : . . 886 *Excursion* 9. 167
What witchcraft, mild enchantress, may with thee S.3. 434 **The doubt* 94
With the mild summons ; inmates though they be K.8. 241 *Recluse* 1.1.194
Hath said, " Be mild and cleave to gentle things, K.8. 256 *Recluse* 1.1.735

Milder. But in the milder grief of pity. . . . . 9 *Collins* 16
When from October clouds a milder light . . . 21 *Desc. Sk.* 626
That, in his milder moods, he has expressed . . 43 *Bord.* 346
And speak with milder voice to his poor beasts. . 61 *Bord.* 1336
But he is milder far than she, ... 130 *Idiot Boy* 395
Or with a milder grace adorning . . . . . 182 *Waggoner* 4. 230
Yet sometimes milder hours she knew, . . . 194 *Ruth* 199
But at the coming of the milder day . . . 203 *Hart-leap* 175
To milder climes ; or rather do ye urge . . . 230 *Clouds* 19
And milder echoes from their cells . . . . 233 *Power of Sound* 39
His milder Genius (thanks to the good God . . 362 **List—'twas* 42
And temples, doomed to milder change, unfold . 367 *Trajan* 3
Here hath a milder doom prevailed ; . . . . 415 *White Doe* 1786
And Russell's milder blood the scaffold wet ; . . 442 *Ecc. Sonn.* 3. 10. 4
Before the path of milder suns ; . . . . . 497 *Lycoris* 32
And open thy sad eyes upon a milder day. . . 581 *Invoc. Earth* 7
Nor was there want of milder thoughts, of love, . 661 *Prelude* 4. 172
And milder breezes,—melancholy lot ! . . . . 678 *Prelude* 6. 241
Brought to such spectacle a milder sadness, . . 693 *Prelude* 7. 394
Put on a milder face ; Terror had ceased, . . . 727 *Prelude* 11. 2
The milder minstrelsies of rural scenes . . . . 737 *Prelude* 12. 200
At distance heard, peopled the milder air. . . 771 *Excursion* 1. 964
Had fixed his milder loyalty, and placed . . . 844 *Excursion* 6. 428
And milder worth : nor need we travel far . . 863 *Excursion* 7. 393
Bishops, of milder Spanish breed, shall boast . . L.1. 89 *Juvenal* 1. 25

Mildest. And peach and citron, in Spring's mildest breeze . . . . 356 *Aquap.* 218
Whom I have left, Love's mildest birth, . . . 403 *White Doe* 617
Or mildest visitations of pure thought, . . . 685 *Prelude* 6. 684
Of universal ferment ; mildest men . . . . 712 *Prelude* 9. 162

Mildew. His drought consumes, his mildew taints with death ; . . . . 328 *Ode 1815* 92

Mild-hearted. Of the mild-hearted Champion, save this stone, ... 872 *Excursion* 7. 966

Mildly. The Sun, that seemed so mildly to retire, . 453 **The Sun, that* 1
Yes, lovely Moon ! if thou so mildly bright . . 459 **Wanderer ! that* 40
Of manly virtues, mildly bright, ... 503 **Like a* 71
To tax you with this journey ; "—mildly said . 779 *Excursion* 2. 487
" Is this," the grey-haired Wanderer mildly said, 789 *Excursion* 3. 225
Mildly, and with a clear and steady tone. . . . 883 *Excursion* 8. 601

Mildly-gleaming. (But seldom trod) of mildly-gleaming ore ; . . . . 264 **Lady ! I* 2

Mildness. And mildness, and spirit both forward and coy. . . . . 482 *Character* 12
With the same ghastly mildness in his look, . . 665 *Prelude* 4. 458
Yet keeping her first mildness, was advanced . . 861 *Excursion* 7. 227

Mile. A long mile thence. While thither they pursued . . . . 30 *Guilt* 332
To travel half a mile alone.—Good Lady ! . . 76 *Bord.* 2240
There's not a house within a mile, ... 126 *Idiot Boy* 22
And she can see a mile of road : . . . . . 129 *Idiot Boy* 278
But pass a mile—and *then* for trial,— . . . . 174 *Waggoner* 1. 72
The fourth part of a mile I ween, ... 296 *Highland Boy* 158
Their pace from mile to mile, ... 543 *Russ. Fug.* 126

Mile—*continued.*
Was set, and visible for many a mile . . . . 638 *Prelude* 1. 426
Beneath the trees, clear footing many a mile— . 716 *Prelude* 9. 436

Miles. A thousand miles. I am in poverty, . . 74 *Bord.* 2078
Until a man might travel twelve stout miles, . . 95 *Brothers* 9
Is distant three short miles, and in the time . . 99 *Brothers* 252
And I have travelled weary miles to see . . . 119 *Sailor's Mother* 23
Ten thousand miles from all his brethren ? . . 242 *P. B.* 515
Two long Scotch miles, through rain or snow, . 246 *P. B.* 898
I travelled round our little lake, five miles . . 647 *Prelude* 2. 331
Where there are no measured miles, ... S.3. 423 *Tinker* 6
Even at the utmost distance of two miles . . . K.8. 225 **I will* 42
Have driven him twenty miles." . . . . . K.8. 228 **I will* 122
Drive one of these poor creatures miles and miles, K.8. 228 **I will* 124

Mile-stone. A mile-stone propped him ; I could also ken . . . . 664 *Prelude* 4. 397

Militant. Under such banners militant, the soul . 684 *Prelude* 6. 609

Military. A coat he wore of military red . . . 24 *Guilt* 8
A military casque he wore, ... 192 *Ruth* 20
A sound of military cheer, ... 401 *White Doe* 432
Of vengeful military force, ... 411 *White Doe* 1383
That he was clothed in military garb, ... 664 *Prelude* 4. 398
Arms flashing, and a military glare . . . . . 681 *Prelude* 6. 424
A march it was of military speed, ... 682 *Prelude* 6. 491
The military Idler, and the Dame, ... 690 *Prelude* 7. 209
A band of military Officers, ... 711 *Prelude* 9. 125
Of Chaplain to a military troop . . . . . . 774 *Excursion* 2. 175
Of military sway. The shifting aims, ... 798 *Excursion* 3. 822

Milk. Round as a pillow, and whiter than milk, . 80 †*Address : Child* 12
I bring thee draughts of milk, warm milk it is and new. . . . . 87 *Pet-lamb* 44
Each with a mess of pottage and skimmed milk, . 132 *Michael* 100
Who fills the mother's breast with innocent milk, 669 *Prelude* 5. 272

Milk-maid. The milk-maid followed with her brimming pail, ... 34 *Guilt* 529
And, in disguise, a Milkmaid with her pail . . 521 *Epist. Beaumont* 42
They not the trip of harmless milkmaid feel. . . 596 *Ev. Wk. Quarto* 226
The milkmaid stops her ballad, and her pail . . 598 *Ev. Wk. Quarto* 355

Milkmaid's. Yon isle, which feels not even the milkmaid's feet, ... 6 *Ev. Wk.* 236
Happy milk-maids, one by one . . . . . . 233 *Power of Sound* 45

Milk-thistle. Then the milk-thistle flourished through the land, ... 17 *Desc. Sk.* 396
Then the milk-thistle bad those herds demand . 611 *Desc. Sk. Quarto* 484

Milk-white. The graceful form of milk-white Steed, 341 *Ital. Itin.* 9
The milk-white Lamb which in a line she led,— . 395 *White Doe: Ded.* 14
Why thus the milk-white Doe is found . . . 398 *White Doe* 202
Not distant far, the milk-white Doe— . . . . 406 *White Doe* 972
And heavenly Una with her milk-white Lamb. . 488 *Pers. Talk* 42
With milk-white clusters hung ; the rod and line, 639 *Prelude* 1. 485
Of milk-white Swans, wherefore are *they* not seen K.8. 243 *Recluse* 1.1.239

Milky. And twinkle on the milky way, ... 187 **I wandered* 8

Mill. *See* **Burn-mill**, **Wind-mill**.
Each clacking mill, that broke the murmuring streams, ... 22 *Desc. Sk.* 630
As loud as any mill, or near it ; . . . . . . 127 *Idiot Boy* 98
By their floating mill, ... 166 *Stray Pleasures* 1
To their mill where it floats, ... 166 *Stray Pleasures* 8
To their house and their mill tethered fast : . . 166 *Stray Pleasures* 9
Clustering, with barn and byre, and spouting mill ! 379 *Duddon* 13. 3
A bridge to copy, or to paint a mill, ... 521 *Epist. Beaumont* 31
Beside the pleasant Mill of Trompington . . . 653 *Prelude* 3. 275
Meanwhile, as if the whole were one vast mill, . 698 *Prelude* 7. 719
To turn a slender mill (that new-made plaything) 789 *Excursion* 3. 205

Mill-dog's. And at long intervals the mill-dog's howl ; . . . . 9 *Ev. Wk.* 376

Miller. The Miller with two Dames, on the breast of the Thames ! . . . . 166 *Stray Pleasures* 4

Millions. Of this too much. Men are there, millions, Oswald, ... 77 *Bord.* 2292
Of happy millions lulled in sleep ; . . . . . 113 *Lament* 26
Millions of waves into itself, and run, ... 442 *Ecc. Sonn.* 3. 9. 2
As millions thus shall do, the Headlands of St. Bees. 466 *St. Bees* 27
Millions from glorious aims. Our chains to sever 516 **Hard task* 6
The servile million bow ; . . . . 628 *Installation* 10
Is joy for tens of millions. Southward thence . 680 *Prelude* 6. 349
Why may not millions be ? What bars are thrown 741 *Prelude* 13. 89
To that inheritance which millions rue . . . . 826 *Excursion* 5. 272
Millions of kneeling Hindoos at this day . . . S.3. 435 **The doubt* 122

Mill-race. In a small mill-race severed from his stream, ... 636 *Prelude* 1. 289

Mills. *See* **Water-mills.**

Milton. And those that Milton loved in youthful years ; . . . . 103 *Artegal* 50
Fell round the path of Milton, in his hand . . 260 **Scorn not* 12
Milton ! thou shouldst be living at this hour : . 307 **Milton ! thou* 1
Young Vane, and others who called Milton friend. 307 **Great men* 4
Which Milton held.—In every thing we are sprung 307 **It is not* 13
The sightless Milton, with his hair . . . . . 341 *Ital. Itin.* 12
Where our Milton was wont lonely vigils to keep . 364 *Vallomb.* 7
Such Milton, to the fountain-head . . . . . 473 *Ossian* 81
Romantic tale by Milton left unsung ; . . . . 634 *Prelude* 1. 169
Shakespeare, or Milton, labourers divine ! . . . 668 *Prelude* 5. 165
And sought *that* beauty, which, as Milton sings, . 749 *Prelude* 14. 245
The divine Milton. Lore of different kind, . . 760 *Excursion* 1. 250

Miltonian. And now, ye Miltonian shades ! under you 364 *Vallomb.* 29

Milton's. Honoured by Milton's name. O temperate Bard ! . . . . 653 *Prelude* 3. 295

Miltons. And, like the Pyms and Miltons of that day, 310 *Invasion* 7

Mimic. The mimic notes, striking upon his ear . . 229 *Cuckoo-clock* 29
To mimic Time's forlorn humanities. . . . . 262 **Mark the* 14

Mimicked 607 **Mind**

Mimic—*continued.*
Ensigns of mimic outrage are unfurled. . . . 504 *Warning* 86
A more substantial name, no mimic show, . . 657 *Prelude* 3. 589
Blew mimic hootings to the silent owls, . . . 671 *Prelude* 5. 373
Their steeds bestriding,—every mimic shape . . 689 *Prelude* 7. 138
Liking ; by rules of mimic art transferred . . . 736 *Prelude* 12. 111
With mimic trees inserted in the turf, ... 778 *Excursion* 2. 427
Mimicked. Like blighted buds ; or clouds that mimicked land . . . . 843 *Excursion* 6. 315
Mimicking. Mimicking a troubled sea, ... 550 *Hermit's Cell* 3. 6
Mimicries. Of April's mimicries ! . . . . . 170 *Rural Ill.* 8
Mimicry. That mimicry should thus disgrace . . 163 *Needlecase* 3
Mimics. Yon rampant cloud mimics a lion's shape ; 348 *Sky-prosp.* 4
A toy that mimics with revolving wings . . . 723 *Prelude* 10. 368
Mina. And Mina, nourished in the studious shade, 320 **They seek* 11
Minarets. Yon minarets, would gladly leave for his worst home." . . . . 140 *Arm. Lady* 42
Mind. A mind that, in a calm angelic mood . . 3 *Ev. Wk.* 80
The soft gloom deepening on the tranquil mind. . 8 *Ev. Wk.* 318
While Slavery, forcing the sunk mind to dwell 13 *Desc. Sk.* 137
The mind condemned, without reprieve, to go 13 *Desc. Sk.* 166
But now with other mind I stand alone . . . 16 *Desc. Sk.* 303
But brings some past enjoyment to his mind ; . 18 *Desc. Sk.* 430
And here the unwilling mind may more than trace 19 *Desc. Sk.* 502
Why does their sad remembrance haunt the mind ? 19 *Desc. Sk.* 519
That break against the shore, shall lull thy mind 22 *Yew-tree* 6
Left his mind still as a deep evening stream. . . 26 *Guilt* 96
He hoped, to calm her mind ; but ill he sped, 27 *Guilt* 169
Which by degrees a confidence of mind . . . 28 *Guilt* 194
And nothing to my mind a sweeter pleasure brought. 28 *Guilt* 207
Is rooted in his mind ; this Band of ours, . . . 38 *Bord.* 60
Out of thy mind ? My dear, my only, Child ; . 40 *Bord.* 163
Something I strike upon which turns my mind 51 *Bord.* 783
Else could so strong a mind have ever known 55 *Bord.* 998
Nor any half so sure. This Stripling's mind . . 58 *Bord.* 1162
The senseless body, and why not the mind ?— 58 *Bord.* 1167
These are strange sights—the mind of man, upturned, ... 58 *Bord.* 1168
I strove to ease my mind, when our two Comrades, 59 *Bord.* 1211
One happy thought has passed across my mind. . 61 *Bord.* 1326
How, when the People's mind was racked with doubt, ... 62 *Bord.* 1383
A mighty evil for a strong-built mind !— . . . 65 *Bord.* 1511
From action up to action with a mind . . . . 69 *Bord.* 1789
'Tis a poor wretch of an unsettled mind, . . . 73 *Bord.* 2033
My wife and children came into my mind. . . 74 *Bord.* 2088
That fettered your nobility of mind— . . . . 77 *Bord.* 2281
Is out of mind—or done. . . . . 84 *Shepherd-boys* 15
And bade them better mind their trade. . . . 85 *Shepherd-boys* 99
And eased his mind with this reply : . . . . 86 *Anecdote* 54
Lest all that passed should melt away in silence from my mind, ... 93 *Poet's Dream* 71
A cheerful mind,—and buffeted with bond, . . 98 *Brothers* 214
And you believe, then, that his mind was easy ?— 101 *Brothers* 387
Thou art reputed wise, but in my mind . . . 104 *Artegal* 166
And his own mind did like a tempest strong . . 108 *Indolence* 35
Heaven grants even to the guiltiest mind . . . 110 *Forsaken* 3
And wicked fancies crossed my mind ; . . . . 115 *Last of Flock* 72
One that will answer to my mind ; . . . . . 117 *Affl. Marg.* 69
Those several qualities of heart and mind . . . 118 *Maternal Grief* 20
From bodings, as might be, that hung upon his mind. . . . . 119 *Sailor's Mother* 30
Of their maturer years, his present mind . . . 122 *V. and J.* 36
Uncharitable crossed his mind, no sense . . . 124 *V. and J.* 168
He suffered—breaking down in heart and mind ! . 124 *V. and J.* 184
His days he wasted, an imbecile mind ! . . . 126 *V. and J.* 306
Was, " Johnny ! Johnny ! mind that you . . 126 *Idiot Boy* 58
" Oh ! Johnny, never mind the Doctor ; . . . 130 *Idiot Boy* 397
And, as her mind grew worse and worse, . . . 130 *Idiot Boy* 415
And, while her mind was fighting thus, . . . 130 *Idiot Boy* 420
And, Johnny, mind you tell us true." . . . . 131 *Idiot Boy* 441
Of an unusual strength : his mind was keen, . . 131 *Michael* 44
So many incidents upon his mind . . . . . 132 *Michael* 68
Of fathers, but with patient mind enforced . . 133 *Michael* 156
Albeit of a stern unbending mind, ... 133 *Michael* 161
And Isabel sat silent, for her mind . . . . . 135 *Michael* 256
Passed quickly through the mind of Isabel, . . 135 *Michael* 272
May'st bear in mind the life thy Fathers lived, . 137 *Michael* 410
My father for slave's work may seek a slave in mind." . . . . 140 *Arm. Lady* 36
That store the mind, the memory feed, . . . 143 †*Lov. and Lik.* 63
Even, as your happy presence to my mind . . 143 **High bliss* 25
Pleasant conviction flashed upon my mind . . 150 **When, to* 58
Each other's mind was fashioned ; and at length, 151 **When, to* 72
That spot which seems so to thy mind ! . . . 159 **Up with me* 7
And so may we, with charmèd mind . . . . 164 **Fair Lady* 21
Ye pulled together with one mind ; . . . . 175 *Waggoner* 1. 133
" Go you your way, and mind not me ; . . . . 176 *Waggoner* 1. 258
Proceeding with a mind at ease ; . . . . . 176 *Waggoner* 2. 14
And in a moment calls to mind . . . . . . 177 *Waggoner* 2. 29
At length the Vision closes ; and the mind, . . 184 *Night-piece* 23
Does, then, a deep and earnest thought the blissful mind employ . . . . 189 *Star-gazers* 25
Ye, who within the blameless mind . . . . 191 *Seq. Beggars* 34
To wander with an easy mind ; . . . . . . 193 *Ruth* 76
Did to his mind impart . . . . 193 *Ruth* 129
Full soon that better mind was gone : . . . . 194 *Ruth* 181
Of mind than body's wretchedness, ... 194 *Ruth* 233
In that decrepit Man so firm a mind. . . . . 197 *Resolution* 138
And in my simple mind we cannot tell . . . 203 *Hart-leap* 146
And passing even into my purer mind, . . . 206 *Tintern* 29

Mind—*continued.*
The picture of the mind revives again : . . . 206 *Tintern* 61
And the blue sky, and in the mind of man : . . 207 *Tintern* 99
The mind that is within us, so impress . . . 207 *Tintern* 126
Into a sober pleasure ; when thy mind . . . 207 *Tintern* 139
Within the mind strong fancies work, ... 214 *Kirkstone* 1
Won from the world of mind, dost thou prepare . 216 *Enterprise* 90
When but a single Mind resolves to crouch no more. 216 *Enterprise* 103
By all that mind invents or hand prepares ; . . 221 *Triad* 64
That truth informing mind and heart, ... 224 *'*Tis gone* 61
By art to unsensualise the mind . . . . . 228 *Devot. Incit.* 47
As if within thee dwelt a glancing mind, . . . 232 *Power of Sound* 2
That taints the purer, better, mind ; . . . . 233 *Power of Sound* 88
What nobler marvels than the mind . . . . 238 *P. B.* 143
Come, Spirits of the Mind ! and try, ... 245 *P. B.* 783
And now the Spirits of the Mind . . . . . 246 *P. B.* 916
Breathless and motionless, the mind . . . . 247 *P. B.* 1017
A holy sense pervades his mind ; . . . . . 248 *P. B.* 1053
As if his mind were sinking deep . . . . . 248 *P. B.* 1093
Yet to my mind this scanty Stream is brought . 251 **There is a little* 6
Do Thou, then, breathe those thoughts into my mind . . . . 257 **The prayers* 9
Love, faithful love, recalled thee to my mind— . 257 **Surprised by* 5
Of nature trusts the Mind that builds for aye ; . 259 **A volant* 6
To elevate the more-than-reasoning Mind, . . 259 **Weak is* 7
Demands the service of a mind and heart, . . 260 **High is* 4
Cool air I breathe ; while the unincumbered Mind, 262 *Retirement* 12
The immortal Mind craves objects that endure : . 263 **Those words* 12
From stain or taint ; in which thy blameless mind 264 **Lady ! I* 11
Just Heaven, contract the compass of my mind . 267 **As the* 9
We rather think, with grateful mind sedate, . . 271 *Henry: Portrait* 11
Strains that recalled to mind a distant day ; . . 271 **Fame tells* 8
By favouring Nature and a saintly Mind . . . 274 **Such age* 3
To thy large heart and humble mind, that cast . 279 **Though I* 13
From mind and spirit, grudge a short-lived fence. 280 *Plea for Auth.* 8
Power in my breast, wings growing in my mind, . 284 *Departure* 14
But heart with heart and mind with mind, . . 285 *Grave of Burns* 44
So have I, not unmoved in mind, ... 288 *Highland Girl* 44
In peace, and peace of mind. . . . . . . 291 *Rob Roy* 36
" All freakishness of mind is checked ; . . . . 291 *Rob Roy* 45
How fairly to his mind ! . . . . 291 *Rob Roy* 76
Beneath worse ailments of the mind. . . . . 294 *Jedbor.* 75
Nor had a melancholy mind ; . . . . . . 295 *Highland Boy* 22
That story flashed upon his mind ; . . . . . 296 *Highland Boy* 142
Upon a mind with love o'erflowing— . . . . 301 *Bran* 116
And cheer my mind in sorrow. . . . . . . 302 *Yarrow V.* 88
'Tis ever thus. Ye men of prostrate mind, . . 303 **Is it* 8
Of that Man's mind—what can it be ? what food 304 **I grieved* 3
And love, and man's unconquerable mind. . . . 305 *Toussaint* 14
That, burning independent of the mind, . . . 306 **We had* 11
Among the many movements of his mind, . . 308 **When I* 13
From van to rear—and with one mind would flee, 314 *Hofer* 10
Like him of noble birth and noble mind ; . . . 315 **And is it* 11
Of *justice* which the human mind can frame, . . 316 **Say, what* 2
To whose all-pondering mind a noble aim, . . 317 **Brave Schill* 12
Say can he think of this with mind serene . . 318 **Is there* 11
Avaunt all specious pliancy of mind . . . . 319 **Avaunt all* 1
Whom no weak hopes deceived ; whose mind ensued, ... 323 **Now that* 6
Go forth with rival youthfulness of mind, . . . 324 *Ode 1814* 43
Of warfare waged with desperate mind . . . 330 *Ode : Thanks.* 105
Mounts to the seat of grace within the mind : . 334 **The Spirit* 5
If clay could think and mind were weight, . . 341 *Ital. Itin.* 15
Of that licentious craving in the mind . . . . 347 *Processions* 65
Nor further outlet left to mind or heart ? . . . 350 *Des. Stanzas* 2
Not, therefore, shall my mind give way to sadness ;— . . . . 352 *Aquap.* 9
Relax, to fix and satisfy the mind . . . . . 353 *Aquap.* 25
To feed his mind with watchful eyes could share . 353 *Aquap.* 55
Preyed upon body and mind—yet not the less . 353 *Aquap.* 59
Of thoughtful sentiment for every mind . . . 355 *Aquap.* 149
So with the internal mind it fares ; and so . . 357 *Aquap.* 333
Else more and more the general mind will droop, 357 *Aquap.* 340
To soberness of mind and peace of heart . . . 358 *Aquap.* 367
Of freedom, with mind grasping the whole theme . 359 **They—who* 10
Of mind, that dread heart-freezing discipline, . . 362 **List—'twas* 44
That everywhere, before the thoughtful mind, . . 364 **What aim* 13
Of that holiest of Bards, and the name for my mind 364 *Vallomb.* 26
The mind, depressed by thought of greatness flown. 365 **Under the* 8
I gladly commune with the mind and heart . . 368 *Trajan* 25
Becomes with all her years a vision of the Mind. . 368 *Trajan* 73
There are whose calmer mind it would content . 377 *Duddon* 7. 11
Body and mind, from molestation freed, . . . 382 *Duddon* 24. 8
The drooping mind of absence, by vows sworn . 383 *Duddon* 28. 12
Prepared, in peace of heart, in calm of mind . . 384 *Duddon* 33. 13
The freeborn mind enthralling, ... 385 *Yarrow Rev.* 22
Into a vacant mind. Can written book . . . 389 *Tyndrum* 8
Concord that elevates the mind, and stills. . . 389 *Breadalb.* 14
In mind the landscape, as if still in sight ; . . 392 *Bothwell* 5
O, that my mind were equal to fulfil . . . . 395 *White Doe: Ded.* 59
Nor to the Child's enquiring mind . . . . . 398 *White Doe* 206
A mutual hope, a common mind ; . . . . . 403 *White Doe* 643
Far back—far back my mind must go . . . . 406 *White Doe* 887
To your nobility of mind ! " . . . . . . 406 *White Doe* 923
This would I beg ; but on my mind . . . . 408 *White Doe* 1086
Rushed through his mind the prophecy . . . 411 *White Doe* 1427
He heard, and with misgiving mind. . . . . 412 *White Doe* 1445
Of mind, to Rylstone back she came ; . . . . 415 *White Doe* 1752
Although with no unwilling mind . . . . . 416 *White Doe* 1861
And bears a memory and a mind . . . . . 416 *White Doe* 1877
Repeatedly his own deep mind he sounds . . . 422 *Ecc. Sonn.* 1. 15. 11

Mirror—*continued.*
And no vain mirror glittered upon the walls, . . 860 *Excursion* 7. 176
Mirrored. Mirrored, yet not too strictly, may refine S.3. 435 **The doubt* 118
Mirror's. Within the mirror's depth, a world at rest— 524 *Epist. Beaumont* 174

Mirrors. Not stripped; not voiceless in the mirrors, 300 *Bran* 20
Mirth. The valley rings with mirth and joy ; . . 84 *Shepherd-boys* 1
The crickets long have ceased their mirth ; . . 118 †*Cottager* 7
Meanwhile, a noise was heard, the busy mirth . 149 **A narrow* 40
Prophet of delight and mirth, ... 160 **Pansies, lilies* 57
Moves all nature to gladness and mirth. . . . 167 *Stray Pleasures* 30
All have laid their mirth aside. . . . . . . 171 *Kitten* 62
And implements of frolic mirth ; . . . . . 191 *Seq. Beggars* 4
The hare is running races in her mirth ; . . . 195 *Resolution* 11
With sighs of self-exhausted mirth . . . . . 225 *Present.* 44
The blind man's gloom, exalts the veteran's mirth ; 233 *Power of Sound* 50
Swift Mercury resounds with mirth, ... 237 *P. B.* 46
Suffices me—her tears, her mirth, ... 238 *P. B.* 134
Her humblest mirth and tears. . . . . . . 238 *P. B.* 135
When, to upset his spiteful mirth, ... 245 *P. B.* 833
Might need for comfort, or for festal mirth ; . . 276 *Filial Piety* 3
With mirth elate, ... 286 *Nith* 34
Beat like the heart of Man : songs, garlands, mirth, 304 **Jones ! as* 7
Should come in frenzy and in drunken mirth, . 308 **One might* 12
We met, while festive mirth ran wild, . . . 348 **Lulled by* 31
Would mirth run round, with generous fare ; . . 409 *White Doe* 1185
To meet the coming hours of festal mirth, . . 445 *Ecc. Sonn.* 3. 20. 10
It is the man of mirth. . . . . 487 *Fountain* 52
Sound sense, and love itself, and mirth and glee . 488 *Pers. Talk* 19
Let easy mirth his social hours inspire, . . . 528 **Those breathing* 96
And jollity, fresh cheerfulness, and mirth ; . . 559 *Cuck.andNight.*155
When link'd with thoughtless Mirth I cours'd the plain, ... 592 *Ev. Wk. Quarto* 31
The night in dancing, gaiety, and mirth, . . . 663 *Prelude* 4. 312
You and your not unwelcome days of mirth . . 675 *Prelude* 6. 15
Along that very Loire, with festal mirth . . 716 *Prelude* 9. 431
For sacrifice, and struggling with fond mirth . . 724 *Prelude* 10. 407
That had no mirth in them ; or with his knife . 764 *Excursion* 1. 570
In their repose, the living in their mirth, . . . 828 *Excursion* 5. 374
Into the troop of mirth, a soldier, sworn . . . 842 *Excursion* 6. 285
Of speech as wild as ever heightened mirth. . . K.8. 301 **And oh* 10
But here's a thought which well our mirth may cross L.1. 95 *Juvenal* 3. 14
Mirth that to aching ribs will not submit . . . L.1. 95 *Juvenal* 3. 19
Mirthful. What shall it be ? a mirthful throng ? or that holy place and calm . . . . . 92 *Poet's Dream* 23
Over their mirthful triumph clapping hands. . . 222 *Triad* 173
Is this a place for mirthful cheer ? . . . . . 294 *Jedbor.* 23
Miry. The boisterous carman, in the miry road, . 61 *Bord.* 1334
And walked with me along the miry road, . . 769 *Excursion* 1. 864
Mirza's. He who stood visible to Mirza's eye, . . 252 **The fairest* 7
Misapplied. And sorceries of talent misapplied. . 425 *Ecc. Sonn.* 1. 28. 14
Misbelievers. Though with misbelievers bred ; but that dark night . . . . 141 *Arm. Lady* 119
Miscellaneous. From miscellaneous converse, ye were taught . . . . 586 *Ch. Lamb* 111
That miscellaneous garland of wild flowers . . 652 *Prelude* 3. 223
Mischance. But, through severe mischance and cruel wrong, ... 28 *Guilt* 228
That would have been a vile mischance. It would. 50 *Bord.* 738
When you had told him the mischance, was troubled 51 *Bord.* 761
Thy Father perished. Perished—by what mischance ? . . . . 76 *Bord.* 2213
Sheds round the transient harm or vague mischance . . . . 222 *Triad* 161
Without a shadow of mischance, ... 296 *Highland Boy* 94
We had not travelled long, ere some mischance . 737 *Prelude* 12. 231
By passion or mischance, or such misrule . . 761 *Excursion* 1. 379
Mischances. Of sad mischances not a few, . . . 128 *Idiot Boy* 178
Mischief. Anxiety lest mischief should befall her . 41 *Bord.* 234
That, wanting not wild grace, are from all mischief free ! . . . . 103 *Artegal* 65
Who shun the mischief which they cannot heal. . 262 *Retirement* 8
Weighing the mischief with the promised gain, . 283 **Proud were* 12
From mischief, caused by spells himself had muttered ; . . . . 370 *Eg. Maid* 68
That shield from mischief and preserve from stains 382 *Duddon* 26. 11
What mischief cleaves to unsubdued regret, . . 458 *Sea-shore* 1
Plotting new mischief—out again he leaps . . 476 *Nunnery* 5
Pondering the mischiefs of these restless times, . 509 *F. Stone* 111
Pride, anger, mischief, poverty, and madness. . 560 *Cuck.andNight.*175
Which, as a deadly mischief, and a foul . . . 717 *Prelude* 9. 551
I spake of mischief by the wise diffused . . . 887 *Excursion* 9. 195
And lifts his wilful hand on mischief bent, . . 889 *Excursion* 9. 317
Misconceived. From honour misconceived, or fancied wrong, ... 389 *Sound of Mull* 7
A spiritual presence, ofttimes misconceived, . . 815 *Excursion* 4. 927
Miscreant. We've solved the riddle—Miscreant ! Do you, ... 46 *Bord.* 515
Misdeem. (Misdeem it not a cankerous change) may grow . . . . 267 **Desponding Father* 11
Where gentlest judgments may misdeem, . . . 285 *Nith* 14
Misdeem most widely, lodging it elsewhere : . . 654 *Prelude* 3. 350
Miser. All treasures hoarded by the miser, Time. . 234 *Power of Sound* 114
Ease from this noble miser of his time . . . . 425 *Ecc. Sonn.* 1. 26. 9
Miserable. And when the miserable work was done 25 *Guilt* 71
" It was indeed a miserable hour . . . . . 28 *Guilt* 235
To join those miserable men he flew, ... 29 *Guilt* 278
And drop, as he once dropped, in miserable trance. 36 *Guilt* 666
And in that miserable place we left him, . . . 68 *Bord.* 1724
And from that hour the miserable man . . . 69 *Bord.* 1754
I have the proofs !— O miserable Father ! . . 75 *Bord.* 2172

Miserable—*continued.*
Of resurrection. Miserable Woman, ... 76 *Bord.* 2232
A miserable rag indeed ! . . . . 82 *Alice Fell* 32
He gave three miserable groans ; . . . . . 241 *P. B.* 447
Of this poor miserable Ass ! " . . . . . . 243 *P. B.* 585
This miserable vision ! . . . . 247 *P. B.* 935
Ever put on ; a miserable crowd, ... 257 **Methought I* 6
O miserable Chieftain ! where and when . . . 305 *Toussaint* 5
Redeemed, from miserable fear set free . . . 326 *Sobieski* 9
And Fear, and Bloodshed, miserable train ! . . 493 *Hap. War.* 13
Mean, miserable, wilfully depraved, ... 714 *Prelude* 9. 286
Were my day-thoughts,—my nights were miserable ; 724 *Prelude* 10. 398
By prejudice, the miserable slave . . . . . 735 *Prelude* 12. 73
And miserable love, that is not pain . . . . 743 *Prelude* 13. 247
In misery near the miserable Thorn ;— . . . 752 *Prelude* 14. 407
If to be weak is to be wretched—miserable, . . 827 *Excursion* 5. 318
And penalties of miserable life, ... 829 *Excursion* 5. 477
Wandering about in miserable search . . . . 836 *Excursion* 5. 932
And miserable hunger. Much, too much, . . . 886 *Excursion* 9. 164
Miserably. Tho' miserably, oft monstrously, abused 429 *Ecc. Sonn.* 2. 2. 13
How miserably deep ! . . . . 580 *John Words.* 34
The Mother followed :—miserably bare . . . 774 *Excursion* 2. 201
Miserere. *Miserere Domine !* . . . . 336 **Jesu ! bless* 24
Miseries. One might believe that natural miseries . 308 **One might* 1
The terrors, pains, and early miseries, ... 637 *Prelude* 1. 345
In painting to ourselves the miseries . . . . 714 *Prelude* 9. 344
Miserrimus. " *Miserrimus !* " and neither name nor date, ... 275 *Gravestone* 1
Miser's. A Miser's Pensioner—behold our lot ! . . 571 **There is a Flower* 22

Misery. Brought from without to inward misery. . 25 *Guilt* 75
Now, on my life, I grieve for you. The misery . 53 *Bord.* 879
Of misery that was not—— Troth, 'tis hard— . 56 *Bord.* 1048
That misery is a sacred thing : for me, . . . 58 *Bord.* 1160
And his new Favorite. Misery !— I knew . . 59 *Bord.* 1207
To fear the virtuous, and reverence misery, . . 61 *Bord.* 1338
Behold thee, and my misery is complete ! " . . 124 *V. and J.* 162
Becomes an echo of man's misery. . . . . . 153 *Morn. Ex.* 6
And mighty Poets in their misery dead. . . . 197 *Resolution* 116
' Oh misery ! oh misery ! . . . . 198 *Thorn* 65
Oh woe is me ! oh misery ! ' . . . . . . 198 *Thorn* 66
' Oh misery ! oh misery ! . . . . 198 *Thorn* 76
Oh woe is me ! oh misery ! ' " . . . . . . 198 *Thorn* 77
' Oh misery ! oh misery ! ' . . . . . . 199 *Thorn* 191
' Oh misery ! oh misery ! ' " . . . . . . 200 *Thorn* 198
' Oh misery ! oh misery ! . . . . 200 *Thorn* 241
Oh woe is me ! oh misery ! ' " . . . . . . 200 *Thorn* 242
What shrieking and what misery ! . . . . . 296 *Highland Boy* 162
In sign of misery relieved, ... 338 **Meek Virgin* 8
Than heartless misery called them to repel. . . 420 *Ecc. Sonn.* 1. 9. 14
And, with that draught, the life-blood : misery, shame, ... 441 *Ecc. Sonn.* 3. 3. 13
" Here Penury oft from misery's mount will guide 613 *Desc.Sk.Quarto* 598
Nor all the misery forced upon my sight, . . . 708 *Prelude* 8. 647
Misery not lightly passed, but sometimes scanned 708 *Prelude* 8. 648
Their happiness or misery, depends . . . . 728 *Prelude* 11. 103
From which it would be misery to stir : . . . 741 *Prelude* 13. 127
In misery near the miserable Thorn ;— . . . 752 *Prelude* 14. 407
A misery to him ; and the Youth resigned . . 761 *Excursion* 1. 314
Could hold vain dalliance with the misery . . 765 *Excursion* 1. 628
Beneath the misery of that wandering life.' . . 766 *Excursion* 1. 681
Misery and shame. But Wisdom of her sons . . 805 *Excursion* 4. 293
Still roll ; where all the aspects of misery . . . 806 *Excursion* 4. 327
' His lot and hers, as misery must be mine ! ' . . 840 *Excursion* 6. 142
Was misery in remembrance ; he was stung, . . 855 *Excursion* 6. 1095
In spite of vice, and misery, and disease, . . . 870 *Excursion* 7. 854
Misery's. And bright will shine in misery's midnight hour ; . . . . 619 **She wept* 10
Misfortune. Proof shalt thou furnish that misfortune, pain, ... 105 *Artegal* 208
Crossed by misfortune, or of doubted faith ? . . 508 *F. Stone* 45
Misfortunes. But unforeseen misfortunes suddenly 134 *Michael* 213
Of your misfortunes, that at least, ... 406 *White Doe* 920
Misgave. My heart misgave me not, nor did mine eye L.2. 318 *Frag. Æneid* 4. 10

Misgiving. Misgiving, while the crimson day . . 223 *Wishing-gate* 65
For he has no misgiving ! . . . . 249 *P. B.* 1110
He heard, and with misgiving mind. . . . . 412 *White Doe* 1445
Where no misgiving is, rely . . . . 492 *Duty* 11
Misgivings. Misgivings, hard to vanquish or control, 112 **O dearer* 5
Blank misgivings of a Creature . . . . . . 589 *Immortality* 148
Misguided. And poor misguided Shame, and witless Fear, ... 657 *Prelude* 3. 598
Misguided, and misguiding. So I fared, . . . 731 *Prelude* 11. 293
Misguiding. Misguided, and misguiding. So I fared, 731 *Prelude* 11. 293
Mishap. Forebodes mishap or seems but to complain ; . . . . 153 *Morn. Ex.* 10
Heaven shield him from mishap and snare ! . . 174 *Waggoner* 1. 46
Their way, without mishap or fault ; . . . . 175 *Waggoner* 1. 208
Nor from mishap be freed. . . . . 374 *Eg. Maid* 370
Mishap by worm and blight ; . . . . . . 507 *May* 66
By this mishap no longer be dismayed, . . . 561 *Cuck.andNight.*232
In its sweet opening ? and what dire mishap . . 575 *Chiabrera* 7. 6
From anxious fear of error or mishap, ... 670 *Prelude* 5. 280
Ceased, when she learned through what mishap I came, ... 834 *Excursion* 5. 756
—Her wedded days had opened with mishap, . 849 *Excursion* 6. 716
Be here retraced ;—enough that, by mishap . . 854 *Excursion* 6. 1088
Mislead. Should animate, but not mislead, the pen. 359 *Plea : Hist.* 14
What less may mislead you, they took it away. . 569 *Farmer* 28
By reason sanctioned— Can the choice mislead, 621 *Recluse* 1. 1. 72

Mislead—*continued.*
How we mislead each other ; above all, 743 *Prelude* 13. 207
How books mislead us, seeking their reward 743 *Prelude* 13. 208
Misleading. For not misleading us. That subtle Grey-beard— 56 *Bord.* 1019
Misleads. *Our* pride misleads, our timid likings kill. 351 *Des. Stanzas* 73
Misled. Or sadly he has been misled, 128 *Idiot Boy* 225
Harboured where none can be misled, 285 *Grave of Burns* 69
" Gone are they, bravely, though misled ; 401 *White Doe* 461
Err not, by hasty zeal misled, 412 *White Doe* 1473
Long-favoured England ! be not thou misled 514 **Long-favoured* 1
My story early—not misled, I trust, 641 *Prelude* 1. 613
Misled in estimating words, not only 676 *Prelude* 6. 107
From sleep awakened, and misled by sound 685 *Prelude* 6. 692
Not pressed upon, nor dazzled or misled 714 *Prelude* 9. 338
May have sustained, that, howsoe'er misled, 748 *Prelude* 14. 149
Though far misled ? Shall men for whom our age 815 *Excursion* 4. 944
Misnamed. Which the sweet Bird, misnamed the melancholy, 217 *Enterprise* 145
May never House, misnamed of Industry, 569 *Cumb. Beg.* 179
A Power misnamed the Spirit of Reform, 626 *Ballot* 2
Misplaced. How sadly is your love misplaced, 366 **Ye Trees* 9
Oh ! if through confidence misplaced 492 *Duty* 15
Nor deem the Poet's hope misplaced, 533 **Blest is* 41
Honour misplaced, and Dignity astray ; 657 *Prelude* 3. 600
Is all too true ; and surely not misplaced : 828 *Excursion* 5. 370
My Sister, here misplaced and desolate, K.8. 248*Recluse* 1.1.428
Misrule. Analogy to uproar and misrule, 707 *Prelude* 8. 516
By passion or mischance, or such misrule 761 *Excursion* 1. 379
Miss. Your piety would not miss its due reward ; 52 *Bord.* 840
I catch at them, and then I miss ; 117 *Affl. Marg.* 13
Amusement, where the Mother does not miss 119 *Maternal Grief* 70
For what I have and what I miss 182 *Waggoner* 4. 207
Such insolent temptations wouldst thou miss, 347 *Processions* 71
For whom the gravest thought of what they miss, 456 *Rydal Mere* 40
From ill we meet or good we miss, 578 **I come* 54
I cannot miss my way. I breathe again ! 632 *Prelude* 1. 18
On the dead letter, miss the spirit of things ; 703 *Prelude* 8. 297
Ye could not miss the funeral train—they yet 779 *Excursion* 2. 535
And I shall miss him ; scanty tribute ! yet, 780 *Excursion* 2. 602
Miss not the humbler good at which they aim, 835 *Excursion* 5. 857
Nor Miss Taylor, Captain Stamp, S.3. 438 **My Lord* 5
Missed. And, caught by glimpses now—now missed, 143 **Driven in* 14
And thus is *missed* the sole true glory 330 *Ode : Thanks.* 83
Missed not the truth, retains a single name 356 *Aquap.* 239
What benefits are missed, what evils bred, 443 *Ecc. Sonn.* 3. 14. 4
Whose virtues called them forth. That aim is missed ; 585 *Ch. Lamb* 43
Who only misses what I missed, who falls 656 *Prelude* 3. 492
And, with the half-shaped road which we had missed, 684 *Prelude* 6. 620
By multitudes was missed, perhaps attained 792 *Excursion* 3. 407
Were missed, I should at least secure my own, 797 *Excursion* 3. 792
—Yet, while the better part is missed, the worse 828 *Excursion* 5. 403
Thus comprehension fails, and truth is missed ; 830 *Excursion* 5. 511
Misses. Who only misses what I missed, who falls 656 *Prelude* 3. 492
Mis-shapen. Stranger! this hillock of mis-shapen stones 548 **Stranger ! this* 1
Or mis-shapen to the sight, 549 *Hermit's Cell* 1. 26
Mis-shapes. Mis-shapes the beauteous forms of things :— 481 *Tables Turned* 27
Missing. But two are missing—two, a lonely pair K.8. 243*Recluse* 1.1.238
Mission. Their transient mission o'er, 300 *Cora Linn* 27
Grants to thy mission a brief term of silence, 363 **List—'twas* 111
Go forth upon a mission best fulfilled 538 **In desultory* 20
Whate'er its mission, the soft breeze can come 632 *Prelude* 1. 5
Or sent on mission to some northern Chief 871 *Excursion* 7. 932
Mississippi. Of Mississippi, or that northern stream 799 *Excursion* 3. 931
Mist. Here, vanish, as in mist, before a flood 4 *Ev. Wk.* 100
A mighty waste of mist the valley fills, 17 *Desc. Sk.* 408
Pines, on the coast, through mist their tops uprear, 17 *Desc. Sk.* 411
One calm September morning, ere the mist 148 **A narrow* 7
While neither mist, nor thickest cloud 167 *Pilgrim's Dream* 38
By breathing mist ; and thine appears to be 173 *InfantDaughter* 63
Blend with the mist—a moving shroud 181 *Waggoner* 4. 104
In pomp of mist or pomp of snow, 182 *Waggoner* 4. 228
The mist and the river, the hill and the shade : 188 *Poor Susan* 14
Raises a mist ; that, glittering in the sun, 195 *Resolution* 13
" 'Twas mist and rain, and storm and rain : 199 *Thorn* 177
Like morning mist : and, where it lay, 225 *Present.* 28
The towering headlands, crowned with mist, 235 *Power of Sound* 185
In naked splendour, clear from mist or haze, 329 *Ode : Thanks.* 9
His head from mist ; and, as the wind sobbed through 360 *Albano* 2
Like sunny mist ;—at length the golden hair, 440 *Ecc. Sonn.* 3. 1. 11
His sides, or wreathe with mist his forehead high : 471 *Ailsa Crag* 4
And, while the mortal mist is gathering, draws 494 *Hap. War.* 82
The mountain top, or breathed the mist 583 **O for a* 47
'Tis storm ; and hid in mist from hour to hour 608 *Desc.Sk.Quarto* 332
Or lost at eve in sudden mist the day 610 *Desc.Sk.Quarto* 460
Mounts thro' the nearer mist the chaunt of birds, 611 *Desc.Sk.Quarto* 506
Mist into air dissolving ! Then a wish, 635 *Prelude* 1. 227
Of curling mist, or from the level plain 640 *Prelude* 1. 565
Straining my eyes intensely, as the mist 738 *Prelude* 12. 303
The noise of wood and water, and the mist 739 *Prelude* 12. 321
The mountain-side. The mist soon girt us round, 746 *Prelude* 14. 15
Rested a silent sea of hoary mist. 746 *Prelude* 14. 42
A cloud of mist, that smitten by the sun 760 *Excursion* 1. 297
By mist and silent rain-drops silvered o'er, 770 *Excursion* 1.944
The mist, the shadows, light of golden suns, 782 *Excursion* 2. 713
Lay shrouded in impenetrable mist ; 784 *Excursion* 2. 809
Through the dull mist, I following—when a step, 784 *Excursion* 2. 829

Mist—*continued.*
When, from the blind mist issuing, I beheld 796 *Excursion* 3. 719
Or through the groves gliding like morning mist 810 *Excursion* 4. 637
Mistake. And you mistake the cause : you hear the woods 40 *Bord.* 146
I now perceive we do mistake our masters, 54 *Bord.* 908
Which, after a short time, by some mistake 125 *V. and J.* 279
And ye—who might mistake for sober sense 310 *Invasion* 13
Deceived, mistake calamities for wrongs ; 505 *Warning* 114
Mistaken. Nay, then—I am mistaken. There's a weakness 64 *Bord.* 1476
Yet not to be mistaken. Hark again ! 361 **List—'twas* 4
A poor mistaken and bewildered offering,— 721 *Prelude* 10. 231
Mistakes. And thus a way was opened for mistakes 730 *Prelude* 11. 181
Mistakes for sorrow darting beams of light K.8. 238*Recluse* 1. 1. 54
Mistaking. Sometimes the ambitious Power of choice, mistaking 634 *Prelude* 1. 166
Mis-timed. Shrinks from the note as from a mis-timed thing, 360 **Long has* 10
Mistress. Been mistress also of a clock, 176 *Waggoner* 2. 5
Of her loved mistress : soon the music died, 267 *St. Cath.* 7
This day, be mistress of a single pearl 358 *Aquap.* 356
And now her sainted Mistress dear ? 414 *White Doe* 1672
Which her dear Mistress once held dear : 416 *White Doe* 1880
Of a kind mistress, fairest of the land, 528 **Those breathing* 65
" Dear child, sweet Mistress, say not so ! 542 *Russ. Fug.* 75
Deign, Sovereign Mistress ! to accept a lay, 628 **Deign, Sovereign* 1
Her eye was not the mistress of her heart ; 736 *Prelude* 12. 153
Left one day mistress of her mother's stores, 781 *Excursion* 2. 655
Sole Mistress of this house, when I am gone ? 849 *Excursion* 6. 755
Mistrust. *See* **Self-mistrust.**
"Whence the undeserved mistrust ? Too wide apart 140 *Arm. Lady* 47
That wretched boon, days lengthened by mistrust. 214 *Dion* 117
Taught to mistrust her flattering horoscope 345 **Ambition—following* 5
Mistrust thyself, vain Country ! cease to cry, 513 *Newspaper* 9
Mistrust and jealousy, despite, debate, 560 *Cuck.andNight.*173
Nor did by habit of her thoughts mistrust 669 *Prelude* 5. 270
Beginning to mistrust their boastful guides, 695 *Prelude* 7. 515
That Man is only weak through his mistrust 720 *Prelude* 10. 161
Ensures to all believers ?—Yet mistrust 803 *Excursion* 4. 161
Mistrusted. Of popular reason, long mistrusted, freed 327 **Emperors and* 10
Mistrusting. Mistrusting her evasive skill, 168 *Wren's Nest* 38
Mists. Where mists, suspended on the expiring gale, 14 *Desc. Sk.* 210
—At once bewildering mists around him close, 16 *Desc. Sk.* 328
Amid the heart of many thousand mists, 132 *Michael* 59
The mists, that o'er the streamlet's bed 180 *Waggoner* 4. 57
Most potent when mists veil the sky, 215 *Kirkstone* 37
Mists that distort and magnify, 215 *Kirkstone* 38
Where mists are breaking up or gone, 233 *Power of Sound* 42
Lo, in the vale, the mists of evening spread ! 252 **The fairest* 9
Which mists and vapours from mine eyes did shroud— 257 **Methought I* 2
Those steps I clomb ; the mists before me gave 257 **Methought I* 9
Like mountain-tops whose mists have rolled away— 326 **The Bard* 8
Did sullen mists hide lake and skies 343 *Eclipse* 71
Toward the mists that hang over the land of my Sires, 345 *Stanzas : Simplon* 19
Reflected through the mists of age, from hours 354 *Aquap.* 112
Rock-built, are hung with rainbow-coloured mists— 388 *Loch Etive* 2
Its perilous front in mists and clouds ? 413 *White Doe* 1563
Nourish the sufferers then ; and mists, that brood 431 *Ecc.Sonn.* 2. 12. 11
Mists rose to hide the Land—that search, though long 469 **Bold words* 6
And mists that spread the flying shroud ; 491 *Fidelity* 30
These mists, and lead you to a safer place, 505 *Warning* 132
Such gentle mists as glide, 508 *May* 78
Into the mists of fabling Time 544 *Russ. Fug.* 193
While mists, suspended on th' expiring gale, 607 *Desc.Sk.Quarto* 265
Ye dewy mists the arid rocks o'er-spread 609 *Desc.Sk.Quarto* 392
Condemn'd, in mists and tempests ever rife, 613 *Desc.Sk.Quarto* 592
And sounding cataracts, ye mists and winds 648 *Prelude* 2. 425
Blown from their favourite resting-place, or mists 699 *Prelude* 8. 16
By mists bewildered, suddenly mine eyes 703 *Prelude* 8. 264
Clouds, mists, streams, watery rocks and emerald turf, 784 *Excursion* 2. 853
Among the many there ; and while the mists 809 *Excursion* 4. 521
The fountain of the mists. The father stooped K.8. 226 **I will* 54
Through some Helvetian dell, when low-hung mists K.8. 249*Recluse* 1.1.476
Misty. Dilated hang the misty pines on high, 14 *Desc. Sk.* 223
And Kirkstone tossed it from his misty head. 147 *Joanna* 65
And let the misty mountain-winds be free 207 *Tintern* 136
Or with the Moon conquering earth's misty air, 274 **Such age* 12
To seize whate'er, through misty air, 301 *Bran* 79
And some we gather from the misty air, 522 *Epist.Beaumont* 83
Of water-lilies veiled in misty steam— 524 *Epist. Beaumont* 182
When, as day broke, the Maid, through misty air, 540 *Grace Darl.* 29
And neither cloud conceal, nor misty air 548 **Stay, bold* 9
By the still borders of the misty lake, 674 *Prelude* 5. 563
Spread like a halo round a misty moon, 775 *Excursion* 2. 261
To lift thee high above the misty air 787 *Excursion* 3. 103
Misuse. And will misuse me, Sir ! No trifling, Woman !— 46 *Bord.* 499
Misused. He had been sore misused ; but he forgave 74 *Bord.* 2070
Raised by remembrances of misused life, 526 **Soon did* 9
Though slighted and too oft misused. Besides, 663 *Prelude* 4. 345
Mithridates. How vanquished Mithridates north-ward passed, 635 *Prelude* 1. 187
Mitigate. Yet frequent transports mitigate the gloom : 139 *Widow* 33

Mitigate—*continued.*
To mitigate and cheer its loneliness. 266 **Even as* 8
Of innocence survive to mitigate distress? 344 **How blest* 65
See, hear, obstruct, or mitigate. 401 *White Doe* 514
Which fellow-feeling doth not mitigate!" 429 *Ecc. Sonn.* 2. 4. 14
To mitigate the injurious sway of place 650 *Prelude* 3. 102
Did also often mitigate the force 716 *Prelude* 9. 497
Which no one dared to oppose or mitigate. 723 *Prelude* 10. 355
To mitigate the fever of his heart. 760 *Excursion* 1. 300
To mitigate, as gently as I could, 854 *Excursion* 6. 1032
Mitigates. And mitigates the harshest clime. 233 *Power of Sound* 56
Whose saintly radiance mitigates the gloom 496 **A little* 46
Mitigation. With little mitigation. They escape, 829 *Excursion* 5. 428
Mitred. *See* **Once-mitred.**
Of mitred Thurston—what a Host 405 *White Doe* 814
Black Demons hovering o'er his mitred head, 428 *Ecc. Sonn.* 1. 38. 1
And Heaven will crown the right."—The mitred Sire 432 *Ecc. Sonn.* 2. 15. 9
Of mitred Prelates, Lords in ermine clad, 688 *Prelude* 7. 108
Mitre's. Small reverence for the mitre's offices, 442 *Ecc. Sonn.* 3. 8. 12
Mix. Mix with the day, and cross the hour of rest; 112 **O dearer* 6
Gathering green weeds to mix with poppy flower, 261 **Fair Prime* 6
Mix strangely; trifles light, and partly vain, 480 *Cordelia* 8
To mix with hymns that Spirits make and hear; 500 *Humanity* 17
Into the human breast, and mix with sleep 501 **Theunremitting* 11
And mix the poison, they themselves must drink. 513 *Newspaper* 8
And hope and fear mix not in further strife. 540 *Grace Darl.* 42
To mix in quarrels; that were far beneath 670 *Prelude* 5. 300
I mix more lowly matter; with the thing 755 *Recluse* 1. 1. 847
The gilded summer flies to mix and weave 807 *Excursion* 4. 446
To mix the manly brown with silver grey, 842 *Excursion* 6. 278
Mixed. Where, mixed with graceful birch, the sombrous pine 5 *Ev. Wk.* 156
Mixed with a faint yet grating sound 173 *Waggoner* 1. 27
Bright Seraphs mixed familiarly with men; 228 *Vernal Ode* 134
Has mixed its current with the limpid flood, 392 *Avon* 11
Among its withering topmost branches mixed, 393 *Hart's-horn* 3
Has with that Parting mixed a filial sigh, 394 *Countess' Pillar* 11
And, mixed with these, to Brancepeth came 403 *White Doe* 628
All that was mixed and reconciled in Thee 434 *Ecc. Sonn.* 2. 25. 12
Green leaves with yellow mixed are torn away, 435 *Ecc. Sonn.* 2. 28. 2
With wonder mixed—that Man could e'er be tied, 497 **Enough of climbing* 9
If, mixed with what appeared of rock, lawn, wood, 524 *Epist. Beaumont* 187
Mixed with the green, some shine not lacking power 529 *Poor Robin* 9
All kinds of pleasure mix'd with sorrowing; 557 *Cuck.and Night.* 29
Mixed with auxiliar Rocks, three hundred Forms; 612 *Desc.Sk.Quarto* 539
Brother to many more. In this mixed sort 653 *Prelude* 3. 321
Mixed something of stern mood, an under-thirst 683 *Prelude* 6. 558
Daily upon me, mixed with pity too 717 *Prelude* 9. 507
Pure, or with no unpleasing sadness mixed; 755 *Recluse* 1. 1. 758
With pity mixed, astonishment with scorn!" 870 *Excursion* 7. 831
A simple blessing, or with evil mixed; 884 *Excursion* 9. 12
Mixture. But, above all, that mixture of earth's mould 842 *Excursion* 6. 273
Mixtures. Unwelcome mixtures as the uncouth noise 382 *Duddon* 23. 10
Mnemosyne. And sage Mnemosyne,—full long debarred 325 *Ode 1814* 112
Revered her Mother, sage Mnemosyne, 359 *Plea: Hist.* 12
Sprung from high Jove, of sage Mnemosyne S.3. 436 **The doubt* 151
Moan. Touched by the beggar's moan of human woes; 15 *Desc. Sk.* 243
Then sank upon her straw with feeble moan. 34 *Guilt* 564
I hurried on, when straight a second moan, 73 *Bord.* 2047
Without a dog to moan for him. Think not of it, 75 *Bord.* 2138
"Whence comes," said I, "'this piteous moan?" 82 *Alice Fell* 18
When list! he hears a piteous moan— 85 *Shepherd-boys* 60
And thus he makes his moan: 110 **'Tis said that some* 10
When thus his moan he made: 110 **'Tis said that some* 12
Is sick, and makes a piteous moan, 126 *Idiot Boy* 20
Repeats a moan o'er moss and stone, 162 *Binnorie* 58
Hovering around with dolorous moan! 243 *P. B.* 650
The caves reply with hollow moan; 299 *Cora Linn* 4
Extended, clasp the winds, with mutual moan 353 *Aquap.* 45
Upon his monstrous urn, the farewell moan 435 *Ecc. Sonn.* 2. 27. 8
Snatch'd from her shoulder with despairing moan, 597 *Ev. Wk. Quarto* 289
A giant moan along the forest swells 605 *Desc.Sk.Quarto* 201
Moaned. She moaned most bitterly. 248 *P. B.* 1025
She prayed, she moaned;—her husband's sister watched 849 *Excursion* 6. 749
Moaning. What an odd moaning that is!— Mighty odd 51 *Bord.* 751
As if there came such moaning from the flood 73 *Bord.* 2019
Returning late, I heard a moaning sound; 73 *Bord.* 2045
In bed she moaning lay, 84 *We are Seven* 50
Moanings. And moanings, or he dwells (as if the wren 516 **Feel for* 5
Moans. Poor Susan moans, poor Susan groans; 127 *Idiot Boy* 142
Poor Susan moans, poor Susan groans; 127 *Idiot Boy* 147
To utter melancholy moans 301 *Bran* 100
But if thou (like Cocytus from the moans 464 **Greta, what* 5
Where moans the blast, or beats the wave, 472 *Ossian* 26
And afflicting moans she fetches, 490 *Incident: Dog* 35
Moated. Where battlement and moated gate 533 **Blest is* 2
Mobs. Mobs, riots, or rejoicings? From these sights 697 *Prelude* 7. 675
Mock. A viewless flight of laughing Demon's mock 11 *Desc. Sk.* 69
Of this mock Father's guilt. The Baron Herbert 49 *Bord.* 664
Who of thy words dost make a mock apparel, 88 *H. C.* 2
Seem not his handy-work to mock 214 *Kirkstone* 8

Mock—*continued.*
To mock the *wandering* Voice beside some haunted stream. 229 *Cuckoo-clock* 33
To mock the Outcast—O ye Heavens, be kind! 306 **We had* 13
That name, a local Phantom proud to mock 358 **Is this* 4
In that announcement, greeting seemed to mock. 367 **As indignation* 12
When I shall scorn thy voice or mock thy mien! 456 **The leaves* 25
Strange apparitions mock the village sight. 595 *Ev. Wk. Quarto* 178
The cross with hideous laughter Demons mock, 603 *Desc.Sk.Quarto* 70
To mock the mind with "desperation's toys"; 610 *Desc.Sk.Quarto* 467
And the red banner mock the sullen breeze; 615 *Desc.Sk.Quarto* 747
Their veteran foes mock as an idle noise; 628 *Eagle and Dove* 14
And mock me with a sky that ripens not 634 *Prelude* 1. 126
Collaterally pourtrayed, as in mock fight, 657 *Prelude* 3. 582
To mock me under such a strange reverse. 725 *Prelude* 10. 510
Rudely to mock the works of toiling Man. 788 *Excursion* 3. 127
Mock-chastisement. Mock-chastisement and partnership in play. 80 **Loving she* 6
Mocked. Strange apparitions mocked the shepherd's sight. 6 *Ev. Wk.* 195
Mocked me with many a strange fantastic shape!— 39 *Bord.* 112
He mocked and treated with disdain 159 *Green Linnet* 38
We were not mocked with glimpse and shadow then, 228 *Vernal Ode* 133
Mockeries. All but the mutual mockeries of body, 59 *Bord.* 1216
Mockery. Some scoffed at him with hellish mockery, 68 *Bord.* 1736
Else these words would come like mockery, 140 *Arm. Lady* 45
But such mockery as the nations 163 *Hint* 21
A song in mockery and despite 186 **O Nightingale* 7
Mockery—or model roughly hewn, 214 *Kirkstone* 10
Now on the water vexed with mockery. 253 **O gentle* 8
For natural rights, a mockery and a shame; 280 *Plea for Auth.* 4
Where mingle, as for mockery combined, 364 **What aim* 10
Exclaimed the King, "a mockery hateful; 372 *Eg. Maid* 212
To the light clouds a mockery! 405 *White Doe* 852
Is but a mockery! when from coast to coast, 501 *Humanity* 84
Betrayed by mockery of holy fear. 514 **Portentous change* 8
As if in scornful mockery of me; 561 *Cuck.andNight.* 223
And mockery of the rustic painter's hand— 644 *Prelude* 2. 153
And ended with such mockery. Be wise, 655 *Prelude* 3. 409
Of life, and life-like mockery beneath, 690 *Prelude* 7. 246
And wedded her, in cruel mockery 691 *Prelude* 7. 301
And not then only, "What a mockery this 712 *Prelude* 9. 168
"What are they but a mockery of a Being 732 *Prelude* 11. 311
In mockery, to wither in the sun, 787 *Excursion* 3. 65
By various mockery of sight and sound; 841 *Excursion* 6. 228
Mocking. The sportive outcry of the mocking owl; 9 *Ev. Wk.* 375
Mocking the Man that keeps the ferry; 179 *Waggoner* 3. 123
And, mocking its own plighted word, 298 *Brownie's Cell* 38
Mocking-bird. Failed not to greet the merry Mocking-bird; 799 *Excursion* 3. 946
Mock-patience. With the worst shape mock-patience ever wore; 505 *Warning* 123
Mocks. Mocks the dull ear of Time with deaf abortive sound. 16 *Desc. Sk.* 315
But now it mocks my steps; its fitful stroke 67 *Bord.* 1652
Or mocks each casual note. 165 *Parrot* 20
When she stands cresting the Clown's head, and mocks 260 **How sweet* 8
And mocks whom he adores. 374 *Eg. Maid* 358
That mocks the gladness of the Spring! 413 *White Doe* 1578
That mocks the recreant age *we* live in, then 654 *Prelude* 3. 400
And mocks the prompter's listening. Marvellous things 688 *Prelude* 7. 102
Profession mocks performance. Earth is sick, 828 *Excursion* 5. 378
Mode. A life and soul, to every mode of being 567 *Cumb. Beg.* 78
Model. Mockery—or model roughly hewn, 214 *Kirkstone* 10
This model of a child is never known 670 *Prelude* 5. 299
By scale exact, in model, wood or clay, 691 *Prelude* 7. 249
Who to the model of his own pure heart 762 *Excursion* 1. 411
Models. In framing models to improve the scheme 791 *Excursion* 3. 336
Moderate. "Bard! moderate your ire; 164 *Needlecase* 18
Thy transports moderate; and meekly mourn 210 *Laod.* 77
Peace, leisure, freedom, moderate desires; 356 *Aquap.* 260
Moderated. Thus moderated, thus composed, I found 740 *Prelude* 13. 48
Moderation. If thou persist, and, scorning moderation, 505 *Warning* 147
And seek through noiseless pains and moderation 516 **As leaves* 7
Modern. Shames the degenerate grasp of modern science, 369 *Eg. Maid* 20
Appears, and none of modern Fortune's care; 376 *Duddon* 3. 11
May try this modern system by its fruits, 670 *Prelude* 5. 295
Of modern Merlins, Wild Beasts, Puppet-shows, 698 *Prelude* 7. 713
And in our high-wrought modern narratives 708 *Prelude* 8. 619
Of modern statists to their proper test, 741 *Prelude* 13. 72
Of modern ingenuity; no town 880 *Excursion* 8. 421
Of modern ingenuity, and made 886 *Excursion* 9. 158
Go, modern Prince, at Henry's tomb proclaim L.1. 94 *Juvenal* 2. 19
Modes. That touch each other to the quick in modes 290 *Kilchurn* 7
Of unknown modes of being; o'er my thoughts 638 *Prelude* 1. 393
On sundry and most widely different modes 698 *Prelude* 7. 738
Modest. He in the preference, modest Youth, might take, 47 *Bord.* 552
As the clear Moon with modest pride 112 **What heavenly* 5
Of modest kindness, that would hide 154 *Flower Garden* 45
Modest, yet withal an Elf 160 **Pansies, lilies* 17
When this in modest guise was said, 167 *Pilgrim's Dream* 49
If Wytheburne's modest House of prayer, 176 *Waggoner* 2. 1
For modest meanings dear. 224 **'Tis gone* 18
From humble violet—modest thyme— 228 *Devot. Incit.* 7
Thou, with ambition modest yet sublime, 252 *Picture* 11

Modesties 615 Moment

Modest—*continued.*
A grateful few, shall love thy modest Lay, . . . 254 Dyer 11
Modest her mien ; and she, whose thoughts keep pace . . . . 256 Marriage : Friend 7
Nor will I then thy modest grace forget, . . . 264 Snowdrop 12
With one calm triumph of a modest pride. . . 265 *The Shepherd 14
One offering, kneel before her modest shrine, . . 270 *Though the bold 13
To pastoral dales, thin-set with modest farms, . 275 *Chatsworth! thy 10
Fresh as the flower, whose modest worth . . . 285 Grave of Burns 19
Yet mark his modest state ! upon his head, . . 314 Hofer 7
To deck your stern Defenders' modest brows ! . 324 Ode 1814 46
As aptly suits therewith that modest pace . . 329 Ode : Thanks. 15
Her modest gratitude. . . . . 348 *Lulled by 60
Modest Savona ! over all did brood . . . . 356 Aquap. 233
Or softly stealing into modest shade. . . . . 367 Trajan 18
Remnants of love whose modest sense . . . . 376 *The Minstrels 57
For great and sacred is the modest claim . . . 392 Avon 5
In thankful bosoms to a modest pride. . . . 456 Rydal Mere 44
And all those attributes of modest grace, . . . 460 *Queen of 13
These modest walls, amid a flock that need, . . 465 *Pastor and 2
But who is He, with modest looks, ... 485 Poet's Epitaph 37
This modest charm of not too much, ... 508 May 95
With modest scorn reject whate'er would blind . 529 *Those breathing 135
Lifting her front with modest grace . . . . 533 *Blest is 23
Modest and sweet, a progeny of earth, ... 539 *Lady ! a 20
Pious and pure, modest and yet so brave, . . . 541 Grace Darl. 94
Yet modest hand of charity, ... 577 *By playful 4
He would have loved thy modest grace, . . . 580 John Words. 51
From out the bosom of a modest home . . . 627 *Son of 12
Humility and modest awe themselves . . . . . 635 Prelude 1. 243
With my own modest pleasures, and have lived . 648 Prelude 2. 429
The Muses' modest nurslings underwent . . . 655 Prelude 3. 460
Of modest meekness, simple-mindedness, . . . 670 Prelude 5. 291
Fierce, moody, patient, venturous, modest, shy ; . 672 Prelude 5. 415
Of modest sympathy. Such aspect now, . . . 676 Prelude 6. 63
With admiration of her modest mien . . . . 691 Prelude 7. 307
Young, modest, meek, and beautiful, I led . . 793 Excursion 3. 514
Gave modest intimation to the mind . . . . 793 Excursion 3. 528
In modest panegyric. " These dim lines, . . . 825 Excursion 5. 205
And yet a modest comrade, led them forth . . 869 Excursion 7. 773
To thy obscure and modest attributes, . . . S.3. 437 *The doubt 205
I and the modest partners of my days . . . . K.8. 255 Recluse 1.1.695
Modesties. In silence and the awful modesties . . 516 *Feel for 7
Modestly. That shunned so modestly the light of praise, ... 583 *With copious 8
Modesty. In reverential modesty demand, . . . 328 Ode 1815 58
Beneath the roof of settled Modesty. . . . . 439 Ecc. Sonn. 2. 41. 8
Ensued a diffidence and modesty, ... 643 Prelude 2. 75
Of modesty, that he, who in his youth . . . 674 Prelude 5. 586
As may be hoped, of real modesty,— . . . 698 Prelude 7. 764
Did of itself in modesty give way, ... 722 Prelude 10. 306
Modulate. And modulate, with subtle reach of skill 271 *Fame tells 33
Modulated. —Say whence that modulated shout ! . 344 *How blest 33
With modulated echoes rang, ... 457 *Had this 10
Modulation. Their modulation with these vocal streams— . . . . 748 Prelude 14. 146
Modulations. Pure modulations flowing from the heart . . . . 234 Power of Sound 110
Avails those modulations to detect, ... 339 Ranz 2
Mogul. Banded beneath the Great Mogul, when he 718 Prelude 10. 18
Mohammedan. Mohammedan and Christian. But enough ; . . . . 37 Bord. 19
Moiety. His moiety in trust, till Joy shall lead . 586 Ch. Lamb 130
Moist. Or blooming thicket moist with morning dews ; 227 Vernal Ode 80
That with moist virtue softly cleaves . . . . 228 Devot. Incit. 15
Which for the loss of that moist gleam atone . . 250 *Happy the 8
Or moist with dews ; what more unsightly now, . 266 *Desponding Father 3
Round the moist marge of Persian fountains cling ; 376 Duddon 1. 6
And his moist eyes were glorified ; . . . . . 400 White Doe 404
Day's grateful warmth, tho' moist with falling dews. 453 *Calm is the 2
Was moist with water-drops, as if the brim . . 762 Excursion 1. 445
Right at the foot of that moist precipice, . . . 787 Excursion 3. 53
Was pallid : seldom hath that eye been moist . 871 Excursion 7. 882
That hangs o'er the moist plain. Again they view K.8. 234 *The order'd 4
Moisten. And moisten the parched lips of thirsty flowers— . . . . 230 Clouds 69
And, all day long, moisten these flowery fields ! '. 812 Excursion 4. 752
Moistened. Herbs moistened by Virginian dew, . 348 *Lulled by 45
Moistened each fleece, beneath the twinkling stars 380 Duddon 17. 9
Dropped from an Angel's wing. With moistened eye 441 Ecc. Sonn. 3. 5. 4
Moistened from age to age by dewy eve, . . . 450 Ecc. Sonn. 3. 39. 2
That moistened Dunkirk's sands with blood and tears, ... L.1. 96 Juvenal 3. 62
Moisture. Oft leaves a saving moisture at its root. . 124 V. and J. 194
The dew whose moisture fell in gentle drops . . 354 Aquap. 134
Scattering this far-fetched moisture from my wings, 582 Invoc. Earth 23
A fertilising moisture,' said the Swain, . . . 835 Excursion 5. 872
Mole. Oh yes, that mole, that viper in the path ; . 60 Bord. 1255
May pierce the earth with the patient mole, . . 142 †Lov. and Lik. 51
The mole contented with her darksome walk . . 807 Excursion 4. 429
Moles. He will destroy. To have been trapped like moles !— . . . . 63 Bord. 1434
Molest. Fearless of all assaults that would her brood molest. . . . . 525 Epist. Beaumont 231
Molest ; may gentle breezes fan thy brow ; . . 548 *Stay, bold 8
Molestation. Body and mind, from molestation freed, 382 Duddon 24. 8
In place from outward molestation free, . . . 844 Excursion 6. 400
Mollified. With hands stretched forth in mollified disdain, ... 435 Ecc. Sonn. 2. 28. 5
Molten. Molten together, and composing thus, . . 784 Excursion 2. 856
Moment. A little moment past so smiling ! . . . 9 Lines : Boat 6
In that glad moment will for you a sigh . . . 20 Desc. Sk. 565
In that glad moment when your hands are prest . 20 Desc. Sk. 567
That died the moment the air breathed upon it. . 47 Bord. 557
'Tis at this moment.—Oswald, I have loved . . 48 Bord. 633
Stoop for a moment ; 'tis an act of justice ; . . 48 Bord. 638
Would wreak on us the passion of the moment. . 49 Bord. 646
Why are you not the man you were that moment ? 52 Bord. 795
From the first moment that I loved the Maid ; . 61 Bord. 1322
That I should ever live to see this moment ! . . 66 Bord. 1598
Subsided in a moment, like a wind . . . . . 69 Bord. 1785
Nor to this moment have I ever wished . . . 75 Bord. 2174
Slips in a moment out of life. . . . . . . 88 H. C. 33
The humour of the moment, lagged behind. . . 101 Brothers 363
At this blest moment led me, if I speak . . . 104 Artegal 152
Death in a moment parted them, and left . . . 118 Maternal Grief 41
Perhaps to himself at that moment he said ; . . 120 Childless Father 17
One moment let me be thy mother ! . . . . 120 EmigrantMother 16
Of some unguarded moment that dissolved . . 122 V. and J. 55
At the first hearing, for a moment took . . . 134 Michael 218
And of this moment ; hither turn thy thoughts, . 137 Michael 407
Years contracting to a moment, ... 141 Arm. Lady 105
You *live* each moment of your day ; . . . . 143 †Lov. and Lik. 60
In a moment lost and found, ... 173 Waggoner 1. 28
And in a moment calls to mind . . . . . 177 Waggoner 2. 29
In a perilous moment threw . . . . 181 Waggoner 4. 111
For what one moment flung aside, ... 191 Seq. Beggars 8
That in this moment there is life and food . . 206 Tintern 64
A moment I was startled at the sight : . . . 208 *It is no 11
Passed in a moment—and as faint again ! . . 218 Recluse 1. 1. 221
By casting on a moment all we dare ? . . . . 220 Triad 31
Glad moment is it when the throng . . . . 221 Triad 80
Alas ! how little can a moment show . . . . 221 Triad 128
One moment, and the next revealed. . . . . 228 Devot. Incit. 37
And in a moment to the verge . . . . . . 242 P. B. 558
The very moment that she died, ... 246 P. B. 929
At the same moment Peter Bell . . . . . 247 P. B. 1014
To one brief moment caught from fleeting time . 252 Picture 13
The moment it has left the virgin's eye, . . . 265 *There is a pleasure 13
Not loth to thank each moment for its boon . . 278 *The most 9
And in a moment charmed my cares to rest. . . 279 *Hark ! 'tis 8
At this dread moment—even so— . . . . . 285 Grave of Burns 51
And, when the moment comes, to part . . . 300 Bran 9
Thought for another moment. Thou art free, . 306 *Here, on our 10
In the worst moment of these evil days ; . . . 321 *Here pause 4
And for a moment meet the soul's desires ! . . 325 Ode 1814 126
For a brief moment, terrible ; . . . . . . 331 Ode : Thanks. 185
And, at one moment, in one rapture, strive . . 331 Ode : Thanks. 198
(At least for one rapt moment) every trace . . 343 Last Sup. 7
What moment in life is so conscious of love, . . 346 Stanzas : Simplon 31
All that I felt this moment doth renew ; . . . 350 Des. Stanzas 12
And, for a moment, filled that empty Throne. . 365 *Under the 14
Then, for a moment, he, in spirit, resumes . . 389 Eagles 12
A moment ends the fervent din, ... 396 White Doe 43
Oh weak, weak moment ! to what end . . . 411 White Doe 1395
Oh, moment ever blest ! O Pair . . . . . 414 White Doe 1665
No moment steals ; pain narrows not his cares. . 425 Ecc. Sonn. 1. 26. 10
Which, at this moment, on my waking sight . . 458 *Had this 75
Smiting, as if each moment were their last. . . 474 *Hope smiled 6
Even for a moment, has our verse deplored . . 474 *On to 7
One moment now may give us more . . . . 483 Sister 25
As at that moment, with a bough . . . . . 487 *We walked 59
Some awful moment to which Heaven has joined . 493 Hap. War. 49
And prostrate at some moment when remorse . 519 Pun. Death 12. 2
The parting moment and its fond regret. . . . 531 *I know 16
Checked, in the moment of its issue, checked . . 539 *Lady ! a 37
The passion of a moment came . . . . . . 545 Russ. Fug. 327
Extinguished in a moment ; total gloom, . . . 548 *Stay, bold 27
Might die in the same moment. Nor in vain . . 551 *If thou in 23
And, the first moment that the sun may shine, . 571 *There is a Flower 3
'Twill be no fruitless moment. I was born . . 573 Chiabrera 3. 3
I learned that one poor moment can suffice . . 574 Chiabrera 4. 23
Not for a moment could I now behold . . . . 578 Peele Castle 37
Can in a moment travel thither, ... 590 Immortality 169
All night the door at every moment ope ; . . . 609 Desc.Sk.Quarto 409
Call back, O Friend ! a moment to thy mind, . . 653 Prelude 3. 309
Not seldom since that moment have I wished . . 682 Prelude 6. 472
Contented, from the moment that the dawn . . 682 Prelude 6. 512
While every moment added doubt to doubt, . . 683 Prelude 6. 578
Not rich one moment to be poor for ever ; . . 686 Prelude 6. 735
Must needs bring back the moment when we first, 691 Prelude 7. 303
And from his work this moment had been stolen) 696 Prelude 7. 614
As in a moment ; yet with Time it dwells, . . 707 Prelude 8. 558
The moment to depart. An Englishman, . . . 712 Prelude 9. 188
Yet at this very moment do tears start . . . 713 Prelude 9. 267
And for a moment, men from far with sound . . 713 Prelude 9. 276
Down to that very moment ; neither lapse . . 722 Prelude 10. 270
The gloom, that, but a moment past, was deepened 733 Prelude 11. 427
A moment, but an inmate of the heart, . . . 750 Prelude 14. 269
As if the thought were but a moment old, . . . 772 Excursion 2. 88
In that one moment when the corse is lifted . . 780 Excursion 2. 556
The moment I was seated here alone, ... 783 Excursion 2. 802
As marvellously seized as in that moment . . 796 Excursion 3. 718
To see the moment, when the righteous cause . 806 Excursion 4. 311
More multitudinous every moment, rend . . . 809 Excursion 4. 530
At every moment—and, with strength, increase . 813 Excursion 4. 794
At every moment softened in its course . . . 818 Excursion 4. 1119
At any moment may the Dame be found, . . . 833 Excursion 5. 706

Moment—*continued.*
Who happier for the moment—who more blithe . 843 *Excursion* 6. 341
Then, reappearing in a moment, quits . 858 *Excursion* 7. 46
In one blest moment. Like a shadow thrown . 861 *Excursion* 7. 283
Came at that moment, ringing noisily. . 865 *Excursion* 7. 545
Is stricken in the moment when her throes . 867 *Excursion* 7. 643
That there should pass a moment of the year, . 877 *Excursion* 8. 194
And at the self-same moment, works its way . 883 *Excursion* 8. 579
(For every moment hath its own to-morrow !) 884 *Excursion* 9. 28
Delusion which a moment may destroy ! . 887 *Excursion* 9. 198
That rapturous moment never shall I forget . 893 *Excursion* 9. 588
A parting moment with her loveliest look, . S.3. 434 **The doubt* 88
Compare ! thy earthly bed a moment past . S.3. 434 **The doubt* 95
The moment I was left behind. . K.8. 219 **The snow-tracks* 8

Momentary. And momentary hope, and worn-out prayer, . 724 *Prelude* 10. 405
A momentary pleasure, never marked . 765 *Excursion* 1. 630
A momentary trance comes over me ; . 768 *Excursion* 1. 784
It was no momentary happiness . 848 *Excursion* 6. 637
Momently. Thou shrink'st as momently thy rays . 167 *Pilgrim's Dream* 36
Of Mountains varying momently their crests— . 388 *Loch Etive* 5
Momentous. Aloft ;—momentous but uneasy bliss ! 123 *V. and J.* 99
Howe'er momentous in itself it be, . 518 *Pun. Death* 5. 2
—Life, death, eternity ! momentous themes . 874 *Excursion* 8. 10
Moment's. Nor voice, nor sound, that moment's pain expressed, . 30 *Guilt* 308
Ha ! ha !—As 'twill be but a moment's work, . 60 *Bord.* 1258
To shield her from a moment's harm. To you, . 78 *Bord.* 2332
A moment's heaviness they feel, . 81 †*Mother's Return* 47
Could lend out of that moment's store . 127 *Idiot Boy* 134
Red, green, and blue ; a moment's sight ! . 180 *Waggoner* 4. 33
To be a moment's ornament ; . 186 **She was* 4
Who, through the portal of one moment's guilt, . 214 *Dion* 104
And then, without a moment's stay, . 243 *P. B.* 598
Moves on without a moment's stop, . 244 *P. B.* 713
Such transport, though but for a moment's space ; 270 **Shame on* 2
Not worth a moment's pains. . 291 *Rob Roy* 72
(Though it were only for a moment's space) . 323 **Now that* 13
Mounts on rapt wing, and with a moment's flight 336 *Danube* 7
Too free to one bright moment's hope ? . 406 *White Doe* 929
There Francis for a moment's space . 412 *White Doe* 1442
Might give to serious thought a moment's sway, . 453 **Calm is the* 31
We breathed together for a moment's space, . 464 **A point* 12
Forbid a moment's rest ; . 499 **This Lawn* 9
Brings not a moment's care. . 577 **I come* 25
For one poor moment's space to Thee, . 580 *John Words.* 8
That I am trifling : 'twas a moment's pause,— . 707 *Prelude* 8. 556
Or deemed it worth a moment's thought to stir, . 711 *Prelude* 9. 137
Would I give a moment's pain ; . S.3. 438 **My Lord* 4
Moments. how could I disturb his last moments ? 72 *Bord.* 1940
What happy moments did I count ! . 111 *A Complaint* 7
My very moments are too full . 113 *Lament* 13
And, in their happiest moments, not content, . 122 *V. and J.* 24
No more than moments of thy life ? . 235 *Power of Sound* 218
To the flying moments, and is seen no more. . 261 **I watch* 9
Think rather of those moments bright . 286 *Nith* 20
Moments, to cast a look behind, . 376 **The Minstrels* 69
In thoughtful moments, wafted by the gales . 438 *Ecc. Sonn.* 2. 39. 13
Blest are the moments, doubly blest, . 506 *Lab. Hymn* 13
By moments thus increaseth in my face, . 565 *Troilus* 156
Long for some moments in a weary life . 568 *Cumb. Beg.* 148
Our noisy years seem moments in the being . 589 *Immortality* 158
Oft in these moments such a holy calm . 647 *Prelude* 2. 348
On those ingenuous moments of our youth . 692 *Prelude* 7. 331
But memorable moments intervened, . 695 *Prelude* 7. 537
Narrowing itself by moments—they, rash men, . 718 *Prelude* 10. 24
O Friend ! few happier moments have been mine 725 *Prelude* 10. 511
(As at some moments might not be unfelt . 729 *Prelude* 11. 119
The pensive moments by this calm fire-side, . 734 *Prelude* 11. 450
The obedient servant of her will. Such moments 737 *Prelude* 12. 223
At other moments—(for through that wide waste 744 *Prelude* 13. 336
And giving to the moments as they pass . K.8. 249 *Recluse* 1.1.466
Moments'. An eager grasp ; and many moments' space— . 779 *Excursion* 2. 519
The moments' [? moment's] humour, rough Tars spend their wit. . K.8. 301 **And oh* 4
Mona. On Mona settle, and the shapes assume . 468 **Ranging the* 5
Mona from our Abode is daily seen, . 522 *Epist. Beaumont* 77
Monarch. Pride of his sister-wives, the monarch stalks ; . 5 *Ev. Wk.* 147
Which from Siberian caves the Monarch freed, . 321 **Humanity, delighting* 28
And strike with reverence. The Monarch leans . 422 *Ecc. Sonn.* 1. 15. 9
Gaz'd by his sister-wives, the monarch stalks ; . 594 *Ev. Wk. Quarto* 130
To his chamber the monarch is led, . 621 *Convict* 26
Monarch and peasant : be the house redeemed . 682 *Prelude* 6. 456
Cased in the gleaming mail the monarch wore, . 689 *Prelude* 7. 139
The prison where the unhappy Monarch lay, . 719 *Prelude* 10. 51
And where the very monarch of the brook, . 882 *Excursion* 8. 564
Monarch's. Cleared for a monarch's progress. Priests might spin . 70 *Bord.* 1837
And lo ! a poniard, at the Monarch's side, . 271 *Henry : Portrait* 5
Like gallant Falkland, by the Monarch's side, . 310 *Invasion* 3
Galled by their monarch's chain. The times were big 695 *Prelude* 7. 534
And prove with endless puns a monarch's power, L.1. 94 *Juvenal* 2. 2
And self-devoted sought the monarch's tent, . L.1. 95 *Juvenal* 3. 8
Monarchs. The haughty towers where monarchs dwell ; . 329 *Ode : Thanks.* 5
The innocent eyes of youthful Monarchs driven . 436 *Ecc. Sonn.* 2. 32. 13
And monarchs surly at the wrongs sustained . 640 *Prelude* 1. 534

Mona's. And visibly engirding Mona's Isle . 219 **This Height* 16
Like Mona's miniature of sovereignty. . 471 *Tynwald* 14
What shall I treat of ? News from Mona's Isle ? . 522 *Epist. Beaumont* 59
Monasteries. For eastern monasteries, sunny mounts 700 *Prelude* 8. 86
Monastery. At early dawn. The monastery bells . 681 *Prelude* 6. 408
Monastic. That, shaped like old monastic turrets, rise 335 *Namur* 13
From Bolton's old monastic tower . 396 *White Doe* 1
Monastic Domes ! following my downward way, . 449 *Ecc. Sonn.* 3. 35. 1
And that monastic castle, 'mid tall trees, . 678 *Prelude* 6. 205
Of the monastic brotherhood, upon rock . 791 *Excursion* 3. 393
Money. A piece of money glittering through the dust ? 45 *Bord.* 435
Of that blind Man. 'Twas not your money, Sir,— 55 *Bord.* 952
And I gave money to the host, . 82 *Alice Fell* 55
To the neighbours he went,—all were free with their money ; . 570 *Farmer* 33
Pieces of money carefully enclosed, . 766 *Excursion* 1. 670
Money's. If money's slack, . S.3. 431 **If money's* 1
Moneys. *See* **Monies.**
The moneys he possessed, and hoard up more, . 672 *Prelude* 5. 471
'Mong. *See* **Among.**
His rank 'mong freeborn creatures that live free, 389 *Eagles* 13
Who, 'mong those thousands, friend hath none, . 404 *White Doe* 755
'Mong Christian folk, a street where Jews might be, 553 *Prioress* 37
'Mong other consolations, we may draw . 752 *Prelude* 14. 428
Monied. These times strike monied worldlings with dismay : . 308 **These times* 1
Monies. *See* **Moneys.**
And left estates and monies to the poor, . 135 *Michael* 268
Behold me rich in monies, and attired . 649 *Prelude* 3. 37
Monition. Divine monition Nature yields, . 228 *Devot. Incit.* 71
Monitor. Discerning Monitor, my faithful Wilfred, 78 *Bord.* 2322
And pensive monitor of fleeting years ! . 264 *Snowdrop* 14
The monitor revives his own sweet strain ; . 455 *Rydal Mere* 4
I thank the silent Monitor, and say . 470 *Bala-Sala* 13
A silent monitor, which on their minds . 568 *Cumb. Beg.* 123
Murmurings, whereby the monitor expressed . 818 *Excursion* 4. 1139
Might wait on thee, a silent monitor, . S.3. 435 **The doubt* 129
Monitors. To catch from Nature's humblest monitors 362 **List—'twas* 72
On a wild coast, rough monitors to feed . 424 *Ecc. Sonn.* 1. 23. 8
Solemn monitors are ours. . 629 *Installation* 76
Monitory. He heard the monitory growl ; . 178 *Waggoner* 2. 154
With vital sounds and monitory gleams . 267 **Though narrow* 7
Can hear the monitory clock . 533 **Blest is* 45
A monitory sound that never failed,— . 723 *Prelude* 10. 324
The monitory voice ? But most of all . 780 *Excursion* 2. 566
Monitress. Then, silent Monitress ! let us—not blind 461 **Queen of* 39
Monk. *Then* might the passing Monk receive a boon 339 *Tell* 16
Thus sensitive must be the Monk, though pale . 362 **List—'twas* 74
Else will the enamoured Monk too surely find . 363 **Grieve for* 12
That to a Monk allots, both in the esteem . 433 *Ecc. Sonn.* 2. 19. 12
Where once came monk and nun with gentle stir, 474 **How sad* 4
One above all, a Monk who waits on God . 509 *F. Stone* 95
"This holy Monk, this Abbot—him mean I, . 556 *Prioress* 219
The ghostly semblance of a hooded monk, . 708 *Prelude* 8. 586
Walks a lone Monk, when service hath expired, . 716 *Prelude* 9. 445
Like a cowled monk who hath forsworn the world, 735 *Prelude* 12. 78
Monkeys. Of monkeys on his back ; a minstrel band 689 *Prelude* 7. 178
With chattering monkeys dangling from their poles, 697 *Prelude* 7. 694
Monkish. When human touch (as monkish books attest) . 267 *St. Cath.* 1
Behold a pupil of the monkish gown, . 425 *Ecc. Sonn.* 1. 26. 1
For solace by dim light of monkish lamps ; . 673 *Prelude* 5. 498
Of that idolatry, through monkish rites . S.3. 435 **The doubt* 127
Monks. The Monks of Fountain's thronged to force 301 *Bran* 58
Defeating, put the Monks to shame, . 301 *Bran* 69
By a few Monks, a stern society, . 362 **List—'twas* 34
What aim had they, the Pair of Monks, in size . 363 **What aim* 1
The Monks still repeat the tradition with pride, . 364 *Vallomb.* 9
While the Monks prayed in Maiden's Bower . 405 *White Doe* 833
His thin autumnal locks where Monks abide . 424 *Ecc. Sonn.* 1. 21. 5
From Monks in Ely chanting service high, . 426 *Ecc. Sonn.* 1. 30. 2
That we the sweet song of the Monks may hear !" 426 *Ecc. Sonn.* 1. 30. 5
The Monks relax or break these iron chains ; . 429 *Ecc. Sonn.* 2. 4. 7
The thoughtful Monks, intent their God to please, 468 *St. Bees* 142
Among a grave fraternity of Monks, . 510 **Among a* 1
As all Monks are, or surely ought to be, . 555 *Prioress* 192
No jarring monks, to gloomy cell confined, . 619 *School Ex.* 49
Monster. Her whom the Monster, Clifford, drove to madness. . 47 *Bord.* 569
Whate'er the monster brooding in your breast . 56 *Bord.* 1014
Contains not such a Monster ! For this purpose 56 *Bord.* 1057
Oh Monster ! Monster ! there are three of us, . 74 *Bord.* 2089
Hast thou pursued the monster ? I have found him.— . 76 *Bord.* 2192
Wrest from the guardian Monster of the tomb . 210 *Laod.* 80
From this dull Monster and her sooty crew ; . 471 **Arran ! a* 7
Let Ignorance o'er the monster swarms preside, . L.1. 88 *Juvenal* 1. 19
Monsters. Among the monsters of the Deep ; . 216 *Enterprise* 74
Where men were monsters. A last grace he craves, 234 *Power of Sound* 133
A Parliament of Monsters. Tents and Booths . 698 *Prelude* 7. 718
Ephemeral monsters, to be seen but once ! . 719 *Prelude* 10. 46
Monstrous. This monstrous crime to be laid open—*here*, . 58 *Bord.* 1118
That monstrous perfidy ! Keep down your wrath. 70 *Bord.* 1833
Of monstrous crime !—that horror-striking blade, 214 *Dion* 107
The pyramid extend its monstrous base, . 313 **Go back* 6
Their monstrous Idol if the dead e'er spake, . 325 *Enghien* 7
Whose monstrous riches threatened. So the shaft 432 *Ecc. Sonn.* 2. 16. 4
Upon his monstrous urn, the farewell moan . 435 *Ecc Sonn.* 2. 27. 8
Man to curse man, (thought monstrous and appalling). . 447 *Ecc. Sonn.* 3. 29. 3

Monstrously 617 **Mood**

Monstrous—*continued.*
By monstrous theories of alien growth, 514 **Long-favoured* 2
Rise up, thou monstrous ant-hill on the plain. 689 *Prelude* 7. 149
Monstrous in colour, motion, shape, sight, sound! 697 *Prelude* 7. 688
Nature's rebellion against monstrous law; 717 *Prelude* 9. 571
And false as monstrous! Can the mother thrive. 878 *Excursion* 8. 285
Strange, then, not less than monstrous, might be deemed 887 *Excursion* 9. 229
Monstrously. Tho' miserably, oft monstrously, abused 429 *Ecc. Sonn.* 2. 2. 13
Mont. Unveiled the summit of Mont Blanc, and grieved 683 *Prelude* 6. 525
And from Mont Martre southward to the Dome. 710 *Prelude* 9. 47
Monte. Of Monte Rosa—*there* on frailer stone 350 *Des. Stanzas* 31
Days passed—and Monte Calvo would not clear. 360 *Albano* 1
Month. A month, sweet Little-ones, is past 81 †*Mother's Return* 1
Sing at thy Mother's breast. Month followed month, 136 *Michael* 349
From month to month, life passing not away: 169 *Love lies Bleeding* 4
From month to month trembling and unassured, 449 *Ecc. Sonn.* 3. 37. 8
Month falls on month with heavier weight; 479 *Somnamb.* 79
From week to week, from month to month, we lived 642 *Prelude* 2. 8
To quit my pleasure, and, from month to month, 654 *Prelude* 3. 357
Month after month. Obscurely did I live, 710 *Prelude* 9. 25
Divided from me by one little month, 719 *Prelude* 10. 74
Through a whole month of calm and glassy days 722 *Prelude* 10. 320
And fed him there, alive, month after month, 733 *Prelude* 11. 447
When the fresh eagle, in the month of May, 807 *Excursion* 4. 397
Which told it was the pleasant month of June; 858 *Excurson* 7. 76
What lamentable change, a year—a month— 878 *Excursion* 8. 256
Monthling. Frail, feeble, Monthling!—by that name, methinks, 172 *Infant Daughter* 16
Monthly. Is hidden, buried in its monthly grave; 460 **Wanderer! that* 64
And from example of thy monthly range 461 **Queen of* 53
The Moon re-entering her monthly round, 532 **Once I* 2
Twelve times her monthly round, 544 *Russ. Fug.* 258
When thou wert hidden in thy monthly grave; 630 [?] **O Moon* 4
For what reward!—The moon her monthly round 783 *Excursion* 2. 774
Months. Chancing to pass this way some six months gone, 47 *Bord.* 573
Comes to this church-yard once in eighteen months; 97 *Brothers* 126
Leonard, the elder by just eighteen months, 99 *Brothers* 249
Three months with one, and six months with another; 100 *Brothers* 344
For two months now in vain we shall be sought; 106 *Farewell* 18
Two burning months let summer overleap, 107 *Farewell* 62
Fresh sprigs of green box-wood, not six months before, 120 *Childless Father* 9
So, many months passed on: and once again 138 *Michael* 437
"They say, full six months after this, 199 *Thorn* 122
To vanish—fleet as days and months and years, 230 *Clouds* 37
Uncounted months are gone, 232 *Jew. Fam.* 22
Months perish with their moons; year treads on year; 251 **There is a little* 9
In painful struggles. Months each other chase, 274 *Infant M.* 4
But many days, and many months, 287 *Ellen Irwin* 41
—Hours, Days, and Months, *have* borne them in the sight 327 *Ode 1815* 11
Few months of life has he in store 483 *Simon Lee* 57
A natural meal—days, months, from Nature's hand; 528 **Those breathing* 85
Months passed in love that failed not to fulfil, 531 **I know* 17
Months passed on, and no Sir Eustace! 535 *Egremont* 57
Months and years went smilingly; 535 *Egremont* 70
That gave them birth:—months passed, and still this hand, 539 **Lady! a* 6
Six months to six years added he remained 576 **Six months* 1
Long months of peace (if such bold word accord 632 *Prelude* 1. 24
Long months of ease and undisturbed delight 632 *Prelude* 1. 26
The months passed on, remissly, not given up 653 *Prelude* 3. 322
Eight months! rolled pleasingly away; the ninth 658 *Prelude* 3. 631
Than pathless wastes. Once, when those summer months 664 *Prelude* 4. 370
To make this book our own. Through several months, 672 *Prelude* 5. 473
A few short months before. I turned my face 675 *Prelude* 6. 9
Through months, through years, long after the last beat 724 *Prelude* 10. 399
That he had disappeared—not two months gone. 766 *Excursion* 1. 661
A course of days composing happy months, 792 *Excursion* 3. 453
Of his day's work. 'Three dark mid-winter months 834 *Excursion* 5. 804
Two months unwearied of severest storm, K.8. 241 *Recluse* 1.1.181
Through these two months of unrelenting storm, K.8. 243 *Recluse* 1.1.244
And months, and let me add the long year through K.8. 265 **Brook, that* 2
Months'. In five months' time, should he be seen, 129 *Idiot Boy* 330
And, after ten months' melancholy, 249 *P. B.* 1134
This Dog, had been through three months' space 492 *Fidelity* 56
Of golden cities ten months' journey deep 688 *Prelude* 7. 83
A sportive infant, who, for six months' space, 692 *Prelude* 7. 337
"Through four months' space the Infant drew its food 852 *Excursion* 6. 939
Montrose. And, like Montrose, make Loyalty your pride— 310 *Invasion* 4
Monument. He died,—this seat his only monument. 23 *Yew-tree* 47
His death will be a monument for ages. 58 *Bord.* 1124
Raise on that dreary Waste a monument 78 *Bord.* 2326
Is neither epitaph nor monument, 95 *Brothers* 13
Another monument shall here be raised; 201 *Hart-leap* 66
Wrinkled Egyptian monument; 214 *Kirkstone* 17
Like a Form sculptured on a monument 273 **When Philoctetes* 2
Your Country rears this sacred Monument! 326 **Intrepid sons* 14
What offering, what transcendent monument 331 *Ode: Thanks.* 169
Monument—*continued.*
Pleased could my verse, a speaking monument, 376 *Duddon* 3. 3
Thou monument of peaceful happiness! 489 *Spade* 24
Will gladly stand a monument of thee. 491 *Tribute: Dog* 10
A lasting monument of words 492 *Fidelity* 52
Uphold a Monument as fair 550 *Hermit's Cell* 2. 11
That yet survive, a shattered monument 636 *Prelude* 1. 284
Some monument behind me which pure hearts 676 *Prelude* 6. 56
The Monument, and that Chamber of the Tower 689 *Prelude* 7. 136
Thy monument of glory will be raised; 752 *Prelude* 14. 432
A token (may it prove a monument!) 753 **Oft, through* 7
To her, a monument of faithful love 841 *Excursion* 6. 210
As their own private monument: for this 845 *Excursion* 6. 499
All buried with me without monument K.8. 255 *Recluse* 1.1.698
Monumental. His church with monumental wreck bestrown; 393 *Inglewood* 10
The monumental pomp of age 404 *White Doe* 737
By plate of monumental brass 417 *White Doe* 1895
That monumental grace 543 *Russ. Fug.* 172
Here let a monumental Stone 581 *John Words.* 63
Of state, equipped in monumental trim; 661 *Prelude* 4. 219
The monumental letters were inscribed 737 *Prelude* 12. 241
The monumental hillocks, and the pomp 744 *Prelude* 13. 334
From monumental hints: and thou, O Friend! 745 *Prelude* 13. 352
To monumental pillars: and, from these 787 *Excursion* 3. 57
That leans upon a monumental urn 825 *Excursion* 5. 216
And now that monumental stone preserves 864 *Excursion* 7. 472
Intent upon a monumental stone, 871 *Excursion* 7. 913
Monuments. These monuments shall all be overgrown. 203 *Hart-leap* 176
And monuments that soon must disappear: 334 **A winged* 9
Feelingly told by living monuments— 346 *Processions* 5
With monuments decayed or overthrown, 360 *Alban Hills* 3
Of things gone by, her meagre monuments 393 **The Lovers* 10
Nor these, nor monuments of eldest name, 419 *Ecc. Sonn.* 1. 5. 9
For other monuments than those of Earth; 421 *Ecc. Sonn.* 1. 11. 10
And Christian monuments, that now must burn 421 *Ecc. Sonn.* 1. 12. 8
Open your gates, ye Monuments of love 451 *Ecc. Sonn.* 3. 42. 11
Are monuments of his unfinished task. 548 **Stranger! this* 13
Where'er I roamed, were speaking monuments. 701 *Prelude* 8. 172
Of evidence from monuments, erect, 708 *Prelude* 8. 612
Religious, 'mid those frequent monuments 716 *Prelude* 9. 493
And marble monuments were here displayed 825 *Excursion* 5. 166
Their monuments and their memory. The vast Frame 872 *Excursion* 7. 999
—A few rude monuments of mountain-stone 894 *Excursion* 9. 710
Mood. A mind that, in a calm angelic mood 3 *Ev. Wk.* 80
His home approaching, but in such a mood 25 *Guilt* 68
I, too, infected by their mood, 81 †*Mother's Return* 51
In careless mood he looked at me, 86 *Anecdote* 33
Bring back a humbler mood! 112 **How rich* 6
Of the dry wreck. And, in our vacant mood, 148 **A narrow* 16
Poets, vain men in their mood! 160 **Pansies, lilies* 33
Though wrought in Vulcan's happiest mood, 163 *Needlecase* 11
While Benjamin in earnest mood 175 *Waggoner* 1. 146
So forth in dauntless mood they fare, 178 *Waggoner* 3. 20
In that sweet mood when pleasure loves to pay 185 *Nutting* 39
In vacant or in pensive mood, 187 **I wandered* 20
As if life's business were a summer mood; 195 *Resolution* 37
Of aspect more sublime; that blessed mood, 206 *Tintern* 37
Is lightened:—that serene and blessed mood, 206 *Tintern* 41
Spake of heroic arts in graver mood 211 *Laod.* 101
Ere shaken by that mood of stern disdain 227 *Vernal Ode* 123
And let some mood of thine in firm array 233 *Power of Sound* 94
All worlds, all natures, mood and measure keep 235 *Power of Sound* 206
But quickly Peter's mood is changed, 240 *P. B.* 346
In quiet uncomplaining mood, 241 *P. B.* 428
It suited Peter's present mood. 245 *P. B.* 830
Her froward mood, and softliest reprehend; 255 **Grief, thou* 4
Of higher mood, which now I meditate;— 259 *Calvert* 12
Those words were uttered as in pensive mood 263 **Those words* 1
Who trembles now at thy capricious mood? 271 *Henry: Portrait* 9
Listening, and listening long, in rapturous mood, 271 **Fame tells* 13
Or in his nobly-pensive mood, 286 *Nith* 35
An outlaw of as daring mood; 291 *Rob Roy* 4
When disenchanted from the mood 300 *Bran* 29
And an unthinking grief! The tenderest mood 304 **I grieved* 2
Roused though it be full often to a mood 307 **It is not* 5
To stillest mood of softest skies, 344 **How blest* 17
By the joint pressure of his musing mood 362 **List—'twas* 81
And thus in joyous mood they hie 396 *White Doe* 15
Or melancholy's sickly mood, 398 *White Doe* 174
Harsh thoughts with her high mood agree— 399 *White Doe* 261
And spake in firm and earnest mood. 406 *White Doe* 896
Walked quick or slowly, every mood 415 *White Doe* 1726
Deafening the region in his ireful mood. 439 *Ecc. Sonn.* 2. 43. 14
And the Land's humblest comforts. Now her mood 439 *Ecc. Sonn.* 2. 44. 6
Of Ocean roused into his fiercest mood, 454 **The Sun, that* 16
To fiercer mood the frenzy-stricken brain, 459 **Wanderer! that* 42
That verse of mine, whate'er its varying mood, 476 *Eden* 3
In that sweet mood when pleasant thoughts 482 *Lines: Spring* 3
Blank ocean and mere sky, support that mood 488 *Pers. Talk* 31
There let me see thee sink into a mood 498 **Enough of climbing* 42
Oft snapping at revenge in sullen mood; 505 *Warning* 116
Charged with those lays, and others of like mood, 538 **In desultory* 15
To speak of Love's true Servants in this mood; 559 *Cuck. and Night.* 148
The kindly mood in hearts which lapse of years, 567 *Cumb. Beg.* 92
No mood, which season takes away, or brings: 578 *Peele Castle* 10
In more than happy mood 579 **Sweet Flower* 24
And serious mood; but after I had seen 638 *Prelude* 1. 390

Moonlight—*continued.*
And, by the moonlight, Betty Foy 126 *Idiot Boy* 38
So through the moonlight lanes they go; 127 *Idiot Boy* 117
And far into the moonlight dale, 127 *Idiot Boy* 118
Appears along the moonlight road ; 128 *Idiot Boy* 174
So, through the moonlight lane she goes, 128 *Idiot Boy* 202
And far into the moonlight dale ; 128 *Idiot Boy* 203
For in the moonlight he had been 131 *Idiot Boy* 445
While hovering o'er the moonlight vale. 235 *Power of Sound* 168
All by the moonlight river-side 238 *P. B.* 191
All by the moonlight river side 241 *P. B.* 446
Thence back into the moonlight creeps ; 243 *P. B.* 639
The open moonlight reach. 244 *P. B.* 675
By moonlight made more faint and wan ; 244 *P. B.* 722
To-night, beneath the moonlight sky, 245 *P. B.* 784
To ivied castles and to moonlight skies, 273 **While Anna's* 12
Unhappy ghosts in troops by moonlight seen ; 361 **For action* 8
In open moonlight doth she lie ; 407 *White Doe* 994
The hour of moonlight solitude. 415 *White Doe* 1750
In frosty moonlight glistening ; 499 *Memory* 26
Like beds of moonlight shifting on the brine. 522 *Epist. Beaumont* 76
For moonlight fascinations mild, 526 **The soaring* 51
At morn, at noon, and under moonlight skies 549 **The massy* 8
Or the first woodcocks roam'd the moonlight hills. 592 *Ev. Wk. Quarto* 26
Or moonlight Upland lifts her hoary breast ; 602 *Desc. Sk. Quarto* 8
Lighted by gleams of moonlight from the sea 644 *Prelude* 2. 136
Looked ghastly in the moonlight : from behind, 664 *Prelude* 4. 396
By moonlight, doubting not that day was nigh, 685 *Prelude* 6. 695
Moonlight and stars, and empty streets, and sounds 697 *Prelude* 7. 661
Along the margin of the moonlight sea— 727 *Prelude* 10. 602
After the perils of his moonlight ride, 752 *Prelude* 14. 405
Motions of moonlight, all come thither—touch, 782 *Excursion* 2. 714

Moonlight-loving. Dwarf Genii, moonlight-loving Fays, 164 *Needlecase* 22

Moonlight's. As touch'd with dawning moonlight's hoary gleams, 598 *Ev. Wk. Quarto* 340

Moonlit. Of distant moon-lit mountains faintly shine, 384 *Duddon* 31. 13
Which moonlit elves, far seen by credulous eyes, 387 **Part fenced* 4

Moon's. Her dawn, far lovelier than the moon's own morn, 8 *Ev. Wk.* 340
By the moon's sullen lamp she first discerned, 27 *Guilt* 183
—The Moon's in heaven, as Betty sees, 127 *Idiot Boy* 154
Is it the moon's distorted face ? 242 *P. B.* 501
Aloft, beneath the moon's pale beam, 300 *Cora Linn* 22
When the East kindles with the full moon's light ; 455 *Rydal Mere* 23
The Moon's fix'd gaze between the opening trees, 596 *Ev. Wk. Quarto* 262
With the moon's beauty and the moon's soft pace, 653 *Prelude* 3. 281

Moons. —And hence, long afterwards, when eighteen moons 148 *Joanna* 77
Months perish with their moons ; year treads on year; 251 **There is a little* 9

Moonshine. Yet standing in the clear moonshine ; 248 *P. B.* 1097
Like moonshine—but the hue was green ; 343 *Eclipse* 26
Still moonshine, without shadow, spread 343 *Eclipse* 27
To memory's shadowy moonshine ! 386 *Yarrow Rev.* 112
The hall-clock in the clear moonshine 406 *White Doe* 960
To open moonshine, where the Doe 407 *White Doe* 1001
Nor feared she in the still moonshine 416 *White Doe* 1815
By moonshine through mere lack of taper light. 656 *Prelude* 3. 478

Moor. *See* **Clifford-moor.**
The bag-pipe dinning on the midnight moor 32 *Guilt* 410
O'er moor and mountain, midnight theft to hatch ! 32 *Guilt* 416
A firmer step than mine. That dismal Moor— 39 *Bord.* 108
The barren Moor, hangs from a beetling rock 49 *Bord.* 658
And therefore chose this solitary Moor, 59 *Bord.* 1209
And he is dead !—that Moor—how shall I cross it ? 76 *Bord.* 2238
She dwelt on a wide moor, 82 *Lucy Gray* 6
That overlooked the moor ; 83 *Lucy Gray* 38
On the moor, and in the wood, 160 **Pansies, lilies* 45
Others slunk to moor and wood, 171 *Kitten* 57
I was a Traveller then upon the moor ; 195 *Resolution* 15
From pond to pond he roamed, from moor to moor ; 196 *Resolution* 103
I'll think of the Leech-gatherer on the lonely moor !" 197 *Resolution* 140
The Knight had ridden down from Wensley Moor 200 *Hart-leap* 1
To barren heath, bleak moor, and quaking fen, 298 *Brownie's Cell* 1
Of fern-thatched hut on heathy moor : 390 *Highland Broach* 22
And southward far, with moor between, 406 *White Doe* 943
Dark moor, and gleam of pool and stream, 409 *White Doe* 1171
Mountain, and moor, and crowded street, where lie 442 *Ecc. Sonn.* 3. 7. 8
The captive Bird was gone ;—to cliff or moor 472 **The captive* 1
The gentle Lady married to the Moor ; 488 *Pers. Talk* 41
In marshalled thousands, darkening street and moor 505 *Warning* 122
Followed each other till a dreary moor 658 *Prelude* 4. 2
Dismounting, down the rough and stony moor 737 *Prelude* 12. 233

Moore. And Moore and Partridge stare me in the face. L.1. 96 *Juvenal* 3. 60

Moored. Till in the sunny bay his fleet was moored ! 449 *Ecc. Sonn.* 3. 37. 4
And, when the ship was moored, I leaped ashore 798 *Excursion* 3. 871
To the lake's margin, where a boat lies moored 890 *Excursion* 9. 425

Mooring-place. There in her mooring-place I left my bark,— 638 *Prelude* 1. 388
Her mooring-place ; where, to the sheltering tree, 895 *Excursion* 9. 766

Moorish. Upon the margin of that moorish flood 196 *Resolution* 74
Against the Moorish crescent. 287 *Ellen Irwin* 40
Unharnessed, naked, troops of Moorish horse 368 *Trajan* 45

Moorland. Yet o'er the moorland will she roam 108 *Louisa* 8
Between two sister moorland rills 165 *Danish Boy* 1
(Foretaste of winter) on the moorland heights ; 394 **No more* 28
Are heard among the moorland dells, 416 *White Doe* 1886
Invested moorland waste, and naked pool, 738 *Prelude* 12. 258
Upon that open moorland stood a grove, 756 *Excursion* 1. 26

Moorland—*continued.*
Paid cheerful tribute to the moorland house. 776 *Excursion* 2. 343
Had clomb aloft to delve the moorland turf 783 *Excursion* 2. 787
Worn in the moorland, till I overtook 823 *Excursion* 5. 62

Moorlands. And, up among the moorlands, see 396 *White Doe* 9
When first, descending from the moorlands, 586 *Hogg* 1

Moors. On the bleak sides of Cumbria's heath-clad moors, 21 *Desc. Sk.* 593
He was in slavery among the Moors 100 *Brothers* 317
Through prickly moors or dusty ways must wind ; 160 **Up with me* 27
The grass is bright with rain-drops ;—on the moors 195 *Resolution* 10
About the weary moors continually, 197 *Resolution* 130
Of mountains and of dreary moors. 239 *P. B.* 295
'Tis not a plover of the moors, 243 *P. B.* 616
And luxuries extract from bleakest moors ; 284 *Departure* 26
Her spirit, while he crosses lonely moors, 463 **Adieu, Rydalian* 13
Who with the ploughshare clove the barren moors, 468 *St. Bees* 136
America, the Hunter-Indian ; Moors, 690 *Prelude* 7. 226
Moors, mountains, headlands, and ye hollow vales, 702 *Prelude* 8. 216

Moping. Whole hours, with idle arms in moping sorrow knit. 32 *Guilt* 432
But, for that moping Son of Idleness, 95 *Brothers* 11
Or spied where thou sitt'st moping in thy mew 456 **The leaves* 18

Moral. Depicted in the dial's moral round ; 2 *Ev. Wk.* 28
Awoke a fainter sense of moral grief ; 22 *Desc. Sk.* 633
The moral shapes of things. His tender cries 57 *Bord.* 1083
Of moral qualities in their diverse aspects ; 59 *Bord.* 1226
I would urge this moral pleading, 90 *Longest Day* 27
Thus spake the moral Muse—her wing 154 *Flower Garden* 49
His genius and his moral frame 194 *Ruth* 151
Of all my moral being. Nor perchance, 207 *Tintern* 111
He left this moral grafted on his Fate ; 214 *Dion* 121
Their moral element, 225 *Primrose* 40
This hides not from the moral Muse 225 *Present.* 17
No scale of moral music—to unite 235 *Power of Sound* 170
He sought his moral creed. 291 *Rob Roy* 20
Of moral prudence, sought through good and ill ; 315 **Alas ! what* 2
It was a *moral* end for which they fought ; 316 **It was a* 1
Nor hath that moral good been *vainly* sought ; 316 **It was a* 5
Than for like scenes in moral vision shown, 360 *Alban Hills* 5
In the delight of moral prudence schooled, 368 *Trajan* 31
That moral sweeten by a heaven-taught lay, 388 *Trosachs* 13
Yet in this moral Strain a power may live, 395 *White Doe: Ded.* 62
Known to the moral world, Imagination, 427 *Ecc. Sonn.* 1. 34. 10
They came,—and, while the moral tempest roars 449 *Ecc. Sonn.* 3. 36. 12
The moral intimations of the sky, 461 **Queen of* 48
How in thy mind and moral frame agree 478 **Lonsdale ! it* 6
Of moral evil and of good, 481 *Tables Turned* 23
But makes his moral being his prime care ; 493 *Hap. War.* 11
Lay on the moral will a withering ban ? 501 *Humanity* 80
Fit retribution, by the moral code 519 *Pun. Death* 8. 1
And fortify the moral sense of all. 519 *Pun. Death* 9. 14
No self-reproach ; who of the moral law 568 *Cumb. Beg.* 136
Awoke a fainter pang of moral grief ; 616 *Desc. Sk. Quarto* 769
Firm in the sacred paths of moral truth, 619 *School Ex.* 78
Reflective acts to fix the moral law 650 *Prelude* 3. 84
I gave a moral life : I saw them feel, 651 *Prelude* 3. 129
One sense for moral judgments, as one eye 709 *Prelude* 8. 671
Given to my moral nature had I known 722 *Prelude* 10. 269
And sundry moral sentiments as props 731 *Prelude* 11. 264
Yielded up moral questions in despair. 731 *Prelude* 11. 305
Was scanned, as I had scanned the moral world ? 735 *Prelude* 12. 92
Of time and season, to the moral power, 736 *Prelude* 12. 119
From moral purpose—early tutored me 740 *Prelude* 13. 44
In moral judgments which from this pure source 748 *Prelude* 14. 128
Apt illustrations of the moral world, 750 *Prelude* 14. 319
And moral notions too intolerant, 751 *Prelude* 14. 340
Of moral strength, and intellectual Power ; 755 *Recluse* 1. 1. 770
The moral properties and scope of things. 758 *Excursion* 1. 169
And every moral feeling of his soul 760 *Excursion* 1. 304
For moral dignity, and strength of mind, 775 *Excursion* 2. 287
The moral interests, the creative might, 798 *Excursion* 3. 823
And intuitions moral and divine) 811 *Excursion* 4. 646
With less intelligence for *moral* things 813 *Excursion* 4. 806
Bestowed ; were gladsome,—and their moral sense 815 *Excursion* 4. 938
Subservient still to moral purposes, 820 *Excursion* 4. 1248
Shall fix, in calmer seats of moral strength, 820 *Excursion* 4. 1272
By act of naked reason. Moral truth 831 *Excursion* 5. 562
Of moral anger previously had tinged 832 *Excursion* 5. 622
And to his moral being appertained : 853 *Excursion* 6. 1014
A labourer, with moral virtue girt, 862 *Excursion* 7. 338
Discoursed of natural or moral truth 865 *Excursion* 7. 512
Upon the moral law. Egyptian Thebes, 877 *Excursion* 8. 216
The excellence of moral qualities 887 *Excursion* 9. 232
The mind with moral and religious truth, 888 *Excursion* 9. 302
Of moral prudence, clothed in images K.8. 227 **I will* 91

Moralise. By wisdom, moralise his pensive road. 11 *Desc. Sk.* 28

Moralised. Had moralised on this, and other truths 845 *Excursion* 6. 442

Moralising. Fade,—and the moralising mind derive S.3. 433 **The doubt* 23

Moralist. She is innocent. Were I a Moralist, 66 *Bord.* 1621
A Moralist perchance appears ; 485 *Poet's Epitaph* 25
Resolve,' the haughty Moralist would say, 817 *Excursion* 4. 1081

Moralists. A whipping to the Moralists who preach 58 *Bord.* 1159
These moralists could act and comprehend : 307 **Great men* 5

Morality. Resound the praise of your morality— 77 *Bord.* 2291
With trite reflections of morality, 739 *Prelude* 12. 314
Else had Morality beheld her line L.1. 97 *Juvenal* 3. 63

Morals. That Shakspeare spake ; the faith and morals hold 307 **It is not* 12
With morals, trusting, in contempt or fear 357 *Aquap.* 334

Most—*continued.*
And into most of these secluded vales — 858 *Excursion* 7. 61
In times when most existence with herself — 885 *Excursion* 9. 103
How with most quiet and most silent death, — 886 *Excursion* 9. 149
We rose together: all were pleased; but most — 890 *Excursion* 9. 427
The most assured seat of [poesy ?] — S.3. 436 **The doubt* 164
But most of all the Birds that haunt the flood — K.8. 241 *Recluse* 1.1.193
Not even the nearest to me and most dear, — K.8. 255 *Recluse* 1.1.688

Mostly. And mostly profitless. And, sooth to say, — 799 *Excursion* 3. 896

Moth. "Rich robes are fretted by the moth; — 372 *Eg. Maid* 217
The busy dor-hawk chases the white moth — 453 **Calm is the* 22
Thanks to the moth that spared it for our eyes; — 526 **Soon did* 5

Mother. *See* **Foster-mother, Giant-mother, Lady-mother, Virgin-mother.**
Press the sad kiss, fond mother! vainly fears — 7 *Ev. Wk.* 275
Close by my mother in their native bowers: — 28 *Guilt* 240
Thy Mother too!—scarce had I gained the door, — 40 *Bord.* 182
Where is she—holla! You are Idonea's Mother?— — 46 *Bord.* 529
And most forlorn, should bribe a Mother, pressed — 56 *Bord.* 1039
Since your dear Mother went away,— — 81 †*Mother's Return* 2
And shouted, "Mqther, come to me!" — 81 †*Mother's Return* 8
Your tender mother cannot hear." — 81 †*Mother's Return* 12
And all "since Mother went away!" — 81 †*Mother's Return* 40
Your mother through the snow." — 83 *Lucy Gray* 16
—When in the snow the mother spied — 83 *Lucy Gray* 43
Dwell near them with my mother." — 83 *We are Seven* 24
Have left the mother and the nest; — 84 *Shepherd-boys* 7
And thy mother from thy side for evermore was gone. — 87 *Pet-lamb* 36
"My Mother," said the Boy, "was born near to a blessèd Tree, — 92 *Poet's Dream* 27
"Hither the Afflicted come, as thou hast heard thy Mother say, — 92 *Poet's Dream* 49
As the dying mother witnessed — 94 *Westmoreland Girl* 39
Was half a mother to them.—If you weep, Sir, — 99 *Brothers* 235
A woman who was not thy mother. — 114 *Ind. Wom.* 32
A little lamb, and then its mother! — 115 *Last of Flock* 62
Heard by his mother unawares! — 117 *Affl. Marg.* 25
Years to a mother bring distress; — 117 *Affl. Marg.* 27
Kind mother have I been, as kind — 117 *Affl. Marg.* 32
The Mother, in her turns of anguish, worse — 118 *Maternal Grief* 42
Amusement, where the Mother does not miss — 119 *Maternal Grief* 70
One moment let me be thy mother! — 120 *Emigrant Mother* 16
An infant thou, a mother I! — 120 *Emigrant Mother* 36
She with her mother crossed the sea; — 121 *Emigrant Mother* 69
The babe and mother near me dwell: — 121 *Emigrant Mother* 70
The promise of a mother. To conceal — 122 *V. and J.* 68
And while the Mother, at the door, — 127 *Idiot Boy* 87
Oh! what a wretched Mother I!" — 129 *Idiot Boy* 266
The Mother mourned, nor ceased her tears to flow, — 139 *Widow* 15
The Mother hails in her descending Son — 139 *Widow* 40
You love your father and your mother, — 143 †*Lov. and Lik.* 55
For I thy own dear mother am: — 145 *Her Eyes* 92
All children of one mother: — 161 *Binnorie* 2
With thankfulness the Mother pressed; — 176 *Waggoner* 1. 246
Not to speak of babe and mother; — 181 *Waggoner* 4. 167
That Mother, whose spirit in fetters is bound, — 189 *Music* 39
Your Mother has had alms of mine." — 191 *Beggars* 40
It was your Mother, as I say!" — 191 *Beggars* 45
Hunt the Mother and the Child. — 204 *Brougham* 60
Blissful Mary, Mother mild, — 204 *Brougham* 69
Maid and Mother undefiled, — 204 *Brougham* 70
Save a Mother and her Child! — 204 *Brougham* 71
The Mother—her thou must have seen, — 232 *Jew. Fam.* 9
And left her mother at sixteen, — 246 *P. B.* 894
"My mother! oh my mother!" — 246 *P. B.* 930
Heard plainly by the wretched Mother— — 247 *P. B.* 1007
And Peter hears the Mother sigh, — 248 *P. B.* 1069
The Mother o'er the threshold flies, — 248 *P. B.* 1083
Dear mother of fresh thoughts and joyous health! — 254 **A flock* 14
How sweet it is, when mother Fancy rocks — 260 **How sweet* 1
Smile on his Mother now with bolder cheer. — 294 **Fly, some* 14
His Mother, too, no doubt, above — 295 *Highland Boy* 26
His Mother often thought, and said, — 296 *Highland Boy* 86
His Mother, she who loved him best, — 296 *Highland Boy* 164
But most of all, his Mother dear, — 297 *Highland Boy* 231
The Mother *then* mourns, as she needs must mourn; — 318 **In due* 12
O Silence! thou wert mother of a shout — 322 *Germans* 5
Meek Virgin Mother, more benign — 338 **Meek Virgin* 1
And hence, O Virgin Mother mild! — 338 **Meek Virgin* 19
And, when thy Mother weeps for Thee, — 348 **Lulled by* 73
Lost Youth! a solitary Mother; — 348 **Lulled by* 74
Revered her Mother, sage Mnemosyne, — 359 *Plea: Hist.* 12
Mother of Heroes, from thy death-like sleep! — 366 **Fair Land* 14
For the distracted Mother to assuage — 378 *Duddon* 11. 8
Sacred Religion! "mother of form and fear," — 380 *Duddon* 18. 1
Mother of Love! (that name best suits thee here) — 380 *Duddon* 18. 5
Mother of Love! for this deep vale, protect — 380 *Duddon* 18. 6
For maid and mother, when despair — 391 *Highland Broach* 53
Again the Mother whispered low, — 398 *White Doe* 184
A fondly-anxious Mother strove — 407 *White Doe* 1030
Mother! whose virgin bosom was uncrost — 434 *Ecc. Sonn.* 2. 25. 1
Do Thou, in truth a second Mother, strive — 445 *Ecc. Sonn.* 3. 21. 5
Belovèd Mother! Thou whose happy hand — 445 *Ecc. Sonn.* 3. 22. 9
In and for whom the pious Mother felt — 446 *Ecc. Sonn.* 3. 24. 3
And such vibration through the Mother went — 446 *Ecc. Sonn.* 3. 24. 8
To courses fit to make a mother rue — 447 *Ecc. Sonn.* 3. 27. 10
Feel with the Mother, think the severed Wife — 476 *Howard* 11
"You look round on your Mother Earth, — 481 *Expost.* 9
But, O Mother! by the close — 502 **Like a* 13

Mother—*continued.*
And, sweet Mother! under warrant — 502 **Like a* 45
Mother! blest be thy calm ease; — 503 **Like a* 60
His Mother leaves him free to taste — 507 *May* 39
Dear Mother! if thou *must* thy steps retrace, — 516 **Young England* 12
The Mother Church in yon sequestered vale; — 534 **When in* 4
To cast their shadows on our mother Earth — 538 **In desultory* 28
"O Mother Maid! O Maid and Mother free! — 552 *Prioress* 15
Of Jesu's Mother, as he had been told, — 553 *Prioress* 54
Our blissful Lady, Jesu's Mother dear, — 553 *Prioress* 58
Of Jesu's Mother?' said this Innocent; — 554 *Prioress* 87
On Jesu's Mother fixed was his intent. — 554 *Prioress* 99
The sweetness of Christ's Mother piercèd so — 554 *Prioress* 104
And ever on Christ's Mother meek and kind — 555 *Prioress* 146
And eke His Mother, honour of Mankind: — 555 *Prioress* 168
His Mother swooning by the body lay: — 555 *Prioress* 174
And, for the worship of His Mother dear, — 556 *Prioress* 203
"'This well of mercy, Jesu's Mother sweet, — 556 *Prioress* 205
Weeping and praising Jesu's Mother dear; — 556 *Prioress* 227
On us, for reverence of His Mother Mary!" — 556 *Prioress* 239
O rest, thou doleful Mother of Mankind!" — 581 *Invoc. Earth* 2
Upon its mother) may be both alike — 586 *Ch. Lamb* 115
His Acidalian mother, by degrees — 625 *Æneid* 90
Queen, Wife and Mother! may All-judging Heaven — 628 **Deign, Sovereign* 5
While she as duteous as the mother dove — 634 *Prelude* 1. 140
My honoured Mother, she who was the heart — 669 *Prelude* 5. 257
Mother and child!—These feelings, in themselves — 692 *Prelude* 7. 329
The mother; but, upon her cheeks diffused, — 692 *Prelude* 7. 344
Contending after showers. The mother now — 692 *Prelude* 7. 365
Some vagrant mother, whose arch little ones, — 705 *Prelude* 8. 402
The mother from the cradle of her babe, — 723 *Prelude* 10. 359
And the lamb's mother, and their tender ways — 748 *Prelude* 14. 173
Urged by his Mother, he essayed to teach — 761 *Excursion* 1. 312
Had from its mother caught the trick of grief, — 768 *Excursion* 1. 830
The Mother followed:—miserably bare — 774 *Excursion* 2. 201
Into his mother earth without such pomp — 780 *Excursion* 2. 597
The Mother now remained; as if in her, — 795 *Excursion* 3. 652
The Wife and Mother pitifully fixing — 798 *Excursion* 3. 854
And to the winds and mother elements, — 811 *Excursion* 4. 677
Of a young fowl beneath one mother hatched, — 843 *Excursion* 6. 367
The Mother oft was seen to stand, or kneel — 850 *Excursion* 6. 813
My Infant! and for that good Mother dear, — 852 *Excursion* 6. 925
The Child whom Ellen and her Mother loved — 852 *Excursion* 6. 931
The Mother, oft as she was sent abroad, — 853 *Excursion* 6. 984
And love, benignant mother of the vale, — 855 *Excursion* 6. 1107
"Here rests a Mother. But from her I turn — 855 *Excursion* 6. 1115
—Thrice happy, then, the Mother may be deemed, — 856 *Excursion* 6. 1188
The warm lap of his mother earth: and so, — 861 *Excursion* 7. 287
Mother and little children, boys and girls, — 877 *Excursion* 8. 181
The Mother left alone,—no helping hand — 878 *Excursion* 8. 267
And false as monstrous! Can the mother thrive — 878 *Excursion* 8. 285
From earth, the common mother of us all. — 879 *Excursion* 8. 357
Have a Mother, once a Statue, — S.3. 437 **I, whose* 3
She being herself a Mother, happy Beast — K.8. 251 *Recluse* 1.1.529
Thy mother to the fold must go — K.8. 262 **Ah! if* 9

Mother-bird. Rest, Mother-bird! and when thy young — 169 *Wren's Nest* 65
Moved we as plunderers where the mother-bird — 637 *Prelude* 1. 327

Mother-church. Grave doctors strenuous for the mother-church, — 825 *Excursion* 5. 176

Mother-earth. The common growth of mother-earth — 238 *P. B.* 133

Mother-ewe. Beneath my shade the mother-ewe — 156 *Oak and Broom* 86

Motherless. I'm fatherless and motherless. — 82 *Alice Fell* 44
And thither took with him his motherless Babe, — 125 *V. and J.* 274

Motherly. Thoughts motherly, and meek as womanhood. — 304 **I grieved* 8
From my old Dame, so kind and motherly, — 658 *Prelude* 4. 28
Of motherly humanity, outspread — 836 *Excursion* 5. 925
Domestic, and in spirit motherly — K.8. 251 *Recluse* 1.1.528

Mother-maid. The Mother-maid, whose countenance bright — 544 *Russ. Fug.* 213

Mother's. *See* **Foster-mother's.**
She, in a mother's care, her beauty's pride — 6 *Ev. Wk.* 228
Fair Swan! by all a mother's joys caressed, — 7 *Ev. Wk.* 250
"Twelve steps or more from my mother's door, — 84 *We are Seven* 39
And, while with all a mother's love — 85 *Shepherd-boys* 73
And placed him at his mother's side; — 85 *Shepherd-boys* 96
That 'tis thy mother's heart which is working so in thee? — 88 *Pet-lamb* 50
And the bleating mother's Young-one — 93 *Westmoreland Girl* 7
Mother's care no more her guide, — 93 *Westmoreland Girl* 30
An orphan could not find his mother's grave: — 98 *Brothers* 169
Are aught of what makes up a mother's heart, — 99 *Brothers* 233
Oh! do not dread thy mother's door; — 117 *Affl. Marg.* 38
Daily before the Mother's watchful eye, — 118 *Maternal Grief* 22
Shrunk from his Mother's presence, shunned with fear — 118 *Maternal Grief* 51
Is gone, and twilight to the Mother's wish — 119 *Maternal Grief* 66
And sure a mother's heart is mine: — 120 *Emigrant Mother* 18
Thy own dear mother's far away, — 120 *Emigrant Mother* 19
Contentment, hope, and mother's glee, — 121 *Emigrant Mother* 87
Upon the Mother's bosom; resting thus — 124 *V. and J.* 214
The sentence, by her mother's lip pronounced, — 124 *V. and J.* 221
No answer, only took the mother's hand — 125 *V. and J.* 232
Sing at thy Mother's breast. Month followed month, — 136 *Michael* 349
Thou art thy mother's only joy; — 145 *Her Eyes* 42
Who might have wandered with thee.—Mother's love, — 172 *Infant Daughter* 28
Nor less than mother's love in other breasts, — 172 *Infant Daughter* 29

Mother's—*continued.*
Thy shelter—and their mother's breast! 182 Waggoner 4. 263
About its mother's heart, and brought 199 Thorn 140
When he had wandered from his mother's side. 203 Hart-leap 152
To sink upon your mother's lap—and rest? 229 Clouds 10
Age faithful to the mother's knee, 232 Jew. Fam. 31
A mother's hope is hers;—but soon 246 P. B. 906
Fine as the mother's softest plumes allow: 254 Wild Duck's Nest 12
A nursling couched upon her mother's knee, 274 Infant M. 13
Whose murmur soothed thy languid Mother's ear 275 Rotha Q. 10
And more than mother's love. 295 Highland Boy 30
His Mother's neck entwine; 342 Ital. Itin. 34
The patriot Mother's weight of anxious cares! 344 *How blest 52
Whose ruddy children, by the mother's eyes 377 Duddon 5. 11
Was buried by her Mother's side. 416 White Doe 1870
Of mother's love with maiden purity, 434 Ecc. Sonn. 2. 25. 13
I saw a Mother's eye intensely bent 446 Ecc. Sonn. 3. 24. 1
Spreading his little palms in his glad Mother's sight) 460 *Queen of 20
Stretched on the dying Mother's lap, lies dead 476 Howard 1
Upon his mother's grave? 485 Poet's Epitaph 20
And hers is a mother's sorrow. 495 Force of Prayer 48
Her Mother's favourite; and the orphan Girl, 509 F. Stone 66
She sits, for that departed Mother's sake. 509 F. Stone 69
The noble-minded Mother's helping hand 541 Grace Darl. 47
"With Mother's pity in her breast enclosed 555 Prioress 142
A third now slumbers at the Mother's side; 576 *By a 10
Fond healing, like a mother's kiss. 578 *I come 56
And the Babe leaps up on his Mother's arm:— 588 Immortality 49
And, even with something of a Mother's mind, 588 Immortality 79
Fretted by sallies of his mother's kisses, 588 Immortality 88
Till Venus cried, "A mother's heart is mine; 620 Birth of Love 3
(Alive to all a mother's pain, 620 Birth of Love 10
Love, at the word, before his mother's sight 624 Æneid 44
On Indian plains, and from my mother's hut 636 Prelude 1. 298
Nursed in his Mother's arms, who sinks to sleep, 645 Prelude 2. 235
Rocked on his Mother's breast; who with his soul 645 Prelude 2. 236
Drinks in the feelings of his Mother's eye! 645 Prelude 2. 237
I held mute dialogues with my Mother's heart, 646 Prelude 2. 268
Who fills the mother's breast with innocent milk, 669 Prelude 5. 272
As ever clung around a mother's neck, 692 Prelude 7. 340
Be tender as a nursing mother's heart; 749 Prelude 14. 228
Left one day mistress of her mother's stores, 781 Excursion 2. 655
Endeared my wanderings; and the mother's kiss 794 Excursion 3. 582
In smoky cabins, from a mother's tongue— 813 Excursion 4. 791
The sheltering hillock is the Mother's grave. 850 Excursion 6. 792
Alone, within her widowed Mother's house. 851 Excursion 6. 854
Thus, in her Mother's hearing Ellen spake, 852 Excursion 6. 917
A mother's loss, but mourned in bitterness 853 Excursion 6. 989
Home to her mother's house. The Youth was fled; 853 Excursion 6. 1005
With which by nature every mother's soul 867 Excursion 7. 642
Affections seated in the mother's breast, 875 Excursion 8. 74
Who, if indeed she own a mother's heart, 889 Excursion 9. 328
He learned to pasture at his mother's side. K.8. 228 *I will 127

Mothers. But there are Mothers who can see the Babe 45 Bord. 440
And looked, as mothers ne'er were known to look, 125 V. and J. 260
Shall mothers breathe a like sweet air 224 *'Tis gone 35
Upon their leading mothers hung— 398 White Doe 165
Sons, mothers, maidens withering on the stalk, 488 Pers. Talk 6
Was as the love of mothers; and when years, 585 Ch. Lamb 88

Mother-spray. And goodly fruitage with the mother-spray; 435 Ecc. Sonn. 2. 28. 3

Motion. The boat's first motion—made with dashing oar; 9 Ev. Wk. 372
Thro' worlds where Life, and Voice, and Motion sleep; 16 Desc. Sk. 310
He fell, and without sense or motion lay; 26 Guilt 89
Which with the motion of a virtuous act 40 Bord. 170
The motion of a muscle—this way or that— 65 Bord. 1540
The breeze-like motion and the self-born carol; 88 H. C. 4
Smiles, that with motion of their own 108 Louisa
Their starts of motion and their fits of rest, 118 Maternal Grief 33
With a leisurely motion the door of his hut. 120 Childless Father 16
From earth to heaven with motion fleet 164 *Fair Lady 25
Slumbers without sense of motion, 166 Wand. Jew 15
No motion has she now, no force; 187 *A slumber 5
With the slow motion of a summer's cloud, 200 Hart-leap 2
And even the motion of our human blood 206 Tintern 44
A motion and a spirit, that impels 207 Tintern 100
With grace of motion that might scarcely seem 218 Recluse 1. 1. 204
And every motion of his starry train 220 Triad 49
Respond with sympathetic motion; 226 Vernal Ode 51
Only the Ass, with motion dull, 241 P. B. 413
—Once more the Ass, with motion dull, 241 P. B. 418
He sees a motion—hears a groan; 242 P. B. 527
And doth with his eternal motion make 258 *It is a 7
Where even the motion of an Angel's wing 259 *A volant 12
Nor could I let one thought—one motion—slip 273 *Wild Redbreast 7
He felt the motion—took his seat; 296 Highland Boy 152
That with a motion overthrow 297 Highland Boy 208
With such invisible motion speed thy flight, 315 *Advance—come 10
In motion rapid as the lightning's gleam; 330 Ode: Thanks. 78
Of nun-like females, with soft motion, glide! 334 *Bruges I 14
Impetuous motion to the Stars above her. 346 Gemmi 8
While they the Church engird with motion slow, 347 Processions 56
The form and motion of a stream to take; 351 Des. Stanzas 62
To that mild breeze with motion and with voice 356 Aquap. 221
Of motion, whether in the embrace 369 Eg. Maid 40
And griefs whose aery motion comes not near 395 White Doe: Ded. 35
To a lingering motion bound, 397 White Doe 149
With the fleet motion of a dove; 411 White Doe 1374

Motion—*continued.*
Crimes that might stop the motion of the sun) 439 Ecc. Sonn. 2. 42. 7
Or down the nave to pace in motion slow; 451 Ecc. Sonn. 3. 42. 6
A tell-tale motion! soon will it be laid, 454 Sea-side 5
But the least motion which they made, 482 Lines: Spring 15
To regulate the motion of our dreams 502 *The unremitting 12
Of motion they renounce, and with the head 508 F. Stone 37
And of all visible motion destitute, 523 Epist. Beaumont 141
To wheel with languid motion round and round, 527 *Those breathing 48
In look and motion, that the cottage curs, 567 Cumb. Beg. 61
No motion but the moving tide, a breeze, 578 Peele Castle 27
Thro' worlds where Life and Sound, and Motion sleep, 609 Desc.Sk.Quarto 375
And the motion unsettles a tear; 621 Convict 42
Of undistinguishable motion, steps 637 Prelude 1. 324
Of earth—and with what motion moved the clouds! 637 Prelude 1. 339
And measured motion like a living thing, 638 Prelude 1. 384
And everlasting motion, not in vain 638 Prelude 1. 404
The rapid line of motion, then at once 639 Prelude 1. 456
With visible motion her diurnal round! 639 Prelude 1. 460
With giddy motion. But the time approached 642 Prelude 2. 48
In motion without pause; but ye have left 685 Prelude 6. 677
Monstrous in colour, motion, shape, sight, sound! 697 Prelude 7. 688
Whose truth is not a motion or a shape 703 Prelude 8. 298
Incited it to motion, and controlled. 705 Prelude 8. 432
Till, every effort, every motion gone, 707 Prelude 8. 574
With motion constant as his own, I went 710 Prelude 9. 39
Unto a heifer's motion, by a cord 717 Prelude 9. 512
The motion of a wind-mill; though the air 723 Prelude 10. 369
But yet no motion of the breast was seen, 768 Excursion 1. 800
Of motion, save the water that descended, 787 Excursion 3. 69
Betray to sight the motion of the stream, 800 Excursion 3. 976
On the first motion of a holy thought; 804 Excursion 4. 217
Be as a presence or a motion—one 809 Excursion 4. 520
Of never-varying motion, to and fro. 833 Excursion 5. 747
—Rocked by the motion of a trusty ass 858 Excursion 7. 72
And constant as the motion of the day; 862 Excursion 7. 325
"I feel at times a motion of despite 866 Excursion 7. 590
That inward motion to disguise, he said 874 Excursion 8. 32
A look or motion of intelligence 880 Excursion 8. 412
Partook of every motion, met, retired, S.3. 434 *The doubt 75
Of ceaseless motion, that might scarcely seem K.8. 242 Recluse 1. 1. 204
And now am landed, and the motion gone, K.8. 244 Recluse 1. 1. 293

Motionless. Stand motionless, to awful silence bound: 17 Desc. Sk. 410
How motionless!—not frozen seas 106 *I've watched 5
More motionless! and then 106 *I've watched 6
The green bough motionless and dead: 127 Idiot Boy 79
Where all things else are still and motionless. 184 Airey-force 7
Motionless as a cloud the old Man stood, 196 Resolution 75
Ascending from behind the motionless brow 229 Clouds 2
Breathless and motionless, the mind 247 P. B. 1017
Of mountains, silent, dreary, motionless: 266 *Even as 5
I listened, motionless and still; 289 Sol. Reap. 29
Yon foaming flood seems motionless as ice; 290 Kilchurn 36
And motionless; and, to the gazer's eye, 456 *Soft as 3
And sultry air, depending motionless. 497 *Enough of climbing 23
Both silent and both motionless alike; 643 Prelude 2. 112
A motionless array of mighty waves, 683 Prelude 6. 531

Motions. Tracking the motions of the fitful gale. 7 Ev. Wk. 296
All motions, sounds, and voices, far and nigh, 17 Desc. Sk. 362
Would watch my motions with suspicious stare, 150 *When, to 28
From the motions that are made, 170 Kitten 11
The feeble motions of thy life, and cheers 173 Infant Daughter 70
And sullen motions long and slow, 175 Waggoner 1. 201
Her household motions light and free, 186 *She was 13
Even in the motions of the Storm 187 *Three years 22
But your smooth motions suit a peaceful aim; 230 Clouds 15
On those revolving motions did await 255 *Grief, thou 11
Motions of thought which elevate the will 281 Chris. Words. 12
He tracks her motions, quick or slow. 294 Jedbor. 57
Hence motions, even amid the vulgar throng, 334 *The Spirit 7
Beauty, and life, and motions as of joy: 337 Aar 11
With intermingling motions soft and still, 338 Engelberg 8
O for those motions only that invite 473 *We saw 5
Motions and Means, on land and sea at war 477 Steamboats 1
Its motions, too, are wild and shy; 491 Fidelity 10
The motions that it graces—and forbear 511 *Who rashly 8
Your motions, glittering Elves! 526 *The soaring 14
Those hallowed and pure motions of the sense 640 Prelude 1. 551
All finite motions overruling, lives 651 Prelude 3. 120
And wavering motions sent he knows not whence, 662 Prelude 4. 269
Attends the motions of the viewless winds, 674 Prelude 5. 596
And sometimes rustling motions nigh at hand, 686 Prelude 6. 719
Motions not treacherous or profane, else why 725 Prelude 10. 458
Had watched all gentle motions, and to these 729 Prelude 11. 133
Ye motions of delight, that haunt the sides 734 Prelude 12. 9
Of music swayed their motions, and the waste 745 Prelude 13. 348
Motions of moonlight, all come thither—touch, 782 Excursion 2. 714
And all the tender motions of the soul, 796 Excursion 3. 683
For consciousness the motions of thy will; 802 Excursion 4. 95
The form, port, motions, of this Cottage-girl 850 Excursion 6. 826
So joyful in its motions, is become 879 Excursion 8. 323
Dull, to the joy of her own motions dead; 879 Excursion 8. 324
As inward motions of the wandering thought K.8. 233 *Along the 2
And not feel motions there? He thought of clouds K.8. 237 Recluse 1. 1.25
With motions of true dignity and grace? K.8. 248 Recluse 1. 1. 411
They try all frolic motions; flutter, plunge, K.8. 251 Recluse 1. 1. 550
Motions of savage instinct, my delight K.8. 256 Recluse 1. 1. 707
Thy motions, intricate and manifold, K.8. 301 *And oh 7

Mountain—*continued.*
Whose skirts the glowing Mountain thirsted to detain. 338 Engelberg 18
Of thy own mountain, set to keep 338 *Meek Virgin 3
Are moved, for me—upon this Mountain named 340 Ranz 10
Thy mountain notes with simple skill; 341 Ital. Itin. 6
A product of that awful Mountain seem, 347 Processions 57
Take, cradled Nursling of the mountain, take 377 Duddon 4. 1
O mountain Stream! the Shepherd and his Cot 379 Duddon 14. 1
Round strath and mountain, stamped by the ancient tongue 389 Sound of Mull 3
The mountain region of the west, 390 Highland Broach 6
The White Doe on the Mountain browsing, 415 White Doe 1732
Praised be the Rivers, from their mountain springs 431 Ecc. Sonn. 2. 13. 1
Then, like the mountain, thundering from above 439 Ecc. Sonn. 2. 44. 4
Mountain, and moor, and crowded street, where lie 442 Ecc. Sonn. 3. 7. 8
So, like the Mountain, may we grow more bright 452 Ecc. Sonn. 3. 46. 12
Herds range along the mountain side; 457 *Had this 30
But when a storm, on sea or mountain bred, 472 Dunolly Eagle 2
Was yielding, on a mountain height 472 Ossian 6
Our own domestic mountain. Thing and thought 480 Cordelia 7
The Dog is not of mountain breed; 491 Fidelity 9
These swan-like specks of mountain snow, 497 Lycoris 16
Or mountain rivers, where they creep 499 Memory 27
Fell on the ground; and the small mountain birds, 566 Cumb. Beg. 19
Let him be free of mountain solitudes; 569 Cumb. Beg. 183
Rises no mountain to mine eyes unknown; 574 Chiabrera 4. 16
The mountain will we cross." 580 John Words. 60
The mountain top, or breathed the mist 583 *O for a 47
Found by the verdant door of mountain farms. 594 Ev. Wk. Quarto 128
Tune in the mountain dells their water lyres. 598 Ev. Wk. Quarto 328
The mountain streams their rising song suspend; 598 Ev. Wk. Quarto 352
Weeping beneath his chill of mountain gloom. 603 Desc. Sk. Quarto 54
She hears, upon the mountain forest's brow, 606 Desc. Sk. Quarto 225
When hums the mountain bee in May's glad ear, 610 Desc. Sk. Quarto 444
Up the green mountain tracking Summer's feet, 610 Desc. Sk. Quarto 452
On the lone mountain top, their chang'd estate. 611 Desc. Sk. Quarto 489
And wild-wood mountain lutes of saddest swell. 611 Desc. Sk. Quarto 509
Alone ascends that mountain nam'd of white 614 Desc. Sk. Quarto 690
—On the slope of a mountain I stood, 620 Convict 2
Thy Church and cottages of mountain stone 622 Recluse 1. 1. 121
Among the windings hid of mountain brooks. 639 Prelude 1. 490
The western mountain touch his setting orb, 645 Prelude 2. 185
I smile, in many a mountain solitude 657 Prelude 3. 568
Nor that unruly child of mountain birth, 659 Prelude 4. 50
Of mountain torrents; or the visible scene 671 Prelude 5. 384
Descending from the mountain to make sport 683 Prelude 6. 539
A lofty mountain. After brief delay 683 Prelude 6. 573
And mountain liberty. It could not be 713 Prelude 9. 238
Yet—compassed round by mountain solitudes, 748 Prelude 14. 139
That makes her dwelling on the mountain rocks! 764 Excursion 1. 565
Among yon mountain fastnesses concealed, 774 Excursion 2. 156
And overlaying them with mountain sods; 777 Excursion 2. 419
And tufts of mountain moss. Mechanic tools 781 Excursion 2. 664
And whortle-berries from the mountain side. 782 Excursion 2. 684
Islanders 'mid a stormy mountain sea, 782 Excursion 2. 735
The mountain infant to the sun comes forth, 786 Excursion 3. 34
Whoe'er hath stood to watch a mountain brook 800 Excursion 3. 969
As if the visible mountain made the cry. 807 Excursion 4. 404
On an unwealthy mountain Benefice." 824 Excursion 5. 132
High on the breast of yon dark mountain, dark 832 Excursion 5. 671
High on that mountain where they long have dwelt 833 Excursion 5. 691
Of mountain turf required the builder's hand 834 Excursion 5. 772
Down a rocky mountain, buried now and lost 849 Excursion 6. 736
That, stretching boldly from the mountain side, 855 Excursion 6. 1117
Along the surface of a mountain pool: 858 Excursion 7. 33
Among the mountain coves. Yon household fir, 866 Excursion 7. 612
Through Cumbrian wilds, in many a mountain cave, S.3. 426 *Through Cumbrian 1
Their own emotions given to mountain air S.3. 436 *The doubt 156
In notes which mountain echoes would take up S.3. 436 *The doubt 157
To lie beside the lonely mountain brooks, K.8. 224 *I will 2
To gather all their mountain family K.8. 224 *I will 9
From mountain ridges peeping as they passed K.8. 225 *I will 36
Against the mountain blasts, and to the heights K.8. 226 *I will 75
Was through that unfenced tract of mountain ground K.8. 228 *I will 130
Began to fall upon the mountain tops, K.8. 228 *I will 135
Up his own mountain grounds, where, as he walked K.8. 229 *I will 164
Of mountain sights, this untaught shepherd stood K.8. 230 *I will 196
And bleatings manifold of mountain sheep, K.8. 245 Recluse 1. 1. 330
Through this their mountain sanctuary. Long, K.8. 249 Recluse 1. 1. 463
Shows like a mountain built of silver light. K.8. 252 Recluse 1. 1. 569
Mountain-ash. Thy image disappear! The Mountain-ash 868 Excursion 7. 714
Mountain-bard's. Here in a Mountain-bard's secure abode, 461 *Giordano, verily 10
Mountain-borders. The mountain-borders of this seat of care, 392 *Though joy 12
Mountain-bounds. "Roll back, sweet Rill! back to thy mountain-bounds, 111 *'Tis said that some 29
Mountain-boy. Yet still the spirit of a mountain-boy 100 Brothers 336
Mountain-chapel. Beside the mountain-chapel, sleeps in earth 692 Prelude 7. 324
Beside the mountain-chapel, undisturbed. 692 Prelude 7. 381
But a mere mountain-chapel, that protects 743 Prelude 13. 230
Mountain-cottage. A single mountain-cottage might be seen. 146 *It was an 36
Mountain-cove. Hurled down a mountain-cove from stage to stage, 424 Ecc. Sonn. 1. 22. 4
Then, in the bosom of yon mountain-cove. 894 Excursion 9. 688
Mountain-coves. And trepidation strikes the blackened mountain-coves. 105 Artegal 201
Mountain-daisy's. That to this mountain-daisy's self were known 511 *So fair 4
Mountain-dew. Up-starting, Cynthia skimmed the mountain-dew 346 Gemmi 6
Mountain-dwelling. Inmate of a mountain-dwelling, 217 *Inmate of 1
Mountain-echoes. Of mountain-echoes did my boat move on; 637 Prelude 1. 363
Mountaineer. The freedom of a Mountaineer: 288 Highland Girl 33
A Mountaineer by habit, would resound 352 Aquap. 4
Teach what *they* learn? Up, hardy Mountaineer! 389 Tyndrum 9
A youthful friend, he too a mountaineer, 680 Prelude 6. 323
Mountaineers. The Helvetian Mountaineers, on ground 342 Ital. Itin. 59
Where, in the guise of mountaineers, we lay, 821 Excursion 4. 1320
Of mountaineers (by nature's self removed 828 Excursion 5. 424
Mountain-farms. Found by the grassy door of mountain-farms. 5 Ev. Wk. 145
Mountain-flock. A few sheep, stragglers from some mountain-flock, 150 *When, to 27
Mountain-ground. Farewell, thou little Nook of mountain-ground, 106 Farewell 1
Mountain-heath. That sucks from mountain-heath her honey fee, 503 Warning 33
Mountain-heights. The hoary mountain-heights were cheered, 224 Primrose 27
Mountain-horse. Bright beams the lonely mountain-horse illume 4 Ev. Wk. 132
Mountain-lamb. A snow-white mountain-lamb with a Maiden at its side. 87 Pet-lamb 4
While to that mountain-lamb she gave its evening meal. 87 Pet-lamb 8
Mountainous. Thou, lodged 'mid mountainous entrenchments deep, 339 Schwytz 12
And northwards, from beneath the mountainous verge 702 Prelude 8. 214
(Spirit attached to regions mountainous 761 Excursion 1. 319
And mountainous retirements, only trod 809 Excursion 4. 516
Mountain-pass. While traversing alone yon mountain-pass. 833 Excursion 5. 735
Mountain-peak. The wind blew from the mountain-peak, 199 Thorn 156
Mountain-plants. Tough moss, and long-enduring mountain-plants, 860 Excursion 7. 181
Mountain-ponies. The mountain-ponies prick their ears, 166 Danish Boy 41
Mountain-quiet. Of mountain-quiet and boon nature's grace; 418 Ecc. Sonn. 1. 1. 4
Mountain-rill. The limpid mountain-rill avoids it not; 390 Highland Hut 5
Mountain-rills. And Peter, by the mountain-rills, 239 P. B. 222
Mountain-road. And Garry, thundering down his mountain-road, 293 Killicranky 6
Mountain's. From lonesome chapel at the mountain's feet 4 Ev. Wk. 138
'Mid groves of clouds that crest the mountain's brow, 7 Ev. Wk. 289
The deepest cleft the mountain's front displays 8 Ev. Wk. 357
Above a melancholy mountain's head, 14 Desc. Sk. 189
Upon the fragrant mountain's purple side: 18 Desc. Sk. 426
Or, when upon the mountain's silent brow 18 Desc. Sk. 465
They sport beneath that mountain's matchless height 21 Desc. Sk. 577
Reflected from the mountain's side 112 *What heavenly 7
Along this mountain's edge, 156 Oak and Broom 22
Sleeping on the mountain's breast. 163 Spinning Wheel 18
"High on a mountain's highest ridge, 197 Thorn 23
I climbed the mountain's height:— 199 Thorn 174
New glory o'er the mountain's head, 224 *'Tis gone 59
Yet sacred is to me this Mountain's head, 252 *The fairest 12
When twilight shades darken the mountain's head. 255 S. H. 6
The effluence from yon distant mountain's head, 263 *How clear 2
If so he might, yon mountain's glittering head— 263 *How clear 7
Each slumbering on some mountain's head), 338 Brientz 8
From yon steep mountain's loftiest stage, 341 San Salv. 2
And on the mountain's head. 343 Eclipse 30
By skeleton arms, that, from the mountain' trunk 353 Aquap. 44
Or torrent from the mountain's brow, 391 Highland Broach 84
The sun, above the mountain's head, 481 Tables Turned 5
On that green mountain's side. 508 May 80
With amber honey from the mountain's breast; 525 Epist. Beaumont 243
Upon the blinded mountain's silent top! 548 *Stay, bold 29
This humble Walk? Yet on the mountain's side 549 *The massy 5
And eyes through tears the mountain's shadeless height; 596 Ev. Wk. Quarto 252
Beyond the mountain's giant reach that hides 598 Ev. Wk. Quarto 337
The deepest dell the mountain's breast displays, 599 Ev. Wk. Quarto 425
Stretch'd on the scented mountain's purple side. 611 Desc. Sk. Quarto 513
Or gazing from the mountain's silent brow, 612 Desc. Sk. Quarto 556
Of a rude cottage at the mountain's base 746 Prelude 14. 7
Sole building on a mountain's dreary edge, 758 Excursion 1. 123
As he expressed: from out the mountain's heart 807 Excursion 4. 406
The mountain's entrails offered to his view 841 Excursion 6. 232
Upon the rugged mountain's stony side, 842 Excursion 6. 247
The length of road that from yon mountain's base 858 Excursion 7. 43
While from the grassy mountain's open side 893 Excursion 9. 609
Not less than half-way up yon Mountain's side K.8. 247 Recluse 1. 1. 384
Mountains. By mountains, glowing till they seem to melt. 15 Desc. Sk. 284
Or steal beneath the mountains, half-deterred, 17 Desc. Sk. 378

Mountains—*continued.*
'Mid the green mountains many a thoughtless song 28 *Guilt* 246
Ran mountains high before the howling blast, . 29 *Guilt* 291
Burst on the mountains with hell-rousing force. . 51 *Bord.* 789
Left among her native mountains . . . . . 93 *Westmoreland Girl* 27
Yes, the wild Girl of the mountains . . . . 94 *Westmoreland Girl* 61
Among the mountains, and he in his heart . . 95 *Brothers* 45
Saw mountains; saw the forms of sheep that grazed 96 *Brothers* 62
Who has been born and dies among the mountains. 98 *Brothers* 183
Among the distant mountains, flower and weed, . 106 *Farewell* 35
Among thy mountains did I feel . . . . . 109 **I travelled* 9
Among the vine-clad mountains of Auvergne, . 121 *V. and J.* 11
The pastoral mountains front you, face to face. . 131 *Michael* 5
The mountains have all opened out themselves, . 131 *Michael* 7
Up to the mountains: he had been alone . . . 132 *Michael* 58
And on the mountains; else I think that thou . 136 *Michael* 351
Of ancient mountains, or my ear was touched . 148 *Joanna* 70
Among the mountains, through the midnight watch 151 **When, to* 100
Yet they find among the mountains . . . . 166 *Wand. Jew* 3
Lambs, that through the mountains went . . . 171 *Kitten* 76
The mountains against heaven's grave weight . 173 *Waggoner* 1. 13
Had seen him through the mountains go, . . . 182 *Waggoner* 4. 227
There's joy in the mountains; . . . . . . 190 *March* 16
" Till the foundations of the mountains fail . . 201 *Hart-leap* 73
Our fields rejoice, our mountains ring, ... 204 *Brougham* 32
Upon the mountains visitant; . . . . . . 205 *Brougham* 129
I bounded o'er the mountains, by the sides . . 206 *Tintern* 68
And mountains; and of all that we behold . . 207 *Tintern* 104
From caves of Indian mountains hoar! . . . 215 *Enterprise* 27
Of the untrodden lunar mountains; . . . . 217 **Inmate of* 27
Gigantic mountains rough with crags; beneath, . 219 **This Height* 12
Leaving this Daughter of the mountains free, . 222 *Triad* 169
Cheering the wakeful tent on Syrian mountains, . 232 *Power of Sound* 19
The shadowy forms of mountains bare, . . . 237 *P. B.* 103
Of mountains and of dreary moors. . . . . 239 *P. B.* 295
Among the mountains far away; . . . . . 241 *P. B.* 477
Among the lonely mountains.—Live, ye trees! . 262 **Mark the* 9
Thus did the waters gleam, the mountains lower, 265 **Hail, Twilight* 5
Of mountains, silent, dreary, motionless: . . . 266 **Even as* 5
Clear tops of far-off mountains we descry, . . 268 **Four fiery* 4
Proud were ye, Mountains, when, in times of old, 283 **Proud were* 1
Mountains, and Vales, and Floods, I call on you . 283 **Proud were* 13
Whose mountains, torrents, lake, and woods, unite 290 *Kilchurn* 27
And the pure mountains, and the gentle Tweed, . 292 **DegenerateDouglas* 13
But this we from the mountains learn, . . . 300 *Cora Linn* 32
One of the mountains; each a mighty Voice: . 306 **Two Voices* 2
Sweet Nymph, O rightly of the mountains named! 314 **Advance—come* 3
Like his own lightning, over mountains high, . . 318 **Ah! where* 13
These venerable mountains now enclose . . . 319 *Biscayan* 8
While the thrill of her fifes thro' the mountains was blown: . . . . 340 *Fort Fuentes* 16
And mountains from your view? . . . . . 343 *Eclipse* 72
The mountains (as ye heard) rejoice . . . . 344 **How blest* 44
When universal sea the mountains overflowed. . 346 *Processions* 27
Of mountains, through a deep ravine, ... 347 **Lulled by* 4
And ye that guard them, Mountains old! . . . 376 **The Minstrels* 60
All hail, ye mountains! hail, thou morning light! 376 *Duddon* 1. 10
As this we look on. Distant Mountains hear, 382 *Duddon* 23. 5
Of distant moon-lit mountains faintly shine, . . 384 *Duddon* 31. 13
Of Mountains varying momently their crests— 388 *Loch Etive* 5
Must walk the sorrowing mountains, drest . . 390 *HighlandBroach* 39
The Relics of the sword flee to the mountains: . 421 *Ecc. Sonn.* 1. 11. 6
Off to the mountains, like a covering . . . . 440 *Ecc. Sonn.* 2. 46. 8
Shall dissipate the seas and mountains hoary. . 445 *Ecc. Sonn.* 3. 19. 14
A sea-born service through the mountains felt . 454 *Sea-side* 27
Dazzling the mountains, but an overflow . . . 455 *Rydal Mere* 25
Of its vague mountains and unreal sky! . . . 456 **Soft as* 5
Seems, 'mid inverted mountains, not unheard. . 456 **The leaves* 13
The aspiring Mountains and the winding Streams, 459 **Wanderer! that* 23
Among the mountains were we nursed, loved Stream! . . . . 464 *Derwent* 1
Beneath stern mountains many a soft vale lies, . 472 **Arran! a* 13
To the bare trees, and mountains bare, . . . 482 *Sister* 7
The mountains looking on. . . . . 498 **The sylvan* 6
Upon the mountains. Look at her, whoe'er . . 508 *F. Stone* 22
Ancient castle, woods, and mountains . . . . 536 *Egremont* 83
Among the mountains) and beneath this roof . . 547 **Rude is* 21
An inmate of these mountains,—if, disturbed 548 **Stranger! this* 27
And from the mountains, to thy rural grave . . 585 *Ch. Lamb* 52
I hear the Echoes through the mountains throng, 588 *Immortality* 27
The mountains, glowing hot, like coals of fire. . 608 *Desc.Sk.Quarto* 347
Or steal beneath loose mountains, half-deterr'd, . 610 *Desc.Sk.Quarto* 468
A solemn sea! whose vales and mountains round 611 *Desc.Sk.Quarto* 496
Forc'd from my native mountains bleak and bare; 615 *Desc.Sk.Quarto* 714
Her bed, his mountains mad Ambition piles; . . 617 *Desc.Sk.Quarto* 799
Of thy renown, from Cambrian mountains, fans . 627 *Eagle and Dove* 6
When he had left the mountains and received . 636 *Prelude* 1. 282
Made all the mountains ring. But, ere nightfall, 644 *Prelude* 2. 164
To speak of you, ye mountains, and ye lakes . . 648 *Prelude* 2. 424
Ye mountains! thine, O Nature! Thou hast fed • 648 *Prelude* 2. 447
And mountains, ranging like a fowl of the air, . 654 *Prelude* 3. 355
The trees, the mountains shared it, and the brooks, 662 *Prelude* 4. 242
Mountains and clouds, reflected in the depth . . 662 *Prelude* 4. 265
The solid mountains shone, bright as the clouds, . 663 *Prelude* 4. 327
With mountains for its neighbours, and in view . 685 *Prelude* 6. 653
Of distant mountains and their snowy tops, . . 685 *Prelude* 6. 654
The mountains more by blackness visible . . . 686 *Prelude* 6. 714
Over still mountains, or appears in dreams; . . 696 *Prelude* 7. 634

Mountains—*continued.*
And mountains over all, embracing all; . . . 700 *Prelude* 8. 95
Moors, mountains, headlands, and ye hollow vales, 702 *Prelude* 8. 216
Ere long, the lonely mountains left, I moved, . 706 *Prelude* 8. 495
Child of the mountains, among shepherds reared, 733 *Prelude* 11. 424
Traditionary round the mountains hung, . . . 758 *Excursion* 1. 164
But in the mountains did he *feel* his faith. . . 759 *Excursion* 1. 226
Before us, mountains stern and desolate; . . . 772 *Excursion* 2. 92
Some secret of the mountains, cavern, fall . . 776 *Excursion* 2. 320
Among the mountains; even as if the spot . . 776 *Excursion* 2. 330
Among the mountains; never one like this; . . 776 *Excursion* 2. 353
In thunder down the mountains; with all your might . . . . 808 *Excursion* 4. 499
On thinly-peopled mountains and wild heaths, . 813 *Excursion* 4. 844
High in these mountains, that allured a band . 841 *Excursion* 6. 215
Upon the mountains gemmed with morning dew, 850 *Excursion* 6. 822
Ranged through the mountains, slept upon the earth, ... 855 *Excursion* 6. 1099
His fields, or mountains by the heath-cock ranged, 859 *Excursion* 7. 158
These mountains echoed to an unknown sound; . 868 *Excursion* 7. 697
And mountains white with everlasting snow!' . 869 *Excursion* 7. 803
And distant mountains echoed with a sound . . 871 *Excursion* 7. 889
The Spirit of its mountains and its seas, . . . 871 *Excursion* 7. 897
Each had his glowing mountains, each his sky, . 890 *Excursion* 9. 447
And mountains bare, or clothed with ancient woods, 891 *Excursion* 9. 506
By rocks impassable and mountains huge. . . 892 *Excursion* 9. 579
Among the mountains, fens which might be drained, K.8. 227 **I will* 103
Whether he loved the mountains, true it is . . K.8. 230 **I will* 179
The fields and mountains, not alone for this . . K.8. 230 **I will* 206
And mountains not less green, and flocks, and herds, K.8. 240 *Recluse* 1.1.128
Sent from the mountains or the sheltered fields; . K.8. 245 *Recluse* 1.1.320
And treads the mountains which his fathers trod. K.8. 247 *Recluse* 1.1.383
These mountains will rejoice with open joy. . . K.8. 254 *Recluse* 1.1.661
Some nursling of the mountains, which she leads K.8. 256 *Recluse* 1.1.729
The mountains too are thine, some clouds there are, K.8. 263 **The Lake* 2
Embowering mountains, and the dome of Heaven K.8. 263 **The Lake* 11

Mountain-shades. Or stops the solemn mountain-shades to view . . . . 12 *Desc. Sk.* 93

Mountain-side. In flakes of light upon the mountain-side; . . . . 10 *Desc. Sk.* 6
Following his plough, along the mountain-side; . 196 *Resolution* 46
The poor Hart toils along the mountain-side: . 201 *Hart-leap* 29
By cottage-door on breezy mountain-side, . . 692 *Prelude* 7. 354
The mountain-side. The mist soon girt us round, 746 *Prelude* 14. 15
In the low vale, or on steep mountain-side; . . 814 *Excursion* 4. 882
The once-bare cottage, on the mountain-side, . 860 *Excursion* 7. 200
Of rural labours; the steep mountain-side . . 863 *Excursion* 7. 419

Mountain-sides. Over the mountain-sides, in contrast bold . . . . 820 *Excursion* 4. 1303

Mountain-slopes. Ten birth-days, when among the mountain-slopes . . . . 636 *Prelude* 1. 307

Mountain-snows. When lightning among clouds and mountain-snows . . . . 13 *Desc. Sk.* 179

Mountain-springs. These waters, rolling from their mountain-springs . . . . 205 *Tintern* 3

Mountain-steeps. Like a black wall, the mountain-steeps appear. . . . . 8 *Ev. Wk.* 314
And mountain-steeps and summits, whereunto . 784 *Excursion* 2. 849

Mountain-stone. Covered the smooth blue slabs of mountain-stone . . . . 860 *Excursion* 7. 189
—A few rude monuments of mountain-stone . . 894 *Excursion* 9. 710

Mountain-storms. For rain and mountain-storms! the like thou need'st not fear, . . . 87 *Pet-lamb* 31

Mountain-streams. The song of mountain-streams, unheard by day, ... 9 *Ev. Wk.* 365

Mountain-summits. Like clouds that rake the mountain-summits, ... 586 *Hogg* 21
Where tipp'd with gold the mountain-summits glow'd. . . . . 592 *Ev. Wk. Quarto* 36

Mountain-sunbeams. Only faint news her mountain-sunbeams yield, ... 522 *Epist.Beaumont* 82

Mountain-top. Thus to the dreary mountain-top . 198 *Thorn* 80
" But wherefore to the mountain-top . . . . 198 *Thorn* 100
She to the mountain-top would go, ... 199 *Thorn* 124
Upon the eastern mountain-top, ... 486 **We walked* 19
Yon star upon the mountain-top . . . . . 581 **Loud is* 7
As the black storm upon the mountain-top . . 696 *Prelude* 7. 619
Of his poor hut, or on the mountain-top, . . . 813 *Excursion* 4. 827
Down from a mountain-top,—say one of those . 885 *Excursion* 9. 58
The shadowy vale, the sunny mountain-top; . . 895 *Excursion* 9. 745

Mountain-tops. Upon the mountain-tops no kinder could have been. . . . . 87 *Pet-lamb* 40
" Alas, the mountain-tops that look so green and fair! . . . . 88 *Pet-lamb* 53
Storms, sallying from the mountain-tops, waylay 264 *Snowdrop* 5
Like mountain-tops whose mists have rolled away— . . . . 326 **The Bard* 8
Be left as silent as the mountain-tops, ... 455 *Rydal Mere* 6
A land whose azure mountain-tops are seats . . 501 *Humanity* 73
And mountain-tops, a barren ridge we scale; . . 524 *Epist. Beaumont* 224
And as round mountain-tops the lightning plays, 584 *Ch. Lamb* 18
On the dear mountain-tops where first he rose. . 706 *Prelude* 8. 475
And clouds, and intermingling mountain-tops, . 725 *Prelude* 10. 518
A Herdsman on the lonely mountain-tops, . . 759 *Excursion* 1. 219
Had fallen in torrents; all the mountain-tops . 783 *Excursion* 2. 782
Retired behind the mountain-tops or veiled . . 893 *Excursion* 9. 594

Mountain-torrents. Of mountain-torrents; or the visible scene . . . . 183 *Prelude* 5. 384

Mountain-turf. In freedom, mountain-turf and river's marge; . . . . 273 **While Anna's* 2

Mouth—*continued.*

I saw, espied its shaded mouth ; . . . . . 169 Wren's Nest 55
The mead is crossed—the quarry's mouth . . . 243 P. B. 607
Into the cavern's mouth he peeps ; . . . . . 243 P. B. 638
When, to the mouth, relenting Death . . . . 374 Eg. Maid 333
But lo ! where darkness seems to guard the mouth 497 *Enough of climbing 20
Though in virtue's proud mouth thy report be a stain, ... 621 Convict 50
Long were his arms, pallid his hands ; his mouth 664 Prelude 4. 395
Pressed closely palm to palm, and to his mouth . 671 Prelude 5. 371
A peasant met us, from whose mouth we learned 683 Prelude 6. 579
A minuet course ; and, winding up his mouth, 695 Prelude 7. 556
Such words of hope from her own mouth as served 766 Excursion 1. 685
To the mine's mouth ; a long and slanting track, 842 Excursion 6. 246
At the mine's mouth under impending rocks ; . 879 Excursion 8. 365

Mouths. For some whose rugged northern mouths would strain . . . . 495 Fact 17
But by the mouths of children, gracious God ! . 552 Prioress 5
By mouths of Innocents, lo ! here Thy might ; . 555 Prioress 157
From mouths of men obscure and lowly, truths . 742 Prelude 13. 183
From other mouths, the language which they speak, 819 Excursion 4. 1227

Move. Move on—a mighty caravan of pain : . . 13 Desc. Sk. 170
Move, as the verdure leads, from stage to stage ; . 17 Desc. Sk. 375
The least of Nature's works, one who might move 23 Yew-tree 57
He saw his Wife's lips move his name to bless . 35 Guilt 616
It seemed to move away from us : and yet . 39 Bord. 114
Are not the enemies that move my fears. . . . 43 Bord. 321
Great actions move our admiration, chiefly . 65 Bord. 1536
The faintest breath that breathes can move a world ; 65 Bord. 1564
And move in terror of the elements ; . . . 75 Bord. 2178
" Oh, move, thou Cottage, from behind that oak ! 110 *'Tis said that some 13
Surcharged, within him, overblest to move . . 122 V. and J. 50
She screams—she cannot move for joy ; . . 130 Idiot Boy 373
My feet might move without concern or care ; . 150 *When, to 38
Then, dearest Maiden, move along these shades . 186 Nutting 54
As on their silent tasks they move ! . . . . 192 Gipsies 24
And moveth all together, if it move at all. . . 196 Resolution 77
Move where the blasted soil is not unworn, . . 213 Dion 88
Star-guided contemplations move . . . . . 225 Present. 31
O'er which they move, wherein they are contained, 230 Clouds 51
They move ; but soon the appointed way . . . 233 Power of Sound 58
Shot from the dancing Graces, as they move . 233 Power of Sound 79
Which they would stifle, move at such a pace ! . 266 *With how 6
And trust that spiritual Creatures round us move, 273 *When Philoctetes 9
Nor dares to move unpropped upon the staff . . 277 *A Poet 2
Divine communion ; both do live and move, . . 280 *Oh what 10
Than will hereafter move them, if they make . . 280 *Intent on 6
With legs that move not, if they can, ... 294 Jedbor. 17
But soon they move with softer pace ; . . . . 297 Highland Boy 186
Your kindred Deities, Ye live and move, . . . 325 Ode 1814 120
What steps so suitable as those that move . . 331 Ode : Thanks. 135
Each step hath its value while homeward we move ;— . . . . 346 Stanzas : Simplon 29
I move at ease ; and meet contending themes . 350 Des. Stanzas 15
To move in sunshine ?—Utter thanks, my Soul ! . 354 Aquap. 88
On the great flood were spared to live and move. 360 *Near Anio's 8
Me did a reverent pity move . . . . . . 409 White Doe 1249
To live and move exempt from all control . . 429 Ecc. Sonn. 2. 4. 13
Move Princes to their duty, peace or war ; . . 429 Ecc. Sonn. 2. 5. 7
Even such the contrast that, where'er we move, . 439 Ecc. Sonn. 2. 44. 1
Concord and Charity in circles move. . . . . 443 Ecc. Sonn. 3. 14. 14
As to the deep fair ships which though they move 444 Ecc. Sonn. 3. 17. 3
Nor has her gentle beauty power to move . . . 455 *Not in the lucid 10
From hill or valley, could not move . . . . 457 *Had this 17
Or crossed by vapoury streaks and clouds that move 459 *Wanderer ! that 35
Of a cloud flat and dense, through which must move 461 *Who but is 12
Can nowhere move uncrossed by some new wall . 469 *Desire we 8
And move around it now as planets run, . . . 476 *Tranquillity ! the 13
Now to mingle and to move . . . . 502 *Like a 17
Its duties ;—prompt to move, but firm to wait,— 514 *Blest Statesman 9
Each takes in this high matter, all may move . 520 Pun. Death 14. 13
Or was it Dian's self that seemed to move . . 532 *Once I 19
Should move the tenor of his song . . . . . 534 *Blest is 87
Delivered and Deliverer move . . . . . . 545 Russ. Fug. 363
They move along the ground ; and, evermore, . 567 Cumb. Beg. 47
A man who does not move with pain, but moves 572 Animal Tran. 6
Together move in fellowship without end.— . . 573 Chiabrera 1. 6
On as we move, a softer prospect opes, . . . 607 Desc.Sk.Quarto 263
In heavenly majesty she seem'd to move. . . . 618 School Ex. 14
That at my beck, mine only, she shall move. . 624 Æneid 26
Of mountain-echoes did my boat move on ; . . 637 Prelude 1. 363
Than move with them in tenderness and love, . 669 Prelude 5. 251
To move along the edges of the hills, . . . 671 Prelude 5. 367
Move us with conscious pleasure. I am sad . . 673 Prelude 5. 545
I seemed to move along them, as a bird . . . 686 Prelude 6. 770
The incarnation of the spirits that move . . . 694 Prelude 7. 478
However multitudinous, to move . . . . . 698 Prelude 7. 760
They move about upon the soft green turf : . . 700 Prelude 8. 58
Of most to move in, but that first I looked . . 703 Prelude 8. 315
For her to move about in, uncontrolled. . . . 727 Prelude 11. 34
Where'er we move, under the diverse shapes . 750 Prelude 14. 327
Pitches her tents before me as I move, . . . 755 Recluse 1. 1. 799
And now, when free to move with lighter pace. . 772 Excursion 2. 27
Rise from that posture :—and in concert move . 780 Excursion 2. 582
Of pleasure move without the aid of hope : . . 792 Excursion 3. 457
Where youth's ambitious feet might move at large ; 794 Excursion 3. 539
Those radiant Mercuries, that seemed to move . 811 Excursion 4. 702
Or move the pity of unthinking minds, . . . 813 Excursion 4. 835

Move—*continued.*

For less important ends those phantoms move, . 813 Excursion 4. 842
The law of duty ; and can therefore move . . 816 Excursion 4. 1036
Shall move unswerving, even as if impelled . . 820 Excursion 4. 1268
Far better not to move at all than move . . 827 Excursion 5. 321
Or so he ought to move. Ah ! why in age . . 884 Excursion 9. 36
The things that live, the things that move ? . . K.8. 219 *The snow-tracks 12
And yet, my friends, you live and move. . . . K.8. 220 *The snow-tracks 22

Moveables. All moveables of wonder, from all parts, 697 Prelude 7. 706

Moved. *See* **Self-moved.**

She could not of herself those wasted limbs have moved. . . . . 34 Guilt 549
Thou know'st me for a Man not easily moved, . 38 Bord. 69
Our melancholy story moved a Stranger . . . 40 Bord. 197
These ten years she has moved her lips all day . 47 Bord. 566
Last night, when moved to lift the avenging steel, 59 Bord. 1213
Time, since Man first drew breath, has never moved 65 Bord. 1531
Too quickly moved, too easily giving way, . . 76 Bord. 2233
Like a Spirit of air she moved, ... 94 Westmoreland Girl 42
He sought his brother Leonard.—You are moved ! 101 Brothers 353
My horse moved on ; hoof after hoof . . . . 109 *Strange fits 21
Yes ! thou art fair, yet be not moved . . . . 111 *Yes ! thou 1
And oft was moved to flee from home, ... 115 Last of Flock 79
Moved not ; meanwhile the galaxy displayed . . 123 V. and J. 97
But when the Pony moved his legs, ... 127 Idiot Boy 72
Gentle pleasures round her moved, ... 142 Arm. Lady 146
Moved like a vessel in the wind ! . . . . . 175 Waggoner 1. 135
Moved to and fro, for his delight. . . . . . 205 Brougham 127
By the just Gods whom no weak pity moved, . 212 Laod. 160
While thus these simple-hearted men are moved ? 283 *Well have 14
But moved by choice ; or, if constrained in part, 284 Departure 23
Was moved ; and in such way expressed . . . 289 Glen-Al. 21
Are moved, for me—upon this Mountain named . 340 Ranz 10
That moved in long array before admiring eyes. . 346 Processions 9
Moved to the chant of sober litanies. . . . . 346 Processions 40
By love of beauty moved, to enshrine in verse . 358 Aquap. 363
Not in like sort the Runic Scald was moved ; . 359 *Complacent Fictions 11
My heart—may have been moved like me to think, 363 *List—'twas 91
The Sabine Bard was moved her praise to sing ; . 376 Duddon 1. 4
Have moved in order, to each other bound . . 394 *No more 4
And sorrow moved him to partake . . . . . 401 White Doe 458
With heart by simple nature moved ; . . . . 401 White Doe 472
Where faith was proved ?—while to battle moved 405 White Doe 817
Moved gently in her soul's soft sleep ; . . . . 415 White Doe 1794
By such examples moved to unbought pains, . . 424 Ecc. Sonn. 1. 24. 1
Might here be moved, till Fancy grows so strong 455 Rydal Mere 14
He moved with stealthy pace ; . . . . . . 479 Somnamb. 119
And Wharf, as he moved along, ... 495 Force of Prayer 58
Shall now by such a gift with joy be moved, . . 504 Warning 51
With indignation, deeply moved we grieve, . . 517 Pun. Death 2. 3
Then, moved by needless fear of past abuse, . . 520 Pun. Death 13. 11
Moved by the touch of kindred sympathies. . . 526 *Soon did 7
And humbler growths as moved with one desire . 529 Poor Robin 3
Thee kindred aspirations moved . . . . . . 533 *Blest is 17
Through the whole land—to Manhood, moved in spite . . . . 540 Grace Darl. 9
He once had a heart which was moved by the wires 572 Avarice 25
To fair Aglaia ; by what envy moved, ... 575 Chiabrera 7. 4
A correspondent breeze, that gently moved . . 632 Prelude 1. 35
Sometimes, more sternly moved, I would relate . 635 Prelude 1. 186
Moved we as plunderers where the mother-bird . 637 Prelude 1. 327
Of earth—and with what motion moved the clouds ! 637 Prelude 1. 339
Like living men, moved slowly through the mind 638 Prelude 1. 399
Even while mine eye hath moved o'er many a league 640 Prelude 1. 577
And every season wheresoe'er I moved . . . 646 Prelude 2. 289
Is moved with feelings of delight, to me . . . 647 Prelude 2. 327
Now here, now there, moved by the straggling wind, 661 Prelude 4. 184
And often looking round was moved to smiles . 661 Prelude 4. 210
His shadow lay, and moved not. From self-blame 664 Prelude 4. 408
But let me now, less moved, in order take . . 693 Prelude 7. 400
For though I was most passionately moved . . 694 Prelude 7. 473
Preserved, I moved about, year after year, . . 704 Prelude 8. 329
Ere long, the lonely mountains left, I moved, . 706 Prelude 8. 495
Even in such sort had I at first been moved, . . 708 Prelude 8. 590
Nor otherwise continued to be moved, ... 708 Prelude 8. 591
To suit my ends ; I moved among mankind . . 729 Prelude 11. 155
That rose in splendour, was alive, and moved . 732 Prelude 11. 365
Acknowledge when thus moved, which Nature thus 747 Prelude 14. 87
The old Man ceased : he saw that I was moved ; . 770 Excursion 1. 917
Of that small valley, singing as they moved ; . . 777 Excursion 2. 390
And moved, a willing Page, as he was bid, . . 782 Excursion 2. 687
So moved he like a shadow that performed . . 783 Excursion 2. 772
And with their freight homeward the shepherds moved . . . . 784 Excursion 2. 828
That did not falter though the heart was moved, 801 Excursion 4. 9
Was suddenly revealed !—the swains moved on, . 808 Excursion 4. 472
As those with which your soul in youth was moved, 809 Excursion 4. 556
Man walked ; and when and wheresoe'er he moved, 810 Excursion 4. 632
And did acknowledge, wheresoe'er they moved, . 815 Excursion 4. 926
Who, at her heart's light bidding, once had moved 850 Excursion 6. 819
Until the Wanderer (whether moved by fear . . 862 Excursion 7. 293
Were all things silent, wheresoe'er he moved. . . 863 Excursion 7. 416
—Those seven fair brothers variously were moved 867 Excursion 7. 657
His finger moved, distinguishing the spots . . 869 Excursion 7. 796
Moved towards the grave ;—instinctively his steps 870 Excursion 7. 819
My grey-haired Friend was moved ; his vivid eye 883 Excursion 8. 588
Moved (shall I say ?) like a dear friend who meets S.3. 434 *The doubt 87

Moveless. Their moveless boughs and leaves like threads of gold; 593 *Ev. Wk. Quarto* 104
Proud of the varying arch and moveless form of snow. 595 *Ev. Wk. Quarto* 206
Moveless o'er-hang the deep secluded vale, 607 *Desc. Sk. Quarto* 266
Movement. A backward movement surely have we here, 489 *Illus. Books* 9
Movements. And their glad animal movements all gone by) 206 *Tintern* 74
If there be movements in the Patriot's soul, 216 *Enterprise* 98
Among the many movements of his mind, 308 **When I* 13
And, in its movements, circumspect and slow. 840 *Excursion* 6. 148
Mover. Prime mover in a plot to damn his Victim. 57 *Bord.* 1064
Moves. With furtive watch pursue her as she moves, 6 *Ev. Wk.* 223
Pleased, as she moves, her pomp of clouds to fold 8 *Ev. Wk.* 329
Moves there a cloud o'er mid-day's flaming eye? 11 *Desc. Sk.* 23
While the pale moon moves near him, on the bound 16 *Desc. Sk.* 319
Nor moves her hands to any needful work: 44 *Bord.* 385
Tied by a woollen cord, moves on before 45 *Bord.* 456
Moves me beyond my bearing.—I will try 52 *Bord.* 801
And, while the Pony moves his legs, 127 *Idiot Boy* 77
Meek as a lamb the Pony moves, 127 *Idiot Boy* 99
"Pluck that rose, it moves my liking," 139 *Arm. Lady* 7
Moves all nature to gladness and mirth. 167 *Stray Pleasures* 30
The Waggon moves—and with its load 176 *Waggoner* 1. 262
Light as the wheeling butterfly she moves; 221 *Triad* 124
Invisible, the long procession moves 230 *Clouds* 46
Moves on without a moment's stop, 244 *P. B.* 713
The unheeding Ass moves slowly on, 246 *P. B.* 866
It moves us not.—Great God! I'd rather be 259 **The world is* 9
And on she moves—with pace how light! 397 *White Doe* 137
Moves, handed on with never-ceasing care, 432 *Ecc. Sonn.* 2. 14. 11
As through a zodiac, moves the ritual year 445 *Ecc. Sonn.* 3. 19. 5
The innocent Procession softly moves:— 448 *Ecc. Sonn.* 3. 32. 12
Where'er he moves along the unclouded sky, 539 **Lady! a* 16
His eyes are turned, and, as he moves along, 567 *Cumb. Beg.* 46
A man who does not move with pain, but moves 572 *Animal Tran.* 6
The talking boat that moves with pensive sound, 597 *Ev. Wk. Quarto* 319
Whole hamlets disappearing as he moves, 617 *Desc. Sk. Quarto* 789
Moves through the vault of heaven, and dissipates the night; 618 *School Ex.* 40
O'er all that moves and all that seemeth still; 648 *Prelude* 2. 402
Moves the great spirit of human knowledge, spare 681 *Prelude* 6. 450
Moves through the air, or as a fish pursues 686 *Prelude* 6. 771
Has failed; too slowly moves the promised work. 687 *Prelude* 7. 15
The Bust that speaks and moves its goggling eyes, 698 *Prelude* 7. 711
Along the line of low-roofed water, moves 706 *Prelude* 8. 461
For that which moves with light and life informed, 748 *Prelude* 14. 161
Bent as he moves, and needing frequent rest; 761 *Excursion* 1. 325
Then from the threshold moves with song of peace, 780 *Excursion* 2. 558
A like glad impulse; and so moves the man 884 *Excursion* 9. 34
Run o'er with gladness; whence the Being moves 886 *Excursion* 9. 135
Our pinnace moves; then, coasting creek and bay, 892 *Excursion* 9. 561
Movest. O Thou who movest onward with a mind 573 *Chiabrera* 3. 1
Moveth. And moveth all together, if it move at all. 196 *Resolution* 77
Moving. *See* **Heart-moving, Slowly-moving, Slow-moving, Soul-moving, Spirit-moving.**
Mounts from the road, and spreads its moving shroud; 4 *Ev. Wk.* 111
I love to mark the quarry's moving trains, 5 *Ev. Wk.* 158
Of horsemen-shadows moving to and fro; 6 *Ev. Wk.* 201
Her lips for ever moving. At her door 47 *Bord.* 579
His lips were moving; and his eyes, upraised to sue for grace, 92 *Poet's Dream* 11
Loth to restrain the moving interview, 104 *Artegal* 126
Its playmate, rather say, its moving soul. 148 **A narrow* 25
At every impulse of the moving breeze, 151 **When, to* 103
Say, when the *moving* creatures saw 154 *Flower Garden* 7
Moving untouched in silver purity, 172 *Infant Daughter* 49
Blend with the mist—a moving shroud 181 *Waggoner* 4. 104
The moving image to detain; 182 *Waggoner* 4. 233
The moving accident is not my trade; 202 *Hart-leap* 97
Of still or moving imagery— 228 *Devot. Incit.* 41
As if the moving time had been 239 *P. B.* 268
When Peter spied the moving thing, 244 *P. B.* 706
Be conscious of Thy moving spirit! 331 *Ode: Thanks.* 193
Look round;—of all the clouds not one is moving; 453 **The Sun, that* 5
And nothing save the moving ship's own light 460 **Wanderer! that* 68
Moving along a tract of morning shade, 524 *Epist. Beaumont* 214
No motion but the moving tide, a breeze, 578 *Peele Castle* 27
Six weeks beneath the moving sea 579 **Sweet Flower* 50
Moving about in worlds not realised, 589 *Immortality* 149
The faces of the moving year, even then 640 *Prelude* 1. 561
Sweet Spenser, moving through his clouded heaven 653 *Prelude* 3. 280
His ghostly figure moving at my side; 665 *Prelude* 4. 434
Moving in heaven; or, of that pleasure tired, 679 *Prelude* 6. 270
Thou endless stream of men and moving things! 689 *Prelude* 7. 151
Amid the moving pageant, I was smitten 696 *Prelude* 7. 637
On all things which the moving seasons brought 758 *Excursion* 1. 151
As one, and moving to one glorious end. 774 *Excursion* 2. 222
Not moving to his mind.'" These serious words 776 *Excursion* 2. 315
From moving spectacles;—but let us on." 779 *Excursion* 2. 491
To regulate the moving spheres, and weigh 815 *Excursion* 4. 949
—Within their moving magazines is lodged 875 *Excursion* 8. 72
The moving waters, and the invisible air. 884 *Excursion* 9. 9
And moving dialogues between this pair, K.8. 248 *Recluse* 1.1.419
Mowbray's. The infant Heir of Mowbray's blood— 405 *White Doe* 823
Mower. In summer, ere the mower was abroad 764 *Excursion* 1. 525
Mower's. A prelibation to the mower's scythe. 669 *Prelude* 5. 245

Mown. He thinks of the fields he so often hath mown, 571 *Farmer* 83
Muccawiss. And, while the melancholy Muccawiss 799 *Excursion* 3. 947
Much. Much done, and much designed, and more desired,— 3 *Ev. Wk.* 83
Much wondering by what fit of crazing care, 11 *Desc. Sk.* 41
Much sorrow ere the fleet its anchor weighed; 29 *Guilt* 281
Much need have ye that time more closely draw 33 *Guilt* 507
I feel myself much bounden to you, Oswald; 38 *Bord.* 52
We, neighbours of the Esk and Tweed: 'tis much 39 *Bord.* 85
Thus much to speak; but think not I forget— 40 *Bord.* 175
After his death. I have been much deceived. 41 *Bord.* 235
Resembled much that cold voluptuary, 42 *Bord.* 279
Ere can be known to you how much a Father 52 *Bord.* 822
That, in my zeal, I have caused you so much pain. 55 *Bord.* 1004
Whether too much for patience, or, like mine, 61 *Bord.* 1339
I have much to say, but for whose ear?—not thine. 66 *Bord.* 1602
And never *can* you know, how much he loved me. 66 *Bord.* 1605
—So much for my remorse! Unhappy Man! 70 *Bord.* 1814
Of this too much. Men are there, millions, Oswald, 77 *Bord.* 2292
Much converse do I find in thee, 79 **Stay near* 3
With so much happiness to spare, 85 *Anecdote* 15
For length of days so much revered, so famous where it stands 92 *Poet's Dream* 35
That chasm is much the same— But, surely, yonder— 97 *Brothers* 137
They, notwithstanding, had much love to spare, 99 *Brothers* 247
Though much disguised by long adversity! 104 *Artegal* 117
I bear it with me, Sir;—he took so much delight in it." 119 *Sailor's Mother* 36
Much how the Youth, in scanty space of time, 124 *V. and J.* 178
Was traversed from without; much, too, of thoughts 124 *V. and J.* 179
This piteous news so much it shocked her, 129 *Idiot Boy* 274
The Housewife answered, talking much of things 136 *Michael* 318
Much she rejoiced, trusting that from that hour 139 *Widow* 23
To thee I know too much I owe; 144 *Her Eyes* 19
Delighted much to listen to those sounds, 149 **A narrow* 42
Much wondering how I could have sought in vain 150 **When, to* 51
The Briar quaked—and much I fear 155 *Waterfall* 55
Much did it taunt the humble Light 167 *Pilgrim's Dream* 25
Be one of much infirmity; 174 *Waggoner* 1. 51
You'll find you've much in little here! 178 *Waggoner* 2. 118
Seen fairly, is not much amiss! 179 *Waggoner* 3. 75
As much as may be of the blame, 181 *Waggoner* 4. 90
And bounty never yields so much but it seems to do her wrong? 189 *Star-gazers* 18
Much witnessing of change and cheer, 192 *Gipsies* 11
So much of earth—so much of heaven, 193 *Ruth* 125
But ill he lived, much evil saw, 194 *Ruth* 145
Whose heart with so much nature played? 194 *Ruth* 161
Who have felt the weight of too much liberty, 250 **Nuns fret* 13
The world is too much with us; late and soon, 259 **The world is* 1
To think how much of this will be thy praise. 260 *Calvert* 14
Much have ye suffered from Time's gnawing tooth: 270 **Ye sacred* 5
Too much from this frail earth we claim, 348 **Lulled by* 29
Much have my books disclosed, but the end is hidden." 371 *Eg. Maid* 174
Ah! if their fluttering hearts should stir too much, 378 *Duddon* 10. 11
Celestial Power, as much with love as light? 392 **Though joy* 14
Much injured Earls! by these preferred, 403 *White Doe* 675
And sift her laws—much wondering that the wrong, 435 *Ecc. Sonn.* 2. 29. 7
We, differing once so much, are now Compeers, 464 **Thou look'st* 3
And much it grieved my heart to think 482 *Lines: Spring* 7
And attention full ten times as much as there needs; 482 *Character* 10
Pride where there's no envy, there's so much of joy; 482 *Character* 11
I am not One who much or oft delight 488 *Pers. Talk* 1
More brave for this, that he hath much to love:— 494 *Hap. War.* 64
This modest charm of not too much, 508 *May* 95
Too much the heroic Daughter feared 544 *Russ. Fug.* 231
On this commodious Seat! for much remains 548 **Stay, bold* 2
Well did I watch, much laboured, nor had power 573 *Chiabrera* 3. 8
For much that truth most urgently required 585 *Ch. Lamb* 44
Much wondering what sad stroke of crazing Care 602 *Desc. Sk. Quarto* 43
A heart, that could not much itself approve, 602 *Desc. Sk. Quarto* 46
With warmth, as much as needed, from a sun 633 *Prelude* 1. 66
Much wanting, so much wanting, in myself, 636 *Prelude* 1. 264
Like a false steward who hath much received 636 *Prelude* 1. 268
Much favoured in my birthplace, and no less 636 *Prelude* 1. 303
Thus far, O Friend! have we, though leaving much 642 *Prelude* 2. 1
And I was taught to feel, perhaps too much, 643 *Prelude* 2. 76
I had received so much, that all my thoughts 648 *Prelude* 2. 398
Much pains and little progress, and at once 660 *Prelude* 4. 112
Earth's paramount Creature! not so much for woes 665 *Prelude* 5. 5
Much I rejoiced, not doubting but a guide 667 *Prelude* 5. 81
As if from Fairy-land. Much I questioned him; 688 *Prelude* 7. 98
Had never much delighted me. And less 708 *Prelude* 8. 622
Awaits us! Oh, how much unlike the past! 710 *Prelude* 9. 22
As much as any that was ever seen, 712 *Prelude* 9. 151
How much the destiny of Man had still 720 *Prelude* 10. 155
Its unsuccessful issue much excite 722 *Prelude* 10. 256
Oh! much have they to account for, who could tear, 722 *Prelude* 10. 300
Much, as it seemed, I was no further changed 732 *Prelude* 11. 343
Was never much my habit—giving way 736 *Prelude* 12. 114
In what the Historian's pen so much delights 740 *Prelude* 13. 42
Enquire," said I, "how much of mental power 741 *Prelude* 13. 95
But much was wanting: therefore did I turn 741 *Prelude* 13. 116
Grandeur as much, and loveliness far more. 742 *Prelude* 13. 156
Yet much hath been omitted, as need was; 750 *Prelude* 14. 312
Of books how much! and even of the other wealth 750 *Prelude* 14. 313
With due regret) how much is overlooked 750 *Prelude* 14. 322
Is nearer now, much nearer; yet even then, 751 *Prelude* 14. 375

Murmur—*continued.*
I heard the murmur and the murmuring sound, . 185 *Nutting* 38
And streams that murmur as they run, . . . 192 *Ruth* 35
And Emont's murmur mingled with the Song.— . 203 *Brougham* 2
With a soft inland murmur.—Once again . . . 205 *Tintern* 4
Faint I, nor mourn nor murmur ; other gifts . . 206 *Tintern* 86
To the soft murmur of the vagrant Bee. . . . 227 *Vernal Ode* 90
A murmur, pent within the earth, ... 245 *P. B.* 834
Will murmur by the hour in foxglove bells : . . 250 **Nuns fret* 7
With green hills fenced, with ocean's murmur lulled ; " . . . . 254 *Dyer* 6
My nerves from no such murmur shrink,—tho' near, 255 *S. H.* 4
Whose murmur soothed thy languid Mother's ear 275 *Rotha Q.* 10
A murmur near the silent lake ; . . . . . 288 *Highland Girl* 8
With omnipresent murmur as they rave . . . 314 **Not 'mid* 7
Roused into fury, murmur a soft tune . . . . 339 *Tell* 14
And murmur sweet songs on the ground of their birth ! . . . . 345 *Stanzas : Simplon* 8
And murmur issuing from yon pendent flood, . 358 *Aquap.* 370
Its murmur how soft ! as it falls down the steep, 364 *Vallomb.* 5
Swoln by that voice—whose murmur musical . 381 *Duddon* 19. 12
With low soft murmur, like a distant bee, . 445 *Ecc. Sonn.* 3. 22. 5
And the habitual murmur that atones . . . 464 **Greta, what* 8
And murmur of the village school. . . . . . 486 *Matthew* 20
'Twill murmur on a thousand years, ... 487 *Fountain* 23
From murmur of a running stream ; . . . . 533 **Blest is* 56
A mournful murmur for *his* sake ; . . . . . 580 **Sweet Flower* 68
Stays it's low murmur in th' unbreathing vale ; . 598 *Ev.Wk.Quarto* 356
All day the floods a deeper murmur pour, . . 608 *Desc.Sk.Quarto* 333
Shall with its murmur lull me into rest ? . . . 632 *Prelude* 1. 13
Murmur (for truth is hated, where not loved) . 695 *Prelude* 7. 532
Its natal murmur ; followed it to light . . . 749 *Prelude* 14. 196
A softened roar, or murmur ; and the sound . . 800 *Excursion* 3. 978
And streams, whose murmur fills this hollow vale, 836 *Excursion* 5. 917
—Vain thought ! but wherefore murmur or repine ? 863 *Excursion* 7. 387
That suits not them. The murmur of the leaves 885 *Excursion* 9. 74
As they shine out ; and *see* the streams whose murmur . . . . K.8. 249 *Recluse* 1.1.483

Murmured. I murmured—but, remembering Him who feeds . . . . 62 *Bord.* 1352
And for us the brook murmured that ran by its side. 116 *Repentance* 12
Waking at morn he murmured not ; . . . . 168 *Pilgrim's Dream* 68
That murmured in the vale. All else was still ; . 664 *Prelude* 4. 384
Murmured the sister streams of Life and Death, . 681 *Prelude* 6. 439
Murmured the labouring bee. When stormy winds 863 *Excursion* 7. 409

Murmuring. Who, murmuring here a later ditty, . 9 *Collins* 14
Each clacking mill, that broke the murmuring streams, ... 22 *Desc. Sk.* 630
And the torrent murmuring by ; . . . . . 90 *Longest Day* 2
Of murmuring, sparkling, living love, ... 111 *A Complaint* 10
Swiftly turn the murmuring wheel ! . . . . 163 *Spinning Wheel* 1
Is murmuring a reproof, ... 168 *Turtledove* 10
With murmuring Greta for her guide. . . . . 180 *Waggoner* 4. 17
Murmuring from Glaramara's inmost caves. . . 185 *Yew-trees* 33
I heard the murmur and the murmuring sound, . 185 *Nutting* 38
And beauty born of murmuring sound . . . 187 **Three years* 29
To hear the earth's soft murmuring . . . . 237 *P. B.* 74
And for the murmuring river Swale. . . . . 240 *P. B.* 335
Murmuring ; the fall of rivers, winds and seas, . 253 **A flock* 3
And these perennial bowers and murmuring pines 264 **Lady ! the* 12
'Mid song of birds, and insects murmuring ; . . 266 **The stars* 11
Murmuring but one smooth story for all years, . 368 *Trajan* 24
For late, as near a murmuring stream . . . . 373 *Eg. Maid* 301
And Thou, blue Streamlet, murmuring yield'st no more . . . . 378 *Duddon* 8. 10
Is the river murmuring near. . . . . . . 396 *White Doe* 48
Return, and to her murmuring floods, ... 402 *White Doe* 561
In concord with his river murmuring by ; . . . 489 *Spade* 14
Was felt near murmuring brooks in earliest time ; 502 **The unremitting* 14
Above a murmuring brook. . . . . 543 *Russ. Fug.* 120
Where murmuring rivers join the song of ev'n ; . 602 *Desc. Sk. Quarto* 4
Danc'd to the murmuring rill on Lomond's wave, 630 [?] **O Moon* 2
Murmuring so sweetly in themselves, obeyed . . 647 *Prelude* 2. 372
Murmuring submission, and bald government, . 657 *Prelude* 3. 602
I sauntered, like a river murmuring . . . . 660 *Prelude* 4. 119
Down by thy side, O Derwent ! murmuring stream, 673 *Prelude* 5. 484
Murmuring of him who, joyous hap, was found, . 752 *Prelude* 14. 404
And turbulence of murmuring cities vast ; . . 787 *Excursion* 3. 104
Like one whose untired ear a murmuring stream . 814 *Excursion* 4. 892
In the grey cottage by the murmuring stream . 848 *Excursion* 6. 670
Soft murmuring) was too weak to overcome, . . 894 *Excursion* 9. 695
There too did *Fancy* prize the murmuring wheel ; S.3.426 **Through Cumbrian* 9

Murmurings. Chirp and song, and murmurings, . 171 *Kitten* 50
" Why, Minstrel, these untuneful murmurings— 252 **Why, Minstrel* 1
Thou hast attuned thy murmurings ; . . . . 399 *White Doe* 327
Murmurings, whereby the monitor expressed . 818 *Excursion* 4. 1139

Murmurs. How sweet its streamlet murmurs in mine ear !) . . . . 8 *Ev. Wk.* 350
The fir-grove murmurs with a sea-like sound, . . 151 **When, to* 104
They are deaf to your murmurs—they care not for you, ... 189 *Music* 43
For grace and goodness lost, thy murmurs melt . 269 **Pure element* 13
In this still place, where murmurs on . . . 288 *Glen-Al.* 3
Where not a torrent murmurs heard by thee. . . 306 **Two Voices* 8
Ocean's o'erpowering murmurs have set free . . 349 *At Dover* 9
But, Harp ! thy murmurs may not cease— . . 399 *White Doe* 330
He murmurs near the running brooks . . . . 485 *Poet's Epitaph* 39
To their own far-off murmurs listening. . . . 499 *Memory* 29
These all to swell the village murmurs blend, . . 597 *Ev. Wk. Quarto* 323
To blend his murmurs with my nurse's song, . . 636 *Prelude* 1. 271

Murmurs—*continued.*
Thy murmurs heard ; and drunk the crystal lymph 812 *Excursion* 4. 750
Murmurs, not idly, o'er his peaceful grave. . . 864 *Excursion* 7. 481
The sleepless ocean murmurs for all ears ; . . . 887 *Excursion* 9. 212
She pondered murmurs that attuned her ear . . S.3. 436 **The doubt* 174

Murtherer's. *See* **Murderer's.**
Of saintly Friends the " murtherer's chain partake, 437 *Ecc. Sonn.* 2. 34. 11

Musæus. Musæus, stationed with his lyre . . . 472 *Ossian* 39

Muscle. The motion of a muscle—this way or that— 65 *Bord.* 1540

Muse. And ever, as we fondly muse, we find . . 8 *Ev. Wk.* 317
Thus spake the moral Muse—her wing . . . 154 *Flower Garden* 49
Or second my weak Muse ? . . . . 168 *Turtledove* 8
This sight to me the Muse imparts ;— . . . . 178 *Waggoner* 3. 42
But the sage Muse the revel heeds . . . . . 180 *Waggoner* 4. 7
The Muse, who scents the morning air, . . . 180 *Waggoner* 4. 12
—Fly also, Muse ! and from the dell . . . . 180 *Waggoner* 4. 36
Yet, trust the Muse, it rather hath . . . . . 181 *Waggoner* 4. 132
Is left to muse upon the solemn scene. . . . 184 *Night-piece* 26
So tripped the Muse, inventress of the dance ; . 221 *Triad* 105
This hides not from the moral Muse . . . . 225 *Present.* 17
Of a too-anxious world, mild pastoral Muse ! . . 227 *Vernal Ode* 76
And the glad Muse at liberty to note . . . 251 **Her only* 4
From trivial cares. But, Fancy and the Muse, . 252 **Her only* 9
Faith in the whispers of the lonely Muse, . . . 260 **High is* 7
There also is the Muse not loth to range, . . . 262 **Not Love* 6
Or muse in solemn grove whose shades protect . 270 **Though the bold* 5
Which the Muse warms ; and I, whose head is grey, 273 **Wild Redbreast* 5
Serving no haughty Muse, my hands have here . 280 *Valedict.* 1
Dear Fellow-travellers ! think not that the Muse, 333 *Ded. Tour* 1
To muse, to creep, to halt at will, to gaze— . . 335 *Rhine* 11
To range through the Temples of PAESTUM, to muse 345 *Stanzas : Simplon* 5
Beloved by every gentle Muse . . . . . . 348 **Lulled by* 49
From Knowledge !—If the Muse, whom I have served . . . . 358 *Aquap.* 355
A Muse, who, not unmindful of her Sire . . . 359 *Plea : Hist.* 10
And let me believe that when nightly the Muse . 364 *Vallomb.* 21
To sit and muse, fanned by its dewy air . . . 367 **If with* 8
Borne by the Muse from rills in shepherds' ears . 368 *Trajan* 23
On, loitering Muse—the swift Stream chides us—on ! . . . . 379 *Duddon* 12. 1
Turn from the sight, enamoured Muse—we must ; 379 *Duddon* 12. 13
Eternal blessings on the Muse, ... 386 *Yarrow Rev.* 41
The blameless Muse, who trains her Sons . . . 386 *Yarrow Rev.* 43
The Muse exclaimed ; but Story now must hide . 388 *Loch Etive* 10
That from a threshold loved by every Muse . . 394 **No more* 20
Tell, if ye may, some star-crowned Muse, or Saint ! 446 *Ecc. Sonn.* 3. 24. 5
In whom the fiery Muse revered . . . . . 473 *Ossian* 59
The Tragic Muse thee served with thoughtful vow ; 476 **Tranquillity! the* 4
Let us break off all commerce with the Muse : . 480 **Most sweet* 10
To yon exulting thrush the Muse . . . . . 507 **While from* 59
—But if there be a Muse who, free to take . . 521 *Epist. Beaumont* 38
Nor chide the Muse that stooped to break a spell 525 *Epist. Beaumont* 276
Where Man and Muse complained of mutual wrong ; 529 **Those breathing* 116
Of those pure Minds that reverence the Muse. . 549 **The massy* 22
Alone, continuing there to muse : the slopes . . 661 *Prelude* 4. 178
(So willed the Muse) a less impetuous stream, . 687 *Prelude* 7. 9
Thy guidance, or a greater Muse, if such . . . 755 *Recluse* 1. 1. 779
And to myself I seem to muse on One . . . . 768 *Excursion* 1. 785
On wings, angelic Spirits ! I could muse . . . 790 *Excursion* 3. 300
To muse, and be saluted by the air . . . . 817 *Excursion* 4. 1046
" Smooth verse, inspired by no unlettered Muse," 846 *Excursion* 6. 522
Of circumstance ; and here the tragic Muse . . 846 *Excursion* 6. 551
" Here," said the Pastor, " do we muse, and mourn 865 *Excursion* 7. 546
Suffice it, therefore, if the rural Muse . . . . 892 *Excursion* 9. 518
The pastoral Muse laments the Wheel—no more . S.3.426 **Through Cumbrian* 2
Whose muse a sure though late revenge hath ta'en S.3. 432 **Critics, right* 3
Mindful that thou (ah ! wherefore by my Muse . S.3. 433 **The doubt* 15
Thanks, and if favours of the heavenly Muse . . K.8. 239 *Recluse* 1.1.100

Mused. Since earth grew calm while angels mused ? 222 *Triad* 200
I mused ; and, thirsting for redress, ... 301 *Bran* 127
While thus I mused, methought, before mine eyes, 618 *School Ex.* 5
Perhaps too there performed. Thus long I mused, 633 *Prelude* 1. 80
Nor e'er lost sight of what I mused upon, . . . 633 *Prelude* 1. 81
I mused ; upon these chiefly : and at length, . . 666 *Prelude* 5. 68
I mused, and thought, and felt, in solitude. . . 694 *Prelude* 7. 485
Or mused, his sword was haunted by his touch . 712 *Prelude* 9. 159
And mused in rocky cell or sylvan tent, . . . 753 **Oft, through* 3
She mused, resolved, adhered to her resolve ; . 849 *Excursion* 6. 720
What will become of him ? ' we said, and mused 861 *Excursion* 7. 265

Muse's. Frowns are on every Muse's face, . . . 163 *Needlecase* 1
How, with the Muse's aid, her love attest ? . . 253 *Aerial Rock* 6
My temples with the Muse's diadem. . . . . 259 *Calvert* 8
For once, the Muse's help will we implore, . . 697 *Prelude* 7. 682
Ventured, at some rash Muse's earnest call, . . 704 *Prelude* 8. 368
The heroic trumpet with the Muse's breath ! . . K.8. 257 *Recluse* 1.1.750
Or spend upon the dead the muse's rage ? . . . L.1. 94 *Juvenal* 2. 8

Muses. Now, gentle Muses, your assistance grant, 103 *Artegal* 61
I to the Muses have been bound . . . . . 129 *Idiot Boy* 337
O gentle Muses ! let me tell . . . . . . 129 *Idiot Boy* 339
O gentle Muses ! is this kind ? . . . . . . 130 *Idiot Boy* 342
Ye Muses ! whom I love so well ? . . . . . 130 *Idiot Boy* 346
With pride, the Muses love it evermore. . . . 251 *Appleth.* 14
By the celestial Muses glorified. . . . . . 251 **Pelion and* 8
A cheerful life is what the Muses love, ... 261 **From the dark* 13
Whom could the Muses else allure to tread . . 265 **There is a pleasure* 3
The Muses, as they loved them in the days . . 353 *Aquap.* 51
He serves the Muses erringly and ill, ... 395 *White Doe:Ded.* 57

Muses—*continued.*
On whom the Muses smile; 499 **Departing summer* 27
You, Muses, books, fields, liberty, and rest! 529 **Those breathing* 125
Then the Muses might deal with me just as they chose, 571 *Avarice* 3
To wait upon the bright and gracious Muses, 573 *Chiabrera* 2. 7
Of the fair Muses. Not a covert path 574 *Chiabrera* 5. 9
Chosen by the Muses for their Page of State— 653 *Prelude* 3. 279
The high and tender Muses shall accept 757 *Excursion* 1. 105
Song of the muses, sage historic tale, 864 *Excursion* 7. 450
For loftier intercourse. The Muses, crowned S.3. 436 **The doubt* 149
Muses'. If these brief Records, by the Muses' art 269 **If these* 1
The Muses' modest nurslings underwent 655 *Prelude* 3. 460
Wet with the Muses' nectar. Thus I soothe 733 *Prelude* 11. 449
Museum. As through a wide museum from whose stores 658 *Prelude* 3. 617
Music. *See* **Eye-music, Music's.**
Blanch, Swift, and Music, noblest of their kind, 201 *Hart-leap* 19
MUSIC has no heart to follow, 490 *Incident: Dog* 27
Little MUSIC, she stops short. 490 *Incident: Dog* 28
While music, stealing round the glimmering deeps, 7 *Ev. Wk.* 303
To catch the spiritual music of the hill, 9 *Ev. Wk.* 368
And amorous music on the water dies. 12 *Desc. Sk.* 106
Soft music o'er the aerial summit steal? 16 *Desc. Sk.* 343
Blend in a music of tranquillity; 17 *Desc. Sk.* 363
That on his marriage day sweet music made! 28 *Guilt* 238
Resound with music, could you see the sun, 40 *Bord.* 147
I never saw. The music of the birds 49 *Bord.* 675
His music, and to view his imagery: 108 *Indolence* 65
Who heard the heart-felt music of his suit 121 *V. and J.* 13
Make subterraneous music, like the noise 132 *Michael* 51
Light to the sun and music to the wind; 134 *Michael* 202
Bright gem instinct with music, vocal spark; 153 *Morn. Ex.* 29
As if with pipes and music rare 155 **A whirl-blast* 19
His ears are by the music thrilled, 177 *Waggoner* 2. 34
While to the music, from on high, 180 *Waggoner* 4. 5
The music stirs in him like wind through a tree. 189 *Music* 36
And music from that pipe could draw 192 *Ruth* 8
To music suddenly: 194 *Ruth* 171
The still, sad music of humanity, 207 *Tintern* 91
Those quivering wings composed, that music still! 209 **Ethereal minstrel* 6
Of music, audible to him alone. 220 *Triad* 51
While there the music runs to waste, 228 *Devot. Incit.* 20
Shall be our *hand* of music; he shall sweep 230 *Clouds* 62
When Music deigned within this grosser sphere 234 *Power of Sound* 117
No scale of moral music—to unite 235 *Power of Sound* 170
Was it the music of the spheres 237 *P. B.* 83
That the poor Harp distempered music yields 252 **Why, Minstrel* 13
Soft is the music that would charm for ever; 262 **Not Love* 13
Be gracious as the music and the bloom 264 **Lady! the* 13
Of her loved mistress: soon the music died, 267 *St. Cath.* 7
Or float with music in the festal barge; 273 **While Anna's* 3
Embodied in the music of this Lay, 275 *Rotha Q.* 8
Music that sorrow comes not near, 285 *Grave of Burns* 81
The music in my heart I bore, 289 *Sol. Reap.* 31
They were thy chosen music, Liberty! 306 **Two Voices* 4
Old songs, the precious music of the heart! 315 **The Land* 10
Their voices into liquid music swell, 333 *Fish-women* 12
Drown the music of a song 336 **Jesu! bless* 4
Of music opened, and there came a blending 371 *Eg. Maid.* 146
Nor check, the music of the strings; 375 **The Minstrels* 10
The greeting given, the music played, 375 **The Minstrels* 15
Of music reached its height, and even when sank 387 *Roslin* 4
While thus he brooded, music sweet 406 *White Doe* 889
Their sabbath music—"God us ayde!" 415 *White Doe* 1762
With vocal music, "God us ayde;" 415 *White Doe* 1774
A pleasant music floats along the Mere, 426 *Ecc. Sonn.* 1. 30. 1
Glad music! yet there be that, worn with pain 447 *Ecc. Sonn.* 3. 28. 2
This day, when, forth by rustic music led, 448 *Ecc. Sonn.* 3. 32. 4
Where light and shade repose, where music dwells 451 *Ecc. Sonn.* 3. 43. 11
The music bursteth into second life; 451 *Ecc. Sonn.* 3. 44. 10
By its soft music whence the waters flow: 453 **Calm is the* 26
The music, and extinct the lay? 473 *Ossian* 44
Of softest music some responsive place. 473 **Thanks for* 14
Fit music for a solemn vale! 478 *Somnamb.* 5
How sweet his music! on my life, 481 *Tables Turned* 11
A music sweeter than their own. 485 *Poet's Epitaph* 40
Than music of the Spring. 498 **The sylvan* 12
Catch the blithe music as it sinks and swells, 504 *Warning* 43
Delicious odours! music sweet, 507 *May* 9
Surpasses sweetest music. There she sits 508 *F. Stone* 11
In music all unversed, nor blessed with skill 521 *Epist. Beaumont* 30
But we, we lacked not music of our own, 523 *Epist. Beaumont* 156
On their quick sense our sweetest music jarred; 527 **Those breathing* 51
Snatches of music taken up and dropt 539 **Lady! a* 32
From soul-felt music, and the treasured page 583 **With copious* 29
List'ning th' aëreal music of the hill, 600 *Ev. Wk. Quarto* 436
Soft music from th' aereal summit steal? 609 *Desc. Sk. Quarto* 421
Would, with its rattling music, come, 621 *Andrew Jones* 4
Would, with its rattling music, come, 621 *Andrew Jones* 34
Make ceaseless music that composed my thoughts 636 *Prelude* 1. 277
Like harmony in music; there is a dark 637 *Prelude* 1. 341
To hear such music. Through the walls we flew 644 *Prelude* 2. 128
With music, incense, festival, and flowers! 674 *Prelude* 5. 583
Where silence dwells if music be not there: 685 *Prelude* 6. 669
Articulate music. Above all, one thought 688 *Prelude* 7. 115
Music, and shifting pantomimic scenes, 691 *Prelude* 7. 262
The other to make music; hither, too, 699 *Prelude* 8. 27

Music—*continued.*
With tutelary music, from all harm 701 *Prelude* 8. 184
That into music touch the passing wind. 708 *Prelude* 8. 638
Of music, martial tunes, and banners spread, 713 *Prelude* 9. 277
Wild blasts of music thus could find their way 725 *Prelude* 10. 461
Oh! that I had a music and a voice 734 *Prelude* 12. 29
And the bleak music from that old stone wall, 739 *Prelude* 12. 320
Of music swayed their motions, and the waste 745 *Prelude* 13. 348
And now the music of my own sad steps, 767 *Excursion* 1. 704
Blithe notes of music, suddenly let loose 773 *Excursion* 2. 118
Said I, "The music and the sprightly scene 773 *Excursion* 2. 138
And instruments of music, some half-made, 781 *Excursion* 2. 669
Music of finer tone; a harmony, 782 *Excursion* 2. 710
And music waits upon your skilful touch, 809 *Excursion* 4. 571
With music lulled his indolent repose: 814 *Excursion* 4. 853
Dispersed, like music that the wind takes up 820 *Excursion* 4. 1284
By music, prank, and laughter-stirring jest; 858 *Excursion* 7. 82
With music?' (for he had not ceased to touch 861 *Excursion* 7. 270
Heart-stirring music! hourly heard that name; 867 *Excursion* 7. 671
Of music, lute or harp, a long delight 883 *Excursion* 8. 597
Light to the sun and music to the wind; K.8. 226 **I will* 82
An art, a music, and a strain of words K.8. 247 *Recluse* 1. 1. 402
Musical. Nor hallowed less with musical delight 254 *Dyer* 3
Notes shrill and wild with art more musical: 336 *Staub-bach* 9
Had a musical charm, which the winter of age 364 *Vallomb.* 27
Swoln by that voice—whose murmur musical 381 *Duddon* 19. 12
A musical but melancholy chime, 449 *Ecc. Sonn.* 3. 34. 4
Was now an Island musical with birds 643 *Prelude* 2. 58
Musician. She sees the Musician, 'tis all that she sees! 188 *Music* 24
As fast as a musician scatters sounds 809 *Excursion* 4. 524
Musician, gardener, builder, mechanist, 861 *Excursion* 7. 274
Music's. And their music's a prey which they seize; 167 *Stray Pleasures* 21
Yield to the Music's touching influence; 340 *Ranz* 13
Disturb the liquid music's equipoise. 455 *Rydal Mere* 12
Of boisterous merriment, and music's roar, 716 *Prelude* 9. 457
Musing. Depress by weight of musing Phantasy: 108 *Indolence* 43
To serious musing and to self-reproach. 149 **A narrow* 70
Nor from this vestige of thy musing hours 151 **When, to* 85
To holy musing, it may enter here. 264 **Lady! I* 14
So Fancy, to the musing Poet's eye, 282 **While beams* 8
Haunts, with sad echoes, musing Fancy's ear: 312 **A Roman* 10
From the Pier's head, musing, and with increase 349 *At Dover* 1
By the joint pressure of his musing mood 362 **List—'twas* 81
Sate musing; on that hill the Bard would rove, 393 **The Lovers* 5
Or musing sits forsaken halls among. 463 **Adieu, Rydalian* 14
While musing here I sit in shadow cool, 527 **Those breathing* 41
Heedless how Pliny, musing here, survey'd 604 *Desc. Sk. Quarto* 116
To vacant musing, unreproved neglect 636 *Prelude* 1. 253
That, musing on them, often do I seem 642 *Prelude* 2. 31
Thus musing, in a wood I sate me down 661 *Prelude* 4. 177
Musing in solitude, I oft perceive 755 *Recluse* 1. 1. 755
In silence musing by my Comrade's side, 777 *Excursion* 2. 371
As choice as musing Leisure can bestow; 799 *Excursion* 3. 906
For ever musing. Sunken were her eyes; 848 *Excursion* 6. 682
Musing, the lone spot with my soul agrees S.3. 417 **Sweet was* 10
Musings. To trust a Poet in still musings bound. 273 **Wild Redbreast* 14
Oft with his musings does thy image blend, 460 **Wanderer! that* 70
Blithe hopes and happy musings soon took flight, 523 *Epist. Beaumont* 120
And independent musings pleased me so 652 *Prelude* 3. 228
Some pensive musings which might well beseem 706 *Prelude* 8. 457
Those musings or diverted, save that once 746 *Prelude* 14. 21
Accompanied these musings; fervent thanks 823 *Excursion* 5. 50
Muslin. And Negro Ladies in white muslin gowns. 690 *Prelude* 7. 228
Must. (*Partial list.*)
And leading Herbert. We must let them pass— 39 *Bord.* 101
You are too fearful; yet must I confess, 39 *Bord.* 106
But when thy Father must lie down and die, 40 *Bord.* 159
Idonea, we must part. Be not alarmed— 41 *Bord.* 223
There must be truth in this. Truth in his story! 41 *Bord.* 239
He must have felt it then, known what it was, 41 *Bord.* 240
A thing worth further notice, we must act 42 *Bord.* 292
We must not part,—I have measured many a league 42 *Bord.* 297
Holla! No, no, the business must be done.— 43 *Bord.* 329
And he must lead me back. You are most lucky; 43 *Bord.* 354
The Vagrant must, no doubt, be loitering somewhere 44 *Bord.* 365
But here he is, it must have been a dream. 44 *Bord.* 415
I must have more of this;—you shall not stir 46 *Bord.* 496
For love of God I must not pass their doors; 46 *Bord.* 524
What must be done? We will conduct her hither; 48 *Bord.* 593
Caution must not be flung aside; remember, 48 *Bord.* 604
As you must needs have deeply felt, it is 48 *Bord.* 615
Must fall in the execution of his office? 48 *Bord.* 640
Could not come after us—he *must* have perished; 51 *Bord.* 755
Over your head twice twenty years must roll, 52 *Bord.* 820
Touch not a finger—— What then must be done? 53 *Bord.* 877
It must be ended!— Softly; do not rouse him; 54 *Bord.* 914
Must never come before a mortal judgment-seat, 55 *Bord.* 1001
But softly! we must look a little nearer. 58 *Bord.* 1132
This last device must end my work.— Methinks 58 *Bord.* 1145
Nay, we must travel in another path, 58 *Bord.* 1151
Who on her journey must proceed alone, 59 *Bord.* 1186
To them I must relate the Tale 238 *P. B.* 169
Turn from the sight, enamoured Muse—we must; 379 *Duddon* 12. 13
Ye, too, must fly before a chasing hand, 434 *Ecc. Sonn.* 2. 24. 1
For the brief course that must for me remain; 454 **The Sun, that* 18
That all must love or die; but I withdraw, 559 *Cuck. and Night.* 137
Now farewell, quoth she, for I hence must wend; 561 *Cuck. and Night.* 252
We must the Palace see of Cresida; 562 *Troilus* 5
Or yonder is it that the tents must be: 564 *Troilus* 152

My—*continued.*

—Did Sabine grace adorn my living line, 3 *Ev. Wk.* 72
(Sole bourn, sole wish, sole object of my way; 8 *Ev. Wk.* 348
Where we, my Friend, to happy days shall rise, 8 *Ev. Wk.* 351
From such romantic dreams, my soul, awake 14 *Desc. Sk.* 226
My heart leaps up when I behold 79 **My heart* 1
So was it when my life began; 79 **My heart* 3
And I could wish my days to be 79 **My heart* 8
Historian of my infancy! 79 **Stay near* 4
A solemn image to my heart, 79 **Stay near* 8
My father's family! 79 **Stay near* 9
My sister Emmeline and I 79 **Stay near* 12
My My Father's house, in wet or dry 79 *Sparrow's Nest* 8
My sister Emmeline and I 79 *Sparrow's Nest* 9
The Blessing of my later years 79 *Sparrow's Nest* 15
Was nigh; and, sitting by my side, 82 *Alice Fell* 50
My thoughts on former pleasures ran; 85 *Anecdote* 9
My boy beside me tripped, so slim 86 *Anecdote* 25
At this my boy hung down his head, 86 *Anecdote* 45
At remembrance whereof my blood sometimes will flag; 86 *Rural Arch.* 22
And for the Subject of my Verse I heaved a pensive sigh. 91 *Poet's Dream* 4
Nor could my heart by second thoughts from heaviness be cleared, 91 *Poet's Dream* 5
For bodied forth before my eyes the cross-crowned hut appeared; 91 *Poet's Dream* 6
But the poor ragged Thing whose ways my human heart had warmed. 92 *Poet's Dream* 16
And bore him high through yielding air my debt of love to pay, 92 *Poet's Dream* 19
I whispered, "Yet a little while, dear Child! thou art my own, 92 *Poet's Dream* 21
Strong as an Eagle with my charge I glided round and round 92 *Poet's Dream* 37
Lest all that passed should melt away in silence from my mind, 93 *Poet's Dream* 71
My trees they are, my Sister's flowers; 106 **I've watched* 11
With quickening pace my horse drew nigh 109 **Strange fits* 11
My horse moved on; hoof after hoof 109 **Strange fits* 21
The joy of my desire; 109 **I travelled* 10
A fountain at my fond heart's door, 111 *A Complaint* 3
My fancy's own creation. 111 **Yes! thou* 4
To feed my heart's devotion, 112 **Yes! thou* 10
Through my very heart they shine; 112 **What heavenly* 2
Trembling, through my unworthiness, with fear 112 **O dearer* 3
Proud was I that my country bred 119 *Sailor's Mother* 9
I looked at her again, nor did my pride abate. 119 *Sailor's Mother* 12
My song the workings of her heart expressed. 120 *EmigrantMother* 14
In silence, though my memory could add 124 *V. and J.* 177
Why will ye thus my suit repel? 130 *Idiot Boy* 343
And with the owls began my song, 131 *Idiot Boy* 435
For passions that were not my own, and think 131 *Michael* 31
Will be my second self when I am gone. 131 *Michael* 39
I roamed in the confusion of my heart, 146 **It was an* 18
My Emma, I will dedicate to thee." 146 **It was an* 39
——Soon did the spot become my other home, 146 **It was an* 40
My dwelling, and my out-of-doors abode. 146 **It was an* 41
Tracing the lofty barrier with my eye 147 *Joanna* 44
Joanna, looking in my eyes, beheld 147 *Joanna* 52
Of ancient mountains, or my ear was touched 148 *Joanna* 70
Hath to this lonely Summit given my Name. 148 **There is an* 17
My Friend, Myself, and She who then received 149 **A narrow* 75
And therefore, my sweet Mary, this still Nook, 150 *M. H.* 23
At a short distance from my cottage, stands 150 **When, to* 8
Would watch my motions with suspicious stare, 150 **When, to* 28
My feet might move without concern or care; 150 **When, to* 38
Pleasant conviction flashed upon my mind 150 **When, to* 58
Year followed year, my Brother! and we two, 151 **When, to* 70
My Brother, and on all which thou hast lost. 151 **When, to* 97
Timing my steps to thine; and, with a store 151 **When, to* 106
But now my own delights I make,— 157 **In youth* 5
My thirst at every rill can slake, 157 **In youth* 6
Then, cheerful Flower! my spirits play 158 **In youth* 59
Hath often eased my pensive breast 158 **In youth* 63
When all my reveries are past, 159 **With little* 42
Their snow-white blossoms on my head, 159 *Green Linnet* 2
To sit upon my orchard-seat! 159 *Green Linnet* 6
My last year's friends together. 159 *Green Linnet* 8
My dazzled sight he oft deceives, 159 *Green Linnet* 33
And to-day my heart is weary; 159 **Up with me* 9
Alas! my journey, rugged and uneven, 160 **Up with me* 26
Serving at my heart's command, 160 **Pansies, lilies* 61
Who will love my little Flower. 161 **Pleasures newly* 56
My half-formed melodies, 168 *Turtledove* 2
Or second my weak Muse? 168 *Turtledove* 8
The spirit of my song: 168 *Turtledove* 20
Love animates my lyre— 168 *Turtledove* 22
That way look, my Infant, lo! 170 *Kitten* 1
O'er my little Dora's face; 171 *Kitten* 104
Thee, Baby, laughing in my arms, 171 *Kitten* 106
And I will have my careless season 171 *Kitten* 111
Find my wisdom in my bliss; 172 *Kitten* 122
I sing of these;—it makes my bliss! 182 *Waggoner* 4. 208
But a shy spirit in my heart, 182 *Waggoner* 4. 210
The same whom in my schoolboy days 183 **O blithe* 17
With a huge wallet o'er my shoulders slung, 185 *Nutting* 6
A nutting-crook in hand; and turned my steps 185 *Nutting* 7
Forcing my way, I came to one dear nook 185 *Nutting* 16
And—with my cheek on one of those green stones 185 *Nutting* 35
Confound my present feelings with the past, 185 *Nutting* 49

My—*continued.*

When first she gleamed upon my sight; 186 **She was* 2
How soon my Lucy's race was run! 187 **Three years* 38
A slumber did my spirit seal; 187 **A slumber* 1
For oft, when on my couch I lie 187 **I wandered* 19
And then my heart with pleasure fills, 187 **I wandered* 23
A humbler bliss would satisfy my heart. 190 **Lyre! though* 14
They dart across my path—but lo, 191 *Beggars* 37
And to my heart are still endeared 191 *Seq. Beggars* 27
The pleasant season did my heart employ: 195 *Resolution* 19
My former thoughts returned: the fear that kills; 197 *Resolution* 113
The moving accident is not my trade; 202 *Hart-leap* 97
'Tis my delight, alone in summer shade, 202 *Hart-leap* 99
And, pulling now the rein my horse to stop, 202 *Hart-leap* 106
Which in my former rhyme I have rehearsed. 202 *Hart-leap* 122
And passing even into my purer mind, 206 *Tintern* 29
Have hung upon the beatings of my heart— 206 *Tintern* 54
How often has my spirit turned to thee! 206 *Tintern* 57
The guide, the guardian of my heart, and soul 207 *Tintern* 110
Of all my moral being. Nor perchance, 207 *Tintern* 111
Suffer my genial spirits to decay: 207 *Tintern* 113
Of this fair river; thou my dearest Friend, 207 *Tintern* 115
My dear, dear Friend; and in thy voice I catch 207 *Tintern* 116
The language of my former heart, and read 207 *Tintern* 117
My former pleasures in the shooting lights 207 *Tintern* 118
My dear, dear Sister! and this prayer I make, 207 *Tintern* 121
When thou shalt be my guide: 215 *Kirkstone* 52
My Soul was grateful for delight 215 *Kirkstone* 61
A peerless Youth expectant at my side, 220 *Triad* 25
And marked it for my own; 224 *Primrose* 10
That sees them, to my soul that owns in them, 230 *Clouds* 49
Here is my body doomed to tread, this path, 230 *Clouds* 54
I pace it unrepining, for my thoughts 230 *Clouds* 58
Admit no bondage and my words have wings. 230 *Clouds* 59
Fast through the clouds my Boat can sail; 236 *P. B.* 8
The woods, my Friends, are round you roaring, 236 *P. B.* 11
Both for my little Boat and me! 236 *P. B.* 15
The pointed horns of my canoe; 236 *P. B.* 17
And, did not pity touch my breast 236 *P. B.* 18
Till my ribs ached I'd laugh at you! 236 *P. B.* 20
Up goes my Boat among the stars 236 *P. B.* 31
Up goes my little Boat so bright! 236 *P. B.* 35
"Shame on you!" cried my little Boat, 237 *P. B.* 76
"My little vagrant Form of light, 237 *P. B.* 111
My gay and beautiful Canoe, 237 *P. B.* 112
As kindly take what from my heart 237 *P. B.* 114
I shall not covet for my dower, 238 *P. B.* 137
"But grant my wishes,—let us now 238 *P. B.* 151
"To the stone-table in my garden, 238 *P. B.* 156
And there my good friend, Stephen Otter; 238 *P. B.* 167
On two poor legs, toward my stone-table 238 *P. B.* 174
But straight, to cover my confusion, 238 *P. B.* 189
Whom in my fear I love so well; 245 *P. B.* 772
My further labour might prevent! 245 *P. B.* 787
Ye waited then on my good pleasure; 245 *P. B.* 793
Whom once it was my luck to see 249 *P. B.* 1127
Those many records of my childish years, 250 **Beloved Vale* 2
Remembrance of myself and of my peers 250 **Beloved Vale* 3
No fleeting Spirit, but my own true Love? 252 **Her only* 14
Am pleased by fits to have thee for my foe, 253 **O gentle* 11
Must hear, first uttered from my orchard trees; 253 **A flock* 7
My nerves from no such murmur shrink,—tho' near, 255 *S. H.* 4
Love, faithful love, recalled thee to my mind— 257 **Surprised by* 5
To my most grievous loss!—That thought's return 257 **Surprised by* 9
Could to my sight that heavenly face restore. 257 **Surprised by* 14
And let my spirit in that power divine 258 **Even so* 13
My temples with the Muse's diadem. 259 *Calvert* 8
In my past verse; or shall be, in the lays 259 *Calvert* 11
Gave it while cares were weighing on my heart, 266 **The stars* 10
I slight my own beloved Cam, to range 270 **Ye sacred* 10
Where silver Isis leads my stripling feet; 270 **Ye sacred* 11
Yet shall my blessing hover o'er thee still, 275 *Rotha Q.* 7
Yet have my thoughts for thee been vigilant— 277 **Why art* 5
And in a moment charmed my cares to rest. 279 **Hark! 'tis* 8
So loud, so clear, my Partner through life's day, 279 **Hark! 'tis* 11
Serving no haughty Muse, my hands have here 280 *Valedict.* 1
(Like influence never may my soul reject), 282 **While beams* 10
Power in my breast, wings growing in my mind, 284 *Departure* 14
And both my wishes and my fear 284 *Grave of Burns* 11
And showed my youth 285 *Grave of Burns* 34
Sons of the Bard, my heart still mourns 286 *Sons of Burns* 3
And yet my eyes are filled with tears. 288 *Highland Girl* 21
My True-love sighed for sorrow; 293 *Yarrow Unv.* 30
Jane hangs her head upon my breast, 295 *Highland Boy* 3
Because, my Darlings, ye must know 295 *Highland Boy* 12
That fills my heart with sadness! 302 *Yarrow V.* 8
Been soothed, in all my wanderings. 302 *Yarrow V.* 12
And on my True-love's forehead plant 302 *Yarrow V.* 67
And gladsome notes my lips can breathe, 302 *Yarrow V.* 79
And cheer my mind in sorrow. 302 *Yarrow V.* 88
For my dear Country, many heartfelt sighs, 303 **Fair Star* 13
My youth here witnessed, in a prouder time; 304 **Festivals have* 10
My Country! and 'tis joy enough and pride 306 **Here, on our* 11
With such a dear Companion at my side. 306 **Here, on our* 14
Verily, in the bottom of my heart, 308 **When I* 7
My Soul, a sorrowful interpreter, 311 **Who rises* 22
And through the human heart explore my way; 314 **Not 'mid* 12
Anon before my sight a palace rose 324 *Ode 1814* 69
And oft my soul hath kindled at the same, 329 *Ode: Thanks.* 45
Such feeling pressed upon my soul, 334 **In Bruges* 33
My ears did listen, 'twas enough to gaze; 338 *Engelberg* 16

My—*continued.*
The dear companion of my lonely walk, . . . K.8. 234 **Witness thou* 2
My hope, my joy, my sister, and my friend, . . K.8. 234 **Witness thou* 3
One of thy lowly dwellings is my Home. . . K.8. 238 *Recluse* 1. 1. 59
Here as it found its way into my heart . . . K.8. 240 *Recluse* 1. 1. 138
Recal my song the ungenerous thought; forgive, . K.8. 244 *Recluse* 1. 1. 269
To regulate my hopes. Pleased with the good, . K.8. 246 *Recluse* 1. 1. 350
A task above my skill; the silent mind . . . K.8. 248 *Recluse* 1. 1. 424
My Sister, here misplaced and desolate, . . . K.8. 248 *Recluse* 1. 1. 428
The more I see the more delight my mind . . K.8. 250 *Recluse* 1. 1. 498
A chosen one of my regards. See there . . . K.8. 251 *Recluse* 1. 1. 523
In my affections. Witness the delight . . . K.8. 251 *Recluse* 1. 1. 544
I and the modest partners of my days . . . . K.8. 255 *Recluse* 1. 1. 695
Love, knowledge, all my manifold delights . . K.8. 255 *Recluse* 1. 1. 697
Motions of savage instinct, my delight . . . . K.8. 256 *Recluse* 1. 1. 707
Brook, that hast been my solace days and weeks, K.8. 265 **Brook, that* 1
I come to thee, thou dost my heart renew; . . K.8. 265 **Brook, that* 3
What wonder? on my soul 'twould split a tub L.1. 95 *Juvenal* 3. 10
Good honest souls!—if right my judgment lies L.1. 95 *Juvenal* 3. 20
My Lord can muster (all but honour spent) . . L.1. 97 *Juvenal* 3. 81
My Lady ne'er approached a thing so coarse . L.1. 98 *Juvenal* 3. 102

Myriads. Myriads of notes attest her subtle skill; . 153 *Morn. Ex.* 14
The leaves in myriads jump and spring, . . . 155 **A whirl-blast* 18
I sang—Let myriads of bright flowers, . . . 225 *Primrose* 31
Their myriads?—endlessly renewed, ... 227 *Vernal Ode* 66
Of knowledge; that whole myriads should unite . 308 **One might* 10
Myriads of daisies have shone forth in flower . . 475 **There! said* 10
That shook the leaves in myriads as it passed;— 583 **With copious* 18
Of myriads and boon nature's lavish help; . . 700 *Prelude* 8. 81
Cased with its several beads, what myriads there K.8. 252 *Recluse* 1. 1. 566
That hang aloft in myriads—nay, far less, . . K.8. 253 *Recluse* 1. 1. 608

Myrtle. And bays with myrtle fringed, the southern breeze . . . . 17 *Desc. Sk.* 367
Which the myrtle would delight in . . . . . 221 *Triad* 113
The Sonnet glittered a gay myrtle leaf . . . 260 **Scorn not* 7
Adorned with wreaths of myrtle; . . . . . . 287 *Ellen Irwin* 4
Of Swains reposing myrtle groves among! . . 389 *Tyndrum* 3
Ye myrtle wreaths, your fragrance shed . . . 498 **Departing summer* 17
The gentle Power that haunts the myrtle plain, . 607 *Desc.Sk.Quarto* 308
When warm from myrtle bays and tranquil seas, 610 *Desc.Sk.Quarto* 442
Leaves of myrtle in her Crown, ... 629 *Installation* 51
Those scattered along Adria's myrtle shores: . . 701 *Prelude* 8. 176
The unendangered myrtle, decked with flowers, . 793 *Excursion* 3. 523
With the green myrtle, to endear the hours . . 793 *Excursion* 3. 530
With the myrtle [? myrtle's] boughs arrayed, . S.3. 442 *Harmodius* 16

Myrtle-braided. With the myrtle-braided sword, . S.3. 442 *Harmodius* 6
With the myrtle-braided sword . . . . . . S.3. 442 *Harmodius* 25

Myrtle-crowned. And some recline on couches, myrtle-crowned, ... 275 **While poring* 5

Myrtle's. While, in the flowering myrtle's neighbourhood, ... 793 *Excursion* 3. 525
With the myrtle's boughs arrayed, ... S.3. 442 *Harmodius* 2

Myrtles. From the climate of myrtles contented I go. 345 *Stanzas: Simplon* 20

Myrtle-wreathed. With myrtle-wreathed tiara on his brow, ... 811 *Excursion* 4. 675

Myself. (*Partial list.*)
Oh! leave me to myself, nor let me feel . . . 2 *Early Youth* 13
With which, though bent on haste, myself I decked; 28 *Guilt* 222
I feel myself much bounden to you, Oswald; . . 38 *Bord.* 52
I dare not trust myself with such a thought— . 42 *Bord.* 289
I'll plant myself before Lord Clifford's Castle, . 60 *Bord.* 1248
Landed with a small troop, myself being one: . 68 *Bord.* 1713
A shadow of myself—made by myself. . . . 73 *Bord.* 2039
This song to myself did I oftentimes repeat; . . 88 *Pet-lamb* 62
"O mercy!" to myself I cried, ... 109 **Strange fits* 27
This Child, I chanted to myself a lay, ... 120 *EmigrantMother* 10
I but repay a gift which I myself . . . . . 136 *Michael* 363
I gazed and gazed, and to myself I said, . . . 146 **It was an* 37
At break of day, Joanna and myself. . . . . 147 *Joanna* 37
And there myself and two beloved Friends, . . 148 **A narrow* 6
My Friend, Myself, and She who then received . 149 **A narrow* 75
By myself a lonely pleasure, ... 161 **Pleasures newly* 26
This Child I to myself will take; . . . . . 187 **Three years* 4
"Myself will to my darling be . . . . . . 187 **Three years* 7
While I these thoughts within myself pursued, . 197 *Resolution* 132
I could have laughed myself to scorn to find . . 197 *Resolution* 137
Remembrance of myself and of my peers . . . 250 **Beloved Vale* 3
And leave me to myself!" . . . . 297 *Highland Boy* 205
Myself so satisfied in heart before. . . . . . 306 **Here, on our* 8
Which I myself could scarcely brook. . . . . 401 *White Doe* 494
I would myself have hung it high, ... 410 *White Doe* 1278
Yet being to myself a guide, ... 492 *Duty* 27
I call thee: I myself commend . . . . . . 492 *Duty* 50
To brace myself to some determined aim, . . . 633 *Prelude* 1. 115
For such an arduous work, I through myself . . 634 *Prelude* 1. 147
Take refuge and beguile myself with trust . . 635 *Prelude* 1. 235
Much wanting, so much wanting, in myself, . . 636 *Prelude* 1. 264
Am worthy of myself! Praise to the end! . . 637 *Prelude* 1. 350
To understand myself, nor thou to know . . . 641 *Prelude* 1. 627
Two consciousnesses, conscious of myself . . . 642 *Prelude* 2. 32
Appeared like something in myself, a dream, . . 647 *Prelude* 2. 351
Of pride and pleasure! to myself I seemed . . 649 *Prelude* 3. 25
Even with myself divided such delight, . . . 652 *Prelude* 3. 237
Inexorably adverse: for myself . . . . . 656 *Prelude* 3. 490
The balance, and with firm hand weighed myself. 660 *Prelude* 4. 159
Myself unseen. He was of stature tall, . . . 664 *Prelude* 4. 391
Peculiar to myself, let that remain . . . . . 668 *Prelude* 5. 195
With one not richer than myself, I made . . . 672 *Prelude* 5. 469

Myself—*continued.*
I to the sport betook myself again. . . . . 673 *Prelude* 5. 490
Recall what then I pictured to myself, ... 688 *Prelude* 7. 107
Nor made unto myself a secret boast . . . . 696 *Prelude* 7. 586
Unto myself, "The face of every one . . . . 696 *Prelude* 7. 628
Myself from frequent perils; nor were tales . . 701 *Prelude* 8. 168
The fold protecting. I myself, mature . . . 701 *Prelude* 8. 185
When to myself it fairly might be said, . . . 707 *Prelude* 8. 548
Less genuine and wrought up within myself— . 716 *Prelude* 9. 472
And in this way I wrought upon myself, . . . 719 *Prelude* 10. 85
A Poet only to myself, to men . . . . . . 721 *Prelude* 10. 234
To yield myself to Nature, when that strong . 724 *Prelude* 10. 417
Upon his tombstone, whispering to myself: . . 726 *Prelude* 10. 547
Review the past, I warred against myself— . . 735 *Prelude* 12. 76
Pampering myself with meagre novelties . . . 736 *Prelude* 12. 117
My brothers and myself. There rose a crag, . . 738 *Prelude* 12. 292
To speak, what I myself have known and felt; . 740 *Prelude* 13. 13
For having given the story of myself, ... 751 *Prelude* 14. 391
And to myself,' said she, 'have done much wrong 768 *Excursion* 1. 768
And to myself I seem to muse on One . . . . 768 *Excursion* 1. 785
"Though now sojourning there, he, like myself, . 774 *Excursion* 2. 164
Upon myself."—The other left these words . . 779 *Excursion* 2. 545
Though comfortless!— Not of myself I speak; . 790 *Excursion* 3. 263
"Yet be it said, in justice to myself, ... 790 *Excursion* 3. 282
Only by records in myself not found. . . . . 796 *Excursion* 3. 705
Once more did I retire into myself. . . . . 798 *Excursion* 3. 830
Lack virtue to receive; what I myself, . . . 800 *Excursion* 3. 960
Within myself, not comfortless.—The tenour . . 800 *Excursion* 3. 967
Joy to myself! but to the heart of her . . . 834 *Excursion* 5. 752
Beneath yon hawthorn, planted by myself . . 854 *Excursion* 6. 1081
Myself have seen, a gateway, last remains . . 872 *Excursion* 7. 963
(If I may venture of myself to speak, ... 873 *Excursion* 7. 1045
We both have witnessed, lot which I myself . . 886 *Excursion* 9. 166
Would lead me, I should whisper to myself; . . K.8. 244 *Recluse* 1. 1. 276
Shall I reprove myself? Ah no, the stream . . K.8. 244 *Recluse* 1. 1. 294

Mysteries. *See* **Heart-mysteries.**
The mysteries that cups of flowers enfold, . . 108 *Indolence* 62
Unbosom their last mysteries. . . . . . . 216 *Enterprise* 88
Point not these mysteries to an Art . . . . 234 *Power of Sound* 108
Whose pen, the mysteries of the rod and line . 254 *Complete Angler* 3
Of mysteries revealed, ... 332 *Ode: Thanks.* 238
And mysteries above her years. . . . . . 407 *White Doe* 1032
Spreads wide; though special mysteries multiply, 438 *Ecc. Sonn.* 2. 41. 4
Of England's Church; stupendous mysteries! . 445 *Ecc. Sonn.* 3. 19. 6
In mysteries of birth and life and death . . . 460 **Queen of* 30
And wedded Life, through scriptural mysteries, . 467 *St. Bees* 115
But these poetic mysteries I withhold; . . . 522 *Epist. Beaumont* 85
Dissevered both from all the mysteries . . . 527 **Those breathing* 19
Diffused through all the mysteries of our Being, . 538 **In desultory* 26
Those mysteries of being which have made, . . 735 *Prelude* 12. 85
Among the mysteries of love and hate, . . . 751 *Prelude* 14. 337
Exemplified by mysteries, that were felt . . . 812 *Excursion* 4. 740
With mysteries;—for, if Faith were left untried, . 846 *Excursion* 6. 563
Would draw out of his heart the mysteries . . K.8. 227 **I will* 95

Mysterious. That dark mysterious gulf ascending, sound . . . . 18 *Desc. Sk.* 415
Within that fabric of mysterious form . . . . 26 *Guilt* 127
So meet extremes in this mysterious world, . . 65 *Bord.* 1529
All die in solitude. Mysterious God, ... 75 *Bord.* 2154
Her fires, that like mysterious pulses beat . . 123 *V. and J.* 98
Mysterious safeguard, that, in spite . . . . 232 *Jew. Fam.* 41
These types mysterious (if the show . . . . 299 *Brownie's Cell* 67
And vanish by mysterious art; . . . . . . 300 *Bran* 10
For the same service, by mysterious ties; . . . 347 *Processions* 50
Brings to thy food, mysterious Sacrament! . . 446 *Ecc. Sonn.* 3. 25. 3
And strive to fathom the mysterious laws . . . 468 **Ranging the* 3
Thou a mysterious intercourse dost hold, . . . 475 **Homeward we* 9
Do still perform mysterious offices! . . . . 500 *Humanity* 10
Their own mysterious groves. . . . . . . 506 **While from* 32
Where'er her course; mysterious Bird! . . . . 511 **Who rashly* 25
Unto Thee, mysterious God! . . . . . . 550 *Hermit's Cell* 4. 4
The Spirit ended his mysterious rite, ... 582 *Invoc. Earth* 35
Bending beneath our life's mysterious weight . 672 *Prelude* 5. 418
To presences of God's mysterious power . . . 713 *Prelude* 9. 234
For admiration and mysterious awe. . . . . 784 *Excursion* 2. 869
Mysterious union with its native sea. . . . . 818 *Excursion* 4. 1140
Guide of our way, mysterious comforter! . . . 864 *Excursion* 7. 483
Mysterious rites were solemnised; and there— . 894 *Excursion* 9. 690

Mysteriously. Mysteriously remote and high; . . 227 *Vernal Ode* 117
Of soul and sense mysteriously allied, ... 798 *Excursion* 3. 843
Of my own cunning, earth mysteriously . . . S.3. 435 **The doubt* 100

Mysteriously-united. "To a mysteriously-united pair 836 *Excursion* 5. 903

Mystery. No—no—the thing stands clear of mystery; 42 *Bord.* 261
O wretched Human-kind!—Until the mystery . 69 *Bord.* 1795
She wars not with the mystery . . . . . . 81 †*Mother's Return* 18
Lady, is a mystery rare; . . . . 140 *Arm. Lady* 62
Depends upon that mystery. . . . . . . 164 **Glad sight* 4
To solve the mystery, not in Nature's laws . . 170 **Never enlivened* 17
A voice, a mystery; . . . . 183 **O blithe* 16
In which the burthen of the mystery, ... 206 *Tintern* 38
Blest times when mystery is laid bare, . . . 226 *Present.* 68
Initiation in that mystery old. . . . . . . 235 *Power of Sound* 180
To tuneful tongues in mystery versed; . . . 237 *P. B.* 123
Yet—though dread Powers, that work in mystery, spin . . . . 280 **Oh what* 2
Nor long this mystery did detain . . . . . 294 *Jedbor.* 70
There let a mystery of joy prevail, ... 294 **Fly, some* 5
Which to this mystery belong, ... 398 *White Doe* 210
This mystery if the Stranger can reveal, . . . 422 *Ecc. Sonn.* 1. 16. 13
A mystery potent human love to endow . . . 447 *Ecc. Sonn.* 3. 26. 12
Or gulf of mystery, which thou alone, ... 469 **Desire we* 9

Mystery—*continued.*
Into the land of mystery. . . . . 472 *Ossian* 36
You would in mystery hide ; . . . . . . 545 *Russ. Fug.* 292
Embodied in the mystery of words : . . . . 674 *Prelude* 5. 597
These courts of mystery, where a step advanced . 681 *Prelude* 6. 451
That passes by me is a mystery ! " . . . . 696 *Prelude* 7. 629
Oh ! mystery of man, from what a depth . . . 738 *Prelude* 12. 272
More rational proportions ; mystery, ... 750 *Prelude* 14. 285
The incumbent mystery of sense and soul, . . 750 *Prelude* 14. 286
The mystery, the life which cannot die ; . . . 759 *Excursion* 1. 225
Of his own mind ; by mystery and hope, . . . 760 *Excursion* 1. 284
That these—and that superior mystery . . . 816 *Excursion* 4. 974
Differ, by mystery not to be explained ; . . . 818 *Excursion* 4. 1108
No mystery is here ! Here is no boon . . . 887 *Excursion* 9. 243
Mystic. The mystic shapes that by thy margin rove 3 *Ev. Wk.* 78
Along the mystic streams of Life and Death. . . 12 *Desc. Sk.* 72
The mystic stirrings that are here, ... 223 *Wishing-gate* 38
A Saint, the Church's Rock, the mystic Keys 357 *Aquap.* 309
Or near that mystic Round of Druid frame . 380 *Duddon* 17. 12
As Menai's foam ; and toward the mystic ring . 419 *Ecc. Sonn.* 1. 3. 2
Broods, visibly portrayed, the mystic Dove, . . 450 *Ecc. Sonn.* 3. 39. 13
In every cell of Fingal's mystic Grot, ... 473 **Ye shadowy* 2
From thence to search the mystic cause of things 619 *School Ex.* 75
Mystical. Obeys a mystical intent ! . . . . . 214 *Dion* 95
Not in a mystical and idle sense, ... 645 *Prelude* 2. 230
Mythologists. The old mythologists, more impressed than we . . . . 170 **Never enlivened* 11

N

Naiad. On Grasmere's beach, than Naiad by the side 149 **A narrow* 36
I will not fetch a Naiad from a flood . . . . 220 *Triad* 8
Channels for tears ; no Naiad shouldst thou be,— 268 **Brook ! whose* 9
The Naiad. Sunbeams, upon distant hills . . 814 *Excursion* 4. 873
Naiads. That ever among Men or Naiads sought . 251 **There is a little* 3
Abodes of Naiads, calm abysses pure, ... 379 *Duddon* 12. 6
Nail. Upon the self-same nail ; his very staff . . 769 *Excursion* 1. 853
Nails. The nails of cart or chariot-wheel have left 567 *Cumb. Beg.* 56
The nails, the thorns, and thy two hands, thy face K.8. 266 **Rid of* 6
Naked. Cheering its naked waste of scattered stone, 4 *Ev. Wk.* 94
The rocks rise naked as a wall, or stretch . . . 14 *Desc. Sk.* 230
Upon the summit of this naked cone, ... 16 *Desc. Sk.* 304
Hoary and naked are its walls, and raise . . . 26 *Guilt* 115
Disclose a naked guide-post's double head, . . 26 *Guilt* 134
And saw a woman in the naked room . . . . 27 *Guilt* 165
With naked feet walked over burning ploughshares. 62 *Bord.* 1385
And he was famished ? Naked was the spot ; . 68 *Bord.* 1721
" Poor Shepherd of the naked Down, a favoured lot is thine, ... 92 *Poet's Dream* 53
And, like a naked Indian, slept himself away. . 107 *Indolence* 27
That, from the dandelion's naked stalk, . . . 123 *V. and J.* 137
That every naked ash, and tardy tree . . . . 146 **It was an* 14
Through border wilds where naked Indians stray, 153 *Morn. Ex.* 13
Of naked instinct, wound about the heart. . . 172 *Infant Daughter* 38
And, lo !—up Castrigg's naked steep . . . . 180 *Waggoner* 4. 61
See, perched upon the naked height . . . . 182 *Waggoner* 4. 254
When fields are naked far and wide, ... 217 *Enterprise* 130
The naked Indian of the wild, ... 225 *Present.* 34
Which by their aid re-clothe the naked lawn . . 230 *Clouds* 67
Re-echoed by a naked rock, ... 247 *P. B.* 942
—By planting on thy naked head the crest . . 253 **Aerial Rock* 7
O'er naked Snowdon's wide aerial waste ; . . . 254 *Dyer* 13
Pure as the naked heavens, majestic, free, . . 307 **Milton ! thou* 11
In Zaragoza, naked to the gales . . . . . . 315 **And is it* 8
In naked splendour, clear from mist or haze, . . 329 *Ode : Thanks.* 9
Of History, stript naked as a rock . . . . . 359 **Those old* 3
Unharnessed, naked, troops of Moorish horse . . 368 *Trajan* 45
How shall I paint thee ?—Be this naked stone . 376 *Duddon* 3. 1
Their prayers out to the wind and naked skies. . 387 **Part fenced* 8
Ours couch on naked rocks,—will cross a brook . 389 *Tyndrum* 4
Unarmed and naked will I go, ... 401 *White Doe* 511
His frame is tied ; firm from the naked feet . . 437 *Ecc. Sonn.* 2. 35. 6
There are the naked clothed, the hungry fed ; . . 467 *St. Bees* 64
Opinion bow before the naked sense . . . . 500 *Humanity* 43
On the smooth surface of this naked stone ! . . 511 **So fair* 6
With which, though slighted, he, on naked hill . 530 *Poor Robin* 25
And naked left this dripping Rock, ... 550 *Hermit's Cell* 2. 27
The skiffs with naked masts at anchor laid, . . 593 *Ev. Wk. Quarto* 105
Tower like a wall the naked rocks, or reach . . 607 *Desc.Sk.Quarto* 287
Nor longer naked be your way-worn feet, . . . 614 *Desc.Sk.Quarto* 667
Wensley's rich Vale and Sedbergh's naked heights. 622 *Recluse* 1. 1. 157
A feeling of their strength. The naked trees, . 622 *Recluse* 1. 1. 165
Nor am I naked of external things, ... 634 *Prelude* 1. 154
A naked savage, in the thunder shower. . . . 636 *Prelude* 1. 300
Shouldering the naked crag, oh, at that time . 637 *Prelude* 1. 335
Or round the naked table, snow-white deal, . . 639 *Prelude* 1. 514
When, in forlorn and naked chambers cooped . 655 *Prelude* 3. 450
The naked recollection of that time, ... 658 *Prelude* 3. 611
Naked, as in the presence of her God. . . . . 660 *Prelude* 4. 152
Of naked pools, and common crags that lay . . 678 *Prelude* 6. 234
By naked huts, wood-built, and sown like tents . 683 *Prelude* 6. 521
And Ossian (doubt not—'tis the naked truth) . 695 *Prelude* 7. 567
In silent beauty on the naked ridge . . . . 706 *Prelude* 8. 465
With that which makes our Reason's naked self . 730 *Prelude* 11. 234
A naked pool that lay beneath the hills, . . . 738 *Prelude* 12. 249
Invested moorland waste, and naked pool, . . . 738 *Prelude* 12. 258
Upon the naked pool and dreary crags, . . . 738 *Prelude* 12. 264
I sate half-sheltered by a naked wall ; . . . . 738 *Prelude* 12. 299

Naked—*continued.*
We almost meet a friend, on naked heaths . . 742 *Prelude* 13. 139
The naked summit of a far-off hill . . . . . 742 *Prelude* 13. 148
The Moon hung naked in a firmament . . . . 746 *Prelude* 14. 40
Appeared a roofless Hut ; four naked walls . . 756 *Excursion* 1. 30
And 'mid the hollow depths of naked crags . . 758 *Excursion* 1. 155
What soul was his, when, from the naked top . 759 *Excursion* 1. 198
The Savoyard to quit his naked rocks, . . . 761 *Excursion* 1. 317
Lofty, and steep, and naked as a tower. . . . 787 *Excursion* 3. 42
On Sarum's naked plain—than pyramid . . . 788 *Excursion* 3. 148
Upon my naked branches :—lively thoughts . . 793 *Excursion* 3. 493
The naked spirit, ceasing to deplore . . . . 820 *Excursion* 4. 1250
By naked rafters intricately crossed, ... 824 *Excursion* 5. 147
By act of naked reason. Moral truth . . . . 831 *Excursion* 5. 562
It is no night-fire of the naked hills, ... 833 *Excursion* 5. 748
Not from the naked *Heart* alone of Man . . . 837 *Excursion* 5. 979
At morn and evening from that naked perch . 851 *Excursion* 6. 865
And naked stood that lowly Parsonage . . . 858 *Excursion* 7. 55
Naked without, and rude within ; a spot . . . 859 *Excursion* 7. 138
Whose shelving sides are red with naked mould. . 868 *Excursion* 7. 700
Naked, and coloured like the soil, the feet . . 879 *Excursion* 8. 354
Nakedness. Driven out in troops to want and nakedness ; . . . . 56 *Bord.* 1032
And in tenderest nakedness, ... 502 **Like a* 4
And not in utter nakedness, ... 588 *Immortality* 63
He clothed the nakedness of austere truth. . . 760 *Excursion* 1. 269
The planet in its nakedness : were this . . . 777 *Excursion* 2. 361
Had almost a forbidding nakedness ; . . . . 781 *Excursion* 2. 640
Name. To which the sage would give a prouder name. 10 *Desc. Sk.* 14
Such further deed in manhood's name forbade ; . 33 *Guilt* 479
He saw his Wife's lips move his name to bless . 35 *Guilt* 616
Out of that deed. My trust, Saviour ! is in thy name ! " . . . . 36 *Guilt* 657
The name of Marmaduke is blown away : . . . 39 *Bord.* 138
My Child, forgetful of the name of Herbert, . . 41 *Bord.* 206
That savoured of aversion to thy name . . . 41 *Bord.* 232
I' th' name of all the Saints, and by the Mass 45 *Bord.* 448
A holier name ; and, under such a mask, . . . 47 *Bord.* 544
That you too should subscribe your name. . . 49 *Bord.* 671
To lisp the name of Father—could he look . . 56 *Bord.* 1052
The name of daughter in his mouth, he prays ! . 62 *Bord.* 1377
That often, when the name of God is uttered, . 63 *Bord.* 1438
Be calm, I pray thee ! Oswald— Name him not. 76 *Bord.* 2237
Will waste her curses on another name. . . . 77 *Bord.* 2276
And said, " My name is Alice Fell ; . . . . 82 *Alice Fell* 43
Tombstone nor name—only the turf we tread . 95 *Brothers* 14
That name through every age, her hatred to declare. 103 *Artegal* 40
I, Brother ! only should be king in name, . . . 105 *Artegal* 182
He bore the lasting name of " pious Elidure ! " . 106 *Artegal* 241
Smile of the Moon !—for so I name . . . . 112 *Lament* 1
Nor sorrow may attend thy name ? . . . . 116 *Affl. Marg.* 7
My sister's child, who bears my name, ... 121 *EmigrantMother* 67
I'll call thee by my darling's name ; . . . . 121 *EmigrantMother* 90
That Julia, wanting yet the name of wife, . . 122 *V. and J.* 66
Then with the father's name she coupled words . 124 *V. and J.* 165
There dwelt a Shepherd, Michael was his name ; . 131 *Michael* 41
The Clipping Tree, a name which yet it bears. . 133 *Michael* 169
May call it by the name of Emma's Dell. . . . 146 **It was an* 47
Some uncouth name upon the native rock, . . 147 *Joanna* 30
Joanna's name deep in the living stone :— . . 148 *Joanna* 83
Hath to this lonely Summit given my Name. . . 148 **There is an* 17
By a memorial name, uncouth indeed . . . . 149 **A narrow* 77
And Point Rash-Judgment is the Name it bears. 149 **A narrow* 80
Could I withhold thy honoured name,—and now. 151 **When, to* 86
Gave the baptismal name each Sister bore. . . 151 **Forth from* 15
And many a fond and idle name . . . . . 158 **With little* 13
Bright *Flower !* for by that name at last, . . . 159 **With little* 41
The bird that by some name or other . . . . 162 **Art thou the* 9
A name with us endeared to hope, ... 164 **Fair Lady* 15
And haply some familiar name . . . . . . 164 **Fair Lady* 29
Whose name is Non-pareil. . . . . 165 *Parrot* 4
With thine, and gave the mournful name which thou wilt ever bear. . . . . 169 *Love lies Bleeding* 24
Frail, feeble, Monthling !—by that name, methinks, 172 *InfantDaughter* 16
Gave to the days a mark and name . . . . 182 *Waggoner* 4. 223
In the street that from Oxford hath borrowed its name. . . . . 188 *Music* 4
Doth she betray us when they're seen ? or are they but a name ? . . . . 189 *Star-gazers* 16
And bore a soldier's name ; . . . . 192 *Ruth* 27
His name in the wild woods. . . . . . . 193 *Ruth* 114
Dim sadness—and blind thoughts, I knew not, nor could name. . . . . 195 *Resolution* 28
Since she (her name is Martha Ray) . . . . 198 *Thorn* 105
Ere I had heard of Martha's name, ... 199 *Thorn* 173
Tell thy name, thou trembling Field ; . . . . 205 *Brougham* 147
" The good Lord Clifford " was the name he bore. 205 *Brougham* 172
Upon the ruins of thy glorious name ; . . . . 214 *Dion* 103
Gives to this savage Pass its name. . . . . 215 *Kirkstone* 48
And Love, when worthiest of his name, . . . 217 *Enterprise* 160
For from the summit of Black Comb (dread name 218 **This Height* 2
The daring thought, forget the name ; . . . . 231 **The gentlest Poet* 6
Or found on earth a name ; . . . . 232 *Jew. Fam.* 12
But field or meadow name it not ; . . . . . 240 *P. B.* 368
From Scripture she a name did borrow ; . . . 246 *P. B.* 908
She calls the poor Ass by his name, ... 248 *P. B.* 1044
Notice or name !—It quivers down the hill, . . 251 **There is a little* 4
Shall live the name of Walton : Sage benign ! . 254 *Complete Angler* 2
Nor heat, at Tam o' Shanter's name, their blood). 255 *Detraction* 6
Who may respect my name that I to thee . . 259 *Calvert* 2
At this late day, its sanctifying name. . . . . 272 *Lady E. B.* 8

Name—*continued.*

After her throes, this Stream of name more dear . 275 *Rotha Q.* 11
" *Miserrimus !* " and neither name nor date, . . 275 *Gravestone* 1
In Heaven ; hence no one blushes for thy name, . 278 *Wellington* 13
Where, Cavendish, *thine* seems nothing but a name ! 283 **Here, where* 14
And of your Father's name will make . . . . 286 *Sons of Burns* 23
At sound of Rob Roy's name. . . . . . . 292 *Rob Roy* 120
Fixed on him an unhallowed name ; . . . . 299 *Brownie's Cell* 54
First open traitor to the German name ! . . . 313 *Prophecy* 14
Anxious an aery name to immortalize. . . . . 313 **Go back* 8
Yet shall thy name, conspicuous and sublime, . 317 **Brave Schill* 6
Temptation ; and whose kingly name and state . 317 **Call not* 4
And utter England's name with sadly-plausive voice. . . . . 327 *Ode 1815* 44
And magnify Thy name, Almighty God ! . . . 328 *Ode 1815* 105
For to a few collected in His name, ... 332 *Ode : Thanks.* 224
And to the enormous labour left his name, . . 335 *Aix* 13
The name of Aloys Reding. . . . . 337 *Thun* 4
Clouds do not name those Visitants ; they were . 338 *Engelberg* 10
Thy very name, O Lady ! flings, ... 338 **Meek Virgin* 27
Thy name, O Schwytz, in happy freedom keep ! . 339 *Schwytz* 14
Of Winter—but a name. . . . . 348 **Lulled by* 18
Oh Goddard !—what art thou ?—a name— . . 348 **Lulled by* 25
Missed not the truth, retains a single name . . 356 *Aquap.* 239
That name, a local Phantom proud to mock . . 358 **Is this* 4
His bitter tears, whose name the Papal Chair . 360 **Long has* 13
Save in this Rill that took from blood the name . 361 **When here* 7
That awful name to Thee, thee, simple Cuckoo, . 363 **List—'twas* 97
Of that holiest of Bards, and the name for my mind 364 *Vallomb.* 26
Of Lago Morto, dreary sight and name, . . . 366 **Fair Land* 7
And took from men her name—The Water Lily 369 *Eg. Maid* 6
But worthy of the name she bore . . . . . 369 *Eg. Maid* 37
And to her name my soul shall cleave in sorrow ; " 374 *Eg. Maid* 326
In honour of each household name, ... 375 **The Minstrels* 16
Mother of Love ! (that name best suits thee here) 380 *Duddon* 18. 5
Derives its name, reflected as the chime . . . 381 *Duddon* 22. 5
Of that serene companion—a good name, . . . 383 *Duddon* 30. 2
Avon—a precious, an immortal name ! . . . 392 *Avon* 1
Shrink from *thy* name, pure Rill, with unpleased ears. . . . . 392 *Avon* 14
Is but a name, no more is Inglewood, ... 392 *Inglewood* 2
A valiant man, and a name of dread . . . . 399 *White Doe* 250
Bethink you of your own good name : . . . . 400 *White Doe* 385
That name—pronounced with a dying fall— . . 400 *White Doe* 400
The name of his only Daughter dear, ... 400 *White Doe* 401
" Thou, Richard, bear'st thy father's name, . . 400 *White Doe* 406
Grave Gentry of estate and name, ... 403 *White Doe* 629
For, with a high and valiant name, ... 404 *White Doe* 793
Shall Percy blush, then, for his name ? . . . 405 *White Doe* 825
Stands single—Norton Tower its name— . . . 409 *White Doe* 1168
Yea, by her brother's very name, ... 409 *White Doe* 1198
But for lost Faith and Christ's dear name, . . 410 *White Doe* 1299
The name untouched, the tear unshed ;— . . . 410 *White Doe* 1306
The Norton name hath been unknown. . . . . 413 *White Doe* 1574
That legend and her Grandsire's name ; . . . 415 *White Doe* 1766
And of that lonely name she thought, ... 415 *White Doe* 1771
Or some of humbler name, to these wild shores . 419 *Ecc. Sonn.* 1. 2. 11
Nor these, nor monuments of eldest name, . . 419 *Ecc. Sonn.* 1. 5. 9
And for the faith ; nor shall his name forsake . 420 *Ecc. Sonn.* 1. 6. 12
Angli by name ; and not an Angel waves . . 421 *Ecc. Sonn.* 1. 13. 5
Who, having learnt that name, salvation craves . 422 *Ecc. Sonn.* 1. 13. 8
These legalized oppressions ! Man—whose name . 429 *Ecc. Sonn.* 2. 4. 10
No—some fierce Maniac hath usurped her name ; 439 *Ecc. Sonn.* 2. 44. 11
Hear also of that name, and mercy cast . . . 440 *Ecc. Sonn.* 2. 46. 7
That bigotry may swallow the good name, . . 441 *Ecc. Sonn.* 3. 3. 12
A holier name ! then lightly do not bear . . . 445 *Ecc. Sonn.* 3. 21. 2
And magnify the glorious name of God, . . . 446 *Ecc. Sonn.* 3. 25. 7
Or like the Alpine Mount, that takes its name . 452 *Ecc. Sonn.* 3. 46. 5
A happy people won for thee that name . . . 463 **They called* 2
Shall be thy rightful name, in prose and rhyme ! 464 **They called* 14
Name that first struck by chance my startled ear) 465 **The cattle* 8
Of old grey stone, and high-born name . . . 472 *Ossian* 24
Repeats but once the sound of thy sweet name : . 476 *Eden* 4
Yet wants heaven knows what to be worthy the name. . . . . 482 *Character* 16
Has travelled down to Matthew's name, . . . 486 *Matthew* 11
Oh ! might my name be numbered among theirs, 489 *Pers. Talk* 55
And, therefore, shalt thou be an honoured name ! 491 *Tribute : Dog* 36
He instantly recalled the name, ... 491 *Fidelity* 46
O Duty ! if that name thou love . . . . . 492 *Duty* 2
My hopes no more must change their name, . . 492 *Duty* 39
And leave a dead unprofitable name— . . . 494 *Hap. War.* 80
A name which it took of yore : . . . . . 494 *Force of Prayer* 22
A thousand years hath it borne that name, . . 494 *Force of Prayer* 23
A name more sad than Yarrow. . . . . . 494 *Force of Prayer* 40
Deserves the name (this truth the billows preach) 495 *Fact* 13
Of humbler name ; whose souls do, like the flood 497 *Fact* 40
Lycoris (if such name befit . . . . . . 497 *Lycoris* 27
The pole, from which thy name . . . . . 506 **While from* 42
A holy name—the Bird of Heaven ! . . . . 511 **Who rashly* 28
Region that crowns her beauty with the name . 512 **Who rashly* 34
Grieve for the land on whose wild woods his name 515 *Penn.* 10
Dead to the very name ? Presumption fed . . 516 **Young England* 3
On empty air ! That name will keep its hold . 516 **Young England* 4
Why bears it then the name of " Weeping Hill " ? 517 *Pun. Death* 1. 8
Shed on their chains ; and hence that doleful name. 517 *Pun. Death* 1. 14
Such name Italian fancy would have given, . . 524 *Epist. Beaumont* 167
All ranks ! What Sovereign, worthy of the name, 528 **Those breathing* 76
And at an hour which nobody could name. . . 535 *Egremont* 64
Asked it by a brother's name, ... 536 *Egremont* 100

Name—*continued.*

And Thou, wild Stream, that giv'st the honoured name . . . . 539 **Lady ! a* 23
Inspired by one whose very name bespeaks . . 540 *Grace Darl.* 4
Yea, to celestial Choirs, Grace Darling's name ! 541 *Grace Darl.* 97
" Thy name in this large world is spread abroad ! 552 *Prioress* 2
Upon the breast Thy name do glorify. . . . . 552 *Prioress* 7
Fie, quoth she, on thy name, Bird ill beseen ! . 560 *Cuck.and Night.* 186
And other Peers whose names are on record ; . . 562 *Cuck.and Night.* 277
Where'er Permessus bears an honoured name, . . 574 *Chiabrera* 5. 22
Francesco was the name the Youth had borne, . 575 *Chiabrera* 8. 6
From nearest kindred, Vernon her new name ; . 576 **By a* 2
This Tablet, hallowed by her name, ... 577 *Cenotaph* 7
Was nothing but a name. . . . . 580 *John Words.* 40
Too long abashed thy Name is like a rose . . 584 **With copious* 46
Had been derived the name he bore—a name, . 584 *Ch. Lamb* 24
Now honour'd Edward's less than Bacon's name. 619 *School Ex.* 56
Pronounced the name of Hope :—The conscious child . . . . 620 *Birth of Love* 26
" At thy name though compassion her nature resign, ... 621 *Convict* 49
And left the Glow-worm, blessing it by name, . 622 **Among all* 15
A Book time-cherished and an honoured name . 626 **Son of* 9
Madly played to win a name : . . . . . . 628 *Installation* 8
" VICTORIA be her name ! " . . . . . . 629 *Installation* 38
How Wallace fought for Scotland ; left the name 635 *Prelude* 1. 214
Far better never to have heard the name . . . 636 *Prelude* 1. 255
By the proud name she bears—the name of Heaven. 650 *Prelude* 3. 111
To inspiration, sort with such a name ; . . . 651 *Prelude* 3. 149
Honoured by Milton's name. O temperate Bard ! 653 *Prelude* 3. 295
A seemly plainness, name it what you will, . . 654 *Prelude* 3. 397
(At least from what we commonly so name,) . . 656 *Prelude* 3. 512
A more substantial name, no mimic show, . . . 657 *Prelude* 3. 589
Can beat never will I forget thy name. . . . 659 *Prelude* 4. 32
My name from piteous rumours, such as wait . 660 *Prelude* 4. 129
That in the name of all inspirèd souls— . . . 668 *Prelude* 5. 201
The wandering beggars propagate his name, . . 670 *Prelude* 5. 305
And knowledge, rightly honoured with that name— 672 *Prelude* 5. 424
Poems withal of name, which at that time . . 674 *Prelude* 5. 549
A name it now deserves, this cowardice, . . . 675 *Prelude* 6. 31
Maintained even by the very name and thought . 676 *Prelude* 6. 58
And hath the name of, God. Transcendent peace 677 *Prelude* 6. 139
With amity and glee ; we bore a name . . . 681 *Prelude* 6. 402
Honoured in France, the name of Englishmen, . 681 *Prelude* 6. 403
Strangers, not knowing each the other's name. . 689 *Prelude* 7. 118
To mention by its name, as in degree, . . . 691 *Prelude* 7. 264
Ere the broad world rang with the maiden's name, 691 *Prelude* 7. 304
One, of whose name from childhood we had heard 694 *Prelude* 7. 495
A Father—for he bore that sacred name— . . 696 *Prelude* 7. 603
Born in a land whose very name appeared . . 712 *Prelude* 9. 189
Of whom I speak. So Beaupuy (let the name 715 *Prelude* 9. 419
Or to that rural castle, name now slipped . . 716 *Prelude* 9. 483
Assumed the body and venerable name . . . 718 *Prelude* 10. 40
A conflict of sensations without name, . . . 722 *Prelude* 10. 290
Nor could have been, without her blessèd name. . 723 *Prelude* 10. 380
Which then was going forward in her name ! . . 729 *Prelude* 11. 116
A Poet, made me seek beneath that name, . . 732 *Prelude* 11. 347
Nor can my tongue give utterance to a name . . 733 *Prelude* 11. 432
Then, near some other spring—which by the name 734 *Prelude* 11. 467
Some unknown hand had carved the murderer's name. . . . . 737 *Prelude* 12. 240
The name of Education, have to do . . . . 742 *Prelude* 13. 171
Known by whatever name, is falsely deemed . . 742 *Prelude* 13. 187
Is but another name for absolute power . . . 749 *Prelude* 14. 190
Poet, or destined for a humbler name ; . . . 750 *Prelude* 14. 292
The name of Calvert—it shall live, if words . 751 *Prelude* 14. 355
And the creation (by no lower name . . . . 755 *Recluse* 1. 1. 822
I cannot *tell* how she pronounced my name :— . 766 *Excursion* 1. 654
Fantastic pomp of structure without name, . . 784 *Excursion* 2. 859
And not less glad, for sake of her good name, . 785 *Excursion* 2. 889
By sounding titles, hath acquired the name . . 788 *Excursion* 3. 130
The substance classes by some barbarous name, . 789 *Excursion* 3. 184
Place worthier still of envy. May I name, . . 789 *Excursion* 3. 196
Which bears the name of action, howsoe'er . . 799 *Excursion* 3. 894
To the dishonour of his holy name. . . . . 801 *Excursion* 4. 27
And when the One, ineffable of name, ... 811 *Excursion* 4. 663
He only knows by name ; and, if he hear, . . 819 *Excursion* 4. 1226
And only then, be worthy of her name : . . . 820 *Excursion* 4. 1253
That shall survive his name and memory. . . . 823 *Excursion* 5. 48
" Philosophy ! and thou more vaunted name . . 827 *Excursion* 5. 331
Is virtue, or no better than a name, ... 829 *Excursion* 5. 472
The vanquished Whig, under a borrowed name, . 845 *Excursion* 6. 451
A century shall hear his name pronounced, . . 862 *Excursion* 7. 354
His name, and unambitiously relates . . . . 864 *Excursion* 7. 473
For in that female infant's name he heard . . 867 *Excursion* 7. 669
The silent name of his departed wife ; . . . . 867 *Excursion* 7. 670
Heart-stirring music ! hourly heard that name ; . 867 *Excursion* 7. 671
No higher name ; in whom our country showed, . 870 *Excursion* 7. 852
Faithless memorial ! and his family name . . 872 *Excursion* 7. 967
These, and the name and title at full length,— . 872 *Excursion* 7. 970
(Or call it comfort, by a humbler name,) . . . 878 *Excursion* 8. 263
The sceptre of his sway ; his country's name, . 880 *Excursion* 8. 429
It bears no sounding name, nor ever bore ; . . 887 *Excursion* 9. 184
" Once, while the Name, Jehovah, was a sound . 894 *Excursion* 9. 682
Of humbler name, whose souls do like the flood S.3. 427 **My Son* 11
Their common sire, thou only bear'st his name. . S.3. 433 **The doubt* 12
Do the name of Paphus bear, ... S.3. 437 **I, whose* 5
Through him the Antipodes in thy name delight. S.3. 442 **Vasco, whose* 14
Let thy name, Harmodius dear, ... S.3. 442 *Harmodius* 21
To that high spring which bears no human name, K.8. 225 **I will* 52

Nations—*continued.*
England ! all nations in this charge agree : 309 **England ! the* 9
With mighty Nations for his underlings, 309 **When, looking* 4
Of Nations wanting virtue to be strong 311 **Who rises* 43
Is won, and by all Nations shall be worn ! 312 *Clarkson* 10
And all the Nations labour to fulfil 329 *Ode 1815* 127
Pride of two nations, wood and lake and plains, 353 *Aquap.* 42
To enslave whole nations on their native soil ; 368 *Trajan* 59
Floating at ease while nations have effaced 452 *Ecc. Sonn.* 3. 47. 7
Nations, and Death has gathered to his fold 452 *Ecc. Sonn.* 3. 47. 8
Of Nations," sacrifice a People's health, 501 *Humanity* 90
And nations sink ; or, struggling to be free, 516 **As leaves* 12
To brood the nations o'er with Nile-like wings ; 617 *Desc.Sk.Quarto* 805
Among the nations, surely would my heart 680 *Prelude* 6. 337
As if awaked from sleep, the Nations hailed 686 *Prelude* 6. 757
Of vanished nations, or more clearly drawn 708 *Prelude* 8. 615
Reading of nations and their works, in faith, 712 *Prelude* 9. 171
Of nations and their passing interests, 712 *Prelude* 9. 202
How quickly mighty Nations have been formed, 715 *Prelude* 9. 376
And management of nations ; what it is 728 *Prelude* 11. 100
Among the fallen of nations, dost abide 732 *Prelude* 11. 376
Abroad on many nations, are no more 733 *Prelude* 11. 411
"The Wealth of Nations," *where* alone that wealth 741 *Prelude* 13. 78
Had never been when throes of mighty Nations 741 *Prelude* 13. 107
By nations sink together, we shall still 752 *Prelude* 14. 437
As makes the nations groan. This active course 761 *Excursion* 1. 381
—'Be joyful all ye nations ; in all lands, 796 *Excursion* 3. 728
Revered among the nations. I implored 798 *Excursion* 3. 863
The groaning nations ; when the impious rule, 805 *Excursion* 4. 298
And, to whole nations bound in servile straits, 870 *Excursion* 7. 825
Break from the maddened nations at the sight 873 *Excursion* 7. 1038
Show to the wretched nations for what end 890 *Excursion* 9. 414
Alas ! the nations, who of yore received 894 *Excursion* 9. 652
Unheard, the savage nations bowed the head 894 *Excursion* 9. 684

Native. Dear native regions, I foretell, 1 *Extract* 1
Sweetly ferocious, round his native walks, 5 *Ev. Wk.* 146
The native Genii walk the mountain green ? 16 *Desc. Sk.* 341
Beyond his native valley seldom stray, 18 *Desc. Sk.* 428
And as his native hills encircle ground 18 *Desc. Sk.* 449
Close by my mother in their native bowers : 28 *Guilt* 240
Green fields before us, and our native shore, 29 *Guilt* 282
Shall sun himself before his native doors ; 66 *Bord.* 1628
And in that dream had left my native land, 70 *Bord.* 1840
Left among her native mountains 93 *Westmoreland Girl* 27
Were brother-shepherds on their native hills. 96 *Brothers* 75
It touches on that piece of native rock 98 *Brothers* 199
His soul was knit to this his native soil. 100 *Brothers* 298
He towards his native country cast a longing look. 103 *Artegal* 89
And sorrow, have confirmed thy native right to reign. 105 *Artegal* 209
Who drag, beneath our native skies, 109 **Ere with* 7
Reached speedily the native threshold, bent 123 *V. and J.* 103
Never see my native land, nor castle towers, 140 *Arm. Lady* 53
Were native to the summer.—Up the brook 146 **It was an* 17
Some uncouth name upon the native rock, 147 *Joanna* 30
These matins mounting towards her native sphere. 154 *Morn. Ex.* 54
Lift men from their native stations, 163 *Hint* 23
Bear for me to my native land 164 **Fair Lady* 39
Shone meekly 'mid their native dust, 168 *Pilgrim's Dream* 63
To his own native greatness to desire 214 *Dion* 116
And, far beyond thy native East, 216 *Enterprise* 37
Affect my native habitations ; 226 *Vernal Ode* 27
Up from their native ground they rise 228 *Devot. Incit.* 5
To its sad Lord, far from his native fields ? 252 **Why, Minstrel* 14
That of its native self can nothing feed : 257 **The prayers* 4
That, in our native isle, and every land, 281 *Chris. Words.* 4
Was walking by her native lake : 289 *Stepping West.* 18
Here, on our native soil, we breathe once more. 306 **Here, on our* 1
Were England's native growth ; and throughout Spain 319 **Avaunt all* 10
Dear native regions where ye wont to rove, 325 *Ode 1814* 115
Doomed as we are our native dust 337 *Cath. Cantons* 1
But heath-bells from thy native ground, 345 **How blest* 71
Say rather, one in native fellowship 356 *Aquap.* 244
That bound it to its native earth—poised high 358 *Pine : Rome* 3
To enslave whole nations on their native soil ; 368 *Trajan* 59
That took thee from thy native hills ; 375 **The Minstrels* 20
I seek the birthplace of a native Stream.— 376 *Duddon* 1. 9
With native Fancy her fresh aid, 386 *Yarrow Rev.* 55
While native song the heroic Past recalls." 388 *Loch Etive* 8
From Oxford come to his native vale, 399 *White Doe* 265
To o'ershadow by no native right 413 *White Doe* 1601
Among her native wilds of Craven ; 414 *White Doe* 1618
His native superstitions melt away. 426 *Ecc. Sonn.* 1. 29. 8
With the inoffensive sword of native wit, 435 *Ecc. Sonn.* 2. 26. 13
Hangs o'er the Arabian Prophet's native Waste, 435 *Ecc. Sonn.* 2. 27. 11
Assumes the accents of our native tongue ; 435 *Ecc. Sonn.* 2. 29. 3
Whose fruit around the sun-burnt Native falls 444 *Ecc. Sonn.* 3. 17. 7
The encircling ground, in native turf arrayed, 450 *Ecc. Sonn.* 3. 41. 1
Beyond her native dell. 478 *Somnamb.* 18
The truth that Britain was his native land ; 504 *Warning* 54
Their native Land, for outrage provident ; 515 **Men of* 4
Frowns deepening visibly his native gloom, 521 *Epist. Beaumont* 6
Half hid in native trees. Alas 'tis not, 524 *Epist. Beaumont* 193
Blest is this Isle—our native Land ; 533 **Blest is* 1
Her Father's native land, 544 *Russ. Fug.* 246
To resume its native light. 549 *Hermit's Cell* 1. 28
And his pure native genius, lead him back 573 *Chiabrera* 2. 6
Round this dear Vale, his native place 578 **I come* 60

Native—*continued.*
Sleeps by his native shore. 579 **Sweet Flower* 7
"It grows upon its native bed 580 *John Words.* 53
Or through her truant pathway's native charms, 603 *Desc.Sk.Quarto* 49
Beyond his native valley hardly stray, 611 *Desc.Sk.Quarto* 515
The native dignity no forms debase, 611 *Desc.Sk.Quarto* 530
Forc'd from my native mountains bleak and bare ; 615 *Desc.Sk.Quarto* 714
Of native rock, left midway in the square 642 *Prelude* 2. 34
Her native instincts : let me dare to speak 650 *Prelude* 3. 99
That having 'mid my native hills given loose 655 *Prelude* 3. 424
Came and returned me to my native hills. 658 *Prelude* 3. 632
And now was travelling towards his native home. 664 *Prelude* 4. 425
Whether by native prose, or numerous verse, 668 *Prelude* 5. 200
In progress from their native continent 673 *Prelude* 5. 537
Of my own native region, and was blest 678 *Prelude* 6. 195
See trees, and meadows, and thy native stream, 679 *Prelude* 6. 272
Cast on the white cliffs of our native shore 680 *Prelude* 6. 343
His comforts, native occupations, cares, 700 *Prelude* 8. 106
Powers of my native region ! Ye that seize 702 *Prelude* 8. 218
To native man. A rambling schoolboy, thus 703 *Prelude* 8. 256
Dear native Regions, wheresoe'er shall close 706 *Prelude* 8. 468
'Tis true, the history of our native land, 708 *Prelude* 8. 617
Of eloquence even in my native speech, 720 *Prelude* 10. 150
Had caught the accents of my native speech 721 *Prelude* 10. 240
Upon our native country's sacred ground. 721 *Prelude* 10. 241
From the retirement of my native hills, 736 *Prelude* 12. 175
As native passion dictates. Others, too, 743 *Prelude* 13. 265
They from their native selves can send abroad 747 *Prelude* 14. 93
Old songs, the product of his native hills ; 757 *Excursion* 1. 67
Foreboding evil. From his native hills 761 *Excursion* 1. 340
But by the native vigour of his mind, 762 *Excursion* 1. 403
This office filling, yet by native power 774 *Excursion* 2. 178
And force of native inclination made 774 *Excursion* 2. 179
Upon earth's native energies ; forgetting 792 *Excursion* 3. 423
Those native plants, the holly and the yew, 793 *Excursion* 3. 527
Of native feeling, grateful to our minds ; 801 *Excursion* 4. 5
Drawn towards her native firmament of heaven, 807 *Excursion* 4. 396
The streams far distant of your native glen ; 809 *Excursion* 4. 551
At a safe distance from our native land, 814 *Excursion* 4. 895
Her native brightness. As the ample moon, 817 *Excursion* 4. 1062
Mysterious union with its native sea. 818 *Excursion* 4. 1140
Who does not love his native soil ?—he prized 824 *Excursion* 5. 116
Of native cordiality, our Friend 829 *Excursion* 5. 443
In early youth, among my native hills, 835 *Excursion* 5. 862
The Poet, fostering for his native land 839 *Excursion* 6. 42
Exchange the shepherd's frock of native grey 846 *Excursion* 6. 548
The native grandeur of the human soul— 848 *Excursion* 6. 666
Restored me to my native valley, here 860 *Excursion* 7. 198
Are brightened round her. In his native vale 868 *Excursion* 7. 722
The red-deer driven along its native heights 870 *Excursion* 7. 864
A native Briton to these inward chains, 878 *Excursion* 8. 298
Of her own native vigour ; thence can hear 884 *Excursion* 9. 40
That when we stand upon our native soil, 886 *Excursion* 9. 129
Within the bosom of his native vale. 888 *Excursion* 9. 280
Of numbers crowded on their native soil, 889 *Excursion* 9. 364
His native vale and patrimonial fields K.8. 231 **I will* 212
Of her own native element, the hand K.8. 246 *Recluse* 1. 1. 370

Nativity. Hope smiled when your nativity was cast, 474 **Hope smiled* 1

Natural. And taught that pain is pleasure's natural heir, 20 *Desc. Sk.* 537
And, to a natural sympathy resigned, 28 *Guilt* 196
Are natural ; and from no one can be learnt 38 *Bord.* 34
Your natural breathing has been troubled. Nay, 39 *Bord.* 105
By mingling natural matter of her own 44 *Bord.* 367
Which to our kind is natural as life, 48 *Bord.* 627
Even to the shedding of some natural tears 51 *Bord.* 762
With all their natural weight of sorrow and pain, 52 *Bord.* 821
Whose natural element was freedom—— Stop— 70 *Bord.* 1819
Were natural enough ; but that, I trust, 77 *Bord.* 2279
Bound each to each by natural piety. 79 **My heart* 9
And a few natural graves." To Jane, his wife, 95 *Brothers* 15
Whose natural affection doubts enslave, 104 *Artegal* 124
I was their natural guardian ; and 'tis just 104 *Artegal* 136
Its natural gifts for purposes of rest, 123 *V. and J.* 139
Of natural objects, led me on to feel 131 *Michael* 30
For the delight of a few natural hearts ; 131 *Michael* 36
First uttering, without words, a natural tune ; 136 *Michael* 347
As if it were a natural shield 143 **Driven in* 7
Or like some natural produce of the air, 146 **It was an* 29
A rude and natural causeway, interposed 148 **A narrow* 2
Along a natural opening, that I stood 150 **When, to* 50
As in a natural temple scattered o'er 185 *Yew-trees* 29
That I might step beyond my natural race 208 **It is no* 13
Where'er he turned, a natural grace 212 *Dion*
Mount Skiddaw ? In his natural sovereignty 251 **Pelion and* 11
Find in the heart of man no natural home : 263 **Those words* 11
These natural council-seats your acrid blood 268 **DogmaticTeachers* 6
For natural rights, a mockery and a shame ; 280 *Plea for Auth.* 4
Some natural sorrow, loss, or pain, 289 *Sol. Reap.* 23
One might believe that natural miseries 308 **One might* 1
Grant to the morn of life its natural blessedness ! 342 *Ital. Itin.* 96
Their natural utterance ? whence this strange release 349 *At Dover* 6
Into a natural port, a tideless sea, 356 *Aquap.* 220
That overpowered their natural green. 375 **The Minstrels* 6
If, *then*, some natural shadows spread 386 *Yarrow Rev.* 37
More than enough ; a fault so natural 394 **No more* 34
The Sons obey a natural lord ; 401 *White Doe* 463
Through force of natural piety ; 409 *White Doe* 1232
Is natural as dreams to feverish sleep. 420 *Ecc. Sonn.* 1. 9. 3

Natural—*continued.*
Death, darkness, danger, are our natural lot ; 423 Ecc. Sonn. 1. 18. 3
Upheave, so seems it, from her natural station 427 Ecc. Sonn. 1. 34.11
With natural smiles of greeting. Bells are dumb ; 427 Ecc. Sonn. 1. 36. 9
Its natural echo ; but hope comes reborn 448 Ecc. Sonn. 3. 31.12
A stir of mind too natural to deceive ; 448 Ecc. Sonn. 3. 33. 4
No natural bond between the boldest schemes 471 *Arran ! a 11
Not by black arts but magic natural ! 474 *Ye shadowy 12
Near the lark's nest, and in their natural hour 475 *There ! said 11
Who, with a natural instinct to discern 493 Hap. War. 8
For me, thy natural leader, once again 496 *A little 14
That quietly restores the natural mien 505 Warning 136
Of natural beauty and life's daily rounds, 522 Epist. Beaumont 53
A natural meal—days, months, from Nature's hand ; 528 *Those breathing 85
What every natural heart enjoys ? 533 *Blest is 54
The sweet and natural hopes that shall not die, 534 *When in 19
Of private life their natural pleasantness, 538 *In desultory 36
The natural heart is touched, and public way 540 Grace Darl. 2
Be his the natural silence of old age ! 569 Cumb. Beg. 182
Yearnings she hath in her own natural kind, 588 Immortality 78
Whence human kind, and brute ; what natural powers 625 Æneid 124
Of natural heroes : or I would record 635 Prelude 1. 202
Her natural sanctuaries, with a local soul 635 Prelude 1. 219
To every natural form, rock, fruit, or flower, 651 Prelude 3. 127
As natural beings in the strength of Nature. 652 Prelude 3. 193
And call of her own natural appetites, 669 Prelude 5. 254
And natural or supernatural fear, 670 Prelude 5. 307
To carry meaning to the natural heart ; 676 Prelude 6. 112
Of natural rights and civil ; and to acts 712 Prelude 9. 201
From the natural inlets of just sentiment, 714 Prelude 9. 350
That nothing hath a natural right to last 721 Prelude 10. 205
To me came rarely charged with natural gifts, 724 Prelude 10. 401
In vision, yet constrained by natural laws 724 Prelude 10. 438
Could through my understanding's natural growth 730 Prelude 11. 200
Of clouds—his glory's natural retinue— 732 Prelude 11. 367
Until that natural graciousness of mind 735 Prelude 12. 50
Among the natural abodes of men, 741 Prelude 13. 102
Dislodged the natural sleep that binds them up 763 Excursion 1. 489
From natural wisdom turn our hearts away ; 765 Excursion 1. 601
To natural comfort shut our eyes and ears ; 765 Excursion 1. 602
The unshackled layman's natural liberty ; 775 Excursion 2. 265
By natural piety ; nor a lofty mind, 790 Excursion 3. 266
Of natural passion, seemingly escaped, 796 Excursion 3. 737
No natural branch ; despondency far less ; 803 Excursion 4. 163
Of observations natural ; and, thus 812 Excursion 4. 708
His natural wings !—To friendship let him turn 817 Excursion 4. 1085
And natural reverence which the place inspired. 824 Excursion 5. 143
Are both a natural process ; and by me 827 Excursion 5. 314
By natural exhalation. With the dead 828 Excursion 5. 373
The natural roof of that dark house in which 831 Excursion 5. 589
The steadfast quiet natural to a mind 840 Excursion 6. 146
The natural crown that sage Experience wears. 842 Excursion 6. 281
Soothed by the natural spirit which they breathe. 847 Excursion 6. 633
A natural dignity on humblest rank ; 850 Excursion 6. 794
The natural feeling of equality 852 Excursion 6. 950
Beyond its natural elevation raised 864 Excursion 7. 445
Discoursed of natural or moral truth 865 Excursion 7. 512
Or dwell in chambers of some natural cave ; 879 Excursion 8. 366
A more than natural vividness of hue 881 Excursion 8. 472
Pursued her voyage, till a natural pier 892 Excursion 9. 567
Erelong, forsaking all her natural haunts, S.3. 436 *The doubt 186
But a glad function natural to man. K.8. 249 Recluse 1.1.470

Naturalise. To naturalise this tawny Lion brood ; 392 Daniel 4

Naturally. To higher things ; more naturally matured, 656 Prelude 3. 528

Nature. *See* **Human-nature.**
Calm is all nature as a resting wheel. 1 Early Youth 1
That clung to Nature with a truant's love, 11 Desc. Sk. 44
Through vacant worlds where Nature never gave 16 Desc. Sk. 307
Of angry Nature to avenge her God. 17 Desc. Sk. 402
Still, Nature, ever just, to him imparts 17 Desc. Sk. 403
Even so, by faithful Nature guarded, here 18 Desc. Sk. 441
All nature smiles, and owns beneath her eyes 21 Desc. Sk. 622
And led by nature into a wild scene 23 Yew-tree 14
When nature had subdued him to herself, 23 Yew-tree 38
Yet Nature, with excess of grief o'er-borne, 30 Guilt 309
There, pains which nature could no more support 31 Guilt 383
The bond of nature, all unkindness cease, 33 Guilt 508
Nature reviving, with a deep-drawn sigh 35 Guilt 572
Nature by sign or sound made no essay ; 35 Guilt 623
And look upon the pleasant face of Nature—— 40 Bord. 148
And learn what nature is from this poor Wretch ! 45 Bord. 444
I would so long have struggled with my Nature, 53 Bord. 872
Work on her nature, and so turn compassion 57 Bord. 1061
Shall Nature be avenged. 'Tis nobly thought ; 58 Bord. 1123
Of Nature, finished with most curious skill ! 60 Bord. 1276
Have roused all Nature up against him—pshaw !— 61 Bord. 1291
And shares the nature of infinity. 65 Bord. 1544
Of Nature, by a cunning usurpation 66 Bord. 1576
By man and nature ;—if a breeze had blown, 68 Bord. 1700
All nature curses me, and in my heart 76 Bord. 2205
By lowly nature reared, as if to make her 78 Bord. 2334
If Nature to her tongue could measured numbers bring, 87 Pet-lamb 19
Nature will either end thee quite ; 88 H. C. 21
Nor kept by Nature for herself, nor made by man his own, 91 Norman Boy 2
With wild Nature to run wild. 93 Westmoreland Girl 28
That, though he was not of a timid nature, 100 Brothers 335

Nature—*continued.*
But One there is, a Child of nature meek. 103 Artegal 45
Aught that my feeble nature could perform, 105 Artegal 179
Be pleased that nature made thee fit 112 *Yes ! thou 9
Which, in her own blest nature, rooted deep, 118 Maternal Grief 21
That Nature prompts them to display, their looks, 118 Maternal Grief 32
Of our weak nature rest not, must be deemed 119 Maternal Grief 76
By ready nature for a life of love, 122 V. and J. 32
To nature for a happy end of all ; 122 V. and J. 63
With ornaments—the prettiest, nature yields 124 V. and J. 200
Of Nature, by the gentle agency 131 Michael 29
By tendency of nature needs must fail. 133 Michael 150
Through a haze of human nature, 141 Arm. Lady 133
In which he swims as taught by nature, 142 †Lov. and Lik. 25
Once more, those creatures thus by nature paired, 143 *High bliss 23
The spot was made by Nature for herself ; 149 M. H. 15
Of nature and of love had made their home 150 *When, to 24
Undying recollections ; Nature there 151 *When, to 77
That their pure joy in nature may survive 152 *Forth from 25
Yet more hath Nature reconciled in thee ; 153 Morn. Ex. 38
Only by art in nature lost. 154 Flower Garden 30
The common life our nature breeds ; 158 *In youth 54
Of Nature, with that homely face, 158 *With little 6
Of thy meek nature ! 159 *With little 48
That is gentle by nature ? 162 *Art thou the 26
(So you fancied) is by nature 163 Hint 27
Moves all nature to gladness and mirth. 167 Stray Pleasures 30
But gentle Nature plays her part 170 Rural Ill. 31
Of the silent heart which Nature 171 Kitten 97
The Sailor, Man by nature gay, 177 Waggoner 2. 83
But Nature might not be gainsaid ; 182 Waggoner 4. 206
Then Nature said, "A lovelier flower 187 *Three years 2
Thus Nature spake—The work was done— 187 *Three years 37
When universal nature breathed 191 Seq. Beggars 15
(By nature transient) than this torpid life ; 192 Gipsies 22
The beauteous forms of nature wrought, 193 Ruth 134
Whose heart with so much nature played ? 194 Ruth 161
And Nature here were willing to decay. 202 Hart-leap 116
This Beast not unobserved by Nature fell ; 203 Hart-leap 163
But Nature, in due course of time, once more 203 Hart-leap 171
Wherever nature led : more like a man 206 Tintern 70
Who sought the thing he loved. For nature then 206 Tintern 72
To look on nature, not as in the hour 207 Tintern 89
In nature and the language of the sense 207 Tintern 108
Knowing that Nature never did betray 207 Tintern 122
A worshipper of Nature, hither came 207 Tintern 152
Dear Child of Nature, let them rail ! 218 Young Lady 1
In languor ; or by Nature, for repose 219 Haunted Tree 14
Nor less, by excellence of nature, fit 220 Triad 53
Of nature, and the lonely elements. 221 Triad 96
Nature, from thy genuine law ! 222 Triad 155
Her procreant vigils Nature keeps 227 Vernal Ode 57
Kind Nature keeps a heavenly door 228 Devot. Incit. 58
Divine monition Nature yields, 228 Devot. Incit. 71
O sovereign Nature ! I appeal to thee, 231 *The gentlest Poet 14
That blend the nature of the star 232 Jew. Fam. 19
But nature ne'er could find the way 239 P. B. 244
Did Nature lead him as before ; 239 P. B. 247
"Though Nature could not touch his heart 239 P. B. 286
Which solitary Nature feeds 239 P. B. 297
—Let good men feel the soul of nature, 245 P. B. 764
And Nature, through a world of death, 248 P. B. 1073
That Nature utters from her rural shrine. 254 Complete Angler 6
Thy nature is not therefore less divine : 258 *It is a 11
Little we see in Nature that is ours ; 259 *The world is 3
Of nature trusts the Mind that builds for aye ; 259 *A volant 6
And, oh ! when Nature sinks, as oft she may, 260 *High is 9
When solitary Nature condescends 262 *Mark the 13
Oft shall the lowly weak, till nature bring 265 *When haughty 3
Produced as lonely Nature or the strife 269 *If these 2
Forgets her nature, opening like a flower 274 Infant M. 2
By favouring Nature and a saintly Mind 274 *Such age 3
So kind is simple Nature, fairly tried ! 275 *Chatsworth ! thy 8
Thy Art be Nature ; the live current quaff, 277 *A Poet 5
Yet Nature seems to them a heavenly guide. 278 *Life with 2
The visual powers of Nature satisfy, 279 *All praise 12
If simple Nature trained by careful Art 281 Valedict. 12
Night after night ? True is it Nature hides 281 *What strong 4
Of nature ; and, if human hearts be dead, 283 Railway 12
That Nature takes, her counter-work pursuing. 283 *Here, where 4
Some barrier with which Nature, from the birth 284 Departure 17
And ask of Nature from what cause 286 Nith 39
Hath Nature strung your nerves to bear 286 Sons of Burns 13
He paid to Nature tuneful vows ; 287 Sons of Burns 32
All that the God of Nature hath conferred, 290 Kilchurn 18
On wrongs, which Nature scarcely seems to heed : 292 *Degenerate Douglas 11
O Nature—in thy changeful visions, 300 Bran 31
Till Nature cannot find her own, 301 Bran 124
Of cultivated nature ; 302 Yarrow V. 52
No grandeur now in nature or in book 307 *O Friend 8
Even rich men, brave by nature, taint the air 308 *These times 2
But the live scales of a portentous nature ; 311 *Who rises 18
Which his own nature hath enjoined ;—and why ? 311 *Who rises 54
Here, mighty Nature ! in this school sublime 314 *Not 'mid 9
And God and Nature say that it is just. 315 *The Land 4
Of pitying human nature ? Once again 318 *Ah ! where 5
To labour, and to prayer, to nature, and to heaven. 320 *O'erweening Statesmen 14
Ye slight not life—to God and Nature true ; 326 *Intrepid sons 5
All nature seems to hear me while I speak, 329 Ode : Thanks. 37

Near—*continued.*

Near—*continued.*

Near-approaching. Of near-approaching good that shall not fail :

Neared. Though danger, as the Wreck is neared, becomes . . . . .

Nearer.

Nearer—*continued.*
And when the Cripple nearer drew, 621 *Andrew Jones* 27
As near and nearer to the spot we drew, 649 *Prelude* 3. 13
In nature somewhat nearer to her own? 666 *Prelude* 5. 47
Or boldly seeking pleasure nearer heaven 735 *Prelude* 12. 36
Nearer ourselves. Such often might be gleaned 741 *Prelude* 13. 113
Is nearer now, much nearer; yet even then, 751 *Prelude* 14. 375
Were now come nearer to her: weeds defaced 769 *Excursion* 1. 834
Wisdom is ofttimes nearer when we stoop 789 *Excursion* 3. 231
On nearer view, a motley spectacle 799 *Excursion* 3. 897
Even were the object nearer to our sight, 855 *Excursion* 6. 1141
Far nearer, in the habit of her soul, 861 *Excursion* 7. 228
To have a nearer view of thee, in heaven. 894 *Excursion* 9. 646
Nearest. Their nearest kin with deadly purpose met) 106 *Artegal* 237
And to the nearest homesteads ran 412 *White Doe* 1509
From nearest kindred, Vernon her new name; 576 **By a* 2
So passed the time; yet to the nearest town 760 *Excursion* 1. 244
The nearest in affection or in blood; 780 *Excursion* 2. 572
Not even the nearest to me and most dear, K.8. 255 *Recluse* 1. 1. 688
Nearing. The echoed hoof nearing the distant shore, 9 *Ev. Wk.* 371
Nearly. How nearly joy and sorrow are allied! 395 *White Doe: Ded.* 24
Too nearly, or intent to reinforce 862 *Excursion* 7. 296
Nearness. Two glow-worms in such nearness that they shared, 143 **High bliss* 18
Neat. When market-morning came, the neat attire 28 *Guilt* 221
'Twas my Son's bird; and neat and trim 119 *Sailor's Mother* 26
To the neat mansion, where, his flock among, 444 *Ecc. Sonn.* 3. 18. 3
Yet is yon neat trim church a grateful speck 474 **How sad* 6
The floor was neither dry nor neat, the hearth 768 *Excursion* 1. 823
Neater. And to the door a neater pathway winds, 615 *Desc.Sk.Quarto* 727
Neatness. Its pride of neatness. Daisy-flowers and thrift 767 *Excursion* 1. 722
Necessary. A necessary maintenance insures, 751 *Prelude* 14. 366
Necessities. Till checked by some necessities severe. 251 *Appleth.* 8
Necessity. And law was from necessity received. 316 **Hail, Zaragoza* 14
Turns his necessity to glorious gain; 493 *Hap. War.* 14
The mild necessity of use compels 567 *Cumb. Beg.* 99
But nature is gracious, necessity kind, 570 *Farmer* 51
But its necessity in being old. 571 **There is a Flower* 16
Through sinful choice; or dread necessity 803 *Excursion* 4. 128
By strict necessity, along the path 820 *Excursion* 4. 1269
Whom a benign necessity compels 831 *Excursion* 5. 594
Necessity, the stationary host 843 *Excursion* 6. 325
Or the necessity that fixed him here; 859 *Excursion* 7. 147
In whom a premature necessity 878 *Excursion* 8. 287
Did, in the time of their necessity, 889 *Excursion* 9. 324
Necessity's. Cold from necessity's continual snow, 613 *Desc.Sk.Quarto* 605
Neck. With forward neck the closing gate to press— 3 *Ev. Wk.* 52
His neck, a varying arch, between his towering wings: 6 *Ev. Wk.* 219
Their frozen arms her neck no more can fold; 7 *Ev. Wk.* 272
Or the swan stirs the reeds, his neck and bill 7 *Ev. Wk.* 283
Shoots upward, darting his long neck before. 7 *Ev. Wk.* 286
With one bright bell a favourite heifer's neck; 19 *Desc. Sk.* 495
Round his wife's neck; the prize of victory laid 25 *Guilt* 61
Like one revived, upon his neck I wept; 29 *Guilt* 258
Fashions his neck into a goodly curve; 212 *Dion*
He stoops the Ass's neck to seize 242 *P. B.* 497
The little Ass his neck extends, 242 *P. B.* 564
And up about his neck he climbs; 249 *P. B.* 1112
Lies fixed for ages on his conscious neck; 278 *Wellington* 4
Of the beautiful countenance, twine round his neck; 340 *Fort Fuentes* 8
His Mother's neck entwine; 342 *Ital. Itin.* 34
"Ere I absolve thee, stoop! that on thy neck 428 *Ecc. Sonn.* 1. 38. 3
Yes, Lady, while about your neck is wound 480 *Cordelia* 10
In a white vest, white as her marble neck 508 *F. Stone* 13
His bridling neck between his tow'ring wings; 595 *Ev. Wk. Quarto* 202
Death, as she turns her neck the kiss to seek, 597 *Ev. Wk. Quarto* 287
As ever clung around a mother's neck, 692 *Prelude* 7. 340
With those that stretch the neck and strain the eyes, 697 *Prelude* 7. 696
Necks. *See* **Serpent-necks.**
From the submissive necks of guiltless men 252 **Why, Minstrel* 9
And their necks play, involved in rings, 374 *Eg. Maid* 322
At his approach, and low-bowed necks entreat 423 *Ecc. Sonn.* 1. 19. 11
From unsubmissive necks the bridle shook 515 **Men of* 5
At peace inverted your lithe necks ye lave, 596 *Ev. Wk. Quarto* 235
Your vassal necks how poor the garter's pride! L.1. 97 *Juvenal* 3. 91
Necromancer. Thus to the Necromancer spake 370 *Eg. Maid* 93
Need. Much need have ye that time more closely draw 33 *Guilt* 507
Hath need of rest; the sight of Hut or Hostel 41 *Bord.* 215
When these old limbs had need of rest,—and now 42 *Bord.* 298
And need repose. Could you but wait an hour? 43 *Bord.* 360
O Lady, you have need to love your Father. 50 *Bord.* 713
I know the need that all men have of mercy, 63 *Bord.* 1406
Yes, you are right, we need not hunt for motives: 63 *Bord.* 1435
As there are daggers here. What need of swearing! 64 *Bord.* 1461
I am your friend. What need of this assurance 64 *Bord.* 1478
We need an inward sting to goad us on. 70 *Bord.* 1859
At my worst need, my crimes have in a net 74 *Bord.* 2091
There will be need of preparation. Master! 74 *Bord.* 2110
Should the country need a heroine, 94 *Westmoreland Girl* 87
We have no need of names and epitaphs; 98 *Brothers* 178
Hast taken gifts which thou dost little need. 107 *Farewell* 40
Of its own bounty, or my need. 111 *A Complaint* 6
Hard labour in a time of need! 115 *Last of Flock* 42
There is no need of boot or spur, 126 *Idiot Boy* 47
There is no need of whip or wand; 126 *Idiot Boy* 48

Need—*continued.*
To any that might need it. 127 *Idiot Boy* 136
That these are things of which I need not speak. 136 *Michael* 360
His flock had need. 'Tis not forgotten yet 138 *Michael* 462
What need there is to be reserved in speech, 149 **A narrow* 72
Why need our Hero then (though frail 174 *Waggoner* 1. 61
Or what need of explanation, 181 *Waggoner* 4. 155
More ragged than need was! O'er pathless rocks, 185 *Nutting* 14
That had no need of a remoter charm, 206 *Tintern* 81
"These given, what more need I desire 238 *P. B.* 141
You need a strong and stormy gale 240 *P. B.* 373
Peter, you need not fear! 240 *P. B.* 390
And with like force, if need there be, 245 *P. B.* 778
What need of clamorous bells, or ribands gay, 256 *Marriage: Friend* 1
Or (if need be) impediment to spurn, 269 *Gordale* 13
Might need for comfort, or for festal mirth; 276 *Filial Piety* 3
What need of fields in some far clime 286 *Nith* 49
There will be need; 286 *Sons of Burns* 18
Remote from men, Thou dost not need 288 *Highland Girl* 29
Said generous Rob, "What need of books? 291 *Rob Roy* 21
A dog, too, had he; not for need, 295 *Highland Boy* 36
England hath need of thee: she is a fen 307 **Milton! thou* 2
And that we need no second victory! 329 *Ode 1815* 124
And that we need no second victory!— 331 *Ode: Thanks.* 182
By gross Utilities enslaved we need 358 *Aquap.* 348
Eternal things; and, if need be, defy 358 **Is this* 13
Farewell!—but go thy way, no need hast thou 363 **List—'twas* 105
What served they in her need? 374 *Eg. Maid* 368
Such wrong; nor need *we* blame the licensed joys, 382 *Duddon* 23. 12
To meet such need as might befall— 391 *HighlandBroach* 57
At need, he stood, advancing high 404 *White Doe* 751
Less would not at our need be due 405 *White Doe* 835
And yet want courage at their need: 406 *White Doe* 903
And said—'We need not stop, my Son! 410 *White Doe* 1257
Help did she give at need, and joined 416 *White Doe* 1862
Tended at need, the adopted Plant may thrive 445 *Ecc. Sonn.* 3. 21. 8
When wisdom stands in need of nature's grace; 456 **Soft as* 21
These modest walls, amid a flock that need, 465 **Pastor and* 2
What need, then, of these finished Strains? 472 *Ossian* 11
And, from invisible worlds at need laid bare, 475 **Here on their* 13
To serve thy need, in union with that Clyde 475 *Greenock* 12
"If there be one who need bemoan 487 *Fountain* 49
Yet seek thy firm support, according to their need. 492 *Duty* 24
Come when it will, is equal to the need: 493 *Hap. War.* 56
Or need, of counsel breathed through lips divine. 498 **Enough of climbing* 31
We need not toil from morn to night; 506 *Lab. Hymn* 10
Nor do they need, our hospitable care, 527 **Those breathing* 6
But gladly would escape; and, if need were, 528 **Those breathing* 66
Crowded with thoughts that need a settled home, 551 **Behold an* 2
What need is there against the truth to strive? 559 *Cuck.andNight.* 145
What need to seek a conquest over me, 563 *Troilus* 68
All trades, as need was, did old Adam assume,— 570 *Farmer* 49
He hath no need. He is by nature led 572 *Animal Tran.* 12
Another's need to suit, 582 **O for a* 27
From fear and grief, and from all need 623 *G. and S. Green* 27
May cling;—hard fate! which haply need not be 626 **Son of* 7
To a servile yoke. What need of many words? 633 *Prelude* 1. 105
Help at his need in Dalecarlia's mines: 635 *Prelude* 1. 213
Of him thou lovest; need I dread from thee 641 *Prelude* 1. 629
That in its broken windings we shall need 646 *Prelude* 2. 274
Ah! need I say, dear Friend! that to the brim 663 *Prelude* 4. 333
No more shall need such garments; and yet man, 666 *Prelude* 5. 24
And now and then, alike from need of theirs 669 *Prelude* 5. 253
A dreary mansion, large beyond all need, 684 *Prelude* 6. 645
I wanted not that joy, I did not need 686 *Prelude* 6. 773
Frugal as there was need, and, though self-willed, 688 *Prelude* 7. 64
Diversified the allurement. Need I fear 691 *Prelude* 7. 263
An ordinary sight; but I should need 738 *Prelude* 12. 254
I chiefly looked (what need to look beyond?) 741 *Prelude* 13. 101
They need not extraordinary calls 747 *Prelude* 14. 104
Emotions which best foresight need not fear, 748 *Prelude* 14. 122
Here, if need be, struggling with storms, and there 750 *Prelude* 14. 299
Yet much hath been omitted, as need was; 750 *Prelude* 14. 312
In holiest mood. Urania, I shall need 755 *Recluse* 1. 1. 778
He had small need of books; for many a tale 758 *Excursion* 1. 163
And, sometimes—to my shame I speak—have need 767 *Excursion* 1. 755
Ministering to our need. In genial mood, 782 *Excursion* 2. 688
Ye need her favours, ye shall find her not; 792 *Excursion* 3. 460
Or, for confession, in the sinner's need, 793 *Excursion* 3. 473
What special record can, or need, be given 795 *Excursion* 3. 607
And orient gems, which, for a day of need, 809 *Excursion* 4. 568
Of the world's interests—such a one hath need 810 *Excursion* 4. 582
Why need such man go desperately astray, 810 *Excursion* 4. 601
That laid their country waste. No need to speak 825 *Excursion* 5. 200
To be deposited, for future need, 825 *Excursion* 5. 223
To those who need the gift. But, after all, 831 *Excursion* 5. 586
The eye of roving plunderer—for their need 833 *Excursion* 5. 700
And recommending for their mutual need, 833 *Excursion* 5. 726
Need a bewildered traveller wish for more? 834 *Excursion* 5. 777
From each day's need, out of each day's least gain. 849 *Excursion* 6. 726
Their spring-time with one love, and that have need 851 *Excursion* 6. 876
An unrelaxing bond, a mutual need; 853 *Excursion* 6. 1017
Nor need the windings of his devious course 854 *Excursion* 6. 1087
Yet, when need was, with no reluctant will, 859 *Excursion* 7. 152
And milder worth: nor need we travel far 863 *Excursion* 7. 393
"Though born a younger brother, need was none 864 *Excursion* 7. 428
And functions dying and produced at need,— 872 *Excursion* 7. 1003
Save at worst need, from bold impetuous force, 873 *Excursion* 7. 1031
In due proportion to their country's need; 877 *Excursion* 8. 213
But for some favour, suited to our need? 885 *Excursion* 9. 84

Need—*continued.*
Declares his due, while he makes known his need. 889 *Excursion* 9. 320
Of urgent need.—Your Country must complete . 890 *Excursion* 9. 407
Defended, and appropriate to man's need. . . S.3. 433 **The doubt* 36
What need of more ? that we shall neither droop, K.8. 254 *Recluse* 1.1.634
Need only blush for what they once have been, . L.1. 96 *Juvenal* 3. 54

Needed. *See* **Much-needed.**
One upward hand, as if she needed rest . . . 278 **Lo ! where she* 2
The heavenly sanction needed to ensure . . . 360 *Albano* 10
Should that be needed for their sacred Charge ; . 432 *Ecc. Sonn.* 2. 13. 13
Alms may be needed) which that House bestowed ? 434 *Ecc. Sonn.* 2. 23. 12
More than is needed, but the precious Art . . 509 *F. Stone* 75
Which Horace needed for his spirit's health ; . 528 **Those breathing* 92
As needed kindness, for this single cause, . . . 568 *Cumb. Beg.* 152
Age might but take the things Youth needed not ! 571 **There is a Flower* 24
With warmth, as much as needed, from a sun . 633 *Prelude* 1. 66
For rest not needed or exchange of love, . . . 702 *Prelude* 8. 240
Guide faithful as is needed—I began . . . . 728 *Prelude* 11. 98
Unutterable love. Sound needed none, . . . 759 *Excursion* 1. 205
Of that which is no longer needed, see . . . . 892 *Excursion* 9. 557

Needest. For rain and mountain-storms ! the like thou need'st not fear, ... 87 *Pet-lamb* 31
"Here thou need'st not dread the raven in the sky ; 88 *Pet-lamb* 57
From body pains and pains of soul thou needest no release, ... 92 *Poet's Dream* 55

Needeth. "God for His service needeth not proud work of human skill ; . . . . . . 93 *Poet's Dream* 65

Needful. Bears not to those he loves their needful food. . . . . 25 *Guilt* 67
Nor moves her hands to any needful work : . . 44 *Bord.* 385
The game is up !— If it be needful, Sir, . . . 73 *Bord.* 2030
Things needful for the journey of her son. . . 135 *Michael* 287
As if all needful things would come unsought . 195 *Resolution* 38
Dawns on a kingdom, and for needful haste . . 233 *Power of Sound* 66
Why throw away a needful day . . . . . . 293 *Yarrow Unv.* 23
Needful when o'er wide realms the tempest breaks, 395 *White Doe: Ded.* 53
Needful amid life's ordinary woes ;— . . . . 395 *White Doe: Ded.* 54
A Cause, which on a needful day . . . . . 405 *White Doe* 860
Or needful sunshine ; prosperous enterprise, . . 424 *Ecc. Sonn.* 1. 24. 6
Was needful round men thirsting to transgress ;— 436 *Ecc. Sonn.* 2. 30. 8
Two aspects bears Truth needful for salvation ; . 447 *Ecc. Sonn.* 3. 29. 9
For needful listening, pledge is here, ... 503 **Like a* 67
A needful journey, under favouring skies, . . . 522 *Epist. Beaumont* 97
And circumspection needful to preserve . . . 568 *Cumb. Beg.* 129
Perhaps some needful service of the State . . . 573 *Chiabrera* 2. 1
And needful to build up a Poet's praise. . . . 634 *Prelude* 1. 157
And that a needful part, in making up . . . 637 *Prelude* 1. 348
Not doing in their stead the needful work. . . 653 *Prelude* 3. 328
That lies before us, needful to be told. . . . 688 *Prelude* 7. 51
Whene'er it comes ! needful in work so long, . . 710 *Prelude* 9. 20
Thrice needful to the argument which now . . 710 *Prelude* 9. 21
With needful knowledge, had abruptly passed . 711 *Prelude* 9. 93
To give her needful help. That very time . . 769 *Excursion* 1. 862
With the few needful things that life requires. . 777 *Excursion* 2. 357
And prudent caution needful to avert . . . . 889 *Excursion* 9. 356
The courage that was needful to leap back . . K.8. 229 **I will* 155

Needing. To greet the traveller needing food and rest ; 21 *Desc. Sk.* 610
Bent as he moves, and needing frequent rest ; . 761 *Excursion* 1. 325

Needle. While needle peaks of granite shooting bare 19 *Desc. Sk.* 468
Even her *own* needle that subdued . . . . 163 *Needlecase* 9
Where needle peaks of granite shooting bare . . 612 *Desc.Sk.Quarto* 558

Needle-case. As a humble Needle-case ; . . . S.3. 437 **I, whose* 20

Needles. Needles for strings in apt gradation ! . . 163 *Needlecase* 6

Needless. 'Tis needless ; spare your violence. His Daughter—— . . . . 74 *Bord.* 2093
Thy sting was needless then, perchance unknown, 227 *Vernal Ode* 125
Excuse is needless when with love sincere . . . 255 *S. H.* 1
As renders needless spells and magic wands, . . 338 *Engelberg* 4
Than toil in needless sleep from dream to dream : 376 *Duddon* 1. 12
Needless renewal of an old delight ? . . . . 392 *Bothwell* 8
Whence idle fears, and needless pain, ... 408 *White Doe* 1121
Then, moved by needless fear of past abuse, . . 520 *Pun. Death* 13. 11
With needless services, from hardship free. . . 762 *Excursion* 1. 385
The attempt was made ;—'tis needless to report . 841 *Excursion* 6. 176

Needlework. And needlework and flowers. . . . . 478 *Somnamb.* 54
Of needle-work ; no bustle at the fire, ... 878 *Excursion* 8. 272

Needs. As you must needs have deeply felt, it is . 48 *Bord.* 615
Must needs step in, and save my life. The look . 54 *Bord.* 919
The feeble and the strong. She needs not here . 57 *Bord.* 1090
I know him well ; there needs no other motive . 63 *Bord.* 1430
For both our needs ; must I, and in thy presence, 75 *Bord.* 2147
A tiny tenement, forsooth, and frail, as needs must be 91 *Norman Boy* 15
"These Tourists, heaven preserve us ! needs must live . . . . 95 *Brothers* 1
'Tis one of those who needs must leave the path . 96 *Brothers* 105
Should come, 'twould needs be a glad day for him ; 100 *Brothers* 326
Imagination needs must stir ; . . . . 112 **Yes ! thou* 5
And one domestic for their common needs, . . 125 *V. and J.* 275
The Shepherd, if he loved himself, must needs . 133 *Michael* 141
By tendency of nature needs must fail. . . . 133 *Michael* 150
He needs not fear the season's rage, ... 144 **Driven in* 67
He needs but look about, and there . . . . 158 **In youth* 38
A wisdom fitted to the needs . . . . . . 158 **In youth* 55
Since we needs must first have met . . . . 160 **Pansies, lilies* 19
Thou must needs, I think, have had, ... 161 **Pleasures newly* 6
And seldom needs a laboured roof ; . . . . 168 *Wren's Nest* 6
No farther than her story needs ; . . . . . 180 *Waggoner* 4. 8
If, as needs he must forbode, ... 181 *Waggoner* 4. 128
Or, if such faith must needs deceive— . . . . 191 *Seq. Beggars* 31
And stately needs must have their share . . . 193 *Ruth* 143

Needs—*continued.*
Sore aches she needs must have ! but less . . 194 *Ruth* 232
Knit every thought the impending issue needs, . 233 *Power of Sound* 95
Pleased if some Souls (for such there needs must be) 250 **Nuns fret* 12
The Mother *then* mourns, as she needs must mourn ; 318 **In due* 12
Our slack devotion needs them all ; . . . . 341 *San Salv.* 15
Must needs be fatal to our cause. . . . . . 408 *White Doe* 1138
Dear be the Church that, watching o'er the needs 445 *Ecc. Sonn.* 3. 20. 1
And attention full ten times as much as there needs; 482 *Character* 10
Must needs be conversant with upward looks, . 508 *F. Stone* 34
Locked in a dungeon needs must eat the heart . 519 *Pun. Death* 11. 2
Must needs impress a transitory thought . . 568 *Cumb. Beg.* 124
Nor needs a warning voice to tame the pride . . 642 *Prelude* 2. 20
Are not so pure by nature that they needs . . 656 *Prelude* 3. 481
Even at that early time, needs must I trust . . 679 *Prelude* 6. 309
Must, in such Temple, needs have offered up . . 686 *Prelude* 6. 741
Must needs bring back the moment when we first, 691 *Prelude* 7. 303
Intent on little but substantial needs, ... 701 *Prelude* 8. 162
Of past and present, such a place must needs . 708 *Prelude* 8. 598
Must needs have given—to the inexperienced mind, 728 *Prelude* 11. 96
By a bequest sufficient for my needs . . . . 751 *Prelude* 14. 359
Have been laid open, needs must make me feel . 752 *Prelude* 14. 422
A Wife and Widow. Needs must it have been . 769 *Excursion* 1. 874
As ye must needs be here ? in such a place . . 780 *Excursion* 2. 609
All that Abstraction furnished for my needs . . 797 *Excursion* 3. 796
I deem not arduous ; but must needs confess . . 803 *Excursion* 4. 135
All weakness fathoms, can supply all needs : . . 817 *Excursion* 4. 1092
No vengeance, and no hatred—needs must feel . 819 *Excursion* 4. 1212
Her dreary pillow, waited on her needs ; . . . 849 *Excursion* 6. 750
To which her frowardness must needs submit. . 862 *Excursion* 7. 322
The will, the instincts, and appointed needs . . 889 *Excursion* 9. 376
This spot to me must needs be dear, ... K.8. 220 **The snow-tracks* 31
Or single. And although it needs must seem . . K.8. 225 **I will* 40
Must needs themselves be hallowed, they require K.8. 244 *Recluse* 1.1.278

Needy. No board inscribed the needy to allure . . 24 *Guilt* 13
Neither checked by the rich nor the needy they roam ; . . . . 572 *Avarice* 41

Ne'er. (*Partial list.*) *See* **Never.**
Be better fed. Ne'er may I own the heart . . 38 *Bord.* 67
I ne'er had heart to separate—my grave, . . . 40 *Bord.* 143

Neglect. All but neglect. The world, for so it thought, ... 23 *Yew-tree* 20
We soon shall meet again. If thou neglect . . 42 *Bord.* 303
Neglect me ! no, I suffered long . . . . . 117 *Affl. Marg.* 29
Want, through neglect of hoar Antiquity. . . 253 **Aerial Rock* 12
Of cold neglect she leaves thy head ungraced, . 254 *Dyer* 9
In no confusion or neglect . . . . 413 *White Doe* 1526
Hear, then, and neglect me not ! . . . . . 535 *Egremont* 21
To vacant musing, unreproved neglect . . . 636 *Prelude* 1. 253
From man, neglect the universal heart. . . . 743 *Prelude* 13. 220
Of sudden overthrow ; and cold neglect . . . 873 *Excursion* 7. 1039
Have not been starved by absolute neglect ; . . 885 *Excursion* 9. 97

Neglected. "There were we long neglected, and we bore . . . . 29 *Guilt* 280
In the blank earth, neglected and forlorn, . . . 383 *Duddon* 29. 10
Shun not this Rite, neglected, yea abhorred, . . 447 *Ecc. Sonn.* 3. 29. 1
For all that seem neglected or bereft ; . . . 530 *Poor Robin* 34
Scorned, or neglected, fear not such a dearth. . 531 *Octogen.* 8
Neglected and ungratefully thrown by . . . 640 *Prelude* 1. 518
Nor is my aim neglected if I tell . . . . 643 *Prelude* 2. 94
Had been neglected ; left a register . . . 646 *Prelude* 2. 292
And lay till now neglected in the grass. . . 665 *Prelude* 4. 430
Which the neglected veteran had dropped, . . 783 *Excursion* 2. 796
How that neglected Pensioner was sent . . . 821 *Excursion* 4. 1313
With the neglected house to which she clung. . 854 *Excursion* 6. 1061
Meek and neglected thing, of no renown ! . . . K.8. 250 *Recluse* 1.1.513

Neglecting. Neglecting in imperial state . . . . 413 *White Doe* 1591

Neglects. His book he prizes, nor neglects his sword ; 18 *Desc. Sk.* 446
Altars that piety neglects ; . . . . 366 **Ye Trees* 2

Negligence. Bespake a sleepy hand of negligence ; 768 *Excursion* 1. 822

Negligent. Not negligent the style ;—the matter ?—good . . . . 254 *Detraction* 2
This parting glance, no negligent adieu ! . . . 377 *Duddon* 4. 2
Are strict observers ; and not negligent . . . 568 *Cumb. Beg.* 138
This generous Youth, too negligent of self, . . 870 *Excursion* 7. 867

Negress. Queen and negress chaste and fair ! . . L.2. 190 **Queen and* 1
Negress excellently bright ! . . . . L.2. 190 **Queen and* 12

Negro. A white-robed Negro, like a lady gay, . . 305 **We had* 3
And Negro Ladies in white muslin gowns. . . 690 *Prelude* 7. 228
The silver-collared Negro with his timbrel, . . 697 *Prelude* 7. 703
Upon the traffickers in Negro blood ; . . . . 721 *Prelude* 10. 249
Negro princess, ebon bright ! . . . . . . L.2. 190 **Queen and* 6

Neighbour. For her good neighbour Susan Gale, . 126 *Idiot Boy* 18
Their ancient neighbour, the old steeple-tower, . 147 *Joanna* 20
His neighbour thus addressed :— . . . . . 156 *Oak and Broom* 20
Each leaf, that and this, his neighbour will kiss ; . 167 *Stray Pleasures* 34
Some willing neighbour must be found. . . . 248 *P. B.* 1060
Arrived a neighbour with his horse ; . . . . 249 *P. B.* 1122
Its neighbour and its namesake—town, and flood 352 *Aquap.* 14
To my life's neighbour dues of neighbourhood ; . 476 *Eden* 10
While, day by day, grim neighbour ! huge Black Comb . . . . 521 *Epist. Beaumont* 5
My neighbour, when with punctual care, each week, 568 *Cumb. Beg.* 155
I was thy neighbour once, thou rugged Pile ! . . 578 *Peele Castle* 1
Her pealing organ was my neighbour too ; . . 650 *Prelude* 3. 57
—The face of every neighbour whom I met . . 659 *Prelude* 4. 67
An hourly neighbour. Paradise, and groves . . 755 *Recluse* 1. 1. 800
Lies guarded by its neighbour ; the small heap . 850 *Excursion* 6. 790

Neighbourhood. My husband lurked about the neighbourhood ; . . . . 35 *Guilt* 605

Night—*continued.*
Worse than the product of that dismal night, . 439 Ecc. Sonn. 2. 42. 12
Last night, without a voice, that Vision spake 440 Ecc. Sonn. 3. 2. 1
Apart—like glow-worms on a summer night ; . 441 Ecc. Sonn. 3. 5. 10
Shine on, until ye fade with coming Night !— 451 Ecc. Sonn. 3. 44. 8
At the approach of all-involving night. . . . 452 Ecc. Sonn. 3. 46. 14
And lays as prompt would hail the dawn of Night : 455 Rydal Mere 21
May the night never come, nor day be seen, . . 456 *The leaves 24
On such a night of June . . . . 457 *The sun has 12
On such a night as this is ! . . . . 457 *The sun has 15
And night approaches with her shades. . . . 458 *Had this 80
Who lov'st with Night and Silence to partake, . 459 *Wanderer ! that 3
Abates the perils of a stormy night ; . . . . 459 *Wanderer ! that 16
Empress of Night ! are gladdened by thy beams : 459 *Wanderer ! that 24
To cheer the long dark hours of vacant night— . 460 *Wanderer ! that 69
Glory of night, conspicuous yet serene, . . . 460 *Queen of 10
Eclipsing or eclipsed, by night or day, ... 461 *Queen of 52
Hope of the dawn and solace of the night, . . 467 St. Bees 83
Concord with oaths ? What differ night and day 475 *Here on their 6
While she dispels the cumbrous shades of Night ; 477 Long Meg 9
Day sickens round her, and the night . . . . 479 Somnamb. 80
By whom on this still night descried ? . . . . 479 Somnamb. 97
Mingling with night, such twilight to compose . 498 *Enough of climbing 27
Like those good Angels whom a dream of night . 500 Humanity 33
We need not toil from morn to night ; . . . . 506 Lab. Hymn 10
And were the Sister-power that shines by night . 511 *So fair 13
They heard, and, starting up, the Brood of Night 513 *Said Secrecy 10
They wore away the night in starless gloom ; . . 528 *Those breathing 55
Lark of the dawn, and Philomel of night, . . . 528 *Those breathing 82
How beautiful the Queen of Night, on high . . 532 *How beautiful the 1
Through unremitting vigils of the night, . . . 534 *When in 7
Night or day, at even or morn ; . . . . . 535 Egremont 66
At night, at morning, and at noon, ... 536 Goody Blake 13
And then her three hours' work at night, . . . 536 Goody Blake 26
The winds at night had made a rout ; . . . . 536 Goody Blake 50
And there, at night, in frost and snow, . . . 537 Goody Blake 71
A-bed or up, by night or day ; . . . . . . 537 Goody Blake 125
All night the storm had raged, nor ceased, nor paused, ... 540 Grace Darl. 28
Stepped One at dead of night, ... 542 Russ. Fug. 10
Erst a religious House, which day and night . . 547 *Beneath yon 5
" Now this poor Widow waiteth all that night . 554 Prioress 135
And it was then the third night of the May. . . 557 Cuck. and Night. 55
Where they had rested them all night ; and they, 558 Cuck. and Night. 68
Luna by night, with heavenly influence . . . 562 Cuck.andNight.313
O Palace whilom day that now art night, . . . 563 Troilus 26
That ever dark in torment, night by night, . . 564 Troilus 122
For which upon the tenth night if thou fail . . 564 Troilus 124
And every night, as was his wont to do, . . . 564 Troilus 129
The day is more, and longer every night . . . 564 Troilus 141
Till fully passed and gone was the ninth night ; . 565 Troilus 163
By night or day, blow foul or fair, ... 577 *I come 12
And through the stormy night they steer ; . . 579 *Sweet Flower 39
But one dear remnant of the night— . . . . 579 *Sweet Flower 48
Oh ! could he on that woeful night . . . . 580 John Words. 6
By night or day, ... 587 Immortality 8
Waters on a starry night . . . . 587 Immortality 14
The sun at morning, and the stars of night, . . 592 Ev. Wk. Quarto 24
Blends with the solemn colouring of the night ; . 598 Ev. Wk. Quarto 330
Where Silence, on her night of wing, o'er-broods . 602 Desc. Sk. Quarto 9
—Heavy, and dull, and cloudy is the night, . . 606 Desc.Sk.Quarto 215
All night the door at every moment ope ; . . . 609 Desc.Sk.Quarto 409
Last night, while by his dying fire, as clos'd . . 613 Desc.Sk.Quarto 596
That dallies with the Sun the summer night. . . 614 Desc.Sk.Quarto 691
The voice of Ruin, day and night, resounds. . . 614 Desc.Sk.Quarto 693
While, as Night bids the startling uproar die, . . 616 Desc.Sk.Quarto 754
And fled indignant to the shades of night ; . . 618 School Ex. 30
Moves through the vault of heaven, and dissipates the night ; . . . . 618 School Ex. 40
The shades of night no more the soul involve, . 618 School Ex. 47
That only wait the darkness of the night . . . 620 *She wept 13
When his fetters at night have so press'd on his limbs, ... 621 Convict 33
'Tis like the solemn shelter of the night. . . . 622 Recluse 1. 1. 113
While riding near her home one stormy night . 622 *Among all 5
To bear it with me through the stormy night : . 622 *Among all 10
At night the Glow-worm shone beneath the Tree : 623 *Among all 18
By night, upon these stormy fells, ... 623 G. and S. Green 5
After that living night— . . . . 623 G. and S. Green 30
The calm of night is powerless to remove . . . 624 Æneid 9
Depends, and torches overcome the night ; . . . 625 Æneid 102
—But, lengthening out the night with converse new, 625 Æneid 132
Old Camus, too, on that prophetic night . . . 629 Installation 63
Or sighed for thy sweet presence some dark night, 630 [?] *O Moon 3
Each night, while I recline within this cell, . . 630 [?] *O Moon 14
To night, unbroken cheerfulness serene. . . . 633 Prelude 1. 113
Among the smooth green turf. Through half the night, ... 636 Prelude 1. 312
In these night wanderings, that a strong desire . 637 Prelude 1. 318
Mine was it in the fields both day and night, . . 638 Prelude 1. 423
If the night blackened with a coming storm, . . 646 Prelude 2. 307
And what the summer shade, what day and night, 647 Prelude 2. 354
Who never let the quarters, night or day, . . . 650 Prelude 3. 54
No longer haunting the dark winter night. . . 653 Prelude 3. 308
The night in dancing, gaiety, and mirth, . . . 663 Prelude 4. 312
When, for the night deserted, it assumes . . . 664 Prelude 4. 368
Were making night do penance for a day . . . 664 Prelude 4. 377
Was never seen before by night or day. . . . 664 Prelude 4. 394
The tales that charm away the wakeful night . 673 Prelude 5. 496
Did I by night frequent the College groves . . 676 Prelude 6. 67

Night—*continued.*
That night our lodging was a house that stood . 684 Prelude 6. 641
A character more stern. The second night, . . 685 Prelude 6. 691
We sate and sate, wondering as if the night . . 685 Prelude 6. 708
These were our food ; and such a summer's night 686 Prelude 6. 723
With an unmeasured welcome. Through the night, 693 Prelude 7. 433
With ominous change, which, night by night, provoked . . . . 695 Prelude 7. 535
That comes with night ; the deep solemnity . . 697 Prelude 7. 655
One night, or haply more than one, through pain 705 Prelude 8. 387
Of one so unimportant ; night by night . . . 711 Prelude 9. 113
And half upbraids their silence. But that night . 719 Prelude 10. 63
Appeared unfit for the repose of night, . . . 719 Prelude 10. 92
Nor day nor night, evening or morn, was free . 724 Prelude 10. 419
From out the bosom of the night, come ye : . . 726 Prelude 10. 581
By day, a quiet sound in silent night ; . . . . 734 Prelude 12. 20
It was a close, warm, breezeless summer night, . 746 Prelude 14. 11
In that wild place and at the dead of night, . . 746 Prelude 14. 26
That vision, given to spirits of the night . . . 747 Prelude 14. 64
At such unthought-of meeting.—For the night 757 Excursion 1. 48
For his dismissal, day and night, compelled . . 774 Excursion 2. 203
All night the storm endured : and, soon as help . 784 Excursion 2. 805
Night is than day more acceptable ; sleep . . 790 Excursion 3. 277
Night hushed as night, and day serene as day ! ' . 791 Excursion 3. 324
Did, in the placid clearness of the night, . . . 798 Excursion 3. 859
From day to night, from night to day, prolonged ! ' " 809 Excursion 4. 539
Wherever fancy leads ; by day, by night, . . . 809 Excursion 4. 554
By day, and all the pomp which night reveals ; . 816 Excursion 4. 973
Of death and night, has caught at every turn 818 Excursion 4. 1125
Of far-off torrents charming the still night, . . 821 Excursion 4. 1322
In peace, from morn to night, from year to year. 825 Excursion 5. 217
And night succeeded with unusual gloom, . . . 833 Excursion 5. 737
Till night lies black upon the ground. ' But come, 834 Excursion 5. 766
With nothing better, in the chill night air, . . 846 Excursion 6. 537
To the Twelfth Night, beneath the frosty stars 851 Excursion 6. 837
Until dark night dismissed her to her bed ! . . 852 Excursion 6. 903
Amid a perilous waste that all night long . . 852 Excursion 6. 912
No quiet in the darkness of the night, ... 855 Excursion 6. 1101
Of night is falling round my steps, then most . 856 Excursion 6. 1174
In utter night ; and of his course remain . . . 862 Excursion 7. 357
Which all acknowledged. The dark winter night, 864 Excursion 7. 448
Seized him, that self-same night ; and through the space . . . . 870 Excursion 7. 871
As that of war, which rests not night or day, . . 875 Excursion 8. 94
Their vigils kept ; where tapers day and night 877 Excursion 8. 188
The journey of another night, ... K.8. 220 *The snow-tracks 39
By night, here only ; or in chosen minds . . . K.8. 240 Recluse 1. 1. 140
A human voice—a Spirit of coming night, . . K.8. 245 Recluse 1. 1. 326
Thou that mak's't [? mak'st] a day of night . . L. 2. 190 *Queen and 17
As little as the unblemish'd Queen of Night, . . [?] *A sad 13

Night-bird. Nor night-bird chambered in the rocks, 243 P: B: 619
The clouds, or night-bird sang from shady bough ; 270 *Shame on 5

Night-calm. Heard by the night-calm of the wat'ry plains. . . . . 599 Ev. Wk. Quarto 378
When Contemplation, like the night-calm felt . 665 Prelude 5. 1
That ever in the night-calm, when the Sheep . . S.3. 427 *Through Cumbrian 12

Night-cap. And one hand rubs his old night-cap. . 128 Idiot Boy 251

Night-duck. No night-duck clamours for his wilder'd mate, ... 598 Ev. Wk. Quarto 357

Nightfall. Ere nightfall—truth that well may claim a sigh, ... 448 Ecc. Sonn. 3. 31. 11
Made all the mountains ring. But, ere nightfall, . 644 Prelude 2. 164

Night-fire. It is no night-fire of the naked hills, 833 Excursion 5. 748

Nightingale. As if nor dove nor nightingale . . 168 Turtledove 15
O Nightingale ! thou surely art . . . . . 186 *O Nightingale 1
Leave to the nightingale her shady wood ; . . . 209 *Ethereal minstrel 7
Groves that inspire the Nightingale to trill . . 271 *Fame tells 2
Or, like the nightingale, her joyous vein . . 279 *'Tis he 5
No Nightingale did ever chaunt . . . . . 289 Sol. Reap. 9
Oft have I heard the Nightingale and Thrush 361 *List—'twas 22
O Nightingale ! Who ever heard thy song . . 455 Rydal Mere 13
Fairer than Tempe ! Yet, sweet Nightingale ! . 455 Rydal Mere 32
A very nightingale. . . . . 486 *We walked 36
That it was good to hear the Nightingale, . . . 557 Cuck. and Night. 49
If I perchance a Nightingale might hear, . . . 557 Cuck. and Night. 53
I heard the lusty Nightingale so sing, ... 558 Cuck. and Night. 98
Ah ! good sweet Nightingale ! for my heart's cheer, 558 Cuck.andNight.101
The Nightingale thus in my hearing spake :— . 558 Cuck.andNight.111
But, Nightingale, so may they not of thee ; . . 559 Cuck.andNight.122
Good Nightingale ! thou speakest wondrous fair, 559 Cuck.andNight.166
And, therefore, Nightingale ! do thou keep nigh, . 560 Cuck.andNight.181
Thou Nightingale ! the Cuckoo said, be still, . . 560 Cuck.andNight.196
Then of the Nightingale did I take note, . . . 560 Cuck.andNight.206
Then straightway came the Nightingale to me, . 561 Cuck.andNight.226
Thus takes the Nightingale her leave of me ; . . 561 Cuck.andNight.256
Forth then she flew, the gentle Nightingale, . . 561 Cuck.andNight.261
Here,—if the solemn nightingale be mute, . . 818 Excursion 4. 1167

Nightingale's. Regretted like the nightingale's last note, ... 782 Excursion 2. 726

Nightingales. And nightingales desert the village grove, ... 21 Desc. Sk. 615

Nightly. And ear still busy on its nightly watch, . 32 Guilt 421
There be who pray nightly before the Altar. . . 67 Bord. 1655
Thence offer nightly sacrifice) . . . . . . 214 Kirkstone 16
Nightly, on human kind . . . . 226 Vernal Ode 46
And nightly tosses on a bed of pain ; . . . . 229 Cuckoo-clock 24
They leave, and speed on nightly embassy . 229 Cuckoo-clock 41
Seen the SEVEN WHISTLERS in their nightly rounds, 267 *Though narrow 10
And let me believe that when nightly the Muse . 364 Vallomb. 21

Nightly—*continued.*
That, calmly couching while the nightly dew . . 380 *Duddon* 17. 8
Till nightly lamentations, like the sweep . . 383 *Duddon* 27. 6
On her last thorn the nightly moon has shone ; . 393 *Inglewood* 4
Come secrets, whispered nightly to his ear ; . . 441 *Ecc. Sonn.* 3. 4. 11
The unremitting voice of nightly streams . . 501 **The unremitting* 1
Hence whole day wanderings, broken nightly sleeps 523 *Epist. Beaumont* 137
Induced by sleeping nightly on the ground . . 705 *Prelude* 8. 439
Was sapped ; and while she slept, the nightly damps 770 *Excursion* 1. 907
That Belus, nightly to his splendid couch . . . 811 *Excursion* 4. 686
The nightly hunter, lifting a bright eye . . . 814 *Excursion* 4. 861
Nightmare. But soft !—how came he forth ? The Nightmare Conscience . . . . . . 53 *Bord.* 866
Night's. Roaring with storms beneath night's starless gloom ; . . . . 26 *Guilt* 139
Of last night's snow, beneath a sky threatening the fall of more, ... 91 *Norman Boy* 10
Or the night's darkness, or its cheerful face . . 172 *Infant Daughter* 23
And one night's diminution of her power, . . . 192 *Gipsies* 18
Profound of night's ethereal blue ; . . . . . 226 *Vernal Ode* 31
Prelude of night's approach with soothing dreams. 453 **The Sun, that* 4
Thinly by a one night's frost ; . . . . 490 *Incident : Dog* 18
The pie, and chattering breaks the night's repose. 606 *Desc.Sk.Quarto* 230
Do thou, but for a single night's brief space, . . 624 *Æneid* 36
The last night's genial feeling overflowed . . . 687 *Prelude* 7. 43
More keenly than elsewhere in night's blue vault, 782 *Excursion* 2. 721
At night's approach bring down the unclouded sky, 818 *Excursion* 4. 1159
Nights. On cold blue nights, in hut or straw-built shed, ... 7 *Ev. Wk.* 257
A stone than what I am.—But two nights gone, . 45 *Bord.* 422
Drove by the place of my retreat : three nights . 69 *Bord.* 1772
Three sleepless nights I passed in sounding on, . 69 *Bord.* 1774
The wolf keeps festival these stormy nights : . . 71 *Bord.* 1887
As is heard often after stormy nights. . . . . 73 *Bord.* 2020
Thy mornings showed, thy nights concealed, . . 109 **I travelled* 13
The days are cold, the nights are long, . . . 117 †*Cottager* 1
By Michael's side, she through the last two nights 135 *Michael* 290
On busy days, with thankful nights, be mine. . 217 *Enterprise* 150
The Beast four days and nights had past ; . . 243 *P. B.* 602
Even thus last night, and two nights more, I lay 253 **A flock* 9
On favouring nights, she loved to go ; . . . . 416 *White Doe* 1812
Seven nights her course renewed, ... 542 *Russ. Fug.* 18
Post seaward,—what impedes the tardy nights. . 625 *Æneid* 129
At noon and 'mid the calm of summer nights, . 638 *Prelude* 1. 419
Of those soft starry nights, and that old Dame . 642 *Prelude* 2. 43
Had lain awake on summer nights to watch . . 659 *Prelude* 4. 87
Relinquished, and your nights of revelry, . . . 675 *Prelude* 6. 16
Than I beheld loitering on calm clear nights . . 676 *Prelude* 6. 93
Were my day-thoughts,—my nights were miserable ; . . . . 724 *Prelude* 10. 398
As at a fountain ; and on winter nights, . . . 739 *Prelude* 12. 326
Tempestuous nights—the conflict and the sounds 760 *Excursion* 1. 290
O, calm contented days, and peaceful nights ! . 817 *Excursion* 4. 1050
A stirring foot, a head which beat at nights . . 860 *Excursion* 7. 211
Of play-thing fire-works, that on festal nights . K.8. 251 *Recluse* 1.1.558
Nightshade. The wild rose, and the poppy, and the nightshade : . . . . 38 *Bord.* 45
Of Nightshade haply yet may tell ;) . . . . . 533 **Blest is* 16
Of Nightshade, to St. Mary's honour built, . . 643 *Prelude* 2. 104
Of Nightshade, and St. Mary's mouldering fane, . 727 *Prelude* 10. 598
Laurels to some, a night-shade wreath to thee, . S.3. 432 **Critics, right* 2
Night-time. None could tell if it were night-time, . 535 *Egremont* 65
Night-watch. My night-watch : nor should e'er the crested fowl . . . . 424 *Ecc. Sonn.* 1. 22. 12
Nile. This was the Flag-ship at the Nile, . . . 178 *Waggoner* 2. 115
Nile trembles at his fountain head ; . . . . 216 *Enterprise* 86
Oftener than Ganges or the Nile ; a thought . . 251 **There is a little* 7
From the Land of Nile did go ; . . . . . . 374 *Eg. Maid* 360
As his own worshippers : and Nile, reclined . . 435 *Ecc. Sonn.* 2. 27. 7
The all-sustaining Nile. No more—the time . . 450 *Ecc. Sonn.* 3. 38. 9
That hides her, like the mighty flood of Nile . . 684 *Prelude* 6. 614
. . . the scaly regent of the Nile. . . . . . L.1. 89 *Juvenal* 1. 24
Nile-like. Brood o'er the long-parched lands with Nile-like wings ! . . . . 22 *Desc. Sk.* 658
To brood the nations o'er with Nile-like wings ; . 617 *Desc.Sk.Quarto* 805
Nimble. But the nimble Hare hath trusted . . . 490 *Incident : Dog* 19
Nina. Nina, the Lady of the Lake, ... 370 *Eg. Maid* 94
Soon did the gentle Nina reach . . . . . . 371 *Eg. Maid* 121
On Nina, as she passed, with hopeful greeting. . 371 *Eg. Maid* 132
Then Nina, stooping down, embraced, ... 371 *Eg. Maid* 139
And Nina heard a sweeter voice . . . . . . 371 *Eg. Maid* 151
Once more did gentle Nina lift . . . . . . 371 *Eg. Maid* 181
Nina, the good Enchantress, shed . . . . . 373 *Eg. Maid* 303
Nine. I see them there, in number nine, . . . 238 *P. B.* 163
Full nine of them or more ! . . . . 238 *P. B.* 180
With glittering finger points at nine. . . . . 406 *White Doe* 961
Nine beats distinctly to each other bound . . . 453 **Calm is the* 12
" Nine summers had she scarcely seen, . . . 486 **We walked* 33
And coats enough to smother nine. . . . . 536 *Goody Blake* 8
Young as I was, a child not nine years old, . . 672 *Prelude* 5. 452
A punctual follower on the stroke of nine, . . 676 *Prelude* 6. 71
Into this tract again. Nine tedious years ; . . 769 *Excursion* 1. 871
From their first separation, nine long years, . . 769 *Excursion* 1. 872
Ninety. There are ninety good seasons of fair and foul weather . . . . 572 *Avarice* 15
Ninth. Till fully passed and gone was the ninth night ; 565 *Troilus* 163
Eight months ! rolled pleasingly away ; the ninth 658 *Prelude* 3. 631
Niphates'. To Niphates' top invited, ... 218 **Inmate of* 29
Nipped. Recalls ! *He* lived not till his locks were nipped . . . . 842 *Excursion* 6. 275
Nipping. My hands are numb. Ha ! ha ! 'tis nipping cold. . . . . 50 *Bord.* 727
That, for protection from the nipping blast, . . 150 **When, to* 17
Or nipping frost remind thee trees are bare, . . 229 *Cuckoo-clock* 13
In brightest sunshine bask ; this nipping air, . . 263 **While not* 3
Hunger, and sultry heat, and nipping blast . . 320 **Hunger, and* 1
A shelter from the nipping wind : . . . . . 404 *White Doe* 775
Their meek heads to the nipping air, ... 503 *Warning* 3
At the first nipping of October frost, ... 770 *Excursion* 1. 902
No, *omitted.*
Nob. Fond lovers ! yet not quite hob nob, . . . 129 *Idiot Boy* 289
Nobility. That fettered your nobility of mind— . 77 *Bord.* 2281
To your nobility of mind ! " . . . . . . 406 *White Doe* 923
If reason be nobility in man, ... 735 *Prelude* 12. 70
Noble. Why, this is noble ! shake her off at once. . 41 *Bord.* 248
So dealt with him. I have a noble Friend . . 71 *Bord.* 1896
In all things worthier of that noble birth, . . 78 *Bord.* 2335
With some, the noble Creature never slept ; . . 139 *Widow* 12
The noble Instrument. . . . . 163 *Needlecase* 4
To noble Clifford ; from annoy . . . . . 180 *Waggoner* 4. 48
By his noble Mastiff's side, ... 181 *Waggoner* 4. 163
Of noble sentiment. . . . . 193 *Ruth* 144
Such garb with such a noble mien ; . . . . 205 *Brougham* 113
The noble Syracusan low in dust ! . . . . . 214 *Dion* 109
That hath in noble tasks been tried ; . . . . 233 *Power of Sound* 90
Sweet tones, and caught by a noble Lady blest . 267 *St. Cath.* 5
Sad tidings to that noble Youth ! . . . . . 287 *Ellen Irwin* 13
To level with the dust a noble horde, ... 292 **Degenerate Douglas* 5
And know that noble feelings, manly powers, . . 308 **There is a bondage* 11
That every gift of noble origin . . . . . . 308 **These times* 10
Like him of noble birth and noble mind ; . . . 315 **And is it* 11
To whose all-pondering mind a noble aim, . . 317 **Brave Schill* 12
Faithfully kept, is as a noble deed ; . . . . 317 **Brave Schill* 13
Might well be styled this noble body's HEAD ; . 339 *Schwytz* 11
As noble as the best endued, ... 342 *Ital. Itin.* 80
Your noble birthright, ye that occupy . . . . 350 *Des. Stanzas* 49
None but a noble people could have loved . . 359 **Complacent Fictions* 9
They—who have seen the noble Roman's scorn . 359 **They—who* 1
My noble fire emits the joyful ray . . . . . 365 **Rapt above* 13
A harvest of high hopes and noble enterprises." . 373 *Eg. Maid* 264
The noble Boy of Egremound. . . . . . . 398 *White Doe* 230
To noble Percy ; and a force . . . . . . 401 *White Doe* 465
" This meeting, noble Lords ! looks fair, . . . 402 *White Doe* 605
" Rise, noble Earls, put forth your might . . . 403 *White Doe* 633
—The noble Francis—wise as brave, ... 408 *White Doe* 1111
" Your noble brother hath been spared ; . . . 409 *White Doe* 1212
Yea, offered up this noble Brood, ... 410 *White Doe* 1302
Unclosed the noble Francis lay— . . . . . 412 *White Doe* 1493
Ease from this noble miser of his time . . . . 425 *Ecc. Sonn.* 1. 26. 9
And they are led by noble HILLARY. . . . . 469 **The feudal* 14
For ever, and to noble deeds give birth, . . . 494 *Hap. War.* 78
Honouring the hope of noble ancestry. . . . . 504 *Warning* 46
A noble instinct ; in all kinds the same, . . . 528 **Those breathing* 75
O Lady ! from a noble line . . . . 533 **Blest is* 11
What thou askest, noble Brother, ... 535 *Egremont* 35
Witness how oft upon my noble Friend . . . . 539 **Lady ! a* 27
And there, 'mid many a noble guest, ... 545 *Russ. Fug.* 371
What noble pomp and frequent have not I . . 574 *Chiabrera* 4. 21
Of noble parents : seventy years and three . . 574 *Chiabrera* 4. 30
Then noble Sandys, inspir'd with great design, . 619 *School Ex.* 65
Would gladly grapple with some noble theme, . 634 *Prelude* 1. 129
Of noble feeling, that those spiritual men, . . 653 *Prelude* 3. 266
Than that most noble attribute of man, . . . 674 *Prelude* 5. 573
With the most noble, but unto the poor . . . 714 *Prelude* 9. 303
Man and his noble nature, as it is . . . . . 714 *Prelude* 9. 355
At times with virtuous wrath and noble scorn, . 716 *Prelude* 9. 496
The noble Living and the noble Dead. . . . 733 *Prelude* 11. 395
To noble raptures ; while my voice proclaims . 755 *Recluse* 1. 1. 815
Wake sometimes to a noble restlessness— . . . 809 *Excursion* 4. 548
For noble purposes of mind : his heart . . . 813 *Excursion* 4. 831
A noble mind to practise on herself, ... 816 *Excursion* 4. 1019
Shall it forget that its most noble use, . . . 820 *Excursion* 4. 1260
An effort only, and a noble aim ; . . . . . 830 *Excursion* 5. 502
" A noble—and, to unreflecting minds, ... 865 *Excursion* 7. 516
On Albion's noble Race in freedom born, . . . 890 *Excursion* 9. 393
Favoured by noble privilege like this, ... K.8. 247 *Recluse* 1.1.379
Between ourselves ! The noble laid aside), . . L.1. 97 *Juvenal* 3. 68
Noble-minded. The noble-minded Mother's helping hand . . . . 541 *Grace Darl.* 47
Nobler. It shall be for a nobler end—to teach . . 65 *Bord.* 1558
A nobler ship did never swim, ... 178 *Waggoner* 2. 119
With nobler zeal I burn ; . . . . 194 *Ruth* 177
Fitter hope, and nobler doom ; . . . . . . 205 *Brougham* 139
A nobler counsellor than my poor heart. . . . 210 *Laod.* 54
What nobler marvels than the mind . . . . 238 *P. B.* 143
Our British Hill is nobler far ; he shrouds . . 251 **Pelion and* 12
And nobler cares than listless summer knew. . . 263 **While not* 14
Knows that the source is nobler whence doth rise 329 *Ode : Thanks.* 53
Blessings and prayers in nobler retinue . . . 387 *Scott* 10
A second and yet nobler birth ; . . . . . 416 *White Doe* 1845
I, who essayed the nobler Stream to trace . . 418 *Ecc. Sonn.* 1. 1. 5
Had mortal action e'er a nobler scope ? . . . 442 *Ecc. Sonn.* 3. 9. 9
Requires for nobler deeds ; . . . . 479 *Somnamb.* 69
Can prop, as you have learnt, our nobler being : . 480 *Cordelia* 9
Who gave us nobler loves, and nobler cares— . . 489 *Pers. Talk* 52
A trophy nobler than a conqueror's sword. . . 489 *Spade* 20
Doth also for our nobler part provide, ... 669 *Prelude* 5. 273
A handmaid to a nobler than herself, ... 749 *Prelude* 14. 260

Noticeable 661 Now

Notice—*continued.*
Sent welcome notice of the rising moon, 640 *Prelude* 1. 571
An artless rustic's notice, this way less, 657 *Prelude* 3. 586
To give me timely notice, and straightway, 660 *Prelude* 4. 124
Would now direct thy notice. Yet in spite 662 *Prelude* 4. 276
Offered to notice by less daring pens, 673 *Prelude* 5. 543
Without a separate notice: many books 675 *Prelude* 6. 23
Due to this timely notice, unawares 687 *Prelude* 7. 27
Of public notice—an offensive light 691 *Prelude* 7. 314
Deserving notice have escaped regard, 709 *Prelude* 9. 13
To notice old forgotten principles, 722 *Prelude* 10. 251
That fragrant notice of a pleasant shore 735 *Prelude* 12. 54
From the world's notice to a rural home. 774 *Excursion* 2. 194
Will force upon his notice; undeterred 781 *Excursion* 2. 629
This notice comes too late.' With joy I saw 783 *Excursion* 2. 793
His countenance gave notice that my zeal 791 *Excursion* 3. 357
With a brief notice when, and how, and where, 816 *Excursion* 4. 1010
Attract your notice; statelier than could else 824 *Excursion* 5. 130
Rise to the notice of a serious mind 828 *Excursion* 5. 372
And notice forced upon incurious ears; 828 *Excursion* 5. 418
Are capable to notice or discern 830 *Excursion* 5. 498
"When to those shining fields our notice first 833 *Excursion* 5. 729
Cannot but notice among men and things) 834 *Excursion* 5. 798
In courting notice; and the ground all paved 847 *Excursion* 6. 626
To such will we restrict our notice, else 848 *Excursion* 6. 659
By notice indirect, or blunt demand 859 *Excursion* 7. 105
Retired from notice, lost in attributes 862 *Excursion* 7. 318
Failed not to notice, inly pleased, and said:— 874 *Excursion* 8. 4
Directing notice, merely from a wish 893 *Excursion* 9. 586
Noticeable. A noticeable Man with large grey eyes, 108 *Indolence* 39
That noticeable kindliness of heart 701 *Prelude* 8. 124
Noticed. Is it possible? One thing you noticed not: 51 *Bord.* 787
He recks not human law; and I have noticed 63 *Bord.* 1437
And unbridged stream, such as you may have noticed 99 *Brothers* 254
Shades of the Past, oft noticed with a sigh, 584 **With copious* 51
You might have noticed, busily engaged, 789 *Excursion* 3. 201
Not wished for; sometimes noticed with a sigh, 795 *Excursion* 3. 618
Notices. Here as elsewhere, to notices that make 525 *Epist. Beaumont* 266
Of these and other kindred notices 658 *Prelude* 3. 609
How arch his notices, how nice his sense 670 *Prelude* 5. 310
My earliest notices; with these compared 741 *Prelude* 13. 104
Closed the preparatory notices 776 *Excursion* 2. 316
Of less particular notices assigned 825 *Excursion* 5. 201
Noting. Of even the least emotion. Noting this, 125 *V. and J.* 229
To the sea-coast, noting that each man frames 304 **Festivals have* 8
And, noting that my eye was on the tree, 769 *Excursion* 1. 844
The old Man, noting this, resumed, and said, 770 *Excursion* 1. 931
Noting that in despite of their commands 853 *Excursion* 6. 993
Notion. No notion have they—not a thought, 178 *Waggoner* 3. 29
Were a vain notion; but the hope is dear 250 **Happy the* 12
Their notion of its perfect rest. 289 *Glen-Al.* 22
Promptly replied—"My notion is the same. 789 *Excursion* 3. 233
By each new upstart notion? In the ports 816 *Excursion* 4. 1026
Notions. *See* **Book-notions.**
With speculative notions rashly sown, 437 *Ecc. Sonn.* 2. 37. 9
Troubled long with warring notions 550 *Hermit's Cell* 4. 1
And heard their notions; nor did they disdain 712 *Prelude* 9. 196
And thought that other notions were as sound, 728 *Prelude* 11. 50
To certain general notions, for the sake 743 *Prelude* 13. 213
And moral notions too intolerant, 751 *Prelude* 14. 340
Of spurious notions—worn as open signs 775 *Excursion* 2. 271
Enough if notions seemed to be high-pitched, 797 *Excursion* 3. 786
His notions to this standard; on this rock 813 *Excursion* 4. 816
How far those erring notions were reformed; 896 *Excursion* 9. 790
Notre. St. Denis, filled with royal tombs, or the Church of Notre Dame? 92 *Poet's Dream* 24
Notwithstanding. They, notwithstanding, had much love to spare, 99 *Brothers* 247
This notwithstanding, being brought more near 706 *Prelude* 8. 510
Nought. *See* **Naught.**
Nought but the *chalets*, flat and bare, on high 16 *Desc. Sk.* 348
Nought round its darling precincts can he find 18 *Desc. Sk.* 429
I yielded up those precious hopes, which nought 66 *Bord.* 1616
If nought in loveliness compare 111 **Let other* 7
Nought but the world-redeeming Cross 113 *Lament* 61
Though nought was left undone which staff, or voice, 134 *Michael* 192
Nor grieved if thou be set at nought: 158 **In youth* 21
Nought is there that you shall not see. 237 *P. B.* 90
This Ship was nought to me, nor I to her, 258 **With Ships* 9
And nought untunes that Infant's voice; no trace 274 *Infant M.* 5
Nought but that word assigned to the unknown, 275 *Gravestone* 3
For nought but what thy happiness could spare. 277 **Why art* 8
To thy beginning nought that doth present 376 *Duddon* 3. 7
Of that rash levy nought remained. 408 *White Doe* 1162
Nought heard, of ocean troubled or serene? 470 **Did pangs* 5
Nought but her changes. Thus, ungrateful Nation! 505 *Warning* 146
Nought equals when the hours are winged with crime) 505 *Warning* 152
Prayer's voiceless service; but now, seeking nought 508 *F. Stone* 35
And shunning nought, their own peculiar life 508 *F. Stone* 36
Nought I perceived within it dull or dim; 532 **Once I* 8
Nought but the heaven-directed spire, 533 **Blest is* 8
Who had been nought, if Love had never been. 560 *Cuck.andNight.*190
Nought wakens or disturbs it's tranquil tides; 597 *Ev. Wk. Quarto* 310
Nought but the char that for the may-fly leaps, 597 *Ev. Wk. Quarto* 311
Nought else of man or life remains behind 598 *Ev. Wk. Quarto* 375
Nought but the herds that pasturing upward creep, 610 *Desc.Sk.Quarto* 426
Striving to hide, what nought could heal, the wounds 730 *Prelude* 11. 215
Nourish. Nourish the hope that memory lacks not power 231 *Clouds* 90
Ere they descend to nourish root and stalk 390 *Glencroe* 8
Nourish the sufferers then; and mists, that brood 431 *Ecc. Sonn.* 2.12. 11
Nourished. A morbid pleasure nourished, tracing here 23 *Yew-tree* 31
I had been nourished by the sickly food 70 *Bord.* 1821
And Mina, nourished in the studious shade, 320 **They seek* 11
Here did not kill, but nourished, Piety. 355 *Aquap.* 169
How nourished here through such long time 492 *Fidelity* 62
Are nourished and invisibly repaired; 737 *Prelude* 12. 215
Nourished Imagination in her growth, 758 *Excursion* 1. 166
Nourishment. With a hard bed and scanty nourishment, 529 *Poor Robin* 8
By nourishment that came unsought; for still 642 *Prelude* 2. 7
And deals it out, their regular nourishment 702 *Prelude* 8. 228
It draws its nourishment imperceptibly— 794 *Excursion* 3. 581
Some nourishment, as trees do by their roots, 879 *Excursion* 8. 356
That gave them nourishment. When frosty winds 881 *Excursion* 8. 445
Novel. With aspects novel to my sight; but still 361 **List—'twas* 13
Prompt transformation works the novel Lore; 422 *Ecc. Sonn.* 1. 17. 1
When novel trusts by folly are betrayed,— 504 *Warning* 69
That flashed upon me from this novel show 652 *Prelude* 3. 202
A novel scene, did often in this way 716 *Prelude* 9. 463
And through the nation spread a novel heat 722 *Prelude* 10. 252
In the French tongue, a Novel of Voltaire, 778 *Excursion* 2. 443
Novelties. Among the novelties of morn, 391 *HighlandBroach* 76
Of novelties in Church and State; 404 *White Doe* 706
Than shaping novelties for times to come, 669 *Prelude* 5. 268
I hasten; there, by novelties in speech, 711 *Prelude* 9. 82
Pampering myself with meagre novelties 736 *Prelude* 12. 117
And all the laboured novelties at best 829 *Excursion* 5. 437
Novelty. Of novelty amid the sacred wreck 474 **How sad* 7
And brooks were like a dream of novelty 672 *Prelude* 5. 429
Of novelty survived for scenes like these; 693 *Prelude* 7. 447
Custom and habit, novelty and change; 714 *Prelude* 9. 325
Worn out in greatness, stripped of novelty, 730 *Prelude* 11. 198
Amusing, yet uneasy, novelty, 764 *Excursion* 1. 575
Was catching at some novelty of spring, 867 *Excursion* 7. 680
November. One beautiful November night, 240 *P. B.* 323
With stinted kindness. In November days, 638 *Prelude* 1. 416
November's. With a step quickened by November's cold, S.3. 433 **The doubt* 44
Novice. An eager Novice robed in fluttering gown! 270 **Ye sacred* 14
Yet many a Novice of the cloistral shade, 434 *Ecc. Sonn.* 2. 23. 1
Even to the rudest novice of the Schools. 696 *Prelude* 7. 597
Teaching some Novice of the sisterhood 856 *Excursion* 6. 1182
Now. (*Partial list.*)
In what alone is ours, the living Now. 360 **Near Anio's* 14
Past, future, shrinking up beneath the incumbent Now; 504 *Warning* 96
When I gave way to your request; and now, 39 *Bord.* 134
Where now we dwell.—For many years I bore 41 *Bord.* 202
It could not be. And yet I now remember 42 *Bord.* 283
Now she is gone, I fain would call her back. 43 *Bord.* 328
Why now—but yesterday I overtook 45 *Bord.* 446
But 'tis all over now. That good old Lady 46 *Bord.* 486
Now I *do* love thee. I am thunderstruck. 46 *Bord.* 528
His voice—methinks I hear it now, his voice 50 *Bord.* 714
That I have been his comforter till now! 50 *Bord.* 720
How now, what mean you? Truly, I was going 51 *Bord.* 765
Why do I tremble now?—Is not the depth 51 *Bord.* 780
It now becomes my duty to resume it. 53 *Bord.* 876
Now, on my life, I grieve for you. The misery 53 *Bord.* 879
Perchance you think so now? I cannot do it: 53 *Bord.* 889
I now perceive we do mistake our masters, 54 *Bord.* 908
With which he gave the boon—I see it now! 54 *Bord.* 920
Now may I perish if this turn do more 55 *Bord.* 991
Now I could laugh till my ribs ached. Oh, Fool! 59 *Bord.* 1218
With understanding spirit now may look 435 *Ecc. Sonn.* 2. 29. 5
Whose blaze is now subdued to tender gleams, 453 **The Sun, that* 3
Now, dazzling Stranger! when thou meet'st my glance, 532 **Once I* 31
Nothing has he now to dread. 535 *Egremont* 62
'Now, certès, I will use my diligence 554 *Prioress* 88
Now may'st thou sing for aye before the throne, 554 *Prioress* 129
"Now this poor Widow waiteth all that night 554 *Prioress* 135
Now against May shall have some stirring—whether 557 *Cuck. and Night.* 23
For now when they may hear the small birds' song, 557 *Cuck. and Night.* 26
In sooth, I speak from feeling, what though now 557 *Cuck. and Night.* 36
Now, God, quoth I, that died upon the rood, 558 *Cuck. and Night.* 93
Full little joy have I now of thy cry. 558 *Cuck. and Night.* 95
But hear you now a wondrous thing, I pray; 558 *Cuck.andNight.*106
What! quoth she then, what is't that ails thee now? 558 *Cuck.andNight.*116
Now say—in such belief I'll live and die; 559 *Cuck.andNight.*162
Not one word have I now, I am so forlorn,— 560 *Cuck.andNight.*209
Now, God of Love! thou help me in some wise, 560 *Cuck.andNight.*214
Now farewell, quoth she, for I hence must wend; 561 *Cuck.andNight.*252
And now I pray you all to do me right 561 *Cuck.andNight.*269
O Palace whilom day that now art night, 563 *Troilus* 26
O ring of which the ruby now is lost, 563 *Troilus* 31
Now, my sweet Troilus, love me well, I pray! 563 *Troilus* 54
Now mercy, Lord! thou know'st well I desire 563 *Troilus* 73
Now, blissful Lord, so cruel do not be 563 *Troilus* 81
Thy horns were old as now upon that morrow, 564 *Troilus* 134
He was so old, he seems not older now; 566 *Cumb. Beg.* 23
Now farewell, old Adam! when low thou art laid, 571 *Farmer* 89
Now standing forth an offering to the blast, 571 **There is a Flower* 11
O now that the genius of Bewick were mine, 571 *Avarice* 1
And now with old Daniel you see how it fares; 572 *Avarice* 31

Now—*continued.*
That patience now doth seem a thing of which . 572 *Animal Tran.* 11
And this alone—the life which now I live . . . 573 *Chiabrera* 1. 4
Now is there not good reason to break forth . . 575 *Chiabrera* 8. 17
Not for a moment could I now behold . . . 578 *Peele Castle* 37
It is not now as it hath been of yore;— . . . 587 *Immortality* 6
Where is it now, the glory and the dream? . . 588 *Immortality* 57
Nowhere. But where the sower dwelt was nowhere to be found. . . . . 24 *Guilt* 27
And nowhere upon earth is place so fit . . . 49 *Bord.* 656
Stirred nowhere without weapons, that full soon . 123 *V. and J.* 124
Up-caught in whirlwinds, nowhere can find rest. . 217 *Enterprise* 132
Stirred nowhere but an urgent equipage . . . 234 *Power of Sound* 123
Would wrong thee nowhere; least of all . . . 292 *Rob Roy* 99
Can nowhere move uncrossed by some new wall . 469 **Desire we* 8
Are found in plenteous store, but nowhere such . 634 *Prelude* 1. 159
Earth, nowhere unembellished by some trace . . 650 *Prelude* 3. 108
Here, nowhere, there, and everywhere at once. . 673 *Prelude* 5. 533
Nowhere, dominion o'er the enlightened spirit . 770 *Excursion* 1. 953
Or nowhere; days unruffled by the gale . . . 777 *Excursion* 2. 365
Words of assurance can be heard; if nowhere . 789 *Excursion* 3. 220
Issuing, however feebly, nowhere flows . . . 804 *Excursion* 4. 220
Seeks, yet can nowhere find, the light of truth. . 810 *Excursion* 4. 630
Upon this sacred ground, if nowhere else." . . 847 *Excursion* 6. 588
Noxious. Scorching blight or noxious dew, . . . 226 *Vernal Ode* 26
The dullest or most noxious, should exist . . . 567 *Cumb. Beg.* 76
Strong to subvert our noxious qualities: . . . 886 *Excursion* 9. 132
Nubian. Than a lone obelisk, 'mid Nubian sands, . 367 *Trajan* 10
Nuisances. To rid the world of nuisances; ye proud, 567 *Cumb. Beg.* 70
Numa. As Numa loved; when, in the Egerian grot, 498 **Enough of climbing* 28
Numb. My hands are numb. Ha! ha! 'tis nipping cold. 50 *Bord.* 727
Shakes her numb arm that slumbers with its weight, 596 *Ev. Wk. Quarto* 251
Number. That absorbs time, space, and number; . 90 *Longest Day* 47
And all day long I number yet, ... 158 **In youth* 65
Yet of their number no one dares to die?' . . 211 *Laod.* 135
Number their signs or instruments? . . . . 225 *Present.* 38
I see them there, in number nine, ... 238 *P. B.* 163
Of number, pure and silent Votaries . . . . 347 *Processions* 52
Ten times their number, man and horse; . . . 405 *White Doe* 856
And strives the towers to number, that recline . 443 *Ecc. Sonn.* 3. 12. 6
Match'd with an equal number of like age, . . 624 *Æneid* 67
Of tenderness, which I may number now . . . 704 *Prelude* 8. 361
With its rich freight; their number he proclaims; 882 *Excursion* 8. 562
—Accomplish, then, their number; and conclude 893 *Excursion* 9. 634
Numbered. Of sheep I numbered a full score, . . 115 *Last of Flock* 29
Oh! might my name be numbered among theirs, 489 *Pers. Talk* 55
Though here the Hermit numbered his last day . 551 **If thou in* 25
Yet *here* at least, though few have numbered days 583 **With copious* 7
Numberless. With glorious forms in numberless array, 282 **While beams* 12
The little rills, and waters numberless, . . . 818 *Excursion* 4. 1173
Numbers. And now to the sea-coast, with numbers more, we drew. . . . . 29 *Guilt* 279
If Nature to her tongue could measured numbers bring, ... 87 *Pet-lamb* 19
Of tones and numbers all things are controlled, . 235 *Power of Sound* 178
While trees, dim-seen, in frenzied numbers, tear . 263 *Storm* 6
Perhaps the plaintive numbers flow . . . 289 *Sol. Reap.* 18
What if our numbers barely could defy . . . 309 **What if* 1
Which, without aid of numbers, I sustain, . . 314 **I dropped* 7
Numbers exceeding credible account . . . . 347 *Processions* 51
Whose were the numbers, where the loss, . . . 405 *White Doe* 827
The foe from numbers courage drew, ... 408 *White Doe* 1153
For One who speaks in numbers; ampler scope . 520 *Pun. Death* 14. 2
With numbers near, alas! no company. . . . 530 **I know* 4
A prophecy: poetic numbers came . . . . 632 *Prelude* 1. 51
In lines and numbers, and, by charm severe, . . 760 *Excursion* 1. 254
The appropriate sense, in Latin numbers couched: 846 *Excursion* 6. 514
Of numbers crowded on their native soil, . . . 889 *Excursion* 9. 364
Where numbers overwhelm humanity, ... K.8. 253*Recluse* 1.1.599
Numerous. Dwarf panniered steeds, and men, and numerous wains: . . . . 5 *Ev. Wk.* 159
Else can ye hope but with such numerous foes . 33 *Guilt* 510
Perchance as numerous, overpeers the rock . . 230 *Clouds* 43
Gave to my charge Urbino's numerous flock. . . 573 *Chiabrera* 3. 7
Forms, images, nor numerous other aids . . . 634 *Prelude* 1. 155
Whether by native prose, or numerous verse, . . 668 *Prelude* 5. 200
I would give utterance in numerous verse. . . 755 *Recluse* 1. 1. 766
His Parents, with their numerous offspring, dwelt; 758 *Excursion* 1. 111
To numerous self-denials, Margaret . . . . 764 *Excursion* 1. 548
Numerous as stars; that, by their onward lapse, . 800 *Excursion* 3. 975
She with a numerous issue filled his house, . . 825 *Excursion* 5. 198
Nun. A nun demure of lowly port; . . . . . 158 **With little* 17
The holy time is quiet as a Nun . . . . . 258 **It is a* 2
And, if the glory reached the Nun, ... 334 **In Bruggès* 23
There Venus sits disguisèd like a Nun,— . . . 433 *Ecc. Sonn.* 2. 20. 3
The lovely Nun (submissive, but more meek . . 434 *Ecc. Sonn.* 2. 22. 1
Where once came monk and nun with gentle stir, 474 **How sad* 4
Pure as the holiest cloistered nun . . . . . 576 *Cenotaph* 4
Dumb creatures find him tender as a nun, . . 670 *Prelude* 5. 306
Veiled nun, or pilgrim resting on his staff: . . 708 *Prelude* 8. 587
Nun-like. Of nun-like females, with soft motion, glide! 334 **Bruggès I* 14
Nunnery. What change shall happen next to Nunnery Dell? . . . . 477 *Nunnery* 13
Nun's. Listening to nun's faint throb of holy fear, 233 *Power of Sound* 30
Of the pure spring (they call it the "Nun's Well," 465 **The cattle* 7
Nuns. Nuns fret not at their convent's narrow room; 250 **Nuns fret* 1
Unhappy Nuns, whose common breath's a sigh . 266 **With how* 5
That voice which soothed the Nuns while on the steeps . . . . 476 *Nunnery* 7

Nuns—*continued.*
To mind the living presences of nuns; . . . . 496 **A little* 44
Nuptial. Their nuptial song, a gladsome air; . . 157 *Oak and Broom* 97
Give, on this well-known couch, one nuptial kiss . 210 *Laod.* 63
Flowers strewed the ground; the nuptial feast . 545 *Russ. Fug.* 369
Nuptials. These humble nuptials to proclaim or grace? . . . . 256 *Marriage: Friend* 2
Not long the Nuptials were delayed; . . . . 374 *Eg. Maid* 349
Nurse. —And let him nurse his fond deceit, . . 9 *Lines: Boat* 13
Could find delight to nurse itself so strangely, . 41 *Bord.* 237
A faithful nurse thou hast; the dam that did thee yean . . . . 87 *Pet-lamb* 39
The nurse said to me, 'Tears should not . . . 121 *EmigrantMother* 41
Both for her Messenger and Nurse; . . . . 130 *Idiot Boy* 414
The anchor of my purest thoughts, the nurse, . 207 *Tintern* 109
Him Virtue's Nurse, Adversity, in vain . . . 441 *Ecc. Sonn.* 3. 3. 3
And "O beloved Nurse," she said, ... 542 *Russ. Fug.* 53
The homely Nurse doth all she can . . . . 588 *Immortality* 81
Oft he descends to nurse the brother pair, . . 612 *Desc.Sk.Quarto* 576
None but myself shall nurse my boy." . . . . 620 *Birth of Love* 4
Wherewith to nurse the child—and still he pin'd. 620 *Birth of Love* 19
Upon the smooth flat stones: the Nurse is here, . 690 *Prelude* 7. 207
More wise desires, and simpler manners;—nurse . 705 *Recluse* 1. 1. 857
And nurse 'the dreadful appetite of death?' . . 810 *Excursion* 4. 602
They soon were proud of; tended it and nursed; 852 *Excursion* 6. 932
The pair, whose infant she was bound to nurse, . 853 *Excursion* 6. 960
Must tune his pipe, insidiously to nurse . . . 863 *Excursion* 7. 371
Nursed. No common soul. In youth by science nursed, ... 23 *Yew-tree* 13
Though at my bosom nursed; this woeful gain . 118 *Maternal Grief* 2
Thee wingèd Fancy took, and nursed . . . . 215 *Enterprise* 24
WhereTrent is nursed,far southward! Cambrian hills 219 **This Height* 6
O, nursed at happy distance from the cares . . 227 *Vernal Ode* 75
But, nursed in mountain solitude, ... 301 *Bran* 77
Have they, who nursed the blossom, seen . . . 344 **How blest* 59
He, nursed 'mid savage passions that defile . . 359 **Complacent Fictions* 12
What dreams encompassed? Was the intruder nursed . . . . 378 *Duddon* 8. 6
Bards, nursed on blue Plinlimmon's still abode, . 421 *Ecc. Sonn.* 1. 10. 12
Among the mountains were we nursed, loved Stream! . . . . 464 *Derwent* 1
Nursed in the quiet Abbey of St. Bees. . . . 467 *St. Bees* 108
Produced you nursed in various climes, . . . 473 *Ossian* 64
From the most gentle creature nursed in fields . 584 *Ch. Lamb* 23
Nursed in his Mother's arms, who sinks to sleep, . 645 *Prelude* 2. 235
Though mutually unknown, yea, nursed and reared 678 *Prelude* 6. 254
In which my early feelings had been nursed— . 708 *Prelude* 8. 634
Tall ash-tree, sown by winds, by vapours nursed, 866 *Excursion* 7. 596
Nurseries. Ye sacred Nurseries of blooming Youth! 270 **Ye sacred* 1
Nurse's. To blend his murmurs with my nurse's song, 636 *Prelude* 1. 271
Nursing. Be tender as a nursing mother's heart; . 749 *Prelude* 14. 228
Nursling. *See* **Flower-pot-nursling.**
A nursling babe her only comforter; . . . . 13 *Desc. Sk.* 176
Upon the nursling which his arms embraced. . . 125 *V. and J.* 261
The softest Nursling of a gorgeous palace . . . 221 *Triad* 68
A nursling couched upon her mother's knee, . . 274 *Infant M.* 13
Take, cradled Nursling of the mountain, take . 377 *Duddon* 4. 1
Whose nursling current brawls o'er mossy stones, 475 *Greenock* 13
Conscious Nursling, to thy breast! . . . . . 503 **Like a* 82
And the besprinkled nursling, unrequired . . . 836 *Excursion* 5. 954
Some nursling of the mountains, which she leads K.8. 256*Recluse* 1.1.729
Nurslings. And that, so placed, my Nurslings may requite . . . . 281 *Valedict.* 6
The Muses' modest nurslings underwent . . . 655 *Prelude* 3. 460
Nurture. Can drink its nurture from the scantiest rill: 222 *Triad* 148
For nurture or repose; . . . . 543 *Russ. Fug.* 148
And all that generous nurture breeds to make . 575 *Chiabrera* 7. 2
Nurtured. Nurtured, as thy mien bespeaks, in high degree, ... 140 *Arm. Lady* 23
Nurtured by hospitable hands: . . . . . . 144 **Driven in* 59
And nurtured in a fickle clime, ... 497 *Lycoris* 11
Nuts. *See* **Earth-nuts.**
With all its mealy clusters of ripe nuts, . . . 99 *Brothers* 270
Nutting-crook. A nutting-crook in hand; and turned my steps . . . . 185 *Nutting* 7
Nymph. *See* **Sea-nymph, Wood-nymph.**
The Patriot nymph starts at imagined sounds, . 15 *Desc. Sk.* 266
Vouchsafes her lessons, bounteous Nymph . . 217 *Enterprise* 141
While to these shades a sister Nymph I call. . . 221 *Triad* 88
Swift as a Thracian Nymph o'er field and height! 221 *Triad* 120
Dear Liberty! stern Nymph of soul untamed; . 314 **Advance—come* 2
Sweet Nymph, O rightly of the mountains named! 314 **Advance—come* 3
And that intrepid Nymph, on Uri's steep descried! 345 **How blest* 78
The thousandth part of what the Nymph bestows; 377 *Duddon* 7. 8
From the sage Nymph appearing at his wish . . 498 **Enough of climbing* 29
Nymph-haunted. Like some Nymph-haunted grot beneath the roaring sea. . . . . . 324 *Ode 1814* 81
Nymph-like. That, nymph-like, she is fleet and strong, 108 *Louisa* 4
Thy nymph-like step swift-bounding o'er the lawn, 496 **A little* 18
A nymph-like liberty, in nymph-like form, . . 540 **Lady! a* 71
Nymphs. *See* **Sea-nymphs, Wood-nymphs.**
Those laureat wreaths ungathered which the Nymphs . . . . 576 *Chiabrera* 9. 13
Gaz'd on thy lovely Nymphs with fond delight, . 630 [?] **O Moon* 8
Thy Nymphs with more than earthly beauty bright; 630 [?] **O Moon* 9
And hence, a beaming Goddess with her Nymphs, 814 *Excursion* 4. 865
Wasting that love the nymphs implored in vain. . S.3. 434 **The doubt* 85
Nysa's. In Nysa's isle, the embellished grot; . . 299 *Brownie's Cell* 92

O

O, *omitted.*

Oak. And round the broad-spread oak, a glimmering scene, ... 3 *Ev. Wk.* 46
And, fronting the bright west, yon oak entwines . 6 *Ev. Wk.* 214
Yes, to my sorrow—under the great oak . . . 47 *Bord.* 538
The torrent would have dashed an oak to splinters. 51 *Bord.* 756
Led by its murmur, to the ancient oak . . . 62 *Bord.* 1357
The Chapel Oak of Allonville ; good Angel, show it me ! " . . . . 92 *Poet's Dream* 28
Forth from his eyes, when first the Boy looked down on that huge oak, ... 92 *Poet's Dream* 34
" Oh, move, thou Cottage, from behind that oak ! 110 *'*Tis said that some* 13
Perhaps he's climbed into an oak, ... 128 *Idiot Boy* 223
Under the large old oak, that near his door . . 133 *Michael* 165
In all the neighbourhood :—yet the oak is left . 138 *Michael* 479
Out of its head an Oak had grown, ... 156 *Oak and Broom* 13
This Oak, a giant and a sage, ... 156 *Oak and Broom* 19
But in the branches of the oak . . . . . 157 *Oak and Broom* 95
The storm had fallen upon the Oak, ... 157 *Oak and Broom* 105
The forehead of a pollard oak, ... 168 *Wren's Nest* 35
More ample than the time-dismantled Oak . . 219 *Haunted Tree* 7
But as an oak in breathless air . . . . . 246 *P. B.* 846
Oak of Guernica ! Tree of holier power . . . 319 *Guernica* 1
When the broad oak drops, a leafless skeleton, . 379 *Duddon* 12. 8
Here stood an Oak, that long had borne affixed . 393 *Hart's-horn* 1
Who sate in the shade of the Prior's Oak ! . . 396 *White Doe* 34
A self-surviving leafless oak . . . . . . 414 *White Doe* 1630
Wide as the oak extends its dewy gloom, . . . 425 *Ecc. Sonn.* 1. 27. 13
We lay beneath a spreading oak, ... 487 *Fountain* 5
This Oak points out thy grave ; the silent tree . 491 *Tribute : Dog* 9
The Druid-priest the hallowed Oak adore ; . . 500 *Humanity* 8
The umbrageous Oak, in pomp outspread, . . 550 *Hermit's Cell* 5. 9
The oak its dark'ning boughs and foliage twines, . 595 *Ev. Wk. Quarto* 194
Beneath an old-grey oak as violets lie, ... 605 *Desc.Sk.Quarto* 172
Stand like an oak whose stag-horn branches start 695 *Prelude* 7. 520
Of sculptured oak stood here, with drapery lined ; 825 *Excursion* 5. 165
A broad oak, stretching forth its leafy arms . . 825 *Excursion* 5. 227
Of contrast and resemblance. To an oak . . . 829 *Excursion* 5. 455
Hardy and grand, a weather-beaten oak, . . . 829 *Excursion* 5. 456
Who trembled, trunk and limbs, like some huge oak 840 *Excursion* 6. 144
The waste of death ; and lo ! the giant oak . . 865 *Excursion* 7. 547
And oak whose roots by noontide dew were damped, 866 *Excursion* 7. 600
And the LORD'S OAK—would plead their several rights . . . . 866 *Excursion* 7. 622

Oak-crowned. The leaves that rustled on this oak-crowned hill, ... 456 **The leaves* 1

Oaken. An oaken staff by me yet unobserved— . 665 *Prelude* 4. 428
Was occupied by oaken benches ranged . . . 824 *Excursion* 5. 155
And oaken leaves that, driven by whirling blasts, S.3. 433 **The doubt* 49

Oak's. Under a hoary oak's thin canopy, . . . 13 *Desc. Sk.* 150

Oaks. Where oaks o'erhang the road the radiance shoots . . . . 5 *Ev. Wk.* 186
Like mountain oaks rocked by the stormy wind. . 57 *Bord.* 1116
Where leafless oaks towered high above, . . . 154 **A whirl-blast* 5
Has entered, by the sturdy oaks unfelt, . . . 184 *Airey-force* 10
Those forest oaks of Druid memory, ... 450 *Ecc. Sonn.* 3. 39. 7
Save when, amid the stately grove of oaks, . . 633 *Prelude* 1. 82

Oaks'. Beneath the oaks' umbrageous covert, sown 643 *Prelude* 2. 60

Oak-staff. With his oak-staff the cottage children played ; . . . . 34 *Guilt* 537

Oar. Coasts, with industrious oar, the charcoal barge. 4 *Ev. Wk.* 127
The boat's first motion—made with dashing oar ; 9 *Ev. Wk.* 372
For *him* suspend the dashing oar ; . . . . . 9 *Collins* 18
The dripping of the oar suspended ! . . . . 9 *Collins* 22
And steals into the shade the lazy oar ; . . . 12 *Desc. Sk.* 104
At midnight listens till his parting oar, . . . 15 *Desc. Sk.* 252
The pictured fane of Tell suspends his oar ; . . 15 *Desc. Sk.* 286
For the tired slave, Song lifts the languid oar, . 233 *Power of Sound* 53
With deftly-lifted oar ; . . . . 297 *Highland Boy* 190
Where'er was dipped the toiling oar, ... 343 *Eclipse* 13
With the next dipping of its slackened oar ; . . 453 **Calm is the* 29
This independence upon oar and sail, ... 466 *St. Bees* 10
Each grasps an oar, and struggling on they go— . 541 *Grace Darl.* 51
Soon follow'd by his hollow-parting oar, . . . 600 *Ev. Wk. Quarto* 439
Below, the echo of his parting oar, ... 607 *Desc.Sk.Quarto* 314
Dropped the light oar his eager hand had seized. . 891 *Excursion* 9. 481

Oar-forgotten. Steal, and compose the oar-forgotten floods ; . . . . 12 *Desc. Sk.* 118

Oars. And quickens the blithe sound of oars that pass . . . . 13 *Desc. Sk.* 125
And, slighting sails and scorning oars, ... 216 *Enterprise* 81
And scarcely conscious of the dashing oars . . 271 **Fame tells* 10
In a frail bark urged by two slender oars . . 354 *Aquap.* 120
Furl we the sails, and pass with tardy oars . . 430 *Ecc. Sonn.* 2. 8. 1
Sung to the Virgin while accordant oars . . . 454 *Sea-side* 25
A summons to the sound of oars, that pass, . . 604 *Desc.Sk.Quarto* 144
I dipped my oars into the silent lake, ... 637 *Prelude* 1. 374
Strode after me. With trembling oars I turned, . 638 *Prelude* 1. 385
With rival oars ; and the selected bourne . . . 643 *Prelude* 2. 57
Had staid his oars, and touched the jutting pier, . 658 *Prelude* 4. 15
Of oars with oars contending, sails with sails, . 664 *Prelude* 4. 372
Was cleared, I dipped, with arms accordant, oars 891 *Excursion* 9. 489
Marshal forth-with a pair of oars in gules. . . L.1. 96 *Juvenal* 3. 36

Oarsmen. " My Oarsmen," quoth the mighty King, " draw near, ... 426 *Ecc. Sonn.* 1. 30. 4

Oaten. Sat round the basket piled with oaten cakes, 132 *Michael* 101

Oaten—*continued.*
That oaten pipe of hers is mute, ... 195 *Ruth* 241
Of dainties,—oaten bread, curd, cheese, and cream ; 781 *Excursion* 2. 677

Oath. " For evil tongues made oath how on that day 35 *Guilt* 604
To the oath of fealty, I well remember, . . . 63 *Bord.* 1445
Had sworn another oath ; . . . . 199 *Thorn* 114
" And some had sworn an oath that she . . . 200 *Thorn* 221
An impious oath confirmed the threat— . . . 241 *P. B.* 461
Words that require no sanction from an oath, . . 515 *Penn.* 4
To be cast off, upon an oath proposed . . . . 816 *Excursion* 4. 1025
Whose oath had virtue to protect the land . . 844 *Excursion* 6. 432

Oaths. Concord with oaths ? What differ night and day . . . . 475 **Here on their* 6
Or, bound by oaths, come forth to tread earth's floor . . . . 505 *Warning* 121
While oaths and laughter and indecent speech . 692 *Prelude* 7. 363
As by some tie invisible, oaths professed . . . 714 *Prelude* 9. 305

Obduracy. Hath softened that obduracy, and made 852 *Excursion* 6. 921

Obdurate. Was a dependant on the obdurate heart 125 *V. and J.* 235
Obdurate, proud, and blind, ... 582 *Invoc. Earth* 20

Obedience. In prompt obedience to spontaneous measures . . . . 331 *Ode : Thanks.* 136
In faith and hope, and dutiful obedience, . . . 362 **List—'twas* 33
Obedience to her Lord, and haste to twine, . . 428 *Ecc. Sonn.* 2. 1. 6
Of strict obedience, serve the Almighty Lord ; . 500 *Humanity* 38
" I look'd obedience : the celestial Fair . . . 619 *School Ex.* 111
In safe obedience ; that a mind, whose rest . . 720 *Prelude* 10. 173
Who, with obedience willing and sincere, . . . 827 *Excursion* 5. 351
And act in that obedience, he shall gain . . . 830 *Excursion* 5. 519
In fond obedience to her private thoughts . . K.8. 247 *Recluse* 1. 1. 400

Obedient. Forthwith, obedient to command, . . 179 *Waggoner* 3. 56
Obedient to my breath." . . . . 292 *Rob Roy* 92
Obedient, as here taught, to thy commands. . . 447 *Ecc. Sonn.* 3. 26. 8
But all might see it float, obedient to the wind ; . 531 †*Float. Isl.* 8
Their painted couches seek, obedient to command. 624 *Æneid* 72
Of passion ; was obedient as a lute . . . . 651 *Prelude* 3. 138
The obedient servant of her will. Such moments 737 *Prelude* 12. 223
Obedient to the strong creative power . . . . 763 *Excursion* 1. 480

Obeisance. Spared for obeisance from perpetual love, 325 *Ode 1814* 121
With mute obeisance gladly paid . . . . . 398 *White Doe* 166
Hence my obeisance, my devotion hence, . . . 647 *Prelude* 2. 375
That justice may be done, obeisance paid . . . 743 *Prelude* 13. 237
Who, offering no obeisance to the world, . . . 846 *Excursion* 6. 531

Obeisances. Won from me those minute obeisances 704 *Prelude* 8. 360

Obelisk. Than a lone obelisk, 'mid Nubian sands, . 367 *Trajan* 10
My Theban obelisk ; and, there, behold . . . 788 *Excursion* 3. 132

Obelisks. 'Mid crowded obelisks and urns . . . 286 *Sons of Burns* 1

Oberon. As if she knew that Oberon king of Faery . 222 *Triad* 170

Obey. Fear not, I will obey you ;—but One so young, 42 *Bord.* 308
Obey you more. Your weakness, to the Band, . 55 *Bord.* 980
That all is well prepared. We will obey you. . 58 *Bord.* 1131
Not unwilling to obey ; . . . . 217 **Inmate of* 6
" Appear !—obey my lyre's command ! . . . 220 *Triad* 15
With fancy, I obey my heart, ... 225 *Present.* 11
Memory, like sleep, hath powers which dreams obey, 392 *Bothwell* 12
The Sons obey a natural lord ; . . . . . . 401 *White Doe* 463
Woe to the Crown that doth the Cowl obey ! . . 425 *Ecc. Sonn.* 1. 29. 1
Her Lord might worship and his word obey . . 443 *Ecc. Sonn.* 3. 13. 8
Which they shall long obey : . . . . . . 483 *Sister* 30
Whose everlasting laws, sea, earth, and heaven obey." . . . . 495 *Fact* 14
For who is loth the God of Love to obey, . . . 559 *Cuck.andNight.* 133
And He will teach thy people to obey. . . . 628 **Deign, Sovereign* 12
Was Man created ; but to obey the law . . . 886 *Excursion* 9. 127
Them who are born to serve her and obey ; . . 888 *Excursion* 9. 298
The high behest, and every heart obey ; . . . 893 *Excursion* 9. 642

Obeyed. Light up this beacon. You shall be obeyed. 64 *Bord.* 1465
You have obeyed the only law that sense . . . 64 *Bord.* 1493
Obeyed a summons covetous of truth. . . . . 222 *Triad* 215
Well obeyed was that command— . . . . . 323 *Ode 1814* 35
Resounded—but the voice obeyed . . . . . 344 **How blest* 38
The Harp in lowliness obeyed ; . . . . . 400 *White Doe* 337
His parting charge—but ill obeyed— . . . . 407 *White Doe* 1064
Rights equal, laws with cheerfulness obeyed, . . 515 *Penn.* 3
As each new Moon obeyed the call of Time, . . 532 **Once I* 26
Rebuke us not !—The mandate is obeyed . . . 584 **With copious* 40
Murmuring so sweetly in themselves, obeyed . . 647 *Prelude* 2. 372
Of conscience—conscience reverenced and obeyed, 804 *Excursion* 4. 225

Obeys. Obeys a mystical intent ! . . . . . . 214 *Dion* 95
Their happy year spins round. The youth obeys . 884 *Excursion* 9. 33

Object. (Sole bourn, sole wish, sole object of my way ; 8 *Ev. Wk.* 348
" To draw, out of the object of his eyes," . . . 110 **Look at* 20
An object beauteous to behold ; . . . . . 117 *Affl. Marg.* 16
A more congenial object. But, as time . . . 118 *Maternal Grief* 54
When the impatient object of his love . . . . 125 *V. and J.* 230
But for one object which you might pass by. . . 131 *Michael* 15
And to that simple object appertains . . . . 131 *Michael* 18
Them and their object : but, meanwhile, prevailed 146 **It was an* 12
To shelter from some object of her fear. . . . 148 *Joanna* 76
Changed countenance, like an object sullied o'er . 173 *InfantDaughter* 62
Object uncouth ! and yet our boast, ... 174 *Waggoner* 1. 89
Around the object of his care . . . . . . 181 *Waggoner* 4. 112
The wished-for object is in sight ; . . . . . 181 *Waggoner* 4. 131
No object higher than my knee. . . . . . 199 *Thorn* 176
Seeking a higher object. Love was given, . . . 211 *Laod.* 146
That to their object cleave like sleet . . . . 217 *Enterprise* 128
A dwindled object, and submits to lie . . . . 219 **This Height* 22
No mortal object did these eyes behold . . . 256 **No mortal* 1
From every object dear to mortal sight, . . . 282 **Wansfell ! this* 10
—Divinest Object which the uplifted eye . . . 329 *Ode : Thanks.* 27

Object—*continued.*
If with his vows this object ill agree ; 363 **The world forsaken* 10
And the first object which he saw, 411 *White Doe* 1389
Again this piteous object see ? 411 *White Doe* 1405
Earth never witnessed object more sublime 437 *Ecc. Sonn.* 2. 34. 13
Conspicuous object in a Nation's eye, 494 *Hap. War.* 66
Though but a simple object, into light 510 **Among a* 14
Not to the object specially designed, 518 *Pun. Death* 5. 1
And in that griesly object recognise 523 *Epist. Beaumont* 130
Affections lose their object ; Time brings forth 531 *Octogen.* 1
Without an object, hope, or fear, 532 †*Float. Isl.* 23
Fix on a lovely object, nor my mind 622 *Recluse* 1. 1. 86
Our object and inglorious, yet the end 637 *Prelude* 1. 329
Paid to the object by prescriptive right. 689 *Prelude* 7. 148
On every object near. The Boy had been 692 *Prelude* 7. 347
Of time, and place, and object ; by his wants, 700 *Prelude* 8. 105
A solitary object and sublime, 703 *Prelude* 8. 272
Object, so seemed it, of superfluous pains, 722 *Prelude* 10. 261
From every object pleasant circumstance 729 *Prelude* 11. 154
Her hand upon her object—evidence 730 *Prelude* 11. 203
The object of its fervour. What delight ! 730 *Prelude* 11. 235
Once more in Man an object of delight, 740 *Prelude* 13. 49
Familiar object as it is, hath wrought 742 *Prelude* 13. 144
Both of the object seen, and eye that sees. 745 *Prelude* 13. 378
The time (our guiding object from the first) 750 *Prelude* 14. 307
Her cottage, then a cheerful object, wore 767 *Excursion* 1. 713
An object that enticed my steps aside ! 777 *Excursion* 2. 411
We there espied the object of our search, 784 *Excursion* 2. 817
Of open court, an object like a throne 784 *Excursion* 2. 862
An object whereunto their souls are tied 790 *Excursion* 3. 294
As the prime object of a wise man's aim, 791 *Excursion* 3. 362
With no determined object, though upheld 795 *Excursion* 3. 632
For any object of his love, removed 803 *Excursion* 4. 156
That one, poor, finite object, in the abyss 816 *Excursion* 4. 993
When they shall meet no object but may teach 819 *Excursion* 4. 1236
Chained to its object in brute slavery ; 820 *Excursion* 4. 1256
The object as it is ; but, for ourselves, 830 *Excursion* 5. 488
An object worthier of regard than he, 840 *Excursion* 6. 132
Even were the object nearer to our sight, 855 *Excursion* 6. 1141
—But to what object shall the lovely Girl 883 *Excursion* 8. 584
Even as an object is sublime or fair, 887 *Excursion* 9. 215
That object is laid open to the view 887 *Excursion* 9. 216

Objects. There, objects, by the searching beams betrayed, 4 *Ev. Wk.* 102
What mighty objects do impress their forms 70 *Bord.* 1809
Of natural objects, led me on to feel 131 *Michael* 30
Nor cheerful, yet with objects and with hopes, 133 *Michael* 121
That objects which the Shepherd loved before 134 *Michael* 199
Such objects as the waves had tossed ashore— 148 **A narrow* 13
And, among fairest objects, some 168 *Wren's Nest* 31
New objects did new pleasure give, 194 *Ruth* 184
" She leaves these objects to a slow decay, 203 *Hart-leap* 173
All thinking things, all objects of all thought, 207 *Tintern* 101
'Mid seas how steadfast ! objects all for the eye 262 **Dark and* 11
The immortal Mind craves objects that endure : 263 **Those words* 12
Than noblest objects utterly decayed. 269 *Malham* 14
Not 'mid the World's vain objects that enslave 313 **Not 'mid* 1
So many objects to which love is due : 326 **Intrepid sons* 4
Objects of false pretence, or meanly true ! 335 *Aix* 8
Amid this dance of objects sadness steals 335 *Rhine* 1
Forth from their coverts ; slighted objects rise ; 350 *Des. Stanzas* 6
In Forms that must perish, frail objects of sense ; 364 *Vallomb.* 34
Objects immense portrayed in miniature, 379 *Duddon* 12. 3
By objects, which might force the soul to abate 493 *Hap. War.* 19
That, softening objects, sometimes even 499 *Memory* 7
All creatures and all objects, in degree, 501 *Humanity* 103
Are objects only for the hand 533 **Blest is* 3
But with high objects, with enduring things— 638 *Prelude* 1. 409
Collateral objects and appearances, 641 *Prelude* 1. 593
My heart to rural objects, day by day 645 *Prelude* 2. 199
Objects through widest intercourse of sense. 645 *Prelude* 2. 240
In objects where no brotherhood exists 647 *Prelude* 2. 385
A freshness in those objects of her love, 654 *Prelude* 3. 362
Objects embossed to catch the general eye, 657 *Prelude* 3. 551
For objects hitherto the absolute wealth 662 *Prelude* 4. 234
Had come among these objects heretofore, 662 *Prelude* 4. 250
And, though full oft the objects of our love 674 *Prelude* 5. 569
Present themselves as objects recognised, 674 *Prelude* 5. 604
To single forms and objects, whence they draw, 696 *Prelude* 7. 623
Of trivial objects, melted and reduced 698 *Prelude* 7. 726
At man through objects that were great or fair ; 703 *Prelude* 8. 316
And Nature and her objects beautified 704 *Prelude* 8. 374
Objects of sport, and ridicule, and scorn, 706 *Prelude* 8. 498
Among new objects serve or give command, 708 *Prelude* 8. 641
With that in which *her* mighty objects lay. 709 *Prelude* 8. 686
To youthful minds, by objects over near 714 *Prelude* 9. 337
That objects, even as they are great, thereby 720 *Prelude* 10. 159
Among the grandest objects of the sense, 729 *Prelude* 11. 129
By present objects, and by reasonings false 731 *Prelude* 11. 288
And makes them all, and the objects with which all 736 *Prelude* 12. 137
With present objects, and the busy dance 740 *Prelude* 13. 30
Of objects that endure ; and by this course 740 *Prelude* 13. 32
Objects unseen before, thou wilt not blame 744 *Prelude* 13. 305
All objects from my sight ; and lo ! again 744 *Prelude* 13. 329
May sort with highest objects, then—dread Power ! 755 *Recluse* 1. 1. 853
So vividly great objects that they lay 758 *Excursion* 1. 137
Which nature's various objects might inspire ; 772 *Excursion* 2. 39
He coloured objects to his own desire 775 *Excursion* 2. 277
Whether to such wild objects he were led 787 *Excursion* 3. 46

Objects—*continued.*
From unknown objects I received ; and those, 798 *Excursion* 3. 857
Quick change of objects ; and, to laugh alone, 799 *Excursion* 3. 903
As individual objects of regard, 806 *Excursion* 4. 360
Lacked not, for love, fair objects whom they wooed 814 *Excursion* 4. 878
Viewing all objects unremittingly 815 *Excursion* 4. 961
Both knows and loves such objects as excite 819 *Excursion* 4. 1210
But seek for objects of a kindred love 819 *Excursion* 4. 1216
Into high objects farther than they may, 831 *Excursion* 5. 598
Unelbowed by such objects as oppress 886 *Excursion* 9. 130
Unsightly objects and uncoveted, S.3. 434 **The doubt* 52
Of objects with internal seeing, S.3. 439 **Avaunt this* 12
That objects which the shepherd lov'd before K.8. 226 **I will* 79
On objects unaccustomed to the gifts K.8. 248 *Recluse* 1.1.433
With objects wanting life, repelling love ; K.8. 253 *Recluse* 1.1.596
On lovely objects, and we wish to part K.8. 254 *Recluse* 1.1.631

Oblation. Can such a vain oblation tend, 411 *White Doe* 1396
Gracious God, the pure oblation 550 *Hermit's Cell* 4. 15

Obligation. Of obligation, what the rule and whence 731 *Prelude* 11. 300
Where is the obligation to enforce ? 732 *Prelude* 11. 317
With obligation charged, with service taxed, 798 *Excursion* 3. 840
The obligation of an anxious mind, 866 *Excursion* 7. 571
An obligation, on her part, to *teach* 888 *Excursion* 9. 297

Oblique. Then would be closed the restless oblique eye 500 *Humanity* 49

Obliquities. Through quaint obliquities I might pursue 705 *Prelude* 8. 392

Oblivion. Oblivion may not cover 234 *Power of Sound* 113
These twinklings of oblivion ? Thou dost love 253 **O gentle* 2
Dust for oblivion ! To the solid ground 259 **A volant* 5
That for oblivion take their daily birth 349 *Sky-prosp.* 13
Tradition, be thou mute ! Oblivion, throw 389 *Sound of Mull* 1
And clears Oblivion from reproach, 391 *Highland Broach* 89
And thus, with short oblivion blest, 404 *White Doe* 776
But if grief, self-consumed, in oblivion would doze, 621 *Convict* 29

Oblivious. From one oblivious winter called 225 *Primrose* 45
Amid oblivious weeds. " *O come to me,* 423 *Ecc. Sonn.* 1. 17. 10
No dull oblivious nook shall hide thy fate. 489 *Spade* 28
To selfishness and cold oblivious cares. 567 *Cumb. Beg.* 95
Which, 'mid the calm oblivious tendencies 770 *Excursion* 1. 928
In creeping sadness, through oblivious shades 818 *Excursion* 4. 1124

Obloquy. Through good and evil, obloquy and scorn, 64 *Bord.* 1500
Than o loquy ; that, if we wish to serve 70 *Bord.* 1828
Whom Obloquy pursues with hideous bark : 432 *Ecc. Sonn.* 2. 14. 8

Obnoxious. We must become obnoxious to its hate, 70 *Bord.* 1830
Not even a zephyr stirs ;—the obnoxious Tree 220 *Haunted Tree* 32
And forced to join in less obnoxious shapes 889 *Excursion* 9. 341

Obolus. Crying, " An obolus, a penny give 656 *Prelude* 3. 473

Obscure. As by enchantment, an obscure retreat 3 *Ev. Wk.* 55
Suffering is permanent, obscure and dark, 65 *Bord.* 1543
Through long-lived pressure of obscure distress, 260 **High is* 10
Obscure not yet these silent avenues 334 **Bruges I* 12
Fills many a damp obscure recess 397 *White Doe* 101
Who near his fountains sought obscure repose, 431 *Ecc. Sonn.* 2. 13. 11
That things obscure and small outlive the great : 546 **Oft is* 4
Of obscure feelings representative 641 *Prelude* 1. 606
Remembering not, retains an obscure sense 646 *Prelude* 2. 317
Was my abiding-place, a nook obscure ; 649 *Prelude* 3. 48
Less strong of wonder and obscure delight. 688 *Prelude* 7. 87
As man ; and, to the mean and the obscure, 714 *Prelude* 9. 307
An insignificant stranger and obscure, 720 *Prelude* 10. 148
From mouths of men obscure and lowly, truths 742 *Prelude* 13. 183
Or obscure records of the path of fire. 760 *Excursion* 1. 279
Than this obscure Itinerant had skill 771 *Excursion* 2. 22
Into a gulf obscure of silent grief, 795 *Excursion* 3. 675
For his obscured condition, an obscure 844 *Excursion* 6. 425
From sire to son, in this obscure retreat 872 *Excursion* 7. 943
To thy obscure and modest attributes, S.3. 437 **The doubt* 205

Obscured. Made weakness a protection, and obscured 57 *Bord.* 1082
Who meekly yields, and is obscured—content 265 **The Shepherd* 13
Fearless (but how obscured !) the golden Power, 527 **Those breathing* 14
For his obscured condition, an obscure 844 *Excursion* 6. 425

Obscurely. Month after month. Obscurely did I live, 710 *Prelude* 9. 25

Obscurest. Slept, with the obscurest, in the low 285 *Grave of Burns* 29

Obscurities. Sigh for the obscurities of happiness. 458 *Sea-shore* 33
Lost, thought I, in the obscurities of time, 834 *Excursion* 5. 787
That in his thoughts there were obscurities, K.8. 230 **I will* 186

Obscurity. Of bright obscurity, hill, lawn, and wood ; 4 *Ev. Wk.* 101
In silence and obscurity. 111 *A Complaint* 16
At last, of hindrance and obscurity, 265 **There is a pleasure* 10
Or left unthought-of in obscurity,— 494 *Hap. War.* 67
Hidden from view in dense obscurity. 532 **How beautiful the* 4
Disquiet, danger, and obscurity. 707 *Prelude* 8. 517
Or fancied in the obscurity of years 745 *Prelude* 13. 351
Obscurity, and undisturbed repose. 823 *Excursion* 5. 28

Obsequies. Fit obsequies the Stranger paid ; 348 **Lulled by* 68
For which, with pain, he caused due obsequies 623 **I find* 4
Permission to attend its obsequies. 853 *Excursion* 6. 972

Obsequious. Obsequious service to the precious child, 125 *V. and J.* 278
Obsequious Grace the winding swan pursue. 595 *Ev. Wk. Quarto* 200
Obsequious to my steps early and late, 660 *Prelude* 4. 107
With an obsequious promptness, yet the storm 694 *Prelude* 7. 475
Into each other their obsequious hues, 700 *Prelude* 8. 89
And her obsequious shadow, peace of mind, 855 *Excursion* 6. 1090

Obsequiously. Obsequiously doth take upon herself 888 *Excursion* 9. 267

Observance. Befriends the observance, readily they join 119 *Maternal Grief* 67
And from affectionate observance gain 212 *Dion* 16
In due observance of an ancient rite, 318 **In due* 1
That all observance, due to them, be paid 328 *Ode 1815* 59

Observance—*continued.*
Vain thoughts, and speed ye, with observance due 372 *Eg. Maid* 239
Cast upon this observance may renew 447 *Ecc. Sonn.* 3. 27. 12
In due observance of her pious wish, 854 *Excursion* 6. 1039
Observances. And shrunk from vain observances, to lurk 815 *Excursion* 4. 922
Of these benign observances prevail: 837 *Excursion* 5. 995
Observant. Observant, studious, thoughtful, and refreshed 762 *Excursion* 1. 394
Observation. By observation of affinities 647 *Prelude* 2. 384
As nicest observation furnished hints 812 *Excursion* 4. 725
From human observation, as if yet 822 *Excursion* 5. 6
With transient observation; and thence caught 871 *Excursion* 7. 934
From sense and observation, it subsists 884 *Excursion* 9. 4
Observations. The observations made in later youth, 741 *Prelude* 13. 105
His observations, and the thoughts his mind 757 *Excursion* 1. 101
By observations transient as the glance 794 *Excursion* 3. 576
Of observations natural; and, thus 812 *Excursion* 4. 708
Observe. Do you observe him, and endeavour 142 †*Lov. and Lik.* 19
It was our occupation to observe 148 **A narrow* 12
Observe each wing!—a tiny van! 227 *Vernal Ode* 114
Observe the faithful flowers! if small to great 265 **When haughty* 9
Observe how dewy Twilight has withdrawn 456 **Soft as* 8
Content to observe, to achieve, and to enjoy. 676 *Prelude* 6. 65
Roaming at large, to observe, and not to feel 799 *Excursion* 3. 892
They act, or they recede, observe, and feel; 806 *Excursion* 4. 323
Observe their ways; and, free from envy, find 807 *Excursion* 4. 383
With vacant mind, not seldom may observe 852 *Excursion* 6. 936
Here reigns the Russian, there the Turk; observe 869 *Excursion* 7. 793
Their tardy steps give leisure to observe, 875 *Excursion* 8. 54
—"Observe," the Vicar said, "yon rocky isle 891 *Excursion* 9. 495
If rightly we observe and justly weigh) K.8. 254 *Recluse* 1.1.646
Observed. Have you observed a tuft of wingèd seed 123 *V. and J.* 136
Of those plain-living people now observed 661 *Prelude* 4. 213
Have seen her,—her discretion have observed, 691 *Prelude* 7. 310
Observed where pastime only had been sought, 693 *Prelude* 7. 403
Who, looking inward, have observed the ties 694 *Prelude* 7. 461
(Though they had long been carefully observed), 704 *Prelude* 8. 359
I felt, observed, and pondered; did not judge, 737 *Prelude* 12. 188
He had observed the progress and decay 761 *Excursion* 1. 375
And, looking round me, now I first observed 767 *Excursion* 1. 742
Have acted, suffered, travelled far, observed 809 *Excursion* 4. 563
Observed the liberating stroke—and blessed. 837 *Excursion* 5. 977
"'Tis strange," observed the Solitary, "strange 844 *Excursion* 6. 376
Or rather, let us say, how least observed, 886 *Excursion* 9. 148
Observers. Are strict observers; and not negligent 568 *Cumb. Beg.* 138
Observes. The one that feels, the other that observes. 751 *Prelude* 14. 347
Obsolete. Reviving obsolete idolatry, 147 *Joanna* 27
Obsolete lamps, whose light no time recalls; 394 **How profitless* 13
Nor is, they feel, its wisdom obsolete— 520 *Pun. Death* 13. 6
Conjuring up scenes as obsolete in freaks 657 *Prelude* 3. 569
Of long-past times, nor obsolete in ours. 846 *Excursion* 6. 547
Obstacle. Our daily raiment seems no obstacle 469 **Why stand* 12
Triumphant over every obstacle 715 *Prelude* 9. 372
Obstacles. What obstacles hath he failed to overcome? 38 *Bord.* 38
O'er chasms with new-fallen obstacles bestrown, 431 *Ecc. Sonn.* 2. 12. 12
Obstinate. The obstinate bolt of a small iron door 59 *Bord.* 1200
The Emathian phalanx, nobly obstinate; 265 **When haughty* 11
Clarkson! it was an obstinate hill to climb: 312 *Clarkson* 1
Revive, their obstinate winter pass away, 363 **List—'twas* 96
The obstinate pride and wanton revelry 365 **The Baptist* 5
But for those obstinate questionings 589 *Immortality* 145
Though obstinate on this way, yet on that 691 *Prelude* 7. 277
But though not deaf, nor obstinate to find 714 *Prelude* 9. 340
Obstinately. Yet obstinately cherishing itself: 796 *Excursion* 3. 677
Obstreperous. But by the obstreperous voice of higher still; 799 *Excursion* 3. 899
The obstreperous city; on the barren seas 806 *Excursion* 4. 369
Obstruct. See, hear, obstruct, or mitigate. 401 *White Doe* 514
And all that they can further or obstruct! 700 *Prelude* 8. 60
Obstructed. Of merry England, are obstructed less 886 *Excursion* 9. 175
Obstruction. Viewless obstruction; whence, all unforewarned, 867 *Excursion* 7. 685
Free from obstruction; and the boat advanced 891 *Excursion* 9. 490
Obstructions. Are these obstructions insurmountable? 741 *Prelude* 13. 92
By these obstructions, 'round the shady stones 835 *Excursion* 5. 871
Of near obstructions, and is privileged 885 *Excursion* 9. 71
Obtain. And such chance food as outlaws can obtain, 103 *Artegal* 10
And something also did my worth obtain; 210 *Laod.* 41
More humble favours may obtain 217 *Enterprise* 136
Obtain reluctant hearing. Plain his garb; 762 *Excursion* 1. 420
Rise with the lark! your matins shall obtain 808 *Excursion* 4. 491
Raising his voice triumphantly, "obtain 815 *Excursion* 4. 942
"The way," said I, "to court, if not obtain 831 *Excursion* 5. 580
The unhappy alien hoping to obtain 844 *Excursion* 6. 398
By ruinous contest, to obtain a seat 845 *Excursion* 6. 447
Fallacious, or shall righteousness obtain 894 *Excursion* 9. 664
Obtained. Full oft, our wish obtained, deeply we sigh; 358 **Is this* 9
"The pledge obtained, the solemn word 410 *White Doe* 1312
Had been obtained;—the Wanderer then resolved 761 *Excursion* 1. 383
From sense and reason less than these obtained, 815 *Excursion* 4. 943
Who, when such good can be obtained, would strive 817 *Excursion* 4. 1051
Began in honour, gradually obtained 849 *Excursion* 6. 707
Obtaining. Obtaining ampler boon, at every step, 353 *Aquap.* 39
Obtains. Where Piety, as they believe, obtains 424 *Ecc. Sonn.* 1. 24. 4
Obtrusive. Or, from the bending rocks, obtrusive cling, 12 *Desc. Sk.* 85
If ever an obtrusive word were dropped 123 *V. and J.* 113

Obvious. Of obvious shelter, as a shipless sea. 62 *Bord.* 1390
By obvious signal to the world's protection 75 *Bord.* 2165
For what was now so obvious. To abide, 150 **When, to* 52
Oft as appears a grove, or obvious hill, 267 **As the* 3
For health, and time in obvious duty spent. 278 **Lo! where she* 14
And for less obvious benefits, that find 459 **Wanderer! that* 17
That obvious emblem giving to the eye 535 **When in* 25
If each most obvious and particular thought, 645 *Prelude* 2. 229
Is scarcely obvious; but, that common sense 670 *Prelude* 5. 294
Gave obvious instance of the sad effect 842 *Excursion* 6. 279
Obviously. Most obviously simplicity and power. 698 *Prelude* 7. 744
More obviously the self-same influence rules 808 *Excursion* 4. 449
Occasion. That thou shouldst ever meet a like occasion 74 *Bord.* 2114
The occasion of his woe, as best he might; 564 *Troilus* 114
All else is nothing.—Did occasion suit 576 *Chiabrera* 9. 6
Such apt occasion that I dread a snare. 624 *Æneid* 22
Pointed upon occasion to the site 716 *Prelude* 9. 480
Oft was occasion given me to perceive 772 *Excursion* 2. 48
Of grief, depart without occasion given 780 *Excursion* 2. 598
As might from that occasion be distilled, 783 *Excursion* 2. 742
For this occasion daintily adorned, 826 *Excursion* 5. 278
Occasion given him to display his skill, 882 *Excursion* 8. 532
Occasional. Occasional, an accidental grace, 704 *Prelude* 8. 355
Occasion's. Meek, yielding to the occasion's call, 486 **Bright Flower* 21
Occasions. Happy occasions oft by self-mistrust 316 **Say, what* 13
On kind occasions I may wait, 401 *White Doe* 513
Is placable—because occasions rise 493 *Hap. War.* 21
Even as the heart's occasions might require, 708 *Prelude* 8. 642
Those helps for his occasions ever near 804 *Excursion* 4. 215
Occult. For practising occult and perilous lore) 369 *Eg. Maid* 22
Occupants. Asks of the clouds what occupants they hide:— 220 *Triad* 29
Through fields whose thrifty occupants abide 275 **Chatsworth! thy* 5
Whose cawing occupants with joy proclaim 283 **Here, where* 12
Occupation. Of occupation led from height to height 101 *Brothers* 360
Where was their occupation and abode. 131 *Michael* 26
It was our occupation to observe 148 **A narrow* 12
I know him and his occupation; 179 *Waggoner* 3. 119
"What occupation do you there pursue? 196 *Resolution* 88
Of occupation, not by fashion led, 255 *S. H.* 2
For occupation of a magic wand, 428 *Ecc. Sonn.* 1. 39. 12
Who lacking occupation looks far forth 656 *Prelude* 3. 514
Hence endless occupation for the Soul, 747 *Prelude* 14. 119
"Seven years of occupation undisturbed 795 *Excursion* 3. 622
Of household occupation; no nice arts 878 *Excursion* 8. 271
Betray their occupation, rising up, K.8. 251 *Recluse* 1.1.554
Occupations. And from their occupations out of doors 132 *Michael* 96
For patriarchal occupations, named 389 *Sound of Mull* 13
Whose occupations really I loved; 661 *Prelude* 4. 193
His comforts, native occupations, cares, 700 *Prelude* 8. 106
And occupations which her beauty adorned, 701 *Prelude* 8. 127
In trivial occupations, and the round 737 *Prelude* 12. 213
These occupations oftentimes deceived 760 *Excursion* 1. 258
The simple occupations of their sires, 878 *Excursion* 8. 260
Of trivial occupations well devised, 892 *Excursion* 9. 520
Occupied. *See* **Self-occupied.**
That occupied his days in solitude 124 *V. and J.* 180
Are occupied with one delight! 397 *White Doe* 72
Of the spectators occupied 410 *White Doe* 1343
Less occupied the mind, and sentiments 730 *Prelude* 11. 199
Perchance too lightly occupied, or lulled 807 *Excursion* 4. 419
Thus occupied in mind I paced along, 823 *Excursion* 5. 60
Was occupied by oaken benches ranged 824 *Excursion* 5. 155
But, while his blindness thus is occupied, 846 *Excursion* 6. 518
Are occupied; and the Soul, that would incline 885 *Excursion* 9. 79
Occupies. It occupies—what consciousness retains 796 *Excursion* 3. 694
Occupy. *See* **Pre-occupy.**
To occupy—both fools, or wise alike, 60 *Bord.* 1238
For life to occupy in love and rest; 266 **The stars* 6
Your noble birthright, ye that occupy 350 *Des. Stanzas* 49
For fickle, short-lived clouds to occupy, 787 *Excursion* 3. 96
To those who occupy and till the ground, 833 *Excursion* 5. 690
That occupy their places, and, though oft 848 *Excursion* 6. 703
Were they, to seize and occupy the sense; 857 *Excursion* 7. 23
And with their parents occupy the skirts 879 *Excursion* 8. 363
Occurrence. The dignities of plain occurrence then 704 *Prelude* 8. 381
Ocean. The very ocean hath its hour of rest. 30 *Guilt* 337
How quiet 'round me ship and ocean were! 30 *Guilt* 339
Is, after conflict, quiet as the ocean, 40 *Bord.* 172
In sky, air, earth, and ocean. 112 **Yes! thou* 12
—Back to the joyless Ocean thou art gone; 151 **When, to* 84
How would it please old Ocean to partake, 154 *Morn. Ex.* 49
And the Sea-horse, though the ocean 166 *Wand. Jew* 13
He 'cross the ocean came. 192 *Ruth* 30
To view the ocean wide and bright, 199 *Thorn* 171
And the round ocean and the living air, 207 *Tintern* 98
Ridge, and gulf, and distant ocean 217 **Inmate of* 15
Main ocean, breaking audibly, and stretched 219 **This Height* 14
Pervade the lonely ocean far 225 *Present.* 56
Renewed throughout the bounds of earth or ocean, 226 *Vernal Ode* 49
That Ocean is a mighty harmonist; 235 *Power of Sound* 187
There spreads the famed Pacific Ocean! 237 *P. B.* 57
Huge Ocean shows, within his yellow strand, 266 **The stars* 4
Sky without cloud—ocean without a wave; 277 **Haydon! let* 6
And Ocean bellow from his rocky shore, 306 **Two Voices* 13
'Tis said, fantastic ocean doth enfold 333 *Fish-women* 1
Like something out of Ocean sprung 370 *Eg. Maid* 45
But Ocean under magic heaves, 370 *Eg. Maid* 49
Sleep fell upon the air, and stilled the ocean. 371 *Eg. Maid* 144
Ye winds of ocean, and the midland sea, 387 *Scott* 13

Ocean—*continued.*
Of ocean for her own domain. . . . . . 397 *White Doe* 66
And angry Ocean roars a vain appeal. . . 428 *Ecc. Sonn.* 1. 37. 14
Into main Ocean they, this deed accurst . 433 *Ecc. Sonn.* 2. 17. 11
Purer than foam on central ocean tost ; . 434 *Ecc. Sonn.* 2. 25. 5
Like Ocean burning with purpureal flame ; . 452 *Ecc. Sonn.* 3. 46. 4
Of Ocean roused into his fiercest mood, . 454 *The Sun, that* 16
Deeper than ocean, in the immensity . . 456 *Soft as* 4
Nought heard, of ocean troubled or serene ? . 470 *Did pangs* 5
Through every clime and ocean did I range, . 470 †*From early* 3
Since risen from ocean, ocean to defy, . . 471 *Ailsa Crag* 1
Ocean has proved its strength, and of its grace . 473 *Thanks for* 12
Blank ocean and mere sky, support that mood . 488 *Pers. Talk* 31
Of Ocean, press right on ; or gently wind, . 495 *Fact* 41
Ocean and Earth contending for regard. . . 497 *Enough of climb-ing* 18

Even though the Atlantic ocean roll between. . 508 *F. Stone* 27
On earth, air, ocean, or the starry sky, . . 511 *So fair* 17
The birds shall sing and ocean make . . 580 *Sweet Flower* 67
From the same beach one ocean to explore . 586 *Ch. Lamb* 103
Sweet as the spring, as ocean deep ; . . 586 *Hogg* 38
Where summer Suns in ocean sink to rest, . 602 *Desc. Sk. Quarto* 7
The Ocean ; not to comfort the oppressed, . 635 *Prelude* 1. 210
From a tumultuous ocean, trees and towers . 643 *Prelude* 2. 110
To the broad ocean and the azure heavens . 651 *Prelude* 3. 161
Old Ocean, in his bed left singed and bare, . 666 *Prelude* 5. 33
Sees annually, if clouds towards either ocean . 699 *Prelude* 8. 15
All over this still ocean ; and beyond, . . 746 *Prelude* 14. 44
Upon the billowy ocean, as it lay . . . 747 *Prelude* 14. 55
Ocean and earth, the solid frame of earth . 759 *Excursion* 1. 201
Of a living ocean ; or, to sink engulfed, . 790 *Excursion* 3. 260
And ocean, and look down upon the works, . 832 *Excursion* 5. 684
The ocean paid him tribute from the stores . 865 *Excursion* 7. 504
The sleepless ocean murmurs that all ears ; . 887 *Excursion* 9. 212
Of ocean press right on, or gently wind, . S.3. 427 *My Son* 12
Ocean's. 'Twas dark and void as ocean's watery realm . . . . 26 *Guilt* 138
And of the ocean's dismal breast . . . 216 *Enterprise* 61
With green hills fenced, with ocean's murmur lulled ; " . . . . . . 254 *Dyer* 6
Upon the battle field, or under ocean's waves ; . 328 *Ode 1815* 82
Ocean's o'erpowering murmurs have set free . 349 *At Dover* 9
We sojourn stunned by Ocean's ceaseless roar ; . 521 *Epist. Beaumont* 4
Bays, gulfs, and ocean's Indian width, shall be, . 527 *Those breathing* 39
So when on Ocean's face the storm subsides, . 618 *School Ex.* 37
And ocean's liquid mass, in gladness lay . 759 *Excursion* 1. 202
Ocean-tide. While rising, like the ocean-tide, . 507 *While from* 55
O'clock. Alas ! 'tis the sound of the eight o'clock bell. . 81 †*Address : Child* 37
'Tis eight o'clock,—a clear March night, . 126 *Idiot Boy* 1
From eight o'clock till five. . . . . 131 *Idiot Boy* 446
October. When from October clouds a milder light . 21 *Desc. Sk.* 626
At the first nipping of October frost, . . 770 *Excursion* 1. 902
October's. (October's workmanship to rival May) . 388 *Trosachs* 11
Odd. What an odd moaning that is !— Mighty odd . 51 *Bord.* 751
Such an odd such a kind happy creature as he. . 482 *Character* 20
Some quaint odd plaything of elaborate skill, . 548 *Stranger ! this* 17
To what odd purpose have the darlings turned . 778 *Excursion* 2. 455
Ode. An Ode, in passion uttered, which foretold . 667 *Prelude* 5. 96
Odin. Odin, the Father of a race by whom . . 635 *Prelude* 1. 189
Odin's. For the blood-thirsty mead of Odin's riotous Hall. . . . 359 *Complacent Fictions* 14
Odious. Odious to me the pomp of regal court, . 104 *Artegal* 158
In odious litigation ; and full long, . . 574 *Chiabrera* 5. 3
Stood almost single ; uttering odious truth— . 653 *Prelude* 3. 284
Formal, and odious, and contemptible. . . 798 *Excursion* 3. 826
Odorous. The tapers burn ; the odorous incense feeds . . . . . 431 *Ecc. Sonn.* 2. 11. 2
Of odorous incense ; while a hundred more . 624 *Æneid* 66
Odours. Exhaled, the essential odours climb, . 228 *Devot. Incit.* 8
With bright jonquils, their odours lavishing . 264 *Snowdrop* 10
Wide-spreading odours from her flowery wreaths. . 367 *Trajan* 22
Like odours, sweet as if the same) . . 407 *White Doe* 1029
Of elevation ; let their odours float . . 423 *Ecc. Sonn.* 1. 18. 7
More sweet than odours caught by him who sails . 438 *Ecc. Sonn.* 2. 39. 9
Delicious odours ! music sweet, . . . 507 *May* 9
O'er. (*Partial list.*) *See* **Over.**
But 'twas an angry night, and o'er our heads . 50 *Bord.* 710
Has peered o'er the beeches, their work is begun : . 572 *Avarice* 34
And One a *Tempest*—and, the voyage o'er, . 574 *Chiabrera* 4. 26
O'erborne, *etc. See* **Overborne,** *etc.*
Yet Nature, with excess of grief o'erborne, . 30 *Guilt* 309
O'er-broods. Where Silence, on her night of wing, o'er-broods . . . . 602 *Desc. Sk. Quarto* 9
O'ercome. O'ercome by humblest prelude of that strain, ... 648 *Prelude* 2. 417
O'er-drowsèd. To lie and listen—till o'er-drowsèd sense . . . . 227 *Vernal Ode* 88
O'erflowed. Of Walter's forefathers o'erflowed the bounds . . . . 98 *Brothers* 205
O'erflowing. Upon a mind with love o'erflowing— . 301 *Bran* 116
Enlivened happiness with joy o'erflowing . 792 *Excursion* 3. 430
O'erflows. Stands fixed, her face with joy o'erflows, . 127 *Idiot Boy* 88
O'ergrown. *See* **Half-o'ergrown.**
By lichens grey, and scanty moss, o'ergrown ; . 4 *Ev. Wk.* 95
"Like rock or stone, it is o'ergrown, . . 197 *Thorn* 12
This heap of earth o'ergrown with moss, . 198 *Thorn* 49
O'erhang. Where oaks o'erhang the road the radiance shoots . . . . 5 *Ev. Wk.* 186
Moveless o'er-hang the deep secluded vale, . 607 *Desc.Sk.Quarto* 266
O'erhanging. Upwards among the o'erhanging rocks ; nor . . . . . K.8. 229 *I will* 171

O'erhung. And soon she reached a spot o'erhung with trees . . . . 34 *Guilt* 538
Rolled over a wide plain o'erhung with clouds, . 649 *Prelu e* 3. 2
O'erlabour'd. Shot stinging through her stark o'er-labour'd bones. . . . 596 *Ev. Wk. Quarto* 246
O'erleap. In scanty strings, had tempted to o'erleap . 763 *Excursion* 1. 458
O'erload. And we will ne'er o'erload thee more." . 129 *Idiot Boy* 301
O'erlook. Where antique roots its bustling course o'erlook, . . . 3 *Ev. Wk.* 67
Where antique roots its bustling path o'erlook, . 593 *Ev. Wk. Quarto* 82
O'erlooks. O'erlooks the torrent breathing showers . 301 *Bran* 121
O'erpowered. O'erpowered my better reason, and the bird . . . . 637 *Prelude* 1. 319
With still increasing weight ; he was o'erpowered . 760 *Excursion* 1. 282
O'erpowering. Ocean's o'erpowering murmurs have set free . . . . 349 *At Dover* 9
O'ershade. The bat, lured forth where trees the lane o'ershade, . . 453 *Calm is the* 20
O'ershades. The eagle of the Alps o'ershades her prey. 16 *Desc. Sk.* 335
Dewy night o'ershades the ground ; . . 163 *Spinning Wheel* 5
The eagle of the Alps o'ershades his prey. . 609 *Desc.Sk.Quarto* 407
O'ershadow. To o'ershadow by no native right . 413 *White Doe* 1601
The thick-ribbèd walls that o'ershadow the gate . 620 *Convict* 9
O'ershadowing. Words cannot paint the o'ershadow-ing yew-tree bough, . 254 *Wild Duck's Nest* 9
O'ershrouds. Thus often, when thick gloom the east o'ershrouds, . . 426 *Ecc. Sonn.* 1. 29. 9
O'erspread. Thou turn'st the Wheel that slept with dust o'erspread ; . 255 *S. H.* 3
Ye dewy mists the arid rocks o'er-spread . 609 *Desc.Sk.Quarto* 392
With cheeks o'erspread by smiles of baleful glow, . 617 *Desc.Sk.Quarto* 790
By which it had been bleached, o'erspread the board ; . . . 781 *Excursion* 2. 675
O'erspreads. Spires, rocks, and lawns a browner night o'erspreads ; . 11 *Desc. Sk.* 64
O'ertake. The post-boy, when his rattling wheels o'ertake . . . 566 *Cumb. Beg.* 37
O'ertasked. Striding along as if o'ertasked by Time, . 649 *Prelude* 3. 9
O'erthrew. Death blasted all. Death suddenly o'er-threw . . . . 774 *Excursion* 2. 199
That violent commotion, which o'erthrew, . 873 *Excursion* 7. 1022
O'erthrown. That was no life for me—I was o'er-thrown, ... 69 *Bord.* 1768
And mortal hopes defeated and o'erthrown . 212 *Laod.* 165
Yet hints at peace to be o'erthrown, . . 344 *How blest* 18
Memento uninscribed of Pride o'erthrown, . 345 *Ambition—follow-ing* 7
This melancholy waste of hopes o'erthrown, . 648 *Prelude* 2. 433
When Englishmen by thousands were o'erthrown, . 722 *Prelude* 10. 286
How they had prospered ; how they were o'erthrown . 761 *Excursion* 1. 378
O'ertook. That a fierce storm o'ertook us, worn with travel, . . . 50 *Bord.* 697
O'ertops. That, carried sceptre-like, o'ertops the head . 448 *Ecc. Sonn.* 3. 32. 8
O'erturn. Strong to o'erturn, strong also to build up. . 77 *Bord.* 2277
O'erturned. She almost has o'erturned the Horse,. . 130 *Idiot Boy* 375
O'erwalk. O'erwalk the slender plank from side to side ; . . . . 5 *Ev. Wk.* 165
O'erwalk the viewless plank from side to side ; . 594 *Ev. Wk. Quarto* 148
O'er-walk the chasmy torrent's foam-lit bed, . 610 *Desc.Sk.Quarto* 464
O'erweening. O'erweening Art was caught as in a snare. . . . . 231 *The gentlest Poet* 26
O'erweening Statesmen have full long relied . 320 *O'erweening States-men* 1
With o'erweening complacence our state to com-pare, ... 621 *Convict* 46
O'erwhelm. And his crime, through the pains that o'erwhelm him, descried, . 621 *Convict* 23
Of, *omitted.*
Off. (*Partial list.*) *See* **Cast-off, Far-off.**
Where leafy shades fence off the blustering gale, . 6 *Ev. Wk.* 234
Like fate ; was hurried off, a helpless prey, . 25 *Guilt* 53
The cock far off sounded his clarion throat ; . 30 *Guilt* 329
Why, this is noble ! shake her off at once. . 41 *Bord.* 248
Cast off by her Betrayer, she dwells alone, . 44 *Bord.* 384
—It may not be—I am cut off from man ; . 61 *Bord.* 1327
Or mourn him dead. A man by men cast off, . 68 *Bord.* 1727
Was off for ever ; and the men, from whom . 70 *Bord.* 1842
The dust from off its wings. . . . . 79 *Stay near* 18
Cut off from all intelligence with man, . . 126 *V. and J.* 300
Then off she hies ; but with a prayer, . . 128 *Idiot Boy* 199
Or hast thou put off wings which thou in heaven dost wear ? . . . 140 *Arm. Lady* 71
Here broke off the dangerous converse : . 140 *Arm. Lady* 73
And starting off again with freak as sudden ; . 148 *A narrow* 21
Off, off ! or, puny Thing ! . . . . 155 *Waterfall* 12
At once far off, and near. . . . . 183 *O blithe* 8
Off to some other play the joyous Vagrants flew ! . 191 *Beggars* 48
A jutting crag,—and off I ran, . . . 199 *Thorn* 182
—Cast off your bonds, awake, arise, . . 228 *Devot. Incit.* 38
Off flew the Boat—away she flees, . . 238 *P. B.* 171
Then clear the weeds from off his Grave, . . 291 *Rob Roy* 6
She rose, and off at once the yoke she threw . . 313 *Prophecy* 8
I saw far off the dark top of a Pine . . 358 *Pine : Rome* 1
Far off and faint, and melting into air, . . 361 *List—'twas* 3
And smote off his head on the stones of the porch ! . 399 *White Doe* 253
Or He, whose bonds dropped off, whose prison doors . . . . 419 *Ecc. Sonn.* 1. 2. 9
Off to the mountains, like a covering . . 440 *Ecc. Sonn.* 2. 46. 8
Set off her brightness with a pleasing shade. . 440 *Ecc. Sonn.* 3. 1. 4
Off with yon cloud, old Snafell ! that thine eye . 471 *Tynwald* 9
For things far off we toil, while many a good . 476 *Eden* 13

Off—*continued.*
Let us break off all commerce with the Muse : 480 **Most sweet* 10
Shakes off that pearly shower. 506 **While from* 8
Of pillars, branching off from year to year, 546 **Ye Lime* 4
Soon as the grain from off thy tongue they take : 556 *Prioress* 217
Turned his back on the country—and off like a bird. 570 *Farmer* 40
Or not far off. Where'er my footsteps turned, 622 *Recluse* 1. 1. 90
Puts off his wings, and walks, with proud delight, 624 *Æneid* 45
Come fast upon me : it is shaken off, 632 *Prelude* 1. 20
On every side fall off, we know not how, 648 *Prelude* 2. 436
Put off her veil, and, self-transmuted, stood 660 *Prelude* 4. 151
The off and on companion of my walk ; 661 *Prelude* 4. 187
There was an inner falling off—I loved, 662 *Prelude* 4. 278
Zealously laboured to cut off my heart 735 *Prelude* 12. 79
For this to last : I shook the habit off 737 *Prelude* 12. 204
Cuts off that hand, with all its world of nerves, 831 *Excursion* 5. 609
Cut off, an island in the dusky waste ; 832 *Excursion* 5. 677
Him, farther off ; the pair, who here are laid ; 842 *Excursion* 6. 272
To shake the burthen off ? Ah ! there was felt, 849 *Excursion* 6. 718
A guardian planted to fence off the blast, 866 *Excursion* 7. 613
The Sage broke off. No sooner had he ceased 890 *Excursion* 9. 417
Shall off, and go to the hammer : S.3. 431 **If money's* 3

Offence. Why, if his heart be tender, that offence 56 *Bord.* 1043
Of my offence. I see you love me still, 67 *Bord.* 1639
His peace hath no offence betrayed ; 247 *P. B.* 937
'Twere no offence to reason ; 302 *Yarrow V.* 70
And guard the way of life from all offence 316 **Say, what* 4
Of trial past without offence 402 *White Doe* 522
In that blest charge ; let us—without offence 461 **Queen of* 44
This perilous bay, stands clear of all offence ; 469 **The feudal* 6
Without offence to God cast out of view ; 567 *Cumb. Beg.* 84
Without offence ; ye who, as if to show 734 *Prelude* 12. 14
Without offence, that fair-faced cottage-boy ? 789 *Excursion* 3. 197
By her offence to lay a twofold weight 852 *Excursion* 6. 943
Heavier, as his offence was heavier far. 854 *Excursion* 6. 1077
Of reconcilement after deep offence— 854 *Excursion* 6. 1084
Let homelier words without offence attest K.8. 301 **And oh* 2

Offences. In part, the offences of their guide) 178 *Waggoner* 3. 11
Of thy offences be a heavy weight : 309 **England ! the* 13
In faith, which fresh offences, were he cast 520 *Pun. Death* 12. 13
Of their offences, punishment to come ; 724 *Prelude* 10. 443

Offend. Tells that these words thy humbleness offend ; 112 **O dearer* 10
Thy forehead as if fearful to offend, 264 *Snowdrop* 3
—No more of this, lest I offend his dust : 870 *Excursion* 7. 859

Offended. Wherein I have offended you ;—last night 60 *Bord.* 1280
And if I have in aught offended you, 61 *Bord.* 1317
Of man, offended, liberty is here, 806 *Excursion* 4. 376
Revolts, offended at the ways of men 816 *Excursion* 4. 985

Offender's. Unsheathed in wrath to strike the offender's head, 447 *Ecc. Sonn.* 3. 29. 6

Offenders. To some offenders ; other penitents, 78 *Bord.* 2341
Offenders, dost put off the gracious look, 454 **The Sun, that* 14
For worst offenders : though the heart will heave 517 *Pun. Death* 2. 2

Offending. *See* **Heaven-offending.**

Offensive. For those offensive creatures shun 299 *Brownie's Cell* 77
On that offensive soil, like waves upon a thousand shores. 331 *Ode : Thanks.* 151
Of public notice—an offensive light 691 *Prelude* 7. 314
And, through dislike and most offensive pain, 707 *Prelude* 8. 525

Offer. What if he mean to offer up our Captain 64 *Bord.* 1456
"Then offer up thy heart to God in thankfulness and praise, 93 *Poet's Dream* 57
That earth can offer to declining man, 133 *Michael* 147
Thence offer nightly sacrifice) 214 *Kirkstone* 16
To thee would offer no presumptuous hymn ! 215 *Enterprise* 13
Memorial tribute offer ? 386 *Yarrow Rev.* 84
Accepted of the offer. 620 *Birth of Love* 37
Presume to offer ; we, who—from the breast 893 *Excursion* 9. 624

Offered. *See* **Self-offered.**
The shady porch ne'er offered a cool seat 15 *Desc. Sk.* 244
Offered a greeting of good ale 174 *Waggoner* 1. 54
Its homage offered up in purity. 222 *Triad* 196
Or they are offered at the door 375 **The Minstrels* 35
Is offered to the Saints, the sigh 403 *White Doe* 676
Yea, offered up this noble Brood, 410 *White Doe* 1302
Strains offered only to the genial Spring. 449 *Ecc. Sonn.* 3. 33. 14
A bowl of state is offered to her hand : 625 *Æneid* 104
Cheap matter offered they to boyish wit, 640 *Prelude* 1. 529
A homage frankly offered up, like that 654 *Prelude* 3. 377
Offered to notice by less daring pens, 673 *Prelude* 5. 543
Must, in such Temple, needs have offered up 686 *Prelude* 6. 741
To their great Father, prayers were offered up, 722 *Prelude* 10. 294
To competence and ease :—to him it offered 761 *Excursion* 1. 336
And offered, far as frailty would allow, 816 *Excursion* 4. 981
The mountain's entrails offered to his view 841 *Excursion* 6. 232
That had been offered to his doubtful choice 859 *Excursion* 7. 135
Reject the incense offered up by him, 866 *Excursion* 7. 580
Within this temple, where is offered up 877 *Excursion* 8. 183
Of human victims, offered up to appease 894 *Excursion* 9. 697
First offered help that the deficient rock S.3. 433 **The doubt* 34
In rites once offered to thy bellowing voice. L.1. 88 *Juvenal* 1. 22

Offerest. Thou offerest up for safe Delivery 447 *Ecc. Sonn.* 3. 27. 7

Offering. A tuneful offering for the weal 113 *Lament* 25
She left that farewell offering, 154 *Flower Garden* 51
One offering, kneel before her modest shrine, 270 **Though the bold* 13
What offering, what transcendent monument 331 *Ode : Thanks.* 169
An offering not unworthy to find place, 332 *Ode : Thanks.* 243
Prompt offering to thy Foster-mother, Earth ! 376 *Duddon* 3. 14
Fit offering of glad victory ! 410 *White Doe* 1279

Offering—*continued.*
With bigotry shall tread the Offering 435 *Ecc. Sonn.* 2. 29. 13
Strawberries from lane or woodland, offering wild 525 *Epist. Beaumont* 244
This humble offering made by Truth to Love, 525 *Epist. Beaumont* 275
Whose offering gladly would accord 534 **Blest is* 89
Now standing forth an offering to the blast, 571 **There is a Flower* 11
Such offering Beaumont dreaded and forbade, 583 **With copious* 5
She spake and shed an offering on the board ; 625 *Æneid* 116
No Laureate offering of elaborate art ; 628 **Deign, Sovereign* 2
To days, each offering some new sight, or fraught 686 *Prelude* 6. 728
A poor mistaken and bewildered offering,— 721 *Prelude* 10. 231
Some pleasure from this offering of my love. 752 *Prelude* 14. 429
The offering, though imperfect, premature. 753 **Oft, through* 14
Who, offering no obeisance to the world, 846 *Excursion* 6. 531
Offering a sunny resting-place to them 850 *Excursion* 6. 781
An offering, or a sacrifice, a tool 886 *Excursion* 9. 115
They see the offering of my lifted hands, 895 *Excursion* 9. 748
Before us with its offering ; not a tree K.8. 248 *Recluse* 1. 1. 441

Offerings. Shrine, Altar, Image, Offerings hung in sign of gratitude ; 92 *Poet's Dream* 47
With first-fruit offerings crowd to bend the knee 303 **Is it* 6
These crowded offerings as they hang 338 **Meek Virgin* 7
In priestly vest, with holy offerings charged, 394 **No more* 15
Charged with these offerings which their fathers bore 448 *Ecc. Sonn.* 3. 32. 10
From holy offerings at noontide. 506 *Lab. Hymn* 6
Mute offerings, tribute from an inward sense 539 **Lady ! a* 28

Offers. Offers the beauty, the magnificence, 333 **Bruges I* 6
When most fantastic, offers to the view. 428 *Ecc. Sonn.* 1. 37. 8
Benign, meek, . . . , offers grace K.8. 266 **Rid of* 7

Office. Must fall in the execution of his office ? 48 *Bord.* 640
My Office is fulfilled—the Man is now 66 *Bord.* 1586
Thy office, thy ambition, be henceforth 78 *Bord.* 2303
She, fulfilling her sire's office, 94 *Westmoreland Girl* 65
And, to his office prematurely called, 134 *Michael* 187
Ambitiously the office tried ; 182 *Waggoner* 4. 190
Exalted office, worthily sustained ! 331 *Ode : Thanks.* 160
But faintly picture, 'twere an office meet 335 *Cologne* 8
Such was her office while she walked with men, 359 *Plea : Hist.* 9
But in the solemn Office which ye sought 444 *Ecc. Sonn.* 3. 16. 9
Is with that wholesome office satisfied, 456 *Rydal Mere* 42
If office help the factious to conspire, 504 *Warning* 105
And Will, whose office, by divine command, 514 **Who ponders* 13
Loving is aye an office of despair, 560 *Cuck. and Night.* 176
And Gaiety the charming office sought ; 620 *Birth of Love* 16
And known authority of office served 656 *Prelude* 3. 538
Such pleasant office have we long pursued 662 *Prelude* 4. 271
Of her new office, blushing restlessly. 699 *Prelude* 8. 43
Higher and higher, him his office leads 702 *Prelude* 8. 232
And that alone, my office upon earth ; 732 *Prelude* 11. 348
Whate'er their office, whether to beguile 739 *Prelude* 12. 333
This office filling, yet by native power 774 *Excursion* 2. 178
His office he relinquished ; and retired 774 *Excursion* 2. 193
A long-suspended office in the House 797 *Excursion* 3. 761
With the same pensive office ; and make known 800 *Excursion* 3. 981
To every class its station and its office, 806 *Excursion* 4. 341
"That for this arduous office you possess 813 *Excursion* 4. 780
Office, alliance, and promotion—all 825 *Excursion* 5. 174
The Priest replied—"An office you impose 832 *Excursion* 5. 658
Sate down ; and to her office, with leave asked, 834 *Excursion* 5. 770
To Nature's care, assisted in her office 841 *Excursion* 6. 183
His office, uninvited, he resumed. 850 *Excursion* 6. 786
A Foster-mother's office. 'Tis, perchance, 852 *Excursion* 6. 948
As with her office would but ill accord) 853 *Excursion* 6. 959
For her soul's good ? Nor was that office vain. 854 *Excursion* 6. 1041
Their place I took—and for a grateful office 891 *Excursion* 9. 483
Called to such office by the peaceful sound 895 *Excursion* 9. 726
Each being has his office, lowly some K.8. 255 *Recluse* 1. 1. 669
All shall survive—though changed their office, all K.8. 257 *Recluse* 1. 1. 743

Officers. And Officers appeared in state 410 *White Doe* 1314
A band of military Officers, 711 *Prelude* 9. 125
Among that band of Officers was one, 714 *Prelude* 9. 288

Offices. Had done so many offices about him, 100 *Brothers* 334
In whom all busy offices unite 227 *Vernal Ode* 107
Of offices dispensing heavenly grace ! 430 *Ecc. Sonn.* 2. 6. 14
Small reverence for the mitre's offices, 442 *Ecc. Sonn.* 3. 8. 12
(As yours above all offices is high) 444 *Ecc. Sonn.* 3. 16. 2
Do still perform mysterious offices ! 500 *Humanity* 10
And offices humane, intent to adore 551 **If thou in* 11
Past deeds and offices of charity, 567 *Cumb. Beg.* 90
To tender offices and pensive thoughts. 568 *Cumb. Beg.* 170
The imperfect offices of prayer and praise, 759 *Excursion* 1. 216
All her accustomed offices and cares S.3. 437 **The doubt* 187
Their healing offices a pure goodwill K.8. 244 *Recluse* 1. 1. 284

Officious. The officious touch that makes me droop again. 2 *Early Youth* 14
To our infirmity. No officious slave 645 *Prelude* 2. 215
And your officious doings bring disgrace 655 *Prelude* 3. 415
A channel paved by man's officious care. 659 *Prelude* 4. 56

Off-sloping. Of that off-sloping outlet, disappeared, 777 *Excursion* 2. 407

Offspring. All are the undying offspring of one Sire : v **If thou indeed* 14
Of their own offspring tired. 170 *Rural Ill.* 24
Mild Offspring of infirm humanity, 172 *Infant Daughter* 2
Ye are their perilous offspring ; and the Sun— 231 *Clouds* 79
From the same gracious will, were both an offspring 354 *Aquap.* 143
The Offspring, haply at the Parent's side ; 446 *Ecc. Sonn.* 3. 25. 4
And You, my Offspring ! that do still remain, 464 **A point* 9

Offspring—*continued.*
Her lawful offspring in Man's art; and Time, . 477 *Steamboats* 11
Offspring of soul-bewitching Art, make me . . 508 *F. Stone* 41
"And must my offspring languish in my sight?" 620 *Birth of Love* 9
His Parents, with their numerous offspring, dwelt; 758 *Excursion* 1. 111
Ephemeral offspring of the unblushing world; . 804 *Excursion* 4. 210
A ragged Offspring, with their upright hair . . 879 *Excursion* 8. 348
Off-taken. Till from my tongue off-taken is the grain; 556 *Prioress* 214
Oft. (*Partial list.*)
Blind as the grave, but, as you oft have told me, 40 *Bord.* 180
That oft have checked their fury at your bidding. 48 *Bord.* 608
The shattered Castle in which Clifford oft . . . 49 *Bord.* 659
Full oft is pleased a wayward dart to throw; . . 153 *Morn. Ex.* 2
And if full oft the Sanctuary save . . . . . 424 *Ecc. Sonn.* 1. 24. 13
Doubtless shall cheat full oft the heart's desires; 429 *Ecc. Sonn.* 2. 3. 9
Whence oft great sickness grows of heart and home; . . . . 557 *Cuck.and Night.* 32
Oft as I say Osee, Osee, I wis, ... 559 *Cuck.andNight.*127
For to th' untrue he oft gives ease and joy; . . 560 *Cuck.andNight.*198
And to himself full oft he said, alas! . . . . 564 *Troilus* 88
And of himself did he imagine oft, ... 564 *Troilus* 99
How oft have I heard in sweet Tilsbury Vale . . 569 *Farmer* 15
Up the Haymarket hill he oft whistles his way, . 570 *Farmer* 81
Oft have I seen it muffled up from harm, . . . 571 **There is a Flower* 7
Old Man! whom so oft I with pity have eyed, . 572 *Avarice* 45
And the broad gulfs I traversed oft and oft. . . 574 *Chiabrera* 4. 17
Use them, full oft, as pioneers to ruin, ... 812 *Excursion* 4. 770
Often. (*Partial list.*)
Well!—he has often spurned me like a toad, . . 45 *Bord.* 470
To seek thee did I often rove . . . . . . 184 **O blithe* 21
Had often been together. . . . . 239 *P. B.* 290
And ye—full often spurned as weeds— . . . 366 **Ye Trees* 12
Which thou prepar'st, full often, to convey . . 440 *Ecc. Sonn.* 2. 45. 11
But often his mind is compelled to demur, . . 570 *Farmer* 59
With a look of such earnestness often will stand, 570 *Farmer* 71
He thinks of the fields he so often hath mown, . 571 *Farmer* 83
Oftener. Appeared but seldom; oftener was he seen 124 *V. and J.* 212
Oftener than Ganges or the Nile; a thought . . 251 **There is a little* 7
Hath oftener left me mourning. . . . . . 484 *Simon Lee* 96
Far oftener then, bad ushering worse event, . . 519 *Pun. Death* 8. 7
In serious mood, but oftener, I confess, . . . 656 *Prelude* 3. 531
My comfort:—would that they were oftener fixed 835 *Excursion* 5. 824
In his suspicious wisdom; oftener still, . . . 859 *Excursion* 7. 104
Oftenest. Whom oftenest she beguiles. . . . . 170 *Rural Ill.* 36
Oftentimes. This song to myself did I oftentimes repeat; . . . . 88 *Pet-lamb* 62
And oftentimes, how long I fear to say, . . . 107 *Indolence* 24
And, oftentimes, hear the church-bell with a sigh, 116 *Repentance* 34
Of blasts of every tone; and oftentimes, . . . 132 *Michael* 49
His heart and his heart's joy! For oftentimes . 133 *Michael* 152
He as a watchman oftentimes was placed . . . 134 *Michael* 185
Dwelt in a tranquil spot. And oftentimes . . 150 **When, to* 26
And oftentimes compelled to halt, ... 175 *Waggoner* 1. 206
And oftentimes, when all are fast asleep, . . . 202 *Hart-leap* 135
Of thoughtless youth; but hearing oftentimes . 207 *Tintern* 90
And counted them: and oftentimes will start— . 267 **Though narrow* 11
Who oftentimes within those narrow bounds . . 354 *Aquap.* 127
And oftentimes before him stood, ... 399 *White Doe* 275
He told; and oftentimes with voice . . . . 411 *White Doe* 1350
And oftentimes the Lady meek . . . . . . 415 *White Doe* 1767
Before my window, oftentimes and long . . . 508 *F. Stone* 5
Not oftentimes, I trust, as we, poor brute! . . 523 *Epist. Beaumont* 139
This oftentimes, that he might be at ease, . . 553 *Prioress* 77
Upon the glassy plain; and oftentimes, . . . 639 *Prelude* 1. 452
At wake or fair. And oftentimes do flit . . 657 *Prelude* 3. 573
That he himself had oftentimes given way . . 666 *Prelude* 5. 55
For oftentimes he cast a backward look, . . . 667 *Prelude* 5. 119
Upon like errand. Oftentimes at least . . . 668 *Prelude* 5. 161
Lay bedded, changing oftentimes its form . . 685 *Prelude* 6. 706
Familiarly perused it; oftentimes, ... 689 *Prelude* 7. 145
Of that huge city, oftentimes was seen . . . 709 *Prelude* 8. 666
Was oftentimes uplifted, and he seemed . . . 713 *Prelude* 9. 282
Was his existence oftentimes *possessed*. . . . 759 *Excursion* 1. 221
These occupations oftentimes deceived . . . 760 *Excursion* 1. 258
That in yon arbour oftentimes she sate . . . 769 *Excursion* 1. 876
At this, not knowing why—as often-times . . K.8. 229 **I will* 168
Oft-recurring. In oft-recurring hours of sober thought 760 *Excursion* 1. 240
Offtimes. Than desolate; for oft-times from the sound . . . . 118 *Maternal Grief* 43
A pair of herons oft-times have I seen, . . . 143 **High bliss* 14
And cheering oft-times their reluctant gloom. . 172 *Infant Daughter* 50
"Yet bitter, oft-times bitter, was the pang . . 211 *Laod.* 127
Checked oft-times in a devious race, ... 285 *Grave of Burns* 74
For gentlest uses, oft-times Nature takes . . . 338 *Engelberg* 1
And oft-times he—who, yielding to the force . . 383 *Duddon* 30. 5
And oft-times in the most forbidding den . . . 429 *Ecc. Sonn.* 2. 5. 8
Witness the Church that oft-times, with effect . 431 *Ecc. Sonn.* 2. 10. 6
Oft-times makes its bounty known . . . . . 502 **Like a* 31
Oft-times from Alpine *chalets* sends a greeting. 524 *Epist. Beaumont* 206
And oft-times hast thou made my griefs thine own. 624 *Æneid* 18
Had ceased to dazzle, ofttimes did I quit . . . 650 *Prelude* 3. 91
With Nature,—hence, ofttimes, with reason too— 727 *Prelude* 11. 30
Who, in her worst distress, had ofttimes felt . . 770 *Excursion* 1. 935
Wisdom is ofttimes nearer when we stoop . . . 789 *Excursion* 3. 231
Should be permitted, ofttimes, to endure . . . 792 *Excursion* 3. 450
A spiritual presence, ofttimes misconceived, . . 815 *Excursion* 4. 927
Are ofttimes not unprofitably shown . . . . 848 *Excursion* 6. 667
Of the rude pile; as ofttimes trunks of trees, . . 871 *Excursion* 7. 916
Do I remember ofttimes to have seen . . . . 879 *Excursion* 8. 376

Ofttimes—*continued.*
And ofttimes Death, avenger of the past, . . . 886 *Excursion* 9. 124
Of the gay mind, as ofttimes splenetic youth . . K.8. 237 *Recluse* 1.1. 53
Are ofttimes to their fellow-men no more . . . K.8. 253 *Recluse* 1.1.606
Oh, *omitted.*
Old. Portentous through her old woods' trackless bounds, ... 12 *Desc. Sk.* 74
There an old man an olden measure scanned . . 13 *Desc. Sk.* 147
Whether some old Swiss air hath checked her haste, 15 *Desc. Sk.* 268
Hung there, no bush proclaimed to old and poor 24 *Guilt* 14
He from his old hereditary nook . . . . . 28 *Guilt* 233
That fear is like a cloak which old men huddle . 38 *Bord.* 22
An image of this old Man still was present, . . 39 *Bord.* 97
For my old age, it doth remain with thee . . . 40 *Bord.* 190
Thy absence, till old age and fresh infirmities . 41 *Bord.* 203
The house is hidden by the shade. Old Man, . 41 *Bord.* 219
When these old limbs had need of rest,—and now 42 *Bord.* 298
Let this old Man find at your hands; poor Leader, 42 *Bord.* 302
A blind old Greybeard and accosted him, . . . 45 *Bord.* 447
But 'tis all over now. That good old Lady . . 46 *Bord.* 486
And see your Friend again. The good old Man . 50 *Bord.* 695
Than twenty armies. How? The old blind Man, 51 *Bord.* 760
May love his Child. Thank you, old Man, for this! 52 *Bord.* 823
When my old Leader slipped into the flood . . 52 *Bord.* 834
How his old heart would leap to hear her steps, . 53 *Bord.* 886
Murder—perhaps asleep, blind, old, alone, . . 54 *Bord.* 901
Are brave: Clifford is brave; and that old Man . 54 *Bord.* 911
For this old venerable Grey-beard—faith . . . 54 *Bord.* 922
Would I could find the old Man and his Daughter. 55 *Bord.* 954
The old Man in that dungeon *is* alive. . . . . 55 *Bord.* 978
Of towns in flames, fields ravaged, young and old 56 *Bord.* 1031
And old, and blind—— Blind, say you? . . 57 *Bord.* 1072
—We recognise in this old Man a victim . . . 57 *Bord.* 1092
But first, how wash our hands of this old Man? . 60 *Bord.* 1254
Old Man! you were a very Lynx, you knew . . 61 *Bord.* 1313
Old Man! my wrath is as a flame burnt out, . . 63 *Bord.* 1402
In his old age—— Patience—Heaven grant me patience!— . . . . 66 *Bord.* 1611
Mutually consecrated. Poor old Man! . . . 70 *Bord.* 1849
To-night I met with an old Man . . . . . 72 *Bord.* 1923
This old Man may have a wife, ... 72 *Bord.* 1999
Have you, good Peasant, seen a blind old Man? . 73 *Bord.* 2041
This old man *had* a Daughter. To the spot . . 74 *Bord.* 2095
Was meek and patient, feeble, old and blind, . . 77 *Bord.* 2253
Of that old Man's forgiveness on thy heart, . . 77 *Bord.* 2297
Like the old Roman, on their own sword's point. 78 *Bord.* 2343
So be it when I shall grow old, ... 79 **My heart* 5
Than when both young and old sit gathered round 80 **Loving she* 9
To buy a new cloak for the old. . . . . . 82 *Alice Fell* 56
She was eight years old, she said; . . . . . 83 *We are Seven* 6
"Down to the stump of yon old yew . . . . 85 *Shepherd-boys* 35
I have a boy of five years old; . . . . . . 85 *Anecdote* 1
She in Grasmere's old church-steeple . . . . 94 *Westmoreland Girl* 59
Of his old cottage,—as it chanced, that day, . . 95 *Brothers* 19
Of carded wool which the old man had piled . . 95 *Brothers* 32
The old house-clock is decked with a new face; . 97 *Brothers* 160
A little—yet a little,—and old Walter, . . . 98 *Brothers* 210
Year after year the old man still kept up . . . 98 *Brothers* 213
His pace was never that of an old man: . . . 98 *Brothers* 220
The old man was a father to the boys, . . . 98 *Brothers* 229
This old Man, in the day of his old age, . . . 99 *Brothers* 234
They loved this good old Man?— They did—and truly: . . . . 99 *Brothers* 240
Live to such end is what both old and young . . 99 *Brothers* 287
But, as I said, old Walter was too weak . . . 100 *Brothers* 299
In old Armorica, whose secret springs . . . . 102 *Artegal* 10
Of old tradition, one particular flower . . . . 103 *Artegal* 58
Of some old cave, or mossy nook, ... 109 *Louisa* 16
Not old, though something past her prime: . . 119 *Sailor's Mother* 4
Old times, thought I, are breathing there; . . 119 *Sailor's Mother* 8
Old Timothy took up his staff, and he shut . . 120 *Childless Father* 15
Old Susan, she who dwells alone, ... 126 *Idiot Boy* 19
Old Susan lies a-bed in pain, ... 126 *Idiot Boy* 24
Or she will die, old Susan Gale. . . . . . 126 *Idiot Boy* 46
To comfort poor old Susan Gale. . . . . . 127 *Idiot Boy* 121
At poor old Susan then she railed, ... 128 *Idiot Boy* 232
And one hand rubs his old night-cap. . . . . 128 *Idiot Boy* 251
To comfort poor old Susan Gale. . . . . . 129 *Idiot Boy* 276
Who is it, but old Susan Gale? . . . . . . 130 *Idiot Boy* 411
An old man, stout of heart, and strong of limb. . 131 *Michael* 42
His Helpmate was a comely matron, old— . . 132 *Michael* 79
To deem that he was old,—in shepherd's phrase, 132 *Michael* 89
And his old Father both betook themselves . . 132 *Michael* 104
There by the light of this old lamp they sate, . 133 *Michael* 124
Both old and young, was named The Evening Star. . . . . 133 *Michael* 139
This son of his old age was yet more dear— . . 133 *Michael* 143
Old Michael, while he was a babe in arms, . . 133 *Michael* 153
Under the large old oak, that near his door . . 133 *Michael* 165
Two steady roses that were five years old; . . 134 *Michael* 179
But soon as Luke, full ten years old, could stand 134 *Michael* 194
And that the old Man's heart seemed born again? 134 *Michael* 203
Had prest upon him; and old Michael now . . 134 *Michael* 214
That any old man ever could have lost. . . . 134 *Michael* 220
What can be gained?" At this the old Man paused, ... 135 *Michael* 255
And her face brightened. The old Man was glad, 135 *Michael* 273
Had to her house returned, the old Man said, . . 136 *Michael* 316
And thus the old Man spake to him:—"My son . . . . 136 *Michael* 331

Old—*continued.*

Old—*continued.*

Old—*continued.*
Old Michael and his son one day went forth — K.8. 224 **I will* 6
Old Michael for this purpose had driven down — K.8. 224 **I will* 12
Of old Helvellyn spread their arms abroad — K.8. 225 **I will* 33
His son had drunk, the old man said to him — K.8. 226 **I will* 58
But soon as Luke, full ten years old, could stand — K.8. 226 **I will* 74
And that the old man's heart seem'd born again? — K.8. 226 ** I will* 83
Old Michael's manners and discourse, and thus — K.8. 228 **I will* 109
The old man afterwards was heard to say— — K.8. 229 **I will* 169
The dupe of history—that "old almanack"; — L.3. 27 **For Lubbock* 2
Olden. There an old man an olden measure scanned — 13 *Desc. Sk.* 147
Older. I am older, Anne, than you. — 79 *Foresight* 8
And older eyes than theirs beheld, — 215 *Kirkstone* 46
He was so old, he seems not older now; — 566 *Cumb. Beg.* 23
Oldest. The oldest and youngest — 190 *March* 6
The oldest man he seemed that ever wore grey hairs. — 196 *Resolution* 56
To oldest time! and, reckless of the storm — 809 *Excursion* 4. 518
The oldest, he was taken last, survived — 861 *Excursion* 7. 259
Old-grey. Beneath an old-grey oak as violets lie, — 605 *Desc.Sk.Quarto* 172
Olive. Of olive green and scarlet bright, — 198 *Thorn* 46
To Albogasio's olive bowers, — 343 *Eclipse* 35
Perched on an olive branch, and heard her cooing — 360 **Near Anio's* 2
But restless Fancy left that olive grove — 360 **Near Anio's* 5
Olive-bough. Where once the Dove and Olive-bough — 174 *Waggoner* 1. 53
There, where the Dove and Olive-bough — 174 *Waggoner* 1. 58
And hope—the Olive-bough and Dove; — 174 *Waggoner* 1. 86
Olive-bower. The vineyard and the olive-bower, — 343 *Eclipse* 65
Olive's. The lightsome Olive's twinkling canopy— — 361 **List—'twas* 21
Olympian. Some God or Hero, from the Olympian clime — 220 *Triad* 3
The Olympian summit hath destroyed for aye — 325 *Ode 1814* 119
Olympus. His ancient dower Olympus hath not sold; — 251 **Pelion and* 3
Her seat upon Olympus, doth forsake — 521 *Epist.Beaumont* 39
Omen. Soft notes, awful as the omen — 328 *Ode 1815* 72
Omen of man's grievous doom! — 502 **Like a* 12
Followed as of good omen, and meek Worth — 658 *Prelude* 3. 607
Weak, and of heartless omen, had not power — 727 *Prelude* 11. 10
Omening. *See* **Ill-omening.**
Ominous. Before the ominous aspect of her spear; — 311 **Who rises* 24
Of rash change, ominous for the public weal. — 394 **No more* 30
With ominous change, which, night by night, provoked — 695 *Prelude* 7. 535
Omission. Prevent omission, help deficiency, — 445 *Ecc. Sonn.* 3. 21. 11
Omit. And made me love them, may I here omit — 640 *Prelude* 1. 547
After an eight-days' absence. For (to omit — 661 *Prelude* 4. 196
Omitted. Yet much hath been omitted, as need was; — 750 *Prelude* 14. 312
Omnipotent. The Covenant. The Omnipotent will raise — 446 *Ecc. Sonn.* 3. 23. 11
Omnipresent. With omnipresent murmur as they rave — 314 **Not 'mid* 7
With no one near save the omnipresent God. — 391 *Brownie* 8
Single and one, the omnipresent God, — 811 *Excursion* 4. 652
Omniscience. To his omniscience will appear — 332 *Ode: Thanks.* 242
Omniscient. Learn thou the beauty of omniscient care! — 505 *Warning* 159
Audible praise, to thee, omniscient Mind, — 895 *Excursion* 9. 753
Omrahs. Rajahs and Omrahs in his train, intent — 718 *Prelude* 10. 20
On, *omitted.*
Once. (*Partial list.*)
By a miraculous finger stilled at once. — 40 *Bord.* 173
Why, this is noble! shake her off at once. — 41 *Bord.* 248
Which pleased him so, that he was hushed at once: — 44 *Bord.* 402
You are wasting words; hear me then once for all: — 48 *Bord.* 625
For once you loved me. You shall back with me — 50 *Bord.* 694
If once they blew a horn this side the Tweed. — 50 *Bord.* 730
Then—all at once the air was still, — 154 **A whirl-blast* 3
Once lived a happy life! — 155 *Waterfall* 24
And birds and flowers once more to greet, — 159 *Green Linnet* 7
Though of a lineage once abhorred, — 232 *Jew. Fam.* 39
So these,—and, heard of once again, are chased — 320 **Hunger, and* 8
Yet never once doth go astray, — 486 *Matthew* 4
For me, thy natural leader, once again — 496 **A little* 14
And once, behind a rick of barley, — 537 *Goody Blake* 73
That once, while there he plied his studious work — 548 **Stay, bold* 21
O house of houses, once so richly dight! — 563 *Troilus* 23
O, of all houses once the crownèd boast! — 563 *Troilus* 29
Where he had felt such perfect pleasure once. — 563 *Troilus* 46
Heard my own Cresid's laugh; and once at play — 563 *Troilus* 51
And yonder once she unto me 'gan say— — 563 *Troilus* 53
For when thy horns begin once more to spring, — 564 *Troilus* 139
He once had a heart which was moved by the wires — 572 *Avarice* 25
Of that delightful fragrance which was once — 575 *Chiabrera* 8. 23
What though the radiance which was once so bright — 590 *Immortality* 179
Once to Our Lady dedicate, and served — 643 *Prelude* 2. 64
"Once," and with wild demeanour, as he spake, — 894 *Excursion* 9. 679
"Once, while the Name, Jehovah, was a sound — 894 *Excursion* 9. 682
Once-bare. The once-bare cottage, on the mountain-side, — 860 *Excursion* 7. 200
Once-bright. And if, amid those once-bright bowers, our fate — 124 *V. and J.* 198
Once-intellectual. The taste of this once-intellectual Land. — 489 *Illus. Books* 8
Once-mitred. Are glorified while this once-mitred pair — 437 *Ecc. Sonn.* 2. 34. 10
One. (*Partial list.*) *See* **Little-one, Young-one.**
No purer essence, than the one that burns, — v **If thou indeed* 9
All are the undying offspring of one Sire: — v **If thou indeed* 14
Be given, not one memorial gleam, — 1 *Extract* 12
Gives one bright glance, and drops behind the hill. — 5 *Ev. Wk.* 191
The form appears of one that spurs his steed — 6 *Ev. Wk.* 196
The *west*, that burns like one dilated sun, — 15 *Desc. Sk.* 282
One I behold who, 'cross the foaming flood, — 17 *Desc. Sk.* 380

One—*continued.*
With one bright bell a favourite heifer's neck; — 19 *Desc. Sk.* 495
One flower of hope—oh, pass and leave it there! — 20 *Desc. Sk.* 552
By one soft impulse saved from vacancy. — 22 *Yew-tree* 7
If Thou be one whose heart the holy forms — 23 *Yew-tree* 48
Is ever on himself doth look on one, — 23 *Yew-tree* 56
But not one dwelling-place his heart to cheer. — 25 *Guilt* 31
From gulf of parting clouds one friendly beam, — 26 *Guilt* 131
All perished—all in one remorseless year, — 30 *Guilt* 302
Husband and children! one by one, by sword — 30 *Guilt* 303
And from her grateful heart a fresh one drew: — 30 *Guilt* 322
Rise various wreaths that into one unite — 33 *Guilt* 462
As the wain fronted her,—wherein lay one, — 34 *Guilt* 544
Though even to die near one she most had loved — 34 *Guilt* 548
Till one was found by stroke of violence dead, — 35 *Guilt* 599
The corse interred, not one hour he remained — 36 *Guilt* 645
Companionship with One of crooked ways, — 37 *Bord.* 8
That cannot feel for one, helpless as he is. — 38 *Bord.* 68
In the same nest, my spring-time one with thine. — 40 *Bord.* 151
Fear not, I will obey you;—but One so young, — 42 *Bord.* 308
And One so fair, it goes against my heart. — 43 *Bord.* 309
By the brook-side: it is the abode of One, — 44 *Bord.* 380
She paces out the hour 'twixt twelve and one— — 44 *Bord.* 392
He was that One so young should pass his youth — 49 *Bord.* 689
Is it possible? One thing you noticed not: — 51 *Bord.* 787
That horn again—'Tis some one of our Troop; — 56 *Bord.* 1016
She weighs them in one scale. The wiles of woman, — 57 *Bord.* 1080
With two Companions; one of them, as seemed, — 58 *Bord.* 1137
Two columns, one for passion, one for proof; — 58 *Bord.* 1148
You take it as it merits—— One a King, — 60 *Bord.* 1228
Floats kingcups in the brook—a Hero one — 60 *Bord.* 1235
And leave his body here, it were all one — 61 *Bord.* 1299
One happy thought has passed across my mind. — 61 *Bord.* 1326
Makes up one damning falsehood. Leave him here — 62 *Bord.* 1398
Might stretch beyond the measure of one moon. — 68 *Bord.* 1711
Landed with a small troop, myself being one: — 68 *Bord.* 1713
We all are of one blood, our veins are filled — 69 *Bord.* 1739
One of Love's simple bondsmen—the soft chain — 70 *Bord.* 1841
Of our distress—and thou art one of them! — 74 *Bord.* 2086
And thus we meet again; one human stay — 75 *Bord.* 2134
Shame! Eldred, shame! The dead have but one face. — 75 *Bord.* 2162
—But hear me. For *one* question, I have a heart — 77 *Bord.* 2255
By One who would have died a thousand times — 78 *Bord.* 2331
Strawberry-blossoms, one and all, — 79 *Foresight* 3
Heaven grant that he spare but that one upright twig — 80 †*Address: Child* 24
Those foot marks, one by one, — 83 *Lucy Gray* 54
A Poet, one who loves the brooks — 85 *Shepherd-boys* 84
One morn we strolled on our dry walk, — 85 *Anecdote* 5
They built him and christened him all in one day, — 86 *Rural Arch.* 8
With one knee on the grass did the little Maiden kneel, — 87 *Pet-lamb* 7
"What ails thee, young One? what? Why pull so at thy cord? — 87 *Pet-lamb* 21
Rest, little young One, rest; what is't that aileth thee? — 87 *Pet-lamb* 24
"Rest, little young One, rest; thou hast forgot the day — 87 *Pet-lamb* 33
That but half of it was hers, and one half of it was *mine*. — 88 *Pet-lamb* 64
Where earth and heaven do make one imagery; — 88 *H. C.* 10
Paid to One who loved her well. — 94 *Westmoreland Girl* 68
Your years make up one peaceful family; — 97 *Brothers* 122
Was rent with lightning—one hath disappeared; — 97 *Brothers* 144
One roaring cataract! a sharp May-storm — 97 *Brothers* 151
And in one night send twenty score of sheep — 97 *Brothers* 153
A pair of diaries,—one serving, Sir, — 97 *Brothers* 163
For the whole dale, and one for each fire-side— — 97 *Brothers* 164
By turning o'er these hillocks one by one, — 98 *Brothers* 191
Two fathers in one father: and if tears, — 99 *Brothers* 230
That venturous foot could reach, to one or both — 99 *Brothers* 275
And that he had one Brother— That is but — 100 *Brothers* 330
Three months with one, and six months with another; — 100 *Brothers* 344
And in the midst is one particular rock — 101 *Brothers* 366
If he had one, the Youth had twenty homes. — 101 *Brothers* 386
But One there is, a Child of nature meek, — 103 *Artegal* 45
Of old tradition, one particular flower — 103 *Artegal* 58
One side of our whole vale with grandeur rare; — 106 *Farewell* 4
We go for One to whom ye will be dear; — 106 *Farewell* 25
Of which I sang one song that will not die. — 107 *Farewell* 56
Within our happy Castle there dwelt One — 107 *Indolence* 1
In one of those sweet dreams I slept, — 109 **Strange fits* 17
—Fair as a star, when only one — 109 **She dwelt* 7
Thou one fair shrub, oh! shed thy flowers, — 111 **'Tis said that some* 39
Is one of giant stature, who could dance — 111 **'Tis said that some* 46
One upright arm sustains the cheek, — 112 **How rich* 14
And one across the bosom lies— — 112 **How rich* 15
Another day, a single one! — 114 *Ind. Wom.* 22
But such a one, on English ground, — 114 *Last of Flock* 5
And from this one, this single ewe, — 115 *Last of Flock* 32
They dwindled, dwindled, one by one; — 115 *Last of Flock* 66
I had but only one: — 116 *Last of Flock* 96
Weeping for him when no one knew. — 117 *Affl. Marg.* 35
One that will answer to my mind; — 117 *Affl. Marg.* 69
Save one *wee*, hungry, nibbling mouse, — 118 †*Cottager* 9
What one short sigh so easily removed?— — 118 *Maternal Grief* 10

One—*continued.*
One spirit animating old and young, 892 *Excursion* 9. 526
Of one day's pleasure, and all mortal joys! 892 *Excursion* 9. 555
Of good from evil; as if one extreme 895 *Excursion* 9. 723
To the one cottage in the lonely dell: 895 *Excursion* 9. 774
Unheard of, save in one small hamlet, here S.3. 433 **The doubt* 9
Entering the cell gave restlessness to one, S.3. 434* *The doubt* 73
The grieved one whom it meant to send away, S.3. 434 **The doubt* 91
On thee, bright Spring, a bashful little one, S.3. 435**The doubt* 130
As one unknown by others, aptly called K.8. 226 **I will* 53
More than one thought of death, and his last hour. K.8. 229 **I will* 158
One of a golden summer holiday, K.8. 236 *Recluse* 1. 1. 4
Scarcely a wish, but one bright pleasing thought, K.8. 237 *Recluse* 1.1.16
One of thy lowly dwellings is my Home. K.8. 238*Recluse* 1.1. 59
The one sensation that is here; 'tis here, K.8. 240*Recluse* 1.1.137
That she should entertain for this one day, K.8. 241*Recluse* 1.1.190
One of a mighty multitude, whose way K.8. 242*Recluse* 1.1.201
One death, and that were mercy given to both. K.8. 244*Recluse* 1.1.268
A chosen one of my regards. See there K.8. 251*Recluse* 1.1.523
To one who holds it dear; with duteous care K.8. 251*Recluse* 1.1.525
First one and then another silver spout, K.8. 251*Recluse* 1.1.555
As one or other takes the fit of glee, K.8. 251*Recluse* 1.1.556
Upon one tree, while all the distant grove K.8. 252*Recluse* 1.1.567
Of many into one incorporate. K.8. 253*Recluse* 1.1.616
One household under God for high and low, K.8. 253*Recluse* 1.1.618
One family, and one mansion; to themselves K.8. 253*Recluse* 1.1.619
Take we at once this one sufficient hope, K.8. 254*Recluse* 1.1.633
And one, like them, a brother of our hearts, K.8. 254*Recluse* 1.1.659
By one, sole keeper of his own intent, K.8. 256*Recluse* 1.1.718
The cry is six to one upon the Duke. L.1. 96 *Juvenal* 3. 30

One-pennied. The one-pennied Boy has his penny to spare. 188 *Music* 28

One's. A criminal in no one's eyes but theirs— 71 *Bord.* 1894
In walks whose boundary is the lost One's grave, 119 *Maternal Grief* 68
Part of her lost One's glory back to trace 446 *Ecc. Sonn.* 3.24. 12
Guid'st the pale Mourner to the lost one's tomb; 459 **Wanderer! that* 28
No one's eye had seen him enter, 535 *Egremont* 67
No one's ear had heard the Horn. 535 *Egremont* 68

Ones. *See* **Little-ones, Young-ones.**
Yet two sweet little ones partook my bed; 35 *Guilt* 596
Smiles hast thou, bright ones of thy own; 121 *EmigrantMother* 61
For *Books!*" Yes, heartless Ones, or be it proved 280 *Plea for Auth.* 10
Bereft Ones, and in lowly anguish weep 387 **Part fenced* 7
Where be the wretched ones, the sights for pity? 475 *Greenock* 4
For if than other rash ones more thou know, 513 *Newspaper* 11
Take those dear young Ones to a fearless nest; 525 **Soon did* 2
Was smitten by the great ones of the world, 574 *Chiabrera* 3. 10
Six little ones at home had left, 623 *G. and S. Green* 7
Food for the hungry ears of little ones, 668 *Prelude* 5. 211
Behold a race of young ones like to those 671 *Prelude* 5. 407
Some vagrant mother, whose arch little ones, 705 *Prelude* 8. 402
(If like desires of innocent little ones 723 *Prelude* 10. 365
And great in large ones, I had oft revolved, 728 *Prelude* 11. 86
Ran in new channels, leaving old ones dry; 730 *Prelude* 11. 185
With an impassioned life, what feeble ones 735 *Prelude* 12. 104
Great truths, than touch and handle little ones. 740 *Prelude* 13. 54

Onion. These seven long years to Grenville's onion head. L.1. 89 *Juvenal* 1. 28

Only. (*Partial list.*)
Though seeking only holiday delight; 10 *Desc. Sk.* 12
Out of thy mind? My dear, my only, Child; 40 *Bord.* 163
As if he were the only Saint on earth, 45 *Bord.* 463
Henceforth it shall be said that bad men only 54 *Bord.* 910
For joy and rest, albeit to find them only 231 *Clouds* 93
Will build their savage fortunes only there; 421 *Ecc. Sonn.* 1. 11. 12
Let both meet only on thy royal shield! 432 *Ecc. Sonn.* 2. 15. 5
How hard, alas! to bear, I only know. 557 *Cuck.and Night.* 40
Is only fit to die, I dare well say, 559 *Cuck.andNight.*134
Of all this town, save only in this place, 565 *Troilus* 159
Only by gold. And now a simple stone 574 *Chiabrera* 5. 16
This only grieves me, for it seems a wrong, 575 *Chiabrera* 6. 10
I only have relinquished one delight 590 *Immortality* 194

Onset. Heed not such onset! nay, if praise of men 255 *Detraction* 11
Whom onset, fiercely urged at Jove's command, 265 **When haughty* 13
Who on that day the word of onset gave! 293 *Killicranky* 12
Of that first memorable onset made 721 *Prelude* 10. 247
For onset, for resistance too inert, 791 *Excursion* 3. 344

Ontario's. The matted forests of Ontario's shore 379 *Duddon* 13. 8

Onward. Right onward to the Scottish strand 161 *Binnorie* 16
I stagger onward—heaven knows how; 179 *Waggoner* 3. 89
—Pass onward (even the glancing deer 221 *Triad* 76
The shepherd struggles with them. Onward thence 353 *Aquap.* 47
I thanked the Leader of my onward way. 383 *Duddon* 28. 14
They come—and onward travel without dread, 422 *Ecc. Sonn.* 1. 14. 7
Ye mariners, that plough your onward way, 454 *Sea-side* 36
Furrowing its way right onward. The most rude, 460 **Wanderer! that* 52
"*A little onward lend thy guiding hand* 496 **A little* 1
O Thou who movest onward with a mind 573 *Chiabrera* 3. 1
And drove us onward like to ships at sea, 622 *Recluse* 1. 1. 160
And help life onward in its noblest aim. 628 **Deign, Sovereign* 28
Onward we drove beneath the Castle; caught, 649 *Prelude* 3. 15
Departs, intent upon his onward quest!— 788 *Excursion* 3. 172
Numerous as stars; that, by their onward lapse, 800 *Excursion* 3. 975
If Stephen's distanced, onward see him strive L.1. 96 *Juvenal* 3. 31

Onward-looking. Me rich in many onward-looking thoughts, K.8. 243*Recluse* 1.1.233

Onwards. Swept onwards, did the vision cross your view? 283 **Proud were* 10

Ooze. Not undistinguished, for of wells that ooze S.3. 433 **The doubt* 10

Oozy. The local Deity, with oozy hair 269 *Gordale* 8

Ope. All night the door at every moment ope; 609 *Desc.Sk.Quarto* 409

Open. *See* **Half-open.**
Thy open beauties, or thy lone retreats; 12 *Desc. Sk.* 108
When, from the sunny breast of open seas, 17 *Desc. Sk.* 366
Dismissed, again on open day I gazed, 31 *Guilt* 400
In open air forgetful would I sit 32 *Guilt* 431
And clear and open soul, so prized in fearless youth. 32 *Guilt* 441
Beneath their roof, but to the open air 36 *Guilt* 646
The truth shall be laid open, his guilt proved 48 *Bord.* 600
A few leagues hence we shall have open ground, 49 *Bord.* 655
The Sheriff read, in open Court, a letter 49 *Bord.* 679
This monstrous crime to be laid open—*here*, 58 *Bord.* 1118
All gathered to the spot, in open day 58 *Bord.* 1122
Henceforth new prospects open on your path; 64 *Bord.* 1497
If e'er I open out this heart of mine 65 *Bord.* 1557
his eyes may yet open upon those that love him. 72 *Bord.* 2002
He will never open them more; 72 *Bord.* 2004
In the open streets, and let him think he sees, 76 *Bord.* 2180
And then an open field they crossed: 83 *Lucy Gray* 49
Weary of the open sky. 90 *Longest Day* 4
Who, in the open air, with due accord 95 *Brothers* 24
Hanging in the open air—but, O good Sir! 100 *Brothers* 314
In open fields; and when the glare of day 119 *Maternal Grief* 65
And in the open sunshine of God's love 134 *Michael* 229
And in the open fields my life was passed 136 *Michael* 350
A length of open space, where to and fro 150 **When, to* 37
Could Father Adam open his eyes 162 **Art thou the* 12
And in this smooth and open dell 165 *Danish Boy* 5
In the broad open eye of the solitary sky, 166 *Stray Pleasures* 16
Of Him who slept upon the open lea: 168 *Pilgrim's Dream* 67
Into open sign of joy: 171 *Kitten* 90
Of open house and ready fare. 174 *Waggoner* 1. 82
Of open door and shining light. 174 *Waggoner* 1 9
Hallooing from an open throat, 179 *Waggoner* 3.1
With careless air and open mien. 181 *Waggoner* 4. 14
Have been a traveller under open sky, 192 *Gipsies* 10
Open, ye thickets! let her fly, 221 *Triad* 119
Who deem that ye from open light 225 *Present.* 2
Wide open for the scattered Poor. 228 *Devot. Incit.* 59
The grave shall open, quench the stars. 235 *Power of Sound* 216
Against the wind and open sky!" 240 *P. B.* 320
Now running o'er the open plains. 243 *P. B.* 645
The open moonlight reach. 244 *P. B.* 675
A length of green and open road— 244 *P. B.* 678
And green vales open out, with grove and field, 268 **Four fiery* 9
Open unto the fields, and to the sky; 269 *Westm. Bridge* 7
O'er hilly path, and open Strath, 293 *Yarrow Unv.* 37
In the open sunshine, or we are unblest: 307 **O Friend* 6
Of British freedom, which, to the open sea 307 **It is not* 2
'Tis his who walks about in the open air, 308 **There is a bondage* 4
First open traitor to the German name! 313 *Prophecy* 14
When he himself was tried in open light. 318 **Is there* 14
For they have learnt to open and to close 320 **They seek* 3
When duty bids you bleed in open war: 326 **Intrepid sons* 7
For victory shaped an open space, 341 *San Salv.* 33
Your council-seats beneath the open sky, 350 *Des. Stanzas* 50
To lay a new world open. Nor less prized 354 *Aquap.* 130
And through each window's open fret-work looked 355 *Aquap.* 157
From all her Sanctuaries!—Open for my feet 357 *Aquap.* 298
And down the path through the open green, 396 *White Doe* 50
Leads through space of open day, 397 *White Doe* 84
Who gave their wishes open vent; 400 *White Doe* 369
He saw her where in open view 401 *White Doe* 446
Appeared, with free and open hate 404 *White Doe* 705
In open victory o'er the weight 404 *White Doe* 741
Then look at them with open eyes! 406 *White Doe* 904
In open field their gathering foes, 406 *White Doe* 907
In open moonlight doth she lie; 407 *White Doe* 994
To open moonshine, where the Doe 407 *White Doe* 1001
The breach is open—on the wall, 408 *White Doe* 1139
Where Francis stood in open sight. 412 *White Doe* 1463
Lies open on the sabbath day; 416 *White Doe* 1888
Flew open, by an Angel's voice unbarred? 419 *Ecc. Sonn.* 1. 2. 10
As oft, 'mid some green plot of open ground, 425 *Ecc. Sonn.* 1. 27. 12
Open a passage to the Romish sword, 431 *Ecc. Sonn.* 2. 12. 8
While through the Convent's gate to open view 434 *Ecc. Sonn.* 2. 22. 7
Unlooked-for outlet to an open sea, 434 *Ecc. Sonn.* 2. 23. 6
Open your gates, ye everlasting Piles! 451 *Ecc. Sonn.* 3. 42. 1
Open your gates, ye Monuments of love 451 *Ecc. Sonn.* 3. 42. 11
And, from the wide and open Baltic, rise 454 *Sea-side* 31
"I come to open out, for fresh display, 456 **Soft as* 25
Then, while the Sailor, 'mid an open sea 460 **Wanderer! that* 65
Of Science laid them open to mankind— 461 **Queen of* 41
To glide in open prospect through clear sky. 461 **Who but is* 8
Now near his master's house in open view 472 *Dunolly Eagle* 5
We talked with open heart, and tongue 487 *Fountain* 1
Rises by open means; and there will stand 493 *Hap. War.* 36
Lie open; and the book of Holy Writ, 496 **A little* 51
To open a bright eye. 506 **While from* 40
Hooded the open brow that overawed 513 **Said Secrecy* 5
With door left open makes a gloomy spot, 524 *Epist. Beaumont* 220
And while thus in open day 535 *Egremont* 77
Open their hearts before Thee, pouring out 539 **Lady! a* 52
"Leave open to my wish the course, 545 *Russ. Fug.* 337
He looks, through the open door-place, toward the lake 547 **Rude is* 27
And open thy sad eyes upon a milder day. 581 *Invoc. Earth* 7
Along a bare and open valley, 586 *Hogg* 3

Open—*continued*.
Now, passing Urseren's open vale serene, 606 *Desc.Sk.Quarto* 243
Now in the clear and open day I feel 622 *Recluse* 1. 1. 111
Recorded: to the open fields I told 632 *Prelude* 1. 50
To range the open heights where woodcocks run 636 *Prelude* 1. 311
The mind lay open, to a more exact 646 *Prelude* 2. 283
Or walks of open scandal, but in vague 653 *Prelude* 3. 324
And open field, through which the pathway wound, 663 *Prelude* 4. 322
Up-turning, then, along an open field, 665 *Prelude* 4. 448
Rich with indigenous produce, open ground 669 *Prelude* 5. 236
One of those open fields, which, shaped like ears, 672 *Prelude* 5. 433
Forth, through some Gothic window's open space, 678 *Prelude* 6. 216
Of darkness, dances in the open air 680 *Prelude* 6. 372
All hearts were open, every tongue was loud 681 *Prelude* 6. 401
Upon the open lawns! Vallombre's groves 682 *Prelude* 6. 480
An open place it was, and overlooked, 685 *Prelude* 6. 703
Saw woman as she is, to open shame 693 *Prelude* 7. 386
Open it out, diffusing thence a smile 695 *Prelude* 7. 560
Him saw I, sitting in an open square, 696 *Prelude* 7. 604
Below, the open space, through every nook 697 *Prelude* 7. 689
Seated, with open door, often and long 705 *Prelude* 8. 411
The curious traveller, who, from open day, 707 *Prelude* 8. 560
Of the Bastille, I sate in the open sun, 710 *Prelude* 9. 68
Which once had been erect and open, now 711 *Prelude* 9. 147
Distinction open lay to all that came, 713 *Prelude* 9. 230
Lofty and over-arched, with open space 716 *Prelude* 9. 435
Should cease; and open accusation lead 717 *Prelude* 9. 537
And open punishment, if not the air 717 *Prelude* 9. 539
Pleased in some open field to exercise 723 *Prelude* 10. 367
Said I forth-pouring on those open sands 726 *Prelude* 10. 579
Had left an interregnum's open space 727 *Prelude* 11. 33
Was my condition, till with open war 729 *Prelude* 11. 174
The open eye of Reason. Then I said, 735 *Prelude* 12. 67
Open; I would approach them, but they close. 738 *Prelude* 12. 280
Were open schools in which I daily read 742 *Prelude* 13. 163
And open day; accompanied its course 749 *Prelude* 14. 197
Have been laid open, needs must make me feel 752 *Prelude* 14. 422
Upon that open moorland stood a grove, 756 *Excursion* 1. 26
His heart lay open; and, by nature tuned 761 *Excursion* 1. 362
Through many a wood and many an open ground, 766 *Excursion* 1. 699
Lay scattered here and there, open or shut, 768 *Excursion* 1. 828
Of spurious notions—worn as open signs 775 *Excursion* 2. 271
They faint not, but advance towards the open grave 780 *Excursion* 2. 586
Of open court, an object like a throne 784 *Excursion* 2. 862
And, with blithe air of open fellowship, 785 *Excursion* 2. 898
Shut out from prospect of the open vale, 786 *Excursion* 3. 38
Through wood or open field, the harmless Man 788 *Excursion* 3. 171
Him, as we entered from the open glen, 789 *Excursion* 3. 200
But, there, lay open to our daily haunt, 794 *Excursion* 3. 537
And acclamation, crowds in open air 797 *Excursion* 3. 750
Idle temptations; open vanities, 804 *Excursion* 4. 209
Lies open: we have heard from you a voice 818 *Excursion* 4. 1118
In open circle seated round, and hushed 820 *Excursion* 4. 1280
Open, and day's pure cheerfulness, but veiled 822 *Excursion* 5. 5
Stood open; and we entered. On my frame, 824 *Excursion* 5. 139
Who there was standing on the open hill, 834 *Excursion* 5. 753
Not less than beautiful; an open brow 834 *Excursion* 5. 780
And receptacle, open to the good 836 *Excursion* 5. 913
Open or covert, be that priesthood still, 839 *Excursion* 6. 55
That open grave is destined." "Died he then 840 *Excursion* 6. 115
No more to open on that irksome world 843 *Excursion* 6. 365
By the last lingering help of the open sky 852 *Excursion* 6. 902
Asked comfort of the open air, and found 855 *Excursion* 6. 1100
Laid open through the blazing window:—there 856 *Excursion* 6. 1178
Of open projects, and his inward hoard 861 *Excursion* 7. 280
To be laid open, and they prophesied. 865 *Excursion* 7. 533
On all sides open to the fanning breeze, 866 *Excursion* 7. 618
Of his bright hearth, and from his open door, 867 *Excursion* 7. 650
Flew open, and a pair of lusty Boys 882 *Excursion* 8. 545
Should open while they range the richer fields 886 *Excursion* 9. 174
That object is laid open to the view 887 *Excursion* 9. 216
So the wide waters, open to the power, 889 *Excursion* 9. 375
While from the grassy mountain's open side 893 *Excursion* 9. 609
Exultingly, in view of open day 894 *Excursion* 9. 706
Why open thus mine eyes? To die K.8. 219 **The snow-tracks* 15
From open ground to covert, from a bed K.8. 237 *Recluse* 1.1. 41
Could see them, nor in that small open space K.8. 243 *Recluse* 1.1.258
Of the fire-side, or of the open field, K.8. 246 *Recluse* 1.1.361
These mountains will rejoice with open joy. K.8. 254 *Recluse* 1.1.661
His Grace's watermen in open race L.1. 96 *Juvenal* 3. 27

Opened. *See* **Half-opened, Re-opened.**
Opened at once, and stayed my devious feet. 3 *Ev. Wk.* 56
A cave that opened to the road presented 50 *Bord.* 699
I lighted—opened with soft touch the chapel's iron door, 92 *Poet's Dream* 41
The mountains have all opened out themselves, 131 *Michael* 7
Is opened of still deeper pain, 180 *Waggoner* 4. 76
Her brow hath opened on me—see it there, 222 *Triad* 187
Had opened on his eager glance; 348 **Lulled by* 52
Of music opened, and there came a blending 371 *Eg. Maid* 146
Is opened round him:—hamlets, towers, and towns, 384 *Duddon* 32. 10
A way first opened; and, with Roman chains, 419 *Ecc. Sonn.* 1. 3. 11
Opened a vision of that blissful place 446 *Ecc. Sonn.* 3. 24.10
On thy wings opened wide for smoothest flight, 456 **The leaves* 15
But now there opened on me other thoughts 662 *Prelude* 4. 239
With conscious pleasure opened to the charm 674 *Prelude* 5. 554
Was opened; tract more exquisitely fair 700 *Prelude* 8. 75
And thus a way was opened for mistakes 730 *Prelude* 11. 181
Of kindred hands that opened out the springs 749 *Prelude* 14. 238
She opened—found no writing, but beheld 766 *Excursion* 1. 669

Opened—*continued*.
A narrow, winding, entry opened out 777 *Excursion* 2. 412
Had opened of itself (for it was swoln 778 *Excursion* 2. 439
That opened from the enclosure of green fields 779 *Excursion* 2. 495
Opened, as she before had done for me, 783 *Excursion* 2. 743
Of the blind vapour, opened to my view 784 *Excursion* 2. 831
Opened, and she re-entered with glad looks, 834 *Excursion* 5. 774
—Her wedded days had opened with mishap, 849 *Excursion* 6. 716
"A kindlier passion opened on her soul 852 *Excursion* 6. 906
Her heart she opened; and no pains were spared 854 *Excursion* 6. 1031
Mines opened, forests planted, and rocks split, K.8. 227 **I will* 104
Are opened. Churlish Winter hath given leave K.8. 241 *Recluse* 1.1.189

Open-hearted. To our confiding, open-hearted, Leader. 37 *Bord.* 10

Opening. Or marks, 'mid opening cliffs, fair dark-eyed maids 12 *Desc. Sk.* 91
And saw the dawn opening the silvery east 30 *Guilt* 313
Of opening out my story; you must hear it, 68 *Bord.* 1683
In their stead each opening flower. 94 *Westmoreland Girl* 80
That, in the gracious opening of thy reign, 105 *Artegal* 192
Could, by the simple opening of a door, 122 *V. and J.* 47
Along a natural opening, that I stood 150 **When, to* 50
Opening daily at thy side, 161 **Pleasures newly* 47
While Faith, from yonder opening cloud, 215 *Kirkstone* 83
And vernal mornings opening bright 217 *Enterprise* 147
That opening—but a look ye cast 224 *'Tis gone* 8
His heart is opening more and more; 248 *P. B.* 1052
Forgets her nature, opening like a flower 274 *Infant M.* 2
Where herbs look up, and opening flowers are seen; 278 **Life with* 11
Fair scenes for childhood's opening bloom, 302 *Yarrow V.* 57
Opening to view the abyss in which she feeds 313 **Clouds, lingering* 10
Opening before the sun's triumphant eye— 323 *Ode 1814* 21
How fearful were it down through opening waves 333 *Fish-women* 6
And opening life to thee? 334 **In Bruges* 32
With golden blossoms opening at the feet 353 *Aquap.* 29
The opening of the year. 483 *Sister* 20
And nearer interests culled from the opening stage 522 *Epist. Beaumont* 90
Ah, Beaumont! when an opening in the road 524 *Epist. Beaumont* 171
In its sweet opening? and what dire mishap 575 *Chiabrera* 7. 6
Thro' craggs, and forest glooms, and opening lakes, 591 *Ev. Wk. Quarto* 4
The Moon's fix'd gaze between the opening trees, 596 *Ev. Wk. Quarto* 262
Opening the peaceful clouds; or she may use 637 *Prelude* 1. 354
In the simplicities of opening life 669 *Prelude* 5. 277
Turn where I might, was opening out its glories, 686 *Prelude* 6. 775
Opening the clouds; or sovereign king, announced 693 *Prelude* 7. 416
Endless, here opening widely out, and there 702 *Prelude* 8. 193
Assisted, led me back through opening day 732 *Prelude* 11. 352
Opening from land to land an easy way 771 *Excursion* 2. 17
A glorious opening, the unlooked-for dawn, 774 *Excursion* 2. 212
Was one small opening, where a heath-clad ridge 776 *Excursion* 2. 335
Are opening round her; those of middle age, 837 *Excursion* 5. 962
Save through a gap high in the hills, an opening 859 *Excursion* 7. 142
Wishful to leave an opening for my choice, 891 *Excursion* 9. 480
The Valley, opening out her bosom, gave 892 *Excursion* 9. 571
Though slowly opening, opens every day K.8. 249 *Recluse* 1.1.473

Openings. 'Mid silver clouds, and openings of blue sky 190 **Lyre! though* 23
And irremoveable) gracious openings lie, 396 **Action is* 8

Openly. Persisted openly that death alone 123 *V. and J.* 116
With us openly abide, 171 *Kitten* 61
Be with them openly displayed. 405 *White Doe* 802
Openly in the eye of earth and heaven, 730 *Prelude* 11. 210

Openness. To bring his charge in openness; whereat, 719 *Prelude* 10. 108

Opens. Opens—a little world of calm delight; 14 *Desc. Sk.* 209
The scene that opens now? 215 *Kirkstone* 64
Opens a way for life, or consonance 449 *Ecc. Sonn.* 3. 36. 5
Hell opens, and the heavens in vengeance crack 475 **Here on their* 8
He opens of his feet the sanguine tides, 609 *Desc.Sk.Quarto* 395
A gulf of gloomy blue, that opens wide 611 *Desc.Sk.Quarto* 498
Where passage opens, but the same shall have 702 *Prelude* 8. 203
That opens, for such sufferers, relief 841 *Excursion* 6. 180
Though slowly opening, opens every day K.8. 249 *Recluse* 1.1.473

Opera. Sets like an Opera phantom. Thus, O Friend! 732 *Prelude* 11. 370

Operation. *See* **Co-operation.**

Operations. On fluent operations a fixed shape; 812 *Excursion* 4. 727

Opes. On as we move, a softer prospect opes, 607 *Desc.Sk.Quarto* 263

Opinion. Opinion bow before the naked sense 500 *Humanity* 43
By false opinion and contentious thought, 737 *Prelude* 12. 211
And tempt opinion to support the wrongs 816 *Excursion* 4. 1020
Opinion, ever changing! I have seen 818 *Excursion* 4. 1132

Opinions. The World's opinions and her usages, 70 *Bord.* 1816
I read, without design, the opinions, thoughts, 661 *Prelude* 4. 212
Her just opinions, delicate reserve, 691 *Prelude* 7. 311
Of passions and opinions, filled the walls 712 *Prelude* 9. 164
By new opinions, scattered tribes have made 715 *Prelude* 9. 378
Of our opinions had been just, we took 728 *Prelude* 11. 48
Of contest, did opinions every day 730 *Prelude* 11. 219
Was given to old opinions; all men's minds 731 *Prelude* 11. 271
The wisest whose opinions stooped the least 775 *Excursion* 2. 257
"Possessions vanish, and opinions change, 802 *Excursion* 4. 69

Opponent. Whose rival sword a like Opponent slew: 434 *Ecc.Sonn.* 2. 24. 10

Opponents. Of these opponents gradually was wrought, 845 *Excursion* 6. 469

Opportune. That, to this opportune recess allured, 150 **When, to* 59
An opportune recess, 168 *Wren's Nest* 14
Studious regard with opportune delight, 281 *Valedict.* 7
Inviting shades of opportune recess, 676 *Prelude* 6. 74

Opportunity. Of servile opportunity to gold; 351 *Des. Stanzas* 79

Ordained—*continued.*
In strife, in tribulation; and ordained, . . . 837 *Excursion* 5. 1014
For those ordained to take their sounding flight . 889 *Excursion* 9. 372
As if some friendly Genius had ordained . . . 892 *Excursion* 9. 522
The works by faith ordained. Pursue thy path, . K.8. 325 [?] **The vestal* 12

Ordaining. New rites ordaining when the old are wrecked, ... 380 *Duddon* 18. 3
Ordains. That bind thee to the path which God ordains . . . . 329 *Ode: Thanks.* 17
Forth for His mercy, as the Church ordains, . . 448 *Ecc. Sonn.* 3. 30. 7
Ordeal. I will commit him to this final *Ordeal!*— . 62 *Bord.* 1393
Idonea! thy blind Father on the Ordeal . . . 77 *Bord.* 2267
Order. Of peace and order. Aged men with tears 48 *Bord.* 612
We come by order of the Band. Belike . . . 56 *Bord.* 1021
But each in solemn order followed each, . . . 196 *Resolution* 93
In seemly order stand, ... 213 *Dion* 33
With Order dwell, in endless youth? . . . 234 *Power of Sound* 112
Advance in order the redoubted Bands, . . . 324 *Ode 1814* 56
Pupils of Heaven, in order stand . . . . . 338 *Brientz* 11
And thus, in order, 'mid the sacred grove . . 346 *Processions* 19
Than the fair Forms, that in long order glide, . 347 *Processions* 62
Knights each in order as ye stand . . . . 373 *Eg. Maid* 267
Have moved in order, to each other bound . . 394 **No more* 4
Justice, and order. Tremblingly escaped, . . 419 *Ecc. Sonn.* 1. 4. 9
Licence and slavish order, dares be free. . . 450 *Ecc. Sonn.* 3. 37. 14
Making of social order a mere dream. . . . 518 *Pun. Death* 7. 14
That public order, private weal, ... 534 **Blest is* 73
Anon, in order mounts a gorgeous show . . . 595 *Ev. Wk. Quarto* 183
As they in order stand, the dainty fare; . . . 624 *Æneid* 64
In scale and order, class the cabinet . . . 645 *Prelude* 2. 22[illegible]
Of words in tuneful order, found them sweet . . 674 *Prelude* 5. 555
But let me now, less moved, in order take . . 693 *Prelude* 7. 400
With order and relation. This, if still, . . . 698 *Prelude* 7. 761
To a religious order. Man he loved . . . . 714 *Prelude* 9. 306
And in the order of sublime behests: . . . . 724 *Prelude* 10. 453
In seemly order, now, with straggling leaves . . 768 *Excursion* 1. 827
Of order and distinctness, not for this . . . 820 *Excursion* 4. 1259
Of order and of good. Whate'er we see, . . . 820 *Excursion* 4. 1270
In lucid order; so that, when his course . . . 823 *Excursion* 5. 43
In order, drawing toward their wished-for home. . 858 *Excursion* 7. 71
He who had seen his own bright order fade, . . 873 *Excursion* 7. 1017
Sobriety, and order, and chaste love, ... 877 *Excursion* 8. 240
The discipline of virtue; order else . . . . 889 *Excursion* 9. 353
Ordered. Winding in ordered pomp their upward way, 6 *Ev. Wk.* 207
Sad or disturbed, is ordered by a Being . . . 801 *Excursion* 4. 14
In beauty of holiness, with ordered pomp, . . 838 *Excursion* 6. 11
The order'd troops . . . . K.8. 234 **The order'd* 1
Orderly. Of orderly respect and awe; . . . . 399 *White Doe* 321
And, one among the orderly array . . . . 783 *Excursion* 2. 766
Order's. Of social Order's care for wretchedness, . 32 *Guilt* 453
By Social Order's watchful arms embraced; . . 463 **Why should the* 10
Come links for social order's awful chain. . . . 475 **Here on their* 14
Orders. Degrees and Orders stood, each under each: 471 *Tynwald* 6
Threatening to lay all Orders at her feet . . . 626 *Ballot* 4
Of orders and degrees, I nothing found . . . 712 *Prelude* 9. 210
Fraternities and orders—heaping high . . . . 872 *Excursion* 7. 989
Ordinance. Oh, 'tis a goodly Ordinance,—the sight, 331 *Ode: Thanks.* 194
By Hebrew ordinance devoutly kept, ... 354 *Aquap.* 136
From Rite and Ordinance abused they fled . . 443 *Ecc. Sonn.* 3. 14. 1
For Rite and Ordinance, Piety is led . . . . 443 *Ecc. Sonn.* 3. 14. 7
Who framed the Ordinance by your lives disowned! 444 *Ecc. Sonn.* 3. 26. 14
This Ordinance, whether loss it would supply, . 445 *Ecc. Sonn.* 3. 21. 10
And ancient ordinance, shall endure, ... 534 **Blest is* 98
And 'tis a common ordinance of fate . . . . 546 **Oft is* 3
By will or by established ordinance, ... 805 *Excursion* 4. 299
Ordinances. Upon the vulgar ordinances of the world; . . . . 782 *Excursion* 2. 737
Ordinary. To its dull round of ordinary cares; . . 122 *V. and J.* 52
And watchful more than ordinary men. . . . 131 *Michael* 47
Of ordinary men; a stately speech; . . . . 196 *Resolution* 96
Like her ordinary cry, ... 209 **Yes, it* 7
And ordinary business without care; . . . . 308 **One might* 7
Needful amid life's ordinary woes;— . . . . 395 *White Doe: Ded.* 54
But theirs the wise man's ordinary lot, . . . 438 *Ecc. Sonn.* 2. 40. 12
Or mild concerns of ordinary life, ... 493 *Hap. War.* 46
And slipped into the ordinary works . . . . 652 *Prelude* 3. 241
For me beyond its ordinary mark, ... 688 *Prelude* 7. 89
And ordinary interests of man, ... 700 *Prelude* 8. 117
On all sides from the ordinary world . . . 704 *Prelude* 8. 321
And all the attire of ordinary life, ... 711 *Prelude* 9. 84
Of ordinary intercourse, our minds . . . . 737 *Prelude* 12. 214
An ordinary sight; but I should need . . . . 738 *Prelude* 12. 254
And, after ordinary travellers' talk . . . . 746 *Prelude* 14. 16
Of ordinary life; unvexed, unwarped . . . . 761 *Excursion* 1. 357
An ordinary sorrow of man's life, ... 765 *Excursion* 1. 637
To implements of ordinary use, ... 784 *Excursion* 2. 865
The ordinary chronicle of birth, ... 825 *Excursion* 5. 173
That lies beyond life's ordinary bounds, . . . 866 *Excursion* 7. 569
Sinking with less than ordinary state, ... 893 *Excursion* 9. 591
Ore. (But seldom trod) of mildly-gleaming ore; . 264 **Lady!* I 2
And far above the mine's most precious ore . . 426 *Ecc. Sonn.* 1. 32. 12
To mould and stamp the ore of thought . . . 629 *Installation* 83
Of virgin ore, that gold which we, by pains . . 832 *Excursion* 5. 632
In search of precious ore: they tried, were foiled— 841 *Excursion* 6. 217
Oread. Oread or Dryad glancing through the shade 850 *Excursion* 6. 829
Oreads. Into fleet Oreads sporting visibly. . . . 814 *Excursion* 4. 876
Organ. Organ of Vision! And a Spirit aërial . . 232 *Power of Sound* 3
Her pealing organ was my neighbour too; . . 650 *Prelude* 3. 57
Under the pealing organ. Empty thoughts! . . 653 *Prelude* 3. 315
The ready Organ of articulate sounds . . . . K.8. 246 *Recluse* 1. 1. 343

Organic. Organic pleasure from the silver wreaths 640 *Prelude* 1. 564
Is gone for ever; and this organic frame, . . . 879 *Excursion* 8. 322
Organist. The wind is now thy organist;—a clank 387 *Roslin* 1
Organs. Even with the organs of his bodily eye, . 96 *Brothers* 60
Whence the main organs of the public power . . 711 *Prelude* 9. 102
Her organs and her members, with decay . . . 872 *Excursion* 7. 1001
Orgies. Has held infernal orgies—with the gloom, . 49 *Bord.* 660
Orient. And colour life's dark cloud with orient rays. 259 **Weak is* 8
While beams of orient light shoot wide and high, . 282 **While beams* 1
Hail, orient Conqueror of gloomy Night! . . 329 *Ode: Thanks.* 1
Though joy attend Thee orient at the birth . . 391 **Though joy* 1
He, whose strong arm the Orient could not check, 428 *Ecc. Sonn.* 1. 38. 6
Mindful of Him Who in the Orient born . . . 534 **When in* 13
More orient in the western cloud, that drew . . 709 *Prelude* 8. 662
And orient gems, which, for a day of need, . . 809 *Excursion* 4. 568
Oriental. An Oriental chain. . . . . 109 **Ere with* 8
At oriental flattery; . . . . 495 *Fact* 18
And with an oriental loathing spurned, . . . 714 *Prelude* 9. 291
Orifice. From time to time, into an orifice . . . 695 *Prelude* 7. 557
Origin. Are yet of no diviner origin, ... v **If thou indeed* 8
Your origin divine. . . . . 225 *Present.* 18
That every gift of noble origin . . . . . 308 **These times* 10
Of subtler origin; how I have felt, ... 640 *Prelude* 1. 549
How shall I seek the origin? where find . . . 647 *Prelude* 2. 346
And in the origin and bounds of power . . . 775 *Excursion* 2. 238
Our origin, what matters it? In lack . . . 789 *Excursion* 3. 238
Original. Interpret that Original, ... 472 *Ossian* 28
There how the Original of human art, ... 496 **A little* 35
In the first warmth of their original sunshine, . 498 **Enough of climbing* 49
What love of nature, what original strength . . 675 *Prelude* 6. 38
In her original self too confident, ... 749 *Prelude* 14. 249
The original stain, the child is there received . 826 *Excursion* 5. 281
There lies the channel, and original bed, . . . 837 *Excursion* 5. 1004
In its original beauty, here restored. . . . . 895 *Excursion* 9. 719
Originates. Whence spiritual dignity originates, . 745 *Prelude* 13. 373
Orion. Orion with his belt, and those fair Seven, . 662 *Prelude* 4. 245
Orisons. Their orisons with voices half-suppressed, 357 *Aquap.* 303
Of foaming torrents.—From thy orisons . . . 496 **A little* 20
Pealed to his orisons, and when he paced . . . 551 **If thou in* 19
Orleans. Of Orleans; coasted round and round the line . . . . 710 *Prelude* 9. 53
Of Orleans eagerly I turned; as yet . . . . 719 *Prelude* 10. 95
Ornament. To be a moment's ornament; . . . 186 **She was* 4
Yet more for love than ornament. . . . . . 221 *Triad* 118
Chosen for ornament—stone matched with stone . 378 *Duddon* 9. 5
And loved to borrow, ornament; . . . . . 390 *Highland Broach* 42
Now rich with mossy ornament? . . . . . 397 *White Doe* 125
That ornament, unblamed. The floweret, held . 509 *F. Stone* 63
That took his station there for ornament: . . . 704 *Prelude* 8. 380
Of use or ornament; and with a strange, . . . 764 *Excursion* 1. 574
Nor wanting ornament of walks between, . . . 778 *Excursion* 2. 426
Whose blue roofs ornament a distant reach . . 844 *Excursion* 6. 408
Which might be lacked for use or ornament. . . 860 *Excursion* 7. 173
Ornamental. Each, in its ornamental scroll, enclosed; 824 *Excursion* 5. 151
Of ornamental interest, and the charm . . . 838 *Excursion* 6. 27
Ornaments. With ornaments—the prettiest, nature yields . . . . 124 *V. and J.* 200
Some ornaments to me are left— . . . . . 155 *Waterfall* 46
And ornaments of seemlier pride, ... 191 *Seq. Beggars* 6
Would, in their turns, lend ornaments and flowers 695 *Prelude* 7. 569
Oppress, far less becoming ornaments . . . . 816 *Excursion* 4. 1002
These ornaments, that fade not with the year, . 856 *Excursion* 6. 1156
One after one, their proudest ornaments. . . . 866 *Excursion* 7. 594
Of all the lighter ornaments attached . . . . 878 *Excursion* 8. 250
Their skeletons, turned to brilliant ornaments. . S.3. 434 **The doubt* 54
Oroonoko. Conspicuous yet where Oroonoko flows; 380 *Duddon* 16. [illegible]
Orphan. The little Orphan then would be your succour, ... 52 *Bord.* 841
Wild words for me to hear, for me, an orphan, . 76 *Bord.* 2198
Who, through most wicked arts, was made an orphan . . . . 78 *Bord.* 2330
The little orphan, Alice Fell! . . . . . . 82 *Alice Fell* 60
Fared this little bright-eyed Orphan . . . . 93 *Westmoreland Girl* 31
An orphan could not find his mother's grave: . 98 *Brothers* 169
To attend upon the orphan, and perform . . . 125 *V. and J.* 277
As hath this little orphan Boy, ... 249 *P. B.* 1109
Too late, I feel, sweet Orphan! was the day . . 275 *Rotha Q.* 5
Her Mother's favourite; and the orphan Girl, . 509 *F. Stone* 66
But chanted by your Orphan Quire . . . . 577 **I come* 31
A younger orphan of a home extinct, ... 622 *Recluse* 1. 1. 78
And for her little orphan boy, she said, . . . 769 *Excursion* 1. 849
Of rustic loneliness: that grey-haired Orphan— . 835 *Excursion* 5. 885
Orphan's. Perhaps is shedding orphan's tears; you also . . . . 779 *Excursion* 2. 541
Orphans. But those two Orphans! Orphans!—Such they were— . . . . 98 *Brothers* 226
Outcasts and homeless orphans—— . . . . 505 *Warning* 157
And I and my three brothers, orphans then, . . 738 *Prelude* 12. 308
Orphean. Where is the Orphean lyre, or Druid harp, 230 *Clouds* 60
Orphean Insight! truth's undaunted lover, . . 234 *Power of Sound* 115
Whose waves the Orphean lyre forbad to meet . 336 *Danube* 9
Thoughtfully fitted to the Orphean lyre; . . . 635 *Prelude* 1. 233
Orpheus. An Orpheus! an Orpheus! yes, Faith may grow bold, ... 188 *Music* 1
One measure, Orpheus! of thy verse; . . . . 472 *Ossian* 38
Orrest-head. Baffle the threat, bright Scene, from Orrest-head . . . . 282 *Railway* 9
Osee. Thou say'st OSEE, OSEE, then how may I . 559 *Cuck. and Night.* 124
Oft as I say OSEE, OSEE, I wis, ... 559 *Cuck. and Night.* 127

Owen. Through life was OWEN LLOYD endeared   577 *By playful 5
Owes. Owes to the fit in which his soul hath tossed   26 Guilt 92
To serve me so, and knowing that he owes   46 Bord. 484
The sky owes somebody a grudge !   176 Waggoner 1. 250
While here sits One whose brightness owes its hues   252 *Her only 12
To whom the wild sequestered region owes,   272 Lady E. B. 7
Maturer Fancy owes to their rough noise   382 Duddon 26. 13
Or aught that watchful Love to Nature owes   471 Ailsa Crag 13
He labours good on good to fix, and owes   493 Hap. War. 33
Owes that presiding aspect which might well   824 Excursion 5. 129
Which to outrageous wrong the sufferer owes,   870 Excursion 7. 840
Owes to alliance with these new-born arts !   876 Excursion 8. 132
Owing. To thee am owing .   158 *In youth 68
Yet to their sturdiness 'tis owing   175 Waggoner 1. 144
Owl. *See* Screech-owl.
The sportive outcry of the mocking owl ;   9 Ev. Wk. 375
But you may love a screaming owl,   142 †Lov. and Lik. 6
Blithe ravens croak of death ; and when the owl   153 Morn. Ex. 7
But save us from yon screeching owl ! "   179 Waggoner 3. 98
" Yon owl !—pray God that all be well !   179 Waggoner 3. 112
This vagrant owl is playing here—   179 Waggoner 3. 127
The presence even of a stuffed Owl for her   273 *While Anna's 10
Crisp, yellow leaves my bed ; the hooting owl   424 Ecc. Sonn. 1. 22. 11
The owl of evening and the woodland fox   433 Ecc. Sonn. 2. 21. 9
Of sapience in thy aspect, headless Owl !   456 *The leaves 27
The tremulous sob of the complaining owl ;   600 Ev. Wk. Quarto 443
Whence the scared Owl on pinions grey   626 †Cento 13
A fearful apprehension from the owl   810 Excursion 4. 616
Where no one dwells but the wide-staring owl   843 Excursion 6. 327
The owl that gives the name to Owlet-Crag   K.8. 251 Recluse 1.1.521
Owlet. The owlet, in the moonlight air,   126 Idiot Boy 3
I'll teach him how the owlet sings.   145 Her Eyes 82
Owlet-Crag. The owl that gives the name to Owlet-Crag   K.8. 251 Recluse 1.1.521
Owlet's. Save when the Owlet's unexpected scream   456 *The leaves 8
Brushed by the owlet's wing ;   497 Lycoris 20
Owlets. The owlets hoot, the owlets curr,   127 Idiot Boy 104
The owlets through the long blue night   129 Idiot Boy 287
Owl's. And the owl's prey ; from these bare haunts, to which .   843 Excursion 6. 328
Owls. The owls have hardly sung their last,   131 Idiot Boy 432
The owls have hooted all night long,   131 Idiot Boy 434
And with the owls began my song,   131 Idiot Boy 435
And with the owls must end.   131 Idiot Boy 436
The owls in tuneful concert strive ;   131 Idiot Boy 443
And owls alone are waking,   479 Somnamb. 92
Blew mimic hootings to the silent owls,   671 Prelude 5. 373
Own. (Partial list.)
Be better fed. Ne'er may I own the heart   38 Bord. 67
Who live in these disputed tracts, that own   48 Bord. 596
Or own we baby Spirits ? Genuine courage   57 Bord. 1073
And Reason's godlike Power be proud to own.   173 Infant Daughter 78
This the Sun's Bird, whom Glendoveers might own   231 *The gentlest Poet 7
Perverse, self-willed to own and to disown,   253 *Fond words 12
And, seeing this, own nothing in its stead.   279 *All praise 8
Own—that the progeny of this fair Isle   325 Ode 1814 139
Of flowers the Virgin without fear may own,   360 Albano 13
Stretched far as earth might own a single lord ;   368 Trajan 30
And all the assembly own a law   399 White Doe 320
And said ; " The Minds of Men will own   403 White Doe 637
And own that Art, triumphant over strife   476 Howard 13
Or waves that own no curbing hand,   586 Hogg 22
Which seem, in their simplicity, to own   640 Prelude 1. 552
Of virtuous feeling. For myself, I own   722 Prelude 10. 253
(How far soe'er a stranger) does not own   780 Excursion 2. 561
A task it was, I own, to hold discourse   783 Excursion 2. 758
From its fantastic birthplace ! And I own,   787 Excursion 3. 87
Its cares and sorrows ; he, though taught to own   809 Excursion 4. 546
To hearts that own not him ? Will showers of grace,   817 Excursion 4. 1096
To use of reason. And, I own that, tired   835 Excursion 5. 849
Who, if indeed she own a mother's heart,   889 Excursion 9. 328
And its own twilight softens the whole scene,   3 Ev. Wk. 61
Her dawn, far lovelier than the morn's own morn,   8 Ev. Wk. 340
And the near heavens impart their own delights.   19 Desc. Sk. 477
Rouse hell's own aid, and wrap thy fields in fire :   22 Desc. Sk. 643
An emblem of his own unfruitful life :   23 Yew-tree 32
Howe'er disguised in its own majesty,   23 Yew-tree 51
The Woman thus retraced her own untoward fate.   28 Guilt 198
I have a house that I can call my own ;   34 Guilt 566
When on his own he cast a rueful look.   36 Guilt 634
By mingling natural matter of her own   44 Bord. 367
Are hushed to sleep, by your own act and deed,   55 Bord. 956
From my own threshold I looked up to Heaven   62 Bord. 1354
Ha ! what is here ? and carved by her own hand !   63 Bord. 1412
Spin motives out of their own bowels, Lacy !   63 Bord. 1428
Some uncouth superstition of its own.   63 Bord. 1441
The prey or masters of our own past deeds.   65 Bord. 1522
But his own crime had brought on him this doom,   69 Bord. 1745
If his own eyes play false with him, these freaks .   73 Bord. 2036
Tranquil as he had died in his own bed.   75 Bord. 2140
Like the old Roman, on their own sword's point.   78 Bord. 2343
He may work his own will, and what shall we care ?   81 †Address : Child 39
That I almost received her heart into my own.   87 Pet-lamb 12
I whispered, " Yet a little while, dear Child ! thou art my own .   92 Poet's Dream 21
Relinquished by his own ;   105 Artegal 223
On his own time here would he float away,   107 Indolence 6
And his own mind did like a tempest strong   108 Indolence 35
Smiles, that with motion of their own   108 Louisa
Of its own bounty, or my need.   111 A Complaint 6
My fancy's own creation.   111 *Yes ! thou 4

Own—continued.
Tears due unto their own.   113 Lament 21
Thy own dear mother's far away,   120 EmigrantMother 19
" My own dear Little-one will sigh,   121 EmigrantMother 45
The Housewife plied her own peculiar work,   133 Michael 126
Here, lay it for me, Luke, with thine own hands.   137 Michael 387
Her own angelic glory seems begun.   139 Widow 42
Of Grasmere safe in its own privacy :   148 *A narrow 5
Wings lovely as his own.   156 Oak and Broom 84
But now my own delights I make,—   157 *In youth 5
Thyself thy own enjoyment.   159 Green Linnet 24
Beside a grotto of their own,   161 Binnorie 2
A crimson as bright as thine own :   163 *Art thou the 36
Even her own needle that subdued   163 Needlecase 9
The lovely dell is all his own.   165 Danish Boy 22
But enjoy their own the more !   177 Waggoner 2. 100
—Blithe spirits of her own impel   180 Waggoner 4. 11
A Lady of my own.   187 *Three years 6
A slighted child, at her own will   192 Ruth 4
She seemed to live ; her thoughts her own ;   192 Ruth 14
Herself her own delight ;   192 Ruth 15
That our own children to our eyes   193 Ruth 89
Or run, my own adopted bride,   193 Ruth 94
To his own powers, and justified   193 Ruth 131
The breezes their own languor lent ;   193 Ruth 136
And gave them back his own.   194 Ruth 150
Over his own sweet voice the Stock-dove broods ;   195 Resolution 5
By our own spirits are we deified :   196 Resolution 47
A Clifford to his own restored !   204 Brougham 23
As in a dream her own renewing.   204 Brougham 43
' My own, my own, thy Fellow-guest   204 Brougham 84
He hath it to himself—'tis all his own.   208 *It is no 8
Their own domain ;—but ever, while intent   218 Recluse 1. 1. 210
Their own fair forms, upon the glimmering plain,   218 Recluse 1. 1. 225
All happiness her own.   223 Wishing-gate 36
And marked it for my own ;   224 Primrose 10
Charms of their own ;—then come with me,   237 P. B. 87
And be thy own delight !   238 P. B. 155
From his own thoughts did Peter start ;   248 P. B. 1078
Its own small pasture, almost its own sky !   250 Admon. 4
No fleeting Spirit, but my own true Love ?   252 *Her only 14
Its own ; though Rulers, with undue respect,   255 S. H. 11
Kind Nature's various wealth was all your own ;   256 Easter 13
Of her own Being is her paramount end ;   262 Retirement 6
The river glideth at his own sweet will :   269 Westm. Bridge 12
I slight my own beloved Cam, to range   270 *Ye sacred 10
Nor doubt that He marked also for his own   275 Gravestone 10
But from its own divine vitality.   277 *A Poet 14
To reverence, suspends his own ; submitting   290 Kilchurn 17
And we our own Rob Roy !   292 Rob Roy 96
Go back to Yarrow, 'tis their own ;   292 Yarrow Unv. 11
We have a vision of our own ;   293 Yarrow Unv. 51
This corner is your own.   295 Highland Boy 5
He in a vessel of his own   296 Highland Boy 98
Each hut, perchance, might have its own ;   296 Highland Boy 113
Till Nature cannot find her own,   301 Bran 124
And what if I enwreathed my own !   302 Yarrow V. 69
Must either win, through effort of his own,   312 *When, far 7
Of thy own mountain, set to keep   338 *Meek Virgin 3
And to his Father give its own unerring aim.   339 Tell 17
Another's first, and then her own ?)   344 *How blest 19
Of my own Fairfield. The glad greeting given,   353 Aquap. 30
Prefiguring his own impendent doom,   357 Aquap. 311
Into thy own prophetic book ;   370 Eg. Maid 112
As thy own Yarrow gave to me   386 Yarrow Rev. 75
Thus, in the net of her own wishes caught,   388 Loch Etive 9
Him his own thoughts did elevate,—   399 White Doe 292
Her own thoughts loved she ; and could bend   416 White Doe 1854
Repeatedly his own deep mind he sounds   422 Ecc. Sonn. 1. 15. 11
By wrong triumphant through its own excess,   426 Ecc. Sonn. 1. 32. 2
Who on the good of others builds his own !   433 Ecc. Sonn. 2. 19. 14
The monitor revives his own sweet strain ;   455 Rydal Mere 4
And nothing save the moving ship's own light   460 *Wanderer ! that 68
On this fair Mount, a Poet of your own,   463 *Adieu, Rydalian 4
To make this Gem their own,   478 Somnamb. 20
Our own domestic mountain. Thing and thought   480 Cordelia 7
Himself his world, and his own God ;   485 Poet's Epitaph 28
A music sweeter than their own.   485 Poet's Epitaph 40
That broods and sleeps on his own heart.   485 Poet's Epitaph 52
Whose mind is but the mind of his own eyes,   488 Pers. Talk 27
And joy its own security.   492 Duty 20
Of my own wish ; and feel past doubt   492 Duty
And in himself possess his own desire ;   493 Hap. War. 38
—O my own Dora, my belovèd child !   496 *A little 11
Making a truth and beauty of her own ;   497 *Enough of climbing 13

Her own Æolian lute.   499 *Departing summer 48

To their own far-off murmurs listening.   499 Memory 29
Less for his own than for thy innocent sake ?   504 Warning 81
Their own mysterious groves.   506 *While from 32
That our own hands have drest,   507 May 46
And shunning nought, their own peculiar life   508 F. Stone 36
In his own storms he hides himself from sight.   521 Epist. Beaumont 9
But we, we lacked not music of our own,   523 Epist. Beaumont 156

And reaped—what hath been, and what is, our own.   524 Epist. Beaumont 202

Have meanings of their own ;   526 *The soaring 12
This child of Nature's own humility,   530 Poor Robin 32
Which from their own blind hearts they draw ;   534 *Blest is 76

Own—continued.
To his own genial instincts ; and was heard — 537 *In desultory 5
Which She is pleased and proud to call her own, — 539 *Lady ! a 26
For some rude beauty of its own, — 549 *In these 4
Assigned to them and given them for their own — 553 Prioress 38
For Love no reason hath but his own will ;— — 560 Cuck.and Night. 197
And unto Pandarus, his own Brother dear, — 562 Troilus 3
Lo, yonder saw I mine own Lady dance, — 563 Troilus 47
Heard my own Cresid's laugh ; and once at play — 563 Troilus 51
Lo ! yonder is my own bright Lady free ; — 564 Troilus 151
Who sits at his own door,—and, like the pear — 568 Cumb. Beg. 117
And is happy as if the rich freight were his own. — 571 Farmer 84
'Tis a look which at this time is hardly his own, — 572 Avarice 23
Like London with its own black wreath, — 586 Hogg 30
Adding immortal labours of his own— — 587 Crosth. 6
Earth fills her lap with pleasures of her own ; — 588 Immortality 77
Yearnings she hath in her own natural kind, — 588 Immortality 78
See, where 'mid work of his own hand he lies, — 588 Immortality 87
Rouze Hell's own aid, and wrap thy hills in fire. — 616 Desc.Sk.Quarto 781
With it's own Virtues springs another earth : — 616 Desc.Sk.Quarto 783
And learn from thence thy own defects to scan ; — 619 School Ex. 86
What a man finds is all his own, — 621 Andrew Jones 29
My own ; and not mine only, for with me — 621 Recluse 1. 1. 75
That hails him for our own ! — 629 Installation 110
Joyous, nor scared at its own liberty, — 632 Prelude 1. 15
That burthen of my own unnatural self, — 632 Prelude 1. 21
Vexing its own creation. Thanks to both, — 632 Prelude 1. 38
My own voice cheered me, and, far more, the mind's — 633 Prelude 1. 55
Though no distress be near him but his own — 634 Prelude 1. 138
A tale from my own heart, more near akin — 635 Prelude 1. 222
To my own passions and habitual thoughts ; — 635 Prelude 1. 223
For so it seemed, with purpose of its own — 638 Prelude 1. 383
A ministration of your own was yours ; — 639 Prelude 1. 500
Delights and exultations of your own. — 639 Prelude 1. 506
For its own pleasure, and I breathed with joy. — 645 Prelude 2. 188
More deeply read in thy own thoughts ; to thee — 645 Prelude 2. 211
A local spirit of his own, at war — 647 Prelude 2. 365
My own enjoyments ; or the power of truth — 647 Prelude 2. 392
With my own modest pleasures, and have lived — 648 Prelude 2. 429
From shop to shop about my own affairs, — 649 Prelude 3. 27
I had a world about me—'twas my own ; — 651 Prelude 3. 141
Symbols or actions, but of my own heart — 651 Prelude 3. 175
Even the great Newton's own ethereal self, — 653 Prelude 3. 267
Its own protection ; a primeval grove, — 655 Prelude 3. 430
With our own inner being are forgot. — 656 Prelude 3. 508
In my own mind remote from social life, — 656 Prelude 3. 511
And many of them seeming yet my own ! — 659 Prelude 4. 43
" An emblem here behold of thy own life ; — 659 Prelude 4. 61
Of my own private being and no more ; — 662 Prelude 4. 235
And Jupiter, my own beloved star ! — 662 Prelude 4. 247
Within the pinfold of his own conceit. — 670 Prelude 5. 336
To make this book our own. Through several months, — 672 Prelude 5. 473
From regulations even of my own — 675 Prelude 6. 34
Of my own native region, and was blest — 678 Prelude 6. 195
On wanderings of my own, that now embraced — 679 Prelude 6. 320
That are their own perfection and reward, — 684 Prelude 6. 612
Wakes in me agitations like its own, — 687 Prelude 7. 47
Yet richly graced with honours of her own, — 691 Prelude 7. 266
From our own ground,—the Maid of Buttermere,— — 691 Prelude 7. 297
Each fondly reared on his own pedestal, — 695 Prelude 7. 577
There, for her own delight had Nature framed — 702 Prelude 8. 189
I felt his presence in his own domain, — 703 Prelude 8. 257
But secondary to my own pursuits — 704 Prelude 8. 343
For her own sake, became my joy, even then— — 704 Prelude 8. 347
With motion constant as his own, I went — 710 Prelude 9. 39
To aspirations then of our own minds — 715 Prelude 9. 380
Of wildest course but treads back his own steps ; — 719 Prelude 10. 79
In the last place of refuge—my own soul. — 724 Prelude 10. 415
Fell from me in my own despite. But now — 726 Prelude 10. 544
To my own history. It hath been told — 728 Prelude 11. 75
My own delights do scarcely seem to me — 733 Prelude 11. 408
My own delights ; the lordly Alps themselves, — 733 Prelude 11. 409
When thinking on my own beloved friend, — 733 Prelude 11. 442
For His own service ; knoweth, loveth us, — 744 Prelude 13. 277
Have each his own peculiar faculty, — 744 Prelude 13. 303
As my own child. Oh, Sir ! the good die first, — 763 Excursion 1. 500
He coloured objects to his own desire — 775 Excursion 2. 277
Were missed, I should at least secure my own, — 797 Excursion 3. 792
Are guardians of their own tranquillity. — 806 Excursion 4. 322
On its own axis restlessly revolving, — 810 Excursion 4. 629
When his own breath was silent, chanced to hear — 814 Excursion 4. 855
The good and evil are our own ; and we — 830 Excursion 5. 490
His own peculiar utterance for distress — 837 Excursion 5. 982
He, taking counsel of his own clear thoughts, — 841 Excursion 6. 219
And trusting only to his own weak hands, — 841 Excursion 6. 220
Forbad her all communion with her own : — 853 Excursion 6. 961
Hath now its own peculiar sanctity ; — 864 Excursion 7. 479
Lived in an age conspicuous as our own — 873 Excursion 7. 1009
Without his own consent, or knowledge, fixed ! — 878 Excursion 8. 300
Dull, to the joy of her own motions dead ; — 879 Excursion 8. 324
Purloined, in times less jealous than our own, — 879 Excursion 8. 371
(For every moment hath its own to-morrow !) — 884 Excursion 9. 28
By women, who have children of their own, — 887 Excursion 9. 193
And each seemed centre of his own fair world : — 890 Excursion 9. 448
For his own careless head. — S.3. 423 Tinker 22
It frustrates its own purpose, and recalls — S.3. 434 *The doubt 90
Of my own cunning, earth mysteriously — S.3. 435 *The doubt 100
Their own emotions given to mountain air — S.3. 436 *The doubt 156
Folly's own hyperbole. — S.3. 438 *My Lord 28
All over their own pastures, and beyond. — K.8. 224 *I will 16

Own—continued.
To his own hills, the spots where when a lamb — K.8. 228 *I will 126
To his own home, and now at the approach — K.8. 229 *I will 160
Up his own mountain grounds, where, as he walked — K.8. 229 *I will 164
Of his own business, and the goings on — K.8. 230 *I will 184
Her own peculiar family of love — K.8. 243 Recluse 1.1.236
Of her own native element, the hand — K.8. 246 Recluse 1.1.370
Has her own treasures, and I think of these, — K.8. 248 Recluse 1.1.425
Calmly they breathe their own undying life — K.8. 249 Recluse 1.1.462
From my own door I shall be free to claim — K.8. 250 Recluse 1.1.519
Not want, for this, your own subordinate place — K.8. 251 Recluse 1.1.543
By one, sole keeper of his own intent, — K.8. 256 Recluse 1.1.718
By flames breathed on her from her own fireside. — K.8. 275 *These vales 4

Owned. I well remember.—He was one who owned — 23 Yew-tree 12
" A little croft we owned—a plot of corn, — 28 Guilt 208
Many flocks were on the hills, but thou wert owned by none, — 87 Pet-lamb 35
If aught which he had owned might still remain for me. — 119 Sailor's Mother 24
Once owned her Father for his Lord ; — 414 White Doe 1691
As will be owned alike by bad and good, — 478 *Lonsdale ! it 12
Tried the Horn,—it owned his power ; — 535 Egremont 14
That least of all can aught—that ever owned — 567 Cumb. Beg. 80
But no one owned them ; meanwhile the calm lake — 672 Prelude 5. 439
That owned him ; living cheerfully abroad — 688 Prelude 7. 74
Whom no one owned, sate silent, shall I add, — 722 Prelude 10. 298
My school-time, an apartment he had owned, — 757 Excursion 1. 54
To see the Man who owned it, dwelling here, — 778 Excursion 2. 462
He wrought not : neither field nor flock he owned : — 863 Excursion 7. 425

Owner. The ducal Owner, in his palace-home — 392 Daniel 3
Restored it to its owner. " Gentle Friend," — 816 Excursion 4. 1015
Whose grateful owner can attest these truths, — 855 Excursion 6. 1140

Owner's. And blanch, without the owner's crime, — 113 Lament 41

Owners. The genuine owners of such Lands and Baronies — 56 Bord. 1025

Ownership. Of restless ownership ! — 214 Kirkstone 24

Owning. At least, not owning to himself an aim — 10 Desc. Sk. 13
Prevents me not from owning, that the law, — 805 Excursion 4. 303

Owns. All nature smiles, and owns beneath her eyes — 21 Desc. Sk. 622
In grange or farm this Hundred scarcely owns — 46 Bord. 522
That the earth owns shall never choose to die, — 75 Bord. 2150
That sees them, to my soul that owns in them, — 230 Clouds 49
Owns not a sylvan bower ; or gorgeous cell — 254 Wild Duck's Nest 2
As if his orb, that owns no curb, — 478 Somnamb. 66

Ox. Or rather like a stallèd ox debarred — 669 Prelude 5. 242

Oxford. In the street that from Oxford hath borrowed its name. — 188 Music 4
Yet, O ye spires of Oxford ! domes and towers ! — 270 *Ye sacred 6
From Oxford come to his native vale, — 399 White Doe 265

P

Pace. On he must pace, perchance till night descend, — 24 Guilt 17
His pace was never that of an old man : — 98 Brothers 220
And travel with the year at a soft pace. — 107 Farewell 48
With quickening pace my horse drew nigh — 109 *Strange fits 11
And, when he thinks, his pace is slack ; — 127 Idiot Boy 113
O blessèd Bird ! the earth we pace — 184 *O blithe 29
Where up and down with easy pace — 194 Ruth 239
And, still as I drew near with gentle pace, — 196 Resolution 73
In my mind's eye I seemed to see him pace — 197 Resolution 129
I pace it unrepining, for my thoughts — 230 Clouds 58
The cherished tenor of his pace — 243 P. B. 658
With weary pace is drawing nigh ; — 249 P. B. 1106
Modest her mien ; and she, whose thoughts keep pace — 256 Marriage: Friend 7
Yes ! hope may with my strong desire keep pace, — 256 *Yes ! hope 1
Which they would stifle, move at such a pace ! — 266 *With how 6
Pace the long avenue, or glide adown — 270 *Ye sacred 12
But soon they move with softer pace ; — 297 Highland Boy 186
As aptly suits therewith that modest pace — 329 Ode : Thanks. 15
Well—let him pace this noted beach once more, — 349 Boulogne 5
Calls me to pace her honoured Bridge—that cheers — 351 Des. Stanzas 56
The best that should keep pace with it, and must, — 357 Aquap. 339
Or there to pace, and mark the summits hoar — 384 Duddon 31. 12
And on she moves—with pace how light ! — 397 White Doe 137
And why she duly loves to pace — 398 White Doe 204
She yielded, and with gentle pace, — 411 White Doe 1361
Of horsemen at an eager pace ! — 412 White Doe 1444
And then advanced with stealth-like pace, — 414 White Doe 1650
The White Doe tracked with faithful pace — 414 White Doe 1686
I, who accompanied with faithful pace — 418 Ecc. Sonn. 1. 1. 1
Shape, limbs, and heavenly features, keeping pace — 440 Ecc. Sonn. 3. 1. 12
Or down the nave to pace in motion slow ; — 451 Ecc. Sonn. 3. 42. 6
He moved with stealthy pace ; — 479 Somnamb. 119
To pace the ground, if path be there or none, — 480 *Most sweet 2
With cherished sullenness of pace — 490 Night Thought 9
Truths of the heart flock in with eager pace, — 503 Warning 24
Pace between door and window muttering rhyme, — 521 Epist. Beaumont 34
Impelled to livelier pace. But now, my Book ! — 538 *In desultory 14
Their pace from mile to mile, — 543 Russ. Fug. 126
Kept pace with his desires ; — 545 Russ. Fug. 346
And, as the Child 'gan to the school to pace, — 554 Prioress 118
Without word uttered, forth he 'gan to pace ; — 563 Troilus 19
Last Industry appear'd with steady pace, — 618 School Ex. 23
With the moon's beauty and the moon's soft pace, — 653 Prelude 3. 281
And freer pace ; but more, far more, I grieved — 656 Prelude 3. 497
He rode, I keeping pace with him ; and now — 667 Prelude 5. 121

Pace—*continued.*
Gathering upon us ; " quickening then the pace — 667 *Prelude* 5. 131
At a slow pace. The immeasurable height — 684 *Prelude* 6. 624
Some Hermit, from his cell forth-strayed, might pace — 716 *Prelude* 9. 442
On which, with a diversity of pace, — 722 *Prelude* 10. 274
With eager pace, and no less eager thoughts. — 746 *Prelude* 14. 31
But still he loved to pace the public roads — 762 *Excursion* 1. 387
And now, when free to move with lighter pace. — 772 *Excursion* 2. 27
Travelling at steadier pace than ours, had risen — 824 *Excursion* 5. 135
Pace to and fro, from morn till eventide, — 831 *Excursion* 5. 599
Keeps pace, a harvest answering to the seed— — K.8. 255 *Recluse* 1. 1. 672

Paced. *See* **Slow-paced, Soft-paced.**
" The roads I paced, I loitered through the fields ; — 32 *Guilt* 433
You paced along, when the bewildering moonlight — 39 *Bord.* 111
He paced along ; and pensively, — 167 *Pilgrim's Dream* 9
Into my spirit, when I paced, enclosed — 355 *Aquap.* 154
While Merlin paced the Cornish sands, — 369 *Eg. Maid* 1
But now, as silently she paced — 407 *White Doe* 1074
Pealed to his orisons, and when he paced — 551 **If thou in* 19
Paced the long Vales—how long they were—and yet — 622 *Recluse* 1. 1. 155
A respite to this passion, I paced on — 633 *Prelude* 1. 60
And as I paced alone the level fields — 650 *Prelude* 3. 93
For ever near us as we paced along : — 680 *Prelude* 6. 363
Then paced the beaten downward way that led — 683 *Prelude* 6. 568
Of the huge town's first presence, and had paced — 688 *Prelude* 7. 67
I paced, a dear companion at my side, — 725 *Prelude* 10. 497
Trackless and smooth, or paced the bare white roads — 744 *Prelude* 13. 316
And ever with me as I paced along. — 756 *Excursion* 1. 25
And, while I paced along the foot-way path, — 766 *Excursion* 1. 693
There, to and fro, she paced through many a day — 769 *Excursion* 1. 884
Before us ; savage region ! which I paced — 776 *Excursion* 2. 326
His judgments, near that lonely house we paced — 805 *Excursion* 4. 241
While, listening, he had paced the noiseless turf, — 814 *Excursion* 4. 891
Thus occupied in mind I paced along, — 823 *Excursion* 5. 60
Or paced the ground—to guide her Husband home, — 834 *Excursion* 5. 760
With prompt yet careful hands. This done, we paced — 895 *Excursion* 9. 768

Paces. She paces out the hour 'twixt twelve and one— — 44 *Bord.* 392
She paces round and round an Infant's grave, — 44 *Bord.* 393
He paces on, a trusty Guide,— — 174 *Waggoner* 1. 31
Which thus assiduously she paces, — 397 *White Doe* 107
Paces softly, or makes halt, — 417 *White Doe* 1893
Paces the deck—no star perhaps in sight, — 460 **Wanderer ! that* 67
Not twenty paces from the door, — 483 *Simon Lee* 42

Pacific. There spreads the famed Pacific Ocean ! — 237 *P. B.* 57
The vast Pacific gladdens with the freight— — 327 *Ode 1815* 23

Pacified. She wept, nor would be pacified. — 82 *Alice Fell* 52
Now pacified ; on them, and on the coves — 784 *Excursion* 2. 848

Pacing. And not in vain, while they went pacing side by side. — 32 *Guilt* 459
Long did I watch, and saw her pacing round — 47 *Bord.* 577
By pacing here, unwearied and alone, — 150 **When, to* 62
Art pacing thoughtfully the vessel's deck — 151 **When, to* 101
Went pacing side by side, this public Way — 304 **Jones ! as* 2
In heart as dull in brain—while pacing ground — 356 *Aquap.* 270
Pacing behind along the silent lane. — 523 *Epist. Beaumon* 119
Pacing, two social pilgrims, or alone — 683 *Prelude* 6. 548
Each evening, pacing by the still sea-shore, — 723 *Prelude* 10. 323
Compared with ours ! who, pacing side by side, — 773 *Excursion* 2. 104

Pack. The pack loud chiming, and the hunted hare. — 638 *Prelude* 1. 437

Packed. To chase mankind, with men in armies packed — 313 **Go back* 12

Paestum. To range through the Temples of Paestum, to muse — 345 *Stanzas : Simplon* 5

Pagan. A Pagan suckled in a creed outworn ; — 259 **The world is* 10
Best of the good—in pagan faith allied — 368 *Trajan* 33
Of Pagan night. Afflicted and dismayed, — 421 *Ecc. Sonn.* 1. 11. 5
Helps to restore and spread a Pagan sway : — 426 *Ecc. Sonn.* 1. 29. 4
Her Temples rose, 'mid pagan gloom ; but why, — 474 **On to* 6
And from Pagan chains had rescued, — 536 *Egremont* 107
To the unenlightened swains of pagan Greece. — 814 *Excursion* 4. 850
Survive, as pagan temples stood of yore, — 870 *Excursion* 7. 843

Pagans. Were those bewildered Pagans of old time. — 815 *Excursion* 4. 934

Page. *See* **Title-page.**
Soon returned a trusty Page — 141 *Arm. Lady* 122
When Fancy was Truth's willing Page ; — 154 *Flower Garden* 54
Knight, squire, and yeoman, page and groom : — 204 *Brougham* 38
—Or I would hail thee when some high-wrought page — 222 *Triad* 183
The snow-white page on which he read, — 244 *P. B.* 744
And on the page, more black than coal, — 244 *P. B.* 752
So shall the characters of that proud page — 325 *Ode 1814* 131
Is then the final page before me spread, — 350 *Des. Stanzas* 1
Yet in his page the records of that worth — 356 *Aquap.* 248
Vallombrosa ! of thee I first heard in the page — 364 *Vallomb.* 25
There is an ampler page for man to quote, — 393 **The Lovers* 12
Who hath a Page her book to hold, — 399 *White Doe* 259
Departed promptly as a Page — 408 *White Doe* 1109
Look only on the Gospel's brighter page : — 447 *Ecc. Sonn.* 3. 29. 11
Which is the attendant Page and which the Queen ? — 459 **The Crescent* 5
Avaunt this vile abuse of pictured page ! — 489 *Illus. Books* 12
Now also shall the page of classic lore, — 496 **A little* 49
And not unhallowed was the page — 499 **Departing summer* 43
Will flow, and on a welcome page appear — 522 *Epist. Beaumont* 57
Noise that brings forth no liveried Page of state, — 525 *Epist. Beaumont* 234
Shall with a thankful tear bedrop its latest page. — 529 **Those breathing* 140
From soul-felt music, and the treasured page — 583 **With copious* 29

Page—*continued.*
Yet, haply, on the printed page received, — 585 *Ch. Lamb* 46
The golden precepts of the classic page ; — 619 *School Ex.* 68
But each of manly sex, a docile page, — 624 *Æneid* 68
Though for brief absence. But farewell ! the page — 627 **The star* 9
Chosen by the Muses for their Page of State— — 653 *Prelude* 3. 279
To think of, to read over, many a page, — 674 *Prelude* 5. 548
When, having closed the mighty Shakspeare's page, — 694 *Prelude* 7. 484
Oh ! laughter for the page that would reflect — 712 *Prelude* 9. 173
Ere yet familiar with the classic page, — 733 *Prelude* 11. 425
And moved, a willing Page, as he was bid, — 782 *Excursion* 2. 687
Give back faint echoes from the historian's page ; — 795 *Excursion* 3. 603
Our little Page : the rustic pair approach ; — 821 *Excursion* 4. 1310
In quality of page among the train — 825 *Excursion* 5. 181

Pageant. Who, from a martial *pageant*, spreads — 233 *Power of Sound* 73
That catch the pageant from the flood — 300 *Bran* 21
The pageant haunts me as it met our eyes ! — 347 *Processions* 47
The pageant glancing to and fro ; — 404 *White Doe* 779
On that proud pageant now at hand or past, — 522 *Epist. Beaumont* 70
No wrack of all the pageant scene remains, — 598 *Ev. Wk. Quarto* 360
Might in this pageant be supposed to hit — 657 *Prelude* 3. 585
Amid the moving pageant, I was smitten — 696 *Prelude* 7. 637
Pageant and revels of blithe elves—to her — S.3. 436 **The doubt* 172
See yonder the same pageant, and again — K.8. 252 *Recluse* 1. 1. 570

Pageantries. Appeared—to govern Christian pageantries : — 346 *Processions* 38

Pageantry. No wreck of all the pageantry remains. — 8 *Ev. Wk.* 306
And the long train of doleful pageantry — 213 *Dion* 85
Do serve with all their changeful pageantry ; — 252 *Picture* 10
The venerable pageantry of Time, — 335 *Rhine* 6
The glittering, floating Pageantry. — 404 *White Doe* 752
This rueful sky, this pageantry of fear ! — 579 *Peele Castle* 48
Of wild ideal pageantry, shaped out — 679 *Prelude* 6. 299
Ere time expire, the pageantry that stirs — K.8. 253 *Recluse* 1. 1. 629

Pageants. Hath fed on pageants floating through the air, — 216 *Enterprise* 93

Pages. (Perchance the pages that relate — 215 *Enterprise* 5
Depicted on these pages smile at time ; — 511 **Who rashly* 10
That on its simplest pages thou wilt look — 628 **Deign, Sovereign* 19

Paid. Except for that abatement which is paid — 68 *Bord.* 1685
Paid to One who loved her well. — 94 *Westmoreland Girl* 68
Until the debt I owe be paid. — 182 *Waggoner* 4. 215
Your seats, and quickly shall be paid — 238 *P. B.* 184
Glory to that eternal Peace is paid, — 256 **Yes ! hope* 7
He paid to Nature tuneful vows ; — 287 *Sons of Burns* 32
A seemly reverence may be paid to power ; — 303 **Is it* 9
Yet shall some tribute of regret be paid — 305 *Ven. Rep.* 11
Look now on that Adventurer who hath paid — 317 **Look now* 1
That all observance, due to them, be paid — 328 *Ode 1815* 59
Fit obsequies the Stranger paid ; — 348 **Lulled by* 68
Paid simple tribute, such as might have flowed — 356 *Aquap.* 242
Flowing of time and place, and paid to both — 358 *Aquap.* 361
And who but listened ?—till was paid — 375 **The Minstrels* 13
With mute obeisance gladly paid — 398 *White Doe* 166
By blind ambition, be this tribute paid. — 429 *Ecc. Sonn.* 2. 2. 14
Of ritual honours to this Fountain paid — 465 **The cattle* 10
Have unto Heaven and You been paid : — 542 *Russ. Fug.* 55
To them and nature paid ! — 545 *Russ. Fug.* 376
He paid what he could with his ill-gotten pelf, — 570 *Farmer* 37
She paid, for in our age the heart is ruled — 574 *Chiabrera* 5. 15
To be performed, and paid all holy fees. — 623 **I find* 5
Wrongs to redress, harmonious tribute paid — 635 *Prelude* 1. 182
Which I had paid to Nature. Toil and pains — 654 *Prelude* 3. 378
Paid to the object by prescriptive right. — 689 *Prelude* 7. 148
Had paid to woman : somewhat vain he was, — 714 *Prelude* 9. 313
The first was service paid to things which lie — 724 *Prelude* 10. 431
That justice may be done, obeisance paid — 743 *Prelude* 13. 237
Paid cheerful tribute to the moorland house. — 776 *Excursion* 2. 343
Are paid to Him upon whose shy retreat — 777 *Excursion* 2. 397
Duly we paid, each after each, and read — 825 *Excursion* 5. 172
Are here deposited, with tribute paid — 837 *Excursion* 5. 971
Various, but unto each some tribute paid ; — 837 *Excursion* 5. 972
Permit, like honours, dance and song, are paid — 851 *Excursion* 6. 836
From those to whom our last regards were paid, — 863 *Excursion* 7. 394
The ocean paid him tribute from the stores — 865 *Excursion* 7. 504
Is paid without reluctance ; but in truth," — 866 *Excursion* 7. 588
To him, thus snatched away, his comrades paid — 870 *Excursion* 7. 874
The guide appointed, and the ransom paid. — 894 *Excursion* 9. 651
And 'tis their due devotion has been paid — L.1. 89 *Juvenal* 1. 27

Pail. Thrice every day, the pail and welcome hand. — 17 *Desc. Sk.* 398
The milk-maid followed with her brimming pail, — 34 *Guilt* 529
Down which she so often has tripped with her pail ; — 188 *Poor Susan* 10
And, in disguise, a Milkmaid with her pail — 521 *Epist. Beaumont* 42
The milkmaid stops her ballad, and her pail — 598 *Ev. Wk. Quarto* 355
Three times a day the pail and welcome hand. — 611 *Desc. Sk. Quarto* 485
For morn and evening service, with her pail, — 832 *Excursion* 5. 641

Pain. Those busy cares that would allay my pain ; — 2 *Early Youth* 12
And hope itself was all I knew of pain ; — 2 *Ev. Wk.* 22
But why, ungrateful, dwell on idle pain ? — 2 *Ev. Wk.* 33
Though grief and pain may come to-morrow ? — 9 *Lines : Boat* 16
Move on—a mighty caravan of pain : — 13 *Desc. Sk.* 170
And taught that pain is pleasure's natural heir, — 20 *Desc. Sk.* 537
As if thenceforth nor pain nor trouble she could know. — 25 *Guilt* 63
In spot so savage, but with shuddering pain ; — 25 *Guilt* 83
Who in his heart had groaned with deadlier pain — 26 *Guilt* 125
The man half raised the stone with pain and sweat, — 27 *Guilt* 178
Beat round to clear the streets of want and pain. — 29 *Guilt* 274
Nor voice, nor sound, that moment's pain expressed, — 30 *Guilt* 308

Pain—*continued.*
A thought resigned with pain, when from the mast 31 *Guilt* 354
Nor pain nor pity in my bosom raised. 31 *Guilt* 398
The Soldier's Widow learned with honest pain 34 *Guilt* 550
The wholesome ministry of pain and evil, 48 *Bord.* 619
With all their natural weight of sorrow and pain, 52 *Bord.* 821
That, in my zeal, I have caused you so much pain. 55 *Bord.* 1004
To cold and hunger !—Pain is of the heart, 62 *Bord.* 1399
In the entire forgetfulness of pain. 65 *Bord.* 1551
He is a puny soul who, feeling pain, 65 *Bord.* 1555
A Man by pain and thought compelled to live, 78 *Bord.* 2351
Till God released her of her pain ; 84 *We are Seven* 51
I could not feel a pain. 85 *Anecdote* 16
I thought of times when Pain might be thy guest, 88 *H. C.* 15
Others saved from lingering pain. 94 *Westmoreland Girl* 56
Proof shalt thou furnish that misfortune, pain, 105 *Artegal* 208
My calmest faith escapes not pain ; 110 *Forsaken* 12
His love was such a grievous pain. 110 *'*Tis said that some* 5
My fire is dead : it knew no pain ; 114 *Ind. Wom.* 11
For strong and without pain I lay, 114 *Ind. Wom.* 29
I should not feel the pain of dying, 114 *Ind. Wom.* 47
In spite of all my weary pain 114 *Ind. Wom.* 53
Think not of me with grief and pain : 117 *Affl. Marg.* 39
And kissed it ; seemingly devoid of pain, 125 *V. and J.* 233
Old Susan lies a-bed in pain, 126 *Idiot Boy* 24
Whether he be in joy or pain, 126 *Idiot Boy* 34
" What can I do to ease your pain ? 128 *Idiot Boy* 193
There's nothing that can ease my pain." 128 *Idiot Boy* 198
Poor Betty ! it would ease her pain 129 *Idiot Boy* 269
How she loved a Christian Slave, and told her pain 139 *Arm. Lady* 5
Eases her pain, and helps her prayers. 144 **Driven in* 36
And in my head a dull, dull pain ; 144 *Her Eyes* 22
Draw from my heart the pain away. 145 *Her Eyes* 34
From weakness now and pain defended, 157 *Sexton* 15
Is opened of still deeper pain, 180 *Waggoner* 4. 76
I felt a sense of pain when I beheld 186 *Nutting* 52
There came a respite to her pain ; 194 *Ruth* 206
The engines of her pain, the tools 194 *Ruth* 217
Solitude, pain of heart, distress, and poverty. 195 *Resolution* 35
As if some dire constraint of pain, or rage 196 *Resolution* 68
Cold, pain, and labour, and all fleshly ills ; 197 *Resolution* 115
From her exceeding pain. 199 *Thorn* 130
If solitude, or fear, or pain, or grief, 207 *Tintern* 143
Hollow excuses, and triumphant pain ; 213 *Dion* 59
And nightly tosses on a bed of pain ; 229 *Cuckoo-clock* 24
Of being, smites with irresistible pain, 234 *Power of Sound* 98
To ease his conscience of its pain. 245 *P. B.* 800
He knew not one forewarning pain ; 248 *P. B.* 1048
I have no pain that calls for patience, no ; 253 **O gentle* 9
No trace of pain or languor could abide 258 **Even so* 5
Of harmony !—a shriek of terror, pain, 274 **Wait, prithee* 11
I shrink with pain ; 284 *Grave of Burns* 10
Some natural sorrow, loss, or pain, 289 *Sol. Reap.* 23
The fate of those old Trees ; and oft with pain 292 **Degenerate Douglas* 9
The strife of happiness and pain, 294 *Jedbor.* 52
That triumph, when the very worst, the pain, 310 *Anticip.* 11
In these usurping times of fear and pain ? 316 **O'er the* 8
Admonished by these truths, and quench all pain 317 **Call not* 13
As though his weakness were disturbed by pain : 321 **Humanity, delighting* 6
And with an infinite pain the spirit aches, 330 *Ode : Thanks.* 102
Pain entered through a ghastly breach— 337 **Oh Life* 7
Her peace from images to pain allied. 361 **For action* 4
A softened remembrance of sorrow and pain, 398 *White Doe* 239
Dismay, and superstitious pain, 405 *White Doe* 867
Hath any sway ? or pain, or fear ? 406 *White Doe* 963
Not unperplexed nor free from pain, 407 *White Doe* 1013
O'ER PAIN AND GRIEF A TRIUMPH PURE. 407 *White Doe* 1072
Whence idle fears, and needless pain, 408 *White Doe* 1121
She shrunk :—with one frail shock of pain 414 *White Doe* 1696
—What now is left for pain or fear ? 415 *White Doe* 1743
No moment steals ; pain narrows not his cares. 425 *Ecc. Sonn.* 1. 26. 10
Or would have taught, by discipline of pain 441 *Ecc. Sonn.* 3. 3. 6
Glad music ! yet there be that, worn with pain 447 *Ecc. Sonn.* 3. 28. 2
Encounters, armed for work of pain and death. 448 *Ecc. Sonn.* 3. 30. 12
If e'er, through fault of mine, in mutual pain 464 **A point* 11
And pain, hath powers to Eternity endeared. 476 *Howard* 14
Such strength as, if ever affliction and pain 482 *Character* 6
" There came from me a sigh of pain 487 **We walked* 53
Who, doomed to go in company with Pain, 493 *Hap. War.* 12
If this great world of joy and pain 505 **If this* 1
And proud deliverance issuing out of pain 514 **Who ponders* 4
They must forbid the State to inflict a pain, 518 *Pun. Death* 7. 13
Amazement rose to pain, 545 *Russ. Fug.* 354
What is peace ?—when pain is over, 550 *Hermit's Cell* 1. 33
Although for pain thou may'st be like to die, 561 *Cuck.andNight.*244
Well hast thou wreaked on me by pain and grief ; 563 *Troilus* 72
Feel I a wind, that soundeth so like pain ; 565 *Troilus* 160
A weary while in pain he tosseth thus, 565 *Troilus* 162
A man who does not move with pain, but moves 572 *Animal Tran.* 6
And buoyant spirit triumphed over pain ; 574 *Chiabrera* 5. 7
Reader ! if to thy bosom cling the pain 576 **By a* 13
Let sorrow overcharged with pain 578 **I come* 51
Sad was I, even to pain deprest, 581 **Loud is* 9
—With backward gaze, lock'd joints, and step of pain, 596 *Ev. Wk. Quarto* 247
By Pain and her sad family unfound, 602 *Desc. Sk. Quarto* 2
Can guess the high resolve, the cherish'd pain 608 *Desc.Sk.Quarto* 360

Pain—*continued.*
Labour, and Pain, and Grief, and joyless Age, 613 *Desc.Sk.Quarto* 639
Where the charm'd worm of pain shall gnaw no more. 614 *Desc.Sk.Quarto* 669
And my full heart was swell'd to dear delicious pain. 619 **She wept* 4
(Alive to all a mother's pain, 620 *Birth of Love* 10
In the pain of my spirit I said, 620 *Convict* 6
A thousand sharp punctures of cold-sweating pain, 621 *Convict* 39
For which, with pain, he caused due obsequies 623 **I find* 4
Both pain and fear, until we recognise 638 *Prelude* 1. 413
Uneasiness, or pain, or jealousy : 643 *Prelude* 2. 67
Issued low muttered sounds, as if of pain 664 *Prelude* 4. 405
To travel without pain, and I beheld, 665 *Prelude* 4. 432
Of pain, and doubt, and fear, yet yielding not 672 *Prelude* 5. 419
A world of pain, ripened a thousand hopes, 679 *Prelude* 6. 285
Without uneasy forethought of the pain, 680 *Prelude* 6. 330
One night, or haply more than one, through pain 705 *Prelude* 8. 387
And, through dislike and most offensive pain, 707 *Prelude* 8. 525
So that he questions the mute leaves with pain, 719 *Prelude* 10. 62
Sorrow for human kind, and pain of heart. 723 *Prelude* 10. 330
Whose souls were sick with pain of what would be 724 *Prelude* 10. 395
A lonely wanderer art gone, by pain 733 *Prelude* 11. 402
And miserable love, that is not pain 743 *Prelude* 13. 247
With the adverse principles of pain and joy— 748 *Prelude* 14. 166
From sources deeper far than deepest pain, 770 *Excursion* 1. 938
With pain the regions of eternity. 774 *Excursion* 2. 205
Of pain were keen as those of better men, 775 *Excursion* 2. 279
Sickness, or accident, or grief, or pain. 777 *Excursion* 2. 369
" To the dark pit ; but he will feel no pain ; 779 *Excursion* 2. 510
The mind is full—and free from pain their pastime." 789 *Excursion* 3. 193
Not as a refuge from distress or pain, 791 *Excursion* 3. 383
By pain of heart—now checked—and now impelled— 796 *Excursion* 3. 699
His mournful narrative—commenced in pain, 801 *Excursion* 4. 2
In pain commenced, and ended without peace : 801 *Excursion* 4. 3
To unsettle or perplex it : yet with pain 804 *Excursion* 4. 199
Divine or human ; exercised in pain, 837 *Excursion* 5. 1013
Of pain and grief ? " the Solitary asked, 840 *Excursion* 6. 116
Resolved to quell his pain, and search for truth 840 *Excursion* 6. 152
Their virtue's humbler mark ; a sigh of *pain* 842 *Excursion* 6. 269
Would I give a moment's pain ; S.3. 438 **My Lord* 4
When I could live without a pain, K.8. 220 **The snow-tracks* 23
Or with immoderate pain. I look for Man, K.8. 246 *Recluse* 1.1.352
All brothers, long endeared by kindred pain, L.1. 95 *Juvenal* 3. 6

Painful. In painful struggles. Months each other chase, 274 *Infant M.* 4
While thus illumined, tells of painful strife 278 **Lo ! where she* 6
Upon the pressure of a painful thing, 311 **Who rises* 47
A few short steps (painful they were) apart 353 *Aquap.* 83
Thy part is done—thy painful part ; 401 *White Doe* 503
Laud, " in the painful art of dying " tried, 440 *Ecc. Sonn.* 2. 45. 3
And painful struggle and deliverance—prayed 460 **Queen of* 31
Enough ;—before us lay a painful road, 520 *Pun. Death* 14. 9
Where the brook brawls along the painful road, 596 *Ev. Wk. Quarto* 271
Threading the painful cragg surmounts the cliff. 607 *Desc.Sk.Quarto* 298
Yea, afterwards—truth most painful to record !— 722 *Prelude* 10. 284
And therefore bold to look on painful things, 731 *Prelude* 11. 277
He had no painful pressure from without 761 *Excursion* 1. 368
Beginning, ends in servitude—still painful, 799 *Excursion* 3. 895
From painful and discreditable shocks 828 *Excursion* 5. 362
Whose visual nerve shrinks from a painful glare 848 *Excursion* 6. 685
The weakness painful and most pitiful, 851 *Excursion* 6. 846
To cast from time to time a painful look K.8. 250 *Recluse* 1.1.493

Painfully. So painfully in the wood ? 162 **Art thou the* 23
No stammerer of a minute, painfully 694 *Prelude* 7. 500
Less fair, I grant, even painfully less fair, 781 *Excursion* 2. 641

Paining. *See* **Hardly-paining.**

Pain's. Pain's wild rebellious burst proclaims her rights aloud. 614 *Desc.Sk.Quarto* 653

Pains. Turning past pleasures into mortal pains ; 19 *Desc. Sk.* 525
" The pains and plagues that on our heads came down, 29 *Guilt* 298
There, pains which nature could no more support, 31 *Guilt* 383
Your pains shall ever with your years increase ? "— 33 *Guilt* 511
Than you have entered, were it worth the pains. 59 *Bord.* 1222
But our joint pains unloosed the cloak, 82 *Alice Fell* 31
The hut stood finished by his pains, nor seemingly lacked aught 91 *Norman Boy* 17
From body pains and pains of soul thou needest no release, 92 *Poet's Dream* 55
With all my care and pains, 115 *Last of Flock* 58
Who told him that his pains were thrown away, 125 *V. and J.* 291
Is worth the best with all their pains ; 178 *Waggoner* 3. 13
God help thee, Ruth !—Such pains she had, 194 *Ruth* 193
Calm pleasures there abide—majestic pains. 210 *Laod.* 72
If some, by ceaseless pains outworn, 223 *Wishing-gate* 44
Him hath he sought with fruitless pains, 243 *P. B.* 642
And once again those ghastly pains, 244 *P. B.* 733
There is a pleasure in poetic pains 265 **There is a pleasure* 1
Slackening the pains of ruthless banishment 273 **When Philoctetes* 7
Upturned with curious pains, the Bard, a Seer, 275 **While poring* 2
Pains which the World inflicts can she requite ? 280 **Intent on* 10
Have I received this proof of pains bestowed 281 *Chris. Words.* 2
Not worth a moment's pains. 291 *Rob Roy* 72
What pains to dazzle and confound ! 300 *Bran* 23
Or pains abstruse—to elevate the will, 315 **Alas ! what* 3
To suffer pains with heathen scorn and hate 357 *Aquap.* 313
Even to the inmost seat of mortal pains, 383 *Duddon* 29. 7
For the departed, built with curious pains 389 *Breadalb.* 8

Pains—*continued.*
By such examples moved to unbought pains, . . 424 *Ecc. Sonn.* 1. 24. 1
The Race of Alfred covet glorious pains . . . 425 *Ecc. Sonn.* 1. 27. 5
And seek through noiseless pains and moderation 516 **As leaves* 7
Lest, capital pains remitting till ye spare . . . 518 *Pun. Death* 4. 7
Laughs at my pains, and seems to say, " Be done." 525 *Epist. Beaumont* 273
Softening the toils and pains that have not ceased 538 **In desultory* 27
With earnest pains unchecked by dread . . . 543 *Russ. Fug.* 113
One wooed the silent Art with studious pains : 546 **The embowering* 5
Not by the sluggish and ungrateful pains . . 546 **Oft is* 11
Old Adam will smile at the pains that have made 570 *Farmer* 75
Faith bore her up through pains in mercy given, . 576 **By a* 7
When, after pains dispensed to prove . . . . 577 **By playful* 9
From many a humble source, to pains . . . . 580 *John Words.* 46
Why with such earnest pains dost thou provoke . 589 *Immortality* 127
And his crime, through the pains that o'erwhelm him, descried, ... 621 *Convict* 23
The terrors, pains, and early miseries, ... 637 *Prelude* 1. 345
Which I had paid to Nature. Toil and pains . 654 *Prelude* 3. 378
That never set the pains against the prize ; . . 657 *Prelude* 3. 596
Much pains and little progress, and at once . . 660 *Prelude* 4. 112
Appeared to recompense the traveller's pains . . 710 *Prelude* 9. 76
Wouldstthou not chide ? Yet deem not my pains lost : . . . . 717 *Prelude* 9. 564
Object, so seemed it, of superfluous pains, . . 722 *Prelude* 10. 261
Caught at a glance, or traced with curious pains. 750 *Prelude* 14. 320
Told what best merits mention, further pains . 751 *Prelude* 14. 370
For the peculiar pains they had required, . . 767 *Excursion* 1. 726
By none, they for the attempt, and pains employed, 792 *Excursion* 3. 408
And they who rather dive than soar, whose pains 815 *Excursion* 4. 951
With her minute and speculative pains, . . . 818 *Excursion* 4. 1131
To them, and to his own judicious pains, . . . 824 *Excursion* 5. 127
May be, through pains and persevering hope, . . 827 *Excursion* 5. 306
Among so many shadows, are the pains . . . 829 *Excursion* 5. 476
So have we argued ; reaping for our pains . . 832 *Excursion* 5. 626
Of virgin ore, that gold which we, by pains . . 832 *Excursion* 5. 632
Of keen adventurers to unite their pains . . . 841 *Excursion* 6. 216
In ceaseless pains—and strictest parsimony . . 849 *Excursion* 6. 724
Her heart she opened ; and no pains were spared 854 *Excursion* 6. 1031
Industrious to destroy ! With fruitless pains . 875 *Excursion* 8. 95
Till perfect mastery crown the pains at last. . . 880 *Excursion* 8. 415
Expect these mighty issues : from the pains . . 890 *Excursion* 9. 394
These fertile fields, that recompense your pains ; . 895 *Excursion* 9. 744
Pains-taking. Pains-taking thoughts, and truth, their dear reward) . . . . 732 *Prelude* 11. 327
Paint. To me was all in all.—I cannot paint . 206 *Tintern* 75
Words cannot paint the o'ershadowing yew-tree bough, ... 254 *Wild Duck's Nest* 9
Thus might *he* paint our lot of mortal days . 259 **Weak is* 5
But 'tis a fruitless task to paint for me, . . . 279 **All praise* 2
Such deeds to paint, such characters to frame, . 359 **Complacent Fictions* 6
To paint this picture of his lady-love : . . . 363 **Grieve for* 4
How shall I paint thee ?—Be this naked stone . 376 *Duddon* 3. 1
What a fair world were ours for verse to paint, . 500 *Humanity* 41
A bridge to copy, or to paint a mill, ... 521 *Epist.Beaumont* 31
To paint these vanities, and how they wrought . 662 *Prelude* 4. 293
Longing for skill to paint a scene so bright . . 726 *Prelude* 10. 569
To paint the visionary dreariness . . . . . . 738 *Prelude* 12. 256
Painted. *See* **Rudely-painted.**
When the rising sun he painted, ... 161 **Pleasures newly* 14
For it was painted by the Host ; . . . . . 174 *Waggoner* 1. 90
Painted more soft and fair as they descend, . . 218 *Recluse* 1. 1. 226
What ! Ossian here—a painted Thrall, . . . 300 *Bran* 5
Hath painted Winter like a traveller old, . . . 321 **Humanity, delighting* 3
Painted on rich men's floors, for one feast-night. . 488 *Pers. Talk* 8
Their painted couches seek, obedient to command. 624 *Æneid* 72
The very gilding, lamps and painted scrolls, . . 693 *Prelude* 7. 408
Are here—Albinos, painted Indians, Dwarfs, . . 697 *Prelude* 7. 707
Less than the painted Magdalene of Le Brun, . . 710 *Prelude* 9. 77
Such as the boy you painted, lineal heirs . . . 886 *Excursion* 9. 179
Or is the painted staffs [? staff's] avenging host . L.1. 97 *Juvenal* 3. 85
Painter. And whom the curious Painter doth pursue 268 **Brook ! whose* 3
Then, and then only, Painter ! could thy Art . 279 **All praise* 11
A British Painter (eminent for truth . . . . 509 *F. Stone* 99
Here may some Painter sit in future days, . . 546 **The embowering* 13
—There, though by right the excelling Painter sleep 547 **Ye Lime* 9
Whether the Painter, whose ambitious skill . . 690 *Prelude* 7. 240
Painter's. Creation of the painter's skill, . . 228 *Devot. Incit.* 35
That to the Painter's skill is here allowed. . . 231 **The gentlest Poet* 4
Hast loved the painter's true Promethean craft . 508 *F. Stone* 24
Triumphs, in that great work, the Painter's skill, 510 **Among a* 3
Ah ! THEN, if mine had been the Painter's hand, . 578 *Peele Castle* 13
Intensely studied with a painter's eye, . . . 583 **With copious* 21
And mockery of the rustic painter's hand— . . 644 *Prelude* 2. 153
Painting. In painting to ourselves the miseries . 714 *Prelude* 9. 344
Paints. That paints, by strength of sorrow, . . 302 *Yarrow V.* 38
Who paints how Britain struggled and prevailed . 330 *Ode : Thanks.* 72
As fades the chequer'd bow that paints the sky. . 619 *School Ex.* 98
Pair. To glance a look upon the well-matched pair ; 19 *Desc. Sk.* 486
Forthwith the pair passed on ; and down they look 33 *Guilt* 514
Their breakfast done, the pair, though loth, must part ; . . . . 34 *Guilt* 532
He breathed for her, and for that merciful pair. . 36 *Guilt* 644
I watched them with delight, they were a lovely pair. . . . . 87 *Pet-lamb* 14
A pair of diaries,—one serving, Sir, ... 97 *Brothers* 163
A pair of Leverets each provoking each . . . 118 *Maternal Grief* 28
If more divided than a sportive pair . . . . 122 *V. and J.* 25

Pair—*continued.*
I pass the raptures of the pair ;—such theme . . 123 *V. and J.* 87
Of that same town, in which the pair had left . 125 *V. and J.* 286
The Pair had but one inmate in their house, . . 132 *Michael* 86
That thrifty Pair had lived. For, as it chanced, . 133 *Michael* 131
Make one being of a pair." . . . . 140 *Arm. Lady* 64
How the pair escaped together, ... 140 *Arm. Lady* 75
A pair of herons oft-times have I seen, . . . 143 **High bliss* 14
In fellowship, the loftiest of the pair . . . 151 **Forth from* 3
Too blest with any one to pair : . . . . . 159 *Green Linnet* 23
If called to choose between the favoured pair, . 165 *Parrot* 42
Even as ye do, thoughtless pair ; . . . . 171 *Kitten* 110
Dread pair that, spite of wind and weather, . . 175 *Waggoner* 1. 178
A little pair that hang in air, ... 176 *Waggoner* 2. 4
Our Travellers are the happiest pair ; . . . . 177 *Waggoner* 2. 79
And with them goes the guardian pair. . . . 178 *Waggoner* 3. 21
To take of this transported pair . . . . . 180 *Waggoner* 4. 13
Another ; then perhaps a pair— . . . . . 182 *Waggoner* 4. 257
A pair of little Boys at play, ... 191 *Beggars* 21
The faith which saw that gladsome pair . . . 191 *Seq. Beggars* 29
The horse and horseman are a happy pair ; . . 200 *Hart-leap* 10
The pair were servants of his eye . . . . . 205 *Brougham* 124
By which the journeying pair are chased ? . . 244 *P. B.* 702
What aim had they, the Pair of Monks, in size . 363 **What aim* 1
Changed, as the pair approached the light, . . 371 *Eg. Maid* 178
Blest Pair ! whate'er befall you, ... 374 *Eg. Maid* 383
Not so that Pair whose youthful spirits dance . 378 *Duddon* 10. 1
Said fearless Norton to the pair . . . . . 402 *White Doe* 603
Oh, moment ever blest ! O Pair . . . . . 414 *White Doe* 1665
They, like a nested pair, reposed ! . . . . 415 *White Doe* 1737
Are glorified while this once-mitred pair . . 437 *Ecc. Sonn.* 2. 34. 10
A pair of friends, though I was young, . . . 487 *Fountain* 3
Four dogs, each pair of different breed, . . . 490 *Incident : Dog* 7
The pair have reached that fearful chasm, . . 494 *Force of Prayer* 17
White as the pair that slid along the plains . . 497 *Lycoris* 17
Which ye feel not, happy pair ! . . . . . 503 *Warning* 4
But turn, my Soul, and from the sleeping pair . 505 *Warning* 158
A Pair who smilingly sat side by side, ... 523 *Epist. Beaumont* 114
Was formed between the solitary pair, . . . 531 **I know* 22
That of the pair—tossed on the waves to bring . 541 *Grace Darl.* 69
The dwelling of this faithful pair . . . . 542 *Russ. Fug.* 89
The pair sally forth hand in hand : ere the sun . 572 *Avarice* 33
Oft he descends to nurse the brother pair, . . 612 *Desc.Sk.Quarto* 576
Of deep and stately vales ! A lonely pair . . 680 *Prelude* 6. 384
Followed that pair of golden days that shed . . 686 *Prelude* 6. 724
Or dromedary, with an antic pair . . . . . 689 *Prelude* 7. 177
With looking on, some ancient wedded pair . . 699 *Prelude* 8. 46
Sometimes methought I saw a pair of knights . 716 *Prelude* 9. 454
The ill-fated pair) in that plain tale will draw . 717 *Prelude* 9. 566
And joyous creatures ; see that pair, the lamb . 748 *Prelude* 14. 172
A pair of falcons wheeling on the wing, . . . 786 *Excursion* 3. 2
Some little space disjoined, a pair were seen, . . 787 *Excursion* 3. 58
If I must take my choice between the pair . . 790 *Excursion* 3. 275
" In privacy we dwelt, a wedded pair, . . . 794 *Excursion* 3. 584
Our little Page : the rustic pair approach ; . . 821 *Excursion* 4. 1310
Each also crowned with wingèd heads—a pair . 824 *Excursion* 5. 152
—For me, I looked upon the pair, well pleased : . 829 *Excursion* 5. 452
A wedded pair in childless solitude. . . . . 833 *Excursion* 5. 692
Hold lower rank than this sequestered pair : . . 833 *Excursion* 5. 718
" To a mysteriously-united pair . . . . . 836 *Excursion* 5. 903
Him, farther off ; the pair, who here are laid ; . 842 *Excursion* 6. 272
Survives, for worthy mention, of a pair . . . 844 *Excursion* 6. 405
The pair, whose infant she was bound to nurse, . 853 *Excursion* 6. 960
Their grave migration, the good pair would tell, . 859 *Excursion* 7. 109
That now divides the pair, or rather say, . . . 861 *Excursion* 7. 239
Flew open, and a pair of lusty Boys . . . . 882 *Excursion* 8. 545
Upon the brighter scene. How blest that pair . 888 *Excursion* 9. 256
With caution we embarked ; and now the pair . 891 *Excursion* 9. 478
But two are missing—two, a lonely pair . . . K.8. 243 *Recluse* 1.1.238
They strangers, and we strangers ; they a pair, . K.8. 243 *Recluse* 1.1.254
And we a solitary pair like them. . . . . . K.8. 243 *Recluse* 1.1.255
And neither pair be broken ? Nay perchance . K.8. 244 *Recluse* 1.1.264
And moving dialogues between this pair, . . . K.8. 248 *Recluse* 1.1.419
Return, Helvellyn's eagles ! with the pair . . K.8. 250 *Recluse* 1.1.518
Marshal forth-with a pair of oars in gules. . . L.1. 96 *Juvenal* 3. 36
Paired. Once more, those creatures thus by nature paired, ... 143 **High bliss* 23
Paired with the ostrich, o'er the plain ; . . . 216 *Enterprise* 33
With its twin notes inseparably paired. . . . 273 **Not the* 4
Where Solitude with Silence paired stops short . 355 *Aquap.* 196
Man, bird, and beast ; then, with a consort paired, 388 *Eagles* 6
And thirst for bloody spoils abroad is paired . . 714 *Prelude* 9. 353
One whom with thee friendship had early paired ; 750 *Prelude* 14. 267
Beneath his ample brow, in darkness paired,— . 865 *Excursion* 7. 508
Pairing. As yon Hawk exhibits, pairing . . . 163 *Hint* 6
Pair's. Wept for that pair's unhappy fate, . . . 623 *G. and S. Green* 3
Pairs. In knots, or pairs, or single. Not a look . 710 *Prelude* 9. 60
Mute or conversing, single or in pairs. . . . 890 *Excursion* 9. 436
Paix. And, kneeling, supplication make to our Lady de la Paix ; . . . . 92 *Poet's Dream* 50
Palace. The finest palace of a hundred realms ! . 202 *Hart-leap* 128
This is our palace,—yonder is thy throne ; . . 210 *Laod.* 33
The softest Nursling of a gorgeous palace . . . 221 *Triad* 68
A palace of the proudest show, ... 297 *Highland Boy* 209
Anon before my sight a palace rose . . . . 324 *Ode 1814* 69
Dashed their white foam against the palace walls 354 *Aquap.* 122
In his ancestral palace, where, from morn . . . 359 **They—who* 4
Palace and tower, are crumbled into dust !— . . 379 *Duddon* 12. 10
Studied alike in palace and in cot. . . . . . 393 **The Lovers* 14
That quench, from hut to palace, lamps and fires, 426 *Ecc. Sonn.* 1. 31. 10

Palace-floor 689 Pan

Palace—*continued.*
To sanctify the Escurial palace. He— . . . 509 *F. Stone* 97
Entering her palace gate ; . . . . 543 *Russ. Fug.* 156
We must the Palace see of Cresida ; . . . . 562 *Troilus* 5
Let us behold her Palace at the least ! . . . . 562 *Troilus* 7
And they right forth to Cresid's Palace went ; . 562 *Troilus* 10
Then said he thus,—O Palace desolate ! . . . 563 *Troilus* 22
O Palace empty and disconsolate ! . . . . . 563 *Troilus* 24
O Palace whilom day that now art night, . . . 563 *Troilus* 26
Palace illumined with the sun of bliss ; . . . 563 *Troilus* 30
And that imperial palace whence he came. . . 588 *Immortality* 84
The King, and the King's Palace, and, not last, . 688 *Prelude* 7. 109
Or palace built by fairies of the rock ; . . . . 705 *Prelude* 8. 418
The Arcades I traversed, in the Palace huge . . 710 *Prelude* 9. 52
In bondage ; and the palace, lately stormed . . 719 *Prelude* 10. 53
Palace or grove, even so could I unsoul . . . 735 *Prelude* 12. 83
Of temple, palace, citadel, and huge . . . . 784 *Excursion* 2. 858
A golden palace rose, or seemed to rise, . . . 796 *Excursion* 3. 714
As from the haughtiest palace. He, whose soul . 887 *Excursion* 9. 247
Palace-floor. And on the palace-floor a lifeless corse She lay. . . . . 211 *Laod.* 157
Palace-home. The ducal Owner, in his palace-home 392 *Daniel* 3
Palaces. The shades of palaces and kings ! . . . 237 *P. B.* 105
Of palaces, or temples, 'mid the wreck . . . 394 **No more* 8
Of airy palaces, and gardens built . . . . . 688 *Prelude* 7. 78
Palace-walk. With early morning towards the Palace-walk . . . . 719 *Prelude* 10. 94
Palafox. By Palafox, and many a brave compeer, . 315 **And is it* 10
Ah ! where is Palafox ? Nor tongue nor pen . 318 **Ah ! where* 1
Pale. The Child she mourned had overstepped the pale . . . . 118 *Maternal Grief* 14
Not wholly rescued from the pale . . . . . 238 *P. B.* 187
Beautiful strangers, stand within the pale . . . 421 *Ecc. Sonn.* 1. 13. 2
This threw me first out of the pale of love ; . . 729 *Prelude* 11. 176
To Britons born and bred within the pale . . . 880 *Excursion* 8. 392
Breathed a pale steam around the glaring hill, . 2 *Ev. Wk.* 38
Cling from the rocks, with pale wood-weeds between ; . . . . 3 *Ev. Wk.* 60
Soft o'er the surface creep those lustres pale . . 7 *Ev. Wk.* 295
While the pale moon moves near him, on the bound 16 *Desc. Sk.* 319
A woman stood with quivering lips and pale, . . 33 *Guilt* 469
Who will turn pale upon you, call you murderer, 64 *Bord.* 1509
—Nay, you are pale. It may be so. Remorse— 65 *Bord.* 1560
Thy vest is torn, thy cheek is deadly pale ; . . 76 *Bord.* 2191
Or like a sinful creature, pale and wan. . . 107 *Indolence* 21
And a pale face that seemed undoubtedly . . . 108 *Indolence* 40
Propping a pale and melancholy face . . . . 124 *V. and J.* 213
So pale you scarcely looked at her : . . . . 130 *Idiot Boy* 404
Ere it wither and grow pale." . . . . . . 139 *Arm. Lady* 10
How pale and wan it else would be. . . . . 145 *Her Eyes* 70
Glimmering through the twilight pale ; . . . 180 *Waggoner* 4. 20
Himself he propped, limbs, body, and pale face, . 196 *Resolution* 71
The aspiring Virgin kneels ; and, pale . . . . 216 *Enterprise* 55
Far into silent regions blue and pale ;— . . . 219 **This Height* 15
He trembles—he is pale as death ; . . . . . 248 *P. B.* 1031
Pale twilight's lingering glooms,—and in the sun 278 **Life with* 5
Aloft, beneath the moon's pale beam, ... 300 *Cora Linn* 22
Our groans, our blushes, our pale cheeks declare . 319 *Spaniard* 13
Pale, ragged, with bare feet and head ; . . . 342 *Ital. Itin.* 88
Thus sensitive must be the Monk, though pale . 362 **List—'twas* 74
That slender Youth, a scholar pale, ... 399 *White Doe* 264
And Neville's cheek grew pale with fear ; . . . 404 *White Doe* 792
In her pale chambers of the west, ... 408 *White Doe* 1161
But now, his Child, with anguish pale, . . . 409 *White Doe* 1188
Under the holy fear of God turns pale ; . . . 446 *Ecc. Sonn.* 3. 23. 8
When each pale brow to dread hosannas bowed . 450 *Ecc. Sonn.* 3. 40. 3
Guid'st the pale Mourner to the lost one's tomb ; 459 **Wanderer ! that* 28
Like that pale Queen whose hands are seen . . 479 *Somnamb.* 84
Trembled the groves, the stars grew pale, . . . 499 **Departing summer* 34
To see Presumption, turning pale, refrain . . . 504 *Warning* 70
As in a posy, with a few pale ears . . . . . 509 *F. Stone* 57
Sends the pale Convict to his last retreat . . 520 *Pun. Death* 13. 3
Would their lost strength restore and freshen the pale cheek ? . . . . 523 *Epist. Beaumont* 117
Pale and trembling Hubert stood. . . . . . 535 *Egremont* 52
This, Ina saw ; and, pale with fear, ... 544 *Russ. Fug.* 269
With face all pale with dread and busy thought, . 554 *Prioress* 138
For which, with changèd, pale, and deadly face, . 563 *Troilus* 18
That he was blighted, pale, and waxen less . . 564 *Troilus* 100
Pale was her hue ; yet mortal cheek . . . . 583 **O for a* 31
Soft o'er the surface creep the lustres pale . . 598 *Ev. Wk. Quarto* 343
Pale Passion, overpower'd, retires and woos . . 604 *Desc.Sk.Quarto* 118
And apple sickens pale in summer's ray, . . . 608 *Desc.Sk.Quarto* 322
Wheel pale and silent her diminish'd round, . . 609 *Desc.Sk.Quarto* 383
Round your pale eyes a wintry lustre wake. . . 614 *Desc.Sk.Quarto* 675
On his pale horse shall fell Consumption go. . . 617 *Desc.Sk.Quarto* 791
With panting breast, now pale as winter snows, . 618 *School Ex.* 19
Pale and bedropped with everflowing tears. . . 710 *Prelude* 9. 80
Through a pale steam ; but all the northern downs, 756 *Excursion* 1. 3
Her face was pale and thin—her figure, too, . . 767 *Excursion* 1. 751
That it could be no other ; a pale face, . . . 779 *Excursion* 2. 499
When issue forth the first pale stars, is heard, . 819 *Excursion* 4. 1176
In their appointed place. The pale Recluse . . 825 *Excursion* 5. 224
The pale Recluse—" praise to the sturdy plough, 831 *Excursion* 5. 602
When he beholds the first pale speck serene . . 852 *Excursion* 6. 914
Creeping his gait and cowering, his lip pale, . . 879 *Excursion* 8. 311
The pale Recluse indignantly exclaimed, . . . 879 *Excursion* 8. 335
Shagged with wild pale green tufts of fragrant hay, S.3. 417 **Sweet was* 3
Pale-blue. These, by the pale-blue rocks that ceaseless ring, ... 5 *Ev. Wk.* 166

Pale-blue—*continued.*
With pale-blue hands, and eyes that fix'd implore, 615 *Desc.Sk.Quarto* 710
Pale-faced. A pale-faced Woman, in disease far gone. 34 *Guilt* 545
The fever of that pale-faced Child ; . . . . 144 **Driven in* 38
Now vacant ; pale-faced babes whom I had left . 661 *Prelude* 4. 203
Paleness. There's thought and no thought, and there's paleness and bloom . . . . 482 *Character* 3
Paler. Chequer with paler red the thicket shades. . 599 *Ev. Wk. Quarto* 398
And bidding paler shades her form conceal, . . 603 *Desc.Sk.Quarto* 77
Bending its apex toward a paler self . . . . S.3. 434 **The doubt* 69
Pales. Wherein were fixed the iron pales that fenced 696 *Prelude* 7. 606
Palestine. In Palestine ? Where he despised alike 37 *Bord.* 18
That when, on our return from Palestine, . . . 40 *Bord.* 192
From Palestine, and brought with me a heart, . 49 *Bord.* 685
Give not to them a thought. From Palestine . 70 *Bord.* 1801
Delivered heart and head ! Let us to Palestine ; 77 *Bord.* 2282
Of Palestine, of glory past, ... 232 *Jew. Fam.* 47
As thence she holds her way to Palestine. . . 427 *Ecc. Sonn.* 1. 35. 8
In Palestine. Advance, indignant Sword ! . . 467 *St. Bees* 105
To Palestine the Brothers took their way. . . 535 *Egremont* 40
Pale-visaged. And the pale-visaged Baker's, with basket on back. . . . . 188 *Music* 16
Palfrey. I have a palfrey and a groom : the lad . 43 *Bord.* 311
Upon her palfrey, or that gentle maid . . . . 716 *Prelude* 9. 452
Palfreys. Of those led palfreys that should bear us home ; . . . . 738 *Prelude* 12. 291
Pall. The land as with a funeral pall ? . . . . 628 *Installation* 20
Hopeful and cheerful :—vanished is the pall . . 830 *Excursion* 5. 547
Pallet. The wretch on his pallet should turn, . . 621 *Convict* 36
Pallid. The mine's dire earthquake, and the pallid host 30 *Guilt* 348
Struck the poor innocent. Pallid with dismay . 33 *Guilt* 475
He totters, pallid as a ghost, ... 85 *Shepherd-boys* 63
Faint colour over both their pallid cheeks, . . 119 *Maternal Grief* 62
Seems changed into a pallid spot. . . . . . 173 *Waggoner* 1. 12
Hurrying the pallid hue away . . . . . . 181 *Waggoner* 4. 152
And pallid brow, a melancholy lustre. . . . 371 *Eg. Maid* 162
Step forth."—To touch the pallid hand . . . 373 *Eg. Maid* 268
And lightened o'er the pallid countenance. . . 383 *Duddon* 29. 8
Breathes out from floor or couch, through pallid lips 541 *Grace Darl.* 90
Long were his arms, pallid his hands ; his mouth 664 *Prelude* 4. 395
Its sustenance, while the girl with pallid hands . 717 *Prelude* 9. 514
Of comfort, spread over his pallid face. . . . 785 *Excursion* 2. 886
On the baptismal font ; his pallid face . . . 825 *Excursion* 5. 212
Was pallid : seldom hath that eye been moist . 871 *Excursion* 7. 882
Palm. But, Cynthia ! should to thee the palm be given, ... 266 **With how* 13
Beneath some shady palm of Galilee. . . . . 274 *Infant M.* 14
Duty's intrepid liegeman, see, the palm . . . 312 *Clarkson* 9
To rest where the lizard may bask in the palm . 340 *Fort Fuentes* 5
Thick boughs of palm, and willows from the brook, 346 *Processions* 11
Palm to palm, on his tranquil breast ; . . . . 397 *White Doe* 131
Scarcely the hand forbears to dip its palm . . 469 **Why stand* 9
Borne in their hands the lily and the palm . . 500 *Humanity* 23
To win the palm of gaiety and wit ; . . . . 528 **Those breathing* 107
Pressed closely palm to palm, and to his mouth . 671 *Prelude* 5. 371
Retained a flashing eye, a burning palm, . . . 860 *Excursion* 7. 210
Palm-groves. With palm-groves shaded at wide intervals, ... 444 *Ecc. Sonn.* 3. 17. 6
Palms. And ensures those palms of honour . . . 90 *Longest Day* 73
On tombs, with palms together prest, ... 301 *Bran* 49
Those palms and amaranthine wreaths . . . 324 *Ode 1814* 50
The uplifted palms, the silent marble lips . . . 343 *Eclipse* 51
Immortal amaranth and palms abound. . . . 418 *Ecc. Sonn.* 1. 1. 14
The Sensual think with reverence of the palms . 424 *Ecc. Sonn.* 1. 24. 9
Spreading his little palms in his glad Mother's sight) 460 **Queen of* 20
Another race hath been, and other palms are won. 590 *Immortality* 203
When so disturbed, whatever palms are won. . 656 *Prelude* 3. 502
Doth melt away ; but for those palms achieved, . 665 *Prelude* 5. 8
Such palms I boast not ;—no ! to me, who find, . 790 *Excursion* 3. 270
Princes, and emperors, and the crowns and palms 872 *Excursion* 7. 981
Palm-tree. Or as a fruitful palm-tree towering high 383 *Duddon* 31. 5
Palmy. On broad Euphrates' palmy shore, . . . 215 *Enterprise* 25
The palmy antlers of a hunted Hart, ... 393 *Hart's-horn* 4
Palmyra. Palmyra, central in the desert, fell ; . . 877 *Excursion* 8. 218
Palpable. A palpable memorial of that day, . . 335 *Aix* 10
Nor only palpable restraints unbind, ... 518 *Pun. Death* 4. 11
More palpable, as best might suit her aim. . . 637 *Prelude* 1. 356
When every hour brings palpable access . . . 646 *Prelude* 2. 286
Of art, this palpable array of sense, ... 812 *Excursion* 4. 730
From palpable oppressions of despair." . . . 817 *Excursion* 4. 1077
Palpable to sight as the dry ground, ... S.3. 435 **The doubt* 96
Palsied. Infirmly grasped within a palsied hand. . 321 **Humanity, delighting* 10
To a palsied, and unconscious hand ; . . . . 411 *White Doe* 1416
And ever, scattered from his palsied hand, . . 566 *Cumb. Beg.* 16
With all the Persons, down to palsied Age, . . 589 *Immortality* 104
Palsy. There is a palsy in his limbs—he shakes. . 49 *Bord.* 673
Palsy-shaken. From a palsy-shaken head. . . . 549 *Hermit's Cell* 1. 16
Paltry. This is a paltry field for enterprise. . . 77 *Bord.* 2283
Would all have seemed but paltry things, . . 291 *Rob Roy* 71
Paly. Shedding, through paly loop-holes mild and small, ... 7 *Ev. Wk.* 293
Thence, from three paly loopholes mild and small, 598 *Ev. Wk. Quarto* 335
Pampered. How, with empurpled cheeks and pampered eyes, ... 364 **What aim* 4
Pampering. Pampering myself with meagre novelties 736 *Prelude* 12. 117
Pamphlets. *See* **Master-pamphlets.**
Pan. The pipe of Pan, to shepherds . . . . . 234 *Power of Sound* 145
Great Pan himself low-whispering through the reeds, 313 **Clouds, lingering* 12

Part—*continued.*
"And must we then part from a dwelling so fair?" 620 *Convict* 5
In contradiction; with no skill to part . . . 635 *Prelude* 1. 238
Within my mind, should e'er have borne a part, . 637 *Prelude* 1. 347
And that a needful part, in making up . . . 637 *Prelude* 1. 348
Itself a living part of a live whole, ... 657 *Prelude* 3. 590
Yet often is perplexed and cannot part . . . 662 *Prelude* 4. 263
How could I ever play an ingrate's part? . . . 668 *Prelude* 5. 173
Though fledged and feathered, and well pleased to part . . . . 669 *Prelude* 5. 247
Doth also for our nobler part provide, ... 669 *Prelude* 5. 273
With a dear friend, and for the better part . . 674 *Prelude* 5. 561
To part from company and take this book . . 677 *Prelude* 6. 149
And part through outward hindrance. But I heard, ... 687 *Prelude* 7. 18
In part by fear to shape a way direct, ... 709 *Prelude* 9. 3
In part lay here, that unto me the events . . . 713 *Prelude* 9. 246
Whereof he was a part: yet this was meek . . 714 *Prelude* 9. 319
He, on his part, accoutred for the worst, . . . 715 *Prelude* 9. 423
The indecision on their part whose aim . . . 720 *Prelude* 10. 130
That I was led to take an eager part . . . . 728 *Prelude* 11. 76
When erring, erring on the better part, . . . 729 *Prelude* 11. 157
Too justly bore a part. A veil had been . . . 731 *Prelude* 11. 266
The sympathies erewhile in part discharged, . . 733 *Prelude* 11. 406
It seemed the better part were gnawed away . . 769 *Excursion* 1. 838
With malady—in part, I fear, provoked . . . 776 *Excursion* 2. 306
And well those lofty brethren bear their part . . 782 *Excursion* 2. 699
Beneath the sun, like Ganges, to make part . . 790 *Excursion* 3. 259
And be in part compensated. For rights, . . 797 *Excursion* 3. 793
Heavenward; and chide the part of me that flags, 803 *Excursion* 4. 127
Sons of the morning. For your nobler part, . . 804 *Excursion* 4. 232
We must not part at this inviting hour." . . 823 *Excursion* 5. 72
—Yet, while the better part is missed, the worse 828 *Excursion* 5. 403
Of earth, and human nature's mortal part. . . 847 *Excursion* 6. 623
And sufferings meekly borne—I, for my part, . 847 *Excursion* 6. 630
Part shaded by cool sycamore, and part . . . 850 *Excursion* 6. 780
As you have seen, bear such conspicuous part . 866 *Excursion* 7. 592
A willing, nay, at times, a forward part; . . . 882 *Excursion* 8. 529
An obligation, on her part, to *teach* . . . . 888 *Excursion* 9. 297
Said he, "shall shine upon us, ere we part; . . 896 *Excursion* 9. 780
Of winds, this deep Vale,—as it doth in part . . K.8. 247 *Recluse* 1. 1. 375
On lovely objects, and we wish to part . . . K.8. 254 *Recluse* 1. 1. 631
On earth we dimly see, and but in part . . . K.8. 275 **These vales* 5

Partake. Alone partake of it?—Belovèd Marmaduke! . . . . 75 *Bord.* 2148
That Leonard would partake his homely fare: . 102 *Brothers* 414
How would it please old Ocean to partake, . . 154 *Morn. Ex.* 49
And the sweet joy which they partake, . . . 156 *Oak and Broom* 89
And gladly Nature's love partake . . . . . 157 **In youth* 7
Their inspiration I partake; . . . . . . 178 *Waggoner* 3. 32
That sullenly refuses to partake . . . . . 230 *Clouds* 44
"Let beeves and home-bred kine partake . . . 293 *Yarrow Unv.* 41
And yet a higher joy partake: . . . . . . 294 *Jedbor.* 44
Sad thoughts, avaunt!—partake we their blithe cheer . . . . 381 *Duddon* 23. 1
Again we wandered, willing to partake . . . 395 *White Doe: Ded.* 39
And sorrow moved him to partake . . . . . 401 *White Doe* 458
Of saintly Friends the "murtherer's chain partake, 437 *Ecc. Sonn.* 2. 34. 11
Yet, my belovèd Country! I partake . . . . 440 *Ecc. Sonn.* 3. 2. 4
Union that shadows forth and doth partake . . 447 *Ecc. Sonn.* 3. 26. 11
Who lov'st with Night and Silence to partake, . 459 **Wanderer! that* 3
Partake its inclination towards earth . . . . 508 *F. Stone* 38
From the Vale's peace which all her fields partake, 521 *Epist. Beaumont* 2
Which they partake at pleasure. Early died . . 669 *Prelude* 5. 256
From kindred, friends, and playmates, to partake 701 *Prelude* 8. 122
Partake of, each in their degree; 'tis mine . . 740 *Prelude* 13. 12
If thou partake the animating faith . . . . 744 *Prelude* 13. 300
To linger I would here with you partake, . . . 773 *Excursion* 2. 141
These may he range, if willing to partake . . . 810 *Excursion* 4. 593
Do tend their flocks) partake man's general lot . 829 *Excursion* 5. 427
Contented to partake the quiet meal . . . . 859 *Excursion* 7. 160
Invited, summoned, to partake the cheer . . . 867 *Excursion* 7. 653
Do, by the almighty Ruler's grace, partake . . 885 *Excursion* 9. 110
Thy lively spirits to partake, ... K.8. 262 **Ah! if* 4

Partakers. Some true Partakers of his loving spirit 362 **List—'twas* 68

Partakes. The infection of the ground partakes, . 223 *Wishing-gate* 34
Of the dull earth partakes not, nor desires? . . 261 **I heard (alas* 12
With sweets that she partakes not some distaste . 382 *Duddon* 25. 11
Now some gloomy nook partakes . . . . . 397 *White Doe* 91
Partakes, in her degree, Heaven's grace; . . . 416 *White Doe* 1876
By her commands partakes not, in degree, . . 429 *Ecc. Sonn.* 2. 2. 10
Partakes a livelier cheer; . . . . 507 *May* 22

Partaking. The faith partaking of those holy times, 837 *Excursion* 5. 1011
Partaking this day's pleasure? From afar . . K.8. 243 *Recluse* 1. 1. 240

Parted. *See* **Death-parted.**
I parted with the Child. Parted with whom? . 46 *Bord.* 508
In such sad service; and he parted with him. . 50 *Bord.* 690
Was sadly crossed.—Poor Leonard! when we parted, ... 100 *Brothers* 321
He would pursue his journey. So they parted. . 102 *Brothers* 417
Death in a moment parted them, and left . . . 118 *Maternal Grief* 41
They parted; and the generous Vaudracour . . 123 *V. and J.* 102
Impelled;—they parted from him there, and stood 125 *V. and J.* 251
Now are they parted, far as Death's cold hand . 152 **Forth from* 16
Was from his team and waggon parted; . . . 182 *Waggoner* 4. 184
Could draw, when we had parted, vain delight, . 211 *Laod.* 113
We parted upon solemn ground . . . . . 348 **Lulled by* 37
Be parted from his ancient ground: . . . . 402 *White Doe* 553
He parted from them; but at their side . . . 409 *White Doe* 1239
They parted.—Well with him it fared . . . . 478 *Somnamb.* 46
Within whose shade they parted. . . . . . 479 *Somnamb.* 103

Parted—*continued.*
They parted, sorrow was at hand . . . . . 579 **Sweet Flower* 34
Parted and re-united by the blast. . . . . . 622 *Recluse* 1. 1. 162
Been parted by the hurrying world, and droop, . 663 *Prelude* 4. 355
And so we parted. Back I cast a look, . . . 665 *Prelude* 4. 467
The widely parted hours; the noise of streams, . 686 *Prelude* 6. 718
The man to come, parted, as by a gulph, . . . 735 *Prelude* 12. 59
Whereby society has parted man . . . . . 743 *Prelude* 13. 219
We parted, nothing willingly; and now . . . 757 *Excursion* 1. 49
We parted.—'Twas the time of early spring; . . 766 *Excursion* 1. 690
That she had parted with her elder child; . . 767 *Excursion* 1. 760
For him whom she had lost. We parted then— 769 *Excursion* 1. 868
Have parted hence; and still that length of road, 770 *Excursion* 1. 912
Discreetly parted to preserve the peace, . . . 845 *Excursion* 6. 479
Parted and re-united: his compeer . . . . 883 *Excursion* 8. 581
And parted them; or haply both are gone . . K.8. 244 *Recluse* 1. 1. 267

Parterre. Each kind in several beds of one parterre; 281 *Valedict.* 4

Parterres. From thy most secret haunts; and ye Parterres, ... 539 **Lady! a* 25
And easy contemplation; gay parterres, . . . 810 *Excursion* 4. 589

Parthenope. Wafting your Charge to soft Parthenope! . . . . 387 *Scott* 14

Parthenope's. Parthenope's Domain—Virgilian haunt, 356 *Aquap.* 265

Partial. If I could think one weak or partial feeling—— . . . . 48 *Bord.* 630
That thou, if not with partial joy elate, . . . 250 **Happy the* 13
Shall a few partial breezes only creep?— . . . 366 **Fair Land* 11
Of custom that prepares a partial scale . . . 737 *Prelude* 12. 195
A partial judgment—and yet why? for *then* . 745 *Prelude* 13. 361
By partial bondage. In his steady course, . . 761 *Excursion* 1. 358
Of angry umpires, partial and unjust; . . . 839 *Excursion* 6. 65
Trust not to partial care a general good; . . . 890 *Excursion* 9. 405

Partially. Of reason partially let in . . . . . 234 *Power of Sound* 104
When into air had partially dissolved . . . . 747 *Prelude* 14. 63

Participate. Seem to participate, the while they view 220 *Haunted Tree* 37
Fade, and participate in man's decline. . . . 308 **There is a bondage* 14
Not seeking those who might participate . . . 652 *Prelude* 3. 234
We all too thanklessly participate, ... 864 *Excursion* 7. 485
Whose lustre we alone participate, ... K.8. 248 *Recluse* 1. 1. 437

Participation. Beyond participation lie . . . . 117 *Affl. Marg.* 71
Than by participation of delight . . . . . 807 *Excursion* 4. 443

Particle. To the least particle of sentient dust; . 500 *Humanity* 46
The particle divine remained unquenched; . . 802 *Excursion* 4. 51

Parti-coloured. *See* **Party-coloured.**
A parti-coloured show of grave and gay, . . . 663 *Prelude* 4. 340

Particular. That, as he knew in what particular spot 96 *Brothers* 81
And in the midst is one particular rock . . . 101 *Brothers* 366
Of old tradition, one particular flower . . . . 103 *Artegal* 58
Huge trunks! and each particular trunk a growth 185 *Yew-trees* 16
There, at the root of one particular tree, . . . 531 **I know* 9
If each most obvious and particular thought, . . 645 *Prelude* 2. 229
The memory of one particular hour . . . . 663 *Prelude* 4. 308
That this particular strife had wanted power . 722 *Prelude* 10. 254
General distress in his particular lot; . . . . 772 *Excursion* 2. 68
That my particular current soon will reach . . 800 *Excursion* 3. 990
Of less particular notices assigned . . . . 825 *Excursion* 5. 201
Was the particular spot, in which they wished . 845 *Excursion* 6. 500
In like low voice to my particular ear, . . . 891 *Excursion* 9. 458
When these particular interests were effaced . . 893 *Excursion* 9. 589
Strangers to all particular amity, ... K.8. 251 *Recluse* 1. 1. 534

Particulars. And all particulars that dull brains require . . . . 58 *Bord.* 1156

Parties. *See* **Treason-parties.**
Friends, enemies, of all parties, ages, ranks, . . 723 *Prelude* 10. 361
Split into parties by the fickle mind. . . . . L.2. 318 *Frag. Æneid* 4. 2

Parting. *See* **Hollow-parting.**
Though to the vale no parting beam . . . . 1 *Extract* 11
Slant watery lights, from parting clouds, apace . 4 *Ev. Wk.* 92
The "parting Genius" sighs with hollow breath . 12 *Desc. Sk.* 71
At midnight listens till his parting oar, . . . 15 *Desc. Sk.* 252
From gulf of parting clouds one friendly beam, . 26 *Guilt* 131
The parting signal streamed—at last the land withdrew. . . . . 29 *Guilt* 288
Peace to my parting soul, the fulness of content." 36 *Guilt* 630
A parting word—though not of grace, ... 176 *Waggoner* 1. 275
Since parting Innocence bequeathed . . . . 191 *Seq. Beggars* 21
The grace of parting Infancy . . . . . . 232 *Jew. Fam.* 29
Gaze on the moon by parting clouds revealed. . 268 **Four fiery* 14
Parting; the casual word had power to reach . 367 **As indignation* 13
This parting glance, no negligent adieu! . . . 377 *Duddon* 4. 2
Has with that Parting mixed a filial sigh, . . . 394 *Countess' Pillar* 11
It is the last, the parting song; . . . . . 397 *White Doe* 158
His parting charge—but ill obeyed— . . . . 407 *White Doe* 1064
(Earth's lingering love to parting reconciled, . . 476 *Howard* 7
Brief parting, for the spirit is all but fled)— . . 476 *Howard* 8
Brings on her parting hour. . . . . 502 *Seasons* 8
And this our parting spring. . . . . . . 530 †*Redbreast* 4
The parting moment and its fond regret. . . . 531 **I know* 16
Where every parting agony is hushed, ... 540 *Grace Darl.* 41
For that last thought of parting Friends . . . 580 *John Words.* 23
That was indeed a parting! oh, ... 580 *John Words.* 41
To the blest world where parting is unknown. . 586 *Ch. Lamb* 131
Below, the echo of his parting oar, ... 607 *Desc. Sk. Quarto* 314
Be mentioned as a parting word, that not . . 686 *Prelude* 6. 732
Added no farewell to his parting counsel, . . . 726 *Prelude* 10. 538
Our final parting; for from that time forth . . 769 *Excursion* 1. 869
A parting tribute to a spot that seemed . . . 822 *Excursion* 5. 15
Insensibly the foretaste of this parting . . . S.3. 433 **The doubt* 13
A parting moment with her loveliest look, . . S.3. 434 **The doubt* 88

Parting-place. Beside our Parting-place; . . . 580 *John Words.* 54
Partings. Glad meetings, tender partings, that upstay . . . 383 *Duddon* 28. 11
Partisan. An active partisan, I thus convoked . . 729 *Prelude* 11. 153
Partition. In union, in partition only such; . . 585 *Ch. Lamb* 99
The union, the partition where, that makes . . 806 *Excursion* 4. 336
Yet, in partition, with their several spheres, . . 890 *Excursion* 9. 450
Partly. Mix strangely; trifles light, and partly vain, 480 *Cordelia* 8
More justly balanced; partly at their feet, . . 488 *Pers. Talk* 24
Partly from voluntary holiday, ... 687 *Prelude* 7. 17
Even as a river,—partly (it might seem) . . . 709 *Prelude* 9. 1
Partner. Stood his dumb partner in this glorious feat; 201 *Hart-leap* 38
As no unworthy Partner in their flight . . . 231 **The gentlest Poet* 8
So loud, so clear, my Partner through life's day, . 279 **Hark! 'tis* 11
I thought of Thee, my partner and my guide, . . 384 *Duddon* 34. 1
Hath yet this faithful Partner left; . . . . 415 *White Doe* 1788
And when the partner of those varied walks . . 716 *Prelude* 9. 479
Her wedded Partner lacked not on his side . . 764 *Excursion* 1. 520
For Nature called my Partner to resign . . 794 *Excursion* 3. 551
And partner of my loss.—O heavy change! . . 795 *Excursion* 3. 669
Of his fond partner, silent in the nest. . . . 851 *Excursion* 6. 868
And where yet dwells her faithful Partner, left . 855 *Excursion* 6. 1120
When the meek Partner of his age, his Son, . . 861 *Excursion* 7. 260
Partners. What ghastly partners hath your call . 225 *Present.* 59
Partners in faith, and brothers in distress, . . 437 *Ecc. Sonn.* 2. 37. 6
Her work and her work's partners she can cheer, 523 *Epist. Beaumont* 162
I and the modest partners of my days . . . . K.8. 255 *Recluse* 1.1.695
Partnership. Mock-chastisement and partnership in play. . . . . 80 **Loving she* 6
To both; and, if that partnership must cease, . 888 *Excursion* 9. 272
Partook. Yet two sweet little ones partook my bed; 35 *Guilt* 596
That sanctifies its confines, and partook . . . 118 *Maternal Grief* 16
Came not, but in a lane partook his bread. . . 531 **I know* 8
Was spread, and we partook a plain repast. . . 882 *Excursion* 8. 519
Merrily seated in a ring, partook . . . . . 892 *Excursion* 9. 529
Partook of every motion, met, retired, . . . S.3. 434 **The doubt* 75
Partridge. And Moore and Partridge stare me in the face. . . . . L.1. 96 *Juvenal* 3. 60
Parts. Were that man, who could draw the line that parts . . . . 63 *Bord.* 1449
Spring parts the clouds with softest airs, . . . 157 **In youth* 11
The Phantom parts—but parts to re-unite, . . 210 *Laod.* 29
As humanising graces, are but parts . . . 420 *Ecc. Sonn.* 1. 8. 13
When a soft summer gale at evening parts . . 465 **Dear to* 7
And in the middle parts the braided hair, . . 508 *F. Stone* 29
Just three parts blown—a cottage-child—if e'er, . 692 *Prelude* 7. 353
All moveables of wonder, from all parts, . . . 697 *Prelude* 7. 706
An under-sense of greatest; sees the parts . . 698 *Prelude* 7. 735
As parts, but with a feeling of the whole. . . . 698 *Prelude* 7. 736
Lying full three parts buried among tufts . . . 784 *Excursion* 2. 818
The veil, or where it parts at once, to spy . . K.8. 249 *Recluse* 1.1.479
That parts the individual from his kind, . . . K.8. 251 *Recluse* 1.1.536
That parts the image from reality; . . . . K.8. 252 *Recluse* 1.1.577
Party. Watchwords of Party, on all tongues are rife; 443 *Ecc. Sonn.* 3. 11. 10
Party-coloured. *See* **Parti-coloured.**
Whose party-coloured garments gay . . . . 180 *Waggoner* 4. 31
Of merriment a party-coloured knot, ... 773 *Excursion* 2. 124
And wreck of party-coloured earthenware, . . 778 *Excursion* 2. 434
Party-strife. That come but as a curse to party-strife; 454 **Not in the lucid* 2
Pass. *See* **Mountain-pass.**
The horse alone, seen dimly as I pass, ... 1 *Early Youth* 3
Nibbling the water lilies as they pass, ... 6 *Ev. Wk.* 226
And quickens the blithe sound of oars that pass . 13 *Desc. Sk.* 125
One flower of hope—oh, pass and leave it there! 20 *Desc. Sk.* 552
And leading Herbert. We must let them pass— 39 *Bord.* 101
For love of God I must not pass their doors; . 46 *Bord.* 524
Chancing to pass this way some six months gone 47 *Bord.* 573
He was that One so young should pass his youth 49 *Bord.* 689
They have no substance. Pass but a few minutes 59 *Bord.* 1172
(For other impulse let it pass) was driven, . . 71 *Bord.* 1863
Despatch him! If I pass beneath a rock . . . 78 *Bord.* 2314
And ever, as they pass away, ... 108 *Louisa*
If human Life do pass away, ... 110 **Look at* 7
The clouds pass on; they from the heavens depart: 110 **'Tis said that some* 17
Pondering that Time to-night will pass . . . 112 *Lament* 10
Have power to shake me as they pass: . . . 117 *Affl. Marg.* 67
I pass the raptures of the pair;—such theme . . 123 *V. and J.* 87
Fond Youth! that mournful solace now must pass 124 *V. and J.* 218
But for one object which you might pass by, . . 131 *Michael* 15
Should pass into a stranger's hand, I think . . 134 *Michael* 231
Startling the timid as they pass, ... 142 †*Lov. and Lik.* 18
But *likings* come, and pass away; . . . . . 143 †*Lov. and Lik.* 65
Amid the smoke of cities did you pass . . . . 147 *Joanna* 1
From heaven to earth our thoughts will pass, . 164 **Fair Lady* 26
Pass high above those fragrant bells . . . . 165 *Danish Boy* 18
But pass a mile—and *then* for trial,— . . . . 174 *Waggoner* 1. 72
And oft, as they pass slowly on, ... 182 *Waggoner* 4. 252
From hill to hill it seems to pass . . . . . 183 **O blithe* 7
Were fellow-travellers in this gloomy Pass, . . 186 *Prelude* 6. 622
Shall pass into her face. . . . . 187 **Three years* 30
What crowd is this? what have we here! we must not pass it by; . . . . 189 *Star-gazers* 1
Pass by her door—'tis seldom shut— . . . . 198 *Thorn* 95
No thoughts hath he but thoughts that pass . . 204 *Brougham* 74
For yet it is broad day-light: clouds pass by; . 208 **It is no* 6
Oft as I pass along the fork . . . . . . 214 *Kirkstone* 3
Gives to this savage Pass its name. . . . . 215 *Kirkstone* 48
—Pass onward (even the glancing deer . . . 221 *Triad* 76
Themselves to lose their light, or pass away . . 226 *Vernal Ode* 43

Pass—*continued.*
Is in the WORD, that shall not pass away. . . 235 *Power of Sound* 224
And through the brain of Peter pass . . . . 243 *P. B.* 582
And through his brain like lightning pass. . . 244 *P. B.* 735
A flock of sheep that leisurely pass by, . . . 253 **A flock* 1
Dull would he be of soul who could pass by . . 269 *Westm. Bridge* 2
Trampling upon his vileness. Stranger, pass . . 275 *Gravestone* 13
The house that cannot pass away be ours. . . 278 **The most* 14
—Would She were now as when she hoped to pass 278 **Lo! where she* 9
Morn into noon did pass, noon into eve, . . . 279 **Though I* 7
Stop here, or gently pass! . . . . 289 *Sol. Reap.* 4
That still invests the guardian Pass, ... 300 *Cora Linn* 40
Europe is yet in bonds; but let that pass, . . 306 **Here, on our* 9
And to the aerial zephyrs as they pass, . . . 322 **Ye Storms* 12
Till, with the heavens and earth, thou pass away! 329 *Ode: Thanks.* 19
Turning, for them who pass, the common dust . 351 *Des. Stanzas* 78
But here am I fast bound; and let it pass, . . 353 *Aquap.* 53
Revive, their obstinate winter pass away, . . . 363 **List—'twas* 96
Both pass into new being,—but the Worm, . . 366 *Lombardy* 11
Upon the signs that pass away or tarry; . . . 374 *Eg. Maid* 338
Or he would pass into her bird, that throws . . 377 *Duddon* 7. 5
With prompt emotion, urging them to pass; . . 378 *Duddon* 10. 2
There's not a nook within this solemn Pass . . 388 *Trosachs* 1
May pass in hope, and, though from mortal bonds 396 **Action is* 11
So the balmy minutes pass, ... 397 *White Doe* 152
Pass, pass who will, yon chantry door; . . . 398 *White Doe* 242
Pass from their Master, sojourned here to guard . 419 *Ecc. Sonn.* 1. 2. 13
Furl we the sails, and pass with tardy oars . . 430 *Ecc. Sonn.* 2. 8. 1
Hope guides the young; but when the old must pass 434 *Ecc. Sonn.* 2. 23. 9
Pass, some through fire—and by the scaffold some— 435 *Ecc. Sonn.* 2. 26. 7
Did pass dependent on maternal care, . . . 447 *Ecc. Sonn.* 3. 27. 4
List, ye who pass by Lyulph's Tower . . . . 478 *Somnamb.* 1
We travelled merrily, to pass . . . . . . 486 **We walked* 11
Too sweet to pass away! . . . . 507 *May* 10
Pass sentence on themselves, confess the fact, . 517 *Pun. Death* 3. 11
Thus gladdened from our own dear Vale we pass . 524 *Epist. Beaumont* 164
Wanting accustomed food, must pass from earth, 531 *Octogen.* 4
In a strait and treacherous pass. . . . . . 549 *Hermit's Cell* 1. 4
From hence my hope and solace forth did pass. . 564 *Troilus* 89
And lifts the latch for him that he may pass. . 566 *Cumb. Beg.* 36
And urchins newly breeched—all pass him by: . 567 *Cumb. Beg.* 65
Then let him pass, a blessing on his head! . . 568 *Cumb. Beg.* 162
—Then let him pass, a blessing on his head! . . 568 *Cumb. Beg.* 171
Yet he watches the clouds that pass over the streets; 570 *Farmer* 70
If you pass by at morning, you'll meet with him there. . . . . 571 *Farmer* 86
And to the few who pass this way, ... 581 *John Words.* 65
A summons to the sound of oars, that pass, . . 604 *Desc.Sk.Quarto* 144
Nor pass unprais'd the robe and veil divine, . . 624 *Æneid* 77
Will pass so soon from human memory; . . . 627 **We gaze* 5
Pass unrecorded, that I still had loved . . . 647 *Prelude* 2. 377
My lordly dressing-gown, I pass it by, . . . 649 *Prelude* 3. 40
Unmoved. I could not always lightly pass . . 652 *Prelude* 3. 261
The day pass lightly on, when foresight sleeps, . 656 *Prelude* 3. 506
That all would come to pass of which the voice . 667 *Prelude* 5. 100
Think not that I could pass along untouched . . 668 *Prelude* 5. 182
Pass we from entertainments, that are such . . 694 *Prelude* 7. 486
Heard as we pass, when no one looks about, . . 697 *Prelude* 7. 667
Of things that pass away, a temperate show . . 740 *Prelude* 13. 31
I pass them unalarmed. Not Chaos, not . . . 755 *Recluse* 1. 1. 788
To pass the remnant of his days, untasked . . 762 *Excursion* 1. 384
Did many seasons pass ere I returned . . . 769 *Excursion* 1. 870
Unfailing: not a hamlet could we pass, . . . 772 *Excursion* 2. 34
Of public news or private; years that pass . . 777 *Excursion* 2. 366
Impatient to pass on, when I exclaimed, . . . 778 *Excursion* 2. 431
Till, chancing on that lofty ridge to pass . . 784 *Excursion* 2. 811
Or to pass through; but rather an abyss . . 787 *Excursion* 3. 97
This universe shall pass away—a work . . . 802 *Excursion* 4. 100
The words he uttered shall not pass away . . 820 *Excursion* 4. 1283
Shall pass uncensured; though the issue prove, . 827 *Excursion* 5. 315
Brush it away, or cloud pass over it; . . . . 832 *Excursion* 5. 674
Pass,' said the Matron, 'and I never see, . . . 834 *Excursion* 5. 805
If so approved and sanctified, to pass, . . . 837 *Excursion* 5. 1015
Shall cause to fade, till ages pass away; . . . 842 *Excursion* 6. 252
And strange disasters; but I pass them by, . . 847 *Excursion* 6. 571
Or shall we overhear him, as we pass, ... 861 *Excursion* 7. 268
"Now from the living pass we once again: . . 867 *Excursion* 7. 632
To all that come, almost to all that pass; . . 867 *Excursion* 7. 652
Over thy last abode, and we may pass . . . 868 *Excursion* 7. 709
Pass with the respirations of the tide, ... 876 *Excursion* 8. 141
That there should pass a moment of the year, . 877 *Excursion* 8. 194
Days will pass on, the year, if years be given, . S.3. 433 **The doubt* 22
Thence northward did they pass by Arthur's seat, K.8. 225 **I will* 23
And giving to the moments as they pass . . . K.8. 249 *Recluse* 1.1.466
Nor let me pass unheeded other loves . . . . K.8. 250 *Recluse* 1.1.502
Them leaving to their joyous hours I pass, . . K.8. 252 *Recluse* 1.1.588
Pass with a thought the life of the whole year . K.8. 252 *Recluse* 1.1.589
That must not die, that must not pass away. . K.8. 255 *Recluse* 1.1.676
And the great name of Troy; now all things pass L.2. 121 *Frag. Æneid* 2. 4

Passage. At once the griding iron passage found; . 33 *Guilt* 493
Through a strait passage intricate and dim? . . 173 *Infant Daughter* 74
Hard passage forcing on, with head . . . . 179 *Waggoner* 3. 81
Where'er the streams a passage find; . . . . 228 *Devot. Incit.* 4
Strict passage, through which sighs are brought, . 232 *Power of Sound* 7
And force their passage to the salt-sea tides! . . 269 *Gordale* 14
Through It have won a passage to thy heart; . . 281 *Valedict.* 13
Through the rocks our passage smooth; . . . 336 **Jesu! bless* 20
And through this wilderness a passage cleave . . 379 *Duddon* 14. 12
And fervent words a passage found. . . . . 401 *White Doe* 460

Pathetic 698 Patience

Path—*continued.*
Up from the lake a zigzag path will creep . . . 14 *Desc. Sk.* 236
Or woodbine wreaths, a smoother path is wound ; 21 *Desc. Sk.* 605
In spite of all the larks that cheered our path, . 39 *Bord.* 109
Nay, we must travel in another path, ... 58 *Bord.* 1151
Oh yes, that mole, that viper in the path ; . . 60 *Bord.* 1255
Henceforth new prospects open on your path ; . 64 *Bord.* 1497
Light to thy path, warmth to thy blood !—Together . . . . 70 *Bord.* 1852
That in the shape of man do cross our path . . 74 *Bord.* 2084
Then pity crossed the path of my resolve : . . 77 *Bord.* 2265
Each in the other locked ; and down the path, . 95 *Brothers* 34
He had forgotten. He had lost his path, . . . 96 *Brothers* 91
'Tis one of those who needs must leave the path . 96 *Brothers* 105
I almost see him tripping down the path . . . 98 *Brothers* 221
I've wet my path with tears like dew, ... 117 *Affl. Marg.* 34
You will suppose that with an upright path . . 131 *Michael* 3
Foes might hang upon their path, snakes rustle near, ... 141 *Arm. Lady* 89
Christian meekness smoothed for all the path of life, 142 *Arm. Lady* 149
Into a path or public way . . . . 142 †*Lov. and Lik.* 16
There was no road, nor any woodman's path ; . 149 *M. H.* 2
And with the sight of this same path—begun, . 150 **When, to* 56
Alone I tread this path ;—for aught I know, . . 151 **When, to* 105
His lonesome path, with unobserving eye . . . 184 *Night-piece* 10
They dart across my path—but lo, ... 191 *Beggars* 37
The glorious path in which he trod. . . . . 192 *Gipsies* 16
Not five yards from the mountain path, . . . 198 *Thorn* 27
The churchyard path to seek : . . . . . . 199 *Thorn* 158
Intent to trace the ideal path of right . . . 213 *Dion* 50
Thou strew'st temptation o'er the path . . . 216 *Enterprise* 108
Here is my body doomed to tread, this path, . . 230 *Clouds* 54
But, chancing to espy a path . . . . . . 240 *P. B.* 336
There's little sign the treacherous path . . . 240 *P. B.* 349
The path grows dim, and dimmer still ; . . . 240 *P. B.* 351
With the green path ; and now he wends . . . 244 *P. B.* 697
Fell round the path of Milton, in his hand . . 260 **Scorn not* 12
Some path of steep ascent and lofty aim ; . . . 261 **Fair Prime* 12
O'er hilly path, and open Strath, ... 293 *Yarrow Unv.* 37
The path that leads them to the grove, . . . 302 *Yarrow V.* 35
Honour that knows the path and will not swerve ; 319 **Avaunt all* 7
That bind thee to the path which God ordains . 329 *Ode : Thanks.* 17
A verdant path before us lies ; . . . . . . 339 **Meek Virgin* 38
Our path that straggled here and there ; . . . 348 **Lulled by* 16
Along his path ? His unprotected bed . . . 378 *Duddon* 8. 5
Yet are allowed to steal my path athwart . . . 381 *Duddon* 21. 5
On road or path, or at the door . . . . . 390 *Highland Broach* 21
Path, or no path, what care they ? . . . . . 396 *White Doe* 14
And down the path through the open green, . . 396 *White Doe* 50
O'er path and road, and plain and dell, . . . 409 *White Doe* 1170
With prayers and blessings we your path will sow ; 427 *Ecc. Sonn.* 1. 33. 5
That can secure for you a path of light . . . 446 *Ecc. Sonn.* 3. 25. 12
Of awe-struck wisdom droops : or let my path . 452 *Ecc. Sonn.* 3. 45. 7
Whate'er the path these mortal feet may trace, . 454 **The Sun, that* 21
Whatever path he chooses ; . . . . 478 *Somnamb.* 65
To pace the ground, if path be there or none, . 480 **Most sweet* 2
That makes the path before him always bright : . 493 *Hap. War.* 7
Before the path of milder suns ; . . . . . 497 *Lycoris* 32
That life—the flowery path that winds by stealth— 528 **Those breathing* 91
Beheld with wonder ; whether floor or path . . 540 **Lady ! a* 72
Will guide me in my forward path ; . . . . 542 *Russ. Fug.* 71
Than treading a path trod by thousands before. . 572 *Avarice* 28
'Twas a path trod by thousands ; but Daniel is one 572 *Avarice* 29
Of the fair Muses. Not a covert path . . . 574 *Chiabrera* 5. 9
Where antique roots its bustling path o'erlook, . 593 *Ev. Wk. Quarto* 82
Oh ! when the bitter showers her path assail, . 597 *Ev. Wk. Quarto* 279
Tracking with silvering path the changeful gale. . 598 *Ev. Wk. Quarto* 344
A zig-zag path from the domestic skiff . . . 607 *Desc.Sk.Quarto* 297
And let thy path be hewn out of the Rock, . . 626 *Rock : Rydal* 3
Augmented and sustained. Yet is a path . . 646 *Prelude* 2. 272
Of all that breathe ?—what in the path of all . 668 *Prelude* 5. 186
Of flitting pleasures tempt him from his path ; . 670 *Prelude* 5. 304
And that meanwhile, by no uncertain path, . . 685 *Prelude* 6. 696
Seemed best, and the straightforward path of those 720 *Prelude* 10. 131
All else was progress on the self-same path . . 722 *Prelude* 10. 273
Would only follow, in the path of shame, . . . 727 *Prelude* 11. 15
Along this intricate and difficult path, . . . 750 *Prelude* 14. 330
Or obscure records of the path of fire. . . . 760 *Excursion* 1. 279
And, while I paced along the foot-way path, . . 766 *Excursion* 1. 693
That made her heart beat quick. You see that path, 769 *Excursion* 1. 882
The little sinuous path of earthly care, . . . 790 *Excursion* 3. 305
Advance, swerving not from the path prescribed ; 795 *Excursion* 3. 612
By strict necessity, along the path . . . . . 820 *Excursion* 4. 1269
—Adown the path that from the glen had led . 821 *Excursion* 4. 1307
And round our path darted oppressive beams. . 824 *Excursion* 5. 137
Thus darkness and delusion round our path . . 830 *Excursion* 5. 512
While tens of thousands falter in their path, . . 835 *Excursion* 5. 833
Each other's path ; but, as the Intruder seemed . 839 *Excursion* 6. 104
The path remains that linked his cottage-door . 842 *Excursion* 6. 245
The Path of Perseverance." "Thou from whom 842 *Excursion* 6. 254
Treading their path in sympathy and linked . . 845 *Excursion* 6. 477
Of the path worn by mournful tread of her . . 850 *Excursion* 6. 818
Oft stretches toward me, like a long straight path 863 *Excursion* 7. 398
—We followed, taking as he led, a path . . . 880 *Excursion* 8. 441
Receiving, took the slender path that leads . . 895 *Excursion* 9. 773
The works by faith ordained. Pursue thy path, . K.8. 325 [?] **The vestal* 12

Pathetic. Of that pathetic story : . . . . . 337 *Thun* 12
Nor of the setting sun's pathetic light . . . . 386 *Scott* 2
Of time's pathetic sanctity ; . . . . 533 **Blest is* 44
And mingling playful with pathetic thoughts. . 657 *Prelude* 3. 558

Pathetic—*continued.*
And balanced by pathetic truth, by trust . . . 750 *Prelude* 14. 296
For the pathetic records which his voice . . . 873 *Excursion* 7. 1053

Pathless. More ragged than need was ! O'er pathless rocks, ... 185 *Nutting* 14
Nor leaf-crowned Dryad from a pathless wood, . 220 *Triad* 10
Now gads the wild vine o'er the pathless ascent :— 340 *Fort Fuentes* 17
By lurking Dernbrook's pathless side, ... 415 *White Doe* 1711
Than pathless wastes. Once, when those summer months . . . . 664 *Prelude* 4. 370
Ships he can guide across the pathless sea, . . 670 *Prelude* 5. 316

Paths. Have far to travel,—and on these rough paths 98 *Brothers* 224
Those paths so dear to me. . . . . 109 **Strange fits* 12
Thy Husband walks the paths of upper air : . . 209 *Laod.* 22
The paths which we had trod—these fountains, flowers ; . . . . 211 *Laod.* 131
Through paths of wickedness and woe, . . . 247 *P. B.* 952
Their smoothest paths, to wear their lightest chains ? 265 **There is a pleasure* 4
Or feed his eye in paths sun-proof . . . . . 342 *Ital. Itin.* 47
Ere, from accustomed paths, familiar fields, . . 353 *Aquap.* 33
Through paths and alleys roofed with darkest green ; 376 *Duddon* 2. 12
These only, Duddon ! with their paths renewed . 379 *Duddon* 14. 7
Fields which they love, and paths they daily trod, 441 *Ecc. Sonn.* 3. 6. 10
Or lured along where green-wood paths he trod. . 461 **Giordano, verily* 14
Through crags, and smoothing paths beset with danger, ... 477 *Nunnery* 10
By paths no human wisdom can foretrace ! . . 505 *Warning* 133
In the bright paths of fair majestic Truth : . . 618 *School Ex.* 12
Firm in the sacred paths of moral truth, . . . 619 *School Ex.* 78
Oft have I said, the paths of Fame pursue, . . 619 *School Ex.* 83
Of that sweet Valley ; when its paths, its shores, 672 *Prelude* 5. 428
So reverenced by us both. O'er paths and fields . 678 *Prelude* 6. 230
And, once, three days successively, through paths 680 *Prelude* 6. 354
Led me to these by paths that, in the main, . . 686 *Prelude* 6. 751
And the wild paths ; and, by the summer's warmth 762 *Excursion* 1. 388
O'er paths they used to deck : carnations, once . 767 *Excursion* 1. 724
And those wild paths were left to me alone. . . 794 *Excursion* 3. 556
To ecstasy ; and all the crooked paths . . . 804 *Excursion* 4. 183
Traversed but by a few irregular paths, . . . 834 *Excursion* 5. 763
With tenderness embosom ; to your paths ; . . S.3. 433 **The doubt* 5

Pathway. The pathway leads, as round the steeps it twines ; . . . . 12 *Desc. Sk.* 87
Our pathway led us on to Rotha's banks ; . . 147 *Joanna* 41
Pathway, and lane, and public road, were clogged 150 **When, to* 6
A hoary pathway traced between the trees, . . 150 **When, to* 48
And there the pathway ends. . . . . . . 240 *P. B.* 355
A fair smooth pathway you discern, ... 244 *P. B.* 677
A gravelled pathway treading, ... 337 *Thun* 2
More than by smoothest pathway may be brought 389 *Tyndrum* 7
Undressed the pathway leading to the door ; . . 390 *Highland Hut* 10
The downward pathway taking, ... 479 *Somnamb.* 94
Pathway, or cultivated land ; . . . . . . 491 *Fidelity* 23
And held the pathway down by a brookside ; . 557 *Cuck. and Night.* 60
Till dipp'd his pathway in the river shade ; . . 592 *Ev. Wk. Quarto* 70
Shot, down the headlong pathway darts his sledge ; 593 *Ev. Wk. Quarto* 112
Chok'd is the pathway, and the pitcher broke. . 596 *Ev. Wk. Quarto* 256
Wild round the steeps the little pathway twines, . 603 *Desc. Sk. Quarto* 90
And to the door a neater pathway winds, . . . 615 *Desc.Sk.Quarto* 727
By road or pathway, or through trackless field, . 632 *Prelude* 1. 28
And open field, through which the pathway wound, 663 *Prelude* 4. 322
Said—"Shall we take this pathway for our guide ?— . . . . 786 *Excursion* 3. 22
And thus the pathway, by perennial green . . 881 *Excursion* 8. 455

Pathway's. Or through her truant pathway's native charms, ... 603 *Desc. Sk. Quarto* 49

Pathways. Or where her pathways straggle as they please . . . . 11 *Desc. Sk.* 48
Let itself in upon him :—pathways, walks, . . 122 *V. and J.* 48
The turf unites, the pathways intertwine ; . . 271 **Where holy* 3
These pathways, yon far-stretching road ! . . 286 *Nith* 32
Trips down the pathways of some winding dale ; . 521 *Epist. Beaumont* 43
Their golden leaves upon the pathways, . . . 586 *Hogg* 7
Thy lofty steeps, and pathways roofed with vines, 685 *Prelude* 6. 665
With those delightful pathways we advanced, . 685 *Prelude* 6. 688
To you, ye pathways, and ye lonely roads ; . . 741 *Prelude* 13. 117
Beside our roads and pathways, though, thank Heaven ! . . . . 788 *Excursion* 3. 176

Patience. *See* **Mock-patience.**
And tears which flowed for ills which patience might not heal. . . . . 29 *Guilt* 270
Whether too much for patience, or, like mine, . 61 *Bord.* 1339
But patience ! Curses on that Traitor, Oswald !— 63 *Bord.* 1417
In his old age—— Patience—Heaven grant me patience !— . . . . 66 *Bord.* 1611
Doth haunt your memory. Patience, hear me further !— . . . . 68 *Bord.* 1704
"Nay, patience ! patience, little boy ; . . . . 81 †*Mother's Return* 11
Listen yet awhile ;—with patience . . . . . 94 *Westmoreland Girl* 57
With patience merit the reward of peace, . . . 143 **High bliss* 3
And, patience coveting yet passion feeding, . . 170 **Never enlivened* 26
With all the patience that he can ; . . . . 181 *Waggoner* 4. 135
Called for *his* patience and *his* skill ;— . . . 182 *Waggoner* 4. 192
Soothe it into patience—stay . . . . . . 233 *Power of Sound* 92
I have no pain that calls for patience, no ; . . 253 **O gentle* 9
Wilt thou find patience ! Yet die not ; do thou . 305 *Toussaint* 6
Patience and temperance with this high reserve, . 319 **Avaunt all* 6
As boundless patience only could endure ? . . 330 *Ode : Thanks.* 97
Labour accomplishes, or patience bears— . . . 363 **The world forsaken* 5

Paused—*continued.*

They paused, and heard a hoarser voice blaspheme, 33 *Guilt* 466
What can be gained ? " At this the old Man paused, ... 135 *Michael* 255
That thou shouldst go." At this the old Man paused ; . . . . . 137 *Michael* 382
Paused not, and through the depth of night she kept 139 *Widow* 10
And when will she return to us ? " he paused ; 147 *Joanna* 24
Alike indulged to all, we paused, one now, . . 148 **A narrow* 27
He paused—for shadows of strange shape, . . 240 *P. B.* 356
Abruptly paused the strife ;—the field throughout 322 *Germans* 1
He paused, and stood entranced by that still face 373 *Eg. Maid* 299
Or some deep chestnut grove, oft have I paused . 537 **In desultory* 2
All night the storm had raged, nor ceased, nor paused, ... 540 *Grace Darl.* 28
Nor paused, till o'er the stag he blew . . 544 *Russ. Fug.* 275
When by the gliding Loire I paused, and cast . 718 *Prelude* 10. 6
Heaved at safe distance, far retired. I paused, . 726 *Prelude* 10. 568
'Made my heart bleed.' " At this the Wanderer paused ; . . . . 765 *Excursion* 1. 591
He paused, as if unwilling to proceed, . . . 807 *Excursion* 4. 413
He paused—and having lifted up his eyes . . 836 *Excursion* 5. 900
The Vicar paused ; and toward a seat advanced, . 850 *Excursion* 6. 778
Fronting the noontide sun. We paused to admire 881 *Excursion* 8. 464
He paused, as if revolving in his soul . . . 888 *Excursion* 9. 290

Pauses. He turns aside his head, he pauses ; . 248 *P. B.* 1033
Catch, in the pauses of their keenest play, . . 281 *Chris. Words.* 11

Pausing. And, wildly pausing, oft she hangs aghast, 15 *Desc. Sk.* 267
The tall sun, pausing on an Alpine spire, . . 20 *Desc. Sk.* 553
Given to the pausing traveller's rapturous glance : 282 *Railway* 10
And heard, the pausing village hum between, . 616 *Desc.Sk.Quarto* 750
Pausing at will—our spirits braced, our thoughts 773 *Excursion* 2. 108
This said, oft pausing, we pursued our way ; . 824 *Excursion* 5. 133

Pave. Of genuine crystals, pure as those that pave 264 **Lady ! I* 4

Paved. (More fair than heaven's broad causeway paved with stars) . . . 213 *Dion* 51
Of its Arcades paved with sepulchral slabs, . . 355 *Aquap.* 156
A channel paved by man's officious care. . . 659 *Prelude* 4. 56
In courting notice ; and the ground all paved . 847 *Excursion* 6. 626

Pavement. By sudden pangs ; what bitter tears have on this pavement dropt ! . 92 *Poet's Dream* 52
That o'er the pavement of the surging streams . 268 **Dogmatic Teachers* 11
Dawns this time-buried pavement. From that mound . . . . 275 **While poring* 8
Heaven's sapphire pavement, yet breathed well content, ... 278 **Lo ! where she* 11
The grass-grown pavement tread. . . . 334 **In Bruges* 4
The Place unfolds, from pavement skinned with moss, ... 355 *Aquap.* 193
" Eke the whole Convent on the pavement lay, . 556 *Prioress* 226
Of houses, pavement, streets, of men and things,— 707 *Prelude* 8. 546
As on the pavement of a Gothic church . . 716 *Prelude* 9. 444

Paves. That paves the brooks, the stationary rocks, 884 *Excursion* 9. 8

Pavilions. From rich pavilions spreading wide, . 372 *Eg. Maid* 191
Uplifted ; here, serene pavilions bright, . . 784 *Excursion* 2. 842

Paw. Would crush the lion's paw with mortal anguish, 70 *Bord.* 1798
Old as the tiger's paw, the lion's mane . . 227 *Vernal Ode* 122

Pawed. While his horse pawed the floor with furious heat ; . . . . 27 *Guilt* 175
Bounced, leapt, and pawed the air ; or mumbling sire, ... 693 *Prelude* 7. 422

Paws. Crouches, stretches, paws, and darts ! . 170 *Kitten* 18
From the brink her paws she stretches, . . 490 *Incident : Dog* 33

Pay. And bore him high through yielding air my debt of love to pay, . 92 *Poet's Dream* 19
In that sweet mood when pleasure loves to pay . 185 *Nutting* 39
Stooped down to pay him fealty ; . . . 205 *Brougham* 121
Shall Fancy pay to thee a grateful vow ? . . 253 **Aerial Rock* 5
Is there no debt to pay, no boon to grant ? . . 277 **Why art* 4
With chastened feelings would I pay . . . 284 *Grave of Burns* 15
To pay the homage ; and with these are joined, . 290 *Kilchurn* 28
Less tribute could she pay than this. . . . 334 **In Bruges* 37
The passing Winds memorial tribute pay ; . . 383 *Duddon* 29. 11
Yet will yourselves to God no service pay ; . . 433 *Ecc. Sonn.* 2. 18. 6
Measuring thy course, fair Stream ! at length I pay 476 *Eden* 9
Instinctive homage pay ; . . . . 506 **While from* 34
It would not pay for candle-light. . . . 536 *Goody Blake* 28
We pay a high and holy debt ; . . . . 582 **O for a* 7
To pay the filial debt, for food to roam, . . 613 *Desc.Sk.Quarto* 615
Have made me pay to science and to arts . . 654 *Prelude* 3. 375
Pay fruitless worship to humanity. . . . 722 *Prelude* 10. 259
Forgetfully ; uncalled upon to pay . . . 777 *Excursion* 2. 367
Upon their knees, and daily homage pay . . 866 *Excursion* 7. 585

Paying. Who, paying deadly hate in kind . . 403 *White Doe* 641
Than slow and torpid ; paying in this wise . 83 *Excursion* 2. 754

Paynim. Flaming till thou from Paynim hands release 467 *St. Bees* 106

Pays. Then pays submissively the appointed debt 261 **I watch* 8
The lonely redbreast pays ! . . . . 498 **Departing summer* 9

Peace. Where peace to Grasmere's lonely island leads, 2 *Ev. Wk.* 5
And breathes in peace the lily of the vale ! . . 6 *Ev. Wk.* 235
A peace enlivened not, disturbed, by wreaths . 9 *Ev. Wk.* 362
Till peace go with him to the tomb. . . . 9 *Lines : Boat* 12
" We lived in peace and comfort ; and were blest 29 *Guilt* 262
But what afflicts my peace with keenest ruth, . 32 *Guilt* 438
And that among so few there still be peace : . . 33 *Guilt* 509
On shipboard, bound till peace or death should set him free. . . . 35 *Guilt* 594
Peace to my parting soul, the fulness of content." 36 *Guilt* 630
She slept in peace,—his pulses throbbed and stopped, 36 *Guilt* 631

Peace—*continued.*

And be at rest. Oh, Sir ! Peace, my good Wilfred ; 38 *Bord.* 40
Receive that letter ? Be at peace.—The tie . . 43 *Bord.* 341
Of peace and order. Aged men with tears . . 48 *Bord.* 612
And every sacrifice his peace requires.— . . 50 *Bord.* 722
But listen, for my peace—— Why, I *believe* you. 59 *Bord.* 1175
Soon would her gentle voice make peace between us. 61 *Bord.* 1318
Remembered terror, there is peace and rest. . 64 *Bord.* 1469
Banish the thought, crush it, and be at peace. . 69 *Bord.* 1750
The earth for sure redemption of lost peace. . 69 *Bord.* 1783
Be at peace ; I am innocent. . . . . 72 *Bord.* 1921
Tranquil—why not ? Oh, peace ! He is at peace 75 *Bord.* 2141
The extremes of suffering meet in absolute peace. 76 *Bord.* 2216
Thy hours as they flow on are spent, if not in joy in peace. . . . 92 *Poet's Dream* 56
They please Him best who labour most to do in peace His will : . . . 93 *Poet's Dream* 66
Peace and rest, as seems, before them . . 93 *Westmoreland Girl* 15
To live in peace upon his father's land, . . 100 *Brothers* 324
The peace which others seek they find ; . . 110 *Forsaken* 1
It robs my heart of peace. . . . . 111 **'Tis said that some* 24
Peace settles where the intellect is meek, . . 112 **O dearer* 13
No peace, no comfort could I find, . . . 115 *Last of Flock* 75
Who must now be a wanderer ! but peace to that strain ! . . . 116 *Repentance* 26
He clove to her who could not give him peace— . 123 *V. and J.* 155
Of suffering or of peace, I know not which : . . 125 *V. and J.* 282
—Hushed was that House in peace, or seeming peace, ... 137 *Michael* 424
Are of inward peace secure : . . . . 140 *Arm. Lady* 32
With patience merit the reward of peace, . . 143 **High bliss* 3
Peace ye deserve ; and may the solid good, . . 143 **High bliss* 4
Ensuring peace to innocence. . . . . 154 *Flower Garden* 48
These died in peace each with the other,— . . 157 *Sexton* 7
May peace come never to his nest, . . . 159 **With little* 39
To peace, or fond regret. . . . . 164 **Fair Lady* 16
In such a heedless peace. Alas ! full soon . . 173 *Infant Daughter* 60
Through accidents of peace or war, . . . 181 *Waggoner* 4. 110
" But if thou goest, I follow—" " Peace ! " he said,— . . . . 211 *Laod.* 91
But in calm peace the appointed Victim slept, . 214 *Dion* 112
" Him only pleasure leads, and peace attends, . 214 *Dion* 122
Peace to embosom and content— . . . 223 *Wishing-gate* 28
All creatures met in peace, from fierceness free, . 227 *Vernal Ode* 127
His peace hath no offence betrayed ; . . . 247 *P. B.* 937
And spreads in steadfast peace her brooding wing. 254 *Wild Duck's Nest* 8
In thoughtful reverence to the Prince of Peace, . 255 *Easter* 7
Glory to that eternal Peace is paid, . . . 256 **Yes ! hope* 7
And hope of endless peace in me grew bold ; . 257 **No mortal* 4
Peace in these feverish times is sovereign bliss : . 262 *Retirement* 9
But where untroubled peace and concord dwell, . 262 **Not Love* 5
To live and die, the peace of heaven his aim ; . 272 *Lady E. B.* 6
To breathe in rural peace, to hear the stream, . 276 *Author's Portrait* 7
Peace let us seek,—to steadfast things attune . 278 **The most* 11
Plead for thy peace, thou beautiful romance . 282 *Railway* 11
Wills that your peace, your beauty, shall be sold, 283 **Proud were* 6
Nor by soft Peace adopted ; though, in place . 290 *Kilchurn* 11
In peace, and peace of mind. . . . . 291 *Rob Roy* 36
To live in peace on shore. . . . . 297 *Highland Boy* 245
How loud ! yet lived in peace with shame. . . 299 *Brownie's Cell* 50
Is gone ; our peace, our fearful innocence, . . 307 **O Friend* 13
Peace that should claim respect from lawless Might. 323 **Now that* 8
In peace of spirit, and sublime content ! . . 324 *Ode 1814* 89
Now, from Heaven-sanctioned victory, Peace is sprung ; . . . 326 **Emperors and* 7
Nor will the God of peace and love . . . 328 *Ode 1815* 87
Thy law, and live henceforth in peace, in pure good will. . . . 329 *Ode 1815* 128
And to the heavenly saints in peace who dwell, . 331 *Ode : Thanks.* 184
For liberty confirmed, and peace restored ! . . 332 *Ode : Thanks.* 204
A deeper peace than that in deserts found ! . . 334 **The Spirit* 14
A portion of God's peace. . . . . 337 **Oh Life* 12
The melodies of Peace in love ! . . . 338 *Brientz* 17
That fosters peace, and gentleness recalls ; . . 339 *Tell* 15
And, therefore, art thou blest with peace, serene . 339 *Schwytz* 6
Yet hints at peace to be o'erthrown, . . . 344 **How blest* 18
Peace greets us ;—rambling on without an aim . 349 *Val. Dover* 5
Hushed to a depth of more than Sabbath peace : . 349 *At Dover* 4
Peace to their Spirits ! why should Poesy . . 354 *Aquap.* 85
Peace, leisure, freedom, moderate desires ; . . 356 *Aquap.* 260
To soberness of mind and peace of heart . . 358 *Aquap.* 358
Striving in peace each other to outshine. . . 358 *Pine : Rome* 5
Now all is sun-bright peace. Of that day's shame, 361 **When here* 5
Her peace from images to pain allied. . . . 361 **For action* 4
How wide a space can part from inward peace . 363 **Grieve for* 13
To Her, as to her opposite in peace, . . . 365 **The Baptist* 10
And now, if men with men in peace abide, . . 383 *Duddon* 27. 11
Prepared, in peace of heart, in calm of mind . . 384 *Duddon* 33. 13
Win rest, and ease, and peace, with bliss that Angels share. . . . 390 *Glencroe* 14
Even to the fountain-head of peace divine." . . 396 **Action is* 13
Lie down in peace, and lovingly, . . . 397 *White Doe* 147
And peace is none, for living or dead ! . . . 399 *White Doe* 307
In solitude, and utter peace : . . . . 399 *White Doe* 329
Of peace on our humanity.— . . . . 400 *White Doe* 388
Then peace to cruelty and scorn, . . . 409 *White Doe* 1241
Peace, peace to all indignity ! ' . . . 409 *White Doe* 1243
Confirmed the deed in peace profound. . . 410 *White Doe* 1335
And with a deeper peace endued . . . . 415 *White Doe* 1749

Peace—*continued.*

But chastisement shall follow peace despised.	420 *Ecc. Sonn.* 1. 9. 7
Justice and peace :—bold faith ! yet also rise	424 *Ecc. Sonn.* 1. 24. 7
Justice and Peace through Her uphold their claims ;	429 *Ecc. Sonn.* 2. 2. 7
Move Princes to their duty, peace or war ;	429 *Ecc. Sonn.* 2. 5. 7
The peace of God within his single breast !	438 *Ecc. Sonn.* 2. 37. 14
For every wave against her peace unites.	439 *Ecc. Sonn.* 2. 41. 14
Her peace destroyed ! her hopes a wilderness !	439 *Ecc. Sonn.* 2. 44. 13
The peace of mind is Virtue's sure effect.	441 *Ecc. Sonn.* 3. 6. 8
To human kind ; though peace be on his tongue,	444 *Ecc. Sonn.* 3. 18. 7
Yield timely fruit of peace and love and joy.	447 *Ecc. Sonn.* 3. 29. 14
In hours of peace, or when the storm is driven	452 *Ecc. Sonn.* 3. 46. 7
As on a bed of death ? Some lodge in peace,	454 *Sea-side* 15
Vain is the pleasure, a false calm the peace,	455 **Not in the lucid* 26
The shadow—and the peace supreme !	457 **Had this* 20
Dread Power ! whom peace and calmness serve	458 **Had this* 69
Love to promote and purity and peace ;	460 **Queen of* 36
Intrudes on peace, I pray the eternal Sire	470 *Bala-Sala* 5
Peace to the Mourner. But when He who wore	476 **Tranquillity! the* 7
Would be rational peace—a philosopher's ease.	482 *Character* 8
That he below may rest in peace,	485 *Poet's Epitaph* 23
In peace fulfilling.	486 **Bright Flower* 24
To breathe Elysian peace in upper air.	501 *Humanity* 76
For the blissful calm, the peace	502 **Like a* 21
Justice and peace to a secure abode,	504 *Warning* 84
Wherever peace is on the brow,	506 **While from* 47
Gleams 'mid the peace of this deep dale	508 *May* 83
Loves it, while there in solitary peace	509 *F. Stone* 68
And love the end, which all through peace must seek.	518 *Pun. Death* 7. 8
From the Vale's peace which all her fields partake,	521 *Epist. Beaumont* 2
And peace among yourselves.	526 **The soaring* 16
Their peace, perhaps, our lightest footfall marred ;	527 **Those breathing* 50
Think of their common peace, their simple play,	531 **I know* 15
All peace depends, all safety rests.	533 **Blest is* 20
Heaven prosper it ! may peace, and love,	534 **Blest is* 91
Came ministers of peace, intent to rear	534 **When in* 3
So may it set in peace, to rise again	540 **Lady ! a* 82
Sent forth her peace to cheer.	544 *Russ. Fug.* 208
With all his ancestry. Then peace to him,	548 **Stranger ! this* 23
What is peace ?—when pain is over,	550 *Hermit's Cell* 1. 33
And asked for peace on suppliant knee ;	550 *Hermit's Cell* 5. 18
And peace was given,—nor peace alone,	550 *Hermit's Cell* 5. 19
Praise be to such, and to their slumbers peace !	568 *Cumb. Beg.* 141
To peace so perfect that the young behold	572 *Animal Tran.* 13
In peace eternal ; where desire and joy	573 *Chiabrera* 1. 5
For peace on earth and bliss in heaven.	577 **By playful* 22
A steadfast peace that might not be betrayed.	578 *Peele Castle* 32
The tender peace of rural thought :	579 **Sweet Flower* 23
To comfort and to peace.	580 *John Words.* 50
In peace is roaring like the Sea ;	581 **Loud is* 6
And thou, O rescued Earth, by peace and love,	582 *Invoc. Earth* 33
At peace inverted your lithe necks ye lave,	596 *Ev. Wk. Quarto* 235
The scene is waken'd, yet its peace unbroke,	599 *Ev. Wk. Quarto* 429
That breath'd a death-like peace these woods around,	603 *Desc. Sk. Quarto* 57
The redbreast peace had bury'd it in wood,	605 *Desc. Sk. Quarto* 169
But deeper lies the heart of peace	623 *G. and S. Green* 21
In bond of peace, in bond of love,	623 *G. and S. Green* 35
The sea, or trod the earth, to peace estrang'd."	625 *Æneid* 143
As bland as the reed of peace,	629 *Installation* 37
Long months of peace (if such bold word accord	632 *Prelude* 1. 24
And seemed to be a trouble to the peace	636 *Prelude* 1. 316
Of quietness or peace ; yet have I stood,	640 *Prelude* 1. 576
Our horses grazed. To more than inland peace,	643 *Prelude* 2. 108
Of peace and quiet and domestic love,	648 *Prelude* 2. 438
In glory immutable. But peace ! enough	651 *Prelude* 3. 121
Of sedentary peace. Those lovely forms	654 *Prelude* 3. 359
But peace to vain regrets ! We see but darkly	656 *Prelude* 3. 479
Intense desire through meditative peace ;	663 *Prelude* 4. 306
And hath the name of, God. Transcendent peace	677 *Prelude* 6. 139
Of peace and self-command. Of rivers, fields,	679 *Prelude* 6. 264
And didst sit down in temperance and peace,	679 *Prelude* 6. 280
Spake with a sense of peace, at intervals	681 *Prelude* 6. 412
Tumult and peace, the darkness and the light—	684 *Prelude* 6. 635
Maiden of Buttermere ! She lives in peace	692 *Prelude* 7. 320
Possession of the faculties,—the peace	697 *Prelude* 7. 654
To thee, and those domains of rural peace,	700 *Prelude* 8. 73
That spreads its leaves in unmolested peace,	711 *Prelude* 9. 89
Justice and peace. But far more sweet such toil—	715 *Prelude* 9. 396
In peace and silence. But if e'er was heard,—	716 *Prelude* 9. 446
Promised soft peace and sweet forgetfulness.	719 *Prelude* 10. 90
Was gentleness and peace. Upon a small	726 *Prelude* 10. 554
March firmly towards righteousness and peace."—	727 *Prelude* 10. 589
Triumphs of unambitious peace at home,	727 *Prelude* 11. 20
Whence grew that genuine knowledge, fraught with peace,	732 *Prelude* 11. 354
So neither were complacency, nor peace,	735 *Prelude* 12. 38
Of peace and excitation, finds in her	740 *Prelude* 13. 6
Where I could meditate in peace, and cull	742 *Prelude* 13. 131
Hope to my hope, and to my pleasure peace	742 *Prelude* 13. 180
May with fit reverence be applied—that peace	748 *Prelude* 14. 126
Strewing in peace life's humblest ground with herbs,	750 *Prelude* 14. 300
Would chant, in lonely peace, the spousal verse	755 *Recluse* 1. 1. 810
The peace required, he scanned the laws of light .	760 *Excursion* 1. 294
Amid the bounties of the year, the peace	761 *Excursion* 1. 352
And ere our lively greeting into peace	762 *Excursion* 1. 447
A Being, who by adding love to peace	764 *Excursion* 1. 518
In peace and comfort ; and a pretty boy	764 *Excursion* 1. 533
Had filled with plenty, and possessed in peace,	764 *Excursion* 1. 567
At this still season of repose and peace,	765 *Excursion* 1. 594

Peace—*continued.*

She sleeps in the calm earth, and peace is here.	770 *Excursion* 1. 941
It could not be more quiet : peace is here	777 *Excursion* 2. 364
" He is departed, and finds peace at last !"	777 *Excursion* 2. 384
Then from the threshold moves with song of peace,	780 *Excursion* 2. 558
To which thou may'st resort for holier peace,—	787 *Excursion* 3. 107
For independent happiness ; craving peace,	791 *Excursion* 3. 381
But for its absolute self ; a life of peace	791 *Excursion* 3. 385
As times of quiet and unbroken peace,	794 *Excursion* 3. 601
Which I had trod in happiness and peace,	797 *Excursion* 3. 802
Against my peace. Within the cabin stood	798 *Excursion* 3. 861
In pain commenced, and ended without peace :	801 *Excursion* 4. 3
Nor rapt, nor craving, but in settled peace,	804 *Excursion* 4. 187
Have still the keeping of their proper peace ;	806 *Excursion* 4. 321
Where peace and happy consciousness should dwell,	810 *Excursion* 4. 628
Peace in ourselves, and union with our God.	818 *Excursion* 4. 1116
And central peace, subsisting at the heart	818 *Excursion* 4. 1146
In peace and meditative cheerfulness ;	819 *Excursion* 4. 1203
In peace, from morn to night, from year to year.	825 *Excursion* 5. 217
Than this, to graze the herb in thoughtless peace,	827 *Excursion* 5. 329
For the mind's government, or temper's peace ;	833 *Excursion* 5. 725
To virtue lost, insensible of peace,	836 *Excursion* 5. 938
Where health abides, and cheerfulness, and peace.'	841 *Excursion* 6. 175
Discreetly parted to preserve the peace,	845 *Excursion* 6. 479
Of Time's eternal Master, and that peace,	846 *Excursion* 6. 520
From peace like exiles on some barren rock,	846 *Excursion* 6. 534
Loth to disturb what Heaven hath hushed in peace.	847 *Excursion* 6. 572
" A woman rests in peace ; surpassed by few .	848 *Excursion* 6. 676
A mind intolerant of lasting peace,	849 *Excursion* 6. 732
Her mind she strictly tutored to find peace	854 *Excursion* 6. 1026
And her obsequious shadow, peace of mind,	855 *Excursion* 6. 1090
Wretched at home, he gained no peace abroad ;	855 *Excursion* 6. 1098
That wears a look so full of peace and hope	855 *Excursion* 6. 1106
From some staid guardian of the public peace,	859 *Excursion* 7. 102
One after one, with intervals of peace.	861 *Excursion* 7. 254
To spend the sabbath of old age in peace,	867 *Excursion* 7. 666
This hallowed grave demands, where rests in peace	870 *Excursion* 7. 849
Impregnable of Liberty and Peace.	876 *Excursion* 8. 147
Oh ! where is now the character of peace,	877 *Excursion* 8. 239
Possessed of health, and strength, and peace of mind ;	887 *Excursion* 9. 204
With what Heaven grants, and die—in peace of mind,	888 *Excursion* 9. 279
Cannot subsist, nor confidence, nor peace.	889 *Excursion* 9. 354
As if preparing for the peace of evening.	890 *Excursion* 9. 422
Seems but a fleeting sunbeam's gift, whose peace	891 *Excursion* 9. 472
Your very poorest rich in peace of thought	895 *Excursion* 9. 734
Of house and field,—to plenty, peace, and love.	S.3.426 **Through Cumbrian* 8
Peace to the sober matron who shall dip	S.3. 435 **The doubt* 135
To be waylaid by her betrothèd, peace	S.3. 436 **The doubt* 143
The greeting " peace be with you " unto them,	K.8. 244 *Recluse* 1.1.281
For peace they have, it cannot but be theirs,	K.8. 244 *Recluse* 1.1.282
To breathe in peace, we shall moreover find	K.8. 254 *Recluse* 1.1.644
—Such is our wealth ; O Vale of Peace, we are	K.8. 254 *Recluse* 1.1.662
From such a desperate breaker of the peace ?	L.1. 97 *Juvenal* 3. 70
Peaceable. —" The peaceable remains of this good Knight	874 *Excursion* 8. 34
A peaceable dominion, wide as earth,	894 *Excursion* 9. 665
Peaceably. Watch also, shifting peaceably their place	230 *Clouds* 73
Thou, chequering peaceably the minster's gloom,	459 **Wanderer ! that* 27
Rocks in its harbour, lodging peaceably.	489 *Pers. Talk* 50
And there we found him breathing peaceably,	784 *Excursion* 2. 821
Peaceful. " Peaceful as this immeasurable plain	30 *Guilt* 334
And end my days upon the peaceful flood.'—	31 *Guilt* 366
Maintained, for peaceful ends beyond our view.	78 *Bord.* 2310
Up to heaven, thro' peaceful ways.	94 *Westmoreland Girl* 92
Your years make up one peaceful family ;	97 *Brothers* 122
Farewell!—we leave thee to Heaven's peaceful care,	106 *Farewell* 7
Thus often would he leave our peaceful home,	107 *Indolence* 10
A habitation in this peaceful Vale,	150 **When, to* 3
Of Silver-how, and Grasmere's peaceful lake	151 **When, to* 91
There close the peaceful lives of flowers ?	154 *Flower Garden* 6
Within that warm and peaceful berth,	177 *Waggoner* 2. 88
Which slowly settles into peaceful calm,	184 *Night-piece* 25
Now sleeping in these peaceful groves.	186 **O Nightingale* 10
Has raised thy spirit to a peaceful stand	222 *Triad* 185
But your smooth motions suit a peaceful aim ;	230 *Clouds* 15
Peaceful striving, gentle play	233 *Power of Sound* 77
Hail, Twilight, sovereign of one peaceful hour !	265 **Hail, Twilight* 1
Breathed forth beside the peaceful mountain Stream	275 *Rotha Q.* 9
Not small like ours, a peaceful flood,	295 *Highland Boy* 52
Now peaceful as the morning,	302 *Yarrow V.* 30
Come forth, ye old men, now in peaceful show	310 *Anticip.* 6
Of peaceful civic virtue : they attest	316 **Hail, Zaragoza* 7
Attire the peaceful corse in vestments white ;	318 **In due* 4
The triumph hail, which from their peaceful clime	326 **The Bard* 13
The peaceful guest advancing from afar.	327 *Ode 1815* 51
That, slowly making way for peaceful night,	333 **Bruges I* 4
Spreading her peaceful ensigns, calls the swains	335 *Namur* 6
Gently wound the peaceful flood,	336 **Jesu ! bless* 10
But with its peaceful majesty content.	355 *Aquap.* 191
Its shining forehead through the peaceful rent	383 *Duddon* 31. 3
Yet peaceful Arts did entrance gain	390 *Highland Broach* 11
" Even she will to her peaceful woods	402 *White Doe* 560
Than from her wily praise, her peaceful gown,	420 *Ecc. Sonn.* 1. 8. 11
And cheering oft his peaceful reveries.	466 *St. Bees* 44
Peaceful abodes, where Justice might uphold .	468 *St. Bees* 129
In peaceful earth : for, doubtless, he was frank,	470 **A youth* 9
A peaceful spot where Nature's gifts abound ;	470 †*From early* 12

Peaceful—*continued.*

Thou monument of peaceful happiness ! . . .	489 *Spade* 24
But from this peaceful centre of delight .	503 *Warning* 30
On the humanities of peaceful fame, ...	529 **Those breathing* 127
Of peaceful years ; a chronicle of heaven ;— .	578 *Peele Castle* 22
A peaceful cradle given :	582 **O for a* 21
When pure Religion rear'd the peaceful breast .	618 *School Ex.* 31
Though peaceful, full of gladness. Thou art pleased,	622 *Recluse* 1. 1. 117
Whereon Britannia rests her peaceful fame. .	629 *Installation* 40
Opening the peaceful clouds ; or she may use .	637 *Prelude* 1. 354
Of boldest projects, and a peaceful end . . .	661 *Prelude* 4. 175
The peaceful scene oft filled me with surprise .	661 *Prelude* 4. 194
And, save the flowing water's peaceful voice, .	664 *Prelude* 4. 386
Those sanctified abodes of peaceful man, . . .	682 *Prelude* 6. 508
Of peaceful houses with unquiet sounds. . . .	712 *Prelude* 9. 165
Of hospitality and peaceful rest.	716 *Prelude* 9. 478
Even here, though less than with the peaceful house	716 *Prelude* 9. 492
And in the region of their peaceful selves ;— .	729 *Prelude* 11. 135
Release from fear ; and cherished peaceful days .	791 *Excursion* 3. 364
O, calm contented days, and peaceful nights ! .	817 *Excursion* 4. 1050
For my own peaceful lot and happy choice ; .	823 *Excursion* 5. 51
Gathered together in their peaceful fold ? " .	836 *Excursion* 5. 899
As if, amid these peaceful hills and groves, . .	837 *Excursion* 5. 973
Intrudes, the peaceful concert to disturb . . .	848 *Excursion* 6. 644
His gentle manners : and his peaceful smiles, .	864 *Excursion* 7. 460
Murmurs, not idly, o'er his peaceful grave. . .	864 *Excursion* 7. 481
In what may now be called a peaceful bed. . .	868 *Excursion* 7. 694
To which his peaceful fancy oft had turned. . .	872 *Excursion* 7. 940
From out the labours of a peaceful Land . . .	875 *Excursion* 8. 91
With peaceful admonitions for the heart . . .	876 *Excursion* 8. 163
Into our hearts ; and charmed the peaceful flood.	892 *Excursion* 9. 537
Called to such office by the peaceful sound . .	895 *Excursion* 9. 726
Yet in this peaceful Vale we will not spend .	K.8. 257 *Recluse* 1.1.751
Unheard-of days, though loving peaceful thoughts.	K.8. 257 *Recluse* 1.1.752

Peacefully.

The breathless corse ; then peacefully resigned	123 *V. and J.* 133
And he gave up the ghost full peacefully ; .	556 *Prioress* 221
Entrenched, say rather peacefully embowered, .	622 *Recluse* 1. 1. 76

Peach.

And peach and citron, in Spring's mildest breeze	356 *Aquap.* 218

Peacock.

The peacock in the broad ash-tree . . .	406 *White Doe* 953

Pea-green.

That turns its goat's-beard flakes of pea-green moss	61 *Bord.* 1295

Peak. *See* **Mountain-peak.**

And, when the stormy wind blows o'er the peak,	73 *Bord.* 2056
A Man on the peak of the Crag.	86 *Rural Arch.* 6
From the peak of the crag blew the giant away. .	86 *Rural Arch.* 16
Along the public way, this Peak, so high . . .	148 **There is an* 5
From snowy peak and cloud, attune	235 *Power of Sound* 200
High as the highest Peak of Furness-fells, . .	250 **Nuns fret* 6
Of the wild Peak ; where new-born waters glide .	275 **Chatsworth! thy* 4
Cloud-piercing peak, and trackless heath, . .	506 **While from* 33
The horizon's bound, a huge peak, black and huge,	637 *Prelude* 1. 378
That is the eagle's birthplace, or some peak . .	760 *Excursion* 1. 275

Peak's.

—To wet the peak's impracticable sides . .	609 *Desc.Sk.Quarto* 394

Peaks.

More high, the snowy peaks with hues of rose. .	17 *Desc. Sk.* 406
While needle peaks of granite shooting bare . .	19 *Desc. Sk.* 468
On the tall peaks the glistening sunbeams play, .	22 *Desc. Sk.* 668
The cliffs and peaks so high that are, . . .	129 *Idiot Boy* 319
To one or other brow of those twin Peaks . . .	151 **Forth from* 8
The hoary peaks of Scotland that give birth . .	219 **This Height* 9
Yon towering Peaks, " Shepherds of Etive Glen ? "	389 *Sound of Mull* 14
Of all her peaks and ridges. What he draws . .	468 **Ranging the* 6
Varying her crowded peaks and ridges blue ; . .	471 **Arran! a* 3
Above sea-clouds, the Peaks of Arran rose . . .	475 **There! said* 6
Where needle peaks of granite shooting bare . .	612 *Desc.Sk.Quarto* 558
Those rosy peaks, from which the Morning looks .	733 *Prelude* 11. 410
To glance an upward look on two huge Peaks, .	782 *Excursion* 2. 692
On th ose high peaks, the first autumnal snow, .	861 *Excursion* 7. 249
High peaks, that bound the vale where now we are.	885 *Excursion* 9. 59

Peal.

There where the peal of swelling torrents fills	18 *Desc. Sk.* 463
Through these wide realms a festive peal . . .	113 *Lament* 23
—No sooner ceased that peal, than on the verge .	324 *Ode 1814* 82
The Sabbath bells renew the inviting peal ; . .	447 *Ecc. Sonn.* 3. 28. 1
Deepening her echoing torrents' awful peal . .	603 *Desc. Sk. Quarto* 76
When the dread peal of swelling torrents fills . .	612 *Desc.Sk.Quarto* 552
There, 'mid a peal of ill-matched sounds and cries,	719 *Prelude* 10. 97
They started at the tributary peal	871 *Excursion* 7. 886
Of waters, with invigorated peal	885 *Excursion* 9. 67

Pealed.

Pealed to his orisons, and when he paced .	551 **If thou in* 19

Pealing.

Hosannas pealing down the long-drawn aisle, ...	232 *Power of Sound* 14
And steeple tower (with pealing bells . . .	533 **Blest is* 9
Her pealing organ was my neighbour too ; . .	650 *Prelude* 3. 57
Under the pealing organ. Empty thoughts ! . .	653 *Prelude* 3. 315

Peals. *See* **Thunder-peals.**

The thunder rolled in peals that would have made	50 *Bord.* 711
With liveliest peals of birth-day harmony : . .	464 **Greta, what* 13
Hark to the peals on this bright May-morn ! . .	628 *Installation* 29
Responsive to his call, with quivering peals, . .	671 *Prelude* 5. 376
To laughter multiplied in louder peals . . .	843 *Excursion* 6. 345

Pear.

And pines the unripened pear in summer's kindliest ray ;	15 *Desc. Sk.* 259
Who sits at his own door,—and, like the pear .	568 *Cumb. Beg.* 117
Dwindles the pear on autumn's latest spray, .	608 *Desc.Sk.Quarto* 321

Pearl.

With pearl or gleaming agate vies . . .	165 *Parrot* 7
This day, be mistress of a single pearl . . .	358 *Aquap.* 356
She cast a Pearl ashore.	374 *Eg. Maid* 374

Pearls.

Lovers lock up as pearls, though oft no better	68 *Bord.* 1680

Pearly.

Green, red, and pearly white ! . . .	198 *Thorn* 48

Pearly—*continued.*

The flowers in pearly dews their bloom renewing !	283 **Here, where* 8
As the pearly car of Amphitrite, ...	296 *Highland Boy* 119
Save where that pearly whiteness	302 *Yarrow V.* 18
Thrilling each pearly cleft and sparry grot, .	333 *Fish-women* 13
Familiar, as the Morn with pearly dews ? . .	335 *Namur* 4
" My pearly Boat, a shining Light, . . .	370 *Eg. Maid* 103
And in the pearly shallop placed, . . .	371 *Eg. Maid* 143
Their pearly lustre—coming but to go ; . .	436 *Ecc. Sonn.* 2. 32. 7
Shakes off that pearly shower. . . .	506 **While from* 8
A pearly crest, like Dian's when it threw . .	532 **Once I* 15
Frosting with hoary light the pearly ground, .	599 *Ev. Wk. Quarto* 393

Peas.

A garden stored with peas, and mint, and thyme, ...	28 *Guilt* 209
But hear the proofs—— Ay, prove that when two peas	59 *Bord.* 1176
Be larger than the peas—prove this—'twere matter	59 *Bord.* 1178
Had twined about her two small rows of peas, .	767 *Excursion* 1. 729

Peasant.

The peasant, from yon cliff of fearful edge .	4 *Ev. Wk.* 130
The kneeling peasant scarcely dares to gaze ; .	14 *Desc. Sk.* 201
No peasant leans upon his pole, to tell . . .	15 *Desc. Sk.* 240
Behind his sail the peasant shrinks, to shun .	15 *Desc. Sk.* 281
Think not the peasant from aloft has gazed .	18 *Desc. Sk.* 421
The peasant, wild in passion, made reply . .	33 *Guilt* 480
I met a peasant near the spot ; he told me, .	47 *Bord.* 570
No traveller, peasant, herdsman ? Not a soul .	61 *Bord.* 1293
Have you, good Peasant, seen a blind old Man ? .	73 *Bord.* 2041
Thus talking of that Peasant, we approached .	149 **A narrow* 55
Peasant and lord, in their appointed seat, . .	319 *Guernica* 13
Where gazed the peasant from his door, . .	343 *Eclipse* 29
To king, to peasant, to rough sailor, dear, . .	455 *Rydal Mere* 29
Peasant and mail-clad Chief with pious awe ; .	467 *St. Bees* 122
He had insulted—Peasant, King, or Thane ? .	475 **Here on their* 11
Whence the blithe hail ? behold a Peasant stand	524 *Epist. Beaumont* 207
Awe struck, the kneeling peasant scarce surveys ;	606 *Desc.Sk.Quarto* 254
Behind his sail the peasant strives to shun .	608 *Desc.Sk.Quarto* 344
Tho' now, where erst the grey-clad peasant stray'd,	615 *Desc.Sk.Quarto* 744
Peasant and king ; when boys and youths, the growth	655 *Prelude* 3. 464
Monarch and peasant : be the house redeemed .	682 *Prelude* 6. 456
A peasant met us, from whose mouth we learned	683 *Prelude* 6. 579
Upon those tidings by the peasant given . . .	684 *Prelude* 6. 618
I knew a Scottish Peasant who possessed . .	835 *Excursion* 5. 863
He was a peasant of the lowest class : . . .	865 *Excursion* 7. 550

Peasantry.

Of that young peasantry, who, in our days, ...	869 *Excursion* 7. 806

Peasant's.

Strong terror checks the female peasant's sighs, ...	11 *Desc. Sk.* 65
By silent cottage-doors, the peasant's home .	13 *Desc. Sk.* 143
I spied him skulking in his peasant's dress. .	46 *Bord.* 491
To look upon you. In a peasant's dress . .	47 *Bord.* 531
Attired in peasant's garb, who stood alone, .	149 **A narrow* 48
Unscorned the peasant's whistling breath, that lightens	233 *Power of Sound* 51
Cheer'st the low threshold of the peasant's cell ! .	329 *Ode : Thanks.* 7
In one meek smile, beneath a peasant's shed, .	359 **They—who* 7
My dull forebodings in a Peasant's ear . .	360 *Albano* 4
And lean upon a peasant's staff. . . .	485 *Poet's Epitaph* 16
The far-off peasant's day-deserted home ; . .	605 *Desc.Sk.Quarto* 167
Was never heard the plodding peasant's tread. .	607 *Desc.Sk.Quarto* 286
But every word that from the peasant's lips .	684 *Prelude* 6. 589

Peasants.

She eats her food which every day the peasants	44 *Bord.* 386
Thrice happy, burghers, peasants, warriors old, .	339 *Tell* 6
Of Peasants in their homely gear. . . .	403 *White Doe* 627
The Wharfdale peasants in their prayers. . .	416 *White Doe* 1863
The peasants of these lonely valleys used . .	784 *Excursion* 2. 815
From dateless usage which our peasants hold .	851 *Excursion* 6. 833

Peasant-youth.

A Peasant-youth, so call him, for he asked	870 *Excursion* 7. 851

Peat-fire.

Our home-amusements by the warm peat-fire	639 *Prelude* 1. 508

Peat-yielding.

From the peat-yielding Moss on Gowdar's head.	523 *Epist. Beaumont* 111

Pebbles.

In the slope-channel floored with pebbles bright, ...	190 **Lyre! though* 34
Did o'er the pebbles play. . . ' . .	194 *Ruth* 204
Among the stones and pebbles he . . .	247 *P. B.* 988
Of wave-worn pebbles, pleading on the shore .	474 **How sad* 3
Grots, pebbles, roots of trees, and fancies more, .	662 *Prelude* 4. 262

Pebbly.

Across the pebbly road a little runnel strayed	34 *Guilt* 540
In a calm hour to kiss the pebbly shore, . .	734 *Prelude* 12. 22
In flower and tree, in every pebbly stone . .	884 *Excursion* 9. 7

Peck.

Then peck or perch, fond Flutterer ! nor forbear	273 **Wild Redbreast* 13
Not venturing yet to peck their destined meal, .	566 *Cumb. Beg.* 20
That peck along the road, regard him not. .	572 *Animal Tran.* 2
That peck along the hedge-rows, or the kite .	764 *Excursion* 1. 564

Pecked.

The red-breast, known for years, which at my casement pecked. · . . .	28 *Guilt* 225
Pecked, as at mine, thus boldly, Love might say, .	272 **Wild Redbreast* 2
While Robin pecked the crumbs upon his knee .	531 **I know* 11

Peculiar.

Her fields peculiar, and peculiar skies. . .	21 *Desc. Sk.* 623
And not hers only, their peculiar charms . .	118 *Maternal Grief* 23
The Housewife plied her own peculiar work, .	133 *Michael* 126
Drawn by what peculiar spell, . . .	161 **Pleasures newly* 41
Or herb that claimed peculiar sympathy, . .	170 **Never enlivened* 13
Now, whether it were by peculiar grace, . .	196 *Resolution* 50
(Each hero following his peculiar bent) . . .	211 *Laod.* 116

Pendent. *See* **Pendant.**
The pendent grapes glittered above the door;— 24 *Guilt* 16
About the pendent nest, did thus espy . . . 123 *V. and J.* 84
Is the light ash! that, pendent from the brow . 184 *Airey-force* 12
And pendent rocks, where'er, in gliding state, . 212 *Dion*
From Cadenabbia's pendent grapes. . . . . 342 *Ital. Itin.* 50
And murmur issuing from yon pendent flood, . 358 *Aquap.* 370
(While from the pendent woodbine came . . . 407 *White Doe* 1028
All, while *he* slept, treading the pendent stairs 500 *Humanity* 35
And the smooth green of many a pendent field, . 524 *Epist. Beaumont* 176
Whose hoary diadem of pendent rocks . . . 788 *Excursion* 3. 145
In the dry crannies of the pendent rocks; . . 866 *Excursion* 7. 597
Pendle-hill. As Pendle-hill or Pennygent . . 409 *White Doe* 1175
Pendragon. How glad Pendragon—though the sleep 204 *Brougham* 40
Penetrable. Hath placed beyond these penetrable bounds, ... 789 *Excursion* 3. 219
Or the least penetrable hiding-place . . . . 829 *Excursion* 5. 450
Penetrate. My heart, could penetrate its inmost core, 48 *Bord.* 632
This long-roofed Vista penetrate—but see, . . 351 *Des. Stanzas* 65
And penetrate the hearts of all; . . . . . 534 **Blest is* 94
Shall penetrate the heart without a wound; . . 584 **With copious* 59
Could never penetrate, yet did there not . . . 652 *Prelude* 3. 244
To penetrate the lofty and the low; . . . . 750 *Prelude* 14. 271
May'st penetrate, wherever truth shall lead; . . 787 *Excursion* 3. 109
These pure sensations; that can penetrate . . 806 *Excursion* 4. 368
Easy and bold, that penetrate the gloom . . . 876 *Excursion* 8. 110
Penetrated. And penetrated all with tender light, . 265 **The Shepherd* 4
Penetrates. Whose softened image penetrates the deep. 5 *Ev. Wk.* 173
And penetrates the glades. . . . . 457 **Had this* 24
And penetrates the forest's inmost shades; . . 459 **Wanderer! that* 26
That penetrates, enables us to mount, ... 737 *Prelude* 12. 217
Penetrating. Of penetrating harps and voices sweet! 335 *Cologne* 14
What penetrating power of sun or breeze, . . . 880 *Excursion* 8. 417
The penetrating bliss; oh surely these . . . K.8.243 *Recluse* 1.1. 234
Penetration. But, to Thy sovereign penetration, fair, 331 *Ode: Thanks.* 186
Penetrative. The penetrative eye which can perceive 842 *Excursion* 6. 257
Peninsulas. Make green peninsulas on Esthwaite's Lake: . . . . 672 *Prelude* 5. 434
Penitent. Earth's noblest penitent; from bondage freed . . . . 105 *Artegal* 229
Some Penitent sincere . . . . 223 *Wishing-gate* 51
For penitent guilt, and innocent distress. . . . 426 *Ecc. Sonn.* 1. 32. 8
On a true Penitent. When breath departs . . 447 *Ecc. Sonn.* 3. 28. 9
Soon the relapsing penitent may boast . . . 519 *Pun. Death* 11. 7
The crime confessed, a kneeling Penitent . . . 520 *Pun. Death* 12. 6
Then did the Penitent adorn . . . . . . 543 *Russ. Fug.* 185
Her own transgression; penitent sincere . . . 853 *Excursion* 6. 990
Penitential. Of penitential anguish, yea with tears. 78 *Bord.* 2305
With brow in penitential sorrow bent! . . . . 270 **Though the bold* 14
A penitential loneliness. . . . . 398 *White Doe* 177
Do penitential cogitations cling; . . . . . 424 *Ecc. Sonn.* 1. 21. 10
Who in the penitential desert met . . . . . 434 *Ecc. Sonn.* 2. 24. 13
With penitential sorrow, and aloft . . . . . 513 *General Fast* 7
Into that world where penitential tear . . . . 519 *Pun. Death* 10. 6
A doleful bower for penitential song, ... 529 **Those breathing* 115
For penitential tears and trembling hopes . . . 682 *Prelude* 6. 454
Grieving for sin, and penitential tears . . . . 850 *Excursion* 6. 799
Penitents. To some offenders; other penitents, . 78 *Bord.* 2341
Of tardy penitents; or for the best . . . . 467 *St. Bees* 67
Penmanmaur. On Cader Idris, or huge Penmanmaur) 857 *Excursion* 7. 8
Penn. All who revere the memory of Penn . . . 515 *Penn.* 9
Penned. Just as those final words were penned, the sun broke out in power, ... 91 *Poet's Dream* 1
Great men have been among us; hands that penned . . . . 307 **Great men* 1
For whom this simple Register was penned. . . 525 **Soon did* 4
Penned these sad lines, nor can forbear to pray . 575 *Chiabrera* 7. 16
In Araby, romances; legends penned . . . . 673 *Prelude* 5. 497
Moses, and he who penned, the other day, . . 695 *Prelude* 7. 563
Are penned in cotes; the chaffering is begun. . 699 *Prelude* 8. 22
Each in his separate cell, or penned in crowds . 724 *Prelude* 10. 406
Who penned, to ridicule confiding faith, . . . 816 *Excursion* 4. 1006
Pennied. *See* **One-pennied.**
Penniless. In penniless poverty. But now to school 643 *Prelude* 2. 84
Pennine. Down from the Pennine Alps how fiercely sweeps . . . . 476 *Nunnery* 2
Penny. The one-pennied Boy has his penny to spare. 188 *Music* 28
A penny on the ground had thrown; . . . . 621 *Andrew Jones* 13
He saw the penny on the ground. . . . . . 621 *Andrew Jones* 25
He stooped and took the penny up: . . . . 621 *Andrew Jones* 26
Crying, "An obolus, a penny give . . . . . 656 *Prelude* 3. 473
Pennygent. As Pendle-hill or Pennygent . . . 409 *White Doe* 1175
Pens. Offered to notice by less daring pens, . . 673 *Prelude* 5. 543
Pensioned. Where, pensioned, they in shelter might sit down, ... 655 *Prelude* 3. 468
Pensioner. Long may you love your pensioner mouse, 142 †*Lov. and Lik.* 39
A Miser's Pensioner—behold our lot! . . . . 571 **There is a Flower* 22
Herself were nothing, a mere pensioner . . . 686 *Prelude* 6. 737
Her doors to admit this homeless Pensioner; . . 783 *Excursion* 2. 744
How that neglected Pensioner was sent . . . 821 *Excursion* 4. 1313
Perhaps yon loose sods cover, the poor Pensioner 835 *Excursion* 5. 881
Pensive. *See* **Nobly-pensive.**
Stay! pensive, sadly-pleasing visions, stay! . . 8 *Ev. Wk.* 319
By wisdom, moralise his pensive road. . . . . 11 *Desc. Sk.* 28
Of pensive Underwalden's pastoral heights. . . 16 *Desc. Sk.* 339
The whilst her comrade to her pensive cheer . . 30 *Guilt* 323
And for the Subject of my Verse I heaved a pensive sigh. . . . . 91 *Poet's Dream* 4

Pensive—*continued.*
Were yet with pensive fear and gentle awe . . 118 *Maternal Grief* 59
But pensive fancies putting by, ... 143 **Driven in* 11
Hath often eased my pensive breast . . . . 158 **In youth* 63
Upon the pensive solitude, ... 180 *Waggoner* 4. 27
Startles the pensive traveller while he treads . 184 *Night-piece* 9
In vacant or in pensive mood, ... 187 **I wandered* 20
Brought from a pensive though a happy place. . 211 *Laod.* 96
And sylvan places heaved a pensive sigh; . . 214 *Dion* 111
Reveal thyself, like pensive Morn . . . . . 222 *Triad* 175
From men of pensive virtue go, ... 245 *P. B.* 773
And students with their pensive citadels; . . . 250 **Nuns fret* 3
For worthless brows, while in the pensive shade . 254 *Dyer* 8
Their pensive light from a departed sun! . . . 256 *Decay of Piety* 14
And thou, grey Stone, the pensive likeness keep . 262 **Mark the* 10
Those words were uttered as in pensive mood . 263 **Those words* 1
And pensive monitor of fleeting years! . . . 264 *Snowdrop* 14
May feed on thoughts though pensive not austere; 264 **Lady! I* 12
Then, pensive Votary! let thy feet repair . . 269 *Gordale* 4
As pensive Evening deepens into night. . . . 274 **Such age* 14
How in thy pensive glooms our hearts found rest. 282 **Wansfell! this* 14
Bear witness many a pensive sigh . . . . . 292 *Rob Roy* 113
My thoughts;—she told in pensive strain . . . 294 *Jedbor.* 71
A pensive recollection. . . . . 302 *Yarrow V.* 24
Touches me not, though pensive as a bird . . 304 **Jones! as* 13
With its grey rocks clustering in pensive shade— 335 *Namur* 12
Like vision, pensive though not cold, ... 343 *Eclipse* 74
Too lovely to be pensive in themselves . . . 355 *Aquap.* 201
The dome of Florence, pensive and alone, . . . 365 **Under the* 2
Fulfil thy pensive duty, ... 386 *Yarrow Rev.* 106
The pensive warbler of the ruddy breast . . . 388 *Trosachs* 12
What harmonious pensive changes . . . . . 397 *White Doe* 79
Ah, pensive Scholar, think not so, ... 399 *White Doe* 308
And one, the pensive Marmaduke, ... 401 *White Doe* 490
To cheer this sad and pensive time; . . . . 410 *White Doe* 1281
The pensive visitant is seen. . . . . . . 417 *White Doe* 1900
And what a pensive Sage doth utter, hear! . . 422 *Ecc. Sonn.* 1. 15. 14
Into the pensive heart ill fortified, ... 427 *Ecc. Sonn.* 1. 36. 13
To all that Earth from pensive hearts is stealing, 455 **Not in the lucid* 20
A tender Spirit broods—the pensive Shade . . 465 **The cattle* 9
A grey-haired, pensive, thankful Refugee; . . 470 *Bala-Sala* 7
A part so charmed the pensive soul: . . . . 472 *Ossian* 4
Came studious Taste; and many a pensive stranger 477 *Nunnery* 11
Sweet is thy voice at pensive even; . . . . 480 *Somnamb.* 160
A gentle, pensive, white-robed sisterhood, . . . 496 **A little* 45
May pensive Autumn ne'er present . . . . 497 *Lycoris* 49
From out the pensive shadows where they lie) . 498 **Enough of climbing* 48
What pensive beauty autumn shows, ... 502 *Seasons* 13
(Surely I do not err) that pensive air . . . . 509 *F. Stone* 71
These groves have heard the Other's pensive strains; . . . . 546 **The embowering* 6
To tender offices and pensive thoughts. . . . 568 *Cumb. Beg.* 170
But if the pensive gloom . . . . 577 *Cenotaph* 9
The talking boat that moves with pensive sound, 597 *Ev. Wk. Quarto* 319
With pensive step to measure my slow way, . . 605 *Desc. Sk. Quarto* 165
A smile sat beaming on her pensive face. . . . 618 *School Ex.* 24
A pensive feeling! It spread far and wide; . . 662 *Prelude* 4. 241
A pensive sky, sad days, and piping winds, . . 677 *Prelude* 6. 174
Some pensive musings which might well beseem . 706 *Prelude* 8. 457
As even their pensive influence drew from mine. . 726 *Prelude* 10. 530
The pensive moments by this calm fireside, . . 734 *Prelude* 11. 450
In pensive idleness. What could he do, . . . 760 *Excursion* 1. 261
By each and all of these the pensive ear . . . 786 *Excursion* 3. 5
The poet fits it to his pensive lyre. . . . . . 792 *Excursion* 3. 445
Where mild enthusiasts tuned a pensive lay . . 797 *Excursion* 3. 754
With the same pensive office; and make known . 800 *Excursion* 3. 981
The feathered kinds; the fieldfare's pensive flock, 808 *Excursion* 4. 450
A gay or pensive tenderness prevailed, . . . 812 *Excursion* 4. 743
Here did our pensive Host put forth his hand . 823 *Excursion* 5. 67
Stretched overhead, and at my pensive feet . . 827 *Excursion* 5. 344
The pensive silence, saying:— "Blest are they . 854 *Excursion* 6. 1069
—Bright garland form they for the pensive brow 855 *Excursion* 6. 1127
Which did to him assign a pensive lot— . . . 873 *Excursion* 7. 1013
The pensive Sceptic of the lonely vale . . . . 874 *Excursion* 8. 1
And pensive quiet, an unnatural light . . . . 876 *Excursion* 8. 167
By virtue.—He, sighing with pensive grief, . . 877 *Excursion* 8. 227
Her pensive beauty; from the breeze her sweets. . 892 *Excursion* 9. 544
A pensive stranger, journeying at his leisure . . K.8.249 *Recluse* 1.1. 475
And oh! dear soother of the pensive breast, . . K.8. 301 **And oh* 1
Pensively. He paced along; and pensively, . . 167 *Pilgrim's Dream* 9
And somewhat pensively he wooed: . . . . 186 **O Nightingale* 16
Faint and somewhat pensively; . . . . . 190 **Lyre! though* 20
As pensively his steps advance, ... 244 *P. B.* 688
Pensively with downcast eyes. . . . . . . 397 *White Doe* 155
In dreams and fictions, pensively composed: . . 683 *Prelude* 6. 550
With our conductor, pensively we sank . . . 746 *Prelude* 14. 17
The grey-haired Wanderer pensively exclaimed, . 872 *Excursion* 7. 977
Pensiveness. In humble grace, and quiet pensiveness 508 *F. Stone* 39
Pent. *See* **Close-pent.**
A lamb, that in the pool is pent . . . . . 85 *Shepherd-boys* 65
The Hamadryad, pent within, bewailed . . . 219 *Haunted Tree* 26
A murmur, pent within the earth, ... 245 *P. B.* 834
Pent in, a Tyrant's solitary Thrall: . . . . 308 **There is a bondage* 3
Than either, pent within her separate sphere, . 357 *Aquap.* 287
For lordly Wharf is there pent in . . . . . 494 *Force of Prayer* 19
And in the sluggish pools where ships are pent: . 495 *Fact* 34
While Ye, in lasting durance pent, ... 526 **The soaring* 5
His soul is pent! How little can be known— . 831 *Excursion* 5. 590
And in the sluggish Ports where ships were pent. S.3. 427 **My Son* 5

Perchance—*continued.*
If I perchance a Nightingale might hear, 557 *Cuck.and Night.* 53
His charters and exemptions ; and, perchance, 568 *Cumb. Beg.* 127
And hence my transport. Nor should this, perchance, 647 *Prelude* 2. 376
Of magic fiction, verse of mine perchance 676 *Prelude* 6. 88
Tricked out for that proud use, if I perchance 694 *Prelude* 7. 450
And, 'mid the simple worshippers, perchance 722 *Prelude* 10. 296
A box, perchance, is from your casement hung 807 *Excursion* 4. 388
Perchance too lightly occupied, or lulled 807 *Excursion* 4. 419
Unseen, perchance above all power of sight— 819 *Excursion* 4. 1180
Perchance, the heavier woes of guilt ; feel not 829 *Excursion* 5. 429
Perchance you not unfrequently have marked 839 *Excursion* 6. 96
A Foster-mother's office. 'Tis, perchance, 852 *Excursion* 6. 948
May cover him ; and by its help, perchance, 862 *Excursion* 7. 353
Ranged round the garden walk, while she perchance 867 *Excursion* 7. 679
The habitations empty ! or perchance 878 *Excursion* 8. 266
"The Father, if perchance he still retain 878 *Excursion* 8. 276
Idlers perchance they were,—but in *his* sight ; 878 *Excursion* 8. 279
To-morrow—nay perchance this very hour 884 *Excursion* 9. 27
Nor yet, perchance, translucent Spring, had tolled S.3. 433 **The doubt* 32
And now 'tis mine, perchance for life, dear Vale, K.8. 238 *Recluse* 1.1. 56
And neither pair be broken ? Nay perchance K.8. 244 *Recluse* 1.1.264
Hath furnished matter for a thought ; perchance, K.8. 248 *Recluse* 1.1.443
Perched. *See* **High-perched.**
Perched on the forehead of a jutting crag, 95 *Brothers* 6
Some, perched on stems of stately port 154 *Flower Garden* 39
Behold him perched in ecstasies, 159 *Green Linnet* 27
Fluttered, perched, into a round 171 *Kitten* 70
See, perched upon the naked height 182 *Waggoner* 4. 254
Perched on an olive branch, and heard her cooing 360 **Near Anio's* 2
Perched on whose top the Danish Raven croaks ; 380 *Duddon* 17. 2
Where he is perched, from yon lone Tower 406 *White Doe* 959
Some scattered o'er the level, others perched 823 *Excursion* 5. 89
Percival. Even for Sir Percival was no disclosure ; 373 *Eg. Maid* 272
Percy. Of Umfraville or Percy ere they marched 184 *Yew-trees* 5
To noble Percy ; and a force 401 *White Doe* 465
Shall Percy blush, then, for his name ? 405 *White Doe* 825
Were such your servant Percy ! (be it tried L.1. 97 *Juvenal* 3. 67
Percy's. In Percy's and in Neville's right, 400 *White Doe* 367
At Percy's voice : and Neville sees 403 *White Doe* 690
Perdita. Or there where Perdita and Florizel 701 *Prelude* 8. 142
Perdition. Led by my hand to save thee from perdition ; 63 *Bord.* 1404
To bring perdition on the universe. 67 *Bord.* 1637
Alive or dead, I'll find him. Alive—perdition ! 71 *Bord.* 1881
Perennial. Of that perennial shade, a cloistral place 150 **When, to* 11
And these perennial bowers and murmuring pines 264 **Lady ! the* 12
With their perennial hills ;—but Crime, 298 *Brownie's Cell* 33
Careless of flowers that in perennial blow 376 *Duddon* 1. 5
For recompense—their own perennial bower. 424 *Ecc. Sonn.* 1. 21. 14
Perennial of the ancient hills ; nor less 698 *Prelude* 7. 757
And thus the pathway, by perennial green 881 *Excursion* 8. 455
Perennially. Perennially—beneath whose sable roof 185 *Yew-trees* 23
Perfect. And clanking chains are perfect liberty. 69 *Bord.* 1778
Their busy limbs in perfect rest, 82 †*Mother's Return* 55
Leans smilingly, and sinks into a perfect rest. 103 *Artegal* 48
But thou art no such perfect thing : 111 **Let other* 3
Due requisites a perfect shepherd's staff, 134 *Michael* 183
I love the fir-grove with a perfect love. 151 **When, to* 87
In perfect fitness for its aim, 168 *Wren's Nest* 10
Hours of perfect gladsomeness. 171 *Kitten* 116
A perfect Woman, nobly planned, 186 **She was* 27
But here is perfect joy and pride 204 *Brougham* 50
In perfect shape (whose beauty Time shall spare 250 **Happy the* 2
And perfect harmony of notes, achieved 261 **I heard (alas* 6
With finished sweep into a perfect round, 269 *Malham* 7
Ripening in perfect innocence. 288 *Highland Girl* 27
Their notion of its perfect rest. 289 *Glen-Al.* 22
Books, leisure, perfect freedom, and the talk 304 **I grieved* 10
For one hour's perfect bliss, to tread the grass 306 **Here, on our* 12
For perfect triumph o'er your Enemies. 316 **It was a* 14
With perfect cunning framed as well 397 *White Doe* 94
And perfect sway, through many a thought 413 *White Doe* 1594
For Faith, more perfect still, with which the Lord 436 *Ecc. Sonn.* 2. 30. 9
Our mortal ken ! Inspire a perfect trust 437 *Ecc. Sonn.* 2. 36. 2
What perfect glory ye in Heaven shall reap !— 444 *Ecc. Sonn.* 3. 16. 8
Glad, through a perfect love, a faith sincere 454 **The Sun, that* 23
No perfect cure grows on that bounded field. 455 **Not in the lucid* 25
And if not so, whose perfect joy makes sleep 458 *Sea-shore* 19
The image of its perfect bow. 472 *Ossian* 10
That, with a perfect will in one accord 500 *Humanity* 37
Infinite Power, perfect Intelligence. 519 *Pun. Death* 10. 14
Where joys are perfect—neither wax nor wane. 533 **Once I* 42
For perfect secrecy. 543 *Russ. Fug.* 112
Where he had felt such perfect pleasure once. 563 *Troilus* 46
To peace so perfect that the young behold 572 *Animal Tran.* 13
How perfect was the calm ! it seemed no sleep ; 578 *Peele Castle* 9
More touching still, more perfect was the pleasure, 626 **The confidence* 9
A perfect stillness. Many were the thoughts 633 *Prelude* 1. 70
Whom I, in perfect confidence, might hope 634 *Prelude* 1. 162
And gratitude, and perfect joy of heart— 660 *Prelude* 4. 135
Having a perfect faith in all that passed. 667 *Prelude* 5. 114
Nor would I praise her but in perfect love. 669 *Prelude* 5. 263
The scene before him stands in perfect view 707 *Prelude* 8. 575
Of that great change wandered in perfect faith, 714 *Prelude* 9. 299
And perfect triumph for the better cause. 718 *Prelude* 10. 30
And through a perfect happiness of soul, 736 *Prelude* 12. 162
Perfect him, made imperfect in himself, 749 *Prelude* 14. 224
In perfect wisdom, guiding mightiest power, 804 *Excursion* 4. 195
And his most perfect image in the world. 804 *Excursion* 4. 227

Perfect—*continued.*
Sweet, perfect, to be wished for ! save that here 861 *Excursion* 7. 256
For their sweet purposes, with perfect skill.) 861 *Excursion* 7. 272
Made perfect, and from injury secure. 864 *Excursion* 7. 454
Till perfect mastery crown the pains at last. 880 *Excursion* 8. 415
Blended in perfect stillness, to our sight ! 890 *Excursion* 9. 451
Reflected all in perfect lineaments— S.3. 434 **The doubt* 70
For rest of body, perfect was the spot, K.8. 237 *Recluse* 1.1. 22
Perfect Contentment, Unity entire. K.8. 240 *Recluse* 1.1.151
Love, perfect love ; of so much majesty K.8. 245 *Recluse* 1.1.313
That satisfies and ends in perfect rest. K.8. 255 *Recluse* 1.1.685
Perfècted. For the perfècted Spirits of the just ! 452 *Ecc. Sonn.* 3. 47. 14
Perfection. Thirsting after all perfection, 141 *Arm. Lady* 117
With whose perfection it consists to ordain 514 **Who ponders* 6
That are their own perfection and reward, 684 *Prelude* 6. 612
Contemplating perfection absolute K.8. 245 *Recluse* 1.1.307
Perfections. Of his perfections ; with habitual dread 801 *Excursion* 4. 24
For her benign perfections ; and yet more 825 *Excursion* 5. 195
Perfectly. Too perfectly his headstrong will : 400 *White Doe* 353
More perfectly of purer creatures ;—yet 735 *Prelude* 12. 69
So lonesome, and so perfectly secure ; 776 *Excursion* 2. 354
Perfidious. How they have scourged old foes, perfidious friends : 421 *Ecc. Sonn.* 1. 10. 2
Perfidy. That monstrous perfidy ! Keep down your wrath. 70 *Bord.* 1833
O matchless perfidy ! portentous lust 214 *Dion* 106
Perforce. Will turn perforce and seek for sympathy 64 *Bord.* 1454
We were perforce connected, men whose sway 656 *Prelude* 3. 537
We shall be wise perforce ; and, while inspired 820 *Excursion* 4. 1266
Perforce ? Are we a creature in whom good 829 *Excursion* 5. 469
Perform. Aught that my feeble nature could perform, 105 *Artegal* 179
To attend upon the orphan, and perform 125 *V. and J.* 277
Or looks, or threatening gestures, could perform. 134 *Michael* 193
—Soon did the Knight perform what he had said ; 202 *Hart-leap* 79
That which we *would* perform in arms—we must ! 315 **The Land* 5
Rite to perform, or boon to ask ? 397 *White Doe* 109
That Courage may find something to perform ; 466 *St. Bees* 15
What knowledge can perform, is diligent to learn ; 493 *Hap. War.* 9
Do still perform mysterious offices ! 500 *Humanity* 10
"O Thou great God that dost perform Thy laud 555 *Prioress* 156
Works which the enthusiast would perform with love. 654 *Prelude* 3. 386
Perform their feats. Nor was it mean delight 691 *Prelude* 7. 274
Where senators, tongue-favoured men, perform, 694 *Prelude* 7. 492
A task he was unable to perform. 761 *Excursion* 1. 315
Reclaiming and extirpating, perform 805 *Excursion* 4. 285
Or could perform ; a zealous actor, hired 842 *Excursion* 6. 284
Whence dire dependence. What could she perform 849 *Excursion* 6. 717
Enables them to be and to perform. 875 *Excursion* 8. 53
As zealously perform ! I cannot share 877 *Excursion* 8. 198
Performance. Profession mocks performance. Earth is sick, 828 *Excursion* 5. 378
Performed. An aged utensil, which had performed 133 *Michael* 115
Performed all kinds of labour for his sheep, 138 *Michael* 458
As were performed in man's heroic prime ; 325 *Ode 1814* 141
Shall be performed at pregnant intervals ; 328 *Ode 1815* 65
The vow performed, in cross-legged effigy, 430 *Ecc. Sonn.* 2. 8. 7
And now, his task performed, the flood stands still, 495 *Fact* 35
Thy worship is performed and precious laud ; 552 *Prioress* 4
To be performed, and paid all holy fees. 623 **I find* 5
Perhaps too there performed. Thus long I mused, 633 *Prelude* 1. 80
As aught by wooden images performed 657 *Prelude* 3. 571
What in those days through Britain was performed 728 *Prelude* 11. 55
How oft high service is performed within, 743 *Prelude* 13. 227
For whom this pious service is performed ; 777 *Excursion* 2. 401
So moved he like a shadow that performed 783 *Excursion* 2. 772
If but with hers performed ; climb once again, 808 *Excursion* 4. 493
"Change wide, and deep, and silently performed, 889 *Excursion* 9. 384
By priestly hands, for sacrifice performed 894 *Excursion* 9. 705
And now, its task performed, the flood stands still S.3. 427 **My Son* 6
That which in stealth by Nature was performed K.8. 256 *Recluse* 1.1.733
Performing. She seems performing as she flies 512 **Who rashly* 31
Performs. Performs these delicate services, and therefore 38 *Bord.* 51
Performs its functions ; rarely competent 879 *Excursion* 8. 327
Perfume. Rich steam of sweetest perfume comes and goes. 16 *Desc. Sk.* 345
Perfumes. A garden-plot the desert air perfumes, 607 *Desc.Sk.Quarto* 295
Perhaps. And still, perhaps, with faithless gleam, 9 *Lines : Boat* 7
By seamen, who perhaps themselves had shared 25 *Guilt* 52
'Gainst all that in *his* heart, or theirs perhaps, said nay. 25 *Guilt* 54
And that he hates you !—Pardon me, perhaps 38 *Bord.* 28
Have power to yield ? perhaps he looks elsewhere.— 42 *Bord.* 259
Would there perhaps have gathered the first fruits 49 *Bord.* 663
Thanks for your care. Perhaps it would be useful 49 *Bord.* 670
In such a night as this. Stop, stop. Perhaps, 51 *Bord.* 770
Murder—perhaps asleep, blind, old, alone, 54 *Bord.* 901
And I have felt, more than perhaps becomes me 57 *Bord.* 1112
Perhaps you are his son ? The All-seeing knows, 74 *Bord.* 2072
Perhaps I might ; and, on a winter evening, 98 *Brothers* 189
Perhaps some dungeon hears thee groan, 117 *Affl. Marg.* 50
Perhaps to himself at that moment he said ; 120 *Childless Father* 17
That Johnny may perhaps be drowned ; 128 *Idiot Boy* 179
Or lost, perhaps, and never found ; 128 *Idiot Boy* 180
Johnny perhaps his horse forsook, 128 *Idiot Boy* 214
Perhaps he's climbed into an oak, 128 *Idiot Boy* 223
Perhaps he's gone along the dell, 129 *Idiot Boy* 305
Perhaps, and no unlikely thought ! 129 *Idiot Boy* 317
Perhaps he's turned himself about, 129 *Idiot Boy* 322
And now, perhaps, is hunting sheep, 129 *Idiot Boy* 327

Perished—*continued.*
When good Jemima perished in her bloom ; . . K.8. 275 **These vales* 2
Perishes. In that which perishes : nor will he lend . 257 **No mortal* 10
Of power that perishes, and rights that fade. . . 393 *Inglewood* 14
Till the world perishes, a field for thee ! . . . 527 **Those breathing* 40
Perisheth. Thou strikest—absence perisheth, . . 583 **O for a* 50
Perishing. Perishing yet more swiftly than the flower, 110 **Look at* 8
Even as if bent on perishing. There lives . . 357 *Aquap.* 341
Through park and field, a perishing . . . . 413 *White Doe* 1577
To save the perishing ; and, henceforth, I breathe 852 *Excursion* 6. 923
Periwinkle. The periwinkle trailed its wreaths ; . 482 *Lines : Spring* 10
Perjured. Then, when before the Perjured on his way 475 **Here on their* 7
Permanence. Of kindred permanence, unchanged in form . . . . 740 *Prelude* 13. 37
Permanent. Suffering is permanent, obscure and dark, 65 *Bord.* 1543
Ran permanent and free ; . . . . 194 *Ruth* 213
Of permanent relations, else unknown. . . . 646 *Prelude* 2. 293
For permanent possession, better fruits, . . . 656 *Prelude* 3. 529
Of permanent and universal sway, ... 677 *Prelude* 6. 131
Of marvels, broad-day wonders permanent : . . 689 *Prelude* 7. 128
But hence to my more permanent abode . . . 711 *Prelude* 9. 81
Hangs permanent, and plentiful as wreaths . . 876 *Excursion* 8. 126
Permessus. Where'er Permessus bears an honoured name, ... 574 *Chiabrera* 5. 22
Twine near their loved Permessus.—Finally, . . 576 *Chiabrera* 9. 14
And his Permessus found on Lebanon. . . . . 576 *Chiabrera* 9. 18
Permission. Must come and ask permission when to blow, ... 428 *Ecc. Sonn.* 1. 39. 2
Permission to attend its obsequies. . . . . 853 *Excursion* 6. 972
Of fruit or flower, permission asked or not, . . 856 *Excursion* 6. 1166
Permit. Permit to visit any but a man . . . . 73 *Bord.* 2028
"But should suspense permit the Foe to cry, . . 211 *Laod.* 133
Nor would permit the thin smoke to escape, . . 252 *Picture* 3
Permit his heart to kindle, and to embrace . . 323 **Now that* 12
Permit not for one hour . . . . 508 *May* 90
Will not permit us ; but pursue the mind, . . 704 *Prelude* 8. 337
Permit, like honours, dance and song, are paid . 851 *Excursion* 6. 836
Permits. Well as the wreck I am permits. And you, Sir ? . . . . 43 *Bord.* 336
Permits a second and a darker shade . . . . 421 *Ecc. Sonn.* 1. 11. 4
How slackly, for the absent mind permits . . . 509 *F. Stone* 55
Whose absolute rule permits not to withstand . 518 *Pun. Death* 4. 13
While solitude permits the mind to feel ; . . . 875 *Excursion* 8. 55
Permitted. *See* **Heaven-permitted.**
Reserved, had fate permitted, for support . . 122 *V. and J.* 35
As in life's morn ; permitted to behold, . . . 272 *Devil's Bridge* 9
On the last skirts of their permitted ground, . . 653 *Prelude* 3. 314
Should be permitted, ofttimes, to endure . . . 792 *Excursion* 3. 450
Permitted to descend, and bless mankind. . . 797 *Excursion* 3. 758
Imagination—not permitted here . . . . 813 *Excursion* 4. 819
They also were permitted to receive . . . . 843 *Excursion* 6. 363
This transfer is permitted,—not alone . . . . 865 *Excursion* 7. 522
Are still permitted to extend their pride, . . . 870 *Excursion* 7. 845
Have been permitted to enjoy the dawn ; . . . 888 *Excursion* 9. 283
Of the frail earth, permitted to behold . . . 893 *Excursion* 9. 625
Pernicious. Might overarch thee, from pernicious heat S.3. 433 **The doubt* 35
Perpetrate. To perpetrate his crimes, serve as a Sanctuary . . . . 57 *Bord.* 1087
Perpetual. Where daylight lingers on perpetual snow ; 21 *Desc. Sk.* 582
Of that perpetual weight which on her spirit lay. 32 *Guilt* 450
His arms have a perpetual holiday ; . . . . 96 *Brothers* 107
Perpetual flight, unchecked by earthly ties, . . 153 *Morn. Ex.* 35
And life be one perpetual growth . . . . 224 **'Tis gone* 53
And before *him* doth dawn perpetual run. . . 277 **Haydon ! let* 14
Perpetual emptiness ! unceasing change ! . . . 307 **Great men* 11
Is breathed upon by Hope's perpetual breath ; . 308 **These times* 11
Spared for obeisance from perpetual love, . . . 325 *Ode 1814* 121
For their great deeds, perpetual memory, . . . 325 *Ode 1814* 147
And a perpetual growth secure . . . . . . 373 *Eg. Maid* 262
Fed by the stream with soft perpetual showers, . 377 *Duddon* 6. 7
Perpetual industry. Sublime Recluse ! . . . 424 *Ecc. Sonn.* 1. 23. 9
Kept in perpetual verdure by the steam . . . 464 *Derwent* 8
Perpetual lessons of forbearance yield ; . . . 501 *Humanity* 106
Laws that lay under Heaven's perpetual ban . . 514 **Portentous change* 12
Of a perpetual dawn from brow and cheek . . 525 *Epist. Beaumont* 253
To the perpetual silence of the grave. . . . . 573 *Chiabrera* 2. 18
Perpetual benediction : not indeed . . . . . 589 *Immortality* 138
Which spake perpetual logic to my soul, . . . 651 *Prelude* 3. 164
In silence visible and perpetual calm. . . . 681 *Prelude* 6. 429
Living amid the same perpetual whirl . . . . 698 *Prelude* 7. 725
In one perpetual progress smooth and bright ?— 748 *Prelude* 14. 135
Or the perpetual warbling that prevails . . . 790 *Excursion* 3. 321
Perpetual sabbath ; come, disease and want ; . 802 *Excursion* 4. 58
Carrying through ether, in perpetual round, . . 811 *Excursion* 4. 703
Perpetual, multitudinous ! Finally, ... 876 *Excursion* 8. 142
Perpetual sacrifice. Even thus of old . . . . 877 *Excursion* 8. 185
What want we ? have we not perpetual streams, K.8. 240 *Recluse* 1. 1. 126
Is a perpetual harmony, and dance . . . . K.8. 242 *Recluse* 1. 1. 202
Perpetually. Is present and perpetually abides . . 118 *Maternal Grief* 4
Perpetually recumbent ; Statues—man, . . . 689 *Prelude* 7. 133
We are not so ;—perpetually we touch . . . 782 *Excursion* 2. 736
To be perpetually attacked by foes . . . . 839 *Excursion* 6. 54
Perplex. Perplex the wise, the strong to overthrow ; 428 *Ecc. Sonn.* 1. 39. 7
Perplex the Church ; but be thou firm,—be true . 465 **Pastor and* 6
With mazy rules perplex the weary mind ; . . 619 *School Ex.* 50
Perplex her mind ; but, wise as women are . . 736 *Prelude* 12. 156
To unsettle or perplex it : yet with pain . . . 804 *Excursion* 4. 199
Perplexed. *See* **Perplext.**
Perplexed and comfortless he gazed around, . . 24 *Guilt* 24

Perplexed—*continued.*
I am perplexed. What hast thou heard or seen ? 42 *Bord.* 260
Which way soe'er I turn, I am perplexed. . . 53 *Bord.* 878
Such as *he* is, and sore perplexed as I am, . . 62 *Bord.* 1392
He listens, puzzled, sore perplexed, ... 81 †*Mother's Return* 15
In such perplexed and intricate array, . . . 150 **When, to* 35
—Perplexed, and longing to be comforted, . . 197 *Resolution* 117
Becoming less and less perplexed, ... 242 *P. B.* 547
Perplexed the good man's gentle soul. . . . 244 *P. B.* 755
Henceforth a humbler course perplexed and slow ; 359 **Those old* 9
Perplexed as if between a splendour lost . . . 392 **Though joy* 5
Perplexed her fingers seem, ... 479 *Somnamb.* 105
At consciences perplexed with scruples nice ! . . 514 **Portentous change* 4
Yet often is perplexed and cannot part . . . 662 *Prelude* 4. 263
That to the spot which had perplexed us first . 683 *Prelude* 6. 580
Now disbelieving ; endlessly perplexed . . . 731 *Prelude* 11. 298
Perplexed the bodily sense. He had received . 758 *Excursion* 1. 139
Struggling against it ; with a soul perplexed, . 772 *Excursion* 2. 70
So saying, round he looked, as if perplexed ; . 786 *Excursion* 3. 20
Perplexed with currents ; of his weakness sick ; 798 *Excursion* 3. 867
At once—or, not recoiling, is perplexed— . . . 810 *Excursion* 4. 625
Perplexing. *See* **Thought-perplexing.**
His guilt a thousand-fold. 'Tis most perplexing : 48 *Bord.* 592
Through what perplexing labyrinths, abrupt . . 800 *Excursion* 3. 982
Perplexity. And somewhat of a sad perplexity, . . 206 *Tintern* 60
Is such perplexity confined : . . . . . . 398 *White Doe* 207
In listlessness from vain perplexity, ... 636 *Prelude* 1. 266
Perplext. *See* **Perplexed.**
The Mastiff wondering, and perplext . . . . 179 *Waggoner* 3. 60
Persecute. As fathers persecute rebellious sons, . 321 **Humanity, delighting* 19
Persecuted. Concealed the persecuted boy, . . . 180 *Waggoner* 4. 49
To whom all persecuted men retreat ; . . . . 327 *Ode 1815* 48
To shelter persecuted men : . . . . 408 *White Doe* 1095
Persecutes. Remembrance persecutes, and Hope betrays ; . . . . 259 **Weak is* 2
Persecuting. Dread of the persecuting sword, remorse, ... 791 *Excursion* 3. 373
Persecution. That persecution, blind with rage extreme, ... 420 *Ecc. Sonn.* 1. 7. 11
He taught, till persecution chased him thence, . 431 *Ecc. Sonn.* 2. 11. 10
Where Persecution decks with ghastly smiles . . 617 *Desc. Sk. Quarto* 798
Of persecution, and the Covenant—times . . . 759 *Excursion* 1. 175
Then, nor till then, shall persecution cease, . . 894 *Excursion* 9. 649
Persepolis. Rites such as yet Persepolis presents . 346 *Processions* 7
Of famed Persepolis ; each following each, . . 394 **No more* 9
Alcairo, Babylon, or Persepolis ; . . . . . 688 *Prelude* 7. 81
Perseverance. Till we by perseverance gain the top 496 **A little* 25
By Roman perseverance, are destroyed, . . . 549 **The massy* 2
By perseverance in this track of life . . . . 761 *Excursion* 1. 335
Not failing, perseverance from their steps . . 820 *Excursion* 4. 1245
By perseverance in the course prescribed." . . 841 *Excursion* 6. 191
The PATH OF PERSEVERANCE." "Thou from whom 842 *Excursion* 6. 254
To dread his perseverance in the chase. . . . 868 *Excursion* 7. 746
A perseverance fed ; almost a soul . . . . . 877 *Excursion* 8. 203
And perseverance their deserved reward. . . . 889 *Excursion* 9. 382
Persevere. Yet still I persevere, and find them where I may." . . . . 197 *Resolution* 126
And strength to persevere. . . . . 224 **'Tis gone* 48
For, strength to persevere and to support, . . 848 *Excursion* 6. 663
And persevere in good, that they shall rise, . . 893 *Excursion* 9. 645
Persevered. Who in the field of contest persevered, 656 *Prelude* 3. 499
Persevering. He urged his persevering suit in vain. 103 *Artegal* 85
The persevering wedge of tyranny . . . . . 124 *V. and J.* 172
Meanwhile the persevering Ass . . . . . 247 *P. B.* 981
Looks forward, persevering to the last, . . . 494 *Hap. War.* 75
It is most serious : persevering rain . . . . 783 *Excursion* 2. 781
May be, through pains and persevering hope, . . 827 *Excursion* 5. 306
Perseveringly. As long and perseveringly to mourn 803 *Excursion* 4. 155
Persian. Of Persian mornings would ye fill, and stand 230 *Clouds* 26
Round the moist marge of Persian fountains cling ; 376 *Duddon* 1. 6
Whether the Persian—zealous to reject . . . 811 *Excursion* 4. 671
Which Persian kings might envy ; and thy meek S.3. 433 **The doubt* 19
Persist. If thou persist, and, scorning moderation, 505 *Warning* 147
Persisted. Persisted openly that death alone . . 123 *V. and J.* 116
Persists. The witless shepherd who persists to drive 655 *Prelude* 3. 406
Person. I think, good Woman, you are the very person . . . . 45 *Bord.* 478
Person, and place—the where, the when, the how, 58 *Bord.* 1155
Who, casting as I thought a guilty Person . . 76 *Bord.* 2210
Majestic in her person, tall and straight ; . . . 119 *Sailor's Mother* 5
His person to the law, was lodged in prison, . . 123 *V. and J.* 134
She towered, fit person for a Queen . . . . 190 *Beggars* 10
And flowers are on his person thrown . . . . 213 *Dion* 37
Thy warlike person with the staff and scrip ; . . 427 *Ecc. Sonn.* 1. 35. 3
And the whole person. Words have something told 509 *F. Stone* 73
His mien and person, nor was free, in sooth, . . 688 *Prelude* 7. 95
The beauty of his person, doing wrong . . . 711 *Prelude* 9. 145
Or person singled out among the rest, ... 713 *Prelude* 9. 279
In person and appearance ; but her house . . 768 *Excursion* 1. 821
Cast out, alike of person and of thing. . . . 775 *Excursion* 2. 242
He answered, "to the Person suited well, . . . 778 *Excursion* 2. 459
A meagre person, tall, and in a garb . . . 779 *Excursion* 2. 500
Personage. Was with this goodly Personage ; . . 404 *White Doe* 738
Personal. Or personal memory of his own deep wrongs, ... 126 *V. and J.* 304
To season my fireside with personal talk,— . . 488 *Pers. Talk* 2
There find I personal themes, a plenteous store, . 488 *Pers. Talk* 37
That did not leave us free from personal fear ; . 686 *Prelude* 6. 720
By personal ambition unenslaved, ... 688 *Prelude* 7. 63

Pity—*continued.*
No pity asking, on the group she gazed . . . 34 *Guilt* 562
He cried—" Do pity me! That thou shouldst live 35 *Guilt* 620
—Pity that our young Chief will have no part . 37 *Bord.* 4
Pity the Maiden did not wait a while; . . . 43 *Bord.* 326
I bore her in my arms; her looks won pity; . . 53 *Bord.* 846
Of doubt is insupportable. Pity, the facts . . 53 *Bord.* 880
Compassion!—pity!—pride can do without them; 65 *Bord.* 1553
I pity, can forgive, you; but those wretches— . 70 *Bord.* 1832
Mercy! I said I know not what—oh pity me— . 77 *Bord.* 2247
Pity me, I am haunted;—thrice this day . . 77 *Bord.* 2249
Then pity crossed the path of my resolve: . . 77 *Bord.* 2265
" He took thee in his arms, and in pity brought thee home: . . . . 87 *Pet-lamb* 37
Dear caresses given in pity, ... 94 *Westmoreland Girl* 37
They pity me, and not my grief. . . . . . 117 *Affl. Marg.* 74
Remain unpitied, pity is not in man. . . . 124 *V. and J.* 199
The pity which was then in every heart . . 138 *Michael* 463
Oh, gracious Heaven, in pity make her thine! . 139 *Widow* 28
Women, in your land, may pity . . . . . 139 *Arm. Lady* 15
No more of pity for regrets . . . . . . 165 *Parrot* 21
Stop," it exclaimed, " and pity me!" . . . . 176 *Waggoner* 1. 220
And less in pity than in wonder, ... 176 *Waggoner* 1. 221
Celestial pity I again implore;— . . . . . 209 *Laod.* 5
By the just Gods whom no weak pity moved, . 212 *Laod.* 160
Where Pity sheds sweet tears—and Love, . . . 215 *Kirkstone* 70
For terror, joy, or pity, ... 234 *Power of Sound* 161
And, did not pity touch my breast . . . . . 236 *P. B.* 18
In pity to this poor drowned man. . . . . . 243 *P. B.* 595
For God took pity on the Boy, ... 295 *Highland Boy* 23
And Pity sanctifies the Verse . . . . . . 302 *Yarrow V.* 37
Of pity pleading from the heart in vain— . . 328 *Ode 1815* 119
Nor pity idly born, ... 334 **In Bruges* 26
And with regret and useless pity haunt . . . 336 *Staub-bach* 13
For unasked alms in pity given. . . . . . 342 *Ital. Itin.* 56
But in sweet pity; and can hear . . . . . 344 **How blest* 12
Vouchsafed in pity or in wrath assigned; . . . 347 *Processions* 70
Destroy in pity, or with care remove. . . . 363 **Grieve for* 8
Part from thee without pity dyed in shame: . . 366 **Fair Land* 3
Still pity to this last retreat . . . . . . 390 *Highland Broach* 45
And meet their pity face to face; . . . . . 401 *White Doe* 487
Me did a reverent pity move . . . . . . 409 *White Doe* 1249
To Marmaduke, cut off from pity! . . . . . 411 *White Doe* 1368
In love and pity at her feet; . . . . . . 416 *White Doe* 1825
Is tender pity then of no avail? . . . . . 423 *Ecc. Sonn.* 1. 20. 3
Of pity or fear; and More's gay genius played . 435 *Ecc. Sonn.* 2. 26. 12
Pity that such a promise e'er should prove . . 461 **Who but is* 9
Looked down with pity upon eyes beguiled . . 465 **The cattle* 13
The heart to pity, train the mind in care . . 468 *St. Bees* 131
Where be the wretched ones, the sights for pity? 475 *Greenock* 4
A mild domestic pity kept its place, ... 523 *Epist. Beaumont* 145
Of heaven in pity visiting the place. . . . . 525 *Epist. Beaumont* 263
Where pity, to the mind conveyed . . . . . 530 *Gleaner* 13
But wonder, pity, soon were quelled; . . . . 545 *Russ. Fug.* 321
" With Mother's pity in her breast enclosed . . 555 *Prioress* 142
Old Man! whom so oft I with pity have eyed, . 572 *Avarice* 45
That outcast of pity behold. . . . . . . 620 *Convict* 12
Of pity cast from inward tenderness . . . . 646 *Prelude* 2. 249
This heard, I said, in pity, " Come with me." . 665 *Prelude* 4. 426
Pity the tree.—Poor human vanity, ... 670 *Prelude* 5. 329
Daily upon me, mixed with pity too . . . . 717 *Prelude* 9. 507
Oh, pity and shame! with those confederate Powers! . . . . 722 *Prelude* 10. 265
Of pity and sorrow to a state of being . . . . 724 *Prelude* 10. 450
With unavailing pity. Rich in love . . . . 772 *Excursion* 2. 54
To my benign Companion,—" Pity 'tis . . . 781 *Excursion* 2. 619
Pity and scorn, and melancholy pride, ... 788 *Excursion* 3. 142
Of scornful pity be the just reward . . . . 791 *Excursion* 3. 334
At others' tears in pity; and in scorn . . . 797 *Excursion* 3. 810
But spare your pity, if there be in me . . . 800 *Excursion* 3. 965
This triumph, yet the pity of my heart . . . 805 *Excursion* 4. 302
Or move the pity of unthinking minds, . . . 813 *Excursion* 4. 835
Though bound to earth by ties of pity and love, . 820 *Excursion* 4. 1296
To pity dead, the oppressor and the opprest; . . 836 *Excursion* 5. 940
Then, Pity could have scarcely found on earth . 840 *Excursion* 6. 131
How would you pity her who yonder rests; . . 842 *Excursion* 6. 271
Where love and pity tenderly unite . . . . 848 *Excursion* 6. 642
Of mutual pity and forgiveness, sweet . . . . 851 *Excursion* 6. 877
Give way to words of pity or complaint, . . . 854 *Excursion* 6. 1044
Abashed, and tender pity overawed." . . . . 865 *Excursion* 7. 515
With pity mixed, astonishment with scorn!" . . 870 *Excursion* 7. 831
Pity away, soon shall ye quake with *fear!* . . 870 *Excursion* 7. 838
For the least boon that pity can bestow. . . . 879 *Excursion* 8. 361
That seemed to pity what he could not spare. . 883 *Excursion* 8. 571
" Ah! what a pity were it to disperse, . . . 890 *Excursion* 9. 452
Ill neighbourhood—pity that this should be— . K.8. 246 *Recluse* 1. 1. 356
Where pity shrinks from unremitting calls, . . K.8. 253 *Recluse* 1. 1. 598

Pitying. No, not the pitying moon! And perish so. 75 *Bord.* 2137
Bright boon of pitying Heaven!—alas, . . . 112 *Lament* 8
For such, by pitying Angels and by Spirits . . 119 *Maternal Grief* 74
Of pitying Heaven, at least were free . . . 192 *Seq. Beggars* 39
Inly illumined by Heaven's pitying love; . . . 280 **Oh what* 12
Love pitying innocence, not long to last, . . . 280 **Oh what* 13
And oh for Thee, by pitying grace . . . . 285 *Grave of Burns* 73
Of pitying human nature? Once again . . . 318 **Ah! where* 5
No pitying voice commands a halt, ... 322 **Humanity, delighting* 32
Wharf shall be to pitying hearts . . . . . 494 *Force of Prayer* 39

Pitying—*continued.*
Can the pitying spirit doubt . . . . . . 502 **Like a* 23
A guardian Spirit sent from pitying Heaven, . . 541 *Grace Darl.* 73
Till pitying Saints conduct her bark . . . . 544 *Russ. Fug.* 235
Weak sinful folk, that God, with pitying eye, . 556 *Prioress* 237
But doubly pitying Nature loves to show'r . . 602 *Desc. Sk. Quarto* 13
Of blessèd angels, pitying human cares. . . . 839 *Excursion* 6. 52
Who saw enough for blame and pitying love. . . 843 *Excursion* 6. 362
Think not, that, pitying him, I could forget . . 886 *Excursion* 9. 161
The fair Narcissus, by some pitying God . . S.3. 434 **The doubt* 81

Pity's. Then, they, for Christian pity's sake, . 412 *White Doe* 1520

Pivot. Upon the pivot of his skull . . . . . 241 *P. B.* 414
Upon the pivot of his skull . . . . 241 *P. B.* 419

Placable. Is placable—because occasions rise . . 493 *Hap. War.* 21
And in the kinder spirit; placable, ... 729 *Prelude* 11. 158

Place. *See* **Abiding-place, Birthplace, Breathing-place, Burial-place, Common-place, Couching-place, Death-place, Door-place, Dwelling-place, Halting-place, Hiding-place, Market-place, Mooring-place, Parting-place, Resting-place, Sheltering-place, Striding-place, Trysting-place.**
Shine, Poet! in thy place, and be content:— . v **If thou indeed* 3
Shine, Poet! in thy place, and be content. . . v **If thou indeed* 16
Feels not the spirit of the place control, . . 15 *Desc. Sk.* 291
From that day forth no place to him could be . 25 *Guilt* 73
Of human shelter in that dreary place. . . . 27 *Guilt* 158
Should hold a place, as if 'twere robbery, . . 38 *Bord.* 57
And nowhere upon earth is place so fit . . . 49 *Bord.* 656
And very superstition of the place, ... 49 *Bord.* 661
The fittest place? He is growing pitiful. . . 51 *Bord.* 750
In such a weary night, and such a place. . . 52 *Bord.* 806
I was alarmed. No wonder; this is a place . . 52 *Bord.* 812
Has been but comfortless; and yet that place, . 53 *Bord.* 860
There are the strangest echoes in that place! . . 55 *Bord.* 962
No! this is not the place to hear the tale: . . 56 *Bord.* 1010
Person, and place—the where, the when, the how, 58 *Bord.* 1155
Commend me to the place. If a man should die . 61 *Bord.* 1298
Oh that I had but strength to reach the place! . 67 *Bord.* 1656
This is a dismal place—well—that is well— . . 67 *Bord.* 1674
And in that miserable place we left him, . . . 68 *Bord.* 1724
Drove by the place of my retreat: three nights . 69 *Bord.* 1772
Their veil, but not for me—'twas in fit place . 70 *Bord.* 1838
Oh! lift me up and carry me to the place. . . 72 *Bord.* 2010
—Yet seek him,—and what shall you find in the place? . . . . 80 †*Address: Child* 16
Kilve, thought I, was a favoured place, . . . 86 *Anecdote* 23
Right towards the lamb she looked; and from a shady place . . . . 87 *Pet-lamb* 17
With soft illumination cheered the dimness of that place. . . . . 92 *Poet's Dream* 12
What shall it be? a mirthful throng? or that holy place and calm . . . . 92 *Poet's Dream* 23
And yet, some changes must take place among you: 97 *Brothers* 127
(It is the loneliest place of all these hills) . . 97 *Brothers* 140
Among these rocks, and every hollow place . . 99 *Brothers* 274
Lay stretched at ease; but, passing by the place 101 *Brothers* 371
A place in which he could not bear to live: . . 102 *Brothers* 426
How changed from him who, born to highest place, 103 *Artegal* 94
Who to this blessed place . . . . 104 *Artegal* 151
Within this realm a place of safe retreat; . . . 104 *Artegal* 163
Did place upon his brother's head the crown, . . 105 *Artegal* 222
And O most constant, yet most fickle Place, . . 107 *Farewell* 41
No livelier love in such a place could be: . . 108 *Indolence* 67
My heart again is in its place! . . . . . . 121 *Emigrant Mother* 84
To some remote and solitary place, ... 123 *V. and J.* 108
Find place within his bosom.—Once again . . 124 *V. and J.* 171
Shocked at his savage aspect, from the place . . 126 *V. and J.* 298
And soon as they had reached the place he stopped, 136 *Michael* 330
When thou return'st, thou in this place wilt see . 137 *Michael* 413
Of her who in my heart still holds her ancient place. 141 *Arm. Lady* 114
When they have cause to speak of this wild place, 146 **It was an* 46
The loneliest place we have among the clouds. . 148 **There is an* 13
With such communion that no place on earth . 148 **There is an* 15
Either to be divided from the place . . . . 149 **A narrow* 30
The same admonishment, have called the place . 149 **A narrow* 76
Of that perennial shade, a cloistral place . . . 150 **When, to* 11
To thy banqueting place in the sky. . . . . 159 **Up with me* 15
They will have a place in story: . . . . . 160 **Pansies, lilies* 6
In the lane;—there's not a place, ... 160 **Pansies, lilies* 46
A *Speedwell* may not want its place. . . . . 164 **Fair Lady* 20
And this vale, so blithe a place; . . . . . 171 *Kitten* 52
The place to Benjamin right well . . . . . 174 *Waggoner* 1. 83
And after farewell to the place, ... 176 *Waggoner* 1. 274
This little place may well be dizzy! . . . . 177 *Waggoner* 2. 63
Back to her place the ship he led; . . . . . 178 *Waggoner* 2. 160
That in this uneventful place, ... 182 *Waggoner* 4. 222
An unsubstantial, faery place; . . . . . . 184 **O blithe* 31
In many a secret place . . . . 187 **Three years* 27
The Showman chooses well his place, 'tis Leicester's busy Square; . . . . 189 *Star-gazers* 5
And there she begs at one steep place . . . . 194 *Ruth* 238
Yet it befell that, in this lonely place, ... 196 *Resolution* 52
This is a lonesome place for one like you." . . 196 *Resolution* 89
While he was talking thus, the lonely place, . . 197 *Resolution* 127
A place of love for damsels that are coy. . . . 201 *Hart-leap* 60
More doleful place did never eye survey; . . . 202 *Hart-leap* 114
And what this place might be I then enquired. . 202 *Hart-leap* 120
" A jolly place," said he, " in times of old! . . 202 *Hart-leap* 123
What cause the Hart might have to love this place, 203 *Hart-leap* 147
Nor did he change; but kept in lofty place . . 205 *Brougham* 167

Place—*continued.*
Around the porch, and seems, in that trim place, 855 Excursion 6. 1150
To place those hillocks in that lonely guise. . . 858 Excursion 7. 41
No wish for wealth had place within his mind ; . 864 Excursion 7. 426
Whose place of rest is near yon ivied porch. . . 864 Excursion 7. 487
From what the place afforded, have been given ; . 874 Excursion 8. 20
Or easier links connecting place with place) . . 876 Excursion 8. 108
—We enter—by the Lady of the place . . . 881 Excursion 8. 500
In awful sovereignty ; a place of power, . . . 885 Excursion 9. 55
Their place ; and genuine piety descend, . . . 889 Excursion 9. 361
Their place I took—and for a grateful office . . 891 Excursion 9. 483
Of some thick wood, her place of covert, cleaves . 891 Excursion 9. 493
They ceased not to surround us ; change of place, 891 Excursion 9. 509
Such product, and such pastime, did the place . 892 Excursion 9. 545
Finds some place or other . . . . S.3. 423 Tinker 21
Smooth summer dreams, old favours of the place, S.3. 436 *The doubt 171
By her side I'll take my place, ... S.3. 437 *I, whose 19
In such a lonely place. . . . . K.8. 223 *There is a shapeless 6
An island in the brook. It was a place . . . K.8. 229 *I will 140
Since that day forth the place to him—*to me* . . K.8. 237 Recluse 1.1. 46
They who are dwellers in this holy place . . . K.8. 244 Recluse 1.1.277
Who here abide, the persons like the place. . . K.8. 245 Recluse 1.1.315
Not want, for this, your own subordinate place . K.8. 251 Recluse 1.1.543
In the bare twigs, each little budding place . . K.8. 252 Recluse 1.1.565

Placed. They placed me—there to end life's pilgrimage, ... 35 Guilt 583
And placed him at his mother's side ; . . . . 85 Shepherd-boys 96
Where he, in his poor self so weak, by Providence was placed. . . . . 91 Norman Boy 28
And on the vacant throne his worthier Brother placed. . . . . 103 Artegal 81
And placed together near our rocky Well. . . . 106 Farewell 24
He as a watchman oftentimes was placed . . . 134 Michael 185
Till a winter's noon-day placed her buried Son 139 Widow 16
—Within our fearless reach are placed . . . . 216 Enterprise 83
And that, so placed, my Nurslings may requite . 281 Valedict. 6
What treasures would have then been placed . . 285 Grave of Burns 55
Their God, and placed their trust in human pride ! 321 *Humanity, delighting 18
All our hope is placed in Thee ; . . . . . . 336 *Jesu ! bless 23
Well judged the Friend who placed it there . . 337 Thun 5
Mercy has placed within our reach . . . . . 337 *Oh Life 11
For dignity not placed beyond her reach, . . . 357 Aquap. 344
Fit to be placed in that pure diadem ; . . . . 358 Aquap. 357
And in the pearly shallop placed, ... 371 Eg. Maid 143
Some Statue, placed amid these regions old . . 379 Duddon 15. 6
Man placed him here, and God, he knows, can save. 392 Daniel 14
Placed there—that he might go before . . . 410 White Doe 1324
Were under her dominion placed. . . . . . 413 White Doe 1582
This Homestead, placed where nothing could be seen, ... 470 *Did pangs 4
Of conscience souls are placed by deeds that lack 475 *Here on their 5
The power of years—pre-eminent, and placed 477 Long Meg 6
Placed in the little boat, then o'er the deep . . 541 Grace Darl. 80
Had placed his staff across the broad smooth stone 566 Cumb. Beg. 7
The Grison gypsey here her tent has plac'd, . . 605 Desc.Sk.Quarto 188
Hast placed me high above my best deserts, . . 653 Prelude 3. 318
Decked with refreshments had this child been placed, ... 692 Prelude 7. 357
Here placed to be the inheritor of heaven, . . . 704 Prelude 8. 336
The gift which God has placed within his power, . 714 Prelude 9. 356
Placed on this earth to love and understand, . . 750 Prelude 14. 278
A folded paper, lying as if placed . . . . . 766 Excursion 1. 667
That must have placed it there ; and ere that day 766 Excursion 1. 673
So placed, to be shut out from all the world ! . 776 Excursion 2. 332
Hath placed beyond these penetrable bounds, . 789 Excursion 3. 219
Placed, among flowery gardens curtained round . 791 Excursion 3. 346
Not placed by fortune within easy reach . . . 794 Excursion 3. 586
Had fixed his milder loyalty, and placed . . . 844 Excursion 6. 428
There, where *they* placed them who in conscience prized . . . . 844 Excursion 6. 430
Not seeking from that source, she placed her trust 849 Excursion 6. 723
"And may it not be hoped, that, placed by age . 885 Excursion 9. 81
When, heretofore, I placed before your sight . . 886 Excursion 9. 156

Places. *See* **Hiding-places, Resting-places.**
When my father found thee first in places far away ; . . . . 87 Pet-lamb 34
Above and round the sacred places . . . . 144 *Driven in 56
Strange places, coverts unendeared, ... 165 Parrot 33
And sylvan places heaved a pensive sigh ; . . 214 Dion 111
When she is, far from these wild places, . . . 222 Triad 152
I see the places where they once were known, . 256 Decay of Piety 9
For sheltered places, bosoms, nooks, and bays, . 292 *Degenerate Douglas 12
Here, there, and in all places at one hour. . . 315 *Advance—come 14
Of consecrated places, ... 324 Ode 1814 101
And, in the desert places of the earth, ... 325 Ode 1814 133
In shady places, to proclaim . . . . . . 348 *Lulled by 59
Places forsaken now, though loving still . . . 353 Aquap. 50
Looks up in all places, for joy or for rest, . . 365 Vallomb. 39
But say, among these holy places, ... 397 White Doe 106
To distant places and unknown. . . . . . 414 White Doe 1616
All Powers and Places that abhor the light . . 513 *Said Secrecy 12
Came as he rode by places of the town . . . 563 Troilus 45
Had in high places built her lodge ; though mean 637 Prelude 1. 328
And Souls of lonely places ! can I think . . . 639 Prelude 1. 466
In lonely places ; if a throng was near . . . . 652 Prelude 3. 231
And all known places and familiar sights . . . 793 Excursion 3. 508
That occupy their places, and, though oft . . . 848 Excursion 6. 703
For men who in such places, feeling there . . . K.8. 226 *I will 70

Placid. Upon the bosom of a placid lake. . . . 80 *Loving she 21
I may not trust thy placid cheer ! . . . . . . 112 Lament 9
For endless constancy, and placid truth ; . . . 122 V. and J. 33
Say, Dora ! tell me, by yon placid moon, . . . 165 Parrot 41
When first they met the placid light of thine, . 256 *No mortal 2
And sage content, and placid melancholy ; . . 262 *Not Love 10
(Which even the placid innocence of death . . 274 Infant M. 9
Could scarcely make more placid, heaven more bright) . . . . 274 Infant M. 10
In the wife's smile ; and in the placid sky ; . . 315 *The Land 7
But hark—the summons !—down the placid lake . 332 Ode : Thanks. 205
Around his placid temples curled ; . . . . . 341 Ital. Itin. 13
Rough as the past ; where Thou, of placid mien, 381 Duddon 20. 8
The day is placid in its going, ... 397 Whit Doe 148
Touched by accordance of thy placid cheer, . . 460 *Wanderer ! that 56
In placid beauty and sublime content ! . . . 495 Fact 37
Thus, gifted Friend, but with the placid brow . 529 *Those breathing 133
The true Ascanius steep'd in placid rest ; . . . 624 Æneid 48
'Twas autumn, and a clear and placid day, . . 633 Prelude 1. 65
And placid under-countenance, first endeared ; . 678 Prelude 6. 227
And placid, and took nothing from the man . . 714 Prelude 9. 320
In strength, reflecting from its placid breast . 749 Prelude 14. 201
Did, in the placid clearness of the night, . . . 798 Excursion 3. 859
To mark *their* placid state, who never heard . . 806 Excursion 4. 378
Embosomed happiness, and placid love ; . . . 828 Excursion 5. 414
Anchors her placid beauty. Not a leaf, . . . 842 Excursion 6. 295
So placid, so inactive, as content ; . . . . . 849 Excursion 6. 731
Sails in smooth weather by the placid coast . . 882 Excursion 8. 507
Who, in some placid day of summer, looks . . 885 Excursion 9. 57
The silvery lake is streaked with placid blue ; . 890 Excursion 9. 421
In placid beauty and entire content. . . . . S.3. 427 *My Son 8
On the broad water's placid breast— . . . . S.3. 438 *My Lord 22
And placid way of life, and constant love . . . K.8. 243 Recluse 1.1.250
And entertained as in a placid sleep. . . . . K.8. 245 Recluse 1.1.308

Placing. And placing trust in privilege confirmed . 872 Excursion 7. 991

Plague. *See* **Pharaoh-plague.**
And ravenous plague, all perished : every tear . 30 Guilt 304
Plague on my memory, him I had forgotten. . . 60 Bord. 1256
Hedge in the life of every pest and plague . . 66 Bord. 1582
Or plague the fancy 'mid the sculptured shows . 380 Duddon 16. 2
To plague her beating heart ; and there is one . 439 Ecc. Sonn. 2. 42. 2
A plague on your languages, German and Norse ! 484 *A plague 1
A worse affliction in the plague of war : . . . 764 Excursion 1. 539
Plague from this union spread, whose subtle bane 775 Excursion 2. 243
For, like a plague, will memory break out ; . . 798 Excursion 3. 847
As by a plague. Yet no rapacious plague . . 861 Excursion 7. 252
Now, when oppression, like the Egyptian plague . 890 Excursion 9. 409

Plagued. Baffled and plagued by a mind that every hour . . . . 636 Prelude 1. 257
Plagued with uncharitable thoughts the church ; . 845 Excursion 6. 467

Plagues. "The pains and plagues that on our heads came down, ... 29 Guilt 298
But passions spread like plagues, and thousands wild . . . . 435 Ecc. Sonn. 2. 29. 12
Into their contraries the petty plagues . . . 835 Excursion 5. 860

Plaid. Against an equal host that wore the plaid, . 293 Killicranky 3
In crimson stockings, tartan plaid, ... 295 Highland Boy 32

Plaided. The old grey stones the plaided chief surveys, ... 608 Desc.Sk.Quarto 359
In plaided vest,—his fellow-countrymen. . . . 774 Excursion 2. 177

Plain. In thoughtless gaiety I coursed the plain, . 2 Ev. Wk. 21
The lone black fir, forsakes the faded plain ; . . 8 Ev. Wk. 310
Where beasts and men together o'er the plain . 13 Desc. Sk. 169
On Zutphen's plain, or on that highland dell, . 15 Desc. Sk. 295
With stern composure watches to the plain— . 19 Desc. Sk. 516
A Traveller on the skirt of Sarum's Plain . . . 24 Guilt 1
Or whistling thro' thin grass along the unfurrowed plain. . . . . 25 Guilt 36
Rolled at his back along the living plain ; . . . 25 Guilt 88
The Plain resounding to the whirlwind's sweep, . 26 Guilt 120
And now the walls are named the "Dead House" of the plain. . . . . 27 Guilt 153
"Peaceful as this immeasurable plain . . . . 30 Guilt 334
And, for yourself, in plain terms he asserts . . 38 Bord. 64
'Tis plain he loves the Maid, and what he said 41 Bord. 231
With which he taints her ear ;—for a plain reason ; 42 Bord. 263
The punishment they merit. All is plain : . . 42 Bord. 267
Twelve honest men, plain men, would set us right ; 53 Bord. 882
These trepidations ? Plain it is that Heaven . 55 Bord. 999
Or on some vast and solitary plain . . . . . 56 Bord. 1012
Then plain it is as day that eyes were made . . 60 Bord. 1273
A plain confession, such as leaves no doubt, . . 63 Bord. 1420
Hard by a Man I met, who, from plain proofs . 75 Bord. 2188
It caught his eye, he saw it plain— . . . . 86 Anecdote 50
No symbols, Sir, to tell us that plain tale : . . 98 Brothers 181
And, scouring toward him o'er the grassy plain, . 104 Artegal 110
And, while they stood upon the plain apart, . . 104 Artegal 128
And their plain home-made cheese. Yet when the meal . . . . 132 Michael 102
But only give some plain directions . . . . 142 †Lov. and Lik. 3
Thrills not the less the bosom of the plain : . . 153 Morn. Ex. 46
And transient feignings with plain truth . . . 170 Rural Ill. 33
Vainly glitter hill and plain, ... 171 Kitten 85
Along the smooth unpathwayed plain, ... 180 Waggoner 4. 24
While Grasmere smoothed her liquid plain . . 182 Waggoner 4. 232
Can lie upon the plain . . . . 184 *O blithe 26
The Girl, in rock and plain, ... 187 *Three years 9
As might from India's farthest plain . . . . 190 *Lyre ! though 2
With plain and manifest intent . . . . . . 197 Thorn 19
Her state to any eye was plain ; . . . . . 199 Thorn 12

Plain—*continued.*
Whene'er you look on it, 'tis plain . . . . . 200 *Thorn* 219
But plain it is the Thorn is bound . . . . . 200 *Thorn* 233
And forth I leapt upon the sandy plain ; . . . 210 *Laod.* 47
The gazers feel ; and, rushing to the plain, . . 213 *Dion* 27
Hope, pointing to the cultured plain, ... 215 *Kirkstone* 78
Paired with the ostrich, o'er the plain ; . . . 216 *Enterprise* 33
Their own fair forms, upon the glimmering plain , 218 *Recluse* I. I. 225
That, as we left the plain, before our sight . . 219 **This Height* 17
A level plain extends. . . . . 244 *P. B.* 700
Into large letters—bright and plain ! . . . . 244 *P. B.* 750
" And, say the best you can, 'tis plain, . . . 245 *P. B.* 811
As void of sunshine, when, from that wide plain, . 268 **Four fiery* 3
Well pleased to skim the plain with wild flowers deckt, ... 270 **Though the bold* 4
But in plain daylight :——She, too, at my side, . 270 **Shame on* 6
Embraced those Brothers upon earth's wide plain ; 276 *Oker Hill* 11
Distinctions that are plain and few : . . . . 291 *Rob Roy* 30
" Since, then, the rule of right is plain, . . . 291 *Rob Roy* 53
Shall walk the Marathonian plain ; . . . . . 300 *Cora Linn* 38
Plain living and high thinking are no more : . . 307 **O Friend* 11
A few strong instincts and a few plain rules, . . 315 **Alas ! what* 11
O'er the wide earth, on mountain and on plain, . 315 **O'er the* 1
In hooded mantle, limping o'er the plain, . . . 321 **Humanity,delighting* 5
Along the surface of a spacious plain . . . . 324 *Ode 1814* 55
From the clear spring of a plain English heart, . 356 *Aquap.* 243
His way to Rome ? Ah, no,—round hill and plain 361 **For action* 12
I choose to saunter o'er the grassy plain, . . . 383 *Duddon* 30. 12
By humble choice of plain old times, are seen . 387 **Part fenced* 10
A glittering ship, that hath the plain . . . . 397 *White Doe* 65
Gone forth to greet him on the plain— . . . 402 *White Doe* 604
He conquered !—Saw we not the Plain . . . 405 *White Doe* 815
O'er path and road, and plain and dell, . . . 409 *White Doe* 1170
Along the plain of York he past ; . . . . . 411 *White Doe* 1378
He went, and traversed plain and hill ; . . . 412 *White Doe* 1437
Along the plain of Sarum, by the ghost . . . 419 *Ecc. Sonn.* I. 5. 4
To the blue ether and bespangled plain ; . . . 420 *Ecc. Sonn.* I. 7. 4
Upwhirled, and flying o'er the ethereal plain . . 435 *Ecc. Sonn.* 2. 28. 8
That in the morning whitened hill and plain . . 449 *Ecc. Sonn.* 3. 34. 9
O'er the wide realm, as o'er the Egyptian plain . 450 *Ecc. Sonn.* 3. 38. 8
The boundless plain of waters seems to lie :— . 453 **The Sun, that* 8
A plain below stretched seaward, while, descried . 475 **There ! said* 5
Yes, proof was plain that, since the day . . . 492 *Fidelity* 58
To this plain truth, or fling it to the wind ; . . 504 *Warning* 94
What on the Plain *we* have of warmth and light, . 521 *Epist. Beaumont* 8
Descend and reach, in Yewdale's depths, a plain . 525 *Epist. Beaumont* 225
And all who see him say, 'tis plain, ... 537 *Goody Blake* 118
Plain Nature's enviable privilege, ... 539 **Lady ! a* 50
For mine's a song that is both true and plain,— . 559 *Cuck.andNight.*118
But tells a plain tale of the days that are flown. . 572 *Avarice* 24
When link'd with thoughtless Mirth I cours'd the plain, ... 592 *Ev. Wk. Quarto* 31
The gentle Power that haunts the myrtle plain, . 607 *Desc.Sk.Quarto* 308
On Zutphen's plain ; or where with soften'd gaze 608 *Desc.Sk.Quarto* 358
Of him whom passion rivets to the plain, . . . 608 *Desc.Sk.Quarto* 361
His last dread pleasure ! watches to the plain— . 613 *Desc.Sk.Quarto* 620
Upon the glassy plain ; and oftentimes, . . . 639 *Prelude* I. 452
The plain and seemly countenance with which . 639 *Prelude* I. 504
Ye dealt out your plain comforts ? Yet had ye . 639 *Prelude* I. 505
Of curling mist, or from the level plain . . . 640 *Prelude* I. 565
The road lies plain before me ;—'tis a theme . 641 *Prelude* I. 640
To sweep along the plain of Windermere . . . 643 *Prelude* 2. 56
Upon a slope surmounted by a plain . . . . 644 *Prelude* 2. 156
Rolled over a wide plain o'erhung with clouds, . 649 *Prelude* 3. 2
No more : for now into a populous plain . . . 652 *Prelude* 3. 194
Of the plain Burghers, who in audience stood . 653 *Prelude* 3. 313
On the plain steeples of our English Church, . . 655 *Prelude* 3. 416
Spare diet, patient labour, and plain weeds. . . 655 *Prelude* 3. 457
He told in few plain words a soldier's tale— . . 664 *Prelude* 4. 421
I saw before me stretched a boundless plain . . 666 *Prelude* 5. 71
Those unclaimed garments telling a plain tale . 672 *Prelude* 5. 443
Lessons of genuine brotherhood, the plain . . 683 *Prelude* 6. 545
And, that our future course, all plain to sight, . 683 *Prelude* 6. 584
To fertilise the whole Egyptian plain. . . . . 684 *Prelude* 6. 616
Rise up, thou monstrous ant-hill on the plain . 689 *Prelude* 7. 149
But imitations, fondly made in plain . . . . 690 *Prelude* 7. 238
And banked with woody risings ; but the Plain . 702 *Prelude* 8. 192
Of plain Imagination and severe, ... 704 *Prelude* 8. 366
The dignities of plain occurrence then . . . . 704 *Prelude* 8. 381
The land all swarmed with passion, like a plain . 712 *Prelude* 9. 175
Far off at Chambord on the plain beneath ; . . 716 *Prelude* 9. 491
The ill-fated pair) in that plain tale will draw . 717 *Prelude* 9. 566
I thought, still traversing that widespread plain, . 726 *Prelude* 10. 545
Not far from that still ruin all the plain . . . 726 *Prelude* 10. 562
The plain straight road, for one no better chosen 728 *Prelude* 11. 71
Suspiciously, to establish in plain day . . . . 731 *Prelude* 11. 296
And plain beneath. Ere we to school returned,— 738 *Prelude* 12. 305
Of Sarum's Plain, my youthful spirit was raised ; 744 *Prelude* 13. 314
Three summer days I roamed) where'er the Plain 745 *Prelude* 13. 337
Alternately, and plain below, while breath . . 745 *Prelude* 13. 347
In the plain presence of his dignity ! . . . . 757 *Excursion* I. 76
Obtain reluctant hearing. Plain his garb ; . . 762 *Excursion* I. 420
A steep ascent ; and reached a dreary plain, . . 776 *Excursion* 2. 324
On Sarum's naked plain—than pyramid . . . 788 *Excursion* 3. 148
Their tribes, till we behold a spacious plain . . 807 *Excursion* 4. 434
And, from the plain, with toil immense, upreared 811 *Excursion* 4. 684
Plain indication that the words, which told . . 821 *Excursion* 4. 1312
An unillumined, blank, and dreary, plain, . . . 830 *Excursion* 5. 537
For our disputes, plain pictures. Say what man 832 *Excursion* 5. 638

Plain—*continued.*
The voice of Deity, on height and plain, . . . 837 *Excursion* 5. 991
A plain blue stone, a gentle Dalesman lies, . . 863 *Excursion* 7. 400
Was spread, and we partook a plain repast. . . 882 *Excursion* 8. 519
Or fret and labour on the Plain below. . . . 885 *Excursion* 9. 92
From that exalted station to the plain . . . 895 *Excursion* 9. 756
That hangs o'er the moist plain. Again they view K.8. 234 **The order'd* 4
Pursue each other through the yielding plain . K.8. 237*Recluse* I.I. 28
Too distant are they for plain view, but lo ! . . K.8. 251*Recluse* I.I.552
All plain blunt sense, all subtlety of thought. . L.I. 88 *Juvenal* I. 8
Plainer. And speak a plainer language. In the woods, ... 761 *Excursion* I. 347
The boy of plainer garb, whose blush survives . 882 *Excursion* 8. 552
Plain-living. Of those plain-living people now observed . . . . 661 *Prelude* 4. 213
Plainly. But there was something which most plainly said . . . . 67 *Bord.* 1634
As, if you look up, you plainly may see ; . . . 80 †*Address : Child* 6
You plainly in her face may read it, ... 127 *Idiot Boy* 133
A wound where plainly might be read . . . . 181 *Waggoner* 4. 175
Some plainly living voices were ; . . . . . 199 *Thorn* 161
The ghostly word, thus plainly seen, ... 245 *P. B.* 756
Did plainly come to Peter's ears ; . . . . . 247 *P. B.* 957
The very word was plainly heard, ... 247 *P. B.* 1006
Heard plainly by the wretched Mother— . . . 247 *P. B.* 1007
In which more plainly I could trace . . . . 288 *Highland Girl* 25
I wondered not, although I plainly saw . . . 667 *Prelude* 5. 111
More plainly still, that poverty and grief . . . 769 *Excursion* I. 833
But the whole plainly wrought by children's hands ! 778 *Excursion* 2. 423
Cheered, plainly, and yet serious. What a wreck 781 *Excursion* 2. 660
Plainness. A seemly plainness, name it what you will, 654 *Prelude* 3. 397
Plains. —The lights are vanished from the watery plains : . . . . 8 *Ev. Wk.* 305
And, rimy without speck, extend the plains : . . 8 *Ev. Wk.* 356
Of purple lights and ever-vernal plains ; . . . 20 *Desc. Sk.* 574
On the blank plains,—the coldness of the night, . 172 *Infant Daughter* 22
I looked upon those hills and plains, ... 194 *Ruth* 172
That skins the plains of Thessaly, ... 213 *Dion* 74
O care ! O guilt !—O vales and plains, . . . 214 *Kirkstone* 33
Now running o'er the open plains. . . . . . 243 *P. B.* 645
The rising sun, and on the plains descend ; . . 264 *Snowdrop* 6
Haunts him belated on the silent plains ! . . . 265 **There is a pleasure* 8
The gentlest Shade that walked Elysian plains . 284 *Departure* 1
Nor less, the stillness of these frosty plains, . . 329 *Ode : Thanks.* 20
Is this the stream, whose cities, heights, and plains, 335 *Namur* 2
Of midnight,—cities, plains, forests, and mighty streams. . . . . 350 *Des. Stanzas* 18
Pride of two nations, wood and lake and plains, . 353 *Aquap.* 42
Heaved less for thy bright plains and hills bestrown 360 *Alban Hills* 2
Covered the plains, and, wandering where they chose, ... 380 *Duddon* 16. 7
Thy waters, Duddon ! 'mid these flowery plains ; 381 *Duddon* 20. 3
And o'er wide plains cheered by the lark that trills 387 *Manse* 5
On them who urge the keel her *plains* to trace . 459 **Wanderer ! that* 51
Upon these happy plains ; . . . . 487 *Fountain* 60
White as the pair that slid along the plains . . 497 *Lycoris* 17
Committed to the silent plains . . . . . . 499 **Departing summer* 32
From high Gibraltar to Siberian plains, . . . 509 *F. Stone* 92
But he could see the woods and plains, . . . 577 **I come* 17
Heard by the night-calm of the wat'ry plains. . 599 *Ev. Wk. Quarto* 378
Of purple lights and even vernal plains. . . . 614 *Desc.Sk.Quarto* 685
To lead the mind to those Elysian plains . . . 619 *School Ex.* 69
On Indian plains, and from my mother's hut . . 636 *Prelude* I. 298
Given out while mid-day heat oppressed the plains. 678 *Prelude* 6. 223
This pretty Shepherd, pride of all the plains, . . 695 *Prelude* 7. 571
That bore it—on the plains of Liberty . . . . 718 *Prelude* 10. 15
Rivers and fertile plains, and sounding shores,— . 812 *Excursion* 4. 719
And O, ye swelling hills, and spacious plains !. . 838 *Excursion* 6. 17
His genius mounted to the plains of heaven. . . 865 *Excursion* 7. 506
That filled her plains, that reached her utmost shores, ... 869 *Excursion* 7. 761
We shall not scatter through the plains and rocks K.8. 248*Recluse* I.I.430
Plaint. Plaint was it ? or prophecy . . . . . 502 **Like a* 10
And heard meanwhile the Psalmist's mournful plaint, ... 780 *Excursion* 2. 576
None ! 'tis the general plaint of human kind . . 792 *Excursion* 3. 440
Plaintive. That plaintive cry ! which up the hill . 85 *Shepherd-boys* 32
Made answer to that plaintive sound. . . . . 85 *Shepherd-boys* 77
Sung to the plaintive lyre in Grecian vales. . . 170 **Never enlivened* 19
Each ready with a plaintive whine ! . . . . 191 *Beggars* 38
Perhaps the plaintive numbers flow . . . . 289 *Sol. Reap.* 18
These crowded streets resound no plaintive ditty :— 475 *Greenock* 5
Gives plaintive ditties to the heedless wind, . . 522 *Epist.Beaumont* 47
(Though not without some plaintive tones between) 537 **In desultory* 6
A Spirit sang in tones more plaintive than the wind : 581 *Invoc. Earth* 3
Singing, and often with more plaintive voice . . 751 *Prelude* 14. 384
Repeated o'er and o'er his plaintive cry, . . . 799 *Excursion* 3. 949
The plaintive spirit of the solitude ! . . . . 807 *Excursion* 4. 412
This plaintive note disturbed not the repose . . 892 *Excursion* 9. 559
Plan. Sufficeth them, the simple plan, ... 291 *Rob Roy* 38
This Temple—Angels governed by a plan . . . 335 *Cologne* 2
Of his best workmanship by plan and tool. . . 473 **Thanks for* 8
If such be Nature's holy plan, ... 482 *Lines : Spring* 22
Upon the plan that pleased his boyish thought : . 493 *Hap. War.* 5
See, at his feet, some little plan or chart, . . . 589 *Immortality* 90
But with no settled plan. I was detached . . 675 *Prelude* 6. 25
And on a frugal plan without more words. . . L.I. 95 *Juvenal* 3. 24
Planet. The planet in its nakedness : were this . 777 *Excursion* 2. 361
Turned towards the planet Jupiter that hung . 849 *Excursion* 6. 761

Pleasant—*continued.*
Amid your pleasant bowers to sit, 227 *Vernal Ode* 73
So might I, standing on this pleasant lea, 259 **The world is* 11
O pleasant transit, Grasmere! to resign 284 *Departure* 19
To them, 'mid Kirtle's pleasant braes, 287 *Ellen Irwin* 19
There's pleasant Tiviot-dale, a land 293 *Yarrow Unv.* 21
And earth with all her pleasant fruits and flowers 308 **There is a bondage* 13
His project crowned, his pleasant travel o'er? 349 *Boulogne* 4
And shrubs, whose pleasant looks gave proof how kind 356 *Aquap.* 214
And pleasant course; flower after flower has blown, 361 **List—'twas* 11
That binds them, pleasant River! to thy side:— 383 *Duddon* 30. 10
This Mansion and these pleasant bowers, 402 *White Doe* 547
A pleasant music floats along the Mere, 426 *Ecc. Sonn.* 1. 30. 1
In that sweet mood when pleasant thoughts 482 *Lines: Spring* 3
Not far from pleasant Ivor-hall, 483 *Simon Lee* 2
This water's pleasant tune 487 *Fountain* 10
And shaped these pleasant walks by Emont's side, 489 *Spade* 2
The leaves of any pleasant tree 543 *Russ. Fug.* 179
To show to her some pleasant meanings writ 562 *Cuck.andNight.*299
The pleasant melody of woodland birds. 569 *Cumb. Beg.* 185
How pleasant, as the yellowing sun declines, 593 *Ev. Wk. Quarto* 97
Of cabins, woods, and lawns a pleasant shore 611 *Desc.Sk.Quarto* 502
A pleasant loitering journey, through three days 633 *Prelude* 1. 106
Remained, no pleasant images of trees, 638 *Prelude* 1. 396
So beautiful among the pleasant fields 639 *Prelude* 1. 502
Within the crescent of a pleasant bay, 644 *Prelude* 2. 139
Of pleasant wandering. Happy time! more dear 647 *Prelude* 2. 332
Beside the pleasant Mill of Trompington 653 *Prelude* 3. 275
And pleasant flowers. The thirst of living praise, 654 *Prelude* 3. 336
With all its pleasant promises, was gone 661 *Prelude* 4. 207
Such pleasant office have we long pursued 662 *Prelude* 4. 271
Her pleasant habitations, and dry up 666 *Prelude* 5. 32
That cannot take long leave of pleasant thoughts. 675 *Prelude* 6. 19
As calmly, underneath the pleasant brows 701 *Prelude* 8. 181
Prepared to sojourn in a pleasant town, 710 *Prelude* 9. 40
Now was I from that pleasant station torn 722 *Prelude* 10. 282
O pleasant exercise of hope and joy! 728 *Prelude* 11. 105
From every object pleasant circumstance 729 *Prelude* 11. 154
A pleasant promise, wafted from her shores, 733 *Prelude* 11. 429
That fragrant notice of a pleasant shore 735 *Prelude* 12. 54
And, when that pleasant toil had ceased to please, 742 *Prelude* 13. 137
Tarrying at will in many a pleasant spot 751 *Prelude* 14. 352
Of bright and pleasant sunshine interposed; 756 *Excursion* 1. 8
To him most pleasant who on soft cool moss 756 *Excursion* 1. 9
We were tried Friends: amid a pleasant vale, 757 *Excursion* 1. 52
What pleasant expectations lured me on 766 *Excursion* 1. 645
Pleasant as roses in the thickets blown, 773 *Excursion* 2. 109
Of winter, and protect that pleasant place. 793 *Excursion* 3. 531
And pleasant awning. On the moss-grown wall 826 *Excursion* 5. 230
And pleasant interests—for the sequel leaving 829 *Excursion* 5. 435
Which told it was the pleasant month of June; 858 *Excursion* 7. 76
Expire; and nature's pleasant robe of green, 872 *Excursion* 7. 997
Tears wipe away, and pleasant tidings bring; 875 *Excursion* 8. 80
And thence let loose, to seek their pleasant homes 888 *Excursion* 9. 261
And pleasant dwellings, to familiar trees S.3. 433 **The doubt* 6
On Armath's pleasant fields. And now they came, K.8. 225 **I will* 51
Discourse both wise and pleasant, shrewd remarks K.8. 227 **I will* 90
What, if I floated down a pleasant Stream K.8. 244 *Recluse* 1.1.292

Pleasantly. But not so pleasantly as now: 179 *Waggoner* 3. 90

Pleasantness. Shall with its pleasantness be past, 144 **Driven in* 64
Of private life their natural pleasantness, 538 **In desultory* 36

Please. Or where her pathways straggle as they please 11 *Desc. Sk.* 48
To the top of GREAT How did it please them to climb: 86 *Rural Arch.* 4
"St. Ouen's golden Shrine? Or choose what else would please thee most 92 *Poet's Dream* 25
They please Him best who labour most to do in peace His will: 93 *Poet's Dream* 66
How would it please old Ocean to partake, 154 *Morn. Ex.* 49
While they dance, crying, "Long as ye please!" 167 *Stray Pleasures* 24
Shall vanish, if ye please, 225 *Present.* 27
Or made with hope to please that inward eye 231 **The gentlest Poet* 34
Meek aspirations please her, lone endeavour, 262 **Not Love* 9
Of these illusions, or they please no more. 270 **Shame on* 14
Change for the worse might please, incursion bold 284 *Departure* 9
Whom mere despite of heart could so far please, 292 **Degenerate Douglas* 2
Spot rich in all things that can soothe and please! 308 **One might* 8
Go forth, and please the gentle and the good; 351 *Des. Stanzas* 88
If that substantial title please thee more, 363 **List—'twas* 104
Or cease to please the fickle worshipper; 380 *Duddon* 18. 4
Their vocal charm; their sparklings cease to please. 382 *Duddon* 25. 14
Then, too, this Song *of mine* once more could please, 395 *WhiteDoe: Ded.* 41
Of pompous horses; whom vain titles please; 433 *Ecc. Sonn.* 2. 18. 4
The thoughtful Monks, intent their God to please, 468 *St. Bees* 142
Let loose their carols when they please, 487 *Fountain* 39
He proud to please, above all rivals, fit 528 **Those breathing* 106
To see or not to see, as best may please 532 **Once I* 29
Power hath been given to please for higher ends 538 **In desultory* 22
Would fill it with his spirit. He, to please 625 *Æneid* 89
Of undulations varying as might please 680 *Prelude* 6. 368
And, when that pleasant toil had ceased to please, 742 *Prelude* 13. 137
Which did not please me, "must be deemed, I fear, 780 *Excursion* 2. 595
Range; if it please them, speed from clime to clime; 789 *Excursion* 3. 192
That soonest fails to please, and quickliest turns 799 *Excursion* 3. 912
Bedropped with tears. 'Twill please you to be told 851 *Excursion* 6. 893

Pleased. *See* **Heart-pleased, Well-pleased.**
Pleased, as she moves, her pomp of clouds to fold 8 *Ev. Wk.* 329
More pleased, my foot the hidden margin roves 12 *Desc. Sk.* 77
Well pleased upon some simple annual feast, 19 *Desc. Sk.* 496
Which pleased him so, that he was hushed at once: 44 *Bord.* 402
As pleased as if the same had been a Maiden-queen. 108 *Indolence* 72
Be pleased that naturè made thee fit 112 **Yes! thou* 9
Which old folk, fondly pleased to trim 144 **Driven in* 50
Full oft is pleased a wayward dart to throw; 153 *Morn. Ex.* 2
Urania's self might welcome with pleased ear 154 *Morn. Ex.* 53
Most pleased when most uneasy; 157 **In youth* 4
Pleased at his greeting thee again; 158 **In youth* 19
And pleased to be admired! 165 *Parrot* 28
That those fond Idlers most are pleased 170 *Rural Ill.* 35
—Pleased by any random toy; 171 *Kitten* 117
Recovering breath, and pleased to win 174 *Waggoner* 1. 44
Well pleased in rustic garb to feed 180 *Waggoner* 4. 50
Pleased some favourite chief to follow 181 *Waggoner* 4. 109
Pleased with herself, nor sad, nor gay; 192 *Ruth* 16
And what perceive; well pleased to recognise 207 *Tintern* 107
And Fancy, not less aptly pleased, compares 230 *Clouds* 16
Then starts the sluggard, pleased to meet 233 *Power of Sound* 70
Upon the pleased and thankful Ass; 243 *P. B.* 597
Pleased if some Souls (for such there needs must be) 250 **Nuns fret* 12
Am pleased by fits to have thee for my foe, 253 **O gentle* 11
Well pleased to skim the plain with wild flowers deckt, 270 **Though the bold* 4
So styled by those fierce Britons, pleased to see 272 *Lady E. B.* 3
Well pleased, her foot should print earth's common grass, 278 **Lo! where she* 12
Pleased to renounce, does this dear Thrush attune 279 **'Tis he* 6
Nor am I loth, though pleased at heart, 288 *Highland Girl* 72
And all were pleased to hear and see, 295 *Highland Boy* 43
Yet more it pleased him, more it stirred, 295 *Highland Boy* 76
Still better pleased as more and more 296 *Highland Boy* 153
Yet he was pleased and reconciled 297 *Highland Boy* 244
Pleased in refreshing dews to steep 299 *Cora Linn* 10
On England's bosom; yet well pleased to rest, 303 **Fair Star* 4
And slaves are pleased to learn that mighty feats are done; 327 *Ode 1815* 38
Passive yet pleased. What! with this Broom in flower 353 *Aquap.* 26
Nor is least pleased, we trust, when golden beams, 354 *Aquap.* 111
—So, pleased with purple clusters to entwine 367 *Trajan* 19
The pleased Enchanter was aware 369 *Eg. Maid* 3
A pleased attention I may win 376 **The Minstrels* 75
Pleased could my verse, a speaking monument, 376 *Duddon* 3. 3
Thy pleased associates:—light as endless May 377 *Duddon* 5. 13
Well pleased that future Bards should chant 386 *Yarrow Rev.* 107
While Tweed, best pleased in chanting a blithe strain, 387 *Scott* 6
Then may we ask, though pleased that thought should range 388 **The pibroch's* 10
Of Lookers-on how pleased and proud! 409 *White Doe* 1181
How pleased, when down the Straggler sank 415 *White Doe* 1734
Pleased with the thanks that in His People's eye 447 *Ecc. Sonn.* 3. 27. 6
The spirit of Laud is pleased in heaven's pure clime, 448 *Ecc. Sonn.* 3. 32. 13
Might both be pleased with, for it suits them both. 453 **Calm is the* 24
Who but is pleased to watch the moon on high 461 **Who but is* 1
All seasons through, is humbly pleased to braid 463 **Adieu, Rydalian* 7
Pleased with your triumphs o'er his brother Space, 477 *Steamboats* 12
Pleased rather with some soft ideal scene, 480 **Most sweet* 5
Yet pleased and willing; 486 **Bright Flower* 20
High will he hang thee up, well pleased to adorn 490 *Spade* 31
Upon the plan that pleased his boyish thought: 493 *Hap. War.* 5
Pleased with the harvest hope that runs 497 *Lycoris* 31
Pleased while the sylvan world displays 497 *Lycoris* 33
Pleased when the sullen winds resound the knell 497 *Lycoris* 35
Best pleased with what is aptliest framed 499 **Departing summer* 29
And if the harp pleased his gay youth, it rings 503 *Warning* 18
And yet how pleased we wander forth 507 *May* 49
Pleased looks around the delicate repast— 525 *Epist. Beaumont* 241
Which She is pleased and proud to call her own, 539 **Lady! a* 26
For which it pleased him in his songs to show 564 *Troilus* 113
Pleas'd thro' the dusk their breaking smiles to view, 596 *Ev. Wk. Quarto* 274
Though peaceful, full of gladness. Thou art pleased, 622 *Recluse* 1. 1. 117
Pleased with thy crags, and woody steeps, thy Lake, 622 *Recluse* 1. 1. 118
Unmanageable thoughts: his mind, best pleased 634 *Prelude* 1. 139
We rested in the shade, all pleased alike, 643 *Prelude* 2. 68
And independent musings pleased me so 652 *Prelude* 3. 228
Among the favourites whom it pleased me well 659 *Prelude* 4. 93
Of a pleased grandame tottering up and down; 661 *Prelude* 4. 205
Her talk, her business, pleased me; and no less 661 *Prelude* 4. 224
Though fledged and feathered, and well pleased to part 669 *Prelude* 5. 247
And phrases pleased me chosen for delight, 674 *Prelude* 5. 557
With Indian awe and wonder, ignorance pleased 677 *Prelude* 6. 121
Or, not less pleased, lay on some turret's head, 678 *Prelude* 6. 220
Pleased (though to hardship born, and compassed round 682 *Prelude* 6. 509
Pleased with his daily task, or, if not pleased, 682 *Prelude* 6. 511
Well pleased to pitch a vagrant tent among 688 *Prelude* 7. 56
In spite of strongest disappointment, pleased 689 *Prelude* 7. 146
With no unthinking mind, well pleased to note 690 *Prelude* 7. 220
Unless itself be pleased, here more than once 691 *Prelude* 7. 269
Although well pleased to be where they were found, 696 *Prelude* 7. 584
Among the crowd, half pleased with, half ashamed 699 *Prelude* 8. 42

Pleased—*continued.*
And Shepherds were the men that pleased me first ; 701 *Prelude* 8. 128
Have pleased me, seeking knowledge at that time 708 *Prelude* 8. 599
That would have pleased me in more quiet times ; 719 *Prelude* 10. 68
Erewhile my tuneful haunt ? It pleased me more 721 *Prelude* 10. 244
Pleased in some open field to exercise . . . . 723 *Prelude* 10. 367
And is half pleased with things that are amiss, . 729 *Prelude* 11. 151
Flattered the young, pleased with extremes, nor least . . . . 730 *Prelude* 11. 233
But through presumption ; even in pleasure pleased 736 *Prelude* 12. 109
Ambitious projects, pleased me less ; I sought . 741 *Prelude* 13. 61
Pleased with some unpremeditated strains . . 745 *Prelude* 13. 353
Into a second place, pleased to become . . . 749 *Prelude* 14. 259
We sate—we walked ; he pleased me with report 757 *Excursion* 1. 63
With gracious smile, deliberately pleased, . . . 758 *Excursion* 1. 106
Or pleased their fancies, with the wares he brought. 761 *Excursion* 1. 332
Not speaking much, pleased rather with the joy . 764 *Excursion* 1. 515
With half a harvest. It pleased Heaven to add . 764 *Excursion* 1. 538
Each with the other pleased, we now pursued . 772 *Excursion* 2. 31
And gardens interposed. Pleased with the sight, 778 *Excursion* 2. 428
Pleasing and pleased, he shared their simple sports, 778 *Excursion* 2. 450
And pleased I looked upon my grey-haired Friend, 781 *Excursion* 2. 658
The antiquarian humour, and am pleased . . 788 *Excursion* 3. 134
By the reflection of your pleasure, pleased. . . 788 *Excursion* 3. 158
Pleased to have been, contented not to be. . . 790 *Excursion* 3. 269
From discontent, indifferent, pleased to sit . . 798 *Excursion* 3. 838
Pleased to perceive his own unshackled life, . . 799 *Excursion* 3. 933
Yet so it pleased a fond, a vain, old Man, . . . 816 *Excursion* 4. 1004
Of unreproved enjoyment ; and is pleased . . 817 *Excursion* 4. 1045
—For me, I looked upon the pair, well pleased : . 829 *Excursion* 5. 452
" Much was I pleased," the grey-haired Wanderer said, ... 833 *Excursion* 5. 728
You turned ; and yet more pleased have from your lips . . . . 833 *Excursion* 5. 730
Was graceful, when it pleased him, smooth and still 842 *Excursion* 6. 292
Of kindred import, pleased and satisfied— . . 845 *Excursion* 6. 443
(And Heaven was pleased to accomplish the desire) 845 *Excursion* 6. 501
Though with the silence pleased that here prevails, 847 *Excursion* 6. 631
Confessed the power of nature.—Pleased though sad, 854 *Excursion* 6. 1063
More pleased than sad, the grey-haired Wanderer sate ; . . . . 854 *Excursion* 6. 1064
To end my days ; well pleased was I to see . . 860 *Excursion* 7. 199
Of rights to him ; but he remained well pleased, . 864 *Excursion* 7. 433
Down on this spot, well pleased would he have seen 871 *Excursion* 7. 880
Failed not to notice, inly pleased, and said :— . 874 *Excursion* 8. 4
Till the spectator, who awhile was pleased . . 874 *Excursion* 8. 26
This ardent sally pleased the mild good Man, . . 880 *Excursion* 8. 434
We rose together : all were pleased ; but most . 890 *Excursion* 9. 427
The fancy pleased by spectacles unlooked for. . S.3. 433 **The doubt* 31
Pleased to detect the dimpling stir of life, . . . S.3. 433 **The doubt* 40
His guests, and make them jocund. They are pleased, ... K.8. 241 *Recluse* 1.1.192
To regulate my hopes. Pleased with the good, . K.8. 246 *Recluse* 1.1.350
How pleased he is where thin and thinner grows . K.8. 249 *Recluse* 1.1.478
Had soothed his ear while *they* were hidden : how pleased . . . . K.8. 249 *Recluse* 1.1.484
And fighting to the death, but I am pleased . . K.8. 256 *Recluse* 1.1.723

Pleasing. *See* **Sadly-pleasing, Self-pleasing.**
Of present pleasure, but with pleasing thoughts . 206 *Tintern* 63
Wrapped in a fit of pleasing indolence, . . . 227 *Vernal Ode* 86
Pleasing remembrance of a thought foregone ; . 258 **Methought I* 13
Of high astonishment and pleasing fear. . . . 267 **Though narrow* 8
Ah, then, Belovèd ! pleasing was the smart, . . 395 *White Doe : Ded.* 9
Set off her brightness with a pleasing shade. . . 440 *Ecc. Sonn.* 3. 1. 4
Through all my frame the pleasing accents ran. . 618 *School Ex.* 28
O ever pleasing Solitude, ... 626 †*Cento* 7
More pleasing, and whose character I deem . . 647 *Prelude* 2. 380
Pleasing and pleased, he shared their simple sports, 778 *Excursion* 2. 450
This pleasing fancy (cherished and upheld . . 834 *Excursion* 5. 794
" Those pleasing works the Housewife's skill produced : . . . . 860 *Excursion* 7. 192
Of pleasing lustre.—But no more of this ; . . . 861 *Excursion* 7. 237
Unknowing and unknown. A pleasing thought . 871 *Excursion* 7. 929
Had learned the art of pleasing, and had now . 882 *Excursion* 8. 531
Scarcely a wish, but one bright pleasing thought, K.8. 237 *Recluse* 1.1. 16
And lap in pleasing rest, and bear us on . . . K.8. 245 *Recluse* 1.1.305

Pleasingly. Eight months ! rolled pleasingly away ; the ninth . . . . 658 *Prelude* 3. 631

Pleasurable. A pleasurable feeling of blind love, . 132 *Michael* 76

Pleasure. To sterner pleasure, where, by Uri's lake, 14 *Desc. Sk.* 227
That virtue languishes and pleasure fails, . . . 21 *Desc. Sk.* 598
A morbid pleasure nourished, tracing here . . 23 *Yew-tree* 31
And hope returned, and pleasure fondly made . 25 *Guilt* 58
Sight which, tho' lost at once, a gleam of pleasure shed. . . . . 26 *Guilt* 135
And nothing to my mind a sweeter pleasure brought. 28 *Guilt* 207
Attends your pleasure. We are ready— Sir ! . 49 *Bord.* 665
Which purported it was the royal pleasure . . 49 *Bord.* 680
I was the pleasure of all hearts, the darling . . 68 *Bord.* 1687
Seemed to feast with head and ears ; and his tail with pleasure shook. . . . . 87 *Pet-lamb* 10
Pleasure on pleasure crowded in, each livelier than the last. . . . . 92 *Poet's Dream* 44
No pleasure now, and no desire. . . . . . 114 *Ind. Wom.* 18
Twins had they been in pleasure ; after strife . 122 *V. and J.* 21
Betty a drunken pleasure quaffs . . . . . 130 *Idiot Boy* 380
The pleasure which there is in life itself. . . . 132 *Michael* 77
Lack any pleasure which a boy can know." . . 136 *Michael* 356
If seen, and with like pleasure stirred . . . . 143 **Driven in* 28
Of common pleasure : beast and bird, the lamb, . 146 **It was an* 25
Devoured like pleasure ere it spreads . . . . 154 *Flower Garden* 15

Pleasure—*continued.*
What pleasure through my veins you spread . . 155 *Waterfall* 26
Of pleasure high and turbulent, ... 157 **In youth* 3
A lowlier pleasure ; . . . . 158 **In youth* 52
By myself a lonely pleasure, ... 161 **Pleasures newly* 26
" Who but hails the sight with pleasure . . . 163 *Hint* 1
And there for gentle pleasure live ; . . . . 164 **Fair Lady* 12
Thus pleasure is spread through the earth . . 167 *Stray Pleasures* 27
Of her own exceeding pleasure ! . . . . . 171 *Kitten* 40
To stand or go is at *their* pleasure ; . . . . 174 *Waggoner* 1. 105
His eyes take pleasure in the road . . . . 177 *Waggoner* 2. 35
In that sweet mood when pleasure loves to pay . 185 *Nutting* 39
And then my heart with pleasure fills, ... 187 **I wandered* 23
Of the pleasure it spreads through so thankful a band ; . . . . 188 *Music* 30
Of pleasure and of fear ; . . . . 192 *Ruth* 45
New objects did new pleasure give, ... 194 *Ruth* 184
And built a house of pleasure in the dell. . . . 202 *Hart-leap* 84
Never to blend our pleasure or our pride . . 203 *Hart-leap* 179
A taste of this great pleasure, viewing . . . . 204 *Brougham* 42
No life is good, no pleasure long. . . . . 204 *Brougham* 88
No life is good, no pleasure long, ... 204 *Brougham* 105
Of unremembered pleasure : such, perhaps, . . 206 *Tintern* 31
Of present pleasure, but with pleasing thoughts . 206 *Tintern* 63
Into a sober pleasure ; when thy mind . . . 207 *Tintern* 139
" Him only pleasure leads, and peace attends, . 214 *Dion* 122
Ask, for its pleasure, screen or canopy . . . . 219 *Haunted Tree* 6
Lucida ! from domes of pleasure, ... 220 *Triad* 36
Pour pleasure forth, and solaces that trace . . 229 *Cuckoo-clock* 36
With more than vernal pleasure feeding, . . . 239 *P. B.* 253
By pleasure running in his head, ... 240 *P. B.* 329
A thought received with languid pleasure ! . . 242 *P. B.* 545
Ye waited then on my good pleasure ; . . . . 245 *P. B.* 793
There is a pleasure in poetic pains . . . . . 265 **There is a pleasure* 1
To pleasure snatched for reckless pleasure's sake. 280 **Intent on* 8
Strike pleasure dead, ... 284 *Grave of Burns* 4
Our pleasure varying at command . . . . . 286 *Nith* 29
O happy pleasure ! here to dwell . . . . . 288 *Highland Girl* 49
To give new pleasure like the past, ... 288 *Highland Girl* 70
A course of lively pleasure ; . . . . 302 *Yarrow V.* 78
Your grandame's ears with pleasure of your noise ! 310 *Anticip.* 9
Of business, care, or pleasure ; or resigned . . 314 **I dropped* 5
Records on which, for pleasure of all eyes, . . 324 *Ode 1814* 108
Of saintly pleasure from these pictured walls, . 339 *Tell* 17
Nor to her was the dance of soft pleasure unknown : 340 *Fort Fuentes* 14
With pleasure dancing through the frame . . . 348 **Lulled by* 14
She seems to work, at pleasure to lie still ;— . . 366 *Lombardy* 7
For some high day of long-expected pleasure. . 372 *Eg. Maid* 192
For pleasure hath not ceased to wait . . . . 375 **The Minstrels* 31
Fair fruit of pleasure and serene content . . . 395 *WhiteDoe : Ded.* 31
Whose aim is pleasure light and fugitive : . . . 395 *WhiteDoe : Ded.* 58
For pleasure made, a goodly spot, ... 407 *White Doe* 984
Through human hearts, and pleasure dead,— . 416 *White Doe* 1843
So have we hurried on with troubled pleasure : . 443 *Ecc. Sonn.* 3. 12. 9
Not in some hour when Pleasure with a sigh . . 454 **Not in the lucid* 3
Vain is the pleasure, a false calm the peace, . . 455 **Not in the lucid* 26
What pleasure once encompassed those sweet names . . . . 459 **Wanderer ! that* 7
Pleasure, or Grief, and Toil that seldom looks . 471 *Ailsa Crag* 10
With pleasure sometimes by this thought restrained— . . . . 476 *Eden* 12
It seemed a thrill of pleasure. . . . . . . 482 *Lines : Spring* 16
That there was pleasure there. . . . . . . 482 *Lines : Spring* 20
And bustle and sluggishness, pleasure and gloom. 482 *Character* 4
And with a living pleasure we describe ; . . . 488 *Pers. Talk* 16
We may find pleasure : wilderness and wood, . . 488 *Pers. Talk* 30
Whose silence, for the pleasure of the ear, . . 508 *F. Stone* 10
Conscious of half the pleasure which they give ; . 511 **So fair* 3
As blameless pleasure, not without some tears, . 526 **Soon did* 14
For mutual pleasure glide ; . . . . 526 **The soaring* 30
The far-fetched worm with pleasure would disown 528 **Those breathing* 73
In pleasure, is the darkest shade . . . . . 530 *Gleaner* 14
Than pleasure only ; gladdening to prepare . . 538 **In desultory* 23
The pleasure was, and no one heard the praise, . 539 **Lady ! a* 36
All kinds of pleasure mix'd with sorrowing ; . . 557 *Cuck. and Night.* 29
Old am I, and to genial pleasure slow ; . . . 557 *Cuck. and Night.* 37
Thence worship comes, content and true heart's pleasure, ... 559 *Cuck. and Night.* 153
Where he had felt such perfect pleasure once. . 563 *Troilus* 46
By that sweet taste of pleasure unpursued, . . 567 *Cumb. Beg.* 103
—Such pleasure is to one kind Being known, . . 568 *Cumb. Beg.* 154
There pleasure crowned his days ; and all his thoughts . . . . 573 *Chiabrera* 2. 12
His last dread pleasure ! watches to the plain— . 613 *Desc. Sk. Quarto* 620
Take pleasure in the midst of happy thoughts, . 622 *Recluse* 1. 1. 87
More touching still, more perfect was the pleasure, 626 **The confidence* 9
Youth, by pleasure unbeguiled . . . . . . 629 *Installation* 47
And troubled pleasure, nor without the voice . . 637 *Prelude* 1. 362
Organic pleasure from the silver wreaths . . 640 *Prelude* 1. 564
New pleasure like a bee among the flowers. . . 640 *Prelude* 1. 580
By pleasure and repeated happiness, ... 641 *Prelude* 1. 604
Even with a weight of pleasure, and the sky, . 644 *Prelude* 2. 172
For its own pleasure, and I breathed with joy. . 645 *Prelude* 2. 188
Of pride and pleasure ! to myself I seemed . . 649 *Prelude* 3. 25
To quit my pleasure, and, from month to month, 654 *Prelude* 3. 357
And simple Pleasure foraging for Death ; . . . 657 *Prelude* 3. 599
Of pleasure won, and knowledge not withheld, . 662 *Prelude* 4. 277
Whose transient pleasure mounted to the head, . 663 *Prelude* 4. 318
Or pleasure sown, or fostered thus, may be . . 668 *Prelude* 5. 194
Which they partake at pleasure. Early died . . 669 *Prelude* 5. 256

Point—*continued.*
Attain a point that showed the valley—stretched 823 *Excursion* 5. 78
A very hero till his point was gained, ... 842 *Excursion* 6. 236
Who from truth's central point serenely views 883 *Excursion* 8. 599
In aspect and forbidding, yet a point . . . 885 *Excursion* 9. 53
The failure, if the Almighty, to this point . . . 887 *Excursion* 9. 230
Shadow and substance kissing point to point . . S.3. 434 **The doubt* 71
At the sword's point, visions conceived in love. . S.3. 437 **The doubt* 193

Pointed. *See* **Iron-pointed.**
The pointed steeple peering forth from the centre of the shade. 92 *Poet's Dream* 40
He pointed towards his dwelling-place, entreating 102 *Brothers* 413
Sharper than the pointed thorn." . . . . . 140 *Arm. Lady* 46
Who the first with pointed rays . . . . . 161 **Pleasures newly* 11
A Telescope upon its frame, and pointed to the sky: 189 *Star-gazers* 2
The pointed horns of my canoe; . . . . . 236 *P. B.* 17
Or rain-drop lingering on the pointed thorn. . . 265 **There is a pleasure* 14
He pointed to a lovely Doe, ... 402 *White Doe* 557
To the Horn Sir Eustace pointed . . . . . 535 *Egremont* 3
With his lance Sir Eustace pointed, ... 535 *Egremont* 17
If e'er they pointed forth the blissful way . . 619 *School Ex.* 105
The road that pointed toward the chosen Vale. . 633 *Prelude* 1. 93
For still we had hopes that pointed to the clouds, 684 *Prelude* 6. 587
Echoes and waterfalls, and pointed crags . . . 708 *Prelude* 8. 637
Pointed upon occasion to the site . . . . . 716 *Prelude* 9. 480

Pointedly. Was pointedly addressed; and to the thoughts . . . . 880 *Excursion* 8. 436

Pointing. And wild Impatience, pointing upward, showed, ... 2 *Ev. Wk.* 25
By pointing to the gliding moon on high. . . . 7 *Ev. Wk.* 259
And, pointing to a little child that lay . . . . 33 *Guilt* 470
Then, pointing to the stones near which they stood, 137 *Michael* 383
And pointing with a feeble hand . . . . . 164 **Fair Lady* 37
Hung—head pointing towards the ground— . . 171 *Kitten* 69
Hope, pointing to the cultured plain, ... 215 *Kirkstone* 78
And drop thy pointing finger bright . . . . 215 *Enterprise* 8
Star-high, and pointing still to something higher; 282 **In my* 12
In the pines pointing heavenward her beauty austere; . . . . 364 *Vallomb.* 12
Pyramid pointing to the stars, ... 472 *Ossian* 32
"There!" said a Stripling, pointing with meet pride . . . . 475 **There! said* 1
By pointing to a shooting star on high: . . . 596 *Ev. Wk. Quarto* 260
Whence Danger leans, and pointing ghastly, joys 610 *Desc.Sk.Quarto* 466
Uplifted, pointing to the starry sky, ... 745 *Prelude* 13. 346
Pointing towards a sweet-briar, bade me climb . 763 *Excursion* 1. 451
Let us proceed." Then, pointing with his staff . 773 *Excursion* 2. 153
He yielded not; but, pointing to a slope . . . 793 *Excursion* 3. 475
"There," said the Vicar, pointing as he spake, . 848 *Excursion* 6. 675
Now pointing this way, and now that.—'Here flows,' . . . . 869 *Excursion* 7. 787

Points. Or from high points of rock looked out for fanning gales; . . . . 3 *Ev. Wk.* 44
With thousand thousand twinkling points of light; 4 *Ev. Wk.* 121
Hunts, where his master points, the intercepted flocks. . . . . 5 *Ev. Wk.* 185
Than feathers clinging to their points of passion. 68 *Bord.* 1681
No leaves it has, no prickly points; . . . . 197 *Thorn* 7
True to the kindred points of Heaven and Home! 209 **Ethereal minstrel* 12
Points she to aught?—the bliss draws near, . . 223 *Wishing-gate* 5
Points heavenward, indicate the end and way. . 281 *Chris. Words.* 14
With glittering finger points at nine. . . . . 406 *White Doe* 961
With points of morning dew. . . . . . . 487 **We walked* 44
This Oak points out thy grave; the silent tree . 491 *Tribute: Dog* 9
Hunts, where he points, the intercepted flocks; . 594 *Ev. Wk. Quarto* 168
Is there a flower, to which he points with hand . 645 *Prelude* 2. 245
Points have we all of us within our souls . . . 651 *Prelude* 3. 185
Of character, in points of wit as broad, . . . 657 *Prelude* 3. 570
These are the points," the Wanderer said, "on which . . . . 829 *Excursion* 5. 480
And spires whose "silent finger points to heaven;" 838 *Excursion* 6. 19
His own discoveries; or to favourite points . . 893 *Excursion* 9. 585

Poise. On wings from broad and steadfast poise let loose by this reply, ... 92 *Poet's Dream* 29
Or on thy head to poise a show . . . . . . 341 *Ital. Itin.* 7

Poised. *See* **Self-poised, Well-poised.**
Self-collected, poised, and steady: . . . . . 181 *Waggoner* 4. 143
Poised like a weary cloud, in middle air . . . 226 *Vernal Ode* 9
High poised—or as the wren that sings . . . 348 **Lulled by* 58
That bound it to its native earth—poised high . 358 *Pine: Rome* 3
Absolute stillness, poised aloft in air, ... 390 *Glencroe* 11
Of pine-tree foliage poised in air, forth darts, . . 465 **Dear to* 6
Vivid as fire; clouds separately poised,— . . . 893 *Excursion* 9. 600

Poising. Poising your splendours high above the heads . . . . 230 *Clouds* 27

Poison. Sweet poison spreads along the listener's veins, ... 19 *Desc. Sk.* 524
Poison, which not a frame of steel can brave, . . 20 *Desc. Sk.* 526
And mix the poison, they themselves must drink. 513 *Newspaper* 8
Strong poison not a form of steel can brave . . 613 *Desc.Sk.Quarto* 630
Instil thy subtle poison, and inspire, ... 624 *Æneid* 42

Poisoned. The world is poisoned at the heart. What mean you? . . . . 56 *Bord.* 1036

Poisonous. At the same poisonous fountain! 'Twas an island . . . . 69 *Bord.* 1740
Grew many a poisonous weed; . . . . 102 *Artegal* 30
Whence thickly-sprouting growth of poisonous weeds; . . . . 438 *Ecc. Sonn.* 2. 37. 10

Poisons. I know the poisons of the shade; . . . 145 *Her Eyes* 95

Poisons—*continued.*
And deadlier poisons in the chalice blend. . . . 330 *Ode: Thanks.* 124

Poker. And the tongs and the poker, instead of that horse . . . . 484 **A plague* 3

Polar. Shall lift his country's fame above the polar star! . . . . 103 *Artegal* 56
In his bark the polar sea; . . . . 161 **Pleasures newly* 52
Thou speak'st—and lo! the polar Seas . . . 216 *Enterprise* 87
Is she for tropic suns, or polar snow? . . . . 258 **Where lies the Land* 4
And temples flashing, bright as polar ice, . . . 420 *Ecc. Sonn.* 1. 8. 4
In polar ice, propitious winds have made . . . 434 *Ecc. Sonn.* 2. 23. 5
Floating or fixed of polar ice, allow. . . . . 586 *Ch. Lamb* 106
Forth like a Polar summer: every word . . . 713 *Prelude* 9. 256
Looked on the polar star, as on a guide . . . 811 *Excursion* 4. 697
Like fields of ice rent by the polar wind, . . . 889 *Excursion* 9. 340
Is known to all beneath the polar star, . . . S.3. 442 **Vasco, whose* 13

Pole. *See* **May-pole.**
No peasant leans upon his pole, to tell . . . 15 *Desc. Sk.* 240
Long is it as a barber's pole, or mast of little boat, 189 *Star-gazers* 3
Lodged above the starry pole; . . . . . . 234 *Power of Sound* 109
That host, when from the regions of the Pole . . 321 **Humanity, delighting* 15
Still loftier, and to climes more near the Pole. . 363 **List—'twas* 102
The pole, from which thy name . . . . . . 506 **While from* 42
To roam from heaven to heaven, from pole to pole, 619 *School Ex.* 74
Beyond the seas, and to the farthest pole, . . 797 *Excursion* 3. 748

Polemic. 'Mid clouds enveloped of polemic dust, . 437 *Ecc. Sonn.* 2. 36. 7

Poles. Sounding with grappling irons and long poles. 672 *Prelude* 5. 447
With chattering monkeys dangling from their poles, 697 *Prelude* 7. 694

Policies. He knows the policies of foreign lands; . 670 *Prelude* 5. 319

Policy. For matched with these shall policy prove vain, ... 320 **Avaunt all* 13

Polish. By breezeless air to smoothest polish, yield 313 **Clouds, lingering* 3
The final polish of the Plasterer's hand. . . . 521 *Epist. Beaumont* 25

Polished. Around its polished strings; . . . . 164 *Needlecase* 32
Of the sea-beach, when, polished with nice care, . 250 **Happy the* 6
We hissed along the polished ice in games . . 638 *Prelude* 1. 434
Polished in arts, and in punctilio versed; . . . 711 *Prelude* 9. 117
Still gleams upon their polish'd plumes—the bright K.8. 234 **The order'd* 6

Politic. There, too, ere wiles and politic dispute . 313 **Go back* 9
Glory, and triumph. Yet with politic skill . . 316 **Say, what* 9

Polity. For Polity was then too strong— . . . 291 *Rob Roy* 63
Of polity which wise men venerate, ... 477 **Lowther! in* 7
Rash Polity begin her maniac dance, ... 504 *Warning* 64
While polity and discipline were weak, . . . 518 *Pun. Death* 7. 2
To reason well of polity or law, ... 712 *Prelude* 9. 199
In arguments of civil polity, ... 728 *Prelude* 11. 77
Of civil polity, and early trained . . . . . 880 *Excursion* 8. 393
The powers of civil polity were given." . . . 890 *Excursion* 9. 415

Pollard. The forehead of a pollard oak, ... 168 *Wren's Nest* 35
Through the stiff lance-like shoots of pollard ash, 379 *Duddon* 13. 6

Pollute. To soothe and cleanse, not madden and pollute! . . . . 378 *Duddon* 8. 14

Polluted. *See* **Too-long-polluted.**
Stained and polluted, brighten as they roll, . . 452 *Ecc. Sonn.* 3. 47. 12
Her fields of carnage, and polluted air. . . . 798 *Excursion* 3. 834

Pollution. Of foul pollution—— The whole visible world . . . . 56 *Bord.* 1056
Pollution tainted all that was most pure. . . . 311 **Who rises* 32

Pomp. Blue pomp of lakes, high cliffs and falling floods, ... 5 *Ev. Wk.* 143
Winding in ordered pomp their upward way, . . 6 *Ev. Wk.* 207
Pleased, as she moves, her pomp of clouds to fold 8 *Ev. Wk.* 329
To see a planet's pomp and steady light . . . 16 *Desc. Sk.* 317
Odious to me the pomp of regal court, . . . 104 *Artegal* 158
In pomp of mist or pomp of snow, ... 182 *Waggoner* 4. 228
Is nothing of that radiant pomp so good as we have here? . . . . 189 *Star-gazers* 13
When they in pomp depart . . . . 216 *Enterprise* 109
Be present at his setting; or the pomp . . . 230 *Clouds* 25
And, though past pomp no changes can restore, . 272 *Ruins* 13
In pomp that fades not; everlasting snows; . . 272 *Devil's Bridge* 11
That, not for Fancy only, pomp hath charms; . 276 **Chatsworth! thy* 12
Would hasten, that such pomp may float on high? 278 **The most* 6
Can pomp and show allay one heart-born grief? . 280 **Intent on* 9
Over the pomp and beauty of a scene . . . . 290 *Kilchurn* 26
With Yarrow winding through the pomp . . . 302 *Yarrow V.* 51
Streamed with the pomp of a too-credulous day. . 304 **Jones! as* 3
Hath flowed, "with pomp of waters, unwithstood," 307 **It is not* 4
An intermingled pomp of vale and hill, . . . 323 *Ode 1814* 8
By visual pomp, and by the tie . . . . . . 328 *Ode 1815* 70
(Whose tranquil pomp and spotless purity . . 329 *Ode: Thanks.* 23
Who knows not pomp, who heeds not pelf; . . 344 **How blest* 7
Of splendour unextinguished, pomp unscathed, . 355 *Aquap.* 183
The pomp, the glory of that hour . . . . . 374 *Eg. Maid* 351
And mausolean pomp? Yet here they stand . 389 *Breadalb.* 9
Nor in broad pomp, or courtly state; . . . . 399 *White Doe* 291
The monumental pomp of age . . . . . . 404 *White Doe* 737
To see her in her pomp arrayed— . . . . . 410 *White Doe* 1274
Of sacred home;—with pomp are others gored . 420 *Ecc. Sonn.* 1. 6. 8
She whose high pomp displaced, as story tells, . 434 *Ecc. Sonn.* 2. 21. 13
An intermingling of Heaven's pomp is spread . 457 **Had this* 39
The power is merged, the pomp a grave has found. 471 *Tynwald* 8
Cathedral pomp and grace, in apt accord . . . 477 **Lowther! in* 2
Whose day departs in pomp, returns with smiles— 501 *Humanity* 70
In pomp foreseen by her creative eye, ... 503 *Warning* 40
And how he rules the pomp of light and shade; . 511 **So fair* 12
Are trivial pomp and city noise, ... 533 **Blest is* 52
Issuing in pomp, shall come to judge mankind. . 534 **When in* 16

Pomp—*continued.*
The umbrageous Oak, in pomp outspread, 550 *Hermit's Cell* 5. 9
And with procession great and pomp of men 555 *Prioress* 172
What noble pomp and frequent have not I 574 *Chiabrera* 4. 21
And, floating there, in pomp serene, 579 **Sweet Flower* 19
Lost gradual o'er the heights in pomp they go, 595 *Ev. Wk. Quarto* 187
—The pomp is fled, and mute the wondrous strains, 598 *Ev. Wk. Quarto* 359
Rejoic'd her solemn pomp of clouds to fold 599 *Ev. Wk. Quarto* 395
—To mark a planet's pomp and steady light 609 *Desc.Sk.Quarto* 380
The God of day, in all the pomp of light, 618 *School Ex.* 39
Or all the gaudy pomp of splendid Vice, 619 *School Ex.* 94
Reclin'd in festal pomp the Tyrian queen. 624 *Æneid* 57
With all its foolish pomp. The garden lay 644 *Prelude* 2. 155
The morning rose, in memorable pomp, 663 *Prelude* 4. 324
For pomp, or love. Oft, in the public roads 674 *Prelude* 5. 558
And the horse under him—in gilded pomp 689 *Prelude* 7. 134
With less regret for its luxurious pomp, 710 *Prelude* 9. 30
Yet in the regal sceptre, and the pomp 712 *Prelude* 9. 209
That legalised exclusion, empty pomp 717 *Prelude* 9. 526
Triumphal pomp for liberty confirmed, 725 *Prelude* 10. 496
In the empyrean. Underneath that pomp 725 *Prelude* 10. 523
In exultation with a living pomp 732 *Prelude* 11. 366
Not like a temple rich with pomp and gold, 743 *Prelude* 13. 229
The monumental hillocks, and the pomp 744 *Prelude* 13. 334
Into his mother earth without such pomp 780 *Excursion* 2. 597
Fantastic pomp of structure without name, 784 *Excursion* 2. 859
With pomp, with glory, with magnificence! 803 *Excursion* 4. 122
By day, and all the pomp which night reveals; 816 *Excursion* 4. 973
Contingencies of pomp; and serve to exalt 817 *Excursion* 4. 1061
He had become invisible,—a pomp 820 *Excursion* 4. 1301
A rural lord might dwell."—"No feudal pomp, 824 *Excursion* 5. 98
Her lavish pomp, and ripe magnificence? 828 *Excursion* 5. 402
That spreads, in gentle pomp, its honied shade. 829 *Excursion* 5. 461
In beauty of holiness, with ordered pomp, 838 *Excursion* 6. 11
The crook into a sceptre; give the pomp 846 *Excursion* 6. 550
Of duke or earl, from scenes of courtly pomp 859 *Excursion* 7. 125
"One day—a summer's day of annual pomp 870 *Excursion* 7. 861
In air high-towering with a boorish pomp, 880 *Excursion* 8. 428
Of thy paternal splendours, and the pomp 893 *Excursion* 9. 620
Yet nothing to be seen but lovely pomp K.8. 252 *Recluse* 1.1.561
Pomp has been a sad deceiver. L.2. 190 **Queen and* 14
Pompeii. In POMPEII preserved by her burial in earth; 345 *Stanzas: Simplon* 6
Pompey's. Of Pompey's pillar; that I gravely style 788 *Excursion* 3. 131
Pompous. A greedy flame; the pompous mass proceeds; 431 *Ecc. Sonn.* 2. 11. 3
Of pompous horses; whom vain titles please; 433 *Ecc. Sonn.* 2. 18. 4
And yet—triumphant o'er this pompous show 812 *Excursion* 4. 729
Pompously. Threatened her foes,—or, pompously at rest, 311 **Who rises* 26
Pomps. Or holy festal pomps adorn, 164 **Fair Lady* 7
Her approbation, and with pomps and games. 304 **Festivals have* 5
And all the Pomps of this frail "spot 341 *San Salv.* 20
Why speak of Roman Pomps? the haughty claims 346 *Processions* 28
The exultations, pomps, and cares of Rome, 368 *Trajan* 37
From the collegiate pomps on Windsor's height 430 *Ecc. Sonn.* 2. 6. 4
Pond. A green-grown pond she just has past, 129 *Idiot Boy* 294
At length, himself unsettling, he the pond 196 *Resolution* 78
From pond to pond he roamed, from moor to moor; 196 *Resolution* 103
You see a little muddy pond 198 *Thorn* 30
This pond, and beauteous hill of moss, 198 *Thorn* 57
And that same pond of which I spoke, 198 *Thorn* 62
The pond—and Thorn, so old and grey; 198 *Thorn* 94
The waters of the pond to shake, 199 *Thorn* 195
"But what's the Thorn? and what the pond? 200 *Thorn* 199
The little pond to stir?" 200 *Thorn* 202
Some say she drowned it in the pond, 200 *Thorn* 205
Some say if to the pond you go, 200 *Thorn* 214
Ponder. Listen, ponder, hold them dear; 209 **Yes, it* 19
To watch and ponder—to discern 301 *Bran* 112
Ponder the blessing they entreat 530 *Gleaner* 31
Gravely to ponder—judging between good 707 *Prelude* 8. 520
Pondered. I pondered patiently your wish and will 39 *Bord.* 133
Of the Unsubstantial, pondered well! 235 *Power of Sound* 176
Have pondered here their country's weal, 629 *Installation* 88
I felt, observed, and pondered; did not judge, 737 *Prelude* 12. 188
Only to be examined, pondered, searched, 816 *Excursion* 4. 977
She pondered murmurs that attuned her ear S.3. 436 **The doubt* 174
Pondering. *See* **All-pondering.**
His looks—for pondering he was mute the while. 32 *Guilt* 452
Pondering that Time to-night will pass 112 *Lament* 10
Pondering the mischiefs of these restless times, 509 *F. Stone* 111
Ponderous. Downward the ponderous timber-wain resounds; 4 *Ev. Wk.* 135
This ponderous block was caught by me, 156 *Oak and Broom* 38
Flings o'er the fen that ponderous knell— 238 *P. B.* 214
And crowded, o'er the ponderous books they hung 655 *Prelude* 3. 451
Journeyed with ponderous folios in their hands; 655 *Prelude* 3. 470
And ponderous loom—resounding while it holds 831 *Excursion* 5. 604
A team of horses, with a ponderous freight 865 *Excursion* 7. 542
Ponders. He looks, he ponders, looks again; 242 *P. B.* 526
Who ponders National events shall find 514 **Who ponders* 1
Ponders this true equality, may walk 887 *Excursion* 9. 248
Ponds. If Betty fifty ponds should see, 129 *Idiot Boy* 309
Poniard. And lo! a poniard, at the Monarch's side, 271 *Henry: Portrait* 5
Ponies. *See* **Mountain-ponies.**
Pontiff. A Pontiff, Trajan *here* the Gods implores, 368 *Trajan* 41
"And shall," the Pontiff asks, "profaneness flow 426 *Ecc. Sonn.* 1. 33. 1
To Cæsar's Successor the Pontiff spake; 428 *Ecc. Sonn.* 1. 38. 2
Pony. Then I'll yoke thee to my cart like a pony in the plough; 88 *Pet-lamb* 46

Pony—*continued.*
Her Pony, that is mild and good; 126 *Idiot Boy* 33
But when the Pony moved his legs, 127 *Idiot Boy* 72
And, while the Pony moves his legs, 127 *Idiot Boy* 77
Meek as a lamb the Pony moves, 127 *Idiot Boy* 99
For of this Pony there's a rumour 127 *Idiot Boy* 108
The Pony had his share. 128 *Idiot Boy* 241
"Oh dear, dear Pony! my sweet joy! 129 *Idiot Boy* 299
The Pony he is mild and good, 129 *Idiot Boy* 303
He with his Pony now doth roam 129 *Idiot Boy* 318
And that's the very Pony, too! 130 *Idiot Boy* 357
And Betty sees the Pony too: 130 *Idiot Boy* 367
She pats the Pony, where or when 130 *Idiot Boy* 392
The little Pony glad may be, 130 *Idiot Boy* 394
The Pony, Betty, and her Boy, 130 *Idiot Boy* 407
Pony's. She gently pats the Pony's side, 126 *Idiot Boy* 69
"Or him that wicked Pony's carried 128 *Idiot Boy* 227
Your Pony's worth his weight in gold: 130 *Idiot Boy* 362
And now she's at the Pony's tail, 130 *Idiot Boy* 382
And now is at the Pony's head,— 130 *Idiot Boy* 383
And gently turned the Pony's head 130 *Idiot Boy* 400
Pool. Of a small pool of water he was laid, 73 *Bord.* 2063
Far as the willow-skirted pool, 81 †*Mother's Return* 35
A lamb, that in the pool is pent 85 *Shepherd-boys* 65
He drew it from the troubled pool, 85 *Shepherd-boys* 89
And you may love him in the pool, 142 †*Lov. and Lik.* 23
All round this pool both flocks and herds might drink 149 *M. H.* 8
Beside a pool bare to the eye of heaven 196 *Resolution* 54
Vividly pictured in some glassy pool, 220 *Haunted Tree* 39
For in the pool a startling sight 242 *P. B.* 499
And let the groveller sip his stagnant pool, 277 **A Poet* 6
Reflected in the pool below. 301 *Bran* 73
And haply from this crystal pool, 302 *Yarrow V.* 29
Came to this hidden pool, whose depths surpass 381 *Duddon* 22. 2
Checking the stream, make a pool smooth and clear 382 *Duddon* 23. 4
And slept in many a crystal pool 385 *Yarrow Rev.* 19
Dark moor, and gleam of pool and stream, 409 *White Doe* 1171
In the soft heaven of a translucent pool; 424 *Ecc. Sonn.* 1. 22. 6
Build, at thy choice, or sing, by pool or fount, 455 *Rydal Mere* 35
Is silent as a standing pool; 486 *Matthew* 18
Loitering in glassy pool: 508 *May* 76
Into Bethesda's pool, with healing virtue 510 *F. Stone* 126
Associate all in the calm Pool beneath, 524 *Epist. Beaumont* 180
An elfin pool so sheltered that its rest 527 **Those breathing* 9
And watch these mute Companions, in the pool, 527 **Those breathing* 42
A flock that thirsts not to a pool disliked? 655 *Prelude* 3. 407
A naked pool that lay beneath the hills, 738 *Prelude* 12. 249
Invested moorland waste, and naked pool, 738 *Prelude* 12. 258
Upon the naked pool and dreary crags, 738 *Prelude* 12. 264
A liquid pool that glittered in the sun, 776 *Excursion* 2. 338
That seek yon pool, and there prolong their stay 808 *Excursion* 4. 457
Dimly reflected in a lonely pool. 808 *Excursion* 4. 488
By weedy pool or pestilential swamp, 847 *Excursion* 6. 597
Along the surface of a mountain pool: 858 *Excursion* 7. 33
How she her station doth adorn: the pool 868 *Excursion* 7. 720
Tells from what pool the noblest had been dragged 882 *Excursion* 8. 563
In a deep pool, by happy chance we saw 890 *Excursion* 9. 439
Like that reflected in yon quiet pool, 891 *Excursion* 9. 471
Down looking on that hollow, where the pool K.8. 225 **I will* 47
Pool's. The garden pool's dark surface, stirred 406 *White Doe* 966
Pools. That shaped her sorrow, rocks and pools, 194 *Ruth* 218
The waters of the pools where they abide. 197 *Resolution* 123
Walks, pools, and arbours, homestead, hall— 402 *White Doe* 548
Pools, terraces, and walks are sown 413 *White Doe* 1570
And in the sluggish pools where ships are pent: 495 *Fact* 34
By rocks and pools shut out from every star, 639 *Prelude* 1. 488
Of naked pools, and common crags that lay 678 *Prelude* 6. 234
In silent pools, now in strong eddies chained; 849 *Excursion* 6. 737
Deep pools, tall trees, black chasms, and dizzy crags, K.8. 256 *Recluse* 1.1.711
Poor. To his spare meal he calls the passing poor; 11 *Desc. Sk.* 30
To soothe and cheer the poor man's solitude. 13 *Desc. Sk.* 142
Hung there, no bush proclaimed to old and poor 24 *Guilt* 14
We reached the western world, a poor devoted crew. 29 *Guilt* 297
Where my poor heart lost all its fortitude: 32 *Guilt* 444
Struck the poor innocent. Pallid with dismay 33 *Guilt* 475
Yet happy thou, poor boy! compared with me, 33 *Guilt* 498
Nor could we live together those poor boys and I; 35 *Guilt* 603
Do we poor mortals cater for ourselves! 41 *Bord.* 243
Let this old Man find at your hands; poor Leader, 42 *Bord.* 302
The heart of living creature.—My poor Babe 44 *Bord.* 398
And learn what nature is from this poor Wretch! 45 *Bord.* 444
What strong temptations press upon the Poor. 46 *Bord.* 504
We've weathered out together. My poor Gilfred! 46 *Bord.* 513
The cruel Viper!—Poor devoted Maid, 46 *Bord.* 527
Oh! the poor tenant of that ragged homestead, 47 *Bord.* 568
Though rich in heavenly, poor in earthly, comfort, 49 *Bord.* 686
Of this poor Babe, and taught its innocent tongue 56 *Bord.* 1051
Poor Victim! not a virtue under heaven 57 *Bord.* 1099
And speak with milder voice to his poor beasts. 61 *Bord.* 1336
A human groan. Ha! what is here? Poor Man— 67 *Bord.* 1667
Mutually consecrated. Poor old Man! 70 *Bord.* 1849
The storm beats hard—Mercy for poor or rich, 71 *Bord.* 1882
What can this mean? Alas, for my poor husband!— 71 *Bord.* 1885
'Tis a poor wretch of an unsettled mind, 73 *Bord.* 2033
Entangled this poor man? Where was it? where? 74 *Bord.* 2092
And say no blame was mine—and so, poor fool, 77 *Bord.* 2275
Of which I have been proud. O my poor Master! 78 *Bord.* 2321

Poor—continued.

Sat the poor girl, and forth did send . . . . 82 *Alice Fell* 38
" It will not, will not rest !—Poor creature, can it be . . . . 88 *Pet-lamb* 49
And the poor Boy was busier still, with work of anxious heed. 91 *Norman Boy* 12
Where he, in his poor self so weak, by Providence was placed. 91 *Norman Boy* 28
But the poor ragged Thing whose ways my human heart had warmed. 92 *Poet's Dream* 16
" Poor Shepherd of the naked Down, a favoured lot is thine, 92 *Poet's Dream* 53
Alas the dream, to thee, poor Boy ! to thee from whom it flowed, 93 *Poet's Dream* 77
Poor Walter ! whether it was care that spurred him . . . . 98 *Brothers* 217
Was sadly crossed.—Poor Leonard ! when we parted, 100 *Brothers* 321
I buried him, poor Youth, and there he lies ! . 101 *Brothers* 382
There is a change—and I am poor ; 111 *A Complaint* 1
Of my fond heart, hath made me poor. 111 *A Complaint* 18
My poor forsaken Child, if I . . . . 114 *Ind. Wom.* 65
They cried, ' what to the poor is due ?' 115 *Last of Flock* 50
My Son, if thou be humbled, poor, . 117 *Affl. Marg.* 36
She begged an alms, like one in poor estate ; . 119 *Sailor's Mother* 11
To a poor neighbouring cottage ; as I found, . 120 *Emigrant Mother* 7
To my poor heart, if thou wouldst be . 120 *Emigrant Mother* 23
These tears—and my poor idle tongue. 121 *Emigrant Mother* 78
There's none to help poor Susan Gale ; 126 *Idiot Boy* 30
Oh ! then for the poor Idiot Boy ! 127 *Idiot Boy* 73
Now, though he knows poor Johnny well, . 127 *Idiot Boy* 114
To comfort poor old Susan Gale. 127 *Idiot Boy* 121
But Betty, poor good woman ! she, . 127 *Idiot Boy* 132
Poor Susan moans, poor Susan groans ; . 127 *Idiot Boy* 142
Poor Susan moans, poor Susan groans ; . 127 *Idiot Boy* 147
" Oh God forbid !" poor Susan cries. 128 *Idiot Boy* 191
That God poor Susan's life would spare, . 128 *Idiot Boy* 200
At poor old Susan then he railed, . 128 *Idiot Boy* 232
Poor Betty, in this sad distemper, . 128 *Idiot Boy* 237
And I have lost my poor dear Boy, . 129 *Idiot Boy* 255
Poor Betty ! it would ease her pain . 129 *Idiot Boy* 269
To comfort poor old Susan Gale. 129 *Idiot Boy* 276
Poor Betty now has lost all hope, . 129 *Idiot Boy* 292
What can be done ? Where every one is poor, . 135 *Michael* 254
And left estates and monies to the poor, . 135 *Michael* 268
Honour ascends among the humblest poor, . 138 *Widow* 2
And what if my poor cheek be brown ? . 145 *Her Eyes* 68
But he, poor man ! is wretched made ; . 145 *Her Eyes* 78
And in thy iteration, " WHIP POOR WILL !" . 153 *Morn. Ex.* 16
Thus threatened a poor Briar-rose, . 179 *Waterfall* 6
Poor pilot I, by snows confounded, . 179 *Waggoner* 3. 91
Poor Susan has passed by the spot, and has heard . 188 *Poor Susan* 3
Poor in estate, of manners base, men of the multitude, 189 *Star-gazers* 22
Deserted his poor Bride, and Ruth . 194 *Ruth* 191
To gather leeches, being old and poor : . 196 *Resolution* 100
And this poor Thorn they clasp it round . 197 *Thorn* 17
To bury this poor Thorn for ever. . 197 *Thorn* 22
Does this poor Woman go ? . 198 *Thorn* 81
Poor Martha ! on that woeful day . 199 *Thorn* 117
For what became of this poor child . 199 *Thorn* 146
With drops of that poor infant's blood ; . 200 *Thorn* 211
The poor Hart toils along the mountain-side ; . 201 *Hart-leap* 29
For shelter, and a poor man's bread ! . 204 *Brougham* 79
Love had he found in huts where poor men lie ; . 205 *Brougham* 161
A nobler counsellor than my poor heart. . 210 *Laod.* 54
How poor, were human life ! . 223 *Wishing-gate* 12
Wide open for the scattered Poor. . 228 *Devot. Incit.* 59
O'er this poor family. . 231 *Jew. Fam.* 8
On two poor legs, toward my stone-table . 238 *P. B.* 174
Groaned the poor Beast—alas ! in vain ; . 238 *P. B.* 192
The poor Ass staggered with the shock ; . 241 *P. B.* 426
" I'm helping this poor dying brute." . 242 *P. B.* 490
And he whom the poor Ass had lost, . 243 *P. B.* 577
Of this poor miserable Ass !" . 243 *P. B.* 585
In pity to this poor drowned man. . 243 *P. B.* 595
Like a poor bird—her plundered nest . 243 *P. B.* 649
And this poor slave who loved him well, . 243 *P. B.* 662
But he hath said, poor gentle wight ! . 245 *P. B.* 758
" This poor man never but for me . 245 *P. B.* 809
Are busy with poor Peter Bell ; . 246 *P. B.* 917
Thought Peter, 'tis the poor man's home. . 247 *P. B.* 996
The poor Ass standing by her side, . 248 *P. B.* 1024
Poor Peter from a thousand causes . 248 *P. B.* 1034
She calls the poor Ass by his name, . 248 *P. B.* 1044
Oh ! would, poor beast, that I had now . 248 *P. B.* 1099
And many years did this poor Ass, . 249 *P. B.* 1126
The very flowers are sacred to the Poor, . 250 *Admon.* 11
That the poor Harp distempered music yields . 252 *Why, Minstrel* 13
Torn from the Poor ! yet shall kind Heaven protect 255 *S. H.* 10
The poor old Man is greater than he seems : . 267 *Though narrow* 2
Whence the poor unregarded Favourite, true . 274 *Wait, prithee* 7
A poor old Dame will bless them for the boon : . 280 *Intent on* 3
Thou " poor Inhabitant below," . 285 *Grave of Burns* 50
For thou wert still the poor man's stay, . 292 *Rob Roy* 109
The poor man's heart, the poor man's hand ; . 292 *Rob Roy* 110
A poor blind Highland Boy. . 295 *Highland Boy* 10
Than did the poor blind Boy. . 295 *Highland Boy* 45
Woe to the poor blind Mariner ! . 296 *Highland Boy* 104
Which he, poor Child, had studied well ; . 296 *Highland Boy* 117
She saw her poor blind Boy. . 296 *Highland Boy* 165

Poor—continued.

And welcomed the poor Child. . 297 *Highland Boy* 225
Of such poor Instruments, with thoughts sublime . 309 *When, looking* 13
Could they, poor Shepherds, have preserved an aim, 316 *It was a* 3
Which shall not fail, though poor men cleave with pride . 320 *O'erweening Statesmen* 4
That guards the lowliest of the poor. . 375 *The Minstrels* 36
But love, as Nature loves, the lonely Poor ; . 390 *Highland Hut* 11
What poor abodes the heirloom hide, . 391 *Highland Broach* 65
And this poor verse, and worthier lays, . 391 *Highland Broach* 81
While the Poor gather round, till the end of time . 393 *Countess' Pillar* 1
—" Even these poor eight of mine would stem—" . 405 *White Doe* 853
To hide her poor afflicted head ? . 413 *White Doe* 1556
Flow to the poor, and freedom to the slave ; . 424 *Ecc. Sonn.* I. 24. 12
(Like a poor bird entangled in a snare . 440 *Ecc. Sonn.* 2. 45. 4
Not in the breathing-times of that poor slave . 454 *Not in the lucid* 5
Poor as thou art. A welcome sacrifice . 465 *Pastor and* 8
For poor to Sea I went, and poor I still remain. . 470 *From early* 5
Though poor to Sea I went, and poor I still remain. 470 *From early* 14
Though poor, yet rich, without the wealth of books, 471 *Ailsa Crag* 12
Eyeing the sea's blue depths. Poor Bird ! even so 472 *Dunolly Eagle* 12
The poor, the lonely, herdsman's joy and pride. . 475 *Greenock* 14
Are poorest of the poor. . 483 *Simon Lee* 44
At which the poor old Man so long . 484 *Simon Lee* 87
Has seduced the poor fool from his winter retreat, 484 *A plague* 9
Led, Heaven knows how ! to this poor sod : . 485 *Poet's Epitaph* 26
Poor Matthew, all his frolics o'er, . 486 *Matthew* 1
Said to his servile Courtiers,—" Poor the reach, . 495 *Fact* 10
For the poor Many, measured out by rules . 501 *Humanity* 87
Soon shall the Rich be levelled down—the Poor . 513 *Newspaper* 2
Where one poor Plane-tree, having as it might . 521 *Epist. Beaumont* 14
Not oftentimes, I trust, as we, poor brute ! . 523 *Epist. Beaumont* 139
From his poor inch or two of daisied sod ? . 527 *Those breathing* 29
Poor Robin is yet flowerless ; but how gay . 529 *Poor Robin* 5
Poor Robin as a sure and crafty friend. . 530 *Poor Robin* 21
When he could creep about, at will, though poor . 531 *I know* 5
Though poor and destitute of friends thou art, . 531 *Octogen.* 9
Old Goody Blake was old and poor ; . 536 *Goody Blake* 21
Might see how poor a hut she had. . 536 *Goody Blake* 24
All day she spun in her poor dwelling : . 536 *Goody Blake* 25
Two poor old Dames, as I have known, . 536 *Goody Blake* 34
But she, poor Woman ! housed alone. . 536 *Goody Blake* 36
And made her poor old bones to ache, . 537 *Goody Blake* 58
And sprang upon poor Goody Blake. . 537 *Goody Blake* 88
" Poor Harry Gill is very cold." . 537 *Goody Blake* 124
As in a cloister. Yet the grateful Poor . 539 *Lady ! a* 48
One is a Woman, a poor earthly sister, . 541 *Grace Darl.* 71
A poor Man's counsel take ; . 542 *Russ. Fug.* 32
To end life here like this poor deer. . 545 *Russ. Fug.* 311
But take it in good part :—alas ! the poor . 547 *Rude is* 5
" Now this poor Widow waiteth all that night . 554 *Prioress* 135
Alas, poor Book ! for thy unworthiness, . 562 *Cuck.and Night.* 298
At distance still the same. Poor Traveller ! . 567 *Cumb. Beg.* 58
—But of the poor man ask, the abject poor ; . 568 *Cumb. Beg.* 142
No—man is dear to man ; the poorest poor . 568 *Cumb. Beg.* 147
For Adam was simple in thought ; and the poor, . 569 *Farmer* 25
Poor winter look fine in such strange masquerade. . 570 *Farmer* 76
I learned that one poor moment can suffice . 574 *Chiabrera* 4. 23
And mourn, thou poor half-witted Boy ! . 577 *I come* 39
For one poor moment's space to Thee, . 580 *John Words.* 8
When the poor heart has all its joys resign'd, . 613 *Desc.Sk.Quarto* 622
For thy poor babes that, hurrying from the door, . 615 *Desc.Sk.Quarto* 709
" Poor victim ! no idle intruder has stood . 621 *Convict* 45
But for the poor dear sake of one . 621 *Andrew Jones* 5
For this poor crawling helpless wretch . 621 *Andrew Jones* 11
But the poor Cripple was alone . 621 *Andrew Jones* 14
Seemed friends, poor simple schoolboys, now hung round . 649 *Prelude* 3. 20
To a poor scholar !"—when illustrious men, . 656 *Prelude* 3. 474
And poor misguided Shame, and witless Fear, . 657 *Prelude* 3. 598
Of trivial pleasures was a poor exchange . 663 *Prelude* 4. 298
Commended him as a poor friendless man, . 665 *Prelude* 4. 451
Poor earthly casket of immortal verse, . 668 *Prelude* 5. 164
Stringed like a poor man's heifer at its feed, . 669 *Prelude* 5. 240
Pity the tree.—Poor human vanity, . 670 *Prelude* 5. 329
Not rich one moment to be poor for ever ; . 686 *Prelude* 6. 735
Eyed the poor babe with love unutterable. . 696 *Prelude* 7. 618
For, born in a poor district, and which yet . 712 *Prelude* 9. 215
With the most noble, but unto the poor . 714 *Prelude* 9. 303
A poor mistaken and bewildered offering,— . 721 *Prelude* 10. 231
A virtuous household, though exceeding poor ! . 758 *Excursion* 1. 112
Hath blessed poor Margaret for her gentle looks, . 763 *Excursion* 1. 503
Sank down, as in a dream, among the poor ; . 764 *Excursion* 1. 544
And of the poor did many cease to be, . 764 *Excursion* 1. 545
Of the poor innocent children. ' Every smile,' . 765 *Excursion* 1. 589
I thought of that poor Woman as of one . 765 *Excursion* 1. 613
Nor how to speak to her. Poor Wretch ! at last . 766 *Excursion* 1. 652
To that poor Woman :—so familiarly . 768 *Excursion* 1. 780
The same sad question. Meanwhile her poor Hut . 770 *Excursion* 1. 900
How the poor brute's condition, forced to run . 772 *Excursion* 2. 51
And, sometimes—where the poor man held dispute . 772 *Excursion* 2. 65
With one poor shepherd, far from all the world !— . 778 *Excursion* 2. 463
And he too hath his comforter. How poor, . 778 *Excursion* 2. 479
" That poor Man taken hence to-day," replied . 780 *Excursion* 2. 593
That the poor Sufferer had escaped with life. . 785 *Excursion* 2. 890
If from my poor retirement ye had gone . 788 *Excursion* 3. 118
Erect himself, how poor ... thing is man !' . 806 *Excursion* 4. 331
Of a poor lamb—left somewhere to itself, . 807 *Excursion* 4. 411
That poor men's children, they, and they alone, . 813 *Excursion* 4. 786
Of his poor hut, or on the mountain-top, . 813 *Excursion* 4. 827

Poor—*continued.*
Which his poor skill could make, his fancy fetched, 814 *Excursion* 4. 857
Beyond their own poor natures and above . . 815 *Excursion* 4. 935
That one, poor, finite object, in the abyss . . . 816 *Excursion* 4. 993
And rich and poor, and young and old, rejoice . 824 *Excursion* 5. 105
Come,' said the Matron, 'to our poor abode ; . . 834 *Excursion* 5. 767
And pride of opportunity made poor ; . . . . 835 *Excursion* 5. 832
Perhaps yon loose sods cover, the poor Pensioner 835 *Excursion* 5. 881
And burthensome ; and lastly, that poor few . . 837 *Excursion* 5. 967
Of poor humanity's afflicted will . . . . 846 *Excursion* 6. 556
"Wish could be ours that you, for such poor gain, 847 *Excursion* 6. 581
To a poor dissolute Son, her only child. . . . 849 *Excursion* 6. 715
Of the fresh shower, but of poor Ellen's tears . 850 *Excursion* 6. 816
To grant, or be received ; while that poor bird— 851 *Excursion* 6. 878
When that poor Child was born. Upon its face . 852 *Excursion* 6. 907
Like a poor singing-bird from distant lands ; . . 852 *Excursion* 6. 934
See him a constant preacher to the poor ! . . . 859 *Excursion* 7. 150
Which her poor treasure-house is content to owe, 862 *Excursion* 7. 320
Behind yon hill, a poor and rugged wild, . . . 862 *Excursion* 7. 348
Of the poor calling which my youth embraced . 873 *Excursion* 7. 1049
Of a poor brotherhood who walk the earth . . 875 *Excursion* 8. 42
For grateful converse : and to these poor men . 875 *Excursion* 8. 58
Of some poor hamlet, rapidly produced . . . 876 *Excursion* 8. 119
How art thou blighted for the poor Man's heart ! 878 *Excursion* 8. 264
Which the poor broom no sooner felt . . . . S.3.431 **The Scottish* 19
You know where my poor bones shall be, . . . K.8. 220 **The snow-tracks* 34
Drive one of these poor creatures miles and miles, K.8. 228 **I will* 124
Your vassal necks how poor the garter's pride ! . L.I. 97 *Juvenal* 3. 91
Poorest. From the old and the young, from the poorest ; and there ! . . . . . . 188 *Music* 27
Proud be this Land ! whose poorest huts are halls 388 *Loch Etive* 6
Are poorest of the poor. . . . . 483 *Simon Lee* 44
No—man is dear to man ; the poorest poor . . 568 *Cumb. Beg.* 147
Your very poorest rich in peace of thought . . 895 *Excursion* 9. 734
Poorly. "Poorly provided, poorly followed," . . 103 *Artegal* 92
And wayworn Wanderers, poorly fed, ... 507 *May* 31
Pope. Happy is he, who, caring not for Pope, . . 304 **Festivals have* 12
And 'tis the Pope that wields it :—whether rough . 428 *Ecc. Sonn.* 1. 39. 13
The vacillating Bondman of the Pope . . . . 442 *Ecc. Sonn.* 3. 9. 13
And seal up all the gains of France, a Pope . . 732 *Prelude* 11. 359
Popinjay. Kept crying, "Farewell !—farewell, Popinjay !" 561 *Cuck.andNight.*222
Popinjays. By chattering popinjays ; the inner heart . . . . 655 *Prelude* 3. 444
Poplar. And swings above the roof the poplar tall. 6 *Ev. Wk.* 241
Poplars. And while those lofty poplars gently wave 272 **Where holy* 11
Poppy. The wild rose, and the poppy, and the nightshade : . . . . 38 *Bord.* 45
Gathering green weeds to mix with poppy flower, 261 **Fair Prime* 6
While rose and poppy, as the glow-worm fades, . 599 *Ev. Wk. Quarto* 397
Popular. Of popular applause. I now perceived . 70 *Bord.* 1822
Not on the breath of popular applause, . . . 213 *Dion* 47
Of popular reason, long mistrusted, freed . . . 327 **Emperors and* 10
With those of Greece compared and popular Rome, 708 *Prelude* 8. 618
From popular government and equality," . . . 725 *Prelude* 10. 473
Thither his popular talents he transferred ; . . 774 *Excursion* 2. 219
A popular equality reigns here, ... 823 *Excursion* 5. 96
Populous. No more : for now into a populous plain 652 *Prelude* 3. 194
Her rivers populous with gliding life ; . . . . 819 *Excursion* 4. 1199
Porch. The shady porch ne'er offered a cool seat . 15 *Desc. Sk.* 244
There, to the porch, belike with jasmine bound . 21 *Desc. Sk.* 604
The roses to the porch which they entwine : . . 250 *Admon.* 12
The cluster round the porch, and the folk . . . 396 *White Doe* 33
And smote off his head on the stones of the porch ! 399 *White Doe* 253
Porch, door-way, or kirk-pillar ; and of youths, . 701 *Prelude* 8. 152
The honeysuckle, crowding round the porch, . . 767 *Excursion* 1. 715
The corner stones, on either side the porch, . . 767 *Excursion* 1. 743
And the wild birds that gather round my porch. . 834 *Excursion* 5. 816
Around the porch, and seems, in that trim place, 855 *Excursion* 6. 1150
Whose place of rest is near yon ivied porch. . . 864 *Excursion* 7. 487
The pillared porch, elaborately embossed ; . . 881 *Excursion* 8. 465
Pore. Whatever be the cause, 'tis sure that they who pry and pore . . . . 189 *Star-gazers* 29
Our minds shall drink at every pore . . . . 483 *Sister* 27
A shadow, a delusion, ye who pore . . . . . 703 *Prelude* 8. 296
That we should pore, and dwindle as we pore, . 815 *Excursion* 4. 960
Of their long twilight, pore upon her book . . 852 *Excursion* 6. 901
Pored. Pored, watched, expected, listened, spread my thoughts . . . . 650 *Prelude* 3. 114
Poring. While poring Antiquarians search the ground . . . . 275 **While poring* 1
Porlezza's. Porlezza's verdant lawn. . . . . 343 *Eclipse* 36
Porringer. I take my little porringer, ... 84 *We are Seven* 47
Demure with porringer and plate . . . . . 127 *Idiot Boy* 129
Port. For me—farthest from earthly port to roam . 31 *Guilt* 359
Some, perched on stems of stately port . . . 154 *Flower Garden* 39
A nun demure of lowly port ; . . . . . . 158 **With little* 17
Erect his port, and firm his going ; . . . . . 181 *Waggoner* 4. 148
Of contemplation, the calm port . . . . . 190 **Lyre ! though* 10
Ere thrice the Moon into her port had steered, . 202 *Hart-leap* 81
Of rainbow colours ; One whose port was bold, . 334 **A winged* 2
Into a natural port, a tideless sea, ... 356 *Aquap.* 220
Her port she could not win it, ... 374 *Eg. Maid* 369
Turn into port ; and, reckless of the gale, . . . 379 *Duddon* 13. 10
Fresh gales to waft them to the far-off port ; . . 454 *Sea-side* 18
Alike to body and to mind : his port, ... 711 *Prelude* 9. 146
The wished-for port to which my course was bound. 756 *Excursion* 1. 27
Within a port of rest had lodged me safe ; . . . 794 *Excursion* 3. 566
The form, port, motions, of this Cottage-girl . . 850 *Excursion* 6. 826
Is that the countenance, and such the port, . . 879 *Excursion* 8. 316

Port—*continued.*
Cordially greeted. Graceful was her port : . . 881 *Excursion* 8. 501
Portal. He rose, and to the ruin's portal went, . 30 *Guilt* 312
He through the portal takes his silent way, . . 211 *Laod.* 156
Who, through the portal of one moment's guilt, . 214 *Dion* 104
Lay hushed ; till—through a portal in the sky . 323 *Ode 1814* 19
Who through the silent portal arch . . . . 386 *Yarrow Rev.* 99
The dark cave's portal gliding by, ... 415 *White Doe* 1740
Portals. Through the year's successive portals ; . 90 *Longest Day* 53
The portals of the dawn ; all Paradise . . . . 122 *V. and J.* 46
Between the portals of the shadowy rocks . . 681 *Prelude* 6. 452
As chanced, the portals of the sacred Pile . . . 824 *Excursion* 5. 138
Portended. And the waves rose, and sky portended danger. . . . . 369 *Eg. Maid* 30
Portending. Portending ruin to each baleful rite . 419 *Ecc. Sonn.* 1. 3. 5
Portent. Whence these opprobrious leaves of dire portent ? . . . . 515 **Men of* 2
Portentous. Portentous through her old woods' trackless bounds, ... 12 *Desc. Sk.* 74
A burning of portentous red ; . . . . . . 175 *Waggoner* 1. 169
O matchless perfidy ! portentous lust . . . . 214 *Dion* 106
But the live scales of a portentous nature ; . . 311 **Who rises* 18
All steeped in this portentous light ! . . . . 343 *Eclipse* 53
Portentous fellowship. Her silver car, . . . 438 *Ecc. Sonn.* 2. 38. 8
Portentous change when History can appear . . 514 **Portentous change* 1
Assumed a voice of deep portentous sound, . . 629 *Installation* 103
Nay brighter shone, by this portentous gloom . 709 *Prelude* 8. 657
Porter. The Porter sits down on the weight which he bore ; . . . . 188 *Music* 21
Like a gaunt shaggy Porter forced to wait . . 523 *Epist. Beaumont* 152
Served as stable-boy, errand-boy, porter, and groom ; . . . . 570 *Farmer* 50
Porter's. Through hours of silence, till the porter's bell, ... 676 *Prelude* 6. 70
Portion. A final portion from his father's hand ; . 123 *V. and J.* 106
A portion of the tale may well be left . . . . 124 *V. and J.* 176
A portion of his patrimonial fields. . . . . . 134 *Michael* 224
On that best portion of a good man's life, . . . 206 *Tintern* 33
Should be thy portion, with what healing thoughts 207 *Tintern* 144
Thy lot, O Man, is good, thy portion fair ! " . . 215 *Kirkstone* 86
And, through the sunny portion of the year, . . 268 **Pure element* 5
Curses are *his* dire portion, scorn, and hate, . . 317 **Look now* 10
A portion of God's peace. . . . . 337 **Oh Life* 12
From wolves your portion of His chosen sheep : . 444 *Ecc. Sonn.* 3. 16. 5
A portion of the gift is won ; . . . . . . 457 **Had this* 38
Therein a portion claim. . . . . 498 **The sylvan* 18
How faint their portion of his vital beams ! . . 528 **Those breathing* 57
"This portion of the river of my mind . . . 645 *Prelude* 2. 209
I cannot say what portion is in truth . . . . 658 *Prelude* 3. 610
That portion of my story I shall leave . . . . 668 *Prelude* 5. 192
In this late portion of my argument, ... 679 *Prelude* 6. 275
So, did a portion of that spirit fall . . . . . 724 *Prelude* 10. 448
That were our daily portion when we first . . 752 *Prelude* 14. 417
And some small portion of his eloquent speech, . 757 *Excursion* 1. 98
The better portion of his time ; and there . . 761 *Excursion* 1. 350
The portion gave of coarse but wholesome fare . 783 *Excursion* 2. 745
And will possess my portion in content ! . . . 802 *Excursion* 4. 65
Can portion out his pleasures, and adapt, . . . 813 *Excursion* 4. 803
To me some portion of a kind regard ; . . . . 824 *Excursion* 5. 107
Shines with some portion of that heavenly lustre 839 *Excursion* 6. 50
Hath issued any portion of the joy . . . . . K.8. 245 *Recluse* 1.1.317
Some portion of its human history . . . . . K.8. 248 *Recluse* 1.1.416
Portioned. Thy scanty breathing-time is portioned out 172 *Infant Daughter* 17
Portions. The last and later portions of this gift . 752 *Prelude* 14. 415
Portland. Near Portland lighthouse in a lonesome creek, ... 35 *Guilt* 592
Portrait. Go, faithful Portrait ! and where long hath knelt . . . . 276 *Author's Portrait* 1
I gaze upon a Portrait whose mild gleam . . . 508 *F. Stone* 6
Domestic Portrait ! have to verse consigned . . 510 *F. Stone* 122
Portrait's. From this fair Portrait's fleshly Archetype, ... 509 *F. Stone* 83
Portraits. Your portraits still may reach the heart 164 **Fair Lady* 11
(Even like their persons in their portraits clothed 653 *Prelude* 3. 270
For, in such portraits, though a vulgar face . . 847 *Excursion* 6. 576
Portraiture. Like portraiture, from loftier source, endears . . . . 351 *Des. Stanzas* 59
With thy memorial flower, meek Portraiture ! . . 510 **Among a* 11
This portraiture is sketched. The great, the good, 862 *Excursion* 7. 341
Portraitures. Their Portraitures, their stone-work glimmers, dyed . . . . 451 *Ecc. Sonn.* 3. 44. 3
Or portraitures for special use designed, . . . 657 *Prelude* 3. 552
Portray. Who rashly strove thy Image to portray ? 511 **Who rashly* 1
Portrayed. *See* **Pourtrayed.**
Is it a gallows there portrayed ? . . . . . 242 *P. B.* 503
All praise the Likeness by thy skill portrayed ; . 279 **All praise* 1
Objects immense portrayed in miniature, . . . 379 *Duddon* 12. 3
Broods, visibly portrayed, the mystic Dove, . . 450 *Ecc. Sonn.* 3. 39. 13
Hath here portrayed with Nature's happiest grace 461 **Giordano, verily* 2
Where Christian Martyrs stand in hues portrayed, 500 *Humanity* 21
Portrayed with happiest pencil, not untrue . . 583 **With copious* 23
On many a staring countenance portrayed . . 858 *Excursion* 7. 96
Have been portrayed, I guess not ; but it chanced 865 *Excursion* 7. 540
Of living nature, cannot be portrayed . . . . 891 *Excursion* 9. 513
Portrays. *See* **Pourtrays.**
A Pastor such as Chaucer's verse portrays ; . . 380 *Duddon* 18. 12
Ports. And navies perish in their ports ; . . . 328 *Ode 1815* 100
By each new upstart notion ? In the ports . . 816 *Excursion* 4. 1026
Of keels that rest within her crowded ports, . . 876 *Excursion* 8. 137

Pouring. *See* **Forth-pouring.**
Thus Hope, first pouring from her blessed horn — 8 *Ev. Wk.* 339
Pouring out praise to the almighty Giver, — 160 **Up with me* 24
Open their hearts before Thee, pouring out — 539 **Lady! a* 52
And pouring deeper blue to Æther's bound; — 599 *Ev. Wk. Quarto* 394
Pouring above his head its radiance down — 799 *Excursion* 3. 942
Pourings. *See* **Out-pourings.**
Pours. And pours a deeper blue to Æther's bound; — 8 *Ev. Wk.* 328
On me such bounty Summer pours, — 156 *Oak and Broom* 75
Pours forth his song in gushes; — 159 *Green Linnet* 36
Pours forth in shady groves, shall plead for me; — 217 *Enterprise* 146
The sweat pours down from Peter's face, — 247 *P. B.* 931
And pours forth streams more sweet than Castaly. — 251 **Pelion and* 14
Pours forth his bounty, like the day doth cheer, — 425 *Ecc. Sonn.* 1. 26. 7
Pours on the surface of the turbid Stream! — 430 *Ecc. Sonn.* 2. 7. 3
Of many-coloured life that Fortune pours — 430 *Ecc. Sonn.* 2. 8. 4
Pours out his choicest beverage high and higher — 433 *Ecc. Sonn.* 2. 20. 5
To cheer the Itinerant on whom she pours — 463 **Adieu, Rydalian* 12
Till pours the wakeful bird her solemn strains — 599 *Ev. Wk. Quarto* 377
Pourtrayed. *See* **Portrayed.**
Collaterally pourtrayed, as in mock fight, — 657 *Prelude* 3. 582
A specimen pourtrayed with faithful hand. — 670 *Prelude* 5. 297
Pourtrays. *See* **Portrays.**
Yet my fancy has pierced to his heart, and pourtrays — 620 *Convict* 19
Poverty. A thousand miles. I am in poverty, — 74 *Bord.* 2078
Dire poverty assailed; — 103 *Artegal* 87
And perish all of poverty. — 115 *Last of Flock* 40
Solitude, pain of heart, distress, and poverty. — 195 *Resolution* 35
Of poverty and wrong, — 232 *Jew. Fam.* 42
To poverty, and grief, and disrespect, — 441 *Ecc. Sonn.* 3. 6. 4
For discontent, and poverty, and crime; — 463 **They called* 11
In liveried poverty. — 483 *Simon Lee* 28
Pride, anger, mischief, poverty, and madness. — 560 *Cuck. and Night.* 175
In penniless poverty. But now to school — 643 *Prelude* 2. 84
Which might not be withstood, that poverty — 717 *Prelude* 9. 520
Their power or weakness, wealth or poverty, — 728 *Prelude* 11. 102
And poverty and labour in excess — 742 *Prelude* 13. 198
Busy in solitude and poverty. — 760 *Excursion* 1. 257
The keen, the wholesome, air of poverty, — 760 *Excursion* 1. 306
And poverty brought on a petted mood — 765 *Excursion* 1. 580
More plainly still, that poverty and grief — 769 *Excursion* 1. 833
It seemed the home of poverty and toil, — 776 *Excursion* 2. 340
Beyond all poverty how destitute, — 778 *Excursion* 2. 480
From childhood up, the ways of poverty; — 802 *Excursion* 4. 48
Of vagrant poverty; from rifted barns — 843 *Excursion* 6. 326
Powdered. The ground was green, with daisy powdered over; — 557 *Cuck. and Night.* 63
Powdered like rimy trees, when frost is keen. — 649 *Prelude* 3. 39
Powdery. Her feet disperse the powdery snow, — 83 *Lucy Gray* 27
Power. *See* **Sister-power.**
Yet still, the sport of some malignant power, — 2 *Ev. Wk.* 31
Where with loud voice the power of water shakes — 10 *Desc. Sk.* 7
Whither is fled that Power whose frown severe — 11 *Desc. Sk.* 54
Yet are thy softer arts with power indued — 13 *Desc. Sk.* 141
Itself all trembling at the torrent's power. — 14 *Desc. Sk.* 185
—And sure there is a secret Power that reigns — 16 *Desc. Sk.* 346
An unknown power connects him with the dead: — 18 *Desc. Sk.* 454
—Yet hast thou found that Freedom spreads her power — 21 *Desc. Sk.* 620
Crowed with ear-piercing power till then unheard; — 21 *Desc. Sk.* 629
Well may we wonder he has gained such power — 37 *Bord.* 13
Has given him power to teach: and then for courage — 38 *Bord.* 36
Have power to yield? perhaps he looks elsewhere.— — 42 *Bord.* 259
Has left a power of riches; and I say it, — 46 *Bord.* 487
Eternal praises on the power that saved her!— — 46 *Bord.* 519
His Power is this way tending. It befits us — 56 *Bord.* 1027
Which haunts this Oswald. Power is life to him — 63 *Bord.* 1432
He was forsaken? There is a power in sounds: — 68 *Bord.* 1732
The tale was spread abroad; my power at once — 69 *Bord.* 1761
That waking life had never power to give. — 69 *Bord.* 1794
Why should a thrust of the arm have such a power, — 77 *Bord.* 2270
God has given a kindlier power — 80 *Foresight* 25
That Cross he now was fastening there, as the surest power and best — 91 *Norman Boy* 21
Just as those final words were penned, the sun broke out in power, — 91 *Poet's Dream* 1
And a steadfast outward power — 94 *Westmoreland Girl* 78
The power of speech. Both left the spot in silence; — 101 *Brothers* 408
And stripped of power! me, feeble, destitute, — 104 *Artegal* 140
Far as in power the eagle doth the worm: — 105 *Artegal* 181
Down would he sit; and without strength or power — 107 *Indolence* 22
What power is in his wildest scream, — 117 *Affl. Marg.* 24
Have power to shake me as they pass: — 117 *Affl. Marg.* 67
To imprint a kiss that lacked not power to spread — 119 *Maternal Grief* 61
Careless of books, yet having felt the power — 131 *Michael* 28
Appeared, and spiritual presence gained a power — 139 *Widow* 26
Hath power to part the Spirits of those who love — 152 **Forth from* 17
In power of wing and never-wearied voice. — 153 *Morn. Ex.* 42
Have I derived from thy sweet power — 158 **In youth* 43
Help, as if from faery power; — 163 *Spinning Wheel* 4
"Mark him, how his power he uses, — 163 *Hint* 9
Gazing she feels its power beguile — 164 **Fair Lady* 33
Hath power to injure mine. — 167 *Pilgrim's Dream* 40
(Sentient by Grecian sculpture's marvellous power), — 169 *Love lies Bleeding* 6
Has it in her power again: — 171 *Kitten* 28
And Reason's godlike Power be proud to own. — 173 *Infant Daughter* 78
His bones, and those of all his Power, — 176 *Waggoner* 1. 213

Power—*continued.*
Had for their joys a killing power. — 180 *Waggoner* 4. 74
Motley accoutrement, of power to smile — 185 *Nutting* 12
Shall feel an overseeing power — 187 **Three years* 11
He fills with his power all their hearts to the brim— — 188 *Music* 7
No, no, this cannot be;—men thirst for power and majesty! — 189 *Star-gazers* 24
Lyre! though such power do in thy magic live — 190 **Lyre! though* 1
A time to overrule the power — 191 *Seq. Beggars* 17
And one night's diminution of her power, — 192 *Gipsies* 18
When our Shepherd in his power, — 205 *Brougham* 151
While with an eye made quiet by the power — 206 *Tintern* 47
Of harmony, and the deep power of joy, — 206 *Tintern* 48
Nor harsh nor grating, though of ample power — 207 *Tintern* 92
And he, whose power restores thee, hath decreed — 210 *Laod.* 57
Was princely Dion, in the power — 212 *Dion* 5
Hath stained the robes of civil power with blood, — 213 *Dion* 56
As variously thy power was shown, — 216 *Enterprise* 39
For the power of hills is on thee, — 218 **Inmate of* 33
Of Britain's calm felicity and power! — 219 **This Height* 34
Pure as herself—(song lacks not mightier power) — 220 *Triad* 9
What spirit-stirring power it gained — 224 **'Tis gone* 10
Suddenly raised by some enchanter's power, — 226 *Vernal Ode* 17
Her darkness splendour gave, her silence power, — 226 *Vernal Ode* 38
And is She brought within the power — 227 *Vernal Ode* 110
The double note, as if with living power, — 229 *Cuckoo-clock* 10
Power, glory, empire, as the world itself, — 230 *Clouds* 39
Nourish the hope that memory lacks not power — 231 *Clouds* 90
Of power ethereal and celestial grace, — 231 **The gentlest Poet* 37
That voice of Freedom, in its power — 233 *Power of Sound* 71
And with a soul of power. — 238 *P. B.* 140
Twined round him by demoniac power, — 241 *P. B.* 474
And if I had the power to say — 243 *P. B.* 632
To bow to some transforming power, — 246 *P. B.* 859
A stifling power compressed his frame, — 246 *P. B.* 873
A gentle, a relaxing, power! — 247 *P. B.* 965
Praised be the Art whose subtle power could stay — 252 *Picture* 1
From her own overflow, what power sedate — 255 **Grief, thou* 10
But in chaste hearts, uninfluenced by the power — 256 **Yes! hope* 12
That I may have the power to sing of Thee, — 257 **The prayers* 13
But how could I forget thee? Through what power, — 257 **Surprised by* 6
And let my spirit in that power divine — 258 **Even so* 13
Rejoice, as, through that power, it ceased to mourn. — 258 **Even so* 14
Imagination is that sacred power, — 259 **Weak is* 9
Thee might thy Minions crown, and chant thy power, — 261 **Fair Prime* 7
While health, power, glory, from their height decline, — 261 **I watch* 11
Yet did the glowing west with marvellous power — 262 **Dark and* 5
Day's mutable distinctions.—Ancient Power! — 265 **Hail, Twilight* 4
At thy meek bidding, shadowy Power! brought forth; — 265 **Hail, Twilight* 11
The power of Merlin, Goddess! this should be: — 266 **With how* 9
Such power possess the family of floods — 272 *Devil's Bridge* 13
That neither feeds nor wastes its vital power — 274 *Infant M.* 3
Like them. The unguilty Power pursues his way, — 277 **Haydon! let* 13
In power, where once he trembled in his weakness; — 281 **What strong* 6
Now, for your shame, a Power, the Thirst of Gold, — 283 **Proud were* 4
Power in my breast, wings growing in my mind, — 284 *Departure* 14
His power survives. — 286 *Nith* 48
Its power was felt; and while my eye — 289 *Stepping West.* 21
Youthful as Spring.—Shade of departed Power, — 290 *Kilchurn* 31
That they should take, who have the power, — 291 *Rob Roy* 39
That there is One who scorns thy power:— — 293 *Jedbor.* 7
When madding Power her bolts had hurled, — 298 *Brownie's Cell* 22
Brought low a Power, which from its home — 298 *Brownie's Cell* 35
Quakes—conscious of thy power; — 299 *Cora Linn* 3
A seemly reverence may be paid to power; — 303 **Is it* 9
True Power doth grow on; and her rights are these. — 304 **I grieved* 14
A span of waters; yet what power is there! — 306 **Inland, within* 7
Strength to the brave, and Power, and Deity; — 306 **Inland, within* 11
And give us manners, virtue, freedom, power. — 307 **Milton! thou* 8
And by the power, of wrong. — 312 **Who rises* 68
All power was given her in the dreadful trance; — 313 *Prophecy* 9
And babble of her pastime!—On, dread Power! — 315 **Advance—come* 9
O joyless power that stands by lawless force! — 317 **Look now* 9
Is there a power that can sustain and cheer — 318 **Is there* 1
Oak of Guernica! Tree of holier power — 319 *Guernica* 1
That he has power to inflict what we lack strength to bear. — 319 *Spaniard* 14
The power of Armies is a visible thing, — 321 **The power* 1
But who the limits of that power shall trace — 321 **The power* 3
That power, that spirit, whether on the wing — 321 **The power* 8
Gathered his power, a manifest ally; — 322 **By Moscow* 11
With starry lustre; yet had power to throw — 324 *Ode 1814* 77
Had power as lofty actions to achieve — 325 *Ode 1814* 140
The power of retribution once was given: — 325 *Enghien* 11
Of irksome change, or threats from saddening power. — 327 *Ode 1815* 16
Thy power and majesty, — 329 *Ode: Thanks.* 12
That less than power unbounded could not tame — 330 *Ode: Thanks.* 94
Not all the light of earthly power could fill; — 330 *Ode: Thanks.* 116
Lodge it within us!—as the power of light — 331 *Ode: Thanks.* 165
Shall lack not power the "meeting soul to pierce!" — 333 *Ded. Tour* 14
(Streamed from the west) as with a robe of power: — 333 **Bruges I* 2
O gentle Power of darkness! these mild hues; — 334 **Bruges I* 11
To a voice of thrilling power. — 334 **In Bruges* 8
Fling the shadow of thy power, — 336 **Jesu! bless* 15
With tutelary power, — 342 *Ital. Itin.* 72
And all-controlling power. — 344 *Eclipse* 84

Powers—*continued.*
Powers that survive but in the faintest dream . 235 *Power of Sound* 171
Getting and spending, we lay waste our powers : 259 **The world is* 2
Unswept, unstained ? Nor shall the aerial Powers 263 **How clear* 10
The dream, to time and nature's blended powers . 264 **Lady ! the* 6
The visual powers of Nature satisfy, ... 279 **All praise* 12
Yet—though dread Powers, that work in mystery, spin . . . . 280 **Oh what* 2
Oh ! there is life that breathes not ; Powers there are . . . . 290 *Kilchurn* 6
Else verily the sober powers 300 *Bran* 37
Powers that will work for thee ; air, earth, and skies ; . . . . 305 *Toussaint* 10
And know that noble feelings, manly powers, . 308 **There is a bondage* 11
Among the lurking powers . . . . 311 **Who rises* 50
By all the blended powers of Earth and Heaven. 312 **A Roman* 14
Powers have they left, an impulse, and a claim . 316 **It was a* 7
Your thrones, ye Powers, from duty fear to swerve ! 327 **Emperors and* 11
With all her armèd Powers, 331 *Ode : Thanks.* 150
Hath failed ; and now, ye Powers ! whose gorgeous wings . . . . 335 *Cologne* 6
Fetch, sympathising Powers of air, ... 348 **Lulled by* 43
Of bounty infinite. Between Powers that aim 354 *Aquap.* 144
By no profane ambition, Powers that thrive . . 354 *Aquap.* 146
And others like in fame, created Powers . . . 357 *Aquap.* 282
Powers manifold we have that intervene . . . 361 **For action* 2
Of evil with good Powers . . . . 374 *Eg. Maid* 356
Which Nature and these rustic Powers, . . . 375 **The Minstrels* 29
To what dread Powers He delegates his part . . 389 *Tyndrum* 13
And prompt a harmony of genuine powers ; . . 389 *Breadalb.* 13
So may the Soul, through powers that Faith bestows, 390 *Glencroe* 13
Fate, fortune, sweep strong powers away, . . . 391 *Highland Broach* 63
Memory, like sleep, hath powers which dreams obey, ... 392 *Bothwell* 12
Or Fancy localises Powers we love. . . . . 393 **The Lovers* 8
A song of Nature's hidden powers ; . . . . 399 *White Doe* 271
Him will I seek : the insurgent Powers . . . 408 *White Doe* 1115
What Powers, presiding o'er the sacred well . . 418 *Ecc. Sonn.* 1. 2. 3
Warbled a while with faint and fainter powers, . 453 **Calm is the* 8
Not one of all those wingèd powers is seen, . . 454 *Sea-side* 20
Of *Powers* endued with visible form, instinct . . 469 **Bold words* 13
For her mute Powers, fixed Forms, or transient Shows. . . . . 471 *Ailsa Crag* 14
And pain, hath powers to Eternity endeared. . . 476 *Howard* 14
" Nor less I deem that there are Powers . . . 481 *Expost.* 21
Whose powers shed round him in the common strife, ... 493 *Hap. War.* 45
Kindles intense desire for powers withheld . . 496 **A little* 27
For deathless powers to verse belong, ... 499 **Departing summer* 25
That wastes so oft, we think, its tuneful powers, . 501 **The unremitting* 2
Thanks to the Powers that yet maintain their sway, 503 *Warning* 22
All Powers and Places that abhor the light . . 513 **Said Secrecy* 12
Is to control and check disordered Powers ? . . 514 **Who ponders* 14
On Love and Fear, their several powers he blends, 518 *Pun. Death* 5. 7
Stript of its frightful powers by slow decay, . . 523 *Epist. Beaumont* 126
To rural incidents, whose genial powers . . . 525 *Epist. Beaumont* 268
Harmonious Powers with Nature work . . . 531 †*Float. Isl.* 1
May Nature's kindliest powers sustain the Tree, . 546 **The embowering* 9
Began to honour May with all their powers. . . 558 *Cuck. and Night.* 70
Those rare accomplishments, and varied powers, . 583 **With copious* 15
All softening, humanising, hallowing powers, . . 585 *Ch. Lamb* 84
The father forc'd by Powers that only deign . . 613 *Desc.Sk.Quarto* 616
Close at her side were all the powers, design'd . 618 *School Ex.* 17
Whence human kind, and brute ; what natural powers . . . . 625 *Æneid* 124
Are haunted by majestic Powers, ... 629 *Installation* 79
And their congenial powers, that, while they join 632 *Prelude* 1. 39
Bear witness Truth, endowed with holy powers . 650 *Prelude* 3. 88
Breathings for incommunicable powers ; . . . 651 *Prelude* 3. 187
The worth I knew of powers that I possessed, . 663 *Prelude* 4. 344
Why, gifted with such powers to send abroad . 666 *Prelude* 5. 48
Their benediction ; speak of them as Powers . . 669 *Prelude* 5. 218
In reconcilement with our stinted powers ; . . 673 *Prelude* 5. 517
Of human forms with superhuman powers, . . 676 *Prelude* 6. 92
Hands of angelic powers had fixed it there, . . 682 *Prelude* 6. 485
The whole creative powers of man asleep !— . . 697 *Prelude* 7. 681
Armies of clouds,—even so, its powers and aspects 698 *Prelude* 7. 753
Man suffering among awful Powers and Forms ; . 701 *Prelude* 8. 165
Powers of my native region ! Ye that seize . . 702 *Prelude* 8. 218
Nor to be heard of more ; yet, they were powers, . 712 *Prelude* 9. 178
Oh, pity and shame ! with those confederate Powers ! . . . . 722 *Prelude* 10. 265
All powers of swiftness, subtilty, and strength . 729 *Prelude* 11. 127
Prevailed among the powers of heaven and earth, . 733 *Prelude* 11. 438
In glorious apparition, Powers on whom . . . 735 *Prelude* 12. 98
For they are Powers ; and hence the highest bliss 747 *Prelude* 14. 113
Suppose my powers so far confirmed, and such . 750 *Prelude* 14. 309
(And the progressive powers perhaps no less . . 755 *Recluse* 1. 1. 817
There mingled, heard or not. The powers of song 797 *Excursion* 3. 752
Upon the tall mast streaming. But, ye Powers . 798 *Excursion* 3. 842
" And what are things eternal ?—powers depart," 802 *Excursion* 4. 66
Restor'st us, daily, to the powers of sense . . . 802 *Excursion* 4. 90
What visionary powers of eye and soul . . . 803 *Excursion* 4. 111
' Vain-glorious Generation ! what new powers . 805 *Excursion* 4. 278
The constitutions, powers, and faculties, . . . 806 *Excursion* 4. 338
Nor let the hallowed powers, that shed from heaven . . . . 808 *Excursion* 4. 483

Powers—*continued.*
—Jehovah—shapeless Power above all Powers, . 811 *Excursion* 4. 651
To waste her powers, as in the worldling's mind, . 813 *Excursion* 4. 820
The forms of Nature, and enlarge her powers ? . 814 *Excursion* 4. 846
Now simply guarded by the sober powers . . . 815 *Excursion* 4. 917
Unbaffled powers of vision hath prepared, . . 815 *Excursion* 4. 945
His privacy to principles and powers . . . . 823 *Excursion* 5. 40
High-titled Powers, am I constrained to ask, . 827 *Excursion* 5. 341
With evening cheerfulness. In powers of mind, . 833 *Excursion* 5. 716
Powers not unjustly likened to those gifts . . 835 *Excursion* 5. 844
" You do not err : the powers, that had been lost 841 *Excursion* 6. 192
Among the first of Powers and Virtues—proved ? 846 *Excursion* 6. 566
And what to higher powers is justly due. . . . 862 *Excursion* 7. 314
The powers of nature : and a few short steps . 864 *Excursion* 7. 465
And to the mind among her powers of sense . . 865 *Excursion* 7. 521
Restless, and restless generation, powers . . . 872 *Excursion* 7. 1002
Measuring the force of those gigantic powers . . 877 *Excursion* 8. 205
Our active powers, those powers themselves become 886 *Excursion* 9. 131
The powers of civil polity were given." . . . 890 *Excursion* 9. 415
Tricks out her blustering powers, ... S.3. 431**The Scottish* 30
By powers celestial tossed on land and sea . . . K.8. 281 **Arms and* 4
Pozzobonnelli. Pozzobonnelli his illustrious house ; 575 *Chiabrera* 8. 7
Practicable. Their practicable way. . . . . . 458 **Had this* 52
Practice. (A practice till this time unknown to him) 100 *Brothers* 350
Your practice prove, faithless though but in thought, 444 *Ecc. Sonn.* 3. 16. 11
—Not He, who from her mellowed practice drew 504 *Warning* 61
Whose practice teaches, spite of names to show . 530 *Poor Robin* 22
The practice flow,—if thence, or from a deep . 847 *Excursion* 6. 618
Doth practice give) that neither in the flocks . K.8. 225 **I will* 44
Practise. To practise games and archery : . . 409 *White Doe* 1179
A noble mind to practise on herself, ... 816 *Excursion* 4. 1019
Practised. *See* **Long-practised.**
Who has so practised on the world's cold sense, . 41 *Bord.* 250
Good Baron, have you ever practised tillage ? . 60 *Bord.* 1277
And an eye practised like a blind man's touch. . 151 **When, to* 83
Six thousand veterans practised in war's game, . 293 *Killicranky* 1
Which practised talent readily affords, . . . 455 **Not in the lucid* 8
The keenness of that practised eye, ... 485 *Poet's Epitaph* 7
Practised to commune with her royal knight . . 716 *Prelude* 9. 488
By nature yielded to his practised hand ;— . . 860 *Excursion* 7. 165
Both understood and practised,—so that none, . 888 *Excursion* 9. 303
A Youth, I practised this delightful art ; . . . 891 *Excursion* 9. 486
Practising. For practising occult and perilous lore) 369 *Eg. Maid* 22
Praise. Bandusia's praise, wild stream, should yield to thine ! . . . . 3 *Ev. Wk.* 73
Have wrought with godlike arm the deeds of praise, 15 *Desc. Sk.* 290
That, when your praise was warm upon my tongue, 42 *Bord.* 284
Your generous qualities have won due praise, . 48 *Bord.* 621
And we too chant the praise of his good deeds. . 54 *Bord.* 907
Is bold, and would relieve itself by praise. . 64 *Bord.* 1483
Resound the praise of your morality— . . . 77 *Bord.* 2291
" Then offer up thy heart to God in thankfulness and praise, ... 93 *Poet's Dream* 57
A Maid whom there were none to praise . . . 109 **She dwelt* 3
Receiving from his Father hire of praise ; . . . 134 *Michael* 191
Thy long-lost praise thou shalt regain ; . . . 158 **In youth* 77
I give to thee, for praise or blame, ... 158 **With little* 14
Pouring out praise to the almighty Giver, . . . 160 **Up with me* 24
Taken praise that should be thine, ... 160 **Pansies, lilies* 55
Hymns in praise of what I love ! . . . . . 160 **Pansies, lilies* 64
Praise of which I nothing know. . . . . . 161 **Pleasures newly* 8
And thy store of other praise. . . . . . 161 **Pleasures newly* 32
Praise it is enough for me, ... 161 **Pleasures newly* 54
Accept, O Friend, for praise or blame, ... 182 *Waggoner* 4. 197
Praise, blame, love, kisses, tears, and smiles. . . 186 **She was* 20
If they speak 'tis to praise, and they praise with a smile. . . . . 188 *Music* 32
—Give Sir Lancelot Threlkeld praise ! . . . . 204 *Brougham* 95
And venture on your praise. . . . . . . 225 *Present.* 12
For praise and ceaseless gratulation, poured . . 235 *Power of Sound* 207
Heed not such onset ! nay, if praise of men . . 255 *Detraction* 11
To think how much of this will be thy praise. . 260 *Calvert* 14
Nor will I praise a cloud, however bright, . . . 263 **Those words* 7
Haydon ! let worthier judges praise the skill . . 277 **Haydon ! let* 1
All praise the Likeness by thy skill portrayed ; . 279 **All praise* 1
Hath sounded (shame upon the Bard !) thy praise 281 **Wansfell ! this* 6
I praise thee, Matron ! and thy due . . . . 294 *Jedbor.* 35
Is praise, heroic praise, and true ! . . . . . 294 *Jedbor.* 36
So be it !—but let praise ascend . . . . . 294 *Jedbor.* 76
Our sires set forth their grateful praise : . . . 301 *Bran* 75
Of the world's praise, from dark antiquity . . 307 **It is not* 3
With deeds of hope and everlasting praise :— . 318 **Is there* 10
Here pause : the poet claims at least this praise, . 321 **Here pause* 1
To rob our Human-nature of just praise . . . 322 **By Moscow* 5
—Chant the Deliverer's praise in every tongue ! . 326 *Sobieski* 11
Songs of victory and praise, ... 328 *Ode 1815* 79
A holy Structure to the Almighty's praise. . . 338 *Engelberg* 14
Another's praise from envy clear. . . . . . 344 **How blest* 13
Not vain is sadly-uttered praise ; . . . . . 348 **Lulled by* 61
Your praise, in meet accordance with your claims 352 *Aquap.* 5
With praise, as genuine admiration prompts. . . 356 *Aquap.* 246
The grief, the praise, are severed from their dust, 356 *Aquap.* 247
Then eased his soul at length by praise . . . 374 *Eg. Maid* 341
The Sabine Bard was moved her praise to sing ; . 376 *Duddon* 1. 4
And tender Goldsmith crowned with deathless praise ! . . . . 380 *Duddon* 18. 14
The Torrents chant their praise, inspiring scorn . 383 *Duddon* 29. 12
Shall yield no light of love or praise ; . . . . 391 *Highland Broach* 82
But Praise can waste her voice on work of tears, 392 *Avon* 9
This Sabbath-day, for praise and prayer. . . . 396 *White Doe* 30
With awful cheer a voice of praise ; . . . . 397 *White Doe* 157

Praise—*continued.*
The light of praise shall shine for ever! . . . 409 *White Doe* 1215
Than from her wily praise, her peaceful gown, . 420 *Ecc. Sonn.* 1. 8. 11
Nor shall the eternal roll of praise reject . . 441 *Ecc. Sonn.* 3. 6. 1
Of praise from Heaven. To Thee, O saintly WHITE, 444 *Ecc. Sonn.* 3. 15. 8
Shall hymns of praise resound at morn and even; 450 *Ecc. Sonn.* 3. 41. 7
By some acknowledgment of thanks and praise, . 454 *Sea-side* 23
With stainless touch, as chaste as when thy praise 460 **Queen of* 25
Of prayer and praise forget their rosaries, . . . 467 *St. Bees* 89
While heaven's vast sea of voices chants their praise. 474 **On to* 14
Her Champion's praise recounted; . . . . . 478 *Somnamb.* 56
Blessings be with them—and eternal praise, . . 489 *Pers. Talk* 51
False praise from true, or, greater from the less, . 489 *Spade* 22
It is not from unwillingness to praise, ... 490 *Tribute: Dog* 3
Who, whether praise of him must walk the earth 494 *Hap. War.* 77
Rich theme of England's fondest praise, . . . 495 *Fact* 25
This hymn of thanks and praise, ... 498 **The sylvan* 21
Their voices mount symbolical of praise— . . 500 *Humanity* 16
The voice of praise at early morn, ... 506 *Lab. Hymn* 2
A song of gratitude and praise. . . . . . . 506 *Lab. Hymn* 8
Should praise thee, genial Power! . . . . . 507 *May* 14
In thy fresh wreaths, than they for praise . . 508 *May* 87
Be Thou to love and praise alike impelled, . . 511 **So fair* 20
A theme for praise and admiration high. . . . 517 *Pun. Death* 3. 4
Accept, mute Captives! thanks and praise; . . 527 **The soaring* 53
Nay, we would simply praise the free good-will . 530 *Poor Robin* 24
That would unite in prayer and praise; . . . 533 **Blest is* 34
The pleasure was, and no one heard the praise, . 539 **Lady! a* 36
To Infancy, that lisps her praise—to Age . . . 540 *Grace Darl.* 11
Blended with praise of that parental love, . . 541 *Grace Darl.* 92
So far runs back the praise . . . . 544 *Russ. Fug.* 194
Self-hidden praise, and Friendship's private tear: 547 **Ye Lime* 12
"Wherefore in praise, the worthiest that I may, . 552 *Prioress* 8
Our Lady I will praise with all my power. . . 554 *Prioress* 92
His heart, that her to praise, to her to pray, . . 554 *Prioress* 105
Praise be to such, and to their slumbers peace! . 568 *Cumb. Beg.* 141
Be lost in thankfulness and praise. . . . . . 578 **I come* 52
That shunned so modestly the light of praise, . 583 **With copious* 8
That said, "Let praise be mute where I am laid;" 584 **With copious* 41
The hermit, exercised in prayer and praise, . . 586 *Ch. Lamb* 122
The song of thanks and praise; . . . . . 589 *Immortality* 144
Hear Britain's sons rehearse thy praise with joy, 619 *School Ex.* 101
And needful to build up a Poet's praise. . . . 634 *Prelude* 1. 157
Am worthy of myself! Praise to the end! . . 637 *Prelude* 1. 350
And pleasant flowers. The thirst of living praise, 654 *Prelude* 3. 336
For its own sake, on glory and on praise . . . 654 *Prelude* 3. 390
And shapes of spurious fame and short-lived praise 657 *Prelude* 3. 592
Nor would I praise her but in perfect love. . . 669 *Prelude* 5. 263
To chant your praise; nor can approach you now 685 *Prelude* 6. 672
Hyperboles of praise comparative; . . . . 686 *Prelude* 6. 734
Of earth-born passions, on the wings of praise . 748 *Prelude* 14. 186
And listening Time reward with sacred praise. . 758 *Excursion* 1. 107
The imperfect offices of prayer and praise, . . 759 *Excursion* 1. 216
Munificent, and love, and ladies' praise; . . . 771 *Excursion* 2. 4
Which kings might envy!"—Praise to this effect 787 *Excursion* 3. 75
Little to praise, and nothing to regret, . . . 790 *Excursion* 3. 272
Yet I will praise thee with impassioned voice: . 802 *Excursion* 4. 39
Vigils of contemplation; praise; and prayer— . 804 *Excursion* 4. 218
Nor is it a mean praise of rural life . . . . 806 *Excursion* 4. 365
With lifted hands invoked, and songs of praise: . 811 *Excursion* 4. 680
And from their fervent lips drew hymns of praise, 815 *Excursion* 4. 931
He sought not praise, and praise did overlook . 823 *Excursion* 5. 45
By sight undazzled with the glare of praise, . . 827 *Excursion* 5. 357
The pale Recluse—"praise to the sturdy plough, . 831 *Excursion* 5. 602
And patient spade; praise to the simple crook, . 831 *Excursion* 5. 603
Preclude forgiveness, from the praise debarred, . 845 *Excursion* 6. 489
Within this ground, were covetous of praise, . . 847 *Excursion* 6. 603
Less gracefully were braided;—but this praise, . 851 *Excursion* 6. 842
Lying insensible to human praise, ... 865 *Excursion* 7. 538
All praise, all safety, and all happiness, . . . 877 *Excursion* 8. 215
Nothing to praise, to teach, or to command! . . 878 *Excursion* 8. 275
Beheld without compassion, yea, with praise! . 887 *Excursion* 9. 194
Fulfilled, the hope accomplished; and thy praise 894 *Excursion* 9. 677
Will find a vent; and thought is praise to him, . 895 *Excursion* 9. 752
Audible praise, to thee, omniscient Mind, . . . 895 *Excursion* 9. 753
Of many a Grecian vale, who sought not praise, . S.3. 436 **The doubt* 154
That your praise appears to me . . . . . S.3. 438 **My Lord* 27
The whip, the cap, and spurs, thy praise attest; . L.1. 94 *Juvenal* 2. 22
Praised. Fervently cried the housewife—"God be praised, ... 34 *Guilt* 565
And it was you, dear Lady! God be praised, . 50 *Bord.* 719
That we are praised, only as men in us . . . 70 *Bord.* 1823
But when the fruit, so often praised . . . . 142 †*Lov. and Lik.* 35
"Oh! God be praised—my heart's at ease— . 248 *P. B.* 1026
Praised be the Art whose subtle power could stay . 252 *Picture* 1
And by the general reverence God is praised: . 283 **Well have* 12
That God might suitably be praised. . . . . 298 *Brownie's Cell* 10
Has ended, though no Clerk, with "God be praised!" . . . . 394 *Countess' Pillar* 14
Praised be the Rivers, from their mountain springs 431 *Ecc. Sonn.* 2. 13. 1
"The blossom you so fondly praised . . . . 542 *Russ. Fug.* 65
Admired for beauty, for her sweetness praised; . 774 *Excursion* 2. 188
The weak were praised, rewarded, and advanced; . 798 *Excursion* 3. 828
Is styled, when most affectionately praised, . . 824 *Excursion* 5. 103
And praised the gallant bearing, of a Knight . . 825 *Excursion* 5. 186
(The same kind Matron whom your tongue hath praised) . . . . 834 *Excursion* 5. 754
Praised the consummate harmony serene . . . 882 *Excursion* 8. 538
Praises. Eternal praises on the power that saved her!— . . . . 46 *Bord.* 519
Thanks and praises, each a gage . . . . . 141 *Arm. Lady* 124

Praises—*continued.*
Let them live upon their praises; . . . . . 160 **Pansies, lilies* 2
The praises of mild Benjamin. . . . . . . 174 *Waggoner* 1. 45
"And, gallant Stag! to make thy praises known, 201 *Hart-leap* 65
O Thou, through whom the temple rings with praises, ... 233 *Power of Sound* 83
And sound thy praises everlastingly. . . . . 257 **The prayers* 14
Ye Storms, resound the praises of your King! . 322 **Ye Storms* 1
Shall praises be poured forth, and thanks ascend, 328 *Ode 1815* 122
Or thanks and praises to His throne ascend . . 331 *Ode: Thanks.* 180
And thanks and praises seemed to run . . . 484 *Simon Lee* 90
Or praises for our country's victories; . . . . 722 *Prelude* 10. 295
Will I record the praises, making verse . . . 743 *Prelude* 13. 234
That still unites them, praises, like heaven's dew, 861 *Excursion* 7. 240
Praiseth. And praiseth Christ that is our heavenly King, ... 555 *Prioress* 167
Praising. Their solemn joy—praising the Eternal Lord . . . . 332 *Ode: Thanks.* 201
Weeping and praising Jesu's Mother dear; . . 556 *Prioress* 227
But, blessing God and praising him, bequeathed . 839 *Excursion* 6. 69
Prancing. Joy sparkled in the prancing courser's eyes; . . . . 200 *Hart-leap* 9
Prank. By music, prank, and laughter-stirring jest; 858 *Excursion* 7. 82
Pranks. Like a bold Girl, who plays her agile pranks 260 **How sweet* 6
At all the merry pranks of Donnerdale! . . . 379 *Duddon* 13. 14
Prate. While clarions prate of kingdoms to be won— 345 **Ambition—following* 3
Prate somewhat loudly of the whereabout . . 693 *Prelude* 7. 428
Prater. This woman is a prater. Pray, good Lady! 45 *Bord.* 436
Prattle. Mid the gay prattle of those infant tongues, 523 *Epist. Beaumont* 158
Or when the prattle of Bandusia's spring . . . 528 **Those breathing* 104
And unaimed prattle flying up and down; . . 663 *Prelude* 4. 315
Articulate prattle—Child as beautiful . . . . 692 *Prelude* 7. 339
Prattled. On which so oft he prattled when a boy. 609 *Desc.Sk.Quarto* 413
Prattler. A little Prattler among men. . . . . 79 *Sparrow's Nest* 14
While yet a prattler on the knee, ... 407 *White Doe* 1038
Prattlers. In arms, now rosy prattlers at the feet . 661 *Prelude* 4. 204
Prattling. A little prattling child, he oft descends, 19 *Desc. Sk.* 485
Prattling upon his knee, to call him Father—— 56 *Bord.* 1042
Bandusia, prattling as when long ago . . . . 376 *Duddon* 1. 3
And later down, in prattling childhood even, . . 668 *Prelude* 5. 171
The wild brooks prattling from invisible haunts; 700 *Prelude* 8. 67
Pray. And pray that never child of song . . . 9 *Collins* 19
I could not pray:—through tears that fell in showers 28 *Guilt* 242
No more, I pray, of this. Three days at farthest 43 *Bord.* 322
This woman is a prater. Pray, good Lady! . . 45 *Bord.* 436
Pray tell me what this land is worth by the acre. . 60 *Bord.* 1278
Near the wood's edge—rest there to-night, I pray you: . . . . 67 *Bord.* 1648
There be who pray nightly before the Altar. . . 67 *Bord.* 1655
And lays it to his heart—. I pray you speak! . . 67 *Bord.* 1670
Be calm, I pray thee! Oswald— Name him not. 76 *Bord.* 2237
Watch over her, I pray—sustain her—— Captain! 78 *Bord.* 2338
"And where are they? I pray you tell." . . 83 *We are Seven* 17
Yet ye are seven! I pray you tell, ... 84 *We are Seven* 27
I only pray to know the worst; . . . . . 110 *Forsaken* 6
My Johnny, do, I pray you, do." . . . . . 126 *Idiot Boy* 61
And all temptation, Luke, I pray that thou . . 137 *Michael* 409
"Tempt me not, I pray; my doom is . . . . 140 *Arm. Lady* 49
I pray thee have no fear of me; . . . . . 144 *Her Eyes* 16
And every day we two will pray . . . . . 145 *Her Eyes* 79
"Yon owl!—pray God that all be well! . . . 179 *Waggoner* 3. 112
Pray in ghostly agonies. . . . . 204 *Brougham* 68
Confirm, I pray, the vision with thy voice: . . 210 *Laod.* 32
Had she; and, in the kirk to pray, ... 246 *P. B.* 897
If Thou the spirit give by which I pray: . . . 257 **The prayers* 2
With earnest feeling I shall pray . . . . . 288 *Highland Girl* 22
Thus did he cry, and thus did pray, ... 297 *Highland Boy* 203
Therefore the wise pray for thee, though the freight 309 **England! the* 12
Intrudes on peace, I pray the eternal Sire . . 470 *Bala-Sala* 5
Edward will come with you;—and, pray, . . . 483 *Sister* 13
Then come, my Sister! come, I pray, ... 483 *Sister* 37
O turn aside,—and take, I pray, ... 485 *Poet's Epitaph* 22
Thus on her knees did Goody pray; . . . . 537 *Goody Blake* 102
Now think, ye farmers all, I pray, ... 537 *Goody Blake* 127
"Tears might be shed, and I might pray, . . . 545 *Russ. Fug.* 289
Of his Companion, he would pray that both . . 551 **If thou in* 21
For sometimes, Lady! ere men pray to thee . . 552 *Prioress* 25
Even so fare I; and therefore, I thee pray, . . 553 *Prioress* 34
Her to salute, and also her to pray . . . . 553 *Prioress* 82
His heart, that her to praise, to her to pray, . . 554 *Prioress* 105
"She asketh, and she piteously doth pray . . 555 *Prioress* 149
Pray also thou for us, while here we tarry . . 556 *Prioress* 236
But hear you now a wondrous thing, I pray; . . 558 *Cuck.andNight.*106
Have knowledge, I thee pray, what this may be? 559 *Cuck.andNight.*125
I pray to God with her always to be, ... 561 *Cuck.andNight.*257
And now I pray you all to do me right . . . 561 *Cuck.andNight.*269
Now, my sweet Troilus, love me well, I pray! . 563 *Troilus* 54
Unto the blood of Troy, I pray of thee, . . . 563 *Troilus* 82
Penned these sad lines, nor can forbear to pray . 575 *Chiabrera* 7. 16
And pray that in his faithful breast the grace . 576 **By a* 21
For which we pray; and for the wants provide . 834 *Excursion* 5. 810
The majesty of both, shall pray for both; . . 838 *Excursion* 6. 13
Where, Sir, I pray you, where are laid the bones . 854 *Excursion* 6. 1078
Then wake me not, I pray you. Hush, speak low. S.3. 441 **Grateful is sleep, more* 4
Prayed. Bidding me trust in God, he stood and prayed;— . . . . 28 *Guilt* 241
Ravage for which no knell was heard. We prayed 29 *Guilt* 284

Prayed—*continued.*
But you prayed by him? 72 *Bord.* 1963
And then I would have prayed, and had no voice. 77 *Bord.* 2251
And what, for my part, I have often prayed: 99 *Brothers* 289
I prayed, yet every day I thought 115 *Last of Flock* 87
Mere slave of them who never for thee prayed, 253 **Fond words* 13
For which it prayed! 285 *Grave of Burns* 78
I to my Father knelt and prayed; 401 *White Doe* 489
And prayed the Earls in self-defence 403 *White Doe* 631
While the Monks prayed in Maiden's Bower 405 *White Doe* 833
With tears, and of his Father prayed— 409 *White Doe* 1236
And painful struggle and deliverance—prayed 460 **Queen of* 31
And the Lady prayed in heaviness 495 *Force of Prayer* 61
By their own daring. But the People prayed 513 *General Fast* 5
And, kneeling on the sticks, she prayed 537 *Goody Blake* 95
She prayed, her withered hand uprearing, 537 *Goody Blake* 97
So prayed he:—as our chronicles report, 551 **If thou in* 24
But to his comrade he repaired, and prayed 553 *Prioress* 74
To cleave unto this man; but when I prayed 667 *Prelude* 5. 116
Was prayed to as a judge; but these were past, 719 *Prelude* 10. 44
Have prayed that throughout earth upon all men, 720 *Prelude* 10. 135
"So prayed, more gaining than he asked, the Bard— 755 *Recluse* 1. 1. 777
The one Survivor stood; he wept, he prayed 774 *Excursion* 2. 202
And with that pang I prayed to be no more!— 785 *Excursion* 2. 877
She prayed, she moaned;—her husband's sister watched 849 *Excursion* 6. 749
Who bore me; and hath prayed for me in vain;— 852 *Excursion* 6. 926

Prayer. While prayer contends with silenced agony, 20 *Desc. Sk.* 549
Died in his arms; and with those thanks a prayer 36 *Guilt* 643
And hear his prayer that I would not forsake him 66 *Bord.* 1610
Is ringing it—'twould stop a Saint in prayer, 67 *Bord.* 1665
The thunder send him on his knees to prayer 75 *Bord.* 2179
With this dear holy shepherd-boy breathe a prayer of earnest heart, 91 *Norman Boy* 30
I saw, within, the Norman Boy kneeling alone in prayer. 91 *Poet's Dream* 8
Yet, not the less, in children's hymns and lonely prayer delights. 93 *Poet's Dream* 64
Prayer that Grace divine may raise 94 *Westmoreland Girl* 90
Why did ye listen to my prayer? 114 *Ind. Wom.* 24
In prayer, yet blending with that solemn rite 119 *Maternal Grief* 72
Then off she hies; but with a prayer, 128 *Idiot Boy* 199
But why that prayer? as if to her could come 139 *Widow* 29
But why so early with this prayer?— 174 *Waggoner* 1. 47
If Wytheburne's modest House of prayer, 176 *Waggoner* 2. 1
And, if they had a prayer to make, 178 *Waggoner* 3. 14
The prayer would be that they may take 178 *Waggoner* 3. 15
My dear, dear Sister! and this prayer I make, 207 *Tintern* 121
That calms all fear; "Such grace hath crowned thy prayer, 209 *Laod.* 20
Nor doth the general voice abstain from prayer, 213 *Dion* 39
Why should it daunt a blameless prayer? 217 *Enterprise* 121
Dwell fruitless day-dreams, lawless prayer, 223 *Wishing-gate* 8
To sailor's prayer breathed from a darkening sea, 233 *Power of Sound* 31
Through the long year the House of Prayer would seek: 256 *Decay of Piety* 4
Yet failed to seek the sure relief of prayer, 263 *Storm* 2
Prayer, text, or symbol, graven upon the stone; 275 *Gravestone* 2
But why to Him confine the prayer, 286 *Nith* 61
(Penance their trust, and prayer their store;) 298 *Brownie's Cell* 6
To labour, and to prayer, to nature, and to heaven. 320 **O'erweening Statesmen* 14
When a whole people shall kneel down in prayer, 331 *Ode: Thanks.* 197
Spiry and dark, around their House of prayer, 347 *Processions* 44
O come, if undishonoured by the prayer, 357 *Aquap.* 297
For converse with God, sought through study and prayer. 364 *Vallomb.* 8
Might else have triumphed, baffling prayer, 391 *Highland Broach* 54
Now toiling, wafted now on wings of prayer— 396 **Action is* 10
This Sabbath-day, for praise and prayer. 396 *White Doe* 30
The pang of unavailing prayer; 398 *White Doe* 228
And sorrow of his fruitless prayer. 401 *White Doe* 440
But said; "The prayer which ye have heard, 403 *White Doe* 674
Sang mass,—and tore the book of prayer,— 404 *White Doe* 713
At length, the issue of a prayer 406 *White Doe* 927
All prayer for this cause or for that; 407 *White Doe* 1066
This dying prayer, and be thou blest!' 410 *White Doe* 1309
Fulfilment of a Father's prayer 411 *White Doe* 1422
Received and followed by a prayer, 414 *White Doe* 1697
Their part in this effectual prayer. 415 *White Doe* 1776
Chanting in barbarous ears a tuneful prayer— 422 *Ecc. Sonn.* 1. 14. 8
For prayer in stillness, or the chanted rite; 430 *Ecc. Sonn.* 2. 6. 8
Wan cheek, and knees indúrated with prayer, 433 *Ecc. Sonn.* 2. 19. 3
And prayer, man's rational prerogative, 436 *Ecc. Sonn.* 2. 33. 13
Source of their liveliest hope, and tenderest prayer!— 438 *Ecc. Sonn.* 2. 40. 8
An apostolic hand, and with prayer seals 446 *Ecc. Sonn.* 3. 23. 10
Beside the afflicted; to sustain with prayer, 447 *Ecc. Sonn.* 3. 28. 6
She knelt in prayer—the waves their wrath appease; 466 *St. Bees* 34
The prayer for them whose hour is past away 467 *St. Bees* 77
Of prayer and praise forget their rosaries, 467 *St. Bees* 89
Above his head uplifted in vain prayer 475 **Here on their* 9
They knelt in prayer, or sang to blissful Mary. 477 *Nunnery* 8
When Prayer is of no avail? 494 *Force of Prayer* 4
May not avail, nor prayer have for God's ear 519 *Pun. Death* 10. 7
And chanted hymns and stiller voice of prayer, 522 *Epist. Beaumont* 73
While they give utterance to the prayer 530 *Gleaner* 33
That would unite in prayer and praise; 533 **Blest is* 34
As my last earnest prayer ere we depart. 535 *Egremont* 24

Prayer—*continued.*
Which came, but it has passed into a prayer— 540 **Lady! a* 77
And inwardly sustained by silent prayer, 541 *Grace Darl.* 49
Be thou my safeguard!"—such her prayer 543 *Russ. Fug.* 163
The prayer is heard, the Saints have seen, 543 *Russ. Fug.* 169
At her own prayer transformed, took root, 543 *Russ. Fug.* 183
The light to us vouchsafing of thy prayer, 553 *Prioress* 27
A prayer to the Redeemer of the world. 576 *Chiabrera* 9. 4
Shall be attended with a bolder prayer— 582 *Invoc. Earth* 29
The hermit, exercised in prayer and praise, 586 *Ch. Lamb* 122
Is hospitable dealing, grant my prayer! 625 *Æneid* 108
Nor wilt thou blame an aged Poet's prayer, 628 **Deign, Sovereign* 21
Ah, with how different spirit might a prayer 692 *Prelude* 7. 373
And momentary hope, and worn-out prayer, 724 *Prelude* 10. 405
Love that adores, but on the knees of prayer, 748 *Prelude* 14. 183
The imperfect offices of prayer and praise, 759 *Excursion* 1. 216
In God's good love, and seek his help by prayer. 768 *Excursion* 1. 808
The unbounded might of prayer; and learned, with soul 770 *Excursion* 1. 936
Foretold, and added prayer to prophecy; 797 *Excursion* 3. 765
Vigils of contemplation; praise; and prayer— 804 *Excursion* 4. 218
The wisdom of the prayer that daily asks 813 *Excursion* 4. 788
Restores not to their prayer! Ah! who would think 836 *Excursion* 5. 934
"That prayer were not superfluous," said the Priest, 842 *Excursion* 6. 262
Which wafts that prayer to heaven, is due to all, 842 *Excursion* 6. 267
The congregation joined with me in prayer 854 *Excursion* 6. 1040
Not to our prayer, but far beyond our prayer; 855 *Excursion* 6. 1136
With each repeating its allotted prayer, 862 *Excursion* 7. 304
And prayer and thought can bring to worst distress 868 *Excursion* 7. 688
The Pastor's mansion with the house of prayer. 881 *Excursion* 8. 458
Urge it is vain; and, therefore, like a prayer 889 *Excursion* 9. 325
—Father of good! this prayer in bounty grant, 894 *Excursion* 9. 647
A prayer both bold and sly S.3.431 **The Scottish* 10

Prayer-bell. Or prayer-bell by the dull cicada drown'd. 603 *Desc. Sk. Quarto* 59
Prayerless. Aghast and prayerless. Into a deep wood 718 *Prelude* 9. 578
Prayer's. Prayer's voiceless service; but now, seeking nought 508 *F. Stone* 35

Prayers. And in his hearing there my prayers I said: 28 *Guilt* 203
In such dismay my prayers and tears were vain: 29 *Guilt* 277
The God in heaven my prayers for you will hear; 35 *Guilt* 575
Hope cheered my dreams, and to my daily prayers 35 *Guilt* 597
And no return have I to make but prayers; 52 *Bord.* 826
Though but a glimpse, it sent me to my prayers. 55 *Bord.* 973
To baffle me—it put me to my prayers. 55 *Bord.* 987
And, by the Mass, to see him at his prayers!— 57 *Bord.* 1096
Give to Him prayers, and many thoughts, in thy most busy days; 93 *Poet's Dream* 58
Came forth with wishes and with farewell prayers, 137 *Michael* 429
Eases her pain, and helps her prayers. 144 **Driven in* 36
The prayers I make will then be sweet indeed 257 **The prayers* 1
Present your prayers—go—and rejoice aloud— 332 *Ode: Thanks.* 229
Blessings and prayers in nobler retinue 387 *Scott* 10
Their prayers out to the wind and naked skies. 387 **Part fenced* 8
Ye multitude, pursue your prayers; 397 *White Doe* 70
All prayers for this cause, or for that! 402 *White Doe* 541
The Wharfdale peasants in their prayers. 416 *White Doe* 1863
And prayers that would undo her forced farewell; 420 *Ecc. Sonn.* 1. 9. 10
The *unarmed* Host who by their prayers would turn 421 *Ecc. Sonn.* 1. 12. 5
Hence, prayers are shaped amiss, and dirges sung 423 *Ecc. Sonn.* 1. 20. 8
With prayers and blessings we your path will sow; 427 *Ecc. Sonn.* 1. 33. 5
The prayers, the contrite struggle, and the trust 451 *Ecc. Sonn.* 3. 41. 13
Alternate; carrying holy thoughts and prayers 500 *Humanity* 30
To like hope our prayers will cling. 503 *Warning* 11
Mid muttering prayers all sounds of torment meet, 614 *Desc. Sk. Quarto* 656
Kneeling at prayers; or watchman on the top 664 *Prelude* 4. 364
To their great Father, prayers were offered up, 722 *Prelude* 10. 294
Our prayers have been accepted; thou wilt stand 734 *Prelude* 11. 453
Of my best prayers to bring me back again.' 767 *Excursion* 1. 756
That spite of the defrauded Kitchen's prayers L.1. 95 *Juvenal* 3. 16

Praying. What I am now— Praying or parleying?—tut! 54 *Bord.* 940
Prays. By cells upon whose image, while he prays, 14 *Desc. Sk.* 200
The name of daughter in his mouth, he prays! 62 *Bord.* 1377
And, as the saint he prays to, still. 342 *Ital. Itin.* 90
So prays the Church, to consecrate a Vow 447 *Ecc. Sonn.* 3. 26. 9
And skyward lift, like one that prays, his hand, 596 *Ev. Wk. Quarto* 264
By cells whose image, trembling as he prays, 606 *Desc. Sk. Quarto* 253
Preach. A whipping to the Moralists who preach 58 *Bord.* 1159
Yet listen, Child!—I would not preach; 142 †*Lov. and Lik.* 2
Copy their beauty more and more, and preach, 387 *Roslin* 13
Ages ere Valdo raised his voice to preach 431 *Ecc. Sonn.* 2. 12. 3
Deserves the name (this truth the billows preach) 495 *Fact* 13
Preached. A river of Blood, and preached that nothing else 726 *Prelude* 10. 584
Preacher. He, too, is no mean preacher: 481 *Tables Turned* 14
St. Mary's Church, the preacher then would cry:— 627 **When Severn's* 2
See him a constant preacher to the poor! 859 *Excursion* 7. 150
Preaching. Is preaching to no heedless flock! 247 *P. B.* 945
—Preaching, administering, in every work 862 *Excursion* 7. 334
Preamble. A glad preamble to this Verse: I sang 687 *Prelude* 7. 4
Precarious. And earth's precarious days. 498 **The sylvan* 24
Precede. And now precede thee, winding to and fro, 496 **A little* 24
Precedent. How little boots that precedent of good, 422 *Ecc. Sonn.* 3. 7. 5
Precedes. That precedes the passing-knell! 550 *Hermit's Cell* 1. 36
While the joy that precedes the calm season of rest 620 *Convict* 3
Preceding. The Cross preceding Him who floats in air, 442 *Ecc. Sonn.* 1. 14. 5
Precept. By precept only, and shed tears by rule. 277 **A Poet* 4
For them whom precept and the pedantry 293 *Killicranky* 9
The precept eye for eye, and tooth for tooth, 518 *Pun. Death* 7. 3

Prelates. " Woe to you, Prelates ! rioting in ease . 433 *Ecc. Sonn.* 2. 18. 1
Of mitred Prelates, Lords in ermine clad, . . . 688 *Prelude* 7. 108
Prelibation. A prelibation to the mower's scythe. . 669 *Prelude* 5. 245
Prelude. And, after prelude of unearthly sound 226 *Vernal Ode* 23
A harp that tuneful prelude made . . . 334 **In Bruges* 7
The notes, in prelude, ROSLIN ! to a blank . 387 *Roslin* 5
Prelude of night's approach with soothing dreams. 453 **The Sun, that* 4
Is the string touched in prelude to a lay . . 529 *Poor Robin* 17
Unconscious prelude to heroic themes. . . 547 **Beneath yon* 13
O'ercome by humblest prelude of that strain, . 648 *Prelude* 2. 417
So might—and with that prelude *did* begin . 717 *Prelude* 9. 557
With words that might be prelude to a tale . 855 *Excursion* 6. 1123
Prelusive. Ere the prelusive hymn is heard :— 396 *White Doe* 36
With step prelusive to a long array . . 465 **Dear to* 11
Some notes prelusive, from the round of songs 523 *Epist. Beaumont*
                         159
For us hath such prelusive vigil ceased ; . 535 **When in* 21
The Poet mutter his prelusive songs . . K.8. 241 *Recluse* 1.1.184
Premature. By twilight premature of cloud and
   rain ; . . . . 279 **Hark ! 'tis* 2
The offering, though imperfect, premature. . 753 **Oft, through* 14
From vice and premature decay preserved . 862 *Excursion* 7. 300
In whom a premature necessity . . . 878 *Excursion* 8. 287
Prematurely. And, to his office prematurely called, 134 *Michael* 187
And prematurely disappeared, . . . 154 *Flower Garden* 14
Before his temples, prematurely forced . 842 *Excursion* 6. 277
Premonished. And undertook premonished, if un-
   sound . . . . 444 *Ecc. Sonn.* 3. 16. 10
'Prentice. That errand-bound 'Prentice was passing
   in haste . . . . 188 *Music* 17
Pre-occupy. From day to day pre-occupy the ground 742 *Prelude* 13. 199
Pre-ordained. By birth and call of nature pre-ordained 659 *Prelude* 4. 96
Preparation. There will be need of preparation.
   Master ! . . . . 74 *Bord.* 2110
Hath left him high in preparation,— . 244 *P. B.* 692
With preparation artful and benign, . 687 *Prelude* 7. 24
Of hopeful preparation, grasped his staff ; . 771 *Excursion* 1. 966
Our Country marked the preparation vast . 869 *Excursion* 7. 759
And earnest preparation.—Forth we went, . 890 *Excursion* 9. 433
Preparatory. Closed the preparatory notices . 776 *Excursion* 2. 316
Announced, as a preparatory act . . 839 *Excursion* 6. 89
Prepare. And solitude prepare the soul for heaven ; 10 *Desc. Sk.* 3
You should prepare to meet him. I have nothing 75 *Bord.* 2131
Those shocks of passion can prepare . . 113 *Lament* 39
Wrought on with her best fingers to prepare . 135 *Michael* 286
This untried world, and to prepare thy way . 173 *Infant Daughter* 73
Won from the world of mind, dost thou prepare . 216 *Enterprise* 90
And whispers to the silent birds, " Prepare . 263 **While not* 7
Such simple gifts prepare, ... 324 *Ode 1814* 47
Dost Thou prepare, whose sign will be the smoke . 465 **Pastor and* 9
Than pleasure only ; gladdening to prepare . 538 **In desultory* 23
This Provost doth for those bad Jews prepare 555 *Prioress* 178
Junonian hospitalities prepare . . . 624 *Æneid* 21
Within are fifty handmaids, who prepare, . 624 *Æneid* 63
When, as becomes a man who would prepare . 634 *Prelude* 1. 146
Prepared. —Well taught by that to feel his rights,
   prepared . . . . 18 *Desc. Sk.* 447
And scorn,—against all enemies prepared, . 23 *Yew-tree* 19
Confirmed of purpose, fearlessly prepared . 36 *Guilt* 649
I have prepared a most apt Instrument— 44 *Bord.* 364
Prepared already for the sacrifice. . . 57 *Bord.* 1093
That all is well prepared. We will obey you. 58 *Bord.* 1131
Here is a Man by Nature's hand prepared . 62 *Bord.* 1386
His wickedness prepared it ; these expedients 69 *Bord.* 1746
That she should be prepared ; I'll go before. . 74 *Bord.* 2109
They for the voyage were prepared, . . 194 *Ruth* 188
Prepared themselves for glorious enterprise . 211 *Laod.* 117
Prepared by one who loves the buoyant swell 254 *Wild Duck's Nest* 6
Heroes !—for instant sacrifice prepared ; . 326 **Intrepid sons* 9
Of hearts and hands alike " prepared . . 342 *Ital. Itin.* 67
The Apostle of the Gentiles ; both prepared . 357 *Aquap.* 312
But for coeval sympathy prepared . . 359 **Complacent Fic-*
                         tions 7
Prepared, in peace of heart, in calm of mind . 384 *Duddon* 33. 13
Mount along ways by man prepared ; . . 391 *Highland Broach* 70
Of years hemmed round, had dwelt, prepared to try 391 *Brownie* 6
And for this issue been prepared . . . 402 *White Doe* 580
Yet came prepared as glorious lights to shine, 432 *Ecc. Sonn.* 2. 13. 12
Approach, come gladly, ye prepared, in sight . 446 *Ecc. Sonn.* 3. 26. 2
Prepared, when each has stood his time, to sink . 464 **Thou look'st* 4
Unfaded, yet prepared to fade, . . . 498 **Departing summer*
                         5
Entering, we find the morning meal prepared : 525 *Epist. Beaumont*
                         239
Have faithfully prepared each other's way— . 538 **In desultory* 19
Prepared to sojourn in a pleasant town, . 710 *Prelude* 9. 40
Of my associates stood prepared for flight . 712 *Prelude* 9. 182
In that unworthy service was prepared . 722 *Prelude* 10. 316
Not safe within its bosom. Thus prepared, . 728 *Prelude* 11. 92
And what would disappear ; prepared to find 741 *Prelude* 13. 65
Have been prepared, not with the buoyant spirits 752 *Prelude* 14. 416
Of Nature, and already was prepared, . 759 *Excursion* 1. 192
Such as might suit a rustic Sire, prepared . 762 *Excursion* 1. 421
By philosophic discipline prepared . . 790 *Excursion* 3. 267
Are ye prepared to urge, that my decrees . 805 *Excursion* 4. 282
Unbaffled powers of vision hath prepared, 815 *Excursion* 4. 945
The generations are prepared ; the pangs, 846 *Excursion* 6. 554
Prepared for never-resting Labour's eyes . 877 *Excursion* 8. 168
Where once the dinner was prepared with pride . 878 *Excursion* 8. 273
Within his mind, he seemed prepared to give . 880 *Excursion* 8. 438
Prepares. By all that mind invents or hand prepares ; 221 *Triad* 64

Prepares—*continued.*
Troubles and toils that every day prepares. . 282 **While beams* 7
That, for the virtuous, Life prepares ; . . 344 **How blest* 50
The woman-hearted Confessor prepares . 426 *Ecc. Sonn.* 1. 31. 1
Our Church prepares not, trusting to the might . 450 *Ecc. Sonn.* 3. 40. 7
Of reason ; yet prepares that after-joy . 567 *Cumb. Beg.* 101
Of custom that prepares a partial scale . 737 *Prelude* 12. 195
Prepar'st. Which thou prepar'st, full often, to convey 440 *Ecc. Sonn.* 2. 45. 11
Preparing. " ' You are preparing as before, . 156 *Oak and Broom* 31
Preparing your deliverance, . . . 545 *Russ. Fug.* 331
As if preparing for the peace of evening. . 890 *Excursion* 9. 422
Preponderates. Preponderates, or evil ? Doth the will 829 *Excursion* 5. 470
Prepossession. Of prepossession, without which the
   soul . . . . 704 *Prelude* 8. 325
Prerogative. And prayer, man's rational prerogative, 436 *Ecc. Sonn.* 2. 33. 13
Presage. And kindlings like the morning—presage
   sure . . . . 666 *Prelude* 5. 36
Presageful. A fixed Abode—keep down presageful
   sighs. . . . . 465 **Pastor and* 4
Prescience. This prescience from on high, . 225 *Primrose* 50
As if with prescience of the coming storm, . 419 *Ecc. Sonn.* 1. 4. 10
Sages who in their prescience would control . 671 *Prelude* 5. 355
Prescient. Of prescient reason ; all conclusions else 837 *Excursion* 5. 1009
Prescribe. And the best ages of the world prescribe. 862 *Excursion* 7. 333
Prescribed. Prescribed to duty :—woeful forfeiture 428 *Ecc. Sonn.* 2. 1. 3
Far less did rules prescribed by passive taste, 736 *Prelude* 12. 154
Advance, swerving not from the path prescribed ; 795 *Excursion* 3. 612
By perseverance in the course prescribed." . 841 *Excursion* 6. 191
Or courtesy prescribed. While question rose . 882 *Excursion* 8. 524
Prescribes. To words the Church prescribes aiding
   the lip . . . . 448 *Ecc. Sonn.* 3. 30. 10
Prescriptive. Prescriptive title to the shattered pile, 283 **Here, where* 13
Paid to the object by prescriptive right. . 689 *Prelude* 7. 148
Presence. See **Self-presence.**
In thy loved presence known, and only there ; . 21 *Desc. Sk.* 600
He dreads the presence of a virtuous man . 42 *Bord.* 264
For both our needs ; must I, and in thy presence, 75 *Bord.* 2147
Shrunk from his Mother's presence, shunned with
   fear . . . . 118 *Maternal Grief* 51
Earth breathed in one great presence of the spring ; 122 *V. and J.* 41
Its presence tempted him to cherish schemes. 124 *V. and J.* 188
Appeared, and spiritual presence gained a power . 139 *Widow* 26
Even, as your happy presence to my mind . 143 **High bliss* 25
A Life, a Presence like the Air, . . . 159 *Green Linnet* 21
In presence of the lyre. . . . . . 164 *Needlecase* 20
Whose presence cheers the drooping frame . 164 **Fair Lady* 31
A presence that disturbs me with the joy . 207 *Tintern* 94
His vital presence ? his corporeal mould ? . 209 *Laod.* 16
In presence of their heedless dams, . . 217 *Enterprise* 139
Appeared, in presence of the spiritual eye . 226 *Vernal Ode* 3
Your presence often have I felt . . . 245 *P. B.* 776
Gardens and groves ! your presence overpowers 270 **Ye sacred* 7
The presence even of a stuffed Owl for her . 273 **While Anna's* 10
In his calm presence ! Him the mighty deed 278 *Wellington* 9
Two Hearts, which in thy presence might be called 290 *Kilchurn* 30
Thy presence turns the scale of doubtful fight, 328 *Ode 1815* 112
Or thou, impartial Sun, with presence bright . 329 *Ode : Thanks.* 6
Springs forth in presence of this gaudy show, . 339 *Tell* 4
His presence to point out the spot where once . 356 *Aquap.* 258
I feel how in their presence doth abide . . 365 **Rapt above* 10
In his pure presence near the trysting thorn— 383 *Duddon* 28. 13
The presence of this wandering Doe . . 397 *White Doe* 100
And yet not faint—a presence bright . . 407 *White Doe* 1034
As thou thy presence hast to me . . . 407 *White Doe* 1049
That Presence, dearer and more dear, . . 415 *White Doe* 1744
Sang in this Presence kindred themes ; .   416 *White Doe* 1841
How beautiful your presence, how benign, . 423 *Ecc. Sonn.* 1. 19. 1
The bright corporeal presence—form and face— 440 *Ecc. Sonn.* 3. 1. 9
Nor shall your presence, howso'er it mar . 477 *Steamboats* 4
In the loved presence of my cottage-fire, . 488 *Pers. Talk* 12
Of their presence tell—too bright . . 502 **Like a* 35
Earth, sea, thy presence feel—nor less, . 507 *May* 17
In thy calm presence those heart-moving words : 510 *F. Stone* 123
Words by thy presence unrestrained may speak . 525 *Epist. Beaumont*
                         252
To one mute Presence, above all, . . . 544 *Russ. Fug.* 209
Saint Nicholas in my presence standeth aye, . 553 *Prioress* 63
A Presence which is not to be put by ; . . 589 *Immortality* 120
Nor by his presence traverse the design. . 624 *Æneid* 35
And that Presence fair and bright, . . 629 *Installation* 113
Or sighed for thy sweet presence some dark night, 630 [?] **O Moon* 3
Your presence, when with slackened step we
   breathed . . . . 644 *Prelude* 2. 134
For him, in one dear Presence, there exists . 645 *Prelude* 2. 238
Grew darker in the presence of my eye : . . 647 *Prelude* 2. 374
Naked, as in the presence of her God. . . 660 *Prelude* 4. 152
Yet would the living Presence still subsist . 666 *Prelude* 5. 34
Had fallen in presence of a studious friend, . 666 *Prelude* 5. 51
And straggle from her presence, still a brood, 669 *Prelude* 5. 248
Risen on mid noon ; blest with the presence,
   Friend ! . . . . 678 *Prelude* 6. 198
From their foundation, strangers to the presence 682 *Prelude* 6. 477
For two days' space, in presence of the Lake, . 685 *Prelude* 6. 689
On outward forms—did we in presence stand . 686 *Prelude* 6. 738
Of the huge town's first presence, and had paced 688 *Prelude* 7. 67
The absolute presence of reality, . . . 690 *Prelude* 7. 233
Thrice welcome Presence ! how can patience e'er 694 *Prelude* 7. 503
I felt his presence in his own domain, . . 703 *Prelude* 8. 257
Was not a punctual presence, but a spirit . 708 *Prelude* 8. 610
Her very presence such a sweetness breathed, 736 *Prelude* 12. 167
In Nature's presence stood, as now I stand, . 737 *Prelude* 12. 206

Preserves. Preserves her beauty 'mid autumnal leaves, ... 169 *Never enlivened 5
And now that monumental stone preserves . 864 Excursion 7. 472
A mighty gain, that Labour here preserves . K.8. 246 Recluse 1.1.359

Preserving. See **Word-preserving.**

Preside. To the just cause ; and, oh ! do thou preside . . . . 22 Desc. Sk. 654
Let Ignorance o'er the monster swarms preside, . L.1. 88 Juvenal 1. 19

Presidents. Ye Presidents and Deans, and, till the spirit . . . . 655 Prelude 3. 410

Presides. Fidelity presides ; . . . . . 222 Triad 143
His lineaments by day, yet there presides, . 269 Gordale 11
Her treasures less and less.—Man now presides . 281 *What strong 5
Supports, adorns, and over all presides ; . . 368 Trajan 52
A gracious spirit o'er this earth presides, . . 673 Prelude 5. 491

Presiding. Presiding Spirit here to-day, . . 159 Green Linnet 14
What Powers, presiding o'er the sacred well . 418 Ecc. Sonn. 1. 2. 3
Presiding ; and severest solitude . . . 703 Prelude 8. 260
Owes that presiding aspect which might well . 824 Excursion 5. 129
In majesty presiding over fields . . . . 892 Excursion 9. 576
Which speaks from a presiding Spirit here, . K.8. 244 Recluse 1.1.275

Presignified. Their purposes. Behold, pre-signified, . 425 Ecc. Sonn. 1. 28. 9
Presignified by that dread strife . . . 503 *Like a 75

Press. With forward neck the closing gate to press— . 3 Ev. Wk. 52
Press the sad kiss, fond mother ! vainly fears . 7 Ev. Wk. 275
That you do press upon me. There—indeed . 39 Bord. 129
What strong temptations press upon the Poor. Speak out. . . . . 46 Bord. 504
Wherefore press this on me ? Because I feel . 64 Bord. 1484
Oh ! press me with thy little hand ; . . 145 Her Eyes 35
Did press this semblance of unpitied smart . 169 Love lies Bleeding 21
Did Peter boldly press his way . . . . 240 P. B. 360
He longs to press her to his heart, . . . 248 P. B. 1079
Will press me down : to think of what is gone . 251 *Beloved Vale 4
Press the point home, or falter and demur, . 268 *Dogmatic Teachers 4
Her doom it is to press a weary bed— . . 273 *While Anna's 5
Off weight—nor press on weight !—away . . 284 Grave of Burns 13
(As the crowd press devoutly down the aisle . 332 Ode : Thanks. 213
That press upon me, crossing the career . . 350 Des. Stanzas 16
Thoughts press, and time is hurrying on'— . 410 White Doe 1258
Thy thundering battle-axe as it cleaves the press . 427 Ecc. Sonn. 1. 35. 10
Shut close the door ; press down the latch ; . 485 Poet's Epitaph 33
I press thee, through the yielding soil, with pride. 489 Spade 4
Of Ocean, press right on ; or gently wind, . 495 Fact 41
In dance, amid a press . . . . . 499 *This Lawn 3
While thoughts press on, and feelings overflow, . 503 Warning 20
Press forward by the teasing dogs unscared. . 525 Epist. Beaumont 238
How Want may press thee down, and with thee sink . 626 *Son of 3
And in the press of twenty thousand thoughts, . 659 Prelude 4. 58
Press forward, in all colours, on the sight ; . 690 Prelude 7. 195
Above the press and danger of the crowd, . 697 Prelude 7. 684
Through meagre lines and colours, and the press . 698 Prelude 7. 769
That from the press of Paris duly brought . 712 Prelude 9. 154
A child of hope ? Do generations press . . 829 Excursion 5. 466
Who sits, is disencumbered from the press . 885 Excursion 9. 70
Of ocean press right on, or gently wind, . . S.3. 427 *My Son 12

Pressed. See **Prest.**
Kindly the housewife pressed, and they in comfort fed. . . . . 34 Guilt 531
And most forlorn, should bribe a Mother, pressed . 56 Bord. 1039
But things substantial have so pressed on me— . 74 Bord. 2087
Proof after proof was pressed upon me ; guilt . 77 Bord. 2258
All pressed on him with such a weight, that now, . 102 Brothers 424
Of agony had pressed the Sufferer down : . . 125 V. and J. 226
Or care, that what so tenderly he pressed . . 125 V. and J. 234
He pressed his Son, he kissèd him and wept ; . 137 Michael 422
With thankfulness the Mother pressed ; . . 176 Waggoner 1. 246
Against the yielding gate he pressed . . . 247 P. B. 984
With his hands pressed against his brow, . . 248 P. B. 1089
Invades a Realm, so pressed that in the scale . 316 *Say, what 6
Such feeling pressed upon my soul, . . . 334 *In Bruges 33
Sighed on the wing as her foot pressed the strand, . 465 *Dear to 10
So spake Sir Eglamore, and pressed . . . 478 Somnamb. 43
" But we are pressed by heavy laws ; . . . 487 Fountain 45
Duly as Friday comes, though pressed herself . 568 Cumb. Beg. 156
When his fetters at night have so press'd on his limbs, ... 621 Convict 33
Pressed closely palm to palm, and to his mouth . 671 Prelude 5. 371
Thus by conflicting passions pressed, my heart . 681 Prelude 6. 440
When, pressed by tragic sufferings, the heart . 694 Prelude 7. 470
Not pressed upon, nor dazzled or misled . . 714 Prelude 9. 338
Harassing both ; until he sank and pressed . . 718 Prelude 9. 574
Pressed on me almost like a fear to come. . 719 Prelude 10. 72
And all the accidents of life were pressed . . 723 Prelude 10. 349
Accumulated feelings pressed his heart . . 760 Excursion 1. 281
The Pastor pressed by thoughts which round his theme . . . . 863 Excursion 7. 361
That pressed upon his brother's house ; for books . 864 Excursion 7. 439
Began to fail, this sheep by hunger pressed . K.8. 229 *I will 144

Presses. A tranquillising spirit presses now . 642 Prelude 2. 27

Press-gang. I wish the press-gang or the drum . 621 Andrew Jones 3
And wish'd the press-gang, or the drum . . 621 Andrew Jones 33

Pressing. Pressing upon his solitary heart. . 60 Bord. 1262
Pressing upon thy heart, and this the hour . . 61 Bord. 1306
Pressing as heavily as it doth on mine. . . 78 Bord. 2298
The foremost prow in pressing to the strand,— . 211 Laod. 125
Time pressing on with starry crest . . . 223 Wishing-gate 70
Of a wide army pressing on to meet . . . 230 Clouds 13

Pressing—continued.
Nor wanted 'mid the pressing crowd . . . 409 White Doe 1227
Pressing behind, adown a rugged slope, . . 865 Excursion 7. 543

Pressure. Through long-lived pressure of obscure distress, ... 260 *High is 10
Upon the pressure of a painful thing, . . . 311 *Who rises 47
Thy sense from pressure of life's common din ; . 349 At Dover 10
By the joint pressure of his musing mood . . 362 *List—'twas 81
Drawn forth by pressure of his gilded chains, . 528 *Those breathing 101
But, under pressure of a private grief, . . . 752 Prelude 14. 419
He had no painful pressure from without . . 761 Excursion 1. 368
Against the pressure of beleaguering war. . . 811 Excursion 4. 693
Who, from the pressure of their several fates, . 844 Excursion 6. 406
Caught from the pressure of elastic turf . . 850 Excursion 6. 821

Pressures. Here, too, were " forms and pressures of the time," . . . . 691 Prelude 7. 288

Prest. See **Pressed.**
Close by her mantling wings' embraces prest. . 6 Ev. Wk. 231
In that glad moment when your hands are prest . 20 Desc. Sk. 567
Had prest upon him ; and old Michael now . 134 Michael 214
I feel thy little fingers prest. . . . . 145 Her Eyes 38
By random footsteps to be prest, ... 154 Flower Garden 32
If she is prest by want of food, ... 194 Ruth 235
On tombs, with palms together prest, . . . 301 Bran 49
Or prest together by the appetite, ... 312 *Who rises 67
And hands in resignation prest, ... 397 White Doe 130
So, when upon sad thoughts had prest . . . 412 White Doe 1516
Prest in the tenderness of virgin love . . . 500 Humanity 26
Than even now await her prest, ... 503 *Like a 81
Perish the grovelling few, who, prest between . 516 *Hard task 4

Presume. " Dost thou presume my course to block ? . 155 Waterfall 11
A very reptile could presume . . . . 167 Pilgrim's Dream 28
Presume those interweavings to reprove . . 220 Triad 3
That doth presume no more than to supply . 253 *Aerial Rock 10
Unless they chasten fancies that presume . . 394 *How profitless 3
Presume to offer ; we, who—from the breast . . 893 Excursion 9. 624

Presumed. Presumed to grapple with their scorn, . 401 White Doe 486
Which words less free presumed not even to touch) . 585 Ch. Lamb 57

Presumes. Dazzling the vision that presumes to gaze. . 329 Ode : Thanks. 13

Presumption. To see Presumption, turning pale, refrain . . . . 504 Warning 70
Dead to the very name ? Presumption fed . . 516 *Young England 3
Had no presumption, no such jealousy, . . 669 Prelude 5. 269
Like engines ; when will their presumption learn, . 671 Prelude 5. 358
Of mortified presumption, I adhered . . . 730 Prelude 11. 216
But through presumption ; even in pleasure pleased . 736 Prelude 12. 109
Presumption, folly, madness, in the men . . 741 Prelude 13. 66
Renown, if their presumption make them such ? . 815 Excursion 4. 955

Presumptuous. Who cries presumptuous, " Here the flood shall stay," . . . . . . 22 Desc. Sk. 660
Been most presumptuous. There is guilt in this, . 55 Bord. 997
I am not of the world's presumptuous judges, . 64 Bord. 1503
Presumptuous above all that ever breathed, . 76 Bord. 2209
Begone, thou fond presumptuous Elf," . . 155 Waterfall 1
To thee would offer no presumptuous hymn ! . 215 Enterprise 13
A sense of seemingly presumptuous wrong . . 231 *The gentlest Poet 27
Presumptuous Book ! too forward to be read, . 350 Des. Stanzas 3
Inherited :—presumptuous thought !—it fled . 352 Aquap. 7
Issues, revealed in no presumptuous vision, . 357 Aquap. 307
Of judgment such presumptuous doom repeat !) . 437 Ecc. Sonn. 2. 35. 3
And for presumptuous wrongs atone ;— . . 472 Ossian 29
For the presumptuous thoughts that would assign . 473 *Thanks for 2
Yet on presumptuous wing as far would fly . 513 Newspaper 12
Who cries, presumptuous, " here their tides shall stay," . . . . 617 Desc. Sk. Quarto 807
Presumptuous cloud, on whose black front was written . . . . 718 Prelude 10. 13
A proud and most presumptuous confidence . 775 Excursion 2. 235
Are abject, vain, presumptuous, and perverse. . 837 Excursion 5. 1010

Presumptuously. Presumptuously) their roots both wide and deep, ... 420 Ecc. Sonn. 1. 9. 2
When we may, not presumptuously, I hope, . 750 Prelude 14. 308
And not presumptuously, I trust, of Age, . . 885 Excursion 9. 51

Presumptuousness. When youth's presumptuousness is mellowed down, ... 816 Excursion 4. 1039

Pretence. Under pretence of violence, be seized. . 59 Bord. 1187
Of haughtiness without pretence, . . . 212 Dion 3
Law but a servile dupe of false pretence, . . 280 Plea for Auth. 5
In men of low degree, all smooth pretence ! . 319 *Avaunt all 2
Objects of false pretence, or meanly true ! . . 335 Aix 8
Before a flying season's rash pretence . . . 471 *Despond who 5
And wherefore fugitive or on what pretence ; . 522 Epist. Beaumont 62

Pretended. But the pretended Father—— Earthly law . . . . 47 Bord. 582

Pretensions. To whose pretensions, sedulously urged, . 730 Prelude 11. 190
Appeared, of high pretensions—unreproved . 799 Excursion 3. 898

Preternatural. That left half-told the preternatural tale, ... 759 Excursion 1. 179

Prettiest. With ornaments—the prettiest, nature yields . . . . 124 V. and J. 200
" The prettiest letters that were ever seen." . 138 Michael 435
The prettiest of the grove ! . . . . . 169 Wren's Nest 44
Prettiest Tumbler ever seen ! . . . . 171 Kitten 73

Prettily. To mark its eddying foam-balls prettily distrest . . . . 190 *Lyre ! though 27

Pretty. Aloft upon the elm-tree. Pretty Maids, . 44 Bord. 371
Smiling in sleep—— A pretty feat of Fancy ! . 55 Bord. 972
A pretty prospect this, a masterpiece . . . 60 Bord. 1275
When the pretty flowerets die ; . . . . 80 Foresight 22
And feats of cunning ; and the pretty round . . 80 *Loving she 4

Priests—*continued.*
Bishops and Priests, think what a gulf profound . 444 *Ecc. Sonn.* 3. 16. 12
'Mid temples, served by sapient priests, and choirs 734 *Prelude* 11. 460
The patron, on the shoulders of his priests, . . 815 *Excursion* 4. 915
Primal. Fit countenance for the soul of primal truth; 221 *Triad* 139
Of disobedience to the primal law. . . . . . 343 *Last Sup.* 8
And still, 'mid yon thick woods, the primal truth 419 *Ecc. Sonn.* 1. 4. 12
On all that marked the primal flight . . . . 472 *Ossian* 34
In the primal sympathy . . . . 590 *Immortality* 185
Whose gracious favour is the primal source . . 755 *Recluse* 1. 1. 854
The primal duties shine aloft—like stars; . . . 887 *Excursion* 9. 238
Prime. The cowslip-gathering in June's dewy prime; 28 *Guilt* 214
Prime mover in a plot to damn his Victim . . 57 *Bord.* 1064
Was, I believed, prime Agent. The wind fell; . 68 *Bord.* 1692
He was among the prime in worth, ... 117 *Affl. Marg.* 15
Not old, though something past her prime : . . 119 *Sailor's Mother* 4
His stripling prime. A town of small repute, . 121 *V. and J.* 10
When the year was in its prime, ... 171 *Kitten* 78
That brought him up to manhood's prime. . . 205 *Brougham* 109
A soaring spirit is their prime delight. . . . 261 **From the dark* 14
Fair Prime of life! were it enough to gild . . 261 **Fair Prime* 1
Fair Prime of life! arouse the deeper heart; . . 261 **Fair Prime* 10
From desolation toward the genial prime; . . 274 **Such age* 11
But thou, who, starting in thy fervent prime, . 312 *Clarkson* 4
As were performed in man's heroic prime; . . 325 *Ode 1814* 141
With a thought he would flee to these haunts of his prime, ... 364 *Vallomb.* 19
And, gazing, saw that Rose, which from the prime 381 *Duddon* 22. 4
Flower than the loveliest of the vernal prime . . 393 *Countess' Pillar* 4
Of a pure faith the vernal prime— . . . . . 396 *White Doe* 41
But Daughter of the Eternal Prime!" . . . . 417 *White Doe* 1910
Both for the adventurer starting in life's prime; . 459 **Wanderer! that* 19
But makes his moral being his prime care; . . 493 *Hap. War.* 11
Luminous region, fair as if the prime . . . . 524 *Epist. Beaumont* 217
Such happy privilege hath life's gay Prime, . . 532 **Once I* 28
Would bring him back in manhood's prime . . 579 **Sweet Flower* 12
Nature, as in her prime, her virgin reign . . 616 *Desc.Sk.Quarto* 784
As her prime teacher, intercourse with man . . 666 *Prelude* 5. 14
On every side, in prime of youthful strength, . 680 *Prelude* 6. 365
When one among the prime of these rose up,— . 694 *Prelude* 7. 494
Was in the prime of manhood, and erewhile . . 711 *Prelude* 9. 140
When I began in youth's delightful prime . . . 724 *Prelude* 10. 416
A prime enchantress—to assist the work, . . . 729 *Prelude* 11. 115
The bliss of walking daily in life's prime . . 741 *Prelude* 13. 122
To love as prime and chief, for there fear ends, . 748 *Prelude* 14. 163
The prime and vital principle is thine . . . . 749 *Prelude* 14. 215
And she was in youth's prime. How free their love, 774 *Excursion* 2. 196
For spendthrift feats, excesses of his prime. . . 783 *Excursion* 2. 756
As the prime object of a wise man's aim, . . . 791 *Excursion* 3. 362
Prime, self-existing cause and end of all . . 802 *Excursion* 4. 80
Hither, in prime of manhood, he withdrew . . 824 *Excursion* 5. 114
Though somewhat past the fulness of his prime, . 829 *Excursion* 5. 459
While she was yet in prime of health and strength, 849 *Excursion* 6. 758
In the prime hour of sweetest scents and airs. . 850 *Excursion* 6. 823
Now, when destruction is a prime pursuit, . . 890 *Excursion* 9. 413
Who in their prime of wedlock, with joint hands . K.8. 248 *Recluse* 1.1.420
Primer. His Primer conning with an earnest cheer, 553 *Prioress* 66
Although I for my Primer shall be shent, . . . 554 *Prioress* 90
Or puzzling through a primer, line by line, . . 880 *Excursion* 8. 414
Primeval. As man in his primeval dower arrayed . 18 *Desc. Sk.* 439
The traces of primeval Man appear; . . . . 18 *Desc. Sk.* 442
Union with those primeval energies . . . . 357 *Aquap.* 289
Far as she may, primeval Nature's style. . . . 463 *Why should the* 8
Since the primeval doom. Such is the grace . . 538 **In desultory* 29
Primeval like its neighbouring cottages, . . . 644 *Prelude* 2. 141
Its own protection; a primeval grove, ... 655 *Prelude* 3. 430
Primeval Nature's child. A creature weak . . 799 *Excursion* 3. 919
Primeval forests wrapped thee round with dark . 822 *Excursion* 5. 7
Primitive. Where I was reared; in Nature's primitive gifts . . . . 700 *Prelude* 8. 99
Primrose. Pull the primrose, sister Anne! . . . 79 *Foresight* 9
While the patient primrose sits . . . . . 161 **Pleasures newly* 35
Had to a Primrose looked for aid . . . . . 168 *Wren's Nest* 39
The Primrose for a veil had spread . . . . . 169 *Wren's Nest* 57
And one coy Primrose to that Rock . . . . 224 *Primrose* 5
And to the Primrose of the Rock . . . . . 224 *Primrose* 29
A primrose by a river's brim . . . . . . 239 *P. B.* 248
A yellow primrose was to him, ... 239 *P. B.* 249
The lonely Primrose yet renews its bloom, . . 381 *Duddon* 22. 13
Upon a primrose bank, her throne . . . . . 413 *White Doe* 1583
Through primrose tufts, in that green bower, . . 482 *Lines: Spring* 9
Or "the rathe primrose as it dies . . . . . 507 *May* 59
Now when the primrose makes a splendid show, . . 529 *Poor Robin* 1
When on its sunny bank the primrose flower . . 768 *Excursion* 1. 815
Soon will peep forth the primrose; ere it fades . K.8. 250 *Recluse* 1.1.514
Primroses. Primroses, the Spring may love them— 79 *Foresight* 17
Here, thronged with primroses, the steep rock's breast . . . . 107 *Farewell* 53
Primroses will have their glory; . . . . . 160 **Pansies, lilies* 4
Primrose-time. Before last primrose-time. Belovèd Friend! . . . . 687 *Prelude* 7. 12
Primrose-tuft. Housed near the growing Primrose-tuft . . . . 169 *Wren's Nest* 71
Since first I spied that Primrose-tuft . . . . 224 *Primrose* 9
Prince. In thoughtful reverence to the Prince of Peace, ... 255 *Easter* 7
O murdered Prince! meek, loyal, pious, brave! . . 325 *Enghien* 10
Better fate have PRINCE and SWALLOW— . . . 490 *Incident: Dog* 25
Prince, in these collegiate bowers, ... 629 *Installation* 73
And the PRINCE whom we greet . . . . . 629 *Installation* 107

Prince—*continued.*
Yet doth remembrance, like a sovereign prince, . 809 *Excursion* 4. 560
Are these the studies that beseem a prince? . . L.1. 94 *Juvenal* 2. 12
Go, modern Prince, at Henry's Tomb proclaim L.1. 94 *Juvenal* 2. 19
Princely. Was princely Dion, in the power . . . 212 *Dion* 5
Released from life and cares of princely state, . 214 *Dion* 120
How Verse may build a princely throne . . . 285 *Grave of Burns* 35
Upon a princely company below, ... 324 *Ode 1814* 79
And softly touched; but, to his princely cheer . 373 *Eg. Maid* 287
Holy as princely, who that looks on thee . . . 392 **Though joy* 10
Princes. More fresh, more bright, than princes wear; 191 *Seq. Beggars* 7
Mirror of Princes! Indigent Renown . . . . 425 *Ecc. Sonn.* 1. 26. 4
Move Princes to their duty, peace or war; . . 429 *Ecc. Sonn.* 2. 5. 7
Whose merchants Princes were, whose decks were thrones; . . . . 475 *Greenock* 10
Not to be tracked or fathered. Princes then . . 655 *Prelude* 3. 454
Princes, and emperors, and the crowns and palms 872 *Excursion* 7. 981
Princess. "Princess fair, I till the ground, but may not take . . . . 139 *Arm. Lady* 11
"Princess, at this burst of goodness, ... 140 *Arm. Lady* 37
"Feeling tunes your voice, fair Princess! . . . 140 *Arm. Lady* 43
Done to the Princess, and her Land . . . . 370 *Eg. Maid* 83
The Princess, passive to all changes: . . . . 371 *Eg. Maid* 182
Here, where the Princess lies, begin the trial; . 373 *Eg. Maid* 266
Negro princess, ebon bright! . . . . . . L.2. 190 **Queen and* 6
Sable princess, ebon bright. . . . . . . L.2. 190 **Queen and* 18
Principalities. —Melt, Principalities, before her melt! 311 **Who rises* 13
Principle. 'Tis that worst principle of ill which dooms . . . . 70 *Bord.* 1812
And sound in principle, I seek repose . . . . 470 *Bala-Sala* 2
If to expedience principle must bow; . . . . 504 *Warning* 95
In the great social principle of life . . . . 647 *Prelude* 2. 389
A never-failing principle of joy . . . . . 648 *Prelude* 2. 450
The prime and vital principle is thine . . . . 749 *Prelude* 14. 215
The thinking principle—shall they in fact . . . 815 *Excursion* 4. 953
The joy of that pure principle of love . . . . 819 *Excursion* 4. 1213
The inward principle that gives effect . . . 831 *Excursion* 5. 572
"An *active* Principle:—howe'er removed . . . 884 *Excursion* 9. 3
Principle's. Of vital principle's controlling law, . 357 *Aquap.* 335
Principles. For in the principles of things . . 291 *Rob Roy* 19
All principles of action that transcend . . . . 514 **Portentous change* 13
Shape for mankind, by principles as fixed, . . 698 *Prelude* 7. 754
To notice old forgotten principles, ... 722 *Prelude* 10. 251
The immediate proof of principles no more . . 730 *Prelude* 11. 196
With the adverse principles of pain and joy— . 748 *Prelude* 14. 166
In their unhallowed principles; the bad . . . 805 *Excursion* 4. 307
Is yet preserved to principles of truth, ... 818 *Excursion* 4. 1127
His privacy to principles and powers . . . . 823 *Excursion* 5. 40
That basis laid, those principles of faith . . . 839 *Excursion* 6. 88
Print. The first whose footsteps print the mountain dew. . . . . 22 *Desc. Sk.* 670
The print of Lucy's feet. . . . . 83 *Lucy Gray* 44
Well pleased, her foot should print earth's common grass, ... 278 **Lo! where she* 12
And yet not utterly. I could not print . . . 652 *Prelude* 3. 258
Printed. Even while he printed kisses on the cheek 56 *Bord.* 1050
Yet, haply, on the printed page received, . . . 585 *Ch. Lamb* 46
Of printed books and authorship, began . . . 676 *Prelude* 6. 59
Prompt as the voice, held forth a printed speech, 719 *Prelude* 10. 102
Printing. Whether printing desert sands . . . 141 *Arm. Lady* 92
Then followed Printing with enlarged command . 489 *Illus. Books* 3
Printless. While, free as air, o'er printless sands we march, ... 819 *Excursion* 4. 1200
Prior. When the Prior of Durham with holy hand 405 *White Doe* 829
Prioress. By which the Prioress beguiled the way, 436 *Ecc. Sonn.* 2. 31. 3
Prior's. Who sate in the shade of the Prior's Oak! 396 *White Doe* 34
Priory. To Bolton's mouldering Priory. . . . . 396 *White Doe* 16
Rose up, this stately Priory! . . . . . . 398 *White Doe* 234
New life in Bolton Priory; . . . . 410 *White Doe* 1271
Bear it to Bolton Priory, ... 410 *White Doe* 1292
In the Churchyard of the Priory. . . . . . 412 *White Doe* 1523
Toward Bolton's ruined Priory. . . . . . . 413 *White Doe* 1542
A stately Priory!" . . . . 495 *Force of Prayer* 56
The stately Priory was reared; . . . . . . 495 *Force of Prayer* 57
Prism. Of Newton with his prism and silent face, . 650 *Prelude* 3. 61
Prismatic. Prismatic colours from the sun; . . 472 *Ossian* 8
Prison. Descending, shuts for aye his prison door. . 16 *Desc. Sk.* 331
His person to the law, was lodged in prison, . . 123 *V. and J.* 134
And in a prison housed; . . . . 194 *Ruth* 195
She from her prison fled; . . . . 194 *Ruth* 207
In truth the prison, unto which we doom . . . 250 **Nuns fret* 8
Ourselves, no prison is: and hence for me, . . 250 **Nuns fret* 9
Slips from his prison walls: and Fancy, free . . 336 *Danube* 5
Even at this hour. And thou Mamertine prison, 357 *Aquap.* 305
While to the prison they are borne, ... 409 *White Doe* 1242
"And so in Prison were they laid— . . . . 409 *White Doe* 1244
Or He, whose bonds dropped off, whose prison doors 419 *Ecc. Sonn.* 1. 2. 9
And in his prison breathes celestial air. . . . 440 *Ecc. Sonn.* 2. 45. 8
Yet might your glassy prison seem . . . . . 526 **The soaring* 9
That from his bauble prison used to cast . . . 527 **Those breathing* 15
From out thy noisome prison; . . . . . . 581 *Invoc. Earth* 9
The prison where the unhappy Monarch lay, . . 719 *Prelude* 10. 51
Their life's appointed prison; not more free . . 846 *Excursion* 6. 535
Prison-bars. Imbue your prison-bars with solemn sheen, ... 451 *Ecc. Sonn.* 3. 44. 7
Prisoner. "Prisoner! pardon youthful fancies, . 140 *Arm. Lady* 55
Nor friendless he, the prisoner of the mine, . . 233 *Power of Sound* 62
Such was this prisoner once; and when his plumes 388 *Eagles* 10
'A Prisoner once, but now set free! . . . . 409 *White Doe* 1230
Canst reach the Prisoner—to his grated cell . . 459 **Wanderer! that* 29

Prisoner—*continued.*
Stone-walls a prisoner make, but not a slave. . . 501 *Humanity* 78
A prisoner of fond fears ; . . . . 507 *May* 36
And oft a Prisoner in the cheerless place, . . . 521 *Epist. Beaumont* 27
He rests a prisoner of the ground. . . . . . 577 **I come* 21
"Ha," quoth I, "pretty prisoner, are you there !" 659 *Prelude* 4. 59
Is still a prisoner ; when the wind is up . . . 878 *Excursion* 8. 303
A prisoner on the island, not without . . . K.8. 229 **I will* 157
Prisoner's. Thanks ; thou hast snapped a fireside Prisoner's chain, ... 279 **Hark ! 'tis* 6
Where he abides, as in a Prisoner's cell, . . . 530 **I know* 3
Prisoners. Behold yon Prisoners three, ... 166 *Stray Pleasures* 3
To lead the prisoners to their fate. . . . . . 410 *White Doe* 1315
Blest Prisoners They, whose spirits were at large ! 432 *Ecc. Sonn.* 2. 13. 14
And by her help ye are my prisoners still. . . . 786 *Excursion* 3. 15
The thriving prisoners of their village-school : . 888 *Excursion* 9. 260
Prison-house. Shades of the prison-house begin to close . . . . 588 *Immortality* 67
Prison's. A Woman rules my prison's key ; . . 113 *Lament* 50
A prison's crown, along this way they past . . 517 *Pun. Death* 1. 10
Pristine. In Nature's pristine majesty outspread, . 14 *Desc. Sk.* 228
Firm in its pristine majesty hath stood . . . 367 *Trajan* 5
Hail, Usages of pristine mould, ... 376 **The Minstrels* 59
We have an image of the pristine earth, . . . 777 *Excursion* 2. 360
Prithee. I prithee, to the harm thou'st done already. 75 *Bord.* 2126
"Wait, prithee, wait !" this answer Lesbia threw 274 **Wait, prithee* 1
And, prithee, let us that can sing dwell here ; . 558 *Cuck.andNight.* 113
Privacy. She might remain shrouded in privacy, . 122 *V. and J.* 72
That lonely union, privacy so deep, ... 143 **High bliss* 11
Of Grasmere safe in its own privacy : . . . . 148 **A narrow* 5
A privacy of glorious light is thine ; . . . . 209 **Ethereal minstrel* 8
That cheered the trellised arbour's privacy, . . 221 *Triad* 102
In cloistered privacy. But not to dwell . . . 424 *Ecc. Sonn.* 1. 21. 6
Designed to rise in humble privacy, ... 524 *Epist. Beaumont* 190
Citadels dear to studious privacy. . . . . . 529 **Those breathing* 119
Of Abyssinian privacy. I spake . . . . . 685 *Prelude* 6. 662
Of privacy is deep enough to hide, ... 778 *Excursion* 2. 472
Of stillness and close privacy, a nook . . . . 793 *Excursion* 3. 471
"In privacy we dwelt, a wedded pair, ... 794 *Excursion* 3. 584
His privacy to principles and powers . . . . 823 *Excursion* 5. 40
Even by his studied depth of privacy, ... 844 *Excursion* 6. 397
With unescutcheoned privacy interred . . . . 844 *Excursion* 6. 412
Private. These narrow bounds contain our private store . . . . 106 *Farewell* 14
Under a private signet of the State. . . . . 123 *V. and J.* 129
For him, by private influence with the Court, . 123 *V. and J.* 150
Of private recollection sweet and still ! . . . 251 **There is a little* 8
And if these Transcripts of the private heart . 269 **If these* 5
No public and no private care . . . . . . 385 *Yarrow Rev.* 21
If, when at home our private weal . . . . . 402 *White Doe* 575
Who in their private cells have yet a care . . . 429 *Ecc. Sonn.* 2. 5. 3
The private hearth ; though keeping thy sole seat 510 **Among a* 16
That public order, private weal, ... 534 **Blest is* 73
Of private life their natural pleasantness, . . . 538 **In desultory* 36
Self-hidden praise, and Friendship's private tear : 547 **Ye Lime* 12
Could private feelings meet for holier rest. . . 587 *Crosth.* 14
The gentler manners of the private dome ; . . 619 *School Ex.* 90
Of poesy, affecting private shades . . . . . 660 *Prelude* 4. 104
Of my own private being and no more ; . . . 662 *Prelude* 4. 235
An English ballad-singer. Private courts, . . 689 *Prelude* 7. 180
In public room or private, park or street, . . . 695 *Prelude* 7. 576
Each into commerce with his private thoughts : . 746 *Prelude* 14. 18
Tamper with conscience from a private aim ; . . 748 *Prelude* 14. 151
But, under pressure of a private grief, ... 752 *Prelude* 14. 419
To private interest dead, and public care. . . . 774 *Excursion* 2. 209
Of private life licentiously displayed . . . . 775 *Excursion* 2. 268
Of public news or private ; years that pass . . 777 *Excursion* 2. 366
And, in the private regions of the mind, . . . 804 *Excursion* 4. 211
Of truth and justice. Turn to private life . . 828 *Excursion* 5. 381
And from the private struggles of mankind . . 835 *Excursion* 5. 852
As their own private monument : for this . . . 845 *Excursion* 6. 499
Whither, as to a little private cell, ... 867 *Excursion* 7. 664
In fond obedience to her private thoughts . . K.8. 247 *Recluse* 1.1.400
Privation. Under privation and restraint ; and what, 124 *V. and J.* 181
And long privation, now dissolves amain, . . . 441 *Ecc. Sonn.* 3. 3. 7
Privation, under sorrow thrive ; . . . . . 473 *Ossian* 58
The sad privation was by him endured. . . . 864 *Excursion* 7. 476
Privation's. Privation's worst extremities, and die 391 *Brownie* 7
Privations. For manifold privations ; he refers . 813 *Excursion* 4. 815
Of these privations, richer in the main !— . . 835 *Excursion* 5. 829
Privilege. Can feel his crimes. I have resigned a privilege ; . . . . 53 *Bord.* 875
And Innocence hath privilege in her . . . . 80 **Loving she* 2
Should abrogate his human privilege . . . . 123 *V. and J.* 117
Handmaid's privilege would leave my purpose free, 140 *Arm. Lady* 59
——And often, trifling with a privilege . . . 148 **A narrow* 26
Yet might'st thou seem, proud privilege ! to sing 153 *Morn. Ex.* 47
And now a stranger's privilege I took ; . . . 196 *Resolution* 82
The heart that loved her ; 'tis her privilege, . . 207 *Tintern* 123
That privilege by virtue.—"Ill," said he, . . . 211 *Laod.* 110
Such privilege ye claim. . . . . 225 *Present.* 6
By Art's bold privilege Warrior and War-horse stand . . . . 278 *Wellington* 1
"What ! lengthened privilege, a lineal tie, . . 280 *Plea for Auth.* 9
For privilege redeemed of godlike sway) . . . 325 *Ode 1814* 122
"An old man's privilege I take : . . . . . . 408 *White Doe* 1078
And privilege of ancient love ; . . . . . . 409 *White Doe* 1250
O yield him back his privilege !—No sea . . . 527 **Those breathing* 30
Such happy privilege hath life's gay Prime, . . 532 **Once I* 28

Privilege—*continued.*
Plain Nature's enviable privilege, ... 539 **Lady ! a* 50
And their high privilege of lasting life, . . . 666 *Prelude* 5. 66
In lightsome mood—such privilege has youth . 675 *Prelude* 6. 18
By special privilege of Nature's love, ... 692 *Prelude* 7. 375
Perhaps was round me than it is the privilege . 703 *Prelude* 8. 314
Old usages and local privilege, ... 706 *Prelude* 8. 508
Whom, in the city, privilege of birth . . . . 711 *Prelude* 9. 115
A stranger, with youth's further privilege, . . 712 *Prelude* 9. 191
Where passions had the privilege to work, . . 730 *Prelude* 11. 230
A privilege whereby a work of his, ... 744 *Prelude* 13. 309
In soul of more than mortal privilege. . . . . 747 *Prelude* 14. 77
"In sooth, with love's familiar privilege, . . . 787 *Excursion* 3. 78
To anticipate the privilege of Age. . . . . . 791 *Excursion* 3. 327
Should be allowed a privilege to have . . . . 823 *Excursion* 5. 30
By immemorial privilege allowed ; . . . . . 824 *Excursion* 5. 158
That privilege, did yet expire too soon, . . . 836 *Excursion* 5. 948
By yet a higher privilege once more . . . . 861 *Excursion* 7. 290
And placing trust in privilege confirmed . . . 872 *Excursion* 7. 991
That not the slender privilege is theirs . . . 877 *Excursion* 8. 229
Possess such privilege, how could we escape . . 877 *Excursion* 8. 233
Beauty, or strength ! Such privilege is theirs, . 888 *Excursion* 9. 270
Favoured by noble privilege like this, ... K.8. 247 *Recluse* 1.1.379
Privileged. *See* **Long-privileged.**
In time's abyss, are privileged to endure . . . 152 **Forth from* 21
Wan cheek at once was privileged to unfold . . 258 **Even so* 7
Like Children, She is privileged to hold . . . 280 **Oh what* 9
Are privileged Inmates of deep solitude ; . . . 379 *Duddon* 14. 2
So privileged, what a countenance of delight . . 511 **So fair* 14
Towards human business, to a privileged world . 656 *Prelude* 3. 520
And every comfort of that privileged ground, . 688 *Prelude* 7. 55
To privileged regions and inviolate, ... 690 *Prelude* 7. 186
Of near obstructions, and is privileged . . . . 885 *Excursion* 9. 71
Be privileged to speak as I have felt . . . . K.8. 255 *Recluse* 1.1.701
Privily. As they went homeward taught him privily 554 *Prioress* 94
Privy. Of Nature's privy council, as thou art, . . 389 *Tyndrum* 11
That in an alley had a privy place, ... 554 *Prioress* 117
Prize. Round his wife's neck ; the prize of victory laid . . . . 25 *Guilt* 61
We seemed still more and more to prize each other ; 28 *Guilt* 249
Seeing that he should lose the prize, ... 85 *Shepherd-boys* 40
And she will prize this Bower, this Indian shed, . 106 *Farewell* 26
Less than I wished to prize, that calm recess. . 150 **When, to* 42
Is gone—returns—and with a prize ; . . . . 177 *Waggoner* 2. 105
"A prize !" cries Peter—but he first . . . . 240 *P. B.* 386
In spots like these it is we prize . . . . . 288 *Highland Girl* 66
The house that held this prize ; and, led . . . 296 *Highland Boy* 137
For dearly must we prize thee ; we who find . . 308 **When I* 9
The prize, or be content to see it worn . . . 312 **When, far* 8
Together we have learned to prize . . . . . 402 *White Doe* 577
Even for our Altars—for the prize . . . . . 403 *White Doe* 652
From showers, or when the prize was won, . . . 409 *White Doe* 1183
One, the most eager for the prize, ... 412 *White Doe* 1490
The least small pittance of bare mould they prize 426 *Ecc. Sonn.* 1. 32. 13
With what entire affection do they prize . . . 438 *Ecc. Sonn.* 2. 40. 3
Denial and restraint I prize . . . . 492 *Duty*
Which, haply, kindred souls may prize . . . 499 **Departing summer* 22
And Strangers even the slighted Scroll may prize, 526 **Soon did* 6
Than the industrious Poet, taught to prize, . . 528 **Those breathing* 88
Trained up through piety and zeal to prize . . 655 *Prelude* 3. 456
That never set the pains against the prize ; . . 657 *Prelude* 3. 596
When first I learnt, that this dear prize of mine . 672 *Prelude* 5. 464
I did not hunt after, nor greatly prize, . . . 696 *Prelude* 7. 585
And twice ten thousand interests, do yet prize . 816 *Excursion* 4. 989
To prize the breath we share with human kind ; . 832 *Excursion* 5. 656
Nor summoned to contend for virtue's prize, . . 835 *Excursion* 5. 856
Fondly to prize the silence which he kept, . . 839 *Excursion* 6. 105
There too did *Fancy* prize the murmuring wheel ; S.3.426 **Through Cumbrian* 9
His Grace and his protection win the prize. . . L.1. 96 *Juvenal* 3. 34
Prized. *See* **High-prized.**
And clear and open soul, so prized in fearless youth. 32 *Guilt* 441
I ceased the shelter to frequent,—and prized, . 150 **When, to* 41
Prized above all buds and bells . . . . . . 161 **Pleasures newly* 46
He knew and prized them all. . . . . . . 296 *Highland Boy* 115
To lay a new world open. Nor less prized . . 354 *Aquap.* 130
Free Fancy prized each specious miracle, . . . 395 *White Doe : Ded.* 19
With heavenly, each more prized for the other's sake ; . . . . 447 *Ecc. Sonn.* 3. 26. 13
But one She prized, and only one ; . . . . . 478 *Somnamb.* 23
The Power least prized is that which thinks and feels. . . . . 501 *Humanity* 94
Known unto few but prized as far as known, . . 540 *Grace Darl.* 7
Yet Adam prized little the feast and the bowl,— 569 *Farmer* 21
So prized, and things inward and outward held . 586 *Ch. Lamb* 117
On knowledge, when sincerely sought and prized 654 *Prelude* 3. 389
Those walks well worthy to be prized and loved— 660 *Prelude* 4. 131
And gradually expired, and Nature, prized . . 704 *Prelude* 8. 346
Prizing but little otherwise than I prized . . . 712 *Prelude* 9. 205
Sought you enriched with everything I prized, . 741 *Prelude* 13. 118
I prized such walks still more, for there I found . 742 *Prelude* 13. 179
The prized memorial of relinquished toils, . . . 762 *Excursion* 1. 436
And prized in his peculiar nook of earth . . . 763 *Excursion* 1. 472
Prized for surpassing beauty, and no less . . . 767 *Excursion* 1. 725
Your prized companions.—Many are the notes . 782 *Excursion* 2. 696
That are not prized according to their worth. . 792 *Excursion* 3. 436
Who does not love his native soil ?—he prized . 824 *Excursion* 5. 116
Of his possessions that which most he prized ; . 841 *Excursion* 6. 204
There, where *they* placed them who in conscience prized . . . . 844 *Excursion* 6. 430

Prized—*continued.*
That, with like burthen of effects most prized . 858 *Excursion* 7. 67
Of a prized visitant, in the jolly hall . . . . 859 *Excursion* 7. 123
In reverence, or in courtesy ; they prized . . . 864 *Excursion* 7. 459
(Prized avenues ere others had been shaped . . 876 *Excursion* 8. 107
Prizes. His book he prizes, nor neglects his sword ; 18 *Desc. Sk.* 446
Prizing. Prizing but little otherwise than I prized . 712 *Prelude* 9. 205
When, prizing knowledge as her noblest wealth . 888 *Excursion* 9. 294
Probation. And, in the long probation that ensues, 673 *Prelude* 5. 515
Probed. Probed, vexed, and criticised ?—Accuse me not . . . . 816 *Excursion* 4. 978
Proceed. Proceed alone. It shall be so ; for strength 41 *Bord.* 226
Who on her journey must proceed alone, . . . 59 *Bord.* 1186
From whom the Race of human kind proceed, . 172 *Infant Daughter* 9
A thousand ghostly fears, and haunting thoughts, proceed ! . . . . 346 *Gemmi* 14
The glorious temple—did alike proceed . . . 354 *Aquap.* 142
By charities and duties that proceed . . . . 510 **Among a* 22
The glorious renovation would proceed. . . . 727 *Prelude* 10. 593
Proceed thy honours. I am lost, but see . . . 738 *Prelude* 12. 273
I will proceed. While thus it fared with them, . 765 *Excursion* 1. 640
Let us proceed." Then, pointing with his staff . 773 *Excursion* 2. 153
Proceed all visible ministers of good . . . 794 *Excursion* 3. 571
" Scorn and contempt forbid me to proceed ! . . 797 *Excursion* 3. 768
He paused, as if unwilling to proceed, ... 807 *Excursion* 4. 413
And to the best affections that proceed . . . 836 *Excursion* 5. 905
Proceeded. —So bad proceeded propagating worse ; 330 *Ode : Thanks.* 121
Proceeding. Proceeding, made the heart rejoice . 168 *Pilgrim's Dream* 66
Proceeding with a mind at ease ; . . . . . 176 *Waggoner* 2. 14
Proceeding under joint command, ... 404 *White Doe* 710
And thus proceeding to Locarno's Lake, . . . 685 *Prelude* 6. 655
Proceeding from a source of untaught things, . 744 *Prelude* 13. 310
Proceeds. Through the still night proceeds again ; 179 *Waggoner* 3. 65
And tremble, seeing whence proceeds the strength 309 **When, looking* 12
But from *within* proceeds a Nation's health ; . . 320 **O'erweening Statesmen* 3
A greedy flame ; the pompous mass proceeds ; . 431 *Ecc. Sonn.* 2. 11. 3
Proceeds from infancy to lusty youth ; . . . 432 *Ecc. Sonn.* 2.16. 12
Fitliest beneath the sacred roof proceeds . . . 445 *Ecc. Sonn.* 3. 20. 5
Proceeds, from some uneasy seat . . . . . 498 **The sylvan* 14
Upon the events of home as life proceeds, . . . 503 *Warning* 13
Sorrow proceeds, which else were not ; at least, . 803 *Excursion* 4. 147
Process. No, not by stroke of arm. But learn the process : . . . . 77 *Bord.* 2257
Appalling process ! I have marked . . . . 245 *P. B.* 826
At like unlovely process in the May . . . . 267 **DespondingFather* 8
But, from the process in that still retreat, . . 456 **Soft as* 6
When I the process have in memory, ... 563 *Troilus* 65
To Nature's laws, and by what process led, . . 677 *Prelude* 6. 124
And in their process unperceivable ; . . . . 795 *Excursion* 3. 617
But, in the process, I began to feel . . . . 797 *Excursion* 3. 790
Are both a natural process ; and by me . . . 827 *Excursion* 5. 314
To impious use—by process indirect . . . . 889 *Excursion* 9. 319
With process not unlike to that which cheers . . K.8. 249 *Recluse* 1.1.474
Processes. Uncaught by processes in show humane, 518 *Pun. Death* 5. 9
On timid man) of Nature's processes . . . . 548 **Stay, bold* 19
Her processes by steadfast laws ; gives birth . . 740 *Prelude* 13. 23
By nature's gradual processes be taught ; . . . 805 *Excursion* 4. 288
The processes of things, and serve the cause . . 820 *Excursion* 4. 1258
By processes minute), even so—when thought . S.3. 435 **The doubt* 112
Procession. Or blest procession (to the Immortals dear) . . . . 213 *Dion* 29
Invisible, the long procession moves . . . . 230 *Clouds* 46
And long procession—there to lie, ... 328 *Ode 1815* 84
The Cross, in calm procession, borne aloft . . . 346 *Processions* 39
Our yesterday's procession did not sue . . . 360 *Albano* 6
Of martial banner, in procession bear ; . . . 422 *Ecc. Sonn.* 1. 14. 4
The innocent Procession softly moves :— . . . 448 *Ecc. Sonn.* 3. 32. 12
And with procession great and pomp of men . . 555 *Prioress* 172
A second-sight procession, such as glides . . . 696 *Prelude* 7. 633
In loose procession through the shallow stream . 726 *Prelude* 10. 566
A mute procession on the houseless road ; . . . 780 *Excursion* 2. 563
That the procession of our fate, howe'er . . . 801 *Excursion* 4. 13
In long procession calm and beautiful. . . . 873 *Excursion* 7. 1016
Proclaim. Our streams proclaim a welcoming ; . 204 *Brougham* 33
These humble nuptials to proclaim or grace ? . . 256 *Marriage: Friend* 2
Whose cawing occupants with joy proclaim . . 283 **Here, where* 12
In words like these : " Up, Voice of song ! proclaim 326 *Sobieski* 4
Why should the Song be tardy to proclaim . . 330 *Ode : Thanks.* 93
Assured that Heaven its justice will proclaim, . 339 *Tell* 26
In shady places, to proclaim . . . . . . 348 **Lulled by* 59
And hear far-off the mellow horn proclaim . . 349 *Val. Dover* 8
Proclaim it, let your Masters hear . . . . . 402 *White Doe* 597
They mount for rapture as their songs proclaim . 462 **Where lies the truth* 9
Prompt answer ; they proclaim the annual Wake, 773 *Excursion* 2. 120
Or purposes ; nor scrupled to proclaim, . . . 797 *Excursion* 3. 797
Go, modern Prince, at Henry's tomb proclaim . L.1. 94 *Juvenal* 2. 19
Proclaimed. Hung there, no bush proclaimed to old and poor . . . . 24 *Guilt* 14
Shall be proclaimed : brave Men, they all shall hear it. . . . . 55 *Bord.* 981
His crime shall be proclaimed ; and for the rest . 58 *Bord.* 1128
For it may be proclaimed with truth, ... 287 *Ellen Irwin* 14
Proclaiming. *See* **Death-proclaiming.**
Hath sought, proclaiming to the ear . . . . 249 *P. B.* 1103
Foretelling and proclaiming, ere thou leave . . 363 **List—'twas* 99
Proclaiming boldly that they never drew . . . 880 *Excursion* 8. 411
Proclaims. That proclaims a genuine queen ; . . 90 *Longest Day* 72
To hill and vale proclaims aloud, ... 215 *Kirkstone* 84

Proclaims—*continued.*
Consul for life. With worship France proclaims . 304 **Festivals have* 4
Assembled, He, by a herald's voice, proclaims . 312 **A Roman* 3
To God proclaims defiance, ... 374 *Eg. Maid* 357
The roving bee proclaims aloud . . . . . . 526 **The soaring* 3
Pain's wild rebellious burst proclaims her rights aloud. . . . . 614 *Desc.Sk.Quarto* 653
That tear proclaims—in thee each virtue dwells, . 619 **She wept* 9
Proclaims it, and the insuperable look . . . . 668 *Prelude* 5. 190
Keen ridicule ; the majesty proclaims . . . . 695 *Prelude* 7. 525
Proclaims to him that hope should be most sure ; 720 *Prelude* 10. 163
To noble raptures ; while my voice proclaims . 755 *Recluse* 1. 1. 815
To the four quarters of the winds, proclaims. . . 837 *Excursion* 5. 993
Or disappearing ; triumph that proclaims . . . 876 *Excursion* 8. 130
With its rich freight ; their number he proclaims ; 882 *Excursion* 8. 562
This sacred right, the lisping babe proclaims . . 888 *Excursion* 9. 311
Proclamation. *See* **Counter-proclamation.**
This was the outside proclamation, ... 177 *Waggoner* 2. 54
Of power usurped ; with proclamation high, . . 383 *Duddon* 29. 13
Glad proclamation make, and heights and dells . 503 *Warning* 42
In sudden proclamation, burst from haunt . . 716 *Prelude* 9. 458
The proclamation that he makes, how far . . . 851 *Excursion* 6. 886
Proclamations. Dumb proclamations of the Prodigies ; . . . . 697 *Prelude* 7. 693
Procrastinating. Where no procrastinating gaze 216 *Enterprise* 49
Procreant. Her procreant vigils Nature keeps . . 227 *Vernal Ode* 57
Procure. " Barred every comfort labour could procure, ... 35 *Guilt* 577
With just enough life's comforts to procure, . . 470 †*From early* 10
Procured. Was pardon gained, and liberty procured ; 123 *V. and J.* 151
Full oft procured, yet may they claim respect, . 875 *Excursion* 8. 51
Prodigal. Like a careless Prodigal ; . . . . . 160 **Pansies, lilies* 30
To feed the insatiate Prodigal ! . . . . . . 214 *Kirkstone* 26
To our own prodigal excess . . . . 497 *Lycoris* 25
For the Prodigal Son, Joseph's Dream and his sheaves, ... 571 *Avarice* 11
A better eye than theirs, most prodigal . . . 671 *Prelude* 5. 361
" Yet, when this Prodigal returned, the rites . . 843 *Excursion* 6. 319
With prodigal communion, the bright hues . . 893 *Excursion* 9. 604
Prodigality. In boundless prodigality ; . . . . 213 *Dion* 38
Or tax high Heaven with prodigality ?) . . . 501 **The unremitting* 9
In Nature's prodigality displayed . . . . . 508 *F. Stone* 4
Prodigally. On that is prodigally bright— . . . 182 *Waggoner* 4. 242
With ripening harvest prodigally fair, ... 263 **While not* 2
Promptly received, as prodigally brought, . . 812 *Excursion* 4. 722
Prodigal's. To be a Prodigal's Favourite—then, worse truth, ... 571 **There is a Flower* 21
Prodigies. Dumb proclamations of the Prodigies ; . 697 *Prelude* 7. 693
Produce. *See* **Dairy-produce.**
Or like some natural produce of the air, . . . 146 **It was an* 29
Springs this indigenous produce far and near ; . 321 **The power* 11
Flowers—or a richer produce (did it suit . . . 529 *Poor Robin* 13
If dairy produce, from his inner hoard, . . . 613 *Desc.Sk.Quarto* 588
The exercise and produce of a toil, ... 647 *Prelude* 2. 378
Rich with indigenous produce, open ground . . 669 *Prelude* 5. 236
More than its timely produce ; rather loved . . 670 *Prelude* 5. 285
But, as a common produce, things that are . . 696 *Prelude* 7. 588
And with the ruddy produce she walks round . . 699 *Prelude* 8. 41
Were the unluxuriant produce of a life . . . 701 *Prelude* 8. 161
A simple produce of the common day. . . . . 755 *Recluse* 1. 1. 808
Hope of a flight celestial, will produce . . . 805 *Excursion* 4. 292
Not for gross good alone which ye produce, . . 831 *Excursion* 5. 616
Of feeling to produce them, without aid . . . 837 *Excursion* 5. 985
He gives it—the boon produce of a soil . . . 855 *Excursion* 6. 1137
And to produce, with appetite as keen . . . 875 *Excursion* 8. 93
With the world's choicest produce. Hence that sum . . . . 876 *Excursion* 8. 136
He may be roused. This Boy the fields produce : . 880 *Excursion* 8. 425
Blush Pride to see a farmer's wife produce . . L.1. 97 *Juvenal* 3. 96
Produced. Almost as vivid as a dream, produced a dream at night ? . . . . 92 *Poet's Dream* 14
As ever were produced by youth and age . . . 98 *Brothers* 202
Produced too slowly ever to decay ; . . . . 184 *Yew-trees* 11
Produced as lonely Nature or the strife . . . 269 **If these* 2
Or, at a touch, produced by happiest transformation. . . . . 369 *Eg. Maid* 18
Produced you nursed in various climes, . . . 473 *Ossian* 64
And joy's excess produced a fear . . . . . 545 *Russ. Fug.* 355
Were tempered ; thus was gradually produced . 643 *Prelude* 2. 71
From the same cause produced, 'mid outward things 677 *Prelude* 6. 155
Therefore, for what is here produced, I ask . . 753 **Oft, through* 12
The breeze how soft ! Can any thing produced . 798 *Excursion* 3. 881
Whom earth, at this late season, hath produced . 815 *Excursion* 4. 948
Produced, when thoughtless Folly hath usurped . 842 *Excursion* 6. 280
" Those pleasing works the Housewife's skill produced : . . . . 860 *Excursion* 7. 192
And functions dying and produced at need,— . . 872 *Excursion* 7. 1003
Of some poor hamlet, rapidly produced . . . 876 *Excursion* 8. 119
Of what this stock hath long produced to enrich . 880 *Excursion* 8. 396
Producing. Different effect producing) is for me . 788 *Excursion* 3. 155
Producing change of beauty ever new. . . . 891 *Excursion* 9. 511
Product. A product of that awful Mountain seem, . 347 *Processions* 57
Worse than the product of that dismal night, . 439 *Ecc. Sonn.* 2. 42. 12
Old songs, the product of his native hills ; . . 757 *Excursion* 1. 67
Than this dull product of a scoffer's pen, . . . 778 *Excursion* 2. 484
That yields such kindly product. He, whose bed 835 *Excursion* 5. 880
Such product, and such pastime, did the place . 892 *Excursion* 9. 545
Productive. Productive day be this of lasting joy . 625 *Æneid* 109
Products. Than Youth's spontaneous products ; and to-day . . . . 48 *Bord.* 623
Profanation. The unclassic profanation. . . . 163 *Needlecase* 8

Prolong—*continued.*
Know, if thou grudge not to prolong thy rest, . 548 **Stay, bold* 12
From memory, prolong their stay . . . . . 578 **I come* 67
That seek yon pool, and there prolong their stay 808 *Excursion* 4. 457
Prolongation. The prolongation of some still response, ... 871 *Excursion* 7. 895
Prolonged. Prolonged beneath the bordering deep ; 299 *Brownie's Cell* 88
Echo prolonged a tell-tale sound . . . . . 342 *Ital. Itin.* 66
Were, in the conscious sea, roused and prolonged 541 *Grace Darl.* 57
Prolonged in summer till the day-light failed : 642 *Prelude* 2. 10
Deftly prolonged, though grey-haired lookers on . 680 *Prelude* 6. 373
Prolonged till sprinklings of autumnal snow . . 686 *Prelude* 6. 730
Their dread vibration to this hour prolonged ? . 725 *Prelude* 10. 460
From day to night, from night to day, prolonged !'" 809 *Excursion* 4. 539
Did, after trials not in vain prolonged, . . . 850 *Excursion* 6. 773
Prolongs. Sole sound, the Sourd prolongs his mournful cry ; . . . . 21 *Desc. Sk.* 619
That vale or hill prolongs or multiplies ! . . . 450 *Ecc. Sonn.* 3. 38. 14
Promethean. Hast loved the painter's true Promethean craft . . . . 508 *F. Stone* 24
All freaks of nature, all Promethean thoughts . 698 *Prelude* 7. 715
Prometheus. That ancient story of Prometheus chained . . . . 846 *Excursion* 6. 539
Prominent. His prominent feature like an eagle's beak ; . . . . 422 *Ecc. Sonn.* 1. 15. 7
In everything that stood most prominent, . . 750 *Prelude* 14. 305
Of luckless rock or prominent stone, disguised . 788 *Excursion* 3. 179
Promiscuous. 'Mid casual tokens and promiscuous shows, ... 511 **Who rashly* 17
Promise. —All cannot be : the promise is too fair 22 *Desc. Sk.* 646
Upon that promise, nor the hope disown ; . . . 22 *Desc. Sk.* 649
With rays of promise, north and southward sent ; 30 *Guilt* 314
And for that promise spare the flower ! . . . 80 *Foresight* 32
The promise of a mother. To conceal . . . . 122 *V. and J.* 68
That wert a promise to me ere thy birth, . . . 136 *Michael* 334
"This morning gives us promise of a glorious day." 196 *Resolution* 84
Even for such promise :—serious is her face, . . 256 *Marriage: Friend* 6
Whose zeal outruns his promise ! Blue-eyed May 264 *Snowdrop* 8
A land of promise and of pride . . . . . . 294 *Jedbor.* 47
Mild dawn of promise ! that excludes . . . . 302 *Yarrow V.* 21
What joy to read the promise of her mien ! . . 311 **Who rises* 3
And to the attendant promise will give heed— . 314 **I dropped* 11
And neither hope nor steadfast promise yield . . 316 **O'er the* 7
Bright be thy course to-day, let not this promise fail ! . . . . 329 *Ode : Thanks.* 35
No breach of promise in the fruit ? . . . . . 344 **How blest* 60
No promise. Still, in more than ear-deep seats, . 353 *Aquap.* 71
Do neither promise ask nor grace implore . . . 360 **Near Anio's* 13
To a sincere repentance promise grace, . . . 366 **Eternal Lord* 7
A timely promise of unlooked-for fruit, . . . 395 *White Doe : Ded.* 30
For promise fails of Howard's aid ; . . . . 408 *White Doe* 1134
Now promise, grant this one request, ... 410 *White Doe* 1308
What hath he done ? what promise made ? . . 411 *White Doe* 1394
The promise in that speaking face ; . . . . 414 *White Doe* 1677
Shall, by regenerate life, the promise claim. . . 423 *Ecc. Sonn.* 1. 17. 14
The solemn promise. Strongest sinews fail, . . 446 *Ecc. Sonn.* 3. 23. 6
Pity that such a promise e'er should prove . . 461 **Who but is* 9
From hope and promise, self-betrayed ; . . . 473 *Ossian* 48
Flattered with promise of escape . . . . . 502 *Seasons* 1
Instinct with light whose sweetest promise lies, . 525 *Epist. Beaumont* 254
Whispering of promise, where no blight . . . 530 *Gleaner* 11
The promise in thy song ; . . . . 530 †*Redbreast* 6
The Promise, with uplifted ear ; . . . . . 533 **Blest is* 38
From tossing boughs, the promise of a calm, . . 537 **In desultory* 8
How treacherous to her promise, is the world ; . 574 *Chiabrera* 3. 18
Comes in the promise from the Cross, . . . 578 **I come* 71
Remembering the bold promise of the past, . . 634 *Prelude* 1. 128
Which Fate, beyond the promise of their birth, . 640 *Prelude* 1. 523
Their highest promise. If the mariner, . . . 656 *Prelude* 3. 483
A promise scarcely earthly. Instantly, . . . 672 *Prelude* 5. 468
The town of Arras, whence with promise high 725 *Prelude* 10. 498
Of promise, nor belying the kind hope . . . 726 *Prelude* 10. 550
The beauty wore of promise—that which sets 729 *Prelude* 11. 118
A pleasant promise, wafted from her shores, . . 733 *Prelude* 11. 429
The promise of the present time retired . . . 740 *Prelude* 13. 59
Who to the letter of the outward promise . . 743 *Prelude* 13. 255
The written promise ! Early had he learned . . 759 *Excursion* 1. 223
But speedily the promise was fulfilled ; . . . 781 *Excursion* 2. 671
When in the sky no promise may be seen, . . 817 *Excursion* 4. 1097
Might, by the promise that is here, be won . . 822 *Excursion* 5. 26
A dedication made, a promise given . . . . 826 *Excursion* 5. 289
Replete with vivid promise, bright as spring." . 831 *Excursion* 5. 557
Of unexpected promise, where a grief . . . . 852 *Excursion* 6. 909
The Christian promise with attentive ear ; . . 866 *Excursion* 7. 578
But turned not without welcome promise made . 895 *Excursion* 9. 775
Promised. And what was boldly promised, truly shall be done. . . . . 220 *Triad* 33
Began the promised Tale. . . . . 238 *P. B.* 190
We've reached at last the promised Tale ;) . . 240 *P. B.* 322
That promised to cut short the way ; . . . . 240 *P. B.* 337
Weighing the mischief with the promised gain, . 283 **Proud were* 12
And, as I promised, I will tell . . . . . . 295 *Highland Boy* 8
No tempest from his breath, their promised rest . 512 **Who rashly* 39
Their fill of promised lustre, wait in vain. . . . 533 **Once I* 36
The promised hiding-place ; . . . . 543 *Russ. Fug.* 132
It promised to defend. . . . . 550 *Hermit's Cell* 5. 12
He promised comfort ; and the flattering thoughts 575 *Chiabrera* 8. 14
Has failed ; too slowly moves the promised work. 687 *Prelude* 7. 15
Promised soft peace and sweet forgetfulness. . . 719 *Prelude* 10. 90
That promised to abstract the hopes of Man . . 730 *Prelude* 11. 225

Promised—*continued.*
Promised, now is ; a far more sober cause . . 733 *Prelude* 11. 387
Of humble industry that promised best . . . 761 *Excursion* 1. 310
That promised everlasting joy to France ! . . 774 *Excursion* 2. 213
I promised also,—with undaunted trust . . . 797 *Excursion* 3. 764
Promises. And for its promises to future years, . 118 *Maternal Grief* 25
Nor for the world's best promises renounced. . . 143 **High bliss* 8
Sweet records, promises as sweet ; . . . . . 186 **She was* 16
Of promises, shrill, wild, and sweet ! . . . . 233 *Power of Sound* 72
And so, His gifts and promises between, . . . 278 **Life with* 13
All promises vouchsafed by Heaven will shine 431 *Ecc. Sonn.* 2. 10. 12
Nor aught that makes men's promises a blank, . 470 **A youth* 12
For airy promises and hopes suborned . . . . 477 **Lowther ! in* 10
Blest the starry promises,— . . . . 503 **Like a* 61
Fields gaily sown when promises were cheap.— . 505 *Warning* 139
With any promises of human life), ... 632 *Prelude* 1. 25
Bring with them vernal promises, the hope . . 632 *Prelude* 1. 41
Conversed with promises, had glimmering views . 660 *Prelude* 4. 164
With all its pleasant promises, was gone . . . 661 *Prelude* 4. 207
Glanced on their promises in restless pride. . . 670 *Prelude* 5. 287
Gladly the highest promises, and hail, ... 713 *Prelude* 9. 241
Its petty promises, to build a tower . . . . 727 *Prelude* 11. 38
With loftiest promises of good and fair. . . . 742 *Prelude* 13. 185
Such grateful promises his youth displayed : . . 774 *Excursion* 2. 170
—With promises the Hebrew Scriptures teem : . 797 *Excursion* 3. 759
Which reason promises, and holy writ . . . . 803 *Excursion* 4. 160
That promises to the end a blest old age ! " . . 828 *Excursion* 5. 389
Smitten while all the promises of life . . . . 836 *Excursion* 5. 961
Yet to the measure of thy promises . . . . S.3. 435 **The doubt* 131
Promising. Hopeful and promising with buds and flowers ; . . . . 828 *Excursion* 5. 397
And promising to keep his hold on earth . . . 867 *Excursion* 7. 626
Or bold adventure ; promising to skill . . . 889 *Excursion* 9. 381
Promontories. Lake, islands, promontories, gleaming bays, ... 658 *Prelude* 4. 8
Promontory. Like a lone shepherd on a promontory 656 *Prelude* 3. 513
In headlands, tongues, and promontory shapes, . 746 *Prelude* 14. 46
Promote. But to promote and fortify the weal . . 262 *Retirement* 5
The Soul's eternal interests to promote : . . . 423 *Ecc. Sonn.* 1. 18. 2
Love to promote and purity and peace ; . . . 460 **Queen of* 36
Good to promote or curb depravity, ... 518 *Pun. Death* 5. 3
Enjoining, as may best promote the aims . . . 721 *Prelude* 10. 186
What countenance to promote this second love ! . 724 *Prelude* 10. 430
Gods which themselves had fashioned, to promote 894 *Excursion* 9. 686
Promotion. Office, alliance, and promotion—all . 825 *Excursion* 5. 174
Prompt. Herbert *is* innocent. What fiend could prompt . . . . 71 *Bord.* 1879
And in his shepherd's calling he was prompt . . 131 *Michael* 46
And prompt to many a gentle deed : . . . . 143 †*Lov. and Lik.* 64
The Waggoner, with prompt command, . . . 176 *Waggoner* 1. 223
'Tis what can be most prompt and eager ; . . 177 *Waggoner* 2. 65
Prompt voyage shall to you reveal . . . . . 237 *P. B.* 108
Prompt, lively, self-sufficing, yet so meek . . . 274 *Infant M.* 7
More prompt, more glad, to fall than drops of dew 276 *Author's Portrait* 11
With prompt embrace all beauty to enfold, . . 284 *Departure* 27
The prompt, the brave, ... 285 *Grave of Burns* 28
And prompt to welcome every gleam . . . . 285 *Nith* 15
In prompt obedience to spontaneous measures 331 *Ode : Thanks.* 136
And prompt self-sacrifice to which I owe . . . 352 *H. C. R.* 8
And enter, with prompt aid from the Most High, 361 *Alban Hills* 13
Of a baptized imagination, prompt . . . . . 362 **List—'twas* 71
To learn thy course ; farewell ! be prompt and steady." . . . . 370 *Eg. Maid* 114
Prompt offering to thy Foster-mother, Earth ! . 376 *Duddon* 3. 14
With prompt emotion, urging them to pass ; . . 378 *Duddon* 10. 2
To prompt the thought ?—Upon the steep rock's breast . . . . 381 *Duddon* 22. 12
And prompt a harmony of genuine powers ; . . 389 *Breadalb.* 13
For prompt forgiveness will not sue in vain. . . 394 **No more* 36
Was then reviewed, and prompt word given, . . 412 *White Doe* 1459
Prompt transformation works the novel Lore ; . 422 *Ecc. Sonn.* 1. 17. 1
And lays as prompt would hail the dawn of Night : 455 *Rydal Mere* 21
Yet none so prompt to succour and protect . . 467 *St. Bees* 91
For the unconscious Babe so prompt a love !)— . 503 *Warning* 29
Its duties ;—prompt to move, but firm to wait,— 514 **Blest Statesman* 9
Then let the Book receive in these prompt lines . 539 **Lady ! a* 57
Still let him prompt the unlettered villagers . . 568 *Cumb. Beg.* 169
And gave to Bitias, urging the prompt lord ; . . 625 *Æneid* 118
Are prompt attendants, 'mid that giddy bliss . . 640 *Prelude* 1. 583
Nor will it seem to thee, O Friend ! so prompt . 641 *Prelude* 1. 617
With prompt rebound seemed fresh as heretofore. 650 *Prelude* 3. 97
So be it, if the pure of heart be prompt . . . 652 *Prelude* 3. 197
Passions more fervent, making me less prompt . 654 *Prelude* 3. 366
Went back to Granta's cloisters, not so prompt . 675 *Prelude* 6. 6
Is prompt, or slow, to feel. What say you, then, 697 *Prelude* 7. 671
Prompt as the voice, held forth a printed speech, 719 *Prelude* 10. 102
But by their quickening impulse made more prompt 747 *Prelude* 14. 107
Prompt answer ; they proclaim the annual Wake, 773 *Excursion* 2. 120
And prompt to exhibit all that he possessed . . 842 *Excursion* 6. 283
To urge unthinkingly their prompt departure, . 853 *Excursion* 6. 975
She stilled them with a prompt reproof, and said, 854 *Excursion* 6. 1045
Her Father's prompt attendant, does for him . 856 *Excursion* 6. 1159
Generous and charitable, prompt to serve ; . . 860 *Excursion* 7. 214
Prompt utterance ; but the Vicar interposed . . 880 *Excursion* 8. 439
The Wanderer ever welcome ! A prompt kiss . 881 *Excursion* 8. 495
Used or abused, as selfishness may prompt. . . 886 *Excursion* 9. 119
With prompt yet careful hands. This done, we paced . . . . 895 *Excursion* 9. 768
Prompt aid, forgiveness speedy and entire. . . K.8. 266 **Rid of* 14
Prompted. *See* **Heaven-prompted, Love-prompted.**
Ere judgment prompted from within . . . . 224 **'Tis gone* 46

Propitious. Propitious to your earth-born light! — 173 *Waggoner* 1. 8
Of the propitious hour, thou may'st perceive — 269 *Gordale* 7
With something more propitious to high aims — 357 *Aquap.* 286
In many a calm propitious hour, — 399 *White Doe* 298
In polar ice, propitious winds have made — 434 *Ecc. Sonn.* 2. 23. 5
Propitious hour! had we, like them, endured — 449 *Ecc. Sonn.* 3. 37. 5
Caught at propitious intervals, may win — 538 **In desultory* 49
Proportion. To fit proportion with my altered state! — 267 **As the* 10
Dependence infinite, proportion just; — 327 *Ode 1815* 54
Of colour and proportion; to the moods — 736 *Prelude* 12. 118
Into its true proportion; sanguine schemes, — 741 *Prelude* 13. 60
Their due proportion, under all the weight — 741 *Prelude* 13. 98
If, in proportion, it be just and meet, — 803 *Excursion* 4. 149
In due proportion to their country's need; — 877 *Excursion* 8. 213
Proportions. Of those proportions where the almighty hand — 473 **We saw* 12
Proportions more harmonious, and approached — 547 **Rude is* 3
That here in dwarf proportions were expressed — 657 *Prelude* 3. 580
More rational proportions; mystery, — 750 *Prelude* 14. 285
Not raised in nice proportions was the pile, — 824 *Excursion* 5. 144
And undisturbed proportions; but a thing — 831 *Excursion* 5. 565
Their fair proportions; nor the blinder rage — 838 *Excursion* 6. 33
Proposed. To be cast off, upon an oath proposed — 816 *Excursion* 4. 1025
Or of the end stops short, proposed to all — 826 *Excursion* 5. 260
Propounds. Toward the pure truths this Delegate propounds, — 422 *Ecc. Sonn.* 1. 15. 10
Propped. We propped his steps, he leaned upon us both. — 70 *Bord.* 1853
Himself he propped, limbs, body, and pale face, — 196 *Resolution* 71
His head upon his elbow propped, — 242 *P. B.* 546
Her body propped against his knee, — 248 *P. B.* 1022
Propped on a staff, and, through the sullen day, — 321 **Humanity, delighting* 4
A mile-stone propped him; I could also ken — 664 *Prelude* 4. 397
Stood, propped against a wall, upon his chest — 696 *Prelude* 7. 640
Propping. Propping a pale and melancholy face — 124 *V. and J.* 213
Proprietor. Thou, thou art king, and sole proprietor. — K.8. 263 **The Lake* 4
Props. Imprisoned 'mid the formal props — 214 *Kirkstone* 23
Whatever props may fail, — 224 *'Tis gone* 57
These humble props disdained not! O green dales! — 255 *Easter* 10
The props of my affections were removed, — 646 *Prelude* 2. 279
Each to the other, and the curious props — 694 *Prelude* 7. 463
And sundry moral sentiments as props — 731 *Prelude* 11. 264
Proscribed. Proscribed the spirit fostered by that rule, — 518 *Pun. Death* 7. 6
Proscription. As merciless proscription ebbs and flows. — 848 *Excursion* 6. 674
Prose. Shall be thy rightful name, in prose and rhyme! — 464 **They called* 14
Now prose and verse sunk into disrepute — 489 *Illus. Books* 6
For I'd take my last leave both of verse and of prose. — 571 *Avarice* 4
With copious eulogy in prose or rhyme — 583 **With copious* 1
Whether by native prose, or numerous verse, — 668 *Prelude* 5. 200
Prosecution. In prosecution of their deadly chase, — 798 *Excursion* 3. 879
Proserpine. Fit for the glimmering brow of Proserpine. — 532 **Once I* 18
Prospect. With towers and woods, a "prospect all on fire;" — 5 *Ev. Wk.* 175
In sea-like reach of prospect round him spread, — 19 *Desc. Sk.* 474
A pretty prospect this, a masterpiece — 60 *Bord.* 1275
Alone amid a prospect wide; — 128 *Idiot Boy* 218
Stood single, with large prospect, north and south, — 133 *Michael* 133
Of unobstructed prospect may be seen — 219 **This Height* 4
Or, in no doubtful prospect, let me see — 220 *Triad* 5
May in life's daily prospect find, — 238 *P. B.* 144
" On a fair prospect some have looked — 239 *P. B.* 266
Of prospect, whereof many thousands tell. — 262 **Dark and* 4
And even the prospect of our brethren slain, — 310 *Anticip.* 12
Fair prospect, such as Britain only shows! — 323 *Ode 1814* 15
She vanished; leaving prospect blank and cold — 334 **A wingèd* 6
How sweet the prospect of yon watery glade, — 335 *Namur* 11
And prospect right below of deep coves shaped — 353 *Aquap.* 43
Conjoined in prospect mutable or fixed — 355 *Aquap.* 175
Here wants not stealthy prospect, that may tempt — 382 *Duddon* 24. 13
Our inward prospect over, — 386 *Yarrow Rev.* 38
But the familiar prospect shed — 405 *White Doe* 864
Upon a prospect without bound. — 409 *White Doe* 1172
Such is the prospect far as sight can range, — 454 *Sea-side* 9
To glide in open prospect through clear sky. — 461 **Who but is* 8
With golden prospect for futurity, — 463 **Why should the* 13
Cheered with the prospect of a brighter day. — 520 *Pun. Death* 14. 14
Rich prospect left behind of stream and vale, — 524 *Epist. Beaumont* 223
Could strip, for aught the prospect yields — 533 **Blest is* 57
Is all his prospect. Thus, from day to day, — 567 *Cumb. Beg.* 51
Where silver rocks the savage prospect chear — 591 *Ev. Wk. Quarto* 7
On as we move, a softer prospect opes, — 607 *Desc.Sk.Quarto* 263
Of weedless herbs a healthier prospect sees, — 615 *Desc.Sk.Quarto* 730
Are mine in prospect; whither shall I turn, — 632 *Prelude* 1. 27
A prospect in the mind. 'Twere long to tell — 647 *Prelude* 2. 352
It was a goodly prospect: for, in sooth, — 652 *Prelude* 3. 226
And giddy prospect of the raving stream, — 684 *Prelude* 6. 633
With distant prospect among gleams of sky — 725 *Prelude* 10. 517
What temper at the prospect did not wake — 729 *Prelude* 11. 122
Prospect so large into futurity; — 729 *Prelude* 11. 167
Gave intermitting prospect of the copse — 738 *Prelude* 12. 304
Vast prospect of the world which I had been — 751 *Prelude* 14. 381
Renowned for splendid prospect far and wide) — 776 *Excursion* 2. 322
Shut out from prospect of the open vale, — 786 *Excursion* 3. 38
But stoop, and place the prospect of the soul — 826 *Excursion* 5. 248

Prospect—*continued.*
Then will a vernal prospect greet your eye, — 830 *Excursion* 5. 545
A dismal prospect yields the wild shore strewn — 836 *Excursion* 5. 930
With prospect of the company within, — 856 *Excursion* 6. 1177
Aloft, in prospect of the shouting field! — 868 *Excursion* 7. 744
With no unworthy prospect. But enough; — 873 *Excursion* 7. 1050
Fair prospect, intercepted less and less, — 892 *Excursion* 9. 572
And doubled (prospect ever bettering) — S.3. 438 **My Lord* 9
With prospect underneath of Striding edge, — K.8. 225 **I will* 29
In prospect far above the denser air — K.8. 234 **The order'd* 3
And yet a growing prospect in the main. — K.8. 250 *Recluse* 1.1.490
Prospective. And by the care prospective of our wise — 837 *Excursion* 5. 997
Prospects. Henceforth new prospects open on your path; — 64 *Bord.* 1497
Unfolding prospects fair as human eyes — 151 **Forth from* 6
And prospects of the inferior Creature! — 416 *White Doe* 1831
—No purple prospects now the mind employ — 599 *Ev. Wk. Quarto* 379
Her prospects, nor did he believe,—he *saw.* — 759 *Excursion* 1. 232
Had vanished from his prospects and desires; — 840 *Excursion* 6. 137
Prosper. Will prosper, though untended and alone: — 106 *Farewell* 12
For the still growths that prosper here? — 154 *Flower Garden* 10
Heaven prosper thee, be hope thy guide! — 341 *Ital. Itin.* 2
Prosper the new-born College of St. Bees! — 468 *St. Bees* 153
Heaven prosper it! may peace, and love, — 534 **Blest is* 91
Go forth and prosper; and, ye purging fires, — 681 *Prelude* 6. 445
And flowers that prosper in the shade. And when — 848 *Excursion* 6. 654
Prospered. And grateful Britain prospered far above — 103 *Artegal* 68
Think how ye prospered, thou and thine, — 169 *Wren's Nest* 69
When Wisdom prospered in his sight — 286 *Nith* 23
That, if France prospered, good men would not long — 722 *Prelude* 10. 258
How they had prospered; how they were o'erthrown — 761 *Excursion* 1. 378
Prosperities. That the prosperities of love and joy — 792 *Excursion* 3. 449
Prosperity. He who in proud prosperity — 406 *White Doe* 955
Prosperity subverted, maddening want, — 791 *Excursion* 3. 376
Prosperous. Oh find me, prosperous or undone! — 116 *Affl. Marg.* 3
In this distress. He is a prosperous man, — 135 *Michael* 249
And so hath gained at length a prosperous height, — 317 **Look now* 6
On prosperous tyrants with a dazzled eye; — 321 **Here pause* 9
Or needful sunshine; prosperous enterprise, — 424 *Ecc. Sonn.* 1. 24. 6
Prosperous or adverse, to his wish or not— — 494 *Hap. War.* 69
This just reproof the prosperous Dane — 495 *Fact* 15
The prosperous and unthinking, they who live — 568 *Cumb. Beg.* 120
Than talents, worth, and prosperous industry. — 713 *Prelude* 9. 232
Of prosperous fortune. On the fields he looked — 842 *Excursion* 6. 238
Prostrate. Though the red Flower, not prostrate, only droops, — 169 *Love lies Bleeding* 2
Have souls which never yet have risen, and therefore prostrate lie? — 189 *Star-gazers* 23
Thy call a prostrate Nation can restore, — 216 *Enterprise* 102
That overwhelmed and prostrate lies, — 242 *P. B.* 557
When haughty expectations prostrate lie, — 265 **When haughty* 1
Not prostrate, not like those that rest — 301 *Bran* 48
'Tis ever thus. Ye men of prostrate mind, — 303 **Is it* 8
—O prostrate Lands, consult your agonies! — 330 *Ode: Thanks.* 126
By admonition from this prostrate Stone! — 345 **Ambition—following* 6
For all that tottering stands or prostrate lies, — 360 *Alban Hills* 4
None bleed, and none lie prostrate but the foe; — 368 *Trajan* 48
Of prostrate altars, shrines defaced, — 416 *White Doe* 1890
The prostrate, then my spring-time is renewed, — 440 *Ecc. Sonn.* 3. 2. 13
When Europe prostrate lay, the Conqueror's aim, — 471 **Despond who* 7
While all lie prostrate, save the tyrant few — 513 *Newspaper* 6
And prostrate at some moment when remorse — 519 *Pun. Death* 12. 2
Not prostrate, overborne, as if the mind — 686 *Prelude* 6. 736
Prostrate, or leaning towards their common rest — 708 *Prelude* 8. 613
Her prostrate frame with unrelaxing power, — 849 *Excursion* 6. 747
Prostrated. How are the mighty prostrated! They first, — 732 *Prelude* 11. 380
Protean. As if some Protean art the change had wrought, — 230 *Clouds* 75
A Protean change seems wrought while I pursue — 377 *Duddon* 4. 3
Protect. May He whose eye is over all protect you! — 38 *Bord.* 43
Will bring me back—protect him, Saints—farewell! — 43 *Bord.* 323
And helpless innocence—do they protect — 57 *Bord.* 1084
But to protect themselves from extirpation?— — 66 *Bord.* 1584
Who lives but to protect the weak or injured. — 71 *Bord.* 1898
Torn from the Poor! yet shall kind Heaven protect — 255 *S. H.* 10
Or muse in solemn grove whose shades protect — 270 **Though the bold* 5
And, strenuous to protect from lawless harms — 276 **Chatsworth! thy* 13
Even so doth God protect us if we be — 306 **Inland, within* 9
Mother of Love! for this deep vale, protect — 380 *Duddon* 18. 6
Protect from beating sunbeams, and the sweep — 395 *White Doe: Ded.* 46
Protect them; and the eternal snow that daunts — 431 *Ecc. Sonn.* 2. 12. 13
Of a shrewd Counsellor, eager to protect — 432 *Ecc. Sonn.* 2. 16. 2
That shall protect from blasphemy the Land. — 450 *Ecc. Sonn.* 3. 39. 14
Yet none so prompt to succour and protect — 467 *St. Bees* 91
Protect us, there deciphering as we may — 498 **Enough of climbing* 33
Shame that our laws at distance still protect — 501 *Humanity* 81
And Love protect it from all injury! — 546 **The embowering* 10
Whose shades protect the hidden wave serene; — 595 *Ev. Wk. Quarto* 222
Of winter, and protect that pleasant place. — 793 *Excursion* 3. 531
Whose oath had virtue to protect the land — 844 *Excursion* 6. 432
Long to protect her own. The man himself — 872 *Excursion* 7. 984
For they protect his walk from sun and shower, — K.8. 253 *Recluse* 1.1.609
Protected. *See* **Long-Protected.**
Kindly have you protected me to-night, — 52 *Bord.* 825
Protected from this cold damp air?" — 119 *Sailor's Mother* 16

Protected—*continued.*
Yon old grey Stone, protected from the ray . . 262 **Mark the* 2
Remaineth one protected part; . . . . . 396 *White Doe* 26
A spear,—and, so protected, watched . . . . 412 *White Doe* 1483
There hears, protected by the woods behind, . . 612 *Desc.Sk.Quarto* 578
He walked—protected from the sword of war . . 771 *Excursion* 2. 13
By this dark hill protected from thy beams! . . 773 *Excursion* 2. 112
How tenderly protected! Far and near . . . 777 *Excursion* 2. 359
That, mutually protected and sustained, . . . 838 *Excursion* 6. 14
Protected, say enlightened, by his ear; . . . 865 *Excursion* 7. 495
And flowering shrubs, protected and adorned: . 881 *Excursion* 8. 470
Protecting. There was a time, when this protecting hand . . . . 76 *Bord.* 2195
For Thy protecting care, ... 331 *Ode: Thanks.* 200
The fold protecting. I myself, mature . . . 701 *Prelude* 8. 185
Protection. But wherefore slight protection such as you . . . . 42 *Bord.* 258
Made weakness a protection, and obscured . . 57 *Bord.* 1082
By obvious signal to the world's protection . . 75 *Bord.* 2165
That, for protection from the nipping blast, . . 150 **When, to* 17
The firm protection she bestows; . . . . . 154 *Flower Garden* 46
A covert for protection . . . . 302 *Yarrow V.* 62
Ah no! though Nature's dread protection fails, . 315 **And is it* 5
For silence and protection; . . . . . . 337 *Thun* 6
To Thy protection for a safe abode. . . . . 366 **Eternal Lord* 4
Sailed" (hear me, Merlin!) "under high protection, 370 *Eg. Maid* 74
Of their protection, gentle virtues thrive; . . . 425 *Ecc. Sonn.* 1. 27. 11
Its own protection; a primeval grove, ... 655 *Prelude* 3. 430
And best protection, this imperial Realm, . . . 888 *Excursion* 9. 295
For the protection of his innocence; . . . . 888 *Excursion* 9. 313
A power and a protection for the mind, . . . K.8. 247 *Recluse* 1. 1. 377
His Grace and his protection win the prize. . . L.I. 96 *Juvenal* 3. 34
Protector. You a protector of humanity! . . . 55 *Bord.* 982
Of a protector, the first filial tie . . . . . 585 *Ch. Lamb* 91
Protectors. I found in you the kindest of Protectors; 60 *Bord.* 1281
Protectress. Merciful protectress, kindling . . . 94 *Westmoreland Girl* 53.
Protects. Protects the lingering dew-drop from the Sun. . . . . 538 **Small service* 4
In that delightful island which protects . . . 722 *Prelude* 10. 321
But a mere mountain-chapel, that protects . . 743 *Prelude* 13. 230
Protending. His staff protending like a hunter's spear, ... 702 *Prelude* 8. 246
Protesiláus. "Protesiláus, lo! thy guide is gone! . 210 *Laod.* 31
Protest. And constant voice, protest against the wrong. . . . . 283 *Railway* 14
Protestants. *See* **Compatriot-protestants.**
Proteus. Have sight of Proteus rising from the sea; 259 **The world is* 13
Protracted. Of gentler thought, protracted till thine eye 498 **Enough of climbing* 43
A blessèd Man! who of protracted days . . . 576 *Chiabrera* 9. 19
Protracted, and the twilight storm foretells, . . 605 *Desc.Sk.Quarto* 202
Protracted yelling, like the noise of wolves . . 640 *Prelude* 1. 542
Protracted among endless solitudes; . . . . 667 *Prelude* 5. 147
I have protracted, in the unwearied heavens . . 751 *Prelude* 14. 383
Near and more near; for this protracted strain . S.3. 437 **The doubt* 196
Protruded. Just half protruded to the light of morn, 523 *Epist. Beaumont* 123
Of yon black Yew-tree, whose protruded boughs . 786 *Excursion* 3. 26
Proud. *See* **Purse-proud.**
And round the west's proud lodge their shadows throw, ... 7 *Ev. Wk.* 290
Pile of Stone-henge! so proud to hint yet keep . 26 *Guilt* 118
But soon, with proud parade, the noisy drum . 29 *Guilt* 273
To a proud Soul.—Nobody loves this Oswald— . 38 *Bord.* 31
To make the proud and vain his tributaries, . . 39 *Bord.* 82
Of which I have been proud. O my poor Master! 78 *Bord.* 2321
That looked up at the sky so proud and big . . 80 †*Address: Child* 25
Proud creature was she the next day, ... 82 *Alice Fell* 59
Of any wonder Normandy, or all proud France, can boast!" . . . . 92 *Poet's Dream* 26
"God for His service needeth not proud work of human skill; . . . . 93 *Poet's Dream* 65
Proud as a rainbow spanning half the vale, . . 111 **'Tis said that some* 38
Can I be proud that jealous fear . . . . . 113 *Lament* 48
Proud was I that my country bred . . . . . 119 *Sailor's Mother* 9
Proud of herself, and proud of him, ... 127 *Idiot Boy* 89
Daughter of the proud Soldàn; . . . . . . 139 *Arm. Lady* 4
Yet might'st thou seem, proud privilege! to sing 153 *Morn. Ex.* 47
"But now proud thoughts are in your breast— . 155 *Waterfall* 41
Proud be the rose, with rains and dews . . . 158 **In youth* 27
With menace proud, and insult loud, ... 162 *Binnorie* 36
That Star, so proud of late, looked wan; . . . 167 *Pilgrim's Dream* 53
Over happy to be proud, ... 171 *Kitten* 38
And Reason's godlike Power be proud to own. . 173 *Infant Daughter* 78
And with proud cause my heart is light: . . . 174 *Waggoner* 1. 111
Thus they, with freaks of proud delight, . . . 180 *Waggoner* 4. 1
Tricked out in proud disguise of cast-off weeds . 185 *Nutting* 9
O blest are the hearers, and proud be the hand . 188 *Music* 29
Is proud to walk the earth with Thee! . . . 217 *Enterprise* 161
Ye daunt the proud array of war, ... 225 *Present.* 55
And would ye, tracking your proud lord the Sun, 230 *Clouds* 24
Full surely, when with such proud gifts of life . 231 **The gentlest Poet* 24
And proud Jerusalem! . . . . 232 *Jew. Fam.* 48
A proud One docile as a managed horse; . . . 234 *Power of Sound* 139
Entering the proud Jerusalem, ... 247 *P. B.* 978
And proud discoveries of the intellect, ... 255 *S. H.* 13
Yet no proud gladness would the Bride display . 256 *Marriage: Friend* 5
Rein the proud steed, or through the dance are led; 273 **While Anna's* 4

Proud—*continued.*
And might of its own beauty have been proud, . 282 **In my* 4
Proud were ye, Mountains, when, in times of old, 283 **Proud were* 1
Proud thoughts that Image overawes, ... 286 *Nith* 37
Proud Gordon, maddened by the thoughts . . 287 *Ellen Irwin* 25
The proud heart flashing through the eyes, . . 292 *Rob Roy* 119
And proud she was of heart, when clad . . . 295 *Highland Boy* 31
Proud Remnant was he of a fearless Race, . . 298 *Brownie's Cell* 31
Which lingering NID is proud to show . . . . 301 *Bran* 72
Stoop their proud heads, but not unto the dust— 316 **Say, what* 11
He, whose heaped waves confounded the proud boast . . . . 322 **By Moscow* 12
So shall the characters of that proud page . . 325 *Ode 1814* 131
Even the proud Realm, from whose distracted borders . . . . 327 *Ode 1815* 39
The very humblest are too proud of heart; . . 330 *Ode: Thanks.* 87
In the proud Isle of liberty! . . . . . . 342 *Ital. Itin.* 30
A sea-green river, proud to lave, ... 348 **Lulled by* 34
Of a proud Ararat! and, thereupon, ... 348 *Sky-prosp.* 2
A shattered Convent, yet rose proud to have . . 355 *Aquap.* 212
That name, a local Phantom proud to mock . . 358 **Is this* 4
And yon resplendent Church are proud to bear. . 360 **Long has* 14
Faith crushed, yet proud of weeds, her gaudy crown; . . . . 360 *Alban Hills* 7
From the proud margin of the Thames, . . . 376 **The Minstrels* 64
Proud tomb is none; but rudely-sculptured knights, ... 387 **Part fenced* 9
Proud be this Land! whose poorest huts are halls 388 *Loch Etive* 6
Proud was the field of Sons and Sire; . . . . 404 *White Doe* 733
He who in proud prosperity . . . . 406 *White Doe* 955
How proud and happy they! the crowd . . . 409 *White Doe* 1180
Of Lookers-on how pleased and proud! . . . 409 *White Doe* 1181
Realms quake by turns: proud Arbitress of grace, 427 *Ecc. Sonn.* 1. 36. 1
At a proud Legate's feet! The spears that line . 428 *Ecc. Sonn.* 1. 37. 12
Proud Glastonbury can no more refuse . . . 433 *Ecc. Sonn.* 2. 21. 11
Proud Tiber grieves, and far-off Ganges, blind . 435 *Ecc. Sonn.* 2. 27. 6
(Proud triumph is it for a sullen Queen!) . . 436 *Ecc. Sonn.* 2. 33. 7
Of proud Self-will, Rapacity, and Lust, . . . 437 *Ecc. Sonn.* 2. 36. 6
Of a proud slavery met by tenets strained . . 442 *Ecc. Sonn.* 3. 11. 2
Of the proud Bearer. To the wide church-door, . 448 *Ecc. Sonn.* 3. 32. 9
Upon the proud enslavers of mankind! . . . 464 *Derwent* 14
Might seem designed to humble man, when proud 473 **Thanks for* 7
Strewn far and wide. Think, proud Philosopher! 474 **How sad* 8
The inviolable God, that tames the proud! . . 477 *Long Meg* 14
In those proud days, he little cared . . . . 483 *Simon Lee* 13
An age hath been when Earth was proud . . 496 *Lycoris* 1
Though of gorgeous drapery proud, ... 502 **Like a* 28
On proud towers, like this humble cottage, blest . 503 *Warning* 37
Can such a One, dear Babe! though glad and proud 504 *Warning* 78
Thou and thy train are proud to look, ... 507 *May* 47
Where sea-nymphs might be proud to dwell: . . 511 **Who rashly* 15
And proud deliverance issuing out of pain . . 514 **Who ponders* 4
On proud temptations, till the victim groaned . 517 *Pun. Death* 2. 7
On that proud pageant now at hand or past, . . 522 *Epist. Beaumont* 70
The soaring lark is blest as proud . . . . 526 **The soaring* 1
He proud to please, above all rivals, fit . . . 528 **Those breathing* 106
Which She is pleased and proud to call her own, . 539 **Lady! a* 26
E'er struggled with a heart so proud, ... 543 *Russ. Fug.* 155
And proud hearts can make tremble in a trice. . 557 *Cuck. and Night.* 15
To rid the world of nuisances; ye proud, . . . 567 *Cumb. Beg.* 70
Where proud Covent-garden, in desolate hours . 570 *Farmer* 73
Obdurate, proud, and blind, ... 582 *Invoc. Earth* 20
However proud and strong. . . . . 583 **O for a* 36
Proud of the varying arch and moveless form of snow. . . . . 595 *Ev. Wk. Quarto* 206
Though in virtue's proud mouth thy report be a stain, ... 621 *Convict* 50
And goblets crown the proud festivity, . . . 624 *Æneid* 41
Puts off his wings, and walks, with proud delight, 624 *Æneid* 45
And, proud of her award, ... 629 *Installation* 70
Proud spring-tide swellings for a regular sea, . 634 *Prelude* 1. 167
Proud of his skill, to reach a chosen point . . . 637 *Prelude* 1. 368
Proud and exulting like an untired horse . . . 638 *Prelude* 1. 432
We from our funds drew largely;—proud to curb, 643 *Prelude* 2. 96
Proud of its own bright fire and sycamore shade. 644 *Prelude* 2. 148
By the proud name she bears—the name of Heaven. 650 *Prelude* 3. 111
And kindred, proud rebellion and unkind. . . . 675 *Prelude* 6. 29
The saucy air. In this proud company . . . 681 *Prelude* 6. 394
Tricked out for that proud use, if I perchance . 694 *Prelude* 7. 450
The times, too sage, perhaps too proud, have dropped . . . . 701 *Prelude* 8. 158
To sanction the proud workings of the soul, . . 713 *Prelude* 9. 237
Who was not lost, abandoned, selfish, proud, . . 713 *Prelude* 9. 285
Spared not the empty throne, and in proud haste 718 *Prelude* 10. 39
When the proud fleet that bears the red-cross flag 722 *Prelude* 10. 315
From her first ground expelled, grew proud once more. . . . . 731 *Prelude* 11. 246
Proud of her own endowments, and rejoiced . . 736 *Prelude* 12. 146
Could scarcely hold a bridle, with proud hopes . 737 *Prelude* 12. 227
A proud and most presumptuous confidence . . 775 *Excursion* 2. 235
Whose skill had thronged the floor with a proud show . . . . 778 *Excursion* 2. 424
Sparkle the stars, as of their station proud. . . 782 *Excursion* 2. 722
A proud communication with the sun . . . . 807 *Excursion* 4. 401
To proud Self-love her own intelligence; . . . 816 *Excursion* 4. 992
And proud insensibility to hope, ... 816 *Excursion* 4. 1030
—Stoop from your height, ye proud, and copy these! . . . . 833 *Excursion* 5. 722
He had descended from the proud saloon, . . . 843 *Excursion* 6. 329
To suit this place; yet built in no proud scorn . 846 *Excursion* 6. 507

Proud—*continued.*
They soon were proud of ; tended it and nursed ; 852 *Excursion* 6. 932
With no engagement, in his thoughts, more proud 859 *Excursion* 7. 156
"All that this world is proud of. From their spheres . . . . 872 *Excursion* 7. 978
Could the proud quest of chivalry do more ?" . 875 *Excursion* 8. 81
Or straggling burgh, of ancient charter proud, . 875 *Excursion* 8. 101
His proud complacency :—yet do I exult, . . . 877 *Excursion* 8. 199
With dignity befitting his proud hope ; . . . 879 *Excursion* 8. 318
In this oppression ; none are proud of it ; . . 887 *Excursion* 9. 183
That now he might be proud, for he that day K.8. 226 **I will* 59
He leapt upon the island, with proud heart, . . K.8. 229 **I will* 148
Of proud Tarentum, proud to share the fame . . L.2. 120 *Frag. Æneid* 1. 2

Prouder. To which the sage would give a prouder name. . . . . 10 *Desc. Sk.* 14
Comfort by prouder mansions unbestowed . . 34 *Guilt* 525
A prouder heart than Luke's. When Isabel . . 136 *Michael* 315
My youth here witnessed, in a prouder time ; . . 304 **Festivals have* 10
Such as at least do wear a prouder face, . . . 694 *Prelude* 7. 466
Prouder itinerant, mountebank, or he . . . . 699 *Prelude* 8. 35
More keen and prouder daring ; yet hath she, . 856 *Excursion* 6. 1161
For prouder service were addrest ; but each, . . 891 *Excursion* 9. 479
Proudest. With the proudest thou art there, . 161 **Pleasures newly* 23
"O Lady, worthy of earth's proudest throne ! . 220 *Triad* 52
A palace of the proudest show, ... 297 *Highland Boy* 209
Was happiest, proudest, of them all ! . . . . 409 *White Doe* 1187
And seemed the proudest thing on earth. . . . 550 *Hermit's Cell* 2. 20
A trifler only in her proudest day ; . . . . . 733 *Prelude* 11. 385
Indifferent judges. 'Spite of proudest boast, . 830 *Excursion* 5. 500
"Amid the noblest relics, proudest dust, . . . 842 *Excursion* 6. 263
One after one, their proudest ornaments. . . . 866 *Excursion* 7. 594
Proudly. "Let him come, with his purse proudly grasped in his hand ; . . . . 116 *Repentance* 6
And proudly shook the bridle too ; . . . . . 126 *Idiot Boy* 64
The treasure proudly did I show . . . . . 169 *Wren's Nest* 45
Bears him on while proudly sailing . . . . . 212 *Dion*
And lo ! with crimson banners proudly streaming, 324 *Ode 1814* 53
And proudly think, beside the chafing sea, . . 349 *Boulogne* 10
Proudly the Horsemen bore away . . . . . 412 *White Doe* 1499
Till the checked torrent, proudly triumphing, . 418 *Ecc. Sonn.* 1. 1. 7
And proudly did its branches wave ; . . . . 495 *Force of Prayer* 50
With help from female hands, that proudly strove 546 **Oft is* 14
Proudly revealed with instantaneous burst, . . 658 *Prelude* 4. 10
Walked proudly at my side : she guided me ; . . 659 *Prelude* 4. 65
The River proudly bridged ; the dizzy top . . 689 *Prelude* 7. 129
They made it proudly, eager as a child, . . . 723 *Prelude* 10. 364
Is worshipped in that idol proudly named . . . 741 *Prelude* 13. 77
For high—yet not for low ; for proudly graced— 887 *Excursion* 8. 244
Prove. But hear the proofs—— Ay, prove that when two peas . . . . 59 *Bord.* 1176
Be larger than the peas—prove this—'twere matter 59 *Bord.* 1178
The Cross, fixed in his soul, may prove an all-sufficing stay. . . . . 91 *Norman Boy* 32
She might prove our Maid of Arc. . . . . 94 *Westmoreland Girl* 88
That self might be annulled : her bondage prove 211 *Laod.* 149
Prove that thy heaven-descended sway . . . 216 *Enterprise* 51
And not unfelt will prove the loss . . . . . 224 **'Tis gone* 37
Yea, veriest reptiles have sufficed to prove . . 273 **When Philoctetes* 11
Rise, tardy Sun ! and let the Songster prove . . 279 **'Tis he* 9
Now is the time to prove your hardiment ! . . 309 *Men of Kent* 4
For matched with these shall policy prove vain, . 320 **Avaunt all* 13
Sad blindness ! but ordained to prove . . . . 344 *Eclipse* 82
My vehicle shall prove—O precious Charge ! . . 371 *Eg. Maid* 172
To rise, and prove their innocence.— . . . . 403 *White Doe* 632
Nor did he turn aside to prove . . . . . . 406 *White Doe* 933
And, if the endeavour prove not vain, ... 410 *White Doe* 1289
And may it prove a fruitful meeting ! . . . . 414 *White Doe* 1668
Your practice prove, faithless though but in thought, ... 444 *Ecc. Sonn.* 3. 16. 11
Prove that her hand has touched responsive chords ; . . . . 455 **Not in the lucid* 9
Pity that such a promise e'er should prove . . 461 **Who but is* 9
Flesh to exalt than prove its nothingness. . . . 469 **Desire we* 14
That, by the unwilling ploughshare, died to prove 475 **There ! said* 13
The loveliness of Nature, prove a bar . . . . 477 *Steamboats* 5
To her I left, shall prove . . . . 479 *Somnamb.* 114
Their gifts she hails (deemed precious, as they prove 503 *Warning* 28
And may this tribute prove . . . . 527 **The soaring* 54
Though it should prove a farewell lay . . . . 530 †*Redbreast* 3
O that the good old Man had power to prove, . 531 **I know* 29
Their constancy to prove, ... 544 *Russ. Fug.* 230
The smoothest seas will sometimes prove, . . . 550 *Hermit's Cell* 5. 5
I prove it thus ; for in no other space . . . . 565 *Troilus* 158
When, after pains dispensed to prove . . . . 577 **By playful* 9
Prove vain, and thus should neither I be taught . 641 *Prelude* 1. 626
Arguments sent from Heaven to prove the cause 713 *Prelude* 9. 283
That prove to what low depth had struck the roots, 717 *Prelude* 9. 549
More firmly to old tenets, and, to prove . . . 730 *Prelude* 11. 217
A token (may it prove a monument !) . . . . 753 **Oft, through* 7
Yet, should this confidence prove vain, the wise . 806 *Excursion* 4. 320
Prove a degraded Race ? and what avails . . 815 *Excursion* 4. 954
His royal state to show, and prove his strength . 825 *Excursion* 5. 183
Shall pass uncensured ; though the issue prove, . 827 *Excursion* 5. 315
The stream, that bears thee forward, prove not, soon 844 *Excursion* 6. 438
Dark as a riddle, prove a favourite theme ; . . K.8. 301 **And oh* 6
And prove with endless puns a monarch's power, L.1. 94 *Juvenal* 2. 2
Proved. True ; and, remembering how the Band have proved . . . . 37 *Bord.* 11

Proved—*continued.*
The truth shall be laid open, his guilt proved . 48 *Bord.* 600
This, one of those small builders proved . . . 168 *Wren's Nest* 33
Proved last year's leaves, pushed from the spray 170 *Rural Ill.* 11
And it was proved in Bosworth-field. . . . . 204 *Brougham* 25
For *Books !*" Yes, heartless Ones, or be it proved 280 *Plea for Auth.* 10
And now their faithfulness is proved : . . . . 401 *White Doe* 473
Where faith was proved ?—while to battle moved 405 *White Doe* 817
Ocean has proved its strength, and of its grace . 473 **Thanks for* 12
That woman's fortitude—so tried, so proved— . 541 *Grace Darl.* 58
Your proved fidelity."— . . . . 542 *Russ. Fug.* 74
In aught to earth pertaining ? Death has proved 581 **Why should we* 6
Proved tedious, and I gradually withdrew . . 711 *Prelude* 9. 121
To re-appear, 'twas proved that not in vain . . 740 *Prelude* 13. 19
From the great City, else it must have proved . 741 *Prelude* 13. 114
Proved that such hope was vain :—for now we stood 786 *Excursion* 3. 37
Proved all unable to support the weight . . . 842 *Excursion* 6. 237
Among the first of Powers and Virtues—proved ? 846 *Excursion* 6. 566
Else had the strongest fastnesses proved weak 868 *Excursion* 7. 750
Proverb. That they were as a proverb in the vale . 132 *Michael* 94
Proverbial. Proverbial words of comfort he applied, 32 *Guilt* 458
Proves. For a brief absence, proves that love is true ; 284 *Departure* 30
Then, the strained heart of fortitude proves weak ; 319 *Spaniard* 12
History that proves by inward evidence . . . 359 **Complacent Fictions* 3
And proves the Lover true ;" . . . . . . 478 *Somnamb.* 42
Like an unshifting weathercock which proves . 521 *Epist. Beaumont* 18
O dread reverse ! if aught *be* so, which proves . 576 **By a* 5
Proves to the most ; and called to make good search 742 *Prelude* 13. 174
Where Fortune led :—and Fortune, who oft proves 774 *Excursion* 2. 185
Provide. Better provide thee with a Cuckoo-clock, 229 *Cuckoo-clock* 7
There lives Who can provide . . . . . . 498 **The sylvan* 27
With every hope that mutual cares provide ; . . 519 *Pun. Death* 11. 4
Doth also for our nobler part provide, ... 669 *Prelude* 5. 273
Her vespers,—Nature fails not to provide . . . 818 *Excursion* 4. 1169
For which we pray ; and for the wants provide . 834 *Excursion* 5. 810
A hardy Girl continues to provide ; . . . . . 856 *Excursion* 6. 1157
Provided. "Poorly provided, poorly followed," . 103 *Artegal* 92
Provided in a calmer hour, ... 391 *Highland Broach* 56
To charity, and love, that have provided, . . . 836 *Excursion* 5. 911
Providence. Our wanderings together. Providence 40 *Bord.* 195
But there's a Providence for them who walk . . 51 *Bord.* 791
In his providence, assigned . . . . 90 *Longest Day* 34
Where he, in his poor self so weak, by Providence was placed. . . . . 91 *Norman Boy* 28
How Providence educeth, from the spring . . 271 *Henry: Portrait* 12
Of Providence, such emptiness at length . . . 309 **When, looking* 9
Of Providence. But now did the Most High . . 322 **By Moscow* 9
Are weighed by Providence, in balance even ; . 331 *Ode : Thanks.* 156
Of all-disposing Providence, ... 411 *White Doe* 1413
And cast the future upon Providence ; . . . 441 *Ecc. Sonn.* 3. 6. 11
But not to them had Providence foreshown . . 443 *Ecc. Sonn.* 3. 14. 3
The glorious work of time and providence, . . 471 **Despond who* 4
Of the great Vision,—faith in Providence ; . . 500 *Humanity* 44
Too late—or, should the providence of God . . 504 *Warning* 82
Servant of Providence, not slave of Fate— . . 514 **Blest Statesman* 13
In Him whose Providence your rage hath served ! 541 *Grace Darl.* 86
Fanned by the breath of angry Providence. . . 681 *Prelude* 6. 447
Forced by the gracious providence of Heaven,— 721 *Prelude* 10. 224
Who doubted not that Providence had times . . 723 *Prelude* 10. 340
Of Providence ; and in reverence for duty, . . 750 *Prelude* 14. 298
(Should Providence such grace to us vouchsafe) 752 *Prelude* 14. 442
That earthly Providence, whose guiding love . 794 *Excursion* 3. 565
Nor unreproved by Providence, thus speaking . 805 *Excursion* 4. 276
In Providence, for solace and support, ... 830 *Excursion* 5. 516
Is in controlling Providence, admit . . . . 846 *Excursion* 6. 561
To Providence submissive, so she thought ; . . 849 *Excursion* 6. 744
The Pastor said : "So Providence is served ; . 870 *Excursion* 7. 833
And Heaven's good providence, preserved from taint ! . . . . 876 *Excursion* 8. 150
Of gratitude to Providence, will grant . . . . 889 *Excursion* 9. 330
Provident. Their native Land, for outrage provident ; 515 **Men of* 4
Providential. Of providential goodness ever nigh ! . 264 *Storm* 14
At providential judgments, undismayed . . . 513 *General Fast* 4
Provides. Of natures, for our wants provides . . 226 *Present.* 76
That Rome provides, less dreading from her frown 420 *Ecc. Sonn.* 1. 8. 10
Of Infancy, provides a timely shower . . . . 445 *Ecc. Sonn.* 3. 20. 2
For the spent hurricane the air provides . . . 719 *Prelude* 10. 80
That in a land where charity provides . . . . 844 *Excursion* 6. 378
Province. Might scan the narrow province with disdain . . . . 231 **The gentlest Poet* 3
Split like a province into round and square ? . . 645 *Prelude* 2. 205
Mounted—from province on to province swept, . 682 *Prelude* 6. 496
Wide as a province, but, the signal given, . . 718 *Prelude* 10. 22
Its most illustrious province, must be found . . 820 *Excursion* 4. 1261
Proving. And thus, experience proving that no few 728 *Prelude* 11. 47
Provision. He followed till provision for his wants 761 *Excursion* 1. 382
For due provision to control and guide, . . . 826 *Excursion* 5. 290
Provocation. Who, on such provocation as this earth 60 *Bord.* 1242
Of provocation. Leave me, with the weight . . 77 *Bord.* 2296
Found dreadful provocation : for at night, . . 123 *V. and J.* 125
This complicated provocation, ... 181 *Waggoner* 4. 178
Provoke. To see him thus provoke her tenderness . 41 *Bord.* 244
Of trespasses, affected to provoke . . . . . 80 **Loving she* 5
If to provoke such doom the Impious dare, . . 217 *Enterprise* 120
Provoke all potent symphonies to raise . . . 328 *Ode 1815* 78
Crimes which the great Avenger's hand provoke, . 345 **Ambition—following* 12
Thy fortunes, twice exalted, might provoke . . 360 *Alban Hills* 10
Thou wilt provoke a heavier penalty. . . . . 513 *Newspaper* 14
Why with such earnest pains dost thou provoke . 589 *Immortality* 127

Pure—*continued.*
So be it, if the pure of heart be prompt . . . 652 *Prelude* 3. 197
Are not so pure by nature that they needs . . 656 *Prelude* 3. 481
Or His pure Word by miracle revealed. . . . 669 *Prelude* 5. 222
This was her creed, and therefore she was pure . 670 *Prelude* 5. 279
Some monument behind me which pure hearts . 676 *Prelude* 6. 56
Created out of pure intelligence. . . . . . 677 *Prelude* 6. 167
Exchanged—to equalise in God's pure sight . . 682 *Prelude* 6. 455
Cerulean ether's pure inhabitants, ... 682 *Prelude* 6. 465
And pure simplicity of wish and will, ... 682 *Prelude* 6. 507
Or mildest visitations of pure thought, . . . 685 *Prelude* 6. 684
And the independent spirit of pure youth . . . 686 *Prelude* 6. 776
Feelings of pure commiseration, grief . . . 693 *Prelude* 7. 395
By pure Imagination : busy Power . . . . 705 *Prelude* 8. 423
In a pure stream of words fresh from the heart : . 706 *Prelude* 8. 467
On the pure bliss, and takes her rest with God. . 709 *Prelude* 8. 675
Good, pure, which no one could stand up against, 713 *Prelude* 9. 224
As just in regulation, and as pure . . . . . 715 *Prelude* 9. 362
To health and joy and pure contentedness ; . . 733 *Prelude* 11. 398
For me that image of pure gladsomeness . . . 733 *Prelude* 11. 412
Or Archimedes, pure abstracted soul ! . . . . 733 *Prelude* 11. 435
Of pure imagination, and of love ; . . . . . 740 *Prelude* 13. 50
The excellence, pure function, and best power . 745 *Prelude* 13. 377
In moral judgments which from this pure source . 748 *Prelude* 14. 128
Pure, or with no unpleasing sadness mixed ; . . 755 *Recluse* 1. 1. 758
My Heart in genuine freedom :—all pure thoughts 755 *Reclus* 1. 1. 858
Still deeper welcome found his pure discourse : . 757 *Excursion* 1. 73
Pure livers were they all, austere and grave, . . 758 *Excursion* 1. 113
Was wanting yet the pure delight of love . . . 759 *Excursion* 1. 187
Who to the model of his own pure heart . . . 762 *Excursion* 1. 411
And pure as dew bathing their crimson leaves. . 773 *Excursion* 2. 110
The seat and bosom of pure innocence, . . . 781 *Excursion* 2. 624
By the example of his own pure course, . . . 781 *Excursion* 2. 630
Her share in the pure freedom of that life, . . 794 *Excursion* 3. 552
Yielded to mortal reflux ; her pure glory, . . . 795 *Excursion* 3. 672
The help desiring of the pure devout. . . . . 797 *Excursion* 3. 767
But that pure archetype of human greatness, . . 799 *Excursion* 3. 951
Of the pure intellect, that stand as laws . . . 802 *Excursion* 4. 97
Of pure, imperishable, blessedness, ... 803 *Excursion* 4. 159
That finds no limits but her own pure will. . . 804 *Excursion* 4. 196
As may support longings of pure desire ; . . . 804 *Excursion* 4. 236
These pure sensations ; that can penetrate . . 806 *Excursion* 4. 368
Tidings of joy and love.—From those pure heights 811 *Excursion* 4. 641
Pure and serene, diffused—to overlook . . . 811 *Excursion* 4. 688
The joy of that pure principle of love . . . . 819 *Excursion* 4. 1213
Less pure and exquisite, he cannot choose . . 819 *Excursion* 4. 1215
Open, and day's pure cheerfulness, but veiled . 822 *Excursion* 5. 5
At the baptismal font. And when the pure . . 826 *Excursion* 5. 279
To the pure heaven, he cast them down again . 836 *Excursion* 5. 901
Of pure imagination ;—above all, ... 836 *Excursion* 5. 910
From the pure soul, the soul sublime and pure ; . 837 *Excursion* 5. 986
Of those pure altars worthy ; ministers . . . 839 *Excursion* 6. 44
Shedding sweet influence from above ; or pure . 841 *Excursion* 6. 187
Your own pure spirit. Not a step we look for . 847 *Excursion* 6. 584
By which a virtuous woman, in pure youth, . . 851 *Excursion* 6. 847
She gazed as on a pure and spotless gift . . 852 *Excursion* 6. 908
Into that pure and unknown world of love . . 854 *Excursion* 6. 1050
Thanks to his pure imaginative soul . . . . 854 *Excursion* 6. 1065
To the pure course of human life which there . 856 *Excursion* 6. 1172
Rose this pure eloquence. And, when the stream 857 *Excursion* 7. 25
—Those transports, with staid looks of pure good-will, ... 860 *Excursion* 7. 224
Yet, by the solace of his own pure thoughts . . 863 *Excursion* 7. 417
By the pure bond of independent love, . . . 864 *Excursion* 7. 434
And in what pure contentedness of mind, . . . 864 *Excursion* 7. 475
Descending, and supporting his pure heart . . 871 *Excursion* 7. 900
And pure good-will, and hospitable cheer ; . . 878 *Excursion* 8. 242
Drink the pure water of its innocent stream . . 878 *Excursion* 8. 261
With lip almost as pure.—Domestic bliss . . . 878 *Excursion* 8. 262
With pure cerulean gravel, from the heights . . 881 *Excursion* 8. 452
Kind wishes, and good actions, and pure thoughts— 887 *Excursion* 9. 242
How pure his spirit ! in what vivid hues . . . 891 *Excursion* 9. 462
Pure, cloudless, ether ; and the star of eve . . 895 *Excursion* 9. 761
And pure, from further intercourse ensued ; . . 896 *Excursion* 9. 792
With beverage pure as ever fixed the choice . . S.3. 433 **The doubt* 17
Of pure affections, shedding upon joy . . . . K.8. 237 *Recluse* 1.1. 51
Inflicted upon confidence so pure. . . . . . K.8. 244 *Recluse* 1.1.272
Their healing offices a pure goodwill . . . . K.8. 244 *Recluse* 1.1.284
Pure and unsullied, flowing from the heart . . K.8. 248 *Recluse* 1.1.410
How goodly, how exceeding fair, how pure . . K.8. 254 *Recluse* 1.1.640
Shine for Clarkson's pure delight . . . . . L.2. 190 **Queen and* 5

Purely. Shall simply feel and purely meditate— 332 *Ode : Thanks.* 233
"*Here Man more purely lives, less oft doth fall*, 429 *Ecc. Sonn.* 2. 3. 1
"The light from past endeavours purely willed . 526 **Soon did* 10

Pure-minded. Flattery in Ancient Rome's pure-minded style : . . . . 359 **Complacent Fictions* 10

Purer. No purer essence, than the one that burns, . v **If thou indeed* 9
While all the future, for thy purer soul, . . . 112 **O dearer* 7
And passing even into my purer mind, . . . 206 *Tintern* 29
That taints the purer, better, mind ; . . . . 233 *Power of Sound* 88
With purer robes than those of flesh and blood, . 268 **Brook ! whose* 12
To something purer and more exquisite . . . 274 **Such age* 4
With gleams of fresher, purer, light ; . . . . 338 **Meek Virgin* 34
Together of a purer faith ; . . . . 402 *White Doe* 569
The Soul to purer worlds : and *who* the line . . 423 *Ecc. Sonn.* 1. 18. 12
Purer than foam on central ocean tost ; . . . 434 *Ecc. Sonn.* 2. 25. 5
Sublimer transport, purer love, ... 457 **Had this* 18
A happier, brighter, purer Heaven than theirs. . 462 **Where lies the truth* 14
The social rights of man breathe purer air ; . . 520 *Pun. Death* 13. 9
That they are kindred to our purer mind . . . 646 *Prelude* 2. 314

Purer—*continued.*
For, ever as a thought of purer birth . . . . 670 *Prelude* 5. 332
For ever in a purer element— . . . . . . 730 *Prelude* 11. 227
More perfectly of purer creatures ;—yet . . . 735 *Prelude* 12. 69
The purer elements of truth involved . . . . 760 *Excursion* 1. 253
Of higher reason and a purer will, ... 811 *Excursion* 4. 669
Their purer service, in this realm at least, . . . 875 *Excursion* 8. 86

Purest. The anchor of my purest thoughts, the nurse, 207 *Tintern* 109
A flaky weight of winter's purest snows ! . . . 212 *Dion*
Large space ('mid dreadful clouds) of purest sky, . 264 *Storm* 11
On the frail heart the purest share . . . . . 286 *Nith* 63
Lovelier—transplanted from heaven's purest clime ! 393 *Countess' Pillar* 5
A pledge of grace from purest heaven. . . . . 397 *White Doe* 78
Uplifted to the purest sky . . . . 402 *White Doe* 586
Uplifted to the purest sky . . . . 416 *White Doe* 1852
We read of faith and purest charity . . . . 441 *Ecc. Sonn.* 3. 5. 5
The purest stream of patient Energy. . . . . 444 *Ecc. Sonn.* 3. 15. 14
As if their lustre flowed from ether's purest blue. 525 *Epist. Beaumont* 257
Drawn from love's purest earthly fount for him . 646 *Prelude* 2. 247
And purest passion. Thou, my Friend ! wert reared . . . . 648 *Prelude* 2. 451
And wedded soul to soul in purest bond . . . 667 *Prelude* 5. 104
Of Grecian art, and purest poesy. . . . . . 672 *Prelude* 5. 459
By means refined attaining purest ends, . . . 690 *Prelude* 7. 237
His best and purest friend ; from her receives . 740 *Prelude* 13. 7
Lifted, in union with the purest, best, ... 748 *Prelude* 14. 185
Associates in the joy of purest minds, ... K.8. 249 *Recluse* 1.1. 460

Purge. Gifted to purge the vapoury atmosphere . 380 *Duddon* 18. 8
And purge from Vice's dross my tender charge. . 619 *School Ex.* 82

Purging. Go forth and prosper ; and, ye purging fires, ... 681 *Prelude* 6. 445

Purified. The faith reformed and purified. . . . 407 *White Doe* 1041
Did first present themselves thus purified, . . 703 *Prelude* 8. 304
Retirement, leisure, language purified . . . . 742 *Prelude* 13. 190

Purify. Thro' Time and Nature's influence, purify . 361 **When here* 11
Can give us inward help, can purify, ... K.8. 245 *Recluse* 1.1.302

Purifying. A purifying instrument—the storm . . 354 *Aquap.* 137
With life and nature—purifying thus . . . . 638 *Prelude* 1. 410

Purity. Moving untouched in silver purity, . . . 172 *Infant Daughter* 49
Its homage offered up in purity. . . . . . 222 *Triad* 196
(Whose tranquil pomp and spotless purity . . . 329 *Ode : Thanks.* 23
Have striven by purity to gain . . . . . . 343 *Eclipse* 47
And purity of nature spread before your sight ! . 350 *Des. Stanzas* 54
Of mother's love with maiden purity, ... 434 *Ecc. Sonn.* 2. 25. 13
And Faith preserved her ancient purity. . . . 441 *Ecc. Sonn.* 3. 7. 4
Love to promote and purity and peace ; . . . 460 **Queen of* 36
And all-enraptured with its purity ?— . . . 469 **Why stand* 3
In purity were such, ... 499 *Memory* 18
With emblematic purity attired . . . . . 508 *F. Stone* 12
In vestal purity. . . . . 544 *Russ. Fug.* 240
And conscious step of purity and pride. . . . 653 *Prelude* 3. 292
Retained its purity inviolate, ... 709 *Prelude* 8. 656
The strong hand of her purity ; and still . . . 762 *Excursion* 1. 399
Now in its morning purity arrayed. . . . . 823 *Excursion* 5. 91
Sublime from present purity and joy ! . . . . 879 *Excursion* 8. 320
Both for the love of purity, and hope . . . . 893 *Excursion* 9. 643

Purlieus. In forest purlieus ; and the like are bred, ... 879 *Excursion* 8. 369

Purloined. Purloined, in times less jealous than our own, ... 879 *Excursion* 8. 371

Purple. Come forth, and here retire in purple shade ; 4 *Ev. Wk.* 103
Feeding 'mid purple heath, "green rings," and broom ; . . . . 4 *Ev. Wk.* 133
A crest of purple tops the warrior's head. . . . 5 *Ev. Wk.* 149
And now that orb has touched the purple steep, . 5 *Ev. Wk.* 172
Of fainter gold, a purple gleam betray. . . . . 5 *Ev. Wk.* 177
Where falls the purple morning far and wide . . 10 *Desc. Sk.* 5
And Silence loves its purple roof of vines. . . . 12 *Desc. Sk.* 88
Upon the fragrant mountain's purple side : . . 18 *Desc. Sk.* 426
Of purple lights and ever-vernal plains ; . . . 20 *Desc. Sk.* 574
Before the purple dawn." . . . . 167 *Pilgrim's Dream* 48
Flung from off the purple pinions, ... 217 **Inmate of* 23
Beneath the shadow of his purple wings . . . 226 *Vernal Ode* 21
Preferr'st a garland culled from purple heath, . 227 *Vernal Ode* 79
While the stars shine, or while day's purple eye . 259 **A volant* 10
With purple of the trellis-roof, ... 342 *Ital. Itin.* 48
Blithe Autumn's purple crown, and Winter's icy mail ! . . . . 350 *Des. Stanzas* 36
—So, pleased with purple clusters to entwine . 367 *Trajan* 19
The thyme her purple, like the blush of Even ; . 377 *Duddon* 6. 11
Tells that their turf drank purple from the veins . 383 *Duddon* 29. 3
The fostered hyacinths spread their purple bloom. 425 *Ecc. Sonn.* 1. 27. 14
The gadding bramble hang her purple fruit ; . . 433 *Ecc. Sonn.* 2. 21. 6
Art thou a Man of purple cheer ? . . . . . 485 *Poet's Epitaph* 9
"Yon cloud with that long purple cleft . . . 486 **We walked* 21
Sky streaked with purple, grove and craggy *bield*, 524 *Epist. Beaumont* 175
With multitude of purple eyes, ... 580 *John Words.* 56
A crest of purple tops his warrior head. . . . 594 *Ev. Wk. Quarto* 132
And now it touches on the purple steep . . . 594 *Ev. Wk. Quarto* 155
—No purple prospects now the mind employ . . 599 *Ev. Wk. Quarto* 379
Stretch'd on the scented mountain's purple side. . 611 *Desc. Sk. Quarto* 513
Of purple lights and even vernal plains. . . . 614 *Desc. Sk. Quarto* 685
Serene he towers, in deepest purple dy'd ; . . . 615 *Desc. Sk. Quarto* 699
She wept.—Life's purple tide began to flow . . 619 **She wept* 1
On couches lie, with purple overspread : . . . 624 *Æneid* 59
Of morning beautified, or purple eve ; . . . . 678 *Prelude* 6. 219
Gathered the purple cups that round them lay, . 705 *Prelude* 8. 405
And beautified with morning's purple beams. . . 773 *Excursion* 2. 96
For robes with regal purple tinged ; convert . . 846 *Excursion* 6. 549

Q

Quenched—*continued.*
The tapers shall be quenched, the belfries mute, . 433 *Ecc. Sonn.* 2. 21. 3
The Senate stood aghast, her prudence quenched, 723 *Prelude* 10. 351
Quenching. Was smitten, and poured forth a quenching stream, ... 852 *Excursion* 6. 920
Quest. Alas ! what boots the long laborious quest . 315 **Alas ! what* 1
In Church or Chapel, if my curious quest . . . 356 *Aquap.* 238
No quest was hers of vague desire, ... 371 *Eg. Maid* 133
Untouched, unbreathed upon. Thrice happy quest, 388 *Trosachs* 9
In quest belike of transmutations . . . . . 399 *White Doe* 303
Subalpine vales, in quest of safe retreats . . . 431 *Ecc. Sonn.* 2. 12. 6
Where good men, disappointed in the quest . . 458 *Sea-shore* 30
In visible quest of immortality, ... 509 *F. Stone* 90
Seeking with indefatigable quest . . . . . 512 **Who rashly* 40
Who foiled an Emperor's eager quest ? . . . 545 *Russ. Fug.* 317
Through ever-changing scenes of votive quest . 634 *Prelude* 1. 181
Forsook their homes, and, errant in the quest . 655 *Prelude* 3. 466
To lure my mind from firm habitual quest . . 662 *Prelude* 4. 287
Have shaped him wandering upon this quest ! . 668 *Prelude* 5. 148
In summer, making quest for works of art, . . 677 *Prelude* 6. 190
Never did I, in quest of right and wrong, . . . 748 *Prelude* 14. 150
Diverging now (as if his quest had been . . 776 *Excursion* 2. 319
With morning we renewed our quest : the wind . 784 *Excursion* 2. 807
Departs, intent upon his onward quest !— . . 788 *Excursion* 3. 172
A Visitor—in quest of herbs and flowers ; . . . 839 *Excursion* 6. 97
Could the proud quest of chivalry do more ? " . 875 *Excursion* 8. 81
Leaving, in quest of other scenes, the shore . . 892 *Excursion* 9. 547
Far went these shepherds in their devious quest, K.8.225 **I will* 35
The longing, the contempt, the undaunted quest, K.8.257*Recluse* 1.1.742
Question. The cold blast struck me. 'Twas a foolish question. . . . . 52 *Bord.* 838
—But hear me. For *one* question, I have a heart 77 *Bord.* 2255
I question things and do not find . . . . . 117 *Affl. Marg.* 68
She answered, soon as she the question heard, . 119 *Sailor's Mother* 17
And thus, to Betty's question, he . . . . . 131 *Idiot Boy* 447
And Benjamin, without a question, ... 176 *Waggoner* 1. 232
My question eagerly did I renew, ... 197 *Resolution* 118
Then question not that, 'mid the austere Band, . 362 **List—'twas* 66
Can question that thy countenance is bright, . . 392 **Though joy* 13
Though question followed question, dear . . . 545 *Russ. Fug.* 343
To question us. " Whence come ye ? to what end ? " . . . . 622 *Recluse* 1. 1. 167
All things are put to question ; he must live . . 670 *Prelude* 5. 323
After strict question, left within my mind . . 726 *Prelude* 10. 574
To watch and question those I met, and speak . 742 *Prelude* 13. 161
The same sad question. Meanwhile her poor Hut 770 *Excursion* 1. 900
Or question deep ? what profits all that earth, . 789 *Excursion* 3. 210
Answering the question which himself had asked, 802 *Excursion* 4. 68
To lower : can you question that the soul . . . 816 *Excursion* 4. 1023
Or courtesy prescribed. While question rose . 882 *Excursion* 8. 524
Strange question, yet it answers not itself. . . K.8. 255*Recluse* 1.1.681
Questionable. To keep this new and questionable road ? . . . . 434 *Ecc. Sonn.* 2. 23. 14
Questioned. *See* **Self-questioned.**
And, as we talked, I questioned him, ... 86 *Anecdote* 27
We questioned him again, and yet again ; . . . 684 *Prelude* 6. 588
As if from Fairy-land. Much I questioned him ; 688 *Prelude* 7. 98
Questioning. Gazing, doubting, questioning ; . . 399 *White Doe* 315
Where Augurs stand, the Future questioning, . 419 *Ecc. Sonn.* 1. 3. 3
Questionings. But for those obstinate questionings 589 *Immortality* 145
Questions. Answer these questions, from our common knowledge, ... 38 *Bord.* 39
Breathless questions followed fast, ... 141 *Arm. Lady* 104
Such fruitless questions may not long beguile . 380 *Duddon* 16. 1
His questions urging, feels, in slender ties . . 422 *Ecc. Sonn.* 1. 13. 10
By noise and strife, and questions wearisome, . 528 **Those breathing* 94
Questions, directions, warnings and advice, . . 649 *Prelude* 3. 23
Sprinkling this talk with questions, better spared, 665 *Prelude* 4. 438
So that he questions the mute leaves with pain, . 719 *Prelude* 10. 62
Yielded up moral questions in despair. . . . 731 *Prelude* 11. 305
Doubts, and determine questions, by the rules . 792 *Excursion* 3. 414
And questions in authoritative tone, ... 859 *Excursion* 7. 101
When, as our questions led, he told at large . . 883 *Excursion* 8. 575
Unusual aspects, or by questions apt . . . . K.8. 230 **I will* 192
Quibble. So patient Senates quibble by the hour . L.1. 94 *Juvenal* 2. 1
Quick. Quick—to the point—if any untold crime . 68 *Bord.* 1703
Alive ! you heard him breathe ? quick, quick— . 73 *Bord.* 2014
Quick was the little Maid's reply, ... 84 *We are Seven* 63
Quick as he in feats of art, ... 171 *Kitten* 31
From quick and eager visitings . . . . . . 288 *Highland Girl* 39
That touch each other to the quick in modes . 290 *Kilchurn* 7
He tracks her motions, quick or slow. . . . . 294 *Jedbor.* 57
(Too quick and keen) incited to disdain . . . 328 *Ode 1815* 118
A startling thunder quick and short ! . . . . 342 *Ital. Itin.* 64
The footsteps of a quick retreat ; . . . . . 406 *White Doe* 891
But quick the turns of chance and change, . . 408 *White Doe* 1119
Walked quick or slowly, every mood . . . . 415 *White Doe* 1726
Deep sighs with quick words blending, . . . 479 *Somnamb.* 83
Less quick the stir when tide and breeze . . . 499 **This Lawn* 7
And quick words round him fall like flakes of snow. 503 *Warning* 21
Bent in quick turns each other to undo, . . . 513 *Newspaper* 7
For lingering durance or quick death with shame, 517 *Pun. Death* 1. 11
Stings to the quick, and, with resistless force, . 519 *Pun. Death* 12. 3
Through the quick turns of many a hollow nook, 523 *Epist. Beaumont* 105
On their quick sense our sweetest music jarred ; . 527 **Those breathing* 51
Or thither thronged for refuge. With quick glance 540 *Grace Darl.* 35
Quick to the secret grotto they retire . . . . 619 *School Ex.* 61
Quick as the pantings of the faithful dog, . . . 661 *Prelude* 4. 186
Had vanity (quick Spirit that appears . . . . 688 *Prelude* 7. 103
On strangers, of all ages ; the quick dance . . 689 *Prelude* 7. 154

Quick—*continued.*
Of reading them with quick and curious eye ; . 696 *Prelude* 7. 587
No vain conceits ; provokes to no quick turns . 740 *Prelude* 13. 26
By which she is made quick to recognise . . . 758 *Excursion* 1. 168
O'er the flat Common !—With quick step I reached . . . . 766 *Excursion* 1. 646
That made her heart beat quick. Yousee that path, 769 *Excursion* 1. 882
Like human life from darkness."—A quick turn . 786 *Excursion* 3. 35
Quick change of objects ; and, to laugh alone, . 799 *Excursion* 3. 903
Of a quick fancy and an active heart, ... 810 *Excursion* 4. 583
For studious fancy, his quick hand bestowed . . 812 *Excursion* 4. 726
Gay, volatile, ingenious, quick to learn, . . . 842 *Excursion* 6. 282
Are yet made desperate by ' too quick a sense . 846 *Excursion* 6. 532
How quick, how vast an increase ! From the germ 876 *Excursion* 8. 118
His respiration quick and audible ; . . . . . 879 *Excursion* 8. 312
Quick-eared. Teach me with quick-eared spirit to rejoice . . . . 454 **The Sun, that* 19
Quicken. Quicken the slothful, and exalt the vile !— 217 *Enterprise* 156
Only ministers to quicken . . . . 222 *Triad* 166
To quicken, and to aggravate—to feed . . . 788 *Excursion* 3. 141
Or feel, shall tend to quicken and refine ; . . . 820 *Excursion* 4. 1271
Power that comes forth to quicken and exalt . . 875 *Excursion* 8. 73
Quickened. Be its depths quickened ; what thou dost inherit . . . . 366 **Fair Land* 12
—From worlds not quickened by the sun . . . 457 **Had this* 37
Were such as might have quickened and inspired 850 *Excursion* 6. 827
With a step quickened by November's cold, . . S.3. 433 **The doubt* 44
Quickener. *See* **Spirit-quickener.**
Quickening. *See* **Soul-quick'ning.**
With quickening pace my horse drew nigh . . 109 **Strange fits* 11
'Tis thine the quickening impulse to control, . . 216 *Enterprise* 100
Divine of words quickening insensate things. . 252 **Why, Minstrel* 8
The quickening spark of this day's sacrifice ; . . 329 *Ode : Thanks.* 52
And her lips, quickening with uncertain red, . . 374 *Eg. Maid* 329
With quickening impulse answered their mute pleas, 466 *St. Bees* 62
A quickening hope, a freshening glee, ... 506 **While from* 5
I saw (ambition quickening at the view) . . . 532 **Once I* 13
With quickening virtue, but is now become . . 632 *Prelude* 1. 36
Lay bedded in a quickening soul, and all . . . 651 *Prelude* 3. 131
Bright was the summer's noon when quickening steps . . . . 658 *Prelude* 4. 1
Gathering upon us ; " quickening then the pace . 667 *Prelude* 5. 131
Poured out (saluted by that quickening breeze . 687 *Prelude* 7. 2
And a new quickening shall succeed, at first . . 707 *Prelude* 8. 578
But by their quickening impulse made more prompt 747 *Prelude* 14. 107
The quickening spindle drew a trustier line. . . S.3.427**Through Cumbrian* 14
Quickens. And quickens the blithe sound of oars that pass . . . . 13 *Desc. Sk.* 125
That quickens only where Thou say'st it may : . 257 **The prayers* 6
Quickens, as now, the withered heath ;— . . . 299 *Brownie's Cell* 84
Quickens the slumbering mind, and aids the thoughts, ... 698 *Prelude* 7. 759
Quicker. In fear) have walked with quicker step ; but why . . . . 742 *Prelude* 13. 159
And, with light steps still quicker than his words, 781 *Excursion* 2. 637
But, in the quicker turns of the discourse, . . 834 *Excursion* 5. 784
Quickliest. That soonest fails to please, and quickliest turns . . . . 799 *Excursion* 3. 912
Quickly. Forgotten ? have my warnings passed so quickly . . . . 40 *Bord.* 162
Of fancy shall be quickly tamed by mine ; . . 73 *Bord.* 2037
Too quickly moved, too easily giving way, . . 76 *Bord.* 2233
Nor rate too high what must so quickly fade, . 110 **Look at* 17
Slew, and as quickly to a second gave . . . . 123 *V. and J.* 131
He quickly will repair this loss, and then . . . 135 *Michael* 252
Passed quickly through the mind of Isabel, . . 135 *Michael* 272
Would mount, too, quickly as he can : . . . 176 *Waggoner* 1. 254
Your seats, and quickly shall be paid . . . . 238 *P. B.* 184
But quickly Peter's mood is changed, ... 240 *P. B.* 346
Never did pulse so quickly throb, ... 242 *P. B.* 516
But then it quickly fled ; . . . . 244 *P. B.* 730
How quickly from that aery hold unbound, . . 259 **A volant* 4
" A lesson that is quickly learned, ... 291 *Rob Roy* 41
And quickly with a silent crew . . . . . . 297 *Highland Boy* 181
Silently disappears, or quickly fades : . . . . 349 *Sky-prosp.* 11
And quickly spread themselves abroad, . . . 398 *White Doe* 160
Stilled by thy voice ! But quickly from afar . . 438 *Ecc. Sonn.* 2. 38. 5
As quickly as he may ; . . . . 491 *Fidelity* 37
" Fear not," quickly answered Hubert ; . . . 535 *Egremont* 33
And as quickly it is gone ; . . . . 549 *Hermit's Cell* 1. 24
Such is Joy—as quickly hidden, ... 549 *Hermit's Cell* 1. 25
Constrain her heart as quickly to return, . . . 563 *Troilus* 78
How quickly mighty Nations have been formed, . 715 *Prelude* 9. 376
But quickly from among our morning thoughts . 773 *Excursion* 2. 114
Without refreshment ! " Quickly had he spoken, 781 *Excursion* 2. 636
The earth-born wanderer hath passed ; and quickly, 800 *Excursion* 3. 984
Quiet. *See* **Mountain-quiet.**
Thy quiet soul on all bestowing, ... 9 *Collins* 6
The leafy wood, or sleeps in quiet lakes. . . . 10 *Desc. Sk.* 8
Suspended 'mid the quiet of the sky ; . . . . 16 *Desc. Sk.* 349
Uplift in quiet their illumined forms, ... 19 *Desc. Sk.* 473
Profounder quiet, when the fit retires, ... 26 *Guilt* 93
And in a quiet home once more my father slept. . 29 *Guilt* 261
How quiet 'round me ship and ocean were ! . . 30 *Guilt* 339
As quiet all within me. I was blest, ... 30 *Guilt* 340
He bore within a breast where dreadful quiet reigned. . . . . 36 *Guilt* 648
Is, after conflict, quiet as the ocean, ... 40 *Bord.* 172
Will give me quiet lodging. You have a boy, good Host, ... 43 *Bord.* 353

Quiet—*continued.*
Made quiet as he is. Why came you down? 55 *Bord.* 957
And did not want glimmerings of quiet hope. 62 *Bord.* 1355
The only quiet heart on earth. In terror, 64 *Bord.* 1468
Our quiet home all full in view, 85 *Anecdote* 6
You live, Sir, in these dales, a quiet life: 97 *Brothers* 121
A mighty wonder bred among our quiet crew. 107 *Indolence* 18
The Babe was drawing in its quiet food. 124 *V. and J.* 216
Who knew not to what quiet depths a weight 125 *V. and J.* 225
Where in forgotten quiet he might dwell, 125 *V. and J.* 269
That I could not lie quiet in my grave. 134 *Michael* 232
From years of quiet industry, to love 147 *Joanna* 3
Its own deep quiet to restore our hearts. 148 **There is an* 8
Lashed out of life, not quiet in the grave. 153 *Morn. Ex.* 18
Let them all in quiet lie, 157 *Sexton* 26
Thy quiet with no ill intent, 169 *Wren's Nest* 62
The horses made a quiet stand; 179 *Waggoner* 3. 57
Sickening into thoughtful quiet; 180 *Waggoner* 4. 72
Their quiet being: and unless I now 185 *Nutting* 48
He sang of love, with quiet blending, 186 **O Nightingale* 17
This heath, this calm, and quiet scene; 187 **Three years* 40
So passed in quiet bliss, 193 *Ruth* 81
The landscape with the quiet of the sky. 205 *Tintern* 8
While with an eye made quiet by the power 206 *Tintern* 47
Of blissful quiet 'mid unfading bowers. 212 *Laod.* 163
Safe through the winter storm in quiet dwells! 227 *Vernal Ode* 109
In listless quiet o'er the ethereal deep 231 *Clouds* 76
Transmute him to a wretch from quiet hurled— 234 *Power of Sound* 101
Less quiet regions to explore, 237 *P. B.* 107
But he flowed quiet and unseen:— 240 *P. B.* 372
Across the deep and quiet spot 240 *P. B.* 381
In quiet uncomplaining mood, 241 *P. B.* 428
And touch more quiet skies. 242 *P. B.* 495
The holy time is quiet as a Nun 258 **It is a* 2
Gently hast sunk into the quiet tomb, 271 *George: Death* 7
Couch near their dams, with quiet satisfied; 278 **Life with* 6
Of glory lavished on our quiet days. 282 **Wansfell! this* 8
For *he* is safe, a quiet bed 285 *Grave of Burns* 67
This little bay; a quiet road 288 *Highland Girl* 9
It is not quiet, is not ease; 289 *Glen-Al.* 25
Still hint that quiet best is found, 301 *Bran* 66
And bloodshed, longed in quiet to be laid 320 **They seek* 13
'Mid the deep quiet of this morning hour, 329 *Ode: Thanks.* 36
Though false to Nature's quiet equipoise: 382 *Duddon* 23. 13
For quiet contemplation: 385 *Yarrow Rev.* 20
Lie quiet in your churchyard bed! 397 *White Doe* 68
What quiet watch she seems to keep, 399 *White Doe* 310
Of quiet to the neighbouring fields; 406 *White Doe* 948
Eager to build the quiet Fortresses 424 *Ecc. Sonn.* 1. 24. 3
Of public quiet; unambitious Men, 429 *Ecc. Sonn.* 2. 5. 4
Not to the golden mean, and quiet flow 443 *Ecc. Sonn.* 3. 11. 13
Seen in her course, nor 'mid this quiet heard; 454 *Sea-side* 21
One, who has watched thee at some quiet hour 459 **Wanderer! that* 33
In kindred quiet I repose my trust. 464 **A point* 4
Nursed in the quiet Abbey of St. Bees. 467 *St. Bees* 108
On woman's quiet hours; 478 *Somnamb.* 51
The harvest of a quiet eye 485 *Poet's Epitaph* 51
Are quiet when they will. 487 *Fountain* 40
Is quiet in its sheath, 507 *May* 38
In humble grace, and quiet pensiveness 508 *F. Stone* 39
Can thy enduring quiet gently raise 510 **Among a* 28
Far from our home by Grasmere's quiet Lake, 521 *Epist. Beaumont* 1
Within your quiet range. 526 **The soaring* 28
Out of the quiet rock the elements 548 **Stranger! this* 29
This quiet spot; and, Stranger! not unmoved 551 **If thou in* 5
The quiet of nature was Adam's delight. 569 *Farmer* 24
To settled quiet: he is one by whom 572 *Animal Tran.* 8
Death is the quiet haven of us all. 574 *Chiabrera* 4. 27
So pure the sky, so quiet was the air! 578 *Peele Castle* 5
Elysian quiet, without toil or strife; 578 *Peele Castle* 26
His quiet heart's selected home. 580 *John Words.* 27
Her quiet is secure; 583 **O for a* 39
O gift divine of quiet sequestration! 586 *Ch. Lamb* 121
—Then Quiet led me up the huddling rill, 592 *Ev. Wk. Quarto* 71
By silver'd wreaths of quiet charcoal smoke, 599 *Ev. Wk. Quarto* 430
In cataracts, or sleeps in quiet lakes. 602 *Desc. Sk. Quarto* 12
By the deep quiet gloom appall'd, she sighs, 606 *Desc.Sk.Quarto* 221
Her quiet streams, and hills of downy green, 606 *Desc.Sk.Quarto* 244
Turning with quiet touch the valley's hay, 607 *Desc.Sk.Quarto* 274
To break the quiet of the village shade 615 *Desc.Sk.Quarto* 745
And quiet *now* are the depths of air, 623 *G. and S. Green* 19
In quiet more profound; 623 *G. and S. Green* 22
A quiet independence of the heart; 643 *Prelude* 2. 72
Under the quiet stars, and at that time 646 *Prelude* 2. 303
Of peace and quiet and domestic love, 648 *Prelude* 2. 438
Health and the quiet of a healthful mind 648 *Prelude* 2. 467
Full oft the quiet and exalted thoughts 652 *Prelude* 3. 207
Come forth, perhaps without one quiet thought. 652 *Prelude* 3. 255
For quiet things to wander in; a haunt 655 *Prelude* 3. 437
And more than pastoral quiet, 'mid the stir 661 *Prelude* 4. 174
I saw the quiet woodman in the woods, 661 *Prelude* 4. 215
Preyed on my strength, and stopped the quiet stream 663 *Prelude* 4. 296
A character of quiet more profound 664 *Prelude* 4. 369
And with a quiet uncomplaining voice, 664 *Prelude* 4. 419
Then sought with quiet heart my distant home. 665 *Prelude* 4. 469
A pleasure quiet and profound, a sense 677 *Prelude* 6. 130
Measuring our steps in quiet, we pursued 681 *Prelude* 6. 416
Quiet and lorded over and possessed 683 *Prelude* 6. 520
Locked up in quiet. For myself, I fear 711 *Prelude* 9. 110
Then from the quiet of that scene passed on, 718 *Prelude* 10. 10

Quiet—*continued.*
That would have pleased me in more quiet times; 719 *Prelude* 10. 68
By day, a quiet sound in silent night; 734 *Prelude* 12. 20
Happy, and quiet in his cheerfulness, 761 *Excursion* 1. 367
And she forgotten in the quiet grave. 763 *Excursion* 1. 510
A quiet treeless nook, with two green fields, 776 *Excursion* 2. 337
It could not be more quiet: peace is here 777 *Excursion* 2. 364
Or introduced at this more quiet time. 787 *Excursion* 3. 49
Through the long year in constant quiet bound, 790 *Excursion* 3. 323
Who, for the sake of sterner quiet, closed 791 *Excursion* 3. 354
Where earth is quiet and her face unchanged 792 *Excursion* 3. 401
As times of quiet and unbroken peace, 794 *Excursion* 3. 601
In the best quiet to her course allowed; 800 *Excursion* 3. 988
That keeps the raven quiet in her nest, 809 *Excursion* 4. 519
Before his time into a quiet grave, 821 *Excursion* 4. 1314
On the hill-sides, a cheerful quiet scene, 823 *Excursion* 5. 90
Here to lie down in lasting quiet, he, 835 *Excursion* 5. 883
The steadfast quiet natural to a mind 840 *Excursion* 6. 146
The visible quiet of this holy ground, 845 *Excursion* 6. 482
No quiet in the darkness of the night, 855 *Excursion* 6. 1101
Amid the quiet of the green recess, 857 *Excursion* 7. 13
Contented to partake the quiet meal 859 *Excursion* 7. 160
That, near the quiet churchyard where we sate, 865 *Excursion* 7. 541
The innocent troubler of their quiet, sleeps 868 *Excursion* 7. 693
And pensive quiet, an unnatural light 876 *Excursion* 8. 167
Quiet and calm. Behold him—in the school 878 *Excursion* 8. 306
How with most quiet and most silent death, 886 *Excursion* 9. 149
Like that reflected in yon quiet pool, 891 *Excursion* 9. 471
Quiet and dark; for through the thick-wove trees, S.3. 417 **Sweet was* 11
In quiet hopelessness I sleep, K.8. 220 **The snow-tracks* 25
Alas! how quiet, and how deep! K.8. 220 **The snow-tracks* 26
Composing darkness, with a quiet load K.8. 241 *Recluse* 1.1.175
And lived so long in quiet, side by side. K.8. 243 *Recluse* 1.1.260
Our beautiful and quiet home, enriched K.8. 254 *Recluse* 1.1.652
Through quiet meadows, after he has learnt K.8. 256 *Recluse* 1.1.730
From frightful storms into a quiet road. K.8. 266 **Rid of* 4

Quieted. And all was calmed and quieted. 179 *Waggoner* 3. 109
And quieted in character—the strife, 290 *Kilchurn* 41
And, quieted and soothed, a torrent small, 524 *Epist. Beaumont* 177
"But all was quieted by iron bonds 798 *Excursion* 3. 821

Quietly. How quietly her Johnny goes. 127 *Idiot Boy* 91
As quietly as spots of sky 193 *Ruth* 71
Is Peter quietly resigned; 242 *P. B.* 572
And quietly passed through. 247 *P. B.* 985
That you can listen quietly: 295 *Highland Boy* 7
Or quietly self-buried in earth's mould, 382 *Duddon* 27. 2
Stood quietly in Rylstone-hall. 400 *White Doe* 379
The same who quietly was feeding 406 *White Doe* 973
That quietly restores the natural mien 505 *Warning* 136
From thy mild manners quietly exhaled.' 575 *Chiabrera* 8. 24
He lay in slumber quietly; 579 **Sweet Flower* 51
Is listening quietly. 581 **Loud is* 8
I went into the Orchard quietly; 622 **Among all* 14
Or sate reclined; admiring quietly 893 *Excursion* 9. 582

Quietness. For shadowy quietness. 168 *Wren's Nest* 16
With quietness and beauty, and so feed 207 *Tintern* 127
In quietness withdraws; 223 *Wishing-gate* 66
What groans! what shrieks! what quietness in death! 345 **Ambition—following* 14
In quietness she lays her down; 397 *White Doe* 142
Of Barden's lowly quietness. 399 *White Doe* 294
Of quietness, she sits alone; 413 *White Doe* 1584
Now with her own deep quietness content; 439 *Ecc. Sonn.* 2. 44. 3
Health, meekness, ardour, quietness secure, 489 *Spade* 9
But in the quietness of thought: 492 *Duty* 36
And quietness pillow his head. 621 *Convict* 28
The heart of quietness is here 623 *G. and S. Green* 23
Of quietness or peace; yet have I stood, 640 *Prelude* 1. 576
The safeguard for repose and quietness. 643 *Prelude* 2. 114
In quietness, without anxiety: 692 *Prelude* 7. 323
Then fading with unusual quietness,— 718 *Prelude* 10. 3
To meditation in that quietness!— 792 *Excursion* 3. 405
For quietness profound!" Upon the side 822 *Excursion* 5. 11
Our thoughts unite in kindred quietness! 868 *Excursion* 7. 704
Of glad emotion and deep quietness; K.8. 243 *Recluse* 1.1.231

Quire. *See* **Choir.**
And while the rest, a ruddy quire, 156 *Oak and Broom* 8
So pleads the town's cathedral quire, 228 *Devot. Incit.* 27
Besprinkled with a careless quire, 233 *Power of Sound* 44
(So might he seem) of all the glittering quire! 261 **I watch* 3
To Nature's tuneful quire, this rustling dry 263 **While not* 10
For I have heard the quire of Richmond hill 271 **Fame tells* 6
Hallows once more the long-deserted Quire 283 **Well have* 6
And add your voices to the quire 286 *Sons of Burns* 26
Can she be grieved for quire or shrine, 397 *White Doe* 112
Till the whole City rings like one vast quire. 442 *Ecc. Sonn.* 3. 8. 8
The silent stars, among the angelic quire, 466 *St. Bees* 57
Supreme among the Elysian quire, 472 *Ossian* 40
But chanted by your Orphan Quire 577 **I come* 31

Quires. *See* **Choirs.**
Mount, tuneful Bird, and join the immortal quires! 261 **I heard (alas* 13
Touch not the tapers of the sacred quires; 426 *Ecc. Sonn.* 1. 31. 11
Have felt it, not the happy Quires of Spring, K.8. 243 *Recluse* 1.1.235

Quit. Let us quit the leafy arbour, 90 *Longest Day* 1
Nor will I quit thy shore 109 **I travelled* 6
All that could quit my grasp, or flee, 113 *Lament* 45
To quit the slow-paced waggon's side, 180 *Waggoner* 4. 15

Quit—*continued.*
Who quit their fold with dance and shout, 193 *Ruth* 50
And quit the flowers that summer brings 204 *Brougham* 91
Mortals, rejoice ! the very Angels quit 227 *Vernal Ode* 71
Or quit the stars with a lingering farewell—how 253 **Aerial Rock* 4
When Heroes are allowed to quit 342 *Ital. Itin.* 70
Or we for ever quit the field. 408 *White Doe* 1132
Or quit with zealous step their knee-worn floors 424 *Ecc. Sonn.* 1. 25. 3
Their altars they forego, their homes they quit, 441 *Ecc. Sonn.* 3. 6. 9
Not loth we quit the newly-hallowed sward 451 *Ecc. Sonn.* 3. 42. 3
For summer wandering quit their household bowers ; 463 **Adieu, Rydalian* 10
Up ! up ! my Friend, and quit your books ; 481 *Tables Turned* 1
To quit the Ship for which he died, 579 **Sweet Flower* 53
Harsh judgments, if the song be loth to quit 641 *Prelude* 1. 630
Had ceased to dazzle, ofttimes did I quit 650 *Prelude* 3. 91
And, therefore, now that we must quit this theme, 651 *Prelude* 3. 189
To quit my pleasure, and, from month to month, 654 *Prelude* 3. 357
The Savoyard to quit his naked rocks, 761 *Excursion* 1. 317
And, if a dog passed by, she still would quit 769 *Excursion* 1. 878
Invite us ; shall we quit our road, and join 773 *Excursion* 2. 139
To quit the beaten track of life, and soar 789 *Excursion* 3. 213
Depresses the soul's vigour. Quit your couch— 808 *Excursion* 4. 481
And, having once espoused, would never quit ; 862 *Excursion* 7. 350

Quite. His sense, in sudden vacancy quite lost, 26 *Guilt* 95
You are quite exhausted. Let us rest awhile 39 *Bord.* 130
Nature will either end thee quite ; 88 *H. C.* 21
He quite forgot his holly whip, 127 *Idiot Boy* 84
By this time is not quite so flurried : 127 *Idiot Boy* 128
But Betty is not quite at ease ; 127 *Idiot Boy* 155
She quite forgot to send the Doctor, 129 *Idiot Boy* 275
Fond lovers ! yet not quite hob nob, 129 *Idiot Boy* 289
Not quite so fair as many are 159 **With little* 35
Hath quite forgotten her—or may be 177 *Waggoner* 2. 86
No wonder if you quite forget 237 *P. B.* 119
Said I, becoming quite collected ; 238 *P. B.* 202
His temper was quite mastered by the times, 711 *Prelude* 9. 143

Quits. Who at the call of summer quits his home, 10 *Desc. Sk.* 10
She quits her house and, in the neighbouring Churchyard 44 *Bord.* 390
And quits the bosom of the deep 344 **How blest* 31
The war-worn Chieftain quits the world—to hide 424 *Ecc. Sonn.* 1. 21. 4
Nor quits the Body when the Soul is freed, 448 *Ecc. Sonn.* 3. 31. 3
Within the old Man's hat ; nor quits him so, 566 *Cumb. Beg.* 29
The aged Beggar coming, quits her work, 566 *Cumb. Beg.* 35
Quits, growling, the white bones that strew his lair ; 606 *Desc.Sk.Quarto* 232
The wanderers choose. For this he quits his home 702 *Prelude* 8. 234
My helpmate's face by light of day. He quits 834 *Excursion* 5. 807
Then, reappearing in a moment, quits 858 *Excursion* 7. 46

Quitted. When thou hadst quitted Esthwaite's pleasant shore, 150 **When, to* 67
Quitted, not loth, the mild magnificence 675 *Prelude* 6. 12
Of gownèd students, quitted hall and bower, 688 *Prelude* 7. 54

Quitting. And, quitting unsubstantial dreams, 416 *White Doe* 1840

Quiver. And Peter's lips with fury quiver ; 241 *P. B.* 457
Upon the stream the moonbeams quiver. 242 *P. B.* 535
Not equipp'd with bow and quiver S.3. 437 **I, whose* 13

Quivered. The startled bird quivered upon the wing. 74 *Bord.* 2105
Quivered and seemed almost to heave, 334 **In Bruges* 19

Quivering. A woman stood with quivering lips and pale, 33 *Guilt* 469
Those quivering wings composed, that music still ! 209 **Ethereal minstrel* 6
The rocks, and quivering trees, and billowy lake, 230 *Clouds* 63
From this deep chasm, where quivering sunbeams play 379 *Duddon* 15. 1
And jealousy, and quivering strife, 498 **The sylvan* 17
Responsive to his call, with quivering peals, 671 *Prelude* 5. 376

Quivers. Notice or name !—It quivers down the hill, 251 **There is a little* 4

Quixote. *See* **Semi-Quixote.**

Quoit. Our unpretending valley.—How the quoit 868 *Excursion* 7. 740

Quondam. The tale of this his quondam Barony 39 *Bord.* 79

Quote. There is an ampler page for man to quote, 393 **The Lovers* 12

Quoth. Quoth Betty, " and will soon be here, 127 *Idiot Boy* 150
Quoth Peter, leaping from his seat, 241 *P. B.* 406
Quoth he, " You little mulish dog, 241 *P. B.* 458
That I am here, they'll think," quoth he, 242 *P. B.* 489
" No doubt," quoth he, " he is the Master 243 *P. B.* 584
" Blood drops—leaves rustle—yet," quoth he, 245 *P. B.* 808
Quoth Merlin, " Even as I was bidden, 371 *Eg. Maid* 170
" My Oarsmen," quoth the mighty King, " draw near, 426 *Ecc. Sonn.* 1. 30. 4
" O Lord, our Lord ! how wondrously," (quoth she) 552 *Prioress* 1
Following the Lamb celestial," quoth she, 554 *Prioress* 130
Now, God, quoth I, that died upon the rood, 558 *Cuck.and Night.* 93
What ! quoth she then, what is't that ails thee now? 558 *Cuck.and Night.*116
Ah, fool ! quoth she, wist thou not what it is ? 559 *Cuck.andNight.*126
Ay, quoth the Cuckoo, that is a quaint law, 559 *Cuck.andNight.*136
What ! quoth she, thou art all out of thy mind, 559 *Cuck.andNight.*146
Then, quoth she, let me never hope for bliss, 559 *Cuck.andNight.*164
Fie, quoth she, on thy name, Bird ill beseen ! 560 *Cuck.andNight.*186
Quoth she, to hear this churlish bird thus speak 560 *Cuck.andNight.*212
Nay, nothing shall me bring thereto, quoth I, 561 *Cuck.andNight.*239
Yea, hath it ? use, quoth she, this medicine ; 561 *Cuck.andNight.*241
Now farewell, quoth she, for I hence must wend ; 561 *Cuck.andNight.*252
Quoth Andrew, " Under half-a-crown, 621 *Andrew Jones* 28
" Ha," quoth I, " pretty prisoner, are you there ! " 659 *Prelude* 4. 59

R

Rabbits. Hares couch, and rabbits burrow ! 292 *Yarrow Unv.* 14

Rabble. The glittering rabble housed to . . and swear L.1. 97 *Juvenal* 3. 83

Rabblement. Amid the uproar of the rabblement, 691 *Prelude* 7. 273

Raby. Had sate together in Raby Hall ! 403 *White Doe* 696

Race. *See* **After-race, Eagle-race, Mill-race.**
The general sorrows of the human race : 19 *Desc. Sk.* 503
They run up stairs in gamesome race ; 81 †*Mother's Return* 50
We'll for our whistles run a race." 85 *Shepherd-boys* 36
—They were the last of all their race : and now, 96 *Brothers* 76
Thou easy-hearted Thing, with thy wild race 107 *Farewell* 46
Figures with armorial signs of race and birth, 142 *Arm. Lady* 155
From whom the Race of human kind proceed, 172 *Infant Daughter* 9
How soon my Lucy's race was run ! 187 **Three years* 38
Such race, I think, was never seen before. 200 *Hart-leap* 16
Where is the throng, the tumult of the race ? 201 *Hart-leap* 25
" For thirteen hours he ran a desperate race ; 203 *Hart-leap* 145
In him the savage virtue of the Race, 205 *Brougham* 165
That I might step beyond my natural race 208 **It is no* 13
Enquire not if the faery race 223 *Wishing-gate* 19
The shadow-casting race of trees survive : 227 *Vernal Ode* 63
High o'er the red-haired race of Mars, 237 *P. B.* 38
As ever ran a felon's race. 239 *P. B.* 275
Running among the clouds a Wood-nymph's race ! 266 **With how* 4
Checked oft-times in a devious race, 285 *Grave of Burns* 74
That Ossian, last of all his race ! 289 *Glen-Al.* 31
Proud Remnant was he of a fearless Race, 298 *Brownie's Cell* 31
And feel, thou Earth, for this afflicted Race ! 306 **We had* 14
For some Aspirant of our short-lived race, 313 **Go back* 7
Ne'er saw a race who held, by right of birth, 325 **Intrepid sons* 3
The blood of Heroes runs its race ! 344 **How blest* 48
To the Valerian, Fabian, Curian Race, 357 *Aquap.* 281
And, though the passions of man's fretful race 367 *Trajan* 7
For the clear waters to pursue their race 378 *Duddon* 9. 7
Yet, though a wild vindictive Race, untamed 389 *Sound of Mull* 9
The Race of Alfred covet glorious pains 425 *Ecc. Sonn.* 1. 27. 5
The turbaned Race are poured in thickening swarms 427 *Ecc. Sonn.* 1. 34. 1
Each with the other in a lingering race 440 *Ecc. Sonn.* 3. 1. 13
Yet may outstrip me in the appointed race, 464 **A point* 10
Far different we—a froward race, 490 *Night Thought* 7
All the four are in the race : 490 *Incident : Dog* 12
Already half his race hath run ; 506 *Lab. Hymn* 22
To Beardless Boys—an imitative race, 516 **Young England* 10
Perhaps the sole survivor of thy race, 531 *Octogen.* 10
When Fermor's race is run ; 582 **O for a* 3
Another race hath been, and other palms are won. 590 *Immortality* 203
Albert, in thy race we cherish 629 *Installation* 95
Odin, the Father of a race by whom 635 *Prelude* 1. 189
And wasted down by glorious death that race 635 *Prelude* 1. 201
Daily with chaunted rites. In such a race 643 *Prelude* 2. 65
In uncouth race, and left the cross-legged knight, 643 *Prelude* 2. 117
And manners finely wrought, the delicate race 657 *Prelude* 3. 560
Behold a race of young ones like to those 671 *Prelude* 5. 407
A race of real children ; not too wise, 671 *Prelude* 5. 411
Humanity, splitting the race of man 693 *Prelude* 7. 390
Feelingly watched, might teach Man's haughty race 734 *Prelude* 12. 12
Of the whole human race one brotherhood. 735 *Prelude* 12. 87
And all will be complete, thy race be run, 752 *Prelude* 14. 431
Yet not the noblest of that honoured Race 771 *Excursion* 2. 19
As sound—blithe race ! whose mantles were bedecked 790 *Excursion* 3. 249
Between the Cherubim—on the chosen Race 811 *Excursion* 4. 657
Prove a degraded Race ? and what avails 815 *Excursion* 4. 954
Of knightly race, nor wanting powerful friends. 824 *Excursion* 5. 113
And noiseless commonwealth. The simple race 828 *Excursion* 5. 423
A race illustrious for heroic deeds, 834 *Excursion* 5. 792
By Tantalus entailed upon his race, 846 *Excursion* 6. 543
She, far behind him in the race of years, 861 *Excursion* 7. 226
A nobler race, the Switzers, and their land, 869 *Excursion* 7. 801
For see the universal Race endowed 887 *Excursion* 9. 208
On Albion's noble Race in freedom born, 890 *Excursion* 9. 393
Issued the blest Redeemer of our race— [?] **A sad* 11
His Grace's watermen in open race L.1. 96 *Juvenal* 3. 27

Raced. I saw the hare that raced about with joy ; 195 *Resolution* 16

Racers. By the fleet Racers, ere the sun be set, 773 *Excursion* 2. 144

Races. The hare is running races in her mirth ; 195 *Resolution* 11

Rachel. My little Rachel, you must run,— 248 *P. B.* 1059
" Make haste—my little Rachel—do, 248 *P. B.* 1061
Away goes Rachel weeping loud ;— 248 *P. B.* 1066
Remove this second Rachel from the bier. 555 *Prioress* 176

Racing. Rushing and racing came to meet me at the waterside ! 28 *Guilt* 216
Or racing o'er your blue ethereal field 229 *Clouds* 7

Rack. And in such wise to rack her gentle heart, 41 *Bord.* 241
But what is colour, if upon the rack 475 **Here on their* 4

Racked. How, when the People's mind was racked with doubt, 62 *Bord.* 1383

Racking. And groans that rage of racking famine spoke ; 30 *Guilt* 344
Of racking malady. And true it is 574 *Chiabrera* 5. 5

Radiance. Strong flakes of radiance on the tremulous stream : 4 *Ev. Wk.* 109
Where oaks o'erhang the road the radiance shoots 5 *Ev. Wk.* 186
Of massy gloom and radiance bold. 180 *Waggoner* 4. 56
Shines with poetic radiance as of old ; 251 **Pelion and* 6
Dwell, clothed in radiance, their immortal vest ; 266 **The stars* 3
Their radiance through the woods—may yet suffice 420 *Ecc. Sonn.* 1. 8. 5
Of beamy radiance, that imbues 457 **Had this* 27

Rainbow-coloured. Rock-built, are hung with rainbow-coloured mists— . . . . . 388 *Loch Etive* 2

Rainbow's. Met by the rainbow's form divine, . . 221 *Triad* 84

Rainbows. "This Land of Rainbows spanning glens whose walls, ... 388 *Loch Etive* 1

Rain-drop. Or rain-drop lingering on the pointed thorn. . . . . 265 **There is a pleasure* 14

Tipped with a rain-drop, Fancy loved to seat, . 705 *Prelude* 8. 399

Rain-drops. Nor by the heaviest rain-drops more depresst, ... 169 **Never enlivened* 3

But soon large rain-drops on his head . . . . 175 *Waggoner* 1. 156

The grass is bright with rain-drops;—on the moors 195 *Resolution* 10

Where dew falls not, where rain-drops seem unknown? . . . . 387 *Roslin* 10

By mist and silent rain-drops silvered o'er, . . 770 *Excursion* 1. 944

Rains. Swoln with incessant rains from hour to hour, ... 15 *Desc. Sk.* 270

Oh! might I kiss the mountain rains . . . . 108 *Louisa* 11

When rains are on thee. . . . . 157 **In youth* 16

Proud be the rose, with rains and dews . . . 158 **In youth* 27

If to a rock from rains he fly, ... 158 **In youth* 33

Swoln with chill rains, nor ever cast a look . . 389 *Tyndrum* 5

From Heaven a *general* blessing; timely rains 424 *Ecc. Sonn.* 1. 24. 5

Rains, that make each rill a torrent, ... 550 *Hermit's Cell* 4. 11

Of winter evenings, when unwholesome rains . . 697 *Prelude* 7. 663

When copious rains have magnified the stream . 787 *Excursion* 3. 47

Ye rains of April, duly wet this earth! . . . 868 *Excursion* 7. 701

The rains at length have ceas'd, the winds are still'd, S.3. 425 **The rains* 1

For neither unremitting rains avail . . . . . S.3. 433 **The doubt* 27

Rainy. When up the lonely brooks on rainy days . 703 *Prelude* 8. 262

Flying, and rainy vapours, call out shapes . . 809 *Excursion* 4. 522

To cheat the sadness of a rainy day; . . . . 859 *Excursion* 7. 118

Raise. *See* **Dunmail-raise.**

—But foes are gathering—Liberty must raise . 22 *Desc. Sk.* 638

Hoary and naked are its walls, and raise . . . 26 *Guilt* 115

Begone, ye Slaves, or I will raise a whirlwind . 54 *Bord.* 944

Nay, think not so: come, let me raise you up: . 67 *Bord.* 1673

Raise on that dreary Waste a monument . . . 78 *Bord.* 2326

Prayer that Grace divine may raise . . . . 94 *Westmoreland Girl* 90

To support, restrain, or raise. . . . . . . 141 *Arm. Lady* 88

Oh! raise us up, return to us again; . . . . 307 **Milton! thou* 7

The unfeeling Elements no claim shall raise . . 322 **By Moscow* 4

Provoke all potent symphonies to raise . . . 328 *Ode 1815* 78

Made known the spot where piety should raise . 338 *Engelberg* 13

Given or acquired, to raise us from the mire, . . 358 *Aquap.* 346

I raise my thoughts, inform my deeds and words, 365 **Rapt above* 7

—But now again the people raise . . . . . 397 *White Doe* 156

And ye must raise her from the dust. . . . . 403 *White Doe* 649

Of good works, mingling with the visions, raise 423 *Ecc. Sonn.* 1. 18. 11

Sits there in sober truth—to raise the low, . 428 *Ecc. Sonn.* 1. 39. 6

Despised by that stern God to whom they raise 440 *Ecc. Sonn.* 2. 46. 11

The Covenant. The Omnipotent will raise . 446 *Ecc. Sonn.* 3. 23. 11

On those bright steps that heavenward raise . . 458 **Had this* 51

Or want of love, that here no Stone we raise; . 490 *Tribute: Dog* 4

Then here reposing let us raise . . . . . 506 *Lab. Hymn* 7

Can thy enduring quiet gently raise . . . . 510 **Among a* 28

That gentle admirations raise . . . . . . 527 **The soaring* 55

Calming to raise; and, by a sapient Art . . 538 **In desultory* 25

They perish;—but the Intellect can raise, . . 547 **Beneath yon* 19

Then shalt thou raise a clamour as do I. . . 560 *Cuck.andNight.* 185

With one accord our voices raise, ... 578 **I come* 50

Not for these I raise . . . . 589 *Immortality* 143

—Tho' Liberty shall soon, indignant, raise . . 616 *Desc.Sk.Quarto* 774

Shall raise them highest in their own esteem— . 655 *Prelude* 3. 403

Of the fleet coursers they bestride, to raise . 773 *Excursion* 2. 100

Aptly disposed, had lent its help to raise . . . 778 *Excursion* 2. 435

Or clustered dwellings, where again they raise . 780 *Excursion* 2. 565

Earthly desires; and raise, to loftier heights . 820 *Excursion* 4. 1273

And raise up a radical clamor! . . . . . . S.3. 431 **If money's* 6

Raised. *See* **Half-raised, Self-raised.**

Raised by yon travelling flock, a dusty cloud . . 4 *Ev. Wk.* 110

From one who mourned in sleep, he raised his head, 27 *Guilt* 164

The man half raised the stone with pain and sweat, 27 *Guilt* 178

Half raised, for well his arm might lose its force . 27 *Guilt* 179

Nor raised my hand at any door to knock. . . 31 *Guilt* 373

Nor pain nor pity in my bosom raised. . . . 31 *Guilt* 398

He ıhand in his, and raised it, but both dropped, 36 *Guilt* 633

Heavier than work, raised it: within that hut . 39 *Bord.* 121

*f*sad spectacle: I raised him up . . . . . 72 *Bord.* 1925

And flung it to the dogs: but I am raised . . 77 *Bord.* 2294

At this the Father raised his hook, ... 83 *Lucy Gray* 21

His head he raised—there was in sight, . . . 86 *Anecdote* 49

That Cross belike he also raised as a standard for the true . . . . 91 *Norman Boy* 25

cıhis paternal Gods, the Trojan raised? . . . 102 *Artegal* 2

He raised, and never stopped: . . . . . . 109 **Strange fits* 22

Born all too high, by wedlock raised . . . . 113 *Lament* 29

And other sheep from her I raised, ... 115 *Last of Flock* 25

Full fifty comely sheep I raised, ... 115 *Last of Flock* 33

For beauty, to your lip is raised, ... 142 †*Lov. and Lik.* 36

Another monument shall here be raised; . . . 201 *Hart-leap* 66

Be thy affections raised and solemnised. . . . 211 *Laod.* 144

Once raised, remains aghast, and will not fall! . 214 *Dion* 93

Has raised thy spirit to a peaceful stand . . . 222 *Triad* 185

Through space, though calm, not raised above . 225 *Present.* 32

Suddenly raised by some enchanter's power, . . 226 *Vernal Ode* 17

The staff was raised to loftier height, ... 238 *P. B.* 193

He raised her up; and while he held . . . . 248 *P. B.* 1021

As if the sun were not. He raised his eye . . 264 *Storm* 9

'Gainst him who raised it,—his last work on earth: 276 *Filial Piety* 7

Raised—*continued.*

That wide-spanned arch, wondering how it was raised, ... 283 **Well have* 9

Or with a new ambition raised; . . . . . . 298 *Brownie's Cell* 9

The thing which ought to be; is raised *above* . . 305 **The Voice* 10

Raised up to sway the world, to do, undo, . . 309 **When, looking* 3

Raised and sustained by memory of Him . . . 354 *Aquap.* 126

From that depression raised, to mount on high . 358 **Is this* 11

Bound him, nor, since he raised yon House, have ceased . . . . 362 **List—'twas* 39

Seated alone, with forehead sky-ward raised, . . 362 **List—'twas* 78

And, while she raised her from the ground, . . 371 *Eg. Maid* 142

That raised, for centuries, a bar . . . . . 390 *Highland Broach* 9

Can such a mighty host be raised . . . . . 404 *White Doe* 789

Raised, as the Vision gave command, ... 405 *White Doe* 830

This Banner raised with joyful pride, ... 405 *White Doe* 846

Raised toward that Imagery once more: . . . 405 *White Doe* 863

But Emily hath raised her head, ... 413 *White Doe* 1535

Raised far above the law of kind; . . . . . 416 *White Doe* 1878

And, while the Host is raised, its elevation . . 431 *Ecc. Sonn.* 2. 11. 5

Ages ere Valdo raised his voice to preach . . . 431 *Ecc. Sonn.* 2. 12. 3

In worship neither raised nor limited . . . . 443 *Ecc. Sonn.* 3. 14. 5

By Him who raised the Tempest and restrains: . 448 *Ecc. Sonn.* 3. 30. 5

With love of God, throughout the Land were raised 467 *St. Bees* 120

Or hindrance raised by sordid purposes, . . . 468 *St. Bees* 134

The dwelling raised,—a veteran Marine. . . . 470 **Did pangs* 8

Of luminous faith, heavenward hath raised that head 476 *Howard* 4

Raised by remembrances of misused life, . . . 526 **Soon did* 9

Raised this frail tribute to his memory; . . . 547 **Ye Lime* 14

Inscribed with this memorial here is raised . . 574 *Chiabrera* 5. 17

I raised, while kneeling by his side, ... 577 **I come* 7

Wherever Christian altars have been raised, . . 584 *Ch. Lamb* 25

Through God, is raised a spirit and soul of love . 585 *Ch. Lamb* 66

Were earlier raised, remain to hear . . . . 586 *Hogg* 26

He rais'd the bowl, and took a long deep draught; 625 *Æneid* 119

Raised by many a hand august, ... 629 *Installation* 78

To a schoolboy's vision, I had raised a pile . . 655 *Prelude* 3. 425

Keen struggles, and black clouds of passion raised; 695 *Prelude* 7. 536

Above the rest raised infinite ascents . . . . 724 *Prelude* 10. 426

Of Sarum's Plain, my youthful spirit was raised; 744 *Prelude* 13. 314

And all affections by communion raised . . . 747 *Prelude* 14. 117

Thy monument of glory will be raised; . . . . 752 *Prelude* 14. 432

And on the third, as wistfully she raised . . . 766 *Excursion* 1. 663

Raised toward those craggy summits, his intent . 773 *Excursion* 2. 154

An overweening trust was raised; and fear . . 775 *Excursion* 2. 241

Is raised from the church-aisle, and forward borne 780 *Excursion* 2. 570

That an appearance which hath raised your minds 788 *Excursion* 3. 153

Raised for enabling this penurious stream . . . 789 *Excursion* 3. 204

"Ah! if the heart, too confidently raised, . . 807 *Excursion* 4. 418

Not raised in nice proportions was the pile, . . 824 *Excursion* 5. 144

To lofty raised; and to the highest, last; . . . 839 *Excursion* 6. 84

So, where the mouldered tree had stood, was raised 846 *Excursion* 6. 503

And saturnine; her head not raised to hold . . 848 *Excursion* 6. 679

As ever raised to heaven a streaming eye! . . . 853 *Excursion* 6. 991

Beyond its natural elevation raised . . . . 864 *Excursion* 7. 445

Raised in the tender passage of the throat . . 867 *Excursion* 7. 684

Raised from his seat within the chosen shade, . 870 *Excursion* 7. 818

Raised by his hands. And now no trace is left . 872 *Excursion* 7. 965

And the Arts died by which they had been raised. 877 *Excursion* 8. 219

—Can hope look forward to a manhood raised . 879 *Excursion* 8. 333

With shouts we raised the echoes;—stiller sounds 892 *Excursion* 9. 533

Where couch the spotted deer; or raised our eyes 892 *Excursion* 9. 563

His beaming eye that had been raised to Heaven, 894 *Excursion* 9. 681

Was raised again: and to a happy few, . . . 895 *Excursion* 9. 718

Thoughts raised above the Earth while here he sits S.3. 435 **The doubt* 140

Raises. *See* **Half-raises.**

Sunward now his flight he raises, ... 163 *Hint* 14

Raises a mist; that, glittering in the sun, . . 195 *Resolution* 13

Raising. *See* **High-raising.**

Thoughts of thy raising: . . . . 158 **With little* 12

Their heads never raising; . . . . 190 *March* 9

Raising his voice triumphantly, "obtain . . . 815 *Excursion* 4. 942

Raising, through just gradation, savage life . . 875 *Excursion* 8. 70

Rajahs. Rajahs and Omrahs in his train, intent . 718 *Prelude* 10. 20

Rake. Will flatter you,—and fool and rake . . . 286 *Sons of Burns* 21

Like clouds that rake the mountain-summits, . 586 *Hogg* 21

His little rake with cunning sidelong look, . . S.3. 417 **Sweet was* 7

Raleigh. Could pause between a Raleigh and a James? . . . . L.1. 96 *Juvenal* 3. 44

Ralph. And so without scruple they called him Ralph Jones. . . . . 86 *Rural Arch.* 10

Now Ralph is renowned for the length of his bones; 86 *Rural Arch.* 11

Ram. The last year's cup whose Ram or Heifer gained, ... 522 *Epist.Beaumont* 67

A snow-white ram, and in the crystal flood . 890 *Excursion* 9. 441

Ramble. Might have fine room to ramble about here, 61 *Bord.* 1303

Wilt ramble over hill and dale, ... 341 *Ital. Itin.* 21

He said that she was used to ramble far.— . . 767 *Excursion* 1. 733

Rambled. On holidays, we rambled through the woods: . . . . 757 *Excursion* 1. 62

Rambles. Our rambles by the swift brook's side . 81 †*Mother's Return* 34

As through the glen it rambles, ... 162 *Binnorie* 57

Rambling. And they go rambling east and west . 84 *Shepherd-boys* 8

Peace greets us;—rambling on without an aim . 349 *Val. Dover* 5

Was a spoiled child, and, rambling like the wind, 654 *Prelude* 3. 352

To native man. A rambling schoolboy, thus . . 703 *Prelude* 8. 256

Rampant. Yon rampant cloud mimics a lion's shape; 348 *Sky-prosp.* 4

Rampart. On rampart, and the banks of all her streams. . . . . 318 **Ah! where* 14

Each beetling rampart, and each tower sublime, . 335 *Rhine* 7

Of long-drawn rampart, witness what they were. 421 *Ecc. Sonn.* 1. 11. 14

Rather—*continued.*
May rather seem — 88 *H. C.* 7
Turn rather, though I love her well: — 121 *Emigrant Mother* 72
Deem rather that the fervent Youth, who saw — 122 *V. and J.* 57
Its playmate, rather say, its moving soul. — 148 **A narrow* 25
Or rather of some gentle maid, — 162 **Who fancied* 8
I rather think the gentle Dove — 168 *Turtledove* 9
Yet, trust the Muse, it rather hath — 181 *Waggoner* 4. 132
Doth rather deepen than disturb the calm — 184 *Airey-force* 6
Or is it rather that Conceit rapacious is and strong, — 189 *Star-gazers* 17
Unwearied in that service: rather say — 207 *Tintern* 153
Exclaimed the Chieftain—" let me rather see — 213 *Dion* 82
Him rather suits it, side by side with thee, — 227 *Vernal Ode* 85
To milder climes; or rather do ye urge — 230 *Clouds* 19
It moves us not.—Great God! I'd rather be — 259 **The world is* 9
At early dawn, or rather when the air — 269 *Gordale* 1
We rather think, with grateful mind sedate, — 271 *Henry: Portrait* 11
Think rather of those moments bright — 286 *Nith* 20
Wear rather in thy bonds a cheerful brow: — 305 *Toussaint* 7
Say rather, one in native fellowship — 356 *Aquap.* 244
Or rather thou appear'st a glistering snake, — 377 *Duddon* 4. 5
Or rather felt, the entrancement that detains — 381 *Duddon* 20. 2
Say, rather, with that generous sympathy — 393 *Hart's-horn* 11
Unbent, which rather seemed to rise, — 404 *White Doe* 740
My feet would rather turn—to some dry nook — 424 *Ecc. Sonn.* 1. 22. 2
Or rather rose the day to antedate, — 432 *Ecc. Sonn.* 2. 14. 3
Which showers of blood seem rather to incite — 437 *Ecc. Sonn.* 2. 36. 8
Nay, rather speak with gratitude; — 458 **Had this* 66
Pleased rather with some soft ideal scene, — 480 **Most sweet* 5
The while a Thrush, urged rather than restrained — 537 **In desultory* 3
Others do rather from their notice shrink, — 539 **Lady! a* 18
Rather than be disgraced, would chuse to die. — 559 *Cuck.and Night.* 160
Ask rather a triumphal strain — 582 **O for a* 2
Was given (say rather thou of later birth — 585 *Ch. Lamb* 78
But turn we rather, let my spirit turn — 586 *Ch. Lamb* 107
Mourn rather for that holy Spirit, — 586 *Hogg* 37
We will grieve not, rather find — 590 *Immortality* 183
Entrenched, say rather peacefully embowered, — 622 *Recluse* 1. 1. 76
I choose it rather at this time, than work — 641 *Prelude* 1. 642
Into the boundless sea, and rather makes — 656 *Prelude* 3. 515
And what may rather have been called to life — 658 *Prelude* 3. 612
Nor have I pitied him; but rather felt — 668 *Prelude* 5. 149
Or rather like a stallèd ox debarred — 669 *Prelude* 5. 242
Fetching her goodness rather from times past, — 669 *Prelude* 5. 267
More than its timely produce; rather loved — 670 *Prelude* 5. 285
This spurious virtue, rather let it bear — 675 *Prelude* 6. 30
Me, rather, it employed, to note, and keep — 696 *Prelude* 7. 598
That dazzled me, but rather what I mourned — 712 *Prelude* 9. 212
A gift that was come rather late than soon. — 713 *Prelude* 9. 248
Of condescension; but did rather seem — 714 *Prelude* 9. 310
Not speaking much, pleased rather with the joy — 764 *Excursion* 1. 515
Or, rather say, sate down by very chance, — 776 *Excursion* 2. 308
Or to pass through; but rather an abyss — 787 *Excursion* 3. 97
Fraught rather with depression than delight, — 788 *Excursion* 3. 156
Breeds love: yet, suited as it rather is — 806 *Excursion* 4. 347
Yet rather would I instantly decline — 810 *Excursion* 4. 613
To this would rather bend than see and hear — 810 *Excursion* 4. 619
And they who rather dive than soar, whose pains — 815 *Excursion* 4. 951
Say rather, all his thoughts now flowing clear, — 819 *Excursion* 4. 1222
Or rather, as we stand on holy earth, — 832 *Excursion* 5. 646
Perhaps incited rather, by these shocks, — 836 *Excursion* 5. 893
Would rather shun than seek the fellowship — 844 *Excursion* 6. 390
Who rather would not envy, men that feel — 847 *Excursion* 6. 616
With its appropriate grace, yet rather seeking — 848 *Excursion* 6. 689
Whose sorrow rather is to suffer wrong — 854 *Excursion* 6. 1070
That now divides the pair, or rather say, — 861 *Excursion* 7. 239
Or rather seemed to have grown into the side — 871 *Excursion* 7. 915
Or rather, let us say, how least observed, — 886 *Excursion* 9. 148
" Then let us rather fix our gladdened thoughts — 888 *Excursion* 9. 255
Through mutual injury! Rather in the law — 889 *Excursion* 9. 366
And neighbourhood serves rather to divide — K.8. 253 *Recluse* 1.1.600
Or rather skulking for the common weal — L.1. 97 *Juvenal* 3. 87
Ratify. Which, with a generous shout, the crowd did ratify. — 142 *Arm. Lady* 144
Rational. Which ill can brook more rational relief: — 423 *Ecc. Sonn.* 1. 20. 7
And prayer, man's rational prerogative, — 436 *Ecc. Sonn.* 2. 33. 13
Of rational and manly sympathy. — 455 **Not in the lucid* 19
Would be rational peace—a philosopher's ease. — 482 *Character* 8
On rational liberty, and hope in man, — 715 *Prelude* 9. 395
Of rational Experience, for the shoots — 727 *Prelude* 11. 5
More rational proportions; mystery, — 750 *Prelude* 14. 285
Human and rational, report of thee — 802 *Excursion* 4. 37
The rational creature, left, to feel the weight — 811 *Excursion* 4. 667
Yet is the creature rational, endowed — 866 *Excursion* 7. 576
Say, what can follow for a rational soul — 886 *Excursion* 9. 120
Rattle. Right in the slates, and with a huge rattle — 81 †*Address: Child* 30
Rattled. Rattled his chain;—'twas all in vain, — 178 *Waggoner* 2. 152
Rattles. Rattles the salt-box, thumps the kettle-drum, — 697 *Prelude* 7. 701
Rattling. And hear the rattling thunder far below; — 17 *Desc. Sk.* 377
The post-boy, when his rattling wheels o'ertake — 566 *Cumb. Beg.* 37
Would, with its rattling music, come, — 621 *Andrew Jones* 4
The voice of spears was heard, the rattling spear — 744 *Prelude* 13. 324
Ravage. Ravage for which no knell was heard. We prayed — 29 *Guilt* 284
And merciless ravage: and the shady nook — 185 *Nutting* 45
Had found, in ravage widely dealt, — 298 *Brownie's Cell* 39
Ravage the world, tranquillity is here!" — 313 **Clouds, lingering* 14
Is stripped; the ravage hath spread wide — 413 *White Doe* 1576
Of ravage saved—sate Emily. — 414 *White Doe* 1632

Ravage—*continued.*
A ravage out of season, made by thoughts — 712 *Prelude* 9. 152
Ravaged. Of towns in flames, fields ravaged, young and old — 56 *Bord.* 1031
Its courts are ravaged; but the tower — 396 *White Doe* 21
Rave. With omnipresent murmur as they rave — 314 **Not 'mid* 7
Until this storm hath ceased to rave: — 408 *White Doe* 1098
Raven. And, hovering, round it often did a raven fly. — 25 *Guilt* 81
Gone is the raven timely rest to seek; — 26 *Guilt* 101
He'd not have robbed the raven of its food. — 35 *Guilt* 610
She was my Raven in the wilderness, — 53 *Bord.* 847
" Here thou need'st not dread the raven in the sky; — 88 *Pet-lamb* 57
If on windy days the Raven — 166 *Wand. Jew* 17
Perched on whose top the Danish Raven croaks; — 380 *Duddon* 17. 2
Aloft the Raven hangs a visible nest, — 525 *Epist. Beaumont* 230
As sent from heav'n the raven of the skies, — 609 *Desc.Sk.Quarto* 403
That keeps the raven quiet in her nest, — 809 *Excursion* 4. 519
One voice—the solitary raven, flying — 819 *Excursion* 4. 1178
The raven lodged in safety.—Many a ship — 866 *Excursion* 7. 602
The raven croaks, and fills the upper air — K.8. 252 *Recluse* 1.1.581
Raven-crag. Of Raven-crag—black as a storm— — 180 *Waggoner* 4. 19
Ravenous. And ravenous plague, all perished: every tear — 30 *Guilt* 304
Ere, pouncing like a ravenous bird of prey, — 118 *Maternal Grief* 40
That would engulph him soon in the ravenous sea— — 709 *Prelude* 9. 4
Raven's. The mountain raven's youngling brood — 84 *Shepherd-boys* 6
In colour like a raven's wing; — 166 *Danish Boy* 28
The crags repeat the raven's croak, — 491 *Fidelity* 27
Above the raven's nest, by knots of grass — 637 *Prelude* 1. 331
Ravens. And fling him to the ravens. But his aspect, — 57 *Bord.* 1067
To feed the ravens; or a shepherd dies — 97 *Brothers* 154
They played like two young ravens on the crags: — 99 *Brothers* 278
Blithe ravens croak of death; and when the owl — 153 *Morn. Ex.* 7
Two ravens now began to croak — 157 *Oak and Broom* 96
Where ravens spread their plumy vans, at ease! — 496 **A little* 32
Raves. Where the whirlpool frets and raves — 336 **Jesu! bless* 21
He raves, or through some moody passage creeps — 476 *Nunnery* 4
Ravine. Of mountains, through a deep ravine, — 347 **Lulled by* 4
Raving. And giddy prospect of the raving stream, — 684 *Prelude* 6. 633
Ravish. She longed to ravish;—shall she plunge, or climb — 381 *Duddon* 22. 8
That down didst ravish from the Deity, — 552 *Prioress* 17
Ravishment. That ravishment of mine, and laughed aloud. — 147 *Joanna* 53
And all the mighty ravishment of spring. — 264 **Lady! the* 14
And filled the illumined groves with ravishment. — 814 *Excursion* 4. 860
Raw. One morning (raw it was and wet— — 119 *Sailor's Mother* 1
For cold and raw the air was, and untuned; — 660 *Prelude* 4. 145
Not only in that raw unpractised time — 674 *Prelude* 5. 589
Ray. Since she (her name is Martha Ray) — 198 *Thorn* 105
That Martha Ray about this time — 199 *Thorn* 153
They had to do with Martha Ray. — 199 *Thorn* 165
Tip their smooth ridges with a softer ray; — 4 *Ev. Wk.* 123
While coves and secret hollows, through a ray — 5 *Ev. Wk.* 176
Gilding that cottage with her fondest ray, — 8 *Ev. Wk.* 347
Blesses the moon that comes with kindly ray, — 11 *Desc. Sk.* 33
'Mid smoking woods gleams hid from morning's ray — 12 *Desc. Sk.* 120
And pines the unripened pear in summer's kindliest ray; — 15 *Desc. Sk.* 259
—Alas! in every clime a flying ray — 19 *Desc. Sk.* 500
Fresh-smitten by the morning ray, — 158 **In youth* 57
Never enlivened with the liveliest ray — 169 **Never enlivened* 1
Are smitten by a silver ray; — 180 *Waggoner* 4. 60
Which, with slant ray, the merry sun — 181 *Waggoner* 4. 106
Wherever strikes the sun's glad ray; — 227 *Vernal Ode* 67
Glisten with a livelier ray: — 233 *Power of Sound* 61
Yon old grey Stone, protected from the ray — 262 **Mark the* 2
Glistening with unparticipated ray, — 267 **As the* 4
His judgment with benignant ray — 287 *Sons of Burns* 37
A ray of fancy still survives— — 302 *Yarrow V.* 75
Dread King of Kings, vouchsafe a ray divine — 323 **Now that* 9
Nor take one ray of light from Thee; — 345 **How blest* 73
My noble fire emits the joyful ray — 365 **Rapt above* 13
Nor lose one ray of glory! — 386 *Yarrow Rev.* 64
Shines in the greeting of the sun's first ray — 390 *Highland Hut* 3
Communication, like the ray — 416 *White Doe* 1829
Most glorious sunset! and a ray — 416 *White Doe* 1871
A guiding ray; or seen—like stars on high, — 441 *Ecc. Sonn.* 3. 5. 12
Cheers these Recluses with a steady ray — 467 *St. Bees* 84
The sun's first greeting, his last farewell ray! — 511 **Who rashly* 23
The hastiest sunrise yields a temperate ray; — 516 **Hard task* 11
Where, sensitive of every ray — 526 **The soaring* 21
And all shall welcome the new ray — 533 **Blest is* 39
His graceful manners, and the temperate ray — 583 **With copious* 9
The ray the cot of morning trav'ling nigh, — 592 *Ev. Wk. Quarto* 47
The coves and secret hollows thro' a ray — 594 *Ev. Wk. Quarto* 159
Who faint, and beat by summer's breathless ray, — 596 *Ev. Wk. Quarto* 243
Delighted, with the glow-worm's harmless ray — 597 *Ev. Wk. Quarto* 276
Blesses the Moon that comes with kindest ray — 602 *Desc.Sk.Quarto* 35
Gleams, streak'd or dappled, hid from morning's ray — 604 *Desc.Sk.Quarto* 139
To throw the " sultry ray " of young Desire; — 604 *Desc.Sk.Quarto* 151
And apple sickens pale in summer's ray, — 608 *Desc.Sk.Quarto* 322
With earlier smile the ray of morn to view — 610 *Desc.Sk.Quarto* 454
Enlivening Hope display'd her cheerful ray, — 618 *School Ex.* 35
With steadfast ray benign — 629 *Installation* 58
Was conscious of the ray; — 629 *Installation* 64
The other, which the ray divine hath touched, — 831 *Excursion* 5. 556
From which it did itself imbibe a ray — 861 *Excursion* 7. 236
Rays. Hope with reflection blends her social rays — 2 *Ev. Wk.* 29
Scarce hides a shadow from her searching rays; — 9 *Ev. Wk.* 358

Rays—*continued.*
Rejoicing in the glory of her rays : 16 *Desc. Sk.* 322
With rays of promise, north and southward sent ; 30 *Guilt* 314
Some amid lingering shade, some touched by the sun's rays. 34 *Guilt* 522
Who the first with pointed rays 161 **Pleasures newly* 11
Thou shrink'st as momently thy rays 167 *Pilgrim's Dream* 36
In ten thousand dewy rays ; 221 *Triad* 130
Lost and recovered, as the rays of light 231 **The gentlest Poet* 22
And colour life's dark cloud with orient rays. 259 **Weak is* 8
To watch while Morn first crowns thee with her rays, 281 **Wansfell ! this* 3
Or cloud approaching to divert the rays, 329 *Ode : Thanks.* 10
Of all its sparkling rays disarmed, 343 *Eclipse* 23
As evening's fondly-lingering rays, 348 **Lulled by* 65
And profit by those kindly rays 376 **The Minstrels* 70
Are edged with golden rays ! 479 *Somnamb.* 157
Whence the tall window drinks the morning rays ; 535 **When in* 24
With Hope Reflexion blends her social rays 592 *Ev. Wk. Quarto* 39
And with long rays and shades the landscape shines ; 593 *Ev. Wk. Quarto* 98
Where fierce the rays of woe collected burn. 613 *Desc.Sk.Quarto* 647
Upon Iulus, dazzled with the rays 624 *Æneid* 74
Of gold, the Maypole shines ; as if the rays 773 *Excursion* 2. 134
Attained his western bound ; but rays of light— 893 *Excursion* 9. 592

Razed. Tents of a camp that never shall be razed— 214 *Kirkstone* 19

Reach. To reach a small wood-hut hung boldly on the steep. 15 *Desc. Sk.* 237
In sea-like reach of prospect round him spread, 19 *Desc. Sk.* 474
Of this Man's crimes beyond the reach of thought? 51 *Bord.* 781
Oh that I had but strength to reach the place ! 67 *Bord.* 1656
That venturous foot could reach, to one or both 99 *Brothers* 275
Fluttering its pinions, almost within reach, 122 *V. and J.* 83
By chance of business coming within reach 125 *V. and J.* 288
Will reach both great and small ; 156 *Oak and Broom* 62
Your portraits still may reach the heart 164 **Fair Lady* 11
Choice word and measured phrase, above the reach 196 *Resolution* 95
—Within our fearless reach are placed 216 *Enterprise* 83
Meanwhile the Ass to reach his home 244 *P. B.* 666
The open moonlight reach. 244 *P. B.* 675
And modulate, with subtle reach of skill 271 **Fame tells* 3
Even on this earth, above the reach of Time ! 272 *Lady E. B.* 14
That cry can reach ; and to the sick man's room 273 **Not the* 7
Pledged till thou reach the verge of womanhood, 274 *Rotha Q.* 3
Within my reach ; of knowledge graced 285 *Grave of Burns* 56
Of thoughts that lie beyond the reach 288 *Highland Girl* 40
Mounting as if to reach the moon, 296 *Highland Boy* 169
—Not work of hands ; but trophies that may reach 331 *Ode : Thanks.* 171
For what strange service, does this concert reach 336 *Staub-bach* 2
Mercy has placed within our reach 337 **Oh Life* 11
For dignity not placed beyond her reach, 357 *Aquap.* 344
Parting ; the casual word had power to reach 367 **As indignation* 13
Soon did the gentle Nina reach 371 *Eg. Maid* 121
Our fate is theirs, will reach them all ; 402 *White Doe* 549
To reach the well-spring of this woe ! 406 *White Doe* 888
Hath typified by reach of daring art 452 *Ecc. Sonn.* 3. 45. 9
Canst reach the Prisoner—to his grated cell 459 **Wanderer ! that* 29
Now, like to things within fate's easiest reach, 471 *Tynwald* 7
Shall place thy virtues out of Envy's reach. 478 **Lonsdale ! it* 14
Said to his servile Courtiers,—" Poor the reach, 495 *Fact* 10
Until they reach the bounds by Heaven assigned." 495 *Fact* 43
Hearts also shall thy lessons reach 507 **While from* 51
And, what ye cannot reach by statute, draw 516 **Feel for* 13
No tidings reach us thence from town or field, 522 *Epist. Beaumont* 81
Descend and reach, in Yewdale's depths, a plain 525 *Epist. Beaumont* 225
Reach the caged lark, within a town-abode, 527 **Those breathing* 28
Can reach the innocent delight ; 530 *Gleaner* 12
Or never hope to reach a second birth. 531 *Octogen.* 5
Who reach this dire extremity ! 534 **Blest is* 80
Of hard ascent before thou reach the top 548 **Stay, bold* 3
To reach a safer shore—how near, 579 **Sweet Flower* 41
Beyond the mountain's giant reach that hides 598 *Ev. Wk. Quarto* 337
Tower like a wall the naked rocks, or reach 607 *Desc.Sk.Quarto* 287
Reach after reach, salute us and depart ; 625 **The confidence* 4
Proud of his skill, to reach a chosen point 637 *Prelude* 1. 368
O'er all that, lost beyond the reach of thought 648 *Prelude* 2. 403
It lies far hidden from the reach of words. 651 *Prelude* 3. 184
Ran, ostrich-like, to reach our chapel door 653 *Prelude* 3. 304
With eager footsteps I advance and reach 658 *Prelude* 4. 25
Reach after reach, succession without end 680 *Prelude* 6. 383
Duly to reach the point marked out by Heaven. 686 *Prelude* 6. 753
Thence back into the throng, until we reach, 690 *Prelude* 7. 189
The reach of common indication, lost 696 *Prelude* 7. 636
Do come within the reach of humblest eyes ; 720 *Prelude* 10. 160
Mortal, or those beyond the reach of death ; 741 *Prelude* 13. 75
Usurped upon far as the sight could reach. 746 *Prelude* 14. 49
From any reach of outward fellowship, 749 *Prelude* 14. 217
The reach of sight ; from whom, as from their source, 794 *Excursion* 3. 570
Not placed by fortune within easy reach 794 *Excursion* 3. 586
That my particular current soon will reach 800 *Excursion* 3. 990
Lies within reach, and one day shall be gained." 827 *Excursion* 5. 308
That speculative height *we* may not reach. 830 *Excursion* 5. 489
Is too infirm to reach. But, waiving this, 830 *Excursion* 5. 522
To reach it, destitute of other hope. 833 *Excursion* 5. 742
I turn, and reach at last the guiding light ; 834 *Excursion* 5. 751
Whose blue roofs ornament a distant reach 844 *Excursion* 6. 408
But to a higher mark than song can reach 857 *Excursion* 7. 24
In excellence less difficult to reach, 863 *Excursion* 7. 392
If consciousness could reach him where he lies 875 *Excursion* 8. 36
Fixed, within reach of every human eye ; 887 *Excursion* 9. 211

Reach—*continued.*
It mounts to reach the State's parental ear ; 889 *Excursion* 9. 327
Until they reach the bounds by Heaven assigned. S.3. 427 **My Son* 14

Reached. We reached the western world, a poor devoted crew. 29 *Guilt* 297
To break my dream the vessel reached its bound ; 31 *Guilt* 367
Near the sea-side I reached a ruined fort ; 31 *Guilt* 382
Ere long they reached that cottage in the dale : 34 *Guilt* 527
And soon she reached a spot o'erhung with trees 34 *Guilt* 538
Would fail you ere our journey's end be reached. 41 *Bord.* 227
Have reached his ear—you have had enemies. 42 *Bord.* 256
Scarcely, by groping, had I reached the Spot, 55 *Bord.* 964
The goal is reached. My Master shall become 73 *Bord.* 2038
But never reached the town. 83 *Lucy Gray* 32
And Leonard, when they reached the church-yard gate, 102 *Brothers* 409
It was not long ere Leonard reached a grove 102 *Brothers* 418
And now we reached the orchard-plot ; 109 **Strange fits* 13
Reached speedily the native threshold, bent 123 *V. and J.* 103
Departed with his infant ; and thus reached 125 *V. and J.* 263
And now, when Luke had reached his eighteenth year, 133 *Michael* 123
And now, when he had reached his eighteenth year, 134 *Michael* 205
And soon as they had reached the place he stopped, 136 *Michael* 330
Began his journey, and, when he had reached 137 *Michael* 426
And now have reached that pile of stones, 176 *Waggoner* 1. 209
Had almost reached the festive door, 177 *Waggoner* 2. 26
Till he had reached a summit sharp and bare, 226 *Vernal Ode* 12
We've reached at last the promised Tale ;) 240 *P. B.* 322
And now has reached the skirting trees ; 240 *P. B.* 383
Is reached ; but there the trusty guide 243 *P. B.* 608
The Beast bestriding thus, he reached 246 *P. B.* 851
Is reached, where, forfeiting his bright attire, 261 **I watch* 6
The wished-for point was reached—but at an hour 262 **Dark and* 2
When her long life hath reached its final day : 305 *Ven. Rep.* 12
The roving Spanish Bands are reached at last, 320 **Hunger, and* 5
And, if the glory reached the Nun, 334 **In Bruges* 23
Hath reached the encincture of that gloomy sea 336 *Danube* 8
We reached a votive Stone that bears 337 *Thun* 3
He reached that ebon car, the bier 373 *Eg. Maid* 274
She reached the destined strand. 374 *Eg. Maid* 382
Of music reached its height, and even when sank 387 *Roslin* 4
Reached by the dews of heavenly grace ; 390 *HighlandBroach* 44
Faint—but it reached that sheltered spot ; 401 *White Doe* 433
They met, when they had reached the door, 410 *White Doe* 1322
She reached the grave, and with her breast 413 *White Doe* 1547
Till they have reached the eternal City—built 452 *Ecc. Sonn.* 3. 47. 13
The pair have reached that fearful chasm, 494 *Force of Prayer* 17
And reached the lonely Isle. 543 *Russ. Fug.* 128
For ye have reach'd at last the happy shore, 614 *Desc.Sk.Quarto* 668
Nor rest till they had reached the very door 633 *Prelude* 1. 73
We reached a cottage. At the door I knocked, 665 *Prelude* 4. 449
Following a band of muleteers, we reached 683 *Prelude* 6. 564
Which, when the spirit of evil reached its height, 735 *Prelude* 12. 42
Have faithfully been pictured ; we have reached 750 *Prelude* 14. 306
Had reached its close ; but Life is insecure, 753 **Oft, through* 10
O'er the flat Common !—With quick step I reached 766 *Excursion* 1. 646
And, ere the stars were visible, had reached 771 *Excursion* 1. 969
Her voice of social transport reached even him ! 774 *Excursion* 2. 214
A steep ascent ; and reached a dreary plain, 776 *Excursion* 2. 324
And, to my feeling, ere we reached the door, 781 *Excursion* 2. 639
And reached a small apartment dark and low, 781 *Excursion* 2. 648
And I descended. Having reached the house, 785 *Excursion* 2. 881
Rises ; but, having reached the thinner air, 803 *Excursion* 4. 144
The Sun, before his place of rest were reached, 820 *Excursion* 4. 1298
Nor reached the village-churchyard till the sun 824 *Excursion* 5. 134
And daily longing that the same were reached, 844 *Excursion* 6. 389
She reached the house, last of the funeral train ; 853 *Excursion* 6. 973
That filled her plains, that reached her utmost shores, 869 *Excursion* 7. 761
Or as a stranger reached this deep recess, 871 *Excursion* 7. 928
Thus having reached a bridge, that overarched 890 *Excursion* 9. 437
Whose low tones reached not to the distant rocks 892 *Excursion* 9. 535
Was reached, the Solitary checked his steps ; 895 *Excursion* 9. 770
Reached her with supernatural mandates charged S.3. 436 **The doubt* 177
And now when he had reached his eighteenth year K.8. 226 **I will* 85
That Shepherd's voice, it may have reached mine ear K.8. 246 *Recluse* 1.1.341
Look back till we had reached the boundary L.2.318 *Frag.Æneid* 4.11

Reaches. Winds far in reaches hidden from our sight, 824 *Excursion* 5. 123
The mazy reaches of Loch Katerine, S.3. 438 **My Lord* 10

Reaching. That, reaching to her gates, spreads east and west, 702 *Prelude* 8. 213

Read. I read, and loved the books in which I read ; 28 *Guilt* 205
The Sheriff read, in open Court, a letter 49 *Bord.* 679
And be disturbed, as I am. I have read 62 *Bord.* 1381
Books have we to read,—but that half-stifled knell, 81 †*Address : Child* 36
If I may dare to cherish hope that gentle eyes will read 93 *Poet's Dream* 79
There too we read of Spenser's fairy themes, 103 *Artegal* 49
You plainly in her face may read it, 127 *Idiot Boy* 133
Of such we in romances read : 130 *Idiot Boy* 355
The letter was read over ; Isabel 136 *Michael* 312
Both parents read them with rejoicing hearts. 138 *Michael* 436
Of which we in the Ballad read. 143 **Driven in* 10
Sighed to think I read a book 161 **Pleasures newly* 27
Only read, perhaps, by me ; 161 **Pleasures newly* 28
A wound where plainly might be read 181 *Waggoner* 4. 175
The language of my former heart, and read 207 *Tintern* 117
Wild as it is, he there can read 243 *P. B.* 653
The snow-white page on which he read, 244 *P. B.* 744
What joy to read the promise of her mien ! 311 **Who rises* 3

Read—*continued.*
We read the dictate in the infant's eye ; . . . 315 *The Land 6
And in its sparkling progress read . . . . . 327 Ode 1815 35
Father of all ! though wilful Manhood read . . 342 Ital. Itin. 94
Presumptuous Book ! too forward to be read, . 350 Des. Stanzas 3
By feet of purse-proud strangers ; they—who have read . . . . 359 *They—who 6
Did we together read in Spenser's Lay . . . 395 White Doe : Ded. 5
And we have in one meaning read ; . . . . 402 White Doe 574
For she hath ventured now to read . . . . 415 White Doe 1714
Had in her childhood read the same ; . . . . 415 White Doe 1768
That confident assurance may be read ; . . . 429 Ecc. Sonn. 2. 3. 6
We read of faith and purest charity . . . . 441 Ecc. Sonn. 3. 5. 5
Read o'er these lines ; and then review . . . 486 Matthew 5
When You might read, my credit would be gone. 522 Epist. Beaumont 88
To read that they, who mark thy course, behold . 539 *Lady ! a 59
That is to say, to sing and read alsò, ... 553 Prioress 48
May read them not without some bitter tears. . 575 Chiabrera 7. 18
Which pious, learned, MURFITT saw and read ;— 582 *To public 5
More deeply read in thy own thoughts ; to thee . 645 Prelude 2. 211
Read lazily in trivial books, went forth . . . 652 Prelude 3. 251
Bucer, Erasmus, or Melancthon, read . . . . 656 Prelude 3. 476
I read, without design, the opinions, thoughts, . 661 Prelude 4. 212
With thoughts unfelt till now I saw her read . . 661 Prelude 4. 227
And can read lectures upon innocence ; . . . 670 Prelude 5. 314
And tell you all their cunning ; he can read . . 670 Prelude 5. 317
And there have read, devouring as I read, . . 673 Prelude 5. 486
To think of, to read over, many a page, . . . 674 Prelude 5. 548
Before our eyes, we could not choose but read . 683 Prelude 6. 544
Like others, I had skimmed, and sometimes read 711 Prelude 9. 96
Into a thousand colours ; while he read, . . . 712 Prelude 9. 158
Shall beat no more. Thou, also, there may'st read, 717 Prelude 9. 568
Being written in a tongue he cannot read, . . 719 Prelude 10. 61
The scale of liberty. I read her doom, . . . 730 Prelude 11. 211
Of whom we read, the man whom we behold . . 741 Prelude 13. 83
Were open schools in which I daily read . . . 742 Prelude 13. 163
Do read the invisible soul ; by men adroit . . 743 Prelude 13. 256
But eagerly he read, and read again, ... 758 Excursion 1. 170
And in their silent faces could he read . . . 759 Excursion 1. 204
While at the stall he read. Among the hills . . 760 Excursion 1. 248
For the meek Sufferer. Why then should we read 770 Excursion 1. 939
And in the silence of his face I read . . . . 772 Excursion 2. 40
And in the Matron's countenance may be read . 821 Excursion 4. 1311
Duly we paid, each after each, and read . . . 825 Excursion 5. 172
I read,—how in his manhood's earlier day . . 825 Excursion 5. 190
This honest sheep-dog's countenance I read ; . . 834 Excursion 5. 817
Thither we turned ; and gathered, as we read, . 846 Excursion 6. 513
And much she read ; and brooded feelingly . . 854 Excursion 6. 1028
The Pastor answered, " You have read him well. 866 Excursion 7. 564
And tottering towers ; I loved to stand and read K.8. 256 Recluse 1.1.712
Their looks forbidding, read and disobey, . . . K.8. 256 Recluse 1.1.713
Yea to this hour I cannot read a tale . . . . K.8. 256 Recluse 1.1.721
The sage has read the stars with skill so true, . L.3. 27 *For Lubbock 3

Re-addressed. To bend, he stoutly re-addressed himself, ... 840 Excursion 6. 151

Reader. (Reader, forgive the intolerable thought) . 36 Guilt 659
Oh Reader ! now that I might tell . . . . . 129 Idiot Boy 312
Reader, farewell ! My last words let them be— . 281 Valedict. 10
My gentle Reader, I perceive . . . . . . 484 Simon Lee 61
O Reader ! had you in your mind . . . . . 484 Simon Lee 65
O gentle Reader ! you would find . . . . . 484 Simon Lee 67
Now, Reader, learn from this my fate, how false, 574 Chiabrera 3. 17
Reader ! if to thy bosom cling the pain . . . 576 *By a 13

Read'st. Think not, O Passenger! who read'st the lines 574 Chiabrera 5. 19
That, deaf and silent, read'st the eternal deep, . 589 Immortality 112

Readier. A readier book of manifold contents, . . 393 *The Lovers 13
Listened with readier patience than to strain . . 883 Excursion 8. 596

Readiest. Through Paris lay my readiest course, and there . . . . 710 Prelude 9. 42

Readily. Befriends the observance, readily they join 119 Maternal Grief 67
Will now so readily be found . . . . . . 224 *'Tis gone 32
More readily the more my years require . . . 366 *Eternal Lord 13
Which practised talent readily affords, . . . 455 *Not in the lucid 8
As readily by syllogistic words . . . . . . 735 Prelude 12. 84
Which my life holds, he readily may conceive . 800 Excursion 3. 968
Or death-watch : and as readily rejoice, . . . 810 Excursion 4. 617
More readily, the more my years require . . . K.8. 266 *Rid of 13

Readiness. Or both, with equal readiness of will, . 772 Excursion 2. 83

Reading. As if he had been reading in a book : . 196 Resolution 81
Like some one reading in a book— . . . . 242 P. B. 519
This man was reading in his room ; . . . . 244 P. B. 740
Conversing, reading, laughing ;—or they sing, . 266 *Even as 13
Reading or thinking ; either to lay up . . . 633 Prelude 1. 116
In which I had been reading, at my side. . . . 667 Prelude 5. 140
On the vague reading of a truant youth . . . 676 Prelude 6. 95
Of reading them with quick and curious eye ; . . 696 Prelude 7. 587
Reading of nations and their works, in faith, . . 712 Prelude 9. 171
Reading at intervals ; the fear gone by . . . 719 Prelude 10. 71
Reading, where'er we turn, of innocent lives, . . 847 Excursion 6. 628
In lonely reading found a meek resource : . . . 852 Excursion 6. 896

Ready. *See* **Ever-ready.**
Brisk toil, alternating with ready ease, . . . 11 Desc. Sk. 17
Attends your pleasure. We are ready— . . . 49 Bord. 665
I have no cases by me ready made . . . . . 65 Bord. 1572
A stern face it puts on, as if ready to say, . . 116 Repentance 19
By ready nature for a life of love, ... 122 V. and J. 32
Make ready Luke's best garments, of the best . 135 Michael 279
Lay thrown together, ready for the work. . . . 136 Michael 328
Was ready with her cavern ; Hammar-scar, . . 147 Joanna 57
So humble, yet so ready to rejoice . . . . . 153 Morn. Ex. 41
A steady to salute the sun . . . . 158 *In youth 75

Ready—*continued.*
Of open house and ready fare. . . . . . . 174 Waggoner 1. 82
Espies—and instantly is ready, ... 181 Waggoner 4. 142
Calm, though impatient, is the crowd ; each stands ready with the fee, ... 189 Star-gazers 7
Each ready with a plaintive whine ! . . . . 191 Beggars 38
With tools for ready wit to guide ; . . . . . 191 Seq. Beggars 5
To freeze the blood I have no ready arts : . . 202 Hart-leap 98
With ready heels his shaggy side ; . . . . . 241 P. B. 399
With ready sunbeams every straggling shower ; . 261 *Fair Prime 2
Hangs ready to be grasped in sympathy . . . 271 Henry : Portrait 6
A boat is ready to pursue ; . . . . 297 Highland Boy 182
Apt language, ready as the tuneful notes . . . 329 Ode : Thanks. 39
Must, when my part is done, be ready ; . . . 370 Eg. Maid 110
She has a world of ready wealth, ... 481 Tables Turned 17
To which I listen with a ready ear ; . . . . 488 Pers. Talk 39
And ready for the gentlest stroke of death. . . 491 Tribute : Dog 20
Are with a ready heart bestowed . . . . . 506 Lab. Hymn 15
The Wain stood ready, at our Cottage-door, . . 522 Epist. Beaumont 93
And couch—all ready to a wish . . . . . 543 Russ. Fug. 147
Here will he gather stores of ready bliss, . . . 549 *The massy 15
For simple infant hath a ready ear. . . . . 553 Prioress 60
Who have a broom still ready in your hands . . 567 Cumb. Beg. 69
On board a ship then ready for the seas. . . . 623 *I find 8
Give ready place to any random seed . . . . 657 Prelude 3. 545
She was, and with her ready pupil turned . . . 705 Prelude 8. 424
That time was ready to set all things right, . . 730 Prelude 11. 192
Found ready welcome. Tempting region *that* 730 Prelude 11. 228
Mild, inoffensive, ready in *his* way, ... 783 Excursion 2. 761
And, with that ready answer satisfied, ... 789 Excursion 3. 183
The internal pangs, are ready ; the dread strife 846 Excursion 6. 555
Were ready comrades whom he could not tire ; . 864 Excursion 7. 440
Instructing simple childhood's ready ear : . . . 890 Excursion 9. 396
So cowardly, so ready to betray, ... K.8. 238 Recluse 1.1. 66
The ready Organ of articulate sounds . . . . K.8. 246 Recluse 1.1.343
Be ready and unwearied without plea . . . . K.8. 246 Recluse 1.1.371

Real. Among the tasks of real life, hath wrought . 493 Hap. War. 4
Or, from long stress of real injuries fly . . . . 505 Warning 117
A race of real children ; not too wise, ... 671 Prelude 5. 411
Or physiognomies of real men. . . . . . . 689 Prelude 7. 164
How casual incidents of real life, ... 693 Prelude 7. 402
As may be hoped, of real modesty,— . . . . 698 Prelude 7. 764
In spite of real fervour, and of that . . . . 716 Prelude 9. 471
With real feeling and just sense ; how vain . . 742 Prelude 13. 172
By courage, to demand from real life . . . . 792 Excursion 3. 417
Your further help ? The mine of real life . . 832 Excursion 5. 630
And real evil, yet be sweet withal, ... K.8. 247 Recluse 1.1.406

Realised. *See* **Realized.**
Europe, a realised romance, ... 348 *Lulled by 51
And the realised vision is clasped to my heart. . 364 Vallomb. 32
Moving about in worlds not realised, ... 589 Immortality 149
No few of which have since been realised ; . . . 675 Prelude 6. 46

Realities. Has spared of sound and grave realities, 359 Plea : Hist. 4
From the hushed vale's realities, transferred . . 456 *The leaves 11
When most enslaved by gross realities ! . . . 512 *Who rashly 42
And reconciled us to realities ; . . . . . . 683 Prelude 6. 533
Save when realities of act and mien, ... 694 Prelude 7. 477
Yes, the realities of life so cold, ... K.8. 238 Recluse 1.1. 65

Reality. Death, life, and sleep, reality and thought, 118 Maternal Grief 11
More like a grave reality : . . . . 288 Highland Girl 54
The absolute presence of reality, ... 690 Prelude 7. 233
Reality too close and too intense, ... 728 Prelude 11. 58
In sober contrast with reality, ... 826 Excursion 5. 249
That parts the image from reality ; . . . . . K.8. 252 Recluse 1.1.577

Realize. To realize the vision, with intense . . . 804 Excursion 4. 176

Realized. *See* **Realised.**
And which, with caution due, may soon be realized." . . . . 105 Artegal 217
And dear Imaginations realized . . . . . . K.8. 239 Recluse 1.1.108

Really. With things that really are ; I, at this time, 647 Prelude 2. 394
Whose occupations really I loved ; . . . . . 661 Prelude 4. 193

Realm. And plods through some wide realm o'er vale and height, ... 10 Desc. Sk. 11
'Twas dark and void as ocean's watery realm . 26 Guilt 138
From realm to realm the humbled Exile went, . 103 Artegal 82
Within this realm a place of safe retreat ; . . . 104 Artegal 163
Of Britain's realm, whose leafy crest . . . . 226 Vernal Ode 19
" Or we'll into the realm of Faery, ... 237 P. B. 101
Whose realm had dwindled to one stately room ; 271 George : Death 2
Invades a Realm, so pressed that in the scale . 316 *Say, what 6
Even the proud Realm, from whose distracted borders . . . . 327 Ode 1815 39
Had freed his Realm, he plighted word . . . 372 Eg. Maid 225
All ancient honour in the realm. . . . . . . 403 White Doe 645
Realm there is none that if controlled or sway'd 429 Ecc. Sonn. 2. 2. 9
For England's shame, O Sister Realm ! from wood, 442 Ecc. Sonn. 3. 7. 7
O'er the wide realm, as o'er the Egyptian plain . 450 Ecc. Sonn. 3. 38. 8
Who shall preserve or prop the tottering Realm ? 504 Warning 87
Stretched forth with trembling hope ?—In every realm, ... 509 F. Stone 91
Through every realm confided to thy sway ; . . 628 *Deign, Sovereign 10
France lured me forth ; the realm that I had crossed . . . . 710 Prelude 9. 34
A mightier river, winds from realm to realm ; . 869 Excursion 7. 790
Of England's realm, this vale he might have seen 871 Excursion 7. 933
Their purer service, in this realm at least, . . 875 Excursion 8. 86
To Gain, the master-idol of the realm, ... 877 Excursion 8. 184
And best protection, this imperial Realm, . . . 888 Excursion 9. 295

Realms. Through these wide realms a festive peal ; 113 Lament 23
The finest palace of a hundred realms ! . . . . 202 Hart-leap 128
Swift, toward the realms that know not earthly day, 211 Laod. 155

Realms—*continued.*
Through the realms of woe and weal : 234 *Power of Sound* 125
In realms where everlasting freshness breathes ! " 324 *Ode 1814* 52
That through the realms of glory shines for aye. 365 **Rapt above* 14
Needful when o'er wide realms the tempest breaks, 395 *White Doe : Ded.* 53
Realms quake by turns : proud Arbitress of grace, 427 *Ecc. Sonn.* 1. 36. 1
Over three Realms may take its widest range ; 471 *Tynwald* 10
More efficaciously than realms outspread, 497 **Enough of climbing* 16
To viewless realms his Spirit towers amain, 612 *Desc.Sk.Quarto* 548
From town to town and through wide scattered realms 655 *Prelude* 3. 469
Darkness is banished from the realms of death, 865 *Excursion* 7. 529
Reanimate. Failed to reanimate and but feebly cheered 354 *Aquap.* 97
With gladsome influence could re-animate 773 *Excursion* 2. 136
Reanimated. Alcestis, a reanimated corse, 210 *Laod.* 81
Reanimating. To the reanimating influence lost 733 *Prelude* 11. 389
Reap. Our hopes such harvest of affliction reap, 29 *Guilt* 295
Or reap an acre of his neighbour's corn. 95 *Brothers* 10
Of years be on her !—She shall reap 204 *Brougham* 41
Whether men sow or reap the fields, 228 *Devot. Incit.* 70
What perfect glory ye in Heaven shall reap !— 444 *Ecc. Sonn.* 3. 16. 8
Else shall your blood-stained hands in frenzy reap 505 *Warning* 138
To reap the whirlwind on a Libyan rock. 628 *Installation* 6
The child, whose love is here, at least, doth reap 670 *Prelude* 5. 345
Saying, " Behold the harvest that we reap 725 *Prelude* 10. 472
And can reap nothing better,—child-like longed 728 *Prelude* 11. 68
That the brief hours, which yet remain, may reap 786 *Excursion* 3. 18
Reaped. And reaped—what hath been, and what is, our own. 524 *Epist. Beaumont* 202
Reaper. There doth the reaper bind the yellow sheaf, 683 *Prelude* 6. 536
Reapers. Of reapers, men and women, boys and girls. 149 **A narrow* 41
While reapers strove, or busy ploughs 287 *Sons of Burns* 35
You might think he'd twelve reapers at work in the Strand. 570 *Farmer* 72
Among the jocund reapers. For himself, 863 *Excursion* 7. 423
Reaping. So, but from toil less sign of profit reaping, 213 *Dion* 77
Reaping and singing by herself ; 289 *Sol. Reap.* 3
So have we argued ; reaping for our pains 832 *Excursion* 5. 626
Re-appear. Even so thy latent worth will re-appear, 105 *Artegal* 204
The violets of five seasons re-appear 185 *Nutting* 31
Takes fire :—The men that have been reappear ; 275 **While poring* 3
Never perhaps to reappear. The Stream 357 *Aquap.* 321
Her countenance, phantom-like, doth re-appear : 445 *Ecc. Sonn.* 3. 22. 12
Will reappear before the uplifted eye 461 **Who but is* 6
Until her fellow sinks to re-appear no more. 490 *Incident : Dog* 40
And all the scenes of childhood reappear, 699 *Prelude* 8. 50
To re-appear, 'twas proved that not in vain 740 *Prelude* 13. 19
Re-appeared. When the green earth re-appeared ; 218 **Inmate of* 32
The bold Arch-despot re-appeared ;—again 331 *Ode : Thanks.* 148
Re-appearing. From his grey re-appearing tower shall soon 8 *Ev. Wk.* 325
Like a re-appearing Star, 205 *Brougham* 154
And, reappearing, she no less 397 *White Doe* 103
He hath hailed it re-appearing— 549 *Hermit's Cell* 1. 23
Then, reappearing in a moment, quits 858 *Excursion* 7. 46
Re-appears. Aloud she shrieked ! for Hermes re-appears ! 211 *Laod.* 151
Reaps. That he, who would sow death, reaps death, or worse, 728 *Prelude* 11. 67
Rear. The rear through iron brown betrays a sullen gleam. 6 *Ev. Wk.* 204
Or hovering over wastes too bleak to rear 15 *Desc. Sk.* 256
Even if thou saw'st the giant wicker rear 26 *Guilt* 122
She strove, and not in vain, her head to rear ; 35 *Guilt* 573
Yet bear me up—else faltering in the rear 112 **O dearer* 11
Rear who will a pyramid ; 161 **Pleasures newly* 53
Shall rear her form to stately height, 187 **Three years* 32
Our shed at night to rear ; 193 *Ruth* 93
Beaumont ! it was thy wish that I should rear 251 *Appleth.* 1
From van to rear—and with one mind would flee, 314 *Hofer* 10
Flinging round van and rear his ghastly net, 321 **Humanity,delighting* 14
But Norton lingered in the rear, 406 *White Doe* 892
Came ministers of peace, intent to rear 534 **When in* 3
And be not slow a stately growth to rear 546 **Ye Lime* 3
The pines that near the coast their summits rear 611 *Desc.Sk.Quarto* 501
If virtue be indeed so hard to rear, 742 *Prelude* 13. 177
To rear for food, for shelter, and delight ; 860 *Excursion* 7. 195
Reared. On tiptoe reared, he strains his clarion throat, 5 *Ev. Wk.* 152
The fountains reared for them amid the waste ! 20 *Desc. Sk.* 560
By lowly nature reared, as if to make her 78 *Bord.* 2334
Through twenty seasons ; but he had been reared 95 *Brothers* 44
The pretty flock which I had reared 115 *Last of Flock* 57
In which this Child of Spring was reared 165 *Parrot* 35
Three pillars of rude stone Sir Walter reared, 202 *Hart-leap* 83
Or fortress, reared at Nature's sage command. 266 **The stars* 8
The ground where we were born and reared ! 375 **The Minstrels* 54
Who saw the Banner reared on high 403 *White Doe* 682
Types of the spiritual Church which God hath reared ; 451 *Ecc. Sonn.* 3. 42. 2
The Pleasure-house is reared, 478 *Somnamb.* 11
The stately Priory was reared ; 495 *Force of Prayer* 57
Firm and unflinching, as the Lighthouse reared 540 *Grace Darl.* 23
But frost had reared the gorgeous Pile 550 *Hermit's Cell* 2. 21
Was reared and taught ; and humbly earned his bread, 584 *Ch. Lamb* 4
When Life rear'd laughing up her morning sun ; 592 *Ev. Wk. Quarto* 28
On tiptoe rear'd he blows his clarion throat, 594 *Ev. Wk.Quarto* 137

Reared—*continued.*
And crosses rear'd to Death on every side, 606 *Desc.Sk.Quarto* 256
The fountains rear'd for you amid the waste ! 614 *Desc.Sk.Quarto* 671
When pure Religion rear'd the peaceful breast 618 *School Ex.* 31
Reared Hawkshead's happy roof, and call'd it mine. 619 *School Ex.* 66
Of that interminable building reared 647 *Prelude* 2. 383
And purest passion. Thou, my Friend ! wert reared 648 *Prelude* 2. 451
That chooses to be reared upon their trunks. 657 *Prelude* 3. 546
Towards that sweet Valley where I had been reared ; 658 *Prelude* 4. 19
Thanks with uplifted heart, that I was reared 669 *Prelude* 5. 226
Though mutually unknown, yea, nursed and reared 678 *Prelude* 6. 254
Upon the spot where she was born and reared ; 692 *Prelude* 7. 321
Each fondly reared on his own pedestal, 695 *Prelude* 7. 577
Though reared upon the base of outward things, 697 *Prelude* 7. 650
Where I was reared ; in Nature's primitive gifts 700 *Prelude* 8. 99
Child of the mountains, among shepherds reared, 733 *Prelude* 11. 424
Thus was he reared ; much wanting to assist 760 *Excursion* 1. 302
Reared by the industrious hand of human art 787 *Excursion* 3. 102
Reared for thy presence : therefore am I bound 802 *Excursion* 4. 45
Cemented ; by the hands of Wisdom reared 838 *Excursion* 6. 10
Of furze-clad commons ; such are born and reared 879 *Excursion* 8. 364
She reared it, and in speaking of her charge K.8.251 *Recluse* 1.1.526
Rearer. A planter, and a rearer from the seed ? 861 *Excursion* 7. 275
Rears. Just where a cloud above the mountain rears 5 *Ev. Wk.* 168
Your Country rears this sacred Monument ! 326 **Intrepid sons* 14
Her heaven-offending trophies Glory rears : 392 *Avon* 12
This tablet, that thus humbly rears 486 *Matthew* 6
Hung o'er a cloud, above the steep that rears 594 *Ev. Wk. Quarto* 151
Reascend. A ladder for thy spirit to reascend 733 *Prelude* 11. 397
Reascending. Then, reascending the bare common, saw 738 *Prelude* 12. 248
Re-ascent. The re-ascent in sanctity ! 416 *White Doe* 1847
Reason. Awed sober Reason till she crouched in fear ? 11 *Desc. Sk.* 55
Confessed no law but what his reason taught, 18 *Desc. Sk.* 437
Yet not for this will sober reason frown 22 *Desc. Sk.* 648
With which he taints her ear ;—for a plain reason ; 42 *Bord.* 263
And craft of age, seducing reason, first 57 *Bord.* 1081
By heaven, his words are reason ! Yes, my Friends, 57 *Bord.* 1094
Where Reason has an eye that she can use, 58 *Bord.* 1119
And you should see how deeply I could reason 59 *Bord.* 1224
To purposes of reason—not a dream 69 *Bord.* 1792
Give me a reason why the wisest thing 75 *Bord.* 2149
There surely must some reason be 86 *Anecdote* 42
And that's the reason why." 86 *Anecdote* 56
From the truths of homely reason 90 *Longest Day* 23
Inclined to both by reason of his age, 99 *Brothers* 245
Over material forms that mastered reason. 139 *Widow* 27
Since reason failed want is her threatened doom, 139 *Widow* 32
Learning from him to find a reason 142 †*Lov. and Lik.* 21
Spite of melancholy reason, 171 *Kitten* 112
The reason firm, the temperate will, 186 **She was* 25
By reason fenced from winds that sigh 190 **Lyre ! though* 11
For the true reason no one knows : 198 *Thorn* 90
In reason, in self-government too slow ; 211 *Laod.* 140
In fixed resolves by Reason justified ; 217 *Enterprise* 127
Though reason might say no. 224 **'Tis gone* 12
When lights of reason fail. 226 *Present.* 78
And type of man's far-darting reason, therefore 231 *Clouds* 81
Of reason partially let in 234 *Power of Sound* 104
And reason govern that audacious flight 261 **From the dark* 8
The soberness of reason ; till, in sooth, 270 **Ye sacred* 8
Griefs to allay which Reason cannot heal ; 273 **When Philoctetes* 10
To Her from heights that Reason may not win. 280 **Oh what* 8
'Twere no offence to reason ; 302 *Yarrow V.* 70
But British reason and the British sword. 310 *Invasion* 20
Of Reason, seated on her sovereign hill ; 315 **Alas ! what* 6
Of popular reason, long mistrusted, freed 327 **Emperors and* 10
That she too lacks not reason to rejoice, 327 *Ode 1815* 43
Imagination feels what Reason fears not 356 *Aquap.* 278
Substantial motive, reason clear, 398 *White Doe* 201
And strength of Reason ; held above 414 *White Doe* 1625
Who with a power like human reason 415 *White Doe* 1718
The lucid shafts of reason to employ, 436 *Ecc. Sonn.* 2. 31. 13
From sense, faith, reason, fancy, of the cause, 468 **Ranging the* 7
And conquering Reason, if self-glorified, 469 **Desire we* 7
Then sure I have no reason to complain, 470 †*From early* 13
Impotent wish ! which reason would despise 471 **Arran ! a* 9
Have I not reason to lament 482 *Lines : Spring* 23
Than years of toiling reason : 483 *Sister* 26
Or on his reason, 485 **Bright Flower* 12
Long hast Thou served a man to reason true ; 489 *Spade* 6
Our tears from passion and from reason came, 491 *Tribute : Dog* 35
The confidence of reason give ; 493 *Duty* 55
—'Tis he whose law is reason ; who depends 493 *Hap. War.* 27
The cause of grateful reason to sustain ; 520 *Pun. Death* 14. 5
To truth and sober reason blind, 530 *Gleaner* 23
A mournful change, should Reason fail to bring 533 **Once I* 38
Who tempt their reason to deny 534 **Blest is* 77
That Reason dictates ; and, as even the wish 538 **In desultory* 32
That Reason *should* control ; 543 *Russ. Fug.* 174
For Love no reason hath but his own will ;— 560 *Cuck.andNight.*197
Of reason ; yet prepares that after-joy 567 *Cumb. Beg.* 101
Which reason cherishes. And thus the soul, 567 *Cumb. Beg.* 102
Now is there not good reason to break forth 575 *Chiabrera* 8. 17
In whom thy reason and intelligent heart 585 *Ch. Lamb* 82
Tam'd " sober Reason " till she crouch'd in fear ? 603 *Desc. Sk. Quarto* 56
By reason sanctioned—Can the choice mislead, 621 *Recluse* 1. 1. 72

Receive—*continued.*
Then might the passing Monk receive a boon . . 339 *Tell* 16
Into that vault receive me from whose depth . . 357 *Aquap.* 306
And what if Duddon's spotless flood receive . . 382 *Duddon* 23. 9
And will not Emily receive . . . . 414 *White Doe* 1673
Receive the faith, and in the hope abide. . . 419 *Ecc. Sonn.* 1. 3. 14
Shall disappear, and grateful earth receive . . 450 *Ecc. Sonn.* 3. 39. 3
Receive whatever good 'tis given thee to dispense. 461 *Queen of 46
From wandering fiends of air receive a yoke, . . 465 *Pastor and 12
Receive the curb of sacred truth, ... 533 *Blest is 36
Which the unsheltered traveller might receive . 537 *In desultory 9
Then let the Book receive in these prompt lines . 539 *Lady ! a 57
Receive him to her breast : . . . . 620 *Birth of Love* 13
And when enraptured Dido shall receive . . . 624 *Æneid* 38
What dwelling shall receive me ? in what vale . 632 *Prelude* 1. 10
By glittering verse ; but further, doth receive, . 674 *Prelude* 5. 591
Receive it daily as a joy of ours ; . . . . . 678 *Prelude* 6. 249
Upon the faculties of man, receive . . . . . 713 *Prelude* 9. 240
Else never canst receive. The days gone by . . 738 *Prelude* 12. 277
Which fits him to receive it when unsought. . . 740 *Prelude* 13. 10
Also, about this time did I receive . . . . . 744 *Prelude* 13. 279
By his intense conceptions, to receive . . . . 759 *Excursion* 1. 193
To feel intensely, cannot but receive. . . . . 759 *Excursion* 1. 196
You will receive, before the hour of noon, . . 774 *Excursion* 2. 157
Lack virtue to receive ; what I myself, . . . 800 *Excursion* 3. 960
They also were permitted to receive . . . . 843 *Excursion* 6. 363
And, without sorrow, will the ground receive . . 863 *Excursion* 7. 389
They had imbibed, and ceased not to receive. . 893 *Excursion* 9. 606
Received. We'll go together, and, such proof received 66 *Bord.* 1594
That I almost received her heart into my own. . 87 *Pet-lamb* 12
That I almost received her heart into my own." . 88 *Pet-lamb* 68
Seven years, alas ! to have received . . . . 117 *Affl. Marg.* 8
Received at others' hands ; for, though now old . 136 *Michael* 364
My Friend, Myself, and She who then received . 149 *A narrow 75
Those wild men's vices he received, ... 194 *Ruth* 149
A cup of stone received the living well ; . . . 202 *Hart-leap* 82
A thought received with languid pleasure ! . . 242 *P. B.* 545
By waking ears have sometimes been received . 261 *I heard (alas 3
Have I received this proof of pains bestowed . . 281 *Chris. Words.* 2
And law was from necessity received. . . . . 316 *Hail, Zaragoza 14
If they received into a conscious ear . . . . 363 *List—'twas 88
Whence half the breathing world received its doom ; 368 *Trajan* 38
The car received her :—then up-went . . . . 371 *Eg. Maid* 183
Given and received in mutual jeopardy, . . . 381 *Duddon* 20. 12
Received the bitterness of woe : . . . . . 409 *White Doe* 1191
Upon the ground received the rest,— . . . . 413 *White Doe* 1548
Received and followed by a prayer, ... 414 *White Doe* 1697
Received the memory of old loves, ... 415 *White Doe* 1754
Received, and fostered in her iron breast : . . 441 *Ecc. Sonn.* 3. 3. 4
Then, when her Child the hallowing touch received, 446 *Ecc. Sonn.* 3. 24. 7
Received the light hers loses. . . . . . . 478 *Somnamb.* 67
Received my proffered aid. . . . . 484 *Simon Lee* 84
Or from like wanderer, haply have received . . 567 *Cumb. Beg.* 111
That his life hath received, to the last will remain. 569 *Farmer* 12
Yet, haply, on the printed page received, . . . 585 *Ch. Lamb* 46
Like a false steward who hath much received . 636 *Prelude* 1. 268
When he had left the mountains and received . 636 *Prelude* 1. 282
I had received so much, that all my thoughts . 648 *Prelude* 2. 398
Its woods, and that uncertain heaven, received . 671 *Prelude* 5. 387
Were all received, the least of them not lost, . 693 *Prelude* 7. 432
Then was the truth received into my heart, . . 725 *Prelude* 10. 464
Within whose solemn temple I received . . . 748 *Prelude* 14. 140
Perplexed the bodily sense. He had received . 758 *Excursion* 1. 139
Which with a look of welcome she received ; . . 768 *Excursion* 1. 806
By many a cottage-hearth, where he received . 772 *Excursion* 2. 59
'Mid much abasement, what he had received . . 775 *Excursion* 2. 273
Which it had unexpectedly received, ... 779 *Excursion* 2. 524
But, though he seemed at first to have received . 785 *Excursion* 2. 891
From unknown objects I received ; and those, . 798 *Excursion* 3. 857
From your progenitors, have ye received, . . . 805 *Excursion* 4. 280
Apart from benefits received or done . . . . 810 *Excursion* 4. 579
Promptly received, as prodigally brought, . . 812 *Excursion* 4. 722
Received a shock of awful consciousness, . . . 818 *Excursion* 4. 1157
The original stain, the child is there received . 826 *Excursion* 5. 281
Was he received, and mutual joy prevailed. . . 829 *Excursion* 5. 445
Or, through illuminating grace, received, . . . 839 *Excursion* 6. 72
From nature's kindliness received a frame . . 839 *Excursion* 6. 100
To grant, or be received ; while that poor bird— 851 *Excursion* 6. 878
Alas ! the nations, who of yore received . . . 894 *Excursion* 9. 652
Of those terrific Idols some received . . . . 894 *Excursion* 9. 692
Receiver. Create, creator and receiver both, . . 646 *Prelude* 2. 258
Receives. Receives a lofty waterfall. . . . . 85 *Shepherd-boys* 55
With awe, receives the hallowed veil, ... 216 *Enterprise* 56
The upturned soil receives the hopeful seed— . 327 *Ode 1815* 31
Ungraciously receives. Too daring choice ! . . 377 *Duddon* 7. 10
That watches and receives. . . . . 482 *Tables Turned* 32
Of their bad influence, and their good receives : . 493 *Hap. War.* 18
Receives at supper hour her tempting hoard ; . . 615 *Desc.Sk.Quarto* 737
Receives no knowledge that can bring forth good, 704 *Prelude* 8. 326
His best and purest friend ; from her receives . 740 *Prelude* 13. 7
Receives, or by reflexion can create. . . . . K.8. 250 *Recluse* 1.1.499
Receiving. Receiving from his Father hire of praise ; 134 *Michael* 191
Receiving, willingly or not, fresh strength . . . 394 *No more 24
Are vomiting, receiving on all sides, ... 698 *Prelude* 7. 720
Of golden expectations, and receiving . . . . 774 *Excursion* 2. 217
Receiving, took the slender path that leads . . 895 *Excursion* 9. 773
Recent. 'Mid recent coolness, such as falls . . 343 *Eclipse* 16
Of innocent delight, remote or recent, ... 354 *Aquap.* 113
Of recent sorrow combated in vain ; . . . . 576 *By a 14
Of the old church, that—though from recent showers . . . . 644 *Prelude* 2. 120

Recent—*continued.*
And recent things yet warm with life ; a sea-fight, 691 *Prelude* 7. 291
In haste, each spot of old or recent fame, . . . 710 *Prelude* 9. 44
Who, by the recent deluge stupefied, ... 727 *Prelude* 11. 36
Recently. The Church, whose power hath recently been checked, ... 432 *Ecc. Sonn.* 2. 16. 3
The same that had been recently pronounced, . 719 *Prelude* 10. 103
Receptacle. The Wanderer seeks that receptacle vast 384 *Duddon* 33. 7
For way and guide, a fluent receptacle . . . 720 *Prelude* 10. 170
And receptacle, open to the good . . . . . 836 *Excursion* 5. 913
Reception. For the reception of far other sounds . S.3.436 *The doubt 175
Recess. The Tale I follow to its last recess . . . 125 *V. and J.* 281
But as a blessing to this calm recess, ... 149 *M. H.* 13
Less than I wished to prize, that calm recess. . 150 *When, to 42
That, to this opportune recess allured, ... 150 *When, to 59
While fluttering o'er this gay Recess, ... 154 *Flower Garden* 2
An opportune recess, ... 168 *Wren's Nest* 14
Beside him in the cool recess . . . . . . 238 *P. B.* 159
So burns yon Taper 'mid a black recess . . . 266 *Even as 4
Tempting recess as ever pilgrim chose, . . . 382 *Duddon* 24. 6
Fills many a damp obscure recess . . . . . 397 *White Doe* 101
Most happy in the shy recess . . . . . . 399 *White Doe* 293
Into a deep recess of years ! . . . . 413 *White Doe* 1567
Of things not seen, drawn forth from their recess, 436 *Ecc. Sonn.* 2. 30. 4
An abbey in its lone recess, ... 472 *Ossian* 13
It was a cove, a huge recess, ... 491 *Fidelity* 17
Cast into that recess—the tender shade, . . . 508 *F. Stone* 16
To make a fair recess more fair ; . . . . . 533 *Blest is 24
In this recess, by thoughtful Fancy built, . . . 654 *Prelude* 3. 379
Inviting shades of opportune recess, ... 676 *Prelude* 6. 74
Down on a green recess, the first I saw . . . 682 *Prelude* 6. 518
Advanced in radiance through a deep recess . . 693 *Prelude* 7. 414
Is the recess, the circumambient world . . . 700 *Prelude* 8. 56
Ah ! what a sweet Recess, thought I, is here ! . 776 *Excursion* 2. 349
And one old moss-grown wall ;—a cool recess, . 777 *Excursion* 2. 415
Amid the quiet of the green recess, ... 857 *Excursion* 7. 13
Or as a stranger reached this deep recess, . . . 871 *Excursion* 7. 928
Of this recess, their legislative hall, ... K.8. 253 *Recluse* 1.1.623
Recesses. From deep recesses of a loyal heart. . . 628 *Deign, Sovereign 4
Recesses in man's heart, immortal verse . . . 635 *Prelude* 1. 232
And intricate recesses, creek or bay . . . . 702 *Prelude* 8. 195
In the recesses of thy nature, far . . . . . 749 *Prelude* 14. 216
Glitter, with dark recesses interposed, ... 773 *Excursion* 2. 129
And blind recesses of the caverned rocks ; . . 818 *Excursion* 4. 1172
With bold projections and recesses deep ; . . 881 *Excursion* 8. 462
Recitals. Among those fair recitals also range, . . 847 *Excursion* 6. 632
Recites. Recites the holy liturgy, ... 396 *White Doe* 46
Reckless. Anglers, bent on reckless pastime, . . 94 *Westmoreland Girl* 49
Reckless of what might come at last . . . . 115 *Last of Flock* 69
The silver shower, whose reckless burthen weighs 124 *V. and J.* 192
"Improvident and reckless," we exclaimed, . . 149 *A narrow 50
If still the reckless change we mourn, ... 224 *'Tis gone 43
From land to land a reckless will . . . . . 246 *P. B.* 864
To pleasure snatched for reckless pleasure's sake. 280 *Intent on 8
Turn into port ; and, reckless of the gale, . . . 379 *Duddon* 13. 10
Reckless of angry Duddon sweeping by, . . . 379 *Duddon* 13. 11
Or whirlwind, reckless what his might . . . . 391 *Highland Broach* 85
Reckless of what impels or leads, ... 411 *White Doe* 1379
Of reckless mastery, hitherto unknown. . . . 435 *Ecc. Sonn.* 2. 28. 14
To slake their thirst, with reckless hoofs have trod 465 *The cattle 2
Reckless audacity extol, and jeer . . . . . 514 *Portentous change 3
Reckless of me : I followed, not unseen, . . . 667 *Prelude* 5. 118
My soul, too reckless of mild grace, had stood . 749 *Prelude* 14. 248
Through the long winter, reckless and alone ; . 770 *Excursion* 1. 905
To oldest time ! and, reckless of the storm . . 809 *Excursion* 4. 518
Recklessness. In recklessness flung out to overturn 538 *In desultory 46
Reckoning. But who (though neither reckoning ills assigned . . . . 504 *Warning* 47
Looked thitherward. One, reckoning by years, . 711 *Prelude* 9. 139
Recks. He recks not human law ; and I have noticed 63 *Bord.* 1437
Reclaimed. Aspiring thoughts, by memory reclaimed, 340 *Ranz* 12
Reclaiming. Reclaiming and extirpating, perform . 805 *Excursion* 4. 283
Recline On withered briars that o'er the crags recline ; . . . . 3 *Ev. Wk.* 63
And yew-tree o'er the silver rocks recline, . . 5 *Ev. Wk.* 157
The wood-crowned cliffs that o'er the lake recline ; 15 *Desc. Sk.* 278
And some recline on couches, myrtle-crowned, . 275 *While poring 5
The tale as fabulous.—Here while I recline, . . 340 *Ranz* 8
Than 'mid that wave-washed Churchyard to recline, 384 *Duddon* 31. 10
You not forbidden to recline . . . . . . 408 *White Doe* 1090
And strives the towers to number, that recline . 443 *Ecc. Sonn.* 3. 12. 6
And yew-trees o'er the silver rocks recline, . . 594 *Ev. Wk. Quarto* 140
While round a vacant board the chiefs recline, . 625 *Æneid* 97
But who shall count the Towers as they recline . 625 *The confidence 6
Each night, while I recline within this cell, . . 630 [?] *O Moon 14
Thou wilt recline of pastoral Arethuse ; . . . 734 *Prelude* 11. 465
Reclined. Reclined, he sees, above him and below, 19 *Desc. Sk.* 466
What keeps her thus reclined upon her lonesome bed ? . . . . 170 *Never enlivened 10
Thou, on thy rock reclined, though kingdoms melt 276 *Author's Portrait* 5
Reclined on flowers and mosses ? . . . . . 287 *Ellen Irwin* 20
To slumber, reclined on the moss-covered floor, . 345 *Stanzas : Simplon* 2
Reclined, shall I have yielded up my soul . . . 358 *Aquap.* 359
To slumber, reclined on the moss-covered floor ! " 364 *Vallomb.* 2
There did she rest, with head reclined, . . . 414 *White Doe* 1633
As his own worshippers : and Nile, reclined . . 435 *Ecc. Sonn.* 2. 27. 7
While in a grove I sate reclined, ... 482 *Lines : Spring* 2
Or, Pilgrim-like, on forest moss reclined, . . . 522 *Epist. Beaumont* 46
Reclin'd in festal pomp the Tyrian queen. . . 624 *Æneid* 57
Standing apart ; with curvèd arm reclined . . 825 *Excursion* 5. 211

Record—*continued.*
Will I record the praises, making verse — 743 *Prelude* 13. 234
Had dealt with—I will here record in verse; — 757 *Excursion* 1. 102
—But why this tedious record?—Age, we know, — 791 *Excursion* 3. 325
What special record can, or need, be given — 795 *Excursion* 3. 607
Or to record; we judge, but cannot be — 830 *Excursion* 5. 499
As books record, and even the careless mind — 834 *Excursion* 5. 797
To oral record, and the silent heart; — 847 *Excursion* 6. 612
Recorded. Sleep fled, and with it fled the dream—recorded in this book, — 93 *Poet's Dream* 70
Recorded: to the open fields I told — 632 *Prelude* 1. 50
Recorded by Cervantes, these same thoughts — 666 *Prelude* 5. 61
That would be found in all recorded time, — 715 *Prelude* 9. 366
And in his mind recorded it with love! — 892 *Excursion* 9. 517
Records. Sweet records, promises as sweet; — 186 **She was* 16
Those many records of my childish years, — 250 **Beloved Vale* 2
As aught that song records of Robin Hood; — 255 *Detraction* 3
If these brief Records, by the Muses' art — 269 **If these* 1
Records on which, for pleasure of all eyes, — 324 *Ode 1814* 108
These records take, and happy should I be — 352 *H. C. R.* 5
Yet in his page the records of that worth — 356 *Aquap.* 248
Thy veil in mercy o'er the records, hung — 389 *Sound of Mull* 2
These Records wrought in pledge of love — 403 *White Doe* 665
Upon her records, listen to her song, — 435 *Ecc. Sonn.* 2. 29. 6
Of Power whose ministers the records keep — 469 **Desire we* 12
Diluvian records; or the sighs of Earth — 498 **Enough of climbing* 34
(As records mouldering in the Dell — 533 **Blest is* 15
Left, 'mid the Records of this Book inscribed, — 538 **Lady! a* 3
Triumphantly displayed in records left — 759 *Excursion* 1. 174
Or obscure records of the path of fire. — 760 *Excursion* 1. 279
Only by records in myself not found. — 796 *Excursion* 3. 705
The tribute by these various records claimed, — 825 *Excursion* 5. 171
So, by your records, may our doubts be solved; — 832 *Excursion* 5. 654
For the pathetic records which his voice — 873 *Excursion* 7. 1053
Recount. "But nay—the fatal wiles, O guest, recount, — 625 *Æneid* 139
Recounted. Ere he his Tale recounted. — 386 *Yarrow Rev.* 104
Her Champion's praise recounted; — 478 *Somnamb.* 56
Recover. Its brightness to recover. — 386 *Yarrow Rev.* 40
Recovered. The Boy recovered heart, and told — 85 *Shepherd-boys* 80
His freedom he recovered on the eve — 124 *V. and J.* 186
Recovered heart. That evening her best fare — 135 *Michael* 301
Lost and recovered, as the rays of light — 231 **The gentlest Poet* 22
For fifty kingdoms by my sword recovered. — 372 *Eg. Maid* 234
And yet again recovered! But descending — 819 *Excursion* 4. 1187
Recovered; or, if hitherto unknown, — 827 *Excursion* 5. 307
Recovering. Recovering heart, like answer did she make; — 27 *Guilt* 186
And he, recovering sense, upon her breast — 103 *Artegal* 47
Recovering breath, and pleased to win — 174 *Waggoner* 1. 44
Recovering, to my Friend I said, "You spake, — 777 *Excursion* 2. 395
Recovers. Recovers not his loss; but walks with shame, — 383 *Duddon* 30. 3
Recreant. "A recreant harp, that sings of fear — 204 *Brougham* 102
Her recreant Brother—he prevailed — 405 *White Doe* 881
The recreant soul, that dares to shun the debt — 424 *Ecc. Sonn.* 1. 23. 10
Turns recreant to her task; takes heart again, — 636 *Prelude* 1. 258
That mocks the recreant age *we* live in, then — 654 *Prelude* 3. 400
Recreation. For recreation, leading into each: — 810 *Excursion* 4. 592
Recross. Of their rich Spoil, ere they recross the Border. — 37 *Bord.* 3
Recruit. Her bane, her vital energies recruit. — 431 *Ecc. Sonn.* 2. 10. 8
Recruited. Wrapped in our cloaks, and, with recruited strength, — 39 *Bord.* 124
May issue thence, recruited for the tasks — 810 *Excursion* 4. 595
Rectify. Father of Mercy! rectify his view, — 363 **The world forsaken* 9
Recumbent.—Recumbent: Him thou may'st behold, who hides — 269 *Gordale* 10
Perpetually recumbent; Statues—man, — 689 *Prelude* 7. 133
Recumbent in the shade, as if asleep; — 756 *Excursion* 1. 36
Recur. Cause should recur, which righteous Heaven avert! — 839 *Excursion* 6. 60
Recurred. Old frailties then recurred:—but lofty thought, — 211 *Laod.* 137
Recurrence. With each recurrence of this glorious morn — 255 *Easter* 1
Recurring. *See* **Oft-recurring.**
Recusants. Half-and-half idlers, hardy recusants, — 650 *Prelude* 3. 67
Red. *See* **Blood-red, Dull-red.**
Tipt with eve's latest gleam of burning red. — 6 *Ev. Wk.* 211
Only the waning moon hangs dull and red — 14 *Desc. Sk.* 188
Tinged like an angel's smile all rosy red— — 19 *Desc. Sk.* 475
Red on the hills her beacon's far-seen blaze; — 22 *Desc. Sk.* 639
A coat he wore of military red — 24 *Guilt* 8
The gathering clouds grew red with stormy fire, — 24 *Guilt* 19
Marks nothing but the red sun's setting round, — 26 *Guilt* 111
No labourer watched his red kiln glaring bright, — 26 *Guilt* 141
Lurking berries, ripe and red, — 80 *Foresight* 29
Though the red Flower, not prostrate, only droops, — 169 *Love lies Bleeding* 2
A burning of portentous red; — 175 *Waggoner* 1. 169
Red, green, and blue; a moment's sight! — 180 *Waggoner* 4. 33
Now deep and red, the colouring of night; — 192 *Gipsies* 6
Green, red, and pearly white! — 198 *Thorn* 48
"I've heard, the moss is spotted red — 200 *Thorn* 210
The red rose is a gladsome flower. — 203 *Brougham* 6
The red rose is revived at last; — 203 *Brougham* 8
Both roses flourish, red and white: — 204 *Brougham* 11
All bright with berries ripe and red, — 243 *P. B.* 637
And though your sins be red as scarlet, — 247 *P. B.* 954
And the red cross on my breast; — 323 *Ode 1814* 32

Red—*continued.*
And her lips, quickening with uncertain red, — 374 *Eg. Maid* 329
A shame-faced blush of glowing red! — 398 *White Doe* 183
In the ruthless wars of the White and Red; — 399 *White Doe* 251
The village Children, while the sky is red — 448 *Ecc. Sonn.* 3. 32. 5
Is red as a ripe cherry. — 483 *Simon Lee* 8
We walked along, while bright and red — 486 **We walked* 1
Towers where red streamers flout the breezy sky. — 503 *Warning* 39
Self-smitten till thy garments reek dyed red — 514 **Long-favoured* 4
With his red stalks upon this sunny day! — 529 *Poor Robin* 6
His cheeks were red as ruddy clover; — 536 *Goody Blake* 19
Of red Morocco folio saw displayed, — 547 **Rude is* 8
On red slow-waving pinions down the vale, — 595 *Ev. Wk. Quarto* 192
Thence red from different heights with restless gleam — 598 *Ev. Wk. Quarto* 373
Checquer with paler red the thicket shades. — 599 *Ev. Wk. Quarto* 398
And red, above her melancholy hill. — 606 *Desc.Sk.Quarto* 220
And his red eyes the slinking water hides; — 606 *Desc.Sk.Quarto* 236
—Red stream the cottage lights; the landscape fades, — 614 *Desc.Sk.Quarto* 688
And the red banner mock the sullen breeze; — 615 *Desc.Sk.Quarto* 747
Red on his hills his beacon's comet blaze; — 616 *Desc.Sk.Quarto* 775
On which a dull red image of the moon — 685 *Prelude* 6. 705
In lineaments, and red with over-toil. — 690 *Prelude* 7. 201
Into a narrower circle of deep red, — 762 *Excursion* 1. 427
With dull red stains discoloured, and stuck o'er — 767 *Excursion* 1. 744
A man whose garments showed the soldier's red, — 769 *Excursion* 1. 888
Of red ripe currants; gift by which he strove, — 779 *Excursion* 2. 505
Chase the wild goat; and if the bold red deer — 808 *Excursion* 4. 500
Whose shelving sides are red with naked mould. — 868 *Excursion* 7. 700
He's got his red ribbon — S.3. 440 **Said red-ribboned* 31
Redbreast. The red-breast, known for years, which at my casement pecked. — 28 *Guilt* 225
The redbreast near me hopped; nor was I loth — 150 **When, to* 15
Wild Redbreast! hadst thou at Jemima's lip — 272 **Wild Redbreast* 1
Some bird (like our own honoured redbreast) may strew — 340 *Fort Fuentes* 11
The redbreast sings from the tall larch — 482 *Sister* 3
The lonely redbreast pays! — 498 **Departing summer* 9
A Redbreast, one that to his cottage door — 531 **I know* 7
Trilled by the redbreast, when autumnal leaves — 539 **Lady! a* 34
And let the redbreast hop from stone to stone. — 549 **Stranger! this* 35
The redbreast peace had bury'd it in wood, — 605 *Desc.Sk.Quarto* 169
The redbreast, ruffled up by winter's cold — 807 *Excursion* 4. 386
For wren and redbreast,—where they sit and sing — 881 *Excursion* 8. 482
Redbreasts. And red-breasts warble when sweet sounds are rare. — 276 *Filial Piety* 14
A choir of redbreasts gathered somewhere near — 687 *Prelude* 7. 21
Red-brown. Upon whose grassless floor of red-brown hue, — 185 *Yew-trees* 21
Red-cross. That, like the Red-cross Knight, they urge their way, — 425 *Ecc. Sonn.* 1. 25. 7
When the proud fleet that bears the red-cross flag — 722 *Prelude* 10. 315
Red-deer. The red-deer driven along its native heights — 870 *Excursion* 7. 864
Redden. Yet we mark it not;—fruits redden, — 90 *Longest Day* 37
Reddened. Reddened the fiery hues, and shot — 385 *Yarrow Rev.* 15
Reddening. Thy reddening orchards, and thy fields of gold; — 615 *Desc.Sk.Quarto* 705
Redeem. That spirit only can redeem mankind; — 806 *Excursion* 4. 317
Redeem by love the individual sense — K.8. 249 *Recluse* 1. 1. 457
Redeemable. If penance be redeemable, thence alms — 424 *Ecc. Sonn.* 1. 24. 11
Redeemed. Nor yet redeemed from scorn. — 232 *Jew. Fam.* 40
Redeemed to baffle that imperial Slave, — 318 **Ah! where* 7
For privilege redeemed of godlike sway) — 325 *Ode 1814* 122
By aught redeemed out of the hollow grave: — 325 *Enghien* 9
Redeemed, from miserable fear set free — 326 *Sobieski* 9
Monarch and peasant: be the house redeemed — 682 *Prelude* 6. 456
Redeemed, according to example given — 721 *Prelude* 10. 220
Do, in my present censure, stand redeemed — 792 *Excursion* 3. 409
That he, from wrath redeemed, therein shall float — 826 *Excursion* 5. 283
Redeemer. That my Redeemer liveth,"—hears each word — 448 *Ecc. Sonn.* 3. 31. 6
A prayer to the Redeemer of the world. — 576 *Chiabrera* 9. 4
To heaven, I know, by my Redeemer taught.' — 835 *Excursion* 5. 826
Issued the blest Redeemer of our race— — [?] **A sad* 11
Redeemer's. At the Redeemer's feet?" In rueful tone, — 817 *Excursion* 4. 1100
Redeeming. *See* **World-redeeming.**
Is God's redeeming love; — 225 *Primrose* 36
Had wakened some redeeming thought — 300 *Bran* 42
Of a redeeming happiness. — 409 *White Doe* 1248
Of holy freedom, by redeeming love — 894 *Excursion* 9. 656
Redemption. The earth for sure redemption of lost peace. — 69 *Bord.* 1783
Of your redemption. Shun the insidious arts — 420 *Ecc. Sonn.* 1. 8. 9
Redemptoris. The *Alma Redemptoris* did he hear; — 553 *Prioress* 68
O *Alma Redemptoris!* high and low: — 554 *Prioress* 103
The *Alma Redemptoris* 'gan to sing — 555 *Prioress* 161
And sang, O *Alma Redemptoris Mater!* — 555 *Prioress* 190
Red-haired. High o'er the red-haired race of Mars, — 237 *P. B.* 38
Red-hot. Like red-hot iron burnt into my heart. — 59 *Bord.* 1183
Reding. The name of Aloys Reding. — 337 *Thun* 4
Redouble. Day and night my toils redouble, — 166 *Wand. Jew* 25
Redoubled. Redoubled and redoubled, concourse wild — 671 *Prelude* 5. 378
Redoubt. (Freedom's impregnable redoubt, — 217 *Enterprise* 152
Redoubted. Redoubted Viriathus breathes again; — 320 **They seek* 10
Advance in order the redoubted Bands, — 324 *Ode 1814* 56
Redoubted King, of courage leonine, — 427 *Ecc. Sonn.* 1. 35. 1

Redounding. Through fancy's heat redounding in the brain, 863 *Excursion* 7. 380
Redounds. To hear of, for the glory that redounds 743 *Prelude* 13. 248
Redress. I mused; and, thirsting for redress, 301 *Bran* 127
What could they gain but shadows of redress? 330 *Ode: Thanks.* 120
By flames, look up to heaven and crave redress 426 *Ecc. Sonn.* 1. 32. 4
Wrongs and the terror of redress, would wean 516 **Hard task* 5
Wrongs to redress, harmonious tribute paid 635 *Prelude* 1. 182
As he must bear, being powerless to redress; 806 *Excursion* 4. 329
Bound by his vow to labour for redress 873 *Excursion* 7. 1042
Red-ribboned. Said red-ribboned Evans: S.3. 440 **Said red-ribboned* 1
Reduced. When threatened war reduced the children's meal: 29 *Guilt* 267
Of trivial objects, melted and reduced 698 *Prelude* 7. 726
Redundancy. Redundancy of youth's contentedness. 677 *Prelude* 6. 178
Redundant. Redundant are thy locks, thy lips as fair 210 *Laod.* 59
There's weakness, and strength both redundant and vain; 482 *Character* 5
Graced with redundant hair, Iopas sings 625 *Æneid* 121
A tempest, a redundant energy, 632 *Prelude* 1. 37
Redundantly. Thus a rich loving-kindness, redundantly kind, 167 *Stray Pleasures* 29
Re-echoed. Re-echoed by a naked rock, 247 *P. B.* 942
Reed. Thou wouldst be leaning on a broken reed— 40 *Bord.* 164
His flock, and pipe on shepherd's reed 180 *Waggoner* 4. 51
And, like the lowly reed, her love 222 *Triad* 147
Is it a reed that's shaken by the wind, 303 **Is it* 1
Farewell the solace of the vagrant reed! 382 *Duddon* 24. 4
As bland as the reed of peace: 629 *Installation* 37
7 *Ev. Wk.* 283
Reeds. Or the swan stirs the reeds, his neck and bill
Or whispering like two reeds that in the cold moonbeam 141 *Arm. Lady* 95
Great Pan himself low-whispering through the reeds, 313 **Clouds, lingering* 12
And all the people bow their heads, like reeds 431 *Ecc. Sonn.* 2. 11. 7
Reedy. 'Mid reedy fens wide-spread and marshes drear, 431 *Ecc. Sonn.* 2. 13. 7
Of joyous comrades. Soon as the reedy marge 891 *Excursion* 9. 488
Reek. Self-smitten till thy garments reek dyed red 514 **Long-favoured* 4
Reeking. *See* **Blood-reeking, Warm-reeking.**
Reel. They themselves make the reel, 167 *Stray Pleasures* 20
Though worlds to their foundations reel 629 *Installation* 93
Reeled. And reeled with visionary stir 167 *Pilgrim's Dream* 54
He reeled, and was stone-blind. 483 *Simon Lee* 20
Reels. Beneath her vine-leaf crown the green Earth reels: 335 *Rhine* 4
(What time a State with madding faction reels) 440 *Ecc. Sonn.* 2. 45. 12
Re-embarked. And season yield; but, as we re-embarked, 892 *Excursion* 9. 546
Re-entered. Opened, and she re-entered with glad looks, 834 *Excursion* 5. 774
Re-entering. The Moon re-entering her monthly round, 532 **Once I* 2
Re-establish. Would re-establish and uphold: 405 *White Doe* 840
Re-established. Were re-established now those watchful thoughts 740 *Prelude* 13. 40
"Thus all was re-established, and a pile 849 *Excursion* 6. 727
Refectory. Graced the Refectory: and there, while both 509 *F. Stone* 106
Refers. For manifold privations; he refers 813 *Excursion* 4. 815
Refine. To soothe or cheer, to soften or refine. 21 *Desc. Sk.* 590
The affections, to exalt them or refine; 172 *Infant Daughter* 35
For wholesome sadness, troubling to refine, 538 **In desultory* 24
Or feel, shall tend to quicken and refine; 820 *Excursion* 4. 1271
Examples efficacious to refine 875 *Excursion* 8. 66
Mirrored, yet not too strictly, may refine S.3. 435 **The doubt* 118
Refine the selfishness from which they spring, K.8.249 *Recluse* 1.1.456
Refined. Harmonious thoughts, a soul by truth refined, 3 *Ev. Wk.* 84
With goodly arts and usages refined; 102 *Artegal* 20
Hues more exalted, "a refinèd Form," 110 **Look at* 22
To the refined indignity? 164 *Needlecase* 16
Refined, as with intent to show 232 *Jew. Fam.* 27
Imagination lofty and refined: 259 **Weak is* 10
Whose mortal lineaments seem all refined 274 **Such age* 2
And a refined rusticity, belong 444 *Ecc. Sonn.* 3. 18. 2
And pleasure-grounds where Taste, refined Co-mate 463 **Why should the* 6
As nature is;—too pure to be refined. 489 *Spade* 12
'Tis not for the unfeeling, the falsely refined, 569 *Farmer* 1
Faith had refined; and to her heart 582 **O for a* 20
By means refined attaining purest ends, 690 *Prelude* 7. 237
Of courteous usages refined by art. 742 *Prelude* 13. 194
Of more refined humanity, thy breath, 750 *Prelude* 14. 264
Malice so subtle, vengeance so refin'd. L.1. 88 *Juvenal* 1. 4
Refines. Long-vanished happiness refines, 499 *Memory* 11
Refitted. In strength, in power refitted, he renewed 843 *Excursion* 6. 332
Reflect. O'er the chilled heart—reflect; far, far within 280 **Oh what* 4
Reflect, in glowing hues that shall not fade, 324 *Ode 1814* 95
Streams that reflect the poetry of things! 500 *Humanity* 20
The glittering waves reflect the dazzling blaze; 618 *School Ex.* 42
Oh! laughter for the page that would reflect 712 *Prelude* 9. 173
Who can reflect, unmoved, upon the round 828 *Excursion* 5. 375
Reflected. Reflected from the mountain's side 112 **What heavenly* 7
Reflected beams of that celestial light 118 *Maternal Grief* 17
Reflected from the years gone by, 144 **Driven in* 80
Reflected in my bosom all too late!— 267 **As the* 12
With light reflected from the invisible sun 277 **Haydon! let* 11
Reflected in the pool below. 301 *Bran* 73
Shine on his soul, reflected from the days 318 **Is there* 13
Reflected in some crystal brook; 344 **How blest* 10

Reflected—*continued.*
Reflected through the mists of age, from hours 354 *Aquap.* 112
Derives its name, reflected as the chime 381 *Duddon* 22. 5
(Among reflected boughs of leafy trees) 527 **Those breathing* 43
Joy?—a moon by fits reflected 549 *Hermit's Cell* 1. 19
Mountains and clouds, reflected in the depth 662 *Prelude* 4. 265
Not hitherto reflected. Call we this 745 *Prelude* 13. 360
Reflected, it appeared to me the type 747 *Prelude* 14. 66
Faintly reflected in a lingering stream. 782 *Excursion* 2. 681
Enriched by mutual and reflected wealth, 796 *Excursion* 3. 732
Dimly reflected in a lonely pool. 808 *Excursion* 4. 488
A character reflected in himself, 824 *Excursion* 5. 120
Like that reflected in yon quiet pool, 891 *Excursion* 9. 471
Reflected all in perfect lineaments— S.3. 434 **The doubt* 70
Reflecting. From a reflecting mind and sorrowing heart 584 *Ch. Lamb* 39
In strength, reflecting from its placid breast 749 *Prelude* 14. 201
Reflection. *See* **Reflexion.**
Hope with reflection blends her social rays 2 *Ev. Wk.* 29
By soft reflection—grateful to the sky, 219 *Haunted Tree* 4
A fond reflection of her own decay, 321 **Humanity, delighting* 2
Where'er, preserved in this most true reflection, 627 **We gaze* 11
By the reflection of your pleasure, pleased. 788 *Excursion* 3. 158
In faint reflection of infinitude 827 *Excursion* 5. 343
A true reflection of the circling year, 828 *Excursion* 5. 394
Reflections. On Johnny vile reflections cast: 127 *Idiot Boy* 158
With trite reflections of morality, 739 *Prelude* 12. 314
The faint reflections only of thy face— 893 *Excursion* 9. 626
Reflective. Reflective acts to fix the moral law 650 *Prelude* 3. 84
Reflects. And now the van reflects the solar beam; 6 *Ev. Wk.* 203
The lake below reflects it not; the sky 266 **Even as* 6
Whose eye reflects it, glistening through a tear 540 *Grace Darl.* 12
No more than as a mirror that reflects 816 *Excursion* 4. 991
Reflex. To cut across the reflex of a star 638 *Prelude* 1. 450
Reflexion. *See* **Reflection.**
But by reflexion made so, which do best 355 *Aquap.* 202
With Hope Reflexion blends her social rays 592 *Ev. Wk. Quarto* 39
Receives, or by reflexion can create. K.8.250 *Recluse* 1.1.499
Reflits. Flits and reflits along the close arcade; 453 **Calm is the* 21
Reflux. Is a reflux from on high, 90 *Longest Day* 30
Yielded to mortal reflux; her pure glory, 795 *Excursion* 3. 672
Reform. To curb, exalt, reform the tender mind: 618 *School Ex.* 18
A Power misnamed the SPIRIT of REFORM, 626 *Ballot* 2
Reformation's. In Reformation's sweeping overthrow. 468 *St. Bees* 148
Reformed. The faith reformed and purified. 407 *White Doe* 1041
Their Church reformed! labouring with earnest care 438 *Ecc. Sonn.* 2. 40. 4
How far those erring notions were reformed; 896 *Excursion* 9. 790
Refract. Refract in rainbow hues the restless fires! 609 *Desc.Sk.Quarto* 391
Refrain. To see Presumption, turning pale, refrain 504 *Warning* 70
"'Wherefore I sing, nor can from song refrain, 556 *Prioress* 212
(Who could refrain?) and feed by stealth my sight 856 *Excursion* 6. 1176
Refresh. For Zeal to enter and refresh herself, 730 *Prelude* 11. 229
With which thou dost refresh the thirsty lip, 812 *Excursion* 4. 751
Fall to refresh a parched and withered land? 817 *Excursion* 4. 1098
Refreshed. I hope you are refreshed.—I have just written 49 *Bord.* 666
Refreshed, the Wanderer rose at morn, 542 *Russ. Fug.* 49
And thou, O Friend! wilt be refreshed. There is 733 *Prelude* 11. 393
Observant, studious, thoughtful, and refreshed 762 *Excursion* 1. 394
By flowers embellished, and by springs refreshed. 790 *Excursion* 3. 306
Beguiled his leisure hours; refreshed his thoughts; 864 *Excursion* 7. 444
Refreshing. Pleased in refreshing dews to steep 299 *Cora Linn* 10
For this refreshing incense from the West!— 327 *Ode 1815* 27
As cool refreshing water, by the care 757 *Excursion* 1. 70
Grateful to sight, refreshing to the soul, 830 *Excursion* 5. 528
Refreshment. Had shaped for their refreshment; nor did sun, 149 *M. H.* 11
Refreshment, strawberries and mellow cream. 644 *Prelude* 2. 160
Then, cheered by short refreshment, sallied forth. 746 *Prelude* 14. 10
When she upheld the cool refreshment drawn 763 *Excursion* 1. 504
Without refreshment!" Quickly had he spoken, 781 *Excursion* 2. 636
Refreshments. Decked with refreshments had this child been placed, 692 *Prelude* 7. 357
Refuge. Could find no refuge from distress 9 *Collins* 15
Where from distress a refuge might be found, 10 *Desc. Sk.* 2
Had taken refuge in this neighbourhood, 49 *Bord.* 682
Of refuge, with an unincumbered floor. 150 **When, to* 12
A solid refuge for distress— 329 *Ode: Thanks.* 49
Or grovelling thought, to seek a refuge here; 451 *Ecc. Sonn.* 3. 45. 3
A Tower of refuge built for the else forlorn. 469 **The feudal* 8
Or thither thronged for refuge. With quick glance 540 *Grace Darl.* 35
Take refuge and beguile myself with trust 635 *Prelude* 1. 235
Yet why take refuge in that plea?—the fault, 677 *Prelude* 6. 188
In the last place of refuge—my own soul. 724 *Prelude* 10. 415
Seeking a place of refuge at the root 786 *Excursion* 3. 25
Not as a refuge from distress or pain, 791 *Excursion* 3. 383
Of levity no refuge can be found, 816 *Excursion* 4. 1027
A thought of refuge, for a mind detained 878 *Excursion* 8. 244
Refugee. A grey-haired, pensive, thankful Refugee; 470 *Bala-Sala* 7
Refulgent. With trampling horses and refulgent cars— 216 *Enterprise* 110
On the refulgent spectacle, diffused 893 *Excursion* 9. 611
Refuse. And though the jealous turf refuse 154 *Flower Garden* 31
Which her Heaven-guided feet refuse to tread. 390 *Highland Hut* 8
Proud Glastonbury can no more refuse 433 *Ecc. Sonn.* 2. 21. 11
To the distempered Intellect refuse 455 **Not in the lucid* 30
Whate'er the senses take or may refuse, 480 **Most sweet* 12
Hush, feeble lyre! weak words refuse 507 **While from* 57
Checking the finer spirits that refuse 773 *Excursion* 2. 150

Remorse—*continued.*
Stung with remorse for broken vows; . . . . 473 *Ossian* 50
—O for a bridle bitted with remorse . . . . 505 *Warning* 129
And prostrate at some moment when remorse . 519 *Pun. Death* 12. 2
Save when the stings of viperous remorse, . . 718 *Prelude* 9. 576
Dread of the persecuting sword, remorse, . . . 791 *Excursion* 3. 373
Diverting evil purposes, remorse . . . . . 813 *Excursion* 4. 839
Is sure, that through remorse and grief he died; . 855 *Excursion* 6. 1111
Ye Thrones that have defied remorse, and cast . 870 *Excursion* 7. 837

Remorseless. All perished—all in one remorseless year, ... 30 *Guilt* 302
On the remorseless hearts of men grown old . . 325 *Enghien* 4
Remorseless, and submissive to no law . . . 800 *Excursion* 3. 954
Remorseless punishment; and so retreads . . 827 *Excursion* 5. 327
To Gods delighting in remorseless deeds; . . . 894 *Excursion* 9. 685

Remote. And *blasted* quarry thunders, heard remote! . . . . 4 *Ev. Wk.* 141
Threatened by faintly-answering farms remote: . 5 *Ev. Wk.* 153
On darling spots remote her tempting smile. . . 8 *Ev. Wk.* 344
Or rumbling, heard remote, of falling snow. . . 17 *Desc. Sk.* 361
That rang down a bare slope not far remote: . 30 *Guilt* 326
In a deep wood remote from any town. . . . 50 *Bord.* 698
From home and company remote and every playful joy, ... 91 *Norman Boy* 3
To some remote and solitary place, ... 123 *V. and J.* 108
And oft alone in nooks remote . . . . . . 158 **In youth* 22
Mysteriously remote and high; . . . . . . 227 *Vernal Ode* 117
Happy Associates breathing air remote . . . 252 **Her only* 8
Remote from men, Thou dost not need . . . 288 *Highland Girl* 29
In this still place, remote from men, ... 288 *Glen-Al.* 1
Or is she swallowed up, remote from ken . . . 318 **Ah! where* 4
Of innocent delight, remote or recent, ... 354 *Aquap.* 113
Child of the clouds! remote from every taint . 376 *Duddon* 2. 1
When here, in this remote alcove, ... 407 *White Doe* 1027
But to remote Northumbria's royal Hall, . . . 422 *Ecc. Sonn.* 1. 15. 1
Of Alfred boasts remote Jerusalem, ... 425 *Ecc. Sonn.* 1. 26. 12
Remote St. Kilda, lone and loved sea-mark . . 475 **Homeward we* 6
Great gains are mine; for thus I live remote . 488 *Pers. Talk* 44
Remote from public road or dwelling, ... 491 *Fidelity* 22
Remote from sheltered village-green, ... 536 *Goody Blake* 29
Of boys that bathe remote the faint uproar, . . 597 *Ev. Wk. Quarto* 321
Near or remote, minute or vast; an eye . . 651 *Prelude* 3. 159
In my own mind remote from social life, . . . 656 *Prelude* 3. 511
To spots remote, and draw his diagrams . . . 677 *Prelude* 6. 151
The Frenchman and the Spaniard; from remote . 690 *Prelude* 7. 225
Remote from view of city spire, or sound . . . 758 *Excursion* 1. 124
To travel in a country far remote; . . . . . 766 *Excursion* 1. 643
Remote from Europe; from her blasted hopes; . 798 *Excursion* 3. 833
"Compatriot, Friend, remote are Garry's hills, . 809 *Excursion* 4. 550
Such as, remote, 'mid savage wilderness, . . . 820 *Excursion* 4. 1277
And far remote the chapel stood,—remote, . . 859 *Excursion* 7. 140
Discoursing on remote imaginations, strong . . K.8. 227 **I will* 100
Remote and deep, piled round with rocks, where foot . . . . K.8. 229 **I will* 141
His lullaby. From crowded streets remote, . . K.8. 253 *Recluse* 1. 1. 612

Remoter. That had no need of a remoter charm, . 206 *Tintern* 81
But for remoter purposes of love . . . . . 865 *Excursion* 7. 524

Remotest. While the remotest hamlets blessings share 21 *Desc. Sk.* 599
From the remotest outskirts of the grove,— . . 150 **When, to* 29
Remotest lands and unborn times shall turn, . . 444 *Ecc. Sonn.* 3. 15. 10
And almost make remotest infancy . . . . 641 *Prelude* 1. 634
Whose worship, 'mid remotest village trees, . . 655 *Prelude* 3. 417
To the remotest corners of the land . . . 720 *Prelude* 10. 126
Of harmony from Heaven's remotest spheres. . . 747 *Prelude* 14. 99
And in remotest vales was heard—to arms! . . 869 *Excursion* 7. 762
With gentle language; in remotest wilds, . . . 875 *Excursion* 8. 79

Remoulds. With cordial transport, moulds it and remoulds, ... 729 *Prelude* 11. 150

Remount. May thence remount at ease. The aged Man . . . . 566 *Cumb. Beg.* 6

Remounted. Our steeds remounted and the summons given, ... 643 *Prelude* 2. 115

Removal. In like removal, tranquil though severe, 885 *Excursion* 9. 82

Remove. The bell is left, which no one dares remove; 73 *Bord.* 2055
Her virtuous scruples to remove, her fears allay. . 141 *Arm. Lady* 126
O Sexton, do not then remove her, ... 157 *Sexton* 31
But studious only to remove from sight . . . 265 **Hail, Twilight* 3
Destroy in pity, or with care remove. . . . . 363 **Grieve for* 8
Speak one of you, my doubts remove, ... 459 **The Crescent* 4
And from vicissitude remove its sting; . . . . 533 **Once I* 40
Remove this second Rachel from the bier. . . . 555 *Prioress* 176
Me, lur'd by hope her sorrows to remove, . . . 602 *Desc. Sk. Quarto* 45
The calm of night is powerless to remove . . . 624 *Æneid* 9
Blots out Sichæus, studious to remove . . . . 625 *Æneid* 91
And, to remove those doubts, my grey-haired Friend . . . . 786 *Excursion* 3. 21
Friendly the weight of leisure to remove, . . . S.3. 426 **Through Cumbrian* 5

Removed. What one short sigh so easily removed?— 118 *Maternal Grief* 10
Meanwhile that veil, removed or thrown aside, . 265 **The Shepherd* 9
Removed in kindness from their glassy Cell . . 527 **Those breathing* 7
And of that famous Youth, full soon removed . 546 **The embowering* 19
And when he was removed from all men's sight, . 564 *Troilus* 117
O blessèd Lord! whose mercy then removed . . 576 **Six months* 3
For such thou wert ere from our sight removed, . 581 **Why should we* 2
The props of my affections were removed, . . 646 *Prelude* 2. 279
With God and Nature communing, removed . . 648 *Prelude* 2. 430
Even when unconsciously, to things removed . . 676 *Prelude* 6. 104
Removed, and to a distance that was fit: . . 703 *Prelude* 8. 305
And loveliness endeared which they removed. . 795 *Excursion* 3. 621
For any object of his love, removed . . . . 803 *Excursion* 4. 156

Removed—*continued.*
Removed from all approach of living sight . . 812 *Excursion* 4. 714
And courteously, as if the act removed, . . . 816 *Excursion* 4. 1012
Of mountaineers (by nature's self removed . . 828 *Excursion* 5. 424
Yet, though such service be, with us, removed . 852 *Excursion* 6. 952
"An *active* Principle:—howe'er removed . . . 884 *Excursion* 9. 3
We are not so removed for utter loss; . . . . 885 *Excursion* 9. 83
And, if that ignorance were removed, which breeds 889 *Excursion* 9. 346

Remuneration. Nor less remuneration waits on him 355 *Aquap.* 178

Rend. Save when the avalanche breaks loose, to rend . . . . 16 *Desc. Sk.* 312
Full oft, when storms the welkin rend, . . . 550 *Hermit's Cell* 5. 10
More multitudinous every moment, rend . . . 809 *Excursion* 4. 530
Was forced to rend away its only hope; . . . 840 *Excursion* 6. 130
With shouts the *assembled* people rend the skies . L.1. 96 *Juvenal* 3. 33

Render. Ill names, can render no ill services, . . 65 *Bord.* 1527
Nor will fail the like to render . . . . . . 94 *Westmoreland Girl* 71
May render back the Highland Broach. . . . 391 *Highland Broach* 90
To render visible her own soft dreams, . . . 524 *Epist. Beaumont* 186
Which it hath witnessed; render back an echo . 850 *Excursion* 6. 809

Rendered. Is rendered vain as love for great. . . 154 *Flower Garden* 24
That Host, which rendered all your bounties vain! 322 **Ye Storms* 14
Her feeling, rendered more compassionate; . . 493 *Hap. War.* 20
And three, were it asked, would be rendered for one. 572 *Avarice* 44
Have rendered prone, can upward look to heaven; 837 *Excursion* 5. 989
Heart-sorrow rendered sweet by gratitude. . . 864 *Excursion* 7. 471

Renders. As renders needless spells and magic wands, 338 *Engelberg* 4
And renders nothing back. Was it for this . . 636 *Prelude* 1. 269

Rendezvous. Strange rendezvous! My mind was at that time . . . . 663 *Prelude* 4. 339
Great rendezvous of worst and best, the walk . 710 *Prelude* 9. 55

Rending. *See* **Heart-rending.**
A rending o'er his head begins the fray again. . 175 *Waggoner* 1. 204

Rends. Save when the startling cliff unfrequent rends: . . . . 609 *Desc. Sk. Quarto* 377

Renew. With a light heart our course we may renew, 22 *Desc. Sk.* 669
Nor only did for him at once renew . . . . 25 *Guilt* 84
You have guessed right. The trees renew their murmur: . . . . 53 *Bord.* 868
Like a scared Bird encouraged to renew . . . 118 *Maternal Grief* 57
My question eagerly did I renew, ... 197 *Resolution* 118
If some have thirsted to renew . . . . . . 223 *Wishing-gate* 46
Their fellowship renew; . . . . 224 *Primrose* 14
Announce a season potent to renew, ... 263 **While not* 12
Intent his wasted spirits to renew; . . . . 268 **Brook! whose* 2
—Fly, wretched Gauls! ere they the charge renew 322 *Germans* 12
That faith which no devotion may renew! . . 335 *Aix* 4
All that I felt this moment doth renew; . . . 350 *Des. Stanzas* 12
His best endeavours to renew, ... 406 *White Doe* 936
Cast upon this observance may renew . . . . 447 *Ecc. Sonn.* 3. 27. 12
The Sabbath bells renew the inviting peal; . . 447 *Ecc. Sonn.* 3. 28. 1
Had three times called us to renew our walk, . 772 *Excursion* 2. 86
She still renewed and could not but renew . . 853 *Excursion* 6. 994
In fresh abodes—their labour to renew; . . . 889 *Excursion* 9. 374
I come to thee, thou dost my heart renew; . . K.8. 265 **Brook, that* 3

Renewal. Needless renewal of an old delight? . . 392 *Bothwell* 8

Renewed. Their way, the Woman thus her mournful tale renewed. . . . . 30 *Guilt* 333
Sight that inspired accordant thoughts; and speech I thus renewed: . . . . 92 *Poet's Dream* 48
Ere sorrow be renewed, ... 112 **How rich* 4
But oft the woods renewed their green, . . . 113 *Lament* 68
Their journey had renewed; . . . . 157 *Oak and Broom* 94
He, having made a pause, the same discourse renewed. . . . . 197 *Resolution* 133
Renewed throughout the bounds of earth or ocean, 226 *Vernal Ode* 49
Their myriads?—endlessly renewed, ... 227 *Vernal Ode* 66
Yet evermore, through years renewed . . . . 228 *Devot. Incit.* 54
Enriched—too transient, were they not renewed . 231 *Clouds* 87
And for the sway of equity renewed, ... 332 *Ode: Thanks.* 203
His soul her daily tasks renewed, ... 348 **Lulled by* 56
These only, Duddon! with their paths renewed . 379 *Duddon* 14. 7
And so to Francis he renewed . . . . . . 410 *White Doe* 1259
Have the survivors of this Storm renewed . . 420 *Ecc. Sonn.* 1. 7. 6
And soft Italia feels renewed alarms; . . . . 427 *Ecc. Sonn.* 1. 34. 4
The prostrate, then my spring-time is renewed, . 440 *Ecc. Sonn.* 3. 2. 13
This glimpse of glory, why renewed? . . . . 458 **Had this* 65
And have renewed the tributary Lay. . . . . 503 *Warning* 23
To thy own conscience gradually renewed; . . 515 **Ah why* 11
Renewed—renewed incessantly— . . . . . . 526 **The soaring* 27
Seven nights her course renewed, ... 542 *Russ. Fug.* 18
Light pleasures, every day renewed; . . . . 578 **I come* 63
Impediments from day to day renewed. . . . . 634 *Prelude* 1. 131
With these blithe friends our voyage we renewed 681 *Prelude* 6. 407
Uprisen betimes, our journey we renewed, . . 684 *Prelude* 6. 649
Of Goslar, once imperial, I renewed . . . . 702 *Prelude* 8. 211
With morning we renewed our quest: the wind . 784 *Excursion* 2. 807
A serious eye, and his speech thus renewed. . . 793 *Excursion* 3. 479
Who lacks not will to use them; vows, renewed . 804 *Excursion* 4. 216
And invitation every hour renewed, ... 806 *Excursion* 4. 377
In strength, in power refitted, he renewed . . 843 *Excursion* 6. 332
She still renewed and could not but renew . . 853 *Excursion* 6. 994
With invitation urgently renewed. . . . . . 880 *Excursion* 8. 440

Renewing. Tasks that are no tasks renewing, . . 160 **Pansies, lilies* 62
As in a dream her own renewing. . . . . . 204 *Brougham* 43
As if he were his grief renewing; . . . . . 243 *P. B.* 590
Erroneously renewing a sad vow . . . . . . 261 **From the dark* 11
The flowers in pearly dews their bloom renewing! 283 **Here, where* 8
To hail the exploratory Bird renewing . . . . 360 **Near Anio's* 6

Renewing—*continued.*
Renewing, when the rosy summits glow — 617 *Desc.Sk.Quarto* 812
Empurpled hills, conspicuously renewing — 807 *Excursion* 4. 400
Renews. Eve renews her calm career; — 90 *Longest Day* 10
Both feel, when he renews the wished-for aid: — 378 *Duddon* 10. 10
The lonely Primrose yet renews its bloom, — 381 *Duddon* 22. 13
Renews. Througn every forest, cave, and den, — 435 *Ecc. Sonn.* 2. 27. 9
Long as the sun his gladsome course renews. — 534 *When in 20
Sole sound, the sourd renews his mournful cry: — 616 *Desc.Sk.Quarto* 755
Renounce. Pleased to renounce, does this dear Thrush attune — 279 *'Tis he 6
Of motion they renounce, and with the head — 508 *F. Stone* 37
Would tempt me to renounce that humble aim. — 521 *Epist.Beaumont* 37
Renounced. Nor for the world's best promises renounced. — 143 *High bliss 8
Forsook his crimes, renounced his folly, — 249 *P. B.* 1133
Renounced, abandoned by degenerate Men — 515 *Penn.* 12
"His sacred function was at length renounced; — 775 *Excursion* 2. 263
Are all renounced; high as the thought of man — 826 *Excursion* 5. 287
—Would I had ne'er renounced it!" A slight flush — 832 *Excursion* 5. 621
Renounces. Renounces, till among the scattered clouds — 461 *Who but is 4
Renouncing. Renouncing here, as worse than dead, — 298 *Brownie's Cell* 47
Renovated. A renovated spirit singled out, — 633 *Prelude* 1. 53
Restored to us in renovated health; — 752 *Prelude* 14. 426
Renovating. A renovating virtue, whence, depressed — 737 *Prelude* 12. 210
Renovation. Hope, and a renovation without end. — 173 *Infant Daughter* 65
When civic renovation — 233 *Power of Sound* 65
In annual renovation thus it stands— — 276 *Filial Piety* 12
A renovation from the dead, — 410 *White Doe* 1263
The glorious renovation would proceed. — 727 *Prelude* 10. 593
Power may be trained, and renovation brought — 831 *Excursion* 5. 585
What renovation had been brought; and what — 896 *Excursion* 9. 785
Renown. O genuine glory, pure renown! — 327 *Ode 1815* 45
Mirror of Princes! Indigent Renown — 425 *Ecc. Sonn.* 1. 26. 4
And Knights of high renown; — 478 *Somnamb.* 22
Whose boyish ear the voice of her renown — 504 *Warning* 57
To works that ne'er shall forfeit their renown, — 587 *Crosth.* 5
Of thy renown, from Cambrian mountains, fans — 627 *Eagle and Dove* 6
Womanhood in pure renown, — 629 *Installation* 49
Renown, if their presumption make them such? — 815 *Excursion* 4. 955
Meek and neglected thing, of no renown! — K.8. 250 *Recluse* 1.1.513
Renowned. *See* **Far-renowned.**
For many a marvellous victory renowned, — 18 *Desc. Sk.* 450
Now Ralph is renowned for the length of his bones; — 86 *Rural Arch.* 11
Or Roy, renowned through many a Scottish dell; — 255 *Detraction* 4
Renowned in Border story. — 302 *Yarrow V.* 56
For Tell's dread archery renowned, — 342 *Ital. Itin.* 60
From this appropriate Court renowned LUCERNE. — 350 *Des. Stanzas* 55
Though King or Knight the most renowned in story. — 373 *Eg. Maid* 318
Renowned in song and story, — 386 *Yarrow Rev.* 62
This People, once so happy, so renowned — 513 *General Fast* 11
A long posterity renowned, — 536 *Egremont* 111
Not mindless of that distant age renowned — 546 *The embowering 15
O seat of Arts! renowned throughout the world! — 655 *Prelude* 3. 458
Or scenes renowned for beauty, I explored — 677 *Prelude* 6. 191
Nor least, Heaven bless him! the renowned Lord Mayor: — 688 *Prelude* 7. 110
Felicity, in Grecian song renowned; — 701 *Prelude* 8. 135
Renowned for splendid prospect far and wide) — 776 *Excursion* 2. 322
Rent. Within that black and frightful rent. — 85 *Shepherd-boys* 66
There *was* he, where of branches rent and withered and decayed, — 91 *Norman Boy* 13
Was rent with lightning—one hath disappeared; — 97 *Brothers* 144
Rent, weeping over him, her golden hair — 169 *Love lies Bleeding* 16
To house and home in many a craggy rent — 275 *Chatsworth! thy 3
Where rocks were rudely heaped, and rent — 288 *Glen-Al.* 9
Towers rent, winds combating with woods, — 299 *Brownie's Cell* 63
Glad acclamation by which air was rent! — 312 *A Roman 6
If foresight could have rent the veil — 348 *Lulled by 19
Its shining forehead through the peaceful rent — 383 *Duddon* 31. 3
Or altar, whence the cross was rent, — 397 *White Doe* 124
Prying into the darksome rent; — 399 *White Doe* 256
Yielded by this craggy rent, — 550 *Hermit's Cell* 4. 6
With tens of thousands rent from off the tree — 582 *Invoc. Earth* 11
And in the narrow rent at every turn — 684 *Prelude* 6. 627
By violence, at one decisive rent, — 722 *Prelude* 10. 301
Like fields of ice rent by the polar wind, — 889 *Excursion* 9. 340
From his wife's Faro-bank a decent rent, — L.1. 97 *Juvenal* 3. 82
Rents. Then rents and factors, rights of chase, — 291 *Rob Roy* 69
Re-opened. Re-opened that inspired my youth; — 410 *White Doe* 1273
Repaid. Repaid thee for that sore distress — 294 *Jedbor.* 80
Rejected, or with slight repaid. — 407 *White Doe* 1019
And mounting spirit, pitiably repaid, — 656 *Prelude* 3. 501
Repair. Repair to Liddesdale, and tell the Band — 38 *Bord.* 41
Good Dame, repair to Liddesdale and wait — 46 *Bord.* 516
Yourself; and many did to him repair,— — 108 *Indolence* 53
Where she was childless, daily would repair — 120 *Emigrant Mother* 6
Wool for the Housewife's spindle, or repair — 132 *Michael* 107
He quickly will repair this loss, and then — 135 *Michael* 252
Did he repair, to build the Fold of which — 138 *Michael* 461
Do thou, as thou art wont, repair — 159 *With little 46
Eager to repair lost time; — 181 *Waggoner* 4. 86
Another could repair; — 191 *Seq. Beggars* 9
As I from Hawes to Richmond did repair, — 202 *Hart-leap* 101
Then, pensive Votary! let thy feet repair — 269 *Gordale* 4
Through reverence, touch it only to repair — 276 *Filial Piety* 10
Did mighty Tell repair of old— — 341 *San Salv.* 27
And thither young and old repair, — 396 *White Doe* 29

Repair—*continued.*
For the old Manx-harvest to the Deep repair, — 522 *Epist.Beaumont* 74
But chiefly to Smithfield he loves to repair,— — 571 *Farmer* 85
Who will gladly repair all the damage that's done; — 572 *Avarice* 43
And with a deep sadness I turned, to repair — 620 *Convict* 7
Its wasted splendour to repair, the door — 834 *Excursion* 5. 773
Repaired. He had repaired to ply a gainful trade: — 29 *Guilt* 254
To Calaterium's forest he repaired. — 103 *Artegal* 93
Repaired, but only found the matron there, — 125 *V. and J.* 290
Hither repaired.—A single beech-tree grew — 150 *When, to 18
But to his comrade he repaired, and prayed — 553 *Prioress* 74
After long absence, thither I repaired, — 642 *Prelude* 2. 37
Are nourished and invisibly repaired; — 737 *Prelude* 12. 215
My expectation, thither I repaired, — 738 *Prelude* 12. 296
To which I oft repaired, and thence would drink, — 739 *Prelude* 12. 325
Of long-continuing winter, he repaired, — 758 *Excursion* 1. 121
He broke from his contracted bounds, repaired — 774 *Excursion* 2. 215
Once every day he duteously repaired — 867 *Excursion* 7. 667
Repairs. Repairs to a road-side; — 194 *Ruth* 237
Repast. By fancy what a rich repast! — 285 *Grave of Burns* 57
Pleased looks around the delicate repast— — 525 *Epist. Beaumont* 241
The vulture, the inexhaustible repast — 846 *Excursion* 6. 541
Was spread, and we partook a plain repast. — 882 *Excursion* 8. 519
A choice repast—served by our young companions — 892 *Excursion* 9. 530
Repay. I but repay a gift which I myself — 136 *Michael* 363
Their union brought, will they repay the debt, — 143 *High bliss 26
That did your cares repay. — 155 *Waterfall* 30
Or to repay the potent Charm, — 221 *Triad* 100
The mighty debt which nothing can repay!" — 324 *Ode 1814* 68
Your scaly panoplies repay — 526 *The soaring 23
The laggard Rustic; and repay with boons — 773 *Excursion* 2. 123
Repayment. A just repayment, both for conscience-sake — 138 *Widow* 7
Repays. When earth repays with golden sheaves — 502 *Seasons* 9
Who repays in season due — 502 *Like a 47
Repealed. All past forgiveness it repealed; — 181 *Waggoner* 4. 180
The tidings passed of servitude repealed, — 312 *When, far 2
Care may be respited, but not repealed; — 455 *Not in the lucid 24
That flowing years repealed not: and distress — 811 *Excursion* 4. 648
Repeat. Three humble bells their rustic chime repeat; — 4 *Ev. Wk.* 139
Repeat her Father's terrible adventures, — 39 *Bord.* 93
To her these tales they will repeat, — 81 †*Mother's Return* 41
This song to myself did I oftentimes repeat; — 88 *Pet-lamb* 62
Again, and once again, did I repeat the song; — 88 *Pet-lamb* 65
He with a smile did then his words repeat; — 197 *Resolution* 120
Does she repeat that doleful cry?" — 198 *Thorn* 88
Repeat the bridal symphony. — 233 *Power of Sound* 40
And long the story will repeat — 297 *Highland Boy* 248
Hast heard the constant Voice its charge repeat, — 312 *Clarkson* 6
This vast design might tempt you to repeat — 335 *Cologne* 11
The Monks still repeat the tradition with pride, — 364 *Vallomb.* 9
Hear and repeat, the turmoil that unites — 382 *Duddon* 23. 6
Hope nothing, I repeat; for we — 402 *White Doe* 532
Of judgment such presumptuous doom repeat!) — 437 *Ecc. Sonn.* 2. 35. 3
The crags repeat the raven's croak, — 491 *Fidelity* 27
From Heaven, and *feel* what they repeat, — 530 *Gleaner* 32
The whilst the rest their anthem-book repeat — 553 *Prioress* 67
Doth the same tale repeat: — 588 *Immortality* 55
It might have well beseemed me to repeat — 668 *Prelude* 5. 177
This I repeat, was mine; mine be the blame. — 677 *Prelude* 6. 189
But I might here, instead, repeat a tale, — 717 *Prelude* 9. 547
Of tender feeling, she might dare repeat — 770 *Excursion* 1. 899
Life, I repeat, is energy of love — 837 *Excursion* 5. 1012
Nature (I but repeat your favourite boast) — 875 *Excursion* 8. 59
Repeat the dictates of her calmer mind, — 890 *Excursion* 9. 402
Take up, the cloud-capped hills repeat, the Name), — K.8. 238 *Recluse* 1.1. 58
Methinks I could repeat in tuneful verse, — K.8. 248 *Recluse* 1.1.413
Repeated. Repeated—heard, and heard no more! — 234 *Power of Sound* 160
Methinks, if audibly repeated now — 457 *Had this 16
Of that same Bard—repeated to and fro — 549 *The massy 7
By pleasure and repeated happiness, — 641 *Prelude* 1. 604
So frequently repeated, and by force — 641 *Prelude* 1. 605
Repeated through his tributary vales, — 699 *Prelude* 8. 13
Like earthquakes, shocks repeated day by day, — 712 *Prelude* 9. 179
Repeated o'er and o'er his plaintive cry, — 799 *Excursion* 3. 949
Old things repeated with diminished grace; — 829 *Excursion* 5. 436
Repeated without loss of simple phrase, — 851 *Excursion* 6. 889
A volley, thrice repeated o'er the Corse — 868 *Excursion* 7. 698
To be repeated thence, but gently sank — 892 *Excursion* 9. 536
Repeated; but with unity sublime! — 893 *Excursion* 9. 608
Repeated, like the whistling of a kite. — K.8. 229 *I will 167
Repeatedly. Repeatedly his own deep mind he sounds — 422 *Ecc. Sonn.* 1. 15. 11
Repeater's. Forbear to covet a Repeater's stroke, — 229 *Cuckoo-clock* 5
Repeating. Repeating the same timid cry, — 492 *Fidelity* 55
Repeating favourite verses with one voice, — 674 *Prelude* 5. 564
With each repeating its allotted prayer, — 862 *Excursion* 7. 304
His yell repeating; yet it was in truth — K.8. 245 *Recluse* 1.1.325
Repeats. Repeats a moan o'er moss and stone, — 162 *Binnorie* 58
Repeats but once the sound of thy sweet name: — 476 *Eden* 4
Repel. Why will ye thus my suit repel? — 130 *Idiot Boy* 343
And, rising to repel or to subdue, — 315 *And is it 3
No courage can repel the dire assault; — 322 *Humanity, delighting 33
That doth the living stars repel, — 397 *White Doe* 98
Than heartless misery called them to repel. — 420 *Ecc. Sonn.* 1. 9. 14
Yet not alone, nor helpless to repel — 441 *Ecc. Sonn.* 3. 4. 9
Even when they rose to check or to repel — 469 *The feudal 2
To welcome thee, repel the fears that crowd — 504 *Warning* 79

Repel—*continued.*
Armed to repel them ? Every hazard faced . . 541 *Grace Darl.* 76
And energy to conquer and repel— . . . . 848 *Excursion* 6. 664
Repelled. Thus far the Opposer, and repelled . . 412 *White Doe* 1455
Rejected, yea repelled ; and, if with scorn . . 840 *Excursion* 6. 121
Repelled the storm and deadened its loud roar. . 860 *Excursion* 7. 179
Repelling. The mortal spear repelling. . . . 287 *Ellen Irwin* 36
With objects wanting life, repelling love ; . . K.8. 253 *Recluse* 1.1.596
Repent. In this deserted Castle—*I repent me.* . . 54 *Bord.* 947
I *do* repent me, Sir ; I fear the curse . . . 54 *Bord.* 951
Yes, be it so ;—repent and be forgiven— . . 63 *Bord.* 1415
" Repent ! repent ! " he cries aloud, . . . 247 *P. B.* 946
" Repent ! repent ! though ye have gone, . . 247 *P. B.* 951
Then I repent not. But my soul hath fears . . 270 **If these* 7
" Make straight a highway for the Lord—repent ! " 365 **The Baptist* 14
He will repent him of his troth ; . . . . . 372 *Eg. Maid* 221
So may I hope, if truly I repent . . . . 464 **A point* 7
From further havoc, but repent in vain,— . . 504 *Warning* 71
Bitterly shall you repent, ... S.3. 438 **I, whose* 29
Repentance. Repentance is a tender Sprite ; . . 238 *P. B.* 148
To a sincere repentance promise grace, . . . 366 **Eternal Lord* 7
Till, by repentance stung, they fear to think ; . 513 *Newspaper* 5
For—save the calm repentance sheds o'er strife . 526 **Soon did* 8
Of meek repentance, wafting wallflower scents . 817 *Excursion* 4. 1047
On much repentance Grace will be bestow'd. . . K.8. 266 **Rid of* 5
Repentant. And while, repentant all too late, . . 370 *Eg. Maid* 69
His last, repentant breath ; and closed his eyes, . 843 *Excursion* 6. 364
Repenting. But, of his scorn repenting soon, he drew 231 **The gentlest Poet* 29
Repents. Oh ! it repents me I have neither wit . 562 *Cuck. and Night.* 302
Repetition. Strange repetition of the deadly wound 33 *Guilt* 491
A vivid repetition of the stars ; . . . . . . 313 **Clouds, lingering* 4
That with blunt repetition of your words . . . K.8. 230 **I will* 180
Repetitions. The repetitions wearisome of sense, . 810 *Excursion* 4. 620
Repine. That almost I could repine . . . . . 171 *Kitten* 107
Yet why repine, created as we are . . . . . 231 *Clouds* 92
Near the bright River's edge. Yet why repine ? . 335 *Rhine* 10
Then why repine that now in vain I crave . . 392 *Bothwell* 7
Lamenting, do not hopelessly repine . . . . 431 *Ecc. Sonn.* 2. 10. 9
Hush, not a voice is here ! but why repine, . . 454 *Sea-side* 33
Repine as if his hour were come too late ? . . 463 **Why should the* 2
—Vain thought ! but wherefore murmur or repine ? 863 *Excursion* 7. 387
Repine not for his cottage-comrade, whom . . 888 *Excursion* 9. 275
Repined. So lived I, and repined not at such fate : 575 *Chiabrera* 6. 9
But he repined not. Though the plough was scared 835 *Excursion* 5. 870
Repines. Yet he repines not, if his thought stand clear, ... 265 **There is a pleasure* 9
Repining. As many do, repining while they look ; . 250 *Admon.* 6
Without repining from the coves and heights . . 675 *Prelude* 6. 10
Not wishing more ; repining not to tread . . 790 *Excursion* 3. 304
Without repining or desire for more, ... 795 *Excursion* 3. 629
From trepidation and repining free. . . . . 866 *Excursion* 7. 583
Replace. That, were power granted to replace them (fetched . . . . 498 **Enough of climbing* 47
Replenished. For his hive had so long been replenished with honey, ... 570 *Farmer* 34
Upborne, at evening, on replenished wing, . . 807 *Excursion* 4. 398
For her defence, replenished with a band . . 839 *Excursion* 6. 56
From cups replenished by his joyous hand. . . 867 *Excursion* 7. 656
Replete. Replete with honour ; sounds in unison 742 *Prelude* 13. 184
Replete with vivid promise, bright as spring." . 831 *Excursion* 5. 557
Replied. The little Maid replied, ... 84 *We are Seven* 38
" I do not blame thee," Elidure replied ; . . . 104 *Artegal* 146
" Exalted Star ! " the Worm replied, ... 167 *Pilgrim's Dream* 33
To courteous Benjamin replied, ... 176 *Waggoner* 1. 257
Ere he replied, a flash of mild surprise . . . . 196 *Resolution* 90
A voice to which the hills replied ! . . . . . 400 *White Doe* 419
The elements have heard, and rock and cave replied. 457 **The leaves* 34
And thus the dear old Man replied, ... 487 *Fountain* 19
To that calm word a shriek replied, ... 579 **Sweet Flower* 44
Replied, and when the Charon of the flood . . 658 *Prelude* 4. 14
He would resume his story. He replied, . . . 765 *Excursion* 1. 625
These festive matins ? "—He replied, " Not loth . 773 *Excursion* 2. 140
" That poor Man taken hence to-day," replied . 780 *Excursion* 2. 593
Promptly replied—" My notion is the same. . . 789 *Excursion* 3. 233
The grey-haired Wanderer steadfastly replied, . . 802 *Excursion* 4. 67
" Methinks," persuasively the Sage replied, . . 813 *Excursion* 4. 779
Or power," replied the Wanderer, " to that House 824 *Excursion* 5. 99
The Priest replied—" An office you impose . . 832 *Excursion* 5. 658
Replies. The Turtledove replies : . . . . . . 168 *Turtledove* 4
Where lurks a Spirit that replies . . . . . 344 **How blest* 16
No voice replies ;—both air and earth are mute ; . 378 *Duddon* 8. 9
And Dacre to our call replies . . . . . . 408 *White Doe* 1135
Reply. The peasant, wild in passion, made reply . 33 *Guilt* 480
Then did the little Maid reply, ... 84 *We are Seven* 29
Quick was the little Maid's reply, ... 84 *We are Seven* 63
He blushed with shame, nor made reply ; . . . 86 *Anecdote* 46
And eased his mind with this reply : . . . . 86 *Anecdote* 54
On wings from broad and steadfast poise let loose by this reply, ... 92 *Poet's Dream* 29
And this was my reply :—" As it befell, . . . 147 *Joanna* 35
He ventured to reply. . . . . 155 *Waterfall* 20
The echoes make a glad reply.— . . . . . 180 *Waggoner* 4. 6
Unsolicited reply . . . . 209 **Yes, it* 5
Of midnight makes reply ; . . . . 223 *Wishing-gate* 69
All light and lustre. Did no heart reply ? . . 268 **Four fiery* 6
Yield to such after-thought the sole reply . . . 271 *George : Death* 11
The caves reply with hollow moan ; . . . . . 299 *Cora Linn* 4
The Council-roof and Clermont's towers reply ;— . 427 *Ecc. Sonn.* 1. 33. 11
And thus I made reply : . . . . 481 *Expost.* 16
To me he made reply : . . . . 486 **We walked* 20

Reply—*continued.*
His history, the veteran, in reply, ... 664 *Prelude* 4. 417
Came in reply, translated by our feelings, . . . 684 *Prelude* 6. 590
We spake—he made reply, but would not stir . 784 *Excursion* 2. 824
Stooped to this apt reply :—" As men from men . 818 *Excursion* 4. 1106
" Our nature," said the Priest, in mild reply, . . 829 *Excursion* 5. 485
—Blest as they are—to furnish a reply, . . . K.8. 255 *Recluse* 1.1.684
Report. And you remember such was my report : . 74 *Bord.* 2119
Who dares report, the tidings to the lord . . . 125 *V. and J.* 223
A good report did from their Kinsman come, . . 138 *Michael* 431
Making report of an invisible breeze . . . . 148 **A narrow* 23
And, if that men report him right, ... 205 *Brougham* 136
To reverend watching of each still report . . . 254 *Complete Angler* 5
Such bold report I venture to gainsay : . . . 271 **Fame tells* 5
With feet, hands, eyes, looks, lips, report your gain ; 322 **Ye Storms* 10
The bold report, transferred to every clime ; . . 325 *Ode 1814* 136
Report of storms gone by . . . . 329 *Ode : Thanks.* 24
Report of comfortless despairs, ... 338 **Meek Virgin* 10
Loud was the rifle-gun's report— . . . . . 342 *Ital. Itin.* 63
So fair, of such divine report . . . . . . 372 *Eg. Maid* 232
But you, at least, may make report . . . . 408 *White Doe* 1104
More could my pen report of grave or gay . . 525 *Epist. Beaumont* 270
Upon the exalted hills. He made report . . . 548 **Stay, bold* 20
So prayed he :—as our chronicles report, . . . 551 **If thou in* 24
Toils long and hard.—The warrior will report . 574 *Chiabrera* 4. 3
Though in virtue's proud mouth thy report be a stain, ... 621 *Convict* 50
Make rigorous inquisition, the report . . . . 634 *Prelude* 1. 148
Of good or ill report ; or those with whom . . 656 *Prelude* 3. 535
Or given upon report by pilgrim friars, . . . 688 *Prelude* 7. 82
Of record or report swept over us ; . . . . . 717 *Prelude* 9. 546
We sate—we walked ; he pleased me with report 757 *Excursion* 1. 63
Human and rational, report of thee . . . . 802 *Excursion* 4. 37
Led on, those shepherds made report of stars . . 812 *Excursion* 4. 709
The silent hours ; and who to that report . . . 813 *Excursion* 4. 802
Gathered this fair report of them who dwell . . 833 *Excursion* 5. 731
If living now, could otherwise report . . . . 835 *Excursion* 5. 884
The attempt was made ;—'tis needless to report . 841 *Excursion* 6. 176
In ears that relished the report ;—but all . . . 843 *Excursion* 6. 360
And feelingly the Sage shall make report . . . 877 *Excursion* 8. 222
Reportest. Have had, as thou reportest, miracles . 733 *Prelude* 11. 440
Reports. Reports of him, his dwelling or his grave ! 318 **Ah ! where* 2
(So fame reports) and die,—his sweet-breathed kine 340 *Ranz* 5
Or fountain, listen to the grave reports . . . 634 *Prelude* 1. 174
A mansion visited (as fame reports) . . . . 678 *Prelude* 6. 207
This covert nook reports not of his hand) . . . 788 *Excursion* 3. 177
Now she is not ; the swelling turf reports . . . 850 *Excursion* 6. 815
For, as reports the dame, whose fire sends up . K.8. 247 *Recluse* 1.1.389
Repose. In rocky basin its wild waves repose, . . 3 *Ev. Wk.* 58
And now the whole wide lake in deep repose . . 4 *Ev. Wk.* 124
And need repose. Could you but wait an hour ? 43 *Bord.* 360
Think of evening's repose when our labour was done, 116 *Repentance* 27
Where He that made them blesses their repose.— 143 **High bliss* 21
Her eggs within the nest repose, ... 168 *Wren's Nest* 27
United worship ; or in mute repose . . . . 185 *Yew-trees* 31
And now, too happy for repose or rest, . . . 201 *Hart-leap* 45
The day is come when I again repose . . . . 205 *Tintern* 9
And she expects the issue in repose. . . . . 209 *Laod.* 12
In languor ; or by Nature, for repose . . . . 219 *Haunted Tree* 14
A canopy, is smoothed for thy repose ! " . . . 221 *Triad* 79
That vision of endurance and repose. . . . . 226 *Vernal Ode* 47
In which some ancient Chieftain finds repose . . 262 **Mark the* 8
In Nature's face the expression of repose ; . . 272 *Lady E. B.* 4
And skies that ne'er relinquish their repose ; . . 272 *Devil's Bridge* 12
Gleams from a world in which the saints repose. . 282 **While beams* 14
Burst, when repose grew wearisome ; . . . . 298 *Brownie's Cell* 36
Repose at length, firm friend of human kind ! . 313 *Clarkson* 14
Sleep, Warriors, sleep ! among your hills repose ! 316 **It was a* 9
Through its wide circuit, that, in deep repose, . 323 *Ode 1814* 17
Where Spirits dwell in undisturbed repose— . . 349 *Sky-prosp.* 10
Friendly ; as here to my repose hath been . . 358 *Aquap.* 368
And folds thy pinions up in blest repose. . . . 363 **List—'twas* 112
The most profound repose his cell can give. . . 363 **Grieve for* 14
I repose, nor am forced from sweet fancy to part, 364 *Vallomb.* 30
On Laura's breast, in exquisite repose ; . . . 377 *Duddon* 7. 4
The still repose, the liquid lapse serene, . . . 381 *Duddon* 20. 4
If we advance unstrengthened by repose, . . . 382 *Duddon* 24. 3
Of valley flowers. Nor, while the limbs repose, . 390 *Glencroe* 9
Of female patience winning firm repose ; . . . 395 *White Doe : Ded.* 50
An undisturbed repose of heart. . . . . . 399 *White Doe* 319
In soft repose he comes. Within his cell, . . . 424 *Ecc. Sonn.* 1. 21. 7
Who near his fountains sought obscure repose, . . 431 *Ecc. Sonn.* 2. 13. 11
Where light and shade repose, where music dwells 451 *Ecc. Sonn.* 3. 43. 11
Hints to the thrush 'tis time for their repose ; . 455 *Rydal Mere* 2
In kindred quiet I repose my trust. . . . . 464 **A point* 4
And sound in principle, I seek repose . . . . 470 *Bala-Sala* 2
And, by that simple notice, the repose . . . 475 **There ! said* 7
Sequestered with repose ; . . . . 478 *Somnamb.* 38
Is empty of repose. . . . . 479 *Somnamb.* 81
In hermits' weeds repose he found, ... 479 *Somnamb.* 149
I long for a repose that ever is the same. . . . 492 *Duty* 40
Such the repose that sage and hero find ; . . . 495 *Fact* 38
Unheeded, and the mute repose . . . . . . 499 **This Lawn* 17
Or seems to charm it, into like repose ; . . . 508 *F. Stone* 9
To circumscribe this Shape in fixed repose ; . . 511 **Who rashly* 18
That yet disturb not its concealed repose . . . 524 *Epist. Beaumont* 169
Day-thoughts while limbs repose ; . . . . . 526 **The soaring* 50
To interrupt the deep repose ! . . . . . . 533 **Blest is* 30
For nurture or repose ; . . . . 543 *Russ. Fug.* 148

Repose—*continued.*
In dark-brown bason its wild waves repose, 592 *Ev. Wk. Quarto* 74
—'Mid the dark steeps repose the shadowy streams, 598 *Ev. Wk. Quarto* 339
There turns for glad repose the weary eye; 598 *Ev. Wk. Quarto* 366
The pie, and chattering breaks the night's repose. 606 *Desc.Sk.Quarto* 230
'Mid tumult and uproar this man must repose; 621 *Convict* 31
To more profound repose! 626 †*Cento* 16
That I recoil and droop, and seek repose 636 *Prelude* 1. 265
The safeguard for repose and quietness. 643 *Prelude* 2. 114
Of innocence, and holiday repose; 661 *Prelude* 4. 173
Assured that now the traveller would repose 665 *Prelude* 4. 453
Whose evening shadows lead him to repose. 682 *Prelude* 6. 516
Hushed in profound repose. We left the town 685 *Prelude* 6. 699
Appeared unfit for the repose of night, 719 *Prelude* 10. 92
And steadiness, and healing and repose 742 *Prelude* 13. 181
Which passeth understanding, that repose 748 *Prelude* 14. 127
Detained for contemplation or repose, 757 *Excursion* 1. 42
He asked repose; and, failing oft to win 760 *Excursion* 1. 293
At this still season of repose and peace, 765 *Excursion* 1. 594
Whose meditative sympathies repose 770 *Excursion* 1. 954
The universal instinct of repose, 792 *Excursion* 3. 397
Repose and hope among eternal things— 802 *Excursion* 4. 63
And sink at evening into sound repose." 808 *Excursion* 4. 504
With music lulled his indolent repose: 814 *Excursion* 4. 853
A grateful couch was spread for our repose; 821 *Excursion* 4. 1319
Obscurity, and undisturbed repose. 823 *Excursion* 5. 28
In their repose, the living in their mirth, 828 *Excursion* 5. 374
"And in your judgment, Sir! the mind's repose 831 *Excursion* 5. 560
Went with me to the place of my repose. 834 *Excursion* 5. 799
And end their journey in the same repose! 836 *Excursion* 5. 921
Its best attainment fits of such repose 849 *Excursion* 6. 739
To hope and love; to confident repose 873 *Excursion* 7. 1056
Might still preserve the beautiful repose 889 *Excursion* 9. 349
This plaintive note disturbed not the repose 892 *Excursion* 9. 559
Such the repose that Sage and Hero find, S.3. 427 **My Son* 9
Sunk down, and lay immersed in dead repose S.3. 434 **The doubt* 50
Of majesty, and beauty, and repose, K.8. 240 *Recluse* 1.1.143

Reposed. Reposed upon the block! 113 *Lament* 70
At which the bearers halted or reposed, 125 *V. and J.* 258
They, like a nested pair, reposed! 415 *White Doe* 1737
Too blindly have reposed my trust: 492 *Duty* 28
And in Death's arms has long reposed the Friend 525 **Soon did* 3
Where she in childhood had reposed, 542 *Russ. Fug.* 39
The day, in luxury my limbs repos'd, 613 *Desc.Sk.Quarto* 597
Reposed in noontide rest, the inner pulse 654 *Prelude* 3. 330
Flung from the setting sun, as they reposed 706 *Prelude* 8. 464
Upon that cottage-bench reposed his limbs, 762 *Excursion* 1. 437

Reposes. The eye reposes on a secret bridge, 3 *Ev. Wk.* 68
Brooding on her eggs reposes 166 *Wand. Jew* 23

Reposeth. Of rock or sand reposeth, there to sun itself; 196 *Resolution* 63

Reposing. On a friendly deck reposing 141 *Arm. Lady* 97
Reposing on a lone sick-bed; 144 **Driven in* 33
They lie like fawns reposing. 161 *Binnorie* 26
And hand reposing on the board in ruth 343 *Last Sup.* 11
Of Swains reposing myrtle groves among! 389 *Tyndrum* 3
Reposing here, and in the aisles beyond 496 **A little* 42
Then here reposing let us raise 506 *Lab. Hymn* 7
Upon her lap reposing, holds—but mark 509 *F. Stone* 54
Along the brighten'd gloom reposing deep. 607 *Desc.Sk.Quarto* 276
Amid reposing knights by a river side 634 *Prelude* 1. 173
Look down upon them; the reposing clouds; 700 *Prelude* 8. 66

Reprehend. Her froward mood, and softliest reprehend; 255 **Grief, thou* 4

Reprehended. And reprehended, by a fancied blush 539 **Lady! a* 38

Represent. Shall represent her labouring with an eye 330 *Ode: Thanks.* 73
Could represent the countenance horrible 574 *Chiabrera* 4. 11
Had dignified, and called to represent 640 *Prelude* 1. 524
Or more mechanic artist represent 691 *Prelude* 7. 248
Shaped by the Druids, so to represent 745 *Prelude* 13. 340

Representative. Of obscure feelings representative 641 *Prelude* 1. 606

Representing. Yet representing, amid wreck and wrong 510 **Among a* 5

Reprieve. The mind condemned, without reprieve, to go 13 *Desc. Sk.* 166
Perish without reprieve for flower or tree! 330 *Ode: Thanks.* 112
To fortitude without reprieve. 402 *White Doe* 545

Reproach. *See* **Self-reproach.**
And I divine the cause. Do not reproach me: 39 *Bord.* 132
None will reproach you, for our truth is known; 124 *V. and J.* 197
"Reproach me not—your fears be still— 238 *P. B.* 181
A contrast and reproach to gross delight, 263 **Those words* 3
From self-reproach, reproach that he must share 308 **There is a bondage* 8
And clears Oblivion from reproach, 391 *Highland Broach* 89
Glad Hearts! without reproach or blot; 492 *Duty* 13
Too full for that reproach. My aged Dame 659 *Prelude* 4. 64
Till with a sudden bound of smart reproach, 673 *Prelude* 5. 488
Which 'tis reproach to hear? Anon I rose 751 *Prelude* 14. 379
Who feels that to exhort is to reproach. 805 *Excursion* 4. 258
Bringing from age to age its own reproach, 827 *Excursion* 5. 316
She was to him a sickness and reproach. 855 *Excursion* 6. 1109
From all reproach is yon ethereal vault, K.8. 254 *Recluse* 1.1.641
By keen reproach or blind ingratitude, K.8. 325 [?] **The vestal* 5

Reproached. *See* **Self-reproached.**
There I reproached him with his treachery. 68 *Bord.* 1714
As Lear reproached the winds—I could almost 725 *Prelude* 10. 507

Reproaches. *See* **Self-reproaches.**
Reproaches from their lips are sent, 163 *Needlecase* 2
And haply meet reproaches too, whose power 641 *Prelude* 1. 623
Tender reproaches, insupportable! 798 *Excursion* 3. 855

Reproachful. 'Twas but one mild, reproachful look, 241 *P. B.* 436

Reproduce. *And reproduce the troubles he destroys.* 846 *Excursion* 6. 517

Reproof. With that reproof I do resign a station 78 *Bord.* 2320
No word of indignation or reproof, 125 *V. and J.* 266
Of fond correction and reproof bestowed 133 *Michael* 173
Apt emblem (for reproof of pride) 154 *Flower Garden* 43
Is murmuring a reproof, 168 *Turtledove* 10
I looked reproof—they saw—but neither hung his head. 191 *Beggars* 42
Their spirit; or, unless they for reproof 361 **When here* 12
This just reproof the prosperous Dane 495 *Fact* 15
Such as his state required. At this reproof, 665 *Prelude* 4. 457
But on the front of his reproof confessed 666 *Prelude* 5. 54
Some words of indirect reproof had been 719 *Prelude* 10. 105
Severe reproof, if we were men whose hearts 765 *Excursion* 1. 627
For the reproof of human vanity, 842 *Excursion* 6. 302
She stilled them with a prompt reproof, and said, 854 *Excursion* 6. 1045
Not for reproof, but high and warm delight, 863 *Excursion* 7. 385

Reprove. My torpor to reprove! 112 *Lament* 7
Who shall reprove thee! 159 **With little* 40
Life which the very stars reprove 192 *Gipsies* 23
Tread there with steps that no one shall reprove! 208 **It is no* 17
Presume those interweavings to reprove 220 *Triad* 20
The selfish to reprove. 223 *Wishing-gate* 30
Than tremblings that reprove 225 *Primrose* 34
Ye feelingly reprove; 225 *Present.* 45
Whose rage the gentle skies in vain reprove, 439 *Ecc. Sonn.* 2. 44. 8
Catching the lustre they in part reprove— 459 **Wanderer! that* 36
To check the erring, and reprove; 492 *Duty* 4
Yet, Beaumont, thou wilt not, I trust, reprove 525 *Epist. Beaumont* 274
In purpose join to hasten or reprove 773 *Excursion* 2. 122
The trailing worm reprove her thoughtless pride? 807 *Excursion* 4. 426
And with soft smile, his consort would reprove. 861 *Excursion* 7. 225
Shall I reprove myself? Ah no, the stream K.8. 244 *Recluse* 1.1.294

Reproved. Reproved his soarings of the night, 180 *Waggoner* 4. 80
Thus, all in vain exhorted and reproved, 212 *Laod.* 158
Profane Despoilers, stand ye not reproved, 283 **Well have* 13
Nor feel the fulness of that joy reproved? 504 *Warning* 52

Reptile. A very reptile could presume 167 *Pilgrim's Dream* 28
And harmless reptile coiling in the sun, 772 *Excursion* 2. 43

Reptiles. Yea, veriest reptiles have sufficed to prove 273 **When Philoctetes* 11

Republic. Of a Republic, where all stood thus far 713 *Prelude* 9. 226
Of a Republic. Lamentable crimes, 718 *Prelude* 10. 41
Life from the young Republic; that new foes 727 *Prelude* 11. 14
Leave this unknit Republic to the scourge 799 *Excursion* 3. 914

Republican. Republican or pious. If these thoughts 654 *Prelude* 3. 398

Repulsive. And a coarse outside of repulsive life 847 *Excursion* 6. 577

Repute. His stripling prime. A town of small repute, 121 *V. and J.* 10
This high repute, with bounteous Nature's aid, 515 *Penn.* 6

Reputed. Thou art reputed wise, but in my mind 104 *Artegal* 166

Request. When I gave way to your request; and now, 39 *Bord.* 134
This last request. You know me, Sire; farewell! 42 *Bord.* 295
But of his father begged, a last request, 125 *V. and J.* 267
Now promise, grant this one request, 410 *White Doe* 1308
For Matthew a request I make 486 *Matthew* 15
Fulfilment of his own request;— 577 **By playful* 12
Fixed on the Suitor; frustrate her request— 626 *Ballot* 10
Turned inward; or at my request would sing 757 *Excursion* 1. 66
No thanks he breathed, he proffered no request; 759 *Excursion* 1. 214
—But your compliance, Sir! with our request 836 *Excursion* 5. 891
Some farewell words—with one, but one, request; 841 *Excursion* 6. 202
The gladsome child bestows at his request; 881 *Excursion* 8. 496

Requested. As I requested; and hereafter, Luke, 137 *Michael* 404
And, as his Father had requested, laid 137 *Michael* 419

Requests. To which, requests were added, that forthwith 136 *Michael* 310

Requiem. A most melodious requiem, a supreme 261 *I heard (alas* 5
Am I deceived? Or is their requiem chanted 430 *Ecc. Sonn.* 2. 8. 9
Requiem which Earth takes up with voice undaunted, 430 *Ecc. Sonn.* 2. 8. 12
Come, and my requiem sing, 530 †*Redbreast* 14
That voice, ill requiem! seldom heard by me 723 *Prelude* 10. 327

Requiem's. Are not, in sooth, their Requiem's sacred ties 467 *St. Bees* 73

Requiems. And requiems answered by the pulse that beats 232 *Power of Sound* 15

Require. And all particulars that dull brains require 58 *Bord.* 1156
Of spirit too capacious to require 214 *Dion* 114
His father!—Him doth he require— 243 *P. B.* 641
More readily the more my years require 366 **Eternal Lord* 13
When I of thee require the same: 400 *White Doe* 408
Words that require no sanction from an oath, 515 *Penn.* 4
No rampart's stern defence require, 533 **Blest is* 7
Even as the heart's occasions might require, 708 *Prelude* 8. 642
Our present purpose seems not to require, 751 *Prelude* 14. 371
What from my fellow-beings I require, 800 *Excursion* 3. 958
Do, with united urgency, require, 802 *Excursion* 4. 78
Among us,—hence the more do we require 889 *Excursion* 9. 352
Impending evil, equally require 889 *Excursion* 9. 357
Must needs themselves be hallowed, they require K.8. 244 *Recluse* 1.1.278
More readily, the more my years require K.8. 266 **Rid of* 13

Required. Beholds, of all from her high powers required, 3 *Ev. Wk.* 82
In recompense for what themselves required. 65 *Bord.* 1528
With such allowance as his wants required; 125 *V. and J.* 270
Of night, my slaughtered Lord have I required[:] 209 *Laod.* 4
Lie in the means required, or ways ordained, 504 *Warning* 91
For much that truth most urgently required 585 *Ch. Lamb* 44

Required—*continued.*
Such as his state required. At this reproof, 665 *Prelude* 4. 457
The peace required, he scanned the laws of light 760 *Excursion* 1. 294
For the peculiar pains they had required, 767 *Excursion* 1. 726
Which appetite required—a blind dull nook, 783 *Excursion* 2. 746
That mine was a condition which required 792 *Excursion* 3. 424
Of mountain turf required the builder's hand 834 *Excursion* 5. 772
Even upon mine, the more are we required 846 *Excursion* 6. 529
Of the time-hallowed minstrelsy) required 857 *Excursion* 7. 21
Requires. To win belief, such as my plot requires. 44 *Bord.* 369
And every sacrifice his peace requires.— 50 *Bord.* 722
And from their secret loyalty requires 104 *Artegal* 104
No door the tenement requires, 168 *Wren's Nest* 5
Requires for nobler deeds; 479 *Somnamb.* 69
Lycoris! life requires an *art* 497 *Lycoris* 39
Survive not Judgment that requires his own? 518 *Pun. Death* 6. 14
Of vulgar nature; that its growth requires 742 *Prelude* 13. 189
With the few needful things that life requires. 777 *Excursion* 2. 357
—Come, labour, when the worn-out frame requires 802 *Excursion* 4. 57
And course of service Truth requires from those 810 *Excursion* 4. 596
Which the salvation of his soul requires. 895 *Excursion* 9. 737
Requiring. O'er high and low, and if requiring rest, 354 *Aquap.* 99
Requisites. Due requisites a perfect shepherd's staff, 134 *Michael* 183
For which peculiar requisites are mine; 832 *Excursion* 5. 659
Requital's. They know the dread requital's source profound; 520 *Pun. Death* 13. 5
Requite. And this good Man, whom Heaven requite, 248 *P. B.* 1064
Pains which the World inflicts can she requite? 280 **Intent on* 10
And that, so placed, my Nurslings may requite 281 *Valedict.* 6
It chastens only to requite 338 **Meek Virgin* 33
With gladness must requite Thee. 386 *Yarrow Rev.* 72
Requited. *See* **Ill-requited.**
And ill requited by this heartfelt sigh! 445 *Ecc. Sonn.* 3. 22. 14
And, in requited passion, all too much 863 *Excursion* 7. 368
Re-salute. I re-salute these sentiments confirmed 831 *Excursion* 5. 570
Rescue. Thee from bondage would I rescue 140 *Arm. Lady* 21
She could not rescue, perished in her sight! 274 **Wait, prithee* 14
"A rescue for the Standard!" cried 408 *White Doe* 1155
And to the tomb for rescue flies 544 *Russ. Fug.* 199
That thou wert near to rescue me; and now, 561 *Cuck.andNight.*228
New stores, or rescue from decay the old 633 *Prelude* 1. 117
Rescued. And the blind Man was told how you had rescued 42 *Bord.* 285
Many a captive hath she rescued, 94 *Westmoreland Girl* 55
Not wholly rescued from the pale 238 *P. B.* 187
The rescued Pine-tree, with its sky so bright 358 *Pine: Rome* 9
The rescued Maiden lay, 479 *Somnamb.* 137
And from Pagan chains had rescued, 536 *Egremont* 107
Was rescued by the Bard: 549 **In these* 5
And thou, O rescued Earth, by peace and love, 582 *Invoc. Earth* 33
Let rescued Europe tell the story. 628 *Installation* 18
I found its rescued inmate safely lodged, 785 *Excursion* 2. 882
And from debasement rescued.—By thy grace 802 *Excursion* 4. 50
Research. Severe research, that in our hearts we know 359 **Those old* 12
The deepest and the best, what keen research, 675 *Prelude* 6. 40
Lost in a gloom of uninspired research; 810 *Excursion* 4. 626
That meditation and research may guide 823 *Excursion* 5. 39
Re-seated. Re-seated on thy throne, 105 *Artegal* 207
Resemblance. Some new resemblance we may trace 164 **Fair Lady* 18
Whose countenance bore resemblance to the sun, 226 *Vernal Ode* 6
A livelier sisterly resemblance show 347 *Processions* 61
Resemblance of that glorious faculty 747 *Prelude* 14. 89
With brotherly resemblance. Turn your steps 809 *Excursion* 4. 553
With a resemblance not to be denied, 828 *Excursion* 5. 405
Of contrast and resemblance. To an oak 829 *Excursion* 5. 455
Are graced with some resemblance. Errant those, 875 *Excursion* 8. 45
Resemblances. Resemblances, or contrasts, that connect, 172 *InfantDaughter* 43
Stood fixed; and fixed resemblances were seen 784 *Excursion* 2. 864
Resemble. The Dames resemble whom we here behold, 333 *Fish-women* 5
Did most resemble him. Degrees and ranks, 872 *Excursion* 7. 988
Resembled. Resembled much that cold voluptuary, 42 *Bord.* 279
But that *their* state so much resembled ours, K.8. 243*Recluse* 1.1.252
Resembles. Where earth resembles most his own domain! 154 *Morn. Ex.* 52
To something that resembles an approach 656 *Prelude* 3. 519
Resembling. Delight resembling love. 527 **The soaring* 56
Is more poetic as resembling more 647 *Prelude* 2. 381
A mass of rock, resembling, as it lay 787 *Excursion* 3. 52
Resented. But not on high, where madness is resented, 582 *Invoc. Earth* 15
Resentment. By sharp resentment, or belike to taunt 718 *Prelude* 10. 35
Of a false prophet. While resentment rose 730 *Prelude* 11. 214
Or cherishing resentment, or in vain 772 *Excursion* 2. 69
Which anger and resentment could not dry. 783 *Excursion* 2. 804
Resentments. When all resentments were at rest, 411 *White Doe* 1424
Reserve. Behold! the mantling spirit of reserve 212 *Dion*
And wise reserve the plea of indolence— 310 *Invasion* 14
Patience and temperance with this high reserve, 319 **Avaunt all* 6
Without reserve to those whom we love well— 522 *Epist.Beaumont* 55
And why that scrupulous reserve? In sooth 539 **Lady! a* 10
From courtesy and delicate reserve; 583 **With copious* 12
Locks every function up in blank reserve, 635 *Prelude* 1. 246
Her just opinions, delicate reserve, 691 *Prelude* 7. 311
From play-house lustres thrown without reserve 692 *Prelude* 7. 346
Without reserve to them, the lonely roads 742 *Prelude* 13. 162
In slight of that forbearance and reserve 847 *Excursion* 6. 585
Without reserve descending upon both. 861 *Excursion* 7. 241
Casting reserve away, exult to see 877 *Excursion* 8. 200

Reserve—*continued.*
And answer flowed, the fetters of reserve 882 *Excursion* 8. 525
Without reserve or veil; and as a power 887 *Excursion* 9. 217
Reserved. Reserved, had fate permitted, for support 122 *V. and J.* 35
What need there is to be reserved in speech, 149 **A narrow* 72
She was reserved by me her life's betrayer; 372 *Eg. Maid* 236
And something, it might be, reserved for himself: 570 *Farmer* 38
For her, who (all too timid and reserved 791 *Excursion* 3. 343
More winningly reserved! If ye enquire 842 *Excursion* 6. 298
Reserves. Reserves for either, sure it is that both 888 *Excursion* 9. 282
Reservoir. But a terrific reservoir of guilt 725 *Prelude* 10. 477
Reservoirs. The sullen reservoirs whence their bold brood— 382 *Duddon* 26. 5
Residence. Within a world, a midway residence 656 *Prelude* 3. 521
Imperial, their chief living residence. 708 *Prelude* 8. 596
'Twixt her high-seated residence and his 716 *Prelude* 9. 490
Truth's consecrated residence, the seat 876 *Excursion* 8. 146
A residence afford them, 'mid the bloom 879 *Excursion* 8. 373
A settled residence, or be from far, K.8. 251*Recluse* 1.1.539
Residue. What are they but a wreck and residue, 350 *Des. Stanzas* 22
Residues. We love, but that the residues of flesh, S.3. 435 **The doubt* 117
Resign. With that reproof I do resign a station 78 *Bord.* 2320
O pleasant transit, Grasmere! to resign 284 *Departure* 19
Make haste, your morning task resign; 482 *Sister* 11
Will not unwillingly their place resign; 546 **The embowering* 2
I resign my soul's emotions 550 *Hermit's Cell* 4. 3
Make slow to feel, and by sure steps resign 567 *Cumb. Beg.* 94
Support us, teach us calmly to resign 576 **Six months* 5
"At thy name though compassion her nature resign, 621 *Convict* 49
Which now we too unwillingly resign 627 **The star* 8
For Nature called my Partner to resign 794 *Excursion* 3. 551
Resignation. The gentlest breath of resignation drew; 169 *Love lies Bleeding* 14
And hands in resignation prest, 397 *White Doe* 130
In resignation to abide 407 *White Doe* 1070
Of resignation find a hallowed place. 576 **By a* 22
A soul by resignation sanctified: 584 *Ch. Lamb* 31
Fearful; but resignation tempers fear, 813 *Excursion* 4. 798
With resignation; and no jarring tone 848 *Excursion* 6. 643
With resignation sink into the grave; 850 *Excursion* 6. 774
Due resignation. Therefore, though some tears 868 *Excursion* 7. 689
Resigned. When long familiar joys are all resigned, 19 *Desc. Sk.* 518
And, to a natural sympathy resigned, 28 *Guilt* 196
A thought resigned with pain, when from the mast 31 *Guilt* 354
Can feel his crimes. I have resigned a privilege; 53 *Bord.* 875
The breathless corse; then peacefully resigned 123 *V. and J.* 133
With many tasks that were resigned to thee: 137 *Michael* 392
Thy votaries, wooingly resigned 233 *Power of Sound* 86
Is Peter quietly resigned; 242 *P. B.* 572
To female hands the treasures were resigned; 264 **Lady! I* 9
Of business, care, or pleasure; or resigned 314 **I dropped* 5
Where the wild waves resigned their prey— 348 **Lulled by* 71
The sweets of earth contentedly resigned, 384 *Duddon* 33. 10
There lived, and on the cross His life resigned, 534 **When in* 14
When the poor heart has all its joys resign'd, 613 *Desc.Sk.Quarto* 622
And ask no record of the hours, resigned 635 *Prelude* 1. 252
A misery to him; and the Youth resigned 761 *Excursion* 1. 314
(Resigned with sadness gently weighing down 793 *Excursion* 3. 509
And He—to whom all tongues resigned their rights 883 *Excursion* 8. 594
To stern Plantagenet resigned her keys) L.I. 95 *Juvenal* 3. 2
Resigns. Where Machination her fell soul resigns, 617 *Desc.Sk.Quarto* 796
Resist. Till no one can resist him.—Now, even now, 124 *V. and J.* 203
If he resist that tempting door, 174 *Waggoner* 1. 74
If he resist those casement panes, 174 *Waggoner* 1. 76
Resist—the thunder quails thee!—crouch—rebuff 428 *Ecc. Sonn.* 1. 39. 9
Resistance. Admitting no resistance, bends alike 57 *Bord.* 1089
Resistance strong as heretofore, I thought 727 *Prelude* 11. 22
For onset, for resistance too inert, 791 *Excursion* 3. 344
Resistless. Stings to the quick, and, with resistless force, 519 *Pun. Death* 12. 3
Resolute. Wert kind as resolute, and good as brave; 210 *Laod.* 56
Till the arched roof, with resolute abuse 433 *Ecc. Sonn.* 2. 20. 12
Informed, were resolute to do his will, 436 *Ecc. Sonn.* 2. 30. 13
Resolute, at all hazards, to fulfil 514 **Blest Statesman* 8
Though young so wise, though meek so resolute— 541 *Grace Darl.* 95
Though resolute when duty called, 576 *Cenotaph* 2
But as a Pilgrim resolute, I took, 633 *Prelude* 1. 91
And, with a resolute mastery shaking off 730 *Prelude* 11. 238
Or by a resolute few who for the sake K.8. 256*Recluse* 1.1.719
Resolution. A resolution, or enlivening thought? 316 **It was a* 4
And resolution competent to take 862 *Excursion* 7. 330
Resolutions. With all my resolutions, all my hopes, 721 *Prelude* 10. 233
Decrees and resolutions of the Gods; 812 *Excursion* 4. 704
Resolve. Should he resolve to taint her Soul by means 56 *Bord.* 1058
Oh, Wisdom! a most wise resolve! and then, 58 *Bord.* 1143
Then pity crossed the path of my resolve: 77 *Bord.* 2265
Such was his first resolve; he thought again, 134 *Michael* 225
With that resolve he boldly mounts 243 *P. B.* 596
Power must resolve to cleave to it through life, 354 *Aquap.* 116
How no one can resolve; but every eye 426 *Ecc. Sonn.* 1. 29. 12
Abides by this resolve, and stops not there, 493 *Hap. War.* 10
And difficulty mastered, with resolve 541 *Grace Darl.* 77
Can guess the high resolve, the cherish'd pain 608 *Desc.Sk.Quarto* 360
A calm resolve of mind, firmly addressed 654 *Prelude* 3. 346
That mood, or undermine my first resolve." 781 *Excursion* 2. 617
A chip or splinter—to resolve his doubts; 789 *Excursion* 3. 182
Resolve,' the haughty Moralist would say, 817 *Excursion* 4. 1081
Grant to the wise *his* firmness of resolve!" 842 *Excursion* 6. 261

Retirement—*continued.*
In that retirement ; whither, by such course 833 *Excursion* 5. 732
Retirements. And mountainous retirements, only trod 809 *Excursion* 4. 516
Retires. Profounder quiet, when the fit retires, 26 *Guilt* 93
The wounded deer retires to solitude, 75 *Bord.* 2152
Now, risen ere the light-footed Chamois retires 345 *Stanzas:Simplon* 17
Where'er they rise, the sylvan waste retires, 429 *Ecc. Sonn.* 2. 3. 13
While, as one kindly growth retires, 507 *May* 63
Pale Passion, overpower'd, retires and woos 604 *Desc.Sk.Quarto* 118
Retiring. By chance retiring from the glare of noon 150 **When, to* 46
Never retiring, in thy large dark eyes, 525 *Epist. Beaumont* 255
Retiring or approaching from afar 716 *Prelude* 9. 448
Retold. That may not be retold to any ear. 59 *Bord.* 1199
Retorted. By the cloud-capt hills retorted ; 324 *Ode 1814* 62
Retrace. By Conscience governed do their steps retrace.— 443 *Ecc. Sonn.* 3. 14. 10
Dear Mother ! if thou *must* thy steps retrace, 516 **Young England* 12
Retrace the Grecian cunning from its source, 625 *Æneid* 140
Unvisited, endeavoured to retrace 642 *Prelude* 2. 2
'Tis not my present purpose to retrace 682 *Prelude* 6. 489
From risk and hardship, inwardly retrace 794 *Excursion* 3. 559
The good man's purposes and deeds ; retrace 863 *Excursion* 7. 376
Retraced. The Woman thus retraced her own untoward fate. 28 *Guilt* 198
In pure compassion she her steps retraced 34 *Guilt* 555
And it seemed, as I retraced the ballad line by line, 88 *Pet-lamb* 63
And here, O Friend ! have I retraced my life 651 *Prelude* 3. 167
Descending, have I faithfully retraced 732 *Prelude* 11. 372
A humbler destiny have we retraced, 748 *Prelude* 14. 136
In bleak December, I retraced this way, 769 *Excursion* 1. 855
Much less, retraced in words. If she, of life 796 *Excursion* 3. 681
The story that retraced the slow decline 854 *Excursion* 6. 1059
Be here retraced ;—enough that, by mishap 854 *Excursion* 6. 1088
Retracing. On tracing and retracing that large round, 218 *Recluse* 1. 1. 211
Retreads. Remorseless punishment ; and so retreads 827 *Excursion* 5. 327
Retreat. As by enchantment, an obscure retreat 3 *Ev. Wk.* 55
Felt the loose walls of this decayed Retreat 27 *Guilt* 173
Drove by the place of my retreat : three nights 69 *Bord.* 1772
Within this realm a place of safe retreat ; 104 *Artegal* 163
Their steps he followed to the Maid's retreat. 122 *V. and J.* 78
That a retreat might be assigned to him, 125 *V. and J.* 268
Sir Lancelot gave a safe retreat 180 *Waggoner* 4. 47
In some complaining, dim retreat, 288 *Glen-Al.* 13
And torn him from his loved retreat, 301 *Bran* 64
To whom all persecuted men retreat ; 327 *Ode 1815* 48
Near that Cell—yon sequestered Retreat high in air— 364 *Vallomb.* 6
O'er hill and valley to this dim retreat ! 382 *Duddon* 25. 8
Still pity to this last retreat 390 *HighlandBroach* 45
The footsteps of a quick retreat ; 406 *White Doe* 891
Then from within the embowered retreat 407 *White Doe* 1057
Is that the Sufferer's last retreat ? 413 *White Doe* 1561
Religion finds even in the stern retreat 430 *Ecc. Sonn.* 2. 6. 2
In their afflictions a divine retreat ; 438 *Ecc. Sonn.* 2. 40. 7
But, from the process in that still retreat, 456 **Soft as* 6
Oh may this work have found its last retreat 461 **Giordano, verily* 9
Has seduced the poor fool from his winter retreat, 484 **A plague* 9
Sends the pale Convict to his last retreat 520 *Pun. Death* 13. 3
The joy in that retreat 544 *Russ. Fug.* 218
Whom chance may lead to this retreat, 550 *Hermit's Cell* 2. 2
Should find an undisturbed retreat 580 **Sweet Flower* 62
Are paid to Him upon whose shy retreat 777 *Excursion* 2. 397
Retreat within retreat, a sheltering-place 778 *Excursion* 2. 446
The loneliness of this sublime retreat !" 806 *Excursion* 4. 372
Withdrew, and fixed me in a still retreat ; 823 *Excursion* 5. 53
Retreat, within this nook of English ground. 844 *Excursion* 6. 426
From sire to son, in this obscure retreat 872 *Excursion* 7. 943
A termination, and a last retreat, K.8. 240 *Recluse* 1.1.147
Their safe retreat. We knew them well, I guess K.8. 243 *Recluse* 1.1.246
Retreated. The snow hath retreated, 190 *March* 12
The tide retreated from the shore, 296 *Highland Boy* 154
Retreated towards a brake of thorn, 412 *White Doe* 1477
Retreating. Such retreating and advancing 180 *Waggoner* 3. 141
For gently each from each retreating 371 *Eg. Maid* 128
Retreats. Thy open beauties, or thy lone retreats ; 12 *Desc. Sk.* 108
True beauty dwells in deep retreats, 111 **Let other* 9
Devoutly, in life's last retreats ! 232 *Power of Sound* 16
Through the beloved retreats your arms enfold ! 283 **Proud were* 8
Subalpine vales, in quest of safe retreats 431 *Ecc. Sonn.* 2. 12. 6
For Gods in council, whose green vales, retreats 501 *Humanity* 74
When up the hills, as now, retreats the light, 595 *Ev. Wk. Quarto* 177
And lurking dimly in their shy retreats, 622 *Recluse* 1. 1. 123
As fierce a successor ; the tide retreats 719 *Prelude* 10. 81
In a few fortunate retreats like this ; 878 *Excursion* 8. 254
Retribution. Will retribution show itself again 55 *Bord.* 969
The power of retribution once was given : 325 *Enghien* 11
And final retribution,— 332 *Ode : Thanks.* 241
Fit retribution, by the moral code 519 *Pun. Death* 8. 1
Of vengeful retribution, theirs who throned 723 *Prelude* 10. 341
Glimpses of retribution, terrible, 724 *Prelude* 10. 452
Provoked a retribution too severe, S.3. 434 **The doubt* 83
Retrim. Their cheerfulness, and busily retrim 420 *Ecc. Sonn.* 1. 7. 2
Retrospect. For ever withered. Through this retrospect 679 *Prelude* 6. 286
Retrospective. The retrospective virtues. Festive songs 873 *Excursion* 7. 1037
Return. Binds her wild wreaths, and whispers his return. 18 *Desc. Sk.* 432

Return—*continued.*
And thou, lost fragrance of the heart, return ! 20 *Desc. Sk.* 531
Seemed to return, dried the last lingering tear, 30 *Guilt* 321
With strength did memory return ; and, thence 31 *Guilt* 399
That when, on our return from Palestine, 40 *Bord.* 192
Exacted thy return, and our reunion. 41 *Bord.* 204
For my return ; be sure you shall have justice. 46 *Bord.* 517
And no return have I to make but prayers ; 52 *Bord.* 826
This instant we'll return to our Companions— 66 *Bord.* 1589
But will return to you by break of day. 67 *Bord.* 1650
let us return, I can help you. 72 *Bord.* 1929
let us return to the spot ; 72 *Bord.* 2000
And she to-morrow will return ; 81 †*Mother's Return* 3
If e'er he should grow rich, he would return, 100 *Brothers* 323
On their return, they found that he was gone. 101 *Brothers* 372
Of weeds and flowers, till we return be slow, 107 *Farewell* 47
The sabbath's return ; and its leisure's soft chain ! 116 *Repentance* 28
Of future happiness. "You shall return, 124 *V. and J.* 189
He may return to us. If here he stay, 135 *Michael* 253
"Humble love in me would look for no return, 140 *Arm. Lady* 65
"Hie thee to the Countess, friend ! return with speed, 141 *Arm. Lady* 107
And when will she return to us ?" he paused ; 147 *Joanna* 24
Where, till the flitting bird's return, 168 *Wren's Nest* 26
The morning doth return." 194 *Ruth* 180
Of sense were able to return as fast 210 *Laod.* 69
Not seldom may the hour return 215 *Kirkstone* 51
Nor will return—but droop not, favoured Youth ; 222 *Triad* 213
Will to the road return ! 240 *P. B.* 350
To my most grievous loss !—That thought's return 257 **Surprised by* 9
The bright assurance, visibly return : 258 **Even so* 12
That winds into itself for sweet return. 284 *Departure* 32
Oh ! raise us up, return to us again ; 307 **Milton ! thou* 7
Return us to the dust from which we came ; 319 *Spaniard* 3
Due recompense, and safe return 342 *Ital. Itin.* 41
Were but the Gift a meet Return to thee 352 *H. C. R.* 6
Return, Content ! for fondly I pursued, 382 *Duddon* 26. 1
May Health return to mellow Age, 386 *Yarrow Rev.* 59
Return, and to her murmuring floods, 402 *White Doe* 561
And must in joy to her return. 403 *White Doe* 655
Their labours end ; or they return to lie, 430 *Ecc. Sonn.* 2. 8. 6
And usages, whose due return invites 448 *Ecc. Sonn.* 3. 33. 3
Since thy return, through days and weeks 507 *May* 25
Return, and sound the Horn, that we 535 *Egremont* 31
Shoot forth with lively power at Spring's return ; 546 **Ye Lime* 2
Constrain her heart as quickly to return, 563 *Troilus* 78
Doth yet again to God return ?— 581 **Loud is* 22
Are conscious ;—may the like return no more ! 582 *Invoc. Earth* 27
Return Delights ! with whom my road begun, 592 *Ev. Wk. Quarto* 27
Of pleasure ebbed but to return as fast 693 *Prelude* 7. 411
London, to thee I willingly return. 707 *Prelude* 8. 532
Or was departing never to return, 708 *Prelude* 8. 630
But to return out of its hiding-place 719 *Prelude* 10. 82
But from these bitter truths I must return 728 *Prelude* 11. 74
To feel it ;—but return we to our course. 731 *Prelude* 11. 258
She whispered still that brightness would return, 732 *Prelude* 11. 345
I saw the Spring return, and could rejoice, 735 *Prelude* 12. 33
Return upon me almost from the dawn 738 *Prelude* 12. 278
Though men return to servitude as fast 752 *Prelude* 14. 435
Where now we sit, I waited her return. 767 *Excursion* 1. 712
And infant's smile awaited my return. 794 *Excursion* 3. 583
So, wearied to your hut shall you return, 808 *Excursion* 4. 503
Thankful for my belovèd child's return. 812 *Excursion* 4. 748
And if heart-rending thoughts would oft return, 852 *Excursion* 6. 929
Deserve the least return of human thanks ; 870 *Excursion* 7. 829
And in return for sympathy bestowed 874 *Excursion* 8. 8
Ne'er to return ! That birthright now is lost. 878 *Excursion* 8. 282
If he can crawl, he will return again K.8. 228 **I will* 125
Return, Helvellyn's eagles ! with the pair K.8. 250 *Recluse* 1.1.518
We who behold thee ! But why *thus* return ? L.2. 318 *Frag. Æneid* 4. 7

Returned. And hope returned, and pleasure fondly made 25 *Guilt* 58
Even in the desert's heart ; but he, returned, 25 *Guilt* 66
You rushed into the murderous flames, returned 40 *Bord.* 179
Filled my dim eyes with tears.—When I returned 49 *Bord.* 684
When from the Holy Land I had returned 52 *Bord.* 828
When I returned with water from the brook, 59 *Bord.* 1181
That bore us through the water—— You returned 68 *Bord.* 1734
To his paternal home he is returned, 96 *Brothers* 68
Feebly returned by daunted Artegal ; 104 *Artegal* 123
Of war, had I returned to claim my right ; 104 *Artegal* 144
To what he saw, he gradually returned, 118 *Maternal Grief* 56
Upbraided him with slackness, he returned 125 *V. and J.* 231
Had to her house returned, the old Man said, 136 *Michael* 316
And to the house together they returned. 137 *Michael* 423
Soon returned a trusty Page 141 *Arm. Lady* 122
The snows dissolved, and genial Spring returned 150 **When, to* 43
And are returned into themselves, they cannot but be sad ? 189 *Star-gazers* 20
My former thoughts returned : the fear that kills ; 197 *Resolution* 113
Returned, to seek a Consort upon earth ; 220 *Triad* 4
Returned to animate an age forlorn ? 314 *Hofer* 4
Given with a voice and by a look returned 353 *Aquap.* 31
Within him, instantly returned : 410 *White Doe* 1255
And when she from the abyss returned 416 *White Doe* 1821
But to the world returned no more, 416 *White Doe* 1860
And oft returned, again, and yet again. 535 *Egremont* 56
Beheld their only Child returned 545 *Russ. Fug.* 359
Threw back my eyes, return'd, and gazed again. 618 *School Ex.* 26
Or centre of these sports ; and when, returned 642 *Prelude* 2. 36

Richly—*continued.*
Yet richly graced with honours of her own, . . 691 *Prelude* 7. 266
Of wedlock richly crowned with Heaven's regard, 825 *Excursion* 5. 197
The cornice, richly fretted, of grey stone ; . . . 881 *Excursion* 8. 467
Richly-laden. Whence they, like richly-laden merchants, come . . . . 425 *Ecc. Sonn.* 1. 25. 5
Richmond. As I from Hawes to Richmond did repair, 202 *Hart-leap* 101
For I have heard the quire of Richmond hill . . 271 **Fame tells* 6
Rick. And once, behind a rick of barley, . . . 537 *Goody Blake* 73
Rid. The plot to rid themselves, at any cost, . . 69 *Bord.* 1758
Ye who are longing to be rid . . . . . . 234 *Power of Sound* 154
To rid the world of nuisances ; ye proud, . . . 567 *Cumb. Beg.* 70
Was busier with his task—to rid, to plant, . . 860 *Excursion* 7. 194
Rid of a vexing and a heavy load, ... K.8. 265 **Rid of* 1
From this curst Pharaoh-plague to rid the land ? L.1. 88 *Juvenal* 1. 16
Ridden. The Knight had ridden down from Wensley Moor . . . . 200 *Hart-leap* 1
Riddle. We've solved the riddle—Miscreant ! Do you, ... 46 *Bord.* 515
And there's a riddle to be guessed, ... 143 **Driven in* 22
Dark as a riddle, prove a favourite theme ; . . . K.8. 301 **And oh* 6
Ride. The spirit of vengeance seemed to ride the air. 51 *Bord.* 794
And there will safely ride when we are gone ; . 106 *Farewell* 10
On which her Idiot Boy must ride, ... 126 *Idiot Boy* 70
The horsemen-travellers ride. . . . . . . 194 *Ruth* 240
When Jesus humbly deigned to ride, ... 247 *P. B.* 977
Come boats and ships that safely ride . . . . 295 *Highland Boy* 67
Does yet the unheard-of vessel ride the wave ? . 318 **Ah ! where* 3
And to the battle ride. . . . . 321 **Humanity, delighting* 31
All horsed and harnessed with him to ride,— . . 400 *White Doe* 418
And through this street who list might ride and wend ; . . . . 553 *Prioress* 41
And on his purpose bent so fast to ride, . . . 563 *Troilus* 20
Yonder I saw her to her Father ride, ... 564 *Troilus* 94
Oh give, great God, to Freedom's waves to ride . 617 *Desc.Sk.Quarto* 792
To ride the ring, or toss the beamy lance ; . . 619 *School Ex.* 58
After the perils of his moonlight ride, ... 752 *Prelude* 14. 405
Or ride at anchor in her sounds and bays ; . . . 876 *Excursion* 8. 138
Rides. He rides over the water, and over the snow, 80 †*Address : Child* 2
Sweeps his harp, the Master rides ; . . . . . 234 *Power of Sound* 141
Rides forth, an armèd man, and hurls a spear . 422 *Ecc. Sonn.* 1. 17. 3
Behind her hill the Moon, all crimson, rides, . . 606 *Desc.Sk.Quarto* 235
Rides high ; then all the upper air they fill . . 782 *Excursion* 2. 701
Rides to and fro : I know them and their ways. . K.8. 250 *Recluse* 1.1.509
Rideth. Forth from the spot he rideth up and down, 563 *Troilus* 43
Ridge. Like an untended watch-fire, on the ridge . v **If thou indeed* 10
Half grey, half shagged with ivy to its ridge ; . 3 *Ev. Wk.* 69
That I may see him. On a ridge of rocks . . 73 *Bord.* 2053
Risen from his seat, beside the snow-white ridge . 95 *Brothers* 31
Beneath yon ridge, the last of those three graves ? 98 *Brothers* 198
Forth from a jutting ridge, around whose base . 151 **Forth from* 1
Mount to the ridge of Nathdale Fell ; . . . . 180 *Waggoner* 4. 37
" High on a mountain's highest ridge, ... 197 *Thorn* 23
Ridge, and gulf, and distant ocean . . . . . 217 **Inmate of* 15
At the spectator's feet.—Yon azure ridge, . . 219 **This Height* 23
Sweeps now along this elevated ridge ; . . . 220 *Haunted Tree* 31
It found no barrier on the ridge . . . . . 327 *Ode 1815* 21
Arch that *here* rests upon the granite ridge . . 350 *Des. Stanzas* 30
O'er which his Fathers urged, to ridge and steep . 380 *Duddon* 16. 10
Beside the ridge of a grassy grave . . . . . 397 *White Doe* 141
Above the loftiest ridge or mound . . . . . 409 *White Doe* 1165
Soft as a cloud is yon blue Ridge—the Mere . . 456 **Soft as* 1
Of some smooth ridge, whose brink precipitous . 496 **A little* 26
And mountain-tops, a barren ridge we scale ; . . 524 *Epist. Beaumont* 224
Beneath yon eastern ridge, the craggy bound, . . 547 **Beneath yon* 1
While on the perilous ridge I hung alone, . . . 637 *Prelude* 1. 336
Upon the summit of a craggy ridge, ... 637 *Prelude* 1. 370
Was crossed, a bare ridge clomb, upon whose top 658 *Prelude* 4. 3
And crept along a ridge of fractured wall, . . . 678 *Prelude* 6. 214
From a bare ridge we also first beheld . . . . 683 *Prelude* 6. 524
In silent beauty on the naked ridge . . . . 706 *Prelude* 8. 465
Upon smooth Quantock's airy ridge we roved . . 751 *Prelude* 14. 396
Was one small opening, where a heath-clad ridge . 776 *Excursion* 2. 335
Till, chancing on that lofty ridge to pass . . . 784 *Excursion* 2. 811
Of that brown ridge, sole outlet of the vale . . 822 *Excursion* 5. 12
Ridge rising gently by the side of ridge, . . . 847 *Excursion* 6. 606
And from her grave.—Behold—upon that ridge, . 855 *Excursion* 6. 1116
The ridge itself may sink into the breast . . . 868 *Excursion* 7. 711
In cyphers on Helvellyn's highest ridge, . . . K.8. 226 **I will* 64
Crams through the arch, and bellies o'er the ridge ? L.1. 95 *Juvenal* 3. 26
Ridges. Tip their smooth ridges with a softer ray ; 4 *Ev. Wk.* 123
Which a thousand ridges yield ; . . . . . 217 **Inmate of* 14
The ridges of grim war ; and at their head . . 320 **They seek* 4
Yon hazy ridges to their eyes . . . . . . 457 **Had this* 43
Of all her peaks and ridges. What he draws . . 468 **Ranging the* 6
Varying her crowded peaks and ridges blue ; . . 471 **Arran ! a* 3
No ridges there appeared of clear black mould, . 769 *Excursion* 1. 836
From mountain ridges peeping as they passed . K.8. 225 **I will* 36
Ridicule. Keen ridicule ; the majesty proclaims 695 *Prelude* 7. 525
Objects of sport, and ridicule, and scorn, . . . 706 *Prelude* 8. 498
Not unamused.—But ridicule demands . . . 799 *Excursion* 3. 902
Who penned, to ridicule confiding faith, . . . 816 *Excursion* 4. 1006
Ridiculous. Of the ridiculous ; not blind is he . . 670 *Prelude* 5. 311
Riding. Less fair is summer riding high . . . . 502 *Seasons* 5
While riding near her home one stormy night 622 **Among all* 5
Riding-coat. That day he wore a riding-coat, . . 537 *Goody Blake* 109
Ridley. See Latimer and Ridley in the might . . 437 *Ecc. Sonn.* 2. 34. 2
Rife. Watchwords of Party, on all tongues are rife ; 443 *Ecc. Sonn.* 3. 11. 10
Condemn'd, in mists and tempests ever rife, . . 613 *Desc.Sk.Quarto* 592

Rife—*continued.*
Were rife about him as the songs of birds . . . 692 *Prelude* 7. 364
Rifled. Lady ! I rifled a Parnassian Cave . . . 264 **Lady ! I* 1
Rifle-gun's. Loud was the rifle-gun's report— . . 342 *Ital. Itin.* 63
Rifles. That rifles blossoms on a tree, ... 221 *Triad* 126
Rift. All meek and silent, save that through a rift— 747 *Prelude* 14. 56
Rifted. Cowering beside her rifted cell, ... 175 *Waggoner* 1. 176
To dwell these rifted rocks between, ... 232 *Jew. Fam.* 11
Enfolds her ?—is a rifted tomb . . . . . . 413 *White Doe* 1558
Or from a rifted crag or ivy tod . . . . . . 456 **The leaves* 20
Of vagrant poverty ; from rifted barns . . . 843 *Excursion* 6. 326
Righi's. On Righi's silent brow. . . . . . . 348 **Lulled by* 66
Right. You have guessed right. The trees renew their murmur : . . . . 53 *Bord.* 868
Twelve honest men, plain men, would set us right ; 53 *Bord.* 882
" She is right willing—strange if she were not !— 59 *Bord.* 1189
Yes, you are right, we need not hunt for motives : 63 *Bord.* 1435
Right in the slates, and with a huge rattle . . 81 †*Address : Child* 30
Right opposite to Dungeon-Ghyll, ... 85 *Shepherd-boys* 39
Right towards the lamb she looked ; and from a shady place . . . . 87 *Pet-lamb* 17
Preserve for thee, by individual right, ... 88 *H. C.* 23
Of war, had I returned to claim my right ; . . . 104 *Artegal* 144
Would balance claim with claim, and right with right ? . . . . 105 *Artegal* 171
And sorrow, have confirmed thy native right to reign. . . . . 105 *Artegal* 209
Sweet heaven forefend ! his was a lawful right ; . 108 *Indolence* 46
Yea, his first word of greeting was,—" All right . 124 *V. and J.* 156
How turn to left, and how to right. . . . . 126 *Idiot Boy* 56
He's at the guide-post—he turns right ; . . . 127 *Idiot Boy* 94
His steed and he right well agree ; . . . . . 127 *Idiot Boy* 107
And while these right affections play, ... 143 †*Lov. and Lik.* 59
Whole Summer-fields are thine by right ; . . . 157 **In youth* 13
Some chime of fancy wrong or right ; . . . . 158 **In youth* 47
Right onward to the Scottish strand . . . . 161 *Binnorie* 16
Away they fly to left, to right— . . . . . 161 *Binnorie* 29
They are happy, for that is their right ! . . . 167 *Stray Pleasures* 36
The Horses have worked with right good-will, . 174 *Waggoner* 1. 40
The place to Benjamin right well . . . . . 174 *Waggoner* 1. 83
Right gladly had the horses stirred, ... 178 *Waggoner* 3. 1
" And now, as fitting is and right, ... 193 *Ruth* 103
Of blessed Angels crowned the right. . . . . 204 *Brougham* 29
Rejoiced is Brough, right glad, I deem, . . . 204 *Brougham* 44
And, if that men report him right, ... 205 *Brougham* 136
Intent to trace the ideal path of right . . . . 213 *Dion* 50
Right at the imperial station's western base, . . 219 **This Height* 13
Ye did not forfeit one dear right, ... 223 *Wishing-gate* 14
Presentiments ! they judge not right . . . . 225 *Present.* 1
Right through the quarry ;—and behold . . . 240 *P. B.* 361
Right in the middle of the thicket ; . . . . 243 *P. B.* 622
As if to vindicate her beauty's right, ... 265 **The Shepherd* 7
When to the consciousness of right . . . . . 286 *Nith* 21
And seemed to give me spiritual right . . . . 289 *Stepping West.* 15
" Since, then, the rule of right is plain, . . . 291 *Rob Roy* 53
And battled for the Right. . . . . 292 *Rob Roy* 108
Both lying right before us ; . . . . 292 *Yarrow Unv.* 18
No right had he but what he made . . . . . 298 *Brownie's Cell* 43
Of a just God for liberty and right. . . . . 309 **What if* 14
That by our own right hands it must be wrought ; 310 **Another year* 7
And daring not to feel the majesty of right ! . . 311 **Who rises* 45
Fixed as a star : such glory is thy right. . . . 317 **Brave Schill* 8
Of virtuous hope, of liberty, and right, . . . 317 **Look now* 3
Of martyrdom, and fortitude, and right. . . . 318 **Ah ! where* 10
Ne'er saw a race who held, by right of birth, . . 325 **Intrepid sons* 3
Upon the future advocates of right ; . . . . 332 *Ode : Thanks.* 237
Of right and wrong, of weal and woe, ... 337 **Oh Life* 2
On Sarnen's Mount, there judge of fit and right, . 350 *Des. Stanzas* 51
And prospect right below of deep coves shaped . 353 *Aquap.* 43
In Percy's and in Neville's right, ... 400 *White Doe* 367
I, by the right of eldest born, ... 401 *White Doe* 484
For holy Church, and the People's right ! " . . 403 *White Doe* 634
Was on his right, from that guardian hand . . 403 *White Doe* 657
And find, find anywhere, a right . . . . . 411 *White Doe* 1399
To o'ershadow by no native right . . . . . 413 *White Doe* 1601
He only judges right who weighs, compares, . . 429 *Ecc. Sonn.* 2. 1. 12
And Heaven will crown the right."—The mitred Sire . . . . 432 *Ecc. Sonn.* 2. 15. 9
To trace right courses for the stubborn blind, . . 438 *Ecc. Sonn.* 2. 40. 13
Furrowing its way right onward. The most rude, 460 **Wanderer ! that* 52
And I for five centuries right gladly would be . 482 *Character* 19
And at the word right gladly he . . . . . 484 *Simon Lee* 83
A rosy Man, right plump to see ? . . . . . 485 *Poet's Epitaph* 10
Matter wherein right voluble I am, ... 488 *Pers. Talk* 38
Doth seldom on a right foundation rest, . . . 493 *Hap. War.* 32
Of Ocean, press right on ; or gently wind, . . 495 *Fact* 41
Of right affections climbing or descending . . . 500 *Humanity* 28
Will not be found. Her right hand, as it lies . 509 *F. Stone* 52
Right gladly answering signals we displayed, . . 524 *Epist. Beaumont* 213
But most the Bard is true to inborn right, . . 528 **Those breathing* 81
Who of right had held the Lordship . . . . 535 *Egremont* 11
So were both right well content : . . . . . 535 *Egremont* 37
He is come to claim his right : . . . . . . 536 *Egremont* 82
Right glad was he when he beheld her : . . . 537 *Goody Blake* 81
—There, though by right the excelling Painter sleep . . . . 547 **Ye Lime* 9
They pruned themselves, and made themselves right gay, ... 558 *Cuck. and Night.* 76
And that was right upon a tree fast by, . . . 558 *Cuck. and Night.* 91
Methought I wist right well what these birds meant, 558 *Cuck. and Night.* 108

Right—*continued.*

And, God of Love, that can right well and may, . 561 *Cuck.andNight.*253
And now I pray you all to do me right . . . 561 *Cuck.andNight.*269
And they right forth to Cresid's Palace went ; . 562 *Troilus* 10
I am right sorry Troilus will die : . . . . . 564 *Troilus* 109
And that the sun did take his course not right, . 564 *Troilus* 143
Where gold determines between right and wrong. 573 *Chiabrera* 2. 4
This to the dead by sacred right belongs ; . . . 576 *Chiabrera* 9. 5
Yea, appertained by a peculiar right . . . . 645 *Prelude* 2. 196
Right underneath, the College kitchens made . . 649 *Prelude* 3. 49
To wilful alienation from the right, ... 653 *Prelude* 3. 323
The head turns round and cannot right itself ; . 658 *Prelude* 3. 623
To see again, was one by ancient right . . . 659 *Prelude* 4. 94
Right to a rough stream's edge, and there broke off ; 683 *Prelude* 6. 569
Paid to the object by prescriptive right. . . . 689 *Prelude* 7. 148
And continence of mind, and sense of right, . . 715 *Prelude* 9. 388
Arbiter undisturbed of right and wrong, . . . 721 *Prelude* 10. 184
That nothing hath a natural right to last . . . 721 *Prelude* 10. 205
Humanity and right, *that* Robespierre, . . . 725 *Prelude* 10. 500
Yea, could not but be right, because we saw . . 728 *Prelude* 11. 51
To turn *all* judgments out of their right course ; . 728 *Prelude* 11. 56
As if they had within some lurking right . . . 729 *Prelude* 11. 131
That time was ready to set all things right, . . 730 *Prelude* 11. 192
With impulse, motive, right and wrong, the ground 731 *Prelude* 11. 299
Upon my right hand couched a single sheep, . . 738 *Prelude* 12. 300
And image of right reason ; that matures . . . 740 *Prelude* 13. 22
My sense of excellence—of right and wrong : . . 740 *Prelude* 13. 58
Never did I, in quest of right and wrong, . . . 748 *Prelude* 14. 150
Honour and shame, looking to right and left, . . 751 *Prelude* 14. 338
Right in the midst, where interspace appeared . 784 *Excursion* 2. 861
Right at the foot of that moist precipice, . . . 787 *Excursion* 3. 53
Established seemingly a right to hold . . . . 795 *Excursion* 3. 623
Right to expect his vigorous decline, ... 828 *Excursion* 5. 388
By right of birth ; within whose spotless breast . 844 *Excursion* 6. 414
—Right toward the sacred Edifice his steps . . 871 *Excursion* 7. 911
Of common right or interest in the end ; . . . 886 *Excursion* 9. 118
This sacred right, the lisping babe proclaims . . 888 *Excursion* 9. 311
—This sacred right is fruitlessly announced, . . 889 *Excursion* 9. 321
Of the still evening. Right across the lake . . 892 *Excursion* 9. 560
Right before the Farmer's door . . . . . . S.3. 423 *Tinker* 9
Right good ale he bowses ; . . . . S.3. 423 *Tinker* 15
Of ocean press right on, or gently wind, . . . S.3. 427 **My Son* 12
Critics, right honourable Bard, decree . . . . S.3. 432 **Critics, right* 1
And Fairfield's highest summit, on the right . . K.8. 225 **I will* 24
Right in the middle of the roaring stream. . . K.8. 229 **I will* 173
Right gladly would I lie awake . . . . . . K.8. 262 **Ah! if* 3
Good honest souls !—if right my judgment lies . L.1. 95 *Juvenal* 3. 20

Righteous. And therefore leave thee to a righteous judgment. . . . . 63 *Bord.* 1407
Upon Heaven's righteous judgment, did become . 76 *Bord.* 2211
All neighbouring countries through his righteous sway ; . . . . 103 *Artegal* 69
That this great Servant of a righteous cause . . 317 **Call not* 10
Of righteous Vengeance side by side appear, . . 318 **Is there* 8
And for Thy righteous purpose they prevail ; . . 328 *Ode 1815* 109
Have chased far off by righteous victory . . . 427 *Ecc. Sonn.* 1. 33. 7
If thou hast fallen, and righteous Heaven restore 440 *Ecc. Sonn.* 3. 2. 12
To righteous Gods when man has ceased to feel, . 500 *Humanity* 2
Exclaimed he : " righteous Heaven, ... 545 *Russ. Fug.* 330
For righteous triumphs are the base . . . . 629 *Installation* 39
The city of Timoleon ! Righteous Heaven ! . . 732 *Prelude* 11. 379
" That righteous cause (such power hath freedom) bound, ... 775 *Excursion* 2. 227
To see the moment, when the righteous cause . 806 *Excursion* 4. 311
Cause should recur, which righteous Heaven avert ! 839 *Excursion* 6. 60
And fear of him who is a righteous judge ; . . 851 *Excursion* 6. 873
With righteous Joshua ; nor appeared in arms . 870 *Excursion* 7. 813

Righteously. Yet trained to judgments righteously severe, ... 326 **The Bard* 2

Righteousness. The towers of righteousness ; . . 329 *Ode : Thanks.* 50
To Christ, the Sun of righteousness, espoused. . 496 **A little* 48
Works not the righteousness of God ? Oh bend, . 514 **Portentous change* 10
Of righteousness, of sins forgiven, ... 577 **By playful* 21
March firmly towards righteousness and peace."— 727 *Prelude* 10. 589
Fallacious, or shall righteousness obtain . . . 894 *Excursion* 9. 664

Rightful. Gorbonian's first-born son, your rightful king restored ! " . . . . 105 *Artegal* 225
Where sits in state our rightful Lord, ... 204 *Brougham* 22
The heroes bless him, him their rightful son. . . 305 **The Voice* 14
In vain who, for a rightful cause, give breath . 448 *Ecc. Sonn.* 3. 30. 9
Shall be thy rightful name, in prose and rhyme ! 464 **They called* 14
Save He who came as rightful Heir . . . . 535 *Egremont* 7
Firm Independence, Bounty's rightful sire ; . . 584 *Ch. Lamb* 9
With a due reverence on earth's rightful lord, . 704 *Prelude* 8. 335
And rightful government subverted, found . . 825 *Excursion* 5. 192

Rightfully. Have rightfully been laid at last . . 288 *Glen-Al.* 8
Taught us how rightfully a nation shone . . . 307 **Great men* 7
Rightfully borne ; for Nature gives thee flowers 476 *Eden* 6

Rightlier. Or were ye rightlier hailed, when first mine eyes . . . . 229 *Clouds* 11

Rightly. Nor seldom, if I rightly guess, while Thou, 151 **When, to* 98
Which only Poets know ;—'twas rightly said ; . . 265 **There is a pleasure* 2
And, therefore, was it rightly said . . . . . 289 *Glen-Al.* 30
Sweet Nymph, O rightly of the mountains named ! 314 **Advance—come* 3
And one brief day is rightly set apart . . . . 330 *Ode : Thanks.* 88
And why shouldst thou ?—If rightly trained and bred, ... 390 *Highland Hut* 6
As one who rightly taught how zeal should burn, 444 *Ecc. Sonn.* 3. 15. 12
Awaits you then, if they were rightly taught . . 444 *Ecc. Sonn.* 3. 16. 13

Rightly—*continued.*

And knowledge, rightly honoured with that name— 672 *Prelude* 5. 424
So different, may rightly be compared), . . . 677 *Prelude* 6. 156
All gratulant, if rightly understood. . . . . 751 *Prelude* 14. 387
Of hopeful nature. Rightly it is said . . . . 885 *Excursion* 9. 48
If rightly we observe and justly weigh) . . . K.8. 254 *Recluse* 1.1.646

Rights. —Well taught by that to feel his rights, prepared . . . . 18 *Desc. Sk.* 447
Where none but those who trampled on my rights 52 *Bord.* 844
Of his own rights restored, his gratitude . . . 66 *Bord.* 1595
Whose long-suspended rights are now on the eve 78 *Bord.* 2336
Urge her powers their rights to shield. . . . . 94 *Westmoreland Girl* 48
Upon the rights of visual sense . . . . . . 246 *P. B.* 918
For natural rights, a mockery and a shame ; . . 280 *Plea for Auth.* 4
And having rights in all that we behold. . . . 284 *Departure* 28
To have my ends, maintain my rights, ... 291 *Rob Roy* 55
Then rents and factors, rights of chase, . . . 291 *Rob Roy* 69
True Power doth grow on ; and her rights are these. 304 **I grieved* 14
In hideous usages, and rights accursed, . . . 378 *Duddon* 8. 7
Nor covets lineal rights in lands and towers. . . 387 *Manse* 14
Of power that perishes, and rights that fade. . 393 *Inglewood* 14
" Rights have you, and may well be bold : . . 408 *White Doe* 1082
Such rights did feeble nature claim ; . . . . 409 *White Doe* 1193
The sons who for thy civil rights have bled ! . . 442 *Ecc. Sonn.* 3. 10. 2
To sound the crystal depth of maiden rights ; . 467 *St. Bees* 114
Ye shadowy Beings, that have rights and claims . 473 **Ye shadowy* 1
Rights to compare and duties to discern ! . . . 501 *Humanity* 102
Rights equal, laws with cheerfulness obeyed, . . 515 *Penn.* 3
Be one fixed mind for all ; thy rights approve . 515 **Ah why* 10
Of all who for her rights watched, toiled and bled, ... 516 **Young England* 7
They urge, " have interwoven claims and rights . 519 *Pun. Death* 10. 10
The social rights of man breathe purer air ; . . 520 *Pun. Death* 13. 9
That all the seasons shared with equal rights ;— . 583 **With copious* 27
By reverence for the rights of all mankind. . . 587 *Crosth.* 12
Pain's wild rebellious burst proclaims her rights aloud. . . . . 614 *Desc.Sk.Quarto* 653
That I should here assert their rights, attest . . 669 *Prelude* 5. 216
Against all systems built on abstract rights, . . 695 *Prelude* 7. 524
Of natural rights and civil ; and to acts . . . 712 *Prelude* 9. 201
As best, the government of equal rights . . . 713 *Prelude* 9. 242
Of ancient loyalty, and chartered rights, . . . 714 *Prelude* 9. 324
When Reason seemed the most to assert her rights 729 *Prelude* 11. 113
Gives rights to error ; and aware, no less, . . 729 *Prelude* 11. 161
Of sex and age, and heaven-descended rights, . . 741 *Prelude* 13. 74
Their rights acknowledging he felt for all. . . 772 *Excursion* 2. 47
And her discernment ; not alone in rights, . . 775 *Excursion* 2. 237
And be in part compensated. For rights, . . 797 *Excursion* 3. 793
That are not lofty as her rights ; aspiring . . 806 *Excursion* 4. 815
Rights that transcend the loftiest heritage . . 826 *Excursion* 5. 276
Had earned for him sure welcome, and the rights 859 *Excursion* 7. 122
Of rights to him ; but he remained well pleased, . 864 *Excursion* 7. 433
And the LORD'S OAK—would plead their several rights . . . . 866 *Excursion* 7. 622
Have fought and perished for Helvetia's rights— 869 *Excursion* 7. 807
Its rights and virtues—by that Deity . . . . 871 *Excursion* 7. 899
Yea, to avenge her violated rights, ... 876 *Excursion* 8. 155
Her equal rights, her churches and her schools— 880 *Excursion* 8. 430
And He—to whom all tongues resigned their rights 883 *Excursion* 8. 594
To vindicate the ideal rights . . . . . . S.3. 439 **Avaunt this* 10

Rigid. The rigid features of a transient smile, . . 273 **When Philoctetes* 5
Not she whose rigid precepts trained the boy . . 618 *School Ex.* 7

Rigorous. Though stern and rigorous, melancholy ! 413 *White Doe* 1597
Vigils, and fastings rigorous as long ; . . . . 433 *Ecc. Sonn.* 2. 19. 4
Those Unconforming ; whom one rigorous day . 441 *Ecc. Sonn.* 3. 6. 2
Make rigorous inquisition, the report . . . . 634 *Prelude* 1. 148
A fervent love of rigorous discipline.— . . . 654 *Prelude* 3. 341
A rigorous student. What a stormy course . . 679 *Prelude* 6. 281

Rigours. Join to the rigours of the sires of Rome . 619 *School Ex.* 89

Rill. *See* **Gold-rill, Mountain-rill.**

Then, while I wandered where the huddling rill . 3 *Ev. Wk.* 53
While thick above the rill the branches close, . 3 *Ev. Wk.* 57
In foamy breaks the rill, with merry song, . . 4 *Ev. Wk.* 136
" Roll back, sweet Rill ! back to thy mountain-bounds, ... 111 *'*Tis said that some* 29
Be anything, sweet Rill, but that which thou art now. . . . . 111 *'*Tis said that some* 36
My thirst at every rill can slake, ... 157 **In youth* 6
Save a little neighbouring rill, ... 171 *Kitten* 82
Can drink its nurture from the scantiest rill : . . 222 *Triad* 148
Save from the trickling household rill ; . . . 247 *P. B.* 998
There is a little unpretending Rill . . . . . 251 **There is a little* 1
Lingers beside that Rill, in vision clear. . . . 251 **There is a little* 14
Save in this Rill that took from blood the name . 361 **When here* 7
Starts from a dizzy steep the undaunted Rill . . 377 *Duddon* 4. 9
The struggling Rill insensibly is grown . . . 378 *Duddon* 9. 1
And Tiber, and each brook and rill . . . . 386 *Yarrow Rev.* 61
Shrink from *thy* name, pure Rill, with unpleased ears. . . . . 392 *Avon* 14
In vain, upon the growing Rill may gaze. . . . 419 *Ecc. Sonn.* 1. 5. 14
Rains, that make each rill a torrent, ... 550 *Hermit's Cell* 4. 11
—Then Quiet led me up the huddling rill, . . 592 *Ev. Wk. Quarto* 71
—Sweet rill, farewel ! To-morrow's noon again, . 593 *Ev. Wk. Quarto* 85
Danc'd to the murmuring rill on Lomond's wave, . 630 [?] **O Moon* 2
Greta, or Derwent, or some nameless rill, . . . 715 *Prelude* 9. 393
That gathers up each petty straggling rill . . . 720 *Prelude* 10. 171
A humming bee—a little tinkling rill— . . . 786 *Excursion* 3. 1
And saw the water, that composed this rill, . . 786 *Excursion* 3. 39
His thirst from rill or gushing fount, and thanked 814 *Excursion* 4. 872
Busy in that enclosure ; while the rill, ... 856 *Excursion* 6. 1170

Rills. *See* **Mountain-rills.**
Or wild Aosta lulled by Alpine rills, — 15 *Desc. Sk.* 294
Beside the babbling rills; — 155 *Oak and Broom* 2
Between two sister moorland rills — 165 *Danish Boy* 1
Crags, woodlands, waterfalls, and rills; — 180 *Waggoner* 4. 53
His daily teachers had been woods and rills, — 205 *Brougham* 162
And drinks up all the pretty rills — 295 *Highland Boy* 59
Borne by the Muse from rills in shepherds' ears — 368 *Trajan* 23
On airy upland, and by forest rills, — 387 *Manse* 4
From Were, and all the little rills — 403 *White Doe* 692
And by the steaming rills, — 486 **We walked* 10
And gurgling rills, assist her in the work — 497 **Enough of climbing* 15
By rills that tumble down the woody steeps, — 595 *Ev. Wk. Quarto* 197
The little rills, and waters numberless, — 818 *Excursion* 4. 1173
Rim. A blue rim borders all the lake's still brink; — 4 *Ev. Wk.* 115
Rime. The longest date do melt like frosty rime, — 449 *Ecc. Sonn.* 3. 34. 8
Rimless. The other wore a rimless crown — 191 *Beggars* 25
Rimmed. *See* **Silver-rimmed, White-rimmed.**
Rimy. And, rimy without speck, extend the plains: — 8 *Ev. Wk.* 356
Powdered like rimy trees, when frost is keen. — 649 *Prelude* 3. 39
Ring. These, by the pale-blue rocks that ceaseless ring, — 5 *Ev. Wk.* 166
The druid-stones a brightened ring unfold; — 5 *Ev. Wk.* 188
Must bid the tocsin ring from tower to tower!— — 22 *Desc. Sk.* 640
A hollow ring; they say it is knee-deep—— — 44 *Bord.* 395
And ring a sharp 'larum;—but, if you should look, — 80 †*Address: Child* 10
Girt round with a bare ring of mossy wall, — 95 *Brothers* 28
To-night the church-tower bells will ring — 113 *Lament* 22
For thee a funeral bell shall ring, — 195 *Ruth* 256
And far and wide the fame thereof did ring. — 202 *Hart-leap* 80
Our fields rejoice, our mountains ring, — 204 *Brougham* 32
How tunefully the forests ring! — 237 *P. B.* 73
"The dragon's wing, the magic ring, — 238 *P. B.* 136
Would have pulled up an iron ring; — 241 *P. B.* 403
Perhaps a ring of shining fairies? — 242 *P. B.* 508
Apart she toils within the chosen ring; — 259 **A volant* 9
Perhaps are seated in domestic ring — 266 **Even as* 11
And thou, too, mingle in the ring! — 293 *Jedbor.* 4
But the ground lay within that ring — 298 *Brownie's Cell* 45
Looks on delighted—meet in festal ring, — 322 **Ye Storms* 4
The spangled turf, and neighbouring thickets ring — 387 **Part fenced* 13
The bells ring loud with gladsome power; — 396 *White Doe* 2
While stand the people in a ring, — 399 *White Doe* 314
Like those eight Sons—who, in a ring, — 404 *White Doe* 720
That used to spread its boughs, and ring — 413 *White Doe* 1588
As Menai's foam; and toward the mystic ring — 419 *Ecc. Sonn.* 1. 3. 2
Sceptre and mantle, sword and ring, laid down — 428 *Ecc. Sonn.* 1. 37. 11
Satellites burning in a lucid ring — 441 *Ecc. Sonn.* 3. 5. 13
With the symbolic ring, and willing hands — 446 *Ecc. Sonn.* 3. 26. 4
'Mid fruitful fields that ring with jocund toil, — 463 **Why should the* 5
By love untaught to ring, — 498 **The sylvan* 9
So loud, that with his voice the place did ring. — 555 *Prioress* 162
O ring of which the ruby now is lost, — 563 *Troilus* 31
Two hundred times around the ring of heaven, — 618 *School Ex.* 2
To ride the ring, or toss the beamy lance; — 619 *School Ex.* 58
Made all the mountains ring. But, ere nightfall, — 644 *Prelude* 2. 164
Found everywhere, but chiefly in the ring — 657 *Prelude* 3. 541
We rose at signal given, and formed a ring — 681 *Prelude* 6. 399
To drive their prey enclosed within a ring — 718 *Prelude* 10. 21
Yet ring with all their voices, or before — 850 *Excursion* 6. 783
Merrily seated in a ring, partook — 892 *Excursion* 9. 529
Ringing. From ringing team apart and grating wain— — 12 *Desc. Sk.* 82
Is ringing it—'twould stop a Saint in prayer, — 67 *Bord.* 1665
With clouds and sky about thee ringing, — 159 **Up with me* 5
To tend their silent boats and ringing wains, — 335 *Namur* 7
—The whistling swain that plods his ringing way — 597 *Ev. Wk. Quarto* 315
To ringing team unknown and grating wain, — 603 *Desc. Sk. Quarto* 85
With hollow ringing ears and darkening gaze, — 603 *Desc. Sk. Quarto* 97
While fill each pause the ringing woods of morn. — 604 *Desc. Sk. Quarto* 147
In every grove were ringing, 'War shall cease; — 796 *Excursion* 3. 723
Came at that moment, ringing noisily. — 865 *Excursion* 7. 545
Ringlets. For us your yellow ringlets comb, — 162 *Binnorie* 41
But the ringlets of that head — 221 *Triad* 107
Ringlet-tossing. Lip-dewing song, and ringlet-tossing dance; — 13 *Desc. Sk.* 132
Rings. Feeding 'mid purple heath, "green rings," and broom; — 4 *Ev. Wk.* 133
Again with his shrill voice the mountain rings, — 5 *Ev. Wk.* 154
Involve their serpent-necks in changeful rings, — 6 *Ev. Wk.* 246
It rings, as if a human hand were there — 73 *Bord.* 2057
The valley rings with mirth and joy; — 84 *Shepherd-boys* 1
O Thou, through whom the temple rings with praises, — 233 *Power of Sound* 83
Upon the Beast the sapling rings; — 241 *P. B.* 441
This cry—that rings along the wood, — 243 *P. B.* 628
The great events with which old story rings — 309 **When, looking* 5
Sees long-drawn files, concentric rings — 343 *Eclipse* 49
And their necks play, involved in rings, — 374 *Eg. Maid* 322
The time is come that rings the knell — 402 *White Doe* 528
A thousand, thousand rings of light — 406 *White Doe* 969
Till the whole City rings like one vast quire. — 442 *Ecc. Sonn.* 3. 8. 8
His drowsy rings. Look forth!—that Stream behold, — 452 *Ecc. Sonn.* 3. 47. 5
And if the harp pleased his gay youth, it rings — 503 *Warning* 18
Whose echo rings through Scotland to this hour! — 759 *Excursion* 1. 176
Riot. And, after their high-minded riot, — 180 *Waggoner* 4. 71
Rioted. We sauntered, played, or rioted; we talked — 652 *Prelude* 3. 248
Rioters. And in their fashion very rioters, — K.8.252 *Recluse* 1.1.585
Rioting. "Woe to you, Prelates! rioting in ease — 433 *Ecc. Sonn.* 2. 18. 1

Rioting—*continued.*
That her clear voice made a loud rioting, — 558 *Cuck. and Night.* 99
Riotous. What means this riotous noise? The villagers — 43 *Bord.* 330
For the blood-thirsty mead of Odin's riotous Hall. — 359 **Complacent Fictions* 14
Of riotous men commissioned to expel — 681 *Prelude* 6. 425
Riots. Mobs, riots, or rejoicings? From these sights — 697 *Prelude* 7. 675
Ripe. Waves the ripe harvest in the autumnal gale; — 21 *Desc. Sk.* 587
Lurking berries, ripe and red, — 80 *Foresight* 29
With all its mealy clusters of ripe nuts, — 99 *Brothers* 270
For youthful faults ripe virtues shall atone; — 105 *Artegal* 206
All bright with berries ripe and red, — 243 *P. B.* 637
Ripe for the hand, or under a thick shade — 361 **List—'twas* 19
Was ripe to send its thousands forth, — 400 *White Doe* 365
The time is ripe. With festive din — 403 *White Doe* 621
(Ripe men, or blooming in life's spring) — 404 *White Doe* 721
Is red as a ripe cherry. — 483 *Simon Lee* 8
The season) sprinklings of ripe strawberry fruit. — 529 *Poor Robin* 14
O'er ripe fruit, seasonably gathered, — 586 *Hogg* 35
Of red ripe currants; gift by which he strove, — 779 *Excursion* 2. 505
Like a ripe date which in the desert falls — 780 *Excursion* 2. 605
Her lavish pomp, and ripe magnificence? — 828 *Excursion* 5. 402
And the ripe corn before his sickle fell — 863 *Excursion* 7. 422
Ripe for the block that might have spared his son, — L.1. 96 *Juvenal* 3. 48
Ripen. There berries ripen, flowerets bloom; — 532 †*Float. Isl.* 14
Ripened. Suspicion ripened into dread; — 241 *P. B.* 421
A world of pain, ripened a thousand hopes, — 679 *Prelude* 6. 285
Did Dion hold with Plato; ripened thus — 715 *Prelude* 9. 409
Had ripened into faith, and faith become — 820 *Excursion* 4. 1294
Ripeness. Its ripeness to the feeding gaze; — 497 *Lycoris* 34
Ripening. And ripening foliage shone with richer gold. — 22 *Desc. Sk.* 637
With ripening harvest prodigally fair, — 263 **While not* 2
Ripening in perfect innocence. — 288 *Highland Girl* 27
The ripening corn beneath it. As mine eyes — 335 *Namur* 9
And ripening fruits and forest leaves — 502 *Seasons* 11
Ripens. And mock me with a sky that ripens not — 634 *Prelude* 1. 126
Riper. For domination at some riper day; — 504 *Warning* 100
That mellower years will bring a riper mind — 635 *Prelude* 1. 236
And stung with injury, at this riper day, — 713 *Prelude* 9. 251
How precious when in riper days I learned — 757 *Excursion* 1. 74
This he remembered in his riper age — 762 *Excursion* 1. 401
In youth, and sanctioned by the riper mind, — 860 *Excursion* 7. 197
Rippled. Fell where the blue flood rippled into white; — 21 *Desc. Sk.* 627
Rippling. Tremble on dancing waves and rippling streams — 460 **Queen of* 24
With darkness, and before a rippling breeze — 661 *Prelude* 4. 180
Eludes perception, not by rippling air — S.3. 435 **The doubt* 97
Rise. Where we, my Friend, to happy days shall rise, — 8 *Ev. Wk.* 351
The rocks rise naked as a wall, or stretch — 14 *Desc. Sk.* 230
Sink with his servile bands, to rise no more! — 22 *Desc. Sk.* 664
Rise various wreaths that into one unite — 33 *Guilt* 462
Without the strength to rise. Well, well, he lives, — 73 *Bord.* 2065
Do spread, and sink, and rise; — 108 *Louisa*
Thus rise and thus descend,— — 111 *'Tis said that some 43
That rose, and now forgets to rise, — 112 **How rich* 16
Did Susan rise up from her bed, — 130 *Idiot Boy* 425
When the wings of genius rise, — 163 *Hint* 2
Rise up, and grow to wondrous height. — 173 *Waggoner* 1. 14
Hung low, begin to rise and spread; — 180 *Waggoner* 4. 58
The stream will not flow, and the hill will not rise, — 188 *Poor Susan* 15
Did incense-bearing altars rise, — 216 *Enterprise* 40
Shall rise, and breathe again; — 225 *Primrose* 46
Up from their native ground they rise — 228 *Devot. Incit.* 5
Full suddenly the Ass doth rise! — 242 *P. B.* 560
Yet round our sea-girt shore they rise in crowds: — 251 **Pelion and* 9
Rise, then, ye votive Towers! and catch a gleam — 253 **Aerial Rock* 13
Rise from the dead, erewhile the Cottage-dame — 255 *Easter* 3
Rise, Gillies, rise: the gales of youth shall bear — 260 **From the dark* 3
Rise into life and in thy train appear: — 268 **Pure element* 4
Rise, tardy Sun! and let the Songster prove — 279 **'Tis he* 9
That, under hills which rise like towers, — 295 *Highland Boy* 13
Though fallen thyself, never to rise again, — 305 *Toussaint* 8
Never to rise again!—the work is done. — 310 *Anticip.* 5
Go back, and see the Tower of Babel rise; — 313 **Go back* 5
Europe breaks forth; then, Shepherds! shall ye rise — 316 **It was a* 13
And let imperishable Columns rise — 324 *Ode 1814* 103
Knows that the source is nobler whence doth rise — 329 *Ode: Thanks.* 53
That, shaped like old monastic turrets, rise — 335 *Namur* 13
Thou sacred Pile! whose turrets rise — 341 *San Salv.* 1
Shouts rise, and storms of sound from lifted trumpets blow! — 346 *Processions* 18
Forth from their coverts; slighted objects rise; — 350 *Des. Stanzas* 6
Rise, and to-morrow greet magnificent Rome. — 358 *Aquap.* 372
Rise as he may, his grandeur scorns the test — 368 *Trajan* 55
And some unbidden tears that rise — 375 **The Minstrels* 45
And thou hast also tempted here to rise, — 377 *Duddon* 5. 9
As golden locks of birch, that rise and fall — 381 *Duddon* 21. 12
Yet undelivered, rise with sure ascent — 396 **Action is* 12
"O Father! rise not in this fray— — 400 *White Doe* 381
To rise, and prove their innocence.— — 403 *White Doe* 632
"Rise, noble Earls, put forth your might — 403 *White Doe* 633
Unbent, which rather seemed to rise, — 404 *White Doe* 740
The delegates of Heaven we rise, — 405 *White Doe* 837
That *he* is unprepared to rise. — 408 *White Doe* 1136
Could see the Tower of Bolton rise. — 412 *White Doe* 1441
That Hill, whose flowery platform seems to rise — 420 *Ecc. Sonn.* 1. 6. 13
Rise!—they *have* risen: of brave Aneurin ask — 421 *Ecc. Sonn.* 1. 10. 1
Justice and peace:—bold faith! yet also rise — 424 *Ecc. Sonn.* 1. 24. 7

Road—*continued.*
Winds neither road nor path for foot to tread : 14 *Desc. Sk.* 229
They looked and saw a lengthening road, and wain 30 *Guilt* 325
They saw and heard, and, winding with the road 34 *Guilt* 523
Across the pebbly road a little runnel strayed. 34 *Guilt* 540
The jolting road and morning air severe. 34 *Guilt* 553
Trotting alone along the beaten road, 44 *Bord.* 411
A cave that opened to the road presented 50 *Bord.* 699
The boisterous carman, in the miry road, 61 *Bord.* 1334
That smile hath life in it ! This road is perilous ; 67 *Bord.* 1646
(For many years ago I passed this road) 97 *Brothers* 132
That overhung the road : he there stopped short, 102 *Brothers* 419
A Woman on the road I met, 119 *Sailor's Mother* 3
And to the road she turns her ears, 127 *Idiot Boy* 139
Appears along the moonlight road ; 128 *Idiot Boy* 174
And she can see a mile of road : 129 *Idiot Boy* 278
That hobbles up the steep rough road ? 130 *Idiot Boy* 410
——Ill suits the road with one in haste ; but we 148 **A narrow* 10
There was no road, nor any woodman's path ; 149 *M. H.* 2
Pathway, and lane, and public road, were clogged 150 **When, to* 6
The splinters took another road— 156 *Oak and Broom* 28
The road we travel, steep, and rough ; 175 *Waggoner* 1. 139
The road is black before his eyes, 175 *Waggoner* 1. 160
The rain rushed down—the road was battered, 175 *Waggoner* 1. 188
Descends along the sloping road ; 176 *Waggoner* 1. 263
His eyes take pleasure in the road 177 *Waggoner* 2. 35
Thou hast been loitering on the road ! 181 *Waggoner* 4. 129
Where the road it fringes, sweet, 181 *Waggoner* 4. 160
Where, save the rugged road, we find 214 *Kirkstone* 5
Aspiring Road ! that lov'st to hide 215 *Kirkstone* 49
Will to the road return ! 240 *P. B.* 350
A length of green and open road— 244 *P. B.* 678
In the dead earth beneath the road, 245 *P. B.* 835
Some lying fast at anchor in the road, 258 **With Ships* 3
By Thee to guide thy Pupils on the road 281 *Chris. Words.* 3
These pathways, yon far-stretching road ! 286 *Nith* 32
This little bay ; a quiet road 288 *Highland Girl* 9
Then hurries back the road it came— 295 *Highland Boy* 61
No master spirit, no determined road ; 307 **Great men* 13
The Arabian desert shapes a willing road 327 *Ode 1815* 25
On road or path, or at the door 390 *Highland Broach* 21
While each pursues his several road. 398 *White Doe* 161
O'er path and road, and plain and dell, 409 *White Doe* 1170
At this he from the beaten road 412 *White Doe* 1476
Mercy and Love have met thee on thy road, 419 *Ecc. Sonn.* 1. 4. 1
To keep this new and questionable road ? 434 *Ecc. Sonn.* 2. 23. 14
And if some traveller, weary of his road, 458 **Had this* 55
Remote from public road or dwelling, 491 *Fidelity* 22
Good aims lie down, and perish in the road 504 *Warning* 72
She plants well-measured terrors in the road 519 *Pun. Death* 8. 4
Enough ;—before us lay a painful road, 520 *Pun. Death* 14. 9
Turn from a spot where neither sheltered road 521 *Epist. Beaumont* 12
Up many a sharply-twining road and down, 523 *Epist. Beaumont* 103
Ah, Beaumont ! when an opening in the road 524 *Epist. Beaumont* 171
And to the fields his road would take ; 537 *Goody Blake* 70
Who lead their horses down the steep rough road 566 *Cumb. Beg.* 5
She turns her wheel, if on the road she sees 566 *Cumb. Beg.* 34
Impressed on the white road,—in the same line, 567 *Cumb. Beg.* 57
That peck along the road, regard him not. 572 *Animal Tran.* 2
Upon this lonely road ; 581 **Loud is* 12
Return Delights ! with whom my road begun, 592 *Ev. Wk. Quarto* 27
Where winds the road along the secret bay ; 595 *Ev. Wk. Quarto* 196
To teach their limbs along the burning road 596 *Ev. Wk. Quarto* 249
Where the brook brawls along the painful road, 596 *Ev. Wk. Quarto* 271
Who plods o'er hills and vales his road forlorn, 602 *Desc. Sk. Quarto* 15
Her road elms rustling thin above my head, 602 *Desc. Sk. Quarto* 48
Starts like a horse beside the flashing road ; 605 *Desc. Sk. Quarto* 208
By road or pathway, or through trackless field, 632 *Prelude* 1. 28
The road that pointed toward the chosen Vale. 633 *Prelude* 1. 93
The road lies plain before me ;—'tis a theme 641 *Prelude* 1. 640
Advancing, we espied upon the road 649 *Prelude* 3. 7
Saluted the chance comer on the road, 656 *Prelude* 3. 472
Upon the road, some busy at their work, 659 *Prelude* 4. 69
Sometimes embodied on a public road, 664 *Prelude* 4. 367
Shown by a sudden turning of the road, 664 *Prelude* 4. 388
All accidents, and to the very road 671 *Prelude* 5. 356
Along the Simplon's steep and rugged road, 683 *Prelude* 6. 563
Crossing the unbridged stream, that road we took, 683 *Prelude* 6. 574
We must descend, and there should find the road, 683 *Prelude* 6. 581
And, with the half-shaped road which we had missed, 684 *Prelude* 6. 620
Entered a narrow chasm. The brook and road 684 *Prelude* 6. 621
The plain straight road, for one no better chosen 728 *Prelude* 11. 71
When the world travels in a beaten road, 728 *Prelude* 11. 97
That did but *cross* a lonely road, and now 732 *Prelude* 11. 338
Faltering and faint, and ignorant of the road : 738 *Prelude* 12. 247
Thither, uncertain on which road to fix 738 *Prelude* 12. 295
And took my rounds along this road again 768 *Excursion* 1. 814
And walked with me along the miry road, 769 *Excursion* 1. 864
That bars the traveller's road, she often stood, 769 *Excursion* 1. 895
Have parted hence ; and still that length of road, 770 *Excursion* 1. 912
And walked along my road in happiness." 770 *Excursion* 1. 956
Now meeting on his road an armed knight, 771 *Excursion* 2. 5
Its course of suffering in the public road, 772 *Excursion* 2. 52
Invite us ; shall we quit our road, and join 773 *Excursion* 2. 139
A mute procession on the houseless road ; 780 *Excursion* 2. 563
For you, assuredly, a hopeful road 818 *Excursion* 4. 1117
Following the rugged road, by sledge or wheel 823 *Excursion* 5. 61

Road—*continued.*
Whence the bare road descended rapidly 823 *Excursion* 5. 65
Dark on my road the autumnal evening fell, 833 *Excursion* 5. 736
—The road is dim, the current unperceived, 851 *Excursion* 6. 845
The length of road that from yon mountain's base 858 *Excursion* 7. 43
By which the road is hidden, also hides 858 *Excursion* 7. 51
From frightful storms into a quiet road. K.8. 266 **Rid of* 4

Road-elms. Her files of road-elms, high above my head 11 *Desc. Sk.* 46

Road's. Where the road's watery surface, to the top 664 *Prelude* 4. 380

Roads. Where'er the dreary roads their bare white lines extend. 24 *Guilt* 18
" The roads I paced, I loitered through the fields ; 32 *Guilt* 433
Met in the roads, would bless us ; little children, 61 *Bord.* 1331
Crossing our roads at every hundred steps, 99 *Brothers* 255
Weep in the public roads, alone. 114 *Last of Flock* 4
Our roads, through many a long year's space, 182 *Waggoner* 4. 219
But we, by different roads, at length have gained 648 *Prelude* 2. 453
For pomp, or love. Oft, in the public roads 674 *Prelude* 5. 558
And window-garlands. On the public roads, 680 *Prelude* 6. 353
With their thin umbrage, on the stately roads 680 *Prelude* 6. 361
I triumphed. Meantime, day by day, the roads 713 *Prelude* 9. 262
That on the line of each of those two roads 739 *Prelude* 12. 322
To you, ye pathways, and ye lonely roads ; 741 *Prelude* 13. 117
Without reserve to them, the lonely roads 742 *Prelude* 13. 162
Trackless and smooth, or paced the bare white roads 744 *Prelude* 13. 316
But still he loved to pace the public roads 762 *Excursion* 1. 387
Hath been the fields, the roads, and rural lanes, 772 *Excursion* 2. 29
Beside our roads and pathways, though, thank Heaven ! 788 *Excursion* 3. 176
Rough and forbidding were the choicest roads 858 *Excursion* 7. 59
Have vanished—swallowed up by stately roads 876 *Excursion* 8. 109

Road-side. Repairs to a road-side ; 194 *Ruth* 237
Turns with less noisy wheels to the road-side, 566 *Cumb. Beg.* 41

Roam. Yet not unrecompensed the man shall roam, 10 *Desc. Sk.* 9
Left vacant for the day, I loved to roam. 13 *Desc. Sk.* 144
For me—farthest from earthly port to roam 31 *Guilt* 359
A blessèd day for thee ! then whither wouldst thou roam ? 87 *Pet-lamb* 38
Friendships that will not break, and love that cannot roam. 102 *Artegal* 24
Out of our Valley's limits did he roam : 107 *Indolence* 12
Yet o'er the moorland will she roam 108 *Louisa* 8
And hide my head where wild beasts roam. 115 *Last of Flock* 80
He with his Pony now doth roam 129 *Idiot Boy* 318
For me, why should I wish to roam ? 156 *Oak and Broom* 65
Cried they, " Your Father loves to roam : 162 *Binnorie* 38
Take flight, and thou art free to roam, 169 *Wren's Nest* 66
Type of the wise who soar, but never roam ; 209 **Ethereal minstrel* 11
Whole ages if I here should roam, 237 *P. B.* 52
Sure never man like him did roam ! 239 *P. B.* 235
These cleave to it ; from these it cannot roam, 263 **Those words* 13
If we, who thus together roam 289 *Stepping West.* 3
Where'er we roam—along the brink 337 *Cath. Cantons* 13
While in far-distant lands we roam, 343 *Eclipse* 68
Their love-songs ; but, where'er my feet might roam, 362 **List—'twas* 24
Else let the dastard backward wend, and roam, 377 *Duddon* 4. 13
(Couched in their den) with those that roam at large 392 *Daniel* 6
Not sedentary all : there are who roam 424 *Ecc. Sonn.* 1. 25. 1
Or through the aisles of Westminster to roam ; 452 *Ecc. Sonn.* 3. 45. 4
While in Judea Fancy loves to roam, 467 *St. Bees* 111
Neither checked by the rich nor the needy they roam ; 572 *Avarice* 41
Direst of savage beasts, would roam in fear, 585 *Ch. Lamb* 70
Long may ye roam these hermit waves that sleep, 595 *Ev. Wk. Quarto* 219
By lonely, silent cottage-doors to roam, 605 *Desc. Sk. Quarto* 166
'Tis his with fearless step at large to roam 609 *Desc. Sk. Quarto* 370
To pay the filial debt, for food to roam, 613 *Desc. Sk. Quarto* 615
To roam from heaven to heaven, from pole to pole, 619 *School Ex.* 74
Did wife and husband roam ; 623 *G. and S. Green* 6
But, like a thirsty wind, to roam about 635 *Prelude* 1. 211
The shepherd roam the hills. With new delight, 661 *Prelude* 4. 216
When but a half-hour's roam through such a place 700 *Prelude* 8. 113
Defenceless as a wood where tigers roam. 719 *Prelude* 10. 93
Here may I roam at large ;—my business is, 799 *Excursion* 3. 891
To roam at large among unpeopled glens 809 *Excursion* 4. 515
Their way before them—what a joy to roam 809 *Excursion* 4. 531

Roamed. Was heard, or woodcocks roamed the moonlight hill. 2 *Ev. Wk.* 20
Yes, as I roamed where Loiret's waters glide 21 *Desc. Sk.* 624
I roamed in the confusion of my heart, 146 **It was an* 18
Had roamed about, with vagrant bands 193 *Ruth* 119
From pond to pond he roamed, from moor to moor ; 196 *Resolution* 103
Once on those steeps *I* roamed at large, and have 392 *Bothwell* 4
Hath roamed in trouble and in grief, 414 *White Doe* 1613
They roamed through Wastes where now the tented Arabs dwell. 522 *Epist. Beaumont* 100
Or the first woodcocks roam'd the moonlight hills. 592 *Ev. Wk. Quarto* 26
I was the Dreamer, they the Dream ; I roamed 649 *Prelude* 3. 30
This was not wanting. Carelessly I roamed 658 *Prelude* 3. 616
Where'er I roamed, were speaking monuments. 701 *Prelude* 8. 172
I roamed from hill to hill, from rock to rock, 736 *Prelude* 12. 143
I roamed, in daily presence of this scene, 738 *Prelude* 12. 263
Three summer days I roamed) where'er the Plain 745 *Prelude* 13. 337
In London chiefly harboured, whence I roamed, 751 *Prelude* 14. 351
In youth I roamed, on youthful pleasures bent ; 753 **Oft, through* 2
Than a soldier among soldiers—lived and roamed 774 *Excursion* 2. 184

Rod—*continued.*
But human vices have provok'd the rod . . . 611 *Desc.Sk.Quarto* 486
With milk-white clusters hung; the rod and line, 639 *Prelude* 1. 485
Haunting with rod and line the craggy brooks? . 861 *Excursion* 7. 267

Rode. And all the happy Souls that rode . . . 168 *Pilgrim's Dream* 60
Aloft, yet in a tilting vessel rode, ... 346 *Processions* 26
Rode full of years to Flodden-field, ... 399 *White Doe* 284
That, while the sun rode high, was lost beneath their dazzling sheen. . . . . . . 456 **Soft as* 11
Her fancy rode the blast; . . . . 544 *Russ. Fug.* 244
Aye as he rode, to Pandarus he told . . . 563 *Troilus* 39
Came as he rode by places of the town . . 563 *Troilus* 45
Whence Cresid rode, as if in haste she was; . 563 *Troilus* 86
He rode, I keeping pace with him; and now . . 667 *Prelude* 5. 121
And, close behind, the comely Matron rode, . . 858 *Excursion* 7. 77
Checking the sober steed on which he rode, . . 859 *Excursion* 7. 103

Roe. Not blither is the mountain roe: . . . 83 *Lucy Gray* 25
I came among these hills; when like a roe . . 206 *Tintern* 67
Look to thy plumage and thy life!—The roe, . 472 *Dunolly Eagle* 9

Roe-bucks. Like roe-bucks they went bounding o'er the hills; . . . . 99 *Brothers* 277

Roland. That ROLAND clove with huge two-handed sway, ... 335 *Aix* 12
The illustrious wife of Roland, in the hour . . 723 *Prelude* 10. 381

Roll. *See* **Bead-roll.**
Like sun-lit tempests, troubled transports roll; . 18 *Desc. Sk.* 458
Over your head twice twenty years must roll, . 52 *Bord.* 820
"Roll back, sweet Rill! back to thy mountain-bounds, ... 111 **'Tis said that some* 29
But they are silent;—still they roll along . . . 184 *Night-piece* 19
Virtuous and wise. Winds blow, and waters roll, 306 **Inland, within* 10
Nor shall the eternal roll of praise reject . . . 441 *Ecc. Sonn.* 3. 6. 1
Stained and polluted, brighten as they roll, . . 452 *Ecc. Sonn.* 3. 47. 12
Even though the Atlantic ocean roll between. . 508 *F. Stone* 27
Roll on, ye spouting whales, who die or keep . . 527 **Those breathing* 33
Like lighted tempests troubled transports roll; . 612 *Desc.Sk.Quarto* 547
Drove far away the savage thoughts that roll . 618 *School Ex.* 33
Voices of gladness roll the walls around; . . . 625 *Æneid* 99
May roll in chariots, or provoke the hoofs . . 773 *Excursion* 2. 99
Still roll; where all the aspects of misery . . . 806 *Excursion* 4. 327
Be your frequented watch-tower; roll the stone . 808 *Excursion* 4. 498
This Land shall witness; and as days roll on, . 890 *Excursion* 9. 385

Rolled. Rolled wantonly between their slippery wings, 6 *Ev. Wk.* 247
With more majestic course the water rolled, . . 22 *Desc. Sk.* 636
Rolled at his back along the living plain; . . . 25 *Guilt* 88
Too little marked how fast they rolled away: . . 28 *Guilt* 227
Rolled fast along the sky his warm and genial moon. 32 *Guilt* 414
The thunder rolled in peals that would have made 50 *Bord.* 711
Rolled round in earth's diurnal course, . . . 187 **A slumber* 7
Rolled audibly!—it swept along, ... 245 *P. B.* 836
Like mountain-tops whose mists have rolled away— 326 **The Bard* 8
Above whose heads the tide so long hath rolled, . 333 *Fish-women* 4
Of wind-swept corn that wide around us rolled . 334 **A winged* 7
Volumes of sound, from the Cathedral rolled, . . 351 *Des. Stanzas* 64
For tutelary service, thence had rolled, . . . 379 *Duddon* 15. 7
Like vapours, years have rolled and spread; . . 391 *Highland Broach* 80
The transport was rolled down the river of Were, 403 *White Doe* 685
Like stars when clouds are rolled away; . . . 410 *White Doe* 1266
Her waves rolled on, respecting his decree . . 495 *Fact* 7
A more majestic tide the water roll'd . . . 616 *Desc.Sk.Quarto* 772
Wheeled by me—even as if the earth had rolled . 639 *Prelude* 1. 459
Rolled over a wide plain o'erhung with clouds, . 649 *Prelude* 3. 2
Eight months! rolled pleasingly away; the ninth 658 *Prelude* 3. 631
Hath rolled along, and this bright innocent, . . 692 *Prelude* 7. 378
And vein of water, glad to be rolled on . . 720 *Prelude* 10. 172
—Methinks I see him—how his eye-balls rolled, . 865 *Excursion* 7. 507
To time and season, as the year rolled round?" . 878 *Excursion* 8. 251

Rolling. Bright sparks his black and rolling eye-ball hurls . . . . 5 *Ev. Wk.* 150
These waters, rolling from their mountain-springs 205 *Tintern* 3
With rolling years thy strength increased; . . 216 *Enterprise* 36
Rolling a solemn sea-like bass, that floats . . . 234 *Power of Sound* 164
Nor has the rolling year twice measured, . . . 586 *Hogg* 13
And hear the mighty waters rolling evermore. . 590 *Immortality* 171
When vapours rolling down the valley made . . 638 *Prelude* 1. 417
The shepherd strays, a rolling hut his home. . . 702 *Prelude* 8. 197

Rolls. And rolls through all things. Therefore am I still . . . . 207 *Tintern* 102
And rolls the planets through the blue profound; 273 **Wild Redbreast* 12
And from the blessed power that rolls . . . 483 *Sister* 33
Save in the rolls of heaven, where hers may live . 540 *Grace Darl.* 16
Upon the beach, rolls back into the sea. . . . 823 *Excursion* 5. 76

Roman. Like the old Roman, on their own sword's point. . . . . 78 *Bord.* 2343
And like a Roman matron's was her mien and gait. 119 *Sailor's Mother* 6
A Roman Master stands on Grecian ground, . . 312 **A Roman* 1
Why speak of Roman Pomps? the haughty claims 346 *Processions* 28
That gave the Roman his triumphal shells; . . . 349 *Boulogne* 6
In every Roman, through all turns of fate, . . 368 *Trajan* 49
Is Roman dignity inviolate; . . . . . . 368 *Trajan* 50
The Roman kilt, degraded to a toy . . . . 388 **The pibroch's* 2
Where the all-conquering Roman feared to tread. 388 *Loch Etive* 14
The clasp that fixed the Roman Gown; . . . 390 *Highland Broach* 16
A way first opened; and, with Roman chains, . . 419 *Ecc. Sonn.* 1. 3. 11
Nor characters of Greek or Roman fame, . . . 419 *Ecc. Sonn.* 1. 5. 11
Of Aboriginal and Roman lore, ... 421 *Ecc. Sonn.* 1. 12. 7
Yes, to thy domination, Roman See, ... 429 *Ecc. Sonn.* 2. 2. 12
How, like a Roman, Sidney bowed his head, . . 442 *Ecc. Sonn.* 3. 10. 3
Meed of some Roman chief—in triumph borne . 464 *Derwent* 11
The Roman Consul doomed his sons to die . . 517 *Pun. Death* 3. 1

Roman—*continued.*
By Roman perseverance, are destroyed, . . . 549 **The massy* 2
To sacred studies; and the Roman Shepherd . 573 *Chiabrera* 3. 6
Is felt, thy Roman burial-place will be . . 581 **Why should we* 13
Old Roman boats and figures thro' the shade, . 604 *Desc.Sk.Quarto* 117
Perished the Roman Empire: how the friends . 635 *Prelude* 1. 190
A more than Roman confidence, a faith . . 648 *Prelude* 2. 443
Life, like that Roman Janus, double-faced; . . 775 *Excursion* 2. 251

Romance. Sole-sitting by the shores of old romance. 149 **A narrow* 38
She bears the stringed lute of old romance, . . 221 *Triad* 101
Plead for thy peace, thou beautiful romance . . 282 *Railway* 11
Europe, a realised romance, ... 348 **Lulled by* 51
Nor deem that localised Romance . . . . . 386 *Yarrow Rev.* 89
Upon the dream-like issues—the romance . . 430 *Ecc. Sonn.* 2. 8. 3
In days of old romance at Archimago's gate. . . 523 *Epist. Beaumont* 153
Of faery land, the forest of romance. . . . . 672 *Prelude* 5. 455
By Genii of romance; or hath in grave . . . 688 *Prelude* 7. 79
Into a dazzling cavern of romance, ... 694 *Prelude* 7. 455
Astonished; like a hero in romance, ... 694 *Prelude* 7. 506
As through a book, an old romance, or tale . . 714 *Prelude* 9. 300
The attraction of a country in romance! . . . 729 *Prelude* 11. 112
Romance of giants, chronicle of fiends, . . . 759 *Excursion* 1. 180

Romances. Of such we in romances read: . . . 130 *Idiot Boy* 355
In Araby, romances; legends penned . . . . 673 *Prelude* 5. 497

Romanist. The Romanist exults; fresh hope he draws 439 *Ecc. Sonn.* 2. 41. 9

Roman's. They—who have seen the noble Roman's scorn . . . . 359 **They—who* 1

Romans. Romans for travel girt, for business gowned; . . . . 275 **While poring* 4

Romantic. From such romantic dreams, my soul, awake . . . . 14 *Desc. Sk.* 226
In those old romantic days . . . . 141 *Arm. Lady* 86
To sweep from many an old romantic strain . . 335 *Aix* 3
Nor is it silver of romantic Spain; . . . . 480 *Cordelia* 5
Fair sights, and visions of romantic joy! . . . 547 **Rude is* 30
No more of old romantic sorrows, ... 586 *Hogg* 41
Romantic tale by Milton left unsung; . . . . 634 *Prelude* 1. 169
Between romantic Dovedale's spiry rocks; . . . 678 *Prelude* 6. 193
Romantic almost, looked at through a space, . . 693 *Prelude* 7. 442
Aught of romantic interest, it is gone. . . . 875 *Excursion* 8. 85
Did we come hither, with romantic hope . . . K.8. 245 *Recluse* 1.1.311

Rome. "Holy as that far seen which crowns the sumptuous Church in Rome . . . . 93 *Poet's Dream* 61
Whom hardy Rome was fearful to oppose; . . 320 **They seek* 7
The beauty of Florence, the grandeur of Rome, . 345 *Stanzas: Simplon* 9
Descend, and, on the brow of ancient Rome . . 357 *Aquap.* 292
Rise, and to-morrow greet magnificent Rome. . 358 *Aquap.* 372
Supplanted the whole majesty of Rome . . . 358 *Pine: Rome* 12
The glory of Infant Rome must disappear, . . 359 **Those old* 5
From ancient Rome, downwards through that bright dream . . . . 359 **They—who* 11
When here with Carthage Rome to conflict came, 361 **When here* 1
His way to Rome? Ah, no,—round hill and plain 361 **For action* 12
The exultations, pomps, and cares of Rome, . . 368 *Trajan* 37
Till Rome, to silent marble unconfined, . . . 368 *Trajan* 72
Aloft, the imperial Bird of Rome invokes . . . 380 *Duddon* 17. 3
Troubling the last holds of ambitious Rome, . . 394 **How profitless* 2
That Rome provides, less dreading from her frown 420 *Ecc. Sonn.* 1. 8. 10
By Rome abandoned; vain are suppliant cries, . 420 *Ecc. Sonn.* 1. 9. 9
Was the supremacy of crafty Rome; . . . . 435 *Ecc. Sonn.* 2. 26. 2
And the vain splendours of Imperial Rome?— . 528 **Those breathing* 95
To moulder in a far-off field of Rome; . . . . 581 **Why should we* 10
Join to the rigours of the sires of Rome . . . 619 *School Ex.* 89
May soothe thy memory of the chains of Rome. . 627 *Eagle and Dove* 4
Authentic history been set forth of Rome, . . 688 *Prelude* 7. 80
In microscopic vision, Rome herself; . . . . 691 *Prelude* 7. 253
With those of Greece compared and popular Rome, 708 *Prelude* 8. 618
The Alban Sites and walls of lofty Rome. . . . K.8. 281 **Arms and* 9
Never did Rome herself so set at naught . . . L.1. 88 *Juvenal* 1. 7

Romeo. Who told of Juliet and her Romeo, . . 123 *V. and J.* 91

Rome's. Rome's earliest legion passed! . . . 215 *Kirkstone* 44
Chosen by Rome's legendary Bards, high minds . 356 *Aquap.* 271
Flattery in Ancient Rome's pure-minded style: . 359 **Complacent Fictions* 10

Romilly. For her youthful Romilly. . . . . . 494 *Force of Prayer* 12
—Young Romilly through Barden woods . . 494 *Force of Prayer* 13
And hither is young Romilly come, ... 494 *Force of Prayer* 25
For never more was young Romilly seen . . 494 *Force of Prayer* 35

Romish. And Romish priest, in priest's attire. . 404 *White Doe* 708
Open a passage to the Romish sword, ... 431 *Ecc. Sonn.* 2. 12. 8
A Romish chapel, where the vested priest . . 726 *Prelude* 10. 559
The weeds of Romish phantasy, in vain . . . 815 *Excursion* 4. 908

Romorentin. Of Romorentin, home of ancient kings, 716 *Prelude* 9. 481

Romped. Have romped enough, my little Boy! . 295 *Highland Boy* 2

Romping. His slender manacles; or romping girl . 693 *Prelude* 7. 421

Rood. Bleeding on that precious Rood; . . . 336 **Jesu! bless* 8
Once more the Rood had been upraised . . . 410 *White Doe* 1268
While clouds of incense mounting veiled the rood, 450 *Ecc. Sonn.* 3. 40. 4
Now God, quoth I, that died upon the rood, . . 558 *Cuck. and Night.* 93
And hangs her garland on the Holy Rood. . . K.8. 325 [?] **The vestal* 8

Roods. Four roods of sheer ascent) Sir Walter found 201 *Hart-leap* 50

Roof. *See* **Cottage-roof, Council-roof, Hawthorn-roof, Trellis-roof.**
And swings above the roof the poplar tall. . . 6 *Ev. Wk.* 241
Weak roof a cowering form two babes to shield, . 7 *Ev. Wk.* 273
And Silence loves its purple roof of vines. . . . 12 *Desc. Sk.* 88
Chequering the canvas roof the sunbeams shone. . 34 *Guilt* 542
Unless beneath your roof I may remain: . . . 35 *Guilt* 584
Beneath their roof, but to the open air . . . 36 *Guilt* 646

Roof—*continued.*
Drops deadened from a roof so thick with leaves. 49 *Bord.* 676
to look up at this roof in storm or fair 72 *Bord.* 1947
The roof, self-moved, unsettling o'er his head ; 76 *Bord.* 2182
Hark ! over the roof he makes a pause, 81 †*Address : Child* 28
Past softly, leading in the Boy ; and while from roof to floor, 92 *Poet's Dream* 42
From floor to roof, all round his eyes the Child with wonder cast, 92 *Poet's Dream* 43
And, when he dwelt beneath our roof, we found 100 *Brothers* 349
Thy couch the dewy earth, thy roof the forest thorn ! " 104 *Artegal* 161
When down behind the cottage roof, 109 **Strange fits* 23
To hasten, for I found, beneath the roof 150 **When, to* 10
A lodging begged beneath a castle's roof ; 167 *Pilgrim's Dream* 3
And seldom needs a laboured roof ; 168 *Wren's Nest* 6
Perennially—beneath whose sable roof 185 *Yew-trees* 23
Beneath her father's roof, alone 192 *Ruth* 13
It seemed—wall, window, roof and tower— 246 *P. B.* 858
Even thine, though few thy wants !—Roof, window, door, 250 *Admon.* 10
Upon that roof, amid embowering gloom, 262 **Mark the* 6
Than his who breathes, by roof, and floor, and wall, 308 **There is a bondage* 2
As if the fretted roof were riven. 332 *Ode : Thanks.* 219
And, high above that length of cloistral roof, 355 *Aquap.* 170
Of silence, how it thrilled thy sumptuous roof, 387 *Roslin* 6
The walls are cracked, sunk is the flowery roof, 390 *Highland Hut* 9
Roof, raiment, bread, or burial : 391 *Highland Broach* 58
A phantasm, in which roof and wall 400 *White Doe* 422
Hath seen again her Father's roof, 414 *White Doe* 1619
Till the arched roof, with resolute abuse 433 *Ecc. Sonn.* 2. 20. 12
Beneath the roof of settled Modesty. 439 *Ecc. Sonn.* 2. 41. 8
Fitliest beneath the sacred roof proceeds 445 *Ecc. Sonn.* 3. 20. 5
These lofty pillars, spread that branching roof 451 *Ecc. Sonn.* 3. 43. 9
Expanding yet precise, the roof embowed, 473 **Thanks for* 6
Towards a low roof with green trees half concealed, 475 **There ! said* 2
Though waves, to every breeze, its high-arched roof, 496 **A little* 38
Its living roof above our heads. 506 *Lab. Hymn* 20
In course of nature under a low roof 510 **Among a* 21
For I have left my Father's roof, 542 *Russ. Fug.* 27
Nor roof, nor window ;—all seemed wild 543 *Russ. Fug.* 135
As shaggy as were wall and roof 543 *Russ. Fug.* 141
Among the mountains) and beneath this roof 547 **Rude is* 21
Here stood his threshold ; here was spread the roof 551 **If thou in* 8
Beneath yon roof began her heavenly reign ? 618 *School Ex.* 4
Reared Hawkshead's happy roof, and call'd it mine. 619 *School Ex.* 66
On Gotha's ducal roof, and on 629 *Installation* 59
Of the huge city, on the leaded roof 679 *Prelude* 6. 267
Entered thy vast dominion ? On the roof 707 *Prelude* 8. 543
Erelong, the massy roof above his head, 707 *Prelude* 8. 566
High was my room and lonely, near the roof 719 *Prelude* 10. 66
Beat on my roof, or, haply, at noon-day, 739 *Prelude* 12. 328
Of virtues bloomed beneath this lowly roof. 763 *Excursion* 1. 512
Of a clear brook ;—beneath an abbey's roof 771 *Excursion* 2. 7
And wholly without roof (the bleached remains 784 *Excursion* 2. 813
Of gay companions, to the natal roof, 793 *Excursion* 3. 507
Save for yon stately House beneath whose roof 824 *Excursion* 5. 97
With pillars crowded, and the roof upheld 824 *Excursion* 5. 146
The natural roof of that dark house in which 831 *Excursion* 5. 589
Danced in the breeze, chequering its mossy roof. 860 *Excursion* 7. 203
But towering high the roof above, as if 866 *Excursion* 7. 614
Altar, and cross, and church of solemn roof, 873 *Excursion* 7. 1024
And uncouth fancy. From behind the roof 881 *Excursion* 8. 477
Use, comfort, do this roof endear ; S. 3. 425 **No whimsy* 3
Beneath our roof. And others whom we love K.8.254 *Recluse* 1.1.657
That humble roof embowered among the trees, K.8.255 *Recluse* 1.1.682

Roofed. *See* **Flat-roofed, Long-roofed, Low-roofed, Sky-roofed.**
In the roofed bridge ; the bridge, in that dread hour, 14 *Desc. Sk.* 184
I spied a Covert walled and roofed with sods— 39 *Bord.* 118
Ceilinged and roofed ; that is so fair a thing 254 *Wild Duck's Nest* 4
Through paths and alleys roofed with darkest green ; 376 *Duddon* 2. 12
In the roof'd bridge, at that despairing hour, 606 *Desc.Sk.Quarto* 209
Thy lofty steeps, and pathways roofed with vines, 685 *Prelude* 6. 665

Roof-high. Roof-high ; the wild pink crowns the garden-wall, 855 *Excursion* 6. 1153

Roofless. Why so ? a roofless rock had been a comfort, 52 *Bord.* 814
Through shattered galleries, 'mid roofless halls, 272 *Ruins* 1
Thou art discovered in a roofless tower, 456 **The leaves* 16
Of art mosaic, in a roofless floor, 472 **The captive* 6
She clasps them at that dim-seen roofless stone.— 597 *Ev. Wk. Quarto* 290
And respirations, from the roofless walls 644 *Prelude* 2. 123
By a brook-side, we came, a roofless pile, 716 *Prelude* 9. 467
Appeared a roofless Hut ; four naked walls 756 *Excursion* 1. 30

Rooflike. Spread rooflike o'er the deep secluded vale, 14 *Desc. Sk.* 211

Roofs. While, from amid the darkened roofs, the spire, 12 *Desc. Sk.* 99
Even while I speak, the sacred roofs of France 449 *Ecc. Sonn.* 3. 36. 1
From the dark sylvan roofs the restless spire, 604 *Desc.Sk.Quarto* 108
Where danger roofs the narrow walks of death ; 606 *Desc.Sk.Quarto* 246
And roofs of temples built by human hands— 811 *Excursion* 4. 673
Whose blue roofs ornament a distant reach 844 *Excursion* 6. 408
And on the very turf that roofs her own, 850 *Excursion* 6. 812

Rooks. The throng of rooks, that now, from twig or nest, 455 *Rydal Mere* 8
The cawing rooks, and sea-mews from afar, 808 *Excursion* 4. 451
The cloud of rooks descending through mid air S.3. 437 **The doubt* 194

Room. *See* **Assembly-room.**
Nor taper glimmered dim from sick man's room ; 26 *Guilt* 142
And saw a woman in the naked room 27 *Guilt* 165
Might have fine room to ramble about here, 61 *Bord.* 1303
The platform is small, but gives room for them all ; 166 *Stray Pleasures* 5
Sky, hill, and dale, one dismal room, 175 *Waggoner* 1. 164
This man was reading in his room ; 244 *P. B.* 740
Nuns fret not at their convent's narrow room ; 250 **Nuns fret* 1
Whose realm had dwindled to one stately room ; 271 *George : Death* 2
That cry can reach ; and to the sick man's room 273 **Not the* 7
His world is in this single room : 294 *Jedbor.* 22
Thus into narrow room withdraws ; 376 **The Minstrels* 58
On you, if room for mortal aid 408 *White Doe* 1088
Made room where wolf and boar were used to range ? 468 *St. Bees* 139
As if green summer grass were the floor of my room, 484 **A plague* 29
Guiding, from cell to cell and room to room, 509 *F. Stone* 98
When fire or taper ceased to cheer the room, 528 **Those breathing* 54
A peopled world it is ; in size a tiny room. 532 †*Float. Isl.* 16
Of College labours, of the Lecturer's room 650 *Prelude* 3. 64
Whom chance had stationed in the very room 653 *Prelude* 3. 294
That—after I had left a flower-decked room 664 *Prelude* 4. 374
In public room or private, park or street, 695 *Prelude* 7. 576
High was my room and lonely, near the roof 719 *Prelude* 10. 66
Seen, from the shady room in which we sate, 882 *Excursion* 8. 536

Rooms. But oft, in lonely rooms, and 'mid the din 206 *Tintern* 25
The rooms, the court, the garden were not left 659 *Prelude* 4. 46
With high and spacious rooms, deafened and stunned 684 *Prelude* 6. 646

Roosted. Aloft is roosted for the night, 406 *White Doe* 954

Root. To the least fibre of their lowest root, 124 *V. and J.* 158
Oft leaves a saving moisture at its root. 124 *V. and J.* 194
Whose moss-grown root might serve for couch or seat, 167 *Pilgrim's Dream* 11
Take root (so seems it) and look up 170 *Rural Ill.* 17
The stems are faithful to the root, 224 *Primrose* 15
And to the rock the root adheres 224 *Primrose* 17
Thy youth to hopeless wasting, root and stem— 259 *Calvert* 5
Down to its root, and, in that freedom, bold ; 277 **A Poet* 11
Take root again, a boundless canopy. 384 *Duddon* 31. 8
All speak of manners withering to the root, 388 **The pibroch's* 8
Ere they descend to nourish root and stalk 390 *Glencroe* 8
The root sincere, the branches bold to strive 425 *Ecc. Sonn.* 1. 27. 9
Where long and deeply hath been fixed the root 431 *Ecc. Sonn.* 2. 10. 1
Root there, and not in forms, her holiness ;— 436 *Ecc. Sonn.* 2. 30. 5
So piety took root ; and Song might tell 466 *St. Bees* 48
To unearth the root of an old tree, 484 *Simon Lee* 75
That at the root of the old tree 484 *Simon Lee* 79
The tangled root I severed, 484 *Simon Lee* 86
And the root of this delightful tree 495 *Force of Prayer* 51
No sheltering stone, no tangled root was near. 528 **Those breathing* 53
There, at the root of one particular tree, 531 **I know* 9
At her own prayer transformed, took root, 543 *Russ. Fug.* 183
For she herself is honour, and the root 552 *Prioress* 13
Illumined ! root of beauty and goodnesse, 562 *Cuck.and Night.* 314
With two collateral stems sprung from one root ; 585 *Ch. Lamb* 97
The yellow stone-crop, suffered to take root 767 *Excursion* 1. 717
Of a young apple-tree, lay at its root ; 769 *Excursion* 1. 841
Seeking a place of refuge at the root 786 *Excursion* 3. 25
Whose fibres cannot, if they would, take root. 799 *Excursion* 3. 890
Whose root is fixed in stable earth, whose head 831 *Excursion* 5. 568
For such example. Almost at the root 863 *Excursion* 7. 395

Rooted. *See* **Fast-rooted.**
Is rooted in his mind ; this Band of ours, 38 *Bord.* 60
Rooted I stood ; for, looking at the woman, 47 *Bord.* 580
And rooted out the intolerable kind ; 102 *Artegal* 18
Which, in her own blest nature, rooted deep, 118 *Maternal Grief* 21
But the winds roar, shaking the rooted trees, 230 *Clouds* 41
Him who is rooted to his chair ! 294 *Jedbor.* 14
Or like a rooted tree, or stone earth-bound ; 429 *Ecc. Sonn.* 2. 4. 5
But, rooted here, I stand and gaze 458 **Had this* 50
And, whether from this habit rooted now 647 *Prelude* 2. 387
Wantoned, fast rooted on the ancient tower 722 *Prelude* 10. 279
Fast rooted at her heart : and here, my Friend,— 770 *Excursion* 1. 914
See, rooted in the earth, her kindly bed, 793 *Excursion* 3. 522
Be rooted out, and virtuous habits take 889 *Excursion* 9. 360

Roots. Where antique roots its bustling course o'erlook, 3 *Ev. Wk.* 67
On tawny earth, wild weeds, and twisted roots ; 5 *Ev. Wk.* 187
And states be torn up by the roots, wilt seem 276 *Author's Portrait* 6
And as it shook, enabling the blind roots 354 *Aquap.* 139
Ye Trees ! whose slender roots entwine 366 **Ye Trees* 1
Presumptuously) their roots both wide and deep, 420 *Ecc. Sonn.* 1. 9. 2
Where antique roots its bustling path o'erlook, 593 *Ev. Wk. Quarto* 82
From the roots of his hair there shall start 621 *Convict* 38
Grots, pebbles, roots of trees, and fancies more, 662 *Prelude* 4. 262
Is shaking to the roots : indifference this 711 *Prelude* 9. 91
When o'er those interwoven roots, moss-clad, 716 *Prelude* 9. 440
That prove to what low depth had struck the roots, 717 *Prelude* 9. 549
Had plucked up mercy by the roots, were glad 723 *Prelude* 10. 332
And oak whose roots by noontide dew were damped, 866 *Excursion* 7. 600
Some nourishment, as trees do by their roots, 879 *Excursion* 8. 356
Of leafy spray, concealed the stems and roots 881 *Excursion* 8. 444

Rope. Leonard had never handled rope or shroud : 100 *Brothers* 295
Six simple burghers—To the rope that tied L.1. 95 *Juvenal* 3. 9

Rosa. Of Monte Rosa—*there* on frailer stone 350 *Des. Stanzas* 31

Rosamond. Fair Rosamond, and the Children of the Wood, 858 *Excursion* 7. 90

Rosaries. Of prayer and praise forget their rosaries, 467 *St. Bees* 89

Rose. *See* **Briar-rose.**
On the dear hills where first he rose. . . . . 1 *Extract* 14
By the lake's edge, she rose—to face the noontide heat; . . . . 7 *Ev. Wk.* 253
More high, the snowy peaks with hues of rose. . 17 *Desc. Sk.* 406
To scent the sweets of Piedmont's breathing rose, 21 *Desc. Sk.* 595
He rose, and to the ruin's portal went, . . . 30 *Guilt* 312
The breathing pestilence that rose like smoke, . 30 *Guilt* 346
She rose and bade farewell! and, while her heart 34 *Guilt* 534
And, when he rose, he thanked her pious care 36 *Guilt* 641
The wild rose, and the poppy, and the nightshade: 38 *Bord.* 45
Lovely as Spring's first rose; a little dog, . . . 45 *Bord.* 455
The Villains rose in mutiny to destroy me; . . 54 *Bord.* 917
Imperious at all times, his temper rose; . . . 68 *Bord.* 1715
Rose from the spot;—the Daughter clapped her hands, ... 74 *Bord.* 2103
Fields smiled, and temples rose, and towns and cities grew. . . . . 103 *Artegal* 73
Rose,—and, to comsummate this just intent, . . 105 *Artegal* 221
Fresh as a rose in June, ... 109 **Strange fits* 6
Her sweets, and triumph o'er the breathing rose? 110 **Look at* 11
That rose, and now forgets to rise, ... 112 **How rich* 16
That rose a brief league distant from the town, . 125 *V. and J.* 248
And when they rose at morning she could see 135 *Michael* 292
"Pluck that rose, it moves my liking," . . . 139 *Arm. Lady* 7
The spring's first rose by you espied, ... 142 †*Lov. and Lik.* 31
The half-blown rose, the lily spare? . . . . 154 *Flower Garden* 12
Proud be the rose, with rains and dews . . . 158 **In youth* 27
Of devastation; but the hazels rose . . . . 185 *Nutting* 19
And on the vacant air. Then up I rose, . . . 185 *Nutting* 43
The red rose is a gladsome flower. . . . . . 203 *Brougham* 6
The red rose is revived at last; . . . . . . 203 *Brougham* 8
With Idalian rose enwreathed? . . . . . . 221 *Triad* 114
Down to that hidden gulf from which they rose . 230 *Clouds* 36
And wild rose tip-toe upon hawthorn stocks, . . 260 **How sweet* 5
A half-blown rose had tempted thee to sip . . 273 **Wild Redbreast* 3
She rose, and toward the close-shut casement drew, 274 **Wait, prithee* 6
Rose out of darkness: the bright Work stood still; 282 **In my* 3
Rose like a star that touching earth, ... 285 *Grave of Burns* 21
Stirred by the breeze; they rose, a Nation, true, 313 *Prophecy* 5
She rose, and off at once the yoke she threw. . 313 *Prophecy* 8
With happy garlands of the pure white rose: . 318 **In due* 7
A garland fashioned of the pure white rose . . 319 *Biscayan* 5
Anon before my sight a palace rose . . . . 324 *Ode 1814* 69
A shattered Convent, yet rose proud to have . . 355 *Aquap.* 212
And the waves rose, and sky portended danger. . 369 *Eg. Maid* 30
"Change me, some God, into that breathing rose!" 377 *Duddon* 7. 1
Of the GREAT WATERS telling how they rose, . 380 *Duddon* 16. 6
And, gazing, saw that Rose, which from the prime 381 *Duddon* 22. 4
I rose while yet the cattle, heat-oppress, . . . 383 *Duddon* 28. 1
Where the wild rose blossoms fair; . . . . 397 *White Doe* 123
Rose up, this stately Priory! . . . . . . 398 *White Doe* 234
He rose not in this quarrel, he, ... 409 *White Doe* 1233
They rose, oh! wherefore should I fear . . . 410 *White Doe* 1316
They rose—embraces none were given— . . . 410 *White Doe* 1318
Rose to the God from whom it came! . . . . 416 *White Doe* 1868
From false assumption rose, and fondly hailed 429 *Ecc. Sonn.* 2. 2. 1
As Po was heard to give where Venice rose . . 431 *Ecc. Sonn.* 2. 13. 9
Or rather rose the day to antedate, ... 432 *Ecc. Sonn.* 2. 14. 3
Has roused the lion; no one plucks the rose, . . 466 *St. Bees* 5
Rose, where she touched the strand, the Chantry of St. Bees. . . . . 466 *St. Bees* 36
Mists rose to hide the Land—that search, though long . . . . 469 **Bold words* 6
Even when they rose to check or to repel . . . 469 **The feudal* 2
Her Temples rose, 'mid pagan gloom; but why, . 474 **On to* 6
Above sea-clouds, the Peaks of Arran rose; . . 475 **There! said* 6
We rose up from the fountain-side; . . . . 488 *Fountain* 65
Till he rose a lifeless corse. . . . . . . 494 *Force of Prayer* 36
That rose, and steadily advanced to fill . . . 495 *Fact* 31
Ere on its banks the few grey cabins rose . . 524 *Epist. Beaumont* 168
Or human habitation rose . . . . 533 **Blest is* 29
He rose, and straight—as by divine command, . 534 **When in* 9
Or loftier pitch if higher rose the theme, . . . 538 **In desultory* 16
Refreshed, the Wanderer rose at morn, . . . 542 *Russ. Fug.* 49
A single Island rose . . . . 543 *Russ. Fug.* 102
Amazement rose to pain, ... 545 *Russ. Fug.* 354
The embowering rose, the acacia, and the pine, . 546 **The embowering* 1
Thy fragments to the bramble and the rose; . . 549 **Stranger! this* 33
And after that they rose, and took their way, . 556 *Prioress* 228
Of the unfaded rose that still blooms on his cheek. 569 *Farmer* 8
Too long abashed thy Name is like a rose . . . 584 **With copious* 46
And lovely is the Rose, ... 587 *Immortality* 11
While rose and poppy, as the glow-worm fades, . 599 *Ev. Wk. Quarto* 397
Now flush'd as Hebe, Emulation rose; . . . 618 *School Ex.* 20
The Rose of England suffers blight, ... 628 *Installation* 21
From that soft couch I rose not, till the sun . 633 *Prelude* 1. 86
But speedily an earnest longing rose . . . 633 *Prelude* 1. 114
And, as I rose upon the stroke, my boat . . 637 *Prelude* 1. 375
Some lovely Image in the song rose up . . . 660 *Prelude* 4. 113
The morning rose, in memorable pomp, . . . 663 *Prelude* 4. 324
He rose, and with a lean and wasted arm . . 664 *Prelude* 4. 413
Beset me, and to height unusual rose, . . . 666 *Prelude* 5. 62
Rose, with his ghastly face, a spectre shape . . 672 *Prelude* 5. 450
We rose at signal given, and formed a ring . . 681 *Prelude* 6. 399
Their noon-tide meal. Hastily rose our guide, . 683 *Prelude* 6. 566
That awful Power rose from the mind's abyss . 684 *Prelude* 6. 594
Whose import then we had not learned, we rose . 685 *Prelude* 6. 694
That we must tread—thy image rose again, . . 692 *Prelude* 7. 319
He was in limb, in cheek a summer rose . . . 692 *Prelude* 7. 352

Rose—*continued.*
Rose to ideal grandeur, or, called forth . . . 694 *Prelude* 7. 480
When one among the prime of these rose up,— . 694 *Prelude* 7. 494
Sparkling from out a copse-clad bank that rose . 705 *Prelude* 8. 409
On the dear mountain-tops where first he rose. . 706 *Prelude* 8. 475
Intended, rose in hardihood, and dared . . 719 *Prelude* 10. 106
The budding rose above the rose full blown. . . 729 *Prelude* 11. 121
Of a false prophet. While resentment rose . . 730 *Prelude* 11. 214
Thus expectation rose again; thus hope, . . . 731 *Prelude* 11. 245
That rose in splendour, was alive, and moved . 732 *Prelude* 11. 365
My brothers and myself. There rose a crag, . . 738 *Prelude* 12. 292
Then given it greeting as it rose once more . . 749 *Prelude* 14. 200
Which 'tis reproach to hear? Anon I rose . . 751 *Prelude* 14. 379
Had newly scooped a running stream. He rose, . 762 *Excursion* 1. 446
I rose; and, having left the breezy shade, . . 765 *Excursion* 1. 620
She rose from off her seat, and then,—O Sir! . 766 *Excursion* 1. 653
The voice was silent. From the bench I rose; . 767 *Excursion* 1. 738
The old Man rose, and, with a sprightly mien . 771 *Excursion* 1. 965
Rose, though reluctantly, and forth we went. . 785 *Excursion* 2. 904
A golden palace rose, or seemed to rise, . . . 796 *Excursion* 3. 714
Upon our brave Progenitors, who rose . . . . 815 *Excursion* 4. 920
Taken from air and sunshine when the rose . . 836 *Excursion* 5. 957
Upon a fickle Ingrate. Thrice he rose, . . . 843 *Excursion* 6. 334
From the maternal breast; then scruples rose; . 852 *Excursion* 6. 940
Against his conscience rose in arms, and, braving 855 *Excursion* 6. 1092
A plant no longer wild; the cultured rose . . 855 *Excursion* 6. 1151
Rose this pure eloquence. And, when the stream 857 *Excursion* 7. 25
These structures rose, commingling old and young, 879 *Excursion* 8. 339
That, in assent or opposition, rose . . . . . 880 *Excursion* 8. 437
And that smooth slope from which the dwelling rose, 881 *Excursion* 8. 468
Rose the slim ash and massy sycamore, . . . 881 *Excursion* 8. 478
Or courtesy prescribed. While question rose . . 882 *Excursion* 8. 524
We rose together: all were pleased; but most . 890 *Excursion* 9. 427
That rose, and steadily advanced to fill . . . S.3. 427 **My Son* 2
Roseate. Upon those roseate lips a Stygian hue. . 210 *Laod.* 66
With the morning's roseate Spirit . . . . . 217 **Inmate of* 19
The roseate bloom on woman's cheek; . . . . 227 *Vernal Ode* 119
From roseate hues, far kenned at morn and even, 452 *Ecc. Sonn.* 3. 46. 6
A roseate fragrance breathed.—O human life, . 573 *Chiabrera* 2. 13
Rose-bud. That lip—a rose-bud from the thorn, . 530 *Gleaner* 5
Enough of rose-bud lips, and eyes . . . . . 541 *Russ. Fug.* 1
Rose's. Within a breeze-fanned rose's breast . 582 **O for a* 23
Roses. On infant cheeks there fresher roses blow; . 21 *Desc. Sk.* 608
While youth's roses are thy crown. . . . . . 90 *Longest Day* 68
Two steady roses that were five years old; . . 134 *Michael* 179
Roses, lilies, side by side, ... 157 *Sexton* 19
Both roses flourish, red and white: . . . . 204 *Brougham* 11
The roses to the porch which they entwine: . . 250 *Admon.* 12
In trellised shed with clustering roses gay, . . 395 *White Doe: Ded.* 1*
With fancied roses, than the unblemished moon . 434 *Ecc. Sonn.* 2. 25. 7
And round this earthly tomb let roses rise, . . 575 *Chiabrera* 8. 21
Her infant's cheeks with fresher roses glow, . . 615 *Desc.Sk.Quarto* 734
Of virgins crowned with roses. Not in vain . 734 *Prelude* 11. 461
Pleasant as roses in the thickets blown, . . . 773 *Excursion* 2. 109
Perish the roses and the flowers of kings, . . . 872 *Excursion* 7. 980
Roslin. The notes, in prelude, ROSLIN! to a blank 387 *Roslin* 5
Roslin's. In the low dell 'mid Roslin's faded grove: 261 **From the dark* 12
Rossland. At length conducted us to Rossland,—there, ... 40 *Bord.* 196
Rostrum. His rostrum, with seraphic glance look up, 695 *Prelude* 7. 553
Rosy. Tinged like an angel's smile all rosy red— . 19 *Desc. Sk.* 475
Glittering and twinkling near yon rosy cloud; . 153 *Morn. Ex.* 28
For Skiddaw-top with rosy light . . . . . 180 *Waggoner* 4. 34
Crag, lawn, and wood—with rosy light. . . . 182 *Waggoner* 4. 243
And a throng of rosy boys . . . . 324 *Ode 1814* 63
Of languor puts his rosy garland by; . . . . 454 **Not in the lucid* 4
A rosy Man, right plump to see? . . . . . 485 *Poet's Epitaph* 10
Fall, rosy garlands, from my head! . . . . . 498 **Departing summer* 16
Renewing, when the rosy summits glow . . . 617 *Desc.Sk.Quarto* 812
A boy, no better, with his rosy cheeks . . . . 653 *Prelude* 3. 290
In arms, now rosy prattlers at the feet . . . 661 *Prelude* 4. 204
Those rosy peaks, from which the Morning looks . 733 *Prelude* 11. 410
He loved me; from a swarm of rosy boys . . 757 *Excursion* 1. 57
His rosy face, a servant only here . . . . . K.8. 246 *Recluse* 1.1.360
Rosy-cheeked. Three rosy-cheeked school-boys, the highest not more . . . . 86 *Rural Arch.* 2
Rotation. In set rotation passing to and fro, . . 812 *Excursion* 4. 710
Rote. Till the first verse he learned it all by rote. . 553 *Prioress* 71
Well did they know that service all by rote, . . 558 *Cuck.and Night.* 71
There also stands a speech-maker by rote, . . 699 *Prelude* 8. 32
Rotha. Above the Rotha, by the forest-side. . . 147 *Joanna* 31
Rotha, my Spiritual Child! this head was grey . 274 *Rotha Q.* 1
Rotha's. Our pathway led us on to Rotha's banks; 147 *Joanna* 41
In the green dales beside our Rotha's stream, . 715 *Prelude* 9. 392
Rotten. With rotten boughs and leaves, such as the winds . . . . 50 *Bord.* 705
A stump of rotten wood. . . . . 484 *Simon Lee* 76
And many a rotten bough about. . . . . . 536 *Goody Blake* 52
And this most rotten branch of human shame, . 722 *Prelude* 10. 260
Rough. In the rough fern-clad park, the herded deer 3 *Ev. Wk.* 47
Dashed o'er the rough rock, lightly leaps along; . 4 *Ev. Wk.* 137
Through which rough Garry cleaves his way, can tell . . . . 15 *Desc. Sk.* 296
Of such rough storm, this happy change to view." 30 *Guilt* 317
"Rough potters seemed they, trading soberly . 32 *Guilt* 406
From the stern breathing of the rough sea-wind; . 61 *Bord.* 1296
From such rough dealing. Ha! what sound is that? . . . . 67 *Bord.* 1661
The first hours of last night were rough with storm: 73 *Bord.* 2043
O'er rough and smooth she trips along, . . . 83 *Lucy Gray* 61

Rough—*continued.*
Have far to travel,—and on these rough paths — 98 *Brothers* 224
In weather rough and bleak; — 108 *Louisa* 9
That hobbles up the steep rough road? — 130 *Idiot Boy* 410
A narrow girdle of rough stones and crags, — 148 **A narrow* 1
" 'If breeze or bird to this rough steep — 156 *Oak and Broom* 41
The road we travel, steep, and rough; — 175 *Waggoner* 1. 139
Rough doings these! as God's my judge, — 176 *Waggoner* 1. 249
And the rough Sailor instantly — 176 *Waggoner* 1. 264
Grinding through rough and smooth our way; — 179 *Waggoner* 3. 94
Gigantic mountains rough with crags; beneath, — 219 **This Height* 12
And glance, while wantonly the rough wind blows, — 262 **Mark the* 4
Where sights were rough, and sounds were wild, — 288 *Glen-Al.* 11
That, rough or smooth, is full of change, — 295 *Highland Boy* 54
The rough Ætolians smiled with bitter scorn. — 312 **When, far* 4
In conflict; whose rough winds forgot their jars — 336 *Danube* 10
Near the rough Falls of Inversneyd! — 344 **How blest* 58
As if, to rough assaults unknown, — 348 **Lulled by* 9
Soft breezes fanning your rough brows—the might — 350 *Des. Stanzas* 53
Over waves rough and deep, that, when they broke, — 354 *Aquap.* 121
Will soon be broken;—a rough course remains, — 381 *Duddon* 20. 7
Rough as the past; where Thou, of placid mien, — 381 *Duddon* 20. 8
Rough ways my steps have trod;—too rough and long — 382 *Duddon* 25. 9
Maturer Fancy owes to their rough noise — 382 *Duddon* 26. 13
Through the rough copse wheel thou with hasty stride; — 383 *Duddon* 30. 11
Of Ignorance, that ran so rough and high — 422 *Ecc. Sonn.* 1. 14. 11
On a wild coast, rough monitors to feed — 424 *Ecc. Sonn.* 1. 23. 8
And 'tis the Pope that wields it:—whether rough — 428 *Ecc. Sonn.* 1.39. 13
That, in rough winter, oft inflicts a fear — 453 **Calm is the* 14
To king, to peasant, to rough sailor, dear, — 455 *Rydal Mere* 29
Here, as 'mid busier scenes, ground steep and rough, — 497 **Enough of climbing* 2
By rough waves on a perilous coast, — 502 **Like a* 2
Rough is the time; and thoughts, that would be free — 521 *Epist. Beaumont* 10
And the rough bed of many an unbridged brook? — 523 *Epist. Beaumont* 106
Is all too rough for Thee to tread. — 534 **Blest is* 84
With thickets rough and blind; — 542 *Russ. Fug.* 94
While I have lodged in this rough hold, — 545 *Russ. Fug.* 299
Who lead their horses down the steep rough road — 566 *Cumb. Beg.* 5
But lately, one rough day, this Flower I passed — 571 **There is a Flower* 9
I knew the force; and hence the rough sea's pride — 574 *Chiabrera* 4. 19
Dash'd down the rough rock, lightly leaps along; — 593 *Ev. Wk. Quarto* 120
In wantonness of heart, through rough and smooth — 644 *Prelude* 2. 130
Our inmate, a rough terrier of the hills; — 659 *Prelude* 4. 95
Right to a rough stream's edge, and there broke off; — 683 *Prelude* 6. 569
That the rough lord had left the surly North — 687 *Prelude* 7. 25
Rough, bold, as Grecian comedy displayed — 691 *Prelude* 7. 289
Dismounting, down the rough and stony moor — 737 *Prelude* 12. 233
A man of kindlier nature. The rough sports — 762 *Excursion* 1. 415
Into the rough uncultivated ground, — 779 *Excursion* 2. 496
A napkin, white as foam of that rough brook — 781 *Excursion* 2. 674
By the rough wind unscattered, at whose call — 808 *Excursion* 4. 453
In spite of many a rough untoward blast, — 828 *Excursion* 5. 396
A rough abode—in colour, shape, and size, — 833 *Excursion* 5. 697
Of a rough precipice; and some, apart, — 835 *Excursion* 5. 867
Sparry and bright, rough scatterings of the hills. — 856 *Excursion* 6. 1155
Rough and forbidding were the choicest roads — 858 *Excursion* 7. 59
Throughout the lofty range of these rough hills, — 865 *Excursion* 7. 499
The moments' humour, rough Tars spend their wit. — K.8. 301 **And oh* 4

Roughened. The main flood roughened into hill and valley. — 369 *Eg. Maid* 42

Rough-hewn. Three several pillars, each a rough-hewn stone, — 201 *Hart-leap* 67

Roughly. Mockery—or model roughly hewn, — 214 *Kirkstone* 10

Round. (*Partial list.*) *See* **Around.**
Depicted in the dial's moral round; — 2 *Ev. Wk.* 28
And round the broad-spread oak, a glimmering scene, — 3 *Ev. Wk.* 46
Sweetly ferocious, round his native walks, — 5 *Ev. Wk.* 146
And round the west's proud lodge their shadows throw, — 7 *Ev. Wk.* 290
While music, stealing round the glimmering deeps, — 7 *Ev. Wk.* 303
—The evening darkness gathers round — 9 *Collins* 23
Of holy rites chanted in measured round? — 11 *Desc. Sk.* 58
The pathway leads, as round the steeps it twines; — 12 *Desc. Sk.* 87
Round undistinguished clouds, and rocks, and snow: — 13 *Desc. Sk.* 161
Of ether, shining with diminished round, — 16 *Desc. Sk.* 320
Of drowsy bells, for ever tinkling round; — 17 *Desc. Sk.* 357
Nought round its darling precincts can he find — 18 *Desc. Sk.* 429
In sea-like reach of prospect round him spread, — 19 *Desc. Sk.* 474
Hears Winter calling all his terrors round, — 19 *Desc. Sk.* 490
With shrill winds whistling round my lonely way, — 21 *Desc. Sk.* 592
Round his wife's neck; the prize of victory laid — 25 *Guilt* 61
And, hovering, round it often did a raven fly. — 25 *Guilt* 81
Marks nothing but the red sun's setting round, — 26 *Guilt* 111
Beat round to clear the streets of want and pain. — 29 *Guilt* 274
How quiet 'round me ship and ocean were! — 30 *Guilt* 339
Roaming the illimitable waters round; — 31 *Guilt* 364
Fretting the fever round the languid heart, — 31 *Guilt* 395
She paces round and round an Infant's grave, — 44 *Bord.* 393
Upon the self-same spot, still round and round, — 47 *Bord.* 578
Three good round years, for playing the fool here — 51 *Bord.* 769
He shall be led, and there, the Country round — 58 *Bord.* 1121
And feats of cunning; and the pretty round — 80 **Loving she* 4
Round as a pillow, and whiter than milk, — 80 †*Address: Child* 12
That clustered round her head. — 83 *We are Seven* 8
Together round her grave we played, — 84 *We are Seven* 55

Round—*continued.*
The lamb, still swimming round and round, — 85 *Shepherd-boys* 76
By those huge rocks encompassed round. — 85 *Shepherd-boys* 88
Birds warbled round me—and each trace — 86 *Anecdote* 21
Strong as an Eagle with my charge I glided round and round — 92 *Poet's Dream* 37
From floor to roof, all round his eyes the Child with wonder cast, — 92 *Poet's Dream* 43
Her large round wheel was turning. Towards the field — 95 *Brothers* 26
Girt round with a bare ring of mossy wall, — 95 *Brothers* 28
And, looking round, imagined that he saw — 96 *Brothers* 96
We two could travel, Sir, through a strange round; — 98 *Brothers* 192
As I remember, looking round these rocks — 99 *Brothers* 264
Long blades of grass, plucked round him as he lay, — 108 *Indolence* 56
To its dull round of ordinary cares; — 122 *V. and J.* 52
In great and small, in round and square, — 128 *Idiot Boy* 208
Like happy people round a Christmas fire. — 135 *Michael* 303
Went forth to show it to the neighbours round; — 136 *Michael* 313
Above and round the sacred places — 144 **Driven in* 56
And showers of hailstones pattered round. — 154 **A whirl-blast* 4
Were seated round their blazing fire, — 156 *Oak and Broom* 9
With brightest sunshine round me spread — 159 *Green Linnet* 3
Turn the swift wheel round and round! — 163 *Spinning Wheel* 6
Eddying round and round they sink — 170 *Kitten* 9
Fluttered, perched, into a round — 171 *Kitten* 70
The buzzing dor-hawk, round and round, is wheeling,— — 173 *Waggoner* 1. 3
Hung round and overhung with gloom; — 175 *Waggoner* 1. 165
Built round by those white clouds, enormous clouds, — 184 *Night-piece* 21
Where rivulets dance their wayward round, — 187 **Three years* 28
Rolled round in earth's diurnal course, — 187 **A slumber* 7
Wreathed round with yellow flowers the gayest of the land. — 191 *Beggars* 24
Sir Walter walked all round, north, south, and west, — 201 *Hart-leap* 47
And the round ocean and the living air, — 207 *Tintern* 98
Round the dear Shade she would have clung—'tis vain: — 211 *Laod.* 152
And hideous aspect, stalking round and round! — 213 *Dion* 68
Where Toil pursues his daily round; — 215 *Kirkstone* 69
On tracing and retracing that large round, — 218 *Recluse* 1. 1. 211
Sheds round the transient harm or vague mischance — 222 *Triad* 161
And listening dolphins gather round. — 234 *Power of Sound* 136
Strains that support the Seasons in their round; — 235 *Power of Sound* 191
The woods, my Friends, are round you roaring, — 236 *P. B.* 11
Had danced his round with Highland lasses; — 239 *P. B.* 223
"A savage wildness round him hung — 239 *P. B.* 291
With rocks encompassed round. — 240 *P. B.* 370
Turns round his long left ear. — 241 *P. B.* 415
Turned round his long left ear. — 241 *P. B.* 420
Twined round him by demoniac power, — 241 *P. B.* 474
And made the good man round him look. — 244 *P. B.* 745
The Ass turned round his head and *grinned.* — 245 *P. B.* 825
Secure foundations. As the year runs round, — 259 **A volant* 8
Fell round the path of Milton, in his hand — 260 **Scorn not* 12
With finished sweep into a perfect round, — 269 *Malham* 7
Close-crowding round the infant-god; — 299 *Brownie's Cell* 3
Meek loveliness is round thee spread, — 302 *Yarrow V.* 45
Wisdom doth live with children round her knees: — 304 **I grieved* 9
Stalks round—abhorred by Heaven, a terror to the Earth! — 311 **Who rises* 20
Round which the elements of worldly might — 317 **Look now* 7
If never more within their shady round — 319 *Guernica* 11
Of the round world, and built, by laws as strong, — 329 *Ode: Thanks.* 48
The waves danced round us as before, — 343 *Eclipse* 14
Marched round the altar—to commemorate — 346 *Processions* 12
They round his altar bore the hornèd God, — 346 *Processions* 24
Historic figures round the shaft embost — 367 *Trajan* 13
Of holy Angels round her hovered: — 372 *Eg. Maid* 230
But Angels round her pillow — 374 *Eg. Maid* 379
Or near that mystic Round of Druid frame — 380 *Duddon* 17. 12
Round strath and mountain, stamped by the ancient tongue — 389 *Sound of Mull* 3
Round and through this Pile of state — 397 *White Doe* 81
Her silence; then his thoughts turned round, — 401 *White Doe* 459
On foot they girt their Father round; — 404 *White Doe* 726
They belt him round with hearts undaunted — 408 *White Doe* 1142
The Assailants, turning round and round; — 412 *White Doe* 1484
Ah, when the Body, round which in love we clung, — 423 *Ecc. Sonn.* 1. 20. 1
Round the decaying trunk of human pride, — 424 *Ecc. Sonn.* 1. 21. 8
Like ivy, round some ancient elm, they twine — 424 *Ecc. Sonn.* 1. 21. 11
With the fierce tempest, while, within the round — 425 *Ecc. Sonn.* 1. 27. 10
Round the Crusaders, till on distant shores — 430 *Ecc. Sonn.* 2. 8. 5
Still round my shattered brow in beauty wave." — 465 **Thou look'st* 14
Each in its orbit round the central Sun. — 476 **Tranquillity! the* 14
That Sisterhood, in hieroglyphic round — 477 *Long Meg* 12
"You look round on your Mother Earth, — 481 *Expost.* 9
When Echo bandied, round and round, — 483 *Simon Lee* 11
In common things that round us lie — 485 *Poet's Epitaph* 49
Round these, with tendrils strong as flesh and blood, — 488 *Pers. Talk* 35
All round, in hollow or on height; — 491 *Fidelity* 14
The emblematic round! — 502 *Seasons* 16
And quick words round him fall like flakes of snow. — 503 *Warning* 21
Some notes prelusive, from the round of songs — 523 *Epist. Beaumont* 159
To Loughrigg-tarn, round clear and bright as heaven, — 524 *Epist. Beaumont* 166
To wheel with languid motion round and round, — 527 **Those breathing* 48

3

Roves. More pleased, my foot the hidden margin roves — 12 *Desc. Sk.* 77
Or by the lazy Seine, the exile roves; — 19 *Desc. Sk.* 521
And, while she roves through St. John's Vale, — 180 *Waggoner* 4. 23
Or where the solitary shepherd roves — 419 *Ecc. Sonn.* 1. 5. 3
Where the slim wild deer roves; — 506 **While from* 30
Lo! by the lazy Seine the exile roves, — 613 *Desc.Sk.Quarto* 624
Roving. While thou art roving, wretched and forlorn, — 104 *Artegal* 160
Land sometimes by the roving shepherd-swain — 219 **This Height* 26
Here roving wild, he laid him down to rest — 265 **Hail, Twilight* 7
The roving Spanish Bands are reached at last, — 320 **Hunger, and* 5
Of roving tired or desultory war— — 444 *Ecc. Sonn.* 3. 17. 8
The roving bee proclaims aloud — 526 **The soaring* 3
A hundred times when, roving high and low, — 660 *Prelude* 4. 110
While I was roving up and down alone, — 672 *Prelude* 5. 431
The roving Indian, on his desert sands: — 698 *Prelude* 7. 747
The eye of roving plunderer—for their need — 833 *Excursion* 5. 700
Than in fantastic conqueror's roving camp, — 848 *Excursion* 6. 671
A roving school-boy; what the Adventurer's age — K.8. 236 *Recluse* 1.1. 2
Row. *See* **Hedge-row.**
Into yon row of willows flit, — 111 *'*Tis said that some* 26
Nor mount the mast, nor row, nor float — 295 *Highland Boy* 83
Of Images in seemly row; — 341 *Ital. Itin.* 8
Not virgin lilies marshalled in bright row, — 347 *Processions* 59
And hither does one Poet sometimes row — 547 **Rude is* 17
Rowed. And rowed off gently, while he blew his flute — 644 *Prelude* 2. 169
Rowing. While-as Canute the King is rowing by: — 426 *Ecc. Sonn.* 1. 30. 3
Rows. *See* **Hedge-rows.**
And cups in seemly rows, — 543 *Russ. Fug.* 146
In brighter rows her table wealth aspires, — 615 *Desc.Sk.Quarto* 732
Of sparkling light. But now, like one who rows, — 637 *Prelude* 1. 367
Had twined about her two small rows of peas, — 767 *Excursion* 1. 729
In seemly rows; the chancel only showed — 824 *Excursion* 5. 156
Who then through rows of weeping comrades went, — L.1. 95 *Juvenal* 3. 7
Roy. Or Roy, renowned through many a Scottish dell; — 255 *Detraction* 4
She has her brave Rob Roy! — 291 *Rob Roy* 5
Heaven gave Rob Roy a dauntless heart — 291 *Rob Roy* 9
Yet was Rob Roy as *wise* as brave; — 291 *Rob Roy* 13
A Poet worthy of Rob Roy — 291 *Rob Roy* 15
Rob Roy had never lingered here, — 291 *Rob Roy* 73
And we our own Rob Roy! — 292 *Rob Roy* 96
Royal. Which purported it was the royal pleasure — 49 *Bord.* 680
St. Denis, filled with royal tombs, or the Church of Notre Dame? — 92 *Poet's Dream* 24
Had swayed the royal mace, — 103 *Artegal* 95
The royal Elidure, who leads the chase, — 104 *Artegal* 114
Thy royal mantle worn: — 104 *Artegal* 135
—It is my royal state that yields — 113 *Lament* 34
Is of royal eastern blood, — 141 *Arm. Lady* 116
Call not the royal Swede unfortunate, — 317 **Call not* 1
"Shame! should a Child of royal line — 370 *Eg. Maid* 91
Ye saw, throughout this royal House, — 372 *Eg. Maid* 201
The royal Guinever looked passing glad — 373 *Eg. Maid* 297
Whether she graced a royal chair, — 390 *HighlandBroach* 26
A Royal army is gone forth — 404 *White Doe* 785
But to remote Northumbria's royal Hall, — 422 *Ecc. Sonn.* 1. 15. 1
The Royal Minstrel, ere the choir is still, — 426 *Ecc. Sonn.* 1. 30. 9
Let both meet only on thy royal shield! — 432 *Ecc. Sonn.* 2. 15. 5
Tax not the royal Saint with vain expense, — 451 *Ecc. Sonn.* 3. 43. 1
The Danish Conqueror, on his royal chair, — 495 *Fact* 1
Some solace under weight of royal care, — 628 **Deign, Sovereign* 23
Oft to royal hearts denied." — 629 *Installation* 56
By royal visages. Meanwhile abroad — 640 *Prelude* 1. 535
Of royal courts, and that voluptuous life — 714 *Prelude* 9. 345
Practised to commune with her royal knight — 716 *Prelude* 9. 488
Baronial court or royal; cheered with gifts — 771 *Excursion* 2. 3
His royal state to show, and prove his strength — 825 *Excursion* 5. 183
To guard the royal brood. The sailing glead, — 868 *Excursion* 7. 751
Do arts like these a royal mind evince? — L.1. 94 *Juvenal* 2. 11
Royally. Of yesterday, which royally did wear — 449 *Ecc. Sonn.* 3. 34. 11
Royalty. Esteeming earthly royalty — 495 *Fact* 22
Roy's. At sound of Rob Roy's name. — 292 *Rob Roy* 120
Rubbed. *See* **Smooth-rubbed.**
Rubbish. Bring down a heap of rubbish, and it crush me, — 78 *Bord.* 2316
And from the rubbish gathered up a stone, — 710 *Prelude* 9. 69
Among more innocent rubbish."—Speaking thus, — 816 *Excursion* 4. 1009
Rubicon. A Cæsar past the Rubicon! — 177 *Waggoner* 2. 81
Rubies. A queen in crown of rubies drest; — 158 **With little* 21
Rubs. And one hand rubs his old night-cap. — 128 *Idiot Boy* 251
To Benjamin, who rubs his eyes, — 177 *Waggoner* 2. 110
Ruby. And eke of martyrdom this ruby bright, — 555 *Prioress* 159
O ring of which the ruby now is lost, — 563 *Troilus* 31
Ruddy. Confiding in his ruddy breast, — 143 **Driven in* 6
And while the rest, a ruddy quire, — 156 *Oak and Broom* 8
Jove, Venus, and the ruddy crest of Mars — 313 **Clouds, lingering* 5
Whose head the ruddy apple tops, while he — 339 *Tell* 22
Whose ruddy children, by the mother's eyes — 377 *Duddon* 5. 11
The pensive warbler of the ruddy breast — 388 *Trosachs* 12
His cheeks were red as ruddy clover; — 536 *Goody Blake* 19
And with the ruddy produce she walks round — 699 *Prelude* 8. 41
Two ruddy children hung, a well-poised freight, — 858 *Excursion* 7. 73
Abruptly broken off. The ruddy boys — 883 *Excursion* 8. 592
Rude. Leads to her bridge, rude church, and cottaged grounds, — 2 *Ev. Wk.* 7
Or, starting up with noise and rude delight, — 6 *Ev. Wk.* 248
—To towns, whose shades of no rude noise complain, — 12 *Desc. Sk.* 81

Rude—*continued.*
On a rude viol touched with withered hand. — 13 *Desc. Sk.* 148
Unmoved with each rude form of peril nigh; — 14 *Desc. Sk.* 205
For supplying all deficiencies, all wants of the rude nest — 91 *Norman Boy* 22
Of this rude church-yard, till the stars appeared — 97 *Brothers* 114
Homely and rude, I will relate the same — 131 *Michael* 35
I chiselled out in those rude characters — 148 *Joanna* 82
A rude and natural causeway, interposed — 148 **A narrow* 2
With the rude shepherd's favoured glance, — 180 *Waggoner* 4. 29
Or must we be constrained to think that these Spectators rude, — 189 *Star-gazers* 21
Three pillars of rude stone Sir Walter reared, — 202 *Hart-leap* 83
Of nether air's rude billows is unknown; — 231 **The gentlest Poet* 10
He was a Carl as wild and rude — 239 *P. B.* 273
To the rude Briton, when, in wolf-skin vest — 265 **Hail, Twilight* 6
Rude Mausoleum! but wrens nestle there, — 276 *Filial Piety* 13
May no rude hand deface it, — 287 *Ellen Irwin* 55
Uncouth the workmanship, and rude! — 301 *Bran* 76
And is it among rude untutored Dales, — 315 **And is it* 1
The rude Biscayans, when their children lie — 318 **In due* 2
On hearts howe'er insensible or rude; — 329 *Ode: Thanks.* 3
Rude Nature's Pilgrims did we go, — 347 **Lulled by* 2
The Patriot's heart with pictures rude and stern, — 351 *Des. Stanzas* 57
'Mid sheltering pines, this Cottage rude and grey; — 377 *Duddon* 5. 10
Into rude shape by fire, with roaring blast — 379 *Duddon* 15. 11
Furrowing its way right onward. The most rude, — 460 **Wanderer! that* 52
When teeming Matrons—yielding to rude faith — 460 **Queen of* 29
There saw, impaved with rude fidelity — 472 **The captive* 5
Back towards caverned life's first rude career. — 489 *Illus. Books* 11
These rude habiliments, and rest — 545 *Russ. Fug.* 319
Rude is this Edifice, and Thou hast seen — 547 **Rude is* 1
Buildings, albeit rude, that have maintained — 547 **Rude is* 2
Than the rude embryo of a little Dome — 548 **Stranger! this* 5
For some rude beauty of its own, — 549 **In these* 4
Unlearned Book and rude, as well I know, — 562 *Cuck.andNight.*291
On a low structure of rude masonry — 566 *Cumb. Beg.* 3
To stately Hall and Cottage rude — 578 **I come* 61
To towns, whose shades of no rude sound complain, — 603 *Desc. Sk. Quarto* 84
Unmov'd with each rude form of Danger nigh, — 607 *Desc.Sk.Quarto* 260
And of some other Being. A rude mass — 642 *Prelude* 2. 33
When at a country-playhouse, some rude barn — 694 *Prelude* 7. 449
When all the external man is rude in show,— — 743 *Prelude* 13. 228
Thus wrongfully of verse, however rude, — 745 *Prelude* 13. 363
Of a rude cottage at the mountain's base — 746 *Prelude* 14. 7
And this rude bench, one torturing hope endeared, — 770 *Excursion* 1. 913
By thrusting two rude staves into the wall — 777 *Excursion* 2. 418
"Farewell, deep Valley, with thy one rude House, — 822 *Excursion* 5. 1
By rude hands built, with rocky knolls in front, — 833 *Excursion* 5. 694
Naked without, and rude within; a spot — 859 *Excursion* 7. 138
Of the rude pile; as ofttimes trunks of trees, — 871 *Excursion* 7. 916
Of their rude homesteads. Here the Warrior dwelt; — 872 *Excursion* 7. 955
Rude intercourse; apt agents to expel, — 875 *Excursion* 8. 67
And the rude boy—who, having overpast — 888 *Excursion* 9. 314
—A few rude monuments of mountain-stone — 894 *Excursion* 9. 710
Rudely. And rudely canopied by leafy boughs, — 172 *Infant Daughter* 20
Where rocks were rudely heaped, and rent — 288 *Glen-Al.* 9
Rudely to mock the works of toiling Man. — 788 *Excursion* 3. 127
Rudely-painted. Of rudely-painted Cherubim. The floor — 824 *Excursion* 5. 153
Rudely-sculptured. Proud tomb is none; but rudely-sculptured knights, — 387 **Part fenced* 9
Ruder. Or ruder weapon which their course might yield, — 212 *Dion* 20
By ruder fancy, that a troubled ghost — 219 *Haunted Tree* 28
The Season's harmless pastime. Ruder sound — 349 *Val. Dover* 9
By ruder hands in homelier vest. — 390 *HighlandBroach* 40
No ruder sound your desart haunts invades, — 596 *Ev. Wk. Quarto* 237
Rudest. That wants not, even in rudest breasts, a seat; — 393 *Hart's-horn* 12
And rudest age are subject to the thrill — 426 *Ecc. Sonn.* 1. 30. 13
As, at this day, the rudest swains who dwell — 502 **The unremitting* 15
Even to the rudest novice of the Schools. — 696 *Prelude* 7. 597
Upon their virtues; saw, in rudest men, — 715 *Prelude* 9. 386
The rudest habitations. Ye might think — 855 *Excursion* 6. 1143
Rudiments. To illustrate Nature's book of rudiments— — 657 *Prelude* 3. 554
The pleasure gathered from the rudiments — 676 *Prelude* 6. 116
While yet he lingered in the rudiments — 760 *Excursion* 1. 270
The rudiments of war; ten—hardy, strong, — 869 *Excursion* 7. 771
The rudiments of letters, and inform — 888 *Excursion* 9. 301
Rue. That we the mercy of the waves should rue: — 29 *Guilt* 296
Full soon this generous purpose thou may'st rue, — 104 *Artegal* 168
And oh, how grievously I rue, — 114 *Ind. Wom.* 26
Which they must both for ever rue. — 128 *Idiot Boy* 181
It must, or we shall rue it: — 293 *Yarrow Unv.* 50
In vain shall rue the broken intercourse. — 383 *Duddon* 30. 8
To courses fit to make a mother rue — 447 *Ecc. Sonn.* 3. 27. 10
That every wight might on his sorrow rue. — 563 *Troilus* 42
To that inheritance which millions rue — 826 *Excursion* 5. 272
Oh no! I do not, cannot rue, — K.8. 220 **The snow-tracks* 27
Rueful. When on his own he cast a rueful look. — 36 *Guilt* 634
That sent this rueful cry, I ween — 85 *Shepherd-boys* 79
In rueful words, with sobs between— — 176 *Waggoner* 1. 227
The rueful conflict, the heart riven — 286 *Nith* 57
Bear witness, rueful Yarrow! — 302 *Yarrow V.* 40
But 'tis a rueful thought that willow bands — 325 *Enghien* 12
And float in rueful company! — 400 *White Doe* 359

Rural—*continued.*
But that the minstrel of the rural shade — 863 *Excursion* 7. 370
Of rural labours; the steep mountain-side — 863 *Excursion* 7. 419
And through the impediment of rural cares, — 868 *Excursion* 7. 736
On rural business passing to and fro — 881 *Excursion* 8. 449
Suffice it, therefore, if the rural Muse — 892 *Excursion* 9. 518
Lively and beautiful, in rural forms, — K.8. 227 **I will* 92
Ruralised. Of city smoke, by distance ruralised; — 633 *Prelude* 1. 89
Rush. Rush in—the villains seize us—— Seize! Yes, they— — 49 *Bord.* 644
Then grasp our swords and rush upon a cure — 56 *Bord.* 1033
A very hunter did I rush — 79 **Stay near* 14
Rush on the fight, to harps preferring swords, — 421 *Ecc. Sonn.* 1. 10. 13
Some with ungovernable impulse rush; — 436 *Ecc. Sonn.* 2. 32. 4
Rush down the living rocks with whirlwind sound. — 612 *Desc.Sk.Quarto* 581
To rush and disappear. But soon broke forth — 687 *Prelude* 7. 8
Rushed. The crows rushed by in eddies, homeward borne. — 25 *Guilt* 40
Deluge of tender thoughts then rushed amain, — 33 *Guilt* 494
You rushed into the murderous flames, returned — 40 *Bord.* 179
That instant rushed between us, and I heard — 40 *Bord.* 186
Rushed in between us: then did I insist — 68 *Bord.* 1718
Rushed o'er the wood with startling sound; — 154 **A whirl-blast* 2
The rain rushed down—the road was battered, — 175 *Waggoner* 1. 188
And forth she rushed into the light, — 247 *P. B.* 1009
Rushed forth, and at the heart of Bruce — 287 *Ellen Irwin* 27
So had they rushed into the grot — 301 *Bran* 62
Rushed through his mind the prophecy — 411 *White Doe* 1427
Rushed in; and—while, O grief to tell! — 412 *White Doe* 1491
Tell what rushed in, from what she was relieved— — 446 *Ecc. Sonn.* 3. 24. 6
The desperate deer rushed on, and near — 544 *Russ. Fug.* 271
Forth rushed from Envy sprung and Self-conceit, — 626 *Ballot* 1
Into my little sanctuary rushed— — 783 *Excursion* 2. 777
A kindling eye:—accordant feelings rushed — 808 *Excursion* 4. 506
Back to my mind rushed all that had been urged — 817 *Excursion* 4. 1102
Rushes. *See* **Water-rushes.**
While the coarse rushes, to the sweeping breeze, — 215 *Kirkstone* 39
Thridding with sinuous lapse the rushes, through — 377 *Duddon* 4. 7
And a far-off wind that rushes, — 457 **The sun has* 6
Fresh water rushes strew the verdant floor; — 596 *Ev. Wk. Quarto* 228
Rushing. Rushing and racing came to meet me at the waterside! — 28 *Guilt* 216
Rushing along in the full tide of play, — 61 *Bord.* 1332
The gazers feel; and, rushing to the plain, — 213 *Dion* 27
Transformed, and rushing on a bold exchange — 270 **Ye sacred* 9
For One, among those rushing deer, — 414 *White Doe* 1642
Of winter rushing in, to close — 502 *Seasons* 15
The Tyrians rushing in, an eager band, — 624 *Æneid* 71
Russ. Plunge with the Russ embrown'd by Terror's breath, — 606 *Desc.Sk.Quarto* 245
Russell's. And Russell's milder blood the scaffold wet; — 442 *Ecc. Sonn.* 3. 10. 4
Russet. And clad in homely russet brown? — 485 *Poet's Epitaph* 38
Blew softly o'er the russet heath, — 550 *Hermit's Cell* 2. 10
Russia. And Russia far inland? — 162 **Art thou the* 8
Russian. Of dreadful sacrifice; by Russian blood — 322 **By Moscow* 2
This Russian vassal plied, — 543 *Russ. Fug.* 106
By Russian usage hung— — 544 *Russ. Fug.* 212
The Swede, the Russian; from the genial south, — 690 *Prelude* 7. 224
Here reigns the Russian, there the Turk; observe — 869 *Excursion* 7. 793
Rustic. Three humble bells their rustic chime repeat; — 4 *Ev. Wk.* 139
It was a rustic inn;—the board was spread, — 34 *Guilt* 528
She had a rustic, woodland air, — 83 *We are Seven* 9
And graceful in his rustic dress! — 86 *Anecdote* 26
Thence in our rustic dialect was called — 133 *Michael* 168
Of whom I sing this rustic lay, — 174 *Waggoner* 1. 94
Well pleased in rustic garb to feed — 180 *Waggoner* 4. 50
The rustic Wishing-gate! — 223 *Wishing-gate* 18
The Rustic sate. — 286 *Nith* 36
Whether the whistling Rustic tend his plough — 305 *Toussaint* 2
The rustic Maidens, every hand — 338 *Brientz* 12
Which Nature and these rustic Powers, — 375 **The Minstrels* 29
Till in the bosom of our rustic Cell — 395 *White Doe: Ded.* 21
As she approached yon rustic Shed — 407 *White Doe* 1022
This day, when, forth by rustic music led, — 448 *Ecc. Sonn.* 3. 32. 4
His rustic chimney with the last of Thee! — 490 *Spade* 32
To mingle in the rustic dance, — 544 *Russ. Fug.* 247
Of Beauties yet unborn—the rustic Lodge — 547 **Rude is* 10
Hence rustic dinners on the cool green ground, — 643 *Prelude* 2. 89
And mockery of the rustic painter's hand— — 644 *Prelude* 2. 153
They hold a rustic fair—a festival, — 699 *Prelude* 8. 11
In rustic sequestration—all dependent — 761 *Excursion* 1. 330
Such as might suit a rustic Sire, prepared — 762 *Excursion* 1. 421
The laggard Rustic; and repay with boons — 773 *Excursion* 2. 123
Of rustic persons, from behind the hut — 777 *Excursion* 2. 387
Not rustic—dull and faded like himself! — 779 *Excursion* 2. 501
Of a most rustic ignorance, and take — 810 *Excursion* 4. 615
Our little Page: the rustic pair approach; — 821 *Excursion* 4. 1310
Of rustic loneliness: that grey-haired Orphan— — 835 *Excursion* 5. 885
Of sweet civility, on rustic wilds. — 839 *Excursion* 6. 41
Of rustic homeliness; they only aimed — 846 *Excursion* 6. 508
This rustic tenement, had gently shed, — 860 *Excursion* 7. 206
So, through a simple rustic garb's disguise, — 868 *Excursion* 7. 735
Hung in his rustic hall. One ivied arch — 872 *Excursion* 7. 962
To rustic, and the rustic to urbane. — 875 *Excursion* 8. 71
The rustic Boy, who walks the fields, untaught; — 886 *Excursion* 9. 162
The chosen rustic urged a warlike steed — S.3. 437 **The doubt* 190
Rusticity. And a refined rusticity, belong — 444 *Ecc. Sonn.* 3. 18. 2
Rustic's. An artless rustic's notice, this way less, — 657 *Prelude* 3. 586
Rusting. Armour rusting in his halls — 205 *Brougham* 142
Rustle. Foes might hang upon their path, snakes rustle near, — 141 *Arm. Lady* 89
"Blood drops—leaves rustle—yet," quoth he, — 245 *P. B.* 808
Thy green leaves rustle or thy torrents roar. — 331 *Ode: Thanks.* 144
Then all is hushed; the bushes rustle near, — 606 *Desc.Sk.Quarto* 237
Rustled. The leaves that rustled on this oak-crowned hill, — 456 **The leaves* 1
Dislodged, through sere leaves rustled, or at once — 633 *Prelude* 1. 84
Of that great kingdom, rustled o'er our heads, — 680 *Prelude* 6. 362
Rustling. *See* **Faintly-rustling.**
Where the duck dabbles 'mid the rustling sedge, — 7 *Ev. Wk.* 281
Hurrying the timid hare through rustling corn; — 9 *Ev. Wk.* 374
In long-drawn vista, rustling in the breeze; — 11 *Desc. Sk.* 47
Through rustling aspens heard from side to side, — 21 *Desc. Sk.* 625
Winds rustling over plots of unripe grain, — 25 *Guilt* 35
And that green corn all day is rustling in thy ears! — 87 *Pet-lamb* 28
In rustling conflict through the skies, — 114 *Ind. Wom.* 5
I dread the rustling of the grass; — 117 *Affl. Marg.* 65
And startled only by the rustling brake, — 262 *Retirement* 11
To Nature's tuneful quire, this rustling dry — 263 **While not* 10
And that soft rustling of invisible wings — 371 *Eg. Maid* 149
Crowded together under rustling trees — 383 *Duddon* 28. 2
Comes that low sound from breezes rustling o'er — 453 **The Sun, that* 9
Hurrying the feeding hare thro' rustling corn; — 600 *Ev. Wk. Quarto* 442
Her road elms rustling thin above my head, — 602 *Desc. Sk. Quarto* 48
Breaks from the rustling boughs, — 626 †*Cento* 14
And sometimes rustling motions nigh at hand, — 686 *Prelude* 6. 719
And rustling leaves. Enchanting age and sweet! — 693 *Prelude* 7. 441
Rusty. Their rusty hats they trim: — 84 *Shepherd-boys* 20
Rusty lance, I ne'er shall grasp thee, — 140 *Arm. Lady* 51
Her eyebrows have a rusty stain, — 144 *Her Eyes* 3
Ruth. But what afflicts my peace with keenest ruth, — 32 *Guilt* 438
When Ruth was left half desolate, — 192 *Ruth* 1
And Ruth, not seven years old, — 192 *Ruth* 3
"Sweet Ruth! and could you go with me — 193 *Ruth* 91
"Beloved Ruth!"—No more he said. — 193 *Ruth* 97
The wakeful Ruth at midnight shed — 193 *Ruth* 98
That to sweet Ruth that happy day — 193 *Ruth* 107
"O Ruth! I have been worse than dead; — 194 *Ruth* 164
Dear Ruth! more happily set free — 194 *Ruth* 176
Deserted his poor Bride, and Ruth — 194 *Ruth* 191
God help thee, Ruth!—Such pains she had, — 194 *Ruth* 193
When Ruth three seasons thus had lain, — 194 *Ruth* 205
And Ruth will, long before her day, — 194 *Ruth* 230
Ill-fated Ruth, in hallowed mould — 195 *Ruth* 254
Assaulting without ruth — 330 *Ode: Thanks.* 107
And hand reposing on the board in ruth — 343 *Last Sup.* 11
Ungentle, or untouched by seemly ruth, — 359 *Plea: Hist.* 2
The consummation, the whole ruth — 413 *White Doe* 1549
That fills the Soul with unavailing ruth. — 419 *Ecc. Sonn.* 1. 4. 14
Ruth does what Simon cannot do; — 483 *Simon Lee* 50
Had of him ruth, and fancied that they said, — 564 *Troilus* 108
Ruthless. Never shall ruthless minister of death — 3 *Ev. Wk.* 74
'Tis done! The ruthless traitor! A rash deed!— — 78 *Bord.* 2319
Had slain his paramour with ruthless sword: — 103 *Artegal* 36
'Tis gone—a ruthless spoiler's prey, — 169 *Wren's Nest* 49
Slackening the pains of ruthless banishment — 273 **When Philoctetes* 7
Pounced,—and the Dove, which from its ruthless beak — 274 **Wait, prithee* 13
And must he too the ruthless change bemoan — 282 *Railway* 6
Where ruthless mortals wage incessant wars. — 313 **Clouds, lingering* 8
By the blind Goddess,—ruthless, undismayed; — 317 **Look now* 5
Of Chiefs triumphant after ruthless wars; — 346 *Processions* 29
She guards thee, ruthless Power! who would not spare — 376 *Duddon* 2. 9
In the ruthless wars of the White and Red; — 399 *White Doe* 251
Hath preyed with ruthless appetite — 472 *Ossian* 33
"Now ruthless Tempest launch thy deadliest dart! — 597 *Ev. Wk. Quarto* 291
"Calm as a frozen lake when ruthless winds — 795 *Excursion* 3. 650
Struggling in vain with ruthless destiny." — 846 *Excursion* 6. 557
Ruthlessly. Won confidence, now ruthlessly betrayed — 515 *Penn.* 7
Rydal. Along the banks of Rydal Mere — 174 *Waggoner* 1. 30
As when he clomb from Rydal Mere; — 174 *Waggoner* 1. 102
Rydal-cove. Down Rydal-cove from Fairfield's side, — 534 **Blest is* 86
Rydale's. Of giant yews that frown on Rydale's mere; — 591 *Ev. Wk. Quarto* 8
Rydal-heights. Though Rydal-heights and Dunmail-raise, — 175 *Waggoner* 1. 140
Rydalian. Adieu, Rydalian Laurels! that have grown — 463 **Adieu, Rydalian* 1
Rylstone. From Rylstone she hath found her way — 398 *White Doe* 186
Among the wastes of Rylstone Fell, — 409 *White Doe* 1164
To Rylstone he the tidings brought; — 409 *White Doe* 1205
Where Rylstone brook with Wharf is blended. — 414 *White Doe* 1693
Of mind, to Rylstone back she came; — 415 *White Doe* 1752
When the bells of Rylstone played — 415 *White Doe* 1761
The bells of Rylstone seemed to say, — 415 *White Doe* 1772
—In Rylstone Church her mortal frame — 416 *White Doe* 1869
Rylstone-hall. Stood quietly in Rylstone-hall. — 400 *White Doe* 379
Herself beloved in Rylstone-hall. — 402 *White Doe* 565
And the stern old Lord of Rylstone-hall — 409 *White Doe* 1186
To Rylstone-hall her way she took. — 411 *White Doe* 1363
—How desolate is Rylstone-hall! — 412 *White Doe* 1511
And forth from Rylstone-hall stepped she,— — 413 *White Doe* 1539
Bore it, or led, to Rylstone-hall — 416 *White Doe* 1809
Rylstone's. Where Rylstone's old sequestered Hall — 406 *White Doe* 946
In Rylstone's woeful neighbourhood, — 411 *White Doe* 1349
O'er Rylstone's fair domain have blown; — 413 *White Doe* 1569

S

Sabbath. For ever broke, the sabbath of her bowers. 12 *Desc. Sk.* 76
An idle voice the sabbath region fills 16 *Desc. Sk.* 354
Or tempt them to an hour of sabbath breach. 99 *Brothers* 272
Free for a sabbath of the heart: 228 *Devot. Incit.* 75
Sad may *I* be who heard your sabbath chime 256 *Easter* 11
To Kirk he on the sabbath day 295 *Highland Boy* 34
Hushed to a depth of more than Sabbath peace: 349 *At Dover* 4
Enter in dance. Of church, or sabbath ties, 387 **Part fenced* 5
'Tis a work for sabbath hours 397 *White Doe* 73
Her sabbath couch has made. 398 *White Doe* 169
Over the hills this sabbath day; 398 *White Doe* 187
Her sabbath morning, foul or fair." 398 *White Doe* 191
Their sabbath music—"𝔊𝔬𝔡 𝔲𝔰 𝔞𝔶𝔡𝔢!" 415 *White Doe* 1762
And every sabbath here is found; 416 *White Doe* 1884
Lies open on the sabbath day; 416 *White Doe* 1888
The Sabbath bells renew the inviting peal; 447 *Ecc. Sonn.* 3. 28. 1
I hear their sabbath bells' harmonious chime 450 *Ecc. Sonn.* 3. 38. 12
And ere the Sabbath he had three. 537 *Goody Blake* 112
Where Death and Glory a joint sabbath keep, 547 **Ye Lime* 10
Again to bend the Sabbath of that time 633 *Prelude* 1. 104
That ran on Sabbath days a fresher course; 661 *Prelude* 4. 226
To break upon the sabbath of her rest 669 *Prelude* 5. 261
For sabbath duties; yet he was a man 762 *Excursion* 1. 422
Alone, through half the vacant sabbath day; 769 *Excursion* 1. 877
Perpetual sabbath; come, disease and want; 802 *Excursion* 4. 58
Save when the sabbath brings its kind release, 834 *Excursion* 5. 806
Which makes the sabbath lovely in the sight 839 *Excursion* 6. 51
With foresight; hears, too, every sabbath day, 866 *Excursion* 7. 577
To spend the sabbath of old age in peace, 867 *Excursion* 7. 666
Like vernal ground to sabbath sunshine left. 869 *Excursion* 7. 781
Where now the beauty of the sabbath kept 878 *Excursion* 8. 246
Of sabbath bells; and ye, who sleep in earth, 895 *Excursion* 9. 727
Sabbath-day. Twice every Sabbath-day. 246 *P. B.* 900
This Sabbath-day, for praise and prayer. 396 *White Doe* 30
Imparted to their sabbath-day. 533 **Blest is* 40
And every sabbath-day its golden sun.'" 835 *Excursion* 5. 837
Sabbath-days. Large measures shall be dealt. Three sabbath-days 808 *Excursion* 4. 468
Sabbath's. The sabbath's return; and its leisure's soft chain! 116 *Repentance* 28
Sabine.—Did Sabine grace adorn my living line, 3 *Ev. Wk.* 72
Or Sabine vales explored inspire a wish 356 *Aquap.* 255
The Sabine Bard was moved her praise to sing; 376 *Duddon* 1. 4
Upon the Sabine farm he loved so well; 528 **Those breathing* 103
Our daily meals were frugal, Sabine fare! 643 *Prelude* 2. 78
Sable. Those fast-receding depths of sable blue 16 *Desc. Sk.* 326
Perennially—beneath whose sable roof 185 *Yew-trees* 23
Broke from the sable orbs of his yet-vivid eyes. 196 *Resolution* 91
Green, sable, shining yellow, shadowy brown, 231 **The gentlest Poet* 18
The heaven of sable night 324 *Ode 1814* 76
Th' interminable sea of sable blue. 609 *Desc.Sk.Quarto* 389
Sable princess, ebon bright. L.2. 190 **Queen and* 18
Sabra. And Sabra in the forest with St. George! 670 *Prelude* 5. 344
Sabrina. Sabrina,—vowing that the stream should bear 103 *Artegal* 39
Sacerdotal. And food cut off by sacerdotal ire, 419 *Ecc. Sonn.* 1. 4. 3
Sackcloth. In sackcloth, and God's anger deprecate 364 **What aim* 7
Sacked. While, to dislodge his game, cities are sacked! 313 **Go back* 14
Sacrament. Brings to thy food, mysterious Sacrament! 446 *Ecc. Sonn.* 3. 25. 3
Before the Altar, where the Sacrament 520 *Pun. Death* 12. 7
Sacred. Which unsubstantial Phantoms sacred keep; 16 *Desc. Sk.* 309
While they are drawing toward the sacred floor 20 *Desc. Sk.* 557
Father, I would not change that sacred feeling 40 *Bord.* 139
That misery is a sacred thing: for me, 58 *Bord.* 1160
Scarcely less than sacred passions, 94 *Westmoreland Girl* 45
Above and round the sacred places 144 **Driven in* 56
Sacred to flowerets of the hills, 165 *Danish Boy* 3
And sacred to the sky. 165 *Danish Boy* 4
But through dependence on the sacred laws 213 *Dion* 48
The very flowers are sacred to the Poor, 250 *Admon.* 11
Yet sacred is to me this Mountain's head, 252 **The fairest* 12
Imagination is that sacred power, 259 **Weak is* 9
Ye sacred Nurseries of blooming Youth! 270 **Ye sacred* 1
When at the sacred font for thee I stood; 274 *Rotha Q.* 2
See how her ivy clasps the sacred Ruin, 283 **Here, where* 5
And, if old judgments keep their sacred course, 318 **Look now* 12
And sacred home—ah! why should hoary Age be bold? 321 **Humanity, delighting* 25
Your Country rears this sacred Monument! 326 **Intrepid sons* 14
With his most sacred wealth, heroic dust. 327 *Ode 1815* 56
Surrendering the whole heart to sacred pleasures? 331 *Ode: Thanks.* 138
The sacred Engelberg, celestial Bands, 338 *Engelberg* 7
Thou sacred Pile! whose turrets rise 341 *San Salv.* 1
And thus, in order, 'mid the sacred grove 346 *Processions* 19
O'er the blank Area of sacred earth 355 *Aquap.* 158
My fault, nor hear it with Thy sacred ear; 366 **Eternal Lord* 10
Sacred Religion! "mother of form and fear," 380 *Duddon* 18. 1
For great and sacred is the modest claim 392 *Avon* 5
Nor will the Power we serve, that sacred Power, 394 **No more* 17
Attuned to words with sacred wisdom fraught; 395 *White Doe: Ded.* 18
The sacred Cross; and figured there 400 *White Doe* 356

Sacred—*continued.*
And the sacred Cross on which Jesus died. 403 *White Doe* 663
The Standard, on the Sacred Wain 405 *White Doe* 818
But, see, the sacred Standard falls!— 408 *White Doe* 1157
Which Emily doth sacred hold 415 *White Doe* 1799
But most to Bolton's sacred Pile, 416 *White Doe* 1811
What Powers, presiding o'er the sacred well 418 *Ecc. Sonn.* 1. 2. 3
Of sacred home;—with pomp are others gored 420 *Ecc. Sonn.* 1. 6. 8
The sacred Structures for less doubtful gains. 424 *Ecc. Sonn.* 1. 24. 8
In sacred converse gifts with Alfred shares. 425 *Ecc. Sonn.* 1. 26. 14
Touch not the tapers of the sacred quires; 426 *Ecc. Sonn.* 1. 31. 11
Scooped from the sacred earth where his dear relics lie. 426 *Ecc. Sonn.* 1. 32. 14
Closes the gates of every sacred place. 427 *Ecc. Sonn.* 1. 36. 4
All sacred things are covered: cheerful morn 427 *Ecc. Sonn.* 1. 36. 6
Should that be needed for their sacred Charge; 432 *Ecc. Sonn.* 2. 13. 13
But they desist not;—and the sacred fire, 432 *Ecc. Sonn.* 2. 14. 9
But, to outweigh all harm, the sacred Book, 435 *Ecc. Sonn.* 2. 29. 1
Upon that circle traced from sacred story 445 *Ecc. Sonn.* 3. 19. 9
Fitliest beneath the sacred roof proceeds 445 *Ecc. Sonn.* 3. 20. 5
Closing the sacred Book which long has fed 448 *Ecc. Sonn.* 3. 32. 1
Even while I speak, the sacred roofs of France 449 *Ecc. Sonn.* 3. 36. 1
Of sacred truth may enter—till it brood 450 *Ecc. Sonn.* 3. 38. 7
Are not, in sooth, their Requiem's sacred ties 467 *St. Bees* 73
Of novelty amid the sacred wreck 474 **How sad* 7
Enraptured Art draws from those sacred springs 500 *Humanity* 19
—Not from a source less sacred is derived 509 *F. Stone* 70
Or sacred wonder, growing with the power 510 **Among a* 25
The sacred limits of humanity. 514 **Portentous change* 14
So sacred, so informed with light divine, 519 *Pun. Death* 10. 3
Receive the curb of sacred truth, 533 **Blest is* 36
Her sacred recompense for many wants) 539 **Lady! a* 51
To sacred studies; and the Roman Shepherd 573 *Chiabrera* 3. 6
This to the dead by sacred right belongs; 576 *Chiabrera* 9. 5
Stand—sacred as a Shrine; 581 *John Words.* 64
This Stone is sacred. Here he lies apart 584 *Ch. Lamb* 2
Your *dual* loneliness. The sacred tie 586 *Ch. Lamb* 128
Since Science first, with all her sacred train, 618 *School Ex.* 3
Fair to the view is sacred Truth display'd, 619 *School Ex.* 71
Firm in the sacred paths of moral truth, 619 *School Ex.* 78
O sacred marriage-bed of death, 623 *G. and S. Green* 33
Guards the sacred heart of youth, 629 *Installation* 75
Of those long vistas, sacred catacombs, 654 *Prelude* 3. 338
As toward the sacred mansion we advanced, 681 *Prelude* 6. 423
A Father—for he bore that sacred name— 696 *Prelude* 7. 603
Upon our native country's sacred ground. 721 *Prelude* 10. 241
Kept sacred to restorative delight, 733 *Prelude* 11. 422
Life, human life, with all its sacred claims 741 *Prelude* 13. 73
And listening Time reward with sacred praise. 758 *Excursion* 1. 107
By virtue of that sacred instrument 771 *Excursion* 2. 14
"His sacred function was at length renounced; 775 *Excursion* 2. 263
And when that sacred spirit shall appear, 806 *Excursion* 4. 318
Men, who, from faction sacred, and unstained 823 *Excursion* 5. 32
His rank and sacred function. This deep vale 824 *Excursion* 5. 122
As chanced, the portals of the sacred Pile 824 *Excursion* 5. 138
That overspread and chilled the sacred turf, 830 *Excursion* 5. 548
A thing most sacred in the eye of Heaven; 841 *Excursion* 6. 179
Upon this sacred ground, if nowhere else." 847 *Excursion* 6. 588
By sacred charter, holden for her use, 856 *Excursion* 6. 1164
To punctual labour in his sacred charge. 859 *Excursion* 7. 149
And lend the echoes of his sacred shell, 863 *Excursion* 7. 365
Whose sacred influence, spread through earth and heaven, 864 *Excursion* 7. 484
May find chance-mention on this sacred ground)— 868 *Excursion* 7. 734
—Right toward the sacred Edifice his steps 871 *Excursion* 7. 911
Proof of the sacred love she bears for all; 885 *Excursion* 9. 100
This sacred right, the lisping babe proclaims 888 *Excursion* 9. 311
—This sacred right is fruitlessly announced, 889 *Excursion* 9. 321
The sacred truth to acknowledge, linger still; 894 *Excursion* 9. 654
My fault, and keep it from thy sacred ear K.8. 266 **Rid of* 10
Sacrifice. *See* **Self-sacrifice.**
A more benignant sacrifice approve— 3 *Ev. Wk.* 79
For sacrifice its throngs of living men, 26 *Guilt* 123
And every sacrifice his peace requires.— 50 *Bord.* 722
Prepared already for the sacrifice. 57 *Bord.* 1093
An expiation and a sacrifice 64 *Bord.* 1457
For, if, by such strange sacrifice restored, 105 *Artegal* 176
A sacrifice of birthright to attain 123 *V. and J.* 105
For every tender sacrifice her heart had made. 141 *Arm. Lady* 138
"With sacrifice before the rising morn 209 *Laod.* 1
Thence offer nightly sacrifice) 214 *Kirkstone* 16
Which caught the blaze of sacrifice, 216 *Enterprise* 41
High sacrifice, and labour without pause, 316 **O'er the* 12
Of dreadful sacrifice; by Russian blood 322 **By Moscow* 2
Heroes!—for instant sacrifice prepared; 326 **Intrepid sons* 9
Which ministered, erewhile, to a sacrifice 326 *Sobieski* 2
The quickening spark of this day's sacrifice; 329 *Ode: Thanks.* 52
To sulphurous bolts a sacrifice, 341 *San Salv.* 5
His acts, his wrongs, his final sacrifice; 351 *Des. Stanzas* 71
Or leading victims drest for sacrifice. 394 **No more* 16
Deserve they further sacrifice?— 406 *White Doe* 905
By Nature decked for holiest sacrifice. 420 *Ecc. Sonn.* 1. 6. 14
No sacrifice avert, no power dispute; 433 *Ecc. Sonn.* 2. 21. 2
Poor as thou art. A welcome sacrifice 465 *Pastor and* 8
So often that demand such sacrifice; 493 *Hap. War.* 22
Of Nations," sacrifice a People's health, 501 *Humanity* 90
(Would that it were!) the sacrifice unmeet 520 *Pun. Death* 13. 7
Drawn from the Sacrifice fulfilled, 533 **Blest is* 27
From the altar of this sacrifice, 544 *Russ. Fug.* 239
Of truth and justice, either sacrifice, 721 *Prelude* 10. 187

Sacrifice—*continued.*
For sacrifice, and struggling with fond mirth . . 724 *Prelude* 10. 407
Presented sacrifice to moon and stars, ... 811 *Excursion* 4. 676
My heart a daily sacrifice to Truth, ... 816 *Excursion* 4. 982
Perpetual sacrifice. Even thus of old . . . . 877 *Excursion* 8. 185
An offering, or a sacrifice, a tool . . . . . 886 *Excursion* 9. 115
By priestly hands, for sacrifice performed . . . 894 *Excursion* 9. 705
They hear my lips present their sacrifice, . . . 895 *Excursion* 9. 749
Sacrificed. Whose nobler will hath long been sacrificed ; . . . . K.8. 253 *Recluse* 1. 1. 602
Sacrificial. To triumphs and to sacrificial rites . . 701 *Prelude* 8. 178
It is the sacrificial altar, fed . . . . 744 *Prelude* 13. 331
Sacrilegious. Her chantry blazed with sacrilegious fire, ... 466 *St. Bees* 58
—"Stay, stay your sacrilegious hands !"—The voice . . . . 681 *Prelude* 6. 430
Sad. Press the sad kiss, fond mother ! vainly fears 7 *Ev. Wk.* 275
With sad congratulation joins the train . . . 13 *Desc. Sk.* 168
Why does their sad remembrance haunt the mind ? 19 *Desc. Sk.* 519
If the sad grave of human ignorance bear . . . 20 *Desc. Sk.* 551
What tender vows our last sad kiss delayed ! . . 29 *Guilt* 256
With bitter insult and revilings sad ; . . . . 33 *Guilt* 481
Far as the cottage. "A sad sight is here," . . 34 *Guilt* 556
Of my sad journey ; and within the wain . . . 35 *Guilt* 582
My husband served in sad captivity . . . . 35 *Guilt* 593
With look as sad as he were dumb ; the cur, . . 45 *Bord.* 457
In such sad service ; and he parted with him. . 50 *Bord.* 690
I bless her with sad spirit,—when of God, . . 62 *Bord.* 1375
lying stretched upon the ground—a sad spectacle : 72 *Bord.* 1924
This is sad talk—they'll never sound for him— . 100 *Brothers* 315
But, whether blithe or sad, 'tis my belief . . . 100 *Brothers* 347
For years to me are sad and dull ; . . . . . 113 *Lament* 12
Sturdy he seemed, though he was sad ; . . . 114 *Last of Flock* 9
"They dwindled, Sir, sad sight to see ! . . . 115 *Last of Flock* 91
With our pastures about us, we could not be sad ; 116 *Repentance* 21
Her sad approach, and stole away to find, . . 118 *Maternal Grief* 52
For ever—sad alternative ! preferred, ... 125 *V. and J.* 237
And Betty's in a sad *quandary* ; . . . . . 128 *Idiot Boy* 168
—She's in a sad *quandary*. . . . . 128 *Idiot Boy* 171
Of sad mischances not a few, ... 128 *Idiot Boy* 178
Poor Betty, in this sad distemper, ... 128 *Idiot Boy* 237
A few sad tears does Betty shed. . . . . . 130 *Idiot Boy* 386
Sad deliverance would it be, and yoked with shame, 140 *Arm. Lady* 29
Full many a sad and doleful thing : . . . . 144 *Her Eyes* 14
Then I must be for ever sad. . . . . . . 145 *Her Eyes* 90
Sending sad shadows after things not sad, . . 153 *Morn. Ex.* 3
Sad thoughts, and breathes with easier breath ; . 164 **Fair Lady* 34
The dying Gladiator. So, sad Flower ! . . . 169 *Lovelies Bleeding* 9
No—sad progress of my story ! . . . . . . 181 *Waggoner* 4. 120
And are returned into themselves, they cannot but be sad ? . . . . 189 *Star-gazers* 20
Pleased with herself, nor sad, nor gay ; . . . 192 *Ruth* 16
Yet often was she sober sad . . . . 199 *Thorn* 129
"Sad case for such a brain to hold . . . . 199 *Thorn* 133
Sad case, as you may think, for one . . . . 199 *Thorn* 135
And somewhat of a sad perplexity, ... 206 *Tintern* 60
The still, sad music of humanity, ... 207 *Tintern* 91
This precious boon ; and blest a sad abode." . . 210 *Laod.* 36
And all the sad and precious things . . . . 216 *Enterprise* 75
Could from sad regions send him to a dear . . 229 *Cuckoo-clock* 31
Your heart would be as sad as his . . . . . 243 *P. B.* 634
To its sad Lord, far from his native fields ? . . 252 **Why, Minstrel* 14
Sad may *I* be who heard your sabbath chime . . 256 *Easter* 11
Erroneously renewing a sad vow . . . . . 261 **From the dark* 11
Of sad mortality's earth-sullying wing, . . . 263 **How clear* 9
With how sad steps, O Moon, thou climb'st the sky, 266 **With how* 1
Conqueror, 'mid some sad thoughts, divinely blest ! 278 *Wellington* 14
His day-break note, a sad vicissitude ! . . . 279 **'Tis he* 3
Some sad delight. . . . . 285 *Grave of Burns* 66
Sad tidings to that noble Youth ! . . . . . 287 *Ellen Irwin* 13
Less deeply sad, with these to blend ! . . . . 301 *Bran* 104
Sad thought, which I would banish, ... 302 *Yarrow V.* 84
Haunts, with sad echoes, musing Fancy's ear : . 312 **A Roman* 10
Must still have sad or vexing thoughts to endure, 317 **Call not* 11
Yet sad as sweet,—for *English* words . . . . 334 **In Bruges* 15
Sad is thy doom, self-solaced dove, ... 334 **In Bruges* 29
Sad blindness ! but ordained to prove . . . . 344 *Eclipse* 82
To which sad course, these wrinkled Sons of Time 350 *Des. Stanzas* 24
To the sad soul give hope of pardon free. . . . 366 **Eternal Lord* 8
Which o'er sad thoughts a sadder colouring threw. 366 **Fair Land* 8
Which she in duty left, sad but not cheerless. . 370 *Eg. Maid* 84
Sad relique, but how fair the while ! . . . . 371 *Eg. Maid* 127
Sad thoughts, avaunt !—partake we their blithe cheer . . . . 381 *Duddon* 23. 1
Union not sad, when sunny daybreak smites . . 387 **Part fenced* 12
Thoughtful and sad, the "narrow house." No style . . . . 389 *Breadalb.* 2
How Una, sad of soul—in sad attire, ... 395 *White Doe : Ded.* 6
Sad words to that mute Animal, ... 405 *White Doe* 876
In one sad sweep of destiny— . . . . . . 406 *White Doe* 980
To cheer this sad and pensive time ; . . . . 410 *White Doe* 1281
By this sad burden—even that thought, . . . 411 *White Doe* 1409
So, when upon sad thoughts had prest . . . 412 *White Doe* 1516
But now, when such sad change was wrought, . 415 *White Doe* 1770
Of a sad market, ranged for public sale, . . . 421 *Ecc. Sonn.* 1. 13. 3
A waste of hope ?—From this sad source have sprung . . . . 423 *Ecc. Sonn.* 1. 20. 5
Grows sad as night—no seemly garb is worn, . . 427 *Ecc. Sonn.* 1. 36. 7
How sad would be their durance, if forlorn . . 430 *Ecc. Sonn.* 2. 6. 13
Totters the Throne ; the new-born Church is sad, 439 *Ecc. Sonn.* 2. 41. 13
With filial love the sad vicissitude ; . . . . 440 *Ecc. Sonn.* 3. 2. 11

Sad—*continued.*
Sad thoughts ; for from above the starry sphere . 441 *Ecc. Sonn.* 3. 4. 10
Who, with sad hearts, of friends and country took 443 *Ecc. Sonn.* 3. 13. 2
O sad it is, in sight of foreign shores, ... 458 *Sea-shore* 9
Sad were our lot : no hunter of the hare . . . 466 *St. Bees* 3
Bewailing his sad fate, when he was laid . . . 470 **A youth* 8
That clings to slavery for its own sad sake. . . 472 *Dunolly Eagle* 14
And friendless, by their own sad choice ! . . . 473 *Ossian* 52
Hence, while in you each sad regret . . . . 473 *Ossian* 67
How sad a welcome ! To each voyager . . . 474 **How sad* 1
Warmed our sad being with celestial light, . . 476 **Tranquillity ! the* 9
Bring sad thoughts to the mind. . . . . . 482 *Lines : Spring* 4
So sad a sigh has brought ? " . . . . . . 486 **We walked* 16
A name more sad than Yarrow. . . . . . 494 *Force of Prayer* 40
Sad fancies do we then affect, ... 497 *Lycoris* 23
So, by chequerings of sad cheer, ... 502 **Like a* 33
We act as if we joyed in the sad tune . . . . 505 *Warning* 144
And eyes that cannot but be sad . . . . . 507 *May* 23
Found at the Widow's feet some sad relief ; . . 523 *Epist. Beaumont* 134
Give *me* the humblest note of those sad strains . 528 **Those breathing* 100
This sad belief, the happiest that is left . . . 531 *Octogen.* 6
While I salute my joys, thoughts sad or stern ; . 533 **Once I* 34
Smitten to the heart, and sad. . . . . . . 536 *Egremont* 92
Sad case it was, as you may think, ... 536 *Goody Blake* 46
Sad theme for every tongue ; . . . . . . 545 *Russ. Fug.* 316
To London—a sad emigration I ween— . . . 570 *Farmer* 45
Penned these sad lines, nor can forbear to pray . 575 *Chiabrera* 7. 16
A sad heart's sunshine) by a soft . . . . . 577 **By playful* 2
Sad was I, even to pain deprest, ... 581 **Loud is* 9
And many thousands now are sad— . . . . 581 **Loud is* 13
And open thy sad eyes upon a milder day. . . 581 *Invoc. Earth* 7
And murder causes some sad tears to flow, . . 582 *Invoc. Earth* 16
Sad doom, at Sorrow's shrine to kneel, . . . 582 **O for a* 13
Sad tides of joy from Melancholy's hand ; . . 592 *Ev. Wk. Quarto* 22
By Pain and her sad family unfound, ... 602 *Desc. Sk. Quarto* 2
No sad vacuities his heart annoy, ... 602 *Desc. Sk. Quarto* 17
Much wondering what sad stroke of crazing Care 602 *Desc. Sk. Quarto* 43
Why does their sad remembrance cleave behind ? 613 *Desc. Sk. Quarto* 623
At morn, our various journey, sad and slow. . . 617 *Desc. Sk. Quarto* 813
And sad experience forbade a thought . . . . 620 *Birth of Love* 22
Their spirit hallowed the sad spectacle . . . 672 *Prelude* 5. 456
Move us with conscious pleasure. I am sad . . 673 *Prelude* 5. 545
Almost to tears I sometimes could be sad . . . 674 *Prelude* 5. 547
A pensive sky, sad days, and piping winds, . . 677 *Prelude* 6. 174
Through sad incompetence of human speech, . . 684 *Prelude* 6. 593
And all the sad etcetera of the wrong, ... 705 *Prelude* 8. 442
From those sad scenes when meditation turned, . 709 *Prelude* 8. 654
Told by my Patriot friend, of sad events, . . 717 *Prelude* 9. 548
Sad opposites out of the inner heart, ... 726 *Prelude* 10. 529
"A sad reverse it was for him who long . . . 764 *Excursion* 1. 566
With the sad news, that he had joined a troop . 766 *Excursion* 1. 676
And now the music of my own sad steps, . . . 767 *Excursion* 1. 704
I sate with sad impatience. From within . . 767 *Excursion* 1. 735
I found her sad and drooping : she had learned . 768 *Excursion* 1. 817
Her heart was still more sad. And by yon gate, 769 *Excursion* 1. 894
The same sad question. Meanwhile her poor Hut 770 *Excursion* 1. 900
Sad contrast ! all too often smote his heart . . 772 *Excursion* 2. 53
And wastes the sad remainder of his hours, . . 776 *Excursion* 2. 310
This sad memorial of their hapless friend !" . . 778 *Excursion* 2. 456
And, of the sad appearance which at once . . 779 *Excursion* 2. 521
From mild to angry, and from sad to gay, . . . 790 *Excursion* 3. 315
Sad or disturbed, is ordered by a Being . . . 801 *Excursion* 4. 14
And sad exclusion through decay of sense ; . . 802 *Excursion* 4. 59
Her sad dependence upon time, and all . . . 807 *Excursion* 4. 422
Grave, and in truth too often sad.—"Is Man . 829 *Excursion* 5. 465
Gave obvious instance of the sad effect . . . 842 *Excursion* 6. 279
Of the sad steps by which it hath been trod ! . . 850 *Excursion* 6. 810
Confessed the power of nature.—Pleased though sad, ... 854 *Excursion* 6. 1063
More pleased than sad, the grey-haired Wanderer sate ; . . . . 854 *Excursion* 6. 1064
In sad conjectures—'Shall we meet him now . . 861 *Excursion* 7. 266
The sad privation was by him endured. . . . 864 *Excursion* 7. 476
To us, with our sad spirits, heavenly-fair— . . 868 *Excursion* 7. 696
In this sad service, less disturbed than we. . . 871 *Excursion* 7. 885
The lot is wretched, the condition sad, . . . 878 *Excursion* 8. 292
Entrust the future.—Not for these sad issues . . 886 *Excursion* 9. 126
Pomp has been a sad deceiver. . . . . . . L.2. 190 **Queen and* 14
A sad and lovely face, with upturn'd eyes, . . [?] **A sad* 1
Saddened. These vales were saddened with no common gloom . . . . K.8. 275 **These vales* 1
Saddening. *See* **Spirit-saddening.**
Of irksome change, or threats from saddening power. . . . . 327 *Ode 1815* 16
Heard them, unchecked by aught of saddening hue, 367 **If with* 12
Saddening the heart. Go forward, and look back ; 830 *Excursion* 5. 539
Saddens. Saddens his voice again, and yet again. . 387 *Scott* 7
Is clasping mine, it saddens me to think . . . 626 **Son of* 2
Sadder. Make sadder transits o'er thought's optic glass . . . . 269 *Malham* 13
Which o'er sad thoughts a sadder colouring threw. 366 **Fair Land* 8
Thoughts sadder still, they deemed it best . . 412 *White Doe* 1517
Through ignorance and false teaching, sadder proof 721 *Prelude* 10. 215
Motive to sadder grief, as we have found ; . . 888 *Excursion* 9. 251
Saddest. I've had the saddest dream that ever troubled . . . . 44 *Bord.* 397
The saddest thought the Creature brings ? . . 414 *White Doe* 1679
And wild-wood mountain lutes of saddest swell. . 611 *Desc. Sk. Quarto* 509

Sails—*continued.*
Whose flaccid sails in forms fantastic droop, . . 604 *Desc.Sk.Quarto* 128
Or where thick sails illume Batavia's groves ; 613 *Desc.Sk.Quarto* 625
And down the lone vale sails away . . . . 626 †*Cento* 15
Of oars with oars contending, sails with sails, 664 *Prelude* 4. 372
The mariner who sails the roaring sea . . . 742 *Prelude* 13. 153
That animating spectacle of sails . . . . 876 *Excursion* 8. 139
Sails in smooth weather by the placid coast . . 882 *Excursion* 8. 507

Saint. *See* **Patron-saint.**
Soon after, the good Abbot of St. Cuthbert's . . 41 *Bord.* 199
'Tis never drought with us—St. Cuthbert and his Pilgrims, ... 43 *Bord.* 324
Your favourite saint—no matter—this good day . 45 *Bord.* 430
As if he were the only Saint on earth, . . . 45 *Bord.* 463
St. Cuthbert speed you on your holy errand. . . 58 *Bord.* 1141
Is ringing it—'twould stop a Saint in prayer, . . 67 *Bord.* 1665
St. Denis, filled with royal tombs, or the Church of Notre Dame ? . . . . 92 *Poet's Dream* 24
" St. Ouen's golden Shrine ? Or choose what else would please thee most . . . . . 92 *Poet's Dream* 25
And, while she roves through St. John's Vale, . 180 *Waggoner* 4. 23
St. George was for us, and the might . . . 204 *Brougham* 28
Or here a saint expired. . . . . 223 *Wishing-gate* 24
That exquisite Saint John. . . . . . . 232 *Jew. Fam.* 24
All anguish ; Saint that evil thoughts and aims . 253 **Fond words* 7
The swan on still St. Mary's Lake . . . . 293 *Yarrow Unv.* 43
And guiding, like the Patmos Saint, ... 299 *Brownie's Cell* 56
Intent to guard St. Robert's cell ; . . . . 301 *Bran* 55
And, through her depths, Saint Mary's Lake . . 302 *Yarrow V.* 13
Saint George himself this Visitant must be ; . . 323 *Ode 1814* 24
And, as the saint he prays to, still. . . . . 342 *Ital. Itin.* 90
Far as St. Maurice, from yon eastern Forks, . . 350 *Des. Stanzas* 37
Of young or old, warrior, or saint, or sage, . . 356 *Aquap.* 240
A Saint, the Church's Rock, the mystic Keys . . 357 *Aquap.* 309
Crowned with St. Peter's everlasting Dome. . . 358 *Pine : Rome* 14
St. Francis, far from Man's resort, to abide . . 362 **List—'twas* 37
Can she, a blessèd saint, the work approve ? . . 363 **Grieve for* 5
Ere the meek Saint, Columba, bore . . . . 390 *HighlandBroach* 3
And the towers of Saint Cuthbert were stirred by the shout ! . . . . 403 *White Doe* 687
And in Saint Cuthbert's ancient seat . . . . 404 *White Doe* 712
Saint Cuthbert's Relic—far and near . . . . 405 *White Doe* 831
Returns to her—that blessèd Saint . . . . . 407 *White Doe* 1035
And lay it on Saint Mary's shrine ; . . . . 410 *White Doe* 1293
To look upon Saint Mary's shrine ; . . . . . 416 *White Doe* 1816
The saint, the scholar, from a circle freed . . . 424 *Ecc. Sonn.* 1. 23. 5
Michael, and thou, St. George, whose flaming brand 434 *Ecc. Sonn.* 2. 24. 8
The Saint or Patriot to the world that heals . . 440 *Ecc. Sonn.* 2. 45. 13
Tell, if ye may, some star-crowned Muse, or Saint ! 446 *Ecc. Sonn.* 3. 24. 5
Tax not the royal Saint with vain expense, . . 451 *Ecc. Sonn.* 3. 43. 1
For some rare plant, yon Headland of St. Bees. . 466 *St. Bees* 9
Firm as the towering Headlands of St. Bees. . . 466 *St. Bees* 18
As millions thus shall do, the Headlands of St. Bees. 466 *St. Bees* 27
Rose, where she touched the strand, the Chantry of St. Bees. . . . . 466 *St. Bees* 36
Like the fixed Light that crowns yon Headland of St. Bees. . . . . 466 *St. Bees* 45
From her religious Mansion of St. Bees. . . . 466 *St. Bees* 54
And lo ! a *statelier* pile, the Abbey of St. Bees. . 466 *St. Bees* 63
Keep watch before the altars of St. Bees. . . . 467 *St. Bees* 72
That best unlock the secrets of St. Bees. . . . 467 *St. Bees* 81
Nor hear the loudest surges of St. Bees. . . . 467 *St. Bees* 90
Brightening the archway of revered St. Bees. . . 467 *St. Bees* 99
Nursed in the quiet Abbey of St. Bees. . . . 467 *St. Bees* 108
Taught by the hooded Celibates of St. Bees. . . 467 *St. Bees* 117
Witness yon Pile that greets us from St. Bees. . 467 *St. Bees* 126
To bear thy part in this good work, St. Bees. . 468 *St. Bees* 135
Poured from the bosom of thy Church, St. Bees ! 468 *St. Bees* 144
Prosper the new-born College of St. Bees ! . . 468 *St. Bees* 153
That furthered the first teaching of St. Bees. . 468 *St. Bees* 162
A St. Helena next—in shape and hue, . . . 471 **Arran ! a* 2
To Saint, or Fiend, or to the Godhead whom . . 475 **Here on their* 10
Remote St. Kilda, lone and loved sea-mark . . 475 **Homeward we* 6
Then, to her Patron Saint a previous rite . . . 534 **When in* 5
The desolate ruins of St. Herbert's Cell. . . . 551 **If thou in* 7
Far from St. Cuthbert his belovèd Friend, . . 551 **If thou in* 26
Saint Nicholas in my presence standeth aye, . . 553 *Prioress* 63
" Of which the great Evangelist, Saint John, . . 554 *Prioress* 131
Upon Saint Valentine's returning day. . . . 558 *Cuck. and Night.* 80
The morrow after Saint Valentine's day, . . . 562 *Cuck.andNight.* 282
Farewell, thou shrine of which the Saint is out ! . 563 *Troilus* 35
St. George of England ! keep a watchful eye . . 626 *Ballot* 9
St. Mary's Church, the preacher then would cry:— 627 **When Severn's* 2
Of Nightshade, to St. Mary's honour built, . . 643 *Prelude* 2. 104
The Evangelist St. John my patron was : . . . 649 *Prelude* 3. 46
And Sabra in the forest with St. George ! . . . 670 *Prelude* 5. 344
She ceased to speak, but while St. Bruno's pines . 681 *Prelude* 6. 436
And Whispering Gallery of St. Paul's ; the tombs 689 *Prelude* 7. 130
St. Peter's Church ; or, more aspiring aim, . . 691 *Prelude* 7. 252
And named of St. Bartholomew ; there, see . . 697 *Prelude* 7. 678
Down to the suburbs of St. Antony, ... 710 *Prelude* 9. 46
Of Nightshade, and St. Mary's mouldering fane, . 727 *Prelude* 10. 598
To good Saint Fillan and to fair Saint Anne ; . . 815 *Excursion* 4. 910
And from long banishment recall Saint Giles, . . 815 *Excursion* 4. 911
Meek Saint ! through patience glorified on earth ! 854 *Excursion* 6. 1034
Leaving St. Sunday's Crag, to Grisdale tarn . . K.8. 225 **I will* 25

Saint Anne, St. Bartholomew, *etc.* *See* **Saint.**

Sainted. The house she dwelt in was a sainted shrine ; . . . . 122 *V. and J.* 44
(Workman worthy to be sainted) . . . . 161 **Pleasures newly* 12
Religion in the sainted grove, ... 341 *San Salv.* 23

Sainted—*continued.*
And now her sainted Mistress dear ? . . . . 414 *White Doe* 1672
Martyr, or King, or sainted Eremite, ... 451 *Ecc. Sonn.* 3. 44. 5
Oft as those sainted Rocks before him spread, . 612 *Desc.Sk.Quarto* 542
To drink the waters of some sainted well, . . . 701 *Prelude* 8. 155

Saint-like. Lo ! where she stands fixed in a saint-like trance, ... 278 **Lo ! where she* 1
Kings, warriors, high-souled poets, saint-like sages, 328 *Ode 1815* 61
How saintlike is the look those features wear ! . [?] **A sad* 3

Saintly. So saintly and so pure !——Harkee, my Friend, ... 60 *Bord.* 1247
And there, a saintly Anchoress, she dwelt . . . 267 *St. Cath.* 13
By favouring Nature and a saintly Mind . . . 274 **Such age* 3
Margaret, the saintly Foundress, take thy place ; 276 *Author's Portrait* 2
Thy saintly rapture with celestial aim : . . . 326 *Sobieski* 5
Of saintly pleasure from these pictured walls, . 339 *Tell* 17
With lustre of a saintly show ; . . . . . 397 *White Doe* 102
Under the saintly ensigns three, ... 405 *White Doe* 822
Might seem a saintly Image from its shrine . . 423 *Ecc. Sonn.* 1. 19. 8
Through saintly habit than from effort due . . 434 *Ecc. Sonn.* 2. 22. 2
Like saintly Fisher, and unbending More. . . . 435 *Ecc. Sonn.* 2. 26. 8
The saintly Youth has ceased to rule, discrowned 436 *Ecc. Sonn.* 2. 33. 1
Of saintly Friends the " murtherer's chain partake, 437 *Ecc. Sonn.* 2. 34. 11
Of praise from Heaven. To Thee, O saintly White, ... 444 *Ecc. Sonn.* 3. 15. 8
By hooded Votaresses with saintly cheer ; . . 465 **The cattle* 11
Whose saintly radiance mitigates the gloom . . 496 **A little* 46
To saintly bosoms !—Glorious is the blending . 500 *Humanity* 27
No saintly anchoress . . . . 543 *Russ. Fug.* 158
Upon my thoughts his saintly Spirit fed ; . . . 582 **To public* 6
And saintly magnanimity ; that—spurning . . 845 *Excursion* 6. 484
And visiting, though not with saintly zeal, . . 859 *Excursion* 7. 151

Saints. *See* **Virgin-saints.**
Will bring me back—protect him, Saints—farewell ! 43 *Bord.* 323
Here's what will comfort you. The Saints reward you . . . . 44 *Bord.* 408
I' th' name of all the Saints, and by the Mass . 45 *Bord.* 448
Forgive me !—Saints forgive me. Had I thought 76 *Bord.* 2241
" Oh saints ! what is become of him ? . . . . 128 *Idiot Boy* 222
And will be our bliss with saints above. . . . 143 †*Lov. and Lik.* 68
To saints accorded in their mortal hour. . . . 272 **Where holy* 14
Gleams from a world in which the saints repose. . 282 **While beams* 14
Or seek, from saints above, miraculous aid— . . 311 **Who rises* 52
And to the heavenly saints in peace who dwell, . 331 *Ode : Thanks.* 184
Saints would not grieve nor guardian angels frown 354 *Aquap.* 118
Imagine (but ye Saints ! who can ?) . . . . 373 *Eg. Maid* 277
Is offered to the Saints, the sigh . . . . . 403 *White Doe* 676
Dear to the saints, strives earnestly to eject . . 431 *Ecc. Sonn.* 2. 10. 7
Angels and Saints, in every hamlet mourned ! . 434 *Ecc. Sonn.* 2. 24. 2
The Saints must govern is their common cry ; . 439 *Ecc. Sonn.* 2. 41. 5
Iona's Saints, forgetting not past days, . . . 474 **On to* 12
And by all the saints in heaven ; . . . . . 536 *Egremont* 101
The prayer is heard, the Saints have seen, . . 543 *Russ. Fug.* 169
Till pitying Saints conduct her bark . . . . 544 *Russ. Fug.* 235
When Saints have passed away. . . . . . 582 **O for a* 12
Stationed above the door, like guardian saints ; . 689 *Prelude* 7. 162
To which the silver wands of saints in Heaven . 725 *Prelude* 10. 485
We were no saints at twenty, be it so ; . . . L.I. 96 *Juvenal* 3. 52

Saith. " I am eyes to the blind, saith the Lord. . 63 *Bord.* 1413
In Patmos wrote, who saith of them that go . . 554 *Prioress* 132
It saith, Alas, why severed are we twain ? . . 565 *Troilus* 161

Sake. *See* **Conscience-sake.**
And think that they were blasted for my sake, . 39 *Bord.* 137
Come, come, for manhood's sake ! These drowsy shiverings, ... 51 *Bord.* 776
Thy secret for its sake, or verily . . . . . 54 *Bord.* 949
For mercy's sake, is nobody in sight ? . . . . 61 *Bord.* 1292
And for his sake I loved her more : these tears— 61 *Bord.* 1323
and will not curse my son for my sake. . . . 72 *Bord.* 1962
The life he had lived there ; both for the sake . 96 *Brothers* 70
And Leonard, chiefly for his Brother's sake, . . 100 *Brothers* 305
For sake of a young Child whose home was there. 120 *Emigrant Mother* 8
And, with yet fonder feeling, for the sake . . . 131 *Michael* 37
From twig or bed an humbler flower, even for your sake ! " . . . . 139 *Arm. Lady* 12
More dear, both for themselves and for thy sake ! 207 *Tintern* 159
A faith that for the dead man's sake, ... 243 *P. B.* 661
And yawn for his unworthy sake, ... 246 *P. B.* 844
To pleasure snatched for reckless pleasure's sake. 280 **Intent on* 8
To spare your failings for his sake, ... 286 *Sons of Burns* 20
Delighted am I for thy sake ; . . . . . . 294 *Jedbor.* 43
For old remembrance sake. And oft—where Spring 361 **List—'twas* 16
And, for this feeling's sake, let no one chide . . 393 *Hart's-horn* 13
All that she suffered for her dear Lord's sake. . 395 *White Doe : Ded.* 40
For these my brethren's sake, for me ; . . . 400 *White Doe* 396
She steeped, but not for Jesu's sake, ... 405 *White Doe* 878
In friendship—strive—for his sake go— . . . 408 *White Doe* 1084
For concord's sake and England's good, . . . 409 *White Doe* 1234
Then, they, for Christian pity's sake, ... 412 *White Doe* 1520
In glory for this Maiden's sake, ... 413 *White Doe* 1554
Of kindred agitations for thy sake ; . . . . 440 *Ecc. Sonn.* 3. 2. 5
With heavenly, each more prized for the other's sake ; . . . . 447 *Ecc. Sonn.* 3. 26. 13
For the heart's sake, ere ship with hostile ship . 448 *Ecc. Sonn.* 3. 30. 11
Life's rule from passion craved for passion's sake ; 455 **Not in the lucid* 13
Thou giv'st, for pastime's sake, by shriek or shout, 456 **The leaves* 22
For Christ's dear sake, by human sympathies . 468 *St. Bees* 143
That clings to slavery for its own sad sake. . . 472 *Dunolly Eagle* 14
My spirit droop for drooping's sake, ... 490 *Night Thought* 14
But hear a wonder, for whose sake . . . . . 492 *Fidelity* 50
Less for his own than for thy innocent sake ? . . 504 *Warning* 81

Sang—*continued.*
Sang mass,—and tore the book of prayer,— . . 404 *White Doe* 713
Sang in this Presence kindred themes ; . . . 416 *White Doe* 1841
While choirs of fervent Angels sang . . 457 **Had this* 11
They knelt in prayer, or sang to blissful Mary. . 477 *Nunnery* 8
And then she sang ;—she would have been . . 486 **We walked* 35
He sang those witty rhymes . . . . . . 488 *Fountain* 70
The haunt of him who sang how spear and shield 546 **The embowering* 17
Sang youthful tales of shepherds and their flocks ; 547 **Beneath yon* 12
And then he sang it well and fearlessly, . . . 554 *Prioress* 95
And sang, O *Alma Redemptoris Mater!* . . . 555 *Prioress* 190
A Spirit sang in tones more plaintive than the wind : . . . . 581 *Invoc. Earth* 3
Her Voice was like a hidden Bird that sang, . . 622 *Recluse* 1. 1. 91
Who sang in ancient Greece his loving lay, . . 623 **I find* 13
That sang and ceased not ; now a Sister Isle . . 643 *Prelude* 2. 59
Which one day sang so sweetly in the nave . . 644 *Prelude* 2. 119
Sang to herself, that there I could have made . 644 *Prelude* 2. 126
One song they sang, and it was audible, . . . 648 *Prelude* 2. 415
Pilfered away, by what the Bard who sang . . 677 *Prelude* 6. 180
A glad preamble to this Verse : I sang . . . 687 *Prelude* 7. 4
A thrush sang loud, and other melodies, . . . 771 *Excursion* 1. 963
We heard the hymn they sang—a solemn sound . 779 *Excursion* 2. 548
With their belief, I sang Saturnian rule . . . 797 *Excursion* 3. 756
Sanguinary. To hear the sanguinary trumpet sounded. 575 *Chiabrera* 6. 8
Sanguine. So drooped Adonis, bathed in sanguine dew . . . . 169 *Love lies Bleeding* 12
And learn how sanguine expectations fade . . . 504 *Warning* 68
He opens of his feet the sanguine tides, . . . 609 *Desc.Sk.Quarto* 395
Into its true proportion ; sanguine schemes, . . 741 *Prelude* 13. 60
Sanguinetto. Of Sanguinetto or broad Thrasymene, 361 **For action* 6
Sanity. His sanity of reason not impaired, . . . 819 *Excursion* 4. 1221
Sank. Of hideous sense, I sank, nor step could crawl: 31 *Guilt* 386
Then sank upon her straw with feeble moan. . . 34 *Guilt* 564
Interest, and mortgages ; at last he sank, . . . 98 *Brothers* 215
They sank, delivered o'er . . . . 102 *Artegal* 6
Swarmed with enchantment, till his spirit sank, . 122 *V. and J.* 49
" Here on the grass perhaps asleep he sank, . . 203 *Hart-leap* 149
Sank in our hearts, we felt as men *should* feel . 334 **A wingèd* 12
Belief sank deep into the crowd . . . . . 373 *Eg. Maid* 311
Of music reached its height, and even when sank 387 *Roslin* 4
Both sank and died, the life-veins of the chased . 393 *Hart's-horn* 7
How pleased, when down the Straggler sank . . 415 *White Doe* 1734
Never before so beautiful, sank down . . . . 644 *Prelude* 2. 173
Harassing both ; until he sank and pressed . . 718 *Prelude* 9. 574
With our conductor, pensively we sank . . . 746 *Prelude* 14. 17
Sank down, as in a dream, among the poor ; . . 764 *Excursion* 1. 544
Sank to decay ; for he was gone, whose hand, . 770 *Excursion* 1. 901
No—they sank into me, the bounteous gift . . 820 *Excursion* 4. 1286
If to the opposite extreme they sank. . . . . 842 *Excursion* 6. 270
Thrice sank as willingly. For he—whose nerves . 843 *Excursion* 6. 335
To be repeated thence, but gently sank . . . 892 *Excursion* 9. 536
Santo. In Pisa's Campo Santo, the smooth floor . 355 *Aquap.* 155
Saone. Upon the bosom of the gentle Saone . . 680 *Prelude* 6. 376
Sap. To sap your hardy virtue, and abate . . . 420 *Ecc. Sonn.* 1. 8. 6
Sapience. Of sapience in thy aspect, headless Owl ! . 456 **The leaves* 27
Conceivèd was the Father's sapience, ... 552 *Prioress* 20
Caused by the wish, as knows your sapience, . . 562 *Cuck.andNight.*309
Sapient. If sapient Germany must lie deprest, . . 315 **Alas! what* 8
Calming to raise ; and, by a sapient Art . . . 538 **In desultory* 25
'Mid temples, served by sapient priests, and choirs 734 *Prelude* 11. 460
Sapless. Kindled and burnt among the sapless twigs 797 *Excursion* 3. 744
Sapling. With his own hand a sapling, which he hooped . . . . 134 *Michael* 181
Of weed and sapling, along soft green turf . . 149 *M. H.* 4
Upon the Beast the sapling rings ; . . . . 241 *P. B.* 441
From Peter's hand the sapling dropped ! . . . 242 *P. B.* 486
His sapling Peter has entwined. . . . . . 242 *P. B.* 575
That to the sapling ash gives birth ; . . . . 397 *White Doe* 121
Sapped. That sapped good thoughts, or scared them with defiance. . . . . 369 *Eg. Maid* 24
Sapped by the very beam that gilds. . . . . 550 *Hermit's Cell* 2. 24
Was sapped; and while she slept, the nightly damps 770 *Excursion* 1. 907
Sapphire. Heaven's sapphire pavement, yet breathed well content, ... 278 **Lo! where she* 11
The trembling eyebright showed her sapphire blue, 377 *Duddon* 6. 10
Clouds of all tincture, rocks and sapphire sky, . 784 *Excursion* 2. 854
Saps. That saps the individual's bodily frame, . . 885 *Excursion* 9. 108
Saracens. There the Saracens were tamed. . . . 535 *Egremont* 44
Sarah. For George and Sarah Green ; . . . . 623 *G. and S. Green* 2
Sarah's. For MARY's humble, SARAH's silent claim, 152 **Forth from* 24
Sarcastic. Well might sarcastic Fancy then have whispered, ... 659 *Prelude* 4. 60
The Solitary, with a faint sarcastic smile . . . 780 *Excursion* 2. 594
Sarnen's. On Sarnen's Mount, there judge of fit and right, ... 350 *Des. Stanzas* 51
Sarum. And well he knew the spire of Sarum ; . 238 *P. B.* 212
Along the plain of Sarum, by the ghost . . 419 *Ecc. Sonn.* 1. 5. 4
Sarum's. A Traveller on the skirt of Sarum's Plain . 24 *Guilt* 1
Of Sarum's Plain, my youthful spirit was raised ; 744 *Prelude* 13. 314
On Sarum's naked plain—than pyramid . . . 788 *Excursion* 3. 148
Sat. Sat the poor girl, and forth did send . . . 82 *Alice Fell* 38
Sat round the basket piled with oaten cakes, . . 132 *Michael* 101
And Isabel sat silent, for her mind . . . . . 135 *Michael* 256
Did she bring forth, and all together sat . . . 135 *Michael* 302
And silent morning, I sat down, and there, . . 148 *Joanna* 80
I sat within an undergrove . . . . . . 154 **A whirl-blast* 6
Who sat a ruler on his throne . . . . . . 167 *Pilgrim'sDream* 31
A Pair who smilingly sat side by side, ... 523 *Epist. Beaumont* 114

Sat—*continued.*
He sat, and ate his food in solitude : . . . . 566 *Cumb. Beg.* 15
A smile sat beaming on her pensive face. . . . 618 *School Ex.* 24
Of his own board, where sat his gentle Mate . . 859 *Excursion* 7. 161
Satan. Whither spiteful Satan steered ; . . . . 218 **Inmate of* 30
" The Serpent, Satan, our first foe, that hath . 554 *Prioress* 107
Satchel. Equipped with satchel, to a school, that stood . . . . 758 *Excursion* 1. 122
Sate. In that forsaken building where they sate . 28 *Guilt* 197
These ten years she had sate all day alone . . 47 *Bord.* 571
We sate us down. The sky grew dark and darker : 50 *Bord.* 703
I sate me down, and cannot but believe— . . 62 *Bord.* 1359
But when she sate within the touch of thee. . . 88 *H. C.* 18
It was a July evening ; and he sate . . . . 95 *Brothers* 17
His wife sate near him, teasing matted wool, . . 95 *Brothers* 21
Or butterfly sate down, they were, I ween, . . 108 *Indolence* 71
Sate yesterday, and made a nest . . . . 120 *EmigrantMother* 30
There by the light of this old lamp they sate, . 133 *Michael* 124
Sate with a fettered sheep before him stretched . 133 *Michael* 164
I who ne'er sate within their bowers, ... 164 **Fair Lady* 3
The banquet ;—or beneath the trees I sate . . 185 *Nutting* 25
High in the breathless Hall the Minstrel sate, . 203 *Brougham* 1
Frail man ne'er sate in such another ; . . . . 236 *P. B.* 22
Have sate and talked where gowans blow, . . 285 *Grave of Burns* 53
The Rustic sate. . . . . 286 *Nith* 36
Fair Ellen Irwin, when she sate . . . . . 287 *Ellen Irwin* 1
While there he sate, alone and blind, ... 296 *Highland Boy* 141
She sate, from notice turning not away, . . . 306 **We had* 6
Sate watching in a forest shed, ... 342 *Ital. Itin.* 87
He sate, and eulogised with earnest pen . . . 356 *Aquap.* 259
Enormous, dragged, while side by side they sate, 363 **What aim* 2
Bold with the thought, in reverence I sate down, 365 **Under the* 13
In moody posture there he sate, ... 370 *Eg. Maid* 70
Sate musing ; on that hill the Bard would rove, . 393 **The Lovers* 5
Who sate in the shade of the Prior's Oak ! . . 396 *White Doe* 34
She sate beneath the spreading yew— . . . . 401 *White Doe* 447
Had sate together in Raby Hall ! . . . . . 403 *White Doe* 696
Of ravage saved—sate Emily. . . . . . . 414 *White Doe* 1632
While she sate listening in the shade, ... 415 *White Doe* 1773
For that she came ; there oft she sate . . . 416 *White Doe* 1819
Your love of Him upon whose forehead sate . . 420 *Ecc. Sonn.* 1. 8. 7
Of daisies, shepherds sate of yore and wove . . 450 *Ecc. Sonn.* 3. 39. 10
His Eagle's favourite perch, while round him sate 457 **The leaves* 30
While in a grove I sate reclined, ... 482 *Lines : Spring* 2
And, as good men do, he sate . . . . . . 535 *Egremont* 74
Once he sate, as old books say, ... 535 *Egremont* 78
The Foster-parents sate ; . . . . 545 *Russ. Fug.* 372
In which he sate alone, with unclosed eyes, . . 548 **Stay, bold* 28
" This little Child, while in the school he sate . 553 *Prioress* 65
There sate I down among the fair fresh flowers, . 558 *Cuck.and Night.* 66
Meanwhile the stream, whose bank I sate upon, . 558 *Cuck.and Night.* 81
And there she sate and sung—upon that tree— . 562 *Cuck.andNight.*288
To a green shady place, where down I sate . . 633 *Prelude* 1. 62
Cherry or maple, sate in close array, ... 639 *Prelude* 1. 515
The labourer, and the old man who had sate . . 642 *Prelude* 2. 13
From whom the stone was named, who there had sate, ... 642 *Prelude* 2. 44
Was audible ; and sate among the woods . . . 647 *Prelude* 2. 342
Here sate in state, and fed with daily alms . . 657 *Prelude* 3. 593
Thus musing, in a wood I sate me down . . . 661 *Prelude* 4. 177
And in the sheltered coppice where I sate, . . 661 *Prelude* 4. 182
While listlessly I sate, and, having closed . . . 666 *Prelude* 5. 63
And in my own unlovely cell sate down . . . 675 *Prelude* 6. 17
And on a rock sate down, to wait for day. . . 685 *Prelude* 6. 702
We sate and sate, wondering as if the night . . 685 *Prelude* 6. 708
Sate on a stone, and heard the bells speak out . 688 *Prelude* 7. 114
One, at whose centre sate a lovely Boy, . . . 692 *Prelude* 7. 336
And there he sate surrounded with a throng . . 692 *Prelude* 7. 359
A spacious grass-plot ; there, in silence, sate . . 696 *Prelude* 7. 607
Of an itinerant vehicle I sate, ... 707 *Prelude* 8. 544
Of the Bastille, I sate in the open sun, . . . 710 *Prelude* 9. 68
He had sate lord in many tender hearts ; . . . 711 *Prelude* 9. 141
Whom no one owned, sate silent, shall I add, . 722 *Prelude* 10. 298
From indiscriminate laughter, nor sate down . . 732 *Prelude* 11. 323
I sate half-sheltered by a naked wall ; . . . . 738 *Prelude* 12. 299
Near the loud waterfall ; or her who sate . . . 752 *Prelude* 14. 406
We sate—we walked ; he pleased me with report 757 *Excursion* 1. 63
He sate, and even in their fixed lineaments, . . 758 *Excursion* 1. 156
Where Fear sate thus, a cherished visitant, . . 759 *Excursion* 1. 186
Where sate the old Man on the cottage-bench ; . 763 *Excursion* 1. 465
I sate with sad impatience. From within . . 767 *Excursion* 1. 735
We sate together, sighs came on my ear, . . . 768 *Excursion* 1. 802
That in yon arbour oftentimes she sate . . . 769 *Excursion* 1. 876
For hours she sate ; and evermore her eye . . 769 *Excursion* 1. 880
The little child who sate to turn the wheel . . 769 *Excursion* 1. 890
We sate on that low bench : and now we felt, . 771 *Excursion* 1. 960
Or, rather say, sate down by very chance, . . 776 *Excursion* 2. 308
Or sate companionless ; and here the book, . . 778 *Excursion* 2. 451
While at our pastoral banquet thus we sate . . 782 *Excursion* 2. 689
While we sate listening with compassion due. . 801 *Excursion* 4. 7
Enkindled by the sun. He sate—and talked . . 811 *Excursion* 4. 638
Sate by my side, had vanished, if a wish . . . 829 *Excursion* 5. 448
Sate down ; and to her office, with leave asked, . 834 *Excursion* 5. 770
But more was given ; I studied as we sate . . 834 *Excursion* 5. 778
Beneath the shade we all sate down ; and there . 850 *Excursion* 6. 785
' Nay, ye must wait my time ! ' and down she sate, 853 *Excursion* 6. 978
In whom, as by her lonely hearth she sate, . . 854 *Excursion* 6. 1035
More pleased than sad, the grey-haired Wanderer sate ; . . . . 854 *Excursion* 6. 1064
By some accomplished Master, while he sate . . 857 *Excursion* 7. 12
That, near the quiet churchyard where we sate, . 865 *Excursion* 7. 541

Sate—*continued.*
—Seven lusty Sons sate daily round the board . 867 *Excursion* 7. 636
Whereon our fathers sate. And mark his brow ! 880 *Excursion* 8. 407
Seen, from the shady room in which we sate, . . 882 *Excursion* 8. 536
Or sate reclined ; admiring quietly . . . . . 893 *Excursion* 9. 582
Round which the Shepherd and his household sate K.8. 228 **I will* 111
Satellites. Satellites burning in a lucid ring . . . 441 *Ecc. Sonn.* 3. 5. 13
Satiate. Beats frequent on thy satiate ear, . . . 376 **The Minstrels* 74
Satiate are *these* ; and stilled to eye and ear ; . 392 *Daniel* 9
Filled with mementos, satiate with its part . . 452 *Ecc. Sonn.* 3. 45. 13
Was never satiate. Their familiar voice, . . 864 *Excursion* 7. 442
Satisfied. Lingers, but Fancy is well satisfied ; . . 251 **Her only* 2
Who, with her heart's experience satisfied, . . 270 **Shame on* 7
Couch near their dams, with quiet satisfied ; . . 278 **Life with* 6
Myself so satisfied in heart before. . . . . . 306 **Here, on our* 8
And with the embrace was satisfied. . . . . 327 *Ode 1815* 7
Be thou then satisfied in heart ! . . . . . . 401 *White Doe* 504
With my condition satisfied ; . . . . 408 *White Doe* 1103
There stopped ; her thirst was satisfied . . . . 416 *White Doe* 1856
Is with that wholesome office satisfied, . . . 456 *Rydal Mere* 42
And who was then ill satisfied but I ? . . . . 558 *Cuck.and Night.* 92
Well satisfied, I thanked her, and she said, . . 561 *Cuck.andNight.*231
(All claims of duty satisfied ;) . . . . . . 579 **Sweet Flower* 54
No longer breathe, but all be satisfied. . . . 622 *Recluse* 1. 1. 82
Enwrought upon thy mantle ; satisfied . . . 707 *Prelude* 8. 534
The earthquake is not satisfied at once ; . . . 719 *Prelude* 10. 84
Of all this glory filled and satisfied. . . . . 737 *Prelude* 12. 190
The humble worth that satisfied her heart : . . 764 *Excursion* 7. 521
And, with that ready answer satisfied, ... 789 *Excursion* 3. 183
So to declare the conscience satisfied : . . . . 839 *Excursion* 6. 67
Of kindred import, pleased and satisfied— . . 845 *Excursion* 6. 443
Until at length her soul was satisfied. . . . . 853 *Excursion* 6. 982
Be satisfied, 'tis well,—the end is gained ; . . . 874 *Excursion* 8. 7
Is satisfied, I cannot but believe, ... 885 *Excursion* 9. 104
Satisfies. That satisfies the simple and the meek, . 468 **Ranging the* 12
By aught that innocently satisfies . . . . . 806 *Excursion* 4. 353
That satisfies and ends in perfect rest. . . . K.8. 255*Recluse* 1.1.685
Satisfy. And nothing less would satisfy him ? No less ; 38 *Bord.* 55
A humbler bliss would satisfy my heart. . . . 190 **Lyre ! though* 14
Their subtle flight could satisfy : . . . . . 228 *Devot. Incit.* 10
Which ever strives in vain itself to satisfy, . . 231 **The gentlest Poet* 35
The visual powers of Nature satisfy, ... 279 **All praise* 12
Alone could satisfy her wide embrace. . . . . 311 **Who rises* 12
Relax, to fix and satisfy the mind . . . . . 353 *Aquap.* 25
Wherewith to satisfy the human soul ? . . . 568 *Cumb. Beg.* 146
Satisfying. *See* **Self-satisfying.**
A satisfying view upon that state . . . . . 803 *Excursion* 4. 158
Saturn. The towns in Saturn are decayed, . . . 237 *P. B.* 41
Not such as Saturn ruled 'mid Latian wilds, . . 701 *Prelude* 8. 129
Saturnian. She smiled ; but Time, the old Saturnian seer, ... 465 **Dear to* 9
With their belief, I sang Saturnian rule . . . 797 *Excursion* 3. 756
Saturnine. And saturnine ; her head not raised to hold 848 *Excursion* 6. 679
Satyrs. While Fauns and Satyrs beat the ground . 234 *Power of Sound* 150
Of Satyrs in some viewless glade, with dance . . 716 *Prelude* 9. 459
These were the lurking Satyrs, a wild brood . . 814 *Excursion* 4. 885
Saucy. Beware of him ! Thou, saucy cockatoo, . 472 *Dunolly Eagle* 8
The saucy air. In this proud company . . . 681 *Prelude* 6. 394
Saunter. Not yet in sight !—We'll saunter here awhile ; . . . . 38 *Bord.* 48
The wayward brain, to saunter through a wood ! 260 **How sweet* 2
I choose to saunter o'er the grassy plain, . . . 383 *Duddon* 30. 12
Sauntered. Sauntered on this retired and difficult way. . . . . 148 **A narrow* 9
We sauntered, played, or rioted ; we talked . . 652 *Prelude* 3. 248
I sauntered, like a river murmuring . . . . 660 *Prelude* 4. 119
Sauntering. " A little idle sauntering Thing ! " . 127 *Idiot Boy* 159
The sauntering Horseman throws not with a slack 566 *Cumb. Beg.* 26
Sauntering to pluck the strawberries wild unseen. S.3. 417 **Sweet was* 8
Savage. Yet here and there, if 'mid the savage scene 14 *Desc. Sk.* 234
Shouts from the echoing hills with savage joy. . 17 *Desc. Sk.* 365
'Mid savage rocks, and seas of snow that shine, . 20 *Desc. Sk.* 540
In spot so savage, but with shuddering pain ; . 25 *Guilt* 83
Upon these savage confines, we have seen you . 48 *Bord.* 606
They say Lord Clifford is a savage man ; . . . 59 *Bord.* 1190
In any corner of this savage Waste . . . . 73 *Bord.* 2040
Left to the mercy of that savage Man ! . . . 76 *Bord.* 2186
By Christian disturbers more savage than Turks, 86 *Rural Arch.* 20
Shocked at his savage aspect, from the place . . 126 *V. and J.* 298
So beautiful, through savage lands . . . . 193 *Ruth* 118
In him the savage virtue of the Race, ... 205 *Brougham* 165
Gives to this savage Pass its name. . . . . 215 *Kirkstone* 48
" A savage wildness round him hung . . . . 239 *P. B.* 291
A savage character was seen . . . . . . 239 *P. B.* 294
Wild Chieftain of a savage Clan ! . . . . . 292 *Rob Roy* 102
He, nursed 'mid savage passions that defile . 359 **Complacent Fictions* 12
Through park, or chase, or savage wood. . . . 407 *White Doe* 998
And bless for both this savage spot ; . . . . 415 *White Doe* 1798
Of Christian Faith, this savage Island blessed 418 *Ecc. Sonn.* 1. 2. 4
Will build their savage fortunes only there ; . . 421 *Ecc. Sonn.* 1. 11. 12
Rekindled thus, from dens and savage woods . . 432 *Ecc. Sonn.* 2. 14. 10
How savage bosoms melted at the sound . . . 466 *St. Bees* 51
A dweller in that savage place. . . . . . . 492 *Fidelity* 57
In life-long exile on a savage coast, ... 519 *Pun. Death* 11. 6
Direst of savage beasts, would roam in fear, . . 585 *Ch. Lamb* 70
Where silver rocks the savage prospect chear . . 591 *Ev. Wk. Quarto* 7
And still, below, where mid the savage scene . 607 *Desc.Sk.Quarto* 291
And savage Nature humbly joins the rite, . . 612 *Desc.Sk.Quarto* 554
Drove far away the savage thoughts that roll . 618 *School Ex.* 33

Savage—*continued.*
A naked savage, in the thunder shower. . . . 636 *Prelude* 1. 300
Before us ; savage region ! which I paced . . 776 *Excursion* 2. 326
Such as, remote, 'mid savage wilderness, . . . 820 *Excursion* 4. 1277
Raising, through just gradation, savage life . . 875 *Excursion* 8. 70
By savage Nature ? Shrivelled are their lips ; . 879 *Excursion* 8. 353
A savage horde among the civilised, ... 888 *Excursion* 9. 309
Unheard, the savage nations bowed the head . . 894 *Excursion* 9. 684
Motions of savage instinct, my delight K.8. 256*Recluse* 1.1.707
Savages. Wild beasts, or uncouth savages impure ! 102 *Artegal* 28
Savannah. Regions of wood and wide savannah, vast 799 *Excursion* 3. 938
Savannahs. The Youth of green savannahs spake, 193 *Ruth* 67
And green savannahs, she should share . . . 193 *Ruth* 112
Save. Save where aloft the subtle sunbeams shine . 3 *Ev. Wk.* 62
Save where, with sparkling foam, a small cascade 3 *Ev. Wk.* 64
Save where, along the shady western marge, . . 4 *Ev. Wk.* 126
Of splendour—save the beacon's spiry head . . 6 *Ev. Wk.* 210
Save when the avalanche breaks loose, to rend . 16 *Desc. Sk.* 312
Save when, a stranger seen below, the boy . . 17 *Desc. Sk.* 364
Save cornfields stretched and stretching without bound ; . . . . 24 *Guilt* 26
Save that the bustard, of those regions bleak . . 26 *Guilt* 104
To save thee from the extreme of penury ; . . 40 *Bord.* 158
That's all—God save you, Sir. Ha ! as I live, . 43 *Bord.* 332
Must needs step in, and save my life. The look . 54 *Bord.* 919
Led by my hand to save thee from perdition ; . 63 *Bord.* 1404
That Woman will come o'er this Waste to save thee. 63 *Bord.* 1411
But what is done will save you from the blank . 71 *Bord.* 1870
Holla ! to bed, good Folks, within ! O save us ! 71 *Bord.* 1884
Outspread, as if to save himself from falling !— . 73 *Bord.* 2025
I hurried back with her.—Oh save me, Sir, . . 74 *Bord.* 2096
Save, in a corner, a heap of dry leaves, . . . 80 †*Address : Child* 18
Save those who to my sorrows lend . . . . 113 *Lament* 20
Save six feet of earth where our forefathers lie ! . 116 *Repentance* 36
Save thee, my pretty Love ! . . . . 117 †*Cottager* 5
Save one *wee*, hungry, nibbling mouse, . . . 118 †*Cottager* 9
Me to save from chance of harm : . . . . . 140 *Arm. Lady* 40
Save a little neighbouring rill, ... 171 *Kitten* 82
Save that above a single height . . . . . . 175 *Waggoner* 1. 166
But save us from yon screeching owl ! " . . . 179 *Waggoner* 3. 98
Save a Mother and her Child ! . . . . . . 204 *Brougham* 71
Or Rival, save the Queen of night . . . . . 212 *Dion*
Where, save the rugged road, we find . . . . 214 *Kirkstone* 5
And save your souls alive ! . . . . 247 *P. B.* 950
Save from the trickling household rill ; . . . . 247 *P. B.* 998
Save one, one only, when I stood forlorn, . . . 257 **Surprised by* 11
Save only far as thought and feeling blend . . 261 *Retirement* 2
Save haply for some feeble glimmering . . . 271 *George : Death* 5
Softly !—To save the contrite, Jesus bled. . . 275 *Gravestone* 14
Save when the wind sweeps by and sounds are caught . . . . 290 *Kilchurn* 4
And perished, save one narrow cell ; . . . . 298 *Brownie's Cell* 24
All, all were dispossessed, save him whose smile . 298 *Brownie's Cell* 41
Save where that pearly whiteness . . . . . 302 *Yarrow V.* 18
Or save this honoured Land from every Lord . 310 *Invasion* 19
Till all is dim, save this bright Stone . . . . 337 *Thun* 15
Save insect-swarms that hum in air afloat, . . 360 **Long has* 6
Save that the Cock is crowing, a shrill note, . . 360 **Long has* 7
Save in this Rill that took from blood the name . 361 **When here* 7
Or aught in Syrian deserts left to save . . . 367 *Trajan* 11
Attended but by thy own voice, save when . . 379 *Duddon* 14. 13
With no one near save the omnipresent God. . . 391 *Brownie* 8
Man placed him here, and God, he knows, can save. 392 *Daniel* 14
"My all save one, a Daughter dear ! . . . . 403 *White Doe* 616
Thought he, may want not skill to save. . . . 408 *White Doe* 1112
For why ?—to save his Father's land ; . . . . 412 *White Doe* 1467
De-irians—he would save them from God's Ire ; 422 *Ecc. Sonn.* 1. 13. 12
And if full oft the Sanctuary save . . . . . 424 *Ecc. Sonn.* 1. 24. 13
Save by Self-will. Lo ! from that distant shore, 443 *Ecc. Sonn.* 3. 14. 6
Save when the Owlet's unexpected scream . . 456 **The leaves* 8
And nothing save the moving ship's own light 460 **Wanderer! that* 68
To *us* save matter for a thoughtful sigh, . . . 474 **On to* 2
And fondly strives her struggling friend to save. . 490 *Incident : Dog* 32
While all lie prostrate, save the tyrant few . . 513 *Newspaper* 6
"Knowledge will save me from the threatened woe." 513 *Newspaper* 10
Not scourge, to save the People—not destroy. 515 **Long-favoured* 14
For—save the calm repentance sheds o'er strife . 526 **Soon did* 8
Save hope that we, yet bound to Earth, may share 526 **Soon did* 12
Is smooth as clear, save where with dimples small 527 **Those breathing* 11
Save He who came as rightful Heir . . . . 535 *Egremont* 7
Save in the rolls of heaven, where hers may live . 540 *Grace Darl.* 16
Of all this town, save only in this place, . . . 565 *Troilus* 159
Save that, atop, the subtle sunbeams shine, . . 593 *Ev. Wk. Quarto* 77
Save when the startling cliff unfrequent rends : . 609 *Desc. Sk.Quarto*377
Save that, the stranger seen below, the boy . . 610 *Desc.Sk.Quarto* 440
Save in the land where all things are forgot, . . 614 *Desc.Sk.Quarto* 677
(What, save thyself, none dares through earth and skies) . . . . 624 *Æneid* 12
Save when, amid the stately grove of oaks, . . 633 *Prelude* 1. 82
To give and take a greeting that might save . . 660 *Prelude* 4. 128
And, save the flowing water's peaceful voice, . . 664 *Prelude* 4. 386
Save when realities of act and mien, ... 694 *Prelude* 7. 477
And stood of all dismantled, save the last . . . 705 *Prelude* 8. 396
(Save only one, hereafter to be named) . . . 711 *Prelude* 9. 132
In anything, save only as the act . . . . . 711 *Prelude* 9. 138
Save when the stings of viperous remorse, . . 718 *Prelude* 9. 576
A revolution, save at this one time ; . . . . 722 *Prelude* 10. 272
Those musings or diverted, save that once . . 746 *Prelude* 14. 21
All meek and silent, save that through a rift— . 747 *Prelude* 14. 56
With rocks encompassed, save that to the south . 776 *Excursion* 2. 334
Was silent ; save the solitary clock . . . . 781 *Excursion* 2. 645

Save—*continued.*
Of motion, save the water that descended, — 787 *Excursion* 3. 69
(Save some remembrances of dream-like joys — 790 *Excursion* 3. 273
Save by the simplest toil of human hands — 792 *Excursion* 3. 402
And such is mine,—save only for a hope — 800 *Excursion* 3. 989
Save for that single cry, the unanswer'd bleat — 807 *Excursion* 4. 410
Save for yon stately House beneath whose roof — 824 *Excursion* 5. 97
Save when the sabbath brings its kind release, — 834 *Excursion* 5. 806
And all desisted, all, save him alone. — 841 *Excursion* 6. 218
Save the contentment of the builder's mind ; — 849 *Excursion* 6. 729
To save the perishing ; and, henceforth, I breathe — 852 *Excursion* 6. 923
Save only those which to their common shame, — 853 *Excursion* 6. 1013
Save through a gap high in the hills, an opening — 859 *Excursion* 7. 142
Sweet, perfect, to be wished for ! save that here — 861 *Excursion* 7. 256
Of the mild-hearted Champion, save this stone, — 872 *Excursion* 7. 966
Save at worst need, from bold impetuous force, — 873 *Excursion* 7. 1031
To save themselves from blank forgetfulness ! " — 877 *Excursion* 8. 230
Save by degrees and steps which thou hast deigned — 893 *Excursion* 9. 616
Unheard of, save in one small hamlet, here — S.3. 433 **The doubt* 9

Saved. By one soft impulse saved from vacancy. — 22 *Yew-tree* 7
You know that you have saved his life. I know it. — 38 *Bord.* 27
Eternal praises on the power that saved her !— — 46 *Bord.* 519
Her, who hath saved me, to this hour, from harm, — 62 *Bord.* 1369
and could he be saved by our means, — 72 *Bord.* 1995
Shout in triumph, both are saved ; — 93 *Westmoreland Girl* 20
Saved by courage that with danger — 93 *Westmoreland Girl* 21
Others saved from lingering pain. — 94 *Westmoreland Girl* 56
Thus was a Brother by a Brother saved ; — 105 *Artegal* 234
Of the dumb animals, whom he had saved, — 132 *Michael* 71
Had saved him from that breach of faith ! — 199 *Thorn* 132
The perilous Deep, the Boy was saved ; — 297 *Highland Boy* 242
Saved from the sordid axe by Beaumont's care, — 358 *Pine : Rome* 7
If saved at all, are saved by stealth. — 391 *Highland Broach* 68
That insult, and the Banner saved, — 410 *White Doe* 1341
Of ravage saved—sate Emily. — 414 *White Doe* 1632
By these Religious saved for all posterity. — 425 *Ecc. Sonn.* 1. 25. 14
Of a storm-shattered Vessel saved from Wreck — 447 *Ecc. Sonn.* 3. 30. 3
Saved by His care who bade the tempest cease ; — 454 *Sea-side* 16
The Power that saved him in his strange distress. — 470 **A youth* 14
A few may yet be saved." The Daughter's words, — 540 *Grace Darl.* 44
Saved out of many by his piety. — 623 **I find* 14
To land a single volume, saved by chance, — 677 *Prelude* 6. 145

Saves. Fixed on the anchor left by Him who saves — 14 *Desc. Sk.* 206
He saves for me my precious soul ; — 145 *Her Eyes* 48
And saves the peopled fields of earth — 227 *Vernal Ode* 59

Saving. Oft leaves a saving moisture at its root. — 124 *V. and J.* 194
No longer : ye, whom to the saving rite — 446 *Ecc. Sonn.* 3. 25. 10
Struggling for life, into its saving arms ! — 469 **The feudal* 10
They fail, thy saving arms, dread Power ! around them cast. — 492 *Duty* 16
Whom, then, shall meekness guard ? What saving skill — 505 *Warning* 149
Maintained for me a saving intercourse — 732 *Prelude* 11. 341

Savings. Till our joint savings had amassed enough — 672 *Prelude* 5. 472
The annual savings of a toilsome life, — 760 *Excursion* 1. 251

Saviour. Out of that deed. My trust, Saviour ! is in thy name ! " — 36 *Guilt* 657
Such wings as, when our Saviour calls, shall bear us up to heaven." — 93 *Poet's Dream* 68
That saw the Saviour in his human frame — 255 *Easter* 2
Saviour, for our warning, seen — 336 **Jesu ! bless* 7
The pictured Saviour !—By Augustin led, — 422 *Ecc. Sonn.* 1. 14. 6
But whence came they who for the Saviour Lord — 431 *Ecc. Sonn.* 2. 12. 1
In which course if Christ our Saviour — 535 *Egremont* 27

Saviour's. The love deep-seated in the Saviour's face, — 342 *Last Sup.* 3
In precincts nearer to the Saviour's tomb, — 355 *Aquap.* 160

Savona. Savona, Queen of territory fair — 355 *Aquap.* 207
Modest Savona ! over all did brood — 356 *Aquap.* 233
Savona was my birthplace, and I sprang — 574 *Chiabrera* 4. 29
Had traced its windings.—This Savona knows, — 574 *Chiabrera* 5. 13
Has from Savona torn her best delight ? — 575 *Chiabrera* 7. 7
The eyes of all Savona streamed with tears. — 575 *Chiabrera* 8. 9

Savona's. Within Savona's walls, of gentle blood. — 573 *Chiabrera* 3. 4

Savour. And loses its sweet savour ! — 331 *Ode : Thanks.* 164

Savoured. That savoured of aversion to thy name . — 41 *Bord.* 232

Savoyard. The Savoyard to quit his naked rocks, — 761 *Excursion* 1. 317

Savoyards. Of Savoyards ; or, single and alone, — 689 *Prelude* 7. 179

Saw. *See* **See-saw.**
He saw and passed a stately inn, full sure — 24 *Guilt* 11
He looked, and saw upon a gibbet high — 25 *Guilt* 78
And saw a woman in the naked room — 27 *Guilt* 165
And saw the dawn opening the silvery east — 30 *Guilt* 313
They looked and saw a lengthening road, and wain — 30 *Guilt* 325
The travellers saw me weep, my fate inquired, — 31 *Guilt* 404
As if he saw—there and upon that ground— — 33 *Guilt* 490
They saw and heard, and, winding with the road — 34 *Guilt* 523
She saw the carman bend to scoop the flood — 34 *Guilt* 543
He saw his Wife's lips move his name to bless — 35 *Guilt* 616
'Tis a strange letter this !—You saw her write it ? — 38 *Bord.* 53
And saw the tears with which she blotted it. — 38 *Bord.* 54
She saw my blasted face—a tide of soldiers — 40 *Bord.* 185
What is your meaning ? Two days gone I saw, — 42 *Bord.* 276
When first I saw him sitting there, alone, — 44 *Bord.* 376
Beat hard upon my head—and yet I saw — 45 *Bord.* 424
Whom, but some few days past, I saw in Eskdale, — 46 *Bord.* 479
You saw, who was it ? Nay, I dare not speak ; — 47 *Bord.* 532
Long did I watch, and saw her pacing round — 47 *Bord.* 577

Saw—*continued.*
I thought I saw the skeleton of Idonea. — 47 *Bord.* 581
(You saw them gathering for the festival) — 48 *Bord.* 643
I never saw. The music of the birds — 49 *Bord.* 675
I saw a distant fire in the north-east ; — 50 *Bord.* 741
Saw him—his face turned toward me ; and I tell thee — 55 *Bord.* 985
By a dim lantern's light I saw that wreaths — 59 *Bord.* 1202
I saw that every possible shape of action — 69 *Bord.* 1780
Might lead to good—I saw it and burst forth, — 69 *Bord.* 1781
To seek for sympathy, because I saw — 71 *Bord.* 1864
I saw the stains of blood upon my clothes— — 72 *Bord.* 1933
I saw it in the wheel entangled, — 82 *Alice Fell* 26
And thence they saw the bridge of wood, — 83 *Lucy Gray* 39
She saw him down the torrent borne ; — 85 *Shepherd-boys* 72
It caught his eye, he saw it plain— — 86 *Anecdote* 50
Him never saw I, nor the spot ; but from an English Dame, — 91 *Norman Boy* 5
I saw, within, the Norman Boy kneeling alone in prayer. — 91 *Poet's Dream* 8
The Stranger, whom he saw still lingering there. — 95 *Brothers* 37
Saw mountains ; saw the forms of sheep that grazed — 96 *Brothers* 62
And, looking round, imagined that he saw — 96 *Brothers* 96
The very brightest Sunday Autumn saw, — 99 *Brothers* 269
You say that he saw many happy years ? — 101 *Brothers* 384
I heard, I saw the flashes drive, — 114 *Ind. Wom.* 6
He saw me, and he turned aside, — 114 *Last of Flock* 11
To what he saw, he gradually returned, — 118 *Maternal Grief* 56
A vision, and adored the thing he saw. — 122 *V. and J.* 38
Deem rather that the fervent Youth, who saw — 122 *V. and J.* 57
I waked, and saw my little boy, — 144 *Her Eyes* 27
To greet us—and we saw a Man worn down — 149 **A narrow* 58
Say, when the *moving* creatures saw — 154 *Flower Garden* 7
" I saw a crag, a lofty stone — 156 *Oak and Broom* 11
I saw a dazzling Belle, — 165 *Parrot* 2
I saw, espied its shaded mouth ; — 169 *Wren's Nest* 55
I saw you, between rage and fear, — 175 *Waggoner* 1. 126
I saw you in that jeopardy : — 175 *Waggoner* 1. 131
For ever ; and I saw the sparkling foam, — 185 *Nutting* 34
The silent trees, and saw the intruding sky.— — 186 *Nutting* 53
I saw her upon nearer view, — 186 **She was* 11
When all at once I saw a crowd, — 187 **I wandered* 3
Ten thousand saw I at a glance, — 187 **I wandered* 11
I looked reproof—they saw—but neither hung his head. — 191 *Beggars* 42
The faith which saw that gladsome pair — 191 *Seq. Beggars* 29
But ill he lived, much evil saw, — 194 *Ruth* 145
I saw the hare that raced about with joy ; — 195 *Resolution* 16
I saw a Man before me unawares : — 196 *Resolution* 55
I looked around, I thought I saw — 199 *Thorn* 181
" I did not speak—I saw her face ; — 199 *Thorn* 188
It chanced that I saw standing in a dell — 202 *Hart-leap* 102
I saw three pillars standing in a line,— — 202 *Hart-leap* 107
Saw, at a long-drawn gallery's dusky bound, — 213 *Dion* 66
—They saw, adventurously impelled, — 215 *Kirkstone* 45
She saw me at the garden-door ; — 238 *P. B.* 177
Of courage you saw little there, — 239 *P. B.* 303
Beneath the clear blue sky he saw — 240 *P. B.* 366
But Peter—when he saw the Ass — 243 *P. B.* 656
She saw—and uttered with a scream, — 247 *P. B.* 1004
And saw it was another ! — 247 *P. B.* 1010
That saw the Saviour in his human frame — 255 *Easter* 2
Methought I saw the footsteps of a throne — 257 **Methought I* 1
Ne'er saw I, never felt, a calm so deep ! — 269 *Westm. Bridge* 11
Fair Ellen saw it as it came, — 287 *Ellen Irwin* 29
For never saw I mien, or face, — 288 *Highland Girl* 24
I saw her singing at her work, — 289 *Sol. Reap.* 27
For many saw ; among the rest — 296 *Highland Boy* 163
She saw her poor blind Boy. — 296 *Highland Boy* 165
Till they, who saw his outward frame, — 299 *Brownie's Cell* 53
And saw, while sea was calm and air was clear, — 306 **Inland, within* 2
I saw, in wondrous pérspective displayed, — 323 *Ode 1814* 5
I saw the banquet spread beneath a Dome of state, — 324 *Ode 1814* 74
Ne'er saw a race who held, by right of birth, — 325 **Intrepid sons* 3
To Heaven ;—who never saw, may heave a sigh ; — 330 *Ode : Thanks.* 100
Bruges I saw attired with golden light — 333 **Bruges I* 1
Saw ye the soft yet awful veil — 344 *Eclipse* 76
That saw the Corsican his cap and bells — 349 *Boulogne* 7
All that I saw returns upon my view, — 350 *Des. Stanzas* 10
I saw far off the dark top of a Pine — 358 *Pine : Rome* 1
He heard a voice, and saw, with half-raised head, — 370 *Eg. Maid* 71
Nor saw of wreck or ruin aught — 371 *Eg. Maid* 124
For in that face they saw the last — 372 *Eg. Maid* 196
Ye saw, throughout this royal House, — 372 *Eg. Maid* 201
I saw them ply their harmless robberies, — 377 *Duddon* 6. 5
And, gazing, saw that Rose, which from the prime — 381 *Duddon* 22. 4
Vexed is he, and screams loud. The last I saw — 388 *Eagles* 4
The Hermit saw the Angel spread his wings — 393 **The Lovers* 3
He saw her where in open view — 401 *White Doe* 446
Who saw the Banner reared on high — 403 *White Doe* 682
He conquered !—Saw we not the Plain — 405 *White Doe* 815
Ill tears she wept ; I saw them fall, — 405 *White Doe* 874
She saw the desperate assault — 408 *White Doe* 1126
The unhappy Banner Francis saw, — 410 *White Doe* 1330
And the first object which he saw, — 411 *White Doe* 1389
Looked round—but saw no cause for fear ; — 414 *White Doe* 1652
She saw the Creature once again ; — 414 *White Doe* 1698
Saw we not Henry scourged at Becket's Shrine ? — 428 *Ecc. Sonn.* 1. 37. 9
I saw the figure of a lovely Maid — 440 *Ecc. Sonn.* 3. 1. 1
I saw a Mother's eye intensely bent — 446 *Ecc. Sonn.* 3. 24. 1

Scaffold—*continued.*	
And Russell's milder blood the scaffold wet; . .	42 *Ecc. Sonn.* 3. 10. 4
Scaffolds. Hath summoned kings to scaffolds, do but give	778 *Excursion* 2. 475
Scald. Not in like sort the Runic Scald was moved;	359 **Complacent Fictions* 11
Scale. Directs his winding dog the cliffs to scale,—	5 *Ev. Wk.* 183
The pastoral Swiss begin the cliffs to scale, . .	17 *Desc. Sk.* 372
She weighs them in one scale. The wiles of woman,	57 *Bord.* 1080
A scale and table of belief—as thus—	58 *Bord.* 1147
Whose wisdom fixed the scale	226 *Present.* 75
No scale of moral music—to unite	235 *Power of Sound* 170
Invades a Realm, so pressed that in the scale .	316 **Say, what* 6
Thy presence turns the scale of doubtful fight, .	328 *Ode 1815* 112
A Vender of the well-wrought Scale, ...	341 *Ital. Itin.* 22
And sink from high to low, along a scale . . .	449 *Ecc. Sonn.* 3. 34 2
Present a glorious scale, ...	457 **Had this* 44
Along a scale of light and life, with cares . .	500 *Humanity* 29
And mountain-tops, a barren ridge we scale; . .	524 *Epist. Beaumont* 224
The pastoral Swiss begins the cliffs to scale, . .	610 *Desc.Sk.Quarto* 450
In scale and order, class the cabinet	645 *Prelude* 2. 224
By scale exact, in model, wood or clay, . . .	691 *Prelude* 7. 249
In my habitual thoughts; the scale of love, . .	709 *Prelude* 8. 684
The scale of liberty. I read her doom, . . .	730 *Prelude* 11. 211
Of custom that prepares a partial scale . . .	737 *Prelude* 12. 195
Measuring through all degrees, until the scale .	787 *Excursion* 3. 110
That in the scale of being fill their place; . .	802 *Excursion* 4. 81
With truth, the scale of intellectual rank?" . .	813 *Excursion* 4. 778
In scale of culture, few among my flock . .	833 *Excursion* 5. 717
Such (we will hope the lowest in the scale) . .	879 *Excursion* 8. 375
Not *there* diminutive, but through a scale . .	S.3. 435 **The doubt* 108
Bred also there, I wanted not a scale	K.8. 246 *Recluse* 1.1.349
Scaled. We scaled, without a track to ease our steps,	776 *Excursion* 2. 323
By unrequited love, he scaled the rocks, . . .	840 *Excursion* 6. 109
Scales. Beholds the unwearied sweep of wood that scales	12 *Desc. Sk.* 109
And benefits were weighed in Reason's scales! .	256 *Easter* 14
But the live scales of a portentous nature; . .	311 **Who rises* 18
Her scales with even hand, and culture mould .	468 *St. Bees* 130
In faithful scales, things and their opposites, .	510 **Among a* 27
Against time present, passion holds the scales: .	516 **As leaves* 10
Th' unwearied sweep of wood thy cliffs that scales,	604 *Desc.Sk.Quarto* 122
Scaly. For all the startled scaly tribes that slink .	383 *Duddon* 28. 6
Your scaly panoplies repay	526 **The soaring* 23
. . . the scaly regent of the Nile.	L.1. 89 *Juvenal* 1. 24
Scampered. The horses scampered through the rain;	82 *Alice Fell* 14
We scampered homewards. Oh, ye rocks and streams, ...	644 *Prelude* 2. 131
Scan. Might scan the narrow province with disdain	231 **The gentlest Poet* 3
And learn from thence thy own defects to scan; .	619 *School Ex.* 86
Scandal. Of feasts, or scandal, eddying like the wind	522 *Epist. Beaumont* 63
Or walks of open scandal, but in vague . . .	653 *Prelude* 3. 324
Scanned. There an old man an olden measure scanned	13 *Desc. Sk.* 147
O may these lessons be with profit scanned . .	281 *Chris. Words.* 7
And, while I scanned them o'er and o'er, . . .	294 *Jedbor.* 65
That heresies should strike (if truth be scanned .	420 *Ecc. Sonn.* 1. 9. 1
And scanned them with a fixed and serious look .	566 *Cumb. Beg.* 11
Are dearest to me *now*; for, having scanned, .	676 *Prelude* 6. 100
After short absence, curiously I scanned . .	688 *Prelude* 7. 94
Misery not lightly passed, but sometimes scanned	708 *Prelude* 8. 648
But seemed there present; and I scanned them all,	710 *Prelude* 9. 62
Was scanned, as I had scanned the moral world?	735 *Prelude* 12. 92
The peace required, he scanned the laws of light .	760 *Excursion* 1. 294
We scanned the various features of the scene: .	788 *Excursion* 3. 114
Scans. He scans the Ass from limb to limb, . .	242 *P. B.* 491
She scans the future with the eye of gods. . .	516 **Hard task* 14
Scant. Of the old grey stone, from her scant board, supplied.	643 *Prelude* 2. 88
Scantiest. Can drink its nurture from the scantiest rill:	222 *Triad* 148
With scantiest knowledge, master of all truth .	895 *Excursion* 9. 736
Scantily. Or scantily rewarded; but all hopes, .	843 *Excursion* 6. 313
Not scantily, bright minutes on the thread . .	862 *Excursion* 7. 307
Scanty. By lichens grey, and scanty moss, o'ergrown;	4 *Ev. Wk.* 95
Appears a scanty plot of smiling green, . . .	14 *Desc. Sk.* 235
To climb the treacherous cliffs for scanty fare. .	17 *Desc. Sk.* 395
Lay in concealment with his scanty train, . .	103 *Artegal* 99
Much how the Youth, in scanty space of time, .	124 *V. and J.* 178
A starveling in a scanty vest;	158 **With little* 22
Thy scanty breathing-time is portioned out . .	172 *Infant Daughter* 17
Within the Sonnet's scanty plot of ground; . .	250 **Nuns fret* 11
Yet to my mind this scanty Stream is brought .	251 **There is a little* 6
Her feeble columns? and that scanty chair! . .	335 *Aix* 6
Nor have I tracked their course for scanty gains;	382 *Duddon* 26. 9
Less scanty measure of those graceful rites . .	448 *Ecc. Sonn.* 3. 33. 2
Albeit labouring for a scanty band	451 *Ecc. Sonn.* 3. 43. 3
For she, with scanty cause for pride, ...	483 *Simon Lee* 51
Tired of my books, a scanty company! . . .	521 *Epist. Beaumont* 32
With a hard bed and scanty nourishment, . .	529 *Poor Robin* 8
To where a scanty knot of verdure peeps, . . .	610 *Desc.Sk.Quarto* 471
For scanty food the treacherous cliffs to dare. .	611 *Desc.Sk.Quarto* 483
In scanty strings, had tempted to o'erleap . .	763 *Excursion* 1. 458
And I shall miss him; scanty tribute! yet, . .	780 *Excursion* 2. 602
A lone pedestrian with a scanty freight, . . .	875 *Excursion* 8. 98
Scar. *See* **Hammar-scar.**	
Intrenched your brows; ye gloried in each scar:	283 **Proud were* 3
Scarce. Where scarce the foxglove peeps, or thistle's beard;	4 *Ev. Wk.* 96
Scarce—*continued.*	
Scarce hides a shadow from her searching rays;	9 *Ev. Wk.* 358
And scarce could any trace of man descry, . .	24 *Guilt* 25
My hen's rich nest through long grass scarce espied;	28 *Guilt* 213
Thy Mother too!—scarce had I gained the door,	40 *Bord.* 182
They cannot be remembered? Scarce a funeral .	97 *Brothers* 125
I'll to the wood."—The word scarce said, . . .	130 *Idiot Boy* 424
Scarce heard; nor word from word could I divide;	197 *Resolution* 108
Where scarce the foxglove peeps, and thistle's beard, ...	593 *Ev. Wk. Quarto* 95
Her seat scarce left, she strives, alas! in vain, .	596 *Ev.Wk. Quarto* 248
Scarce heard, their chattering lips her shoulder chill, ...	597 *Ev. Wk. Quarto* 283
Awe struck, the kneeling peasant scarce surveys;	606 *Desc.Sk.Quarto* 254
Scarce peeps the curious star, till solemn gleams .	S.3. 417 **Sweet was* 12
Towards him, bade him leap, which word scarce said	K.8. 230 **I will* 176
Your friend the country-Justice scarce would fail	L.1. 97 *Juvenal* 3. 71
Scarce-appearing. In the least star of scarce-appearing night;	16 *Desc. Sk.* 318
Scarcely. The kneeling peasant scarcely dares to gaze;	14 *Desc. Sk.* 201
At morn my sick heart hunger scarcely stung, .	31 *Guilt* 377
Of scarcely seven years' growth, beneath the Elm	39 *Bord.* 90
In grange or farm this Hundred scarcely owns .	46 *Bord.* 522
I scarcely can believe it. Myself, I heard . .	49 *Bord.* 678
Scarcely, by groping, had I reached the Spot, .	55 *Bord.* 964
Can scarcely be the work of human hands. . .	67 *Bord.* 1653
'Tis scarcely afternoon—	83 *Lucy Gray* 18
The rain and storm are things that scarcely can come here.	87 *Pet-lamb* 32
Was nothing, scarcely can be aught, yet 'twas bounteously bestowed, ...	93 *Poet's Dream* 78
(Ten years scarcely had she told)	93 *Westmoreland Girl* 10
Scarcely less than sacred passions, ...	94 *Westmoreland Girl* 45
On the hill top. His eyes he scarcely took, . .	125 *V. and J.* 253
Scarcely a soul is out of bed;	126 *Idiot Boy* 12
So pale you scarcely looked at her:	130 *Idiot Boy* 404
Has scarcely been more diligent than I; . . .	134 *Michael* 234
Her tread that would scarcely crush a worm, . .	142 †*Lov. and Lik.* 46
Listen! you can scarcely hear!	174 *Waggoner* 1. 32
Sees nothing, and can scarcely hear them. . .	175 *Waggoner* 1. 193
With grace of motion that might scarcely seem .	218 *Recluse* 1. 1. 204
O'er timid waters that have scarcely left . . .	221 *Triad* 134
And scarcely conscious of the dashing oars . .	271 **Fame tells* 10
Could scarcely make more placid, heaven more bright)	274 *Infant M.* 10
On wrongs, which Nature scarcely seems to heed:	292 **Degenerate Douglas* 11
Whose overburthened hand could scarcely hold .	334 **A winged* 3
Even yet my heart can scarcely brook, . . .	342 *Ital. Itin.* 53
This scarcely spoken, she again	371 *Eg. Maid* 115
And scarcely have they disappeared	396 *White Doe* 35
And scarcely could the Father hear	400 *White Doe* 399
Which I myself could scarcely brook.	401 *White Doe* 494
Thus scarcely given, a noise was heard, . . .	410 *White Doe* 1313
By men yet scarcely conscious of a care . . .	421 *Ecc. Sonn.* 1. 11. 9
Of infant passion, scarcely dare to show . . .	436 *Ecc. Sonn.* 2. 32. 6
Their Country's woes. But scarcely have they met,	437 *Ecc. Sonn.* 2. 37. 5
Scarcely the hand forbears to dip its palm . .	469 **Why stand* 9
Of shame scarcely seeming to know that she's there,	482 *Character* 14
"Nine summers had she scarcely seen, . . .	486 **We walked* 33
Found scarcely anywhere in like degree! . . .	491 *Tribute: Dog* 26
In scarcely conscious fingers, was, she knows, .	509 *F. Stone* 64
Can scarcely trust his eyes, when he perceives .	541 *Grace Darl.* 68
A little scholar, scarcely seven years old, . . .	553 *Prioress* 51
And scarcely could the people that were near .	555 *Prioress* 175
His staff trails with him; scarcely do his feet .	567 *Cumb. Beg.* 59
In him it was scarcely a business of art, . . .	570 *Farmer* 43
Had scarcely flowered: and at this early time, .	575 *Chiabrera* 8. 11
A breath, a sound, and scarcely heard. . . .	580 *John Words.* 36
Whence he had landed scarcely three weeks past;	664 *Prelude* 4. 423
Is scarcely obvious; but, that common sense .	670 *Prelude* 5. 294
A promise scarcely earthly. Instantly, . . .	672 *Prelude* 5. 468
May never tread; but scarcely Spenser's self .	676 *Prelude* 6. 89
No absence scarcely can there be, for those . .	678 *Prelude* 6. 246
That scarcely, as my term of pupilage . . .	679 *Prelude* 6. 276
A stripling, scarcely of the household then . .	686 *Prelude* 6. 766
Trite, do yet scarcely seem so when I think . .	692 *Prelude* 7. 330
Four rapid years had scarcely then been told .	693 *Prelude* 7. 382
And yet not shaped, had seen and scarcely seen, .	694 *Prelude* 7. 483
Distinguished. Scarcely was a year thus spent .	710 *Prelude* 9. 28
It was my fortune scarcely to have seen, . . .	713 *Prelude* 9. 218
And I, who at that time was scarcely dipped .	714 *Prelude* 9. 331
My own delights do scarcely seem to me . . .	733 *Prelude* 11. 408
Could scarcely hold a bridle, with proud hopes .	737 *Prelude* 12. 227
May scarcely see at all; and I would give, . .	738 *Prelude* 12. 282
With strictness scarcely known on English ground.	758 *Excursion* 1. 117
Can scarcely bear it now in mind, there came .	764 *Excursion* 1. 536
Youth's season yet with him was scarcely past, .	774 *Excursion* 2. 195
This scarcely spoken, and those holy strains . .	777 *Excursion* 2. 385
Have scarcely disappeared." "This blooming Child,"	779 *Excursion* 2. 536
Had scarcely closed this high-wrought strain of rapture	782 *Excursion* 2. 727
That scarcely seem to have belonged to me) . .	790 *Excursion* 3. 274
To struggle in as scarcely would allow . . .	795 *Excursion* 3. 640
Are scarcely told, since, on a service bent . .	808 *Excursion* 4. 469
Amid the deafening tumult, scarcely heard . .	809 *Excursion* 4. 534
Then, Pity could have scarcely found on earth .	840 *Excursion* 6. 131

Scarcely—*continued.*
It seems, and scarcely less than pitiful, . . . 844 *Excursion* 6. 377
And, on the burial-day, could scarcely gain . . 853 *Excursion* 6. 971
For me, the emotion scarcely was less strong . . 854 *Excursion* 6. 1055
(Ye scarcely can) amid its sheltering trees . 858 *Excursion* 7. 53
And scarcely could you fancy that a gleam . . 879 *Excursion* 8. 313
Scarcely a wish, but one bright pleasing thought, K.8. 237 *Recluse* 1.1. 16
Of ceaseless motion, that might scarcely seem . K.8. 242 *Recluse* 1.1.204
With impulses that scarcely were by these . . K.8. 256 *Recluse* 1.1.715
Scare. To scare him as a trespasser, ... 144 **Driven in* 72
Thou art!—a friend at hand, to scare . . . . 158 **In youth* 39
I am not sent to scare thee or deceive; . . . 210 *Laod.* 39
The flame-eyed eagle oft wouldst scare . . . 215 *Enterprise* 30
Scare-crow. From any garden scare-crow dangled. 82 *Alice Fell* 28
A scare-crow pattern of old age dressed up . . 693 *Prelude* 7. 423
Scared. Scared by the fife and rumbling drum's alarms, ... 21 *Desc. Sk.* 616
He landed; and by many dangers scared, . . 103 *Artegal* 91
Like a scared Bird encouraged to renew . . . 118 *Maternal Grief* 57
Scared them, while they lay still beneath the shears. 134 *Michael* 176
That sapped good thoughts, or scared them with defiance. . . . . 369 *Eg. Maid* 24
Whence the scared Owl on pinions grey . . . 626 †*Cento* 13
Joyous, nor scared at its own liberty, . . . 632 *Prelude* 1. 15
Whose white belt scared him thence, or wind that blew . . . . 656 *Prelude* 3. 489
Her wisdom stifled, and her justice scared, . . 723 *Prelude* 10. 352
But he repined not. Though the plough was scared . . . . 835 *Excursion* 5. 870
Scarf. Of stole and doublet, hood and scarf, . . 396 *White Doe* 5
Scarlet.—Of coats and of jackets grey, scarlet, and green, ... 120 *Childless Father* 5
Rich store of scarlet hips is mine, ... 155 *Waterfall* 47
The pious bird with the scarlet breast, . . . 162 **Art thou the* 2
—Of flowers that with one scarlet gleam . . . 193 *Ruth* 64
Of olive green and scarlet bright, ... 198 *Thorn* 46
A Woman in a scarlet cloak, ... 198 *Thorn* 63
And there sits in a scarlet cloak, ... 199 *Thorn* 168
And though your sins be red as scarlet, . . . 247 *P. B.* 954
Ye wrangling Schoolmen, of the scarlet hood! . 268 **DogmaticTeachers* 2
To rival summer's brightest scarlet flower; . . 529 *Poor Robin* 10
The shepherd's grey to martial scarlet changed, . 869 *Excursion* 7. 764
And, in his scarlet coat, ... S.3. 423 *Tinker* 17
Scars. And, while he talked of blows and scars, . 180 *Waggoner* 3. 138
Covered from top to toe with scars; . . . . 237 *P. B.* 39
Among the rocks and winding *scars*; . . . 239 *P. B.* 227
And to his grave will go with scars, ... 398 *White Doe* 221
By scars which his activity has left . . . . 788 *Excursion* 3. 175
Scathed. (Blighted or scathed tho' many branches be, 431 *Ecc. Sonn.* 2. 10. 3
Scatter. Along—and scatter and divide, . . . 180 *Waggoner* 4. 63
To scatter seeds of life on barbarous shores; . . 424 *Ecc. Sonn.* 1. 25. 2
Oh may the Almighty scatter with His grace . 505 *Warning* 131
Scatter the colours from the plumes that bear . 528 **Those breathing* 67
We shall not scatter through the plains and rocks K.8. 248 *Recluse* 1.1.430
I heard her scatter some endearing words . . . K.8. 251 *Recluse* 1.1.527
Scattered. *See* **Loosely-scattered, Thinly-scattered, Widely-scattered.**
Cheering its naked waste of scattered stone, . . 4 *Ev. Wk.* 94
Deep yellow beams the scattered stems illume, . 5 *Ev. Wk.* 180
Of scattered herds, that in the meadow graze, . 34 *Guilt* 521
And if they had care, it has scattered their cares 167 *Stray Pleasures* 23
But where the scattered stars are seen . . . 173 *Waggoner* 1. 9
As in a natural temple scattered o'er . . . 185 *Yew-trees* 29
Lay round me, scattered like a flock of sheep— . 185 *Nutting* 37
Wide open for the scattered Poor. . . . . 228 *Devot. Incit.* 59
Scattered, a Cyclades of various shapes . . . 231 *Clouds* 77
Among the scattered stars. . . . . . . 236 *P. B.* 30
Where they bloomed singly, or in scattered knots,) 280 *Valedict.* 3
Here scattered, like a random seed, ... 288 *Highland Girl* 28
Of scattered quails by signs do reunite, . . . 320 **Hunger, and* 7
And scattered rural farms of aspect bright; . . 323 *Ode 1814* 12
Scattered on all sides by the hideous jars . . 346 *Processions* 34
Influence, at least among a scattered few, . . 358 *Aquap.* 366
Scattered all Britain over, through deep glen, . 387 *Manse* 3
Renounces, till among the scattered clouds . . 461 **Who but is* 4
Among the scattered rocks: . . . . 491 *Fidelity* 4
Laid one by one, or scattered on the ground. . . 531 **I know* 12
Her way pursuing among scattered clouds, . . 532 **How beautiful the* 2
And scattered many a lusty splinter . . . . 536 *Goody Blake* 51
And ever, scattered from his palsied hand, . . 566 *Cumb. Beg.* 16
Some scattered leaf, or marks which, in one track, 567 *Cumb. Beg.* 55
Deep yellow beams the scatter'd boles illume, . 594 *Ev.Wk. Quarto* 163
From town to town and through wide scattered realms . . . . 655 *Prelude* 3. 469
Among my schoolfellows I scattered round . . 659 *Prelude* 4. 72
Or sleeping nameless in their scattered graves, . 668 *Prelude* 5. 215
As scattered birds troop to the fowler's lure, . . 675 *Prelude* 6. 5
Exposed on the bare fell, were scattered love, . 678 *Prelude* 6. 235
A sort of alien scattered from the clouds. . . . 692 *Prelude* 7. 350
Are scattered everywhere, no rarities, ... 696 *Prelude* 7. 596
Those scattered along Adria's myrtle shores: . . 701 *Prelude* 8. 176
In earth, the widely scattered wreck sublime . . 708 *Prelude* 8. 614
By new opinions, scattered tribes have made . . 715 *Prelude* 9. 378
Small islands scattered amid stormy waves, . . 725 *Prelude* 10. 482
Are scattered everywhere, taking their date . . 737 *Prelude* 12. 224
All but a scattered few, live out their time, . . 757 *Excursion* 1. 89
Lay scattered here and there, open or shut, . . 768 *Excursion* 1. 828
Had we about us! scattered was the floor, . . 781 *Excursion* 2. 661
By nature's care from wreck of scattered stones, 805 *Excursion* 4. 243
Uncensured, and subsist, a scattered few . . . 823 *Excursion* 5. 34

Scattered—*continued.*
Some scattered o'er the level, others perched . . 823 *Excursion* 5. 89
Scattered about under the mouldering walls . . 835 *Excursion* 5. 866
That all the scattered subjects which compose . 836 *Excursion* 5. 935
Are scattered at the feet of Man—like flowers. . 887 *Excursion* 9. 240
Wild tracts of forest-ground, and scattered groves, 891 *Excursion* 9. 505
Scattered through half the circle of the sky; . . 893 *Excursion* 9. 602
Certes were self-taught damsels, scattered births . S.3. 436 **The doubt* 153
Then to be greeted by the scattered huts, . . . K.8. 249 *Recluse* 1.1.482
Scattered about us, nor through dearth of aught . K.8. 254 *Recluse* 1.1.636
Scattereth. Who scattereth lustres o'er noon-day, . 506 **While from* 11
Scattering. *See* **Leaf-scattering.**
Scattering thy gladness without care, ... 159 *Green Linnet* 22
Scattering fresh flowers; though happier far, I ween, 191 *Beggars* 35
Scattering a ditty each to her desire, ... 233 *Power of Sound* 46
By scattering gleams, through your distress, . . 409 *White Doe* 1247
Scattering, like birds escaped the fowler's net, . 437 *Ecc. Sonn.* 2. 37. 1
No longer, scattering to the heedless winds . . 549 **The massy* 11
Scattering this far-fetched moisture from my wings, 582 *Invoc. Earth* 23
While in soft gloom the scattering bowers recede, 607 *Desc.Sk.Quarto* 271
Scatterings. Deep, gloomy were they, and severe; the scatterings . . . . 662 *Prelude* 4. 252
Sparry and bright, rough scatterings of the hills. 856 *Excursion* 6. 1155
Scatters. While thro' the stillness scatters wild dismay, ... 606 *Desc.Sk.Quarto* 241
As fast as a musician scatters sounds . . . . 809 *Excursion* 4. 524
Scavenger. The begging scavenger, with hat in hand; 690 *Prelude* 7. 213
Scawfell. Ranging the heights of Scawfell or Black-comb, ... 468 **Ranging the* 1
Scawfell's. *See* **Scafell's.**
Scene. And round the broad-spread oak, a glimmering scene, ... 3 *Ev. Wk.* 46
And its own twilight softens the whole scene, . 3 *Ev. Wk.* 61
Even now she decks for me a distant scene, . . 8 *Ev. Wk.* 345
How blest, delicious scene! the eye that greets . 12 *Desc. Sk.* 107
Gently illuminate a sober scene:— . . . . . 14 *Desc. Sk.* 213
Yet here and there, if 'mid the savage scene . . 14 *Desc. Sk.* 234
A scene more fair than what the Grecian feigns . 20 *Desc. Sk.* 573
And led by nature into a wild scene . . . . 23 *Yew-tree* 14
On the more distant scene,—how lovely 'tis . . 23 *Yew-tree* 34
The world, and human life, appeared a scene . . 23 *Yew-tree* 41
Into a narrow valley's pleasant scene . . . . 34 *Guilt* 515
But for the scene which we by chance have witnessed. . . . . 42 *Bord.* 275
Of the dark firs, a visionary scene! . . . . 151 **When, to* 93
Involved and restless all—a scene . . . . . 178 *Waggoner* 3. 39
Is left to muse upon the solemn scene. . . . 184 *Night-piece* 26
A virgin scene!—A little while I stood, . . . 185 *Nutting* 21
This heath, this calm, and quiet scene; . . . 187 **Three years* 40
That on a wild secluded scene impress . . . . 205 *Tintern* 6
The scene that opens now? . . . . 215 *Kirkstone* 64
Might stop before this favoured scene, . . . 223 *Wishing-gate* 58
A thing as steadfast as the scene . . . . . 239 *P. B.* 269
A scene of soft and lovely hue! . . . . . 240 *P. B.* 362
Together make as sweet a scene . . . . . 240 *P. B.* 364
Build up a wild fantastic scene; . . . . . 244 *P. B.* 682
Baffle the threat, bright Scene, from Orrest-head 282 *Railway* 9
Over the pomp and beauty of a scene . . . . 290 *Kilchurn* 26
O froward Fancy! 'mid a scene . . . . . 299 *Brownie's Cell* 75
And yet how fair the rural scene! . . . . . 299 *Cora Linn* 7
Strange scene, fantastic and uneasy . . . . 300 *Bran* 27
Filling from morn to night the heroic scene . . 318 **Is there* 9
Oh Life! without thy chequered scene . . . 337 **Oh Life* 1
My spirit is the scene of such wild art . . . 350 *Des. Stanzas* 7
These are before me; and the varied scene . . 352 *Aquap.* 23
By aught that mingled with the tragic scene . . 435 *Ecc. Sonn.* 2. 26. 11
Pleased rather with some soft ideal scene, . . . 480 **Most sweet* 5
Upon a soothing scene, ... 499 *Memory* 22
Or book regardless, and of that fair scene . . . 508 *F. Stone* 3
In a deep vision's intellectual scene, ... 528 **Those breathing* 111
More than theatric force to Shakspeare's scene;— 583 **With copious* 33
And round the humming elm, a glimmering scene! 592 *Ev. Wk. Quarto* 62
While, by the scene compos'd, the breast subsides, 597 *Ev. Wk. Quarto* 309
No wrack of all the pageant scene remains, . . 598 *Ev. Wk. Quarto* 360
The scene is waken'd, yet its peace unbroke, . . 599 *Ev. Wk. Quarto* 429
Light up of tranquil joy a sober scene; . . . 607 *Desc.Sk.Quarto* 268
And still, below, where mid the savage scene . . 607 *Desc.Sk.Quarto* 291
—When the Sun bids the gorgeous scene farewell, 612 *Desc.Sk.Quarto* 562
So fair; and while upon the fancied scene . . 633 *Prelude* 1. 76
A lonely scene more lonesome, among woods, . 638 *Prelude* 1. 418
A visible scene, on which the sun is shining? . . 641 *Prelude* 1. 635
A holy scene!—Along the smooth green turf . . 643 *Prelude* 2. 107
—Of that external scene which round me lay, . 660 *Prelude* 4. 160
The peaceful scene oft filled me with surprise . . 661 *Prelude* 4. 194
Of mountain torrents; or the visible scene . . 671 *Prelude* 5. 384
At last, the dead man, 'mid that beauteous scene 672 *Prelude* 5. 448
Led, as before, we should behold the scene, . . 685 *Prelude* 6. 698
And now I looked upon the living scene; . . . 689 *Prelude* 7. 144
Some half-frequented scene, where wider streets . 690 *Prelude* 7. 191
To have, for instance, brought upon the scene . 691 *Prelude* 7. 279
With the ever-shifting figures of the scene, . . 693 *Prelude* 7. 412
And yielded to all changes of the scene . . . 694 *Prelude* 7. 474
The scene before him stands in perfect view . . 707 *Prelude* 8. 575
A novel scene, did often in this way . . . . 716 *Prelude* 9. 463
Then from the quiet of that scene passed on, . . 718 *Prelude* 10. 10
Was laid with tears. Then suddenly the scene . 724 *Prelude* 10. 409
Longing for skill to paint a scene so bright . . 726 *Prelude* 10. 569
To a comparison of scene with scene, ... 736 *Prelude* 12. 115
Whate'er the scene presented to her view . . . 736 *Prelude* 12. 159
I roamed, in daily presence of this scene, . . . 738 *Prelude* 12. 263

Scene—*continued.*
With side-long eye looks out upon the scene, . . 756 *Excursion* 1. 15
Said I, "The music and the sprightly scene . . 773 *Excursion* 2. 138
We scanned the various features of the scene : 788 *Excursion* 3. 114
To a proficient of the tragic scene . . . . 793 *Excursion* 3. 466
On the hill-sides, a cheerful quiet scene, . . . 823 *Excursion* 5. 90
Is either fair and tempting, a soft scene . . . 830 *Excursion* 5. 527
The words he uttered, and the scene that lay . . 857 *Excursion* 7. 2
The agitated scene before his eye . . . . 863 *Excursion* 7. 414
Upon the brighter scene. How blest that pair . 888 *Excursion* 9. 256
The general aspect of the scene ; but each . . 893 *Excursion* 9. 583
Yet happy they who in life's later scene. . . . L.1. 96 *Juvenal* 3. 53

Scenes. Fair scenes, erewhile, I taught, a happy child, ... 2 *Ev. Wk.* 13
Than those soft scenes through which thy childhood strayed, ... 254 *Dyer* 4
That animates the scenes of public life . . . 269 **If these* 3
Fair scenes for childhood's opening bloom, . . 302 *Yarrow V.* 57
Than for like scenes in moral vision shown, . . 360 *Alban Hills* 5
Withered at eve. From scenes of art which chase 388 *Trosachs* 5
To homefelt pleasures and to gentle scenes ; . . 494 *Hap. War.* 60
Here, as 'mid busier scenes, ground steep and rough, 497 **Enough of climbing* 2
To scenes Arcadian, whispering, through soft air, 530 *Gleaner* 7
Fair scenes ! with other eyes, than once, I gaze, . 591 *Ev. Wk. Quarto* 17
Through ever-changing scenes of votive quest . 634 *Prelude* 1. 181
The scenes which were a witness of that joy . . 641 *Prelude* 1. 599
Of things forgotten, these same scenes so bright, . 641 *Prelude* 1. 607
And tranquil scenes, that universal power . . 647 *Prelude* 2. 324
In the great city, 'mid far other scenes ; . . . 648 *Prelude* 2. 452
Conjuring up scenes as obsolete in freaks . . . 657 *Prelude* 3. 569
Or scenes renowned for beauty, I explored . . 677 *Prelude* 6. 191
Music, and shifting pantomimic scenes, . . . 691 *Prelude* 7. 262
Are now my theme ; and, foremost of the scenes, 692 *Prelude* 7. 334
Of novelty survived for scenes like these ; . . . 693 *Prelude* 7. 447
Builds for herself ; scenes different there are, . 697 *Prelude* 7. 652
And all the scenes of childhood reappear, . . . 699 *Prelude* 8. 50
From those sad scenes when meditation turned, . 709 *Prelude* 8. 654
Which they were wont to be. Through kindred scenes, ... 733 *Prelude* 11. 413
The milder minstrelsies of rural scenes . . . 737 *Prelude* 12. 200
And journey far, revisiting the scenes . . . . 762 *Excursion* 1. 390
Of duke or earl, from scenes of courtly pomp . . 859 *Excursion* 7. 125
Leaving, in quest of other scenes, the shore . . 892 *Excursion* 9. 547

Scent. To scent the sweets of Piedmont's breathing rose, ... 21 *Desc. Sk.* 595
God, who instructs the brutes to scent . . . . 226 *Present.* 73
Distinguished two for scent, and two for speed. . 490 *Incident : Dog* 8

Scented. Stretch'd on the scented mountain's purple side. . . . . 611 *Desc.Sk.Quarto* 513

Scents. The Muse, who scents the morning air, . . 180 *Waggoner* 4. 12
A loathsome pit, whence noisome scents exhale ; . 554 *Prioress* 122
Whence fragrance scents the water's desart gale, . 596 *Ev. Wk.Quarto* 223
When fragrant scents beneath th' enchanted tread 610 *Desc.Sk.Quarto* 448
Of meek repentance, wafting wallflower scents . 817 *Excursion* 4. 1047
In the prime hour of sweetest scents and airs. . 850 *Excursion* 6. 823
Shadows or breezes, scents or sounds. Nor deem K.8. 249 *Recluse* 1. 1. 448

Sceptic. The Sceptic somewhat haughtily exclaimed: 812 *Excursion* 4. 767
Exclaimed the Sceptic, "and the strain of thought 846 *Excursion* 6. 523
The pensive Sceptic of the lonely vale . . . . 874 *Excursion* 8. 1

Sceptre. Choose her thistle for thy sceptre, . . . 90 *Longest Day* 67
The British sceptre, here would I to thee . . . 104 *Artegal* 155
Humbling that lily-stem, thy sceptre meek, . . 220 *Triad* 58
The chosen sceptre is a withered bough, . . . 321 **Humanity,delighting* 9
Sceptre and mantle, sword and ring, laid down . 428 *Ecc. Sonn.* 1. 37. 11
And near the golden sceptre grasped by Jove, . 457 **The leaves* 29
Then, will the sceptre be a straw, the crown . 504 *Warning* 107
Bore a light switch, her sceptre of command . 523 *Epist. Beaumont* 108
His staff is a sceptre—his grey hairs a crown ; . 569 *Farmer* 6
Yet in the regal sceptre, and the pomp . . . 712 *Prelude* 9. 209
Wielded the sceptre of the Atheist crew. . . . 725 *Prelude* 10. 502
The crook into a sceptre ; give the pomp . . . 846 *Excursion* 6. 550
The sceptre of his sway ; his country's name, . 880 *Excursion* 8. 429

Sceptred. And grant that every sceptred child of clay . . . . 22 *Desc. Sk.* 659
Than sceptred king or laurelled conqueror knows, 387 *Scott* 11
Must bend the sceptred Potentates of earth. . . 574 *Chiabrera* 3. 20
While England's sceptred Line . . . . . . 629 *Installation* 97

Sceptre-like. That, carried sceptre-like, o'ertops the head . . . . 448 *Ecc. Sonn.* 3. 32. 8

Scheme. *See* **Counter-scheme.**
Most tunable. In faith, a pleasant scheme ; . . 60 *Bord.* 1251
And thus resumed :—" Well, Isabel ! this scheme 135 *Michael* 274
That round it clung, and tempting scheme . . 223 *'Tis gone* 2
Ye wandering Utterances, has earth no scheme, . 235 *Power of Sound* 169
Of ruin shall not touch. Innocent scheme ! . . 253 **Aerial Rock* 9
And crossed by many a shattered scheme, . . 342 *Ital. Itin.* 28
So far that, if consistent in their scheme, . . 518 *Pun. Death* 7. 12
To every scheme of holiday delight . . . . 642 *Prelude* 2. 52
When she would enter on her tender scheme . . 657 *Prelude* 3. 556
Nor had, in truth, the scheme been formed by me 680 *Prelude* 6. 329
Connected in a mighty scheme of truth, . . . 744 *Prelude* 13. 302
In framing models to improve the scheme . . 791 *Excursion* 3. 336
Such was their scheme : and though the wished-for end . . . . 792 *Excursion* 3. 406
How, think you, would they tolerate this scheme 814 *Excursion* 4. 905
A fancy pregnant with resource and scheme . . 859 *Excursion* 7. 117
She vanished—eager to impart the scheme . . 890 *Excursion* 9. 430
To scheme and counter-scheme for purse and plate. L.1. 94 *Juvenal* 2. 16

Schemed. Where once his airy helpers schemed and planned . . . . 435 *Ecc. Sonn.* 2. 27. 12
We schemed and puzzled, head opposed to head . 639 *Prelude* 1. 512

Schemers. Had fitted their own thoughts, schemers more mild, ... 729 *Prelude* 11. 134

Schemes. Shrunk from me ; plans and schemes, and lofty hopes— . . . . 69 *Bord.* 1762
The sage enchanter Merlin's subtle schemes ; . . 103 *Artegal* 51
Its presence tempted him to cherish schemes . . 124 *V. and J.* 188
From rash assault ? Schemes of retirement sown 282 *Railway* 2
He listens (all past conquests and all schemes . 426 *Ecc. Sonn.* 1. 30. 6
No natural bond between the boldest schemes . 471 **Arran ! a* 11
Our schemes ; the faith and honour, never yet . 513 **Said Secrecy* 6
Rash schemes, to abjure all selfish agitation, . . 516 **As leaves* 6
Of heady schemes jostling each other, gawds, . 662 *Prelude* 4. 281
Out of the bowels of those very schemes . . . 673 *Prelude* 5. 502
Then schemes I framed more calmly, when and how . . . . 727 *Prelude* 10. 590
To depravation, speculative schemes— . . . 730 *Prelude* 11. 224
Into its true proportion ; sanguine schemes, . . 741 *Prelude* 13. 60
Wishes and endless schemes ; by daylight walked 842 *Excursion* 6. 240
Upon its pillow with a thousand schemes. . . . 860 *Excursion* 7. 212
Conceits, devices, plans, and schemes, ... K.8. 227 **I will* 101
Then farewell to the Warrior's schemes, farewell . K.8. 257 *Recluse* 1. 1. 745

Schill. Brave Schill ! by death delivered, take thy flight . . . . 317 **Brave Schill* 1

Scholar. There's never a scholar in England knows. 80 †*Address : Child* 8
That slender Youth, a scholar pale, ... 399 *White Doe* 264
Ah, pensive Scholar, think not so, ... 399 *White Doe* 308
The saint, the scholar, from a circle freed . . . 424 *Ecc. Sonn.* 1. 23. 5
A little scholar, scarcely seven years old, . . . 553 *Prioress* 51
To a poor scholar ! "—when illustrious men, . . 656 *Prelude* 3. 474

Scholar's. Familiarly, and in his scholar's dress . 653 *Prelude* 3. 288
In him revealed a scholar's genius shone ; . . . 868 *Excursion* 7. 737

Scholars. Of white-robed Scholars only—this immense . . . . 451 *Ecc. Sonn.* 3. 43. 4
Scholars and gentlemen ; where, furthermore, . 713 *Prelude* 9. 229

Scholastic. Of our scholastic studies ; could have wished . . . . 656 *Prelude* 3. 495
Of strenuous champions, in scholastic arts . . 839 *Excursion* 6. 57

School. *See* **Village-school.**
That casts its shade over our village school, . . 39 *Bord.* 91
I had as lief turn to the Friar's school . . . . 45 *Bord.* 467
To hear, to meet them !—From their house the school . . . . 99 *Brothers* 251
That is for him a happy school, ... 142 †*Lov. and Lik.* 24
Are pupils of your school. . . . . 225 *Present.* 36
A Poet !—He hath put his heart to school, . . 277 **A Poet* 1
Here, mighty Nature ! in this school sublime . 314 **Not 'mid* 9
Where thoughtful Edwin, tutored in the school . 422 *Ecc. Sonn.* 1. 15. 2
Thanks for the lessons of this Spot—fit school . 473 **Thanks for* 1
And murmur of the village school. . . . . 486 *Matthew* 20
Not seeking in the school of pride . . . . . 492 *Duty*
Patience *his* law, long-suffering *his* school, . . 518 *Pun. Death* 7. 7
" A little school of Christian people stood . . . 553 *Prioress* 43
That learnèd in that school from year to year . 553 *Prioress* 46
Who day by day unto this school hath gone, . . 553 *Prioress* 52
" This little Child, while in the school he sate . 553 *Prioress* 65
And, as the Child 'gan to the school to pace, . . 554 *Prioress* 118
She at the School and elsewhere him hath sought, 554 *Prioress* 139
In penniless poverty. But now to school . . . 643 *Prelude* 2. 84
Were early ;—oft before the hours of school . . 647 *Prelude* 2. 330
Of Patron, famous school or friendly nook, . . 655 *Prelude* 3. 467
Of manners put to school I took small note, . . 663 *Prelude* 4. 302
Upon a slope above the village school, . . . 671 *Prelude* 5. 393
That, from the rural school ascending, play . . 671 *Prelude* 5. 405
Of that wide edifice, thy school and home, . . 679 *Prelude* 6. 268
Summoned from school to London ; fortunate . 688 *Prelude* 7. 92
And plain beneath. Ere we to school returned,— 738 *Prelude* 12. 305
Equipped with satchel, to a school, that stood . 758 *Excursion* 1. 122
What wonder, then, if I, whose favourite school . 772 *Excursion* 2. 28
But, for disciples of the inner school, ... 775 *Excursion* 2. 255
Youngest apprentice in the school of art ! . . . 789 *Excursion* 3. 199
A pupil in the many-chambered school, . . . 810 *Excursion* 4. 609
Quiet and calm. Behold him—in the school . . 878 *Excursion* 8. 306
How throngs the crowd to yon theatric school . L.1. 97 *Juvenal* 3. 89

Schoolboy. But thou, a School-boy, to the sea hadst carried . . . . 151 **When, to* 76
The same whom in my schoolboy days . . . 183 **O blithe* 17
One to whom, yet a School-boy, Cynthia showed 461 **Giordano,verily* 11
Who, yet a liveried schoolboy, in the depths . . 679 *Prelude* 6. 266
To native man. A rambling schoolboy, thus . 703 *Prelude* 8. 256
The thinking, thoughtless, school-boy ; the bold youth . . . . 836 *Excursion* 5. 959
Young was I then, a schoolboy of eight years ; . 858 *Excursion* 7. 69
A roving school-boy ; what the Adventurer's age K.8. 236 *Recluse* 1. 1. 2

Schoolboy's. To a schoolboy's vision, I had raised a pile . . . . 655 *Prelude* 3. 425

Schoolboys. When school-boys stretched their length upon the green ; . . . . . 3 *Ev. Wk.* 45
Three rosy-cheeked school-boys, the highest not more . . . . 86 *Rural Arch.* 2
And what did these school-boys ? The very next day . . . . 86 *Rural Arch.* 17
Seemed friends, poor simple schoolboys, now hung round . . . . 649 *Prelude* 3. 20
Of schoolboys hastening to their distant home . 727 *Prelude* 10. 601

School-day. Through the whole tenour of my school-day time, ... 713 *Prelude* 9. 219

Schooled. In the delight of moral prudence schooled, 368 *Trajan* 31
O'er men in dauntless virtues schooled, . . . 390 *Highland Broach* 8

Schoolfellow 823 Scorn

Schoolfellow. " His Schoolfellow, who elder was than he, 553 *Prioress* 79
" His Schoolfellow, whom he had so besought, 554 *Prioress* 93
Schoolfellows. Among my schoolfellows I scattered round 659 *Prelude* 4. 72
As one of many schoolfellows compelled, 750 *Prelude* 14. 332
Schoolmaster. A village schoolmaster was he, 486 **We walked* 5
His Schoolmaster supplied ; books that explain 760 *Excursion* 1. 252
Schoolmen. Ye wrangling Schoolmen, of the scarlet hood ! 268 **Dogmatic Teachers* 2
Among the schoolmen, and Platonic forms 679 *Prelude* 6. 298
Schools. I could fetch lessons out of wiser schools 59 *Bord.* 1221
Framed in the schools where Wisdom dwelt retired, 213 *Dion* 49
That shames the Schools. 286 *Nith* 42
Beneath the brutal sword ?—Her haughty Schools 315 **Alas ! what* 9
Alas ! the Genius of our age, from Schools 468 *St. Bees* 154
In heathen schools of philosophic lore ; 476 **Tranquillity! the* 2
And storms the pillars rock. But we such schools 496 **A little* 39
Fetched with cupidity from heartless schools, 501 *Humanity* 88
Such course he held ! Bologna's learned schools 573 *Chiabrera* 2. 9
Let them parade among the Schools at will, 655 *Prelude* 3. 404
Even to the rudest novice of the Schools. 696 *Prelude* 7. 597
That are the commonplaces of the schools— 721 *Prelude* 10. 192
Were open schools in which I daily read 742 *Prelude* 13. 163
Amid the wrangling schools—a SPIRIT hung, 812 *Excursion* 4. 735
Her equal rights, her churches and her schools— 880 *Excursion* 8. 430
And faithful care of unambitious schools 890 *Excursion* 9. 395
School-time. My school-time, an apartment he had owned, 757 *Excursion* 1. 54
Schoolward. Homeward or schoolward, ape what ye behold ; 339 *Tell* 8
Homeward and schoolward whensoe'er he went, 554 *Prioress* 98
Schwytz. To dignity—in thee, O SCHWYTZ ! are seen 339 *Schwytz* 2
Thy name, O SCHWYTZ, in happy freedom keep ! 339 *Schwytz* 14
Science. No common soul. In youth by science nursed, 23 *Yew-tree* 13
Science advances with gigantic strides ; 281 **What strong* 7
Stood Science waiting for the hour 343 *Eclipse* 2
Science, wide-spread and spreading still as be 357 *Aquap.* 331
Shames the degenerate grasp of modern science, 329 *Eg. Maid* 20
Of solitude, with love of science strong, 429 *Ecc. Sonn.* 2. 5. 9
Isis and Cam, to patient Science dear ! 451 *Ecc. Sonn.* 3. 42. 14
Of Science laid them open to mankind— 461 **Queen of* 41
Truths whose thick veil Science has drawn aside ? 469 **Desire we* 3
Enough of Science and of Art ; 482 *Tables Turned* 29
Surpass all science and all utterance ; 552 *Prioress* 24
Since Science first, with all her sacred train, 618 *School Ex.* 3
Science with joy saw Superstition fly 618 *School Ex.* 43
Where, throned in gold, immortal Science reigns ; 619 *School Ex.* 70
Where science, leagued with holier truth, 629 *Installation* 74
Science appears but what in truth she is, 645 *Prelude* 2. 212
Have made me pay to science and to arts 654 *Prelude* 3. 375
Suffers for this. Even Science, too, at hand 655 *Prelude* 3. 418
Of geometric science. Though advanced 676 *Prelude* 6. 117
But turned to abstract science, and there sought 732 *Prelude* 11. 328
Of science, and among her simplest laws, 760 *Excursion* 1. 271
Of science, and philosophy, and sense ! " 815 *Excursion* 4. 918
The burthen of existence. Science then 820 *Excursion* 4. 1251
O'er which enchained by science he had loved 840 *Excursion* 6. 150
Science severe, or word of holy Writ 864 *Excursion* 7. 451
Lodged in her bosom ; and, by science led, 865 *Excursion* 7. 505
Scientific. A miracle of scientific lore, 670 *Prelude* 5. 315
Scilly. Forth-looking toward the rocks of Scilly, 369 *Eg. Maid* 2
A bare rock of the Scilly cluster ; 371 *Eg. Maid* 158
Scimitar. His icy scimitar, a foretaste yields 263 **While not* 5
The scimitar, that yields not to the charms 427 *Ecc. Sonn.* 1. 34. 5
Scoff. The insinuated scoff of coward tongues, 648 *Prelude* 2. 456
Scoffed. Some scoffed at him with hellish mockery, 68 *Bord.* 1736
The last of their humanity, and scoffed 513 *General Fast* 3
And re-confirmed—are scoffed at with a smile 872 *Excursion* 7. 992
Scoffer's. Than this dull product of a scoffer's pen, 778 *Excursion* 2. 484
Scoffers. Was taken up by scoffers in their pride, 725 *Prelude* 10. 471
With scoffers, seeking light and gay revenge 732 *Prelude* 11. 322
Scoffs. With scoffs and taunts, like Vulcan out of heaven : 640 *Prelude* 1. 531
Scolding. Of sharp command and scolding intermixed. 650 *Prelude* 3. 52
Scoop. *See* **Scroop.**
She saw the carman bend to scoop the flood 34 *Guilt* 543
Of Patriots scoop their freedom out, with hand 272 *Devil's Bridge* 5
Of hermit, dubious where to [? scoop] his cell ; S.3. 433 **The doubt* 18
Scooped. When giants scooped from out the rocky ground, 269 *Malham* 2
Scooped out of living rock, and near a brook 424 *Ecc. Sonn.* 1. 22. 3
Scooped from the sacred earth where his dear relics lie. 426 *Ecc. Sonn.* 1. 32. 14
Self-poised, and scooped into ten thousand cells, 451 *Ecc. Sonn.* 3. 43. 10
That it was scooped within the living stone,— 546 **Oft is* 10
Nor aught of blinder vacancy, scooped out 755 *Recluse* 1. 1. 790
Had newly scooped a running stream. He rose, 762 *Excursion* 1. 446
From the beginning, hollowed out and scooped 837 *Excursion* 5. 1005
Fresh as the freshest field, scoop'd out, and green K.8. 263 **The Lake* 6
Scoops. Death's hireling, who scoops out his neighbour's grave, 826 *Excursion* 5. 235
Scope. While Fancy ranging with free scope 164 **Fair Lady* 13
When some great change gives boundless scope 225 *Present.* 49
Buried in glory, far beyond the scope 226 *Vernal Ode* 28
To which our fancies, mingling, gave free scope 251 *Appleth.* 7
That virtuous Liberty hath been the scope 321 **Here pause* 2
With wishes of still bolder scope 403 *White Doe* 650
Which love had prompted, yielding scope 406 *White Doe* 928
Had mortal action e'er a nobler scope ? 442 *Ecc. Sonn.* 3. 9. 9

Scope—*continued.*
Meek, patient, steadfast, and with loftier scope, 461 **Queen of* 55
But Sculpture here, with the divinest scope 476 *Howard* 3
Yes, for them whose souls have scope 503 **Like a* 64
Into those jarring fractions.—Let thy scope 515 **Ah why* 9
For One who speaks in numbers ; ampler scope 520 *Pun. Death* 14. 2
From all that lies within the scope 534 **Blest is* 67
Others of wider scope, where living men, 691 *Prelude* 7. 261
The moral properties and scope of things. 758 *Excursion* 1. 169
May yet have scope to range among her own, 803 *Excursion* 4. 107
That, far as kindly Nature hath free scope 885 *Excursion* 9. 105
Scorch. Be wrenched, or fire come down from far to scorch 666 *Prelude* 5. 31
Scorched. Had summer scorched the fields ; not twice had fallen, 861 *Excursion* 7. 248
Scorching. Scorching blight or noxious dew, 226 *Vernal Ode* 26
And from the scorching noon-tide sun, 409 *White Doe* 1182
Score. *See* **Eight-score.**
And in one night send twenty score of sheep 97 *Brothers* 153
Of sheep I numbered a full score, 115 *Last of Flock* 29
(Take from him what you will upon the score 813 *Excursion* 4. 829
Scored. Have scored thine age, and punctually timed 172 *Infant Daughter* 26
The cross upon thy shoulder scored, 247 *P. B.* 973
Scorn. Be scorn and fear and hope alike forgot 22 *Desc. Sk.* 666
And scorn,—against all enemies prepared, 23 *Yew-tree* 19
The wise man to that scorn which wisdom holds 23 *Yew-tree* 58
Asked him in scorn what business there he had ; 33 *Guilt* 482
We call, and scorn the other as Time's spendthrift ; 60 *Bord.* 1236
Through good and evil, obloquy and scorn, 64 *Bord.* 1500
Or fear disguised in simulated scorn. 70 *Bord.* 1831
To me a kingdom ! spare the bitter scorn : 104 *Artegal* 141
But scorn with scorn outbrave ; 110 **Ere with* 18
To scorn the declaration, 111 **Yes ! thou* 2
And your brow is free from scorn, 140 *Arm. Lady* 44
Who first, weighed down by scorn, in some lone bower 169 *Love lies Bleeding* 20
In scorn I speak not ;—they are what their birth 192 *Gipsies* 26
I could have laughed myself to scorn to find 197 *Resolution* 137
Smile if thou wilt, but not in scorn, 223 *Wishing-gate* 43
As his distress is sharp, would scorn my theme, 229 *Cuckoo-clock* 28
But, of his scorn repenting soon, he drew 231 **The gentlest Poet* 29
Nor yet redeemed from scorn. 232 *Jew. Fam.* 40
His scorn returns—his hate revives ; 242 *P. B.* 496
Scorn not the Sonnet ; Critic, you have frowned, 260 **Scorn not* 1
Have killed him, Scorn should write his epitaph. 277 **A Poet* 8
Must scorn a timid song. 291 *Rob Roy* 16
—Strange words they seemed of slight and scorn ; 293 *Yarrow Unv.* 29
That less should scorn the abandoned clay ; 301 *Bran* 83
Whether the mighty beam, in scorn upheld, 311 **Who rises* 25
The rough Ætolians smiled with bitter scorn. 312 **When, far* 4
Curses are *his* dire portion, scorn, and hate, 317 **Look now* 10
But mighty Winter the device shall scorn. 321 **Humanity, delighting* 12
With impious thanksgiving, the Almighty's scorn ! 326 **Emperors and* 2
Opposed to hopes that battened upon scorn, 330 *Ode : Thanks.* 114
To suffer pains with heathen scorn and hate 357 *Aquap.* 313
Of what is won, we overlook or scorn 357 *Aquap.* 338
They—who have seen the noble Roman's scorn 359 **They—who* 1
But not in scorn :—the Matron's Faith may lack 360 *Albano* 9
Due audience, how for aught but scorn defy 365 **The Baptist* 4
Gay June would scorn us. But when bleak winds roar 379 *Duddon* 13. 5
The Torrents chant their praise, inspiring scorn 383 *Duddon* 29. 12
'Tis meet that I endure your scorn ; 400 *White Doe* 389
Presumed to grapple with their scorn, 401 *White Doe* 486
Thus to become at once the scorn 405 *White Doe* 849
I scorn your Chiefs—men who would lead, 406 *White Doe* 902
Then peace to cruelty and scorn, 409 *White Doe* 1241
Aloft in sign of taunting scorn, 410 *White Doe* 1326
The oppression of the tumult—wrath and scorn— 421 *Ecc. Sonn.* 1. 12. 1
Nor scorn the aid which Fancy oft doth lend 423 *Ecc. Sonn.* 1. 18. 1
With scorn, invoking a vindictive ban 428 *Ecc. Sonn.* 1. 38. 12
Be lost, through apathy, or scorn, or fear, 442 *Ecc. Sonn.* 3. 10. 10
When I shall scorn thy voice or mock thy mien ! 456 **The leaves* 25
Ah ! scorn not hastily their rule who try 467 *St. Bees* 86
Greedy ambition, armed to treat with scorn 469 **The feudal* 4
Speak Thou, whose massy strength and stature scorn 477 *Long Meg* 5
His thrift thy uselessness will never scorn ; 490 *Spade* 29
Witness those glances of indignant scorn 501 *Humanity* 64
Thy gifts, thy beauty scorn ; 507 *May* 4
With modest scorn reject whate'er would blind 529 **Those breathing* 135
May season apathy with scorn, 534 **Blest is* 63
That seemed to play with it in love or scorn, 538 **In desultory* 11
Of humblest Friends, bright Creature ! scorn not one : 538 **Small service* 2
Earth wants not beauty that may scorn 541 *Russ. Fug.* 5
Of slighted love, and scorn, and jealous rage, 547 **Beneath yon* 15
With thy own scorn of tyrants they advance, 628 *Eagle and Dove*
Objects of sport, and ridicule, and scorn, 706 *Prelude* 8. 498
At times with virtuous wrath and noble scorn, 716 *Prelude* 9. 496
Of scorn and condemnation personal, 728 *Prelude* 11. 60
And vexed, and chafed, by levity and scorn, 776 *Excursion* 2. 298
An eye of scorn :—" The lover," said he, " doomed 778 *Excursion* 2. 470
Pity and scorn, and melancholy pride, 788 *Excursion* 3. 142
" Scorn and contempt forbid me to proceed ! 797 *Excursion* 3. 768
At others' tears in pity ; and in scorn 797 *Excursion* 3. 810
To keep the secret of a poignant scorn, 799 *Excursion* 3. 908

Scorn—*continued.*
And those illusions, which excite the scorn . . 813 *Excursion* 4. 834
In deadly scorn of superstitious rites, ... 814 *Excursion* 4. 903
Fearfully low ; nor will your judgment scorn . . 827 *Excursion* 5. 296
Rejected, yea repelled ; and, if with scorn . . 840 *Excursion* 6. 121
To suit this place ; yet built in no proud scorn . 846 *Excursion* 6. 507
Had crossed her only to be shunned with scorn. . 848 *Excursion* 6. 694
Bound—by vexation, and regret, and scorn, . . 849 *Excursion* 6. 712
With pity mixed, astonishment with scorn ! " . 870 *Excursion* 7. 831
Would be disturbed, I fear, with wrathful scorn, . 874 *Excursion* 8. 35
Yield not, to scorn, or sorrow, living men . . . K.8.253 *Recluse* 1.1.605
No self, and whom the selfish scorn— . . . . K.8.325[?]**The vestal* 2
Scorned. As if they scorned both resting-place and rest ! . . . . 218 *Recluse* 1. 1. 229
The future scorned, the past defied ; . . . . 298 *Brownie's Cell* 28
Could gentleness be scorned by those fierce Men, . 389 *Sound of Mull* 11
Scorned or forgotten, Thou canst testify, . . . 442 *Ecc. Sonn.* 3. 7. 6
The strength of backward-looking thoughts is scorned. . . . . 477 **Lowther ! in* 11
Scorned, or neglected, fear not such a dearth. . 531 *Octogen.* 8
So low as to be scorned without a sin ; . . . 567 *Cumb. Beg.* 83
Nor arduous, yet will not be scorned by them, . 694 *Prelude* 7. 460
I scorned indifference ; but, inflamed with thirst . 731 *Prelude* 11. 248
His scorned, or unacknowledged, sovereignty. . 811 *Excursion* 4. 662
Scorner. Thou wert a scorner of the fields, my Friend, 585 *Ch. Lamb* 50
Scornful. As if in scornful mockery of me ; . . . 561 *Cuck.and Night.*223
Of scornful pity be the just reward . . . . 791 *Excursion* 3. 334
Scorning. Thou art laughing and scorning ; . . 159 **Up with me* 17
And, slighting sails and scorning oars, ... 216 *Enterprise* 81
Dead to the world and scorning earth-born joys. . 362 **List—'twas* 35
Scorning that world whose blindness makes her strong ? . . . . 433 *Ecc. Sonn.* 2. 19. 8
If thou persist, and, scorning moderation, . . 505 *Warning* 147
Scorning love-whispers shrinks from love itself . S.3. 436 **The doubt* 146
Scorns. Who scorns a false utilitarian lure . . . 282 *Railway* 7
That there is One who scorns thy power :— . . 293 *Jedbor.* 7
But this swift travel scorns the company . . . 327 *Ode 1815* 15
Rise as he may, his grandeur scorns the test . . 368 *Trajan* 55
That scorns temptation ; power defies . . . . 544 *Russ. Fug.* 197
Scorpion. The Crab, the Scorpion, and the Bull— . 236 *P. B.* 36
Scorpions. Ay, in the word a thousand scorpions lodge : . . . . 74 *Bord.* 2094
Scot. 'Quell the Scot,' exclaims the Lance— . . 205 *Brougham* 144
Scotch. Of those Scotch Rovers echo through the vale. 64 *Bord.* 1463
Two long Scotch miles, through rain or snow, . 246 *P. B.* 898
Scotland. Such as grave Livers do in Scotland use, 196 *Resolution* 97
The hoary peaks of Scotland that give birth . 219 **This Height* 9
And Scotland has a thief as good, ... 291 *Rob Roy* 3
We'll wander Scotland thorough ; . . . . . 293 *Yarrow Unv.* 38
How Wallace fought for Scotland ; left the name 635 *Prelude* 1. 214
Whose echo rings through Scotland to this hour ! 759 *Excursion* 1. 176
Among the wilds of Scotland, in a tract . . 774 *Excursion* 2. 166
Who swept from Scotland, in a flame of zeal, . . 814 *Excursion* 4. 898
Scotland's. Or where dank sea-weed lashes Scotland's shores ; . . . . 21 *Desc. Sk.* 594
Of Scotland's rocky wilds, did seem . . . . 113 *Lament* 17
Ere the tired head of Scotland's Queen . . . 113 *Lament* 69
To Scotland's heaths ; or those that crossed the sea 184 *Yew-trees* 6
The fatal end of Scotland's King, ... 399 *White Doe* 287
To Scotland's court in service of his Queen, . . 871 *Excursion* 7. 931
Scott. For thee, O Scott ! compelled to change . 386 *Yarrow Rev.* 49
Scottish. Back to our post, and strip the Scottish Foray . . . . 37 *Bord.* 2
Would drive those Scottish Rovers to their dens . 50 *Bord.* 729
Right onward to the Scottish strand . . . . 161 *Binnorie* 16
Or Roy, renowned through many a Scottish dell ; 255 *Detraction* 4
The Scottish Church, both on himself and those . 762 *Excursion* 1. 397
I knew a Scottish Peasant who possessed . . . 835 *Excursion* 5. 863
In which the Scottish Laird had long possessed . 845 *Excursion* 6. 456
The Scottish Broom on Bird-nest brae . . . . S.3. 431 **The Scottish* 1
Scoured. Alternate, all a summer's day, or scoured 636 *Prelude* 1. 292
Scourge. Who, while they struggle from the scourge to flee, ... 213 *Dion* 87
Of vain conceit, an iron scourge ! . . . . . 298 *Brownie's Cell* 30
Not scourge, to save the People—not destroy. . 515 **Long-favoured* 14
Leave this unknit Republic to the scourge . . 799 *Excursion* 3. 914
Whose country groan'd under a foreign scourge ? S.3. 436 **The doubt* 173
Scourged. That should be scourged, not pitied. Restless Minds, ... 63 *Bord.* 1451
How they have scourged old foes, perfidious friends : 421 *Ecc. Sonn.* 1. 10. 2
Saw we not Henry scourged at Becket's Shrine ? 428 *Ecc. Sonn.* 1. 37. 9
Scourges. And the winds roused the Deep with fiercer scourges. . . . . 369 *Eg. Maid* 36
And scourges England struggling to be free : . . 439 *Ecc. Sonn.* 2. 44. 12
Scouring. A look of mine would send him scouring back, ... 43 *Bord.* 318
And, scouring toward him o'er the grassy plain, . 104 *Artegal* 110
Scours. *See* **Scow'rs.**
Or Boreas when he scours the snow . . . . 213 *Dion* 73
Scout. With breath suspended, like a listening scout. 322 *Germans* 4
Scout-like. Scout-like, and gained the summit ; 'twas a day . . . . 738 *Prelude* 12. 297
Scow'rs. *See* **Scours.**
To break, the vales where Death with Famine scow'rs, ... 617 *Desc.Sk.Quarto* 794
Scrap. A scrap of land they have, but they . . 483 *Simon Lee* 43
This scrap of land he from the heath . . . . 483 *Simon Lee* 45
Scraped. That scraped the chords with strenuous hand ! . . . . 375 **The Minstrels* 21
Scraps. He drew his scraps and fragments, one by one ; 566 *Cumb. Beg.* 10
Lay intermixed with scraps of paper, some . . 781 *Excursion* 2. 665

Scratch. Throughout the landscape ; tuft, stone, scratch minute— . . . . 691 *Prelude* 7. 258
Scratches. She scratches, ransacks up the earth for food, ... 669 *Prelude* 5. 255
Scream. Fair spectacle,—but instantly a scream . 33 *Guilt* 464
What power is in his wildest scream, ... 117 *Affl. Marg.* 24
She saw—and uttered with a scream, ... 247 *P. B.* 1004
Both when he heard the eagles scream, . . . 295 *Highland Boy* 47
Save when the Owlet's unexpected scream . . 456 **The leaves* 8
That had been ours. There let the fiddle scream, 642 *Prelude* 2. 40
Thrilled by some female vendor's scream, belike . 690 *Prelude* 7. 182
Screamed. While plovers screamed with tumult harsh . . . . 544 *Russ. Fug.* 267
Screaming. But you may love a screaming owl, . 142 †*Lov. and Lik.* 6
Ye screaming Sea-mews, in the concert join ! . . 541 *Grace Darl.* 87
Grimacing, writhing, screaming,—him who grinds 697 *Prelude* 7. 699
Screams. From Bruno's forest screams the affrighted jay, ... 11 *Desc. Sk.* 67
She screams—she cannot move for joy ; . . . 130 *Idiot Boy* 373
Vexed is he, and screams loud. The last I saw . 388 *Eagles* 4
Screams round the Arch-druid's brow the sea-mew —white . . . . 419 *Ecc. Sonn.* 1. 3. 1
From Bruno's forest screams the frighted jay, . 603 *Desc.Sk.Quarto* 68
And long halloos and screams, and echoes loud, . 671 *Prelude* 5. 377
Screeching. But save us from yon screeching owl ! " 179 *Waggoner* 3. 98
Screech-owl. "Yon screech-owl," says the Sailor, turning . . . . 179 *Waggoner* 3. 110
Screen. Interposed so bright a screen— . . . . 181 *Waggoner* 4. 114
No screen, no fence could I discover ; . . . . 199 *Thorn* 178
Ask, for its pleasure, screen or canopy . . . . 219 *Haunted Tree* 6
To serve—an unsuspected screen . . . . . 300 *Bran* 7
That screen the morning dew. . . . . . . 343 *Eclipse* 18
To stir the heart that would too closely screen . 361 **For action* 3
Those mighty forests, once the bison's screen, . 376 *Duddon* 2. 10
Or behind a rocky screen— . . . . 407 *White Doe* 1006
Nor hedge-row screen invites my steps abroad ; . 521 *Epist.Beaumont* 13
Is here—how grateful this impervious screen ! . 881 *Excursion* 8. 447
Screened. Screened from the sun. Supine the Wanderer lay, ... 762 *Excursion* 1. 438
Whose battlements were screened by tufted trees. 823 *Excursion* 5. 81
Screened by its parent, so that little mound . . 850 *Excursion* 6. 789
Screen'd from assault of every bitter blast ; . . 860 *Excursion* 7. 201
Screes. *See* **Glenridding-screes.**
Scribble. Will look and scribble, scribble on and look, 95 *Brothers* 8
Scribbled. With crosses and with cyphers scribbled o'er, ... 639 *Prelude* 1. 511
Scribbled with verse : a broken angling-rod . . 781 *Excursion* 2. 666
Scribe. But History, time's slavish scribe, will tell . 797 *Excursion* 3. 769
Scrip. You from my shoulder took my scrip and threw it . . . . 60 *Bord.* 1283
The scrip that held his food, and I forgot . . . 67 *Bord.* 1643
Thy warlike person with the staff and scrip ; . . 427 *Ecc. Sonn.* 1. 35. 3
Sustained by what her scrip might yield, . . . 542 *Russ. Fug.* 19
Takes one unsparing handful for the scrip . . 568 *Cumb. Beg.* 158
But now, relinquishing the scrip and staff, . . 710 *Prelude* 9. 36
Scriptural. And wedded Life, through scriptural mysteries, ... 467 *St. Bees* 115
Scripture. From Scripture she a name did borrow ; 246 *P. B.* 908
The whole design of Scripture history ; . . . 351 *Des. Stanzas* 67
And that most awful scripture which declares . 780 *Excursion* 2. 577
The voice of wisdom whispering scripture texts . 833 *Excursion* 5. 724
In Scripture sanctified—the patient brute, . . K.8. 250 *Recluse* 1.1.507
Scriptures. Have long borne witness as the Scriptures teach ?— . . . . 431 *Ecc. Sonn.* 2. 12. 2
—With promises the Hebrew Scriptures teem : . 797 *Excursion* 3. 759
Scroll. One precious, tender-hearted, scroll . . . 499 **Departing summer* 53
And Strangers even the slighted Scroll may prize, 526 **Soon did* 6
Each, in its ornamental scroll, enclosed ; . . . 824 *Excursion* 5. 151
Scrolls. The very gilding, lamps and painted scrolls, 693 *Prelude* 7. 408
Is thronged with staring pictures and huge scrolls, 697 *Prelude* 7. 692
Scroop. *See* **Scoop.**
Of hermit, dubious where to scroop [*sic*] his cell ; S.3.433 **The doubt* 18
Scrub. To see the arch grimace of Marquis Scrub, . L.I. 95 *Juvenal* 3. 11
Scrub lives a genuine Marquess above stairs, . . L.I. 95 *Juvenal* 3. 17
Scruple. And so without scruple they called him Ralph Jones. . . . . 86 *Rural Arch.* 10
If cloistered Avarice scruple not, to wrong . . . 433 *Ecc. Sonn.* 2. 19. 5
No just remembrance, scruple, or wise doubt ? . 873 *Excursion* 7. 1029
Scrupled. Or purposes ; nor scrupled to proclaim, 797 *Excursion* 3. 797
Scruples. Their verdict would abolish these weak scruples. . . . . 53 *Bord.* 883
Her virtuous scruples to remove, her fears allay. . 141 *Arm. Lady* 126
Though timid scruples checked me long ; . . . 182 *Waggoner* 4. 200
The Stranger sighs, nor scruples to upbraid . . 272 *Ruins* 3
For this Adventurer scruples not . . . . . 342 *Ital. Itin.* 39
And doubts and scruples seldom teased the brain, 468 **Bold words* 2
At consciences perplexed with scruples nice ! . . 514 **Portentous change* 4
Of forward youth—that scruples not to solve . . 792 *Excursion* 3. 413
Or what their scruples construed to be such— . 814 *Excursion* 4. 904
From the maternal breast ; then scruples rose ; . 852 *Excursion* 6. 940
Scrupulous. Would that our scrupulous Sires had dared to leave . . . . 448 *Ecc. Sonn.* 3. 33. 1
Unchecked by pride or scrupulous doubt, . . . 486 **Bright Flower* 18
And why that scrupulous reserve ? In sooth . 539 **Lady ! a* 10
To forward reason's else too scrupulous march. . 708 *Prelude* 8. 643
With scrupulous care ; but these restrictions soon 711 *Prelude* 9. 120
Other support, not scrupulous whence it came ; . 797 *Excursion* 3. 784
How many scrupulous worshippers fall down . . 866 *Excursion* 7. 584
Scudding. Of trusty anchorage, or scudding o'er . 369 *Eg. Maid* 41

Sea—*continued.*
And the sea breeze as innocently breathes, 793 *Excursion* 3. 517
His brightness o'er a tract of sea and land 794 *Excursion* 3. 542
Which thou includest, as the sea her waves : 802 *Excursion* 4. 93
And holiest love ; as earth, sea, air, with light, 803 *Excursion* 4. 121
Spread like a sea, in boundless solitude, 811 *Excursion* 4. 696
Mysterious union with its native sea. 818 *Excursion* 4. 1140
City, and town, and tower,—and sea with ships 819 *Excursion* 4. 1197
Upon the beach, rolls back into the sea. 823 *Excursion* 5. 76
In anger blowing from the distant sea. 833 *Excursion* 5. 703
Of friends or kindred, whom the angry sea 836 *Excursion* 5. 933
They may endure long as the sea surrounds 838 *Excursion* 6. 15
Eastward, the Danube toward this inland sea, 869 *Excursion* 7. 789
—Hence is the wide sea peopled,—hence the shores 876 *Excursion* 8. 133
To the flat margin of the Baltic sea, 889 *Excursion* 9. 337
A never-resting Pilgrim of the Sea, K.8. 254 *Recluse* 1.1.655
As is the greenest billow of the sea. K.8. 263 **The Lake* 7
By powers celestial tossed on land and sea K.8. 281 **Arms and* 4
Sea-beach. Of the sea-beach, when, polished with nice care, 250 **Happy the* 6
Sea-beast. Like a sea-beast crawled forth, that on a shelf 196 *Resolution* 62
Sea-beat. I slight them all ; and, on this sea-beat shore 459 **Wanderer! that* 10
Sea-blast. The sea-blast ruffles as the storm comes on, 388 *Eagles* 11
Sea-blasts. Where from sea-blasts the hawthorns lean, 536 *Goody Blake* 31
Sea-born. A sea-born service through the mountains felt 454 *Sea-side* 27
As the sun mounts, by sea-born breezes fanned ; 501 *Humanity* 72
Sea-cave. And back with her to this sea-cave ;— 370 *Eg. Maid* 106
Sea-clouds. Above sea-clouds, the Peaks of Arran rose ; 475 **There ! said* 6
Sea-coast. And now to the sea-coast, with numbers more, we drew. 29 *Guilt* 279
To the sea-coast, noting that each man frames 304 **Festivals have* 8
Seafaring. Such gifts had those seafaring men 296 *Highland Boy* 111
Sea-fight. And recent things yet warm with life ; a sea-fight, 691 *Prelude* 7. 291
Sea-fights. Tried in the sea-fights of the second Charles. 825 *Excursion* 5. 187
Sea-flashes. Breasts the sea-flashes, and huge waves 370 *Eg. Maid* 47
Sea-flower. Was this Sea-flower, this buoyant Galley ; 369 *Eg. Maid* 38
Sea-fowl. Of sea-fowl, conscious both that they are hovering 122 *V. and J.* 26
The sun is couched, the sea-fowl gone to rest, 454 *Sea-side* 1
Sea-girt. Yet round our sea-girt shore they rise in crowds : 251 **Pelion and* 9
Nor lacks this sea-girt Isle a timely share 432 *Ecc. Sonn.* 2. 14. 13
Within the circuit of this sea-girt isle 894 *Excursion* 9. 683
Sea-green. A sea-green river, proud to lave, 348 **Lulled by* 34
Sea-gull. The sportive sea-gull dancing with the waves, 869 *Excursion* 7. 753
Sea-horse. And the Sea-horse, though the ocean 166 *Wand. Jew* 13
Seal. A slumber did my spirit seal ; 187 **A slumber* 1
That pardon, from God's throne, may set its seal 447 *Ecc. Sonn.* 3. 28. 8
Her seal, the mortal tear his cheek has wet ; 613 *Desc.Sk.Quarto* 629
The State, as if to stamp the final seal 718 *Prelude* 10. 31
And seal up all the gains of France, a Pope 732 *Prelude* 11. 359
To shake ; but only to bind up and seal ; 795 *Excursion* 3. 656
Sealed. he kept them firmly sealed, as if he had been blind. 72 *Bord.* 2006
Sleep sealed her eyes, and stole 542 *Russ. Fug.* 46
Sea-like. In sea-like reach of prospect round him spread, 19 *Desc. Sk.* 474
The fir-grove murmurs with a sea-like sound, 151 **When, to* 104
Rolling a solemn sea-like bass, that floats 234 *Power of Sound* 164
Seals. An apostolic hand, and with prayer seals 446 *Ecc. Sonn.* 3. 23. 10
Why should we break Time's charitable seals ? 449 *Ecc. Sonn.* 3. 35. 12
Hath ruled my steps, and seals me to thy side, S.3. 433 **The doubt* 14
Seaman. A seaman, a grey-headed Mariner. 102 *Brothers* 435
Sea-mark. Remote St. Kilda, lone and loved sea-mark 475 **Homeward we* 6
Seamen. By seamen, who perhaps themselves had shared 25 *Guilt* 52
Sea-mew. Screams round the Arch-druid's brow the sea-mew—white 419 *Ecc. Sonn.* 1. 3. 1
Sea-mews. Ye screaming Sea-mews, in the concert join ! 541 *Grace Darl.* 87
The cawing rooks, and sea-mews from afar, 808 *Excursion* 4. 451
Sea-nymph. Nor Sea-nymph glistening from her coral bower ; 220 *Triad* 11
Sea-nymphs. The undisturbed abodes where Sea-nymphs dwell ! 333 *Fish-women* 14
Had perished. Then might Sea-nymphs (and with sighs 470 **A youth* 6
Where sea-nymphs might be proud to dwell : 511 **Who rashly* 15
Search. And search the affections to their inmost cell ; 19 *Desc. Sk.* 523
Like you ; he knows your eye would search his heart, 42 *Bord.* 265
I had been out in search of a stray heifer ; 73 *Bord.* 2044
In search of nothing that this earth can give, 78 *Bord.* 2349
In search of their own food ; 84 *Shepherd-boys* 9
And search the fibres of the caves, and they 230 *Clouds* 64
How art thou named ? In search of what strange land, 272 *Devil's Bridge* 1
The lordly eagle-race through hostile search 273 **Not the* 9
While poring Antiquarians search the ground 275 **While poring* 1
The silent thoughts that search for steadfast light, 280 **Intent on* 12

Search—*continued.*
To go in search of Yarrow ? 293 *Yarrow Unv.* 24
Search, for their worth, some gentle heart wrong-proof, 390 *Highland Hut* 12
Merry and loud and safe from prying search, 449 *Ecc. Sonn.* 3. 33. 13
Mists rose to hide the Land—that search, though long 469 **Bold words* 6
Now back to the tiles, then in search of the wall, 484 **A plague* 14
In never-wearied search of Paradise— 512 **Who rashly* 33
From thence to search the mystic cause of things 619 *School Ex.* 75
Where still it works, though hidden from all search 668 *Prelude* 5. 196
Far art thou wandered now in search of health 678 *Prelude* 6. 240
Endowed with various power to search the soul ; 695 *Prelude* 7. 548
Long time in search of knowledge did I range 740 *Prelude* 13. 16
Proves to the most ; and called to make good search 742 *Prelude* 13. 174
We there espied the object of our search, 784 *Excursion* 2. 817
Or for progressive virtue, by the search 789 *Excursion* 3. 222
Wandering about in miserable search 836 *Excursion* 5. 932
Resolved to quell his pain, and search for truth 840 *Excursion* 6. 152
In search of precious ore : they tried, were foiled— 841 *Excursion* 6. 217
Where Fact with heartless search explored S.3. 439 **Avaunt this* 3
In search of a stray sheep. It was the time K.8. 224 **I will* 7
Far did they go that morning : with their search K.8. 224 **I will* 18
Was busy in his search, until at length K.8. 229 **I will* 138
Searched. Searched to its heart. Share with me, Friend ! the wish 731 *Prelude* 11. 282
Only to be examined, pondered, searched, 816 *Excursion* 4. 977
Searches. Searches pasture after pasture, 490 *Incident : Dog* 3
He halts—and searches with his eyes 491 *Fidelity* 3
Searching. There, objects, by the searching beams betrayed, 4 *Ev. Wk.* 102
Scarce hides a shadow from her searching rays ; 9 *Ev. Wk.* 358
More searching than the breath of spring. 248 *P. B.* 1075
Tho' searching damps and many an envious flaw 342 *Last Sup.* 1
To worlds unthought of till the searching mind 461 **Queen of* 40
That searching test thy public course has stood ; 478 **Lonsdale ! it* 11
Was searching out the lines of difference 651 *Prelude* 3. 157
With searching damp, and seemingly had lain 778 *Excursion* 2. 440
And so, not searching higher, we may learn 832 *Excursion* 5. 655
A baffled conqueror's deeply searching rage, L.1. 95 *Juvenal* 3. 4
Sea-river's. In a sea-river's bed at ebb of tide, 652 *Prelude* 3. 216
Sea-rock's. When o'er the sea-rock's edge we go ; 145 *Her Eyes* 44
Sea's. Eyeing the sea's blue depths. Poor Bird ! even so 472 *Dunolly Eagle* 12
I knew the force ; and hence the rough sea's pride 574 *Chiabrera* 4. 19
Seas. When, from the sunny breast of open seas, 17 *Desc. Sk.* 366
'Mid savage rocks, and seas of snow that shine, 20 *Desc. Sk.* 540
Stand like an isthmus 'twixt two stormy seas 48 *Bord.* 607
A band of Pirates in the Norway seas ; 63 *Bord.* 1443
When seas and continents shall lie between us — 78 *Bord.* 2306
Was half a shepherd on the stormy seas. 95 *Brothers* 46
A thriving man, and trafficked on the seas : 100 *Brothers* 293
Resolved to try his fortune on the seas. 100 *Brothers* 306
How motionless !—not frozen seas 106 **I've watched* 5
Sailed on the seas, but he is dead ; 119 *Sailor's Mother* 21
Beyond the seas ; where he grew wondrous rich, 135 *Michael* 267
To seek a hiding-place beyond the seas. 138 *Michael* 447
While the old Familiar of the seas, 176 *Waggoner* 2. 15
Thou speak'st—and lo ! the polar Seas 216 *Enterprise* 87
Through seas of ether, where the ruffling sway 231 **The gentlest Poet* 9
Nor the green Islands, nor the shining Seas ; 252 **The fairest* 11
Murmuring ; the fall of rivers, winds and seas, 253 **A flock* 3
'Mid seas how steadfast ! objects all for the eye 262 **Dark and* 11
Breaking the silence of the seas 289 *Sol. Reap.* 15
Fetch, ye that post o'er seas and lands, 348 **Lulled by* 44
Lo ! ships, from seas by nature barred, 391 *Highland Broach* 69
Seek other seas, their canvass gleams. 391 *Highland Broach* 72
Ploughs her bold course across the wondering seas; 432 *Ecc. Sonn.* 2. 15.11
Of Severn, Severn to the narrow seas, 432 *Ecc. Sonn.* 2. 17. 10
Shall dissipate the seas and mountains hoary. 445 *Ecc. Sonn.* 3. 19. 14
At Danger's bidding, may confront the seas, 466 *St. Bees* 17
Guiding the mariner through troubled seas, 466 *St. Bees* 43
Oh may that Power who hushed the stormy seas, 468 *St. Bees* 151
Encounter, and to narrow seas 499 **This Lawn* 8
The smoothest seas will sometimes prove, 550 *Hermit's Cell* 5. 5
When warm from myrtle bays and tranquil seas, 610 *Desc.Sk.Quarto* 44
O'er Anet's hopeless seas of marsh to stray, 615 *Desc.Sk.Quarto* 715
On board a ship then ready for the seas. 623 **I find* 8
Voyaging through strange seas of Thought, alone. 650 *Prelude* 3. 63
Her seas yet smiling, her once happy vales ; 733 *Prelude* 11. 431
Beyond the seas, and to the farthest pole, 797 *Excursion* 3. 748
That spreads into successive seas, he walks ; 799 *Excursion* 3. 932
Of heart, the sailor fights with roaring seas. 804 *Excursion* 4. 204
The obstreperous city ; on the barren seas 806 *Excursion* 4. 369
Of the eighth Henry, when he crossed the seas 825 *Excursion* 5. 182
The Spirit of its mountains and its seas, 871 *Excursion* 7. 897
Sea-shells. On sea-shells that bestrew the sandy beach, 696 *Prelude* 7. 592
Sea-shore. And went to the sea-shore, 194 *Ruth* 189
Each evening, pacing by the still sea-shore, 723 *Prelude* 10. 323
Sea-side. Near the sea-side I reached a ruined fort ; 31 *Guilt* 382
Of wonder, I have watched this sea-side Town, 349 *At Dover* 2
By the sea-side, perusing, so it chanced, 666 *Prelude* 5. 59
Season. Whose season was, and cannot be recalled. 20 *Desc. Sk.* 535
" But the calm summer season now was past. 29 *Guilt* 289
Which for a season I have stooped to wear, 71 *Bord.* 1861
Or, lengthening out thy season of delight, 88 *H. C.* 22
Yet, at this impressive season, 90 *Longest Day* 2
A season after Julia had withdrawn 125 *V. and J.* 241
But the Transfigured, in and out of season, 139 *Widow* 25

Season—*continued.*

For a light heart in a dull season.	142 †*Lov. and Lik.* 22
—'Twas that delightful season when the broom, .	147 *Joanna* 38
Sharp season followed of continual storm . . .	150 **When, to* 4
By the season multiplied ?	161 **Pleasures newly* 48
Of the dreary season near ?	171 *Kitten* 92
And I will have my careless season	171 *Kitten* 111
Which, when the appointed season hath arrived, .	173 *InfantDaughter* 76
The pleasant season did my heart employ : . .	195 *Resolution* 19
Which at this season, with their unripe fruits,	206 *Tintern* 12
And in due season send the mandate forth ; . .	216 *Enterprise* 101
Which at no season fade, ...	218 *Young Lady* 9
Announce a season potent to renew, ...	263 **While not* 12
Glad thought for every season ! but the Spring .	266 **The stars* 9
Freely as in youth's season bland, ...	286 *Nith* 26
To meet the wintry season.	302 *Yarrow V.* 72
With a hope (and no more) for a season to come,	345 *Stanzas : Simplon* 11
Discerns the favourable season, ...	415 *White Doe* 1719
Glad to expand ; and, for a season, free . . .	454 **The Sun, that* 25
Full happy season, when was known, ...	478 *Somnamb.* 25
The spirit of the season.	483 *Sister* 28
And every season ?	485 **Bright Flower* 16
Which that sweet season gave, ...	486 **We walked* 30
To season my fireside with personal talk,— . .	488 *Pers. Talk* 2
Who repays in season due	502 **Like a* 47
Season of fancy and of hope, ...	508 *May* 89
For time and season, rules that work to cheer— .	515 **Long-favoured* 13
The season) sprinklings of ripe strawberry fruit. .	529 *Poor Robin* 14
May season apathy with scorn, ...	534 **Blest is* 63
Of summer, in the season of sere leaves ; . . .	539 **Lady ! a* 61
And every season has soft arms	545 *Russ. Fug.* 303
The respite of the season, he, at least, ...	568 *Cumb. Beg.* 131
At length, what to most is a season of sorrow, .	569 *Farmer* 31
Nor in life's vigorous season did I shun . . .	575 *Chiabrera* 6. 4
No mood, which season takes away, or brings : .	578 *Peele Castle* 10
Sets sail :—in season due, ...	579 **Sweet Flower* 31
No more shall grief of mine the season wrong ; .	588 *Immortality* 26
Hence in a season of calm weather	590 *Immortality* 165
Then Summer lengthen'd out his season bland .	611 *Desc.Sk.Quarto* 476
While the joy that precedes the calm season of rest	620 *Convict* 3
And in the frosty season, when the sun . . .	638 *Prelude* 1. 425
And every season wheresoe'er I moved . . .	646 *Prelude* 2. 289
Of life's sweet season—could have seen unmoved	652 *Prelude* 3. 222
If in the season of unperilous choice, ...	669 *Prelude* 5. 234
Nor with impatience from the season asked . .	670 *Prelude* 5. 284
Who, summoned by that season, reunite . . .	675 *Prelude* 6. 4
And at a later season, or preserved ;	675 *Prelude* 6. 37
A gladness o'er that season, then to me, . . .	678 *Prelude* 6. 225
Called forth, at every season, new delights . .	686 *Prelude* 6. 777
It slept, even in the pregnant season of youth. .	694 *Prelude* 7. 472
How Fancy, in a season when she wove . . .	706 *Prelude* 8. 454
A ravage out of season, made by thoughts . .	712 *Prelude* 9. 152
Withal a season dangerous and wild, ...	722 *Prelude* 10. 311
Of time and season, to the moral power, . . .	736 *Prelude* 12. 119
At every season green, sweet at all hours. . .	750 *Prelude* 14. 301
(Which, in the docile season of their youth, . .	757 *Excursion* 1. 81
Than in his earlier season did he love . . .	760 *Excursion* 1. 289
The hardships of that season : many rich . . .	764 *Excursion* 1. 543
At this still season of repose and peace, . . .	765 *Excursion* 1. 594
To lag behind the season, and had lost . . .	767 *Excursion* 1. 721
Which the bright season favours.—Tabor and pipe	773 *Excursion* 2. 121
Youth's season yet with him was scarcely past, .	774 *Excursion* 2. 195
Whom earth, at this late season, hath produced .	815 *Excursion* 4. 948
In some calm season, when these lofty rocks . .	818 *Excursion* 4. 1158
In man's autumnal season is set forth	828 *Excursion* 5. 404
Of life's autumnal season.—Shall I tell . . .	849 *Excursion* 6. 742
It was the season of unfolding leaves, ...	851 *Excursion* 6. 855
Drawn by the sunshine—at that hopeful season .	867 *Excursion* 7. 682
To time and season, as the year rolled round ? " .	878 *Excursion* 8. 251
Its very spring a season of decay !	878 *Excursion* 8. 291
And season yield ; but, as we re-embarked, . .	892 *Excursion* 9. 546
And season favours." To enfeebled Power, . .	896 *Excursion* 9. 783
Bleak season was it, turbulent and bleak, . . .	K.8. 240 *Recluse* 1.1.152

Seasonable. Give seasonable rest, for 'tis a sound .	655 *Prelude* 3. 413
When wisdom shows her seasonable fruit, . . .	816 *Excursion* 4. 1041
By seasonable frost of age ; nor died	842 *Excursion* 6. 276
Seasonably. O'er ripe fruit, seasonably gathered, .	586 *Hogg* 35
Seasoned. That had been seasoned in the wars, and all	711 *Prelude* 9. 128
Seasoning. Seasoning his wickedness. The Debauchee	49 *Bord.* 662
Season's. *He* needs not fear the season's rage, . .	144 **Driven in* 67
The Season's harmless pastime. Ruder sound .	349 *Val. Dover* 9
The time's and season's influence disown ; . .	453 **Calm is the* 11
Before a flying season's rash pretence	471 **Despond who* 5
In spite of season's change, its own demand, . .	531 **I know* 18
And season's difference—a double tree	585 *Ch. Lamb* 96
Or season's difference ; the immortal Soul . .	792 *Excursion* 3. 403
Seasons. Here all the seasons revel hand in hand :	20 *Desc. Sk.* 575
Through twenty seasons ; but he had been reared	95 *Brothers* 44
All seasons through, another debt, ...	158 **In youth* 66
The violets of five seasons re-appear	185 *Nutting* 31
When Ruth three seasons thus had lain, . . .	194 *Ruth* 205
Of seasons balancing their flight	228 *Devot. Incit.* 56
Strains that support the Seasons in their round ; .	235 *Power of Sound* 191
The sweet-souled Poet of the Seasons stood— .	271 **Fame tells* 12
Time *loves* Thee ! at his call the Seasons twine .	272 *Ruins* 11
Like thine, shall gladden, as in seasons past, . .	279 **Hark ! 'tis* 13
And ye mild Seasons—in a sunny clime, . . .	322 **Ye Storms* 2
Cliffs, fountains, rivers, seasons, times— . . .	341 *San Salv.* 13

Seasons—*continued.*

(Life's three first seasons having passed away) .	394 **No more* 26
All seasons through, is humbly pleased to braid .	463 **Adieu,Rydalian* 7
Hence have I genial seasons, hence have I . .	489 *Pers. Talk* 47
Inviting, at all seasons, ears and eyes	500 *Humanity* 13
How happy at all seasons, could like aim . . .	512 **Who rashly* 36
For seasons and for hours.	541 *Russ. Fug.* 8
There are ninety good seasons of fair and foul weather	572 *Avarice* 15
That all the seasons shared with equal rights ;— .	583 **With copious* 27
Which, through all seasons, on a child's pursuits .	640 *Prelude* 1. 582
Until maturer seasons called them forth . . .	641 *Prelude* 1. 595
And sorrow is not there ! The seasons came, .	646 *Prelude* 2. 288
And seasons serve ; all Faculties to whom . .	673 *Prelude* 5. 530
With danger, varying as the seasons change), .	682 *Prelude* 6. 510
The elements, and seasons as they change, . .	700 *Prelude* 8. 102
Forgot, at seasons, whence they had their being ;	723 *Prelude* 10. 376
The later seasons owed to thee no less ; . . .	749 *Prelude* 14. 236
On all things which the moving seasons brought .	758 *Excursion* 1. 151
Two blighting seasons, when the fields were left .	764 *Excursion* 1. 537
Did many seasons pass ere I returned	769 *Excursion* 1. 870
Or solace, varying as the seasons change. . . .	810 *Excursion* 4. 587
With all its seasons. Grant that Spring is there,	828 *Excursion* 5. 395
—But when the lord of seasons had matured . .	841 *Excursion* 6. 230
Through all the seasons of the changeful year, .	888 *Excursion* 9. 266
Seasons'. And thus through many seasons' space .	532 †*Float. Isl.* 17

Seat. *See* **Cloud-seat, Judgment-seat, Mercy-seat, Orchard-seat, Stone-seat, Window-seat.**

At times, while young Content forsook her seat, .	2 *Ev. Wk.* 24
When with her infants, from some shady seat .	7 *Ev. Wk.* 252
The shady porch ne'er offered a cool seat . . .	15 *Desc. Sk.* 244
He died, —this seat his only monument. . . .	23 *Yew-tree* 47
His seat beneath the honied sycamore	28 *Guilt* 219
So in they bear her to the chimney seat, . . .	34 *Guilt* 568
And down from off her seat she leapt.	82 *Alice Fell* 24
Risen from his seat, beside the snow-white ridge .	95 *Brothers* 31
In Troynovant, his seat by silver Thames's side !	103 *Artegal* 97
We can behold it from our orchard seat ; . . .	148 **There is an* 3
Whose moss-grown root might serve for couch or seat, ...	167 *Pilgrim'sDream* 11
Your favourite seat of empire find—	191 *Seq. Beggars* 35
And though his favourite seat be feeble woman's breast.	210 *Laod.* 90
Quoth Peter, leaping from his seat, ...	241 *P. B.* 406
Take, then, thy seat, Vicegerent unreproved ! .	290 *Kilchurn* 22
There ! take your seat, and let me see	295 *Highland Boy* 6
He felt the motion—took his seat ;	296 *Highland Boy* 152
Where altar-stone and rock-hewn seat	301 *Bran* 65
Which, out of thy young heart's oracular seat, .	312 *Clarkson* 7
Peasant and lord, in their appointed seat, . .	319 *Guernica* 13
Mounts to the seat of grace within the mind : .	334 **The Spirit* 5
That we approached the Seat of Charlemaine ? .	335 *Aix* 2
Studious that *He* might not disdain the seat . .	335 *Cologne* 4
Seat Sandal, a fond suitor of the clouds, . . .	353 *Aquap.* 36
Of Commonwealths, each city a starlike seat . .	359 **They—who* 12
The laurelled Dante's favourite seat. A throne, .	365 **Under the* 5
The marvel of the PERILOUS SEAT, ...	373 *Eg. Maid* 316
My seat, while I give way to such intent ; . .	376 *Duddon* 3. 2
From her unworthy seat, the cloudy stall . . .	381 *Duddon* 21. 9
With tenderest love ;—or, if a safer seat . . .	382 *Duddon* 25. 5
Close to the vital seat of human clay ;	383 *Duddon* 28. 10
Even to the inmost seat of mortal pains, . . .	383 *Duddon* 29. 7
Clove fondly ; to his favourite seat	390 *HighlandBroach* 46
The mountain-borders of this seat of care, . .	392 **Though joy* 12
That wants not, even in rudest breasts, a seat ; .	393 *Hart's-horn* 12
To have no seat for thought were better doom, .	394 **How profitless* 6
And in Saint Cuthbert's ancient seat	404 *White Doe* 712
Where she had found a grateful seat	407 *White Doe* 1058
Within the wilderness her seat ?	413 *White Doe* 1559
Of toil stupendous, in a hallowed seat	424 *Ecc. Sonn.* 1. 23. 6
Of feudal sway her own appropriate seat ; . .	430 *Ecc. Sonn.* 2. 6. 3
(O God of mercy, may no earthly Seat . . .	437 *Ecc. Sonn.* 2. 35. 2
That Church, the unperverted Gospel's seat ; . .	438 *Ecc. Sonn.* 2. 40. 6
Fixed, by her smile, upon some rocky seat ; . .	461 **Giordano,verily* 13
Beside a mossy seat ;	487 *Fountain* 6
Proceeds, from some uneasy seat	498 **The sylvan* 14
Within her lonely seat.	499 *Memory* 16
Up to the sovereign seat of the Most High ; . .	500 *Humanity* 31
The private hearth ; though keeping thy sole seat	510 **Among a* 16
Her seat upon Olympus, doth forsake	521 *Epist.Beaumont* 39
An easy seat this worn-out Labourer found . .	531 **I know* 10
She led the Lady to a seat	542 *Russ. Fug.* 33
On this commodious Seat ! for much remains .	548 **Stay, bold* 2
A form discover'd at the well-known seat, . .	592 *Ev. Wk. Quarto* 45
Her seat scarce left, she strives, alas ! in vain,	596 *Ev. Wk. Quarto* 248
The grassy seat beneath their casement shade .	607 *Desc.Sk.Quarto* 305
Of passion at the bosom's inmost seat. . . .	624 *Æneid* 6
O seat of Arts ! renowned throughout the world !	655 *Prelude* 3. 458
Long unsaluted, nor the sunny seat	659 *Prelude* 4. 47
Taking my seat, I saw (nor blush to add, . .	691 *Prelude* 7. 270
Tipped with a rain-drop, Fancy loved to seat, .	705 *Prelude* 8. 399
In silence of all present, from his seat . . .	720 *Prelude* 10. 110
She rose from off her seat, and then,—O Sir ! .	766 *Excursion* 1. 653
Man's only dwelling, sole appointed seat, . . .	777 *Excursion* 2. 362
To weather-fend a little turf-built seat . . .	777 *Excursion* 2. 420
The seat and bosom of pure innocence, . . .	781 *Excursion* 2. 624
Delivering her decisions from the seat : . . .	792 *Excursion* 3. 412
The priest announces from his holy seat : . . .	792 *Excursion* 3. 443
Approach the embowered abode—our chosen seat—	793 *Excursion* 3. 521
From some dark seat of fatal power was urged .	795 *Excursion* 3. 637
The appointed seat of equitable law	796 *Excursion* 3. 715

Seat—*continued.*
—The darts of anguish *fix* not where the seat . 801 *Excursion* 4. 18
And passions hold a fluctuating seat : . . . . 802 *Excursion* 4. 70
These helps solicit ; and a steadfast seat . . . 804 *Excursion* 4. 229
Meanwhile, the heart within the heart, the seat . 810 *Excursion* 4. 627
And guardian rocks !—Farewell, attractive seat ! 822 *Excursion* 5. 3
Gone forth already to the far-off seat . . . . 834 *Excursion* 5. 803
Continued, " 'tis not in the vital seat . . . . 837 *Excursion* 5. 984
Whose steps are equity, whose seat is law. . . 838 *Excursion* 6. 5
By ruinous contest, to obtain a seat . . . . 845 *Excursion* 6. 447
The Vicar paused ; and toward a seat advanced, 850 *Excursion* 6. 778
And by the unclosed coffin kept her seat . . . 853 *Excursion* 6. 979
Fixed at their seat, the centre of the Mere, . . 869 *Excursion* 7. 755
Raised from his seat within the chosen shade, . 870 *Excursion* 7. 818
Truth's consecrated residence, the seat . . . 876 *Excursion* 8. 146
The most assured seat of [poesy ?] . . . . . S.3. 436 **The doubt* 164
Thence northward did they pass by Arthur's seat, K.8. 225 **I will* 23
Seated. *See* **Deep-seated, High-seated, Re-seated.**
He shall be seated in his Barony, ... 54 *Bord.* 906
If you were seated at my chimney's nook, . . 98 *Brothers* 190
While I was seated, now some ten days past, . 147 *Joanna* 18
That ancient Woman seated on Helm-crag . . 147 *Joanna* 56
Were seated round their blazing fire, ... 156 *Oak and Broom* 9
A Woman seated on the ground. . . . . . 199 *Thorn* 187
By martial sports,—or, seated in the tent, . . 211 *Laod.* 118
Perhaps are seated in domestic ring . . . . 266 **Even as* 11
Of Reason, seated on her sovereign hill ; . . 315 **Alas ! what* 6
Seated alone, with forehead sky-ward raised, . 362 **List—'twas* 78
Was seated in her gleaming shallop, ... 371 *Eg. Maid* 116
Seated alone beneath a darksome tree, . . . 440 *Ecc. Sonn.* 3. 1. 2
And he was seated, by the highway side, . . . 566 *Cumb. Beg.* 2
Seated on her lineal throne ; . . . . . . 629 *Installation* 50
To shepherd swains, or seated harp in hand, . . 634 *Prelude* 1. 172
Be it confest that, for the first time, seated . 653 *Prelude* 3. 296
While I was seated in a rocky cave . . . . 666 *Prelude* 5. 58
Almost as deeply seated and as strong . . . 688 *Prelude* 7. 104
Seated, with open door, often and long . . . 705 *Prelude* 8. 411
That he was often seated at his loom, ... 764 *Excursion* 1. 524
The moment I was seated here alone, ... 783 *Excursion* 2. 802
In open circle seated round, and hushed . . . 820 *Excursion* 4. 1280
Their courtly figures, seated on the stump . . 845 *Excursion* 6. 492
When seated near my venerable Friend, . . . 854 *Excursion* 6. 1057
A grave assemblage, seated while they shear . . 866 *Excursion* 7. 619
Stretched on the grass, or seated in the shade, . 869 *Excursion* 7. 783
Affections seated in the mother's breast, . . . 875 *Excursion* 8. 74
Merrily seated in a ring, partook . . . . . 892 *Excursion* 9. 529
Seated in a British chair. . . . . L.2. 190 **Queen and* 3
Seats. *See* **Council-seats, Judgment-seats, Sod-seats.**
Your seats, and quickly shall be paid . . . . 238 *P. B.* 184
No promise. Still, in more than ear-deep seats, . 353 *Aquap.* 71
Seats of glad instinct and love's carolling, . . 464 **Greta, what* 11
A land whose azure mountain-tops are seats . . 501 *Humanity* 73
While Faith aspires to seats in that domain . . 533 **Once I* 41
May she, who once disturbed the seats of bliss . 582 *Invoc. Earth* 30
The seats of learning brave the distant skies. . 619 *School Ex.* 64
Farewell for ever to the sheltered seats . . . 688 *Prelude* 7. 53
Greeted us all day long ; we took our seats . . 772 *Excursion* 2. 58
From seats of power divine ; and hope, or trust, . 790 *Excursion* 3. 257
And mossy seats, detained us side by side, . . 794 *Excursion* 3. 547
Doth most debase the mind ; the genuine seats . 813 *Excursion* 4. 776
In seats of wisdom, not to be approached . . . 818 *Excursion* 4. 1129
Shall fix, in calmer seats of moral strength, . . 820 *Excursion* 4. 1272
Our seats ; and thus the Solitary spake, . . . 826 *Excursion* 5. 232
Seat-sandal. *See* **Sandal.**
And all Seat-Sandal was laid bare ! . . . . 176 *Waggoner* 1. 230
Seat-Sandal, a fond lover of the clouds ; . . . K.8. 225 **I will* 27
Seaward. Sloped seaward, turf whose tender April green, ... 356 *Aquap.* 225
A plain below stretched seaward, while, descried . 475 **There ! said* 5
Post seaward,—what impedes the tardy nights. . 625 *Æneid* 129
Sea-water. The great Sea-water finds its way . 295 *Highland Boy* 57
Sea-weed. Or where dank sea-weed lashes Scotland's shores ; . . . . 21 *Desc. Sk.* 594
Sea-wind. From the stern breathing of the rough sea-wind ; . . . . 61 *Bord.* 1296
Sebeto. For her heart's grief, she will entreat Sebeto 575 *Chiabrera* 7. 10
Not to withhold his bounteous aid, Sebeto . . 575 *Chiabrera* 7. 11
Secluded. *See* **Self-secluded.**
In these secluded vales, if village fame, . . . 5 *Ev. Wk.* 192
Spread rooflike o'er the deep secluded vale, . . 14 *Desc. Sk.* 211
That on a wild secluded scene impress . . . 205 *Tintern* 6
Moveless o'er-hang the deep secluded vale, . . 607 *Desc.Sk.Quarto* 266
In this secluded glen, and eagerly . . . . 699 *Prelude* 8. 19
From sight of One who lives secluded there, . . 774 *Excursion* 2. 159
Aerial, or in green secluded vale, ... 792 *Excursion* 3. 394
To our secluded vale) it may be told— . . . 793 *Excursion* 3. 501
Secluded, but not buried ; and with song . . . 823 *Excursion* 5. 55
And into most of these secluded vales . . . 858 *Excursion* 7. 61
He turned to this secluded chapelry ; . . . . 859 *Excursion* 7. 134
Seclusion. O happy Garden ! whose seclusion deep 107 *Farewell* 57
Thoughts of more deep seclusion ; and connect . 205 *Tintern* 7
" O blest seclusion ! when the mind admits . . 816 *Excursion* 4. 1035
At sight of this seclusion, he forgot . . . . K.8. 236 *Recluse* 1. 1. 8
Seclusions. And audible seclusions, dashing lakes, . 708 *Prelude* 8. 636
Second. " So passed a second day ; and, when the third 31 *Guilt* 379
Joy's second spring and Hope's long-treasured smile, ... 32 *Guilt* 455
I think I see a second range of Towers ; . . . 50 *Bord.* 731
I hurried on, when straight a second moan, . . 73 *Bord.* 2047
Nor could my heart by second thoughts from heaviness be cleared, ... 91 *Poet's Dream* 5

Second—*continued.*
Possess a kind of second life : no doubt . . . 98 *Brothers* 185
A second time ; for still I seem . . . . . . 109 **I travelled* 7
Slew, and as quickly to a second gave . . . . 123 *V. and J.* 131
Will be my second self when I am gone. . . . 131 *Michael* 39
On human nature's second infancy. . . . . 144 **Driven in* 81
A second time, in Grasmere's happy Vale. . . . 151 **When, to* 110
Or second my weak Muse ? . . . . 168 *Turtledove* 8
A second darted by ;—and lo ! . . . . . . 170 *Rural Ill.* 3
The second glory of the Heavens ?—Thou hast ; . 172 *Infant Daughter* 5
But there is matter for a second rhyme, . . . 202 *Hart-leap* 95
To me, this day, a second time thy bride ! " . . 210 *Laod.* 64
Into a second swoon ! . . . . 242 *P. B.* 540
Breathes into him a second breath, ... 248 *P. B.* 1074
Its second twilight, and looks gay ; . . . . 294 *Jedbor.* 46
Hath called for thee a second spring ; . . . . 294 *Jedbor.* 79
And Rover whine, as at a second sight . . . 294 **Fly, some* 7
With second life the deed of Marathon . . . 324 *Ode 1814* 97
And that we need no second victory ! . . . . 329 *Ode 1815* 124
And that we need no second victory !—— . . . 331 *Ode : Thanks.* 182
And in a second father's place, ... 401 *White Doe* 485
A second and yet nobler birth ; . . . . . . 416 *White Doe* 1845
Permits a second and a darker shade . . . . 421 *Ecc. Sonn.* 1. 11. 4
The Infant's notice of his second birth— . . . 445 *Ecc. Sonn.* 3. 20. 12
Do Thou, in truth a second Mother, strive . . 445 *Ecc. Sonn.* 3. 21. 5
The music bursteth into second life ; . . . . 451 *Ecc. Sonn.* 3. 44. 10
Look up a second time, and, one by one, . . . 453 **Calm is the* 4
Hark to that second larum !—far and wide . . 457 **The leaves* 33
Rejoices in a second birth ! . . . . 458 **Had this* 78
A second time did Matthew stop ; . . . . . 486 **We walked* 17
No farther than they breed a second Will more wise.] . . . . 492 *Duty*
Or never hope to reach a second birth. . . . 531 *Octogen.* 5
No second look she cast, ... 542 *Russ. Fug.* 30
Remove this second Rachel from the bier. . . . 555 *Prioress* 176
Upon the second step of that small pile, . . . 566 *Cumb. Beg.* 13
Such was the tenour of the second act . . . . 652 *Prelude* 3. 256
A character more stern. The second night, . . 685 *Prelude* 6. 691
In the great deep ; all things have second birth ; 719 *Prelude* 10. 83
What countenance to promote this second love ! . 724 *Prelude* 10. 430
And hopeful blossoms of a second spring : . . 727 *Prelude* 11. 6
Into a second place, pleased to become . . . 749 *Prelude* 14. 259
With cheerful hope, until the second autumn, . . 764 *Excursion* 1. 550
Was all consumed. A second infant now . . . 764 *Excursion* 1. 556
This second visitation had no power . . . . 795 *Excursion* 3. 655
Tried in the sea-fights of the second Charles. . 825 *Excursion* 5. 187
Into the second ark, Christ's church, with trust . 826 *Excursion* 5. 282
An inmate of a second family ; . . . . . . 864 *Excursion* 7. 435
Thence, journeying on a second time, they passed K.8. 226 **I will* 62
I will go back and range a second time . . . K.8. 228 **I will* 116
And waters in the midst, a Second Heaven. . . K.8. 263 **The Lake* 12
Secondary. Of secondary birth, the Jung-frau's cone ; . . . . 350 *Des. Stanzas* 32
To transports from the secondary founts . . . 358 *Aquap.* 360
And secondary, now at length was sought . . . 645 *Prelude* 2. 202
Art thou of that false secondary power . . . 645 *Prelude* 2. 216
Bur secondary to my own pursuits . . . . . 704 *Prelude* 8. 343
No secondary hand can intervene . . . . . 749 *Prelude* 14. 213
Far more : for Nature's secondary grace . . . 750 *Prelude* 14. 315
Second-sight. In second-sight appearances, or crost 523 *Epist. Beaumont* 149
A second-sight procession, such as glides . . . 696 *Prelude* 7. 633
Secrecy. Said Secrecy to Cowardice and Fraud, . 513 **Said Secrecy* 1
For perfect secrecy. . . . . 543 *Russ. Fug.* 112
Secret. The eye reposes on a secret bridge, . . . 3 *Ev. Wk.* 68
While coves and secret hollows, through a ray . 5 *Ev. Wk.* 176
Where, winding on along some secret bay, . . 6 *Ev. Wk.* 217
By lonely farms and secret villages. . . . . 11 *Desc. Sk.* 49
—And sure there is a secret Power that reigns . 16 *Desc. Sk.* 346
Thy secret for its sake, or verily . . . . . 54 *Bord.* 949
In old Armorica, whose secret springs . . . . 102 *Artegal* 10
And from their secret loyalty requires . . . . 104 *Artegal* 104
Carried about her for a secret grief . . . . . 122 *V. and J.* 67
To secret 'spousals meanly disavowed. . . . . 125 *V. and J.* 239
Be violets in their secret mews . . . . . . 158 **In youth* 25
In many a secret place . . . . 187 **Three years* 27
In secret, like a smothered flame ? . . . . . 204 *Brougham* 77
The shell from out its secret nook, ... 296 *Highland Boy* 144
Trembling, I look upon the secret springs . . . 347 *Processions* 64
The secret thou art bent on keeping : . . . . 372 *Eg. Maid* 248
In secret revels—haply after theft . . . . . 378 *Duddon* 11. 6
Into the secret of to-morrow's fare ; . . . . 471 *Ailsa Crag* 11
Yet sometimes, when the secret cup . . . . 486 *Matthew* 25
That winds through secret wards ; . . . . . 499 *Memory* 2
Not unadvisedly those secret springs . . . . 525 *Epist. Beaumont* 264
From thy most secret haunts ; and ye Parterres, 539 **Lady ! a* 25
To undermine with secret guile, ... 550 *Hermit's Cell* 2. 23
Of which the rivers in their secret springs, . . 582 *Invoc. Earth* 25
The coves and secret hollows thro' a ray . . 594 *Ev. Wk. Quarto* 159
Where winds the road along the secret bay ; . . 595 *Ev. Wk. Quarto* 196
By secret villages and lonely farms, ... 603 *Desc. Sk. Quarto* 50
Far o'er the secret water dark with beach, . . 607 *Desc.Sk.Quarto* 288
While strives a secret Power to hush the croud, 614 *Desc.Sk.Quarto* 652
Ev'n by the secret cottage far away . . . . 615 *Desc.Sk.Quarto* 722
Quick to the secret grotto they retire . . . . 619 *School Ex.* 61
And follow Nature to her secret springs ; . . . 619 *School Ex.* 76
In secret did, we trust, her loss bemoan. . . . 627 **When Severn's* 8
Nor made unto myself a secret boast . . . . 696 *Prelude* 7. 586
Maintained for me a secret happiness. . . . . 735 *Prelude* 12. 43
That secret spirit of humanity . . . . . . 770 *Excursion* 1. 927

Sees—*continued.*
When the lone shepherd sees the morning spread 508 *F. Stone* 21
Sees that, apart from magnanimity, 514 **Blest Statesman* 3
Who sees, foresees; who cannot judge amiss, 519 *Pun. Death* 11. 13
She turns her wheel, if on the road she sees 566 *Cumb. Beg.* 34
And seldom knowing that he sees, some straw, 567 *Cumb. Beg.* 54
—A few (my soul oft sees that sight) 579 **Sweet Flower* 46
He sees it in his joy; 588 *Immortality* 70
I hear, while in the forest depth he sees, 596 *Ev. Wk. Quarto* 261
The viewless lingerer hence, at evening, sees 603 *Desc. Sk. Quarto* 92
Of weedless herbs a healthier prospect sees, 615 *Desc. Sk. Quarto* 730
And to the God who sees into the heart. 651 *Prelude* 3. 143
Sees many beauteous sights—weeds, fishes, flowers, 662 *Prelude* 4. 261
All that the traveller sees when he is there. 691 *Prelude* 7. 259
An under-sense of greatest; sees the parts 698 *Prelude* 7. 735
Sees annually, if clouds towards either ocean 699 *Prelude* 8. 15
For gains, and who that sees her would not buy? 699 *Prelude* 8. 39
Or sees in his day's march; himself he feels, 703 *Prelude* 8. 251
Yordas; he looks around and sees the vault 707 *Prelude* 8. 564
Widening on all sides; sees, or thinks he sees, 707 *Prelude* 8. 565
Both of the object seen, and eye that sees. 745 *Prelude* 13. 378
The bond of brotherhood, when he sees them go, 780 *Excursion* 2. 562
With mind that sheds a light on what he sees; 799 *Excursion* 3. 940
Oh! no, the innocent Sufferer often sees 804 *Excursion* 4. 174
Who sees all suffering, comprehends all wants, 817 *Excursion* 4. 1091
What sees he but a creature too perturbed; 830 *Excursion* 5. 506
He sees the barren wilderness erased, 876 *Excursion* 8. 129
Even as he sees; but when his voice hath ceased, 891 *Excursion* 9. 466
Heavens! who sees majesty in George's face? L.1. 88 *Juvenal* 1. 9
Till Egypt sees her antient fame outvied. L.1. 88 *Juvenal* 1. 20

See-saw. The hard dry see-saw of his horrible bray! 241 *P. B.* 480

Seest. Thou seest,—and he would gaze till it became 23 *Yew-tree* 35
And, as thou see'st, under the arch of heaven 62 *Bord.* 1343
Thou seest me what I am. It was most heinous, 75 *Bord.* 2124
Thou see'st a homely Pile, yet to these walls 547 **Rude is* 14
When, looking back, thou seest, in clearer view 751 *Prelude* 14. 393

Seignories. The seignories of Herbert are in Devon; 39 *Bord.* 84

Seignory. He who will gain his Seignory when Idonea 55 *Bord.* 976

Seine. Or by the lazy Seine, the exile roves; 19 *Desc. Sk.* 521
Who rises on the banks of Seine, 311 **Who rises* 1
Lo! by the lazy Seine the exile roves, 613 *Desc. Sk. Quarto* 624

Seize. Rush in—the villains seize us—— Seize! Yes, they— 49 *Bord.* 644
Was made to seize him by three armèd men, 123 *V. and J.* 127
And their music's a prey which they seize; 167 *Stray Pleasures* 21
He stoops the Ass's neck to seize 242 *P. B.* 497
To seize (while on the Deep it slept) 297 *Highland Boy* 192
To seize whate'er, through misty air, 301 *Bran* 79
The humid precipice, and seize the guest 381 *Duddon* 22. 9
Then did he seize the staff, and say: 400 *White Doe* 405
Back therefore will they hie to seize 405 *White Doe* 797
Seized it, as hunters seize their prey; 412 *White Doe* 1494
What rapture! could ye seize 499 **Departing summer* 51
Lest alien frenzy seize thee, waxing wroth, 514 **Long-favoured* 3
He watched to seize old Goody Blake. 537 *Goody Blake* 72
Powers of my native region! Ye that seize 702 *Prelude* 8. 218
Were they, to seize and occupy the sense; 857 *Excursion* 7. 23

Seized. As, in these long commotions, have been seized. 56 *Bord.* 1026
Under pretence of violence, be seized. 59 *Bord.* 1187
When Benjamin had seized the bowl, 178 *Waggoner* 2. 149
Of him whom sudden death had seized 244 *P. B.* 731
He should be seized, alive or dead. 412 *White Doe* 1461
Seized it, as hunters seize their prey; 412 *White Doe* 1494
Once more the Church is seized with sudden fear, 432 *Ecc. Sonn.* 2. 17. 1
Was fondly seized by Sculpture, to restore 476 **Tranquillity! the* 6
Is seized with strong incitement to push forth 496 **A little* 29
And whither could they dart, if seized with fear? 528 **Those breathing* 52
This cruel Jew him seized, and held him fast. 554 *Prioress* 119
Sleep seized me, and I passed into a dream. 666 *Prelude* 5. 70
As marvellously seized as in that moment 796 *Excursion* 3. 718
I spake with vehemence; and promptly seized 797 *Excursion* 3. 795
Ruefully seized, and shedding bitter tears, 827 *Excursion* 5. 339
"A sudden illness seized her in the strength 849 *Excursion* 6. 741
Seized him, that self-same night; and through the space 870 *Excursion* 7. 871
Dropped the light oar his eager hand had seized. 891 *Excursion* 9. 481

Seizes. Till madness seizes on the whole wide Flood, 439 *Ecc. Sonn.* 2. 43. 9
A bolder transport seizes. From the side 867 *Excursion* 7. 649

Seizing. The halter seizing, Peter leapt 241 *P. B.* 397
And mighty forms, seizing a youthful fancy, 680 *Prelude* 6. 334

Seizure. Oswald, Oswald! This is some sudden seizure! 52 *Bord.* 798

Seldom. Beyond his native valley seldom stray, 18 *Desc. Sk.* 428
For better lore would seldom yearn, 86 *Anecdote* 58
Appeared but seldom; oftener was he seen 124 *V. and J.* 212
Not seldom did we stop to watch some tuft 148 **A narrow* 17
Nor seldom, if I rightly guess, while Thou, 151 **When, to* 98
And seldom needs a laboured roof; 168 *Wren's Nest* 6
Pass by her door—'tis seldom shut— 198 *Thorn* 95
Not seldom may the hour return 215 *Kirkstone* 51
Bear witness ye who seldom passed 224 **'Tis gone* 7
And, verily, have seldom met 245 *P. B.* 828
Are seldom free to touch the moss that grows 262 **Mark the* 5
(But seldom trod) of mildly-gleaming ore; 264 **Lady! I* 2
No one knows how; nor seldom is put forth 357 *Aquap.* 319
Not seldom, when with heat the valleys faint, 376 *Duddon* 2. 4
And seldom hath ear listened to a tune 381 *Duddon* 19. 10
Not seldom foremost in the way; 402 *White Doe* 572
Though bleak and bare, and seldom free 409 *White Doe* 1174

Seldom—*continued.*
Though seldom heard by busy human kind)— 432 *Ecc. Sonn.* 2. 17. 7
And doubts and scruples seldom teased the brain, 468 **Bold words* 2
Pleasure, or Grief, and Toil that seldom looks 471 *Ailsa Crag* 10
Doth seldom on a right foundation rest, 493 *Hap. War.* 32
Or changed and changing, I not seldom gaze 510 *F. Stone* 113
Not seldom, clad in radiant vest, 550 *Hermit's Cell* 5. 1
Not seldom Evening in the west 550 *Hermit's Cell* 5. 3
Within this court full seldom Truth avails, 560 *Cuck. and Night.* 204
And seldom knowing that he sees, some straw, 567 *Cumb. Beg.* 54
Of Lybia; and not seldom, on the banks 575 *Chiabrera* 6. 6
By duty chained. Not seldom did those tasks 584 *Ch. Lamb* 6
Such as start forth, not seldom, to approve 627 **The star* 11
Not seldom from the uproar I retired 638 *Prelude* 1. 447
Not seldom even in that tempestuous time, 640 *Prelude* 1. 550
Nor seldom did I lift our cottage latch 647 *Prelude* 2. 339
Not seldom differed from my taste in books, 676 *Prelude* 6. 97
Not seldom since that moment have I wished 682 *Prelude* 6. 472
Of vigour seldom utterly allayed: 683 *Prelude* 6. 559
But seldom led, or wished to go; in truth 693 *Prelude* 7. 398
That voice, ill requiem! seldom heard by me 723 *Prelude* 10. 327
Not seldom, and his own uneasy heart: 734 *Prelude* 12. 28
Her goodness, that, not seldom, in my walks 768 *Excursion* 1. 783
Of stream and headlong flood that seldom fails; 782 *Excursion* 2. 705
And suffer now, not seldom, from the thought 793 *Excursion* 3. 486
One spirit seldom failed to extend its sway 845 *Excursion* 6. 480
With vacant mind, not seldom may observe 852 *Excursion* 6. 936
As seen not seldom on some gusty day, 861 *Excursion* 7. 231
Was pallid: seldom hath that eye been moist 871 *Excursion* 7. 882
Not seldom over anxious to make known 893 *Excursion* 9. 584
Of man or beast was seldom used to tread. K.8. 229 **I will* 142

Select. This Height a ministering Angel might select: 218 **This Height* 1
Appeared more touching. One will I select; 696 *Prelude* 7. 602
In Nature's presence: thence may I select 743 *Prelude* 13. 245
He now was summoned to select the course 760 *Excursion* 1. 309
And such as my best judgment could select 874 *Excursion* 8. 19

Selected. Which selected spirits wear, 90 *Longest Day* 74
The Bruce had been selected; 287 *Ellen Irwin* 10
As a selected treasure thy one cliff, 355 *Aquap.* 210
Was once selected as the corner-stone 548 **Stranger! this* 15
His quiet heart's selected home. 580 *John Words.* 27
With rival oars; and the selected bourne 643 *Prelude* 2. 57
Who shall be first selected from my flock 836 *Excursion* 5. 898

Self. Is that I have my inner self abused, 32 *Guilt* 439
In you a mirror of my youthful self; 71 *Bord.* 1865
Where he, in his poor self so weak, by Providence was placed. 91 *Norman Boy* 28
Unfolded,—beauty, for its present self, 118 *Maternal Grief* 24
The Doctor's self could hardly spare: 128 *Idiot Boy* 238
Will be my second self when I am gone. 131 *Michael* 39
That for my single self I looked at them, 149 **A narrow* 61
Urania's self might welcome with pleased ear 154 *Morn. Ex.* 53
"Nor dare to thrust thy foolish self 155 *Waterfall* 3
Minerva's self would stigmatize 163 *Needlecase* 7
That self might be annulled: her bondage prove 211 *Laod.* 149
A type of her capacious self and all 230 *Clouds* 52
Softer than Nature's self could mould. 234 *Power of Sound* 120
Of fire his desperate self is tethering? 242 *P. B.* 512
His very self in form and feature, 246 *P. B.* 924
What was the great Parnassus' self to Thee, 251 **Pelion and* 10
That of its native self can nothing feed: 257 **The prayers* 4
For others; for thy future self, a spell 275 *Rotha Q.* 13
Hence lives He, to his inner self endeared; 317 **Call not* 6
Askance upon her pretty Self 344 **How blest* 9
Although invisible as Echo's self, 361 **List—'twas* 6
Yea, what were mighty Nature's self? 386 *Yarrow Rev.* 85
For self, and struggles with himself alone, 433 *Ecc. Sonn.* 2. 19. 10
And to Religion's self no friendly will, 442 *Ecc. Sonn.* 3. 8. 13
Her very self stood there. 479 *Somnamb.* 130
That to this mountain-daisy's self were known 511 **So fair* 4
When Nature's self, amid such blending, seems 524 *Epist. Beaumont* 185
Or was it Dian's self that seemed to move 532 **Once I* 19
And an habitual disregard of self 539 **Lady! a* 65
From earth, perhaps by Shakespeare's self approved, 546 **The embowering* 20
That burthen of my own unnatural self, 632 *Prelude* 1. 21
Even the great Newton's own ethereal self, 653 *Prelude* 3. 267
As far as doth concern my single self, 654 *Prelude* 3. 349
Than Nature's self, which is the breath of God, 669 *Prelude* 5. 221
This verse is dedicate to Nature's self, 669 *Prelude* 5. 230
May never tread; but scarcely Spenser's self 676 *Prelude* 6. 89
Love for the human creature's absolute self, 701 *Prelude* 8. 123
Not in my single self alone I found, 722 *Prelude* 10. 266
With that which makes our Reason's naked self 730 *Prelude* 11. 234
With my true self; for, though bedimmed and changed 732 *Prelude* 11. 342
If willing audience fail not, Nature's self, 732 *Prelude* 11. 350
Of the affections, and to Nature's self 743 *Prelude* 13. 200
In her original self too confident, 749 *Prelude* 14. 249
But for its absolute self; a life of peace, 791 *Excursion* 3. 385
Of mountaineers (by nature's self removed 828 *Excursion* 5. 424
As virtue's self; like virtue is beset 830 *Excursion* 5. 494
From visible nature, or the inner self 831 *Excursion* 5. 584
This generous Youth, too negligent of self, 870 *Excursion* 7. 867
By the division of her inward self 875 *Excursion* 8. 57
The mansion's self displayed;—a reverend pile 881 *Excursion* 8. 461
Bending its apex toward a paler self S.3. 434 **The doubt* 69
No self, and whom the selfish scorn— K.8. 325 [?] **The vestal* 2
Self judged, can with such discipline dispense, L.1. 97 *Juvenal* 3. 76

Senses—*continued.*
This tyranny, summons all the senses each 736 *Prelude* 12. 135
Sensibility. Whereby this infant sensibility, 646 *Prelude* 2. 270
My first creative sensibility ; 647 *Prelude* 2. 360
Whom he had sensibility to love, 774 *Excursion* 2. 189
With shrinking sensibility endued, 808 *Excursion* 4. 510
Sensible. By sensible impressions not enthralled, 747 *Prelude* 14. 106
(Whether of actual vision, sensible 811 *Excursion* 4. 642
Sensibly. Did breathe its sweetness out most sensibly, 714 *Prelude* 9. 296
Sensitive. But to its gentle touch how sensitive 184 *Airey-force* 11
Though sensitive, yet, in their weakest part, 260 **High is* 5
Or creeping worm, with sensitive respect. 270 **Though the bold* 8
Thus sensitive must be the Monk, though pale 362 **List—'twas* 74
Be duly mindful : still more sensitive 445 *Ecc. Sonn.* 3. 21. 4
That there's a sensitive, a tender, part 459 **Wanderer! that* 44
A household small and sensitive,—whose love, 510 **Among a* 29
So fair, so sweet, withal so sensitive, 511 **So fair* 1
Where, sensitive of every ray 526 **The soaring* 21
I was as sensitive as waters are 651 *Prelude* 3. 136
A sensitive being, a *creative* soul. 737 *Prelude* 12. 207
That men, least sensitive, see, hear, perceive, 747 *Prelude* 14. 85
A sensitive existence, and a God, 811 *Excursion* 4. 679
Sensual. In a sensual creed that trampled 141 *Arm. Lady* 81
The Sensual think with reverence of the palms 424 *Ecc. Sonn.* 1. 24. 9
Wrapt closely in thy sensual fleece, 485 *Poet's Epitaph* 21
Abolished, sensual state and cruel power, 717 *Prelude* 9. 527
Would I arouse the sensual from their sleep 755 *Recluse* 1. 1. 813
Sensuous. Sensuous or intellectual, wrought by men, 666 *Prelude* 5. 43
Sent. And so he sent a feeble shout—in vain ; 25 *Guilt* 33
With rays of promise, north and southward sent ; 30 *Guilt* 314
" Be blest : by sight of thee from heaven was sent 36 *Guilt* 629
Our little fire sent forth a cheering warmth 50 *Bord.* 708
Sent after him. I have loved you ever since. 52 *Bord.* 836
Though but a glimpse, it sent me to my prayers. 55 *Bord.* 973
Dissolved the Barons' League, and sent abroad 56 *Bord.* 1023
Hailed us as if he had been sent from heaven, 62 *Bord.* 1366
Sent forth a cry forlorn, 85 *Shepherd-boys* 75
That sent this rueful cry, I ween 85 *Shepherd-boys* 79
While half an hour went by, the Priest had sent 95 *Brothers* 29
Sent to his heart ! he lifted up his eyes, 96 *Brothers* 95
A daughter sent to service, a web spun, 97 *Brothers* 159
Well born, well bred ; I sent him forth 117 *Affl. Marg.* 17
With marble, which he sent from foreign lands. 135 *Michael* 270
He might be sent to him. Ten times or more 136 *Michael* 311
Sent forth such sallies of glad sound, that all 146 **It was an* 23
And the tall Steep of Silver-how, sent forth 147 *Joanna* 58
Reproaches from their lips are sent, 163 *Needlecase* 2
A lovely Apparition, sent 186 **She was* 3
The stars had feelings, which they sent 193 *Ruth* 137
Or like a man from some far region sent, 197 *Resolution* 111
Into her soul was sent ; 190 *Thorn* 119
Sent up, in silence, from among the trees ! 206 *Tintern* 18
To a babbling wanderer sent ; 209 **Yes, it* 6
I am not sent to scare thee or deceive ; 210 *Laod.* 39
And east and west, the Ass sent forth 241 *P. B.* 464
Sent from some distant clime where Winter wields 263 **While not* 4
Which from the crowd on shore was sent, 297 *Highland Boy* 177
To France be words of invitation sent ! 309 *Men of Kent* 5
And sent him forth, with squadrons of his kind, 321 **Humanity, delighting* 29
Of Justice sent to earth from highest Heaven ! 325 *Enghien* 14
Of a good wish sent after thee ; from bower 363 **List—'twas* 106
To Her and to all Lands its warning sent, 365 **The Baptist* 12
Sent upon embassies of fear ; 407 *White Doe* 1048
They come, by cruel Sussex sent ; 412 *White Doe* 1447
One (like those prophets whom God sent of old) 437 *Ecc. Sonn.* 2. 34. 4
A voice, from long-expecting thousands sent, 442 *Ecc. Sonn.* 3. 8. 1
With flying haste, I might have sent, 457 **Had this* 2
If this belief from heaven be sent, 482 *Lines : Spring* 21
By thee, thee only, could be sent 508 *May* 77
And vocal wishes sent of like good will 524 *Epist. Beaumont* 215
By message sent through air or visible token, 531 **I know* 30
A guardian Spirit sent from pitying Heaven, 541 *Grace Darl.* 73
Sent forth her peace to cheer. 544 *Russ. Fug.* 208
A shout thrice sent from one who chased 544 *Russ. Fug.* 261
The Emperor sent a pledge as strong 545 *Russ. Fug.* 351
And hastily they for the Provost sent ; 555 *Prioress* 165
A summons to the Cuckoo shall be sent, 562 *Cuck.andNight.*278
Our common Friend and Father sent. 577 **I come* 4
That Man, who is from God sent forth, 581 **Loud is* 21
As sent from heav'n the raven of the skies, 609 *Desc.Sk.Quarto* 403
And from his fords and shallows, sent a voice 636 *Prelude* 1. 273
Into the tumult sent an alien sound 638 *Prelude* 1. 443
Or, from the meadows sent on gusty days, 639 *Prelude* 1. 496
Sent welcome notice of the rising moon, 640 *Prelude* 1. 571
And wavering motions sent he knows not whence, 662 *Prelude* 4. 269
Of that imaginative impulse sent 682 *Prelude* 6. 462
Sent in on Winter's service, to announce, 687 *Prelude* 7. 23
Seemed sent on the same errand with the choir 687 *Prelude* 7. 40
Arguments sent from Heaven to prove the cause 713 *Prelude* 9. 283
The rapture of the hallelujah sent 750 *Prelude* 14. 294
From one who by my husband had been sent 766 *Excursion* 1. 675
Called out, and sent a blessing after me, 766 *Excursion* 1. 694
From yon huge breast of rock, a voice sent forth 807 *Excursion* 4. 403
How that neglected Pensioner was sent 821 *Excursion* 4. 1313
By impulse sent from such illusive power,— 827 *Excursion* 5. 322
The Mother, oft as she was sent abroad, 853 *Excursion* 6. 984
Sent by the ancient Soul of this wide land, 871 *Excursion* 7. 896
Or sent on mission to some northern Chief 871 *Excursion* 7. 932
Sent from the jocund hearts of those two Boys, 891 *Excursion* 9. 475

Sent—*continued.*
And sent ' warm-reeking, rich and sweet,' S.3. 432 **A German* 3
Sent from the mountains or the sheltered fields ; K.8. 245 *Recluse* 1.1.320
Sentence. " O welcome sentence which will end though late," 36 *Guilt* 655
When will my sentence be reversed ? 110 *Forsaken* 5
The sentence, by her mother's lip pronounced, 124 *V. and J.* 221
And, in the sternest sentence which his voice 429 *Ecc. Sonn.* 2. 1. 13
To take his sentence from the balanced Block, 500 *Humanity* 5
Pass sentence on themselves, confess the fact, 517 *Pun. Death* 3. 11
The sentence rule by mercy's heaven-born lights." 519 *Pun. Death* 10. 12
To sentence in the hearing of the world, 717 *Prelude* 9. 538
Resolved the dubious point ; and sentence gave 772 *Excursion* 2. 78
His sentence to the axe would doom them all. 867 *Excursion* 7. 624
Sentient. (Sentient by Grecian sculpture's marvellous power), 169 *Love lies Bleeding* 6
Whose sentient tube instructs to time 342 *Ital. Itin.* 23
To the least particle of sentient dust ; 500 *Humanity* 46
Sentiment. Of noble sentiment. 193 *Ruth* 144
Of thoughtful sentiment for every mind 355 *Aquap.* 149
I felt the sentiment of Being spread 648 *Prelude* 2. 401
From the natural inlets of just sentiment, 714 *Prelude* 9. 350
Nor turn of sentiment that might be named 722 *Prelude* 10. 271
Of pious sentiment diffused afar, 838 *Excursion* 6. 28
With little change of general sentiment, 845 *Excursion* 6. 470
Sentiments. Filling the soul with sentiments august— 351 *Des. Stanzas* 80
Those human sentiments that make this earth 648 *Prelude* 2. 422
For, images, and sentiments, and words, 674 *Prelude* 5. 579
My sentiments ; was not, as hitherto, 730 *Prelude* 11. 178
Less occupied the mind, and sentiments 730 *Prelude* 11. 199
And sundry moral sentiments as props 731 *Prelude* 11. 264
I re-salute these sentiments confirmed 831 *Excursion* 5. 570
His gentler sentiments of love and hate, 844 *Excursion* 6. 429
Sentinel. From its dull sheath—stern sentinel 301 *Bran* 54
Spread through all ranks ; and lo ! the Sentinel 442 *Ecc. Sonn.* 3. 11. 4
Sentinels. Than sentinels, between two armies, set, 846 *Excursion* 6. 536
Separate. I ne'er had heart to separate—my grave, 40 *Bord.* 143
Two separate Creatures in their several gifts 118 *Maternal Grief* 30
And makes each soul a separate heaven, 225 *Primrose* 53
Might overwhelm, but could not separate ! 265 **When haughty* 14
That solitary word—to separate 275 *Gravestone* 4
Than either, pent within her separate sphere, 357 *Aquap.* 287
Through pregnant vision, separate or conjoined. 663 *Prelude* 4. 353
Without a separate notice : many books 675 *Prelude* 6. 23
Each in his separate cell, or penned in crowds 724 *Prelude* 10. 406
A separate record. Over the smooth sands 725 *Prelude* 10. 514
Separated. Hath separated from its kind, 414 *White Doe* 1636
Like separated stars with clouds between. 622 *Recluse* 1. 1. 125
Separately. Vivid as fire ; clouds separately poised,— 893 *Excursion* 9. 600
Separation. " Some mighty gulf of separation passed, 31 *Guilt* 352
Achieved their separation : and once more 124 *V. and J.* 173
The separation that is here 289 *Glen-Al.* 27
Sure, when the separation has been tried, 383 *Duddon* 30. 13
Now, after separation desolate, 678 *Prelude* 6. 201
At dearest separation, patriot love 713 *Prelude* 9. 272
In wholesome separation the two natures, 751 *Prelude* 14. 346
From their first separation, nine long years, 769 *Excursion* 1. 872
Their lenient term of separation past, 861 *Excursion* 7. 288
Of mortal separation, could intrude K.8. 236 *Recluse* 1.1.13
September. One calm September morning, ere the mist 148 **A narrow* 7
I thought of those September massacres, 719 *Prelude* 10. 73
Sepulchral. Sullenly glaring through sepulchral damp, 266 **Even as* 3
And thrills the old sepulchral earth, around. 283 **Well have* 7
Of its Arcades paved with sepulchral slabs, 355 *Aquap.* 156
To whose dear memories his sepulchral verse 356 *Aquap.* 241
Of fond sepulchral flattery can beguile 389 *Breadalb.* 3
Yet no sepulchral honours to her Son 574 *Chiabrera* 5. 14
Sepulchral stones appeared, with emblems graven 825 *Excursion* 5. 168
From interruption of sepulchral stones, 847 *Excursion* 6. 608
Sepulture. Honoured with costliest sepulture. 550 *Hermit's Cell* 2. 16
Sequel. Easily may the sequel be divined— 122 *V. and J.* 79
The doleful sequel. But our little bark 717 *Prelude* 9. 559
And pleasant interests—for the sequel leaving 829 *Excursion* 5. 435
Sequence. In drowsy sequence—how unlike the sound 453 **Calm is the* 13
Sequestered. *See* **Cloud-sequestered, Far-sequestered.**
With suit that I would speak in verse of that sequestered child 91 *Norman Boy* 7
We who in this sequestered spot 155 *Waterfall* 23
In this sequestered nook how sweet 159 *Green Linnet* 5
Or in sequestered lanes they build, 168 *Wren's Nest* 25
Are thridding a sequestered lane ; 245 *P. B.* 797
To whom the wild sequestered region owes, 272 *Lady E. B.* 7
Near that Cell—yon sequestered Retreat high in air— 364 *Vallomb.* 6
Where Rylstone's old sequestered Hall 406 *White Doe* 946
That one sequestered hillock green, 417 *White Doe* 1899
Sequestered with repose ; 478 *Somnamb.* 38
The Mother Church in yon sequestered vale ; 534 **When in* 4
And there, sequestered from the sight, 542 *Russ. Fug.* 97
Then, stretcht at ease in some sequestered cave, 630 [?]**O Moon* 7
In that sequestered valley may be seen, 643 *Prelude* 2. 111
Among sequestered villages we walked 680 *Prelude* 6. 356
Abruptly into some sequestered nook, 689 *Prelude* 7. 170
Sequestered, handed down among themselves 701 *Prelude* 8. 134
Sequestered from the rest, societies 711 *Prelude* 9. 116
Is not sequestered—what a change is here ! 724 *Prelude* 10. 428
Hold lower rank than this sequestered pair : 833 *Excursion* 5. 718
Brought yesterday from our sequestered dell 835 *Excursion* 5. 882

Sequestered—*continued.*
Unsociably sequestered, and encroaching — 858 *Excursion* 7. 36
And fixed his home in this sequestered vale. — 871 *Excursion* 7. 926
In town and city and sequestered glen, — 873 *Excursion* 7. 1023
True; as the mightiest; upon thee sequestered — S.3. 435 **The doubt* 132
Sequestration. In dusty sequestration wrapt too long, — 435 *Ecc. Sonn.* 2. 29. 2
O gift divine of quiet sequestration! — 586 *Ch. Lamb* 121
In rustic sequestration—all dependent — 761 *Excursion* 1. 330
Seraph. King, child, and seraph, blended in the mien — 436 *Ecc. Sonn.* 2. 31. 7
Seraph-haunted. And rapt Cecilia, seraph-haunted Queen — 434 *Ecc. Sonn.* 2. 24. 11
Seraphic. His rostrum, with seraphic glance look up, — 695 *Prelude* 7. 553
Seraphim. The six-days' Work by flaming Seraphim — 235 *Power of Sound* 203
By Seraphim. — 285 *Grave of Burns* 84
Even like the radiant Seraphim, — 498 **The sylvan* 29
Seraph's. May Discord—for a Seraph's care — 582 *Invoc. Earth* 28
Are they—and might demand a seraph's tongue, — 874 *Excursion* 8. 11
Seraphs. Bright Seraphs mixed familiarly with men; — 228 *Vernal Ode* 134
Or crown of burning seraphs as they sit — 725 *Prelude* 10. 522
Sere. In gentle bosoms, while sere leaves — 385 *Yarrow Rev.* 11
Me, conscious that my leaf is sere, — 498 **Departing summer* 14
Hopeless of further growth, and brown and sere — 521 *Epist. Beaumont* 16
Of summer, in the season of sere leaves; — 539 **Lady! a* 61
Dislodged, through sere leaves rustled, or at once — 633 *Prelude* 1. 84
Serenade. Tears brightened by the serenade — 375 **The Minstrels* 47
Serene. Long may they float upon this flood serene; — 6 *Ev. Wk.* 232
How bright, how solemn, how serene! — 9 *Collins* 12
Appalling havoc! but serene his brow, — 21 *Desc. Sk.* 581
Like a dead Boy he is serene. — 166 *Danish Boy* 55
Of a sky serene and pure; — 171 *Kitten* 88
Earth, spangled sky, and lake serene, — 178 *Waggoner* 3. 38
And now I see with eye serene — 186 **She was* 21
Is lightened:—that serene and blessed mood, — 206 *Tintern* 41
Serene, and fitted to embrace, — 212 *Dion* 1
But an old age serene and bright, — 218 *Young Lady* 16
In depth, in height, in circuit, how serene — 219 **This Height* 29
In this serene and solemn hour, — 241 *P. B.* 473
Of aspect winning and serene; — 299 *Brownie's Cell* 76
Say can he think of this with mind serene — 318 **Is there* 11
And, even to sadness, lonely and serene, — 323 *Ode 1814* 18
Or top serene of unmolested mountain, — 325 *Ode 1814* 124
Where their serene progenitors are laid; — 328 *Ode 1815* 60
From the smooth meadow-ground, serene and still! — 335 *Namur* 14
For faith, 'mid ruined hopes, serene? — 337 **Oh Life* 5
And, therefore, art thou blest with peace, serene — 339 *Schwytz* 6
The still repose, the liquid lapse serene, — 381 *Duddon* 20. 4
Of that serene companion—a good name, — 383 *Duddon* 30. 2
Fair fruit of pleasure and serene content — 395 *White Doe: Ded.* 31
Comes gliding in serene and slow, — 396 *White Doe* 56
And carrying inward a serene — 413 *White Doe* 1593
Wonder that aught of aspect so serene — 439 *Ecc. Sonn.* 2. 43. 4
Glory of night, conspicuous yet serene, — 460 **Queen of* 10
Nought heard, of ocean troubled or serene? — 470 **Did pangs* 5
Extracting from clear skies and air serene, — 475 **Homeward we* 10
Serene will be our days and bright, — 492 *Duty* 17
Contented and serene; — 499 *Memory* 24
She may look for serene weather; — 503 **Like a* 77
Crescent in simple loveliness serene, — 509 *F. Stone* 47
From whose serene companionship I passed — 510 **Among a* 12
Once I could hail (howe'er serene the sky) — 532 **Once I* 1
Resolves devotedly serene; — 543 *Russ. Fug.* 171
This, which I know, I speak with mind serene. — 578 *Peele Castle* 40
And, floating there, in pomp serene, — 579 **Sweet Flower* 19
Whose shades protect the hidden wave serene; — 595 *Ev.Wk. Quarto* 222
Now, passing Urseren's open vale serene, — 606 *Desc.Sk.Quarto* 243
O'er azure pikes serene and still, they go, — 610 *Desc.Sk.Quarto* 458
Lift, all serene, their still, illumin'd forms, — 612 *Desc.Sk.Quarto* 565
Serene he towers, in deepest purple dy'd; — 615 *Desc.Sk.Quarto* 699
Stern was her forehead, but a smile serene — 618 *School Ex.* 15
Confiding in that Star serene, — 629 *Installation* 71
To night, unbroken cheerfulness serene. — 633 *Prelude* 1. 113
A sober hour, not winning or serene, — 660 *Prelude* 4. 144
Your beauty with me, a serene accord — 685 *Prelude* 6. 678
Though under skies less generous, less serene: — 702 *Prelude* 8. 188
Interposition—a serene delight — 750 *Prelude* 14. 289
Serene it was, unclouded by the cares — 761 *Excursion* 1. 356
The most serene, with most undaunted eye!— — 780 *Excursion* 2. 590
Uplifted; here, serene pavilions bright, — 784 *Excursion* 2. 842
And in serene possession of himself, — 785 *Excursion* 2. 883
Night hushed as night, and day serene as day!' — 791 *Excursion* 3. 324
But no—for the serene was also bright; — 792 *Excursion* 3. 429
Pure and serene, diffused—to overlook — 811 *Excursion* 4. 688
Capacious and serene. Like power abides — 817 *Excursion* 4. 1070
He stood; or if not so, whose top serene — 827 *Excursion* 5. 300
To your serene authorities conform; — 827 *Excursion* 5. 352
When he beholds the first pale speck serene — 852 *Excursion* 6. 914
Capacious and serene; his blameless life, — 854 *Excursion* 6. 1066
Praised the consummate harmony serene — 882 *Excursion* 8. 538
That combinations so serene and bright — 891 *Excursion* 9. 468
Serenely. Or when along thy breast serenely float — 281 **Wansfell! this* 4
—But hers are eyes serenely bright, — 397 *White Doe* 136
Who from truth's central point serenely views — 883 *Excursion* 8. 599
Serenity. Blended in absolute serenity, — 226 *Vernal Ode* 35
Serious. Is a most serious thing. Not I alone, — 55 *Bord.* 995
To serious musing and to self-reproach. — 149 **A narrow* 70
Of serious faith, and inward glee; — 186 **O Nightingale* 19
Even for such promise:—serious is her face, — 256 *Marriage: Friend* 6
Might give to serious thought a moment's sway, — 453 **Calm is the* 31
And make the serious happier than the gay? — 459 **Wanderer! that* 39
Of still and serious thought went round, — 486 *Matthew* 26

Serious—*continued.*
And scanned them with a fixed and serious look — 566 *Cumb. Beg.* 11
And serious mood; but after I had seen — 638 *Prelude* 1. 390
In serious mood, but oftener, I confess, — 656 *Prelude* 3. 531
Set forth, too serious theme for that light place— — 691 *Prelude* 7. 295
Not moving to his mind.'" These serious words — 776 *Excursion* 2. 315
Cheered, plainly, and yet serious. What a wreck — 781 *Excursion* 2. 660
It is most serious: persevering rain — 783 *Excursion* 2. 781
On serious minds: then, as the Hindoos draw — 790 *Excursion* 3. 254
A serious eye, and his speech thus renewed. — 793 *Excursion* 3. 479
And undisguised, and strong and serious thought; — 824 *Excursion* 5. 119
Rise to the notice of a serious mind — 828 *Excursion* 5. 372
While in this serious mood we held discourse, — 829 *Excursion* 5. 440
—Serious and thoughtful was her mind; and yet, — 850 *Excursion* 6. 824
Inspire the serious song, and gentle Hearts — 896 *Excursion* 9. 794
Serpent. "The Serpent, Satan, our first foe, that hath — 554 *Prioress* 107
And, like a serpent, shows his glittering back — 869 *Excursion* 7. 791
Serpentine. Of intertwisted fibres serpentine — 185 *Yew-trees* 17
In grisly folds and strictures serpentine; — 424 *Ecc. Sonn.* 1. 21. 12
Mounts, as you see, in mazes serpentine, — 858 *Excursion* 7. 48
Serpent-like. And ye, Beliefs! coiled serpent-like about — 518 *Pun. Death* 6. 9
Serpent-necks. Involve their serpent-necks in changeful rings, — 6 *Ev. Wk.* 246
Serpent's. The dry leaves stir as with the serpent's walk, — 606 *Desc.Sk.Quarto* 233
Serpents. In waves, like two enormous serpents, wind — 615 *Desc.Sk.Quarto* 696
Sertorius. And followers of Sertorius, out of Spain — 635 *Prelude* 1. 191
Servant. Swiftly went that grey-haired Servant, — 141 *Arm. Lady* 121
(High Servant of paternal Love) — 299 *Brownie's Cell* 94
That this great Servant of a righteous cause — 317 **Call not* 10
While on each head his lawn-robed servant lays — 446 *Ecc. Sonn.* 3. 23. 9
Thee his loved servant, his inspiring mate! — 489 *Spade* 26
Servant of Providence, not slave of Fate— — 514 **Blest Statesman* 13
With this tried Servant of a thankless Court, — 529 **Those breathing* 121
For he that faithfully Love's servant is, — 559 *Cuck.and Night.* 159
The obedient servant of her will. Such moments — 737 *Prelude* 12. 223
An ancient servant of my father's house — 737 *Prelude* 12. 229
The faithful servant, who must hide his head — 778 *Excursion* 2. 476
His rosy face, a servant only here — K.8. 246 *Recluse* 1. 1. 360
Thou good and faithful servant of the Cross." — K.8. 325 [?] **The vestal* 14
Were such your servant Percy! (be it tried — L. 1. 97 *Juvenal* 3. 67
Servant's. The Master died, his drooping servant's grief — 523 *Epist. Beaumont* 133
Servants. The pair were servants of his eye — 205 *Brougham* 124
Upon those servants of another world — 298 *Brownie's Cell* 21
Thy servants, who can trifle thus; — 300 *Bran* 36
And taught her faithful servants how the lyre — 359 *Plea: Hist.* 13
Servants of God! who not a thought will share — 423 *Ecc. Sonn.* 1. 19. 2
To speak of Love's true Servants in this mood; — 559 *Cuck.and Night.* 148
For evermore his servants Love amendeth, — 560 *Cuck.and Night.* 191
Such hope, entreats that servants may abound — 839 *Excursion* 6. 43
Serve. Let me have leave to serve you! My Companion — 41 *Bord.* 214
To serve me so, and knowing that he owes — 46 *Bord.* 484
To perpetrate his crimes, serve as a Sanctuary — 57 *Bord.* 1087
Than obloquy; that, if we wish to serve — 70 *Bord.* 1828
His words and tones and gestures, did but serve — 77 *Bord.* 2262
To serve them for a guide. — 83 *Lucy Gray* 36
Whose moss-grown root might serve for couch or seat, — 167 *Pilgrim's Dream* 11
All powers that serve the bright-eyed Queen — 223 *Wishing-gate* 2
Serve Thee, invisible Spirit, with untired powers; — 232 *Power of Sound* 18
Do serve with all their changeful pageantry; — 252 *Picture* 10
And earth below, they best can serve true gladness — 280 **'Tis he* 13
To serve—an unsuspected screen — 300 *Bran* 7
Here only serve a feeling to invite — 349 *Val. Dover* 12
And fitliest serve to crown with fragrant wreaths — 355 *Aquap.* 203
Oft for a holy warning may it serve, — 360 **Long has* 11
Or warning serve, thus let them all, on ground — 361 **When here* 13
To live, and act, and serve the future hour; — 384 *Duddon* 34. 11
Nor will the Power we serve, that sacred Power, — 394 **No more* 17
How can I serve you? point the way." — 408 *White Doe* 1081
What serve they? if, on transitory good — 450 *Ecc. Sonn.* 3. 38. 3
Dread Power! whom peace and calmness serve — 458 **Had this* 69
And under one blest ensign serve the Lord — 467 *St. Bees* 104
To serve thy need, in union with that Clyde — 475 *Greenock* 12
But thee I now would serve more strictly, if I may. — 492 *Duty* 32
Of those terrestrial fabrics, where they serve, — 496 **A little* 47
Of strict obedience, serve the Almighty Lord; — 500 *Humanity* 38
To serve the glorious Henry, King of France, — 574 *Chiabrera* 3. 14
Though but a doubting hope, that they might serve — 585 *Ch. Lamb* 41
To serve in Nature's temple, thou hast been — 648 *Prelude* 2. 463
As some might seem, so aptly do they serve — 657 *Prelude* 3. 553
And seasons serve; all Faculties to whom — 673 *Prelude* 5. 530
Duly to serve the mind of earth-born man; — 677 *Prelude* 6. 126
For all things serve them; them the morning light — 700 *Prelude* 8. 63
Among new objects serve or give command, — 708 *Prelude* 8. 641
Therefore to serve was high beatitude; — 724 *Prelude* 10. 433
Serve to exalt; they build up greatest things — 747 *Prelude* 14. 101
And something that may serve to set in view — 757 *Excursion* 1. 99
Who would forbid them, if their presence serve, — 813 *Excursion* 4. 843
Contingencies of pomp; and serve to exalt — 817 *Excursion* 4. 1061
The processes of things, and serve the cause — 820 *Excursion* 4. 1258
Discerning Mortal! do thou serve the will — 846 *Excursion* 6. 519
Generous and charitable, prompt to serve; — 860 *Excursion* 7. 214
To serve the will of feeble-bodied Man. — 877 *Excursion* 8. 207
Them who are born to serve her and obey; — 888 *Excursion* 9. 298

Served. My husband's arms now only served to strain 29 *Guilt* 275
" These things just served to stir the slumbering sense, 31 *Guilt* 397
My husband served in sad captivity 35 *Guilt* 593
Served, tending a few sheep and goats, a ragged Norman Boy. 91 *Norman Boy* 4
And while he served the Gods with reverence due, 103 *Artegal* 72
Laid down his whip—and served no more.— 182 *Waggoner* 4. 186
That served my turn, when following still 246 *P. B.* 863
From Knowledge !—If the Muse, whom I have served 358 *Aquap.* 355
As a true man, who long had served the lyre, 365 **Under the* 9
His Father served Jehovah ; but how win 365 **The Baptist* 3
What served they in her need ? 374 *Eg. Maid* 368
He served in folly. Woden falls, and Thor 423 *Ecc. Sonn.* 1. 17. 5
Who will be served by others on their knees, 433 *Ecc. Sonn.* 2. 18. 5
Like those the Heathen served ; and mass is sung ; 436 *Ecc. Sonn.* 2. 33. 12
Tides of aggressive war, oft served as well 469 **The feudal* 3
The Tragic Muse thee served with thoughtful vow ; 476 **Tranquillity! the* 4
Long hast Thou served a man to reason true ; 489 *Spade* 6
And served in depths where fishes haunt 506 **While from* 31
In Him whose Providence your rage hath served ! 541 *Grace Darl.* 86
Served as stable-boy, errand-boy, porter, and groom ; 570 *Farmer* 50
Once to Our Lady dedicate, and served 643 *Prelude* 2. 64
And known authority of office served 656 *Prelude* 3. 538
That in the Tropic Islands he had served, 664 *Prelude* 4. 422
'Mid temples, served by sapient priests, and choirs 734 *Prelude* 11. 460
That served those wanderings to beguile, hast said 745 *Prelude* 13. 354
Such words of hope from her own mouth as served 766 *Excursion* 1. 685
Was served by rival advocates that came 775 *Excursion* 2. 230
That served my Fellow-traveller to beguile 776 *Excursion* 2. 317
Between their several births than served for one 794 *Excursion* 3. 593
Metal or stone, idolatrously served. 812 *Excursion* 4. 728
Whom I have served, that their DIVINITY 816 *Excursion* 4. 984
But we are kindly welcomed—promptly served 821 *Excursion* 4. 1316
The Pastor said : " So Providence is served ; 870 *Excursion* 7. 833
A choice repast—served by our young companions 892 *Excursion* 9. 530
Serves. A Sister serves with slacker hand ; 344 **How blest* 25
He serves the Muses erringly and ill, 395 *White Doe: Ded.* 5
That serves the steadfast hours, 499 **This Lawn* 15
Voice but serves for one brief cry ; 502 **Like a* 9
Just serves to show how delicate a soil 508 *F. Stone* 30
Serves as a solemn background, or relief, 696 *Prelude* 7. 622
A domineering instinct, serves at once 720 *Prelude* 10. 169
For some one, serves as a familiar friend. K.8.248 *Recluse* 1.1.444
And neighbourhood serves rather to divide K.8.253 *Recluse* 1.1.600
Service. *See* **Vesper-service, Villain-service.**
Owed him no service ; wherefore he at once 23 *Yew-tree* 21
Of service done with cold formality, 31 *Guilt* 394
Nor was I then for toil or service fit ; 32 *Guilt* 429
In this good service. Rather let us grieve 37 *Bord.* 5
A lucky woman !—go, you have done good service. 46 *Bord.* 518
In such sad service ; and he parted with him. 50 *Bord.* 690
And do good service, though she knew it not. 52 *Bord.* 842
To thank me for this service. Rainbow arches, 54 *Bord.* 930
Woman, I've lent my body to the service 74 *Bord.* 2112
Hereafter you will thank me for this service. 75 *Bord.* 2127
And faithful service of his heart in the worst that might ensue 91 *Norman Boy* 26
" God for His service needeth not proud work of human skill ; 93 *Poet's Dream* 65
On that service she went forth ; 94 *Westmoreland Girl* 70
A daughter sent to service, a web spun, 97 *Brothers* 159
Of glad or willing service to thy share would fall." 105 *Artegal* 185
That gave it birth : in service meek 112 **How rich* 13
Obsequious service to the precious child, 125 *V. and J.* 278
Service beyond all others of its kind. 133 *Michael* 116
Had done him female service, not alone 133 *Michael* 154
To melancholy service—hark ! O hark ! 153 *Morn. Ex.* 24
Into the service of his constant heart, 169 *Lovelies Bleeding* 22
Which for that service had been husbanded, 185 *Nutting* 10
Unwearied in that service : rather say 207 *Tintern* 153
Altars for Druid service fit ; 214 *Kirkstone* 13
Who, for thy service trained in lonely woods, 216 *Enterprise* 92
That on the service wait concealed 228 *Devot. Incit.* 36
For service hung behind thy chamber-door ; 229 *Cuckoo-clock* 8
Nor hushed be service from the lowing mead, 235 *Power of Sound* 197
Demands the service of a mind and heart, 260 **High is* 4
Bound to thy service with unceasing care, 277 **Why art* 6
With service meet ; 286 *Sons of Burns* 28
Such martial service disapprove. 328 *Ode 1815* 88
Do with the service of this Day accord. 329 *Ode : Thanks.* 26
The outward service of this day ; 331 *Ode : Thanks.* 177
Gracious to service hallowed by its aim ;— 332 *Ode : Thanks.* 226
For what strange service, does this concert reach 336 *Staub-bach* 2
Where haply (kind service to Piety due !) 340 *Fort Fuentes* 9
For the same service, by mysterious ties ; 347 *Processions* 50
" On Christian service this frail Bark 370 *Eg. Maid* 73
For tutelary service, thence had rolled, 379 *Duddon* 15. 7
To mark some change of service. As the swell 387 *Roslin* 3
They sing a service which they feel : 396 *White Doe* 39
Or service, it must lie elsewhere. 397 *White Doe* 135
The white Doe, to her service true, 398 *White Doe* 168
Whom to this service I commend ; 402 *White Doe* 612
And, in your service making bold, 409 *White Doe* 1251
Such Priest, when service worthy of his care 423 *Ecc. Sonn.* 1. 19. 6
Is chilled by death, does mutual service fail ? 423 *Ecc. Sonn.* 1. 20. 2
The last dear service of thy passing breath ! 424 *Ecc. Sonn.* 1. 23. 14
From Monks in Ely chanting service high, 426 *Ecc. Sonn.* 1. 30. 2
Service—*continued.*
Yet will yourselves to God no service pay ; 433 *Ecc. Sonn.* 2. 18. 6
As the high service pledges now, now pleads. 445 *Ecc. Sonn.* 3. 20. 8
A sea-born service through the mountains felt 454 *Sea-side* 27
Who, to that service bound by venial fees, 467 *St. Bees* 71
No; their dread service nerves the heart it warms, 469 **The feudal* 13
And, when Thou art past service, worn away, 489 *Spade* 27
Upon the service of our God ! 506 *Lab. Hymn* 16
The service to prolong ! 507 **While from* 58
Prayer's voiceless service ; but now, seeking nought 508 *F. Stone* 35
Came, in that service, to a glorious work, 509 *F. Stone* 103
Grateful to Thee, while service pure, 534 **Blest is* 97
" On good service we are going 535 *Egremont* 25
Small service is true service while it lasts : 538 **Small service* 1
Well did they know that service all by rote, 558 *Cuck. and Night.* 71
For in this world no service is so good 559 *Cuck. and Night.* 149
Thee she accepts as for her service fit ! 562 *Cuck. and Night.* 301
And 'tis no vulgar service, makes them felt. 568 *Cumb. Beg.* 132
Perhaps some needful service of the State 573 *Chiabrera* 2. 1
Vain service ! yet not vainly done 579 **Sweet Flower* 57
Slow swells the service o'er the water born, 604 *Desc. Sk. Quarto* 146
Abstruse, nor wanting punctual service high, 632 *Prelude* 1. 44
Even for the very service they had wrought, 640 *Prelude* 1. 519
To instantaneous service ; should at once 654 *Prelude* 3. 374
At home in pious service, to your bells 655 *Prelude* 3. 412
Far different service in those homely days 655 *Prelude* 3. 459
Into a gentler service. And when first 660 *Prelude* 4. 100
Sent in on Winter's service, to announce, 687 *Prelude* 7. 23
In those vast regions where his service lies, 703 *Prelude* 8. 252
Among mankind he was in service bound, 714 *Prelude* 9. 304
Walks a lone Monk, when service hath expired, 716 *Prelude* 9. 445
Service however dangerous. I revolved, 720 *Prelude* 10. 154
In that unworthy service was prepared 722 *Prelude* 10. 316
Into one service, busy with one work. 723 *Prelude* 10. 350
The first was service paid to things which lie 724 *Prelude* 10. 431
How oft high service is performed within, 743 *Prelude* 13. 227
For His own service ; knoweth, loveth us, 744 *Prelude* 13. 277
And their hard service, deemed debasing now, 761 *Excursion* 1. 327
Intoxicating service ! I might say 775 *Excursion* 2. 223
A happy service ; for he was sincere 775 *Excursion* 2. 224
For whom this pious service is performed ; 777 *Excursion* 2. 401
Substantial service. Mark me now, and learn 783 *Excursion* 2. 773
Some, tired of honest service ; these, outdone, 797 *Excursion* 3. 772
With obligation charged, with service taxed, 798 *Excursion* 3. 840
Are scarcely told, since, on a service bent 808 *Excursion* 4. 469
And course of service Truth requires from those 810 *Excursion* 4. 596
Of inward conscience ? with whose service charged 813 *Excursion* 4. 837
For acts of service ? Can his love extend 817 *Excursion* 4. 1095
For morn and evening service, with her pail, 832 *Excursion* 5. 641
Is by domestic service unimpaired ; 852 *Excursion* 6. 951
Yet, though such service be, with us, removed 852 *Excursion* 6. 952
To most laborious service, though to them 869 *Excursion* 7. 778
In this sad service, less disturbed than we. 871 *Excursion* 7. 885
To Scotland's court in service of his Queen, 871 *Excursion* 7. 931
Their virtue, service, happiness, and state 872 *Excursion* 7. 996
Their purer service, in this realm at least, 875 *Excursion* 8. 86
When in their land the Almighty's service ceased. 877 *Excursion* 8. 195
For prouder service were addrest ; but each, 891 *Excursion* 9. 479
Such dismal service, that the loudest voice 894 *Excursion* 9. 693
For whom like service, now and then his choice, S.3.435 **The doubt* 138
Oh ! shame ! is this thy service boastful plume ? L.I. 94 *Juvenal* 2. 18
Services. Performs these delicate services, and therefore 38 *Bord.* 51
Ill names, can render no ill services, 65 *Bord.* 1527
Join me in thanks for their blind services. 70 *Bord.* 1844
By some weak aims at services assigned 262 *Retirement* 13
Each linked to each for kindred services ; 444 *Ecc. Sonn.* 3. 17. 10
Of Love, and of his holy services ; 560 *Cuck. and Night.* 213
And came her services to proffer : 620 *Birth of Love* 34
Such hope was mine, for holy services. 633 *Prelude* 1. 54
With needless services, from hardship free. 762 *Excursion* 1. 385
Those services, whereby attempt is made 827 *Excursion* 5. 297
Servile. Sink with his servile bands, to rise no more ! 22 *Desc. Sk.* 664
Ye Gods, thought He, that servile Implement 214 *Dion* 94
Law but a servile dupe of false pretence, 280 *Plea for Auth.* 5
Wise, upright, valiant ; not a servile band, 310 **Another year* 12
Of servile opportunity to gold ; 351 *Des. Stanzas* 79
Impetuous thoughts that brook not servile reins. 382 *Duddon* 26. 14
The fond heart proffered it—the servile heart ; 434 *Ecc. Sonn.* 2. 24. 6
Said to his servile Courtiers,—" Poor the reach, 495 *Fact* 10
The servile million bow ; 628 *Installation* 10
To a servile yoke. What need of many words ? 633 *Prelude* 1. 105
And, to whole nations bound in servile straits, 870 *Excursion* 7. 825
A servile band among the lordly free ! 888 *Excursion* 9. 310
Servilely. Nor will she servilely attend 180 *Waggoner* 4. 9
Serving. A pair of diaries,—one serving, Sir, 97 *Brothers* 163
Serving at my heart's command, 160 **Pansies, lilies* 61
Serving no haughty Muse, my hands have here 280 *Valedict.* 1
Though serving sage philosophy), 341 *Ital. Itin.* 20
So fare they—the Man serving as her Slave. 366 *Lombardy* 9
To his high charge, and truly serving God, 387 *Manse* 11
And, serving Truth, the heart more strongly beats 520 *Pun. Death* 14. 6
Betray me, serving often for a cloak 635 *Prelude* 1. 244
Beheld her serving at the cottage inn ; 691 *Prelude* 7. 305
Of ancient inspiration serving me, 797 *Excursion* 3. 763
Serving as doth a spindle or a wheel ; 886 *Excursion* 9. 160
Servitude. The tidings passed of servitude repealed, 312 **When, far* 2
And instruments of deadliest servitude ! 420 *Ecc. Sonn.* 1. 8. 14
That long-lived servitude must last for ever. 515 **Hard task* 3
Led through the lanes in forlorn servitude ; 669 *Prelude* 5. 241
Though men return to servitude as fast 752 *Prelude* 14. 435

Seven—*continued.*

And, in seven days' space, will to York be led !— . 404 *White Doe* 788
Seven days she lurked in brake and field, . 542 *Russ. Fug.* 17
Seven nights her course renewed, . 542 *Russ. Fug.* 18
A little scholar, scarcely seven years old, . 553 *Prioress* 51
Orion with his belt, and those fair Seven, . 662 *Prelude* 4. 245
" Seven years of occupation undisturbed . 795 *Excursion* 3. 622
—Seven lusty Sons sate daily round the board . 867 *Excursion* 7. 636
—Those seven fair brothers variously were moved 867 *Excursion* 7. 657
These seven long years to Grenville's onion head. L.1. 89 *Juvenal* 1. 28

Sevens. Were at sixes and sevens ; . S.3. 440 **Said red-rib-boned* 3

Seventeenth. To passive minds. My seventeenth year was come ; . 647 *Prelude* 2. 386

Seventh. So shall the seventh be truly blest, . 228 *Devot. Incit.* 76
For now, till this seventh summer have ye rang'd 625 *Æneid* 142

Seventy. " I have been toiling more than seventy years, . 134 *Michael* 228
The weight of more than seventy years, . 293 *Jedbor.* 10
Of seventy years, to loftier height ; . 404 *White Doe* 742
Of noble parents : seventy years and three . 574 *Chiabrera* 4. 30
Full seventy winters hath he lived, and mark ! . 780 *Excursion* 2. 600
The still contentedness of seventy years. . 783 *Excursion* 2. 750

Seventy-two. And Matthew seventy-two. . 487 *Fountain* 4

Sever. Millions from glorious aims. Our chains to sever . 516 *Hard task 6
And of the bounds which sever it from good, . 728 *Prelude* 11. 94

Several. Those several qualities of heart and mind . 118 *Maternal Grief* 20
Two separate Creatures in their several gifts . 118 *Maternal Grief* 30
With but a step between their several homes, . 122 *V. and J.* 20
Three several hoof-marks which the hunted Beast . 201 *Hart-leap* 51
Three several pillars, each a rough-hewn stone, . 201 *Hart-leap* 67
Their several features, mingled like the sound . 271 *Where holy 7
Each kind in several beds of one parterre ; . 281 *Valedict.* 4
Was the beginning ; yet the several Lays . 394 *No more 3
While each pursues his several road. . 398 *White Doe* 161
On Love and Fear, their several powers he blends, . 518 *Pun. Death* 5. 7
The more endeared. Their several memories here 653 *Prelude* 3. 269
Each in his several melancholy walk . 669 *Prelude* 5. 239
To make this book our own. Through several months, . 672 *Prelude* 5. 473
As if in several elements, we were framed . 678 *Prelude* 6. 255
And while below, along their several beds, . 681 *Prelude* 6. 438
And with them did we journey several hours . 684 *Prelude* 6. 623
Of the spectators, and each several nook . 693 *Prelude* 7. 435
And all the several frames of things, like stars, . 706 *Prelude* 8. 481
Or several voices in one solemn sound, . 777 *Excursion* 2. 374
Fearless of winds and waves. Three several stones 787 *Excursion* 3. 55
Between their several births than served for one . 794 *Excursion* 3. 593
Two several souls alternately had lodged, . 842 *Excursion* 6. 288
Who, from the pressure of their several fates, . 844 *Excursion* 6. 406
And the LORD'S OAK—would plead their several rights . 866 *Excursion* 7. 622
Or posy, girding round the several fronts . 872 *Excursion* 7. 973
Blest in their several and their common lot ! . 888 *Excursion* 9. 258
Within the compass of their several shores . 889 *Excursion* 9. 347
Yet, in partition, with their several spheres . 890 *Excursion* 9. 450
Cased with its several beads, what myriads there K.8. 252 *Recluse* 1.1.566

Severally. Than those which they had severally sustained, . 845 *Excursion* 6. 461

Severe. Whither is fled that Power whose frown severe . 11 *Desc. Sk.* 54
Rouses the soul from her severe delight. . 16 *Desc. Sk.* 353
But, through severe mischance and cruel wrong, . 28 *Guilt* 228
The jolting road and morning air severe. . 34 *Guilt* 553
Profound his forehead was, though not severe ; . 108 *Indolence* 44
But, surely, if severe afflictions borne . 143 *High bliss 2
Know—that, for him whose waking thoughts, severe . 229 *Cuckoo-clock* 27
A look more tender than severe ; . 241 *P. B.* 437
Till checked by some necessities severe. . 251 *Appleth.* 8
That I, if frugal and severe, might stray . 259 *Calvert* 6
Yet trained to judgments righteously severe, . 326 *The Bard 2
Helvellyn's brow severe ? . 344 *Eclipse* 78
Severe research, that in our hearts we know . 359 *Those old 12
That made us) over those severe restraints . 362 **List—'twas* 43
Neither put forth that way Thy arm severe ; . 366 *Eternal Lord 11
To agitations less severe . 376 *The Minstrels 76
His Spirit, when most severe, is oft most kind ; . 518 *Pun. Death* 5. 5
Where now is fled that Power whose frown severe 603 *Desc. Sk. Quarto* 55
While flash her upward eyes severe delight. . 612 *Desc. Sk. Quarto* 555
Deep, gloomy were they, and severe ; the scatterings . 662 *Prelude* 4. 252
Of plain Imagination and severe, . 704 *Prelude* 8. 366
Thou canst put on an aspect most severe ; . 707 *Prelude* 8. 531
Of life and death, in majesty severe . 721 *Prelude* 10. 185
Retained too long a countenance severe ; . 749 *Prelude* 14. 250
Or haply by a temper too severe, . 757 *Excursion* 1. 84
In lines and numbers, and, by charm severe, . 760 *Excursion* 1. 254
Severe reproof, if we were men whose hearts . 765 *Excursion* 1. 627
That losses and vexations, less severe . 845 *Excursion* 6. 460
To impose severe restraints and laws unjust, . 852 *Excursion* 6. 955
Against all trials ; industry severe . 862 *Excursion* 7. 324
Science severe, or word of holy Writ . 864 *Excursion* 7. 451
In like removal, tranquil though severe, . 885 *Excursion* 9. 82
Provoked a retribution too severe, . S.3. 434 *The doubt 83

Severed. The grief, the praise, are severed from their dust, . 356 *Aquap.* 247
What force had severed. Thence they fetched the seed . 444 *Ecc. Sonn.* 3. 15. 6
Feel with the Mother, think the severed Wife . 476 *Howard* 11

Severed—*continued.*

The tangled root I severed, . 484 *Simon Lee* 86
It saith, Alas, why severed are we twain ? . 565 *Troilus* 161
On severed love, and only sink . 582 *O for a 17
Oh ! severed, too abruptly, from delights . 583 *With copious 26
In a small mill-race severed from his stream, . 636 *Prelude* 1. 289
The space that severed us ! But, as the sight . 795 *Excursion* 3. 661
Thus would the Votary say—' this severed hair, . 812 *Excursion* 4. 746
Such ties will not be severed : but, when we . S.3. 433 *The doubt 37

Severely. Severely honest, break no plighted trust, . 619 *School Ex.* 87

Severer. Vowed to severer discipline ; . 216 *Enterprise* 58
When thousands, by severer doom, . 473 *Ossian* 45
Severer interventions, ministry . 637 *Prelude* 1. 355

Severest. Presiding ; and severest solitude . 703 *Prelude* 8. 260
Two months unwearied of severest storm, . K.8. 241 *Recluse* 1.1.181

Severing. And of the streaks that laced the severing clouds . 123 *V. and J.* 93
" People ! your chains are severing link by link ; . 513 *Newspaper* 1
Forebode not any severing of our loves ! . 590 *Immortality* 192
Th' insuperable rocks and severing tide, . 607 *Desc. Sk. Quarto* 310
Her mandates, severing whom true love had joined, . 718 *Prelude* 9. 573
What more than that the severing should confer . 885 *Excursion* 9. 85

Severings. Domestic severings, female fortitude . 713 *Prelude* 9. 721

Severity. Untouched through all severity of cold ; . 276 *Filial Piety* 1

Severn. Then into Severn hideously defiled, . 103 *Artegal* 37
Of Severn, Severn to the narrow seas, . 432 *Ecc. Sonn.* 2. 17. 10

Severn's. When Severn's sweeping flood had overthrown . 627 **When Severn's* 1

Sex. For her sex, of every age. . 94 *Westmoreland Girl* 84
But each of manly sex, a docile page, . 624 *Æneid* 68
Of sex and age, and heaven-descended rights, . 741 *Prelude* 13. 74
Graced mutually by difference of sex, . 794 *Excursion* 3. 591
Indignantly, the weakness of her sex. . 849 *Excursion* 6. 719
And unripe sex with sex, for mutual taint ; . 879 *Excursion* 8. 340

Sexton. Wherefore, Sexton, piling still . 157 *Sexton* 2
O Sexton, do not remove her, . 157 *Sexton* 31
Him from that posture did the Sexton rouse ; . 825 *Excursion* 5. 218

Sexton's. And soon, full soon, the lonely Sexton's spade . 450 *Ecc. Sonn.* 3. 41. 8

Shade. *See Nightshade.*

He knows but from its shade the present hour. . 2 *Ev. Wk.* 32
Illumines, from within, the leafy shade ; . 3 *Ev. Wk.* 65
Come forth, and here retire in purple shade ; . 4 *Ev. Wk.* 103
Wins on the shade, the shade upon the light. . 7 *Ev. Wk.* 298
Where but a mass of shade the sight can trace, . 8 *Ev. Wk.* 333
In golden light ; half hides itself in shade : . 12 *Desc. Sk.* 98
And steals into the shade the lazy oar ; . 12 *Desc. Sk.* 104
Ye lovely maidens that in noontide shade . 13 *Desc. Sk.* 129
The still vale lengthens underneath its shade . 14 *Desc. Sk.* 217
Some amid lingering shade, some touched by the sun's rays. . 34 *Guilt* 522
And banks of ragged earth ; beneath the shade . 34 *Guilt* 539
That casts its shade over our village school, . 39 *Bord.* 91
We left the willow shade by the brook-side, . 39 *Bord.* 104
The house is hidden by the shade. Old Man, . 41 *Bord.* 219
A grove of darker and more lofty shade . 49 *Bord.* 674
I came ; and when I felt its cooling shade, . 62 *Bord.* 1358
No food was there, no drink, no grass, no shade, . 68 *Bord.* 1707
Behold, within the leafy shade, . 79 *Sparrow's Nest* 1
From shade to sunshine, and as fleet . 85 *Anecdote* 19
From sunshine back to shade. . 85 *Anecdote* 20
The pointed steeple peering forth from the centre of the shade. . 92 *Poet's Dream* 40
Retired in that sunshiny shade he lay ; . 107 *Indolence* 26
I met Louisa in the shade, . 108 *Louisa* 1
Or sit in the shade of my grandfather's tree, . 116 *Repentance* 18
Accomplished under friendly shade of night. . 123 *V. and J.* 86
Or for the summer shade. It was the first . 131 *Michael* 21
Stood single, and, from matchless depth of shade, . 133 *Michael* 166
There, while they two were sitting in the shade, . 133 *Michael* 170
I know the poisons of the shade ; . 145 *Her Eyes* 95
Of that perennial shade, a cloistral place . 150 **When, to* 11
Though entering but as Fancy's Shade. . 154 *Flower Garden* 56
Along the floor, beneath the shade . 155 *A whirl-blast 16
Beneath my shade the mother-ewe . 156 *Oak and Broom* 86
The Seven are laid, and in the shade . 161 *Binnorie* 25
(In the sun or under shade, . 171 *Kitten* 47
Lurking in a double shade, . 180 *Waggoner* 4. 44
On this side with a sober shade ; . 182 *Waggoner* 4. 241
That threaten the profane ; a pillared shade, . 185 *Yew-trees* 20
The mist and the river, the hill and the shade : . 188 *Poor Susan* 14
Shade upon the sunshine lying . 190 **Lyre ! though* 19
By such a Youth, in the green shade, . 192 *Ruth* 47
In sunshine or in shade . 193 *Ruth* 75
'Tis my delight, alone in summer shade, . 202 *Hart-leap* 99
" Now, here is neither grass nor pleasant shade ; . 203 *Hart-leap* 157
Round the dear Shade she would have clung—'tis vain : . 211 *Laod.* 152
Or under leaves of thickest shade, . 222 *Triad* 198
Resume, my Friends ! within the shade . 238 *P. B.* 183
Along the shade with footsteps true . 244 *P. B.* 673
Into a shade of darksome trees, . 248 *P. B.* 1087
This Peter sees, while in the shade . 249 *P. B.* 1116
For worthless brows, while in the pensive shade . 254 *Dyer* 8
When, haply under shade of that same wood, . 271 *Fame tells 9
Light deepening the profoundest sleep of shade. . 272 *Ruins* 8
The gentlest Shade that walked Elysian plains . 284 *Departure* 1
Youthful as Spring.—Shade of departed Power, . 290 *Kilchurn* 31
To this small spot, his leafy shade ; . 298 *Brownie's Cell* 44
And, to the patriot-warrior's Shade, . 299 *Cora Linn* 16

Shade—*continued.*
Men are we, and must grieve when even the Shade 305 *Ven. Rep.* 13
And Mina, nourished in the studious shade, 320 **They seek* 11
Of pencil ever clothed with light and shade ; 323 *Ode 1814* 7
There heard we, halting in the shade 334 **In Bruges* 5
With its grey rocks clustering in pensive shade— 335 *Namur* 12
Nor falls that intermingling shade 338 **Meek Virgin* 31
Halting beneath the chestnut shade 344 **How blest* 22
A sunbeam followed by a shade ! 348 **Lulled by* 26
—How lovely robed in forenoon light and shade, 355 *Aquap.* 205
To meet the shade of Horace by the side 356 *Aquap.* 256
Ripe for the hand, or under a thick shade 361 **List—'twas* 19
Or softly stealing into modest shade. 367 *Trajan* 18
The sun in heaven !—but now, to form a shade 377 *Duddon* 5. 5
Nor wants the holy Abbot's gliding Shade 393 *Inglewood* 9
Who sate in the shade of the Prior's Oak ! 396 *White Doe* 34
And first we sang of the greenwood shade 400 *White Doe* 338
He led her from the yew-tree shade, 402 *White Doe* 589
His last words in the yew-tree shade, 406 *White Doe* 976
Emerging from a cedar shade 407 *White Doe* 1000
To Emily in the yew-tree shade : 411 *White Doe* 1429
While she sate listening in the shade, 415 *White Doe* 1773
Permits a second and a darker shade 421 *Ecc. Sonn.* 1. 11. 4
Thy hovering Shade, O venerable Bede ! 424 *Ecc. Sonn.* 1. 23. 4
Yet many a Novice of the cloistral shade, 434 *Ecc. Sonn.* 2. 23. 1
With the least shade of thought to sin allied ; 434 *Ecc. Sonn.* 2. 25. 2
Set off her brightness with a pleasing shade. 440 *Ecc. Sonn.* 3. 1. 4
Through gloomiest shade ; put on (nor dread its weight) 446 *Ecc. Sonn.* 3. 25. 13
Where light and shade repose, where music dwells 451 *Ecc. Sonn.* 3. 43. 11
Of light with shade in beauty reconciled— 454 *Sea-side* 8
To sue the God ; but, haunting your green shade 463 **Adieu, Rydalian* 6
A tender Spirit broods—the pensive Shade 465 **The cattle* 9
To cast a soul-subduing shade on me, 470 *Bala-Sala* 6
A shade—but with some sparks of heavenly fire 470 *Bala-Sala* 8
Yon light shapes forth a Bard, that shade a Chief. 474 **Ye shadowy* 14
Within whose shade they parted. 479 *Somnamb.* 103
Or boding Shade, or if the Maid 479 *Somnamb.* 129
Where clouds that spread in solemn shade, 479 *Somnamb.* 156
Sing here beneath the shade, 487 *Fountain* 14
Could fearlessly approach the shade ? 497 *Lycoris* 8
That calls from yonder leafy shade 498 **Departing summer* 4
Forsaken " in the shade ! 507 *May* 60
Cast into that recess—the tender shade, 508 *F. Stone* 16
The shade and light, both there and everywhere, 508 *F. Stone* 17
And how he rules the pomp of light and shade ; 511 **So fair* 12
Moving along a tract of morning shade, 524 *Epist. Beaumont* 214
Under a fancied yew-tree's luckless shade ; 528 **Those breathing* 114
In pleasure, is the darkest shade 530 *Gleaner* 14
A shade upon the future cast, 533 **Blest is* 43
Loving the dewy shade,—a humble band, 539 **Lady ! a* 19
And pine-trees made a heavy shade 542 *Russ. Fug.* 95
They shrank not into shade ; 545 *Russ. Fug.* 374
Leads to the dear Parnassian forest's shade, 574 *Chiabrera* 5. 10
Urged less for this Yew's shade, though he 577 **By playful* 13
Till dipp'd his pathway in the river shade ; 592 *Ev. Wk. Quarto* 70
Illumes with sparkling foam the twilight shade. 593 *Ev. Wk. Quarto* 80
Before the boat-house peeping thro' the shade ; 593 *Ev. Wk. Quarto* 106
Breaks on the shade, the shade upon the light, 598 *Ev. Wk. Quarto* 346
Bright as the moon, half hides itself in shade. 604 *Desc.Sk.Quarto* 107
Old Roman boats and figures thro' the shade, 604 *Desc.Sk.Quarto* 117
Farewel ! those forms that, in thy noon-tide shade, 604 *Desc.Sk.Quarto* 148
The still vale lengthens underneath the shade ; 607 *Desc.Sk.Quarto* 270
Shade above shade the desert pines ascend, 607 *Desc.Sk.Quarto* 290
The grassy seat beneath their casement shade 607 *Desc.Sk.Quarto* 305
The casement shade more luscious woodbine binds, 615 *Desc.Sk.Quarto* 726
To break the quiet of the village shade 615 *Desc.Sk.Quarto* 745
With breathing flowers embraced, and fragrant shade. 624 *Æneid* 52
Shade of Caractacus, if spirits love 627 *Eagle and Dove* 1
That he might wake to clasp thee in the shade : 630 [?] **O Moon* 13
How, when the Sea threw off his evening shade 640 *Prelude* 1. 569
We rested in the shade, all pleased alike, 643 *Prelude* 2. 68
Proud of its own bright fire and sycamore shade. 644 *Prelude* 2. 148
And what the summer shade, what day and night, 647 *Prelude* 2. 354
I laughed with Chaucer in the hawthorn shade ; 653 *Prelude* 3. 276
So near that, slipping back into the shade 664 *Prelude* 4. 389
Sit in the shade together, while they gaze, 699 *Prelude* 8. 47
Of Arden—amid sunshine or in shade 701 *Prelude* 8. 139
With length of shade so thick, that whoso glides 706 *Prelude* 8. 460
As in a cloister. Once—while, in that shade 706 *Prelude* 8. 462
Or in wide forests of continuous shade, 716 *Prelude* 9. 434
Lived in the shade ; and to Harmodius known 721 *Prelude* 10. 198
A twilight of its own, an ample shade, 756 *Excursion* 1. 12
Under a shade as grateful I should find 756 *Excursion* 1. 19
Recumbent in the shade, as if asleep ; 756 *Excursion* 1. 36
Of my approaching steps, and in the shade 762 *Excursion* 1. 442
Withdrawing, straightway to the shade returned 763 *Excursion* 1. 464
I rose ; and, having left the breezy shade, 765 *Excursion* 1. 620
In sunshine and in shade, in wet and fair, 766 *Excursion* 1. 700
I found that she was absent. In the shade, 767 *Excursion* 1. 711
The shade, and look abroad. On this old bench 769 *Excursion* 1. 879
Upon those silent walls, we left the shade ; 771 *Excursion* 1. 968
The shade of discontent which on his brow 786 *Excursion* 3. 12
Where arbours of impenetrable shade, 794 *Excursion* 3. 546
I worshipped thee, and find thee but a Shade !' 797 *Excursion* 3. 777
Roaming, or resting under grateful shade 819 *Excursion* 4. 1202
Impenetrable shade ; once more farewell, 822 *Excursion* 5. 8

Shade—*continued.*
All withered by the depth of shade above. 824 *Excursion* 5. 149
Where sun and shade were intermixed ; for there 825 *Excursion* 5. 226
That spreads, in gentle pomp, its honied shade. 829 *Excursion* 5. 461
And gathering all within their tender shade, 836 *Excursion* 5. 926
And not a flower, that droops in the green shade, 842 *Excursion* 6. 297
To the deep shade of those untravelled Wilds ; 845 *Excursion* 6. 455
And flowers that prosper in the shade. And when 848 *Excursion* 6. 654
Beneath the shade we all sate down ; and there 850 *Excursion* 6. 785
Oread or Dryad glancing through the shade 850 *Excursion* 6. 829
Stern self-denial round him spread, with shade 862 *Excursion* 7. 326
But that the minstrel of the rural shade 863 *Excursion* 7. 370
Within its shade, as in a stately tent 866 *Excursion* 7. 617
Yet, like the sweet-breathed violet of the shade, 868 *Excursion* 7. 731
Stretched on the grass, or seated in the shade, 869 *Excursion* 7. 783
Raised from his seat within the chosen shade, 870 *Excursion* 7. 818
Cherished in shade though peeped at by the sun ; S.3. 437 **The doubt* 202
Let not " Willy's " holy shade L.2. 190 **Queen and* 7

Shaded. *See* **Laurel-shaded.**
I saw, espied its shaded mouth ; 169 *Wren's Nest* 55
No bonnet shaded, but she wore 190 *Beggars* 3
With palm-groves shaded at wide intervals, 444 *Ecc. Sonn.* 3. 17. 6
This shaded valley leaves ; and leaves the dark 807 *Excursion* 4. 399
Part shaded by cool sycamore, and part 850 *Excursion* 6. 780
(Yon cottage shaded by the woody crags) 864 *Excursion* 7. 467

Shadeless. And eyes through tears the mountain's shadeless height ; 596 *Ev. Wk. Quarto* 252
Shadeless and shelterless, by driving showers 859 *Excursion* 7. 143

Shades. *See* **Mountain-shades.**
And shades of deep-embattled clouds were seen, 3 *Ev. Wk.* 39
'Cross the calm lake's blue shades the cliffs aspire, 5 *Ev. Wk.* 174
Where leafy shades fence off the blustering gale, 6 *Ev. Wk.* 234
And start the astonished shades at female eyes. 11 *Desc. Sk.* 66
—To towns, whose shades of no rude noise complain, 12 *Desc. Sk.* 81
Freshening the wilderness with shades and springs. 13 *Desc. Sk.* 172
'Mid lawns and shades by breezy rivulets fanned, 21 *Desc. Sk.* 576
And, while shades to shades succeeding 90 *Longest Day* 25
" O ! what a weight is in these shades ! Ye leaves, 111 **'Tis said that some* 21
Rouse him : but in those solitary shades 126 *V. and J.* 305
Then, dearest Maiden, move along these shades 186 *Nutting* 54
Of shades, and dews, and silent night ; 186 **O Nightingale* 8
And from the infernal Gods, 'mid shades forlorn 209 *Laod.* 3
Our blest re-union in the shades below. 211 *Laod.* 142
Your once sweet memory, studious walks and shades ! 213 *Dion* 45
While to these shades a sister Nymph I call. 221 *Triad* 88
Among the lovely shades of things ; 237 *P. B.* 102
The shades of palaces and kings ! 237 *P. B.* 105
When twilight shades darken the mountain's head. 255 *S. H.* 6
Dark and more dark the shades of evening fell ; 262 **Dark and* 1
Dim shades—for reliques, upon Lethe's shore, 264 **Lady ! I* 7
Or muse in solemn grove whose shades protect 270 **Though the bold* 5
Through twilight shades of good and ill 286 *Sons of Burns* 7
From shades, her chosen place of short-lived rest. 311 **Who rises* 38
While the Sun rules, and cross the shades of night— 327 *Ode 1815* 32
Yet all is harmless—as the Elysian shades 349 *Sky-prosp.* 9
For them who in the shades of sorrow dwell, 354 *Aquap.* 90
And now, ye Miltonian shades ! under you 364 *Vallomb.* 29
Not envying Latian shades—if yet they throw 376 *Duddon* 1. 1
With lawns and beds of flowers, and shades 407 *White Doe* 985
Soft shades and dews have shed their blended power 456 **The leaves* 4
And night approaches with her shades. 458 **Had this* 80
And penetrates the forest's inmost shades ; 459 **Wanderer ! that* 26
Alternate empire in the shades below— 460 **Queen of* 5
While she dispels the cumbrous shades of Night ; 477 *Long Meg* 9
To heights more glorious still, and into shades 496 **A little* 53
And moss-grown alleys, circumscribing shades, 497 **Enough of climbing* 14
Fit for the shades of heroes, mingling there 501 *Humanity* 75
Shades of past bliss, or phantoms that, to gain 533 **Once I* 35
Shades of the Past, oft noticed with a sigh, 584 **With copious* 51
Shades of the prison-house begin to close 588 *Immortality* 67
Gazing the tempting shades to them deny'd, 592 *Ev. Wk. Quarto* 57
And with long rays and shades the landscape shines ; 593 *Ev. Wk. Quarto* 98
Whose shades protect the hidden wave serene ; 595 *Ev. Wk. Quarto* 222
Than waters dashing wild, or rocking shades. 596 *Ev. Wk. Quarto* 238
Checquer with paler red the thicket shades. 599 *Ev. Wk. Quarto* 398
And bidding paler shades her form conceal, 603 *Desc.Sk.Quarto* 77
To towns, whose shades of no rude sound complain, 603 *Desc.Sk.Quarto* 84
Freshening the waste of sand with shades and springs. 605 *Desc.Sk.Quarto* 198
Here lawns and shades by breezy rivulets fann'd, 614 *Desc.Sk.Quarto* 686
Erroneous wavering mid the twilight shades. 614 *Desc.Sk.Quarto* 689
And fled indignant to the shades of night ; 618 *School Ex.* 30
The shades of night no more the soul involve, 618 *School Ex.* 47
She sheds her beam, and, lo ! the shades dissolve ; 618 *School Ex.* 48
Thy shades, thy silence, now be mine, 626 †*Cento* 9
Through shades that solemnize Life's calm decline, 627 **The star* 5
And, from his alder shades and rocky falls, 636 *Prelude* 1. 272
Hath beautified that flower ; already shades 646 *Prelude* 2. 248
Where, though the shades with cheerfulness were filled, 655 *Prelude* 3. 431
Of poesy, affecting private shades 660 *Prelude* 4. 104
Inviting shades of opportune recess, 676 *Prelude* 6. 74
Will chant together." Thereafter, as the shades 687 *Prelude* 7. 31
Such conversation, under Attic shades, 715 *Prelude* 9. 408
Rouse him ; but, hidden in those gloomy shades, 718 *Prelude* 9. 584
Into communion with her sylvan shades, 721 *Prelude* 10. 243
Oh ! wrap him in your shades, ye giant woods, 733 *Prelude* 11. 418
To interpose the covert of your shades, 734 *Prelude* 12. 25

Shades—*continued.*
And roaring waters, and in lights and shades . . 735 *Prelude* 12. 96
From me, those dark impervious shades, that hang 790 *Excursion* 3. 296
Whose shades have never felt the encroaching axe, 799 *Excursion* 3. 916
In creeping sadness, through oblivious shades . 818 *Excursion* 4. 1124
Through shades and silent rest, to endless joy." . 837 *Excursion* 5. 1016
"Behold the shades of afternoon have fallen . . 890 *Excursion* 9. 419

Shadiest. Vallombrosa! I longed in thy shadiest wood 345 *Stanzas: Simplon* 1
"Vallombrosa—I longed in thy shadiest wood . 364 *Vallomb.* 1

Shadings. Whatever shadings of mortality, . . . 662 *Prelude* 4. 248

Shadow. *See* **Hill-shadow.**
Scarce hides a shadow from her searching rays; . 9 *Ev. Wk.* 358
Whose very shadow gnaws us to the vitals. . . 65 *Bord.* 1567
A shadow of myself—made by myself. . . . 73 *Bord.* 2039
A shadow in a hated land, while all . . . . 105 *Artegal* 184
A shadow, never, never to be displaced . . . 118 *Maternal Grief* 5
And, like a shadow, glided out of view. . . . 126 *V. and J.* 297
The shadow of a Danish Boy. . . . . . . 165 *Danish Boy* 11
So feebly spread that not a shadow falls, . . . 184 *Night-piece* 6
And Time the Shadow;—there to celebrate, . . 185 *Yew-trees* 28
The shadow of a babe you trace, ... 200 *Thorn* 216
"No Spectre greets me,—no vain Shadow this; . 210 *Laod.* 61
Beneath the shadow of his purple wings . . . 226 *Vernal Ode* 21
We were not mocked with glimpse and shadow then, 228 *Vernal Ode* 133
Couched in the shadow of Mænalian pines, . . 234 *Power of Sound* 146
The meagre shadow that looks on— . . . . 243 *P. B.* 586
Ward of the Law!—dread Shadow of a King! . 271 *George: Death* 1
Or gambol—each with his shadow at his side, . 278 **Life with* 7
Float double, swan and shadow! . . . . . 293 *Yarrow Unv.* 44
Without a shadow of mischance, ... 296 *Highland Boy* 94
The shadow and the song. . . . . 334 **In Bruges* 12
Fling the shadow of thy power, ... 336 **Jesu! bless* 15
Still moonshine, without shadow, spread . . . 343 *Eclipse* 27
In the Tower's shadow, of decline and fall . . 355 *Aquap.* 180
Under the shadow of a stately Pile, ... 365 **Under the* 1
No zephyr breathes, no cloud its shadow throws: 382 *Duddon* 24. 2
Flung from yon cliff a shadow large and cold. . 383 *Duddon* 27. 4
Now doth a delicate shadow fall, ... 397 *White Doe* 87
"'A shadow of such thought remains . . . . 410 *White Doe* 1280
The shadow—and the peace supreme! . . . 457 **Had this* 20
By its shadow round him thrown; . . . . . 502 **Like a* 32
But for the shadow by the drooping chin . . . 508 *F. Stone* 15
The beauty of its star-shaped shadow, thrown . 511 **So fair* 5
While musing here I sit in shadow cool, . . . 527 **Those breathing* 41
The Daisy, by the shadow that it casts, . . . 538 **Small service* 3
There, under shadow of the neighbouring rocks, . 547 **Beneath yon* 11
Such is life; and death a shadow . . . . 550 *Hermit's Cell* 3. 7
That flings his shadow on the pictur'd deep. . . 594 *Ev. Wk. Quarto* 156
On his smooth breast the shadow of those towers 636 *Prelude* 1. 283
A random choice, could shadow forth a place . . 654 *Prelude* 3. 371
The shadow from the substance, rocks and sky, . 662 *Prelude* 4. 264
His shadow lay, and moved not. From self-blame 664 *Prelude* 4. 408
A shadow, a delusion, ye who pore . . . . 703 *Prelude* 8. 296
Substance and shadow, light and darkness, all . 707 *Prelude* 8. 568
His shadow stretching towards Syracuse, . . . 732 *Prelude* 11. 378
—Beyond the limits of the shadow cast . . . 773 *Excursion* 2. 126
He was all fire: no shadow on his brow . . . 779 *Excursion* 2. 516
So moved he like a shadow that performed . . 783 *Excursion* 2. 772
Glorious! because the shadow of thy might, . . 803 *Excursion* 4. 101
The shadow falls to note the stealthy hours, . . 846 *Excursion* 6. 511
For, like a shadow, he was passed away . . . 853 *Excursion* 6. 1010
And her obsequious shadow, peace of mind, . . 855 *Excursion* 6. 1090
In one blest moment. Like a shadow thrown . 861 *Excursion* 7. 283
Of that tall pine, the shadow of whose bare . . 863 *Excursion* 7. 396
A type and shadow of an awful truth; . . . 865 *Excursion* 7. 527
Shadow and substance kissing point to point . . S.3. 434 **The doubt* 71
Darkened beneath the shadow of her thoughts . S.3. 436 **The doubt* 182

Shadow-casting. The shadow-casting race of trees survive: . . . . 227 *Vernal Ode* 63

Shadowed. Boldly assembled,—here is shadowed forth . . . . 707 *Prelude* 8. 582
Had Nature shadowed there, by putting forth, . 747 *Prelude* 14. 79
Have condescendingly been shadowed forth . . 811 *Excursion* 4. 644

Shadowing. *See* **Forth-shadowing.**
The Church, by mandate shadowing forth the power . . . . 427 *Ecc. Sonn.* 1. 36. 2

Shadows. *See* **Horsemen-shadows.**
Now, while the solemn evening shadows sail, . . 6 *Ev. Wk.* 212
And round the west's proud lodge their shadows throw, ... 7 *Ev. Wk.* 290
And o'er the whitened wave their shadows fling— 12 *Desc. Sk.* 86
And when a gathering weight of shadows brown . 19 *Desc. Sk.* 470
I did believe all things were shadows—yea, . . 59 *Bord.* 1214
The very shadows of the clouds . . . . 117 *Affl. Marg.* 66
Sending sad shadows after things not sad, . . . 153 *Morn. Ex.* 3
Shadows and sunny glimmerings, ... 159 *Green Linnet* 31
But neither veil thy head in shadows dim, . . . 215 *Enterprise* 10
Lo! the clouds, the solemn shadows, ... 217 **Inmate of* 11
A face o'er which a thousand shadows go! . . 221 *Triad* 131
Ye Voices, and ye Shadows . . . . 233 *Power of Sound* 33
He paused—for shadows of strange shape, . . . 240 *P. B.* 356
Entanglings of the brain; though shadows stretch 280 **Oh what* 3
What could they gain but shadows of redress? . 330 *Ode: Thanks.* 120
A way with shadows overspread; . . . . . 344 **How blest* 67
If, *then*, some natural shadows spread . . . . 386 *Yarrow Rev.* 37
Of Time and shadows of Tradition crost; . . . 419 *Ecc. Sonn.* 1. 5. 5
Union that shadows forth and doth partake . . 447 *Ecc. Sonn.* 3. 26. 11
From out the pensive shadows where they lie) . 498 **Enough of climbing* 48
With shadows flung from leaves—to strive . . 499 **This Lawn* 2
They are in truth the Substance, we the Shadows." 510 *F. Stone* 117

Shadows—*continued.*
To cast their shadows on our mother Earth . . 538 **In desultory* 28
Fleet as the shadows, over down or field, . . . 540 **Lady! a* 74
Of horsemen shadows winding to and fro; . . . 595 *Ev.Wk. Quarto* 184
So vanish those fair Shadows, human joys, . . 598 *Ev.Wk. Quarto* 361
Grew dark with all the shadows on its breast, . 672 *Prelude* 5. 440
Whose evening shadows lead him to repose. . . 682 *Prelude* 6. 516
A surface dappled o'er with shadows flung . . 756 *Excursion* 1. 5
From brooding clouds; shadows that lay in spots 756 *Excursion* 1. 6
The shadows of the breezy elms above . . . 762 *Excursion* 1. 440
Even at her threshold. Deeper shadows fell . . 767 *Excursion* 1. 748
The mist, the shadows, light of golden suns, . . 782 *Excursion* 2. 713
Gliding apace, with shadows in their train, . . 814 *Excursion* 4. 874
With ample shadows, seemingly, no less . . 821 *Excursion* 4. 1304
Among so many shadows, are the pains . . . 829 *Excursion* 5. 476
We met, and passed, like shadows. I have heard, 839 *Excursion* 6. 107
While the dark shadows of the summer leaves . 860 *Excursion* 7. 202
Of sunbeams, shadows, butterflies and birds, . . K.8. 237 *Recluse* 1.1.32
Shadows or breezes, scents or sounds. Nor deem K.8. 249 *Recluse* 1.1.448

Shadowy. Now shows a shadowy speck, and now is lost entire. . . . . 4 *Ev. Wk.* 113
A pregnant dream, within whose shadowy bounds 167 *Pilgrim's Dream* 19
For shadowy quietness. . . . . 168 *Wren's Nest* 16
Vanish inverted hill, and shadowy wood, . . . 212 *Dion*
Fetched from the shadowy world. . . . . . 225 *Present.* 60
Green, sable, shining yellow, shadowy brown, . 231 **The gentlest Poet* 18
The shadowy forms of mountains bare, . . . 237 *P. B.* 103
At thy meek bidding, shadowy Power! brought forth; 265 **Hail, Twilight* 11
Glimmers with fading light, and shadowy Eve 269 *Gordale* 2
Yon trophied Mound shrinks to a shadowy speck 278 *Wellington* 8
Or thrid the shadowy gloom, ... 300 *Cora Linn* 39
A tender sense of shadowy fear, ... 338 **Meek Virgin* 29
This spot—his shadowy death-cup in his hand. . 361 **For action* 14
Amid the sunny, shadowy, Colosseum; . . . 367 **If with* 11
To memory's shadowy moonshine! . . . . 386 *Yarrow Rev.* 112
And when thy beauty in the shadowy cave . . 460 **Wanderer! that* 63
From the close confines of a shadowy vale. . . 460 **Queen of* 9
Ye shadowy Beings, that have rights and claims . 473 **Ye shadowy* 1
From shadowy fountains of the Infinite, . . . 476 **Tranquillity! the* 11
A shadowy link 'tween wakefulness and sleep, . 524 *Epist. Beaumont* 184
Those shadowy recollections, ... 589 *Immortality* 153
—'Mid the dark steeps repose the shadowy streams, 598 *Ev. Wk. Quarto* 339
Those shadowy breasts in love's soft light array'd, 604 *Desc.Sk.Quarto* 154
No shadowy forms entice the soul aside, . . . 619 *School Ex.* 51
And all the shadowy banks on either side . . . 639 *Prelude* 1. 454
Over the shadowy lake, and to the beach . . . 644 *Prelude* 2. 166
Of shadowy exultation: not for this, ... 646 *Prelude* 2. 313
Of shadowy things work endless changes,—there, 674 *Prelude* 5. 599
Between the portals of the shadowy rocks . . 681 *Prelude* 6. 452
For I must tread on shadowy ground, must sink . 755 *Recluse* 1. 1. 781
Some shadowy intimations haunt me here, . . 787 *Excursion* 3. 88
Sends inspiration from the shadowy heights, . . 818 *Excursion* 4. 1171
Amid the groves, under the shadowy hills, . . 846 *Excursion* 6. 553
When, in the hollow of some shadowy vale, . . 857 *Excursion* 7. 5
Shadowy, yet gay and lightsome as it stood . . 881 *Excursion* 8. 463
Beneath him, showed his shadowy counterpart. . 890 *Excursion* 9. 446
The shadowy vale, the sunny mountain-top; . . 895 *Excursion* 9. 745
In mute composure, o'er the shadowy lake, . . 895 *Excursion* 9. 758
The bright array of shadowy thoughts from times K.8. 253 *Recluse* 1.1.627

Shady. Save where, along the shady western marge, 4 *Ev. Wk.* 126
When with her infants, from some shady seat . 7 *Ev. Wk.* 252
The shady porch ne'er offered a cool seat . . . 15 *Desc. Sk.* 244
Right towards the lamb she looked; and from a shady place . . . . 87 *Pet-lamb* 17
Shady as night, and beautiful as heaven, . . . 123 *V. and J.* 109
Begun and ended, in the shady grove, . . . 150 **When, to* 57
Some, inmates lodged in shady nests, ... 154 *Flower Garden* 38
Halting beneath a shady tree, ... 167 *Pilgrim's Dream* 10
Beneath the shady tree. . . . . 168 *Pilgrim's Dream* 72
That, fleeced with moss, under the shady trees, . 185 *Nutting* 36
And merciless ravage: and the shady nook . . 185 *Nutting* 45
Leave to the nightingale her shady wood; . . 209 **Ethereal minstrel* 7
Pours forth in shady groves, shall plead for me; . 217 *Enterprise* 146
To be descried through shady groves. . . . . 222 *Triad* 190
Across a shady lane; his chest . . . . . . 247 *P. B.* 983
Ere they were lost within the shady wood; . . 252 *Picture* 6
The cowslip-bank and shady willow-tree; . . . 254 *Complete Angler* 12
The clouds, or night-bird sang from shady bough; 270 **Shame on* 5
With shady night. Soft airs, from shrub and flower, ... 271 **Where holy* 9
Beneath some shady palm of Galilee. . . . . 274 *Infant M.* 14
Of travellers in some shady haunt, ... 289 *Sol. Reap.* 11
If never more within their shady round . . . 319 *Guernica* 11
In shady places, to proclaim . . . . . . 348 **Lulled by* 59
To shady rest withdrawing or withdrawn . . . 360 **Long has* 4
He rested 'mid an arbour green and shady, . . 373 *Eg. Maid* 302
To live and die in a shady bower, ... 414 *White Doe* 1637
Where shady hamlet, town that breathes . . . 533 **Blest is* 5
Adorned, and shady boughs. . . . . . . 543 *Russ. Fug.* 104
To a green shady place, where down I sate . . 633 *Prelude* 1. 62
Or shady fountain's, while among the leaves . . 643 *Prelude* 2. 91
I left the shady nook where I had stood . . . 664 *Prelude* 4. 411
Of eglantine, and through the shady woods, . . 678 *Prelude* 6. 232
Of pleasure sprinkled over, shady dells . . . 700 *Prelude* 8. 85
The shady forest of its green attire,— . . . 790 *Excursion* 3. 309
And shady groves in studied contrast—each, . . 810 *Excursion* 4. 591
By these obstructions, 'round the shady stones . 835 *Excursion* 5. 871
Under those shady elms, from him I heard . . 854 *Excursion* 6. 1058

Shady—*continued.*
That little shady spot, that sylvan tuft, 858 *Excursion* 7. 50
Seen, from the shady room in which we sate, 882 *Excursion* 8. 536
That, disentangled from the shady boughs 891 *Excursion* 9. 492
Shaft. But smiles—the hesitating shaft to free; 339 *Tell* 25
Historic figures round the shaft embost 367 *Trajan* 13
Was pierced by whizzing shaft of hunter keen! 376 *Duddon* 2. 14
Whose monstrous riches threatened. So the shaft 432 *Ecc. Sonn.* 2. 16. 4
That never fowler's gun, nor shaft 543 *Russ. Fug.* 107
And hence, this upright shaft of unhewn stone, 788 *Excursion* 3. 128
Shafts. For you, on these unfinished shafts to try 335 *Cologne* 9
The lucid shafts of reason to employ, 436 *Ecc. Sonn.* 2. 31. 13
Shagged. Half grey, half shagged with ivy to its ridge; 3 *Ev. Wk.* 69
Shagged with wild pale green tufts of fragrant hay, S.3. 417 **Sweet was* 3
Shaggy. Dim from the twilight water's shaggy side, 12 *Desc. Sk.* 116
Lo, where she sits beneath yon shaggy rock, 13 *Desc. Sk.* 177
With ready heels his shaggy side; 241 *P. B.* 399
From year to year this shaggy Mortal went 299 *Brownie's Cell* 51
Where stalked the huge deer to his shaggy lair 376 *Duddon* 2. 11
Like a gaunt shaggy Porter forced to wait 523 *Epist. Beaumont* 152
As shaggy as were wall and roof 543 *Russ. Fug.* 141
Shaggy and grey, had meanings which it brought 762 *Excursion* 1. 429
From depth of shaggy covert peeping forth 814 *Excursion* 4. 881
Under whose shaggy canopy are set 880 *Excursion* 8. 408
Shaggy and bold, and wreathèd horns superb, 890 *Excursion* 9. 444
To shaggy steeps on which the careless goat 892 *Excursion* 9. 564
Shake. Why, this is noble! shake her off at once. 41 *Bord.* 248
Is left me still in thee. Nay, shake not so. 75 *Bord.* 2135
Or shake his high desert. 105 *Artegal* 231
Have power to shake me as they pass: 117 *Affl. Marg.* 67
The waters of the pond to shake, 199 *Thorn* 195
His staring bones all shake with joy, 242 *P. B.* 561
Bright shines the Sun—and not a breeze to shake 332 *Ode: Thanks.* 209
Haughtily shake, a dreaming Conqueror!— 349 *Boulogne* 8
England's first Martyr, whom no threats could shake; 420 *Ecc. Sonn.* 1. 6. 10
Oh then how her old bones would shake! 536 *Goody Blake* 42
Those trumpet-tones of harmony that shake 668 *Prelude* 5. 205
A punctual visitant, to shake this man, 712 *Prelude* 9. 156
To shake; but only to bind up and seal; 795 *Excursion* 3. 656
To shake the burthen off? Ah! there was felt, 849 *Excursion* 6. 718
Shaken. *See* **Palsy-shaken, Self-shaken.**
To light him shaken by his rugged way. 11 *Desc. Sk.* 34
Is shaken till the dregs float on the surface; 58 *Bord.* 1163
Ere shaken by that mood of stern disdain 227 *Vernal Ode* 123
Is it a reed that's shaken by the wind, 303 **Is it* 1
Of tortured hope and purpose shaken! 371 *Eg. Maid* 134
"To look on tempests, and be never shaken;" 461 **Queen of* 50
To light him shaken by his viewless way. 602 *Desc.Sk.Quarto* 36
Come fast upon me: it is shaken off, 632 *Prelude* 1. 20
Shaken by arms of mighty bone, in strength, 744 *Prelude* 13. 325
By a fierce tempest shaken, soon resumed 840 *Excursion* 6. 145
Shakes. Where with loud voice the power of water shakes 10 *Desc. Sk.* 7
Her shameless timbrel shakes on Como's marge, 13 *Desc. Sk.* 139
There is a palsy in his limbs—he shakes. 49 *Bord.* 673
He shakes the green bough in his hand. 126 *Idiot Boy* 51
He shrugs his shoulders, shakes his head, 174 *Waggoner* 1. 66
But the foundation of our nature shakes, 330 *Ode: Thanks.* 101
Shakes off that pearly shower. 506 **While from* 8
Shakes her numb arm that slumbers with its weight, 596 *Ev. Wk. Quarto* 251
Where rocks and groves the power of waters shakes 602 *Desc.Sk.Quarto* 11
Her shameless timbrel shakes along thy marge, 605 *Desc.Sk.Quarto* 160
Shakes from behind the clouds his flashing shield. 608 *Desc.Sk.Quarto* 337
The Tinker shakes his head, S.3. 424 *Tinker* 43
Shakespeare.
Shakspeare unlocked his heart; the melody 260 **Scorn not* 3
That Shakspeare spake; the faith and morals hold 307 **It is not* 12
And Shakspeare at his side—a freight, 341 *Ital. Itin.* 14
Shakespeare, or Milton, labourers divine! 668 *Prelude* 5. 165
Boyle, Shakspeare, Newton, or the attractive head 689 *Prelude* 7. 166
The Death of Abel, Shakspeare, and the Bard 695 *Prelude* 7. 564
Shakespeare's. From earth, perhaps by Shakespeare's self approved, 546 **The embowering* 20
More than theatric force to Shakspeare's scene;— 583 **With copious* 33
When, having closed the mighty Shakspeare's page, 694 *Prelude* 7. 484
Entered, with Shakspeare's genius, the wild woods 701 *Prelude* 8. 138
Shaking. *See* **Hand-shaking.**
But the winds roar, shaking the rooted trees, 230 *Clouds* 41
Shaking the dust and ashes from her head! 331 *Ode: Thanks.* 130
Such shaking doth the fever in me keep 557 *Cuck. and Night.* 41
Is shaking to the roots: indifference this 711 *Prelude* 9. 91
And, with a resolute mastery shaking off 730 *Prelude* 11. 238
Shakspeare. *See* **Shakespeare.**
Shakspeare's. *See* **Shakespeare's.**
Shall. (*Partial list.*)
I shall be with them in two days at farthest. 38 *Bord.* 42
There cannot come a day when I shall cease 39 *Bord.* 88
You seem worn out with travel—shall I support you? 41 *Bord.* 220
We soon shall meet again. If thou neglect 42 *Bord.* 303
Shall give me half. What's this?—I fear, good Woman, 46 *Bord.* 489
I must have more of this;—you shall not stir 46 *Bord.* 496
These walls shall witness it—from first to last 48 *Bord.* 594
He shall reveal himself. Happy are we, 48 *Bord.* 595
The truth shall be laid open, his guilt proved 48 *Bord.* 600
A few leagues hence we shall have open ground, 49 *Bord.* 655
For once you loved me. You shall back with me 50 *Bord.* 694

Shall—*continued.*
Shall it be law to stab the petty robber 53 *Bord.* 894
We'll lead him to the Convent. He shall live, 54 *Bord.* 904
And she shall love him. With unquestioned title 54 *Bord.* 905
He shall be seated in his Barony, 54 *Bord.* 906
Henceforth it shall be said that bad men only 54 *Bord.* 910
That wretched life of thine shall be the forfeit. 54 *Bord.* 950
He shall be led, and there, the Country round 58 *Bord.* 1121
I thank you for that hint. He shall be brought 58 *Bord.* 1125
It shall be done as Wisdom shall decide: 58 *Bord.* 1129
In some a hideous one—hem! shall I stop? 58 *Bord.* 1170
Shall feign a sudden illness, and the Girl, 59 *Bord.* 1185
—Yet seek him,—and what shall you find in the place? 80 †*Address: Child* 16
A yearning survives which few hearts shall withstand: 345 *Stanzas: Simplon* 28
Guide thou my song which I of thee shall say. 553 *Prioress* 35
Although I for my Primer shall be shent, 554 *Prioress* 90
And shall be beaten three times in an hour, 554 *Prioress* 91
'Is it an honest thing? Shall this be so? 554 *Prioress* 110
That such a Boy where'er he lists shall go 554 *Prioress* 111
Who will do evil, evil shall he bear; 555 *Prioress* 181
Yet if I live it shall amended be, 561 *Cuck.andNight.*234
Nay, nothing shall me bring thereto, quoth I, 561 *Cuck.andNight.*239
A summons to the Cuckoo shall be sent, 562 *Cuck.andNight.*278
Failing, we finally shall make accord. 562 *Cuck.andNight.*280
And all this shall be done, without a nay, 562 *Cuck.andNight.*281
"For term of life Love shall have hold of me"— 562 *Cuck.andNight.*289
I shall be glad if all the world be true. 564 *Troilus* 133
And live as long as its pure stream shall flow. 574 *Chiabrera* 5. 23
Yet haply Arno shall be spared all cause 575 *Chiabrera* 6. 13
Shallop. Was seated in her gleaming shallop, 371 *Eg. Maid* 116
And in the pearly shallop placed, 371 *Eg. Maid* 143
Shallow. A fence far stretched into the shallow lake, 3 *Ev. Wk.* 42
A shallow project;—you of late have seen 65 *Bord.* 1574
Here, in safe covert, on the shallow snow, 150 **When, to* 13
And each day's shallow grief; 224 **'Tis gone* 39
Furrowing its shallow way with dubious will; 251 **There is a little* 5
Whate'er to shallow Faith their ways unfold, 280 **Oh what* 11
To sight so shallow, with a bather's glee, 469 **A youth* 3
Long rails into the shallow lake extend; 592 *Ev. Wk. Quarto* 60
Her clear though shallow stream of piety 661 *Prelude* 4. 225
In loose procession through the shallow stream 726 *Prelude* 10. 566
True as the stock-dove to her shallow nest 833 *Excursion* 5. 707
Shallows. And from his fords and shallows, sent a voice 636 *Prelude* 1. 273
Shalt. (*Partial list.*)
Shalt show us how divine a thing 218 *Young Lady* 11
Shalt change thy temper; and, with many a shock 381 *Duddon* 20. 11
Then shalt thou raise a clamour as do I. 560 *Cuck.andNight.*185
Shame. That either e'er existed is my shame: 47 *Bord.* 555
To cover him from punishment? Shame!—Justice, 57 *Bord.* 1088
False Shame discarded, spurious Fame despised, 70 *Bord.* 1834
Shame! Eldred, shame! The dead have but one face. 75 *Bord.* 2162
He blushed with shame, nor made reply; 86 *Anecdote* 46
And govern to my shame; 105 *Artegal* 183
—"Shame on me, Sir! this lusty Lamb, 115 *Last of Flock* 17
The threatened shame, the parents of the Maid 122 *V. and J.* 69
To evil courses: ignominy and shame 138 *Michael* 445
Sad deliverance would it be, and yoked with shame, 140 *Arm. Lady* 29
Knowing what cause there is for shame, 181 *Waggoner* 4. 88
A boaster that, when he is tried, fails, and is put to shame? 189 *Star-gazers* 10
Whose just reward is shame. 223 *Wishing-gate* 42
Retire in fear of shame; 225 *Present.* 3
"Shame on you!" cried my little Boat, 237 *P. B.* 76
I stood, of simple shame the blushing Thrall; 251 **Beloved Vale* 10
Shame on this faithless heart! that could allow 270 **Shame on* 1
For natural rights, a mockery and a shame; 280 *Plea for Auth.* 4
Hath sounded (shame upon the Bard!) thy praise 281 **Wansfell! this* 6
Now, for your shame, a Power, the Thirst of Gold, 283 **Proud were* 4
Of the dead bodies.—'Twas a day of shame 293 *Killicranky* 8
How loud! yet lived in peace with shame. 299 *Brownie's Cell* 50
Defeating, put the Monks to shame, 301 *Bran* 69
Shame on you, feeble Heads, to slavery prone! 303 **Is it* 14
Shame followed shame, and woe supplanted woe— 311 **Who rises* 39
—Woe to them all! but heaviest woe and shame 313 *Prophecy* 11
Else how, when mighty Thrones were put to shame, 316 **It was a* 2
And guilt and shame, from which is no defence, 319 *Biscayan* 13
And Christendom respires; from guilt and shame 326 *Sobieski* 8
And, with the guilt, the shame is fled; 330 *Ode: Thanks.* 128
And, with the guilt and shame, the Woe hath vanished, 330 *Ode: Thanks.* 129
And filled our hearts with grief for England's shame? 349 *Val. Dover* 4
Now all is sun-bright peace. Of that day's shame, 361 **When here* 5
Part from thee without pity dyed in shame: 366 **Fair Land* 3
"Shame! should a Child of royal line 370 *Eg. Maid* 91
Recovers not his loss; but walks with shame, 383 *Duddon* 30. 3
Must Westmoreland be asked with shame 405 *White Doe* 826
A spot of shame to the sun's bright eye, 405 *White Doe* 851
But marks of infamy and shame— 409 *White Doe* 1225
Temple and Altar sink, to hide their shame 423 *Ecc. Sonn.* 1. 17. 9
And cumbrous wealth—the shame of your estate; 433 *Ecc. Sonn.* 2. 18. 2
Her blessings cursed—her glory turned to shame! 439 *Ecc. Sonn.* 2. 44. 14
And, with that draught, the life-blood: misery, shame, 441 *Ecc. Sonn.* 3. 3. 13
For England's shame, O Sister Realm! from wood, 442 *Ecc. Sonn.* 3. 7. 7
Shame if the consecrated Vow be found 445 *Ecc.Sonn.* 3. 21. 13

Shame—*continued.*
Should fall; that She, whose virtue put to shame, 471 **Despond who* 6
By glimpses only, and confess with shame 476 *Eden* 2
Of shame scarcely seeming to know that she's there, 482 *Character* 14
Hence, if we wept, it was not done in shame; 491 *Tribute: Dog* 34
Shame that our laws at distance still protect 501 *Humanity* 81
For lingering durance or quick death with shame, 517 *Pun. Death* 1. 11
Though these dull hours (mine is it, or their shame?) 521 *Epist. Beaumont* 36
Might any common friendship shame, 544 *Russ. Fug.* 219
And dread of shame that will not do amiss; 559 *Cuck. and Night.* 158
Dishonour, shame, envy importunate, 560 *Cuck. and Night.* 174
A judgment too harsh of the sin and the shame; 570 *Farmer* 42
And, in spite of the shame that may lurk in his mind, 570 *Farmer* 52
Shame follow'd after with reverted eye, 618 *School Ex.* 21
Oh! in the past if cause there was for shame, 627 **When Severn's* 13
Look was there none within these walls to shame 654 *Prelude* 3. 343
And poor misguided Shame, and witless Fear, 657 *Prelude* 3. 598
But with more shame, for my habiliments, 659 *Prelude* 4. 75
Such as an idler deals with in his shame, 673 *Prelude* 5. 489
A march of glory, which doth put to shame 679 *Prelude* 6. 315
Saw woman as she is, to open shame 693 *Prelude* 7. 386
And this most rotten branch of human shame, 722 *Prelude* 10. 260
Oh, pity and shame! with those confederate Powers! 722 *Prelude* 10. 265
Would only follow, in the path of shame, 727 *Prelude* 11. 15
Was now a shame; my likings and my loves 730 *Prelude* 11. 184
But not dismayed, nor taking to the shame 730 *Prelude* 11. 213
Through times of honour and through times of shame 732 *Prelude* 11. 371
Honour and shame, looking to right and left, 751 *Prelude* 14. 338
As the tide ebbs, to ignominy and shame 752 *Prelude* 14. 436
Or a nice backwardness afraid of shame) 757 *Excursion* 1. 85
And, sometimes—to my shame I speak—have need 767 *Excursion* 1. 755
Though shame it were, could I not look around, 788 *Excursion* 3. 157
And self-indulgence—without shame pursued. 794 *Excursion* 3. 561
Misery and shame. But Wisdom of her sons 805 *Excursion* 4. 293
Through manifold degrees of guilt and shame; 818 *Excursion* 4. 1111
We should recoil, stricken with sorrow and shame, 826 *Excursion* 5. 254
(With shame I speak it) to her guilty bowers 843 *Excursion* 6. 352
A man like this should choose to bring his shame 844 *Excursion* 6. 380
And tears, in pride suppressed, in shame concealed— 849 *Excursion* 6. 714
May be delivered to distress and shame. 851 *Excursion* 6. 848
The rash betrayer could not face the shame 853 *Excursion* 6. 1006
Save only those which to their common shame, 853 *Excursion* 6. 1013
Nor could endure the weight of his own shame. 855 *Excursion* 6. 1114
To his worn cheek; or with uneasy shame 871 *Excursion* 7. 906
Ah! sleep not there in shame! Shall Wisdom's voice 890 *Excursion* 9. 400
More grateful still: while wrong and shame shall last, S.3 441 **Grateful is sleep; my* 2
Issuing when shame hath ceased to check the brawls K.8. 246 *Recluse* 1.1.345
What has this blessed earth to do with shame L.1. 88 *Juvenal* 1. 11
Oh! shame! is this thy service boastful plume? L.1. 94 *Juvenal* 2. 18
Who pushed by thoughtless youth to deeds of shame L.1. 96 *Juvenal* 3. 55
Shame of such dye, but worse remains behind. L.1. 97 *Juvenal* 3. 80

Shame-faced. A shame-faced blush of glowing red! 398 *White Doe* 183
Shamefacedness. And maidenly shamefacedness: 288 *Highland Girl* 31
Shameful. Into a shameful grave. Among thy youth, 514 **Long-favoured* 9
"Torment and shameful death to every one 555 *Prioress* 177
Of shameful imbecility uprisen, 715 *Prelude* 9. 384
Brave hearts! to shameful flight. It was a grief,— 722 *Prelude* 10. 288
Shamefully. That shamefully they one and all were slain, 559 *Cuck. and Night.* 129
Shameless. Her shameless timbrel shakes on Como's marge, 13 *Desc. Sk.* 139
Her shameless timbrel shakes along thy marge, 605 *Desc. Sk. Quarto* 160
And shameless women, treated and caressed; 692 *Prelude* 7. 361
Of marble; for while shameless wrong and woe S.3. 441 **Grateful is sleep, more* 2
Shame's. And to inflict shame's salutary stings 325 *Enghien* 3
Shames. That shames the Schools. 286 *Nith* 42
Shames the degenerate grasp of modern science, 369 *Eg. Maid* 20
Shame-stricken. Hers is not a cheek shame-stricken, 222 *Triad* 163
Shanks. With long and ghostly shanks—forms which once seen 759 *Excursion* 1. 184
Shape. A cowering shape half hid in curling smoke! 13 *Desc. Sk.* 178
And when that shape, with eyes in sleep half drowned, 27 *Guilt* 182
Mocked me with many a strange fantastic shape!— 39 *Bord.* 112
To constitute the spiritless shape of Fact, 58 *Bord.* 1157
With carcasses, in lineament and shape 60 *Bord.* 1231
That bears the shape of man; and for what purpose, 66 *Bord.* 1583
I saw that every possible shape of action 69 *Bord.* 1780
That in the shape of man do cross our path 74 *Bord.* 2084
You see yon precipice;—it wears the shape 101 *Brothers* 364
To deck your slender shape; 156 *Oak and Broom* 32
The shape will vanish—and behold 159 **With little* 29
And still impatient of the shape she wears. 172 *Infant Daughter* 55
"I like," said Benjamin, "her shape and stature: 179 *Waggoner* 3. 72
A dancing Shape, an Image gay, 186 **She was* 9
By ever-changing shape and want of rest; 190 **Lyre! though* 28
The old Man's shape, and speech—all troubled me: 197 *Resolution* 128
In his deportment, shape, and mien, appeared 211 *Laod.* 94
A Shape of more than mortal size 213 *Dion* 67
Is so unearthly, and what shape so fair? 231 **The gentlest Poet* 16
In shape a very crescent-moon: 236 *P. B.* 7

Shape—*continued.*
He paused—for shadows of strange shape, 240 *P. B.* 356
In perfect shape (whose beauty Time shall spare 250 **Happy the* 2
Yon cloud, and fix it in that glorious shape; 252 *Picture* 2
Grove, isle, with every shape of sky-built dome, 263 **Those words* 9
Varying its shape wherever he may run. 278 **Life with* 8
What strife of colour, shape and sound 300 *Bran* 24
To fix in heaven her shape distinct with stars. 336 *Danube* 14
Yon rampant cloud mimics a lion's shape; 348 *Sky-prosp.* 4
And every shape of creature they sustain, 362 **List—'twas* 53
Upon this wingèd Shape so fair 369 *Eg. Maid* 13
Into rude shape by fire, with roaring blast 379 *Duddon* 15. 11
The Fibula, whose shape, I ween, 390 *Highland Broach* 17
No shape of man in all the array 404 *White Doe* 735
That shape themselves and disappear 406 *White Doe* 970
Shape, limbs, and heavenly features, keeping pace 440 *Ecc. Sonn.* 3. 1. 12
Forbear to shape due channels which the Flood 450 *Ecc. Sonn.* 3. 38. 6
A St. Helena next—in shape and hue, 471 **Arran! a* 2
Whom neither shape of danger can dismay, 494 *Hap. War.* 72
Spring takes, O sprightly May! thy shape, 502 *Seasons* 3
Nor turn aside, unless to shape a way 504 *Warning* 99
With the worst shape mock-patience ever wore; 505 *Warning* 123
To circumscribe this Shape in fixed repose; 511 **Who rashly* 18
Of hue and altering shape that charmed all eyes. 527 **Those breathing* 20
The dusky Shape within her arms imbound, 532 **Once I* 4
And when I learned to mark the spectral Shape 532 **Once I* 25
In woman's shape. But why prolong the tale, 541 *Grace Darl.* 74
And growing still in stature the grim shape 637 *Prelude* 1. 381
Sound there was none—but, lo! an uncouth shape, 664 *Prelude* 4. 387
Close at my side, an uncouth shape appeared 666 *Prelude* 5. 75
Stretched forth the shell, so beautiful in shape, 667 *Prelude* 5. 90
Rose, with his ghastly face, a spectre shape 672 *Prelude* 5. 450
These spread like day, and something in the shape 673 *Prelude* 5. 504
Their steeds bestriding,—every mimic shape 689 *Prelude* 7. 138
And, on the shape of that unmoving man, 697 *Prelude* 7. 647
Monstrous in colour, motion, shape, sight, sound! 697 *Prelude* 7. 688
Shape for mankind, by principles as fixed, 698 *Prelude* 7. 754
Whose truth is not a motion or a shape 703 *Prelude* 8. 298
Of shapes and forms and tendencies to shape 707 *Prelude* 8. 570
A variegated landscape,—there the shape 708 *Prelude* 8. 584
In part by fear to shape a way direct, 709 *Prelude* 9. 3
The shape of theirs, my understanding bend 713 *Prelude* 9. 253
In action, give it outwardly a shape, 715 *Prelude* 9. 402
Past outrages, and shape the way for new, 723 *Prelude* 10. 354
That wisdom could, in any shape, come near 728 *Prelude* 11. 45
That is the visible quality and shape 740 *Prelude* 13. 21
Urn-like it was in shape, deep as an urn; 776 *Excursion* 2. 333
And have an answer—thither come, and shape 782 *Excursion* 2. 715
Stood empty of all shape of life, and silent 807 *Excursion* 4. 409
For influence undefined a personal shape; 811 *Excursion* 4. 683
On fluent operations a fixed shape; 812 *Excursion* 4. 727
One that hath barely learned to shape a smile, 826 *Excursion* 5. 263
And Man," said I, "be in his noblest shape 828 *Excursion* 5. 366
And which, once built, retains a steadfast shape 831 *Excursion* 5. 564
Both ye that shapè and build, and ye that force, 831 *Excursion* 5. 612
Dig for us; and present us, in the shape 832 *Excursion* 5. 631
A rough abode—in colour, shape, and size, 833 *Excursion* 5. 697
Masses of every shape and size, that lay 835 *Excursion* 5. 865
Yet walked beneath the sun, in human shape, 879 *Excursion* 8. 344
A bondage lurking under shape of good,— 887 *Excursion* 9. 188
While thitherward we shape our course; or while 891 *Excursion* 9. 497
Such delicate caress as in the shape S.3. 434 **The doubt* 77
And borrowing more their spirit, and their shape K.8. 249 *Recluse* 1.1.451

Shaped. *See* **Cone-shaped, Half-shaped, Star-shaped, Well-shaped.**
Had shaped for their refreshment; nor did sun, 149 *M. H.* 11
That shaped her sorrow, rocks and pools, 194 *Ruth* 218
By something cognizably shaped; 214 *Kirkstone* 9
Shaped like the crescent-moon. 236 *P. B.* 5
That, shaped like old monastic turrets, rise 335 *Namur* 13
A mortal hymn, or shaped the choir, 338 *Brientz* 4
For victory shaped an open space, 341 *San Salv.* 33
And prospect right below of deep coves shaped 353 *Aquap.* 43
Knowledge no help; Imagination shaped 353 *Aquap.* 70
That intimation when the stars were shaped; 419 *Ecc. Sonn.* 1. 4. 11
Hence, prayers are shaped amiss, and dirges sung 423 *Ecc. Sonn.* 1. 20. 8
Was shaped that traced the lives of these good men, 441 *Ecc. Sonn.* 3. 5. 3
And shaped these pleasant walks by Emont's side, 489 *Spade* 2
Were shaped to cheer dark winter's lonely hours. 546 **Oft is* 16
A POET'S hand first shaped it; and the steps 549 **The massy* 6
Shaped by himself with newly-learned art; 589 *Immortality* 92
Have shaped him wandering upon this quest! 668 *Prelude* 5. 148
One of those open fields, which, shaped like ears, 672 *Prelude* 5. 433
Of wild ideal pageantry, shaped out 679 *Prelude* 6. 299
As at a glance, the things which I had shaped, 694 *Prelude* 7. 482
And yet not shaped, had seen and scarcely seen, 694 *Prelude* 7. 483
Shaped by the Druids, so to represent 745 *Prelude* 13. 340
Seemed infinite; and there his spirit shaped 759 *Excursion* 1. 231
Shaped his belief, as grace divine inspired, 762 *Excursion* 1. 412
They shaped their course along the sloping side 777 *Excursion* 2. 389
Hail to the crown by Freedom shaped—to gird 838 *Excursion* 6. 1
And skill in letters—every fancy shaped 843 *Excursion* 6. 309
Of the lark's flight,—or shaped a rainbow curve, 868 *Excursion* 7. 743
(Prized avenues ere others had been shaped 876 *Excursion* 8. 107
—Not shaped by simple wearing of the foot 881 *Excursion* 8. 448

Shapeless. Through dark and shapeless fear of things to come, 124 *V. and J.* 182
Fallen, and diffused into a shapeless heap, 382 *Duddon* 27. 1
With shapeless ruin spread around! 550 *Hermit's Cell* 2. 28
Wilt thou behold this shapeless heap of stones, 551 **If thou in* 6
Fair greetings to this shapeless eagerness, 710 *Prelude* 9. 19

Shapeless—*continued.*
And new and shapeless wishes, would allow. . . 775 *Excursion* 2. 226
—Jehovah—shapeless Power above all Powers, . 811 *Excursion* 4. 651
There is a shapeless crowd of unhewn stones . . K.8. 223 **There is a shapeless* 1

Shapen. *See* **Mis-shapen.**
Shapes. *See* **Mis-shapes.**
The mystic shapes that by thy margin rove . . 3 *Ev. Wk.* 78
In solemn shapes before the admiring eye . . . 14 *Desc. Sk.* 222
The moral shapes of things. His tender cries 57 *Bord.* 1083
Of love in all its shapes, beginnings, ends ; . . 59 *Bord.* 1225
That shapes in heaven its murky shroud, . . . 167 *Pilgrim's Dream* 39
With unrejoicing berries—ghostly Shapes . . . 185 *Yew-trees* 25
In darkness and amid the many shapes . . . 206 *Tintern* 51
But Shapes, that come not at an earthly call, 214 *Dion* 90
Scattered, a Cyclades of various shapes . . . 231 *Clouds* 77
These Shapes of awful phantasy ? . . . . . 300 *Cora Linn* 29
The Arabian desert shapes a willing road . . . 327 *Ode 1815* 25
Still, with those white-robed Shapes—a living Stream, ... 347 *Processions* 48
Bear to the glacier band—those Shapes aloft descried. . . . . 347 *Processions* 63
Wild shapes for many a strange comparison ! . 379 *Duddon* 12. 4
Though unapparent—like those Shapes distinct . 394 **No more* 6
'Twas said that She all shapes could wear ; . . 399 *White Doe* 274
Fit haunt of shapes whose glorious equipage . . 424 *Ecc. Sonn.* 1. 22. 8
Let not your radiant Shapes desert the Land : . 434 *Ecc. Sonn.* 2. 24. 4
On Mona settle, and the shapes assume . . 468 **Ranging the* 5
Yon light shapes forth a Bard, that shade a Chief. 474 **Ye shadowy* 14
By spectral shapes of guilt, or to the ground, . . 523 *Epist. Beaumont* 150
Or blank desertion. No familiar shapes . . . 638 *Prelude* 1. 395
And shapes of spurious fame and short-lived praise 657 *Prelude* 3. 592
Shapes fairer or less doubtfully discerned . . . 662 *Prelude* 4. 274
The untransmuted shapes of many worlds, . . 682 *Prelude* 6. 464
There, allegoric shapes, female or male, . . . 689 *Prelude* 7. 163
See, among less distinguishable shapes, . . . 690 *Prelude* 7. 212
Commingled—shapes which met me in the way . 692 *Prelude* 7. 318
Of these, and of the living shapes they wear, . . 696 *Prelude* 7. 582
Until the shapes before my eyes became . . . 696 *Prelude* 7. 632
Among the simple shapes of human life . . . 704 *Prelude* 8. 372
Engrafted far-fetched shapes on feelings bred 705 *Prelude* 8. 422
Begirt, from day to day, with temporal shapes 706 *Prelude* 8. 496
Mean shapes on every side : but, at the instant, . 707 *Prelude* 8. 547
Of shapes and forms and tendencies to shape . . 707 *Prelude* 8. 570
That some dramatic tale, endued with shapes 731 *Prelude* 11. 283
Advanced in such indisputable shapes ; . . . 739 *Prelude* 12. 323
In headlands, tongues, and promontory shapes, . 746 *Prelude* 14. 46
Where'er we move, under the diverse shapes . . 750 *Prelude* 14. 327
All his remembrances, thoughts, shapes, and forms ; 758 *Excursion* 1. 142
At my own door. The shapes before our eyes 788 *Excursion* 3. 124
Flying, and rainy vapours, call out shapes . . 809 *Excursion* 4. 522
Than of this breath, which shapes itself in words . 863 *Excursion* 7. 359
With all the shapes over their surface spread : . 885 *Excursion* 9. 62
And forced to join in less obnoxious shapes . . 889 *Excursion* 9. 341
Shaping. Their curious pastime, shaping in mid air, 218 *Recluse* 1. 1. 206
While I was shaping beds for winter flowers ; . 264 **Lady ! the* 2
Than shaping novelties for times to come, . . 669 *Prelude* 5. 268
Was busy in the distance, shaping things . . . 769 *Excursion* 1. 881
Share. Till our small share of hardly-paining sighs 8 *Ev. Wk.* 352
While the remotest hamlets blessings share . . 21 *Desc. Sk.* 599
To share your triumph ? Yes, her very look, 55 *Bord.* 971
That they should share the banquet with their Lord . . . . 59 *Bord.* 1206
Of glad or willing service to thy share would fall." 105 *Artegal* 185
The Pony had his share. . . . . 128 *Idiot Boy* 241
My heart with gladness, and a share . . . . 159 **With little* 47
His own dejection, downcast Flower ! could share 169 *LoveliesBleeding* 23
Share their empyreal spirits—yea, ... 178 *Waggoner* 3. 33
And green savannahs, she should share . . . 193 *Ruth* 112
And stately needs must have their share . . . 193 *Ruth* 143
I turned to share the transport—Oh ! with whom 257 **Surprised by* 2
Or share with me, fond thought ! that inward eye, 279 **All praise* 10
To share the passion of a just disdain. . . . . 283 **Proud were* 14
On the frail heart the purest share . . . . 286 *Nith* 63
But if the Poet's wit ye share, ... 286 *Sons of Burns* 15
The blind Boy always had his share ; . . . . 295 *Highland Boy* 72
From self-reproach, reproach that he must share . 308 **There is a bondage* 8
And in due time shall share . . . . 324 *Ode 1814* 49
To share his wanderings ! him whose look . . 342 *Ital. Itin.* 52
For in my Fancy thou dost share . . . . . 345 **How blest* 74
To feed his mind with watchful eyes could share 353 *Aquap.* 55
Or wish to share it ?—One there surely was, . . 353 *Aquap.* 56
If with old love of you, dear Hills ! I share . 367 **If with* 1
Share with their sculptured fellows, that, green-grown, ... 387 *Roslin* 12
Win rest, and ease, and peace, with bliss that Angels share. . . . . 390 *Glencroe* 14
In your indignant thoughts my share ; . . . 406 *White Doe* 899
Servants of God ! who not a thought will share 423 *Ecc. Sonn.* 1. 19. 2
Nor lacks this sea-girt Isle a timely share . . 432 *Ecc. Sonn.* 2. 14. 13
The amplest share of heavenly favour gives ; . . 433 *Ecc. Sonn.* 2. 19. 11
His own humanity with Thee will share, . . . 447 *Ecc. Sonn.* 3. 27. 5
Tired with its daily share of earth's unrest,— 460 **Wanderer! that* 59
God's glory ; and acknowledging thy share . . 461 **Queen of* 43
Follow the fortunes which they may not share. . 467 *St. Bees* 110
Rejoiced in—take, whate'er thou be, a share, . 472 **The captive* 12
Old household thoughts, in which thou hadst thy share ; . . . . 491 *Tribute : Dog* 24
Approaching Waters of the deep, that share . . 495 *Fact* 4

Share—*continued.*
And, with cloud-streaks lightest and loftiest, share 511 **Who rashly* 22
Slow be the Statutes of the land to share . . . 518 *Pun. Death* 6. 6
Save hope that we, yet bound to Earth, may share 526 **Soon did* 12
Those silent Inmates now no longer share, . . 527 **Those breathing* 5
Life's daily tasks with them to share . . . . 530 *Gleaner* 28
To thousands, share not Thou ; howe'er bereft, . 531 *Octogen.* 7
And the least welfare cometh to their share ; . . 559 *Cuck.andNight.* 144
Share his chance-gathered meal ; and, finally, . 569 *Cumb. Beg.* 195
And bids her soldier come her woes to share, . . 596 *Ev.Wk. Quarto* 253
—Yes, were it mine, the cottage meal to share . 615 *Desc.Sk.Quarto* 713
While Freedom's farthest hamlets blessings share, 615 *Desc.Sk.Quarto* 724
Is come as a brother thy sorrows to share. . . 621 *Convict* 48
To share his enterprise, he hurried on . . . . 667 *Prelude* 5. 117
Or heaven made manifest, that I could share . 668 *Prelude* 5. 159
Share with us thy fresh spirits, whether gift . . 678 *Prelude* 6. 250
Not slow to share my wishes, took his staff, . . 680 *Prelude* 6. 324
And no one seems to want his share.—Immense . 700 *Prelude* 8. 55
Searched to its heart. Share with me, Friend ! the wish . . . . 731 *Prelude* 11. 282
Your heart had borne a pitiable share . . . . 793 *Excursion* 3. 484
Her share in the pure freedom of that life, . . 794 *Excursion* 3. 552
That timely light, to share his joyous sport : . . 814 *Excursion* 4. 864
To prize the breath we share with human kind ; . 832 *Excursion* 5. 656
As zealously perform ! I cannot share . . . . 877 *Excursion* 8. 198
A wide compassion which with you I share. . . 886 *Excursion* 9. 155
That he would share the pleasures and pursuits . 895 *Excursion* 9. 776
Her captivity to share. . . . . S.3. 437 **I, whose* 16
Come, share my couch, nor speedily depart ; . . S.3. 441 **Come, gentle* 2
Of proud Tarentum, proud to share the fame . . L.2. 120 *Frag. Æneid* 1. 2

Shared. By seamen, who perhaps themselves had shared . . . . 25 *Guilt* 52
From this time forth he never shared a smile . . 125 *V. and J.* 284
Two glow-worms in such nearness that they shared, 143 **High bliss* 18
And on the joys we shared in mortal life,— . . 211 *Laod.* 130
A holy sadness shared. . . . . 343 *Eclipse* 60
While not one joy of ours by them was shared. . 528 **Those breathing* 59
And universal Moscow shared . . . . . . 545 *Russ. Fug.* 367
That all the seasons shared with equal rights ;— . 583 **With copious* 27
The trees, the mountains shared it, and the brooks, 662 *Prelude* 4. 242
Hadst shared, when, from profane regards apart, 682 *Prelude* 6. 474
Pleasing and pleased, he shared their simple sports, 778 *Excursion* 2. 450
Who shared at first the illusion ; but was soon . 805 *Excursion* 4. 273
Shared, though in mild and merciful degree : . . 886 *Excursion* 9. 167
For social interest such as I have shared. . . S.3. 435* *The doubt* 134
Something within which yet is shared by none, . K.8. 255 *Recluse* 1.1.687
Sharer. And frequent sharer of their calm delight . 151 **Forth from* 13
Sharers. The sharers of her golden couch, was seen . 624 *Æneid* 56
Shares. Contentment shares the desolate domain . 15 *Desc. Sk.* 260
And shares the nature of infinity. . . . . . 65 *Bord.* 1544
In sacred converse gifts with Alfred shares. . . 425 *Ecc. Sonn.* 1. 26. 14
And bright the Lady is who shares his bed. . . 535 *Egremont* 72
Shares with her species, nature's grace sometimes 835 *Excursion* 5. 846
Even as she shares the pride and joy of both. . 883 *Excursion* 8. 587
Sharing. Sharing in the ecstasy ; . . . . . 171 *Kitten* 120
Sharing the strong emotion of the crowd, . . 450 *Ecc. Sonn.* 3. 40. 2
Sharp. While the sharp slope the slackened team confounds, ... 4 *Ev. Wk.* 134
And the sharp wind his head he oft hath bared ; . 25 *Guilt* 47
And ring a sharp 'larum ;—but, if you should look, 80 †*Address : Child* 10
One roaring cataract ! a sharp May-storm . . 97 *Brothers* 151
Sharp season followed of continual storm . . . 150 **When, to* 4
And sharp, and bright, along the dark abyss . . 184 *Night-piece* 16
Till he had reached a summit sharp and bare, . 226 *Vernal Ode* 12
As his distress is sharp, would scorn my theme, . 229 *Cuckoo-clock* 28
And, if the virtuous feel a pang too sharp, . . 233 *Power of Sound* 91
And sharp his staring bones ! . . . . . . 241 *P. B.* 450
Yet, in some fit of anger sharp, ... 301 *Bran* 98
With love too true, a love with pangs too sharp, 373 *Eg. Maid* 293
Of the sharp winds ;—fair Creatures !—to whom Heaven . . . . 395 *White Doe:Ded.* 47
Stung with sharp thoughts ; and, ere the last . 406 *White Doe* 893
Claim for the pilgrim : and, though chidings sharp 467 *St. Bees* 95
With the sharp wind, and seem to court the shower, 539 **Lady ! a* 13
A thousand sharp punctures of cold-sweating pain, 621 *Convict* 39
Of sharp command and scolding intermixed. . . 650 *Prelude* 3. 52
Of that sharp rising, glittered to the moon . 664 *Prelude* 4. 381
By sharp resentment, or belike to taunt . . . 718 *Prelude* 10. 35
Sharp contradictions may arise, by doom . . . 792 *Excursion* 3. 447
By reason : if, with sharp recoil, from one . . 805 *Excursion* 4. 269
And, with this change, sharp air and falling leaves, 828 *Excursion* 5. 409
Along the sharp edge of yon lofty crags, . . . 863 *Excursion* 7. 413
Whose sharp descent confounded their array, . 865 *Excursion* 7. 544
Sharp-edged. But now, when every sharp-edged blast . . . . 507 *May* 37
Sharp-elbowed. Sharp-kneed, sharp-elbowed, and lean-ankled too, ... 759 *Excursion* 1. 183
Sharpen. Sharpen the keenest edge of present ill,— 267 **As the* 7
Sharpening. Driven in by Autumn's sharpening air . 143 **Driven in* 1
Sharper. Sharper than the pointed thorn." . . . 140 *Arm. Lady* 46
With sharper grief is Yarrow smitten, ... 586 *Hogg* 43
Sharpest. Woven out of passion's sharpest agonies, 467 *St. Bees* 74
Sharp-kneed. Sharp-kneed, sharp-elbowed, and lean-ankled too, ... 759 *Excursion* 1. 183
Sharply-twining. Up many a sharply-twining road and down, ... 523 *Epist. Beaumont* 103
Sharp-toothed. And the fierce sharp-toothed pike. . 94 *Westmoreland Girl* 52
Shatter. Then shatter the delusion, break it up . . 54 *Bord.* 934

Sheep—*continued.*
And in one night send twenty score of sheep . . 97 *Brothers* 153
The estate and house were sold; and all their sheep, 100 *Brothers* 301
And other sheep from her I raised, ... 115 *Last of Flock* 25
As healthy sheep as you might see; . . . . 115 *Last of Flock* 26
Of sheep I numbered a full score, ... 115 *Last of Flock* 29
Full fifty comely sheep I raised, ... 115 *Last of Flock* 33
My sheep upon the uplands fed, ... 115 *Last of Flock* 46
"I sold a sheep, as they had said, ... 115 *Last of Flock* 51
Looking down on the kine, and our treasure of sheep 116 *Repentance* 31
And now, perhaps, is hunting sheep, ... 129 *Idiot Boy* 327
With a few sheep, with rocks and stones, and kites 131 *Michael* 11
Sate with a fettered sheep before him stretched . 133 *Michael* 164
Upon the Child, if he disturbed the sheep . . . 134 *Michael* 174
Performed all kinds of labour for his sheep, . . 138 *Michael* 458
A few sheep, stragglers from some mountain-flock, 150 **When, to* 27
Thick as sheep in shepherd's fold! . . . . . 161 **Pleasures newly* 22
Couch the widely-scattered sheep;— . . . . 163 *Spinning Wheel* 8
Lay round me, scattered like a flock of sheep— . 185 *Nutting* 37
"There's neither dog nor heifer, horse nor sheep, 202 *Hart-leap* 133
A flock of sheep that leisurely pass by, . . . 253 **A flock* 1
From wolves your portion of His chosen sheep: . 444 *Ecc. Sonn.* 3. 16. 5
Sheep and cattle eyes with care; . . . . . 490 *Incident: Dog* 4
Spreads out his limbs, while, yet unshorn, the Sheep, ... 547 **Rude is* 23
Below Eve's listening Star the sheep walk stills . 598 *Ev. Wk. Quarto* 353
From byre or field the kine were brought; the sheep . . . . 699 *Prelude* 8. 21
His sheep like Greenland bears; or, as he stepped 703 *Prelude* 8. 267
Upon my right hand couched a single sheep, . . 738 *Prelude* 12. 300
The single sheep, and the one blasted tree, . . 739 *Prelude* 12. 319
With tufts and hairs of wool, as if the sheep, . . 767 *Excursion* 1. 745
The bark was nibbled round by truant sheep. . 769 *Excursion* 1. 842
That ever in the night-calm, when the Sheep . . S.3. 427 **Through Cumbrian* 12
In search of a stray sheep. It was the time . . K.8. 224 **I will* 7
A single sheep was wanting. They had sought . K.8. 224 **I will* 14
. . . and many a sheep . . . . K.8. 225 **I will* 38
Nor in the single sheep was what they sought. . K.8. 225 **I will* 45
He spied the sheep upon a plot of grass, . . . K.8. 229 **I will* 139
Began to fail, this sheep by hunger pressed . . K.8. 229 **I will* 144
The sheep sprang forward to the further shore, . K.8. 229 **I will* 150
And bleatings manifold of mountain sheep, . . K.8. 245 *Recluse* 1.1.330
Their sheep might neither want (from perilous storms . . . . K.8. 247 *Recluse* 1.1.394
To tend the sheep and kine. . . . . K.8. 262 **Ah! if* 10
Sheep-boy. The Sheep-boy whistled loud, and lo! . 580 *John Words.* 1
Sheep-cot-cove. Of Sheep-cot-cove, and those two other coves, ... K.8. 225 **I will* 31
Sheep-dog. The famous sheep-dog, first in all the Vale, ... K.8. 250 *Recluse* 1.1.510
Sheep-dog's. This honest sheep-dog's countenance I read; . . . . 834 *Excursion* 5. 817
Sheep-dogs. With two brave sheep-dogs tried in many a storm, ... 132 *Michael* 91
Sheep-fold. To build a Sheep-fold; and, before he heard . . . . 136 *Michael* 324
The first stone of the Sheep-fold. At the sight . 137 *Michael* 420
Wrought at the Sheep-fold. Meantime Luke began 138 *Michael* 442
There, by the Sheep-fold, sometimes was he seen . 138 *Michael* 467
He at the building of this Sheep-fold wrought, . 138 *Michael* 471
Of the unfinished Sheep-fold may be seen . . 138 *Michael* 481
Sheepfold-wise. Into a platform—that lay, sheepfold-wise, ... 777 *Excursion* 2. 413
Sheep-track. By sheep-track or through cottage lane, 180 *Waggoner* 4. 25
Of the green sheep-track did we glide; . . . 488 *Fountain* 67
Sheepwalks. Her rocky sheepwalks, and her woodland bounds; . . . . 2 *Ev. Wk.* 8
Sheer. Four roods of sheer ascent) Sir Walter found 201 *Hart-leap* 50
Through half the summer, stands with top cut sheer, ... 521 *Epist. Beaumont* 17
Sheet. *See* **Winding-sheet.**
Your young on winter's winding sheet of snow. . 596 *Ev. Wk. Quarto* 240
Sheets. Smooth fields, white sheets of water, and pure sky; . . . . 253 **A flock* 4
Shelf. Like a sea-beast crawled forth, that on a shelf 196 *Resolution* 62
Whate'er the minister's old shelf supplied; . . 759 *Excursion* 1. 171
And, in like sort, chair, window-seat, and shelf, . 781 *Excursion* 2. 662
Shell. *See* **Turtle-shell.**
And voice and shell drew forth a tear . . . . 234 *Power of Sound* 119
With emerald floored, and with purpureal shell . 254 *Wild Duck's Nest* 3
Not these *alone* inspire the tuneful shell; . . . 262 **Not Love* 4
A shell of ample size, and light . . . . . . 296 *Highland Boy* 118
This shell upon the deep would swim, ... 296 *Highland Boy* 123
Had heard, how in a shell like this . . . . . 296 *Highland Boy* 128
In his delightful shell. . . . . 296 *Highland Boy* 135
The shell from out its secret nook, ... 296 *Highland Boy* 144
Erewhile within the dancing shell, ... 297 *Highland Boy* 194
Notes could we hear as of a faery shell . . . 395 *White Doe: Ded.* 17
Are here, and likenesses of many a shell . . . 511 **Who rashly* 12
A stone, and in the opposite hand a shell . . . 666 *Prelude* 5. 79
Stretched forth the shell, so beautiful in shape, . 667 *Prelude* 5. 90
The one to be a stone, the other a shell; . . . 667 *Prelude* 5. 112
The convolutions of a smooth-lipped shell; . . 818 *Excursion* 4. 1135
Even such a shell the universe itself . . . . 818 *Excursion* 4. 1141
And lend the echoes of his sacred shell, . . . 863 *Excursion* 7. 365
Shell-grot. Green-house, shell-grot, and moss-lined hermitage. . . . . 547 **Rude is* 13
Shells. *See* **Sea-shells.**
Have shells to fit their tiny hands . . . . . 164 *Needlecase* 23
That gave the Roman his triumphal shells; . . . 349 *Boulogne* 6

Shells—*continued.*
(With shells encrusted, dark with briny weeds) . 726 *Prelude* 10. 557
Shelter. *See* **Self-shelter.**
Their brow sublime: in shelter there to bide . . 26 *Guilt* 116
Than he who, tempest-driven, thy shelter now would gain? . . . . 26 *Guilt* 126
Of human shelter in that dreary place. . . . 27 *Guilt* 158
Through which his Wife, to that kind shelter brought, ... 36 *Guilt* 642
For shelter to their banners. But it is, . . . 48 *Bord.* 614
A friendly shelter, and we entered in. . . . . 50 *Bord.* 700
Of obvious shelter, as a shipless sea. . . . . 62 *Bord.* 1390
Than a tight case of dungeon walls for shelter . 67 *Bord.* 1660
the hope that we might shelter and restore him. . 72 *Bord.* 1926
Shelter and daily bread,—the sum of his desires. . 104 *Artegal* 105
The traveller to a shelter, summoned him . . . 132 *Michael* 57
To shelter from some object of her fear. . . . 148 *Joanna* 76
Should sleep beneath the shelter of its trees, . . 149 *M. H.* 19
I ceased the shelter to frequent,—and prized, . 150 **When, to* 41
Thy shelter—and their mother's breast! . . . 182 *Waggoner* 4. 263
Her shelter and her bread. . . . . 194 *Ruth* 210
The shelter of the crag to gain; . . . . . . 199 *Thorn* 184
A leafy shelter from the sun and wind. . . . 202 *Hart-leap* 88
For shelter, and a poor man's bread! . . . . 204 *Brougham* 79
The shelter—that the përspective . . . . . 215 *Kirkstone* 67
In whose collegiate shelter England's Flowers . 270 **Ye sacred* 2
That holds in shelter thy Abode— . . . . . 288 *Highland Girl* 10
Though home or shelter he had none, ... 289 *Stepping West.* 7
And here once again a kind shelter be found. . . 364 *Vallomb.* 20
A shelter from the nipping wind: . . . . . 404 *White Doe* 775
A place of shelter, till the rage . . . . . . 406 *White Doe* 915
To shelter persecuted men: . . . . 408 *White Doe* 1095
And, to like shelter, from the world have fled . 429 *Ecc. Sonn.* 2. 3. 7
Shall long survive, to shelter the Abode . . . 450 *Ecc. Sonn.* 3. 39. 8
When ye would shelter in a happy home, . . . 463 **Adieu, Rydalian* 3
Whose proffered beauty in safe shelter blows . . 466 *St. Bees* 6
A shelter under every wind, ... 485 **Bright Flower* 14
Food, shelter, safety, there they find; . . . . 532 †*Float. Isl.* 13
The new-dropped lamb finds shelter from the wind. 547 **Rude is* 16
What avails the kindly shelter . . . . . . 550 *Hermit's Cell* 4. 5
She seeks a shelter from the battering show'r. . 606 *Desc. Sk. Quarto* 210
'Tis like the solemn shelter of the night. . . . 622 *Recluse* 1. 1. 113
Flying, found shelter in the Fortunate Isles, . . 635 *Prelude* 1. 192
Such the deep shelter that is there, and such . . 643 *Prelude* 2. 113
Where, pensioned, they in shelter might sit down, 655 *Prelude* 3. 468
Sheltered within a shelter, where at large . . . 702 *Prelude* 8. 196
Within how deep a shelter! He had fits, . . . 778 *Excursion* 2. 447
There in commodious shelter may we rest. . . . 786 *Excursion* 3. 29
No shelter, for a spirit in distress. . . . . . 816 *Excursion* 4. 1028
Lurks in safe shelter from the winds of March, . 850 *Excursion* 6. 788
To rear for food, for shelter, and delight; . . . 860 *Excursion* 7. 195
Here, resting in cool shelter, we beguiled . . . 882 *Excursion* 8. 520
To shelter innocence, and cherish love; . . . 887 *Excursion* 9. 202
Sheltered. *See* **Half-sheltered, Ill-sheltered.**
The home and sheltered bed, ... 79 *Sparrow's Nest* 6
Had fed or sheltered, linking to such acts . . . 132 *Michael* 72
I sheltered you with leaves and flowers; . . . 155 *Waterfall* 36
Than his coevals in the sheltered vale . . . . 220 *Haunted Tree* 36
For sheltered places, bosoms, nooks, and bays, . 292 **Degenerate Douglas* 12
Faint—but it reached that sheltered spot; . . . 401 *White Doe* 433
And in their common birthplace sheltered it . . 509 *F. Stone* 59
Turn from a spot where neither sheltered road . 521 *Epist. Beaumont* 12
Where sheltered from the north and bleak northwest . . . . 525 *Epist. Beaumont* 229
An elfin pool so sheltered that its rest . . . . 527 **Those breathing* 9
Remote from sheltered village-green, ... 536 *Goody Blake* 29
That sheltered him, a self-secluded Man, . . . 551 **If thou in* 9
Sheltered, and flourish in a little grove . . . 568 *Cumb. Beg.* 121
And in the sheltered and the sheltering grove . 633 *Prelude* 1. 69
And in the sheltered coppice where I sate, . . 661 *Prelude* 4. 182
Farewell for ever to the sheltered seats . . . 688 *Prelude* 7. 53
Still as a sheltered place when winds blow loud! 689 *Prelude* 7. 171
Sheltered within a shelter, where at large . . . 702 *Prelude* 8. 196
Where many a sheltered and well-tended plant . 774 *Excursion* 2. 167
On Devon's leafy shores;—a sheltered hold, . . 793 *Excursion* 3. 518
Sheltered, but not to social duties lost, . . . 823 *Excursion* 5. 54
Were of one species with the sheltered few, . . 836 *Excursion* 5. 943
Of bees around their range of sheltered hives . 856 *Excursion* 6. 1169
Sent from the mountains or the sheltered fields; . K.8. 245 *Recluse* 1.1.320
Sheltering. How fair its lawns and sheltering woods appear! . . . . 8 *Ev. Wk.* 349
From France to sheltering England came; . . . 121 *Emigrant Mother* 68
Slip'st into thy sheltering hold; . . . . . 161 **Pleasures newly* 38
A spot where, in a sheltering cove, ... 246 *P. B.* 852
For ever anchored in her sheltering bay. . . . 252 *Picture* 8
And sheltering wall; and still, as Fancy wove . 264 **Lady! the* 5
'Mid sheltering pines, this Cottage rude and grey; 377 *Duddon* 5. 10
On Duddon's margin, in the sheltering nest; . . 383 *Duddon* 28. 5
And Chastity finds many a sheltering bower. . . 429 *Ecc. Sonn.* 2. 2. 8
Ritual restraints, within some sheltering nook . 443 *Ecc. Sonn.* 3. 13. 7
Or in the haven rest, or sheltering bay, . . . 454 *Sea-side* 37
No sheltering stone, no tangled root was near. . 528 **Those breathing* 53
Within the sheltering Lighthouse.—Shout, ye Waves! . . . . 541 *Grace Darl.* 83
Beside their sheltering cross of wall, the flock . 593 *Ev. Wk. Quarto* 117
And in the sheltered and the sheltering grove . 633 *Prelude* 1. 69
To mark some sheltering bower or sunny nook, . 661 *Prelude* 4. 201
Or in some sheltering vale, was seen a babe . . 692 *Prelude* 7. 355
Sagacious, into sheltering coves he drives . . . 702 *Prelude* 8. 225
Upon the boughs of sheltering leisure hung . . 816 *Excursion* 4. 1042

Shines—*continued.*
As now it shines, when we are laid in earth . . 849 *Excursion* 6. 765
How temptingly the landscape shines ! The air . 890 *Excursion* 9. 423
Which shines dependent upon us alone, . . . K.8. 248 *Recluse* 1.1.438
Shining. *See* **Clear-shining.**
The shining glow-worm ; or, in heedless play, . 7 *Ev. Wk.* 265
Like Una shining on her gloomy way, ... 7 *Ev. Wk.* 291
Of ether, shining with diminished round, . . . 16 *Desc. Sk.* 320
" If the sun be shining hot, do but stretch thy woollen chain, ... 87 *Pet-lamb* 29
At mid-day when the sun was shining bright ; . 107 *Indolence* 16
Is shining in the sky. . . . . 109 **She dwelt* 8
Beneath the moon, yet shining fair, ... 130 *Idiot Boy* 349
Some shining notice will be *there*, ... 174 *Waggoner* 1. 81
Of open door and shining light. . . . . . . 174 *Waggoner* 1. 98
Green, sable, shining yellow, shadowy brown, . 231 **The gentlest Poet* 18
When the full moon was shining bright . . . 240 *P. B.* 324
His shining hazel eye. . . . . 241 *P. B.* 435
Perhaps a ring of shining fairies ? . . . . . 242 *P. B.* 508
Where, shining like the smoothest sea, . . . 244 *P. B.* 698
His shining horn tobacco-box ; . . . . . . 245 *P. B.* 817
Beneath the full moon shining bright, ... 247 *P. B.* 1012
Nor the green Islands, nor the shining Seas ; . 252 **The fairest* 11
Or shining slope where he must never stray ; . 267 **As the* 5
All turn, and court the shining and the green, . 278 **Life with* 10
" My pearly Boat, a shining Light, ... 370 *Eg. Maid* 103
To lifted eyelids, and a doubtful shining. . . 374 *Eg. Maid* 336
Its shining forehead through the peaceful rent . 383 *Duddon* 31. 3
Only the centre of the shining cot . . . . 524 *Epist. Beaumont* 219
The moon was full and shining clearly, . . . 537 *Goody Blake* 75
O Man, that from thy fair and shining youth . . 571 **There is a Flower* 23
Shining upon thy happy grave. . . . . . . 578 **I come* 72
Were shining o'er my head. I was alone, . . 636 *Prelude* 1. 315
Of shining water, gathering as it seemed, . . 640 *Prelude* 1. 578
A visible scene, on which the sun is shining ? . 641 *Prelude* 1. 635
Such sights before, among the shining streams . 672 *Prelude* 5. 454
From these majestic floods, yon shining cliffs, . 682 *Prelude* 6. 463
Of Summer, lingering, shining, by herself, . . 687 *Prelude* 7. 38
Than he lies down upon some shining rock, . . 702 *Prelude* 8. 237
Under a shining canopy of state . . . . 784 *Excursion* 2. 863
By a faint shining from the heart, a gleam . . 785 *Excursion* 2. 885
A tall and shining holly, that had found . . 787 *Excursion* 3. 62
The shining giver of the day diffuse . . . 794 *Excursion* 3. 541
And shining effigies of brass inlaid. . . . . 825 *Excursion* 5. 170
With stony barrenness, a shining speck . . . 832 *Excursion* 5. 672
" When to those shining fields our notice first . 833 *Excursion* 5. 729
For you each evening hath its shining star, . . 835 *Excursion* 5. 836
Struggling and bold, and shining from the west . 861 *Excursion* 7. 232
And graced with shining weapons, weekly marched, 869 *Excursion* 7. 767
Or when the sun is shining in the east, . . . 878 *Excursion* 8. 305
This goodly Matron, shining in the beams . . . 882 *Excursion* 8. 517
Of heavenly bodies shining in their spheres. . . 889 *Excursion* 9. 350
Hayti's shining queen was made . . . . L.2. 190 **Queen and* 9
Ship. *See* **Flag-ship.**
A British ship I waked, as from a trance restored." 30 *Guilt* 306
How quiet 'round me ship and ocean were ! . . 30 *Guilt* 339
The gallant ship is borne ; . . . . 161 *Binnorie* 17
With what ?—a Ship of lusty size ; . . . . 177 *Waggoner* 2. 106
A nobler ship did never swim, ... 178 *Waggoner* 2. 119
Back to her place the ship he led ; . . . . . 178 *Waggoner* 2. 160
Thy ship will travel without harm ; . . . . 179 *Waggoner* 3. 71
And the ship, in all her pride, ... 181 *Waggoner* 4. 165
That Figure, like a ship with snow-white sail ! . 220 *Triad* 42
Where lies the Land to which yon Ship must go ? 258 **Where lies the Land* 1
This Ship was nought to me, nor I to her, . . 258 **With Ships* 9
This Ship to all the rest did I prefer : . . . . 258 **With Ships* 11
In sailor's ship, or fisher's boat, ... 295 *Highland Boy* 84
His father's ship, and had sailed far— . . . . 296 *Highland Boy* 133
To join that gallant ship of war, ... 296 *Highland Boy* 134
When the first Ship sailed for the Golden Fleece— 336 *Danube* 12
While, in a ship begirt with silver bells, . . . 346 *Processions* 23
And grasp of purpose, long ere sailed his ship . 354 *Aquap.* 129
Of a bright Ship that seemed to hang in air, . . 369 *Eg. Maid* 4
A Ship to Christ devoted . . . . 374 *Eg. Maid* 359
Alas ! the bright Ship floated, ... 374 *Eg. Maid* 361
Or like a ship some gentle day . . . . . . 397 *White Doe* 63
A glittering ship, that hath the plain . . . . 397 *White Doe* 65
Yea, like a ship at random blown . . . . . 414 *White Doe* 1615
And see love-emblems streaming from thy ship, . 427 *Ecc. Sonn.* 1. 35. 7
For the heart's sake, ere ship with hostile ship . 448 *Ecc. Sonn.* 3. 30. 11
Bright ship of heaven ! . . . . 490 *Night Thought* 16
Clinging about the remnant of this Ship, . . . 540 *Grace Darl.* 37
My ship and me Charybdis will devour. . . . 564 *Troilus* 126
When to that Ship he bent his way, ... 579 **Sweet Flower* 9
While that stout Ship at anchor lay . . . . 579 **Sweet Flower* 16
That Ship was goodly to be seen, ... 579 **Sweet Flower* 20
But hark the word !—the ship is gone ;— . . . 579 **Sweet Flower* 29
To quit the Ship for which he died, ... 579 **Sweet Flower* 53
Sea—Ship—drowned—Shipwreck—so it came, . 580 *John Words.* 37
On board a ship then ready for the seas. . . . 623 **I find* 8
Remained behind ; the ship the following day . 623 **I find* 10
Eager as birds of prey, or as a ship . . . . 682 *Prelude* 6. 498
Or in a ship on waters, with a world . . . . 690 *Prelude* 7. 245
Toss like a ship at anchor, rocked by storms ; . 710 *Prelude* 9. 51
Of a ship struggling with a hideous storm) . . 721 *Prelude* 10. 228
A stranded ship, with keel upturned, that rests . 787 *Excursion* 3. 54
The ship went gliding with her thoughtless crew ; 798 *Excursion* 3. 836

Ship—*continued.*
And, when the ship was moored, I leaped ashore 798 *Excursion* 3. 871
While the ship glides before a steady breeze. . . 805 *Excursion* 4. 250
The raven lodged in safety.—Many a ship . . 866 *Excursion* 7. 602
And wisdom loves.—But when a stately ship . . 882 *Excursion* 8. 506
Shipboard. On shipboard, bound till peace or death should set him free. . . . . . . 35 *Guilt* 594
This done, he went on shipboard, and is now . . 102 *Brothers* 434
I, who on shipboard lived from earliest youth, . 574 *Chiabrera* 4. 10
Shipless. Of obvious shelter, as a shipless sea. . . 62 *Bord.* 1390
Ship's. And nothing save the moving ship's own light . . . . 460 **Wanderer! that* 68
Ships. That like to leaning masts of stranded ships appear. . . . . 18 *Desc. Sk.* 412
Of ships to ships and guns to guns ; . . . . 178 *Waggoner* 2. 141
And, almost as it was when ships were rare, . . 258 **Where lies the Land* 10
With Ships the sea was sprinkled far and nigh, . 258 **With Ships* 1
Ships, towers, domes, theatres, and temples lie . 269 *Westm. Bridge* 6
Come boats and ships that safely ride . . . . 295 *Highland Boy* 67
Are brought in ships from far. . . . . . . 296 *Highland Boy* 110
Lo ! ships, from seas by nature barred, . . . 391 *Highland Broach* 69
Like ships before whose keels, full long embayed . 434 *Ecc. Sonn.* 2. 23. 4
As to the deep fair ships which though they move 444 *Ecc. Sonn.* 3. 17. 3
Where now the ships that drove before the blast, 454 *Sea-side* 11
Traversed by gleaming ships, looked up to thee . 460 **Queen of* 7
Towering above the sea and little ships ; . . . 471 *Ailsa Crag* 7
And in the sluggish pools where ships are pent : . 495 *Fact* 34
And harboured ships, whose pride is on the sea, . 504 *Warning* 44
Like leaning masts of stranded ships appear . . 611 *Desc.Sk.Quarto* 500
And drove us onward like two ships at sea, . . 622 *Recluse* 1. 1. 160
Ships he can guide across the pathless sea, . . 670 *Prelude* 5. 316
City, and town, and tower,—and sea with ships . 819 *Excursion* 4. 1197
Of Britain are resorted to by ships . . . . . 876 *Excursion* 8. 134
And in the sluggish Ports where ships were pent. S.3. 427 **My Son* 5
Ship-soldier. A tired Ship-soldier on paternal land, 470 **Did pangs* 6
Shipwreck. Murdered, like one ashore by shipwreck cast, ... 317 **The martial* 12
Where she by shipwreck had been thrown ; . . 372 *Eg. Maid* 209
Sea—Ship—drowned—Shipwreck—so it came, . 580 *John Words.* 37
With fellow-sufferers by the shipwreck spared, . 677 *Prelude* 6. 143
Shipwreck, or some domestic incident . . . 691 *Prelude* 7. 292
Shipwrecked. Like a shipwrecked Sailor tost . 502 **Like a* 1
Or, shipwrecked, kindles on the coast . . . . 534 **Blest is* 69
Shire. All through the bonny shire of Ayr ; . . 239 *P. B.* 219
Thought Peter, in the shire of Fife . . . . . 246 *P. B.* 862
In the sweet shire of Cardigan, ... 483 *Simon Lee* 1
Shirt. Mortification with the shirt of hair, . . . 433 *Ecc. Sonn.* 2. 19. 2
The shirt on my back . . . . S.3. 431 **If money's* 2
Though I sell shirt and skin, ... S.3. 431 **If money's* 4
Shirts. In white-sleeved shirts are playing ; and the roar . . . . 306 **Here, on our* 4
Shiver. Alas ! 'tis cold—I shiver in the sunshine— 60 *Bord.* 1265
I shiver, Spirit fierce and bold, ... 284 *Grave of Burns* 1
Shivering. How cattle pine, and droop the shivering fowl, ... 229 *Cuckoo-clock* 14
Of shivering flesh ; and warbled air, ... 232 *Power of Sound* 10
(Above it shivering aspens play) . . . . . 246 *P. B.* 922
And shivering wolves, surprised with darkness, howl . . . . 264 *Storm* 8
Shiverings. Come, come, for manhood's sake ! These drowsy shiverings, ... 51 *Bord.* 776
Shoal. From these I turned to travel with the shoal 656 *Prelude* 3. 503
Shoals. *See* **Herring-shoals.**
In shoals and bands, a morrice train, ... 158 **In youth* 17
Its currents ; magnifies its shoals of life . . . 698 *Prelude* 7. 751
With care and sorrow : shoals of artisans . . . 764 *Excursion* 1. 559
Shock. Stole forth, unsettled by the shock ; . . . 113 *Lament* 67
And in due time the soft spontaneous shock, . . 229 *Cuckoo-clock* 9
The poor Ass staggered with the shock ; . . . 241 *P. B.* 426
Had past a sudden shock of dread, ... 248 *P. B.* 1082
The shock, nor quell the inevitable rout, . . . 309 **What if* 10
O Liberty ! they stagger at the shock ! . . . 314 *Hofer* 9
Whose desperate shock the Carthaginian fled. . 320 **They seek* 8
As if all Germany had felt the shock ! . . . . 322 *Germans* 11
—*The shock is given—the Adversaries bleed*— . . 327 *Ode 1815* 17
An earthquake, mingling with the battle's shock, 361 **When here* 2
I feign not ; witness that unwelcome shock . . 367 **As indignation* 9
Shalt change thy temper ; and, with many a shock 381 *Duddon* 20. 11
Hath suffered from the shock of zeal, ... 402 *White Doe* 576
A shock of intimations vain, ... 405 *White Doe* 866
The shock, AND FINALLY SECURE . . . . . 407 *White Doe* 1071
She shrunk :—with one frail shock of pain . . 414 *White Doe* 1696
Or, whirling with reiterated shock, ... 464 **Greta, what* 3
'Mid your fierce shock like men afraid to die ? . 469 **The feudal* 12
By shock of circumstance, or lapse of years, . . 510 *F. Stone* 115
Sound o'er the lake with gentle shock . . . . 533 **Blest is* 46
And, while I gazed, with sudden shock . . . 550 *Hermit's Cell* 2. 25
Ill-fated Vessel !—ghastly shock ! . . . . . 579 **Sweet Flower* 36
That instant, startled by the shock, ... 580 *John Words.* 2
Feeds on in light, nor thinks of winter's shock ; . 593 *Ev. Wk. Quarto* 118
Too long insulted by the Spoiler's shock, . . . 628 *Installation* 3
Listening, a gentle shock of mild surprise . . 671 *Prelude* 5. 382
Since I had felt in heart and soul the shock . . 688 *Prelude* 7. 66
Upon some showman's platform. What a shock 697 *Prelude* 7. 685
However potent their first shock, with me . . 710 *Prelude* 9. 75
Change and subversion from that hour. No shock 722 *Prelude* 10. 268
The shock ; most woeful for those few who still . 723 *Prelude* 10. 387
Or, seeing, had forgotten ! A strong shock . . 731 *Prelude* 11. 270
Amid conflicting interests, and the shock . . . 751 *Prelude* 14. 334
Security from shock of accident, ... 791 *Excursion* 3. 363

Shock—continued.

And mild paternal sway. The potent shock . .	796 *Excursion* 3. 716
Received a shock of awful consciousness, . .	818 *Excursion* 4. 1157

Shocked. Shocked at his savage aspect, from the

place	126 *V. and J.* 298
This piteous news so much it shocked her, . .	129 *Idiot Boy* 274

Shocks. Ill fitted to sustain unkindly shocks, . . 88 *H. C.* 28

Those shocks of passion can prepare	113 *Lament* 39
Desperate as thine ? Or come the incessant shocks	272 *Devil's Bridge* 6
'Mid direst shocks of mortal accident— . . .	326 *Intrepid sons* 11
Thither, in time of adverse shocks, ...	341 *San Salv.* 25
Doth deaden, shocks of tumult, shrieks of crime,	349 *At Dover* 13
Is by these shocks exhausted, spiritual truth . .	432 *Ecc. Sonn.* 2. 16. 10
To stoop her head before these desperate shocks—	433 *Ecc. Sonn.* 2. 21. 12
Through life's worst trials, whether shocks or snares, ...	462 *Where lies the truth* 13
But did not fal' ; for Virtue braves all shocks, .	574 *Chiabrera* 3. 11
Slight shocks of young love-liking interspersed, .	663 *Prelude* 4. 317
Like earthquakes, shocks repeated day by day, .	712 *Prelude* 9. 179
Cast from the pedestal of pride by shocks . .	805 *Excursion* 4. 274
From painful and discreditable shocks . . .	828 *Excursion* 5. 362
Perhaps incited rather, by these shocks, . .	836 *Excursion* 5. 893
Forefathers, who, to guard against the shocks, .	837 *Excursion* 5. 998

Shod. As if with felt his hoofs were shod. . . 247 *P. B.* 990

That cares not for his home. All shod with steel,	638 *Prelude* 1. 433

Shone. And ripening foliage shone with richer gold. 22 *Desc. Sk.* 637

Chequering the canvas roof the sunbeams shone. .	34 *Guilt* 542
The moon shone clear, the air was still, so still .	47 *Bord.* 575
While sweetly shone the evening sun . . .	81 *Mother's Return* 31
For never sun on living creature shone . . . '	107 *Indolence* 3
Shone meekly 'mid their native dust, ...	168 *Pilgrim's Dream* 63
" Before me shone a glorious world— . . .	194 *Ruth* 169
When all the stars shone clear and bright, . .	200 *Thorn* 239
The sun on drearier hollow never shone ; . .	203 *Hart-leap* 158
The apparition that before thee shone . . .	222 *Triad* 214
The Virgin, as she shone with kindred light ; .	274 *Infant M.* 12
How oft, to elevate our spirits, shone . . .	282 *Wansfell ! this* 12
Whose light I hailed when first it shone, . .	285 *Grave of Burns* 33
With which his soul had shone so bright— . .	297 *Highland Boy* 212
Taught us how rightfully a nation shone . . .	307 *Great men* 7
On her last thorn the nightly moon has shone ; .	393 *Inglewood* 4
Black as the clouds its beams dispersed, while stars	438 *Ecc. Sonn.* 2. 38. 13
That orb whose beams round Saxon Alfred shone :	471 *Despond who* 11
Of time) shone like the morning-star, farewell !—	475 *Homeward we* 4
Myriads of daisies have shone forth in flower . .	475 *There ! said* 10
Alas ! they pined, they languished while they shone ;	527 *Those breathing* 21
Young, like the Crescent that above me shone, .	532 *Once I* 7
To the Traveller's eye it shone :	549 *Hermit's Cell* 1. 22
And, ever as the sun shone forth, ...	550 *Hermit's Cell* 2. 18
And, as before, it shone without dismay ; . .	622 *Among all* 11
At night the Glow-worm shone beneath the Tree :	623 *Among all* 18
That eve, the Star of Brunswick shone . . .	629 *Installation* 57
Unfelt shone brightly round us in our joy. . .	643 *Prelude* 2. 93
The solid mountains shone, bright as the clouds, .	663 *Prelude* 4. 327
Shone mutually indebted, or half lost . . .	706 *Prelude* 8. 483
Nay brighter shone, by this portentous gloom .	709 *Prelude* 8. 657
In him revealed a scholar's genius shone ; . .	868 *Excursion* 7. 737

Shook. Shook the still-twinkling tail and glancing

ear ;	3 *Ev. Wk.* 48
All night from time to time under him shook .	36 *Guilt* 637
Seemed to feast with head and ears ; and his tail with pleasure shook.	87 *Pet-lamb* 10
And proudly shook the bridle too ;	126 *Idiot Boy* 64
The grass—it shook upon the ground ! . . .	200 *Thorn* 228
Their habitation shook—it fell, ...	298 *Brownie's Cell* 23
And of that joy which shook the Isthmian Field,	312 *When, far* 3
Green boughs were borne, while, for the blast that shook	346 *Processions* 16
That shook on Lebanon the cedar's top, . .	354 *Aquap.* 138
And as it shook, enabling the blind roots . .	354 *Aquap.* 139
Shook, tottered, swam before his sight ; . .	400 *White Doe* 423
Clapped hands, and shook with glee their matted locks ;	513 *Said Secrecy* 11
From unsubmissive necks the bridle shook . .	515 *Men of* 5
And fiercely by the arm he shook her, . . .	537 *Goody Blake* 91
With which his genius shook the buskined stage. .	547 *Beneath yon* 16
That shook the leaves in myriads as it passed ;—	583 *With copious* 18
And shook the mind's simplicity.—And yet . .	652 *Prelude* 3. 213
For this to last : I shook the habit off . . .	737 *Prelude* 12. 204
And shook their tenants out into the fields, . .	873 *Excursion* 7. 1026

Shoon. But a thing " beneath our shoon : " . . 161 *Pleasures newly* 50

Which staff and cockle hat and sandal shoon .	467 *St. Bees* 94

Shoot. To shoot and circulate ; smiles have there

been seen ;	173 *Infant Daughter* 68
Shoot to and through heart and reins, . . .	244 *P. T.* 734
While beams of orient light shoot wide and high,	282 *Wh e beams* 1
Shoot but a little way—'tis all they can— . .	354 *Aquap.* 114
And give the timid herbage leave to shoot, . .	395 *White Doe: Ded.* 28
Put forth to wither, many a hopeful shoot) . .	431 *Ecc. Sonn.* 2. 10. 4
Shoot forth with lively power at Spring's return ;	546 *Ye Lime* 2

Shooting. Thy torrents shooting from the clear-blue

sky ;	12 *Desc. Sk.* 113
While needle peaks of granite shooting bare . .	19 *Desc. Sk.* 468
My former pleasures in the shooting lights . .	207 *Tintern* 118
Downcast, or shooting glances far, . . .	232 *Jew. Fam.* 17
By pointing to a shooting star on high : . .	596 *Ev. Wk. Quarto* 260
Where needle peaks of granite shooting bare . .	612 *Desc.Sk.Quarto* 558
The torrents shooting from the clear blue sky, .	684 *Prelude* 6. 629

Shoots. Where oaks o'erhang the road the radiance

shoots	5 *Ev. Wk.* 186

Shoots—continued.

Shoots upward, darting his long neck before. . .	7 *Ev. Wk.* 286
Through the stiff lance-like shoots of pollard ash,	379 *Duddon* 13. 6
She shoots the tidings forth to distant friends ; .	503 *Warning* 27
Of rational Experience, for the shoots . . .	727 *Prelude* 11. 5

Shop. From shop to shop about my own affairs,

	649 *Prelude* 3. 27
Shop after shop, with symbols, blazoned names, .	689 *Prelude* 7. 158
Court, theatre, conventicle, or shop, . . .	695 *Prelude* 7. 575
Of Tavern, Brothel, Gaming-house, and Shop, .	710 *Prelude* 9. 54

Shops. *See* **Sedition-shops.**

While faction Blue from shops and booths . .	S.3. 431 *The Scottish* 29

Shore. *See* **Sea-shore.**

Where twilight glens endear my Esthwaite's shore,	2 *Ev. Wk.* 11
And heron, as resounds the trodden shore, . .	7 *Ev. Wk.* 285
The echoed hoof nearing the distant shore, . .	9 *Ev. Wk.* 371
Slow glides the sail along the illumined shore, .	12 *Desc. Sk.* 103
Thy lowly cots that sprinkle all the shore, . .	12 *Desc. Sk.* 111
Or, swept in anger from the insulted shore, . .	22 *Desc. Sk.* 663
That break against the shore, shall lull thy mind	22 *Yew-tree* 6
Green fields before us, and our native shore, . .	29 *Guilt* 282
I thought of Kilve's delightful shore, . . .	85 *Anecdote* 10
" On Kilve's smooth shore, by the green sea, . .	86 *Anecdote* 31
There's George Fisher, Charles Fleming, and Reginald Shore, ...	86 *Rural Arch.* 1
Ere Julius landed on her white-cliffed shore, . .	102 *Artegal* 5
Gladdening the people's heart from shore to shore ;	105 *Artegal* 205
Our boat is safely anchored by the shore, . .	106 *Farewell* 7
Nor will I quit thy shore	109 *I travelled* 6
Of copse and thicket, leaves the eastern shore .	148 *A narrow* 4
Along the indented shore ; when suddenly, . .	149 *A narrow* 44
When thou hadst quitted Esthwaite's pleasant shore, ...	150 *When, to* 67
A lake was near ; the shore was steep ; . .	162 *Binnorie* 49
From the shore come the notes	166 *Stray Pleasures* 7
There came a Youth from Georgia's shore— . .	192 *Ruth* 19
By doubt, propelled thee to the fatal shore ; . .	210 *Laod.* 52
On broad Euphrates' palmy shore, ...	215 *Enterprise* 25
That beautifies the fairest shore, ...	233 *Power of Sound* 55
" The vain distress-gun," from a leeward shore, .	234 *Power of Sound* 159
On farthest Cornwall's rocky shore, . . .	238 *P. B.* 209
Yet round our sea-girt shore they rise in crowds :	251 *Pelion and* 9
Dim shades—for reliques, upon Lethe's shore, .	264 *Lady ! I* 7
And heard the water beat the shore	295 *Highland Boy* 49
May human creature leave the shore ! . . .	296 *Highland Boy* 102
Had stoutly launched from shore ;	296 *Highland Boy* 130
The tide retreated from the shore, ...	296 *Highland Boy* 154
Which from the crowd on shore was sent, . .	297 *Highland Boy* 177
And from the shore their course they take, . .	297 *Highland Boy* 183
To live in peace on shore.	297 *Highland Boy* 245
To what untrodden shore ?	300 *Cora Linn* 30
Of the waves breaking on the chalky shore ;— .	306 *Here, on our* 5
And Ocean bellow from his rocky shore, . . .	306 *Two Voices* 13
We all are with you now from shore to shore ;— .	309 *Men of Kent* 13
High on the shore of silver Thames—to greet .	327 *Ode 1815* 50
On jutting rock, and crowd the shore, . . .	343 *Eclipse* 28
Asleep on ZURICH's shore !	348 *Lulled by* 24
Why cast ye back upon the Gallic shore, . .	349 *Boulogne* 1
Expanding ; and, along the smooth shore curved	356 *Aquap.* 219
This sea of life without a visible shore, . . .	360 *Near Anio's* 12
Within its depths, and to the shore we came . .	366 *Fair Land* 6
O winds without remorse ! O shore ungrateful !	372 *Eg. Maid* 216
The matted forests of Ontario's shore . . .	379 *Duddon* 13. 8
Glad tidings to Iona's shore, ...	390 *Highland Broach* 4
Blest be the unconscious shore on which ye tread,	422 *Ecc. Sonn.* 1. 14. 2
Save by Self-will. Lo ! from that distant shore,	443 *Ecc. Sonn.* 3. 14. 6
One boat there was, but it will touch the shore .	453 *Calm is the* 28
The grass-crowned headland that conceals the shore ?	453 *The Sun, that* 10
I slight them all ; and, on this sea-beat shore .	459 *Wanderer ! that* 10
And to the throng, that on the Cumbrian shore .	465 *Dear to* 3
Appears, on Morven's lonely shore, . . .	473 *Ossian* 7
Of wave-worn pebbles, pleading on the shore . .	474 *How sad* 3
Here on the bleakest point of Cumbria's shore .	521 *Epist. Beaumont* 3
Might see it, from the mossy shore	531 *Float.* 11. 9
That from the shore a full-grown man might wade,	548 *Stranger ! this* 9
On a flat and lazy shore.	549 *Hermit's Cell* 1. 32
Bold settlers on some foreign shore, . . .	577 *I come* 46
This sea in anger, and that dismal shore. . .	579 *Peele Castle* 44
Sleeps by his native shore.	579 *Sweet Flower* 7
To reach a safer shore—how near, ...	579 *Sweet Flower* 41
And see the Children sport upon the shore, . .	590 *Immortality* 170
Glanc'd oft upturn'd along the breezy shore, . .	593 *Ev. Wk. Quarto* 102
Along the " wild meand'ring " shore to view, . .	595 *Ev. Wk. Quarto* 199
And restless piper wearying out the shore ; . .	597 *Ev. Wk. Quarto* 322
And echo'd hoof approaching the far shore, . .	600 *Ev. Wk. Quarto* 440
Insinuated, sprinkling all the shore, . . .	604 *Desc.Sk.Quarto* 126
Of cabins, woods, and lawns a pleasant shore . .	611 *Desc.Sk.Quarto* 502
For ye have reach'd at last the happy shore, . .	614 *Desc.Sk.Quarto* 668
Swept in their anger from th' affrighted shore, .	617 *Desc.Sk.Quarto* 808
Pushed from the shore. It was an act of stealth	637 *Prelude* 1. 361
Midway on long Winander's eastern shore, . .	644 *Prelude* 2. 138
His bark to land upon the wished-for shore, . .	656 *Prelude* 3. 487
Appeared distinctly on the opposite shore, . .	672 *Prelude* 5. 436
In passive expectation from the shore, . . .	672 *Prelude* 5. 445
Cast on the white cliffs of our native shore . .	680 *Prelude* 6. 343
Beat against Albion's shore, since ear of mine .	721 *Prelude* 10. 239
Along that very shore which I had skimmed . .	727 *Prelude* 10. 596
In a calm hour to kiss the pebbly shore, . .	734 *Prelude* 12. 22
That fragrant notice of a pleasant shore . . .	735 *Prelude* 12. 54
Not distant from the shore whereon we stood, .	747 *Prelude* 14. 57

Shore—*continued.*
To fly, for safeguard, to some foreign shore, — 798 *Excursion* 3. 832
And waves have wafted to this distant shore, — 799 *Excursion* 3. 888
A dismal prospect yields the wild shore strewn — 836 *Excursion* 5. 930
Besprent from shore to shore with steeple-towers, — 838 *Excursion* 6. 18
Deposited upon the silent shore — 857 *Excursion* 7. 28
On every shore whose aspect favours hope — 889 *Excursion* 9. 380
We seek that other, on the western shore ; — 891 *Excursion* 9. 498
A gipsy-fire we kindled on the shore — 892 *Excursion* 9. 527
Leaving, in quest of other scenes, the shore — 892 *Excursion* 9. 547
And thus the bark, meandering with the shore, — 892 *Excursion* 9. 566
The sheep sprang forward to the further shore, — K.8. 229 **I will* 150
From shore to island, and from isle to shore, — K.8. 237 *Recluse* 1.1. 40
Harmonious landscape ; all along the shore — K.8. 252 *Recluse* 1.1.575
His course to Latium from the Trojan shore, — K.8. 281 **Arms and* 2

Shores. Or where dank sea-weed lashes Scotland's shores ; — 21 *Desc. Sk.* 594
Sole-sitting by the shores of old romance. — 149 **A narrow* 38
And from the shores of Erin, — 161 *Binnorie* 13
Keep faith with Time on distant shores ? — 216 *Enterprise* 82
Her habitable shores, but now appears — 219 **This Height* 21
Plied steadily between those willowy shores, — 271 **Fame tells* 11
To cull contentment upon wildest shores, — 284 *Departure* 25
On that offensive soil, like waves upon a thousand shores. — 331 *Ode : Thanks.* 151
Deeply embosomed, and your winding shores — 352 *Aquap.* 2
More than fulfilled, as gay Campania's shores — 353 *Aquap.* 78
There greets an Embassy from Indian shores ; — 368 *Trajan* 42
Or some of humbler name, to these wild shores — 419 *Ecc. Sonn.* 1. 2. 11
To scatter seeds of life on barbarous shores ; — 424 *Ecc. Sonn.* 1. 25. 2
Round the Crusaders, till on distant shores — 430 *Ecc. Sonn.* 2. 8. 5
Near spicy shores of Araby the blest, — 438 *Ecc. Sonn.* 2. 39. 10
Throughout the Country they have left, our shores — 449 *Ecc. Sonn.* 3. 36. 13
Urge the slow bark along Calabrian shores ; — 454 *Sea-side* 26
O sad it is, in sight of foreign shores, — 458 *Sea-shore* 9
And to green meadows changed the swampy shores ? — 468 *St. Bees* 137
These shores if he approached them bent on wrong ; — 468 **Bold words* 4
The shores and channels, working Nature's will — 495 *Fact* 32
Or, like a Mermaid, warbles on the shores — 522 *Epist. Beaumont* 44
Beside the shores of Wight ; — 579 **Sweet Flower* 17
Its one green Island and its winding shores ; — 622 *Recluse* 1. 1. 119
Our shores in England,—from those loftiest notes — 668 *Prelude* 5. 206
Of that sweet Valley ; when its paths, its shores, — 672 *Prelude* 5. 428
Those scattered along Adria's myrtle shores : — 701 *Prelude* 8. 176
A pleasant promise, wafted from her shores, — 733 *Prelude* 11. 429
From rocks, woods, caverns, heaths, and dashing shores ; — 782 *Excursion* 2. 698
On Devon's leafy shores ;—a sheltered hold, — 793 *Excursion* 3. 518
From my unguarded heart.—The tranquil shores — 797 *Excursion* 3. 812
Rivers and fertile plains, and sounding shores,— — 812 *Excursion* 4. 719
From that disastrous rout, to foreign shores — 844 *Excursion* 6. 422
That filled her plains, that reached her utmost shores, — 869 *Excursion* 7. 761
—Hence is the wide sea peopled,—hence the shores — 876 *Excursion* 8. 133
Within the compass of their several shores — 889 *Excursion* 9. 347
The shores and channels, working Nature's will — S.3. 427 **My Son* 3

Shorn. *See* **Self-shorn.**
Shorn of its beams, insufferably white, — 16 *Desc. Sk.* 324
Then thus exclaimed : " To me, of titles shorn, — 104 *Artegal* 139
Domestic hands the home-bred wool had shorn, — 255 *Easter* 5
Which whosoe'er approached of strength was shorn, — 373 *Eg. Maid* 317
And 'mid his bright locks never shorn — 543 *Russ. Fug.* 187
Shorn of his beams, insufferably white, — 609 *Desc.Sk.Quarto* 387
And napkins of smooth texture, finely shorn. — 624 *Æneid* 62
Whose very sorrow is, that time hath shorn — 817 *Excursion* 4. 1084

Short. A few short steps to totter with their load. — 7 *Ev. Wk.* 255
And the short thunder, and the flash of arms ; — 21 *Desc. Sk.* 617
And, after many interruptions short — 31 *Guilt* 385
With a few drops of blood cut short the business ; — 71 *Bord.* 1868
Stopped short,—and thence, at leisure, limb by limb — 96 *Brothers* 102
Is distant three short miles, and in the time — 99 *Brothers* 252
That overhung the road : he there stopped short, — 102 *Brothers* 419
And yet they leave it short, and fears — 110 *Forsaken* 10
They mount—how short a voyage brings — 117 *Affl. Marg.* 45
What one short sigh so easily removed ?— — 118 *Maternal Grief* 10
Which, after a short time, by some mistake — 125 *V. and J.* 279
Which, if at such short notice he should go, — 136 *Michael* 319
Thus, after a short silence, he resumed : — 137 *Michael* 384
And on a summit, distant a short space, — 146 **It was an* 34
And, after short exchange of village news, — 147 *Joanna* 25
That eastward looks, I there stopped short—and stood — 147 *Joanna* 43
At a short distance from my cottage, stands — 150 **When, to* 8
His short domain upon the vessel's deck, — 150 **When, to* 65
You could not say in one short day — 161 *Binnorie* 3
That promised to cut short the way ; — 240 *P. B.* 337
The Ass is startled—and stops short — 243 *P. B.* 621
He found the longest summer day too short, — 254 *Complete Angler* 8
A startling thunder quick and short ! — 342 *Ital. Itin.* 64
Of three short days—but hush—no more ! — 348 **Lulled by* 20
A few short steps (painful they were) apart — 353 *Aquap.* 83
Where Solitude with Silence paired stops short — 355 *Aquap.* 196
Short leisure even in busiest days ; — 376 **The Minstrels* 68
And thus, with short oblivion blest, — 404 *White Doe* 776
And, if dissevered thence, its course is short. — 442 *Ecc. Sonn.* 3.10. 14
What more I have to say is short, — 484 *Simon Lee* 69

Short—*continued.*
And, to the churchyard come, stopped short — 486 **We walked* 31
Little Music, she stops short. — 490 *Incident : Dog* 28
Help with thy grace, through life's short day, — 506 *Lab. Hymn* 29
Caught at the point where it stops short of sadness. — 508 *F. Stone* 40
Old Daniel begins ; he stops short—and his eye, — 572 *Avarice* 21
Lelius ! has death cut short thy brilliant day — 575 *Chiabrera* 7. 5
Short while a Pilgrim in our nether world, — 575 *Chiabrera* 8. 19
Deluded Hope for one short hour — 620 *Birth of Love* 39
A few short steps were the chain that bound — 623 *G. and S. Green* 15
Stopped short ; yet still the solitary cliffs — 639 *Prelude* 1. 458
Though short of mortal combat ; and whate'er — 657 *Prelude* 3. 584
'Twas but a short hour's walk, ere veering round — 658 *Prelude* 4. 20
Short velvet cloak, (her bonnet of the like), — 661 *Prelude* 4. 220
A few short months before. I turned my face — 675 *Prelude* 6. 9
Among Tartarian wilds—fell short, far short, — 688 *Prelude* 7. 84
After short absence, curiously I scanned — 688 *Prelude* 7. 94
A travelling cripple, by the trunk cut short, — 690 *Prelude* 7. 203
That after a short space works less and less, — 707 *Prelude* 8. 573
He who thereafter, and in how short time ! — 725 *Prelude* 10. 501
Then, cheered by short refreshment, sallied forth. — 746 *Prelude* 14. 10
Oh ! yet a few short years of useful life, — 752 *Prelude* 14. 430
In the short course of one undreaded year, — 774 *Excursion* 2. 198
This simple Child will mourn his one short hour, — 780 *Excursion* 2. 601
Soon showed itself : he lingered three short weeks; — 785 *Excursion* 2. 894
With what short interval of time between, — 795 *Excursion* 3. 646
Or of the end stops short, proposed to all — 826 *Excursion* 5. 260
In social converse, or by some short space — 845 *Excursion* 6. 478
This Dwelling charms me ; often I stop short, — 856 *Excursion* 6. 1175
The powers of nature : and a few short steps — 864 *Excursion* 7. 465
Short was his life, and a brief tale remains. — 870 *Excursion* 7. 860
Till their short holiday of childhood ceased, — 878 *Excursion* 8. 281
A few short hours of each returning day — 888 *Excursion* 9. 259
Or should you even stop short of Woolwich docks — L.1. 97 *Juvenal* 3. 73

Shorten. Nor shorten the sweet life, too fugitive, — 501 *Humanity* 109

Shorten'd. When stood the shorten'd herds amid the tide, — 592 *Ev. Wk. Quarto* 58

Shortening. Of their near neighbours ; and, when shortening fast — 686 *Prelude* 6. 762

Shortest. Take thy bliss, while longest, shortest, — 90 *Longest Day* 15
I'll take the shortest way." — 291 *Rob Roy* 56

Short-flighted. This is no trifler, no short-flighted wit, — 694 *Prelude* 7. 499

Short-lived. Short-lived likings may be bred — 163 *Spinning Wheel* 13
It gladdens me, O worthy, short-lived, Youth ! — 260 *Calvert* 13
From mind and spirit, grudge a short-lived fence. — 280 *Plea for Auth.* 8
From shades, her chosen place of short-lived rest. — 311 **Who rises* 38
For some Aspirant of our short-lived race, — 313 **Go back* 7
—There is a radiant though a short-lived flame, — 329 *Ode : Thanks.* 43
The wretch, the short-lived vision of an hour ; — 619 *School Ex.* 96
And shapes of spurious fame and short-lived praise — 657 *Prelude* 3. 592
Of short-lived transport, like a torrent bursting, — 687 *Prelude* 7. 6
Who were content to barter short-lived pangs — 723 *Prelude* 10. 344
With many a short-lived thought that passed between, — 767 *Excursion* 1. 705
For fickle, short-lived clouds to occupy, — 787 *Excursion* 3. 96

Shortly. " Thy limbs will shortly be twice as stout as they are now, — 88 *Pet-lamb* 45

Short-sighted. Solid and light, short-sighted and profound ; — 663 *Prelude* 4. 341

Shot. *See* **Far-shot.**
Shot, down the headlong path darts with his sledge ; — 4 *Ev. Wk.* 131
Shot from the dancing Graces, as they move — 233 *Power of Sound* 79
We pry among them all ; have shot — 236 *P. B.* 37
Shot lightning through this lonely Isle ! — 298 *Brownie's Cell* 42
Reddened the fiery hues, and shot — 385 *Yarrow Rev.* 15
Till the fatal bolt is shot ! — 549 *Hermit's Cell* 1. 8
Shot, down the headlong pathway darts his sledge ; — 593 *Ev. Wk. Quarto* 112
Shot stinging through her stark o'erlabour'd bones. — 596 *Ev. Wk. Quarto* 246
Whether the bolt of childhood's Fancy shot — 688 *Prelude* 7. 88
The gooseberry trees that shot in long lank slips, — 763 *Excursion* 1. 456
He ceased. Ere long the sun declining shot — 771 *Excursion* 1. 957
By the dense air—shot upwards to the crown — 893 *Excursion* 9. 595
They shot, and over that cloud-loving hill, — K.8. 225 **I will* 26

Should. (*Partial list.*)
Nay, but I grieve that we should part. This Stranger, — 38 *Bord.* 24
Should hold a place, as if 'twere robbery, — 38 *Bord.* 57
Should *yet* be true ? Would it were possible ! — 38 *Bord.* 73
I comprehend thee—I should be as cheerful — 40 *Bord.* 149
That I should leave you at this house, and thence — 41 *Bord.* 225
Anxiety lest mischief should befall her — 41 *Bord.* 234
Should in his love admit no rivalship, — 42 *Bord.* 269
I never should have thought of it again — 42 *Bord.* 274
That you should travel unattended, Lady !— — 43 *Bord.* 310
Why, if a wolf should leap from out a thicket, — 43 *Bord.* 317
He should have used me better !—Charity ! — 45 *Bord.* 449
He is a man, if it should come to his ears — 47 *Bord.* 533
That you too should subscribe your name. — 49 *Bord.* 671
The wind should pipe a little, while we stand — 51 *Bord.* 752
We should deserve to wear a cap and bells, — 51 *Bord.* 768
You'd better like we should descend together, — 51 *Bord.* 771
Three of us—we should keep each other warm : — 51 *Bord.* 773
Fallen should I be indeed— — 54 *Bord.* 900
It should be told you pinioned in your bed, — 56 *Bord.* 1011
When he should give her up, a Woman grown, — 56 *Bord.* 1054
Should he resolve to taint her Soul by means — 56 *Bord.* 1058
Should he, by tales which would draw tears from iron, — 57 *Bord.* 1060
That half a word should blow it to the winds ! — 58 *Bord.* 1144
That they should share the banquet with their Lord — 59 *Bord.* 1206

Show—*continued.*
Whose practice teaches, spite of names to show . 530 *Poor Robin* 22
That he the meaning of this song would show, . 553 *Prioress* 75
To show to her some pleasant meanings writ . . 562 *Cuck.andNight.*299
For which it pleased him in his songs to show . 564 *Troilus* 113
But more in show than truth ; and from the fields, 585 *Ch. Lamb* 51
Anon, in order mounts a gorgeous show . . . 595 *Ev. Wk. Quarto* 183
There have I loved to show the tender age . . 619 *School Ex.* 67
Oft when the dazzling show no longer new . . 650 *Prelude* 3. 90
That flashed upon me from this novel show . . 652 *Prelude* 3. 202
A more substantial name, no mimic show, . . 657 *Prelude* 3. 589
A parti-coloured show of grave and gay, . . . 663 *Prelude* 4. 340
Were flown, and autumn brought its annual show 664 *Prelude* 4. 371
Kept holiday, a never-ending show, ... 674 *Prelude* 5. 582
Between thy lofty rocks. Enchanting show . . 680 *Prelude* 6. 380
And what earth is, and what she has to show. . 690 *Prelude* 7. 235
Our argument. Enough is said to show . . . 693 *Prelude* 7. 401
Between the show, and many-headed mass . . 693 *Prelude* 7. 434
What grandeur not unfelt, what pregnant show . 698 *Prelude* 7. 748
Leads, though by sinuous ways, if here I show . 706 *Prelude* 8. 453
A chronicle that might suffice to show . . . . 711 *Prelude* 9. 101
Show what she was, a high and fearless soul, . . 718 *Prelude* 10. 33
Things that could only show themselves and die. 719 *Prelude* 10. 47
Without offence ; ye who, as if to show . . . 734 *Prelude* 12. 14
Of things that pass away, a temperate show . . 740 *Prelude* 13. 31
When all the external man is rude in show,— . 743 *Prelude* 13. 228
Whose skill had thronged the floor with a proud show . . . . 778 *Excursion* 2. 424
Great show of joy the housewife made, and truly 785 *Excursion* 2. 887
And what a marvellous and heavenly show . . 808 *Excursion* 4. 471
And yet—triumphant o'er this pompous show . 812 *Excursion* 4. 729
His royal state to show, and prove his strength . 825 *Excursion* 5. 183
Show to his eye an image of the pangs . . . 850 *Excursion* 6. 808
When the next village hears the show announced 858 *Excursion* 7. 93
Show to the wretched nations for what end . . 890 *Excursion* 9. 414
Imaged in downward show ; the flower, the herbs, S.3. 435 **The doubt* 106
Wedged in with blacklegs at a boxer's show . . L.1. 94 *Juvenal* 2. 13

Showed. And wild Impatience, pointing upward, showed, ... 2 *Ev. Wk.* 25
Yet when faint beams of light that ruin showed, . 27 *Guilt* 156
It came with sleep and showed the Boy, no cherub, not transformed, ... 92 *Poet's Dream* 15
For, deftly framed within the trunk, the sanctuary showed, ... 92 *Poet's Dream* 45
Thy mornings showed, thy nights concealed, . . 109 **I travelled* 13
Yet leafless, showed as if the countenance . . 146 **It was an* 15
He in jocose defiance showed— . . . . . 245 *P. B.* 832
And showed the Bark upon the glassy flood . . 252 *Picture* 7
Like stars in heaven, and joyously it showed ; . 258 **With Ships* 2
She cast away, and showed her fulgent head . . 265 **The Shepherd* 5
And showed my youth . . . . 285 *Grave of Burns* 34
Showed little of his state ; . . . . . . 334 **In Bruges* 22
And more than all, that Eminence which showed 353 *Aquap.* 81
The trembling eyebright showed her sapphire blue, 377 *Duddon* 6. 10
And taught him signs, and showed him sights, . 399 *White Doe* 278
That like a place of vantage showed ; . . . . 412 *White Doe* 1478
The wounds the broidered Banner showed, . . 412 *White Doe* 1497
Nor on the lonely turf that showed . . . . 416 *White Doe* 1817
One to whom, yet a School-boy, Cynthia showed 461 **Giordano, verily* 11
Who taught, and showed by deeds, that gentler chains . . . . 468 *St. Bees* 140
Stopped me at once by charm of what it showed, 524 *Epist. Beaumont* 172
The sun above the pine-trees showed . . . . 543 *Russ. Fug.* 129
And wild Impatience, panting upward, show'd . 592 *Ev. Wk. Quarto* 35
In clearest air ascending, showed far off . . . 756 *Excursion* 1. 4
A man whose garments showed the soldier's red, . 769 *Excursion* 1. 888
That showed like happiness. But, in despite . 775 *Excursion* 2. 284
Soon showed itself : he lingered three short weeks ; 785 *Excursion* 2. 894
Attain a point that showed the valley—stretched 823 *Excursion* 5. 78
In seemly rows ; the chancel only showed . . 824 *Excursion* 5. 156
No higher name ; in whom our country showed, . 870 *Excursion* 7. 852
Beneath him, showed his shadowy counterpart. . 890 *Excursion* 9. 446

Shower. *See* **Thunder-shower.**
She seeks a covert from the battering shower . . 14 *Desc. Sk.* 183
And be it so—for to the chill night shower . . 25 *Guilt* 46
Sunshine and shower be with you, bud and bell ! 106 *Farewell* 17
The silver shower, whose reckless burthen weighs 124 *V. and J.* 192
Spangled with drops of that celestial shower. . . 169 *Love lies Bleeding* 17
Three years she grew in sun and shower, . . . 187 **Three years* 1
The lagging shower, and force coy Phœbus out, . 221 *Triad* 83
Waves high, embellished by a gleaming shower ! . 226 *Vernal Ode* 20
Delightful land of verdure, shower and gleam, . 229 *Cuckoo-clock* 32
And fast they fell, a plenteous shower ! . . . 247 *P. B.* 962
Wreaths that endure affliction's heaviest shower, 259 **Weak is* 13
With ready sunbeams every straggling shower ; . 261 **Fair Prime* 2
When sunshine follows shower, the breast can thrill . . . . 273 **Not the* 2
Sweet Highland Girl, a very shower . . . . 287 *Highland Girl* 1
In haste, nor springing with a transient shower : . 303 **Is it* 11
The dews of morn, or April's tender shower ? . . 319 *Guernica* 8
Of mortals, hurrying like a sudden shower . . 327 *Ode 1815* 12
Warbling a farewell to a vernal shower. . . . 329 *Ode : Thanks.* 42
To wet with many a bitter shower, ... 337 *Cath. Cantons* 2
" Sweet Highland Girl ! a very shower . . . 344 **How blest* 53
Darling of England ! many a bitter shower . . 425 *Ecc. Sonn.* 1. 27. 2
Of Infancy, provides a timely shower . . . . 445 *Ecc. Sonn.* 3. 20. 2
Shakes off that pearly shower. . . . . . 506 **While from* 8
—*There* swims, of blazing sun and beating shower 527 **Those breathing* 13
With the sharp wind, and seem to court the shower, 539 **Lady ! a* 13

Shower—*continued.*
" It doth not love the shower, nor seek the cold : 571 **There is a Flower* 14
But doubly pitying Nature loves to show'r . . 602 *Desc. Sk. Quarto* 13
She seeks a shelter from the battering show'r. . 606 *Desc.Sk.Quarto* 210
Shower with a bounteous hand on Thee and Thine 628 **Deign, Sovereign* 6
A naked savage, in the thunder shower. . . . 636 *Prelude* 1. 300
Its simple worshippers from sun and shower. . . 743 *Prelude* 13. 231
The burning sunshine, or a transient shower ; . 777 *Excursion* 2. 422
Without remission of the blast or shower, . . . 783 *Excursion* 2. 799
Bright as a sunbeam sleeping till a shower . . 832 *Excursion* 5. 673
Of the fresh shower, but of poor Ellen's tears . 850 *Excursion* 6. 816
They seemed to say ; " What would ye," said the shower, ... K.8. 241 *Recluse* 1.1.168
For they protect his walk from sun and shower, . K.8. 253 *Recluse* 1.1.609

Showered. Unblest distinction ! showered on me . 113 *Lament* 43
Showered equally on city and on field, . . . 316 **O'er the* 6
Showered miracles, and ceased not to dispense . 811 *Excursion* 4. 658
As if the moon had showered them down in spite. 835 *Excursion* 5. 869
Conscious of that abundant favour showered . . 895 *Excursion* 9. 738

Showering. Showering down a silver light, . . . 212 *Dion*

Shower-proof. Or lofty wood, shower-proof. . . 167 *Pilgrim's Dream* 8

Showers. *See* **May-showers.**
Oh ! when the sleety showers her path assail, . 7 *Ev. Wk.* 269
And antique castles seen through gleamy showers. 14 *Desc. Sk.* 225
In copious showers, from earth by wholesome springs, ... 22 *Desc. Sk.* 657
I could not pray :—through tears that fell in showers . . . . 28 *Guilt* 242
" Thou Eglantine, so bright with sunny showers, 111 *'*Tis said that some* 37
With frequent showers of snow. Upon a hill, . 150 **When, to* 7
And showers of hailstones pattered round. . . 154 **A whirl-blast* 4
The showers of the spring . . . . . . 167 *Stray Pleasures* 31
Their course, or genial showers descend ! . . . 227 *Vernal Ode* 70
Loves his own glory in their looks, and showers . 231 *Clouds* 84
O'erlooks the torrent breathing showers . . . 301 *Bran* 121
Of Winter's breath surcharged with sleety showers, 322 **Ye Storms* 7
Fed by the stream with soft perpetual showers, . 377 *Duddon* 6. 7
Dewy and fresh, till showers again shall fall. . 381 *Duddon* 19. 14
From showers, or when the prize was won, . . 409 *White Doe* 1183
Which showers of blood seem rather to incite . 437 *Ecc. Sonn.* 2. 36. 8
Like showers of manna, if they come at all : . 493 *Hap. War.* 44
Their first look—blinded as tears fell in showers . 517 *Pun. Death* 1. 13
To utter, above showers of blossom swept . . 537 **In desultory* 7
His salt tears trickled down like showers of rain ; 556 *Prioress* 223
Was baffled still, the crumbs in little showers . 566 *Cumb. Beg.* 18
Could hear the wind and mark the showers . . 577 **I come* 18
Oh ! when the bitter showers her path assail, . 597 *Ev.Wk. Quarto* 279
And antique castles seen thro' drizzling show'rs. . 607 *Desc.Sk.Quarto* 282
Through bursts of sunshine and through flying showers, ... 622 *Recluse* 1. 1. 154
Engender lightning, whence are falling showers. . 625 *Æneid* 125
Of the old church, that—though from recent showers . . . . 644 *Prelude* 2. 120
Contending after showers. The mother now . . 692 *Prelude* 7. 365
To hearts that own not him ? Will showers of grace, ... 817 *Excursion* 4. 1096
Shadeless and shelterless, by driving showers . . 859 *Excursion* 7. 143

Showery. And when, upon some showery day, . . 142 †*Lov. and Lik.* 15

Showing. By showing that you look beyond the instant. . . . . 49 *Bord.* 654
Her ground-flowers shrink, afraid of showing . . 503 *Warning* 2

Showman. The Showman chooses well his place, 'tis Leicester's busy Square ; . . . . . . 189 *Star-gazers* 5
Yet, Showman, where can lie the cause ? Shall thy Implement have blame, ... 189 *Star-gazers* 9

Showman's. Accomplished in the showman's part ; 178 *Waggoner* 2. 126
Upon some showman's platform. What a shock 697 *Prelude* 7. 685

Shown. That you have shown, and by a signal instance, ... 64 *Bord.* 1485
As variously thy power was shown, ... 216 *Enterprise* 39
Hath shown that nothing human can be clear . 256 *Marriage: Friend* 12
Here by thy pencil shown in truth of lines . . 277 **Haydon ! let* 2
The genial spot had *ever* shown . . . . . 348 **Lulled by* 10
Than for like scenes in moral vision shown, . . 360 *Alban Hills* 5
Things that recoil from language ; that, if shown 368 *Trajan* 39
Aught that was ever shown in magic glass ; . . 369 *Eg. Maid* 16
Its will unquestionably shown— . . . . . 411 *White Doe* 1414
On her departure waits, no tongue hath shown ; . 422 *Ecc. Sonn.* 1. 16.12
By confidence supplied and mercy shown, . . 459 **Wanderer! that* 14
In character, and depth of feeling, shown . . . 509 *F. Stone* 100
In the full might they hitherto have shown, . . 518 *Pun. Death* 6. 12
" Thus, Christian people, God his might hath shown . . . . 627 **When Severn's* 3
Shown by a sudden turning of the road, . . . 664 *Prelude* 4. 388
And, lastly, as hereafter will be shown, . . . 732 *Prelude* 11. 349
A casual glance had shown them, and I fled, . 738 *Prelude* 12. 246
And, having shown in study forward zeal, . . 774 *Excursion* 2. 171
Be shown ? her glorious excellence—that ranks . 846 *Excursion* 6. 565
Are ofttimes not unprofitably shown . . . . 848 *Excursion* 6. 667
In this one Man is shown a temperance—proof . 862 *Excursion* 7. 323
Been shown, alike to body and to mind." . . . 888 *Excursion* 9. 289

Shows. *See* **Puppet-shows.**
Now shows a shadowy speck, and now is lost entire. 4 *Ev. Wk.* 113
Even now she shows, half-veiled, her lovely face : 8 *Ev. Wk.* 334
The Doctor at the casement shows . . . . . 128 *Idiot Boy* 249
This delicate Enclosure shows . . . . . . 154 *Flower Garden* 44
Not such the World's illusive shows ; . . . . 170 *Rural Ill.* 25
The very bacon shows its feeling, ... 177 *Waggoner* 2. 68
The Cherry Tree shows proof of this ; . . . . 177 *Waggoner* 2. 77

Sight—*continued.*
Lost sight of it bewildered and engulphed; . . 749 *Prelude* 14. 199
Than any liveliest sight of yesterday, ... 751 *Prelude* 14. 394
Unrecognised; but, stricken by the sight, . . 757 *Excursion* 1. 45
Silver and gold. 'I shuddered at the sight,' . . 766 *Excursion* 1. 671
By the broad hill, glistened upon our sight . . 773 *Excursion* 2. 127
From sight of One who lives secluded there, . . 774 *Excursion* 2. 159
Before whose sight the troubles of this world . 775 *Excursion* 2. 291
From his own sight—this gone, he forfeited . . 776 *Excursion* 2. 296
Before his sight in power or fame, and won, . . 776 *Excursion* 2. 301
And gardens interposed. Pleased with the sight, 778 *Excursion* 2. 428
This wanting, he would leave the sight of men, . 780 *Excursion* 2. 603
I would not willingly, methinks, lose sight . . 780 *Excursion* 2. 610
Oh, 'twas an unimaginable sight! . . . . . 784 *Excursion* 2. 852
The reach of sight; from whom, as from their source, ... 794 *Excursion* 3. 570
The space that severed us! But, as the sight . 795 *Excursion* 3. 661
"Long wished-for sight, the Western World appeared; . . . . 798 *Excursion* 3. 870
Betray to sight the motion of the stream, . . . 800 *Excursion* 3. 976
If the dear faculty of sight should fail, . . . 803 *Excursion* 4. 109
This deep abiding place, before your sight . . 807 *Excursion* 4. 391
Of God; and Angels to his sight appeared . . 810 *Excursion* 4. 635
To sight and feeling, or that in this sort . . 811 *Excursion* 4. 643
Removed from all approach of living sight . . 812 *Excursion* 4. 714
Unseen, perchance above all power of sight— . 819 *Excursion* 4. 1180
To sight restored, and glittering in the sun. . 823 *Excursion* 5. 86
Winds far in reaches hidden from our sight, . . 824 *Excursion* 5. 123
By sight undazzled with the glare of praise, . . 827 *Excursion* 5. 357
Within the very faculty of sight. . . . . . 830 *Excursion* 5. 514
Grateful to sight, refreshing to the soul, . . . 830 *Excursion* 5. 528
To that green pasture; place before our sight . 832 *Excursion* 5. 642
That they whom death has hidden from our sight 832 *Excursion* 5. 662
The lofty sight, by nature framed to tempt . . 832 *Excursion* 5. 679
Which makes the sabbath lovely in the sight . . 839 *Excursion* 6. 51
With hostile din, and combating in sight . . . 839 *Excursion* 6. 64
By various mockery of sight and sound; . . . 841 *Excursion* 6. 228
Whom sight of this green hillock to my mind . 842 *Excursion* 6. 274
Of Man degraded in his Maker's sight . . . . 847 *Excursion* 6. 574
To sight or mind. Nor less than care divine . 850 *Excursion* 6. 770
More holy in the sight of God or Man; . . . 850 *Excursion* 6. 803
—So near! yet not allowed upon that sight . . 853 *Excursion* 6. 963
Beholding her condition, at the sight . . . . 854 *Excursion* 6. 1043
Even were the object nearer to our sight, . . . 855 *Excursion* 6. 1141
(Who could refrain?) and feed by stealth my sight 856 *Excursion* 6. 1176
—Once more look forth, and follow with your sight 858 *Excursion* 7. 42
A sight that kindled pleasure in all hearts . . 868 *Excursion* 7. 724
And so, not wholly hidden from men's sight, . . 868 *Excursion* 7. 738
Break from the maddened nations at the sight . 873 *Excursion* 7. 1038
—But let us hence! my dwelling is in sight, . . 874 *Excursion* 8. 29
Idlers perchance they were,—but in *his* sight; . 878 *Excursion* 8. 279
A splendid sight, together thus exposed; . . . 883 *Excursion* 8. 569
To the still lake, whose stillness is to sight . . 883 *Excursion* 8. 582
When, heretofore, I placed before your sight . . 886 *Excursion* 9. 156
Blended in perfect stillness, to our sight! . . . 890 *Excursion* 9. 451
Faintly, too faint almost for sight; and some . 895 *Excursion* 9. 763
Palpable to sight as the dry ground, ... S.3. 435 **The doubt* 96
With sight of now and then a straggling gleam . K.8. 225 **I will* 50
Thus in his Father's sight the Boy grew up; . . K.8. 226 **I will* 84
At sight of this seclusion, he forgot . . . . K.8. 236 *Recluse* 1. 1. 8
Ah, if I wished to follow where the sight . . . K.8. 244 *Recluse* 1.1.273
Of tears that have been shed at sight of it, . . K.8. 248 *Recluse* 1.1.418
Philosopher and Poet, in whose sight . . . . K.8. 254 *Recluse* 1.1.660
Have walked within her sight? It cannot be. . K.8. 257 **Shall he* 10

Sighted. *See* **Clear-sighted, Short-sighted.**

Sight-eluding. She moulds her sight-eluding den . 543 *Russ. Fug.* 119

Sightless. Sightless, and from my heritage was driven, ... 52 *Bord.* 829
But for the child, the sightless Boy, ... 296 *Highland Boy* 166
All fervour to the sightless eye; . . . . . 301 *Bran* 95
The sightless Milton, with his hair . . . . . 341 *Ital. Itin.* 12
His steadfast face and sightless eyes, I gazed, . 697 *Prelude* 7. 648
A sightless labourer, whistles at his work— . . 813 *Excursion* 4. 797

Sights. These are strange sights—the mind of man, upturned, ... 58 *Bord.* 1168
The devils at such sights do clap their hands. . 76 *Bord.* 2190
And all the gorgeous sights which fairies do behold. 108 *Indolence* 63
With sights the ruefullest that flesh and bone . 257 **Methought I* 5
Where sights were rough, and sounds were wild, . 288 *Glen-Al.* 11
Avoid these sights; nor brood o'er Fable's dark abyss! . . . . 347 *Processions* 72
And taught him signs, and showed him sights, . 399 *White Doe* 278
Where be the wretched ones, the sights for pity? 475 *Greenock* 4
Induces, for its old familiar sights, ... 497 **Enough of climbing* 7
Thoughts, chances, sights, or doings, which we tell 522 *Epist. Beaumont* 54
Fair sights, and visions of romantic joy! . . . 547 **Rude is* 30
And frequent sights of what is to be borne! . . 579 *Peele Castle* 58
Such sights, or worse, as are before me here.— . 579 *Peele Castle* 59
Far from those lovely sights and sounds sublime . 650 *Prelude* 3. 94
Sees many beauteous sights—weeds, fishes, flowers, 662 *Prelude* 4. 261
Such sights before, among the shining streams . 672 *Prelude* 5. 454
And sights and sounds that come at intervals, . 689 *Prelude* 7. 173
From every clime; and, next, those sights that ape 690 *Prelude* 7. 232
In memory, those individual sights . . . . 696 *Prelude* 7. 599
Mobs, riots, or rejoicings? From these sights . 697 *Prelude* 7. 675
For 'tis most certain, that these various sights, . 710 *Prelude* 9. 74
And fellowships of men, and see ill sights . . 755 *Recluse* 1. 1. 827
And all known places and familiar sights . . . 793 *Excursion* 3. 508
Of mountain sights, this untaught shepherd stood K.8. 230 **I will* 196

Sign. Nature by sign or sound made no essay; . 35 *Guilt* 623

Sign—*continued.*
What is become of you.—You'll sit down and sign it; . . . . 49 *Bord.* 668
Shrine, Altar, Image, Offerings hung in sign of gratitude; . . . . 92 *Poet's Dream* 47
Composed and silent, without visible sign . . . 125 *V. and J.* 228
As gave sure sign that they, who in that house . 150 **When, to* 23
Into open sign of joy: . . . . 171 *Kitten* 90
As used to be that sign of love . . . . . 174 *Waggoner* 1. 85
Drooped with its withered leaves, ungracious sign 185 *Nutting* 18
That doth reject all show of pride, admits no outward sign, ... 189 *Star-gazers* 27
So, but from toil less sign of profit reaping, . . 213 *Dion* 77
There's little sign the treacherous path . . . 240 *P. B.* 349
Until no sign of life he makes, ... 248 *P. B.* 1092
From me the sign of life and death: . . . . 292 *Rob Roy* 90
His master's hands in sign of bliss, ... 297 *Highland Boy* 229
No sign of answer made by word or face: . . . 306 **We had* 9
And, in like sign of cloudless triumph bright, . 318 **In due* 5
Their heads in sign of worship, Nature's God, . 337 *Aar* 13
In sign of misery relieved, ... 338 **Meek Virgin* 8
So may all trace and sign of deeds aloof . . 361 **When here* 9
With thrilling word, and potent sign . . . . 369 *Eg. Maid* 31
Though on her prow a sign of heathen power . . 370 *Eg. Maid* 75
Sir Agravaine advanced; no sign he won . . . 373 *Eg. Maid* 269
And high expectancy, no sign was granted. . . 373 *Eg. Maid* 288
A sign he craved, tired slave of vain contrition; . 373 *Eg. Maid* 296
No sign of hoar Antiquity's esteem . . . . 376 *Duddon* 3. 10
Aloft in sign of taunting scorn, ... 410 *White Doe* 1326
As winter trees, yield no fallacious sign . . . 423 *Ecc. Sonn.* 1. 19. 4
Weeds on whose front the world had fixed her sign. 428 *Ecc. Sonn.* 2. 1. 8
Dost Thou prepare, whose sign will be the smoke 465 **Pastor and* 9
Thee, thee my life's celestial sign!) . . . . 497 *Lycoris* 28
Shall hoist their topmost flags in sign of glee, . 504 *Warning* 45
But not a hint from under-ground, no sign . . 532 **Once I* 17
They, who had waited for that sign to trace . . 534 **When in* 10
From sign to sign, its steadfast course, . . . 586 *Hogg* 14
Look up for sign of havoc, Fire and Sword, . . 617 *Desc.Sk.Quarto* 803
High on the topmost pinnacle, a sign . . . . 716 *Prelude* 9. 476
Remained, nor sign of sickness on his face. . . 779 *Excursion* 2. 517
With golden grasshoppers, in sign that they . . 790 *Excursion* 3. 250
In sign of conquest by his wit achieved . . . 816 *Excursion* 4. 999
In sign of farewell. "Nay," the old Man said, . 823 *Excursion* 5. 68
Within the heart no outward sign appeared . . 840 *Excursion* 6. 155
In memory and for warning, and in sign . . . 854 *Excursion* 6. 1082

Signal. The parting signal streamed—at last the land withdrew. . . . . 29 *Guilt* 288
That you have shown, and by a signal instance, . 64 *Bord.* 1485
By obvious signal to the world's protection . . 75 *Bord.* 2165
some signal judgment has befallen the man . . 76 *Bord.* 2218
A signal this which all can see! . . . . . 291 *Rob Roy* 42
We rose at signal given, and formed a ring . . 681 *Prelude* 6. 399
Wide as a province, but, the signal given, . . 718 *Prelude* 10. 22
By that unwearied signal, kenned afar; . . . 834 *Excursion* 5. 761

Signals. Expressive signals of a glorious strife, . . 324 *Ode 1814* 105
Right gladly answering signals we displayed, . . 524 *Epist. Beaumont* 213

Signature. 'Twill glad her heart to see her father's signature. . . . . 49 *Bord.* 669
now with me, as his signature will show: . . . 76 *Bord.* 2220
The writing Oswald's; the signature my Father's: 76 *Bord.* 2225

Sign-board. No swinging sign-board creaked from cottage elm . . . . 26 *Guilt* 136
Will see an ash from which a sign-board hangs; . 41 *Bord.* 218
Set the sign-board in a blaze, ... 161 **Pleasures newly* 13
Spread o'er the spangled sign-board, had dislodged 644 *Prelude* 2. 151

Signet. Under a private signet of the State. . . 123 *V. and J.* 129

Significance. Their own significance for hearts awake, 525 *Epist. Beaumont* 267

Significant. Union significant of God adored, . . 477 **Lowther! in* 4

Significants. And in my glass significants there are 372 *Eg. Maid* 251

Signified. *See* **Presignified.**
We signified a wish to leave that place . . . 793 *Excursion* 3. 470

Signifying. And, by their aspects, signifying works . 812 *Excursion* 4. 705

Signs. Figures with armorial signs of race and birth, 142 *Arm. Lady* 155
Peopling the harmless fields with signs of woe: . 153 *Morn. Ex.* 4
Such are they; and the same are tokens, signs, . 173 *Infant Daughter* 75
Number their signs or instruments? . . . . 225 *Present.* 38
And charm of colours; *I* applaud those signs . 277 **Haydon! let* 3
Of scattered quails by signs do reunite, . . . 320 **Hunger, and* 7
Guided by signs which ne'er the sky forsook, . . 346 *Processions* 14
O bounteous Heaven! signs true as dove and bough 360 **Near Anio's* 9
Upon the signs that pass away or tarry; . . . 374 *Eg. Maid.* 338
And taught him signs, and showed him sights, . 399 *White Doe* 278
And with dread signs the nascent Stream invest? 418 *Ecc. Sonn.* 1. 2. 8
Distinct with signs, through which in set career, . 445 *Ecc. Sonn.* 3. 19. 4
If he should speak, by fancy touched, of signs . 477 **Lonsdale! it* 3
For Christian Faith. But hopeful signs abound; . 520 *Pun. Death* 13. 8
What signs of mutual gladness when they met! . 531 **I know* 14
With other signs of manhood that supplied . . 649 *Prelude* 3. 41
Done visibly for other minds, words, signs, . . 651 *Prelude* 3. 174
Of an event so dire, by signs in earth . . . 668 *Prelude* 5. 158
Of spurious notions—worn as open signs . . . 775 *Excursion* 2. 271
For signs and tokens of a mutual bond; . . . 806 *Excursion* 4. 362

Silence. *That* Silence, once in deathlike fetters bound, 11 *Desc. Sk.* 56
And Silence loves its purple roof of vines. . . . 12 *Desc. Sk.* 88
Leaving to silence the deserted vale; . . . . 17 *Desc. Sk.* 373
Stand motionless, to awful silence bound: . . . 17 *Desc. Sk.* 410
One day in silence did we drift at noon . . . 68 *Bord.* 1705
No more of that; in silence hear my doom: . . 78 *Bord.* 2339
Nothing but silence and empty space; . . . 80 †*Address: Child* 17

Silence—*continued.*
Lest all that passed should melt away in silence from my mind, 93 *Poet's Dream* 71
The power of speech. Both left the spot in silence; 101 *Brothers* 408
That silence only should inhabit there, 102 *Artegal* 27
In silence and obscurity. 111 *A Complaint* 16
In silence, though my memory could add 124 *V. and J.* 177
The silence of her Idiot Boy, 127 *Idiot Boy* 92
'Tis silence all on every side; 128 *Idiot Boy* 244
Thus, after a short silence, he resumed: 137 *Michael* 384
Doth in its silence of past sorrow tell, 141 *Arm. Lady* 131
In silence deeper far than that of deepest noon! 173 *Waggoner* 1. 6
And the silence makes it sweet. 173 *Waggoner* 1. 21
Of yon dim cave, in seeming silence makes 184 *Airey-force* 13
Silence and Foresight; Death the Skeleton 185 *Yew-trees* 27
And hers the silence and the calm 187 **Three years* 17
In the silence of morning the song of the Bird. 188 *Poor Susan* 4
There is a doleful silence in the air. 200 *Hart-leap* 12
The silence that is in the starry sky, 205 *Brougham* 163
Sent up, in silence, from among the trees! 206 *Tintern* 18
Which there in ghastly silence sleep? 216 *Enterprise* 76
Is mute; and, in his silence, would look down, 220 *Haunted Tree* 33
And in its silence even, no heart is proof; 221 *Triad* 66
Her darkness splendour gave, her silence power, 226 *Vernal Ode* 38
O Silence! are Man's noisy years 235 *Power of Sound* 217
Would break the silence of this Dell: 289 *Glen-Al.* 24
Breaking the silence of the seas 289 *Sol. Reap.* 15
And chase this silence from the air, 302 *Yarrow V.* 7
O Silence! thou wert mother of a shout 322 *Germans* 5
And what, 'mid silence deep, with faith sincere, 332 *Ode: Thanks.* 231
For silence and protection; 337 *Thun* 6
O silence of Nature, how deep is thy sway, 340 *Fort Fuentes* 18
From social noise—silence elsewhere unknown?— 349 *At Dover* 7
Where Solitude with Silence paired stops short 355 *Aquap.* 196
Grants to thy mission a brief term of silence, 363 **List—'twas* 111
Silence, and holiness, and innocence, 365 **The Baptist* 11
In silence did King Arthur gaze 374 *Eg. Maid* 337
In silence watched the gentle strife 374 *Eg. Maid* 339
And into silence hush the timorous flocks, 380 *Duddon* 17. 7
Gliding in silence with unfettered sweep! 384 *Duddon* 32. 8
Of silence, how it thrilled thy sumptuous roof, 387 *Roslin* 6
Her silence; then his thoughts turned round, 401 *White Doe* 459
'Tis night: in silence looking down, 406 *White Doe* 938
And vows, that bind the will, in silence made. 423 *Ecc. Sonn.* 1. 19. 14
But, from the arms of silence—list! O list! 451 *Ecc. Sonn.* 3. 44. 9
Who lov'st with Night and Silence to partake, 459 **Wanderer! that* 3
In silence Matthew lay, and eyed 487 *Fountain* 17
Better than such discourse doth silence long, 488 *Pers. Talk* 9
Long, barren silence, square with my desire; 488 *Pers. Talk* 10
And, for silence or for talk, 490 *Incident: Dog* 5
Whose silence, for the pleasure of the ear, 508 *F. Stone* 10
In silence and the awful modesties 516 **Feel for* 7
And thought in silence, with regret too keen, 524 *Epist. Beaumont* 196
That haply flowed from me, by fits of silence 538 **In desultory* 13
Endure that silence, and broke out in song, 539 **Lady! a* 31
Her silence to endear; 544 *Russ. Fug.* 206
Where silence yields reluctantly 550 *Hermit's Cell* 2. 3
Broke silence, or I heard him in my thought. 558 *Cuck.andNight.* 90
My sighs breathed forth in silence,—comfort give! 562 *Cuck.andNight.* 316
Be his the natural silence of old age! 569 *Cumb. Beg.* 182
To the perpetual silence of the grave. 573 *Chiabrera* 2. 18
"Silence!" the brave Commander cried; 579 **Sweet Flower* 43
Of the eternal Silence: truths that wake, 589 *Immortality* 159
She lifts in silence up her lovely face; 599 *Ev. Wk. Quarto* 402
Where Silence, on her night of wing, o'er-broods 602 *Desc. Sk. Quarto* 9
Where Silence still her death-like reign extends, 609 *Desc.Sk.Quarto* 376
To silence leaving the deserted vale, 610 *Desc.Sk.Quarto* 451
The silence of sorrow it seems to supply, 621 *Convict* 43
—Oh if such silence be not thanks to God 622 *Recluse* 1. 1. 83
Silence ensued. "O Jupiter, whose care 625 *Æneid* 107
Thy shades, thy silence, now be mine, 626 †*Cento* 9
And lastly utter silence! "Be it so; 633 *Prelude* 1. 99
Suffered in silence for Truth's sake; or tell, 635 *Prelude* 1. 205
In silence, or with keen devouring noise 655 *Prelude* 3. 453
In silence through a wood gloomy and still. 665 *Prelude* 4. 447
Of silence came and baffled his best skill, 671 *Prelude* 5. 380
Then sometimes, in that silence while he hung 671 *Prelude* 5. 381
Through hours of silence, till the porter's bell, 676 *Prelude* 6. 70
And silence did await upon these thoughts 677 *Prelude* 6. 140
In silence visible and perpetual calm. 681 *Prelude* 6. 429
Where silence dwells if music be not there: 685 *Prelude* 6. 669
Through a thick forest. Silence touched me here 687 *Prelude* 7. 36
Whom the fifth Harry talks of. Silence! hush! 694 *Prelude* 7. 498
A spacious grass-plot; there, in silence, sate 696 *Prelude* 7. 607
Helvellyn, in the silence of his rest, 699 *Prelude* 8. 14
In peace and silence. But if e'er was heard,— 716 *Prelude* 9. 446
And half upbraids their silence. But that night 719 *Prelude* 10. 63
In silence of all present, from his seat 720 *Prelude* 10. 110
In silence as before. With forehead bent 746 *Prelude* 14. 28
And in the silence of his face I read 772 *Excursion* 2. 40
In silence musing by my Comrade's side, 777 *Excursion* 2. 371
Said the old man, abruptly breaking silence,— 777 *Excursion* 2. 383
In silence, with a hush of decency; 780 *Excursion* 2. 557
Of silence, though there be no voice;—the clouds, 782 *Excursion* 2. 712
Was greeted, in the silence that ensued, 786 *Excursion* 3. 6
A pause of silence followed; then, with voice 801 *Excursion* 4. 8
Through consciousness that silence in such place 807 *Excursion* 4. 414
That neither she nor Silence lack the power 816 *Excursion* 4. 1033
To which, in silence hushed, his very soul 818 *Excursion* 4. 1136

Silence—*continued.*
Fondly to prize the silence which he kept, 839 *Excursion* 6. 105
Though with the silence pleased that here prevails, 847 *Excursion* 6. 631
The pensive silence, saying:—"Blest are they 854 *Excursion* 6. 1069
And silence waited on these closing words; 862 *Excursion* 7. 292
Thus silence broke:—"Behold a thoughtless Man 862 *Excursion* 7. 299
We gazed, in silence hushed, with eyes intent 893 *Excursion* 9. 610
Of solitude, and silence in the sky? K.8. 240 *Recluse* 1.1.133
Among the silence of the woods and hills; K.8. 241 *Recluse* 1.1.186
Silenced. While prayer contends with silenced agony, 20 *Desc. Sk.* 549
Silent. While silent stands the admiring crowd below, 6 *Ev. Wk.* 205
Silent the visionary warriors go, 6 *Ev. Wk.* 206
Turn to a silent smile their sleepy cry, 7 *Ev. Wk.* 258
Silent the hedge or steamy rivulet's bed, 8 *Ev. Wk.* 324
The boat her silent course pursues! 9 *Lines: Boat* 4
By silent cottage-doors, the peasant's home 13 *Desc. Sk.* 143
That faded silent from the upward eye 14 *Desc. Sk.* 204
Where silent Hours their death-like sway extend, 16 *Desc. Sk.* 311
Or, when upon the mountain's silent brow 18 *Desc. Sk.* 465
Gay lark of hope, thy silent song resume! 20 *Desc. Sk.* 528
Who, in the silent hour of inward thought, 23 *Yew-tree* 62
The empty loom, cold hearth, and silent wheel, 29 *Guilt* 269
And looked, and fed upon the silent air 30 *Guilt* 341
The silent sea. From the sweet thoughts of home 31 *Guilt* 357
His ears were never silent; sleep forsook 36 *Guilt* 635
On this green bank. Idonea, you are silent, 39 *Bord.* 131
The blind Man—at the silent Girl he looked 47 *Bord.* 540
The trees were silent as the graves beneath them. 47 *Bord.* 576
Stood silent as we passed them! I have heard 61 *Bord.* 1333
My voice was silent, but my heart hath joined thee. 76 *Bord.* 2185
Silent he stood; then laughed amain,— 81 †*Mother's Return* 7
O weary struggle! silent years 110 *Forsaken* 8
That silent greeting from above; 112 *Lament* 2
Composed and silent, without visible sign 125 *V. and J.* 228
Is silent as the skies. 128 *Idiot Boy* 246
All silent as a horseman-ghost, 129 *Idiot Boy* 325
Making the cottage through the silent hours 133 *Michael* 127
And Isabel sat silent, for her mind 135 *Michael* 256
And silent morning, I sat down, and there, 148 *Joanna* 80
A *silent* Poet; from the solitude 151 **When, to* 80
For Mary's humble, Sarah's silent claim, 152 **Forth from* 24
Sweet silent creature! 159 **With little* 44
Though silent as a leaf before, 168 *Turtledove* 5
Or by the silent lapse of fountain clear, 170 **Never enlivened* 14
Of the silent heart which Nature 171 *Kitten* 97
Close-treading on the silent flashes— 175 *Waggoner* 1. 198
(The vale now silent, hushed, I ween, 176 *Waggoner* 2. 12
And, while they coast the silent lake, 178 *Waggoner* 3. 31
The silent company betray: 180 *Waggoner* 4. 32
But they are silent;—still they roll along 184 *Night-piece* 19
The silent trees, and saw the intruding sky.— 186 *Nutting* 53
Of shades, and dews, and silent night; 186 **O Nightingale* 8
By silent sympathy. 187 **Three years* 24
Because not of this noisy world, but silent and divine! 189 *Star-gazers* 28
As on their silent tasks they move! 192 *Gipsies* 24
By day, and in the silent night, 200 *Thorn* 238
But gazed upon the spoil with silent joy. 201 *Hart-leap* 36
A festal strain that hath been silent long:— 203 *Brougham* 4
The oracle, upon the silent sea; 211 *Laod.* 122
He through the portal takes his silent way, 211 *Laod.* 156
Nor grieves—tho' doomed thro' silent night to bear 216 *Enterprise* 95
Far into silent regions blue and pale;— 219 **This Height* 15
Speak, silent creatures.—They are gone, are fled, 230 *Clouds* 30
In silent rapture, credulous desire 231 *Clouds* 89
In memory, through silent night. 234 *Power of Sound* 144
'Tis lodged within her silent tear. 238 *P. B.* 150
These silent raptures found no place; 239 *P. B.* 272
By lovely forms, and silent weather, 239 *P. B.* 287
Over the silent stream. 240 *P. B.* 395
All, all is silent—rocks and woods, 241 *P. B.* 411
All still and silent—far and near! 241 *P. B.* 412
Is silent as a silent cricket. 243 *P. B.* 625
Whom seeks he—whom?—the silent dead: 243 *P. B.* 640
In agony of silent grief— 248 *P. B.* 1077
But Thee, deep buried in the silent tomb, 257 **Surprised by* 3
Of silent hills, and more than silent sky. 259 **A volant* 14
Of silent rapture; but we felt the while 262 **Dark and* 12
And whispers to the silent birds, "Prepare 263 **While not* 7
Haunts him belated on the silent plains! 265 **There is a pleasure* 8
Of mountains, silent, dreary, motionless: 266 **Even as* 5
The beauty of the morning; silent, bare, 269 *Westm. Bridge* 5
In this deep knell, silent for threescore years, 271 *George: Death* 13
Waft fragrant greetings to each silent grave; 272 **Where holy* 10
Why art thou silent! Is thy love a plant 277 **Why art* 1
The silent thoughts that search for steadfast light, 280 **Intent on* 12
And silent grave. 285 *Grave of Burns* 30
A murmur near the silent lake; 288 *Highland Girl* 8
Is come, and thou art silent in thy age; 290 *Kilchurn* 3
And the green silent pastures, yet remain. 292 **Degenerate Douglas* 14
And quickly with a silent crew 297 *Highland Boy* 181
And left them lying in the silent sun, 310 *Anticip.* 4
And, at our feet, amid the silent dust 315 **The Land* 8
And silent fetters? Yes, if visions bright 318 **Is there* 12
Victorious England! bid the silent Art 324 *Ode 1814* 94
Their utter stillness, and the silent grace 329 *Ode: Thanks.* 21
Obscure not yet these silent avenues 334 **Bruges I* 12
When silent were both voice and chords, 334 **In Bruges* 13
And horror breathing from the silent ground! 335 **A winged* 14

Silver—*continued.*
And beauteous as the silver moon . . . . 396 White Doe 60
Bright locks of silver hair, thick spread, . . . 404 White Doe 746
The smoke, and mounts in silver wreaths. . . 406 White Doe 950
And blest the silver Cross, which ye, instead . 422 Ecc. Sonn. 1. 14. 3
Over the bowl, whose silver lip hath won . . 433 Ecc. Sonn. 2. 20. 7
Portentous fellowship. Her silver car, . . . 438 Ecc. Sonn. 2. 38. 8
When darkness creeping o'er thy silver brow . 460 *Queen of 3
Nor is it silver of romantic Spain ; . . . . 480 Cordelia 5
Planting his favourite silver diadem, . . . 496 *A little 6
Till the first silver star appear, ... 507 *While from 63
A silver line, that runs from brow to crown . 508 F. Stone 28
Had from the east her silver star withdrawn, . 522 Epist. Beaumont 92
Where golden flash and silver gleam . . . 526 *The soaring 11
The silver Tenant of the crystal dome ; . . 527 *Those breathing 18
A silver boat launched on a boundless flood ; . 532 *Once I 14
Where silver rocks the savage prospect chear . 591 Ev. Wk. Quarto 7
And yew-trees o'er the silver rocks recline, . 594 Ev. Wk. Quarto 140
Thin silver hairs, and ancient hamlet fame ; . 595 Ev. Wk. Quarto 176
A silver cross enchased with Flowers of France 628 Eagle and Dove 11
With silver clouds, and sunshine on the grass, 633 Prelude 1. 68
Organic pleasure from the silver wreaths . . 640 Prelude 1. 564
'Twas now for me a burnished silver shield . 705 Prelude 8. 414
To which the silver wands of saints in Heaven 725 Prelude 10. 485
Silver and gold. 'I shuddered at the sight,' . 766 Excursion 1. 671
Half-veiled in vapoury cloud, the silver steam 773 Excursion 2. 131
With alabaster domes, and silver spires, . . 784 Excursion 2. 840
Darken the silver bosom of the crag, . . . 786 Excursion 3. 27
Her silver voice was heard upon the earth, . . 793 Excursion 3. 482
To mix the manly brown with silver grey, . . 842 Excursion 6. 278
Light as the silver fawn, a radiant Girl ; . . 881 Excursion 8. 493
As if they from a silver tree had fallen— . . S.3. 433 *The doubt 48
First one and then another silver spout, . . K.8. 251 Recluse 1.1.555
Shows like a mountain built of silver light. . K.8. 252 Recluse 1.1.569
When envious clouds shut out her silver light. . [?] *A sad 14
Silver-bright. A radiant creature, silver-bright ! . 414 White Doe 1647
Silver-collared. The silver-collared Negro with his timbrel, ... 697 Prelude 7. 703
Silvered. While, near the midway cliff, the silvered kite . . . . 3 Ev. Wk. 90
On as he floats, the silver'd waters glow, . . . 595 Ev. Wk. Quarto 205
By silver'd wreaths of quiet charcoal smoke, . . 599 Ev. Wk. Quarto 430
By mist and silent rain-drops silvered o'er, . . 770 Excursion 1. 944
Silver-how. And the tall Steep of Silver-how, sent forth . . . . 147 Joanna 58
Of Silver-how, and Grasmere's peaceful lake . 151 *When, to 91
Silvering. Tracking with silvering path the changeful gale. . . . . 598 Ev. Wk. Quarto 344
Silver-rimmed. Of the silver-rimmed horn whence he dealt his mild ale ! . . . . . . 569 Farmer 16
Silvery. From the dark-blue faint silvery threads divide . . . . 9 Ev. Wk. 359
And saw the dawn opening the silvery east . . 30 Guilt 313
Yet why ?—a silvery current flows . . . . 302 Yarrow V. 9
You mark them twinkling out with silvery light, . 453 *Calm is the 5
That lit the dark slant woods with silvery white ! 593 Ev. Wk. Quarto 100
How fair it's lawn and silvery woods appear ! . . 599 Ev. Wk. Quarto 417
The silvery lake is streaked with placid blue ; . 890 Excursion 9. 421
Similar. Have been possessed by similar desire ; . 680 Prelude 6. 338
Similes. I sit, and play with similes, ... 158 *With little 10
Simon. The halloo of Simon Lee. . . . . . 483 Simon Lee 12
To blither tasks did Simon rouse . . . . 483 Simon Lee 15
Old Simon to the world is left . . . . . 483 Simon Lee 27
Ruth does what Simon cannot do ; . . . . 483 Simon Lee 50
" You're overtasked, good Simon Lee, . . . 484 Simon Lee 81
Simonides. Of pure Simonides. . . . . . . 499 *Departing summer 54
I find it written of Simonides . . . . . 623 *I find 1
Simonides, admonished by the ghost, ... 623 *I find 9
Simon's. Simon's sickly daughter lies, ... 157 Sexton 14
Simple. And, like the Patriarchs in their simple age, 17 Desc. Sk. 374
For as the pleasures of his simple day . . . 18 Desc. Sk. 427
The simple dignity no forms debase ; . . . 18 Desc. Sk. 443
Well pleased upon some simple annual feast, . . 19 Desc. Sk. 496
How in a simple freak of thoughtless play . . 33 Guilt 472
A deep and simple meekness : and that Soul, . 40 Bord. 169
One of Love's simple bondsmen—the soft chain . 70 Bord. 1841
——A simple Child, ... 83 We are Seven 1
Stranger to me and yet my friend, a simple notice came, ... 91 Norman Boy 6
In verse, which to thy ear might come, would treat this simple theme, ... 93 Poet's Dream 75
Nor can the winds restore his simple gift. . . 103 Artegal 44
Whe while on thee they gaze in simple truth, . 110 *Look at 21
" A simple burthen, Sir, a little Singing-bird." 119 Sailor's Mother 18
Could, by the simple opening of a door, . . . 122 V. and J. 47
And to that simple object appertains . . . 131 Michael 18
While in this sort the simple household lived . 134 Michael 207
Smiled in my face) this were in simple truth . 147 Joanna 68
Beneath her sway, a simple forest cry . . . 153 Morn. Ex. 5
His simple truths did Andrew glean . . . 155 Oak and Broom 1
A simple flower deceives. . . . . . . 169 Wren's Nest 60
A simple water-drinking Bard ; . . . . . 174 Waggoner 1. 60
For transient sorrows, simple wiles, . . . 186 *She was 19
To pipe a simple song for thinking hearts. . . 202 Hart-leap 100
And in my simple mind we cannot tell . . . 203 Hart-leap 146
Yet lacks not friends for simple glee, . . . 205 Brougham 116
And was it granted to the simple ear . . . 227 Vernal Ode 82
In simple truth I cannot tell ; . . . . . 239 P. B. 283
I stood, of simple shame the blushing Thrall ; . 251 *Beloved Vale 10
A simple answer ! but even so forth springs, . . 252 *Why, Minstrel 5

Simple—*continued.*
Meek, nobly versed in simple discipline— . . . 254 Complete Angler 7
So kind is simple Nature, fairly tried ! . . . 275 *Chatsworth ! thy 8
If simple Nature trained by careful Art . . . 281 Valedict. 12
Sufficeth them, the simple plan, ... 291 Rob Roy 38
That simple crest, a heron's plume, is worn. . 314 Hofer 8
Such simple gifts prepare, ... 324 Ode 1814 47
The measure, simple truth to tell, ... 334 *In Bruges 9
Where simple Sufferers bend, in trust . . . 337 Cath. Cantons 5
A simple, but a touching, song ; . . . . 338 Brientz 15
Mindful how others by this simple Strain . . 340 Ranz 9
Thy mountain notes with simple skill ; . . . 341 Ital. Itin. 6
Her simple cares to magnify ; . . . . . 344 *How blest 4
In simple democratic majesty ; . . . . . 350 Des. Stanzas 52
These simple efforts of Helvetian skill, . . . 351 Des. Stanzas 75
The simple rapture ;—who that travels far . . 353 Aquap. 54
Paid simple tribute, such as might have flowed . 356 Aquap. 242
That awful name to Thee, thee, simple Cuckoo, . 363 *List—'twas 97
In simple childhood, spread through ours ! . . 375 *The Minstrels 30
Though simple thy companions were and few ; . 379 Duddon 14. 11
For simple hearts thy beauty ; . . . . . 386 Yarrow Rev. 108
This brief this simple wayside Call can slight, . 389 Glencroe 3
With heart by simple nature moved ; . . . . 401 White Doe 472
In meek and simple infancy, what joy . . . 436 Ecc. Sonn. 2. 31. 9
Of simple truth with grace divine imbued ; . . 450 Ecc. Sonn. 3. 40. 8
May sage and simple, catching with one eye . . 461 *Queen of 47
Thanks to the austere and simple Devotees, . . 467 St. Bees 70
That satisfies the simple and the meek, . . . 468 *Ranging the 12
And, by that simple notice, the repose . . . 475 *There ! said 7
Crescent in simple loveliness serene, . . . 509 F. Stone 47
And are endeared to simple cottagers)— . . . 509 F. Stone 102
Though but a simple object, into light . . . 510 *Among a 14
And simple honesty a common growth— . . . 515 Penn. 5
Where simple art with bounteous nature vied, . 525 Epist. Beaumont 248
For whom this simple Register was penned. . . 525 *Soon did 4
Think of their common peace, their simple play, . 531 *I know 15
And on that simple bed, ... 542 Russ. Fug. 38
For simple infant hath a ready ear. . . . 553 Prioress 60
But, Lord, this simple Troilus was woe, . . . 562 Troilus 11
For Adam was simple in thought ; and the poor, 569 Farmer 25
Only by gold. And now a simple stone . . . 574 Chiabrera 5. 16
Those simple lines flowed with an earnest wish, . 585 Ch. Lamb 40
Delight and liberty, the simple creed . . . 589 Immortality 140
Content upon some simple annual feast, . . . 613 Desc.Sk.Quarto 586
The simple ways in which my childhood walked ; 642 Prelude 2. 3
Seemed friends, poor simple schoolboys, now hung round . . . . 649 Prelude 3. 20
And wild outlandish walks of simple youth . . 656 Prelude 3. 518
And simple Pleasure foraging for Death ; . . . 657 Prelude 3. 599
Our simple childhood, sits upon a throne . . 673 Prelude 5. 508
O, wond'rous power of words, by simple faith . 689 Prelude 7. 119
And sorrows of the world. Those simple days . 692 Prelude 7. 333
Among the simple shapes of human life . . . 704 Prelude 8. 372
With that amusement, and a simple look . . . 707 Prelude 8. 535
And, 'mid the simple worshippers, perchance . . 722 Prelude 10. 296
And as, by simple waving of a wand, . . . 735 Prelude 12. 81
In simple childhood something of the base . . 738 Prelude 12. 274
With human kindnesses and simple joys. . . . 741 Prelude 13. 119
Its simple worshippers from sun and shower. . 743 Prelude 13. 231
A simple produce of the common day. . . . 755 Recluse 1. 1. 808
Exist more simple in their elements, . . . 761 Excursion 1. 346
All recollection ; and that simple tale . . . 765 Excursion 1. 609
The simple pastimes of the day and place. . . 773 Excursion 2. 143
Smooth words he had to wheedle simple souls ; . 775 Excursion 2. 254
Pleasing and pleased, he shared their simple sports, 778 Excursion 2. 450
This simple Child will mourn his one short hour, . 780 Excursion 2. 601
The simple shepherd's awe-inspiring God ! " . . 814 Excursion 4. 887
Of simple manners, feelings unsuppress . . . 824 Excursion 5. 118
And noiseless commonwealth. The simple race . 828 Excursion 5. 423
And patient spade ; praise to the simple crook, . 831 Excursion 5. 603
" Yet—in less simple districts, where we see . . 847 Excursion 6. 624
Over her comrades ; else their simple sports, . . 848 Excursion 6. 692
One of God's simple children that yet know not . 851 Excursion 6. 881
Repeated without loss of simple phrase, . . . 851 Excursion 6. 889
Unknown to you that in these simple vales . . 852 Excursion 6. 949
A simple curiosity to ease : . . . . . . 859 Excursion 7. 107
Frolicked industriously, a simple Clerk . . . 859 Excursion 7. 129
Our simple shepherds, speaking from the heart, . 862 Excursion 7. 345
That lowly, great, good Man. A simple stone . 862 Excursion 7. 352
So, through a simple rustic garb's disguise, . . 868 Excursion 7. 735
Carrying relief for nature's simple wants. . . 875 Excursion 8. 48
Her simple manners, and the stable worth . . 877 Excursion 8. 237
The simple occupations of their sires, ... 878 Excursion 8. 260
—Not shaped by simple wearing of the foot . . 881 Excursion 8. 448
A simple blessing, or with evil mixed ; . . . 884 Excursion 9. 12
Instructing simple childhood's ready ear : . . . 890 Excursion 9. 396
The lovely Girl supplied—a simple song, . . . 892 Excursion 9. 534
So long unthanked) hast cheered a simple board . S.3. 433 *The doubt 16
Six simple burghers—To the rope that tied . . L.1. 95 Juvenal 3. 9
Simple-hearted. While thus these simple-hearted men are moved ? . . . . 283 *Well have 14
Simple-mindedness. Of modest meekness, simple-mindedness, ... 670 Prelude 5. 291
Simpler. More wise desires, and simpler manners ;—nurse . . . . 755 Recluse 1. 1. 857
Gained merited respect in simpler times ; . . . 761 Excursion 1. 328
That, 'mid the simpler forms of rural life, . . 761 Excursion 1. 345
Simples. This wood is rich in plants and curious simples. . . . . 38 Bord. 44
Simplest. Not undelightful are the simplest charms, 5 Ev. Wk. 144

Sing—*continued.*
Thus, thought I, to her lamb that little Maid might sing: . . . . 87 Pet-lamb 20
Or sing another song, or choose another tree. . . 111 *'Tis said that some 28
Let other bards of angels sing, ... 111 *Let other 1
Sing at thy Mother's breast. Month followed month, ... 136 Michael 349
Used to sing in heavenly tone, ... 144 *Driven in 55
And I am happy when I sing . . . . . . 144 Her Eyes 13
My pretty thing! then thou shalt sing . . . 145 Her Eyes 59
Yet might'st thou seem, proud privilege! to sing 153 Morn. Ex. 47
I will sing, as doth behove, ... 160 *Pansies, lilies 63
Sing, mournfully, oh! mournfully, ... 161 Binnorie 10
Sing, mournfully, oh! mournfully, ... 161 Binnorie 21
Sing, mournfully, oh! mournfully, ... 162 Binnorie 32
Sing, mournfully, oh! mournfully, ... 162 Binnorie 43
Sing, mournfully, oh! mournfully, ... 162 Binnorie 54
Sing, mournfully, oh! mournfully, ... 162 Binnorie 65
Fair Lady! can I sing of flowers . . . . . 164 *Fair Lady 1
Rouse the birds, and they sing; . . . . . 167 Stray Pleasures 32
Of whom I sing this rustic lay, ... 174 Waggoner 1. 94
I sing of these;—it makes my bliss! . . . . 182 Waggoner 4. 208
I heard a Stock-dove sing or say . . . . . 186 *O Nightingale 11
And all the congregation sing . . . . . . 195 Ruth 257
He heard the birds their morning carols sing; . 203 Hart-leap 154
And into caves where Faeries sing . . . . . 205 Brougham 131
—I sing in vain;—the pines have hushed their waving: . . . . 220 Triad 24
Can draw, and sing his griefs to rest. . . . . 233 Power of Sound 64
That I may have the power to sing of Thee, . . 257 *The prayers 13
Conversing, reading, laughing;—or they sing, . 266 *Even as 13
That we may sing together, if thou wilt, . . . 279 *Hark! 'tis 10
The lintwhites sing in chorus; . . . . . . 292 Yarrow Unv. 20
And bid them dance, and bid them sing; . . . 293 Jedbor. 3
And she will dance and sing with thee. . . . 293 Jedbor. 12
Of them that were before us.—Sing aloud . . . 315 *The Land 9
And loud and long of Winter's triumph sing! . . 322 *Ye Storms 5
Sing ye, with blossoms crowned, and fruits, and flowers, ... 322 *Ye Storms 6
Of Britain's acts would sing, ... 330 Ode: Thanks. 68
But that they sing and that they love?" . . . 338 Brientz 2
The Sabine Bard was moved her praise to sing; . 376 Duddon 1. 4
They sing a service which they feel: . . . . 396 White Doe 39
And psalms they sing—a holy sound . . . . 413 White Doe 1533
A mortal Song we sing, by dower . . . . . 416 White Doe 1832
And loved with spirit ruled by his to sing . . 418 Ecc. Sonn. 1. 1. 3
Subjects of Saxon Ælla—they shall sing . . . 422 Ecc. Sonn. 1. 13. 13
Early awake, by Siloa's brook, to sing . . . . 440 Ecc. Sonn. 2. 46. 5
In which the linnet or the thrush might sing, . . 449 Ecc. Sonn. 3. 33. 12
Build, at thy choice, or sing, by pool or fount, . 455 Rydal Mere 35
Sing here beneath the shade, ... 487 Fountain 14
I live and sing my idle songs . . . . . . 487 Fountain 59
Here often hast Thou heard the Poet sing . . . 489 Spade 13
And at my casement sing, ... 530 †Redbreast 2
Come, and my requiem sing, ... 530 †Redbreast 14
That is to say, to sing and read also, ... 553 Prioress 48
And unto him declare why men sing so; . . . 553 Prioress 76
Full merrily then would he sing and cry, . . . 554 Prioress 102
In your despite, and sing his hymns and saws, . 554 Prioress 112
Now may'st thou sing for aye before the throne, . 554 Prioress 129
The Alma Redemptoris 'gan to sing . . . . 555 Prioress 161
Tell me the cause why thou dost sing this hymn, . 555 Prioress 196
Yet may I sing, O Alma! loud and clear. . . 556 Prioress 204
'Thou in thy dying sing this holy lay,' . . . 556 Prioress 209
"'Wherefore I sing, nor can from song refrain, . 556 Prioress 212
And some did sing all out with the full throat. . 558 Cuck. and Night. 75
I heard the lusty Nightingale so sing, ... 558 Cuck. and Night. 98
And, prithee, let us that can sing dwell here; . 558 Cuck.andNight.113
It seems to me I sing as well as thou; 558 Cuck.andNight.117
And I will sing one song, of many new, . . . 561 Cuck.andNight.247
That absent was, 'gan sing as ye may hear. . . 564 Troilus 119
That I sing of old Adam, the pride of old men. . 569 Farmer 4
The birds shall sing and ocean make . . . . 580 *Sweet Flower 67
Now, while the birds thus sing a joyous song, . 588 Immortality 19
Then sing, ye Birds, sing, sing a joyous song! . 590 Immortality 172
Glad from their airy baskets hang and sing. . . 594 Ev. Wk. Quarto 150
Sing notes of greeting to strange fields or groves, 742 Prelude 13. 135
I sing:—'fit audience let me find though few!' . 755 Recluse 1. 1. 776
Turned inward; or at my request would sing . . 757 Excursion 1. 66
For wren and redbreast,—where they sit and sing 881 Excursion 8. 482
Sonorous squadrons sing their evening hymn. . K.8. 234 *The order'd 7
Arms and the Man I sing, the first who bore . . K.8. 281 *Arms and 1
Singed. Old Ocean, in his bed left singed and bare, 666 Prelude 5. 33
Singer. *See* **Ballad-singer.**
Singer's. *See* **Ballad-singer's.**
Singest. Thou Thrush, that singest loud—and loud and free, ... 111 *'Tis said that some 25
Thou sing'st as if the God of wine . . . . . 186 *O Nightingale 5
Singing. Wert thou among them, singing as they shine! . . . . 154 Morn. Ex. 60
Singing, singing, ... 159 *Up with me 4
The birds are singing in the distant woods; . . 195 Resolution 4
And singing, while the accordant hand . . . 234 Power of Sound 140
And knows she not, singing as he inspires, . . 261 *I heard (alas 10
Reaping and singing by herself; . . . . . 289 Sol. Reap. 3
I saw her singing at her work, ... 289 Sol. Reap. 27
He cannot stop his singing by the way. . . . 554 Prioress 106
Before the Lamb singing continually, ... 554 Prioress 133
Was taken up, singing his song alway; . . . . 555 Prioress 171
Some, singing loud, as if they had complained; . 558 Cuck. and Night. 73

Singing—*continued.*
Such uncouth singing verily dost thou make. . . 558 Cuck.andNight.115
Singing so well, so goodly, and so clear, . . . 563 Troilus 60
Singing, and often with more plaintive voice . 751 Prelude 14. 384
Of that small valley, singing as they moved; . . 777 Excursion 2. 390
And small birds singing happily to mates . . . 851 Excursion 6. 857
Singing-bird. "A simple burthen, Sir, a little Singing-bird." . . . . 119 Sailor's Mother 18
The singing-bird had gone with him; . . . . 119 Sailor's Mther 28
Like a poor singing-bird from distant lands; . . 852 Excursion 6. 934
Single. If in that hour a single tie . . . . . 1 Extract 5
A single chasm, a gulf of gloomy blue, ... 18 Desc. Sk. 413
Your single virtue has transformed a Band . . 48 Bord. 610
What do they mean? were this my single body . 51 Bord. 778
A single tree; she thought it was her Father.— . 74 Bord. 2098
Of their inheritance, that single cottage— . . 98 Brothers 206
Another day, a single one! . . . . 114 Ind. Wom. 22
"When I was young, a single man, ... 115 Last of Flock 21
And from this one, this single ewe, ... 115 Last of Flock 32
There's not a single soul abroad." . . . . . 129 Idiot Boy 281
Stood single, with large prospect, north and south, 133 Michael 133
Stood single, and, from matchless depth of shade, 133 Michael 166
And never lifted up a single stone. . . . . . 138 Michael 466
A single mountain-cottage might be seen. . . . 146 *It was an 36
That for my single self I looked at them, . . . 149 *A narrow 61
Hither repaired.—A single beech-tree grew . . 150 *When, to 18
Save that above a single height . . . . . . 175 Waggoner 1. 166
A single traveller—and there . . . . 182 Waggoner 4. 256
Which to this day stands single, in the midst . . 184 Yew-trees 2
And a single small cottage, a nest like a dove's, . 188 Poor Susan 11
When but a single Mind resolves to crouch no more. 216 Enterprise 103
There's not a single house in sight, ... 240 P. B. 388
Behold her, single in the field, ... 289 Sol. Reap. 1
O for a single hour of that Dundee, ... 293 Killicranky 11
His world is in this single room: . . . . . 294 Jedbor. 22
No single volume paramount, no code, ... 307 *Great men 12
Left single, in bold parley, ye, of yore, . . . 309 Men of Kent 9
Or were conducted home in single state, . . . 328 Ode 1815 83
Into his single breast, a sheaf . . . . . . 341 San Salv. 35
Missed not the truth, retains a single name . . 356 Aquap. 239
This day, be mistress of a single pearl . . . 358 Aquap. 356
Stretched far as earth might own a single lord; . 368 Trajan 30
Stands single—Norton Tower its name— . . . 409 White Doe 1168
Single on the gladsome earth. . . . . . . 414 White Doe 1638
A single One, in mid career . . . . 414 White Doe 1643
But chiefly by that single grave, ... 417 White Doe 1898
The peace of God within his single breast! . . 438 Ecc. Sonn. 2. 37. 14
I struck, and with a single blow . . . . . . 484 Simon Lee 85
A single human life have wrongly taken, . . . 517 Pun. Death 3. 10
Go, single—yet aspiring to be joined . . . . 538 *In desultory 17
A single Act endears to high and low . . . . 540 Grace Darl. 8
A single Island rose . . . . 543 Russ. Fug. 102
As needed kindness, for this single cause, . . . 568 Cumb. Beg. 152
All vanished in a single word, ... 580 John Words. 35
A single Field which I have looked upon, . . . 588 Immortality 52
Clustered like stars some few, but single most, . 622 Recluse 1. 1. 122
A single Glow-worm did I chance to espy; . . . 622 *Among all 6
Do thou, but for a single night's brief space, . . 624 Æneid 36
Went single in his ministry across . . . . . 635 Prelude 1. 209
Single and of determined bounds; and hence . . 641 Prelude 1. 641
And the stone-abbot, and that single wren . . 644 Prelude 2. 118
As of a single independent thing. . . . . . . 645 Prelude 2. 227
Where all stand single; this I feel, and make . 651 Prelude 3. 186
Stood almost single; uttering odious truth— . . 653 Prelude 3. 284
As far as doth concern my single self, ... 654 Prelude 3. 349
Unpeaceful in itself. A single tree . . . . . 676 Prelude 6. 76
To land a single volume, saved by chance, . . . 677 Prelude 6. 145
And single cottages and lurking towns, ... 680 Prelude 6. 382
Of Savoyards; or, single and alone, ... 689 Prelude 7. 179
To single forms and objects, whence they draw, . 696 Prelude 7. 623
In knots, or pairs, or single. Not a look . . . 710 Prelude 9. 60
Of single spirits that catch the flame from Heaven, 715 Prelude 9. 368
Was not this single confidence enough . . . . 717 Prelude 9. 533
Louvet walked single through the avenue, . . . 720 Prelude 10. 111
Hung upon single persons; that there was, . . 720 Prelude 10. 156
Not in my single self alone I found, ... 722 Prelude 10. 266
In single or in social eminence, ... 724 Prelude 10. 425
Stands single in her only sanctuary; . . . . . 733 Prelude 11. 401
Upon my right hand couched a single sheep, . . 738 Prelude 12. 300
The single sheep, and the one blasted tree, . . 739 Prelude 12. 319
A single Briton clothed in wolf-skin vest, . . . 744 Prelude 13. 322
All strength—all terror, single or in bands, . . 755 Recluse 1. 1. 784
—There crows the cock, single in his domain: . 776 Excursion 2. 344
First, last, and single, in the breathing world, . 777 Excursion 2. 363
Or passing by some single tenement . . . . . 780 Excursion 2. 564
A single step, that freed me from the skirts . . 784 Excursion 2. 830
Save for that single cry, the unanswer'd bleat . 807 Excursion 3. 410
Single and one, the omnipresent God, ... 811 Excursion 4. 652
'This single act is all that we demand.' . . . 817 Excursion 4. 1082
Fair dwellings, single, or in social knots; . . . 823 Excursion 5. 88
Mute or conversing, single or in pairs. . . . . 890 Excursion 9. 436
A single sheep was wanting. They had sought . K.8. 224 *I will 14
Or single. And although it needs must seem . . K.8. 225 *I will 40
Nor in the single sheep was what they sought. . K.8. 225 *I will 45
By the grey moss, but not a single stone . . . K.8. 226 *I will 66
Single at chase among the lonely woods, . . . K.8. 245 Recluse 1. 1. 324
Six which themselves must single from a train, . L.1. 95 Juvenal 3. 5
A single word on Kings, and sons of Kings, . . L.1. 96 Juvenal 3. 40
Single-crested. Arran! a single-crested Teneriffe, . 471 *Arran! a 1
Singled. (I speak of one from many singled out) . 185 Nutting 2
A renovated spirit singled out, ... 633 Prelude 1. 53

Singled—*continued.*
As may be singled out with steady choice; 634 *Prelude* 1. 160
A casual rarity is singled out 658 *Prelude* 3. 618
Or person singled out among the rest, 713 *Prelude* 9. 279
Singled out me, as he in sport would say, 757 *Excursion* 1. 58
Or fell, those only shall be singled out 848 *Excursion* 6. 656
Singleness. His days had not been passed in singleness. 132 *Michael* 78
Yet, in aërial singleness, so free; 153 *Morn. Ex.* 40
And singleness her lot, 165 *Parrot* 18
Keeps faithful with a singleness of aim; 493 *Hap. War.* 40
In singleness, and little tried by time, 510 **Among a* 17
To life-long singleness; but happier far 586 *Ch. Lamb* 125
Ah! surely not in singleness of heart 679 *Prelude* 6. 306
Here keepest thou in singleness thy state: 749 *Prelude* 14. 211
Singly. Where they bloomed singly, or in scattered knots,) 280 *Valedict.* 3
And singly thine O vanquished Chief! whose corse, 361 **For action* 9
Sings. And sings a solitary song 83 *Lucy Gray* 63
The north-wind sings a doleful song; 117 †*Cottager* 2
I'll teach him how the owlet sings. 145 *Her Eyes* 82
While in the dell he sings alone 166 *Danish Boy* 43
Hangs a Thrush that sings loud, it has sung for three years: 187 *Poor Susan* 2
"A recreant harp, that sings of fear 204 *Brougham* 102
And sings a melancholy strain; 289 *Sol. Reap.* 6
Will no one tell me what she sings?— 289 *Sol. Reap.* 17
Delicious is the Lay that sings 302 *Yarrow V.* 33
High poised—or as the wren that sings 348 **Lulled by* 58
Not mute, where now the linnet only sings: 393 **The Lovers* 6
And hark! how blithe the throstle sings! 481 *Tables Turned* 13
The redbreast sings from the tall larch 482 *Sister* 3
When at heaven's gate she sings; 526 **The soaring* 2
And with strange tinglings sings her fainting ear. 606 *Desc.Sk.Quarto* 238
Graced with redundant hair, Iopas sings 625 *Æneid* 121
O'er all that leaps and runs, and shouts and sings, 648 *Prelude* 2. 406
And sought *that* beauty, which, as Milton sings, 749 *Prelude* 14. 245
The universal Parent, how he sings 851 *Excursion* 6. 882
He sings the sun to bed; S.3. 423 *Tinker* 19
Athens sings 'tis thine to rest S.3. 442 *Harmodius* 11
Singularity. And all the strife of singularity, 695 *Prelude* 7. 580
Sink. Into a gradual calm the breezes sink, 4 *Ev. Wk.* 114
Or sink, with heart alive like Memnon's lyre; 11 *Desc. Sk.* 32
Soon with despair's whole weight his spirits sink; 16 *Desc. Sk.* 332
Sink with his servile bands, to rise no more! 22 *Desc. Sk.* 664
No.—Thoughts and feelings will sink deep, but then 58 *Bord.* 1171
I let him sink again to the ground. 72 *Bord.* 1935
Your limbs sink under you, shall I support you? 74 *Bord.* 2111
Do spread, and sink, and rise; 108 *Louisa*
And busy throat whose sink and swell 143 **Driven in* 24
Eddying round and round they sink 170 *Kitten* 9
Through dream and vision did she sink, 193 *Ruth* 109
In our dejection do we sink as low; 195 *Resolution* 25
And oft his cogitations sink as low 213 *Dion* 60
Or, tired with sport, wouldst sink asleep 216 *Enterprise* 34
Sink, to attain a loftier flight; 228 *Devot. Incit.* 29
To sink upon your mother's lap—and rest? 229 *Clouds* 10
To sink, perhaps, where he is lying, 242 *P. B.* 539
Thou hangest, stooping, as might seem, to sink 303 **Fair Star* 3
He must sink down to languish 311 **Who rises* 56
Whole legions sink—and, in one instant, find 322 **Humanity, delighting* 35
Darkens the sun, hath bade the forest sink, 328 *Ode 1815* 95
To sink, and meet them in their fretted caves, 333 *Fish-women* 7
Sink (if thou must) as heretofore, 341 *San Salv.* 4
To hear—and sink again to sleep! 375 **The Minstrels* 39
Sink, and forget their nature—*now* expands 384 *Duddon* 32. 6
Exhaust itself and sink to rest; 406 *White Doe* 917
Temple and Altar sink, to hide their shame 423 *Ecc. Sonn.* 1. 17. 9
But for what gain? if England soon must sink 441 *Ecc. Sonn.* 3. 3. 10
And sink from high to low, along a scale 449 *Ecc. Sonn.* 3. 34. 2
Prepared, when each has stood his time, to sink 464 **Thou look'st* 4
His spindles sink under him, foot, leg, and thigh! 484 **A plague* 21
There let me see thee sink into a mood 498 **Enough of climbing* 42
That into breezes sink; impetuous minds 500 *Humanity* 52
When we shall sink to final rest. 506 *Lab. Hymn* 32
They thus would rise, must low and lower sink 513 *Newspaper* 4
And nations sink; or, struggling to be free, 516 **As leaves* 12
Make the heart sink, then wilt thou reverence 551 **If thou in* 4
Which man is born to—sink, howe'er depressed, 567 *Cumb. Beg.* 82
On severed love, and only sink 582 **O for a* 17
Where summer Suns in ocean sink to rest, 602 *Desc. Sk. Quarto* 7
Then with despair's whole weight his spirits sink, 609 *Desc.Sk.Quarto* 404
With all his creatures sink—to rise no more. 617 *Desc.Sk.Quarto* 809
Slow sink the Spires,—and up again they start! 625 **The confidence* 5
How Want may press thee down, and with thee sink 626 **Son of* 3
Meek men, whose very souls perhaps would sink 744 *Prelude* 13. 269
By nations sink together, we shall still 752 *Prelude* 14. 437
For I must tread on shadowy ground, must sink 755 *Recluse* 1. 1. 781
Which, if with truth it correspond, and sink 757 *Excursion* 1. 103
That I should follow with my babes, and sink 766 *Excursion* 1. 680
Of the unblest; for he will surely sink 780 *Excursion* 2. 596
Of a living ocean; or, to sink engulfed, 790 *Excursion* 3. 260
Sink, with a retinue of flaming clouds 803 *Excursion* 4. 117
For who could sink and settle to that point 803 *Excursion* 4. 153
And sink at evening into sound repose." 808 *Excursion* 4. 504
And as we fall by various ways, and sink 818 *Excursion* 4. 1109
And sink, through utter want of cheering light; 835 *Excursion* 5. 834
Whoe'er may sink, or rise—to sink again, 848 *Excursion* 6. 673

Sink—*continued.*
With resignation sink into the grave; 850 *Excursion* 6. 774
The ridge itself may sink into the breast 868 *Excursion* 7. 711
Sink'st. Thou sink'st, the image of thy rest 158 **In youth* 62
Sinking. *See* **Slowly-sinking.**
Sinking. Sinking, rising, on they go, 93 *Westmoreland Girl* 14
The sinking moon to Lucy's cot 109 **Strange fits* 15
Whose goodness, sinking deep, would reconcile 221 *Triad* 67
As if his mind were sinking deep 248 *P. B.* 1093
Is sinking down in its tranquillity; 258 **It is a* 4
He sets, his sinking yields a type 337 *Thun* 11
Tardily sinking by its proper weight 380 *Duddon* 17. 13
Preserve thy heart from sinking! 386 *Yarrow Rev.* 56
Sees spires fast sinking—up again to start! 443 *Ecc. Sonn.* 3. 12. 5
The linnet's warble, sinking towards a close, 455 *Rydal Mere* 1
And innocent victims sinking under fear, 724 *Prelude* 10. 404
The sun was sinking in the west; and now 767 *Excursion* 1. 734
A wilderness of building, sinking far 784 *Excursion* 2. 836
Far sinking into splendour—without end! 784 *Excursion* 2. 838
Of Margaret, sinking on the lonely heath 854 *Excursion* 6. 1060
Sinking with less than ordinary state, 893 *Excursion* 9. 591
Sinkings. Ha! why these sinkings of despair? 244 *P. B.* 723
Which, through the later sinkings of this cause, 732 *Prelude* 11. 355
Sinks. Thus, while the Sun sinks down to rest 1 *Extract* 9
She hath an eye that sinks into all hearts, 61 *Bord.* 1316
Leans smilingly, and sinks into a perfect rest. 103 *Artegal* 48
And feeling sinks as deep! See there the door 138 *Widow* 3
Sinks, hardly conscious of the influence— 227 *Vernal Ode* 89
And, oh! when Nature sinks, as oft she may, 260 **High is* 9
For human-kind sinks out of sight, is gone, 357 *Aquap.* 318
Transfigured, sinks into a hopeless grave; 366 *Lombardy* 12
Sinks, when the summer breeze hath died, 397 *White Doe* 144
Until her fellow sinks to re-appear no more. 490 *Incident: Dog* 40
Catch the blithe music as it sinks and swells, 504 *Warning* 43
Sinks smilingly forsworn. 550 *Hermit's Cell* 5. 4
Gives one bright glance, and sinks behind the hill. 595 *Ev. Wk. Quarto* 174
Nursed in his Mother's arms, who sinks to sleep, 645 *Prelude* 2. 235
Sinless. And first;—thy sinless progress, through a world 172 *Infant Daughter* 46
Dead in the sinless time of infancy, 318 **In due* 3
Like sinless snakes in Eden's happy land;— 374 *Eg. Maid* 323
Pure minds with sinless envy, than the Abode 387 *Manse* 9
A calm and sinless life, with love, hath given. 395 *WhiteDoe: Ded.* 48
The sinless age, by conscience is enrolled, 888 *Excursion* 9. 315
Sinner. And, to the sinner, mercifully bent; 464 **A point* 6
Sinner's. Or, for confession, in the sinner's need, 793 *Excursion* 3. 473
Sinners. But in His glory who for Sinners died. 443 *Ecc. Sonn.* 3. 13. 14
Fountain of Grace, whose Son for sinners died. 446 *Ecc. Sonn.* 3. 25. 8
To sinners whom their sins oppress and goad. K.8. 266 **Rid of* 8
Sinning. Of common sense you're surely sinning; 238 *P. B.* 197
Was given, that I should be, else sinning greatly, 663 *Prelude* 4. 336
Sins. And though your sins be red as scarlet, 247 *P. B.* 954
In them—in Her our sins and sorrows past. 280 **Oh what* 14
This Minstrel lead, his sins forgiven; 286 *Nith* 56
And sins, that point their terrors, 328 *Ode 1815* 103
Wash with Thy blood my sins; thereto incline 366 **Eternal Lord* 12
Cares entangle, sins beset, 503 **Like a* 54
Of righteousness, of sins forgiven, 577 **By playful* 21
Charity, 'mid the multitude of sins 584 *Ch. Lamb* 35
The one by which a creature, whom his sins 837 *Excursion* 5. 988
To sinners whom their sins oppress and goad. K.8. 266 **Rid of* 8
Cleanse with thy blood my sins, to this incline K.8. 266 **Rid of* 12
Sinuous. A grace the sinuous vale and roaring stream 253 **Aerial Rock* 11
Thridding with sinuous lapse the rushes, through 377 *Duddon* 4. 7
Decks, on thy sinuous banks, her thousand thrones, 464 **Greta, what* 10
With sinuous trunk, boughs exquisitely wreathed, 676 *Prelude* 6. 77
Leads, though by sinuous ways, if here I show 706 *Prelude* 8. 453
The little sinuous path of earthly care, 790 *Excursion* 3. 305
That creep along the ground with sinuous trail, 860 *Excursion* 7. 182
Sion. Did waft him to Sion, the glorified hill, 364 *Vallomb.* 22
Or, out of Sion, thundering from his throne 811 *Excursion* 4. 656
Sion's. Which Sion's Kings did consecrate of old; 576 *Chiabrera* 9. 17
Sip. A half-blown rose had tempted thee to sip 273 **Wild Redbreast* 3
And let the groveller sip his stagnant pool, 277 **A Poet* 6
As soon it must, a sense to sip, 497 *Lycoris* 43
Sipp'd. Then sipp'd the bowl whence she the wine had pour'd 625 *Æneid* 117
Sir. And be at rest. Oh, Sir! Peace, my good Wilfred; 38 *Bord.* 40
Sir Host! by all the love you bear to courtesy, 42 *Bord.* 306
Shall squire you, (would it not be better, Sir?) 43 *Bord.* 312
You know, Sir, I have been too long your guard 43 *Bord.* 315
She could not, Sir, have failed of company. 43 *Bord.* 327
That's all—God save you, Sir. Ha! as I live, 43 *Bord.* 332
Well as the wreck I am permits. And you, Sir? 43 *Bord.* 336
Oh, Sir, you would not talk thus, if you knew 45 *Bord.* 418
Has made amends. Thanks to you both; but, Oh Sir! 45 *Bord.* 431
Do you tell fortunes? Oh Sir, you are like the rest. 45 *Bord.* 437
But you, Sir, should be kinder. Come hither, Fathers, 45 *Bord.* 443
Ay, Sir, there's nobody that feels for us. 45 *Bord.* 445
But to your story. I was saying, Sir— 45 *Bord.* 469
And will misuse me, Sir! No trifling, Woman!— 46 *Bord.* 499
And I will tell you all!—You know not, Sir, 46 *Bord.* 503
Speak out. Oh, Sir, I've been a wicked Woman. 46 *Bord.* 505
Wife, Sir! his wife—not I; my husband, Sir, 46 *Bord.* 511
I'll be his Godfather. Oh Sir, you are merry with me. 46 *Bord.* 521

Sir—*continued.*
With such a look—it makes me tremble, Sir, 47 *Bord.* 541
Attends your pleasure. We are ready— Sir! 49 *Bord.* 665
Heavens! my good Friend! Forgive me, gracious Sir!— 54 *Bord.* 943
I *do* repent me, Sir; I fear the curse 54 *Bord.* 951
Of that blind Man. 'Twas not your money, Sir,—— 55 *Bord.* 952
The worm was in her—— Mercy! Sir, what mean you? 61 *Bord.* 1314
The game is up!— If it be needful, Sir, 73 *Bord.* 2030
My heart was willing, Sir, but I am one 74 *Bord.* 2080
I hurried back with her.—Oh save me, Sir, 74 *Bord.* 2096
Oh Sir, I would not see that hour again 74 *Bord.* 2099
Dead, dead!— A dismal matter, Sir, for me, 74 *Bord.* 2106
"And I to Durham, Sir, belong." 82 *Alice Fell* 45
"And often after sun-set, Sir, 84 *We are Seven* 45
You live, Sir, in these dales, a quiet life: 97 *Brothers* 121
Which then it had! Nay, Sir, for aught I know, 97 *Brothers* 136
A pair of diaries,—one serving, Sir, 97 *Brothers* 163
Why, there, Sir, is a thought that's new to me! 98 *Brothers* 174
No symbols, Sir, to tell us that plain tale: 98 *Brothers* 181
You, Sir, could help me to the history 98 *Brothers* 186
We two could travel, Sir, through a strange round; 98 *Brothers* 192
Was half a mother to them.—If you weep, Sir, 99 *Brothers* 235
Hanging in the open air—but, O good Sir! 100 *Brothers* 314
As any that should meet him— Happy! Sir— 100 *Brothers* 328
Ay, Sir, that passed away: we took him to us; 100 *Brothers* 342
Forgive me, Sir: before I spoke to you, 101 *Brothers* 354
—"Shame on me, Sir! this lusty Lamb, 115 *Last of Flock* 17
"Six Children, Sir! had I to feed; 115 *Last of Flock* 41
"Sir! 'twas a precious flock to me, 115 *Last of Flock* 81
"They dwindled, Sir, sad sight to see! 115 *Last of Flock* 91
"A simple burthen, Sir, a little Singing-bird." 119 *Sailor's Mother* 18
I bear it with me, Sir;—he took so much delight in it." 119 *Sailor's Mother* 36
"Oh Sir! you know I'm Betty Foy, 129 *Idiot Boy* 254
Sir Lancelot gave a safe retreat 180 *Waggoner* 4. 47
"She has been dead, Sir, many a day."— 191 *Beggars* 43
Sir Walter mounted him; he was the third 200 *Hart-leap* 7
But, though Sir Walter like a falcon flies, 200 *Hart-leap* 11
A rout this morning left Sir Walter's Hall, 200 *Hart-leap* 13
Sir Walter, restless as a veering wind, 200 *Hart-leap* 17
Sir Walter and the Hart are left alone. 201 *Hart-leap* 28
Close to the thorn on which Sir Walter leaned 201 *Hart-leap* 37
Sir Walter walked all round, north, south, and west, 201 *Hart-leap* 47
Four roods of sheer ascent) Sir Walter found 201 *Hart-leap* 50
Sir Walter wiped his face, and cried, "Till now 201 *Hart-leap* 53
Three pillars of rude stone Sir Walter reared, 202 *Hart-leap* 83
Sir Walter led his wondering Paramour; 202 *Hart-leap* 90
The Knight, Sir Walter, died in course of time, 202 *Hart-leap* 93
Are but three bounds—and look, Sir, at this last— 203 *Hart-leap* 143
—Give Sir Lancelot Threlkeld praise! 204 *Brougham* 95
———"A Potter, Sir, he was by trade," 238 *P. B.* 201
Sir Agravaine advanced; no sign he won 373 *Eg. Maid* 269
From Heaven or earth;—Sir Kaye had like denial. 373 *Eg. Maid* 270
Abashed, Sir Dinas turned away; 373 *Eg. Maid* 271
Even for Sir Percival was no disclosure; 373 *Eg. Maid* 272
While drawing toward the car Sir Gawaine, mailed 373 *Eg. Maid* 285
Sir Tristram, dear to thousands as a brother, 373 *Eg. Maid* 290
Not so Sir Launcelot;—from Heaven's grace 373 *Eg. Maid* 295
When his touch failed.—Next came Sir Galahad; 373 *Eg. Maid* 298
Sir Galahad! a treasure, that God giveth, 374 *Eg. Maid* 344
—'Tis Sir George Bowes who leads the Band: 412 *White Doe* 1446
Sir Eglamore was he; 478 *Somnamb.* 24
So spake Sir Eglamore, and pressed 478 *Somnamb.* 43
By thee, Sir Eglamore! 479 *Somnamb.* 99
To the Horn Sir Eustace pointed 535 *Egremont* 3
Which good Sir Eustace sounded, was the last. 535 *Egremont* 16
With his lance Sir Eustace pointed, 535 *Egremont* 17
"Sir!" the Ruffians said to Hubert, 535 *Egremont* 49
Months passed on, and no Sir Eustace! 535 *Egremont* 57
'Tis the breath of good Sir Eustace! 536 *Egremont* 81
'Tis Sir Eustace; if it be 536 *Egremont* 93
But Sir Eustace, whom good angels 536 *Egremont* 105
"From your deportment, Sir! I deem 544 *Russ. Fug.* 281
But, as it chanced, Sir William having learned 548 **Stranger! this* 8
For old Sir William was a gentle Knight, 548 **Stranger! this* 21
By old Sir William and his quarry, leave 549 **Stranger! this* 32
As my own child. Oh, Sir! the good die first, 763 *Excursion* 1. 500
She rose from off her seat, and then,—O Sir! 766 *Excursion* 1. 653
Your very soul to see her. Sir, I feel 768 *Excursion* 1. 777
I said, "My thoughts, agreeing, Sir, with yours, 791 *Excursion* 3. 332
I ceased, and he resumed.—"Ah! gentle Sir, 791 *Excursion* 3. 359
Revered Compatriot—and to you, kind Sir, 793 *Excursion* 3. 498
Our inquest turns.—Accord, good Sir! the light 829 *Excursion* 5. 481
"And in your judgment, Sir! the mind's repose 831 *Excursion* 5. 560
—But your compliance, Sir! with our request 836 *Excursion* 5. 891
Where, Sir, I pray you, where are laid the bones 854 *Excursion* 6. 1078
But you, Sir, know that in a neighbouring vale 862 *Excursion* 7. 315
Sir Alfred Irthing, with appropriate words 872 *Excursion* 7. 971
From Venice to Sir Walter's table. S.3. 432 **A German* 4

Sire. All are the undying offspring of one Sire: v **If thou indeed* 14
The image of his glorious Sire displayed, 18 *Desc. Sk.* 440
The bending body of my active sire; 28 *Guilt* 218
When, from the last hill-top, my sire surveyed, 28 *Guilt* 236
And thee, my Child! Believe me, honoured Sire! 40 *Bord.* 144
This last request. You know me, Sire; farewell! 42 *Bord.* 295
They toiled and wrought, and still, from sire to son, 98 *Brothers* 208
Who comes her Sire to seek; 103 *Artegal* 46
But how unworthy of that sire was he! 103 *Artegal* 75
Oh, ill-judging sire of an innocent son 116 *Repentance* 25

Sire—*continued.*
How will her Sire be reconciled 164 *Needlecase* 15
Yon slowly-sinking star—immortal Sire 261 **I watch* 2
There seek the genius of your Sire, 286 *Sons of Burns* 29
Cast off—abandoned by thy rugged Sire, 290 *Kilchurn* 10
A Muse, who, not unmindful of her Sire 359 *Plea: Hist.* 10
That bearded, staff-supported Sire— 398 *White Doe* 217
And, in his place, among son and sire, 399 *White Doe* 248
"Might ever son *command* a sire, 401 *White Doe* 450
This sympathy of Sire and Sons; 401 *White Doe* 470
Stood by their Sire, on Clifford-moor, 404 *White Doe* 724
Proud was the field of Sons and Sire; 404 *White Doe* 733
The Sire, unconscious of his age, 408 *White Doe* 1108
And others follow;—Sire and Son 408 *White Doe* 1143
Ancient of days! that to the eternal Sire, 419 *Ecc. Sonn.* 1. 4. 6
For Them, and for their Land. The earnest Sire, 422 *Ecc. Sonn.* 1. 13. 9
And Heaven will crown the right."—The mitred Sire 432 *Ecc. Sonn.* 2. 15. 9
Intrudes on peace, I pray the eternal Sire 470 *Bala-Sala* 5
Daughter and Sire through optic-glass discern, 540 *Grace Darl.* 36
For the grey-headed Sire has a daughter at home, 572 *Avarice* 42
Firm Independence, Bounty's rightful sire; 584 *Ch. Lamb* 9
There, by the door a hoary-headed sire 605 *Desc.Sk.Quarto* 170
"'So shall thy sire, whilst hope his breast inspires, 619 *School Ex.* 99
These children claim thee for their sire; the breath 627 *Eagle and Dove* 5
Bounced, leapt, and pawed the air; or mumbling sire, 693 *Prelude* 7. 422
Such as might suit a rustic Sire, prepared 762 *Excursion* 1. 421
Like harshness,—that the old grey-headed Sire, 861 *Excursion* 7. 258
From sire to son, in this obscure retreat 872 *Excursion* 7. 943
Their common sire, thou only bear'st his name. S.3. 433 **The doubt* 12
No longer greeted—to the tottering sire, S.3. 435 **The doubt* 137

Siren's. Arise superior to the Siren's power, 619 *School Ex.* 95

Sire's. She, fulfilling her sire's office, 94 *Westmoreland Girl* 65
Embroidered (such her Sire's command) 400 *White Doe* 355

Sires. Sons haply of extinguished sires, 226 *Vernal Ode* 42
Matrons and Sires—who, punctual to the call 256 *Decay of Piety* 2
Our sires set forth their grateful praise: 301 *Bran* 75
And grey-haired sires, on staffs supported, 324 *Ode 1814* 65
Toward the mists that hang over the land of my Sires, 345 *Stanzas: Simplon* 19
Would that our scrupulous Sires had dared to leave 448 *Ecc. Sonn.* 3. 33. 1
Join to the rigours of the sires of Rome 619 *School Ex.* 89
(A theme for boys, too hackneyed for their sires,) 721 *Prelude* 10. 193
To meet such trial) from their spiritual sires 839 *Excursion* 6. 61
The simple occupations of their sires, 878 *Excursion* 8. 260

Sirius. White Sirius glittering o'er the southern crags, 662 *Prelude* 4. 244

Sirs. For this good deed!—Well, Sirs, this passed away: 44 *Bord.* 409
I overtook him, Sirs, my Babe and I, 45 *Bord.* 472
We've overslept ourselves.—Sirs, have you seen him? 46 *Bord.* 495
What can I do? believe me, gentle Sirs, 47 *Bord.* 535

Sister. *See* **Twin-sister.**
My sister Emmeline and I 79 **Stay near* 12
My sister Emmeline and I 79 *Sparrow's Nest* 9
Pull the primrose, sister Anne! 79 *Foresight* 9
My sister and my brother; 83 *We are Seven* 22
"The first that died was sister Jane; 84 *We are Seven* 49
A sister Queen, against the bent 113 *Lament* 51
Thy little sister is at play;— 120 *Emigrant Mother* 21
His little sister thou shalt be; 121 *Emigrant Mother* 93
Reverenced, like a sister loved. 142 *Arm. Lady* 148
You love your sister and your friends, 143 †*Lov. and Lik.* 57
Gave the baptismal name each Sister bore. 151 **Forth from* 15
Father, sister, friend, and brother. 157 *Sexton* 8
Between two sister moorland rills 165 *Danish Boy* 1
Thee and thy mate and sister of the sky. 172 *Infant Daughter* 45
My dear, dear Sister! and this prayer I make, 207 *Tintern* 121
While to these shades a sister Nymph I call. 221 *Triad* 88
And to her sister Clio's laurel wreath, 227 *Vernal Ode* 78
When thou, dear Sister! wert become Death's Bride: 258 **Even so* 4
Well might such thoughts, dear Sister, throng 285 *Nith* 7
A Sister serves with slacker hand; 344 **How blest* 25
Thou, chiefly thou, my Sister dear, 401 *White Doe* 496
—O Sister, I could prophesy! 402 *White Doe* 527
—But thou, my Sister, doomed to be 402 *White Doe* 566
Should bear him to his Sister dear 411 *White Doe* 1373
For England's shame, O Sister Realm! from wood, 442 *Ecc. Sonn.* 3. 7. 7
Shall disappear from both the sister Isles, 474 **On to* 11
My sister! ('tis a wish of mine) 482 *Sister* 9
Then come, my Sister! come, I pray, 483 *Sister* 37
Like a fair sister of the sky, 498 **The sylvan* 4
One is a Woman, a poor earthly sister, 541 *Grace Darl.* 71
Wert given to her) a Sister—'tis a word 585 *Ch. Lamb* 79
The heart-affianced sister of our love! 627 **The star* 14
That sang and ceased not; now a Sister Isle 643 *Prelude* 2. 59
Bowing her head before her sister Faith 650 *Prelude* 3. 86
Of that sole Sister, her who hath been long 678 *Prelude* 6. 199
Murmured the sister streams of Life and Death, 681 *Prelude* 6. 439
That the belovèd Sister in whose sight 732 *Prelude* 11. 335
Are sister horns that constitute her strength. 740 *Prelude* 13. 4
Child of my parents! Sister of my soul! 749 *Prelude* 14. 232
Dear Sister! was a kind of gentler spring 750 *Prelude* 14. 265
She prayed, she moaned;—her husband's sister watched 849 *Excursion* 6. 749
My hope, my joy, my sister, and my friend, K.8. 234 **Witness thou*

Six—*continued.*	
The village clock tolled six,—I wheeled about,	638 *Prelude* 1. 431
Six changeful years have vanished since I first	687 *Prelude* 7. 1
A sportive infant, who, for six months' space,	692 *Prelude* 7. 337
Those six fair Daughters, budding yet—not one,	855 *Excursion* 6. 1129
Six which themselves must single from a train,	L.1. 95 *Juvenal* 3. 5
Six simple burghers—To the rope that tied	L.1. 95 *Juvenal* 3. 9
The cry is six to one upon the Duke.	L.1. 96 *Juvenal* 3. 30
Six-days'. The six-days' Work by flaming Seraphim	235 *Power of Sound* 203
Sixes. Were at sixes and sevens;	S.3. 440 **Said red-ribboned* 3
Sixpenny. By sixpenny sedition-shops engrossed,	L.1. 97 *Juvenal* 3. 86
Sixteen. And left her mother at sixteen,	246 *P. B.* 894
Full sixteen thousand fair to see;"	404 *White Doe* 717
Sixteenth. A Shepherd-lad; who ere his sixteenth year	95 *Brothers* 39
Sixth. I married my sixth wife!	246 *P. B.* 865
From his sixth year, the Boy of whom I speak,	758 *Excursion* 1. 118
Sixty. Assiduous, through the length of sixty years.	642 *Prelude* 2. 46
"At length, when sixty years and five were told,	864 *Excursion* 7. 463
Size. *See* **Giant-size.**	
Of formidable size had chiselled out	147 *Joanna* 29
A very Harp in all but size!	163 *Needlecase* 5
With what?—a Ship of lusty size;	177 *Waggoner* 2. 106
Is like an infant's grave in size,	198 *Thorn* 52
So like an infant's grave in size,	198 *Thorn* 61
A Shape of more than mortal size	213 *Dion* 67
But one of mighty size, and strange;	295 *Highland Boy* 53
A shell of ample size, and light	296 *Highland Boy* 118
What aim had they, the Pair of Monks, in size	363 **What aim* 1
A stature undepressed in size,	404 *White Doe* 739
Fays, Genii of gigantic size!	526 **The soaring* 33
A peopled world it is; in size a tiny room.	532 †*Float. Isl.* 16
A six years' Darling of a pigmy size!	588 *Immortality* 86
And their own size, than any outward light;	686 *Prelude* 6. 715
In size a giant, stalking through thick fog,	703 *Prelude* 8. 266
But vast in size, in substance glorified;	784 *Excursion* 2. 866
Stood near, of smaller size, and not unlike	787 *Excursion* 3. 56
A rough abode—in colour, shape, and size,	833 *Excursion* 5. 697
Masses of every shape and size, that lay	835 *Excursion* 5. 865
Skeleton. I thought I saw the skeleton of Idonea.	47 *Bord.* 581
Silence and Foresight; Death the Skeleton	185 *Yew-trees* 27
Skeleton of unfleshed humanity,	290 *Kilchurn* 32
By skeleton arms, that, from the mountain's trunk	353 *Aquap.* 44
When the broad oak drops, a leafless skeleton,	379 *Duddon* 12. 8
Hath still his castle, though a skeleton,	393 *Inglewood* 12
A human skeleton on the ground;	491 *Fidelity* 39
Skeletons. Their skeletons, turned to brilliant ornaments.	S.3. 434 **The doubt* 54
Huge skeletons of crags which from the coast	K.8. 225 **I will* 32
Sketched. This portraiture is sketched. The great, the good,	862 *Excursion* 7. 341
Skiddaw. And Skiddaw is glad with the cry of the hounds."	120 *Childless Father* 4
Carried the Lady's voice,—old Skiddaw blew	147 *Joanna* 62
Old Skiddaw will look down upon the Spot	251 *Appleth.* 13
Mount Skiddaw? In his natural sovereignty	251 **Pelion and* 11
By Skiddaw seen,—	285 *Grave of Burns* 40
Skiddaw's. From Skiddaw's top; but he to heaven was vowed	587 *Crosth.* 16
The woods, and distant Skiddaw's lofty height,	636 *Prelude* 1. 295
Skiddaw-top. For Skiddaw-top with rosy light	180 *Waggoner* 4. 34
Skies. Exulting 'mid the winter of the skies,	15 *Desc. Sk.* 262
Her fields peculiar, and peculiar skies.	21 *Desc. Sk.* 623
Who drag, beneath our native skies,	109 **Ere with* 7
Mute strains from worlds beyond the skies,	112 **How rich* 19
In rustling conflict through the skies,	114 *Ind. Wom.* 5
Is silent as the skies.	128 *Idiot Boy* 246
And see this sight beneath the skies,	162 **Art thou the* 13
The stormy skies!	163 *Hint* 8
Erected in the skies.	167 *Pilgrim's Dream* 32
But, till the warmth of summer skies	194 *Ruth* 224
When the blue daylight's in the skies,	198 *Thorn* 72
Whatever star is in the skies,	198 *Thorn* 102
Unless the glow-worm to the skies	214 *Kirkstone* 15
From suppliants panting for the skies!	216 *Enterprise* 42
Where flower-breathed incense to the skies	228 *Devot. Incit.* 60
With that of summer skies!	232 *Jew. Fam.* 20
Fair is that land as evening skies,	237 *P. B.* 98
And touch more quiet skies.	242 *P. B.* 495
And skies that ne'er relinquish their repose;	272 *Devil's Bridge* 12
To ivied castles and to moonlight skies,	273 **While Anna's* 12
Powers that will work for thee; air, earth, and skies;	305 *Toussaint* 10
Of gratitude, beneath Italian skies,	326 *Sobieski* 3
Than aught dependent on the fickle skies.	329 *Ode: Thanks.* 56
Afloat beneath Italian skies,	343 *Eclipse* 7
Did sullen mists hide lake and skies	343 *Eclipse* 71
To stillest mood of softest skies,	344 **How blest* 17
Gay vision under sullen skies,	344 **How blest* 56
Till the bright Star appeared in eastern skies,	351 *Des. Stanzas* 69
That might have drawn down Clio from the skies	359 *Plea: Hist.* 7
This thy last haunt beneath Italian skies	363 **List—'twas* 100
Mounts, in this fine illusion, toward the skies:	368 *Trajan* 69
Their prayers out to the wind and naked skies.	387 **Part fenced* 8
Brighter than eastern skies at daybreak strewn	434 *Ecc. Sonn.* 2. 25. 6
Whose rage the gentle skies in vain reprove,	439 *Ecc. Sonn.* 2. 44. 8
Extracting from clear skies and air serene,	475 **Homeward we* 10
The skies will weep o'er old men desolate:	505 *Warning* 155
Over the earth and through the skies	512 **Who rashly* 32
A needful journey, under favouring skies,	522 *Epist. Beaumont* 97
Skies—*continued.*	
Those locks from summer's golden skies,	530 *Gleaner* 2
At morn, at noon, and under moonlight skies	549 **The massy* 8
Lapp'd by the panting tongue of thirsty skies.	609 *Desc.Sk.Quarto* 397
As sent from heav'n the raven of the skies,	609 *Desc.Sk.Quarto* 403
The seats of learning brave the distant skies.	619 *School Ex.* 64
(What, save thyself, none dares through earth and skies)	624 *Æneid* 12
Though under skies less generous, less serene:	702 *Prelude* 8. 188
On wings that navigate cerulean skies.	735 *Prelude* 12. 37
That summer, under whose indulgent skies,	751 *Prelude* 14. 395
Our journey, under favourable skies.	772 *Excursion* 2. 32
In Arcady, beneath unaltered skies,	790 *Excursion* 3. 322
Beneath the concave of unclouded skies	811 *Excursion* 4. 695
The forkèd weapon of the skies can send	870 *Excursion* 7. 834
His fame touched the skies,	S.3. 440 **Said red-ribboned* 22
With shouts the *assembled* people rend the skies	L.1. 96 *Juvenal* 3. 33
A spirit that can look through clouded skies,	[?] **A sad* 8
Skiff. *See* **Pleasure-skiff.**	
Gambol like a dancing skiff,	166 *Wand. Jew* 18
Then take thy way, adventurous Skiff,	238 *P. B.* 153
In her light skiff, the tossing waves,	344 **How blest* 30
Who but must covet a cloud-seat, or skiff	471 **Arran! a* 4
A zig-zag path from the domestic skiff	607 *Desc.Sk.Quarto* 297
Skiffs. The skiffs, at anchor where with umbrage wide	4 *Ev. Wk.* 106
The skiffs with naked masts at anchor laid,	593 *Ev. Wk. Quarto* 105
Skilful. —O, would that some more skilful voice	245 *P. B.* 786
Bard of the Fleece, whose skilful genius made	254 *Dyer* 1
And, 'mid the works of skilful hands,	390 *HighlandBroach* 13
More skilful in self-knowledge, even more pure,	493 *Hap. War.* 23
Skilful and bold, the horse and burthened *sled*	523 *Epist. Beaumont* 110
A skilful distribution of sweet sounds,	757 *Excursion* 1. 68
And music waits upon your skilful touch,	809 *Excursion* 4. 571
Skill. Of Nature, finished with most curious skill!	60 *Bord.* 1276
That skill or means of his could add, but the architect had wrought	91 *Norman Boy* 18
"God for His service needeth not proud work of human skill;	93 *Poet's Dream* 65
In more delightful verse than skill of mine	123 *V. and J.* 89
And all his skill in horsemanship:	127 *Idiot Boy* 85
Of hardship, skill or courage, joy or fear;	132 *Michael* 69
The Man was using his best skill to gain	149 **A narrow* 64
Myriads of notes attest her subtle skill;	153 *Morn. Ex.* 14
Beholding what your skill has wrought,	164 **Fair Lady* 22
And, smoothed by Nature's skill,	165 *Parrot* 6
Mistrusting her evasive skill,	168 *Wren's Nest* 38
Called for *his* patience and *his* skill;—	182 *Waggoner* 4. 192
Endurance, foresight, strength, and skill;	186 **She was* 26
Whose skill can speed the day with lively cares,	221 *Triad* 62
Flow from your visionary skill,	225 *Present.* 23
Creation of the painter's skill,	228 *Devot. Incit.* 35
That to the Painter's skill is here allowed.	231 **The gentlest Poet* 4
Was for belief no dream:—thy skill, Arion!	234 *Power of Sound* 131
Of skill, upon the sounding hide	241 *P. B.* 424
And modulate, with subtle reach of skill	271 **Fame tells* 3
Which to the work surpassing skill hath dealt,	276 *Author's Portrait* 4
Haydon! let worthier judges praise the skill	277 **Haydon! let* 1
All praise the Likeness by thy skill portrayed;	279 **All praise* 1
Through Nature's skill,	285 *Grave of Burns* 46
And more than common strength and skill	286 *Sons of Burns* 9
The free-born Soul—that World whose vaunted skill	313 **Not 'mid* 2
What is it but a vain and curious skill,	315 **Alas! what* 7
Glory, and triumph. Yet with politic skill	316 **Say, what* 9
A landscape more august than happiest skill	323 *Ode 1814* 6
Shall show her clothed with strength and skill	330 *Ode: Thanks.* 75
Opposed to dark, deep plots of patient skill,	330 *Ode: Thanks.* 117
Her skill she tried with less ambitious views.	333 *Ded. Tour* 8
Nor such fine skill as did the meed bestow	339 *Tell* 2
Thy mountain notes with simple skill;	341 *Ital. Itin.* 6
These simple efforts of Helvetian skill,	351 *Des. Stanzas* 75
With all who want not skill to couple grief	356 *Aquap.* 245
Through marvellous felicity of skill,	357 *Aquap.* 285
Impelled by thirst of all but Heaven-taught skill.	358 **Is this* 8
Nor grieve the less that skill to him was left	363 **Grieve for* 3
Now, though a Mechanist, whose skill	369 *Eg. Maid* 19
Esteem me, Liege! if I, whose skill	372 *Eg. Maid* 244
Such as the heaven-taught skill of Herbert drew;	380 *Duddon* 18. 13
If, undeceived, my skill can trace	398 *White Doe* 211
Thought he, may want not skill to save.	408 *White Doe* 1112
Urged by Ambition, who with subtlest skill	425 *Ecc. Sonn.* 1. 28. 1
Ye have no skill to teach, or if ye know	433 *Ecc. Sonn.* 2. 18. 9
Giordano, verily thy Pencil's skill	461 **Giordano, verily* 1
Nor be it e'er forgotten how by skill	467 *St. Bees* 118
Boastful Idolatress of formal skill	468 *St. Bees* 158
Which a fine skill, of Indian growth, has wrought	480 *Cordelia* 3
And, though you with your utmost skill	483 *Simon Lee* 53
The best of his skill he has tried;	484 **A plague* 17
If he be one that feels, with skill to part	489 *Spade* 21
A skill—to balance and supply;	497 *Lycoris* 41
Whom, then, shall meekness guard? What saving skill	505 *Warning* 149
Nor gain, from past or future, skill	505 **If this* 7
Broad, clear, and toned harmoniously, with skill	508 *F. Stone* 19
Triumphs, in that great work, the Painter's skill,	510 **Among a* 3
Wisdom exists not; nor the humbler skill	514 **Blest Statesman* 4
In music all unversed, nor blessed with skill	521 *Epist.Beaumont* 30
Is it that ye with conscious skill	526 **The soaring* 29
Some quaint odd plaything of elaborate skill,	548 **Stranger! this* 17

Skill—*continued.*
To gladden or to grieve, he hath like skill; . . 557 *Cuck. and Night.* 19
And the skill which he learned on the banks of the Tyne, ... 571 *Avarice* 2
Commemorating genius, talent, skill; . . . . 584 **With copious* 61
With skill and power that might not be withstood, 635 *Prelude* 1. 199
In contradiction; with no skill to part . . . 635 *Prelude* 1. 238
Proud of his skill, to reach a chosen point . . 637 *Prelude* 1. 368
And the vain-glory of superior skill, ... 643 *Prelude* 2. 70
On the smooth platform, whether skill prevailed . 644 *Prelude* 2. 162
Some skill, and longer time than may be spared, . 662 *Prelude* 4. 292
Was present, one who with unerring skill . . 667 *Prelude* 5. 82
Tamed to their bidding; they who have the skill 671 *Prelude* 5. 350
Of silence came and baffled his best skill, . . 671 *Prelude* 5. 380
Whether the Painter, whose ambitious skill . . 690 *Prelude* 7. 240
Of lowly thyme, by Nature's skill enwrought . . 702 *Prelude* 8. 243
Longing for skill to paint a scene so bright . . 726 *Prelude* 10. 569
Were called upon to exercise their skill, . . 729 *Prelude* 11. 139
I summoned my best skill, and toiled, intent . 731 *Prelude* 11. 279
Of many Beings, he had wondrous skill . . 762 *Excursion* 1. 431
Than this obscure Itinerant had skill . . . 771 *Excursion* 2. 22
Ambition to attempt, and skill to win. . . . 774 *Excursion* 2. 190
Whose skill had thronged the floor with a proud show . . . . 778 *Excursion* 2. 424
As skill and graceful nature might suggest . . 793 *Excursion* 3. 465
Of all adventurers. With unrivalled skill, . . 812 *Excursion* 4. 724
Which his poor skill could make, his fancy fetched, 814 *Excursion* 4. 857
And skill in letters—every fancy shaped . . . 843 *Excursion* 6. 309
Charming the air with skill of hand or voice, . 843 *Excursion* 6. 356
That skill in this or other household work, . . 856 *Excursion* 6. 1183
"Those pleasing works the Housewife's skill produced: . . . . 860 *Excursion* 7. 192
For their sweet purposes, with perfect skill.) . . 861 *Excursion* 7. 272
Towards one, whose bold contrivances and skill, . 866 *Excursion* 7. 591
Occasion given him to display his skill, . . . 882 *Excursion* 8. 532
Or bold adventure; promising to skill . . . . 889 *Excursion* 9. 381
By words, nor by the pencil's silent skill; . . 891 *Excursion* 9. 514
Shall pause, the skill admiring that can work . S.3. 433 **The doubt* 45
A task above my skill; the silent mind . . K.8. 248 *Recluse* 1.1.424
The sage has read the stars with skill so true, . L.3. 27 **For Lubbock* 3

Skilled. About this ground; she hath a tongue well skilled, ... 44 *Bord.* 366
Hail, blest above all kinds!—Supremely skilled . 153 *Morn. Ex.* 31
Skilled to approach or to retire,— . . . . . 415 *White Doe* 1720
Thy heart! what hopes inspired thy genius, skilled, 436 *Ecc. Sonn.* 2. 31. 11
And thou wilt doubt, with me less aptly skilled . 645 *Prelude* 2. 222
By poets skilled in nature's secret ways . . . 840 *Excursion* 6. 162

Skim. And Truth would skim the flowery glade, . 154 *Flower Garden* 55
Well pleased to skim the plain with wild flowers deckt, ... 270 **Though the bold* 4
Whose fancy had a thousand fields to skim; . . 532 **Once I* 10
To skim along the surfaces of things, . . . 788 *Excursion* 3. 135

Skimmed. Each with a mess of pottage and skimmed milk, ... 132 *Michael* 100
That skimmed the surface of the dead calm lake, 148 **A narrow* 19
Up-starting, Cynthia skimmed the mountain-dew 346 *Gemmi* 6
Were skimmed, devoured, or studiously perused, . 675 *Prelude* 6. 24
Like others, I had skimmed, and sometimes read 711 *Prelude* 9. 96
Along that very shore which I had skimmed . . 727 *Prelude* 10. 596
The turf of yon large pasture will be skimmed; . 773 *Excursion* 2. 145
Launched from our hands the smooth stone skimmed the lake; . . . . 892 *Excursion* 9. 532

Skims. Smoothly skims the meadows wide; . . 215 *Kirkstone* 82
While his free Barge skims the smooth flood along, 426 *Ecc. Sonn.* 1. 30. 10

Skin. *See* **Wolf-skin.**
Between my breast-plate and my skin than make 63 *Bord.* 1424
Her skin was of Egyptian brown: . . . . . 190 *Beggars* 7
She wrapped thee in a panther's skin; . . . . 215 *Enterprise* 28
The smooth transparent skin, ... 232 *Jew. Fam.* 26
Her tawny skin, dark eyes, and glossy locks, . . 605 *Desc.Sk.Quarto* 190
Though I sell shirt and skin, ... S.3. 431 **If money's* 4

Skinned. The Place unfolds, from pavement skinned with moss, ... 355 *Aquap.* 193

Skins. That skins the plains of Thessaly, . . . 213 *Dion* 74

Skip. The withered leaves all skip and hop; . . 155 **A whirl-blast* 13

Skipton. "How glad is Skipton at this hour—. . 204 *Brougham* 36

Skirt. A Traveller on the skirt of Sarum's Plain 24 *Guilt* 1
And downward by the skirt of Greenside fell, . 353 *Aquap.* 48
To teach the skirt of thy dark cloud to shine; . 615 *Desc.Sk.Quarto* 708

Skirted. *See* **Forest-skirted, Willow-skirted.**

Skirting. And now has reached the skirting trees; 240 *P. B.* 383

Skirts. And to the waggon's skirts was tied . . 179 *Waggoner* 3. 58
Even while I speak, their skirts of grey . . . 180 *Waggoner* 4. 59
Whose skirts the glowing Mountain thirsted to detain. . . . . 338 *Engelberg* 18
On the last skirts of their permitted ground, . . 653 *Prelude* 3. 314
A single step, that freed me from the skirts . 784 *Excursion* 2. 830
And with their parents occupy the skirts . . . 879 *Excursion* 8. 363

Skulk. Would stoop to skulk about a Cottage door— 42 *Bord.* 282

Skulking. I spied him skulking in his peasant's dress. 46 *Bord.* 491
Or rather skulking for the common weal . . . L.1. 97 *Juvenal* 3. 87

Skull. Cross-bones nor skull,—type of our earthly state . . . . 98 *Brothers* 171
Upon the pivot of his skull . . . . . . 241 *P. B.* 414
Upon the pivot of his skull . . . . . . 241 *P. B.* 419
Like this old helmet, or the eyeless skull . . 394 **How profitless* 7

Skulls. Where three thousand skulls are laid; . . 157 *Sexton* 6

Sky. O'er vale, and mountain, and the starless sky. 1 *Early Youth* 6
Thy torrents shooting from the clear-blue sky; . 12 *Desc. Sk.* 113
The sky is veiled, and every cheerful sight: . . 15 *Desc. Sk.* 272
Suspended 'mid the quiet of the sky; . . . . 16 *Desc. Sk.* 349

Sky—*continued.*
Was lost, though still he looked, in the blank sky. 24 *Guilt* 23
Rolled fast along the sky his warm and genial moon. 32 *Guilt* 414
When into storm the evening sky is wrought, . 36 *Guilt* 664
Shine calmly as if nothing ailed the sky: . . . 45 *Bord.* 426
We sate us down. The sky grew dark and darker: 50 *Bord.* 703
On a dead sea under a burning sky, ... 68 *Bord.* 1698
That drops down dead out of a sky it vexed. . . 69 *Bord.* 1786
A rainbow in the sky: . . . . 79 **My heart* 2
That looked up at the sky so proud and big . . 80 †*Address: Child* 25
All newly born! both earth and sky . . . . 84 *Shepherd-boys* 28
"Here thou need'st not dread the raven in the sky; 88 *Pet-lamb* 57
Suspended in a stream as clear as sky, . . . 88 *H. C.* 9
Weary of the open sky. . . . . 90 *Longest Day* 4
Of last night's snow, beneath a sky threatening the fall of more, ... 91 *Norman Boy* 10
Air blackened, thunder growled, fire flashed from clouds that hid the sky, ... 91 *Poet's Dream* 3
The sky, the gay green field, ... 105 *Artegal* 199
Glittered at evening like a starry sky; . . . 107 *Farewell* 54
Is shining in the sky. . . . . 109 **She dwelt* 8
May mount into the sky! . . . . 110 **'Tis said that some* 16
I look—the sky is empty space; . . . . . 110 **'Tis said that some* 18
In sky, air, earth, and ocean. . . . . . . 112 **Yes! thou* 12
The moon is up,—the sky is blue, ... 126 *Idiot Boy* 2
That overhead are sailing in the sky. . . . . 131 *Michael* 12
Helvellyn far into the clear blue sky . . . . 147 *Joanna* 61
And when the Frost is in the sky, ... 156 *Oak and Broom* 77
Or, some bright day of April sky, ... 158 **In youth* 34
With clouds and sky about thee ringing, . . . 159 **Up with me* 5
To thy banqueting place in the sky. . . . . 159 **Up with me* 15
Beneath the summer sky . . . . 163 **Art thou the* 27
Now, beneath the starry sky, ... 163 *Spinning Wheel* 7
Vain is the glory of the sky, ... 164 **Glad sight* 5
And sacred to the sky. . . . . 165 *Danish Boy* 4
Nor ever was a cloudless sky . . . . . . 166 *Danish Boy* 47
In the broad open eye of the solitary sky, . . 166 *Stray Pleasures* 16
Then from the tenant of the sky . . . . . 167 *Pilgrim's Dream* 13
Of a sky serene and pure; . . . . 171 *Kitten* 88
Thee and thy mate and sister of the sky. . . . 172 *Infant Daughter* 45
Is it for threatenings in the sky? . . . . . 174 *Waggoner* 1. 48
Black is the sky—and every hill, ... 175 *Waggoner* 1. 162
Up to the sky, is blacker still— . . . . . 175 *Waggoner* 1. 163
Sky, hill, and dale, one dismal room, ... 175 *Waggoner* 1. 164
The sky owes somebody a grudge! . . . . . 176 *Waggoner* 1. 250
The utmost anger of the sky: . . . . . . 177 *Waggoner* 2. 73
Earth, spangled sky, and lake serene, ... 178 *Waggoner* 3. 38
In bush, and tree, and sky. . . . . 183 **O blithe* 20
——The sky is overcast . . . . 184 *Night-piece* 1
The silent trees, and saw the intruding sky.— . 186 *Nutting* 53
A Telescope upon its frame, and pointed to the sky: 189 *Star-gazers* 2
Blue sky prevailing; . . . . 190 *March* 19
'Mid silver clouds, and openings of blue sky . 190 **Lyre! though* 23
Sailed through the sky—the brooks ran clear; . 191 *Seq. Beggars* 24
Have been a traveller under open sky, . . . 192 *Gipsies* 10
As quietly as spots of sky . . . . 193 *Ruth* 71
The tumult of a tropic sky, ... 193 *Ruth* 122
Like the whole sky when to the east . . . . 194 *Ruth* 179
The sky rejoices in the morning's birth; . . . 195 *Resolution* 9
I heard the sky-lark warbling in the sky; . . . 195 *Resolution* 29
When the blue daylight's in the sky . . . . 198 *Thorn* 83
Through half the clear blue sky will go; . . . 199 *Thorn* 193
The silence that is in the starry sky, ... 205 *Brougham* 163
The landscape with the quiet of the sky. . . . 205 *Tintern* 8
And the blue sky, and in the mind of man: . . 207 *Tintern* 99
A few are near him still—and now the sky, . . 208 **It is no* 7
Ethereal minstrel! pilgrim of the sky! . . . 209 **Ethereal minstrel* 1
Most potent when mists veil the sky, ... 215 *Kirkstone* 37
By soft reflection—grateful to the sky, . . . 219 *Haunted Tree* 4
Beneath the concave of an April sky, ... 226 *Vernal Ode* 1
Thus, in their stations, lifting tow'rd the sky . 227 *Vernal Ode* 61
As if no space below the sky . . . . . . 228 *Devot. Incit.* 9
Streaming from founts above the starry sky, . . 229 *Cuckoo-clock* 39
Appear; a calm descent of sky conducting . . 230 *Clouds* 34
Beneath their little patch of sky . . . . . 239 *P. B.* 229
The soft blue sky did never melt . . . . . 239 *P. B.* 263
The witchery of the soft blue sky! . . . . . 239 *P. B.* 265
Against the wind and open sky!" . . . . . 240 *P. B.* 320
Beneath the clear blue sky he saw . . . . . 240 *P. B.* 366
To-night, beneath the moonlight sky, ... 245 *P. B.* 784
Its own small pasture, almost its own sky! . . . 250 *Admon.* 4
Smooth fields, white streets of water, and pure sky; 253 **A flock* 4
That, struggling through the western sky, have won 256 *Decay of Piety* 13
Of silent hills, and more than silent sky. . . . 259 **A volant* 14
We should forget them; they are of the sky, . . 262 **Dark and* 13
Through leaves yet green, and yon crystalline sky, 263 **While not* 11
Which, strewn with snow smooth as the sky can shed, ... 263 **How clear* 3
Large space ('mid dreadful clouds) of purest sky, 264 *Storm* 11
With how sad steps, O Moon, thou climb'st the sky, 266 **With how* 1
The lake below reflects it not; the sky . . . 266 **Even as* 6
Whirled us o'er sunless ground beneath a sky . 268 **Four fiery* 2
Open unto the fields, and to the sky; . . . . 269 *Westm. Bridge* 7
Their tops, between them comes and goes a sky . 272 **Where holy* 12
Sky without cloud—ocean without a wave; . . . 277 **Haydon! let* 6
The most alluring clouds that mount the sky . . 277 **The most* 1
That mounts not toward the radiant morning sky, 282 **While beams* 4
With such a sky to lead him on? . . . . . 289 *Stepping West.* 8
Was fixed upon the glowing Sky, ... 289 *Stepping West.* 22

Slain—continued.
Unburied, lay hid under heaps of slain : . . . 361 *For action 10
Like the brave Lion slain in her defence. . 395 White Doe : Ded. 16
Earl Pembroke, slain so impiously ! . . 399 White Doe 263
O'er heaps of slain ;—from Cambrian wood and
  moss . . . . 421 Ecc. Sonn. 1. 10. 10
Slain by Compatriot-protestants that draw . 442 Ecc. Sonn. 3. 7. 10
That shamefully they one and all were slain, . 559 Cuck.andNight.129
Now they're famished or slain : . . . . S.3. 440 *Said red-rib-
  boned 4
Slake. Their thirst they slake :—they wash their
  toil-worn feet, ... 20 Desc. Sk. 561
My thirst at every rill can slake, . . . 157 *In youth 6
Here, with no thirst but what the stream can slake, 262 Retirement 10
To slake their thirst, with reckless hoofs have trod 465 *The cattle 2
Slaked. In this pellucid Current slaked his thirst ? 378 Duddon 8. 3
My thirst I slaked, and, from the cheerless spot . 763 Excursion 1. 463
When winds are blowing strong. The traveller
  slaked . . . . 814 Excursion 4. 871
Had slaked his thirst out of a famous well, . K.8. 226 *I will 60
Slander. (As you have said) he coins himself the
  slander . . . . 42 Bord. 262
Slanderous. Bewildered whether ye, by slanderous
  tongues . . . . 505 Warning 113
Slant. Slant watery lights, from parting clouds, apace 4 Ev. Wk. 92
Shed from their sides, that face the sun's slant beam, 4 Ev. Wk. 108
Together smoking in the sun's slant beam, . . 33 Guilt 461
Which, with slant ray, the merry sun . . . 181 Waggoner 4. 106
That lit the dark slant woods with silvery white ! 593 Ev. Wk. Quarto 100
A slant and mellow radiance, which began . 771 Excursion 1. 958
From under thee hath vanished, and slant beams, S.3. 435 *The doubt 101
Slanting. To the mine's mouth ; a long and slanting
  track, ... 842 Excursion 6. 246
Slap-dash. Slap-dash, tail foremost, as his arms shall
  drive. . . . . L.1. 96 Juvenal 3. 32
Slate. At evening, when with pencil, and smooth slate 639 Prelude 1. 509
Slates. Right in the slates, and with a huge rattle. . 81 †Address : Child 30
Slaughter. Swords that are with slaughter wild . 204 Brougham 59
The Highlanders, the slaughter spread like flame ; 293 Killicranky 5
To you who fell, and you whom slaughter spared . 326 *Intrepid sons 12
Of civil slaughter. Yet, while temporal power . 432 Ecc. Sonn. 2. 16. 9
Of civil slaughter, was our frequent walk ; . 716 Prelude 9. 433
In stillness left when slaughter is no more, . 836 Excursion 5. 928
Slaughtered. Of night, my slaughtered Lord have I
  required [:] . . . . 209 Laod. 4
For slaughtered Youth or love-lorn Maid ! . 586 Hogg 42
Slave. See **Bond-slave.**
The slave of none, of beasts alone the lord, . 18 Desc. Sk. 445
That thou, the slave of slaves, art doomed to pine 21 Desc. Sk. 588
She is," continued the detested Slave, . . 59 Bord. 1788
A subject, not a slave ! . . . . . 110 *Ere with 20
How she loved a Christian Slave, and told her pain 139 Arm. Lady 5
My father for slave's work may seek a slave in
  mind." . . . . 140 Arm. Lady 36
Is heard the spirit of a toil-worn slave, . . 153 Morn. Ex. 17
The slave of low desires : . . . . . 194 Ruth 153
A melancholy slave ; . . . . . . 218 Young Lady 15
Not Fortune's slave is Man : our state . . 224 *'Tis gone 49
And whispers for the heart, their slave ; . . 232 Power of Sound 8
For the tired slave, Song lifts the languid oar, . 233 Power of Sound 53
And this poor slave who loved him well, . . 243 P. B. 662
Mere slave of them who never for thee prayed, . 253 *Fond words 13
The slave of business, time, or care for life, . 284 Departure 22
And let no Slave his head incline, . . . 300 Cora Linn 43
Redeemed to baffle that imperial Slave, . . 318 *Ah ! where 7
Becomes not one whose father is a slave : . . 319 Biscayan 6
Forth slips, like an enfranchised slave, . . 348 *Lulled by 33
So fare they—the Man serving as her Slave. . 366 Lombardy 9
A sign he craved, tired slave of vain contrition ; . 373 Eg. Maid 296
Flow to the poor, and freedom to the slave ; . 424 Ecc. Sonn. 1. 24. 12
Not in the breathing-times of that poor slave . 454 *Not in the lucid 5
Philosopher !—a fingering slave, . . . 485 Poet's Epitaph 18
He is a Slave ; the meanest we can meet ! . 488 Pers. Talk 28
From some high-minded Slave, impelled to spurn 501 Humanity 65
Stone-walls a prisoner make, but not a slave ; . 501 Humanity 78
Though fettered slave be none, her floors and soil . 501 Humanity 85
Servant of Providence, not slave of Fate— . 514 *Blest Statesman 13
Broods like the Day, a Master o'er a Slave, . 589 Immortality 119
To our infirmity. No officious slave . . 645 Prelude 2. 215
The dupe of folly, or the slave of crime." . 732 Prelude 11. 320
By prejudice, the miserable slave . . . 735 Prelude 12. 73
Of contradictions infinite the slave, . . 843 Excursion 6. 373
He is a slave to whom release comes not, . . 878 Excursion 8. 301
The slave of ignorance, and oft of want, . . 886 Excursion 9. 163
Slavery. While Slavery, forcing the sunk mind to
  dwell . . . . 13 Desc. Sk. 137
A slavery compared to which the dungeon . . 69 Bord. 1777
In slavery ; all is slavery ; we receive . . 70 Bord. 1857
He was in slavery among the Moors . . . 100 Brothers 317
Shame on you, feeble Heads, to slavery prone ! 303 *Is it 14
Of a proud slavery met by tenets strained . 442 Ecc. Sonn. 3. 11. 2
That clings to slavery for its own sad sake. . 472 Dunolly Eagle 14
Chained to its object in brute slavery ; . . 820 Excursion 4. 1256
—The discipline of slavery is unknown . . 889 Excursion 9. 351
Slave's. My father for slave's work may seek a slave
  in mind." . . . . 140 Arm. Lady 36
Slaves. That thou, the slave of slaves, art doomed to
  pine . . . . 21 Desc. Sk. 588
That things will work to ends the slaves o' the
  world . . . . 54 Bord. 936
Begone, ye Slaves, or I will raise a whirlwind . 54 Bord. 944

Slaves—continued.
Slaves of folly, love, or strife— . . . . 209 *Yes, it 11
For human-kind, weak slaves of cumbrous pride ! 254 Wild Duck's Nest
  14
Slaves, vile as ever were befooled by words, . . 309 *What if 3
And slaves are pleased to learn that mighty feats
  are done ; . . . . 327 Ode 1815 38
Thro' what men see and touch,—slaves wandering
  on, ... 358 *Is this 7
Was it by mortals sculptured ?—weary slaves . 379 Duddon 15. 9
A bright-haired company of youthful slaves, . 421 Ecc. Sonn. 1. 13. 1
" Slaves cannot breathe in England "—yet that
  boast . . . . 501 Humanity 83
Ethereal natures and the worst of slaves ; . 775 Excursion 2. 229
And slaves who will consent to be destroyed— . 836 Excursion 5. 942
Slavish. Licence and slavish order, dares be free. . 450 Ecc. Sonn. 3. 37. 14
Groan underneath a weight of slavish toil, . 501 Humanity 86
But History, time's slavish scribe, will tell . 797 Excursion 3. 769
Sled. Skilful and bold, the horse and burthened sled 523 Epist. Beaumont
  110
Sledge. Shot, down the headlong path darts with his
  sledge ; . . . . 4 Ev. Wk. 131
That he might pull the sledge for me : . . 114 Ind. Wom. 38
Shot, down the headlong pathway darts his sledge ; 593 Ev. Wk. Quarto 112
Following the rugged road, by sledge or wheel . 823 Excursion 5. 61
Sleep. There doth the twinkling aspen's foliage sleep, 4 Ev. Wk. 116
Or shout that wakes the ferry-man from sleep, . 9 Ev. Wk. 370
Here, on the brown wood-cottages they sleep, . 14 Desc. Sk. 214
Thro' worlds where Life, and Voice, and Motion
  sleep ; . . . . 16 Desc. Sk. 310
In timely sleep ; and when, at break of day, . 22 Desc. Sk. 667
Here shall much-needed sleep his frame embrace. 27 Guilt 160
From one who mourned in sleep, he raised his head, 27 Guilt 164
And when that shape, with eyes in sleep half
  drowned, ... 27 Guilt 182
We gazed with terror on their gloomy sleep, . 29 Guilt 293
His ears were never silent ; sleep forsook . 36 Guilt 635
'Tis too disorderly for sleep or rest. . . 43 Bord. 351
When next inclined to sleep, take my advice . 44 Bord. 416
What life is this of ours, how sleep will master . 45 Bord. 419
Are hushed to sleep, by your own act and deed, . 55 Bord. 956
In a deep sleep. I whispered to him thrice. . 55 Bord. 961
Smiling in sleep— A pretty feat of Fancy ! . 55 Bord. 972
Have I lived many days—my sleep was bound . 69 Bord. 1791
Doth lodge, and feed, and coil, and sleep, in safety. 70 Bord. 1799
as if he wished to settle into sleep. . . . 72 Bord. 1941
Or sleep, or rest : but over waste and wild, . 78 Bord. 2348
Sleep—and at break of day I will come to thee
  again ! ". . . . . 88 Pet-lamb 60
It came with sleep and showed the Boy, no cherub,
  not transformed, ... 92 Poet's Dream 15
Sleep fled, and with it fled the dream—recorded in
  this book, ... 93 Poet's Dream 70
He in his sleep would walk about, and sleeping . 101 Brothers 352
He there had fallen asleep ; that in his sleep . 101 Brothers 398
I know not if you sleep or feed. . . . 106 *I've watched 4
What matter ? if the waters sleep . . . 111 A Complaint 15
Of happy millions lulled in sleep ; . . . 113 Lament 26
In sleep I heard the northern gleams ; . . 113 Ind. Wom. 3
And in sickness, if night had been sparing of sleep, 116 Repentance 29
An incommunicable sleep. . . . . . 117 Affl. Marg. 56
Then little Darling ! sleep again, . . . 118 †Cottager 14
Death, life, and sleep, reality and thought, . 118 Maternal Grief 11
Heard him, how he was troubled in his sleep : . 135 Michael 291
To new-born infants—thou didst sleep away . 136 Michael 341
Both of them sleep together : here they lived, . 136 Michael 367
The Rock, like something starting from a sleep, . 147 Joanna 54
Should sleep beneath the shelter of its trees, . 149 M. H. 19
For not an eyelid could to sleep incline . . 154 Morn. Ex. 59
And there together sleep. . . . . . 162 Binnorie 64
For the spindle, while they sleep, . . . 163 Spinning Wheel 10
A boding sound—for aught but sleep unfit ! . 167 Pilgrim's Dream 51
How glad Pendragon—though the sleep . . 204 Brougham 40
The sleep that is among the lonely hills. . . 205 Brougham 164
Which there in ghastly silence sleep ? . . 216 Enterprise 76
To filial sleep upon the breast . . . . 223 Wishing-gate 71
Wouldst thou be taught, when sleep has taken
  flight, ... 229 Cuckoo-clock 1
In sleep, and intermingling with his dream, . 229 Cuckoo-clock 30
In his last sleep securely bound ! . . . 242 P. B. 552
O gentle Sleep ! do they belong to thee, . . 253 *O gentle 1
This tiresome night, O Sleep ! thou art to me . 253 *O gentle 5
Fond words have oft been spoken to thee, Sleep ! 253 *Fond words 1
And could not win thee, Sleep ! by any stealth : . 254 *A flock 10
Of a dark chamber where the Mighty sleep : . 262 *Mark the 11
Of a bedimming sleep, or as a lamp . . . 266 *Even as 2
Light deepening the profoundest sleep of shade. . 272 Ruins 8
Does then the Bard sleep here indeed ? . . 289 Glen-Al. 17
Of sleep took import terrible ;— . . . 299 Brownie's Cell 66
Or calls the lily from her sleep . . . . 299 Brownie's Cell 87
In glory will they sleep and endless sanctity. . 310 Anticip. 14
How long shall vengeance sleep ? Ye patient
  Heavens, how long ? . . . . . 311 *Who rises 41
To timely sleep. Thought I, the impassioned
  strain, ... 314 *I dropped 6
Have roused her from her sleep : and forest-lawn, 314 *Advance—come 7
Sleep, Warriors, sleep ! among your hills repose ! 316 *It was a 9
When the soft hand of sleep had closed the latch 323 Ode 1814 1
And exquisite, that sleep alone bestows . . 324 Ode 1814 71
When the captivity of sleep had ceased ; . . 329 Ode : Thanks. 46
Else we sleep among the dead ; . . . . 336 *Jesu ! bless 16

Slender—*continued.*
To bend as doth a slender blade of grass . . . 705 *Prelude* 8. 398
Those slender cords, to guide the unconscious Boy 706 *Prelude* 8. 455
Which had been twined about the slender stem . 769 *Excursion* 1. 840
The Housewife, tempted by such slender gains . 783 *Excursion* 2. 741
How gracefully that slender shrub looks forth 787 *Excursion* 3. 86
To turn a slender mill (that new-made plaything) 789 *Excursion* 3. 205
Their slender means: so, to that parent's care . 852 *Excursion* 6. 945
For a life's stay (slender it was, but sure) . . 859 *Excursion* 7. 133
And slender stem, while here I sit at eve, . . 863 *Excursion* 7. 397
That not the slender privilege is theirs . . . 877 *Excursion* 8. 229
Their slender ditties when the trees are bare. . 881 *Excursion* 8. 483
Receiving, took the slender path that leads . . 895 *Excursion* 9. 773
Slept. And in a quiet home once more my father slept. 29 *Guilt* 261
In the calm sunshine slept the glittering main; . 30 *Guilt* 336
She slept in peace,—his pulses throbbed and stopped, ... 36 *Guilt* 631
Came to my child as by my side he slept, . . . 44 *Bord.* 412
And, like a naked Indian, slept himself away. . 107 *Indolence* 27
In one of those sweet dreams I slept, ... 109 **Strange fits* 17
The vacant city slept; the busy winds, . . . 123 *V. and J.* 95
With some, the noble Creature never slept; . . 139 *Widow* 12
Of Him who slept upon the open lea: . . . . 168 *Pilgrim's Dream* 67
But in calm peace the appointed Victim slept, . 214 *Dion* 112
Thou turn'st the Wheel that slept with dust o'er-spread; . . . . 255 *S. H.* 3
Slept, with the obscurest, in the low . . . . 285 *Grave of Burns* 29
To seize (while on the Deep it slept) . . . . 297 *Highland Boy* 192
Slept amid that lone Camp on Hardknot's height, 380 *Duddon* 17. 10
And slept in many a crystal pool . . . . . 385 *Yarrow Rev.* 19
The heroic Age expired—it slept . . . . . 390 *Highland Broach* 31
And for two days unnoticed slept. . . . . . 412 *White Doe* 1502
Where Francis slept in his last abode. . . . . 416 *White Doe* 1818
Hath slept since noon-tide on the grassy ground, . 458 **Had this* 56
Among the good (when love might else have slept, 467 *St. Bees* 68
All, while *he* slept, treading the pendent stairs . 500 *Humanity* 35
Forgot her functions, and slept undisturbed. . . 648 *Prelude* 2. 418
In this new life. Imagination slept, ... 652 *Prelude* 3. 257
Through the same gateways, sleep where they had slept, ... 652 *Prelude* 3. 262
Languish within me; even then it slept, . . . 694 *Prelude* 7. 469
It slept, even in the pregnant season of youth. . 694 *Prelude* 7. 472
To him who slept at noon and wakes at eve." . 700 *Prelude* 8. 52
To the cold grave in which her husband slept, . 704 *Prelude* 8. 386
And to this helpless infant. I have slept . . . 768 *Excursion* 1. 769
Was sapped; and while she slept, the nightly damps . . . . 770 *Excursion* 1. 907
Ranged through the mountains, slept upon the earth, ... 855 *Excursion* 6. 1099
A golden lustre slept upon the hills; . . . . 871 *Excursion* 7. 877
Slew. Slew, and as quickly to a second gave . . 123 *V. and J.* 131
Whose rival sword a like Opponent slew: . . . 434 *Ecc. Sonn.* 2. 24. 10
Where her thousands Fate slew, ... S.3. 440 **Said red-ribboned* 19
Slid. White as the pair that slid along the plains . 497 *Lycoris* 17
Slide. And I could run and slide, ... 84 *We are Seven* 58
What fond and wayward thoughts will slide . . 109 **Strange fits* 25
Old Daniel his hand to the treasure will slide! . 572 *Avarice* 19
Sliding. *See* **Smoothly-sliding.**
Slight. But wherefore slight protection such as you 42 *Bord.* 258
But what has brought you hither? A slight affair, 43 *Bord.* 339
As have no slight or trivial influence . . . . 206 *Tintern* 32
A veil is lifted—can she slight . . . . . . 215 *Kirkstone* 63
I slight my own beloved Cam, to range . . . 270 **Ye sacred* 10
—Strange words they seemed of slight and scorn; 293 *Yarrow Unv.* 29
His vows to Fortune; who, in cruel slight . . 317 **Look now* 2
Ye slight not life—to God and Nature true; . . 326 **Intrepid sons* 5
This brief this simple wayside Call can slight, . 389 *Glencroe* 3
And ne'er did Genius slight them, as they go, . 392 *Avon* 7
Rejected, or with slight repaid. . . . . . . 407 *White Doe* 1019
I slight them all; and, on this sea-beat shore . 459 **Wanderer! that* 10
Thy Spirit triumphs o'er the slight; . . . . 506 **While from* 23
The old Lion and usurped his place, in slight . 644 *Prelude* 2. 152
Slight shocks of young love-liking interspersed, . 663 *Prelude* 4. 317
Bound to the distant Alps. A hardy slight . . 680 *Prelude* 6. 326
Ere we have learnt by use to slight the crimes . 692 *Prelude* 7. 332
Upon these uncouth Forms a slight regard . . 788 *Excursion* 3. 164
Slight, if you will, the *means*; but spare to slight 791 *Excursion* 3. 360
—Would I had ne'er renounced it!" A slight flush . . . . 832 *Excursion* 5. 621
In slight of that forbearance and reserve . . . 847 *Excursion* 6. 585
And, in this unpremeditated slight . . . . . 892 *Excursion* 9. 556
Slighted. We slighted them all,—and our birth-right was lost. . . . . 116 *Repentance* 24
A slighted child, at her own will . . . . . 192 *Ruth* 4
Is in the mirror slighted. . . . . 302 *Yarrow V.* 16
Who slighted fear; rejected steadfastly . . . 317 **Call not* 3
Forth from their coverts; slighted objects rise; . 350 *Des. Stanzas* 6
Words which she slighted at that day; . . . 415 *White Doe* 1769
And Strangers even the slighted Scroll may prize, 526 **Soon did* 6
In lonely spots, become a slighted thing;) . . 527 **Those breathing* 4
With which, though slighted, he, on naked hill . 530 *Poor Robin* 25
Of slighted love, and scorn, and jealous rage, . 547 **Beneath yon* 15
Not that I slighted books,—that were to lack . 654 *Prelude* 3. 364
To deck some slighted playmate's homely cheek. 661 *Prelude* 4. 208
Though slighted and too oft misused. Besides, . 663 *Prelude* 4. 345
And slighted Hope *will* be avenged; and, when . 792 *Excursion* 3. 459
His flock he slighted: his paternal fields . . 855 *Excursion* 6. 1103
Slightest. Maintains inviolate its slightest vow! . 270 **Shame on* 8
Even by an innocent fancy's slightest freak . . 509 *F. Stone* 84
Slighting. And, slighting sails and scorning oars, . 216 *Enterprise* 81
Slightly. With firmness, hitherto but slightly touched 675 *Prelude* 6. 54
Slights. And, tired with slights his pride no more could brook, ... 103 *Artegal* 88
The passing traveller slights; . . . . . . 224 *Primrose* 2
And, if there be a joy that slights the claim . 261 **Fair Prime* 13
That slights this passion, or condemns; . . . 376 **The Minstrels* 62
Hardening a heart that loathes or slights . . . 533 **Blest is* 53
Slim. My boy beside me tripped, so slim . . 86 *Anecdote* 25
Where the slim wild deer roves; . . . . . 506 **While from* 30
Rose the slim ash and massy sycamore, . . . 881 *Excursion* 8. 478
Slimy. Upon the slimy foot-stone I espied . . 763 *Excursion* 1. 492
Slink. For all the startled scaly tribes that slink 383 *Duddon* 28. 6
Slinking. And his red eyes the slinking water hides; 606 *Desc.Sk.Quarto* 236
Slip. Each slip of lawn the broken rocks between . 5 *Ev. Wk.* 178
I put a slip of foxglove in his hand, ... 44 *Bord.* 401
A track, that brought us to a slip of lawn, . . 149 *M. H.* 6
Yon tawny slip is Libya's sands; . . . . . 237 *P. B.* 61
Nor could I let one thought—one motion—slip . 273 **Wild Redbreast* 7
To let slip upon buck or doe. . . . . . . 494 *Force of Prayer* 16
Once did I see a slip of earth . . . . . 531 †*Float. Isl.* 5
Slip by him unproclaimed, and told the hours . 650 *Prelude* 3. 55
An unproductive slip of rugged ground, . . . 758 *Excursion* 1. 110
When she could slip into the cottage-barn, . . 852 *Excursion* 6. 898
Slip'st. Slip'st into thy sheltering hold; . . . 161 **Pleasures newly* 38
Slipped. When my old Leader slipped into the flood 52 *Bord.* 834
The lamb had slipped into the stream, . . . 85 *Shepherd-boys* 67
And slipped into the ordinary works . . . . 652 *Prelude* 3. 241
From earnest dialogues I slipped in thought, . . 716 *Prelude* 9. 438
Or to that rural castle, name now slipped . . . 716 *Prelude* 9. 483
Slippers. With freight of slippers piled beneath his arm! . . . . 690 *Prelude* 7. 218
Slippery. Rolled wantonly between their slippery wings, ... 6 *Ev. Wk.* 247
At home, go staggering through the slippery fords, 99 *Brothers* 258
Along the loose rocks, or the slippery verge . . 496 **A little* 19
Or slippery even to peril! and each step, . . 497 **Enough of climbing* 3
Whose slippery face derides his deathful tread! . 609 *Desc.Sk.Quarto* 393
And half-inch fissures in the slippery rock . . 637 *Prelude* 1. 332
With languid steps that by the slippery turf . . 756 *Excursion* 1. 22
Slipping. And beams of evening, slipping in between, 14 *Desc. Sk.* 212
Of meditation, slipping in between . . . . . 480 **Most sweet* 7
The beams of evening, slipping soft between, . . 607 *Desc.Sk.Quarto* 267
So near that, slipping back into the shade . . 664 *Prelude* 4. 389
Slips. Slips in a moment out of life. . . . . 88 *H. C.* 33
Slips from his prison walls: and Fancy, free . 336 *Danube* 5
Forth slips, like an enfranchised slave, . . . 348 **Lulled by* 33
Life slips from underneath us, like that arch . 351 *Des. Stanzas* 84
Tumbles, the wildering Thunder slips abroad; . 605 *Desc.Sk.Quarto* 204
Of the suspicious, slips of the indiscreet, . . . 723 *Prelude* 10. 348
The gooseberry trees that shot in long lank slips, 763 *Excursion* 1. 456
All England through, where nooks and slips of ground . . . . 879 *Excursion* 8. 370
Slope. While the sharp slope the slackened team confounds, ... 4 *Ev. Wk.* 134
Long had he fancied each successive slope . . 25 *Guilt* 37
That rang down a bare slope not far remote: . 30 *Guilt* 326
Between the water and a winding slope . . . 148 **A narrow* 3
Are tempted to this sunny slope! . . . . . 154 *Flower Garden* 36
Here was it—on this rugged slope, ... 175 *Waggoner* 1. 124
That mossy slope, o'er which the woodbine throws 221 *Triad* 78
But now, while down that slope he wends, . . 247 *P. B.* 938
Or shining slope where he must never stray; . . 267 **As the* 5
Ambition—following down this far-famed slope . 345 **Ambition—following* 1
"And just above yon slope of corn . . . . 486 **We walked* 25
—On the slope of a mountain I stood, ... 620 *Convict* 2
Upon a slope surmounted by a plain . . . . 644 *Prelude* 2. 156
Upon a slope above the village school, . . . 671 *Prelude* 5. 393
Strewing the turf's green slope. A diamond light 705 *Prelude* 8. 406
He yielded not; but, pointing to a slope . . . 793 *Excursion* 3. 475
Pressing behind, adown a rugged slope, . . . 865 *Excursion* 7. 543
And that smooth slope from which the dwelling rose, ... 881 *Excursion* 8. 468
Upon this flowery slope; and see—beyond— . 890 *Excursion* 9. 420
Slope-channel. In the slope-channel floored with pebbles bright, ... 190 **Lyre! though* 34
Sloped. Sloped seaward, turf whose tender April green, ... 356 *Aquap.* 225
Slopes. *See* **Mountain-slopes.**
Far to the western slopes with hamlets white; . 8 *Ev. Wk.* 336
Embowered in walnut slopes and citron isles: . 13 *Desc. Sk.* 155
A structure stands, which two bare slopes enclose. 27 *Guilt* 147
On the slopes of the pastures all colours were seen; 120 *Childless Father* 6
Ye ploughshares sparkling on the slopes! . . . 214 *Kirkstone* 21
For warm Vesuvio's vine-clad slopes; . . . . 386 *Yarrow Rev.* 51
The sylvan slopes with corn-clad fields . . . 498 **The sylvan* 1
What slopes are planted, or what mosses drained: 522 *Epist. Beaumont* 68
Calm huts, and lawns between, and sylvan slopes. 607 *Desc.Sk.Quarto* 264
Alone, continuing there to muse: the slopes . . 661 *Prelude* 4. 178
The vine-clad hills and slopes of Burgundy, . . 680 *Prelude* 6. 375
In this delicious region."—Cultured slopes, . . 891 *Excursion* 9. 504
Sloping. *See* **Off-sloping.**
There, over rock or sloping pasture creep. . . . 14 *Desc. Sk.* 215
Descends along the sloping road; . . . . . 176 *Waggoner* 1. 263
They shaped their course along the sloping side . 777 *Excursion* 2. 389
Sloth. And, though little troubled with sloth, . . 159 **Up with me* 19
With burring note, which Industry and Sloth . 453 **Calm is the* 23
Be plighted, not to ease but sullen sloth, . . . 514 **Long-favoured* 7
Days undefiled by luxury or sloth, ... 515 *Penn.* 1
Of intellect; such sloth I could not brook, . . 732 *Prelude* 11. 325

Slumbrous. Induced a soft and slumbrous dream, . 167 Pilgrim's Dream 18
Slung. A harp is from his shoulder slung ; . . . 166 Danish Boy 34
With a huge wallet o'er my shoulders slung, . . 185 Nutting 6
From far, with basket, slung upon her arm, . . 699 Prelude 8. 28
With store of household goods, in panniers slung . 858 Excursion 7. 64
Slunk. Others slunk to moor and wood, . . . 171 Kitten 57
And by a postern-gate he slunk away. . . . . 536 Egremont 96
That he was glad to lose) slunk from the world . 845 Excursion 6. 454
Sly. Declining Manhood learns to note the sly . . 378 Duddon 9. 12
Through the lost look of dotage, is cunning and sly : 572 Avarice 22
Sly subterfuge, if the adventure's bound . . . 643 Prelude 2. 100
A prayer both bold and sly . . . . S.3. 431 *The Scottish 10
Of the sly boatmen of Killarney, ... S.3. 438 *My Lord 14
Smacked. The boy then smacked his whip, and fast 82 Alice Fell 13
Small. Save where, with sparkling foam, a small cascade . . . . 3 Ev. Wk. 64
Toil, small as pygmies in the gulf profound ; . . 5 Ev. Wk. 163
Shedding, through paly loop-holes mild and small, 7 Ev. Wk. 293
Till our small share of hardly-paining sighs . . 8 Ev. Wk. 352
Tend the small harvest of their garden glades ; . 12 Desc. Sk. 92
To reach a small wood-hut hung boldly on the steep. . . . . 15 Desc. Sk. 237
To him the day-star glitters small and bright, . 16 Desc. Sk. 323
Small help ; and, after marriage such as mine, . 32 Guilt 427
That Oswald finds small favour in our sight, . . 37 Bord. 12
I struck my flint, and built up a small fire . . 50 Bord. 704
The obstinate bolt of a small iron door . . . 59 Bord. 1200
Landed with a small troop, myself being one : . 68 Bord. 1713
Of a small pool of water he was laid, ... 73 Bord. 2063
Look at it—the flower is small, ... 79 Foresight 5
Small and low, though fair as any : . . . . 79 Foresight 6
They tracked the footmarks small ; . . . . 83 Lucy Gray 46
And, in a basin black and small, ... 85 Shepherd-boys 54
To be engrafted on the top of his small edifice. . 91 Norman Boy 20
And in His sight the fragile Cross, on thy small hut, will be . . . . 93 Poet's Dream 59
From perils manifold, with some small wealth . 96 Brothers 66
His stripling prime. A town of small repute, . 121 V. and J. 10
In great and small, in round and square, . . . 128 Idiot Boy 208
That small, for flax ; and, if one wheel had rest, . 132 Michael 84
And for the land, his small inheritance. . . . 138 Michael 459
But small and fugitive our gain . . . . . 143 *Driven in 30
And a small bed of water in the woods. . . . 149 M. H. 7
At such small elevation from the ground . . . 150 *When, to 22
A small Cascade fresh swoln with snows . . . 155 Waterfall 5
Will reach both great and small ; . . . . . 156 Oak and Broom 62
Methinks you take small heed ! . . . . . . 161 Binnorie 31
The platform is small, but gives room for them all ; 166 Stray Pleasures 5
To the small wooden isle where, their work to beguile, ... 166 Stray Pleasures 10
This, one of those small builders proved . . . 168 Wren's Nest 33
Where fancy hath small liberty to grace . . . 172 Infant Daughter 34
And see, beyond that hamlet small . . . . 180 Waggoner 4. 42
Followed by multitudes of stars, that, small . . 184 Night-piece 15
And a single small cottage, a nest like a dove's, . 188 Poor Susan 11
Or gives a thing but small delight that never can be dear ? . . . . 189 Star-gazers 14
The small birds twitter, ... 190 March 3
Small clouds are sailing, ... 190 March 18
Such small machinery as she turned . . . . 195 Ruth 250
Though but of compass small, and bare . . . 198 Thorn 32
And a small arbour, made for rural joy ; . . . 201 Hart-leap 58
Small difference lies between thy creed and mine : 203 Hart-leap 162
"Small change it made in Peter's heart . . . 239 P. B. 251
In city or in village small, ... 239 P. B. 278
Call it of earth a small green plot, ... 240 P. B. 369
Small cause of dire effect ! for, surely, . . . 246 P. B. 841
The Ass in that small meadow-ground ; . . . 248 P. B. 1037
Its own small pasture, almost its own sky ! . . 250 Admon. 4
So narrow seemed the brooks, the fields so small ! 251 *Beloved Vale 11
Why have I crowded this small bark with you . 252 *Her only 10
Sleepless ! and soon the small birds' melodies . 253 *A flock 6
Of this small lute gave ease to Petrarch's wound ; 260 *Scorn not 4
Observe the faithful flowers ! if small to great . 265 *When haughty 9
Watching the least small bird that round her hops, 270 *Though the bold 7
As I do now, the cabin small, ... 288 Highland Girl 76
Not small like ours, a peaceful flood ; . . . . 295 Highland Boy 52
To this small spot, his leafy shade ; . . . . 298 Brownie's Cell 44
Exalt his still small voice ;—to quell that Host . 322 *By Moscow 10
On the small hyssop destined to become, . . . 354 Aquap. 135
Appears his lot, to the small Worm's compared, . 366 Lombardy 3
Where small birds warbled to their paramours ; . 377 Duddon 6. 3
And one small hamlet, under a green hill . . . 379 Duddon 13. 2
One small possession lacked not power, . . . 391 Highland Broach 55
A falchion, and a buckler small, ... 404 White Doe 723
The bright Moon sees that valley small . . . 406 White Doe 945
Breaks into dimples small and bright ; . . . 406 White Doe 968
Though small his kingdom as a spark or gem, . 425 Ecc. Sonn. 1. 26. 11
The least small pittance of bare mould they prize 426 Ecc. Sonn. 1. 32. 13
Seek in domestic oratory small, ... 430 Ecc. Sonn. 2. 6. 7
Small reverence for the mitre's offices, . . . 442 Ecc. Sonn. 3. 8. 12
Shall wound the tender sod. Encincture small, . 451 Ecc. Sonn. 3. 41. 9
And whispers caught, and speeches small, . . 479 Somnamb. 122
Yet, God is my witness, thou small helpless Thing ! 484 *A plague 31
Nor form, nor feeling, great or small ; . . . . 485 Poet's Epitaph 30
Through dewy grass, nor small birds hushed in bowers, ... 501 *The unremitting 4
A household small and sensitive,—whose love, . 510 *Among a 29
And quieted and soothed, a torrent small, . . 524 Epist. Beaumont 177

Small—*continued.*
Like a small Hamlet, with its bashful head . . 524 Epist. Beaumont 192
Is smooth as clear, save where with dimples small 527 *Those breathing 11
Will often live in one small cottage ; . . . . 536 Goody Blake 35
Small service is true service while it lasts : . . 538 *Small service 1
That things obscure and small outlive the great : 546 *Oft is 4
His pinnace, a small vagrant barge, up-piled . . 547 *Rude is 18
Along the beach of this small isle and thought . 551 *If thou in 20
Song do I learn,—small grammar I have got.' . 553 Prioress 85
For now when they may hear the small birds' song, 557 Cuck.and Night. 26
Upon the second step of that small pile, . . . 566 Cumb. Beg. 13
Fell on the ground ; and the small mountain birds, 566 Cumb. Beg. 19
Of some small blessings ; have been kind to such . 568 Cumb. Beg. 151
And the small critic wielding his delicate pen, . 569 Farmer 3
And there, with small wealth but his legs and his hands, ... 570 Farmer 47
Small cause there is for that fond wish of ours . 573 Chiabrera 1. 9
Sole light admitted here, a small cascade, . . . 593 Ev. Wk. Quarto 79
Small circles of green radiance gleam around. . . 597 Ev. Wk. Quarto 278
While in sweet cadence rising small and still . . 598 Ev. Wk. Quarto 325
Thence, from three paly loopholes mild and small, 598 Ev. Wk. Quarto 335
Small cottage lights across the water stream, . 598 Ev. Wk. Quarto 374
Her babe's small cry, that leads him to his prey. 606 Desc.Sk.Quarto 242
And hangs his small wood-hut upon the steeps. . 607 Desc.Sk.Quarto 294
Small as a bird the chamois-chaser fly. . . . 609 Desc.Sk.Quarto 369
The star of noon that glitters small and bright, . 609 Desc.Sk.Quarto 386
In a small mill-race severed from his stream, . . 636 Prelude 1. 289
Small circles glittering idly in the moon, . . . 637 Prelude 1. 365
Of our small market village, was the goal . . 642 Prelude 2. 35
And now a third small Island, where survived . 643 Prelude 2. 62
Of a small bowling-green ; beneath us stood . . 644 Prelude 2. 157
Of some small island steered our course with one, 644 Prelude 2. 167
Small jealousies, and triumphs good or bad— . 650 Prelude 3. 72
Of manners put to school I took small note, . . 663 Prelude 4. 302
There small birds warble from the leafy trees, . 683 Prelude 6. 534
How small, of intervening years ! For then, . . 693 Prelude 7. 443
Most delicate, a lurking eyelet, small, ... 695 Prelude 7. 558
Full-formed, that take, with small internal help, . 697 Prelude 7. 653
That I both was and must be of small weight, . 721 Prelude 10. 226
Small islands scattered amid stormy waves, . . 725 Prelude 10. 482
Was gentleness and peace. Upon a small . . . 726 Prelude 10. 554
Benevolent in small societies, ... 728 Prelude 11. 85
This small adventure, for even such it seemed . 746 Prelude 14. 25
And some small portion of his eloquent speech, . 757 Excursion 1. 98
Where, on a small hereditary farm, ... 758 Excursion 1. 109
He had small need of books ; for many a tale . 758 Excursion 1. 163
He duly went with what small overplus . . . 760 Excursion 1. 245
Had twined about her two small rows of peas, . 767 Excursion 1. 729
Was comfortless, and her small lot of books, . . 768 Excursion 1. 824
Was one small opening, where a heath-clad ridge 776 Excursion 2. 335
The small birds find in spring no thicket there . 776 Excursion 2. 345
Of that small valley, singing as they moved ; . 777 Excursion 2. 390
"Can it be thus among so small a band . . . 780 Excursion 2. 608
And reached a small apartment dark and low, . 781 Excursion 2. 648
Our table, small parade of garden fruits, . . . 782 Excursion 2. 683
Of a small chapel, where, in ancient time, . . . 784 Excursion 2. 814
Small space ! but, for reiterated steps, . . . 805 Excursion 4. 245
For the small wren to build in ;—not in vain, . 807 Excursion 4. 389
Small creature as she is, from earth's bright flowers, 807 Excursion 4. 393
To his small island in the ethereal deep . . . 811 Excursion 4. 640
Might, with small help from fancy, be transformed 814 Excursion 4. 875
Of the small Cottage in the lonely Dell . . . 821 Excursion 4. 1318
And its small lot of life-supporting fields, . . . 822 Excursion 5. 2
And foot-worn epitaphs, and some with small . 825 Excursion 5. 169
Small space of that green churchyard with a light 826 Excursion 5. 229
A few small crofts of stone-encumbered ground ; . 835 Excursion 5. 864
Of that small town encountering thus, they filled, 845 Excursion 6. 465
Or the pellucid lake." "Small risk," said I, . . 847 Excursion 6. 599
Lies guarded by its neighbour ; the small heap . 850 Excursion 6. 790
And small birds singing happily to mates . . . 851 Excursion 6. 857
To a small Chapel in the vale beyond) . . . . 858 Excursion 7. 57
To help the small but certain comings-in . . . 860 Excursion 7. 166
To whom the small inheritance had fallen. . . 864 Excursion 7. 437
Forth with small leave-taking : . . . . . . S.3. 424 Tinker 26
Unheard of, save in one small hamlet, here . . S.3. 433 *The doubt 9
Those small flat stones, which, ranged by traveller's hands . . . . K.8. 226 *I will 63
Whole hours with but small interchange of speech, K.8. 227 *I will 88
This small abiding-place of many men, . . . K.8. 240 Recluse 1.1.146
Could see them, nor in that small open space . K.8. 243 Recluse 1.1.258
A liking for the small grey horse that bears . . K.8. 250 Recluse 1.1.505
Smaller. Stood near, of smaller size, and not unlike 787 Excursion 3. 56
That seems still smaller than it is. This grove . K.8. 247 Recluse 1.1.386
Smallest. Even till the smallest habitable rock, . 890 Excursion 9. 387
Smart. Did press this semblance of unpitied smart 169 Love lies Bleeding 21
And chaser bursting here with one dire smart. . 393 Hart's-horn 8
Ah, then, Belovèd ! pleasing was the smart, . . 395 White Doe : Ded. 9
A smart Assembly-room usurped the ground . . 642 Prelude 2. 39
Till with a sudden bound of smart reproach, . . 673 Prelude 5. 488
Smell. By what charm of sight or smell, . . . 161 *Pleasures newly 42
A subtle smell that Spring unbinds, ... 225 Present. 40
The flower of sweetest smell is shy and lowly. . 262 *Not Love 14
Smells. Thrusts his hands in a waggon, and smells at the hay ; . . . . 570 Farmer 82
Smile. *See* **Half-smile.**
Turn to a silent smile their sleepy cry, . . . 7 Ev. Wk. 258
On darling spots remote her tempting smile. . . 8 Ev. Wk. 344
Tinged like an angel's smile all rosy red— . . 19 Desc. Sk. 475

Smile—*continued.*
Joy's second spring and Hope's long-treasured smile, ... 32 Guilt 455
Might tempt me to a smile ; but what of him ? . 38 Bord. 26
That smile hath life in it ! This road is perilous ; 67 Bord. 1646
Smile of the Moon !—for so I name . . . . 112 Lament 1
There was a smile or two—yet—yet . . . . 121 EmigrantMother 56
That last, that sweetest smile of his ? . . . . 121 EmigrantMother 64
From this time forth he never shared a smile . . 125 V. and J. 284
Heart-pleased we smile upon the Bird . . . . 143 *Driven in 27
" Oh ! smile on me, my little lamb ! . . . . 145 Her Eyes 91
Alas ! that meek that tender smile . . . . 164 *Fair Lady 35
For the undeceived, smile as they may, ... 170 Rural Ill. 29
—That smile forbids the thought ; for on thy face 173 InfantDaughter 66
The VANGUARD—you may smirk and smile, . . 178 Waggoner 2. 116
Motley accoutrement, of power to smile . . . 185 Nutting 12
If they speak 'tis to praise, and they praise with a smile. . . . . 188 Music 32
He with a smile did then his words repeat ; . . 197 Resolution 120
Keep for the Young the impassioned smile . . 215 Enterprise 1
Ah, spare the exulting smile, ... 215 Enterprise 7
O Thou, against whose lip, without its smile . . 221 Triad 65
Smile if thou wilt, but not in scorn, ... 223 Wishing-gate 43
The chains of frenzy, or entice a smile . . . . 232 Power of Sound 12
Wilt smile upon this gift with more than mild content ! . . . . 250 *Happy the 14
If the heavens smile, and leave us free to glide, . 252 *Her only 7
Might smile on work, O Lady, once so dear . . 255 S. H. 8
Then may that heaven-revealing smile of thine, . 258 *Even so 11
No mightier work had gained the plausive smile . 269 Malham 8
The rigid features of a transient smile, . . . 273 *When Philoctetes 5
Sends gladness, by no languid smile declared. . 273 *Not the 8
Even as I speak the rising Sun's first smile . . 283 *Here, where 10
Smile on his Mother now with bolder cheer. . . 294 *Fly, some 14
All, all were dispossessed, save him whose smile . 298 Brownie's Cell 41
In the wife's smile ; and in the placid sky ; . . 315 *The Land 7
To sadness not their own, when, with faint smile . 353 Aquap. 74
In one meek smile, beneath a peasant's shed, . . 359 *They—who 7
Of a Divinity, that seemed to smile . . . . 371 Eg. Maid 131
There would the Indian answer with a smile . . 380 Duddon 16. 4
Looks down upon her with a smile, ... 417 White Doe 1907
A gracious smile, that seems to say— . . . . 417 White Doe 1908
The gift exalting, and with playful smile : . . . 437 Ecc. Sonn. 2. 39. 5
Like men ashamed : the Sun with his first smile . 450 Ecc. Sonn. 3. 40. 10
Fixed, by her smile, upon some rocky seat ; . . 461 *Giordano,verily 13
Antiquity salutes him with a smile, ... 463 *Why should the 4
Knew not the double-dealing of a smile ; . . . 470 *A youth 11
For Fortune on me never deigned to smile ; . . 470 †From early 8
As is the smile upon thy face : . . . . . . 492 Duty 44
On whom the Muses smile ; . . . . 499 *Departing summer 27
With its soft smile the truth express, ... 507 May 19
Depicted on these pages smile at time ; . . . 511 *Who rashly 10
And she would deign this day to smile on me . . 522 Epist.Beaumont 51
Thy smile is sure, Thy plighted word . . . . 550 Hermit's Cell 5. 15
Old Adam will smile at the pains that have made . 570 Farmer 75
Beside a sea that could not cease to smile ; . . 578 Peele Castle 19
Or charms that smile on Tusa's evening stream, . 605 Desc.Sk.Quarto 178
With earlier smile the ray of morn to view . . 610 Desc.Sk.Quarto 454
Found still beneath her smile, and only there. . 615 Desc.Sk.Quarto 725
Stern was her forehead, but a smile serene . . 618 School Ex. 15
A smile sat beaming on her pensive face. . . . 618 School Ex. 24
With rapture she beheld Britannia smile, . . . 618 School Ex. 45
Dear Valley, having in thy face a smile . . . 622 Recluse 1. 1. 116
I smile, in many a mountain solitude . . . . 657 Prelude 3. 568
He with a smile made answer, that in truth . . 666 Prelude 5. 52
Open it out, diffusing thence a smile . . . . 695 Prelude 7. 560
" A cheerful smile unbends the wrinkled brow, . . 699 Prelude 8. 48
With gracious smile, deliberately pleased, . . . 758 Excursion 1. 106
Of the poor innocent children. 'Every smile,' . . 765 Excursion 1. 589
An amicable smile retained the life . . . . . 779 Excursion 2. 523
The Solitary, with a faint sarcastic smile . . . 780 Excursion 2. 594
Ere with inviting smile the Wanderer said : . . 782 Excursion 2. 728
And infant's smile awaited my return. . . . . 794 Excursion 3. 583
Let him build systems of his own, and smile . . 810 Excursion 4. 605
He with a smile exclaimed :— " 'Tis well you speak . . . . 814 Excursion 4. 894
One that hath barely learned to shape a smile, . 826 Excursion 5. 263
" Yet," with a smile of triumph thus exclaimed . 828 Excursion 5. 390
" Yes ! " said the Solitary with a smile . . . 835 Excursion 5. 838
Till he begins to smile upon the breast . . . 836 Excursion 5. 955
A woman of soft speech and gracious smile, . . 858 Excursion 7. 78
And with soft smile, his consort would reprove. . 861 Excursion 7. 225
And he returned our greeting with a smile. . . 866 Excursion 7. 555
Of his employment, with a courteous smile . . 871 Excursion 7. 920
And re-confirmed—are scoffed at with a smile . 872 Excursion 7. 992
Insatiate Charlotte's tears, and Charlotte's smile. L.1. 89 Juvenal 1. 23

Smiled. Usurping where the fairest herbage smiled : 17 Desc. Sk. 393
Fields smiled, and temples rose, and towns and cities grew. . . . . 103 Artegal 73
Smiled in my face) this were in simple truth . . 147 Joanna 68
Were oft among the first that smiled . . . . 224 *'Tis gone 41
I looked, I stared, I smiled, I laughed ; and all . 251 *Beloved Vale 13
The rough Ætolians smiled with bitter scorn. . . 312 *When, far 4
So touchingly he smiled— . . . . 342 Ital. Itin. 54
A countenance that as sweetly smiled— . . . 348 *Lulled by 11
Thanks to our Lady's grace." I smiled to hear, . 360 Albano 8
Hung back, and smiled, and blushed for joy, . . 398 White Doe 182
She smiled ; but Time, the old Saturnian seer, . 465 *Dear to 9
Hope smiled when your nativity was cast, . . . 474 *Hope smiled 1
Have smiled upon thy flowers. . . . . . . 507 May 32

Smiled—*continued.*
" Have you forgot "—and here she smiled— . . 542 Russ. Fug. 57
She sought in vain, the Woodman smiled ; . . . 543 Russ. Fug. 133
And, in my spleen, I smiled that it was grey. . . 571 *There is a Flower 20
Smiled like the morn, and vanish'd into air." . . 619 School Ex. 112
Stretched forth his little arms and smil'd. . . . 620 Birth of Love 27
And while the fearless infant smiled, ... 629 Installation 43
I looked at him and smiled, and smiled again, . . 659 Prelude 4. 57
O fostering Nature ! I rejected—smiled . . . 797 Excursion 3. 809
To cure his malady ! " The Vicar smiled,— . . 840 Excursion 6. 112
His suit to Fortune ; and she smiled again . . 843 Excursion 6. 333
Or bounty tires—and every face, that smiled . . 880 Excursion 8. 387

Smileless. Ingrates who wear a smileless face . . 490 Night Thought 11

Smiles. Where sparkling eyes and breaking smiles illume . . . . 13 Desc. Sk. 133
But let us hence ; for fair Locarno smiles . . . 13 Desc. Sk. 154
All nature smiles, and owns beneath her eyes . . 21 Desc. Sk. 622
And often, viewing their sweet smiles, I sighed, . 29 Guilt 265
Tears down his cheek, or solitary smiles . . . 97 Brothers 110
[And she hath smiles to earth unknown ; . . . 108 Louisa
Smiles, that with motion of their own . . . . 108 Louisa
What heavenly smiles ! O Lady mine, ... 112 *What heavenly 1
Oh ! had he but thy cheerful smiles, ... 121 EmigrantMother 49
The smiles, worth all the world to me. . . . . 121 EmigrantMother 58
Smiles hast thou, bright ones of thy own ; . . . 121 EmigrantMother 61
She smiles as if a martyr's crown were won : . . 139 Widow 37
Smiles are beginning, like the beams of dawn, . . 173 Infant Daughter 67
To shoot and circulate ; smiles have there been seen ; . . . . 173 Infant Daughter 68
Thy loneliness : or shall those smiles be called . 173 Infant Daughter 71
Praise, blame, love, kisses, tears, and smiles. . . 186 *She was 20
Behold her how She smiles to-day . . . . . 204 Brougham 17
Amid their smiles and dimples dignified— . . . 221 Triad 138
Is Harmony, blest queen of smiles and tears, . . 235 Power of Sound 219
And smiles that from their birthplace ne'er shall flee 279 *All praise 6
Soft smiles, by human kindness bred ! . . . . 288 Highland Girl 35
But smiles—the hesitating shaft to free ; . . . 339 Tell 25
And smiles, that dared to take their place, . . . 401 White Doe 499
Meek filial smiles, upon thy face, ... 401 White Doe 500
With natural smiles of greeting. Bells are dumb ; 427 Ecc. Sonn. 1. 36. 9
Just limits ; but yon Tower, whose smiles adorn . 469 *The feudal 5
Of hope, and smiles on you with cheer sublime. . 477 Steamboats 14
Whose smiles, diffused o'er land and sea, . . . 497 Lycoris 46
Whose day departs in pomp, returns with smiles— 501 Humanity 70
And jocund smiles, and toward the lowly Grange . 525 Epist. Beaumont 237
And smiles, fond efforts of distress . . . . . 543 Russ. Fug. 167
Every face in the village is dimpled with smiles. . 572 Avarice 40
Its Sister-twin survives, whose smiles afford . . 576 *By a 11
By playful smiles, (alas ! too oft . . . . . 577 *By playful 1
Inspired—works potent over smiles and tears. . 584 Ch. Lamb 17
Pleas'd thro' the dusk their breaking smiles to view, ... 596 Ev. Wk. Quarto 274
And smiles to Solitude and Want impart. . . . 605 Desc.Sk.Quarto 163
Hence shall we seek where fair Locarno smiles . 605 Desc.Sk.Quarto 176
With cheeks o'erspread by smiles of baleful glow, 617 Desc.Sk.Quarto 790
Where Persecution decks with ghastly smiles . . 617 Desc.Sk.Quarto 798
What Genius smiles on yonder flood ? . . . . 626 †Cento 4
And often looking round was moved to smiles . . 661 Prelude 4. 210
Smiles of good-will from faces that he knew . . 772 Excursion 2. 57
Would push this censure farther ;—for, if smiles . 791 Excursion 3. 333
She smiles, including in her wide embrace . . . 819 Excursion 4. 1196
Stung by his inward thoughts, and by the smiles 855 Excursion 6. 1096
His gentle manners : and his peaceful smiles, . . 864 Excursion 7. 460
Reason, and, with that reason, smiles and tears ; 887 Excursion 9. 222

Smiling. A little moment past so smiling ! . . . 9 Lines : Boat 6
Appears a scanty plot of smiling green, ... 14 Desc. Sk. 235
Smiling in sleep—— A pretty feat of Fancy ! . 55 Bord. 972
Ay, thought the Vicar, smiling to himself, . . . 96 Brothers 104
Look round, and by their smiling seem to say, . 324 Ode 1814 66
Of April, smiling high in upper air ? . . . . 381 Duddon 22. 10
Though smiling on the last hill-top ! . . . . 473 Ossian 72
A smiling sea, and be what I have been : . . . 578 Peele Castle 38
Peeps out a little speck of smiling green, . . . 607 Desc.Sk.Quarto 292
Ev'n here Content has fix'd her smiling reign . . 608 Desc.Sk.Quarto 323
Fair smiling lights the purpled hills illume ! . . 613 Desc.Sk.Quarto 633
Her seas yet smiling, her once happy vales ; . . 733 Prelude 11. 431
The rainbow smiling on the faded storm ; . . . 808 Excursion 4. 463
To trust the smiling aspect of this fair . . . . 828 Excursion 5. 422
His little smiling Grandchild, were no more. . . 861 Excursion 7. 262
To his Compatriot, smiling as he spake ; . . . 874 Excursion 8. 33
Lo ! Smiling Nature's lavish hand . . . . . S.3. 431 *The Scottish 31

Smilingly. Leans smilingly, and sinks into a perfect rest. . . . . 103 Artegal 48
Hark, how thy Country triumphs !—Smilingly . 318 *Ah ! where 11
A Pair who smilingly sat side by side, ... 523 Epist. Beaumont 114
Months and years went smilingly ; . . . . . 535 Egremont 70
Sinks smilingly forsworn. . . . . 550 Hermit's Cell 5. 4

Smirk. The VANGUARD—you may smirk and smile, 178 Waggoner 2. 116

Smit. With wonder smit by its transparency, . . 469 *Why stand 2

Smite. Whether thy punctual visitations smite . . 329 Ode : Thanks. 4

Smites. Of being, smites with irresistible pain, . . 234 Power of Sound 98
From that young Stream, that smites the throbbing rocks, ... 272 Devil's Bridge 7
Union not sad, when sunny daybreak smites . . 387 *Part fenced 12
That smites this tiny sea, ... 526 *The soaring 22
Stumping upon a cane with which he smites, . . 693 Prelude 7. 426
He who with pocket-hammer smites the edge . . 788 Excursion 3. 178

Smithfield. But chiefly to Smithfield he loves to repair,— 571 *Farmer* 85
That Smithfield should sustain so vast a loss, L.1. 95 *Juvenal* 3. 15
Smiting. Smiting with fury ; and a deeper dread 346 *Processions* 33
Smiting, as if each moment were their last. 474 *Hope smiled 6
The winds of March, smiting insidiously, 867 *Excursion* 7. 683
Smitten. *See* **Fresh-smitten, Heart-smitten, Joy-smitten, Self-smitten, Soul-smitten, Terror-smitten.**
Was smitten with a startling sound. 82 *Alice Fell* 4
Are smitten by a silver ray ; 180 *Waggoner* 4. 60
He trembles, smitten to the core 246 *P. B.* 884
And nod their helmets, smitten by the wing 265 *When haughty 7
While, smitten by a lofty moon, 375 *The Minstrels 3
It rages ;—some are smitten in the field— 420 *Ecc. Sonn.* 1. 6. 6
Smitten to the heart, and sad. 536 *Egremont* 92
Was smitten by the great ones of the world, 574 *Chiabrera* 3. 10
With sharper grief is Yarrow smitten, 586 *Hogg* 43
Smitten, the precipices rang aloud ; 638 *Prelude* 1. 440
Is smitten thence with an unnatural taint, 655 *Prelude* 3. 420
Amid the moving pageant, I was smitten 696 *Prelude* 7. 637
For the sun's light. The soul when smitten thus 709 *Prelude* 8. 672
A cloud of mist, that smitten by the sun 760 *Excursion* 1. 297
Smitten with perilous fever. In disease 764 *Excursion* 1. 552
By the strong sunbeams smitten. Like a mast 773 *Excursion* 2. 133
Smitten while all the promises of life 836 *Excursion* 5. 961
Hastily smitten by a fever's force ; 841 *Excursion* 6. 198
Was smitten, and poured forth a quenching stream, 852 *Excursion* 6. 920
Smoke. *See* **Battle-smoke, Charcoal-smoke.**
Last evening sight, the cottage smoke, no more, 8 *Ev. Wk.* 311
A cowering shape half hid in curling smoke ! 13 *Desc. Sk.* 178
The breathing pestilence that rose like smoke, 30 *Guilt* 346
That rises up like smoke. 83 *Lucy Gray* 28
That in some other way yon smoke 110 *'Tis said that some 15
Amid the smoke of cities did you pass 147 *Joanna* 1
It thundered down, with fire and smoke, 156 *Oak and Broom* 36
And the smoke and respiration, 181 *Waggoner* 4. 102
Green to the very door ; and wreaths of smoke 206 *Tintern* 17
Nor would permit the thin smoke to escape, 252 *Picture* 3
Watching the twilight smoke of cot or grange, 262 *Not Love 7
The cock that crows, the smoke that curls, that sound 306 *Here, on our 2
Whose smoke, forth-issuing whence and how it may, 390 *Highland Hut* 2
The smoke, and mounts in silver wreaths. 406 *White Doe* 950
Again with frankincense the altars smoke 436 *Ecc. Sonn.* 2. 33. 11
Blasts of tempestuous smoke—wherewith he tries 439 *Ecc. Sonn.* 2. 43. 11
Dost Thou prepare, whose sign will be the smoke 465 *Pastor and 9
Its busy smoke in social wreaths, 533 *Blest is 6
Let them smoke, let them burn, not a straw would he care ! 571 *Avarice* 10
And curling from the trees the cottage smoke. 593 *Ev. Wk. Quarto* 108
By silver'd wreaths of quiet charcoal smoke, 599 *Ev. Wk. Quarto* 430
Bend o'er the smoke that curls beneath the rocks. 605 *Desc. Sk. Quarto* 191
Of city smoke, by distance ruralised ; 633 *Prelude* 1. 89
Yon azure smoke betrays the lurking town ; 658 *Prelude* 4. 24
Smoke round him, as from hill to hill he hies, 702 *Prelude* 8. 245
Breathed up its smoke, an image of his ghost 705 *Prelude* 8. 449
Like smoke, along the level of the blast, 782 *Excursion* 2. 703
Want due consistence ; like a pillar of smoke, 803 *Excursion* 4. 142
Below, from which the curling smoke ascends. 832 *Excursion* 5. 645
O'er which the smoke of unremitting fires 876 *Excursion* 8. 125
Yet not for meek of heart. The smoke ascends 887 *Excursion* 9. 245
Bedimmed with smoke, in wreaths voluminous, 894 *Excursion* 9. 702
Yon curling smoke from the grey cot below, K.8. 247 *Recluse* 1.1.390
Smokeless. All bright and glittering in the smokeless air. 269 *Westm. Bridge* 8
Behold a smokeless sky, 506 *While from 38
The smokeless chimney-top.— All unembowered 858 *Excursion* 7. 54
Smoke-wreath. Far earlier, ere one smoke-wreath had risen 647 *Prelude* 2. 340
Smoking. 'Mid smoking woods gleams hid from morning's ray 12 *Desc. Sk.* 120
He turned, while rain poured down smcking on every side. 26 *Guilt* 117
Together smoking in the sun's slant beam, 33 *Guilt* 461
The smoking steam-boat eager in pursuit, 388 *The pibroch's 5
One chimney smoking and its azure wreath, 524 *Epist. Beaumont* 179
—Thy lake, mid smoking woods, that blue and grey 604 *Desc. Sk. Quarto* 138
Fall on his shifting hut that gleams mid smoking dew ; 610 *Desc. Sk. Quarto* 455
Smoky. Swinging from the smoky ceiling ! 177 *Waggoner* 2. 69
In smoky cabins, from a mother's tongue— 813 *Excursion* 4. 791
Smooth. Tip their smooth ridges with a softer ray ; 4 *Ev. Wk.* 123
From the green vale of Urseren smooth and wide 14 *Desc. Sk.* 196
And laughed so loud it seemed that the smooth sea 68 *Bord.* 1737
Life stretched before me smooth as some broad way 70 *Bord.* 1836
O'er rough and smooth she trips along, 83 *Lucy Gray* 61
"On Kilve's smooth shore, by the green sea, 86 *Anecdote* 31
"For here are woods, hills smooth and warm : 86 *Anecdote* 41
Rock the cradle of joy, smooth the death-bed of strife. 143 †*Lov. and Lik.* 54
Runs with speed more smooth and fine, 163 *Spinning Wheel* 11
And in this smooth and open dell 165 *Danish Boy* 5
Grinding through rough and smooth our way ; 179 *Waggoner* 3. 94
Along the smooth unpathwayed plain, 180 *Waggoner* 4. 24
Not undiversified though smooth and even ; 228 *Vernal Ode* 132
But your smooth motions suit a peaceful aim ; 230 *Clouds* 15
The smooth transparent skin, 232 *Jew. Fam.* 26
With her smooth tones and discords just, 235 *Power of Sound* 220

Smooth—*continued.*
Towards the smooth river deep and clear. 241 *P. B.* 440
A fair smooth pathway you discern, 244 *P. B.* 677
Smooth fields, white sheets of water, and pure sky ; 253 *A flock 4
Smooth way ; and I beheld the face of one 257 *Methought I 10
Which, strewn with snow smooth as the sky can shed, 263 *How clear 3
That, rough or smooth, is full of change, 295 *Highland Boy* 54
Smooth, graceful, tender, or sublime— 300 *Bran* 33
His bed perchance was yon smooth mound 302 *Yarrow V.* 27
In men of low degree, all smooth pretence ! 319 *Avaunt all 2
From the smooth meadow-ground, serene and still ! 335 *Namur* 14
Through the rocks our passage smooth ; 336 *Jesu ! bless 20
From the smooth breast of gay Winandermere ? 344 *Eclipse* 75
In Pisa's Campo Santo, the smooth floor 355 *Aquap.* 155
Expanding ; and, along the smooth shore curved 356 *Aquap.* 219
Smooth space of turf which from the guardian fort 356 *Aquap.* 224
Murmuring but one smooth story for all years, 368 *Trajan* 24
And, as they traversed the smooth brine, 371 *Eg. Maid* 159
The Birds with progress smooth and swift 371 *Eg. Maid* 185
Which tiny Elves impressed ;—on that smooth stage 378 *Duddon* 11. 4
Deep into patient Earth, from whose smooth breast it came ! 380 *Duddon* 17. 14
Checking the stream, make a pool smooth and clear 382 *Duddon* 23. 4
Majestic Duddon, over smooth flat sands 384 *Duddon* 32. 7
Rocks, rivers, and smooth lakes more clear than glass 388 *Trosachs* 8
Thence marching southward smooth and free 404 *White Doe* 715
For Souls whose doom is fixed ! The way is smooth 423 *Ecc. Sonn.* 1. 20. 9
While his free Barge skims the smooth flood along, 426 *Ecc. Sonn.* 1. 30. 10
Or smooth his front, our world is in his hand ! 428 *Ecc. Sonn.* 1. 39. 14
If good can smooth the way to evil choice, 428 *Ecc. Sonn.* 2. 1. 10
And in our caverns smooth thy ruffled wings !" 431 *Ecc. Sonn.* 2. 13. 4
Can link with desolation. Smooth and green, 439 *Ecc. Sonn.* 2. 43. 5
On the smooth bottom of this clear bright sea, 469 *A youth 2
Her brow was smooth and white : 487 *We walked 46
And down the smooth descent 488 *Fountain* 66
Smooth passions, smooth discourse, and joyous thought : 489 *Pers. Talk* 48
Of some smooth ridge, whose brink precipitous 496 *A little 26
Along a channel smooth and deep, 499 *Memory* 28
On the smooth surface of this naked stone ! 511 *So fair 6
And the smooth green of many a pendent field, 524 *Epist. Beaumont* 176
Is smooth as clear, save where with dimples small 527 *Those breathing 11
So smooth was all within, air-proof, 543 *Russ. Fug.* 143
Had placed his staff across the broad smooth stone 566 *Cumb. Beg.* 7
Thus thirty smooth years did he thrive on his farm : 569 *Farmer* 29
And napkins of smooth texture, finely shorn. 624 *Æneid* 62
A smooth free course along the watery gleam, 626 *The confidence 12
On his smooth breast the shadow of those towers 636 *Prelude* 1. 283
Among the smooth green turf. Through half the night, 636 *Prelude* 1. 312
At evening, when with pencil, and smooth slate 639 *Prelude* 1. 509
A holy scene !—Along the smooth green turf 643 *Prelude* 2. 107
In wantonness of heart, through rough and smooth 644 *Prelude* 2. 130
On the smooth platform, whether skill prevailed 644 *Prelude* 2. 162
Smooth housekeeping within, and all without 649 *Prelude* 3. 44
That this first transit from the smooth delights 656 *Prelude* 3. 517
Their smooth enthralment ; " but the heart was full, 659 *Prelude* 4. 63
Wore in old time. Her smooth domestic life, 661 *Prelude* 4. 222
From smooth Cam's silent waters : had we met, 679 *Prelude* 6. 308
Upon the smooth flat stones : the Nurse is here, 690 *Prelude* 7. 207
Smooth life had flock and shepherd in old time, 701 *Prelude* 8. 173
Smooth life had herdsman, and his snow-white herd 701 *Prelude* 8. 177
A smooth rock wet with constant springs) was seen 705 *Prelude* 8. 408
And smooth as marble or a waveless sea, 716 *Prelude* 9. 441
A separate record. Over the smooth sands 725 *Prelude* 10. 514
Smooth task ! for words find easy way, inspired 740 *Prelude* 13. 14
Trackless and smooth, or paced the bare white roads 744 *Prelude* 13. 316
In one perpetual progress smooth and bright ?— 748 *Prelude* 14. 135
Upon smooth Quantock's airy ridge we roved 751 *Prelude* 14. 396
Smooth words he had to wheedle simple souls ; 775 *Excursion* 2. 254
O'er the smooth surface of an ample crag, 787 *Excursion* 3. 41
A fragment, like an altar, flat and smooth : 787 *Excursion* 3. 60
On their smooth surface, evidence was none : 794 *Excursion* 3. 536
Smooth and commodious ; as a stately deck 805 *Excursion* 4. 246
Of smooth and solemnized complacencies, 828 *Excursion* 5. 376
Even at the worst, a smooth stream of content, 833 *Excursion* 5. 712
Whether their course be turbulent or smooth, 836 *Excursion* 5. 918
Was graceful, when it pleased him, smooth and still 842 *Excursion* 6. 292
"Smooth verse, inspired by no unlettered Muse," 846 *Excursion* 6. 522
For the smooth glozings of the indulgent world ; 854 *Excursion* 6. 1086
On the smooth playground of the village-school ?" 858 *Excursion* 7. 37
Covered the smooth blue slabs of mountain-stone 860 *Excursion* 7. 189
Smooth task, with *his* compared, whose mind could string, 862 *Excursion* 7. 306
Conciliatory manners and smooth speech ; 875 *Excursion* 8. 64
And that smooth slope from which the dwelling rose, 881 *Excursion* 8. 468
Sails in smooth weather by the placid coast 882 *Excursion* 8. 507
Between his hands he holds a smooth blue stone, 882 *Excursion* 8. 556
Fraught with their burthens ; and a way as smooth 889 *Excursion* 9. 371
Launched from our hands the smooth stone skimmed the lake ; 892 *Excursion* 9. 532
Of the smooth lake, in compass seen :—far off, 892 *Excursion* 9. 574
Smooth summer dreams, old favours of the place, S.3. 436 *The doubt 171
Tempt the smooth water, or the gleaming ice, K.8. 242 *Recluse* 1.1.223
Smoothed. Christian meekness smoothed for all the path of life, 142 *Arm. Lady* 149
And, smoothed by Nature's skill, 165 *Parrot* 6
While Grasmere smoothed her liquid plain 182 *Waggoner* 4. 232
A canopy, is smoothed for thy repose !" 221 *Triad* 79

Soft—*continued.*

But soft !—how came he forth ? The Nightmare Conscience — 53 Bord. 866
One of Love's simple bondsmen—the soft chain — 70 Bord. 1841
Of the soft breeze ruffling the meadow-flowers, — 80 *Loving she 18
Thy plot of grass is soft, and green as grass can be; — 87 Pet-lamb 23
With soft illumination cheered the dimness of that place. — 92 Poet's Dream 12
I lighted—opened with soft touch the chapel's iron door, — 92 Poet's Dream 41
On the soft heath,—and, waiting for his comrades, — 101 Brothers 397
And travel with the year at a soft pace. — 107 Farewell 48
And to soft slumbers, that did gently steep — 107 Farewell 59
The sabbath's return ; and its leisure's soft chain ! — 116 Repentance 28
Blessings upon that soft, warm face, — 121 Emigrant Mother 83
Soft as a guiding star that cheers, but cannot burn." — 140 Arm. Lady 66
Soft as the dying throb of the lyre. — 142 †Lov. and Lik. 48
As seemed, their soft self-satisfying light, — 143 *High bliss 19
If the soft voice he throws about — 143 *Driven in 16
Recalling now, with descant soft — 144 *Driven in 41
Of weed and sapling, along soft green turf — 149 M. H. 4
This moss-lined shed, green, soft, and dry, — 165 Parrot 29
Induced a soft and slumbrous dream, — 167 Pilgrim's Dream 18
Is it to teach her own soft lore, — 168 Turtledove 7
Soft darkness o'er its latest gleams is stealing ; — 173 Waggoner 1. 2
Green pasture and the soft warm air — 176 Waggoner 1. 268
Soft and cool to way-worn feet ; — 181 Waggoner 4. 161
A soft eye-music of slow-waving boughs, — 184 Airey-force 14
As soft almost and deep as her cerulean eye. — 190 *Lyre ! though 24
Soft clouds, the whitest of the year, — 191 Seq. Beggars 23
With a soft inland murmur.—Once again — 205 Tintern 4
A soft and tender Heroine — 216 Enterprise 57
Painted more soft and fair as they descend, — 218 Recluse 1. 1. 226
By soft reflection—grateful to the sky, — 219 Haunted Tree 4
As pure a sunshine and as soft a gale — 220 Triad 45
But air breathed soft that day, — 224 Primrose 26
To the soft murmur of the vagrant Bee. — 227 Vernal Ode 90
And in due time the soft spontaneous shock, — 229 Cuckoo-clock 9
To hear the earth's soft murmuring — 237 P. B. 74
The soft blue sky did never melt — 239 P. B. 263
The witchery of the soft blue sky ! — 239 P. B. 265
A scene of soft and lovely hue ! — 240 P. B. 362
Upon this soft and fertile nook ? — 240 P. B. 379
Her only pilot the soft breeze, the boat — 251 *Her only 1
Than those soft scenes through which thy childhood strayed, — 254 Dyer 4
Soft as the Dorhawk's to a distant ear, — 255 S. H. 5
Soft is the music that would charm for ever ; — 262 *Not Love 13
On the soft west-wind and his frolic peers ; — 264 Snowdrop 11
With shady night. Soft airs, from shrub and flower, — 271 *Where holy 9
His lenient touches, soft as light that falls, — 272 Ruins 6
To rouse the dawn, soft gales shall speed thy wing, — 274 *Not the 13
Speak—though this soft warm heart, once free to hold — 277 *Why art 9
Soft smiles, by human kindness bred ! — 288 Highland Girl 35
The voice was soft, and she who spake — 289 Stepping West. 17
Nor by soft Peace adopted ; though, in place — 290 Kilchurn 11
Built up by soft seducing harmonies ; — 312 *Who rises 66
Or the soft breezes from the Atlantic sea, — 319 Guernica 7
Knit the blithe dance upon the soft green grass ; — 322 *Ye Storms 9
When the soft hand of sleep had closed the latch . — 323 Ode 1814 1
Breathed from a soft and lonely instrument, — 324 Ode 1814 84
Soft notes, awful as the omen — 328 Ode 1815 72
Floats the soft cadence of the church-tower bells ; — 332 Ode : Thanks. 206
Of nun-like females, with soft motion, glide ! — 334 *Bruges I 14
By one soft trickling tear that stole — 334 *In Bruges 35
With intermingling motions soft and still, — 338 Engelberg 8
Roused into fury, murmur a soft tune — 339 Tell 14
Nor to her was the dance of soft pleasure unknown : — 340 Fort Fuentes 14
Saw ye the soft yet awful veil — 344 Eclipse 76
When, from the soft couch of her sleeping Lover, — 346 Gemmi 5
At length a Spirit more subdued and soft — 346 Processions 37
Soft breezes fanning your rough brows—the might — 350 Des. Stanzas 53
'Mid new-born blossoms that soft airs were wooing, — 360 *Near Anio's 3
Its murmur how soft ! as it falls down the steep, — 364 Vallomb. 5
Mingling with thy soft breath ! That morning too, — 367 *If with 9
Soft was the wind, that landward blew ; — 369 Eg. Maid 7
And that soft rustling of invisible wings — 371 Eg. Maid 149
If this be sleep, how soft ! if death, how fair ! — 371 Eg. Maid 173
Allowed a soft and flower-like breath, — 374 Eg. Maid 334
Fed by the stream with soft perpetual showers, — 377 Duddon 6. 7
Than a soft record, that, whatever fruit — 378 Duddon 8. 11
And countenanced like a soft cerulean sky, — 381 Duddon 20. 10
For her companionship ; here dwells soft ease : — 382 Duddon 25. 10
Wafting your Charge to soft Parthenope ! — 387 Scott 14
Love wound his way by soft approach, — 391 Highland Broach 47
—But, as soft gales dissolve the dreary snow, — 395 White Doe : Ded. 27
—When soft !—the dusky trees between, — 396 White Doe 49
Soft and silent as a dream, — 396 White Doe 57
In soft and breeze-like visitings, — 399 White Doe 332
A soft and lulling sound is heard — 406 White Doe 964
With a soft spring-day of holy, — 415 White Doe 1757
Moved gently in her soul's soft sleep ; — 415 White Doe 1794
In soft repose he comes. Within his cell, — 424 Ecc. Sonn. 1. 21. 7
In the soft heaven of a translucent pool ; — 424 Ecc. Sonn. 1. 22. 6
And soft Italia feels renewed alarms ; — 427 Ecc. Sonn. 1. 34. 4
To a soft breeze, in lowly adoration. — 431 Ecc. Sonn. 2. 11. 8
With low soft murmur, like a distant bee, — 445 Ecc. Sonn. 3. 22. 5
By THEM who blessed the soft and happy gale — 449 Ecc. Sonn. 3. 37. 2

Soft—*continued.*

In the soft chequerings of a sleepy light. — 451 Ecc. Sonn. 3. 44. 4
By its soft music whence the waters flow: — 453 *Calm is the 26
Soft in its temper as those vesper lays — 454 Sea-side 24
Soft as a cloud is yon blue Ridge—the Mere — 456 *Soft as 1
Soft shades and dews have shed their blended power — 456 *The leaves 4
With that beautiful soft half-moon, — 457 *The sun has 13
Of thy soft breath !—Less vivid wreath entwined — 464 Derwent 9
Into the shedding of "too soft a tear." — 465 *The cattle 14
When a soft summer gale at evening parts — 465 *Dear to 7
Beneath stern mountains many a soft vale lies, — 472 *Arran ! a 13
The soft touch snapped the thread — 479 Somnamb. 132
Pleased rather with some soft ideal scene, — 480 *Most sweet 5
Could pierce through a temper that's soft to disease, — 482 Character 7
—Enough for one soft vernal day, — 497 Lycoris 9
Unchecked is that soft harmony : — 498 *The sylvan 26
With its soft smile the truth express, — 507 May 19
Soft and capacious as a cloudless sky — 508 F. Stone 32
As with one voice ; their flinty heart grew soft — 513 General Fast 6
Nay, said a voice, soft as the south wind's breath, — 515 *Men of 9
To render visible her own soft dreams, — 524 Epist. Beaumont 186
For day-dreams soft as e'er beguiled — 526 *The soaring 49
To scenes Arcadian, whispering, through soft air, — 530 Gleaner 7
'Mid that soft air, those long-lost bowers, — 530 Gleaner 24
In phrase that now with echoes soft — 544 Russ. Fug. 251
And every season has soft arms — 545 Russ. Fug. 303
Than he was wont ; and that in whispers soft — 564 Troilus 101
With a soft voice, he of his Lady dear, — 564 Troilus 118
With a thousand soft pictures his memory will teem, — 570 Farmer 79
On the soft down of my paternal home. — 575 Chiabrera 6. 12
A sad heart's sunshine) by a soft — 577 *By playful 2
I sprinkle thee with soft celestial dews, — 582 Invoc. Earth 21
Whose fragrance, by soft dews and rain unbound, — 584 *With copious 58
Say, will my friend, with soft affection's ear, — 592 Ev. Wk. Quarto 51
Soft o'er the surface creep the lustres pale — 598 Ev. Wk. Quarto 343
Soft on his wounded heart her healing pow'r, — 602 Desc. Sk. Quarto 14
Those shadowy breasts in love's soft light array'd, — 604 Desc. Sk. Quarto 154
The beams of evening, slipping soft between, — 607 Desc. Sk. Quarto 267
While in soft gloom the scattering bowers recede, — 607 Desc. Sk. Quarto 271
Soft music from th' aereal summit steal ? — 609 Desc. Sk. Quarto 421
Soft o'er the waters mournful measures swell, — 613 Desc. Sk. Quarto 626
Soft gales and dews of life's delicious morn, — 613 Desc. Sk. Quarto 634
Spurn the soft fetters of lethargic rest. — 619 School Ex. 108
As the soft star of dewy evening tells — 619 *She wept 11
All soothers of sense their soft virtue shall yield, — 621 Convict 27
And soft, and gay, and beautiful thou art, — 622 Recluse 1. 1. 115
Him now the generous Dido by soft chains — 624 Æneid 19
Where he on soft amaracus is laid, — 624 Æneid 51
O Moon ! if e'er I joyed when thy soft light — 630 [?] *O Moon 1
Soft as the gentle kiss of amorous maid — 630 [?] *O Moon 11
Whate'er its mission, the soft breeze can come — 632 Prelude 1. 5
From that soft couch I rose not, till the sun — 633 Prelude 1. 86
That came with soft alarm, like hurtless light . — 637 Prelude 1. 353
Of those soft starry nights, and that old Dame — 642 Prelude 2. 43
Soft airs were stirring, and the mid-day sun — 643 Prelude 2. 92
With the moon's beauty and the moon's soft pace, — 653 Prelude 3. 281
Of those glad respites, though a soft west wind — 673 Prelude 5. 481
Yet still in me with those soft luxuries — 683 Prelude 6. 557
They move about upon the soft green turf : — 700 Prelude 8. 58
Promised soft peace and sweet forgetfulness. — 719 Prelude 10. 90
Of the green hills ; ye breezes and soft airs, — 734 Prelude 12. 10
In soft forgetfulness the livelong hours, — 752 Prelude 14. 403
To him most pleasant who on soft cool moss — 756 Excursion 1. 9
To the soft handling of the elements : — 763 Excursion 1. 495
Was yellow ; and the soft and bladed grass, — 767 Excursion 1. 708
And whose soft gloom, and boundless depth, might tempt — 787 Excursion 3. 99
On these soft beds of thyme-besprinkled turf, — 789 Excursion 3. 247
Of soft Epicureans, taught—if they — 791 Excursion 3. 348
In a soft clime encouraging the soil — 793 Excursion 3. 519
On whose soft leaves it hangs, and from whose cup — 794 Excursion 3. 580
At those, which thy soft influence sometimes drew — 797 Excursion 3. 811
The breeze how soft ! Can any thing produced — 798 Excursion 3. 881
And, in soft tone of speech, thus he resumed. — 807 Excursion 4. 417
Their soft indulgences, and in due time — 810 Excursion 4. 594
On the soft grass through half a summer's day, — 814 Excursion 4. 852
Soft, as may seem, but, under that disguise, — 817 Excursion 4. 1053
And the soft woodlark here did never chant — 818 Excursion 4. 1168
Inviting sleep and soft forgetfulness. — 821 Excursion 4. 1324
With whisper soft my venerable Friend — 825 Excursion 5. 208
Is either fair and tempting, a soft scene — 830 Excursion 5. 527
And with such soft materials line, her nest — 835 Excursion 5. 841
Accords with nature's language ;—the soft voice — 846 Excursion 6. 524
An interchange of soft or solemn tunes, — 857 Excursion 7. 15
A woman of soft speech and gracious smile, — 858 Excursion 7. 78
What, though no soft and costly sofa there — 860 Excursion 7. 174
And with soft smile, his consort would reprove. — 861 Excursion 7. 225
She was a soft attendant cloud, that hung — 861 Excursion 7. 234
And like the soft infections of the heart, — 863 Excursion 7. 381
That many, sweet to hear of in soft verse, — 880 Excursion 8. 401
With feminine allurement soft and fair, — 881 Excursion 8. 460
Soft heath this elevated spot supplied, — 892 Excursion 9. 580
Soft murmuring) was too weak to overcome, — 894 Excursion 9. 695
The station whence he looked was soft and green, — K.8. 237 Recluse 1.1. 19

Soften. Soften their glare before the mellow light ; — 4 Ev. Wk. 105
To soothe or cheer, to soften or refine. — 21 Desc. Sk. 590
Of truths that soften hatred, temper strife. — 443 Ecc. Sonn. 3. 11. 14
Hath terror in it. Thou didst soften down — 749 Prelude 14. 246
—But time hath power to soften all regrets, — 868 Excursion 7. 687

Softened. Whose softened image penetrates the deep. — 5 Ev. Wk. 173

Softened—*continued.*
Softened till it becomes a gift of mercy. . . . 61 *Bord.* 1340
Softened her pangs, and reconciled the child . . 118 *Maternal Grief* 55
So that it shall be softened, and our loves . . 124 *V. and J.* 210
Was softened down into a vernal tone. . . . 146 **It was an* 5
Was softened into feeling, soothed, and tamed. 205 *Brougham* 160
Thy fierce beginnings, softened and subdued . . 290 *Kilchurn* 40
A softened remembrance of sorrow and pain, . . 398 *White Doe* 239
That soften'd from the water-head descend. . . 597 *Ev. Wk. Quarto* 324
On Zutphen's plain ; or where with soften'd gaze 608 *Desc.Sk.Quarto* 358
'Soften'd the terrors of her awful mien.' . . . 618 *School Ex.* 16
Of mighty names was softened down and seemed 676 *Prelude* 6. 61
Was welcome, softened, if not solemnised. . . 706 *Prelude* 8. 509
With softened spirit, even when it condemned. 772 *Excursion* 2. 80
A softened roar, or murmur ; and the sound . . 800 *Excursion* 3. 978
At every moment softened in its course . . . 818 *Excursion* 4. 1119
His feelings of aversion softened down ; . . . 819 *Excursion* 4. 1219
Was into meekness softened and subdued ; . . . 850 *Excursion* 6. 772
Hath softened that obduracy, and made . . . 852 *Excursion* 6. 921
In softened perspective ; and more than once . 882 *Excursion* 8. 537

Softening. Softening their inbred dignity austere— 212 *Dion* 11
(Softening that bright effulgence by degrees) . . 226 *Vernal Ode* 11
By Nature, softening and concealing, ... 397 *White Doe* 118
Then Arts, which still had drawn a softening grace 476 **Tranquillity!the* 10
That, softening objects, sometimes even . . . 499 *Memory* 7
Softening the toils and pains that have not ceased 538 **In desultory* 27
That, while it only spreads a softening charm 539 **Lady ! a* 42
All softening, humanising, hallowing powers, . . 585 *Ch. Lamb* 84
But why no softening thought of gratitude, . . 873 *Excursion* 7. 1028

Softens. And its own twilight softens the whole scene, ... 3 *Ev. Wk.* 61
Softens his heart, till from his eyes outwell . . 520 *Pun. Death* 12. 8
Softens its evening uproar towards a close . . S.3. 437 **The doubt* 195

Softer. Tip their smooth ridges with a softer ray ; . 4 *Ev. Wk.* 123
Yet are thy softer arts with power indued . . 13 *Desc. Sk.* 141
And softer than if it were covered with silk. . . 80 †*Address : Child* 13
Softer than Nature's self could mould. . . . . 234 *Power of Sound* 120
With warmer suns and softer gales, ... 295 *Highland Boy* 74
But soon they move with softer pace ; . . . . 297 *Highland Boy* 186
On as we move, a softer prospect opes, . . . 607 *Desc.Sk.Quarto* 263
Boldly and bear away to softer life ; . . . . S.3. 436 **The doubt* 158

Softest. The streams with softest sound are flowing, 129 *Idiot Boy* 284
The leaves that make the softest bed : . . . 145 *Her Eyes* 56
Spring parts the clouds with softest airs, . . . 157 **In youth* 11
The softest Nursling of a gorgeous palace . . . 221 *Triad* 68
Fine as the mother's softest plumes allow : . . 254 *WildDuck'sNest* 12
To stillest mood of softest skies, ... 344 **How blest* 17
The fairest, softest, liveliest of them all ! . . . 381 *Duddon* 19. 9
With its softest summer sound : . . . . . 397 *White Doe* 151
Her inmost, softest, tenderest harmonies ; . . . 430 *Ecc. Sonn.* 2. 8. 11
In admonitions of thy softest voice ! . . . . 454 **The Sun, that* 20
Of softest music some responsive place. . . . 473 **Thanks for* 14
With their softest whispers vouch, ... 502 **Like a* 52
The softest breeze to fairest flowers gives birth : . 516 **Hard task* 12
The bed we give him, though of softest down ; . 528 **Those breathing* 74
Their fairest, softest, happiest influence. . . . 686 *Prelude* 6. 726
The idle breath of softest pipe attuned . . . K.8. 247 *Recluse* 1.1.408

Softliest. Her froward mood, and softliest reprehend ; 255 **Grief, thou* 4

Softly. Time softly treads ; throughout the landscape breathes . . . . 9 *Ev. Wk.* 361
Softly he stroked the child, who lay outstretched 33 *Guilt* 487
Have I been waiting for him. Well, but softly, . 45 *Bord.* 452
It must be ended !— Softly ; do not rouse him ; 54 *Bord.* 914
But softly ! we must look a little nearer. . . . 58 *Bord.* 1132
Past softly, leading in the Boy ; and while from roof to floor, ... 92 *Poet's Dream* 42
Softly, slowly : one might think, ... 170 *Kitten* 10
"It is my Husband," softly said . . . . . 176 *Waggoner* 1. 241
That downy prow, and softly cleaves . . . . 212 *Dion*
Softly she treads, as if her foot were loth . . 222 *Triad* 201
That with moist virtue softly cleaves . . . . 228 *Devot. Incit.* 15
Tints softly with each other blended, ... 231 **Thegentlest Poet* 19
No ghost more softly ever trod ; . . . . . 247 *P. B.* 987
Softly resounded through this rocky glade ; . . 252 **The fairest* 4
The Shepherd, looking eastward, softly said, . . 265 **The Shepherd* 1
Softly !—To save the contrite, Jesus bled. . . 275 *Gravestone* 14
From rapture, lying softly on her breast ! . . . 278 **Lo ! where she* 3
Provokes no echoes, but must softly tread ; . . 355 *Aquap.* 195
Softly responsive ; and, attuned to all . . . . 356 *Aquap.* 222
Thy course and sport around thee softly fan— . 363 **List—'twas* 109
And softly sleeps within the thread she spins. . 366 *Lombardy* 8
Or softly stealing into modest shade. . . . . 367 *Trajan* 18
And softly touched ; but, to his princely cheer 373 *Eg. Maid* 287
To whom the words were softly said, ... 398 *White Doe* 181
Drew softly near her, and more near— . . . 414 *White Doe* 1657
Paces softly, or makes halt, ... 417 *White Doe* 1893
Softly she glides, another home to seek. . . . 434 *Ecc. Sonn.* 2. 22. 8
The innocent Procession softly moves :— . . . 448 *Ecc. Sonn.* 3. 32. 12
And, through the cottage-lattice softly peeping, . 459 **Wanderer ! that* 5
Softly embosoming the timid light ! . . . . 473 **We saw* 8
At eve ; how softly then . . . . 478 *Somnamb.* 2
Softly as morning vapours glide . . . . . 534 **Blest is* 85
He softly creeps—'tis Goody Blake ; . . . . 537 *Goody Blake* 79
Blew softly o'er the russet heath, ... 550 *Hermit's Cell* 2. 10
One word he softly uttered, ... 629 *Installation* 33
The softly flowing Leine, ... 629 *Installation* 60
—In rugged arms how softly does it lie, . . . 777 *Excursion* 2. 358
And softly creeping, like a breath of air, . . . 787 *Excursion* 3. 71
Softly accompanied the tuneful harp, . . . 843 *Excursion* 6. 337
Softly and lightly from a passing cloud, . . . 861 *Excursion* 7. 284
May creep (I wish that they would softly creep) . 868 *Excursion* 7. 708

Softly-gliding. Of fluttering Sylphs, and softly-gliding Fays, ... K.8. 237 *Recluse* 1.1. 33

Softly-moulded. Bright, speckless, as a softly-moulded tear . . . . 265 **There is a pleasure* 12

Softly-stealing. Did only softly-stealing hours . . 154 *Flower Garden* 5

Softness. A softness still and holy ; . . . . . 302 *Yarrow V.* 46
To more than infant softness, giving me . . . 636 *Prelude* 1. 278
Of female softness shall his life be full, . . . 749 *Prelude* 14. 229
Of aspect, with aerial softness clad, ... 773 *Excursion* 2. 95

Soft-paced. Attended by the soft-paced Doe ; . . 416 *White Doe* 1814

Soil. His soul was knit to this his native soil. . . 100 *Brothers* 298
Move where the blasted soil is not unworn, . . 213 *Dion* 88
The casual treasure from the furrowed soil. . . 275 **While poring* 14
Upturned the soil ; . . . . 287 *Sons of Burns* 36
Here, on our native soil, we breathe once more. . 306 **Here, on our* 1
But 'tis a chosen soil, where sun and breeze . . 308 **One might* 5
Ye children of a Soil that doth advance . . . 309 *Men of Kent* 2
Rising like water from the soil, to find . . . 321 **The power* 13
Fixed in the depths of this courageous soil ; . . 324 *Ode 1814* 104
The upturned soil receives the hopeful seed— . 327 *Ode 1815* 31
On that offensive soil, like waves upon a thousand shores. . . . . 331 *Ode : Thanks.* 151
Hath cherished on a healthful soil ; . . . . 344 **How blest* 6
To enslave whole nations on their native soil ; . 368 *Trajan* 59
A barren and ungrateful soil. . . . . . . 375 **The Minstrels* 24
Of villain-service, passing with the soil . . . 429 *Ecc. Sonn.* 2. 4. 3
In the blest soil of gospel truth, the Tree, . . 431 *Ecc. Sonn.* 2. 10. 2
Methinks that I could trip o'er heaviest soil, . . 438 *Ecc. Sonn.* 2. 39. 1
I press thee, through the yielding soil, with pride. 489 *Spade* 4
Though *fettered* slave be none, her floors and soil . 501 *Humanity* 85
And saw, thereafter, on the soil of France . . 504 *Warning* 63
Just serves to show how delicate a soil . . . 508 *F. Stone* 30
Before this rugged soil was tilled, ... 533 **Blest is* 28
We might have fed upon a fatter soil . . . . 671 *Prelude* 5. 409
Upon that meagre soil, helped out by talk . . 711 *Prelude* 9. 99
The soil of common life, was, at that time, . . 712 *Prelude* 9. 166
The hardened soil, and knots of withered grass : . 769 *Excursion* 1. 835
Had sprung, like those bright creatures, from the soil . . . . 790 *Excursion* 3. 251
In a soft clime encouraging the soil . . . . 793 *Excursion* 3. 519
Or soil endured a transfer in the mart . . . . 799 *Excursion* 3. 917
And, 'mid the wild weeds of a rugged soil, . . 802 *Excursion* 4. 52
Who does not love his native soil ?—he prized 824 *Excursion* 5. 116
The mutual aptitude of seed and soil . . . . 835 *Excursion* 5. 879
This favoured Land, or sunshine warms her soil. . 838 *Excursion* 6. 16
And, in the centre of a world whose soil . . . 848 *Excursion* 6. 634
He gives it—the boon produce of a soil . . . 855 *Excursion* 6. 1137
By useful habits, to a fitter soil . . . . . 862 *Excursion* 7. 301
Measuring the soil beneath their happy feet . . 869 *Excursion* 7. 776
Naked, and coloured like the soil, the feet . . 879 *Excursion* 8. 354
That when we stand upon our native soil, . . 886 *Excursion* 9. 129
Of those who once were vassals of her soil, . . 886 *Excursion* 9. 180
For all the children whom her soil maintains . 888 *Excursion* 9. 300
Of numbers crowded on their native soil, . . . 889 *Excursion* 9. 364

Soiling. Or to be trailed along the soiling earth ; . 88 *H. C.* 29

Sojourn. *See* **After-sojourn.**
When I depart, for brief is my sojourn—" . . 210 *Laod.* 78
We sojourn stunned by Ocean's ceaseless roar ; . 521 *Epist. Beaumont* 4
Shall sojourn in this fair domain ; . . . . . 534 **Blest is* 96
Then know I well that she would not sojourn. . 563 *Troilus* 80
Prepared to sojourn in a pleasant town, . . . 710 *Prelude* 9. 40
We sojourn, have I lifted up my soul, ... 895 *Excursion* 9. 741
They came, to sojourn here in solitude, . . . K.8. 243 *Recluse* 1.1.241

Sojourned. Once in a lonely hamlet I sojourned . 120 *Emigrant Mother* 1
Pass from their Master, sojourned here to guard . 419 *Ecc. Sonn.* 1. 2. 13
The father sojourned in a distant land) . . . 575 *Chiabrera* 8. 3

Sojourner. A discontented sojourner : now free, . 632 *Prelude* 1. 8
Have I been now a sojourner on earth, . . . 675 *Prelude* 6. 49
I saw them in their rest, a sojourner . . . 722 *Prelude* 10. 319

Sojourners. Sojourners in my father's house, he died, 738 *Prelude* 12. 307

Sojourning. Sojourning a few days, I visited . . 710 *Prelude* 9. 43
"Though now sojourning there, he, like myself, . 774 *Excursion* 2. 164

Sol. When Sol was destined to endure . . . . 343 *Eclipse* 3

Solace. Fond Youth ! that mournful solace now must pass . . . . 124 *V. and J.* 218
Loving and liking are the solace of life, . . . 142 †*Lov. and Lik.* 53
He finds no solace in his course ; . . . . . 246 *P. B.* 882
Should find brief solace there, as I have found. . 250 **Nuns fret* 14
One solace yet remains for us who came . . . 359 **Those old* 10
Farewell the solace of the vagrant reed ! . . . 382 *Duddon* 24. 4
Belovèd Wife ? such solace to impart . . . . 395 *White Doe : Ded.* 63
Find solace which a busy world disdains. . . . 444 *Ecc. Sonn.* 3. 17. 14
Hope of the dawn and solace of the night, . . 467 *St. Bees* 83
The solace beads and masses yield, ... 478 *Somnamb.* 53
A solace she might borrow . . . . 494 *Force of Prayer* 42
From hence my hope and solace forth did pass. . 564 *Troilus* 89
A trembling solace to her widowed Lord. . . . 576 **By a* 12
Such solace find we for our loss ; . . . . . 578 **I come* 69
Some solace under weight of royal care, . . . 628 **Deign, Sovereign* 23
For solace by dim light of monkish lamps ; . . 673 *Prelude* 5. 498
That doth not yield a solace to my grief : . . . 733 *Prelude* 11. 436
Find solace—knowing what we have learnt to know, ... 752 *Prelude* 14. 438
Or solace, varying as the seasons change. . . . 810 *Excursion* 4. 587
One only solace—that he had espoused . . . 825 *Excursion* 5. 193
In Providence, for solace and support, ... 830 *Excursion* 5. 516
For noontide solace on the summer grass, . . . 861 *Excursion* 7. 286
Yet, by the solace of his own pure thoughts . . 863 *Excursion* 7. 417
Solace and self-excuse, had sometimes urged . . 871 *Excursion* 7. 909
Excuse and solace for her own defects ; . . . 896 *Excursion* 9. 789

Solitude—*continued.*

In solitude and solitary thought	761 *Excursion* 1. 354
Some other tenant of the solitude."	777 *Excursion* 2. 402
What stuff the Dwellers in a solitude,	781 *Excursion* 2. 622
Is garrulous ; and solitude is apt	791 *Excursion* 3. 326
In solitude : and mutually addressed	792 *Excursion* 3. 441
Our solitude. It soothes me to perceive,	794 *Excursion* 3. 598
And, in the blank and solitude of things,	798 *Excursion* 3. 848
And solitude, that they do favour most,	806 *Excursion* 4. 366
The plaintive spirit of the solitude !	807 *Excursion* 4. 412
Alone or mated, solitude was not.	810 *Excursion* 4. 633
Of destitution ;—solitude was not.	811 *Excursion* 4. 650
Spread like a sea, in boundless solitude,	811 *Excursion* 4. 696
The face which rural solitude might wear	814 *Excursion* 4. 849
Affronts the eye of Solitude, shall learn	816 *Excursion* 4. 1031
A wedded pair in childless solitude.	833 *Excursion* 5. 692
In life, in death, what solitude can breed	836 *Excursion* 5. 888
Flows on in solitude. But, when the gloom	856 *Excursion* 6. 1173
A solitude, unchosen, unprofessed ;	862 *Excursion* 7. 309
From their shy solitude, to face the world,	869 *Excursion* 7. 774
While solitude permits the mind to feel ;	875 *Excursion* 8. 55
No chasm, no solitude ; from link to link	884 *Excursion* 9. 14
To breathe in solitude, above the host	885 *Excursion* 9. 72
Of solitude, and silence in the sky ?	K.8. 240 *Recluse* 1.1.133
They came, to sojourn here in solitude,	K.8. 243 *Recluse* 1.1.241
Say boldly then that solitude is not	K.8. 252 *Recluse* 1.1.592

Solitudes. Unfruitful solitudes, that seemed to upbraid . . . . .   377 *Duddon* 5. 4

Let him be free of mountain solitudes ;	569 *Cumb. Beg.* 183
Protracted among endless solitudes ;	667 *Prelude* 5. 147
Gathered among those solitudes sublime	683 *Prelude* 6. 554
Companionless your awful solitudes !	702 *Prelude* 8. 222
Yet—compassed round by mountain solitudes,	748 *Prelude* 14. 139
Or Cambrian solitudes. A youth—(he bore	751 *Prelude* 14. 354
Hovering above these inland solitudes,	808 *Excursion* 4. 452
Dispensed indeed to other solitudes,	K.8. 247 *Recluse* 1.1.378

Solstitial. In fierce solstitial power, . .   502 *Seasons* 6

Solve. To solve the mystery, not in Nature's laws   170 **Never enlivened* 17
Of forward youth—that scruples not to solve . 792 *Excursion* 3. 413

Solved. We've solved the riddle—Miscreant ! Do
you, . . .   46 *Bord.* 515

Of all this world is solved, well may we envy	69 *Bord.* 1796
Have solved the elements, or analysed	815 *Excursion* 4. 952
So, by your records, may our doubts be solved ;	832 *Excursion* 5. 654

Solway's. 'Mid the deep holds of Solway's mossy
waste, . .   48 *Bord.* 609

Sombre. The cypress waves her sombre plume . 343 *Eclipse* 63
Of sombre foliage, seem to imitate . 891 *Excursion* 9. 501

Sombrous. Where, mixed with graceful birch, the
sombrous pine . 5 *Ev. Wk.* 156

Bright'ning with water-breaks the sombrous gill ;	592 *Ev. Wk. Quarto* 72
Bright'ning the cliffs between where sombrous pine,	594 *Ev. Wk. Quarto* 139

Some. (*Partial list.*)

Of some dark deed to which in early life	37 *Bord.* 15
A miniature ; belike some Shepherd-boy,	39 *Bord.* 119
Whom, but some few days past, I saw in Eskdale,	46 *Bord.* 479
That haunt some barren island of the north,	47 *Bord.* 559
Chancing to pass this way some six months gone,	47 *Bord.* 573
Even to the shedding of some natural tears	51 *Bord.* 762
Oswald, Oswald ! This is some sudden seizure !	52 *Bord.* 798
That well may put some fears into *your* heart.	52 *Bord.* 813
Or on some vast and solitary plain	56 *Bord.* 1012
That horn again—'Tis some one of our Troop	56 *Bord.* 1016
In some a hideous one—hem ! shall I stop ?	58 *Bord.* 1170
Shall on some lovely Alien set	164 **Fair Lady* 14
Midway on some high hill, while father Time	322 **Ye Storms* 3
Now against May shall have some stirring—whether	557 *Cuck. and Night.* 23
To joy, or be it to some mourning ; never	557 *Cuck. and Night.* 24
Some, singing loud, as if they had complained ;	558 *Cuck. and Night.* 73
Some with their notes another manner feigned ;	558 *Cuck. and Night.* 74
And some did sing all out with the full throat.	558 *Cuck. and Night.* 75
Good Cuckoo, seek some other bush or brake,	558 *Cuck. and Night.* 112
Now, God of Love ! thou help me in some wise,	560 *Cuck. and Night.* 214
Some scattered leaf, or marks which, in one track,	567 *Cumb. Beg.* 55
Long for some moments in a weary life	568 *Cumb. Beg.* 148
That not without some effort they behold	569 *Cumb. Beg.* 188
Perhaps some needful service of the State	573 *Chiabrera* 2. 1
May read them not without some bitter tears.	575 *Chiabrera* 7. 18
Than Fancy gave assurance of some work	633 *Prelude* 1. 78
An insight that in some sort he possesses,	744 *Prelude* 13. 308
That yet survive, a work, as some divine,	745 *Prelude* 13. 339
Pleased with some unpremeditated strains	745 *Prelude* 13. 353
Some pleasure from this offering of my love.	752 *Prelude* 14. 429
Each being has his office, lowly some	K.8. 255 *Recluse* 1.1.669

Somebody. The sky owes somebody a grudge ! 176 *Waggoner* 1. 250

Something. 'Tis but a word and then—— Something is here . .   41 *Bord.* 253

But vigorous Spirits look for something more	48 *Bord.* 622
A comforter of sorrow ;—there is something	48 *Bord.* 635
Something I strike upon which turns my mind	51 *Bord.* 783
And something shall be done which Memory	59 *Bord.* 1173
But there was something which most plainly said	67 *Bord.* 1634
while he was muttering something about his	
Child—	72 *Bord.* 1956
I am sure I heard something breathing—	72 *Bord.* 1970
Something must stay to tell us of the rest.	107 *Farewell* 52
Through his whole body something ran,	114 *Ind. Wom.* 35
Not old, though something past her prime ;	119 *Sailor's Mother* 4
Something between a hindrance and a help ;	134 *Michael* 189
It loosens something at my chest ;	145 *Her Eyes* 36
The Rock, like something starting from a sleep,	147 *Joanna* 54

Something—*continued.*

And yet with something of a grace	158 **With little* 7
Nor doubt that something of their spirit swayed	170 **Never enlivened* 20
With something of angelic light.	186 **She was* 30
A leading from above, a something given,	196 *Resolution* 51
With something of a lofty utterance drest—	196 *Resolution* 94
But something ails it now : the spot is curst.	202 *Hart-leap* 124
Flying from something that he dreads than one	206 *Tintern* 71
Of something far more deeply interfused,	207 *Tintern* 96
And something also did my worth obtain ;	210 *Laod.* 41
By something cognizably shaped ;	214 *Kirkstone* 9
There's something in a flying horse,	236 *P. B.* 1
There's something in a huge balloon ;	236 *P. B.* 2
Was something Peter did not like.	241 *P. B.* 470
"Oh, mercy ! something must be done,	248 *P. B.* 1058
Crossing the waters) doubt, and something dark,	258 **Where lies the Land* 12
To something purer and more exquisite	274 **Such age* 4
Star-high, and pointing still to something higher ;	282 **In my* 12
Like something fashioned in a dream ;	288 *Highland Girl* 12
But something deeper far than these :	289 *Glen-Al.* 26
Of something without place or bound ;	289 *Stepping West.* 14
That earth hath something yet to show,	293 *Yarrow Unv.* 63
This do I see ; and something more ;	294 *Jedbor.* 41
A flash of something over-bright !	294 *Jedbor.* 69
Hath something in it which the heart enjoys :—	310 *Anticip.* 13
Or something night and day between,	343 *Eclipse* 25
With something more propitious to high aims	357 *Aquap.* 286
Like something out of Ocean sprung	370 *Eg. Maid* 45
Enough, if something from our hands have power	384 *Duddon* 34. 10
Spurned it, like something that would stand	401 *White Doe* 518
That Courage may find something to perform ;	466 *St. Bees* 15
Have ever in them something of benign ;	469 **Why stand* 5
And still there's something in the world	483 *Simon Lee* 21
With something, as the Shepherd thinks,	491 *Fidelity* 11
But something whispers to my heart	497 *Lycoris* 37
Something like the faintest breath	502 **Like a* 41
And the whole person. Words have something told	509 *F. Stone* 73
Through peopled Vales ; yet something in the guise	522 *Epist. Beaumont* 98
For something more than dull content,	526 **The soaring* 7
Of something void and vain ;	545 *Russ. Fug.* 356
And something, it might be, reserved for himself :	570 *Farmer* 38
Who went something farther than others have gone,	572 *Avarice* 30
Both of them speak of something that is gone :	588 *Immortality* 53
And, even with something of a Mother's mind,	588 *Immortality* 79
Is something that doth live,	589 *Immortality* 134
Have something to pursue. And not alone,	646 *Prelude* 2. 322
Appeared like something in myself, a dream,	647 *Prelude* 2. 351
To something that resembles an approach	656 *Prelude* 3. 519
Yet to the memory something cleaves at last,	658 *Prelude* 3. 627
Yes, I had something of a subtler sense,	661 *Prelude* 4. 209
" Is something of more worth ;" and at the word	667 *Prelude* 5. 89
These spread like day, and something in the shape	673 *Prelude* 5. 504
That wish for something loftier, more adorned,	674 *Prelude* 5. 575
Mixed something of stern mood, an under-thirst	683 *Prelude* 6. 558
And something evermore about to be.	684 *Prelude* 6. 608
Yet something of a girlish child-like gloss	693 *Prelude* 7. 446
But something must have felt. Call ye these appearances—	703 *Prelude* 8. 293
Alone, that something of a better life	703 *Prelude* 8. 313
Descending slow with something heavenly fraught.	709 *Prelude* 8. 664
I looked for something that I could not find,	710 *Prelude* 9. 72
And rules, that they held something up to view	713 *Prelude* 9. 225
And intermixed with something, in my mind,	728 *Prelude* 11. 59
Of something false and weak, that could not stand	735 *Prelude* 12. 66
In simple childhood something of the base	738 *Prelude* 12. 274
Yes, something of the grandeur which invests	742 *Prelude* 13. 152
Whate'er was wanting, something had I gained,	750 *Prelude* 14. 331
And something that may serve to set in view	757 *Excursion* 1. 99
To human life, or something very near	768 *Excursion* 1. 788
To establish something of a leader's sway ;	794 *Excursion* 3. 594
If grief be something hallowed and ordained,	803 *Excursion* 4. 148
And something also of his inner mind	824 *Excursion* 5. 108
Suffused with something of a feminine hue ;	834 *Excursion* 5. 782
Upon whose lapse, or error, something more	848 *Excursion* 6. 657
Was something which to mortal sense might sound	861 *Excursion* 7. 257
Wins help from something greater than herself—	S.3. 435 **The doubt* 113
Or something dearer still, if reason knows .	K.8. 234 **Witness thou* 4
Something that makes this individual Spot,	K.8. 240 *Recluse* 1.1.145
Yet is it something gained, it is in truth	K.8. 246 *Recluse* 1.1.358
Something on every side concealed from view,	K.8. 250 *Recluse* 1.1.486
In every quarter something visible,	K.8. 250 *Recluse* 1.1.487
For that end only ; something must be done.	K.8. 255 *Recluse* 1.1.665
Something within which yet is shared by none,	K.8. 255 *Recluse* 1.1.687
Something which power and effort may impart,	K.8. 255 *Recluse* 1.1.689

Sometimes. And sometimes, as from rock to rock she
bounds, . .   15 *Desc. Sk.* 265

Contentedly, yet sometimes self-accused,	32 *Guilt* 434
For sometimes, in despite of my conviction,	41 *Bord.* 229
Indeed we meant no harm ; we lodge sometimes	54 *Bord.* 946
Sometimes he'll hide in the cave of a rock,	80† *Address: Child* 14
At remembrance whereof my blood sometimes will flag ;	86 *Rural Arch.* 22
Sometimes frowns, or seems to frown ;	90 *Longest Day* 66
That sometimes I in thee have loved	111 **Yes ! thou* 3
Sometimes with thoughts of very bliss !	117 *Affl. Marg.* 12
Sometimes when he could find a leisure hour	138 *Michael* 440
There, by the Sheep-fold, sometimes was he seen	138 *Michael* 467
And sometimes, just as listening ends	144 **Driven in* 47
To whom I sometimes in our idle talk	146 **It was an* 43

Songs—*continued.*
Began to spin, with toil, my earliest songs. . . 726 Prelude 10. 552
Old songs, the product of his native hills ; . . 757 Excursion 1. 67
—The Poets, in their elegies and songs . . . 763 Excursion 1. 475
With lifted hands invoked, and songs of praise : . 811 Excursion 4. 680
Tell in their idle songs of wandering gods, . . 868 Excursion 7. 729
The retrospective virtues. Festive songs . . . 873 Excursion 7. 1037
Beaten by lonely billows, hear the songs . . . 890 Excursion 9. 388
The Poet mutter his prelusive songs . . . . K.8. 241 Recluse 1.1.184
Songster. Rise, tardy Sun ! and let the Songster prove 279 *'Tis he 9
Songsters. As if we two were twins ; two songsters bred . . . . 40 Bord. 150
And thickets full of songsters, and the voice . . K.8. 240 Recluse 1.1.129
Songstress. Of that shy songstress, whose love-tale 235 Power of Sound 166
That all this May I will thy songstress be. 561 Cuck.and Night.230
No solemn songstress lull the fading green, . . 616 Desc.Sk.Quarto 751
Sonnet. Scorn not the Sonnet ; Critic, you have frowned, ... 260 *Scorn not 1
The Sonnet glittered a gay myrtle leaf . . . 260 *Scorn not 7
Sonnet's. Within the Sonnet's scanty plot of ground ; . . . . 250 *Nuns fret 11
Sonorous. A clear sonorous voice, inaudible . . 885 Excursion 9. 89
Sonorous squadrons sing their evening hymn. K.8. 234 *The order'd 7
Son's. 'Twas my Son's bird ; and neat and trim . 119 Sailor's Mother 26
For by her Son's blest hand the seed was sown. . 360 Albano 14
For her son's use, some tokens of regard, . . . 768 Excursion 1. 805
Sons. Full oft the father, when his sons have grown 19 Desc. Sk. 512
Drives, eagle-like, those sons as he was driven ; . 19 Desc. Sk. 515
The reasoning Sons of Men, ... 225 Primrose 44
Sons haply of extinguished sires, ... 226 Vernal Ode 42
Your patriot sons, to stem invasive war, . . . 283 *Proud were 2
Sons of the Bard, my heart still mourns . . . 286 Sons of Burns 3
Her sons were bursting forth, to dwell at ease. . 308 *One might 4
And greet your sons ! drums beat and trumpets blow ! . . . . 310 Anticip. 7
Sons of the brave who fought at Marathon, . . 312 *When, far 10
As fathers persecute rebellious sons, ... 321 *Humanity,delighting 19
Intrepid sons of Albion ! not by you . . . . 325 *Intrepid sons 1
England's illustrious sons of long, long ages ; . . 328 Ode 1815 62
Where their sons' sons, and all posterity, . . . 328 Ode 1815 85
To which sad course, these wrinkled Sons of Time 350 Des. Stanzas 24
The blameless Muse, who trains her Sons . . . 386 Yarrow Rev. 43
Grew on the floors his sons had trod : . . . . 390 HighlandBroach 34
He spake, and eight brave sons straightway . . 400 White Doe 412
Thus, with his sons, when forth he came . . . 400 White Doe 414
The Sons obey a natural lord ; . . . . . . 401 White Doe 463
This sympathy of Sire and Sons ; . . . . . . 401 White Doe 470
—Stand forth, my Sons !—these eight are mine, . 402 White Doe 611
Like those eight Sons—who, in a ring, ... 404 White Doe 720
Proud was the field of Sons and Sire ; . . . . 404 White Doe 733
Where Norton and his sons are laid ! . . . . 408 White Doe 1129
—'Twas done : his Sons were with him—all ; . . 408 White Doe 1141
These sons of Amalek, or laid them low !"— . . 427 Ecc. Sonn. 1 .33. 8
The sons who for thy civil rights have bled ! . . 442 Ecc. Sonn. 3. 10. 2
Still on her sons the beams of mercy shine ; . . 474 *How sad 10
Sons, mothers, maidens withering on the stalk, . 488 Pers. Talk 6
The Roman Consul doomed his sons to die . . 517 Pun. Death 3. 1
Likewise he had sons and daughters ; . . . . 535 Egremont 73
Sons he had, saw sons of theirs : . . . . . 536 Egremont 109
Thus does the father to his sons relate, . . . 611 Desc.Sk.Quarto 488
Drives, eagle-like, his sons as he was driven, . . 613 Desc.Sk.Quarto 619
And beam'd on Britain's sons a brighter day ; . 618 School Ex. 36
Her sons no more in listed fields advance . . . 619 School Ex. 57
Hear Britain's sons rehearse thy praise with joy, 619 School Ex. 101
To thousands upon thousands of her sons, . . 698 Prelude 7. 724
Sons of the morning. For your nobler part, . . 804 Excursion 4. 232
Misery and shame. But Wisdom of her sons . . 805 Excursion 4. 293
—Seven lusty Sons sate daily round the board 867 Excursion 7. 636
On which the sons of mighty Germany . . . 869 Excursion 7. 799
No longer led or followed by the Sons ; . . . 878 Excursion 8. 278
By the destruction of her innocent sons . . . 878 Excursion 8. 286
In mercy grant it, to thy wretched sons. . . . 894 Excursion 9. 648
A single word on Kings, and sons of Kings, . . L.1. 96 Juvenal 3. 40
Sons'. Where their sons' sons, and all posterity, . 328 Ode 1815 85
Soon. From his grey re-appearing tower shall soon 8 Ev. Wk. 325
But soon a peopled region on the sight . . . 14 Desc. Sk. 208
Soon with despair's whole weight his spirits sink ; 16 Desc. Sk. 332
But soon his voice and words of kind intent . . 27 Guilt 190
And I believe that, soon as I began . . . . 28 Guilt 201
But soon, with proud parade, the noisy drum . 29 Guilt 273
Untaught that soon such anguish must ensue, . 29 Guilt 294
And soon with crimson fire kindled the firmament. 30 Guilt 315
Their wearied frames, she hoped, would soon regale. 34 Guilt 526
And soon she reached a spot o'erhung with trees 34 Guilt 538
May my end be ! Soon will this voice be dumb : 35 Guilt 588
Is he not valiant ? Am I then so soon . . . 40 Bord. 161
Soon after, the good Abbot of St. Cuthbert's . . 41 Bord. 199
We soon shall meet again. If thou neglect . . 42 Bord. 303
That will be soon despatched. Did Marmaduke . 43 Bord. 340
Who soon grew weary of her ; but, alas ! . . . 44 Bord. 382
The cloud will soon disperse—farewell—but stay, 49 Bord. 647
Soon would her gentle voice make peace between us. 61 Bord. 1318
But they will soon be lightened. Ay, look up— . 65 Bord. 1533
This is a happy day. My Father soon . . . 66 Bord. 1627
Hither soon as spring is fled . . . . . . 80 Foresight 27
As soon as 'tis daylight to-morrow, with me . . 80 †Address : Child 20
But, hearing soon upon the blast . . . . . 82 Alice Fell 15
The little colour that he had was soon . . . . 100 Brothers 339
Hence, and how soon ! that war of vengeance waged 103 Artegal 33

Soon—*continued.*
Was darkened soon by foul iniquity. . . . . 103 Artegal 77
Full soon this generous purpose thou may'st rue, 104 Artegal 168
And which, with caution due, may soon be realized." 105 Artegal 217
So soon be lost. . . . . 110 *Look at 18
Too soon I yielded to despair ; . . . . . . 114 Ind. Wom. 23
Too soon, my friends, ye went away ; . . . . 114 Ind. Wom. 49
She answered, soon as she the question heard, 119 Sailor's Mother 17
Chafed like a wild beast in the toils ; but soon . 122 V. and J. 76
Stirred nowhere without weapons, that full soon . 123 V. and J. 124
Quoth Betty, " and will soon be here, ... 127 Idiot Boy 150
But I shall soon be back again." . . . . . 128 Idiot Boy 196
But soon as Luke, full ten years old, could stand 134 Michael 194
As soon as he had armed himself with strength . 134 Michael 221
And soon as they had reached the place he stopped, 136 Michael 330
Soon returned a trusty Page . . . . . . 141 Arm. Lady 122
——Soon did the spot become my other home, . 146 *It was an 40
Both you and he, Heaven knows how soon ! . . 156 Oak and Broom 49
Soon as gentle breezes bring . . . . . . 161 *Pleasures newly 17
In such a heedless peace. Alas ! full soon . . 173 Infant Daughter 60
But soon large rain-drops on his head . . . . 175 Waggoner 1. 156
For soon, of all the happy there, ... 177 Waggoner 2. 78
Which soon the morning shall enfold, ... 180 Waggoner 4. 54
Which, they foresee, must soon alight . . . . 181 Waggoner 4. 91
How soon my Lucy's race was run ! . . . . 187 *Three years 38
And soon before me did espy . . . . . . 191 Beggars 20
Full soon that better mind was gone : . . . . 194 Ruth 181
And soon with this he other matter blended, . . 197 Resolution 134
—Soon did the Knight perform what he had said ; 202 Hart-leap 79
Which soon composed a little sylvan hall, . . . 202 Hart-leap 87
Soon to be swallowed by the briny surge ; . . 216 Enterprise 111
To crush the mountain dew-drops—soon to melt . 222 Triad 202
But, of his scorn repenting soon, he drew . . . 231 *The gentlest Poet 29
They move ; but soon the appointed way . . . 233 Power of Sound 58
Look up—and you shall see me soon ! . . . . 236 P. B. 10
To a thick wood he soon is brought . . . . 240 P. B. 341
He will be turned to iron soon, ... 242 P. B. 522
Convinced that he, or soon or late, ... 244 P. B. 693
A mother's hope is hers ;—but soon . . . . 246 P. B. 906
Sleepless ! and soon the small birds' melodies . 253 *A flock 6
The world is too much with us ; late and soon, . 259 *The world is 1
Shall soon behold this border thickly set . . . 264 Snowdrop 9
Of her loved mistress : soon the music died, . . 267 St. Cath. 7
Yon busy Little-ones rejoice that soon . . . 280 *Intent on 2
As soon we shall be, may these words attest . . 282 *Wansfell ! this 11
Full soon the Aspirant of the plough, ... 285 Grave of Burns 27
And Bruce, as soon as he had slain . . . . 287 Ellen Irwin 37
Or shall we say an age too soon ? . . . . . 291 Rob Roy 65
Ye soon shall know how this befell) . . . . 296 Highland Boy 97
But soon they move with softer pace ; . . . . 297 Highland Boy 186
They melt, and soon must vanish ; . . . . . 302 Yarrow V. 82
But soon, through Christian faith, is grief subdued : 318 *In due 13
And monuments that soon must disappear : . . 334 *A winged 9
Her sisters, soon like her to be attired . . . . 353 Aquap. 28
Soon witnessed, and the city of seven hills, . . 353 Aquap. 79
Fear that soon vanishes before the sight . . . 355 Aquap. 182
Soon will the Knights of Arthur's Table . . . 370 Eg. Maid 86
Soon did the gentle Nina reach . . . . . 371 Eg. Maid 121
And soon Caerleon's towers appeared, ... 372 Eg. Maid 189
Soon, like a lingering star forlorn . . . . . 391 HighlandBroach 75
Full soon to be uplifted high, ... 400 White Doe 358
Almost as soon as seen :—and lo ! . . . . . 406 White Doe 971
But Francis, soon as he had braved . . . . 410 White Doe 1340
Soon to become more dreaded enemies . . . . 420 Ecc. Sonn. 1. 9. 13
Fierceness and rage ; and soon the cruel Dane . 426 Ecc. Sonn. 1. 29. 6
How soon—alas ! did Man, created pure— . . 428 Ecc. Sonn. 2. 1. 1
Men, who have ceased to reverence, soon defy . 438 Ecc. Sonn. 2. 41. 1
But for what gain ? if England soon must sink . 441 Ecc. Sonn. 3. 3. 10
And soon, full soon, the lonely Sexton's spade . 450 Ecc. Sonn. 3. 41. 8
A tell-tale motion ! soon will it be laid, . . . 454 Sea-side 5
But both will soon be mastered, and the copse . 455 Rydal Mere 5
One with its kindling edge declares that soon . . 461 *Who but is 5
God's bounty, soon forgotten ; or indeed, . . . 462 *Where lies the truth 5
Soon may the punctual sea in vain respire . . 475 Greenock 11
The floods are roused, and will not soon be weary ; 476 Nunnery 1
Soon as the measuring of life's little span . . . 478 *Lonsdale ! it 13
Is it that Man is soon depress ? . . . . . . 485 *Bright Flower 9
As soon it must, a sense to sip, ... 497 Lycoris 43
Too soon—thou com'st into this breathing world ; 504 Warning 85
—Soon shall the widow (for the speed of Time . 505 Warning 151
Soon shall the Rich be levelled down—the Poor . 513 Newspaper 2
"The frost of England's pride will soon be thawed ; 513 *Said Secrecy 4
Soon the relapsing penitent may boast . . . 519 Pun. Death 11. 7
Soon as the herring-shoals at distance shine . . 522 Epist.Beaumont 75
Blithe hopes and happy musings soon took flight, 523 Epist. Beaumont 120
And soon approach Diana's Looking-glass ! . . 524 Epist. Beaumont 165
Soon did the Almighty Giver of all rest . . . 525 *Soon did 1
Not soon does aught to which mild fancies cling 527 *Those breathing 3
A brightening edge will indicate that soon . . 532 *How beautiful the 6
And soon again was dight . . . . 542 Russ. Fug. 50
And soon shall you be led . . . . 542 Russ. Fug. 86
But wonder, pity, soon were quelled ; . . . . 545 Russ. Fug. 321
Soon gratitude gave way to love . . . . . 545 Russ. Fug. 361
And of that famous Youth, full soon removed 546 *The embowering 19
Of thy trim Mansion destined soon to blaze . . 548 *Stranger ! this 30
As ye have heard ; and soon as I had sung . . 556 Prioress 210
Soon as the grain from off thy tongue they take : 556 Prioress 217

Soon—*continued.*
And soon as I a glimpse of day espied, . . . 557 *Cuck.and Night.* 56
He may full soon go with an old man's hair. . . 560 *Cuck.andNight.*180
And soon as she had sung it to the end, . . . 561 *Cuck.andNight.*251
That Cresida again thou send me soon. . . . 563 *Troilus* 77
And shall, unless I see her soon in Troy. . . . 564 *Troilus* 98
As soon as he this song had thus sung through, . 564 *Troilus* 127
A Tuscan audience : but full soon was called . 573 *Chiabrera* 2. 17
Full soon in sorrow did I weep, ... 580 *John Words.* 31
Foreboding not how soon he must depart ; . . 582 **To public* 8
Full soon thy Soul shall have her earthly freight, 589 *Immortality* 130
Soon shall the Light'ning hold before thy head . 597 *Ev. Wk. Quarto* 297
Soon follow'd by his hollow-parting oar, . . . 600 *Ev. Wk. Quarto* 439
Soon fading "silent" from her upward eye, . . 607 *Desc.Sk.Quarto* 259
Soon flies the little joy to man allow'd, . . . 613 *Desc.Sk.Quarto* 636
—Tho' Liberty shall soon, indignant, raise . . 616 *Desc.Sk.Quarto* 774
Soon fades her cheek, her blushing beauties fly, . 619 *School Ex.* 97
But soon upon her breast he sunk—to wake no more. . . . . 620 *Birth of Love* 45
Soon after, this man's Ghost unto him came . . 623 **I find* 6
Will pass so soon from human memory ; . . . 627 **We gaze* 5
Was soon defrauded, and the banded host . . 633 *Prelude* 1. 97
But from this awful burthen I full soon . . . 635 *Prelude* 1. 234
The famous brook, who, soon as he was boxed . 659 *Prelude* 4. 51
Our cottage door, and evening soon brought on . 660 *Prelude* 4. 143
Soon ended, and together on we passed . . . 665 *Prelude* 4. 446
Too soon, while yet the very flash and gleam . 682 *Prelude* 6. 502
Of Chamouny stretched far below, and soon . . 683 *Prelude* 6. 529
Was soon dislodged. Downwards we hurried fast, 684 *Prelude* 6. 619
Of Gravedona with this hope ; but soon . . . 685 *Prelude* 6. 700
To rush and disappear. But soon broke forth . 687 *Prelude* 7. 8
Returned from that excursion, soon I bade . . 688 *Prelude* 7. 52
With this last relic, soon itself to fall, ... 705 *Prelude* 8. 401
Or spirit that full soon must take her flight. . . 705 *Prelude* 8. 450
That would engulph him soon in the ravenous sea— 709 *Prelude* 9. 4
With scrupulous care ; but these restrictions soon 711 *Prelude* 9. 120
A gift that was come rather late than soon. . . 713 *Prelude* 9. 248
That Liberty, and Life, and Death would soon . 720 *Prelude* 10. 125
But said to me, "My head will soon lie low ;" . 726 *Prelude* 10. 539
Hard by, soon after that fell deed was wrought, . 737 *Prelude* 12. 239
The mountain-side. The mist soon girt us round, 746 *Prelude* 14. 15
At large and unrestrained, nor damped too soon . 751 *Prelude* 14. 361
From hope that thou art near, and wilt be soon . 752 *Prelude* 14. 425
Far other lot, yet with good hope that soon . . 756 *Excursion* 1. 18
With slackened footsteps I advanced, and soon . 757 *Excursion* 1. 46
Dies with him, or is changed ; and very soon . . 763 *Excursion* 1. 473
But this endured not ; his good humour soon . . 764 *Excursion* 1. 578
To me soon tasteless. In my own despite, . . 765 *Excursion* 1. 612
Then, when the body, soon to be consigned . . 780 *Excursion* 2. 568
It were your lot to dwell, would soon become . . 782 *Excursion* 2. 695
All night the storm endured : and, soon as help . 784 *Excursion* 2. 805
Soon showed itself : he lingered three short weeks ; 785 *Excursion* 2. 894
And soon the Tenant of that lonely vale . . . 788 *Excursion* 3. 115
—With even as brief a warning—and how soon, . 795 *Excursion* 3. 645
Hath overpowered his forefathers, and soon . . 799 *Excursion* 3. 926
That my particular current soon will reach . . 800 *Excursion* 3. 990
Who shared at first the illusion ; but was soon . 805 *Excursion* 4. 273
But soon his thoughts returned upon themselves, 807 *Excursion* 4. 416
Listened intensely ; and his countenance soon . 818 *Excursion* 4. 1137
In whose dark vaults my own shall soon be laid, . 827 *Excursion* 5. 346
A general greeting was exchanged ; and soon . . 829 *Excursion* 5. 462
That privilege, did yet expire too soon, . . . 836 *Excursion* 5. 948
By a fierce tempest shaken, soon resumed . . 840 *Excursion* 6. 145
The wreck of gaiety ! But soon revived . . . 843 *Excursion* 6. 331
The stream, that bears thee forward, prove not, soon . . . . 844 *Excursion* 6. 438
She bore a secret burthen ; and full soon . . . 851 *Excursion* 6. 851
They soon were proud of ; tended it and nursed ; 852 *Excursion* 6. 932
There blossoms, strong in health, and will be soon 855 *Excursion* 6. 1152
Pity away, soon shall ye quake with *fear !* . . 870 *Excursion* 7. 838
Departs ; and soon is spent the line of those . . 872 *Excursion* 7. 985
To which (and who can tell where or how soon ?) 880 *Excursion* 8. 424
Of unexpected pleasure.—Soon the board . . . 882 *Excursion* 8. 518
Of joyous comrades. Soon as the reedy marge . 891 *Excursion* 9. 488
But soon as Luke, full ten years old, could stand K.8. 226 **I will* 74
Soon will peep forth the primrose ; ere it fades K.8.250 *Recluse* 1.1.514
Have I heard whooping, and he soon will be . . K.8.251 *Recluse* 1.1.522
Soon as the cock begins to crow . . . . K.8. 262 **Ah ! if* 8

Sooner. —No sooner ceased that peal, than on the verge . . . . 324 *Ode 1814* 82
Of thy new hearth ; and sooner shall its wreaths, 465 **Pastor and* 10
No sooner stand attired . . . . 508 *May* 86
By deluge, now at hand. No sooner ceased . . 667 *Prelude* 5. 98
Else sooner ended, I have borne in mind . . . 679 *Prelude* 6. 260
At day-spring, and no sooner doth the sun . . 702 *Primrose* 8. 235
Which was no sooner entered than our Host . . 781 *Excursion* 2. 649
The Sage broke off. No sooner had he ceased . 890 *Excursion* 9. 417
Which the poor broom no sooner felt . . . . S.3. 431 **The Scottish* 19

Soonest. That soonest fails to please, and quickliest turns . . . . 799 *Excursion* 3. 912

Sooth. And I had heard the like before : in sooth . 38 *Bord.* 78
I owe him no ill will, but in good sooth . . . 45 *Bord.* 458
And, sooth, these two were each to the other dear: 108 *Indolence* 66
And, sooth to say, an apter Mate . . . . . 165 *Parrot* 13
Yet, sooth, those little starry specks, ... 170 *Rural Ill.* 19
And sooth for Benjamin a vein . . . . . . 180 *Waggoner* 4. 75
And then the wind ! in sooth, it was . . . . 199 *Thorn* 179
It was in sooth a happy thought . . . . . 224 **'Tis gone* 19
The soberness of reason ; till, in sooth, . . . 270 **Ye sacred* 8
As welcome, and as beautiful—in sooth . . . 279 **Though I* 9

Sooth—*continued.*
Of him the most ; and, sooth to say, ... 404 *White Doe* 734
For, sooth to say, ambition, in the breast . . . 432 *Ecc. Sonn.* 2. 15. 12
Are not, in sooth, their Requiem's sacred ties . 467 *St. Bees* 73
And, sooth to say, yon vocal grove, ... 498 **The sylvan* 7
And why that scrupulous reserve ? In sooth . 539 **Lady ! a* 10
In sooth, I speak from feeling, what though now . 557 *Cuck.and Night.* 36
For he, in sooth, is blind, and may not see, . . 560 *Cuck.andNight.*202
And glad, in sooth, was I when he was gone. . . 560 *Cuck.andNight.*220
And, in good sooth, the Cuckoo here is not ; . . 562 *Cuck.andNight.*274
It was a goodly prospect : for, in sooth, . . . 652 *Prelude* 3. 226
His mien and person, nor was free, in sooth, . . 688 *Prelude* 7. 95
Uplifted ; why deceive ourselves ? in sooth, . . 731 *Prelude* 11. 267
"In sooth, with love's familiar privilege, . . . 787 *Excursion* 3. 78
Leaving this nook unvisited : but, in sooth, . . 788 *Excursion* 3. 119
And mostly profitless. And, sooth to say, . . 799 *Excursion* 3. 896

Soothe. To soothe and cheer the poor man's solitude. 13 *Desc. Sk.* 142
To soothe or cheer, to soften or refine. . . . . 21 *Desc. Sk.* 590
No brook to wet his lip or soothe his ear ; . . 24 *Guilt* 29
To stay the wanderer's steps and soothe his thoughts. . . . . 184 *Airey-force* 16
Soothe it into patience—stay . . . . . . 233 *Power of Sound* 92
To stir, to soothe, or elevate ? . . . . . . 238 *P. B.* 142
Assiduously—to soothe her aching breast ; . . 255 **Grief, thou* 12
'Twill soothe us in our sorrow, ... 293 *Yarrow Unv.* 62
Spot rich in all things that can soothe and please ! 308 **One might* 8
Let Thy love its anger soothe : . . . . . . 336 **Jesu ! bless* 22
To soothe and cleanse, not madden and pollute ! 378 *Duddon* 8. 14
Confession ministers the pang to soothe . . . 423 *Ecc. Sonn.* 1. 20. 11
And soothe the heart confession hath laid bare— 447 *Ecc. Sonn.* 3. 28. 7
Or like those hymns that soothe with graver sound 454 *Sea-side* 29
Or fancies stealing forth to soothe the breast . . 460 **Wanderer! that* 58
Words that can soothe, more than they agitate ; . 510 *F. Stone* 124
Might soothe in human breasts the sense of ill, . 517 *Pun. Death* 1. 4
Or soothe it with a healing power . . . . . 533 **Blest is* 26
May soothe thy memory of the chains of Rome. . 627 *Eagle and Dove* 4
To exhilarate the spirit, and to soothe, . . . 667 *Prelude* 5. 108
To soothe regret, though deepening what it soothed, 718 *Prelude* 10. 5
Wet with the Muses' nectar. Thus I soothe . . 733 *Prelude* 11. 449
But neither could divert nor soothe my thoughts. 767 *Excursion* 1. 739
To soothe a Child, who walked beside him, weeping 779 *Excursion* 2. 507
The charities that soothe, and heal, and bless, . 887 *Excursion* 9. 239
Thus do we soothe ourselves, and when the thought K.8. 244 *Recluse* 1.1.290
And elevate, and harmonise, and soothe, . . . K.8.245 *Recluse* 1.1.303

Soothed. *See* **Heart-soothed.**
—Now o'er the soothed accordant heart we feel . 8 *Ev. Wk.* 315
Sympathy that soothed his grief, ... 94 *Westmoreland Girl* 38
Which, soothed and sweetened by the grace of Heaven . . . . 119 *Maternal Grief* 79
Was softened into feeling, soothed, and tamed. . 205 *Brougham* 160
And soothed war-wearied knights in raftered hall. 221 *Triad* 103
With it Camöens soothed an exile's grief ; . . . 260 **Scorn not* 6
Whose murmur soothed thy languid Mother's ear 275 *Rotha Q.* 10
Been soothed, in all my wanderings. . . . . 302 *Yarrow V.* 12
Or let me loiter, soothed with what is given, . . 356 *Aquap.* 263
Soothed by the unseen River's gentle roar. . . 384 *Duddon* 31. 14
It soothed us—it beguiled us—then, to hear . . 395 *White Doe:Ded.* 33
Yet Emily is soothed ;—the breeze . . . . . 407 *White Doe* 1020
Yes, she is soothed : an Image faint, ... 407 *White Doe* 1033
How soothed, when in thick bower enclosed, . . 415 *White Doe* 1736
That voice which soothed the Nuns while on the steeps . . . . 476 *Nunnery* 7
And, quieted and soothed, a torrent small, . . 524 *Epist. Beaumont* 177
Her soothed affections clung, ... 544 *Russ. Fug.* 210
Transported, my soothed spirit hovers o'er . . 585 *Ch. Lamb* 53
But o'er the sooth'd accordant heart we feel . . 599 *Ev. Wk. Quarto* 381
And swellings of the spirit, was rapt and soothed, 660 *Prelude* 4. 163
Would with an influence benign have soothed, . 679 *Prelude* 6. 312
To soothe regret, though deepening what it soothed, 718 *Prelude* 10. 5
To happy contemplation soothed his walk ; . . 772 *Excursion* 2. 50
In me, a meekly-bending spirit soothed . . . 790 *Excursion* 3. 265
These with a soothed or elevated heart, . . . 807 *Excursion* 4. 381
Soothed by the natural spirit which they breathe. 847 *Excursion* 6. 633
—Thus soothed at home, thus busy in the field, . 864 *Excursion* 7. 455
More joyful if it be with sorrow sooth'd. . . . K.8. 233 **Along the* 7
Had soothed his ear while *they* were hidden : how pleased . . . . K.8. 249 *Recluse* 1.1.484

Soother. And oh ! dear soother of the pensive breast, ... K.8. 301 **And oh* 1

Soothers. All soothers of sense their soft virtue shall yield, ... 621 *Convict* 27

Soothes. That did bewitch me then, and soothes me now. . . . . 668 *Prelude* 5. 180
And dear remembrances, whose presence soothes 755 *Recluse* 1. 1. 760
Our solitude. It soothes me to perceive, . . . 794 *Excursion* 3. 598

Soothing. *See* **Soul-soothing.**
And with that voice accords the soothing sound . 16 *Desc. Sk.* 356
And her soothing song by the winter fire, . . . 142 †*Lov. and Lik.* 47
Most soothing was it for a welcome Friend, . . 143 **High bliss* 9
A soothing recompense, his gift, is thine ! . . . 272 *Ruins* 14
A soothing spirit follows in the way . . . . 283 **Here, where* 3
Prelude of night's approach with soothing dreams. 453 **The Sun, that* 4
The soothing recompense, the welcome change. . 454 *Sea-side* 10
Upon a soothing scene, ... 499 *Memory* 22
If neither soothing to the worm that gleams . . 501 **The unremitting* 3
In the soothing thoughts that spring . . . . 590 *Immortality* 187
If Pleasure's soothing song thy soul entice, . . 619 *School Ex.* 93
Half conscious of the soothing melody, . . . 756 *Excursion* 1. 14
Though soothing, and the little floating isles . . 800 *Excursion* 3. 979

Soothing—continued.

And breathed its soothing air ;—the spirit of hope	845 Excursion 6. 483
A soothing comforter, although forlorn ;	852 Excursion 6. 933
For England's bane.—When soothing darkness spreads	876 Excursion 8. 156

Sooty. From this dull Monster and her sooty crew ; — 471 *Arran! a 7
Those sooty knaves, precipitated down — 640 Prelude 1. 530
And visage grim and sooty, — S.3. 424 Tinker 36

Sorcerer. Traced on the beach, his work the Sorcerer urges ; — 369 Eg. Maid 32

Sorceress. A gentle Sorceress, and benign, — 370 Eg. Maid 95

Sorceries. And sorceries of talent misapplied. — 425 Ecc. Sonn. 1. 28. 14

Sordid. We have given our hearts away, a sordid boon ! — 259 *The world is 4
Saved from the sordid axe by Beaumont's care, — 358 Pine : Rome 7
Of sordid industry thy lot is cast ; — 376 Duddon 2. 2
Or hindrance raised by sordid purposes, — 468 St. Bees 134

Sore. Such as he is, and sore perplexed as I am, — 62 Bord. 1392
He had been sore misused ; but he forgave — 74 Bord. 2070
He listens, puzzled, sore perplexed, — 81 †Mother's Return 15
God cursed me in my sore distress ; — 115 Last of Flock 86
A thought with which her heart is sore— — 128 Idiot Boy 213
Sore aches she needs must have ! but less — 194 Ruth 232
Limped on with sore vexation. — 238 P. B. 175
Is crippled sore in his narration. — 248 P. B. 1035
Repaid thee for that sore distress — 294 Jedbor. 80
Sore stress of apprehension, with a mind — 449 Ecc. Sonn. 3. 37. 6
Into a grievous sore of self-tormenting earth. — 504 Warning 77
With a sore heart well ought I to bewail, — 564 Troilus 121
Is of my Lady's sighs heavy and sore ; — 565 Troilus 157
With anger vexed, with disappointment sore, — 730 Prelude 11. 212
And a sore temper : day by day he drooped, — 765 Excursion 1. 581
A sore heart-wasting ! I have heard, my Friend, — 769 Excursion 1. 875

Sorely. And sorely puzzled are the twain, — 126 Idiot Boy 25

Sorento's. For mild Sorento's breezy waves ; — 386 Yarrow Rev. 53

Sorrow. See **Heart-sorrow.**
And what if he must die in sorrow ! — 9 Lines : Boat 14
Bows his young head with sorrow to the grave. — 20 Desc. Sk. 527
Much sorrow ere the fleet its anchor weighed ; — 29 Guilt 281
" No help I sought ; in sorrow turned adrift, — 31 Guilt 370
Whole hours, with idle arms in moping sorrow knit. — 32 Guilt 432
Struggled with tears nor could its sorrow ease, — 34 Guilt 535
Yes, to my sorrow—under the great oak — 47 Bord. 538
A comforter of sorrow ;—there is something — 48 Bord. 635
With all their natural weight of sorrow and pain, — 52 Bord. 821
The Stranger had some pitiable sorrow — 60 Bord. 1261
In this deep sorrow, trust, that I am thine — 76 Bord. 2201
What hast thou to do with sorrow, — 88 H. C. 25
Tribute, by her hand, in sorrow, — 94 Westmoreland Girl 67

A fellow-tale of sorrow. From his youth — 100 Brothers 331
Is a true friend to sorrow ; and, unless — 101 Brothers 389
And sorrow, have confirmed thy native right to reign. — 105 Artegal 209
Ere sorrow be renewed ; — 112 *How rich 4
Nor sorrow may attend thy name ? — 116 Affl. Marg. 7
And all those tokens of a cherished sorrow, — 119 Maternal Grief 78
Had been no sorrow. I forgive him ;—but — 134 Michael 240
Of sorrow in her heart while through her father's door, — 140 Arm. Lady 77
Doth in its silence of past sorrow tell, — 141 Arm. Lady 131
Even from things by sorrow wrought, — 172 Kitten 125
By sorrow darkened and by care disturbed, — 172 Infant Daughter 47
That shaped her sorrow, rocks and pools, — 194 Ruth 218
With sorrow of the meanest thing that feels." — 203 Hart-leap 180
For sorrow that had bent — 225 Primrose 38
" A potent wand doth Sorrow wield ; — 238 P. B. 146
And straight in sorrow, not in dread, — 241 P. B. 438
Benoni, or the child of sorrow, — 246 P. B. 909
Was the worst pang that sorrow ever bore, — 257 *Surprised by 10
And, like mine eyes that stream with sorrow, blind ! " — 267 *As the 14
With brow in penitential sorrow bent ! — 270 *Though the bold 14
Why should we bend in grief, to sorrow cling, — 271 George : Death 8
Nor aught of mutual joy or sorrow knew — 276 Oker Hill 12
Music that sorrow comes not near, — 285 Grave of Burns 81
Enough of sorrow, wreck, and blight ; — 286 Nith 19
With sorrow true ; — 286 Sons of Burns 4
And there his sorrow ended. — 287 Ellen Irwin 48
Some natural sorrow, loss, or pain, — 289 Sol. Reap. 23
My True-love sighed for sorrow ; — 293 Yarrow Unv. 30
'Twill soothe us in our sorrow, — 293 Yarrow Unv. 62
That paints, by strength of sorrow, — 302 Yarrow V. 38
And cheer my mind in sorrow. — 302 Yarrow V. 88
For, high-souled Maid, what sorrow would it be — 306 *Two Voices 11
I tremble at the sorrow of the time. — 309 *When, looking 14
Shall blush ; and may not we with sorrow say, — 315 *Alas ! what 10
We can approach, thy sorrow to behold, — 316 *Hail, Zaragoza 2
And sorrow that to fruitless sorrow clung ! — 326 *Emperors and 6
If sickness, sorrow, or distress — 344 Eclipse 80
From sorrow, like the sky above our heads. — 353 Aquap. 65
For them who in the shades of sorrow dwell, — 354 Aquap. 90
To mortals, joy is turned to sorrow ; — 372 Eg. Maid 206
A Father's sorrow for her fate ? — 372 Eg. Maid 220
And to her name my soul shall cleave in sorrow ; " — 372 Eg. Maid 326
By tales of love and sorrow, — 386 Yarrow Rev. 66
How nearly joy and sorrow are allied ! — 395 White Doe : Ded. 24
Of sorrow, or of reverence ? — 397 White Doe III
A softened remembrance of sorrow and pain, — 398 White Doe 239
And sorrow of his fruitless prayer. — 401 White Doe 440
And sorrow moved him to partake — 401 White Doe 458

Sorrow—continued.
The sorrow, through the Villages, — 411 White Doe 1381
And sorrow of this final truth ! — 413 White Doe 1550
The mighty sorrow hath been borne, — 414 White Doe 1621
By sorrow lifted towards her God ; — 416 White Doe 1851
Of sorrow, still maintains a heathen rule, — 422 Ecc. Sonn. 1. 15. 3
Their eyes away in sorrow, others burn — 428 Ecc. Sonn. 1. 38. 11
Where frauds were hatched of old, hath sorrow past— — 435 Ecc. Sonn. 2. 27. 10
Merciless act of sorrow infinite ! — 439 Ecc. Sonn. 2. 42. 11
And sorrow bartered for exceeding joy. — 440 Ecc. Sonn. 3. 2. 14
Thy own, if sorrow for thy sin be dead, — 447 Ecc. Sonn. 3. 29. 7
Must Man, with labour born, awake to sorrow — 462 *Where lies the truth 6
To fix a wiser sorrow in the heart ? — 467 St. Bees 76
Privation, under sorrow thrive ; — 473 Ossian 58
Sorrow seems here excluded ; and that knell, — 475 Greenock 7
Though minister of sorrow ; — 480 Somnamb. 159
And, sorrow for him ! the dull treacherous heat — 484 *A plague 8
Of joy and sorrow ; — 485 *Bright Flower 4
And she made answer "ENDLESS SORROW ! " — 494 Force of Prayer 7
And long, unspeaking, sorrow ; — 494 Force of Prayer 38
Old Wharf might heal her sorrow. — 494 Force of Prayer 44
And hers is a mother's sorrow. — 495 Force of Prayer 48
Oh ! there is never sorrow of heart — 495 Force of Prayer 65
Of sorrow that will surely come ? — 502 *Like a 11
Lead, through dark ways by sin and sorrow trod, — 504 Warning 83
With penitential sorrow, and aloft — 513 General Fast 7
Joy based on sorrow, good with ill combined, — 514 *Who ponders 3
Of sorrow ;—feel for all, as brother Men ! — 516 *Feel for 8
His face was gloom, his heart was sorrow, — 537 Goody Blake 116
Most feeling have of sorrow, woe and care, — 559 Cuck.and Night.143
Well nigh for sorrow down he 'gan to fall. — 562 Troilus 14
Both his new sorrow and his joys of old, — 563 Troilus 40
That every wight might on his sorrow rue. — 563 Troilus 42
That cause is of my torment and my sorrow ; — 564 Troilus 136
Of the tenth day will come, and end his sorrow. — 565 Troilus 168
Where want and sorrow were. The easy man — 568 Cumb. Beg. 116
At length, what to most is a season of sorrow, — 569 Farmer 31
Of recent sorrow combated in vain ; — 576 *By a 14
Let sorrow overcharged with pain — 578 *I come 51
They parted, sorrow was at hand — 579 *Sweet Flower 34
Full soon in sorrow did I weep, — 580 John Words. 31
In sorrow, but for higher trust, — 580 John Words. 33
Bows his young hairs with sorrow to the grave. — 613 Desc.Sk.Quarto 631
'Tis sorrow enough on that visage to gaze, — 620 Convict 17
The silence of sorrow it seems to supply, — 621 Convict 43
Of sorrow and affright ? — 623 G. and S. Green 32
And sorrow is not there ! The seasons came, — 646 Prelude 2. 288
That fails not, in all sorrow my support, — 648 Prelude 2. 444
When sorrow damps it, or, whatever look — 660 Prelude 4. 147
By sorrow not unsmitten ; yet for me — 675 Prelude 6. 50
Did oft beguile his sorrow, and almost — 677 Prelude 6. 153
There is no grief, no sorrow, no despair, — 678 Prelude 6. 244
Oh ! sorrow for the youth who could have seen — 682 Prelude 6. 504
From formal gardens of the lady Sorrow, — 683 Prelude 6. 555
The sorrow of the passion stopped me there. — 693 Prelude 7. 399
My sorrow ; for I brought with me the faith — 722 Prelude 10. 257
Sorrow for human kind, and pain of heart. — 723 Prelude 10. 330
Of pity and sorrow to a state of being — 724 Prelude 10. 450
That, under heaviest sorrow earth can bring, — 725 Prelude 10. 465
'Twas even so ; and sorrow for the man — 731 Prelude 11. 268
Thine eyes must see of sorrow in a land, — 733 Prelude 11. 388
With sorrow, disappointment, vexing thoughts, — 734 Prelude 12. 4
With all the sorrow that it brought, appeared — 739 Prelude 12. 310
Sorrow, that is not sorrow, but delight ; — 743 Prelude 13. 246
Of sorrow, barricadoed evermore — 755 Recluse 1. 1. 832
Unoccupied by sorrow of its own, — 761 Excursion 1. 361
With care and sorrow : shoals of artisans — 764 Excursion 1. 559
An ordinary sorrow of man's life, — 765 Excursion 1. 637
By sorrow laid asleep ; or borne away, — 768 Excursion 1. 786
Of sorrow. Yet I saw the idle loom — 769 Excursion 1. 851
" My Friend ! enough to sorrow you have given, — 770 Excursion 1. 932
That what we feel of sorrow and despair, — 770 Excursion 1. 949
A day of sorrow. I have here a charge "— — 779 Excursion 2. 528
Loved with such love, and with such sorrow mourned ! " — 780 Excursion 2. 592
From doubt and sorrow, than the senseless grave ? " — 789 Excursion 3. 224
Sorrow proceeds, which else were not ; at least, — 803 Excursion 4. 147
An agonizing sorrow to transmute ; — 803 Excursion 4. 168
Whose very sorrow is, that time hath shorn — 817 Excursion 4. 1084
We should recoil, stricken with sorrow and shame, — 826 Excursion 5. 254
Or sorrow which his senseless guilt had caused ; — 853 Excursion 6. 1007
Whose sorrow rather is to suffer wrong — 854 Excursion 6. 1070
Of sorrow and dejection ; but I feel — 855 Excursion 6. 1124
By tender sorrow for our mortal state) — 862 Excursion 7. 298
And, without sorrow, will the ground receive — 863 Excursion 7. 389
Oft as they hear of sorrow like their own, — 868 Excursion 7. 691
Her sorrow for that multitude in whom — 886 Excursion 9. 140
And sorrow and care blow over him, — S.3. 424 Tinker 49
Through joy and sorrow ; if my lot be joy — K.8. 233 *Along the 6
More joyful if it be with sorrow sooth'd. — K.8. 233 *Along the 7
Mistakes for sorrow darting beams of light — K.8. 238 Recluse I.I. 54
Joy spreads, and sorrow spreads ; and this whole Vale, — K.8. 248 Recluse I.I.445
Yield not, to scorn, or sorrow, living men — K.8. 253 Recluse I.I.605
The theme is fruitful ; nor can sorrow find — L.I. 97 Juvenal 3. 79
Such sorrow is more lovely in its guise — [?] *A sad 4

Sorrowful. This cannot be a sorrowful grove ; — 121 Emigrant Mother 86
How sorrowful the wanderer is, — 243 P. B. 633
Of night his grief and sorrowful fear— — 249 P. B. 1104

Sorrowful—*continued.*
My Soul, a sorrowful interpreter, 311 *Who rises 22
Him thought his sorrowful heart would break in two; 562 Troilus 12
This sorrowful reverse for all mankind. 733 Prelude 11. 404
—Oh! pang of sorrowful regret for those 848 Excursion 6. 695
Sorrowing. Must walk the sorrowing mountains, drest 390 Highland Broach 39
On thee I look, not sorrowing; fare thee well, 510 F. Stone 130
All kinds of pleasure mix'd with sorrowing; 557 Cuck. and Night. 29
From a reflecting mind and sorrowing heart 584 Ch. Lamb 39
We know, yet faith sustains the sorrowing heart; K.8. 275 *These vales 6
Sorrowings. Long past, delights and sorrowings? 414 White Doe 1675
Sorrow's. And do not shrink from sorrow's keenest wind. 259 *Weak is 14
For Her, who, pierced by sorrow's thrilling dart, 395 White Doe: Ded. 11
And there was Sorrow's guest; 479 Somnamb. 148
And to abridge my sorrow's violence, 562 Cuck. and Night. 308
Sad doom, at Sorrow's shrine to kneel, 582 *O for a 13
Sorrows. May know that Poet's sorrows more. 9 Collins 20
The general sorrows of the human race: 19 Desc. Sk. 503
Save those who to my sorrows lend 113 Lament 20
And wild-wood sorrows, speedily 143 *Driven in 12
For transient sorrows, simple wiles, 186 *She was 19
In them—in Her our sins and sorrows past. 280 *Oh what 14
A dirge devoutly breathed o'er sorrows past; 314 *I dropped 10
A Soul, by force of sorrows high, 402 White Doe 585
For deepest sorrows that aspire 411 White Doe 1352
And some break forth when others' sorrows crush 436 Ecc. Sonn. 2. 32. 8
He fell again into his sorrows old; 564 Troilus 128
No more of old romantic sorrows, 586 Hogg 41
Me, lur'd by hope her sorrows to remove, 602 Desc. Sk. Quarto 45
Is come as a brother thy sorrows to share. 621 Convict 48
And sorrows of the world. Those simple days 692 Prelude 7. 333
Its cares and sorrows; he, though taught to own 809 Excursion 4. 546
And the dark sorrows of the line of Thebes? 846 Excursion 6. 544
And safe from all our sorrows.' With a sigh 849 Excursion 6. 766
Sorrow-stricken. Its impulse took—that sorrow-stricken door, 394 *No more 21
Sorry. And thinking it but sorry cheer 179 Waggoner 3. 62
Eight sorry carts, no less a train! 182 Waggoner 4. 249
For we have had the sorry Cuckoo here, 558 Cuck. and Night. 103
I am right sorry Troilus will die: 564 Troilus 109
This sorry Legend; which by chance we found 816 Excursion 4. 1007
Sort. But life of happier sort set forth to me, 32 Guilt 408
Expedients, too, of simplest sort he tried: 108 Indolence 55
While in this sort the simple household lived 134 Michael 207
These thoughts, and many others of like sort, 135 Michael 271
Not in like sort the Runic Scald was moved; 359 *Complacent Fictions 11
Dealt in like sort with feeble human kind 514 *Who ponders 8
Such sort of doctrine as men usèd there, 553 Prioress 47
"Young Hew of Lincoln! in like sort laid low 556 Prioress 233
Nor general Truths, which are themselves a sort 634 Prelude 1. 151
Communing in this sort through earth and heaven 648 Prelude 2. 411
To inspiration, sort with such a name; 651 Prelude 3. 149
Brother to many more. In this mixed sort 653 Prelude 3. 321
A sort of alien scattered from the clouds. 692 Prelude 7. 350
These fictions, as in some sort, in their turn, 704 Prelude 8. 375
Even in such sort had I at first been moved, 708 Prelude 8. 590
In some sort seeing with my proper eyes 720 Prelude 10. 124
An insight that in some sort he possesses, 744 Prelude 13. 308
May sort with highest objects, then—dread Power! 755 Recluse 1. 1. 853
Such intercourse was his, and in this sort 759 Excursion 1. 220
Heedless how far; and, in such piteous sort 769 Excursion 1. 865
Then, speaking in like careless sort, he said 781 Excursion 2. 618
And, in like sort, chair, window-seat, and shelf, 781 Excursion 2. 662
To sight and feeling, or that in this sort 811 Excursion 4. 643
To drink of the cold well. When in like sort K.8. 226 *I will 57
Sorted. *See* **Ill-sorted.**
Sottish. Of sottish vice or desperate breach of law, 880 Excursion 8. 423
Sought. The spirit sought not then, in cherished sadness, 2 Ev. Wk. 15
Thus warned he sought some shepherd's spreading thorn 25 Guilt 41
But sought in vain; for now, all wild, forlorn, 25 Guilt 43
For books in every neighbouring house I sought, 28 Guilt 206
"Ho help I sought; in sorrow turned adrift, 31 Guilt 370
The lanes I sought, and, as the sun retired, 31 Guilt 402
Could gaze, as on a show by idlers sought; 36 Guilt 661
His absence, he hath sought, whate'er his aim, 37 Bord. 7
He sought his brother Leonard.—You are moved! 101 Brothers 353
Then Artegal thus spake: "I only sought 104 Artegal 162
For two months now in vain we shall be sought; 106 Farewell 18
Sought by a wise though late exchange, and here 143 *High bliss 5
I've sought thy father far and wide. 145 Her Eyes 94
Much wondering how I could have sought in vain 150 *When, to 51
Though she appear not, and be sought in vain. 165 Parrot 40
By bird or beast made vocal, sought a cause 170 *Never enlivened 16
And where it liked her best she sought 194 Ruth 209
With spades they would have sought. 200 Thorn 224
Who sought the thing he loved. For nature then 206 Tintern 72
Him hath he sought with fruitless pains, 243 P. B. 642
But He—who deviously hath sought 249 P. B. 1101
Hath sought, proclaiming to the ear 249 P. B. 1103
That ever among Men or Naiads sought 251 *There is a little 3
Warned in a dream, the Wanderer long had sought 267 St. Cath. 9
I sought the untimely grave of Burns; 286 Sons of Burns 2
He sought his moral creed. 291 Rob Roy 20
Suns that through blood their western harbour sought, 299 Brownie's Cell 61

Sought—*continued.*
That in ourselves our safety must be sought; 310 *Another year 6
Of moral prudence, sought through good and ill; 315 *Alas! what 2
Nor hath that moral good been vainly sought; 316 *It was a 5
They seek, are sought; to daily battle led, 320 *They seek 1
He sought the regions of humanity, 323 Ode 1814 26
For converse with God, sought through study and prayer. 364 Vallomb. 8
Landing, she found not what she sought, 371 Eg. Maid 123
Whate'er they sought, shunned, loved, or deified! 380 Duddon 16. 14
That charge, impatient Norton sought 405 White Doe 807
Then on this height the Maid had sought, 409 White Doe 1206
Enough—if eyes, that sought the fountain-head 419 Ecc. Sonn. 1. 5. 13
Who near his fountains sought obscure repose, 431 Ecc. Sonn. 2. 13. 11
In doctrine and communion they have sought 438 Ecc. Sonn. 2. 40. 10
Yet Truth is keenly sought for, and the wind 441 Ecc. Sonn. 3. 4. 1
But in the solemn Office which ye sought 444 Ecc. Sonn. 3. 16. 9
As bravely as the foe was keenly sought. 458 Sea-shore 24
When Bega sought of yore the Cumbrian coast, 466 St. Bees 32
Not sought, because too near, is never gained. 476 Eden 14
You say, Cordelia, was the metal sought, 480 Cordelia 2
From evil-speaking; rancour, never sought, 488 Pers. Talk 45
Of good or bad (whate'er be sought for or profest) 504 Warning 90
Knowing, things rashly sought are rarely found; 514 *BlestStatesman 10
And guidance have I sought in duteous love 520 Pun. Death 14. 10
She sought in vain, the Woodman smiled; 543 Russ. Fug. 133
She at the School and elsewhere him hath sought, 554 Prioress 139
And him among the accursèd Jews she sought. 555 Prioress 148
Yet then, when called ashore, he sought 579 *Sweet Flower 22
Clapp'd her strong wings, and sought the cheerful isle, 618 School Ex. 46
And Gaiety the charming office sought; 620 Birth of Love 16
Here, in the Founder's Spirit sought 629 Installation 82
I sought thy golden vale with dancing flight, 630 [?] *O Moon 6
Withering the Oppressor: how Gustavus sought 635 Prelude 1. 212
And secondary, now at length was sought 645 Prelude 2. 202
Of beauty and of love. For thou hast sought 648 Prelude 2. 460
Such glory was but little sought by me, 650 Prelude 3. 74
On knowledge, when sincerely sought and prized 654 Prelude 3. 389
Then sought with quiet heart my distant home. 665 Prelude 4. 469
Observed where pastime only had been sought, 693 Prelude 7. 403
Sought or unsought, and influxes of power 708 Prelude 8. 601
Elsewhere will safety now be sought, and earth 727 Prelude 10. 588
As could not be impeached, was sought elsewhere. 730 Prelude 11. 205
But turned to abstract science, and there sought 732 Prelude 11. 328
(Such as they were) were sought insatiably. 736 Prelude 12. 141
Ambitious projects, pleased me less; I sought 741 Prelude 13. 61
Sought you enriched with everything I prized, 741 Prelude 13. 118
Must come, or will by man be sought in vain. 748 Prelude 14. 129
And sought *that* beauty, which, as Milton sings, 749 Prelude 14. 245
Sought in the Atlantic Main—why should they be 755 Recluse 1. 1. 802
The Friend I sought; a Man of reverend age, 756 Excursion 1. 33
Sought daily bread from public charity, 764 Excursion 1. 561
Then, not less idly, sought, through every nook 764 Excursion 1. 572
A stranger passed; and, guessing whom I sought, 767 Excursion 1. 732
And long and hopelessly we sought in vain: 784 Excursion 2. 810
Such the reward he sought; and wore out life, 791 Excursion 3. 388
In timid selfishness withdrew, I sought 797 Excursion 3. 783
He sought not praise, and praise did overlook 823 Excursion 5. 45
Sought for his weariness a place of rest 843 Excursion 6. 322
Those troubles had appeased, he sought and gained, 844 Excursion 6. 424
—What though no higher recompense be sought 875 Excursion 8. 49
Of many a Grecian vale, who sought not praise, S.3. 436 *The doubt 154
A single sheep was wanting. They had sought K.8. 224 *I will 14
Nor in the single sheep was what they sought. K.8. 225 *I will 45
Or sought with courage; enterprize forlorn K.8. 256 Recluse 1. 1. 717
And self-devoted sought the monarch's tent, L.1. 95 Juvenal 3. 8
Mid such bad daring sought a coward's name. L.1. 96 Juvenal 3. 56
Soul. My soul will cast the backward view, 1 Extract 7
Harmonious thoughts, a soul by truth refined, 3 Ev. Wk. 84
Thy quiet soul on all bestowing, 9 Collins 6
And solitude prepare the soul for heaven; 10 Desc. Sk. 3
To all that binds the soul in powerless trance, 13 Desc. Sk. 131
Breathes o'er the failing soul voluptuous dreams, 13 Desc. Sk. 136
From such romantic dreams, my soul, awake 14 Desc. Sk. 226
Or rouse and agitate his labouring soul? 15 Desc. Sk. 292
Rouses the soul from her severe delight. 16 Desc. Sk. 353
And heard with heart unmoved, with soul unraised: 18 Desc. Sk. 422
Fitfully, and in flashes, through his soul, 18 Desc. Sk. 457
No common soul. In youth by science nursed, 23 Yew-tree 13
And with the food of pride sustained his soul 23 Yew-tree 23
Owes to the fit in which his soul hath tossed 26 Guilt 92
And clear and open soul, so prized in fearless youth. 32 Guilt 441
Peace to my parting soul, the fulness of content." 36 Guilt 630
From whose perverted soul can come no good 37 Bord. 9
To a proud Soul.—Nobody loves this Oswald— 38 Bord. 31
A deep and simple meekness: and that Soul, 40 Bord. 169
Appeared the genuine colour of his soul— 41 Bord. 233
Which looks like a transition in my soul, 48 Bord. 636
Should he resolve to taint her Soul by means 56 Bord. 1058
Both soul and body—— 'Tis too horrible; 57 Bord. 1065
He talks of a transition in his Soul, 58 Bord. 1165
No traveller, peasant, herdsman? Not a soul: 61 Bord. 1293
He is a puny soul who, feeling pain, 65 Bord. 1555
A hideous plot, against the soul of man: 75 Bord. 2143
The Cross, fixed in his soul, may prove an all-sufficing stay. 91 Norman Boy 32
From body pains and pains of soul thou needest no release, 92 Poet's Dream 55
His soul was knit to this his native soil. 100 Brothers 298
For happier soul no living creature has 108 Indolence 30

Soul—*continued.*
While all the future, for thy purer soul, 112 *O dearer 7
Thy dissolution brings, that in my soul 118 *Maternal Grief* 3
Not a soul in the village this morning will stay ; 119 *Childless Father* 2
Scarcely a soul is out of bed ; 126 *Idiot Boy* 12
Her life and soul were buried. 127 *Idiot Boy* 131
There's not a single soul abroad." 129 *Idiot Boy* 281
And like the very soul of evil, 129 *Idiot Boy* 333
Body, heart, and soul in union, 140 *Arm. Lady* 63
He saves for me my precious soul ; 145 *Her Eyes* 48
Its playmate, rather say, its moving soul. 148 *A narrow 25
With a soul as strong as a mountain river 160 *Up with me 23
Of the Wanderer in my soul. 166 *Wand. Jew* 28
Was to the Pilgrim's soul endeared, 168 *Pilgrim's Dream* 70
Keep the sprightly soul awake, 172 *Kitten* 123
He heard not, too intent of soul ; 175 *Waggoner* 1. 153
Who can or will !—my honest soul, 177 *Waggoner* 2. 45
Thinks her the luckiest soul on earth, 177 *Waggoner* 2. 87
For Benjamin, triumphant soul ! 178 *Waggoner* 2. 153
And the guilt-burthened soul is no longer opprest. 188 *Music* 12
Would seek what the degraded soul 194 *Ruth* 155
My soul from darkness is released, 194 *Ruth* 178
The sleepless Soul that perished in his pride ; 195 *Resolution* 44
Into her soul was sent ; 199 *Thorn* 119
In body, and become a living soul : 206 *Tintern* 46
The guide, the guardian of my heart, and soul 207 *Tintern* 110
My Soul, an Apparition in the place, 208 *It is no 16
The depth, and not the tumult, of the soul ; 210 *Laod.* 75
Yet there the Soul shall enter which hath earned 211 *Laod.* 109
In soul I swept the indignity away : 211 *Laod.* 136
The spots that to my soul adhere ; 214 *Dion* 97
The soul of Dion, instantly dissolved. 214 *Dion* 119
My Soul was grateful for delight 215 *Kirkstone* 61
If there be movements in the Patriot's soul, 216 *Enterprise* 98
His soul with but a *glimpse* of heavenly day ? 221 *Triad* 72
Fit countenance for the soul of primal truth ; 221 *Triad* 139
And makes each soul a separate heaven, 225 *Primrose* 53
Doth to the *Soul* exalt it with the chime 227 *Vernal Ode* 92
That sees them, to my soul that owns in them, 230 *Clouds* 49
Shout, cuckoo !—let the vernal soul 233 *Power of Sound* 25
Terrible for sense and soul ! 234 *Power of Sound* 106
And with a soul of power. 238 *P. B.* 140
The soul of happy sound was spread, 239 *P. B.* 257
I've heard of one, a gentle Soul, 244 *P. B.* 736
Perplexed the good man's gentle soul. 244 *P. B.* 755
—Let good men feel the soul of nature, 245 *P. B.* 764
How ye, that play with soul and sense, 245 *P. B.* 767
To him, a jovial soul, I ween, 246 *P. B.* 878
No disproportion in her soul, no strife : 256 *Marriage : Friend* 10
And my Soul felt her destiny divine, 256 *No mortal 3
Heaven-born, the Soul a heavenward course must hold ; 257 *No mortal 5
That kills the soul : love betters what is best, 257 *No mortal 13
And in the soul admit of no decay, 260 *High is 12
One who was suffering tumult in his soul 263 *Storm* 1
It seems the Eternal Soul is clothed in thee 268 *Brook ! whose 11
In man's perturbèd soul thy sway benign ; 269 *Pure element 10
Dull would he be of soul who could pass by 269 *Westm. Bridge* 2
Then I repent not. But my soul hath fears 270 *If these 7
And head that droops because the soul is meek, 274 *Such age 8
(Like influence never may my soul reject), 282 *While beams 10
Let no mean hope your souls enslave ; 287 *Sons of Burns* 43
No soul to dream of. What art Thou, from care 290 *Kilchurn* 9
In bitterness of soul. 291 *Rob Roy* 28
With which his soul had shone so bright— 297 *Highland Boy* 212
His soul into the briar-rose ; 299 *Brownie's Cell* 86
The man of abject soul in vain 300 *Cora Linn* 37
Spake laws to *them*, and said that by the soul 306 *Inland, within 13
Thy soul was like a Star, and dwelt apart ; 307 *Milton ! thou 9
To have one Soul, and perish to a man, 310 *Invasion* 18
My Soul, a sorrowful interpreter, 311 *Who rises 22
The free-born Soul—that World whose vaunted skill 313 *Not 'mid 2
Dear Liberty ! stern Nymph of soul untamed ; 314 *Advance—come 2
There is a bulwark in the soul. This knew 315 *And is it 6
Dwells in the affections and the soul of man 315 *O'er the 2
Of awful prudence, keep the unvanquished soul : 316 *It was a 11
Shine on his soul, reflected from the days 318 *Is there 13
With firmer soul, yet labour to regain 318 *Biscayan* 2
A Soul by contemplation sanctified. 320 *O'erweening Statesmen 8
Upon his inner soul in mercy shine ; 323 *Now that 11
The Bard—whose soul is meek as dawning day, 326 *The Bard 1
And oft my soul hath kindled at the same, 329 *Ode : Thanks.* 45
That soul of Evil—which, from Hell let loose, 330 *Ode : Thanks.* 95
To highest Heaven—the labour of the Soul ; 331 *Ode : Thanks.* 172
Shall lack not power the "meeting soul to pierce!" 333 *Ded. Tour* 14
Such feeling pressed upon my soul, 334 *In Bruges 33
Let all remind the soul of heaven ; 341 *San Salv.* 14
The Soul transported sees, from hint of thine, 345 *Ambition—following 11
His soul her daily tasks renewed, 348 *Lulled by 56
Filling the soul with sentiments august— 351 *Des. Stanzas* 80
To move in sunshine ?—Utter thanks, my Soul ! 354 *Aquap.* 88
No faculty within us which the Soul 357 *Aquap.* 342
Reclined, shall I have yielded up my soul 358 *Aquap.* 359
Assent is power, belief the soul of fact. 359 *Those old 14
To be ; by Faith, not sight, his soul must live ; 363 *Grieve for 11
Give him a soul that cleaveth unto Thee. 363 *The world forsaken 14

Soul—*continued.*
Unblamed—if the Soul be intent on the day 364 *Vallomb.* 35
To the sad soul give hope of pardon free. 366 *Eternal Lord 8
And to her name my soul shall cleave in sorrow ;" 374 *Eg. Maid* 326
Then eased his soul at length by praise 374 *Eg. Maid* 341
And soul, to mingle with Eternity ! 384 *Duddon* 33. 14
So may the Soul, through powers that Faith bestows, 390 *Glencroe* 13
How Una, sad of soul—in sad attire, 395 *White Doe : Ded.* 6
By which the soul—with patient steps of thought 396 *Action is 9
To the grief of her soul that doth come and go, 398 *White Doe* 236
That soul of conscientious daring. 401 *White Doe* 475
Of love on which his soul was bent. 401 *White Doe* 520
And be in heart and soul the same 402 *White Doe* 562
A Soul, by force of sorrows high, 402 *White Doe* 585
Her soul doth in itself stand fast, 414 *White Doe* 1623
Into a soul which now was blest 415 *White Doe* 1756
Thy soul, exalted Emily, 416 *White Doe* 1866
That fills the Soul with unavailing ruth. 419 *Ecc. Sonn.* 1. 4. 14
The human Soul ; not utterly unknown 422 *Ecc. Sonn.* 1. 16. 9
The Soul to purer worlds : and *who* the line 423 *Ecc. Sonn.* 1. 18. 12
That the firm soul is clothed with fruit divine ! 423 *Ecc. Sonn.* 1. 19. 5
The recreant soul, that dares to shun the debt 424 *Ecc. Sonn.* 1. 23. 10
When thy great soul was freed from mortal chains, 425 *Ecc. Sonn.* 1. 27. 1
And comfortless despairs the soul benumb. 427 *Ecc. Sonn.* 1. 36. 14
And nature God disdained not ; Man—whose soul 429 *Ecc. Sonn.* 2. 4. 11
The unconverted soul with awe submit. 430 *Ecc. Sonn.* 2. 9. 14
From rites that trample upon soul and sense. 431 *Ecc. Sonn.* 2. 11. 14
Than that the Soul, freed from the bonds of Sense, 436 *Ecc. Sonn.* 2. 30. 2
Fear to my Soul, and sadness which might seem 440 *Ecc. Sonn.* 3. 2. 2
Shines through his soul—" that he may see and tell 441 *Ecc. Sonn.* 3. 4. 13
But who would force the Soul tilts with a straw 442 *Ecc. Sonn.* 3. 7. 13
Recall the wandering Soul to sympathy 445 *Ecc. Sonn.* 3. 20. 13
By chain yet stronger must the Soul be tied : 446 *Ecc. Sonn.* 3. 25. 1
Nor quits the Body when the Soul is freed, 448 *Ecc. Sonn.* 3. 31. 3
Long lines of mighty Kings—look forth, my Soul ! 452 *Ecc. Sonn.* 3. 47. 9
Breathe through my soul the blessing of thy grace, 454 *The Sun, that 22
The soul of Genius, if he dare to take 455 *Not in the lucid 12
In classic ages men perceived a soul 456 *The leaves 26
As may attune his soul to meet the dower 458 *Had this 59
My soul, though yet confined to earth, 458 *Had this 77
A part so charmed the pensive soul : 472 *Ossian* 4
Brothers in soul ! though distant times 473 *Ossian* 63
May be discovered what in soul ye are. 477 *Steamboats* 8
The human soul that through me ran ; 482 *Lines : Spring* 6
Thy ever-dwindling soul, away ! 485 *Poet's Epitaph* 24
One to whose smooth-rubbed soul can cling 485 *Poet's Epitaph* 29
—Thou soul of God's best earthly mould ! 486 *Matthew* 29
Thou happy Soul ! and can it be 486 *Matthew* 30
A soul of love, love's intellectual law :— 491 *Tribute : Dog* 33
Through no disturbance of my soul, 492 *Duty* 33
By objects, which might force the soul to abate 493 *Hap. War.* 19
Is yet a Soul whose master-bias leans 494 *Hap. War.* 59
And from the love which was in her soul 494 *Force of Prayer* 11
Transparent as the soul of innocent youth, 496 *A little 22
To calm the affections, elevate the soul, 496 *A little 56
Be hopeful Spring the favourite of the Soul ! 497 *Lycoris* 54
Or, if the soul to bondage be subdued, 501 *Humanity* 67
Body and mind and soul ; a thirst so keen 501 *Humanity* 91
Whose infant soul was tutored to confide 504 *Warning* 55
But turn, my Soul, and from the sleeping pair 505 *Warning* 158
The soul to love the more ; 506 *While from 50
Thou be that, kindling with a poet's soul, 508 *F. Stone* 23
Humbling the body, to exalt the soul ; 510 *Among a 4
And, to atone for it, with soul unshaken 517 *Pun. Death* 3. 12
And keep vindictive thirstings from the soul, 518 *Pun. Death* 7. 11
And wafts at will the contrite soul to bliss. 519 *Pun. Death* 11. 14
A soul so pitiably forlorn, 534 *Blest is 61
Do my sinful soul demand, 535 *Egremont* 28
And trouble from the soul. 542 *Russ. Fug.* 48
A statue of the soul. 543 *Russ. Fug.* 176
As his own soul. And, when with eye upraised 551 *If thou in 16
That in my soul methinks I yet do hear 563 *Troilus* 61
That in my soul I feel the joy of it. 564 *Troilus* 154
A life and soul, to every mode of being 567 *Cumb. Beg.* 78
Which reason cherishes. And thus the soul, 567 *Cumb. Beg.* 102
Wherewith to satisfy the human soul ? 568 *Cumb. Beg.* 146
The fields better suited the ease of his soul : 569 *Farmer* 22
More of soul in his face than of words on his tongue ; 570 *Farmer* 66
Youth amiable ; O friend so true of soul 575 *Chiabrera* 7. 3
Into a passionate lament ?—O Soul ! 575 *Chiabrera* 8. 18
She came, though meek of soul, in seemly pride 576 *By a 3
And seen the soul of truth in every part, 578 *Peele Castle* 31
A deep distress hath humanised my Soul. 578 *Peele Castle* 36
—A few (my soul oft sees that sight) 579 *Sweet Flower 46
For such a gentle Soul and sweet, 580 *Sweet Flower 61
A soul by resignation sanctified : 584 *Ch. Lamb* 31
Through God, is raised a spirit and soul of love 585 *Ch. Lamb* 66
Calmed in his soul the fear of change and death. 587 *Crosth.* 18
The Soul that rises with us, our life's Star, 588 *Immortality* 59
Full soon thy Soul shall have her earthly freight, 589 *Immortality* 130
Binding the charmed soul in powerless trance, 604 *Desc. Sk. Quarto* 98
Breathe o'er the failing soul voluptuous dreams ; 605 *Desc.Sk.Quarto* 157
Felt only there, oppress his labouring soul, 608 *Desc.Sk.Quarto* 353
But now with other soul I stand alone 609 *Desc.Sk.Quarto* 366
Uncertain thro' his fierce uncultur'd soul 612 *Desc.Sk.Quarto* 546
—And thou ! fair favoured region ! which my soul 615 *Desc.Sk.Quarto* 740
Where Machination her fell soul resigns, 617 *Desc.Sk.Quarto* 796
In the dark mansions of the bigot's soul, 618 *School Ex.* 34
The shades of night no more the soul involve, 618 *School Ex.* 47
No shadowy forms entice the soul aside, 619 *School Ex.* 51

Soul-illumination. Of soul-illumination) calls him forth . . . 682 *Prelude* 6. 514
Soul-inflamed. And Gideon blew the trumpet, soul-inflamed, . . . 870 *Excursion* 7. 815
Soulless. To have a soulless image on the eye . . 683 *Prelude* 6. 526
Soul-moving. Soul-moving sight! . . . . . 285 *Grave of Burns* 64
By the deep soul-moving sense . . . . . . 328 *Ode 1815* 68
Soul-quick'ning. Let Bacchus, donor of soul-quick'ning cheer, . . . 625 *Æneid* 112
Soul's. Mighty were the soul's commandments . 141 *Arm. Lady* 87
And, to my soul's content, I find . . . . 174 *Waggoner* 1. 114
And for a moment meet the soul's desires! . . 325 *Ode 1814* 126
Clasping her beauty in my soul's embrace. . . 365 **Rapt above* 8
The soul's deep valley was not slow . . . 386 *Yarrow Rev.* 39
Moved gently in her soul's soft sleep; . . . 415 *White Doe* 1794
The Soul's eternal interests to promote: . . 423 *Ecc. Sonn.* 1. 18. 2
The shrouded Body to the Soul's command . . 437 *Ecc. Sonn.* 2. 35. 8
Come not to speed the Soul's deliverance; . . 455 **Not in the lucid* 29
Her intercessions made for the soul's rest . . 467 *St. Bees* 66
The soul's desire—a lay . . . . . 507 *May* 12
The soul's pure brightness he beheld . . . 545 *Russ. Fug.* 323
I resign my soul's emotions . . . . . 550 *Hermit's Cell* 4. 3
Of goodness, next her Son, our soul's best boot. . 552 *Prioress* 14
Thy Soul's immensity; . . . . . . 589 *Immortality* 109
Of her soul's beauty; farther I was then . . 693 *Prelude* 7. 397
This the soul's last and lowest ebb; I drooped, . 731 *Prelude* 11. 307
Conceptions equal to the soul's desires; . . 803 *Excursion* 4. 137
Depresses the soul's vigour. Quit your couch— . 808 *Excursion* 4. 481
For her soul's good? Nor was that office vain. . 854 *Excursion* 6. 1041
The household lost their pride and soul's delight. 868 *Excursion* 7. 686
Souls. Where Souls are self-defended, free to grow 57 *Bord.* 1115
Of our emasculated souls, the tyranny . . . 64 *Bord.* 1490
And all the happy Souls that rode . . . . 168 *Pilgrim's Dream* 60
"Blithe souls and lightsome hearts have we . 177 *Waggoner* 2. 52
Here are twenty souls happy as souls in a dream: 189 *Music* 42
Or is it that, when human Souls a journey long have had . . . . . . 189 *Star-gazers* 19
Have souls which never yet have risen, and therefore prostrate lie? . . . . . . 189 *Star-gazers* 23
The birds pour forth their souls in notes . . 228 *Devot. Incit.* 17
Yea, both for souls who God's forbearance try, 229 *Cuckoo-clock* 43
Art, daring because souls could feel, . . . 234 *Power of Sound* 122
And save your souls alive! . . . . . 247 *P. B.* 950
Pleased if some Souls (for such there needs must be) 250 **Nuns fret* 12
Takest away, and into souls dost creep, . . 253 **Fond words* 8
With heaven, our souls more fit for future glory, . 281 **What strong* 12
Hath brought forth no such souls as we had then. 307 **Great men* 10
Their fetters in their souls. For who could be, . 308 **There is a bondage* 6
Never may from our souls one truth depart— . 321 **Here pause* 7
And strength of love our souls shall elevate: . . 332 *Ode: Thanks.* 223
How blest the souls who when their trials come . 339 *Tell* 19
Whose souls take pride in freedom, virtue, fame, 366 **Fair Land* 2
For Souls familiar with the eternal Voice; . . 391 *Brownie* 12
For Souls whose doom is fixed! The way is smooth 423 *Ecc. Sonn.* 1. 20. 9
Their feeble Souls; and bear with *his* regrets, . 446 *Ecc. Sonn.* 3. 23. 12
Of cloistered Architects, free their souls to fill 467 *St. Bees* 119
Of conscience souls are placed by deeds that lack 475 **Here on their* 5
We'll frame the measure of our souls: . . . 483 *Sister* 35
Of humbler name; whose souls do, like the flood 495 *Fact* 40
To which our souls must bend; . . . . 497 *Lycoris* 40
Which, haply, kindred souls may prize . . . 499 **Departing summer* 22
Yes, for them whose souls have scope . . . 503 **Like a* 64
Was to your souls, and, to the thoughts of others, 586 *Ch. Lamb* 126
Our Souls have sight of that immortal sea . . 590 *Immortality* 167
In that stern countenance, for our souls thence drew . . . . 622 *Recluse* 1. 1. 164
And Souls of lonely places! can I think . . 639 *Prelude* 1. 466
O Heavens! how awful is the might of souls, . 651 *Prelude* 3. 177
Points have we all of us within our souls . . 651 *Prelude* 3. 185
That in the name of all inspirèd souls— . . 668 *Prelude* 5. 201
Whose souls were sick with pain of what would be 724 *Prelude* 10. 395
With their whole souls went culling from the day 727 *Prelude* 11. 37
There saw into the depth of human souls, . . 742 *Prelude* 13. 166
Souls that appear to have no depth at all . . 742 *Prelude* 13. 167
Meek men, whose very souls perhaps would sink . 744 *Prelude* 13. 269
Words are but under-agents in their souls; . . 744 *Prelude* 13. 273
Smooth words he had to wheedle simple souls; . 775 *Excursion* 2. 254
An object whereunto their souls are tied . . 790 *Excursion* 3. 294
The crown of wisdom—to yield up their souls . 791 *Excursion* 3. 350
Soul of our Souls, and safeguard of the world! . 801 *Excursion* 4. 28
That harboured them,—the souls retaining yet . 814 *Excursion* 4. 900
Of our own souls! And if indeed there be . . 815 *Excursion* 4. 968
Do, in the constitution of their souls, . . . 818 *Excursion* 4. 1107
But whom, I ask, of individual Souls, . . . 827 *Excursion* 5. 353
Two several souls alternately had lodged, . . 842 *Excursion* 6. 288
Though with her plumes impaired. If they, whose souls . . . . 886 *Excursion* 9. 173
Who in the anguish of their souls bewail . . 894 *Excursion* 9. 659
Of humbler name, whose souls do like the flood S.3. 427 **My Son* 11
Good honest souls!—if right my judgment lies L.I. 95 *Juvenal* 3. 20
Soul-shattered. Soul-shattered was the Knight, nor knew . . . . 479 *Somnamb.* 127
Soul-sick. Of soul-sick flesh and weary bones; . . 301 *Bran* 102
Soul-smitten. Soul-smitten; for, that instant did appear . . . . 264 *Storm* 10
Soul-soothing. Soul-soothing Art! whom Morning, Noon-tide, Even, ... 252 *Picture* 9
Soul-strengthening. Soul-strengthening patience, and sublime content. . . . . . 813 *Excursion* 4. 818
Soul-subduing. Their soul-subduing looks might cheat . . . . 232 *Jew. Fam.* 35
Watch, and be firm! for soul-subduing vice, . . 420 *Ecc. Sonn.* 1. 8. 1
To cast a soul-subduing shade on me, ... 470 *Bala-Sala* 6
Soul-sustaining. With virtuous friendship's soul-sustaining aid, ... 823 *Excursion* 5. 58
Sound. Some (hear you not their chisels' clinking sound?) . . . . 5 *Ev. Wk.* 162
Sound of closed gate, across the water borne, . . 9 *Ev. Wk.* 373
How calm! how still! the only sound, . . . 9 *Collins* 21
Chains that were loosened only by the sound . . 11 *Desc. Sk.* 57
And quickens the blithe sound of oars that pass . 13 *Desc. Sk.* 125
His children's children listened to the sound; . 13 *Desc. Sk.* 152
Mocks the dull ear of Time with deaf abortive sound. . . . . 16 *Desc. Sk.* 315
How still! no irreligious sound or sight . . 16 *Desc. Sk.* 352
And with that voice accords the soothing sound . 16 *Desc. Sk.* 356
That dark mysterious gulf ascending, sound . . 18 *Desc. Sk.* 415
And, blest within himself, he shrinks not from the sound. . . . . 19 *Desc. Sk.* 491
Sole sound, the Sourd prolongs his mournful cry; 21 *Desc. Sk.* 619
A sound of chains along the desert rang; . . . 25 *Guilt* 77
Nor any friendly sound his footsteps led; . . . 26 *Guilt* 132
Her he addressed in words of cheering sound; . 27 *Guilt* 185
Nor voice, nor sound, that moment's pain expressed, 30 *Guilt* 308
Nature by sign or sound made no essay; . . . 35 *Guilt* 623
And never heard a sound so terrible. . . . 53 *Bord.* 888
A sound of laughter, too!—'tis well—I feared 60 *Bord.* 1260
From such rough dealing. Ha! what sound is that? . . . . 67 *Bord.* 1661
And that—what is it? never was sound so like . 67 *Bord.* 1666
Returning late, I heard a moaning sound; . . 73 *Bord.* 2045
To climb up to the spot whence the sound came; 73 *Bord.* 2060
Alas! 'tis the sound of the eight o'clock bell. . 81 †*Address: Child* 37
Was smitten with a startling sound. . . . 82 *Alice Fell* 4
I heard the sound,—and more and more; . . . 82 *Alice Fell* 6
But there was neither sound nor sight . . . 83 *Lucy Gray* 35
Made answer to that plaintive sound. . . . 85 *Shepherd-boys* 77
To their echoes gave the sound, ... 94 *Westmoreland Girl* 62
This is sad talk—they'll never sound for him— . 100 *Brothers* 315
"It is the king, my brother!" and, by sound . 104 *Artegal* 120
Your sound my heart of rest bereaves, . . . 111 **'Tis said that some* 23
Within the sound of Emma's voice, nor know . 111 **'Tis said that some* 51
No sound *here* sweeps away the will . . . 112 **How rich* 12
Than desolate; for oft-times from the sound . . 118 *Maternal Grief* 43
And thence full many a sound she hears, . . 127 *Idiot Boy* 140
The streams with softest sound are flowing, . . 129 *Idiot Boy* 284
Murmur as with the sound of summer flies. . . 133 *Michael* 128
Sent forth such sallies of glad sound, that all . 146 **It was an* 23
The fir-grove murmurs with a sea-like sound, . . 151 **When, to* 104
Rushed o'er the wood with startling sound; . . 154 **A whirl-blast* 2
A boding sound—for aught but sleep unfit! . . 167 *Pilgrim's Dream* 51
Strikes a solitary sound. . . . . . . 171 *Kitten* 84
Mixed with a faint yet grating sound . . . 173 *Waggoner* 1. 27
Thence the sound—the light is there— . . . 176 *Waggoner* 2. 23
He hears a sound and sees the light, . . . 177 *Waggoner* 2. 28
Hushed was by this the fiddle's sound, . . . 178 *Waggoner* 2. 135
And little other sound was heard; . . . . 182 *Waggoner* 4. 237
I heard the murmur and the murmuring sound, . 185 *Nutting* 38
And beauty born of murmuring sound . . . . 187 **Three years* 29
While she dandles the Babe in her arms to the sound. 189 *Music* 40
Irregular in sight or sound . . . . . 193 *Ruth* 128
Giving to her sound for sound! . . . . . 209 **Yes, it* 4
He hears an uncouth sound— . . . . . 213 *Dion* 64
Faint, faint at first; and then an eager sound . 218 *Recluse* 1. 1. 220
Blows keenly, it sends forth a creaking sound . 219 *Haunted Tree* 22
And, after prelude of unearthly sound . . . 226 *Vernal Ode* 23
—A slender sound! yet hoary Time . . . 227 *Vernal Ode* 91
That, answering to thy touch, will sound the hour; 229 *Cuckoo-clock* 6
Regent of sound, have dangerous Passions trod! 233 *Power of Sound* 82
Leave for one chant;—the dulcet sound . . 234 *Power of Souud* 134
Stern Winter loves a dirge-like sound. . . . 235 *Power of Sound* 192
The soul of happy sound was spread, . . . 239 *P. B.* 257
Or whence the might of this strange sound? . . 241 *P. B.* 482
The river's depth to sound. . . . . . 242 *P. B.* 555
When hark a burst of doleful sound! . . . 243 *P. B.* 611
But whence this faintly-rustling sound . . . 244 *P. B.* 701
A muffled noise—a rumbling sound!— . . . 245 *P. B.* 837
Over that dull and dreary sound. . . . . 246 *P. B.* 875
For well did Peter know the sound; . . . 246 *P. B.* 876
He listens—not a sound is heard . . . . 247 *P. B.* 997
One after one; the sound of rain, and bees . . 253 **A flock* 2
And sound thy praises everlastingly. . . . 257 **The prayers* 14
A sound like thunder—everlastingly. . . . 258 **It is a* 8
A thousand times this pipe did Tasso sound; . . 260 **Scorn not* 5
A home that by such miracle of sound . . . 267 *St. Cath.* 10
Their several features, mingled like the sound . 271 **Where holy* 7
And from one voice a Hymn with tuneful sound . 283 **Well have* 5
I liked the greeting; 'twas a sound . . . . 289 *Stepping West.* 13
The very sound of courtesy: . . . . . 289 *Stepping West.* 20
Is overflowing with the sound. . . . . . 289 *Sol. Reap.* 8
At sound of Rob Roy's name. . . . . . 292 *Rob Roy* 120
With sound the least that can be made, . . . 297 *Highland Boy* 196
With sound like lamentation. . . . . . 297 *Highland Boy* 230
What strife of colour, shape and sound . . . 300 *Bran* 24
To sound the depths of every Art . . . . 301 *Bran* 117
A homeless sound of joy was in the sky: . . . 304 **Jones! as* 5
Consul, or King, can sound himself to know . . 304 **Festivals have* 13

Sovereign's. An English Sovereign's brow! and to the throne — 838 *Excursion* 6. 2
Sovereigns. Where England's sovereigns sit in long array, — 689 *Prelude* 7. 137
From sovereigns deep in pedigree intrenched. — L.I. 97 *Juvenal* 3. 93
Sovereignty. If it confined the robe of sovereignty. — 104 *Artegal* 157
Mount Skiddaw? In his natural sovereignty — 251 **Pelion and* 11
An ample sovereignty of eye and ear. — 267 **Though narrow* 4
Proofs of a higher sovereignty I claim; — 270 **Shame on* 10
And, wheresoe'er she spread her sovereignty, — 311 **Who rises* 31
From Love's uneasy sovereignty— — 344 **How blest* 2
Of visual sovereignty—hills multitudinous, — 353 *Aquap.* 40
But manly sovereignty its hold retains; — 425 *Ecc. Sonn.* 1. 27. 8
Hence, with the spiritual sovereignty transferred — 435 *Ecc. Sonn.* 2. 28. 12
Feels through her lowest depths thy sovereignty; — 459 **Wanderer! that* 49
Like Mona's miniature of sovereignty. — 471 *Tynwald* 14
Mustering a face of haughty sovereignty, — 495 *Fact* 2
The sovereignty of May. — 507 **While from* 64
Is gone who held us both in sovereignty. — 563 *Troilus* 28
As thou art wont, thy sovereignty adorn — 628 **Deign, Sovereign* 13
Made manifest in Nature's sovereignty, — 713 *Prelude* 9. 235
His scorned, or unacknowledged, sovereignty. — 811 *Excursion* 4. 662
In awful sovereignty; a place of power, — 885 *Excursion* 9. 55
Meantime the sovereignty of these fair Isles — 889 *Excursion* 9. 344
Sow. Build for him, sow for him, and at his call — 195 *Resolution* 41
Whether men sow or reap the fields, — 228 *Devot. Incit.* 70
With prayers and blessings we your path will sow; — 427 *Ecc. Sonn.* 1. 33. 5
That he, who would sow death, reaps death, or worse, — 728 *Prelude* 11. 67
Far as it might be urged, to sow afresh — 815 *Excursion* 4. 907
Falsehood and guile, be left to sow their seed; — 894 *Excursion* 9. 662
Sower. But where the sower dwelt was nowhere to be found. — 24 *Guilt* 27
Sown. *See* **Self-sown.**
On earth was never sown; — 187 **Three years* 3
The seeds of malice were not sown; — 227 *Vernal Ode* 126
Has sown as yields, we trust, the fruit of fame — 278 *Wellington* 12
From rash assault? Schemes of retirement sown — 282 *Railway* 2
In stiff confusion set or sown, — 301 *Bran* 123
But that's a loyal virtue, never sown — 303 **Is it* 10
For by her Son's blest hand the seed was sown. — 360 *Albano* 14
Came those live herbs? by what hand were they sown — 387 *Roslin* 9
Pools, terraces, and walks are sown — 413 *White Doe* 1570
With speculative notions rashly sown, — 437 *Ecc. Sonn.* 2. 37. 9
Had sown the spot, that witnessed them, with seeds — 466 *St. Bees* 60
Fields gaily sown when promises were cheap.— — 505 *Warning* 139
And let us utter thanks for blessings sown — 524 *Epist. Beaumont* 201
Are sown in every human breast, to beauty — 538 **In desultory* 38
But that the precious love this friend hath sown — 627 **We gaze* 2
Beneath the oaks' umbrageous covert, sown — 643 *Prelude* 2. 60
His habits were first sown, even as a seed? — 645 *Prelude* 2. 207
Nothing but a wild field where they were sown. — 651 *Prelude* 3. 180
Or pleasure sown, or fostered thus, may be — 668 *Prelude* 5. 194
By naked huts, wood-built, and sown like tents — 683 *Prelude* 6. 521
Oh, joy to him who here hath sown, hath laid — 749 *Prelude* 14. 219
Oh! many are the Poets that are sown — 757 *Excursion* 1. 77
Even here, where her amenities are sown — 819 *Excursion* 4. 1192
But thinly sown these natures; rare, at least, — 835 *Excursion* 5. 878
Tall ash-tree, sown by winds, by vapours nursed, — 866 *Excursion* 7. 596
We look for health from seeds that have been sown — 886 *Excursion* 9. 141
Space. His prey, through tracts abrupt of desolate space, — 16 *Desc. Sk.* 306
The wider space the better—we may find — 78 *Bord.* 2307
Nothing but silence and empty space; — 80 †*Address: Child* 17
That absorbs time, space, and number; — 90 *Longest Day* 47
What space hath Virgin's beauty to disclose — 110 **Look at* 10
I look—the sky is empty space; — 110 **'Tis said that some* 18
Much how the Youth, in scanty space of time, — 124 *V. and J.* 178
Large space beneath, as duly as the light — 133 *Michael* 113
And on a summit, distant a short space, — 146 **It was an* 34
—When I had gazed perhaps two minutes' space, — 147 *Joanna* 51
A length of open space, where to and fro — 150 **When, to* 37
Made this orchard's narrow space, — 171 *Kitten* 51
Our roads, through many a long year's space, — 182 *Waggoner* 4. 219
He comes to tarry with thee three hours' space; — 209 *Laod.* 23
That, for a brief space, checks the hurrying stream! — 220 *Haunted Tree* 40
Through space, though calm, not raised above — 225 *Present.* 32
As if no space below the sky — 228 *Devot. Incit.* 9
Large space ('mid dreadful clouds) of purest sky, — 264 *Storm* 11
Such transport, though but for a moment's space; — 270 **Shame on* 2
Formal, and circumscribed in time and space; — 321 **The power* 2
(Though it were only for a moment's space) — 323 **Now that* 13
For victory shaped an open space, — 341 *San Salv.* 33
Smooth space of turf which from the guardian fort — 356 *Aquap.* 224
How wide a space can part from inward peace — 363 **Grieve for* 13
Leads through space of open day, — 397 *White Doe* 84
And, in seven days' space, will to York be led!— — 404 *White Doe* 788
There Francis for a moment's space — 412 *White Doe* 1442
Apart, some little space, was made — 412 *White Doe* 1524
False in the issue, that yon seeming space — 461 **Who but is* 10
We breathed together for a moment's space, — 464 **A point* 12
Pleased with your triumphs o'er his brother Space, — 477 *Steamboats* 12
He comes not back; an ampler space — 479 *Somnamb.* 68
I marvel how Nature could ever find space — 482 *Character* 1
This Dog, had been through three months' space — 492 *Fidelity* 56
Yet cool the space within, and not uncheered — 497 **Enough of climbing* 24

Space—*continued.*
What, is there then no space for golden mean — 516 **Hard task* 8
—This Dwelling's Inmate more than three weeks' space — 521 *Epist. Beaumont* 26
And thus through many seasons' space — 532 †*Float. Isl.* 17
Gave to her thought, that in a little space — 555 *Prioress* 153
I prove it thus; for in no other space — 565 *Troilus* 158
For one poor moment's space to Thee, — 580 *John Words.* 8
Do thou, but for a single night's brief space, — 624 *Æneid* 36
Had also left less space within my mind, — 654 *Prelude* 3. 360
And lingered near the door a little space, — 665 *Prelude* 4. 468
Of reason, undisturbed by space or time; — 667 *Prelude* 5. 105
Space like a heaven filled up with northern lights, — 673 *Prelude* 5. 532
Which—to the boundaries of space and time, — 677 *Prelude* 6. 135
Of melancholy space and doleful time, — 677 *Prelude* 6. 136
Forth, through some Gothic window's open space, — 678 *Prelude* 6. 216
For two days' space, in presence of the Lake, — 685 *Prelude* 6. 689
A little space of intermediate time — 688 *Prelude* 7. 60
A sportive infant, who, for six months' space, — 692 *Prelude* 7. 337
Romantic almost, looked at through a space, — 693 *Prelude* 7. 442
Below, the open space, through every nook — 697 *Prelude* 7. 689
Nook is there none, nor tract of that vast space — 702 *Prelude* 8. 202
That after a short space works less and less, — 707 *Prelude* 8 573
Diffused through time and space, with aid derived — 708 *Prelude* 8' 611
Lofty and over-arched, with open space — 716 *Prelude* 9' 435
Had left an interregnum's open space — 727 *Prelude* 1.1. 33
Where the disturbances of space and time— — 732 *Prelude* 11. 30
Was like an invitation into space — 742 *Prelude* 13. 350
Unnoticed did I stand some minutes' space. — 762 *Excursion* 1.1443
An eager grasp; and many moments' space— — 779 *Excursion* 2. 519
Some little space disjoined, a pair were seen, — 787 *Excursion* 3. 58
Through time or space—if neither in the one, — 789 *Excursion* 3. 216
The space that severed us! But, as the sight — 795 *Excursion* 3. 661
Whose kingdom is, where time and space are not. — 802 *Excursion* 4. 76
Small space! but, for reiterated steps, — 805 *Excursion* 4. 245
Filling a space, else vacant, to exalt — 814 *Excursion* 4. 845
Small space of that green churchyard with a light — 826 *Excursion* 5. 229
Earth's melancholy vision through the space — 836 *Excursion* 5. 936
The fruits of earth through space of twice ten years, — 841 *Excursion* 6. 231
In social converse, or by some short space — 845 *Excursion* 6. 478
"Through four months' space the Infant drew its food — 852 *Excursion* 6. 939
Begun and ended within three days' space, — 853 *Excursion* 6. 967
For her own flowers and favourite herbs, a space, — 856 *Excursion* 6. 1163
Had never come, through space of forty years; — 861 *Excursion* 7. 245
Ten summers and ten winters of a space — 866 *Excursion* 7. 568
Seized him, that self-same night; and through the space — 870 *Excursion* 7. 871
Through earth, sky, water, and all visible space, — 893 *Excursion* 9. 612
Thick storm, and heavy, which for three hours' space — K.8. 228 **I will* 136
Could see them, nor in that small open space — K.8. 243 *Recluse* 1.1.258
Legions of devils through a key-hole's space. — L.I. 94 *Juvenal* 2. 4
Spaces. And be the guardian spaces — 324 *Ode 1814* 100
Or grass-grown spaces, where the heaviest foot — 355 *Aquap.* 194
Spacious. The spacious landscape change in form and hue! — 4 *Ev. Wk.* 99
From year to year the spacious floor — 154 **A whirl-blast* 9
Stand in the spacious firmament of time, — 317 **Brave Schill* 7
Along the surface of a spacious plain — 324 *Ode 1814* 55
Is life despised; ah no, the spacious earth — 325 **Intrepid sons* 2
Where now—within this spacious plot — 407 *White Doe* 983
Through woods and spacious forests,—to behold — 496 **A little* 34
Spread like a spacious Mere, we there could measure — 626 **The confidence* 11
Upon Winander's spacious breast, it chanced — 664 *Prelude* 4. 373
With high and spacious rooms, deafened and stunned — 684 *Prelude* 6. 646
A spacious grass-plot; there, in silence, sate — 696 *Prelude* 7. 607
The spacious city, and in progress passed — 719 *Prelude* 10. 50
Their tribes, till we behold a spacious plain — 807 *Excursion* 4. 434
To range her blooming bowers, and spacious fields, — 819 *Excursion* 4. 1194
And O, ye swelling hills, and spacious plains! — 838 *Excursion* 6. 17
Like trees in forests,—spread through spacious tracts, — 876 *Excursion* 8. 124
When, on thy bosom, spacious Windermere! — 891 *Excursion* 9. 485
Of this fair Vale, and o'er its spacious heights — K.8. 248 *Recluse* 1.1.431
Spade. Then, by the spade, or cleaving plough, — 391 *HighlandBroach* 83
And soon, full soon, the lonely Sexton's spade — 450 *Ecc. Sonn.* 3. 41. 8
Spade! with which Wilkinson hath tilled his lands, — 489 *Spade* 1
That man will have a trophy, humble Spade! — 489 *Spade* 19
Might hear his busy spade, which he would ply, — 764 *Excursion* 1. 529
With spade and mattock o'er his shoulder hung; — 825 *Excursion* 5. 222
And patient spade; praise to the simple crook, — 831 *Excursion* 5. 603
His spade and hoe, mattock and glittering scythe, — 880 *Excursion* 8. 426
Spades. With spades they would have sought. — 200 *Thorn* 224
Ironic diamonds,—clubs, hearts, diamonds, spades, — 640 *Prelude* 1. 527
Spain. Like a Sierra of cerulean Spain, — 268 **Four fiery* 5
The Gordon, sailed away to Spain; — 287 *Ellen Irwin* 38
I weigh the hopes and fears of suffering Spain; — 314 **Not 'mid* 10
Spain may be overpowered, and he possess, — 319 *Spaniard* 6
Were England's native growth; and throughout Spain — 319 **Avaunt all* 10
The Crescent glitters on the towers of Spain; — 427 *Ecc. Sonn.* 1. 34. 3
Nor is it silver of romantic Spain; — 480 *Cordelia* 5
And followers of Sertorius, out of Spain — 635 *Prelude* 1. 191
'My legions in Spain — S.3. 440 **Said red-ribboned* 2
Spake. He waked her—spake in tone that would not fail, — 27 *Guilt* 168
In converse that ensued she nothing spake; — 27 *Guilt* 188
And spake to you, why did you give no answer? — 55 *Bord.* 959

Spake—*continued.*
He only spake to me of a dear Daughter, . . . 74 *Bord.* 2067
" My cloak ! " no other word she spake, . . . 82 *Alice Fell* 21
For she looked with such a look, and she spake with such a tone, ... 88 *Pet-lamb* 67
The Child, as if the thunder's voice spake with articulate call, ... 92 *Poet's Dream* 9
Thus spake the homely Priest of Ennerdale. . . 95 *Brothers* 16
Then Artegal thus spake : " I only sought . . 104 *Artegal* 162
Admittance was denied. The young man spake . 125 *V. and J.* 265
Of those domestic tales that spake to me . . . 131 *Michael* 22
And thus the old Man spake to him :—" My son, 136 *Michael* 331
Thus spake the moral Muse—her wing . . . 154 *Flower Garden* 49
I spake, when whispered a low voice, ... 164 *Needlecase* 17
Thus Nature spake—The work was done— . . 187 **Three years* 37
But no ! he spake the English tongue, . . . 192 *Ruth* 26
He spake of plants that hourly change . . . 193 *Ruth* 55
The Youth of green savannahs spake, ... 193 *Ruth* 67
Mild Hermes spake—and touched her with his wand . . . . 209 *Laod.* 19
He spake of love, such love as Spirits feel . . . 211 *Laod.* 97
Spake of heroic arts in graver mood . . . . 211 *Laod.* 101
I spake with faltering voice, like one . . . . 238 *P. B.* 186
The voice was soft, and she who spake . . . 289 *Stepping West.* 17
As if a dead man spake it ! Yet despair . . . 304 **Jones ! as* 12
Spake laws to *them*, and said that by the soul . 306 **Inland, within* 13
That Shakspeare spake ; the faith and morals hold 307 **It is not* 12
Their monstrous Idol if the dead e'er spake, . . 325 *Enghien* 7
That spake of bards and minstrels ; and his spirit 353 *Aquap.* 61
Therefore the Voice spake from the Desert, thence 365 **The Baptist* 9
Spake bitter words ; words that did ill agree . . 367 **As indignation* 2
Thus to the Necromancer spake . . . . . 370 *Eg. Maid* 93
He spake ; and gliding into view . . . . . 371 *Eg. Maid* 175
He spake, and eight brave sons straightway . . 400 *White Doe* 412
She heard, but looked not up, nor spake ; . . . 401 *White Doe* 457
He spake bare truth ; for far and near . . . 403 *White Doe* 625
And thus abruptly spake ;—" We yield . . . 405 *White Doe* 809
He spake—" would stem, or quell, a force . . 405 *White Doe* 855
I overheard her as she spake . . . . . 405 *White Doe* 875
And spake in firm and earnest mood. . . . . 406 *White Doe* 896
Approached, and, greeting her, thus spake ; . . 408 *White Doe* 1077
She spake—and from the Lady's sight . . . 408 *White Doe* 1107
Coldly we spake. The Saxons, overpowered . . 426 *Ecc. Sonn.* 1. 32. 1
To Cæsar's Successor the Pontiff spake ; . . . 428 *Ecc. Sonn.* 1. 38. 2
Thus spake—and lo ! a Fleet, for Gaul addrest, 432 *Ecc. Sonn.* 2. 15. 10
Last night, without a voice, that Vision spake 440 *Ecc. Sonn.* 3. 2. 1
Some spake, by thought-perplexing fears betrayed ; 445 *Ecc. Sonn.* 3. 22. 6
So spake Sir Eglamore, and pressed . . . . 478 *Somnamb.* 43
To me my good friend Matthew spake, . . . 481 *Expost.* 15
So spake the mild Jeronymite, his griefs . . . 510 *F. Stone* 118
Yet spake this Child when sprinkled was the water ; 555 *Prioress* 189
The Nightingale thus in my hearing spake :— 558 *Cuck.andNight.* 111
Then spake one Bird, and full assent all gave ; 562 *Cuck.andNight.* 271
She spake and shed an offering on the board ; 625 *Æneid* 116
And common face of Nature spake to me . . . 641 *Prelude* 1. 587
Which spake perpetual logic to my soul, . . . 651 *Prelude* 3. 164
Spake with a sense of peace, at intervals . . 681 *Prelude* 6. 412
Black drizzling crags that spake by the way-side 684 *Prelude* 6. 631
Of Abyssinian privacy. I spake . . . . . 685 *Prelude* 6. 662
He spake with somewhat of a solemn tone : . . 765 *Excursion* 1. 605
So busy, that the things of which he spake . . 765 *Excursion* 1. 617
If I had seen her husband. As she spake . . 766 *Excursion* 1. 658
Recovering, to my Friend I said, " You spake, . 777 *Excursion* 2. 395
This had I seen, and saw ; but, till she spake, . 783 *Excursion* 2. 784
We spake—he made reply, but would not stir . 784 *Excursion* 2. 824
With courteous voice thus spake— " I should have grieved . . . . 788 *Excursion* 3. 116
But, while he spake, look, gesture, tone of voice, 793 *Excursion* 3. 463
To appear and answer ; to the grave I spake . . 796 *Excursion* 3. 689
I spake with vehemence ; and promptly seized . 797 *Excursion* 3. 795
That spake was capable to lift the soul . . . 805 *Excursion* 4. 252
With some impatience in his mien, he spake : . 817 *Excursion* 4. 1101
Our seats ; and thus the Solitary spake, . . . 826 *Excursion* 5. 232
With a complacent animation spake, ... 831 *Excursion* 5. 559
You," to the Pastor turning thus he spake, . . 832 *Excursion* 5. 628
Upon the earth beneath his feet ; and spake :— . 836 *Excursion* 5. 902
Then to the Solitary turned, and spake. . . . 839 *Excursion* 6. 94
" There," said the Vicar, pointing as he spake, . 848 *Excursion* 6. 675
She spake, yet, I believe, not unsustained . . . 849 *Excursion* 6. 767
Thus, in her Mother's hearing Ellen spake, . . 852 *Excursion* 6. 917
She spake, nor was the assurance unfulfilled ; . 852 *Excursion* 6. 928
When he had passed, the Solitary spake ; . . . 866 *Excursion* 7. 556
—And, surely, he, that spake with kindling brow, 869 *Excursion* 7. 804
While he advanced, thus spake : " Tradition tells 871 *Excursion* 7. 923
To his Compatriot, smiling as he spake ; . . . 874 *Excursion* 8. 33
That spake the Norman Conqueror's stern behest— 877 *Excursion* 8. 172
Thus calmly spake the venerable Sage, . . . 884 *Excursion* 9. 2
I spake of mischief by the wise diffused . . . 887 *Excursion* 9. 195
" Yes," he continued, kindling as he spake, . . 889 *Excursion* 9. 383
" Once," and with wild demeanour, as he spake, . 894 *Excursion* 9. 679

Span. And fixed an infant's span above . . . 169 *Wren's Nest* 42
Around those happy fields we span . . . . 237 *P. B.* 67
And she who span it culled the daintiest fleece, . 255 *Easter* 6
Impassioned dreams, that strove to span . . . 299 *Brownie's Cell* 59
A span of waters ; yet what power is there ! . . 306 **Inland, within* 7
And all the thoughts that lengthened out a span . 373 *Eg. Maid* 281
With but a span of sky between— . . . . . 459 **The Crescent* 3
Soon as the measuring of life's little span . . . 478 **Lonsdale ! it* 13
And the blue sky, one little span of earth . . . 567 *Cumb. Beg.* 50
We ran a boisterous course ; the year span round 642 *Prelude* 2. 47
A span above man's common measure, tall, . . 664 *Prelude* 4. 392

Spangled. Fire raged : and, when the spangled floor 168 *Pilgrim'sDream* 57
Spangled with drops of that celestial shower. . . 169 *Love lies Bleeding* 17
Earth, spangled sky, and lake serene, ... 178 *Waggoner* 3. 38
Thy handmaid Frost with spangled tissue quaint 376 *Duddon* 2. 5
The spangled turf, and neighbouring thickets ring 387 **Part fenced* 13
Spread o'er the spangled sign-board, had dislodged 644 *Prelude* 2. 151
Spangled with kindred multitudes of stars, . . 651 *Prelude* 3. 162
Whose genius spangled o'er a gloomy theme . . 695 *Prelude* 7. 565

Spangling. Spangling a cushion green like moss ; . 580 *John Words.* 57

Spaniard. The Frenchman and the Spaniard ; from remote . . . . 690 *Prelude* 7. 225

Spaniards. Spaniards of every rank, by whom the good 320 **O'erweeningStatesmen* 10

Spanish. You have heard " a Spanish Lady . . 139 *Arm. Lady* 1
The roving Spanish Bands are reached at last, . 320 **Hunger, and* 5
A mantle such as Spanish Cavaliers . . . . 561 *Prelude* 4. 221
Bishops, of milder Spanish breed, shall boast . L.1. 89 *Juvenal* 1. 25

Spanned. *See* **Wide-spanned.**
And through a rainbow-arch that spanned the street, ... 725 *Prelude* 10. 495

Spanning. Proud as a rainbow spanning half the vale, 111 *'*Tis said that some* 38
" This Land of Rainbows spanning glens whose walls, ... 388 *Loch Etive* 1

Spans. He leaned upon the bridge that spans the glen, ... 73 *Bord.* 2015
That work of kindred frame, which spans the lake 351 *Des. Stanzas* 60
And mark that daisied hillock, three spans long ! 867 *Excursion* 7. 635

Spare. To his spare meal he calls the passing poor ; 11 *Desc. Sk.* 30
She is gone before, to spare my weariness. . . 43 *Bord.* 338
Reverence for life so deeply, that they spare . . 48 *Bord.* 586
The verminous brood, and cherish what they spare 48 *Bord.* 587
Spare me awhile that greeting. It may be . . 64 *Bord.* 1507
'Tis needless ; spare your violence. His Daughter—— . . . . 74 *Bord.* 2093
We must spare them—here are many : . . . 79 *Foresight* 4
Only spare the strawberry-blossom ! . . . . 79 *Foresight* 16
And for that promise spare the flower ! . . . 80 *Foresight* 32
Heaven grant that he spare but that one upright twig . . . . 80 †*Address : Child* 24
With so much happiness to spare, ... 85 *Anecdote* 15
Spare your blame,—remembrance makes him . 93 *Westmoreland Girl* 33
They, notwithstanding, had much love to spare, . 99 *Brothers* 247
To me a kingdom ! spare the bitter scorn : . . 104 *Artegal* 141
That God poor Susan's life would spare, . . . 128 *Idiot Boy* 200
The Doctor's self could hardly spare : . . . . 128 *Idiot Boy* 238
The half-blown rose, the lily spare ? . . . . 154 *Flower Garden* 12
The one-pennied Boy has his penny to spare. . 188 *Music* 28
Ah, spare the exulting smile, ... 215 *Enterprise* 7
In perfect shape (whose beauty Time shall spare . 250 **Happy the* 2
And, if Time spare the colours for the grace . . 276 *Author's Portrait* 3
For nought but what thy happiness could spare. . 277 **Why art* 8
Oh ! spare to sweep, thou mournful blast, . . 285 *Grave of Burns* 59
To spare your failings for his sake, ... 286 *Sons of Burns* 20
Of future war. Advance not—spare to hide, . . 334 **Bruges I* 10
Can spare, and humblest earthly Weal demands, . 357 *Aquap.* 343
And cannot spare the Thing he cherished : . . 370 *Eg. Maid* 50
She guards thee, ruthless Power ! who would not spare . . . . 376 *Duddon* 2. 9
Prejudged by foes determined not to spare, . . 440 *Ecc. Sonn.* 2. 45. 1
Spare it, ye waves, and lift the mariner, . . . 469 **The feudal* 9
Spare, too, the human helpers ! Do they stir . 469 **The feudal* 11
Into his English breast, and spare to quake . . 504 *Warning* 80
Lest, capital pains remitting till ye spare . . . 518 *Pun. Death* 4. 7
How venture then to hope that Time will spare . 549 **The massy* 4
Such wickedness his judgments cannot spare ; . 555 *Prioress* 180
But will the Lightning glance aside to spare . . 628 *Installation* 11
I spare to tell of what ensued, the life . . . 633 *Prelude* 1. 108
But spare the House of God. Was ever known . 655 *Prelude* 3. 405
Spare diet, patient labour, and plain weeds. . . 655 *Prelude* 3. 457
Moves the great spirit of human knowledge, spare 681 *Prelude* 6. 450
Slight, if you will, the *means* ; but spare to slight 791 *Excursion* 3. 360
But spare your pity, if there be in me . . . 800 *Excursion* 3. 965
Spare them, they shall continue to bestow, . . 838 *Excursion* 6. 36
Of that spare benefice. Yet not the less . . 860 *Excursion* 7. 167
Spare, burning sun of midsummer, these sods, . 868 *Excursion* 7. 702
That seemed to pity what he could not spare. . 883 *Excursion* 8. 571

Spared. Whose life and limbs the flood had spared ; 85 *Shepherd-boys* 94
Nor spared the reverend blood that feebly runs ; . 321 **Humanity,delighting* 23
Spared for obeisance from perpetual love, . . . 325 *Ode 1814* 121
To you who fell, and you whom slaughter spared 326 **Intrepid sons* 12
Have spared my Dwelling to this hour ; . . . 344 *Eclipse* 81
Whom grief hath spared—who sheds no tear . . 344 **How blest* 11
Has spared of sound and grave realities, . . . 359 *Plea : Hist.* 4
On the great flood were spared to live and move. 360 **Near Anio's* 8
A votive Column, spared by fire and flood :— . 367 *Trajan* 6
Like a lone criminal whose life is spared. . . . 388 *Eagles* 3
" Your noble brother hath been spared ; . . . 409 *White Doe* 1212
Thanks to the moth that spared it for our eyes ; . 526 **Soon did* 5
Is not a Ruin spared or made by time, . . . 548 **Stranger ! this* 2
At Wordsworth's suit been spared ; . . . . 549 **In these* 2
Yet haply Arno shall be spared all cause . . . 575 *Chiabrera* 6. 13
Some skill, and longer time than may be spared, . 662 *Prelude* 4. 292
Sprinkling this talk with questions, better spared, 665 *Prelude* 4. 438
With fellow-sufferers by the shipwreck spared, . 677 *Prelude* 6. 143
Of circumstances might to thee have spared . . 679 *Prelude* 6. 284
Spared not the empty throne, and in proud haste 718 *Prelude* 10. 39
Him, sleeping or awake, the robber spared ; . . 771 *Excursion* 2. 12

Speak—*continued.*
Creative agency. The song would speak — 647 *Prelude* 2. 382
To speak of you, ye mountains, and ye lakes — 648 *Prelude* 2. 424
I speak, unapprehensive of contempt, — 648 *Prelude* 2. 455
Let others that know more speak as they know. — 650 *Prelude* 3. 73
For (not to speak of Reason and her pure — 650 *Prelude* 3. 83
Her native instincts : let me dare to speak — 650 *Prelude* 3. 99
Why should I speak of what a thousand hearts — 659 *Prelude* 4. 44
And speak of war, battle, and pestilence, — 665 *Prelude* 4. 437
By these remembrances. Yet wherefore speak ? — 668 *Prelude* 5. 183
Their benediction ; speak of them as Powers — 669 *Prelude* 5. 218
In these enquiries, with regret I speak, — 676 *Prelude* 6. 118
By change of accidents, or even, to speak — 677 *Prelude* 6. 186
And groves I speak to thee, my Friend ! to thee, — 679 *Prelude* 6. 265
She ceased to speak, but while St. Bruno's pines — 681 *Prelude* 6. 436
Sate on a stone, and heard the bells speak out — 688 *Prelude* 7. 114
As hitherto, in freedom I may speak, — 698 *Prelude* 7. 762
It might be told (but wherefore speak of things — 707 *Prelude* 8. 518
To speak (as I must be compelled to do) — 711 *Prelude* 9. 112
Of whom I speak. So Beaupuy (let the name — 715 *Prelude* 9. 419
Of which I speak, only as they were storm — 720 *Prelude* 10. 121
" Go to the Poets, they will speak to thee — 735 *Prelude* 12. 68
I speak in recollection of a time — 736 *Prelude* 12. 127
To speak, what I myself have known and felt ; — 740 *Prelude* 13. 13
To watch and question those I met, and speak — 742 *Prelude* 13. 161
And sanctity of passion, speak of these, — 743 *Prelude* 13. 236
They do not breathe among them : this I speak — 744 *Prelude* 13. 275
We were as strangers ; and I may not speak — 745 *Prelude* 13. 362
Who know not what they speak. By love subsists — 748 *Prelude* 14. 168
Finally, and above all, O Friend ! (I speak — 750 *Prelude* 14. 321
Prophets of Nature, we to them will speak — 752 *Prelude* 14. 444
Which speak of nothing more than what we are, — 755 *Recluse* 1. 1. 812
From his sixth year, the Boy of whom I speak, — 758 *Excursion* 1. 118
And speak a plainer language. In the woods, — 761 *Excursion* 1. 347
Thus did he speak. " I see around me here — 763 *Excursion* 1. 469
And senseless rocks ; nor idly ; for they speak, — 763 *Excursion* 1. 478
" I speak," continued he, " of One whose stock — 763 *Excursion* 1. 511
One while he would speak lightly of his babes, — 765 *Excursion* 1. 585
Nor how to speak to her. Poor Wretch ! at last — 766 *Excursion* 1. 652
And, sometimes—to my shame I speak—have need — 767 *Excursion* 1. 755
I interposed, though loth to speak, and said, — 780 *Excursion* 2. 607
Though comfortless !— Not of myself I speak ; — 790 *Excursion* 3. 263
To speak the word—with rapture ! Nature's boon, — 792 *Excursion* 3. 432
He with a smile exclaimed :—" 'Tis well you speak — 814 *Excursion* 4. 894
Do speak, at Heaven's command, to eye and ear, — 819 *Excursion* 4. 1205
And speak to social reason's inner sense, — 819 *Excursion* 4. 1206
From other mouths, the language which they speak, — 819 *Excursion* 4. 1227
So shall they learn, while all things speak of man, — 820 *Excursion* 4. 1239
Stirs in the mighty woods.—So did he speak : — 820 *Excursion* 4. 1282
Hath he imparted—but I speak of him — 824 *Excursion* 5. 109
That laid their country waste. No need to speak — 825 *Excursion* 5. 200
Of what it holds could speak, and every grave — 826 *Excursion* 5. 251
(With shame I speak it) to her guilty bowers — 843 *Excursion* 6. 352
I speak of such among my flock as swerved — 848 *Excursion* 6. 655
Strike the deserted to the heart ; I speak — 851 *Excursion* 6. 860
To speak of him, and instantly dissolves." — 863 *Excursion* 7. 360
(If I may venture of myself to speak, — 873 *Excursion* 7. 1045
Yet have I thought that we might also speak, — 885 *Excursion* 9. 50
His folly. Thus (I feel it while I speak), — S.3. 434 **The doubt* 60
I would not speak in snarling tone ; — S.3. 438 **My Lord* 2
Ah then, lest you awaken me, speak low. — S.3. 441 **Grateful is sleep ; my* 5
Then wake me not, I pray you. Hush, speak low. — S.3. 441 **Grateful is sleep, more* 4
Had ever more abundant cause to speak — K.8. 239 *Recluse* 1.1. 99
To speak of her dead husband. Is there not — K.8. 247 *Recluse* 1.1.401
Shall speak of what is done among the fields, — K.8. 247 *Recluse* 1.1.404
Be privileged to speak as I have felt — K.8. 255 *Recluse* 1.1.701
A voice shall speak, and what will be the theme ? — K.8. 257 *Recluse* 1.1.753
How little dost thou speak of earthly gloom ! — [?] **A sad* 12

Speaker. Broke in upon the Speaker with a frank — 779 *Excursion* 2. 513

Speaker's. Or stem the current of the speaker's thoughts, — 793 *Excursion* 3. 469

Speak'st. Thou speak'st—and lo ! the polar Seas — 216 *Enterprise* 87
Good Nightingale ! thou speakest wondrous fair, — 559 *Cuck.andNight.*166

Speaking. *See* **Evil-speaking.**
'Tis of the elder brother I am speaking : — 99 *Brothers* 291
While they were speaking, Vaudracour approached; — 126 *V. and J.* 294
We had a speaking diary, — 182 *Waggoner* 4. 221
So speaking, and by fervent love endowed — 209 *Laod.* 7
In picture, speaking with heroic tongue, — 334 **The Spirit* 3
Speaking of death alone, beneath a clime — 350 *Des. Stanzas* 26
Pleased could my verse, a speaking monument, — 376 *Duddon* 3. 3
—So speaking, he his reverend head — 405 *White Doe* 862
The promise in that speaking face ; — 414 *White Doe* 1677
Time-honoured Chaucer speaking through that Lay — 436 *Ecc. Sonn.* 2. 31. 2
His voice—beheld his speaking face ; — 479 *Somnamb.* 142
Of things for ever speaking, — 481 *Expost.* 26
Speaking through Law's dispassionate voice the State — 519 *Pun. Death* 9. 9
I have been speaking, for my theme has been — 651 *Prelude* 3. 172
Have I been speaking, and my youthful mind. — 651 *Prelude* 3. 176
Upon the speaking face of earth and heaven — 666 *Prelude* 5. 13
Where'er I roamed, were speaking monuments. — 701 *Prelude* 8. 172
This faithful guide, speaking from his death-bed, — 726 *Prelude* 10. 537
But, speaking more in charity, the dream — 730 *Prelude* 11. 232
Those days were passed, now speaking in a voice — 732 *Prelude* 11. 336
Speaking no dream, but things oracular ; — 743 *Prelude* 13. 253
Not speaking much, pleased rather with the joy — 764 *Excursion* 1. 515
So speaking, on he went, and at the word — 779 *Excursion* 2. 492
And, speaking thus, he patted tenderly — 779 *Excursion* 2. 529

Speaking—*continued.*
Then, speaking in like careless sort, he said — 781 *Excursion* 2. 618
I, speaking now from such disorder free, — 804 *Excursion* 4. 186
Nor unreproved by Providence, thus speaking — 805 *Excursion* 4. 276
Among more innocent rubbish."—Speaking thus, — 816 *Excursion* 4. 1009
Our simple shepherds, speaking from the heart, — 862 *Excursion* 7. 345
While he is speaking, I have power to see — 891 *Excursion* 9. 465
For, though in whispers speaking, the full heart — 895 *Excursion* 9. 751
But speaking of the vale in which he dwelt, — K.8. 230 **I will* 199
She reared it, and in speaking of her charge — K.8. 251 *Recluse* 1.1.526

Speaking-trumpet. His speaking-trumpet ;—back out of the clouds — 147 *Joanna* 63

Speaks. And never speaks ! Who is it ? I have seen her. — 47 *Bord.* 567
What can this mean ? There is a psalm that speaks — 60 *Bord.* 1266
So speaks the Chronicle, and tells of Lear — 103 *Artegal* 41
As the dread Voice that speaks from out the sea — 349 *At Dover* 11
That hourly speaks within us ? — 386 *Yarrow Rev.* 88
This tragic Story cheered us ; for it speaks — 395 *White Doe: Ded.* 49
Thus speaks (that Voice which walks upon the wind, — 432 *Ecc. Sonn.* 2. 17. 6
For One who speaks in numbers ; ampler scope — 520 *Pun. Death* 14. 2
With which she speaks when storms are gone, — 581 **Loud is* 2
These cares, and thus she speaks to winged Love : — 624 *Æneid* 10
The Bust that speaks and moves its goggling eyes, — 698 *Prelude* 7. 711
Speaks, less distinctly, to the same effect. — 846 *Excursion* 6. 526
To have *one* Enclosure where the voice that speaks — 848 *Excursion* 6. 638
Speaks for itself ; an Infant there doth rest ; — 850 *Excursion* 6. 791
Vouchsafe sweet influence, while her Poet speaks — 892 *Excursion* 9. 519
Which speaks from a presiding Spirit here, — K.8. 244 *Recluse* 1.1.275

Spear. " Were this same spear, which in my hand I grasp, — 104 *Artegal* 154
" They came with banner, spear, and shield ; — 204 *Brougham* 24
Each crowned with flowers, and armed with spear and shield, — 212 *Dion* 19
And armed with living spear for mortal fight ; — 227 *Vernal Ode* 104
Old Andes thrusts yon craggy spear — 237 *P. B.* 58
And hart and hind and hunter with his spear — 268 **Pure element* 8
The mortal spear repelling. — 287 *Ellen Irwin* 36
Before the ominous aspect of her spear ; — 311 **Who rises* 24
A golden spear to swallow ! and that brown — 349 *Sky-prosp.* 6
And hence when he, with spear and shield, — 399 *White Doe* 283
Kenned on the point of a lofty spear ; — 405 *White Doe* 832
A spear,—and, so protected, watched — 412 *White Doe* 1483
But all shall be fulfilled ;—the Julian spear — 419 *Ecc. Sonn.* 1. 3. 10
Rides forth, an armêd man, and hurls a spear — 422 *Ecc. Sonn.* 1. 17. 3
Lord of the harp and liberating spear ; — 425 *Ecc. Sonn.* 1. 26. 3
Though faint, compared with spear and shield, — 478 *Somnamb.* 52
The spear, yet gave to works divine — 533 **Blest is* 13
When in the antique age of bow and spear — 534 **When in* 1
The haunt of him who sang how spear and shield — 546 **The embowering* 17
Pierced by thy spear in glorious victory. — 626 *Ballot* 14
Where spear encountered spear, and sword with sword — 634 *Prelude* 1. 177
His staff protending like a hunter's spear, — 702 *Prelude* 8. 246
Before the point of the life-threatening spear — 718 *Prelude* 10. 23
The voice of spears was heard, the rattling spear — 744 *Prelude* 13. 324
The Knight arrived, with spear and shield, and borne — 872 *Excursion* 7. 944
The spear and shield are vanished, which the Knight — 872 *Excursion* 7. 961

Spear-grass. Those weeds, and the high spear-grass on that wall, — 770 *Excursion* 1. 943

Spearman. A Spearman brought him to the ground. — 412 *White Doe* 1486

Spear's. Within the Vault, a spear's length to the left. — 54 *Bord.* 916

Spears. Of fatal Austrian spears. — 341 *San Salv.* 36
At a proud Legate's feet ! The spears that line — 428 *Ecc. Sonn.* 1. 37. 12
The voice of spears was heard, the rattling spear — 744 *Prelude* 13. 324

Spears'. Which two spears' length of level ground — 398 *White Doe* 171

Special. Oswald my special enemy, if you — 63 *Bord.* 1425
That to the Kind by special grace — 168 *Wren's Nest* 11
Unquiet Childhood here by special grace — 274 *Infant M.* 1
Spreads wide ; though special mysteries multiply, — 438 *Ecc. Sonn.* 2. 41. 4
Or portraitures for special use designed, — 657 *Prelude* 3. 552
By special privilege of Nature's love, — 692 *Prelude* 7. 375
What special record can, or need, be given — 795 *Excursion* 3. 607
Though with the Encincture's special sanctity — 824 *Excursion* 5. 159
Rejoice !—and ye have special cause for joy. — 889 *Excursion* 9. 368

Specially. Not to the object specially designed, — 518 *Pun. Death* 5. 1
And specially delightful unto me — 677 *Prelude* 6. 161

Species. Of the whole species) to the external World — 755 *Recluse* 1. 1. 818
Shares with her species, nature's grace sometimes — 835 *Excursion* 5. 846
Were of one species with the sheltered few, — 836 *Excursion* 5. 943

Specimen. A specimen pourtrayed with faithful hand. — 670 *Prelude* 5. 297
His specimen, if but haply interveined — 789 *Excursion* 3. 186

Specimens. Among the crowd all specimens of man, — 690 *Prelude* 7. 221

Specious. Gave specious colouring to aim and act, — 313 **Go back* 10
Avaunt all specious pliancy of mind — 319 **Avaunt all* 1
Free Fancy prized each specious miracle, — 395 *White Doe: Ded.* 19
Subduing my heart's specious cowardice, — 664 *Prelude* 4. 410
By specious wonders, and too slow to tell — 694 *Prelude* 7. 513

Speck. Now shows a shadowy speck, and now is lost entire. — 4 *Ev. Wk.* 113
And, rimy without speck, extend the plains : — 8 *Ev. Wk.* 356
And sometimes on a speck of visible earth, — 150 **When, to* 14
Yon trophied Mound shrinks to a shadowy speck — 278 *Wellington* 8
Of his half-open hand pure from blemish or speck ; — 340 *Fort Fuentes* 6
Yet is yon neat trim church a grateful speck — 474 **How sad* 6
Each speck of lawn the broken rocks between ; — 594 *Ev. Wk. Quarto* 162

Speed—*continued.*
To speed their errand by the wings they wore. . 500 *Humanity* 40
—Soon shall the widow (for the speed of Time . 505 *Warning* 151
Oh, speed the blessed hour, Almighty God! . . 520 *Pun. Death* 13. 14
At speed a wounded deer, ... 544 *Russ. Fug.* 262
Along the midway cliffs with violent speed; . . 595 *Ev. Wk. Quarto* 180
Without a cordial greeting. Thence with speed . 658 *Prelude* 4. 17
Who love as we do. Speed thee well! divide . 678 *Prelude* 6. 247
A march it was of military speed, ... 682 *Prelude* 6. 491
To speed my voyage; every sound or sight, . . 686 *Prelude* 6. 746
That asks not speed, a traveller might bestow . 696 *Prelude* 7. 591
With speed and echoes loud of trampling hoofs . 716 *Prelude* 9. 449
Range; if it please them, speed from clime to clime; . . . . 789 *Excursion* 3. 192
Loud echoing, add your speed to the pursuit; . 808 *Excursion* 4. 502
Has wrought, if not with speed of magic, yet . 875 *Excursion* 8. 88
Nothing to speed the day, or cheer the mind; . 878 *Excursion* 8. 274
Fixing a steady eye, maintain their speed; . . 880 *Excursion* 8. 384
To a bold brook that splits for better speed, . 883 *Excursion* 8. 578
Speediest. Of speediest wing, should he appear. . 411 *White Doe* 1376
Speedily. More speedily than you belike would wish. 44 *Bord.* 374
Reached speedily the native threshold, bent . . 123 *V. and J.* 103
Full speedily resounded, public hope, ... 126 *V. and J.* 303
And wild-wood sorrows, speedily . . . . . 143 **Driven in* 12
Go, and I'll follow speedily!" . . . . . . 176 *Waggoner* 1. 261
But speedily an earnest longing rose . . . . 633 *Prelude* 1. 114
The cottage door was speedily unbarred, . . . 665 *Prelude* 4. 461
Full speedily resounded, public hope, ... 718 *Prelude* 9. 582
But speedily the promise was fulfilled; . . . 781 *Excursion* 2. 671
Come, share my couch, nor speedily depart; . . S.3. 441 **Come, gentle* 2
Speeds. Each wave, one and t'other, speeds after his brother; . . . . 167 *Stray Pleasures* 35
Speedwell. A *Speedwell* may not want its place. . 164 **Fair Lady* 20
Speedy. What speedy help her Boy will bring, . . 127 *Idiot Boy* 124
Help, and forgiveness speedy and entire. . . . 366 **Eternal Lord* 14
Prompt aid, forgiveness speedy and entire. . . K.8. 266 **Rid of* 14
Spell. *See* **Love-spell.**
The Swallow, twittered subject to like spell; . . 153 *Morn. Ex.* 22
Drawn by what peculiar spell, ... 161 **Pleasures newly* 41
Is known, and by as strong a spell . . . . . 174 *Waggoner* 1. 84
As if intent on magic spell;— . . . . . . 175 *Waggoner* 1. 177
Potent was the spell that bound thee . . . . 217 **Inmate of* 5
—Yielding to this gentle spell, ... 220 *Triad* 35
If here a warrior left a spell, ... 223 *Wishing-gate* 22
Ungrieved, with charm and spell; . . . . . 224 **'Tis gone* 63
Rejoiced that clamorous spell and magic verse . 234 *Power of Sound* 127
What spell so strong as guilty Fear! . . . . 238 *P. B.* 147
More terrible than magic spell. . . . . . . 246 *P. B.* 920
For others; for thy future self, a spell . . . 275 *Rotha Q.* 13
And beast and bird that from the spell . . . 299 *Brownie's Cell* 65
Once more of troubles wrought by magic spell; . 395 *White Doe: Ded.* 34
Nor chide the Muse that stooped to break a spell. 525 *Epist. Beaumont* 276
I ask what warrant fixed them (like a spell . . 527 **Those breathing* 46
The inside of the earth, and spell the stars; . . 670 *Prelude* 5. 318
Spells. Medea's spells dispersed the weight of years, 210 *Laod.* 83
As renders needless spells and magic wands, . . 338 *Engelberg* 4
From mischief, caused by spells himself had muttered; . . . . 370 *Eg. Maid* 68
On which he stood, by spells unnatural bound, . 523 *Epist. Beaumont* 151
That spells seemed on me when I was alone, . . 652 *Prelude* 3. 229
Amid the fiery furnace. Charms and spells . . 692 *Prelude* 7. 370
When spells forbade the voyager to land, . . . 735 *Prelude* 12. 53
Spend. To spend the sabbath of old age in peace, . 867 *Excursion* 7. 666
Yet in this peaceful Vale we will not spend . . K.8. 257 *Recluse* 1. 1. 751
The moments' humour, rough Tars spend their wit. K.8. 301 **And oh* 4
Or spend upon the dead the muse's rage? . . L.1. 94 *Juvenal* 2. 8
Spending. Getting and spending, we lay waste our powers: . . . . 259 **The world is* 2
Spendthrift. We call, and scorn the other as Time's spendthrift; . . . . 60 *Bord.* 1236
For spendthrift feats, excesses of his prime. . . 783 *Excursion* 2. 756
Spenser. It cheered mild Spenser, called from Faery-land . . . . 260 **Scorn not* 10
Sweet Spenser, moving through his clouded heaven 653 *Prelude* 3. 280
Nor such as Spenser fabled. True it is, . . . 701 *Prelude* 8. 144
Spenser's. There too we read of Spenser's fairy themes, ... 103 *Artegal* 49
Did we together read in Spenser's Lay . . . 395 *White Doe: Ded.* 5
May never tread; but scarcely Spenser's self . . 676 *Prelude* 6. 89
Spent. In fainter howlings told its *rage* was spent: 27 *Guilt* 192
Thy hours as they flow on are spent, if not in joy in peace. . . . . 92 *Poet's Dream* 56
Entering, when evening was far spent, the house 101 *Brothers* 374
Drooped and pined till life was spent, ... 141 *Arm. Lady* 110
'Tis spent—this burning day of June! . . . 173 *Waggoner* 1. 1
For health, and time in obvious duty spent. . . 278 **Lo! where she* 14
The picture of a life well spent: . . . . . 294 *Jedbor.* 40
When the whirlwind of human destruction is spent, 340 *Fort Fuentes* 19
Taught by his summer spent, his autumn gone, . 388 *Trosachs* 3
"My faithful followers, lo! the tide is spent . . 495 *Fact* 30
Feeling from limbs with travel spent, ... 542 *Russ. Fug.* 47
To con it all ere Christmas-tide be spent; . . . 554 *Prioress* 89
Tease, and the thought of time so spent depress, . 584 *Ch. Lamb* 7
Spent in a round of strenuous idleness— . . . 664 *Prelude* 4. 378
—To time thus spent, add multitudes of hours . 677 *Prelude* 6. 179
Distinguished. Scarcely was a year thus spent . 710 *Prelude* 9. 28
For the spent hurricane the air provides . . . 719 *Prelude* 10. 80
In the dark hedges. So their days were spent . 764 *Excursion* 1. 532
By choice were spent in constant fellowship; . . 845 *Excursion* 6. 472

Spent—*continued.*
Departs; and soon is spent the line of those . . 872 *Excursion* 7. 985
My Son! behold the Tide already spent . . . S.3. 427 **My Son* 1
Yet, having spent a summer's day . . . . . S.3. 438 **My Lord* 7
My Lord can muster (all but honour spent) . . L.1. 97 *Juvenal* 3. 81
Sphere. Though half a sphere be conscious of their brightness) . . . . v **If thou indeed* 7
These matins mounting towards her native sphere. 154 *Morn. Ex.* 54
Of Plato's genius, from its lofty sphere, . . . 212 *Dion* 9
While traversing this nether sphere, ... 215 *Enterprise* 18
The earth is constant to her sphere; . . . . 224 *Primrose* 21
When Music deigned within this grosser sphere . 234 *Power of Sound* 117
Is it a mirror?—or the nether Sphere . . . . 313 **Clouds, lingering* 9
Than either, pent within her separate sphere, . 357 *Aquap.* 287
Spirits that crowd the intellectual sphere . . . 429 *Ecc. Sonn.* 2. 5. 12
Sad thoughts; for from above the starry sphere . 441 *Ecc. Sonn.* 3. 4. 10
Down to the green earth fetch thee from thy sphere, 460 **Queen of* 15
The Star of Bethlehem from its sphere invites . 467 *St. Bees* 113
For love of God, run fast above thy sphere; . . 564 *Troilus* 138
From star to star, from kindred sphere to sphere, 677 *Prelude* 6. 127
Throughout the nether sphere!—And if with this 755 *Recluse* 1. 1. 846
But all within the sphere of little things; . . 795 *Excursion* 3. 609
For different lot, or change to higher sphere, . . 795 *Excursion* 3. 630
But others, far beyond this narrow sphere, . . 806 *Excursion* 4. 363
Between the orbs of our apparent sphere . . . 812 *Excursion* 4. 711
Spheres. Learned from the tuneful spheres that glide 220 *Triad* 22
Was it the music of the spheres . . . . . 237 *P. B.* 83
Shall live enrolled above the starry spheres. . . 330 *Ode: Thanks.* 66
These perishable spheres have wrought . . . 343 *Eclipse* 56
Beyond these transient spheres, doth wear a crown 354 *Aquap.* 109
These mortal spheres above, ... 582 *Invoc. Earth* 31
For know we not that from celestial spheres, . . 628 **Deign, Sovereign* 25
Of harmony from Heaven's remotest spheres. . . 747 *Prelude* 14. 99
To regulate the moving spheres, and weigh . . 815 *Excursion* 4. 949
"All that this world is proud of. From their spheres . . . . 872 *Excursion* 7. 978
Of heavenly bodies shining in their spheres. . . 889 *Excursion* 9. 350
Yet, in partition, with their several spheres, . . 890 *Excursion* 9. 450
Spicy. Through India's spicy regions wing their way, 231 **The gentlest Poet* 12
Near spicy shores of Araby the blest, ... 438 *Ecc. Sonn.* 2. 39. 10
Spider's. Or a spider's web adorning . . . . 549 *Hermit's Cell* 1. 3
Spied. I spied a Covert walled and roofed with sods— 39 *Bord.* 118
I spied him skulking in his peasant's dress. . . 46 *Bord.* 491
—When in the snow the mother spied . . . . 83 *Lucy Gray* 43
Since first I spied that Primrose-tuft . . . . 224 *Primrose* 9
When Peter spied the moving thing, ... 244 *P. B.* 706
The Woman waked—and when she spied . . . 248 *P. B.* 1023
Near Anio's stream I spied a gentle Dove . . . 360 **Near Anio's* 1
She spied the lonely Cast-away, ... 371 *Eg. Maid* 136
Or spied where thou sitt'st moping in thy mew . 456 **The leaves* 18
Of twilight deepened, going forth, I spied . . . 687 *Prelude* 7. 32
He spied the sheep upon a plot of grass, . . . K.8. 229 **I will* 139
Spies. She spies her Friends, she shouts a greeting; 130 *Idiot Boy* 429
Says nothing—till at last he spies . . . . 181 *Waggoner* 4. 173
At length he spies a bleeding wound, ... 244 *P. B.* 726
Spikes. In spikes, in branches, and in stars, . . 198 *Thorn* 47
Spiky. The dark pines thrusting forth their spiky heads; . . . . K.8. 249 *Recluse* 1. 1. 480
Spilt. For whose dire ends tears flow, and blood is spilt, ... 321 **Here pause* 11
Blood would be spilt that in his dark abode . . 519 *Pun. Death* 8. 8
Spin. Spin motives out of their own bowels, Lacy! 63 *Bord.* 1428
Cleared for a monarch's progress. Priests might spin . . . . 70 *Bord.* 1837
Even She who toils to spin our vital thread . . 255 *S. H.* 7
Yet—though dread Powers, that work in mystery, spin . . . . 280 **Oh what* 2
Spin in his eyesight, *that* contents him not, . . 723 *Prelude* 10. 371
Began to spin, with toil, my earliest songs. . . 726 *Prelude* 10. 552
And spin—and pant—and overhead again, . . 880 *Excursion* 8. 385
Spindle. He fed the spindle of his youngest child, . 95 *Brothers* 23
Wool for the Housewife's spindle, or repair . . 132 *Michael* 107
For the spindle, while they sleep, ... 163 *Spinning Wheel* 10
Serving as doth a spindle or a wheel; . . . . 886 *Excursion* 9. 160
The quickening spindle drew a trustier line. . . S.3. 427 **Through Cumbrian* 14
Spindles. His spindles sink under him, foot, leg, and thigh! . . . . 484 **A plague* 21
That whirls (how slow itself!) ten thousand spindles: . . . . 866 *Excursion* 7. 607
Spinners. For cottagers and spinners at the wheel, 668 *Prelude* 5. 208
Spinning. Of antique form; this large, for spinning wool; . . . . 132 *Michael* 83
Came sweeping through the darkness, spinning still 639 *Prelude* 1. 455
By spinning hemp, a pittance for herself; . . . 769 *Excursion* 1. 860
That girt her waist, spinning the long-drawn thread 769 *Excursion* 1. 886
Spinning amain, as if to overtake . . . . . 856 *Excursion* 6. 1180
Spinning-wheel. Now that the cottage Spinning-wheel is mute; . . . . 255 **Grief, thou* 2
Spins. And softly sleeps within the thread she spins. 366 *Lombardy* 8
Their happy year spins round. The youth obeys 884 *Excursion* 9. 33
Spinster. There safe as a Spinster . . . . . S.3. 440 **Said red-ribboned* 27
Spiral. The woodbine so, with spiral grace, and breathes . . . . 367 *Trajan* 21
In spiral circles mount aloft, and soar . . . . K.8. 234 **The order'd* 2
Spire. *See* **Cypress-spire.**
And peeps the far-off spire, his evening bourn! . 11 *Desc. Sk.* 20
While, from amid the darkened roofs, the spire, . 12 *Desc. Sk.* 99
The tall sun, pausing on an Alpine spire, . . . 20 *Desc. Sk.* 553

Spirit—continued.

Her spirit finds its centre ;	479	Somnamb. 74
Her faithful Spirit flew,	479	Somnamb. 141
Up ! up ! and drink the spirit breathed	481	Expost. 7
And mildness, and spirit both forward and coy.	482	Character 12
The spirit of the season.	483	Sister 28
He felt with spirit so profound.	486	Matthew 28
My spirit droop for drooping's sake,	490	Night Thought 14
Live in the spirit of this creed ;	492	Duty 23
The spirit of self-sacrifice ;	493	Duty 54
—It is the generous Spirit, who, when brought	493	Hap. War. 3
My spirit seems to mount above	498	*The sylvan 22
Can the pitying spirit doubt	502	*Like a 23
Thus, while the ruminating spirit feeds	503	Warning 12
Thy Spirit triumphs o'er the slight ;	506	*While from 23
Whose spirit, like the angel that went down	510	F. Stone 125
Their spirit mounted, crying, " God us aid ! "	513	General Fast 8
And thy grieved Spirit brighten strong in faith.	515	*Men of 14
For ever.—The Spirit of Alfred, at the head	516	*Young England 6
His Spirit, when most severe, is oft most kind ;	518	Pun. Death 5. 5
Proscribed the spirit fostered by that rule,	518	Pun. Death 7. 6
Of an immortal spirit, is a gift	519	Pun. Death 10. 2
My passing Spirit cheer.	530	†Redbreast 12
A buoyant Spirit, and a heart at ease.	532	*Once I 30
By what evil spirit brought ?	535	Egremont 46
With thankful spirit. The descant, and the wind	538	*In desultory 10
By Youth's surviving spirit ? What agile grace !	540	*Lady ! a 70
A guardian Spirit sent from pitying Heaven,	541	Grace Darl. 73
And set her Spirit free	544	Russ. Fug. 238
Yet not the less his Spirit would hold dear	547	*Ye Lime 11
If my spirit toss and welter	550	Hermit's Cell 4. 7
Through humbleness, the Spirit that did alight	552	Prioress 18
Divorced from good—a spirit and pulse of good,	567	Cumb. Beg. 77
And buoyant spirit triumphed over pain ;	574	Chiabrera 5. 7
That every gentle Spirit hither led	575	Chiabrera 7. 17
Pause, courteous Spirit !—Balbi supplicates	575	Chiabrera 9. 1
Exalt thy spirit, hear the voice	577	Cenotaph 11
Had been that pious spirit, a tide	577	*By playful 7
Oh true of heart, of spirit gay,	578	*I come 65
Well chosen is the spirit that is here ;	579	Peele Castle 46
A Spirit sang in tones more plaintive than the wind ;	581	Invoc. Earth 3
The Spirit ended his mysterious rite.	582	Invoc. Earth 35
Upon my thoughts his saintly Spirit fed ;	582	*To public 6
Was ever Spirit that could bend	582	*O for a 25
A spirit meek in self-abasement clad.	583	*With copious 6
If thou hast heard me—if thy Spirit know	583	*With copious 34
His spirit, but the recompense was high ;	584	Ch. Lamb 8
Transported, my soothed spirit hovers o'er	585	Ch. Lamb 53
Through God, is raised a spirit and soul of love	585	Ch. Lamb 66
But turn we rather, let my spirit turn	586	Ch. Lamb 107
Mourn rather for that holy Spirit,	586	Hogg 37
And mournful sounds, as of a Spirit lost,	608	Desc.Sk.Quarto 334
To viewless realms his Spirit towers amain,	612	Desc.Sk.Quarto 548
That guides the spirit to eternal day,	619	School Ex. 106
In the pain of my spirit I said,	620	Convict 6
Would fill it with his spirit. He, to please	625	Æneid 89
A Power misnamed the SPIRIT of REFORM,	626	Ballot 2
But now her Spirit hath put forth its claim	627	*When Severn's 9
Here, in the Founder's Spirit sought	629	Installation 82
A renovated spirit singled out,	633	Prelude 1. 53
Dust as we are, the immortal spirit grows.	637	Prelude 1. 340
Wisdom and Spirit of the universe !	638	Prelude 1. 401
A tranquillising spirit presses now	642	Prelude 2. 27
And that still spirit shed from evening air !	644	Prelude 2. 132
Poetic spirit of our human life,	646	Prelude 2. 261
By its own spirit ! All that I beheld	646	Prelude 2. 281
To feed the spirit of religious love	647	Prelude 2. 357
A local spirit of his own, at war	647	Prelude 2. 365
My spirit was up, my thoughts were full of hope ;	649	Prelude 3. 18
Ye Presidents and Deans, and, till the spirit	655	Prelude 3. 410
Informed with such a spirit as might be	655	Prelude 3. 429
And mounting spirit, pitiably repaid,	656	Prelude 3. 501
The boyish spirit flagged, and day by day	660	Prelude 4. 101
And swellings of the spirit, was rapt and soothed,	660	Prelude 4. 163
Which I had loved, even as a blessed spirit	662	Prelude 4. 236
A dedicated Spirit. On I walked	663	Prelude 4. 337
To the end and written spirit of God's works,	663	Prelude 4. 351
A deathless spirit. Thou also, man ! hast wrought,	666	Prelude 5. 18
Her spirit, must it lodge in shrines so frail ?	666	Prelude 5. 49
To exhilarate the spirit, and to soothe,	667	Prelude 5. 108
A wiser spirit is at work for us,	671	Prelude 5. 360
Their spirit hallowed the sad spectacle	672	Prelude 5. 456
A gracious spirit o'er this earth presides,	673	Prelude 5. 491
That other spirit, Coleridge ! who is now	678	Prelude 6. 228
The spirit of pleasure, and youth's golden gleam.	678	Prelude 6. 236
Moves the great spirit of human knowledge, spare	681	Prelude 6. 450
And the independent spirit of pure youth	686	Prelude 6. 776
A spirit friendly to the Poet's task,	687	Prelude 7. 48
Had vanity (quick Spirit that appears	688	Prelude 7. 103
To a meek spirit suffering inwardly,	691	Prelude 7. 315
Ah, with how different spirit might a prayer	692	Prelude 7. 373
Structures like these the excited spirit mainly	697	Prelude 7. 651
The Spirit of Nature was upon me there ;	698	Prelude 7. 766
On the dead letter, miss the spirit of things ;	703	Prelude 8. 297
My spirit to that gentleness of love	704	Prelude 8. 358
Great Spirit as thou art, in endless dreams	705	Prelude 8. 435
Or spirit that full soon must take her flight.	705	Prelude 8. 450
Was not a punctual presence, but a spirit	708	Prelude 8. 610
One spirit over ignorance and vice	709	Prelude 8. 669
One spirit ruling in each heart ; alike	711	Prelude 9. 131
That a benignant spirit was abroad	717	Prelude 9. 519

Spirit—continued.

There dwelt, weakened in spirit more and more ;	718	Prelude 9. 580
Preclude conviction, that a spirit strong	720	Prelude 10. 165
A spirit thoroughly faithful to itself,	720	Prelude 10. 167
Without a spirit overcast by dark	723	Prelude 10. 328
So, did a portion of that spirit fall	724	Prelude 10. 448
And in the kinder spirit ; placable,	729	Prelude 11. 158
A ladder for thy spirit to reascend	733	Prelude 11. 397
Which, when the spirit of evil reached its height,	735	Prelude 12. 42
The affections and the spirit of the place,	736	Prelude 12. 120
This efficacious spirit chiefly lurks	737	Prelude 12. 219
A spirit of pleasure and youth's golden gleam ;	738	Prelude 12. 266
Such is my hope, the spirit of the Past	738	Prelude 12. 285
In a strong wind, some working of the spirit,	739	Prelude 12. 331
But greater, though in spirit more subdued—	741	Prelude 13. 86
Of Sarum's Plain, my youthful spirit was raised ;	744	Prelude 13. 314
This is the very spirit in which they deal	747	Prelude 14. 91
And yet a spirit, there for me enshrined	750	Prelude 14. 270
In the self-haunting spirit learned to take	750	Prelude 14. 284
Descend, prophetic Spirit ! that inspir'st	755	Recluse 1. 1. 836
Nor any voice of joy ; his spirit drank	759	Excursion 1. 206
Seemed infinite ; and there his spirit shaped	759	Excursion 1. 231
Her forms, and with the spirit of her forms,	760	Excursion 1. 268
That stern yet kindly Spirit, who constrains	761	Excursion 1. 316
(Spirit attached to regions mountainous	761	Excursion 1. 319
'Tis long and tedious ; but my spirit clings	768	Excursion 1. 779
That secret spirit of humanity	770	Excursion 1. 927
Nowhere, dominion o'er the enlightened spirit	770	Excursion 1. 953
His overflowing spirit. Birds and beasts,	772	Excursion 2. 41
With softened spirit, even when it condemned.	772	Excursion 2. 80
But if the spirit be oppressed by sense	788	Excursion 3. 137
In me, a meekly-bending spirit soothed	790	Excursion 3. 265
Her whose submissive spirit was to me	794	Excursion 3. 563
And spirit—interrupted and relieved	794	Excursion 3. 575
To what an alien spirit had acquired	795	Excursion 3. 625
The eminence whereon her spirit stood,	795	Excursion 3. 659
Of the departed spirit—what abode	796	Excursion 3. 693
Despise, as senseless : for my spirit relished	798	Excursion 3. 816
Upon his spirit, with a fever's strength,	798	Excursion 3. 849
For the gross spirit of mankind,—the one	799	Excursion 3. 911
Is human Life ; and so the Spirit fares	800	Excursion 3. 987
Attended ; then, my spirit was entranced,	803	Excursion 4. 118
Was less upraised in spirit than abashed ;	805	Excursion 4. 256
That spirit only can redeem mankind ;	806	Excursion 4. 317
And when that sacred spirit shall appear,	806	Excursion 4. 318
Sincere, and humble spirit, teaches love :	806	Excursion 4. 345
The plaintive spirit of the solitude !	807	Excursion 4. 412
What other spirit can it be that prompts	807	Excursion 4. 445
As if it were a spirit !—How divine,	809	Excursion 4. 513
Amid the wrangling schools—a SPIRIT hung,	812	Excursion 4. 735
An all-pervading Spirit, upon whom	815	Excursion 4. 969
No shelter, for a spirit in distress.	816	Excursion 4. 1028
In sober plenty ; when the spirit stoops	816	Excursion 4. 1043
In man's celestial spirit ; virtue thus	817	Excursion 4. 1071
Or shall the groaning Spirit cast her load	817	Excursion 4. 1099
Who, in this spirit, communes with the Forms	819	Excursion 4. 1208
The naked spirit, ceasing to deplore	820	Excursion 4. 1250
With undistempered and unclouded spirit,	830	Excursion 5. 487
To the confiding spirit of his own	836	Excursion 5. 895
Of reverence done to the spirit of the place,	839	Excursion 6. 90
Than this fallen Spirit ? in those dreary holds	843	Excursion 6. 342
One spirit seldom failed to extend its sway	845	Excursion 6. 480
And breathed its soothing air ;—the spirit of hope	845	Excursion 6. 483
Your own pure spirit. Not a step we look for	847	Excursion 6. 584
Soothed by the natural spirit which they breathe.	847	Excursion 6. 633
That held her spirit, in its own despite,	849	Excursion 6. 711
The air with cheerful spirit, for thy sake,	852	Excursion 6. 924
' Nay,' said she, with commanding look, a spirit	853	Excursion 6. 976
Had swept away ; and now her Spirit longed	853	Excursion 6. 1022
So, through the cloud of death, her Spirit passed	854	Excursion 6. 1049
Her tender spirit, and her contrite heart,	854	Excursion 6. 1074
Became a clog to him, whose spirit wished	855	Excursion 6. 1104
And how, her Spirit yet survives on earth ! "	856	Excursion 6. 1191
Of his own spirit urged,—now, as a voice	857	Excursion 7. 17
A generous spirit, and a body strong	859	Excursion 7. 120
His own firm spirit in degree deprest	862	Excursion 7. 297
His introverted spirit ; and bestowed	864	Excursion 7. 446
But each instinct with spirit ; and the frame	865	Excursion 7. 509
By man's imperishable spirit, quelled.	865	Excursion 7. 530
In him the spirit of a hero walked	868	Excursion 7. 739
The inner spirit keeping holiday,	869	Excursion 7. 780
The Spirit of its mountains and its seas,	871	Excursion 7. 897
Glares, like a troubled spirit, in its bed	877	Excursion 8. 179
Spirit that knows no insulated spot,	884	Excursion 9. 13
Of one maternal spirit, bringing forth	885	Excursion 9. 111
The Spirit capable of heaven, assured.	887	Excursion 9. 228
How pure his spirit ! in what vivid hues	891	Excursion 9. 462
One spirit animating old and young,	892	Excursion 9. 526
" Eternal Spirit ! universal God !	893	Excursion 9. 614
Degree of healing to a wounded spirit,	896	Excursion 9. 786
And hopeless pangs the spirit of that youth,	S.3. 434	*The doubt 80
To Spirit ; for the idealising Soul	S.3. 435	*The doubt 119
At once what spirit of love was in his heart.	K.8. 230	*I will 204
But stirring to the spirit. Who could gaze	K.8. 237	Recluse1.1.24
Which speaks from a presiding Spirit here,	K.8. 244	Recluse1.1.275
A human voice—a Spirit of coming night,	K.8. 245	Recluse1.1.326
Is haunted—by what ghost ? a gentle spirit	K.8. 247	Recluse1.1.387
And borrowing more their spirit, and their shape	K.8. 249	Recluse1.1.451
Domestic, and in spirit motherly	K.8. 251	Recluse1.1.528
A spirit that can look through clouded skies,	[?]	*A sad 8

Spiritless. To constitute the spiritless shape of Fact,   58 Bord. 1157

Spiritless—*continued.*
Distracted, spiritless, benumbed, and blind, 322 **Humanity, delighting* 34
Maimed, spiritless ; and, in their weakness strong, 713 *Prelude* 9. 261
A dreamer yet more spiritless and dull ? 791 *Excursion* 3. 340
In disconnection dead and spiritless ; 815 *Excursion* 4. 962
Spirit-moving. From all its spirit-moving imagery, 583 **With copious* 20
Spirit-quickener. The spirit-quickener of the flowers, 228 *Devot. Incit.* 14
Spirit's. Rocked on the surge, there tried his spirit's strength 354 *Aquap.* 128
Christian Traditions ! at my Spirit's call 357 *Aquap.* 291
Has touched thee—and a Spirit's hand : 399 *White Doe* 333
Which Horace needed for his spirit's health ; 528 **Those breathing* 92
But Heaven is now, blest Child, thy Spirit's home : 581 **Why should we* 11
Spirits. *See* **Water-spirits.**
When gentle Spirits urged a sportive chase, 7 *Ev. Wk.* 301
Soon with despair's whole weight his spirits sink ; 16 *Desc. Sk.* 332
But vigorous Spirits look for something more 48 *Bord.* 622
Or own we baby Spirits ? Genuine courage 57 *Bord.* 1073
" I hold of Spirits, and the Sun in heaven." 63 *Bord.* 1447
Their spirits are in heaven ! " 84 *We are Seven* 66
Spirits busy to do and undo : 86 *Rural Arch.* 21
Which selected spirits wear, 90 *Longest Day* 74
So let us strive to live, and to our Spirits will be given 93 *Poet's Dream* 67
Our spirits, carrying with them dreams of flowers, 107 *Farewell* 60
As happy spirits as were ever seen ; 108 *Indolence* 69
For such, by pitying Angels and by Spirits 119 *Maternal Grief* 74
Fields, where with cheerful spirits he had breathed 132 *Michael* 65
Hath power to part the Spirits of those who love 152 **Forth from* 17
Then, cheerful Flower ! my spirits play 158 **In youth* 59
Spirits of all degrees rejoice 164 *Needlecase* 19
Share their empyreal spirits—yea, 178 *Waggoner* 3. 33
—Blithe spirits of her own impel 180 *Waggoner* 4. 11
Then, Spirits of beauty and of grace, 191 *Seq. Beggars* 32
Kind Spirits ! may we not believe 191 *Seq. Beggars* 36
By our own spirits are we deified : 196 *Resolution* 47
Suffer my genial spirits to decay : 207 *Tintern* 113
He spake of love, such love as Spirits feel 211 *Laod.* 97
Then why should conscious Spirits fear 223 *Wishing-gate* 37
The spirits at your bidding play 225 *Present.* 29
Sage Spirits ! by your grace. 226 *Present.* 72
The Spirits of the new-born flowers ? 228 *Devot. Incit.* 2
Thy spirits will seem to feed on balmy air : 229 *Cuckoo-clock* 15
Like bands of ministering Spirits, or when they lie, 230 *Clouds* 74
Dread Spirits ! to confound the meek 245 *P. B.* 761
Yet, potent Spirits ! well I know, 245 *P. B.* 766
Come, Spirits of the Mind ! and try, 245 *P. B.* 783
And now the Spirits of the Mind 246 *P. B.* 916
And, haply, there the spirits of the blest 266 **The stars* 2
Intent his wasted spirits to renew ; 268 **Brook ! whose* 2
Of central earth, where tortured Spirits pine 269 **Pure element* 12
Until their spirits mingled in the sea 276 *Oker Hill* 13
But delegated Spirits comforts fetch 280 **Oh what* 7
How oft, to elevate our spirits, shone 282 **Wansfell ! this* 12
Should life be dull, and spirits low, 293 *Yarrow Unv.* 61
For them whose timid Spirits clung 298 *Brownie's Cell* 18
Of Spirits, and the undying Lay, 300 *Bran* 40
Weak Spirits are there—who would ask, 311 **Who rises* 46
Your feeble spirits ! Greece her head hath bowed, 312 **When, far* 11
Where Spirits dwell in undisturbed repose— 349 *Sky-prosp.* 10
Peace to their Spirits ! why should Poesy 354 *Aquap.* 85
God reigns above, and Spirits strong 370 *Eg. Maid* 81
Not so that Pair whose youthful spirits dance 378 *Duddon* 10. 1
Spirits of Power, assembled there, complain 386 *Scott* 4
His weary spirits gather rest. 404 *White Doe* 777
If there be prophets on whose spirits rest 418 *Ecc. Sonn.* 1. 2. 1
And evil Spirits *may* our walk attend 423 *Ecc. Sonn.* 1. 18. 4
Then be *good* Spirits free to breathe a note 423 *Ecc. Sonn.* 1. 18. 6
Spirits that crowd the intellectual sphere 429 *Ecc. Sonn.* 2. 5. 12
Blest Prisoners They, whose spirits were at large ! 432 *Ecc. Sonn.* 2. 13. 14
Demons and Spirits, many a dolorous groan 435 *Ecc. Sonn.* 2. 27. 4
Holy and heavenly Spirits as they are, 438 *Ecc. Sonn.* 2. 40. 1
Blest while their Spirits from the woods ascend 443 *Ecc. Sonn.* 3. 13. 12
For the perfected Spirits of the just ! 452 *Ecc. Sonn.* 3. 47. 14
And with immortal Spirits blend ! 458 **Had this* 48
Of heaven contemplated by Spirits pure 474 **Hope smiled* 10
To mix with hymns that Spirits make and hear ; 500 *Humanity* 17
But our immortal Spirits may. 506 *Lab. Hymn* 24
Uphold our Spirits urged to kindred flight 512 **Who rashly* 37
In angry spirits for her old free range, 519 *Pun. Death* 8. 13
Devoted thus, their spirits did unite 546 **The embowering* 7
Fair Spirits are abroad ; in sportive chase 598 *Ev. Wk. Quarto* 347
Thro' wastes, of Spirits wing'd the solemn home, 609 *Desc. Sk. Quarto* 371
Then with despair's whole weight his spirits sink, 609 *Desc. Sk. Quarto* 404
Shade of Caractacus, if spirits love 627 *Eagle and Dove* 1
My easy spirits, and discountenance 654 *Prelude* 3. 344
Spirits upon the stretch, and here and there 663 *Prelude* 4. 316
To a late hour), and spirits overwrought 664 *Prelude* 4. 376
Of the same isthmus, which our spirits cross 673 *Prelude* 5. 536
Share with us thy fresh spirits, whether gift 678 *Prelude* 6. 250
The songs of spirits ! Nor had Fancy fed 689 *Prelude* 7. 126
Like that of angels or commissioned spirits, 690 *Prelude* 7. 243
The incarnation of the spirits that move 694 *Prelude* 7. 478
And all the promptest of her spirits, linked 713 *Prelude* 9. 264
Of single spirits that catch the flame from Heaven, 715 *Prelude* 9. 368
Worthy of liberty, all spirits filled 720 *Prelude* 10. 137
Of the two spirits then at strife remained 727 *Prelude* 11. 25
That vision, given to spirits of the night 747 *Prelude* 14. 64
Have been prepared, not with the buoyant spirits 752 *Prelude* 14. 416

Spirits—*continued.*
Which craft of delicate Spirits hath composed 755 *Recluse* 1. 1. 797
—Vigorous in health, of hopeful spirits, undamped 762 *Excursion* 1. 392
Pausing at will—our spirits braced, our thoughts 773 *Excursion* 2. 108
Checking the finer spirits that refuse 773 *Excursion* 2. 150
And idle spirits :—there the sun himself, 782 *Excursion* 2. 717
Of Spirits in beatitude : my heart 784 *Excursion* 2. 874
My spirits, that they were bent on enterprise ; 788 *Excursion* 3. 121
On wings, angelic Spirits ! I could muse 790 *Excursion* 3. 300
Gay as our spirits, free as our desires ; 794 *Excursion* 3. 543
Restore their languid spirits, and recall 801 *Excursion* 4. 30
Art everlasting, and the blessed Spirits, 802 *Excursion* 4. 92
Which, to your overweening spirits, yields 805 *Excursion* 4. 291
Be joyless as the blind ? Ambitious spirits— 815 *Excursion* 4. 947
Which hostile spirits silently allow ; 820 *Excursion* 4. 1289
Of subterranean Spirits feeding hope 841 *Excursion* 6. 227
If gladsome spirits, and benignant looks, 850 *Excursion* 6. 795
Of cordial spirits and vital temperament, 862 *Excursion* 7. 313
To the assembled spirits of just men 864 *Excursion* 7. 453
To us, with our sad spirits, heavenly-fair— 868 *Excursion* 7. 696
Thy lively spirits to partake, K.8. 262 **Ah ! if* 4
Thy changes, which to wiser Spirits seem K.8. 301 **And oh* 5
Spirit-saddening. Happy as they. With spirit-saddening power 851 *Excursion* 6. 858
Spirit-stirring. What spirit-stirring power it gained 224 **'Tis gone* 10
Nor such the spirit-stirring note 499 **Departing summer* 37
Was then a spirit-stirring sound indeed, 686 *Prelude* 6. 759
Spiritual. To catch the spiritual music of the hill, 9 *Ev. Wk.* 368
Appeared, and spiritual presence gained a power 139 *Widow* 26
Than fairest spiritual creature of the groves, 219 *Haunted Tree* 17
Appeared, in presence of the spiritual eye 226 *Vernal Ode* 3
And trust that spiritual Creatures round us move, 273 **When Philoctetes* 9
Rotha, my Spiritual Child ! this head was grey 274 *Rotha Q.* 1
And seemed to give me spiritual right 289 *Stepping West.* 15
To bind his spiritual Progeny, with rules 362 **List—'twas* 40
The Might of spiritual sway ! his thoughts, his dreams, 425 *Ecc. Sonn.* 1. 28. 10
She daunts, forth-thundering from her spiritual tower 429 *Ecc. Sonn.* 2. 2. 5
Is by these shocks exhausted, spiritual truth 432 *Ecc. Sonn.* 2. 16. 10
Hence, with the spiritual sovereignty transferred 435 *Ecc. Sonn.* 2. 28. 12
(Grave this within thy heart !) if spiritual things 442 *Ecc. Sonn.* 3. 10. 9
Both names conjoined, but of thy spiritual care 445 *Ecc. Sonn.* 3. 21. 3
Types of the spiritual Church which God hath reared ; 451 *Ecc. Sonn.* 3. 42. 2
Of noble feeling, that those spiritual men, 653 *Prelude* 3. 266
Meanwhile this creature—spiritual almost 703 *Prelude* 8. 282
Less spiritual, with microscopic view 735 *Prelude* 12. 91
Whence spiritual dignity originates, 745 *Prelude* 13. 373
To hold fit converse with the spiritual world, 747 *Prelude* 14. 108
This spiritual Love acts not nor can exist 749 *Prelude* 14. 188
The strain continued, spiritual as before ; 777 *Excursion* 2. 379
A spiritual presence, ofttimes misconceived, 815 *Excursion* 4. 927
The spiritual presences of absent things. 819 *Excursion* 4. 1234
Under his spiritual sway. He hath vouchsafed 824 *Excursion* 5. 106
Made to the spiritual fabric of her Church ; 838 *Excursion* 6. 8
To meet such trial) from their spiritual sires 839 *Excursion* 6. 61
As to a spiritual comforter and friend, 854 *Excursion* 6. 1030
With spiritual graces, like a glory, crowned." 862 *Excursion* 7. 339
Spiritually. Communications spiritually maintained, 811 *Excursion* 4. 645
Spiry. Of splendour—save the beacon's spiry head 6 *Ev. Wk.* 210
A knot of spiry trees for ages grew 212 *Laod.* 169
Spiry and dark, around their House of prayer, 347 *Processions* 44
That tips with eve's last gleam his spiry head. 595 *Ev. Wk. Quarto* 190
Between romantic Dovedale's spiry rocks ; 678 *Prelude* 6. 193
Stationed alone upon a spiry rock 703 *Prelude* 8. 274
Spital. A lonely Spital, the belated swain 27 *Guilt* 150
Spite. In spite of all the larks that cheered our path, 39 *Bord.* 109
In spite of all my weary pain 114 *Ind. Wom.* 53
Mine art thou—spite of these my tears, 120 *Emigrant Mother* 38
Of blameless debt. On evil Fortune's spite 138 *Widow* 5
Or spite, if cause be given ; 165 *Parrot* 24
Spite of melancholy reason, 171 *Kitten* 112
Spite of care, and spite of grief, 172 *Kitten* 127
Dread pair that, spite of wind and weather, 175 *Waggoner* 1. 178
For, spite of rumbling of the wheels, 176 *Waggoner* 2. 19
Untouched ;—in spite of many a gleam 182 *Waggoner* 4. 202
Mysterious safeguard, that, in spite 232 *Jew. Fam.* 41
Against the injuries of time, the spite 333 **Bruges I* 8
For, spite of sober Truth that sees 398 *White Doe* 208
Yea, many overcome in spite 399 *White Doe* 316
And, spite of change, for me thou keep'st the same 463 **They called* 4
In spite of all that beauty may disown 477 *Steamboats* 9
Yet, spite of all this eager strife, 499 **This Lawn* 13
That haunted us in spite of what we knew. 523 *Epist. Beaumont* 147
Whose practice teaches, spite of names to show 530 *Poor Robin* 22
In spite of season's change, its own demand, 531 **I know* 18
Through the whole land—to Manhood, moved in spite 540 *Grace Darl.* 9
For trust me well, in spite of thy quaint cry, 560 *Cuck. and Night.* 182
That countenance there fashioned, which, spite of a stain 569 *Farmer* 11
And, in spite of the shame that may lurk in his mind, 570 *Farmer* 52
Would now direct thy notice. Yet in spite 662 *Prelude* 4. 276
In spite of all temptation, we preserved 672 *Prelude* 5. 474
In spite of strongest disappointment, pleased 689 *Prelude* 7. 146
In spite of those heart-bracing colloquies, 716 *Prelude* 9. 470
In spite of real fervour, and of that 716 *Prelude* 9. 471

Sport—*continued.*
Snug as a child that hides itself in sport — 784 *Excursion* 2. 822
The sport of Nature, aided by blind Chance — 788 *Excursion* 3. 126
Is still the sport! Here Nature was my guide, — 797 *Excursion* 3. 807
That timely light, to share his joyous sport: — 814 *Excursion* 4. 864
That sport among green leaves, a blither train. — K.8. 243 *Recluse* 1. 1. 237
Sported. Thus innocently sported, breaking forth — 584 *Ch. Lamb* 19
Where silent zephyrs sported with the dust — 710 *Prelude* 9. 67
Sportest. Dora! sport, as now thou sportest, — 90 *Longest Day* 13
Sporting. I see him sporting on the sunny lawn; — 124 *V. and J.* 204
Sporting with the leaves that fall, — 170 *Kitten* 4
Piping on boughs, or sporting on fresh fields, — 735 *Prelude* 12. 35
Into fleet Oreads sporting visibly. — 814 *Excursion* 4. 876
Sportive. When gentle Spirits urged a sportive chase, — 7 *Ev. Wk.* 301
The sportive outcry of the mocking owl; — 9 *Ev. Wk.* 375
If more divided than a sportive pair — 122 *V. and J.* 25
In all its sportive wanderings, all the while, — 148 **A narrow* 22
Arch, volatile, a sportive bird — 165 *Parrot* 25
"She shall be sportive as the fawn — 187 **Three years* 13
Their daring wiles, their sportive cheer? — 191 *Seq. Beggars* 12
This Stripling, sportive, gay, and bold, — 193 *Ruth* 116
Of sportive wood run wild: these pastoral farms, — 206 *Tintern* 16
And kindle sportive wit— — 222 *Triad* 168
Wherever sportive breezes bend — 227 *Vernal Ode* 69
Light plaything for the sportive wind — 244 *P. B.* 704
That sportive dolphins drew. — 296 *Highland Boy* 120
For sportive youth to stray in; — 302 *Yarrow V.* 58
Urged o'er the wilderness in sportive gallop. — 371 *Eg. Maid* 120
It is not then when, swept with sportive ease, — 467 *St. Bees* 97
Too weak to stand against its sportive breath, — 491 *Tribute: Dog* 19
Such shout as many a sportive echo meeting — 524 *Epist. Beaumont* 205
And fiction animate his sportive lyre, — 528 **Those breathing* 97
Fair Spirits are abroad; in sportive chase — 598 *Ev. Wk. Quarto* 347
A sportive infant, who, for six months' space, — 692 *Prelude* 7. 337
Turned this way—that way! sportive and alert — 693 *Prelude* 7. 438
(The sportive bird's companion in the grove) — 799 *Excursion* 3. 948
The sportive sea-gull dancing with the waves, — 869 *Excursion* 7. 753
More had she said—but sportive shouts were heard — 891 *Excursion* 9. 474
Sportively. Into a silent bay, or sportively — 638 *Prelude* 1. 448
Sports. (Fancy that sports more desperately with minds — 121 *V. and J.* 6
By martial sports,—or, seated in the tent, — 211 *Laod.* 118
Frank are the sports, the stains are fugitive. — 382 *Duddon* 23. 14
For sports of wider range. Ere I had told — 636 *Prelude* 1. 306
Haunting me thus among my boyish sports, — 639 *Prelude* 1. 469
Or centre of these sports; and when, returned — 642 *Prelude* 2. 36
And sports and games (too grateful in themselves, — 662 *Prelude* 4. 283
Mad at their sports like withered leaves in winds; — 672 *Prelude* 5. 416
A man of kindlier nature. The rough sports — 762 *Excursion* 1. 415
Pleasing and pleased, he shared their simple sports, — 778 *Excursion* 2. 450
Their sports together in the solar beam, — 808 *Excursion* 4. 447
Loving the sports which once he gloried in. — 809 *Excursion* 4. 549
Over her comrades; else their simple sports, — 848 *Excursion* 6. 692
Or the clear moon. The queen of these gay sports, — 851 *Excursion* 6. 838
Spot. Were there, below, a spot of holy ground — 10 *Desc. Sk.* 1
Sure, nature's God that spot to man had given — 10 *Desc. Sk.* 4
Of him whom passion rivets to the spot, — 15 *Desc. Sk.* 298
Here, where no trace of man the spot profanes, — 16 *Desc. Sk.* 347
The tempting spot with every sinew strained; — 17 *Desc. Sk.* 383
In spot so savage, but with shuddering pain; — 25 *Guilt* 83
It was a spot where, ancient vows fulfilled, — 27 *Guilt* 148
Was best, could I but shun the spot where man might come. — 31 *Guilt* 360
And soon she reached a spot o'erhung with trees — 34 *Guilt* 538
Upon the self-same spot, in rain or storm, — 44 *Bord.* 391
I met a peasant near the spot; he told me, — 47 *Bord.* 570
Upon the self-same spot, still round and round, — 47 *Bord.* 578
Scarcely, by groping, had I reached the Spot, — 55 *Bord.* 964
All gathered to the spot, in open day — 58 *Bord.* 1122
To dig for water on the spot, the Captain — 68 *Bord.* 1712
And he was famished? Naked was the spot; — 68 *Bord.* 1721
That both are guiltless, without spot or stain, — 70 *Bord.* 1848
let us return to the spot; — 72 *Bord.* 2001
I'll lead you to the spot. — 72 *Bord.* 2013
To climb up to the spot whence the sound came; — 73 *Bord.* 2060
This old man *had* a Daughter. To the spot — 74 *Bord.* 2095
Rose from the spot;—the Daughter clapped her hands, — 74 *Bord.* 2103
It was a spot which you may see — 85 *Shepherd-boys* 49
Him never saw I, nor the spot; but from an English Dame, — 91 *Norman Boy* 5
That, as he knew in what particular spot — 96 *Brothers* 81
The power of speech. Both left the spot in silence; — 101 *Brothers* 408
The loveliest spot that man hath ever found, — 106 *Farewell* 6
Dear Spot! which we have watched with tender heed, — 106 *Farewell* 33
Bright suns without a spot; — 111 **Let other* 2
Alas! before I left the spot, — 121 *Emigrant Mother* 39
And unforewarned, that in some distant spot — 122 *V. and J.* 71
——Soon did the spot become my other home, — 146 **It was an* 40
Close to the spot where with his rod and line — 149 **A narrow* 56
The spot was made by Nature for herself; — 149 *M. H.* 15
Dwelt in a tranquil spot. And oftentimes — 150 **When, to* 26
Of this fair Spot her flowers may bind, — 154 *Flower Garden* 20
We who in this sequestered spot — 155 *Waterfall* 23
This spot is my paternal home, — 156 *Oak and Broom* 66
Mark the spot to which I point! — 157 *Sexton* 9
That spot which seems so to thy mind! — 159 **Up with me* 7
There is a spot that seems to lie — 165 *Danish Boy* 2
And, till life's journey closed, the spot — 168 *Pilgrim's Dream* 69

Spot—*continued.*
Seems changed into a pallid spot. — 173 *Waggoner* 1. 12
With such a charge in such a spot; — 175 *Waggoner* 1. 195
Poor Susan has passed by the spot, and has heard — 188 *Poor Susan* 3
Of human Beings, in the self-same spot! — 192 *Gipsies* 2
But would you gladly view the spot, — 198 *Thorn* 91
The spot to which she goes; — 198 *Thorn* 92
Then to the spot away! — 198 *Thorn* 97
Approach the spot when she is there." — 198 *Thorn* 99
And gazed and gazed upon that darling spot. — 201 *Hart-leap* 48
"I'll build a pleasure-house upon this spot, — 201 *Hart-leap* 57
But something ails it now: the spot is curst. — 202 *Hart-leap* 124
That grafted, on so fair a spot, — 224 *'Tis gone* 20
To that green spot, so calm and green! — 240 *P. B.* 375
Across the deep and quiet spot — 240 *P. B.* 381
Upon the spot where he had stood, — 241 *P. B.* 429
A spot where, in a sheltering cove, — 246 *P. B.* 852
Old Skiddaw will look down upon the Spot — 251 *Appleth.* 13
That spot which no vicissitude can find? — 257 **Surprised by* 4
In ours, the Vale of Friendship, let *this* spot — 272 *Lady E. B.* 10
Thou com'st to man's abode the spot grew dearer — 281 **What strong* 3
Of things, has fenced this fairest spot on earth. — 284 *Departure* 18
Whose Fancy in this lonely Spot — 289 *Glen-Al.* 20
To this small spot, his leafy shade; — 298 *Brownie's Cell* 44
Wild Relique! beauteous as the chosen spot — 299 *Brownie's Cell* 91
More worthy of this favoured Spot; — 300 *Bran* 43
In thy fresh beauty. There! that dusky spot — 303 **Fair Star* 9
Spot rich in all things that can soothe and please! — 308 **One might* 8
Hovered in air above the far-famed Spot. — 334 **A wingèd* 5
Made known the spot where piety should raise — 338 *Engelberg* 13
And all the Pomps of this frail "spot — 341 *San Salv.* 20
The genial spot had *ever* shown — 348 **Lulled by* 10
Which hath not left the spot unknown — 348 **Lulled by* 70
His presence to point out the spot where once — 356 *Aquap.* 258
This spot—his shadowy death-cup in his hand. — 361 **For action* 14
To dignify the spot that gives thee birth — 376 *Duddon* 3. 9
Of tillage-ground, that seemeth like a spot — 379 *Duddon* 14. 5
Humanity is humble, finds no spot — 390 *Highland Hut* 7
Turn towards the spot where, full in view, — 398 *White Doe* 167
Faint—but it reached that sheltered spot; — 401 *White Doe* 433
Of rising ground, yon heathy spot! — 404 *White Doe* 763
A spot of shame to the sun's bright eye, — 405 *White Doe* 851
But calmly from the spot withdrew; — 406 *White Doe* 935
For pleasure made, a goodly spot, — 407 *White Doe* 984
Of people, sees them in one spot— — 413 *White Doe* 1545
And bless for both this savage spot; — 415 *White Doe* 1798
Had sown the spot, that witnessed them, with seeds — 466 *St. Bees* 60
A peaceful spot where Nature's gifts abound; — 470 †*From early* 12
Thanks for the lessons of this Spot—fit school — 473 **Thanks for* 1
Where are ye? Driven or venturing to the spot, — 473 **Ye shadowy* 3
So from the spot whereon he stood, — 479 *Somnamb.* 118
The Dog had watched about the spot, — 492 *Fidelity* 60
Each field is then a hallowed spot, — 506 *Lab. Hymn* 17
Whether conducted to the spot by sighs — 516 **Feel for* 4
This Spot—at once unfolding sight so fair — 517 *Pun. Death* 1. 1
Turn from a spot where neither sheltered road — 521 *Epist. Beaumont* 12
Nor ever was; I sighed, and left the spot — 524 *Epist. Beaumont* 194
With door left open makes a gloomy spot, — 524 *Epist. Beaumont* 220
Thus in the chosen spot a tie so strong — 531 **I know* 21
At this time, and on this spot, — 535 *Egremont* 22
A sanctuary seemed the spot — 543 *Russ. Fug.* 109
And when those rites had ceased, the Spot gave birth — 547 **Beneath yon* 7
A favourite spot of tournament and war! — 548 **Stay, bold* 6
And make himself a freeman of this spot — 548 **Stranger! this* 10
This quiet spot; and, Stranger! not unmoved — 551 **If thou in* 5
She for her Son in that same spot did cry — 555 *Prioress* 154
Come to the spot in wonder at the thing; — 555 *Prioress* 164
Forth from the spot he rideth up and down, — 563 *Troilus* 43
A spot, that angles at the riv'let's feet, — 592 *Ev. Wk. Quarto* 46
And emerald isles to spot the heights appear, — 610 *Desc. Sk. Quarto* 445
That made the calmest, fairest spot of earth, — 621 *Recluse* 1. 1. 73
I led my Lucy to the spot, "Look here!" — 623 **Among all* 19
Yet, to this hour, the spot to me is dear — 644 *Prelude* 2. 154
As near and nearer to the spot we drew, — 649 *Prelude* 3. 13
To a floating island, an amphibious spot — 654 *Prelude* 3. 333
And spot in which she lived, and through a grace — 670 *Prelude* 5. 290
Fair is the spot, most beautiful the vale — 671 *Prelude* 5. 391
Drew to the spot an anxious crowd; some looked — 672 *Prelude* 5. 444
Let this one temple last, be this one spot — 681 *Prelude* 6. 434
That to the spot which had perplexed us first — 683 *Prelude* 6. 580
Upon the spot where she was born and reared; — 692 *Prelude* 7. 321
The spectacle, by visiting the spot. — 705 *Prelude* 8. 420
In haste, each spot of old or recent fame, — 710 *Prelude* 9. 44
Of ancient Story, thought of each bright spot, — 715 *Prelude* 9. 365
He walks about and looks upon the spot — 729 *Prelude* 11. 149
From this last spot of earth, where Freedom now — 733 *Prelude* 11. 400
Tarrying at will in many a pleasant spot — 751 *Prelude* 14. 352
My thirst I slaked, and, from the cheerless spot — 763 *Excursion* 1. 463
The spot, though fair, was very desolate— — 767 *Excursion* 1. 740
She loved this wretched spot, nor would for worlds — 770 *Excursion* 1. 911
He thus imparted:—"In a spot that lies — 773 *Excursion* 2. 155
Among the mountains; even as if the spot — 776 *Excursion* 2. 330
Upon a bed of heath;—full many a spot — 776 *Excursion* 2. 351
Led toward the Cottage. Homely was the spot; — 781 *Excursion* 2. 638
In spot so parsimoniously endowed, — 786 *Excursion* 3. 17
And a few steps may bring us to the spot — 786 *Excursion* 3. 32
Loth to forsake the spot, and still more loth — 791 *Excursion* 3. 330
A parting tribute to a spot that seemed — 822 *Excursion* 5. 15

Spot—*continued.*
From academic bowers. He loved the spot— 824 *Excursion* 5. 115
Withdrew; and straight we followed,—to a spot 825 *Excursion* 5. 225
For, from this pregnant spot of ground, such thoughts 828 *Excursion* 5. 371
A house of stones collected on the spot, 833 *Excursion* 5. 693
While in a spot like this we breathe and walk, 836 *Excursion* 5. 923
Lodged, in a dear appropriated spot, 836 *Excursion* 5. 945
Was the particular spot, in which they wished 845 *Excursion* 6. 500
If these may make a hallowed spot of earth 850 *Excursion* 6. 802
Could field or grove, could any spot of earth, 850 *Excursion* 6. 807
" You see the Infant's Grave; and to this spot, 853 *Excursion* 6. 983
That little shady spot, that sylvan tuft, 858 *Excursion* 7. 50
Naked without, and rude within; a spot 859 *Excursion* 7. 138
From this lone valley, to a central spot 869 *Excursion* 7. 768
Down on this spot, well pleased would he have seen 871 *Excursion* 7. 880
Of human nature, in a spot like this, 874 *Excursion* 8. 15
Spirit that knows no insulated spot, 884 *Excursion* 9. 13
Of that wild spot, the Solitary said 892 *Excursion* 9. 548
Soft heath this elevated spot supplied, 892 *Excursion* 9. 580
Musing, the lone spot with my soul agrees S.3. 417 **Sweet was* 10
On unknown snows, a spot unknown. K.8. 220 **The snow-tracks* 30
This spot to me must needs be dear, K.8. 220 **The snow-tracks* 31
For rest of body, perfect was the spot, K.8. 237 *Recluse* 1.1. 22
Something that makes this individual Spot, K.8. 240 *Recluse* 1.1.145
Behold a dusky spot, a grove of Firs, K.8. 247 *Recluse* 1.1.385

Spotless. To lead a Spirit, spotless as the blessed, 47 *Bord.* 545
And make the spotless spirit of filial love 57 *Bord.* 1063
Whose means are fair and spotless as his ends." 214 *Dion* 124
Wrapt in a winding-sheet of spotless snows! 217 *Enterprise* 118
White, radiant, spotless, exquisitely pure, 263 **How clear* 12
Her spotless limbs; and ventured to explore 264 **Lady! I* 6
From Calais with us, spotless in array,— 305 **We had* 2
Now, on the margin of some spotless fountain, 325 *Ode 1814* 123
(Whose tranquil pomp and spotless purity 329 *Ode: Thanks.* 23
Whose memory, spotless as the crystal beads 330 *Ode: Thanks.* 64
And what if Duddon's spotless flood receive 382 *Duddon* 23. 9
Is spotless, and holy, and gentle, and bright; 398 *White Doe* 240
(A spotless Youngling white as foam) 416 *White Doe* 1806
Spotless in life, and eloquent as wise, 438 *Ecc. Sonn.* 2. 40. 2
By right of birth; within whose spotless breast 844 *Excursion* 6. 414
The spotless ether of a maiden life; 850 *Excursion* 6. 801
She gazed as on a pure and spotless gift 852 *Excursion* 6. 908

Spots. Into blue spots, and slowly lengthening streaks; 4 *Ev. Wk.* 119
On darling spots remote her tempting smile. 8 *Ev. Wk.* 344
As quietly as spots of sky 193 *Ruth* 71
The spots that to my soul adhere; 214 *Dion* 97
Such tempting spots as into vision come 268 **Four fiery* 11
Disposed some cultured Flowerets (drawn from spots 280 *Valedict.* 2
In spots like these it is we prize 288 *Highland Girl* 66
Upon the spots with undelighted eye, 356 *Aquap.* 274
Spots where a word, ghost-like, survives to show 389 *Sound of Mull* 5
Herself, in spots unseen before. 415 *White Doe* 1709
Haunting the spots with lonely cheer 416 *White Doe* 1879
Surely, from fairest spots of favoured lands, 455 *Rydal Mere* 17
With fancied spots contending; 479 *Somnamb.* 85
In lonely spots, become a slighted thing;) 527 **Those breathing* 4
To spots remote, and draw his diagrams 677 *Prelude* 6. 151
Some miniature of famous spots or things,— 691 *Prelude* 7. 251
And on these spots with many gleams I looked 716 *Prelude* 9. 500
On this and other spots, as doth a man 719 *Prelude* 10. 58
And as the desert hath green spots, the sea 725 *Prelude* 10. 481
Not favoured spots alone, but the whole Earth, 729 *Prelude* 11. 117
There are in our existence spots of time, 737 *Prelude* 12. 208
From brooding clouds; shadows that lay in spots 756 *Excursion* 1. 6
The spots where such abide! But happier still 823 *Excursion* 5. 37
His finger moved, distinguishing the spots 869 *Excursion* 7. 796
Where nature works in wild and craggy spots, 871 *Excursion* 7. 917
To his own hills, the spots where when a lamb K.8. 228 **I will* 126

Spotted. *See* **Crimson-spotted, Star-spotted.**
When into one of those same spotted bells 44 *Bord.* 403
" I've heard, the moss is spotted red 200 *Thorn* 210
Lay spotted with a variegated crowd 726 *Prelude* 10. 563
Where couch the spotted deer; or raised our eyes 892 *Excursion* 9. 563

Spotting. Spotting the northern cliffs with lights between; 3 *Ev. Wk.* 40
Spotting the steaming deeps, to early mass; 604 *Desc. Sk. Quarto* 145

Spousal. The spousal trembling, and the "dust to dust," 451 *Ecc. Sonn.* 3. 41. 12
Would chant, in lonely peace, the spousal verse 755 *Recluse* 1. 1. 810

Spousals. To secret 'spousals meanly disavowed. 125 *V. and J.* 239
From the great spousals newly solemnized 681 *Prelude* 6. 389

Spout. *See* **Water-spout.**
First one and then another silver spout, K.8. 251 *Recluse* 1.1.555

Spouting. Clustering, with barn and byre, and spouting mill! 379 *Duddon* 13. 3
Roll on, ye spouting whales, who die or keep 527 **Those breathing* 33

Spouts. By spouts and fountains wild 195 *Ruth* 249
Fountains and spouts, yet somewhat in the guise K.8. 251 *Recluse* 1.1.557

Sprang. The happiest bird that sprang out of the Ark! 153 *Morn. Ex.* 30
Forth sprang the impassioned Queen her Lord to clasp; 210 *Laod.* 25
Sprang up, and spread their fragrance wide around; 466 *St. Bees* 50
He sprang in glee,—for what cared he 494 *Force of Prayer* 29
And sprang upon poor Goody Blake. 537 *Goody Blake* 88
Savona was my birthplace, and I sprang 574 *Chiabrera* 4. 29
Sprang out of fountains, there abounding most, 701 *Prelude* 8. 125

Sprang—*continued.*
Sprang from a stock of lowly parentage 774 *Excursion* 2. 165
Borne by yon clustering cottages, that sprang 872 *Excursion* 7. 968
Sprang like a gust of wind: [and with a heart K.8. 228 **I will* 119
The sheep sprang forward to the further shore, K.8. 229 **I will* 150

Spray. *See* **Mother-spray.**
Where the green apple shrivels on the spray, 15 *Desc. Sk.* 258
Of green leaves on the hawthorn spray, 81 †*Mother's Return* 38
Proved last year's leaves, pushed from the spray 170 *Rural Ill.* 11
With holly spray, 285 *Nith* 4
If from a golden perch of aspen spray 388 *Trosachs* 10
While blossoms and the budding spray 497 *Lycoris* 51
Dancing and leaping light upon the spray; 558 *Cuck. and Night.* 77
Dwindles the pear on autumn's latest spray, 608 *Desc. Sk. Quarto* 321
And outer spray profusely tipped with seeds 676 *Prelude* 6. 83
Of leafy spray, concealed the stems and roots 881 *Excursion* 8. 444

Spread. *See* **Broad-spread, O'erspread, Outspread, Wide-spread.**
Steal down the hill, and spread along the flood. 9 *Ev. Wk.* 364
Spread rooflike o'er the deep secluded vale, 14 *Desc. Sk.* 211
In sea-like reach of prospect round him spread, 19 *Desc. Sk.* 474
No sparkling rivulet spread the verdant herb? 22 *Yew-tree* 3
And vacant, a huge waste around him spread; 25 *Guilt* 44
It was a rustic inn;—the board was spread, 34 *Guilt* 528
The tale was spread abroad; my power at once 69 *Bord.* 1761
Do spread, and sink, and rise; 108 *Louisa*
To imprint a kiss that lacked not power to spread 119 *Maternal Grief* 61
What pleasure through my veins you spread 155 *Waterfall* 26
Spread here his careless blossoms, here 156 *Oak and Broom* 69
With brightest sunshine round me spread 159 *Green Linnet* 3
Thus pleasure is spread through the earth 167 *Stray Pleasures* 27
Across the welkin seemed to spread 167 *Pilgrim's Dream* 50
The Primrose for a veil had spread 169 *Wren's Nest* 57
Sails spread, as if to catch the wind! 179 *Waggoner* 3. 69
Against the storm, and canvas spread. 179 *Waggoner* 3. 82
Hung low, begin to rise and spread; 180 *Waggoner* 4. 58
So feebly spread that not a shadow falls, 184 *Night-piece* 6
He told of the magnolia, spread 193 *Ruth* 61
Trust in that sovereign law can spread 224 *'*Tis gone* 58
And vapours magnify and spread 228 *Devot. Incit.* 66
The soul of happy sound was spread, 239 *P. B.* 257
And rocks that spread a hoary gleam, 240 *P. B.* 392
Lo, in the vale, the mists of evening spread! 252 **The fairest* 9
Forthwith that little cloud, in ether spread 265 **The Shepherd* 3
The Highlanders, the slaughter spread like flame; 293 *Killicranky* 5
Spread round that haven in the glen; 296 *Highland Boy* 112
Meek loveliness is round thee spread, 302 *Yarrow V.* 45
And, wheresoe'er she spread her sovereignty, 311 **Who rises* 31
I saw the banquet spread beneath a Dome of state, 324 *Ode 1814* 74
And fame as largely spread as land and sea, 325 *Ode 1814* 148
The Cross shall spread, the Crescent hath waxed dim; 326 *Sobieski* 12
In unambitious compass round thee spread. 339 *Schwytz* 8
Still moonshine, without shadow, spread 343 *Eclipse* 27
Spread over Grasmere's lovely dale, 344 *Eclipse* 77
Is then the final page before me spread, 350 *Des. Stanzas* 1
And purity of nature spread before your sight! 350 *Des. Stanzas* 54
Where now the haughty Empire that was spread 368 *Trajan* 65
More glorious, with spread sail and streaming pendant. 369 *Eg. Maid* 12
In simple childhood, spread through ours! 375 **The Minstrels* 30
What hopes came with him? what designs were spread 378 *Duddon* 8. 4
That rises here, and humbly spread, the sail; 384 *Duddon* 33. 4
If, *then*, some natural shadows spread 386 *Yarrow Rev.* 37
As eagerly pursued; the umbrella spread 388 **The pibroch's* 6
Who, to spread wide the reverence they claimed 389 *Sound of Mull* 12
Like vapours, years have rolled and spread; 391 *Highland Broach* 80
Fair parks spread wide where Adam Bell might deign 393 *Inglewood* 6
The Hermit saw the Angel spread his wings 393 **The Lovers* 3
Of stone, and ivy, and the spread 397 *White Doe* 95
And quickly spread themselves abroad, 398 *White Doe* 160
Bright locks of silver hair, thick spread, 404 *White Doe* 746
Hung with late-flowering woodbine, spread 407 *White Doe* 1023
Confusion through the Camp spread wide: 408 *White Doe* 1158
To spread its arms, and stand for aye. 410 *White Doe* 1269
Spread by triumphant cruelties 411 *White Doe* 1382
Is stripped; the ravage hath spread wide 413 *White Doe* 1576
That used to spread its boughs, and ring 413 *White Doe* 1588
Distress and desolation spread 416 *White Doe* 1842
They come—they spread—the weak, the suffering, hear; 419 *Ecc. Sonn.* 1. 3. 13
The fostered hyacinths spread their purple bloom. 425 *Ecc. Sonn.* 1. 27. 14
Helps to restore and spread a Pagan sway: 426 *Ecc. Sonn.* 1. 29. 4
By superstition, spread the Papal power; 429 *Ecc. Sonn.* 2. 2. 2
By truth, shall spread, throughout the world dispersed." 433 *Ecc. Sonn.* 2. 17. 14
But passions spread like plagues, and thousands wild 435 *Ecc. Sonn.* 2. 29. 12
Spread through all ranks; and lo! the Sentinel 442 *Ecc. Sonn.* 3. 11. 4
How widely spread the interests of our theme. 443 *Ecc. Sonn.* 3. 12. 14
These lofty pillars, spread that branching roof 451 *Ecc. Sonn.* 3. 43. 9
The silent Cross, among the stars shall spread 452 *Ecc. Sonn.* 3. 45. 11
For sway profoundly felt as widely spread; 455 *Rydal Mere* 28
An intermingling of Heaven's pomp is spread 457 **Had this* 39
And spread as if ye knew that days might come 463 **Adieu, Rydalian* 2
Sprang up, and spread their fragrance wide around; 466 *St. Bees* 50
So patiently; and through one hand has spread 476 *Howard* 5
His fame may spread, but in the past 479 *Somnamb.* 73
Where clouds that spread in solemn shade, 479 *Somnamb.* 156

Sprinkled. *See* **Cottage-sprinkled, Dew-sprinkled, Holly-sprinkled.**
And juniper and thistle, sprinkled o'er, — 23 *Yew-tree* 29
His flock, along the woodland's edge with relics sprinkled o'er — 91 *Norman Boy* 9
With Ships the sea was sprinkled far and nigh, — 258 **With Ships* 1
Hail to the fields—with Dwellings sprinkled o'er, — 379 *Duddon* 13. 1
Yet spake this Child when sprinkled was the water; — 555 *Prioress* 189
Of pleasure sprinkled over, shady dells — 700 *Prelude* 8. 85
A kerchief sprinkled with his master's blood, — 778 *Excursion* 2. 478
Sprinkled;—be our Companion while we track — 819 *Excursion* 4. 1198
Sprinkles. Covers, or sprinkles o'er, yon village green? — 699 *Prelude* 8. 5
Sprinkles these little pastures but the same — K.8. 248 *Recluse* 1.1.442
Sprinkling. Thy hand here sprinkling tiny flowers, — 170 *Rural Ill.* 15
The little sprinkling of cold earth that fell — 234 *Power of Sound* 156
Insinuated, sprinkling all the shore, — 604 *Desc.Sk.Quarto* 126
Sprinkling this talk with questions, better spared, — 665 *Prelude* 4. 438
Sprinklings. Leaf-scattering winds; and hoar-frost sprinklings fell — 394 **No more* 27
What sprinklings of blithe company! — 396 *White Doe* 10
The season) sprinklings of ripe strawberry fruit. — 529 *Poor Robin* 14
Prolonged till sprinklings of autumnal snow — 686 *Prelude* 6. 730
Bright sprinklings of all human excellence, — 725 *Prelude* 10. 484
Sprite. "Trust, angry Bard! a knowing Sprite, — 164 *Needlecase* 37
Where is he that giddy Sprite, — 171 *Kitten* 63
Repentance is a tender Sprite; — 238 *P. B.* 148
The kitten frolic, like a gamesome sprite, — 294 **Fly, some* 6
And Care waylays their steps—a Sprite — 386 *Yarrow Rev.* 47
Sprites. Glance to and fro, like aery Sprites — 499 **This Lawn* 11
Sprout. The leafy antlers sprout; — 168 *Wren's Nest* 36
Sprouting. *See* **Thickly-sprouting.**
Sprung. From which her graces and her honours sprung: — 122 *V. and J.* 16
From Indian blood you deem him sprung: — 192 *Ruth* 25
From Hebrew fountains sprung; — 232 *Jew. Fam.* 44
Conscious of blessedness, but, whence it sprung, — 279 **Though I* 5
Of admiration sprung from truth; — 301 *Bran* 114
Which Milton held.—In every thing we are sprung — 307 **It is not* 13
And ye, Pierian Sisters, sprung from Jove — 325 *Ode 1814* 111
Now, from Heaven-sanctioned victory, Peace is sprung; — 326 **Emperors and* 7
Though sprung from bleeding war, is one of pure delight; — 331 *Ode: Thanks.* 195
Like something out of Ocean sprung — 370 *Eg. Maid* 45
What crimes from hate, or desperate love, have sprung; — 389 *Sound of Mull* 6
A waste of hope?—From this sad source have sprung — 423 *Ecc. Sonn.* 1. 20. 5
As if a Church, though sprung from heaven, must owe — 443 *Ecc. Sonn.* 3. 11. 11
If loves and joys, while up they sprung, — 507 *May* 69
Or haply sprung from vaunting Cowardice — 514 **Portentous change* 7
Of chieftains sprung, who stoutly bore — 533 **Blest is* 12
"From Gallic parents sprung, — 545 *Russ. Fug.* 314
With two collateral stems sprung from one root; — 585 *Ch. Lamb* 97
Forth rushed from Envy sprung and Self-conceit, — 626 *Ballot* 1
From its Hero is sprung. — 629 *Installation* 108
To duty, *might* have sprung up of itself — 677 *Prelude* 6. 185
Had sprung, their transmigrations, when and how — 711 *Prelude* 9. 103
Of mortal power unquestionably sprung) — 788 *Excursion* 3. 144
Had sprung, like those bright creatures, from the soil — 790 *Excursion* 3. 251
Sprung from the desert? And behold a city — 799 *Excursion* 3. 884
Though from another sprung, different in kind: — 843 *Excursion* 6. 368
That it had sprung self-raised from earth, or grown. — 855 *Excursion* 6. 1144
Sprung from high Jove, of sage Mnemosyne — S.3. 436 **The doubt* 151
Already hath sprung up within my heart — K.8. 250 *Recluse* 1.1.504
Spun. A daughter sent to service, a web spun, — 97 *Brothers* 159
"For there," said he, "are spun — 193 *Ruth* 87
Indulgent centuries spun a thread, — 224 **'Tis gone* 23
Unhallowed threads of revelry are spun; — 433 *Ecc. Sonn.* 2. 20. 2
All day she spun in her poor dwelling: — 536 *Goody Blake* 25
Or Reason's? No—hopes spun in timid line — 626 **Son of* 11
By youthful squires; adventures endless, spun — 673 *Prelude* 5. 500
A leprous stain! ere half his thread was spun — L.1. 96 *Juvenal* 3. 47
Spur. There is no need of boot or spur, — 126 *Idiot Boy* 47
Stoops willingly to animate and spur — 268 **Dogmatic Teachers* 8
May spur me on, in manhood now mature, — 641 *Prelude* 1. 624
And eager to spur on, the galloping steed; — 643 *Prelude* 2. 97
With whip and spur we through the chauntry flew — 643 *Prelude* 2. 116
Spur-clad. Spur-clad his nervous feet, and firm his tread; — 5 *Ev. Wk.* 148
Spurious. False Shame discarded, spurious Fame despised, — 70 *Bord.* 1834
And shapes of spurious fame and short-lived praise — 657 *Prelude* 3. 592
This spurious virtue, rather let it bear — 675 *Prelude* 6. 30
Of spurious notions—worn as open signs — 775 *Excursion* 2. 271
Spurn. Or (if need be) impediment to spurn, — 269 *Gordale* 13
Less than divine command they spurn; — 300 *Cora Linn* 31
From some high-minded Slave, impelled to spurn — 501 *Humanity* 65
Spurn Reason's law and humour Passion's rage; — 618 *School Ex.* 10
Spurn the soft fetters of lethargic rest. — 619 *School Ex.* 108
Spurned. Well!—he has often spurned me like a toad, — 45 *Bord.* 470
With haughty indignation, spurned the thought — 122 *V. and J.* 18
But him the haughty Warder spurned; — 167 *Pilgrim's Dream* 4
And humours change, are spurned like weeds: — 228 *Devot. Incit.* 49

Spurned—*continued.*
And ye—full often spurned as weeds— — 366 **Ye Trees* 12
Spurned it, like something that would stand — 401 *White Doe* 518
Ah! if the old idolatry be spurned, — 434 *Ecc. Sonn.* 2. 24. 3
I spurned his lawless suit, — 542 *Russ. Fug.* 68
Sweet honey out of spurned or dreaded weeds. — 669 *Prelude* 5. 278
And with an oriental loathing spurned, — 714 *Prelude* 9. 291
Spurning. Spurning her freight with indignation! — 238 *P. B.* 172
Spurning the unprofitable yoke of care, — 260 **From the dark* 2
Which, spurning God, had flung away remorse— — 330 *Ode: Thanks.* 119
And saintly magnanimity; that—spurning — 845 *Excursion* 6. 484
Spurns. Which spurns the check of salutary bands, — 307 **It is not* 6
Spurred. Poor Walter! whether it was care that spurred him — 98 *Brothers* 217
Spurring. In former days, when—spurring from the Vale — 727 *Prelude* 10. 597
Spurs. The form appears of one that spurs his steed — 6 *Ev. Wk.* 196
A desperate form appears, that spurs his steed, — 595 *Ev. Wk. Quarto* 179
The whip, the cap, and spurs, thy praise attest; — L.1. 94 *Juvenal* 2. 22
Spy. Of the sun peeping through the clouds can spy, — 21 *Desc. Sk.* 602
You yet may spy the fawn at play, — 83 *Lucy Gray* 9
Joys to spy thee near her home; — 160 **Pansies, lilies* 39
There sits he; in his face you spy — 166 *Danish Boy* 45
Must spy about him far and near: — 240 *P. B.* 387
That looks for evil like a treacherous spy; — 500 *Humanity* 50
Should sometimes think, where'er they chance to spy — 530 *Poor Robin* 31
The veil, or where it parts at once, to spy — K.8. 249 *Recluse* 1.1.479
Squadrons. Your squadrons to an endless flight of birds — 230 *Clouds* 17
And sent him forth, with squadrons of his kind, — 321 **Humanity, delighting* 29
Sonorous squadrons sing their evening hymn. — K.8. 234 **The order'd* 7
Squalid. A creature, squalid, vengeful, and impure; — 800 *Excursion* 3. 95
Square. In great and small, in round and square, — 128 *Idiot Boy* 208
From this platform, eight feet square, — 157 *Sexton* 10
Mantling in the tiny square. — 161 **Pleasures newly* 24
The Showman chooses well his place, 'tis Leicester's busy Square; — 189 *Star-gazers* 5
Three aspens at three corners of a square; — 202 *Hart-leap* 103
Half wasted the square mound of tawny green; — 202 *Hart-leap* 110
Long, barren silence, square with my desire; — 488 *Pers. Talk* 10
In square divisions parcelled out and all — 639 *Prelude* 1. 510
Of native rock, left midway in the square — 642 *Prelude* 2. 34
Split like a province into round and square? — 645 *Prelude* 2. 205
Him saw I, sitting in an open square, — 696 *Prelude* 7. 604
I crossed the square (an empty area then!) — 719 *Prelude* 10. 55
Squares. Adorning flowery gardens, 'mid vast squares; — 689 *Prelude* 7. 135
Squeak. A grand domain to squeak and gibber in. — 61 *Bord.* 1304
The fiddle's *squeak*—that call to bliss, — 177 *Waggoner* 2. 97
Squeamish. That some there are, squeamish half-thinking cowards, — 64 *Bord.* 1508
The squeamish in taste, and the narrow of mind, — 569 *Farmer* 2
Squire. *See* **Esquire.**
Shall squire you, (would it not be better, Sir?) — 43 *Bord.* 312
Knight, squire, and yeoman, page and groom: — 204 *Brougham* 38
The Squire is come: his daughter Bess — 238 *P. B.* 158
"Hold!" cried the Squire, "against the rules — 238 *P. B.* 196
When squire, and priest, and they who round them dwelt — 761 *Excursion* 1. 329
Of country 'squire; or at the statelier board — 859 *Excursion* 7. 124
Squires. From many knights and many squires — 287 *Ellen Irwin* 9
Lords, lawyers, statesmen, squires of low degree, — 303 **Is it* 3
By youthful squires; adventures endless, spun — 673 *Prelude* 5. 500
Squirrel. As light and beauteous as a squirrel, — 246 *P. B.* 889
St. *See* **Saint.**
Stab. Where he can stab you deepest. Clifford never — 42 *Bord.* 281
Shall it be law to stab the petty robber — 53 *Bord.* 894
But how, what say you, Oswald? Stab him, were it — 57 *Bord.* 1069
Stability. Heaved over ruin with stability — 474 **On to* 3
Stability without regret or fear; — 791 *Excursion* 3. 386
Stable. Undaunted, lofty, calm, and stable, — 414 *White Doe* 1627
Could cleanse the Augean stable, by the might — 726 *Prelude* 10. 585
Whose root is fixed in stable earth, whose head — 831 *Excursion* 5. 568
Her simple manners, and the stable worth — 877 *Excursion* 8. 237
Stable-boy. Served as stable-boy, errand-boy, porter, and groom; — 570 *Farmer* 50
'Stablished. *See* **Established.**
"O Martyr 'stablished in virginity! — 554 *Prioress* 128
Stack. *See* **Hay-stack.**
Stacks. *See* **Corn-stacks.**
Staff. *See* **Banner-staff, Oak-staff.**
Help from the staff he bore; for mien and air — 24 *Guilt* 4
"The staff I well remember which upbore — 28 *Guilt* 217
That staff of yours, I could almost have heart — 39 *Bord.* 126
His staff—his figure—Murder!—what, of whom? — 54 *Bord.* 926
Sit unmolested on his staff.—Innocent! — 62 *Bord.* 1379
God and that staff are now thy only guides. — 63 *Bord.* 1416
His staff had dropped, and close upon the brink — 73 *Bord.* 2062
With staff in hand across the cleft — 85 *Shepherd-boys* 56
His shepherd's staff; for on that Pillar of rock — 101 *Brothers* 403
"Up, Timothy, up with your staff and away! — 119 *Childless Father* 1
Old Timothy took up his staff, and he shut — 120 *Childless Father* 15
Due requisites a perfect shepherd's staff, — 134 *Michael* 183
Though nought was left undone which staff, or voice, — 134 *Michael* 192
Upon a long grey staff of shaven wood: — 196 *Resolution* 72
Stirred with his staff, and fixedly did look — 196 *Resolution* 79
The staff was raised to loftier height, — 238 *P. B.* 193

Staff—*continued.*
His staff high-raising, in the pride . . . . . 241 *P. B.* 423
He lifts his head, he sees his staff ; . . . . 242 *P. B.* 541
And downward thrust his staff, intent . . . . 242 *P. B.* 554
Nor dares to move unpropped upon the staff . . 277 **A Poet* 2
Propped on a staff, and, through the sullen day, . 321 **Humanity, delighting* 4
That Wisdom wears, or take his treacherous staff 358 *Aquap.* 354
Then did he seize the staff, and say : . . . . 400 *White Doe* 405
Or staff more harmless than a shepherd's crook, . 423 *Ecc. Sonn.* 1. 21. 3
Thy warlike person with the staff and scrip ; . . 427 *Ecc. Sonn.* 1. 35. 3
Were mine the trusty staff that Jewel gave . . 438 *Ecc. Sonn.* 2. 39. 3
Which staff and cockle hat and sandal shoon . . 467 *St. Bees* 94
And lean upon a peasant's staff. . . . . . 485 *Poet's Epitaph* 16
Upon a living staff, with borrowed sight. . . . 496 **A little* 10
What is truth ?—a staff rejected ; . . . . . 549 *Hermit's Cell* 1. 17
Had placed his staff across the broad smooth stone 566 *Cumb. Beg.* 7
Approached within the length of half his staff. . 566 *Cumb. Beg.* 21
His staff trails with him ; scarcely do his feet . 567 *Cumb. Beg.* 59
His staff is a sceptre—his grey hairs a crown ; . 569 *Farmer* 6
So with his staff the Cripple wrought . . . . 621 *Andrew Jones* 18
And blind Authority beating with his staff . . 657 *Prelude* 3. 605
No dog attending, by no staff sustained, . . . 664 *Prelude* 4. 400
An oaken staff by me yet unobserved— . . . 665 *Prelude* 4. 428
A staff which must have dropt from his slack hand 665 *Prelude* 4. 429
With a long staff upon the sand, and thus . . 677 *Prelude* 6. 152
Not slow to share my wishes, took his staff, . . 680 *Prelude* 6. 324
His staff protending like a hunter's spear, . . . 702 *Prelude* 8. 246
Veiled nun, or pilgrim resting on his staff : . . 708 *Prelude* 8. 587
But now, relinquishing the scrip and staff, . . 710 *Prelude* 9. 36
An iron-pointed staff lay at his side. . . . . 756 *Excursion* 1. 37
Turned toward the sun then setting, while that staff 756 *Excursion* 1. 40
Who now, with no appendage but a staff, . . . 762 *Excursion* 1. 435
I took my staff, and, when I kissed her babe, . 768 *Excursion* 1. 809
Upon the self-same nail ; his very staff . . . 769 *Excursion* 1. 853
Of hopeful preparation, grasped his staff ; . . . 771 *Excursion* 1. 966
Accoutred with his burthen and his staff ; . . . 772 *Excursion* 2. 26
Let us proceed." Then, pointing with his staff . 773 *Excursion* 2. 153
Ascended, with his staff and faithful dog ; . . 863 *Excursion* 7. 420
The outcry of his son : he stretched his staff . . K.8. 230 **I will* 175

Staffs. And grey-haired sires, on staffs supported, . 324 *Ode 1814* 65
Or is the painted staffs [? staff's] avenging host . L.1. 97 *Juvenal* 3. 85

Staff-supported. That bearded, staff-supported Sire— 398 *White Doe* 217

Stag. "And, gallant Stag ! to make thy praises known, ... 201 *Hart-leap* 65
Nor paused, till o'er the stag he blew . . . . 544 *Russ. Fug.* 275

Stage. Move, as the verdure leads, from stage to stage; 17 *Desc. Sk.* 375
But sickness stopped me in an early stage . . . 35 *Guilt* 581
What time his injured country is a stage . . . 318 **Is there* 6
From yon steep mountain's loftiest stage, . . . 341 *San Salv.* 2
On the third stage of thy great destiny. . . . 361 *Alban Hills* 14
Which tiny Elves impressed ;—on that smooth stage . . . . 378 *Duddon* 11. 4
Hurled down a mountain-cove from stage to stage, 424 *Ecc. Sonn.* 1. 22. 4
One duty more, last stage of this ascent, . . . 446 *Ecc. Sonn.* 3. 25. 2
Stage above stage) would sit this Island's King, . 470 *Tynwald* 3
Nothing ? Heaven keep us from a lower stage ! . 489 *Illus. Books* 14
And nearer interests culled from the opening stage 522 *Epist. Beaumont* 90
Though sure of plaudits on his costly stage, . . 528 **Those breathing* 63
With which his genius shook the buskined stage. 547 **Beneath yon* 16
Filling from time to time his " humorous stage " 589 *Immortality* 103
The summer long to feed from stage to stage ; . 610 *Desc. Sk. Quarto* 457
He dons his coat of darkness : on the stage . . 691 *Prelude* 7. 281
His little stage in the vast theatre, ... 692 *Prelude* 7. 358
And measured passions of the stage, albeit . . 693 *Prelude* 7. 405
Before the ermined judge, or that great stage . . 694 *Prelude* 7. 491
Upwards through every stage of the tall stem, . 705 *Prelude* 8. 394
Into a theatre, whose stage was filled . . . . 711 *Prelude* 9. 94
When the bodily eye, in every stage of life . . 736 *Prelude* 12. 128
" A child of earth, I rested, in that stage . . 792 *Excursion* 3. 421
Big passions strutting on a petty stage ; . . . 799 *Excursion* 3. 900
Of the ostentatious world—a swelling stage . . 835 *Excursion* 5. 850
Heels over head, like tumblers on a stage. . . 880 *Excursion* 8. 381

Stagger. I stagger onward—heaven knows how ; . 179 *Waggoner* 3. 89
O Liberty ! they stagger at the shock . . . . 314 *Hofer* 9
I saw thee stagger in the summer breeze, . . . 491 *Tribute : Dog* 18

Staggered. The poor Ass staggered with the shock ; 241 *P. B.* 426
And the rocks staggered all around— . . . . 241 *P. B.* 485

Staggering. At home, go staggering through the slippery fords, ... 99 *Brothers* 258
Then, if a widow, staggering with the blow . . 704 *Prelude* 8. 384

Stag-horn. We call stag-horn, or fox's tail, . . . 84 *Shepherd-boys* 19
Stand like an oak whose stag-horn branches start 695 *Prelude* 7. 520

Stagnant. From her sunk eyes a stagnant tear . . 113 *Lament* 66
And let the groveller sip his stagnant pool, . . 277 **A Poet* 6
Of stagnant waters : altar, sword, and pen, . . 307 **Milton ! thou* 3

Stagnates. Nor stagnates, nor precipitates his course, 357 *Aquap.* 316

Stagyrite. And all the wisdom of the Stagyrite, . 576 *Chiabrera* 9. 9

Staid. *See* **Stayed.**
Clear-sighted Honour, and his staid Compeers, . . 329 *Ode : Thanks.* 61
To reassume a staid simplicity. . . . . . . 456 **Soft as* 19
Firm self-denial, manners grave and staid, . . 515 *Penn.* 2
With woman's gentleness, yet firm and staid ; . 628 **Deign, Sovereign* 14
Had staid his oars, and touched the jutting pier, 658 *Prelude* 4. 15
Of maids and youths, old men, and matrons staid, 663 *Prelude* 4. 310
From some staid guardian of the public peace, . 859 *Excursion* 7. 102
—Those transports, with staid looks of pure good-will, ... 860 *Excursion* 7. 224

Stain. That both are guiltless, without spot or stain, 70 *Bord.* 1848
Her eyebrows have a rusty stain, ... 144 *Her Eyes* 3

Stain—*continued.*
Fair are ye both, and both are free from stain : . 172 *Infant Daughter* 51
Or in the dust, a crimson stain. . . . . . 244 *P. B.* 720
A stain—as of a drop of blood . . . . . . 244 *P. B.* 721
So snugly for that crimson stain, ... 245 *P. B.* 803
From stain or taint ; in which thy blameless mind 264 **Lady ! I* 11
Like wreaths of vapour without stain or blot. . 390 *Highland Hut* 4
Stain her cheek in future years— . . . . . 503 **Like a* 56
Plumes that might catch, but cannot keep, a stain ; 511 **Who rashly* 21
That countenance there fashioned, which, spite of a stain . . . . 569 *Farmer* 11
Shall stain this votive lay ; . . . . 582 **O for a* 9
Britain, who thought to stain the field was fame, 619 *School Ex.* 55
Though in virtue's proud mouth thy report be a stain, ... 621 *Convict* 50
The original stain, the child is there received . 826 *Excursion* 5. 281
Of all dishonour, cleansed from mortal stain. . 893 *Excursion* 9. 633
A leprous stain ! ere half his thread was spun . L.1. 96 *Juvenal* 3. 47

Stained. *See* **Blood-stained.**
Desperate the Maid—the Youth is stained with blood ; . . . . 123 *V. and J.* 146
Hath stained the robes of civil power with blood, 213 *Dion* 56
The grove, and stained the turf with gore ; . . 215 *Enterprise* 23
Stained and polluted, brighten as they roll, . . 452 *Ecc. Sonn.* 3. 47. 12
The rivers stained so oft with human gore, . . 582 *Invoc. Earth* 26
Was in the limpid age of this stained world . . S.3. 436 **The doubt* 163

Stainless. With stainless touch, as chaste as when thy praise . . . . 460 **Queen of* 25

Stains. *See* **Weather-stains.**
there are stains in that frock . . . . . . 71 *Bord.* 1904
I saw the stains of blood upon my clothes— . . 72 *Bord.* 1933
But, for the stains of blood—— . . . . . 72 *Bord.* 1942
Is gone ;—but not the subtle stains . . . . 113 *Lament* 46
War's favourite playground, are with crimson stains . . . . 335 *Namur* 3
Frank are the sports, the stains are fugitive. . . 382 *Duddon* 23. 14
That shield from mischief and preserve from stains 382 *Duddon* 26. 11
I come—thy stains to wash away, ... 581 *Invoc. Earth* 5
With dull red stains discoloured, and stuck o'er . 767 *Excursion* 1. 744

Stair. The wide-spread boughs, for view of door, window, and stair that wound . . . 92 *Poet's Dream* 38
Thou rocky corner in the lowest stair . . . . 106 *Farewell* 2
And clomb the winding stair that once . . . 386 *Yarrow Rev.* 101
The darksome windings of a broken stair, . . . 678 *Prelude* 6. 213

Stairs. *See* **Cottage-stairs.**
They run up stairs in gamesome race ; . . . . 81 †*Mother's Return* 50
And up the cottage stairs she hies, ... 248 *P. B.* 1084
All, while *he* slept, treading the pendent stairs . 500 *Humanity* 35
Scrub lives a genuine Marquess above stairs, . . L.1. 95 *Juvenal* 3. 17

Stake. Of life's uneasy game the stake, ... 214 *Kirkstone* 30
Is it a fiend that to a stake . . . . 242 *P. B.* 511
Corded, and burning at the social stake : " . . 437 *Ecc. Sonn.* 2. 34. 12
Firm as the stake to which with iron band . . 437 *Ecc. Sonn.* 2. 35. 5

Stale. In which the meagre, stale, forbidding ways 729 *Prelude* 11. 110

Stalk. Thence issuing often with unwieldy stalk, . 6 *Ev. Wk.* 242
Then will hang on every stalk, ... 80 *Foresight* 30
That, from the dandelion's naked stalk, . . . 123 *V. and J.* 137
This flute, made of a hemlock stalk, ... 195 *Ruth* 244
By which true Sway doth mount ; this is the stalk 304 **I grieved* 13
Ere they descend to nourish root and stalk . . 390 *Glencroe* 8
Sons, mothers, maidens withering on the stalk, . 488 *Pers. Talk* 6
Thence issuing oft, unwieldly as ye stalk, . . . 596 *Ev. Wk. Quarto* 231
But the green stalk of Ellen's life was snapped, . 853 *Excursion* 6. 1000

Stalked. Where stalked the huge deer to his shaggy lair . . . . 376 *Duddon* 2. 11

Stalking. And hideous aspect, stalking round and round ! . . . . 213 *Dion* 68
And stalking pillars built of fiery sand. . . . 435 *Ecc. Sonn.* 2. 27. 14
In size a giant, stalking through thick fog, . . 703 *Prelude* 8. 266

Stalks. Pride of his sister-wives, the monarch stalks ; 5 *Ev. Wk.* 147
Stalks round—abhorred by Heaven, a terror to the Earth ! . . . . 311 **Who rises* 20
With his red stalks upon this sunny day ! . . . 529 *Poor Robin* 6
Gaz'd by his sister-wives, the monarch stalks ; . 594 *Ev. Wk. Quarto* 130
Bare steeps, where Desolation stalks, afraid, . . 606 *Desc. Sk. Quarto* 251
Where Discord stalks dilating, every hour, . . 617 *Desc. Sk. Quarto* 800

Stall. They came to lowly bench or sculptured stall, 256 *Decay of Piety* 7
From her unworthy seat, the cloudy stall . . . 381 *Duddon* 21. 9
Booths are there none ; a stall or two is here ; . 699 *Prelude* 8. 25
While at the stall he read. Among the hills . . 760 *Excursion* 1. 248

Stallèd. Or rather like a stallèd ox debarred . . 669 *Prelude* 5. 242

Stalls. *See* **Book-stalls.**

Stammerer. No stammerer of a minute, painfully . 694 *Prelude* 7. 500

Stamp. Your justice stamp upon his evil deeds . . 42 *Bord.* 266
To mould and stamp the ore of thought . . . 629 *Installation* 83
Of the whole place should bear a stamp of awe ; . 655 *Prelude* 3. 434
Some element to stamp her image on . . . . 666 *Prelude* 5. 46
The State, as if to stamp the final seal . . . 718 *Prelude* 10. 31
Nor Miss Taylor, Captain Stamp, ... S.3. 438 **My Lord* 5

Stamped. Round strath and mountain, stamped by the ancient tongue . . . . 389 *Sound of Mull* 3
And twice five summers on my mind had stamped 640 *Prelude* 1. 560

Stand. But now with other mind I stand alone . 16 *Desc. Sk.* 303
Stand motionless, to awful silence bound : . . 17 *Desc. Sk.* 410
Thy secrets, thou that lov'st to stand and hear . 26 *Guilt* 119
How wilt thou stand alone ? Is he not strong ? . 40 *Bord.* 160
Stand like an isthmus 'twixt two stormy seas . 48 *Bord.* 607
Here where we stand—that tribe of vulgar wretches 48 *Bord.* 642
The wind should pipe a little, while we stand . . 51 *Bord.* 752
To stand upon our guard, and with our swords . 56 *Bord.* 1028
But that they cannot stand up of themselves ; . 60 *Bord.* 1233

Stand—*continued.*
Here do I stand, alone, to helplessness, 62 *Bord.* 1344
That she revealed the truth. Stand by me now ; 63 *Bord.* 1422
The weakest of God's creatures, stand resolved 65 *Bord.* 1518
Whose good deeds will not stand by their own light ; 74 *Bord.* 2081
Why stand you thus, good Betty Foy ? 130 *Idiot Boy* 368
But soon as Luke, full ten years old, could stand 134 *Michael* 194
And that herself and hers should stand upright 138 *Widow* 8
Suddenly halting now—a lifeless stand ! 148 **A narrow* 20
Some nook where they had made their final stand, 150 **When, to* 30
To stand or go is at *their* pleasure ; 174 *Waggoner* 1. 105
Whether they should stand or go ; 175 *Waggoner* 1. 191
Summons his horses to a stand. 176 *Waggoner* 1. 224
Stand back, and you shall see her gratis ! 177 *Waggoner* 2. 114
The horses made a quiet stand ; 179 *Waggoner* 3. 57
They stand the wonder of the bowers 193 *Ruth* 59
While here I stand, not only with the sense 206 *Tintern* 62
In seemly order stand, 213 *Dion* 33
Shed from thy countenance, as I see thee stand 215 *Enterprise* 2
Has raised thy spirit to a peaceful stand 222 *Triad* 185
Of Persian mornings would ye fill, and stand 230 *Clouds* 26
As flowers, stand side by side ; 232 *Jew. Fam.* 34
Will stand though to the centre hewn ; 246 *P. B.* 847
Yet he repines not, if his thought stand clear, 265 **There is a pleasure* 9
May lead the thoughts, thus struggling used to stand 265 **When haughty* 10
Of Viamala ? There I seem to stand, 272 *Devil's Bridge* 8
By Art's bold privilege Warrior and War-horse stand 278 *Wellington* 1
Profane Despoilers, stand ye not reproved, 283 **Well have* 13
" All kinds, and creatures, stand and fall 291 *Rob Roy* 49
There where you see his Image stand 301 *Bran* 70
How they with dignity may stand ; or fall, 305 **The Voice* 5
Were with herself at strife, would take your stand, 310 *Invasion* 2
That we must stand unpropped, or be laid low. 310 **Another year* 8
To think that such assurance can stand fast ! 317 **The martial* 14
Stand in the spacious firmament of time, 317 **Brave Schill* 7
But Thou art foremost in the field :—there stand : 331 *Ode: Thanks.* 153
Pupils of Heaven, in order stand 338 *Brientz* 11
Knights each in order as ye stand 373 *Eg. Maid* 267
And mausolean pomp ? Yet here they stand 389 *Breadalb.* 9
Belike less happy.—Stand no more aloof ! 390 *Highland Hut* 14
The Claphams and Mauleverers stand ; 399 *White Doe* 247
While stand the people in a ring, 399 *White Doe* 314
And now before this Pile we stand 399 *White Doe* 328
Spurned it, like something that would stand 401 *White Doe* 518
—Stand forth, my Sons !—these eight are mine, 402 *White Doe* 611
Behold ! "—and from his Son whose stand 403 *White Doe* 656
He takes alone his far-off stand, 404 *White Doe* 764
Her duty is to stand and wait ; 407 *White Doe* 1069
Against a thousand cannot stand ;— 408 *White Doe* 1152
To spread its arms, and stand for aye. 410 *White Doe* 1269
He felt—and made a sudden stand. 411 *White Doe* 1392
Her soul doth in itself stand fast, 414 *White Doe* 1623
Where Augurs stand, the Future questioning, 419 *Ecc. Sonn.* 1. 3. 3
Lo ! Discord at the altar dares to stand 420 *Ecc. Sonn.* 1. 9. 4
Beautiful strangers, stand within the pale 421 *Ecc. Sonn.* 1. 13. 2
Of Faith stand coupled for a common flight ! 437 *Ecc. Sonn.* 2. 34. 3
Amid the shuddering throng doth Cranmer stand ; 437 *Ecc. Sonn.* 2. 35. 4
May-garlands, there let the holy altar stand 450 *Ecc. Sonn.* 3. 39. 11
But, rooted here, I stand and gaze 458 **Had this* 50
Why stand we gazing on the sparkling Brine, 469 **Why stand* 1
And by *one* Votary who at will might stand 473 **We saw* 9
Methinks, I see him stand, 487 **We walked* 58
Will gladly stand a monument of thee. 491 *Tribute : Dog* 10
Too weak to stand against its sportive breath, 491 *Tribute : Dog* 19
Rises by open means ; and there will stand 493 *Hap. War.* 36
Who, not content that former worth stand fast, 494 *Hap. War.* 74
Before the Stone of Power no longer stand— 500 *Humanity* 4
Where Christian Martyrs stand in hues portrayed, 500 *Humanity* 21
If generous Loyalty must stand in awe 504 *Warning* 101
No sooner stand attired 508 *May* 86
Whence the blithe hail ? behold a Peasant stand 524 *Epist. Beaumont* 207
Thus looking out did Harry stand : 537 *Goody Blake* 74
Stand yet, but, Stranger ! hidden from thy view, 547 **Beneath yon* 3
With a look of such earnestness often will stand, 570 *Farmer* 71
Or stand between his knees again. 577 **I come* 15
Once more on English earth they stand : 579 **Sweet Flower* 32
Stand—sacred as a Shrine ; 581 *John Words.* 64
Shall stand a votive Tablet, haply free, 584 **With copious* 52
The imperfect record, there, may stand unblamed 585 *Ch. Lamb* 47
But now with other soul I stand alone 609 *Desc.Sk.Quarto* 366
As they in order stand, the dainty fare ; 624 *Æneid* 64
Or image unprofaned ; and I would stand, 646 *Prelude* 2. 306
All studded round, as thick as chairs could stand, 650 *Prelude* 3. 65
Where all stand single ; this I feel, and make 651 *Prelude* 3. 186
Though I had learnt betimes to stand unpropped, 652 *Prelude* 3. 227
Rising or setting, would he stand alone 671 *Prelude* 5. 368
The cross of Jesus stand erect, as if 682 *Prelude* 6. 484
On outward forms—did we in presence stand 686 *Prelude* 6. 738
Stand like an oak whose stag-horn branches start 695 *Prelude* 7. 520
Good, pure, which no one could stand up against, 713 *Prelude* 9. 284
Stand near the worthiest of Antiquity) 715 *Prelude* 9. 420
Between the sovereign and the people stand, 717 *Prelude* 9. 505
Our prayers have been accepted ; thou wilt stand 734 *Prelude* 11. 453
Of something false and weak, that could not stand 735 *Prelude* 12. 66
In Nature's presence stood, as now I stand, 737 *Prelude* 12. 206
And so shall stand for ever. Dearest Friend ! 744 *Prelude* 13. 299

Stand—*continued.*
For they are each in each, and cannot stand 749 *Prelude* 14. 208
In hardy independence, to stand up 751 *Prelude* 14. 333
Unnoticed did I stand some minutes' space. 762 *Excursion* 1. 443
I followed, till he made a sudden stand : 779 *Excursion* 2. 493
Should the tale tire you, let this challenge stand 782 *Excursion* 2. 731
I stand—the chasm of sky above my head 787 *Excursion* 3. 94
The place where now we stand) that certain men 789 *Excursion* 3. 241
Do, in my present censure, stand redeemed 792 *Excursion* 3. 409
Had been supplanted, could I hope to stand— 796 *Excursion* 3. 684
Of the pure intellect, that stand as laws 802 *Excursion* 4. 97
And stand in freedom loosened from this world, 803 *Excursion* 4. 134
" Life's autumn past, I stand on winter's verge ; 810 *Excursion* 4. 611
Of endless agitation. Here you stand, 818 *Excursion* 4. 1147
Or rather, as we stand on holy earth, 832 *Excursion* 5. 646
And hindrances with which they stand beset. 835 *Excursion* 5. 861
Cast down while confident in strength they stand, 837 *Excursion* 5. 963
Upon its site, a dial, that might stand 845 *Excursion* 6. 497
The Mother oft was seen to stand, or kneel 850 *Excursion* 6. 813
But that the heaven-born poet must stand forth, 863 *Excursion* 7. 364
In him to stand before my swimming eyes, 870 *Excursion* 7. 857
Of greedy foretaste, from the secret stand 872 *Excursion* 7. 993
On which they stand ; as if thereby they drew 879 *Excursion* 8. 355
Till the swift vehicle approach, they stand ; 880 *Excursion* 8. 378
That when we stand upon our native soil, 886 *Excursion* 9. 129
Such as they are who in thy presence stand 893 *Excursion* 9. 628
But soon as Luke, full ten years old, could stand K.8. 226 **I will* 74
No, we are not alone, we do not stand, K.8. 248 *Recluse* 1.1.427
I would stand clear, but yet to me I feel K.8. 255 *Recluse* 1.1.674
And tottering towers ; I loved to stand and read K.8. 256 *Recluse* 1.1.712
Standard. That Cross belike he also raised as a standard for the true 91 *Norman Boy* 25
" Uplift the Standard ! " was the cry 403 *White Doe* 670
To guard the Standard which he bore. 404 *White Doe* 725
The Standard trusting to the care 405 *White Doe* 805
The Standard, on the Sacred Wain 405 *White Doe* 818
" A rescue for the Standard ! " cried 408 *White Doe* 1155
But, see, the sacred Standard falls !— 408 *White Doe* 1157
The Standard ; and where Francis lay 412 *White Doe* 1500
A standard, often usefully applied, 676 *Prelude* 6. 103
His notions to this standard ; on this rock 813 *Excursion* 4. 816
Standards. Tempt the vague will tried standards to disown ; 518 *Pun. Death* 4. 10
Standers-by. Of a thousand standers-by, 171 *Kitten* 34
Though he, and all the standers-by, 398 *White Doe* 198
By all the standers-by revered. 412 *White Doe* 1453
Standeth. Saint Nicholas in my presence standeth aye, 553 *Prioress* 63
As one that standeth betwixt hope and dread. 564 *Troilus* 112
Standing. *See* **Low-standing, Sole-standing.**
But standing, walking, stretching forth his arms, 68 *Bord.* 1729
This beech is standing by, its covert thou canst gain ; 87 *Pet-lamb* 30
It chanced that I saw standing in a dell 202 *Hart-leap* 102
I saw three pillars standing in a line,— 202 *Hart-leap* 107
The poor Ass standing by her side, 248 *P. B.* 1024
Yet standing in the clear moonshine ; 248 *P. B.* 1097
So might I, standing on this pleasant lea, 259 **The world is* 11
Here standing by thy grave. 292 *Rob Roy* 100
And standing upright and alone, 301 *Bran* 51
Is standing with a voice of power, 396 *White Doe* 22
Who, standing on this old church tower, 399 *White Doe* 297
An unblest work ; which, standing by, 400 *White Doe* 349
Is silent as a standing pool ; 486 *Matthew* 18
Lie in forbearance, strength in standing still ? 505 *Warning* 150
Now standing forth an offering to the blast, 571 **There is a Flower* 11
And this huge Castle, standing here sublime, 579 *Peele Castle* 49
Standing alone, and at his feet 621 *Andrew Jones* 24
Standing to gaze upon her while she hung 645 *Prelude* 2. 193
Standing alone, as from a rampart's edge, 658 *Prelude* 4. 4
France standing on the top of golden hours, 680 *Prelude* 6. 340
Too fine to be pursued ; or standing forth 700 *Prelude* 8. 91
If nature then be standing on the brink 715 *Prelude* 9. 398
I yet was standing, freely to respire, 763 *Excursion* 1. 467
I talk—and ye are standing in the sun 781 *Excursion* 2. 635
Standing before the multitude, beset 793 *Excursion* 3. 467
Standing apart ; with curvèd arm reclined 825 *Excursion* 5. 211
Standing before us :—" Did you note the mien 826 *Excursion* 5. 233
Here standing, with the unvoyageable sky 827 *Excursion* 5. 342
Who there was standing on the open hill, 834 *Excursion* 5. 753
A standing grievance, an indigenous vice 887 *Excursion* 9. 185
Stands. While silent stands the admiring crowd below, 6 *Ev. Wk.* 205
Within a temple stands an awful shrine, 20 *Desc. Sk.* 542
Nay, Traveller ! rest. This lonely Yew-tree stands 22 *Yew-tree* 1
A structure stands, which two bare slopes enclose. 27 *Guilt* 147
No—no—the thing stands clear of mystery ; 42 *Bord.* 261
I will attend you to a Hut that stands 67 *Bord.* 1647
A lonesome Chapel stands, deserted now : 73 *Bord.* 2054
For length of days so much revered, so famous where it stands 92 *Poet's Dream* 35
Which stands the universal empire's boast ; 105 *Artegal* 189
Stands fixed, her face with joy o'erflows, 127 *Idiot Boy* 88
She stops, she stands, she looks about ; 129 *Idiot Boy* 267
At a short distance from my cottage, stands 150 **When, to* 8
Which to this day stands single, in the midst 184 *Yew-trees* 2
So He, where he stands, is a centre of light ; 188 *Music* 14
He stands, backed by the wall ;—he abates not his din ; 188 *Music* 25
Calm, though impatient, is the crowd ; each stands ready with the fee, 189 *Star-gazers* 7

Stands—*continued.*
It stands erect, this aged Thorn ; . . . . . 197 *Thorn* 6
It stands erect, and like a stone . . . . . 197 *Thorn* 10
'Tis Hesperus—there he stands with glittering crown, ... 208 **It is no* 4
The councils of both worlds she stands, . . . 226 *Present.* 71
And close by Peter's side he stands : . . . . 242 *P. B.* 562
A little chapel stands alone, ... 246 *P. B.* 853
Upon the Beast that near her stands ; . . . . 248 *P. B.* 1042
Beside the Woman Peter stands ; . . . . . . 248 *P. B.* 1051
When she stands cresting the Clown's head, and mocks . . . . 260 **How sweet* 8
In annual renovation thus it stands— . . . . 276 *Filial Piety* 12
Lo ! where she stands fixed in a saint-like trance, 278 **Lo ! where she* 1
Or stands, in warlike vest, ... 300 *Cora Linn* 21
And stands on tiptoe, conscious she is fair, . . 311 **Who rises* 9
And stands amidst you now an armèd creature, . 311 **Who rises* 16
A Roman Master stands on Grecian ground, . . 312 **A Roman* 1
O joyless power that stands by lawless force ! . 317 **Look now* 9
For lo ! the Imperial City stands released . . . 326 *Sobieski* 6
Expectant stands beneath the linden tree : . . 339 *Tell* 23
Who having left the Cemetery stands . . . . 355 *Aquap.* 179
For all that tottering stands or prostrate lies, . 360 *Alban Hills* 4
He stands upon the grassy sod, ... 404 *White Doe* 730
He there stands fixed from hour to hour : . . . 404 *White Doe* 769
Stands single—Norton Tower its name— . . . 409 *White Doe* 1168
Stands at the Bar, absolved by female eyes . . 442 *Ecc. Sonn.* 3. 11. 6
The Vested Priest before the Altar stands ; . . 446 *Ecc. Sonn.* 3. 26. 1
When wisdom stands in need of nature's grace ; . 456 **Soft as* 21
This perilous bay, stands clear of all offence ; . 469 **The feudal* 6
Survive, and once again the Pile stands fast : . 474 **Hope smiled* 8
With mute astonishment, it stands sustained . . 474 **Hope smiled* 11
That stands beside our door. . . . . 482 *Sister* 4
Stock-still there he stands like a traveller bemazed : 484 **A plague* 16
And now, his task performed, the flood stands still, 495 *Fact* 35
From this corporeal frame ; whereon who stands 496 **A little* 28
Hath not departed, stands forlorn . . . . . 506 **While from* 43
Through half the summer, stands with top cut sheer, ... 521 *Epist. Beaumont* 17
If but the Cedar thrive that near them stands, . 546 **The embowering* 3
While silent stands th' admiring vale below ; . . 595 *Ev. Wk. Quarto* 188
Stands yet a mouldering pile with fractured arch, 643 *Prelude* 2. 105
When the great tide of human life stands still ; . 697 *Prelude* 7. 657
There also stands a speech-maker by rote, . . 699 *Prelude* 8. 32
The scene before him stands in perfect view . . 707 *Prelude* 8. 575
Their madness stands declared and visible ; . . 726 *Prelude* 10. 587
Stands single in her only sanctuary ; . . . . 733 *Prelude* 11. 401
On which thy greatness stands ; but this I feel, . 738 *Prelude* 12. 275
Before the threshold stands to welcome us ! . . 793 *Excursion* 3. 524
Stands in our valley, named THE JOYFUL TREE ; . 851 *Excursion* 6. 832
Stands a tall ash-tree ; to whose topmost twig . 851 *Excursion* 6. 863
Now, by experience taught, he stands assured, . 855 *Excursion* 6. 1133
And now, its task performed, the flood stands still S.3. 427 **My Son* 6
At least so seems it to a man who stands . . . K.8. 223 **There is a shapeless* 5

St. Antony, St. Bartholomew, *etc.* *See* **Saint.**
Star. *See* **Day-star, Morning-star.**
—When low-hung clouds each star of summer hide, 7 *Ev. Wk.* 260
Heard by calm lakes, as peeps the folding star, . 7 *Ev. Wk.* 280
When not a star supplies the comfort of its light ; 14 *Desc. Sk.* 187
In the least star of scarce-appearing night ; . . 16 *Desc. Sk.* 318
Beheld a star twinkling above my head, . . . 55 *Bord.* 989
Till that same star summoned me back again. . 59 *Bord.* 1217
—But see, the evening star comes forth ! . . . 81 †*Mother's Return* 45
Through the bounds which many a star . . . 90 *Longest Day* 54
Shall lift his country's fame above the polar star ! 103 *Artegal* 56
—Fair as a star, when only one . . . . . 109 **She dwelt* 7
Is fairer than the fairest star in heaven ! . . . 121 *V. and J.* 4
To lay his hands upon a star, ... 129 *Idiot Boy* 320
Both old and young, was named THE EVENING STAR. 133 *Michael* 139
The Cottage which was named the EVENING STAR 138 *Michael* 476
Soft as a guiding star that cheers, but cannot burn." 140 *Arm. Lady* 66
The star of Jove, so beautiful and large . . . 148 **There is an* 10
But *He* is risen, a later star of dawn, ... 153 *Morn. Ex.* 27
And then thou art a pretty star ; . . . . . 159 **With little* 34
Yet like a star, with glittering crest, ... 159 **With little* 37
For the finding of a star ; . . . . 160 **Pansies, lilies* 10
Fixed on a Star his upward eye ; . . . . . 167 *Pilgrim's Dream* 12
He recognised the earth-born Star, ... 167 *Pilgrim's Dream* 20
"Exalted Star ! " the Worm replied, ... 167 *Pilgrim's Dream* 33
That Star, so proud of late, looked wan ; . . . 167 *Pilgrim's Dream* 53
The most forlorn—one life of that bright star, . 172 *Infant Daughter* 4
And she is known to every star, ... 198 *Thorn* 69
Whatever star is in the skies, ... 198 *Thorn* 102
Like a re-appearing Star, ... 205 *Brougham* 154
O most ambitious Star ! an inquest wrought . . 208 **It is no* 9
Of magic potent over sun and star, ... 210 *Laod.* 88
The brightest star of ages yet to be, ... 220 *Triad* 6
Insight as keen as frosty star . . . . . . 222 *Triad* 149
But wandering star and fixed, to mortal eye, . . 226 *Vernal Ode* 34
That blend the nature of the star . . . . . 232 *Jew. Fam.* 19
Yon slowly-sinking star—immortal Sire . . . 261 **I watch* 2
In this, how different, lost Star, from thine, . . 261 **I watch* 13
Fresh as the star that crowns the brow of morn ; 265 **There is a pleasure* 11
Aught dost thou see, bright Star ! of pure and wise 281 **What strong* 9
That rules o'er Britain like a baneful star, . . 283 **Proud were* 5
Rose like a star that touching earth, ... 285 *Grave of Burns* 21
Fair Star of evening, Splendour of the west, . . 303 **Fair Star* 1
Star of my Country !—on the horizon's brink . 303 **Fair Star* 2
Bright Star ! with laughter on her banners, drest . 303 **Fair Star* 8

Star—*continued.*
Thy soul was like a Star, and dwelt apart ; . . 307 **Milton ! thou* 9
Fixed as a star : such glory is thy right. . . . 317 **Brave Schill* 8
Bright be the Fabric, as a star . . . . . . 327 *Ode 1815* 52
Than fairest Star, upon the height . . . . . 338 **Meek Virgin* 2
Then, glittering like a star, she joins the festal band. 344 **How blest* 26
Till the bright Star appeared in eastern skies, . 351 *Des. Stanzas* 69
Is welcome as a star, that doth present . . . 383 *Duddon* 31. 2
Soon, like a lingering star forlorn . . . . . 391 *Highland Broach* 75
Emboldened by thy guidance, holy Star, . . . 392 **Though joy* 9
As shepherds watch a lonely star, ... 404 *White Doe* 759
One star of aspect heavenly bright ; . . . . 411 *White Doe* 1357
Beneath the light of sun and star ; . . . . . 413 *White Doe* 1612
(O great Precursor, genuine morning Star) . . 436 *Ecc. Sonn.* 2. 31. 12
The star of Liberty to rise. Nor yet . . . . 442 *Ecc. Sonn.* 3. 10. 8
As star that shines dependent upon star . . . 444 *Ecc. Sonn.* 3. 17. 1
Now when the star of eve comes forth to shine . 454 *Sea-side* 34
Ere some commanding star dismiss to rest . . 455 *Rydal Mere* 7
On chance dependent, and the fickle star . . . 458 *Sea-shore* 7
The Crescent-moon, the Star of Love, ... 459 **The Crescent* 1
When not a twinkling star or beacon's light . . 459 **Wanderer! that* 15
Paces the deck—no star perhaps in sight, . . 460 **Wanderer! that* 67
And like a Star (that, from a heavy cloud . . 465 **Dear to* 5
The Star of Bethlehem from its sphere invites . 467 *St. Bees* 113
The star that led the dawn, ... 506 **While from* 2
Till the first silver star appear, ... 507 **While from* 63
Had from the east her silver star withdrawn, . . 522 *Epist. Beaumont* 92
Your star, your gem, your flower ; . . . . . 542 *Russ. Fug.* 62
That would emulate a star. . . . . 549 *Hermit's Cell* 1. 12
O star, of which I lost have all the light, . . . 564 *Troilus* 120
Yon star upon the mountain-top . . . . . 581 **Loud is* 7
As Vesper, ere the star hath kissed . . . . . 583 **O for a* 46
The Soul that rises with us, our life's Star, . . 588 *Immortality* 59
By pointing to a shooting star on high : . . . 596 *Ev. Wk. Quarto* 260
His father views that good, that kindly star ; . 596 *Ev. Wk. Quarto* 266
Below Eve's listening Star the sheep walk stills . 598 *Ev. Wk. Quarto* 353
If peep between the clouds a star on high, . . 598 *Ev. Wk. Quarto* 365
No star supplies the comfort of it's light, . . . 606 *Desc. Sk. Quarto* 216
The star of noon that glitters small and bright, . 609 *Desc. Sk. Quarto* 386
As the soft star of dewy evening tells . . . . 619 **She wept* 11
Of sun or guiding star. . . . . 623 *G. and S. Green* 28
The star which comes at close of day to shine . 627 **The star* 1
That eve, the Star of Brunswick shone . . . 629 *Installation* 57
Confiding in that Star serene, ... 629 *Installation* 71
To cut across the reflex of a star . . . . . 638 *Prelude* 1. 450
By rocks and pools shut out from every star, . . 639 *Prelude* 1. 488
And Jupiter, my own beloved star ! . . . . . 662 *Prelude* 4. 247
From star to star, from kindred sphere to sphere, 677 *Prelude* 6. 127
Unhoused beneath the evening star we saw . . 680 *Prelude* 6. 370
Fresh as the morning star. Elate we looked . . 715 *Prelude* 9. 385
Is fairer than the fairest star in Heaven ! . . . 717 *Prelude* 9. 556
The horse is taught his manage, and no star . . 719 *Prelude* 10. 78
Ere the last star had vanished.—They who passed 764 *Excursion* 1. 527
If fixed or wandering star could tidings yield . . 796 *Excursion* 3. 692
In this deep Hollow, like a sullen star . . . . 808 *Excursion* 4. 487
Looked on the polar star, as on a guide . . . 811 *Excursion* 4. 697
The torch, the star, the anchor ; nor except . . 827 *Excursion* 5. 336
On the north star, or watch-tower's distant lamp, 833 *Excursion* 5. 744
For you each evening hath its shining star, . . 835 *Excursion* 5. 836
Roused me, her voice ; it said, ' That glorious star 849 *Excursion* 6. 763
Like a bright star, amid the lowly band . . . 872 *Excursion* 7. 954
Pure, cloudless, ether ; and the star of eve . . 895 *Excursion* 9. 761
Scarce peeps the curious star, till solemn gleams . S.3. 417 **Sweet was* 12
Is known to all beneath the polar star, . . . S.3. 442 **Vasco, whose* 13
Though yet the star *some hearts* at court may charm L.1. 96 *Juvenal* 3. 37
Star-bright. And he, with his preserver, shine star-bright . . . . 234 *Power of Sound* 143
Star-crowned. Tell, if ye may, some star-crowned Muse, or Saint ! . . . . 446 *Ecc. Sonn.* 3. 24. 5
Stare. Would watch my motions with suspicious stare, ... 150 **When, to* 28
Clapping hands with shout and stare, ... 171 *Kitten* 35
There's freedom, and sometimes a diffident stare . 482 *Character* 13
Two eyes—not dim, but of a healthy stare— . . 880 *Excursion* 8. 409
And Moore and Partridge stare me in the face. . L.1. 96 *Juvenal* 3. 60
Stared. I looked, I stared, I smiled, I laughed ; and all . . . . 251 **Beloved Vale* 13
I stared and listened, with a stranger's ears, . . 710 *Prelude* 9. 57
That stared upon each other !—I looked round, . 756 *Excursion* 1. 31
He might have stared at you, and said that they K.8. 230 **I will* 181
Star-guided. Star-guided contemplations move . 225 *Present.* 31
Star-high. Star-high, and pointing still to something higher ; . . . . 282 **In my* 12
Staring. *See* **Wide-staring.**
Staring to threaten and defy, ... 159 **With little* 26
And sharp his staring bones ! . . . . . . 241 *P. B.* 450
His staring bones all shake with joy, ... 242 *P. B.* 561
Nor veil, with restless film, his staring eyes. . . 273 **While Anna's* 14
Is thronged with staring pictures and huge scrolls, 697 *Prelude* 7. 692
On many a staring countenance portrayed . . 858 *Excursion* 7. 96
Stark. Shot stinging through her stark o'erlabour'd bones. . . . . 596 *Ev. Wk. Quarto* 246
Starless. O'er vale, and mountain, and the starless sky. . . . . 1 *Early Youth* 6
Roaring with storms beneath night's starless gloom; 26 *Guilt* 139
They wore away the night in starless gloom ; . . 528 **Those breathing* 55
Star-light. By day or star-light thus from my first dawn . . . . 638 *Prelude* 1. 405
Should lie beneath the cold starlight ! . . . . K.8. 220 **The snow-tracks* 37

Stateliest—*continued.*
Of stateliest architecture, where the Forms . . 334 **Bruges I* 13
Stately. He saw and passed a stately inn, full sure 24 *Guilt* 11
So stately, of the Queen Osmunda named ; . . 149 **A narrow* 34
A stately Fir-grove, whither I was wont . . . 150 **When, to* 9
Some, perched on stems of stately port . . . 154 *Flower Garden* 39
If stately passions in me burn, ... 158 **In youth* 49
A gallant stately Man-of-war, ... 177 *Waggoner* 2. 107
The stately waggon is ascending, ... 180 *Waggoner* 4. 65
And of his stately Charge, which none . . . . 182 *Waggoner* 4. 268
Shall rear her form to stately height, ... 187 **Three years* 32
Near the stately Pantheon you'll meet with the same . . . . 188 *Music* 3
And stately needs must have their share . . . 193 *Ruth* 143
Of ordinary men ; a stately speech ; . . . . 196 *Resolution* 96
But stately in the main ; and, when he ended, . 197 *Resolution* 136
Great Jove is full of stately bowers ; . . . . 237 *P. B.* 47
Whose realm had dwindled to one stately room ; 271 *George : Death* 2
Chatsworth ! thy stately mansion, and the pride 275 **Chatsworth ! thy* 1
And stately forest where the wild deer rove ; . . 323 *Ode 1814* 10
Under the shadow of a stately Pile, ... 365 **Under the* 1
Into a Brook of loud and stately march, . . . 378 *Duddon* 9. 2
In stately mien to sovereign Thames allied . . 384 *Duddon* 32. 12
As might beseem a stately embassy, ... 394 **No more* 10
Rose up, this stately Priory ! . . . . . . 398 *White Doe* 234
And Castle like a stately crown . . . . . 406 *White Doe* 941
Herself most like a stately flower, ... 414 *White Doe* 1634
Thou, stately York ! and Ye, whose splendours cheer 451 *Ecc. Sonn.* 3. 42. 13
CROGLIN, the stately Eden's tributary ! . . . 476 *Nunnery* 3
A stately Priory ! " . . . . 495 *Force of Prayer* 56
The stately Priory was reared ; . . . . . . 495 *Force of Prayer* 57
Her temples, fearless for the stately work, . . 496 **A little* 37
And all its stately trees, are passed away, . . . 546 **Oft is* 7
And be not slow a stately growth to rear . . . 546 **Ye Lime* 3
To stately Hall and Cottage rude . . . . . 578 **I come* 61
Stately, and burning in his pride, divides . . . 595 *Ev. Wk. Quarto* 203
Save when, amid the stately grove of oaks, . . 633 *Prelude* 1. 82
Should spread from heart to heart ; and stately groves, ... 654 *Prelude* 3. 380
A stately air of mild indifference, ... 664 *Prelude* 4. 420
With their thin umbrage, on the stately roads . 680 *Prelude* 6. 361
Of deep and stately vales ! A lonely pair . . 680 *Prelude* 6. 384
The Jew ; the stately and slow-moving Turk, . 690 *Prelude* 7. 217
Washed by the current of the stately Loire. . . 710 *Prelude* 9. 41
—Hail Contemplation ! from the stately towers, . 787 *Excursion* 3. 101
That our existence winds her stately course . . 790 *Excursion* 3. 258
Smooth and commodious ; as a stately deck . . 805 *Excursion* 4. 246
For you a stately gallery maintain . . . . . 809 *Excursion* 4. 561
O'er stately Edinborough throned on crags ? . . 815 *Excursion* 4. 913
Save for yon stately House beneath whose roof . 824 *Excursion* 5. 97
The other—like a stately sycamore, ... 829 *Excursion* 5. 460
Beneath the battlements and stately trees . . 844 *Excursion* 6. 440
Within its shade, as in a stately tent . . . 866 *Excursion* 7. 617
From out the ruins of his stately lodge : . . . 872 *Excursion* 7. 969
Have vanished—swallowed up by stately roads . 876 *Excursion* 8. 109
The stately fence accompanied our steps ; . . . 881 *Excursion* 8. 454
And wisdom loves.—But when a stately ship . . 882 *Excursion* 8. 506
On stately terraces of Como, ... S.3. 438 **My Lord* 18
State's. Determined, lies beyond the State's embrace, ... 519 *Pun. Death* 8. 2
For the State's guidance, or the Church's weal, . 587 *Crosth.* 8
It mounts to reach the State's parental ear ; . . 889 *Excursion* 9. 327
States. And states be torn up by the roots, wilt seem 276 *Author's Portrait* 6
Endangered States may yield to terms unjust ; . 316 **Say, what* 10
Of states and kingdoms, to their joy or woe, . . 323 **Now that* 3
All States have glorified themselves ;—their claims 331 *Ode : Thanks.* 155
For future states of being ; and the wings . . 826 *Excursion* 5. 245
Which States and Kingdoms utter when they talk 828 *Excursion* 5. 380
Statesman. In Statesman, Priest, and humble Citizen: 441 *Ecc. Sonn.* 3. 5. 6
Blest Statesman He, whose Mind's unselfish will . 514 **Blest Statesman* 1
Statesmen. Lords, lawyers, statesmen, squires of low degree, ... 303 **Is it* 3
O'erweening Statesmen have full long relied . . 320 **O'erweening Statesmen* 1
But deem not this Man useless.—Statesmen ! ye 567 *Cumb. Beg.* 67
State-whirlwind. And rage of one State-whirlwind, insecure. . . . . 682 *Prelude* 6. 488
Station. With that reproof I do resign a station . 78 *Bord.* 2320
An Angel from his station ; . . . . 112 **How rich* 8
Each, in his station twinkling not, ... 173 *Waggoner* 1. 11
I know that Wanton's noisy station, ... 179 *Waggoner* 3. 118
His station is there ; and he works on the crowd, 188 *Music* 5
But still the Ass his station kept. . . . . . 241 *P. B.* 400
Holding a central station of command, . . . 339 *Schwytz* 10
The watchmen from their station high . . . . 402 *White Doe* 599
Upheave, so seems it, from her natural station . 427 *Ecc. Sonn.* 1. 34. 11
—Who, if he rise to station of command, . . . 493 *Hap. War.* 35
Of lofty station, female goodness walks, . . . 539 **Lady ! a* 46
Thus, dishonouring not her station, ... 550 *Hermit's Cell* 4. 13
Take up a station calmly on the perch . . . 654 *Prelude* 3. 358
His station as before ; and when I asked . . . 664 *Prelude* 4. 416
That took his station there for ornament : . . 704 *Prelude* 8. 380
And took his station in the Tribune, saying, . . 720 *Prelude* 10. 112
Now was I from that pleasant station torn . . 722 *Prelude* 10. 282
A silent station in this beauteous world. . . . 740 *Prelude* 13. 47
To take a station among men, the step . . . 751 *Prelude* 14. 342
Sparkle the stars, as of their station proud. . . 782 *Excursion* 2. 722
Their station under a cerulean sky. . . . . 784 *Excursion* 2. 851
To every class its station and its office, . . . 806 *Excursion* 4. 341
How she her station doth adorn : the pool . . 868 *Excursion* 7. 720
In heart or soul, in station or pursuit, ... 872 *Excursion* 7. 987

Station—*continued.*
From that exalted station to the plain . . . 895 *Excursion* 9. 756
To all the charms this Station shows, ... S.3. 438 **My Lord* 24
The station whence he looked was soft and green, K.8. 237 *Recluse* 1. 1. 19
Stationary. Firm as a rock in stationary fight ; . 330 *Ode : Thanks.* 77
Of stationary sunshine :—thou hast viewed . . 379 *Duddon* 14. 6
The stationary blasts of waterfalls, ... 684 *Prelude* 6. 626
Necessity, the stationary host . . . . . . 843 *Excursion* 6. 325
That paves the brooks, the stationary rocks, . . 884 *Excursion* 9. 8
Stationed. *See* **Self-stationed.**
Musæus, stationed with his lyre . . . . . . 472 *Ossian* 39
Whom chance had stationed in the very room . 653 *Prelude* 3. 294
Stationed above the door, like guardian saints ; . 689 *Prelude* 7. 162
Stationed alone upon a spiry rock . . . . . 703 *Prelude* 8. 274
Then stationed in the city, were the chief . . . 711 *Prelude* 9. 126
And stationed in the public way, with face . . 756 *Excursion* 1. 39
In youth were mine ; when, stationed on the top 803 *Excursion* 4. 112
Station's. Right at the imperial station's western base, ... 219 **This Height* 13
Stations. Lift men from their native stations, . . 163 *Hint* 23
Thus, in their stations, lifting tow'rd the sky . 227 *Vernal Ode* 61
If multiplied, and in their stations set, . . . 839 *Excursion* 6. 78
That, through all stations, human life abounds . 846 *Excursion* 6. 562
Statist. Where She—a statist prudent to confer . 227 *Vernal Ode* 101
Art thou a Statist in the van . . . . . . 485 *Poet's Epitaph* 1
Statists. Of modern statists to their proper test, . 741 *Prelude* 13. 72
Statue. Meet Statue for the court of Fear ! . . 242 *P. B.* 523
Some Statue, placed amid these regions old . . 379 *Duddon* 15. 6
A statue of the soul. . . . . 543 *Russ. Fug.* 176
The antechapel where the statue stood . . . 650 *Prelude* 3. 60
Have a Mother, once a Statue ; . . . . . . S.3. 437 **I, whose* 3
Statues. Perpetually recumbent ; Statues—man, . 689 *Prelude* 7. 133
Statues and temples, and memorial tombs ; . . 812 *Excursion* 4. 737
Stature. Is one of giant stature, who could dance . 111 **'Tis said that some* 46
I like," said Benjamin, " her shape and stature : . 179 *Waggoner* 3. 72
And, near the fountain, flowers of stature tall . 202 *Hart-leap* 85
Her bosom heaves and spreads, her stature grows ; 209 *Laod.* 11
And ever, when such stature they had gained . 212 *Laod.* 171
Disordering colour, form, and stature ! . . . 245 *P. B.* 763
The imperial Stature, the colossal stride, . . . 270 *Henry : Portrait* 1
Rich groves of lofty stature, ... 302 *Yarrow V.* 50
A stature undepressed in size, ... 404 *White Doe* 739
Mark him, of shoulders curved, and stature tall, . 422 *Ecc. Sonn.* 1. 15. 5
Speak Thou, whose massy strength and stature scorn . . . . 477 *Long Meg* 5
Attained a stature twice a tall man's height, . . 521 *Epist. Beaumont* 15
And growing still in stature the grim shape . . 637 *Prelude* 1. 381
Myself unseen. He was of stature tall, . . . 664 *Prelude* 4. 391
There, too, conspicuous for stature tall . . . 692 *Prelude* 7. 342
Tall was her stature ; her complexion dark . . 848 *Excursion* 6. 678
A lofty stature undepressed by time, ... 881 *Excursion* 8. 502
Statute. And, what ye cannot reach by statute, draw . . . . 516 **Feel for* 13
Of custom, law, and statute, took at once . . . 729 *Prelude* 11. 111
Binding herself by statute to secure . . . . 888 *Excursion* 9. 299
Statutes. Burn all the statutes and their shelves : . 291 *Rob Roy* 22
His statutes like the chambers of the deep. . . 440 *Ecc. Sonn.* 2. 46. 14
Slow be the Statutes of the land to share . . . 518 *Pun. Death* 6. 6
Fixed on the statutes of Eternity, ... 519 *Pun. Death* 9. 7
Did Justice mould the Statutes of the Land. . . 626 **Son of* 8
Staunch. No fond hand left to staunch th' unclosing vein, ... 613 *Desc.Sk.Quarto* 611
Stave. And let us chant a passing stave, . . . 291 *Rob Roy* 7
Staves. Their forms are broken staves ; their passions, steeds . . . . 438 *Ecc. Sonn.* 2. 37. 11
By thrusting two rude staves into the wall . . 777 *Excursion* 2. 418
Stay. *See* **Up-stay.**
Stay ! pensive, sadly-pleasing visions, stay ! . . 8 *Ev. Wk.* 319
Or rather stay to taste the mild delights . . . 16 *Desc. Sk.* 338
Who cries presumptuous, " Here the flood shall stay," . . . . 22 *Desc. Sk.* 660
To stay his steps with faintness overcome ; . . 26 *Guilt* 137
The little fool is loth to stay behind. . . . . 42 *Bord.* 305
The cloud will soon disperse—farewell—but stay, 49 *Bord.* 647
To stay behind !—Hearing at first no answer, . 52 *Bord.* 811
Stay you behind ; and, when the sun is down, . 64 *Bord.* 1464
And thus we meet again ; one human stay . . 75 *Bord.* 2134
Stay near me—do not take thy flight ! . . . 79 **Stay near* 1
A little longer stay in sight ! . . . . . . 79 **Stay near* 2
But ere ten yards were gone her footsteps did she stay. . . . . 87 *Pet-lamb* 16
Think how pitiful that stay, ... 90 *Longest Day* 62
The Cross, fixed in his soul, may prove an all-sufficing stay. . . . . 91 *Norman Boy* 32
Something must stay to tell us of the rest. . . 107 *Farewell* 52
As one that lived ungrateful for the stay . . 118 *Maternal Grief* 47
Not a soul in the village this morning will stay ; . 119 *Childless Father* 2
" Oh ! how I love thee !—we will stay . . . 121 *EmigrantMother* 65
Each other's advocate, each other's stay ; . . . 122 *V. and J.* 23
If she must go, or she must stay ! . . . . . 128 *Idiot Boy* 170
" Susan, I'd gladly stay with you. . . . . . 128 *Idiot Boy* 186
Good Susan tell me, and I'll stay ; . . . . . 128 *Idiot Boy* 194
Where he will stay till he is dead ; . . . . . 128 *Idiot Boy* 224
He may return to us. If here he stay, ... 135 *Michael* 253
Many a stop and stay he makes, ... 174 *Waggoner* 1. 36
Thus, after two hours' hearty stay, ... 178 *Waggoner* 2. 165
To stay the wanderer's steps and soothe his thoughts. . . . . 184 *Airey-force* 16
" God," said I, " be my help and stay secure ; . 197 *Resolution* 139
Hovering until the petals stay . . . . . . 227 *Vernal Ode* 112

Still. (*Partial list.*) *See* **Stock-still.**

That grief for which the senses still supply . . 1 Early Youth 9
Yet still, the sport of some malignant power, . . 2 Ev. Wk. 31
When, in the south, the wan noon, brooding still, 2 Ev. Wk. 37
A blue rim borders all the lake's still brink ; . . 4 Ev. Wk. 115
Sunk to a curve, the day-star lessens still, . . 5 Ev. Wk. 190
Theirs be these holms untrodden, still, and green, 6 Ev. Wk. 233
Wetting, that drip upon the water still ; . . . 7 Ev. Wk. 284
Gleams that upon the lake's still bosom fall ; . . 7 Ev. Wk. 294
Still the cold cheek its shuddering tear retains. . 8 Ev. Wk. 322
Air listens, like the sleeping water, still, . . . 9 Ev. Wk. 367
And still, perhaps, with faithless gleam, . . . 9 Lines : Boat 7
How calm ! how still ! the only sound, . . . 9 Collins 21
Nor is she more at ease on some *still* night, . . 14 Desc. Sk. 186
The still vale lengthens underneath its shade . . 14 Desc. Sk. 217
How still ! no irreligious sound or sight . . . 16 Desc. Sk. 352
Still, Nature, ever just, to him imparts . . . 17 Desc. Sk. 403
We still confide in more than we can know ; . . 20 Desc. Sk. 538
Still have I found, where Tyranny prevails, . . 21 Desc. Sk. 597
Can still suspect, and still revere himself, . . . 23 Yew-tree 63
Left his mind still as a deep evening stream. . . 26 Guilt 96
Struck, and still struck again, the troubled horse : 27 Guilt 177
We seemed still more and more to prize each other ; 28 Guilt 249
Of feet still bustling round with busy glee, . . 31 Guilt 392
And ear still busy on its nightly watch, . . . 32 Guilt 421
Besides, on griefs so fresh my thoughts were brooding still. . . . . 32 Guilt 423
An image of this old Man still was present, . . 39 Bord. 97
The moon shone clear, the air was still, so still 47 Bord. 575
I still will be your friend, will cleave to you . . 64 Bord. 1499
The labours of my hand are still your joy ; . . 67 Bord. 1640
When all that multitude of hearts was still, . . 70 Bord. 1803
And still I heard it as before. . . . . . . 82 Alice Fell 8
The marks were still the same ; . . . . . . 83 Lucy Gray 50
While still I held him by the arm, ... 86 Anecdote 34
The Stranger, whom he saw still lingering there. . 95 Brothers 37
The other, left behind, is flowing still. . . . . 97 Brothers 145
His absent Brother still was at his heart. . . . 100 Brothers 348
The morning came, and still he was unheard of : . 101 Brothers 377
Thus fares it still with all that takes its birth . 102 Artegal 31
Came near, and nearer still. . . . . 109 *Strange fits 16
But hand and voice alike are still ; . . . . . 112 *How rich 11
" Another still ! and still another ! . . . . . 115 Last of Flock 61
Is not more still and mute than he. . . . . . 127 Idiot Boy 81
And Betty's still at Susan's side. . . . . . 128 Idiot Boy 176
And, still and mute, in wonder lost, ... 129 Idiot Boy 324
Though yet their tongues were still. . . . . 130 Idiot Boy 406
Her body still grew better. . . . . 130 Idiot Boy 421
Scared them, while they lay still beneath the shears. 134 Michael 176
And still I loved thee with increasing love. . . 136 Michael 344
But still be true till I am dead, ... 145 Her Eyes 58
My little babe ! thy lips are still, ... 145 Her Eyes 83
And therefore, my sweet MARY, this still Nook, . . 150 M. H. 23
Come forth at evening, keeps Thee still and mute ; 154 Morn. Ex. 58
For the still growths that prosper here ? . . . 154 Flower Garden 10
Then—all at once the air was still, ... 154 *A whirl-blast 3
Yet seeming still to hover ; . . . . 159 Green Linnet 28
That lies dead and still, ... 166 Stray Pleasures 2
A canopy in some still nook ; . . . . . . 168 Wren's Nest 18
If you listen, all is still, ... 171 Kitten 81
He marked not that 'twas still as death. . . . 175 Waggoner 1. 155
Still sit upon Helm-crag together ! . . . . . 175 Waggoner 1. 179
Still mounting to a higher height ; . . . . . 178 Waggoner 3. 25
And higher still—a greedy flight ! . . . . . 178 Waggoner 3. 26
Through the still night proceeds again ; . . . 179 Waggoner 3. 65
Like pleasant sunbeams shifting still . . . . 182 Waggoner 4. 204
And thou wert still a hope, a love ; . . . . 184 *O blithe 23
Still longed for, never seen. . . . . 184 *O blithe 24
Still deepens its unfathomable depth. . . . . 184 Night-piece 22
Where all things else are still and motionless. . 184 Airey-force 7
And yet a Spirit still, and bright . . . . . 186 *She was 29
Can he keep himself still, if he would ? oh, not he ! 189 Music 35
The vernal leaves—she loved them still ; . . . 194 Ruth 220
To genial faith, still rich in genial good ; . . . 195 Resolution 39
Yet still I persevere, and find them where I may." 197 Resolution 126
Or frosty air is keen and still, ... 198 Thorn 74
Or frosty air is keen and still, ... 198 Thorn 85
Yet all do still aver . . . . 200 Thorn 229
The waters of the spring were trembling still. . . 201 Hart-leap 44
The still, sad music of humanity, ... 207 Tintern 91
And rolls through all things. Therefore am I still 207 Tintern 102
Those quivering wings composed, that music still ! 209 *Ethereal minstrel 6
And to unfold a still magnificence, ... 212 Dion 4
From source still deeper, and of higher worth, . 216 Enterprise 99
Then all is still ; . . . . 217 Enterprise 116
Mere Mortals, bodied forth in vision still, . . . 220 Triad 12
Around angelic Forms, the still . . . . . . 228 Devot. Incit. 34
Of still or moving imagery— . . . . . . 228 Devot. Incit. 41
Still constant in her worship, still . . . . . 228 Devot. Incit. 68
Two lovely Sisters, still and sweet . . . . . 232 Jew. Fam. 33
At the still hour to Mercy dear, ... 233 Power of Sound 28
The heavens, whose aspect makes our minds as still 235 Power of Sound 181
" Reproach me not—your fears be still— . . . 238 P. B. 181
But still the Ass his station kept. . . . . . 241 P. B. 400
All still and silent—far and near ! . . . . . 241 P. B. 412
The meagre beast lay still as death ; . . . . 241 P. B. 456
That served my turn, when following still . . . 246 P. B. 863
Of private recollection sweet and still ! . . . 251 *There is a little 8
In his still haunt on Bagdad's summit high ; . . 252 *The fairest 6
Still last to come where thou art wanted most ! . 253 *Fond words 14
To reverend watching of each still report . . . 254 Complete Angler 5

Still—*continued.*

Yet pure and powerful minds, hearts meek and still, 254 Dyer 10
Thy countenance—the still rapture of thy mien— 258 *Even so 3
Still to be strenuous for the bright reward, . . 260 *High is 11
And all that mighty heart is lying still ! . . . 269 Westm. Bridge 14
To trust a Poet in still musings bound. . . . 273 *Wild Redbreast 14
Nor one look more exchanging, grief to still . . 276 Oker Hill 3
That unencumbered whole of blank and still, . . 277 *Haydon ! let 5
Rose out of darkness : the bright Work stood still ; 282 *In my 3
More closely still. . . . . 285 Grave of Burns 48
Sons of the Bard, my heart still mourns . . . 286 Sons of Burns 3
In this still place, remote from men, ... 288 Glen-Al. 1
In this still place, where murmurs on . . . . 288 Glen-Al. 3
I listened, motionless and still ; . . . . . . 289 Sol. Reap. 29
For thou wert still the poor man's stay, . . . 292 Rob Roy 109
The swan on still St. Mary's Lake . . . . . 293 Yarrow Unv. 43
Still sounding with the sounding tide, ... 296 Highland Boy 92
Are stifled—all is still. . . . . 297 Highland Boy 180
Still do they keep the Turtle-shell ; . . . . . 297 Highland Boy 247
A softness still and holy ; . . . . 302 Yarrow V. 46
Down their steep beds, that never shall be still : . 314 *Not 'mid 8
Exalt his still small voice ;—to quell that Host . 322 *By Moscow 10
He puts the Earthquake on her still design, . . 328 Ode 1815 94
From the smooth meadow-ground, serene and still ! 335 Namur 14
With intermingling motions soft and still, . . . 338 Engelberg 8
And, as the saint he prays to, still. . . . . . 342 Ital. Itin. 90
Still moonshine, without shadow, spread . . . 343 Eclipse 27
Still in the vivid freshness of a dream, ... 347 Processions 46
Still, with those white-robed Shapes—a living Stream, ... 347 Processions 48
Science, wide-spread and spreading still as be . 357 Aquap. 331
Still loftier, and to climes more near the Pole. . 363 *List—'twas 102
The Monks still repeat the tradition with pride, . 364 Vallomb. 9
She seems to work, at pleasure to lie still ;— . . 366 Lombardy 7
Still as he turns, the charmed spectator sees . . 367 Trajan 15
How in still air the balance trembled— . . . 373 Eg. Maid 278
He paused, and stood entranced by that still face 373 Eg. Maid 299
By blazing fire, the still suspense . . . . . 375 *The Minstrels 41
The still repose, the liquid lapse serene, . . . 381 Duddon 20. 4
Still glides the Stream, and shall for ever glide ; . 384 Duddon 34. 5
Still shy of human neighbourhood ; . . . . . 398 White Doe 175
Nor feared she in the still moonshine . . . . 416 White Doe 1815
Bards, nursed on blue Plinlimmon's still abode, . 421 Ecc. Sonn. 1. 10. 12
Black tempests bursting, blacker still in view ! . 425 Ecc. Sonn. 1. 27. 7
The Royal Minstrel, ere the choir is still, . . . 426 Ecc. Sonn. 1. 30. 9
Methinks their very names shine still and bright ; 441 Ecc. Sonn. 3. 5. 9
The Fathers urge the People to be still, . . . 442 Ecc. Sonn. 3. 8. 9
Through the still churchyard, each with garland gay, 448 Ecc. Sonn. 3. 32. 7
Once ye were holy, ye are holy still ; . . . . 449 Ecc. Sonn. 3. 35. 13
'Tis the still hour of thinking, feeling, loving. . . 453 *The Sun, that 6
But, from the process in that still retreat, . . . 456 *Soft as 6
And sky that danced among those leaves, are still ; 456 *The leaves 2
To the still lake) the imaginative Bird . . . . 456 *The leaves 12
And, with his sleep, that beauty calm and still. . 461 *Giordano, verily 8
Still round my shattered brow in beauty wave." . 465 *Thou look'st 14
(Still marked with green turf circles narrowing . 470 Tynwald 2
Still is he seen, in lone sublimity, ... 471 Ailsa Crag 6
If eyes be still sworn vassals of belief, ... 474 *Ye shadowy 13
Through this still medium, are consoled and cheered ; . . . . 476 Howard 10
By whom on this still night descried ? . . . . 479 Somnamb. 97
We cannot bid the ear be still ; . . . . . . 481 Expost. 18
But we must still be seeking ? . . . . 481 Expost. 28
And still the centre of his cheek . . . . . . 483 Simon Lee 7
With coldness still returning ; . . . . 484 Simon Lee 94
Of still and serious thought went round, . . . 486 Matthew 26
And fixing still his eye . . . . 486 *We walked 18
" Thus fares it still in our decay : . . . . . 487 Fountain 33
Even be it so : yet still among your tribe, . . . 488 Pers. Talk 21
And now, his task performed, the flood stands still, 495 Fact 35
In the still summer noon, while beams of light, . 496 *A little 41
With flaccid threads of ivy, in the still . . . 497 *Enough of climbing 22
Lie in forbearance, strength in standing still ? . 505 Warning 150
Be strong in faith, bid anxious thoughts lie still ; 505 Warning 160
And hums the balmy air to still . . . . . . 506 *While from 15
Queen art thou still for each gay plant . . . 506 *While from 29
That still he loves the Bird, and still must love ; . 531 *I know 31
Still shall be left some corner of the heart . . . 531 Octogen. 13
Chatter, chatter, chatter still ! . . . . 536 Goody Blake 4
Their arms still strengthening with the strengthening heart, ... 541 Grace Darl. 61
And still he lay as if he had been bound. . . . 556 Prioress 225
Thou Nightingale ! the Cuckoo said, be still, . . 560 Cuck. and Night. 196
That, still attempting to prevent the waste, . . 566 Cumb. Beg. 17
At distance still the same. Poor Traveller ! . . 567 Cumb. Beg. 58
Disturb the summer dust ; he is so still . . . 567 Cumb. Beg. 60
Who have a broom still ready in your hands . . 567 Cumb. Beg. 69
Knocked here—and knocked there, pounds still adding to pounds. . . . . 570 Farmer 36
Whene'er I looked, thy Image still was there ; . . 578 Peele Castle 7
I spoke (but let that pang be still) . . . . . 580 John Words. 12
And still we struggle when a good man dies. . . 583 *With copious 4
Still they were faithful ; like two vessels launched 586 Ch. Lamb 102
And in its depth of gratitude is still. . . . . 586 Ch. Lamb 120
Must travel, still is Nature's Priest, ... 588 Immortality 72
With new-fledged hope still fluttering in his breast :— . . . . 589 Immortality 142
These fairy holms untrodden, still, and green, . . 595 Ev. Wk. Quarto 221
While in sweet cadence rising small and still . . 598 Ev. Wk. Quarto 325
Slow lights upon the lake's still bosom fall, . . 598 Ev. Wk. Quarto 336

Still—*continued.*
All air is, as the sleeping water, still, ... 600 *Ev. Wk. Quarto* 435
While, opposite, the waning moon hangs still, . 606 *Desc.Sk.Quarto* 219
The still vale lengthens underneath the shade ; . 607 *Desc.Sk.Quarto* 270
By whose unpathway'd margin still and dread . 607 *Desc.Sk.Quarto* 285
And still, below, where mid the savage scene . 607 *Desc.Sk.Quarto* 291
Where Silence still her death-like reign extends, . 609 *Desc.Sk.Quarto* 376
O'er azure pikes serene and still, they go, . . . 610 *Desc.Sk.Quarto* 458
Bounds calm and clear the chaos still and hoar ; . 611 *Desc.Sk.Quarto* 503
Lift, all serene, their still, illumin'd forms, . . 612 *Desc.Sk.Quarto* 565
Still have my pilgrim feet unfailing found, . . 615 *Desc.Sk.Quarto* 720
Unbreathing Justice her still beam surveys : . . 616 *Desc.Sk.Quarto* 787
And growing still in stature the grim shape . . 637 *Prelude* 1. 381
That fled, and, flying still before me, gleamed . 638 *Prelude* 1. 451
Stopped short ; yet still the solitary cliffs . . . 639 *Prelude* 1. 458
And that still spirit shed from evening air ! . . 644 *Prelude* 2. 132
And dead still water lay upon my mind . . . 644 *Prelude* 2. 171
With faculties still growing, feeling still . . . 646 *Prelude* 2. 320
Pass unrecorded, that I still had loved . . . 647 *Prelude* 2. 377
O'er all that moves and all that seemeth still ; . 648 *Prelude* 2. 402
Is still with Innocence its own reward, . . . 658 *Prelude* 3. 615
Are still, the creature trotted on before ; . . . 660 *Prelude* 4. 121
Of a still water, solacing himself . . . . . 662 *Prelude* 4. 258
That murmured in the vale. All else was still ; . 664 *Prelude* 4. 384
In silence through a wood gloomy and still. . . 665 *Prelude* 4. 447
Yet would the living Presence still subsist . . 666 *Prelude* 5. 34
Where still it works, though hidden from all search 668 *Prelude* 5. 196
Some intermeddler still is on the watch . . . 670 *Prelude* 5. 334
By the still borders of the misty lake, ... 674 *Prelude* 5. 563
Sweet meditations, the still overflow . . . . 675 *Prelude* 6. 43
For still we had hopes that pointed to the clouds, 684 *Prelude* 6. 587
Still as a sheltered place when winds blow loud ! . 689 *Prelude* 7. 171
Add to these exhibitions, mute and still, . . . 691 *Prelude* 7. 260
Over still mountains, or appears in dreams ; . . 696 *Prelude* 7. 634
When the great tide of human life stands still ; . 697 *Prelude* 7. 657
Stretched and still stretching far and wide, exalt 698 *Prelude* 7. 746
The streets were still ; not so those long Arcades ; 719 *Prelude* 10. 96
Each evening, pacing by the still sea-shore, . . 723 *Prelude* 10. 323
Not far from that still ruin all the plain . . 726 *Prelude* 10. 562
She whispered still that brightness would return, 732 *Prelude* 11. 345
Hath still upheld me, and upholds me now . . 732 *Prelude* 11. 356
Still craving combinations of new forms, . . . 736 *Prelude* 12. 144
All over this still ocean ; and beyond, ... 746 *Prelude* 14. 44
Unless this love by a still higher love . . . 748 *Prelude* 14. 181
(Still to the very going-out of youth) . . . 749 *Prelude* 14. 243
Still deeper welcome found his pure discourse : . 757 *Excursion* 1. 73
Rapt into still communion that transcends . . 759 *Excursion* 1. 215
At this still season of repose and peace, . . . 765 *Excursion* 1. 594
That, wheresoe'er I went, I still would ask . . 769 *Excursion* 1. 867
So still an image of tranquillity, ... 770 *Excursion* 1. 946
So calm and still, and looked so beautiful . . . 770 *Excursion* 1. 947
Stood still, though but a casual passenger, . . 780 *Excursion* 2. 554
And, with light steps still quicker than his words, 781 *Excursion* 2. 637
The still contentedness of seventy years. . . . 783 *Excursion* 2. 750
To brush the still breast of a crystal lake. . . 787 *Excursion* 3. 73
I left not uninvoked ; and, in still groves, . . 797 *Excursion* 3. 753
In some still passage of its course, and seen, . . 800 *Excursion* 3. 970
The unfathomable gulf, where all is still ! " . . 800 *Excursion* 3. 991
And still dividing, and dividing still, ... 815 *Excursion* 4. 963
Subservient still to moral purposes, ... 820 *Excursion* 4. 1248
Of far-off torrents charming the still night, . . 821 *Excursion* 4. 1322
To the still influx of the morning light . . . 822 *Excursion* 5. 4
Withdrew, and fixed me in a still retreat ; . . 823 *Excursion* 5. 53
" The fragrant air its coolness still retains ; . . 823 *Excursion* 5. 69
And still remain self-governed, and apart, . . 828 *Excursion* 5. 386
Still to be courted—never to be won. . . . 830 *Excursion* 5. 504
Was graceful, when it pleased him, smooth and still 842 *Excursion* 6. 292
She still renewed and could not but renew . . 853 *Excursion* 6. 994
And still his harsher passions kept their hold— . 860 *Excursion* 7. 215
To that still region whither all are bound. . . 861 *Excursion* 7. 229
Are still permitted to extend their pride, . . . 870 *Excursion* 7. 845
Through the still air, the closing of the Grave ; . 871 *Excursion* 7. 888
The prolongation of some still response, . . . 871 *Excursion* 7. 895
Accompanied, still extant, in a wreath . . . 872 *Excursion* 7. 972
Such have been, and still are in their degree, . . 875 *Excursion* 8. 65
Our ancestors, within the still domain . . . . 877 *Excursion* 8. 186
To the still lake, whose stillness is to sight . . 883 *Excursion* 8. 582
Gathered together, all in still delight, . . . 891 *Excursion* 9. 456
Of the still evening. Right across the lake . . 892 *Excursion* 9. 560
Or hushed ; the roaring waters, and the still— . 895 *Excursion* 9. 747
And now, its task performed, the flood stands still S.3. 427 **My Son* 6
War's tincture, 'mid the forest green and still, . S.3. 436 **The doubt* 184
Or something dearer still, if reason knows . . . K.8. 234**Witness thou* 4
Still gleams upon their polish'd plumes—the bright K.8. 234 **The order'd* 6
From high to low, from low to high, yet still . . K.8. 237 *Recluse* 1.1.43
Not only for their beauty, and their still . . . K.8. 243*Recluse* 1.1.249
That seems still smaller than it is. This grove . K.8. 247*Recluse* 1.1.386
Must honour still to Lonsdale's tail be bound ? . L.1. 88 *Juvenal* 1. 13

Stilled. *See* **Self-stilled.**
By a miraculous finger stilled at once. . . . . 40 *Bord.* 173
And stilled his tremulous lip. Thus they were calmed . . . . 119 *Maternal Grief* 63
This explanation stilled the alarm, ... 179 *Waggoner* 3. 130
Stilled the pantings of dismay. . . . . . . 217 **Inmate of* 8
Unpitied by the wise, all censure stilled. . . . 261 **Fair Prime* 8
(Stilled from afar—such marvel story tells— . . 362 **List—'twas* 55
Sleep fell upon the air, and stilled the ocean. . 371 *Eg. Maid* 144
Satiate are *these ;* and stilled to eye and ear ; . 392 *Daniel* 9
Her fate there measuring ;—all is stilled,— . . 415 *White Doe* 1781
Stilled by thy voice ! But quickly from afar . . 438 *Ecc. Sonn.* 2. 38. 5
Stilled by the ensanguined block of Fotheringay ! 465 **Dear to* 14

Stilled—*continued.*
The choristers in every grove had stilled ; . . . 523 *Epist. Beaumont* 155
His violence is stilled. . . . . 545 *Russ. Fug.* 336
Can never utterly be charmed or stilled ; . . . 721 *Prelude* 10. 204
The Child, who long ere this had stilled his sobs, . 782 *Excursion* 2. 685
That frets, or languishes, be stilled and cheered." 829 *Excursion* 5. 484
She stilled them with a prompt reproof, and said, 854 *Excursion* 6. 1045
The rains at length have ceas'd, the winds are still'd, ... S.3. 425 **The rains* 1

Stiller. And chanted hymns and stiller voice of prayer, ... 522 *Epist.Beaumont* 73
With shouts we raised the echoes ;—stiller sounds 892 *Excursion* 9. 533

Stillest. To stillest mood of softest skies, . . . 344 **How blest* 17

Stilling. And lifted from the grassy floor, stilling his faint alarms, ... 92 *Poet's Dream* 18

Stillness. Yet rage suppressed itself ;—to a deep stillness . . . . 68 *Bord.* 1696
And such the stillness of the house, ... 178 *Waggoner* 2. 137
Stillness, solitude, and calm, ... 182 *Waggoner* 4. 239
Was such a stillness e'er diffused . . . . . 222 *Triad* 199
In stillness or in storm. . . . . 295 *Highland Boy* 80
Nor less, the stillness of these frosty plains, . . 329 *Ode : Thanks.* 20
Their utter stillness, and the silent grace . . . 329 *Ode : Thanks.* 21
When the stillness of evening hath deepened its roar ; . . . . 345 *Stanzas : Simplon* 4
And makes this rural stillness more profound. . 349 *Val. Dover* 14
Absolute stillness, poised aloft in air, ... 390 *Glencroe* 11
A passive stillness is enjoined. . . . . . . 408 *White Doe* 1087
For prayer in stillness, or the chanted rite ; . . 430 *Ecc. Sonn.* 2. 6. 8
Now, ruin, beauty, ancient stillness, all . . . 449 *Ecc. Sonn.* 3. 35. 3
Now there is stillness in the vale, ... 494 *Force of Prayer* 37
The common light ; whose stillness charms the air, ... 508 *F. Stone* 8
What wonder at this hour of stillness deep, . . 524 *Epist. Beaumont* 183
While thro' the stillness scatters wild dismay, . 606 *Desc.Sk.Quarto* 241
A perfect stillness. Many were the thoughts . . 633 *Prelude* 1. 70
That once in the stillness of a summer's noon, . 666 *Prelude* 5. 57
The breathless stillness. The succeeding day, . 672 *Prelude* 5. 442
From her that happy stillness of the mind . . 740 *Prelude* 13. 9
And from the stillness of abstracted thought . . 760 *Excursion* 1. 292
In mortal stillness ; and they ministered . . . 763 *Excursion* 1. 490
The careless stillness of a thinking mind . . . 768 *Excursion* 1. 797
Ended ; and, from the stillness that ensued . . 777 *Excursion* 2. 394
Feelingly sweet is stillness after storm, . . . 790 *Excursion* 3. 280
Of stillness and close privacy, a nook . . . . 793 *Excursion* 3. 471
Stillness prevailed around us : and the voice . . 805 *Excursion* 4. 251
Stillness and rest, with disapproving eye . . . 808 *Excursion* 4. 484
In the deep stillness of a summer even . . . 817 *Excursion* 4. 1063
Did never break the stillness that prevails . . 818 *Excursion* 4. 1166
In stillness left when slaughter is no more, . . 836 *Excursion* 5. 928
Whispering those truths in stillness, which the Word, ... 837 *Excursion* 5. 992
To the profounder stillness of the grave. . . . 864 *Excursion* 7. 468
To the still lake, whose stillness is to sight . . 883 *Excursion* 8. 582
Blended in perfect stillness, to our sight ! . . . 890 *Excursion* 9. 451
In mutual stillness ; or, if some faint breeze . . S.3. 434 **The doubt* 72
There is a stillness, and they seem to make . . K.8. 252*Recluse* 1.1.586

Stills. Ere the storm its fury stills, ... 166 *Wand. Jew* 6
Concord that elevates the mind, and stills. . . . 389 *Breadalb.* 14
Drops at his feet, and stills his droning horn. . 597 *Ev. Wk. Quarto* 314
Below Eve's listening Star the sheep walk stills . 598 *Ev. Wk. Quarto* 353

Still-twinkling. Shook the still-twinkling tail and glancing ear ; . . . . 3 *Ev. Wk.* 48

Sting. We need an inward sting to goad us on. . 70 *Bord.* 1859
To feed remorse, to welcome every sting . . . 78 *Bord.* 2304
Thy sting was needless then, perchance unknown, 227 *Vernal Ode* 125
Charged with remembrance of *his* sudden sting, . 360 **Long has* 12
Grief of her sting ; nor cheat, where he detains . 389 *Breadalb.* 4
Where is thy Sting ?—O Grave, where is thy Victory ? " . . . . 448 *Ecc. Sonn.* 3. 31. 14
And from vicissitude remove its sting ; . . . 533 **Once I* 40
And when our hearts shall feel a sting . . . . 578 **I come* 53
The sting of self-reproach, with healing words. . 854 *Excursion* 6. 1033
The sting of human nature. Spread the law, . 893 *Excursion* 9. 639

Stinging. Shot stinging through her stark o'er-labour'd bones. . . . . 596 *Ev. Wk. Quarto* 246

Stings. And to inflict shame's salutary stings . . 325 *Enghien* 3
Stings to the quick, and, with resistless force, . 519 *Pun. Death* 12. 3
But *could not* sleep, tormented by the stings . . 685 *Prelude* 6. 711
Save when the stings of viperous remorse, . . 718 *Prelude* 9. 576

Stinted. And minds not stinted or untilled are given, 308 **These times* 6
With stinted kindness. In November days, . . 638 *Prelude* 1. 416
In reconcilement with our stinted powers ; . . 673 *Prelude* 5. 517
So stinted in the measure of their grace . . . K.8. 238 *Recluse* 1.1. 67

Stints. Thy bounty stints, nor can thy beauty mar, S.3. 433 **The doubt* 29

Stipend. A little weekly stipend, and we lived . . 643 *Prelude* 2. 82

Stir. " These things just served to stir the slumbering sense, ... 31 *Guilt* 397
And stir the pulse of lazy charity. . . . . . 39 *Bord.* 83
And long as I can stir I'll dog him.—Yesterday, . 46 *Bord.* 483
I must have more of this ;—you shall not stir . 46 *Bord.* 496
Unthought-of, unexpected, as the stir . . . . 80 **Loving she* 17
And stir not in the gale. . . . . 111 **'Tis said that some* 40
Imagination needs must stir ; . . . . 112 **Yes ! thou* 5
The little birds began to stir, ... 130 *Idiot Boy* 405
Think how it would stir against you . . . . 140 *Arm. Lady* 27
Though some may frown and make a stir, . . . 144 **Driven in* 71
Little Flower—I'll make a stir, ... 160 **Pansies, lilies* 15

Stood—*continued.*

How cheerful, at sunrise, the hill where I stood, . 116 *Repentance* 30
Impelled;—they parted from him there, and stood 125 *V. and J.* 251
For wishes he had none. To a lodge that stood . 125 *V. and J.* 271
Stood single, with large prospect, north and south, 133 *Michael* 133
Stood single, and, from matchless depth of shade, 133 *Michael* 166
There stood the urchin, as you will divine, . . 134 *Michael* 188
Then, pointing to the stones near which they stood, 137 *Michael* 383
On which it stood; great changes have been wrought . . . . 138 *Michael* 478
Were only hindrances that stood between . . . 146 **It was an* 11
That eastward looks, I there stopped short—and stood . . . . 147 *Joanna* 43
Attired in peasant's garb, who stood alone, . . 149 **A narrow* 48
He stood alone; whereat he turned his head . . 149 **A narrow* 57
Along a natural opening, that I stood . . . . 150 **When, to* 50
Who, while each stood companionless and eyed . 170 **Never enlivened* 22
On which brave Admiral Nelson stood— . . . 178 *Waggoner* 2. 129
Of its own darkness, as it stood of yore: . . . 184 *Yew-trees* 3
A virgin scene!—A little while I stood, . . . 185 *Nutting* 21
Motionless as a cloud the old Man stood, . . . 196 *Resolution* 75
The old Man still stood talking by my side; . . 197 *Resolution* 106
Stood his dumb partner in this glorious feat; . 201 *Hart-leap* 38
I stood in various thoughts and fancies lost, . . 202 *Hart-leap* 117
These were the bower; and here a mansion stood, 202 *Hart-leap* 127
We stood together; and that I, so long . . 207 *Tintern* 151
And Æson stood a youth 'mid youthful peers. . 210 *Laod.* 84
Stood like a lofty mount, uplifting slowly . . . 219 **This Height* 18
Alighted, there the Stranger stood alone; . . . 226 *Vernal Ode* 15
Stood just as he had stood before! . . . . 241 *P. B.* 405
Upon the spot where he had stood, ... 241 *P. B.* 429
He stood beside the cottage-door; . . . . . 249 *P. B.* 1117
I stood, of simple shame the blushing Thrall; . 251 **Beloved Vale* 10
He who stood visible to Mirza's eye, ... 252 **The fairest* 7
Save one, one only, when I stood forlorn, . . . 257 **Surprised by* 11
Salute us; there stood Indian citadel, ... 262 **Dark and* 6
The sweet-souled Poet of the Seasons stood— . 271 **Fame tells* 12
When at the sacred font for thee I stood; . . 274 *Rotha Q.* 2
Rose out of darkness: the bright Work stood still; 282 **In my* 3
Near which their cottage stood. . . . . . 295 *Highland Boy* 50
Beside a lake their cottage stood, ... 295 *Highland Boy* 51
A while he stood upon his feet; . . . . . 296 *Highland Boy* 151
There stood a consecrated Pile; . . . . . 298 *Brownie's Cell* 16
Who stood and flourished face to face . . . . 298 *Brownie's Cell* 32
Where stood, sublime, Leonidas . . . . . . 300 *Cora Linn* 41
Inland, within a hollow vale, I stood; . . . . 306 **Inland, within* 1
Resting upon his arms each warrior stood, . . 322 *Germans* 2
For them who bravely stood unhurt, or bled . . 328 *Ode 1815* 80
But, where we stood, the setting sun . . . . 334 **In Bruges* 21
Before the target stood—to claim . . . . 342 *Ital. Itin.* 61
Stood Science waiting for the hour . . . . . 343 *Eclipse* 2
Of airy workmanship whereon we stood, . . . 351 *Des. Stanzas* 85
We stood rejoicing, as if earth were free . . 353 *Aquap.* 64
Her splendours, seen, not felt, the while he stood 353 *Aquap.* 82
Of that high Convent-crested cliff I stood, . . 356 *Aquap.* 232
I stood, and gazed upon a marble stone, . . . 365 **Under the* 4
Firm in its pristine majesty hath stood . . . 367 *Trajan* 5
Merlin, as fixed in thought he stood, ... 371 *Eg. Maid* 166
Awe-stricken stood both Knights and Dames . . 372 *Eg. Maid* 193
He paused, and stood entranced by that still face 373 *Eg. Maid* 299
And stood, far-kenned by mantle furred with ermine, ... 373 *Eg. Maid* 308
I stood, looked, listened, and with Thee, . . . 385 *Yarrow Rev.* 7
Here stood an Oak, that long had borne affixed . 393 *Hart's-horn* 1
And oftentimes before him stood, ... 399 *White Doe* 275
The Friend, who stood before her sight, . . . 400 *White Doe* 342
Stood quietly in Rylstone-hall. . . . . . . 400 *White Doe* 379
As on the banner which stood near . . . . 400 *White Doe* 402
Stood silent under dreary weight,— . . . . 400 *White Doe* 421
There stood he, leaning on a lance . . . . . 401 *White Doe* 435
There stood he, cleansed from the despair . . 401 *White Doe* 439
Stood Richard, Ambrose, Christopher, ... 401 *White Doe* 477
Stood He, whose arm yet lacks the power . . 401 *White Doe* 482
From all the listeners that stood round, . . . 403 *White Doe* 671
Stood by their Sire, on Clifford-moor, ... 404 *White Doe* 724
At need, he stood, advancing high . . . . . 404 *White Doe* 751
And with those grey-haired champions stood, . 405 *White Doe* 821
Before his Father, Francis stood, ... 406 *White Doe* 895
Beside the lonely watch-tower stood . . . . 409 *White Doe* 1200
They stood like trees when earth and heaven . 410 *White Doe* 1319
And all the people that stood round . . . . 410 *White Doe* 1334
And hearing passed of Him who stood . . . . 411 *White Doe* 1347
Where Francis stood in open sight. . . . . 412 *White Doe* 1463
And there stood bravely, though forlorn. . . . 412 *White Doe* 1479
He stood,—nor weaponless was now; . . . . 412 *White Doe* 1481
And where full many a brave tree stood, . . . 413 *White Doe* 1587
Went forth, the Doe stood there in sight. . . . 414 *White Doe* 1695
We stood before this ruined Pile, ... 416 *White Doe* 1839
And stood apart from human cares: . . . . 416 *White Doe* 1859
We stood, a trembling, earnest Company! . . 445 *Ecc. Sonn.* 3. 22. 4
Cut off from home and country, may have stood— 460 **Wanderer! that* 53
Prepared, when each has stood his time, to sink . 464 **Thou look'st* 4
Degrees and Orders stood, each under each: . . 471 *Tynwald* 6
That searching test thy public course has stood; . 478 **Lonsdale! it* 11
So from the spot whereon he stood, ... 479 *Somnamb.* 118
Her very self stood there. . . . . 479 *Somnamb.* 130
The Shepherd stood; then makes his way . . 491 *Fidelity* 35
He was a tree that stood alone, ... 495 *Force of Prayer* 49
Stood with eyes fixed upon that masterpiece, . . 509 *F. Stone* 107
In after-thought, for Him who stood in awe . . 517 *Pun. Death* 2. 4
The Wain stood ready, at our Cottage-door, . . 522 *Epist. Beaumont* 93

Stood—*continued.*

On a green bank a creature stood forlorn . . . 523 *Epist. Beaumont* 122
On which he stood, by spells unnatural bound, . 523 *Epist. Beaumont* 151
Pale and trembling Hubert stood. . . . . . 535 *Egremont* 52
He stood behind a bush of elder, ... 537 *Goody Blake* 83
In a straggling village stood, ... 542 *Russ. Fug.* 90
Here stood his threshold; here was spread the roof 551 **If thou in* 8
"A little school of Christian people stood . . . 553 *Prioress* 43
Troilus stood the bright moon to behold; . . . 564 *Troilus* 130
And ever at his side stood Pandarus, ... 565 *Troilus* 164
As lonely he stood as a crow on the sands. . . 570 *Farmer* 48
Mourn, Italy, the loss of him who stood . . . 573 *Chiabrera* 2. 19
When stood the shorten'd herds amid the tide, . 592 *Ev. Wk. Quarto* 58
When horses in the wall-girt intake stood, . . 592 *Ev. Wk. Quarto* 65
Once did I pierce to where a cabin stood, . . . 605 *Desc.Sk.Quarto* 168
—On the slope of a mountain I stood, ... 620 *Convict* 2
"Poor victim! no idle intruder has stood . . 621 *Convict* 45
Were bronzed with deepest radiance, stood alone 636 *Prelude* 1. 296
Feebler and feebler, and I stood and watched . 639 *Prelude* 1. 462
In which ye stood? or can I here forget . . . 639 *Prelude* 1. 503
How I have stood, to fancies such as these . . 640 *Prelude* 1. 572
Of quietness or peace; yet have I stood, . . . 640 *Prelude* 1. 576
A tavern stood; no homely-featured house, . . 644 *Prelude* 2. 140
Of a small bowling-green; beneath us stood . . 644 *Prelude* 2. 157
And yet the building stood, as if sustained . . 646 *Prelude* 2. 280
The antechapel where the statue stood . . . 650 *Prelude* 3. 60
Stood almost single; uttering odious truth— . . 653 *Prelude* 3. 284
Of the plain Burghers, who in audience stood . 653 *Prelude* 3. 313
To utter waste. Hitherto I had stood . . . 656 *Prelude* 3. 510
Of a tall ash, that near our cottage stood; . . 659 *Prelude* 4. 89
Put off her veil, and, self-transmuted, stood . . 660 *Prelude* 4. 151
He stood, and in his very dress appeared . . . 664 *Prelude* 4. 401
I left the shady nook where I had stood . . . 664 *Prelude* 4. 411
A long half hour together I have stood . . . 671 *Prelude* 5. 396
Stirred them, not voiceless. Often have I stood . 676 *Prelude* 6. 85
That night our lodging was a house that stood . 684 *Prelude* 6. 641
And large dark eyes, beside her infant stood . . 692 *Prelude* 7. 343
Stood, propped against a wall, upon his chest . 696 *Prelude* 7. 640
And stood of all dismantled, save the last . . . 705 *Prelude* 8. 396
Of life and glory. In the midst stood Man, . . 706 *Prelude* 8. 485
I stood, 'mid those concussions, unconcerned, . 711 *Prelude* 9. 86
Of my associates stood prepared for flight . . 712 *Prelude* 9. 182
Of a Republic, where all stood thus far . . . 713 *Prelude* 9. 226
The Senate stood aghast, her prudence quenched, 723 *Prelude* 10. 351
And rocky island near, a fragment stood . . . 726 *Prelude* 10. 555
For mighty were the auxiliars which then stood . 728 *Prelude* 11. 106
In Nature's presence stood, as now I stand, . . 737 *Prelude* 12. 206
Upon my left a blasted hawthorn stood; . . . 738 *Prelude* 12. 301
Became more firm in feelings that had stood . . 740 *Prelude* 13. 56
Wherever Nature leads; that he hath stood . . 744 *Prelude* 13. 297
Not distant from the shore whereon we stood, . 747 *Prelude* 14. 57
My soul, too reckless of mild grace, had stood . 749 *Prelude* 14. 248
In everything that stood most prominent, . . 750 *Prelude* 14. 305
Upon that open moorland stood a grove, . . . 756 *Excursion* 1. 26
Graceful support; his countenance as he stood . 757 *Excursion* 1. 43
Equipped with satchel, to a school, that stood . 758 *Excursion* 1. 122
And grow with thought. Beside yon spring I stood, 763 *Excursion* 1. 484
This lonely Cottage. At the door he stood, . . 764 *Excursion* 1. 568
Stood drinking comfort from the warmer sun, . 765 *Excursion* 1. 621
The tears stood in her eyes. I left her then . . 768 *Excursion* 1. 810
—Margaret stood near, her infant in her arms, . 769 *Excursion* 1. 843
Stood undisturbed behind the door. And when, . 769 *Excursion* 1. 854
That bars the traveller's road, she often stood, . 769 *Excursion* 1. 895
I stood, and leaning o'er the garden wall . . . 770 *Excursion* 1. 921
The one Survivor stood; he wept, he prayed . . 774 *Excursion* 2. 202
Stood waiting for my Comrade. When behold . . 777 *Excursion* 2. 410
Stood still, though but a casual passenger, . . 780 *Excursion* 2. 554
By cobwebs, stood within a dusty nook; . . . 781 *Excursion* 2. 668
Stood fixed; and fixed resemblances were seen . 784 *Excursion* 2. 864
I then forgot him:—there I stood and gazed: . . 785 *Excursion* 2. 879
And, deep within that lonesome valley, stood . 786 *Excursion* 3. 8
Proved that such hope was vain:—for now we stood 786 *Excursion* 3. 37
Stood near, of smaller size, and not unlike . . 787 *Excursion* 3. 56
A hospitable chink, and stood upright, . . . 787 *Excursion* 3. 63
The eminence whereon her spirit stood, . . . 795 *Excursion* 3. 659
And, by what compromise it stood, not nice? . . 797 *Excursion* 3. 785
Against my peace. Within the cabin stood . . 798 *Excursion* 3. 861
Whoe'er hath stood to watch a mountain brook . 800 *Excursion* 3. 969
Stood empty of all shape of life, and silent . . 807 *Excursion* 4. 409
To us who stood low in that hollow dell, . . . 820 *Excursion* 4. 1300
Stood open; and we entered. On my frame, . . 824 *Excursion* 5. 139
Of sculptured oak stood here, with drapery lined; 825 *Excursion* 5. 165
In some abstraction;—gracefully he stood, . . 825 *Excursion* 5. 214
He stood; or if not so, whose top serene . . . 827 *Excursion* 5. 300
Awhile they stood in conference, and I guess . . 829 *Excursion* 5. 446
Bearing a lantern in her hand she stood, . . . 834 *Excursion* 5. 759
Before me stood that day; on holy ground . . 839 *Excursion* 6. 81
While both, embellishing each other, stood . . 843 *Excursion* 6. 306
So, where the mouldered tree had stood, was raised 846 *Excursion* 6. 503
Hither she came; here stood, and sometimes knelt 853 *Excursion* 6. 986
And naked stood that lowly Parsonage . . . 858 *Excursion* 7. 55
And far remote the chapel stood,—remote, . . 859 *Excursion* 7. 140
This old Man stood, the patriarch of the Vale! . 861 *Excursion* 7. 243
That, in his presence, humbler knowledge stood . 865 *Excursion* 7. 514
Survive, as pagan temples stood of yore, . . . 870 *Excursion* 7. 843
And, when that eulogy was ended, stood . . . 871 *Excursion* 7. 893
Where not a habitation stood before, ... 876 *Excursion* 8. 122
Shadowy, yet gay and lightsome as it stood . . 881 *Excursion* 8. 463
The breathing creature stood; as beautiful, . . 890 *Excursion* 9. 445

Store—continued.

The sword from Bangor's walls, and guard the store	421 Ecc. Sonn. 1. 12. 6
Yet, while each useful Art augments her store, .	466 St. Bees 28
Some ragged child holds up for sale a store .	474 *How sad 2
Came Barons bold, with store of gold, . . .	478 Somnamb. 21
Few months of life has he in store	483 Simon Lee 57
There find I personal themes, a plenteous store, .	488 Pers. Talk 37
Thoughtfully freighted with a various store ; . .	522 Epist. Beaumont 94
What recompense is kept in store or left . .	530 Poor Robin 33
With plenteous store of heath and withered fern,	547 *Rude is 19
By her own wants, she from her store of meal .	568 Cumb. Beg. 157
And gave, in handfuls gave, the treacherous store:	620 Birth of Love 43
And fume the household deities with store . .	624 Æneid 65
In common things—the endless store of things, .	633 Prelude 1. 109
Are found in plenteous store, but nowhere such .	634 Prelude 1. 159
With store of springes o'er my shoulder hung .	636 Prelude 1. 310
Want store of leafy arbours where the light . .	652 Prelude 3. 245
That golden store of books which I had left, . .	673 Prelude 5. 479
For he was busy, dealing, from a store . . .	779 Excursion 2. 503
And was itself half-covered with a store . . .	781 Excursion 2. 676
Than that accumulated store of gold . . .	809 Excursion 4. 567
With store of household goods, in panniers slung	858 Excursion 7. 64
Year after year is added to his store . . .	866 Excursion 7. 565
Large store of gleaming crimson-spotted trouts : .	882 Excursion 8. 558

Stored. A garden stored with peas, and mint, and

thyme, ...	28 Guilt 209
Into a garden stored with Poesy ;	103 Artegal 63
Is ample, and some little might be stored . .	149 *A narrow 53
He found the little he had stored, to meet . .	764 Excursion 1. 554
A cabinet stored with gems and pictures—draws .	874 Excursion 8. 23

Storehouse. The wide earth's storehouse fenced
about . . . . 217 Enterprise 153

Storehouses. Which God's ethereal storehouses
afford : . . . . 419 Ecc. Sonn. 1. 6. 4

Stores. Nor Winter yet his frozen stores had piled,

	17 Desc. Sk. 392
Her stores, and sighed to find them insecure ! .	311 *Who rises 36
What stores for years to come !	348 *Lulled by 54
With those rich stores of Nature's imagery, . .	367 *As indignation 3
Such stores as silent thought can bring, . . .	484 Simon Lee 66
Here will he gather stores of ready bliss, . .	549 *The massy 15
New stores, or rescue from decay the old . .	633 Prelude 1. 117
As through a wide museum from whose stores .	658 Prelude 3. 617
Left one day mistress of her mother's stores, . .	781 Excursion 2. 655
From Fancy, willing to set off her stores . .	788 Excursion 3. 129
The ocean paid him tribute from the stores . .	865 Excursion 7. 504

Stories. Quaint stories of the bird's attraction ! . 174 Waggoner 1. 96

Storm. See May-storm, Snow-storm.

Triumphant on the bosom of the storm, . . .	15 Desc. Sk. 275
Till storm and driving ice blockade him there. .	19 Desc. Sk. 487
Or hovel from the storm to shield his head, . .	25 Guilt 42
And, from the perilous ground dislodged, through storm	26 Guilt 129
Of such rough storm, this happy change to view."	30 Guilt 317
When into storm the evening sky is wrought, . .	36 Guilt 664
Upon the self-same spot, in rain or storm, . .	44 Bord. 391
That a fierce storm o'ertook us, worn with travel,	50 Bord. 697
Meanwhile the storm fell heavy on the woods ; .	50 Bord. 707
Or till the storm abate. He has restored you,	53 Bord. 864
And, in the storm and anguish of the heart, .	58 Bord. 1164
The storm beats hard—Mercy for poor or rich,	71 Bord. 1882
to look up at this roof in storm or fair . .	72 Bord. 1947
The first hours of last night were rough with storm :	73 Bord. 2043
The storm came on before its time : . . .	83 Lucy Gray 29
The rain and storm are things that scarcely can come here.	87 Pet-lamb 32
And while around it storm as fierce seemed troubling earth and air, ...	91 Poet's Dream 7
Of storm and thaw, when every water-course .	99 Brothers 253
And, truly, at all times, the storm, that drives .	132 Michael 56
With two brave sheep-dogs tried in many a storm,	132 Michael 91
So when the rain is over, the storm laid, . .	143 *High bliss 13
Sharp season followed of continual storm . .	150 *When, to 4
Of me and of the storm. Full many an hour .	150 *When, to 32
Was fettered, and the air by storm disturbed, .	150 *When, to 40
The storm had fallen upon the Oak, . . .	157 Oak and Broom 105
A thing no storm can e'er destroy, . . .	165 Danish Boy 10
But in the storm 'tis fresh and blue . . .	166 Danish Boy 30
Ere the storm its fury stills, ...	166 Wand. Jew 6
A storm, which had been smothered long, . .	175 Waggoner 1. 148
As if a storm had never been)	176 Waggoner 2. 13
Against the storm, and canvas spread. . .	179 Waggoner 3. 82
Of Raven-crag—black as a storm— . . .	180 Waggoner 4. 19
Even in the motions of the Storm	187 *Three years 22
A storm came on, and I could see . . .	199 Thorn 175
" 'Twas mist and rain, and storm and rain : .	199 Thorn 177
Safe through the winter storm in quiet dwells ! .	227 Vernal Ode 109
Beat back the roaring storm—but how subdued	279 *'Tis he 2
In stillness or in storm.	295 Highland Boy 80
Brighter than brightest loop-hole, in a storm, .	323 Ode 1814 20
Bend that way her desires. The dew, the storm—	354 Aquap. 133
A purifying instrument—the storm	354 Aquap. 137
Shun, like a shattered bark, the storm, and flee	366 *Eternal Lord 3
Lo ! he harangues his cohorts—there the storm	368 Trajan 43
The storm has stripped her of her leaves ; . .	370 Eg. Maid 53
The sea-blast ruffles as the storm comes on, .	388 Eagles 11
Until this storm hath ceased to rave : . .	408 White Doe 1098
As if with prescience of the coming storm, .	419 Ecc. Sonn. 1. 4. 10
As, when a storm hath ceased, the birds regain	420 Ecc. Sonn. 1. 7. 1
Have the survivors of this Storm renewed .	420 Ecc. Sonn. 1. 7. 6
Thus is the storm abated by the craft . .	432 Ecc. Sonn. 2. 16. 1
And ploughing storm, the spirit of Nassau . .	442 Ecc. Sonn. 3. 9. 4

Storm—continued.

In hours of peace, or when the storm is driven	452 Ecc. Sonn. 3. 46. 7
And the wild storm hath somewhere found a nest ;	454 Sea-side 2
Depress the hours. Up, Spirit of the storm ! .	466 St. Bees 14
Perchance had flown, delivered by the storm ; .	472 *The captive 2
But when a storm, on sea or mountain bred, .	472 Dunolly Eagle 2
While a dark storm before my sight . . .	472 Ossian 5
And faculty for storm and turbulence, . . .	493 Hap. War. 58
By gusts of vernal storm, attuned his song . .	537 *In desultory 4
All night the storm had raged, nor ceased, nor paused, ...	540 Grace Darl. 28
And buffeted at will by rain and storm. . .	571 *There is a Flower 12
Protracted, and the twilight storm foretells, .	605 Desc.Sk.Quarto 202
'Tis storm ; and hid in mist from hour to hour .	608 Desc.Sk.Quarto 332
So when on Ocean's face the storm subsides, .	618 School Ex. 37
And through the astonished Island swept in storm,	626 Ballot 3
Dashed headlong, and rejected by the storm. .	639 Prelude 1. 498
If the night blackened with a coming storm, . .	646 Prelude 2. 307
A like dominion, and the midnight storm . .	647 Prelude 2. 373
With an obsequious promptness, yet the storm .	694 Prelude 7. 475
As the black storm upon the mountain-top . .	696 Prelude 7. 619
Moreover, the first storm was overblown, . .	711 Prelude 9. 108
Joust underneath the trees, that as in storm .	716 Prelude 9. 455
Of which I speak, only as they were storm .	720 Prelude 10. 121
Of a ship struggling with a hideous storm) . .	721 Prelude 10. 228
Under a long-lived storm of great events— .	732 Prelude 11. 374
Not mute, and then retire, fearing no storm ; .	734 Prelude 12. 23
Down to this very time, when storm and rain .	739 Prelude 12. 327
Through storm and darkness, early in my mind .	742 Prelude 13. 154
Brooding above the fierce confederate storm .	755 Recluse 1. 1. 831
The history of many a winter storm, . . .	760 Excursion 1. 278
Through hot and dusty ways, or pelting storm, .	761 Excursion 1. 323
In the wild concert—chiefly when the storm .	782 Excursion 2. 700
Lay at the mercy of this raging storm. . .	783 Excursion 2. 790
All night the storm endured : and, soon as help .	784 Excursion 2. 805
To baffle, as he might, the watery storm : . .	784 Excursion 2. 820
Upon the dark materials of the storm . . .	784 Excursion 2. 847
Feelingly sweet is stillness after storm, . .	790 Excursion 3. 280
The rainbow smiling on the faded storm ; . .	808 Excursion 4. 463
To oldest time ! and, reckless of the storm . .	809 Excursion 4. 518
Swept in the storm of chase ; as moon and stars .	814 Excursion 4. 869
Who throve, like plants, uninjured by the storm .	825 Excursion 5. 199
Hath harassed him toiling through fearful storm,	852 Excursion 6. 913
Repelled the storm and deadened its loud roar. .	860 Excursion 7. 179
That the dread storm is weathered by them both.	867 Excursion 7. 647
" I know where I shall find him, though the storm	K.8. 228 *I will 121
For ye must know] that though the storm . .	K.8. 228 *I will 123
Thick storm, and heavy, which for three hours' space	K.8. 228 *I will 136
Begins to love us ! By a sullen storm, . .	K.8. 241 Recluse 1.1.180
Two months unwearied of severest storm, . .	K.8. 241 Recluse 1.1.181
Through these two months of unrelenting storm,	K.8. 243 Recluse 1.1.244
Conceal us from the storm,—so here abides .	K.8. 247 Recluse 1.1.376

Storm-beaten. Storm-beaten and bewildered as we
were ; . . . . 52 Bord. 815

Storm-driven. Storm-driven ; who, having seen the
cup of woe . . . . 419 Ecc. Sonn. 1. 2. 12

Stormed. In bondage ; and the palace, lately
stormed . . . . 719 Prelude 10. 53

Storm-proof. Impervious, and storm-proof. . 168 Wren's Nest 8

Storms. See Mountain-storms.

And Pikes, of darkness named and fear and storms,	19 Desc. Sk. 472
And from his nest amid the storms of heaven .	19 Desc. Sk. 514
Roaring with storms beneath night's starless gloom ;	26 Guilt 139
Had heard of one who, forced from storms to shroud, ...	27 Guilt 172
The heaviest storms not longest last ; . . .	110 Forsaken 2
Up to the heights, and in among the storms, . .	137 Michael 393
Derived from clouds and storms !) the amplest range	219 *This Height 3
Founder amid fanatic storms.	228 Devot. Incit. 53
'Mid summer storms or winter's ice, . . .	239 P. B. 298
Storms, sallying from the mountain-tops, waylay	264 Snowdrop 5
We watch their splendour, shall we covet storms,	277 *The most 4
Doth yet frequent the hill of storms, . . .	300 Bran 3
Ye Storms, resound the praises of your King ! .	322 *Ye Storms 1
Report of storms gone by	329 Ode : Thanks. 24
Of fortune, and the desolating storms . . .	333 *Bruges I 9
Of Winter, but the storms of life, . . .	338 *Meek Virgin 22
Shouts rise, and storms of sound from lifted trumpets blow !	346 Processions 18
And alien storms with home-bred ferments claim	438 Ecc. Sonn. 2. 38. 7
Of winter storms, yet budding cheerfully ; . .	450 Ecc. Sonn. 3. 39. 6
And storms the pillars rock. But we such schools	496 *A little 39
But list !—though winter storms be nigh, . .	498 *The sylvan 25
Then, amid the storms of life	503 *Like a 74
Storms make in rising, valued in the moon . .	505 Warning 145
In his own storms he hides himself from sight. .	521 Epist. Beaumont 9
And, to far-travelled storms of sea and land, .	548 *Stay, bold 5
Full oft, when storms the welkin rend, . . .	550 Hermit's Cell 5. 10
With which she speaks when storms are gone, .	581 *Loud is 2
Hath seen in grim array amid their Storms .	612 Desc.Sk.Quarto 538
Huge Pikes of Darkness named, of Fear and Storms, ...	612 Desc.Sk.Quarto 564
From his bare nest amid the storms of heaven .	613 Desc.Sk.Quarto 618
Memorial reverenced by a thousand storms ; .	682 Prelude 6. 486
When storms are raging. Happy are they both—	692 Prelude 7. 328
To wait upon the storms : of their approach . .	702 Prelude 8. 224
Such as the storms and angry elements . .	706 Prelude 8. 514

Strangers—*continued.*
For strangers who have travelled far perhaps, . K.8. 226 **I will* 69
They strangers, and we strangers; they a pair, . K.8. 243 *Recluse* I.I.254
Strangers to me, and all men, or at least . . . K.8. 251 *Recluse* I.I.533
Strangers to all particular amity, ... K.8. 251 *Recluse* I.I.534
Strangest. There are the strangest echoes in that place! . . . . 55 *Bord.* 962
Strangle. Yet, while they strangle, a fair growth they bring, ... 424 *Ecc. Sonn.* I. 21. 13
Strangled. And strangled by a merciless force; . . 494 *Force of Prayer* 34
Strath. O'er hilly path, and open Strath, . . . 293 *Yarrow Unv.* 37
Round strath and mountain, stamped by the ancient tongue . . . . 389 *Sound of Mull* 3
Straw. From her bare straw the Woman half upraised . . . . 34 *Guilt* 560
Then sank upon her straw with feeble moan. . . 34 *Guilt* 564
Their bed of straw and blanket-walls. . . . . 192 *Gipsies* 8
And she had made a pipe of straw, ... 192 *Ruth* 7
But who would force the Soul tilts with a straw . 442 *Ecc. Sonn.* 3. 7. 13
Then, will the sceptre be a straw, the crown . 504 *Warning* 107
And seldom knowing that he sees, some straw, . 567 *Cumb. Beg.* 54
'Mid coaches and chariots, a waggon of straw, . 570 *Farmer* 77
Let them smoke, let them burn, not a straw would he care! . . . . 571 *Avarice* 10
Or trampled into earth; a chain of straw, . . 769 *Excursion* I. 839
Closed up each chink, and with fresh bands of straw 770 *Excursion* I. 903
Strawberries. To gather strawberries all day long; 193 *Ruth* 52
Strawberries from lane or woodland, offering wild 525 *Epist. Beaumont* 244
Refreshment, strawberries and mellow cream. . 644 *Prelude* 2. 160
Sauntering to pluck the strawberries wild unseen. S.3. 417 **Sweet was* 8
Strawberry. And love the strawberry in its bower; 142 *†Lov. and Lik.* 34
There bloomed the strawberry of the wilderness; 377 *Duddon* 6. 9
The season) sprinklings of ripe strawberry fruit. . 529 *Poor Robin* 14
Strawberry-blossom. Only spare the strawberry-blossom! . . . . 79 *Foresight* 16
Strawberry-blossoms. Strawberry-blossoms, one and all, ... 79 *Foresight* 3
Strawberry-flower. To the favoured strawberry-flower. . . . . 80 *Foresight* 26
And you may love the strawberry-flower, . . . 142 *†Lov. and Lik.* 33
Straw-built. On cold blue nights, in hut or straw-built shed, ... 7 *Ev. Wk.* 257
Straws. While winds are eddying round her, among straws . . . . 693 *Prelude* 7. 440
Stray. 'Tis pleasant near the tranquil lake to stray 6 *Ev. Wk.* 216
Beyond his native valley seldom stray, . . . 18 *Desc. Sk.* 428
Hail Freedom! whether it was mine to stray, . 21 *Desc. Sk.* 591
To waken our stray Baron. Were there not . . 51 *Bord.* 766
I had been out in search of a stray heifer; . . 73 *Bord.* 2044
On windy days, in one of those stray brooks, . . 99 *Brothers* 260
Through border wilds where naked Indians stray, 153 *Morn. Ex.* 13
Or stray invention. . . . . 158 **In youth* 48
In stray gifts to be claimed by whoever shall find; 167 *Stray Pleasures* 28
Where'er the subtle waters stray; . . . . . 227 *Vernal Ode* 68
Where human foot did never stray; . . . . 237 *P. B.* 97
With sympathetic heart may stray, ... 238 *P. B.* 139
Long as the shepherd's bleating flock shall stray . 254 *Dyer* 12
That I, if frugal and severe, might stray . . . 259 *Calvert* 6
Or shining slope where he must never stray; . . 267 **As the* 5
We wont to stray, ... 286 *Nith* 28
For sportive youth to stray in; . . . . . . 302 *Yarrow V.* 58
Thoughts that would stray from Heaven? The dream must cease . . . . 363 **Grieve for* 10
The task, in smoother walks to stray; . . . . 492 *Duty* 31
I love beside the flowing lake to stray, . . . 595 *Ev. Wk. Quarto* 195
Where solitary forms illumin'd stray . . . . 607 *Desc.Sk.Quarto* 273
Beyond his native valley hardly stray, . . . 611 *Desc.Sk.Quarto* 515
At such an hour there are who love to stray, . . 614 *Desc.Sk.Quarto* 664
O'er Anet's hopeless seas of marsh to stray, . . 615 *Desc.Sk.Quarto* 715
Ah! better far than this, to stray about . . . 635 *Prelude* I. 250
To drive him back, and pound him, like a stray, . 670 *Prelude* 5. 335
No more shall stray where meditation leads, . . 803 *Excursion* 4. 104
The clouded moon, and calls me forth to stray . S.3. 417 **Sweet was* 13
In search of a stray sheep. It was the time . K.8. 224 **I will* 7
Awful as ever stray Demoniac uttered, . . . K.8. 246 *Recluse* I.I.337
Strayed. *See* **Forth-strayed.**
Across the pebbly road a little runnel strayed. . 34 *Guilt* 540
By chance had thither strayed; . . . . . 85 *Shepherd-boys* 86
While across her virgin cheek pure blushes strayed, 141 *Arm. Lady* 137
Nor through their sunny lawns have strayed? . 164 **Fair Lady* 4
Nor Anguish strayed from her Tartarean den; . 227 *Vernal Ode* 130
Than those soft scenes through which thy childhood strayed, ... 254 *Dyer* 4
Have sunk, at Nature's call; or strayed . . . 473 *Ossian* 47
He strayed through the fields like an indolent wight, 569 *Farmer* 23
Tho' now, where erst the grey-clad peasant stray'd, 615 *Desc.Sk.Quarto* 744
Straying. Who has a trick of straying from his keepers; . . . . 73 *Bord.* 2034
And, if a breeze be straying, ... 311 **Who rises* 7
A few steps distant, feeding, straying; . . . 402 *White Doe* 558
While they, side by side, were straying, . . . 415 *White Doe* 1745
Strays. The weary eye—which, wheresoe'er it strays, 26 *Guilt* 110
Of thoughtful Herdsman when he strays . . . 292 *Rob Roy* 114
The shepherd strays, a rolling hut his home. . . 702 *Prelude* 8. 197
Streak. Above Helm-crag—a streak half dead, . 175 *Waggoner* I. 168
Into clear view the cultured fields that streak . 219 **This Height* 20
Wish not for a richer streak; . . . . . . 222 *Triad* 192
All colours,—and the liveliest streak . . . . 299 *Brownie's Cell* 99
For not a tinge or flowery streak . . . . . 342 *Ital. Itin.* 83
Whereat a tender twilight streak . . . . . 374 *Eg. Maid* 327

Streak—*continued.*
And his bright eyes look brighter, set off by the streak . . . . 569 *Farmer* 7
Ne'er kindled with a livelier streak . . . . . 583 **O for a* 32
Streaked. —Thy lake that, streaked or dappled, blue or grey, ... 12 *Desc. Sk.* 119
Sky streaked with purple, grove and craggy *bield*, 524 *Epist. Beaumont* 175
Gleams, streak'd or dappled, hid from morning's ray 604 *Desc.Sk.Quarto* 139
The silvery lake is streaked with placid blue; . 890 *Excursion* 9. 421
Streaks. *See* **Cloud-streaks.**
Into blue spots, and slowly lengthening streaks; . 4 *Ev. Wk.* 119
In streaks diverging wide and mounting high; . 24 *Guilt* 20
And of the streaks that laced the severing clouds 123 *V. and J.* 93
Or crossed by vapoury streaks and clouds that move 459 **Wanderer! that* 35
Long streaks of fairy light the wave illume . . 598 *Ev. Wk. Quarto* 341
Stream. There, bending o'er the stream, the listless swain . . . . 3 *Ev. Wk.* 70
Bandusia's praise, wild stream, should yield to thine! . . . . 3 *Ev. Wk.* 73
Strong flakes of radiance on the tremulous stream: 4 *Ev. Wk.* 109
At intervals imperial banners stream, ... 6 *Ev. Wk.* 202
And see how dark the backward stream! . . . 9 *Lines: Boat* 5
O glide, fair stream! for ever so, ... 9 *Collins* 5
Or seek at eve the banks of Tusa's stream, . . 13 *Desc. Sk.* 156
Flings o'er the wilderness a stream of fire: . . 20 *Desc. Sk.* 554
Over the mighty stream now spreading wide: . . 22 *Desc. Sk.* 655
Left his mind still as a deep evening stream. . . 26 *Guilt* 96
And rain he wildered on, no moon to stream . . 26 *Guilt* 130
Thanks to them, are to us a stream of comfort: . 43 *Bord.* 325
The lamb had slipped into the stream, . . . 85 *Shepherd-boys* 67
To brood on air than on an earthly stream; . . 88 *H. C.* 8
Suspended in a stream as clear as sky, . . . 88 *H. C.* 9
And the mazy stream unravelled . . . . . 90 *Longest Day* 59
And unbridged stream, such as you may have noticed . . . . 99 *Brothers* 254
Sabrina,—vowing that the stream should bear . 103 *Artegal* 39
Bend with the breeze their heads, beside a crystal stream. . . . . 141 *Arm. Lady* 96
The Stream, so ardent in its course before, . . 146 **It was an* 22
O'er lake and stream, mountain and flowery mead, 151 **Forth from* 5
The stream that flows out of the lake, ... 162 *Binnorie* 56
The murmur of a neighbouring stream . . . 167 *Pilgrim's Dream* 17
The stream will not flow, and the hill will not rise, 188 *Poor Susan* 15
Now, coaches and chariots! roar on like a stream; 189 *Music* 41
The stream is flowing, ... 190 *March* 2
Cast up the Stream or down at her beseeching, . 190 **Lyre! though* 26
But now his voice to me was like a stream . . 197 *Resolution* 107
You see the stones, the fountain, and the stream; 202 *Hart-leap* 130
Beside her little humble stream; . . . . . 204 *Brougham* 45
That on the banks of this delightful stream . . 207 *Tintern* 150
To Tiviot's stream, to Annan, Tweed, and Clyde:— 219 **This Height* 10
That, for a brief space, checks the hurrying stream! 220 *Haunted Tree* 40
To mock the *wandering* Voice beside some haunted stream. . . . . 229 *Cuckoo-clock* 33
A stream as if from one full heart. . . . . . 233 *Power of Sound* 48
Over the silent stream. . . . . 240 *P. B.* 395
Upon the stream the moonbeams quiver. . . . 242 *P. B.* 535
So toward the stream his head he bent, . . . 242 *P. B.* 553
By an immeasurable stream . . . . 247 *P. B.* 979
Yet to my mind this scanty Stream is brought . 251 **There is a little* 6
A grace the sinuous vale and roaring stream . . 253 **Aerial Rock* 11
And leap at once from the delicious stream. . . 260 **How sweet* 14
Wafted adown the wind from lake or stream; . . 261 **I heard (alas* 4
Here, with no thirst but what the stream can slake, 262 *Retirement* 10
And, like mine eyes that stream with sorrow, blind!" . . . . 267 **As the* 14
A Stream, to mingle with your favourite Dee, . 272 *Lady E. B.* I
From that young Stream, that smites the throbbing rocks, ... 272 *Devil's Bridge* 7
Breathed forth beside the peaceful mountain Stream 275 *Rotha Q.* 9
After her throes, this Stream of name more dear . 275 *Rotha Q.* 11
To breathe in rural peace, to hear the stream, . 276 *Author's Portrait* 7
Let us beside the limpid Stream . . . . . 285 *Nith* 17
Child of loud-throated War! the mountain Stream 290 *Kilchurn* I
"Be Yarrow stream unseen, unknown! . . . 293 *Yarrow Unv.* 49
Or fish in stream, or bird in bower, ... 295 *Highland Boy* 19
A Champion worthy of the stream, ... 300 *Cora Linn* 23
Of rock that frowns, and stream that roars, . . 300 *Bran* 38
And is this—Yarrow?—*This* the Stream . . . 301 *Yarrow V.* I
That this most famous Stream in bogs and sands 307 **It is not* 7
The unconquerable Stream his course pursue. . 322 *Germans* 14
City, and naval stream, suburban grove, . . . 323 *Ode 1814* 9
From many a hallowed stream and grove, . . . 325 *Ode 1814* 114
That stream in blithe succession from the throats 329 *Ode: Thanks.* 40
Sully the limpid stream of thankfulness. . . . 331 *Ode: Thanks.* 132
Is this the stream, whose cities, heights, and plains, 335 *Namur* 2
Doth DANUBE spring to life! The wandering Stream . . . . 336 *Danube* 2
Still, with those white-robed Shapes—a living Stream, ... 347 *Processions* 48
The form and motion of a stream to take.; . . 351 *Des. Stanzas* 62
Struggling against the stream of destiny, . . . 355 *Aquap.* 190
Never perhaps to reappear. The Stream . . . 357 *Aquap.* 321
Near Anio's stream I spied a gentle Dove . . . 360 **Near Anio's* I
Which yet it bears, sweet Stream! as crystal pure. 361 **When here* 8
For late, as near a murmuring stream . . . 373 *Eg. Maid* 301
I seek the birthplace of a native Stream.— . . 376 *Duddon* I. 9
Fed by the stream with soft perpetual showers, . 377 *Duddon* 6. 7
On, loitering Muse—the swift Stream chides us—on! 379 *Duddon* 12. I
O mountain Stream! the Shepherd and his Cot . 379 *Duddon* 14. I

Stream—*continued.*
Checking the stream, make a pool smooth and clear 382 *Duddon* 23. 4
And may thy Poet, cloud-born Stream! be free— 384 *Duddon* 33. 9
Still glides the Stream, and shall for ever glide; 384 *Duddon* 34. 5
For busy thoughts the Stream flowed on 385 *Yarrow Rev.* 17
Flow on for ever, Yarrow Stream! 386 *Yarrow Rev.* 105
For us the stream of fiction ceased to flow, 395 *White Doe: Ded.* 25
Like the crystal stream now flowing 397 *White Doe* 150
Dark moor, and gleam of pool and stream, 409 *White Doe* 1171
I, who essayed the nobler Stream to trace 418 *Ecc. Sonn.* 1. 1. 5
And with dread signs the nascent Stream invest? 418 *Ecc. Sonn.* 1. 2. 8
Only perchance some melancholy Stream 421 *Ecc. Sonn.* 1. 12. 12
Where Tiber's stream the immortal City laves: 421 *Ecc. Sonn.* 1. 13. 4
As with the Stream our voyage we pursue, 428 *Ecc. Sonn.* 1. 37. 1
Pours on the surface of the turbid Stream! 430 *Ecc. Sonn.* 2. 7. 3
Down a swift Stream, thus far, a bold design 443 *Ecc. Sonn.* 3. 12. 1
Henceforth, as on the bosom of a stream 443 *Ecc. Sonn.* 3. 12. 10
The purest stream of patient Energy. 444 *Ecc. Sonn.* 3. 15. 14
His drowsy rings. Look forth!—that Stream behold, 452 *Ecc. Sonn.* 3. 47. 5
THAT STREAM upon whose bosom we have passed 452 *Ecc. Sonn.* 3. 47. 6
A stream is heard—I see it not, but know 453 **Calm is the* 25
Where wood or stream by thee was never greeted. 455 *Rydal Mere* 16
Were wont to stream before mine eye, 458 **Had this* 62
Among the mountains were we nursed, loved Stream! 464 *Derwent* 1
Measuring thy course, fair Stream! at length I pay 476 *Eden* 9
Flung from her to the stream. 479 *Somnamb.* 108
And the Stream whirled her down the dell 479 *Somnamb.* 134
Wild stream of Aira, hold thy course, 479 *Somnamb.* 154
Rich prospect left behind of stream and vale, 524 *Epist. Beaumont* 223
From murmur of a running stream; 533 **Blest is* 56
And Thou, wild Stream, that giv'st the honoured name 539 **Lady! a* 23
See studied kindness flow with easy stream, 539 **Lady! a* 63
She heard the ancestral stream; 544 *Russ. Fug.* 254
Meanwhile the stream, whose bank I sate upon, 558 *Cuck. and Night.* 81
And live as long as its pure stream shall flow. 574 *Chiabrera* 5. 23
Less for the love of stream and rock, 577 **By playful* 15
I saw the Stream of Yarrow glide 586 *Hogg* 2
There was a time when meadow, grove, and stream, 587 *Immortality* 1
Small cottage lights across the water stream, 598 *Ev. Wk. Quarto* 374
Or charms that smile on Tusa's evening stream, 605 *Desc.Sk.Quarto* 178
There hang in fear, when growls the frozen stream, 607 *Desc.Sk.Quarto* 315
—Red stream the cottage lights; the landscape fades, 614 *Desc.Sk.Quarto* 688
When hurrying forward till the slack'ning stream 626 **The confidence* 10
Waves o'er the gloomy stream; 626 †*Cento* 12
Shall I take up my home? and what clear stream 632 *Prelude* 1. 12
In a small mill-race severed from his stream, 636 *Prelude* 1. 289
Her clear though shallow stream of piety 661 *Prelude* 4. 225
Preyed on my strength, and stopped the quiet stream 663 *Prelude* 4. 296
And bore the semblance of another stream 664 *Prelude* 4. 382
Down by thy side, O Derwent! murmuring stream, 673 *Prelude* 5. 484
Low-standing by the margin of the stream, 678 *Prelude* 6. 206
See trees, and meadows, and thy native stream, 679 *Prelude* 6. 272
We glided forward with the flowing stream. 680 *Prelude* 6. 377
Crossing the unbridged stream, that road we took, 683 *Prelude* 6. 574
Which in the stony channel of the stream 683 *Prelude* 6. 582
Was downwards, with the current of that stream. 684 *Prelude* 6. 585
And giddy prospect of the raving stream, 684 *Prelude* 6. 633
The rapid stream whose margin we had trod; 684 *Prelude* 6. 644
Led by the stream, ere noon-day magnified 685 *Prelude* 6. 650
I saw, or heard, or felt, was but a stream 686 *Prelude* 6. 743
That flowed into a kindred stream; a gale, 686 *Prelude* 6. 744
(So willed the Muse) a less impetuous stream, 687 *Prelude* 7. 9
Thou endless stream of men and moving things! 689 *Prelude* 7. 151
Devoted, on the inviolable stream 701 *Prelude* 8. 179
In a pure stream of words fresh from the heart: 706 *Prelude* 8. 467
In the green dales beside our Rotha's stream, 715 *Prelude* 9. 392
In loose procession through the shallow stream 726 *Prelude* 10. 566
In one continuous stream; a mind sustained 747 *Prelude* 14. 74
Of our long labour: we have traced the stream 749 *Prelude* 14. 194
He cleared a passage for me, and the stream 751 *Prelude* 14. 368
Had newly scooped a running stream. He rose, 762 *Excursion* 1. 446
And the mute fish that glances in the stream, 772 *Excursion* 2. 42
Faintly reflected in a lingering stream. 782 *Excursion* 2. 681
Of stream and headlong flood that seldom fails; 782 *Excursion* 2. 705
When copious rains have magnified the stream 787 *Excursion* 3. 47
—Voiceless the stream descends into the gulf 787 *Excursion* 3. 92
Raised for enabling this penurious stream 789 *Excursion* 3. 204
Even so deduce the stream of human life 790 *Excursion* 3. 256
And majesty with this gigantic stream, 799 *Excursion* 3. 883
Of Mississippi, or that northern stream 799 *Excursion* 3. 931
Betray to sight the motion of the stream, 800 *Excursion* 3. 976
Must he again encounter.—Such a stream 800 *Excursion* 3. 986
By flowing stream, through wood, or craggy wild, 803 *Excursion* 4. 105
A stream, which, from the fountain of the heart 804 *Excursion* 4. 219
Upon the flowing stream, a thought arose 812 *Excursion* 4. 754
Like one whose untired ear a murmuring stream 814 *Excursion* 4. 892
To drink with gratitude the crystal stream 817 *Excursion* 4. 1044
Poured forth with fervour in continuous stream, 820 *Excursion* 4. 1276
A copious stream with boldly-winding course; 823 *Excursion* 5. 84
Even at the worst, a smooth stream of content, 833 *Excursion* 5. 712
As the mute swan that floats adown the stream, 842 *Excursion* 6. 293
The stream, that bears thee forward, prove not, soon 844 *Excursion* 6. 438
In the grey cottage by the murmuring stream 848 *Excursion* 6. 670
Was smitten, and poured forth a quenching stream, 852 *Excursion* 6. 920
Rose this pure eloquence. And, when the stream 857 *Excursion* 7. 25

Stream—*continued.*
Thus would he say, 'the Rhine, that famous stream! 869 *Excursion* 7. 788
Of a green hill or bank of rugged stream. 876 *Excursion* 8. 104
And in the courts—and where the rumbling stream, 877 *Excursion* 8. 177
Drink the pure water of its innocent stream 878 *Excursion* 8. 261
And hear the mighty stream of tendency 885 *Excursion* 9. 87
In their vast stream, and if an age hath been S.3. 435 **The doubt* 124
Down the deep channel of the stream he went, K.8. 228 **I will* 133
Right in the middle of the roaring stream. K.8. 229 **I will* 173
What, if I floated down a pleasant Stream K.8. 244 *Recluse* 1.1.292
Shall I reprove myself? Ah no, the stream K.8. 244 *Recluse* 1.1.294
And I shall float upon that stream again. K.8. 244 *Recluse* 1.1.296
To pastoral fancies? Is there such a stream, K.8. 248 *Recluse* 1.1.409
Or must we seek that stream where Man is not? K.8. 248 *Recluse* 1.1.412
Hath dealt with me as with a turbulent stream, K.8. 256 *Recluse* 1.1.728

Streamed. Till his eye streamed with tears. In this deep vale 23 *Yew-tree* 46
From lamp of lonely toll-gate streamed athwart the night. 27 *Guilt* 144
The parting signal streamed—at last the land withdrew. 29 *Guilt* 288
Streamed with the pomp of a too-credulous day. 304 **Jones! as* 3
(Streamed from the west) as with a robe of power: 333 **Bruges I* 2
The blood of Huguenots through Paris streamed. 439 *Ecc. Sonn.* 2. 42. 14
Or Cupid's sparkling arrow streamed 497 *Lycoris* 6
The eyes of all Savona streamed with tears. 575 *Chiabrera* 8. 9
Imperishable majesty streamed forth 893 *Excursion* 9. 630

Streamers. We want your streamers, friend, you know; 179 *Waggoner* 3. 76
Towers where red streamers flout the breezy sky. 503 *Warning* 39
With nets and sails outspread and streamers gay, 522 *Epist. Beaumont* 72
Play on her streamers, fails she to assume 882 *Excursion* 8. 514

Streaming. Streaming from founts above the starry sky, 229 *Cuckoo-clock* 39
And lo! with crimson banners proudly streaming, 324 *Ode 1814* 53
Entered, with streaming thousands, through the gate, 324 *Ode 1814* 73
Who sees, may lift a streaming eye 330 *Ode: Thanks.* 99
More glorious, with spread sail and streaming pendant. 369 *Eg. Maid* 12
And see love-emblems streaming from thy ship, 427 *Ecc. Sonn.* 1. 35. 7
Flung back from distant climes a streaming fire, 453 **The Sun, that* 2
Come streaming down the streaming panes. 577 **I come* 19
Upon the tall mast streaming. But, ye Powers 798 *Excursion* 3. 842
As ever raised to heaven a streaming eye! 853 *Excursion* 6. 991

Streamlet. How sweet its streamlet murmurs in mine ear!) 8 *Ev. Wk.* 350
And by the busy streamlet both 168 *Wren's Nest* 23
But one meek streamlet, only one: 288 *Glen-Al.* 4
And Thou, blue Streamlet, murmuring yield'st no more 378 *Duddon* 8. 10
"No check, no stay, this Streamlet fears; 487 *Fountain* 21
There, on the margin of a streamlet wild, 547 **Beneath yon* 9
That streamlet whose blue current works its way 678 *Prelude* 6. 192
Or let us trace this streamlet to its source; 786 *Excursion* 3. 30

Streamlet's. A heap of stones, which by the streamlet's edge 136 *Michael* 327
The mists, that o'er the streamlet's bed 180 *Waggoner* 4. 57
And down the vale along the streamlet's edge 890 *Excursion* 9. 434

Stream-like. The stream-like windings of that glorious street— 270 **Ye sacred* 13

Stream's. Right to a rough stream's edge, and there broke off; 683 *Prelude* 6. 569
On the stream's bank, and everywhere, appeared 823 *Excursion* 5. 87

Streams. *See* **Mountain-streams.**
Along the mystic streams of Life and Death. 12 *Desc. Sk.* 72
—Alas! the very murmur of the streams 13 *Desc. Sk.* 135
While pastoral pipes and streams the landscape lull, 14 *Desc. Sk.* 220
Those lofty cliffs a hundred streams unfold, 15 *Desc. Sk.* 279
Innumerable streams with roar profound. 18 *Desc. Sk.* 416
Five streams of ice amid her cots descend, 20 *Desc. Sk.* 571
Each clacking mill, that broke the murmuring streams, 22 *Desc. Sk.* 630
Into deep chasms troubled by roaring streams; 70 *Bord.* 1805
And from the headlong streams. 112 **What heavenly* 8
The streams with softest sound are flowing, 129 *Idiot Boy* 284
That the green valleys, and the streams and rocks, 132 *Michael* 63
And make dear friendships with the streams and groves. 147 *Joanna* 8
And streams that murmur as they run, 192 *Ruth* 35
Our streams proclaim a welcoming; 204 *Brougham* 33
Of the deep rivers, and the lonely streams, 206 *Tintern* 69
In happier beauty; more pellucid streams, 211 *Laod.* 104
Where'er the streams a passage find; 228 *Devot. Incit.* 4
The headlong streams and fountains 232 *Power of Sound* 17
And streams, and bowers, and ladies fair, 237 *P. B.* 104
"He roved among the vales and streams, 239 *P. B.* 241
And pours forth streams more sweet then Castaly. 251 **Pelion and* 14
That o'er the pavement of the surging streams 268 **Dogmatic Teachers* 11
Of lawless will, unlooked-for streams of good, 271 *Henry: Portrait* 13
Be turned; and streams of truth dried up, even at their source! 280 *Plea for Auth.* 14
Streams on the walls, and torrent-foam 300 *Bran* 17
On rampart, and the banks of all her streams. 318 **Ah! where* 14
Free were the streams and green the bowers; 348 **Lulled by* 8
Of midnight,—cities, plains, forests, and mighty streams. 350 *Des. Stanzas* 18
With ambient streams more pure and bright 375 **The Minstrels* 50
To humbler streams, and greener bowers. 376 **The Minstrels* 66

Strength—*continued.*
A feeling of their strength. The naked trees, . 622 *Recluse* 1. 1. 165
" O son, my strength, my power! who dost despise 624 *Æneid* 11
A Nation's strength that will not perish . . . 629 *Installation* 96
Once more made trial of her strength, nor lacked 633 *Prelude* 1. 95
Conquered and conqueror. Thus the pride of strength, ... 643 *Prelude* 2. 69
Of vigorous hunger—hence corporeal strength . 643 *Prelude* 2. 80
As natural beings in the strength of Nature. . . 652 *Prelude* 3. 193
Strength came where weakness was not known to be, 660 *Prelude* 4. 155
His being armed with strength that cannot fail. . 661 *Prelude* 4. 171
Preyed on my strength, and stopped the quiet stream . . . . 663 *Prelude* 4. 296
What love of nature, what original strength . 675 *Prelude* 6. 38
With us thy pleasure; thy returning strength, . 678 *Prelude* 6. 248
And all the strength and plumage of thy youth, . 679 *Prelude* 6. 296
On every side, in prime of youthful strength, . 680 *Prelude* 6. 365
" I recognise thy glory:" in such strength . . 684 *Prelude* 6. 599
That flowed awhile with unabating strength, . 687 *Prelude* 7. 10
To try her strength among harmonious words; . 704 *Prelude* 8. 369
Such is the strength and glory of our youth! . 708 *Prelude* 8. 607
Trying their strength, enforced him to start up, . 718 *Prelude* 9. 577
Britain put forth her freeborn strength in league, 722 *Prelude* 10. 264
If new strength be not given nor old restored, . 725 *Prelude* 10. 469
All powers of swiftness, subtilty, and strength . 729 *Prelude* 11. 127
Matured, and in the summer of their strength. . 733 *Prelude* 11. 417
From all the sources of her former strength; . . 735 *Prelude* 12. 80
When thou wert in thy strength! Nor this through stroke . . . . 736 *Prelude* 12. 106
Such strength in *me* as often held my mind . . 736 *Prelude* 12. 130
Of feeling, and diversity of strength . . . . 738 *Prelude* 12. 270
Are sister horns that constitute her strength. . 740 *Prelude* 13. 4
And intellectual strength so rare a boon— . . 742 *Prelude* 13. 178
That whoso feels such passion in its strength . 742 *Prelude* 13. 192
When they are grasping with their greatest strength, 744 *Prelude* 13. 274
Shaken by arms of mighty bone, in strength, . . 744 *Prelude* 13. 325
In strength, reflecting from its placid breast . 749 *Prelude* 14. 201
Of moral strength, and intellectual Power; . . 755 *Recluse* 1. 1. 770
All strength—all terror, single or in bands, . . 755 *Recluse* 1. 1. 784
He lingered long; and, when his strength returned, 764 *Excursion* 1. 553
For moral dignity, and strength of mind, . . . 775 *Excursion* 2. 287
Upon his spirit, with a fever's strength, . . . 798 *Excursion* 3. 849
(Submission constituting strength and power) . 802 *Excursion* 4. 98
As soldiers live by courage; as, by strength . . 804 *Excursion* 4. 203
Without access of unexpected strength. . . . 804 *Excursion* 4. 221
Of the contiguous torrent, gathering strength . 813 *Excursion* 4. 793
At every moment—and, with strength, increase . 813 *Excursion* 4. 794
Shall fix, in calmer seats of moral strength, . . 820 *Excursion* 4. 1272
His royal state to show, and prove his strength . 825 *Excursion* 5. 183
Fresh in the strength and majesty of age, . . . 829 *Excursion* 5. 457
Cast down while confident in strength they stand, 837 *Excursion* 5. 963
Will cover him, in the fulness of his strength, . 841 *Excursion* 6. 197
Man has his strength," exclaimed the Wanderer, " oh! . . . . 842 *Excursion* 6. 255
In strength, in power refitted, he renewed . . 843 *Excursion* 6. 332
For, strength to persevere and to support, . . 848 *Excursion* 6. 663
" A sudden illness seized her in the strength . 849 *Excursion* 6. 741
While she was yet in prime of health and strength, 849 *Excursion* 6. 758
The trunk and body of its marvellous strength, . 866 *Excursion* 7. 610
Though strength decay, to breathe in such estate 885 *Excursion* 9. 46
And strength in evil? Hence an after-call . 886 *Excursion* 9. 122
Possessed of health, and strength, and peace of mind; . . . . 887 *Excursion* 9. 204
Beauty, or strength! Such privilege is theirs, . 888 *Excursion* 9. 270
(Such strength of vision to the shepherd's eye . K.8. 225 **I will* 43
Surpassed in strength, I heard of danger, met . K.8. 256 *Recluse* 1.1.716
His strength, and had his triumph and his joy, . K.8. 256 *Recluse* 1.1.731
A calmness that betokens strength to bear . . [?] **A sad* 6

Strengthen. And God will strengthen thee: amid all fear . . . . 137 *Michael* 408
May learn, if judgment strengthen with his growth, 275 **Chatsworth! thy* 11
And strengthen love, rejoicing secretly . . . 804 *Excursion* 4. 237

Strengthened. Came strengthened with a superadded soul, ... 647 *Prelude* 2. 328
Strengthened and braced, by breathing in content 760 *Excursion* 1. 305
When, strengthened, yet not dazzled, by the might 877 *Excursion* 8. 210

Strengtheners. Be these the daily strengtheners of their minds; . . . . 672 *Prelude* 5. 422

Strengthening. *See* **Ever-strengthening, Soul-strengthening.**
Haunts of a strengthening amity . . . . . 415 *White Doe* 1712
Their arms still strengthening with the strengthening heart, ... 541 *Grace Darl.* 61
To strengthening love for things that we have seen; 673 *Prelude* 5. 541
The illusion strengthening as he gazed, he felt . K.8. 237 *Recluse* 1.1. 36

Strengthens. The faith Heaven strengthens where *he* moulds the Creed. . . . . . . 112 **O dearer* 16

Strenuous. That strenuous action follow both, . . 224 **'Tis gone* 52
Yet *strenuous* was the infant Age: . . . . . 234 *Power of Sound* 121
The strenuous Animal hath clomb . . . . . 244 *P. B.* 696
Still to be strenuous for the bright reward, . 260 **High is* 11
And, strenuous to protect from lawless harms . 276 **Chatsworth! thy* 13
That scraped the chords with strenuous hand! . 375 **The Minstrels* 12
Of strenuous idleness; . . . . 499 **This Lawn* 6
Spent in a round of strenuous idleness— . . . 664 *Prelude* 4. 378
Grave doctors strenuous for the mother-church, . 825 *Excursion* 5. 176
Of strenuous champions, in scholastic arts . . 839 *Excursion* 6. 57
Wanting all relish for her strenuous mind, . . 848 *Excursion* 6. 693

Stress. Even as a dragon's eye that feels the stress 266 **Even as* 1
Sore stress of apprehension, with a mind . . . 449 *Ecc. Sonn.* 3. 37. 6
Or, from long stress of real injuries fly . . . . 505 *Warning* 117

Stress—*continued.*
The wealthy, the luxurious, by the stress . . . 773 *Excursion* 2. 97

Stretch. Attend, at every stretch, his headlong fall. 6 *Ev. Wk.* 199
Stretch o'er the pictured mirror broad and blue, . 12 *Desc. Sk.* 94
The rocks rise naked as a wall, or stretch . . . 14 *Desc. Sk.* 230
Where, if a famishing man stretch forth his hand, 47 *Bord.* 560
To stretch her arms, and dim the gladsome light . 56 *Bord.* 1046
Might stretch beyond the measure of one moon. . 68 *Bord.* 1711
" If the sun be shining hot, do but stretch thy woollen chain, ... 87 *Pet-lamb* 29
To see thy arch thus stretch and bend, . . . 111 **'Tis said that some* 42
Full often make you stretch and strain, . . . 175 *Waggoner* 1. 142
But the horses stretch and pull; . . . . . 180 *Waggoner* 4. 84
That stretch a thousand thousand sails) . . . 217 *Enterprise* 155
More urgent called, will stretch his wings at large, 273 **While Anna's* 7
Entanglings of the brain; though shadows stretch 280 **Oh what* 3
Here stretch thy body at full length; . . . . 485 *Poet's Epitaph* 59
Stretch, o'er their pictur'd mirror, broad and blue, 604 *Desc.Sk.Quarto* 103
Behind me did they stretch in solemn train, . . 639 *Prelude* 1. 461
Spirits upon the stretch, and here and there . . 663 *Prelude* 4. 316
Upon the stretch, when winds are blowing fair: . 682 *Prelude* 6. 499
With those that stretch the neck and strain the eyes, ... 697 *Prelude* 7. 696
Stretch from the western marge of Thurston-mere, 706 *Prelude* 8. 459
Of amity, whose living threads should stretch . 797 *Excursion* 3. 747
To stretch his limbs, bemocking, as might seem, . 826 *Excursion* 5. 267

Stretched. *See* **Far-stretched, Outstretched, Stretcht.**
A fence far stretched into the shallow lake, . . 3 *Ev. Wk.* 42
When school-boys stretched their length upon the green; . . . . 3 *Ev. Wk.* 45
Stretched at his feet, with steadfast upward eye, 13 *Desc. Sk.* 151
Far stretched beneath the many-tinted hills, . . 17 *Desc. Sk.* 407
Save cornfields stretched and stretching without bound; . . . . 24 *Guilt* 26
Stretched on the ground, began a piteous tale; . 33 *Guilt* 471
His burning eyelids stretched and stiff as lead; . 36 *Guilt* 636
Life stretched before me smooth as some broad way 70 *Bord.* 1836
an old Man lying stretched upon the ground— . 72 *Bord.* 1924
Lay stretched at ease; but, passing by the place 101 *Brothers* 371
And then he stretched his arms, how wild! . . 114 *Ind. Wom.* 39
Sate with a fettered sheep before him stretched . 133 *Michael* 164
They stretched in never-ending line . . . . 187 **I wandered* 9
Advancing, forth she stretched her hand . . . 191 *Beggars* 13
The dogs are stretched among the mountain fern. 201 *Hart-leap* 24
Upon his side the Hart was lying stretched: . . 201 *Hart-leap* 41
With breathless nostrils stretched above the spring. 202 *Hart-leap* 78
Main ocean, breaking audibly, and stretched . 219 **This Height* 14
With legs stretched out and stiff he lay:— . . 241 *P. B.* 451
And stretched beneath the furze he sees . . . 246 *P. B.* 926
Stretched on the block the glittering axe recoils; 252 **Why, Minstrel* 10
No vapour stretched its wings; no cloud . . . 343 *Eclipse* 19
Earth stretched below, heaven in our neighbourhood. . . . . 351 *Des. Stanzas* 86
Stretched far as earth might own a single lord; . 368 *Trajan* 30
Among the thick weeds, stretched alone; . . . 397 *White Doe* 127
Stretched, herdsman-like, as if to bask . . . 404 *White Doe* 772
Stretched in the sunny light of victory bask . 421 *Ecc. Sonn.* 1. 10. 8
Devoutly stretched upon their chancel floors. . 430 *Ecc. Sonn.* 2. 8. 8
With hands stretched forth in mollified disdain, . 435 *Ecc. Sonn.* 2. 28. 5
An Eagle with stretched wings, but beamless eye— 472 **The captive* 7
A plain below stretched seaward, while, descried . 475 **There! said* 5
Stretched on the dying Mother's lap, lies dead . 476 *Howard* 1
Stretched forth with trembling hope?—In every realm, ... 509 *F. Stone* 91
Stretched out for my acceptance,—but Death came. . . . . 574 *Chiabrera* 3. 16
Now stretched beneath his grass-green mound . 577 **I come* 20
Stretch'd on the scented mountain's purple side. . 611 *Desc.Sk.Quarto* 513
Stretched forth his little arms and smil'd. . . . 620 *Birth of Love* 27
I saw before me stretched a boundless plain . . 666 *Prelude* 5. 71
Stretched forth the shell, so beautiful in shape, . 667 *Prelude* 5. 90
Stretched under wayside hedge-rows, ballad tunes, 668 *Prelude* 5. 210
Of Chamouny stretched far below, and soon . . 683 *Prelude* 6. 529
At last we stretched our weary limbs for sleep, . 685 *Prelude* 6. 710
Stretched and still stretching far and wide, exalt 698 *Prelude* 7. 746
Ascending, overlooked them both, far stretched; 738 *Prelude* 12. 294
Far, far beyond, the solid vapours stretched, . . 746 *Prelude* 14. 45
As if on wings, and saw beneath me stretched . 751 *Prelude* 14. 380
—In that fair clime, the lonely herdsman, stretched 814 *Excursion* 4. 851
Stretched upon fragrant heath, and lulled by sound 821 *Excursion* 4. 1321
Attain a point that showed the valley—stretched 823 *Excursion* 5. 78
Stretched overhead, and at my pensive feet . . 827 *Excursion* 5. 344
Insidiously stretched out its lazy length, . . . 860 *Excursion* 7. 175
Stretched on his bier—that massy timber wain; . 865 *Excursion* 7. 548
Stretched on the grass, or seated in the shade, . 869 *Excursion* 7. 783
Of darkness, stretched o'er guilty Europe, makes . 890 *Excursion* 9. 410
The outcry of his son: he stretched his staff . . K.8. 230 **I will* 175

Stretches. Crouches, stretches, paws, and darts! . 170 *Kitten* 18
As stretches a blue bar of solid cloud . . . . 311 **Who rises* 28
That landward stretches from the sea, ... 327 *Ode 1815* 13
From the brink her paws she stretches, . . . 490 *Incident: Dog* 33
Through bare enclosures stretches, 'till its line . 858 *Excursion* 7. 44
Oft stretches toward me, like a long straight path 863 *Excursion* 7. 398

Stretching. *See* **Far-stretching.**
Dark with bat-haunted ashes stretching broad, . 7 *Ev. Wk.* 263
Save cornfields stretched and stretching without bound; . . . . 24 *Guilt* 26
But standing, walking, stretching forth his arms, . 68 *Bord.* 1729
Like a vast river, stretching in the sun. . . . 658 *Prelude* 4. 6
That, stretching far among the Alps, assumed . 685 *Prelude* 6. 690

Stretching—*continued.*
Above, behind, far stretching and before; . . . 690 *Prelude* 7. 247
Stretched and still stretching far and wide, exalt 698 *Prelude* 7. 746
His shadow stretching towards Syracuse, . . . 732 *Prelude* 11. 378
A broad oak, stretching forth its leafy arms . . 825 *Excursion* 5. 227
That, stretching boldly from the mountain side, . 855 *Excursion* 6. 1117

Stretcht. *See* **Stretched.**
Then, stretcht at ease in some sequestered cave, . 630 [?]**O Moon* 7

Strew. And gives, where woods the chequered upland strew, ... 8 *Ev. Wk.* 337
And without wrong are cropped the marble tomb to strew. . . . . 222 *Triad* 211
Some bird (like our own honoured redbreast) may strew . . . . 340 *Fort Fuentes* 11
A most untimely grave to strew, ... 348 **Lulled by* 46
While your leaves I behold and the brooks they will strew, ... 364 *Vallomb.* 31
Fresh water rushes strew the verdant floor; . . 596 *Ev. Wk. Quarto* 228
And gives, where woods the chequer'd upland strew, ... 599 *Ev. Wk. Quarto* 405
Quits, growling, the white bones that strew his lair; 606 *Desc. Sk. Quarto* 232

Strewed. Flowers strewed the ground; the nuptial feast . . . . 545 *Russ. Fug.* 369

Strew'st. Thou strew'st temptation o'er the path . 216 *Enterprise* 108

Strewing. With chips is the carpenter strewing his floor? . . . . 572 *Avarice* 17
With the green bottom strewing o'er the wave; . 596 *Ev. Wk. Quarto* 236
Strewing the turf's green slope. A diamond light 705 *Prelude* 8. 406
Strewing in peace life's humblest ground with herbs, 750 *Prelude* 14. 300

Strewn. *See* **Strown.**
And cracked the branches, and strewn them about; 80 †*Address: Child* 23
And left as if by earthquake strewn, ... 214 *Kirkstone* 11
Which, strewn with snow smooth as the sky can shed, ... 263 **How clear* 3
On ground yet strewn with their last battle's wreck; . . . . 278 *Wellington* 2
Strewn with grey rocks, and on the horizon's verge, 352 *Aquap.* 17
Brighter than eastern skies at daybreak strewn . 434 *Ecc. Sonn.* 2. 25. 6
Strewn far and wide. Think, proud Philosopher! 474 **How sad* 8
Strewn on the frozen snow. And when the spring 702 *Prelude* 8. 229
Of heath-plant, under and above him strewn, . 784 *Excursion* 2. 819
A dismal prospect yields the wild shore strewn . 836 *Excursion* 5. 930
Had marked the line, and strewn its surface o'er. 881 *Excursion* 8. 451

Strews. Strews twenty acres of good meadow-ground 60 *Bord.* 1230

Stricken. *See* **Awe-stricken, Confusion-stricken, Conscience-stricken, Fancy-stricken, Frenzy-stricken, Heart-stricken, Planet-stricken, Shame-stricken, Sorrow-stricken, Tempest-stricken.**
Been stricken by a twofold stroke; . . . . 294 *Jedbor.* 73
Poet! that, stricken as both are by years, . . 464 **Thou look'st* 2
Stricken by this ill assurance, ... 535 *Egremont* 51
Behold," she said, "a stricken Hind . . . . 544 *Russ. Fug.* 279
Both stricken, as she entered or withdrew, . . 691 *Prelude* 7. 306
Unrecognised; but, stricken by the sight, . . 757 *Excursion* 1. 45
This happy Land was stricken to the heart! . . 764 *Excursion* 1. 540
We should recoil, stricken with sorrow and shame, 826 *Excursion* 5. 254
Is stricken in the moment when her throes . . 867 *Excursion* 7. 643

Strict. Duty, like a strict preceptor, ... 90 *Longest Day* 65
Loth to rule by strict command; . . . . . 93 *Westmoreland Girl* 34
Long, strict, and tender was the embrace he gave, 104 *Artegal* 122
Strict passage, through which sighs are brought, . 232 *Power of Sound* 7
Of strict obedience, serve the Almighty Lord; . 500 *Humanity* 38
Are strict observers; and not negligent . . 568 *Cumb. Beg.* 138
To the strict labours of the merchant's desk . . 584 *Ch. Lamb* 5
From strict analogies by thought supplied . . 651 *Prelude* 3. 125
As is their wont, a pittance from strict time, . . 702 *Prelude* 8. 239
After strict question, left within my mind . . 726 *Prelude* 10. 574
And function, or, through strict vicissitude . . 740 *Prelude* 13. 38
For by superior energies; more strict . . . 805 *Excursion* 4. 305
And a strict love of fellowship, combined. . . 807 *Excursion* 4. 444
By strict necessity, along the path . . . . 820 *Excursion* 4. 1269

Stricter. *More promptly rises, walks with stricter heed,* 429 *Ecc. Sonn.* 2. 3. 2

Strictest. In ceaseless pains—and strictest parsimony . . . . 849 *Excursion* 6. 724

Strictliest. The will to reason's law, can strictliest live . . . . 830 *Excursion* 5. 518

Strictly. But thee I now would serve more strictly, if I may. . . . . 492 *Duty* 32
Subservient strictly to external things . . . . 647 *Prelude* 2. 367
Her mind she strictly tutored to find peace . . 854 *Excursion* 6. 1026
Mirrored, yet not too strictly, may refine . . S.3. 435 **The doubt* 118

Strictness. With strictness scarcely known on English ground. . . . . 758 *Excursion* 1. 117

Strictures. In grisly folds and strictures serpentine; 424 *Ecc. Sonn.* 1. 21. 12

Strid. The striding-place is called The Strid, . . 494 *Force of Prayer* 21
Shall bound across The Strid? . . . . . . 494 *Force of Prayer* 28

Stride. The imperial Stature, the colossal stride, . 270 *Henry: Portrait* 1
Through the rough copse wheel thou with hasty stride; . . . . 383 *Duddon* 30. 11
I had been travelling: this a stride at once . . 722 *Prelude* 10. 275
With shield and stone-axe, stride across the wold; 744 *Prelude* 13. 323

Strides. Science advances with gigantic strides; . 281 **What strong* 7

Striding. Striding with shattered crests his eye athwart. . . . . 443 *Ecc. Sonn.* 3. 12. 8
Striding, with shattered crests, the eye athwart? 625 **The confidence* 8
Striding along as if o'ertasked by Time, . . . 649 *Prelude* 3. 9
With prospect underneath of Striding edge, . . K.8. 225 **I will* 29

Striding-place. The striding-place is called The Strid, ... 494 *Force of Prayer* 21

Strife. *See* **Party-strife.**
Powers that support an unremitting strife . . 19 *Desc. Sk.* 510
No strife disturbs his sister's breast; . . . . 81 †*Mother's Return* 17
But, at the touch of wrong, without a strife . . 88 *H. C.* 32
Twins had they been in pleasure; after strife . 122 *V. and J.* 21
Who, loving most, should wiseliest love, their only strife. . . . . 142 *Arm. Lady* 150
Rock the cradle of joy, smooth the death-bed of strife. . . . . 143 †*Lov. and Lik.* 54
Why should we dwell in strife? . . . . . 155 *Waterfall* 22
He thinks not of his long, long, strife;— . . 177 *Waggoner* 2. 82
Of thoughts with better thoughts at strife, . . 191 *Seq. Beggars* 19
Regard not her:—oh, better wrong and strife . 192 *Gipsies* 21
The two that were at strife are blended, . . . 204 *Brougham* 13
Slaves of folly, love, or strife— . . . . . 209 **Yes, it* 11
No fears to beat away—no strife to heal— . . 211 *Laod.* 99
And thoughts with things at strife; . . . . 223 *Wishing-gate* 9
Began the pencil's strife, ... 231 **The gentlest Poet* 25
Tempered into rapturous strife, ... 235 *Power of Sound* 221
No disproportion in her soul, no strife: . . . 256 *Marriage: Friend* 10
Great is the glory, for the strife is hard! . . 260 **High is* 14
Produced as lonely Nature or the strife . . . 269 **If these* 2
While thus illumined, tells of painful strife . . 278 **Lo! where she* 6
With rival earnestness; far other strife . . . 280 **Intent on* 5
Not like an outcast with himself at strife; . . 284 *Departure* 21
A bondage sweetly brooked, a strife . . . . 288 *Highland Girl* 42
And quieted in character—the strife, ... 290 *Kilchurn* 41
With them no strife can last; they live . . . 291 *Rob Roy* 35
The strife of happiness and pain, ... 294 *Jedbor.* 52
What strife of colour, shape and sound . . . 300 *Bran* 24
For ever with yourselves at strife; . . . . . 301 *Bran* 106
Were with herself at strife, would take your stand, 310 *Invasion* 2
We know the arduous strife, the eternal laws . . 316 **O'er the* 10
There are who cannot languish in this strife, . . 320 **O'erweening Statesmen* 9
With that great Leader vies, who, sick of strife . 320 **They seek* 12
"Finish the strife by deadliest victory!" . . 322 **By Moscow* 14
Abruptly paused the strife;—the field throughout 322 *Germans* 1
Expressive signals of a glorious strife, ... 324 *Ode 1814* 105
Not only from the dreary strife . . . . . . 338 **Meek Virgin* 21
Things in their very essences at strife, ... 364 **What aim* 11
In silence watched the gentle strife . . . . 374 *Eg. Maid* 339
And sunshine to a dangerous strife; . . . . 400 *White Doe* 377
Of strife and factions desperate; . . . . . 403 *White Doe* 640
And, under cover of this woeful strife, ... 432 *Ecc. Sonn.* 2. 16. 13
Of truths that soften hatred, temper strife. . . 443 *Ecc. Sonn.* 3. 11. 14
By sound, or ghost of sound, in mazy strife; . . 451 *Ecc. Sonn.* 3. 44. 12
Extracts from Nature's elemental strife; . . . 458 *Sea-shore* 22
That hung between two callings. May no strife . 470 **Did pangs* 11
And own that Art, triumphant over strife . . 476 *Howard* 13
Books! 'tis a dull and endless strife: . . . . 481 *Tables Turned* 9
A foolish strife; they see . . . . 487 *Fountain* 42
And calm'st the weary strife of frail humanity! . 492 *Duty* 8
Whose powers shed round him in the common strife, ... 493 *Hap. War.* 45
And jealousy, and quivering strife, ... 498 **The sylvan* 17
Yet, spite of all this eager strife, ... 499 **This Lawn* 13
Presignified by that dread strife . . . . . 503 **Like a* 75
That civic strife can turn the happiest hearth . 504 *Warning* 76
And being, to preclude or quell the strife . . 519 *Pun. Death* 9. 11
For—save the calm repentance sheds o'er strife . 526 **Soon did* 8
By noise and strife, and questions wearisome, . 528 **Those breathing* 94
And hope and fear mix not in further strife. . . 540 *Grace Darl.* 42
Elysian quiet, without toil or strife; . . . . 578 *Peele Castle* 26
Which checked discussion ere it warmed to strife; 583 **With copious* 14
To dialogues of business, love, or strife; . . . 589 *Immortality* 98
Thus blindly with thy blessedness at strife? . . 589 *Immortality* 129
Yet more; the tyrant Genius, still at strife . . 613 *Desc. Sk. Quarto* 608
If e'er these precepts quell'd the passions' strife, 619 *School Ex.* 103
When first, above the yells of bigot strife, . . 629 *Installation* 101
That the shield bore, so glorious was the strife; . 634 *Prelude* 1. 179
In strife too humble to be named in verse: . . 639 *Prelude* 1. 513
And all the strife of singularity, ... 695 *Prelude* 7. 580
Were agitated; and commotions, strife . . . 712 *Prelude* 9. 163
Uppermost in the midst of fiercest strife. . . . 715 *Prelude* 9. 389
That this particular strife had wanted power . . 722 *Prelude* 10. 254
Of the two spirits then at strife remained . . 727 *Prelude* 11. 25
Amid the turns and counterturns, the strife . . 736 *Prelude* 12. 148
Shy, and unpractised in the strife of phrase; . . 743 *Prelude* 13. 268
So charactered did I maintain a strife . . . 797 *Excursion* 3. 788
Of strife and folly, though it be a treat . . . 799 *Excursion* 3. 905
But for the impertinent and ceaseless strife . . 831 *Excursion* 5. 617
In strife, in tribulation; and ordained, . . . 837 *Excursion* 5. 1014
And while the uproar of that desperate strife . . 845 *Excursion* 6. 449
Daily, its bowling-green with harmless strife; . 845 *Excursion* 6. 466
The internal pangs, are ready; the dread strife . 846 *Excursion* 6. 555
For strife and ferment in the minds of men; . . 873 *Excursion* 7. 1010
Shall it endure?—Shall enmity and strife, . . 894 *Excursion* 9. 661
Flattery and double-dealing, strife and wrong. . K.8. 246 *Recluse* 1.1.357

Strifeful. And sick at heart of strifeful Christendom, 268 **Four fiery* 13

Strifes. Great God! by whom the strifes of men are weighed . . . . 22 *Desc. Sk.* 652
Our tumults appeased, and our strifes passed away! 340 *Fort Fuentes* 20
The limbs of the great world; its eager strifes . 657 *Prelude* 3. 581

Strike. Something I strike upon which turns my mind . . . . 51 *Bord.* 783
Betrayed, in darkness! Here to strike the blow— 54 *Bord.* 902
Seems like a note of joy to strike,— . . . . 241 *P. B.* 467
Strike pleasure dead, ... 284 *Grave of Burns* 4
These times strike monied worldlings with dismay: 308 **These times* 1

Strokes. Twelve strokes that clock would have been telling . . . . 176 *Waggoner* 2. 7
And where'er their strokes alighted, ... 535 *Egremont* 43
Of the church clock telling the hours with strokes 685 *Prelude* 6. 693

Stroll. We'll stroll into the wood ; lean on my arm. 43 *Bord.* 363
I will stroll on ; you follow when 'tis done. . . 60 *Bord.* 1259

Strolled. One morn we strolled on our dry walk, . 85 *Anecdote* 5
Played with our time ; and, as we strolled along, 148 **A narrow* 11
Of two delightful hours we strolled along . . . 674 *Prelude* 5. 562
And strolled into her garden. It appeared . . 767 *Excursion* 1. 720

Strollers. Or Strollers are they, furnished to enact 858 *Excursion* 7. 89

Strolling. May sometimes greet the strolling minstrel's harp, ... 467 *St. Bees* 96
Awed have I been by strolling Bedlamites ; . . 742 *Prelude* 13. 157

Strong. Strong flakes of radiance on the tremulous stream : . . . . 4 *Ev. Wk.* 109
Strong terror checks the female peasant's sighs, . 11 *Desc. Sk.* 65
" And oft I thought (my fancy was so strong) . 31 *Guilt* 361
I honour him. Strong feelings to his heart . . 38 *Bord.* 33
Strong to destroy, is also strong to heal— . . 38 *Bord.* 47
How wilt thou stand alone ? Is he not strong ? . 40 *Bord.* 160
More than we see, or whence this strong aversion ? 41 *Bord.* 254
What strong temptations press upon the Poor. . 46 *Bord.* 504
Else could so strong a mind have ever known . 55 *Bord.* 998
The feeble and the strong. She needs not here . 57 *Bord.* 1090
Strong to o'erturn, strong also to build up. . . 77 *Bord.* 2277
Her very heart, her grief grew strong ; . . . 82 *Alice Fell* 47
And carols loud and strong. . . . . 84 *Shepherd-boys* 26
Thy limbs, are they not strong ? And beautiful thou art : . . . . 87 *Pet-lamb* 26
On her pinions swift and strong ? . . . . . . 90 *Longest Day* 20
Strong as an Eagle with my charge I glided round and round . . . . 92 *Poet's Dream* 37
And his own mind did like a tempest strong . . 108 *Indolence* 35
Like branches when strong winds the trees annoy. 108 *Indolence* 49
That, nymph-like, she is fleet and strong, . . . 108 *Louisa* 4
And hopes are strong and will prevail. . . . . 110 *Forsaken* 11
For strong and without pain I lay, ... 114 *Ind. Wom.* 29
And what, through strong compunction for the past, ... 124 *V. and J.* 183
These fourteen years, by strong indentures : . . 129 *Idiot Boy* 338
An old man, stout of heart, and strong of limb. . 131 *Michael* 42
Strong hold on his affections, were to him . . 132 *Michael* 75
I still am strong and hale ;—do thou thy part ; . 137 *Michael* 390
With such a strong devotion, that your heart . 147 *Joanna* 5
Shine hot, or wind blows troublesome and strong ; 151 **When, to* 89
The Flood was tyrannous and strong ; . . . . 155 *Waterfall* 15
Wise, foolish, weak, or strong. . . . . . . 156 *Oak and Broom* 60
For thy song, Lark, is strong ; . . . . . . 159 **Up with me* 2
With a soul as strong as a mountain river . . 160 **Up with me* 23
That prompts such work, a Spirit strong, . . . 162 **Who fancied* 16
Though strong, is, in the main, a joyless tie . . 172 *Infant Daughter* 37
He was patient, they were strong, ... 174 *Waggoner* 1. 42
Is known, and by as strong a spell . . . . . 174 *Waggoner* 1. 84
Was growing inwardly more strong ; . . . . 175 *Waggoner* 1. 149
And now the same strong voice more near . . 176 *Waggoner* 1. 247
Or is it rather that Conceit rapacious is and strong, ... 189 *Star-gazers* 17
" Alas ! when evil men are strong . . . . . 204 *Brougham* 87
I said, when evil men are strong, ... 204 *Brougham* 104
Some ground not mine ; and, strong her strength above, ... 208 **It is no* 15
" And Thou, though strong in love, art all too weak 211 *Laod.* 139
Within the mind strong fancies work, ... 214 *Kirkstone* 1
His strong hand on the wind, if it were bent . . 221 *Triad* 74
Of warblers in full concert strong . . . . . 221 *Triad* 81
What spell so strong as guilty Fear ! . . . . 238 *P. B.* 147
You need a strong and stormy gale . . . . 240 *P. B.* 373
By strong compunction and remorse. . . . . 246 *P. B.* 885
When thankfulness of heart is strong and deep ! . 253 **Fond words* 4
Yes ! hope may with my strong desire keep pace, 256 **Yes ! hope* 1
Thence has it, with the Son, so strong a hold . 276 *Filial Piety* 8
What strong allurement draws, what spirit guides, 281 **What strong* 1
Speak, passing winds ; ye torrents, with your strong . . . . 283 *Railway* 13
Forgive me if the phrase be strong ;— . . . . 291 *Rob Roy* 14
Thus nothing here provokes the strong . . . 291 *Rob Roy* 43
For Polity was then too strong— . . . . . 291 *Rob Roy* 63
Broke from the Matron's strong black eye— . 294 *Jedbor.* 67
And rivers large and strong : . . . . . . 295 *Highland Boy* 60
Beneficent as strong ; . . . . 299 *Cora Linn* 9
Of Nations wanting virtue to be strong . . . 311 **Who rises* 43
A few strong instincts and a few plain rules, . 315 **Alas ! what* 11
Like the strong wind, or sleeping like the wind . 321 **The power* 9
That host, as huge and strong as e'er defied . . 321 **Humanity,delighting* 17
Of the round world, and built, by laws as strong, 329 *Ode : Thanks.* 48
Wandering, he haunts, at fancy's strong command, 361 **For action* 13
My heart, and filled that heart with conflict strong. 367 **As indignation* 14
God reigns above, and Spirits strong . . . . 370 *Eg. Maid* 81
Fate, fortune, sweep strong powers away, . . . 391 *HighlandBroach* 63
And superstitious fancies strong, ... 398 *White Doe* 215
Had blindly grasped in that strong trance, . . 401 *White Doe* 437
Which he had grasped in that strong trance ; . . 401 *White Doe* 517
Be strong ;—be worthy of the grace . . . . 402 *White Doe* 583
Eyes dark and strong ; and on his head . . . 404 *White Doe* 745
A strong Hold on the banks of Tees ; . . . . 405 *White Doe* 798
To vacancy, and horror strong : . . . . . 411 *White Doe* 1388
Exciting self-suspicion strong, ... 411 *White Doe* 1410
Whose self-reproaches are too strong ! " . . . 412 *White Doe* 1475
Was to the harp a strong command, ... 413 *White Doe* 1552

Strong—*continued.*
He, whose strong arm the Orient could not check, 428 *Ecc. Sonn.* 1. 38. 6
Perplex the wise, the strong to overthrow ; . . 428 *Ecc. Sonn.* 1. 39. 7
Of solitude, with love of science strong, . . . 429 *Ecc. Sonn.* 2. 5. 9
Scorning that world whose blindness makes her strong ? . . . . 433 *Ecc. Sonn.* 2. 19. 8
With equal wrath the steps of strong and weak) . 434 *Ecc. Sonn.* 2. 22. 4
Calm as an under-current, strong to draw . . . 442 *Ecc. Sonn.* 3. 9. 1
Sharing the strong emotion of the crowd, . . . 450 *Ecc. Sonn.* 3. 40. 2
Might here be moved, till Fancy grows so strong . 455 *Rydal Mere* 14
The strong were merciless, without hope the weak ; 466 *St. Bees* 39
Bold words affirmed, in days when faith was strong 468 **Bold words* 1
Round these, with tendrils strong as flesh and blood, ... 488 *Pers. Talk* 35
Or strong compunction in me wrought, . . . 492 *Duty* 34
And the most ancient heavens, through Thee, are fresh and strong. . . . . 492 *Duty* 48
That the river was strong, and the rocks were steep ?— . . . . 494 *Force of Prayer* 30
Is seized with strong incitement to push forth . 496 **A little* 29
And they like Demi-gods are strong . . . . 499 **Departing summer* 26
Be strong in faith, bid anxious thoughts lie still ; 505 *Warning* 160
Strong by her charters, free because imbound, . 514 **Blest Statesman* 12
And thy grieved Spirit brighten strong in faith. . 515 **Men of* 14
Strong as could then be borne. A Master meek . 518 *Pun. Death* 7. 5
Thus in the chosen spot a tie so strong . . . 531 **I know* 21
Driven by strong winds at play among the clouds. 540 **Lady ! a* 75
The Emperor sent a pledge as strong . . . . 545 *Russ. Fug.* 351
And he was strong to follow in the steps . . . 574 *Chiabrera* 5. 8
To public notice, with reluctance strong, . . . 582 **To public* 1
However proud and strong. . . . . 583 **O for a* 36
And I again am strong : . . . . 588 *Immortality* 24
And who but feels a power of strong controul, . . 608 *Desc.Sk.Quarto* 352
Strong poison not a form of steel can brave . . 613 *Desc.Sk.Quarto* 630
Clapp'd her strong wings, and sought the cheerful isle, ... 618 *School Ex.* 46
With passion for Æneas, such strong love . . . 624 *Æneid* 25
By the strong mind, and tales of warlike feats, . 634 *Prelude* 1. 176
In these night wanderings, that a strong desire . 637 *Prelude* 1. 318
True symbol of hope's foolishness, whose strong . 639 *Prelude* 1. 486
And strong book-mindedness ; and over all . . 654 *Prelude* 3. 395
Were, in the main, of mood less tender : strong, . 662 *Prelude* 4. 251
Me hath such strong entrancement overcome, . 668 *Prelude* 5. 162
Such was she—not from faculties more strong . 670 *Prelude* 5. 288
And yet a power is on me, and a strong . . . 678 *Prelude* 6. 238
Strong in herself and in beatitude . . . . . 684 *Prelude* 6. 613
As if to make the strong wind visible, ... 687 *Prelude* 7. 46
Less strong of wonder and obscure delight. . . 688 *Prelude* 7. 87
Almost as deeply seated and as strong . . . . 688 *Prelude* 7. 104
Behold, turned upwards, a face hard and strong . 690 *Prelude* 7. 200
In no discordant opposition, strong . . . . 700 *Prelude* 8. 92
With strong sensations teeming as it did . . . 708 *Prelude* 8. 597
And the strong hand of outward violence . . . 711 *Prelude* 9. 109
Maimed, spiritless ; and, in their weakness strong, 713 *Prelude* 9. 261
Should see the people having a strong hand . . 717 *Prelude* 9. 530
On a strong river boldly hath been launched ; . 717 *Prelude* 9. 560
Who in attack or in defence were strong . . . 720 *Prelude* 10. 132
Preclude conviction, that a spirit strong . . . 720 *Prelude* 10. 165
Strong and perturbed, not doubting at that time 721 *Prelude* 10. 210
By a strong levy of humanity . . . . . . 721 *Prelude* 10. 248
Of this new enemy. Tyrants, strong before . . 723 *Prelude* 10. 333
In wicked pleas, were strong as demons now ; . 723 *Prelude* 10. 334
To yield myself to Nature, when that strong . . 724 *Prelude* 10. 417
Resistance strong as heretofore, I thought . . 727 *Prelude* 11. 22
Upon our side, us who were strong in love ! . . 728 *Prelude* 11. 107
Is lost in light, the weak in the more strong. . 729 *Prelude* 11. 172
Or, seeing, had forgotten ! A strong shock . . 731 *Prelude* 11. 270
This was the crisis of that strong disease, . . 731 *Prelude* 11. 306
Thine be such converse strong and sanative, . . 733 *Prelude* 11. 396
Although a strong infection of the age, . . . 736 *Prelude* 12. 113
By the strong wind. When, in the blessèd hours 738 *Prelude* 12. 261
Attends us, if but once we have been strong. . 738 *Prelude* 12. 271
In a strong wind, some working of the spirit, . 739 *Prelude* 12. 331
There are who think that strong affection, love 742 *Prelude* 13. 186
Convictions still more strong than heretofore, 744 *Prelude* 13. 280
The strong hand of her purity ; and still . . 762 *Excursion* 1. 399
Obedient to the strong creative power . . . 763 *Excursion* 1. 480
By the strong sunbeams smitten. Like a mast . 773 *Excursion* 2. 133
Impulse and motive to that strong discourse, . . 805 *Excursion* 4. 255
Predominate ; whose strong effects are such . . 806 *Excursion* 4. 328
The tiny creatures strong by social league ; . . 807 *Excursion* 4. 432
When winds are blowing strong. The traveller slaked . . . . 814 *Excursion* 4. 871
And undisguised, and strong and serious thought ; 824 *Excursion* 5. 119
Strong and unbounded to embrace, and firm . . 831 *Excursion* 5. 575
Of their most dreaded foe, the strong South-west 833 *Excursion* 5. 702
" Such was that strong concussion ; but the Man, 840 *Excursion* 6. 143
How hopelessly ; but innocence is strong, . . . 841 *Excursion* 6. 177
In silent pools, now in strong eddies chained ; . 849 *Excursion* 6. 737
For me, the emotion scarcely was less strong . . 854 *Excursion* 6. 1055
There blossoms, strong in health, and will be soon 855 *Excursion* 6. 1152
A generous spirit, and a body strong . . . . 859 *Excursion* 7. 120
Her strong knee-timbers, and the mast that bears 866 *Excursion* 7. 604
The rudiments of war ; ten—hardy, strong, . . 869 *Excursion* 7. 771
And strong in hatred of idolatry." . . . . . 870 *Excursion* 7. 816
Strong to subvert our noxious qualities : . . . 886 *Excursion* 9. 132
Through a strong net, and mounts upon the wind, 886 *Excursion* 9. 172
And the strong wind have reverenced. . . . . K.8. 226 **I will* 73
Discoursing on remote imaginations, strong . . K.8. 227 **I will* 100

Strong-abodes. Our strong-abodes and castles see . 204 *Brougham* 34

Strong-built. A mighty evil for a strong-built mind!— 65 *Bord.* 1511
Stronger. Its darkening boughs and leaves in stronger lines; 6 *Ev. Wk.* 215
Did not admit of stronger evidence; 53 *Bord.* 881
When ye were gone my limbs were stronger; 114 *Ind. Wom.* 25
With stronger wing, more clearly to discern 358 **Is this* 12
Still stronger, bends him to his course. 401 *White Doe* 466
By chain yet stronger must the Soul be tied: 446 *Ecc. Sonn.* 3. 25. 1
Enclosed when he was stronger; 483 *Simon Lee* 46
And, fronting the bright west in stronger lines, 595 *Ev. Wk. Quarto* 193
Far stronger, now, grew the desire I felt 667 *Prelude* 5. 115
His helper and not theirs, laid stronger hold 717 *Prelude* 9. 506
More dignified, and stronger in himself; 799 *Excursion* 3. 923
Strongest. Are at work with the strongest; 190 *March* 7
The solemn promise. Strongest sinews fail, 446 *Ecc. Sonn.* 3. 23. 6
Amid my strongest workings evermore 651 *Prelude* 3. 156
In spite of strongest disappointment, pleased 689 *Prelude* 7. 146
Must labour, whence the strongest are not free. 698 *Prelude* 7. 730
And go to the grave, unthought of. Strongest minds 757 *Excursion* 1. 91
The strongest did not easily escape; 775 *Excursion* 2. 244
Else had the strongest fastnesses proved weak 868 *Excursion* 7. 750
Strong-hold. Entrance I gained to that strong-hold. 409 *White Doe* 1252
Strongly. Should beat too strongly, both may be betrayed. 378 *Duddon* 10. 12
And, serving Truth, the heart more strongly beats 520 *Pun. Death* 14. 6
Strove. She strove, and not in vain, her head to rear; 35 *Guilt* 573
I strove to ease my mind, when our two Comrades, 59 *Bord.* 1211
he strove to turn from me 72 *Bord.* 1940
—As if he strove to be a man, 114 *Ind. Wom.* 37
She wasted no complaint, but strove to make 138 *Widow* 6
While reapers strove, or busy ploughs 287 *Sons of Burns* 35
Impassioned dreams, that strove to span 299 *Brownie's Cell* 59
Which Superstition strove to chase, 343 *Eclipse* 5
Suffice it that the Son, who strove 406 *White Doe* 930
A fondly-anxious Mother strove 407 *White Doe* 1030
And strove in filial love to reunite 444 *Ecc. Sonn.* 3. 15. 5
Year after year I strove, but strove in vain, 470 †*From early* 6
Who rashly strove thy Image to portray? 511 **Who rashly* 1
Assaults the pride she strove in vain to quell. 519 *Pun. Death* 12. 4
With help from female hands, that proudly strove 546 **Oft is* 14
Through fond ambition of that hour, I strove 685 *Prelude* 6. 671
Of them who strove against us, more delight 714 *Prelude* 9. 342
In long orations, which I strove to plead 724 *Prelude* 10. 411
And ought to be; and strove to learn how far 728 *Prelude* 11. 101
And vainly by all other means, he strove 760 *Excursion* 1. 299
Of red ripe currants; gift by which he strove, 779 *Excursion* 2. 505
Who strove to instil this truth into his mind, 840 *Excursion* 6. 165
Which Age, with many a slow stoop, strove to gain; S.3. 417 **Sweet was* 5
Strown. *See* **Strewn.**
But all the steps and ground about were strown 257 **Methought I* 4
Struck. *See* **Awe-struck.**
Struck, and still struck again, the troubled horse: 27 *Guilt* 177
Struck the poor innocent. Pallid with dismay 33 *Guilt* 475
'Tis but for a few days—a thought has struck me. 41 *Bord.* 224
It struck me at the time—yet I believe 42 *Bord.* 273
It struck upon my heart I know not how. 44 *Bord.* 377
I struck my flint, and built up a small fire 50 *Bord.* 704
The cold blast struck me. 'Twas a foolish question. 52 *Bord.* 838
He struck me; and that instant had I killed him, 68 *Bord.* 1716
But that was a vain hope. You have struck home, 71 *Bord.* 1867
A human voice distinct, struck on my ear. 73 *Bord.* 2048
My conscience made me wish to be struck blind; 77 *Bord.* 2250
The minster-clock has just struck two, 83 *Lucy Gray* 19
That struck perchance the farthest cone 113 *Lament* 16
And struck him with a mighty stroke, 157 *Oak and Broom* 106
As Peter struck—and struck again. 238 *P. B.* 195
Where he had struck the Ass's head; 244 *P. B.* 727
Of winds—though winds were silent—struck a deep 383 *Duddon* 27. 7
Of victory, that struck through heart and reins 383 *Duddon* 29. 6
Was on the wing; stooping, he struck with awe 388 *Eagles* 5
Which struck with terror friends and foes! 408 *White Doe* 1148
Name that first struck by chance my startled ear) 465 **The cattle* 8
Have struck thy sides, too many ghastly decks 466 *St. Bees* 22
While he struck his desolate harp without hopes or aims. 474 **Ye shadowy* 8
I struck, and with a single blow 484 *Simon Lee* 85
Awe struck, the kneeling peasant scarce surveys; 606 *Desc.Sk.Quarto* 254
Upreared its head. I struck and struck again, 637 *Prelude* 1. 380
That prove to what low depth had struck the roots, 717 *Prelude* 9. 549
Would but have touched the judgment, struck more deep 730 *Prelude* 11. 187
From these tall elms; the cottage-clock struck eight;— 767 *Excursion* 1. 749
Structure. A structure stands, which two bare slopes enclose. 27 *Guilt* 147
The structure of her laden thigh, 227 *Vernal Ode* 115
As this low structure, for the tasks of Spring 254 *Wild Duck's Nest* 5
Oh, had this vast theatric structure wound 269 *Malham* 6
Man left this Structure to become Time's prey, 283 **Here, where* 2
A holy Structure to the Almighty's praise. 338 *Engelberg* 14
A pious structure, fair to see, 398 *White Doe* 233
The flattered structure glistened, blazed, 550 *Hermit's Cell* 2. 19
On a low structure of rude masonry 566 *Cumb. Beg.* 3
Lofty, but the unsubstantial structure melts 635 *Prelude* 1. 225
Of a dilapidated structure, once 726 *Prelude* 10. 558
Fantastic pomp of structure without name, 784 *Excursion* 2. 859
Is no mechanic structure, built by rule; 831 *Excursion* 5. 563
Yon structure, framing, with the ascent of steps 846 *Excursion* 6. 504
Structure's. Of tide and tempest on the Structure's base, 473 **Thanks for* 10
And flashing to that Structure's topmost height, 473 **Thanks for* 11
Structures. The sacred Structures for less doubtful gains. 424 *Ecc. Sonn.* 1. 24. 8
Structures like these the excited spirit mainly 697 *Prelude* 7. 651
One of those petty structures. "His it must be!" 778 *Excursion* 2. 436
What in those holy structures ye possess 838 *Excursion* 6. 26
These structures rose, commingling old and young, 879 *Excursion* 8. 339
Struggle. O weary struggle! silent years 110 *Forsaken* 8
Were but the bitter struggle past. 115 *Last of Flock* 70
Your feet must struggle; in such bold ascent 131 *Michael* 4
Who, while they struggle from the scourge to flee, 213 *Dion* 87
Or struggle in the net-work of thy dreams! 216 *Enterp,rise* 97
Sun, moon, and stars, all struggle in the toils 252 **Why Minstrel* 11
To struggle through dark ways; and when a damp 260 **Scorn not* 11
Angels and gods! We struggle with our fate, 261 **I watch* 10
The last that dare to struggle with the Foe. 310 **Another year* 4
The struggle, clap their wings for victory! 378 *Duddon* 10. 14
To stir in useless struggle) hath relied 440 *Ecc. Sonn.* 2. 45. 6
The prayers, the contrite struggle, and the trust 451 *Ecc. Sonn.* 3. 41. 13
And painful struggle and deliverance—prayed 460 **Queen of* 31
Struggle with frosty air and winter snows; 568 *Cumb. Beg.* 174
Graven on the tomb we struggle against Time, 583 **With copious* 2
And still we struggle when a good man dies. 583 **With copious* 4
To struggle, to be lost within himself 682 *Prelude* 6. 469
To struggle in as scarcely would allow 795 *Excursion* 3. 640
Yet cease I not to struggle, and aspire 803 *Excursion* 4. 126
After long struggle, had escaped at last— 882 *Excursion* 8. 565
Fret, burn, and struggle, and in soul am there; K.8. 256 *Recluse* 1. 1. 725
Struggled. We toiled and struggled, hoping for a day 28 *Guilt* 230
Struggled with tears nor could its sorrow ease, 34 *Guilt* 535
I would so long have struggled with my Nature, 53 *Bord.* 872
Struggled with the flood in vain: 93 *Westmoreland Girl* 8
Each struggled, and each yielded as before 98 *Brothers* 209
Who paints how Britain struggled and prevailed 330 *Ode: Thanks.* 72
Not vainly struggled in the might 409 *White Doe* 1218
Who in these Wilds then struggled for command; 466 *St. Bees* 38
E'er struggled with a heart so proud, 543 *Russ. Fug.* 155
And all who struggled with the Sea, 580 *John Words.* 9
The capital City; what was struggled for, 720 *Prelude* 10. 128
Which they had struggled for: up mounted now, 730 *Prelude* 11. 209
Through which I struggled, not without distress 886 *Excursion* 9. 169
Struggles. With a hard-hearted ignorance; your struggles 64 *Bord.* 1505
And, in its struggles to get free, 175 *Waggoner* 1. 150
In painful struggles. Months each other chase, 274 *Infant M.* 4
The toils and struggles of thy infant years! 290 *Kilchurn* 35
The shepherd struggles with them. Onward thence 353 *Aquap.* 47
Out of her early struggles well inspired 356 *Aquap.* 272
And, in her struggles, cast ashore; 370 *Eg. Maid* 64
For self, and struggles with himself alone, 433 *Ecc. Sonn.* 2. 19. 10
With its own struggles, did I meditate 677 *Prelude* 6. 122
Seeks for no trophies, struggles for no spoils 684 *Prelude* 6. 610
Keen struggles, and black clouds of passion raised; 695 *Prelude* 7. 536
And from the private struggles of mankind 835 *Excursion* 5. 852
His struggles, his discomfitures deplore, 863 *Excursion* 7. 377
Struggling. as I was struggling on, by the light of the moon 72 *Bord.* 1932
Thus Elidure, by words, relieved his struggling heart. 104 *Artegal* 129
Or awed he weeps, struggling to quell dismay. 234 *Power of Sound* 107
That, struggling through the western sky, have won 256 *Decay of Piety* 13
She soared—and I awoke, struggling in vain to follow. 261 **I heard (alas* 14
Nor Duty struggling with afflictions strange— 262 **Not Love* 3
May lead the thoughts, thus struggling used to stand 265 **When haughty* 10
The struggling heart, where be they now?— 285 *Grave of Burns* 26
He, struggling in the net of pride, 298 *Brownie's Cell* 27
Struggling for liberty, while undismayed 353 *Aquap.* 46
Struggling against the stream of destiny, 355 *Aquap.* 190
The struggling Rill insensibly is grown 378 *Duddon* 9. 1
Of heroes, fallen, or struggling to advance, 383 *Duddon* 29. 4
And scourges England struggling to be free: 439 *Ecc. Sonn.* 2. 44. 12
Struggling for life, into its saving arms! 469 **The feudal* 10
And fondly strives her struggling friend to save. 490 *Incident: Dog* 32
In nature's struggling frame, 498 **The sylvan* 15
Instrument of struggling Nature 502 **Like a* 20
And nations sink; or, struggling to be free, 516 **As leaves* 12
We shall behold the struggling Moon 532 **How beautiful the* 7
Each grasps an oar, and struggling on they go— 541 *Grace Darl.* 51
The pent-up air, struggling to free itself, 640 *Prelude* 1. 540
All side by side, and struggling face to face, 710 *Prelude* 9. 65
By struggling with the crowd for present ends. 714 *Prelude* 9. 339
Of a ship struggling with a hideous storm) 721 *Prelude* 10. 228
For sacrifice, and struggling with fond mirth 724 *Prelude* 10. 407
Here, if need be, struggling with storms, and there 750 *Prelude* 14. 299
Went struggling on through those calamitous years 764 *Excursion* 1. 549
Struggling against it; with a soul perplexed, 772 *Excursion* 2. 70
Struggling against the strange reverse with zeal 775 *Excursion* 2. 283
That, in a struggling and distempered world, 797 *Excursion* 3. 804
Struggling in vain with ruthless destiny." 846 *Excursion* 6. 557
Struggling and bold, and shining from the west 861 *Excursion* 7. 232
Strung. *See* **New-strung.**
Hath Nature strung your nerves to bear 286 *Sons of Burns* 13
Strung on slender blades of grass; 549 *Hermit's Cell* 1. 2
Struts. So struts yon cock that now is crowing; 181 *Waggoner* 4. 149
Strutting. Big passions strutting on a petty stage; 799 *Excursion* 3. 900
Stuart. The Stuart, landing to resume, by force 844 *Excursion* 6. 417

Summer's—*continued.*
Those locks from summer's golden skies, 530 *Gleaner* 2
For summer's heat exchanged, 545 *Russ. Fug.* 298
Who faint, and beat by summer's breathless ray, 596 *Ev. Wk. Quarto* 243
And apple sickens pale in summer's ray, 608 *Desc.Sk.Quarto* 322
Up the green mountain tracking Summer's feet, 610 *Desc.Sk.Quarto* 452
Made one long bathing of a summer's day; 636 *Prelude* 1. 290
Alternate, all a summer's day, or scoured 636 *Prelude* 1. 292
Bright was the summer's noon when quickening steps 658 *Prelude* 4. 1
That once in the stillness of a summer's noon, 666 *Prelude* 5. 57
These were our food; and such a summer's night 686 *Prelude* 6. 723
Laden with summer's thickest foliage, rock 739 *Prelude* 12. 330
And the wild paths; and, by the summer's warmth 762 *Excursion* 1. 388
At the calm close of summer's longest day, 782 *Excursion* 2. 718
Throughout a long and lonely summer's day 813 *Excursion* 4. 804
On the soft grass through half a summer's day, 814 *Excursion* 4. 852
Yet where is glowing Summer's long rich day, 828 *Excursion* 5. 398
The summer's day, and winter's; with success 833 *Excursion* 5. 710
"One day—a summer's day of annual pomp 870 *Excursion* 7. 861
Or foot, or lip, in summer's warmth—perceived. 879 *Excursion* 8. 332
Of yet another summer's day, not loth 895 *Excursion* 9. 777
Yet, having spent a summer's day S.3. 438 **My Lord* 7
Of winter, nor from summer's sultry heat) K.8. 247*Recluse* 1.1.395
Summers. Of thrice ten summers dignify the board. 19 *Desc. Sk.* 499
"The suns of twenty summers danced along,— 28 *Guilt* 226
Do not touch it! summers two 79 *Foresight* 7
Of four-and-twenty summers he withdrew; 125 *V. and J.* 273
Five years have past; five summers, with the length 205 *Tintern* 1
"Nine summers had she scarcely seen, 486 **We walked* 33
Of thrice ten summers consecrate the board. 613 *Desc.Sk.Quarto* 589
And twice five summers on my mind had stamped 640 *Prelude* 1. 560
Than two-and-twenty summers had been told— 704 *Prelude* 8. 349
With *silent* increase: summers, winters—past, 866 *Excursion* 7. 566
Ten summers and ten winters of a space 866 *Excursion* 7. 568
Summer-tide. Lulled by the fountain in the summer-tide; 203 *Hart-leap* 150
Summer-time. "And in the summer-time, when days are long, 201 *Hart-leap* 69
Summit. Upon the summit of this naked cone, 16 *Desc. Sk.* 304
Soft music o'er the aerial summit steal? 16 *Desc. Sk.* 343
Upon its aëry summit crowned with heath, 101 *Brothers* 369
Had walked, and from the summit had fallen headlong: 101 *Brothers* 400
And on a summit, distant a short space, 146 **It was an* 34
From base to summit; such delight I found 147 *Joanna* 45
Hath to this lonely Summit given my Name. 148 **There is an* 17
The summit of a cumbrous freight, 182 *Waggoner* 4. 255
For from the summit of BLACK COMB (dread name 218 **This Height* 2
Till he had reached a summit sharp and bare, 226 *Vernal Ode* 12
In his still haunt on Bagdad's summit high; 252 **The fairest* 6
The Olympian summit hath destroyed for aye 325 *Ode 1814* 119
From the dread summit of the Queen 347 **Lulled by* 3
With fractured summit, no indifferent sight 352 *Aquap.* 20
Or pause) the summit of the Leaning-tower. 355 *Aquap.* 177
The summit of this bold ascent— 409 *White Doe* 1173
Attained a summit whence his eyes 412 *White Doe* 1440
Close to the summit of this height, 416 *White Doe* 1802
That on the summit whither thou art bound, 548 **Stay, bold* 13
Soft music from th' aereal summit steal? 609 *Desc.Sk.Quarto* 421
Upon the summit of a craggy ridge, 637 *Prelude* 1. 370
In the dark summit of the waving tree 659 *Prelude* 4. 91
Unveiled the summit of Mont Blanc, and grieved 683 *Prelude* 6. 525
Up to thy summit, through the depth of air 699 *Prelude* 8. 2
On Etna's summit, above earth and sea, 734 *Prelude* 11. 454
The beacon on the summit, and, more near, 738 *Prelude* 12. 250
Scout-like, and gained the summit; 'twas a day 738 *Prelude* 12. 297
The naked summit of a far-off hill 742 *Prelude* 13. 148
And Fairfield's highest summit, on the right K.8. 225 **I will* 24
That rises to the summit of the steep K.8. 252*Recluse* 1.1.568
Summits. *See* **Mountain-summits.**
And far and wide the icy summits blaze, 16 *Desc. Sk.* 321
The trees' tall summits withered at the sight; 212 *Laod.* 173
Of yon ethereal summits white with snow, 329 *Ode: Thanks.* 22
Or there to pace, and mark the summits hoar 384 *Duddon* 31. 12
On the high summits Darkness comes and goes, 605 *Desc.Sk.Quarto* 205
While far and wide the icy summits blaze 609 *Desc.Sk.Quarto* 384
The pines that near the coast their summits rear 611 *Desc.Sk.Quarto* 501
Renewing, when the rosy summits glow 617 *Desc.Sk.Quarto* 812
Raised toward those craggy summits, his intent 773 *Excursion* 2. 154
And mountain-steeps and summits, whereunto 784 *Excursion* 2. 849
Above the summits of the highest hills, 824 *Excursion* 5. 136
Summon. To summon fancies out of Time's dark cell. 275 *Rotha Q.* 14
When the Being of Beings shall summon her hence. 364 *Vallomb.* 36
Thus saying, 'O dear Child! I summon thee 555 *Prioress* 194
To summon back from lonesome banishment, 634 *Prelude* 1. 163
Did summon us in his delightful round. 639 *Prelude* 1. 478
To either bank, nor could he summon up K.8. 229 **I will* 154
Summoned. Till that same star summoned me back again. 59 *Bord.* 1217
And when the King of Denmark summoned him 63 *Bord.* 1444
Or hast been summoned to the deep, 117 *Affl. Marg.* 54
The traveller to a shelter, summoned him 132 *Michael* 57
Was summoned to discharge the forfeiture, 134 *Michael* 215
Summoned the Sailor to rejoice; 179 *Waggoner* 3. 133
And therefore are ye summoned to depart, 434 *Ecc. Sonn.* 2. 24. 7
Summoned the Chiefs to lay their feuds aside, 467 *St. Bees* 103
As if awakened, summoned, roused, constrained, 650 *Prelude* 3. 105
Who, summoned by that season, reunite 675 *Prelude* 6. 4

Summoned—*continued.*
Summoned from school to London; fortunate 688 *Prelude* 7. 92
Summoned from streamy Morven—each and all 695 *Prelude* 7. 568
We summoned up the honourable deeds 715 *Prelude* 9. 364
I summoned my best skill, and toiled, intent 731 *Prelude* 11. 279
Is summoned in to crown an Emperor— 732 *Prelude* 11. 360
Beneath them, summoned to such intercourse: 744 *Prelude* 13. 270
He now was summoned to select the course 760 *Excursion* 1. 309
Hath summoned kings to scaffolds, do but give 778 *Excursion* 2. 475
I was abruptly summoned by the sound 826 *Excursion* 5. 239
Nor summoned to contend for virtue's prize, 835 *Excursion* 5. 856
The earliest summoned and the longest spared— 837 *Excursion* 5. 970
Invited, summoned, to partake the cheer 867 *Excursion* 7. 653
Summons. Must part; the summons came;—our final leave we took. 28 *Guilt* 234
Summons his horses to a stand. 176 *Waggoner* 1. 224
Obeyed a summons covetous of truth. 222 *Triad* 215
The iterated summons loud, 228 *Devot. Incit.* 42
The convict's summons in the steeple's knell; 234 *Power of Sound* 158
Like the first summons, Cuckoo! of thy bill, 273 **Not the* 3
But hark—the summons!—down the placid lake 332 *Ode: Thanks.* 205
Trooping to that summons holy. 396 *White Doe* 8
They heard the summons;—and, furthermore, 403 *White Doe* 702
Of war, but duty summons her away 427 *Ecc. Sonn.* 1. 35. 11
Ye, who have duly weighed the summons, pause 446 *Ecc. Sonn.* 3. 25. 9
A summons to the Cuckoo shall be sent, 562 *Cuck.and Night.* 278
A summons to the sound of oars, that pass, 604 *Desc.Sk.Quarto* 144
I heeded not their summons: happy time 638 *Prelude* 1. 428
Our steeds remounted and the summons given, 643 *Prelude* 2. 115
Inexorable summons! Lofty elms, 676 *Prelude* 6. 73
This tyranny, summons all the senses each 736 *Prelude* 12. 135
To which she summons him; although the works 744 *Prelude* 13. 293
With startling summons; not for his delight 863 *Excursion* 7. 407
A local summons to unceasing toil! 877 *Excursion* 8. 173
Withdrew, on summons to their well-earned meal; 883 *Excursion* 8. 593
With the mild summons; inmates though they be K.8. 241*Recluse* 1.1.194
Their summons, and are gathering round for food, K.8. 245*Recluse* 1.1.332
Sumptuous. "Holy as that far seen which crowns the sumptuous Church in Rome 93 *Poet's Dream* 61
And pleasure's sumptuous bowers; 102 *Artegal* 22
In sumptuous buildings, vocal in sweet song, 334 **The Spirit* 2
Whether the rich man's sumptuous gate 375 **The Minstrels* 33
Of silence, how it thrilled thy sumptuous roof, 387 *Roslin* 6
That sumptuous Pile, with all its peers, 396 *White Doe* 18
And humble altar, 'mid your sumptuous aisles 451 *Ecc. Sonn.* 3. 42. 4
A sumptuous dream of flowery lawns, with domes 700 *Prelude* 8. 84
A work of art more sumptuous than might seem 846 *Excursion* 6. 506
Sumptuously. One evening sumptuously lodged; the next, 771 *Excursion* 2. 8
Came on a war-horse sumptuously attired, 871 *Excursion* 7. 925
Sun. Thus, while the Sun sinks down to rest 1 *Extract* 9
The sun at morning, and the stars at night, 2 *Ev. Wk.* 18
But now the sun has gained his western road, 3 *Ev. Wk.* 88
How pleasant, as the sun declines, to view 4 *Ev. Wk.* 98
An edge all flame, the broadening sun appears; 5 *Ev. Wk.* 169
He views the sun uplift his golden fire, 11 *Desc. Sk.* 31
Toy with the sun and glitter from afar. 11 *Desc. Sk.* 51
The *west*, that burns like one dilated sun, 15 *Desc. Sk.* 282
And he can look beyond the sun, and view 16 *Desc. Sk.* 325
Falls on the valleys as the sun goes down; 19 *Desc. Sk.* 471
The tall sun, pausing on an Alpine spire, 20 *Desc. Sk.* 553
Of the sun peeping through the clouds can spy, 21 *Desc. Sk.* 602
The lanes I sought, and, as the sun retired, 31 *Guilt* 402
"Through tears the rising sun I oft have viewed, 32 *Guilt* 442
Have hailed the morning sun. But cheerily, Father,— 39 *Bord.* 125
Resound with music, could you see the sun, 40 *Bord.* 147
Are here, to send the sun into the west 44 *Bord.* 373
Another sits i' th' sun, and by the hour 60 *Bord.* 1234
"I hold of Spirits, and the Sun in heaven." 63 *Bord.* 1447
Stay you behind; and, when the sun is down, 64 *Bord.* 1464
Shall sun himself before his native doors; 66 *Bord.* 1628
Methinks I see it now—how in the sun 68 *Bord.* 1722
While sweetly shone the evening sun 81 †*Mother's Return* 31
Two boys are sitting in the sun; 84 *Shepherd-boys* 13
"If the sun be shining hot, do but stretch thy woollen chain, 87 *Pet-lamb* 29
For the sun is in his harbour, 90 *Longest Day* 3
Just as those final words were penned, the sun broke out in power, 91 *Poet's Dream* 1
Into his face, until the setting sun 97 *Brothers* 111
Under a cloudless sun—till he, at length, 101 *Brothers* 361
Of things earth makes, and sun doth shine upon; 106 *Farewell* 15
For never sun on living creature shone 107 *Indolence* 3
At mid-day when the sun was shining bright; 107 *Indolence* 16
I shall not see another sun; 114 *Ind. Wom.* 62
Beneath a sun that wakes a weary world 122 *V. and J.* 51
And the sun did shine so cold!" 131 *Idiot Boy* 451
Chosen for the Shearer's covert from the sun, 133 *Michael* 167
Light to the sun and music to the wind; 134 *Michael* 202
Our lot is a hard lot; the sun himself 134 *Michael* 233
He went, and still looked up to sun and cloud, 138 *Michael* 456
Drying their feathers in the sun, at ease; 143 **High bliss* 16
The sun has burnt her coal-black hair; 144 *Her Eyes* 2
The last that parleys with the setting sun; 148 **There is an* 2
Had altogether yielded to the sun, 148 **A narrow* 8
Had shaped for their refreshment; nor did sun, 149 *M. H.* 11
A bosom to the sun endeared? 154 *Flower Garden* 16
And should I live through sun and rain 157 *Sexton* 29
That she may sun thee; 157 **In youth* 12
As ready to salute the sun 158 **In youth* 75

Superior. He, all superior but his God disdained, . 18 *Desc. Sk.* 435
Charms superior to decay. . . . . 90 *Longest Day* 64
Of a far superior garden. . . . . 157 *Sexton* 24
Superior ? Help to virtue does she give ? . . 388 **The pibroch's* 13
Arise superior to the Siren's power, ... 619 *School Ex.* 95
And the vain-glory of superior skill, ... 643 *Prelude* 2. 70
Superior, and incapable of change, ... 677 *Prelude* 6. 137
Superior, magisterially adopts . . . . . 731 *Prelude* 11. 242
On her—at once superior to my woes . . . . 795 *Excursion* 3. 668
For by superior energies ; more strict . . . . 805 *Excursion* 4. 305
That these—and that superior mystery . . . 816 *Excursion* 4. 974
Superior, insusceptible of pride, ... 839 *Excursion* 6. 46
Ascending ! For on that superior height . . . 885 *Excursion* 9. 69
Thence up Helvellyn, a superior mount, . . . K.8. 225 **I will* 28
Supernatural. Rich are his walks with supernatural cheer ; . . . . 267 **Though narrow* 5
Do in the supernatural world abide : . . . . 425 *Ecc. Sonn.* 1. 28. 11
An awe and supernatural horror breeds ; . . . 431 *Ecc. Sonn.* 2. 11. 6
And natural or supernatural fear, ... 670 *Prelude* 5. 307
Reached her with supernatural mandates charged S.3. 436 **The doubt* 177
Supersedes. That aids or supersedes our grosser sight, 226 *Vernal Ode* 4
Superstition. And very superstition of the place, . 49 *Bord.* 661
Some uncouth superstition of its own. . . . . 63 *Bord.* 1441
Which Superstition strove to chase, ... 343 *Eclipse* 5
By superstition, spread the Papal power ; . . . 429 *Ecc. Sonn.* 2. 2. 2
Might leap, the weakest nerve of superstition start ; 456 **The leaves* 7
" ' When Superstition left the golden light . . 618 *School Ex.* 29
Science with joy saw Superstition fly . . . . 618 *School Ex.* 43
By superstition of the neighbourhood, ... 737 *Prelude* 12. 243
Where superstition weaves her airy dreams. . . 810 *Excursion* 4. 610
Superstitions. Ye superstitions of the *heart*, . . 223 *Wishing-gate* 11
His native superstitions melt away. . . . . 426 *Ecc. Sonn.* 1. 29. 8
Superstitious. And superstitious fancies strong, . 398 *White Doe* 215
Dismay, and superstitious pain, ... 405 *White Doe* 867
Glimmers through many a superstitious form . . 419 *Ecc. Sonn.* 1. 4. 13
And with a superstitious eye of love. . . . . 760 *Excursion* 1. 243
But superstitious fear, and abject sloth. . . . 800 *Excursion* 3. 955
In deadly scorn of superstitious rites, ... 814 *Excursion* 4. 903
Of superstitious fancy, might have seemed . . K.8. 246 *Recluse* 1.1.336
Superstitiously. Whose footsteps superstitiously avoid 219 *Haunted Tree* 20
Supine. The couch his fate had made for him ; supine, ... 718 *Prelude* 9. 575
Screened from the sun. Supine the Wanderer lay, 762 *Excursion* 1. 438
Supper. And eat my supper there. . . . . . 84 *We are Seven* 48
The lamb, while from her hand he thus his supper took, ... 87 *Pet-lamb* 9
Our Lord's Last Supper, beautiful as when first . 509 *F. Stone* 104
Receives at supper hour her tempting hoard ; . 615 *Desc.Sk.Quarto* 737
To Abraham of old. The supper done, . . . 681 *Prelude* 6. 397
Supper-board. Turned to the cleanly supper-board, and there, ... 132 *Michael* 99
Suppers. With invitations, suppers, wine and fruit, 649 *Prelude* 3. 43
Supplant. Would supplant the weeds, and cherish . 94 *Westmoreland Girl* 79
Supplanted. Shame followed shame, and woe supplanted woe— . . . . 311 **Who rises* 39
Supplanted the whole majesty of Rome . . . 358 *Pine : Rome* 12
To others, all supplanted in their turn ; . . . 658 *Prelude* 3. 620
Had been supplanted, could I hope to stand— . 796 *Excursion* 3. 684
Supplanted, not for treacherous vacancy . . . S.3. 435 **The doubt* 115
Supple. Why, friend, to deck her supple twigs . . S.3. 431 **The Scottish* 7
Suppliant. Suppliant for aid his kingdom to regain ; 103 *Artegal* 83
Then crouch no more on suppliant knee, . . . 110 **Ere with* 17
With suppliant gestures and upbraidings stern ; . 201 *Hart-leap* 22
With faith, the Suppliant heavenward lifts her hands ; . . . . 209 *Laod.* 8
" Though here I bend a suppliant knee . . . 406 *White Doe* 897
By Rome abandoned ; vain are suppliant cries, . 420 *Ecc. Sonn.* 1. 9. 9
Not unforgiven the suppliant knee might bend, . 434 *Ecc. Sonn.* 2. 25. 10
Their suppliant hands ; but holy is the feast . . 440 *Ecc. Sonn.* 2. 46. 12
When Alpine Vales threw forth a suppliant cry, . 441 *Ecc. Sonn.* 3. 7. 1
And asked for peace on suppliant knee ; . . . 550 *Hermit's Cell* 5. 18
O son, a suppliant to thy deity ! . . . . . 624 *Æneid* 14
Suppliant's. Unquestionable lines of that wild Suppliant's face. . . . . 191 *Beggars* 30
Suppliants. From suppliants panting for the skies ! 216 *Enterprise* 42
Disregard Thy Suppliants now ! . . . . . 336 **Jesu ! bless* 12
Suppliants ! the God to whom your cause ye trust . . . . 448 *Ecc. Sonn.* 3. 30. 13
Supplicants. And whining voice denote them supplicants . . . . 879 *Excursion* 8. 360
Supplicate. I supplicate for thy control ; . . . 492 *Duty* 35
Supplicates. Pause, courteous Spirit !—Balbi supplicates . . . . 575 *Chiabrera* 9. 1
Supplication. And, kneeling, supplication make to our Lady de la Paix ; . . . . 92 *Poet's Dream* 50
The Woman urged her supplication, ... 176 *Waggoner* 1. 226
In supplication to the Child began . . . . . 555 *Prioress* 193
Supplied. So shall its waters, from the heavens supplied . . . . 22 *Desc. Sk.* 656
With daily bread, by constant toil supplied. . . 29 *Guilt* 263
Supplied my helplessness with food and raiment, 41 *Bord.* 200
Of waters which the winter had supplied . . . 146 **It was an* 4
By thought supplied, nor any interest . . . . 206 *Tintern* 82
With what this innocent spring supplied : . . . 416 *White Doe* 1857
On hope that conscious innocence supplied, . . 440 *Ecc. Sonn.* 2. 45. 7
By confidence supplied and mercy shown, . . . 459 **Wanderer ! that* 14
Will to the woman be supplied ! . . . . . 503 **Like a* 59
By cautious love supplied. . . . . 543 *Russ. Fug.* 152
With books supplied and instruments of art, . . 548 **Stay, bold* 15
With all his wants supplied. . . . . 579 **Sweet Flower* 14

Supplied—*continued.*
Of the old grey stone, from her scant board, supplied. . . . . 643 *Prelude* 2. 88
Supplied our want, we haply might employ . . 643 *Prelude* 2. 99
With other signs of manhood that supplied . . 649 *Prelude* 3. 41
From strict analogies by thought supplied . . 651 *Prelude* 3. 125
Whate'er the minister's old shelf supplied ; . . 759 *Excursion* 1. 171
His Schoolmaster supplied ; books that explain . 760 *Excursion* 1. 252
Upon the PEDLAR's toil—supplied their wants, . 761 *Excursion* 1. 331
Supplied a boundary less abrupt and close ; . . 776 *Excursion* 2. 336
His morbid humour, with delight supplied . . 810 *Excursion* 4. 586
Was put to proof, and exercise supplied . . . 859 *Excursion* 7. 99
The lovely Girl supplied—a simple song, . . . 892 *Excursion* 9. 534
Soft heath this elevated spot supplied, . . . 892 *Excursion* 9. 580
Supplies. When not a star supplies the comfort of its light ; . . . . 14 *Desc. Sk.* 187
Which the kindly wool supplies, ... 163 *Spinning Wheel* 16
A Barn her *winter* bed supplies ; . . . . . 194 *Ruth* 223
Nor more, for aught that time supplies, . . . 348 **Lulled by* 27
No star supplies the comfort of it's light, . . . 606 *Desc.Sk.Quarto* 216
Which an abstract intelligence supplies ; . . . 802 *Excursion* 4. 75
There doth he rest. No theme his fate supplies . 854 *Excursion* 6. 1085
Supply. That grief for which the senses still supply 1 *Early Youth* 9
Is able to supply my loss, ... 113 *Lament* 62
That doth presume no more than to supply . . 253 **Aerial Rock* 10
For You she wrought : Ye only can supply . . 333 *Ded. Tour* 9
This Ordinance, whether loss it would supply, . 445 *Ecc. Sonn.* 3. 21. 10
A skill—to balance and supply ; . . . . . 497 *Lycoris* 41
The silence of sorrow it seems to supply, . . . 621 *Convict* 43
His earnings might supply, and brought away . 760 *Excursion* 1. 246
A grateful recollection must supply . . . . 813 *Excursion* 4. 782
All weakness fathoms, can supply all needs : . . 817 *Excursion* 4. 1092
The voice of gladness, less and less supply . . 828 *Excursion* 5. 407
Instructs, and prompts her to supply defects . . 875 *Excursion* 8. 56
Their succour would supply ; . . . . . . S.3. 431 **The Scottish* 14
Supplying. For supplying all deficiencies, all wants of the rude nest . . . . 91 *Norman Boy* 22
Support. Powers that support an unremitting strife 19 *Desc. Sk.* 510
There, pains which nature could no more support, 31 *Guilt* 383
You seem worn out with travel—shall I support you ? . . . . 41 *Bord.* 220
Deny me your support. We have been fooled— 63 *Bord.* 1426
And your support—my hut is not far off. . . . 67 *Bord.* 1676
Your limbs sink under you, shall I support you ? 74 *Bord.* 2111
Of a steep march : support me to the end. . . 112 **O dearer* 12
My burthen to support. . . . . 113 *Lament* 63
Reserved, had fate permitted, for support . . 122 *V. and J.* 35
To support, restrain, or raise. . . . . . . 141 *Arm. Lady* 88
Strains that support the Seasons in their round ; . 235 *Power of Sound* 191
Support their mighty theme from age to age ; . 325 *Ode 1814* 132
Support, and whom the forest shields ; . . . 416 *White Doe* 1874
Shalt thou thy humbler franchises support, . . 442 *Ecc. Sonn.* 3. 10. 11
Blank ocean and mere sky, support that mood . 488 *Pers. Talk* 31
Yet seek thy firm support, according to their need. 492 *Duty* 24
Support us, teach us calmly to resign . . . . 576 **Six months* 5
That fails not, in all sorrow my support, . . . 648 *Prelude* 2. 444
Support, as heretofore, my fainting steps. . . 652 *Prelude* 3. 200
On whose support harmoniously conjoined . . 681 *Prelude* 6. 449
Weighed with me, could support the test of thought ; . . . . 708 *Prelude* 8. 628
Nor the support of good or evil men . . . . 721 *Prelude* 10. 202
Guide, and support, and cheer me to the end ! " . 755 *Recluse* 1. 1. 860
Graceful support ; his countenance as he stood . 757 *Excursion* 1. 43
Declined their languid heads, wanting support. . 767 *Excursion* 1. 727
By theories with suitable support)— . . . . 795 *Excursion* 3. 633
Other support, not scrupulous whence it came ; . 797 *Excursion* 3. 784
Its guidance ; but the infallible support . . . 798 *Excursion* 3. 864
The Wanderer said :— " One adequate support . 801 *Excursion* 4. 10
For our support, the measures and the forms, . 802 *Excursion* 4. 74
As may support longings of pure desire ; . . . 804 *Excursion* 4. 236
Their town, and foodful region for support . . 811 *Excursion* 4. 692
And tempt opinion to support the wrongs . . 816 *Excursion* 4. 1020
In furnishing clear guidance, a support . . . 820 *Excursion* 4. 1262
In Providence, for solace and support, ... 830 *Excursion* 5. 516
But, above all, my thoughts are my support, . . 835 *Excursion* 5. 823
That, for support, rests on them ; the decayed . 837 *Excursion* 5. 966
Proved all unable to support the weight . . . 842 *Excursion* 6. 237
For, strength to persevere and to support, . . 848 *Excursion* 6. 663
Were they not equal to their own support ; . . 874 *Excursion* 8. 12
Her sole support, she languishes and dies. . . 884 *Excursion* 9. 22
Supported. *See* **Self-supported.**
And grey-haired sires, on staffs supported, . . 324 *Ode 1814* 65
From flower to flower supported ; but to curb . 496 **A little* 17
Supporters. That he and his supporters all were fallen. 726 *Prelude* 10. 575
Four dear supporters of one senseless weight, . 780 *Excursion* 2. 584
Supporting. *See* **Life-supporting.**
Supporting life by water from the spring, . . . 103 *Artegal* 100
Descending, and supporting his pure heart . . 871 *Excursion* 7. 900
Supporting gracefully a massy dome . . . . 891 *Excursion* 9. 500
Supports. Tranquil assurances that Heaven supports 173 *Infant Daughter* 69
That ill supports the luscious fig ; . . . . . 342 *Ital. Itin.* 46
Supports, adorns, and over all presides ; . . . 368 *Trajan* 52
Supports the generations, multiplies . . . . 807 *Excursion* 4. 433
That, while it binds, invigorates and supports. . 813 *Excursion* 4. 825
Suppose. I suppose you would have had me lend my bonnet . . . . 72 *Bord.* 1984
You will suppose that with an upright path . . 131 *Michael* 3
And grossly that man errs, who should suppose . 132 *Michael* 62
Suppose my powers so far confirmed, and such . 750 *Prelude* 14. 309
Supposed. The Baron Herbert, who, as was supposed, 49 *Bord.* 681

Surface—*continued.*
Along the surface of a mountain pool : 858 *Excursion* 7. 33
Had marked the line, and strewn its surface o'er . 881 *Excursion* 8. 451
On whose capacious surface see outspread 882 *Excursion* 8. 557
With all the shapes over their surface spread : 885 *Excursion* 9. 62
Surfaces. But at the surfaces of things ; we hear . 56 *Bord.* 1030
The surfaces of artificial life 657 *Prelude* 3. 559
To skim along the surfaces of things, 788 *Excursion* 3. 135
Surge. Soon to be swallowed by the briny surge ; . 216 *Enterprise* 111
Is lifted of a foaming surge— 242 *P. B.* 559
Above the tossing surge. 296 *Highland Boy* 125
Rocked on the surge, there tried his spirit's strength 354 *Aquap.* 128
Or, in the hollow surge, at anchor rocked 454 *Sea-side* 14
His hoary crown, since I had seen the surge 721 *Prelude* 10. 238
Surges. Had heard the Atlantic surges roar 238 *P. B.* 208
Nor hear the loudest surges of St. Bees. 467 *St. Bees* 90
Said I, " like surges heaving in the wind 858 *Excursion* 7. 32
Surging. That o'er the pavement of the surging streams 268 **DogmaticTeachers* 11
Surly. The eye sublime, and surly lion-grace : 18 *Desc. Sk.* 444
To charm the surly house-dog's faithful bark, 32 *Guilt* 417
A surly mastiff kennels at the gate, 60 *Bord.* 1249
Sour and surly as the north ; 181 *Waggoner* 4. 124
And monarchs surly at the wrongs sustained 640 *Prelude* 1. 534
That the rough lord had left the surly North 687 *Prelude* 7. 25
Surmise. The man who had an ill surmise of him 719 *Prelude* 10. 107
The cloud of fancy and uncouth surmise 858 *Excursion* 7. 84
Surmount. Here to elude and there surmount, they watch 541 *Grace Darl.* 53
Surmounted. Upon a slope surmounted by a plain 644 *Prelude* 2. 156
Surmounting. Slowly surmounting some invidious hill, 282 **In my* 2
Surmounts. Threading the painful cragg surmounts the cliff. 607 *Desc.Sk.Quarto* 298
Surpass. Her chamber-window did surpass in glory 122 *V. and J.* 45
Her lineaments, thought he, surpass 369 *Eg. Maid* 15
Came to this hidden pool, whose depths surpass . 381 *Duddon* 22. 2
Surpass all science and all utterance ; 552 *Prioress* 24
Would seem in no distinction to surpass 855 *Excursion* 6. 1142
Surpassed. *See* **Self-surpast.**
That we are not to be surpassed 291 *Rob Roy* 83
For those examples, in no age surpassed, 725 *Prelude* 10. 487
" A woman rests in peace ; surpassed by few . 848 *Excursion* 6. 676
Surpassed in strength, I heard of danger, met K.8. 256 *Recluse* 1.1.716
Surpasses. Surpasses aught these elements can show. 139 *Widow* 22
Surpasses sweetest music. There she sits 508 *F. Stone* 11
Surpassing. Or even conceive ; surpassing me in love 105 *Artegal* 180
Which to the work surpassing skill hath dealt, 276 *Author's Portrait* 4
Of a surpassing brightness. At the sight 667 *Prelude* 5. 80
Supreme Existence, the surpassing life 677 *Prelude* 6. 134
Surpassing the most fair ideal Forms 755 *Recluse* 1. 1. 796
Prized for surpassing beauty, and no less 767 *Excursion* 1. 725
The boon is absolute ; surpassing grace K.8. 239 *Recluse* 1.1.103
Surpast. *See* **Self-surpast, Surpassed.**
Surplice. My surplice, through the inferior throng I clove 653 *Prelude* 3. 312
Surprise. Surprise to all, but most surprise 177 *Waggoner* 2. 109
Ere he replied, a flash of mild surprise 196 *Resolution* 90
Though I beheld at first with blank surprise 279 **Though I* 1
Full ten times a day takes his heart by surprise. 570 *Farmer* 64
The peaceful scene oft filled me with surprise 661 *Prelude* 4. 194
Listening, a gentle shock of mild surprise 671 *Prelude* 5. 382
A strange surprise and fear came to my heart, 766 *Excursion* 1. 659
" Me," said I, " most doth it surprise, to find 778 *Excursion* 2. 457
Surprised. A sudden joy surprised expiring thought, 35 *Guilt* 624
" Be not surprised if you hear that some signal judgment 76 *Bord.* 2217
Surprised by joy—impatient as the Wind 257 **Surprised by* 1
And shivering wolves, surprised with darkness, howl 264 *Storm* 8
Did tremble like a guilty Thing surprised : 589 *Immortality* 151
Surrender. Unwilling to surrender 386 *Yarrow Rev.* 78
And to the elements surrender it 809 *Excursion* 4. 512
Surrendering. Went forth—his course surrendering to the care 263 *Storm* 3
Surrendering the whole heart to sacred pleasures ? 331 *Ode : Thanks.* 138
Surround. Thee, and the Cottage which thou dost surround. 106 *Farewell* 8
The barriers disregarding that surround 807 *Excursion* 4. 390
They ceased not to surround us ; change of place, 891 *Excursion* 9. 509
Surrounded. And many a foundrous pit surrounded ! 179 *Waggoner* 3. 92
And ask, surrounded even by kneeling crowds, 256 *Decay of Piety* 10
At his board by these surrounded, 535 *Egremont* 75
Surrounded by those wild unpeopled hills, 566 *Cumb. Beg.* 14
And there he sate surrounded with a throng 692 *Prelude* 7. 359
Surrounded by adventurers in arms, 715 *Prelude* 9. 413
Surrounded, too, the wanderers of the earth ; 742 *Prelude* 13. 155
Surrounded us ; and, as we held our way 891 *Excursion* 9. 507
Surrounding. And blend with the surrounding trees. 246 *P. B.* 860
'Mid those surrounding Worthies, haughty King, 271 *Henry : Portrait* 10
Though little suited to surrounding things : 778 *Excursion* 2. 460
From the surrounding countries at the choice 812 *Excursion* 4. 723
Of the surrounding district, they might learn 869 *Excursion* 7. 770
Surrounds. Blue ether still surrounds him—yet—and yet ; 261 **I watch* 4
Darkness surrounds us ; seeking, we are lost 419 *Ecc. Sonn.* 1. 5. 1
They may endure long as the sea surrounds 838 *Excursion* 6. 15
Survey. A sage survey of his condition. 175 *Waggoner* 1. 159
More doleful place did never eye survey ; 202 *Hart-leap* 114
Earth knows, is all unworthy to survey. 211 *Laod.* 108
Or survey their bright dominions 217 **Inmate of* 21
Could imitate for indolent survey, 511 **Who rashly* 19

Survey—*continued.*
Edward, the flower of chivalry, survey L.1. 94 *Juvenal* 2. 24
Surveyed. And death's dire aspect daily he surveyed, 25 *Guilt* 56
When, from the last hill-top, my sire surveyed, 28 *Guilt* 236
Or from the top of Lebanon surveyed 70 *Bord.* 1806
That Lucy's eyes surveyed. 109 **I travelled* 16
He had surveyed it with a finer eye, 150 **When, to* 60
He cautiously surveyed. 241 *P. B.* 410
And long, with wistful gaze, his walk survey'd 592 *Ev. Wk. Quarto* 69
Heedless how Pliny, musing here, survey'd 604 *Desc.Sk.Quarto* 116
Enough ;—the mighty concourse I surveyed 690 *Prelude* 7. 219
Surveying. *See* **Far-surveying.**
Surveys. Left by gigantic arms—at length surveys 26 *Guilt* 113
Or, led by distant warbling notes, surveys, 603 *Desc. Sk. Quarto* 96
Awe struck, the kneeling peasant scarce surveys ; 606 *Desc.Sk.Quarto* 254
The old grey stones the plaided chief surveys, 608 *Desc.Sk.Quarto* 359
Unbreathing Justice her still beam surveys : 616 *Desc.Sk.Quarto* 787
Intruder ne'er beheld, he thence surveys 799 *Excursion* 3. 937
Survive. Survive of local sympathy, 1 *Extract* 6
Survive her Husband : at her death the estate 138 *Michael* 474
Its image would survive among his thoughts : 149 *M. H.* 22
That their pure joy in nature may survive 152 **Forth from* 25
Nor could the waggon long survive, 182 *Waggoner* 4. 187
The shadow-casting race of trees survive : 227 *Vernal Ode* 63
Powers that survive but in the faintest dream 235 *Power of Sound* 171
Survive, and Fortune's utmost anger try ; 265 **When haughty* 5
Say not that we have vanquished—but that we survive. 330 *Ode : Thanks.* 91
Of innocence survive to mitigate distress ? 344 **How blest* 65
Survives for me, and cannot but survive 353 *Aquap.* 72
Survive, uninjured ;—glory then to words, 356 *Aquap.* 249
Do still survive, and, with those gentle hearts 362 **List—'twas* 69
Where they survive, of wholesome laws ; 376 **The Minstrels* 56
That yet survive ensculptured on the walls 394 **No more* 7
Which yet survive on bleak Iona's coast. 419 *Ecc. Sonn.* 1. 5. 8
Shall long survive, to shelter the Abode 450 *Ecc. Sonn.* 3. 39. 8
Whose lofty genius could survive 473 *Ossian* 57
Survive, and once again the Pile stands fast : 474 **Hope smiled* 8
Survive not Judgment that requires his own ? 518 *Pun. Death* 6. 14
This little Island may survive ; 532 †*Float. Isl.* 18
For benefits that still survive, by faith 538 **In desultory* 54
Perchance may still survive. And be it known 546 **Oft is* 9
Survive upon the tall mast's height ; 579 **Sweet Flower* 47
Whose flower with us will vanish, must survive. 627 **We gaze* 14
That yet survive, a shattered monument 636 *Prelude* 1. 284
Nor be himself extinguished, but survive, 666 *Prelude* 5. 27
Which yet survive in memory, appears 692 *Prelude* 7. 335
Survive for inspiration, shall attract 734 *Prelude* 11. 463
That yet survive, a work, as some divine, 745 *Prelude* 13. 339
With joy, and—oh ! that memory should survive 792 *Excursion* 3. 431
Duty exists ;—immutably survive, 802 *Excursion* 4. 73
That shall survive his name and memory. 823 *Excursion* 5. 48
For public use preserved, and thus survive 845 *Excursion* 6. 498
Hamlet, and town ; and piety survive 863 *Excursion* 7. 383
Survive, as pagan temples stood of yore, 870 *Excursion* 7. 843
Whether a pining discontent survive, 878 *Excursion* 8. 293
Survive ; all else is swept away.—How bright 894 *Excursion* 9. 711
Long as Heaven and Earth survive, S.3. 442 *Harmodius* 23
All shall survive—though changed their office, all K.8. 257 *Recluse* 1.1.743
Survived. And others who survived the wreck, beheld 38 *Bord.* 75
he could not have survived an hour. 72 *Bord.* 1980
———Hast thou then survived— 172 *Infant Daughter* 1
Already hast survived that great decay, 172 *Infant Daughter* 6
Then, then—had I survived to see 410 *White Doe* 1279
Survived, 'twas only in my dreams. 458 **Had this* 68
Survived, and, when the European came 635 *Prelude* 1. 198
And now a third small Island, where survived 643 *Prelude* 2. 62
(Whose in-door pastime, lighted up, survived 664 *Prelude* 4. 375
And of old men who have survived their joys— 668 *Prelude* 5. 212
Of novelty survived for scenes like these ; 693 *Prelude* 7. 447
A woeful time for them whose hopes survived 723 *Prelude* 10. 386
Survived, but daring sympathies with power, 725 *Prelude* 10. 457
Lived long enough, nor in the least survived 737 *Prelude* 12. 181
And silent overgrowings, still survived. 770 *Excursion* 1. 930
The oldest, he was taken last, survived 861 *Excursion* 7. 259
Of yew, in which survived some traces, here 881 *Excursion* 8. 475
Survives. In a Saxon church survives, 142 *Arm. Lady* 152
His power survives. 286 *Nith* 48
A ray of fancy still survives— 302 *Yarrow V.* 75
Made to the Twelve, survives : lip, forehead, cheek, 343 *Last Sup.* 10
A yearning survives which few hearts shall withstand : 345 *Stanzas : Simplon* 28
Survives for me, and cannot but survive 353 *Aquap.* 72
As she survives in ruin, manifest 357 *Aquap.* 293
Of him who thus survives by classic art, 368 *Trajan* 26
Survives imagination—to the change 388 **The pibroch's* 12
Spots where a word, ghost-like, survives to show 389 *Sound of Mull* 5
For what survives of house where God 397 *White Doe* 114
Survives—the twilight of this day— 416 *White Doe* 1872
Where that pure Church survives, though summer heats 431 *Ecc. Sonn.* 2. 12. 7
Only a heaving of the deep survives, 454 *Sea-side* 4
Or deadly snare : and He survives to bless 470 **A youth* 13
Its Sister-twin survives, whose smiles afford 576 **By a* 11
In thankful blessedness, which yet survives. 663 *Prelude* 4. 338
And hang it round with garlands. Love survives ; 701 *Prelude* 8. 156
With the great family that still survives 735 *Prelude* 12. 62
That in these shows a chronicle survives 787 *Excursion* 3. 89
Survives, for worthy mention, of a pair 844 *Excursion* 6. 405
And how, her Spirit yet survives on earth ! " 856 *Excursion* 6. 1191
The memory of the just survives in heaven : 863 *Excursion* 7. 388

Survives—*continued.*
The boy of plainer garb, whose blush survives — 882 *Excursion* 8. 552
Surviving. *See* **Self-surviving.**
Surviving comrade of uncounted hours, — 133 *Michael* 118
Surviving near the public way, — 223 *Wishing-gate* 17
By Youth's surviving spirit ? What agile grace ! — 540 **Lady ! a* 70
Surviving—they for us, and we for them— — K.8. 244 *Recluse* 1.1.263
Survivor. He is the sole survivor. — 483 *Simon Lee* 32
Perhaps the sole survivor of thy race, — 531 *Octogen.* 10
The one Survivor stood ; he wept, he prayed — 774 *Excursion* 2. 202
And this Survivor, with his cheerful throng — 861 *Excursion* 7. 279
Survivor's. Of the survivor's sweetest voice (dear child, — 118 *Maternal Grief* 44
Survivors. Have the survivors of this Storm renewed — 420 *Ecc. Sonn.* 1. 7. 6
Of the survivors—to the clouds might bear— — 541 *Grace Darl.* 91
Should frail survivors heave a sigh ? — 586 *Hogg* 36
Susan. For her good neighbour Susan Gale, — 126 *Idiot Boy* 18
Old Susan, she who dwells alone, — 126 *Idiot Boy* 19
Old Susan lies a-bed in pain, — 126 *Idiot Boy* 24
There's none to help poor Susan Gale ; — 126 *Idiot Boy* 30
Or she will die, old Susan Gale. — 126 *Idiot Boy* 46
Away she hies to Susan Gale : — 127 *Idiot Boy* 102
To comfort poor old Susan Gale. — 127 *Idiot Boy* 121
Which she to Susan will not tell. — 127 *Idiot Boy* 141
Poor Susan moans, poor Susan groans ; — 127 *Idiot Boy* 142
Poor Susan moans, poor Susan groans ; — 127 *Idiot Boy* 147
And Susan has a dreadful night. — 127 *Idiot Boy* 156
Susan ! they'll both be here anon." — 128 *Idiot Boy* 166
And Susan now begins to fear — 128 *Idiot Boy* 177
At the first word that Susan said — 128 *Idiot Boy* 184
" Susan, I'd gladly stay with you. — 128 *Idiot Boy* 186
Susan, we must take care of him, — 128 *Idiot Boy* 189
" Oh God forbid ! " poor Susan cries. — 128 *Idiot Boy* 191
Good Susan tell me, and I'll stay ; — 128 *Idiot Boy* 194
At poor old Susan then she railed, — 128 *Idiot Boy* 232
" If Susan had not been so ill, — 128 *Idiot Boy* 234
To comfort poor old Susan Gale. — 129 *Idiot Boy* 276
Who is it, but old Susan Gale ? — 130 *Idiot Boy* 411
Long time lay Susan lost in thought ; — 130 *Idiot Boy* 412
Did Susan rise up from her bed, — 130 *Idiot Boy* 425
Andrew there, and Susan here, — 157 *Sexton* 27
Poor Susan has passed by the spot, and has heard — 188 *Poor Susan* 3
Susan's. And Betty, now at Susan's side, — 127 *Idiot Boy* 122
And Betty, still at Susan's side, — 127 *Idiot Boy* 127
She sits, as if in Susan's fate — 127 *Idiot Boy* 130
And Susan's growing worse and worse, — 128 *Idiot Boy* 167
And Betty's still at Susan's side. — 128 *Idiot Boy* 176
That God poor Susan's life would spare, — 128 *Idiot Boy* 200
Suspect. Can still suspect, and still revere himself, — 23 *Yew-tree* 63
Marmaduke ! I suspect unworthy tales — 41 *Bord.* 255
We see not nor suspect a bound, — 154 *Flower Garden* 27
(Suspect not, Anna, that their fate is hard ; — 527 **Those breathing* 2
Forgive me if I venture to suspect — 880 *Excursion* 8. 400
Suspected. Now Harry he had long suspected — 537 *Goody Blake* 65
On men suspected to be crazed in brain. — 660 *Prelude* 4. 130
Suspend. For *him* suspend the dashing oar ; — 9 *Collins* 18
The mountain streams their rising song suspend ; — 598 *Ev. Wk. Quarto* 352
Suspended. *See* **Long-suspended.**
The dripping of the oar suspended ! — 9 *Collins* 22
Where mists, suspended on the expiring gale, — 14 *Desc. Sk.* 210
Suspended 'mid the quiet of the sky ; — 16 *Desc. Sk.* 349
Suspended in a stream as clear as sky, — 88 *H. C.* 9
Almost suspended, we are laid asleep — 206 *Tintern* 45
With breath suspended, like a listening scout. — 322 *Germans* 4
While mists, suspended on th' expiring gale, — 607 *Desc.Sk.Quarto* 265
Think not, suspended from the cliff on high — 611 *Desc.Sk.Quarto* 510
Suspended by the blast that blew amain, — 637 *Prelude* 1. 334
Suspended over a knight's tomb, who lay — 705 *Prelude* 8. 415
His harp, suspended at the traveller's side ; — 771 *Excursion* 2. 15
Suspending. In rapture,—yet suspending her embrace, — 461 **Giordano, verily* 5
Suspends. The pictured fane of Tell suspends his oar; — 15 *Desc. Sk.* 286
To reverence, suspends his own ; submitting — 290 *Kilchurn* 17
Suspense. " But should suspense permit the Foe to cry, — 211 *Laod.* 133
By blazing fire, the still suspense — 375 **The Minstrels* 41
Suspicion. *See* **Self-suspicion.**
A dire suspicion drove us from our shed ; — 35 *Guilt* 601
You will do well ; unjust suspicion may — 75 *Bord.* 2158
Suspicion ripened into dread ; — 241 *P. B.* 421
Collateral suspicion, else unknown. — 655 *Prelude* 3. 422
To no perverse suspicion he gave way, — 864 *Excursion* 7. 456
Suspicious. Would watch my motions with suspicious stare, — 150 **When, to* 28
Of the suspicious, slips of the indiscreet, — 723 *Prelude* 10. 348
In his suspicious wisdom ; oftener still, — 859 *Excursion* 7. 104
Suspiciously. Suspiciously, to establish in plain day — 731 *Prelude* 11. 296
Sussex. So cruel Sussex, unrestrained — 410 *White Doe* 1328
They come, by cruel Sussex sent ; — 412 *White Doe* 1447
Sustain. Far lovelier, and his heart could not sustain — 23 *Yew-tree* 36
Why thus that worn-out wretch must there sustain — 34 *Guilt* 552
That will sustain me. Did you murder him ? — 77 *Bord.* 2256
Watch over her, I pray—sustain her——Captain ! — 78 *Bord.* 2338
Ill fitted to sustain unkindly shocks, — 88 *H. C.* 28
She hardly can sustain her fears ; — 130 *Idiot Boy* 359
Two losses had we to sustain, — 182 *Waggoner* 4. 195
Which, without aid of numbers, I sustain, — 314 **I dropped* 7
Or fortitude be wanting to sustain, — 317 **The martial* 4
Is there a power that can sustain and cheer — 318 **Is there* 1
And every shape of creature they sustain, — 362 **List—'twas* 53
Sustain the heart in feeling — 386 *Yarrow Rev.* 94

Sustain—*continued.*
Which, though seemingly doomed in its breast to sustain — 398 *White Doe* 238
Beside the afflicted ; to sustain with prayer, — 447 *Ecc. Sonn.* 3. 28. 6
His crown of weeds, but could not even sustain — 449 *Ecc. Sonn.* 3. 34. 12
Thy life I would gladly sustain — 484 **A plague* 32
Extended and extending to sustain — 511 **Who rashly* 7
The cause of grateful reason to sustain ; — 520 *Pun. Death* 14. 5
May Nature's kindliest powers sustain the Tree, — 546 **The embowering* 9
That I the weight of it may not sustain ; — 553 *Prioress* 31
Issued, on delegation to sustain — 725 *Prelude* 10. 499
Sustain, thou only canst, the sick of heart ; — 801 *Excursion* 4. 29
Which, when they should sustain themselves aloft, — 803 *Excursion* 4. 141
Most frequently call forth, and best sustain, — 806 *Excursion* 4. 367
Durance to sustain, be over ; — S.3. 438 **I, whose* 25
That Smithfield should sustain so vast a loss, — L.1. 95 *Juvenal* 3. 15
Sustained. *See* **Ill-sustained.**
And with the food of pride sustained his soul — 23 *Yew-tree* 23
A burthen, now with fortitude sustained, — 36 *Guilt* 647
That cannot be sustained ; — 111 *'*Tis said that some* 32
Sustained by delicate illusion ? — 143 **Driven in* 19
Forgetful of the body they sustained.— — 149 **A narrow* 62
At length, by Peter's arm sustained, — 248 *P. B.* 1056
Dread trials ! yet encountered and sustained — 316 **Hail, Zaragoza* 12
Exalted office, worthily sustained ! — 331 *Ode : Thanks.* 160
That, while the Creature is sustained, — 341 *San Salv.* 11
Raised and sustained by memory of Him — 354 *Aquap.* 126
Sustained by memory of the past — 414 *White Doe* 1624
With mute astonishment, it stands sustained — 474 **Hope smiled* 11
To be sustained ; and Mortals bowed — 496 *Lycoris* 3
Espied him on his legs sustained, blank, mute, — 523 *Epist. Beaumont* 140
And inwardly sustained by silent prayer, — 541 *Grace Darl.* 49
Sustained by what her scrip might yield, — 542 *Russ. Fug.* 19
But ill sustained, and almost (so it seemed) — 637 *Prelude* 1. 333
And monarchs surly at the wrongs sustained — 640 *Prelude* 1. 534
Was in its birth, sustained as might befall — 642 *Prelude* 2. 6
Augmented and sustained. Yet is a path — 646 *Prelude* 2. 272
And yet the building stood, as if sustained — 646 *Prelude* 2. 280
No dog attending, by no staff sustained, — 664 *Prelude* 4. 400
Exists and is sustained. More lofty themes, — 694 *Prelude* 7. 465
(Sustained by worthier as by wiser thoughts) — 731 *Prelude* 11. 256
Sustained and governed, still dost overflow — 735 *Prelude* 12. 103
In one continuous stream ; a mind sustained — 747 *Prelude* 14. 74
May have sustained, that, howsoe'er misled, — 748 *Prelude* 14. 149
The life and death of martyrs, who sustained, — 759 *Excursion* 1. 172
Must have sustained a loss."—" The hand of Death," — 779 *Excursion* 2. 542
Set and sustained ;—thou, who didst wrap the cloud — 802 *Excursion* 4. 83
That, mutually protected and sustained, — 838 *Excursion* 6. 14
Than those which they had severally sustained, — 845 *Excursion* 6. 461
Which it sustained. But no one takes delight — 887 *Excursion* 9. 182
Sustaining. *See* **All-sustaining, Soul-sustaining.**
Each desperately sustaining, till at last — 393 *Hart's-horn* 6
Faith in life endless, the sustaining thought — 749 *Prelude* 14. 204
Sustains. One upright arm sustains the cheek, — 112 **How rich* 14
A solemn fancy yet sustains — 410 *White Doe* 1282
Fulfilled, and she sustains her part ! — 415 *White Doe* 1784
That tempts, emboldens—for a time sustains, — 827 *Excursion* 5. 325
We know, yet faith sustains the sorrowing heart ; — K.8. 275 **These vales* 6
Sustenance. The self-created sustenance of a mind — 679 *Prelude* 6. 301
Its sustenance, while the girl with pallid hands — 717 *Prelude* 9. 514
From which she draws her meagre sustenance. — 786 *Excursion* 3. 28
Swain. *See* **Shepherd-swain.**
There, bending o'er the stream, the listless swain — 3 *Ev. Wk.* 70
A lonely Spital, the belated swain — 27 *Guilt* 150
Crouded behind the swain, in mute distress, — 592 *Ev. Wk. Quarto* 67
—The whistling swain that plods his ringing way — 597 *Ev. Wk. Quarto* 315
" Here," cried a swain, whose venerable head — 613 *Desc.Sk.Quarto* 594
A fertilising moisture,' said the Swain, — 835 *Excursion* 5. 872
A world, his rich discovery ! But our Swain, — 841 *Excursion* 6. 235
Swains. Spreading her peaceful ensigns, calls the swains — 335 *Namur* 6
Of Swains reposing myrtle groves among ! — 389 *Tyndrum* 3
As, at this day, the rudest swains who dwell — 502 **The unremitting* 15
To shepherd swains, or seated harp in hand, — 634 *Prelude* 1. 172
Those shepherd swains whom I had lately left, — 657 *Prelude* 3. 548
Was suddenly revealed !—the swains moved on, — 808 *Excursion* 4. 472
To the unenlightened swains of pagan Greece. — 814 *Excursion* 4. 850
Swale. The joy of them who till the fields of Swale, — 202 *Hart-leap* 75
Upon the rapid river Swale, — 240 *P. B.* 325
And for the murmuring river Swale. — 240 *P. B.* 335
The Swale flowed under the grey rocks, — 240 *P. B.* 371
To bring the noises of the Swale — 240 *P. B.* 374
Have helped us : Ure we crossed, and Swale, — 402 *White Doe* 608
Swallow. And as a swallow, at the hour of rest, — 19 *Desc. Sk.* 482
Who would stop the swallow, wheeling — 90 *Longest Day* 19
Is busy at her casement as the swallow — 122 *V. and J.* 82
The Swallow, twittered subject to like spell ; — 153 *Morn. Ex.* 22
A golden spear to swallow ! and that brown — 349 *Sky-prosp.* 6
That bigotry may swallow the good name, — 441 *Ecc. Sonn.* 3. 3. 12
Better fate have Prince and Swallow— — 490 *Incident : Dog* 25
The sugh of swallow flocks that twittering sweep, — 597 *Ev. Wk. Quarto* 317
The wheeling swallow, and the darting snipe, — 868 *Excursion* 7. 752
Swallowed. Soon to be swallowed by the briny surge ; — 216 *Enterprise* 111
Or is she swallowed up, remote from ken — 318 **Ah ! where* 4
Had vanished, swallowed up with all that there — 540 *Grace Darl.* 33
All melted into him ; they swallowed up — 759 *Excursion* 1. 208
And swallowed up 'mid deserts infinite ! — 837 *Excursion* 5. 1007
Have vanished—swallowed up by stately roads — 876 *Excursion* 8. 109
Swallowing. A swallowing up of lesser things in great, — 730 *Prelude* 11. 179

Symphonies 966 **Take**

Sympathy—*continued.*
But for coeval sympathy prepared — 359 **Complacent Fictions* 7
Say, rather, with that generous sympathy — 393 *Hart's-horn* 11
This sympathy of Sire and Sons; — 401 *White Doe* 470
From every sympathy that Man bestowed! — 419 *Ecc. Sonn.* 1. 4. 4
In abject sympathy with power is lost. — 428 *Ecc. Sonn.* 1. 38. 14
Recall the wandering Soul to sympathy — 445 *Ecc. Sonn.* 3. 20. 13
Of rational and manly sympathy. — 455 **Not in the lucid* 19
A less imperious sympathy is due, — 458 *Sea-shore* 26
Pause with no common sympathy. — 486 *Matthew* 12
A tender sympathy, which did thee bind — 491 *Tribute: Dog* 30
Converse with Nature in pure sympathy; — 511 **So fair* 18
Is sympathy with the unforewarned, who died — 517 *Pun. Death* 2. 12
And sympathy with man's substantial griefs— — 538 **In desultory* 41
That first mild touch of sympathy and thought, — 568 *Cumb. Beg.* 114
Flowed in a course of sympathy divine;— — 583 **With copious* 25
As from a cloud of some grave sympathy, — 584 *Ch. Lamb* 20
In the primal sympathy — 590 *Immortality* 185
In sympathy, that I have lengthened out — 641 *Prelude* 1. 618
Coercing all things into sympathy, — 647 *Prelude* 2. 390
Of modest sympathy. Such aspect now, — 676 *Prelude* 6. 63
From a familiar sympathy.—In fine, — 676 *Prelude* 6. 105
Of sympathy, inspiring and inspired, — 706 *Prelude* 8. 479
I did, by human sympathy impelled; — 707 *Prelude* 8. 524
From lowly sympathy and chastening truth: — 714 *Prelude* 9. 351
And truths of individual sympathy — 741 *Prelude* 13. 112
To sympathy with man, he was alive — 761 *Excursion* 1. 364
To his fraternal sympathy addressed, — 762 *Excursion* 1. 419
Yet left them joined by sympathy in age; — 794 *Excursion* 3. 595
But a discriminating sympathy — 818 *Excursion* 4. 1105
Treading their path in sympathy and linked — 845 *Excursion* 6. 477
That sympathy which you for others ask; — 847 *Excursion* 6. 568
Were met with answering sympathy and love. — 864 *Excursion* 7. 462
And in return for sympathy bestowed — 874 *Excursion* 8. 8
And met again. Such playful sympathy, — S.3. 434 **The doubt* 76
Symphonies. Provoke all potent symphonies to raise — 328 *Ode 1815* 78
Symphony. Repeat the bridal symphony. — 233 *Power of Sound* 40
In symphony austere; — 491 *Fidelity* 28
Synod. Welter and flash, a synod might detain — 268 **Dogmatic Teachers* 12
A synod of his Councillors:—give ear, — 422 *Ecc. Sonn.* 1. 15. 13
When from the dark synod, or blood-reeking field, — 621 *Convict* 25
Startling the Synod. Could a youth, and one — 695 *Prelude* 7. 540
The National Synod and the Jacobins, — 710 *Prelude* 9. 49
Synthesis. Was that clear synthesis built up aloft — 677 *Prelude* 6. 162
Syracusan. The noble Syracusan low in dust! — 214 *Dion* 109
Syracuse. To Syracuse advance in bright array. — 212 *Dion* 21
His shadow stretching towards Syracuse, — 732 *Prelude* 11. 378
Upon the grave of vanished Syracuse, — 877 *Excursion* 8. 221
Syria. That I embarked for Syria. On our voyage — 68 *Bord.* 1689
We marched to Syria: oft I left the Camp, — 70 *Bord.* 1802
Syrian. Cheering the wakeful tent on Syrian mountains, — 232 *Power of Sound* 19
Or aught in Syrian deserts left to save — 367 *Trajan* 11
Syria's. Or Syria's marble ruins towering high — 788 *Excursion* 3. 150
System. May try this modern system by its fruits, — 670 *Prelude* 5. 295
From system on to system without end. — 677 *Prelude* 6. 128
The *end* of those, who did, by system, rank, — 791 *Excursion* 3. 361
Our system is not fashioned to preclude — 847 *Excursion* 6. 567
Systems. Against all systems built on abstract rights, — 695 *Prelude* 7. 524
If tired with systems, each in its degree — 810 *Excursion* 4. 603
Let him build systems of his own, and smile — 810 *Excursion* 4. 605

T

Tabby. What would little Tabby care — 171 *Kitten* 36
Tabby's. And, by that whiskered tabby's aid, set forth — 858 *Excursion* 7. 91
Tabernacle. Comes from that tabernacle—List! — 247 *P. B.* 943
That made His human tabernacle shine — 452 *Ecc. Sonn.* 3. 46. 3
Table. *See* **Stone-table.**
A scale and table of belief—as thus— — 58 *Bord.* 1147
O'er table *lilt*, or perch on chair, — 144 **Driven in* 70
Soon will the Knights of Arthur's Table — 370 *Eg. Maid* 86
With plenty was his table spread; — 535 *Egremont* 71
In brighter rows her table wealth aspires, — 615 *Desc.Sk.Quarto* 732
Or round the naked table, snow-white deal, — 639 *Prelude* 1. 514
And watched her table with its huckster's wares — 642 *Prelude* 2. 45
Round the stone table under the dark pine, — 659 *Prelude* 4. 48
At our domestic table: and, dear Friend! — 659 *Prelude* 4. 78
And, when she at her table gave me food, — 768 *Excursion* 1. 793
Our table, small parade of garden fruits, — 782 *Excursion* 2. 683
From Venice to Sir Walter's table. — S.3. 432 **A German* 4
Tables. And near a thousand tables pined and wanted food. — 31 *Guilt* 369
On tables set, as if for rites divine;— — 213 *Dion* 34
Tablet. To gild the total tablet of his days; — 2 *Ev. Wk.* 30
This tablet, that thus humbly rears — 486 *Matthew* 6
This Tablet, hallowed by her name, — 577 *Cenotaph* 7
Shall stand a votive Tablet, haply free, — 584 **With copious* 52
Barren the tablet, yet thereon appeared — 787 *Excursion* 3. 61
Another tablet registered the death, — 825 *Excursion* 5. 185
Tablets. One after one, its tablets, that unfold — 351 *Des. Stanzas* 66
Tabor. Which the bright season favours.—Tabor and pipe — 773 *Excursion* 2. 121
Tabor's. As to the tabor's sound, — 588 *Immortality* 21
As to the tabor's sound! — 590 *Immortality* 174
Tackling. Her tackling rich, and of apparel high. — 258 **With Ships* 8
Ta'en. *See* **Taken.**
Whose muse a sure though late revenge hath ta'en — S.3. 432 **Critics, right* 3
Tail. Shook the still-twinkling tail and glancing ear; — 3 *Ev. Wk.* 48
Afar, his tail he closes and unfurls; — 5 *Ev. Wk.* 151
We call stag-horn, or fox's tail, — 84 *Shepherd-boys* 19
Seemed to feast with head and ears; and his tail with pleasure shook. — 87 *Pet-lamb* 10
His face unto his horse's tail, — 129 *Idiot Boy* 323
And now she's at the Pony's tail, — 130 *Idiot Boy* 382
Tethered to the waggon's tail: — 181 *Waggoner* 4. 164
Must honour still to Lonsdale's tail be bound? — L.1. 88 *Juvenal* 1. 13
Slap-dash, tail foremost, as his arms shall drive. — L.1. 96 *Juvenal* 3. 32
To give a hint of whips and the cart's tail, — L.1. 97 *Juvenal* 3. 72
Tailor. To Tutor or to Tailor, as befell, — 649 *Prelude* 3. 28
Tails. Lashed the cool water with their restless tails, — 3 *Ev. Wk.* 43
Taint. Which genius did not hallow; 'gainst the taint — 23 *Yew-tree* 17
Should he resolve to taint her Soul by means — 56 *Bord.* 1058
To taint the health which ye infuse; — 225 *Present.* 16
From stain or taint; in which thy blameless mind — 264 **Lady! I* 11
Him, free from all malicious taint, — 299 *Brownie's Cell* 55
Even rich men, brave by nature, taint the air — 308 **These times* 2
Child of the clouds! remote from every taint — 376 *Duddon* 2. 1
Unhurt by violence, from menaced taint — 438 *Ecc. Sonn.* 2. 38. 10
Is smitten thence with an unnatural taint, — 655 *Prelude* 3. 420
That their best virtues were not free from taint — 735 *Prelude* 12. 65
And He, what wonder! took a mortal taint. — 775 *Excursion* 2. 245
And Heaven's good providence, preserved from taint! — 876 *Excursion* 8. 150
And unripe sex with sex, for mutual taint; — 879 *Excursion* 8. 340
With the least taint and injury to the air — 886 *Excursion* 9. 150
Tainted. Pollution tainted all that was most pure. — 311 **Who rises* 32
Straight from the sun and tainted air's embrace — 427 *Ecc. Sonn.* 1. 36. 5
Our tainted nature's solitary boast; — 434 *Ecc. Sonn.* 2. 25. 4
Taints. With which he taints her ear;—for a plain reason; — 42 *Bord.* 263
That taints the purer, better, mind; — 233 *Power of Sound* 88
His drought consumes, his mildew taints with death; — 328 *Ode 1815* 92
Take. To take thee to her home—and for myself, — 40 *Bord.* 198
Take care of him, and feed the truant well. — 42 *Bord.* 307
And, while you take your rest, think not of us; — 43 *Bord.* 362
When next inclined to sleep, take my advice — 44 *Bord.* 416
He in the preference, modest Youth, might take, — 47 *Bord.* 552
With those who take the spirit of their rule — 48 *Bord.* 584
You take it as it merits—— One a King, — 60 *Bord.* 1228
But take your sword along with you, for that — 60 *Bord.* 1252
But take me to your arms—this breast, alas! — 66 *Bord.* 1619
I was too fearful—take me for your guide — 67 *Bord.* 1675
let us take heart; this Man may be rich; — 72 *Bord.* 1993
I would take care she never woke again; — 77 *Bord.* 2273
Come, let us take a peep at both together, — 77 *Bord.* 2289
Stay near me—do not take thy flight! — 79 **Stay near* 1
—Here are daisies, take your fill; — 79 *Foresight* 11
And take delight in its activity; — 80 **Loving she* 10
And take a lantern, Child, to light — 83 *Lucy Gray* 15
I take my little porringer, — 84 *We are Seven* 47
Take thy bliss, while longest, shortest, — 90 *Longest Day* 15
And yet, some changes must take place among you: — 97 *Brothers* 127
We'll take another: who is he that lies — 98 *Brothers* 197
Take all that's mine "beneath the moon," — 109 *Louisa* 13
The humblest rivulet will take — 110 **Ere with* 13
"The key I must take, for my Ellen is dead." — 120 *Childless Father* 18
Susan, we must take care of him, — 128 *Idiot Boy* 189
"The devil take his wisdom!" said — 129 *Idiot Boy* 258
And said, "Nay, do not take it so—I see — 136 *Michael* 359
"Princess fair, I till the ground, but may not take — 139 *Arm. Lady* 11
To take the intruder into favour; — 142 †*Lov. and Lik.* 20
Good friends he has to take his part; — 144 **Driven in* 74
From him no harm my babe can take; — 145 *Her Eyes* 77
"'From me this friendly warning take'— — 156 *Oak and Broom* 51
Take not even a finger-joint: — 157 *Sexton* 11
Methinks you take small heed! — 161 *Binnorie* 31
They from morning to even take whatever is given;— — 166 *Stray Pleasures* 11
Take flight, and thou art free to roam, — 169 *Wren's Nest* 66
Take root (so seems it) and look up — 170 *Rural Ill.* 17
And have faculties to take, — 172 *Kitten* 124
Take her at once—for good and evil!" — 176 *Waggoner* 1. 240
His eyes take pleasure in the road — 177 *Waggoner* 2. 35
The prayer would be that they may take — 178 *Waggoner* 3. 15
To take of this transported pair — 180 *Waggoner* 4. 13
Is touched—and all the band take flight. — 180 *Waggoner* 4. 35
His fears, his doubts, may now take flight— — 181 *Waggoner* 4. 130
This Child I to myself will take; — 187 **Three years* 4
And take to herself all the wonders of old;— — 188 *Music* 2
One after One they take their turn, nor have I one espied — 189 *Star-gazers* 31
So vivid that they take from keenest sight — 190 **Lyre! though* 36
Love him, who for himself will take no heed at all? — 195 *Resolution* 42
You must take care and choose your time — 198 *Thorn* 58
Who will take them from the light? — 204 *Brougham* 61
Maiden! now take flight;—inherit — 217 **Inmate of* 17
To take thee in thy majesty away? — 221 *Triad* 75
Her flight, and take its voice away!— — 227 *Vernal Ode* 113
As kindly take what from my heart — 237 *P. B.* 114
Take with you some ambitious Youth! — 237 *P. B.* 128
Then take thy way, adventurous Skiff, — 238 *P. B.* 153
And then, as if to take his ease, — 241 *P. B.* 427

Take—*continued.*
Take from *her* brow the withering flowers of eve, 270 **Shame on* 11
Margaret, the saintly Foundress, take thy place ; 276 *Author's Portrait* 2
For honest men delight will take . . . . . 286 *Sons of Burns* 19
Take, then, thy seat, Vicegerent unreproved ! . 290 *Kilchurn* 22
That they should take, who have the power, . . 291 *Rob Roy* 39
I'll take the shortest way." . . . . 291 *Rob Roy* 56
" I, too, will have my kings that take . . . . 292 *Rob Roy* 89
Take to thy heart a new delight ; . . . . . 293 *Jedbor.* 5
There ! take your seat, and let me see . . . . 295 *Highland Boy* 6
This Child will take no harm. . . . . . . 296 *Highland Boy* 175
And from the shore their course they take, . . 297 *Highland Boy* 183
Live, and take comfort. Thou hast left behind . 305 *Toussaint* 9
Were with herself at strife, would take your stand, 310 *Invasion* 2
Brave Schill ! by death delivered, take thy flight 317 **Brave Schill* 1
Nor take one ray of light from Thee ; . . . . 345 **How blest* 73
That for oblivion take their daily birth . . . 349 *Sky-prosp.* 13
The form and motion of a stream to take ; . . 351 *Des. Stanzas* 62
These records take, and happy should I be . . 352 *H. C. R.* 5
Forced by intent to take from speech its edge, . 353 *Aquap.* 75
That Wisdom wears, or take his treacherous staff 358 *Aquap.* 354
Chanting her low-voiced hymn, take pride . . 366 **Ye Trees* 7
Whose souls take pride in freedom, virtue, fame, 366 **Fair Land* 2
Then said he, " Take her to thy heart, . . . 374 *Eg. Maid* 343
Take, cradled Nursling of the mountain, take . 377 *Duddon* 4. 1
Take root again, a boundless canopy. . . . . 384 *Duddon* 31. 8
Were only History licensed to take note . . . 393 **The Lovers* 9
And smiles, that dared to take their place, . . 401 *White Doe* 499
Bare breast I take and an empty hand."— . . 401 *White Doe* 515
The invisible God, and take for guide . . . . 407 *White Doe* 1040
" An old man's privilege I take : . . . . . 408 *White Doe* 1078
To take his life they have not dared ; . . . . 409 *White Doe* 1213
Oh take her anguish and her fears . . . . . 413 *White Doe* 1566
And in the churchyard he must take his bride . 427 *Ecc. Sonn.* 1. 36. 11
Your ministry ; that, as ye rise and take . . 430 *Ecc. Sonn.* 2. 9. 10
Pastors who neither take nor point the way . 433 *Ecc. Sonn.* 2. 18. 7
The soul of Genius, if he dare to take . . . 455 **Not in the lucid* 12
He will take with him to the silent tomb. . . . 468 **Ranging the* 8
Over three Realms may take its widest range ; . 471 *Tynwald* 10
Rejoiced in—take, whate'er thou be, a share, . 472 **The captive* 12
Gazing and take into his mind and heart, . . . 473 **We saw* 10
Shalt take thy place with Yarrow ! . . . . . 480 *Somnamb.* 162
Whate'er the senses take or may refuse, . . . 480 **Most sweet* 12
We for the year to come may take . . . . . 483 *Sister* 31
And you must kindly take it : . . . . . . 484 *Simon Lee* 70
O turn aside,—and take, I pray, ... 485 *Poet's Epitaph* 22
A counter impulse let me take . . . . . . 490 *Night Thought* 17
To take his sentence from the balanced Block, . 500 *Humanity* 5
Vague sympathies have urged her to take flight : 503 *Warning* 31
Intensely—from Imagination take . . . . . 508 *F. Stone* 25
High as the Sun, that he could take account . . 511 **So fair* 8
Take from the horror due to a foul deed, . . . 519 *Pun. Death* 8. 10
—But if there be a Muse who, free to take . . 521 *Epist. Beaumont* 38
Take those dear young Ones to a fearless nest ; . 525 **Soon did* 2
On which the warbling birds their pastime take. . 531 †*Float. Isl.* 12
Will take away, may cease to give. . . . . 532 †*Float. Isl.* 20
And take the radiance from the clouds . . . 533 **Blest is* 59
Oh ! can a brave Man wish to take . . . . 535 *Egremont* 47
" Take your earnings."—Oh ! that I . . . . 535 *Egremont* 53
That he on her would vengeance take. . . . . 537 *Goody Blake* 68
And to the fields his road would take ; . . . 537 *Goody Blake* 70
The by-way back again to take ; . . . . . 537 *Goody Blake* 86
A poor Man's counsel take ; . . . . . . 542 *Russ. Fug.* 82
But take it in good part :—alas ! the poor . . 547 **Rude is* 5
Soon as the grain from off thy tongue they take : 556 *Prioress* 217
And for that cause Oser I cry ; take heed ! . . 559 *Cuck.and Night.* 135
And take my leave of all such company, . . . 559 *Cuck.and Night.* 138
Then of the Nightingale did I take note, . . . 560 *Cuck.and Night.* 206
And that the sun did take his course not right, . 564 *Troilus* 143
Age might but take the things Youth needed not ! 571 **There is a Flower* 24
For I'd take my last leave both of verse and of prose. 571 *Avarice* 4
Take pride in him !—O Passenger, farewell ! . . 576 *Chiabrera* 9. 22
Alas ! what idle words ; but take . . . . . 577 **I come* 26
Which good men take with them from earth to heaven. . . . . 582 **To public* 10
Do take a sober colouring from an eye . . . 590 *Immortality* 201
Take pleasure in the midst of happy thoughts, . 622 *Recluse* 1. 1. 87
Him will I take, and in close covert keep, . . . 624 *Æneid* 31
Shall I take up my home ? and what clear stream 632 *Prelude* 1. 12
Take refuge and beguile myself with trust . . 635 *Prelude* 1. 235
Take up a station calmly on the perch . . . 654 *Prelude* 3. 358
Not less delighted did I take my place . . . 659 *Prelude* 4. 77
To give and take a greeting that might save . . 660 *Prelude* 4. 128
Enow there are on earth to take in charge . . 668 *Prelude* 5. 153
Leave let me take to place before her sight . . 670 *Prelude* 5. 296
Take firmer hold of us, and words themselves . 673 *Prelude* 5. 544
That cannot take long leave of pleasant thoughts. 675 *Prelude* 6. 19
To part from company and take this book . . 677 *Prelude* 6. 149
Yet why take refuge in that plea ?—the fault, . 677 *Prelude* 6. 188
Licensed to take the meaning that we love ! . . 689 *Prelude* 7. 120
We take our way. A raree-show is here, . . 689 *Prelude* 7. 174
But let me now, less moved, in order take . . 693 *Prelude* 7. 400
Full-formed, that take, with small internal help, . 697 *Prelude* 7. 653
Take one,—that ancient festival, the Fair, . . 697 *Prelude* 7. 676
Or spirit that full soon must take her flight. . . 705 *Prelude* 8. 450
With them to take a troubled human heart, . . 724 *Prelude* 10. 439
I knew that wound external could not take . . 727 *Prelude* 11. 13
That I was led to take an eager part . . . . 728 *Prelude* 11. 76
For manna, take a lesson from the dog . . . 732 *Prelude* 11. 363
How withouti njury to take, to give . . . . 734 *Prelude* 12. 13

Take—*continued.*
Take note of this ? When I began to enquire, . 742 *Prelude* 13. 160
May boldly take his way among mankind . . . 744 *Prelude* 13. 296
Was uttered, midnight darkness seemed to take . 744 *Prelude* 13. 328
In the self-haunting spirit learned to take . . . 750 *Prelude* 14. 284
To take a station among men, the step . . . 751 *Prelude* 14. 342
By circumstance to take unto the height . . . 757 *Excursion* 1. 87
The silent stars ! Oft did he take delight . . 760 *Excursion* 1. 273
To take a farewell of me ; for he feared . . . 766 *Excursion* 1. 679
To give her comfort, and was glad to take . . 766 *Excursion* 1. 684
The yellow stone-crop, suffered to take root . . 767 *Excursion* 1. 717
Said—"Shall we take this pathway for our guide?— 786 *Excursion* 3. 22
If I must take my choice between the pair . . 790 *Excursion* 3. 275
Take the live herbage from the mead, and strip . 790 *Excursion* 3. 308
Whose fibres cannot, if they would, take root. . 799 *Excursion* 3. 890
Take flight ; while with their clang the air resounds. 808 *Excursion* 4. 459
Take courage, and withdraw yourself from ways . 808 *Excursion* 4. 489
Of a most rustic ignorance, and take . . . 810 *Excursion* 4. 615
—'Take, running river, take these locks of mine'— 812 *Excursion* 4. 745
(Take from him what you will upon the score . 813 *Excursion* 4. 829
And have the dead around us, take from them . 832 *Excursion* 5. 647
Will mercifully take me to himself.' . . . . 854 *Excursion* 6. 1048
Of what he seems to take ; or gives it back, . . 855 *Excursion* 6. 1135
And resolution competent to take . . . . . 862 *Excursion* 7. 330
Obsequiously doth take upon herself . . . . 888 *Excursion* 9. 267
Be rooted out, and virtuous habits take . . . 889 *Excursion* 9. 360
For those ordained to take their sounding flight . 889 *Excursion* 9. 372
Oh ! let thy Word prevail, to take away . . . 893 *Excursion* 9. 638
In notes which mountain echoes would take up . S.3. 436 **The doubt* 157
By her side I'll take my place, ... S.3. 437 **I, whose* 19
And take up my Uncle's bow. . . . . . . S.3. 438 **I, whose* 31
" I only touch—not take—don't fear, ... S.3. 441 **The ball* 3
Take up, the cloud-capped hills repeat, the Name), K.8. 238 *Recluse* 1. 1. 58
That take it with them hence, where'er they go. . K.8. 240 *Recluse* 1. 1. 141
I cannot take possession of the sky, ... K.8. 242 *Recluse* 1. 1. 199
Take from us at your pleasure—yet shall ye . . K.8. 251 *Recluse* 1. 1. 542
—Take we at once this one sufficient hope, . . K.8. 254 *Recluse* 1. 1. 633

Taken. *See* **Off-taken, Ta'en.**
This garb was taken up that indolence . . . 38 *Bord.* 65
Had taken refuge in this neighbourhood, . . . 49 *Bord.* 682
Which thou hast taken to thee as thy own, . . 106 *Farewell* 36
Hast taken gifts which thou dost little need. . . 107 *Farewell* 40
And taken thy first leave of those green hills . . 151 **When, to* 68
Some memory that had taken flight ; . . . . 158 **In youth* 46
Taken praise that should be thine, ... 160 **Pansies, lilies* 55
Wouldst thou be taught, when sleep has taken flight, 229 *Cuckoo-clock* 1
Learn from thy course, where'er their own be taken, 461 **Queen of* 49
A single human life have wrongly taken, . . . 517 *Pun. Death* 3. 10
Snatches of music taken up and dropt . . . . 539 **Lady ! a* 32
Was taken up, singing his song alway ; . . . 555 *Prioress* 171
Have I been taken ; this is genuine life . . . 573 *Chiabrera* 1. 3
Be now for ever taken from my sight, ... 590 *Immortality* 180
This Boy was taken from his mates, and died . . 671 *Prelude* 5. 389
In mind, as when I thence had taken flight . . 675 *Prelude* 6. 8
Dejection taken up for pleasure's sake, . . . 683 *Prelude* 6. 551
Was taken up by scoffers in their pride, . . . 725 *Prelude* 10. 471
From her maternal cares, had taken up . . . 769 *Excursion* 1. 858
" That poor Man taken hence to-day," replied . 780 *Excursion* 2. 593
Taken from air and sunshine when the rose . . 836 *Excursion* 5. 957
The oldest, he was taken last, survived . . . 861 *Excursion* 7. 259

Takes. Which the goat cannot climb, takes his sounding flight ; . . . . 80 †*Address : Child* 4
Her brother now takes up the note, ... 81 †*Mother's Return* 25
Thus fares it still with all that takes its birth . 102 *Artegal* 31
Of moon or stars he takes no heed ; . . . . 130 *Idiot Boy* 354
Many a breathing-fit he takes ; . . . . . . 174 *Waggoner* 1. 37
He starts—and takes, at the admonition, . . . 175 *Waggoner* 1. 158
Takes down the canvas overhead ; . . . . . 176 *Waggoner* 1. 273
Takes delight to play upon. . . . . 181 *Waggoner* 4. 107
He through the portal takes his silent way, . . 211 *Laod.* 156
With malice—that again takes flight ; . . . . 242 *P. B.* 498
So from his pocket Peter takes . . . . . . 245 *P. B.* 816
Takes fire :—The men that have been reappear ; . 275 **While poring* 3
That to itself takes all, Eternity. . . . . . 276 *Oker Hill* 14
That Nature takes, her counter-work pursuing. . 283 **Here, where* 4
For gentlest uses, oft-times Nature takes . . . 338 *Engelberg* 1
He takes alone his far-off stand, ... 404 *White Doe* 764
Requiem which Earth takes up with voice undaunted, ... 430 *Ecc. Sonn.* 2. 8. 12
Or like the Alpine Mount, that takes its name . 452 *Ecc. Sonn.* 3. 46. 5
Mourns less for what age takes away . . . . 487 *Fountain* 35
But, like an arrow, to the river takes. . . . . 490 *Incident : Dog* 16
Spring takes, O sprightly May ! thy shape, . . 502 *Seasons* 3
Another takes its place. . . . . 507 *May* 64
Each takes in this high matter, all may move . 520 *Pun. Death* 14. 13
Thus takes the Nightingale her leave of me ; . . 561 *Cuck.and Night.* 256
Where'er the aged Beggar takes his rounds, . . 567 *Cumb. Beg.* 98
Takes one unsparing handful for the scrip . . 568 *Cumb. Beg.* 158
Full ten times a day takes his heart by surprise. . 570 *Farmer* 64
No mood, which season takes away, or brings : . 578 *Peele Castle* 10
His wizard course where hoary Derwent takes . 591 *Ev. Wk. Quarto* 3
Turns recreant to her task ; takes heart again, . 636 *Prelude* 1. 258
That field-ward takes her walk with decent steps. 690 *Prelude* 7. 210
On the pure bliss, and takes her rest with God. . 709 *Prelude* 8. 675
Hope takes, or Doubt or Fear is forced to wear, . 710 *Prelude* 9. 61
Of time and change disdaining, takes its course . 804 *Excursion* 4. 184
Dispersed, like music that the wind takes up . . 820 *Excursion* 4. 1284
That God, who takes away, yet takes not half . 855 *Excursion* 6. 1134
Which it sustained. But no one takes delight . 887 *Excursion* 9. 182
In manner of a bird that takes delight . . . K.8. 245 *Recluse* 1. 1. 322
As one or other takes the fit of glee, ... K.8. 251 *Recluse* 1. 1. 556

Takest. Which now thou tak'st upon thee. God forbid . . . . 74 *Bord.* 2113
Takest away, and into souls dost creep, . . . 253 **Fond words* 8
Thou takest not away, O Death ! . . . . . 583 **O for a* 49
Thou tak'st thy way, carrying the heart and soul 733 *Prelude* 11. 415

Taking. *See* **Leave-taking, Pains-taking.**
And flow it did ; not taking heed . . . . . 111 *A Complaint* 5
Taking her for some way-worn rover, ... 176 *Waggoner* 1. 233
He hath kenned them taking wing : . . . . 205 *Brougham* 130
And, taking impulse from the sword, ... 298 *Brownie's Cell* 37
Who, taking counsel of unbending Truth, . . . 305 **The Voice* 3
For they are taking the baptismal Vow . . . 446 *Ecc. Sonn.* 3. 23. 4
The downward pathway taking, ... 479 *Somnamb.* 94
And taking up a voice shall speak (tho' still . . 585 *Ch. Lamb* 55
But salutation taking its glad way . . . . . 628 **Deign, Sovereign* 3
Full often, taking from the world of sleep . . . 667 *Prelude* 5. 141
By whom we were encompassed. Taking leave . 681 *Prelude* 6. 414
Submits to nothing less than taking in . . . 690 *Prelude* 7. 241
Taking my seat, I saw (nor blush to add, . . 691 *Prelude* 7. 270
But not dismayed, nor taking to the shame . . 730 *Prelude* 11. 213
Are scattered everywhere, taking their date . . 737 *Prelude* 12. 224
The vapours had receded, taking there . . . 784 *Excursion* 2. 850
" Yes," said the Wanderer, taking from my lips . 809 *Excursion* 4. 540
He, taking counsel of his own clear thoughts, . . 841 *Excursion* 6. 219
In works of havoc ; taking from these vales, . . 866 *Excursion* 7. 593
To endure for aye. The Vicar, taking note . . 871 *Excursion* 7. 919
—We followed, taking as he led, a path . . . 880 *Excursion* 8. 441

Tale. *See* **Fellow-tale, Love-tale, Tell-tale.**
Alas ! the idle tale of man is found . . . . 2 *Ev. Wk.* 27
Confused the Marathonian tale appears, . . . 15 *Desc. Sk.* 287
For of that ruin she had heard a tale . . . . 27 *Guilt* 170
Such tale of this lone mansion she had learned, . 27 *Guilt* 181
She knew not what dire pangs in him such tale could wake. . . . . 27 *Guilt* 189
Their way, the Woman thus her mournful tale renewed. . . . . 30 *Guilt* 333
As if because her tale was at an end, ... 32 *Guilt* 448
Stretched on the ground, began a piteous tale ; . . 33 *Guilt* 471
To end her wrongs. But if the blind Man's tale . 38 *Bord.* 72
The tale of this his quondam Barony . . . . 39 *Bord.* 79
No ! this is not the place to hear the tale : . . 56 *Bord.* 1010
Here to impart the tale, of which, last night, . . 59 *Bord.* 1210
The tale was spread abroad ; my power at once . 69 *Bord.* 1761
Nay ; hear my tale, 'tis fit that you should hear it— 74 *Bord.* 2101
No symbols, Sir, to tell us that plain tale : . . 98 *Brothers* 181
Tell seemingly no doubtful tale ; . . . . . 110 *Forsaken* 9
A portion of the tale may well be left . . . . 124 *V. and J.* 176
The Tale I follow to its last recess . . . . 125 *V. and J.* 281
Would surely be a tedious tale. . . . . . . 128 *Idiot Boy* 206
A most delightful tale pursuing ! . . . . . 129 *Idiot Boy* 316
And hence this Tale, while I was yet a Boy . . 131 *Michael* 27
This Tale the Shepherd told. . . . . . . 156 *Oak and Broom* 10
Then, when the Hero of my tale . . . . . 176 *Waggoner* 2. 10
Thou bringest unto me a tale . . . . . . 183 **O blithe* 11
His homely tale, this very day ; . . . . . 186 **O Nightingale* 12
(And all do in this tale agree) . . . . . 194 *Ruth* 226
And I to this would add another tale. . . . . 202 *Hart-leap* 96
To them I must relate the Tale . . . . . . 238 *P. B.* 169
Began the promised Tale. . . . . 238 *P. B.* 190
We've reached at last the promised Tale ;) . . 240 *P. B.* 322
His tale did Peter tell. . . . . 248 *P. B.* 1030
—Here ends my Tale : for in a trice . . . . 249 *P. B.* 1121
The tale I have been telling, ... 287 *Ellen Irwin* 50
But chiefly let one Cottage hear the tale ; . . 294 **Fly, some* 4
And for the boldest tale belief commands. . . 338 *Engelberg* 5
The tale as fabulous.—Here while I recline, . . 340 *Ranz* 8
Ere he his Tale recounted. . . . . 386 *Yarrow Rev.* 104
That Life is but a tale of morning grass . . . 388 *Trosachs* 4
A tale of tears, a mortal story ! . . . . . . 399 *White Doe* 336
'Tis well that she hath heard the tale, ... 409 *White Doe* 1190
The spirit of a mournful tale, ... 478 *Somnamb.* 8
Some tale will be related. . . . . 484 *Simon Lee* 64
A tale in every thing. . . . . 484 *Simon Lee* 68
It is no tale ; but, should you think, ... 484 *Simon Lee* 71
Perhaps a tale you'll make it. . . . . . . 484 *Simon Lee* 72
This lamentable tale I tell ! . . . . 492 *Fidelity* 51
With these dark words begins my Tale ; . . . 494 *Force of Prayer* 2
In woman's shape. But why prolong the tale, . 541 *Grace Darl.* 74
How among them it was a common tale, . . . 557 *Cuck.and Night.* 48
And thus it was that she began her tale. . . . 561 *Cuck.and Night.* 265
Oh, what would they be to my tale of two Thieves ? 571 *Avarice* 12
But tells a plain tale of the days that are flown. . 572 *Avarice* 24
Doth the same tale repeat : . . . . 588 *Immortality* 55
Romantic tale by Milton left unsung ; . . . . 634 *Prelude* 1. 169
A tale from my own heart, more near akin . . 635 *Prelude* 1. 222
With fond and feeble tongue a tedious tale. . . 641 *Prelude* 1. 619
Up to an eminence, and told a tale . . . . 651 *Prelude* 3. 168
Whose tale is only of himself ; even so, . . . 652 *Prelude* 3. 196
Than these to which the Tale, indulgent Friend ! 662 *Prelude* 4. 275
He told in few plain words a soldier's tale— . . 664 *Prelude* 4. 421
Whose tale Cervantes tells ; yet not the knight, . 667 *Prelude* 5. 123
Some simply fashioned tale, to tell again, . . 668 *Prelude* 5. 178
In slender accents of sweet verse, some tale . . 668 *Prelude* 5. 179
Those unclaimed garments telling a plain tale . 672 *Prelude* 5. 443
Of sound humanity to which our Tale . . . . 706 *Prelude* 8. 452
Almost indifferent, even the historian's tale . . 712 *Prelude* 9. 204
As through a book, an old romance, or tale . . 714 *Prelude* 9. 300
But I might here, instead, repeat a tale, . . 717 *Prelude* 9. 547
The ill-fated pair) in that plain tale will draw . 717 *Prelude* 9. 566
That some dramatic tale, endued with shapes . 731 *Prelude* 11. 283
He had small need of books ; for many a tale . 758 *Excursion* 1. 163

Tale—*continued.*
That left half-told the preternatural tale, . . . 759 *Excursion* 1. 179
Of garrulous age ; nor did the sick man's tale, . 762 *Excursion* 1. 418
All recollection ; and that simple tale . . . . 765 *Excursion* 1. 609
Her homely tale with such familiar power, . . 765 *Excursion* 1. 615
An idle dreamer ! 'Tis a common tale, . . . 765 *Excursion* 1. 636
A tale of silent suffering, hardly clothed . . . 765 *Excursion* 1. 638
" This tale did Margaret tell with many tears : . 766 *Excursion* 1. 682
To thank him for the tale which he had told. . . 770 *Excursion* 1. 920
Some way-beguiling tale. Nor less regard . . 772 *Excursion* 2. 37
" Now for the tale with which you threatened us ! " 782 *Excursion* 2. 729
Should the tale tire you, let this challenge stand . 782 *Excursion* 2. 731
" So ends my dolorous tale, and glad I am . . 785 *Excursion* 2. 896
Is fashioned like an ill-constructed tale ; . . . 829 *Excursion* 5. 432
This tale gives proof that Heaven most gently deals 854 *Excursion* 6. 1072
With words that might be prelude to a tale . . 855 *Excursion* 6. 1123
Song of the muses, sage historic tale, ... 864 *Excursion* 7. 450
Short was his life, and a brief tale remains. . . 870 *Excursion* 7. 860
I will relate a tale for those who love . . . . K.8. 224 **I will* 1
Yea to this hour I cannot read a tale . . . . K.8. 256 *Recluse* 1.1.721

Talent. And sorceries of talent misapplied. . . 425 *Ecc. Sonn.* 1. 28. 14
Which practised talent readily affords, . . . 455 **Not in the lucid* 8
Commemorating genius, talent, skill, ... 584 **With copious* 61

Talents. Your talents, power, or wisdom, deem him not . . . . 567 *Cumb. Beg.* 72
Than talents, worth, and prosperous industry. . 713 *Prelude* 9. 232
Thither his popular talents be transferred ; . . 774 *Excursion* 2. 219
His talents lending to exalt the freaks . . . . 843 *Excursion* 6. 343

Tales. At times, and tales unsought beguile the day, 15 *Desc. Sk.* 247
With tales of weakness and infirmity ! . . . . 41 *Bord.* 245
Marmaduke ! I suspect unworthy tales . . . 41 *Bord.* 255
We joined our tales of wretchedness together, . 50 *Bord.* 691
Should he, by tales which would draw tears from iron, ... 57 *Bord.* 1060
Such tales of your dead Father !—God is my judge, 77 *Bord.* 2244
To her these tales they will repeat, ... 81 †*Mother's Return* 41
Help us to tell Her tales of years gone by, . . 107 *Farewell* 49
I'll tell him many tales of Thee." . . . . . 121 *Emigrant Mother* 95
Of those domestic tales that spake to me . . . 131 *Michael* 22
Telling tales about the sun, ... 160 **Pansies, lilies* 31
But in Man's fortunes. Hence a thousand tales . 170 **Never enlivened* 18
And with him many tales he brought . . . . 192 *Ruth* 44
Such tales as told to any maid . . . . . . 192 *Ruth* 46
Bring tales of distant lands. . . . . . . 295 *Highland Boy* 70
And of those tales, whate'er they were, . . . 295 *Highland Boy* 71
By tales of love and sorrow, ... 386 *Yarrow Rev.* 66
And heard old tales by the convent-fire, . . . 398 *White Doe* 220
No tales of Runagates fresh landed, whence . . 522 *Epist. Beaumont* 61
Sang youthful tales of shepherds and their flocks ; 547 **Beneath yon* 12
By the strong mind, and tales of warlike feats, . 634 *Prelude* 1. 176
Heard him, while birds were warbling, tell his tales 653 *Prelude* 3. 277
A slender abstract of the Arabian tales ; . . . 672 *Prelude* 5. 462
The tales that charm away the wakeful night . . 673 *Prelude* 5. 496
Forgers of daring tales ! we bless you then, . . 673 *Prelude* 5. 524
Tales of the May-pole dance, and wreaths that decked . . . . 701 *Prelude* 8. 151
Myself from frequent perils ; nor were tales . . 701 *Prelude* 8. 168
Tales of the poets, as it made the heart . . . 712 *Prelude* 9. 206

Taliesin. The song of Taliesin ;—Ours shall mourn 421 *Ecc. Sonn.* 1. 12. 4

Taliesin's. Nor Taliesin's unforgotten lays, . . . 419 *Ecc. Sonn.* 1. 5. 10

Talk. Talk, laughter, and perchance a church-tower knell : . . . . 18 *Desc. Sk.* 420
To traveller who might talk of any casual theme. 26 *Guilt* 99
Oh, Sir, you would not talk thus, if you knew . 45 *Bord.* 418
Lord Clifford—did you see him talk with Herbert ? 47 *Bord.* 537
I talk familiarly to you, sweet Lady ! . . . . 50 *Bord.* 693
Would lead me to talk fondly. Do not fear ; . 52 *Bord.* 831
Blown to you from a trumpet. Why talk thus ? 56 *Bord.* 1013
About you still ; you talk of solitude— . . . 64 *Bord.* 1477
And held such intermitted talk . . . . . 85 *Anecdote* 7
We talk about the dead by our fire-sides. . . 98 *Brothers* 179
This is sad talk—they'll never sound for him— . 100 *Brothers* 315
We'll talk of sunshine and of song, ... 106 **I've watched* 16
'Twere better to be dumb than to talk thus. . . 134 *Michael* 241
To whom I sometimes in our idle talk . . . . 146 **It was an* 43
That they, with whom you once were happy, talk 147 *Joanna* 16
Daisy ! again I talk to thee, ... 158 **With little* 3
Among the Ruins, but no idle talk . . . . . 283 **Well have* 3
Books, leisure, perfect freedom, and the talk . . 304 **I grieved* 10
And rests not thankful ? Whether cheered by talk 389 *Glencroe* 4
To season my fireside with personal talk,— . . 488 *Pers. Talk* 2
And, for silence or for talk, ... 490 *Incident : Dog* 5
And ever thus he to himself would talk :— . . 564 *Troilus* 150
And, far beneath, Banditti voices talk ; . . . 606 *Desc.Sk.Quarto* 234
Unprofitable talk at morning hours ; . . . . 652 *Prelude* 3. 249
Her talk, her business, pleased me ; and no less . 661 *Prelude* 4. 224
Sprinkling this talk with questions, better spared, 665 *Prelude* 4. 438
Upon that meagre soil, helped out by talk . . 711 *Prelude* 9. 99
To ruminate, with interchange of talk, . . . 715 *Prelude* 9. 394
And, after ordinary travellers' talk . . . . 746 *Prelude* 14. 16
I talk—and ye are standing in the sun . . . 781 *Excursion* 2. 635
Which States and Kingdoms utter when they talk 828 *Excursion* 5. 380
With him can talk ; nor blush to waste a word . 834 *Excursion* 5. 818
The mid-day hours with desultory talk ; . . . 882 *Excursion* 8. 521
Can talk and speechify) . . . . S.3. 431 **The Scottish* 12
With any who could talk of common things . . . K.8. 230 **I will* 190

Talked. We talked of marriage and our marriage day ; 29 *Guilt* 250
And we were comforted, and talked of comfort ; . 50 *Bord.* 709
We talked of change, of winter gone, ... 81 †*Mother's Return* 37
And, as we talked, I questioned him . . . . 86 *Anecdote* 27

Talked—*continued.*
Shed when he talked of them where they were not, 99 *Brothers* 231
He talked about him with a cheerful love. . . 101 *Brothers* 391
And all that to herself she talked, ... 128 *Idiot Boy* 205
Unworthy things she talked, and wild ; . . . 128 *Idiot Boy*.239
She talked and sung the woods among, . . . 144 *Her Eyes* 9
And, while he talked of blows and scars, . . . 180 *Waggoner* 3. 138
Last Christmas-eve we talked of this, ... 199 *Thorn* 137
Have sate and talked where gowans blow, . . 285 *Grave of Burns* 53
We talked with open heart, and tongue . . . 487 *Fountain* 1
We sauntered, played, or rioted ; we talked . . 652 *Prelude* 3. 248
With these defenders of the Crown, and talked, . 712 *Prelude* 9. 195
To cheer us both. But long we had not talked . 766 *Excursion* 1. 686
Enkindled by the sun. He sate—and talked . . 811 *Excursion* 4. 638
The sound of titled names, and talked in glee . 860 *Excursion* 7. 217
Talking. To hear a stranger talking about strangers, 99 *Brothers* 236
The Housewife answered, talking much of things 136 *Michael* 318
Thus talking of that Peasant, we approached . . 149 **A narrow* 55
The old Man still stood talking by my side ; . . 197 *Resolution* 106
While he was talking thus, the lonely place, . . 197 *Resolution* 127
The talking boat that moves with pensive sound, 597 *Ev. Wk. Quarto* 319
And talking voices, and the low of herds, . . . 611 *Desc.Sk.Quarto* 507
And talking to itself when all things else . . . 660 *Prelude* 4. 120
A correspondence with the talking world . . . 742 *Prelude* 13. 173
To tread for pastime, talking with his mates, . . 805 *Excursion* 4. 248
Talks. He talks of a transition in his Soul, . . . 58 *Bord.* 1165
In loving words he talks to him, ... 249 *P. B.* 1113
Dreams on the banks, and to the river talks. . . 477 *Nunnery* 12
Whom the fifth Harry talks of. Silence ! hush ! 694 *Prelude* 7. 498
Tall. And swings above the roof the poplar tall. 6 *Ev. Wk.* 241
Charmed the tall circle of the enchanted steeps. . 7 *Ev. Wk.* 304
The tall sun, pausing on an Alpine spire, . . . 20 *Desc. Sk.* 553
On the tall peaks the glistening sunbeams play, . 22 *Desc. Sk.* 668
Lank as a ghost and tall, his shoulders bent, . . 45 *Bord.* 461
That does not play you false.—On that tall pike . 97 *Brothers* 139
Majestic in her person, tall and straight ; . . . 119 *Sailor's Mother* 5
And, when we came in front of that tall rock . . 147 *Joanna* 42
And the tall Steep of Silver-how, sent forth . . 147 *Joanna* 58
Fair ferns and flowers, and chiefly that tall fern, . 149 **A narrow* 33
The tall and upright figure of a Man . . . . 149 **A narrow* 47
Of tallest hollies, tall and green ; . . . . . 154 **A whirl-blast* 7
And Ghimmer-crag, his tall twin brother, . . . 180 *Waggoner* 4. 21
Tall and erect, with tempting clusters hung, . . 185 *Nutting* 20
That tall Man, a giant in bulk and in height, . . 189 *Music* 33
She had a tall man's height or more ; . . . . 190 *Beggars* 1
And, near the fountain, flowers of stature tall 202 *Hart-leap* 85
Haunted me like a passion : the tall rock, . . 206 *Tintern* 77
The trees' tall summits withered at the sight ; . 212 *Laod.* 173
Of that tall rock, as from a hidden world, . . . 229 *Clouds* 3
Tall trees, green arbours, and ground-flowers in flocks ; . . . . 260 **How sweet* 4
Gleams on the grass-crowned top of yon tall Tower, 283 **Here, where* 11
Each with a lance, erect and tall, ... 404 *White Doe* 722
Of close-clipt foliage green and tall, ... 407 *White Doe* 988
Mark him, of shoulders curved, and stature tall, . 422 *Ecc. Sonn.* 1. 15. 5
Watching, with upward eye, the tall tower grow . 451 *Ecc. Sonn.* 3. 42. 7
Him found we not : but, climbing a tall tower, . 472 **The captive* 4
The redbreast sings from the tall larch . . . 482 *Sister* 3
'Tis said he once was tall. . . . . 483 *Simon Lee* 4
Attained a stature twice a tall man's height, . . 521 *Epist.Beaumont* 15
Whence the tall window drinks the morning rays ; 535 **When in* 24
Tall were the flowers, the grove a lofty cover, 557 *Cuck.and Night.* 64
Survive upon the tall mast's height ; . . . . 579 **Sweet Flower* 47
Charms the tall circle of th' enchanted steeps. . 598 *Ev. Wk. Quarto* 350
—The tall Sun, tip-toe on an Alpine spire, . . 614 *Desc.Sk.Quarto* 662
Of a tall ash, that near our cottage stood ; . . 659 *Prelude* 4. 89
Myself unseen. He was of stature tall, . . . 664 *Prelude* 4. 391
A span above man's common measure, tall, . . 664 *Prelude* 4. 392
And that monastic castle, 'mid tall trees, . . . 678 *Prelude* 6. 205
There, too, conspicuous for stature tall . . . 692 *Prelude* 7. 342
Upwards through every stage of the tall stem, . 705 *Prelude* 8. 394
To measure the altitude of some tall crag . . . 760 *Excursion* 1. 274
Where two tall hedge-rows of thick alder boughs . 763 *Excursion* 1. 460
From these tall elms ; the cottage-clock struck eight ;— . . . . 767 *Excursion* 1. 749
A meagre person, tall, and in a garb . . . . 779 *Excursion* 2. 500
Of a tall rock, their airy citadel— . . . . . 786 *Excursion* 3. 4
A tall and shining holly, that had found . . . 787 *Excursion* 3. 62
Upon the tall mast streaming. But, ye Powers . 798 *Excursion* 3. 842
Tall was her stature ; her complexion dark . . 848 *Excursion* 6. 678
Stands a tall ash-tree ; to whose topmost twig . 851 *Excursion* 6. 863
Of that tall pine, the shadow of whose bare . . 863 *Excursion* 7. 396
—And yon tall pine-tree, whose composing sound 864 *Excursion* 7. 477
Tall ash-tree, sown by winds, by vapours nursed, 866 *Excursion* 7. 596
Along a hedge of hollies dark and tall, ... 880 *Excursion* 8. 442
Through tall green silent woods and ruins grey. . S.3. 417 **Sweet was* 14
Deep pools, tall trees, black chasms, and dizzy crags, ... K.8. 256 *Recluse* 1.1.711
Taller. How 'twill burn down the taller ; and they all 65 *Bord.* 1514
Was two years taller : 'twas a joy to see, . . . 99 *Brothers* 250
The taller followed with his hat in hand, . . . 191 *Beggars* 23
Tallest. Shall prey upon the tallest. Solitude !— . 65 *Bord.* 1515
Of tallest hollies, tall and green ; . . . . . 154 **A whirl-blast* 7
For dwarfs the tallest seem while sailing by, . . 471 *Ailsa Crag* 8
Tam. Nor heat, at Tam o'Shanter's name, their blood) . . . . 255 *Detraction* 6
Tame. Did my pride tame my pride ;—for many days, 68 *Bord.* 1697
That less than power unbounded could not tame 330 *Ode : Thanks.* 94
" My Art shall help to tame her pride— " . . 369 *Eg. Maid* 28
Kennelled and chained. Ye tame domestic fowl, . 472 *Dunolly Eagle* 7
Of Faith, which doth all passions tame . . . 543 *Russ. Fug.* 173

Tame—*continued.*
Nor needs a warning voice to tame the pride . . 642 *Prelude* 2. 20
Too weak for suffering, and for hope too tame) . 791 *Excursion* 3. 345
Tamed. *See* **Well-tamed.**
Of fancy shall be quickly tamed by mine ; . . 73 *Bord.* 2037
My pride was tamed, and in our grief . . . . 115 *Last of Flock* 43
Was softened into feeling, soothed, and tamed. . 205 *Brougham* 160
He tamed, who foolishly aspires ; . . . . . 291 *Rob Roy* 46
When I have borne in memory what has tamed . 307 **When I* 1
By fortune crushed, or tamed by grief ; . . . 473 *Ossian* 76
There the Saracens were tamed. . . . . . 535 *Egremont* 44
What birds she tamed, what flowers the ground . 544 *Russ. Fug.* 207
Tam'd " sober Reason " till she crouch'd in fear ? 603 *Desc.Sk.Quarto* 56
Great joy by horror tam'd dilates his heart, . . 612 *Desc.Sk.Quarto* 560
Tamed to their bidding ; they who have the skill 671 *Prelude* 5. 350
To custom, mettlesome, and not yet tamed . . 673 *Prelude* 5. 521
But had not tamed his eye ; that, under brows . 762 *Excursion* 1. 428
But me hath Nature tamed, and bade to seek K.8. 256 *Recluse* 1.1.726
Tamer. Nor checked by aught of tamer argument, 688 *Prelude* 7. 50
To gather, ranging through the tamer ground . 771 *Excursion* 2. 23
Tames. In rich reward all suffering ; Balm that tames 253 **Fond words* 6
Last lingering look of clay, that tames . . . 372 *Eg. Maid* 197
Brute rapine, or with gentle lure she tames. . 429 *Ecc. Sonn.* 2. 2. 6
The inviolable God, that tames the proud ! . . 477 *Long Meg* 14
Tamper. Tamper with conscience from a private aim; 748 *Prelude* 14. 151
Tangled. Through beds of matted fern, and tangled thickets, ... 185 *Nutting* 15
Through tangled woods, impending rocks between ; 382 *Duddon* 26. 3
The tangled root I severed, ... 484 *Simon Lee* 86
No sheltering stone, no tangled root was near. . 528 **Those breathing* 53
The tangled covert fell. . . . . 544 *Russ. Fug.* 272
Tankards. What tankards foaming from the tap ! 177 *Waggoner* 2. 58
Tantalus. By Tantalus entailed upon his race, . . 846 *Excursion* 6. 543
Tap. What tankards foaming from the tap ! . . 177 *Waggoner* 2. 58
Taper. Nor taper glimmered dim from sick man's room ; . . . . 26 *Guilt* 142
To show her taper in the gloom, ... 167 *Pilgrim's Dream* 29
—The light had left the lonely taper, ... 244 *P. B.* 748
So burns yon Taper 'mid a black recess . . . 266 **Even as* 4
And this forgotten Taper to the last . . . . 391 *Brownie* 13
When fire or taper ceased to cheer the room, . . 528 **Those breathing* 54
By clearer taper lit a cleanlier board . . . . 615 *Desc.Sk.Quarto* 736
By moonshine through mere lack of taper light. . 656 *Prelude* 3. 478
Clear-shining, like a hermit's taper seen . . . 687 *Prelude* 7. 35
Grieved, and the twilight taper, and the cross 716 *Prelude* 9. 475
With unextinguished taper I kept watch, . . . 719 *Prelude* 10. 70
Look down upon your taper, through a watch . 808 *Excursion* 4. 485
The unguarded taper where the guarded faints ? . 813 *Excursion* 4. 773
Tapering. Left at the tapering ladder's top, that seemed . . . . 705 *Prelude* 8. 397
Taper-light. And, communed with by taper-light, . 544 *Russ. Fug.* 215
Taper-lights. The taper-lights, and curls in clouds . 228 *Devot. Incit.* 33
Taper's. It chanced that by a taper's light . . . 244 *P. B.* 739
To guide his dangerous tread the taper's gleam. . 607 *Desc.Sk.Quarto* 316
Tapers. Join twenty tapers of unequal height . . 65 *Bord.* 1512
Where tapers burned, and mass was sung, . . 298 *Brownie's Cell* 17
Touch not the tapers of the sacred quires ; . . 426 *Ecc. Sonn.* 1. 31. 11
The tapers burn ; the odorous incense feeds . . 431 *Ecc. Sonn.* 2. 11. 2
The tapers shall be quenched, the belfries mute, . 433 *Ecc. Sonn.* 2. 21. 3
Or lonely tapers when from far they fling . . 441 *Ecc. Sonn.* 3. 5. 11
See how dying tapers fare ! . . . . 549 *Hermit's Cell* 1. 10
And glancing forms, and tapers glittering, . . 663 *Prelude* 4. 314
Their vigils kept ; where tapers day and night 877 *Excursion* 8. 188
Tar. Nor did the battered Tar forget, ... 178 *Waggoner* 2. 157
" Ay," said the Tar, " through fair and foul— 179 *Waggoner* 3. 97
Taranis. To Taranis erected on the heights . . . 894 *Excursion* 9. 704
Tardily. Tardily sinking by its proper weight . . 380 *Duddon* 17. 13
Tardy. Approaching, and upbraid the tardy gale ; 15 *Desc. Sk.* 251
That every naked ash, and tardy tree . . . . 146 **It was an* 14
Rise, tardy Sun ! and let the Songster prove . . 279 **'Tis he* 9
Why should the Song be tardy to proclaim . . 330 *Ode : Thanks.* 93
Furl we the sails, and pass with tardy oars . . 430 *Ecc. Sonn.* 2. 8. 1
Of tardy penitents ; or for the best . . . . 467 *St. Bees* 67
Post seaward,—what impedes the tardy nights. . 625 *Æneid* 129
A tardy apprehension. From a fount . . . . 834 *Excursion* 5. 786
Their tardy steps give leisure to observe, . . . 875 *Excursion* 8. 54
Tarentum. Of proud Tarentum, proud to share the fame . . . . L.2. 120 *Frag.Æneid* 1.2
Target. Before the target stood—to claim . . . 342 *Ital. Itin* 61
The target mouldering like ungathered fruit ; . . 388 **The pibroch's* 4
Tarn. *See* **Bowscale-tarn, Loughrigg-tarn.**
A silent tarn below ! . . . . 491 *Fidelity* 20
Send through the tarn a lonely cheer ; . . . . 491 *Fidelity* 26
By a brook-side or solitary tarn, ... 868 *Excursion* 7. 719
Leaving St. Sunday's Crag, to Grisdale tarn . K.8. 225 **I will* 25
Tarpeian. Tarpeian named of yore, and keeping still 358 **Is this* 3
Tarried. They tarried in the wood together. . . 414 *White Doe* 1683
Where hast thou tarried, Hector ? from what coast L.2. 318 *Frag. Æneid* 4. 3
Tarries. Why tarries then thy chariot ? Wherefore stay, ... 440 *Ecc. Sonn.* 2. 45. 9
Tarry. Why can he tarry *yonder* ?—In our church-yard 95 *Brothers* 12
He comes to tarry with thee three hours' space ; . 209 *Laod.* 23
Upon the signs that pass away or tarry ; . . . 374 *Eg. Maid* 338
Balanced in ether he will never tarry, ... 472 *Dunolly Eagle* 11
I may not tarry here ! . . . . 542 *Russ. Fug.* 72
Pray also thou for us, while here we tarry . . 556 *Prioress* 236
Tarrying. No tarrying ; where She comes the winds must stir : . . . . 258 **With Ships* 13
Immediately he came, not tarrying, ... 555 *Prioress* 166
Tarrying at will in many a pleasant spot . . . 751 *Prelude* 14. 352

Taught—*continued.*
Of soft Epicureans, taught—if they 791 *Excursion* 3. 348
By nature's gradual processes be taught ; 805 *Excursion* 4. 288
Its cares and sorrows ; he, though taught to own 809 *Excursion* 4. 546
By their condition taught, can understand 813 *Excursion* 4. 787
And from the mansions where our youth was taught. 814 *Excursion* 4. 896
But taught with patient interest to watch 820 *Excursion* 4. 1257
To heaven, I know, by my Redeemer taught.' 835 *Excursion* 5. 826
Now, by experience taught, he stands assured, 855 *Excursion* 6. 1133
Were taught a base submission.—' Here behold 869 *Excursion* 7. 800
That the whole people should be taught and trained. 889 *Excursion* 9. 358
It must not be, if I, divinely taught, K.8. 255 *Recluse* 1.1.700
Taunt. Much did it taunt the humble Light 167 *Pilgrim's Dream* 25
By sharp resentment, or belike to taunt 718 *Prelude* 10. 35
The blame is ours, not Nature's. When a taunt 725 *Prelude* 10. 470
Triumphantly dispersing with the taunt 786 *Excursion* 3. 11
Taunting. Aloft in sign of taunting scorn, 410 *White Doe* 1326
Parading with a song of taunting rhymes, 701 *Prelude* 8. 148
Tauntingly. His outstretched hand He tauntingly withdraws— 378 *Duddon* 10. 7
Taunts. " Dread not their taunts, my little Life ; 145 *Her Eyes* 71
With scoffs and taunts, like Vulcan out of heaven : 640 *Prelude* 1. 531
Tavern. A tavern stood ; no homely-featured house, 644 *Prelude* 2. 140
Of Tavern, Brothel, Gaming-house, and Shop, 710 *Prelude* 9. 54
Tavern-door. Up to the tavern-door we post ; 82 *Alice Fell* 53
Tawny. On tawny earth, wild weeds, and twisted roots ; 5 *Ev. Wk.* 187
The lion roars and gluts his tawny brood 25 *Guilt* 65
Half wasted the square mound of tawny green ; 202 *Hart-leap* 110
Yon tawny slip is Libya's sands ; 237 *P. B.* 61
To naturalise this tawny Lion brood ; 392 *Daniel* 4
Her tawny skin, dark eyes, and glossy locks, 605 *Desc. Sk. Quarto* 190
Tax. Heaven will not tax our thoughts with pride 228 *Devot. Incit.* 11
Tax not the royal Saint with vain expense, 451 *Ecc. Sonn.* 3. 43. 1
Or tax high Heaven with prodigality ?) 501 **The unremitting* 9
Through courteous self-submission, as a tax 689 *Prelude* 7. 147
To tax you with this journey ; "—mildly said 779 *Excursion* 2. 487
Taxed. Nor ever taxed them with the ill 194 *Ruth* 221
Days of sweet leisure, taxed with patient thought 632 *Prelude* 1. 43
With obligation charged, with service taxed, 798 *Excursion* 3. 840
Nor crowded city can be taxed with aught 880 *Excursion* 8. 422
Taxes. Fame taxes him,) that he could send forth word 292 **Degenerate Douglas* 4
Tay. Had trod the banks of Clyde, and Tay, 292 *Yarrow Unv.* 3
On the green margin of Loch Tay, S.3. 438 **My Lord* 8
Taylor. Nor Miss Taylor, Captain Stamp, S.3. 438 **My Lord* 5
Te. Chant in full choir their innocent Te Deum. 367 **If with* 14
Teach. Has given him power to teach : and then for courage 38 *Bord.* 36
And most despise the men who best can teach us : 54 *Bord.* 909
An instrument of falsehood, should he teach her 56 *Bord.* 1045
Had strength to teach ;—and therefore gratitude 64 *Bord.* 1482
It shall be for a nobler end—to teach 65 *Bord.* 1558
Could I but teach the hundredth part 86 *Anecdote* 59
Then shall love teach some virtuous Youth 110 **Look at* 19
O teach me calm submission to thy Will ! 118 *Maternal Grief* 13
There's more in words than I can teach : 142 †*Lov. and Lik.* 1
" I'll teach my boy the sweetest things : 145 *Her Eyes* 81
I'll teach him how the owlet sings. 145 *Her Eyes* 82
Is it to teach her own soft lore, 168 *Turtledove* 7
And teach us to beware. 225 *Present.* 24
When will your trials teach you to be wise ? 330 *Ode : Thanks.* 125
That builds, as thy unerring precepts teach, 331 *Ode : Thanks.* 173
" May teach him to bewail his loss ; 373 *Eg. Maid* 259
Teach what *they* learn ? Up, hardy Mountaineer ! 389 *Tyndrum* 9
To teach her salutary fears 407 *White Doe* 1031
Who teach the intrepid guardians of the place— 430 *Ecc. Sonn.* 2. 6. 10
Have long borne witness as the Scriptures teach ?— 431 *Ecc. Sonn.* 2. 12. 2
Ye have no skill to teach, or if ye know 433 *Ecc. Sonn.* 2. 18. 9
Teach me with quick-eared spirit to rejoice 454 **The Sun, that* 19
And if the Motto on thy 'scutcheon teach 478 **Lonsdale ! it* 9
May teach you more of man, 481 *Tables Turned* 22
And Thou wouldst teach him how to find 485 **Bright Flower* 13
Yes ! where Love nestles thou canst teach 506 **While from* 49
Thought that should teach the zealot to forego 516 **As leaves* 5
Support us, teach us calmly to resign 576 **Six months* 5
To teach their limbs along the burning road 596 *Ev. Wk. Quarto* 249
To teach the skirt of thy dark cloud to shine ; 615 *Desc. Sk. Quarto* 708
To teach, on rapid wings, the curious soul 619 *School Ex.* 73
Teach from the heart the tender tear to flow ; 619 *School Ex.* 92
And He will teach thy people to obey. 628 **Deign, Sovereign* 12
I called on both to teach me what they might ; 650 *Prelude* 3. 112
And things that teach as Nature teaches : then, 669 *Prelude* 5. 231
Could teach, admonish ; suffered with the rest 703 *Prelude* 8. 290
Feelingly watched, might teach Man's haughty race 734 *Prelude* 12. 12
Where it is due : thus haply shall I teach, 743 *Prelude* 13. 238
And teach the little birds to build their nests 749 *Prelude* 14. 255
Others will love, and we will teach them how ; 752 *Prelude* 14. 447
Urged by his Mother, he essayed to teach 761 *Excursion* 1. 312
Above what rules can teach, or fancy feign ; 792 *Excursion* 3. 434
When they shall meet no object but may teach 819 *Excursion* 4. 1236
Nothing to praise, to teach, or to command ! 878 *Excursion* 8. 275
An obligation, on her part, to *teach* 888 *Excursion* 9. 297
Why do they teach me whom I thus revere ? K.8. 255 *Recluse* 1.1.680
Teacher. Young as I am, I might go forth a teacher, 59 *Bord.* 1223
Enlightened Teacher, gladly from thy hand 281 *Chris. Words.* 1

Teacher—*continued.*
When this low Pile a Gospel Teacher knew, 380 *Duddon* 18. 10
Let Nature be your Teacher. 481 *Tables Turned* 16
Long yet may'st thou live ! for a teacher we see 572 *Avarice* 47
As her prime teacher, intercourse with man 666 *Prelude* 5. 14
Grave Teacher, stern Preceptress ! for at times 707 *Prelude* 8. 530
An honoured teacher of my youth was laid, 726 *Prelude* 10. 534
From which the gallant teacher would discourse, 869 *Excursion* 7. 786
To stop, and yield our gracious Teacher thanks 873 *Excursion* 7. 1052
Teacher's. How the bold Teacher's Doctrine, sanctified 433 *Ecc. Sonn.* 2. 17. 13
Teachers. His daily teachers had been woods and rills, 205 *Brougham* 162
Dogmatic Teachers, of the snow-white fur ! 268 **Dogmatic Teachers* 1
Beheld long-bearded teachers, with white wands 745 *Prelude* 13. 345
Teaches. Whose practice teaches, spite of names to show 530 *Poor Robin* 22
And things that teach as Nature teaches : then, 669 *Prelude* 5. 231
Sincere, and humble spirit, teaches love : 806 *Excursion* 4. 345
It teaches less to love, than to adore ; 806 *Excursion* 4. 349
Teaching. Or watch, with mutual teaching, 190 **Lyre ! though* 29
Teaching the docile waters how to turn, 269 *Gordale* 12
Teaching us to forget them or forgive. 449 *Ecc. Sonn.* 3. 35. 10
That furthered the first teaching of St. Bees. 468 *St. Bees* 162
Of teaching comprehension with delight, 657 *Prelude* 3. 557
Through ignorance and false teaching, sadder proof 721 *Prelude* 10. 215
Teaching some Novice of the sisterhood 856 *Excursion* 6. 1182
Team. While the sharp slope the slackened team confounds, 4 *Ev. Wk.* 134
From ringing team apart and grating wain— 12 *Desc. Sk.* 82
And with his team is gentle here 174 *Waggoner* 1. 101
My jolly team, he finds that ye 174 *Waggoner* 1. 118
Then grieve not, jolly team ! though tough 175 *Waggoner* 1. 138
Apparent now beside his team— 180 *Waggoner* 4. 67
Was from his team and waggon parted ; 182 *Waggoner* 4. 184
To ringing team unknown and grating wain, 603 *Desc. Sk. Quarto* 85
A team of horses, with a ponderous freight 865 *Excursion* 7. 542
Nor fail to note the Man who guides the team." 865 *Excursion* 7. 549
Tear. Still the cold cheek its shuddering tear retains. 8 *Ev. Wk.* 322
And watered duly with the pious tear, 14 *Desc. Sk.* 203
And ravenous plague, all perished : every tear 30 *Guilt* 304
Seemed to return, dried the last lingering tear, 30 *Guilt* 321
Nor could his sunken eyes the starting tear restrain. 33 *Guilt* 495
Ere *I* can shed a tear. I was a woman ; 66 *Bord.* 1613
Long did he reign ; and, when he died, the tear 105 *Artegal* 232
From her sunk eyes a stagnant tear 113 *Lament* 66
And he went to the chase with a tear on his cheek. 120 *Childless Father* 20
Blest, though every tear that falls 141 *Arm. Lady* 130
A solitary tear : 193 *Ruth* 99
Brush the too happy tear ? 220 *Triad* 60
No unavailing tear. 223 *Wishing-gate* 54
Fame sheds the exulting tear ; 224 **'Tis gone* 15
The tear whose source I could not guess, 225 *Present.* 7
And voice and shell drew forth a tear 234 *Power of Sound* 119
'Tis lodged within her silent tear. 238 *P. B.* 150
Intruders—who would tear from Nature's book 250 *Admon.* 7
While trees, dim-seen, in frenzied numbers, tear 263 *Storm* 6
Bright, speckless as a softly-moulded tear 265 **There is a pleasure* 12
Disperse the tear, or to the sigh give vent, 273 **When Philoctetes* 6
Unrecognised through many a household tear 276 *Author's Portrait* 10
The tear will start, and let it flow ; 285 *Grave of Burns* 49
Would keep, perhaps with many a fruitless tear, 310 *Invasion* 11
Such spectacle demands not tear or sigh. 316 **Hail, Zaragoza* 4
By one soft trickling tear that stole 334 **In Bruges* 35
On Marathonian valour, yet the tear 339 *Tell* 3
Now that the farewell tear is dried, 341 *Ital. Itin.* 1
Whom grief hath spared—who sheds no tear 344 **How blest* 11
And the tear precious in compassion shed 395 *White Doe : Ded.* 10
The stifled sigh, the hidden tear, 401 *White Doe* 498
The name untouched, the tear unshed ;— 410 *White Doe* 1306
Heart-touched, and haply not without a tear. 426 *Ecc. Sonn.* 1. 30. 8
So huge a host !)—to tear from the Unbeliever 427 *Ecc. Sonn.* 1. 34. 13
O lost too early for the frequent tear, 445 *Ecc. Sonn.* 3. 22. 13
Into the shedding of " too soft a tear." 465 **The cattle* 14
The tear in answer flows ; 479 *Somnamb.* 78
And if a sleeping tear should wake, 486 *Matthew* 13
Let fall a brightened tear. 507 *May* 24
——But why this stealing tear ? Companion mute, 510 *F. Stone* 129
Into that world where penitential tear 519 *Pun. Death* 10. 6
Shall with a thankful tear bedrop its latest page. 529 **Those breathing* 140
Whose eye reflects it, glistening through a tear 540 *Grace Darl.* 12
Self-hidden praise, and Friendship's private tear : 547 **Ye Lime* 12
One heart-relieving tear may claim ; 577 *Cenotaph* 8
When Transport kiss'd away my april tear, 592 *Ev. Wk. Quarto* 29
Starts at the simplest sight th' unbidden tear, 592 *Ev. Wk. Quarto* 44
And, bending, water'd with the human tear, 606 *Desc. Sk. Quarto* 258
Her seal, the mortal tear his cheek has wet ; 613 *Desc. Sk. Quarto* 629
Teach from the heart the tender tear to flow ; 619 *School Ex.* 92
That tear proclaims—in thee each virtue dwells, 619 **She wept* 9
And the motion unsettles a tear ; 621 *Convict* 42
Wherever man is found ? The trickling tear 668 *Prelude* 5. 188
Oh ! much have they to account for, who could tear, 722 *Prelude* 10. 300
Why should a tear be on an old Man's cheek ? 765 *Excursion* 1. 598
With tiny finger—to let fall a tear ; 826 *Excursion* 5. 265
Tearful. —Now with joy's tearful kiss each other greet, 614 *Desc. Sk. Quarto* 666
Tear-glazed. And, fastening on those lines an eye tear-glazed, 394 *Countess' Pillar* 13

Tearing. Tearing their bleeding ties leaves Age to groan . . . . 613 Desc.Sk.Quarto 612
Tearless. Urns without ashes, tearless lacrymals ! . 394 *How profitless 14
Tearless, yet full of grief. —How heavenly fair . [?] *A sad 2
Tears. Thy flooded cheek to wet them with its tears ; 7 Ev. Wk. 276
No tears can chill them, and no bosom warms, . 7 Ev. Wk. 277
Bent o'er the groaning flood that sweeps away his tears. . . . . 11 Desc. Sk. 62
While his eyes sparkle with heroic tears. . . . 15 Desc. Sk. 288
And some with tears of joy each other greet. . . 20 Desc. Sk. 562
Till his eye streamed with tears. In this deep vale 23 Yew-tree 46
In her full lap, he sees such sweet tears flow . . 25 Guilt 62
I could not pray :—through tears that fell in showers . . . . 28 Guilt 242
What tears of bitter grief, till then unknown, . 29 Guilt 255
And tears which flowed for ills which patience might not heal. . . . . 29 Guilt 270
In such dismay my prayers and tears were vain : 29 Guilt 277
" Through tears the rising sun I oft have viewed, 32 Guilt 442
Through tears have seen him towards that world descend . . . . 32 Guilt 443
The stranger's looks and tears of wrath beguiled . 33 Guilt 500
Struggled with tears nor could its sorrow ease, . 34 Guilt 535
And saw the tears with which she blotted it. . . 38 Bord. 54
Of peace and order. Aged men with tears . . 48 Bord. 612
Filled my dim eyes with tears.—When I returned 49 Bord. 684
Even to the shedding of some natural tears . . 51 Bord. 762
Should he, by tales which would draw tears from iron, ... 57 Bord. 1060
And for his sake I loved her more : these tears— 61 Bord. 1323
And said, with tears, that he would be our guide : 62 Bord. 1367
Eleanor, I have shed tears to-night, ... 71 Bord. 1913
Of penitential anguish, yea with tears. . . . 78 Bord. 2305
A heart, the fountain of sweet tears ; . . . . 79 Sparrow's Nest 19
By sudden pangs ; what bitter tears have on this pavement dropt ! . . . . 92 Poet's Dream 52
Tears down his cheek, or solitary smiles . . . 97 Brothers 110
Two fathers in one father : and if tears, . . . 99 Brothers 230
Had mingled tears of thine, ... 109 *Ere with 2
Tears due unto their own. . . . . 113 Lament 21
His cheeks with tears were wet : . . . . . 114 Last of Flock 8
To wipe those briny tears away. . . . . . 114 Last of Flock 14
He makes my tears to flow. . . . . 115 Last of Flock 18
I've wet my path with tears like dew, ... 117 Affl. Marg. 34
Those willing tears, and unforbidden sighs, . . 119 Maternal Grief 77
Mine art thou—spite of these my tears. . . . 120 EmigrantMother 38
The nurse said to me, ' Tears should not . . . 121 EmigrantMother 41
These tears—and my poor idle tongue. . . . 121 EmigrantMother 78
Such tears she never shed before ; . . . . . 129 Idiot Boy 298
A few sad tears does Betty shed. . . . . . 130 Idiot Boy 386
The Mother mourned, nor ceased her tears to flow, 139 Widow 15
If it end in tears and sighs ; . . . . 140 Arm. Lady 20
Tears not wanting, nor a knell . . . . . . 140 Arm. Lady 76
By the heart of Man, his tears, ... 157 Sexton 21
The voice of tears that fell unseen ; . . . . 176 Waggoner 1. 228
What tears of rapture, what vow-making, . . 179 Waggoner 3. 44
Praise, blame, love, kisses, tears, and smiles. . 186 *She was 20
O'er whom such thankful tears were shed . . . 204 Brougham 78
While tears were thy best pastime, day and night ; 211 Laod. 114
—Yet tears to human suffering are due ; . . . 212 Laod. 164
Where Pity sheds sweet tears—and Love, . . . 215 Kirkstone 70
—Tears had not broken from their source ; . . 227 Vernal Ode 129
Is Harmony, blest queen of smiles and tears, . . 235 Power of Sound 219
Suffices me—her tears, her mirth, ... 238 P. B. 134
Her humblest mirth and tears. . . . . . . 238 P. B. 135
Till you had kissed his tears away ! . . . . . 243 P. B. 635
He melted into tears. . . . . 247 P. B. 960
Sweet tears of hope and tenderness ! . . . . 247 P. B. 961
Distressed me ; from mine eyes escaped no tears ; 251 *Beloved Vale 7
Channels for tears ; no Naiad shouldst thou be,— 268 *Brook ! whose 9
Have gained a sanction from thy falling tears ; . 270 *If these 6
When thankfulness were best ?—Fresh-flowing tears, ... 271 George : Death 9
Or, where tears flow not, sigh succeeding sigh, . 271 George : Death 10
Tears of delight, that testified how true . . . 277 Author's Portrait 13
By precept only, and shed tears by rule. . . . 277 *A Poet 4
And yet my eyes are filled with tears. . . . . 288 Highland Girl 21
Tears flowed in torrents from her eyes ; . . . 297 Highland Boy 238
For whose dire ends tears flow, and blood is spilt, 321 *Here pause 11
And, though some tears the strain attended, . . 324 Ode 1814 87
Of love in the heart made more happy by tears ? 346 Stanzas:Simplon 32
His bitter tears, whose name the Papal Chair . 360 *Long has 13
Yet is there cause for gushing tears ; . . . . 370 Eg. Maid 61
And some unbidden tears that rise . . . . . 375 *The Minstrels 45
Tears brightened by the serenade . . . . . 375 *The Minstrels 47
Unsanctified our tears—made sport . . . . . 386 Yarrow Rev. 91
For woman, even of tears bereft, ... 391 HighlandBroach 59
But Praise can waste her voice on work of tears, 392 Avon 9
A tale of tears, a mortal story ! . . . . . . 399 White Doe 336
This said, our tears to-day may fall . . . . 401 White Doe 467
Ill tears she wept ; I saw them fall, ... 405 White Doe 874
This Cross in tears : by her, and One . . . . 405 White Doe 879
With tears, and of his Father prayed— . . . . 409 White Doe 1236
She melted into tears— . . . . 414 White Doe 1662
A flood of tears that flowed apace . . . . . 414 White Doe 1663
If tears are shed, they do not fall . . . . . 415 White Doe 1791
A few tears down her cheek descend . . . . . 415 White Doe 1795
O wretched Land ! whose tears have flowed like fountains ; . . . . 421 Ecc. Sonn. 1. 11. 7
Pride to be washed away by bitter tears ! . . . 432 Ecc. Sonn. 2. 16. 7
The tears of man in various measure gush . . 436 Ecc. Sonn. 2. 32. 1

Tears—continued.
That tears burst forth amain. Did gleams appear ? 446 Ecc. Sonn. 3. 24. 9
Deep in the thankful heart ;—yet tears will flow. 448 Ecc. Sonn. 3. 31. 8
Though it can wet with tears the hardiest cheek. 460 *Wanderer ! that 62
Bedewed with meditative tears . . . . . . 473 Ossian 61
The tears into his eyes were brought, ... 484 Simon Lee 89
The tears which came to Matthew's eyes . . . 486 Matthew 23
Were tears of light, the dew of gladness. . . . 486 Matthew 24
" My eyes are dim with childish tears, ... 487 Fountain 29
It came, and we were glad ; yet tears were shed ; 491 Tribute : Dog 21
Our tears from passion and from reason came, . 491 Tribute : Dog 35
Audible tears, from some invisible source . . . 498 *Enough of climbing 37
This thy First-born, and with tears . . . . 503 *Like a 55
With thy own blood, which tears in torrents shed 514 *Long-favoured 5
Fail to wash out, tears flowing ere thy troth . . 514 *Long-favoured 6
Their first look—blinded as tears fell in showers . 517 Pun. Death 1. 13
Tears of salvation. Welcome death ! while Heaven 520 Pun. Death 12. 9
Let me not ask what tears may have been wept . 525 Epist. Beaumont 258
As blameless pleasure, not without some tears, . 526 *Soon did 14
All that they think and feel, with tears of joy ; . 539 *Lady ! a 53
" My thanks with silent tears . . . . . . 542 Russ. Fug. 54
" Tears might be shed, and I might pray, . . . 545 Russ. Fug. 289
Kindled 'mid rapturous tears ; . . . . . . 545 Russ. Fug. 326
Heart-breaking tears, and melancholy dreams . 547 *Beneath yon 14
His salt tears trickled down like showers of rain ; 556 Prioress 223
And with that word, she into tears burst out. . 560 Cuck.and Night. 210
And tears of fifteen will come into his eyes. . . 570 Farmer 68
May read them not without some bitter tears. . 575 Chiabrera 7. 18
The eyes of all Savona streamed with tears. . . 575 Chiabrera 8. 9
And murder causes some sad tears to flow, . . 582 Invoc. Earth 16
No tears of passionate regret . . . . . . 582 *O for a 8
Inspired—works potent over smiles and tears. . 584 Ch. Lamb 17
Thoughts that do often lie too deep for tears. . 590 Immortality 207
And eyes through tears the mountain's shadeless height ; . . . . 596 Ev. Wk. Quarto 252
And swells the groaning torrent with his tears. . 603 Desc. Sk. Quarto 67
While burn in his full eyes the glorious tears. . 608 Desc.Sk.Quarto 351
And tears before him travel like a cloud. . . . 613 Desc.Sk.Quarto 637
Glimmers before my sight through thankful tears, 627 *The star 10
(Oh were it mine !) to hallow saddest tears, . . 628 *Deign, Sovereign 27
Glad welcome had I, with some tears, perhaps, . 658 Prelude 4. 27
Almost to tears I sometimes could be sad . . . 674 Prelude 5. 547
For penitential tears and trembling hopes . . . 682 Prelude 6. 454
Was more than full ; amid my sobs and tears . 694 Prelude 7. 471
Wetting the turf with never-ending tears. . . . 705 Prelude 8. 391
Pale and bedropped with everflowing tears. . . 710 Prelude 9. 80
Yet at this very moment do tears start . . . 713 Prelude 9. 267
I wept not then,—but tears have dimmed my sight, 713 Prelude 9. 269
Tears from the hearts of others, when their own . 717 Prelude 9. 567
Was laid with tears. Then suddenly the scene . 724 Prelude 10. 409
Came back upon me, so that some few tears . . 726 Prelude 10. 543
Whether by words, looks, sighs, or tears, revealed ; 742 Prelude 13. 165
When, after the first mingling of our tears . . 752 Prelude 14. 427
" This tale did Margaret tell with many tears : . 766 Excursion 1. 682
As if she had been shedding tears of joy. . . . 766 Excursion 1. 689
Weeping, and weeping have I waked ; my tears . 768 Excursion 1. 770
The tears stood in her eyes. I left her then . . 768 Excursion 1. 810
Perhaps is shedding orphan's tears ; you also . 779 Excursion 2. 541
Honour my little cell with some few tears . . . 783 Excursion 2. 803
At others' tears in pity ; and in scorn . . . 797 Excursion 3. 810
Ruefully seized, and shedding bitter tears, . . 827 Excursion 5. 339
As the sole spring and fountain-head of tears, . 837 Excursion 5. 981
And tears, in pride suppressed, in shame concealed— 849 Excursion 6. 714
Grieving for sin, and penitential tears . . . . 850 Excursion 6. 799
Of the fresh shower, but of poor Ellen's tears . 850 Excursion 6. 816
Bedropped with tears. 'Twill please you to be told 851 Excursion 6. 893
Of many tears, virtuous and thoughtful grief ; . 864 Excursion 7. 470
Due resignation. Therefore, though some tears . 868 Excursion 7. 689
With tears, that wept not then ; nor were the few, 871 Excursion 7. 883
Tears wipe away, and pleasant tidings bring ; . 875 Excursion 8. 80
Reason, and, with that reason, smiles and tears ; 887 Excursion 9. 222
Of tears that have been shed at sight of it, . . K.8. 248 Recluse 1.1.418
Insatiate Charlotte's tears, and Charlotte's smile. L.1. 89 Juvenal 1. 23
That moistened Dunkirk's sands with blood and tears, ... L.1. 96 Juvenal 3. 62
Tease. Our watchful house-dog, that would tease and tire . . . . 28 Guilt 223
Tease, and the thought of time so spent depress, . 584 Ch. Lamb 7
Teased. And doubts and scruples seldom teased the brain, ... 468 *Bold words 2
Had to his joy unearthed a hedgehog, teased . . 746 Prelude 14. 23
Teasing. His wife sate near him, teasing matted wool, 95 Brothers 21
Checked in your course by many a teasing burr ; 268* Dogmatic Teachers 5
Press forward by the teasing dogs unscared. . . 525 Epist. Beaumont 238
And teasing ways of children vexed not him ; . 762 Excursion 1. 416
Tedious. Would surely be a tedious tale. . . . 128 Idiot Boy 206
" Rocking as in a dream the tedious year ; " . . 592 Ev. Wk. Quarto 30
With fond and feeble tongue a tedious tale. . . 641 Prelude 1. 619
Grows tedious even in a young man's ear. . . 694 Prelude 7. 511
Proved tedious, and I gradually withdrew . . 711 Prelude 9. 121
'Tis long and tedious ; but my spirit clings . . 768 Excursion 1. 779
Into this tract again. Nine tedious years ; . . 769 Excursion 1. 871
—But why this tedious record ?—Age, we know, 791 Excursion 3. 325
Twelve tedious years ago, ... S.3. 431 *The Scottish 2
Relieves the tedious holiday of age—— . . . S.3. 435 *The doubt 139
Tedium. The tedium of fantastic idleness : . . . 829 Excursion 5. 430

Tenderly. Or care, that what so tenderly he pressed 125 *V. and J.* 234
Of him whom tenderly she loved. . . . . . 198 *Thorn* 110
With friends and kindred tenderly beloved ; . . 381 *Duddon* 21. 3
An aspect tenderly illumed, ... 498 **Departing summer* 2
Tenderly do we feel by Nature's law . . . . 517 *Pun. Death* 2. 1
A brother's Child, most tenderly beloved ! . . 575 *Chiabrera* 8. 5
How tenderly protected ! Far and near . . . 777 *Excursion* 2. 359
And, speaking thus, he patted tenderly . . . 779 *Excursion* 2. 529
To that same child, addressing tenderly . . . 789 *Excursion* 3. 227
A virtuous Lady tenderly beloved . . . . . 825 *Excursion* 5. 194
Where love and pity tenderly unite . . . . 848 *Excursion* 6. 642
Tenderness. To see him thus provoke her tenderness 41 *Bord.* 244
Words which tenderness can speak . . . . . 90 *Longest Day* 22
With a more fond, familiar, tenderness ; . . . 99 *Brothers* 246
Less from instinctive tenderness, the same . . 133 *Michael* 144
To acts of tenderness ; and he had rocked . . 133 *Michael* 157
Who look upon the hills with tenderness, . . . 147 *Joanna* 7
Sweet tears of hope and tenderness ! . . . . 247 *P. B.* 961
Of tenderness—the Wolf, whose suckling Twins 275 **While poring* 12
Oh, what a gush of tenderness was mine ! . . . 358 *Pine : Rome* 8
With tenderness and mild emotion, ... 371 *Eg. Maid* 140
With hopes in tenderness concealed, ... 408 *White Doe* 1113
Thence, also, more alive to tenderness. . . . 493 *Hap. War.* 26
Prest in the tenderness of virgin love . . . . 500 *Humanity* 26
Thanks to its tenderness, its joys, and fears, . 590 *Immortality* 205
Then TENDERNESS with CANDOUR join'd, . . . 620 *Birth of Love* 15
This tenderness of mind ? . . . . 626 †*Cento* 3
Of pity cast from inward tenderness . . . . 646 *Prelude* 2. 249
Than move with them in tenderness and love, . 669 *Prelude* 5. 251
To grandeur or to tenderness,—to the one . . 686 *Prelude* 6. 748
And the whole year breathed tenderness and love. 687 *Prelude* 7. 42
Or tenderness, which there, set off by foil, . 696 *Prelude* 7. 601
Of tenderness, which I may number now . . . 704 *Prelude* 8. 361
Pour rapture, tenderness, and hope,—my theme . 743 *Prelude* 13. 240
Shall want no humbler tenderness ; his heart . . 749 *Prelude* 14. 227
Poured out for all the early tenderness . . . 749 *Prelude* 14. 234
Even to the last, of genuine tenderness, . . . 778 *Excursion* 2. 448
Beyond the tenderness of human hearts : . . . 804 *Excursion* 4. 193
A gay or pensive tenderness prevailed, . . . 812 *Excursion* 4. 743
By tenderness of heart ; have seen your eye, . . 818 *Excursion* 4. 1120
A holy tenderness pervade his frame. . . . . 819 *Excursion* 4. 1220
With self-forgetting tenderness of heart . . . 831 *Excursion* 5. 577
Time to look back with tenderness on her . . . 841 *Excursion* 6. 200
And if religious tenderness of heart, ... 850 *Excursion* 6. 798
Glistened with tenderness ; his mind, I knew, . 883 *Excursion* 8. 589
With tenderness embosom ; to your paths ; . . S.3. 433 **The doubt* 5
But not betrayed by tenderness of mind . . . K.8. 245 *Recluse* 1. 1. 309
Tending. His Power is this way tending. It befits us 56 *Bord.* 1027
Tending to the darksome hollows . . . . . 90 *Longest Day* 31
Served, tending a few sheep and goats, a ragged Norman Boy. . . . . 91 *Norman Boy* 4
Sylph or Faery hither tending,— . . . . . 170 *Kitten* 13
By the silent thanks, now tending . . . . . 502 **Like a* 15
Kindly emotion tending to console . . . . . 538 **In desultory* 51
Nor shall we not be tending towards that point . 705 *Prelude* 8. 451
This was the time, when, all things tending fast . 730 *Prelude* 11. 223
Of all infirmity, and tending all . . . . . 818 *Excursion* 4. 1114
Should breathe a word tending to violate . . . 847 *Excursion* 6. 583
Tending to patience when affliction strikes ; . . 873 *Excursion* 7. 1055
Tendrils. Round these, with tendrils strong as flesh and blood, ... 488 *Pers. Talk* 35
Tends. So to the homestead, where the grandsire tends . . . . 19 *Desc. Sk.* 484
And tends a flock from hill to hill : . . . . 205 *Brougham* 111
And, wheresoe'er the stealing footstep tends, . . 271 **Where holy* 4
Alas ! where'er the current tends, ... 285 *Grave of Burns* 37
Sidelong, and half-reverted. She who tends . . 566 *Cumb. Beg.* 32
Of fine propensities, that tends, if urged . . . 815 *Excursion* 4. 906
Tenement. A tiny tenement, forsooth, and frail, as needs must be . . . . 91 *Norman Boy* 15
No door the tenement requires, ... 168 *Wren's Nest* 5
Of minster clock ! From that bleak tenement . 758 *Excursion* 1. 125
Or passing by some single tenement . . . . 780 *Excursion* 2. 564
This rustic tenement, had gently shed, . . . 860 *Excursion* 7. 206
—From the low tenement, his own abode, . . . 867 *Excursion* 7. 663
Teneriffe. Arran ! a single-crested Teneriffe, . . 471 **Arran ! a* 1
Tenets. Of a proud slavery met by tenets strained 442 *Ecc. Sonn.* 3. 11. 2
More firmly to old tenets, and, to prove . . . 730 *Prelude* 11. 217
Tenfold. Had been a tenfold cruelty. Strange pleasures . . . . 41 *Bord.* 242
The social hour—of tenfold care . . . . . 286 *Sons of Burns* 17
Tenor. *See* **Tenour.**
The cherished tenor of his pace . . . . . . 243 *P. B.* 658
Its even tenor, and the foe was quelled, . . . 325 *Ode 1814* 143
Should move the tenor of *his* song . . . . . 534 **Blest is* 87
—Yet, in its general tenor, your complaint . . 828 *Excursion* 5. 369
Tenour. *See* **Tenor.**
Such was the tenour of the second act . . . . 652 *Prelude* 3. 256
Through the whole tenour of my school-day time, 713 *Prelude* 9. 219
Within myself, not comfortless.—The tenour . . 800 *Excursion* 3. 967
(For thus the tenour of complaint hath run) . . 829 *Excursion* 5. 475
—Such the too frequent tenour of his boast . . 843 *Excursion* 6. 359
Tens. Which then, when tens of thousands were deprest . . . . 210 *Laod.* 51
While tens of thousands, thinking on the affray, . 308 **These times* 4
Of tens of thousands, secretly." . . . . . 403 *White Doe* 677
With tens of thousands rent from off the tree . 582 *Invoc. Earth* 11
Is joy for tens of millions. Southward thence . 680 *Prelude* 6. 349
While tens of thousands falter in their path, . . 835 *Excursion* 5. 833
"And tens of thousands suffer wrong as deep. . 879 *Excursion* 8. 336

Tens—*continued.*
For tens of thousands uninformed as he ? . . . 880 *Excursion* 8. 432
That tens of thousands at this day exist . . . 886 *Excursion* 9. 178
Tent. In many a court, and many a warrior's tent, 103 *Artegal* 84
Turns to a little tent hard by : . . . . . . 176 *Waggoner* 1. 265
By martial sports,—or, seated in the tent, . . 211 *Laod.* 118
Green moss-grown tower ; or hoary tent ; . . . 214 *Kirkstone* 18
Cheering the wakeful tent on Syrian mountains, . 232 *Power of Sound* 19
O'er the parched waste beside an Arab's tent ; . 383 *Duddon* 31. 6
A geographic Labourer pitched his tent, . . . 548 **Stay, bold* 14
The Grison gypsey here her tent has plac'd, . . 605 *Desc.Sk.Quarto* 188
Well pleased to pitch a vagrant tent among . . 688 *Prelude* 7. 56
And mused in rocky cell or sylvan tent, . . . 753 **Oft, through* 3
Within its shade, as in a stately tent . . . . 866 *Excursion* 7. 617
And self-devoted sought the monarch's tent, . . L.1. 95 *Juvenal* 3. 8
Tented. The Stripling seeks the tented field ; . . 216 *Enterprise* 54
They roamed through Wastes where now the tented Arabs dwell. . . . . 522 *Epist. Beaumont* 100
Tenth. For which upon the tenth night if thou fail 564 *Troilus* 124
Of the tenth day will come, and end his sorrow. . 565 *Troilus* 168
Tents. I'll look upon your tents again. . . . . 114 *Ind. Wom.* 54
Tents of a camp that never shall be razed— . . 214 *Kirkstone* 19
She hastens to the tents . . . . 221 *Triad* 95
They lodged in leafy tents and cabins low ; . . 346 *Processions* 15
Their tents, and check the current of their arms. 427 *Ecc. Sonn.* 1. 34. 8
Or yonder is it that the tents must be ; . . . 564 *Troilus* 152
By naked huts, wood-built, and sown like tents . 683 *Prelude* 6. 521
A Parliament of Monsters. Tents and Booths . 698 *Prelude* 7. 718
Pitches her tents before me as I move, . . . 755 *Recluse* 1. 1. 799
Who pitch their tents under the green-wood tree ? 858 *Excursion* 7. 88
Tenure. Wisely ; and by such tenure do we hold . 822 *Excursion* 5. 23
Tepid. Long springs and tepid winters, on the banks 701 *Prelude* 8. 174
Term. That I—so near the term to human life . 354 *Aquap.* 91
Grants to thy mission a brief term of silence, . . 363 **List—'twas* 111
"For term of life Love shall have hold of me"— 562 *Cuck.and Night.* 289
The dangerous craft of culling term and phrase . 676 *Prelude* 6. 110
That scarcely, as my term of pupilage . . . . 679 *Prelude* 6. 276
Familiarly, a household term, like those, . . . 694 *Prelude* 7. 496
A gift, to use a term which they would use, . . 742 *Prelude* 13. 188
Their lenient term of separation past, ... 861 *Excursion* 7. 288
Till the Term, for which she's fated . . . . S.3. 438 **I, whose* 24
Terminate. The sweetest notes must terminate and die ; . . . . 252 **The fairest* 2
That in itself may terminate, or lead . . . . 888 *Excursion* 9. 285
Termination. O Friend ! The termination of my course . . . . 751 *Prelude* 14. 374
And termination of his mortal course ; . . . . 885 *Excursion* 9. 95
A termination, and a last retreat, ... K.8. 240 *Recluse* 1. 1. 147
Terms. And, for yourself, in plain terms he asserts 38 *Bord.* 64
His speech with uncouth terms of art, ... 178 *Waggoner* 2. 125
On friendly terms with this Machine : . . . . 182 *Waggoner* 4. 217
Endangered States may yield to terms unjust ; . 316 **Say, what* 10
On honourable terms, or else retire, ... 493 *Hap. War.* 37
"Though," said the Priest in answer, "these be terms . . . . 846 *Excursion* 6. 558
No doubt if you in terms direct had asked . . K.8. 230 **I will* 178
Terrace. Along the margin of our terrace walk ; . 636 *Prelude* 1. 286
And blazing terrace upon terrace, high . . . . 784 *Excursion* 2. 841
Terraces. O'er villas, terraces, and towers ; . . 343 *Eclipse* 34
And terraces in trim array— . . . . . . 407 *White Doe* 990
Pools, terraces, and walks are sown . . . . 413 *White Doe* 1570
On stately terraces of Como, ... S.3. 438 **My Lord* 18
Terraqueous. Bedim, the grand terraqueous spectacle, 548 **Stay, bold* 10
Terrene. Of high with low, celestial with terrene ! . 434 *Ecc. Sonn.* 2. 25. 14
Terrestrial. For creatures doomed to breathe terrestrial air : . . . . 22 *Desc. Sk.* 647
Terrestrial, but a surface, by the flight . . . 263 **How clear* 8
Of those terrestrial fabrics, where they serve, . 496 **A little* 47
And self-devotion, and terrestrial hope, . . . 713 *Prelude* 9. 273
Terrible. Repeat her Father's terrible adventures, . 39 *Bord.* 93
And never heard a sound so terrible. . . . . 53 *Bord.* 888
Are terrible, yet ours is not the fault. . . . . 69 *Bord.* 1747
Some terrible phantom I believe is now . . . 73 *Bord.* 2026
And then I heard a shriek so terrible . . . . 74 *Bord.* 2104
Coming on with a terrible pother, ... 86 *Rural Arch.* 15
Terrible for sense and soul ! . . . . 234 *Power of Sound* 106
More terrible than magic spell. . . . . . . 246 *P. B.* 920
Of sleep took import terrible ;— . . . . . 299 *Brownie's Cell* 66
For a brief moment, terrible ; . . . . . . 331 *Ode : Thanks.* 185
Earth cannot check. O terrible excess . . . 439 *Ecc. Sonn.* 2. 44. 9
More terrible images there. . . . . 620 *Convict* 20
Glimpses of retribution, terrible, ... 724 *Prelude* 10. 452
That her mild nature can be terrible ; . . . . 816 *Excursion* 4. 1032
Terrier. Our inmate, a rough terrier of the hills ; . 659 *Prelude* 4. 95
Terrific. "Ah ! how unlike those late terrific sleeps, ... 30 *Guilt* 343
With that terrific sword . . . . 103 *Artegal* 54
To Gordale-chasm, terrific as the lair . . . . 269 *Gordale* 5
But a terrific reservoir of guilt . . . . . 725 *Prelude* 10. 477
Of those terrific Idols some received . . . . 894 *Excursion* 9. 692
Terrified. Nay, be not terrified—it does me good . 47 *Bord.* 530
Was almost terrified. That's excellent !— . . 61 *Bord.* 1288
his wound terrified me— . . . . 72 *Bord.* 1967
Crouching and terrified, ... 545 *Russ. Fug.* 290
Terrifying. Ungovernable, and your terrifying winds, 702 *Prelude* 8. 220
Territory. Savona, Queen of territory fair . . . 355 *Aquap.* 207
Laws overturned ; and territory split, ... 889 *Excursion* 9. 339
Terror. Strong terror checks the female peasant's sighs, ... 11 *Desc. Sk.* 65
We gazed with terror on their gloomy sleep, . . 29 *Guilt* 293
Flashes a look of terror upon guilt, ... 40 *Bord.* 171

Terror—*continued.*
The only quiet heart on earth. In terror, 64 *Bord.* 1468
Remembered terror, there is peace and rest. 64 *Bord.* 1469
And move in terror of the elements; 75 *Bord.* 2178
Conceived a terror; and, by night or day 123 *V. and J.* 123
A twelvemonth's terror and distress!" 176 *Waggoner* 1. 252
Terror over, 177 *Waggoner* 2. 90
And terror of that marvellous night! 178 *Waggoner* 2. 144
O terror! what hath she perceived?—O joy! 209 *Laod.* 13
For terror, joy, or pity, 234 *Power of Sound* 161
Of harmony!—a shriek of terror, pain, 274 **Wait, prithee* 11
Of Terror, bear us to the ground, and tie 309 **What if* 5
Stalks round—abhorred by Heaven, a terror to the Earth! 311 **Who rises* 20
Yield not to terror or despondency, 339 *Tell* 20
And lasting terror through that ancient Hold. 383 *Duddon* 27. 8
The wind with terror while they roar for food. 392 *Daniel* 8
Which struck with terror friends and foes! 408 *White Doe* 1148
Wrongs and the terror of redress, would wean 516 **Hard task* 5
In terror of the Czar." 542 *Russ. Fug.* 28
And terror shall leap at his heart. 621 *Convict* 40
Add that whate'er of Terror or of Love 651 *Prelude* 3. 133
In chase of him; whereat I waked in terror, 667 *Prelude* 5. 138
Of terror; yet no soul-debasing fear, 672 *Prelude* 5. 451
With an indefinite terror and dismay, 706 *Prelude* 8. 513
In terror. Disappointment and dismay 718 *Prelude* 10. 27
Put on a milder face; Terror had ceased, 727 *Prelude* 11. 2
Hath terror in it. Thou didst soften down 749 *Prelude* 14. 246
All strength—all terror, single or in bands, 755 *Recluse* 1. 1. 784
In such communion, not from terror free, 758 *Excursion* 1. 133
What terror doth it strike into the mind 864 *Excursion* 7. 491
He's the terror of boys in the midst of their noise. S.3. 424 *Tinker* 31

Terror's. Plunge with the Russ embrown'd by Terror's breath, 606 *Desc.Sk.Quarto* 245

Terrors. Hears Winter calling all his terrors round, 19 *Desc. Sk.* 490
From the night terrors of that waste to shield: 27 *Guilt* 151
Concentres all the terrors of the Universe: 51 *Bord.* 785
Then calm your terrors, Betty Foy! 130 *Idiot Boy* 363
On all sides doubts and terrors met her; 130 *Idiot Boy* 418
My heart with terrors? Am I not 156 *Oak and Broom* 73
Illusive cataracts! of their terrors 300 *Bran* 19
And sins, that point their terrors, 328 *Ode 1815* 103
Yet as the terrors of the lordly bell, 426 *Ecc. Sonn.* 1. 31. 9
And clothe thyself with terrors like the flood 454 **The Sun, that* 15
When empty terrors overawe; 492 *Duty* 6
She plants well-measured terrors in the road 519 *Pun. Death* 8. 4
'Soften'd the terrors of her awful mien.' 618 *School Ex.* 16
The terrors, pains, and early miseries, 637 *Prelude* 1. 345

Terror-smitten. Unwedded Julia, terror-smitten, hears 124 *V. and J.* 220

Test. I felt that merit has no surer test 70 *Bord.* 1827
Your visitations are a test 225 *Present.* 47
When she applies her annual test 299 *Brownie's Cell* 82
Rise as he may, his grandeur scorns the test 368 *Trajan* 55
From both sides; veteran thunders (the brute test 437 *Ecc. Sonn.* 2. 36. 10
Of true compassion greet them. Creed and test 449 *Ecc. Sonn.* 3. 36. 9
That searching test thy public course has stood; 478 **Lonsdale! it* 11
" A conquering lance is beauty's test, 478 *Somnamb.* 41
If in the aims of men the surest test 504 *Warning* 89
Weighed with me, could support the test of thought; 708 *Prelude* 8. 628
Who hath in no concerns of his a test 732 *Prelude* 11. 312
The test of such a trial; clearer far 740 *Prelude* 13. 57
Of modern statists to their proper test, 741 *Prelude* 13. 72
The test of act and suffering, to provoke 792 *Excursion* 3. 418

Testament. More than on written testament or deed, 393 *Countess' Pillar* 7

Testified. Tears of delight, that testified how true 277 *Author's Portrait* 13
Of humble mourners testified, 577 **By playful* 8
Hath, in my hearing, often testified 813 *Excursion* 4. 785

Testify. And every passing breeze will testify. 21 *Desc. Sk.* 603
This can thy own experience testify: 105 *Artegal* 190
To testify of Love and Grace divine. 226 *Vernal Ode* 39
Which even in deepest winter testify 329 *Ode: Thanks.* 11
Scorned or forgotten, Thou canst testify, 442 *Ecc. Sonn.* 3. 7. 6
Did they together testify of time 585 *Ch. Lamb* 95
That ye to him your love may testify; 627 **When Severn's* 4

Testimony. The testimony there displayed; 410 *White Doe* 1297

Tethered. And by a slender cord was tethered to a stone; 87 *Pet-lamb* 6
To their house and their mill tethered fast: 166 *Stray Pleasures* 9
If he were tethered to the waggon, 179 *Waggoner* 3. 52
Tethered to the waggon's tail: 181 *Waggoner* 4. 164

Tethering. Of fire his desperate self is tethering? 242 *P. B.* 512

Text. Prayer, text, or symbol, graven upon the stone; 275 *Gravestone* 2

Texts. Admonitory texts inscribed the walls, 824 *Excursion* 5. 150
The voice of wisdom whispering scripture texts 833 *Excursion* 5. 724

Texture. With a continuous cloud of texture close, 184 *Night-piece* 2
That through the texture of yon azure dome 322 *Germans* 6
And napkins of smooth texture, finely shorn. 624 *Æneid* 62
Unsound, of spongy texture, yet withal 654 *Prelude* 3. 334
Of texture midway between life and books. 657 *Prelude* 3. 578
Through their ethereal texture pierced—ere we, 893 *Excursion* 9. 598
These not of earthly texture, and the vault S.3. 435 **The doubt* 107

Th'. (*Partial list.*)
Starts at the simplest sight th' unbidden tear, 592 *Ev. Wk. Quarto* 44
While silent stands th' admiring vale below; 595 *Ev. Wk. Quarto* 188
Broke only by th' unvaried torrent's sound, 603 *Desc. Sk. Quarto* 58

Thames. O Thames! that other bards may see 9 *Collins* 2
The Miller with two Dames, on the breast of the Thames! 166 *Stray Pleasures* 4
High on the shore of silver Thames—to greet 327 *Ode 1815* 50
From the proud margin of the Thames, 376 **The Minstrels* 64

Thames—*continued.*
In stately mien to sovereign Thames allied 384 *Duddon* 32. 12
Emblem and instrument, from Thames to Tyne, 426 *Ecc. Sonn.* 1. 31. 7
Up, down, the busy Thames—rapid as fire 442 *Ecc. Sonn.* 3. 8. 5

Thames's. In Troynovant, his seat by silver Thames's side! 103 *Artegal* 97
Some little pleasure-skiff, that doth on Thames's waters float. 189 *Star-gazers* 4

Than. (*Partial list.*)
More of man's thoughts and ways than his experience 38 *Bord.* 35
A firmer step than mine. That dismal Moor— 39 *Bord.* 108
More than we see, or whence this strong aversion? 41 *Bord.* 254
And for less fee than I would let him run 43 *Bord.* 313
More speedily than you belike would wish. 44 *Bord.* 374
But yesterday was worse than all; at last 45 *Bord.* 471
More of contempt than hatred; both are flown; 47 *Bord.* 554
Yes. More than ever Parent loved a Child? 53 *Bord.* 849
Whom he to more than filial love and duty 53 *Bord.* 898
Than make me change my course. Dear Marmaduke, 55 *Bord.* 992
And I have felt, more than perhaps becomes me 57 *Bord.* 1112
Than what it leaves behind. 487 *Fountain* 36
" His Schoolfellow, who elder was than he, 553 *Prioress* 79
Rather than be disgraced, would chuse to die. 559 *Cuck.andNight.* 160
For thou art worse than mad a thousand fold; 560 *Cuck.andNight.* 188
By longer way than he was wont to go; 564 *Troilus* 144
(A thing more precious far than all that books 568 *Cumb. Beg.* 112
More of soul in his face than of words on his tongue; 570 *Farmer* 66
His Grandsire that age more than thirty times told; 572 *Avarice* 14
Who went something farther than others have gone, 572 *Avarice* 30

Thane. He had insulted—Peasant, King, or Thane? 475 **Here on their* 11

Thank. Then said—" I thank you all; if I must die, 35 *Guilt* 574
I thank you; but, a resting-place so near, 41 *Bord.* 221
Ah! what is here? Oh! Gentlemen, I thank you; 44 *Bord.* 396
God bless and thank you both, my gentle Masters. 46 *Bord.* 526
May love his Child. Thank you, old Man, for this! 52 *Bord.* 823
To thank me for this service. Rainbow arches, 54 *Bord.* 930
I thank you for that hint. He shall be brought 58 *Bord.* 1125
Of what I have been—yes, I thank thee, Heaven! 61 *Bord.* 1325
Hereafter you will thank me for this service. 75 *Bord.* 2127
Do I dare to thank the God, 140 *Arm. Lady* 68
Will thank you. Faultless does the Maid appear; 256 *Marriage: Friend* 9
Not loth to thank each moment for its boon 278 **The most* 9
Better to thank a dear and long-past day 392 *Bothwell* 9
I thank the silent Monitor, and say 470 *Bala-Sala* 13
And said, Forsooth, my friend, do I thank thee, 561 *Cuck.andNight.* 227
Good cause would oft be his to thank the surf 656 *Prelude* 3. 488
It seemed she did not thank me. I returned, 768 *Excursion* 1. 813
To thank him for the tale which he had told. 770 *Excursion* 1. 920
As if to thank him; he returned that look, 781 *Excursion* 2. 659
Beside our roads and pathways, though, thank Heaven! 788 *Excursion* 3. 176
There, undisturbed, could think of and could thank 794 *Excursion* 3. 562
The Sage rejoined, " I thank you—you have spared 886 *Excursion* 9. 153

Thanked. And, when he rose, he thanked her pious care 36 *Guilt* 641
Then God be thanked—— 72 *Bord.* 1922
The Stranger would have thanked him, but he felt 101 *Brothers* 406
The other thanked him with an earnest voice; 102 *Brothers* 415
I thanked the Leader of my onward way. 383 *Duddon* 28. 14
The bay; and conquerors thanked the Gods, 543 *Russ. Fug.* 191
Well satisfied, I thanked her, and she said, 561 *Cuck.andNight.* 231
She thankèd them; and then her leave she took, 562 *Cuck.andNight.* 286
Till then unfelt, he thanked me; I returned 665 *Prelude* 4. 465
When God, the giver of all joy, is thanked 685 *Prelude* 6. 685
She thanked me for my wish;—but for my hope 768 *Excursion* 1. 812
His thirst from rill or gushing fount, and thanked 814 *Excursion* 4. 872

Thankful. In mute devotion on the thankful breast! 20 *Desc. Sk.* 568
All that breathe are thankful debtors 90 *Longest Day* 7
To her thankful mind's relief. 94 *Westmoreland Girl* 40
And send a thankful spirit back to you, 143 **High bliss* 27
With thankful heart, to either Eminence 151 **Forth from* 14
Of the pleasure it spreads through so thankful a band; 188 *Music* 30
O'er whom such thankful tears were shed 204 *Brougham* 78
And thankful through a weary time, 205 *Brougham* 108
Be thankful, even though tired and faint, 215 *Kirkstone* 57
On busy days, with thankful nights, be mine. 217 *Enterprise* 150
Be thankful we again have met;— 238 *P. B.* 182
Upon the pleased and thankful Ass; 243 *P. B.* 597
Lived thankful for day's light, for daily bread, 278 **Lo! where she* 13
" Be thankful, thou; for, if unholy deeds 313 **Clouds, lingering* 13
In thankful joy and gratulation pure. 317 **Call not* 14
And rests not thankful? Whether cheered by talk 389 *Glencroe* 4
O suffering Earth! be thankful; sternest clime 426 *Ecc. Sonn.* 1. 30. 12
Deep in the thankful heart;—yet tears will flow. 448 *Ecc. Sonn.* 3. 31. 8
And now with thankful heart to bed doth creep, 453 **Calm is the* 18
In thankful bosoms to a modest pride. 456 *Rydal Mere* 44
A grey-haired, pensive, thankful Refugee; 470 *Bala-Sala* 7
Is in the thankful Creature's power. 506 *Lab. Hymn* 12
Shall with a thankful tear bedrop its latest page. 529 **Those breathing* 140
With thankful spirit. The descant, and the wind 538 **In desultory* 10
Glimmers before my sight through thankful tears, 627 **The star* 10
In thankful blessedness, which yet survives. 663 *Prelude* 4. 338
Happy, and now most thankful that my walk 704 *Prelude* 8. 330
The thankful captive of maternal bonds; 794 *Excursion* 3. 555
Thankful for my belovèd child's return. 812 *Excursion* 4. 748
They looked; were humbly thankful for the good 815 *Excursion* 4. 936

Thee—*continued.*
One whom with thee friendship had early paired ; 750 *Prelude* 14. 267
Coleridge ! with this my argument, of thee . 750 *Prelude* 14. 276
It will be known, by thee at least, my Friend ! . 752 *Prelude* 14. 411
To thee the work shall justify itself. . . . . 752 *Prelude* 14. 414
Theft. O'er moor and mountain, midnight theft to hatch ! . . . . 32 *Guilt* 416
In secret revels—haply after theft . . . . . 378 *Duddon* 11. 6
Their, *omitted.*
Theirs. (*Partial list.*)
'Gainst all that in *his* heart, or theirs perhaps, said nay. . . . . 25 *Guilt* 54
It plays not for them,—what matter ? 'tis theirs ; 167 *Stray Pleasures* 22
Them, *omitted.*
Theme. To traveller who might talk of any casual theme. . . . . 26 *Guilt* 99
In verse, which to thy ear might come, would treat this simple theme, ... 93 *Poet's Dream* 75
I pass the raptures of the pair ;—such theme . . 123 *V. and J.* 87
They checked me—and I left the theme . . 182 *Waggoner* 4. 201
As his distress is sharp, would scorn my theme, . 229 *Cuckoo-clock* 28
Since thou dost bear it,—a memorial theme . . 275 *Rotha Q.* 12
But, leaving each unquiet theme . . . . 285 *Nith* 13
Whate'er the theme, the Maiden sang . . . . 289 *Sol. Reap.* 25
Support their mighty theme from age to age ; . 325 *Ode 1814* 132
All-ruling Jove, whate'er the theme might be . 359 *Plea : Hist.* 11
Of freedom, with mind grasping the whole theme 359 **They—who* 10
For Duddon, long-loved Duddon, is my theme ! . 376 *Duddon* 1. 14
Wholly dissevered from our present theme ; . . 440 *Ecc. Sonn.* 3. 2. 3
How widely spread the interests of our theme. . 443 *Ecc. Sonn.* 3. 12. 14
Rich theme of England's fondest praise, . . . 495 *Fact* 25
A theme for praise and admiration high. . . . 517 *Pun. Death* 3. 4
Or loftier pitch if higher rose the theme, . . 538 **In desultory* 16
The blameless cause lay in the Theme itself. . . 539 **Lady ! a* 11
A theme for angels, when they celebrate . . . 540 *Grace Darl.* 17
Sad theme for every tongue ; . . . . . . 545 *Russ. Fug.* 316
Thy charms my only theme ; . . . . . . 626 †*Cento* 10
Would gladly grapple with some noble theme, . 634 *Prelude* 1. 129
Will settle on some British theme, some old . . 634 *Prelude* 1. 168
Some imperfection in the chosen theme, . . . 636 *Prelude* 1. 262
Might I pursue this theme through every change 639 *Prelude* 1. 476
The road lies plain before me ;—'tis a theme . . 641 *Prelude* 1. 640
I have been speaking, for my theme has been . . 651 *Prelude* 3. 172
And, therefore, now that we must quit this theme, 651 *Prelude* 3. 189
Knowing too well the importance of his theme, . 665 *Prelude* 4. 444
Set forth, too serious theme for that light place— 691 *Prelude* 7. 295
From this memorial tribute to my theme . . . 691 *Prelude* 7. 316
Are now my theme ; and, foremost of the scenes, 692 *Prelude* 7. 334
Whose genius spangled o'er a gloomy theme . . 695 *Prelude* 7. 565
Now in connection with so great a theme . . . 711 *Prelude* 9. 111
(A theme for boys, too hackneyed for their sires,) 721 *Prelude* 10. 193
And tell, since juvenile errors are my theme, . . 728 *Prelude* 11. 54
Pour rapture, tenderness, and hope,—my theme . 743 *Prelude* 13. 240
Imagination having been our theme, ... 749 *Prelude* 14. 206
Couched in the dewy grass. With such a theme, 750 *Prelude* 14. 275
Theme this but little heard of among men— . . 755 *Recluse* 1. 1. 820
Be not this labour useless. If such theme . . 755 *Recluse* 1. 1. 852
To be diverted from our present theme, . . . 791 *Excursion* 3. 331
And I could tell, not travelling for my theme . 847 *Excursion* 6. 569
There doth he rest. No theme his fate supplies . 854 *Excursion* 6. 1085
While thus from theme to theme the Historian passed, ... 857 *Excursion* 7. 1
The Pastor pressed by thoughts which round his theme . . . . 863 *Excursion* 7. 361
The hallowed theme) will rise and celebrate . . 863 *Excursion* 7. 375
Upon this impulse, to the theme—erewhile . . 883 *Excursion* 8. 591
A voice shall speak, and what will be the theme ? K.8. 257 *Recluse* 1.1.753
Dark as a riddle, prove a favourite theme ; . . K.8. 301 **And oh* 6
The theme is fruitful ; nor can sorrow find . . L.1. 97 *Juvenal* 3. 79
Theme's. Awed by the theme's peculiar sanctity . 585 *Ch. Lamb* 56
Themes. There too we read of Spenser's fairy themes, 103 *Artegal* 49
The domination of his glorious themes, . . . 216 *Enterprise* 96
But some (who brook those hackneyed themes full well, ... 255 *Detraction* 5
But surely less so than your far-fetched themes ! 268 **Dogmatic Teachers* 14
I move at ease ; and meet contending themes . 350 *Des. Stanzas* 15
Sang in this Presence kindred themes ; . . . 416 *White Doe* 1841
There find I personal themes, a plenteous store, . 488 *Pers. Talk* 37
Of undiscordant themes ; . . . . 499 **Departing summer* 21
Let more substantial themes the pen engage, . . 522 *Epist. Beaumont* 89
Unconscious prelude to heroic themes, ... 547 **Beneath yon* 13
To transitory themes ; yet I rejoice, ... 669 *Prelude* 5. 224
Exists and is sustained. More lofty themes, . . 694 *Prelude* 7. 465
With vice at home. We added dearest themes— 714 *Prelude* 9. 354
Exalting tender themes, by just degrees . . . 839 *Excursion* 6. 83
—Life, death, eternity ! momentous themes . . 874 *Excursion* 8. 10
From trivial themes to general argument . . . 882 *Excursion* 8. 522
Beget strange themes ; and to freaks give birth . K.8. 301 **And oh* 9
Themselves. By seamen, who perhaps themselves had shared . . . . 25 *Guilt* 52
But that they cannot stand up of themselves ; . . 60 *Bord.* 1233
In recompense for what themselves required. . . 65 *Bord.* 1528
But to protect themselves from extirpation ?— . 66 *Bord.* 1584
The plot to rid themselves, at any cost, . . . 69 *Bord.* 1758
Do recognise some image of themselves, . . . 70 *Bord.* 1824
And everlasting hills themselves were changed. . 96 *Brothers* 99
The mountains have all opened out themselves, . 131 *Michael* 7
Who journey thither find themselves alone . . 131 *Michael* 10
And his old Father both betook themselves . . 132 *Michael* 104

Themselves—*continued.*
She said to Luke, while they two by themselves . 135 *Michael* 294
Helmet-like themselves will fasten . . . . . 166 *Wand. Jew* 7
They themselves make the reel, ... 167 *Stray Pleasures* 20
And are returned into themselves, they cannot but be sad ? . . . . 189 *Star-gazers* 20
Are clad in one green hue, and lose themselves . 206 *Tintern* 13
More dear, both for themselves and for thy sake ! . 207 *Tintern* 159
Prepared themselves for glorious enterprise . . 211 *Laod.* 117
To show them a fair image ; 'tis themselves, . . 218 *Recluse* 1. 1. 224
That flowers themselves, whate'er their hue, . . 222 *Triad* 204
Themselves to lose their light, or pass away . . 226 *Vernal Ode* 43
As they themselves appear to be, ... 235 *Power of Sound* 182
On which they gazed themselves away. . . . 239 *P. B.* 270
More like themselves the rocks appear . . . . 242 *P. B.* 494
Yet in themselves are nothing ! One decree . . 306 **Inland, within* 12
To work against themselves such fell despite : . 308 **One might* 11
Who have seen—themselves now casting off the yoke— . . . . 322 *Germans* 13
Like dreams themselves ; and sweetest sound— . 324 *Ode 1814* 91
All States have glorified themselves ;—their claims 331 *Ode : Thanks.* 155
However humble in themselves, with thoughts . 354 *Aquap.* 125
Too lovely to be pensive in themselves . . . 355 *Aquap.* 201
And feeble, of themselves, decay ; . . . . . 391 *Highland Broach* 64
And quickly spread themselves abroad, . . . 398 *White Doe* 160
That shape themselves and disappear . . . . 406 *White Doe* 970
Sung for themselves, and those whom they would free ! . . . . 422 *Ecc. Sonn.* 1. 14. 9
Which of themselves our minds impress ; . . . 481 *Expost.* 22
And mix the poison, they themselves must drink. 513 *Newspaper* 8
Pass sentence on themselves, confess the fact, . 517 *Pun. Death* 3. 11
Then sped themselves to bury him full fast ; . . 555 *Prioress* 187
They pruned themselves, and made themselves right gay, ... 558 *Cuck. and Night.* 76
Themselves, the fathers and the dealers-out . . 568 *Cumb. Beg.* 150
Give themselves up to jollity, ... 588 *Immortality* 31
Nor general Truths, which are themselves a sort . 634 *Prelude* 1. 151
Humility and modest awe themselves . . . . 635 *Prelude* 1. 243
So beautiful, so majestic in themselves, . . . 641 *Prelude* 1. 608
Murmuring so sweetly in themselves, obeyed . . 647 *Prelude* 2. 372
And what they do within themselves while yet . 651 *Prelude* 3. 178
And sports and games (too grateful in themselves, 662 *Prelude* 4. 283
Yet in themselves less grateful, I believe, . . . 662 *Prelude* 4. 284
Take firmer hold of us, and words themselves . 673 *Prelude* 5. 544
Present themselves as objects recognised, . . . 674 *Prelude* 5. 604
Mother and child !—These feelings, in themselves 692 *Prelude* 7. 329
Sequestered, handed down among themselves . 701 *Prelude* 8. 134
Did first present themselves thus purified, . . 703 *Prelude* 8. 304
Came, of themselves, or at her call derived . . 708 *Prelude* 8. 602
Blown back upon themselves ; their reason seemed 713 *Prelude* 9. 258
Things that could only show themselves and die. 719 *Prelude* 10. 47
Who to themselves are false. But these are things 720 *Prelude* 10. 120
Could be entrusted, while the events themselves, 730 *Prelude* 11. 197
My own delights ; the lordly Alps themselves, . 733 *Prelude* 11. 409
To counteract the other, and themselves, . . . 736 *Prelude* 12. 136
Who thrust themselves upon the passive world . 741 *Prelude* 13. 67
To men as they are men within themselves. . . 743 *Prelude* 13. 226
Who are their own upholders, to themselves . . 743 *Prelude* 13. 262
Of Nature have a passion in themselves, . . . 744 *Prelude* 13. 291
Kindred mutations ; for themselves create . . 747 *Prelude* 14. 94
The measure of themselves, these favoured Beings, 757 *Excursion* 1. 88
Which, when they should sustain themselves aloft, 803 *Excursion* 4. 141
But soon his thoughts returned upon themselves, 807 *Excursion* 4. 416
Of a good shepherd tended, as themselves . . 829 *Excursion* 5. 426
With mute astonishment, themselves to see . . 843 *Excursion* 6. 347
For all that can no longer feed themselves, . . 844 *Excursion* 6. 379
Than to do wrong, albeit themselves have erred. . 854 *Excursion* 6. 1071
Present themselves at once to all men's view : . 874 *Excursion* 8. 16
To save themselves from blank forgetfulness ! " . 877 *Excursion* 8. 230
These, bred to little pleasure in themselves, . . 880 *Excursion* 8. 390
Our active powers, those powers themselves become 886 *Excursion* 9. 131
That works but by extinction ? On themselves . 886 *Excursion* 9. 143
Arts, in themselves beneficent and kind, . . . 887 *Excursion* 9. 189
To eyes and ears of parents who themselves . . 889 *Excursion* 9. 323
Gods which themselves had fashioned, to promote 894 *Excursion* 9. 686
In lines, that seem to keep themselves alive . . K.8. 223 **There is a shapeless* 3
There to defend themselves the winter long. . . K.8. 224 **I will* 11
Must needs themselves be hallowed, they require K.8. 244 *Recluse* 1.1.278
They lift the animal being, do themselves . . . K.8. 249 *Recluse* 1.1.454
Reveal themselves ; not therefore is my heart . K.8. 250 *Recluse* 1.1.495
One family, and one mansion ; to themselves . K.8. 253 *Recluse* 1.1.619
Six which themselves must single from a train, . L.1. 95 *Juvenal* 3. 5
Then. (*Partial list.*)
His passion drove him—then a Voyager . . . 37 *Bord.* 16
He must have felt it then, known what it was, . 41 *Bord.* 240
'Tis but a word and then—— Something is here 41 *Bord.* 253
And are you going then ? Come, come, Idonea, . 42 *Bord.* 296
And, fondling, licked his face, then on a sudden . 44 *Bord.* 413
Well then, says I—I'll out with it ; at which . . 45 *Bord.* 475
You are wasting words ; hear me then once for all : 48 *Bord.* 625
I met your Father, then a wandering Outcast : . 49 *Bord.* 687
But you were then a tottering Little-one— . . 50 *Bord.* 702
Touch not a finger—— What then must be done ? 53 *Bord.* 877
Then shatter the delusion, break it up . . . . 54 *Bord.* 934
Then grasp our swords and rush upon a cure . . 56 *Bord.* 1033
But all our thoughts were *then* of Earth, . . . 348 **Lulled by* 39
And then he sang it well and fearlessly, . . . 554 *Prioress* 95
" This Child with piteous lamentation then . . 555 *Prioress* 170
Then sped themselves to bury him full fast ; . . 555 *Prioress* 187
Touched then his tongue, and took away the grain; 556 *Prioress* 220

Then—*continued.*
And then I thought anon as it was day, . . . 557 *Cuck.and Night.* 51
And it was then the third night of the May. . . 557 *Cuck.and Night.* 55
Then, quoth she, let me never hope for bliss, . . 559 *Cuck.andNight.*164
Then shalt thou raise a clamour as do I. . . . 560 *Cuck.andNight.*185
Then of the Nightingale did I take note, . . . 560 *Cuck.andNight.*206
Then straightway came the Nightingale to me, . 561 *Cuck.andNight.*226
Then spake one Bird, and full assent all gave ; . 562 *Cuck.andNight.*271
She thankèd them ; and then her leave she took, 562 *Cuck.andNight.*286
Then let him pass, a blessing on his head ! . . 568 *Cumb. Beg.* 162
Then the Muses might deal with me just as they chose, ... 571 *Avarice* 3

Thence. (*Partial list.*)
Thence issuing often with unwieldy stalk, . . . 6 *Ev. Wk.* 242
And downward thence a knot of grass he throws, 17 *Desc. Sk.* 384
So lonely, but that thence might come a pang . 25 *Guilt* 74
A long mile thence. While thither they pursued 30 *Guilt* 332
Thence bursting shrill did all remark prevent ; . 33 *Guilt* 465
And thence they saw the bridge of wood, . . . 83 *Lucy Gray* 39
Stopped short,—and thence, at leisure, limb by limb 96 *Brothers* 102
And it was fit that thence I took . . . . . 115 *Last of Flock* 47
And thence full many a sound she hears, . . . 127 *Idiot Boy* 140
Thence in our rustic dialect was called . . . 133 *Michael* 168
And took no note of the hour while thence they gazed, ... 151 **Forth from* 10
And that bright gleam which thence will fall . . 174 *Waggoner* 1. 77
Thence the sound—the light is there— . . . 176 *Waggoner* 2. 23
Thence look thou forth o'er wood and lawn . . 180 *Waggoner* 4. 38
Thence offer nightly sacrifice) . . . . . . 214 *Kirkstone* 16
Thence back into the moonlight creeps ; . . . 243 *P. B.* 639
Thence has it, with the Son, so strong a hold . . 276 *Filial Piety* 8
The shepherd struggles with them. Onward thence 353 *Aquap.* 47
To thee, a woman, and thence weak : . . . . 402 *White Doe* 531
Thence marching southward smooth and free . . 404 *White Doe* 715
He thence may learn, ere fall of night, . . . 404 *White Doe* 781
Thence creeping under sylvan arches cool, . . 424 *Ecc. Sonn.* 1. 22. 7
As thence she holds her way to Palestine. . . . 427 *Ecc. Sonn.* 1. 35. 8
He taught, till persecution chased him thence, . 431 *Ecc. Sonn.* 2. 11. 10
Thence, also, more alive to tenderness. . . . 493 *Hap. War.* 26
All gentleness and honour thence come forth ; . . 559 *Cuck.andNight.*152
Thence worship comes, content and true heart's pleasure, ... 559 *Cuck.andNight.*153
Thence sickness comes, and overwhelming sadness, 560 *Cuck.andNight.*172
Men thence a book might make, a history ; . . 563 *Troilus* 67
Thence issuing oft, unwieldly as ye stalk, . . 596 *Ev. Wk. Quarto* 231
Thence, from three paly loopholes mild and small, 598 *Ev. Wk. Quarto* 335
Thence red from different heights with restless gleam . . . . 598 *Ev. Wk. Quarto* 373
Thence down the steep a pile of grass he throws . 610 *Desc.Sk.Quarto* 472
From thence to search the mystic cause of things 619 *School Ex.* 75
And learn from thence thy own defects to scan ; . 619 *School Ex.* 86
In that stern countenance, for our souls thence drew 622 *Recluse* 1. 1. 164
Thence did I drink the visionary power ; . . . 646 *Prelude* 2. 311
Is smitten thence with an unnatural taint, . . 655 *Prelude* 3. 420
Whose white belt scared him thence, or wind that blew . . . . 656 *Prelude* 3. 489
Thence back into the throng, until we reach, . . 690 *Prelude* 7. 189
A patriot, thence rejected by the rest, ... 714 *Prelude* 9. 290
And thence let loose, to seek their pleasant homes 888 *Excursion* 9. 261
Thence look for these magnificent results ! . . 890 *Excursion* 9. 397
That flattering breezes blowing thence . . . . S.3. 431 **The Scottish* 13
Thence northward did they pass by Arthur's seat, K.8. 225 **I will* 23
Thence up Helvellyn, a superior mount, . . . K.8. 225 **I will* 28
Thence, journeying on a second time, they passed K.8. 226 **I will* 62

Thenceforth. As if thenceforth nor pain nor trouble she could know. . . . . 25 *Guilt* 63
Of vice—thenceforth unable to subvert . . . 105 *Artegal* 230
Out of his feelings, to be fixed thenceforth . . 730 *Prelude* 11. 226

Theocritus. And, O Theocritus, so far have some . 733 *Prelude* 11. 437

Theoretic. Lost people, trained to theoretic feud ! . 505 *Warning* 111
But stop ! these theoretic fancies jar . . . . 790 *Excursion* 3. 253

Theories. By monstrous theories of alien growth, . 514 **Long-favoured* 2
As from the first, wild theories were afloat, . . 730 *Prelude* 11. 189
Plans without thought, or built on theories . . 741 *Prelude* 13. 70
By theories with suitable support)— . . . 795 *Excursion* 3. 633

Theory. The Sage's theory ? the Poet's lay ?— . 394 **How profitless* 11
Of the strange sight, nor hide his theory . . . 468 **Ranging the* 11
Exploding upstart Theory, insists . . . . 695 *Prelude* 7. 529

There, *omitted.*

Thereafter. And saw, thereafter, on the soil of France 504 *Warning* 63
And when thereafter to my father's house . . 672 *Prelude* 5. 477
Will chant together." Thereafter, as the shades . 687 *Prelude* 7. 31
He who thereafter, and in how short time ! . . 725 *Prelude* 10. 501
That went before my steps. Thereafter came . 750 *Prelude* 14. 266
And did, thereafter, bathe their hands in fire, . 839 *Excursion* 6. 66

Thereat. And thereat shall the Eagle be our Lord, 562 *Cuck.andNight.*276

Thereby. Swayed, and thereby enabled to contend 442 *Ecc. Sonn.* 3. 9. 6
That objects, even as they are great, thereby . . 720 *Prelude* 10. 159
And with amazement smote ;—thereby to assert . 811 *Excursion* 4. 661
On which they stand ; as if thereby they drew . 879 *Excursion* 8. 355

Therefore. (*Partial list.*)
And therefore chose this solitary Moor, . . . 59 *Bord.* 1209
Therefore I bless her : when I think of Man, . . 62 *Bord.* 1374
And therefore leave thee to a righteous judgment. 63 *Bord.* 1407
To be alone, and therefore we must part. . . . 64 *Bord.* 1475
Therefore through me alone must be revealed . 75 *Bord.* 2170
—Therefore, unwilling to forget that day, . . . 149 **A narrow* 74
And therefore, my sweet MARY, this still Nook, . 150 *M. H.* 23
Have souls which never yet have risen, and therefore prostrate lie ? . . . . 189 *Star-gazers* 23

Therefore—*continued.*
And rolls through all things. Therefore am I still 207 *Tintern* 102
Thy nature is not therefore less divine : . . . 258 **It is a* 11
Her functions are they therefore less divine, . . 270 **Though the bold* 9
And, therefore, was it rightly said . . . . . 289 *Glen-Al.* 30
Therefore the wise pray for thee, though the freight 309 **England ! the* 12
And, therefore, art thou blest with peace, serene 339 *Schwytz* 6
And therefore are betrayed. . . . . 348 **Lulled by* 30
Not, therefore, shall my mind give way to sadness ;— 352 *Aquap.* 9
Sounder and therefore holier than the ends . . 358 *Aquap.* 351
Therefore the Voice spake from the Desert, thence 365 **The Baptist* 9
Back therefore will they hie to seize . . . . 405 *White Doe* 797
And therefore now she deems it good . . . . 414 *White Doe* 1702
And therefore are ye summoned to depart, . . 434 *Ecc. Sonn.* 2. 24. 7
And, therefore, shalt thou be an honoured name ! 491 *Tribute : Dog* 36
And therefore does not stoop, nor lie in wait . . 493 *Hap. War.* 41
Them therefore with wild horses did he draw, . 555 *Prioress* 182
And, therefore, Nightingale ! do thou keep nigh, 560 *Cuck.andNight.*181
And therefore we a Parliament will have. . . . 562 *Cuck.andNight.*275
And, therefore, now that we must quit this theme, 651 *Prelude* 3. 189
This was her creed, and therefore she was pure . 670 *Prelude* 5. 279
Therefore to serve was high beatitude ; . . . 724 *Prelude* 10. 433
Tumult was therefore gladness, and the fear . . 724 *Prelude* 10. 434
And therefore bold to look on painful things, . . 731 *Prelude* 11. 277
But much was wanting : therefore did I turn 741 *Prelude* 13. 116
With toil, be therefore yoked with ignorance ; . 742 *Prelude* 13. 176
Therefore, for what is here produced, I ask . . 753 **Oft, through* 12
Disgusted therefore, or appalled, by aims . . 797 *Excursion* 3. 773
Therefore, not unconsoled, I wait—in hope . 806 *Excursion* 4. 310
Extinguished, do not, *therefore,* cease to be. . . 865 *Excursion* 7. 520
And therefore no incompetence of mine . . . 874 *Excursion* 8. 13
To whom kind Nature, therefore, may afford . 885 *Excursion* 9. 99
Whose birthright Reason, therefore, may ensure. 885 *Excursion* 9. 101
Urge it in vain ; and, therefore, like a prayer . 889 *Excursion* 9. 325
Suffice it, therefore, if the rural Muse . . . 892 *Excursion* 9. 518
Beauty not therefore wanting change to stir . . S.3.433 **The doubt* 30
—What Being, therefore, since the birth of man . K.8. 239*Recluse* 1.1. 98
A freeman, therefore, sound and unimpaired ; . K.8. 246*Recluse*1.1. 362
Unworthy therefore, and unhallowed : no, . . K.8. 249*Recluse*1.1.453
Reveal themselves ; not therefore is my heart . K.8. 250*Recluse*1.1.495
Dismissing, therefore, all Arcadian dreams, . . K.8. 253*Recluse*1.1.625

Therefrom. Therefrom to human kind, and what we are. . . . . 743 *Prelude* 13. 249

Therein. Therein for ever you must yield to me. . 71 *Bord.* 1869
Lest she should drown herself therein. . . . . 129 *Idiot Boy* 296
To drown herself therein. . . . . 129 *Idiot Boy* 311
Therein a portion claim. . . . . 498 **The sylvan* 18
And one thing is therein which is not fair ; . . 560 *Cuck.andNight.*177
Therein, with our simplicity awhile . . . . 802 *Excursion* 4. 85
That he, from wrath redeemed, therein shall float 826 *Excursion* 5. 283
From those two Brothers who were drowned therein); K.8. 225 **I will* 22

Thereof. But thereof come in the end despondency and madness. . . . . 196 *Resolution* 49
And far and wide the fame thereof did ring. . . 202 *Hart-leap* 80
For thereof comes all goodness and all worth ; . 559 *Cuck.andNight.*151
For thereof come all contraries to gladness ; . . 560 *Cuck.andNight.*171

Thereon. Of fancy which thereon was shed, . . 182 *Waggoner* 4. 203
Nor view of who might sit thereon allowed ; . . 257 **Methought I* 3
Swiftly thereon a rainbow arch to build . . . 261 **Fair Prime* 4
As if the wreath of liberty thereon . . . . 312 **When, far* 12
Can hope the general eye thereon would gaze, . . 333 *Ded. Tour* 3
From this bare eminence thereon have cast . . 517 *Pun. Death* 1. 12
And built thereon my hopes of good to come. . 741 *Prelude* 13. 63
Barren the tablet, yet thereon appeared . . . 787 *Excursion* 3. 61

There's. (*Partial list.*)
Ay, Sir, there's nobody that feels for us. . . . 45 *Bord.* 445
You have been insolent. And there's the Baron, 46 *Bord.* 490
But there's a Providence for them who walk . . 51 *Bord.* 791
There's witchery in 't. I never knew a maid . 59 *Bord.* 1193
There's George Fisher, Charles Fleming, and Reginald Shore, ... 86 *Rural Arch.* 1
Now there's a grave—your foot is half upon it,— 98 *Brothers* 194
There's not a house within a mile, ... 126 *Idiot Boy* 22
There's none to help poor Susan Gale ; . . . 126 *Idiot Boy* 30
For of this Pony there's a rumour . . . . . 127 *Idiot Boy* 108
" As sure as there's a moon in heaven," . . . 127 *Idiot Boy* 143
There's neither horse nor man abroad, ... 128 *Idiot Boy* 175
There's nothing that can ease my pain." . . . 128 *Idiot Boy* 198
There's neither Johnny nor his Horse . . . . 128 *Idiot Boy* 219
There's neither Doctor nor his Guide. . . . . 128 *Idiot Boy* 221
There's not a single soul abroad." . . . . . 129 *Idiot Boy* 281
There's Richard Bateman, thought she to herself, 135 *Michael* 258
And there's a riddle to be guessed, ... 143 **Driven in* 22
There's not a breeze—no breath of air— . . . 155 **A whirl-blast* 14
Long as there's a sun that sets, ... 160 **Pansies, lilies* 3
There's a flower that shall be mine, ... 160 **Pansies, lilies* 7
There's joy in the mountains ; . . . . . . 190 *March* 16
There's life in the fountains ; . . . . . . 190 *March* 17
" There's neither dog nor heifer, horse nor sheep, 202 *Hart-leap* 133
There's something in a flying horse, ... 236 *P. B.* 1
There's something in a huge balloon ; . . . . 236 *P. B.* 2
There's nothing that I would not do ; . . . . 237 *P. B.* 89
" There's Galla Water, Leader Haughs, . . . 292 *Yarrow Unv.* 17
There's pleasant Tiviot-dale, a land . . . . 293 *Yarrow Unv.* 21
There's such a place as Yarrow. . . . . . 293 *Yarrow Unv.* 48
There's not a breathing of the common wind . . 305 *Toussaint* 11
There's not a nook within this solemn Pass . . 388 *Trosachs* 1
There's a cuckoo, and one or two thrushes, . . 457 **The sun has* 5
There's more of wisdom in it. . . . . . . 481 *Tables Turned* 12
There's thought and no thought, and there's paleness and bloom . . . . 482 *Character* 3

There's—*continued.*
There's weakness, and strength both redundant and vain; 482 *Character* 5
There's indifference, alike when he fails or succeeds, 482 *Character* 9
Pride where there's no envy, there's so much of joy; 482 *Character* 11
There's freedom, and sometimes a diffident stare 482 *Character* 13
There's virtue, the title it surely may claim, 482 *Character* 15
But, Babe! there's none to work for me, K.8. 262 **Ah! if* 6

Thereto. Wash with Thy blood my sins; thereto incline 366 **Eternal Lord* 12
Nay, nothing shall me bring thereto, quoth I, 561 *Cuck.and Night.*239

Thereupon. Of a proud Ararat! and, thereupon, 348 *Sky-prosp.* 2

Therewith. As aptly suits therewith that modest pace 329 *Ode: Thanks.* 15
Therewith he threw away the lance, 401 *White Doe* 516
Therewith when this true Lover 'gan behold, 562 *Troilus* 15
Therewith he cast on Pandarus an eye, 563 *Troilus* 36
By timely interference: and therewith 633 *Prelude* 1. 118
This was their rest and only hope; therewith 711 *Prelude* 9. 134
That they may knit together, and therewith 868 *Excursion* 7. 703
They blend therewith congenially: meanwhile, K.8. 249 *Recluse* 1.1.461

Therewithal. And therewithal to cover his intent 562 *Troilus* 8

These. (*Partial list.*)
Answer these questions, from our common knowledge, 38 *Bord.* 39
Performs these delicate services, and therefore 38 *Bord.* 51
'Tis weariness that breeds these gloomy fancies, 40 *Bord.* 145
When these old limbs had need of rest,—and now 42 *Bord.* 298
—These fools of feeling are mere birds of winter 47 *Bord.* 558
These ten years she has moved her lips all day 47 *Bord.* 566
These ten years she had sate all day alone 47 *Bord.* 571
These walls shall witness it—from first to last 48 *Bord.* 594
These joyful tidings from no lips but mine. 50 *Bord.* 724
These are strange sights—the mind of man, upturned, 58 *Bord.* 1168
"Among these children was a Widow's son, 553 *Prioress* 50
Methought I wist right well what these birds meant, 558 *Cuck.and Night.*108
And these inevitable charities, 568 *Cumb. Beg.* 145
Penned these sad lines, nor can forbear to pray 575 *Chiabrera* 7. 16

Thespian. As in a fit of Thespian jollity, 335 *Rhine* 3

Thessalian. As when their breath enriched Thessalian air. 210 *Laod.* 60
He veiled, attendant on Thessalian flocks) 521 *Epist.Beaumont* 41

Thessaly. That skins the plains of Thessaly, 213 *Dion* 74

They. *omitted.*

They'd. As if they'd fall asleep embracing! 179 *Waggoner* 3. 47

They'll. This is sad talk—they'll never sound for him— 100 *Brothers* 315
'He pines,' they'll say, 'it is his doom, 121 *EmigrantMother* 47
They'll both be here—'tis almost ten— 127 *Idiot Boy* 145
Susan! they'll both be here anon." 128 *Idiot Boy* 166

They're. And they're dancing merrily. 166 *Stray Pleasures* 6
Doth she betray us when they're seen? or are they but a name? 189 *Star-gazers* 16
Now they're famished or slain: S.3. 440 **Said red-ribboned* 4

They've. What they've been doing all this time, 129 *Idiot Boy* 314

Thick. *See* **Inch-thick.**
While thick above the rill the branches close, 3 *Ev. Wk.* 57
Forced hard against the wind a thick unwieldy flight. 26 *Guilt* 108
Down a thick wood, they dropt into the vale; 34 *Guilt* 524
Drops deadened from a roof so thick with leaves. 49 *Bord.* 676
Her hair was thick with many a curl 83 *We are Seven* 7
But a thick umbrage—checking the wild growth 149 *M. H.* 3
Thick as sheep in shepherd's fold! 161 **Pleasures newly* 22
And fears and fancies thick upon me came; 195 *Resolution* 27
To a thick wood he soon is brought 240 *P. B.* 341
Darkness as thick as life o'er life could fling, 271 *George: Death* 4
The dullest leaf in this thick wood 299 *Cora Linn* 2
Where towns and cities thick as stars appear, 327 *Ode 1815* 29
Her beauty dazzles the thick wood; 344 **How blest* 40
Thick boughs of palm, and willows from the brook, 346 *Processions* 11
Ripe for the hand, or under a thick shade 361 **List—'twas* 19
The encircling laurels, thick with leaves, 375 **The Minstrels* 4
Among the thick weeds, stretched alone; 397 *White Doe* 127
Amid the trees of some thick wood, 399 *White Doe* 276
Bright locks of silver hair, thick spread, 404 *White Doe* 746
How soothed, when in thick bower enclosed, 415 *White Doe* 1736
And still, 'mid yon thick woods, the primal truth 419 *Ecc. Sonn.* 1. 4. 12
Thus often, when thick gloom the east o'ershrouds, 426 *Ecc. Sonn.* 1. 29. 9
Truths whose thick veil Science has drawn aside? 469 **Desire we* 3
Rests upon ankles swoln and thick; 483 *Simon Lee* 35
To where, while thick above the branches close, 592 *Ev. Wk. Quarto* 73
Bright'ning the gloom where thick the forests stoop; 604 *Desc.Sk.Quarto* 129
Or where thick sails illume Batavia's groves; 613 *Desc.Sk.Quarto* 625
All studded round, as thick as chairs could stand, 650 *Prelude* 3. 65
Of a thick hawthorn, I could mark him well, 664 *Prelude* 4. 390
Through a thick forest. Silence touched me here 687 *Prelude* 7. 36
Of thick entangled forest, like the moon 693 *Prelude* 7. 415
With fancies thick as his inspiring stars, 695 *Prelude* 7. 566
In size a giant, stalking through thick fog, 703 *Prelude* 8. 266
With length of shade so thick, that whoso glides 706 *Prelude* 8. 460
Low-hung and thick that covered all the sky; 746 *Prelude* 14. 13
Where two tall hedge-rows of thick alder boughs 763 *Excursion* 1. 460
Rising behind a thick and lofty grove, 817 *Excursion* 4. 1064
Like leafless underboughs, in some thick wood, 824 *Excursion* 5. 148
While all the undergrove is thick with leaves, 851 *Excursion* 6. 866
Of ivy, flourishing and thick, that clasped 881 *Excursion* 8. 480
Of some thick wood, her place of covert, cleaves 891 *Excursion* 9. 493

Thick—*continued.*
Thick storm, and heavy, which for three hours' space K.8. 228 **I will* 136

Thickened. Lost in the thickened darkness, glimmers hoar; 8 *Ev. Wk.* 312

Thickening. The turbaned Race are poured in thickening swarms 427 *Ecc. Sonn.* 1. 34. 1
Proofs thickening round her that on public ends 504 *Warning* 74
Now homeward through the thickening hubbub, where 690 *Prelude* 7. 211

Thickens. Thickens, the pastoral River will forgive 382 *Duddon* 23. 11
That thickens, spreads, and, mingling fold with fold, 475 **Homeward we* 12

Thickest. While neither mist, nor thickest cloud 167 *Pilgrim's Dream* 38
Or under leaves of thickest shade, 222 *Triad* 198
Laden with summer's thickest foliage, rock 739 *Prelude* 12. 330

Thicket. This thicket will conceal us. 39 *Bord.* 102
Why, if a wolf should leap from out a thicket, 43 *Bord.* 317
Of copse and thicket, leaves the eastern shore 148 **A narrow* 4
Or blooming thicket moist with morning dews; 227 *Vernal Ode* 80
Into a thicket turns aside, 243 *P. B.* 609
Right in the middle of the thicket; 243 *P. B.* 622
To couch in this thicket of brambles alone, 340 *Fort Fuentes* 4
Checquer with paler red the thicket shades. 599 *Ev. Wk. Quarto* 398
The thicket, where th' unlisten'd stock-dove coos. 604 *Desc.Sk.Quarto* 119
The small birds find in spring no thicket there 776 *Excursion* 2. 345

Thickets. Through beds of matted fern, and tangled thickets, 185 *Nutting* 15
Open, ye thickets! let her fly, 221 *Triad* 119
But the green thickets plenteously shall yield 323 *Ode 1814* 39
And blooming thickets; nor by rocky bands 384 *Duddon* 32. 3
The spangled turf, and neighbouring thickets ring 387 **Part fenced* 13
With thickets rough and blind; 542 *Russ. Fug.* 94
Pleasant as roses in the thickets blown, 773 *Excursion* 2. 109
Glades we behold, and into thickets peep, 892 *Excursion* 9. 562
And thickets full of songsters, and the voice K.8. 240 *Recluse* 1.1.129

Thickly. Had been so thickly planted and had thriven 150 **When, to* 34
Shall soon behold this border thickly set 264 *Snowdrop* 9
Shall find such toys of fancy thickly set: 379 *Duddon* 12. 12
Who dares be wedded! Fancies thickly come 427 *Ecc. Sonn.* 1. 36. 12

Thickly-glittering. From thickly-glittering spires the matin-bell 604 *Desc.Sk.Quarto* 142

Thickly-sprouting. Whence thickly-sprouting growth of poisonous weeds; 438 *Ecc. Sonn.* 2. 37. 10

Thick-ribbed. And dark Oppression builds her thick-ribb'd tow'rs; 617 *Desc.Sk.Quarto* 795
The thick-ribbèd walls that o'ershadow the gate 620 *Convict* 9
A thick-ribbed army; not, as in the world, 639 *Prelude* 1. 517

Thick-wove. Quiet and dark; for through the thick-wove trees S.3. 417 **Sweet was* 11

Thief. If a thief could be here he might pilfer at ease; 188 *Music* 23
And Scotland has a thief as good, 291 *Rob Roy* 3

Thieves. What do they here? Listen! What; dogged like thieves! 56 *Bord.* 1017
That he's left, for a bed, to beggars or thieves! 80 †*Address: Child* 19
Oh, what would they be to my tale of two Thieves? 571 *Avarice* 12

Thigh. The structure of her laden thigh, 227 *Vernal Ode* 115
His spindles sink under him, foot, leg, and thigh! 484 **A plague* 21
Start at the reliques of that very thigh, 609 *Desc.Sk.Quarto* 412

Thin. Under a hoary oak's thin canopy, 13 *Desc. Sk.* 150
Down fell in straggling locks his thin grey hair; 24 *Guilt* 7
Or whistling thro' thin grass along the unfurrowed plain. 25 *Guilt* 36
Through a thin veil of glittering haze was seen 149 **A narrow* 45
Nor would permit the thin smoke to escape, 252 *Picture* 3
Time cannot thin thy flowing hair, 345 **How blest* 72
His thin autumnal locks where Monks abide 424 *Ecc. Sonn.* 1. 21. 5
Remaining still distinct grew thin and rare, 440 *Ecc. Sonn.* 3. 1. 10
Our fathers glimpses caught of your thin Frames, 474 **Ye shadowy* 4
His legs are thin and dry. 483 *Simon Lee* 36
That thin memento of effulgence lost 532 **Once I* 5
Are thin upon the bough. Mine, only mine, 539 **Lady! a* 35
Thin silver hairs, and ancient hamlet fame; 595 *Ev. Wk. Quarto* 176
Her road elms rustling thin above my head, 602 *Desc. Sk. Quarto* 48
With their thin umbrage, on the stately roads 680 *Prelude* 6. 361
At leisure, thence, through tracts of thin resort, 689 *Prelude* 7. 172
Her face was pale and thin—her figure, too, 767 *Excursion* 1. 751
Of winter cannot thin; the fresh air lodged 865 *Excursion* 7. 553
Of ever-humming insects, 'mid thin air 885 *Excursion* 9. 73
How pleased he is where thin and thinner grows K.8. 249 *Recluse* 1.1.478

Thine. (*Partial list.*)
In the same nest, my spring-time one with thine. 40 *Bord.* 151
This charge of thine, then ill befall thee!—Look, 42 *Bord.* 304
That wretched life of thine shall be the forfeit. 54 *Bord.* 950
The triumphs of this hour; for they are THINE! 323 **Now that* 14
Cities and towns—'tis Thou—the work is Thine!— 328 *Ode 1815* 97
For Thou art angry with Thine enemies! 328 *Ode 1815* 101
Thine arm from peril guards the coasts 328 *Ode 1815* 110
Dread Lord! so fearful when provoked, thine ire 563 *Troilus* 71

Thing. *See* **Plaything.**
For any living thing, hath faculties 23 *Yew-tree* 53
Alas! the thing she told with labouring breath 35 *Guilt* 613
It is no common thing when one like you 38 *Bord.* 50
No—no—the thing stands clear of mystery; 42 *Bord.* 261
A thing worth further notice, we must act 42 *Bord.* 292
Unless I differ from the thing I am 43 *Bord.* 319
Is it possible? One thing you noticed not: 51 *Bord.* 787
These fifteen years—*Ha! speak*—what Thing art thou? 54 *Bord.* 942
Is a most serious thing. Not I alone, 55 *Bord.* 995
A thing dependent for its casual birth 57 *Bord.* 1075
That misery is a sacred thing: for me, 58 *Bord.* 1160

Thither—continued.

Thither do I withdraw when cloudless suns	151 *When, to 88
But, when they thither came, the Youth	194 Ruth 190
By what means it could thither come, and whence ;	196 Resolution 60
This wretched Woman thither goes ;	198 Thorn 68
And thither, when the summer days were long,	202 Hart-leap 89
By choice or chance, did thither come	296 Highland Boy 138
Thither, in time of adverse shocks,	341 San Salv. 25
No vestige now remains ; yet thither creep	387 *Part fenced 6
And thither young and old repair,	396 White Doe 29
Thither the rainbow comes—the cloud—	491 Fidelity 29
Thither your eyes may turn—the Isle is passed away ;	532 †Float. Isl. 24
Or thither thronged for refuge. With quick glance	540 Grace Darl. 35
Can in a moment travel thither,	590 Immortality 169
After long absence, thither I repaired,	642 Prelude 2. 37
When thou wert thither guided. From the heart	679 Prelude 6. 278
That, thither driven from some unsheltered place,	692 Prelude 7. 326
Upon his knee, whom he had thither brought	696 Prelude 7. 609
Thither he comes with spring-time, there abides .	702 Prelude 8. 198
His flock, and thither from the homestead bears .	702 Prelude 8. 226
Who thither comes to find in it his home ?	729 Prelude 11. 148
Thither, uncertain on which road to fix	738 Prelude 12. 295
My expectation, thither I repaired,	738 Prelude 12. 296
Thither I came, and there, amid the gloom	756 Excursion 1. 28
That fed upon the Common, thither came	767 Excursion 1. 746
Thither his popular talents he transferred ;	774 Excursion 2. 219
Motions of moonlight, all come thither—touch,	782 Excursion 2. 714
And have an answer—thither come, and shape	782 Excursion 2. 715
That from your garden thither soars, to feed .	808 Excursion 4. 496
Thither we turned ; and gathered, as we read, .	846 Excursion 6. 513
By nature only ; but, if thither led,	855 Excursion 6. 1146
Said she, " for thither as the trees grew up,	K.8. 247 Recluse 1.1.397

Thitherward. With Luke that evening thitherward he walked .   136 Michael 329

Looked thitherward. One, reckoning by years, .	711 Prelude 9. 139
With this persuasion thitherward my steps	833 Excursion 5. 750
While thitherward we shape our course ; or while	891 Excursion 9. 497

Tho'. (Partial list.) See **Although, Though.**

Dreading, tho' wishing, to be near it :	79 Sparrow's Nest 12
With patient care. What tho' assaults run high,	514 *Blest Statesman 6
Where, tho' her far-off twilight ditty steal,	596 Ev. Wk. Quarto 225
'Tho' now no more thy maids their voices suit .	615 Desc.Sk.Quarto 748

Thomas. Their Thomas in Finland, .   162 *Art thou the 7

Thong. And what is Penance with her knotted thong;   433 Ecc. Sonn. 2. 19. 1

Thor. He served in folly. Woden falls, and Thor .   423 Ecc. Sonn. 1. 17. 5

Thorn. Thus warned he sought some shepherd's spreading thorn   25 Guilt 41

Thy couch the dewy earth, thy roof the forest thorn ! "	104 Artegal 161
Sharper than the pointed thorn."	140 Arm. Lady 46
The yew, the holly, and the bright green thorn, .	146 *It was an 32
" There is a Thorn—it looks so old,	197 Thorn 1
It stands erect, this aged Thorn,	197 Thorn 6
And this poor Thorn they clasp it round	197 Thorn 17
To bury this poor Thorn for ever.	197 Thorn 22
This Thorn you on your left espy ;	198 Thorn 28
" And, close beside this aged Thorn,	198 Thorn 34
Which close beside the Thorn you see, .	198 Thorn 50
" Now would you see this aged Thorn,	198 Thorn 56
And there, beside the Thorn, she sits	198 Thorn 71
And why sits she beside the Thorn ?	198 Thorn 82
The pond—and Thorn, so old and grey ;	198 Thorn 94
" But that she goes to this old Thorn, .	199 Thorn 166
The Thorn which I described to you,	199 Thorn 167
" But what's the Thorn ? and what the pond ? .	200 Thorn 199
But plain it is the Thorn is bound .	200 Thorn 233
Dismounting, then, he leaned against a thorn ;	201 Hart-leap 33
Close to the thorn on which Sir Walter leaned .	201 Hart-leap 37
" In April here beneath the flowering thorn	203 Hart-leap 153
Beneath the broom or budding thorn, .	239 P. B. 259
Whose temples bled beneath the platted thorn. .	255 Easter 8
Or rain-drop lingering on the pointed thorn. .	265 *There is a pleasure 14
The Gordon, couched behind a thorn, .	287 Ellen Irwin 22
In his pure presence near the trysting thorn—	383 Duddon 28. 13
On her last thorn the nightly moon has shone ;	393 Inglewood 4
Retreated towards a brake of thorn, .	412 White Doe 1477
Its hinder part concealed by hedge-row thorn. .	523 Epist. Beaumont 124
That lip—a rose-bud from the thorn, .	530 Gleaner 5
Whose curtain pine or thorn, .	542 Russ. Fug. 42
In misery near the miserable Thorn ;—	752 Prelude 14. 407
She seeks a wilderness of weed and thorn, .	K.8. 325[?]*The vestal 3

Thorns. At thorns, and brakes, and brambles,—and in truth .   185 Nutting 13

The crown of thorns, hands pierced upon the tree,	366 *Eternal Lord 5
The crown of thorns ; whose life-blood flowed, the price	420 Ecc. Sonn. 1. 8. 8
The crown of thorns around his bleeding brow	476 *Tranquillity! the 8
No thorns can pierce her tender feet,	583 *O for a 40
That the thorns wound her not ; they only guard.	835 Excursion 5. 843
'Mid thorns and brambles ; or a bird that breaks	886 Excursion 9. 171
The nails, the thorns, and thy two hands, thy face	K.8. 266 *Rid of 6

Thorny. And backward wanderings along thorny ways :   748 Prelude 14. 138

Stuffed with the thorny substance of the past	817 Excursion 4. 1054

Thorough. We'll wander Scotland thorough ;   293 Yarrow Unv. 38

The forest thorough !	485 *Bright Flower 8
Echoing thorough all the green wood wide. .	558 Cuck.andNight.100

Thorough-bred. For a Sempstress thorough-bred. .   S.3. 437 *I, whose 22

Thoroughly. With gratulation thoroughly benign !   324 Ode 1814 110

And she is thoroughly forlorn :	414 White Doe 1622
A spirit thoroughly faithful to itself,	720 Prelude 10. 167
Felt deeply, but not thoroughly understood .	728 Prelude 11. 87
Of suffering hath been thoroughly fortified . .	801 Excursion 4. 19
Inspired, and thoroughly fortified ?—If the heart	827 Excursion 5. 355
Thoroughly disciplined ; nor (if in course .	839 Excursion 6. 58

Thorp. From thorp or vill his matins sound for me,   424 Ecc. Sonn. 1. 22. 13

Thorpe. Among the tenantry of thorpe and vill ; .   875 Excursion 8. 100

Those. (Partial list.)

Those eyeballs dark—dark beyond hope of light,	39 Bord. 136
When into one of those same spotted bells	44 Bord. 403
Within those empty walls. I too have seen her ;	47 Bord. 572
With those who take the spirit of their rule .	48 Bord. 584
Would drive those Scottish Rovers to their dens .	50 Bord. 729
Where none but those who trampled on my rights	52 Bord. 844
This Provost doth for those bad Jews prepare .	555 Prioress 178
Surrounded by those wild unpeopled hills,	566 Cumb. Beg. 14
In acts of love to those with whom they dwell, .	568 Cumb. Beg. 139
Those life-consuming sounds that clog the air, .	569 Cumb. Beg. 181
With fondness on those sweet Nestorian strains. .	573 Chiabrera 2. 11
Those laureat wreaths ungathered which the Nymphs .	576 Chiabrera 9. 13

Thou, omitted.

Though. (Partial list.) See **Tho'**.

Though I have never seen his face, methinks, .	39 Bord. 87
Though at a distance and he was disguised, . .	42 Bord. 277
I love her, though I dare not call her daughter. .	47 Bord. 536
You will be firm : but though we well may trust	48 Bord. 602
Though rich in heavenly, poor in earthly, comfort,	49 Bord. 686
And do good service, though she knew it not. .	52 Bord. 842
Though but a glimpse, it sent me to my prayers. .	55 Bord. 973
Faithful, though swift as lightning, the meek dove ;	153 Morn. Ex. 37
In sooth, I speak from feeling, what though now	557 Cuck. and Night. 36
Though thou the Cuckoo heard, ere thou heard'st me ;	561 Cuck.andNight.233
Though I be far from her I reverence,	562 Cuck.andNight.306
Though he to no one give the fortitude	568 Cumb. Beg. 128
Duly as Friday comes, though pressed herself	568 Cumb. Beg. 156
And recognised it, though an altered form, .	571 *There is a Flower 10

Thought. See **After-thought.**

Vain thought !—Yet be as now thou art, .	9 Collins 9
What high resolves exalt the tenderest thought	15 Desc. Sk. 297
Rocked the charmed thought in more delightful dreams ;	22 Desc. Sk. 631
All but neglect. The world, for so it thought,	23 Yew-tree 20
Which he has never used ; that thought with him	23 Yew-tree 54
Who, in the silent hour of inward thought,	23 Yew-tree 62
Some labourer, thought he, may perchance be near;	25 Guilt 32
Nor, if accosted now, in thought engrossed, .	26 Guilt 97
Banished that dismal thought ; and now the wind	27 Guilt 191
Here paused she, of all present thought forlorn, .	30 Guilt 307
A thought resigned with pain, when from the mast	31 Guilt 354
" And oft I thought (my fancy was so strong)	31 Guilt 361
A sudden joy surprised expiring thought, .	35 Guilt 624
(Reader, forgive the intolerable thought) .	36 Guilt 659
He seemed to quarrel with the very thought. .	38 Bord. 58
I thought the Convent never would appear ; .	39 Bord. 113
'Tis but for a few days—a thought has struck me.	41 Bord. 224
I never should have thought of it again .	42 Bord. 274
I dare not trust myself with such a thought—	42 Bord. 289
Was crying, as I thought, crying for bread .	44 Bord. 399
I thought I saw the skeleton of Idonea. .	47 Bord. 581
Of this Man's crimes beyond the reach of thought ?	51 Bord. 781
At this audacious blasphemy, I thought .	51 Bord. 793
A wretched Outcast—but this strain of thought .	52 Bord. 830
You thought his voice the echo of Idonea's. .	53 Bord. 887
A thought that's worth a thousand worlds ! I grieve	55 Bord. 1003
That flatters us, because it asks not thought ;	56 Bord. 1034
Shall Nature be avenged. 'Tis nobly thought ; .	58 Bord. 1123
One happy thought has passed across my mind. .	61 Bord. 1326
Deep, deep and vast, vast beyond human thought,	64 Bord. 1466
It cannot live with thought ; think on, think on,	65 Bord. 1561
That she is innocent. Leave that thought awhile	67 Bord. 1678
Banish the thought, crush it, and be at peace. .	69 Bord. 1750
Give not to them a thought. From Palestine	70 Bord. 1801
I thought he grasped my hand .	72 Bord. 1955
A single tree ; she thought it was her Father.— .	74 Bord. 2098
In some degree. Between us stood, I thought, .	75 Bord. 2145
Alas, the thought of such a cruel death .	75 Bord. 2156
Who, casting as I thought a guilty Person	76 Bord. 2210
Forgive me !—Saints forgive me. Had I thought	76 Bord. 2241
I thought there was no harm : but that bad Man,	77 Bord. 2245
Within the compass of a mortal thought, .	78 Bord. 2300
A Man by pain and thought compelled to live, .	78 Bord. 2351
And love, and thought, and joy. .	79 Sparrow's Nest 20
O blessèd tidings ! thought of joy ! .	81 †Mother's Return 5
Again, as if the thought would choke .	82 Alice Fell 46
I thought of Kilve's delightful shore, .	85 Anecdote 10
Kilve, thought I, was a favoured place, .	86 Anecdote 23
Thus, thought I, to her lamb that little Maid might sing	87 Pet-lamb 20
And fittest to unutterable thought .	88 H. C. 3
I thought of times when Pain might be thy guest,	88 H. C. 15
Leave that thought ; and here be uttered .	94 Westmoreland Girl 89
Ay, thought the Vicar, smiling to himself, .	96 Brothers 104
Why, there, Sir, is a thought that's new to me ! .	98 Brothers 174
The thought of death sits easy on the man	98 Brothers 182

Thought—*continued.*

Why fix upon his wealth or want a thought ?	529 *Poor Robin* 16
A charm, *that* thought can not destroy,	530 †*Redbreast* 7
With this day's work, in thought and word.	534 *Blest is* 90
Whence, then, could it come—the thought—	535 *Egremont* 45
Thus Hubert thought in his dismay,	536 *Egremont* 95
Deliberate traces, registers of thought	539 *Lady ! a* 4
A thought for your dear sake :	542 *Russ. Fug.* 84
But when she of her Parents thought,	544 *Russ. Fug.* 225
Along the beach of this small isle and thought	551 *If thou in* 20
With face all pale with dread and busy thought,	554 *Prioress* 138
Gave to her thought, that in a little space	555 *Prioress* 153
I of a token thought which Lovers heed ;	557 *Cuck.and Night.* 47
And then I thought anon as it was day,	557 *Cuck.and Night.* 51
Broke silence, or I heard him in my thought..	558 *Cuck.and Night.* 90
Him thought his sorrowful heart would break in two ;	562 *Troilus* 12
Like frost he thought his heart was icy cold ; .	563 *Troilus* 17
Than they were wont to be—for he thought so ; .	564 *Troilus* 142
That first mild touch of sympathy and thought, .	568 *Cumb. Beg.* 114
Must needs impress a transitory thought	568 *Cumb. Beg.* 124
For Adam was simple in thought ; and the poor,	569 *Farmer* 25
With thought.—He is insensibly subdued	572 *Animal Tran.* 7
Himself above each lower thought uplifting,	576 *Chiabrera* 9. 15
And what beyond this thought we crave	578 *I come* 70
The tender peace of rural thought :	579 *Sweet Flower* 23
For that last thought of parting Friends	580 *John Words.* 23
But hushed be every thought that springs	583 *O for a* 37
Tease, and the thought of time so spent depress, .	584 *Ch. Lamb* 7
To me alone there came a thought of grief ;	588 *Immortality* 22
A timely utterance gave that thought relief,	588 *Immortality* 23
A place of thought where we in waiting lie ;] .	589 *Immortality* 124
The thought of our past years in me doth breed .	589 *Immortality* 137
We in thought will join your throng,	590 *Immortality* 175
Britain, who thought to stain the field was fame,	619 *School Ex.* 55
And sad experience forbade a thought .	620 *Birth of Love* 22
The thought of her was like a flash of light, .	622 *Recluse* 1. 1. 92
Bids every thought be kind ?	626 †*Cento* 6
To mould and stamp the ore of thought	629 *Installation* 83
Trances of thought and mountings of the mind	632 *Prelude* 1. 19
Days of sweet leisure, taxed with patient thought	632 *Prelude* 1. 43
Then feels immediately some hollow thought	636 *Prelude* 1. 259
Thou Soul that art the eternity of thought,	638 *Prelude* 1. 402
The elements of feeling and of thought,	638 *Prelude* 1. 411
If each most obvious and particular thought,	645 *Prelude* 2. 229
Evening and morning, sleep and waking, thought	647 *Prelude* 2. 355
O'er all that, lost beyond the reach of thought	648 *Prelude* 2. 403
Voyaging through strange seas of Thought, alone.	650 *Prelude* 3. 63
From strict analogies by thought supplied	651 *Prelude* 3. 125
Come forth, perhaps without one quiet thought.	652 *Prelude* 3. 255
Upon the cypress spire in lonely thought	655 *Prelude* 3. 440
Or been more often thought of with regret ;	659 *Prelude* 4. 84
Then into solemn thought I passed once more.	661 *Prelude* 4. 190
Or some uneasy thought ; yet still his form	664 *Prelude* 4. 406
Of study and hard thought ; there, there, it is	665 *Prelude* 5. 10
A thought is with me sometimes, and I say,—	666 *Prelude* 5. 29
By love and feeling, and internal thought	667 *Prelude* 5. 146
And thought that, in the blind and awful lair	668 *Prelude* 5. 151
With any thought that looks at others' blame ;	669 *Prelude* 5. 262
For, ever as a thought of purer birth	670 *Prelude* 5. 332
Who make our wish, our power, our thought a deed,	673 *Prelude* 5. 528
At thought of raptures now for ever flown ; .	673 *Prelude* 5. 546
By such a daring thought, that I might leave	676 *Prelude* 6. 55
Maintained even by the very name and thought .	676 *Prelude* 6. 58
Rebuild it to his liking. I have thought .	679 *Prelude* 6. 294
Such grief for thee would be the weakest thought	679 *Prelude* 6. 317
That had usurped upon a living thought .	683 *Prelude* 6. 527
Or mildest visitations of pure thought,	685 *Prelude* 6. 684
And thought of London—held me by a chain	688 *Prelude* 7. 86
Articulate music. Above all, one thought	688 *Prelude* 7. 115
Of daylight, the bare thought of where I was .	694 *Prelude* 7. 453
By which the world of memory and thought .	694 *Prelude* 7. 464
I mused, and thought, and felt, in solitude. .	694 *Prelude* 7. 485
To steady me : each airy thought revolved .	705 *Prelude* 8. 430
As well they might, the impersonated thought,	706 *Prelude* 8. 501
I trembled,—thought, at times, of human life	706 *Prelude* 8. 512
Upon my heart ; no thought embodied, no .	707 *Prelude* 8. 553
Weighed with me, could support the test of thought ;	708 *Prelude* 8. 628
Or deemed it worth a moment's thought to stir, .	711 *Prelude* 9. 137
Of ancient Story, thought of each bright spot, .	715 *Prelude* 9. 365
And fan each other ; thought of sects, how keen .	715 *Prelude* 9. 370
From earnest dialogues I slipped in thought, .	716 *Prelude* 9. 438
A thought to human welfare,—that, henceforth .	717 *Prelude* 9. 535
In thought or conversation, public acts, .	717 *Prelude* 9. 543
Earth free from them for ever, as was thought,—	719 *Prelude* 10. 45
I thought of those September massacres, .	719 *Prelude* 10. 73
Yet did I grieve, nor only grieved, but thought	720 *Prelude* 10. 146
I thought, still traversing that widespread plain, .	726 *Prelude* 10. 545
Resistance strong as heretofore, I thought .	727 *Prelude* 11. 22
And thought that other notions were as sound, .	728 *Prelude* 11. 50
That Nature gives to Poets, now by thought .	733 *Prelude* 11. 416
Yea, never thought of judging ; with the gift .	737 *Prelude* 12. 189
By false opinion and contentious thought, .	737 *Prelude* 12. 211
Plans without thought, or built on theories .	741 *Prelude* 13. 70
The thought, the image, and the silent joy : .	744 *Prelude* 13. 272
And three chance human wanderers, in calmthought	747 *Prelude* 14. 65
Through every image and through every thought,	747 *Prelude* 14. 116
Faith in life endless, the sustaining thought .	749 *Prelude* 14. 204
Of genial thought in childhood, and in spite .	749 *Prelude* 14. 239
Or by predominance of thought oppressed, .	758 *Excursion* 1. 159

Thought—*continued.*

Thought was not ; in enjoyment it expired. .	759 *Excursion* 1. 213
In oft-recurring hours of sober thought .	760 *Excursion* 1. 240
And from the stillness of abstracted thought .	760 *Excursion* 1. 292
In dreams, in study, and in ardent thought, .	760 *Excursion* 1. 301
In solitude and solitary thought	761 *Excursion* 1. 354
He had imbibed of fear or darker thought	762 *Excursion* 1. 407
And grow with thought. Beside yon spring I stood,	763 *Excursion* 1. 484
I thought of that poor Woman as of one .	765 *Excursion* 1. 613
With many a short-lived thought that passed between, .	767 *Excursion* 1. 705
As if the thought were but a moment old, .	772 *Excursion* 2. 88
Ah ! what a sweet Recess, thought I, is here ! .	776 *Excursion* 2. 349
Not worth the trouble of a thought ?—alas ! .	783 *Excursion* 2. 792
Thought I, if master of a vacant hour, .	787 *Excursion* 3. 44
With the American (a thought which suits .	789 *Excursion* 3. 240
And utter darkness : thought which may be faced,	790 *Excursion* 3. 262
In feeding thought, wherever thought could feed)	790 *Excursion* 3. 289
And suffer now, not seldom, from the thought .	793 *Excursion* 3. 486
" What followed cannot be reviewed in thought ;	796 *Excursion* 3. 680
That which is veiled from waking thought ; conjured	796 *Excursion* 3. 687
In the old World compare, thought I, for power .	799 *Excursion* 3. 882
On the first motion of a holy thought ; .	804 *Excursion* 4. 217
Carried so high, that every thought, which looked	805 *Excursion* 4. 263
To thought and to the climbing intellect, .	806 *Excursion* 4. 348
Nor wanting here, to entertain the thought .	807 *Excursion* 4. 439
Of his own reason, without sense or thought .	811 *Excursion* 4. 668
Upon the flowing stream, a thought arose .	812 *Excursion* 4. 754
Pious beyond the intention of your thought ; .	818 *Excursion* 4. 1149
He is compassionate ; and has no thought, .	819 *Excursion* 4. 1228
How vain, thought I, is it by change of place .	822 *Excursion* 5. 20
Cheering my days, and with industrious thought ;	823 *Excursion* 5. 56
And undisguised, and strong and serious thought ;	824 *Excursion* 5. 119
Are all renounced ; high as the thought of man	826 *Excursion* 5. 287
Thought I—some friendly covert must be near. .	833 *Excursion* 5. 749
Lost, thought I, in the obscurities of time, .	834 *Excursion* 5. 787
With an unsettled liberty of thought, .	842 *Excursion* 6. 239
Abundant exercise for thought and speech, .	844 *Excursion* 6. 385
Exclaimed the Sceptic, " and the strain of thought	846 *Excursion* 6. 523
Wrinkled and furrowed with habitual thought	848 *Excursion* 6. 683
To Providence submissive, so she thought ; .	849 *Excursion* 6. 744
Or dread was all that had been thought of,—joy.	852 *Excursion* 6. 910
Of such excitement and divided thought, .	852 *Excursion* 6. 958
And pleasure in endurance. Much she thought, .	854 *Excursion* 6. 1027
Forbearance, charity in deed and thought, .	862 *Excursion* 7. 329
—Vain thought ! but wherefore murmur or repine ?	863 *Excursion* 7. 387
Of the whole countenance alive with thought, .	865 *Excursion* 7. 510
Futurity was thought, in ancient times, .	865 *Excursion* 7. 532
By any one more thought of than by him .	866 *Excursion* 7. 574
And prayer and thought can bring to worst distress	868 *Excursion* 7. 688
Unknowing and unknown. A pleasing thought .	871 *Excursion* 7. 929
But why no softening thought of gratitude, .	873 *Excursion* 7. 1028
Foreseen, had dared to couple, even in thought, .	875 *Excursion* 8. 39
That made the very thought of country-life .	878 *Excursion* 8. 243
A thought of refuge, for a mind detained .	878 *Excursion* 8. 244
Thrives by the forfeiture—unfeeling thought, .	878 *Excursion* 8. 284
Yet have I thought that we might also speak, .	885 *Excursion* 9. 50
Uttering, for elevation of our thought, .	885 *Excursion* 9. 88
Power inaccessible to human thought, .	893 *Excursion* 9. 615
Your very poorest rich in peace of thought .	895 *Excursion* 9. 734
Will find a vent ; and thought is praise to him, .	895 *Excursion* 9. 752
By processes minute), even so—when thought .	S.3. 435 *The doubt* 112
More than one thought of death, and his last hour.	K.8. 229 *I will* 158
As inward motions of the wandering thought .	K.8. 233 *Along the* 2
A dearer thought, or in the heart of love .	K.8. 234 *Witness thou* 5
And, (if a thought of dying, if a thought .	K.8. 236 *Recluse* 1.1. 12
Scarcely a wish, but one bright pleasing thought,	K.8. 237 *Recluse* 1.1. 16
And not feel motions there ? He thought of clouds	K.8. 237 *Recluse* 1.1.25
As beautiful to thought, as it had been, .	K.8. 237 *Recluse* 1.1.49
Which had been sighed for, ancient thought ful-filled	K.8. 239 *Recluse* 1.1.107
Recal my song the ungenerous thought ; forgive,	K.8. 244 *Recluse* 1.1.269
Thus we do soothe ourselves, and when the thought	K.8. 244 *Recluse* 1.1.290
Hath furnished matter for a thought ; perchance,	K.8. 248 *Recluse* 1.1.443
Their little boons of animating thought .	K.8. 249 *Recluse* 1.1.467
Pass with a thought the life of the whole year	K.8. 252 *Recluse* 1.1.589
Sometimes in act, and evermore in thought, .	K.8. 256 *Recluse* 1.1.714
All plain blunt sense, all subtlety of thought. .	L.1. 88 *Juvenal* 1. 8
But here's a thought which well our mirth may cross	L.1. 95 *Juvenal* 3. 14

Thoughtful.

With joyousness, and with a thoughtful cheer,	106 *Farewell* 30
Sickening into thoughtful quiet ; .	180 *Waggoner* 4. 72
A Being breathing thoughtful breath, .	186 *She was* 23
In thoughtful reverence to the Prince of Peace, .	255 *Easter* 7
The piercing eye, the thoughtful brow, .	285 *Grave of Burns* 25
Of thoughtful Herdsman when he strays .	292 *Rob Roy* 114
Yet were the thoughtful grieved ; and still that voice .	312 *A Roman* 9
Of thoughtful sentiment for every mind .	355 *Aquap.* 149
That everywhere, before the thoughtful mind, .	364 *What aim* 13
Thoughtful and sad, the " narrow house." No style	389 *Breadalb.* 2
And then a thoughtful pause ensued : .	403 *White Doe* 679
A little thoughtful pause it made ; .	414 *White Doe* 1649
Where thoughtful Edwin, tutored in the school .	422 *Ecc. Sonn.* 1. 15. 2
In thoughtful moments, wafted by the gales .	438 *Ecc. Sonn.* 2. 39. 13
The thoughtful Monks, intent their God to please,	468 *St. Bees* 142
To *us* save matter for a thoughtful sigh, .	474 *On to* 2
The Tragic Muse thee served with thoughtful vow ;	476 *Tranquillity ! the* 4
Hence thoughtful Mercy, Mercy sage and pure, .	519 *Pun. Death* 11. 9

Thoughtful—*continued.*
Exalt the sense of thoughtful gratitude . . . 538 **In desultory* 53
And poured out truth in works by thoughtful love 584 *Ch. Lamb* 16
In this recess, by thoughtful Fancy built, . . . 654 *Prelude* 3. 379
For my grave looks, too thoughtful for my years. 757 *Excursion* 1. 59
Observant, studious, thoughtful, and refreshed 762 *Excursion* 1. 394
Even as a thoughtful shepherd by a flash . . . 796 *Excursion* 3. 707
—Serious and thoughtful was her mind ; and yet, 850 *Excursion* 6. 824
Of many tears, virtuous and thoughtful grief ; . 864 *Excursion* 7. 470
Of all-beholding Man, earth's thoughtful lord ; . 876 *Excursion* 8. 164
" So fare the many ; and the thoughtful few, 894 *Excursion* 9. 658
Thoughtfully. Art pacing thoughtfully the vessel's deck . . . . 151 **When, to* 101
Thoughtfully freighted with a various store ; . . 522 *Epist. Beaumont* 94
Thoughtfully fitted to the Orphean lyre ; . . . 635 *Prelude* 1. 233
Thoughtfulness. Of thoughtfulness and beauty, yield 222 *Triad* 195
If steady moods of thoughtfulness matured . . 651 *Prelude* 3. 148
Thoughtless. In thoughtless gaiety I coursed the plain, ... 2 *Ev. Wk.* 21
'Mid the green mountains many a thoughtless song 28 *Guilt* 246
How in a simple freak of thoughtless play . . 33 *Guilt* 472
And the light dancing of the thoughtless heart ; . 65 *Bord.* 1547
'Cross the brook its thoughtless dam. . . . . 93 *Westmoreland Girl* 4
Even as ye do, thoughtless pair ! . . . . . 171 *Kitten* 110
In thoughtless freedom, bold. . . . . . . 192 *Ruth* 6
Of thoughtless youth ; but hearing oftentimes . 207 *Tintern* 90
A thoughtless Thing ! who, once unblest, . . . 485 **Bright Flower* 10
When link'd with thoughtless Mirth I cours'd the plain, ... 592 *Ev. Wk. Quarto* 31
In many a thoughtless hour, when, from excess . 645 *Prelude* 2. 186
With their own thoughtless melodies ; at least . 668 *Prelude* 5. 176
A course of vain delights and thoughtless guilt, . 794 *Excursion* 3. 560
The ship went gliding with her thoughtless crew ; 798 *Excursion* 3. 836
The trailing worm reprove her thoughtless pride ? 807 *Excursion* 4. 426
Than this, to graze the herb in thoughtless peace, 827 *Excursion* 5. 329
The thinking, thoughtless, school-boy ; the bold youth . . . . 836 *Excursion* 5. 959
Produced, when thoughtless Folly hath usurped . 842 *Excursion* 6. 280
" Ah ! what a warning for a thoughtless man, . 850 *Excursion* 6. 806
Thus silence broke :—" Behold a thoughtless Man 862 *Excursion* 7. 299
Mount with a thoughtless impulse, and wheel there, K.8. 242 *Recluse* 1. 1. 200
Who pushed by thoughtless youth to deeds of shame . . . . L.1. 96 *Juvenal* 3. 55
Thoughtlessly. Her beauty thoughtlessly disparaged. 265 **The Shepherd* 8
Thought-perplexing. Some spake, by thought-perplexing fears betrayed ; . . . . . 445 *Ecc. Sonn.* 3. 22. 6
Thought's. To my most grievous loss !—That thought's return . . . . 257 **Surprised by* 9
Make sadder transits o'er thought's optic glass . 269 *Malham* 13
Charged with rich words poured out in thought's defence ; . . . . 441 *Ecc. Sonn.* 3. 4. 2
Unlocking bleeding Thought's " memorial cell ; " 613 *Desc. Sk. Quarto* 627
Thoughts. *See* **Day-thoughts.**
Harmonious thoughts, a soul by truth refined, . 3 *Ev. Wk.* 84
While chastening thoughts of sweetest use, bestowed 11 *Desc. Sk.* 27
And *there* are those fond thoughts which Solitude, 15 *Desc. Sk.* 248
His thoughts, the central point of all his joys. . 19 *Desc. Sk.* 481
Surely in other thoughts contempt may die. . . 20 *Desc. Sk.* 550
Which now with freezing thoughts did all her powers assail ; . . . . 27 *Guilt* 171
The silent sea. From the sweet thoughts of home 31 *Guilt* 357
Besides, on griefs so fresh my thoughts were brooding still. . . . . 32 *Guilt* 423
Yet calm he seemed as thoughts so poignant would allow. . . . . 33 *Guilt* 486
Deluge of tender thoughts then rushed amain, . 33 *Guilt* 494
The father, and relenting thoughts awoke ; . . 33 *Guilt* 501
More of man's thoughts and ways than his experience . . . . 38 *Bord.* 35
Garlands and flowers, and cakes and merry thoughts, ... 44 *Bord.* 372
'Twas this that put it in my thoughts—that countenance— . . . . 54 *Bord.* 925
No.—Thoughts and feelings will sink deep, but then 58 *Bord.* 1171
All thoughts whose idle composition lives . . . 65 *Bord.* 1550
Of thoughts that fail, and a decaying heart ; . . 66 *Bord.* 1631
My thoughts on former pleasures ran ; . . . 85 *Anecdote* 9
Yet by some grave thoughts attended . . . . 90 *Longest Day* 9
Nor could my heart by second thoughts from heaviness be cleared, ... 91 *Poet's Dream* 5
Sight that inspired accordant thoughts ; and speech I thus renewed : . . . . . 92 *Poet's Dream* 48
Give to Him prayers, and many thoughts, in thy most busy days ; . . . . 93 *Poet's Dream* 58
Your Dalesmen, then, do in each other's thoughts 98 *Brothers* 184
His thoughts were turned on Leonard's luckless fortune, ... 101 *Brothers* 390
And thoughts which had been his an hour before, 102 *Brothers* 423
What fond and wayward thoughts will slide . . 109 **Strange fits* 25
My thoughts are all that I possess, ... 113 *Lament* 55
Sometimes with thoughts of very bliss ! . . . 117 *Affl. Marg.* 12
When from these lofty thoughts I woke, . . . 119 *Sailor's Mother* 13
Was traversed from without ; much, too, of thoughts . . . . 124 *V. and J.* 179
Her thoughts are bent on deadly sin, . . . 129 *Idiot Boy* 293
The last of all her thoughts would be . . . . 129 *Idiot Boy* 310
Were things indifferent to the Shepherd's thoughts. 132 *Michael* 64
Brings hope with it, and forward-looking thoughts, 133 *Michael* 148
These thoughts, and many others of like sort, . 135 *Michael* 271
And of this moment ; hither turn thy thoughts, . 137 *Michael* 407
With confident and cheerful thoughts ; and now . 138 *Michael* 439

Thoughts—*continued.*
Sweet thoughts of angels hovering nigh, . . . 144 **Driven in* 43
" Our thoughts at least are ours ; and this wild nook, ... 146 **It was an* 38
What thoughts immediately were ours, nor how . 149 **A narrow* 67
And temper all our thoughts with charity. . . 149 **A narrow* 73
Its image would survive among his thoughts : . 149 *M. H.* 22
" But now proud thoughts are in your breast— . 155 *Waterfall* 41
Thoughts of thy raising : . . . . 158 **With little* 12
From heaven to earth our thoughts will pass, . 164 **Fair Lady* 26
Sad thoughts, and breathes with easier breath ; . 164 **Fair Lady* 34
From bloody deeds his thoughts are far ; . . . 166 *Danish Boy* 51
Within the region of a father's thoughts, . . . 172 *Infant Daughter* 44
He thus pursues his thoughts at leisure. . . . 174 *Waggoner* 1. 109
Who, to his inward thoughts confined, . . . 176 *Waggoner* 2. 25
To *seek* for thoughts of a gloomy cast, ... 177 *Waggoner* 2. 74
Which called their thoughts another way : . . 179 *Waggoner* 3. 100
To stay the wanderer's steps and soothe his thoughts. . . . . 184 *Airey-force* 16
Such thoughts to Lucy I will give . . . . . 187 **Three years* 34
Of thoughts with better thoughts at strife, . . 191 *Seq. Beggars* 19
The thoughts with which it then was cheered ; . 191 *Seq. Beggars* 28
She seemed to live ; her thoughts her own ; . . 192 *Ruth* 14
Fond thoughts about a father's love : . . . . 193 *Ruth* 86
False thoughts, thoughts bold and vain, . . . 194 *Ruth* 165
Dim sadness—and blind thoughts, I knew not, nor could name. . . . . 195 *Resolution* 28
When I with these untoward thoughts had striven, 196 *Resolution* 53
My former thoughts returned : the fear that kills ; 197 *Resolution* 113
While I these thoughts within myself pursued, . 197 *Resolution* 132
I stood in various thoughts and fancies lost, . . 202 *Hart-leap* 117
" What thoughts must through the creature's brain have past ! . . . . 203 *Hart-leap* 141
No thoughts hath he but thoughts that pass . . 204 *Brougham* 74
Revenge, and all ferocious thoughts were dead : . 205 *Brougham* 166
Thoughts of more deep seclusion ; and connect . 205 *Tintern* 7
Of present pleasure, but with pleasing thoughts . 206 *Tintern* 63
Of elevated thoughts ; a sense sublime . . 207 *Tintern* 95
The anchor of my purest thoughts, the nurse, . 207 *Tintern* 109
With lofty thoughts, that neither evil tongues, . 207 *Tintern* 128
Should be thy portion, with what healing thoughts 207 *Tintern* 144
In thoughts whose sternness makes them sweet ; 217 *Enterprise* 126
Thy thoughts and feelings shall not die, . . . 218 *Young Lady* 13
And thoughts with things at strife ; . . . . 223 *Wishing-gate* 9
And not in vain, when thoughts are cast . . . 223 *Wishing-gate* 49
Heaven will not tax our thoughts with pride . . 228 *Devot. Incit.* 11
Know—that, for him whose waking thoughts, severe . . . . 229 *Cuckoo-clock* 27
I pace it unrepining, for my thoughts . . . . 230 *Clouds* 58
The gentlest Poet, with free thoughts endowed, . 231 **The gentlest Poet* 1
" To all the unshaped half-human thoughts . . 239 *P. B.* 296
From human thoughts and purposes, ... 246 *P. B.* 857
I cannot well express the thoughts . . . . 246 *P. B.* 871
But many good and pious thoughts . . . . 246 *P. B.* 896
From his own thoughts did Peter start ; . . . 248 *P. B.* 1078
To thy regard, with thoughts so fortunate, . . 250 **Happy the* 11
All anguish ; Saint that evil thoughts and aims . 253 **Fond words* 7
Dear mother of fresh thoughts and joyous health ! 254 **A flock* 14
Modest her mien ; and she, whose thoughts keep pace . . . . 256 *Marriage : Friend* 7
Do Thou, then, breathe those thoughts into my mind . . . . 257 **The prayers* 9
Or map of the whole world : thoughts, link by link, 260 **How sweet* 11
May feed on thoughts though pensive not austere ; 264 **Lady ! I* 12
Becoming thoughts, I trust, of solemn gloom . . 264 **Lady ! the* 10
May lead the thoughts, thus struggling used to stand 265 **When haughty* 10
Her thoughts less deep, or void of grave intent . 270 **Though the bold* 10
But from that bondage when her thoughts were freed . . . . 274 **Wait, prithee* 5
That child of winter, prompting thoughts that climb 274 **Such age* 10
Yet have my thoughts for thee been vigilant— . 277 **Why art* 5
Conqueror, 'mid some sad thoughts, divinely blest ! 278 *Wellington* 14
The silent thoughts that search for steadfast light, 280 **Intent on* 12
Dark thoughts !—they came, but not to stay ; . 284 *Grave of Burns* 14
Well might such thoughts, dear Sister, throng . 285 *Nith* 7
Proud thoughts that Image overawes, ... 286 *Nith* 37
When kindred thoughts and yearnings bear . . 286 *Nith* 62
Proud Gordon, maddened by the thoughts . . 287 *Ellen Irwin* 25
Of thoughts that lie beyond the reach . . . . 288 *Highland Girl* 40
For Thou, although with some wild thoughts, . 292 *Rob Roy* 101
My thoughts ;—she told in pensive strain . . . 294 *Jedbor.* 71
Stepped into it—his thoughts all free . . . . 296 *Highland Boy* 148
That loves on sullen thoughts to brood ! . . . 300 *Bran* 30
Of tender thoughts, that nestle there— . . . 302 *Yarrow V.* 63
Thoughts motherly, and meek as womanhood. . 304 **I grieved* 8
Great Nations, how ennobling thoughts depart . 307 **When I* 2
Of such poor Instruments, with thoughts sublime 309 **When, looking* 13
Triumph, and thoughts no bondage can restrain. 314 **Not 'mid* 14
Must still have sad or vexing thoughts to endure, 317 **Call not* 11
Aspiring thoughts, by memory reclaimed, . . . 340 *Ranz* 12
With thoughts which no delights can chase, . . 342 *Ital. Itin.* 32
My thoughts become bright like yon edging of Pines 345 *Stanzas : Simplon* 21
A thousand ghostly fears, and haunting thoughts, proceed ! . . . . 346 *Gemmi* 14
But all our thoughts were *then* of Earth, . . . 348 **Lulled by* 39
However humble in themselves, with thoughts . 354 *Aquap.* 125
And cloud-like beauty, rich in thoughts of home, 358 *Pine : Rome* 10
Thoughts that would stray from Heaven ? The dream must cease . . . . 363 **Grieve for* 10
I raise my thoughts, inform my deeds and words, 365 **Rapt above* 7
Which o'er sad thoughts a sadder colouring threw. 366 **Fair Land* 8

Thoughts—*continued*
Than their own thoughts to comfort them. Say why 846 *Excursion* 6. 538
And if heart-rending thoughts would oft return, . 852 *Excursion* 6. 929
Thoughts, which the rich are free from, came and crossed . . . . 852 *Excursion* 6. 941
From Ellen's thoughts ; had perished to her mind 853 *Excursion* 6. 1011
Stung by his inward thoughts, and by the smiles 855 *Excursion* 6. 1096
Of memory, images and precious thoughts, . . 857 *Excursion* 7. 29
With no engagement, in his thoughts, more proud 859 *Excursion* 7. 156
The Pastor pressed by thoughts which round his theme . . . . 863 *Excursion* 7. 361
Yet, by the solace of his own pure thoughts . . 863 *Excursion* 7. 417
Beguiled his leisure hours; refreshed his thoughts ; 864 *Excursion* 7. 444
From Age," the Priest continued, " turn your thoughts ; . . . . 867 *Excursion* 7. 633
Each by the thoughts best suited to his years : . 867 *Excursion* 7. 658
Our thoughts unite in kindred quietness ! . . . 868 *Excursion* 7. 704
To be the awakener of divinest thoughts, . . . 870 *Excursion* 7. 823
Darkening the sun. But less impatient thoughts, 870 *Excursion* 7. 847
" Vague thoughts are these ; but, if belief may rest 872 *Excursion* 7. 941
—Thoughts crowd upon me—and 'twere seemlier now . . . . 873 *Excursion* 7. 1051
Was pointedly addressed ; and to the thoughts . 880 *Excursion* 8. 436
Of every country under heaven. My thoughts . 887 *Excursion* 9. 186
Kind wishes, and good actions, and pure thoughts— 887 *Excursion* 9. 242
" Then let us rather fix our gladdened thoughts . 888 *Excursion* 9. 255
Thus, with the fibres of these thoughts it fares ; . S.3. 434 **The doubt* 61
Thoughts raised above the Earth while here he sits S.3. 435 **The doubt* 140
Darkened beneath the shadow of her thoughts S.3. 436 **The doubt* 182
That in his thoughts there were obscurities, . . K.8. 230 **I will* 186
Me rich in many onward-looking thoughts, . . K.8. 243 *Recluse* 1.1.233
In fond obedience to her private thoughts K.8. 247 *Recluse* 1.1.400
The bright array of shadowy thoughts from times K.8. 253 *Recluse* 1.1.627
Unheard-of days, though loving peaceful thoughts. K.8. 257 *Recluse* 1.1.752
Thought-tempered. Thought-tempered wrongs, for each humane respect . . . 501 *Humanity* 62
Thou'lt. Thou'lt be as others that forsaken are ; . 560 *Cuck.andNight.*184
Thousand. With thousand thousand twinkling points of light ; . . . . 4 *Ev. Wk.* 121
And homeless near a thousand homes I stood, . 31 *Guilt* 368
And near a thousand tables pined and wanted food. 31 *Guilt* 369
Her last death-shriek, distinct among a thousand. 40 *Bord.* 187
This is true comfort, thanks a thousand times !— 43 *Bord.* 343
A thought that's worth a thousand worlds ! I grieve 55 *Bord.* 1003
A thousand miles. I am in poverty, ... 74 *Bord.* 2078
Ay, in the word a thousand scorpions lodge : . . 74 *Bord.* 2094
By One who would have died a thousand times . 78 *Bord.* 2331
A thousand lambs are on the rocks, ... 84 *Shepherd-boys* 27
Had clothed the Ewbanks for a thousand years :— 100 *Brothers* 303
And should he live a thousand years, ... 127 *Idiot Boy* 110
Amid the heart of many thousand mists, . . . 132 *Michael* 59
There are ten thousand to whom loss like this 134 *Michael* 239
Where three thousand skulls are laid ; . . . . 157 *Sexton* 6
But in Man's fortunes. Hence a thousand tales . 170 **Never enlivened* 18
Of a thousand standers-by, ... 171 *Kitten* 34
A thousand years are but as yesterday ; . . . 172 *Infant Daughter* 10
Not less capacious than a thousand years. . . 172 *Infant Daughter* 12
A thousand, if they cross our way. . . . . . 179 *Waggoner* 3. 117
Which made me look a thousand ways . . . 183 **O blithe* 19
Ten thousand saw I at a glance, ... 187 **I wandered* 11
That, of a thousand vessels, mine should be . . 211 *Laod.* 124
Five thousand warriors—O the rapturous day ! . 212 *Dion* 18
On which four thousand years have gazed ! . . 214 *Kirkstone* 20
That stretch a thousand thousand sails) . . . 217 *Enterprise* 155
Which a thousand ridges yield ; . . . . . . 217 **Inmate of* 14
In ten thousand dewy rays ; . . . . 221 *Triad* 130
A face o'er which a thousand shadows go ! . . 221 *Triad* 131
Of rapture from a thousand throats— . . . . 228 *Devot. Incit.* 18
They lull perchance ten thousand thousand flowers. 232 *Power of Sound* 20
And ye have all a thousand fears . . . . . 236 *P. B.* 14
Leaving ten thousand stars beneath her : . . . 236 *P. B.* 34
Ten thousand miles from all his brethren ? . . 242 *P. B.* 515
Poor Peter from a thousand causes . . . . 248 *P. B.* 1034
He kisses him a thousand times ! . . . . . 249 *P. B.* 1115
By doubts and thousand petty fancies crost . . 251 **Beloved Vale* 9
That, while ten thousand pleasures disappear, . 251 **There is a little* 11
A thousand times this pipe did Tasso sound ; . . 260 **Scorn not* 5
The thousand links of that ethereal chain ; . . 268 **Four fiery* 8
A thousand tender pleasures, thine and mine, . 277 **Why art* 10
There are a thousand such elsewhere . . . . 293 *Yarrow Unv.* 27
Six thousand veterans practised in war's game, . 293 *Killicranky* 1
A thousand like it, white as snow— . . . . 300 *Bran* 16
On that offensive soil, like waves upon a thousand shores. . . . . 331 *Ode : Thanks.* 151
A thousand ghostly fears, and haunting thoughts, proceed ! . . . . 346 *Gemmi* 14
Clinging to its steep sides a thousand herbs . . 355 *Aquap.* 213
Full sixteen thousand fair to see ;" . . . . 404 *White Doe* 717
A thousand, thousand rings of light . . . 406 *White Doe* 969
Against a thousand cannot stand ;— . . . . 408 *White Doe* 1152
A thousand times more exquisitely sweet, . . 438 *Ecc. Sonn.* 2. 39. 11
Self-poised, and scooped into ten thousand cells, . 451 *Ecc. Sonn.* 3. 43. 10
Decks, on thy sinuous banks, her thousand thrones, 464 **Greta, what* 10
I heard a thousand blended notes, ... 482 *Lines : Spring* 1
'Twill murmur on a thousand years, ... 487 *Fountain* 23
Not only for a thousand thoughts that were, . . 491 *Tribu : Dog* 23
A thousand years hath it borne that name, . . 494 *Force of Prayer* 23
And shall a thousand more. . . . . 494 *Force of Prayer* 24
That, when a thousand years are told, ... 507 *May* 13
But while a thousand pleasures come unsought, . 529 *Poor Robin* 15
Whose fancy had a thousand fields to skim ; . . 532 **Once I* 10

Thousand—*continued.*
For thou art worse than mad a thousand fold ; . 560 *Cuck.andNight.*188
With a thousand soft pictures his memory will teem, 570 *Farmer* 79
A thousand times more beautiful appeared, . . 586 *Ch. Lamb* 127
In a thousand valleys far and wide, ... 588 *Immortality* 47
While twice ten thousand corselets at the view . 612 *Desc.Sk.Quarto* 540
Six thousand years amid his lonely bounds . . 614 *Desc.Sk.Quarto* 692
Havoc and Chaos blast a thousand vales, . . . 615 *Desc.Sk.Quarto* 695
And on ten thousand hearths his shout rebound ; 616 *Desc.Sk.Quarto* 777
A thousand sharp punctures of cold-sweating pain, 621 *Convict* 39
Why should I speak of what a thousand hearts . 659 *Prelude* 4. 44
And in the press of twenty thousand thoughts, . 659 *Prelude* 4. 58
A world of pain, ripened a thousand hopes, . . 679 *Prelude* 6. 285
Memorial reverenced by a thousand storms ; . . 682 *Prelude* 6. 486
Leaving a thousand others, that, in hall, . . . 695 *Prelude* 7. 574
Than that famed paradise of ten thousand trees, . 700 *Prelude* 8. 76
Into a thousand colours ; while he read, . . . 712 *Prelude* 9. 158
And find a thousand bounteous images . . . 734 *Prelude* 11. 451
One only in ten thousand ? What one is, . . 741 *Prelude* 13. 88
Shines, in the brightest of ten thousand stars, . 750 *Prelude* 14. 273
A thousand times more beautiful than the earth . 752 *Prelude* 14. 449
Among ten thousand innocents, enrolled . . . 810 *Excursion* 4. 608
Be of a thousand faculties composed, ... 816 *Excursion* 4. 988
And twice ten thousand interests, do yet prize . 816 *Excursion* 4. 989
Upon its pillow with a thousand schemes. . . . 860 *Excursion* 7. 212
Into a thousand thousand sparkling waves, . . 863 *Excursion* 7. 411
That whirls (how slow itself !) ten thousand spindles : . . . . 866 *Excursion* 7. 607
Of Tell came trooping from a thousand huts, . . 869 *Excursion* 7. 810
This he is freed from, and from thousand notes . 885 *Excursion* 9. 76
These have we, and a thousand nooks of earth . K.8. 240 *Recluse* 1.1.134
Are hung with thousand thousand diamond drops K.8. 252 *Recluse* 1.1.563
Thousand-fold. His guilt a thousand-fold. 'Tis most perplexing : . . . . 48 *Bord.* 592
Thousands. Where thousands meet to worship God under a mighty Dome ; . . . . . . 93 *Poet's Dream* 62
Which then, when tens of thousands were deprest 210 *Laod.* 51
Of prospect, whereof many thousands tell. . . 262 **Dark and* 4
I mourned with thousands, but as one . . . . 285 *Grave of Burns* 31
While tens of thousands, thinking on the affray, . 308 **These times* 4
Entered, with streaming thousands, through the gate, ... 324 *Ode 1814* 73
Sir Tristram, dear to thousands as a brother, . . 373 *Eg. Maid* 290
Thousands of years before the silent air . . 376 *Duddon* 2. 13
Was ripe to send its thousands forth, ... 400 *White Doe* 365
Of tens of thousands, secretly." . . . . . 403 *White Doe* 677
Who sees him ?—thousands see, and One . . . 404 *White Doe* 753
Who, 'mong those thousands, friend hath none, . 404 *White Doe* 755
Would breed us thousands brave as they." . . 405 *White Doe* 861
Heard near fresh streams ; and thousands, who rejoice . . . . 423 *Ecc. Sonn.* 1. 17. 12
But passions spread like plagues, and thousands wild . . . . 435 *Ecc. Sonn.* 2. 29. 12
A voice, from long-expecting thousands sent, . . 442 *Ecc. Sonn.* 3. 8. 1
When thousands, by severer doom, ... 473 *Ossian* 45
Thousands though rich in Fortune's grace . . 490 *Night Thought* 8
In marshalled thousands, darkening street and moor 505 *Warning* 122
Thousands, in each variety of tongue . . . . 509 *F. Stone* 93
Thousands, as toward yon old Lancastrian Towers, 517 *Pun. Death* 1. 9
To thousands, share not Thou ; howe'er bereft, . 531 *Octogen.* 7
Than treading a path trod by thousands before. . 572 *Avarice* 28
'Twas a path trod by thousands ; but Daniel is one 572 *Avarice* 29
Made not, as thousands do, a vulgar sleep ; . . 576 *Chiabrera* 9. 20
And many thousands now are sad— . . . . 581 **Loud is* 13
With tens of thousands rent from off the tree . 582 *Invoc. Earth* 11
To thousands upon thousands of her sons, . . 698 *Prelude* 7. 724
When Englishmen by thousands were o'erthrown, 722 *Prelude* 10. 286
Thousands of cities, in the desert place . . . 807 *Excursion* 4. 437
While thankless thousands are opprest and clogged 835 *Excursion* 5. 830
While tens of thousands falter in their path, . . 835 *Excursion* 5. 833
" And tens of thousands suffer wrong as deep. . 879 *Excursion* 8. 336
For tens of thousands uninformed as he ? . . . 880 *Excursion* 8. 432
That tens of thousands at this day exist . . . 886 *Excursion* 9. 178
Where her thousands Fate slew, ... S.3. 440 **Said red-ribboned* 19
Com'st thou long-wished for? After thousands lost, L.2. 318 *Frag.Æneid* 4.4
Thousandth. The thousandth part of what the Nymph bestows ; . . . . 377 *Duddon* 7. 8
Thou'st. I prithee, to the harm thou'st done already. . . . . 75 *Bord.* 2126
Thracian. Swift as a Thracian Nymph o'er field and height ! . . . . 221 *Triad* 120
Thraldom. O be my spirit, like my thraldom, strait ; 267 **As the* 13
Even so a thraldom, studious to expel . . . . 426 *Ecc. Sonn.* 1. 31. 12
As we grow up, such thraldom of that sense . . 736 *Prelude* 12. 150
And a strange thraldom of maternal love, . . . 849 *Excursion* 6. 710
Thrall. I stood, of simple shame the blushing Thrall ; 251 **Beloved Vale* 10
What ! Ossian here—a painted Thrall, . . . 300 *Bran* 5
Pent in, a Tyrant's solitary Thrall : . . . . 308 **There is a bondage* 3
And Faith—so oft of sense the thrall, ... 341 *San Salv.* 16
So beautiful the timid Thrall . . . . . . 416 *White Doe* 1805
A mortal beauty, their unhappy thrall. . . . 716 *Prelude* 9. 461
By others dreaded as the luckless thrall . . . 841 *Excursion* 6. 226
Thralls. Old Time, though he, gentlest among the Thralls . . . . 272 *Ruins* 4
Thrasymene. Of Sanguinetto or broad Thrasymene, 361 **For action* 6
Thread. The bird, who ceased, with fading light, to thread . . . . 8 *Ev. Wk.* 323
But true love is like the thread . . . . . . 163 *Spinning Wheel* 15
Though by a slender thread,) . . . . 169 *Lovelies Bleeding* 11

Thread—*continued.*
Indulgent centuries spun a thread, 224 *'Tis gone* 23
That silver thread the river Dnieper; 237 *P. B.* 62
Even She who toils to spin our vital thread 255 *S. H.* 7
And softly sleeps within the thread she spins. 366 *Lombardy* 8
The soft touch snapped the thread 479 *Somnamb.* 132
The bird, with fading light who ceas'd to thread 599 *Ev. Wk. Quarto* 389
Upon a gossamer thread; he sifts, he weighs; 670 *Prelude* 5. 322
That girt her waist, spinning the long-drawn thread 769 *Excursion* 1. 886
Not scantily, bright minutes on the thread 862 *Excursion* 7. 307
Furnish'd too with dainty thread, S.3. 437 **I, whose* 21
A leprous stain! ere half his thread was spun L.1. 96 *Juvenal* 3. 47
Threading. Threading the painful cragg surmounts the cliff. 607 *Desc.Sk.Quarto* 298
Threads. From the dark-blue faint silvery threads divide 9 *Ev. Wk.* 359
With threads that seem part of his own silver hair. 345 *Stanzas: Simplon* 24
How subtly glide its finest threads along! 429 *Ecc. Sonn.* 2. 5. 11
Unhallowed threads of revelry are spun; 433 *Ecc. Sonn.* 2. 20. 2
With flaccid threads of ivy, in the still 497 **Enough of climbing* 22
Their moveless boughs and leaves like threads of gold; 593 *Ev. Wk. Quarto* 104
Of amity, whose living threads should stretch 797 *Excursion* 3. 747
Threat. Should die; but me the threat could not withhold: 210 *Laod.* 45
An impious oath confirmed the threat— 241 *P. B.* 461
Threat has he none to execute; 242 *P. B.* 487
Baffle the threat, bright Scene, from Orrest-head 282 *Railway* 9
The wrath consummate and the threat fulfilled; 724 *Prelude* 10. 446
"In truth the threat escaped me unawares: 782 *Excursion* 2. 730
Threaten. Staring to threaten and defy, 159 **With little* 26
That threaten the profane; a pillared shade, 185 *Yew-trees* 20
When dangers threaten, dangers ever new! 425 *Ecc. Sonn.* 1. 27. 6
Threatened. Threatened by faintly-answering farms remote: 5 *Ev. Wk.* 153
When threatened war reduced the children's meal: 29 *Guilt* 267
The threatened shame, the parents of the Maid 122 *V. and J.* 69
Since reason failed want is her threatened doom, 139 *Widow* 32
Thus threatened a poor Briar-rose, 155 *Waterfall* 6
Threatened her foes,—or, pompously at rest, 311 **Who rises* 26
From bondage threatened by the embattled East, 326 *Sobieski* 7
Whose monstrous riches threatened. So the shaft 432 *Ecc. Sonn.* 2. 16. 4
From altars threatened, levelled, or defiled, 449 *Ecc. Sonn.* 3. 36. 3
Threatened by angry breakers as they passed; 454 *Sea-side* 12
"Knowledge will save me from the threatened woe." 513 *Newspaper* 10
"Now for the tale with which you threatened us!" 782 *Excursion* 2. 729
Threatening. *See* **Life-threatening.**
For threatening clouds the moon had drowned; 82 *Alice Fell* 2
Of last night's snow, beneath a sky threatening the fall of more, 91 *Norman Boy* 10
Or looks, or threatening gestures, could perform. 134 *Michael* 193
That wore a threatening brow; 215 *Kirkstone* 62
Though threatening still to fall; 224 *Primrose* 20
Against the threatening foe your trustiest shields." 263 **While not* 8
Bare to the sky, with threatening brand 301 *Bran* 71
Of sweet and threatening harmony; 328 *Ode 1815* 71
Turn from the fortified and threatening hill, 335 *Namur* 10
They suck—from breath that, threatening to destroy, 337 *Aar* 9
No less than Nature's threatening voice, 458 **Had this* 70
Threatening to lay all Orders at her feet 626 *Ballot* 4
In bitterness, and with a threatening eye 860 *Excursion* 7. 222
Threateningly. Broke threateningly, in sparkles dire 499 **Departing summer* 41
Threatenings. Is it for threatenings in the sky? 174 *Waggoner* 1. 48
With the keen threatenings of that fulgent eye, 271 *Henry: Portrait* 7
Loud its threatenings—let them not 336 **Jesu! bless* 3
Go thou and hear the threatenings of the *Lord*; 447 *Ecc. Sonn.* 3. 29. 4
Threats. Of irksome change, or threats from saddening power. 327 *Ode 1815* 16
England's first Martyr, whom no threats could shake; 420 *Ecc. Sonn.* 1. 6. 10
Threats come which no submission may assuage, 433 *Ecc. Sonn.* 2. 21. 1
Threats, which the unthinking only can despise, 465 **Pastor and* 5
Of France a boastful Tyrant hurled his threats; 869 *Excursion* 7. 758
Three. Three humble bells their rustic chime repeat; 4 *Ev. Wk.* 139
Three lovely babes had lain upon my breast; 29 *Guilt* 264
Three years a wanderer now my course I bend— 32 *Guilt* 445
No more, I pray, of this. Three days at farthest 43 *Bord.* 322
Three good round years, for playing the fool here 51 *Bord.* 769
Three of us—we should keep each other warm: 51 *Bord.* 773
Drove by the place of my retreat: three nights 69 *Bord.* 1772
Three sleepless nights I passed in sounding on, 69 *Bord.* 1774
Oh Monster! Monster! there are three of us, 74 *Bord.* 2089
And three times to the child I said, 86 *Anecdote* 47
Three rosy-cheeked school-boys, the highest not more 86 *Rural Arch.* 2
Beneath yon ridge, the last of those three graves? 98 *Brothers* 198
Is distant three short miles, and in the time 99 *Brothers* 252
Three months with one, and six months with another; 100 *Brothers* 344
With two or three companions, whom their course 101 *Brothers* 359
Three years had Barbara in her grave been laid 110 **'Tis said that some* 1
From ten to five, from five to three, 115 *Last of Flock* 92
And then at last from three to two; 115 *Last of Flock* 94
Was made to seize him by three armèd men, 123 *V. and J.* 127
—The clock strikes three—a dismal knell! 129 *Idiot Boy* 271

Three—*continued.*
And till these three weeks past the land was free. 137 *Michael* 378
Three years, or little more, did Isabel 138 *Michael* 473
And fiendish faces, one, two, three, 144 *Her Eyes* 23
Have told this fancy, two or three, perhaps, 146 **It was an* 44
And yet, just three years back—no more— 156 *Oak and Broom* 33
Where three thousand skulls are laid; 157 *Sexton* 6
If there be but three or four 161 **Pleasures newly* 55
Behold yon Prisoners three, 166 *Stray Pleasures* 3
They dance,—there are three, as jocund as free, 166 *Stray Pleasures* 17
Just three days after, passing by 169 *Wren's Nest* 53
Withered leaves—one—two—and three— 170 *Kitten* 5
Now she works with three or four, 171 *Kitten* 29
Three years she grew in sun and shower, 187 **Three years* 1
Hangs a Thrush that sings loud, it has sung for three years: 187 *Poor Susan* 2
When Ruth three seasons thus had lain, 194 *Ruth* 205
And to the left, three yards beyond, 198 *Thorn* 29
Three several hoof-marks which the hunted Beast 201 *Hart-leap* 51
Three leaps have borne him from this lofty brow 201 *Hart-leap* 55
Three several pillars, each a rough-hewn stone, 201 *Hart-leap* 67
Three pillars of rude stone Sir Walter reared, 202 *Hart-leap* 83
Three aspens at three corners of a square; 202 *Hart-leap* 103
I saw three pillars standing in a line,— 202 *Hart-leap* 107
Are but three bounds—and look, Sir, at this last— 203 *Hart-leap* 143
He comes to tarry with thee three hours' space; 209 *Laod.* 23
Come, youngest of the lovely Three, 221 *Triad* 90
"Last of the Three, though eldest born, 222 *Triad* 174
And one of the bright Three become thy happy Bride. 222 *Triad* 218
He gave three miserable groans; 241 *P. B.* 447
(Not three weeks past the Stripling died,) 285 *Grave of Burns* 62
Of three short days—but hush—no more! 348 **Lulled by* 20
(Life's three first seasons having passed away) 394 **No more* 26
Under the saintly ensigns three, 405 *White Doe* 822
Over three Realms may take its widest range; 471 *Tynwald* 10
This Dog, had been through three months' space 492 *Fidelity* 56
—This Dwelling's Inmate more than three weeks' space 521 *Epist. Beaumont* 26
Filled with delight three summer morning hours. 525 *Epist. Beaumont* 269
His voice was like the voice of three. 536 *Goody Blake* 20
And then her three hours' work at night, 536 *Goody Blake* 26
Enough to warm her for three days. 536 *Goody Blake* 56
And ere the Sabbath he had three. 537 *Goody Blake* 112
And shall be beaten three times in an hour, 554 *Prioress* 91
The One, yet unbreeched, is not three birthdays old, 572 *Avarice* 13
And three, were it asked, would be rendered for one. 572 *Avarice* 44
Of noble parents: seventy years and three 574 *Chiabrera* 4. 30
Thence, from three paly loopholes mild and small, 598 *Ev. Wk. Quarto* 335
Three times a day the pail and welcome hand. 611 *Desc.Sk.Quarto* 485
Mixed with auxiliar Rocks, three hundred Forms; 612 *Desc.Sk.Quarto* 539
A pleasant loitering journey, through three days 633 *Prelude* 1. 106
Through three divisions of the quartered year 643 *Prelude* 2. 83
Three Gothic courts are his, and in the first 649 *Prelude* 3. 47
Whence he had landed scarcely three weeks past; 664 *Prelude* 4. 423
And, once, three days successively, through paths 680 *Prelude* 6. 354
From dangerous passions free. Three years had flown 688 *Prelude* 7. 65
Just three parts blown—a cottage-child—if e'er, 692 *Prelude* 7. 353
And I and my three brothers, orphans then, 738 *Prelude* 12. 308
Three summer days I roamed) where'er the Plain 745 *Prelude* 13. 337
And three chance human wanderers, in calm thought 747 *Prelude* 14. 65
Had three times called us to renew our walk, 772 *Excursion* 2. 86
Lying full three parts buried among tufts 784 *Excursion* 2. 818
Soon showed itself: he lingered three short weeks; 785 *Excursion* 2. 894
Fearless of winds and waves. Three several stones 787 *Excursion* 3. 55
Large measures shall be dealt. Three sabbath-days 808 *Excursion* 4. 468
Of his day's work. 'Three dark mid-winter months 834 *Excursion* 5. 804
Begun and ended within three days' space, 853 *Excursion* 6. 967
And three fair Children, plentifully fed 860 *Excursion* 7. 162
And mark that daisied hillock, three spans long! 867 *Excursion* 7. 635
Of three clear-sounding and harmonious bells, 872 *Excursion* 7. 974
Fond looks on colours three or four S. 3. 431 **The Scottish* 23
Thick storm, and heavy, which for three hours' space K.8. 228 **I will* 136
Threes. The stars are out by twos and threes, 457 **The sun has* 2
Threescore. And see, that with our threescore years and ten 97 *Brothers* 130
"O cruel! I'm almost threescore; 129 *Idiot Boy* 279
And see so little gain from threescore years. 137 *Michael* 373
Our threescore years and ten. 225 *Primrose* 48
In this deep knell, silent for threescore years, 271 *George: Death* 13
Of threescore years, and to thy latest hour, 585 *Ch. Lamb* 60
If, having walked with Nature threescore years, 816 *Excursion* 4. 980
Three-striped. Thy three-striped banner fluctuate on the breeze; 21 *Desc. Sk.* 613
Three-years'. Men, Women, three-years' Children, Babes in arms. 698 *Prelude* 7. 721
Threlkeld. —Give Sir Lancelot Threlkeld praise! 204 *Brougham* 95
Threlkeld-hall. The ruined towers of Threlkeld-hall, 180 *Waggoner* 4. 43
Threshold. *See* **Cottage-threshold.**
I have good business there. I met you at the threshold, 46 *Bord.* 481
From my own threshold I looked up to Heaven 62 *Bord.* 1354
The threshold of another year; 112 *Lament* 11
A coffin through Timothy's threshold had past; 120 *Childless Father* 11
Reached speedily the native threshold bent 123 *V. and J.* 103

Throes—*continued.*	
Had never been when throes of mighty Nations .	741 *Prelude* 13. 107
Is stricken in the moment when her throes . .	867 *Excursion* 7. 643
Throne. And on the vacant throne his worthier Brother placed.	103 *Artegal* 81
Re-seated on thy throne, ...	105 *Artegal* 207
Who sat a ruler on his throne	167 *Pilgrim's Dream* 31
This is our palace,—yonder is thy throne ; . .	210 *Laod.* 33
" O Lady, worthy of earth's proudest throne ! .	220 *Triad* 52
Mercy from her twilight throne	233 *Power of Sound* 29
Methought I saw the footsteps of a throne . .	257 **Methought I* 1
How Verse may build a princely throne . . .	285 *Grave of Burns* 35
Austria a Daughter of her Throne hath sold ! .	317 **The martial* 10
O wretched man, the throne of tyranny ! . . .	321 **Here pause* 14
Or thanks and praises to His throne ascend . .	331 *Ode : Thanks.* 180
On this high DAY of THANKS, before the Throne of Grace !	332 *Ode : Thanks.* 244
The laurelled Dante's favourite seat. A throne, .	365 **Under the* 5
And, for a moment, filled that empty Throne. .	365 **Under the* 14
Or gift to be presented at the throne	394 **No more* 13
Upon a primrose bank, her throne	413 *White Doe* 1583
'Mid woods and wilds, on Nature's craggy throne, .	431 *Ecc. Sonn.* 2. 11. 13
Upon his throne ; " unsoftened, undismayed . .	435 *Ecc. Sonn.* 2. 26. 10
Totters the Throne ; the new-born Church is sad,	439 *Ecc. Sonn.* 2. 41. 13
Woman ! the Power who left His throne on high,	447 *Ecc. Sonn.* 3. 27. 1
That pardon, from God's throne, may set its seal	447 *Ecc. Sonn.* 3. 28. 8
In progress toward the fount of Love,—the throne	469 **Desire we* 11
She heard, ere to the throne of grace	479 *Somnamb.* 140
Your Master's throne is set."—Deaf was the Sea ;	495 *Fact* 6
—Then Canute, rising from the invaded throne, .	495 *Fact* 9
From his everlasting throne, ...	502 **Like a* 50
Up to the throne of God is borne	506 *Lab. Hymn* 1
I bent before Thy gracious throne, ...	550 *Hermit's Cell* 5. 17
Now may'st thou sing for aye before the throne, .	554 *Prioress* 129
So promptly from her lofty throne ?— . . .	582 **O for a* 28
Seated on her lineal throne ;	629 *Installation* 50
For the Church, the State, the Throne ! . . .	629 *Installation* 112
Our simple childhood, sits upon a throne . . .	673 *Prelude* 5. 508
Was Nature's, uttered from her Alpine throne ; .	681 *Prelude* 6. 431
Bound to the fierce Metropolis. From his throne	718 *Prelude* 10. 11
Spared not the empty throne, and in proud haste	718 *Prelude* 10. 39
Bearing a tribute to the Almighty's Throne. . .	748 *Prelude* 14. 187
Of open court, an object like a throne	784 *Excursion* 2. 862
Who tend her altars, wait upon her throne, . .	810 *Excursion* 4. 597
Or, out of Sion, thundering from his throne . .	811 *Excursion* 4. 656
An English Sovereign's brow ! and to the throne	838 *Excursion* 6. 2
How, from his lofty throne, the sun can fling .	847 *Excursion* 6. 595
A throne, that may be likened unto his, . . .	885 *Excursion* 9. 56
From thy empyreal throne, the elect of earth	893 *Excursion* 9. 631
The brightest jewel of a George's throne. . . .	L.1. 97 *Juvenal* 3. 95
Throned. Throned in the hearts of men. Should Heaven ordain	317 **Call not* 9
Where, throned in gold, immortal Science reigns ;	619 *School Ex.* 70
Throned in the Sun's descending car	626 †*Cento* 1
Sit like a thronèd Lady, sending out	658 *Prelude* 4. 22
(The thronèd Lady whom erewhile we hailed)	671 *Prelude* 5. 400
Of vengeful retribution, theirs who throned . .	723 *Prelude* 10. 341
O'er stately Edinborough throned on crags ? . .	815 *Excursion* 4. 913
Thrones. Else how, when mighty Thrones were put to shame, ...	316 **It was a* 2
Your thrones, ye Powers, from duty fear to swerve !	327 **Emperors and* 11
The ancient thrones of Christendom are stuff . .	428 *Ecc. Sonn.* 1. 39. 11
Decks, on thy sinuous banks, her thousand thrones,	464 **Greta, what* 10
Whose merchants Princes were, whose decks were thrones ;	475 *Greenock* 10
For temples, towers, and thrones	628 *Installation* 2
Of shouting Angels, and the empyreal thrones— .	755 *Recluse* 1. 1. 787
Ye Thrones that have defied remorse, and cast .	870 *Excursion* 7. 837
Throng. What shall it be ? a mirthful throng ? or that holy place and calm	92 *Poet's Dream* 23
Where is the throng, the tumult of the race ? .	201 *Hart-leap* 25
On this great throng, this bright array ! . . .	204 *Brougham* 18
Glad moment is it when the throng	221 *Triad* 80
Nor wholly lost upon the throng	228 *Devot. Incit.* 44
Thou wilt salute old memories as they throng .	229 *Cuckoo-clock* 17
And melancholy Spectres throng them ;— . .	237 *P. B.* 42
They cried, and all around me throng, ...	238 *P. B.* 179
Well might such thoughts, dear Sister, throng	285 *Nith* 7
What He—who, mid the kindred throng . . .	300 *Bran* 1
And a throng of rosy boys	324 *Ode 1814* 63
Hence motions, even amid the vulgar throng, .	334 **The Spirit* 7
Was fit for some gay throng ;	334 **In Bruges* 10
From Wood-nymph of Diana's throng ? . . .	344 **How blest* 34
And from the temple forth they throng, . . .	397 *White Doe* 159
So vaunt a throng of Followers, filled with pride .	425 *Ecc. Sonn.* 1. 28. 12
With orb and cycle girds the starry throng. . .	429 *Ecc. Sonn.* 2. 5. 14
Amid the shuddering throng doth Cranmer stand ;	437 *Ecc. Sonn.* 2. 35. 4
The throng of rooks, that now, from twig or nest,	455 *Rydal Mere* 8
And to the throng, that on the Cumbrian shore .	465 **Dear to* 3
It charms a feast-day throng of all degrees, . .	467 *St. Bees* 98
That when his fate had housed him 'mid a throng	531 **I know* 23
And see the budding leaves the branches throng,	557 *Cuck.and Night.* 27
In the throng of the town like a stranger is he, .	570 *Farmer* 61
I hear the Echoes through the mountains throng,	588 *Immortality* 27
We in thought will join your throng, ...	590 *Immortality* 175
Glanced sideway, leaving the tumultuous throng,	638 *Prelude* 1. 449
In lonely places ; if a throng was near	652 *Prelude* 3. 231
My surplice, through the inferior throng I clove .	653 *Prelude* 3. 312
Doth here rise up against me. 'Mid a throng .	663 *Prelude* 4. 309
May not come near him, nor the little throng .	670 *Prelude* 5. 303

Throng—*continued.*	
Of this glad throng, foot-travellers side by side, .	681 *Prelude* 6. 415
Thence back into the throng, until we reach, . .	690 *Prelude* 7. 189
And there he sate surrounded with a throng . .	692 *Prelude* 7. 359
Shrill voices from the hawkers in the throng, . .	719 *Prelude* 10. 99
To seek the ground where, 'mid a throng of graves,	726 *Prelude* 10. 533
We saw a throng of people ;—wherefore met ? .	773 *Excursion* 2. 117
Where on the labours of the happy throng . .	819 *Excursion* 4. 1195
And this Survivor, with his cheerful throng . .	861 *Excursion* 7. 279
Plunged—'mid a gay and busy throng convened .	870 *Excursion* 7. 868
That is to come, the throng of woodland flowers,	K.8. 252 *Recluse* 1. 1. 590
Thronged. Here, thronged with primroses, the steep rock's breast	107 *Farewell* 53
And vacant doth the region which they thronged	230 *Clouds* 33
The Monks of Fountain's thronged to force . .	301 *Bran* 58
In the thronged city, from the walks of gain, . .	320 **O'erweening Statesmen* 6
The streets and quays are thronged, but why disown	349 *At Dover* 5
Thronged yesterday by airy ghosts ;	391 *HighlandBroach* 74
Or thither thronged for refuge. With quick glance	540 *Grace Darl.* 35
The Heavens are thronged with martyrs that have risen	581 *Invoc. Earth* 8
Is thronged with staring pictures and huge scrolls,	697 *Prelude* 7. 692
Was thronged with impregnations like the Wilds	708 *Prelude* 8. 633
Whose skill had thronged the floor with a proud show	778 *Excursion* 2. 424
Upon the thronged abodes of busy men . . .	838 *Excursion* 6. 37
From the thronged hive, and settle where they list	889 *Excursion* 9. 373
Of the thronged world, Society is here	K.8. 253 *Recluse* 1. 1. 614
Thronging. Unscared by thronging fancies of strange hue	523 *Epist. Beaumont* 146
Thronging the walls ; and on the floor beneath .	825 *Excursion* 5. 167
Throngs. For sacrifice its throngs of living men, .	26 *Guilt* 123
And hither throngs of birds resort ;	154 *Flower Garden* 37
Throngs of celestial visages, ...	343 *Eclipse* 58
How throngs the crowd to yon theatric school .	L.1. 97 *Juvenal* 3. 89
Throstle. And hark ! how blithe the throstle sings !	481 *Tables Turned* 13
Throttled. And throttled with an infant godhead's might	724 *Prelude* 10. 392
Through. (*Partial list.*) *See* **Thorough, Thro'.**	
And, through all converse of our later years, . .	39 *Bord.* 96
A glow-worm, through the covert of the furze, .	45 *Bord.* 425
A piece of money glittering through the dust ? .	45 *Bord.* 435
And will be so through every change of fortune .	50 *Bord.* 721
Upwards I cast my eyes, and, through a crevice,	55 *Bord.* 988
With its first bounty. Wandering through the west, ...	418 *Ecc. Sonn.* 1. 2. 5
By wrong triumphant through its own excess, .	426 *Ecc. Sonn.* 1. 32. 2
Renews. Through every forest, cave, and den, .	435 *Ecc. Sonn.* 2. 27. 9
Through humbleness, the Spirit that did alight .	552 *Prioress* 18
Upon thy heart, whence, through that glory's might, ...	552 *Prioress* 19
And through this street who list might ride and wend ;	553 *Prioress* 41
Twice in a day it passèd through his throat ; . .	554 *Prioress* 97
" Through all the Jewry (this before said I) . .	554 *Prioress* 100
" The Christian folk that through the Jewry went	555 *Prioress* 163
Yet have I felt of sickness through the May, . .	557 *Cuck.and Night.* 38
Through all this May that I have little sleep ; .	557 *Cuck.and Night.* 42
He lets them perish through that grievous ill. .	560 *Cuck.andNight.* 200
In winning words, since through her gentiless, .	562 *Cuck.andNight.* 300
As soon as he this song had thus sung through, .	564 *Troilus* 127
He strayed through the fields like an indolent wight, ...	569 *Farmer* 23
And Nature, while through the great city he hies,	570 *Farmer* 63
Will hear the wind sigh through the leaves of a tree.	571 *Farmer* 92
Through the lost look of dotage, is cunning and sly :	572 *Avarice* 22
They hunt through the streets with deliberate tread, ...	572 *Avarice* 37
Throughout. Time softly treads ; throughout the landscape breathes	9 *Ev. Wk.* 361
From age to age, throughout his lonely bounds .	21 *Desc. Sk.* 579
Throughout that journey, from the vehicle . .	125 *V. and J.* 254
With iron, making it throughout in all . . .	134 *Michael* 182
Which, as the Housewife phrased it, were throughout	138 *Michael* 434
Evening spreads throughout the west !	217 **Inmate of* 24
Renewed throughout the bounds of earth or ocean,	226 *Vernal Ode* 49
Were England's native growth ; and throughout Spain	319 **Avaunt all* 10
Abruptly paused the strife ;—the field throughout	322 *Germans* 1
Ye saw, throughout this royal House, ...	372 *Eg. Maid* 210
By truth, shall spread, throughout the world dispersed."	433 *Ecc. Sonn.* 2. 17. 14
Throughout the Country they have left, our shores	449 *Ecc. Sonn.* 3. 36. 13
With love of God, throughout the Land were raised	467 *St. Bees* 120
[Yet not the less would I throughout	492 *Duty*
Throughout the live-long day, ...	507 **While from* 62
But evermore throughout thy reign	507 *May* 7
O seat of Arts ! renowned throughout the world !	655 *Prelude* 3. 458
One happiness. Throughout this narrative, . .	679 *Prelude* 6. 259
Throughout the landscape ; tuft, stone, scratch minute—	691 *Prelude* 7. 258
Have prayed that throughout earth upon all men,	720 *Prelude* 10. 135
Throughout the nether sphere !—And if with this	755 *Recluse* 1. 1. 846
Throughout a long and lonely summer's day . .	813 *Excursion* 4. 804
Throughout the lofty range of these rough hills, .	865 *Excursion* 7. 499
Into all hearts. Throughout the world of sense, .	887 *Excursion* 9. 214
Throughout all lands : let every nation hear . .	893 *Excursion* 9. 641
Throve. They throve, and we at home did thrive :	115 *Last of Flock* 36
Best throve the fire of chaste desire, ...	478 *Somnamb.* 39

Thus—*continued.*
Quoth she, to hear this churlish bird thus speak . 560 *Cuck.andNight.*212
Thus takes the Nightingale her leave of me ; 561 *Cuck.andNight.*256
And thus a day or two drove wearily ; 564 *Troilus* 110
A weary while in pain he tosseth thus, 565 *Troilus* 162
Thus thirty smooth years did he thrive on his farm : 569 *Farmer* 29
Thwart. And thus from year to year his walk they thwart, 320 **Hunger, and* 13
Or if thy cherished grief have failed to thwart 576 **By a* 15
Which Nature studiously employs to thwart 736 *Prelude* 12. 134
Thwarted. His coming step has thwarted, 479 *Somnamb.* 101
Thwarting. Winds thwarting winds, bewildered and forlorn, 684 *Prelude* 6. 628
Thy. (*Partial list.*)
Of thy kind Patroness, which to receive 40 *Bord.* 156
But when thy Father must lie down and die, 40 *Bord.* 159
Thy Mother too !—scarce had I gained the door, 40 *Bord.* 182
I felt thy infant brother in her arms ; 40 *Bord.* 184
Exacted thy return, and our reunion. 41 *Bord.* 204
That savoured of aversion to thy name 41 *Bord.* 232
We'll not insult thy majesty by time, 58 *Bord.* 1154
" Thy name in this large world is spread abroad ! 552 *Prioress* 2
Thy worship is performed and precious laud ; 552 *Prioress* 4
Thy goodness is set forth ; they when they lie 552 *Prioress* 6
Upon the breast Thy name do glorify. 552 *Prioress* 7
Help me to tell it in thy reverence ! 552 *Prioress* 21
" Lady ! thy goodness, thy magnificence, 552 *Prioress* 22
Thy virtue, and thy great humility, 552 *Prioress* 23
Thou goest before in thy benignity, 552 *Prioress* 26
To be our guide unto thy Son so dear. 553 *Prioress* 28
To tell abroad thy mighty worthiness, 553 *Prioress* 30
" O Thou great God that dost perform Thy laud 555 *Prioress* 156
By mouths of Innocents, lo ! here Thy might ; 555 *Prioress* 157
Since that thy throat is cut, as it doth seem.' 555 *Prioress* 197
If long time from thy mate thou be, or far, 560 *Cuck.andNight.*183
That all this May I will thy songstress be. 561 *Cuck.andNight.*230
And live and die I will in thy belief ; 563 *Troilus* 75
With thy bright beams to guide me but one hour, 564 *Troilus* 125
Thy horns were old as now upon that morrow, 564 *Troilus* 134
I love thee, and love the sweet Boy at thy side : 572 *Avarice* 46
Lelius ! has death cut short thy brilliant day 575 *Chiabrera* 7. 5
—Thy fragrant gales and lute-resounding streams, 605 *Desc.Sk.Quarto* 156
Thyme. A garden stored with peas, and mint, and thyme, 28 *Guilt* 209
From humble violet—modest thyme— 228 *Devot. Incit.* 7
The thyme her purple, like the blush of Even ; 377 *Duddon* 6. 11
Of lowly thyme, by Nature's skill enwrought 702 *Prelude* 8. 243
Thyme-besprinkled. On these soft beds of thyme-besprinkled turf, 789 *Excursion* 3. 247
Thyrsus. Tossing her frantic thyrsus wide and high ! 381 *Duddon* 20. 14
Thyself. Now couch thyself where, heard with fear afar, 16 *Desc. Sk.* 336
Fair in thyself and beautiful alone, 107 *Farewell* 39
Thyself thy own enjoyment. 159 *Green Linnet* 24
Bold, and lavish of thyself ; 160 **Pansies, lilies* 18
Till, like thyself, I disappear 167 *Pilgrim'sDream* 47
Reveal thyself, like pensive Morn 222 *Triad* 175
Thee, and not thee thyself, I would not do 268 **Brook ! whose* 7
As if it were thyself that's here 284 *Grave of Burns* 9
Thou wouldst have nobly stirred thyself, 292 *Rob Roy* 107
Though fallen thyself, never to rise again, 305 *Toussaint* 8
Yet thou thyself hast round thee shed a gleam 376 *Duddon* 3. 12
And clothe thyself with terrors like the flood 454 **The Sun, that* 15
Spread for thyself the snares of tribulation, 505 *Warning* 148
Mistrust thyself, vain Country ! cease to cry, 513 *Newspaper* 9
And yet more often living with thyself, 648 *Prelude* 2. 469
And for thyself, so haply shall thy days 648 *Prelude* 2. 470
That from thyself it comes, that thou must give, 738 *Prelude* 12. 276
Power to thyself ; no Helper hast thou here ; 749 *Prelude* 14. 210
Of infancy around us, that thyself, 802 *Excursion* 4. 84
To furnish ; for this effluence of thyself, 893 *Excursion* 9. 617
Tiara. With myrtle-wreathed tiara on his brow, 811 *Excursion* 4. 675
Tiber. And Tiber, and each brook and rill 386 *Yarrow Rev.* 61
Proud Tiber grieves, and far-off Ganges, blind 435 *Ecc. Sonn.* 2. 27. 6
From gladdened Elbe to startled Tiber heard. 629 *Installation* 104
Tiber's. Where Tiber's stream the immortal City laves : 421 *Ecc. Sonn.* 1. 13. 4
On Tiber's banks my youth was dedicate 573 *Chiabrera* 3. 5
Ticked. That on mine ear ticked with a mournful sound.— 781 *Excursion* 2. 646
Ticking. All day the house-clock ticking in mine ear, 834 *Excursion* 5. 814
Tickings. Nor lose ten tickings of thy watch 485 *Poet's Epitaph* 35
Tide. *See* **Christmas-tide, Eventide, Noontide, Ocean-tide, Spring-tide, Summer-tide.**
The hills, while gleams below the azure tide ; 9 *Ev. Wk.* 360
She saw my blasted face—a tide of soldiers 40 *Bord.* 185
Rushing along in the full tide of play, 61 *Bord.* 1332
As I have done. A fresh tide of Crusaders 69 *Bord.* 1771
Does joy approach ? they meet the coming tide ; 278 **Life with* 3
And, with the coming of the tide, 295 *Highland Boy* 66
Still sounding with the sounding tide, 296 *Highland Boy* 92
The tide retreated from the shore, 296 *Highland Boy* 154
Above whose heads the tide so long hath rolled, 333 *Fish-women* 4
Not swans descending with the stealthy tide, 347 *Processions* 60
Impervious to the tide of war : 390 *HighlandBroach* 10
Which way the tide is doomed to flow. 404 *White Doe* 782
Athwart the unresisting tide 410 *White Doe* 1342
Into the Avon, Avon to the tide 432 *Ecc. Sonn.* 2. 17. 9
And by the tide alone the water swayed. 454 *Sea-side* 6
Of tide and tempest on the Structure's base, 473 **Thanks for* 10
"My faithful followers, lo ! the tide is spent 495 *Fact* 30

Tide—*continued.*
Less quick the stir when tide and breeze 499 **This Lawn* 7
Our hope confirming that the salt-sea tide, 523 *Epist. Beaumont* 115
The tide of things has borne him, he appears 568 *Cumb. Beg.* 164
Had been that pious spirit, a tide 577 **By playful* 7
No motion but the moving tide, a breeze, 578 *Peele Castle* 27
But we will see it, joyful tide ! 580 *John Words.* 58
When stood the shorten'd herds amid the tide, 592 *Ev. Wk. Quarto* 58
Th' insuperable rocks and severing tide, 607 *Desc.Sk.Quarto* 310
And bottomless, divides the midway tide. 611 *Desc.Sk.Quarto* 499
—No vulgar joy is his, at even tide 611 *Desc.Sk.Quarto* 512
Ev'n to the summer door his icy tide, 613 *Desc.Sk.Quarto* 599
A more majestic tide the water roll'd 616 *Desc.Sk.Quarto* 772
She wept.—Life's purple tide began to flow 619 **She wept* 1
In a sea-river's bed at ebb of tide, 652 *Prelude* 3. 216
Following the tide that slackens by degrees, 690 *Prelude* 7. 190
But with its universal freight the tide 692 *Prelude* 7. 377
Wanted not animation, when the tide 693 *Prelude* 7. 410
When the great tide of human life stands still ; 697 *Prelude* 7. 657
As fierce a successor ; the tide retreats 719 *Prelude* 10. 81
Who crossed the sands with ebb of morning tide. 726 *Prelude* 10. 561
As the tide ebbs, to ignominy and shame 752 *Prelude* 14. 436
Pass with the respirations of the tide, 876 *Excursion* 8. 141
My Son ! behold the Tide already spent S.3. 427 **My Son* 1
Tideless. Into a natural port, a tideless sea, 356 *Aquap.* 220
Tide's. *See* **Noon-tide's.**
Tides. And breaks the spreading of its golden tides ; 5 *Ev. Wk.* 171
Or adverse tides and currents headed, 216 *Enterprise* 77
But over his great tides 222 *Triad* 142
And force their passage to the salt-sea tides ! 269 *Gordale* 14
Tides of aggressive war, oft served as well 469 **The feudal* 3
Sad tides of joy from Melancholy's hand ; 592 *Ev. Wk. Quarto* 28
And glorying looks around, the silent tides : 595 *Ev. Wk. Quarto* 204
Nought wakens or disturbs it's tranquil tides ; 597 *Ev. Wk. Quarto* 310
In deep determin'd gloom his subject tides. 598 *Ev. Wk. Quarto* 338
Those lips, whose tides of fragrance come, and go, 604 *Desc.Sk.Quarto* 152
He opens of his feet the sanguine tides, 609 *Desc.Sk.Quarto* 395
Who cries, presumptuous, " here their tides shall stay," 617 *Desc.Sk.Quarto* 807
Hush'd are the winds and silent are the tides ; 618 *School Ex.* 38
Of tides, and when the moon will be eclipsed, 840 *Excursion* 6. 172
Tidings. These joyful tidings from no lips but mine. 50 *Bord.* 724
With the glad tidings which this day hath brought ; 66 *Bord.* 1593
O blessed tidings ! thought of joy ! 81 †*Mother's Return* 5
Tidings of one so long and dearly loved, 96 *Brothers* 79
Twelve years are past since we had tidings from him. 100 *Brothers* 307
No tidings of an only child ; 117 *Affl. Marg.* 9
Some tidings that my woes may end ; 117 *Affl. Marg.* 76
Who dares report, the tidings to the lord 125 *V. and J.* 223
Distressful tidings. Long before the time 134 *Michael* 209
The tidings of his melancholy loss, 136 *Michael* 325
Watched for tidings from the East, beheld his Lord, 141 *Arm. Lady* 101
And they such joyful tidings were, 247 *P. B.* 958
In hopes some tidings there to gather : 247 *P. B.* 1002
Sad tidings to that noble Youth ! 287 *Ellen Irwin* 13
The tidings passed of servitude repealed, 312 **When, far* 2
Bear through the world these tidings of delight ! 327 *Ode 1815* 10
To carry thy glad tidings over heights 363 **List—'twas* 101
Glad tidings to Iona's shore, 390 *Highland Broach* 4
And every day brought with it tidings new 394 **No more* 29
To Rylstone he the tidings brought ; 409 *White Doe* 1205
The tidings come of Jesus crucified ; 419 *Ecc. Sonn.* 1. 3. 12
She shoots the tidings forth to distant friends ; 503 *Warning* 27
No tidings reach us thence from town or field, 522 *Epist.Beaumont* 81
Nor of him were tidings heard ; 535 *Egremont* 58
Upon those tidings by the peasant given 684 *Prelude* 6. 618
No tidings of her husband ; if he lived, 768 *Excursion* 1. 818
Shouteth faint tidings of some gladder place. 776 *Excursion* 2. 348
If fixed or wandering star could tidings yield 796 *Excursion* 3. 692
Tidings of joy and love.—From those pure heights 811 *Excursion* 4. 641
Authentic tidings of invisible things ; 818 *Excursion* 4. 1144
The tidings came that she whom he had wooed 840 *Excursion* 6. 128
Tears wipe away, and pleasant tidings bring ; 875 *Excursion* 8. 80
These tidings, and in Christian temples meet 894 *Excursion* 9. 653
Tie. If in that hour a single tie 1 *Extract* 5
Receive that letter ? Be at peace.—The tie 43 *Bord.* 341
Chains tie us down by land and sea ; 117 *Affl. Marg.* 47
Is joined through some dear homeborn tie ; 164 **Glad sight* 2
Though strong, is, in the main, a joyless tie 172 *Infant Daughter* 37
" What ! lengthened privilege, a lineal tie, 280 *Plea for Auth.* 9
Of Terror, bear us to the ground, and tie 309 **What if* 5
So often tie the thunder-wielding hands 325 *Enghien* 13
By visual pomp, and by the tie 328 *Ode 1815* 70
Look like a cloud—a slender stem the tie 358 *Pine : Rome* 2
By a continuous and acknowledged tie 394 **No more* 5
Had bound the flowers I wore, with faithful tie : 445 *Ecc. Sonn.* 3. 22. 10
Thus in the chosen spot a tie so strong 531 **I know* 21
Of a protector, the first filial tie 585 *Ch. Lamb* 91
Your *dual* loneliness. The sacred tie 586 *Ch. Lamb* 128
As by some tie invisible, oaths professed 714 *Prelude* 9. 305
" What other yearning was the master tie 791 *Excursion* 3. 392
Tied. Tied by a woollen cord, moves on before 45 *Bord.* 456
And to the waggon's skirts was tied 179 *Waggoner* 3. 58
What, Lady, if their feet were tied ; 409 *White Doe* 1223
(A vest with woollen cincture tied, 413 *White Doe* 1607
At length, thus faintly, faintly tied 416 *White Doe* 1864
His frame is tied ; firm from the naked feet 437 *Ecc. Sonn.* 2. 35. 6
By chain yet stronger must the Soul be tied : 446 *Ecc. Sonn.* 3. 25. 1
With wonder mixed—that Man could e'er be tied, 497 **Enough of climbing* 9

Tied—*continued.*
A little boat tied to a willow tree . . . . . 637 *Prelude* 1. 358
Tied to her arm, and picking thus from the lane . 717 *Prelude* 9. 513
An object whereunto their souls are tied . . . 790 *Excursion* 3. 294
Six simple burghers—To the rope that tied . . L.1. 95 *Juvenal* 3. 9
Tier. Tier under tier, this semicirque profound ? . 269 *Malham* 3
Ties. Perpetual flight, unchecked by earthly ties, . 153 *Morn. Ex.* 35
Around the heart such tender ties, ... 193 *Ruth* 88
For the same service, by mysterious ties ; . . . 347 *Processions* 50
Bound by indissoluble ties to thee . . . . . 374 *Eg. Maid* 345
Enter in dance. Of church, or sabbath ties, . . 387 **Part fenced* 5
His questions urging, feels, in slender ties . . 422 *Ecc. Sonn.* 1. 13. 10
And if there be whom broken ties . . . . . 457 **Had this* 41
Are not, in sooth, their Requiem's sacred ties . 467 *St. Bees* 73
Upon frail ties dissolving or dissolved . . . . 510 **Among a* 31
Tearing their bleeding ties leaves Age to groan . 613 *Desc.Sk.Quarto* 612
Who, looking inward, have observed the ties . . 694 *Prelude* 7. 461
Declares the vital power of social ties . . . . 695 *Prelude* 7. 527
Though bound to earth by ties of pity and love, . 820 *Excursion* 4. 1296
By ties of daily interest, to maintain . . . . 875 *Excursion* 8. 63
Such ties will not be severed : but, when we . . S.3. 433 **The doubt* 37
Tiger-leap. With a tiger-leap half-way . . . 171 *Kitten* 25
Tiger's. Old as the tiger's paw, the lion's mane . 227 *Vernal Ode* 122
Tigers. Defenceless as a wood where tigers roam. . 719 *Prelude* 10. 93
Tight. When round my wrist I felt a cord drawn tight, ... 55 *Bord.* 965
Than a tight case of dungeon walls for shelter . 67 *Bord.* 1660
About that tight and deadly band . . . . . 145 *Her Eyes* 37
The whole world over, tight as beads of dew . . 670 *Prelude* 5. 321
Tiles. Now back to the tiles, then in search of the wall, ... 484 **A plague* 14
Till. (*Partial list.*)
" Princess fair, I till the ground, but may not take 139 *Arm. Lady* 11
The joy of them who till the fields of Swale, . . 202 *Hart-leap* 75
Which he can till no longer ? . . . . . . 483 *Simon Lee* 48
And labourers going forth to till the fields. . . 663 *Prelude* 4. 332
To those who occupy and till the ground, . . . 833 *Excursion* 5. 690
Which our endeavours have refused to till, . . 855 *Excursion* 6. 1138
Of every clime, to till the lonely field, . . . 894 *Excursion* 9. 671
Till the last banner of their long array . . . 6 *Ev. Wk.* 208
Till higher mounted, strives in vain to cheer . . 8 *Ev. Wk.* 341
Till our small share of hardly-paining sighs . . 8 *Ev. Wk.* 352
Till peace go with him to the tomb. . . . . 9 *Lines : Boat* 12
Till all our minds for ever flow . . . . . 9 *Collins* 7
Awed sober Reason till she crouched in fear ? . . 11 *Desc. Sk.* 55
By mountains, glowing till they seem to melt. . 15 *Desc. Sk.* 284
Till storm and driving ice blockade him there. . 19 *Desc. Sk.* 487
That cease not till night falls, when far and nigh, 21 *Desc. Sk.* 618
Crowed with ear-piercing power till then unheard ; 21 *Desc. Sk.* 629
Till his eye streamed with tears. In this deep vale 23 *Yew-tree* 46
On he must pace, perchance till night descend, . 24 *Guilt* 17
Till to his flock the early shepherd goes, . . . 27 *Guilt* 159
Till then he hoped his bones might there be laid . 28 *Guilt* 239
What tears of bitter grief, till then unknown, . 29 *Guilt* 255
Till now I did not think my end had been so near. 35 *Guilt* 576
On shipboard, bound till peace or death should set him free. . . . . 35 *Guilt* 594
Till one was found by stroke of violence dead, . 35 *Guilt* 599
Till all the band of playmates wept together ; . 39 *Bord.* 94
A Maiden innocent till ensnared by Clifford, . . 44 *Bord.* 381
And under covert rest till break of day, . . . 53 *Bord.* 863
Tut ! let them gabble till the day of doom. . . 55 *Bord.* 963
Till that same star summoned me back again. . . 59 *Bord.* 1217
Now I could laugh till my ribs ached. Oh, Fool ! 59 *Bord.* 1218
Drooped and pined till life was spent, ... 141 *Arm. Lady* 110
Till the waggon gains the top ; . . . . . . 181 *Waggoner* 4. 139
" Till the foundations of the mountains fail . . 201 *Hart-leap* 73
Till trees, and stones, and fountain, all are gone." 203 *Hart-leap* 160
Till he had reached a summit sharp and bare, . 226 *Vernal Ode* 12
Till the whole air is overcharged ; . . . . . 228 *Devot. Incit.* 22
Till my ribs ached I'd laugh at you ! . . . . 236 *P. B.* 20
For I, methinks, till I grow old, ... 288 *Highland Girl* 74
Till, with the heavens and earth, thou pass away ! 329 *Ode : Thanks.* 19
Till the bright Star appeared in eastern skies, . 351 *Des. Stanzas* 69
Till Night, descending upon hill and vale, . . . 363 **List—'twas* 110
Even till long gazing hath bedimmed his eye, . 460 **Wanderer! that* 54
Till from his couch the wished-for Sun uprose. . 534 **When in* 8
Till she had filled her apron full. . . . . . 537 *Goody Blake* 84
Till they have crossed the quaking marsh, . . 543 *Russ. Fug.* 127
Till Daphne, desperate with pursuit . . . . 543 *Russ. Fug.* 181
Till pitying Saints conduct her bark . . . . 544 *Russ. Fug.* 235
Till they have learned to frame a darksome aisle ;— 546 **Ye Lime* 5
Till the fatal bolt is shot ! . . . . 549 *Hermit's Cell* 1. 8
Till the first verse he learned it all by rote. . . 553 *Prioress* 71
She cried, till to the Jewry she was brought, . . 555 *Prioress* 147
Till from my tongue off-taken is the grain ; . . 556 *Prioress* 214
Till to a lawn I came all white and green, . . 557 *Cuck.and Night.* 61
Till he was far, all out of sight, away. . . . 561 *Cuck.andNight.* 225
Till fully passed and gone was the ninth night ; . 565 *Troilus* 163
Till dipp'd his pathway in the river shade ; . . 592 *Ev. Wk. Quarto* 70
Till, but the lonely beacon all is fled, ... 595 *Ev. Wk. Quarto* 189
Nor rest till they had reached the very door . . 633 *Prelude* 1. 73
Till all was tranquil as a dreamless sleep. . . . 639 *Prelude* 1. 463
Till he was left an arrow's flight behind. . . . 649 *Prelude* 3. 12
Libations, to thy memory drank, till pride . . 653 *Prelude* 3. 299
Till 'mid this crowded neighbourhood of things . 658 *Prelude* 3. 621
Till, every effort, every motion gone, ... 707 *Prelude* 8. 574
Till the whole cave, so late a senseless mass, . . 707 *Prelude* 8. 580
I followed, till he made a sudden stand : . . . 779 *Excursion* 2. 493
Till, chancing on that lofty ridge to pass . . . 784 *Excursion* 2. 811
Till nature rested from her work in death. . . 870 *Excursion* 7. 873

Till—*continued.*
Scarce peeps the curious star, till solemn gleams . S.3. 417 **Sweet was* 12
Till thou with crystal bead-drops didst encrust . S.3. 434 **The doubt* 53
Till the Term, for which she's fated . . . . S.3. 438 **I, whose* 24
Till, at the last, thou hear the voice—" Well done, K.8. 325 [?] **The vestal* 13
Till Egypt sees her antient fame outvied. . . . L.1. 88 *Juvenal* 1. 20
Look back till we had reached the boundary . . L.2. 318 *Frag. Æneid* 4. 11
'Till. (*Partial list.*) *See* **Until.**
'Till higher mounted, strives in vain to chear . . 599 *Ev. Wk. Quarto* 409
'Till our small share of hardly-paining sighs . . 599 *Ev. Wk. Quarto* 420
Tillage. Good Baron, have you ever practised tillage ? 60 *Bord.* 1277
For husbandry or tillage ; . . . . 483 *Simon Lee* 14
Tillage-ground. Of tillage-ground, that seemeth like a spot . . . . 379 *Duddon* 14. 5
Tilled. *See* **Half-tilled.**
Spade ! with which Wilkinson hath tilled his lands, 489 *Spade* 1
Before this rugged soil was tilled, ... 533 **Blest is* 28
He was her vassal of all labour, tilled . . . . 783 *Excursion* 2. 764
Tiller's. The tiller's hand, a hermit might have chosen, ... 832 *Excursion* 5. 681
Tillers. Shepherds and tillers of the ground—betimes 699 *Prelude* 8. 8
Tills. Though public care full often tills . . . 375 **The Minstrels* 22
Deplorable his lot who tills the ground, . . . 429 *Ecc. Sonn.* 2. 4. 1
His whole life long tills it, with heartless toil . 429 *Ecc. Sonn.* 2. 4. 2
Is prevalent, where he who tills the field, . . K.8.247 *Recluse* 1.1.381
Tilsbury. How oft have I heard in sweet Tilsbury Vale . . . . 569 *Farmer* 15
And his heart all the while is in Tilsbury Vale. . 571 *Farmer* 88
Tilt. Away with feast and tilt and tourney ! . . 372 *Eg. Maid* 200
Tilth. Upon his rich domains, vineyard and tilth, . 718 *Prelude* 10. 7
Tilting. Aloft, yet in a tilting vessel rode, . . . 346 *Processions* 26
Tilts. But who would force the Soul tilts with a straw 442 *Ecc. Sonn.* 3. 7. 13
Timber. *See* **Cross-timber.**
Stretched on his bier—that massy timber wain ; . 865 *Excursion* 7. 548
Timbers. *See* **Knee-timbers.**
Timber-wain. Downward the ponderous timber-wain resounds ; . . . . 4 *Ev. Wk.* 135
Timbrel. Her shameless timbrel shakes on Como's marge, ... 13 *Desc. Sk.* 139
Her shameless timbrel shakes along thy marge, . 605 *Desc.Sk.Quarto* 160
The silver-collared Negro with his timbrel, . . 697 *Prelude* 7. 703
Time. *See* **Breathing-time, Budding-time, Christmas-time, Couching-time, Curfew-time, May-time, Night-time, Primrose-time, School-time, Seedtime, Spring-time, Summer-time.**
(For dark and broad the gulf of time between) . 8 *Ev. Wk.* 346
Time softly treads ; throughout the landscape breathes . . . . 9 *Ev. Wk.* 361
Mocks the dull ear of Time with deaf abortive sound. . . . . 16 *Desc. Sk.* 315
Food for his beasts in time of winter snows. . . 17 *Desc. Sk.* 385
The beauty, still more beauteous ! Nor, that time, 23 *Yew-tree* 37
Both of the time to come, and time long fled : . 24 *Guilt* 6
Can I forget our freaks at shearing time ! . . . 28 *Guilt* 212
" 'Twas a hard change ; an evil time was come ; . 29 *Guilt* 271
Much need have ye that time more closely draw . 33 *Guilt* 507
All night from time to time under him shook . . 36 *Guilt* 637
Dear Daughter ! precious relic of that time— . 40 *Bord.* 189
It struck me at the time—yet I believe . . . 42 *Bord.* 273
We have no time for this, my babbling Gossip ; . 44 *Bord.* 407
This is a time, said he, when guilt may shudder ; 51 *Bord.* 790
How goes the night. 'Tis hard to measure time . 52 *Bord.* 805
To the unnatural harvest of that time . . . . 56 *Bord.* 1053
Tell where you found us. At some future time . 58 *Bord.* 1133
We'll not insult thy majesty by time, ... 58 *Bord.* 1154
Thou wilt have time to breathe and think——Oh, Mercy ! . . . . 63 *Bord.* 1405
At any time ? and why given now ? Because . 64 *Bord.* 1479
As time advances either we become . . . . . 65 *Bord.* 1521
Time, since Man first drew breath, has never moved 65 *Bord.* 1531
So used to suit his language to the time, . . . 65 *Bord.* 1569
There was a time, when this protecting hand . . 76 *Bord.* 2195
The time, when in our childish plays, ... 79 **Stay near* 11
Of time and distance, night and day ; . . . . 81 †*Mother's Return* 19
The storm came on before its time : . . . . 83 *Lucy Gray* 29
Those Shepherds wear the time away. . . . . 84 *Shepherd-boys* 22
That absorbs time, space, and number ; . . . 90 *Longest Day* 47
Thus when thou with Time hast travelled . . . 90 *Longest Day* 57
Time passed on ; the Child was happy, . . . 94 *Westmoreland Girl* 41
In all his hardships, since that happy time . . 96 *Brothers* 73
To chronicle the time, we all have here . . . 97 *Brothers* 162
And went into his grave before his time. . . . 98 *Brothers* 216
Is distant three short miles, and in the time . . 99 *Brothers* 252
They had an uncle ;—he was at that time . . 99 *Brothers* 292
(A practice till this time unknown to him) . . 100 *Brothers* 350
Which at that time was James's home, there learned . . . . 101 *Brothers* 375
Yes, long before he died, he found that time . . 101 *Brothers* 388
On his own time here would he float away, . . 107 *Indolence* 6
Full many a time, upon a stormy night, . . . 107 *Indolence* 13
A second time ; for still I seem . . . . . 109 **I travelled* 7
Pondering that Time to-night will pass . . . 112 *Lament* 10
That kill the bloom before its time ; . . . . 113 *Lament* 40
Hard labour in a time of need ! . . . . . . 115 *Last of Flock* 42
A woeful time it was for me, ... 115 *Last of Flock* 55
And I may say, that many a time . . . . . 115 *Last of Flock* 67
Alas ! it was an evil time ; . . . . 115 *Last of Flock* 85

Time—*continued.*
And so I waste my time: for I am changed; . . 768 *Excursion* 1. 767
To give her needful help. That very time 769 *Excursion* 1. 862
Our final parting; for from that time forth . . 769 *Excursion* 1. 869
Of business roused, or pleasure, ere their time, . 773 *Excursion* 2. 98
Had been from eldest time by wish of theirs . 776 *Excursion* 2. 331
Of a small chapel, where, in ancient time, . . . 784 *Excursion* 2. 814
Or introduced at this more quiet time. . . . 787 *Excursion* 3. 49
Of time and conscious nature disappear, . . . 788 *Excursion* 3. 111
Through time or space—if neither in the one, . 789 *Excursion* 3. 216
O'er what from eldest time we have been told . 790 *Excursion* 3. 301
" O happy time! still happier was at hand; . . 794 *Excursion* 3. 550
And with no wider interval of time . . . . 794 *Excursion* 3. 592
Caught in the gripe of death, with such brief time 795 *Excursion* 3. 639
With what short interval of time between, . . 795 *Excursion* 3. 646
Of time, else lost;—existing unto me . . . . 796 *Excursion* 3. 704
Who, in old time, attired with snakes and whips . 798 *Excursion* 3. 851
For time and for eternity; by faith, ... 801 *Excursion* 4. 21
Whose kingdom is, where time and space are not. 802 *Excursion* 4. 76
Ah! if the time must come, in which my feet . 803 *Excursion* 4. 103
Of time and change disdaining, takes its course . 804 *Excursion* 4. 184
Is matched unequally with custom, time, . . . 804 *Excursion* 4. 206
What all the slowly-moving years of time, . . 805 *Excursion* 4. 286
Her sad dependence upon time, and all . . 807 *Excursion* 4. 422
To oldest time! and, reckless of the storm . . 809 *Excursion* 4. 518
The tranquillizing power of time, shall wake, . 809 *Excursion* 4. 547
Their soft indulgences, and in due time . . . 810 *Excursion* 4. 594
Of time and nature, girded by a zone . . . 813 *Excursion* 4. 824
Were those bewildered Pagans of old time. . . 815 *Excursion* 4. 934
Whose very sorrow is, that time hath shorn . . 817 *Excursion* 4. 1084
Trust me, that for the instructed, time will come 819 *Excursion* 4. 1235
Of one whom time and nature had made wise, . 820 *Excursion* 4. 1287
Before his time into a quiet grave, ... 821 *Excursion* 4. 1314
A faded hatchment hung, and one by time . . 825 *Excursion* 5. 163
To Youth or Maiden gone before their time, . . 825 *Excursion* 5. 202
That they were ever born to! In due time . . 826 *Excursion* 5. 273
That tempts, emboldens—for a time sustains, . 827 *Excursion* 5. 325
Lost, thought I, in the obscurities of time, . . 834 *Excursion* 5. 787
—Thus never shall the indignities of time . . . 838 *Excursion* 6. 30
Time to look back with tenderness on her . . . 841 *Excursion* 6. 200
Mute register, to him, of time and place, . . . 841 *Excursion* 6. 208
Unseconded, uncountenanced; then, as time . . 841 *Excursion* 6. 222
He fled; and when the lenient hand of time . . 844 *Excursion* 6. 423
" *Time flies; it is his melancholy task* . . . . 846 *Excursion* 6. 515
What time the hunter's earliest horn is heard 850 *Excursion* 6. 830
Such fate was hers.—The last time Ellen danced, 851 *Excursion* 6. 849
' Nay, ye must wait my time!' and down she sate, 853 *Excursion* 6. 978
The never-halting time; or, in her turn, . . . 856 *Excursion* 6. 1181
(What time the splendour of the setting sun . 857 *Excursion* 7. 6
Time, which had thus afforded willing help . . 860 *Excursion* 7. 204
And thus divides and thus relieves the time; . . 862 *Excursion* 7. 305
—But time hath power to soften all regrets, . . 868 *Excursion* 7. 687
—Then, for the first time, here you might have seen 869 *Excursion* 7. 763
Ah, not in vain!—or those who, in old time, . . 869 *Excursion* 7. 808
The animating hope that time may come . . . 877 *Excursion* 8. 209
To time and season, as the year rolled round?" . 878 *Excursion* 8. 251
A lofty stature undepressed by time, ... 881 *Excursion* 8. 502
Country, society, and time itself, ... 885 *Excursion* 9. 107
Whether regarded as a jocund time, ... 888 *Excursion* 9. 284
" O for the coming of that glorious time . . . 888 *Excursion* 9. 293
Did, in the time of their necessity, ... 889 *Excursion* 9. 324
Pregnant with recollections of the time . . . 891 *Excursion* 9. 484
If time, with free consent, be yours to give, . . 896 *Excursion* 9. 782
And since that time has cast . . . . . . S.3. 431 **The Scottish* 22
Time wears the features of Eternity; . . . . S.3. 435 **The doubt* 120
On me can Time no happier state bestow . . . S.3. 441 **Grateful is sleep; my* 3
When in Athens' festal time . . . . . . S.3. 442 *Harmodius* 19
In search of a stray sheep. It was the time . . K.8. 224 **I will* 7
Thence, journeying on a second time, they passed K.8. 226 **I will* 62
I will go back and range a second time . . . K.8. 228 **I will* 116
Abated not; and all that time the boy . . . K.8. 229 **I will* 137
Childless, until the time when he began . . . K.8. 231 **I will* 214
To cast from time to time a painful look . . . K.8. 250 *Recluse* 1. 1. 493
That were before all time, or is to be . . . . K.8. 253 *Recluse* 1. 1. 628
Ere time expire, the pageantry that stirs . . . K.8. 253 *Recluse* 1. 1. 629
And exaltation. Nothing at that time . . . K.8. 256 *Recluse* 1. 1. 708
A fugitive of fate. Long time was he . . . . K.8. 281 **Arms and* 3
The nation's hope shall shew the present time . L.1. 94 *Juvenal* 2. 9

Time-beguiling. A time-beguiling ditty, for delight 851 *Excursion* 6. 867

Time-buried. Dawns this time-buried pavement. From that mound . . . . 275 **While poring* 8

Time-cemented. Yon time-cemented Tower! . . 299 *Cora Linn* 6

Time-cherished. A Book time-cherished and an honoured name . . . . 626 **Son of* 9

Timed. *See* **Ill-timed, Mis-timed.**
Would have been better timed. Alone, I see; . 64 *Bord.* 1471
Have scored thine age, and punctually timed . . 172 *Infant Daughter* 26
" Nor could your coming have been better timed; 779 *Excursion* 2. 526

Time-dismantled. More ample than the time-dismantled Oak . . . . 219 *Haunted Tree* 7

Time-hallowed. Of the time-hallowed minstrelsy) required . . . . 857 *Excursion* 7. 21

Time-honoured. And Durham, the time-honoured Durham, did hear, ... 403 *White Doe* 686
Time-honoured Chaucer speaking through that Lay 436 *Ecc. Sonn.* 2. 31. 2

Timely. In timely sleep; and when, at break of day, 22 *Desc. Sk.* 667
Gone is the raven timely rest to seek; . . . . 26 *Guilt* 101
Fade and are shed, that from their timely fall . 267 **DespondingFather* 10

Timely—*continued.*
So timely Grace the immortal wing may heal, . 270 **If these* 13
To timely sleep. Thought I, the impassioned strain, ... 314 **I dropped* 6
A timely promise of unlooked-for fruit, . . . 395 *White Doe: Ded.* 30
—The courts are hushed;—for timely sleep . . 406 *White Doe* 951
From Heaven a *general* blessing; timely rains . 424 *Ecc. Sonn.* 1. 24. 5
Nor lacks this sea-girt Isle a timely share . . 432 *Ecc. Sonn.* 2. 14. 13
Some seek with timely flight a foreign strand; . 437 *Ecc. Sonn.* 2. 37. 2
Of Infancy, provides a timely shower . . . 445 *Ecc. Sonn.* 3. 20. 2
Yield timely fruit of peace and love and joy. . 447 *Ecc. Sonn.* 3. 29. 14
Leapt from this rock, and but for timely aid . . 469 **A youth* 4
Thy timely mandate, I deferred . . . . . 492 *Duty* 30
That shall lack a timely end, ... 495 *Force of Prayer* 66
A timely carolling. . . . . 498 **Departing summer* 6
Though to give timely warning and deter . . . 519 *Pun. Death* 9. 1
The timely insight that can temper fears, . . 533 **Once I* 39
A timely utterance gave that thought relief, . . 588 *Immortality* 23
By timely interference: and therewith . . . 633 *Prelude* 1. 118
To give me timely notice, and straightway, . . 660 *Prelude* 4. 124
But ask for timely furtherance and help . . . 665 *Prelude* 4. 456
More than its timely produce; rather loved . . 670 *Prelude* 5. 285
Due to this timely notice, unawares . . . . 687 *Prelude* 7. 27
Learns from such timely exercise to keep . . 751 *Prelude* 14. 345
" Such timely warning," said the Wanderer, " gave 805 *Excursion* 4. 295
That timely light, to share his joyous sport: . . 814 *Excursion* 4. 864
To rise from timely sleep, and meet the day . . 859 *Excursion* 7. 155
Nor wanted timely treat of fish or fowl . . . 860 *Excursion* 7. 164
But, timely warned, *He* would have stayed his steps, 865 *Excursion* 7. 494
By timely culture unsustained; or run . . . 888 *Excursion* 9. 305

Time-proof. Pillars, and arches,—not in vain time-proof, ... 387 *Roslin* 7

Time's. Of Time's sure help to calm and reconcile, 32 *Guilt* 454
We call, and scorn the other as Time's spendthrift; 60 *Bord.* 1236
In time's abyss, are privileged to endure . . . 152 **Forth from* 21
To Time's first step across the bound . . . . 223 *Wishing-gate* 68
To mimic Time's forlorn humanities. . . . . 262 **Mark the* 14
Much have ye suffered from Time's gnawing tooth: 270 **Ye sacred* 5
To summon fancies out of Time's dark cell. . . 275 *Rotha Q.* 14
Man left this Structure to become Time's prey, . 283 **Here, where* 2
Who, gathering up all that Time's envious tooth . 359 *Plea: Hist.* 3
Man's headstrong violence and Time's fleetness, . 366 **Ye Trees* 16
By ghostly power:—but Time's unsparing hand . 383 *Duddon* 27. 10
Why should we break Time's charitable seals? . 449 *Ecc. Sonn.* 3. 35. 12
The time's and season's influence disown; . . 453 **Calm is the* 11
Fair Land! by Time's parental love made free, . 463 **Why should the* 9
(Thy Paramount, mighty Nature! and Time's Lord) . . . . 474 **On to* 5
Of time's pathetic sanctity; . . . . 533 **Blest is* 44
Time's vanities, light fragments of earth's dream— 584 **With copious* 39
Culled the best fruits of Time's uncounted hours, 701 *Prelude* 8. 140
That through the time's exceeding fierceness saw 724 *Prelude* 10. 451
Time's fetters are composed; and life was put 796 *Excursion* 3. 697
But History, time's slavish scribe, will tell . . 797 *Excursion* 3. 769
Of Time's eternal Master, and that peace, . . . 846 *Excursion* 6. 520
From disregard of time's destructive power, . . 847 *Excursion* 6. 621
Time's weary course! Or if, by thy decree, . . 893 *Excursion* 9. 635
For Time's invisible tooth to prey upon, . . . S.3. 434 **The doubt* 51

Times. *See* **Breathing-times, Ofttimes, Oftentimes.**
At times, while young Content forsook her seat, . 2 *Ev. Wk.* 24
At times, and tales unsought beguile the day, . 15 *Desc. Sk.* 247
Transmits of happier lot in times of yore! . . 17 *Desc. Sk.* 387
This is true comfort, thanks a thousand times!— 43 *Bord.* 343
Imperious at all times, his temper rose; . . . 68 *Bord.* 1715
By One who would have died a thousand times . 78 *Bord.* 2331
Dead times revive in thee: . . . . 79 **Stay near* 6
And three times to the child I said, ... 86 *Anecdote* 47
I thought of times when Pain might be thy guest, 88 *H. C.* 15
Old times, thought I, are breathing there; . . 119 *Sailor's Mother* 8
And, truly, at all times, the storm, that drives 132 *Michael* 56
Was busy, looking back into past times. . . . 135 *Michael* 257
He might be sent to him. Ten times or more . 136 *Michael* 311
Familiarly of you and of old times. . . . . 147 *Joanna* 17
A hundred times, by rock or bower, ... 158 **In youth* 41
Yet, while he thinks on times of old, ... 174 *Waggoner* 1. 64
Of sickness felt by him in times long past, . . 196 *Resolution* 69
" At all times of the day and night . . . . 198 *Thorn* 67
A wind full ten times over. . . . . 199 *Thorn* 180
" A jolly place," said he, " in times of old! . . 202 *Hart-leap* 123
Ten times and more, I fancied it had ceased; . 218 *Recluse* 1. 1. 217
Blest times when mystery is laid bare, . . . 226 *Present.* 68
Full twenty times was Peter feared . . . . 238 *P. B.* 204
He kisses him a thousand times! . . . . . 249 *P. B.* 1115
A thousand times this pipe did Tasso sound; . . 260 **Scorn not* 5
Peace in these feverish times is sovereign bliss: . 262 *Retirement* 9
More than in humbler times graced human story; 281 **What strong* 10
Proud were ye, Mountains, when, in times of old, 283 **Proud were* 1
But thought how wide the world, the times . . 291 *Rob Roy* 75
The treasured dreams of times long past, . . . 293 *Yarrow Unv.* 53
With all its bravery on; in times . . . . . 294 *Jedbor.* 31
These times strike monied worldlings with dismay: 308 **These times* 1
In these usurping times of fear and pain? . . . 316 **O'er the* 8
This sword that one of our weak times might wear! 335 *Aix* 7
Cliffs, fountains, rivers, seasons, times— . . . 341 *San Salv.* 13
Accordant meditations, which in times . . . 358 *Aquap.* 364
By humble choice of plain old times, are seen . 387 **Part fenced* 10
Immured in Bothwell's towers, at times the Brave 392 *Bothwell* 1
Ten times their number, man and horse; . . . 405 *White Doe* 856
And what melodious sounds at times prevail! . 430 *Ecc. Sonn.* 2. 7. 1
A thousand times more exquisitely sweet, . . . 438 *Ecc. Sonn.* 2. 39. 11

Tiny. A tiny tenement, forsooth, and frail, as needs must be — 91 *Norman Boy* 15
Both for tiny harmless minnow — 94 *Westmoreland Girl* 51
Mantling in the tiny square. — 161 **Pleasures newly* 24
Have shells to fit their tiny hands — 164 *Needlecase* 23
Thy hand here sprinkling tiny flowers, — 170 *Rural Ill.* 15
Observe each wing !—a tiny van ! — 227 *Vernal Ode* 114
What are they to that tiny grain, — 237 *P. B.* 49
Which tiny Elves impressed ;—on that smooth stage — 378 *Duddon* 11. 4
That smites this tiny sea, — 526 **The soaring* 22
Spread, tiny nautilus, the living sail ; — 527 **Those breathing* 35
Or when his tiny gems shall deck his brow : — 530 *Poor Robin* 28
A peopled world it is ; in size a tiny room. — 532 †*Float. Isl.* 16
The tiny creatures strong by social league ; — 807 *Excursion* 4. 432
With tiny finger—to let fall a tear ; — 826 *Excursion* 5. 265
Of melted hoar-frost, every tiny knot — K.8. 252 *Recluse* 1.1.564
Tip. Tip their smooth ridges with a softer ray ; — 4 *Ev. Wk.* 123
The drops that tip the melting icicles. — 332 *Ode : Thanks.* 210
Tipped. *See* **Tipt.**
Those holy turrets tipped with evening gold, — 20 *Desc. Sk.* 564
Where tipp'd with gold the mountain-summits glow'd. — 592 *Ev. Wk. Quarto* 36
Those turrets tipp'd by hope with morning gold, — 614 *Desc.Sk.Quarto* 673
And outer spray profusely tipped with seeds — 676 *Prelude* 6. 83
Tipped with a rain-drop, Fancy loved to seat, — 705 *Prelude* 8. 399
Tipple. Through the long day to swear and tipple ; — 621 *Andrew Jones* 7
Tips. That tips with eve's last gleam his spiry head. — 595 *Ev.Wk. Quarto* 190
Tipstaffs. And *worship* Mayors, Tipstaffs, Aldermen and all. — L.1. 88 *Juvenal* 1. 18
Tipt. *See* **Tipped.**
Tipt with eve's latest gleam of burning red. — 6 *Ev. Wk.* 211
Tiptoe. On tiptoe reared, he strains his clarion throat, — 5 *Ev. Wk.* 152
Or hang on tip-toe at the lifted latch. — 32 *Guilt* 418
And wild rose tip-toe upon hawthorn stocks, — 260 **How sweet* 5
And stands on tiptoe, conscious she is fair, — 311 **Who rises* 9
Again ?—on tip-toe down the hill — 537 *Goody Blake* 78
On tiptoe rear'd he blows his clarion throat, — 594 *Ev. Wk. Quarto* 137
—The tall Sun, tip-toe on an Alpine spire, — 614 *Desc.Sk.Quarto* 662
Tire. Our watchful house-dog, that would tease and tire — 28 *Guilt* 223
When we began to tire of childish play, — 28 *Guilt* 248
Should the tale tire you, let this challenge stand — 782 *Excursion* 2. 731
Were ready comrades whom he could not tire ; — 864 *Excursion* 7. 440
Tired. And, tired with slights his pride no more could brook, — 103 *Artegal* 88
Ere the tired head of Scotland's Queen — 113 *Lament* 69
Of their own offspring tired. — 170 *Rural Ill.* 24
Comes a tired and sultry breeze — 173 *Waggoner* 1. 17
Calls to the few tired dogs that yet remain : — 200 *Hart-leap* 18
Be thankful, even though tired and faint, — 215 *Kirkstone* 57
Or, tired with sport, wouldst sink asleep — 216 *Enterprise* 34
While thy tired lute hangs on the hawthorn-tree, — 227 *Vernal Ode* 87
For the tired slave, Song lifts the languid oar, — 233 *Power of Sound* 53
Here, where, of havoc tired and rash undoing, — 283 **Here, where* 1
Now we are tired of boisterous joy, — 295 *Highland Boy* 1
On the tired household of corporeal sense, — 323 *Ode 1814* 2
A sign he craved, tired slave of vain contrition ; — 373 *Eg. Maid* 296
Tired of the world and all its industry. — 424 *Ecc. Sonn.* 1. 22. 14
Of roving tired or desultory war— — 444 *Ecc. Sonn.* 3. 17. 8
Tired with its daily share of earth's unrest,— — 460 **Wanderer ! that* 59
A tired Ship-soldier on paternal land, — 470 **Did pangs* 6
Of one tired out with fun and madness ; — 486 *Matthew* 22
Tired of my books, a scanty company ! — 521 *Epist.Beaumont* 32
And tired of listening to the boisterous sea— — 521 *Epist.Beaumont* 33
Tired, and uneasy at the halts I made. — 660 *Prelude* 4. 109
Sick of its business, of its pleasures tired, — 663 *Prelude* 4. 356
And sun-burnt travellers resting their tired limbs, — 668 *Prelude* 5. 209
Moving in heaven ; or, of that pleasure tired, — 679 *Prelude* 6. 270
Feverish, and tired, and restless, I went forth — 738 *Prelude* 12. 289
Some, tired of honest service ; these, outdone, — 797 *Excursion* 3. 772
Of vain endeavours tired ; and by his own, — 798 *Excursion* 3. 868
If tired with systems, each in its degree — 810 *Excursion* 4. 603
And, to tired limbs and over-busy thoughts, — 821 *Excursion* 4. 1323
A tired way-faring man, once *I* was brought — 833 *Excursion* 5. 734
To use of reason. And, I own that, tired — 835 *Excursion* 5. 849
By all that breathe in Troy, how tired and worn — L.2. 318 *Frag.Æneid* 4.6
Tires. Me this unchartered freedom tires ; — 492 *Duty* 37
Or bounty tires—and every face, that smiled — 880 *Excursion* 8. 387
That tires not, nor betrays. Our life is turned — 885 *Excursion* 9. 113
Tiresome. Of tiresome indolence, would often hang — 96 *Brothers* 54
This tiresome night, O Sleep ! thou art to me — 253 **O gentle* 5
'Tis. (*Partial list.*)
'Tis a strange letter this !—You saw her write it ? — 38 *Bord.* 53
'Tis weariness that breeds these gloomy fancies, — 40 *Bord.* 145
'Tis but for a few days—a thought has struck me. — 41 *Bord.* 224
'Tis plain he loves the Maid, and what he said — 41 *Bord.* 231
'Tis but a word and then—— Something is here — 41 *Bord.* 253
'Tis never drought with us—St. Cuthbert and his Pilgrims, — 43 *Bord.* 324
'Tis too disorderly for sleep or rest. — 43 *Bord.* 351
'Tis Herbert and no other ! 'Tis a feast to see him, — 45 *Bord.* 460
Yes, loves him ; 'tis a truth that multiplies — 48 *Bord.* 591
His guilt a thousand-fold. 'Tis most perplexing : — 48 *Bord.* 592
Stoop for a moment ; 'tis an act of justice ; — 48 *Bord.* 638
My hands are numb. Ha ! ha ! 'tis nipping cold. — 50 *Bord.* 727
And tell me if 'tis fit for such a work. — 52 *Bord.* 797
How goes the night. 'Tis hard to measure time — 52 *Bord.* 805
'Tis his own fault if he hath got a face — 54 *Bord.* 923

'Tis—*continued.*
Think not of that ! 'tis over—we are safe. — 55 *Bord.* 1005
That horn again—'Tis some one of our Troop ; — 56 *Bord.* 1016
Both soul and body—— 'Tis too horrible ; — 57 *Bord.* 1065
Tissue. On silken tissue, might diffuse his limbs — 219 *Haunted Tree* 13
Thy handmaid Frost with spangled tissue quaint — 376 *Duddon* 2. 5
Titian's. The appropriate Picture, fresh from Titian's hand, — 509 *F. Stone* 105
A Titian's hand, addrest to picture forth — 850 *Excursion* 6. 828
Title. To manhood, seems their title to disown ; — 19 *Desc. Sk.* 513
And she shall love him. With unquestioned title — 54 *Bord.* 905
And came to—what's your title—eh ? your claims — 62 *Bord.* 1349
" Gracious Allah ! by such title — 140 *Arm. Lady* 67
Prescriptive title to the shattered pile, — 283 **Here, where* 13
If that substantial title please thee more, — 363 **List—'twas* 104
Endearing title, a responsive chime — 463 **They called* 5
There's virtue, the title it surely may claim, — 482 *Character* 15
And even a title higher still, — 512 **Who rashly* 29
These, and the name and title at full length,— — 872 *Excursion* 7. 970
Titled. *See* **High-titled.**
Professedly, to others titled higher, — 694 *Prelude* 7. 487
The sound of titled names, and talked in glee — 860 *Excursion* 7. 217
Title-page. Here, fronts of houses, like a title-page, — 689 *Prelude* 7. 160
Titles. Then thus exclaimed : " To me, of titles shorn, — 104 *Artegal* 139
To thee, by varying titles known — 216 *Enterprise* 38
Those titles vanish, and that strength decay ; — 305 *Ven. Rep.* 10
Of Earth's first blood, have titles manifold. — 307 **It is not* 14
Of pompous horses ; whom vain titles please ; — 433 *Ecc. Sonn.* 2. 18. 4
And wealth and titles were in less esteem — 713 *Prelude* 9. 231
Her titles and her honours ; now believing, — 731 *Prelude* 11. 297
By sounding titles, hath acquired the name — 788 *Excursion* 3. 130
Establish sounder titles of esteem — 791 *Excursion* 3. 342
' What titles will he keep ? will he remain — 861 *Excursion* 7. 273
These titles emperors and chiefs have borne, — 862 *Excursion* 7. 343
Long-reverenced titles cast away as weeds ; — 889 *Excursion* 9. 338
Tittle. Nor for the moon cared he a tittle, — 240 *P. B.* 333
Titus. Drew Titus from the depth of studious bowers, — 573 *Chiabrera* 2. 2
Tiviot. And leave thy Tweed and Tiviot — 386 *Yarrow Rev.* 52
Tiviot-dale. There's pleasant Tiviot-dale, a land — 293 *Yarrow Unv.* 21
Tiviot's. To Tiviot's stream, to Annan, Tweed, and Clyde :— — 219 **This Height* 10
Tivoli. Of Tivoli ; and, high upon that steep, — 691 *Prelude* 7. 255
To, *omitted.*
Toad. Well !—he has often spurned me like a toad, — 45 *Bord.* 470
And, if you can, the unwieldy toad — 142 †*Lov. and Lik.* 7
How disappeared He ?—ask the newt and toad, — 299 *Brownie's Cell* 71
" How disappeared he ? " Ask the newt and toad ; — 391 *Brownie* 1
Tobacco-box. His shining horn tobacco-box ; — 245 *P. B.* 817
Tocsin. Must bid the tocsin ring from tower to tower !— — 22 *Desc. Sk.* 640
Tod. Or from a rifted crag or ivy tod — 456 **The leaves* 20
To-day. To-day will clear up all.—You marked a Cottage, — 44 *Bord.* 378
Than Youth's spontaneous products ; and to-day — 48 *Bord.* 623
To-day you have thrown off a tyranny — 64 *Bord.* 1488
But go to-morrow, or belike to-day, — 107 *Indolence* 8
Such happiness as I have known to-day. — 111 *'*Tis said that some* 52
To-day I fetched him from the rock ; — 115 *Last of Flock* 19
To-day I fetched it from the rock ; — 116 *Last of Flock* 99
Presiding Spirit here to-day, — 159 *Green Linnet* 14
And to-day my heart is weary ; — 159 **Up with me* 9
Behold her how She smiles to-day — 204 *Brougham* 17
Familiar matter of to-day ? — 289 *Sol. Reap.* 22
To-day, nor yet to-morrow ; — 293 *Yarrow Unv.* 46
Bright be thy course to-day, let not this promise fail ! — 329 *Ode : Thanks.* 35
The act were justified to-day." — 401 *White Doe* 451
This said, our tears to-day may fall — 401 *White Doe* 467
We who were led to-day down a grim dell, — 475 *Greenock* 2
We from to-day, my Friend, will date — 483 *Sister* 19
Our temper from to-day. — 483 *Sister* 32
That what has been unveiled to-day, — 545 *Russ. Fug.* 291
Ye that through your hearts to-day — 590 *Immortality* 177
To-day, to-morrow will be, took of them — 696 *Prelude* 7. 589
The children now are rich, for the old to-day — 699 *Prelude* 8. 44
You look at me, and you have cause ; to-day — 767 *Excursion* 1. 763
He knows not wherefore ;—but the boy to-day, — 779 *Excursion* 2. 540
" That poor Man taken hence to-day," replied — 780 *Excursion* 2. 593
And he, whom this our cottage hath to-day — 782 *Excursion* 2. 738
And from the cottage hath been borne to-day. — 785 *Excursion* 2. 895
Toe. *See* **Tiptoe.**
Covered from top to toe with scars ; — 237 *P. B.* 39
With letters huge inscribed from top to toe, — 689 *Prelude* 7. 161
Together. Where beasts and men together o'er the plain — 13 *Desc. Sk.* 169
Together smoking in the sun's slant beam, — 33 *Guilt* 461
Nor could we live together those poor boys and I ; — 35 *Guilt* 603
Till all the band of playmates wept together ; — 39 *Bord.* 94
Our wanderings together. Providence — 40 *Bord.* 195
We've weathered out together. My poor Gilfred ! — 46 *Bord.* 513
We joined our tales of wretchedness together, — 50 *Bord.* 691
You'd better like we should descend together, — 51 *Bord.* 771
Come, let us house together. Had I not — 53 *Bord.* 869
We'll go together, and, such proof received — 66 *Bord.* 1594
Light to thy path, warmth to thy blood !—Together — 70 *Bord.* 1852
And we shall howl together. I am deserted — 74 *Bord.* 2090
Come, let us take a peep at both together, — 77 *Bord.* 2289
Together chased the butterfly ! — 79 **Stay near* 13

To-night—*continued.*
have kept me abroad to-night till this hour ? . . 72 *Bord.* 1950
To-night along these lonesome ways ? " . . . 82 *Alice Fell* 34
" To-night will be a stormy night— . . . 83 *Lucy Gray* 13
Unless our Landlord be your host to-night, . . 98 *Brothers* 223
Pondering that Time to-night will pass . . . 112 *Lament* 10
To-night the church-tower bells will ring . . . 113 *Lament* 22
The wolf has come to me to-night, ... 114 *Ind. Wom.* 57
To-morrow, or the next day, or to-night : . . . 135 *Michael* 281
If he *could* go, the Boy should go to-night." . . 135 *Michael* 282
Now am I fairly safe to-night— . . . . . 174 *Waggoner* 1. 110
We shall be meeting ghosts to-night ! " . . . 179 *Waggoner* 3. 115
To-night, beneath the moonlight sky, ... 245 *P. B.* 784
Ask him to lend his horse to-night, ... 248 *P. B.* 1063
So do not let me wear to-night away : . . . . 254 **A flock* 11
Must blow to-night his bugle horn. Had I . . 266 **With how* 8
To-night beneath my cottage-eaves ; . . . . 375 **The Minstrels* 2

Too, *omitted.*

Too-anxious. Of a too-anxious world, mild pastoral Muse ! . . . . 227 *Vernal Ode* 76

Too-credulous. Streamed with the pomp of a too-credulous day. . . . . 304 **Jones ! as* 3

Took. Vain hope ! for fraud took all that he had earned. . . . . 25 *Guilt* 64
Must part ; the summons came ;—our final leave we took. . . . . 28 *Guilt* 234
Breathless he gazed upon her face,—then took . 36 *Guilt* 632
I took thee in my arms, and we began . . . 40 *Bord.* 194
I took it for the blaze of Cheviot Beacon : . . 50 *Bord.* 742
You from my shoulder took my scrip and threw it 60 *Bord.* 1283
It took effect—and yet I baffled it, ... 75 *Bord.* 2144
He plied his work ;—and Lucy took . . . . 83 *Lucy Gray* 23
The other took him at his word, ... 85 *Shepherd-boys* 47
Into their arms the lamb they took, ... 85 *Shepherd-boys* 93
I said, and took him by the arm, ... 86 *Anecdote* 30
The lamb, while from her hand he thus his supper took, ... 87 *Pet-lamb* 9
" He took thee in his arms, and in pity brought thee home : . . . . 87 *Pet-lamb* 37
Me had the dream equipped with wings, so I took him in my arms, ... 92 *Poet's Dream* 17
He took his way, impatient to accost . . . . 95 *Brothers* 36
He took me by the hand, and said to me, . . . 100 *Brothers* 322
Ay, Sir, that passed away : we took him to us ; . 100 *Brothers* 342
A gushing from his heart, that took away . . . 101 *Brothers* 407
Who more devout enjoyment with us took : . . 107 *Indolence* 4
When from my arms my Babe they took, . . . 114 *Ind. Wom.* 33
And it was fit that thence I took . . . . . 115 *Last of Flock* 47
I bear it with me, Sir ;—he took so much delight in it." . . . . 119 *Sailor's Mother* 36
Old Timothy took up his staff, and he shut . . 120 *Childless Father* 15
No answer, only took the mother's hand . . . 125 *V. and J.* 232
On the hill top. His eyes he scarcely took, . . 125 *V. and J.* 253
And thither took with him his motherless Babe, . 125 *V. and J.* 274
She took the reins, when this was said, . . . 130 *Idiot Boy* 399
At the first hearing, for a moment took . . . 134 *Michael* 218
He to that valley took his way, and there . . 138 *Michael* 441
Took up the Lady's voice, and laughed again ; . 147 *Joanna* 55
And took no note of the hour while thence they gazed, ... 151 **Forth from* 10
The splinters took another road— . . . . . 156 *Oak and Broom* 28
Took the fancy from a glance . . . . . 161 **Pleasures newly* 15
Their Father, took of them no thought, . . . 161 *Binnorie* 8
Her Father took another Mate ; . . . . . 192 *Ruth* 2
But of the Vagrant none took thought ; . . . 194 *Ruth* 208
And now a stranger's privilege I took ; . . . 196 *Resolution* 82
Thee wingèd Fancy took, and nursed . . . . 215 *Enterprise* 24
Thankfully took an effort that was meant . . 231**The gentlest Poet* 32
And took it in most grievous part ; . . . . 246 *P. B.* 912
On went She, and due north her journey took. . 258 **With Ships* 14
Forth to her Dove, and took no further heed. . 274 **Wait, prithee* 2
For God took pity on the Boy, ... 295 *Highland Boy* 23
A bold thought roused him, and he took . . . 296 *Highland Boy* 143
He felt the motion—took his seat ; . . . . 296 *Highland Boy* 152
The blind Boy's little dog took part ; . . . . 297 *Highland Boy* 227
Of sleep took import terrible ;— . . . . . 299 *Brownie's Cell* 66
And, when she took unto herself a Mate, . . . 305 *Ven. Rep.* 7
How, when their course they through the desert took, ... 346 *Processions* 13
Save in this Rill that took from blood the name . 361 **When here* 7
And took from men her name—The Water Lily. 369 *Eg. Maid* 6
That took thee from thy native hills ; . . . . 375 **The Minstrels* 20
In which the castle once took pride ! . . . . 391 *HighlandBroach* 66
The Lovers took within this ancient grove . . . 393 **The Lovers* 1
Its impulse took—that sorrow-stricken door, . . 394 **No more* 21
He took the Banner, and unfurled . . . . . 403 *White Doe* 658
And took a place in all men's sight ; . . . . 410 *White Doe* 1301
He took it from the soldier's hand ; . . . . 410 *White Doe* 1333
To Rylstone-hall her way she took. . . . . 411 *White Doe* 1363
Who, with sad hearts, of friends and country took 443 *Ecc. Sonn.* 3. 13. 2
Blest Pilgrims, surely, as they took for guide . . 443 *Ecc. Sonn.* 3. 13. 10
So piety took root ; and Song might tell . . . 466 *St. Bees* 48
Was glorified, and took its place, above . . . 466 *St. Bees* 56
A name which it took of yore : . . . . . . 494 *Force of Prayer* 22
Blithe hopes and happy musings soon took flight, 523 *Epist. Beaumont* 120
To Palestine the Brothers took their way. . . 535 *Egremont* 40
And fiercely by the arm he took her, ... 537 *Goody Blake* 89
E'er took possession of her cell . . . . . . 543 *Russ. Fug.* 159
At her own prayer transformed, took root, . . 543 *Russ. Fug.* 183
The fainting creature took the marsh, ... 544 *Russ. Fug.* 265

Took—*continued.*
Touched then his tongue, and took away the grain ; 556 *Prioress* 220
And after that they rose, and took their way, . 556 *Prioress* 228
She thankèd them ; and then her leave she took, 562 *Cuck.andNight.*286
My Lady first me took unto her grace. . . . 563 *Troilus* 63
Alas, and there I took of her my leave ; . . . 564 *Troilus* 93
Another time he took into his head, ... 564 *Troilus* 106
What less may mislead you, they took it away. . 569 *Farmer* 28
Was I, Roberto Dati, and I took . . . . . 575 *Chiabrera* 6. 2
Lord of the air, he took his flight ; . . . . . 580 *John Words.* 5
Of Innocence the garb she took, ... 620 *Birth of Love* 32
He stooped and took the penny up : . . . . 621 *Andrew Jones* 26
He rais'd the bowl, and took a long deep draught ; 625 *Æneid* 119
But as a Pilgrim resolute, I took, ... 633 *Prelude* 1. 91
Were wanting here, I took what might be found . 657 *Prelude* 3. 566
Up the familiar hill I took my way . . . . 658 *Prelude* 4. 18
Of unacknowledged weariness. I took . . . 660 *Prelude* 4. 158
Of manners put to school I took small note, . . 663 *Prelude* 4. 302
He stooped, and straightway from the ground took up . . . . 665 *Prelude* 4. 427
Not slow to share my wishes, took his staff, . . 680 *Prelude* 6. 324
We landed—took with them our evening meal, . 681 *Prelude* 6. 395
A halting-place, where all together took . . . 683 *Prelude* 6. 565
Crossing the unbridged stream, that road we took, 683 *Prelude* 6. 574
To-day, to-morrow will be, took of them . . . 696 *Prelude* 7. 589
He took no heed ; but in his brawny arms . . 696 *Prelude* 7. 612
Thus early took a place pre-eminent ; . . . . 704 *Prelude* 8. 341
That took his station there for ornament : . . 704 *Prelude* 8. 380
All that took place within me came and went . 707 *Prelude* 8. 557
And placid, and took nothing from the man . . 714 *Prelude* 9. 320
We took, and let this freely be confessed, . . 714 *Prelude* 9. 343
And took his station in the Tribune, saying, . . 720 *Prelude* 10. 112
Of our opinions had been just, we took . . . 728 *Prelude* 11. 48
Of custom, law, and statute, took at once . . 729 *Prelude* 11. 111
Thoughts over busy in the course they took, . . 739 *Prelude* 12. 334
Again I took the intellectual eye . . . . . 740 *Prelude* 13. 52
And westward took my way, to see the sun . . 746 *Prelude* 14. 5
I took my staff, and, when I kissed her babe, . 768 *Excursion* 1. 809
And took my rounds along this road again . . 768 *Excursion* 1. 814
Greeted us all day long ; we took our seats . . 772 *Excursion* 2. 58
And He, what wonder ! took a mortal taint. . . 775 *Excursion* 2. 245
Took their last farewell of the sun and stars, . 791 *Excursion* 3. 371
My ancient Friend and I together took . . . 826 *Excursion* 5. 231
Their place I took—and for a grateful office . . 891 *Excursion* 9. 483
Receiving, took the slender path that leads . . 895 *Excursion* 9. 773
And Childhood, seeming still more busy, took . S.3. 417 **Sweet was* 6
That from Venus took her life. . . . . . . S.3. 437 **I, whose* 8
E'er took such delight in . . . . S.3. 440 **Said red-ribboned* 11
Had stayed so long. The shepherd took his way K.8. 229 **I will* 163

Tool. His tool, the wandering Beggar, made last night . . . . 63 *Bord.* 1419
Of his best workmanship by plan and tool. . . 473 **Thanks for* 8
Give me your tool," to him I said ; . . . . 484 *Simon Lee* 82
Thou art a tool of honour in my hands ; . . . 489 *Spade* 3
Yet, like a tool of Fancy, works . . . . . 499 *Memory* 13
A tool of murder ; they who ruled the State,— . 728 *Prelude* 11. 65
And let the light mechanic tool be hailed . . . 831 *Excursion* 5. 606
An offering, or a sacrifice, a tool . . . . . 886 *Excursion* 9. 115

Too-long-polluted. And this too-long-polluted land imbued . . . . 102 *Artegal* 19

Tools. With tools for ready wit to guide ; . . . 191 *Seq. Beggars* 5
The engines of her pain, the tools . . . . . 194 *Ruth* 217
I left her busy with her garden tools ; . . . . 766 *Excursion* 1. 691
And tufts of mountain moss. Mechanic tools . 781 *Excursion* 2. 664
We sallied forth together ; found the tools . . 783 *Excursion* 2. 795
Of intellectual implements and tools ; . . . . 888 *Excursion* 9. 308
Now, Norfolk set thy heralds to their tools, . . L.1. 96 *Juvenal* 3. 35

Tooth. Much have ye suffered from Time's gnawing tooth : . . . . 270 **Ye sacred* 5
He called on Frost's inexorable tooth . . . . 321 **Humanity,delighting* 21
Who, gathering up all that Time's envious tooth . 359 *Plea : Hist.* 3
The precept eye for eye, and tooth for tooth, . 518 *Pun. Death* 7. 3
Raged bitterly, with keen and silent tooth ; . . 640 *Prelude* 1. 537
For Time's invisible tooth to prey upon, . . . S.3. 434 **The doubt* 51

Toothed. *See* **Sharp-toothed.**
While, from the twin cards toothed with glittering wire, ... 95 *Brothers* 22

Top. *See* **Chimney-top, Hill-top, House-top, Mountain-top, Skiddaw-top.**
Or from the top of Lebanon surveyed . . . . 70 *Bord.* 1806
To the top of Great How did it please them to climb : . . . . 86 *Rural Arch.* 4
Then, light-hearted Boys, to the top of the crag ; 86 *Rural Arch.* 23
To be engrafted on the top of his small edifice. . 91 *Norman Boy* 20
On the hill top. His eyes he scarcely took, . . 125 *V. and J.* 253
And so have gained the top of the hill ; . . . 174 *Waggoner* 1. 41
He's at the top of his enjoyment ! " . . . . 179 *Waggoner* 3. 129
Till the waggon gains the top ; . . . . . . 181 *Waggoner* 4. 139
On the top of the bare hill ; . . . . 190 *March* 14
Couched on the bald top of an eminence ; . . . 196 *Resolution* 58
With lichens to the very top, ... 197 *Thorn* 13
To Niphates' top invited, ... 218 **Inmate of* 29
Covered from top to toe with scars ; . . . . 237 *P. B.* 39
Gleams on the grass-crowned top of yon tall Tower, 283 **Here, where* 11
Huge Criffel's hoary top ascends . . . . . 285 *Grave of Burns* 39
Which, at Jove's will, descends on Pelion's top." 312 **When, far* 14
Or top serene of unmolested mountain, . . . 325 *Ode 1814* 124
Hung round its top, on wings that changed their hues at will. . . . . 338 *Engelberg* 9

Toss. Toss it from hand to hand, disquieted ; 7 *Ev. Wk.* 266
His limbs would toss about him with delight, 108 *Indolence* 48
How the fast-rooted trees can toss 109 **Ere with* 11
Aloft, where pines their branches toss ! 337 *Cath. Cantons* 10
Toss in the fanning wind a humbler plume." 471 **Despond who* 14
If my spirit toss and welter 550 *Hermit's Cell* 4. 7
To ride the ring, or toss the beamy lance ; 619 *School Ex.* 58
Toss like a ship at anchor, rocked by storms ; 710 *Prelude* 9. 51
Tossed. *See* **Tost.**
Owes to the fit in which his soul hath tossed 26 *Guilt* 92
To loathsome vaults, where heart-sick anguish tossed, 30 *Guilt* 350
She turned, she tossed herself in bed, 130 *Idiot Boy* 417
And Kirkstone tossed it from his misty head. 147 *Joanna* 65
Such objects as the waves had tossed ashore— 148 **A narrow* 13
A Juggler's balls old Time about him tossed ; 251 **Beloved Vale* 12
If one—while tossed, as was my lot to be, 354 *Aquap.* 119
Or, tossed about along a waste of foam, 458 *Sea-shore* 12
Tossed ashore by restless waves, 511 **Who rashly* 13
Tossed on the bosom of a stormy sea. 516 **As leaves* 14
That of the pair—tossed on the waves to bring 541 *Grace Darl.* 69
Toss'd light from hand to hand ; while on the ground 597 *Ev. Wk. Quarto* 277
And tossed about in whirlwind. I rejoiced, 722 *Prelude* 10. 283
The female and her garments vexed and tossed 738 *Prelude* 12. 260
He tossed them with a false unnatural joy : 765 *Excursion* 1. 587
On stormy waters, tossed in a little boat 817 *Excursion* 4. 1087
Tossed on the waves alone, or 'mid a crew 891 *Excursion* 9. 487
By powers celestial tossed on land and sea K.8. 281 **Arms and* 4
Tosses. He tosses about in every bare tree, 80 †*Address : Child* 5
And nightly tosses on a bed of pain ; 229 *Cuckoo-clock* 24
Tosseth. A weary while in pain he tosseth thus, 565 *Troilus* 162
Tossing. *See* **Ringlet-tossing.**
Tossing their heads in sprightly dance. 187 **I wandered* 12
Above the tossing surge. 296 *Highland Boy* 125
In her light skiff, the tossing waves, 344 **How blest* 30
A sea of foliage, tossing with the gale, 350 *Des. Stanzas* 35
Tossing her frantic thyrsus wide and high ! 381 *Duddon* 20. 14
From tossing boughs, the promise of a calm, 537 **In desultory* 8
But tossing lately on a sleepless bed, 557 *Cuck.and Night.* 46
Tossing in sunshine its dark boughs aloft, 687 *Prelude* 7. 45
Are vain, as billows in a tossing sea. 775 *Excursion* 2. 292
Floats on the tossing waves. With joy sincere 831 *Excursion* 5. 569
Tost. *See* **Tossed.**
That sang of trees up-torn and vessels tost— 314 **I dropped* 2
Of hallelujahs tost from hill to hill— 421 *Ecc. Sonn.* 1. 11. 2
Purer than foam on central ocean tost ; 434 *Ecc. Sonn.* 2. 25. 5
Like a shipwrecked Sailor tost 502 **Like a* 1
Total. To gild the total tablet of his days ; 2 *Ev. Wk.* 30
Then sets. In total gloom the Vagrant sighs, 14 *Desc. Sk.* 190
But total darkness came anon, 175 *Waggoner* 1. 182
Extinguished in a moment ; total gloom, 548 **Stay, bold* 27
To fill the total measure of his soul ! 867 *Excursion* 7. 662
T'other. Each wave, one and t'other, speeds after his brother ; 167 *Stray Pleasures* 35
Totter. A few short steps to totter with their load. 7 *Ev. Wk.* 255
—Just as the Child could totter on the floor, 867 *Excursion* 7. 677
Tottered. Shook, tottered, swam before his sight ; 400 *White Doe* 423
The mattock tottered in his hand ; 484 *Simon Lee* 77
His stooping body tottered with wreaths of flowers 816 *Excursion* 4. 1001
Tottering. But you were then a tottering Little-one— 50 *Bord.* 702
Tottering upon the very verge of life, 57 *Bord.* 1071
Though it were tottering over a man's head, 67 *Bord.* 1659
And tottering spirit. And full oft the Boy, 118 *Maternal Grief* 49
For all that tottering stands or prostrate lies, 360 *Alban Hills* 4
A tottering infant, with compliant stoop 496 **A little* 16
Who shall preserve or prop the tottering Realm ? 504 *Warning* 87
Shall tottering Age, bent earthward, hear 533 **Blest is* 37
Age ?—a drooping, tottering willow 549 *Hermit's Cell* 1. 31
And the bridge vibrates, tottering to its fall. 606 *Desc.Sk.Quarto* 214
Of a pleased grandame tottering up and down ; 661 *Prelude* 4. 205
That feeds him ; and the tottering little-one 836 *Excursion* 5. 956
And tottering hovels, whence do issue forth 879 *Excursion* 8. 347
No longer greeted—to the tottering sire, S.3. 435 **The doubt* 137
And tottering towers ; I loved to stand and read K.8. 256 *Recluse* 1.1.712
Totters. He totters, pallid as a ghost, 85 *Shepherd-boys* 63
Totters the Throne ; the new-born Church is sad, 439 *Ecc. Sonn.* 2. 41. 13
Touch. The officious touch that makes me droop again. 2 *Early Youth* 14
To flat-roofed towns, that touch the water's bound, 12 *Desc. Sk.* 83
Touch not a finger—— What then must be done ? 53 *Bord.* 877
May touch, whene'er her Vassals are at work. 59 *Bord.* 1174
Few must they be, and delicate in their touch 78 *Bord.* 2328
Do not touch it ! summers two 79 *Foresight* 7
But when she sate within the touch of thee. 88 *H. C.* 18
But, at the touch of wrong, without a strife 88 *H. C.* 32
I lighted—opened with soft touch the chapel's iron door, 92 *Poet's Dream* 41
When thou art from me, even if I should touch 136 *Michael* 338
And an eye practised like a blind man's touch. 151 **When, to* 83
That, as they touch the green, 170 *Rural Ill.* 16
But to its gentle touch how sensitive 184 *Airey-force* 11
Touch—for there is a spirit in the woods. 186 *Nutting* 56
The touch of earthly years. 187 **A slumber* 4
From touch of *deadly* injury ? 192 *Seq. Beggars* 40
Almost to touch ;—then up again aloft, 218 *Recluse* 1. 1. 227
All *heaven-born* Instincts shun the touch 225 *Present.* 4
That, answering to thy touch, will sound the hour ; 229 *Cuckoo-clock* 6
So shall he touch at length a friendly strand, 234 *Power of Sound* 142
And, did not pity touch my breast 236 *P. B.* 18

Touch—*continued.*
" Though Nature could not touch his heart 239 *P. B.* 286
And touch more quiet skies. 242 *P. B.* 495
Memorial of his touch—that day 247 *P. B.* 976
Of ruin shall not touch. Innocent scheme ! 253 **Aerial Rock* 9
Are seldom free to touch the moss that grows 262 **Mark the* 5
When human touch (as monkish books attest) 267 *St. Cath.* 1
Through reverence, touch it only to repair 276 *Filial Piety* 10
That touch each other to the quick in modes 290 *Kilchurn* 7
And touch from rising suns in vain 301 *Bran* 96
Oh, for a kindling touch from that pure flame 326 *Sobieski* 1
Thro' what men see and touch,—slaves wandering on, 358 **Is this* 7
Not injured more by touch of meddling hands 367 *Trajan* 9
Or, at a touch, produced by happiest transformation. 369 *Eg. Maid* 18
Thy Knights must touch the cold hand of the Virgin ; 372 *Eg. Maid* 254
Step forth."—To touch the pallid hand 373 *Eg. Maid* 268
When his touch failed.—Next came Sir Galahad ; 373 *Eg. Maid* 298
Chidden she chides again ; the thrilling touch 378 *Duddon* 10. 9
The Banner touch not, stay your hand, 400 *White Doe* 393
Touch not the tapers of the sacred quires ; 426 *Ecc. Sonn.* 1. 31. 11
Then, when her Child the hallowing touch received, 446 *Ecc. Sonn.* 3. 24. 7
Or the unimaginable touch of Time. 449 *Ecc. Sonn.* 3. 34. 14
Power at whose touch the sluggard shall unfold 452 *Ecc. Sonn.* 3. 47. 4
One boat there was, but it will touch the shore 453 **Calm is the* 28
Which thou canst touch in every human heart, 459 **Wanderer! that* 45
With stainless touch, as chaste as when thy praise 460 **Queen of* 25
Of her most timid touch his sleep would chase, 461 **Giordano, verily* 7
A touch so tender for the insensate Child— 476 *Howard* 6
The soft touch snapped the thread 479 *Somnamb.* 132
With finest touch of passion swayed 499 **Departing summer* 47
Should fear that pencil's touch ! 499 *Memory* 20
As, at his touch, it rocks, or seems to rock ; 500 *Humanity* 6
With hoary Winter, and Life touch, 502 *Seasons* 19
To his grave touch with no unready strings, 503 *Warning* 19
Keep, lovely May, as if by touch 508 *May* 93
Perhaps for touch profane, 511 **Who rashly* 20
I—of whose touch the fiddle would complain, 521 *Epist.Beaumont* 28
Moved by the touch of kindred sympathies. 526 **Soon did* 7
That first mild touch of sympathy and thought, 568 *Cumb. Beg.* 114
Which words less free presumed not even to touch) 585 *Ch. Lamb* 57
Turning with quiet touch the valley's hay, 607 *Desc.Sk.Quarto* 274
Till Death's cold touch her cistern-wheel assail, 615 *Desc.Sk.Quarto* 742
At every touch, an unsuspected fire." 624 *Æneid* 43
The western mountain touch his setting orb, 645 *Prelude* 2. 185
In which, a Babe, by intercourse of touch 646 *Prelude* 2. 267
This genuine prowess, which I wished to touch 651 *Prelude* 3. 182
While on I walked, a comfort seemed to touch 660 *Prelude* 4. 153
From touch of growing grass, that may not taste 669 *Prelude* 5. 243
A passing word erewhile did lightly touch 679 *Prelude* 6. 319
They burnished her. From touch of this new power 704 *Prelude* 8. 376
That into music touch the passing wind. 708 *Prelude* 8. 638
Or mused, his sword was haunted by his touch 712 *Prelude* 9. 159
And not by reverential touch of Time 716 *Prelude* 9. 468
And, with a touch, shift the stupendous clouds 734 *Prelude* 12. 17
Great truths, than touch and handle little ones. 740 *Prelude* 13. 54
Shall touch thee to the heart ; thou callest this love, 748 *Prelude* 14. 174
For, spite of thy sweet influence and the touch 749 *Prelude* 14. 237
When, every day, the touch of human hand 763 *Excursion* 1. 488
Motions of moonlight, all come thither—touch, 782 *Excursion* 2. 714
We are not so ;—perpetually we touch 782 *Excursion* 2. 736
And touch as gentle as the morning light, 802 *Excursion* 4. 89
And music waits upon your skilful touch, 809 *Excursion* 4. 571
At the fond work, demolished with a touch ; 810 *Excursion* 4. 606
With music ? ' (for he had not ceased to touch 861 *Excursion* 7. 270
And, at the touch of every wandering breeze, 864 *Excursion* 7. 480
Upon his touch. The bowels of the earth 865 *Excursion* 7. 502
Yet free from touch of envious discontent, 872 *Excursion* 7. 952
And even the touch, so exquisitely poured 879 *Excursion* 8. 325
—What kindly warmth from touch of fostering hand, 880 *Excursion* 8. 416
" I only touch—not take—don't fear, S.3. 441 **The ball* 3
Touched. *See* **Heart-touched.**
And now that orb has touched the purple steep, 5 *Ev. Wk.* 172
On a rude viol touched with withered hand. 13 *Desc. Sk.* 148
Touched by the beggar's moan of human woes ; 15 *Desc. Sk.* 243
Some amid lingering shade, some touched by the sun's rays. 34 *Guilt* 522
The guilt—have touched it—felt it at your heart— 69 *Bord.* 1770
By the returning substance, seen or touched, 118 *Maternal Grief* 6
Is, by innumerable poets, touched 123 *V. and J.* 88
Of ancient mountains, or my ear was touched 148 *Joanna* 70
Is touched—and all the band take flight. 180 *Waggoner* 4. 35
His nostril touched a spring beneath a hill, 201 *Hart-leap* 42
Mild Hermes spake—and touched her with his wand 209 *Laod.* 19
That the first Greek who touched the Trojan strand 210 *Laod.* 44
Touched by the skylark's earliest note, 222 *Triad* 176
Rested a golden harp ;—he touched the strings ; 226 *Vernal Ode* 22
Glance on the conscious plumes touched here and there ? 231 **ThegentlestPoet* 23
On which it should be touched, would melt away. 250 *Admon.* 14
Nor—touched with due abhorrence of *their* guilt 321 **Here pause* 10
Touched by his golden finger. 337 *Thun* 16
But, touched from behind by the Sun, it now shines 345 *Stanzas:Simplon* 23
And softly touched ; but, to his princely cheer 373 *Eg. Maid* 287
He touched with hesitating hand— 374 *Eg. Maid* 319
Has touched thee—and a Spirit's hand : 399 *White Doe* 333
Prove that her hand has touched responsive chords ; 455 **Not in the lucid* 9

Touched—*continued.*
Touched by accordance of thy placid cheer, . . 460 **Wanderer ! that* 56
Rose, where she touched the strand, the Chantry of St. Bees. . . . . 466 *St. Bees* 36
If he should speak, by fancy touched, of signs . 477 **Lonsdale ! it* 3
He touched ; what followed who shall tell ? . . 479 *Somnamb.* 131
By labours that have touched the hearts of kings, 509 *F. Stone* 101
Is the string touched in prelude to a lay . . . 529 *Poor Robin* 17
The natural heart is touched, and public way . 540 *Grace Darl.* 2
Touched then his tongue, and took away the grain ; 556 *Prioress* 220
And his hearing is touched with the sounds of a dream. . . . . 570 *Farmer* 80
As touch'd with dawning moonlight's hoary gleams, 598 *Ev. Wk. Quarto* 340
Touch'd with his wither'd hand an aged lyre ; . 605 *Desc.Sk.Quarto* 171
Had almost touched the horizon ; casting then . 633 *Prelude* 1. 87
The earth was comfortless, and, touched by faint 644 *Prelude* 2. 121
Alas ! such high emotion touched not me. . . 654 *Prelude* 3. 342
Had staid his oars, and touched the jutting pier, 658 *Prelude* 4. 15
And now the soldier touched his hat once more . 665 *Prelude* 4. 462
Cloud-like it mounts, or touched with light divine 665 *Prelude* 5. 7
With firmness, hitherto but slightly touched . . 675 *Prelude* 6. 54
Nor touched by welterings of passion—is, . . . 677 *Prelude* 6. 138
Was touched, but with no intimate concern ; . . 686 *Prelude* 6. 769
Through a thick forest. Silence touched me here 687 *Prelude* 7. 36
Is no where touched by one memorial gleam) . . 706 *Prelude* 8. 472
Saw them and touched : the rest was conjured up 719 *Prelude* 10. 75
Would but have touched the judgment, struck more deep . . . . 730 *Prelude* 11. 187
Hath hitherto been barely touched upon, . . . 750 *Prelude* 14. 316
Of things which he had seen ; and often touched 757 *Excursion* 1. 64
Beneath him :—Far and wide the clouds were touched, ... 759 *Excursion* 1. 203
A beardless Youth, who touched a golden lute, . 814 *Excursion* 4. 859
The Solitary by these words was touched . . . 817 *Excursion* 4. 1078
The other, which the ray divine hath touched, . 831 *Excursion* 5. 556
Society were touched with kind concern, . . . 837 *Excursion* 5. 974
By the nice finger of fair ladies touched . . . 843 *Excursion* 6. 338
Was hapless Ellen.—No one touched the ground . 851 *Excursion* 6. 840
That might have touched the sick heart of his Friend . . . . 862 *Excursion* 7. 295
Whizzed from the Stripling's arm ! If touched by him, ... 868 *Excursion* 7. 741
His fame touched the skies, ... S.3. 440 **Said red-ribboned* 22
Inverted, all its sun-bright features touched . . K.8. 252 *Recluse* 1. 1. 572

Touches. Touches of her infant hand, ... 93 *Westmoreland Girl* 36
It touches on that piece of native rock . . . 98 *Brothers* 199
He touches—'tis to him a treasure ! . . . . 242 *P. B.* 542
He touches here—he touches there— . . . . 242 *P. B.* 573
With touches irresistible. . . . . 243 *P. B.* 655
His lenient touches, soft as light that falls, . . 272 *Ruins* 6
And touches the blind Boy. . . . . 297 *Highland Boy* 235
Touches me not, though pensive as a bird . . 304 **Jones ! as* 13
May touches of his memory bring . . . . 578 **I come* 55
And now it touches on the purple steep . . 594 *Ev. Wk. Quarto* 155
That waits upon the touches of the wind. . . . 651 *Prelude* 3. 139
Touches him not. To enhance the wonder, see . 670 *Prelude* 5. 309
It touches, it confirms, and elevates, ... 780 *Excursion* 2. 567

Touching. Touching the matter of his passion, still, 123 *V. and J.* 114
Which they are touching ; yea far brighter, even 139 *Widow* 20
A sight so touching in its majesty : . . . . 269 *Westm. Bridge* 3
Rose like a star that touching earth, ... 285 *Grave of Burns* 21
A simple, but a touching, song ; . . . . . 338 *Brientz* 15
Yield to the Music's touching influence ; . . . 340 *Ranz* 13
More touching far than aught which on the walls 355 *Aquap.* 165
How touching, when, at midnight, sweep . . . 375 **The Minstrels* 37
Touching, as now, in thy humility . . . . . 392 **Though joy* 11
Will make a touching melody. . . . . . . 577 **I come* 32
More touching still, more perfect was the pleasure, 626 **The confidence* 9
Put on a lowly and a touching grace . . . . 653 *Prelude* 3. 272
Touching the heart amid the boisterous crew . . 681 *Prelude* 6. 413
Appeared more touching. One will I select ; . 696 *Prelude* 7. 602
Brightness and touching beauty of her own, . . 882 *Excursion* 8. 515

Touchingly. So touchingly he smiled— . . . . 342 *Ital. Itin.* 54
Do but more touchingly recall . . . . . . 366 **Ye Trees* 15
Her landing hailed, how touchingly she bowed ! . 465 **Dear to* 4
That touchingly bespeaks thee born . . . . 530 *Gleaner* 27

Tough. Then grieve not, jolly team ! though tough 175 *Waggoner* 1. 138
Tough moss, and long-enduring mountain-plants, 860 *Excursion* 7. 181

Tourists. "These Tourists, heaven preserve us ! needs must live . . . . 95 *Brothers* 1

Tournament. For tournament, his beaver vailed, . 373 *Eg. Maid* 286
A favourite spot of tournament and war ! . . . 548 **Stay, bold* 6
A tournament of blows, some hardly dealt . . 657 *Prelude* 3. 583
Whether for gorgeous tournament addressed, . . 689 *Prelude* 7. 140
In tournament, upon the fields of France. . . . 825 *Excursion* 5. 184

Tourney. Away with feast and tilt and tourney ! . 372 *Eg. Maid* 200

Toussaint. Toussaint, the most unhappy man of men ! . . . . 305 *Toussaint* 1

Toward. While they are drawing toward the sacred floor . . . . 20 *Desc. Sk.* 557
Saw him—his face turned toward me ; and I tell thee . . . . 55 *Bord.* 985
Toward the mighty gulf of things, ... 90 *Longest Day* 58
And, scouring toward him o'er the grassy plain, . 104 *Artegal* 110
No, passing through strange sufferings toward the tomb, ... 139 *Widow* 36
Tow'rd some far-distant wood, a Figure quaint, . 185 *Nutting* 8
Swift, toward the realms that know not earthly day, 211 *Laod.* 155
Thus, in their stations, lifting tow'rd the sky . . 227 *Vernal Ode* 61

Toward—*continued.*
On two poor legs, toward my stone-table . . . 238 *P. B.* 174
So toward the stream his head he bent, . . . 242 *P. B.* 553
She rose, and toward the close-shut casement drew, 274 **Wait, prithee* 6
From desolation toward the genial prime ; . . 274 **Such age* 11
That mounts not toward the radiant morning sky, 282 **While beams* 4
Driving some vessel toward a dangerous beach— 336 *Staub-bach* 6
Mounts, in this fine illusion, toward the skies : . 368 *Trajan* 69
Forth-looking toward the rocks of Scilly, . . . 369 *Eg. Maid* 2
While drawing toward the car Sir Gawaine, mailed 373 *Eg. Maid* 285
When toward the altar from her bower . . . 374 *Eg. Maid* 352
Held ; but in radiant progress toward the Deep . 384 *Duddon* 32. 4
And if, as toward the silent tomb we go, ... 384 *Duddon* 34. 12
Raised toward that Imagery once more : . . . 405 *White Doe* 863
Toward Bolton's ruined Priory. . . . . . . 413 *White Doe* 1542
As Menai's foam ; and toward the mystic ring . 419 *Ecc. Sonn.* 1. 3. 2
Uplifting toward high Heaven her fiery brand, . 420 *Ecc. Sonn.* 1. 9. 5
Toward the pure truths this Delegate propounds, 422 *Ecc. Sonn.* 1. 15. 10
In progress toward the fount of Love,—the throne 469 **Desire we* 11
Who, with a toward or untoward lot, ... 494 *Hap. War.* 68
Mount toward the empire of the fickle clouds, . 497 **Enough of climbing* 5
Drawn toward the centre whence those sighs creep forth . . . . 498 **Enough of climbing* 39
Thousands, as toward yon old Lancastrian Towers, 517 *Pun. Death* 1. 9
And jocund smiles, and toward the lowly Grange 525 *Epist. Beaumont* 237
And bore her toward the fields of France, . . . 544 *Russ. Fug.* 245
And toward the Island fled, ... 544 *Russ. Fug.* 266
He looks, through the open door-place, toward the lake . . . . 547 **Rude is* 27
Toward my death with wind I steer and sail ; . 564 *Troilus* 123
The road that pointed toward the chosen Vale. . 633 *Prelude* 1. 93
With yearning toward some philosophic song . . 635 *Prelude* 1. 229
Unprofitably travelling toward the grave, . . . 636 *Prelude* 1. 267
The book, had turned my eyes toward the wide sea. 666 *Prelude* 5. 64
Rises to lead him toward a better clime, . . . 670 *Prelude* 5. 333
As toward the sacred mansion we advanced, . . 681 *Prelude* 6. 423
I had my face turned toward the truth, began . 704 *Prelude* 8. 323
So lately, journeying toward the snow-clad Alps. 710 *Prelude* 9. 35
Turned toward the sun then setting, while that staff 756 *Excursion* 1. 40
We started—and he led me toward the hills, . . 772 *Excursion* 2. 90
'Twas chased away : for, toward the western side 773 *Excursion* 2. 115
Raised toward those craggy summits, his intent . 773 *Excursion* 2. 154
Led toward the Cottage. Homely was the spot ; 781 *Excursion* 2. 638
"So, westward, tow'rd the unviolated woods . . 799 *Excursion* 3. 944
His bounteous gift ! or saw him toward the deep 803 *Excursion* 4. 116
Toward regions yet more tranquil. But, methought, 805 *Excursion* 4. 253
The Solitary lifted toward the hills . . . . . 808 *Excursion* 4. 505
To lift the creature toward that eminence . . . 827 *Excursion* 5. 298
The reverend Pastor toward the church-yard gate 829 *Excursion* 5. 441
The Vicar paused ; and toward a seat advanced, 850 *Excursion* 6. 778
Of days advancing toward their utmost length, . 851 *Excursion* 6. 856
In order, drawing toward their wished-for home. . 858 *Excursion* 7. 71
Oft stretches toward me, like a long straight path 863 *Excursion* 7. 398
Straight toward some precipice's airy brink ! . . 864 *Excursion* 7. 493
Eastward, the Danube toward this inland sea, . 869 *Excursion* 7. 789
—Right toward the sacred Edifice his steps . . 871 *Excursion* 7. 911
Undaunted, toward the imperishable heavens, . 885 *Excursion* 9. 43
However gently, toward the vulgar air, . . . S.3. 434 **The doubt* 57
Bending its apex toward a paler self . . . . S.3. 434 **The doubt* 69
Toward the beleaguered city, in the might . . S.3. 437 **The doubt* 191
Pursued his way toward a brook, whose course . K.8. 228 **I will* 129

Towards. Through tears have seen him towards that world descend . . . . 32 *Guilt* 443
And it had led him towards the precipice, . . . 73 *Bord.* 2059
Upon this arm. You led him towards the Convent ? 76 *Bord.* 2228
Right towards the lamb she looked ; and from a shady place . . . . 87 *Pet-lamb* 17
Her large round wheel was turning. Towards the field . . . . 95 *Brothers* 26
He pointed towards his dwelling-place, entreating 102 *Brothers* 413
He towards his native country cast a longing look. 103 *Artegal* 89
These matins mounting towards her native sphere. 154 *Morn. Ex.* 54
Hung—head pointing towards the ground— . . 171 *Kitten* 69
That make the good, tow'rds which he's yearning, 177 *Waggoner* 2. 39
Towards the smooth river deep and clear. . . . 241 *P. B.* 440
And deftly ambles towards the south. . . . . 243 *P. B.* 610
Turned towards a gate that hung in view . . . 247 *P. B.* 982
And piety towards God. Such men of old . . 319 **Avaunt all* 9
Forth towards empyreal Heaven, ... 332 *Ode : Thanks.* 218
Far-lifted towards the unfading sky ; . . . . 348 **Lulled by* 38
Turn towards the spot where, full in view, . . 398 *White Doe* 167
Retreated towards a brake of thorn, ... 412 *White Doe* 1477
By sorrow lifted towards her God ; . . . . . 416 *White Doe* 1851
The linnet's warble, sinking towards a close, . . 455 *Rydal Mere* 1
While he, uplifted towards thee, laughs outright, 460 **Queen of* 19
Towards a low roof with green trees half concealed, 475 **There ! said* 2
Back towards caverned life's first rude career. . 489 *Illus. Books* 11
Partake its inclination towards earth . . . . 508 *F. Stone* 38
Two hours declined towards the west ; a day . . 633 *Prelude* 1. 67
Towards the Uncreated with a countenance . . 648 *Prelude* 2. 413
Towards human business, to a privileged world . 656 *Prelude* 3. 520
Towards that sweet Valley where I had been reared ; . . . . 658 *Prelude* 4. 19
And now was travelling towards his native home. 664 *Prelude* 4. 425
Of hardy disobedience towards friends . . . . 675 *Prelude* 6. 28
Sees annually, if clouds towards either ocean . . 699 *Prelude* 8. 15
Nor shall we not be tending towards that point . 705 *Prelude* 8. 451
Prostrate, or leaning towards their common rest . 708 *Prelude* 8. 613
With early morning towards the Palace-walk . . 719 *Prelude* 10. 94

Towards—*continued.*
March firmly towards righteousness and peace."— 727 *Prelude* 10. 589
His shadow stretching towards Syracuse, . . . 732 *Prelude* 11. 378
Towards them and to all creatures. God delights 736 *Prelude* 12. 171
I mounted, and we journeyed towards the hills : . 737 *Prelude* 12. 228
Pointing towards a sweet-briar, bade me climb . 763 *Excursion* 1. 451
Then towards the cottage I returned ; and traced 770 *Excursion* 1. 925
And confidential yearnings, tow'rds its home, . 780 *Excursion* 2. 559
They faint not, but advance towards the open grave 780 *Excursion* 2. 586
Drawn towards her native firmament of heaven, . 807 *Excursion* 4. 396
Up towards the crescent moon, with grateful heart 814 *Excursion* 4. 862
And towards a crystal Mere, that lay beyond . . 823 *Excursion* 5. 82
Such leaning towards each other, that their days 845 *Excursion* 6. 471
Converse with heaven, nor yet deprest towards earth, ... 848 *Excursion* 6. 680
Turned towards the planet Jupiter that hung 849 *Excursion* 6. 761
Led towards an easy outlet of the vale. . . . 858 *Excursion* 7. 49
Towards one, whose bold contrivances and skill, . 866 *Excursion* 7. 591
Moved towards the grave ;—instinctively his steps 870 *Excursion* 7. 819
Softens its evening uproar towards a close . . S.3. 437 **The doubt* 195
Beginning towards the south, where from Dove Crag K.8. 224 **I will* 19
Towards him, bade him leap, which word scarce said . . . . K.8. 230 **I will* 176
To look towards the shutting in of life. . . . K.8. 231 **I will* 215

Tower. *See* **Church-tower, Convent-tower, Leaning-tower, Steeple-tower, Village-tower, Watch-tower.**
From his grey re-appearing tower shall soon . . 8 *Ev. Wk.* 325
Tower, bare or sylvan, from the narrow deeps. . 12 *Desc. Sk.* 80
Must bid the tocsin ring from tower to tower !— 22 *Desc. Sk.* 640
Peering above the trees, the steeple tower 28 *Guilt* 237
O'er town and tower we fled, and fields in May's fresh verdure drest ; . . . . 92 *Poet's Dream* 31
In tree and tower was Johnny seen, 128 *Idiot Boy* 209
Her bulwark and her tower of strength ! " . . 178 *Waggoner* 2. 148
Chequering the ground—from rock, plant, tree, or tower. . . . . 184 *Night-piece* 7
Mark that Cripple who leans on his crutch ; like a tower . . . . 189 *Music* 37
" From town to town, from tower to tower, . . 203 *Brougham* 5
Though lonely, a deserted Tower ; . . . . . 204 *Brougham* 37
Though each is but a lonely Tower :— . . . 204 *Brougham* 49
Green moss-grown tower ; or hoary tent ; . . . 214 *Kirkstone* 18
Where nothing was ; and firm as some old Tower 226 *Vernal Ode* 18
Piping through cave and battlemented tower ; . 233 *Power of Sound* 69
The rocks that tower on either side . . . . 244 *P. B.* 681
It seemed—wall, window, roof and tower— . . 246 *P. B.* 858
Temple of Greece, and minster with its tower 262 **Dark and* 7
Gleams on the grass-crowned top of yon tall Tower, 283 **Here, where* 11
But dance ! for under Jedborough Tower . . . 293 *Jedbor.* 8
He is as mute as Jedborough Tower : . . . . 294 *Jedbor.* 29
Yon time-cemented Tower ! . . . . 299 *Cora Linn* 6
Go back, and see the Tower of Babel rise ; . . 313 **Go back* 5
Each beetling rampart, and each tower sublime, . 335 *Rhine* 7
Hither, like yon ancient Tower . . . . . . 336 **Jesu ! bless* 13
High on her speculative tower . . . . . . 343 *Eclipse* 1
More cheerily ; and town and tower, ... 343 *Eclipse* 64
" And to Caerleon's loftiest tower . . . . . 370 *Eg. Maid* 85
Palace and tower, are crumbled into dust !— . 379 *Duddon* 12. 10
From Bolton's old monastic tower . . . . . 396 *White Doe* 1
Its courts are ravaged ; but the tower . . . . 396 *White Doe* 21
Who, standing on this old church tower, . . . 399 *White Doe* 297
Where he is perched, from yon lone Tower . . 406 *White Doe* 959
Stands single—Norton Tower its name— . . . 409 *White Doe* 1168
They to the Tower withdrew, and there . . . 409 *White Doe* 1184
Could see the Tower of Bolton rise. . . . . 412 *White Doe* 1441
Up would she climb to Norton Tower, ... 415 *White Doe* 1779
She daunts, forth-thundering from her spiritual tower . . . . 429 *Ecc. Sonn.* 2. 2. 5
Shatters the air, and troubles tower and spire ; . 442 *Ecc. Sonn.* 3. 8. 2
And is no more ; drop like the tower sublime . 449 *Ecc. Sonn.* 3. 34. 10
Watching, with upward eye, the tall tower grow . 451 *Ecc. Sonn.* 3. 42. 7
Thou art discovered in a roofless tower, . . . 456 **The leaves* 16
Of beamy lustre from a tower of strength ; . . 466 *St. Bees* 42
Just limits ; but yon Tower, whose smiles adorn . 469 **The feudal* 5
A Tower of refuge built for the else forlorn. . 469 **The feudal* 8
Him found we not : but, climbing a tall tower, . 472 **The captive* 4
List, ye who pass by Lyulph's Tower . . . . 478 *Somnamb.* 1
And steeple tower (with pealing bells . . . . 533 **Blest is* 9
Or, under rocks that from the water tow'r . . 604 *Desc.Sk.Quarto* 125
Tower like a wall the naked rocks, or reach . 607 *Desc.Sk.Quarto* 287
The Monument, and that Chamber of the Tower . 689 *Prelude* 7. 136
In chains of mutual passion, from the tower, . . 716 *Prelude* 9. 486
Wantoned, fast rooted on the ancient tower . . 722 *Prelude* 10. 279
Its petty promises, to build a tower . . . . 727 *Prelude* 11. 38
Lofty, and steep, and naked as a tower. . . . 787 *Excursion* 3. 42
Tower eight times planted on the top of tower, . 811 *Excursion* 4. 685
City, and town, and tower,—and sea with ships . 819 *Excursion* 4. 1197

Towered. Where leafless oaks towered high above, 154 **A whirl-blast* 5
She towered, fit person for a Queen . . . . 190 *Beggars* 10
Towered up between me and the stars, and still, . 637 *Prelude* 1. 382
Towered like the imperial thistle, not unfurnished 848 *Excursion* 6. 688

Towering. *See* **High-towering, Lately-towering.**
His neck, a varying arch, between his towering wings : . . . . 6 *Ev. Wk.* 219
And, towering from the sullen dark-brown mere, . 8 *Ev. Wk.* 313
On the heads of towering hills. . . . . . . 166 *Wand. Jew* 8
The towering headlands, crowned with mist, . . 235 *Power of Sound* 185
The towering maize, and prop the twig . . . 342 *Ital. Itin.* 45
Like vapour, like a towering cloud, dissolved. . 352 *Aquap.* 8
Or as a fruitful palm-tree towering high . . . 383 *Duddon* 31. 5

Towering—*continued.*
Yon towering Peaks, " Shepherds of Etive Glen ? " 389 *Sound of Mull* 14
Amazement runs before the towering casque . . 421 *Ecc. Sonn.* 1. 10. 5
That to the towering lily doth not yield ? . . . 432 *Ecc. Sonn.* 2. 15. 4
Firm as the towering Headlands of St. Bees. . . 466 *St. Bees* 18
Towering above the sea and little ships ; . . . 471 *Ailsa Crag* 7
And of the towering courage which past times . 472 **The captive* 11
His bridling neck between his tow'ring wings ; . 595 *Ev. Wk. Quarto* 202
High towering from the sullen dark-brown mere, 598 *Ev. Wk. Quarto* 371
Or Syria's marble ruins towering high . . . . 788 *Excursion* 3. 150
But towering high the roof above, as if . . . 866 *Excursion* 7. 614

Tower's. *See* **Watch-tower's.**
Yon grey tower's living crest ! . . . . . . 300 *Cora Linn* 24
In the Tower's shadow, of decline and fall . . 355 *Aquap.* 180
The old Tower's brow yellowed as with the beams 470 *Bala-Sala* 10

Towers. *See* **Steeple-towers, Watch-towers.**
With towers and woods, a " prospect all on fire ; " 5 *Ev. Wk.* 175
Where, 'mid dim towers and woods, her waters gleam. . . . . 13 *Desc. Sk.* 157
Huge convent domes with pinnacles and towers, . 14 *Desc. Sk.* 224
His bosom heaves, his Spirit towers amain, . . 18 *Desc. Sk.* 459
When, Antioch blazing to her topmost towers, . 40 *Bord.* 178
I think I see a second range of Towers ; . . . 50 *Bord.* 731
Whence golden harvests, cities, warlike towers, . 102 *Artegal* 21
Never see my native land, nor castle towers, . . 140 *Arm. Lady* 53
The ruined towers of Threlkeld-hall, ... 180 *Waggoner* 4. 43
My new-planned cities, and unfinished towers. . 211 *Laod.* 132
" And he had seen Caernarvon's towers, . . . 238 *P. B.* 211
Rise, then, ye votive Towers ! and catch a gleam 253 **Aerial Rock* 13
Ships, towers, domes, theatres, and temples lie . 269 *Westm. Bridge* 6
Yet, O ye spires of Oxford ! domes and towers ! . 270 **Ye sacred* 6
From the wan Moon, upon the towers and walls, 272 *Ruins* 7
And Love her towers of dread foundation laid . 282 **In my* 10
Leaving an ancient dome, and towers like these, . 292 **Degenerate Douglas* 7
That, under hills which rise like towers, . . . 295 *Highland Boy* 13
Towers rent, winds combating with woods, . . 299 *Brownie's Cell* 63
The shattered front of Newark's Towers, . . . 302 *Yarrow V.* 55
The haughty towers where monarchs dwell ; . . 329 *Ode : Thanks.* 5
The towers of righteousness ; . . . . . . 329 *Ode : Thanks.* 50
O'er villas, terraces, and towers ; . . . . . 343 *Eclipse* 34
The towers of old Lucerne. . . . . . . 348 **Lulled by* 36
Forth from the towers of that huge Pile, wherein 365 **The Baptist* 2
Where towers are crushed, and unforbidden weeds 367 *Trajan* 1
And soon Caerleon's towers appeared, ... 372 *Eg. Maid* 189
Towers, temples, fall by stroke of thunder ; . . 372 *Eg. Maid* 218
And Lambeth's venerable towers, ... 376 **The Minstrels* 65
Is opened round him :—hamlets, towers, and towns, 384 *Duddon* 32. 10
Nor covets lineal rights in lands and towers. . . 387 *Manse* 14
Immured in Bothwell's towers, at times the Brave 392 *Bothwell* 1
Now joy for you who from the towers . . . . 402 *White Doe* 594
And the towers of Saint Cuthbert were stirred by the shout ! . . . . 403 *White Doe* 687
Are now besieging Barnard's Towers,— . . . 408 *White Doe* 1116
" This night yon faithless Towers must yield, . 408 *White Doe* 1131
The Council-roof and Clermont's towers reply ;— 427 *Ecc. Sonn.* 1. 33. 11
The Crescent glitters on the towers of Spain ; . 427 *Ecc. Sonn.* 1. 34. 3
And strives the towers to number, that recline . 443 *Ecc. Sonn.* 3. 12. 6
Calm as the Universe, from specular towers . . 474 **Hope smiled* 9
Fall if ye must, ye Towers and Pinnacles, . . . 477 **Lowther ! in* 12
On proud towers, like this humble cottage, blest . 503 *Warning* 37
Towers where red streamers flout the breezy sky . 503 *Warning* 39
Of sea and land, with yon grey towers that still . 517 *Pun. Death* 1. 2
Thousands, as toward yon old Lancastrian Towers, 517 *Pun. Death* 1. 9
And antique towers nodded their foreheads high, 529 **Those breathing* 118
High-born Augusta ! Witness, Towers and Groves ! 539 **Lady ! a* 22
The Kremlin and its haughty towers . . . . 544 *Russ. Fug.* 255
When temples, columns, towers, are laid in dust ; 546 **Oft is* 2
When towers and temples fall, to speak of Thee ! 584 **With copious* 53
While mid dim towers and woods her waters gleam : 605 *Desc.Sk.Quarto* 179
To viewless realms his Spirit towers amain, . . 612 *Desc.Sk.Quarto* 548
Serene he towers, in deepest purple dy'd ; . . . 615 *Desc.Sk.Quarto* 699
And dark Oppression builds her thick-ribb'd tow'rs ; 617 *Desc.Sk.Quarto* 795
But who shall count the Towers as they recline . 625 **The confidence* 6
For temples, towers, and thrones . . . . . 628 *Installation* 2
These reverend aisles, these hallowed towers, . . 629 *Installation* 77
On his smooth breast the shadow of those towers 636 *Prelude* 1. 283
From a tumultuous ocean, trees and towers . . 643 *Prelude* 2. 110
Courts, cloisters, flocks of churches, gateways, towers : . . . . 649 *Prelude* 3. 33
Inspired ;—that river and those mouldering towers 678 *Prelude* 6. 211
Up to the loftiest towers of Pride ascend, . . . 681 *Prelude* 6. 446
In avenues disposed ; there, towers begirt . . . 784 *Excursion* 2. 843
—Hail Contemplation ! from the stately towers, . 787 *Excursion* 3. 101
With all the chambers in his horrid towers, . . 796 *Excursion* 3. 710
And dignified by battlements and towers . . . 875 *Excursion* 8. 102
And tottering towers ; I loved to stand and read K.8. 256 *Recluse* 1.1.712

To-whoo. *See* **Tu-whoo.**
" The cocks did crow to-whoo, to-whoo, . . . 131 *Idiot Boy* 450

Town. " Two years were passed since to a distant town . . . . 29 *Guilt* 253
In wood or wilderness, in camp or town, . . . 29 *Guilt* 300
But town, or farm, or hamlet, none they viewed, 30 *Guilt* 330
In a deep wood remote from any town. . . . 50 *Bord.* 698
You to the town must go ; . . . . 83 *Lucy Gray* 14
But never reached the town. . . . . . . 83 *Lucy Gray* 32
To show thee some delightful thing, in country or in town. . . . . 92 *Poet's Dream* 22
O'er town and tower we fled, and fields in May's fresh verdure drest ; . . . . . . 92 *Poet's Dream* 31

Trained—*continued.*
Yet trained to judgments righteously severe, 326 *The Bard 2
And why shouldst thou ?—If rightly trained and bred, 390 Highland Hut 6
Of public conflicts trained and bred ? 485 Poet's Epitaph 2
Lost people, trained to theoretic feud ! 505 Warning 111
Not she whose rigid precepts trained the boy 618 School Ex. 7
Will all be train'd to waste and pillage ; 621 Andrew Jones 32
Trained to health and artless beauty ; 629 Installation 46
Of ancient times revive, and youth be trained 655 Prelude 3. 411
Trained up through piety and zeal to prize 655 Prelude 3. 456
Full early trained to worship seemliness, 670 Prelude 5. 298
In hope, and trained to noble aspirations, 720 Prelude 10. 166
Which on thy young imagination, trained 745 Prelude 13. 364
Power may be trained, and renovation brought 831 Excursion 5. 585
Among her higher creatures born and trained 835 Excursion 5. 848
Of civil polity, and early trained 880 Excursion 8. 393
That the whole people should be taught and trained. 889 Excursion 9. 358

Trainer. For this unnatural growth the trainer blame, 670 Prelude 5. 328

Training. Easily a pious training 94 Westmoreland Girl 77

Trains. I love to mark the quarry's moving trains, 5 Ev. Wk. 158
The blameless Muse, who trains her Sons 386 Yarrow Rev. 43
You, on whose progress dazzling trains await 433 Ecc. Sonn. 2. 18. 3
But she who trains the generous British youth 618 School Ex. 11
Of self-applauding intellect ; but trains 740 Prelude 13. 27
Fair trains of imagery before me rise, 755 Recluse 1. 1. 756

Traitor. Traitor to both. Oh, could you hear his voice ! 41 Bord. 210
But patience ! Curses on that Traitor, Oswald !— 63 Bord. 1417
'Tis done ! The ruthless traitor ! A rash deed !— 78 Bord. 2319
First open traitor to the German name ! 313 Prophecy 14
Worst Traitor of them all is he, 412 White Doe 1468
A Traitor dark and cowardly ! " 412 White Doe 1469
" I am no Traitor," Francis said, 412 White Doe 1470

Traitors. Fell not the wrath of Heaven upon those traitors ? 70 Bord. 1800

Trajan. And study Trajan as by Pliny seen ; 368 Trajan 28
A Pontiff, Trajan *here* the Gods implores, 368 Trajan 41
And Trajan still, through various enterprise, 368 Trajan 68

Trajans. Hoards may come forth of Trajans, Maximins, 275 *While poring 9

Trample. From rites that trample upon soul and sense. 431 Ecc. Sonn. 2. 11. 14

Trampled. Where none but those who trampled on my rights 52 Bord. 844
In a sensual creed that trampled 141 Arm. Lady 81
Or trampled into earth ; a chain of straw, 769 Excursion 1. 839

Trampling. With trampling horses and refulgent cars— 216 Enterprise 110
Trampling upon his vileness. Stranger, pass 275 Gravestone 13
The lightning, the fierce wind, and trampling waves. 579 Peele Castle 52
With speed and echoes loud of trampling hoofs 716 Prelude 9. 449

Trance. To all that binds the soul in powerless trance, 13 Desc. Sk. 131
But, when the trance was gone, feebly pursued his way. 26 Guilt 90
A British ship I waked, as from a trance restored." 30 Guilt 306
And drop, as he once dropped, in miserable trance. 36 Guilt 666
A shepherd-lad, ere yet my trance was gone, 62 Bord. 1365
We left our Hero in a trance, 242 P. B. 531
The trance is passed away—he wakes ; 248 P. B. 1095
Lo ! where she stands fixed in a saint-like trance, 278 *Lo ! where she 1
All power was given her in the dreadful trance ; 313 Prophecy 9
The Damsel, in that trance embound ; 371 Eg. Maid 141
Till doubtful combat issued in a trance 383 Duddon 29. 5
Had blindly grasped in that strong trance, 401 White Doe 437
Which he had grasped in that strong trance ; 401 White Doe 517
Binding the charmed soul in powerless trance, 604 Desc. Sk. Quarto 98
To the whole city, " sleep no more." The trance 719 Prelude 10. 87
A momentary trance comes over me ; 768 Excursion 1. 784

Trances. Trances of thought and mountings of the mind 632 Prelude 1. 19

Tranquil. 'Tis pleasant near the tranquil lake to stray 6 Ev. Wk. 216
The soft gloom deepening on the tranquil mind. 8 Ev. Wk. 318
Creep hushed into the tranquil breast of death. 8 Ev. Wk. 354
Tranquil as he had died in his own bed. 75 Bord. 2140
Tranquil—why not ? Oh, peace ! He is at peace ; 75 Bord. 2141
And guarded in their tranquil state of life, 143 *High bliss 24
Dwelt in a tranquil spot. And oftentimes 150 *When, to 26
Tranquil assurances that Heaven supports 173 Infant Daughter 69
With tranquil restoration :—feelings too 206 Tintern 30
(Whose tranquil pomp and spotless purity 329 Ode : Thanks. 23
Once more beneath the kind Earth's tranquil light ; 381 Duddon 21. 7
Palm to palm, on his tranquil breast ; 397 White Doe 131
Thine is the tranquil hour, purpureal Eve ! 457 *Had this 33
Fondly embosomed in the tranquil flood, 524 Epist. Beaumont 188
On tranquil land, beneath a sky of bliss. 578 Peele Castle 20
Nought wakens or disturbs it's tranquil tides ; 597 Ev. Wk. Quarto 310
Light up of tranquil joy a sober scene ; 607 Desc. Sk. Quarto 268
When warm from myrtle bays and tranquil seas, 610 Desc. Sk. Quarto 442
Till all was tranquil as a dreamless sleep. 639 Prelude 1. 463
And tranquil scenes, that universal power 647 Prelude 2. 324
Of the Upholder of the tranquil soul, 650 Prelude 3. 117
Hollow as ever vexed the tranquil air ; 655 Prelude 3. 414
Could have more tranquil visions in his youth, 676 Prelude 6. 90
Faint, but more tranquil, like the changing sun 699 Prelude 8. 51
Tranquil almost, and careless as a flower 711 Prelude 9. 87
More tranquil, yet perhaps of kindred birth, 763 Excursion 1. 482

Tranquil—*continued.*
Upon that tranquil Ruin, I returned, 765 Excursion 1. 623
From my unguarded heart.—The tranquil shores 797 Excursion 3. 812
Toward regions yet more tranquil. But, methought, 805 Excursion 4. 253
In like removal, tranquil though severe, 885 Excursion 9. 82

Tranquillised. The madding factions might be tranquillised, 727 Prelude 10. 591

Tranquillising. *See* **Tranquillizing.**
A tranquillising spirit presses now 642 Prelude 2. 27
Into the soul its tranquillising power, 665 Prelude 5. 3

Tranquillity. Blend in a music of tranquillity ; 17 Desc. Sk. 363
Is sinking down in its tranquillity ; 258 *It is a 4
Would interrupt the intense tranquillity 259 *A volant 13
An azure disc—shield of Tranquillity ; 264 Storm 12
A more entire tranquillity. 289 Glen-Al. 16
Ravage the world, tranquillity is here ! " 313 *Clouds, lingering 14
Links in the chain of Thy tranquillity ! 331 Ode : Thanks. 189
The blest tranquillity that sunk so deep 355 Aquap. 153
Tranquillity ! the sovereign aim wert thou 476 *Tranquillity ! the 1
Of divine tranquillity ! 550 Hermit's Cell 4. 16
In the tranquillity of nature, came 723 Prelude 10. 326
So still an image of tranquillity, 770 Excursion 1. 946
Tranquillity to all things. Or is she," 791 Excursion 3. 352
The longing for confirmed tranquillity, 792 Excursion 3. 398
Are guardians of their own tranquillity. 806 Excursion 4. 322
Conquered, and in tranquillity retained ! 841 Excursion 6. 211

Tranquillizing. *See* **Tranquillising.**
The tranquillizing power of time, shall wake, 809 Excursion 4. 547

Tranquilly. For though the priest, more tranquilly, 396 White Doe 45

Transacted. Of aught transacted there in bay or creek ; 522 Epist. Beaumont 80

Transactions. 'Mid the transactions of the bustling crowd ; 810 Excursion 4. 580

Transatlantic. He left his Transatlantic home : 348 *Lulled by 50

Transcend. All principles of action that transcend 514 *Portentous change 13
Rights that transcend the loftiest heritage 826 Excursion 5. 276
By faith in glory that shall far transcend 850 Excursion 6. 768
His darkness doth transcend our fickle light ! ' 851 Excursion 6. 887

Transcendent. And lead us on to that transcendent rest 315 *Alas ! what 4
What offering, what transcendent monument 331 Ode : Thanks. 169
Through love, through hope, and faith's transcendent dower, 384 Duddon 34. 13
Transcendent Boon ! noblest that earthly King 435 Ecc. Sonn. 2. 29. 9
Transcendent over time, unbound by place, 443 Ecc. Sonn. 3. 14. 13
Bestowed on this transcendent hour ! 458 *Had this 60
And hath the name of, God. Transcendent peace 677 Prelude 6. 139
Transcendent, superhuman as it seemed, 694 Prelude 7. 510
Transcendent to all local patrimony, 720 Prelude 10. 157
By recognitions of transcendent power, 747 Prelude 14. 75
In the transcendent wisdom of the age, 775 Excursion 2. 236
For apprehension those transcendent truths 802 Excursion 4. 96
This soul, and the transcendent universe, 816 Excursion 4. 990

Transcends. Rapt into still communion that transcends 759 Excursion 1. 215

Transcripts. And if these Transcripts of the private heart 269 *If these 5

Transfer. Or soil endured a transfer in the mart 799 Excursion 3. 917
This transfer is permitted,—not alone 865 Excursion 7. 522
Transfer not to futurity a work 890 Excursion 9. 406

Transferred. To be transferred to thee. When I'm dishonoured ! 49 Bord. 652
Transferred to regions upon which the clouds 119 Maternal Grief 75
The bold report, transferred to every clime ; 325 Ode 1814 136
Transferred to bowers imperishably green, 381 Duddon 20. 5
Hence, with the spiritual sovereignty transferred 435 Ecc. Sonn. 2. 28. 12
From the hushed vale's realities, transferred 456 *The leaves 11
To unorganic natures were transferred 647 Prelude 2. 391
Transferred a courtesy which had no air 714 Prelude 9. 309
Liking ; by rules of mimic art transferred 736 Prelude 12. 111
Thither his popular talents he transferred ; 774 Excursion 2. 219
Could have transferred him to the flying clouds, 829 Excursion 5. 449

Transfigurations. And bold transfigurations, more untrue 428 Ecc. Sonn. 1. 37. 5

Transfigured. But the Transfigured, in and out of season, 139 Widow 25
Transfigured through that fresh abode 168 Pilgrim's Dream 61
Transfigured, sinks into a hopeless grave ; 366 Lombardy 12
Transfigured, from this kindling hath foretold 437 Ecc. Sonn. 2. 34. 5

Transformation. That transformation through the wide earth felt, 172 Infant Daughter 7
Or, at a touch, produced by happiest transformation. 369 Eg. Maid 18
Prompt transformation works the novel Lore ; 422 Ecc. Sonn. 1. 17. 1
Recalls the transformation of the flood, 439 Ecc. Sonn. 2. 44. 7
The transformation wrought by gay attire. 659 Prelude 4. 76
I felt : the transformation I perceived, 796 Excursion 3. 717

Transformed. Your single virtue has transformed a Band 48 Bord. 610
It came with sleep and showed the Boy, no cherub, not transformed, 92 Poet's Dream 15
Transformed, and rushing on a bold exchange 270 *Ye sacred 9
At her own prayer transformed, took root, 543 Russ. Fug. 183
Might, with small help from fancy, be transformed 814 Excursion 4. 875

Transforming. To bow to some transforming power, 246 P. B. 859

Transgress. Was needful round men thirsting to transgress ;— 436 Ecc. Sonn. 2. 30. 8
Or rule which they are tempted to transgress : 807 Excursion 4. 380

Transgressed. If we have faltered or transgressed, 506 Lab. Hymn 26

Travel—*continued.*
How willingly we travel, and how far! 691 *Prelude* 7. 278
To travel independent of her help, 709 *Prelude* 8. 681
How far they travel, and how long endure; 715 *Prelude* 9. 375
Must turn elsewhere—to travel near the tribes 755 *Recluse* 1. 1. 826
But stout and hale, for travel unimpaired. 756 *Excursion* 1. 34
To travel in a country far remote; 766 *Excursion* 1. 643
Had yet to travel far, but unto us, 820 *Excursion* 4. 1299
And milder worth: nor need we travel far 863 *Excursion* 7. 393

Travelled. *See* **Far-travelled.**
Thus when thou with Time hast travelled 90 *Longest Day* 57
He travelled back to Egremont: and thence, 102 *Brothers* 428
I travelled among unknown men, 109 **I travelled* 1
And I have travelled weary miles to see 119 *Sailor's Mother* 23
Travelled into distant lands; 171 *Kitten* 56
He travelled; stirring thus about his feet 197 *Resolution* 122
He travelled here, he travelled there;— 239 *P. B.* 238
And with the Tweed had travelled; 292 *Yarrow Unv.* 4
Has travelled down to Matthew's name, 486 *Matthew* 11
We travelled merrily, to pass 486 **We walked* 11
Not far we travelled ere a shout of glee, 524 *Epist. Beaumont* 203
I travelled round our little lake, five miles 647 *Prelude* 2. 331
We had not travelled long, ere some mischance 737 *Prelude* 12. 231
And travelled through the wood, with no one near 758 *Excursion* 1. 130
Have acted, suffered, travelled far, observed 809 *Excursion* 4. 563
For strangers who have travelled far perhaps, K.8. 226 **I will* 69

Traveller. *See* **Fellow-traveller.**
The loitering traveller hence, at evening, sees 12 *Desc. Sk.* 89
The face of traveller passing to and fro,) 15 *Desc. Sk.* 239
To greet the traveller needing food and rest; 21 *Desc. Sk.* 610
And oh, fair France! though now the traveller sees 21 *Desc. Sk.* 612
Nay, Traveller! rest. This lonely Yew-tree stands 22 *Yew-tree* 1
A Traveller on the skirt of Sarum's Plain 24 *Guilt* 1
He met a traveller, robbed him, shed his blood; 25 *Guilt* 70
To traveller who might talk of any casual theme. 26 *Guilt* 99
You are a lusty Traveller. But how fare you? 43 *Bord.* 335
No traveller, peasant, herdsman? Not a soul: 61 *Bord.* 1293
Made answer, like a traveller bold, 131 *Idiot Boy* 448
The traveller to a shelter, summoned him 132 *Michael* 57
Thou greet'st the traveller in the lane; 158 **In youth* 18
To be such a traveller as I. 160 **Up with me* 21
A single traveller—and there 182 *Waggoner* 4. 256
Startles the pensive traveller while he treads 184 *Night-piece* 9
A Traveller between life and death; 186 **She was* 24
Have been a traveller under open sky, 192 *Gipsies* 10
I was a Traveller then upon the moor; 195 *Resolution* 15
Nor Traveller gone from earth the heavens to espy! 208 **It is no* 3
The passing traveller slights; 224 *Primrose* 2
Yes, Traveller! fifty winters have been told 276 *Filial Piety* 5
The traveller, at this day, will stop and gaze 292 **Degenerate Douglas* 10
The bravest traveller in balloon, 296 *Highland Boy* 168
Hath painted Winter like a traveller old, 321 **Humanity, delighting* 3
And if some traveller, weary of his road, 458 **Had this* 55
The forlorn traveller, or sailor wrecked 467 *St. Bees* 92
While a fair region round the traveller lies 480 **Most sweet* 3
Stock-still there he stands like a traveller bemazed: 484 **A plague* 16
On which the Traveller passed this way. 491 *Fidelity* 49
When this ill-fated Traveller died, 492 *Fidelity* 59
To the sun-burnt traveller, 502 **Like a* 29
Which the unsheltered traveller might receive 537 **In desultory* 9
Pause, Traveller! whosoe'er thou be 550 *Hermit's Cell* 2. 1
At distance still the same. Poor Traveller! 567 *Cumb. Beg.* 58
The traveller would hang his wet clothes on a chair; 571 *Avarice* 9
Traveller or Shepherd, let it say, 581 *John Words.* 66
Besiege the traveller whom they half affright. 615 *Desc.Sk.Quarto* 712
We must descend. A Traveller I am, 652 *Prelude* 3. 195
Assured that now the traveller would repose 665 *Prelude* 4. 453
At once, some lonely traveller. I was lost; 684 *Prelude* 6. 596
And envied traveller! When the Boy returned, 688 *Prelude* 7. 93
All that the traveller sees when he is there. 691 *Prelude* 7. 259
That asks not speed, a traveller might bestow 696 *Prelude* 7. 591
For spring or fountain, which the traveller finds, 702 *Prelude* 8. 207
The curious traveller, who, from open day, 707 *Prelude* 8. 560
Or as a traveller, who has gained the brow 709 *Prelude* 9. 9
Heard, though unseen,—a devious traveller, 716 *Prelude* 9. 447
Or well-spring where the weary traveller rests. 742 *Prelude* 13. 141
A youthful traveller, and see daily now 743 *Prelude* 13. 222
Its final home on earth. What traveller—who— 780 *Excursion* 2. 560
When winds are blowing strong. The traveller slaked 814 *Excursion* 4. 871
Need a bewildered traveller wish for more? 834 *Excursion* 5. 777
Far livelier than bewildered traveller feels, 852 *Excursion* 6. 911
From traveller halting in his own despite, 859 *Excursion* 7. 106
And, wheresoe'er the traveller turns his steps, 876 *Excursion* 8. 128
Herein less happy than the Traveller K.8. 250 *Recluse* 1.1. 492

Traveller's. 'Twill be the traveller's shed, the pilgrim's cot, 201 *Hart-leap* 59
Strikes through the Traveller's frame with deadlier chill, 267 **As the* 2
Given to the pausing traveller's rapturous glance: 282 *Railway* 10
If from a traveller's fortune I might claim 335 *Aix* 9
The Traveller's expectation?—Could our Will 358 **Is this* 5
To the Traveller's eye it shone: 549 *Hermit's Cell* 1. 22
Appeared to recompense the traveller's pains. 710 *Prelude* 9. 76
(How welcome to the weary traveller's eyes!) 716 *Prelude* 9. 477
That bars the traveller's road, she often stood, 769 *Excursion* 1. 895
His harp, suspended at the traveller's side; 771 *Excursion* 2. 15

Traveller's—*continued.*
Those small flat stones, which, ranged by traveller's hands K.8. 226 **I will* 63

Travellers. *See* **Fellow-travellers, Foot-travellers, Horsemen-travellers.**
The travellers saw me weep, my fate inquired, 31 *Guilt* 404
Two Travellers! The woman is Idonea. 39 *Bord.* 100
While our four travellers homeward wend; 131 *Idiot Boy* 433
The travellers know it not, and 'twill remain 149 *M. H.* 16
Our Travellers are the happiest pair; 177 *Waggoner* 2. 79
While thus our jocund Travellers fare, 177 *Waggoner* 2. 101
Like travellers shouting for a boat. 179 *Waggoner* 3. 125
Our Travellers, ye remember well, 245 *P. B.* 796
Which stopped that band of travellers on their way, 252 *Picture* 5
Of travellers in some shady haunt, 289 *Sol. Reap.* 11
To travellers, from such comforts as are thine, 352 *Aquap.* 21
And sun-burnt travellers resting their tired limbs, 668 *Prelude* 5. 209
Of travellers, chiefly delegates returning 681 *Prelude* 6. 388
Of vehicles and travellers, horse and foot, 726 *Prelude* 10. 564
Yet do such travellers find their own delight; 761 *Excursion* 1. 326

Travellers'. And, after ordinary travellers' talk 746 *Prelude* 14. 16

Travellest. Thou travellest so contentedly, and sleep'st 173 *Infant Daughter* 59

Travelling. *See* **Slow-travelling.**
Raised by yon travelling flock, a dusty cloud 4 *Ev. Wk.* 110
And he is all in travelling trim,— 126 *Idiot Boy* 37
She sees him in his travelling trim, 127 *Idiot Boy* 90
For, while they all were travelling home, 131 *Idiot Boy* 437
Peter was travelling all alone;— 240 *P. B.* 327
That through his brain are travelling, 287 *Ellen Irwin* 26
Of travelling through the world that lay 289 *Stepping West.* 25
Travelling where she from time to time enshrouds 461 **Who but is* 2
At length, in darkness travelling on, 542 *Russ. Fug.* 21
The ray the cot of morning trav'ling nigh, 592 *Ev. Wk. Quarto* 47
A friendless Man, a travelling Cripple! 621 *Andrew Jones* 10
That travelling in strange countries once he found 623 **I find* 2
Unprofitably travelling toward the grave, 636 *Prelude* 1. 267
And now was travelling towards his native home. 664 *Prelude* 4. 425
While I was travelling back among those days, 668 *Prelude* 5. 172
A travelling cripple, by the trunk cut short, 690 *Prelude* 7. 203
Since, travelling southward from our pastoral hills, 693 *Prelude* 7. 383
I had been travelling: this a stride at once 722 *Prelude* 10. 275
I have been travelling far; and many days 767 *Excursion* 1. 764
Travelling at steadier pace than ours, had risen 824 *Excursion* 5. 135
And I could tell, not travelling for my theme 847 *Excursion* 6. 569

Travel's. And that was all his travel's story. 131 *Idiot Boy* 453
Its warfare's bourn, its travel's belt! 298 *Brownie's Cell* 40

Travels. He travels slowly down the vale. 129 *Idiot Boy* 326
Mounts with a tune, that travels like a blast 233 *Power of Sound* 68
Diaphanous because it travels slowly; 262 **Not Love* 12
Of locusts travels on his breath; 328 *Ode 1815* 90
The simple rapture;—who that travels far 353 *Aquap.* 54
For Power that travels with the human heart: 423 *Ecc. Sonn.* 1. 20. 10
And flung into the brook that travels near; 432 *Ecc. Sonn.* 2. 17. 4
Which whoso travels in her bosom eyes, 445 *Ecc. Sonn.* 3. 19. 7
He travels on, a solitary Man, 566 *Cumb. Beg.* 24
He travels on, a solitary Man; 567 *Cumb. Beg.* 44
He travels on, and in his face, his step, 572 *Animal Tran.* 3
When the world travels in a beaten road, 728 *Prelude* 11. 97

Traverse. Nor by his presence traverse the design. 624 *Æneid* 35
Who, with their burthen, traverse hill and dale, 875 *Excursion* 8. 47

Traversed. Was traversed from without; much, too, of thoughts 124 *V. and J.* 179
And, as they traversed the smooth brine, 371 *Eg. Maid* 159
He went, and traversed plain and hill; 412 *White Doe* 1437
Traversed by gleaming ships, looked up to thee 460 **Queen of* 7
And the broad gulfs I traversed oft and oft. 574 *Chiabrera* 4. 17
The torrent, travers'd by the lustre broad, 605 *Desc.Sk.Quarto* 207
The Arcades I traversed, in the Palace huge 710 *Prelude* 9. 52
Of the glad times when first I traversed France 725 *Prelude* 10. 491
If Angels traversed their cerulean floors, 796 *Excursion* 3. 691
Traversed but by a few irregular paths, 834 *Excursion* 5. 763

Traverses. That respite o'er, like traverses and toils 800 *Excursion* 3. 985

Traversing. While traversing this nether sphere, 215 *Enterprise* 18
I thought, still traversing that widespread plain, 726 *Prelude* 10. 545
While traversing alone yon mountain-pass. 833 *Excursion* 5. 735

Treacherous. To climb the treacherous cliffs for scanty fare. 17 *Desc. Sk.* 395
There's little sign the treacherous path 240 *P. B.* 349
His hope is treacherous only whose love dies 256 **Yes! hope* 10
Of such weak fibre that the treacherous air 277 **Why art* 2
That Wisdom wears, or take his treacherous staff 358 *Aquap.* 354
But from behind with treacherous wound 412 *White Doe* 1485
Triumphant, snatched from many a treacherous wile! 438 *Ecc. Sonn.* 2. 38. 2
And, sorrow for him! the dull treacherous heat 484 **A plague* 7
That looks for evil like a treacherous spy; 500 *Humanity* 50
Was spread a treacherous swamp, 542 *Russ. Fug.* 98
In a strait and treacherous pass. 549 *Hermit's Cell.* 1. 4
They can be treacherous too. 550 *Hermit's Cell.* 5. 8
How treacherous to her promise, is the world; 574 *Chiabrera* 3. 18
From intricate cabals of treacherous friends. 574 *Chiabrera* 4. 9
For scanty food the treacherous cliffs to dare. 611 *Desc.Sk.Quarto* 483
And gave, in handfuls gave, the treacherous store: 620 *Birth of Love* 43
She dreads the treacherous house, the double tongue; 624 *Æneid* 7
Gave treacherous sanction to that over-love 675 *Prelude* 6. 32
Leaves far behind life's treacherous vanities, 682 *Prelude* 6. 453
Death-like, of treacherous desertion, felt 724 *Prelude* 10. 414
Motions not treacherous or profane, else why 725 *Prelude* 10. 458
Not treacherous, to the mind's *excursive* power. 820 *Excursion* 4. 1263

Treacherous—continued.
Supplanted, not for treacherous vacancy . . . S.3. 435 *The doubt 115
Treachery. There I reproached him with his treachery. . 68 Bord. 1714
Falsehood and Treachery, in close council met, . 513 *Said Secrecy 2
A treachery that foils it or defeats ; . 720 Prelude 10. 178
Tread. Spur-clad his nervous feet, and firm his tread ; 5 Ev. Wk. 148
The hound, the horse's tread, and mellow horn ; . 6 Ev. Wk. 245
And dear the velvet green-sward to his tread : . 11 Desc. Sk. 22
Winds neither road nor path for foot to tread ; . 14 Desc. Sk. 229
From the unpretending ground we mortals tread ;— 54 Bord. 933
Come on, and tread where I shall tread." . . 85 Shepherd-boys 46
Tombstone nor name—only the turf we tread . 95 Brothers 14
Her tread that would scarcely crush a worm, . 142 †Lov. and Lik. 46
Alone I tread this path ;— . . 151 *When, to 105
Tread there with steps that no one shall reprove ! 208 *It is no 17
Here is my body doomed to tread, this path, . 230 Clouds 54
That in thy holy footsteps I may tread ; . 257 *The prayers 11
And all her twinkling stars. Who now would tread, 263 *How clear 6
Whom could the Muses else allure to tread . 265 *There is a pleasure 3

While Anna's peers and early playmates tread, . 273 *While Anna's 1
That every foot might fall with heavier tread, . 275 Gravestone 12
At God's appointed hour to them who tread . 278 *Lo! where she 10
For one hour's perfect bliss, to tread the grass . 306 *Here, on our 12
She gave, if Faith might tread the beaten ways . 322 *By Moscow 8
To us who tread below), . 329 Ode : Thanks. 25
The grass-grown pavement tread. . 334 *In Bruges 4
But from our course why turn—to tread . 344 *How blest 66
Provokes no echoes, but must softly tread ; . 355 Aquap. 195
Who breathe the air he breathed, tread where he trod, . 362 *List—'twas 67
Where the all-conquering Roman feared to tread. 388 Loch Etive 14
Which her Heaven-guided feet refuse to tread. . 390 Highland Hut 8
Blest be the unconscious shore on which ye tread, 422 Ecc. Sonn. 1. 14. 2
Levelled with earth this foot of mine may tread." 428 Ecc. Sonn. 1. 38. 4
With bigotry shall tread the Offering . 435 Ecc. Sonn. 2. 29. 13
Though doomed to tread in solitary ways, . 441 Ecc. Sonn. 3. 4. 7
Wheels and the tread of hoofs are heard no more ; 453 *Calm is the 27
On ground which British shepherds tread ! . 457 *Had this 40
That, if thy new-born Charge shall tread . 503 *Like a 68
Or, bound by oaths, come forth to tread earth's floor 505 Warning 121
Under a rock too steep for man to tread, . 525 Epist. Beaumont 228

Is all too rough for Thee to tread. . 534 *Blest is 84
Thou tread ; or sweep—borne on the managed steed— 540 *Lady! a 73
Where never foot doth tread." . 542 Russ. Fug. 88
The household floor to tread. . 545 Russ. Fug. 360
They hunt through the streets with deliberate tread, 572 Avarice 37
And dear the green-sward to his velvet tread ; . 602 Desc. Sk. Quarto 24
Was never heard the plodding peasant's tread. . 607 Desc. Sk. Quarto 286
To guide his dangerous tread the taper's gleam. . 607 Desc. Sk. Quarto 316
Whose slippery face derides his deathful tread ! . 609 Desc. Sk. Quarto 393
When fragrant scents beneath th' enchanted tread 610 Desc. Sk. Quarto 448
Rock'd on the dizzy larch's narrow tread, . 610 Desc. Sk. Quarto 465
May never tread ; but scarcely Spenser's self . 676 Prelude 5. 89
That we must tread—thy image rose again, . 692 Prelude 7. 319
Too hot to tread upon. Oft said I then, . 712 Prelude 9. 167
That I have dared to tread this holy ground, . 743 Prelude 13. 252
Then, though (too weak to tread the ways of truth) 752 Prelude 14. 433
For I must tread on shadowy ground, must sink . 755 Recluse 1. 1. 781
Not wishing more ; repining not to tread . 790 Excursion 3. 304
Not doomed to ignorance, though forced to tread, 802 Excursion 4. 47
To tread for pastime, talking with his mates, . 805 Excursion 4. 248
The earth we tread, the sky that we behold . 816 Excursion 4. 972
Delight exhaling from the ground they tread." . 841 Excursion 6. 188
Of the path worn by mournful tread of her . 850 Excursion 6. 818
Of man or beast was seldom used to tread. . K.8. 229 *I will 142
Tread'st. Speak, and the floor thou tread'st on will rejoice. . 210 Laod. 34
Treading. See **Close-treading.**
And treading among flowers of joy . 218 Young Lady 8
A gravelled pathway treading, . 337 Thun 2
All, while he slept, treading the pendent stairs . 500 Humanity 35
Than treading a path trod by thousands before. . 572 Avarice 28
Is treading, where no other face is seen) . 664 Prelude 4. 363
Treading their path in sympathy and linked . 845 Excursion 6. 477
Breathing fresh air, and treading the green earth ; 878 Excursion 8. 280
Treads. Time softly treads ; throughout the landscape breathes . 9 Ev. Wk. 361
Startles the pensive traveller while he treads . 184 Night-piece 9
Softly she treads, as if her foot were loth . 222 Triad 201
Months perish with their moons ; year treads on year ; . 251 *There is a little 9
And treads in solitary ways. . 404 White Doe 756
And fragrance in thy footing treads ; . 492 Duty 46
Enough of climbing toil !—Ambition treads . 497 *Enough of climbing 1
That howl so dismally for him who treads . 702 Prelude 8. 221
Of wildest course but treads back his own steps ; 719 Prelude 10. 79
And treads the mountains which his fathers trod. K.8. 247 Recluse 1. 1. 383
Treason. Of subtle Treason, in his mask of law, 504 Warning 102
Treasonable. And, worst of all, a treasonable growth 652 Prelude 3. 211
Treason-parties. Round fire-side treason-parties en famille? . L.1. 97 Juvenal 3. 88
Treason's. From subterraneous Treason's darkling power : . 439 Ecc. Sonn. 2. 42. 10
Treasons. For treasons, tumults, and for wars ? . 236 P. B. 27
Treasure. Looking down on the kine, and our treasure of sheep . 116 Repentance 31

Treasure—continued.
But whatsoe'er of such rare treasure lay . 122 V. and J. 34
The treasure proudly did I show . 169 Wren's Nest 45
Over wealthy in the treasure . 171 Kitten 39
To Nelson, England's pride and treasure, . 178 Waggoner 2. 147
Of treasure sucked from buds and bells, . 227 Vernal Ode 99
To keep the treasure unimpaired. Vain thought ! 231 Clouds 91
He touches—'tis to him a treasure ! . 242 P. B. 542
Knowing my heart's best treasure was no more : . 257 *Surprised by 12
The casual treasure from the furrowed soil. . 275 *While poring 14
And give the treasure to our British tongue ! . 325 Ode 1814 130
As a selected treasure thy one cliff, . 355 Aquap. 210
Sir Galahad ! a treasure, that God giveth, . 374 Eg. Maid 344
The starry treasure from the blue profound . 381 Duddon 22. 7
The treasure,—what mine eyes behold see thou, . 508 F. Stone 26
Old Daniel his hand to the treasure will slide ! . 572 Avarice 19
Love, the treasure worth possessing . 629 Installation 53
Grasping his twofold treasure.—Lance in rest, . 667 Prelude 5. 120
A precious treasure had I long possessed, . 672 Prelude 5. 460
And Como ! thou, a treasure whom the earth . 685 Prelude 6. 660
Within whose silent chambers treasure lies . 809 Excursion 4. 565
Treasured. See **Long-treasured.**
Hangs that day's treasured sword, how firm a check 278 Wellington 6
The treasured dreams of times long past, . 293 Yarrow Unv. 53
Dreams treasured up from early days, . 386 Yarrow Rev. 79
From soul-felt music, and the treasured page . 583 *With copious 29
A treasured and luxurious gloom of choice . 677 Prelude 6. 176
Treasure-house. Thou shouldst have seemed a treasure-house divine . 578 Peele Castle 21
Which her poor treasure-house is content to owe, 862 Excursion 7. 320
Treasures. Heart-blessings—outward treasures too which the eye . 21 Desc. Sk. 601
All treasures hoarded by the miser, Time. . 234 Power of Sound 114
To female hands the treasures were resigned ; . 264 *Lady! I 9
Her treasures less and less.—Man now presides . 281 *What strong 5
What treasures would have then been placed . 285 Grave of Burns 55
Into whose bosom earth's best treasures flow, . 327 Ode 1815 47
The treasures they enjoy to guard ! " . 342 Ital. Itin. 68
That treasures, yet untouched, may grace some future Lay. . 351 Des. Stanzas 90
Treasures I gained with zeal that neither feared . 352 H. C. R. 3
His treasures forth, soliciting regard . 874 Excursion 8. 24
Has her own treasures, and I think of these, . K.8. 248 Recluse 1.1.425
Treasuring. Relinquishing, but treasuring every law S.3. 437 *The doubt 188
Treat. See **Baby-treat.**
The Arch-impostor—— Treat him gently, Oswald ; 39 Bord. 86
In verse, which to thy ear might come, would treat this simple theme, . 93 Poet's Dream 75
Say not you love the delicate treat, . 142 †Lov. and Lik. 37
Our treat shall be a friendly bowl ! " . 177 Waggoner 2. 46
They—who have heard some learned Patriot treat 359 *They—who 9
Greedy ambition, armed to treat with scorn . 469 *The feudal 4
What shall I treat of ? News from Mona's Isle ? 522 Epist. Beaumont 59
I treat the matter lightly, but, alas ! . 783 Excursion 2. 780
Of strife and folly, though it be a treat . 799 Excursion 3. 905
Frank conversation, made the evening's treat : . 834 Excursion 5. 776
—Still less, far less, am I inclined to treat . 847 Excursion 6. 573
Nor wanted timely treat of fish or fowl . 860 Excursion 7. 164
Treated. He mocked and treated with disdain . 159 Green Linnet 38
And shameless women, treated and caressed ; . 692 Prelude 7. 361
Then let both be kindly treated, . S.3. 438 *I, whose 23
Treatise. A treatise of Geometry, he wont, . 677 Prelude 6. 146
Treats. To furnish treats more costly than the Dame 643 Prelude 2. 87
The Pharasaic [sic] sneer that treats as dross . K.8. 325 [?] *The vestal 11
Treble. Voice to a rueful treble humanised. . 783 Excursion 2. 778
Tree. See **Apple-tree, Ash-tree, Axle-tree, Beech-tree, Birch-tree, Elder-tree, Elm-tree, Fir-tree, Forest-tree, Fruit-tree, Hawthorn-tree, Palm-tree, Pine-tree, Plane-tree, Willow-tree, Yew-tree.**
First covered, and here taught this aged Tree . 23 Yew-tree 10
No tree was there, no meadow's pleasant green, . 24 Guilt 28
Sigh at the deed ? Hew down a withered tree, . 54 Bord. 928
Here is a tree, ragged, and bent, and bare, . 61 Bord. 1294
No tree, nor jutting eminence, nor form . 68 Bord. 1708
From such a journey !——there was a black tree, 74 Bord. 2097
A single tree ; she thought it was her Father.— 74 Bord. 2098
He tosses about in every bare tree, . 80 †Address : Child 5
Beneath the church-yard time." . 84 We are Seven 32
" My Mother," said the Boy, " was born near to a blessèd Tree, . 92 Poet's Dream 27
Holy as that which long hath crowned the Chapel of this Tree ; . 93 Poet's Dream 60
Or lay upon the moss by brook or tree, . 108 Indolence 38
Or let the aged tree uprooted lie, . 110 *'Tis said that some 14
Or sing another song, or choose another tree. . 111 *'Tis said that some 28
Or sit in the shade of my grandfather's tree, . 116 Repentance 18
And under every hospitable tree . 125 V. and J. 257
In tree and tower was Johnny seen, . 128 Idiot Boy 209
The CLIPPING TREE, a name which yet it bears. . 133 Michael 169
The breeze I see is in the tree, . 145 Her Eyes 39
And underneath the spreading tree . 145 Her Eyes 73
That every naked ash, and tardy tree . 146 *It was an 14
To note in shrub and tree, in stone and flower, . 147 Joanna 46
Under the branches of the tree : . 162 *Art thou the 18
There is a tempest-stricken tree ; . 165 Danish Boy 6
Beside the tree and corner-stone. . 166 Danish Boy 44
Halting beneath a shady tree, . 167 Pilgrim's Dream 10

Trojan—*continued.*
His course to Latium from the Trojan shore, . K.8. 281 **Arms and* 2
Trojans. The Trojans too (Æneas at their head), . 624 *Æneid* 58
Loud shouts,—the Trojans echo the applause. . 625 *Æneid* 131
Hath come ! we *have* been Trojans, Ilium *was* . L.2. 121 *Frag. Æneid* 2. 3
Trompington. Beside the pleasant Mill of Trompington 653 *Prelude* 3. 275
Troop. The Troop will be impatient ; let us hie . 37 *Bord.* 1
That horn again—'Tis some one of our Troop ; . 56 *Bord.* 1016
You are found at last, thanks to the vagrant Troop 56 *Bord.* 1018
Landed with a small troop, myself being one : . 68 *Bord.* 1713
'Twas by a troop of miners made, ... 245 *P. B.* 838
The troop of horse have gained the height . . 412 *White Doe* 1462
A troop of deer came sweeping by ; . . . . 414 *White Doe* 1640
The Minstrel of the Troop, and left him there, 644 *Prelude* 2. 168
As scattered birds troop to the fowler's lure, . 675 *Prelude* 6. 5
With the sad news, that he had joined a troop 766 *Excursion* 1. 676
Of Chaplain to a military troop . . . . 774 *Excursion* 2. 175
Into the troop of mirth, a soldier, sworn . . 842 *Excursion* 6. 285
Trooping. Trooping to that summons holy. . . 396 *White Doe* 8
Trooping together. Little suits it me . . . . 669 *Prelude* 5. 260
Of Tell came trooping from a thousand huts, . . 869 *Excursion* 7. 810
Troops. Driven out in troops to want and nakedness ; 56 *Bord.* 1032
About your Daughter ! Troops of armed men, . 61 *Bord.* 1330
Army of Clouds ! ye wingèd Host in troops . . 229 *Clouds* 1
Unhappy ghosts in troops by moonlight seen ; . 361 **For action* 8
Unharnessed, naked, troops of Moorish horse . . 368 *Trajan* 45
Howling in troops along the Bothnic Main. . . 640 *Prelude* 1. 543
By annual custom, issuing forth in troops, . . 701 *Prelude* 8. 154
The order'd troops . . . . K.8. 234 **The order'd* 1
Trope. Vanity's hieroglyphic ; a choice trope . . 345 **Ambition—following* 8
Trophied. Yon trophied Mound shrinks to a shadowy speck . . . . 278 *Wellington* 8
Trophies. These desolate remains are trophies high 316 **Hail, Zaragoza* 5
Trophies that led the good and wise to mourn . 326 **Emperors and* 4
—Not work of hands ; but trophies that may reach 331 *Ode : Thanks.* 171
Her trophies, Fancy crouch ; the course of pride 388 *Loch Etive* 11
Her heaven-offending trophies Glory rears : . . 392 *Avon* 12
Bright trophies of the sun ! . . . . 498 **The sylvan* 3
Seeks for no trophies, struggles for no spoils . . 684 *Prelude* 6. 610
There hang thy trophies ; bid the jockey's vest, . L.1. 94 *Juvenal* 2. 21
Trophy. High was the trophy hung with pitiless pride ; . . . . 393 *Hart's-horn* 10
That man will have a trophy, humble Spade ! . 489 *Spade* 19
A trophy nobler than a conqueror's sword. . 489 *Spade* 20
Tropic. Upon the tropic sea. . . . . . . 192 *Ruth* 42
The tumult of a tropic sky, ... 193 *Ruth* 122
Is she for tropic suns, or polar snow ? . . . . 258 **Where lies the Land* 4
Yet still her eyes retained their tropic fire, . . 306 **We had* 10
Thou buoyant minion of the tropic air ; . . . 511 **Who rashly* 2
That in the Tropic Islands he had served, . . 664 *Prelude* 4. 422
Bedded among rich plumes of tropic birds ; . . 700 *Prelude* 8. 94
Tropics. Between the tropics filled the steady sail, 96 *Brothers* 50
Troth. Of misery that was not—— Troth, 'tis hard— . . . . 56 *Bord.* 1048
Each in his way ? Troth, I begin to think so. . 60 *Bord.* 1239
Had pledged his troth before the altar . . . 246 *P. B.* 904
Yet He whose heart in childhood gave her troth . 275 **Chatsworth ! thy* 9
He will repent him of his troth ; . . . . . 372 *Eg. Maid* 221
Of God and chosen friends, your troth to plight . 446 *Ecc. Sonn.* 3. 26. 3
Fail to wash out, tears flowing ere thy troth . 514 **Long-favoured* 6
At will, your power the measure of your troth !— 515 *Penn.* 8
And hope that kept with me her plighted troth. . 532 **Once I* 12
No chief, on my troth, ... S.3. 440 **Said red-ribboned* 10
Trotted. Are still, the creature trotted on before ; . 660 *Prelude* 4. 121.
Trotting. Trotting alone along the beaten road, . 44 *Bord.* 411
And now the 'trotting brooks' and whispering trees, 767 *Excursion* 1. 703
Trouble. (For sighs will ever trouble human breath) 8 *Ev. Wk.* 353
As if thenceforth nor pain nor trouble she could know. . . . . 25 *Guilt* 63
Then, with a voice which inward trouble broke . 33 *Guilt* 503
'Twere wrong to trouble you. God speed you both. 41 *Bord.* 222
Would trouble us ; if he were here again, . . . 51 *Bord.* 758
To look his trouble in the face, it seemed . . . 134 *Michael* 222
What trouble, surely, will be bred ; . . . . 156 *Oak and Broom* 26
Night and day, I feel the trouble . . . . . 166 *Wand. Jew* 27
—Such din shall trouble them no more. . . . 237 *P. B.* 85
Are not unused to trouble friends . . . . . 245 *P. B.* 768
Some inward trouble suddenly . . . . . . 294 *Jedbor.* 66
Of trouble—but the fluttering breeze ; . . . 348 **Lulled by* 17
A trouble, not of clouds, or weeping rain, . . . 386 *Scott* 1
Hath roamed in trouble and in grief, ... 414 *White Doe* 1613
To trouble hours that winged their way, . . . 478 *Somnamb.* 34
Why all this toil and trouble ? . . . . . . 481 *Tables Turned* 4
And trouble from the soul. . . . . 542 *Russ. Fug.* 48
That trouble still is near. . . . . 544 *Russ. Fug.* 228
Nor yet of trouble and alarms : . . . . . 545 *Russ. Fug.* 301
And all his trouble to the moon he told, . . . 564 *Troilus* 131
That drive her as in trouble through the groves ; 634 *Prelude* 1. 143
And seemed to be a trouble to the peace . . . 636 *Prelude* 1. 316
By day, and were a trouble to my dreams. . . 638 *Prelude* 1. 400
For now a trouble came into my mind . . . 646 *Prelude* 2. 276
That thou, O Friend ! the trouble or the calm . 682 *Prelude* 6. 473
Like one in trouble, for returning light, . . . 766 *Excursion* 1. 665
Not worth the trouble of a thought ?—alas ! . . 783 *Excursion* 2. 792
Doubt shall be quelled and trouble chased away ; 804 *Excursion* 4. 234
Their foot-marks do not trouble me, ... K.8. 219 **The snow-tracks* 2
Troubled. Cloud-piercing pine-trees nod their troubled heads, ... 11 *Desc. Sk.* 63
Like sun-lit tempests, troubled transports roll ; . 18 *Desc. Sk.* 458
On the mute Image and the troubled walls. . . 20 *Desc. Sk.* 544
Moody, or inly troubled, would he seem . . . 26 *Guilt* 98
Struck, and still struck again, the troubled horse : 27 *Guilt* 177
Of many things which never troubled me— . . 31 *Guilt* 391
Your natural breathing has been troubled. Nay, 39 *Bord.* 105
I've had the saddest dream that ever troubled . 44 *Bord.* 397
When you had told him the mischance, was troubled 51 *Bord.* 761
Into deep chasms troubled by roaring streams ; . 70 *Bord.* 1805
The wrong and the wrong-doer. You are troubled— 74 *Bord.* 2071
He drew it from the troubled pool, ... 85 *Shepherd-boys* 89
Yet as the troubled seed and tortured bough . . 123 *V. and J.* 148
Heard him, how he was troubled in his sleep : . 135 *Michael* 291
And, though little troubled with sloth, . . . 159 **Up with me* 19
The old Man's shape, and speech—all troubled me : 197 *Resolution* 128
By ruder fancy, that a troubled ghost . . . 219 *Haunted Tree* 28
The throbbing pulse—else troubled without end : 255 **Grief, thou* 8
Owe to a troubled element their forms, . . . 277 **The most* 2
Where these troubled waters roar ! . . . . 336 **Jesu ! bless* 6
So have we hurried on with troubled pleasure : . 443 *Ecc. Sonn.* 3. 12. 9
Guiding the mariner through troubled seas, . . 466 *St. Bees* 43
Nought heard, of ocean troubled or serene ? . . 470 **Did pangs* 5
Mimicking a troubled sea, ... 550 *Hermit's Cell* 3. 6
Troubled long with warring notions . . . . 550 *Hermit's Cell* 4. 1
For me with sighs be troubled. Not from life . 573 *Chiabrera* 1. 2
In the brown park, in flocks, the troubl'd deer . 592 *Ev. Wk. Wuarto* 63
Nod the cloud-piercing pines their troubl'd heads, 603 *Desc. Sk. Quarto* 62
—Bursts from the troubl'd Larch's giant boughs . 606 *Desc.Sk.Quarto* 229
Like lighted tempests troubled transports roll ; . 612 *Desc.Sk.Quarto* 547
And ebbs uncertain on the troubled walls, . . 614 *Desc.Sk.Quarto* 649
And troubled pleasure, nor without the voice . 637 *Prelude* 1. 362
With them to take a troubled human heart, . . 724 *Prelude* 10. 439
Was most inviting to a troubled mind ; . . . 797 *Excursion* 3. 803
Like the fixed centre of a troubled world. . . 822 *Excursion* 5. 16
He craved a substitute in troubled joy ; . . . 855 *Excursion* 6. 1091
Glares, like a troubled spirit, in its bed . . . 877 *Excursion* 8. 179
From out the bosom of these troubled times . . 890 *Excursion* 9. 401
Trouble-haunted. All now was trouble-haunted ground ; . . . . 414 *White Doe* 1701
Troubler. The innocent troubler of their quiet, sleeps 868 *Excursion* 7. 693
Troubles. Have you forgot your own troubles . 72 *Bord.* 1976
My troubles, and beyond relief : . . . . . 117 *Affl. Marg.* 72
Should troubles overflow on her from whom it came." 140 *Arm. Lady* 30
And all old troubles now are ended.— . . . 204 *Brougham* 14
So were the hopeless troubles, that involved . . 214 *Dion* 118
Troubles and toils that every day prepares. . . 282 **While beams* 7
Nor aught that troubles us, the fools of Nature. . 370 *Eg. Maid* 60
Once more of troubles wrought by magic spell ; . 395 *White Doe: Ded.* 34
Shatters the air, and troubles tower and spire ; . 442 *Ecc. Sonn.* 3. 8. 2
And troubles that were each a step to Heaven : . 576 **By a* 8
Provoked out of herself by troubles strange, . . 584 *Ch. Lamb* 28
And outward troubles, between man himself, . . 734 *Prelude* 12. 27
Was added to the troubles of a time . . . . 764 *Excursion* 1. 557
Before whose sight the troubles of this world . . 775 *Excursion* 2. 291
Those troubles had appeased, he sought and gained, 844 *Excursion* 6. 424
And reproduce the troubles he destroys. . . . . 846 *Excursion* 6. 517
Troublesome. When the troublesome Tempter beset us, said I, ... 116 *Repentance* 5
Shine hot, or wind blows troublesome and strong ; 151 **When, to* 89
And, for hunger and thirst and such troublesome calls, ... 571 *Avarice* 7
Over the billows of this troublesome world . . 826 *Excursion* 5. 284
Troublest. Thou troublest me with strange alarms ; 121 *Emigrant Mother* 60
Troubling. And while around it storm as fierce seemed troubling earth and air, . . . 91 *Poet's Dream* 7
And the green, gilded snake, without troubling the calm . . . . 340 *Fort Fuentes* 7
Troubling the last holds of ambitious Rome, . . 394 **How profitless* 2
For wholesome sadness, troubling to refine, . . 538 **In desultory* 24
Troubling a heart that had been long at rest. . 625 *Æneid* 94
Trouts. Large store of gleaming crimson-spotted trouts ; . . . . 882 *Excursion* 8. 558
Trow. I'm as great as they, I trow, ... 160 **Pansies, lilies* 13
" ' My throat is cut unto the bone, I trow,' . . 556 *Prioress* 198
And said, I am in constant dread I trow, . . . 564 *Troilus* 145
Troy. Her Hero slain upon the beach of Troy ? . 209 *Laod.* 15
Unto the blood of Troy, I pray of thee, . . . 563 *Troilus* 82
I might her see again coming to Troy ! . . . 564 *Troilus* 91
And shall, unless I see her soon in Troy. . . 564 *Troilus* 98
To Tyrians, and these exiles driven from Troy ; . 625 *Æneid* 110
And the great name of Troy ; now all things pass L.2. 121 *Frag. Æneid* 2. 4
By all that breathe in Troy, how tired and worn . L.2. 318 *Frag. Æneid* 4. 6
Troynovant. In Troynovant, his seat by silver Thames's side ! . . . . 103 *Artegal* 97
Truant. Take care of him, and feed the truant well. 42 *Bord.* 307
So, truant in waste woods, the blithe Euphrosyne ! 221 *Triad* 106
And if to lure the truant back be well, . . . 229 *Cuckoo-clock* 4
They taught me random cares and truant joys, . 382 *Duddon* 26. 10
Or through her truant pathway's native charms, 603 *Desc. Sk. Quarto* 49
And glorifies the truant youth of Vannes. . . . 627 *Eagle and Dove* 8
Keen as a Truant or a Fugitive, ... 633 *Prelude* 1. 90
On the vague reading of a truant youth . . . 676 *Prelude* 6. 95
The bark was nibbled round by truant sheep. . 769 *Excursion* 1. 842
Truant's. That clung to Nature with a truant's love, 11 *Desc. Sk.* 44
Truce. Even Joy could tell, Joy craving truce and rest 255 **Grief, thou* 9
A breathing-time, vacation, or a truce, . . . 791 *Excursion* 3. 384
Trudge. Might trudge it alongside each other ! " . 179 *Waggoner* 3. 55

Trudged. " And he had trudged through Yorkshire dales, 239 P. B. 226
He trudged along through copse and brake 240 P. B. 331
He trudged along o'er hill and dale; 240 P. B. 332

True. Instructed that true knowledge leads to love; 23 Yew-tree 60
True dignity abides with him alone 23 Yew-tree 61
True sympathy the Sailor's looks expressed, 32 Guilt 451
True; and, remembering how the Band have proved 37 Bord. 11
Should *yet* be true? Would it were possible! 38 Bord. 73
He tempted me to think the Story true; 41 Bord. 230
This is true comfort, thanks a thousand times!— 43 Bord. 343
That could withstand it. True," continued he, 59 Bord. 1194
That we can suffer greatly. Very true. 65 Bord. 1538
My faithful true and only Comforter. 76 Bord. 2186
That Cross belike he also raised as a standard for the true 91 Norman Boy 25
The stone-cutters, 'tis true, might beg their bread 98 Brothers 175
Is a true friend to sorrow; and, unless 101 Brothers 389
True beauty dwells in deep retreats, 111 *Let other 9
But, Allan, be true to me, Allan,—we'll die 116 Repentance 7
As ever breathed:" and that is true; 117 Aff. Marg. 33
Of true domestic loyalty, did e'er 124 V. and J. 170
With, " God forbid it should be true!" 128 Idiot Boy 183
And, Johnny, mind you tell us true." 131 Idiot Boy 441
But still be true till I am dead. 145 Her Eyes 58
Engendered between malice and true love, 147 Joanna 33
In memory of affections old and true, 148 Joanna 81
Last night I heard a crash—'tis true, 156 Oak and Broom 27
That more than what you say is true 156 Oak and Broom 56
But true love is like the thread 163 Spinning Wheel 15
This precious Flower, true love's last token. 164 *Fair Lady 40
Now, heroes, for the true commotion, 178 Waggoner 3. 22
For the true reason no one knows: 198 Thorn 90
Gave with a maiden's true good-will 198 Thorn 106
I will be sworn is true. 199 Thorn 169
True to the kindred points of Heaven and Home! 209 *Ethereal minstrel 12
And though for bridal wreaths and tokens true 222 Triad 207
A broken vow, or bind a true, 223 Wishing-gate 47
In every fibre true. 224 Primrose 18
And a true master of the glowing strain, 231 *The gentlest Poet 2
Along the shade with footsteps true 244 P. B. 673
No fleeting Spirit, but my own true Love? 252 *Her only 14
'Tis sense, unbridled will, and not true love, 257 *No mortal 12
Unless Thou show to us thine own true way 257 *The prayers 7
Whence the poor unregarded Favourite, true 274 *Wait, prithee 7
Tears of delight, that testified how true 277 Author's Portrait 13
Of thought, that give the true poetic thrill; 277 *Haydon! let 4
Why to God's goodness cannot We be true, 278 *Life with 12
And earth below, they best can serve true gladness 280 *'Tis he 13
Night after night? True is it Nature hides 281 *What strong 4
Yes, ye were startled;—and, in balance true, 283 *Proud were 11
For a brief absence, proves that love is true; 284 Departure 30
True friends though diversely inclined; 285 Grave of Burns 43
His course was true, 286 Nith 22
With sorrow true; 286 Sons of Burns 4
Is praise, heroic praise, and true! 294 Jedbor. 36
And he a story strange yet true 296 Highland Boy 127
By which true Sway doth mount; this is the stalk 304 *I grieved 13
True Power doth grow on; and her rights are these. 304 *I grieved 14
First roused thee.—O true yoke-fellow of Time, 312 Clarkson 8
Stirred by the breeze; they rose, a Nation, true, 313 Prophecy 5
True to herself—the mighty Germany, 313 Prophecy 6
There, and there only, that the heart is true? 315 *And is it 2
Ye slight not life—to God and Nature true; 326 *Intrepid sons 5
And thus is *missed* the sole true glory 330 Ode: Thanks. 83
Objects of false pretence, or meanly true! 335 Aix 8
And that the past might have its true intents 346 Processions 4
Whose only business is to perish!—true 350 Des. Stanzas 23
O bounteous Heaven! signs true as dove and bough 360 *Near Anio's 9
From the true guidance of humanity, 361 *When here 10
Some true Partakers of his loving spirit 362 *List—'twas 68
That earthly love may to herself be true, 363 *The world forsaken 13
Who, gathering true pleasures wherever they grow, 365 Vallomb. 38
As a true man, who long had served the lyre, 365 *Under the 9
" Ask not for whom, O Champions true! 372 Eg. Maid 235
With love too true, a love with pangs too sharp, 373 Eg. Maid 293
A true revival of the light 375 *The Minstrels 28
Follow this wondrous Potentate. Be true, 387 Scott 12
And echoes from old verse speak true, 390 Highland Broach 2
The white Doe, to her service true, 398 White Doe 168
And seven as true as thou, I see, 400 White Doe 410
Then well may their accord be true, 415 White Doe 1728
In Liberty's behalf. Fears, true or feigned, 442 Ecc. Sonn. 3. 11. 3
On a true Penitent. When breath departs 447 Ecc. Sonn. 3. 28. 9
Of true compassion greet them. Creed and test 449 Ecc. Sonn. 3. 36. 9
The Mourner, thy true nature was defamed, 464 *Greta, what 7
Perplex the Church; but be thou firm,—be true 465 *Pastor and 6
And as a cresset true that darts its length 466 St. Bees 43
And proves the Lover true;" 478 Somnamb. 42
She felt that he was true. 479 Somnamb. 144
Affectionate and true, 487 Fountain 2
Our daily world's true Worldlings, rank not me! 488 Pers. Talk 28
Long hast Thou served a man to reason true; 489 Spade 6
False praise from true, or, greater from the less, 489 Spade 22
Them who have, like thee, been true 502 *Like a 48
His social sense of just, and fair, and true, 504 Warning 62
Hast loved the painter's true Promethean craft 508 F. Stone 24
True freedom where for ages they have lain 515 *Ah why 3
In the true filial bosom's inmost fold 516 *Young England 5

True—*continued.*
Dark but to every gentle feeling true, 525 Epist. Beaumont 256
But most the Bard is true to inborn right, 528 *Those breathing 81
The remnant of his days at least was true; 529 *Those breathing 123
Small service is true service while it lasts: 538 *Small service 1
Of tremulous admiration. Such true fame 540 Grace Darl. 13
May brighten more and more! True to the mark, 541 Grace Darl. 59
But Thou art true, incarnate Lord, 550 Hermit's Cell 5. 13
For every true heart, gentle heart and free, 557 Cuck. and Night. 21
For mine's a song that is both true and plain,— 559 Cuck. and Night. 118
To speak of Love's true Servants in this mood; 559 Cuck. and Night. 148
Thence worship comes, content and true heart's pleasure, 559 Cuck. and Night. 153
True lovers doth so bitterly annoy, 560 Cuck. and Night. 199
And mind always that thou be good and true, 561 Cuck. and Night. 246
Therewith when this true Lover 'gan behold, 562 Troilus 15
I shall be glad if all the world be true. 564 Troilus 133
To virtue and true goodness. Some there are, 567 Cumb. Beg. 105
Then (what is too true) without hinting a word, 570 Farmer 39
True is it that Ambrosio Salinero 574 Chiabrera 5. 1
Of racking malady. And true it is 574 Chiabrera 5. 5
Youth amiable; O friend so true of soul 575 Chiabrera 7. 3
Oh true of heart, of spirit gay, 578 *I come 65
True, as inexorable winds, or bars 586 Ch. Lamb 105
The true Ascanius steep'd in placid rest; 624 Æneid 48
Where'er, preserved in this most true reflection, 627 *We gaze 11
True disciples, good as great, 629 Installation 87
True to the King of Kings is found; 629 Installation 98
True symbol of hope's foolishness, whose strong 639 Prelude 1. 486
Rememberable things; sometimes, 'tis true, 641 Prelude 1. 588
Yet true it is, that I had made a change 652 Prelude 3. 204
In their true dwelling; now is crossed by gleam 662 Prelude 4. 267
'Tis true, some casual knowledge might be gained 663 Prelude 4. 300
Dear to thee also, thy true friend and mine, 678 Prelude 6. 200
Oh, blank confusion! true epitome 698 Prelude 7. 722
Nor such as Spenser fabled. True it is, 701 Prelude 8. 144
'Tis true, the history of our native land, 708 Prelude 8. 617
True personal dignity, abideth not; 714 Prelude 9. 348
Her mandates, severing whom true love had joined, 718 Prelude 9. 573
'Tis true, had gone before this hour, dire work 718 Prelude 10. 42
From tragic fictions or true history, 719 Prelude 10. 76
Enough, 'tis true—could such a plea excuse 731 Prelude 11. 259
With my true self; for, though bedimmed and changed 732 Prelude 11. 342
Into its true proportion; sanguine schemes, 741 Prelude 13. 60
True is it, where oppression worse than death 742 Prelude 13. 195
Actual, divine, and true. To fear and love, 748 Prelude 14. 162
Which I from thee imbibed: and 'tis most true 749 Prelude 14. 235
Rich in true happiness if allowed to be 752 Prelude 14. 439
Was melted all away; so true was this, 762 Excursion 1. 408
True, the intelligence of social art 799 Excursion 3. 925
The true descendants of those godly men 814 Excursion 4. 897
Of true philanthropy. The light of love 820 Excursion 4. 1244
To king and people true. A brazen plate, 825 Excursion 5. 178
Is all too true; and surely not misplaced: 828 Excursion 5. 370
A true reflection of the circling year, 828 Excursion 5. 394
Would be most grateful. True indeed it is 832 Excursion 5. 661
True as the stock-dove to her shallow nest 833 Excursion 5. 707
But true humility descends from heaven; 833 Excursion 5. 719
That true succession fail of English hearts, 838 Excursion 6. 24
Spread true religion and her genuine fruits) 839 Excursion 6. 80
True to their choice; and gave their bones in trust 844 Excursion 6. 410
" True," said the Solitary, " be it far 847 Excursion 6. 589
Was a true patriot, hopeful as the best 869 Excursion 7. 805
Learning, though late, that all true glory rests, 877 Excursion 8. 214
Ponders this true equality, may walk 887 Excursion 9. 248
" Whence but from thee, the true and only God, 895 Excursion 9. 720
True; as the mightiest; upon thee sequestered S.3. 435 *The doubt 132
A true knight of his kidney. S.3. 440 *Said red-ribboned 8
Whether he loved the mountains, true it is K.8. 230 *I will 179
'Tis true, hath in my walks been often heard, K.8. 245 Recluse 1. 1. 319
With motions of true dignity and grace? K.8. 248 Recluse 1. 1. 411
A true Community, a genuine frame K.8. 253 Recluse 1. 1. 615
The sage has read the stars with skill so true, L.3. 27 *For Lubbock 3

True-love. Thus, from the heart of her True-love, 287 Ellen Irwin 35
My True-love sighed for sorrow; 293 Yarrow Unv. 30
And on my True-love's forehead plant 302 Yarrow V. 67

Truly. With Herbert or his Daughter? Daughter! truly— 46 Bord. 493
How now, what mean you? Truly, I was going 51 Bord. 765
They loved this good old Man?— They did—and truly: 99 Brothers 240
And, truly, at all times, the storm, that drives 132 Michael 56
Made all their household. I may truly say, 132 Michael 93
The noon-tide hour: though truly some there are 219 Haunted Tree 19
And what was boldly promised, truly shall be done. 220 Triad 33
So shall the seventh be truly blest, 228 Devot. Incit. 76
To his high charge, and truly serving God, 387 Manse 11
But is she truly what she seems? 398 White Doe 194
Of all the truly great and all the innocent. 455 *Not in the lucid 15
So may I hope, if truly I repent 464 *A point 7
The neighbours tell, and tell you truly, 536 Goody Blake 11
But truly did *He* live his life. Urbino, 576 Chiabrera 9. 21
Which he could truly love; but how escape? 670 Prelude 5. 331
Such minds are truly from the Deity, 747 Prelude 14. 112
Great show of joy the housewife made, and truly 785 Excursion 2. 887
Loved fondly, truly, fervently; and dared 840 Excursion 6. 119
And truly might be said to die of joy! 842 Excursion 6. 243

Truly—*continued.*
Of earth and sky, then truly had you seen — K.8. 230 *I will 185
Done truly there, or felt, of solid good — K.8. 247 Recluse 1.1.405
Where these things are. He truly is alone, — K.8. 252 Recluse 1.1.593
Trumpery. The "trumpery" that ascends in bare display— — 435 *Ecc. Sonn.* 2. 28. 6
Trumpet. *See* **Speaking-trumpet.**
Blown to you from a trumpet. Why talk thus? — 56 *Bord.* 1013
The trumpet (we, intoxicate with pride, — 235 *Power of Sound* 213
The Thing became a trumpet; whence he blew — 260 **Scorn not* 13
The trumpet blew a universal blast! — 331 *Ode: Thanks.* 152
But word was given, and the trumpet sounded: — 405 *White Doe* 842
To hear the sanguinary trumpet sounded. — 575 *Chiabrera* 6. 8
The trumpet of the Living Word — 629 *Installation* 102
Sounding through Christian lands her trumpet, roused — 655 *Prelude* 3. 463
With flourishing trumpet, came in full-blown state — 693 *Prelude* 7. 417
And him who at the trumpet puffs his cheeks, — 697 *Prelude* 7. 702
By blast of trumpet?' Plenteous was the growth — 858 *Excursion* 7. 94
And Gideon blew the trumpet, soul-inflamed, — 870 *Excursion* 7. 815
The heroic trumpet with the Muse's breath! — K.8. 257 *Recluse* 1.1.750
Trumpet's. As clear and bold as the trumpet's clang, — 629 *Installation* 36
Trumpets. And greet your sons! drums beat and trumpets blow! — 310 *Anticip.* 7
Shouts rise, and storms of sound from lifted trumpets blow! — 346 *Processions* 18
And blast of trumpets. He who hath been doomed — 574 *Chiabrera* 4. 5
The cataracts blow their trumpets from the steep; — 588 *Immortality* 25
Trumpet-tones. Those trumpet-tones of harmony that shake — 668 *Prelude* 5. 205
Trumpet-wearied. And to the soldier's trumpet-wearied ear; — 455 *Rydal Mere* 30
Trunk. Gracefully up the gnarled trunk; nor left we unsurveyed — 92 *Poet's Dream* 39
For, deftly framed within the trunk, the sanctuary showed, — 92 *Poet's Dream* 45
Huge trunks! and each particular trunk a growth — 185 *Yew-trees* 16
Haunts the old trunk; lamenting deeds of which — 219 *Haunted Tree* 29
And useless arms, a trunk of man, — 294 *Jedbor.* 18
By skeleton arms, that, from the mountain's trunk — 353 *Aquap.* 44
Further to force their way, endowed its trunk — 354 *Aquap.* 140
Upon a pine-tree's storm-uprooted trunk, — 362 **List—'twas* 77
To his huge trunk, or, with more subtle art, — 393 *Hart's-horn* 2
Round the decaying trunk of human pride, — 424 *Ecc. Sonn.* 1. 21. 8
That, round his trunk and branches, might have clung — 585 *Ch. Lamb* 75
With sinuous trunk, boughs exquisitely wreathed, — 676 *Prelude* 6. 77
The trunk and every master branch were green — 676 *Prelude* 6. 81
A travelling cripple, by the trunk cut short, — 690 *Prelude* 7. 203
Who trembled, trunk and limbs, like some huge oak — 840 *Excursion* 6. 144
By dances round its trunk.—And if the sky — 851 *Excursion* 6. 835
The trunk and body of its marvellous strength, — 866 *Excursion* 7. 610
Around whose trunk the maidens dance in May— — 866 *Excursion* 7. 621
Trunk's. High on the trunk's projecting brow, — 169 *Wren's Nest* 41
Trunks. Huge trunks! and each particular trunk a growth — 185 *Yew-trees* 16
That chooses to be reared upon their trunks. — 657 *Prelude* 3. 546
Of the rude pile; as ofttimes trunks of trees, — 871 *Excursion* 7. 916
Trust. Bidding me trust in God, he stood and prayed;— — 28 *Guilt* 241
Out of that deed. My trust, Saviour! is in thy name!" — 36 *Guilt* 657
I dare not trust myself with such a thought— — 42 *Bord.* 289
You will be firm': but though we well may trust — 48 *Bord.* 602
But yet I trust, Idonea, thou art safe. — 57 *Bord.* 1101
He that puts his trust in me shall not fail!" — 63 *Bord.* 1414
In this deep sorrow, trust, that I am thine — 76 *Bord.* 2201
Were natural enough; but that, I trust, — 77 *Bord.* 2279
That now I should restore what hath been held in trust." — 104 *Artegal* 137
I trust it is,—and never dry: — 111 *A Complaint* 14
I may not trust thy placid cheer! — 112 *Lament* 9
Urged her steps; she shrunk from trust — 141 *Arm. Lady* 80
And trust me, on some sultry noon, — 156 *Oak and Broom* 48
"Trust, angry Bard! a knowing Sprite, — 164 *Needlecase* 37
Had heretofore, in humble trust, — 168 *Pilgrim's Dream* 62
Yet, trust the Muse, it rather hath — 181 *Waggoner* 4. 132
Of kindness and of love. Nor less, I trust, — 206 *Tintern* 35
Trust in that sovereign law can spread — 224 *'*Tis gone* 58
Becoming thoughts, I trust, of solemn gloom — 264 **Lady! the* 10
To trust a Poet in still musings bound. — 273 **Wild Redbreast* 14
And trust that spiritual Creatures round us move, — 273 **When Philoctetes* 9
Has sown as yields, we trust, the fruit of fame — 278 *Wellington* 12
The Child; when she can trust her eyes, — 297 *Highland Boy* 234
(Penance their trust, and prayer their store;) — 298 *Brownie's Cell* 6
With local sanctities in trust, — 301 *Bran* 90
The Land we from our fathers had in trust, — 315 **The Land* 1
Their God, and placed their trust in human pride! — 321 **Humanity, delighting* 18
A Pile that Grace approves, and Time can trust — 327 *Ode 1815* 55
Where simple Sufferers bend, in trust — 337 *Cath. Cantons* 5
Nor is least pleased, we trust, when golden beams, — 354 *Aquap.* 111
By conflict, and their opposites, that trust — 355 *Aquap.* 147
Fulfilment; but, we trust, her upward track — 360 *Albano* 11
All trust abandoned in the healing might — 363 **The world forsaken* 3
Drove from itself, we trust, all frightful gloom. — 391 *Brownie* 14
Our noblest blood is given in trust, — 403 *White Doe* 647
"Then Francis answered—'Trust thy Son, — 410 *White Doe* 1310
Our mortal ken! Inspire a perfect trust — 437 *Ecc. Sonn.* 2. 36. 2
Suppliants! the God to whom your cause ye trust — 448 *Ecc. Sonn.* 3. 30. 13
The prayers, the contrite struggle, and the trust — 451 *Ecc. Sonn.* 3. 41. 13

Trust—*continued.*
(Nor in this vision be thou slow to trust) — 452 *Ecc. Sonn.* 3. 47. 10
In kindred quiet I repose my trust. — 464 **A point* 4
Too blindly have reposed my trust: — 492 *Duty* 28
Who comprehends his trust, and to the same — 493 *Hap. War.* 39
On earth, will be revived, we trust, in heaven. — 510 **Among a* 32
Then trust thy cause to the arm of Fortitude, — 515 **Ah why* 13
Patience, with trust that, whatsoe'er the way — 520 *Pun. Death* 14. 12
Not oftentimes, I trust, as we, poor brute! — 523 *Epist. Beaumont* 139
Yet, Beaumont, thou wilt not, I trust, reprove — 525 *Epist. Beaumont* 274
Can scarcely trust his eyes, when he perceives — 541 *Grace Darl.* 68
Oft is the medal faithful to its trust — 546 **Oft is* 1
What is friendship?—do not trust her, — 549 *Hermit's Cell* 1. 13
And, if she trust the stars above — 550 *Hermit's Cell* 5. 7
And full-assurèd trust, joy without measure, — 559 *Cuck.and Night.* 154
For trust me well, in spite of thy quaint cry, — 560 *Cuck.and Night.* 182
The Cuckoo trust not thou, nor his Love's saw; — 561 *Cuck.and Night.* 237
And trust in God—to whose eternal doom — 574 *Chiabrera* 3. 19
In sorrow, but for higher trust, — 580 *John Words.* 33
The holier deprecation, given in trust — 584 **With copious* 42
His moiety in trust, till Joy shall lead — 586 *Ch. Lamb* 130
Severely honest, break no plighted trust, — 619 *School Ex.* 87
In secret did, we trust, her loss bemoan. — 627 **When Severn's* 8
Before thy Majesty, in humble trust — 628 **Deign, Sovereign* 18
Who, faithful to a pious trust, — 629 *Installation* 81
Take refuge and beguile myself with trust — 635 *Prelude* 1. 235
My story early—not misled, I trust, — 641 *Prelude* 1. 613
He said, "My trust is in the God of Heaven, — 665 *Prelude* 4. 459
Or draws for minds that are left free to trust — 669 *Prelude* 5. 276
Which also first emboldened me to trust — 675 *Prelude* 6. 53
Even at that early time, needs must I trust — 679 *Prelude* 6. 309
Most feelingly, could overthrow my trust — 709 *Prelude* 8. 649
To trust in; that the godhead which is ours — 721 *Prelude* 10. 203
Were flattered, and had trust in human kind: — 723 *Prelude* 10. 388
Thus far our trust is verified; behold! — 726 *Prelude* 10. 582
To daunt me; in the People was my trust, — 727 *Prelude* 11. 11
Trust the elevation which had made me one — 735 *Prelude* 12. 61
Knowledge was given accordingly; my trust — 740 *Prelude* 13. 55
With overweening trust alone we give — 742 *Prelude* 13. 170
Most worthy then of trust when most intense. — 748 *Prelude* 14. 123
And balanced by pathetic truth, by trust — 750 *Prelude* 14. 296
Of firmer trust, joint labourers in the work — 752 *Prelude* 14. 441
And I exhorted her to place her trust — 768 *Excursion* 1. 807
An overweening trust was raised; and fear — 775 *Excursion* 2. 241
From seats of power divine; and hope, or trust, — 790 *Excursion* 3. 257
I promised also,—with undaunted trust — 797 *Excursion* 3. 764
Be left him, trust the freight of his distress — 798 *Excursion* 3. 845
But leave me unabated trust in thee— — 802 *Excursion* 4. 60
Trust me, pronouncing on your own desert, — 808 *Excursion* 4. 478
Guides to destruction? Is it well to trust — 812 *Excursion* 4. 771
With sparing hand. Then trust yourself abroad — 819 *Excursion* 4. 1193
Trust me, that for the instructed, time will come — 819 *Excursion* 4. 1235
When they, who for this Minor hold in trust — 826 *Excursion* 5. 275
Into the second ark, Christ's church, with trust — 826 *Excursion* 5. 282
Doubt to cast off and weariness; in trust — 827 *Excursion* 5. 304
Of safest guidance or of firmest trust— — 827 *Excursion* 5. 335
To trust the smiling aspect of this fair — 828 *Excursion* 5. 422
True to their choice; and gave their bones in trust — 844 *Excursion* 6. 410
We, whose established and unfailing trust — 846 *Excursion* 6. 560
And everlasting flowers. These Dalesmen trust — 847 *Excursion* 6. 610
Not seeking from that source, she placed her trust — 849 *Excursion* 6. 723
And her uncharitable acts, I trust, — 850 *Excursion* 6. 775
Nor will, I trust, the Majesty of Heaven — 866 *Excursion* 7. 579
And placing trust in privilege confirmed — 872 *Excursion* 7. 991
And not presumptuously, I trust, of Age, — 885 *Excursion* 9. 51
Trust not to partial care a general good; — 890 *Excursion* 9. 405
Trusted. Trusted my life to what chance bounty yields, — 32 *Guilt* 435
I should at once be trusted, not defied, — 104 *Artegal* 148
When trusted to another's care. — 175 *Waggoner* 1. 123
But the nimble Hare hath trusted — 490 *Incident: Dog* 19
Him who too boldly trusted them, I felt — 720 *Prelude* 10. 181
Far less than once I trusted and believed— — 835 *Excursion* 5. 854
Trustier. Gathering up a trustier line. — 163 *Spinning Wheel* 12
The quickening spindle drew a trustier line. — S.3. 427 **Through Cumbrian* 14
Trustiest. Against the threatening foe your trustiest shields." — 263 **While not* 8
Trusting. Much she rejoiced, trusting that from that hour — 139 *Widow* 23
Trusting to crowded factory and mart — 255 *S. H.* 12
The Church, when trusting in divine command — 281 *Chris. Words.* 5
In whose experience trusting, day by day — 352 *H. C. R.* 2
With morals, trusting, in contempt or fear — 357 *Aquap.* 334
Yea, trusting in God's holy aid, — 401 *White Doe* 488
Trusting himself to the earth, and God. — 404 *White Doe* 731
The Standard trusting to the care — 405 *White Doe* 805
Trusting in hope that Others may advance — 445 *Ecc. Sonn.* 3. 19. 11
Our Church prepares not, trusting to the might — 450 *Ecc. Sonn.* 3. 40. 7
Now dupes me, trusting to an anxious eye — 635 *Prelude* 1. 247
Thy favour; trusting that thou wilt not deem — 753 **Oft, through* 13
Trusting ourselves, we wound from crag to crag, — 777 *Excursion* 2. 404
And trusting only to his own weak hands, — 841 *Excursion* 6. 220
Trusting her child, she left their common home, — 852 *Excursion* 6. 946
Trusting that not incongruously I blend — 873 *Excursion* 7. 1046
Trusts. Of nature trusts the Mind that builds for aye; — 259 **A volant* 6
Trusts to your love and vivid memory; — 333 *Ded. Tour* 12
His volant Spirit will, he trusts, ascend — 366 *Lombardy* 13

Truth—*continued.*
He with a smile made answer, that in truth 666 *Prelude* 5. 52
On poetry and geometric truth, 666 *Prelude* 5. 65
In gratitude, and for the sake of truth, 669 *Prelude* 5. 265
Simplicity in habit, truth in speech, 672 *Prelude* 5. 421
With kindred matter, 'twas to me, in truth, 672 *Prelude* 5. 467
When sober truth and steady sympathies, 673 *Prelude* 5. 542
Working within us,—nothing less, in truth, 674 *Prelude* 5. 572
To tell us what is passion, what is truth, 676 *Prelude* 6. 113
Of gentleness, simplicity, and truth, 679 *Prelude* 6. 262
Nor had, in truth, the scheme been formed by me 680 *Prelude* 6. 329
Upon the word of heaven-imparted truth, 682 *Prelude* 6. 460
Divulged by Truth and magnified by Fame; 691 *Prelude* 7. 293
But seldom led, or wished to go; in truth 693 *Prelude* 7. 398
Murmur (for truth is hated, where not loved) 695 *Prelude* 7. 532
And Ossian (doubt not—'tis the naked truth) 695 *Prelude* 7. 567
Of courage, or integrity, or truth, 696 *Prelude* 7. 600
Whose truth is not a motion or a shape 703 *Prelude* 8. 298
I had my face turned toward the truth, began 704 *Prelude* 8. 323
Was to the truth conducted; of this faith 707 *Prelude* 8. 526
Of an enthusiast; yet, in honest truth, 710 *Prelude* 9. 71
In his own body. 'Twas in truth an hour 712 *Prelude* 9. 161
Hater perverse of equity and truth. 714 *Prelude* 9. 287
From lowly sympathy and chastening truth: 714 *Prelude* 9. 351
Capable of clear truth, the one to break 714 *Prelude* 9. 358
Of truth preserved and error passed away; 715 *Prelude* 9. 367
Then doubt is not, and truth is more than truth,— 715 *Prelude* 9. 404
Of truth and justice, either sacrifice, 721 *Prelude* 10. 187
Yea, afterwards—truth most painful to record!— 722 *Prelude* 10. 284
Then was the truth received into my heart, 725 *Prelude* 10. 464
What then I learned, or think I learned, of truth, 731 *Prelude* 11. 286
Pains-taking thoughts, and truth, their dear reward) 732 *Prelude* 11. 327
Or, if that fountain be in truth no more, 734 *Prelude* 11. 466
Dispensing truth, and, over men and things, 735 *Prelude* 12. 46
In truth, the degradation—howsoe'er 737 *Prelude* 12. 193
Against the blowing wind. It was, in truth, 738 *Prelude* 12. 253
That energy by which he seeks the truth, 740 *Prelude* 13. 8
By gratitude, and confidence in truth. 740 *Prelude* 13. 15
Effeminately level down the truth 743 *Prelude* 13. 212
Deal boldly with substantial things; in truth 743 *Prelude* 13. 235
Connected in a mighty scheme of truth, 744 *Prelude* 13. 302
Do I declare—in accents which, from truth 748 *Prelude* 14. 144
Without Imagination, which, in truth, 749 *Prelude* 14. 189
And balanced by pathetic truth, by trust 750 *Prelude* 14. 296
Then, though (too weak to tread the ways of truth) 752 *Prelude* 14. 433
Of Truth, of Grandeur, Beauty, Love, and Hope, 755 *Recluse* 1. 1. 767
Which, if with truth it correspond, and sink 757 *Excursion* 1. 103
The purer elements of truth involved 760 *Excursion* 1. 253
He clothed the nakedness of austere truth. 760 *Excursion* 1. 269
But, in good truth, I've wandered much of late; 767 *Excursion* 1. 754
But let us hence, that we may learn the truth: 777 *Excursion* 2. 399
"In truth the threat escaped me unawares: 782 *Excursion* 2. 730
May'st penetrate, wherever truth shall lead; 787 *Excursion* 3. 109
Irksome sensations; but by love of truth 790 *Excursion* 3. 287
From each to all, for wisdom's sake:—This truth 792 *Excursion* 3. 442
These hoards of truth you can unlock at will: 809 *Excursion* 4. 570
—Truth has her pleasure-grounds, her haunts of ease 810 *Excursion* 4. 588
And course of service Truth requires from those 810 *Excursion* 4. 596
Seeks, yet can nowhere find, the light of truth. 810 *Excursion* 4. 630
With truth, the scale of intellectual rank?" 813 *Excursion* 4. 778
Which to the sun of truth he can apply, 813 *Excursion* 4. 809
My heart a daily sacrifice to Truth, 816 *Excursion* 4. 982
I now affirm of Nature and of Truth, 816 *Excursion* 4. 983
Is yet preserved to principles of truth, 818 *Excursion* 4. 1127
Through his acquaintance with the ways of truth, 823 *Excursion* 5. 42
In holiness and truth." "You cannot blame," 826 *Excursion* 5. 292
Of truth and justice. Turn to private life 828 *Excursion* 5. 381
Grave, and in truth too often sad.—"Is Man 829 *Excursion* 5. 465
Thus comprehension fails, and truth is missed; 830 *Excursion* 5. 511
By act of naked reason. Moral truth 831 *Excursion* 5. 562
Founded in truth; by blood of Martyrdom 838 *Excursion* 6. 9
—And, as on earth it is the doom of truth 839 *Excursion* 6. 53
Resolved to quell his pain, and search for truth 840 *Excursion* 6. 152
Who strove to instil this truth into his mind, 840 *Excursion* 6. 165
Temptation here is none to exceed the truth; 847 *Excursion* 6. 601
Truth every day exemplified, no less 848 *Excursion* 6. 669
His knowledge, wisdom, love of truth, and love 854 *Excursion* 6. 1067
(For such in truth it is, and appertains 858 *Excursion* 7. 56
Discoursed of natural or moral truth 865 *Excursion* 7. 512
A type and shadow of an awful truth; 865 *Excursion* 7. 527
Is paid without reluctance; but in truth," 866 *Excursion* 7. 588
Hath here delivered; words of heartfelt truth, 873 *Excursion* 7. 1054
I said, "And, did in truth those vaunted Arts 877 *Excursion* 8. 232
Upon the steadfast 'vantage-ground of truth. 882 *Excursion* 8. 533
From common understanding; leaving truth 887 *Excursion* 9. 233
The mind with moral and religious truth, 888 *Excursion* 9. 302
The sacred truth to acknowledge, linger still; 894 *Excursion* 9. 654
With scantiest knowledge, master of all truth 895 *Excursion* 9. 736
Emblem of equanimity and truth, S.3. 437 **The doubt* 198
(For I who live to register the truth K.8. 237 *Recluse* 1.1. 47
That feared, or wholly overlooked the truth, K.8. 245 *Recluse* 1.1.310
His yell repeating; yet it was in truth K.8. 245 *Recluse* 1.1.325
Yet is it something gained, it is in truth K.8. 246 *Recluse* 1.1.358
Truth justifies herself, and as she dwells K.8. 250 *Recluse* 1.1.500
And Truth had blest the logic of his sword. L.1. 97 *Juvenal* 3. 66
Truth's. When Fancy was Truth's willing Page; 154 *Flower Garden* 54
Orphean Insight! truth's undaunted lover, 234 *Power of Sound* 115
The words of truth's memorial vow 348 **Lulled by* 62
Truth's holy lamp pure source of bright effect, 380 *Duddon* 18. 7

Truth's—*continued.*
Suffered in silence for Truth's sake; or tell, 635 *Prelude* 1. 205
Were tasteless, and truth's golden mean, a point 704 *Prelude* 8. 382
With zeal expanding in Truth's holy light, 720 *Prelude* 10. 138
Which, for truth's sake, yet in remembrance too 781 *Excursion* 2. 626
Truth's consecrated residence, the seat 876 *Excursion* 8. 146
Who from truth's central point serenely views 883 *Excursion* 8. 599
Truths. From the truths of homely reason 90 *Longest Day* 23
Hear the homely truths I tell, 94 *Westmoreland Girl* 58
His simple truths did Andrew glean 155 *Oak and Broom* 1
Admonished by these truths, and quench all pain 317 **Call not* 13
Diluvian truths, and patriarchal lore. 419 *Ecc. Sonn.* 1. 3. 7
Toward the pure truths this Delegate propounds, 422 *Ecc. Sonn.* 1. 15. 10
Of truths that soften hatred, temper strife. 443 *Ecc. Sonn.* 3. 11. 14
Truths whose thick veil Science has drawn aside? 469 **Desire we* 3
Some random truths he can impart,— 485 *Poet's Epitaph* 50
Truths of the heart flock in with eager pace, 503 *Warning* 24
On whom those truths do rest, 589 *Immortality* 115
Of the eternal Silence: truths that wake, 589 *Immortality* 159
Nor general Truths, which are themselves a sort 634 *Prelude* 1. 151
Of contemplation, what intuitive truths, 675 *Prelude* 6. 39
(Then first a self-taught pupil in its truths) 677 *Prelude* 6. 150
The truths of young and old. Nor, side by side 683 *Prelude* 6. 547
The awful truths delivered thence by tongues 695 *Prelude* 7. 547
On the other side, I called to mind those truths 721 *Prelude* 10. 191
But from these bitter truths I must return 728 *Prelude* 11. 74
Great truths, than touch and handle little ones. 740 *Prelude* 13. 54
And truths of individual sympathy 741 *Prelude* 13. 112
From mouths of men obscure and lowly, truths 742 *Prelude* 13. 183
For apprehension those transcendent truths 802 *Excursion* 4. 96
The clearest apprehension of those truths, 830 *Excursion* 5. 520
Whispering those truths in stillness, which the Word, 837 *Excursion* 5. 992
Embodied and established these high truths 837 *Excursion* 5. 1000
The head and mighty paramount of truths,— 839 *Excursion* 6. 85
Had moralised on this, and other truths 845 *Excursion* 6. 442
Fictions in form, but in their substance truths, 846 *Excursion* 6. 545
Tremendous truths! familiar to the men 846 *Excursion* 6. 546
Whose grateful owner can attest these truths, 855 *Excursion* 6. 1140
To gloom imperishable. So (if truths S.3. 435 **The doubt* 110
Try. In vain to find a friendly face we try, 35 *Guilt* 602
Moves me beyond my bearing.—I will try 52 *Bord.* 801
Resolved to try his fortune on the seas. 100 *Brothers* 306
'Twere worth a wise man's while to try 177 *Waggoner* 2. 72
His force on Caspian foam to try; 213 *Dion* 72
Yea, both for souls who God's forbearance try, 229 *Cuckoo-clock* 43
Come, Spirits of the Mind! and try, 245 *P. B.* 783
Survive, and Fortune's utmost anger try; 265 **When haughty* 5
For you, on these unfinished shafts to try 335 *Cologne* 9
Of years hemmed round, had dwelt, prepared to try 391 *Brownie* 6
And has a Champion risen in arms to try 426 *Ecc. Sonn.* 1. 32. 9
Ah! scorn not hastily their rule who try 467 *St. Bees* 86
May try this modern system by its fruits, 670 *Prelude* 5. 295
To try her strength among harmonious words; 704 *Prelude* 8. 369
They try all frolic motions; flutter, plunge, K.8. 251 *Recluse* 1.1.550
Are called to try their prowess with his Grace. L.1. 96 *Juvenal* 3. 28
Trying. Nearer and nearer comes the trying hour! 22 *Desc. Sk.* 641
And Peter many tricks is trying, 245 *P. B.* 798
Trying their strength, enforced him to start up. 718 *Prelude* 9. 577
Trysting. In his pure presence near the trysting thorn— 383 *Duddon* 28. 13
Trysting-place. Here may the aspirant find a trysting-place S.3. 436 **The doubt* 148
Tub. What wonder? on my soul 'twould split a tub L.1. 95 *Juvenal* 3. 10
Tube. The thundering tube the aged angler hears, 11 *Desc. Sk.* 61
Whose sentient tube instructs to time 342 *Ital. Itin.* 23
The Dalesmen may have aimed the deadly tube, K.8. 244 *Recluse* 1.1.266
Tubed. While the tubed engine feels the inspiring blast, 332 *Ode: Thanks.* 216
Tuft. *See* **Primrose-tuft.**
Have you observed a tuft of wingèd seed 123 *V. and J.* 136
Not seldom did we stop to watch some tuft 148 **A narrow* 17
Amid yon tuft of hazel trees, 159 *Green Linnet* 25
Like yon Tuft of Fern; 163 *Hint* 24
Spreads o'er this tuft of heath, which now, attired 219 *Haunted Tree* 8
Yon tuft conceals your home, your cottage bow'r, 596 *Ev. Wk. Quarto* 227
Throughout the landscape; tuft, stone, scratch minute— 691 *Prelude* 7. 258
Is lost within a little tuft of trees; 858 *Excursion* 7. 45
That little shady spot, that sylvan tuft, 858 *Excursion* 7. 50
Of meadow-flowers into a tuft of wood, K.8. 237 *Recluse* 1.1. 42
Tufted. And tufted with an ivy grove; 246 *P. B.* 855
A hut, by tufted trees defended, 414 *White Doe* 1692
Whose battlements were screened by tufted trees. 823 *Excursion* 5. 81
Tufts. *See* **Orchard-tufts.**
Where tufts of herbage tempted each, were busy at their feed, 91 *Norman Boy* 11
And hung with heavy tufts of moss, 197 *Thorn* 14
With heavy tufts of moss that strive 200 *Thorn* 234
Through primrose tufts, in that green bower, 482 *Lines: Spring* 9
And, as his tufts of leaves he spreads, content 529 *Poor Robin* 7
Catching from tufts of grass and hare-bell flowers 678 *Prelude* 6. 221
Hung down in heavier tufts; and that bright weed, 767 *Excursion* 1. 716
With tufts and hairs of wool, as if the sheep, 767 *Excursion* 1. 745
And tufts of mountain moss. Mechanic tools 781 *Excursion* 2. 664
Lying full three parts buried among tufts 784 *Excursion* 2. 818
Shagged with wild pale green tufts of fragrant bay, S.3. 417 **Sweet was* 3
Tugging. Tugging at the iron chain, 181 *Waggoner* 4. 98
Tugging all with might and main, 181 *Waggoner* 4. 99
Tumble. By rills that tumble down the woody steeps, 595 *Ev. Wk. Quarto* 197

Turn—*continued.*

Which way soe'er I turn, I am perplexed. . . . 53 *Bord.* 878
Now may I perish if this turn do more . . . 55 *Bord.* 991
Work on her nature, and so turn compassion . . 57 *Bord.* 1061
Will turn perforce and seek for sympathy . . . 64 *Bord.* 1454
Who will turn pale upon you, call you murderer, 64 *Bord.* 1509
Substitutes, turn our faces where we may, . . 65 *Bord.* 1525
he strove to turn from me . . . . . . 72 *Bord.* 1940
Ay—you may turn that way—it is a grave . . 99 *Brothers* 238
Turn from me, gentle Love! nor let me walk 111 *'Tis said that some* 50
Turn rather, though I love her well: . . . . 121 *EmigrantMother* 72
And all uncertain whither he should turn, . . 122 *V. and J.* 75
How turn to left, and how to right. . . . . 126 *Idiot Boy* 56
Which way to turn she cannot tell. . . . . 129 *Idiot Boy* 268
If from the public way you turn your steps . . 131 *Michael* 1
At gate or gap, to stem or turn the flock; . . 134 *Michael* 186
And of this moment; hither turn thy thoughts, . 137 *Michael* 407
And one chance look to Thee should turn, . . 158 **In youth* 50
Swiftly turn the murmuring wheel! . . . . 163 *Spinning Wheel* 1
Turn the swift wheel round and round! . . . 163 *Spinning Wheel* 6
Can turn to little things; but once . . . . 169 *Wren's Nest* 47
One after One they take their turn, nor have I one espied . . . . 189 *Star-gazers* 31
Nor turn thy face away . . . . 215 *Enterprise* 11
From turmoil, who would turn or speed . . . 223 *Wishing-gate* 56
A reconciling thought may turn . . . . . 224 **'Tis gone* 44
Not only stop but turn, and change . . . . 243 *P. B.* 657
And, grinning in his turn, his teeth . . . . 245 *P. B.* 831
That served my turn, when following still . . . 246 *P. B.* 863
Turn to him, seek him day and night, ... 247 *P. B.* 949
When will she turn, and whither? She will brook 258 **With Ships* 12
Teaching the docile waters how to turn, . . . 269 *Gordale* 12
All turn, and court the shining and the green, . . 278 **Life with* 10
Do thou, in turn, be paramount; and rule . . 290 *Kilchurn* 25
"Whate'er betide, we'll turn aside, ... 292 *Yarrow Unv.* 7
Nor turn aside to Yarrow. . . . . 292 *Yarrow Unv.* 16
But, though so near, we will not turn . . . . 293 *Yarrow Unv.* 39
To the paternal floor; or turn aside, ... 320 **O'erweening Statesmen* 5
Turn from the fortified and threatening hill, . . 335 *Namur* 10
But from our course why turn—to tread . . . 344 **How blest* 66
—Oh what a spectacle at every turn . . . . 355 *Aquap.* 192
Thus, if from two fair eyes mine cannot turn, . . 365 **Rapt above* 9
And loosened from the world, I turn to Thee; . 366 **Eternal Lord* 2
That he would turn to Christ our Lord, . . . 372 *Eg. Maid* 226
Of things that may to gladness turn this weeping. 372 *Eg. Maid* 252
Turn from the sight, enamoured Muse—we must; 379 *Duddon* 12. 13
Turn into port; and, reckless of the gale, . . . 379 *Duddon* 13. 10
That thought away, turn, and with watchful eyes 388 *Trosachs* 6
Turn towards the spot where, full in view, . . 398 *White Doe* 167
Nor did he turn aside to prove . . . . . 406 *White Doe* 933
All efforts that would turn aside . . . . . 407 *White Doe* 1067
Turn from us all the coming woe: . . . . . 408 *White Doe* 1085
How happy in its turn to meet . . . . . . 416 *White Doe* 1826
The *unarmed* Host who by their prayers would turn 421 *Ecc. Sonn.* 1. 12. 5
My feet would rather turn—to some dry nook 424 *Ecc. Sonn.* 1. 22. 2
And turn the instruments of good to ill, . . . 425 *Ecc. Sonn.* 1. 28. 4
Amazement strikes the crowd: while many turn 428 *Ecc. Sonn.* 1. 38. 10
The threshold, whither shall they turn to find 434 *Ecc. Sonn.* 2. 23. 10
Remotest lands and unborn times shall turn, . 444 *Ecc. Sonn.* 3. 15. 10
Turn to minuter changes at our feet; . . . . 456 **Soft as* 7
Homeward we turn. Isle of Columba's Cell, . . 475 **Homeward we* 1
O turn aside,—and take, I pray, ... 485 *Poet's Epitaph* 22
Her hope is near: no turn she makes; . . . 490 *Incident: Dog* 15
If but to God we turn, and ask . . . . . . 495 *Force of Prayer* 67
That civic strife can turn the happiest hearth 504 *Warning* 76
Nor turn aside, unless to shape a way . . . . 504 *Warning* 99
But turn, my Soul, and from the sleeping pair 505 *Warning* 158
Nor will he turn his ear aside . . . . . . 506 *Lab. Hymn* 5
Fond fancies! wheresoe'er shall turn thine eye 511 **So fair* 16
As oft befalls, prevent or turn aside . . . . 517 *Pun. Death* 2. 10
Deed and intent, should turn the Being adrift 519 *Pun. Death* 10. 5
Turn from a spot where neither sheltered road 521 *Epist. Beaumont* 12
Thither your eyes may turn—the Isle is passed away; . . . . 532 †*Float. Isl.* 24
May turn indifference to pride; . . . . . . 534 **Blest is* 64
But turn we from these "bold bad" men; . . 534 **Blest is* 81
Turn a broad front full on his flattering beams: . 539 **Lady! a* 17
Ere he has passed the door, will turn away, . . 567 *Cumb. Beg.* 62
And each, in his turn, becomes leader or led; . 572 *Avarice* 38
But turn we rather, let my spirit turn . . . 586 *Ch. Lamb* 107
Turn wheresoe'er I may, ... 587 *Immortality* 7
Hence shall we turn where, heard with fear afar, . 609 *Desc.Sk.Quarto* 414
Last let us turn to where Chamouny shields, . . 614 *Desc.Sk.Quarto* 680
The wretch on his pallet should turn, ... 621 *Convict* 36
Then every chief in turn the beverage quaff'd. 625 *Æneid* 120
Are mine in prospect; whither shall I turn, . . 632 *Prelude* 1. 27
Of a known Vale, whither my feet should turn, . 633 *Prelude* 1. 72
To others, all supplanted in their turn; . . . 658 *Prelude* 3. 620
A passenger approaching, he would turn . . . 660 *Prelude* 4. 123
To turn from present hardships to the past, . . 665 *Prelude* 4. 436
Of freedom which encouraged me to turn . . . 675 *Prelude* 6. 33
And in the narrow rent at every turn . . . . 684 *Prelude* 6. 627
Turn where I might, was opening out its glories, . 686 *Prelude* 6. 775
Escaped as from an enemy, we turn . . . . 689 *Prelude* 7. 169
In turn its visitant, telling there his hours . . 702 *Prelude* 8. 204
These fictions, as in some sort, in their turn, . . 704 *Prelude* 8. 375
And from the driving current should we turn . . 717 *Prelude* 9. 561
Nor turn of sentiment that might be named . . 722 *Prelude* 10. 271
To turn *all* judgments out of their right course; . 728 *Prelude* 11. 56

Turn—*continued.*

But now, become oppressors in their turn, . . 730 *Prelude* 11. 206
Is seen, heard, felt, and caught at every turn, . 732 *Prelude* 11. 339
Are conversant, subservient in their turn . . . 736 *Prelude* 12. 138
But much was wanting: therefore did I turn 741 *Prelude* 13. 116
Which lacked not voice to welcome me in turn: . 742 *Prelude* 13. 136
When thou dost to that summer turn thy thoughts, 752 *Prelude* 14. 408
Must turn elsewhere—to travel near the tribes 755 *Recluse* 1. 1. 826
Incessantly to turn his ear and eye . . . . 758 *Excursion* 1. 150
That made him turn aside from wretchedness 761 *Excursion* 1. 369
Would turn without an errand his slack steps; 765 *Excursion* 1. 583
From natural wisdom turn our hearts away; . . 765 *Excursion* 1. 601
The little child who sate to turn the wheel . 769 *Excursion* 1. 890
Turn wheresoe'er we would, he was a light . 772 *Excursion* 2. 33
Like human life from darkness."—A quick turn . 786 *Excursion* 3. 35
To turn a slender mill (that new-made plaything) 789 *Excursion* 3. 205
Their aspects lend, and mingle in their turn . . 809 *Excursion* 4. 537
With brotherly resemblance. Turn your steps 809 *Excursion* 4. 553
Substantial, and all crumbling in their turn, . . 810 *Excursion* 4. 604
Or, if the mind turn inward, she recoils . . . 810 *Excursion* 4. 624
His natural wings!—To friendship let him turn 817 *Excursion* 4. 1085
Of death and night, has caught at every turn 818 *Excursion* 4. 1125
By war, might, if so minded, turn aside . . 823 *Excursion* 5. 33
Of truth and justice. Turn to private life . 828 *Excursion* 5. 381
The old Man's cheek; but, at this closing turn 832 *Excursion* 5. 623
I turn, and reach at last the guiding light; . . 834 *Excursion* 5. 751
The edge of adverse circumstance, and turn . 835 *Excursion* 5. 859
Reading, where'er we turn, of innocent lives, . 847 *Excursion* 6. 628
"Here rests a Mother. But from her I turn . 855 *Excursion* 6. 1115
The never-halting time; or, in her turn, . . . 856 *Excursion* 6. 1181
This keen Destroyer, in his turn, must fall. . . 867 *Excursion* 7. 631
From Age," the Priest continued, "turn your thoughts; . . . . 867 *Excursion* 7. 633
Are profitless to others. Turn we then . . . 880 *Excursion* 8. 391
They cannot lean, nor turn to their own hearts 886 *Excursion* 9. 144
To labour for them; bringing each in turn . . 888 *Excursion* 9. 268
"Turn where we may," said I, "we cannot err . 891 *Excursion* 9. 503
Fainted with fear. Thrice did he turn his face K.8. 229 **I will* 153
Like a frail Bark, weary I turn to Thee,— . . K.8. 266 **Rid of* 3

Turned. At once to pillars turned that flame with gold: . . . . 15 *Desc. Sk.* 280
With indignation turned himself away, ... 23 *Yew-tree* 22
He turned, while rain poured down smoking on every side. . . . . 26 *Guilt* 117
To him we turned:—we had no other aid: . . 29 *Guilt* 257
"No help I sought; in sorrow turned adrift, . . 31 *Guilt* 370
Have I."—She ceased, and weeping turned away; 32 *Guilt* 447
With face to earth; and, as the boy turned round 33 *Guilt* 488
What she had seen and suffered turned her brain. 44 *Bord.* 383
I turned me from the dwellings of my Fathers, . 52 *Bord.* 843
Saw him—his face turned toward me; and I tell thee . . . . 55 *Bord.* 985
And, wheresoe'er I turned me, I beheld . . . 69 *Bord.* 1776
When from these forms I turned to contemplate . 70 *Bord.* 1815
Now with her empty can the Maiden turned away: 87 *Pet-lamb* 15
He to the solitary church-yard turned; . . . . 96 *Brothers* 80
His thoughts were turned on Leonard's luckless fortune, ... 101 *Brothers* 390
As the Priest lifted up the latch, turned round,— 102 *Brothers* 410
By his ungrateful daughters turned adrift. . . 103 *Artegal* 42
And she I cherished turned her wheel . . . . 109 **I travelled* 11
He saw me, and he turned aside, ... 114 *Last of Flock* 11
Turned upon her who bore him, she would stoop 118 *Maternal Grief* 60
Life turned the meanest of her implements, . . 122 *V. and J.* 42
Perhaps he's turned himself about, ... 129 *Idiot Boy* 322
And gently turned the Pony's head . . . . 130 *Idiot Boy* 400
She turned, she tossed herself in bed, ... 130 *Idiot Boy* 417
Turned to the cleanly supper-board, and there, 132 *Michael* 99
He stood alone; whereat he turned his head . 149 **A narrow* 57
And from the gate the Pilgrim turned, . . . 167 *Pilgrim's Dream* 5
He turned, and watched with kindred look . . 167 *Pilgrim's Dream* 14
Can destiny be turned aside? . . . . . . 181 *Waggoner* 4. 119
A nutting-crook in hand; and turned my steps 185 *Nutting* 7
Ere from the mutilated bower I turned . . . 185 *Nutting* 50
Such small machinery as she turned . . . . 195 *Ruth* 250
I turned about and heard her cry, ... 199 *Thorn* 190
Be turned to heaviness and fear. . . . . . 204 *Brougham* 94
How oft, in spirit, have I turned to thee, . . . 206 *Tintern* 55
How often has my spirit turned to thee! . . . 206 *Tintern* 57
Where'er he turned, a natural grace . . . . 212 *Dion*
Where'er he turned, a swan-like grace . . . . 212 *Dion* 2
And turned the thistles of a curse . . . . . 225 *Primrose* 41
Turned round his long left ear. . . . . . . 241 *P. B.* 420
The patient Beast on Peter turned . . . . . 241 *P. B.* 434
He turned the eye-ball in his head . . . . . 241 *P. B.* 439
To the blind work he turned again. . . . . 241 *P. B.* 475
He will be turned to iron soon, ... 242 *P. B.* 522
That earnest Creature turned away, ... 243 *P. B.* 599
And to his book he turned again; . . . . . 244 *P. B.* 747
The Ass turned round his head and *grinned*. . . 245 *P. B.* 825
Now, turned adrift into the past, ... 246 *P. B.* 881
Turned towards a gate that hung in view . . . 247 *P. B.* 982
I turned to share the transport—Oh! with whom 257 **Surprised by* 2
We turned, departing from that solemn sight: . 263 **Those words* 2
Back turned, arms folded, the unapparent face . 277 **Haydon! let* 9
Be turned; and streams of truth dried up, even at their source! . . . . 280 *Plea for Auth.* 14
Sighing I turned away; but ere . . . . . 285 *Grave of Burns* 79
Twice-glorified fields! if in sadness I turned . . 345 *Stanzas: Simplon* 15
Of his last going from Tweed side, thought turned, 353 *Aquap.* 67

Turned—*continued.*
Turned to humbler delights, in which youth might confide, ... 364 *Vallomb.* 14
And turned his eagles back with deep-drawn sighs : 368 *Trajan* 63
To mortals, joy is turned to sorrow ; . . . . 372 *Eg. Maid* 206
Abashed, Sir Dinas turned away ; . . . . . 373 *Eg. Maid* 271
Her silence ; then his thoughts turned round, . 401 *White Doe* 459
To him the Lady turned ; " You said . . . . 409 *White Doe* 1210
And turned away from thee, my Son ! . . . . 410 *White Doe* 1304
Turned to a fearful Thing whose nostrils breathe 439 *Ecc. Sonn.* 2. 43. 10
Her blessings cursed—her glory turned to shame ! 439 *Ecc. Sonn.* 2. 44. 14
He, in disgust, turned from the neighbouring sea 470 **Did pangs* 9
Who faltered not, nor turned aside ; . . . . 473 *Ossian* 56
When with her load she turned about, . . . 537 *Goody Blake* 85
And icy cold he turned away. . . . . . . 537 *Goody Blake* 104
His eyes are turned, and, as he moves along, . . 567 *Cumb. Beg.* 46
Turned his back on the country—and off like a bird. 570 *Farmer* 40
Who checked or turned thy headstrong youth, . 577 **I come* 42
Give, when your thoughts are turned this way, . 577 **I come* 47
And with a deep sadness I turned, to repair . . 620 *Convict* 7
Or not far off. Where'er my footsteps turned, . 622 *Recluse* 1. 1. 90
Strode after me. With trembling oars I turned, . 638 *Prelude* 1. 385
From these I turned to travel with the shoal . . 656 *Prelude* 3. 503
I turned my head to look if he were there ; . . 661 *Prelude* 4. 189
The book, had turned my eyes toward the wide sea. 666 *Prelude* 5. 64
A few short months before. I turned my face . 675 *Prelude* 6. 9
When from the Vallais we had turned, and clomb 683 *Prelude* 6. 562
At full command, to London first I turned, . . 688 *Prelude* 7. 61
Behold, turned upwards, a face hard and strong . 690 *Prelude* 7. 200
Turned this way—that way ! sportive and alert . 693 *Prelude* 7. 438
Caught by the spectacle my mind turned round . 696 *Prelude* 7. 643
I had my face turned toward the truth, began . 704 *Prelude* 8. 323
Of her distress, was known to have turned her steps 704 *Prelude* 8. 385
She was, and with her ready pupil turned . . 705 *Prelude* 8. 424
From those sad scenes when meditation turned, . 709 *Prelude* 8. 654
Turned and returned with intricate delay. . . 709 *Prelude* 9. 8
Exposed to eye and hand where'er I turned. . . 710 *Prelude* 9. 33
To animate the mind that ever turned . . . 717 *Prelude* 9. 534
Had seen the anticipated quarry turned . . . 718 *Prelude* 10. 25
Of Orleans eagerly I turned ; as yet . . . . 719 *Prelude* 10. 95
That very morning had I turned aside . . . 726 *Prelude* 10. 532
Oft, as my thoughts were turned to human kind, 731 *Prelude* 11. 247
Out of a heart that had been turned aside . . 731 *Prelude* 11. 290
But turned to abstract science, and there sought 732 *Prelude* 11. 328
And, turned into a gewgaw, a machine, . . . 732 *Prelude* 11. 369
That, with believing eyes, where'er I turned, . . 745 *Prelude* 13. 344
Turned toward the sun then setting, while that staff 756 *Excursion* 1. 40
Turned inward ; or at my request would sing 757 *Excursion* 1. 66
From ill-requited labour turned adrift . . . . 764 *Excursion* 1. 560
A little while ; then turned her head away 766 *Excursion* 1. 649
Blinding the lower panes. I turned aside, . . 767 *Excursion* 1. 719
Was wasted.—Back I turned my restless steps ; . 767 *Excursion* 1. 731
I turned, and saw her distant a few steps. . . 767 *Excursion* 1. 750
I turned aside in weakness, nor had power . . 770 *Excursion* 1. 919
Upon the breast of Faith. I turned away, . . 770 *Excursion* 1. 955
To what odd purpose have the darlings turned 778 *Excursion* 2. 455
That it is ended." At these words he turned— . 785 *Excursion* 2. 897
Who to the Solitary turned, and said, ... 787 *Excursion* 3. 77
Full on that tender-hearted Man he turned . . 793 *Excursion* 3. 478
Turned inward,—to examine of what stuff . . 796 *Excursion* 3. 696
Which turned an angry beak against the down . 798 *Excursion* 3. 818
Were turned on me—the face of her I loved ; . 798 *Excursion* 3. 853
This answer followed.—" You have turned my thoughts . . . . 815 *Excursion* 4. 919
You turned ; and yet more pleased have from your lips . . . . 833 *Excursion* 5. 730
Then to the Solitary turned, and spake. . . . 839 *Excursion* 6. 94
Thither we turned ; and gathered, as we read, . 846 *Excursion* 6. 513
Turned towards the planet Jupiter that hung 849 *Excursion* 6. 761
I turned, that ye in mind might witness where, . 856 *Excursion* 6. 1190
He turned to this secluded chapelry ; . . . . 859 *Excursion* 7. 134
The pining Solitary turned aside ; . . . . . 871 *Excursion* 7. 903
To which his peaceful fancy oft had turned. . . 872 *Excursion* 7. 940
That tires not, nor betrays. Our life is turned . 885 *Excursion* 9. 113
Were turned to evils that are new and chosen, . 887 *Excursion* 9. 187
Nor think that they are victims—turned to wrongs, 887 *Excursion* 9. 192
I grieve not," to the Pastor here he turned, . . 888 *Excursion* 9. 273
On us the venerable Pastor turned . . . . 894 *Excursion* 9. 680
But turned not without welcome promise made . 895 *Excursion* 9. 775
Their skeletons, turned to brilliant ornaments. . S.3. 434 **The doubt* 54
Turned into blood before her heart-sick eye. . . S.3. 436 **The doubt* 185

Turn'st. Thou turn'st the Wheel that slept with dust o'erspread ; . . . . 255 *S. H.* 3

Turning. *See* **Up-turning.**
Turning past pleasures into mortal pains ; . . 19 *Desc. Sk.* 525
Outstretched, and turning on a restless bed : . 27 *Guilt* 166
They wept—and, turning homeward, cried, . . 83 *Lucy Gray* 41
Her large round wheel was turning. Towards the field . . . . 95 *Brothers* 26
By turning o'er these hillocks one by one, . . 98 *Brothers* 191
At length I to a sudden turning came . . . . 146 **It was an* 20
Turning blossoms inside out ; . . . . . . 171 *Kitten* 68
" Yon screech-owl," says the Sailor, turning . . 179 *Waggoner* 3. 110
Turning them inside out with arch audacity. . . 221 *Triad* 127
When, turning round his head, he sees . . . 240 *P. B.* 384
Two Brothers clomb, and, turning face from face, 276 *Oker Hill* 2
She sate, from notice turning not away, . . . 306 **We had* 6
Turning, for them who pass, the common dust . 351 *Des. Stanzas* 78
The Assailants, turning round and round ; . . 412 *White Doe* 1484
" And, turning from her grave, I met, ... 487 **We walked* 41
To see Presumption, turning pale, refrain . . . 504 *Warning* 70

Turning—*continued.*
Turning with quiet touch the valley's hay, . . 607 *Desc.Sk.Quarto* 274
More often turning to some gentle place . . . 634 *Prelude* 1. 170
Or turning the mind in upon herself, ... 650 *Prelude* 3. 113
Shown by a sudden turning of the road, . . . 664 *Prelude* 4. 388
You," to the Pastor turning thus he spake, . . 832 *Excursion* 5. 628

Turnings. And, through the turnings intricate of verse, ... 674 *Prelude* 5. 603

Turnips. And turnips, and corn-land, and meadow, and lea, ... 569 *Farmer* 19

Turns. Winds met in conflict, each by turns supreme ; 26 *Guilt* 128
He turns his face to heaven. But why so violent 45 *Bord.* 464
Something I strike upon which turns my mind . 51 *Bord.* 783
That turns its goat's-beard flakes of pea-green moss 61 *Bord.* 1295
The Mother, in her turns of anguish, worse . . 118 *Maternal Grief* 42
He's at the guide-post—he turns right ; . . . 127 *Idiot Boy* 94
And to the road she turns her ears, ... 127 *Idiot Boy* 139
Turns to a little tent hard by : . . . . . 176 *Waggoner* 1. 265
The various turns of Crusoe's fate)— . . . . 215 *Enterprise* 6
Turns round his long left ear. . . . . . . 241 *P. B.* 415
Into a thicket turns aside, ... 243 *P. B.* 609
So with his freight the Creature turns . . . 244 *P. B.* 671
Nor once turns round his head to crop . . . 244 *P. B.* 714
He turns aside his head, he pauses ; . . . . 248 *P. B.* 1033
And Peter turns his steps aside . . . . . 248 *P. B.* 1086
I have thought of all by turns, and yet do lie . 253 **A flock* 5
And more would grieve, but that it turns . . 286 *Sons of Burns* 5
Thy presence turns the scale of doubtful fight, . 328 *Ode 1815* 112
Nor turns, nor winds, as doth the liquid flood ; . 351 *Des. Stanzas* 83
Still as he turns, the charmed spectator sees . 367 *Trajan* 15
In every Roman, through all turns of fate, . . 368 *Trajan* 49
From chosen comrade turns, or faithful friend— . 383 *Duddon* 30. 7
But quick the turns of chance and change, . . 408 *White Doe* 1119
Realms quake by turns : proud Arbitress of grace, 427 *Ecc. Sonn.* 1. 36. 1
Under the holy fear of God turns pale ; . . . 446 *Ecc. Sonn.* 3. 23. 8
That we, who contemplate the turns of life . . 476 *Howard* 9
Turns his necessity to glorious gain ; . . . . 493 *Hap. War.* 14
Bent in quick turns each other to undo, . . . 513 *Newspaper* 7
Through the quick turns of many a hollow nook, 523 *Epist. Beaumont* 105
She turns her wheel, if on the road she sees . . 566 *Cumb. Beg.* 34
Turns with less noisy wheels to the roadside, . . 566 *Cumb. Beg.* 41
Death, as she turns her neck the kiss to seek, . 597 *Ev. Wk. Quarto* 287
There turns for glad repose the weary eye ; . . 598 *Ev. Wk. Quarto* 366
She views the gifts ; upon the child then turns . 624 *Æneid* 81
Vain is her wish ; where'er she turns she finds . 634 *Prelude* 1. 130
Turns recreant to her task ; takes heart again, . 636 *Prelude* 1. 258
The head turns round and cannot right itself ; . 658 *Prelude* 3. 623
Would, in their turns, lend ornaments and flowers 695 *Prelude* 7. 569
Turns, and will measure back his course, far back, 709 *Prelude* 9. 5
Amid the turns and counterturns, the strife . . 736 *Prelude* 12. 148
No vain conceits ; provokes to no quick turns . 740 *Prelude* 13. 26
That soonest fails to please, and quickliest turns . 799 *Excursion* 3. 912
Their leafy umbrage, turns the dusky veil . . 817 *Excursion* 4. 1067
Our inquest turns.—Accord, good Sir ! the light . 829 *Excursion* 5. 481
But, in the quicker turns of the discourse, . . 834 *Excursion* 5. 784
And, wheresoe'er the traveller turns his steps, . 876 *Excursion* 8. 128
That turns the multitude of dizzy wheels, . . 877 *Excursion* 8. 178
And cannot come. The boy, where'er he turns, . 878 *Excursion* 8. 302
Or turns the godlike faculty of speech . . . 889 *Excursion* 9. 318

Turret. Though from the same grim turret fell 334 **In Bruges* 11
But from the Castle turret blew . . . . . S.3.431 **The Scottish* 17

Turreted. Of Cybelè was seen, sublimely turreted ! 346 *Processions* 36
And one a turreted manorial hall . . . . . 824 *Excursion* 5. 124

Turret's. Drops on the mouldering turret's head, . 507 *May* 55
Or, not less pleased, lay on some turret's head, . 678 *Prelude* 6. 220

Turrets. Those holy turrets tipped with evening gold, 20 *Desc. Sk.* 564
That, shaped like old monastic turrets, rise . . 335 *Namur* 13
Thou sacred Pile ! whose turrets rise . . . . 341 *San Salv.* 1
Of turrets, and a clash of swords . . . . . 372 *Eg. Maid* 203
Those turrets tipp'd by hope with morning gold, . 614 *Desc.Sk.Quarto* 673
Turrets and pinnacles in answering files, . . . 649 *Prelude* 3. 5

Turtledove. The Turtledove replies : . . . . . 168 *Turtledove* 4

Turtle-shell. The rarest was a Turtle-shell . . . 296 *Highland Boy* 116
Still do they keep the Turtle-shell ; . . . . 297 *Highland Boy* 247

Tusa's. Or seek at eve the banks of Tusa's stream, 13 *Desc. Sk.* 156
Or charms that smile on Tusa's evening stream, . 605 *Desc.Sk.Quarto* 178

Tuscan. A Tuscan audience : but full soon was called 573 *Chiabrera* 2. 17

Tusculum. Shall range of philosophic Tusculum ; . 356 *Aquap.* 254

Tusky. From which the tusky wild boar flies in fear ; 104 *Artegal* 109

Tut. What I am now— Praying or parleying ?—tut ! . . . . 54 *Bord.* 940
Tut ! let them gabble till the day of doom. . . 55 *Bord.* 963

Tutelary. Like a tutelary spirit . . . . . . 142 *Arm. Lady* 147
Invoking Dion's tutelary care, ... 213 *Dion* 40
With tutelary power, ... 342 *Ital. Itin.* 72
For tutelary service, thence had rolled, . . . 379 *Duddon* 15. 7
While, like a tutelary Power, ... 404 *White Doe* 768
With tutelary music, from all harm . . . . . 701 *Prelude* 8. 184
To watch again with tutelary love . . . . . 815 *Excursion* 4. 912

Tutor. Of light was there ;—and thus did I, thy Tutor, ... 465 **Thou look'st* 9
To Tutor or to Tailor, as befell, ... 649 *Prelude* 3. 28

Tutored. *See* **Ill-tutored.**
She trills her song with tutored powers, . . . 165 *Parrot* 19
A light unknown to tutored elegance : . . . 222 *Triad* 162
To the first leagues of tutored passion climb, . . 234 *Power of Sound* 116
Where thoughtful Edwin, tutored in the school . 422 *Ecc. Sonn.* 1. 15. 2
Whose infant soul was tutored to confide . . 504 *Warning* 55
Here tutored for eternity. . . . . 533 **Blest is* 50
May in these tutored days no more be seen . . 651 *Prelude* 3. 153

Tutored—*continued.*
But that one tutored thus should look with awe — 713 *Prelude* 9. 239
From moral purpose—early tutored me — 740 *Prelude* 13. 44
Her mind she strictly tutored to find peace — 854 *Excursion* 6. 1026
Nor would their reason, tutored to aspire — 877 *Excursion* 8. 192
Tu-whit. *Tu-whit—Tu-whoo!* the unsuspecting fowl — 153 *Morn. Ex.* 9
Tu-whoo. *See* **To-whoo.**
Tu-whit—Tu-whoo! the unsuspecting fowl — 153 *Morn. Ex.* 9
Twain. And sorely puzzled are the twain, — 126 *Idiot Boy* 25
From the Cathedral pile; and with the twain — 355 *Aquap.* 174
The twain ere break of day — 543 *Russ. Fug.* 122
It saith, Alas, why severed are we twain? — 565 *Troilus* 161
He chaunts Arcturus,—that fraternal twain — 625 *Æneid* 126
In twain, yet leaving the same outward form. — 693 *Prelude* 7. 391
The twain within our happy cottage born, — 794 *Excursion* 3. 589
'Twas. (*Partial list.*)
'Twas my delight to sit and hear Idonea — 39 *Bord.* 92
'Twas a dull spark—a most unnatural fire — 47 *Bord.* 556
But 'twas an angry night, and o'er our heads — 50 *Bord.* 710
'Twas this that put it in my thoughts—that countenance— — 54 *Bord.* 925
'Twas dark—dark as the grave; yet did I see, — 55 *Bord.* 984
'Twas Johnny, Johnny, everywhere. — 128 *Idiot Boy* 211
And what if he cherished his purse? 'Twas no more — 572 *Avarice* 27
Tweed. Along the confines of the Esk and Tweed — 38 *Bord.* 62
We, neighbours of the Esk and Tweed: 'tis much — 39 *Bord.* 85
Who here, upon the borders of the Tweed, — 41 *Bord.* 208
If once they blew a horn this side the Tweed. — 50 *Bord.* 730
To Tiviot's stream, to Annan, Tweed, and Clyde:— — 219 **This Height* 10
And the pure mountains, and the gentle Tweed, — 292 **Degenerate Douglas* 13
And with the Tweed had travelled; — 292 *Yarrow Unv.* 4
But we will downward with the Tweed, — 292 *Yarrow Unv.* 15
And Dryborough, where with chiming Tweed — 292 *Yarrow Unv.* 19
And leave thy Tweed and Tiviot — 386 *Yarrow Rev.* 52
While Tweed, best pleased in chanting a blithe strain, — 387 *Scott* 6
In warlike trim from Tweed to Tyne, — 403 *White Doe* 689
Or let them cross the River Tweed, — 408 *White Doe* 1099
Tweed-side. Of his last going from Tweed-side, thought turned, — 353 *Aquap.* 67
'Tween. A shadowy link 'tween wakefulness and sleep, — 524 *Epist. Beaumont* 184
Twelfth. To the Twelfth Night, beneath the frosty stars — 851 *Excursion* 6. 837
Twelve. But every night at the first stroke of twelve — 44 *Bord.* 389
She paces out the hour 'twixt twelve and one— — 44 *Bord.* 392
Twelve honest men, plain men, would set us right; — 53 *Bord.* 882
"Twelve steps or more from my mother's door, — 84 *We are Seven* 39
Until a man might travel twelve stout miles, — 95 *Brothers* 9
Twelve years are past since we had tidings from him. — 100 *Brothers* 307
(It will be twelve years since when Spring returns) — 101 *Brothers* 357
The clock is on the stroke of twelve, — 127 *Idiot Boy* 152
Twelve strokes that clock would have been telling — 176 *Waggoner* 2. 7
—Twelve hours, twelve bounteous hours are gone, while I — 192 *Gipsies* 9
"Nay, start not!—wedded wives—and twelve! — 239 *P. B.* 281
Made to the Twelve, survives: lip, forehead, cheek, — 343 *Last Sup.* 10
Twelve years had reigned, a Sovereign dread; — 400 *White Doe* 361
Twelve times her monthly round, — 544 *Russ. Fug.* 258
You might think he'd twelve reapers at work in the Strand. — 570 *Farmer* 72
In childhood, ere he was full twelve years old. — 671 *Prelude* 5. 390
Of twelve ensuing days his frame was wrenched, — 870 *Excursion* 7. 872
Twelve tedious years ago, — S.3. 431 **The Scottish* 2
Twelvemonth. For any lady I have seen this twelvemonth. — 43 *Bord.* 314
Twelvemonth's. A twelvemonth's terror and distress!" — 176 *Waggoner* 1. 252
Twelvemonths. But as a child of twelvemonths old or less, — 553 *Prioress* 32
Twentieth. Alas! the twentieth April of his life — 575 *Chiabrera* 8. 10
Twenty. *See* **Four-and-twenty, Two-and-twenty.**
"The suns of twenty summers danced along,— — 28 *Guilt* 226
I'd wager on his life for twenty years. — 41 *Bord.* 246
Than twenty armies. How? The old blind Man, — 51 *Bord.* 760
Over your head twice twenty years must roll, — 52 *Bord.* 820
Strews twenty acres of good meadow-ground — 60 *Bord.* 1230
As he were twenty fathoms underground. — 61 *Bord.* 1300
Join twenty tapers of unequal height — 65 *Bord.* 1512
For twenty lives. The daylight dawned, and now— — 74 *Bord.* 2100
Through twenty seasons; but he had been reared — 95 *Brothers* 44
And in one night send twenty score of sheep — 97 *Brothers* 153
If he had one, the Youth had twenty homes. — 101 *Brothers* 386
As twenty days are now. — 106 **I've watched* 19
Though younger than himself full twenty years. — 132 *Michael* 80
Whom he twenty winters tended. — 157 *Sexton* 16
Here are twenty souls happy as souls in a dream: — 189 *Music* 42
"Full twenty years are past and gone — 198 *Thorn* 104
Full twenty times was Peter feared — 238 *P. B.* 204
Some twenty fathoms under ground. — 245 *P. B.* 840
Not twenty paces from the door, — 483 *Simon Lee* 42
Like a maiden of twenty he trembles and sighs, — 570 *Farmer* 67
And in the press of twenty thousand thoughts, — 659 *Prelude* 4. 58
"Not twenty years ago, but you I think — 764 *Excursion* 1. 535
Tricks he has twenty, — S.3. 424 *Tinker* 29
Have driven him twenty miles." — K.8. 228 **I will* 122
We were no saints at twenty, be it so; — L.1. 96 *Juvenal* 3. 52
'Twere. (*Partial list.*)
Should hold a place, as if 'twere robbery, — 38 *Bord.* 57
'Twere wrong to trouble you. God speed you both. — 41 *Bord.* 222
'Twere—*continued.*
'Twere well in little, as in great, to pause, — 501 *Humanity* 99
Twice. Over your head twice twenty years must roll, — 52 *Bord.* 820
Twice did I spring to grasp his withered throat, — 53 *Bord.* 890
Twice had he been to me a father, twice — 66 *Bord.* 1606
"Thou know'st that twice a day I have brought thee in this can — 87 *Pet-lamb* 41
And twice in the day, when the ground is wet with dew, — 87 *Pet-lamb* 43
"Thy limbs will shortly be twice as stout as they are now, — 88 *Pet-lamb* 45
Twice every Sabbath-day. — 246 *P. B.* 900
Went twice two hundred yards or more, — 247 *P. B.* 992
Twice seven consenting years have shed — 287 *Highland Girl* 3
Thy fortunes, twice exalted, might provoke — 360 *Alban Hills* 10
Attained a stature twice a tall man's height, — 521 *Epist. Beaumont* 15
Twice in a day it passèd through his throat; — 554 *Prioress* 97
Twice as fast as before does his blood run about; — 570 *Farmer* 54
Nor has the rolling year twice measured, — 586 *Hogg* 13
While twice ten thousand corselets at the view — 612 *Desc. Sk. Quarto* 540
And twice five summers on my mind hād stamped — 640 *Prelude* 1. 560
Twice over with a male and female voice. — 650 *Prelude* 3. 56
Fresh emptied of spectators. Twice five years — 674 *Prelude* 5. 552
Our journey, and ere twice the sun had set — 681 *Prelude* 6. 417
To thee unknown! Twice had the trees let fall — 721 *Prelude* 10. 236
And twice ten thousand interests, do yet prize — 816 *Excursion* 4. 989
The fruits of earth through space of twice ten years, — 841 *Excursion* 6. 231
Suddenly then they disappeared: not twice — 861 *Excursion* 7. 247
Had summer scorched the fields; not twice had fallen, — 861 *Excursion* 7. 248
Twice-glorified. Twice-glorified fields! if in sadness I turned — 345 *Stanzas: Simplon* 15
Twig. Heaven grant that he spare but that one upright twig — 80 †*Address: Child* 24
From twig or bed an humbler flower, even for your sake!" — 139 *Arm. Lady* 12
The towering maize, and prop the twig — 342 *Ital. Itin.* 45
The throng of rooks, that now, from twig or nest, — 455 *Rydal Mere* 8
Stands a tall ash-tree; to whose topmost twig — 851 *Excursion* 6. 863
Twigs. Some limber twigs into a Cross, well-shaped with fingers nice, — 91 *Norman Boy* 19
For you and your green twigs decoy — 156 *Oak and Broom* 45
Were only blossoms dropped from twigs — 170 *Rural Ill.* 23
Green twigs would pluck, as rapidly — 479 *Somnamb.* 107
The budding twigs spread out their fan, — 482 *Lines: Spring* 17
With clustering ivy, and the lightsome twigs — 676 *Prelude* 6. 82
Kindled and burnt among the sapless twigs — 797 *Excursion* 3. 744
Stripped of their leaves and twigs by hoary age, — 814 *Excursion* 4. 880
Why, friend, to deck her supple twigs — S.3. 431 **The Scottish* 7
Upon thy chance-defilements—withered twigs — S.3. 433 **The doubt* 46
In the bare twigs, each little budding place — K.8. 252 *Recluse* 1.1.565
Twilight. Where twilight glens endear my Esthwaite's shore, — 2 *Ev. Wk.* 11
And its own twilight softens the whole scene, — 3 *Ev. Wk.* 61
The half-seen form of Twilight roams astray; — 7 *Ev. Wk.* 292
A sympathetic twilight slowly steal, — 8 *Ev. Wk.* 316
Dim from the twilight water's shaggy side, — 12 *Desc. Sk.* 116
Is gone, and twilight to the Mother's wish — 119 *Maternal Grief* 66
Glimmering through the twilight pale; — 180 *Waggoner* 4. 20
By trees and lingering twilight made! — 180 *Waggoner* 4. 45
Her eyes as stars of Twilight fair; — 186 **She was* 5
Mercy from her twilight throne — 233 *Power of Sound* 29
When twilight shades darken the mountain's head. — 255 *S. H.* 6
Watching the twilight smoke of cot or grange, — 262 **Not Love* 7
Hail, Twilight, sovereign of one peaceful hour! — 265 **Hail, Twilight* 1
By twilight premature of cloud and rain; — 279 **Hark! 'tis* 2
Through twilight shades of good and ill — 286 *Sons of Burns* 7
Its second twilight, and looks gay; — 294 *Jedbor.* 46
Whereat a tender twilight streak — 374 *Eg. Maid* 327
O'er twilight fields the autumnal gossamer? — 378 *Duddon* 11. 14
Survives—the twilight of this day— — 416 *White Doe* 1872
Observe how dewy Twilight has withdrawn — 456 **Soft as* 8
Then, Twilight is preferred to Dawn, — 497 *Lycoris* 21
Mingling with night, such twilight to compose — 498 **Enough of climbing* 27
And gradual progress?—Twilight leads to day, — 516 **Hard task* 9
And now, in twilight dim, — 526 **The soaring* 34
Illumes with sparkling foam the twilight shade. — 593 *Ev. Wk. Quarto* 80
Where, tho' her far-off twilight ditty steal, — 596 *Ev. Wk. Quarto* 225
Protracted, and the twilight storm foretells, — 605 *Desc. Sk. Quarto* 202
Each twilight earlier call'd the Sun to meet, — 610 *Desc. Sk. Quarto* 453
Erroneous wavering mid the twilight shades. — 614 *Desc. Sk. Quarto* 689
To the low-warbled breath of twilight lute, — 615 *Desc. Sk. Quarto* 749
The cottage windows blazed through twilight gloom, — 638 *Prelude* 1. 427
Twilight was coming on, yet through the gloom — 672 *Prelude* 5. 435
That twilight when we first begin to see — 673 *Prelude* 5. 513
The twilight more than dawn, autumn than spring; — 677 *Prelude* 6. 175
Of twilight deepened, going forth, I spied — 687 *Prelude* 7. 32
Grieved, and the twilight taper, and the cross — 716 *Prelude* 9. 475
A twilight of its own, an ample shade, — 756 *Excursion* 1. 12
Or in the gloom of twilight hum their joy? — 808 *Excursion* 4. 448
Of their long twilight, pore upon her book — 852 *Excursion* 6. 901
Then, shall the slowly-gathering twilight close — 862 *Excursion* 7. 356
Twilight's. Like Twilight's, too, her dusky hair; — 186 **She was* 6
Pale twilight's lingering glooms,—and in the sun — 278 **Life with* 5
'Twill. (*Partial list.*) *See* **Will.**
'Twill glad her heart to see her father's signature. — 49 *Bord.* 669
'Twill be between us; but, whatever fate — 137 *Michael* 415
'Twill make a thing endurable, which else — 138 *Michael* 449
'Twill be the traveller's shed, the pilgrim's cot, — 201 *Hart-leap* 59
'Twill be no fruitless moment. I was born — 573 *Chiabrera* 3. 3

Two—*continued.*
That hung between two callings. May no strife 470 **Did pangs* 11
Is stouter of the two. 483 *Simon Lee* 52
And his two pretty pinions of blue dusky gauze 484 **A plague* 24
Its history of two hundred years. 486 *Matthew* 8
That these two words of glittering gold 486 *Matthew* 31
Two shall be named, pre-eminently dear,— 488 *Pers. Talk* 40
Distinguished two for scent, and two for speed. 490 *Incident : Dog* 8
We two have known such happy hours together 498 **Enough of climbing* 46
From his poor inch or two of daisied sod? 527 **Those breathing* 29
Two poor old Dames, as I have known, 536 *Goody Blake* 34
And ever two and two together were, 558 *Cuck. and Night.* 78
Him thought his sorrowful heart would break in two; 562 *Troilus* 12
And thus a day or two drove wearily; 564 *Troilus* 110
Oh, what would they be to my tale of two Thieves? 571 *Avarice* 12
Two Babes were laid in earth before she died; 576 **By a* 9
With two collateral stems sprung from one root; 585 *Ch. Lamb* 97
Still they were faithful; like two vessels launched 586 *Ch. Lamb* 102
In waves, like two enormous serpents, wind 615 *Desc.Sk.Quarto* 696
Two hundred times around the ring of heaven, 618 *School Ex.* 2
And drove us onward like two ships at sea, 622 *Recluse* 1. 1. 160
Or like two birds, companions in mid air, 622 *Recluse* 1. 1. 161
Two hours declined towards the west; a day 633 *Prelude* 1. 67
Two consciousnesses, conscious of myself 642 *Prelude* 2. 32
Was going then to bury those two books: 667 *Prelude* 5. 102
Where had we been, we two, belovèd Friend! 669 *Prelude* 5. 233
Of two delightful hours we strolled along 674 *Prelude* 5. 562
More to myself. Two winters may be passed 675 *Prelude* 6. 22
Predestined, if two beings ever were, 679 *Prelude* 6. 257
Pacing, two social pilgrims, or alone 683 *Prelude* 6. 548
For two days' space, in presence of the Lake, 685 *Prelude* 6. 689
Fresh from a toilette of two hours, ascend 695 *Prelude* 7. 552
Booths are there none; a stall or two is here; 699 *Prelude* 8. 25
When those two vessels with their daring freight, 715 *Prelude* 9. 414
Of the two spirits then at strife remained 727 *Prelude* 11. 25
That, from the meeting-point of two highways 738 *Prelude* 12. 293
That on the line of each of those two roads 739 *Prelude* 12. 322
This is her glory; these two attributes 740 *Prelude* 13. 3
And with a step or two seemed brighter still; 746 *Prelude* 14. 36
In wholesome separation the two natures, 751 *Prelude* 14. 346
Where two tall hedge-rows of thick alder boughs 763 *Excursion* 1. 460
Two blighting seasons, when the fields were left 764 *Excursion* 1. 537
That he had disappeared—not two months gone. 766 *Excursion* 1. 661
He left his house: two wretched days had past, 766 *Excursion* 1. 662
Had twined about her two small rows of peas, 767 *Excursion* 1. 729
Two lovely Children—all that they possessed! 774 *Excursion* 2. 200
A quiet treeless nook, with two green fields, 776 *Excursion* 2. 337
By thrusting two rude staves into the wall 777 *Excursion* 2. 418
To glance an upward look on two huge Peaks, 782 *Excursion* 2. 692
On these two pillars rested as in air 794 *Excursion* 3. 597
The two extremes are equally disowned 805 *Excursion* 4. 268
If two auspicious magpies crossed my way;— 810 *Excursion* 4. 618
My two Associates, in the morning sunshine 823 *Excursion* 5. 63
With her two faculties of eye and ear, 837 *Excursion* 5. 987
Two several souls alternately had lodged, 842 *Excursion* 6. 288
Two sets of manners could the Youth put on; 842 *Excursion* 6. 289
Two doughty champions; flaming Jacobite 845 *Excursion* 6. 458
Than sentinels, between two armies, set, 846 *Excursion* 6. 536
"Two passions, both degenerate, for they both 849 *Excursion* 6. 706
To keep two hearts together, that began 851 *Excursion* 6. 875
Two ruddy children hung, a well-poised freight, 858 *Excursion* 7. 73
"Yet, by the good Knight's leave, the two estates 875 *Excursion* 8. 44
Two eyes—not dim, but of a healthy stare— 880 *Excursion* 8. 409
Of those two boys! yea in the very words 883 *Excursion* 8. 573
Sent from the jocund hearts of those two Boys, 891 *Excursion* 9. 475
From those two Brothers who were drowned therein); K.8. 225 **I will* 22
Of Sheep-cot-cove, and those two other coves, K.8. 225 **I will* 31
Even at the utmost distance of two miles K.8. 225 **I will* 42
Two months unwearied of severest storm, K.8. 241 *Recluse* 1.1.181
But two are missing—two, a lonely pair K.8. 243 *Recluse* 1.1.238
Through these two months of unrelenting storm, K.8. 243 *Recluse* 1.1.244
Of two brave vessels matched in deadly fight, K.8. 256 *Recluse* 1.1.722
The nails, the thorns, and thy two hands, thy face K.8. 266 **Rid of* 6

Two-and-thirty. "He, two-and-thirty years or more, 238 *P. B.* 206

Two-and-twenty. Than two-and-twenty summers had been told— 704 *Prelude* 8. 349

Twofold. For twofold hallowing—Nature's care, and work of human hands? 92 *Poet's Dream* 36
Thy twofold shout I hear; 183 **O blithe* 6
Been stricken by a twofold stroke; 294 *Jedbor.* 73
And lamentably wrapped in twofold night, 323 **Now that* 5
Grasping his twofold treasure.—Lance in rest, 667 *Prelude* 5. 120
He heeded not; but, with his twofold charge 667 *Prelude* 5. 134
A twofold frame of body and of mind. 736 *Prelude* 12. 126
Death and its two-fold aspect! wintry—one, 831 *Excursion* 5. 554
By her offence to lay a twofold weight 852 *Excursion* 6. 943
A twofold image; on a grassy bank 890 *Excursion* 9. 440

Two-handed. That ROLAND clove with huge two-handed sway, 335 *Aix* 12

Twos. The stars are out by twos and threes, 457 **The sun has* 2

'Twould. Is ringing it—'twould stop a Saint in prayer, 67 *Bord.* 1665
Should come, 'twould needs be a glad day for him; 100 *Brothers* 326
Methinks 'twould heighten joy, to overleap 284 *Departure* 5
—'Twould be a *wildish* destiny, 289 *Stepping West.* 2
What wonder? on my soul 'twould split a tub L.1. 95 *Juvenal* 3. 10

Tydides. And the brave Tydides meet. S.3. 442 *Harmodius* 14

Tyne. In warlike trim from Tweed to Tyne, 403 *White Doe* 689

Tyne—*continued.*
Emblem and instrument, from Thames to Tyne, 426 *Ecc. Sonn.* 1. 31. 7
And the skill which he learned on the banks of the Tyne, 571 *Avarice* 2

Tynwald's. Once on the top of Tynwald's formal mound 470 *Tynwald* 1

Type. Cross-bones nor skull,—type of our earthly state 98 *Brothers* 171
Type of the wise who soar, but never roam; 209 **Ethereal minstrel* 11
A type of her capacious self and all 230 *Clouds* 52
And type of man's far-darting reason, therefore 231 *Clouds* 81
If wish were mine some type of thee to view, 268 **Brook! whose* 6
He sets, his sinking yields a type 337 *Thun* 11
A type of age in man, upon its front 355 *Aquap.* 187
Type of a sunny human breast 526 **The soaring* 17
Affecting type of him I mourn! 580 *John Words.* 17
A type, for finite natures, of the one 677 *Prelude* 6. 133
As with the might of waters; an apt type 696 *Prelude* 7. 644
Reflected, it appeared to me the type 747 *Prelude* 14. 66
A type and shadow of an awful truth; 865 *Excursion* 7. 527
Vouchsafed; this local transitory type 893 *Excursion* 9. 619
If I some type of thee did wish to view, K.8. 265 **Brook, that* 6
And see the blue beyond.—Type of that grace [?] **A sad* 9

Types. Loose types of things through all degrees, 158 **With little* 11
To types beneficent. 225 *Primrose* 42
These types mysterious (if the show 299 *Brownie's Cell* 67
Types of the spiritual Church which God hath reared; 451 *Ecc. Sonn.* 3. 42. 2
Faint types of suffering in thy beamless face. 460 **Queen of* 38
The types and symbols of Eternity, 684 *Prelude* 6. 639

Typified. Hath typified by reach of daring art 452 *Ecc. Sonn.* 3. 45. 9

Tyrannic. Of a tyrannic Master whom they loathed. 69 *Bord.* 1759
Tyrannic, keep the Bird of Jove embarred 388 *Eagles* 2
How, in tyrannic times, some high-souled man, 635 *Prelude* 1. 203
To Brutus—that tyrannic power is weak, 721 *Prelude* 10. 200
With abject mind—from a tyrannic lord 798 *Excursion* 3. 875
Said I, "once happy, ere tyrannic power, 823 *Excursion* 5. 93

Tyrannous. The Flood was tyrannous and strong; 155 *Waterfall* 15

Tyranny. Still have I found, where Tyranny prevails, 21 *Desc. Sk.* 597
To-day you have thrown off a tyranny 64 *Bord.* 1488
Of our emasculated souls, the tyranny 64 *Bord.* 1490
The persevering wedge of tyranny 124 *V. and J.* 172
O wretched man, the throne of tyranny! 321 **Here pause* 14
For tyranny subdued, 332 *Ode : Thanks.* 202
Of checked ambition, tyranny controlled, 349 *Boulogne* 11
And Tyranny is balked of her desire: 442 *Ecc. Sonn.* 3. 8. 4
And not alone *harsh* tyranny would cease, 500 *Humanity* 58
To mutual tyranny a deadlier look? 515 **Men of* 8
Through tyranny of sense. 526 **The soaring* 44
And tyranny, and implements of death; 724 *Prelude* 10. 403
This tyranny, summons all the senses each 736 *Prelude* 12. 135

Tyrant. With a vexed people, and the tyrant chased; 103 *Artegal* 80
Call thee worst Tyrant by which Flesh is crost? 253 **Fond words* 11
That day the Tyrant fell. 300 *Cora Linn* 48
There came a Tyrant, and with holy glee 306 **Two Voices* 5
The Tyrant, and confound his cruelty. 314 *Hofer* 14
While all lie prostrate, save the tyrant few 513 *Newspaper* 6
Yet more; the tyrant Genius, still at strife 613 *Desc.Sk.Quarto* 608
Up starts some tyrant, Earth and Heaven to dare, 628 *Installation* 9
Of France a boastful Tyrant hurled his threats; 869 *Excursion* 7. 758
The tyrant felt their arm sublime. S.3. 442 *Harmodius* 20
To hated worth no Tyrant ere design'd L.1. 88 *Juvenal* 1. 3

Tyrant's. Pent in, a Tyrant's solitary Thrall: 308 **There is a bondage* 3
The captive chieftain, by a tyrant's doom, 318 **Is there* 2
Such food a Tyrant's appetite demands; 319 *Spaniard* 4
For the Sicilian Tyrant's overthrow, 715 *Prelude* 9. 415
When the tyrant's heart they gor'd S.3. 442 *Harmodius* 5
Ye the tyrant's bosom gor'd, S.3. 442 *Harmodius* 26

Tyrants. On prosperous tyrants with a dazzled eye; 321 **Here pause* 9
Tyrants exult to hear of kingdoms won, 327 *Ode 1815* 37
Woe! woe to Tyrants! from the lyre 499 **Departing summer* 40
With thy own scorn of tyrants they advance, 628 *Eagle and Dove* 9
Of this new enemy. Tyrants, strong before 723 *Prelude* 10. 333
Tyrants who utter the destroying word, 836 *Excursion* 5. 941

Tyre. That would lament her;—Memphis, Tyre, are gone 425 *Ecc. Sonn.* 1. 25. 12
Alas! too busy Rival of old Tyre, 475 *Greenock* 9
Tyre, by the margin of the sounding waves, 877 *Excursion* 8. 217

Tyrian. And hue far deeper than the Tyrian dye; 618 *School Ex.* 22
His young Ascanius to the Tyrian walls; 624 *Æneid* 28
Reclin'd in festal pomp the Tyrian queen. 624 *Æneid* 57
The learned song from Tyrian hearers draws 625 *Æneid* 130

Tyrians. The Tyrians rushing in, an eager band, 624 *Æneid* 71
To Tyrians, and these exiles driven from Troy; 625 *Æneid* 110
And, Tyrians, may your choicest favours wait 625 *Æneid* 114

Tyrolean. Advance—come forth from thy Tyrolean ground, 314 **Advance—come* 1
And her Tyrolean Champion we behold 317 **The martial* 11

Tyrolese. By whom the undaunted Tyrolese are led? 314 *Hofer* 2

U

Udder. And forced the full-swoln udder to demand, 17 *Desc. Sk.* 397

Ugly. Some ugly witchcraft must be here! 241 *P. B.* 417

Uhlans. With Guards and Uhlans run along the Rhine, L.1. 97 *Juvenal* 3. 64

Under—*continued.*
Under a growing weight of vulgar sense, 748 *Prelude* 14. 159
But, under pressure of a private grief, 752 *Prelude* 14. 419
Under a shade as grateful I should find 756 *Excursion* 1. 19
Under the covert of these clustering elms. 757 *Excursion* 1. 51
Of heath-plant, under and above him strewn, 784 *Excursion* 2. 819
Under a shining canopy of state 784 *Excursion* 2. 863
With answering constellations, under earth, 812 *Excursion* 4. 713
Under a cope of sky more variable, 812 *Excursion* 4. 720
Under his spiritual sway. He hath vouchsafed 824 *Excursion* 5. 106
The vanquished Whig, under a borrowed name, 845 *Excursion* 6. 451
Who pitch their tents under the green-wood tree? 858 *Excursion* 7. 88
Under whose shaggy canopy are set 880 *Excursion* 8. 408
Under a sheltering tree."—Upon this hint 890 *Excursion* 9. 426
Under a faded sky. No trace remained 895 *Excursion* 9. 759
From under thee hath vanished, and slant beams, S.3. 435 **The doubt* 101
And ye as happy under Nature's care, K.8. 251 *Recluse* 1.1.532
Who must inhabit, under a black sky, K.8. 253 *Recluse* 1.1.603
One household under God for high and low, K.8. 253 *Recluse* 1.1.618
By which, and under which, we are enclosed K.8. 254 *Recluse* 1.1.643
Under-agents. Words are but under-agents in their souls; 744 *Prelude* 13. 273
Underboughs. Like leafless underboughs, in some thick wood, 824 *Excursion* 5. 148
Under-countenance. And placid under-countenance, first endeared; 678 *Prelude* 6. 227
Under-coverts. In under-coverts, yet the countenance 655 *Prelude* 3. 433
Under-current. Calm as an under-current, strong to draw 442 *Ecc. Sonn.* 3. 9. 1
Undergo. Through every change its aspects undergo— 455 **Not in the lucid* 23
For you should undergo a sudden change; 805 *Excursion* 4. 283
Undergoes. Or beautifies, like changes undergoes, S.3. 434 **The doubt* 63
Undergone. Debasement undergone by body or mind, 708 *Prelude* 8. 646
And, since their date, my soul hath undergone 803 *Excursion* 4. 124
Is undergone; the transit made that shows 832 *Excursion* 5. 666
And hardship undergone in various climes, 882 *Excursion* 8. 509
Underground. As he were twenty fathoms underground. 61 *Bord.* 1300
Deep underground? Or in the upper air, 378 *Duddon* 11. 12
But not a hint from under-ground, no sign 532 **Once I* 17
Undergrove. I sat within an undergrove 154 **A whirl-blast* 6
While all the undergrove is thick with leaves, 851 *Excursion* 6. 866
Underived. Of fragrance, underived from earth, 371 *Eg. Maid* 147
Underlings. With mighty Nations for his underlings, 309 **When, looking* 4
Undermine. To undermine with secret guile, 550 *Hermit's Cell* 2. 23
Than if their wish had been to undermine 728 *Prelude* 11. 72
That mood, or undermine my first resolve." 781 *Excursion* 2. 617
Undermined. (By throbbing waves long undermined) 531 †*Float. Isl.* 6
Underneath. The still vale lengthens underneath its shade 14 *Desc. Sk.* 217
The worm, that, underneath a stone whose weight 69 *Bord.* 1797
And underneath the hay-stack warm, 144 *Her Eyes* 7
And underneath the spreading tree 145 *Her Eyes* 73
Life slips from underneath us, like that arch 351 *Des. Stanzas* 84
As she passes underneath: 397 *White Doe* 90
Groan underneath a weight of slavish toil, 501 *Humanity* 86
To the great current flowing underneath; 515 **Men of* 11
The still vale lengthens underneath the shade; 607 *Desc.Sk.Quarto* 270
Shall be my harbour? underneath what grove 632 *Prelude* 1. 11
Right underneath, the College kitchens made. 649 *Prelude* 3. 49
A lance he bore, and underneath one arm 666 *Prelude* 5. 78
A glow-worm underneath a dusky plume 687 *Prelude* 7. 33
Rests underneath the little rock-like pile 692 *Prelude* 7. 327
As calmly, underneath the pleasant brows 701 *Prelude* 8. 181
Joust underneath the trees, that as in storm 716 *Prelude* 9. 455
In the empyrean. Underneath that pomp 725 *Prelude* 10. 523
With prospect underneath of Striding edge, K.8. 225 **I will* 29
Than joy itself—for underneath it lies [?] **A sad* 5
Under-powers. Of Elements and Agents, Under-powers, 634 *Prelude* 1. 152
Under-sense. An under-sense of greatest; sees the parts 698 *Prelude* 7. 735
Undersong. Or kettle whispering its faint undersong. 488 *Pers. Talk* 14
Understand. You understand me—I was comforted; 69 *Bord.* 1779
Which Betty well could understand. 126 *Idiot Boy* 66
And honour which they do not understand. 310 **Another year* 14
Whence grace, through which the heart can understand, 423 *Ecc. Sonn.* 1. 19. 13
The things which others understand. 485 *Poet's Epitaph* 56
Of culture, even to feel or understand 626 **Son of* 5
To understand myself, nor thou to know 641 *Prelude* 1. 627
Placed on this earth to love and understand, 750 *Prelude* 14. 278
Self-questioned where it did not understand, 760 *Excursion* 1. 242
"Happy is he who lives to understand, 806 *Excursion* 4. 332
By their condition taught, can understand 813 *Excursion* 4. 787
Understanding. With understanding spirit now may look 435 *Ecc. Sonn.* 2. 29.5
All men may understanding have of me, 559 *Cuck.andNight.*121
Baffled my understanding: how men lived 688 *Prelude* 7. 116
And understanding, I should learn to love 707 *Prelude* 8. 528
The shape of theirs, my understanding bend 713 *Prelude* 9. 253
Than human understanding, their discourse 713 *Prelude* 9. 260
The human Understanding paramount 723 *Prelude* 10. 342
Which passeth understanding, that repose 748 *Prelude* 14. 127
Who, with an understanding heart, allayed 772 *Excursion* 2. 76
Of nature, who with understanding heart 819 *Excursion* 4. 1209
Fancy, and understanding; while the voice 865 *Excursion* 7. 511
From common understanding; leaving truth 887 *Excursion* 9. 233
Understanding's. Could through my understanding's natural growth 730 *Prelude* 11. 200
Understood. The truth should now be better understood; 309 **England! the* 3
Of such high course was felt and understood; 320 **O'erweening Statesmen* 11
In its degree was understood; 415 *White Doe* 1727
So shall the truth be better understood, 515 **Men of* 13
Which yet I understood, articulate sounds, 667 *Prelude* 5. 94
Least understood. Yet, 'mid the fervent swarm 705 *Prelude* 8. 426
Felt deeply, but not thoroughly understood 728 *Prelude* 11. 87
Of being understood at once, or else 743 *Prelude* 13. 214
What was not understood, though known to be; 751 *Prelude* 14. 336
All gratulant, if rightly understood. 751 *Prelude* 14. 387
The individual known and understood; 874 *Excursion* 8. 18
Both understood and practised,—so that none, 888 *Excursion* 9. 303
Undertaken. Have undertaken for a cause so great 720 *Prelude* 10. 153
Undertakes. 'Twas Nature's will; who sometimes undertakes, 842 *Excursion* 6. 301
Undertaking. That, in the undertaking which has caused 37 *Bord.* 6
Under-thirst. Mixed something of stern mood, an under-thirst 683 *Prelude* 6. 558
Undertook. And undertook premonished, if unsound 444 *Ecc. Sonn.* 3. 16. 10
Who promptly undertook the Wain to guide 522 *Epist. Beaumont* 102
Filled with vague hopes, he undertook the charge 774 *Excursion* 2. 174
And undertook with dutiful content 852 *Excursion* 6. 947
Underwalden's. Of pensive Underwalden's pastoral heights. 16 *Desc. Sk.* 339
Underwent. The Muses' modest nurslings underwent 655 *Prelude* 3. 460
Underwood. Of nature's unambitious underwood, 848 *Excursion* 6. 653
Undeserted. In which a cabin undeserted stood; 13 *Desc. Sk.* 146
Undeserved. "Whence the undeserved mistrust? Too wide apart 140 *Arm. Lady* 47
Not undeserved, of the memorial rhymes 472 **The captive* 13
These gashes whence? This undeserved disgrace! L.2. 318 *Frag. Æneid* 4. 8
Undetermined. Worked with a dim and undetermined sense 638 *Prelude* 1. 392
Yet, undetermined to what course of life 688 *Prelude* 7. 58
Undeterred. Will force upon his notice; undeterred 781 *Excursion* 2. 629
My words too long have hindered." Undeterred, 836 *Excursion* 5. 892
Who, by humiliation undeterred, 843 *Excursion* 6. 321
Undevoutly. To cope with Sages undevoutly free. 468 **Ranging the* 14
Undiminished. With undiminished glee, in hoary age. 859 *Excursion* 7. 110
Undimmed. That views, undimmed, Einsiedlen's wretched fane. 20 *Desc. Sk.* 546
Undiscerning. Not dull art Thou as undiscerning Night; 265 **Hail, Twilight* 2
Undischarged. Still undischarged; yet doth she little more 669 *Prelude* 5. 250
Undisciplined. Hard task! exclaim the undisciplined, to lean 515 **Hard task* 1
While yet a youth undisciplined in verse, 685 *Prelude* 6. 670
Undiscoloured. Yet undiscoloured. A capacious pew 825 *Excursion* 5. 164
Undiscordant. Of undiscordant themes; 499 *Departing summer* 21
Undiscouraged. But, undiscouraged, we began to climb 746 *Prelude* 14. 14
Undiscover'd. Unfathom'd dells and undiscover'd woods; 602 *Desc. Sk. Quarto* 10
Undiscriminating. Yet then, from the undiscriminating sweep 682 *Prelude* 6. 487
Undisguised. The undisguised extent, of mortal sway! 495 *Fact* 11
This was their undisguised intent, and they 712 *Prelude* 9. 186
And undisguised, and strong and serious thought; 824 *Excursion* 5. 119
Undishonoured. O come, if undishonoured by the prayer, 357 *Aquap.* 297
Undismantled. Rapt in the grace of undismantled age, 583 **With copious* 28
Undismayed. By the blind Goddess,—ruthless, undismayed; 317 **Look now* 5
Struggling for liberty, while undismayed 353 *Aquap.* 46
Upon his throne;" unsoftened, undismayed 435 *Ecc. Sonn.* 2. 26. 10
At providential judgments, undismayed 513 *General Fast* 4
Undisordered. With undisordered sight. But leaving this, 651 *Prelude* 3. 154
Undisputed. Were undisputed! Like a mendicant, 62 *Bord.* 1350
An undisputed symbol of command, 321 **Humanity, delighting* 8
Enthroned aloft in undisputed power, 459 **Wanderer! that* 34
Undisquieted. Where she may work, safe, undisquieted, 626 *Ballot* 7
Undissolved. Was undissolved; and, in or out of sight, 585 *Ch. Lamb* 92
Of Egypt, unsubverted, undissolved— 788 *Excursion* 3. 149
And conglobated bubbles undissolved, 800 *Excursion* 3. 974
Undissolving. To form, an undissolving cloud; 181 *Waggoner* 4. 105
An undissolving fellowship?—What but this, 792 *Excursion* 3. 396
Undistempered. With undistempered and unclouded spirit, 830 *Excursion* 5. 487
Undistinguishable. An undistinguishable style appears 118 *Maternal Grief* 34
Of undistinguishable sympathies, 151 **When, to* 107
Of undistinguishable motion, steps 637 *Prelude* 1. 324
Amid the undistinguishable crowd K.8. 257 **Shall he* 2
Undistinguished. Round undistinguished clouds, and rocks, and snow: 13 *Desc. Sk.* 161
Not undistinguished, for of wells that ooze S.3. 433 **The doubt* 10
Undistinguishing. Liberal and undistinguishing, should hide 887 *Excursion* 9. 231

Ungrateful—*continued.*
For his ungrateful cause ; no,—I have heard . . 845 *Excursion* 6. 463
Ungratefully. Neglected and ungratefully thrown by 640 *Prelude* 1. 518
Ungreeted. Ungreeted by a more melodious Song, 685 *Prelude* 6. 673
Ungrieved. Ungrieved, with charm and spell ; . . 224 *'Tis gone* 63
Unguarded. Of some unguarded moment that dissolved 122 *V. and J.* 55
Give birth, full often, to unguarded words , . 793 *Excursion* 3. 494
From my unguarded heart.—The tranquil shores 797 *Excursion* 3. 812
The unguarded taper where the guarded faints ? . 813 *Excursion* 4. 773
Unguided. Unrectified, unguided, unsustained, 357 *Aquap.* 329
Unguilty. Like them. The unguilty Power pursues his way, 277 *Haydon! let* 13
Still tempering, from the unguilty forge . . . 298 *Brownie's Cell* 29
Of what it utters, while the unguilty seek . . 343 *Last Sup.* 12
Unhallowed. He could not come to an unhallowed end ! 101 *Brothers* 392
In the cold north's unhallowed ground, . . . 110 *'Tis said that some* 3
Where holy ground begins, unhallowed ends, . . 271 *Where holy* 1
Fixed on him an unhallowed name ; . . . . 299 *Brownie's Cell* 54
As that unhallowed Banner grew . . . . 401 *White Doe* 501
Unhallowed threads of revelry are spun ; . . . 433 *Ecc. Sonn.* 2. 20. 2
And not unhallowed was the page . . . . 499 *Departing summer* 43
And things of holy use unhallowed lie . . . 547 *Beneath yon* 18
Unhallowed actions—planted like a crown . . . 775 *Excursion* 2. 269
In their unhallowed principles ; the bad . . . 805 *Excursion* 4. 307
Unworthy therefore, and unhallowed : no, . . K.8. 249 *Recluse* 1.1.453
Unhappy. Unhappy Woman ! Nay, it was my duty 40 *Bord.* 174
Each word of that unhappy letter fell . . . 66 *Bord.* 1600
—So much for my remorse ! Unhappy Man ! . 70 *Bord.* 1814
that is the blood of an unhappy Man. . . . 71 *Bord.* 1909
In an unhappy home. . . . . . . 155 *Waterfall* 10
That unhappy Figure near him, ... 181 *Waggoner* 4. 158
Am grieved for that unhappy sin . . . . 182 *Waggoner* 4. 266
Can this unhappy Woman go, ... 198 *Thorn* 101
That it was all for that unhappy Hart. . . . 203 *Hart-leap* 140
Dismounts in most unhappy plight. . . . . 247 *P. B.* 1015
Unhappy Nuns, whose common breath's a sigh 266 *With how* 5
For old, unhappy, far-off things, ... 289 *Sol. Reap.* 19
Toussaint, the most unhappy man of men ! . 305 *Toussaint* 1
More for mankind at this unhappy day . . . 315 *Alas ! what* 13
Unhappy ghosts in troops by moonlight seen ; . 361 *For action* 8
The unhappy Banner Francis saw, ... 410 *White Doe* 1330
" Though this unhappy freight I bear ; . . . 412 *White Doe* 1471
Wept for that pair's unhappy fate. . . . . 623 *G. and S. Green* 3
Large draughts of love unhappy Dido drew ; . 625 *Æneid* 133
Of some unhappy woman, now and then . . 697 *Prelude* 7. 666
Upon the borders of the unhappy Loire, . . . 715 *Prelude* 9. 425
A mortal beauty, their unhappy thrall. . . . 716 *Prelude* 9. 461
The prison where the unhappy Monarch lay, . 719 *Prelude* 10. 51
His famous Optimist. " Unhappy Man ! " . 778 *Excursion* 2. 444
The unhappy alien hoping to obtain . . . 844 *Excursion* 6. 398
Of this unhappy lot, in early youth . . . . 886 *Excursion* 9. 165
Unharnessed. Unharnessed, naked, troops of Moorish horse . . . . 368 *Trajan* 45
Unhealthy. Unhealthy and vexatious. With the hour, 712 *Prelude* 9. 153
Unheard. The song of mountain-streams, unheard by day, 9 *Ev. Wk.* 365
Crowed with ear-piercing power till then unheard ; 21 *Desc. Sk.* 629
The morning came, and still he was unheard of : . 101 *Brothers* 377
All unheard of as thou art, ... 161 *Pleasures newly* 5
Unheard of is, like this, a book . . . . . 224 *'Tis gone* 17
Calvert ! it must not be unheard by them . . 259 *Calvert* 1
Unheard by them, their deeds shall celebrate ! . 328 *Ode 1815* 86
Even when a child, the Streams—unheard, unseen ; 382 *Duddon* 26. 2
Seems, 'mid inverted mountains, not unheard. 456 *The leaves* 13
Long, and long was he unheard of : . . . 536 *Egremont* 97
And benedictions not unheard in heaven : . 539 *Lady! a* 54
Left to herself unheard of and unknown. . 658 *Prelude* 3. 608
Unheard by her, that she, not falsely taught, . 669 *Prelude* 5. 266
Unheard, the savage nations bowed the head . 894 *Excursion* 9. 684
Unheard of, save in one small hamlet, here . S.3. 433 *The doubt* 9
Unheard-of. Does yet the unheard-of vessel ride the wave ? 318 *Ah ! where* 3
Like this unheard-of, and their channels wear 392 *Avon* 3
Unheard-of days, though loving peaceful thoughts. K.8. 257 *Recluse* 1.1.752
Unheeded. Unheeded night has overcome the vales : 8 *Ev. Wk.* 307
Unheeded, and the mute repose . . . . 499 *This Lawn* 17
Nor let me pass unheeded other loves . . . K.8. 250 *Recluse* 1.1.502
Unheeding. The unheeding Ass moves slowly on, . 246 *P. B.* 866
Unhelped. Unhelped by the poetic voice . . . 386 *Yarrow Rev.* 87
Unhewn. Appears a straggling heap of unhewn stones ! 131 *Michael* 17
And hence, this upright shaft of unhewn stone, . 788 *Excursion* 3. 128
There is a shapeless crowd of unhewn stones . K.8. 223 *There is a shapeless* 1
Unhidden. Unhidden faces : he that suffers most, . 780 *Excursion* 2. 588
Unholy. For no unholy visitings, ... 216 *Enterprise* 73
" Be thankful, thou ; for, if unholy deeds . 313 *Clouds, lingering* 13
And as I lay, the Cuckoo, bird unholy, . 558 *Cuck. and Night.* 89
Unhoped. Must come unhoped for, if they come again ; 229 *Cuckoo-clock* 26
Unhoused. Unhoused beneath the evening star we saw 680 *Prelude* 6. 370
Unhurt. Unhurt pursues his lengthened flight, while all 6 *Ev. Wk.* 198
For them who bravely stood unhurt, or bled . 328 *Ode 1815* 80

Unhurt—*continued.*
Unhurt by violence, from menaced taint . . 438 *Ecc. Sonn.* 2. 38. 10
Unhurt, the assault of Time with all his hours, . 474 *Hope smiled* 13
Uniform. By uniform control of after years, . . 646 *Prelude* 2. 262
Unillumined. An unillumined, blank, and dreary, plain, 830 *Excursion* 5. 537
Unimaginable. Or the unimaginable touch of Time. 449 *Ecc. Sonn.* 3. 34. 14
Oh, 'twas an unimaginable sight ! . . . 784 *Excursion* 2. 852
Unimaginative. Of these our unimaginative days ; 771 *Excursion* 2. 24
Unimagined. With unimagined beauty shine, . 386 *Yarrow Rev.* 63
Unimpaired. To keep the treasure unimpaired. Vain thought ! 231 *Clouds* 91
And beauty unimpaired. Grand in itself, . 355 *Aquap.* 184
All genuine admiration unimpaired. . . . 653 *Prelude* 3. 274
Yet, in me, confidence was unimpaired ; . 727 *Prelude* 11. 7
But stout and hale, for travel unimpaired. . 756 *Excursion* 1. 34
Of Life continuous, Being unimpaired ; . . 812 *Excursion* 4. 755
Is by domestic service unimpaired ; . . . 852 *Excursion* 6. 951
The dear memorial footsteps unimpaired . 884 *Excursion* 9. 39
A freeman, therefore, sound and unimpaired ; K.8. 246 *Recluse* 1.1.362
Unimpeded. From unimpeded commerce with the Sun, 452 *Ecc. Sonn.* 3. 46. 13
Unimplored. Guilt unrepented, pardon unimplored. 447 *Ecc. Sonn.* 3. 29. 8
Unimportant. Of one so unimportant ; night by night 711 *Prelude* 9. 113
Unimposed. Toil unimposed, vicisitude unknown, 465 *St. Bees* 2
Unimprisoned. Loved haunts like these ; the unimprisoned Mind, 803 *Excursion* 4. 106
Air unimprisoned, and had lived at large ; . 879 *Excursion* 8. 343
Unincited. And unincited by a wish to look . . 831 *Excursion* 5. 597
Unincumbered. See **Unencumbered.**
Of refuge, with an unincumbered floor . . 150 *When, to* 12
Cool air I breathe ; while the unincumbered Mind, 262 *Retirement* 12
Uninfluenced. But in chaste hearts, uninfluenced by the power 256 *Yes ! hope* 12
Uninformed. Nor uninformed with Phantasy, and looks 185 *Yew-trees* 19
Indulgent, as not uninformed that men . . 729 *Prelude* 11. 159
Nor uninformed by books, good books, though few— 743 *Prelude* 13. 244
For tens of thousands uninformed as he ? . 880 *Excursion* 8. 432
Uninjured. With uninjured plumes ! " . . . 163 *Hint* 16
Survive, uninjured ;—glory then to words, . 356 *Aquap.* 249
Unblamed, uninjured, let him bear about . 568 *Cumb. Beg.* 166
Who throve, like plants, uninjured by the storm . 825 *Excursion* 5. 199
From this communion with uninjured Minds, 896 *Excursion* 9. 784
Uninscribed. Memento uninscribed of Pride o'erthrown, 345 *Ambition—following* 7
Uninspired. Minutely linked with diligence uninspired, 357 *Aquap.* 328
Albeit uninspired by love, ... 498 *The sylvan* 8
Not uninspired appear their simplest ways ; . 500 *Humanity* 15
Sit, see, and hear, unthankful, uninspired ? . 695 *Prelude* 7. 543
Lost in a gloom of uninspired research ; . 810 *Excursion* 4. 626
Unintelligible. Of all this unintelligible world, . 206 *Tintern* 40
That unintelligible cry . . . . . 244 *P. B.* 691
That told, with unintelligible voice, . . . 686 *Prelude* 6. 717
Of unintelligible chastisement, ... 724 *Prelude* 10. 455
Uninvited. I only, like an uninvited guest . 722 *Prelude* 10. 297
His office, unrelaxing, he resumed. . . . 850 *Excursion* 6. 786
Uninvoked. I left not uninvoked ; and, in still groves, 797 *Excursion* 3. 753
Union. See **Reunion.**
In union with the employment of his heart, . 96 *Brothers* 58
Such union, in the lovely Girl maintained . . 118 *Maternal Grief* 38
Body, heart, and soul in union, ... 140 *Arm. Lady* 63
Mute memento of that union . . . . 142 *Arm. Lady* 151
That lonely union, privacy so deep, . . . 143 *High bliss* 1
Their union brought, will they repay the debt, . 143 *High bliss* 26
In endless union, earth and sea above." . . 220 *Triad* 23
Union with those primeval energies . . . 357 *Aquap.* 289
Union not sad, when sunny daybreak smites . 387 *Part fenced* 12
Ere hope declines :—their union is beset . 437 *Ecc. Sonn.* 2. 37. 8
Union that shadows forth and doth partake . 447 *Ecc. Sonn.* 3. 26. 11
With unexampled union meet in these, . . 463 *Why should the* 11
If the mind knew no union of extremes, . 471 *Arran! a* 10
To serve thy need, in union with thy Clyde . 475 *Greenock* 12
That union ceased : then, cleaving easy walks 477 *Nunnery* 9
Union significant of God adored, . . . 477 *Lowther ! in* 4
In union, in partition only such ; . . . 585 *Ch. Lamb* 99
The bond of union between life and joy. . 640 *Prelude* 1. 558
Union that cannot be :—who would not give, 642 *Prelude* 2. 24
Vouchsafed for union or communion, feeds 709 *Prelude* 8. 674
Lifted, in union with the purest, best, . . 748 *Prelude* 14. 185
Plague from this union spread, whose subtle bane 775 *Excursion* 2. 243
(And that is intercourse, and union, too,) . 795 *Excursion* 3. 665
The union, the partition where, that makes . 806 *Excursion* 4. 336
Peace in ourselves, and union with our God. 818 *Excursion* 4. 1116
Mysterious union with its native sea. . . 818 *Excursion* 4. 1140
Wise in that union, and without it blind ! " . 831 *Excursion* 5. 579
Unions. (Like those ill-sorted unions, work supposed 641 *Prelude* 1. 590
Unison. But every awful note in unison . . 227 *Vernal Ode* 97
Of aery voices locked in unison,— . . . 346 *Gemmi* 11
A mighty unison of streams ! . . . . 581 *Loud is* 3
Replete with honour ; sounds in unison . 742 *Prelude* 13. 184
Unit. Passion a unit and *against* us—proof— . 58 *Bord.* 1150
Shall be a unit *for* us ; proof—no, passion ! . 58 *Bord.* 1153
Unite. See **Reunite.**
Rise various wreaths that into one unite . . 33 *Guilt* 462
Where flowers and herbs unite, and haply some weeds be, ... 103 *Artegal* 64
In whom all busy offices unite . . . . 227 *Vernal Ode* 107
No scale of moral music—to unite . . . 235 *Power of Sound* 170
Unite, to magnify the Ever-living, . . . 235 *Power of Sound* 195

Unreproved—*continued.*
Of unreproved enjoyment ; and is pleased   817 *Excursion* 4. 1045
Decent and unreproved. The voice, that greets   838 *Excursion* 6. 12
I must not walk in unreproved delight   K.8. 255 *Recluse* 1.1.666
Unrequired. And the besprinkled nursling, unre-
quired   836 *Excursion* 5. 954
Unrequited. By unrequited love, he scaled the rocks,   840 *Excursion* 6. 109
Unresentful. Not unresentful where self-justified ; .   672 *Prelude* 5. 414
Unreserved. Vanish before the unreserved embrace   449 *Ecc. Sonn.* 3. 36. 10
Unresisting. Athwart the unresisting tide   410 *White Doe* 1342
Unrest. Tired with its daily share of earth's unrest,—   460 **Wanderer ! that* 59
Unrestrained. So cruel Sussex, unrestrained   410 *White Doe* 1328
Words by thy presence unrestrained may speak .   525 *Epist. Beaumont* 252
At large and unrestrained, nor damped too soon .   751 *Prelude* 14. 361
Unrestricted. Range unrestricted as the wind, . .   407 *White Doe* 997
Of unrestricted and unthinking man.   682 *Prelude* 6. 478
Unreturned. Friendship betrayed, affection unre-
turned,   791 *Excursion* 3. 377
Unrevealed. His graces unrevealed and unpro-
claimed.   757 *Excursion* 1. 94
Unripe. Winds rustling over plots of unripe grain,   25 *Guilt* 35
And though of unripe years, a stripling only, .   100 *Brothers* 297
Which at this season, with their unripe fruits, .   206 *Tintern* 12
Our unripe years, not wasted, should be taught .   654 *Prelude* 3. 384
Or heard, was fitted to our unripe state   683 *Prelude* 6. 542
Nature herself was, at this unripe time, .   704 *Prelude* 8. 342
So, with more ardour than an unripe girl .   781 *Excursion* 2. 654
And unripe sex with sex, for mutual taint ; .   879 *Excursion* 8. 340
Unripened. And pines the unripened pear in sum-
mer's kindliest ray   15 *Desc. Sk.* 259
Unrivalled. That not for thy reward, unrivall'd Vale !   21 *Desc. Sk.* 586
This fair unrivalled Brotherhood,   410 *White Doe* 1303
Of all adventurers. With unrivalled skill, .   812 *Excursion* 4. 724
Unroll. Some Theban fragment, or unroll . .   499 **Departing summer* 52
Unrolled. How fast the Marian death-list is unrolled !   437 *Ecc. Sonn.* 2. 34. 1
Unroofed. And, 'mid their choirs unroofed by selfish
rage,   433 *Ecc. Sonn.* 2. 21. 4
Unruffled. The unruffled Innocent,—I see thy face,   124 *V. and J.* 161
And when the keen unruffled weather, .   144 **Driven in* 62
To which, on some unruffled morning, clings .   212 *Dion*
On Grasmere's clear unruffled breast   297 *Highland Boy* 188
On the mute sea in this unruffled bay ;   458 *Sea-shore* 28
Unruffled doth the blue lake lie,   498 **The sylvan* 5
Or nowhere ; days unruffled by the gale .   777 *Excursion* 2. 365
Or, on the waters of the unruffled lake, .   842 *Excursion* 6. 294
The other, glassed in thy unruffled breast, .   S.3. 434 **The doubt* 74
I came not dreaming of unruffled life, .   K.8. 246 *Recluse* 1.1.347
Unruliness. Some vapoured in the unruliness of joy,   681 *Prelude* 6. 392
To license some unruliness of mind ; . . . .   712 *Prelude* 9. 190
Unruly. In her breast, unruly fire, . .   94 *Westmoreland Girl* 74
Hath, like the Lover, his unruly times ; . .   634 *Prelude* 1. 136
Nor that unruly child of mountain birth, . .   659 *Prelude* 4. 50
Unsafe. And midway in the unsafe morass, .   543 *Russ. Fug.* 101
Such as in unsafe times of border-war. .   833 *Excursion* 5. 698
Unsaid. And left—but be the rest unsaid, . .   410 *White Doe* 1305
Unsaluted. Long unsaluted, nor the sunny seat .   659 *Prelude* 4. 47
Unsanctifies. Unsanctifies our tears—made sport .   386 *Yarrow Rev.* 91
Unsanctioned. Bodings unsanctioned by the will .   225 *Present.* 22
To some unsanctioned fear ? " " If this be so, .   828 *Excursion* 5. 365
Unsapped. Unsapped by delicate viands ; for, ex-
clude   643 *Prelude* 2. 81
Unsatisfied. And, being still unsatisfied with aught   758 *Excursion* 1. 143
Break down all grandeur, still unsatisfied . .   815 *Excursion* 4. 964
So deeply, that, unsatisfied with aught . . .   819 *Excursion* 4. 1214
Unscared. Of Easter winds, unscared, from hut or
hall   256 *Decay of Piety* 6
Unscared by thronging fancies of strange hue .   523 *Epist. Beaumont* 146
Press forward by the teasing dogs unscared. . .   525 *Epist. Beaumont* 238
Associates, and, unscared by blustering winds, .   687 *Prelude* 7. 30
Unscathed. Of splendour unextinguished, pomp un-
scathed,   355 *Aquap.* 183
Unscattered. By the rough wind unscattered, at
whose call   808 *Excursion* 4. 453
Unscorned. Unscorned the peasant's whistling
breath, that lightens   233 *Power of Sound* 51
Unscoured. Of the grave Elders, men unscoured,
grotesque   657 *Prelude* 3. 542
Unsealed. A hoard of grievances unsealed ; " .   181 *Waggoner* 4. 179
Unsearchable. Lost in unsearchable eternity ! " .   788 *Excursion* 3. 112
Unsearched. I leave unsearched : enough that
memory clings,   525 *Epist. Beaumont* 265
Unseasonably. Of midnight hours, unseasonably
twinkling   808 *Excursion* 4. 486
Unseconded. Unseconded, uncountenanced ; then,
as time   841 *Excursion* 6. 222
Unsedentary. Meanwhile the unsedentary Master's
hand   860 *Excursion* 7. 193
Unseduced. ' Unshaken, unseduced, unterrified ; ' .   842 *Excursion* 6. 260
Unseen. While others, not unseen, are free to shed   7 *Ev. Wk.* 267
They cannot mount the hill, by us unseen. .   38 *Bord.* 49
Unseen by Leonard, at the church-yard gate .   96 *Brothers* 101
The Astrologer was not unseen   175 *Waggoner* 1. 180
The voice of tears that fell unseen ; .   176 *Waggoner* 1. 228
And fade, unseen by any human eye ; . . .   185 *Nutting* 32
But he flowed quiet and unseen :— . . .   240 *P. B.* 372
" Be Yarrow stream unseen, unknown ! . . .   293 *Yarrow Unv.* 49

Unseen—*continued.*
Could I leave them unseen, and not yield to regret ?   345 *Stanzas : Simplon* 10
Even when a child, the Streams—unheard, unseen ;   382 *Duddon* 26. 2
Soothed by the unseen River's gentle roar. . .   384 *Duddon* 31. 14
And streams unknown, hills yet unseen, . .   386 *Yarrow Rev.* 69
To dream-light dear while yet unseen, . . .   386 *Yarrow Rev.* 109
With some loved friend, or by the unseen hawk .   389 *Glencroe* 5
Herself, in spots unseen before. . .   415 *White Doe* 1709
Whoe'er ye be, that thus, yourselves unseen, .   451 *Ecc. Sonn.* 3. 44. 6
More imminent. Not unseen do they approach ;   541 *Grace Darl.* 63
Or an *unseen* companionship, a breath, . .   622 *Recluse* 1. 1. 93
What Power unseen diffuses far . . .   626 †*Cento* 2
Above the babe, unseen ; .   628 *Installation* 32
Was kindling, not unseen, from humble copse .   663 *Prelude* 4. 321
Myself unseen. He was of stature tall, . .   664 *Prelude* 4. 391
Reckless of me : I followed, not unseen, . .   667 *Prelude* 5. 118
Heard, though unseen,—a devious traveller, .   716 *Prelude* 9. 447
Celestial, lay unseen the pastoral vales . .   725 *Prelude* 10. 524
Objects unseen before, thou wilt not blame .   744 *Prelude* 13. 305
Unseen, perchance above all power of sight— .   819 *Excursion* 4. 1180
Himself unseen ! But no tradition tells . .   833 *Excursion* 5. 686
Sauntering to pluck the strawberries wild unseen.   S.3. 417 **Sweet was* 8
Unselfish. Blest Statesman He, whose Mind's un-
selfish will   514 **Blest Statesman* 1
Unsensualise. By art to unsensualise the mind .   228 *Devot. Incit.* 47
Unsettle. Disarmed of power to unsettle present good   586 *Ch. Lamb* 116
To unsettle or perplex it : yet with pain . .   804 *Excursion* 4. 199
Unsettled. 'Tis a poor wretch of an unsettled mind,   73 *Bord.* 2033
Stole forth, unsettled by the shock ; . . .   113 *Lament* 67
Old things have been unsettled ; we have seen .   309 **England ! the* 4
To human life's unsettled atmosphere ; . .   459 **Wanderer ! that* 2
Uneasy and unsettled, yoke-fellows . .   673 *Prelude* 5. 520
Had been erewhile unsettled and disturbed, .   795 *Excursion* 3. 654
With an unsettled liberty of thought, . .   842 *Excursion* 6. 239
Unsettled by a wanton blow from foot . .   K.8. 226 **I will* 67
Unsettles. And the motion unsettles a tear ; .   621 *Convict* 42
That instantly unsettles and recedes,— . .   707 *Prelude* 8. 567
Unsettling. The roof, self-moved, unsettling o'er his
head ;   76 *Bord.* 2182
At length, himself unsettling, he the pond .   196 *Resolution* 78
Unshackled. The unshackled layman's natural
liberty ;   775 *Excursion* 2. 265
Pleased to perceive his own unshackled life, .   799 *Excursion* 3. 933
Unshaded. There, all unshaded, blazing forests throw   12 *Desc. Sk.* 101
Unshaded, eying far below, the flood, . .   592 *Ev. Wk. Quarto* 66
Unshaken. And, to atone for it, with soul unshaken   517 *Pun. Death* 3. 12
But, by the storms of circumstance unshaken, .   802 *Excursion* 4. 71
Suffices ; and unshaken bears the assault . .   833 *Excursion* 5. 701
' Unshaken, unseduced, unterrified ; ' . .   842 *Excursion* 6. 260
Unshaped. " To all the unshaped half-human
thoughts   239 *P. B.* 296
Unshared. To impart a joy, imperfect while un-
shared.   893 *Excursion* 9. 587
Unsheath. 'Mid thy soft glooms the glittering steel
unsheath ;   3 *Ev. Wk.* 75
Unsheathed. Unsheathed in wrath to strike the of-
fender's head,   447 *Ecc. Sonn.* 3. 29. 6
Unshed. The name untouched, the tear unshed ;—   410 *White Doe* 1306
Unsheltered. Which the unsheltered traveller might
receive   537 **In desultory* 9
Where, from the barren wall's unshelter'd end, .   592 *Ev. Wk. Quarto* 59
That, thither driven from some unsheltered place,   692 *Prelude* 7. 326
Unshifting. Like an unshifting weathercock which
proves   521 *Epist. Beaumont* 18
Unshorn. Who gathered in betimes the unshorn flock   381 *Duddon* 23. 2
Spreads out his limbs, while, yet unshorn, the Sheep,   547 **Rude is* 23
Unshrouded. Daily exposed, woe that unshrouded
lies ;   516 **Feel for* 2
Dissolved, have left him an unshrouded head. .   699 *Prelude* 8. 17
Unsighed. The past unsighed for, and the future sure ;   211 *Laod.* 100
Unsightly. Or moist with dews ; what more un-
sightly now,   266 **Desponding Father* 3
Unsightly marks of violence or harm. . . .   646 *Prelude* 2. 251
Gloomy as coffins, and unsightly lanes . .   689 *Prelude* 7. 181
Unsightly objects and uncoveted, . . .   S.3. 434 **The doubt* 52
Unsinged. Walk through the fire with unsinged hair.   191 *Seq. Beggars* 30
Like one of those who walked with hair unsinged   692 *Prelude* 7. 369
Unskill'd. Nor unskill'd his darts to ply ; . .   S.3. 437 **I, whose* 10
Unsleeping. Yet, arts are thine that rock th' un-
sleeping heart,   605 *Desc.Sk.Quarto* 162
Unsmitten. By wasteful steel unsmitten—then
would I   379 *Duddon* 13. 9
By sorrow not unsmitten ; yet for me . .   675 *Prelude* 6. 50
Unsociably. Unsociably sequestered, and encroach-
ing   858 *Excursion* 7. 36
Unsocial. Of all unsocial courses, is least fit .   799 *Excursion* 3. 910
Unsoftened. Upon his throne ; " unsoftened, undis-
mayed   435 *Ecc. Sonn.* 2. 26. 10
Unsolicited. Unsolicited reply . . . .   209 **Yes, it* 5
Unsought. At times, and tales unsought beguile the
day,   15 *Desc. Sk.* 247
Unsought for was the help that did my life recall.   31 *Guilt* 387
As if all needful things would come unsought .   195 *Resolution* 38
By unsought means for gracious purposes ; .   362 **List—'twas* 46
A grace by thee unsought and unpossest, . .   474 **How sad* 12
The fount of feeling, if unsought elsewhere, .   509 *F. Stone* 51
But while a thousand pleasures come unsought, .   529 *Poor Robin* 15
Whether withheld, or for her sake unsought— .   585 *Ch. Lamb* 85
By nourishment that came unsought ; for still .   642 *Prelude* 2. 7
Sought or unsought, and influxes of power .   708 *Prelude* 8. 601

Unsought—*continued.*
Which fits him to receive it when unsought. . . 740 *Prelude* 13. 10
And unsought pleasures springing up by chance ; 892 *Excursion* 9. 521
Unsoul. Palace or grove, even so could I unsoul . 735 *Prelude* 12. 83
Unsound. And undertook premonished, if unsound 444 *Ecc. Sonn.* 3. 16. 10
Perilous is sweeping change, all chance unsound. . 514 **Blest Statesman* 14
Unsound as those which Fortune builds— . . 550 *Hermit's Cell* 2. 22
Unsound, of spongy texture, yet withal . . 654 *Prelude* 3. 334
Vague and unsound ; and having brought the books 741 *Prelude* 13. 71
Fleeting as health or beauty, and unsound ? . . 829 *Excursion* 5. 473
Unsparing. By ghostly power :—but Time's unsparing hand . . . . 383 *Duddon* 27. 10
Grant that by this unsparing hurricane . . . 435 *Ecc. Sonn.* 2. 28. 1
Takes one unsparing handful for the scrip . . 568 *Cumb. Beg.* 158
Unspeaking. And long, unspeaking, sorrow : . . 494 *Force of Prayer* 38
Unspiritual. And life's unspiritual pleasures daily wooed ! . . . . 263 **Those words* 4
Unspoiled. Unspoiled by commendation and the excess . . . . 691 *Prelude* 7. 313
Unstable. It is unstable as a dream of night ; . . 263 **Those words* 6
From this unstable world, if he could fix . . . 803 *Excursion* 4. 157
Unstained. Unstained by envy, discontent, and pride ; 19 *Desc. Sk.* 493
Unswept, unstained ? Nor shall the aerial Powers 263 **How clear* 10
Because the unstained, the clear, the crystalline, . 469 **Why stand* 4
Yet, being inwardly unstained, ... 542 *Russ. Fug.* 79
Upon this sinful earth, by sin unstained : . . . 576 **Six months* 2
Men, who, from faction sacred, and unstained . 823 *Excursion* 5. 32
Unsteadfast. Unsteadfast, by a blasted yew upstay'd ; . . . . 606 *Desc.Sk.Quarto* 252
Unsteadied. By books unsteadied, by his pastoral care 859 *Excursion* 7. 115
Unstigmatized. Nor left unstigmatized those fatal fields . . . . 869 *Excursion* 7. 798
Unstrengthened. If we advance unstrengthened by repose, ... 382 *Duddon* 24. 3
Unstripped. Unmarred, unstripped of her attire, . 371 *Eg. Maid* 137
Unsubdued. Thy gladness unsubdued and bold : . 294 *Jedbor.* 38
What mischief cleaves to unsubdued regret, . . 458 *Sea-shore* 1
My soul was unsubdued. A plastic power . . 647 *Prelude* 2. 362
Unchastened, unsubdued, unawed, unraised . . 682 *Prelude* 6. 505
Even to the last ! '—Such was he, unsubdued. . 861 *Excursion* 7. 277
Unsubmissive. From unsubmissive necks the bridle shook . . . . 515 **Men of* 5
Unsubstantial. Which unsubstantial Phantoms sacred keep ; . . . . 16 *Desc. Sk.* 309
An unsubstantial, faery place ; . . . . . . 184 **O blithe* 31
But unsubstantial Form eludes her grasp . . . 210 *Laod.* 27
Upon that unsubstantial brotherhood . . . . 231 *Clouds* 85
Of the Unsubstantial, pondered well ! . . . . 235 *Power of Sound* 176
He sees an unsubstantial creature, ... 246 *P. B.* 923
And, quitting unsubstantial dreams, ... 416 *White Doe* 1840
Of unsubstantial imagery, the dream, ... 456 **The leaves* 10
Lofty, but the unsubstantial structure melts . . 635 *Prelude* 1. 225
Unsubstantialized. All unsubstantialized,—how loud the voice . . . . 885 *Excursion* 9. 66
Unsubverted. Of Egypt, unsubverted, undissolved— 788 *Excursion* 3. 149
Unsuccessful. Its unsuccessful issue much excite . 722 *Prelude* 10. 256
Unsued. Which, though unsued for, fails not to descend . . . . 538 **In desultory* 30
Unsuitable. —This contrast, not unsuitable to life, 831 *Excursion* 5. 552
Unsuited. Of words unsuited to the place . . . 550 *Hermit's Cell* 2. 7
Unsullied. May the unsullied Goddess of the chase, 104 *Artegal* 150
Unsullied did it meet the day, ... 550 *Hermit's Cell* 2. 13
Unsullied, incorruptible, and drink . . . . 893 *Excursion* 9. 629
Pure and unsullied, flowing from the heart . . K.8. 248 *Recluse* 1.1.410
Unsung. Romantic tale by Milton left unsung ; . 634 *Prelude* 1. 169
Unsunned. The captive 'mid damp vaults unsunned, unaired, ... 273 **Not the* 5
Of unsunned griefs, too many and too keen, . . 861 *Excursion* 7. 281
Unsuppressed. He gazed, with admiration unsuppressed, ... 882 *Excursion* 8. 534
Unsupprest. Of simple manners, feelings unsupprest 824 *Excursion* 5. 118
Unsurpast. Gleams by the richest jewel unsurpast ; 527 **Those breathing* 16
Unsurveyed. Gracefully up the gnarled trunk ; nor left we unsurveyed . . . . . . 92 *Poet's Dream* 39
Unsusceptible. Their mansions unsusceptible of change, ... 227 *Vernal Ode* 72
Unsuspected. To serve—an unsuspected screen . 300 *Bran* 7
At every touch, an unsuspected fire." . . . 624 *Æneid* 43
Unsuspecting. *Tu-whit—Tu-whoo!* the unsuspecting fowl . . . . 153 *Morn. Ex.* 9
Her unsuspecting eye, perchance, ... 180 *Waggoner* 4. 28
Dear as they are to unsuspecting Youth, . . . 359 *Plea : Hist.* 6
Her docile, unsuspecting Child : . . . . . 405 *White Doe* 886
Unsuspended. While unsuspended wheels the village dance, ... 11 *Desc. Sk.* 39
Unsustained. Unrectified, unguided, unsustained, . 357 *Aquap.* 329
She spake, yet, I believe, not unsustained . . 849 *Excursion* 6. 767
By timely culture unsustained ; or run . . . 888 *Excursion* 9. 305
Unswept. Unswept, unstained ? Nor shall the aerial Powers . . . . 263 **How clear* 10
Unswerving. With an unswerving line, I fixed my view . . . . 637 *Prelude* 1. 369
Shall move unswerving, even as if impelled . . 820 *Excursion* 4. 1268
Untainted. And honest dealing, and untainted speech, 878 *Excursion* 8. 241
Untainted manners ; born among the hills, . . K.8. 246 *Recluse* 1.1.348
Untamed. By blushes yet untamed ; . . . . 232 *Jew. Fam.* 30
Dear Liberty ! stern Nymph of soul untamed ; . 314 **Advance—come* 2
Yet, though a wild vindictive Race, untamed . 389 *Sound of Mull* 9
Untasked. To pass the remnant of his days, untasked 762 *Excursion* 1. 384
Untaught. Untaught that soon such anguish must ensue, ... 29 *Guilt* 294

Untaught—*continued.*
Untaught that meekness is the cherished bent . 455 **Not in the lucid* 14
Haply the untaught Philosopher may speak . . 468 **Ranging the* 10
By love untaught to ring, ... 498 **The sylvan* 9
To watch crude Nature work in untaught minds ; 691 *Prelude* 7. 275
But though untaught by thinking or by books . 712 *Prelude* 9. 198
Proceeding from a source of untaught things, . 744 *Prelude* 13. 310
The rustic Boy, who walks the fields, untaught ; . 886 *Excursion* 9. 162
Of mountain sights, this untaught shepherd stood K.8. 230 **I will* 196
Untempted. For those, who, yet untempted to forsake 878 *Excursion* 8. 259
Untended. Like an untended watch-fire, on the ridge v **If thou indeed* 10
And, not untended, climb the dangerous steep. . 16 *Desc. Sk.* 351
Nor shall she perish there, untended and alone ! " 34 *Guilt* 567
Will prosper, though untended and alone : . . 106 *Farewell* 12
Unterrified. ' Unshaken, unseduced, unterrified ; ' . 842 *Excursion* 6. 260
Unthanked. Nor be unthanked, unless I fondly err. 281 *Valedict.* 8
Nor be unthanked their final lingerings— . . . 431 *Ecc. Sonn.* 2. 13. 5
And dearest helpers, left unthanked, unpraised, . 668 *Prelude* 5. 169
So long unthanked) hast cheered a simple board . S.3. 433 **The doubt* 16
Unthankful. Sit, see, and hear, unthankful, uninspired ? . . . . 695 *Prelude* 7. 543
Unthankfully. You judge unthankfully : distempered nerves . . . . 808 *Excursion* 4. 479
Unthinking. Unthinking Stephen went— . . . 199 *Thorn* 116
Hear not we, unthinking Creatures ! . . . . 209 **Yes, it* 10
And an unthinking grief ! The tenderest mood . 304 **I grieved* 2
Threats, which the unthinking only can despise, . 465 **Pastor and* 5
The prosperous and unthinking, they who live . 568 *Cumb. Beg.* 120
Of more unthinking natures, easy minds . . . 656 *Prelude* 3. 504
Of unrestricted and unthinking man. . . . . 682 *Prelude* 6. 478
With no unthinking mind, well pleased to note . 690 *Prelude* 7. 220
Among the unthinking masters of the earth . . 761 *Excursion* 1. 380
Or move the pity of unthinking minds, . . . 813 *Excursion* 4. 835
Unthinkingly. To urge unthinkingly their prompt departure, ... 853 *Excursion* 6. 975
Unthought. A strength unthought of heretofore ! . 294 *Jedbor.* 42
To worlds unthought of till the searching mind . 461 **Queen of* 40
Unthought of—this may surely claim a sigh. . . 627 **We gaze* 8
Unknown, unthought of, yet I was most rich— . 651 *Prelude* 3. 140
Unthought of : in their woodland beds the flowers 670 *Prelude* 5. 339
To happiness unthought of ? The inert . . . 729 *Prelude* 11. 123
And go to the grave, unthought of. Strongest minds . . . . 757 *Excursion* 1. 91
" Oh ! pang unthought of, as the precious boon . 867 *Excursion* 7. 674
Unthought-of. Unthought-of, unexpected, as the stir 80 **Loving she* 17
For this unthought-of greeting ! While allured . 361 **List—'twas* 8
Or left unthought-of in obscurity,— . . . . 494 *Hap. War.* 67
Unwooed, unthought-of even—simplicity, . . 700 *Prelude* 8. 109
At such unthought-of meeting.—For the night . 757 *Excursion* 1. 48
By an unthought-of patron. Bleak and bare . 859 *Excursion* 7. 136
Unthreatened. Had darkness fallen—unthreatened, unproclaimed— . . . . 548 **Stay, bold* 25
Unthwarted. Unthwarted in her wish to recompense 717 *Prelude* 9. 523
Untie. And busily, though yet with fear, untie . 34 *Guilt* 569
Untied. That may not be untied ! . . . . . 623 *G. and S. Green* 36
Unties. By voices never mute when Heaven unties 430 *Ecc. Sonn.* 2. 8. 10
Until. (*Partial list.*) *See* **'Till.**
Until the breath of this corporeal frame . . . 206 *Tintern* 43
Until I have a little Boat, ... 236 *P. B.* 4
Until thus far she learned, that he had been . . 554 *Prioress* 140
Untilled. And minds not stinted or untilled are given, 308 **These times* 6
Untimely. If such their harsh untimely doom, . . 154 *Flower Garden* 17
" O wretched loss—untimely stroke ! . . . . 248 *P. B.* 1046
Insidiously, untimely thunders growl ; . . . 263 *Storm* 5
I sought the untimely grave of Burns ; . . . 286 *Sons of Burns* 2
By no untimely joyousness ; . . . . . . 294 *Jedbor.* 81
A most untimely grave to strew, ... 348 **Lulled by* 46
Untired. Serve Thee, invisible Spirit, with untired powers ; . . . . 232 *Power of Sound* 18
Yet, helped by Genius—untired comforter, . . 273 **While Anna's* 9
And with untired humility forbore . . . . 500 *Humanity* 39
Proud and exulting like an untired horse . . . 638 *Prelude* 1. 432
Untired, the better, surely, would preserve . . 727 *Prelude* 11. 26
That course unchecked, unerring, and untired, . 748 *Prelude* 14. 134
Like one whose untired ear a murmuring stream . 814 *Excursion* 4. 892
Unto. Be known unto you, you will love this Woman, ... 48 *Bord.* 628
With horror is this world) am unto thee . . . 75 *Bord.* 2168
That unto him, where'er shall lie his life's appointed way, ... 91 *Norman Boy* 31
Unto the few whom he esteems his friends . . 104 *Artegal* 102
Tears due unto their own. . . . . 113 *Lament* 21
Such things as she unto the Babe might say : . 120 *Emigrant Mother* 12
Thou bringest unto me a tale . . . . . . 183 **O blithe* 11
In truth the prison, unto which we doom . . . 250 **Nuns fret* 8
Open unto the fields, and to the sky ; . . . . 269 *Westm. Bridge* 7
And, when she took unto herself a Mate, . . . 305 *Ven. Rep.* 7
Men unto whom sufficient for the day . . . . 308 **These times* 5
Stoop their proud heads, but not unto the dust— 316 **Say, what* 11
Unto their martyred Countrymen decreed, . . 324 *Ode 1814* 51
Give him a soul that cleaveth unto Thee. . . . 363 **The world forsaken* 14
Which yet do unto some impart . . . . . 399 *White Doe* 318
Inversion strange ! that, unto One who lives . . 433 *Ecc. Sonn.* 2. 19. 9
Unto itself, the Crown assumes a voice . . . 435 *Ecc. Sonn.* 2. 28. 13
Known unto few but prized as far as known, . . 540 *Grace Darl.* 7
Have unto Heaven and You been paid : . . . 542 *Russ. Fug.* 55
Unto Thee, mysterious God ! . . . . . . 550 *Hermit's Cell* 4. 4
To be our guide unto thy Son so dear. . . . 553 *Prioress* 28
Who day by day unto this school hath gone, . . 553 *Prioress* 52

Unto—*continued.*
And unto him declare why men sing so; — 553 *Prioress* 76
"'My throat is cut unto the bone, I trow,' — 556 *Prioress* 198
And after that thus said she unto me; — 556 *Prioress* 215
He can make low, and unto death bring nigh; — 556 *Cuck. and Night.* 4
This unto their rememberance doth bring — 557 *Cuck. and Night.* 28
And also 'tis not likely unto me, — 557 *Cuck. and Night.* 43
Unto the God of Love I make a vow, — 561 *Cuck.andNight.* 229
Send unto thee as mickle joy this day, — 561 *Cuck.andNight.* 254
Nor leisure unto thee more worth to give; — 562 *Cuck.andNight.* 303
And unto Pandarus, his own Brother dear, — 562 *Troilus* 3
And yonder once she unto me 'gan say— — 563 *Troilus* 53
That hers unto the death my heart I hold. — 563 *Troilus* 56
My Lady first me took unto her grace. — 563 *Troilus* 63
Unto the blood of Troy, I pray of thee, — 563 *Troilus* 82
As Juno was unto the Theban blood, — 563 *Troilus* 83
Enriching and adorning. Unto thee, — 585 *Ch. Lamb* 76
And unto this he frames his song: — 589 *Immortality* 96
From transitory passion, unto this — 651 *Prelude* 3. 135
To cleave unto this man; but when I prayed — 667 *Prelude* 5. 116
And specially delightful unto me — 677 *Prelude* 6. 161
Compelled to be a life unto herself, — 679 *Prelude* 6. 303
Nor made unto myself a secret boast — 696 *Prelude* 7. 586
The human nature unto which I felt — 708 *Prelude* 8. 608
Accomplished, giving thus unto events — 711 *Prelude* 9. 104
Add unto this, subservience from the first — 713 *Prelude* 9. 233
In part lay here, that unto me the events — 713 *Prelude* 9. 246
With the most noble, but unto the poor — 714 *Prelude* 9. 303
The width of those huge forests, unto me — 716 *Prelude* 9. 462
Unto a heifer's motion, by a cord — 717 *Prelude* 9. 512
Brought less encouragement, and unto these — 730 *Prelude* 11. 195
By circumstance to take unto the height — 757 *Excursion* 1. 87
Their lost affections unto thee and thine!" — 801 *Excursion* 4. 31
Had yet to travel far, but unto us, — 820 *Excursion* 4. 1299
Various, but unto each some tribute paid; — 837 *Excursion* 5. 972
Unto the men who see not as we see — 865 *Excursion* 7. 531
A throne, that may be likened unto his, — 885 *Excursion* 9. 56
The greeting "peace be with you" unto them, — K.8. 244 *Recluse* 1.1.281
Or profit unto any but ourselves. — K.8. 255 *Recluse* 1.1.699

Untold. Quick—to the point—if any untold crime — 68 *Bord.* 1703
Nor leave untold our happy flight in that adventurous dream. — 93 *Poet's Dream* 76
A Poet's history, may I leave untold — 659 *Prelude* 4. 80
'Tis left untold if here he first drew breath, — 871 *Excursion* 7. 927
My future labours may not leave untold. — 896 *Excursion* 9. 796

Untouched. Untouched by his breath see the candle shines bright, — 81 †*Address: Child* 34
Moving untouched in silver purity, — 172 *Infant Daughter* 49
Untouched;—in spite of many a gleam — 182 *Waggoner* 4. 202
If thou appear untouched by solemn thought, — 258 **It is a* 10
Untouched through all severity of cold; — 276 *Filial Piety* 1
That treasures, yet untouched, may grace some future Lay. — 351 *Des. Stanzas* 90
Ungentle, or untouched by seemly ruth, — 359 *Plea: Hist.* 2
Untouched memento of her hapless doom! — 381 *Duddon* 22. 14
Untouched, unbreathed upon. Thrice happy quest, — 388 *Trosachs* 9
The name untouched, the tear unshed;— — 410 *White Doe* 1306
Emblem of faith untouched, miraculous attestation! — 437 *Ecc. Sonn.* 2. 35. 14
Untouched by due regret I marked your fall! — 449 *Ecc. Sonn.* 3. 35. 2
Untouched the hawthorn bough, — 506 **While from* 22
Think not that I could pass along untouched — 668 *Prelude* 5. 182
Hath left no corner of the land untouched: — 680 *Prelude* 6. 359
Nor must I leave untouched (the picture else — 881 *Excursion* 8. 484

Untoward. The Woman thus retraced her own untoward fate. — 28 *Guilt* 198
By some untoward death among the rocks: — 97 *Brothers* 155
When I with these untoward thoughts had striven, — 196 *Resolution* 53
Untoward or unfit; — 222 *Triad* 158
Who, with a toward or untoward lot, — 494 *Hap. War.* 68
Unconscious of its own untoward lot, — 524 *Epist. Beaumont* 195
With an untoward fate was long involved — 574 *Chiabrera* 5. 2
Alas! to few in this untoward world, — 741 *Prelude* 13. 121
Why should we thus, with an untoward mind, — 765 *Excursion* 1. 599
Precipitations, and untoward straits, — 800 *Excursion* 3. 983
In spite of many a rough untoward blast, — 828 *Excursion* 5. 396
Imposes, whensoe'er untoward chance — 834 *Excursion* 5. 764

Untowardness. But through untowardness of fate; — 291 *Rob Roy* 62

Untraced. A length of journey yet remains untraced: — 773 *Excursion* 2. 152
Wholly untraced a more forbidding way. — 848 *Excursion* 6. 662

Untrained. Men who, to business of the world untrained, — 721 *Prelude* 10. 197

Untransmuted. The untransmuted shapes of many worlds, — 682 *Prelude* 6. 464

Untravelled. To the deep shade of those untravelled Wilds; — 845 *Excursion* 6. 455
By those untravelled Dalesmen. With less pride, — 872 *Excursion* 7. 951

Untrembling. And shows in the untrembling frame — 543 *Russ. Fug.* 175

Untried. This untried world, and to prepare thy way — 173 *Infant Daughter* 73
Untried our Brothers have been loved — 401 *White Doe* 471
I, loving freedom, and untried; — 492 *Duty* 25
Implores the dreadful untried sleep of Death. — 613 *Desc.Sk.Quarto* 643
Arts yet untried, upon new counsels bent, — 624 *Æneid* 2
Of settling time in this untried abode, — 650 *Prelude* 3. 76
With some untried adventure, in a course — 686 *Prelude* 6. 729
To exercise their untried faculties) — 809 *Excursion* 4. 527
With mysteries;—for, if Faith were left untried, — 846 *Excursion* 6. 563

Untrod. A track pursuing, not untrod before, — 651 *Prelude* 3. 124

Untrodden. Theirs be these holms untrodden, still, and green, — 6 *Ev. Wk.* 233
She dwelt among the untrodden ways — 109 **She dwelt* 1

Untrodden—*continued.*
Of the untrodden lunar mountains; — 217 **Inmate of* 27
To what untrodden shore? — 300 *Cora Linn* 30
Of morning dew upon the untrodden meads, — 330 *Ode: Thanks.* 65
Its green untrodden turf, and blowing flowers; — 585 *Ch. Lamb* 54
These fairy holms untrodden, still, and green, — 595 *Ev. Wk. Quarto* 221
So to th' untrodden floor, where round him looks — 612 *Desc.Sk.Quarto* 574
Amid the untrodden desert, tells his beads, — 862 *Excursion* 7. 303

Untroubled. With angels when their own untroubled home — 229 *Cuckoo-clock* 40
Meanwhile untroubled I admire — 236 *P. B.* 16
But where untroubled peace and concord dwell, — 262 **Not Love* 5
Untroubled at the sight? — 338 **Meek Virgin* 6
Love ebb and flow untroubled by caprice; — 500 *Humanity* 57
And more than eighty, of untroubled life, — 659 *Prelude* 4. 37
In its untroubled element will shine — 849 *Excursion* 6. 764

Untrue. Silent, and to the gazer's eye untrue, — 377 *Duddon* 4. 6
To us, who war against the Untrue;— — 405 *White Doe* 836
And bold transfigurations, more untrue — 428 *Ecc. Sonn.* 1. 37. 5
To the confiding Bark, untrue; — 550 *Hermit's Cell* 5. 6
For to th' untrue he oft gives ease and joy; — 560 *Cuck.andNight.* 198
"Beshrew all them that are in love untrue." — 561 *Cuck.andNight.* 250
Portrayed with happiest pencil, not untrue — 583 **With copious* 23

Untruth. A weak and cowardly untruth! — 205 *Brougham* 106

Untuned. For cold and raw the air was, and untuned; — 660 *Prelude* 4. 145

Untuneful. "Why, Minstrel, these untuneful murmurings— — 252 **Why, Minstrel* 1

Untunes. And nought untunes that Infant's voice; no trace — 274 *Infant M.* 5
Untunes full oft the pleasures of the day; — 773 *Excursion* 2. 149

Untutored. And is it among rude untutored Dales, — 315 **And is it* 1
Though yet untutored and inordinate, — 674 *Prelude* 5. 574
"The untutored bird may found, and so construct, — 835 *Excursion* 5. 840
Home of untutored shepherds as it is, — K.8. 248 *Recluse* 1.1.446

Unuplifted. Most sweet it is with unuplifted eyes — 480 **Most sweet* 1
In silent grief their unuplifted heads, — 780 *Excursion* 2. 575

Unused. Are not unused to trouble friends — 245 *P. B.* 768
But, though to such demands unused, — 247 *P. B.* 1019
Though not unused to mutter lonesome songs, — 652 *Prelude* 3. 236

Unusual. Of an unusual strength: his mind was keen, — 131 *Michael* 44
Of an unusual strength. Among the rocks — 138 *Michael* 455
Unusual in its cry: — 491 *Fidelity* 12
Beset me, and to height unusual rose, — 666 *Prelude* 5. 62
Then fading with unusual quietness,— — 718 *Prelude* 10. 3
And night succeeded with unusual gloom, — 833 *Excursion* 5. 737
Keen anglers with unusual spoil elated. — 882 *Excursion* 8. 550
In an unusual way, and give to them — K.8. 230 **I will* 191
Unusual aspects, or by questions apt — K.8. 230 **I will* 192

Unutterable. And fittest to unutterable thought — 88 *H. C.* 3
Unutterable woe. — 580 *John Words.* 44
Eyed the poor babe with love unutterable. — 696 *Prelude* 7. 618
Unutterable love. Sound needed none, — 759 *Excursion* 1. 205

Unutterably. Unutterably helpless, and a look — 766 *Excursion* 1. 656

Unvanquished. Of awful prudence, keep the unvanquished soul: — 316 **It was a* 11

Unvaried. Such have we, but unvaried in its style; — 522 *Epist.Beaumont* 60
Broke only by th' unvaried torrent's sound, — 603 *Desc. Sk. Quarto* 58

Unveiled. That what has been unveiled to-day, — 545 *Russ. Fug.* 291
From centre to circumference, unveiled! — 548 **Stay, bold* 11
Unveiled the summit of Mont Blanc, and grieved — 683 *Prelude* 6. 525

Unveiling. Goes forth—unveiling timidly a cheek — 434 *Ecc. Sonn.* 2. 22. 5

Unversed. In music all unversed, nor blessed with skill — 521 *Epist.Beaumont* 30
A mind in all heart-mysteries unversed. — 840 *Excursion* 6. 166

Unvexed. Here, 'mid his own unvexed domains, — 214 *Kirkstone* 34
Of ordinary life; unvexed, unwarped — 761 *Excursion* 1. 357

Unviolated. Amid the unviolated grove — 169 *Wren's Nest* 70
"So, westward, tow'rd the unviolated woods — 799 *Excursion* 3. 944

Unvisited. Unvisited, where not a broken bough — 185 *Nutting* 17
Unvisited, endeavoured to retrace — 642 *Prelude* 2. 2
Leaving this nook unvisited: but, in sooth, — 788 *Excursion* 3. 119

Unvouchsafed. Not unvouchsafed—a light that warmed and cheered — 118 *Maternal Grief* 19

Unvoyageable. Here standing, with the unvoyageable sky — 827 *Excursion* 5. 342

Unwarped. Of ordinary life; unvexed, unwarped — 761 *Excursion* 1. 357

Unwary. And deluding the unwary — 549 *Hermit's Cell* 1. 7

Unwatched. So, unwatched by love maternal, — 93 *Westmoreland Girl* 29

Unwatchful. Perceived in things, where, to the unwatchful eye, — 646 *Prelude* 2. 300

Unwealthy. On an unwealthy mountain Benefice." — 824 *Excursion* 5. 132

Unweaponed. Thrilling the unweaponed crowd with plumeless heads?— — 233 *Power of Sound* 75
With breast unmailed, unweaponed hand. — 404 *White Doe* 765

Unwearied. *See* **Unweary'd.**
Beholds the unwearied sweep of wood that scales — 12 *Desc. Sk.* 109
By pacing here, unwearied and alone, — 150 **When, to* 62
Unwearied in that service: rather say — 207 *Tintern* 153
Chime forth unwearied canticles, — 228 *Devot. Incit.* 65
Unwearied joy, and life without its cares. — 268 **Brook! whose* 14
A pen unwearied—to indite, — 299 *Brownie's Cell* 57
The unwearied arrow hath pursued its flight! — 327 *Ode 1815* 33
Th' unwearied glance of woodman's echo'd stroke; — 593 *Ev. Wk. Quarto* 107
Th' unwearied sweep of wood thy cliffs that scales, — 604 *Desc.Sk.Quarto* 122
With pulseless hand, and fix'd unwearied gaze, — 616 *Desc.Sk.Quarto* 786
Checked our unwearied steps. Let this alone — 686 *Prelude* 6. 731
I have protracted, in the unwearied heavens — 751 *Prelude* 14. 383
By that unwearied signal, kenned afar; — 834 *Excursion* 5. 761
Two months unwearied of severest storm, — K.8. 241 *Recluse* 1.1.181
Be ready and unwearied without plea — K.8. 246 *Recluse* 1.1.371

Used—*continued.*
And we have always used him well; 129 *Idiot Boy* 304
Used to sing in heavenly tone, 144 **Driven in* 55
As used to be that sign of love 174 *Waggoner* 1. 85
To kirk she had been used to go, 246 *P. B.* 899
For he, with tongue not used to falter, 246 *P. B.* 903
And Love—a charmer's voice, that used to lend, 255 **Grief, thou* 5
May lead the thoughts, thus struggling used to stand 265 **When haughty* 10
That used to spread its boughs, and ring 413 *White Doe* 1588
Made room where wolf and boar were used to range? 468 *St. Bees* 139
That from his bauble prison used to cast 527 **Those breathing* 15
But Fortune, who had long been used to sport 529 **Those breathing* 120
Such sort of doctrine as men usèd there, 553 *Prioress* 47
Thus far, O Friend! did I, not used to make 632 *Prelude* 1. 46
Or suited to those years. Yet I, though used 654 *Prelude* 3. 368
Like a sick Lover, then this dog was used 660 *Prelude* 4. 105
Where an old man had used to sit alone, 661 *Prelude* 4. 202
Wert used to lie and gaze upon the clouds 679 *Prelude* 6. 269
Than other intellects had mine been used 708 *Prelude* 8. 623
The wondrous influence of power gently used, 734 *Prelude* 12. 15
O'er paths they used to deck: carnations, once 767 *Excursion* 1. 724
He said that she was used to ramble far.— 767 *Excursion* 1. 733
The peasants of these lonely valleys used 784 *Excursion* 2. 815
Which to and fro the mariner is used 805 *Excursion* 4. 247
Were used to thrill with pleasure, while his voice 843 *Excursion* 6. 336
Used or abused, as selfishness may prompt. 886 *Excursion* 9. 119
Of man or beast was seldom used to tread. K.8. 229 **I will* 142
Useful. Thanks for your care. Perhaps it would be useful 49 *Bord.* 670
Whether thou choose this useful part, 342 *Ital. Itin.* 25
The pious, humble, useful Secular, 433 *Ecc. Sonn.* 2. 19. 6
Yet, while each useful Art augments her store, 466 *St. Bees* 28
Oh! yet a few short years of useful life, 752 *Prelude* 14. 430
By useful habits, to a fitter soil 862 *Excursion* 7. 301
Usefully. A standard, often usefully applied, 676 *Prelude* 6. 103
Useless. Fallen am I, and worn out, a useless Man; 52 *Bord.* 824
he waved his hand, as if it were all useless; 72 *Bord.* 1935
And useless arms, a trunk of man, 294 *Jedbor.* 18
And with regret and useless pity haunt 336 *Staub-bach* 13
To stir in useless struggle) hath relied 440 *Ecc. Sonn.* 2. 45. 6
'Twas all in vain, a useless matter, 537 *Goody Blake* 113
But deem not this Man useless.—Statesmen! ye 567 *Cumb. Beg.* 67
Useless, and even, beloved Friend! a soul 721 *Prelude* 10. 235
Be not this labour useless. If such theme 755 *Recluse* 1. 1. 852
The useless fragment of a wooden bowl, 763 *Excursion* 1. 493
Uselessly. Work like a sea? Not uselessly employed, 639 *Prelude* 1. 475
Uselessness. His thrift thy uselessness will never scorn; 490 *Spade* 29
Uses. "Mark him, how his power he uses, 163 *Hint* 9
For gentlest uses, oft-times Nature takes 338 *Engelberg* 1
To finer uses. They for me must cease; S.3. 433 **The doubt* 21
Useth. Who most it useth, him 'twill most impair. 559 *Cuck.andNight.*170
Usher. —Well does thine aspect usher in this Day; 329 *Ode: Thanks.* 14
Ushering. Far oftener then, bad ushering worse event, 519 *Pun. Death* 8. 7
Using. The Man was using his best skill to gain 149 **A narrow* 64
Usual. Within a rocky cave, its usual home. 637 *Prelude* 1. 359
Went through his usual tasks, a silent change 785 *Excursion* 2. 893
Usurp. Dare to usurp;—thou hast a sword to wield, 432 *Ecc. Sonn.* 2. 15. 8
Usurpation. Of Nature, by a cunning usurpation 66 *Bord.* 1576
Of usurpation, when the light of sense 684 *Prelude* 6. 600
Usurpations. And over fancied usurpations brood, 505 *Warning* 115
Usurped. I found how my domains had been usurped, 40 *Bord.* 193
Of power usurped; with proclamation high, 383 *Duddon* 29. 13
No—some fierce Maniac hath usurped her name; 439 *Ecc. Sonn.* 2. 44. 11
A smart Assembly-room usurped the ground 642 *Prelude* 2. 39
The old Lion and usurped his place, in slight 644 *Prelude* 2. 152
That had usurped upon a living thought 683 *Prelude* 6. 527
Usurped upon far as the sight could reach. 746 *Prelude* 14. 49
Widely—inveterately usurped upon, 797 *Excursion* 3. 794
Produced, when thoughtless Folly hath usurped 842 *Excursion* 6. 280
Usurping. Usurping where the fairest herbage smiled: 17 *Desc. Sk.* 393
Usurping, with a prevalence 246 *P. B.* 919
In these usurping times of fear and pain? 316 **O'er the* 8
Meek eve shuts up the whole usurping host 456 **Soft as* 16
Usury. The loan with usury. 526 **The soaring* 24
By a great Lord, for gain and usury, 553 *Prioress* 39
Utensil. An aged utensil, which had performed 133 *Michael* 115
Utilitarian. Who scorns a false utilitarian lure 282 *Railway* 7
Utilities. By gross Utilities enslaved we need 358 *Aquap.* 348
Utmost. Yea, from the utmost corners of the earth, 63 *Bord.* 1410
His utmost for the welfare of the Boy; 136 *Michael* 309
—Even to the utmost I have been to thee 136 *Michael* 361
Intent to use his utmost haste, 176 *Waggoner* 2. 16
The utmost anger of the sky: 177 *Waggoner* 2. 73
And does his utmost to display 178 *Waggoner* 2. 142
To the utmost of his force! 181 *Waggoner* 4. 101
Of joy, that from her utmost walls 235 *Power of Sound* 202
Survive, and Fortune's utmost anger try; 265 **When haughty* 5
Their utmost bounty on thy head: 287 *Highland Girl* 4
Snows, torrents;—to the region's utmost bound, 350 *Des. Stanzas* 42
Have perished?—Verily, to her utmost depth, 356 *Aquap.* 277
And, though you with your utmost skill 483 *Simon Lee* 53
The utmost solitude of age to face, 531 *Octogen.* 12
The horizon's utmost boundary; far above 637 *Prelude* 1. 371
This label seemed of the utmost we can know, 696 *Prelude* 7. 645
And helpful to his utmost power: and there 783 *Excursion* 2. 762
Which unassisted reason's utmost power 830 *Excursion* 5. 521
Of days advancing toward their utmost length, 851 *Excursion* 6. 856
That filled her plains, that reached her utmost shores, 869 *Excursion* 7. 761
Even at the utmost distance of two miles K.8. 225 **I will* 42
Utopia. Not in Utopia,—subterranean fields,— 729 *Prelude* 11. 140
Utter. But did he utter nothing? See him there! 73 *Bord.* 2021
It is in truth an utter solitude; 131 *Michael* 13
Nor did he utter groan or sigh, 155 *Waterfall* 17
Clouds and utter glooms! 163 *Hint* 12
Her voice would utter, aught ensue 222 *Triad* 157
Than these, and utter your devotion there 230 *Clouds* 22
To utter melancholy moans 301 *Bran* 100
To utter notes of gladness, 302 *Yarrow V.* 6
And utter England's name with sadly-plausive voice. 327 *Ode 1815* 44
Their utter stillness, and the silent grace 329 *Ode: Thanks.* 21
To move in sunshine?—Utter thanks, my Soul! 354 *Aquap.* 88
In solitude, and utter peace: 399 *White Doe* 329
Of utter desolation made 411 *White Doe* 1428
And what a pensive Sage doth utter, hear! 422 *Ecc. Sonn.* 1. 15. 14
And let, for them, thy fountains utter strange 471 *Tynwald* 11
And let us utter thanks for blessings sown 524 *Epist. Beaumont* 201
To utter, above showers of blossom swept 537 **In desultory* 7
"I cannot bring to utter woe 542 *Russ. Fug.* 73
In utter solitude.—But he had left 551 **If thou in* 14
And not in utter nakedness, 588 *Immortality* 63
And lastly utter silence! "Be it so; 633 *Prelude* 1. 99
Yet slumbering, lay in utter solitude. 647 *Prelude* 2. 345
To utter waste. Hitherto I had stood 656 *Prelude* 3. 510
The voice of woman utter blasphemy— 693 *Prelude* 7. 385
Through utter weakness pitiably dear, 700 *Prelude* 8. 61
Of utter ruin. How might we believe 728 *Prelude* 11. 44
In reconcilement with an utter waste 732 *Prelude* 11. 324
I feel for thee, must utter what I feel: 733 *Prelude* 11. 405
And, lastly, utter loss of hope itself 734 *Prelude* 12. 6
Or dear voice utter, to complete the man, 749 *Prelude* 14. 223
Didst utter of the Lady Christabel; 752 *Prelude* 14. 401
And utter darkness: thought which may be faced, 790 *Excursion* 3. 262
Which States and Kingdoms utter when they talk 828 *Excursion* 5. 380
"That which we feel we utter; as we think 832 *Excursion* 5. 625
And sink, through utter want of cheering light; 835 *Excursion* 5. 834
Tyrants who utter the destroying word, 836 *Excursion* 5. 941
In utter night; and of his course remain 862 *Excursion* 7. 357
We are not so removed for utter loss; 885 *Excursion* 9. 83
Utterance. With something of a lofty utterance drest— 196 *Resolution* 94
With that faint utterance, which tells 227 *Vernal Ode* 98
Their natural utterance? whence this strange release 349 *At Dover* 6
She sues for help with piteous utterance! 378 *Duddon* 10. 8
Deep feeling, that found utterance loud, 409 *White Doe* 1228
Utterance of thanks that we have past with ease, 466 *St. Bees* 26
His utterance finds; and, conscious of the gain, 520 *Pun. Death* 14. 3
While they give utterance to the prayer 530 *Gleaner* 33
Surpass all science and all utterance; 552 *Prioress* 24
A timely utterance gave that thought relief, 588 *Immortality* 23
With what strange utterance did the loud dry wind 637 *Prelude* 1. 337
For utterance, to think what easy change 679 *Prelude* 6. 283
Nor can my tongue give utterance to a name 733 *Prelude* 11. 432
I would give utterance in numerous verse. 755 *Recluse* 1. 1. 766
By vocal utterance, or blaze of light, 811 *Excursion* 4. 653
Impulse and utterance. The whispering air 818 *Excursion* 4. 1170
Which then were silent; but crave utterance now. 826 *Excursion* 5. 241
To which the lips give public utterance 827 *Excursion* 5. 313
His own peculiar utterance for distress 837 *Excursion* 5. 982
Prompt utterance; but the Vicar interposed 880 *Excursion* 8. 439
My voice the utterance of a keen regret, 886 *Excursion* 9. 154
Utterances. Ye wandering Utterances, has earth no scheme, 235 *Power of Sound* 169
Uttered. *See* **Sadly-uttered.**
That often, when the name of God is uttered, 63 *Bord.* 1438
The cries he uttered might have stopped the boat 68 *Bord.* 1733
Leave that thought; and here be uttered 94 *Westmoreland Girl* 89
For that her Master never uttered word 125 *V. and J.* 292
Cheerfully uttered, with demeanour kind, 197 *Resolution* 135
Loud voice the Land has uttered forth, 204 *Brougham* 30
She saw—and uttered with a scream, 247 *P. B.* 1004
Must hear, first uttered from my orchard trees; 253 **A flock* 7
Those words were uttered as in pensive mood 263 **Those words* 1
And tongues that uttered wisdom—better none: 307 **Great men* 2
Uttered to Heaven in ecstasy devout! 322 *Germans* 8
Uttered by whom, or how inspired—designed 336 *Staub-bach* 1
A Visitant by whom these words were uttered:— 370 *Eg. Maid* 72
No sound is uttered,—but a deep 457 **Had this* 21
The words are uttered from my heart, 535 *Egremont* 23
A blast was uttered from the Horn, 535 *Egremont* 79
Ere the vile Cuckoo's note be utterèd. 557 *Cuck. and Night.* 50
Without word uttered, forth he 'gan to pace; 563 *Troilus* 19
Timidly uttered, for she *lives*, the meek, 585 *Ch. Lamb* 80
One word he softly uttered, 629 *Installation* 33
An Ode, in passion uttered, which foretold 667 *Prelude* 5. 96
Was Nature's, uttered from her Alpine throne; 681 *Prelude* 6. 431
And every word he uttered, on my ears 688 *Prelude* 7. 99
They uttered was a dart, by counter-winds 713 *Prelude* 9. 257
Was uttered, midnight darkness seemed to take 744 *Prelude* 13. 328
The words he uttered shall not pass away 820 *Excursion* 4. 1283
The words he uttered, and the scene that lay 857 *Excursion* 7. 2
Awful as ever stray Demoniac uttered, K.8. 246 *Recluse* 1. 1. 337
Uttering. First uttering, without words, a natural tune; 136 *Michael* 347
Fell down and clasped his knees for joy, not uttering word. 141 *Arm. Lady* 102
When Francis, uttering to the Maid 406 *White Doe* 975
While Mercy, uttering, through their voice, a sound 429 *Ecc. Sonn.* 2. 4. 8

Valdo—*continued.*

Ages ere Valdo raised his voice to preach . . . 431 Ecc. Sonn. 2. 12. 3
Vale. Though to the vale no parting beam . . . 1 Extract 11
O'er vale, and mountain, and the starless sky. . 1 Early Youth 6
Waving his hat, the shepherd, from the vale, . . 5 Ev. Wk. 182
On slowly-waving pinions, down the vale ; . . 6 Ev. Wk. 213
And breathes in peace the lily of the vale ! . . 6 Ev. Wk. 235
Ah no ! as fades the vale, they fade away : . . 8 Ev. Wk. 320
And plods through some wide realm o'er vale and height, ... 10 Desc. Sk. 11
From the green vale of Urseren smooth and wide 14 Desc. Sk. 196
Spread rooflike o'er the deep secluded vale, . . 14 Desc. Sk. 211
The still vale lengthens underneath its shade . . 14 Desc. Sk. 217
Leaving to silence the deserted vale ; . . . . 17 Desc. Sk. 373
Through Nature's vale his homely pleasures glide, 19 Desc. Sk. 492
That not for thy reward, unrivall'd Vale ! . . 21 Desc. Sk. 586
Wound in more welcome cadence down the vale ; 22 Desc. Sk. 635
Till his eye streamed with tears. In this deep vale 23 Yew-tree 46
Down a thick wood, they dropt into the vale ; . 34 Guilt 524
Of those Scotch Rovers echo through the vale. . 64 Bord. 1463
Through wood, and through vale ; and o'er rocky height, ... 80 †Address : Child 3
As up the vale, that afternoon, he walked . . 96 Brothers 92
That rises like a column from the vale, . . . 101 Brothers 367
This vale, where he had been so happy, seemed . 102 Brothers 425
One side of our whole vale with grandeur rare ; . 106 Farewell 4
Proud as a rainbow spanning half the vale, . . 111 *'Tis said that some 38
That follows the thought—We've no land in the vale, ... 116 Repentance 35
A woodman in the distant vale ; . . . . . . 126 Idiot Boy 29
He travels slowly down the vale. . . . . . 129 Idiot Boy 326
Upon the forest-side in Grasmere Vale . . . 131 Michael 40
That they were as a proverb in the vale . . . 132 Michael 94
Who dwelt within the limits of the vale, . . . 133 Michael 138
A habitation in this peaceful Vale, ... 150 *When, to 3
When once again we met in Grasmere Vale, . . 151 *When, to 73
A second time, in Grasmere's happy Vale. . . 151 *When, to 110
Winds our deep Vale, two heath-clad Rocks ascend 151 *Forth from 2
And this vale, so blithe a place ; . . . . . 171 Kitten 52
If you look to vale or hill, ... 171 Kitten 80
To all who entered Grasmere Vale ; . . . . 174 Waggoner 1. 55
Was passing by, and, down the vale . . . . 176 Waggoner 2. 11
(The vale now silent, hushed, I ween, ... 176 Waggoner 2. 12
And, while she roves through St. John's Vale, . 180 Waggoner 4. 23
Though babbling only to the Vale, ... 183 *O blithe 9
There is a Yew-tree, pride of Lorton Vale, . . 184 Yew-trees 1
And a river flows on through the vale of Cheapside. 188 Poor Susan 8
It sweeps from vale to vale ; . . . . 197 Thorn 26
And his bones lie in his paternal vale.— . . . 202 Hart-leap 94
To hill and vale proclaims aloud, ... 215 Kirkstone 84
Than his coevals in the sheltered vale . . . . 220 Haunted Tree 36
Fresh beauty through the vale. . . . . . . 224 *'Tis gone 60
The sunny vale looked gay ; . . . . 224 Primrose 28
Children, thus post ye over vale and height . . 229 Clouds 9
Luminous or gloomy, welcome to the vale . . . 230 Clouds 47
While hovering o'er the moonlight vale. . . . 235 Power of Sound 168
" Beloved Vale ! " I said, " when I shall con . 250 *Beloved Vale 1
But, when into the Vale I came, no fears . . 251 *Beloved Vale 6
Lo, in the vale, the mists of evening spread ! . 252 *The fairest 9
A grace the sinuous vale and roaring stream . . 253 *Aerial Rock 11
Shed on the chosen vale a sun-bright day ! . . 256 Marriage: Friend 4
Along the VALE OF MEDITATION flows ; . . . 272 Lady E. B. 2
In ours, the VALE OF FRIENDSHIP, let *this* spot 272 Lady E. B. 10
Deep in the vale a little rural Town . . . . 282 *While beams 2
O listen ! for the Vale profound . . . . . 289 Sol. Reap. 7
And, far and near, through vale and hill, . . 292 Rob Roy 117
It roused the Vale to holiday. . . . . . . 294 Jedbor. 34
Lord of the vale ! astounding Flood ; . . . . 299 Cora Linn 1
Lord of the vale ! to Heroes laid . . . . . 299 Cora Linn 17
A blue sky bends o'er Yarrow vale, ... 302 Yarrow V. 17
Of Yarrow Vale lay bleeding ? . . . . . . 302 Yarrow V. 26
That region left, the vale unfolds . . . . . 302 Yarrow V. 49
Inland, within a hollow vale, I stood ; . . . . 306 *Inland, within 1
And hollow vale which foaming torrents fill . . 314 *Not 'mid 6
An intermingled pomp of vale and hill, . . . 323 Ode 1814 8
Meek lustre, nor forget'st the humble Vale ; . . 329 Ode : Thanks. 30
Through Alpine vale, or champaign wide, . . . 337 Cath. Cantons 15
And, from that arch, down-looking on the Vale . 350 Des. Stanzas 33
From vale to hill, from hill to vale led on, . . 361 *List—'twas 9
Till Night, descending upon hill and vale, . . . 363 *List—'twas 110
But fill the hollow vale with joy ! . . . . . 376 *The Minstrels 78
Mother of Love ! for this deep vale, protect . . 380 Duddon 18. 6
While, less disturbed than in the narrow Vale . 384 Duddon 33. 5
Through the Vale retired and lowly, ... 396 White Doe 7
From Oxford come to his native vale, ... 399 White Doe 265
And up the vale of Wharf his way . . . . . 412 White Doe 1438
That hill and vale with sadness hear. . . . . 413 White Doe 1534
She comes, and in the vale hath heard . . . . 413 White Doe 1543
The White Doe followed up the vale, ... 414 White Doe 1705
That vale or hill prolongs or multiplies ! . . . 450 Ecc. Sonn. 3. 38. 14
How welcome wouldst thou be to this green Vale 455 Rydal Mere 31
The hollow vale from steep to steep, ... 457 *Had this 23
From the close confines of a shadowy vale. . . 460 *Queen of 9
On mortal notice.—Glory of the vale, ... 464 Derwent 6
Beneath stern mountains many a soft vale lies, . 472 *Arran ! a 13
Fit music for a solemn vale ! . . . . 478 Somnamb. 5
The pride of all the vale ; . . . . 486 *We walked 34
Now there is stillness in the vale, ... 494 Force of Prayer 37
Thus gladdened from our own dear Vale we pass . 524 Epist. Beaumont 164

Vale—*continued.*

Rich prospect left behind of stream and vale, . 524 Epist. Beaumont 223
Hot sunbeams fill the steaming vale ; but hark, 525 Epist. Beaumont 232
To build, within a vale beloved, ... 533 *Blest is 18
The Mother Church in yon sequestered vale ; . . 534 *When in 4
Bred in this vale, to which he appertained . . 548 *Stranger ! this 22
How oft have I heard in sweet Tilsbury Vale . . 569 Farmer 15
And his heart all the while is in Tilsbury Vale. . 571 Farmer 88
Round this dear Vale, his native place. . . . 578 *I come 60
Hidden was Grasmere Vale from sight, . . . 580 John Words. 25
Loud is the Vale ! the Voice is up . . . . . 581 *Loud is 1
Loud is the Vale ;—this inland Depth . . . . 581 *Loud is 5
That from the vale ascends. . . . . 583 *O for a 48
Waving his hat, the shepherd in the vale . . . 594 Ev. Wk. Quarto 165
While silent stands th' admiring vale below ; . . 595 Ev. Wk. Quarto 188
On red slow-waving pinions down the vale, . . 595 Ev. Wk. Quarto 192
The violet, and the lily of the vale ; . . . . 596 Ev. Wk. Quarto 224
Stays it's low murmur in th' unbreathing vale ; . 598 Ev. Wk. Quarto 356
And one sole light shifts in the vale profound ; . 606 Desc. Sk. Quarto 218
Now, passing Urseren's open vale serene, . . . 606 Desc. Sk. Quarto 243
Moveless o'er-hang the deep secluded vale, . . 607 Desc. Sk. Quarto 266
The still vale lengthens underneath the shade ; . 607 Desc. Sk. Quarto 270
To silence leaving the deserted vale, ... 610 Desc. Sk. Quarto 451
That not for thee, delicious vale ! unfold . . . 615 Desc. Sk. Quarto 704
Winded in sweeter cadence down the vale ; . . 616 Desc. Sk. Quarto 771
Wensley's rich Vale and Sedbergh's naked heights. 622 Recluse 1. 1. 157
And down the lone vale sails away . . . . . 626 †Cento 15
I sought thy golden vale with dancing flight, . . 630 [?] *O Moon 6
What dwelling shall receive me ? in what vale . 632 Prelude 1. 10
Of a known Vale, whither my feet should turn, . 633 Prelude 1. 72
The road that pointed toward the chosen Vale. . 633 Prelude 1. 93
In that belovèd Vale to which erelong . . . . 636 Prelude 1. 304
Nor less when spring had warmed the cultured Vale, 637 Prelude 1. 326
Of that large abbey, where within the Vale . . 643 Prelude 2. 103
To thee and thy grey huts, thou one dear Vale ! . 645 Prelude 2. 197
At the first gleam of dawn-light, when the Vale, . 647 Prelude 2. 344
A narrow Vale where each was known to all, . . 661 Prelude 4. 199
That murmured in the vale. All else was still ; . 664 Prelude 4. 384
Across the watery vale, and shout again, . . . 671 Prelude 5. 375
Fair is the spot, most beautiful the vale . . . 671 Prelude 5. 391
From hill to vale we dropped, from vale to hill . 682 Prelude 6. 495
Of those deep haunts, an aboriginal vale, . . . 683 Prelude 6. 519
That never more could be. The wondrous Vale . 683 Prelude 6. 528
Or in some sheltering vale, was seen a babe . . 692 Prelude 7. 355
Even as this setting sun (albeit the Vale . . . 706 Prelude 8. 471
In former days, when—spurring from the Vale . 727 Prelude 10. 597
Deep vale, or anywhere, the home of both, . . 741 Prelude 13. 126
We were tried Friends : amid a pleasant vale, . 757 Excursion 1. 52
The listless hours, while in the hollow vale, . . 760 Excursion 1. 259
Up through an ample vale, with higher hills . . 772 Excursion 2. 91
Of the broad vale, casting a casual glance, . . 773 Excursion 2. 116
The way, while we advanced up that wide vale. . 776 Excursion 2. 318
Beneath our feet, a little lowly vale, ... 776 Excursion 2. 328
A lowly vale, and yet uplifted high . . . . 776 Excursion 2. 329
Down whose steep sides we dropped into the vale, 779 Excursion 2. 547
That from some other vale peered into this. . . 782 Excursion 2. 693
Her husband enter—from a distant vale. . . . 783 Excursion 2. 794
Had been collected from the neighbouring vale, . 784 Excursion 2. 806
This little Vale, a dwelling-place of Man, . . . 784 Excursion 2. 870
Shut out from prospect of the open vale, . . . 786 Excursion 3. 38
And soon the Tenant of that lonely vale . . . 788 Excursion 3. 115
Aerial, or in green secluded vale, ... 792 Excursion 3. 394
To our secluded vale) it may be told— . . . . 793 Excursion 3. 501
Here closed the Tenant of that lonely vale . . 801 Excursion 4. 1
In the low vale, or on steep mountain-side ; . . 814 Excursion 4. 882
Of that brown ridge, sole outlet of the vale . . 822 Excursion 5. 12
To the green meadows of another vale. . . . 823 Excursion 5. 66
His rank and sacred function. This deep vale . 824 Excursion 5. 122
I saw the Tenant of the lonely vale . . . . 825 Excursion 5. 210
And streams, whose murmur fills this hollow vale, 836 Excursion 5. 917
Of this far-winding vale, remained as friends . . 844 Excursion 6. 409
She, 'mid the humble flowerets of the vale, . . 848 Excursion 6. 687
Above the centre of the Vale, a voice . . . . 849 Excursion 6. 762
Tho', in this Vale, remembered with deep awe." . 850 Excursion 6. 777
Of one who died within this vale, by doom . . 854 Excursion 6. 1076
And love, benignant mother of the vale, . . . 855 Excursion 6. 1107
Carries into the centre of the vale . . . . . 855 Excursion 6. 1118
When, in the hollow of some shadowy vale, . . 857 Excursion 7. 5
Led towards an easy outlet of the vale. . . . 858 Excursion 7. 49
To a small Chapel in the vale beyond) . . . 858 Excursion 7. 57
This old Man stood, the patriarch of the Vale ! . 861 Excursion 7. 243
But you, Sir, know that in a neighbouring vale . 862 Excursion 7. 315
Are brightened round her. In his native vale . 868 Excursion 7. 722
And fixed his home in this sequestered vale. . 871 Excursion 7. 926
Of England's realm, this vale he might have seen 871 Excursion 7. 933
The pensive Sceptic of the lonely vale . . . . 874 Excursion 8. 1
O'er hill and vale," the Wanderer thus expressed 876 Excursion 8. 157
Fetched by a neighbouring brook.—Across the vale 881 Excursion 8. 453
Upon the landscape of the sun-bright vale, . . 882 Excursion 8. 535
That Man descends into the VALE of years ; . . 885 Excursion 9. 49
High peaks, that bound the vale where now we are. 885 Excursion 9. 59
From the full river in the vale below, . . . 885 Excursion 9. 68
Within the bosom of his native vale. . . . . 888 Excursion 9. 280
And down the vale along the streamlet's edge . 890 Excursion 9. 434
(Her flowers were shed) the lily of the vale, . . 892 Excursion 9. 542
The shadowy vale, the sunny mountain-top ; . . 895 Excursion 9. 745
The Vale is by a mighty sound possess'd. . . . S.3. 425 *The rains 4
Of many a Grecian vale, who sought not praise, . S.3. 436 *The doubt 154
His flock into the vale, but as it chanced. . . K.8. 224 *I will 13

Vale—continued.
And Grisdale's houseless vale, along the brink — K.8. 225 *I will 30
But speaking of the vale in which he dwelt, — K.8. 230 *I will 199
His native vale and patrimonial fields — K.8. 231 *I will 212
Of vale below, a height of hills above. — K.8. 237 Recluse 1.1. 21
And now 'tis mine, perchance for life, dear Vale, — K.8. 238 Recluse 1.1. 56
The sunbeam said, "Be happy." When this Vale — K.8. 241 Recluse 1.1.170
It loves us now, this Vale so beautiful — K.8. 241 Recluse 1.1.179
Of winds, this deep Vale,—as it doth in part — K.8. 247 Recluse 1.1.375
Of this fair Vale, and o'er its spacious heights — K.8. 248 Recluse 1.1.431
Joy spreads, and sorrow spreads; and this whole Vale, — K.8. 248 Recluse 1.1.445
The famous sheep-dog, first in all the Vale, — K.8. 250 Recluse 1.1.510
And this deep vale, its earthly counterpart, — K.8. 254 Recluse 1.1.642
—Such is our wealth; O Vale of Peace, we are — K.8. 254 Recluse 1.1.662
Yet in this peaceful Vale we will not spend — K.8. 257 Recluse 1.1.751
A moon among her stars, a mighty vale, — K.8. 263 *The Lake 5

Valentine. Had helped thee to a Valentine; — 186 *O Nightingale 6
To the blank margin of a Valentine, — 851 Excursion 6. 892

Valentine's. Upon Saint Valentine's returning day. — 558 Cuck. and Night. 80
The morrow after Saint Valentine's day, — 562 Cuck. and Night. 282

Valerian. To the Valerian, Fabian, Curian Race, — 357 Aquap. 281

Vale's. From the hushed vale's realities, transferred — 456 *The leaves 11
From the Vale's peace which all her fields partake, — 521 Epist. Beaumont 2

Vales. In these secluded vales, if village fame, — 5 Ev. Wk. 192
Unheeded night has overcome the vales: — 8 Ev. Wk. 307
Thy cliffs; the endless waters of thy vales; — 12 Desc. Sk. 110
And long, long vales to travel through; — 81 †Mother's Return 14
Sung to the plaintive lyre in Grecian vales. — 170 *Never enlivened 19
That floats on high o'er vales and hills, — 187 *I wandered 2
The silver moon with all her vales, and hills of mightiest fame, — 189 Star-gazers 15
Glad were the vales, and every cottage-hearth; — 205 Brougham 169
O care! O guilt!—O vales and plains, — 214 Kirkstone 33
"He roved among the vales and streams, — 239 P. B. 241
Has filled the laughing vales with welcome flowers. — 263 *How clear 14
And green vales open out, with grove and field, — 268 *Four fiery 9
Mountains, and Vales, and Floods, I call on you — 283 *Proud were 13
To these few meagre Vales confined; — 291 Rob Roy 74
Whether of mighty towns, or vales — 295 Highland Boy 73
With joy in Kent's green vales; but never found — 306 *Here, on our 7
Through the green vales and through the herdsman's bower— — 315 *Advance—come 12
And all its branchy vales, and all that lurks — 350 Des. Stanzas 39
Ye Apennines! with all your fertile vales — 352 Aquap. 1
Or Sabine vales explored inspire a wish — 356 Aquap. 255
And in far-stretching vales, whose streams — 391 Highland Broach 71
Subalpine vales, in quest of safe retreats — 431 Ecc. Sonn. 2. 12. 6
And the green vales lie hushed in sober light! — 434 Ecc. Sonn. 2. 22. 14
When Alpine Vales threw forth a suppliant cry, — 441 Ecc. Sonn. 3. 7. 1
Then laugh, ye innocent Vales! ye Streams, sweep on, — 471 *Despond who 12
For Gods in council, whose green vales, retreats — 501 Humanity 74
Through peopled Vales; yet something in the guise — 522 Epist. Beaumont 98
In these fair vales hath many a Tree — 549 *In these 1
Ye vales and hills whose beauty hither drew — 587 Crosth. 1
Alike, when first the vales the bittern fills, — 592 Ev. Wk. Quarto 25
In these lone vales, if aught of faith may claim, — 595 Ev. Wk. Quarto 175
Who plods o'er hills and vales his road forlorn, — 602 Desc. Sk. Quarto 15
The never-ending waters of thy vales; — 604 Desc. Sk. Quarto 123
A solemn sea! whose vales and mountains round — 611 Desc. Sk. Quarto 496
Havoc and Chaos blast a thousand vales, — 615 Desc. Sk. Quarto 695
No more, along thy vales and viny groves, — 617 Desc. Sk. Quarto 788
To break, the vales where Death with Famine scow'rs, — 617 Desc. Sk. Quarto 794
Paced the long Vales—how long they were—and yet — 622 Recluse 1. 1. 155
Beheld not vales more beautiful than ours; — 639 Prelude 1. 480
In lieu of wandering, as we did, through vales — 669 Prelude 5. 235
Of deep and stately vales! A lonely pair — 680 Prelude 6. 384
Repeated through his tributary vales, — 699 Prelude 8. 13
Moors, mountains, headlands, and ye hollow vales, — 702 Prelude 8. 216
Celestial, lay unseen the pastoral vales — 725 Prelude 10. 524
Her seas yet smiling, her once happy vales; — 733 Prelude 11. 431
Of rural England's cultivated vales — 751 Prelude 14. 353
The freeborn Swiss to leave his narrow vales, — 761 Excursion 1. 318
To shroud them; only from the neighbouring vales — 776 Excursion 2. 346
His course, on errands bound, to other vales, — 783 Excursion 2. 769
Up through the trenches of the long-drawn vales — 808 Excursion 4. 454
Unknown to you that in these simple vales — 852 Excursion 6. 949
And into most of these secluded vales — 858 Excursion 7. 61
In works of havoc; taking from these vales, — 866 Excursion 7. 593
And in remotest vales was heard—to arms! — 869 Excursion 7. 762
Vales deeper far than these of ours, huge woods, — 869 Excursion 7. 802
To wander with us through the fertile vales, — 895 Excursion 9. 778
These vales were saddened with no common gloom — K.8. 275 *These vales 1

Valiant. Is he not valiant? Am I then so soon — 40 Bord. 161
The Effigies of a valiant Wight — 301 Bran 46
Wise, upright, valiant; not a servile band, — 310 *Another year 12
But if the valiant of this land — 328 Ode 1815 57
A valiant man, and a name of dread — 399 White Doe 250
For, with a high and valiant name, — 404 White Doe 793
The Dragon quelled; and valiant Margaret — 434 Ecc. Sonn. 2. 24. 9
And valiant; but young Oswald, like a chief — 869 Excursion 7. 772

Vallais. When from the Vallais we had turned, and clomb — 683 Prelude 6. 562

Valley. See **Mountain-valley.**
Across the gloomy valley flings her light, — 8 Ev. Wk. 335
When shouts and lowing herds the valley fill, — 17 Desc. Sk. 370
A mighty waste of mist the valley fills, — 17 Desc. Sk. 408
Beyond his native valley seldom stray, — 18 Desc. Sk. 428
The valley rings with mirth and joy; — 84 Shepherd-boys 1

Valley—continued.
Far and wide on hill and valley — 93 Westmoreland Girl 5
In this our valley all of us have wished, — 99 Brothers 288
Whenever from our Valley he withdrew; — 108 Indolence 29
Yon valley, now so trim and green, — 129 Idiot Boy 329
And made a hidden valley of their own. — 131 Michael 8
In that deep valley, Michael had designed — 136 Michael 323
He to that valley took his way, and there — 138 Michael 441
While yet the valley is arrayed, — 182 Waggoner 4. 240
All that the fertile valley shields; — 214 Kirkstone 28
Shouting through one valley calls, — 235 Power of Sound 205
In his first splendour, valley, rock, or hill; — 269 Westm. Bridge 10
But down the irriguous valley hies, — 338 *Meek Virgin 26
Across thy long deep Valley, furious Rhone! — 350 Des. Stanzas 29
The main flood roughened into hill and valley. — 369 Eg. Maid 42
Through hill and valley every breeze — 375 *The Minstrels 7
O'er hill and valley to this dim retreat! — 382 Duddon 25. 8
The soul's deep valley was not slow — 386 Yarrow Rev. 39
Of valley flowers. Nor, while the limbs repose, — 390 Glencroe 9
And down the valley then pursued, — 402 White Doe 592
The bright Moon sees that valley small — 406 White Doe 945
From hill or valley, could not move — 457 *Had this 17
And hill and valley rang with glee — 483 Simon Lee 10
Of hill and valley, he has viewed; — 485 Poet's Epitaph 46
Or in warm valley, seeks his part to fill; — 530 Poor Robin 26
Along a bare and open valley, — 586 Hogg 3
Above the gloomy valley flings her light, — 599 Ev. Wk. Quarto 403
And tempt the icy valley yawning deep, — 610 Desc. Sk. Quarto 463
Beyond his native valley hardly stray, — 611 Desc. Sk. Quarto 515
Dear Valley, having in thy face a smile — 622 Recluse 1. 1. 116
When vapours rolling down the valley made — 638 Prelude 1. 417
With lilies of the valley like a field; — 643 Prelude 2. 61
In that sequestered valley may be seen, — 643 Prelude 2. 111
And down the valley, and, a circuit made — 644 Prelude 2. 129
Towards that sweet Valley where I had been reared; — 658 Prelude 4. 19
Of that sweet Valley; when its paths, its shores, — 672 Prelude 5. 428
Alone, within the valley, at a point — 684 Prelude 6. 642
Sets off the sunbeam in the valley, so — 696 Prelude 7. 620
Some sweet lass of the valley, looking out — 699 Prelude 8. 38
Where Etna, over hill and valley, casts — 732 Prelude 11. 377
Of that small valley, singing as they moved; — 777 Excursion 2. 390
And, deep within that lonesome valley, stood — 786 Excursion 3. 8
This shaded valley leaves; and leaves the dark — 807 Excursion 4. 399
"Farewell, deep Valley, with thy one rude House, — 822 Excursion 5. 1
Attain a point that showed the valley—stretched — 823 Excursion 5. 78
"As 'mid some happy valley of the Alps," — 823 Excursion 5. 92
This fertile valley! Not a house but seems — 828 Excursion 5. 412
Stands in our valley, named The Joyful Tree; — 851 Excursion 6. 832
Restored me to my native valley, here — 860 Excursion 7. 198
Nor so the Valley shall forget her loss. — 868 Excursion 7. 705
Our unpretending valley.—How the quoit — 868 Excursion 7. 740
From this lone valley, to a central spot — 869 Excursion 7. 768
The Valley, opening out her bosom, gave — 892 Excursion 9. 571
Through the valley, up the hill; — S.3. 424 Tinker 27
Must be his home, this Valley be his world. — K.8. 237 Recluse 1.1. 45
Choosing this Valley, they who had the choice — K.8. 243 Recluse 1.1.242
That the whole Valley knew them; but to us — K.8. 243 Recluse 1.1.247
Delightful Valley, habitation fair! — K.8. 245 Recluse 1.1.300

Valley-clock. On viewless fingers counts the valley-clock, — 606 Desc. Sk. Quarto 227

Valley's. Into a narrow valley's pleasant scene — 34 Guilt 515
Out of our Valley's limits did he roam: — 107 Indolence 12
Turning with quiet touch the valley's hay, — 607 Desc. Sk. Quarto 274
In his own valley's rocky guardianship. — 829 Excursion 5. 451

Valleys. And fireless are the valleys far and wide, — 7 Ev. Wk. 261
Falls on the valleys as the sun goes down; — 19 Desc. Sk. 471
When vapours rolling down the valleys made — 89 Prelude 1. 417
Commend me to these valleys! Yet your Churchyard — 98 Brothers 166
Of Shepherds, dwellers in the valleys, men — 131 Michael 23
That the green valleys, and the streams and rocks, — 132 Michael 63
And this the valleys show; — 300 Cora Linn 33
Not seldom, when with heat the valleys faint, — 376 Duddon 2. 4
The freshness of the valleys; let his blood — 568 Cumb. Beg. 173
In a thousand valleys far and wide, — 588 Immortality 47
Enticing valleys, greeted them and left — 682 Prelude 6. 501
Bare hills and valleys, full of caverns, rocks, — 708 Prelude 8. 635
The peasants of these lonely valleys used — 784 Excursion 2. 815

Vallombre. Vallombre, 'mid her falling fanes, deplores, — 12 Desc. Sk. 75

Vallombre's. Upon the open lawns! Vallombre's groves — 682 Prelude 6. 480

Vallombrosa. Vallombrosa! I longed in thy shadiest wood — 345 Stanzas: Simplon 1
"Vallombrosa—I longed in thy shadiest wood — 364 Vallomb. 1
Vallombrosa! of thee I first heard in the page — 364 Vallomb. 25

Valour. Nor discipline nor valour can withstand — 309 *What if 9
Whereon deliberate Valour and the rage — 318 *Is there 7
On Marathonian valour, yet the tear — 339 Tell 3
Of valour, truth, and love. — 479 Somnamb. 117
Were a line for valour famed) — 535 Egremont 42

Value. But not the value of a hair — 239 P. B. 239
Each step hath its value while homeward we move;— — 346 Stanzas: Simplon 29
Where what he most doth value must be won: — 494 Hap. War. 71
In what she most doth value, love of God — 781 Excursion 2. 633

Valued. Storms make in rising, valued in the moon — 505 Warning 145
And yet the books which then I valued most — 676 Prelude 6. 99

Van. And now the van reflects the solar beam; — 6 Ev. Wk. 203
Observe each wing!—a tiny van! — 227 Vernal Ode 114
From van to rear—and with one mind would flee — 314 Hofer 10

Van—*continued.*
Flinging round van and rear his ghastly net, . . 321 **Humanity, delighting* 14
Art thou a Statist in the van . . . . . . 485 *Poet's Epitaph* 1
And now the van is gilt with evening's beam, . 595 *Ev.Wk.Quarto* 185
Vane. A broad and gilded vane. . . . . . . 86 *Anecdote* 52
Young Vane, and others who called Milton friend. 307 **Great men* 4
Nor to you, good Lady Vane, ... S.3. 438 **My Lord* 3
Vanes. Her Spires, her Steeple-towers with glittering vanes . . . . 444 *Ecc. Sonn.* 3. 17. 11
Do of itself blow fresh, and make the vanes . . 723 *Prelude* 10. 370
Vanguard. The Vanguard—you may smirk and smile, ... 178 *Waggoner* 2. 116
The Vanguard, following close behind, . . . 179 *Waggoner* 3. 68
Vanguard of Liberty, ye men of Kent, ... 309 *Men of Kent* 1
Vanish. Here, vanish, as in mist, before a flood 4 *Ev. Wk.* 100
The shape will vanish—and behold . . . . 159 **With little* 29
Yet vanish not!—the wind is in the tree, . . 184 *Night-piece* 18
Must vanish, and his careless cheer . . . . 204 *Brougham* 93
And surely as they vanish. Earth destroys . . 210 *Laod.* 70
Vanish inverted hill, and shadowy wood, . . . 212 *Dion*
Would gladly vanish from a Stranger's sight; . 221 *Triad* 122
Shall vanish, if ye please, ... 225 *Present.* 27
To vanish—fleet as days and months and years, . 230 *Clouds* 37
And vanish, though the heavens dissolve, her stay 235 *Power of Sound* 223
When earth shall vanish from our closing eyes, . 281 **What strong* 13
And vanish by mysterious art; . . . . . . 300 *Bran* 10
They melt, and soon must vanish; . . . . . 302 *Yarrow V.* 82
Those titles vanish, and that strength decay; . 305 *Ven. Rep.* 10
Her morning splendours vanish, and their place . 359 **Those old* 6
That gave them being, vanish to a sound. . . 361 **When here* 14
Like spiteful Fiends that vanish, crossed . . . 369 *Eg. Maid* 34
Ill sight! but grief may vanish ere the morrow." 372 *Eg. Maid* 210
The elements, must vanish;—be it so! . . . . 384 *Duddon* 34. 9
Will vanish the last Highland Broach. . . . 391 *Highland Broach* 78
But see—they vanish one by one, ... 399 *White Doe* 322
From their known course, or vanish like a dream; 421 *Ecc. Sonn.* 1. 12. 10
Vanish before the unreserved embrace . . . 449 *Ecc.Sonn.* 3. 36. 10
So vanish those fair Shadows, human joys, . . 598 *Ev. Wk. Quarto* 361
Whose flower with us will vanish, must survive. . 627 **We gaze* 14
That shift and vanish, change and interchange . 707 *Prelude* 8. 571
If not, then others vanish into air. . . . . 741 *Prelude* 13. 93
"Possessions vanish, and opinions change, . . 802 *Excursion* 4. 69
Vanished. *See* **Long-vanished.**
—The lights are vanished from the watery plains: 8 *Ev. Wk.* 305
O'er all its vanished dells, and lawns, and woods; 8 *Ev. Wk.* 332
All vanished. I gave way—do you attend? . . 69 *Bord.* 1763
Are vanished; gladness ceases in the groves, . . 105 *Artegal* 200
But horse and man are vanished, one and all; . 200 *Hart-leap* 15
But lo! the vanished company again . . . . 218 *Recluse* 1. 1. 218
All vanished;—'twas a heartfelt cross . . . . 297 *Highland Boy* 213
And, with the guilt and shame, the Woe hath vanished, ... 330 *Ode: Thanks.* 129
She vanished; leaving prospect blank and cold . 334 **A wingèd* 6
Effigy of the Vanished—(shall I dare . . . . 472 **The captive* 9
Vanished ye are, but subject to recall; . . . 474 **Ye shadowy* 9
Had vanished, swallowed up with all that there . 540 *Grace Darl.* 33
All vanished in a single word, ... 580 *John Words.* 35
Oh, fled for ever! vanished like a blast . . . 583 **With copious* 17
Has vanished from his lonely hearth. . . . . 586 *Hogg* 20
His joys, his griefs, have vanished like a cloud . 587 *Crosth.* 15
Smiled like the morn, and vanish'd into air." . 619 *School Ex.* 112
Features which else had vanished like a dream. . 626 **The confidence* 14
Six changeful years have vanished since I first . 687 *Prelude* 7. 1
Had vanished, leaving others in their stead: . . 689 *Prelude* 7. 143
Vanished and vanishing in subtle chase, . . . 700 *Prelude* 8. 90
Of vanished nations, or more clearly drawn . . 708 *Prelude* 8. 615
Ere the last star had vanished.—They who passed 764 *Excursion* 1. 527
Had vanished, much was come and coming back— 779 *Excursion* 2. 522
Sate by my side, had vanished, if a wish . . . 829 *Excursion* 5. 448
Hopeful and cheerful:—vanished is the pall . . 830 *Excursion* 5. 547
Vanished or hidden; and the whole domain, . . 830 *Excursion* 5. 549
Had vanished from his prospects and desires; . 840 *Excursion* 6. 137
He vanished; but conspicuous to this day . . 842 *Excursion* 6. 244
"'All gone, all vanished! he deprived and bare, 861 *Excursion* 7. 263
The spear and shield are vanished, which the Knight 872 *Excursion* 7. 961
Have vanished—swallowed up by stately roads . 876 *Excursion* 8. 109
Upon the grave of vanished Syracuse, ... 877 *Excursion* 8. 221
She vanished—eager to impart the scheme . . 890 *Excursion* 9. 430
From under thee hath vanished, and slant beams, S.3. 435 **The doubt* 101
Vanishes. Fear that soon vanishes before the sight . 355 *Aquap.* 182
Vanishing. News of winter's vanishing, ... 161 **Pleasures newly* 18
Of future vanishing like empty dreams) . . . 426 *Ecc. Sonn.* 1. 30. 7
Whose vanishing was rumoured wide, ... 545 *Russ. Fug.* 315
Vanished and vanishing in subtle chase, . . . 700 *Prelude* 8. 90
Vanishings. Fallings from us, vanishings; . . . 589 *Immortality* 147
Vanities. Of pious faith the vanities of grief; . . 119 *Maternal Grief* 73
Prompting the world's audacious vanities! . . . 313 **Go back* 4
From all the fuming vanities of Earth! . . . 349 *Sky-prosp.* 14
To Heaven; for, either lost in vanities . . . 433 *Ecc. Sonn.* 2. 18. 8
The elastic vanities of yesterday?" . . . . 456 **Soft as* 26
Time's vanities, light fragments of earth's dream— 584 **With copious* 39
In some of its unworthy vanities, ... 653 *Prelude* 3. 320
To paint these vanities, and how they wrought . 662 *Prelude* 4. 293
Leaves far behind life's treacherous vanities, . . 682 *Prelude* 6. 453
Idle temptations; open vanities, ... 804 *Excursion* 4. 209
Vanity. The bound of all his vanity, to deck, . . 19 *Desc. Sk.* 494
Among the restless sails of vanity. . . . . . 190 **Lyre! though* 12
Pity the tree.—Poor human vanity, ... 670 *Prelude* 5. 329
Had vanity (quick Spirit that appears . . . . 688 *Prelude* 7. 103
Faith given to vanity and emptiness; . . . . 712 *Prelude* 9. 172

Vanity—*continued.*
Or seemed so, yet it was not vanity, ... 714 *Prelude* 9. 314
Of insolent tempers, the light vanity . . . . 723 *Prelude* 10. 346
Of social vanity, he walked the world, . . . 774 *Excursion* 2. 181
As vanity and fondness for applause, ... 775 *Excursion* 2. 225
The little flower her vanity shall check; . . . 807 *Excursion* 4. 425
For the reproof of human vanity, ... 842 *Excursion* 6. 302
As Fancy's snare for female vanity, ... S.3. 436 **The doubt* 147
Vanity's. Vanity's hieroglyphic; a choice trope . 345 **Ambition—following* 8
Vannes. And glorifies the truant youth of Vannes. 627 *Eagle and Dove* 8
Vanquish. Misgivings, hard to vanquish or control, 112 **O dearer* 5
Vanquished. Say not that we have vanquished—but that we survive. . . . . 330 *Ode: Thanks.* 91
And singly thine, O vanquished Chief! whose corse, 361 **For action* 9
How vanquished Mithridates northward passed, . 635 *Prelude* 1. 187
The vanquished Whig, under a borrowed name, . 845 *Excursion* 6. 451
Vans. Where ravens spread their plumy vans, at ease! 496 **A little* 32
Vantage. On "coignes of vantage" hang their nests of clay; . . . . 259 **A volant* 3
That like a place of vantage showed; . . . . 412 *White Doe* 1478
Vantage-ground. On me uplifted from the vantage-ground . . . . 724 *Prelude* 10. 449
Upon the steadfast 'vantage-ground of truth. . 882 *Excursion* 8. 533
Vapour. Of low-hung vapour: on the freshened mead 14 *Desc. Sk.* 218
Where wreaths of vapour tracked a winding brook, 34 *Guilt* 516
Bright volumes of vapour through Lothbury glide, 188 *Poor Susan* 7
No vapour stretched its wings; no cloud . . 343 *Eclipse* 19
Like vapour, like a towering cloud, dissolved. . 352 *Aquap.* 8
Not with a grief that, like a vapour, rises . . . 373 *Eg. Maid* 260
Like wreaths of vapour without stain or blot. . 390 *Highland Hut* 4
Like an unfathered vapour that enwraps, . . . 684 *Prelude* 6. 595
Of the blind vapour, opened to my view . . 784 *Excursion* 2. 831
Of vapour glittering in the morning sun. . . . 876 *Excursion* 8. 127
Vapoured. Some vapoured in the unruliness of joy, 681 *Prelude* 6. 392
Vapours. Amid tempestuous vapours driving by, . 15 *Desc. Sk.* 255
Mount through the nearer vapours notes of birds, 18 *Desc. Sk.* 417
Or through the glittering vapours dart . . . 84 *Shepherd-boys* 10
(Where, smoothly urged, the vapours sweep . . 180 *Waggoner* 4. 62
And vapours magnify and spread . . . . . 228 *Devot. Incit.* 66
Which mists and vapours from mine eyes did shroud— . . . . 257 **Methought I* 2
As vapours breathed from dungeons cold . . . 284 *Grave of Burns* 3
The vapours linger round the Heights, . . . 302 *Yarrow V.* 81
Like vapours, years have rolled and spread; . . 391 *Highland Broach* 80
From wind, or frost, or vapours wet— . . . 409 *White Doe* 1176
Through Alpine vapours. Such appalling rite . 450 *Ecc. Sonn.* 3. 40. 6
Loose vapours have I watched, that won . . . 472 *Ossian* 7
Softly as morning vapours glide . . . . . . 534 **Blest is* 85
'Mid stormy vapours ever driving by, ... 608 *Desc.Sk.Quarto* 317
When vapours rolling down the valley made . . 638 *Prelude* 1. 417
Dews, vapours, and the melody of birds, . . . 663 *Prelude* 4. 331
Far, far beyond, the solid vapours stretched, . . 746 *Prelude* 14. 45
Were hidden, and black vapours coursed their sides; 783 *Excursion* 2. 783
The vapours had receded, taking there . . . 784 *Excursion* 2. 850
Flying, and rainy vapours, call out shapes . . 809 *Excursion* 4. 522
Tall ash-tree, sown by winds, by vapours nursed, 866 *Excursion* 7. 596
Vapoury. Thy daring in a vapoury bourn, . . . 215 *Kirkstone* 50
Gifted to purge the vapoury atmosphere . . . 380 *Duddon* 18. 8
Or crossed by vapoury streaks and clouds that move 459 **Wanderer! that* 35
Half-veiled in vapoury cloud, the silver steam . 773 *Excursion* 2. 131
The vapoury phantoms of futurity? . . . . 817 *Excursion* 4. 1057
That virtue, like the fumes and vapoury clouds . 863 *Excursion* 7. 379
Variable. Under a cope of sky more variable, . . 812 *Excursion* 4. 720
Varied. These are before me; and the varied scene 352 *Aquap.* 23
And all the varied landscape. Let us now . . 358 *Aquap.* 371
Those rare accomplishments, and varied powers, . 583 **With copious* 15
Of ampler or more varied argument, ... 641 *Prelude* 1. 643
And that more varied and elaborate, ... 668 *Prelude* 5. 204
A gift then first bestowed. The varied banks . 678 *Prelude* 6. 203
And when the partner of those varied walks . . 716 *Prelude* 9. 479
The varied functions and high attributes . . . 798 *Excursion* 3. 824
Variegated. So richly decked in variegated down, . 231 **The gentlest Poet* 17
But some—a variegated band . . . . . . 398 *White Doe* 162
Some variegated story, in the main . . . . 635 *Prelude* 1. 224
That variegated journey step by step. . . . . 682 *Prelude* 6. 490
A variegated landscape,—there the shape . . . 708 *Prelude* 8. 584
Lay spotted with a variegated crowd . . . . 726 *Prelude* 10. 563
Whose variegated feelings were in this . . . 736 *Prelude* 12. 163
Varies. Varies its rainbow hues. But vainly thus, 760 *Excursion* 1. 298
Varieties. And rapture, with varieties of fear . . 541 *Grace Darl.* 64
By all varieties of human love . . . . . . 732 *Prelude* 11. 351
No wild varieties of joy and grief. . . . . . 761 *Excursion* 1. 360
Variety. Thousands, in each variety of tongue . . 509 *F. Stone* 93
Lives only by variety of disease. . . . . . 721 *Prelude* 10. 208
Various. While Echo dallies with its various din! . 5 *Ev. Wk.* 161
Meanwhile discourse ensued of various kind, . . 27 *Guilt* 193
Rise various wreaths that into one unite . . . 33 *Guilt* 462
The steps of June; as if their various hues . . 146 **It was an* 10
I stood in various thoughts and fancies lost, . . 202 *Hart-leap* 117
The various turns of Crusoe's fate)— . . . . 215 *Enterprise* 6
Like stars, at various heights; . . . . . . 224 *Primrose* 4
Scattered, a Cyclades of various shapes . . . 231 *Clouds* 77
Kind Nature's various wealth was all your own; 256 *Easter* 13
We have pursued, through various lands, a long . 361 **List—'twas* 10
And Trajan still, through various enterprise, . . 368 *Trajan* 68
And various climes, was not unknown . . . 390 *Highland Broach* 15
The tears of man in various measure gush . . 436 *Ecc. Sonn.* 2. 32. 1
From various sources; gently overflow . . . 436 *Ecc. Sonn.* 2. 32. 2
Produced you nursed in various climes . . . 473 *Ossian* 64

Various—continued.
Thoughtfully freighted with a various store ; . . 522 Epist. Beaumont 94
To honourable Men of various worth : . . . . 547 *Beneath yon 8
While Echo dallies with the various din ! . . . 594 Ev. Wk. Quarto 144
At morn, our various journey, sad and slow. . . 617 Desc. Sk. Quarto 813
Endowed with various power to search the soul ; 695 Prelude 7. 548
For 'tis most certain, that these various sights, . 710 Prelude 9. 74
Whether in matters various, properties . . . 732 Prelude 11. 331
And various trials of our complex being, . . . 736 Prelude 12. 149
Of various tempers ; to endure and note . . . 751 Prelude 14. 335
For hence, minutely, in his various rounds, . . 761 Excursion 1. 374
He mingled, where he might, the various tasks . 764 Excursion 1. 576
Which nature's various objects might inspire ; . 772 Excursion 2. 39
We scanned the various features of the scene : . 788 Excursion 3. 114
Of various intercourse, nor wishing aught . . . 794 Excursion 3. 587
Are various engines working, not the same . . 809 Excursion 4. 555
And as we fall by various ways, and sink . . . 818 Excursion 4. 1109
So manifold and various are the ways . . . . 818 Excursion 4. 1112
He shall discern, how, through the various means 819 Excursion 4. 1232
The tribute by these various records claimed, . 825 Excursion 5. 171
Various, but unto each some tribute paid ; . . 837 Excursion 5. 972
And various fluctuations in the breast ; . . . 841 Excursion 6. 209
By various mockery of sight and sound ; . . . 841 Excursion 6. 228
Various and vast. A memorable age ! . . . 873 Excursion 7. 1012
Kind nature's various wealth is all their own. . 875 Excursion 8. 61
And hardship undergone in various climes, . . 882 Excursion 8. 509
And in the various conversation bore . . . . 882 Excursion 8. 528
His mind gives back the various forms of things, 891 Excursion 9. 463
Variously. As variously thy power was shown, . . 216 Enterprise 39
—Those seven fair brothers variously were moved 867 Excursion 7. 657
Varlet. Ay, come to me and weep. Yes, Varlet, look, 76 Bord. 2189
Varnish. As with the varnish, and the gloss of dreams ; . . . . K.8. 252 Recluse 1.1.573
Vary. That vary to the heart within. . . . . 415 White Doe 1723
Varying. See **Ever-varying, Never-varying, Slow-varying.**
His neck, a varying arch, between his towering wings : . . . . 6 Ev. Wk. 219
To thee, by varying titles known . . . . . 216 Enterprise 38
With beauty, which is varying every hour ; . . 256 *Yes ! hope 11
Varying its shape wherever he may run. . . . 278 *Life with 8
Our pleasure varying at command . . . . . 286 Nith 29
Of Mountains varying momently their crests— . 388 Loch Etive 5
Varying her crowded peaks and ridges blue ; . . 471 *Arran ! a 3
That verse of mine, whate'er its varying mood, . 476 Eden 3
Our varying moods, on human kind or brute, . 501 Humanity 98
Proud of the varying arch and moveless form of snow. . . . . 595 Ev. Wk. Quarto 206
Wooing her varying charms from eve to morn. . 602 Desc. Sk. Quarto 16
Of undulations varying as might please . . . 680 Prelude 6. 368
With danger, varying as the seasons change), . 682 Prelude 6. 510
Varying their composition and their hue, . . . 750 Prelude 14. 326
Expression ever varying ! Thus informed, . . 758 Excursion 1. 162
Or solace, varying as the seasons change. . . . 310 Excursion 4. 587
Varying its tincture with the changeful light, . 824 Excursion 5. 161
Expression slowly varying, that evinced . . . 834 Excursion 5. 785
Tender or blithe ; now, as the varying mood . . 857 Excursion 7. 16
—Ah ! that such beauty, varying in the light . 891 Excursion 9. 512
Vase. And, by the beauty of the vase beguil'd, . 620 Birth of Love 7
Vassal. "Another horse !"—That shout the vassal heard . . . . 200 Hart-leap 5
Should bind the vassal to his lord's domains ? . 468 St. Bees 141
This Russian vassal plied, ... 543 Russ. Fug. 106
He was her vassal of all labour, tilled . . . . 783 Excursion 2. 764
Your vassal necks how poor the garter's pride ! . L.1. 97 Juvenal 3. 91
Vassalage. A potent vassalage, to fight . . . . 400 White Doe 366
And all the heavy or light vassalage . . . . 501 Humanity 96
To endure this state of meagre vassalage, . . . 673 Prelude 5. 518
The vassalage that binds her to the earth, . . 807 Excursion 4. 421
Vassal's. And now, as he approached a vassal's door, 200 Hart-leap 3
Vassals. May touch, whene'er her Vassals are at work. 59 Bord. 1174
If eyes be still sworn vassals of belief, ... 474 *Ye shadowy 13
Mad Fancy's favourite vassals ? Does not life . 812 Excursion 4. 769
Of those who once were vassals of her soil, . . 886 Excursion 9. 180
Vast. Or on some vast and solitary plain . . . 56 Bord. 1012
Deep, deep and vast, vast beyond human thought, 64 Bord. 1466
Of a vast building made of many crags ; . . . 101 Brothers 365
Along so vast a surface, all at once, ... 147 Joanna 48
Of the vast sea didst bring a watchful heart . . 151 *When, to 81
Of vast circumference and gloom profound . . 184 Yew-trees 9
What a vast abyss is there ! . . . . . . 217 *Inmate of 10
Vast is the compass and the swell of notes : . . 234 Power of Sound 162
Each other in the vast abyss, ... 237 P. B. 44
Oh, had this vast theatric structure wound . . 269 Malham 6
The vast Pacific gladdens with the freight— . . 327 Ode 1815 23
The city one vast temple, dedicate . . . . . 334 *The Spirit 10
With such vast hoards of hidden carnage near, . 335 *A winged 13
This vast design might tempt you to repeat . . 335 Cologne 11
"Though vast thy power, thy words are weak," . 372 Eg. Maid 211
The Wanderer seeks that receptacle vast . . . 384 Duddon 33. 7
Till the whole City rings like one vast quire. . . 442 Ecc. Sonn. 3. 8. 8
Thy domination ; as the whole vast Sea . . . 459 *Wanderer ! that 48
While heaven's vast sea of voices chants their praise. 474 *On to 14
Apart, to overlook the circle vast— . . . . 477 Long Meg 7
For thought—dominion vast and absolute . . 489 Illus. Books 4
Is ever urging on the vast machine . . . . 501 Humanity 92
And while in that vast solitude to which . . . 568 Cumb. Beg. 163
And neighbouring moon, that coasts the vast profound, ... 609 Desc. Sk. Quarto 382
Devoted, strives in vain her vast desires to fill ; . 624 Æneid 80
From the vast city, where I long had pined . . 632 Prelude 1. 7

Vast—continued.
Near or remote, minute or vast ; an eye . . . 651 Prelude 3. 159
A creek in the vast sea ; for, all degrees . . . 657 Prelude 3. 591
Like a vast river, stretching in the sun. . . . 658 Prelude 4. 6
Votary (in vast cathedral, where no foot . . . 664 Prelude 4. 362
Five rivers broad and vast, made rich amends, . 683 Prelude 6. 532
Adorning flowery gardens, 'mid vast squares ; . 689 Prelude 7. 135
His little stage in the vast theatre, ... 692 Prelude 7. 358
Meanwhile, as if the whole were one vast mill, . 698 Prelude 7. 719
This did I feel, in London's vast domain. . . . 698 Prelude 7. 765
Nook is there none, nor tract of that vast space . 702 Prelude 8. 202
In those vast regions where his service lies, . . 703 Prelude 8. 252
Entered thy vast dominion ? On the roof . . 707 Prelude 8. 543
As I explored the vast metropolis, ... 708 Prelude 8. 592
Vast prospect of the world which I had been . . 751 Prelude 14. 381
But vast in size, in substance glorified ; . . . 784 Excursion 2. 866
And turbulence of murmuring cities vast ; . . 787 Excursion 3. 104
Eddying within its vast circumference, . . . 788 Excursion 3. 147
Regions of wood and wide savannah, vast . . 799 Excursion 3. 938
And the vast hills, in fluctuation fixed . . . 802 Excursion 4. 35
Winding Euphrates, and the city vast . . . . 811 Excursion 4. 689
A temple framing of dimensions vast, ... 818 Excursion 4. 1161
And the vast engine labouring in the mine, . . 866 Excursion 7. 608
Our Country marked the preparation vast . . 869 Excursion 7. 759
Their monuments and their memory. The vast Frame . . . . 872 Excursion 7. 999
Various and vast. A memorable age ! . . . . 873 Excursion 7. 1012
How quick, how vast an increase ! From the germ 876 Excursion 8. 118
Of vast cathedral or conventual church, . . . 877 Excursion 8. 187
To the vast multitude ; whose doom it is . . . 885 Excursion 9. 90
The senseless member of a vast machine, . . . 886 Excursion 9. 159
—Vast the circumference of hope—and ye . . 890 Excursion 9. 398
In their vast stream, and if an age hath been . S.3. 435 *The doubt 124
How vast the compass of this theatre, ... K.8. 252 Recluse 1.1.560
He by the vast Metropolis immured, ... K.8. 253 Recluse 1.1.597
That Smithfield should sustain so vast a loss, . L.1. 95 Juvenal 3. 15
Vaudracour. The high-born Vaudracour was brought, by years . . . . 121 V. and J. 8
They parted ; and the generous Vaudracour . . 123 V. and J. 102
In his stern father's hearing, Vaudracour . . . 123 V. and J. 115
This was the manner in which Vaudracour . . 125 V. and J. 262
While they were speaking, Vaudracour approached ; 126 V. and J. 294
For Vaudracour and Julia (so were named . . 717 Prelude 9. 565
Vault. Within the Vault, a spear's length to the left. 54 Bord. 916
There in a black-blue vault she sails along, . . 184 Night-piece 14
Immeasurably distant ; and the vault, . . . 184 Night-piece 20
Their eyes, or minds ? or, finally, is yon resplendent vault ? . . . . 189 Star-gazers 12
Warbling in each sparry vault . . . . . . 217 *Inmate of 26
All that we see—is dome, or vault, or nest, . . 266 *The stars 7
While the vault rang with choral harmony, . . 324 Ode 1814 80
Into that vault receive me from whose depth . 357 Aquap. 306
High-ribbed vault of stone, or cell, ... 397 White Doe 93
A vault where the bodies are buried upright ! . 398 White Doe 245
But dark and dismal is the vault . . . . . 408 White Doe 1128
By fractured cell, or tomb, or vault ; . . . . 417 White Doe 1894
Pierces the ethereal vault ; and ('mid the gleam . 456 *The leaves 9
Moves through the vault of heaven, and dissipates the night ; . . . . 618 School Ex. 40
In the comfortless vault of disease. . . . . 621 Convict 32
Yordas ; he looks around and sees the vault . . 707 Prelude 8. 564
Not so the ethereal vault ; encroachment none . 746 Prelude 14. 50
More keenly than elsewhere in night's blue vault, 782 Excursion 2. 721
Or heaven's blue vault, is suffered to put forth . 789 Excursion 3. 211
And, over all, in that ethereal vault, ... 808 Excursion 4. 460
To breathe beneath a vault of ignorance ? . . 831 Excursion 5. 588
From the far-distant quarry's vault returns ; . . 833 Excursion 5. 714
Far from the family vault.—A Chieftain one . . 844 Excursion 6. 413
Of those celestial splendours ; grey the vault— . 895 Excursion 9. 760
These not of earthly texture, and the vault . . S.3. 435 *The doubt 107
From all reproach is yon ethereal vault, . . . K.8. 254 Recluse 1.1.641
Vaulted. Or shed, within a vaulted hall, . . . 390 Highland Broach 27
Silent, and steadfast as the vaulted sky, . . . 453 *The Sun, that 7
Known and familiar, which the vaulted sky . . 798 Excursion 3. 858
Vault's. And the vault's hoary sides to which they cling, ... S.3. 435 *The doubt 105
Vaults. To loathsome vaults, where heart-sick anguish tossed, ... 30 Guilt 350
The mouldy vaults of the dull idiot's brain, . . 234 Power of Sound 100
The captive 'mid damp vaults unsunned, unaired, 273 *Not the 5
Poured from his vaults of everlasting snow ; . . 347 Processions 58
In whose dark vaults my own shall soon be laid, . 827 Excursion 5. 346
Ere we descend into these silent vaults, . . . 832 Excursion 5. 669
Vaunt. So vaunt a throng of Followers, filled with pride . . . . 425 Ecc. Sonn. 1. 28. 12
Vaunted. The free-born Soul—that World whose vaunted skill . . . . 313 *Not 'mid 2
"Philosophy ! and thou more vaunted name . 827 Excursion 5. 331
I said, "And, did in truth those vaunted Arts . 877 Excursion 8. 232
Vaunting. Or haply sprung from vaunting Cowardice 514 *Portentous change 7
Vauxhall. Vauxhall and Ranelagh ! I then had heard . . . . 689 Prelude 7. 121
Veering. Sir Walter, restless as a veering wind, . 200 Hart-leap 17
His richest splendour—when his veering gait . . 220 Triad 48
Some veering up and down, one knew not why. . 258 *With Ships 4
'Twas but a short hour's walk, ere veering round . 658 Prelude 4. 20
Vehemence. I spake with vehemence ; and promptly seized . . . . 797 Excursion 3. 795
Vehement. And met a man who foamed with anger vehement. . . . . 33 Guilt 468

Voiceless—*continued.*
Where it begins to stir, *yet* voiceless as a snake. 351 *Des. Stanzas* 63
Told, also, how the voiceless heavens declare 461 **Queen of* 42
Prayer's voiceless service ; but now, seeking nought 508 *F. Stone* 35
Stirred them, not voiceless. Often have I stood 676 *Prelude* 6. 85
The voiceless worm on the unfrequented hills, 687 *Prelude* 7. 39
—Voiceless the stream descends into the gulf 787 *Excursion* 3. 92
Voices. Whence lutes and voices down the enchanted woods 12 *Desc. Sk.* 117
All motions, sounds, and voices, far and nigh, 17 *Desc. Sk.* 362
Tries his two voices for a favourite strain— 153 *Morn. Ex.* 8
Some plainly living voices were ; 199 *Thorn* 161
Were voices of the dead : 199 *Thorn* 163
By Voices how men lived of old. 205 *Brougham* 133
Voices of two different natures ? 209 **Yes, it* 12
Will not depart when mortal voices bid ; 214 *Dion* 91
Ye Voices, and ye Shadows 233 *Power of Sound* 33
Innumerable voices fill 235 *Power of Sound* 183
While hearts and voices in the song unite. 266 **Even as* 14
And add your voices to the quire 286 *Sons of Burns* 26
Two Voices are there ; one is of the sea, 306 **Two Voices* 1
Until all voices in one voice are drowned ; 312 **A Roman* 5
Give, herds and flocks, your voices to the wind ! 315 **The Land* 11
From voices into zealous passion stung, 332 *Ode : Thanks.* 215
Their voices into liquid music swell, 333 *Fish-women* 12
Of penetrating harps and voices sweet ! 335 *Cologne* 14
Of aery voices locked in unison,— 346 *Gemmi* 11
Their orisons with voices half-suppressed, 357 *Aquap.* 303
By voices never mute when Heaven unties 430 *Ecc. Sonn.* 2. 8. 10
Voices, thy winds break forth in prophecy, 471 *Tynwald* 12
Sweet voices for the passing wind ; 473 *Ossian* 70
While heaven's vast sea of voices chants their praise. 474 **On to* 14
He dearly loves their voices ! 483 *Simon Lee* 24
Their voices mount symbolical of praise— 500 *Humanity* 16
What are fears but voices airy ? 549 *Hermit's Cell* 1. 5
With one accord our voices raise, 578 **I come* 50
Of all her Voices, One ! 581 **Loud is* 4
And, far beneath, Banditti voices talk ; 606 *Desc.Sk.Quarto* 234
And talking voices, and the low of herds, 611 *Desc.Sk.Quarto* 507
'Tho' now no more thy maids their voices suit 615 *Desc.Sk.Quarto* 748
Voices of gladness roll the walls around ; 625 *Æneid* 99
Those gladsome voices from the courts rebound ; 625 *Æneid* 100
Had voices more than all the winds, with power 667 *Prelude* 5. 107
Shrill voices from the hawkers in the throng, 719 *Prelude* 10. 99
Its voices issuing forth to silent light 747 *Prelude* 14. 73
Or several voices in one solemn sound, 777 *Excursion* 2. 374
Yet ring with all their voices, or before 850 *Excursion* 6. 783
And hear the voices of the winds and flowers. K.8. 224 **I will* 3
Void. 'Twas dark and void as ocean's watery realm 26 *Guilt* 138
As void of sunshine, when, from that wide plain, 268 **Four fiery* 3
Her thoughts less deep, or void of grave intent 270 **Though the bold* 10
Of something void and vain ; 545 *Russ. Fug.* 356
Of sandy wilderness, all black and void, 666 *Prelude* 5. 72
Or from its death-like void, with punctual care, 802 *Excursion* 4. 88
What place so destitute and void—but there 807 *Excursion* 4. 424
Volant. A volant Tribe of Bards on earth are found, 259 **A volant* 1
His volant Spirit will, he trusts, ascend 366 *Lombardy* 13
Volatile. Arch, volatile, a sportive bird 165 *Parrot* 25
And volatile their love of transient bowers, 278 **The most* 13
Hurried and hurrying, volatile and loud. 473 **We saw* 4
Gay, volatile, ingenious, quick to learn, 842 *Excursion* 6. 282
Volcanic. The ground beneath thee with volcanic force : 316 **Hail, Zaragoza* 11
Volcanic burst, earthquake, and hurricane, 514 **Who ponders* 7
Volcano's. He springs the hushed Volcano's mine, 328 *Ode 1815* 93
Volley. A volley, thrice repeated o'er the Corse 868 *Excursion* 7. 698
Voltaire. In the French tongue, a Novel of Voltaire, 778 *Excursion* 2. 443
Voluble. Matter wherein right voluble I am, 488 *Pers. Talk* 38
Of their sensations, and in voluble phrase 645 *Prelude* 2. 225
Volume. A slender volume grasping in thy hand— 215 *Enterprise* 4
Of a closed volume lingering in thy hand 222 *Triad* 184
No single volume paramount, no code, 307 **Great men* 12
Was like a volume to me ; some were hailed 659 *Prelude* 4. 68
When I have held a volume in my hand, 668 *Prelude* 5. 163
To land a single volume, saved by chance, 677 *Prelude* 6. 145
Upon a volume whose contents he knows 719 *Prelude* 10. 59
A straggling volume, torn and incomplete, 759 *Excursion* 1. 178
To reverence the volume that displays 759 *Excursion* 1. 224
That volume—as a compass for the soul— 798 *Excursion* 3. 862
Were as a volume, shut, yet capable 826 *Excursion* 5. 252
Volumes. Bright volumes of vapour through Lothbury glide, 188 *Poor Susan* 7
Volumes of sound, from the Cathedral rolled, 351 *Des. Stanzas* 64
That there were four large volumes, laden all 672 *Prelude* 5. 466
Voluminous. In fleecy folds voluminous, enwrapped. 784 *Excursion* 2. 860
Bedimmed with smoke, in wreaths voluminous, 894 *Excursion* 9. 702
Voluntary. Drives from their Cures, a voluntary prey 441 *Ecc. Sonn.* 3. 6. 3
As if with voluntary power instinct 637 *Prelude* 1. 379
Partly from voluntary holiday, 687 *Prelude* 7. 17
Volunteer. Blind Chance, a volunteer ally, 391 *Highland Broach* 87
Voluptuary. Resembled much that cold voluptuary, 42 *Bord.* 279
Voluptuous. Breathes o'er the failing soul voluptuous dreams, 13 *Desc. Sk.* 136
Voluptuous, fearless of a rival, eyed 185 *Nutting* 24
Nor less, to feed voluptuous thought, 193 *Ruth* 133
To a voluptuous influence 233 *Power of Sound* 87
Of a voluptuous indolence, should meet 424 *Ecc. Sonn.* 1. 23. 3
Breathe o'er the failing soul voluptuous dreams ; 605 *Desc. Sk. Quarto* 157
On the wild Goddess of Voluptuous Joy. 620 *Birth of Love* 23

Voluptuous—*continued.*
Of royal courts, and that voluptuous life 714 *Prelude* 9. 345
To a voluptuous unconcern, preferring 791 *Excursion* 3. 351
Hired minstrel of voluptuous blandishment ; 843 *Excursion* 6. 355
Voluptuously. Voluptuously through fields and rural walks, 635 *Prelude* 1. 251
Voluptuousness. Its own voluptuousness ;—on this resolved, 776 *Excursion* 2. 312
Vomit. Returning to his vomit ; when the sun 732 *Prelude* 11. 364
Vomiting. Are vomiting, receiving on all sides, 698 *Prelude* 7. 720
Vortex. Within the vortex of a foaming flood, 123 *V. and J.* 143
Votaress. Our Lady's laggard Votaress, 344 **How blest* 21
The Votaress by Lugano's side ; 345 **How blest* 77
To aid the Votaress, miracles believed 466 *St. Bees* 46
To this fair Votaress a fate 544 *Russ. Fug.* 201
Votaresses. By hooded Votaresses with saintly cheer ; 465 **The cattle* 11
Votaries. Thy votaries, wooingly resigned 233 *Power of Sound* 86
Thee have thy Votaries aptly styled, 338 **Meek Virgin* 23
Of number, pure and silent Votaries 347 *Processions* 52
Which the chaste Votaries seek, beyond the grave ; 424 *Ecc. Sonn.* 1. 24. 10
And cleared a way for the first Votaries, 468 *St. Bees* 152
With its unworldly votaries, for the sake 682 *Prelude* 6. 457
Votary. For thy contented Votary. 217 *Enterprise* 137
Of thy contented Votary 227 *Vernal Ode* 83
For is she not the votary of Apollo ? 261 **I heard (alas* 9
Then, pensive Votary ! let thy feet repair 269 *Gordale* 4
Aspiring Votary, ere thy hand present 270 **Though the bold* 12
And by *one* Votary who at will might stand 473 **We saw* 9
Votary (in vast cathedral, where no foot 664 *Prelude* 4. 362
I see thee linger a glad votary, 734 *Prelude* 11. 469
Thus would the Votary say—' this severed hair, 812 *Excursion* 4. 746
Votary's. Comes she with a votary's task, 397 *White Doe* 108
Vote. For Lubbock vote—no legislative hack L.3. 27 **For Lubbock* 1
Votive. By many a votive death-cross planted near, 14 *Desc. Sk.* 202
Rise, then, ye votive Towers ! and catch a gleam 253 **Aerial Rock* 13
Or kneel, before the votive shrine 300 *Cora Linn* 44
If a new Temple lift her votive brow 327 *Ode 1815* 49
We reached a votive Stone that bears 337 *Thun* 3
A votive Column, spared by fire and flood :— 367 *Trajan* 6
Whose votive burthen is—"Our Kingdom's here !" 433 *Ecc. Sonn.* 2. 20. 14
Extinct that echoed to the votive strains ; 460 **Queen of* 34
Shall stain this votive lay ; 582 **O for a* 9
Shall stand a votive Tablet, haply free, 584 **With copious* 52
Through ever-changing scenes of votive quest 634 *Prelude* 1. 181
(As books and haply votive altars vouch) S.3. 435 **The doubt* 125
Vouch. I will not call on Heaven to vouch for me, 41 *Bord.* 211
And for the fact will vouch,—one night 244 *P. B.* 738
With their softest whispers vouch, 502 **Like a* 52
Exults in freedom, can with rapture vouch 528 **Those breathing* 83
(As books and haply votive altars vouch) S.3. 435 **The doubt* 125
Vouchsafe. Dread King of Kings, vouchsafe a ray divine 323 **Now that* 9
Who didst vouchsafe for man to die ; 550 *Hermit's Cell* 5. 14
(Should Providence such grace to us vouchsafe) 752 *Prelude* 14. 442
Vouchsafe sweet influence, while her Poet speaks 892 *Excursion* 9. 519
Vouchsafed. Then, to the measure of the light vouchsafed, v **If thou indeed* 15
Was such bright Spectacle vouchsafed to me ? 227 *Vernal Ode* 81
Vouchsafed no sparrow falleth to the ground ? 273 **Wild Redbreast* 10
Vouchsafed in pity or in wrath assigned ; 347 *Processions* 70
Vouchsafed in gentleness to brood 403 *White Doe* 668
Vouchsafed, in radiant ministry 407 *White Doe* 1050
All promises vouchsafed by Heaven will shine 431 *Ecc. Sonn.* 2. 10. 12
Once to these cells vouchsafed. And when I note 470 *Bala-Sala* 9
But for some precious boons vouchsafed to thee, 491 *Tribute : Dog* 25
Nor was this fellowship vouchsafed to me 638 *Prelude* 1. 415
Vouchsafed her inspiration, and diffused, 698 *Prelude* 7. 768
Vouchsafed for union or communion, feeds 709 *Prelude* 8. 674
Oh ! next to one dear state of bliss, vouchsafed 741 *Prelude* 13. 120
That unto him hath also been vouchsafed 744 *Prelude* 13. 307
Of much exalted good by Heaven vouchsafed 813 *Excursion* 4. 783
Under his spiritual sway. He hath vouchsafed 824 *Excursion* 5. 106
Gifts nobler are vouchsafed alike to all ; 887 *Excursion* 9. 221
Vouchsafed ; this local transitory type 893 *Excursion* 9. 619
To me hath been vouchsafed ; among the bowers K.8. 239 *Recluse* 1. 1. 104
That an internal brightness is vouchsafed K.8. 255 *Recluse* 1. 1. 675
Vouchsafes. Vouchsafes her lessons, bounteous Nymph 217 *Enterprise* 141
Vouchsafing. The light to us vouchsafing of thy prayer, 553 *Prioress* 27
Vow. *See* **Marriage-vow.**
A broken vow, or bind a true, 223 *Wishing-gate* 47
Is fragrant with a humbler vow ; 228 *Devot. Incit.* 63
Shall Fancy pay to thee a grateful vow ? 253 **Aerial Rock* 5
Erroneously renewing a sad vow 261 **From the dark* 11
Maintains inviolate its slightest vow ! 270 **Shame on* 8
Too frail to keep the lofty vow 285 *Nith* 1
The words of truth's memorial vow 348 **Lulled by* 62
And habit of his vow. That ancient Man— 362 **List—'twas* 82
This Banner (for such vow I made) 410 *White Doe* 1275
The vow performed, in cross-legged effigy, 430 *Ecc. Sonn.* 2. 8. 7
Shame if the consecrated Vow be found 445 *Ecc. Sonn.* 3. 21. 13
For they are taking the baptismal Vow 446 *Ecc. Sonn.* 3. 23. 4
So prays the Church, to consecrate a Vow 447 *Ecc. Sonn.* 3. 26. 9
And, from her vow well weighed in Heaven's decrees, 466 *St. Bees* 35
The Tragic Muse thee served with thoughtful vow ; 476 **Tranquillity! the* 4
Still from the village-green a vow 506 **While from* 45
Out of the bosom of a wiser vow. 510 **Among a* 23
That woman ne'er should forfeit, keep *thy* vow ; 529 **Those breathing* 134

W

Wait—*continued.*
Good Dame, repair to Liddesdale and wait . . 46 *Bord.* 516
Shall blessings wait upon a deed of mine. . . . 76 *Bord.* 2197
That he should wait thy coming till the day . . 76 *Bord.* 2231
Dismiss thy followers ;—let them calmly wait . 105 *Artegal* 214
Of him I wait for day and night, ... 117 *Affl. Marg.* 62
The Doctor, he has made him wait ; . . . . 128 *Idiot Boy* 165
Wait—and you shall see how hollow . . . 163 *Hint* 31
Through Bowscale-tarn did wait on him ; . . . 205 *Brougham* 123
And what pure homage *then* did wait . . . . 212 *Dion* 7
Upon her coming wait . . . . 220 *Triad* 44
That on the service wait concealed . . . . . 228 *Devot. Incit.* 36
" Wait, prithee, wait ! " this answer Lesbia threw 274 **Wait, prithee* 1
For, if good Angels love to wait . . . . . 296 *Highland Boy* 173
What hardship had it been to wait an hour ? . . 303 **Is it* 13
Of Brethren who, here fixed, on Jesu wait . . 364 **What aim* 6
From honoured Instruments that round him wait ; 368 *Trajan* 54
For pleasure hath not ceased to wait . . . . 375 **The Minstrels* 31
Wait upon her as she ranges . . . . . . 397 *White Doe* 80
On kind occasions I may wait, ... 401 *White Doe* 513
There wait a favourable hour, ... 405 *White Doe* 799
Her duty is to stand and wait ; . . . . . . 407 *White Doe* 1069
But element and orb on *acts* did wait . . . . 469 **Bold words* 12
And therefore does not stoop, nor lie in wait . . 493 *Hap. War.* 41
Its duties ;—prompt to move, but firm to wait,— 514 **Blest Statesman* 9
Like a gaunt shaggy Porter forced to wait . . 523 *Epist. Beaumont* 152
But the whole household, that our coming wait. . 525 *Epist. Beaumont* 235
Their fill of promised lustre, wait in vain. . . . 533 **Once I* 36
To wait upon the bright and gracious Muses, . . 573 *Chiabrera* 2. 7
Wait the fulfilment of their fear ; . . . . . 581 **Loud is* 14
That only wait the darkness of the night . . . 620 **She wept* 13
And, Tyrians, may your choicest favours wait . 625 *Æneid* 114
My name from piteous rumours, such as wait . 660 *Prelude* 4. 129
And on a rock sate down, to wait for day. . . 685 *Prelude* 6. 702
To wait upon the storms : of their approach . . 702 *Prelude* 8. 224
Therefore, not unconsoled, I wait—in hope . . 806 *Excursion* 4. 310
Who tend her altars, wait upon her throne, . . 810 *Excursion* 4. 597
By all the elements that round her wait . . . 841 *Excursion* 6. 184
' Nay, ye must wait my time ! ' and down she sate, 853 *Excursion* 6. 978
Might wait on thee, a silent monitor, ... S.3. 435 **The doubt* 129
Waited. you waited the hour of his release ? . . 72 *Bord.* 1964
" We've waited anxiously and long," . . . . 238 *P. B.* 178
Ye waited then on my good pleasure ; . . . . 245 *P. B.* 793
How patiently you've waited, ... 484 *Simon Lee* 62
They, who had waited for that sign to trace . . 534 **When in* 10
Have waited—till the affections could no more . 539 **Lady ! a* 30
Had waited on some Fairy's wand, at once . . 649 *Prelude* 3. 36
I daily waited, now all eye and now . . . . 735 *Prelude* 12. 99
Gladly would I have waited till my task . . . 753 **Oft, through* 9
He by appointment waited for me here, . . . 757 *Excursion* 1. 50
Where now we sit, I waited her return. . . . 767 *Excursion* 1. 712
' It grieves me you have waited here so long, . . 767 *Excursion* 1. 753
Her dreary pillow, waited on her needs ; . . . 849 *Excursion* 6. 750
And silence waited on these closing words ; . . 862 *Excursion* 7. 292
Waiteth. " Now this poor Widow waiteth all that night . . . . 554 *Prioress* 135
Waiting. I have been waiting in the wood hard by 43 *Bord.* 355
Have I been waiting for him. Well, but softly, . 45 *Bord.* 452
On the soft heath,—and, waiting for his comrades, 101 *Brothers* 397
Stood Science waiting for the hour . . . . . 343 *Eclipse* 2
That Banner, waiting for the Call, ... 400 *White Doe* 378
A place of thought where we in waiting lie ;] . . 589 *Immortality* 124
Were waiting with the whole of their desires . 712 *Prelude* 9. 187
Stood waiting for my Comrade. When behold . 777 *Excursion* 2. 410
Waits. While he the issue waits, at early morn 104 *Artegal* 106
Yet a rich guerdon waits on minds that dare, 261 **From the dark* 7
Nor less remuneration waits on him . . . . 355 *Aquap.* 178
Rich conquest waits them :—the tempestuous sea 422 *Ecc. Sonn.* 1. 14. 10
On her departure waits, no tongue hath shown ; . 422 *Ecc. Sonn.* 1. 16. 12
One above all, a Monk who waits on God . . . 509 *F. Stone* 95
To the cold marble, waits upon thy dust ; . . 584 **With copious* 43
That waits upon the touches of the wind. . . . 651 *Prelude* 3. 139
With a conviction of the power that waits . . 654 *Prelude* 3. 388
From earth's materials—waits upon my steps ; . 755 *Recluse* 1. 1. 798
And music waits upon your skilful touch, . . 809 *Excursion* 4. 571
Waiving. Is too infirm to reach. But, waiving this, 830 *Excursion* 5. 522
Wake. She knew not what dire pangs in him such tale could wake. . . . . 27 *Guilt* 189
But she WILL wake, and she will weep for me, . 77 *Bord.* 2274
And wake when it is day. . . . . 118 †*Cottager* 15
He leaves behind a moon-illumined wake : . . 212 *Dion*
Bright shines the Sun, as if his beams would wake 332 *Ode : Thanks.* 207
Called the submissive strings to wake . . . . 413 *White Doe* 1553
And wake him with such gentle heed . . . . 458 **Had this* 58
So might it seem, the cares of them that wake ; . 459 **Wanderer ! that* 4
And if a sleeping tear should wake, ... 486 *Matthew* 13
From Fancy following in thy wake, ... 490 *Night Thought* 15
And Thou, sweet Flower, shalt sleep and wake . 580 **Sweet Flower* 69
Of the eternal Silence : truths that wake, . . . 589 *Immortality* 159
Round your pale eyes a wintry lustre wake. . . 614 *Desc.Sk.Quarto* 675
To court majestic truth, or wake the golden lyre ; 619 *School Ex.* 62
But soon upon her breast he sunk—to wake no more. 620 *Birth of Love* 45
That he might wake to clasp thee in the shade : . 630 [?] **O Moon* 13
Wake where they waked, range that inclosure old, 653 *Prelude* 3. 263
At wake or fair. And oftentimes do flit . . . 657 *Prelude* 3. 573
What temper at the prospect did not wake . . 729 *Prelude* 11. 122
Prompt answer ; they proclaim the annual Wake, 773 *Excursion* 2. 120
Are glorified ; or, if they sleep, shall wake . . 804 *Excursion* 4. 189
The tranquillizing power of time, shall wake, . . 809 *Excursion* 4. 547

Wake—*continued.*
Wake sometimes to a noble restlessness— . . . 809 *Excursion* 4. 548
Then wake me not, I pray you. Hush, speak low. S.3. 441 **Grateful is sleep, more* 4
Wake sudden recognitions, that were like . . . K.8. 230 **I will* 193
Waked. He waked her—spake in tone that would not fail, ... 27 *Guilt* 168
A British ship I waked, as from a trance restored." 30 *Guilt* 306
I waked, and saw my little boy, ... 144 *Her Eyes* 27
The Woman waked—and when she spied . . . 248 *P. B.* 1023
An Infant, waked by her distress, ... 248 *P. B.* 1067
And, when he waked, his languid eye . . . . 400 *White Doe* 427
Wake where they waked, range that inclosure old, 653 *Prelude* 3. 263
In chase of him ; whereat I waked in terror, . . 667 *Prelude* 5. 138
Weeping, and weeping have I waked ; my tears . 768 *Excursion* 1. 770
Wakeful. A heart more wakeful ; and had worn the track . . . . 150 **When, to* 61
The wakeful Ruth at midnight shed . . . . 193 *Ruth* 98
Cheering the wakeful tent on Syrian mountains, . 232 *Power of Sound* 19
A sleeping infant's brow, or wakeful eye . . . 469 **Why stand* 7
Till pours the wakeful bird her solemn strains . 599 *Ev. Wk. Quarto* 377
The tales that charm away the wakeful night . 673 *Prelude* 5. 496
Wakefulness. A shadowy link 'tween wakefulness and sleep, ... 524 *Epist. Beaumont* 184
Waken. To waken our stray Baron. Were there not 51 *Bord.* 766
Feared you to waken him ? he must have been . 55 *Bord.* 960
If they can waken one pang of remorse ? . . . 62 *Bord.* 1401
Come ye—whate'er your creed—O waken all, . 310 *Invasion* 15
Wakened. Had wakened some redeeming thought 300 *Bran* 42
And hope is wakened by the sight, ... 404 *White Doe* 780
The scene is waken'd, yet its peace unbroke, . 599 *Ev. Wk. Quarto* 429
Wakens. Nought wakens or disturbs it's tranquil tides ; . . . . 597 *Ev. Wk. Quarto* 310
Wakes. Or shout that wakes the ferry-man from sleep, ... 9 *Ev. Wk.* 370
Beneath a sun that wakes a weary world . . . 122 *V. and J.* 51
That wakes the breeze, the sparkling lymph . . 217 *Enterprise* 142
Wakes with glazed eye, and feebly sighing— . . 242 *P. B.* 538
The trance is passed away—he wakes ; . . . 248 *P. B.* 1095
At Wakes and Fairs with wandering Mountebanks,— . . . . 260 **How sweet* 7
Through the bleak concave, wakes this wondrous chime . . . . 346 *Gemmi* 10
And wakes anew life's glimmering trembling fires, 619 *School Ex.* 100
Wakes in me agitations like its own, ... 687 *Prelude* 7. 47
To him who slept at noon and wakes at eve." . 700 *Prelude* 8. 52
Waking. That waking life had never power to give. 69 *Bord.* 1794
But who shall show, to waking sense, the gleam of light that broke . . . . 92 *Poet's Dream* 33
Waking at morn he murmured not ; . . . . . 168 *Pilgrim's Dream* 68
Know—that, for him whose waking thoughts, severe 229 *Cuckoo-clock* 27
By waking ears have sometimes been received . 261 **I heard (alas* 3
For he hath waking empire, wide as dreams ; . . 267 **Though narrow* 3
Hangs o'er its Parent waking to the cares . . . 282 **While beams* 6
Rejoiced when waking she espies . . . . . 297 *Highland Boy* 233
So faithfully, a waking dream ? . . . . . . 301 *Yarrow V.* 3
Meet on the solid ground of waking life. . . . 364 **What aim* 14
And, at her call, a waking dream . . . . . 373 *Eg. Maid* 305
Which, at this moment, on my waking sight . . 458 **Had this* 75
And owls alone are waking, ... 479 *Somnamb.* 92
Not all asleep and yet not waking wholly ; . . 558 *Cuck. and Night.* 88
Evening and morning, sleep and waking, thought 647 *Prelude* 2. 355
And waking thoughts more rich than happiest dreams. . . . . 724 *Prelude* 10. 436
Into a waking dream, a reverie . . . . . . 745 *Prelude* 13. 343
To meet her waking eyes. This tremblingly . . 766 *Excursion* 1. 668
By waking sense or by the dreaming soul ! . . 784 *Excursion* 2. 833
A better state than waking ; death than sleep : . 790 *Excursion* 3. 279
That which is veiled from waking thought ; conjured 796 *Excursion* 3. 687
Thus did a waking fancy sometimes lose . . . 852 *Excursion* 6. 904
Waldensian. Then followed the Waldensian bands, whom Hate . . . . 432 *Ecc. Sonn.* 2. 14. 6
Walk. *See* **O'erwalk, Palace-walk.**
They crush with broad black feet their flowery walk ; . . . . 6 *Ev. Wk.* 243
The native Genii walk the mountain green ? . . 16 *Desc. Sk.* 341
But there's a Providence for them who walk . . 51 *Bord.* 791
And you will walk in solitude among them. . . 65 *Bord.* 1510
But had he strength to walk ? I could have borne him 74 *Bord.* 2077
You and Charles and I will walk ; . . . . . 80 *Foresight* 28
One morn we strolled on our dry walk, . . . 85 *Anecdote* 5
He in his sleep would walk about, and sleeping . 101 *Brothers* 352
Turn from me, gentle Love ! nor let me walk . 111 *'*Tis said that some* 50
When I walk by the hedge on a bright summer's day, 116 *Repentance* 17
Were wasted, as I chanced to walk alone . . . 148 *Joanna* 78
And, when at evening we pursue our walk . . . 148 **There is an* 4
Our walk was far among the ancient trees : . . 149 *M. H.* 1
Will walk through life in such a way . . . . 171 *Kitten* 113
Walk through the fire with unsinged hair. . . 191 *Seq. Beggars* 30
At evening in his homeward walk . . . . . 195 *Ruth* 245
Far from the world I walk, and from all care ; . 195 *Resolution* 33
Shine on thee in thy solitary walk ; . . . . 207 *Tintern* 135
Is proud to walk the earth with Thee ! . . . 217 *Enterprise* 161
Her restless progeny. A humble walk . . . 230 *Clouds* 53
" He had a dark and sidelong walk, ... 240 *P. B.* 306
Withdrawn for noontide rest. They sit, they walk 283 **Well have* 2
Shall walk the Marathonian plain ; . . . . . 300 *Cora Linn* 38
Man holds with week-day man in the hourly walk 304 **I grieved* 11
And thus from year to year his walk they thwart, 320 **Hunger, and* 13
Walk in the light of day, pertain full surely . . 357 *Aquap.* 324

Walk—*continued.*
Ah ! not like me who walk in the world's ways, 363 **List—'twas* 92
Doubling and doubling with laborious walk, 389 *Glencroe* 1
Must walk the sorrowing mountains, drest 390 *Highland Broach* 39
And evil Spirits *may* our walk attend 423 *Ecc. Sonn.* 1. 18. 4
From fields where good men walk, or bowers wherein they rest. 438 *Ecc. Sonn.* 2. 39. 14
Of thy fond hopes hereafter walk inclined 447 *Ecc. Sonn.* 3. 27. 9
That ever walk content with Nature's way, 456 *Rydal Mere* 38
Of friends, who live within an easy walk, 488 *Pers. Talk* 3
He hath comrades in his walk ; 490 *Incident : Dog* 6
Who, whether praise of him must walk the earth 494 *Hap. War.* 77
The bad man's restless walk, and haunt his bed— 518 *Pun. Death* 6. 2
Break forth,—again to walk the clear blue sky. 532 **How beautiful the* 8
In desultory walk through orchard grounds, 537 **In desultory* 1
This humble Walk ? Yet on the mountain's side 549 **The massy* 5
This Walk, his loved possession, to the care 549 **The massy* 21
Upon the walls fast also would he walk, 564 *Troilus* 148
I saw an aged Beggar in my walk ; 566 *Cumb. Beg.* 1
And long, with wistful gaze, his walk survey'd 592 *Ev. Wk. Quarto* 69
Ye crush with broad black feet your flow'ry walk ; 596 *Ev. Wk. Quarto* 232
Below Eve's listening Star the sheep walk stills 598 *Ev. Wk. Quarto* 353
The dry leaves stir as with the serpent's walk, 606 *Desc.Sk.Quarto* 233
Along the margin of our terrace walk ; 636 *Prelude* 1. 286
Sublimer joy ; for I would walk alone, 646 *Prelude* 2. 302
'Twas but a short hour's walk, ere veering round 658 *Prelude* 4. 20
Though often of such dilatory walk 660 *Prelude* 4. 108
The off and on companion of my walk ; 661 *Prelude* 4. 187
Each in his several melancholy walk 669 *Prelude* 5. 239
That field-ward takes her walk with decent steps. 690 *Prelude* 7. 210
My daily walk along that wide champaign, 702 *Prelude* 8. 212
Happy, and now most thankful that my walk 704 *Prelude* 8. 330
Great rendezvous of worst and best, the walk 710 *Prelude* 9. 55
Of civil slaughter, was our frequent walk ; 716 *Prelude* 9. 433
Depressed, bewildered thus, I did not walk 732 *Prelude* 11. 321
Walk on this earth ! how feeble have I been 735 *Prelude* 12. 105
While in a grove I walk, whose lofty trees, 739 *Prelude* 12. 329
Enabled me to pause for choice, and walk 751 *Prelude* 14. 360
To happy contemplation soothed his walk ; 772 *Excursion* 2. 50
Had three times called us to renew our walk, 772 *Excursion* 2. 86
That walk the earth—Father of heaven and earth, 794 *Excursion* 3. 572
For its own sake ; but farthest from the walk 797 *Excursion* 3. 801
The mole contented with her darksome walk 807 *Excursion* 4. 429
You walk, you live, you speculate alone ; 809 *Excursion* 4. 559
To the blind walk of mortal accident ; 812 *Excursion* 4. 758
Who walk this favoured ground. But chance-regards, 828 *Excursion* 5. 417
Your walk conduct you hither, ere the sun 830 *Excursion* 5. 533
While in a spot like this we breathe and walk, 836 *Excursion* 5. 923
Art to outstrip in her peculiar walk. 842 *Excursion* 6. 303
Ranged round the garden walk, while she perchance 867 *Excursion* 7. 679
Of a poor brotherhood who walk the earth 875 *Excursion* 8. 42
Was the commodious walk : a careful hand 881 *Excursion* 8. 450
Ponders this true equality, may walk 887 *Excursion* 9. 248
Breathes invitation ; easy is the walk 890 *Excursion* 9. 424
Sweet was the walk along the narrow lane S.3. 417 **Sweet was* 1
The dear companion of my lonely walk, K.8. 234 **Witness thou* 2
For they protect his walk from sun and shower, K.8. 253 *Recluse* 1.1.609
I must not walk in unreproved delight K.8. 255 *Recluse* 1.1.666

Walked. Walked none restraining, and by none restrained : 18 *Desc. Sk.* 436
With naked feet walked over burning ploughshares. 62 *Bord.* 1385
As up the vale, that afternoon, he walked 96 *Brothers* 92
Had walked, and from the summit had fallen headlong : 101 *Brothers* 400
With him there often walked in friendly guise, 108 *Indolence* 37
And how she ran, and how she walked, 128 *Idiot Boy* 204
With Luke that evening thitherward he walked : 136 *Michael* 329
One summer morning we had walked abroad 147 *Joanna* 36
I have walked through wildernesses dreary, 159 **Up with me* 8
Of Him who walked in glory and in joy 196 *Resolution* 45
Sir Walter walked all round, north, south, and west, 201 *Hart-leap* 47
The gentlest Shade that walked Elysian plains 284 *Departure* 1
Such was her office while she walked with men, 359 *Plea : Hist.* 9
Walked round, affronting the daylight ; 406 *White Doe* 957
He did not arm, he walked aloof ! 412 *White Doe* 1466
Walked quick or slowly, every mood 415 *White Doe* 1726
In sleep She sometimes walked abroad, 479 *Somnamb.* 82
We walked along, while bright and red 486 **We walked* 1
The simple ways in which my childhood walked ; 642 *Prelude* 2. 3
In which I walked with Nature. But let this 647 *Prelude* 2. 358
Walked proudly at my side : she guided me ; 659 *Prelude* 4. 65
While on I walked, a comfort seemed to touch 660 *Prelude* 4. 153
A dedicated Spirit. On I walked 663 *Prelude* 4. 337
Among sequestered villages we walked 680 *Prelude* 6. 356
Like one of those who walked with hair unsinged 692 *Prelude* 7. 369
Had been inspired, and walked about in dreams. 709 *Prelude* 8. 653
Louvet walked single through the avenue, 720 *Prelude* 10. 111
In fear) have walked with quicker step ; but why 742 *Prelude* 13. 159
We sate—we walked ; he pleased me with report 757 *Excursion* 1. 63
And walked with me along the miry road, 769 *Excursion* 1. 864
And walked along my road in happiness." 770 *Excursion* 1. 956
He walked—protected from the sword of war 771 *Excursion* 2. 13
Of social vanity, he walked the world, 774 *Excursion* 2. 181
To soothe a Child, who walked beside him, weeping 779 *Excursion* 2. 507
Man walked ; and when and wheresoe'er he moved, 810 *Excursion* 4. 632
If, having walked with Nature threescore years, 816 *Excursion* 4. 980
Wishes and endless schemes ; by daylight walked 842 *Excursion* 6. 240
But in projection carried, as she walked 848 *Excursion* 6. 681
In him the spirit of a hero walked 868 *Excursion* 7. 739
Yet walked beneath the sun, in human shape, 879 *Excursion* 8. 344

Walked—*continued.*
Up his own mountain grounds, where, as he walked K.8. 229 **I will* 164
Have walked within her sight ? It cannot be. K.8. 257 **Shall he* 10

Walkest. Dear Child ! dear Girl ! that walkest with me here, 258 **It is a* 9

Walking. But standing, walking, stretching forth his arms, 68 *Bord.* 1729
Was walking by her native lake : 289 *Stepping West.* 18
'Till the Sun walking on his western field 608 *Desc.Sk.Quarto* 336
The bliss of walking daily in life's prime 741 *Prelude* 13. 122

Walks. Sweetly ferocious, round his native walks, 5 *Ev. Wk.* 146
And who, that walks where men of ancient days 15 *Desc. Sk.* 289
In walks whose boundary is the lost One's grave, 119 *Maternal Grief* 68
Let itself in upon him :—pathways, walks, 122 *V. and J.* 48
Walks to and fro—watchings at every hour ; 122 *V. and J.* 80
The Danish Boy walks here alone : 165 *Danish Boy* 21
Beyond his wish he walks secure ; 174 *Waggoner* 1. 71
How he, long forced in humble walks to go, 205 *Brougham* 159
Thy Husband walks the paths of upper air : 209 *Laod.* 22
Your once sweet memory, studious walks and shades ! 213 *Dion* 45
Rich are his walks with supernatural cheer ; 267 **Though narrow* 5
'Tis his who walks about in the open air, 308 **There is a bondage* 4
In the thronged city, from the walks of gain, 320 **O'erweening Statesmen* 6
The Bard who walks with Duddon for his guide, 379 *Duddon* 12. 11
Recovers not his loss ; but walks with shame, 383 *Duddon* 30. 3
Enjoys the walks his predecessors trod, 387 *Manse* 13
Together,—'mid trim walks and artful bowers, 389 *Breadalb.* 10
Walks, pools, and arbours, homestead, hall— 402 *White Doe* 548
Converging walks, and fountains gay, 407 *White Doe* 989
Upon the height walks to and fro ; 409 *White Doe* 1189
Now walks in unanimity. 409 *White Doe* 1240
Pools, terraces, and walks are sown 413 *White Doe* 1570
Here walks amid the mournful waste 416 *White Doe* 1889
More promptly rises, walks with stricter heed, 429 *Ecc. Sonn.* 2. 3. 2
Thus speaks (that Voice which walks upon the wind, 432 *Ecc. Sonn.* 2. 17. 6
That union ceased : then, cleaving easy walks 477 *Nunnery* 9
And shaped these pleasant walks by Emont's side, 489 *Spade* 2
The task, in smoother walks to stray ; 492 *Duty* 31
Of lofty station, female goodness walks, 539 **Lady ! a* 46
To aid the work, what time these walks and bowers 546 **Oft is* 15
Where danger roofs the narrow walks of death ; 606 *Desc.Sk.Quarto* 246
Who walks, where honour'd men of ancient days 608 *Desc.Sk.Quarto* 354
Secure she walks, Philosophy her guide. 619 *School Ex.* 52
If e'er they smooth'd the rugged walks of life, 619 *School Ex.* 104
Puts off his wings, and walks, with proud delight, 624 *Æneid* 45
Voluptuously through fields and rural walks, 635 *Prelude* 1. 251
A virtue not its own. My morning walks 647 *Prelude* 2. 329
Drifted about along the streets and walks, 652 *Prelude* 3. 250
Or walks of open scandal, but in vague 653 *Prelude* 3. 324
And wild outlandish walks of simple youth 656 *Prelude* 3. 518
Those walks well worthy to be prized and loved— 660 *Prelude* 4. 131
Those walks in all their freshness now came back 660 *Prelude* 4. 136
And tributary walks ; the last, and oft 676 *Prelude* 6. 68
While Winter like a well-tamed lion walks, 683 *Prelude* 6. 538
Sole link that binds them to each other ; walks, 685 *Prelude* 6. 667
Look out on waters, walks, and gardens green. 690 *Prelude* 7. 188
Walks, and achieves his wonders, from the eye 691 *Prelude* 7. 282
And with the ruddy produce she walks round 699 *Prelude* 8. 41
Walks a lone Monk, when service hath expired, 716 *Prelude* 9. 445
And when the partner of those varied walks 716 *Prelude* 9. 479
He walks about and looks upon the spot 729 *Prelude* 11. 149
I prized such walks still more, for there I found 742 *Prelude* 13. 179
There are among the walks of homely life 743 *Prelude* 13. 266
Her goodness, that, not seldom, in my walks 768 *Excursion* 1. 783
Nor wanting ornament of walks between, 778 *Excursion* 2. 426
—Wild were the walks upon those lonely Downs, 793 *Excursion* 3. 532
That spreads into successive seas, he walks ; 799 *Excursion* 3. 932
And labyrinthine walks, her sunny glades 810 *Excursion* 4. 590
And puissant to range the solemn walks 813 *Excursion* 4. 823
" A favourite boundary to their lengthened walks 845 *Excursion* 6. 475
Of his sublime vocation, in the walks 862 *Excursion* 7. 335
Do we revert so fondly to the walks 884 *Excursion* 9. 37
The rustic Boy, who walks the fields, untaught ; 886 *Excursion* 9. 162
Admonishing the man who walks below K.8. 240 *Recluse* 1.1.132
'Tis true, hath in my walks been often heard, K.8. 245 *Recluse* 1.1.319

Wall. *See* **Garden-wall, Stone-wall.**
Long grass and willows form the woven wall, 6 *Ev. Wk.* 240
Like a black wall, the mountain-steeps appear. 8 *Ev. Wk.* 314
The rocks rise naked as a wall, or stretch 14 *Desc. Sk.* 230
Or you might drive your head against that wall. 56 *Bord.* 1009
Girt round with a bare ring of mossy wall, 95 *Brothers* 28
Left in the church-yard wall. That's Walter Ewbank. 98 *Brothers* 200
Within the mossy garden wall 142 †*Lov. and Lik.* 9
See the Kitten on the wall, 170 *Kitten* 3
The pewter clatters on the wall ; 177 *Waggoner* 2. 67
He stands, backed by the wall ;—he abates not his din ; 188 *Music* 25
By this blank wall, from every eye, 223 **'Tis gone* 5
It seemed—wall, window, roof and tower— 246 *P. B.* 858
And sheltering wall ; and still, as Fancy wove 264 **Lady ! the* 5
Mute fixture on a stuccoed wall ; 300 *Bran* 6
Than his who breathes, by roof, and floor, and wall, 308 **There is a bondage* 2
From fractured arch and mouldering wall— 366 **Ye Trees* 14
No fancied lustre on the wall 390 *Highland Broach* 28
From some lofty arch or wall, 397 *White Doe* 89
A phantasm, in which roof and wall 400 *White Doe* 422

Wall—*continued.*
And cirque and crescent framed by wall . . . 407 *White Doe* 987
The breach is open—on the wall, ... 408 *White Doe* 1139
A brighter crown."—On yon Cistertian wall . . 429 *Ecc. Sonn.* 2. 3. 5
Can nowhere move uncrossed by some new wall . 469 **Desire we* 8
Now back to the tiles, then in search of the wall, 484 **A plague* 14
As shaggy as were wall and roof . . . . . 543 *Russ. Fug.* 141
A picture on the cabin wall . . . . 544 *Russ. Fug.* 211
That overhangs his head from the green wall, . 568 *Cumb. Beg.* 118
Beside their sheltering cross of wall, the flock 593 *Ev. Wk. Quarto* 117
Tower like a wall the naked rocks, or reach . . 607 *Desc.Sk.Quarto* 287
And crept along a ridge of fractured wall, . . 678 *Prelude* 6. 214
In the old wall, an unexpected glimpse . . . 694 *Prelude* 7. 452
Upon a corner-stone of that low wall, ... 696 *Prelude* 7. 605
Stood, propped against a wall, upon his chest 696 *Prelude* 7. 640
(Beyond that mighty wall, not fabulous, . . . 700 *Prelude* 8. 79
I sate half-sheltered by a naked wall ; . . . . 738 *Prelude* 12. 299
And the bleak music from that old stone wall, 739 *Prelude* 12. 320
The broken wall. I looked around, and there, . 763 *Excursion* 1. 459
I stood, and leaning o'er the garden wall . . . 770 *Excursion* 1. 921
Those weeds, and the high spear-grass on that wall, 770 *Excursion* 1. 943
And one old moss-grown wall ;—a cool recess, . 777 *Excursion* 2. 415
And fanciful ! For where the rock and wall . . 777 *Excursion* 2. 416
By thrusting two rude staves into the wall . . 777 *Excursion* 2. 418
And pleasant awning. On the moss-grown wall . 826 *Excursion* 5. 230
That he, who now upon the mossy wall . . . 829 *Excursion* 5. 447
A long stone-seat, fixed in the Church-yard wall; 850 *Excursion* 6. 779
"In that green nook, close by the Church-yard wall, 854 *Excursion* 6. 1080
Whose uncouth form was grafted on the wall, . 871 *Excursion* 7. 914

Wallace. Why art thou here ? Wallace, upon these Borders, ... 78 *Bord.* 2323
Wallace and Wilfred, I commend the Lady, . . 78 *Bord.* 2333
Of Sherwood's Archer, or in caves of Wallace— . 221 *Triad* 70
Sweeps visibly the Wallace Wight ; . . . . 300 *Cora Linn* 20
How Wallace fought for Scotland ; left the name 635 *Prelude* 1. 214
Of Wallace to be found, like a wild flower, . . 635 *Prelude* 1. 215
Of Wallace, like a family of Ghosts, ... 635 *Prelude* 1. 217

Walled. I spied a Covert walled and roofed with sods— . . . . 39 *Bord.* 118
That walled a city with its melody . . . . . 234 *Power of Sound* 130

Wallet. With a huge wallet o'er my shoulders slung, 185 *Nutting* 6

Wallflower. Of meek repentance, wafting wallflower scents . . . . 817 *Excursion* 4. 1047

Wall-girt. When horses in the wall-girt intake stood, 592 *Ev. Wk. Quarto* 65

Wallowing. On towns and cities, wallowing in the abyss . . . . 724 *Prelude* 10. 442

Wall's. Where, from the barren wall's unshelter'd end, ... 592 *Ev. Wk. Quarto* 59

Walls. *See* **Abbey-walls, Blanket-walls, Castle-walls, Stone-walls.**
On the mute Image and the troubled walls. . . 20 *Desc. Sk.* 544
Hoary and naked are its walls, and raise . . . 26 *Guilt* 115
And now the walls are named the "Dead House" of the plain. . . . . 27 *Guilt* 153
Felt the loose walls of this decayed Retreat . . 27 *Guilt* 173
Within those empty walls. I too have seen her ; 47 *Bord.* 572
These walls shall witness it—from first to last . 48 *Bord.* 594
Than a tight case of dungeon walls for shelter . 67 *Bord.* 1660
May sit beneath the walls . . . . 109 *Louisa* 15
To those religious walls. He, too, departs— . . 125 *V. and J.* 242
That Ilium's walls were subject to their view, . 212 *Laod.* 172
Shuddered the walls—the marble city wept— . 214 *Dion* 110
Of joy, that from her utmost walls . . . . 235 *Power of Sound* 202
The chamber walls were dark all round,— . . 244 *P. B.* 746
From the wan Moon, upon the towers and walls, . 272 *Ruins* 7
And, on the mouldered walls, how bright, how gay, 283 **Here, where* 7
Streams on the walls, and torrent-foam . . . 300 *Bran* 17
Upon Athenian walls ; . . . . 324 *Ode 1814* 98
Within the circuit of those Gothic walls, . . . 328 *Ode 1815* 64
Slips from his prison walls : and Fancy, free . . 336 *Danube* 5
Of saintly pleasure from these pictured walls, . 339 *Tell* 17
At noontide from umbrageous walls . . . . 343 *Eclipse* 17
Graven on her cankered walls, solemnities . . 346 *Processions* 8
Down to the earth the walls of Jericho, . . . 346 *Processions* 17
Dashed their white foam against the palace walls 354 *Aquap.* 122
More touching far than aught which on the walls . 355 *Aquap.* 165
"This Land of Rainbows spanning glens whose walls, ... 388 *Loch Etive* 1
The walls are cracked, sunk is the flowery roof, . 390 *Highland Hut* 9
That yet survive ensculptured on the walls . . 394 **No more* 7
Along the walls and overhead, ... 407 *White Doe* 1024
The Father from within the walls ; . . . . . 408 *White Doe* 1156
The sword from Bangor's walls, and guard the store 421 *Ecc. Sonn.* 1. 12. 6
These modest walls, amid a flock that need, . . 465 **Pastor and* 2
Whose rugged walls may still for years demand . 521 *Epist.Beaumont* 24
Thou see'st a homely Pile, yet to these walls . . 547 **Rude is* 14
Upon the walls fast also would he walk, . . . 564 *Troilus* 148
Every ale-house should then have a feast on its walls. . . . . 571 *Avarice* 8
Within Savona's walls, of gentle blood. . . . 573 *Chiabrera* 3. 4
And ebbs uncertain on the troubled walls, . . . 614 *Desc.Sk.Quarto* 649
The thick-ribbèd walls that o'ershadow the gate . 620 *Convict* 9
His young Ascanius to the Tyrian walls ; . . . 624 *Æneid* 28
Voices of gladness roll the walls around ; . . . 625 *Æneid* 99
The Druids worshipped, or the antique walls . . 643 *Prelude* 2. 102
And respirations, from the roofless walls . . . 644 *Prelude* 2. 123
To hear such music. Through the walls we flew . 644 *Prelude* 2. 128
Look was there none within these walls to shame 654 *Prelude* 3. 343
When all who dwelt within these famous walls . 655 *Prelude* 3. 448
Which met me issuing from the City's walls) . . 687 *Prelude* 7. 3
Here files of ballads dangle from dead walls ; . . 690 *Prelude* 7. 193

Walls—*continued.*
I saw when, from the melancholy walls . . . 702 *Prelude* 8. 210
Of passions and opinions, filled the walls . . . 712 *Prelude* 9. 164
Within the walls of cities—may these sounds . . 755 *Recluse* 1. 1. 833
Appeared a roofless Hut ; four naked walls . . 756 *Excursion* 1. 30
Last human tenant of these ruined walls ! " . . 770 *Excursion* 1. 916
Upon those silent walls, we left the shade ; . . 771 *Excursion* 1. 968
Some in disgrace, hung dangling from the walls, . 781 *Excursion* 2. 670
A heap of ruin—almost without walls . . . . 784 *Excursion* 2. 812
Too, too contracted are these walls of flesh, . . 804 *Excursion* 4. 179
Altar and image, and the inclusive walls . . . 811 *Excursion* 4. 672
To rest upon their circumambient walls ; . . . 818 *Excursion* 4. 1160
Admonitory texts inscribed the walls, ... 824 *Excursion* 5. 150
Thronging the walls ; and on the floor beneath . 825 *Excursion* 5. 167
Scattered about under the mouldering walls . . 835 *Excursion* 5. 866
May I not mention—that, within those walls, . . 854 *Excursion* 6. 1038
And no vain mirror glittered upon the walls, . . 860 *Excursion* 7. 176
All cares forgotten, round its hallowed walls ! . . 895 *Excursion* 9. 728
The Alban Sites and walls of lofty Rome. . . . K.8. 281 **Arms and* 9

Walnut. Embowered in walnut slopes and citron isles : . . . . 13 *Desc. Sk.* 155

Walter. Said Walter, leaping from the ground, . 85 *Shepherd-boys* 34
"Stop !" to his comrade Walter cries— . . . 85 *Shepherd-boys* 41
Said Walter then, exulting ; "Here . . . . 85 *Shepherd-boys* 43
Left in the church-yard wall. That's Walter Ewbank. . . . . 98 *Brothers* 200
A little—yet a little,—and old Walter, . . . 98 *Brothers* 210
Poor Walter ! whether it was care that spurred him 98 *Brothers* 217
Yet not while Walter lived :—for, though their parents . . . . 98 *Brothers* 227
Though from the cradle they had lived with Walter, 99 *Brothers* 243
But, as I said, old Walter was too weak . . . 100 *Brothers* 299
Sir Walter mounted him ; he was the third . . 200 *Hart-leap* 7
But, though Sir Walter like a falcon flies, . . . 200 *Hart-leap* 11
Sir Walter, restless as a veering wind, ... 200 *Hart-leap* 17
Sir Walter and the Hart are left alone. . . . 201 *Hart-leap* 28
Close to the thorn on which Sir Walter leaned . 201 *Hart-leap* 37
Sir Walter walked all round, north, south, and west, 201 *Hart-leap* 47
Four roods of sheer ascent) Sir Walter found . . 201 *Hart-leap* 50
Sir Walter wiped his face, and cried, "Till now . 201 *Hart-leap* 53
Three pillars of rude stone Sir Walter reared, . . 202 *Hart-leap* 83
Sir Walter led his wondering Paramour ; . . . 202 *Hart-leap* 90
The Knight, Sir Walter, died in course of time, . 202 *Hart-leap* 93

Walter's. Of Walter's forefathers o'erflowed the bounds . . . . 98 *Brothers* 205
A rout this morning left Sir Walter's Hall, . . 200 *Hart-leap* 13
From Venice to Sir Walter's table. . . . . . S.3. 432 **A German* 4

Waltham. For their abode the shrines of Waltham choose : . . . . 433 *Ecc. Sonn.* 2. 21. 10

Walton. Shall live the name of Walton : Sage benign ! 254 *Complete Angler* 2

Walton's. Around meek Walton's heavenly memory. 441 *Ecc. Sonn.* 3. 5. 14

Wan. When, in the south, the wan noon, brooding still, ... 2 *Ev. Wk.* 37
The moon a wan dead light around her shed. . . 27 *Guilt* 167
Her bony visage—gaunt and deadly wan ; . . . 34 *Guilt* 561
Or like a sinful creature, pale and wan. . . . 107 *Indolence* 21
How pale and wan it else would be. . . . . 145 *Her Eyes* 70
That Star, so proud of late, looked wan ; . . . 167 *Pilgrim's Dream* 53
Heavy and wan, all whitened by the Moon, . . 184 *Night-piece* 3
That love which changed—for wan disease, . . 225 *Primrose* 37
Her wan disasters could disperse. . . . . . 234 *Power of Sound* 128
By moonlight made more faint and wan ; . . . 244 *P. B.* 722
Wan cheek at once was privileged to unfold . . 258 **Even so* 7
"How silently, and with how wan a face !" . . 266 **With how* 2
From the wan Moon, upon the towers and walls, . 272 *Ruins* 7
Shed, on the Slumberer's cold wan cheek . . . 371 *Eg. Maid* 161
Wan cheek, and knees indúrated with prayer, . 433 *Ecc. Sonn.* 2. 19. 3
How many wan and faded cheeks . . . . . 507 *May* 27
Or wan despair—the ghost of false hope fled . . 514 **Long-favoured* 8
Wan, dull, and glaring, with a dripping fog . . 746 *Prelude* 14. 12

Wand. There is no need of whip or wand ; . . . 126 *Idiot Boy* 48
Mild Hermes spake—and touched her with his wand 209 *Laod.* 19
"A potent wand doth Sorrow wield ; . . . . 238 *P. B.* 146
For occupation of a magic wand, ... 428 *Ecc. Sonn.* 1. 39. 12
Who that shall point as with a wand and say . 645 *Prelude* 2. 208
Had waited on some Fairy's wand, at once . . 649 *Prelude* 3. 36
And as, by simple waving of a wand, ... 735 *Prelude* 12. 81
Is Common-sense asleep ? has she no wand . . L.1. 88 *Juvenal* 1. 15

Wander. Should child of mine e'er wander hither, speak . . . . 35 *Guilt* 589
But expiation, will I wander on— . . . . . 78 *Bord.* 2350
For folks that wander up and down like you, . . 97 *Brothers* 149
And wander down yon hawthorn dell, ... 180 *Waggoner* 4. 16
To wander with an easy mind ; . . . . . . 193 *Ruth* 76
They wander with the breeze, they wind . . . 228 *Devot. Incit.* 3
Why wander from your course so far, ... 245 *P. B.* 762
We'll wander Scotland thorough ; . . . . . 293 *Yarrow Unv.* 38
Shall wander, chiefly let me cull with care . . 355 *Aquap.* 199
To wander, and drink inspiration at will. . . . 364 *Vallomb.* 24
Wander the Ministers of God, as chance . . . 449 *Ecc. Sonn.* 3. 36. 4
And wander forth, in forest glades . . . . . 506 **While from* 19
And yet how pleased we wander forth . . . . 507 *May* 49
And, long as he can wander, let him breathe . 568 *Cumb. Beg.* 172
While, Memory at my side, I wander here, . . 592 *Ev. Wk. Quarto* 43
For quiet things to wander in ; a haunt . . . 655 *Prelude* 3. 437
Or wander here and there among the fields. . . 765 *Excursion* 1. 584
About the fields I wander, knowing this . . . 768 *Excursion* 1. 765
To wander with us through the fertile vales, . . 895 *Excursion* 9. 778

Wandered. Then, while I wandered where the huddling rill . . . . 3 *Ev. Wk.* 53

Warm—*continued.*
I bring thee draughts of milk, warm milk it is and new. . . . . 87 *Pet-lamb* 44
That, as the day was warm, he had lain down . 101 *Brothers* 396
Blessings upon that soft, warm face, ... 121 *EmigrantMother* 83
My long-frozen heart grows warm!" . . . . 140 *Arm. Lady* 38
And underneath the hay-stack warm, ... 144 *Her Eyes* 7
Breathed gently from the warm south-west: . . 156 *Oak and Broom* 17
So warm, so beautiful withal, ... 168 *Wren's Nest* 9
Green pasture and the soft warm air . . . 176 *Waggoner* 1. 268
Within that warm and peaceful berth, . . . 177 *Waggoner* 2. 88
"Thy wife and child are snug and warm, . . . 179 *Waggoner* 3. 70
Made the warm earth his lazy bed. . . . 239 *P. B.* 260
And shrubs—to hang upon the warm alcove, . . 264 **Lady! the* 4
Speak—though this soft warm heart, once free to hold . . . . 277 **Why art* 9
Thou who dost warm Earth's universal mould, . 329 *Ode: Thanks.* 31
A Patriot's heart, warm with undying fire. . . 365 **Under the* 12
While the warm hearth exalts the mantling ale, . 379 *Duddon* 13. 12
For warm Vesuvio's vine-clad slopes; . . . . 386 *Yarrow Rev.* 51
Of a once warm Abode, and that *new* Pile, . . 389 *Breadalb.* 7
But not before the warm life-blood . . . 412 *White Doe* 1495
While in the Body lodged, her warm abode; . . 422 *Ecc. Sonn.* 1. 16. 10
From the warm breeze that bears thee on, alight 455 *Rydal Mere* 33
And dissolution and decay, the warm . . . . 510 **Among a* 6
With Young and Old warm greetings we exchange, 525 *Epist. Beaumont* 236
Or in warm valley, seeks his part to fill; . . . 530 *Poor Robin* 26
The long, warm, lightsome summer-day, . . . 536 *Goody Blake* 38
Enough to warm her for three days. . . . . 536 *Goody Blake* 56
And oft from his warm fire he'd go, . . . 537 *Goody Blake* 69
O may he never more be warm!" . . . . 537 *Goody Blake* 100
He never will be warm again. . . . . . 537 *Goody Blake* 120
Affections, warm as sunshine, free as air; . . 584 *Ch. Lamb* 10
Fresh flowers; while the sun shines warm. . . 588 *Immortality* 48
Of day or the warm light, ... 589 *Immortality* 123
When warm from myrtle bays and tranquil seas, 610 *Desc.Sk.Quarto* 442
Our home-amusements by the warm peat-fire . 639 *Prelude* 1. 508
And recent things yet warm with life; a sea-fight, 691 *Prelude* 7. 291
It was a close, warm, breezeless summer night, . 746 *Prelude* 14. 11
Of the warm summer, from a belt of hemp . . 769 *Excursion* 1. 885
Nor lacked, for more delight on that warm day, . 782 *Excursion* 2. 682
By the warm sunshine, and the jocund voice . . 789 *Excursion* 3. 245
Which the warm sun solicited, and earth . . 815 *Excursion* 4. 937
The warm lap of his mother earth: and so, . . 861 *Excursion* 7. 287
Not for reproof, but high and warm delight, . . 863 *Excursion* 7. 385
Warm woods, and sunny hills, and fresh green fields, K.8. 240 *Recluse* 1.1.127
What arts had better claim with wrath to warm . L.1. 94 *Juvenal* 2. 5

Warm-clad. Will, among us warm-clad and warmly housed, ... 172 *Infant Daughter* 30

Warmed. But the poor ragged Thing whose ways my human heart had warmed. . . . 92 *Poet's Dream* 16
Not unvouchsafed—a light that warmed and cheered . . . . 118 *Maternal Grief* 19
Is warmed thro' winter by her feathery breast. . 165 *Parrot* 36
So beautiful of late, with sunshine warmed, . . 266 **DespondingFather* 2
Warmed our sad being with celestial light, . . 476 **Tranquillity! the* 9
Warmed by thy influence, creeping things . . 506 **While from* 27
Which checked discussion ere it warmed to strife; 583 **With copious* 14
Nor less when spring had warmed the cultured Vale, 637 *Prelude* 1. 326
For all; and yet how few are warmed or cheered! 828 *Excursion* 5. 384

Warmer. With warmer love—oh! with far deeper zeal . . . . 207 *Tintern* 154
With warmer suns and softer gales, ... 295 *Highland Boy* 74
But not a whit the warmer he: . . . . . . 537 *Goody Blake* 110
And when the flock, with warmer weather, climbs 702 *Prelude* 8. 231
Stood drinking comfort from the warmer sun, . 765 *Excursion* 1. 621

Warmest. Even for the man who wears the warmest fleece; . . . . 33 *Guilt* 506

Warmly. Will, among us warm-clad and warmly housed, ... 172 *Infant Daughter* 30

Warm-reeking. And sent 'warm-reeking, rich and sweet,' . . . . S.3. 432 **A German* 3

Warms. No tears can chill them, and no bosom warms, ... 7 *Ev. Wk.* 277
Which the Muse warms; and I, whose head is grey, 273 **Wild Redbreast* 5
No; their dread service nerves the heart it warms, 469 **The feudal* 13
Does that benignity pervade, that warms . . . 807 *Excursion* 4. 428
This favoured Land, or sunshine warms her soil. . 838 *Excursion* 6. 16

Warmth. Our little fire sent forth a cheering warmth 50 *Bord.* 708
Light to thy path, warmth to thy blood!—Together 70 *Bord.* 1852
For clothes, for warmth, for food, and fire; . . 114 *Ind. Wom.* 16
What warmth, what comfort would it yield . . 120 *Emigrant Mother* 22
When we've little warmth, or none. . . . . 160 **Pansies, lilies* 32
But, till the warmth of summer skies . . . . 194 *Ruth* 224
His mid-day warmth abate not, seeming less . . 219 *Haunted Tree* 2
Seemed from each other a faint warmth to borrow. 374 *Eg. Maid* 330
Day's grateful warmth, tho' moist with falling dews. . . . . 453 **Calm is the* 2
Can draw warmth from the cheek of my Love; . 484 **A plague* 27
In the first warmth of their original sunshine, . 498 **Enough of climbing* 49
The light of Knowledge, and the warmth of Love. 515 **Ah why* 14
What on the Plain *we* have of warmth and light, 521 *Epist. Beaumont* 8
With warmth, as much as needed, from a sun . 633 *Prelude* 1. 66
And the wild paths; and, by the summer's warmth 762 *Excursion* 1. 388
When, in the warmth of midsummer, the wheat . 767 *Excursion* 1. 707
Beside a fire whose genial warmth seemed met . 785 *Excursion* 2. 884
This vital warmth too cold, these visual orbs, . 804 *Excursion* 4. 180

Warmth—*continued.*
Of outward sunshine and internal warmth; . . 828 *Excursion* 5. 408
How thankful for the warmth of summer days, . 852 *Excursion* 6. 897
For seemliness and warmth, on festal days, . . 860 *Excursion* 7. 188
Or foot, or lip, in summer's warmth—perceived. . 879 *Excursion* 8. 332
—What kindly warmth from touch of fostering hand, ... 880 *Excursion* 8. 416
Howl from the north, what kindly warmth, methought, ... 881 *Excursion* 8. 446

Warn. To warn, to comfort, and command; . . 186 **She was* 28
To warn the living; if truth were ever told . . 325 *Enghien* 8
Thy whereabout, to warn the approaching sail. . 475 **Homeward we* 14

Warned. Stranger! henceforth be warned; and know that pride, ... 23 *Yew-tree* 50
Thus warned he sought some shepherd's spreading thorn . . . . 25 *Guilt* 41
Warned in a dream, the Wanderer long had sought 267 *St. Cath.* 9
Be warned"—His zeal the Chiefs confounded, . 405 *White Doe* 841
Warned thee these upper regions to forego, . . 460 **Queen of* 4
Shouts to him from behind; and, if thus warned 566 *Cumb. Beg.* 39
But, timely warned, *He* would have stayed his steps, ... 865 *Excursion* 7. 494

Warning. The black disguise, the warning whistle shrill, ... 32 *Guilt* 420
Warning solemn and profound. . . . . . . 94 *Westmoreland Girl* 64
The clock gives warning for eleven; . . . . 127 *Idiot Boy* 148
The Shepherd, at such warning, of his flock . . 132 *Michael* 53
"'From me this friendly warning take'— . . 156 *Oak and Broom* 51
And gave his doleful warning. . . . . . 302 *Yarrow V.* 32
Saviour, for our warning, seen . . . . . 336 **Jesu! bless* 7
Oft for a holy warning may it serve, . . . 360 **Long has* 11
Or warning serve, thus let them all, on ground . 361 **When here* 13
To Her and to all Lands its warning sent, . . 365 **The Baptist* 12
My Country! if such warning be held dear, . . 515 **Long-favoured* 10
Though to give timely warning and deter . . 519 *Pun. Death* 9. 1
Nor needs a warning voice to tame the pride . . 642 *Prelude* 2. 20
—With even as brief a warning—and how soon, . 795 *Excursion* 3. 645
"Such timely warning," said the Wanderer, "gave 805 *Excursion* 4. 295
Or with too brief a warning, to admit . . . 836 *Excursion* 5. 949
"Ah! what a warning for a thoughtless man, . 850 *Excursion* 6. 806
In memory and for warning, and in sign . . . 854 *Excursion* 6. 1082
A warning not unwelcome. Fare thee well! . . S.3. 437 **The doubt* 197

Warnings. Forgotten? have my warnings passed so quickly . . . . 40 *Bord.* 162
'Tis said that warnings ye dispense, ... 225 *Present.* 61
Of warnings—from the unprecedented might, . . 332 *Ode: Thanks.* 234
How shall your ancient warnings work for good . 518 *Pun. Death* 6. 11
Upheld by warnings heeded not too late . . . 529 **Those breathing* 130
Questions, directions, warnings and advice, . . 649 *Prelude* 3. 23

Warrant. Leonard and James! I warrant, every corner . . . . 99 *Brothers* 273
The warrant hail, exulting to be free; . . . . 434 *Ecc. Sonn.* 2. 23. 3
Their warrant. Bodies fall by wild sword-law; . 442 *Ecc. Sonn.* 3. 7. 12
The thirst of fame his warrant: . . . . . 478 *Somnamb.* 49
And, sweet Mother! under warrant . . . . 502 **Like a* 45
I ask what warrant fixed them (like a spell . . 527 **Thosebreathing* 46
Parching Summer hath no warrant . . . . 550 *Hermit's Cell* 4. 9
But from Him I crav'd no warrant, ... S.3. 437 **I, whose* 11

Warred. Review the past, I warred against myself— 735 *Prelude* 12. 76

Warring. Troubled long with warring notions . . 550 *Hermit's Cell* 4. 1
And lull'd the warring passions into rest, . . . 618 *School Ex.* 32

Warrior. If here a warrior left a spell, . . . 223 *Wishing-gate* 22
Upon the common weal; a warrior bold, . . . 227 *Vernal Ode* 102
By Art's bold privilege Warrior and War-horse stand . . . . 278 *Wellington* 1
High lodged the *Warrior*, like a bird of prey; . 298 *Brownie's Cell* 11
Descends:—beneath this godlike Warrior, see! . 314 *Hofer* 12
He smote the blossoms of their warrior youth; . 321 **Humanity,delighting* 20
Resting upon his arms each warrior stood, . . 322 *Germans* 2
Of young or old, warrior, or saint, or sage, . . 356 *Aquap.* 240
—She sees a warrior carved in stone, ... 397 *White Doe* 126
A warrior, with his shield of pride . . . . 397 *White Doe* 128
Who is the happy Warrior? Who is he . . . 493 *Hap. War.* 1
This is the happy Warrior; this is He . . . . 494 *Hap. War.* 84
Toils long and hard.—The warrior will report 574 *Chiabrera* 4. 3
A crest of purple tops his warrior head. . . . 594 *Ev. Wk. Quarto* 132
By the dismantled warrior in old age, ... 673 *Prelude* 5. 501
Of some gigantic warrior clad in mail, ... 708 *Prelude* 8. 585
The warrior from the field—all perished, all— 723 *Prelude* 10. 360
Sage, warrior, patriot, hero; for it seemed . . 735 *Prelude* 12. 64
And armèd warrior; and in every grove . . . 812 *Excursion* 4. 742
Of their rude homesteads. Here the Warrior dwelt; . . . . 872 *Excursion* 7. 955

Warrior-chief. The feudal Warrior-chief, a Ghost unlaid, ... 393 *Inglewood* 11

Warrior's. *See* **Patriot-warrior's.**
A crest of purple tops the warrior's head. . . . 5 *Ev. Wk.* 149
In many a court, and many a warrior's tent, . . 103 *Artegal* 84
The frith that glittered like a warrior's shield, . 105 *Artegal* 198
As faith thus sanctified the warrior's crest . . 430 *Ecc. Sonn.* 2. 9. 1
Of Thirlmere flashes like a warrior's shield . . K.8. 225 **I will* 48
Then farewell to the Warrior's schemes, farewell . K.8. 257 *Recluse* 1.1.745

Warriors. *See* **Land-warriors.**
Silent the visionary warriors go, ... 6 *Ev. Wk.* 206
The warriors leap upon the land, ... 161 *Binnorie* 18
Five thousand warriors—O the rapturous day! . 212 *Dion* 18
Sleep, Warriors, sleep! among your hills repose! 316 **It was a* 9
Kings, warriors, high-souled poets, saint-like sages, 328 *Ode 1815* 61

Weight—*continued.*
All pressed on him with such a weight, that now, 102 *Brothers* 424
Deprest by weight of musing Phantasy ; . . . 108 *Indolence* 43
" O ! what a weight is in these shades ! Ye leaves, 111 *'Tis said that some* 21
Who knew not to what quiet depths a weight . 125 *V. and J.* 225
Your Pony's worth his weight in gold : . . . 130 *Idiot Boy* 362
Of One, a Widow, left beneath a weight . . . 138 *Widow* 4
The mountains against heaven's grave weight . 173 *Waggoner* 1. 13
Fell with the weight of drops of lead ;— . . . 175 *Waggoner* 1. 157
Among the rocks ; with weight of rain, . . . 175 *Waggoner* 1. 200
The Porter sits down on the weight which he bore ; 188 *Music* 21
A more than human weight upon his frame had cast. 196 *Resolution* 70
In which the heavy and the weary weight . . 206 *Tintern* 39
Medea's spells dispersed the weight of years, . . 210 *Laod.* 83
A flaky weight of winter's purest snows ! . . 212 *Dion*
And the blows fell with heavier weight . . . 238 *P. B.* 194
Who have felt the weight of too much liberty, . 250 **Nuns fret* 13
The weight of sadness was in wonder lost. . . 251 **Beloved Vale* 14
If the whole weight of what we think and feel, . 261 *Retirement* 1
Does the hour's drowsy weight his glee restrain ? 279 **'Tis he* 4
Off weight—nor press on weight !—away . . . 284 *Grave of Burns* 13
The weight of more than seventy years, . . . 293 *Jedbor.* 10
A weight of languid speech, or to the same . . 306 **We had* 8
Of thy offences be a heavy weight : . . . . 309 **England ! the* 13
A weight of hostile corses : drenched with gore . 317 **The martial* 7
If clay could think and mind were weight, . . 341 *Ital. Itin.* 15
The patriot Mother's weight of anxious cares ! . 344 **How blest* 52
How patiently the weight of wrong is borne ; . 359 **They—who* 8
Tardily sinking by its proper weight . . . . 380 *Duddon* 17. 13
Stood silent under dreary weight,— . . . . 400 *White Doe* 421
In open victory o'er the weight . . . . . 404 *White Doe* 741
This weight of anguish and despair. . . . . 412 *White Doe* 1515
Under the weight of mortal wretchedness ! . . 435 *Ecc. Sonn.* 2. 29. 11
Tempest, or length of way, or weight of toil ?— . 438 *Ecc. Sonn.* 2. 39. 8
Through gloomiest shade ; put on (nor dread its weight) . . . . 446 *Ecc. Sonn.* 3. 25. 13
The mortal weight cast off to be laid low. . . . 448 *Ecc. Sonn.* 3. 31. 4
Down-bearing with his whole Atlantic weight . 473 **Thanks for* 9
A weight of awe, not easy to be borne, . . . 477 *Long Meg* 1
Month falls on month with heavier weight ; . . 479 *Somnamb.* 79
In thee had yielded to the weight of years ; . . 491 *Tribute : Dog* 14
I feel the weight of chance-desires : . . . . 492 *Duty* 38
Groan underneath a weight of slavish toil, . . 501 *Humanity* 86
That I the weight of it may not sustain ; . . . 553 *Prioress* 31
And custom lie upon thee with a weight, . . . 589 *Immortality* 131
Shakes her numb arm that slumbers with its weight, 596 *Ev. Wk. Quarto* 251
Then with despair's whole weight his spirits sink, 609 *Desc.Sk.Quarto* 404
That the weight can no longer be borne, . . . 621 *Convict* 34
Some solace under weight of royal care, . . . 628 **Deign, Sovereign* 23
The heavy weight of many a weary day . . . 632 *Prelude* 1. 22
—And if the vulgar joy by its own weight . . 641 *Prelude* 1. 597
Even with a weight of pleasure, and the sky, . . 644 *Prelude* 2. 172
A weight must surely hang on days begun . . 655 *Prelude* 3. 408
That thou endurest; heavy though that weight be, 665 *Prelude* 5. 6
Bending beneath our life's mysterious weight . . 672 *Prelude* 5. 418
Under the weight of classic eloquence, ... 695 *Prelude* 7. 542
Against the weight of meanness, selfish cares, . 703 *Prelude* 8. 319
A weight of ages did at once descend . . . . 707 *Prelude* 8. 552
Distinct remembrances, but weight and power,— 707 *Prelude* 8. 554
Power growing under weight : alas ! I feel . . 707 *Prelude* 8. 555
That I both was and must be of small weight, . 721 *Prelude* 10. 226
Or aught of heavier or more deadly weight, . . 737 *Prelude* 12. 212
Their due proportion, under all the weight . . 741 *Prelude* 13. 98
Under a growing weight of vulgar sense, . . . 748 *Prelude* 14. 159
With still increasing weight ; he was o'erpowered 760 *Excursion* 1. 282
Became a weight in which no pleasure was : . . 765 *Excursion* 1. 579
Four dear supporters of one senseless weight, . 780 *Excursion* 2. 584
Even to the dust ; apparently, through weight . 803 *Excursion* 4. 166
The rational creature, left, to feel the weight . 811 *Excursion* 4. 667
And more secure, by very weight of all . . . 837 *Excursion* 5. 965
Proved all unable to support the weight . . . 842 *Excursion* 6. 237
By her offence to lay a twofold weight . . . 852 *Excursion* 6. 943
Nor could endure the weight of his own shame. . 855 *Excursion* 6. 1114
—Nor deem that his mild presence was a weight . 864 *Excursion* 7. 438
Whose flexile boughs low bending with a weight . 881 *Excursion* 8. 443
Friendly the weight of leisure to remove, . . . S.3.426 **Through Cumbrian* 5
That they who want, are not too great a weight . K.8. 246 *Recluse* 1.1.366
To be no arbitrary weight imposed, ... K.8. 249 *Recluse* 1.1.469

Weightier. We came with weightier purses, that sufficed . . . . 643 *Prelude* 2. 86

Weightiest. Of perilous war her weightiest armies fail, 316 **Say, what* 7

Weighty. Some weighty matter ; then, with fervent voice . . . . 888 *Excursion* 9. 291

Welcome. *See* **Ever-welcome.**
Host of his welcome inn, the noon-tide bower, . 11 *Desc. Sk.* 29
Thrice every day, the pail and welcome hand. . 17 *Desc. Sk.* 398
Wound in more welcome cadence down the vale ; 22 *Desc. Sk.* 635
That welcome in such house for him was none. . 24 *Guilt* 12
And gave me food—and rest, more welcome, more desired. . . . . 31 *Guilt* 405
" O welcome sentence which will end though late," 36 *Guilt* 655
Would be most welcome. Yon white hawthorn gained, ... 41 *Bord.* 216
(Not the less welcome to my Lord for that) . . 59 *Bord.* 1196
The lame, the hungry, will be welcome there. . 66 *Bord.* 1629
Gave me a hearty welcome ; they had laid . . 69 *Bord.* 1757
To feed remorse, to welcome every sting . . . 78 *Bord.* 2304
To welcome in the May. . . . . 84 *Shepherd-boys* 4

Welcome—*continued.*
And who would grieve and fret, if, welcome come 97 *Brothers* 123
And welcome gone, they are so like each other, . 97 *Brothers* 124
Runs a deafening noise of welcome !— . . . 141 *Arm. Lady* 129
Most soothing was it for a welcome Friend, . . 143 **High bliss* 9
Urania's self might welcome with pleased ear . . 154 *Morn. Ex.* 53
That nod to welcome transient guests ; . . . 154 *Flower Garden* 40
Night has brought the welcome hour, ... 163 *Spinning Wheel* 2
A welcome greeting he can hear ;— . . . . 176 *Waggoner* 2. 20
Thrice welcome, darling of the Spring ! . . . 183 **O blithe* 13
Luminous or gloomy, welcome to the vale . . 230 *Clouds* 47
Which they are entering, welcome to mine eye . 230 *Clouds* 48
A gladsome and a welcome noise. . . . . . 246 *P. B.* 880
Has filled the laughing vales with welcome flowers. 263 **How clear* 14
Yet art thou welcome, welcome as a friend . . 264 *Snowdrop* 7
Thee with the welcome Snowdrop I compare ; . 274 **Such age* 9
And the old day was welcome as the young, . . 279 **Though I* 8
As welcome, and as beautiful—in sooth . . . 279 **Though I* 9
And prompt to welcome every gleam . . . . 285 *Nith* 15
More welcome notes to weary bands . . . . 289 *Sol. Reap.* 10
The chronicle were welcome that should call . 290 *Kilchurn* 33
Stroke merciful and welcome would that be . . 319 *Guernica* 9
That will be welcome, if by you entwined ; . . 324 *Ode 1814* 41
Angels might welcome with a choral shout ! . . 326 **The Bard* 14
Most fair, most welcome, when they drank the dew 361 **List—'twas* 14
Is welcome as a star, that doth present . . . 383 *Duddon* 31. 2
A gracious welcome shall be thine, ... 386 *Yarrow Rev.* 73
And welcome, as a gift of grace, ... 414 *White Doe* 1678
His be a welcome cordially bestowed ! " . . . 422 *Ecc. Sonn.* 1. 16. 14
Of faith invites. More welcome to no land . . 449 *Ecc. Sonn.* 3. 36. 6
The soothing recompense, the welcome change. . 454 *Sea-side* 10
How welcome wouldst thou be to this green Vale 455 *Rydal Mere* 31
And welcome glory won in battles fought . . . 458 *Sea-shore* 23
Welcome, though silent and intangible !— . . 459 **Wanderer ! that* 30
Poor as thou art. A welcome sacrifice . . . 465 **Pastor and* 8
Should here be welcome, and in verse enwrought : 466 *St. Bees* 24
How sad a welcome ! To each voyager . . . 474 **How sad* 1
Welcome !—but lay thy sword aside, ... 485 *Poet's Epitaph* 15
Thee will he welcome to his hand and heart, . . 489 *Spade* 23
Be ours to welcome it ; . . . . 497 *Lycoris* 30
Then welcome, above all, the Guest . . . . 497 *Lycoris* 45
To welcome thee, repel the fears that crowd . . 504 *Warning* 79
Tears of salvation. Welcome death ! while Heaven 520 *Pun. Death* 12. 9
Will flow, and on a welcome page appear . . . 522 *Epist. Beaumont* 57
Of our migration.—Ere the welcome dawn . . 522 *Epist. Beaumont* 91
Put on, to welcome spring, their best attire, . . 529 *Poor Robin* 4
And all shall welcome the new ray . . . . . 533 **Blest is* 39
But welcome fortitude, and patient cheer, . . 579 *Peele Castle* 57
I welcome thee once more : . . . . 579 **Sweet Flower* 3
Three times a day the pail and welcome hand. . 611 *Desc.Sk.Quarto* 485
I gave a fervent welcome to the sight, ... 622 **Among all* 7
That hope hath been discouraged ; welcome light 634 *Prelude* 1. 124
Sent welcome notice of the rising moon, . . . 640 *Prelude* 1. 571
This labour will be welcome, honoured Friend ! . 641 *Prelude* 1. 646
Of welcome faces up and down I roved ; . . . 649 *Prelude* 3. 22
Friendships, acquaintances, were welcome all. . 652 *Prelude* 3. 247
Glad welcome had I, with some tears, perhaps, . 658 *Prelude* 4. 27
In my accustomed bed, more welcome now . . 659 *Prelude* 4. 82
Guests welcome almost as the angels were . . 681 *Prelude* 6. 396
With an unmeasured welcome. Through the night, 693 *Prelude* 7. 433
Thrice welcome Presence ! how can patience e'er 694 *Prelude* 7. 503
They give it welcome. Long ere heat of noon, . 699 *Prelude* 8. 20
Was welcome, softened, if not solemnised. . . 706 *Prelude* 8. 509
(How welcome to the weary traveller's eyes !) . 716 *Prelude* 9. 477
Found ready welcome. Tempting region *that* . 730 *Prelude* 11. 228
Which lacked not voice to welcome me in turn : . 742 *Prelude* 13. 136
Still deeper welcome found his pure discourse : . 757 *Excursion* 1. 73
A daughter's welcome gave me, and I loved her . 763 *Excursion* 1. 499
But he was welcome ; no one went away . . . 763 *Excursion* 1. 506
Which with a look of welcome she received ; . . 768 *Excursion* 1. 806
The welcome of an Inmate from afar, ... 772 *Excursion* 2. 60
Conducted hither your most welcome feet, . . 779 *Excursion* 2. 534
Following the guidance of these welcome feet . 793 *Excursion* 3. 500
Before the threshold stands to welcome us ! . . 793 *Excursion* 3. 524
Where now that boasted liberty ? No welcome . 798 *Excursion* 3. 856
I guess that, welcome to your lonely hearth, . . 807 *Excursion* 4. 385
A welcome interruption to discourse . . . . 829 *Excursion* 5. 464
Of giving welcome to the first of May . . . . 851 *Excursion* 6. 834
Had earned for him sure welcome, and the rights 859 *Excursion* 7. 122
Wished-for, or welcome, wheresoe'er he came— . 875 *Excursion* 8. 99
The Wanderer ever welcome ! A prompt kiss . 881 *Excursion* 8. 495
Of Man may rise, as to a welcome close . . . 885 *Excursion* 9. 94
But turned not without welcome promise made . 895 *Excursion* 9. 775
So welcome, no temptation half so dear . . . K.8. 256 *Recluse* 1.1.709

Welcomed. Welcomed wisely ; though a growth . 222 *Triad* 208
And welcomed the poor Child. . . . . . . 297 *Highland Boy* 225
She welcomed what was given, and craved no more ; 736 *Prelude* 12. 158
Rest, and be welcomed there to livelier joy. . . 756 *Excursion* 1. 20
But we are kindly welcomed—promptly served . 821 *Excursion* 4. 1316

Welcomes. All Nature welcomes Her whose sway . 506 **While from* 9
Welcomes the Consort of a happy Queen. . . . 629 *Installation* 72

Welcoming. To the new year a welcoming ; . . 113 *Lament* 24
Our streams proclaim a welcoming ; . . . . 204 *Brougham* 33
That faced us with a passionate welcoming, . . K.8. 241 *Recluse* 1.1.172

Welcomings. Their own creation. Such glad welcomings . . . . 431 *Ecc. Sonn.* 2. 13. 8

Welfare. His utmost for the welfare of the Boy ; . 136 *Michael* 309
And the least welfare cometh to their share ; . . 559 *Cuck.and Night.* 144
A thought to human welfare,—that, henceforth . 717 *Prelude* 9. 535
Even when the public welfare is their aim, . . 741 *Prelude* 13. 69

Welkin. Across the welkin seemed to spread . . 167 *Pilgrim's Dream* 50

Welkin—*continued.*
Full oft, when storms the welkin rend . . . 550 *Hermit's Cell* 5. 10

Well. *See* **Fare-thee-well, Mountain-well.**
Of banished bliss, by fancy loved too well. . . 17 *Desc. Sk.* 400
—Well taught by that to feel his rights, prepared 18 *Desc. Sk.* 447
Well pleased upon some simple annual feast, . . 19 *Desc. Sk.* 496
I well remember.—He was one who owned . . 23 *Yew-tree* 12
Half raised, for well his arm might lose its force . 27 *Guilt* 179
And well it was that of the corse there found . . 27 *Guilt* 187
"The staff I well remember which upbore . . 28 *Guilt* 217
He well could love in grief; his faith he kept; . 29 *Guilt* 260
Well met from far with revelry secure . . . . 32 *Guilt* 412
The carman wet her lips as well behoved; . . 34 *Guilt* 546
The Sailor knew too well. That wickedness . . 35 *Guilt* 614
Well may we wonder he has gained such power . 37 *Bord.* 13
May well deceive his Child—What! leave her thus, 41 *Bord.* 251
Take care of him, and feed the truant well. . 42 *Bord.* 307
Well as the wreck I am permits. And you, Sir? 43 *Bord.* 336
About this ground; she hath a tongue well skilled, 44 *Bord.* 366
For this good deed!—Well, Sirs, this passed away; 44 *Bord.* 409
Well! they might turn a beggar from their doors, 45 *Bord.* 439
Have I been waiting for him. Well, but softly, . 45 *Bord.* 452
Well!—he has often spurned me like a toad, . . 45 *Bord.* 470
Well then, says I—I'll out with it; at which . . 45 *Bord.* 475
And he seemed angry. Angry! well he might; . 46 *Bord.* 482
You will be firm: but though we well may trust . 48 *Bord.* 602
I hope Idonea is well housed. That horseman, . 50 *Bord.* 734
As well indeed it might. And this you deem . . 51 *Bord.* 749
That well may put some fears into *your* heart. . 52 *Bord.* 813
That all is well prepared. We will obey you. . 58 *Bord.* 1131
A sound of laughter, too!—'tis well—I feared . 60 *Bord.* 1260
Feed on her leaves. You knew her well—ay, there, 61 *Bord.* 1312
Knowing what otherwise we know too well, . . 63 *Bord.* 1421
I know him well; there needs no other motive . 63 *Bord.* 1430
To the oath of fealty, I well remember, . . . 63 *Bord.* 1445
I know not what I said—all may be well. . . . 67 *Bord.* 1645
This is a dismal place—well—that is well— . . 67 *Bord.* 1674
Of all this world is solved, well may we envy . . 69 *Bord.* 1796
Without the strength to rise. Well, well, he lives, 73 *Bord.* 2065
You will do well; unjust suspicion may . . . 75 *Bord.* 2158
All last summer, as well you know, ... 80 †*Address: Child* 26
It is not well with thee? well both for bed and board? . . . . 87 *Pet-lamb* 22
Paid to One who loved her well. . . . . . 94 *Westmoreland Girl* 68
'Twas one well known to him in former days, . 95 *Brothers* 38
Through fields which once had been well known to him: . . . . 96 *Brothers* 93
Was known as well as to the flowers that grow there. 99 *Brothers* 276
Then they could write, ay, and speak too, as well 99 *Brothers* 279
Well—all was gone, and they were destitute, . . 100 *Brothers* 304
Ay, that he did— And all went well with him?— 101 *Brothers* 385
And placed together near our rocky Well. . . . 106 *Farewell* 24
A comfortless and hidden well. . . . . . . 111 *A Complaint* 12
A well of love—it may be deep— . . . . . 111 *A Complaint* 13
When I was well, I wished to live, ... 114 *Ind. Wom.* 15
Well born, well bred; I sent him forth . . . 117 *Aff. Marg.* 17
Turn rather, though I love her well: . . . . 121 *Emigrant Mother* 72
A portion of the tale may well be left . . . 124 *V. and J.* 176
Which Betty well could understand. . . . . 126 *Idiot Boy* 66
His steed and he right well agree; . . . . . 127 *Idiot Boy* 107
Now, though he knows poor Johnny well, . . . 127 *Idiot Boy* 114
With Betty all was not so well; . . . . . 127 *Idiot Boy* 138
And we have always used him well; . . . . 129 *Idiot Boy* 304
Ye Muses! whom I love so well? . . . . . 130 *Idiot Boy* 346
And thus resumed:—"Well, Isabel! this scheme 135 *Michael* 274
As well thou knowest, in us the old and young . 136 *Michael* 354
Bestir them in good deeds. Now, fare thee well— 137 *Michael* 412
I have conversed with more than one who well . 138 *Michael* 451
'Tis well for me thou canst not see . . . . 145 *Her Eyes* 69
My love for thee has well been tried: . . . . 145 *Her Eyes* 93
Among the woods and fields, we love you well, . 147 *Joanna* 11
On its firm margin, even as from a well, . . . 149 *M. H.* 9
'Tis well that some sage instinct, when the stars . 154 *Morn. Ex.* 57
He loved the wars so well. . . . . 161 *Binnorie* 9
To each and all might well belong: . . . . 162 **Who fancied* 14
And felt that all was well. . . . . 169 *Wren's Nest* 56
The place to Benjamin right well . . . . . 174 *Waggoner* 1. 83
Well! that is past—and in despite . . . . . 174 *Waggoner* 1. 97
And near that lurid light, full well . . . . . 175 *Waggoner* 1. 170
This little place may well be dizzy! . . . . 177 *Waggoner* 2. 63
He'd drag as well what he is dragging; . . . 179 *Waggoner* 3. 53
"Yon owl!—pray God that all be well! . . . 179 *Waggoner* 3. 112
Well pleased in rustic garb to feed . . . . . 180 *Waggoner* 4. 50
The Showman chooses well his place, 'tis Leicester's busy Square; . . . . 189 *Star-gazers* 5
Might well be dangerous food . . . . . . 193 *Ruth* 123
But some remember well . . . . 199 *Thorn* 152
From this day forth, shall call it HART-LEAP WELL. 201 *Hart-leap* 64
A cup of stone received the living well; . . . 202 *Hart-leap* 82
And one, not four yards distant, near a well. . 202 *Hart-leap* 104
But as to the great Lodge! you might as well . 202 *Hart-leap* 131
And come and make his death-bed near the well. 203 *Hart-leap* 148
"Grey-headed Shepherd, thou hast spoken well; 203 *Hart-leap* 161
And what perceive; well pleased to recognise . 207 *Tintern* 107
But her humility is well content . . . . . 221 *Triad* 115
And if to lure the truant back be well, . . . 229 *Cuckoo-clock* 4
Well may our hearts have faith that blessings come, 229 *Cuckoo-clock* 38
Of the Unsubstantial, pondered well! . . . . 235 *Power of Sound* 176
Well have you played your friendly part: . . 237 *P. B.* 113
And I, as well as I was able, ... 238 *P. B.* 173

Well—*continued.*
And well he knew the spire of Sarum; . . . 238 *P. B.* 212
"As well might Peter in the Fleet . . . . . 239 *P. B.* 236
Must mount, he shows well as he can: . . . 243 *P. B.* 592
Well may you tremble and look grave! . . . 243 *P. B.* 627
The listening Ass conjectures well; . . . . 243 *P. B.* 652
And this poor slave who loved him well, . . . 243 *P. B.* 662
Yet, potent Spirits! well I know, ... 245 *P. B.* 766
Whom in my fear I love so well; . . . . . 245 *P. B.* 772
Our Travellers, ye remember well, ... 245 *P. B.* 796
I cannot well express the thoughts . . . . 246 *P. B.* 871
For well did Peter know the sound; . . . . 246 *P. B.* 876
For he is dead—I know it well!" . . . . . 248 *P. B.* 1027
Well may'st thou halt—and gaze with brightening eye! . . . . 250 *Admon.* 1
Lingers, but Fancy is well satisfied; . . . . 251 **Her only* 2
But some (who brook those hackneyed themes full well, ... 255 *Detraction* 5
Well pleased to skim the plain with wild flowers deckt, ... 270 **Though the bold* 4
Heaven's sapphire pavement, yet breathed well content, ... 278 **Lo! where she* 11
Well pleased, her foot should print earth's common grass, ... 278 **Lo! where she* 12
Well have yon Railway Labourers to THIS ground 283 **Well have* 1
Well might such thoughts, dear Sister, throng . 285 *Nith* 7
The picture of a life well spent: . . . . . 294 *Jedbor.* 40
When one day (and now mark me well, . . . 296 *Highand Boy* 96
Which he, poor Child, had studied well; . . . 296 *Highland Boy* 117
On England's bosom; yet well pleased to rest, . 303 **Fair Star* 4
'Tis well! from this day forward we shall know . 310 **Another year* 5
Well obeyed was that command— . . . . . 323 *Ode 1814* 35
And well might it beseem that mighty Town . . 327 *Ode 1815* 46
—Well does thine aspect usher in this Day; . . 329 *Ode: Thanks.* 14
Well judged the Friend who placed it there . . 337 *Thun* 5
Might well be styled this noble body's HEAD; . 339 *Schwytz* 11
Well—let him pace this noted beach once more, . 349 *Boulogne* 5
May well suffice, till noon-tide's sultry heat . . 352 *Aquap.* 24
Out of her early struggles well inspired . . . 356 *Aquap.* 272
Humanity, sang feats that well might call . . 359 **Complacent Fictions* 13
So well, that by its help and through His grace . 365 **Rapt above* 6
Lo! by a destiny well known . . . . . . 372 *Eg. Maid* 205
Well pleased that future Bards should chant . . 386 *Yarrow Rev.* 107
Well sang the Bard who called the grave, in strains 389 *Breadalb.* 1
And fresh with rivers, well did it become . . . 392 *Daniel* 2
With perfect cunning framed as well . . . . 397 *White Doe* 94
Of all we loved, and loved so well: . . . . 402 *White Doe* 529
"Rights have you, and may well be bold: . . . 408 *White Doe* 1082
'Tis well that she hath heard the tale, ... 409 *White Doe* 1190
'Tis well, for he the worst defied . . . . . 409 *White Doe* 1231
Then well may their accord be true, ... 415 *White Doe* 1728
What Powers, presiding o'er the sacred well . . 418 *Ecc. Sonn.* 1. 2. 3
Hail countless Temples! that so well befit . . 430 *Ecc. Sonn.* 2. 9. 9
Well worthy to be magnified are they . . . . 443 *Ecc. Sonn.* 3. 13. 1
Ere nightfall—truth that well may claim a sigh, . 448 *Ecc. Sonn.* 3. 31. 11
'Tis well—but what are helps of time and place, . 456 **Soft as* 20
Through cloudy umbrage, well might that fair face, 460 **Queen of* 12
Of the pure spring (they call it the "Nun's Well," 465 **The cattle* 7
And, from her vow well weighed in Heaven's decrees, ... 466 *St. Bees* 35
Tides of aggressive war, oft served as well . . . 469 **The feudal* 3
And fare thee well, to Fancy visible, ... 475 **Homeward we* 5
There set, and guarded well; . . . . . . 478 *Somnamb.* 15
They parted.—Well with him it fared . . . . 478 *Somnamb.* 46
"Our work," said I, "was well begun, . . . 486 **We walked* 13
This wonder merits well. . . . . 492 *Fidelity* 53
From well to better, daily self-surpast: . . . 494 *Hap. War.* 76
May well afford to mortal ear . . . . . . 498 **The sylvan* 10
Are well assigned to Memory . . . . . . 499 *Memory* 3
'Twere well in little, as in great, to pause, . . 501 *Humanity* 99
On thee I look, not sorrowing; fare thee well, . 510 *F. Stone* 130
Yes, though He well may tremble at the sound . 520 *Pun. Death* 13. 1
Without reserve to those whom we love well— . 522 *Epist. Beaumont* 55
Of those old Patriarchs when from well to well . 522 *Epist. Beaumont* 99
As well we knew, together had grown grey. . . 523 *Epist. Beaumont* 132
To the fresh waters of a living Well— . . . . 527 **Those breathing* 8
Upon the Sabine farm he loved so well; . . . . 528 **Those breathing* 103
And flowers they well might seem to passers-by . 529 *Poor Robin* 11
Well may the villagers rejoice! . . . . . . 533 **Blest is* 31
So were both right well content: . . . . . 535 *Egremont* 37
'Twas well enough, when summer came, . . . 536 *Goody Blake* 37
Yet never had she, well or sick, ... 536 *Goody Blake* 53
To consume this crystal Well; . . . . . . 550 *Hermit's Cell* 4. 10
And then he sang it well and fearlessly, . . . 554 *Prioress* 95
"'This well of mercy, Jesu's Mother sweet, . . 556 *Prioress* 205
By cursèd Jews—thing well and widely known, . . 556 *Prioress* 234
Well did they know that service all by rote, . . 558 *Cuck. and Night.* 71
Methought I wist right well what these birds meant, 558 *Cuck. and Night.* 108
It seems to me I sing as well as thou; . . . . 558 *Cuck. and Night.* 117
Is only fit to die, I dare well say, ... 559 *Cuck. and Night.* 134
For trust me well, in spite of thy quaint cry, . . 560 *Cuck. and Night.* 182
Well satisfied, I thanked her, and she said, . . 561 *Cuck. and Night.* 231
And, God of Love, that can right well and may, . 561 *Cuck. and Night.* 253
The Cuckoo—'tis not well that I should hide . . 561 *Cuck. and Night.* 266
Under a maple that is well beseen, ... 562 *Cuck. and Night.* 283
Unlearned Book and rude, as well I know, . . . 562 *Cuck. and Night.* 291
Well nigh for sorrow down he 'gan to fall. . . 562 *Troilus* 14
Now, my sweet Troilus, love me well, I pray! . 563 *Troilus* 54

Well—*continued.*
Singing so well, so goodly, and so clear, 563 *Troilus* 60
Well hast thou wreaked on me by pain and grief; 563 *Troil us* 72
Now mercy, Lord! thou know'st well I desire 563 *Troil us* 73
Then know I well that she would not sojourn. 563 *Troil us* 80
With a sore heart well ought I to bewail, 564 *Troil us* 121
Well did I watch, much laboured, nor had power 573 *Chia brera* 3. 8
O 'tis a passionate Work!—yet wise and well, 579 *Peel e Castle* 45
Well chosen is the spirit that is here; 579 *Peele Castle* 46
But they as well as I have gains;— 580 *John Words.* 45
For hope's deserted well why wistful look? 596 *Ev. Wk. Quarto* 255
Had noted well the stars, all flowers that grew 622 **Among all* 2
Guide hither, O sweet Moon, the maid I love so well. 630 [?] **O Moon* 15
His fits when he is neither sick nor well, 634 *Prelude* 1. 137
In this our deep devotion. Fare thee well! 648 *Prelude* 2. 466
To in-door study than was wise or well. 654 *Prelude* 3. 367
And yet the spectacle may well demand 657 *Prelude* 3. 588
Well might sarcastic Fancy then have whispered, 659 *Prelude* 4. 60
Among the favourites whom it pleased me well 659 *Prelude* 4. 93
Those walks well worthy to be prized and loved— 660 *Prelude* 4. 131
Of a thick hawthorn, I could mark him well, 664 *Prelude* 4. 390
Knowing too well the importance of his theme, 665 *Prelude* 4. 444
It might have well beseemed me to repeat 668 *Prelude* 5. 177
Though fledged and feathered, and well pleased to part 669 *Prelude* 5. 247
There was a Boy: ye knew him well, ye cliffs 671 *Prelude* 5. 364
Well do I call to mind the very week 672 *Prelude* 5. 426
That round us chaunted. Well might we be glad, 674 *Prelude* 5. 566
Who love as we do. Speed thee well! divide 678 *Prelude* 6. 247
Well might a stranger look with bounding heart 682 *Prelude* 6. 517
Well pleased to pitch a vagrant tent among 688 *Prelude* 7. 56
An idler's place; an idler well content 688 *Prelude* 7. 72
With no unthinking mind, well pleased to note 690 *Prelude* 7. 220
False tints too well accorded with the glare 692 *Prelude* 7. 345
Although well pleased to be where they were found, 696 *Prelude* 7. 584
To drink the waters of some sainted well, 701 *Prelude* 8. 155
Some pensive musings which might well beseem 706 *Prelude* 8. 457
As well they might, the impersonated thought, 706 *Prelude* 8. 501
Never forsaken, that, by acting well, 707 *Prelude* 8. 527
To reason well of polity or law, 712 *Prelude* 9. 199
Less than might well befit my youth, the cause 713 *Prelude* 9. 245
"I, Robespierre, accuse thee!" Well is known 720 *Prelude* 10. 113
Well might my wishes be intense, my thoughts 721 *Prelude* 10. 209
The snakes about her cradle; that was well, 724 *Prelude* 10. 393
As well of License as of Liberty; 729 *Prelude* 11. 163
(Too well I loved, in that my spring of life, 732 *Prelude* 11. 326
And their impassioned sounds, which well might make 737 *Prelude* 12. 199
From our first childhood. I remember well, 737 *Prelude* 12. 225
Witness and judge; and I remember well 745 *Prelude* 13. 367
And drinking from the well of homely life. 760 *Excursion* 1. 307
Joined in a cold damp nook, espied a well 763 *Excursion* 1. 461
And well remember, o'er that fence she looked, 766 *Excursion* 1. 692
I well remember that those very plumes, 770 *Excursion* 1. 942
He answered, "to the Person suited well, 778 *Excursion* 2. 459
He answered, "has been here; but could not well 779 *Excursion* 2. 543
And well those lofty brethren bear their part 782 *Excursion* 2. 699
Our housewife knew full well what she possessed! 783 *Excursion* 2. 763
And, even as these are well and widely fixed, 812 *Excursion* 4. 764
Guides to destruction? Is it well to trust 812 *Excursion* 4. 771
He with a smile exclaimed:—"'Tis well you speak 814 *Excursion* 4. 894
With such embellishment as well beseems 824 *Excursion* 5. 121
Owes that presiding aspect which might well 824 *Excursion* 5. 129
—For me, I looked upon the pair, well pleased: 829 *Excursion* 5. 452
Full well I recollect. We often crossed 839 *Excursion* 6. 103
I well remember, while I passed her door 849 *Excursion* 6. 759
To end my days; well pleased was I to see 860 *Excursion* 7. 199
Of rights to him; but he remained well pleased, 864 *Excursion* 7. 433
The Pastor answered, "You have read him well. 866 *Excursion* 7. 564
Down on this spot, well pleased would he have seen 871 *Excursion* 7. 880
Be satisfied, 'tis well,—the end is gained; 874 *Excursion* 8. 7
Of trivial occupations well devised, 892 *Excursion* 9. 520
And wild-flowers known as well as if our hands S.3. 433 **The doubt* 7
A warning not unwelcome. Fare thee well! S.3. 437 **The doubt* 197
Hernani knows well S.3. 440 **Said red-ribboned* 15
Hard to believe, yet could they well discern K.8. 225 **I will* 41
To drink of the cold well. When in like sort K.8. 226 **I will* 57
Had slaked his thirst out of a famous well, K.8. 226 **I will* 60
Before the boy knew well what he had seen K.8. 229 **I will* 147
He well remembers, though the year be gone. K.8. 236 *Recluse* 1. 1. 5
Their safe retreat. We knew them well, I guess K.8. 243 *Recluse* 1. 1. 246
They were more dear than may be well believed, K.8. 243 *Recluse* 1. 1. 248
A friendly covert. "And they knew it well," K.8. 247 *Recluse* 1. 1. 396
Till, at the last, thou hear the voice—"Well done, K.8. 325 [?] **The vestal* 13
But here's a thought which well our mirth may cross L.1. 95 *Juvenal* 3. 14

We'll. Not yet in sight!—We'll saunter here awhile; 38 *Bord.* 48
We'll not complain of that. My limbs are stiff 43 *Bord.* 359
We'll stroll into the wood; lean on my arm. 43 *Bord.* 363
We'll lead him to the Convent. He shall live, 54 *Bord.* 904
We'll not insult thy majesty by time, 58 *Bord.* 1154
We'll have a counting of our flocks to-morrow; 71 *Bord.* 1886
—Come now we'll to bed! and when we are there 81 †*Address: Child* 38
He may knock at the door,—we'll not let him in; 81 †*Address: Child* 40
May drive at the windows,—we'll laugh at his din; 81 †*Address: Child* 41
We'll for our whistles run a race." 85 *Shepherd-boys* 36
We'll take another: who is he that lies 98 *Brothers* 197
We'll talk of sunshine and of song, 106 **I've watched* 16
But, Allan, be true to me, Allan,—we'll die 116 *Repentance* 7

We'll—*continued.*
We'll sport amid the boreal morning; 237 *P. B.* 92
"Or we'll into the realm of Faery, 237 *P. B.* 101
We'll show that we can help to frame 291 *Rob Roy* 87
"Whate'er betide, we'll turn aside, 292 *Yarrow Unv.* 7
We'll wander Scotland thorough; 293 *Yarrow Unv.* 38
We'll keep them, winsome Marrow! 293 *Yarrow Unv.* 54
We'll give to idleness. 483 *Sister* 16
We'll frame the measure of our souls: 483 *Sister* 35
We'll give to idleness. 483 *Sister* 40

Well-a-day. Ah, well-a-day for Peter Bell! 242 *P. B.* 521
Well-appointed. Of well-appointed chivalry. 403 *White Doe* 699
Well-beloved. The well-beloved, the fortunate, the wise,— 862 *Excursion* 7. 342
Well-born. Were men well-born; the chivalry of France. 711 *Prelude* 9. 129
Well-deserving. Calm is the well-deserving brute, 247 *P. B.* 936
Well-doing. Of Luke and his well-doing: and the Boy 138 *Michael* 432
Well-earned. Withdrew, on summons to their well-earned meal; 883 *Excursion* 8. 593
Well-formed. Of well-formed characters, with chalk inscribed 690 *Prelude* 7. 206
Well-girt. Has on the well-girt saddle set 126 *Idiot Boy* 39
Welling. Continual waters welling cheered the waste, 17 *Desc. Sk.* 390
Continual fountains welling chear'd the waste, 611 *Desc. Sk. Quarto* 478
Well-known. Give, on this well-known couch, one nuptial kiss 210 *Laod.* 63
A form discover'd at the well-known seat, 592 *Ev. Wk. Quarto* 45
And sail that glides the well-known alders by. 592 *Ev. Wk. Quarto* 48
I did not step into the well-known boat 658 *Prelude* 4. 16
Beside the well-known charnel-house had then 704 *Prelude* 8. 378
Well-matched. To glance a look upon the well-matched pair; 19 *Desc. Sk.* 486
From things well-matched or ill, and words for things, 679 *Prelude* 6. 300
Well-measured. She plants well-measured terrors in the road 519 *Pun. Death* 8. 4
Well-pleased. Well-pleased, the armèd Company 402 *White Doe* 601
Well-poised. Two ruddy children hung, a well-poised freight, 858 *Excursion* 7. 73
Well-remembered. The well-remembered debt." 238 *P. B.* 185
Wells. Fed in the Libyan waste by gushing wells, 346 *Processions* 20
Half-rural Sadler's Wells? Though at that time 691 *Prelude* 7. 267
Uprooted; would re-consecrate our wells 815 *Excursion* 4. 909
Not undistinguished, for of wells that ooze S.3. 433 **The doubt* 10
Well-shaped. Some limber twigs into a Cross, well-shaped with fingers nice, 91 *Norman Boy* 19
Well-spring. Who from the well-spring of his own clear breast 233 *Power of Sound* 63
To reach the well-spring of this woe! 406 *White Doe* 888
Or well-spring where the weary traveller rests. 742 *Prelude* 13. 141
Assisting, lucid well-spring! thou revealest S.3. 435 **The doubt* 103
Well-steered. Over the well-steered galleys did I rule:— 574 *Chiabrera* 4. 14
Well-tamed. While Winter like a well-tamed lion walks, 683 *Prelude* 6. 538
Well-tended. Where many a sheltered and well-tended plant 774 *Excursion* 2. 167
Well-wrought. A Vender of the well-wrought Scale, 341 *Ital. Itin.* 22
Welter. Welter and flash, a synod might detain 268 **Dogmatic Teachers* 12
If my spirit toss and welter 550 *Hermit's Cell* 4. 7
Weltering. There, waves that, hardly weltering, die away, 4 *Ev. Wk.* 122
Welterings. Nor touched by welterings of passion—is, 677 *Prelude* 6. 138
Wend. While our four travellers homeward wend; 131 *Idiot Boy* 433
Else let the dastard backward wend, and roam, 377 *Duddon* 4. 13
And through this street who list might ride and wend; 553 *Prioress* 41
Now farewell, quoth she, for I hence must wend; 561 *Cuck. and Night.* 252
Wends. Now up, now down, the Rover wends, 240 *P. B.* 352
With the green path; and now he wends 244 *P. B.* 697
But now, while down that slope he wends, 247 *P. B.* 938
Wensley. The Knight had ridden down from Wensley Moor 200 *Hart-leap* 1
Wensley's. Wensley's rich Vale and Sedbergh's naked heights. 622 *Recluse* 1. 1. 157

Went. *See* **Up-went.**
Of lofty hopes, he to the world went forth 23 *Yew-tree* 15
He rose, and to the ruin's portal went, 30 *Guilt* 312
And not in vain, while they went pacing side by side. 32 *Guilt* 459
A minute past, he went to fetch a draught 52 *Bord.* 808
Since your dear Mother went away,— 81 †*Mother's Return* 2
And all "since Mother went away!" 81 †*Mother's Return* 40
Went shouting far and wide; 83 *Lucy Gray* 34
And then she went away. 84 *We are Seven* 52
They went and they built up another. 86 *Rural Arch.* 18
—As homeward through the lane I went with lazy feet, 88 *Pet-lamb* 61
On that service she went forth; 94 *Westmoreland Girl* 70
While half an hour went by, the Priest had sent 95 *Brothers* 29
And went into his grave before his time. 98 *Brothers* 216
And it all went into each other's hearts. 99 *Brothers* 248
Like roe-bucks they went bounding o'er the hills; 99 *Brothers* 277
The very night before he went away, 99 *Brothers* 281
Ay, that he did— And all went well with him?— 101 *Brothers* 385
This done, he went on shipboard, and is now 102 *Brothers* 434
From realm to realm the humbled Exile went, 103 *Artegal* 82
Too soon, my friends, ye went away; 114 *Ind. Wom.* 49
I went my work about; 115 *Last of Flock* 78

Went—*continued.*
And he went to the chase with a tear on his cheek. 120 *Childless Father* 20
And, grumbling, he went back to bed ! . . . 129 *Idiot Boy* 261
He with his Father daily went, and they . . . 134 *Michael* 197
Went up to London, found a master there, . . 135 *Michael* 264
Here Michael ceased, and to the fields went forth 135 *Michael* 283
Went forth to show it to the neighbours round ; . 136 *Michael* 313
The Shepherd went about his daily work . . . 138 *Michael* 438
He went, and still looked up to sun and cloud, . 138 *Michael* 456
That many and many a day he thither went, . . 138 *Michael* 465
Was sold, and went into a stranger's hand. . . 138 *Michael* 475
Swiftly went that grey-haired Servant, . . 141 *Arm. Lady* 121
Went circling, like a multitude of sounds. . . . 146 **It was an* 8
In youth from rock to rock I went, . . . 157 **In youth* 1
Lambs, that through the mountains went . . . 171 *Kitten* 76
The way the Waggon went before. . . . . 176 *Waggoner* 1. 277
Went wandering over dale and hill, . . . 192 *Ruth* 5
And went to the sea-shore, ... 194 *Ruth* 189
My old remembrances went from me wholly ; . 195 *Resolution* 20
Unthinking Stephen went— . . . . 199 *Thorn* 116
Then home he went, and left the Hart stone-dead, 202 *Hart-leap* 77
Of that which went before the brother, . . . 241 *P. B.* 444
Went twice two hundred yards or more, . . . 247 *P. B.* 992
Peter went forth with him straightway ; . . . 249 *P. B.* 1123
On went She, and due north her journey took. . 258 **With Ships* 14
Went forth—his course surrendering to the care . 263 *Storm* 3
Went floating from her, darkening as it went ; . 265 **The Shepherd* 10
Since suddenly the dart of death went forth . . 276 *Filial Piety* 6
Went hand in hand with her. . . . . . . 295 *Highland Boy* 35
From year to year this shaggy Mortal went . . 299 *Brownie's Cell* 51
Went pacing side by side, this public Way . . 304 **Jones ! as* 2
Joyful annunciation !—it went forth— . . . 327 *Ode 1815* 19
To seek her Knight went wandering o'er the earth. 395 *White Doe : Ded.* 8
Went Norton, and resumed his post. . . . . 405 *White Doe* 844
And reverently the Band went forth. . . . . 410 *White Doe* 1321
He went, and traversed plain and hill ; . . . 412 *White Doe* 1437
To seek her Brother forth she went, ... 413 *White Doe* 1540
Went forth, the Doe stood there in sight. . . . 414 *White Doe* 1695
Coursing a train of gunpowder—it went, . . . 442 *Ecc. Sonn.* 3. 8. 6
And such vibration through the Mother went . . 446 *Ecc. Sonn.* 3. 24. 8
For poor to Sea I went, and poor I still remain. . 470 †*From early* 5
Though poor to Sea I went, and poor I still remain. 470 †*From early* 14
Of still and serious thought went round, . . . 486 *Matthew* 26
And through the wood we went ; . . . . . 488 *Fountain* 68
Among the mazy streams that backward went, . 495 *Fact* 33
Whose spirit, like the angel that went down . . 510 *F. Stone* 125
Forth they from the Castle went, ... 535 *Egremont* 38
Months and years went smilingly ; . . . . . 535 *Egremont* 70
Then in a convent went to hide . . . . . 536 *Egremont* 103
He went complaining all the morrow . . . . 537 *Goody Blake* 105
As they went homeward taught him privily . . 554 *Prioress* 94
Homeward and schoolward whensoe'er he went, . 554 *Prioress* 98
" The Christian folk that through the Jewry went 555 *Prioress* 163
And they right forth to Cresid's Palace went ; . 562 *Troilus* 10
And up and down there went, and to and fro, . 564 *Troilus* 87
To the neighbours he went,—all were free with their money ; . . . . 570 *Farmer* 33
With his grey hairs he went from the brook and the green ; . . . . 570 *Farmer* 46
Who went something farther than others have gone, 572 *Avarice* 30
I went into the Orchard quietly ; . . . . . 622 **Among all* 14
Went single in his ministry across . . . . 635 *Prelude* 1. 209
Went heaving through the water like a swan ; . 637 *Prelude* 1. 376
And through the meadows homeward went, in grave 638 *Prelude* 1. 389
Beneath the gloomy hills homeward I went . . 638 *Prelude* 1. 421
Edged the black clouds, home and to bed we went, 642 *Prelude* 2. 17
A man of business and expense, and went . . 649 *Prelude* 3. 26
The lack of beard.—The weeks went roundly on, 649 *Prelude* 3. 42
Read lazily in trivial books, went forth . . . 652 *Prelude* 3. 251
Went hurrying o'er the illimitable waste, . . 667 *Prelude* 5. 136
Was yellowing the hill tops, I went abroad . . 674 *Prelude* 5. 560
Angling I went, or trod the trackless hills . . 703 *Prelude* 8. 263
All that took place within me came and went . 707 *Prelude* 8. 557
With motion constant as his own, I went . . . 710 *Prelude* 9. 39
Erewhile went forth from Agra or Lahore, . . 718 *Prelude* 10. 19
The sunset cannon. While the orb went down . 723 *Prelude* 10. 325
With their whole souls went culling from the day 727 *Prelude* 11. 37
Feverish, and tired, and restless, I went forth . 738 *Prelude* 12. 289
That went before my steps. Thereafter came . 750 *Prelude* 14. 266
He duly went with what small overplus . . . 760 *Excursion* 1. 245
To all that was enjoyed where'er he went, . . 761 *Excursion* 1. 365
But he was welcome ; no one went away . . . 763 *Excursion* 1. 506
Went struggling on through those calamitous years 764 *Excursion* 1. 549
That, wheresoe'er I went, I still would ask . . 769 *Excursion* 1. 867
His dear companion wheresoe'er he went . . . 771 *Excursion* 2. 16
So speaking, on he went, and at the word . . 779 *Excursion* 2. 492
He went about his hospitable task. . . . . 781 *Excursion* 2. 656
Went through his usual tasks, a silent change . 785 *Excursion* 2. 893
Rose, though reluctantly, and forth we went. . 785 *Excursion* 2. 904
Went sounding on, a dim and perilous way ! . . 796 *Excursion* 3. 701
The ship went gliding with her thoughtless crew ; 798 *Excursion* 3. 836
Went with me to the place of my repose. . . . 834 *Excursion* 5. 799
Capacious field forth went the Adventurer, there 843 *Excursion* 6. 311
Prevailed ; and, from those bonds released, she went 853 *Excursion* 6. 1004
And earnest preparation.—Forth we went, . . 890 *Excursion* 9. 433
Among the mazy streams that backward went, . S.3. 427 **My Son* 4
Old Michael and his son one day went forth . . K.8. 224 **I will* 6
Far went these shepherds in their devious quest, . K.8. 225 **I will* 35
So to Helvellyn's eastern side they went, . . . K.8. 225 **I will* 46
He with his Father daily went, and they . . . K.8. 226 **I will* 77
Down the deep channel of the stream he went, . K.8. 228 **I will* 133

Went—*continued.*
Of evening he went forth to meet his son, . . . K.8. 229 **I will* 161
Down to the brook he went, and tracked its course K.8. 229 **I will* 170
Who then through rows of weeping comrades went, L.1. 95 *Juvenal* 3. 7
Wept. Like one revived, upon his neck I wept ; . 29 *Guilt* 258
She wept ; because she had no more to say . . 32 *Guilt* 449
Till all the band of playmates wept together ; . 39 *Bord.* 94
" When we arranged the affair, she wept a little . 59 *Bord.* 1195
But loud and bitterly she wept, ... 82 *Alice Fell* 22
She wept, nor would be pacified. . . . . . 82 *Alice Fell* 52
They wept—and, turning homeward, cried, . . 83 *Lucy Gray* 41
He pressed his Son, he kissèd him and wept ; . . 137 *Michael* 422
Ere she had wept, ere she had mourned, . . . 195 *Ruth* 251
Shuddered the walls—the marble city wept— . 214 *Dion* 110
—At this she wept a bitter flood ; . . . . . 248 *P. B.* 1028
She led him home, and wept amain, ... 297 *Highland Boy* 236
Ill tears she wept ; I saw them fall, ... 405 *White Doe* 874
Both man and woman wept when thou wert dead ; 491 *Tribute : Dog* 22
Hence, if we wept, it was not done in shame ; . 491 *Tribute : Dog* 34
If for a Lover the Lady wept, ... 494 *Force of Prayer* 41
Let me not ask what tears may have been wept . 525 *Epist. Beaumont* 258
She wept.—Life's purple tide began to flow . . 619 **She wept* 1
Who weeps for strangers ? Many wept . . . 623 *G. and S. Green* 1
Wept for that pair's unhappy fate, ... 623 *G. and S. Green* 3
I wept not then,—but tears have dimmed my sight, 713 *Prelude* 9. 269
Wept bitterly. I wist not what to do, . . . 766 *Excursion* 1. 651
The one Survivor stood ; he wept, he prayed . . 774 *Excursion* 2. 202
Of what I suffered, when I wept that loss, . . 793 *Excursion* 3. 485
With tears, that wept not then ; nor were the few, 871 *Excursion* 7. 883
Were. (*Partial list.*)
Marching down the banks of Were. . . . . 402 *White Doe* 602
The transport was rolled down the river of Were, 403 *White Doe* 685
From Were, and all the little rills . . . . . 403 *White Doe* 692
We're. (*Partial list.*)
We build up the fire, we're snug and warm ; . . 81 †*Address : Child* 33
For when we're there, although 'tis fair, . . . 293 *Yarrow Unv.* 55
Were't. A power to virtue friendly ; were't not so, 765 *Excursion* 1. 634
Wert. (*Partial list.*)
Many flocks were on the hills, but thou wert owned by none, ... 87 *Pet-lamb* 35
And thou wert still a hope, a love; . . . . 184 **O blithe* 23
Wert kind as resolute, and good as brave ; . . 210 *Laod.* 56
For thou wert still the poor man's stay, . . . 292 *Rob Roy* 109
West. *See* **North-west, South-west.**
Far in the regions of the west, ... 1 *Extract* 10
And, fronting the bright west, yon oak entwines . 6 *Ev. Wk.* 214
While, facing thus the crimson west, ... 9 *Lines : Boat* 3
The *west*, that burns like one dilated sun, . . . 15 *Desc. Sk.* 282
Are here, to send the sun into the west . . . 44 *Bord.* 373
And they go rambling east and west . . . . 84 *Shepherd-boys* 8
Ye, gentle breezes from the west, ... 154 *Flower Garden* 34
From east to west, in ample vest . . . . . 180 *Waggoner* 4. 55
Then issued Vesper from the fulgent west, . . 192 *Gipsies* 14
Of Indians in the West. . . . . 193 *Ruth* 120
Sir Walter walked all round, north, south, and west, 201 *Hart-leap* 47
Evening spreads throughout the west ! . . . 217 **Inmate of* 24
Of Dawn—or Eve, fair vision of the west, . . 222 *Triad* 179
And east and west, the Ass sent forth . . . . 241 *P. B.* 464
Yet did the glowing west with marvellous power . 262 **Dark and* 5
Fair Star of evening, Splendour of the west, . . 303 **Fair Star* 1
And was the safeguard of the west : the worth . 304 *Ven. Rep.* 2
Across the setting sun and all the fiery west. . . 311 **Who rises* 29
Through the grey west ; and lo ! these waters, steeled . . . . 313 **Clouds, lingering* 2
For this refreshing incense from the West !— . 327 *Ode 1815* 27
(Streamed from the west) as with a robe of power : 333 **Bruges I* 2
The Sun regards it from the West ; . . . . 337 *Thun* 9
Lo ! in the burning west, the craggy nape . . 348 *Sky-prosp.* 1
The mountain region of the west, ... 390 *Highland Broach* 6
In her pale chambers of the west, ... 408 *White Doe* 1161
With its first bounty. Wandering through the west, ... 418 *Ecc. Sonn.* 1. 2. 5
Along the west ; though driven from Aquitaine, . 427 *Ecc. Sonn.* 1. 34. 2
Diffused thro' all the regions of the West ; . . 430 *Ecc. Sonn.* 2. 9. 4
Fleet as the west wind, is for *him* no quarry ; . 472 *Dunolly Eagle* 10
Fallen though she be, this Glory of the west, . . 474 **How sad* 9
To the east and the west, to the south and the north, 484 **A plague* 19
And glorify for us the west, ... 506 *Lab. Hymn* 31
Not seldom Evening in the west . . . . . 550 *Hermit's Cell* 5. 3
And, fronting the bright west in stronger lines, . 595 *Ev. Wk. Quarto* 193
The glory of evening was spread through the west ; 620 *Convict* 1
Two hours declined towards the west ; a day . . 633 *Prelude* 1. 67
Eastward were sparkling clear, and in the west . 638 *Prelude* 1. 445
Left by the west wind sweeping overhead . . . 643 *Prelude* 2. 109
Of those glad respites, though a soft west wind . 673 *Prelude* 5. 481
That, reaching to her gates, spreads east and west, 702 *Prelude* 8. 213
The sun was sinking in the west ; and now . . 767 *Excursion* 1. 734
From east to west, before you will appear . . 830 *Excursion* 5. 536
Struggling and bold, and shining from the west . 861 *Excursion* 7. 232
Western. But now the sun has gained his western road, ... 3 *Ev. Wk.* 88
Save where, along the shady western marge, . . 4 *Ev. Wk.* 126
Far to the western slopes with hamlets white ; . 8 *Ev. Wk.* 336
Slow-travelling down the western hills, to enfold . 12 *Desc. Sk.* 121
We reached the western world, a poor devoted crew. 29 *Guilt* 297
Fresh blows the wind, a western wind, . . . 161 *Binnorie* 12
Right at the imperial station's western base, . . 219 **This Height* 13
That, struggling through the western sky, have won 256 *Decay of Piety* 13
Suns that through blood their western harbour sought, ... 299 *Brownie's Cell* 61

Whate'er—*continued.*
Of order and of good. Whate'er we see, . . . 820 *Excursion* 4. 1270
Yet cause was none, whate'er regret might hang . 859 *Excursion* 7. 145
What'er exists hath properties that spread . . 884 *Excursion* 9. 10

Whatever. *See* **Whate'er.**
'Twill be between us; but, whatever fate . . . 137 *Michael* 415
They from morning to even take whatever is given;— . . . . 166 *Stray Pleasures* 11
With him whatever comes in course, ... 178 *Waggoner* 3. 16
Whatever be the cause, 'tis sure that they who pry and pore . . . . 189 *Star-gazers* 29
Whatever in those climes he found . . . . . 193 *Ruth* 127
Whatever star is in the skies, ... 198 *Thorn* 102
Whatever wind may blow?" . . . . 198 *Thorn* 103
Whatever props may fail, ... 224 *'Tis gone 57
Had Peter joined whatever vice . . . . . 239 *P. B.* 299
Than a soft record, that, whatever fruit . . . 378 *Duddon* 8. 11
Whatever fate remain behind, ... 406 *White Doe* 921
Whatever discipline thy Will ordain . . . . 454 **The Sun, that* 17
Receive whatever good 'tis given thee to dispense. 461 **Queen of* 46
Whatever path he chooses; . . . . 478 *Somnamb.* 65
That—whatever griefs may fret, ... 503 **Like a* 53
Whatever boon is granted or withheld. . . . 511 **So fair* 21
And yet, into whatever sin they may fall, . . 572 *Avarice* 35
Whatever formal gait of discipline . . . . . 655 *Prelude* 3. 402
When so disturbed, whatever palms are won. . . 656 *Prelude* 3. 502
When sorrow damps it, or, whatever look . . . 660 *Prelude* 4. 147
Whatever shadings of mortality, ... 662 *Prelude* 4. 248
Whatever imports from the world of death . . 662 *Prelude* 4. 249
There registered: whatever else of power . . . 668 *Prelude* 5. 193
Known by whatever name, is falsely deemed . . 742 *Prelude* 13. 187
Whom Nature, by whatever means, has taught . 759 *Excursion* 1. 195
—These, and whatever else the garden bears . . 856 *Excursion* 6. 1165
At least, whatever fate the noon of life . . . 888 *Excursion* 9. 281
And to whatever else of outward form . . . . K.8. 245 *Recluse* 1.1.301

What's. Shall give me half. What's this?—I fear, good Woman, ... 46 *Bord.* 489
How say you? in disguise?— But what's your business . . . . 46 *Bord.* 492
"But what's the Thorn? and what the pond? . 200 *Thorn* 199
"What's Yarrow but a river bare, ... 293 *Yarrow Unv.* 25
What's a tempest to him, or the dry parching heats? 570 *Farmer* 69

Whatsoe'er. *See* **Whatsoever.**
But whatsoe'er of such rare treasure lay . . . 122 *V. and J.* 34
Whatsoe'er we feel and know . . . . . . 171 *Kitten* 99
Patience, with trust that, whatsoe'er the way . 520 *Pun. Death* 14. 12
There was a time when whatsoe'er is feigned . . 688 *Prelude* 7. 77
Induced, effect, in whatsoe'er degree, ... 737 *Prelude* 12. 194
Of passion: whatsoe'er be felt or feared, . . . 816 *Excursion* 4. 1021
Choose for your emblems whatsoe'er ye find . . 827 *Excursion* 5. 334

Whatsoever. *See* **Whatsoe'er.**
Whatsoever check they bring, ... 503 *Warning* 9
That whatsoever point they gain, they yet . . 646 *Prelude* 2. 321
Or whatsoever else the heart holds dear; . . . 668 *Prelude* 5. 155
In whatsoever place, but seemed in this . . . 692 *Prelude* 7. 349
To watch their goings, whatsoever track . . . 702 *Prelude* 8. 233
From whatsoever region of our cares . . . . 721 *Prelude* 10. 188
And dealt with whatsoever they found there . . 729 *Prelude* 11. 130
That, whatsoever falls my better mind, . . . 748 *Prelude* 14. 147
Henceforth in whatsoever nook he may, . . . 778 *Excursion* 2. 477
On whatsoever errand, urged her steps: . . . 853 *Excursion* 6. 985

Wheat. When, in the warmth of midsummer, the wheat . . . . 767 *Excursion* 1. 707

Wheaten. Rest near your little plots of wheaten glade; . . . . 13 *Desc. Sk.* 130
Rest, near their little plots of wheaten glade; . 604 *Desc.Sk.Quarto* 149

Wheedle. Smooth words he had to wheedle simple souls; . . . . 775 *Excursion* 2. 254

Wheel. *See* **Chariot-wheel, Cistern-wheel, Spinning-wheel.**
Calm is all nature as a resting wheel. . . . . 1 *Early Youth* 1
The empty loom, cold hearth, and silent wheel, . 29 *Guilt* 269
I saw it in the wheel entangled, ... 82 *Alice Fell* 26
And they were butterflies to wheel about . . . 95 *Brothers* 4
Her large round wheel was turning. Towards the field . . . . 95 *Brothers* 26
And she I cherished turned her wheel . . . . 109 **I travelled* 11
That small, for flax; and, if one wheel had rest, . 132 *Michael* 84
Swiftly turn the murmuring wheel! . . . . 163 *Spinning Wheel* 1
Turn the swift wheel round and round! . . . 163 *Spinning Wheel* 6
Man and Maidens wheel, ... 167 *Stray Pleasures* 19
Drive as she drives: how fast they wheel away, . 184 *Night-piece* 17
Maids at the wheel, the weaver at his loom, . . 250 **Nuns fret* 4
Thou turn'st the Wheel that slept with dust o'er-spread; . . . . 255 *S. H.* 3
Is but a glimmering spoke in the swift wheel . . 270 **If these* 10
The clouds, and wheel around the mountain tops . 270 **Though the bold* 2
Through the rough copse wheel thou with hasty stride; . . . . 383 *Duddon* 30. 11
To wheel with languid motion round and round, . 527 **Those breathing* 48
She turns her wheel, if on the road she sees . . 566 *Cumb. Beg.* 34
Wheel pale and silent her diminish'd round, . . 609 *Desc.Sk.Quarto* 383
For cottagers and spinners at the wheel, . . . 668 *Prelude* 5. 208
The little child who sate to turn the wheel . . 769 *Excursion* 1. 890
Following the rugged road, by sledge or wheel . 823 *Excursion* 5. 61
Dependants, comforters—my wheel, my fire, . . 834 *Excursion* 5. 813
I see the eldest Daughter at her wheel . . . . 856 *Excursion* 6. 1179
No daughters round her, busy at the wheel, . . 878 *Excursion* 8. 269
Serving as doth a spindle or a wheel; . . . . 886 *Excursion* 9. 160
The pastoral Muse laments the Wheel—no more . S.3. 426 **Through Cumbrian* 2

Wheel—*continued.*
There too did *Fancy* prize the murmuring wheel; S.3. 426 **Through Cumbrian* 9
Mount with a thoughtless impulse, and wheel there, K.8. 242 *Recluse* 1.1.200
Wheel through the sky, and see them now at rest, K.8. 251 *Recluse* 1.1.546

Wheel-barrow. Let thy wheel-barrow alone— . . 157 *Sexton* 1

Wheeled. Wheeled her back in full apparel; . . 178 *Waggoner* 2. 161
The village clock tolled six,—I wheeled about, . 638 *Prelude* 1. 431
Wheeled by me—even as if the earth had rolled . 639 *Prelude* 1. 459

Wheeling. Glances the wheeling eagle's glorious form! . . . . 15 *Desc. Sk.* 276
Who would stop the swallow, wheeling . . . 90 *Longest Day* 19
Watchful as a wheeling eagle, ... 94 *Westmoreland Girl* 85
The buzzing dor-hawk, round and round, is wheeling,— . . . . 173 *Waggoner* 1. 3
Light as the wheeling butterfly she moves; . . 221 *Triad* 124
Is wheeling hitherward. Thanks, happy Creature, 361 **List—'twas* 7
Glances the fire-clad eagle's wheeling form; . . 608 *Desc.Sk.Quarto* 339
A pair of falcons wheeling on the wing, . . . 786 *Excursion* 3. 2
The wheeling swallow, and the darting snipe, . . 868 *Excursion* 7. 752

Wheels. In many a whistling circle wheels her flight; 4 *Ev. Wk.* 91
While unsuspended wheels the village dance, . . 11 *Desc. Sk.* 39
And slow the insulted eagle wheels away. . . . 11 *Desc. Sk.* 68
Whose heart was in her house: two wheels she had 132 *Michael* 82
There he wheels in downward mazes; . . . . 163 *Hint* 13
For, spite of rumbling of the wheels, ... 176 *Waggoner* 2. 19
He wheels—and, making many stops, ... 180 *Waggoner* 3. 136
The Lass with her barrow wheels hither her store;— 188 *Music* 22
Backward, in rapid evanescence, wheels . . . 335 *Rhine* 5
O Death! the ensanguined yet triumphant wheels, 440 *Ecc. Sonn.* 2. 45. 10
Wheels and the tread of hoofs are heard no more; 453 **Calm is the* 27
Of sleepless Labour, 'mid whose dizzy wheels . . 501 *Humanity* 93
The post-boy, when his rattling wheels o'ertake . 566 *Cumb. Beg.* 37
Turns with less noisy wheels to the roadside, . . 566 *Cumb. Beg.* 41
It was a dreary morning when the wheels . . . 649 *Prelude* 3. 1
Of a congenial future, that the wheels . . . . 792 *Excursion* 3. 456
That turns the multitude of dizzy wheels, . . . 877 *Excursion* 8. 178

Whelming. Alike in whelming snows and roaring waves. . . . . 14 *Desc. Sk.* 207

Whelps. They *cannot* rest, they gambol like young whelps; . . . . K.8. 251 *Recluse* 1.1.548

When. (*Partial list.*)
Person, and place—the where, the when, the how, 58 *Bord.* 1155
It is no common thing when one like you . . . 38 *Bord.* 50
There cannot come a day when I shall cease . . 39 *Bord.* 88
When I had been most happy. Pardon me . . 39 *Bord.* 98
You paced along, when the bewildering moonlight 39 *Bord.* 111
When I behold the ruins of that face, ... 39 *Bord.* 135
But when thy Father must lie down and die, . . 40 *Bord.* 159
When, Antioch blazing to her topmost towers, . 40 *Bord.* 178
That when, on our return from Palestine, . . . 40 *Bord.* 192
When first I saw him sitting there, alone, . . . 44 *Bord.* 376
When I had none to give him; whereupon . . 44 *Bord.* 400
When into one of those same spotted bells . . 44 *Bord.* 403
When next inclined to sleep, take my advice . . 44 *Bord.* 416
When, after a broad flash that filled the cave, . 50 *Bord.* 715
When you had told him the mischance, was troubled 51 *Bord.* 761
In helplessness, when innocence is with them. . 51 *Bord.* 792
When from the Holy Land I had returned . . 52 *Bord.* 828
When my old Leader slipped into the flood . . 52 *Bord.* 834
But when you were an Outcast?—Heaven is just; 52 *Bord.* 839
When the tempestuous wind first drove us hither, 53 *Bord.* 861
When such a sudden weakness fell upon me, . . 53 *Bord.* 891
This Boy—when he comes forth with bloody hands— . . . . 54 *Bord.* 938
When round my wrist I felt a cord drawn tight, . 55 *Bord.* 965
When he should give her up, a Woman grown, . 56 *Bord.* 1054
When my heart does not ache to think of it!— . 57 *Bord.* 1098
When I returned with water from the brook, . . 59 *Bord.* 1181
"When we arranged the affair, she wept a little . 59 *Bord.* 1195
And eke, when he the image did behold . . . 553 *Prioress* 53
Calling to mind this matter when I may, . . . 553 *Prioress* 62
And, when they holy water on him cast, . . . 555 *Prioress* 188
Yet spake this Child when sprinkled was the water; 555 *Prioress* 189
And, when the Abbot had this wonder seen, . . 556 *Prioress* 222
And, when it likes him, joy enough them sendeth. 560 *Cuck.andNight.*195
And knows not when he hurts and when he heals; 560 *Cuck.andNight.*203
When next May comes, if I am not afraid. . . 561 *Cuck.andNight.*235
For when he saw her doors fast bolted all, . . 562 *Troilus* 13
And when he might his time aright espy, . . . 563 *Troilus* 38
When I the process have in memory, ... 563 *Troilus* 65
Dread Lord! so fearful when provoked, thine ire 563 *Troilus* 71
And said: I wis, when thou art horn'd anew, . 564 *Troilus* 132
When hence did journey my bright Lady dear, . 564 *Troilus* 135
When they can know and feel that they have been, 568 *Cumb. Beg.* 149
And let him, *where* and *when* he will, sit down . 569 *Cumb. Beg.* 192
Of the fields, he collected that bloom, when a boy; 569 *Farmer* 10
When hailstones have been falling, swarm on swarm, 571 **There is a Flower* 5
And, when beneath this stone the Corse was laid, 575 *Chiabrera* 8. 8

Whence. (*Partial list.*)
Whence lutes and voices down the enchanted woods 12 *Desc. Sk.* 117
Thy glittering steeples, whence the matin bell . 12 *Desc. Sk.* 123
More than we see, or whence this strong aversion? 41 *Bord.* 254
Laws, but we ask not whence those laws have come; 70 *Bord.* 1858
"Whence comes," said I, "this piteous moan?" 82 *Alice Fell* 18
Whence by our shepherds it is called The Pillar. 101 *Brothers* 368
Whence golden harvests, cities, warlike towers, . 102 *Artegal* 21
Whence all the fixed delights of house and home, 102 *Artegal* 23
"Whence the undeserved mistrust? Too wide apart . . . . 140 *Afm. Lady* 47

Whence—*continued.*
Coming one knows not how, nor whence, . . . 158 *In youth 71
" Whence strains to love-sick maiden dear, . . 164 Needlecase 33
By what means it could thither come, and whence ; 196 Resolution 60
Answers, and we know not whence ; . . . . 209 *Yes, it 14
Whence thou dost pour upon the world a flood . 209 *Ethereal minstrel 9
Whence doubts that came too late, and wishes vain 213 Dion 58
But whence that sudden check ? that fearful start ! 213 Dion 63
Whence angry perturbations,—and that look . . 214 Dion 100
Whence oft invigorating transports flow . . . 215 Kirkstone 59
Whence, whence, ye Clouds ! this eagerness of speed ? . . . . 230 Clouds 29
Or whence the might of this strange sound ? . . 241 P. B. 482
But whence this faintly-rustling sound . . . 244 P. B. 701
Whence I have risen, uplifted on the breeze . . 252 *The fairest 13
The Thing became a trumpet ; whence he blew . 260 *Scorn not 13
Whence the poor unregarded Favourite, true . . 274 *Wait, prithee 7
And tremble, seeing whence proceeds the strength 309 *When, looking 12
And look and listen—gathering, whence I may, . 314 *Not 'mid 13
Whence bright days of festive beauty ; . . . 323 Ode 1814 36
Whence busy life hath fled ; . . . . 334 *In Bruges 2
Or whence could virtue flow ? . . . . 337 *Oh Life 6
—Say whence that modulated shout ! . . . . 344 *How blest 33
To the Fountain whence Time and Eternity flow. 365 Vallomb. 40
Whence half the breathing world received its doom ; 368 Trajan 38
Whence that low voice ?—A whisper from the heart, ... 381 Duddon 21. 1
(We know not whence) ministers for a bell . . 387 Roslin 2
Whose smoke, forth-issuing whence and how it may, 390 Highland Hut 2
Whence, as a current from its fountain-head, . . 394 *No more 22
Whence idle fears, and needless pain, ... 408 White Doe 1121
As to the one sole fount whence wisdom flowed, . 419 Ecc. Sonn. 1. 4. 8
But whence it came we know not, nor behold . 422 Ecc. Sonn. 1. 16. 7
Whence grace, through which the heart can understand, ... 423 Ecc. Sonn. 1. 19. 13
Whence they, like richly-laden merchants, come . 425 Ecc. Sonn. 1. 25. 5
But whence came they who for the Saviour Lord 431 Ecc. Sonn. 2. 12. 1
Whence thickly-sprouting growth of poisonous weeds ; . . . . 438 Ecc. Sonn. 2. 37. 10
And who he was, and whence he came ; . . . 491 Fidelity 47
Whence, in a state where men are tempted still . 493 Hap. War. 29
And their meaning is, whence can comfort spring 494 Force of Prayer 3
Whence ye have escaped together, ... 503 *Like a 76
Whence these opprobrious leaves of dire portent ? 515 *Men of 2
Whence the blithe hail ? behold a Peasant stand 524 Epist. Beaumont 207
Whence the tall window drinks the morning rays ; 535 *When in 24
Whence, then, could it come—the thought— . . 535 Egremont 45
A loathsome pit, whence noisome scents exhale ; . 554 Prioress 122
Whence oft great sickness grows of heart and home ; 557 Cuck. and Night. 32
From whence to Thebes came griefs in multitude. 563 Troilus 84
Whence Cresid rode, as if in haste she was ; . . 563 Troilus 86
But He beholds the light, and whence it flows, . 588 Immortality 69
And that imperial palace whence he came. . . 588 Immortality 84
Whence fragrance scents the water's desart gale, . 596 Ev. Wk. Quarto 223
Whence Danger leans, and pointing ghastly, joys 610 Desc. Sk. Quarto 466
To question us. " Whence come ye ? to what end ? " . . . . 622 Recluse 1. 1. 167
Whence human kind, and brute ; what natural powers . . . . 625 Æneid 124
Whence inspiration for a song that winds . . . 634 Prelude 1. 180
Of that first Paradise whence man was driven ; . 650 Prelude 3. 109
Whence profit may be drawn in times to come. . 658 Prelude 3. 628
That lowly bed whence I had heard the wind . 659 Prelude 4. 85
And wavering motions sent he knows not whence, 662 Prelude 4. 269
Whence he had landed scarcely three weeks past ; 664 Prelude 4. 423
His story, whence he came, and who he was. . . 696 Prelude 7. 642
Must labour, whence the strongest are not free. . 698 Prelude 7. 730
Whence the main organs of the public power . . 711 Prelude 9. 102
Whence, and from deeper causes, all discourse . 711 Prelude 9. 118
Forgot, at seasons, whence they had their being ; 723 Prelude 10. 376
Of obligation, what the rule and whence . . . 731 Prelude 11. 300
Whence grew that genuine knowledge, fraught with peace, ... 732 Prelude 11. 354
Whence spiritual dignity originates, ... 745 Prelude 13. 373
I knew not how, and hardly whence they came. . 768 Excursion 1. 803
Whence, unmolested wanderers, we beheld . . 794 Excursion 3. 540
" But how begin ? and whence ?—' The Mind is free— . . . . 817 Excursion 4. 1080
Whence the bare road descended rapidly . . . 823 Excursion 5. 65
—' Whence do they come ? and with what errand charged ? . . . . 858 Excursion 7. 86
Whence alteration in the forms of things, . . . 873 Excursion 7. 1011
And whence that difference ? Whence but from himself ? . . . . 887 Excursion 9. 207
The station whence he looked was soft and green, K.8. 237 Recluse 1. 1. 19
Whence flows the Latin people, whence have come K.8. 281 *Arms and 8
But whence yon swarm that loads the western bridge, ... L.1 95 Juvenal 3. 25
But whence this gall, this lengthened face of woe ? L.1. 96 Juvenal 3. 51
These gashes whence ? This undeserved disgrace ! L.2. 318 Frag. Æneid 4. 8

Whencesoe'er. By a sublime *idea*, whencesoe'er . 709 Prelude 8. 673
—To these emotions, whencesoe'er they come, . 755 Recluse 1. 1. 763

Whene'er. *See* **Whenever.**
May touch, whene'er her Vassals are at work. . 59 Bord. 1174
And the fair Captive, who, whene'er she may, . 122 V. and J. 81
Whene'er you look on it, 'tis plain . . . . . 200 Thorn 219
Than flesh and blood ; whene'er thou meet'st my sight, ... 274 *Such age 5
O joy for her ! whene'er in winter . . . . . 536 Goody Blake 49

Whene'er—*continued.*
Whene'er I looked, thy Image still was there ; . 578 Peele Castle 7
Such was his custom ; but whene'er he met . . 660 Prelude 4. 122
(Whene'er the summer sun, declining, smote . . 705 Prelude 8. 407
Whene'er it comes ! needful in work so long, . . 710 Prelude 9. 20
A like existence ; and, whene'er it dawns . . . 747 Prelude 14. 95
Or pride of heart abating : and, whene'er . . . 813 Excursion 4. 841

Whenever. *See* **Whene'er.**
Whenever from our Valley he withdrew ; . . . 108 Indolence 29
All winter long, whenever free to choose, . . . 676 Prelude 6. 66

Whensoe'er. And whensoe'er my course shall end, 1 Extract 4
Of pure delight, come whensoe'er it may, . . . 278 *The most 10
Homeward and schoolward whensoe'er he went, . 554 Prioress 98
Imposes, whensoe'er untoward chance . . . 834 Excursion 5. 764

Where. (*Partial list.*)
Person, and place—the where, the when, the how, 58 Bord. 1155
Is no where touched by one memorial gleam) . 706 Prelude 8. 472
Where now we dwell.—For many years I bore . 41 Bord. 202
Where he can stab you deepest. Clifford never . 42 Bord. 281
Here at my breast, and ask me where I bought it : 45 Bord. 441
Where is she—holla ! You are Idonea's Mother ?— 46 Bord. 529
Where, if a famishing man stretch forth his hand, 47 Bord. 560
Here where we stand—that tribe of vulgar wretches 48 Bord. 642
Give me your hand ; where are you, Friends ? and tell me . . . . 52 Bord. 804
Where none but those who trampled on my rights 52 Bord. 844
Where Souls are self-defended, free to grow . . 57 Bord. 1115
Where Reason has an eye that she can use, . . 58 Bord. 1119
'Mong Christian folk, a street where Jews might be, 553 Prioress 37
Where he was cast into a pit hard by. . . . . 555 Prioress 155
There, where with mangled throat he lay upright, 555 Prioress 160
Where they had rested them all night ; and they, 558 Cuck. and Night. 68
Where he had felt such perfect pleasure once. . 563 Troilus 46
Where want and sorrow were. The easy man . 568 Cumb. Beg. 116
And let him, *where* and *when* he will, sit down . 569 Cumb. Beg. 192
Where proud Covent-garden, in desolate hours . 570 Farmer 73
In peace eternal ; where desire and joy . . . 573 Chiabrera 1. 5
Where gold determines between right and wrong. 573 Chiabrera 2. 4

Whereabout. A puzzling notice of thy whereabout— 456 *The leaves 23
Thy whereabout, to warn the approaching sail. . 475 *Homeward we 14
Prate somewhat loudly of the whereabout . . 693 Prelude 7. 428

Whereat. He stood alone ; whereat he turned his head 149 *A narrow 57
Whereat from the earth on which he lay . . . 241 P. B. 462
Whereat a tender twilight streak . . . . . 374 Eg. Maid 327
Whereat from all the multitude . . . . . 403 White Doe 681
In chase of him ; whereat I waked in terror, . . 667 Prelude 5. 138
To bring his charge in openness ; whereat, . . 719 Prelude 10. 108

Whereby. Whereby this infant sensibility, . . . 646 Prelude 2. 270
Whereby society has parted man . . . . . 743 Prelude 13. 219
A privilege whereby a work of his, ... 744 Prelude 13. 309
To rules and habits, whereby much was done, . 795 Excursion 3. 608
Murmurings, whereby the monitor expressed . . 818 Excursion 4. 1139
Those services, whereby attempt is made . . . 827 Excursion 5. 297

Where'er. *See* **Wherever.**
Where'er the dreary roads their bare white lines extend. . . . . 24 Guilt 18
That unto him, where'er shall lie his life's appointed way, ... 91 Norman Boy 31
In his known haunts of joy where'er he might, . 118 Maternal Grief 53
But see ! where'er the hailstones drop . . . 155 *A whirl-blast 12
While, borrowing helps where'er he may, . . . 178 Waggoner 2. 139
Field of death, where'er thou be, ... 205 Brougham 148
And pendent rocks, where'er, in gliding state, . 212 Dion
Where'er he turned, a natural grace . . . . 212 Dion
Where'er he turned, a swan-like grace . . . . 212 Dion 2
Where'er the subtle waters stray ; . . . . . 227 Vernal Ode 68
Where'er the streams a passage find ; . . . . 228 Devot. Incit. 4
Where'er I liked ; and finally array . . . . 259 Calvert 7
But that I know, where'er I go, ... 302 Yarrow V. 85
Wherever fruits are gathered, and where'er . . 327 Ode 1815 30
Where'er we roam—along the brink . . . . 337 Cath. Cantons 13
Where'er was dipped the toiling oar, ... 343 Eclipse 13
In keen pursuit—and gave, where'er she flew, . 346 Gemmi 7
Decay submits not. But where'er my steps . . 355 Aquap. 198
Their love-songs ; but, where'er my feet might roam, 362 *List—'twas 24
Of Streams to Nature's love, where'er they flow ; 392 Avon 6
Where'er their march : no steed will he . . . 404 White Doe 728
Where'er they rise, the sylvan waste retires, . . 429 Ecc. Sonn. 2. 3. 13
Even such the contrast that, where'er we move, . 439 Ecc. Sonn. 2. 44. 1
Where'er it wandered in the morn . . . . . 458 *Had this 63
Learn from thy course, where'er their own be taken, 461 *Queen of 49
That animate my way where'er it leads ! . . . 472 *The captive 14
Our bodies feel, where'er they be, ... 481 Expost. 19
Where'er her course ; mysterious Bird ! . . . 511 *Who rashly 25
Should sometimes think, where'er they chance to spy . . . . 530 Poor Robin 31
And where'er their strokes alighted, ... 535 Egremont 43
Where'er he moves along the unclouded sky, . . 539 *Lady ! a 16
That such a Boy where'er he lists shall go . . 554 Prioress 111
Where'er he be, God grant us him to meet ! . . 556 Prioress 232
Where'er the aged Beggar takes his rounds, . . 567 Cumb. Beg. 98
Where'er Permessus bears an honoured name, . 574 Chiabrera 5. 22
But yet I know, where'er I go, ... 587 Immortality 17
Or not far off. Where'er my footsteps turned, . 622 Recluse 1. 1. 90
Where'er, preserved in this most true reflection, . 627 *We gaze 11
Vain is her wish ; where'er she turns she finds . 634 Prelude 1. 130
Where'er I roamed, were speaking monuments. . 701 Prelude 8. 172
Exposed to eye and hand where'er I turned. . . 710 Prelude 9. 33
Three summer days I roamed) where'er the Plain 745 Prelude 13. 337
That, with believing eyes, where'er I turned, . . 745 Prelude 13. 344
Where'er we move, under the diverse shapes . . 750 Prelude 14. 327

Whither—*continued.*
Now, whither are you wandering ? That a man, . 65 Bord. 1568
But whither did you carry him ? He was torn, . 74 Bord. 2074
But how he will come, and whither he goes, . . 80 †Address : Child 7
" And whither are you going, child, ... 82 Alice Fell 33
A blessèd day for thee ! then whither wouldst thou roam ? . . . . 87 Pet-lamb 38
Seek for him,—he is fled ; and whither none can say. 107 Indolence 9
And all uncertain whither he should turn, . . 122 V. and J. 75
A stately Fir-grove, whither I was wont . . . 150 *When, to 9
Nor whither going. . . . . 158 *In youth 72
Whither spiteful Satan steered ; . . . . . 218 *Inmate of 30
Oh whither with such eagerness of speed ? . . 229 Clouds 4
When will she turn, and whither ? She will brook 258 *With Ships 12
Whither, at length, a Wretch retired . . . . 298 Brownie's Cell 25
Whither, by care of Libyan Jove, ... 299 Brownie's Cell 93
If fall they must. Now, whither doth it tend ? . 305 *The Voice 6
Say, Spirit ! whither hath she fled . . . . . 413 White Doe 1555
Whither it goes. Even such, that transient Thing, 422 Ecc. Sonn. 1. 16. 8
The threshold, whither shall they turn to find . 434 Ecc. Sonn. 2. 23. 10
And no one can tell whither. Dearest Friend ! . 498 *Enough of climbing 45
And whither could they dart, if seized with fear ? 528 *Thosebreathing 52
" But whither would you, could you, flee ? . . 542 Russ. Fug. 81
That on the summit whither thou art bound, . . 548 *Stay, bold 13
Whither is fled the visionary gleam ? . . . . 588 Immortality 56
Are mine in prospect ; whither shall I turn, . . 632 Prelude 1. 27
Of a known Vale, whither my feet should turn, . 633 Prelude 1. 72
By thoughts of what and whither, when and how, 696 Prelude 7. 631
Upon the region whither we are bound, . . . 790 Excursion 3. 297
In that retirement ; whither, by such course . . 833 Excursion 5. 732
To fly—but whither ! And this gracious Church, 855 Excursion 6. 1105
To that still region whither all are bound. . . 861 Excursion 7. 229
Whither, as to a little private cell, ... 867 Excursion 7. 664
" Wild wanderers, whither through my dark domain ? " . . . . K.8. 241 Recluse 1.1.169
Let grandeur tell thee whither now is flown . . L.1. 97 Juvenal 3. 94

Whittington. A change of purpose in young Whittington, ... 688 Prelude 7. 112
The lucky venture of sage Whittington, . . . 858 Excursion 7. 92

Whizzed. Whizzed from the Stripling's arm ! If touched by him, ... 868 Excursion 7. 741
The Ball whizz'd by,—it grazed his ear, . . . S.3. 441 *The ball 1

Whizzing. Was pierced by whizzing shaft of hunter keen ! . . . . 376 Duddon 2. 14
What is pride ?—a whizzing rocket . . . . 549 Hermit's Cell 1. 11

Who. (*Partial list.*) *See* **Who's.**
And others who survived the wreck, beheld . . 38 Bord. 75
Who might have found a nothing-doing hour . . 39 Bord. 120
Who here, upon the borders of the Tweed, . . 41 Bord. 208
Who has so practised on the world's cold sense, . 41 Bord. 250
Who soon grew weary of her ; but, alas ! . . . 44 Bord. 382
Who is it that hath wronged you ? Mark you me ; 45 Bord. 453
You saw, who was it ? Nay, I dare not speak ; . 47 Bord. 532
With those who take the spirit of their rule . . 48 Bord. 584
Who live in these disputed tracts, that own . . 48 Bord. 596
The majesty of Him who rules the world. . . . 48 Bord. 617
Men who are little given to sift and weigh— . . 49 Bord. 645
Who at full speed swept by us where the wood . 50 Bord. 735
But there's a Providence for them who walk . . 51 Bord. 791
Where none but those who trampled on my rights 52 Bord. 844
Who aims but at our purse ; and shall this Parricide— . . . . 53 Bord. 895
And most despise the men who best can teach us : 54 Bord. 909
Is he alive ? What mean you ? who alive ? . . 55 Bord. 974
Were there a Man who, being weak and helpless . 56 Bord. 1038
To him who bid the highest in the market . . 56 Bord. 1055
Who are we, Friends ? Do we not live on ground . 57 Bord. 1114
A whipping to the Moralists who preach . . . 58 Bord. 1159
Who on her journey must proceed alone, . . . 59 Bord. 1186
And through this street who list might ride and wend ; . . . . 553 Prioress 41
Who day by day unto this school hath gone, . . 553 Prioress 52
Who will do evil, evil shall he bear ; . . . . 555 Prioress 181
Them who are whole in body and in mind, . . 556 Cuck. and Night. 8
Who were so joyful at the light of day, . . . 558 Cuck.and Night. 69
And who was then ill satisfied but I ? . . . . 558 Cuck.and Night. 92
Who do not think in love their life to lead ; . . 559 Cuck.andNight.132
Who most it useth, him 'twill most impair. . . 559 Cuck.andNight.170
Who had been nought, if Love had never been. . 560 Cuck.andNight.190
That every wight, who in the way passed by, . 564 Troilus 107
Who lead their horses down the steep rough road 566 Cumb. Beg. 5
Who have a broom still ready in your hands . . 567 Cumb. Beg. 69
Who sits at his own door,—and, like the pear . 568 Cumb. Beg. 117
Who live a life of virtuous decency, ... 568 Cumb. Beg. 134
Men who can hear the Decalogue and feel . . . 568 Cumb. Beg. 135
Who went something farther than others have gone, 572 Avarice 30
Who will gladly repair all the damage that's done ; 572 Avarice 43
O Thou who movest onward with a mind . . . 573 Chiabrera 3. 1
There never breathed a man who, when his life . 574 Chiabrera 4. 1

Whoe'er. A female voice :—" Whoe'er you be, . . 176 Waggoner 1. 219
Captive, whoe'er thou be ! . . . . 334 *In Brugès 30
Whoe'er ye be, that thus, yourselves unseen, . . 451 Ecc. Sonn. 3. 44. 6
Upon the mountains. Look at her, whoe'er . . 508 F. Stone 22
Whoe'er hath stood to watch a mountain brook . 800 Excursion 3. 969
Whoe'er may sink, or rise—to sink again, . . . 848 Excursion 6. 673

Whoever. In stray gifts to be claimed by whoever shall find ; . . . . 167 Stray Pleasures 28
Whoever against Love mean aught amiss. . . 559 Cuck.andNight.130

Whole. And its own twilight softens the whole scene, 3 Ev. Wk. 61
And now the whole wide lake in deep repose . . 4 Ev. Wk. 124

Whole—*continued.*
Soon with despair's whole weight his spirits sink ; 16 Desc. Sk. 332
' Here will I dwell,' said I, ' my whole life long, . 31 Guilt 363
Whole hours, with idle arms in moping sorrow knit. 32 Guilt 432
How would you like to travel on whole hours . 45 Bord. 432
Of foul pollution—— The whole visible world . 56 Bord. 1056
And in this desert ? If never—then the whole . 62 Bord. 1396
You are safe ; the whole world shall not harm you. 72 Bord. 2011
For the whole dale, and one for each fire-side— . 97 Brothers 164
One side of our whole vale with grandeur rare ; . 106 Farewell 4
Through his whole body something ran, . . . 114 Ind. Wom. 35
For the whole house is Robin's cage. . . . . 144 *Driven in 68
Andrew's whole fire-side is there. . . . . . 157 Sexton 12
Whole Summer-fields are thine by right ; . . . 157 *In youth 13
Of the whole spectacle the same ! . . . . . 192 Gipsies 4
Like the whole sky when to the east . . . . 194 Ruth 179
My whole life I have lived in pleasant thought, . 195 Resolution 36
And the whole body of the Man did seem . . . 197 Resolution 109
In the whole fulness of its bloom, affords . . . 219 Haunted Tree 9
Till the whole air is overcharged ; . . . . . 228 Devot. Incit. 22
Whole ages if I here should roam, ... 237 P. B. 52
In his whole figure and his mien . . . . . 239 P. B. 293
Or map of the whole world : thoughts, link by link, 260 *How sweet 11
While the whole world seems adverse to desert. . 260 *High is 8
If the whole weight of what we think and feel, . 261 Retirement 1
Not the whole warbling grove in concert heard . 273 *Not the 1
That unencumbered whole of blank and still, . . 277 *Haydon ! let 5
Of knowledge ; that whole myriads should unite . 308 *One might 10
Whole legions sink—and, in one instant, find . . 322 *Humanity, delighting 35
And the whole world, not envious but admiring, . 325 Ode 1814 137
Surrendering the whole heart to sacred pleasures ? 331 Ode : Thanks. 138
Her hope of lasting glory for the whole. . . . 331 Ode : Thanks. 175
When a whole people shall kneel down in prayer, 331 Ode : Thanks. 197
The whole design of Scripture history ; . . . 351 Des. Stanzas 67
The whole world's Darling—free to rove at will . 354 Aquap. 98
Supplanted the whole majesty of Rome . . . 358 Pine : Rome 12
Of freedom, with mind grasping the whole theme . 359 *They—who 10
To enslave whole nations on their native soil ; . 368 Trajan 59
Of the whole world's good wishes with him goes ; 387 Scott 9
His whole bold carriage (which had quelled . . 412 White Doe 1454
The consummation, the whole ruth . . . . 413 White Doe 1549
" God willeth it," the whole assembly cry ; . . 427 Ecc. Sonn. 1. 33. 9
His whole life long tills it, with heartless toil . . 429 Ecc. Sonn. 2. 4. 2
Till madness seizes on the whole wide Flood, . . 439 Ecc. Sonn. 2. 43. 9
Till the whole City rings like one vast quire. . . 442 Ecc. Sonn. 3. 8. 8
Meek eve shuts up the whole usurping host . . 456 *Soft as 16
Thy domination ; as the whole vast Sea . . . 459 *Wanderer ! that 48
If the whole State must suffer mortal change, . 471 Tynwald 13
With ear not coveting the whole, ... 472 Ossian 3
Down-bearing with his whole Atlantic weight . 473 *Thanks for 9
And whole artillery of the western blast, . . . 474 *Hope smiled 4
The whole year through. . . . . 490 Night Thought 12
And the whole person. Words have something told 509 F. Stone 73
Hence whole day wanderings, broken nightly sleeps 523 Epist. Beaumont 137
The whole day long, and all days of the year. . 523 Epist. Beaumont 163
But the whole household, that our coming wait. . 525 Epist. Beaumont 235
Through the whole land—to Manhood, moved in spite . . . . 540 Grace Darl. 9
And the whole surface of the out-spread map, . 548 *Stay, bold 23
Fell the whole Fabric to the ground ; . . . . 550 Hermit's Cell 2. 26
" Eke the whole Convent on the pavement lay, . 556 Prioress 226
He can make sick folk whole and fresh and sound ; 556 Cuck. and Night. 7
Them who are whole in body and in mind, . . 556 Cuck. and Night. 8
In brief, the whole of what he will, he may ; . . 557 Cuck. and Night. 16
As if his whole vocation . . . . 589 Immortality 106
Then with despair's whole weight his spirits sink, 609 Desc.Sk.Quarto 404
Whole hamlets disappearing as he moves, . . . 617 Desc.Sk.Quarto 789
The whole next day, I hoped, and hoped with fear ; 623 *Among all 17
Of the whole place should bear a stamp of awe ; . 655 Prelude 3. 434
Itself a living part of a live whole, ... 657 Prelude 3. 590
Should the whole frame of earth by inward throes 666 Prelude 5. 30
The whole world over, tight as beads of dew . . 670 Prelude 5. 321
For a whole day together, have I lain . . . . 673 Prelude 5. 483
To fertilise the whole Egyptian plain. . . . . 684 Prelude 6. 616
Of this whole Song is written that my heart . . 686 Prelude 6. 740
Through the whole summer have I been at rest, . 687 Prelude 7. 16
And the whole year breathed tenderness and love. 687 Prelude 7. 42
A whole horizon's circuit, do with power, . . . 690 Prelude 7. 242
The whole creative powers of man asleep !— . . 697 Prelude 7. 681
Meanwhile, as if the whole were one vast mill, . 698 Prelude 7. 719
As parts, but with a feeling of the whole. . . . 698 Prelude 7. 736
She must be visitant the whole year through, . 705 Prelude 8. 390
Till the whole cave, so late a senseless mass, . . 707 Prelude 8. 580
Were waiting with the whole of their desires . . 712 Prelude 9. 187
Through the whole tenour of my school-day time, 713 Prelude 9. 219
A living confirmation of the whole . . . . . 715 Prelude 9. 382
To the whole city, " sleep no more." The trance 719 Prelude 10. 87
Through a whole month of calm and glassy days 722 Prelude 10. 320
Domestic carnage now filled the whole year . . 723 Prelude 10. 356
With their whole souls went culling from the day 727 Prelude 11. 37
Not favoured spots alone, but the whole Earth, . 729 Prelude 11. 117
Yea, the whole body of society . . . . . . 731 Prelude 11. 281
Through the whole compass of the sky ; ye brooks, 734 Prelude 12. 18
Of the whole human race one brotherhood. . . 735 Prelude 12. 87
With the whole compass of the universe : . . . 747 Prelude 14. 92
Oh ! who is he that hath his whole life long . . 748 Prelude 14. 130
Of the whole species) to the external World . . 755 Recluse 1. 1. 818

Wholesome 1097 **Why**

Whole—*continued.*
And his whole figure breathed intelligence. . . 762 *Excursion* 1. 425
But the whole plainly wrought by children's hands! 778 *Excursion* 2. 423
And unenlivened; who exists whole years . . 810 *Excursion* 4. 578
And the whole circle of the heavens, for him . . 811 *Excursion* 4. 678
The Vicar's dwelling, and the whole domain, . . 824 *Excursion* 5. 128
How idly, how perversely, life's whole course, . 826 *Excursion* 5. 258
Vanished or hidden; and the whole domain, . . 830 *Excursion* 5. 549
And the whole house seems filled with gaiety. . 856 *Excursion* 6. 1187
Of the whole countenance alive with thought, . 865 *Excursion* 7. 510
Was given, the crowning bounty of the whole; . 867 *Excursion* 7. 639
And, to whole nations bound in servile straits, . 870 *Excursion* 7. 825
And by this law the mighty whole subsists: . . 872 *Excursion* 7. 1004
Through the whole body, with a languid will . . 879 *Excursion* 8. 326
Around the mansion and its whole domain; . . 882 *Excursion* 8. 540
That the whole people should be taught and trained. 889 *Excursion* 9. 358
Whole hours with but small interchange of speech, K.8. 227 **I will* 88
A whole without dependence or defect, . . . K.8. 240*Recluse* 1.1.149
Of the whole world. We saw them day by day, . K.8. 243*Recluse* 1.1.243
That the whole Valley knew them; but to us . K.8. 243*Recluse* 1.1.247
Joy spreads, and sorrow spreads; and this whole Vale, ... K.8. 248*Recluse* 1.1.445
Dreamlike the blending also of the whole . . . K.8. 252*Recluse* 1.1.574
Pass with a thought the life of the whole year . K.8. 252*Recluse* 1.1.589
Achilles—but, O Queen, the whole relate. . . . L.2. 123 *Frag. Æneid* 3. 4

Wholesome. And plants were wholesome, now of deadly taste: . . . . 17 *Desc. Sk.* 391
In copious showers, from earth by wholesome springs, ... 22 *Desc. Sk.* 657
The wholesome ministry of pain and evil, . . . 48 *Bord.* 619
Where they survive, of wholesome laws; . . . 376 **The Minstrels* 56
Is with that wholesome office satisfied, . . . 456 *Rydal Mere* 42
For wholesome sadness, troubling to refine, . . 538 **In desultory* 24
In wholesome separation the two natures, . . 751 *Prelude* 14. 346
The keen, the wholesome, air of poverty, . . . 760 *Excursion* 1. 306
The portion gave of coarse but wholesome fare . 783 *Excursion* 2. 745
To earn, by wholesome labour in the field, . . 880 *Excursion* 8. 394
Wholly. That I do not wholly fare . . . . . 171 *Kitten* 109
My old remembrances went from me wholly; . . 195 *Resolution* 20
Nor wholly lost upon the throng . . . . . . 228 *Devot. Incit.* 44
Not wholly rescued from the pale . . . . . 238 *P. B.* 187
Ambiguous, neither wholly thine nor theirs. . . 290 *Kilchurn* 5
A midnight harmony; and wholly lost . . . 314 **I dropped* 3
Wholly dissevered from our present theme; . . 440 *Ecc. Sonn.* 3. 2. 3
That this magnificence is wholly thine! . . . 457 **Had this* 36
Not all asleep and yet not waking wholly; . . 558 *Cuck. and Night.* 88
Since I am wholly at thy will? what joy . . . 563 *Troilus* 69
All which he of himself conceited wholly . . 564 *Troilus* 104
What we possessed, and now is wholly thine! . 576 **Six months* 6
Not wholly free, I watched him thus; at length . 664 *Prelude* 4. 409
It is not wholly so to him who looks . . . . 698 *Prelude* 7. 733
Nor was it wholly without pleasure then. . . . 719 *Prelude* 10. 69
Was wholly ignorant that my ancient Friend— . 783 *Excursion* 2. 785
And wholly without roof (the bleached remains . 784 *Excursion* 2. 813
And of design not wholly worn away. . . . 787 *Excursion* 3. 84
Upon our hearts, not wholly lost, I grant, . . 846 *Excursion* 6. 528
A heaving surface, almost wholly free . . . . 847 *Excursion* 6. 607
Wholly untraced a more forbidding way. . . . 848 *Excursion* 6. 662
And so, not wholly hidden from men's sight, . . 868 *Excursion* 7. 738
Whose visitation had not wholly spared . . . 881 *Excursion* 8. 503
As shall divide them wholly from the stir. . . 885 *Excursion* 9. 47
That feared, or wholly overlooked the truth, . . K.8. 245*Recluse* 1.1.310
Half-seen or wholly, lost and found again, . . K.8. 250*Recluse* 1.1.488
And would not wholly perish even in this, . . K.8. 255*Recluse* 1.1.693
Whom. (*Partial list.*)
Whom, but some few days past, I saw in Eskdale, 46 *Bord.* 479
I parted with the Child. Parted with whom? . 46 *Bord.* 508
Her whom the Monster, Clifford, drove to madness. 47 *Bord.* 569
His staff—his figure—Murder!—what, of whom? 54 *Bord.* 926
"His Schoolfellow, whom he had so besought, . 554 *Prioress* 93
Of that false Bird whom Love can not abide. . 561 *Cuck.andNight.* 270
In acts of love to those with whom they dwell, . 568 *Cumb. Beg.* 139
Old Man! whom so oft I with pity have eyed, . 572 *Avarice* 45
Whom he had early loved. And not in vain . . 573 *Chiabrera* 2. 8
On whom the duty fell (for at that time . . . 575 *Chiabrera* 8. 2
Return Delights! with whom my road begun, . 592 *Ev. Wk. Quarto* 27
Whome'er. To humble or afflict whome'er he will, 557 *Cuck. and Night.* 18
Whoo. *See* **To-whoo, Tu-whoo.**
Whoop. Shout after shout—reiterated whoop . . K.8. 245*Recluse* 1.1.321
Whooping. The Ploughboy is whooping—anon—anon: . . . . 190 *March* 15
Each whooping with a merry shout, ... 191 *Beggars* 28
Have I heard whooping, and he soon will be . . K.8. 251*Recluse* 1.1.522
Whortle-berries. And whortle-berries from the mountain side. . . . . 782 *Excursion* 2. 684
Who's. Who's yon, that, near the waterfall, . 130 *Idiot Boy* 347
Whose. (*Partial list.*)
From whose perverted soul can come no good . 37 *Bord.* 9
May He whose eye is over all protect you! . . 38 *Bord.* 43
Has marked out this foul Wretch as one whose crimes . . . . 55 *Bord.* 1000
Meanwhile the stream, whose bank I sate upon, . 558 *Cuck.and Night.* 81
And other Peers whose names are on record; . . 562 *Cuck.andNight.* 277
Reverence the hope whose vital anxiousness . . 568 *Cumb. Beg.* 177
Like one whose own country's far over the sea; . 570 *Farmer* 62
And trust in God—to whose eternal doom . . 574 *Chiabrera* 3. 19
No—he was One whose memory ought to spread . 574 *Chiabrera* 5. 21
Whoso. Which whoso travels in her bosom eyes, . 445 *Ecc. Sonn.* 3. 19. 7
(As whoso enters shall ere long perceive) . . . 497 **Enough of climbing* 25
Whoso—*continued.*
For whoso gets of love a little bliss, ... 560 *Cuck.andNight.* 178
With length of shade so thick, that whoso glides . 706 *Prelude* 8. 460
That whoso feels such passion in its strength . . 742 *Prelude* 13. 192
Whosoe'er. Whosoe'er the man might be, . . . 161 **Pleasures newly* 10
Which whosoe'er approached of strength was shorn, 373 *Eg. Maid* 317
Pause, Traveller! whosoe'er thou be . . . . 550 *Hermit's Cell* 2. 1
The strain of transport, "whosoe'er in youth . . 809 *Excursion* 4. 541
Why. (*Partial list.*)
But why, ungrateful, dwell on idle pain? . . . 2 *Ev. Wk.* 33
Why does their sad remembrance haunt the mind? 19 *Desc. Sk.* 519
Why thus that worn-out wretch must there sustain 34 *Guilt* 552
Why, this is noble! shake her off at once. . . 41 *Bord.* 248
Why, if a wolf should leap from out a thicket, . 43 *Bord.* 317
Why now—but yesterday I overtook . . . . 45 *Bord.* 446
Why are you not the man you were that moment? 52 *Bord.* 795
Why so? a roofless rock had been a comfort, . 52 *Bord.* 814
And spake to you, why did you give no answer? 55 *Bord.* 959
Why, if his heart be tender, that offence . . 56 *Bord.* 1043
The senseless body, and why not the mind?— . 58 *Bord.* 1167
But listen, for my peace—— Why, I *believe* you. 59 *Bord.* 1175
Why else have I been led to this bleak Waste? . 62 *Bord.* 1388
And was his guide; if once, why not again, . . 62 *Bord.* 1395
Why dost thou come to me with words like these? 75 *Bord.* 2122
Why may we speak these things, and do no more; 77 *Bord.* 2269
Why should a thrust of the arm have such a power, 77 *Bord.* 2270
She is not dead. Why!—if I loved this Woman, 77 *Bord.* 2272
"Now, little Edward, say why so: . . . . . 86 *Anecdote* 37
My little Edward, tell me why."— . . . . . 86 *Anecdote* 38
"Why, this is strange," said I; . . . . . 86 *Anecdote* 40
Why you would change sweet Liswyn farm . . 86 *Anecdote* 43
"Why, Edward, tell me why?" . . . . . . 86 *Anecdote* 48
And that's the reason why." . . . . 86 *Anecdote* 56
"What ails thee, young One? what? Why pull so at thy cord? . . . . 87 *Pet-lamb* 21
Why, there, Sir, is a thought that's new to me! . 98 *Brothers* 174
Why should I fear to say . . . . 108 *Louisa* 3
Why did ye listen to my prayer? . . . . . 114 *Ind. Wom.* 24
Why am I ignorant of the same . . . . . 116 *Affl. Marg.* 5
—Why bustle thus about your door, ... 126 *Idiot Boy* 7
Why are you in this mighty fret? . . . . . 126 *Idiot Boy* 9
And why on horseback have you set . . . . 126 *Idiot Boy* 10
Why will ye thus my suit repel? . . . . . 130 *Idiot Boy* 343
Why of your further aid bereave me? . . . . 130 *Idiot Boy* 344
Cried out, "Good brother, why so fast? . . . 176 *Waggoner* 1. 237
And why sits she beside the Thorn . . . . 198 *Thorn* 82
O wherefore? wherefore? tell me why . . . 198 *Thorn* 87
Why should it daunt a blameless prayer? . . . 217 *Enterprise* 121
Why are they ungarlanded? . . . . 221 *Triad* 108
Yet why repine, created as we are . . . . 231 *Clouds* 92
Why wander from your course so far, ... 245 *P. B.* 762
Why have I crowded this small bark with you . 252 **Her only* 10
"Why, Minstrel, these untuneful murmurings— . 252 **Why, Minstrel* 1
Some veering up and down, one knew not why. . 258 **With Ships* 4
Why art thou silent! Is thy love a plant . . 277 **Why art* 1
Why to God's goodness cannot We be true, . . 278 **Life with* 12
But why go on?— . . . . 285 *Grave of Burns* 58
But why to Him confine the prayer, ... 286 *Nith* 61
"For why?—because the good old rule . . . 291 *Rob Roy* 37
Why throw away a needful day . . . . . 293 *Yarrow Unv.* 23
A *Highland* Boy!—why call him so? . . . . 295 *Highland Boy* 11
Yet why?—a silvery current flows . . . . . 302 *Yarrow V.* 9
Which his own nature hath enjoined;—and why? 311 **Who rises* 54
For why—unless for liberty enrolled . . . . 321 **Humanity, delighting* 24
Why should the Song be tardy to proclaim . . 330 *Ode: Thanks.* 93
Why does this puny Church present to view . . 335 *Aix* 5
Why leap the fountains from their cells . . . 341 *San Salv.* 9
Why speak of Roman Pomps? the haughty claims 346 *Processions* 28
Peace to their Spirits! why should Poesy . . . 354 *Aquap.* 85
For why?—to save his Father's land; . . . . 412 *White Doe* 1467
—Why tell of mossy rock, or tree, ... 415 *White Doe* 1710
Why should we break Time's charitable seals? . 449 *Ecc. Sonn.* 3. 35. 12
Why sleeps the future, as a snake enrolled, . . 452 *Ecc. Sonn.* 3. 47. 1
Why do good thoughts, invoked or not, descend, 456 **Soft as* 22
Why should the Enthusiast, journeying through this Isle, ... 463 **Why should the* 1
Why stand we gazing on the sparkling Brine, . 469 **Why stand* 1
Why grieve for these, though past away . . . 473 *Ossian* 43
Why keep *we* else the instincts whose dread law . 474 **Ye shadowy* 10
"Why, William, on that old grey stone, . . . 481 *Expost.* 1
Why, William, sit you thus alone, ... 481 *Expost.* 3
When life was sweet, I knew not why, . . . 481 *Expost.* 14
Why all this toil and trouble? . . . . . 481 *Tables Turned* 4
Why is the Past belied with wicked art, . . . 505 *Warning* 140
Ah why deceive ourselves! by no mere fit . . 515 **Ah why* 1
Why bears it then the name of "Weeping Hill"? 517 *Pun. Death* 1. 8
Why fix upon his wealth or want a thought? . 529 *Poor Robin* 16
Tell me the cause why thou dost sing this hymn, 555 *Prioress* 196
Why Troilus hath all this heaviness? . . . . 564 *Troilus* 103
Why should we weep or mourn, Angelic boy, . . 581 **Why should we* 1
O for a dirge! But why complain? . . . . 582 **O for a* 1
Is broken; yet why grieve? for Time but holds . 586 *Ch. Lamb* 129
Why with such earnest pains dost thou provoke . 589 *Immortality* 127
Why does their sad remembrance cleave behind? 613 *Desc.Sk.Quarto* 623
Why think of anything but present good?" . . 633 *Prelude* 1. 100
Seeking the visible world, nor knowing why. . 646 *Prelude* 2. 278
Why should I speak of what a thousand hearts . 659 *Prelude* 4. 44
Why is this glorious creature to be found . . 741 *Prelude* 13. 87
Why may not millions be? What bars are thrown 741 *Prelude* 13. 89
Why should a tear be on an old Man's cheek? . 765 *Excursion* 1. 598

Wide—*continued.*
A wide compassion which with you I share. . . 886 *Excursion* 9. 155
So wide a difference between man and man. . . 888 *Excursion* 9. 254
So the wide waters, open to the power, . . . 889 *Excursion* 9. 375
" Change wide, and deep, and silently performed, 889 *Excursion* 9. 384
Of the blue firmament—aloft, and wide : . . . 893 *Excursion* 9. 596
A peaceable dominion, wide as earth, ... 894 *Excursion* 9. 665
So wide the difference, a willing mind . . . 895 *Excursion* 9. 715
I would impart it, I would spread it wide, . . K.8. 255 *Recluse* 1. 1. 690
Widely. Should thus so widely differ from himself— 65 *Bord.* 1570
Had found, in ravage widely dealt, ... 298 *Brownie's Cell* 39
How widely spread the interests of our theme. . 443 *Ecc. Sonn.* 3. 12. 14
For sway profoundly felt as widely spread ; . . 455 *Rydal Mere* 28
By cursèd Jews—thing well and widely known, . 556 *Prioress* 234
Misdeem most widely, lodging it elsewhere : . . 654 *Prelude* 3. 350
Through earth and sky, spreads widely, and sends deep . . . . 665 *Prelude* 5. 2
The widely parted hours ; the noise of streams, . 686 *Prelude* 6. 718
On sundry and most widely different modes . . 698 *Prelude* 7. 738
Endless, here opening widely out, and there . . 702 *Prelude* 8. 193
In earth, the widely scattered wreck sublime . . 708 *Prelude* 8. 614
How widely spread the boughs, of that old tree . 717 *Prelude* 9. 550
Widely—inveterately usurped upon, ... 797 *Excursion* 3. 794
And, even as these are well and widely fixed, . . 812 *Excursion* 4. 764
Widely-scattered. Couch the widely-scattered sheep ;— 163 *Spinning Wheel* 8
Widely-sweeping. Though, from the widely-sweeping blow, ... 582 *Invoc. Earth* 17
Widening. Of green isles widening on each snow-clad height ; . . . . 17 *Desc. Sk.* 369
And widening circuit of ethereal sky. . . . . 426 *Ecc. Sonn.* 1. 29. 14
Widening on all sides ; sees, or thinks he sees, . 707 *Prelude* 8. 565
Widening its circle as the storms advance. . . 775 *Excursion* 2. 262
Widens. Widens the fatal web, its lines extend, . 330 *Ode : Thanks.* 123
Wider. The wider space the better—we may find . 78 *Bord.* 2307
And wider range to passions turbulent, . . . 515 **Men of* 7
For sports of wider range. Ere I had told . . 636 *Prelude* 1. 306
And spread them with a wider creeping ; felt . . 650 *Prelude* 3. 115
With livelier hope a region wider far. . . . . 679 *Prelude* 6. 321
Some half-frequented scene, where wider streets . 690 *Prelude* 7. 191
Others of wider scope, where living men, . . . 691 *Prelude* 7. 261
Diffusing only those affections wider . . . . 729 *Prelude* 11. 169
New pleasure, wider empire for the sight, . . . 736 *Prelude* 12. 145
And with no wider interval of time . . . . 794 *Excursion* 3. 592
Wide-ruling. To the wide-ruling eagle, and his hand 868 *Excursion* 7. 748
Wide-spanned. That wide-spanned arch, wondering how it was raised, ... 283 **Well have* 9
Wide-spread. The wide-spread boughs, for view of door, window, and stair that wound . . 92 *Poet's Dream* 38
Then, on the wide-spread wings . . . . . 104 *Artegal* 143
How sweet to rest her wide-spread wings beneath ! 311 **Who rises* 4
Science, wide-spread and spreading still as be . 357 *Aquap.* 331
And Christian India, through her wide-spread clime, ... 425 *Ecc. Sonn.* 1. 26. 13
'Mid reedy fens wide-spread and marshes drear, . 431 *Ecc. Sonn.* 2. 13. 7
A Bard, who, lately near the wide-spread sea . . 460 **Queen of* 6
Through wide-spread regions errant ; . . . . . 478 *Somnamb.* 47
I thought, still traversing that widespread plain, . 726 *Prelude* 10. 545
Calm did he sit under the wide-spread tree . . 783 *Excursion* 2. 751
Startling the golden hills. A wide-spread elm . 850 *Excursion* 6. 831
Where wide-spread conflict then most fiercely raged ; . . . . 869 *Excursion* 7. 797
Wide-spreading. Wide-spreading odours from her flowery wreaths. . . . . 367 *Trajan* 22
Patriarch of a wide-spreading family, ... 444 *Ecc. Sonn.* 3. 15. 9
Wide-spreading, steady, calm, contemplative. . 660 *Prelude* 4. 141
Widest. Over three Realms may take its widest range ; . . . . 471 *Tynwald* 10
Objects through widest intercourse of sense. . . 645 *Prelude* 2. 240
There, in a clime from widest empire chosen, . . 700 *Prelude* 8. 82
Of joy in widest commonalty spread ; . . . . 755 *Recluse* 1. 1. 771
Wide-staring. Where no one dwells but the wide-staring owl . . . . 843 *Excursion* 6. 327
Wide-wasted. —Wide-wasted regions—cities wrapt in flame— . . . . 330 *Ode : Thanks.* 98
Wide-wasting. The hostile purpose of wide-wasting Time— . . . . 325 *Ode 1814* 145
Widow. The Soldier's Widow heard and stood aghast ; . . . . 33 *Guilt* 476
The Soldier's Widow learned with honest pain . 34 *Guilt* 550
The Soldier's Widow lingered in the cot ; . . . 36 *Guilt* 640
Of One, a Widow, left beneath a weight . . . 138 *Widow* 4
A piercing look the Widow cast . . . . . 248 *P. B.* 1041
The Widow and her family. . . . . 249 *P. B.* 1130
—Soon shall the widow (for the speed of Time . 505 *Warning* 151
Widow, or wife, implore on tremulous knee, . . 505 *Warning* 153
" This Widow thus her little Son hath taught . 553 *Prioress* 57
" Now this poor Widow waiteth all that night . 554 *Prioress* 135
Then, if a widow, staggering with the blow . . 704 *Prelude* 8. 384
A Wife and Widow. Needs must it have been . 769 *Excursion* 1. 874
Widowed. Nor Her who thinking of me there counts widowed hours." . . . . 140 *Arm. Lady* 54
Seven widowed years without my Jane, . . . 157 *Sexton* 30
A trembling solace to her widowed Lord. . . . 576 **By a* 12
Alone, within her widowed Mother's house. . . 851 *Excursion* 6. 854
Widowhood. She lingered in unquiet widowhood ; 769 *Excursion* 1. 873
Of their undrooping Father's widowhood, . . . 855 *Excursion* 6. 1128
Widow's. " A sailor's wife I knew a widow's cares, 35 *Guilt* 595
Or widow's cottage-lullaby. . . . . . . 233 *Power of Sound* 32
Found at the Widow's feet some sad relief ; . . 523 *Epist. Beaumont* 134

Widow's—*continued.*
" Among these children was a Widow's son, . . 553 *Prioress* 50
The widow's lonely shriek. . . . . 623 *G. and S. Green* 12
Width. Bays, gulfs, and ocean's Indian width, shall be, ... 527 **Those breathing* 39
Locarno ! spreading out in width like Heaven, . 685 *Prelude* 6. 657
The width of those huge forests, unto me . . . 716 *Prelude* 9. 462
Wield. These base implements to wield ; . . . 140 *Arm. Lady* 50
" A potent wand doth Sorrow wield ; . . . . 238 *P. B.* 146
While Soldiers, weary of the arms they wield, . 268 **Four fiery* 12
—Not loth the sleepy lance to wield, ... 403 *White Doe* 700
Dare to usurp ;—thou hast a sword to wield, . 432 *Ecc. Sonn.* 2. 15. 8
To wield it ;—they, too, who of gentle mood . . 729 *Prelude* 11. 132
Degenerate ; who, constrained to wield the sword 839 *Excursion* 6. 62
Wielded. Wielded the sceptre of the Atheist crew. . 725 *Prelude* 10. 502
Wielding. *See* **Thunder-wielding.**
And the small critic wielding his delicate pen, . 569 *Farmer* 3
Wielding her potent enginery to frame . . . 875 *Excursion* 8. 92
Wields. Sent from some distant clime where Winter wields . . . . 263 **While not* 4
And 'tis the Pope that wields it :—whether rough . 428 *Ecc. Sonn.* 1. 39. 13
And he who guides the plough, or wields the crook, 435 *Ecc. Sonn.* 2. 29. 4
Discerning sword that Justice wields, do thou . 681 *Prelude* 6. 444
Wife. " A sailor's wife I knew a widow's cares, . 35 *Guilt* 595
Through which his Wife, to that kind shelter brought, ... 36 *Guilt* 642
Is mine. Yours, Woman ! are you Herbert's wife ? 46 *Bord.* 510
Wife, Sir ! his wife—not I ; my husband, Sir, . 46 *Bord.* 511
This old Man may have a wife, ... 72 *Bord.* 1999
My wife and children came into my mind. . . 74 *Bord.* 2088
Point to his wife the blood-drops on his pillow ! . 76 *Bord.* 2184
And a few natural graves." To Jane, his wife, . 95 *Brothers* 15
His wife sate near him, teasing matted wool, . . 95 *Brothers* 21
That Julia, wanting yet the name of wife, . . 122 *V. and J.* 66
I am thy father's wedded wife ; . . . . . 145 *Her Eyes* 72
And he hath now forgot his Wife, ... 177 *Waggoner* 2. 85
" Thy wife and child are snug and warm, . . . 179 *Waggoner* 3. 70
Or ruling Bandit's wife among the Grecian isles. . 190 *Beggars* 12
A husband and a wife." . . . . 193 *Ruth* 105
When of thy loss I thought, belovèd Wife ! . . 211 *Laod.* 128
Where thou, a Wife and Friend, shalt see . . . 218 *Young Lady* 4
But how one wife could e'er come near him, . . 239 *P. B.* 282
I married my sixth wife ! . . . . 246 *P. B.* 865
To love her as his wedded wife. . . . . . 246 *P. B.* 905
From frailty, for that insight may the Wife . . 256 *Marriage : Friend* 13
Belovèd Wife ? such solace to impart . . . . 395 *White Doe: Ded.* 63
Feel with the Mother, think the severed Wife . 476 *Howard* 11
His wife, an aged woman, ... 483 *Simon Lee* 38
Widow, or wife, implore on tremulous knee, . . 505 *Warning* 153
Wife, children, kindred, they were dead and gone ; 531 **I know* 25
—Meanwhile his wife and child with cruel hope . 609 *Desc.Sk.Quarto* 408
Did wife and husband roam ; . . . . . . 623 *G. and S. Green* 6
The husband to the wife. . . . . 623 *G. and S. Green* 16
Queen, Wife and Mother ! may All-judging Heaven 628 **Deign,Sovereign* 5
And how, unfaithful to a virtuous wife . . . 691 *Prelude* 7. 298
Associate with his children and his wife . . . 719 *Prelude* 10. 52
The illustrious wife of Roland, in the hour . . 723 *Prelude* 10. 381
A Wife and Widow. Needs must it have been . 769 *Excursion* 1. 874
The Wife and Mother pitifully fixing . . . . 798 *Excursion* 3. 854
Of wife and children stung to agony. . . . . 855 *Excursion* 6. 1098
The Wife, from whose consolatory grave . . . 856 *Excursion* 6. 1189
The silent name of his departed wife ; . . . . 867 *Excursion* 7. 670
Not too old to have a wife ; . . . . . . S.3. 423 *Tinker* 3
By that wondrous marble wife . . . . . . S.3. 437 **I, whose* 7
Blush Pride to see a farmer's wife produce . . L.1. 97 *Juvenal* 3. 96
Wife's. Round his wife's neck ; the prize of victory laid . . . . 25 *Guilt* 61
He saw his Wife's lips move his name to bless . 35 *Guilt* 616
In the wife's smile ; and in the placid sky ; . . 315 **The Land* 7
From his wife's Faro-bank a decent rent, . . . L.1. 97 *Juvenal* 3. 82
Wight. Come to him thus, and drove the weary Wight along. . . . . 108 *Indolence* 36
And Autumn, melancholy Wight ! . . . . . 157 **In youth* 14
But he hath said, poor gentle wight ! . . . . 245 *P. B.* 758
Sweeps visibly the Wallace Wight ; . . . . . 300 *Cora Linn* 20
The Effigies of a valiant Wight . . . . . . 301 *Bran* 46
Against him dare not any wight say nay ; . . . 557 *Cuck. and Night.* 17
For every wight eschews thy song to hear, . . 558 *Cuck. and Night.* 114
To every wight that gentle is of kind. . . . . 559 *Cuck. and Night.* 150
That no wight his continuance espied. . . . . 563 *Troilus* 21
That every wight might on his sorrow rue. . . 563 *Troilus* 42
That every wight, who in the way passed by, . . 564 *Troilus* 107
He strayed through the fields like an indolent wight, ... 569 *Farmer* 23
Beside the shores of Wight ; . . . . 579 **Sweet Flower* 17
Wild. The echoes of your rocks my carols wild : . 2 *Ev. Wk.* 14
And wild Impatience, pointing upward, showed, . 2 *Ev. Wk.* 25
In rocky basin its wild waves repose, ... 3 *Ev. Wk.* 58
Bandusia's praise, wild stream, should yield to thine ! . . . . 3 *Ev. Wk.* 73
On tawny earth, wild weeds, and twisted roots ; . 5 *Ev. Wk.* 187
Or wild Aosta lulled by Alpine rills, ... 15 *Desc. Sk.* 294
From out the rocks, the wild bees' safe abode : . 17 *Desc. Sk.* 389
Binds her wild wreaths, and whispers his return. . 18 *Desc. Sk.* 432
Once, Man entirely free, alone and wild, . . . 18 *Desc. Sk.* 433
And with wild flowers and blooming orchards blend ;— . . . . 20 *Desc. Sk.* 572
And led by nature into a wild scene . . . . 23 *Yew-tree* 14
But sought in vain ; for now, all wild, forlorn, . 25 *Guilt* 43

Wild—*continued.*
Had been irregular, I might say, wild ; 859 *Excursion* 7. 114
Or the wild brooks ; from which he now returned 859 *Excursion* 7. 159
Behind yon hill, a poor and rugged wild, 862 *Excursion* 7. 348
Yet, of the wild brooks ask if he complained ; 864 *Excursion* 7. 488
Where nature works in wild and craggy spots, 871 *Excursion* 7. 917
Like wild beasts without home ! Their hour was come ; 873 *Excursion* 7. 1027
The foot-path faintly marked, the horse-track wild, 876 *Excursion* 8. 105
Wild pursuivants ! until their breath is lost, 880 *Excursion* 8. 386
Into a wild disorder ; or be forced 888 *Excursion* 9. 306
Wild tracts of forest-ground, and scattered groves, 891 *Excursion* 9. 505
Of that wild spot, the Solitary said 892 *Excursion* 9. 548
" Once," and with wild demeanour, as he spake, 894 *Excursion* 9. 679
Though aided by wild winds, the groans and shrieks 894 *Excursion* 9. 696
Shagged with wild pale green tufts of fragrant hay, S.3. 417 **Sweet was* 3
Sauntering to pluck the strawberries wild unseen. S.3. 417 **Sweet was* 8
" Wild wanderers, whither through my dark domain ? " K.8. 241 *Recluse* 1.1.169
Wild creatures, and of many homes, that come K.8. 251 *Recluse* 1.1.540
Among wild appetites and blind desires, K.8. 256 *Recluse* 1.1.706
Of speech as wild as ever heightened mirth. K.8. 301 **And oh* 10
Wild-bird's. A Chapel, like a wild-bird's nest, 396 *White Doe* 27
Wild-cat. Nor wild-cat in a woody glen ! 243 *P. B.* 620
Wild-duck's. A youngling of the wild-duck's nest 297 *Highland Boy* 189
Wilder. And wilder graces sport around their brow ; 615 *Desc.Sk.Quarto* 735
Wildered. And rain he wildered on, no moon to stream 26 *Guilt* 130
No night-duck clamours for his wilder'd mate, 598 *Ev. Wk. Quarto* 357
To call from other worlds the wilder'd mind, 598 *Ev. Wk. Quarto* 376
Wildering. Tumbles, the wildering Thunder slips abroad ; 605 *Desc.Sk.Quarto* 204
Wilderness. Freshening the wilderness with shades and springs. 13 *Desc. Sk.* 172
Flings o'er the wilderness a stream of fire : 20 *Desc. Sk.* 554
In wood or wilderness, in camp or town, 29 *Guilt* 300
She was my Raven in the wilderness, 53 *Bord.* 847
In such a wilderness—to see no thing, 75 *Bord.* 2136
A desert wilderness will be ! 129 *Idiot Boy* 331
Of Eden's blissful wilderness, 154 *Flower Garden* 4
The panther in the wilderness 192 *Ruth* 38
The wilderness shall hear the lion roar ; 273 **Not the* 11
And in the wilderness were bound 298 *Brownie's Cell* 7
Recoiled into the wilderness. 301 *Bran* 128
For his delight, a solemn wilderness 319 *Spaniard* 7
Crying amid the wilderness, and given, 363 **List—'twas* 94
Urged o'er the wilderness in sportive gallop. 371 *Eg. Maid* 120
There bloomed the strawberry of the wilderness ; 377 *Duddon* 6. 9
And through this wilderness a passage cleave 379 *Duddon* 14. 12
Over the burning wilderness, and charge 392 *Daniel* 7
Within the wilderness her seat ? 413 *White Doe* 1559
" What beast in wilderness or cultured field 432 *Ecc. Sonn.* 2. 15. 1
Her peace destroyed ! her hopes a wilderness ! 439 *Ecc. Sonn.* 2. 44. 13
A look of thine the wilderness pervades, 459 **Wanderer! that* 25
A temple of the wilderness, 472 *Ossian* 14
We may find pleasure : wilderness and wood, 488 *Pers. Talk* 30
But with a wilderness of waves between ; 522 *Epist.Beaumont* 78
A wilderness is rich with liberty. 527 **Those breathing* 32
Kneeling amid the wilderness 543 *Russ. Fug.* 165
" From Moscow to the Wilderness 545 *Russ. Fug.* 305
Deep in the bosom of the wilderness ; 664 *Prelude* 4. 361
Of sandy wilderness, all black and void, 666 *Prelude* 5. 72
Saw, over half the wilderness diffused, 667 *Prelude* 5. 128
The breathless wilderness of clouds ; the clock 686 *Prelude* 6. 716
Of your green groves, and wilderness of lamps 689 *Prelude* 7. 122
To me a heart-depressing wilderness ; 741 *Prelude* 13. 115
A wilderness of building, sinking far 784 *Excursion* 2. 836
For thy own glory, in the wilderness ! 802 *Excursion* 4. 42
In the waste wilderness : the Soul ascends 807 *Excursion* 4. 395
Such as, remote, 'mid savage wilderness, 820 *Excursion* 4. 1277
Amid a wilderness of rocks and stones 832 *Excursion* 5. 680
He sees the barren wilderness erased, 876 *Excursion* 8. 129
His steps to govern in the Wilderness ; K.8. 246 *Recluse* 1.1.338
Far from the living and dead wilderness K.8. 253 *Recluse* 1.1.613
She seeks a wilderness of weed and thorn, K.8. 325 [?] **The vestal* 3
Wildernesses. I have walked through wildernesses dreary, 159 **Up with me* 8
Wilders. All blind she wilders o'er the lightless heath, 597 *Ev. Wk. Quarto* 285
Wildest. What power is in his wildest scream, 117 *Affl. Marg.* 24
He was the wildest far of all ;— 239 *P. B.* 279
Had been the wildest of his clan, 249 *P. B.* 1132
To cull contentment upon wildest shores, 284 *Departure* 25
Of wildest course but treads back his own steps ; 719 *Prelude* 10. 79
Wild-flower. No firmer grasp—a little wild-flower, joined 509 *F. Stone* 56
Wild-flowers. This way and that, with wild-flowers crowned. 234 *Power of Sound* 152
And wild-flowers known as well as if our hands S.3. 433 **The doubt* 7
Wild-hearted. " How fares Joanna, that wild-hearted Maid ! 147 *Joanna* 23
Wilding. Of wilding in his hand. 487 **We walked* 60
Wildish. —'Twould be a *wildish* destiny, 289 *Stepping West.* 2
Wildly. And, wildly pausing, oft she hangs aghast, 15 *Desc. Sk.* 267
And she was wildly clad : 83 *We are Seven* 10
Wildness. " A savage wildness round him hung 239 *P. B.* 291
Wilds. —Is there who 'mid these awful wilds has seen 16 *Desc. Sk.* 340
Of Scotland's rocky wilds, did seem 113 *Lament* 17
Through border wilds where naked Indians stray, 153 *Morn. Ex.* 13
For thy unblest coevals, amid wilds 172 *Infant Daughter* 33
In Craven's Wilds is many a den, 408 *White Doe* 1094

Wilds—*continued.*
Among her native wilds of Craven ; 414 *White Doe* 1618
On Snowdon's wilds, amid Brigantian coves, 419 *Ecc. Sonn.* 1. 5. 2
'Mid woods and wilds, on Nature's craggy throne, 431 *Ecc. Sonn.* 2. 11. 13
To Wilds where both were utterly unknown ; 443 *Ecc. Sonn.* 3. 14. 2
Who in these Wilds then struggled for command ; 466 *St. Bees* 38
Among Tartarian wilds—fell short, far short, 688 *Prelude* 7. 84
Not such as Saturn ruled 'mid Latian wilds, 701 *Prelude* 8. 129
Was thronged with impregnations like the Wilds 708 *Prelude* 8. 633
Not less ambitious once among the wilds 744 *Prelude* 13. 313
The employment common through these wilds, and gained, 769 *Excursion* 1. 859
Among the wilds of Scotland, in a tract 774 *Excursion* 2. 166
" These craggy regions, these chaotic wilds, 807 *Excursion* 4. 427
Of sweet civility, on rustic wilds. 839 *Excursion* 6. 41
Amid these wilds, this answer may suffice ; 842 *Excursion* 6. 300
To the deep shade of those untravelled Wilds ; 845 *Excursion* 6. 455
By which our northern wilds could then be crossed ; 858 *Excursion* 7. 60
With gentle language ; in remotest wilds, 875 *Excursion* 8. 79
Through Cumbrian wilds, in many a mountain cave, S.3. 426 **Through Cumbrian* 1
Wild-wood. Shall hide me, wooing long thy wildwood strain ; 3 *Ev. Wk.* 87
And wild-wood sorrows, speedily 143 **Driven in* 12
The wild-wood fruits to gather, 302 *Yarrow V.* 66
And wild-wood mountain lutes of saddest swell. 611 *Desc.Sk.Quarto* 509
Wile. Triumphant, snatched from many a treacherous wile ! 438 *Ecc. Sonn.* 2. 38. 2
Wiles. She weighs them in one scale. The wiles of woman, 57 *Bord.* 1080
Thy looks, thy cunning, and thy wiles, 121 *EmigrantMother* 51
With ever-varying wiles, 170 *Rural Ill.* 32
For transient sorrows, simple wiles, 186 **She was* 19
Their daring wiles, their sportive cheer ? 191 *Seq. Beggars* 12
There, too, ere wiles and politic dispute 313 **Go back* 9
And mount, at every step, with living wiles 451 *Ecc. Sonn.* 3. 42. 8
And, wherever they carry their plots and their wiles, 572 *Avarice* 39
Would I, by previous wiles, inflame the queen 624 *Æneid* 24
" But nay—the fatal wiles, O guest, recount, 625 *Æneid* 139
Wilfred. For such he is— Your busy fancies, Wilfred, 38 *Bord.* 25
And be at rest. Oh, Sir ! Peace, my good Wilfred ; 38 *Bord.* 40
Discerning Monitor, my faithful Wilfred, 78 *Bord.* 2322
Wallace and Wilfred, I commend the Lady, 78 *Bord.* 2333
And grey-haired Wilfred of the glen 199 *Thorn* 138
Of Wilfred Armathwaite ? " The Vicar answered, 854 *Excursion* 6. 1079
Wilful. Your Father, Lady, from a wilful hand 74 *Bord.* 2117
She perished ; and, as for a wilful crime, 212 *Laod.* 159
Father of all ! though wilful Manhood read 342 *Ital. Itin.* 94
He made by wilful breach of law divine. 428 *Ecc. Sonn.* 2. 1. 4
And some, we know, when they by wilful act 517 *Pun. Death* 3. 9
To wilful alienation from the right, 653 *Prelude* 3. 323
Thus wilful Fancy, in no hurtful mood, 705 *Prelude* 8. 421
Too oft by wilful forfeiture, have lost 800 *Excursion* 3. 961
He, who by wilful disesteem of life 816 *Excursion* 4. 1029
And lifts his wilful hand on mischief bent, 889 *Excursion* 9. 317
Wilfully. Mean, miserable, wilfully depraved, 714 *Prelude* 9. 286
To loiter wilfully within a creek, 717 *Prelude* 9. 562
Wilfully to mean cares or low pursuits, 748 *Prelude* 14. 154
Wilfulness. So diverse in his wilfulness is he. 560 *Cuck.andNight.* 205
A wilfulness of fancy and conceit : 704 *Prelude* 8. 373
Wilkinson. Spade ! with which Wilkinson hath tilled his lands, 489 *Spade* 1
Will. (*Partial list.*) *See* **Good-will, Self-will, 'Twill.**
And in thy iteration, " Whip poor Will ! " 153 *Morn. Ex.* 16
the Troop will be impatient ; let us hie 37 *Bord.* 1
—Pity that our young Chief will have no part 37 *Bord.* 4
I will not call on Heaven to vouch for me, 41 *Bord.* 211
You will look down into a dell, and there 41 *Bord.* 217
Will see an ash from which a sign-board hangs ; 41 *Bord.* 218
We will not waste an hour in such a cause. 41 *Bord.* 247
I will not play the sluggard. Nay, sit down. 42 *Bord.* 299
Fear not, I will obey you ;—but One so young, 42 *Bord.* 308
Is broken, you will hear no more of *him*. 43 *Bord.* 342
To-day will clear up all.—You marked a Cottage, 44 *Bord.* 378
And I will tell you all !—You know not, Sir, 46 *Bord.* 503
What must be done ? We will conduct her hither ; 48 *Bord.* 593
You will not disappoint them ; and hereafter—— 48 *Bord.* 624
The deed is done—if you will have it so— 48 *Bord.* 641
The cloud will soon disperse—farewell—but stay, 49 *Bord.* 647
And will be so through every change of fortune 50 *Bord.* 721
Moves me beyond my bearing.—I will try 52 *Bord.* 801
You will forgive me, but my heart runs over. 52 *Bord.* 833
I will not murmur ; blasted as I have been, 53 *Bord.* 851
He will deny it to the last. He lies 54 *Bord.* 915
Begone, ye Slaves, or I will raise a whirlwind 54 *Bord.* 944
Will retribution show itself again 55 *Bord.* 969
Herbert ! since you will have it, Baron Herbert ; 55 *Bord.* 975
Henceforth, then, will I never in camp or field 55 *Bord.* 979
Or duty sanctions. We will have ample justice. 57 *Bord.* 1113
His death will be a monument for ages. 58 *Bord.* 1124
That all is well prepared. We will obey you. 58 *Bord.* 1131
I will explain the cause. 58 *Bord.* 1134
And said, ' My Father he will have it so.' 59 *Bord.* 1197
But she will wake, and she will weep for me, 77 *Bord.* 2274
Seek who will delight in fable, 93 *Westmoreland Girl* 1
Seeking less bold achievement, where he will ! 377 *Duddon* 4. 14
To tell a story I will use my power ; 552 *Prioress* 11
' Now, certès, I will use my diligence 554 *Prioress* 88
Our Lady I will praise with all my power. 554 *Prioress* 92

Willing—*continued.*
When Fancy was Truth's willing Page; 154 *Flower Garden* 54
('Tis Fancy guides me willing to be led, 169 *Love lies Bleeding* 10
And long shall be so yet—God willing!" 179 *Waggoner* 3. 96
And Nature here were willing to decay, 202 *Hart-leap* 116
Back flows the willing current of my Song: 217 *Enterprise* 119
Steals from the deck o'er willing waves, 234 *Power of Sound* 135
Some willing neighbour must be found. 248 *P. B.* 1060
Yet ever willing to be reconciled: 253 **O gentle* 12
In willing admiration and respect, 290 *Kilchurn* 29
The Arabian desert shapes a willing road 327 *Ode 1815* 25
Unfolds a willing breast) with infant glee 336 *Danube* 4
The work of Fancy from her willing hands; 338 *Engelberg* 2
Again we wandered, willing to partake 395 *White Doe: Ded.* 39
With the symbolic ring, and willing hands 446 *Ecc. Sonn.* 3. 26. 4
Yet pleased and willing; 486 **Bright Flower* 20
To hope, and makes truth willing to be seen! 505 *Warning* 137
I willing, nay—nay, wishing to be led. 659 *Prelude* 4. 66
And wise men, willing to grow wiser, caught, 695 *Prelude* 7. 516
Such willing note, as, on some errand bound 696 *Prelude* 7. 590
Yet would I at this time with willing heart 720 *Prelude* 10. 152
If willing audience fail not, Nature's self, 732 *Prelude* 11. 350
Willing to work and to be wrought upon, 747 *Prelude* 14. 103
And moved, a willing Page, as he was bid, 782 *Excursion* 2. 687
From Fancy, willing to set off her stores 788 *Excursion* 3. 129
How can you droop, if willing to be upraised? 810 *Excursion* 4. 574
These may he range, if willing to partake 810 *Excursion* 4. 593
Who, with obedience willing and sincere, 827 *Excursion* 5. 351
On a kind parent willing to forget 852 *Excursion* 6. 944
Time, which had thus afforded willing help 860 *Excursion* 7. 204
A willing, nay, at times, a forward part; 882 *Excursion* 8. 529
So wide the difference, a willing mind 895 *Excursion* 9. 715
Is fled; we must depart, willing or not; S.3. 432 **The doubt* 2

Willingly. Most willingly!—Come, let me lead you in, 43 *Bord.* 361
Stoops willingly to animate and spur 268 **DogmaticTeachers* 8
Now ye, who willingly have heard 287 *Ellen Irwin* 49
Receiving, willingly or not, fresh strength 394 **No more* 24
And willingly have laid thee here at last: 491 *Tribute: Dog* 12
Willingly or unwillingly revealed, 657 *Prelude* 3. 564
How willingly we travel, and how far! 691 *Prelude* 7. 278
That to devotion willingly would rise, 704 *Prelude* 8. 338
London, to thee I willingly return. 707 *Prelude* 8. 532
Thou gratulatest, willingly deceived— 734 *Prelude* 11. 468
We parted, nothing willingly; and now 757 *Excursion* 1. 49
Most willingly she put her work aside, 769 *Excursion* 1. 863
I would not willingly, methinks, lose sight 780 *Excursion* 2. 610
Here would not linger, willingly detained? 787 *Excursion* 3. 45
How willingly their aid they would unite 793 *Excursion* 3. 529
And I as willingly did cherish mine, 839 *Excursion* 6. 106
Thrice sank as willingly. For he—whose nerves 843 *Excursion* 6. 335
The Pastor said, "I willingly confine 848 *Excursion* 6. 646

Willingness. With willingness, to whom the general ear 883 *Excursion* 8. 595

Willow. We left the willow shade by the brook-side, 39 *Bord.* 104
To her; for her the willow bend; 187 **Three years* 20
But 'tis a rueful thought that willow bands 325 *Enghien* 12
Age?—a drooping, tottering willow 549 *Hermit's Cell* 1. 31
A little boat tied to a willow tree 637 *Prelude* 1. 358
Back to the covert of the willow tree; 638 *Prelude* 1. 387
And gilded sympathies, the willow wreath, 683 *Prelude* 6. 552

Willow-flowers. Shrouded with willow-flowers and plumy fern. 763 *Excursion* 1. 462

Willow-pannier. One bears a willow-pannier on his back, 882 *Excursion* 8.551

Willows. Long grass and willows form the woven wall, 6 *Ev. Wk.* 240
Into yon row of willows flit, 111 **'Tis said that some* 26
Thick boughs of palm, and willows from the brook, 346 *Processions* 11
Dwarf willows gliding, and by ferny brake. 377 *Duddon* 4. 8
The willows weeping trees, that twinkling hoar, 593 *Ev. Wk. Quarto* 101
And his willows whispered in its light, 629 *Installation* 65

Willow-skirted. Far as the willow-skirted pool, 81 †*Mother's Return* 35

Willow-tree. The cowslip-bank and shady willow-tree; 254 *Complete Angler* 12

Willowy. To willowy hedge-rows, and to emerald meads; 2 *Ev. Wk.* 6
Lo! where through flat Batavia's willowy groves, 19 *Desc. Sk.* 520
Plied steadily between those willowy shores, 271 **Fame tells* 11

Wills. Wills that your peace, your beauty, shall be sold, 283 **Proud were* 6
Of fainting hopes and backward wills, 341 *San Salv.* 26
And sometimes, so relenting justice wills, 817 *Excursion* 4. 1076
To Argos. So wills angry Jupiter, L.2. 121 *Frag. Æneid* 2. 5

Willy's. Let not "Willy's" holy shade L.2. 190 **Queen and* 7

Wilt. (*Partial list.*)
To make it what thou wilt. Thou hast been told, 40 *Bord.* 191
Thou wilt relate the story. Am I neither 49 *Bord.* 648
Thou wilt come with half a call, 160 **Pansies, lilies* 28
Of tender joy wilt thou remember me, 207 *Tintern* 145
Of holier love. Nor wilt thou then forget 207 *Tintern* 155
Thou wilt be eased, and less wilt droop and pine. 561 *Cuck.and Night.* 245

Wily. And thy arch and wily ways, 161 **Pleasures newly* 31
Or as the wily sailors crept 297 *Highland Boy* 191
Loose Idless to forego her wily mask. 382 *Duddon* 24. 14
Than from her wily praise, her peaceful gown, 420 *Ecc. Sonn.* 1. 8. 11
This wily interchange of snaky hues, 657 *Prelude* 3. 563

Wimple. The Queen drew back the wimple that she wore; 465 **Dear to* 2

Win. To win belief, such as my plot requires. 44 *Bord.* 369
Shall by his beauty win his grandsire's heart, 124 *V. and J.* 209
Recovering breath, and pleased to win 174 *Waggoner* 1. 44
And Thou, thy favourite food to win, 215 *Enterprise* 29
And could not win thee, Sleep! by any stealth: 254 **A flock* 10
To Her from heights that Reason may not win. 280 **Oh what* 8
She trained her Burns to win applause 286 *Nith* 41
Did from the Norman win a gallant wreath; 309 *Men of Kent* 10
Must either win, through effort of his own, 312 **When, far* 7
To win me at first sight: and be there joined 319 **Avaunt all* 5
To win a happier hour. 337 *Cath. Cantons* 6
His Father served Jehovah; but how win 365 **The Baptist* 3
Her port she could not win it, 374 *Eg. Maid* 369
A pleased attention I may win 376 **The Minstrels* 75
Her features, could they win us, 386 *Yarrow Rev.* 86
Win rest, and ease, and peace, with bliss that Angels share. 390 *Glencroe* 14
To win some look of love, or gain 407 *White Doe* 1016
To win this bright Bird from her cage, 478 *Somnamb.* 19
Provoking punishment, to win reward; 504 *Warning* 104
To win the palm of gaiety and wit; 528 **Those breathing* 107
Caught at propitious intervals, may win 538 **In desultory* 49
Madly played to win a name: 628 *Installation* 8
That win their way into the heart by stealth, 749 *Prelude* 14. 242
Of Death, and win the vacant and the vain 755 *Recluse* 1. 1. 814
He asked repose; and, failing oft to win 760 *Excursion* 1. 293
Ambition to attempt, and skill to win. 774 *Excursion* 2. 190
The ends of being would secure, and win 791 *Excursion* 3. 349
That the bereft their recompense may win; 865 *Excursion* 7. 523
His Grace and his protection win the prize. L.1. 96 *Juvenal* 3. 34

Winander. Where, undisturbed by winds, Winander sleeps; 2 *Ev. Wk.* 9
Where, bosom'd deep, the shy Winander peeps 591 *Ev. Wk. Quarto* 13
And islands of Winander!—many a time 671 *Prelude* 5. 365

Winandermere. *See* **Windermere.**
From the smooth breast of gay Winandermere 344 *Eclipse* 75

Winander's. Midway on long Winander's eastern shore, 644 *Prelude* 2. 138
Upon Winander's spacious breast, it chanced 664 *Prelude* 4. 373

Wind. *See* **North-wind, Sea-wind, Thaw-wind, West-wind.**
He hears the chiding of the baffled wind, 19 *Desc. Sk.* 489
Yet, if the wind breathe soft, the curling waves, 22 *Yew-tree* 5
And the sharp wind his head he oft hath bared; 25 *Guilt* 47
Forced hard against the wind a thick unwieldy flight. 26 *Guilt* 108
Banished that dismal thought; and now the wind 27 *Guilt* 191
And, whistling, called the wind that hardly curled 31 *Guilt* 356
The darkness overtook me—wind and rain 45 *Bord.* 423
For sight of a warm fire. The wind blows keen; 50 *Bord.* 726
The wind should pipe a little, while we stand 51 *Bord.* 752
When the tempestuous wind first drove us hither, 53 *Bord.* 861
Like mountain oaks rocked by the stormy wind. 57 *Bord.* 1116
Hush!—'tis the feeble and earth-loving wind 60 *Bord.* 1263
My Child—my Child—dark—dark—I faint—this wind— 67 *Bord.* 1657
Trees creaking in the wind (but none are here) 67 *Bord.* 1662
Was, I believed, prime Agent. The wind fell; 68 *Bord.* 1692
It is a dismal night—how the wind howls! 69 *Bord.* 1765
Subsided in a moment, like a wind 69 *Bord.* 1785
And, when the stormy wind blows o'er the peak, 73 *Bord.* 2056
What way does the Wind come? What way does he go? 80 †*Address: Child* 1
As if the wind blew many ways, 82 *Alice Fell* 5
That whistles in the wind. 83 *Lucy Gray* 64
Just half a week after, the wind sallied forth, 86 *Rural Arch.* 13
My playmate thou shalt be; and when the wind is cold 88 *Pet-lamb* 47
For covert from the keen north wind, his hands a hut had made. 91 *Norman Boy* 14
Of caves and trees:—and when the regular wind 95 *Brothers* 49
Fair blew the wished-for wind—the voyage sped; 103 *Artegal* 90
A pipe on which the wind would deftly play; 108 *Indolence* 58
And, when against the wind she strains, 108 *Louisa* 10
O wind, that o'er my head art flying 114 *Ind. Wom.* 45
Wind slowly through the woody dale; 130 *Idiot Boy* 408
Light to the sun and music to the wind; 134 *Michael* 202
He shall possess it, free as is the wind 135 *Michael* 246
And listened to the wind; and, as before, 138 *Michael* 457
Or wind from any quarter, ever come, 149 *M. H.* 12
Shine hot, or wind blows troublesome and strong; 151 **When, to* 89
The wind was roaring, on his knees 155 *Oak and Broom* 6
Through prickly moors or dusty ways must wind; 160 **Up with me* 27
Fresh blows the wind, a western wind, 161 *Binnorie* 12
It fears not rain, nor wind, nor dew; 166 *Danish Boy* 29
If the wind do but stir for his proper delight, 167 *Stray Pleasures* 33
Moved like a vessel in the wind! 175 *Waggoner* 1. 135
Dread pair that, spite of wind and weather, 175 *Waggoner* 1. 178
Sails spread, as if to catch the wind! 179 *Waggoner* 3. 69
Regales them as they wind along; 180 *Waggoner* 4. 4
Come straggling through the wind and rain: 182 *Waggoner* 4. 251
Yet vanish not!—the wind is in the tree, 184 *Night-piece* 18
The music stirs in him like wind through a tree. 189 *Music* 36
The wind, the tempest roaring high, 193 *Ruth* 121
There was a roaring in the wind all night; 195 *Resolution* 1
And every wind that blows; 198 *Thorn* 70
Whatever wind may blow?" 198 *Thorn* 103
The wind blew from the mountain-peak, 199 *Thorn* 156

Window—*continued.*
On the window pane bedropped with rain : 118 †Cottager 13
My father from the window sees him too ; 124 V. and J. 205
It seemed—wall, window, roof and tower— 246 P. B. 858
Even thine, though few thy wants !—Roof, window, door, 250 Admon. 10
Before my window, oftentimes and long 508 F. Stone 5
Darkening the window, ill defends the door 521 Epist. Beaumont 21
Pace between door and window muttering rhyme, 521 Epist. Beaumont 34
Whence the tall window drinks the morning rays ; 535 *When in 24
Nor roof, nor window ;—all seemed wild 543 Russ. Fug. 135
How shut was every window of the place, 562 Troilus 16
Fronting the window of that little cell, 782 Excursion 2. 690
Whose window, somewhat sadly, it adorns. 852 Excursion 6. 938
Laid open through the blazing window :—there 856 Excursion 6. 1178
Windowed. *See* **Many-windowed.**
Window-garlands. And window-garlands. On the public roads, 680 Prelude 6. 353
Window's. And through each window's open fret-work looked 355 Aquap. 157
Forth, through some Gothic window's open space, 678 Prelude 6. 216
Along the window's edge, profusely grew 767 Excursion 1. 718
Windows. *See* **Abbey-windows, Cottage-windows.**
May drive at the windows,—we'll laugh at his din ; 81 †Address: Child 41
When windows flap and chimney roars, 182 Waggoner 4. 246
Beneath my windows, one by one, 182 Waggoner 4. 253
With gradual stealth the lateral windows hide 451 Ecc. Sonn. 3. 44. 2
The cottage windows blazed through twilight gloom, 638 Prelude 1. 427
Before the doors or windows of their cells 656 Prelude 3. 477
That eventide, when under windows bright 725 Prelude 10. 493
Yet were the windows of the low abode 860 Excursion 7. 177
The low wide windows with their mullions old ; 881 Excursion 8. 466
Window-seat. And, in like sort, chair, window-seat, and shelf, 781 Excursion 2. 662
Wind's. Nay, said a voice, soft as the south wind's breath, 515 *Men of 9
His tongue, and give it the wind's freedom ; then, K.8. 227 *I will 99
Winds. *See* **Autumn-winds, Counter-winds, Cross-winds, March-winds, Mountain-winds.**
Where, undisturbed by winds, Winander sleeps ; 2 Ev. Wk. 9
Winds neither road nor path for foot to tread : 14 Desc. Sk. 229
With shrill winds whistling round my lonely way, 21 Desc. Sk. 592
Winds rustling over plots of unripe grain, 25 Guilt 35
Winds met in conflict, each by turns supreme ; 26 Guilt 128
With rotten boughs and leaves, such as the winds 50 Bord. 705
That half a word should blow it to the winds ! 58 Bord. 1144
Only by sufferance of the winds and waves, 69 Bord. 1741
I've heard of fearful winds and darkness that come there ; 88 Pet-lamb 54
His expectations to the fickle winds 95 Brothers 41
Nor can the winds restore his simple gift. 103 Artegal 44
Like branches when strong winds the trees annoy. 108 Indolence 49
When up she winds along the brook 109 Louisa 17
The vacant city slept ; the busy winds, 123 V. and J. 95
Hence had he learned the meaning of all winds, 131 Michael 48
" The winds are now devising work for me ! " 132 Michael 55
Winds our deep Vale, two heath-clad Rocks ascend 151 *Forth from 2
To the bleak winds she sometimes gives 165 Parrot 37
Escaped from boisterous winds that rage without, 184 Airey-force 9
By reason fenced from winds that sigh 190 *Lyre ! though 11
Like sounds of winds and floods ; 192 Ruth 9
That heareth not the loud winds when they call ; 196 Resolution 76
Winds the mute Creature without visible Mate 212 Dion
Where winds and waters cease to strive— 216 Enterprise 72
FLOWER OF THE WINDS, beneath her bosom worn— 221 Triad 117
Dead pause abrupt of midnight winds, 225 Present. 41
But the winds roar, shaking the rooted trees, 230 Clouds 41
Whether among the winds we strive, 236 P. B. 23
Murmuring ; the fall of rivers, winds and seas, 253 *A flock 3
Of Easter winds, unscared, from hut or hall 256 Decay of Piety 6
No tarrying ; where She comes the winds must stir : 258 *With Ships 13
The winds that will be howling at all hours, 259 *The world is 6
To winds abandoned and the prying stars, 272 Ruins 10
Faith had her arch—her arch, when winds blow loud, 282 *In my 8
Speak, passing winds ; ye torrents, with your strong 283 Railway 13
That winds into itself for sweet return. 284 Departure 32
Towers rent, winds combating with woods, 299 Brownie's Cell 63
Virtuous and wise. Winds blow, and waters roll, 306 *Inland, within 10
In conflict ; whose rough winds forgot their jars 336 Danube 10
(While all the ruffling winds are fled— 338 Brientz 7
Nor turns, nor winds, as doth the liquid flood ; 351 Des. Stanzas 83
Extended, clasp the winds, with mutual moan 353 Aquap. 45
They follow their dear Lord ! Time flows—nor winds, 357 Aquap. 315
And the winds roused the Deep with fiercer scourges. 369 Eg. Maid 36
O winds without remorse ! O shore ungrateful ! 372 Eg. Maid 216
Snow-muffled winds, and all is dark, 375 *The Minstrels 38
Gay June would scorn us. But when bleak winds roar 379 Duddon 13. 5
Of winds—though winds were silent—struck a deep 383 Duddon 27. 7
The passing Winds memorial tribute pay ; 383 Duddon 29. 11
Ye winds of ocean, and the midland sea, 387 Scott 13
Leaf-scattering winds; and hoar-frost sprinklings fell 394 *No more 27
Of the sharp winds ;—fair Creatures !—to whom Heaven 395 White Doe: Ded. 47
Of babbling winds as they go by, 405 White Doe 850
In polar ice, propitious winds have made 434 Ecc. Sonn. 2. 23. 5
Tempestuous winds her holy errand crossed : 466 St. Bees 33
Voices, thy winds break forth in prophecy, 471 Tynwald 12

Winds—*continued.*
Pleased when the sullen winds resound the knell 497 Lycoris 35
Be calm as water when the winds are gone, 498 *Enough of climbing 44
That winds through secret wards ; 499 Memory 2
Disputes would then relax, like stormy winds 500 Humanity 51
List, the winds of March are blowing ; 503 Warning 1
From sunshine, clouds, winds, waves, 507 May 54
No winds disturb ; the mirror of whose breast 527 *Those breathing 10
That life—the flowery path that winds by stealth— 528 *Those breathing 91
The winds at night had made a rout ; 536 Goody Blake 50
Driven by strong winds at play among the clouds. 540 *Lady ! a 75
Has witnessed. Oh ! that winds and waves could speak 540 Grace Darl. 19
Send forth a song of triumph. Waves and Winds, 541 Grace Darl. 84
No longer, scattering to the heedless winds 549 *The massy 11
(Winds behind, and rocks before !) 549 Hermit's Cell 1. 30
True, as inexorable winds, or bars 586 Ch. Lamb 105
The Winds come to me from the fields of sleep, 588 Immortality 28
Where winds the road along the secret bay ; 595 Ev. Wk. Quarto 196
Where the slow waggon winds along the bay ; 597 Ev. Wk. Quarto 316
And winds between thine isles the vocal barge. 605 Desc. Sk. Quarto 161
Her shrill winds roaring round my lonely way ; 615 Desc. Sk. Quarto 716
And to the door a neater pathway winds, 615 Desc. Sk. Quarto 727
Hush'd are the winds and silent are the tides ; 618 School Ex. 38
Whence inspiration for a song that winds 634 Prelude 1. 180
Or make their dim abode in distant winds. 646 Prelude 2. 310
And sounding cataracts, ye mists and winds 648 Prelude 2. 425
Ye winds and sounding cataracts ! 'tis yours, 648 Prelude 2. 446
Had voices more than all the winds, with power 667 Prelude 5. 107
Mad at their sports like withered leaves in winds ; 672 Prelude 5. 416
Attends the motions of the viewless winds, 674 Prelude 5. 596
A pensive sky, sad days, and piping winds, 677 Prelude 6. 174
Upon the stretch, when winds are blowing fair : 682 Prelude 6. 499
Winds thwarting winds, bewildered and forlorn, 684 Prelude 6. 628
Associates, and, unscared by blustering winds, 687 Prelude 7. 30
Still as a sheltered place when winds blow loud ! 689 Prelude 7. 171
While winds are eddying round her, among straws 693 Prelude 7. 440
He winds away his never-ending horn ; 694 Prelude 7. 507
As the winds fret within the Æolian cave, 695 Prelude 7. 533
Ungovernable, and your terrifying winds, 702 Prelude 8. 220
Within the breast, as ever-varying winds 717 Prelude 9. 545
From the four quarters of the winds to do 720 Prelude 10. 140
As Lear reproached the winds—I could almost 725 Prelude 10. 507
Rejoiced through early youth, before the winds 735 Prelude 12. 95
Full often wished he that the winds might rage 760 Excursion 1. 287
My best companions now the driving winds, 766 Excursion 1. 702
Upward it winds, as if, in summer heats, 786 Excursion 3. 23
Fearless of winds and waves. Three several stones 787 Excursion 3. 55
That our existence winds her stately course 790 Excursion 3. 258
—' Blow winds of autumn !—let your chilling breath 790 Excursion 3. 307
" Calm as a frozen lake when ruthless winds 795 Excursion 3. 650
To One by storms annoyed and adverse winds ; 798 Excursion 3. 866
As he desires that they should be, whom winds 799 Excursion 3. 887
And to the winds and mother elements, 811 Excursion 4. 677
When winds are blowing strong. The traveller slaked 814 Excursion 4. 871
Winds far in reaches hidden from our sight, 824 Excursion 5. 123
To the four quarters of the winds, proclaims. 837 Excursion 5. 993
Winds an inscriptive legend."—At these words 846 Excursion 6. 512
Lurks in safe shelter from the winds of March, 850 Excursion 6. 788
Winds pipe through fading woods; but those blithe notes 851 Excursion 6. 859
Frequented, and beset with howling winds. 859 Excursion 7. 144
Murmured the labouring bee. When stormy winds 863 Excursion 7. 409
Tall ash-tree, sown by winds, by vapours nursed, 866 Excursion 7. 596
The winds of March, smiting insidiously, 867 Excursion 7. 683
A mightier river, winds from realm to realm ; 869 Excursion 7. 790
That gave them nourishment. When frosty winds 881 Excursion 8. 445
Though aided by wild winds, the groans and shrieks 894 Excursion 9. 696
The rains at length have ceas'd, the winds are still'd, S.3. 425 *The rains 1
And hear the voices of the winds and flowers. K.8. 224 *I will 3
And make a stormy harbour for the winds. K.8. 225 *I will 34
That sail on winds, of breezes that delight K.8. 237 Recluse 1. 1. 26
Made visible, amid a noise of winds K.8. 245 Recluse 1. 1. 329
Of winds, this deep Vale,—as it doth in part K.8. 247 Recluse 1. 1. 375
The gift of winds, and whom the winds again K.8. 251 Recluse 1. 1. 541
Windsor's. From the collegiate pomps on Windsor's height 430 Ecc. Sonn. 2. 6. 4
Wind-swept. Of wind-swept corn that wide around us rolled 334 *A wingèd 7
Such are thoughts !—A wind-swept meadow 550 Hermit's Cell 3. 5
Windy. On windy days, in one of those stray brooks, 99 Brothers 260
If on windy days the Raven 166 Wand. Jew 17
Wine. Thou sing'st as if the God of wine 186 *O Nightingale 5
Down the long street, rich goblets filled with wine 213 Dion 32
Huge goblets are brought forth ; they crown the wine ; 625 Æneid 98
From Belus, filled it to the brim with wine ; 625 Æneid 106
Then sipp'd the bowl whence she the wine had pour'd 625 Æneid 117
Decanters, glasses, and the blood-red wine. 644 Prelude 2. 144
With invitations, suppers, wine and fruit, 649 Prelude 3. 43
Never excited by the fumes of wine 653 Prelude 3. 301
More bright than madness or the dreams of wine ; 674 Prelude 5. 568
Brought from the cupboard wine and stouter cheer, 785 Excursion 2. 899
Wing. Where hum on busier wing her happy bees ; 21 Desc. Sk. 607
The startled bird quivered upon the wing. 74 Bord. 2105
Now cooling, with his passing wing, 144 *Driven in 39

Wing—*continued.*
In power of wing and never-wearied voice. 153 *Morn. Ex.* 42
Thus spake the moral Muse—her wing 154 *Flower Garden* 49
Soaring on undaunted wing, 163 *Hint* 26
In colour like a raven's wing ; 166 *Danish Boy* 28
He hath kenned them taking wing : 205 *Brougham* 130
And sometimes with ambitious wing that soars 218 *Recluse* I. I. 207
Observe each wing !—a tiny van ! 227 *Vernal Ode* 114
Through India's spicy regions wing their way, 231 **ThegentlestPoet* 12
"The dragon's wing, the magic ring, 238 *P. B.* 136
And spreads in steadfast peace her brooding wing. 254 *Wild Duck's Nest* 8
Where even the motion of an Angel's wing 259 **A volant* 12
Of sad mortality's earth-sullying wing, 263 **How clear* 9
And nod their helmets, smitten by the wing 265 **When haughty* 7
So timely Grace the immortal wing may heal, 270 **If these* 13
To rouse the dawn, soft gales shall speed thy wing, 274 **Not the* 13
With flapping wing for entrance. What a shriek 274 **Wait, prithee* 9
Fly upon swiftest wing round field and height, 294 **Fly, some* 3
The lion's sinews, or the eagle's wing ; 311 **Who rises* 48
That power, that spirit, whether on the wing 321 **The power* 8
And the dire flapping of his hoary wing ! 322 **Ye Storms* 8
Mounts on rapt wing, and with a moment's flight 336 *Danube* 7
With stronger wing, more clearly to discern 358 **Is this* 12
Was on the wing ; stooping, he struck with awe 388 *Eagles* 5
Of speediest wing, should he appear. 411 *White Doe* 1376
His wing who could seem lovelier to man's eye 421 *Ecc. Sonn.* 1. 13. 6
Here did it enter ; there, on hasty wing, 422 *Ecc. Sonn.* 1. 16. 5
Dropped from an Angel's wing. With moistened eye 441 *Ecc. Sonn.* 3. 5. 4
I, of his bold wing floating on the gale, 464 *Derwent* 3
Sighed on the wing as her foot pressed the strand, 465 **Dear to* 10
While on the wing the Urchin played, 497 *Lycoris* 7
Brushed by the owlet's wing ; 497 *Lycoris* 20
Yet on presumptuous wing as far would fly 513 *Newspaper* 12
Have lent his wing, my Brother dear, 580 *John Words.* 7
Where Silence, on her night of wing, o'er-broods 602 *Desc. Sk. Quarto* 9
The chamois' sinews, and the eagle's wing : 646 *Prelude* 2. 275
Like angels stopped upon the wing by sound 747 *Prelude* 14. 98
A pair of falcons wheeling on the wing, 786 *Excursion* 3. 2
Upborne, at evening, on replenished wing, 807 *Excursion* 4. 398
Did I look forth in vain, nor on the wing K.8. 243 *Recluse* 1.1.257

Winged. Buzz, buzz, ye black and winged free-booters ; 73 *Bord.* 2022
—Waft her to glory, wingèd Powers, 112 **How rich* 3
Have you observed a tuft of wingèd seed 123 *V. and J.* 136
They guard, with wingèd baby-faces. 144 **Driven in* 57
And a God leads him, wingèd Mercury ! 209 *Laod.* 18
Thee wingèd Fancy took, and nursed 215 *Enterprise* 24
Army of Clouds ! ye wingèd Host in troops 229 *Clouds* 1
Thy genius forward like a wingèd steed. 260 **From the dark* 4
A wingèd Goddess—clothed in vesture wrought 334 **A wingèd* 1
Upon this wingèd Shape so fair 369 *Eg. Maid* 13
Not one of all those wingèd powers is seen, 454 *Sea-side* 20
While thou wert chasing the winged butterfly 465 **Thou look'st* 11
Consume with zeal, in wingèd ecstasies 467 *St. Bees* 88
Built for the air, or wingèd Hippogriff ? 471 **Arran ! a* 5
To trouble hours that winged their way, 478 *Somnamb.* 34
By wingèd Love inscribed, to assuage 499 **Departing summer* 44
Ample for a wingèd hope, 503 **Like a* 65
Nought equals when the hours are winged with crime) 505 *Warning* 152
The ethereal eyesight, cramp the wingèd mind ! 529 **Those breathing* 136
Thro' wastes, of Spirits wing'd the solemn home, 609 *Desc.Sk.Quarto* 371
These cares, and thus she speaks to winged Love : 624 *Æneid* 10
With wingèd Messengers ; who daily brought 811 *Excursion* 4. 639
Each also crowned with wingèd heads—a pair 824 *Excursion* 5. 152
Genii, and winged Angels that are Lords K.8. 237 *Recluse* 1.1. 34

Wingless. *Her* wingless flutterings, 170 *Rural Ill.* 26

Wings. While, flapped with conscious pride, resound his wings ! 5 *Ev. Wk.* 155
His neck, a varying arch, between his towering wings : 6 *Ev. Wk.* 219
Rolled wantonly between their slippery wings, 6 *Ev. Wk.* 247
Brood o'er the long-parched lands with Nile-like wings ! 22 *Desc. Sk.* 658
With such a weight upon his wings as now ; 65 *Bord.* 1532
The dust from off its wings. 79 **Stay near* 18
Me had the dream equipped with wings, so I took him in my arms, 92 *Poet's Dream* 17
On wings from broad and steadfast poise let loose by this reply, 92 *Poet's Dream* 29
The wings they did not flag ; the Child, though grave, was not deprest. 92 *Poet's Dream* 32
Such wings as, when our Saviour calls, shall bear us up to heaven." 93 *Poet's Dream* 68
Then, on the wide-spread wings 104 *Artegal* 143
Here rest your wings when they are weary ; 106 **I've watched* 12
Alas ! the fowls of heaven have wings, 117 *Affl. Marg.* 43
Then up she springs as if on wings ; 129 *Idiot Boy* 307
Or hast thou put off wings which thou in heaven dost wear ? 140 *Arm. Lady* 71
That was its wings, its chariot, and its horse, 148 **A narrow* 24
Wings lovely as his own. 156 *Oak and Broom* 84
There ! where the flutter of his wings 159 *Green Linnet* 29
Had I now the wings of a Faery, 159 **Up with me* 10
His beautiful wings in crimson are drest, 163 **Art thou the* 35
When the wings of genius rise, 163 *Hint* 2
Made vocal by their brushing wings, 164 *Needlecase* 30
That with stir of feet and wings 171 *Kitten* 46
Wings let them have, and they might flit 191 *Beggars* 33
Give her wings that she may fly, 204 *Brougham* 57

Wings—*continued.*
Or, while the wings aspire, are heart and eye 209 **Ethereal minstrel* 3
Those quivering wings composed, that music still ! 209 **Ethereal minstrel* 6
An arch thrown back between luxuriant wings 212 *Dion*
Ascending, they approach—I hear their wings 218 *Recluse* 1. 1. 219
Of history, Glory claps her wings, 224 **'Tis gone* 14
Beneath the shadow of his purple wings 226 *Vernal Ode* 21
On the swift wings of day and night, 228 *Devot. Incit.* 57
Admit no bondage and my words have wings. 230 *Clouds* 59
Genius of Raphael ! if thy wings 231 *Jew. Fam.* 1
Fanned by the plausive wings of Love. 233 *Power of Sound* 80
Though the bold wings of Poesy affect 270 **Though the bold* 1
Who gives his Angels wings to speed through air, 273 **Wild Redbreast* 11
More urgent called, will stretch his wings at large, 273 **While Anna's* 7
Power in my breast, wings growing in my mind, 284 *Departure* 14
Folds up his wings ? 286 *Nith* 54
How sweet to rest her wide-spread wings beneath ! 311 **Who rises* 4
Hath failed ; and now, ye Powers ! whose gorgeous wings 335 *Cologne* 6
Hung round its top, on wings that changed their hues at will. 338 *Engelberg* 9
No vapour stretched its wings ; no cloud 343 *Eclipse* 19
Each narrowing above each ;—the wings, 343 *Eclipse* 50
Blithe as the lark on sun-gilt wings 348 **Lulled by* 57
Recoiled—and wings alone could travel—there 350 *Des. Stanzas* 14
In gloom on wings with confidence outspread 354 *Aquap.* 87
And that soft rustling of invisible wings 371 *Eg. Maid* 149
The Swans, in triumph clap their wings ; 374 *Eg. Maid* 321
Had sunk to rest with folded wings : 375 **The Minstrels* 8
The struggle, clap their wings for victory ! 378 *Duddon* 10. 14
Atween his downy wings be furnished, there 382 *Duddon* 25. 6
The Hermit saw the Angel spread his wings 393 **The Lovers* 3
Now toiling, wafted now on wings of prayer— 396 **Action is* 10
A Spirit, with his angelic wings, 399 *White Doe* 331
Whose voice we heard, whose hand and wings 416 *White Doe* 1836
And in our caverns smooth thy ruffled wings !" 431 *Ecc. Sonn.* 2. 13. 4
Whose heart still flutters, though his wings forbear 440 *Ecc. Sonn.* 2. 45. 5
There, should vain thoughts outspread their wings and fly 445 *Ecc. Sonn.* 3. 20. 9
(After a steady flight on home-bound wings, 455 *Rydal Mere* 9
On thy wings opened wide for smoothest flight, 456 **The leaves* 15
—Wings at my shoulders seem to play ; 458 **Had this* 49
An Eagle with stretched wings, but beamless eye— 472 **The captive* 7
Wings have we,—and as far as we can go 488 *Pers. Talk* 29
To speed their errand by the wings they wore. 500 *Humanity* 40
Thy feathered Lieges bill and wings 506 **While from* 25
On wings that fear no glance of God's pure sight, 512 **Who rashly* 38
Their wings to guard the unconscious Innocent— 518 *Pun. Death* 6. 5
Her flight by vocal wings ; 526 **The soaring* 4
In wings of Cherubim, 526 **The soaring* 36
From his smoothly gliding wings. 530 *Gleaner* 16
As on the wings of years. 545 *Russ. Fug.* 328
Scattering this far-fetched moisture from my wings, 582 *Invoc. Earth* 23
His bridling neck between his tow'ring wings ; 595 *Ev. Wk. Quarto* 202
To brood the nations o'er with Nile-like wings ; 617 *Desc.Sk.Quarto* 805
Clapp'd her strong wings, and sought the cheerful isle, 618 *School Ex.* 46
To teach, on rapid wings, the curious soul 619 *School Ex.* 73
Puts off his wings, and walks, with proud delight, 624 *Æneid* 45
If e'er, on wings which active fancy gave, 630 [?] **O Moon* 5
Swift Rhone ! thou wert the *wings* on which we cut 680 *Prelude* 6. 378
But oh ! if Past and Future be the wings 681 *Prelude* 6. 448
And she shall lodge us, wafted on her wings, 697 *Prelude* 7. 683
A toy that mimics with revolving wings 723 *Prelude* 10. 368
And spread abroad the wings of Liberty, 731 *Prelude* 11. 253
On wings that navigate cerulean skies. 735 *Prelude* 12. 37
Of earth-born passions, on the wings of praise 748 *Prelude* 14. 186
As if on wings, and saw beneath me stretched 751 *Prelude* 14. 380
On wings, angelic Spirits ! I could muse 790 *Excursion* 3. 300
Of disencumbering thus her fretful wings. 798 *Excursion* 3. 820
The Zephyrs fanning, as they passed, their wings, 814 *Excursion* 4. 877
His natural wings !—To friendship let him turn 817 *Excursion* 4. 1085
For future states of being ; and the wings 826 *Excursion* 5. 245
That all beneath us by the wings are covered 836 *Excursion* 5. 924
With correspondent wings the abyss of air. 891 *Excursion* 9. 494
And beat the passive water with their wings. K.8. 251 *Recluse* 1.1.551

Wings'. Close by her mantling wings' embraces prest. 6 *Ev. Wk.* 231

Wink. Shouldst be my Country's emblem ; and shouldst wink, 303 **Fair Star* 7
And then for cold not sleep a wink. 536 *Goody Blake* 48

Winning. Of aspect winning and serene ; 299 *Brownie's Cell* 76
Of female patience winning firm repose ; 395 *White Doe: Ded.* 50
In winning words, since through her gentiless, 562 *Cuck.and Night.* 300
For calmer pleasures, when the winning forms 642 *Prelude* 2. 50
A winning power, beyond all other power. 654 *Prelude* 3. 363
A sober hour, not winning or serene, 660 *Prelude* 4. 144
Triumphant, winning from the invaded heavens 734 *Prelude* 11. 455
The admiration winning of the crowd ; 797 *Excursion* 3. 766
Winning no recompense but deadly hate 870 *Excursion* 7. 830
Holy and blest ? and where the winning grace 878 *Excursion* 8. 249

Winningly. Winningly meek or venerably calm, 783 *Excursion* 2. 753
More winningly reserved ! If ye enquire 842 *Excursion* 6. 298

Winnow. From men who winnow charity from Faith K.8. 325 [?] **The vestal* 10

Wins. Wins on the shade, the shade upon the light. 7 *Ev. Wk.* 298
The unlettered ploughboy pities when he wins 275 **While poring* 13
See, where his difficult way that Old Man wins 366 *Lombardy* 1
From *silent* admiration wins relief. 584 **With copious* 45
Wins from the courteous ; I, who had been else 712 *Prelude* 9. 193
Of craggy fountain ; what he hopes for wins, 788 *Excursion* 3. 167
Wins help from something greater than herself— S.3. 435 **The doubt* 113

Wont—*continued.*
A treatise of Geometry, he wont, ... 677 *Prelude* 6. 146
As is their wont, a pittance from strict time, . . 702 *Prelude* 8. 239
Enrapt; but brightest things are wont to draw . 726 *Prelude* 10. 528
Which they were wont to be. Through kindred scenes, ... 733 *Prelude* 11. 413
Wonted. Enter, and each the wonted task resumes 877 *Excursion* 8. 182
Woo. Some thought he was a lover, and did woo: 108 *Indolence* 32
I thine—the conscience-stricken must not woo . 124 *V. and J.* 160
Wood. *See* **Box-wood, Chestnut-wood, Greenwood, Wild-wood.**
Through bare grey dell, high wood, and pastoral cove; . . . . 2 *Ev. Wk.* 2
Of bright obscurity, hill, lawn, and wood; . . 4 *Ev. Wk.* 101
Of charcoal-smoke, that, o'er the fallen wood, . 9 *Ev. Wk.* 363
The leafy wood, or sleeps in quiet lakes. . . 10 *Desc. Sk.* 8
Beholds the unwearied sweep of wood that scales 12 *Desc. Sk.* 109
But once I pierced the mazes of a wood . . . 13 *Desc. Sk.* 145
In some dense wood or gulf of snow profound, . 16 *Desc. Sk.* 314
In wood or wilderness, in camp or town, . . . 29 *Guilt* 300
Down a thick wood, they dropt into the vale; . 34 *Guilt* 524
And *he* had done the deed in the dark wood— . 35 *Guilt* 607
This wood is rich in plants and curious simples. . 38 *Bord.* 44
I have been waiting in the wood hard by . . . 43 *Bord.* 355
We'll stroll into the wood; lean on my arm. . . 43 *Bord.* 363
In a deep wood remote from any town. . . . 50 *Bord.* 698
Who at full speed swept by us where the wood . 50 *Bord.* 735
Through wood, and through vale; and o'er rocky height, ... 80 †*Address: Child* 3
And thence they saw the bridge of wood, . . . 83 *Lucy Gray* 39
The thrush is busy in the wood, ... 84 *Shepherd-boys* 25
A wood is felled:—and then for our own homes! 97 *Brothers* 157
And Betty's husband's at the wood, ... 126 *Idiot Boy* 27
Or bringing fagots from the wood. . . . . . 126 *Idiot Boy* 36
And carried Johnny to the wood. . . . . . 129 *Idiot Boy* 306
I'll to the wood."—The word scarce said, . . . 130 *Idiot Boy* 424
And to the wood at length is come; . . . . 130 *Idiot Boy* 428
We'll find thy father in the wood. . . . . . 145 *Her Eyes* 98
Rushed o'er the wood with startling sound; . . 154 **A whirl-blast* 2
On the moor, and in the wood, ... 160 **Pansies, lilies* 45
So painfully in the wood? . . . . 162 **Art thou the* 23
Nor herd-boy of the wood. . . . . 165 *Danish Boy* 26
Or lofty wood, shower-proof. . . . . . . 167 *Pilgrim's Dream* 8
Others slunk to moor and wood, ... 171 *Kitten* 57
Thence look thou forth o'er wood and lawn . . 180 *Waggoner* 4. 38
Crag, lawn, and wood—with rosy light. . . . 182 *Waggoner* 4. 243
Tow'rd some far-distant wood, a Figure quaint, . 185 *Nutting* 8
At the corner of Wood Street, when daylight appears, ... 187 *Poor Susan* 1
She from her dwelling in the wood . . . . 194 *Ruth* 236
Upon a long grey staff of shaven wood: . . . . 196 *Resolution* 72
"You see these lifeless stumps of aspen wood— . 202 *Hart-leap* 125
Of sportive wood run wild: these pastoral farms, 206 *Tintern* 16
The mountain, and the deep and gloomy wood, . 206 *Tintern* 78
Leave to the nightingale her shady wood; . . 209 **Ethereal minstrel* 7
Vanish inverted hill, and shadowy wood, . . . 212 *Dion*
Nor leaf-crowned Dryad from a pathless wood, . 220 *Triad* 10
In the green wood and hollow dell; . . . . 239 *P. B.* 242
To a thick wood he soon is brought . . . . 240 *P. B.* 341
Sky-ward he looks—to rock and wood— . . . 242 *P. B.* 548
This cry—that rings along the wood, ... 243 *P. B.* 628
The like on heath, in lonely wood; . . . . . 245 *P. B.* 827
Ere they were lost within the shady wood; . . . 252 *Picture* 6
The wayward brain, to saunter through a wood! 260 **How sweet* 2
When, haply under shade of that same wood, . 271 **Fame tells* 9
While we have wandered over wood and wild— . 294 **Fly, some* 13
The dullest leaf in this thick wood . . . . 299 *Cora Linn* 2
Thundering adown a rocky wood. . . . . . 300 *Bran* 22
Not there; but in dark wood and rocky cave, . 314 **Not 'mid* 5
In dreary billows, wood, and meagre cot, . . . 334 **A wingèd* 8
Her beauty dazzles the thick wood; . . . . 344 **How blest* 40
Vallombrosa! I longed in thy shadiest wood . . 345 *Stanzas: Simplon* 1
Pride of two nations, wood and lake and plains, . 353 *Aquap.* 42
"Vallombrosa—I longed in thy shadiest wood . 364 *Vallomb.* 1
Amid a fertile region green with wood . . . . 392 *Daniel* 1
Amid the trees of some thick wood, ... 399 *White Doe* 276
Through park, or chase, or savage wood. . . . 407 *White Doe* 998
Among the ruins of a wood, ... 413 *White Doe* 1585
They tarried in the wood together. . . . . . 414 *White Doe* 1683
O'er heaps of slain;—from Cambrian wood and moss . . . . 421 *Ecc. Sonn.* 1. 10. 10
Their Gods of wood and stone; and, at the sound 436 *Ecc. Sonn.* 2. 33. 5
Of dread Jehovah; then should wood and waste 440 *Ecc. Sonn.* 2. 46. 6
For England's shame, O Sister Realm! from wood, 442 *Ecc. Sonn.* 3. 7. 7
Where wood or stream by thee was never greeted. 455 *Rydal Mere* 16
That shines aloft, while through the wood . . 479 *Somnamb.* 88
One impulse from a vernal wood . . . . . 481 *Tables Turned* 21
A stump of rotten wood. . . . . 484 *Simon Lee* 76
And through the wood we went; . . . . . 488 *Fountain* 68
We may find pleasure: wilderness and wood, . 488 *Pers. Talk* 30
If, mixed with what appeared of rock, lawn, wood, 524 *Epist. Beaumont* 187
Its brightest splendour round a leafy wood; . . 532 **Once I* 16
To cheerful intercourse with wood and field, . . 538 **In desultory* 40
Or berries of the wood; . . . . 542 *Russ. Fug.* 20
And where the wood was clear. . . . . . . 544 *Russ. Fug.* 264
But straightway to a wood that was hard by, . 557 *Cuck.and Night.* 58
Echoing thorough all the green wood wide. . . 558 *Cuck.andNight.*100
Thou Woodman, in the distant wood! . . . 577 **I come* 36
That, o'er the ruins of the fallen wood, . . . 599 *Ev. Wk. Quarto* 431
Th' unwearied sweep of wood thy cliffs that scales, 604 *Desc.Sk.Quarto* 122

Wood—*continued.*
The redbreast peace had bury'd it in wood, . . 605 *Desc.Sk.Quarto* 169
—Fierce comes the river down; the crashing wood 606 *Desc.Sk.Quarto* 211
Winding it's dark-green wood and emerald glade, 607 *Desc.Sk.Quarto* 269
Rang loud through the meadow and wood. . . 620 *Convict* 4
What God in whispers from the wood . . . . 626 †*Cento* 5
Thus musing, in a wood I sate me down . . . 661 *Prelude* 4. 177
In silence through a wood gloomy and still. . . 665 *Prelude* 4. 447
A frame locked up in wood and stone, doth still, . 679 *Prelude* 6. 292
By scale exact, in model, wood or clay, . . . 691 *Prelude* 7. 249
Inglorious, buried in the dusky wood: . . . . 705 *Prelude* 8. 416
Aghast and prayerless. Into a deep wood . . 718 *Prelude* 9. 578
Defenceless as a wood where tigers roam. . . . 719 *Prelude* 10. 93
In wood or echoing cave, for discipline . . . 734 *Prelude* 11. 458
The noise of wood and water, and the mist . . 739 *Prelude* 12. 321
And travelled through the wood, with no one near 758 *Excursion* 1. 130
Through many a wood and many an open ground, 766 *Excursion* 1. 699
Or with some merry outlaws of the wood; . . 771 *Excursion* 2. 10
Through wood or open field, the harmless Man . 788 *Excursion* 3. 171
Regions of wood and wide savannah, vast . . 799 *Excursion* 3. 938
By flowing stream, through wood, or craggy wild, 803 *Excursion* 4. 105
Like leafless underboughs, in some thick wood, . 824 *Excursion* 5. 148
Fair Rosamond, and the Children of the Wood, . 858 *Excursion* 7. 90
His old employments, goes to field or wood, . . 878 *Excursion* 8. 277
Of some thick wood, her place of covert, cleaves . 891 *Excursion* 9. 493
Of meadow-flowers into a tuft of wood, . . . K.8. 237*Recluse* 1.1. 42
Woodbine. Or woodbine wreaths, a smoother path is wound; . . . . 21 *Desc. Sk.* 605
In woodbine bower or birchen grove, ... 215 *Kirkstone* 71
That mossy slope, o'er which the woodbine throws 221 *Triad* 78
The woodbine so, with spiral grace, and breathes 367 *Trajan* 21
This Nook—with woodbine hung and straggling weed, ... 382 *Duddon* 24. 5
Hung with late-flowering woodbine, spread . . 407 *White Doe* 1023
(While from the pendent woodbine came . . 407 *White Doe* 1028
The casement shade more luscious woodbine binds, 615 *Desc.Sk.Quarto* 726
Woodbines. And woodbines were hanging above. . 484 **A plague* 30
Wood-boy. I see a blooming Wood-boy there, . . 243 *P. B.* 631
Wood-built. By naked huts, wood-built, and sown like tents . . . . 683 *Prelude* 6. 521
Woodcocks. Was heard, or woodcocks roamed the moonlight hill. . . . . 2 *Ev. Wk.* 20
Or the first woodcocks roam'd the moonlight hills. 592 *Ev. Wk. Quarto* 26
To range the open heights where woodcocks run . 636 *Prelude* 1. 311
Wood-cottages. Here, on the brown wood-cottages they sleep, ... 14 *Desc. Sk.* 214
Wood-crowned. The wood-crowned cliffs that o'er the lake recline; . . . . 15 *Desc. Sk.* 278
Wooden. To the small wooden isle where, their work to beguile, ... 166 *Stray Pleasures* 10
As aught by wooden images performed . . . 657 *Prelude* 3. 571
Profuse in garniture of wooden cuts . . . . 759 *Excursion* 1. 181
The useless fragment of a wooden bowl, . . . 763 *Excursion* 1. 493
The wooden stools for everlasting use, ... 880 *Excursion* 8. 406
Wood-hut. To reach a small wood-hut hung boldly on the steep. . . . . 15 *Desc. Sk.* 237
And hangs his small wood-hut upon the steeps. . 607 *Desc.Sk.Quarto* 294
Wood-huts. On the low brown wood-huts delighted sleep . . . . 607 *Desc.Sk.Quarto* 275
Woodland. Her rocky sheepwalks, and her woodland bounds; . . . . 2 *Ev. Wk.* 8
She had a rustic, woodland air, ... 83 *We are Seven* 9
Had been a wild and woodland rover; . . . . 238 *P. B.* 207
The owl of evening and the woodland fox . . 433 *Ecc. Sonn.* 2. 21. 9
Come, hear the woodland linnet, ... 481 *Tables Turned* 10
Put on with speed your woodland dress; . . . 483 *Sister* 14
With speed put on your woodland dress; . . . 483 *Sister* 38
Strawberries from lane or woodland, offering wild 525 *Epist. Beaumont* 244
The pleasant melody of woodland birds. . . . 569 *Cumb. Beg.* 185
And woodland pleasures,—the resounding horn, . 638 *Prelude* 1. 436
Unthought of: in their woodland beds the flowers 670 *Prelude* 5. 339
Of happy instinct which the woodland bird . . 835 *Excursion* 5. 845
That is to come, the throng of woodland flowers, K.8.252*Recluse*1.1.590
Woodland's. His flock, along the woodland's edge with relics sprinkled o'er . . . . 91 *Norman Boy* 9
Woodlands. Crags, woodlands, waterfalls, and rills; 180 *Waggoner* 4. 53
Far as the woodlands—with the trill to blend . 235 *Power of Sound* 165
Woodlark. And the soft woodlark here did never chant . . . . 818 *Excursion* 4. 1168
Woodman. Calls forth the woodman from his desert cell, ... 12 *Desc. Sk.* 124
A woodman in the distant vale; . . . . . . 126 *Idiot Boy* 29
The Quantock woodman hears. . . . . . . 195 *Ruth* 246
The Woodman knew, for such the craft . . . 543 *Russ. Fug.* 105
She sought in vain, the Woodman smiled; . . 543 *Russ. Fug.* 133
Thou Woodman, in the distant wood! . . . 577 **I come* 36
Calling the woodman from his desert cell, . . . 604 *Desc.Sk.Quarto* 143
I saw the quiet woodman in the woods, . . . 661 *Prelude* 4. 215
If, when the woodman languished with disease . 705 *Prelude* 8. 438
Woodman's. There was no road, nor any woodman's path; . . . . 149 *M. H.* 2
No woodman's hut, no cottage light— . . . . 240 *P. B.* 389
Th' unwearied glance of woodman's echo'd stroke; 593 *Ev. Wk.Quarto* 107
Wood-nymph. Of panting Wood-nymph, wearied with the chase. . . . . 219 *Haunted Tree* 15
From Wood-nymph of Diana's throng? . . . 344 **How blest* 34
Wood-nymph's. Running among the clouds a Wood-nymph's race! . . . . 266 **With how* 4
Wood's. *See* **Pine-wood's.**
Near the wood's edge—rest there to-night, I pray you: 67 *Bord.* 1648

Woods. Even here, amid the sweep of endless woods, 5 *Ev. Wk.* 142
With towers and woods, a "prospect all on fire ;" 5 *Ev. Wk.* 175
O'er all its vanished dells, and lawns, and woods ; 8 *Ev. Wk.* 332
And gives, where woods the chequered upland strew, 8 *Ev. Wk.* 337
How fair its lawns and sheltering woods appear ! 8 *Ev. Wk.* 349
Or yell, in the deep woods, of lonely hound. 9 *Ev. Wk.* 378
Whence lutes and voices down the enchanted woods 12 *Desc. Sk.* 117
'Mid smoking woods gleams hid from morning's ray 12 *Desc. Sk.* 120
Where, 'mid dim towers and woods, her waters gleam. 13 *Desc. Sk.* 157
There, safely guarded by the woods behind, 19 *Desc. Sk.* 488
With rocks and gloomy woods her fertile fields : 20 *Desc. Sk.* 570
And you mistake the cause : you hear the woods 40 *Bord.* 146
Meanwhile the storm fell heavy on the woods ; 50 *Bord.* 707
And followed on, through woods of gloomy cedar, 70 *Bord.* 1804
"For here are woods, hills smooth and warm : 86 *Anecdote* 41
Among the woods and fields, and that the rocks, 96 *Brothers* 38
But oft the woods renewed their green, 113 *Lament* 68
Enriched the earth, or Faery of the woods 124 *V. and J.* 207
From half-stripped woods and pastures bare, 143 **Driven in* 2
She talked and sung the woods among, 144 *Her Eyes* 9
Now laugh and be gay, to the woods away ! 145 *Her Eyes* 99
Among the woods and fields, we love you well, 147 *Joanna* 11
And a small bed of water in the woods. 149 *M. H.* 7
Among the woods and hills. 155 *Oak and Broom* 4
Through woods and on the green ; 184 **O blithe* 22
Touch—for there is a spirit in the woods. 186 *Nutting* 56
An infant of the woods. 192 *Ruth* 12
My helpmate in the woods to be, 193 *Ruth* 92
His name in the wild woods. 193 *Ruth* 114
The birds are singing in the distant woods ; 195 *Resolution* 4
I heard the woods and distant waters roar ; 195 *Resolution* 17
And them who dwell among the woods of Ure !" 202 *Hart-leap* 76
His daily teachers had been woods and rills, 205 *Brougham* 162
Of vagrant dwellers in the houseless woods, 206 *Tintern* 20
O sylvan Wye ! thou wanderer thro' the woods, 206 *Tintern* 56
A lover of the meadows and the woods, 207 *Tintern* 103
Of absence, these steep woods and lofty cliffs, 207 *Tintern* 157
Who, for thy service trained in lonely woods, 216 *Enterprise* 92
Lo ! the dwindled woods and meadows ; 217 **Inmate of* 9
To rocks, fields, woods. Nor doth our human sense 219 *Haunted Tree* 5
(Above the general roar of woods and crags) 219 *Haunted Tree* 23
So, truant in waste woods, the blithe Euphrosyne ! 221 *Triad* 106
With annual verdure, and revive the woods, 230 *Clouds* 68
The woods, my Friends, are round you roaring, 236 *P. B.* 11
There's nothing to be seen but woods, 240 *P. B.* 391
All, all is silent—rocks and woods, 241 *P. B.* 411
His Father through the lonesome woods, 249 *P. B.* 1102
From the dread chasm, woods climbing above woods, 272 *Devil's Bridge* 10
Whose mountains, torrents, lake, and woods, unite 290 *Kilchurn* 27
Between the woods and lofty rocks ; 295 *Highland Boy* 68
Towers rent, winds combating with woods, 299 *Brownie's Cell* 63
Hills, torrents, woods, embodied to bemock 314 *Hofer* 13
Cliffs, woods and caves, her viewless steps resound 315 **Advance—come* 8
Is it by rocks and woods that man prevails ? 315 **And is it* 4
Through tangled woods, impending rocks between ; 382 *Duddon* 26. 3
And if, as Yarrow, through the woods 386 *Yarrow Rev.* 33
The river glides, the woods before me wave ; 392 *Bothwell* 6
"Even she will to her peaceful woods 402 *White Doe* 560
And still, 'mid yon thick woods, the primal truth 419 *Ecc. Sonn.* 1. 4. 12
Their radiance through the woods—may yet suffice 420 *Ecc. Sonn.* 1. 8. 5
Who, as the fields and woods have given them birth, 421 *Ecc. Sonn.* 1. 11. 11
'Mid woods and wilds, on Nature's craggy throne, 431 *Ecc. Sonn.* 2. 11. 13
Rekindled thus, from dens and savage woods 432 *Ecc. Sonn.* 2. 14. 10
Blest while their Spirits from the woods ascend 443 *Ecc. Sonn.* 3. 13. 12
To sit in leafy woods by fountains clear ! 460 **Queen of* 16
Thinned the rank woods ; and for the cheerful grange 468 *St. Bees* 138
—Young Romilly through Barden woods 494 *Force of Prayer* 13
Through woods and spacious forests,—to behold 496 **A little* 34
The umbrageous woods are left—how far beneath ! 497 **Enough of climbing* 19
Grieve for the land on whose wild woods his name 515 *Penn.* 10
Into strange woods, where he at large may live 528 **Those breathing* 69
How fondly will the woods embrace 533 **Blest is* 21
Ancient castle, woods, and mountains 536 *Egremont* 83
But he could see the woods and plains, 577 **I come* 17
That lit the dark slant woods with silvery white ! 593 *Ev. Wk. Quarto* 100
—As thro' th' astonish'd woods the notes ascend, 598 *Ev. Wk. Quarto* 351
And gives, where woods the checquer'd upland strew, 599 *Ev. Wk. Quarto* 405
How fair it's lawn and silvery woods appear ! 599 *Ev. Wk. Quarto* 417
Unfathom'd dells and undiscover'd woods ; 602 *Desc. Sk. Quarto* 10
That breath'd a death-like peace these woods around, 603 *Desc. Sk. Quarto* 57
—Thy lake, mid smoking woods, that blue and grey 604 *Desc. Sk. Quarto* 138
While fill each pause the ringing woods of morn. 604 *Desc. Sk. Quarto* 147
I lov'd, mid thy most desert woods astray, 605 *Desc. Sk. Quarto* 164
While mid dim towers and woods her waters gleam : 605 *Desc. Sk. Quarto* 179
And insect buzz, that stuns the sultry woods, 606 *Desc. Sk. Quarto* 224
Of cabins, woods, and lawns a pleasant shore 611 *Desc. Sk. Quarto* 502
There hears, protected by the woods behind, 612 *Desc. Sk. Quarto* 578
Bosom'd in gloomy woods, her golden fields, 614 *Desc. Sk. Quarto* 681
The woods, and distant Skiddaw's lofty height, 636 *Prelude* 1. 295
A lonely scene more lonesome, among woods, 638 *Prelude* 1. 418
On caves and trees, upon the woods and hills, 639 *Prelude* 1. 470
The woods of autumn, and their hazel bowers 639 *Prelude* 1. 484
Of rivers, woods, and fields. The passion yet 642 *Prelude* 2. 5

Woods—*continued.*
Or in the woods, or by a river's side 643 *Prelude* 2. 90
Was audible ; and sate among the woods 647 *Prelude* 2. 342
I saw the quiet woodman in the woods, 661 *Prelude* 4. 215
Its woods, and that uncertain heaven, received 671 *Prelude* 5. 387
A daily wanderer among woods and fields 674 *Prelude* 5. 587
Of eglantine, and through the shady woods, 678 *Prelude* 6. 232
Those woods and farms and orchards did present, 680 *Prelude* 6. 381
Of woods decaying, never to be decayed, 684 *Prelude* 6. 625
Of thee, thy chestnut woods, and garden plots 685 *Prelude* 6. 663
Were lost, bewildered among woods immense, 685 *Prelude* 6. 701
Filled all the woods : the cry of unknown birds ; 685 *Prelude* 6. 713
My threshold,—minstrels from the distant woods 687 *Prelude* 7. 22
Think, how the everlasting streams and woods, 698 *Prelude* 7. 745
Entered, with Shakspeare's genius, the wild woods 701 *Prelude* 8. 138
If not already from the woods retired 705 *Prelude* 8. 444
It was Angelica thundering through the woods 716 *Prelude* 9. 451
Green meadow-ground, and many-coloured woods, 718 *Prelude* 10. 8
Oh ! wrap him in your shades, ye giant woods, 733 *Prelude* 11. 418
That is collected among woods and fields, 750 *Prelude* 14. 314
On holidays, we rambled through the woods : 757 *Excursion* 1. 62
And many a legend, peopling the dark woods, 758 *Excursion* 1. 165
And speak a plainer language. In the woods, 761 *Excursion* 1. 347
Self-taught, as of a dreamer in the woods ; 762 *Excursion* 1. 410
From rocks, woods, caverns, heaths, and dashing shores ; 782 *Excursion* 2. 698
"So, westward, tow'rd the unviolated woods 799 *Excursion* 3. 944
Which Nature gently gave, in woods and fields ; 805 *Excursion* 4. 275
Who fled to woods, caverns, and jutting rocks, 814 *Excursion* 4. 902
In woods, and dwell under impending rocks 815 *Excursion* 4. 923
Or pierce the gloom of her majestic woods ; 819 *Excursion* 4. 1201
Stirs in the mighty woods.—So did he speak : 820 *Excursion* 4. 1282
Among steep hills and woods embosomed, flowed 823 *Excursion* 5. 83
Dived into caves, and pierced the matted woods, 840 *Excursion* 6. 110
Court the fresh air, explore the heaths and woods ; 840 *Excursion* 6. 169
Winds pipe through fading woods ; but those blithe notes 851 *Excursion* 6. 859
Its rocks and woods—the Cottage where she dwelt ; 855 *Excursion* 6. 1119
"Brought from the woods the honeysuckle twines 855 *Excursion* 6. 1149
Nor in the woods, that could from him conceal 865 *Excursion* 7. 500
That flashed uncouthly through the woods and fields. 869 *Excursion* 7. 765
Vales deeper far than these of ours, huge woods, 869 *Excursion* 7. 802
Among the clouds, and roars through the ancient woods ; 878 *Excursion* 8. 304
And mountains bare, or clothed with ancient woods, 891 *Excursion* 9. 506
Amid impending rocks and gloomy woods— 894 *Excursion* 9. 691
Woods waving in the wind their lofty heads, 895 *Excursion* 9. 746
Through tall green silent woods and ruins grey. S.3. 417 **Sweet was* 14
When in the woods the little Fowles S.3. 424 *Tinker* 23
Warm woods, and sunny hills, and fresh green fields, K.8. 240 *Recluse* 1.1.127
Among the silence of the woods and hills ; K.8. 241 *Recluse* 1.1.186
Single at chase among the lonely woods, K.8. 245 *Recluse* 1.1.324
And silent majesty ; the birch-tree woods K.8. 252 *Recluse* 1.1.562

Woods'. Portentous through her old woods' trackless bounds, 12 *Desc. Sk.* 74

Woodstock. At Woodstock, on the meadow green and gay. 562 *Cuck. and Night.* 285

Wood-weeds. Cling from the rocks, with pale wood-weeds between ; 3 *Ev. Wk.* 60

Woody. Or lurk in woody sunless glens profound, 12 *Desc. Sk.* 84
Wind slowly through the woody dale ; 130 *Idiot Boy* 408
Nor wild-cat in a woody glen ! 243 *P. B.* 620
But, while he climbs the woody hill, 244 *P. B.* 668
Resounding from the woody glade : 247 *P. B.* 940
Skyward ascending from a woody dell. 262 **Not Love* 8
Around a wild and woody hill 337 *Thun* 1
Lingering in a woody glade 407 *White Doe* 1005
Speak from the woody glen ! 478 *Somnamb.* 4
The aged Beggar in the woody lane, 566 *Cumb. Beg.* 38
By rills that tumble down the woody steeps, 595 *Ev. Wk. Quarto* 197
Pleased with thy crags, and woody steeps, thy Lake, 622 *Recluse* 1. 1. 118
And banked with woody risings ; but the Plain 702 *Prelude* 8. 192
(Yon cottage shaded by the woody crags) 864 *Excursion* 7. 467
Glistening along the low and woody dale ; 876 *Excursion* 8. 114

Wooed. Was the Youth's birth-place. There he wooed a Maid 121 *V. and J.* 12
How she wooed an English man ;" 139 *Arm. Lady* 2
And somewhat pensively he wooed : 186 **O Nightingale* 16
Had wooed the Maiden, day and night 194 *Ruth* 158
And life's unspiritual pleasures daily wooed ! 263 **Those words* 4
No change ;—the fair Izonda he had wooed 373 *Eg. Maid* 292
One wooed the silent Art with studious pains : 546 **The embowering* 5
And wooed the artless daughter of the hills, 691 *Prelude* 7. 300
By the first Francis wooed, and bound to him 716 *Prelude* 9. 485
Lacked not, for love, fair objects whom they wooed 814 *Excursion* 4. 878
The tidings came that she whom he had wooed 840 *Excursion* 6. 128

Wooers. That they all are wanton wooers ; 160 **Pansies, lilies* 36

Wooing. *See* **Cloud-Wooing.**
Shall hide me, wooing long thy wildwood strain ; 3 *Ev. Wk.* 87
The death that he was wooing. 287 *Ellen Irwin* 44
'Mid new-born blossoms that soft airs were wooing, 360 **Near Anio's* 3
Wooing her varying charms from eve to morn. 602 *Desc. Sk. Quarto* 16

Wooingly. Thy votaries, wooingly resigned 233 *Power of Sound* 86
Shall wooingly embrace it ; and green moss 450 *Ecc. Sonn.* 3. 40. 13

Wool. *See* **Mountain-wool.**
His wife sate near him, teasing matted wool, 95 *Brothers* 21
Of carded wool which the old man had piled 95 *Brothers* 32
Of antique form ; this large, for spinning wool ; 132 *Michael* 83
Wool for the Housewife's spindle, or repair 132 *Michael* 107
Which the kindly wool supplies, 163 *Spinning Wheel* 16

Words—*continued.*
Divine of words quickening insensate things. . . 252 **Why, Minstrel* 8
Fond words have oft been spoken to thee, Sleep ! 253 **Fond words* 1
Words cannot paint the o'ershadowing yew-tree bough, ... 254 *Wild Duck's Nest* 9
(Whether the instrument of words she use, . . 260 **High is* 2
Those words were uttered as in pensive mood . 263 **Those words* 1
Reader, farewell ! My last words let them be— . 281 *Valedict.* 10
As soon we shall be, may these words attest . . 282 **Wansfell ! this* 11
Of thy few words of English speech : . . . . 288 *Highland Girl* 41
—Strange words they seemed of slight and scorn ; 293 *Yarrow Unv.* 29
With words of apprehension and despair : . . 308 **These times* 3
To France be words of invitation sent ! . . . 309 *Men of Kent* 5
Slaves, vile as ever were befooled by words, . . 309 **What if* 3
The Liberty of Greece :—the words rebound . 312 **A Roman* 4
Ah ! that a *Conqueror's* words should be so dear : 312 **A Roman* 11
In words like these : "Up, Voice of song ! proclaim 326 *Sobieski* 4
Inviting words—perchance already flung . . . 332 *Ode : Thanks.* 212
Yet sad as sweet,—for *English* words . . . . 334 **In Bruges* 15
The words of truth's memorial vow . . . . 348 **Lulled by* 62
Had his sunk eye kindled at those dear words . 353 *Aquap.* 60
The tone of voice which wedded borrowed words 353 *Aquap.* 73
Survive, uninjured ;—glory then to words, . . 356 *Aquap.* 249
By casual outbreak of his passionate words, . . 362 **List—'twas* 56
I raise my thoughts, inform my deeds and words, 365 **Rapt above* 7
Spake bitter words ; words that did ill agree . 367 **As indignation* 2
A Visitant by whom these words were uttered :— 370 *Eg. Maid* 72
" Though vast thy power, thy words are weak," . 372 *Eg. Maid* 211
Attuned to words with sacred wisdom fraught ; . 395 *White Doe : Ded.* 18
To whom the words were softly said, ... 398 *White Doe* 181
And fervent words a passage found. . . . . 401 *White Doe* 460
And even this Creature ! " which words saying, . 402 *White Doe* 556
Sad words to that mute Animal, ... 405 *White Doe* 876
His last words in the yew-tree shade, ... 406 *White Doe* 976
His farewell words ; and by the same, ... 409 *White Doe* 1197
His words, more calmly thus pursued. . . . . 410 *White Doe* 1260
Words which she slighted at that day ; . . . . 415 *White Doe* 1769
But here her Brother's words have failed ; . . 415 *White Doe* 1785
His words remains for her, and loves. . . . . 415 *White Doe* 1790
And everlasting deeds to burning words ! . . . 421 *Ecc. Sonn.* 1. 10. 14
These good men humble by a few bare words, . . 422 *Ecc. Sonn.* 1. 14. 13
Charged with rich words poured out in thought's defence ; . . . . 441 *Ecc. Sonn.* 3. 4. 2
So shall the fearful words of Commination . . 447 *Ecc. Sonn.* 3. 29. 13
To words the Church prescribes aiding the lip . 448 *Ecc. Sonn.* 3. 30. 10
Is Nature felt, or can be ; nor do words, . . . 455 **Not in the lucid* 7
Bold words affirmed, in days when faith was strong 468 **Bold words* 1
Authentic words be given, or none ! . . . . 472 *Ossian* 30
Black in the people's minds and words, yet they . 474 **Here on their* 2
Deep sighs with quick words blending, . . . 479 *Somnamb.* 83
Brief words may speak the rest ; . . . . . 479 *Somnamb.* 146
That these two words of glittering gold . . 486 *Matthew* 31
And written words the glory of his hand ; . . . 489 *Illus. Books* 2
A lasting monument of words . . . . . . 492 *Fidelity* 52
With these dark words begins my Tale ; . . . 494 *Force of Prayer* 2
She knew it by the Falconer's words, ... 494 *Force of Prayer* 9
And her first words were, " Let there be . . . 495 *Force of Prayer* 54
And quick words round him fall like flakes of snow. 503 *Warning* 21
Hush, feeble lyre ! weak words refuse . . . . 507 **While from* 57
And the whole person. Words have something told 509 *F. Stone* 73
Breathed out these words :—" Here daily do we sit, 509 *F. Stone* 109
In thy calm presence those heart-moving words : 510 *F. Stone* 123
Words that can soothe, more than they agitate ; . 510 *F. Stone* 124
Words that require no sanction from an oath, . 515 *Penn.* 4
Then haply, Beaumont ! words in current clear . 522 *Epist. Beaumont* 56
Words by thy presence unrestrained may speak . 525 *Epist. Beaumont* 252
The words are uttered from my heart, ... 535 *Egremont* 23
Encouraged and endeared the strain of words . 538 **In desultory* 12
Or into anger roused by venal words . . . . 538 **In desultory* 45
Words which the virtues of thy Lord inspired, . 539 **Lady ! a* 8
A few may yet be saved." The Daughter's words, 540 *Grace Darl.* 44
Casting weak words amid a host of thoughts . . 541 *Grace Darl.* 75
Light words, that were more lightly heard . . 542 *Russ. Fug.* 63
Few words they speak, nor dare to slack . . . 543 *Russ. Fug.* 125
And words, not breathed in vain, ... 544 *Russ. Fug.* 204
The Czar full oft in words and deeds . . . . 545 *Russ. Fug.* 333
From airy words alone, a Pile that ne'er decays. . 547 **Beneath yon* 20
Of words unsuited to the place . . . . . . 550 *Hermit's Cell* 2. 7
And hearkened to the words and to the note, . 553 *Prioress* 70
In winning words, since through her gentileness, 562 *Cuck.andNight.*300
And made a fitting song, of words but few, . . 564 *Troilus* 115
More of soul in his face than of words on his tongue ; 570 *Farmer* 66
Alas ! what idle words ; but take . . . . . 577 **I come* 26
The vivid flashes of his spoken words. . . . . 584 *Ch. Lamb* 22
Which words less free presumed not even to touch) 585 *Ch. Lamb* 57
To a servile yoke. What need of many words ? . 633 *Prelude* 1. 105
But in the words of Reason deeply weighed, . . 645 *Prelude* 2. 231
Done visibly for other minds, words, signs, . . 651 *Prelude* 3. 174
It lies far hidden from the reach of words. . . 651 *Prelude* 3. 184
He told in few plain words a soldier's tale— . 664 *Prelude* 4. 421
Why alle upon a few weak words to say . . . 668 *Prelude* 5. 184
Take firmer hold of us, and words themselves 673 *Prelude* 5. 544
Of words in tuneful order, found them sweet . 674 *Prelude* 5. 555
For, images, and sentiments, and words, . . . 674 *Prelude* 5. 579
Embodied in the mystery of words : . . . . 674 *Prelude* 5. 597
I was a better judge of thoughts than words, . . 676 *Prelude* 6. 106
Misled in estimating words, not only . . . . 676 *Prelude* 6. 107
From things well-matched or ill, and words for things, ... 679 *Prelude* 6. 300
O, wond'rous power of words, by simple faith . 689 *Prelude* 7. 119

Words—*continued.*
Of love and marriage bonds. These words to thee 691 *Prelude* 7. 302
Words follow words, sense seems to follow sense : 694 *Prelude* 7. 508
Broke forth in armour of resplendent words, . . 695 *Prelude* 7. 539
To try her strength among harmonious words ; . 704 *Prelude* 8. 369
In a pure stream of words fresh from the heart : . 706 *Prelude* 8. 467
Had burst innocuous. Say in bolder words, . . 718 *Prelude* 10. 16
Some words of indirect reproof had been . . . 719 *Prelude* 10. 105
And gave it vent in her last words. O Friend ! . 723 *Prelude* 10. 383
After the lapse of full eight years, those words, . 726 *Prelude* 10. 541
Livelier, and flinging out less guarded words . 731 *Prelude* 11. 284
As readily by syllogistic words . . . . . . 735 *Prelude* 12. 84
Colours and words that are unknown to man, . 738 *Prelude* 12. 255
While yet we may, as far as words can give, . . 738 *Prelude* 12. 283
Smooth task ! for words find easy way, inspired . 740 *Prelude* 13. 14
Whether by words, looks, sighs, or tears, revealed ; 742 *Prelude* 13. 165
That framed them ; flattering self-conceit with words, ... 743 *Prelude* 13. 216
Expressing liveliest thoughts in lively words . . 743 *Prelude* 13. 264
Words are but under-agents in their souls ; . . 744 *Prelude* 13. 273
Our hearts—if here the words of Holy Writ . . 748 *Prelude* 14. 125
The name of Calvert—it shall live, if words . . 751 *Prelude* 14. 355
Thou in bewitching words, with happy heart, . 751 *Prelude* 14. 398
Of this great consummation :—and, by words . 755 *Recluse* 1. 1. 811
To weigh with care his words, and to rejoice . . 757 *Excursion* 1. 75
Such words of hope from her own mouth as served 766 *Excursion* 1. 685
Smooth words he had to wheedle simple souls ; . 775 *Excursion* 2. 254
Not moving to his mind.' " These serious words 776 *Excursion* 2. 315
These words :—" *Shall in the grave thy love be known,* 777 *Excursion* 2. 381
With intermixture of endearing words, . . . 779 *Excursion* 2. 506
Upon myself."—The other left these words . . 779 *Excursion* 2. 545
And, with light steps still quicker than his words, 781 *Excursion* 2. 637
That it is ended." At these words he turned— . 785 *Excursion* 2. 897
Words of assurance can be heard ; if nowhere . 789 *Excursion* 3. 220
These were your words ; and, verily, methinks . 789 *Excursion* 3. 230
Give birth, full often, to unguarded words ; . . 793 *Excursion* 3. 494
Your courtesy withholds not from my words . . 794 *Excursion* 3. 599
Much less, retraced in words. If she, of life . 796 *Excursion* 3. 681
The intellectual power, through words and things, 796 *Excursion* 3. 700
Into my bosom, whence these words broke forth : 808 *Excursion* 4. 507
The Solitary by these words was touched . . . 817 *Excursion* 4. 1078
The words he uttered shall not pass away . . . 820 *Excursion* 4. 1283
Plain indication that the words, which told . . 821 *Excursion* 4. 1312
And Heaven is weary, of the hollow words . . 828 *Excursion* 5. 379
My words too long have hindered." Undeterred, 836 *Excursion* 5. 892
Some farewell words—with one, but one, request ; 841 *Excursion* 6. 202
Winds an inscriptive legend."—At these words . 846 *Excursion* 6. 512
' Why do not words, and kiss, and solemn pledge, 851 *Excursion* 6. 870
Which I perused, even as the words had been . 851 *Excursion* 6. 890
The sting of self-reproach, with healing words. . 854 *Excursion* 6. 1033
Give way to words of pity or complaint, . . . 854 *Excursion* 6. 1044
With words that might be prelude to a tale . . 855 *Excursion* 6. 1123
The words he uttered, and the scene that lay . . 857 *Excursion* 7. 2
And silence waited on these closing words ; . . 862 *Excursion* 7. 292
Than of this breath, which shapes itself in words 863 *Excursion* 7. 359
By charm of measured words may spread o'er field, 863 *Excursion* 7. 382
The Pastor, even as if by these last words . . 870 *Excursion* 7. 817
And, at the last of those memorial words, . . . 871 *Excursion* 7. 902
Sir Alfred Irthing, with appropriate words . . 872 *Excursion* 7. 971
Hath here delivered ; words of heartfelt truth, . 873 *Excursion* 7. 1054
When from the Wanderer's lips these words had fallen, ... 877 *Excursion* 8. 231
To whom the appeal couched in its closing words 880 *Excursion* 8. 435
The words escaped his lip, with a tender sigh . . 882 *Excursion* 8. 543
Of those two boys ! yea in the very words . . 883 *Excursion* 8. 573
And yet a breath can do it ! " These few words . 891 *Excursion* 9. 454
By words, nor by the pencil's silent skill ; . . . 891 *Excursion* 9. 514
Its silent laboratory ! Words should say . . . S.3. 434 **The doubt* 65
Not with a waste of words, but for the sake . . K.8. 228 **I will* 106
That with blunt repetition of your words . . . K.8. 230 **I will* 180
Words cannot say, how beautiful. Then hail, . K.8. 244 *Recluse* 1. 1. 298
An art, a music, and a strain of words . . . . K.8. 247 *Recluse* 1. 1. 402
I heard her scatter some endearing words . . . K.8. 251 *Recluse* 1. 1. 527
Let homelier words without offence attest . . K.8. 301 **And oh* 2
And on a frugal plan without more words. . . L.1. 95 *Juvenal* 3. 24

Wordsworth's. Planted by Beaumont's and by Wordsworth's hands. . . . . . . 546 **The embowering* 4
At Wordsworth's suit been spared ; . . . . 549 **In these* 2

Wore. A coat he wore of military red . . . . 24 *Guilt* 8
And wore the fetters of a criminal. . . . . . 123 *V. and J.* 135
No bonnet shaded, but she wore . . . . . 190 *Beggars* 3
The other wore a rimless crown . . . . . . 191 *Beggars* 25
A military casque he wore, ... 192 *Ruth* 20
The oldest man he seemed that ever wore grey hairs. . . . . 196 *Resolution* 56
A woman's garb the Phantom wore, ... 213 *Dion* 69
That wore a threatening brow ; . . . . . . 215 *Kirkstone* 62
Against an equal host that wore the plaid, . . 293 *Killicranky* 3
That, while it wore for melancholy crest . . . 355 *Aquap.* 211
Hands clasped above the crucifix he wore . . . 362 **List—'twas* 79
Had bound the flowers I wore, with faithful tie : . 445 *Ecc. Sonn.* 3. 22. 10
The Queen drew back the wimple that she wore ; 465 **Dear to* 2
Peace to the Mourner. But when He who wore . 476 **Tranquillity ! the* 7
To speed their errand by the wings they wore. . 500 *Humanity* 40
Of Saxon liberty that Alfred wore, ... 504 *Warning* 59
With the worst shape mock-patience ever wore ; . 505 *Warning* 123
They wore away the night in starless gloom ; . . 528 **Those breathing* 55
That day he wore a riding-coat, ... 537 *Goody Blake* 109
What arms the son of bright Aurora wore ;— . 625 *Æneid* 135
Wore in old time. Her smooth domestic life, . 661 *Prelude* 4. 222
It seemed the very garments that I wore . . . 663 *Prelude* 4. 295

Worked 1119 **World**

Work—*continued.*
Of his day's work. 'Three dark mid-winter months 834 *Excursion* 5. 804
Urged unremittingly the stubborn work, 841 *Excursion* 6. 221
A work of art more sumptuous than might seem 846 *Excursion* 6. 506
That work a summer flood with hasty swell 853 *Excursion* 6. 1021
Ye would discover, then, a studious work 855 *Excursion* 6. 1147
That skill in this or other household work, 856 *Excursion* 6. 1183
Were nicely braided; and composed a work 860 *Excursion* 7. 183
—Preaching, administering, in every work 862 *Excursion* 7. 334
For work of happier issue, to the side 869 *Excursion* 7. 809
Till nature rested from her work in death. 870 *Excursion* 7. 873
This torpor is no pitiable work 880 *Excursion* 8. 420
Transfer not to futurity a work 890 *Excursion* 9. 406
And while the work is going on S.3. 423 *Tinker* 14
And thus with work or none, S.3. 424 *Tinker* 46
Shall pause, the skill admiring that can work S.3. 433 **The doubt* 45
But, Babe! there's none to work for me, K.8. 262 **Ah! if* 6
Were Kings a free born work, a people's choice. L.1. 96 *Juvenal* 3. 41
Worked. The Horses have worked with right good-will, 174 *Waggoner* 1. 40
He might have worked for ever. 484 *Simon Lee* 80
Worked with a dim and undetermined sense 638 *Prelude* 1. 392
Worketh. That worketh out of view; 224 *Primrose* 16
Working. *See* **Inly-working.**
That 'tis thy mother's heart which is working so in thee? 88 *Pet-lamb* 50
A most strange working did I see; 114 *Ind. Wom.* 36
On working out an ill intent? 181 *Waggoner* 4. 118
In working out a pure intent; 328 *Ode 1815* 107
And each tumultuous working left behind 384 *Duddon* 33. 11
Oft, working by her Husband's side, 483 *Simon Lee* 49
The shores and channels, working Nature's will 495 *Fact* 32
Working but in alliance with the works 646 *Prelude* 2. 259
Working within us,—nothing less, in truth, 674 *Prelude* 5. 572
Man free, man working for himself, with choice 700 *Prelude* 8. 104
In a strong wind, some working of the spirit, 739 *Prelude* 12. 331
Are various engines working, not the same 809 *Excursion* 4. 555
Were working the broad bosom of the lake 863 *Excursion* 7. 410
Working through love, such conquest shall it gain, 894 *Excursion* 9. 673
The shores and channels, working Nature's will S.3. 427 **My Son* 3
Workings. I unobserved could see the workings of her face: 87 *Pet-lamb* 18
My song the workings of her heart expressed. 120 *EmigrantMother* 14
The workings of his heart. 193 *Ruth* 132
Amid my strongest workings evermore 651 *Prelude* 3. 156
Were all like workings of one mind, the features 684 *Prelude* 6. 636
To sanction the proud workings of the soul, 713 *Prelude* 9. 237
Workman. (Workman worthy to be sainted) 161 **Pleasures newly* 12
Workmanship. Uncouth the workmanship, and rude! 301 *Bran* 76
Of airy workmanship whereon we stood, 351 *Des. Stanzas* 85
(October's workmanship to rival May) 388 *Trosachs* 11
Of his best workmanship by plan and tool. 473 **Thanks for* 8
Inscrutable workmanship that reconciles 637 *Prelude* 1. 342
Of nicest workmanship; that once had held 881 *Excursion* 8. 487
Workmen. These mighty workmen of our later age, 671 *Prelude* 5. 347
Work's. Her work and her work's partners she can cheer, 523 *Epist. Beaumont* 162
Their work's foundation, gave with careful hand 534 **When in* 11
Works. *See* **Fireworks.**
Abortive joy, and hope that works in fear; 20 *Desc. Sk.* 548
The least of Nature's works, one who might move 23 *Yew-tree* 57
His good works will be balm and life to him. 67 *Bord.* 1632
—Some little I've seen of blind boisterous works 86 *Rural Arch.* 19
Fond spirit that blindly works in the blood of all— 133 *Michael* 145
All works which I was wont to do alone, 137 *Michael* 395
Now she works with three or four, 171 *Kitten* 29
His station is there; and he works on the crowd, 188 *Music* 5
The spectacle, how pure!—Of Nature's works, 219 **This Height* 30
Of good and pious works Thou art the seed, 257 **The prayers* 5
Now and for ever, She, to works that came 280 *Plea for Auth.* 7
Shed gentle favours: rural works are there, 308 **One might* 6
By Works of spirit high and passion pure! 325 *Ode 1814* 149
—Long may these homely Works devised of old, 351 *Des. Stanzas* 74
Doth sometimes here predominate, and works 362 **List—'twas* 45
How subtly works man's weakness, sighs may heave 363 **The world forsaken* 7
Which Angels make, on works of love descending. 371 *Eg. Maid* 150
Whose good works formed an endless retinue: 380 *Duddon* 18. 11
On Earth, who works in the heaven of heavens, alone. 389 *Tyndrum* 14
And, 'mid the works of skilful hands, 390 *HighlandBroach* 13
But they and their good works are fled, 399 *White Doe* 305
Works busy as the lightning; but instinct 419 *Ecc. Sonn.* 1. 6. 2
Prompt transformation works the novel Lore; 422 *Ecc. Sonn.* 1. 17. 1
Of good works, mingling with the visions, raise 423 *Ecc. Sonn.* 1. 18. 11
By works of Art, that shed, on the outward frame 430 *Ecc. Sonn.* 2. 9. 6
To her fair works did Nature link 482 *Lines: Spring* 5
For still, the more he works, the more 483 *Simon Lee* 59
Yet, like a tool of Fancy, works 499 *Memory* 13
Works not the righteousness of God? Oh bend, 514 **Portentous change* 10
Imagination works with bolder hope 520 *Pun. Death* 14. 4
The spear, yet gave to works divine 533 **Blest is* 13
Of fields with rural works, of hill and dale, 567 *Cumb. Beg.* 49
By their good works exalted, lofty minds, 567 *Cumb. Beg.* 106
In works of love, in these alone, 582 **O for a* 29
And poured out truth in works by thoughtful love 584 *Ch. Lamb* 16
Inspired—works potent over smiles and tears. 584 *Ch. Lamb* 17
To works that ne'er shall forfeit their renown, 587 *Crosth.* 5

Works—*continued.*
Not with the mean and vulgar works of man, 638 *Prelude* 1. 408
Which, like a tempest, works along the blood 640 *Prelude* 1. 584
Working but in alliance with the works 646 *Prelude* 2. 259
And slipped into the ordinary works 652 *Prelude* 3. 241
To minister to works of high attempt— 654 *Prelude* 3. 385
Works which the enthusiast would perform with love. 654 *Prelude* 3. 386
To the end and written spirit of God's works, 663 *Prelude* 4. 351
The consecrated works of Bard and Sage, 666 *Prelude* 5. 42
Where still it works, though hidden from all search 668 *Prelude* 5. 196
'Tis just that in behalf of these, the works, 668 *Prelude* 5. 213
A dignity, a smoothness, like the works 672 *Prelude* 5. 458
It comes, to works of unreproved delight, 673 *Prelude* 5. 493
From the great Nature that exists in works 674 *Prelude* 5. 594
In summer, making quest for works of art, 677 *Prelude* 6. 190
That streamlet whose blue current works its way 678 *Prelude* 6. 192
Crowded with Genii busy among works 694 *Prelude* 7. 456
From early converse with the works of God 698 *Prelude* 7. 742
That after a short space works less and less, 707 *Prelude* 8. 573
Reading of nations and their works, in faith, 712 *Prelude* 9. 171
And all the homely in their homely works, 714 *Prelude* 9. 308
On works of love or freedom, or revolved 714 *Prelude* 9. 317
But indignation works where hope is not, 733 *Prelude* 11. 392
Fields with their rural works; recalled to mind 741 *Prelude* 13. 103
That intermingles with those works of man 744 *Prelude* 13. 292
To which she summons him; although the works 744 *Prelude* 13. 293
The works of man and face of human life; 749 *Prelude* 14. 202
Her works, as they present to Fancy's choice 750 *Prelude* 14. 318
Wisdom, which works thro' patience; thence he learned 759 *Excursion* 1. 239
By loneliness, and goodness, and kind works, 762 *Excursion* 1. 405
Rudely to mock the works of toiling Man. 788 *Excursion* 3. 127
And, by their aspects, signifying works 812 *Excursion* 4. 705
And ocean, and look down upon the works, 832 *Excursion* 5. 684
"Those pleasing works the Housewife's skill produced: 860 *Excursion* 7. 192
In works of havoc; taking from these vales, 866 *Excursion* 7. 593
Where nature works in wild and craggy spots, 871 *Excursion* 7. 917
And at the self-same moment, works its way 883 *Excursion* 8. 579
That works but by extinction? On themselves 886 *Excursion* 9. 143
And in good works; and him, who is endowed 895 *Excursion* 9. 735
And of his works: or, yielding to the bent K.8. 227 **I will* 97
The works by faith ordained. Pursue thy path, K.8. 325 [?] **The vestal* 12

World. Opens—a little world of calm delight; 14 *Desc. Sk.* 209
Of lofty hopes, he to the world went forth 23 *Yew-tree* 15
All but neglect. The world, for so it thought, 23 *Yew-tree* 20
The world, and human life, appeared a scene 23 *Yew-tree* 41
We reached the western world, a poor devoted crew. 29 *Guilt* 297
I seemed transported to another world; 31 *Guilt* 353
Through tears have seen him towards that world descend 32 *Guilt* 443
"Bad is the world, and hard is the world's law 33 *Guilt* 505
For all this world can give. Nay, be composed: 40 *Bord.* 140
The majesty of Him who rules the world. 48 *Bord.* 617
Seemed to remember me. To the wide world 52 *Bord.* 845
That things will work to ends the slaves o' the world 54 *Bord.* 936
The world is poisoned at the heart. What mean you? 56 *Bord.* 1036
But in a world like ours—— This self-same Man— 56 *Bord.* 1049
Of foul pollution—— The whole visible world 56 *Bord.* 1056
But have they not a world of common ground 60 *Bord.* 1237
So meet extremes in this mysterious world, 65 *Bord.* 1529
For such a world as this. The wise abjure 65 *Bord.* 1549
The faintest breath that breathes can move a world; 65 *Bord.* 1564
Of all this world is solved, well may we envy 69 *Bord.* 1796
The world in substance, not deceive by show, 70 *Bord.* 1829
I am spited by the world— 72 *Bord.* 1967
You are safe; the whole world shall not harm you. 72 *Bord.* 2011
With horror is this world) am unto thee 75 *Bord.* 2168
Yet all in the broad highway of the world. 98 *Brothers* 193
That God who made the great book of the world 99 *Brothers* 266
Seems the wide world, far brighter than before! 105 *Artegal* 203
And all the world appears unkind. 117 *Affl. Marg.* 70
The smiles, worth all the world to me. 121 *Emigrant Mother* 58
Arabian fiction never filled the world 122 *V. and J.* 39
Beneath a sun that wakes a weary world 122 *V. and J.* 51
First cam'st into the world—as oft befalls 136 *Michael* 340
And from her narrow world, she passed for evermore. 140 *Arm. Lady* 78
When, to the attractions of the busy world 150 **When, to* 1
Of things that in the great world be, 158 **With little* 2
To this lower world descending, 170 *Kitten* 14
And first;—thy sinless progress, through a world 172 *Infant Daughter* 46
This untried world, and to prepare thy way 173 *Infant Daughter* 73
Because not of this noisy world, but silent and divine! 189 *Star-gazers* 28
That we were in a world of woe, 193 *Ruth* 83
"Before me shone a glorious world— 194 *Ruth* 169
Far from the world I walk, and from all care; 195 *Resolution* 33
Of all this unintelligible world, 206 *Tintern* 40
Unprofitable, and the fever of the world, 206 *Tintern* 53
From this green earth; of all the mighty world 207 *Tintern* 105
Whence thou dost pour upon the world a flood 209 **Ethereal minstrel* 9
The invisible world with thee hath sympathised; 211 *Laod.* 143
How beautiful the world below; 215 *Kirkstone* 74
'Mid the blank world of snow and ice, 216 *Enterprise* 63
Won from the world of mind, dost thou prepare 216 *Enterprise* 90

Wreaths—*continued.*
In thy fresh wreaths, than they for praise . . 508 May 87
Its busy smoke in social wreaths, ... 533 *Blest is 6
Those laureat wreaths ungathered which the Nymphs . . . . 576 Chiabrera 9. 13
By silver'd wreaths of quiet charcoal smoke, . . 599 Ev. Wk. Quarto 430
Organic pleasure from the silver wreaths . . . 640 Prelude 1. 564
Tales of the May-pole dance, and wreaths that decked . . . . 701 Prelude 8. 151
The cumbrous bind-weed, with its wreaths and bells, 767 Excursion 1. 728
His stooping body tottered with wreaths of flowers 816 Excursion 4. 1001
Hangs permanent, and plentiful as wreaths . . 876 Excursion 8. 126
Bedimmed with smoke, in wreaths voluminous, . 894 Excursion 9. 702
Has furnished wreaths for ours. . . . . . S.3. 431 *The Scottish 32
With wreaths that have not faded to this hour, . S.3. 436 *The doubt 150

Wreck. *See* **Wrack.**
No wreck of all the pageant remains. . . . 8 Ev. Wk. 306
And others who survived the wreck, beheld . . 38 Bord. 75
Well as the wreck I am permits. And you, Sir ? . 43 Bord. 336
Of the dry wreck. And, in our vacant mood, . 148 *A narrow 16
In Heaven ; for, 'mid the wreck of IS and WAS, . 269 Malham 11
Relic of Kings ! Wreck of forgotten wars, . . 272 Ruins 9
On ground yet strewn with their last battle's wreck ; . . . . 278 Wellington 2
Oh what a Wreck ! how changed in mien and speech ! . . . . 280 *Oh what 1
Enough of sorrow, wreck, and blight ; . . . . 286 Nith 19
Till not a wreck of help or hope remained, . . 316 *Hail, Zaragoza 13
What are they but a wreck and residue, . . . 350 Des. Stanzas 22
Nor saw of wreck or ruin aught . . . . . 371 Eg. Maid 124
His church with monumental wreck bestrown ; . . 393 Inglewood 10
Of palaces, or temples, 'mid the wreck . . . 394 *No more 8
Of a storm-shattered Vessel saved from Wreck . 447 Ecc. Sonn. 3. 30. 3
Or the bare wreck of faith's solemnities, . . . 467 St. Bees 124
Of novelty amid the sacred wreck . . . . 474 *How sad 7
—When through this little wreck of fame, . . 486 Matthew 9
The wreck of Herculanean lore, ... 499 *Departing summer 50
Yet representing, amid wreck and wrong . . . 510 *Among a 5
Espies far off a Wreck, amid the surf, ... 540 Grace Darl. 30
Though danger, as the Wreck is neared, becomes 541 Grace Darl. 62
In earth, the widely scattered wreck sublime . . 708 Prelude 8. 614
Though with the wreck of loftier years bestrewn. 733 Prelude 11. 391
And wreck of party-coloured earthen-ware, . . 778 Excursion 2. 434
Cheered, plainly, and yet serious. What a wreck 781 Excursion 2. 660
The crash it made in falling ! From the wreck . 796 Excursion 3. 713
By nature's care from wreck of scattered stones, . 805 Excursion 4. 243
The wreck of gaiety ! But soon revived . . . 843 Excursion 6. 331

Wrecked. New rites ordaining when the old are wrecked, ... 380 Duddon 18. 3
And some to want—as if by tempests wrecked . 441 Ecc. Sonn. 3. 6. 5
The forlorn traveller, or sailor wrecked . . . 467 St. Bees 92
Set sail, was wrecked, and all on board was lost. . 623 *I find 11

Wrecks. Of civil conflict, nor the wrecks of change, 262 *Not Love 2
Memorial Pillar ! 'mid the wrecks of Time . . 368 Trajan 35
Breathed the same element ; too many wrecks . 466 St. Bees 21
Wrecks though they be, announce with feeling . 472 Ossian 15
With wrecks, and trod by feet of young and old . 836 Excursion 5. 931

Wren. Harbours a self-contented Wren, . . . 165 Parrot 30
Nor Autumn, when the viewless wren . . . . 299 Brownie's Cell 89
High poised—or as the wren that sings . . . 348 *Lulled by 58
Fearless of plough and scythe ; or darkling wren 377 Duddon 7. 13
The warbling wren shall find a leafy cage ; . . 433 Ecc. Sonn. 2. 21. 5
And moanings, or he dwells (as if the wren . . 516 *Feel for 5
Heart-soothed, and busy as a wren, ... 543 Russ. Fug. 117
And the stone-abbot, and that single wren . . 644 Prelude 2. 118
Where the wren warbles, while the dreaming man, 756 Excursion 1. 13
For the small wren to build in ;—not in vain, . 807 Excursion 4. 389
For wren and redbreast,—where they sit and sing 881 Excursion 8. 482

Wrenched. Be wrenched, or fire come down from far to scorch . . . . 666 Prelude 5. 31
Of twelve ensuing days his frame was wrenched, . 870 Excursion 7. 872
Plebeian hands the . . . mace have wrenched . L.1. 97 Juvenal 3. 92

Wren-like. Down to the low and wren-like warblings, made . . . . 668 Prelude 5. 207

Wren's. Felt warm as a wren's nest. You'd better turn 53 Bord. 862
Is none that with the little Wren's . . . . 168 Wren's Nest 3

Wrens. Rude Mausoleum ! but wrens nestle there, . 276 Filial Piety 13

Wrest. Wrest from the guardian Monster of the tomb 210 Laod. 80

Wrested. On earth could else have wrested from me ;—if erring, ... 66 Bord. 1617

Wrestle. To wrestle with, and victory to complete, K.8. 256 Recluse 1.1.739

Wrestlers. There, too, the lusty Wrestlers shall contend : . . . . 773 Excursion 2. 146

Wretch. Haply some wretch has eyed, and called thee blessed ; . . . . 7 Ev. Wk. 251
Before thy face did ever wretch appear, . . . 26 Guilt 124
Why thus that worn-out wretch must there sustain 34 Guilt 552
Bring to her hut ; and so the Wretch has lived . 44 Bord. 387
And learn what nature is from this poor Wretch ! 45 Bord. 444
Has marked out this foul Wretch as one whose crimes . . . . 55 Bord. 1000
Restore him, Heaven ! The desperate Wretch !—A Flower, ... 61 Bord. 1308
No answer—hush—lost wretch, he lifts his hand . 67 Bord. 1669
'Tis a poor wretch of an unsettled mind, . . . 73 Bord. 2033
Transmute him to a wretch from quiet hurled— . 234 Power of Sound 101
She is not what she seems, a forlorn wretch, . . 280 *Oh what 6
Whither, at length, a Wretch retired . . . . 298 Brownie's Cell 25
Lost wretch, a horrible device enthroned . . . 517 Pun. Death 2. 6

Wretch—*continued.*
Nor that vile wretch who bade the tender age . 618 School Ex. 9
The wretch, the short-lived vision of an hour ; . 619 School Ex. 96
To cheer the wand'ring wretch with hospitable light. . . . . 620 *She wept 14
The wretch on his pallet should turn, ... 621 Convict 36
For this poor crawling helpless wretch . . . . 621 Andrew Jones 11
Nor how to speak to her. Poor Wretch ! at last 766 Excursion 1. 652

Wretched. That views, undimmed, Einsiedlen's wretched fane. . . . . 20 Desc. Sk. 546
A Sailor he, who many a wretched hour . . . 25 Guilt 48
A wretched Outcast—but this strain of thought . 52 Bord. 830
That wretched life of thine shall be the forfeit. . 54 Bord. 950
O wretched Human-kind !—Until the mystery . 69 Bord. 1795
The wretched parents all that night . . . . 83 Lucy Gray 33
Him, in whose wretched heart ambition failed, . 103 Artegal 86
While thou art roving, wretched and forlorn, . . 104 Artegal 160
Because the wretched man himself had slain, . . 110 *'Tis said that some 4
Go with the child.—You have been wretched ; yet 124 V. and J. 191
Oh ! what a wretched Mother I ! " . . . . 129 Idiot Boy 266
But he, poor man ! is wretched made ; . . . 145 Her Eyes 78
A wretched thing forlorn. . . . . 197 Thorn 9
This wretched Woman thither goes ; . . . . 198 Thorn 68
That wretched boon, days lengthened by mistrust. 214 Dion 117
Heard plainly by the wretched Mother— . . . 247 P. B. 1007
" O wretched loss—untimely stroke ! . . . . 248 P. B. 1046
Of him who lies beneath. Most wretched one, . 275 Gravestone 6
This wretched Knight did vainly seek . . . . 287 Ellen Irwin 43
O wretched man, the throne of tyranny ! . . . 321 *Here pause 14
—Fly, wretched Gauls ! ere they the charge renew 322 Germans 12
Thou wretched Outcast, from the gift of fire . . 419 Ecc. Sonn. 1. 4. 2
O wretched Land ! whose tears have flowed like fountains ; . . . . 421 Ecc. Sonn. 1. 11. 7
Where be the wretched ones, the sights for pity ? 475 Greenock 4
Among the wretched and the falsely gay, . . . 692 Prelude 7. 368
He left his house : two wretched days had past, . 766 Excursion 1. 662
She loved this wretched spot, nor would for worlds 770 Excursion 1. 911
Wretched ambition drops astounded, fell . . . 795 Excursion 3. 674
O, never let the Wretched, if a choice . . . . 798 Excursion 3. 844
If to be weak is to be wretched—miserable, . . 827 Excursion 5. 318
Of all her climes—these wretched, these depraved, 836 Excursion 5. 937
Sincerely wretched hearts, or falsely gay. . . . 843 Excursion 6. 358
Wretched at home, he gained no peace abroad ; . 855 Excursion 6. 1098
The lot is wretched, the condition sad, . . . 878 Excursion 8. 292
Show to the wretched nations for what end . . 890 Excursion 9. 414
In mercy grant it, to thy wretched sons. . . . 894 Excursion 9. 648

Wretchedness. Of social Order's care for wretchedness, ... 32 Guilt 453
We joined our tales of wretchedness together, . 50 Bord. 691
Less patient in their wretchedness, have fallen, . 78 Bord. 2342
Of mind than body's wretchedness, ... 194 Ruth 233
To fettered wretchedness that no Bastille . . . 273 *When Philoctetes 12
Under the weight of mortal wretchedness ! . . 435 Ecc. Sonn. 2. 29. 11
And beyond common wretchedness depressed, . 677 Prelude 6. 148
Or chased away, the airy wretchedness . . . 679 Prelude 6. 313
From vice and folly, wretchedness and fear ; . . 703 Prelude 8. 291
To vice and guilt, forerunning wretchedness, . . 706 Prelude 8. 511
That made him turn aside from wretchedness . 761 Excursion 1. 369
And cold and hunger's abject wretchedness, . . K.8. 246 Recluse 1.1.364

Wretches. Here where we stand—that tribe of vulgar wretches . . . . 48 Bord. 642
I pity, can forgive, you ; but those wretches— . 70 Bord. 1832

Wrings. And wrings, and wrings her hands. . . 248 P. B. 1045

Wrinkled. Wrinkled Egyptian monument ; . . . 214 Kirkstone 17
" His forehead wrinkled was and furred ; . . 240 P. B. 311
To which sad course, these wrinkled Sons of Time 350 Des. Stanzas 24
" A cheerful smile unbends the wrinkled brow, . 699 Prelude 8. 48
Wrinkled and furrowed with habitual thought . 848 Excursion 6. 683

Wrinkles. From the projections, wrinkles, cavities, 707 Prelude 8. 583

Wrist. When round my wrist I felt a cord drawn tight, ... 55 Bord. 965
Across the slender wrist of the left arm . . . 509 F. Stone 53

Writ. Form spirit and character from holy writ, . 430 Ecc. Sonn. 2. 9. 11
And so they labour, deeming Holy Writ . . . 439 Ecc. Sonn. 2. 41. 6
Lie open ; and the book of Holy Writ, . . . 496 *A little 51
To show to her some pleasant meanings writ . . 562 Cuck. and Night. 299
Our hearts—if here the words of Holy Writ . . 748 Prelude 14. 125
An infidel contempt of holy writ . . . . . 775 Excursion 2. 249
Which reason promises, and holy writ . . . . 803 Excursion 4. 160
Science severe, or word of holy Writ . . . . 864 Excursion 7. 451

Write. 'Tis a strange letter this !—You saw her write it ? . . . . 38 Bord. 53
Write fool upon his forehead.—Planted thus . . 97 Brothers 112
Then they could write, ay, and speak too, as well 99 Brothers 279
Have killed him. Scorn should write his epitaph. . 277 *A Poet 8
Was yet not bold enough to write of Thee. . . 539 *Lady ! a 9
Write, and allay by your beneficence, ... 562 Cuck. and Night. 315

Writhe. And doth in more conspicuous torment writhe, ... 439 Ecc. Sonn. 2. 43. 13

Writhes. That writhes and chatters in her wiry cage, 842 Excursion 6. 291

Writhing. Grimacing, writhing, screaming,—him who grinds . . . . 697 Prelude 7. 699

Writing. The writing Oswald's ; the signature my Father's : . . . . 76 Bord. 2225
The blood-stained Writing is for ever torn ; . . 312 Clarkson 11
All things, responsive to the writing, there . . 759 Excursion 1. 227
She opened—found no writing, but beheld . . 766 Excursion 1. 669

Written. I hope you are refreshed.—I have just written . . . . 49 Bord. 666

Written—*continued.*

Into a vacant mind. Can written book . . . 389 Tyndrum 8
More than on written testament or deed, . . . 393 Countess' Pillar 7
And written words the glory of his hand . . 489 Illus. Books 2
—Without one hope her written griefs to blot, . 614 Desc.Sk.Quarto 676
I find it written of Simonides . . . . . . 623 *I find 1
And written lore, acknowledged my liege lord, . 654 Prelude 3. 376
To the end and written spirit of God's works, . 663 Prelude 4. 351
What is already written in the hearts . . . . 668 Prelude 5. 185
Of this whole Song is written that my heart . . 686 Prelude 6. 740
Wearing a written paper, to explain . . . . 696 Prelude 7. 641
Exposed, and lifeless as a written book !— . . 707 Prelude 8. 576
Presumptuous cloud, on whose black front was written . . . . 718 Prelude 10. 13
Being written in a tongue he cannot read, . . 719 Prelude 10. 61
Disgrace, of which, custom and written law, . . 731 Prelude 11. 263
The written promise ! Early had he learned . . 759 Excursion 1. 223
As it is written in thy holy book, ... 893 Excursion 9. 640

Wrong. But, through severe mischance and cruel wrong, ... 28 Guilt 228
'Twere wrong to trouble you. God speed you both. 41 Bord. 222
The wrong and the wrong-doer. You are troubled— 74 Bord. 2071
But, at the touch of wrong, without a strife . . 88 H. C. 32
Nor to my wishes lost ;—forgive the wrong, . . 104 Artegal 133
Come oft'n to us, fear no wrong ; . . . . . 106 *I've watched 14
Some thought far worse of him, and judged him wrong ; . . . . 108 Indolence 33
Said, " Pride shall help me in my wrong : . . . 117 Affl. Marg. 31
I weep—I know they do thee wrong, ... 121 EmigrantMother 77
Some chime of fancy wrong or right ; . . . . 158 *In youth 47
Sweet Bird ! to do me wrong ; . . . . . . 168 Turtledove 18
Indignant at the wrong. . . . . 169 Wren's Nest 52
And bounty never yields so much but it seems to do her wrong ? . . . . 189 Star-gazers 18
Regard not her :—oh, better wrong and strife . 192 Gipsies 21
Made of wild words, her cup of wrong . . . . 194 Ruth 197
Some bitter wrong. Nor is it unbelieved, . . . 219 Haunted Tree 27
And without wrong are cropped the marble tomb to strew. . . . . 222 Triad 211
And breathe as in a world where nothing can go wrong. . . . . 229 Cuckoo-clock 22
A sense of seemingly presumptuous wrong . . 231 *The gentlest Poet 27
Of poverty and wrong, ... 232 Jew. Fam. 42
O, my Belovèd ! I have done thee wrong, . . 279 *Though I 4
And constant voice, protest against the wrong. . 283 Railway 14
Indulged as if it were a wrong . . . . . . 285 Nith 11
I would not wrong thee, Champion brave ! . . 292 Rob Roy 98
Would wrong thee nowhere ; least of all . . . 292 Rob Roy 99
And by the power, of wrong. . . . . . . 312 *Who rises 68
Triumphant wrong, battle of battle born, . . . 326 *Emperors and 5
Of contemplation, by no sense of wrong . . . 328 Ode 1815 117
Of right and wrong, of weal and woe, ... 337 *Oh Life 2
How patiently the weight of wrong is borne ; . . 359 *They—who 8
May gather to avenge this wrong . . . . . 370 Eg. Maid 82
Such wrong ; nor need we blame the licensed joys, 382 Duddon 23. 12
Mingles, and lurking consciousness of wrong ; . 382 Duddon 25. 12
From honour misconceived, or fancied wrong, . 389 Sound of Mull 7
The bitterness of wrong and waste : . . . . 396 White Doe 20
Which do the gentle Creature wrong. . . . . 398 White Doe 216
Swayed the brave man to his wrong. . . . . 411 White Doe 1411
Nor do a suffering Spirit wrong, ... 412 White Doe 1474
By wrong triumphant through its own excess, . 426 Ecc. Sonn. 1. 32. 2
If cloistered Avarice scruple not to wrong . . . 433 Ecc. Sonn. 2. 19. 5
And sift her laws—much wondering that the wrong, 435 Ecc. Sonn. 2. 29. 7
Though pride's least lurking thought appear a wrong . . . . 444 Ecc. Sonn. 3. 18. 6
The wrong, by love provoked, let love arraign, . 464 *A point 13
These shores if he approached them bent on wrong ; 468 *Bold words 4
Thou dost preserve the stars from wrong ; . . 492 Duty 47
Inflamed by sense of wrong ; . . . . . . 499 *Departing summer 39
Yet representing, amid wreck and wrong . . . 510 *Among a 5
What could go wrong with such a Charioteer . . 523 Epist. Beaumont 112
Where Man and Muse complained of mutual wrong ; 529 *Those breathing 116
Who means to charity no wrong ; . . . . . 534 *Blest is 88
He sued :—heart-smitten by the wrong, . . . 545 Russ. Fug. 349
Evil light on her ! she hath done me wrong. . . 558 Cuck.andNight.105
Where gold determines between right and wrong. 573 Chiabrera 2. 4
This only grieves me, for it seems a wrong, . . 575 Chiabrera 6. 10
When aught had suffered wrong,— . . . . 583 *O for a 33
So genius triumphed over seeming wrong, . . . 584 Ch. Lamb 15
No more shall grief of mine the season wrong ; . 588 Immortality 26
Though doing wrong and suffering, and full oft . 672 Prelude 5. 417
And all the sad etcetera of the wrong, ... 705 Prelude 8. 442
The beauty of his person, doing wrong . . . 711 Prelude 9. 145
I could not but bewail a wrong so harsh, . . . 716 Prelude 9. 473
Arbiter undisturbed of right and wrong, . . . 721 Prelude 10. 184
With impulse, motive, right and wrong, the ground 731 Prelude 11. 299
My sense of excellence—of right and wrong : . . 740 Prelude 13. 58
Never did I, in quest of right and wrong, . . . 748 Prelude 14. 150
And to myself,' said she, ' have done much wrong 768 Excursion 1. 768
I do not wish to wrong him ; though the course 775 Excursion 2. 267
Had done to her humanity no wrong : . . . . 821 Excursion 4. 1315
Whose sorrow rather is to suffer wrong . . . 854 Excursion 6. 1070
Than to do wrong, albeit themselves have erred. . 854 Excursion 6. 1071
Which to outrageous wrong the sufferer owes, . 870 Excursion 7. 840
Of all who suffer wrong, and to enact . . . . 873 Excursion 7. 1043
Could do them wrong. The universal forms . . 874 Excursion 8. 14

Wrong—*continued.*

" And tens of thousands suffer wrong as deep. . 879 Excursion 8. 336
He can't go wrong go where he will : . . . . S.3. 424 Tinker 28
More grateful still : while wrong and shame shall last, ... S.3. 441 *Grateful is sleep ; my 2
Of marble ; for while shameless wrong and woe . S.3. 441 *Grateful is sleep, more 2
As we pronounce them, doing them much wrong, K.8. 238 Recluse 1.1. 68
Flattery and double-dealing, strife and wrong. . K.8. 246 Recluse 1.1.357

Wrong-doer. The wrong and the wrong-doer. You are troubled— . . . . 74 Bord. 2071

Wronged. (I wot not what ill tongue has wronged him with you) . . . . 40 Bord. 167
Who is it that hath wronged you ? Mark you me ; 45 Bord. 453
Impossible ! The man had never wronged me. . 69 Bord. 1749
Wronged, or distrest ; . . . . 285 Grave of Burns 70
Nor art thou wronged, sweet May ! when I compare 367 *If with 4
Thus wronged in woman's breast : in vain I pleaded— . . . . 853 Excursion 6. 999

Wrongful. Of wrongful acts. Downward it is and broad, ... 519 Pun. Death 8. 5

Wrongfully. Thus wrongfully of verse, however rude, 745 Prelude 13. 363

Wrongly. A single human life have wrongly taken, 517 Pun. Death 3. 10
Regrets, or trembles, wrongly, or too much ; . 830 Excursion 5. 508

Wrong-proof. Search, for their worth, some gentle heart wrong-proof, ... 390 Highland Hut 12

Wrongs. Me and all worldly harms and wrongs however keen." . . . . 35 Guilt 612
To end her wrongs. But if the blind Man's tale . 38 Bord. 72
Or personal memory of his own deep wrongs, . . 126 V. and J. 304
On wrongs, which Nature scarcely seems to heed : 292 *Degenerate Douglas 11
His acts, his wrongs, his final sacrifice ; . . . 351 Des. Stanzas 71
And for presumptuous wrongs atone ;— . . . 472 Ossian 29
Their wrongs, since they fulfilled their destiny ? . 474 *On to 8
" Now both himself and me he wrongs, . . . 487 Fountain 57
Thought-tempered wrongs, for each humane respect 501 Humanity 62
Deceived, mistake calamities for wrongs ; . . . 505 Warning 114
Wrongs and the terror of redress, would wean . 516 *Hard task 5
Feel for the wrongs to universal ken . . . . 516 *Feel for 1
Wrongs to redress, harmonious tribute paid . . 635 Prelude 1. 182
And monarchs surly at the wrongs sustained . . 640 Prelude 1. 534
Or personal memory of his own worst wrongs, . 718 Prelude 9. 583
Hence, amid ills that vex and wrongs that crush . 748 Prelude 14. 124
Wrongs unredressed, or insults unavenged . . 791 Excursion 3. 374
And tempt opinion to support the wrongs . . 816 Excursion 4. 1020
Nor think that they are victims—turned to wrongs, 887 Excursion 9. 192

Wrote. That night, he wrote a letter to the Priest, 102 Brothers 429
Wrote loving letters, full of wondrous news, . . 138 Michael 433
In Patmos wrote, who saith of them that go . . 554 Prioress 132

Wroth. Waxed wroth, and with foul claws, a harpy brood, ... 255 Detraction 7
Lest alien frenzy seize thee, waxing wroth, . . 514 *Long-favoured 3

Wrought. *See* **High-wrought, New-wrought, Well-wrought.**
Have wrought with godlike arm the deeds of praise, 15 Desc. Sk. 290
His hand had wrought ; and when, in the hour of death, ... 35 Guilt 615
To tell the change that Voice within her wrought 35 Guilt 622
When into storm the evening sky is wrought, . 36 Guilt 664
That skill or means of his could add, but the architect had wrought . . . . . . 91 Norman Boy 18
Flashed round him images and hues that wrought 96 Brothers 57
Strange alteration wrought on every side . . . 96 Brothers 97
They toiled and wrought, and still, from sire to son, 98 Brothers 208
With half the wonders that were wrought for him. 122 V. and J. 40
Wrought in the field, or on his shepherd's stool . 133 Michael 163
Wrought on with her best fingers to prepare . . 135 Michael 286
Wrought at the Sheep-fold. Meantime Luke began 138 Michael 442
He at the building of this Sheep-fold wrought, . 138 Michael 471
On which it stood; great changes have been wrought 138 Michael 478
The Frost hath wrought both night and day, . . 156 Oak and Broom 23
A garland of seven lilies wrought ! . . . . . 161 Binnorie 5
Though wrought in Vulcan's happiest mood, . . 163 Needlecase 11
Beholding what your skill has wrought, . . . 164 *Fair Lady 22
Even from things by sorrow wrought, ... 172 Kitten 125
The beauteous forms of nature wrought, . . . 193 Ruth 134
Held that the unborn infant wrought . . . . 199 Thorn 139
O most ambitious Star ! an inquest wrought . . 208 *It is no 9
In act embodied, my deliverance wrought. . . . 211 Laod. 138
As if some Protean art the change had wrought, . 230 Clouds 75
It wrought in him conviction strange ; . . . 243 P. B. 660
No doubt the devil in me wrought ; . . . . 245 P. B. 813
That by our own right hands it must be wrought ; 310 *Another year 7
Among the herdsmen of the Alps, have wrought . 315 *Alas ! what 12
For You she wrought : Ye only can supply . . 333 Ded. Tour 9
A wingèd Goddess—clothed in vesture wrought . 334 *A wingèd 1
What though the Italian pencil wrought not here, 339 Tell 1
We gaily passed,—till Nature wrought . . . 343 Eclipse 9
These perishable spheres have wrought . . . 343 Eclipse 56
Was wrought her punishment. . . . . . . 374 Eg. Maid 366
A Protean change seems wrought while I pursue . 377 Duddon 4. 3
Once more of troubles wrought by magic spell ; . 395 White Doe: Ded. 34
For She it was—this Maid, who wrought . . 400 White Doe 346
And be no farther wrought upon : . . . . . 402 White Doe 539
These Records wrought in pledge of love . . . 403 White Doe 665
Of her by whom the work was wrought :— . . 405 White Doe 869
But now, when such sad change was wrought, . 415 White Doe 1770
In days when Fancy wrought unchecked by fear, 460 *Queen of 14
Wrought in men's minds, like miracles achieved ; 466 St. Bees 47
In her esteem the thirst that wrought man's fall, 469 *Desire we 5

Wrought—*continued.*
Of stormy weather-stains that semblance wrought, 470 *Bala-Sala* 12
Which a fine skill, of Indian growth, has wrought 480 *Cordelia* 3
Or strong compunction in me wrought, . . . 492 *Duty* 34
Among the tasks of real life, hath wrought . . 493 *Hap. War.* 4
Of Death and Time, the marvels it hath wrought. 509 *F. Stone* 78
Exult in this deliverance wrought through faith . 541 *Grace Darl.* 85
But by an industry that wrought in love ; . . 546 **Oft is* 13
Otherwise wrought the will of the Most High ; . 585 *Ch. Lamb* 100
So with his staff the Cripple wrought . . . . 621 *Andrew Jones* 18
Even for the very service they had wrought, . 640 *Prelude* 1. 519
Which, wrought upon instinctively, had found . 654 *Prelude* 3. 361
And manners finely wrought, the delicate race . 657 *Prelude* 3. 560
The transformation wrought by gay attire. . . 659 *Prelude* 4. 76
To paint these vanities, and how they wrought . 662 *Prelude* 4. 293
A deathless spirit. Thou also, man! hast wrought, 666 *Prelude* 5. 18
Sensuous or intellectual, wrought by men, . . 666 *Prelude* 5. 43
Delusion bold ! and how can it be wrought ? . . 691 *Prelude* 7. 285
A beauty exquisitely wrought, with hair . . 710 *Prelude* 9. 78
Of Fairy, or some dream of actions wrought . 714 *Prelude* 9. 301
Less genuine and wrought up within myself— . 716 *Prelude* 9. 472
And public persons, and emotions wrought . . 717 *Prelude* 9. 544
And in this way I wrought upon myself, . . . 719 *Prelude* 10. 85
Her innocent authority was wrought, ... 723 *Prelude* 10. 379
Wrought for them in old time : yea, not unmoved, 733 *Prelude* 11. 441
Hard by, soon after that fell deed was wrought, . 737 *Prelude* 12. 239
Familiar object as it is, hath wrought . . . . 742 *Prelude* 13. 144
Willing to work and to be wrought upon, . . . 747 *Prelude* 14. 103
But the whole plainly wrought by children's hands ! 778 *Excursion* 2. 423
By earthly nature had the effect been wrought . 784 *Excursion* 2. 846
But wrought with mightier arm than now prevails. 787 *Excursion* 3. 91
If you imagine changes slowly wrought, . . . 795 *Excursion* 3. 616
Listen who would, be wrought upon who might, . 843 *Excursion* 6. 357
Of these opponents gradually was wrought, . . 845 *Excursion* 6. 469
But fretted, vexed, and wrought upon, almost . 849 *Excursion* 6. 745
He wrought not : neither field nor flock he owned : 863 *Excursion* 7. 425
Has wrought, if not with speed of magic, yet . . 875 *Excursion* 8. 88
Wonder, and admiration, things that wrought . K.8. 230 **I will* 187

Wrung. With hard contempt his heart was wrung, 241 *P. B.* 454
Wye. O sylvan Wye ! thou wanderer thro' the woods, ... 206 *Tintern* 56
Wytheburne's. If Wytheburne's modest House of prayer, ... 176 *Waggoner* 2. 1

Y

Yard. *See* **Churchyard, Graveyard.**
Yards. But ere ten yards were gone her footsteps did she stay. . . . . 87 *Pet-lamb* 16
That, till full fifty yards were gone, ... 127 *Idiot Boy* 83
So said, so done ; and masts, sails, yards, . . . 178 *Waggoner* 2. 123
Not five yards from the mountain path, . . . 198 *Thorn* 27
And to the left, three yards beyond, ... 198 *Thorn* 29
And, for full fifty yards around, ... 200 *Thorn* 227
And one, not four yards distant, near a well. . 202 *Hart-leap* 104
Not four yards from the broad highway : . . . 246 *P. B.* 925
Went twice two hundred yards or more, . . . 247 *P. B.* 992
Yarrow. And see the Braes of Yarrow." . . . 292 *Yarrow Unv.* 8
" Let Yarrow folk, *frae* Selkirk town, . . . 292 *Yarrow Unv.* 9
Go back to Yarrow, 'tis their own ; . . . . 292 *Yarrow Unv.* 11
Nor turn aside to Yarrow. . . . . 292 *Yarrow Unv.* 16
To go in search of Yarrow ? . . . . 293 *Yarrow Unv.* 24
" What's Yarrow but a river bare, ... 293 *Yarrow Unv.* 25
I thus could speak of Yarrow ! . . . . . . 293 *Yarrow Unv.* 32
And sweet is Yarrow flowing ! . . . . . . 293 *Yarrow Unv.* 34
Into the dale of Yarrow. . . . . 293 *Yarrow Unv.* 40
There's such a place as Yarrow. . . . . . 293 *Yarrow Unv.* 48
" Be Yarrow stream unseen, unknown ! . . . 293 *Yarrow Unv.* 49
'Twill be another Yarrow ! . . . . 293 *Yarrow Unv.* 56
The bonny holms of Yarrow ! " . . . . . . 293 *Yarrow Unv.* 64
And is this—Yarrow ?—*This* the Stream . . . 301 *Yarrow V.* 1
A blue sky bends o'er Yarrow vale, ... 302 *Yarrow V.* 17
Of Yarrow Vale lay bleeding ? . . . . . . 302 *Yarrow V.* 26
Bear witness, rueful Yarrow ! . . . . . . 302 *Yarrow V.* 40
With Yarrow winding through the pomp . . . 302 *Yarrow V.* 51
Loved Yarrow, have I won thee ; . . . . . 302 *Yarrow V.* 74
Thy genuine image, Yarrow ! . . . . . . 302 *Yarrow V.* 86
'Twill be another Yarrow." Prophecy . . . 353 *Aquap.* 77
When first I looked on Yarrow ; . . . . . 385 *Yarrow Rev.* 4
And if, as Yarrow, through the woods . . . . 386 *Yarrow Rev.* 33
Hast shed the power of Yarrow ; . . . . . 386 *Yarrow Rev.* 68
As thy own Yarrow gave to me . . . . . . 386 *Yarrow Rev.* 75
Flow on for ever, Yarrow Stream ! . . . . . 386 *Yarrow Rev.* 105
Shalt take thy place with Yarrow ! . . . . 480 *Somnamb.* 162
A name more sad than Yarrow. . . . . . 494 *Force of Prayer* 40
I saw the Stream of Yarrow glide . . . . . 586 *Hogg* 2
And death upon the braes of Yarrow, ... 586 *Hogg* 11
With sharper grief is Yarrow smitten, ... 586 *Hogg* 43
Yarrow's. On Yarrow's banks let herons feed, . 292 *Yarrow Unv.* 13
" Oh ! green," said I, " are Yarrow's holms, . . 293 *Yarrow Unv.* 33
In Yarrow's groves were centred ; . . . . . 386 *Yarrow Rev.* 98
Yawn. And yawn for his unworthy sake, . . . 246 *P. B.* 844
Yawning. And through the yawning fissures old, . 240 *P. B.* 359
And tempt the icy valley yawning deep, . . . 610 *Desc.Sk.Quarto* 463
Ye, *omitted.*
Yea. I did believe all things were shadows—yea, . 59 *Bord.* 1214
Yea, from the utmost corners of the earth, . . 63 *Bord.* 1410
Of penitential anguish, yea with tears. . . . 78 *Bord.* 2305

Yea—*continued.*
Yea, his first word of greeting was,—" All right . 124 *V. and J.* 156
Which they are touching ; yea far brighter, even 139 *Widow* 20
Share their empyreal spirits—yea, ... 178 *Waggoner* 3. 33
Men, women, children, yea the frame . . . . 192 *Gipsies* 3
Yea ! even the Stranger from afar, ... 223 *Wishing-gate* 31
Yea, both for souls who God's forbearance try, . 229 *Cuckoo-clock* 43
Yea, all, that now enchants thee, from the day . 250 *Admon.* 13
Yea, veriest reptiles have sufficed to prove . . 273 **When Philoctetes* 11
" *What, you are stepping westward ?* "—" *Yea.*" . 289 *Stepping West.* 1
Yea, let our Mary's one companion child— . . 294 **Fly, some* 10
Yea, what were mighty Nature's self ? . . . 386 *Yarrow Rev.* 85
The Boy had seen her, yea, more bright ; . . . 398 *White Doe* 193
Yea, many overcome in spite . . . . . . 399 *White Doe* 316
Yea, trusting in God's holy aid, ... 401 *White Doe* 488
Yea, by her brother's very name, ... 409 *White Doe* 1198
Yea, offered up this noble Brood, ... 410 *White Doe* 1302
Yea, like a heavenly messenger . . . . . . 411 *White Doe* 1375
Yea, like a ship at random blown . . . . . 414 *White Doe* 1615
Yea, his dry bones to ashes are consumed . . . 432 *Ecc. Sonn.* 2. 17. 3
Yea, many, haply wont to entertain . . . . 442 *Ecc. Sonn.* 3. 8. 11
Shun not this Rite, neglected, yea abhorred, . . 447 *Ecc. Sonn.* 3. 29. 1
Yea, for thy fellow-brutes in thee we saw . . . 491 *Tribute : Dog* 32
Or charm it out of memory ; yea, might fill . . 517 *Pun. Death* 1. 5
Yea, to celestial Choirs, Grace Darling's name ! 541 *Grace Darl.* 97
Yea, to the stars, if they were born . . . . 541 *Russ. Fug.* 7
I should have died, yea many hours ago ; . . . 556 *Prioress* 200
Yea, hath it ? use, quoth she, this medicine ; . . 561 *Cuck.and Night.* 241
Yea, appertained by a peculiar right . . . . 645 *Prelude* 2. 196
Beneath the wave, yea, in the wave itself, . . 648 *Prelude* 2. 408
Yea, our blind Poet, who, in his later day, . . 653 *Prelude* 3. 283
Yea, all the adamantine holds of truth . . . 666 *Prelude* 5. 39
The other that was a god, yea many gods, . . 667 *Prelude* 5. 106
Enow to stir for these ; yea, will I say, . . . 668 *Prelude* 5. 156
Though mutually unknown, yea, nursed and reared 678 *Prelude* 6. 254
Yea, when a glimpse of those imperial bowers . 700 *Prelude* 8. 111
Was agitated ; yea, I could almost . . . . . 720 *Prelude* 10. 134
Yea, afterwards—truth most painful to record !— 722 *Prelude* 10. 284
Yea, could not but be right, because we saw . . 728 *Prelude* 11. 51
Yea, the whole body of society . . . . . . 731 *Prelude* 11. 281
Wrought for them in old time : yea, not unmoved, 733 *Prelude* 11. 441
Yea, never thought of judging ; with the gift . 737 *Prelude* 12. 189
Yea, by the very mourners who had knelt . . 780 *Excursion* 2. 573
Yea, with her own incorporated, by power . . 817 *Excursion* 4. 1069
Rejected, yea repelled ; and, if with scorn . . 840 *Excursion* 6. 121
Past or to come ; yea, boldly might I say, . . 866 *Excursion* 7. 567
Yea, to avenge her violated rights, ... 876 *Excursion* 8. 155
Of those two boys ! yea in the very words . . 883 *Excursion* 8. 573
Yea almost on the Mind herself, and seems . . 885 *Excursion* 9. 65
Beheld without compassion, yea, with praise ! . 887 *Excursion* 9. 194
Up to their highest measure, yea and more. . . K.8. 239 *Recluse* 1.1.109
Yea to this hour I cannot read a tale . . . . K.8. 256 *Recluse* 1.1.721
Yean. A faithful nurse thou hast ; the dam that did thee yean . . . . 87 *Pet-lamb* 39
Yeaned. Weak as a lamb the hour that it is yeaned ; 201 *Hart-leap* 39
Year. Remembered half the year and hoped the rest, 19 *Desc. Sk.* 497
Inmate of lonesome Nature's endless year ; . . 26 *Guilt* 121
All perished—all in one remorseless year, . . . 30 *Guilt* 302
Pluck them, and another year . . . . . . 80 *Foresight* 23
You'll find a task for half a year. . . . . . 85 *Shepherd-boys* 44
A long, long year before. . . . . 85 *Anecdote* 12
Is the longest of the year. . . . . 90 *Longest Day* 12
Lord of heaven's unchanging year ! . . . . 90 *Longest Day* 76
A Shepherd-lad ; who ere his sixteenth year . . 95 *Brothers* 39
Year after year the old man still kept up . . . 98 *Brothers* 213
And travel with the year at a soft pace. . . . 107 *Farewell* 48
The threshold of another year ; . . . . . . 112 *Lament* 11
To the new year a welcoming ; . . . . . . 113 *Lament* 24
Hark ! the death-note of the year . . . . . 113 *Lament* 64
And every year increased my store. . . . . 115 *Last of Flock* 30
" Year after year my stock it grew ; . . . . 115 *Last of Flock* 31
So lived he till his eightieth year was past. . . 132 *Michael* 61
Which, going by from year to year, had found, . 133 *Michael* 119
And now, when Luke had reached his eighteenth year, ... 133 *Michael* 123
And now, when he had reached his eighteenth year, 134 *Michael* 205
Year followed year, my Brother ! and we two, . 151 **When, to* 70
From year to year the spacious floor . . . . 154 **A whirl-blast* 9
And all the year the bower is green. . . . . 154 **A whirl-blast* 11
My father many a happy year . . . . . . 156 *Oak and Broom* 68
Child of the Year ! that round dost run . . . 158 **In youth* 73
When the year was in its prime, ... 171 *Kitten* 78
Through " heaven's eternal year."—Yet hail to Thee, ... 172 *Infant Daughter* 15
Through all the changes of the year, ... 182 *Waggoner* 4. 226
Soft clouds, the whitest of the year, ... 191 *Seq. Beggars* 23
That she in half a year was mad, ... 194 *Ruth* 194
The hour that in a distant year . . . . . . 226 *Present.* 65
" In vain, through every changeful year, . . . 239 *P. B.* 246
That undivided we from year to year . . . . 251 *Appleth.* 5
Months perish with their moons ; year treads on year ; . . . . 251 **There is a little* 9
Through the long year the House of Prayer would seek : . . . . 256 *Decay of Piety* 4
Thou liest in Abraham's bosom all the year ; . . 258 **It is a* 12
Secure foundations. As the year runs round, . 259 **A volant* 8
And, through the sunny portion of the year, . . 268 **Pure element* 5
As if its hues were of the passing year, . . . 275 **While poring* 7
From year to year this shaggy Mortal went . . 299 *Brownie's Cell* 51
Another year !—another deadly blow ! . . . 310 **Another year* 1

Year—*continued.*
A dungeon dark! where he must waste the year, 318 **Is there* 4
And thus from year to year his walk they thwart, 320 **Hunger, and* 13
Within its awful caves.—From year to year . . 321 **The power* 10
Lulling the year, with all its cares, to rest! . . 388 *Trosachs* 14
Thus doth she keep, from year to year, . . . 398 *White Doe* 190
Equal to *his* deserts, who, like the year, . . . 425 *Ecc. Sonn.* 1. 26. 6
As through a zodiac, moves the ritual year . . 445 *Ecc. Sonn.* 3. 19. 5
Year after year I strove, but strove in vain, . . 470 †*From early* 6
The opening of the year. 483 *Sister* 20
We for the year to come may take . . . . . 483 *Sister* 31
And all the long year through the heir . . . 485 **Bright Flower* 3
The whole year through. . . . . 490 *Night Thought* 12
Shall find thee through all changes of the year: . 490 *Tribute: Dog* 8
These vespers of another year, ... 498 **The sylvan* 20
In flows the joyous year. . . . . 507 **While from* 56
"Another year is ours;" . . . . 507 *May* 30
The whole day long, and all days of the year. . 523 *Epist. Beaumont* 163
With thy Forerunners that through many a year 538 **In desultory* 18
Was like the crowding of the year . . . . . 544 *Russ. Fug.* 223
Of pillars, branching off from year to year, . . 546 **Ye Lime* 4
Through the vicissitudes of many a year— . . 549 **The massy* 9
That learnèd in that school from year to year 553 *Prioress* 46
For yet had I heard none, of all that year, . . 557 *Cuck.and Night.* 54
The same as they had chosen for the year, . . 558 *Cuck.and Night.* 79
Nor has the rolling year twice measured, . . . 586 *Hogg* 13
"Rocking as in a dream the tedious year;" . . 592 *Ev. Wk. Quarto* 30
Such ministry, when ye through many a year . 639 *Prelude* 1. 468
Of exercise and play, to which the year . . . 639 *Prelude* 1. 477
The faces of the moving year, even then . . 640 *Prelude* 1. 561
We ran a boisterous course; the year span round 642 *Prelude* 2. 47
Through three divisions of the quartered year . 643 *Prelude* 2. 83
To passive minds. My seventeenth year was come; 647 *Prelude* 2. 386
Far distant, thus beheld from year to year . . 679 *Prelude* 6. 273
And the whole year breathed tenderness and love. 687 *Prelude* 7. 42
Year after year, a punctual visitant! . . . . 699 *Prelude* 8. 31
Preserved, I moved about, year after year, . . 704 *Prelude* 8. 329
She must be visitant the whole year through, . 705 *Prelude* 8. 390
Distinguished. Scarcely was a year thus spent . 710 *Prelude* 9. 28
Domestic carnage now filled the whole year . . 723 *Prelude* 10. 356
In times long past; but still, from year to year, . 737 *Prelude* 12. 242
From his sixth year, the Boy of whom I speak, . 758 *Excursion* 1. 118
And thus before his eighteenth year was told, . 760 *Excursion* 1. 280
Amid the bounties of the year, the peace . . . 761 *Excursion* 1. 352
In the short course of one undreaded year, . . 774 *Excursion* 2. 198
Through the long year in constant quiet bound, . 790 *Excursion* 3. 323
Abides, from year to year, a genuine Priest, . . 824 *Excursion* 5. 101
In peace, from morn to night, from year to year. 825 *Excursion* 5. 217
A true reflection of the circling year, ... 828 *Excursion* 5. 394
These ornaments, that fade not with the year, . 856 *Excursion* 6. 1156
From year to year in loneliness of soul; . . . 863 *Excursion* 7. 403
Year after year is added to his store . . . . 866 *Excursion* 7. 565
That there should pass a moment of the year, . 877 *Excursion* 8. 194
To time and season, as the year rolled round?". 878 *Excursion* 8. 251
What lamentable change, a year—a month— . 878 *Excursion* 8. 256
Their happy year spins round. The youth obeys . 884 *Excursion* 9. 33
And make the chalice of the big round year . . 886 *Excursion* 9. 134
Through all the seasons of the changeful year, . 888 *Excursion* 9. 266
Days will pass on, the year, if years be given, . S.3. 433 **The doubt* 22
Live through Heaven's eternal year: . . . . S.3. 442 *Harmodius* 22
And now when he had reached his eighteenth year, K.8. 226 **I will* 85
Year after year, with many a sleep between, . K.8. 233 **Along the* 5
He well remembers, though the year be gone. . K.8. 236 *Recluse* 1. 1. 5
Faithful companions, yet another year . . . K.8. 243 *Recluse* 1.1.262
From year to year, not shunning Man's abode, . K.8. 251 *Recluse* 1.1.538
Pass with a thought the life of the whole year . K.8. 252 *Recluse* 1.1.589
And months, and let me add the long year through, ... K.8. 265 **Brook, that* 2

Yearly. *See* **Half-yearly.**

Yearn. For better lore would seldom yearn, . . 86 *Anecdote* 58

Yearned. Which men call Earth," have yearned to seek, ... 341 *San Salv.* 21

Yearning. Yet does my yearning heart to thee . . 121 *EmigrantMother* 71
That make the good, tow'rds which he's yearning, 177 *Waggoner* 2. 39
"Learn, by a mortal yearning, to ascend— . . 211 *Laod.* 145
A yearning survives which few hearts shall withstand: . . . . 345 *Stanzas: Simplon* 28
Out of a farewell yearning—favoured more . . 549 **The massy* 18
With yearning toward some philosophic song . . 635 *Prelude* 1. 229
Appeased his yearning:—in the after-day . . 758 *Excursion* 1. 153
"What other yearning was the master tie . . 791 *Excursion* 3. 392
And over-constant yearning;—there—there lies . 804 *Excursion* 4. 177
Shall he feel yearning to those lifeless forms, . . K.8. 257 **Shall he* 7

Yearnings. When kindred thoughts and yearnings bear . . . . 286 *Nith* 62
Yearnings she hath in her own natural kind, . . 588 *Immortality* 78
In later youth to yearnings of a love . . . . 662 *Prelude* 4. 254
And damp those yearnings which had once been mine— . . . . 662 *Prelude* 4. 289
Dumb yearnings, hidden appetites, are ours, . . 673 *Prelude* 5. 506
Nor tender yearnings, wanting for my good . . 735 *Prelude* 12. 39
And confidential yearnings, tow'rds its home, . 780 *Excursion* 2. 559

Yearns. That is transported to excess; that yearns, 830 *Excursion* 5. 507

Year's. Through the year's successive portals; . . 90 *Longest Day* 53
A last year's nest, conspicuously built . . . . 150 **When, to* 21
My last year's friends together. . . . . . . 159 *Green Linnet* 8
Proved last year's leaves, pushed from the spray 170 *Rural Ill.* 11
Our roads, through many a long year's space, . 182 *Waggoner* 4. 219
And while the youthful year's prolific art— . . 266 **The stars* 12
Aught of the fading year's inclemency! . . . 381 *Duddon* 21. 14

Year's—*continued.*
When Nature marks the year's decline, . . . 497 *Lycoris* 29
Tempers the year's extremes; . . . . 506 **While from* 10
The last year's cup whose Ram or Heifer gained, 522 *Epist.Beaumont* 67

Years. *See* **Half-years.**
For years the work of carnage did not cease, . . 25 *Guilt* 55
The red-breast, known for years, which at my casement pecked. . . . . 28 *Guilt* 225
"Two years were passed since to a distant town . 29 *Guilt* 253
Three years a wanderer now my course I bend— 32 *Guilt* 445
Your pains shall ever with your years increase?"— 33 *Guilt* 511
And, through all converse of our later years, . . 39 *Bord.* 96
Where now we dwell.—For many years I bore . 41 *Bord.* 202
I'd wager on his life for twenty years. . . . . 41 *Bord.* 246
Ten years; and no one ever heard her voice; . 44 *Bord.* 388
He has been two years in his grave. Enough. . 46 *Bord.* 514
These ten years she has moved her lips all day . 47 *Bord.* 566
These ten years she had sate all day alone . . 47 *Bord.* 571
Three good round years, for playing the fool here 51 *Bord.* 769
Over your head twice twenty years must roll, . 52 *Bord.* 820
These fifteen years—— *Ha! speak*—what Thing art thou . . . . 54 *Bord.* 942
Where, hid from me, he counted many years, . 71 *Bord.* 1893
The Blessing of my later years . . . . . . 79 *Sparrow's Nest* 15
She was eight years old, she said; . . . . . 83 *We are Seven* 6
I have a boy of five years old; . . . . . . 85 *Anecdote* 1
For what may be thy lot in future years. . . . 88 *H. C.* 14
(Ten years scarcely had she told) . . . . . 93 *Westmoreland Girl* 10
Your years make up one peaceful family; . . . 97 *Brothers* 122
And see, that with our threescore years and ten . 97 *Brothers* 130
(For many years ago I passed this road) . . . 97 *Brothers* 132
Was two years taller: 'twas a joy to see, . . . 99 *Brothers* 250
And though of unripe years, a stripling only, . . 100 *Brothers* 297
Had clothed the Ewbanks for a thousand years:— 100 *Brothers* 303
Twelve years are past since we had tidings from him. 100 *Brothers* 307
(It will be twelve years since when Spring returns) 101 *Brothers* 357
You say that he saw many happy years? . . . 101 *Brothers* 384
It had been caught mid-way; and there for years 101 *Brothers* 404
All that the Priest had said: his early years . . 102 *Brothers* 421
And those that Milton loved in youthful years; . 103 *Artegal* 50
Help us to tell Her tales of years gone by, . . 107 *Farewell* 49
O weary struggle! silent years . . . . . . 110 *Forsaken* 8
And there is one whom I five years have known; 110 **'Tis said that some* 6
Three years had Barbara in her grave been laid . 110 **'Tis said that some* 11
For years to me are sad and dull; . . . . . 113 *Lament* 12
Seven years, alas! to have received . . . . 117 *Aff. Marg.* 8
Years to a mother bring distress; . . . . . 117 *Aff. Marg.* 27
And for its promises to future years, ... 118 *Maternal Grief* 25
The high-born Vaudracour was brought, by years 121 *V. and J.* 8
Of their maturer years, his present mind . . . 122 *V. and J.* 36
And should he live a thousand years, ... 127 *Idiot Boy* 110
Five years of happiness or more . . . . . 127 *Idiot Boy* 135
These fourteen years, by strong indentures: . . 129 *Idiot Boy* 338
Though younger than himself full twenty years. . 132 *Michael* 80
When Michael, telling o'er his years, began . . 132 *Michael* 88
Thus living on through such a length of years, . 133 *Michael* 140
Two steady roses that were five years old; . . 134 *Michael* 179
But soon as Luke, full ten years old, could stand 134 *Michael* 194
"I have been toiling more than seventy years, . 134 *Michael* 228
And see so little gain from threescore years. . 137 *Michael* 373
Till I was forty years of age, not more . . . 137 *Michael* 375
Years after he had heard this heavy news. . . 138 *Michael* 453
The length of full seven years, from time to time, 138 *Michael* 470
Three years, or little more, did Isabel . . . . 138 *Michael* 473
Years contracting to a moment, ... 141 *Arm. Lady* 105
Reflected from the years gone by, ... 144 **Driven in* 80
Years after we are gone and in our graves, . . 146 **It was an* 45
From years of quiet industry, to love . . . . 147 *Joanna* 3
So distant from us now for two long years, . . 147 *Joanna* 13
And yet, just three years back—no more— . . 156 *Oak and Broom* 33
Seven widowed years without my Jane, . . . 157 *Sexton* 30
Thirty years or more, and yet . . . . . . 160 **Pansies, lilies* 21
A thousand years are but as yesterday; . . . 172 *Infant Daughter* 10
Not less capacious than a thousand years. . . 172 *Infant Daughter* 12
From hiding-places ten years deep; . . . . 182 *Waggoner* 4. 212
Three years she grew in sun and shower, . . . 187 **Three years* 1
The touch of earthly years. . . . . 187 **A slumber* 4
Hangs a Thrush that sings loud, it has sung for three years: . . . . 187 *Poor Susan* 2
And Ruth, not seven years old, ... 192 *Ruth* 3
"What days and what bright years! Ah me! . 193 *Ruth* 79
"Full twenty years are past and gone . . . . 198 *Thorn* 104
Her thirty years of winter past, ... 203 *Brougham* 7
Of years be on her!—She shall reap . . . . 204 *Brougham* 41
Five years have past; five summers, with the length . . . . 205 *Tintern* 1
For future years. And so I dare to hope, . . 206 *Tintern* 65
Through all the years of this our life, to lead . 207 *Tintern* 124
To blow against thee: and, in after years, . . 207 *Tintern* 137
That after many wanderings, many years . . . 207 *Tintern* 156
Medea's spells dispersed the weight of years, . . 210 *Laod.* 83
The hours are past—too brief had they been years; 211 *Laod.* 153
On which four thousand years have gazed! . . 214 *Kirkstone* 20
With rolling years thy strength increased; . . 216 *Enterprise* 36
As doth with mellowing years agree, ... 217 *Enterprise* 134
Our threescore years and ten. . . . . . . 225 *Primrose* 48
Of all his years;—a company . . . . . 227 *Vernal Ode* 93
The golden years maintained a course . . . . 228 *Vernal Ode* 131

Yellow—*continued.*
The yellow stone-crop, suffered to take root .   767 *Excursion* 1. 717
Leaving behind of yellow radiance spread .   . 820 *Excursion* 4. 1302
With *yellow* in full blow. . . . . . . S.3. 431 **The Scottish* 8
A flag of *yellow* dye. . . . . S.3. 431 **The Scottish* 16
Her *wished-for* yellow she foreswore, . . S.3. 431 **The Scottish* 21
Is clad with yellow flowers. . . . . . S.3. 431 **The Scottish* 28

Yellowed. The old Tower's brow yellowed as with the beams . . . . 470 *Bala-Sala* 10
Yellowing. Of yellowing corn, the same that over-topped . . . 509 *F. Stone* 58
With haycocks studded, striped with yellowing grain— 525 *Epist. Beaumont* 226
How pleasant, as the yellowing sun declines, . 593 *Ev. Wk. Quarto* 97
Was yellowing the hill tops, I went abroad . 674 *Prelude* 5. 560
Yells. When first, above the yells of bigot strife, . 629 *Installation* 101
Yeoman. Knight, squire, and yeoman, page and groom : . . . . 204 *Brougham* 38
Knight, burgher, yeoman, and esquire, . . 404 *White Doe* 707
Yeomanry. The best part of their Yeomanry ! . 402 *White Doe* 610
Yes. (*Partial list.*)
Yes, I must see you when ye first behold . 20 *Desc. Sk.* 563
Yes, as I roamed where Loiret's waters glide . 21 *Desc. Sk.* 624
Yes, to my sorrow—under the great oak . . 47 *Bord.* 538
Yes, loves him ; 'tis a truth that multiplies . 48 *Bord.* 591
Yes, yes. I will not murmur, merciful God ! . 53 *Bord.* 850
By heaven, his words are reason ! Yes, my Friends, . 57 *Bord.* 1094
Carry him to the Camp ! Yes, to the Camp. . . 58 *Bord.* 1142
Oh yes, that mole, that viper in the path ; . 60 *Bord.* 1255
Of what I have been—yes, I thank thee, Heaven ! . 61 *Bord.* 1325
Yes, be it so ;—repent and be forgiven— . . 63 *Bord.* 1415
Yes, you are right, we need not hunt for motives : . 63 *Bord.* 1435
Ay, come to me and weep. Yes, Varlet, look, . 76 *Bord.* 2189
Yes, the wild Girl of the mountains . . . 94 *Westmoreland Girl* 61
They were such darlings of each other. Yes, 99 *Brothers* 242
Yes, long before he died, he found that time . 101 *Brothers* 388
Yes ! thou art fair, it need not be moved . . 111 **Yes !* 1
With many hopes ; it should be so—yes—yes— 137 *Michael* 398
" Yes, kind Lady ! otherwise man could not bear 140 *Arm. Lady* 17
Yes, the sight so stirs and charms . . . 171 *Kitten* 105
Yes, let my master fume and fret, . . . 174 *Waggoner* 1. 116
—Yes, without me, up hills so high . . . 175 *Waggoner* 1. 136
To vibrate between yes and no ; . . . 177 *Waggoner* 2. 42
—Yes, I, and all about me here, . . . 182 *Waggoner* 4. 225
An Orpheus ! an Orpheus ! yes, Faith may grow bold, 188 *Music* 1
Yes, it was the mountain Echo, . . . 209 **Yes, it* 1
Have not *we* too ?—yes, we have . . . 209 **Yes, it* 13
Yes ! hope may with my strong desire keep pace, 256 **Yes ! hope* 1
Yes ! when the sun of life more feebly shines, . 264 **Lady ! the* 9
Yes, there was One ;—for One, asunder fly . 268 **Four fiery* 7
Yes, Traveller ! fifty winters have been told . 276 *Filial Piety* 5
Yes, I will forth, bold Bird ! and front the blast, 279 **Hark ! 'tis* 9
Yes, ye were startled ;—and, in balance true, . 283 **Proud were* 11
Yes, freely let our hearts expand, . . 286 *Nith* 25
Yes, they can make, who fail to find, . . 376 **The Minstrels* 67
Yes, she is soothed : an Image faint, . . 407 *White Doe* 1033
" Yes—God is rich in mercy," said . . 411 *White Doe* 1354
Yes, to thy domination, Roman See, . . 429 *Ecc. Sonn.* 2. 2. 12
Yes, if the intensities of hope and fear . . 445 *Ecc. Sonn.* 3. 19. 1
Yes, lovely Moon ! if thou so mildly bright . 459 **Wanderer ! that* 40
Yes, Lady, while about your neck is wound . 480 *Cordelia* 10
Yes, proof was plain that, since the day . . 492 *Fidelity* 58
Yes, for them whose souls have scope . . 503 **Like a* 64
Yes ! where Love nestles thou canst teach . 506 **While from* 49
Yes, though He well may tremble at the sound . 520 *Pun. Death* 13. 1
Yes I will see you when ye first behold . . 614 *Desc.Sk.Quarto* 672
—Yes, were it mine, the cottage meal to share . 615 *Desc.Sk.Quarto* 713
Yes, I remember when the changeful earth, . 640 *Prelude* 1. 559
Yes, I had something of a subtler sense, . . 661 *Prelude* 4. 209
Yes ; for even then no other than a place . . 681 *Prelude* 6. 420
Yes, something of the grandeur which invests . 742 *Prelude* 13. 152
—Yes, in those wanderings deeply did I feel . 743 *Prelude* 13. 206
Yes, shall the fine immunities she boasts . . 791 *Excursion* 3. 341
" Yes," said the Sage, resuming the discourse . 806 *Excursion* 4. 373
" Yes," said the Wanderer, taking from my lips 809 *Excursion* 4. 540
—Yes, you have felt, and may not cease to feel. . 818 *Excursion* 4. 1151
" Yes !" said the Solitary with a smile . . 835 *Excursion* 5. 838
" Yes," said the Priest, " the Genius of our hills— 844 *Excursion* 6. 392
" Yes," he continued, kindling as he spake, . 889 *Excursion* 9. 383
Yes, the realities of life so cold, . . K.8.238 *Recluse* 1.1. 65
Yesterday. Our march of yesterday had better suited 39 *Bord.* 107
Why now—but yesterday I overtook . . 45 *Bord.* 446
But yesterday was worse than all ; at last . 45 *Bord.* 471
And long as I can stir I'll dog him.—Yesterday, 46 *Bord.* 483
Will be rejoiced to greet you. It seems but yesterday 50 *Bord.* 696
As I have told you : He left us yesterday . . 58 *Bord.* 1136
And, of my fifty, yesterday . . . 115 *Last of Flock* 95
Sate yesterday, and made a nest . . . 120 *Emigrant Mother* 30
A thousand years are but as yesterday ; . 172 *Infant Daughter* 10
Startling the flight of timid Yesterday ! . 379 *Duddon* 15. 8
Thronged yesterday by airy ghosts ; . . 391 *Highland Broach* 74
Of yesterday, which royally did wear . . 449 *Ecc. Sonn.* 3. 34. 11
The elastic vanities of yesterday ?" . . 456 **Soft as* 26
Creation, as it were, of yesterday— . . 510 **Among a* 18

Yesterday—*continued.*
As if but yesterday departed, ... 586 *Hogg* 33
Than any liveliest sight of yesterday, . . 751 *Prelude* 14. 394
" Much, yesterday, was said in glowing phrase 826 *Excursion* 5. 243
Brought yesterday from our sequestered dell . 835 *Excursion* 5. 882
Yesterday's. Our yesterday's procession did not sue 360 *Albano* 6
Yesterdays. " A Man he seems of cheerful yesterdays 866 *Excursion* 7. 557
Yester-even. After the hour of sunset yester-even, 687 *Prelude* 7. 19
Yester-evening's. 'Tis He whose yester-evening's high disdain . . . . 279 **'Tis he* 1
Yet. (*Partial list.*)
Are yet of no diviner origin, . . . v **If thou indeed* 8
Through passes yet unreached, a brighter road. . 2 *Ev. Wk.* 26
Yet still, the sport of some malignant power, . 2 *Ev. Wk.* 31
To show what pleasures yet to me remain, . 2 *Ev. Wk.* 34
Yet still the tender, vacant gloom remains ; . 8 *Ev. Wk.* 321
Yet does she still, undaunted, throw the while . 8 *Ev. Wk.* 343
Yet not unrecompensed the man shall roam, . 10 *Desc. Sk.* 9
Yet are thy softer arts with power indued . 13 *Desc. Sk.* 141
Howls near and nearer yet the famished wolf. . 14 *Desc. Sk.* 195
Yet here and there, if 'mid the savage scene . 14 *Desc. Sk.* 234
Yet more ;—compelled by Powers which only deign 19 *Desc. Sk.* 508
—Yet hast thou found that Freedom spreads her power 21 *Desc. Sk.* 620
Yet not for this will sober reason frown . . 22 *Desc. Sk.* 648
Yet, if the wind breathe soft, the curling waves, . 22 *Yew-tree* 5
Yet when faint beams of light that ruin showed, . 27 *Guilt* 156
Yet happy thou, poor boy ! compared with me, . 33 *Guilt* 498
Should *yet* be true ? Would it were possible ! . 38 *Bord.* 73
And long beard white with age—yet evermore, . 45 *Bord.* 462
And yet I had within me evermore . . 69 *Bord.* 1787
Yet loathing life—till anger is appeased . 78 *Bord.* 2352
You yet may spy the fawn at play, . . 83 *Lucy Gray* 9
Yet by some grave thoughts attended . . 90 *Longest Day* 9
Yet, at this impressive season, . . 90 *Longest Day* 21
I whispered, " Yet a little while, dear Child ! thou art my own, 92 *Poet's Dream* 21
Listen yet awhile ;—with patience . . 94 *Westmoreland Girl* 57
Yet all in the broad highway of the world. . 98 *Brothers* 193
Which yet he brandishes for future war, . . 103 *Artegal* 55
Yet some did think that he had little business here : 108 *Indolence* 45
Yet bear me up—else faltering in the rear . 112 **O dearer* 11
And yet they are upon my eyes, . . 114 *Ind. Wom.* 7
And yet I am alive ! . . . . . 114 *Ind. Wom.* 8
Yet is it dead, and I remain : . . . 114 *Ind. Wom.* 12
Were yet with pensive fear and gentle awe . 118 *Maternal Grief* 59
In prayer, yet blending with that solemn rite . 119 *Maternal Grief* 72
There was a smile or two—yet—yet . . 121 *Emigrant Mother* 56
Yet as the troubled seed and tortured bough . 123 *V. and J.* 148
Beneath the moon, yet shining fair, . . 130 *Idiot Boy* 349
The CLIPPING TREE, a name which yet it bears. 133 *Michael* 169
Entrance and exit both *yet* free ; . . . 144 **Driven in* 61
And all day long I number yet, . . . 158 **In youth* 65
Yet seeming still to hover ; . . . 159 *Green Linnet* 28
Yet, whate'er enjoyments dwell . . 171 *Kitten* 95
While yet the valley is arrayed, . . 182 *Waggoner* 4. 240
Even yet thou art to me . . . 183 **O blithe* 14
A Spirit, yet a Woman too ! . . . 186 **She was* 12
And yet a Spirit still, and bright . . 186 **She was* 29
Yet still I persevere, and find them where I may." 197 *Resolution* 126
Yet there the Soul shall which hath earned . 211 *Laod.* 109
—Yet tears to human suffering are due ; . . 212 *Laod.* 164
And whistling loud may yet be heard, . . 240 *P. B.* 343
Yet standing in the clear moonshine ; . . 248 *P. B.* 1097
Blue ether still surrounds him—yet—and yet ; . 261 **I watch* 4
Yet have my thoughts for thee been vigilant— . 277 **Why art* 5
And the green silent pastures, yet remain. . 292 **Degenerate Douglas* 14
And yet be melancholy ; . . . 293 *Yarrow Unv.* 60
Doth yet frequent the hill of storms, . . 300 *Bran* 3
On England's bosom ; yet well pleased to rest, . 303 **Fair Star* 4
In cheerful godliness ; and yet thy heart . 307 **Milton ! thou* 13
Dread trials ! yet encountered and sustained . . 316 **Hail, Zaragoza* 12
Yet, yet, Biscayans ! we must meet our Foes . 318 *Biscayan* 1
With firmer soul, yet labour to regain . . . 318 *Biscayan* 2
Where it begins to stir, *yet* voiceless as a snake. . 351 *Des. Stanzas* 63
One solace yet remains for us who came . . 359 **Those old* 10
Which yet it bears, sweet Stream ! as crystal pure. 361 **When here* 8
Where Man, yet mortal, rarely finds a place. . 365 **Rapt above* 4
Yet glorious Art the power of Time defies, . 368 *Trajan* 67
Conspicuous yet where Oroonoko flows ; . . 380 *Duddon* 16. 3
The lonely Primrose yet renews its bloom, . 381 *Duddon* 24. 1
Albeit sickness, lingering yet, . . 386 *Yarrow Rev.* 45
A solemn fancy yet sustains . . . 410 *White Doe* 1282
" Yet, Lady ! shines, through this black night, 411 *White Doe* 1356
Who in their private cells have yet a care . . . 429 *Ecc. Sonn.* 2. 5. 3
Yet Truth is keenly sought for, and the wind . 441 *Ecc. Sonn.* 3. 4. 1
Yet will we not conceal the precious Cross, . 450 *Ecc. Sonn.* 3. 40. 9
If yet To-morrow, unbelied, may say, . . 456 **Soft as* 2
Which yet in thy behalf the Poet claims, . 459 **Wanderer ! that* 8
Yet pleased and willing : . . . 486 **Bright Flower* 20
Yet seek thy firm support, according to their need. 492 *Duty* 24
Yet being to myself a guide, . . . 492 *Duty* 27
Stern Lawgiver ! yet thou dost wear . . 492 *Duty* 41
Is yet a Soul whose master-bias leans . . 494 *Hap. War.* 59
And oft returned, again, and yet again. . . 535 *Egremont* 56
Thou see'st a homely Pile, yet to these walls . 547 **Rude is* 14
Yet spake this Child when sprinkled was the water ; 555 *Prioress* 189
Yet may I sing, O *Alma* ! loud and clear. . . 556 *Prioress* 204

Yields. Trusted my life to what chance bounty yields, ... 32 *Guilt* 435
Yields, could not chuck his babe beneath the chin, 60 *Bord.* 1243
—It is my royal state that yields . . . . . 113 *Lament* 34
With ornaments—the prettiest, nature yields . . 124 *V. and J.* 200
And bounty never yields so much but it seems to do her wrong? . . . . 189 *Star-gazers* 18
Divine monition Nature yields, ... 228 *Devot. Incit.* 71
That the poor Harp distempered music yields . 252 **Why, Minstrel* 13
His icy scimitar, a foretaste yields . . . . . 263 **While not* 5
Who meekly yields, and is obscured—content . 265 **The Shepherd* 13
Has sown as yields, we trust, the fruit of fame . 278 *Wellington* 12
Yields every thing to discipline of swords? . . 309 **What if* 7
He sets, his sinking yields a type . . . . . 337 *Thun* 11
Yields to the Stranger's eye. Remembrance holds 355 *Aquap.* 209
A venerable image yields . . . . 406 *White Doe* 947
The scimitar, that yields not to the charms . . 427 *Ecc. Sonn.* 1. 34. 5
An emblem yields to friends and enemies . . 433 *Ecc. Sonn.* 2. 17. 12
Ah! wherefore yields it to a foul constraint . . 438 *Ecc. Sonn.* 2. 38. 12
Yields, if with unpresumptuous faith explored, . 452 *Ecc. Sonn.* 3. 47. 3
Such as my verse now yields, while moonbeams play 458 *Sea-shore* 27
Than thy revival yields, for gladsome hope! . . 461 **Queen of* 56
Of sunshine, an apt emblem yields . . . . 499 **This Lawn* 4
The hastiest sunrise yields a temperate ray; . . 516 **Hard task* 11
Could strip, for aught the prospect yields . . 533 **Blest is* 57
Where silence yields reluctantly . . . . . 550 *Hermit's Cell* 2. 3
Which, to your overweening spirits, yields . . 805 *Excursion* 4. 291
Yields no peculiar reason of complaint . . . 822 *Excursion* 5. 25
That yields such kindly product. He, whose bed 835 *Excursion* 5. 880
A dismal prospect yields the wild shore strewn . 836 *Excursion* 5. 930

Yoke. Then I'll yoke thee to my cart like a pony in the plough; . . . . 88 *Pet-lamb* 46
Spurning the unprofitable yoke of care, . . . 260 **From the dark* 2
That she had borne a heavy yoke, ... 294 *Jedbor.* 72
She rose, and off at once the yoke she threw. . . 313 *Prophecy* 8
Who have seen—themselves now casting off the yoke— . . . . 322 *Germans* 13
When thou, uprisen, shalt break thy double yoke, 361 *Alban Hills* 12
How patiently the yoke of thought they bear! . 429 *Ecc. Sonn.* 2. 5. 10
From wandering fiends of air receive a yoke, . . 465 **Pastor and* 12
Nor ever while I live Love's yoke to draw. . . 559 *Cuck.andNight.*140
The years to bring the inevitable yoke, . . . 589 *Immortality* 128
To a servile yoke. What need of many words? . 633 *Prelude* 1. 105
The yoke of earth is new to them, the world . . 651 *Prelude* 3. 179
And if, at times, they fretted with the yoke, . . 845 *Excursion* 6. 473

Yoked. *See* **Re-yoked.**
Sad deliverance would it be, and yoked with shame, 140 *Arm. Lady* 29
Delivered. No! the Orator hath yoked . . . 694 *Prelude* 7. 501
If man's estate, by doom of Nature yoked . . 742 *Prelude* 13. 175
With toil, be therefore yoked with ignorance; . 742 *Prelude* 13. 176
Even he, who yoked the living to the dead, . . L.I. 88 *Juvenal* 1. 5

Yoke-fellow. First roused thee.—O true yoke-fellow of Time, ... 312 *Clarkson* 8

Yoke-fellows. Uneasy and unsettled, yoke-fellows 673 *Prelude* 5. 520

Yon. Yon chestnuts half the latticed boat-house hide, ... 4 *Ev. Wk.* 107
Raised by yon travelling flock, a dusty cloud . . 4 *Ev. Wk.* 110
The peasant, from yon cliff of fearful edge . . 4 *Ev. Wk.* 130
And, fronting the bright west, yon oak entwines . 6 *Ev. Wk.* 214
Yonisle, which feels not even the milk-maid's feet, 6 *Ev. Wk.* 236
Yon isle conceals their home, their hut-like bower; 6 *Ev. Wk.* 238
Above yon eastern hill, where darkness broods . 8 *Ev. Wk.* 331
Lo, where she sits beneath yon shaggy rock, . . 13 *Desc. Sk.* 177
Would be most welcome. Yon white hawthorn gained, ... 41 *Bord.* 216
"Down to the stump of yon old yew . . . . 85 *Shepherd-boys* 35
Beneath yon ridge, the last of those three graves? 98 *Brothers* 198
You see yon precipice;—it wears the shape . . 101 *Brothers* 364
That in some other way yon smoke . . . . 110 **'Tis said that some* 15
Into yon row of willows flit, ... 111 **'Tis said that some* 26
Headlong yon waterfall must come, ... 111 **'Tis said that some* 34
Yon valley, now so trim and green, ... 129 *Idiot Boy* 329
Who's yon, that, near the waterfall, ... 130 *Idiot Boy* 347
Yon minarets, would gladly leave for his worst home." . . . . 140 *Arm. Lady* 42
Glittering and twinkling near yon rosy cloud; . 153 *Morn. Ex.* 28
Down from yon cliff a fragment broke; . . . 156 *Oak and Broom* 35
Amid yon tuft of hazel trees, ... 159 *Green Linnet* 25
As yon Hawk exhibits, pairing . . . . . . 163 *Hint* 6
Like yon Tuft of fern; . . . . 163 *Hint* 24
Say, Dora! tell me, by yon placid moon, . . . 165 *Parrot* 41
Behold yon Prisoners three, ... 166 *Stray Pleasures* 3
But save us from yon screeching owl!" . . . . 179 *Waggoner* 3. 98
"Yon screech-owl," says the Sailor, turning . . 179 *Waggoner* 3. 110
"Yon owl!—pray God that all be well! . . . 179 *Waggoner* 3. 112
And wander down yon hawthorn dell, ... 180 *Waggoner* 4. 16
Across yon meadowy bottom look, ... 180 *Waggoner* 4. 40
So struts yon cock that now is crowing; . . . 181 *Waggoner* 4. 149
Of yon dim cave, in seeming silence makes . . 184 *Airey-force* 13
Their eyes, or minds? or, finally, is yon resplendent vault? . . . . 189 *Star-gazers* 12
This block—and yon, whose church-like frame . 215 *Kirkstone* 47
At the spectator's feet.—Yon azure ridge, . . . 219 **This Height* 23
Buried together in yon gloomy mass . . . . 230 *Clouds* 31
Yon pilgrims see—in lagging file . . . . . 233 *Power of Sound* 57
Old Andes thrusts yon craggy spear . . . . 237 *P. B.* 58
Yon tawny slip is Libya's sands; . . . . . 237 *P. B.* 61
Yon cloud, and fix it in that glorious shape; . . 252 *Picture* 2

Yon—*continued.*
Where lies the Land to which yon Ship must go? 258 **Where lies the Land* 1
Yon slowly-sinking star—immortal Sire . . . 261 **I watch* 2
Yon old grey Stone, protected from the ray . . 262 **Mark the* 2
Through leaves yet green, and yon crystalline sky, 263 **While not* 11
The effluence from yon distant mountain's head, . 263 **How clear* 2
If so he might, yon mountain's glittering head— . 263 **How clear* 7
So burns yon Taper 'mid a black recess . . . 266 **Even as* 4
Yon eddying balls of foam, these arrowy gleams . 268 **Dogmatic Teachers* 10
'Tis said that to the brow of yon fair hill . . . 276 *Oker Hill* 1
Yon trophied Mound shrinks to a shadowy speck 278 *Wellington* 8
Life with yon Lambs, like day, is just begun, . 278 **Life with* 1
His voice to suit the temper of yon Moon . . . 279 **'Tis he* 7
Yon busy Little-ones rejoice that soon . . . 280 **Intent on* 2
Gleams on the grass-crowned top of yon tall Tower, 283 **Here, where* 11
Well have yon Railway Labourers to this ground 283 **Well have* 1
These pathways, yon far-stretching road! . . 286 *Nith* 32
Yon solitary Highland Lass! . . . . . . 289 *Sol. Reap.* 2
But a mere footstool to yon sovereign Lord, . . 290 *Kilchurn* 13
Yon foaming flood seems motionless as ice; . . 290 *Kilchurn* 36
Yon time-cemented Tower! . . . . 299 *Cora Linn* 6
Yon grey tower's living crest! . . . . . . 300 *Cora Linn* 24
His bed perchance was yon smooth mound . . 302 *Yarrow V.* 27
Yon cottage seems a bower of bliss, ... 302 *Yarrow V.* 61
Of bells;—those boys who in yon meadow-ground 306 **Here, on our* 3
That through the texture of yon azure dome . . 322 *Germans* 6
Of yon ethereal summits white with snow, . . 329 *Ode: Thanks.* 22
How sweet the prospect of yon watery glade, . 335 *Namur* 11
And splendid aspect yon emblazonings . . . 335 *Cologne* 7
Hither, like yon ancient Tower . . . . . 336 **Jesu! bless* 13
Nor doubt but He to whom yon Pine-trees nod . 337 *Aar* 12
From yon steep mountain's loftiest stage, . . . 341 *San Salv.* 2
Such, haply, yon Italian Maid, ... 344 **How blest* 20
My thoughts become bright like yon edging of Pines 345 *Stanzas: Simplon* 21
Yon rampant cloud mimics a lion's shape; . . 348 *Sky-prosp.* 4
And massy grove, so near yon blazing town, . . 349 *Sky-prosp.* 7
Far as St. Maurice, from yon eastern Forks, . 350 *Des. Stanzas* 37
Yon snow-white torrent-fall, plumb down it drops 352 *Aquap.* 10
And murmur issuing from yon pendent flood, . 358 *Aquap.* 370
Yon petty Steep in truth the fearful Rock, . . 358 **Is this* 2
And yon resplendent Church are proud to bear. . 360 **Long has* 14
Bound him, nor, since he raised yon House, have ceased . . . . 362 **List—'twas* 39
Near that Cell—yon sequestered Retreat high in air— . . . . 364 *Vallomb.* 6
The frolic Loves, who, from yon high rock, see . 378 *Duddon* 10. 13
A dark plume fetch me from yon blasted yew, . 380 *Duddon* 17. 1
Of yon pure waters, from their aery height . . 380 *Duddon* 19. 4
Flung from yon cliff a shadow large and cold. . 383 *Duddon* 27. 4
Yon towering Peaks, "Shepherds of Etive Glen?" 389 *Sound of Mull* 14
For instant flight; the Sage in yon alcove . . 393 **The Lovers* 4
And through yon gateway, where is found, . . 396 *White Doe* 52
Pass, pass who will, yon chantry door; . . . 398 *White Doe* 242
Of rising ground, yon heathy spot! . . . . 404 *White Doe* 763
Yon multitude must melt away;) . . . . . 406 *White Doe* 909
Where he is perched, from yon lone Tower . . 406 *White Doe* 959
Beneath yon cypress spiring high, ... 407 *White Doe* 991
As she approached yon rustic Shed . . . . 407 *White Doe* 1022
"This night yon faithless Towers must yield, . 408 *White Doe* 1131
Finds entrance through yon arch, where way . . 416 *White Doe* 1887
And still, 'mid yon thick woods, the primal truth . 419 *Ecc. Sonn.* 1. 4. 12
A brighter crown."—On yon Cistertian wall . . 429 *Ecc. Sonn.* 2. 3. 5
Yon reverend hawthorns, hardened to the rod . 450 *Ecc. Sonn.* 3. 39. 5
Soft as a cloud is yon blue Ridge—the Mere . 456 **Soft as* 1
Yon hazy ridges to their eyes . . . . . . 457 **Had this* 43
False in the issue, that yon seeming space . . 461 **Who but is* 10
For some rare plant, yon Headland of St. Bees. . 466 *St. Bees* 9
Like the fixed Light that crowns yon Headland of St. Bees. . . . . 466 *St. Bees* 45
Witness yon Pile that greets us from St. Bees. . 467 *St. Bees* 126
Just limits; but yon Tower, whose smiles adorn . 469 **The feudal* 5
Off with yon cloud, old Snafell! that thine eye . 471 *Tynwald* 9
Yon light shapes forth a Bard, that shade a Chief. 474 **Ye shadowy* 14
Yet is yon neat trim church a grateful speck . . 474 **How sad* 6
"Yon cloud with that long purple cleft . . . 486 **We walked* 21
"And just above yon slope of corn . . . . 486 **We walked* 25
Of yon wild cave, whose jaggèd brows are fringed 497 **Enough of climbing* 21
And, sooth to say, yon vocal grove, ... 498 **The sylvan* 7
To yon exulting thrush the Muse . . . . . 507 **While from* 59
If yon ethereal blue . . . . 507 *May* 18
Through which yon house of God . . . . . 508 *May* 82
Of sea and land, with yon grey towers that still . 517 *Pun. Death* 1. 2
Thousands, as toward yon old Lancastrian Towers, 517 *Pun. Death* 1. 9
The Mother Church in yon sequestered vale; . . 534 **When in* 4
Hence, when yon mansion and the flowery trim . 546 **Oft is* 5
Beneath yon eastern ridge, the craggy bound, . 547 **Beneath yon* 1
Yon star upon the mountain-top . . . . . 581 **Loud is* 7
Yon tuft conceals your home, your cottage bow'r, 596 *Ev.Wk. Quarto* 227
Beneath yon roof began her heavenly reign? . . 618 *School Ex.* 4
Under yon orchard, in yon humble cot, . . . 622 *Recluse* 1. 1. 77
From the green fields, and from yon azure sky. . 632 *Prelude* 1. 4
Came from yon fountain?" Thou, my Friend! art one . . . . 645 *Prelude* 2. 210
Yon azure smoke betrays the lurking town; . . 658 *Prelude* 4. 24
From these majestic floods, yon shining cliffs, . 682 *Prelude* 6. 463
Covers, or sprinkles o'er, yon village green? . . 699 *Prelude* 8. 5
And grow with thought. Beside yon spring I stood, 763 *Excursion* 1. 484
That in yon arbour oftentimes she sate . . . 769 *Excursion* 1. 876

Young—*continued.*
And hither is young Romilly come, — 494 *Force of Prayer* 25
For never more was young Romilly seen — 494 *Force of Prayer* 35
Such is the lot of all the young, — 507 *May* 71
Young ENGLAND—what is then become of Old, — 516 **Young England* 1
With Young and Old warm greetings we exchange, — 525 *Epist. Beaumont* 236
Take those dear young Ones to a fearless nest; — 525 **Soon did* 2
Young, like the Crescent that above me shone, — 532 **Once I* 7
Issued forth with old and young, — 535 *Egremont* 2
What is't that ails young Harry Gill? — 536 *Goody Blake* 2
Young Harry was a lusty drover, — 536 *Goody Blake* 17
Young Harry heard what she had said: — 537 *Goody Blake* 103
A-bed or up, to young or old; — 537 *Goody Blake* 122
And reconcile; and both with young and old — 538 **In desultory* 52
Though young so wise, though meek so resolute— — 541 *Grace Darl.* 95
For he so young to Christ did reverence. — 553 *Prioress* 64
Said this young Child, 'and by the law of kind — 556 *Prioress* 199
"Young Hew of Lincoln! in like sort laid low — 556 *Prioress* 233
For Love in young folk is but rage, I wis; — 559 *Cuck.andNight.* 168
Feeds in the sunshine; the robust and young, — 568 *Cumb. Beg.* 119
This gives him the fancy of one that is young, — 570 *Farmer* 65
To peace so perfect that the young behold — 572 *Animal Tran.* 13
To young and old; and how revered — 577 **By playful* 6
And while the young lambs bound — 588 *Immortality* 20
And let the young Lambs bound — 590 *Immortality* 173
Your young on winter's winding sheet of snow. — 596 *Ev.Wk.Quarto* 240
To throw the "sultry ray" of young Desire; — 604 *Desc.Sk.Quarto* 151
Bows his young hairs with sorrow to the grave. — 613 *Desc.Sk.Quarto* 631
Think all, he is the God of young delight." — 620 *Birth of Love* 14
To young Ascanius, should assume his place; — 624 *Æneid* 4
His young Ascanius to the Tyrian walls; — 624 *Æneid* 28
Like young Iulus; but the gentlest dews — 624 *Æneid* 46
The shrill defiance of the young crusade — 628 *Eagle and Dove* 13
When Time was young, an inspiration came — 628 **Deign, Sovereign* 26
On the closed eyes of young Endymion fell, — 630 [?] **O Moon* 12
Ah! is there one who ever has been young, — 642 *Prelude* 2. 19
Slight shocks of young love-liking interspersed, — 663 *Prelude* 4. 317
Behold a race of young ones like to those — 671 *Prelude* 5. 407
Young as I was, a child not nine years old, — 672 *Prelude* 5. 452
The truths of young and old. Nor, side by side — 683 *Prelude* 6. 547
There harbours; whether we be young or old, — 684 *Prelude* 6. 603
And all my young affections out of doors. — 688 *Prelude* 7. 76
A change of purpose in young Whittington, — 688 *Prelude* 7. 112
When Art was young; dramas of living men, — 691 *Prelude* 7. 290
The Hours, like young Aurora, to his car: — 694 *Prelude* 7. 502
Grows tedious even in a young man's ear. — 694 *Prelude* 7. 511
Are generous as the young; and, if content — 699 *Prelude* 8. 45
Spreading from young to old, from old to young, — 700 *Prelude* 8. 54
Here then my young imagination found — 708 *Prelude* 8. 639
Life from the young Republic; that new foes — 727 *Prelude* 11. 14
But to be young was very Heaven! O times, — 728 *Prelude* 11. 109
Flattered the young, pleased with extremes, nor least — 730 *Prelude* 11. 233
A young enthusiast, who escaped these bonds; — 736 *Prelude* 12. 152
While yet our hearts are young, while yet we breathe — 741 *Prelude* 13. 124
Which on thy young imagination, trained — 745 *Prelude* 13. 364
Of a young apple-tree, lay at its root; — 769 *Excursion* 1. 841
Too young for any profitable task. — 783 *Excursion* 2. 771
Young, modest, meek, and beautiful, I led — 793 *Excursion* 3. 514
And rich and poor, and young and old, rejoice — 824 *Excursion* 5. 105
With wrecks, and trod by feet of young and old — 836 *Excursion* 5. 931
Of a young fowl beneath one mother hatched, — 843 *Excursion* 6. 367
Young was I then, a schoolboy of eight years; — 858 *Excursion* 7. 69
Sparing both old and young in that abode. — 861 *Excursion* 7. 246
Dear Youth, by young and old alike beloved, — 868 *Excursion* 7. 706
Were subject to young Oswald's steady aim, — 869 *Excursion* 7. 756
And valiant; but young Oswald, like a chief — 869 *Excursion* 7. 772
Of that young peasantry, who, in our days, — 869 *Excursion* 7. 806
These structures rose, commingling old and young, — 879 *Excursion* 8. 339
With which the young narrator was inspired, — 883 *Excursion* 8. 574
One spirit animating old and young, — 892 *Excursion* 9. 526
A choice repast—served by our young companions — 892 *Excursion* 9. 530
Was that same young and happy being) became — K.8. 237 *Recluse* 1.1.48
They *cannot* rest, they gambol like young whelps; — K.8. 251 *Recluse* 1.1.548

Younger. Though younger than himself full twenty years. — 132 *Michael* 80
Were younger;—but this hope is a good hope. — 135 *Michael* 278
Lead to that younger Pile, whose sky-like dome — 452 *Ecc. Sonn.* 3. 45. 8
Around a younger brow! — 498 **Departing summer* 18
He seems ten birthdays younger, is green and is stout; — 570 *Farmer* 53
A younger orphan of a home extinct, — 622 *Recluse* 1. 1. 78
The younger brethren of the grove. But some— — 695 *Prelude* 7. 522
"Though born a younger brother, need was none — 864 *Excursion* 7. 428

Youngest. He fed the spindle of his youngest child, — 95 *Brothers* 23
His youngest born did Andrew hold: — 156 *Oak and Broom* 7
The oldest and youngest — 190 *March* 6
Come, youngest of the lovely Three, — 221 *Triad* 90
Of man, our youngest, fairest flower! — 401 *White Doe* 483
Her youngest Brother brought it home; — 416 *White Doe* 1807
The youngest, then a lusty boy, — 416 *White Doe* 1808
Youngest apprentice in the school of art! — 789 *Excursion* 3. 199

Youngling. The mountain raven's youngling brood — 84 *Shepherd-boys* 6
A youngling of the wild-duck's nest — 297 *Highland Boy* 189
(A spotless Youngling white as foam) — 416 *White Doe* 1806

Young-one. And the bleating mother's Young-one — 93 *Westmoreland Girl* 7

Young-one—*continued.*
Ah! little doth the young-one dream, — 117 *Affl. Marg.* 22
To have the Young-one in his sight, when he — 133 *Michael* 162

Young-ones. The Young-ones gathered in from hill and dale, — 446 *Ecc. Sonn.* 3. 23. 1

Your, *omitted.*

You're. I fear you're in a dreadful way, — 128 *Idiot Boy* 195
"Hush, boys! you're telling me a lie; — 191 *Beggars* 44
But, while these pleasures you're pursuing — 237 *P. B.* 117
"You're overtasked, good Simon Lee, — 484 *Simon Lee* 81

Yours. (*Partial list.*)
That staff of yours, I could almost have heart — 39 *Bord.* 126
Yours, Woman! are you Herbert's wife? — 46 *Bord.* 510
Yours is no common life. Self-stationed here, — 48 *Bord.* 605
Shall then be yours among the happy few — 804 *Excursion* 4. 230

Yourself. Yourself, you do not love him. I do more, — 38 *Bord.* 32
And, for yourself, in plain terms he asserts — 38 *Bord.* 64
From your own Children, if yourself were sick, — 42 *Bord.* 301
Into the court, my Friend, and perch yourself — 44 *Bord.* 370
The Crew deceived you? Nay, command yourself. — 69 *Bord.* 1764
Yourself; and many did to him repair,— — 108 *Indolence* 53
Take courage, and withdraw yourself from ways — 808 *Excursion* 4. 489
With sparing hand. Then trust yourself abroad — 819 *Excursion* 4. 1193

Yourselves. Beautiful in yourselves, and richly graced — 152 **Forth from* 22
For ever with yourselves at strife; — 301 *Bran* 106
Yet will yourselves to God no service pay; — 433 *Ecc. Sonn.* 2. 18. 6
Whoe'er ye be, that thus, yourselves unseen, — 451 *Ecc. Sonn.* 3. 44. 6
And peace among yourselves. — 526 **The soaring* 16
Or waxen image which yourselves have made, — 703 *Prelude* 8. 300
Henceforth, whate'er is wanting to yourselves — 796 *Excursion* 3. 730

Youth. *See* **Peasant-youth.**
No common soul. In youth by science nursed, — 23 *Yew-tree* 13
"There was a Youth whom I had loved so long, — 28 *Guilt* 244
And clear and open soul, so prized in fearless youth. — 32 *Guilt* 441
He in the preference, modest Youth, might take, — 47 *Bord.* 552
He was that One so young should pass his youth — 49 *Bord.* 689
And without further preface.—In my youth, — 68 *Bord.* 1684
As ever were produced by youth and age — 98 *Brothers* 202
Before it ended in his death, the Youth — 100 *Brothers* 320
A fellow-tale of sorrow. From his youth — 100 *Brothers* 331
I judged you most unkindly. But this Youth, — 101 *Brothers* 355
I buried him, poor Youth, and there he lies! — 101 *Brothers* 382
If he had one, the Youth had twenty homes. — 101 *Brothers* 386
And so no doubt he perished. When the Youth — 101 *Brothers* 401
I grieved, fond Youth! that thou shouldst sue — 109 **Ere with* 3
Then shall love teach some virtuous Youth — 110 **Look at* 19
And beauty, for confiding youth, — 113 *Lament* 38
That besprinkled the field; 'twas like youth in my blood! — 116 *Repentance* 32
And hence the father of the enamoured Youth, — 122 *V. and J.* 17
Deem rather that the fervent Youth, who saw — 122 *V. and J.* 57
Deem that by such fond hope the Youth was swayed, — 122 *V. and J.* 64
Muttered the Father.—From these words the Youth — 123 *V. and J.* 122
Desperate the Maid—the Youth is stained with blood; — 123 *V. and J.* 146
For innocence and youth, for weal and woe?" — 124 *V. and J.* 164
Of vehement indignation; but the Youth — 124 *V. and J.* 166
Much how the Youth, in scanty space of time, — 124 *V. and J.* 178
Fond Youth! that mournful solace now must pass — 124 *V. and J.* 218
The visitor retired. Thus lived the Youth — 126 *V. and J.* 299
His bodily frame had been from youth to age — 131 *Michael* 43
The Youth made answer with a jocund voice; — 135 *Michael* 299
Remember them who loved me in my youth. — 136 *Michael* 366
His bodily frame had been from youth to age — 138 *Michael* 454
The time of early youth; and there you learned, — 147 *Joanna* 2
And rocks that were the play-ground of thy youth, — 151 **When, to* 69
In youth from rock to rock I went, — 157 **In youth* 1
The fancy-stricken Youth or heart-sick Maid, — 170 **Never enlivened* 21
There came a Youth from Georgia's shore— — 192 *Ruth* 19
In finest tones the Youth could speak: — 192 *Ruth* 32
He was a lovely Youth! I guess — 192 *Ruth* 37
By such a Youth, in the green shade, — 192 *Ruth* 47
The Youth of green savannahs spake, — 193 *Ruth* 67
For him, a Youth to whom was given — 193 *Ruth* 124
But, when they thither came, the Youth — 194 *Ruth* 190
We Poets in our youth begin in gladness; — 196 *Resolution* 48
Our Clifford was a happy Youth, — 205 *Brougham* 107
Of thoughtless youth; but hearing oftentimes — 207 *Tintern* 90
And Æson stood a youth 'mid youthful peers. — 210 *Laod.* 84
—Bold Goddess! range our Youth among; — 217 *Enterprise* 122
Show me the noblest Youth of present time, — 220 *Triad* 1
A peerless Youth expectant at my side, — 220 *Triad* 25
The bland composure of eternal youth! — 221 *Triad* 140
Nor will return—but droop not, favoured Youth; — 222 *Triad* 213
With Order dwell, in endless youth? — 234 *Power of Sound* 112
Take with you some ambitious Youth! — 237 *P. B.* 128
A loveliness to living youth denied. — 258 **Even so* 8
Thy youth to hopeless wasting, root and stem— — 259 *Calvert* 5
It gladdens me, O worthy, short-lived, Youth! — 260 *Calvert* 13
Rise, GILLIES, rise: the gales of youth shall bear — 260 **From the dark* 3
Ye sacred Nurseries of blooming Youth! — 270 **Ye sacred* 1
Thanks to thy virtues, to the eternal youth — 279 **Though I* 11
In youth, and 'mid the busy world kept pure — 282 *Railway* 3
And showed my youth — 285 *Grave of Burns* 34
Sad tidings to that noble Youth! — 287 *Ellen Irwin* 13
The Youth, her chosen lover. — 287 *Ellen Irwin* 32
The freshness, the everlasting youth, — 301 *Bran* 113
For sportive youth to stray in; — 302 *Yarrow V.* 58
'Tis not in battles that from youth we train — 304 **I grieved* 5
My youth here witnessed, in a prouder time; — 304 **Festivals have* 10

Z

THE END